DAMAGE TO PROPERTY —B8

OFFENCES AFFECTING PUBLIC ORDER—B11

OFFENCES AGAINST THE ADMINISTRATION OF JUSTICE—B14

OFFENCES UNDER CUSTOMS AND EXCISE LEGISLATION—B17

OFFENCES RELATED TO DRUGS—B20

OFFENCES RELATING TO THE PROCEEDS OF CRIMINAL CONDUCT—B22

BLACKSTONE'S

CRIMINAL PRACTICE

2008

GENERAL EDITORS

THE RIGHT HONOURABLE LORD JUSTICE HOOPER QC

DAVID ORMEROD, PROFESSOR OF CRIMINAL JUSTICE,
QUEEN MARY UNIVERSITY OF LONDON;
BARRISTER, 18 RED LION COURT

EMERITUS EDITOR

PETER MURPHY MA, LLB

CONSULTANT EDITOR

HIS HONOUR JUDGE JOHN PHILLIPS CBE

ADVISORY EDITORIAL BOARD

HHJ PETER BEAUMONT QC, HHJ ERIC STOCKDALE, TIM OWEN QC,
DAVID PERRY QC, ROBERT SMITH QC

CONTRIBUTORS

DUNCAN ATKINSON, ALEX BAILIN, DIANE BIRCH,
ED CAPE, ADINA EZEKIEL, RUDI FORTSON, MICHAEL HIRST,
PETER HUNGERFORD-WELCH, ADRIAN KEANE, ANDREW KEOGH,
MICHAEL LEREGO QC, RICHARD McMAHON, TIM MOLONEY,
STEPHEN PARKINSON, EDWARD REES QC, HIS HONOUR JUDGE
PETER ROOK QC, KEIR STARMER QC, RICHARD D. TAYLOR,
MARTIN WASIK, FRANCES WEBER

UNIVERSITY PRESS

OXFORD
UNIVERSITY PRESS

Great Clarendon Street, Oxford OX2 6DP

Oxford University Press is a department of the University of Oxford.
It furthers the University's objective of excellence in research, scholarship,
and education by publishing worldwide in

Oxford New York

Auckland Cape Town Dar es Salaam Hong Kong Karachi
Kuala Lumpur Madrid Melbourne Mexico City Nairobi
New Delhi Shanghai Taipei Toronto

With offices in

Argentina Austria Brazil Chile Czech Republic France Greece
Guatemala Hungary Italy Japan Poland Portugal Singapore
South Korea Switzerland Thailand Turkey Ukraine Vietnam

Published in the United States
by Oxford University Press Inc., New York

First edition published by Blackstone Press 1991
Eighteenth edition published by Oxford University Press 2007

British Library Cataloguing in Publication Data
Data available

Library of Congress Cataloging in Publication Data
Data available

Typeset in Adobe Garamond by
RefineCatch Limited, Bungay, Suffolk
Printed in Italy
on acid-free paper by
Legoprint S.p.A.

ISBN 978–0–19–922814–0 (Hardback)
978–0–19–922815–7 (CD-ROM)
978–0–19–922816–4 (Book & CD)

1 3 5 7 9 10 8 6 4 2

Preface

It is sixteen years since the first edition of *Blackstone's Criminal Practice* and the Editorial board membership had remained relatively constant throughout that period. Under the General Editorship of Peter Murphy, the book progressed, established its strong reputation and gained respect from practitioners and the judiciary alike. In this our first year as editors we record our warm and grateful thanks for his efforts over the years, and for making our succession as smooth as possible. Our joint editorship reflects what we see as the core strengths underpinning the entire book: a unique blend of academic scholarship and comment with practical experience and insight.

This year also saw the departure of a number of contributing authors who had been with *Blackstone's* from the outset: Leonard Leigh, Michael Gunn and John Sprack. Each has made a significant contribution over the years and should be proud of their part in nurturing the book to the acclaimed position it has attained.

We have been extremely fortunate in replacing these contributors with a number of established and widely repsected authors and we welcome them to the team: Rudi Forston who has substantially rewritten the important and heavily used chapters on Drugs offences and Weapons; Duncan Atkinson who has contributed new chapters on criminal procedure which, in light of the continued changes with the Criminal Procedure Rules, have also been substantially rewritten; Professor Ed Cape who has brought his unrivalled expertise to bear in a comprehensive revision of the chapter on police powers; Tim Moloney who has completely rewritten the terrorism chapter, contributed to chapters on sexual offences as well as overhauling all the chapters on appeal; Stephen Parkinson of Kingsley Napley who has revised and refocused the chapter on disclosure; Michael Lerego QC who has revised the chapters on company and insolvency offences, revenue, social security and customs offences, Alex Bailin, who has updated the chapter on offences affecting security. Welcoming these new members, each selected to write in areas of their particular expertise, has also allowed some members of the existing team of contributors to focus more on their own specialist topics. In short, we believe that the new team strikes a better balance between academic and practitioner input, optimises the wealth of expertise this superbly talented range of authors can offer, and remains true to the objectives *Blackstone's* espoused from the outset striving for an authoritative comprehensive and accessible manual.

We have continued the significant improvement of the structure and content of the book. Indeed, readers will notice that this edition contains probably the greatest degree of reorganization and inclusion of additional material in the last sixteen years. We have endeavoured to keep pace with the alarming rate of change in the English criminal justice system. There is a relentless torrent of legislation coupled with an increasing volume of appeals in criminal justice, particularly from the House of Lords. In addition, a new species of material in the form of the 'Protocol' has appeared in recent years and we have incorporated discussion of these important documents on disclosure, terrorism and heavy fraud, in the relevant chapters. All of this means of course that there is more relevant material than ever to incorporate if the book is to maintain its comprehensive coverage. Notable developments this year include several significant statutes: the Fraud Act 2006, the Police and Justice Act 2006, the Road Safety Act 2006, the Violent Crime Reduction Act 2006, the Companies Act 2006, new Criminal Procedure Rules as well as a massive increase in the number and importance of sentencing guidelines. There is also a vast number of new cases digested in the edition including: *Rahman* on joint enterprise, *Bree* on consent in sexual offences, *Heard* on intoxication, *Ramzan* on conspiracy and money laundering, *Carey* on manslaughter, *Ashton* and *Clark and McDaid* on criminal procedure.

We are grateful, as always for the many helpful comments and suggestions received from users of *Blackstone's*. It remains our goal to provide readers with the best possible service, and your input is invaluable to us in pursuing that goal. Please continue to supply us with this valuable feedback. We have established a website to facilitate this at www.oup.com/blackstones/criminal. Alternatively you can send us your comments by email at blackstonescriminal@oup.com.

Readers have begun to take advantage of the free updating services accompanying *Blackstone's*, with a quarterly bulletin and a monthly alerter to key developments which are to be found at www.oup.com/blackstones/criminal.

It is a very sincere pleasure to thank our outstanding team of editors and authors and our distinguished editorial advisory board. Particular thanks, of course, go to our editorial coordinator, Laurence Eastham. More than the 'steady hand on the tiller' as has been previously suggested, he is a dynamic driving force without whom this edition would never have appeared on time nor in such great shape. Last but by no means least, thanks to the excellent production team at OUP, whose quiet competence and professionalism make our work possible.

We have tried to state the law as at 1 August 2007.

Rt Honourable Lord Justice Hooper

Professor David Ormerod

Preface to the First Edition

The last time it happened, George IV was on the throne, and Great Britain still harboured lingering pretensions to sovereignty over the United States. The Judicature Act 1875 was still over a half-century away, the common-law courts sat in Westminster Hall, imprisonment was a remedy for debt and Doctors' Commons was a flourishing institution. Felonies were capital offences, yet the accused enjoyed no right to counsel and was not permitted to testify in his own defence. Times have changed, and even given the conservative attitude of lawyers to innovation, it is time it happened again.

The 'it' referred to is the publication of a wholly new work in the field of criminal law dealing as comprehensively as practicable with all the law, evidence and procedure practitioners need to know. It was in 1822 that J. F. Archbold first published his celebrated work. The editors of its 43rd edition, published 166 years later, in announcing that it had 'exploded' into two volumes, recalled that the original was some 440 pages long, and that its author claimed to have 'taken infinite pains . . . to compress the whole into the smallest possible compass consistent with perspicuity'. It is no criticism of the stalwart efforts of those editors, or those of their many equally distinguished predecessors, that there is now a clear and widely recognised need for a new work that returns to J. F.'s elegant aspiration.

Blackstone's Criminal Practice is designed to fill, in the later years of the 20th century, the need that J. F.'s prototype was designed to fill in the earlier years of the 19th. Its constitution is, we hope, simple and apt to the work of both branches of our legal profession in the field of modern criminal law. The principal articles of that constitution are:

- A single volume of manageable size and expense.
- An annual edition, giving up-to-date service without the cost and inconvenience of supplements.
- In areas of general principle, writing of uncompromising and rigorous scholarly quality.
- In more specific areas, meticulous attention to detail.
- Everywhere, emphasis on the practice of the courts.
- Critical scrutiny of content to promote maximum utility and minimum confusion.

The pursuit of these ideals has led us to some novel approaches. An early decision was that *Blackstone's Criminal Practice* would not attempt to be a portable library. No one book can contain the whole of the law and practice in any field without imitating those stars whose own density causes them to collapse inwards. It is neither necessary nor desirable, in these days of increasingly available and convenient research tools, to give new meaning to the expression 'the weight of authority' by trying to compress the totality of information within the framework of a single treatise. Such lack of discrimination would be apt to produce a work both physically and professionally unmanageable.

We have striven to include everything reasonably necessary from a practical perspective to the everyday work of the practitioner. But we have omitted, without apology, certain obsolete, rarely encountered or antiquated offences and materials of minor importance. Among the casualties are the form of indictment for keeping a puma and two male leopards on the highway to the terror and alarm of the Queen's subjects, and the finer points of assaulting a clergyman of the established Church in the performance of divine worship. These must be sought elsewhere. We have also omitted some areas of law of a more specialised nature, such as offences under the Factories Acts, licensing laws and immigration statutes, the attempted inclusion of which in a general work on criminal law might prove simply to be a disservice.

This selectivity is not, however, entirely exclusive in character. On the contrary, it has created space for the most thorough treatment in a single, well cross-referenced volume of all the material which is truly essential to criminal practice, and much besides that is useful and informative. It is designed to be useful to solicitors as well as barristers, to practitioners in the magistrates' courts as well as those in the Crown Court, to those who prosecute as well as those who defend. This is accomplished by a division of the book into six well defined parts, each consisting of thoughtfully constructed sections.

Part A contains a treatise on the general principles of criminal law. In this part, we have unashamedly requested our authors to write a rigorous and challenging scholarly work that will equip the reader for argument before even the most demanding of appellate tribunals, and will commend itself to the profession as a leading source of academic criticism and opinion.

In part B of the book, which deals with the substantive criminal law, all important criminal offences are fully dealt with and analysed. Due regard is paid to summary offences. The substantive offences are helpfully classified into sections by subject-matter. Each indictable offence is then described, as appropriate, in relation to its definition, applicable procedural rules, range of sentence and any sentencing guidelines, form of indictment, alternative verdicts, elements and defences.

The most significant summary offences in each section are dealt with alongside the indictable offences. A separate part of the book, part C, covers all the most important road traffic offences.

Parts D, E and F deal respectively with criminal procedure, sentencing and evidence, providing a thorough and detailed treatment of the realities of practice, both at the trial level and at the appellate level, and in relation both to summary trial and trial on indictment. The procedural material runs the whole gamut, beginning with police investigative powers, and ending with exhaustion of the final appeal. As mentioned above, this is in addition to the relevant procedural, evidential and sentencing material appended to the treatment of the individual substantive offences.

The authors and editors of this work are a select group and represent the accumulated experience of the Bench, the Bar, the solicitors' profession and the academic world. They have produced a work of high and enduring quality. Tragically, two of those who contributed most to this work will not share the joy of holding it in their hands in its completed form. Within the space of just a few weeks, death claimed both Chris Emmins and Pat Brown while the book was still in preparation.

As a lecturer at the Council of Legal Education, and as a practitioner at the criminal Bar, Christopher Emmins established himself as the undisputed master of criminal procedure. His book *A Practical Approach to Criminal Procedure* was, at the time of his death, preeminent in its field. Chris possessed the rare gift of being able to write with the same clarity with which he thought. He was responsible for almost all the material in this work on procedure. Reading his manuscript as editor-in-chief was a delight comparable to that of a conductor pondering the perfection of a score of Bach or Mozart. Thorough yet readable, complex yet comprehensible, methodical yet imaginative, diverse yet harmonious, the love for the subject and for the work unmistakable. Chris was also the most likeable, modest and unassuming of men, and the most conscientious. It is typical of the man that he had taken the manuscript with him to revise even on the holiday during which he met his death.

Pat Brown brought to her work as an editor not only a keen eye for detail and an innate feel for the overall needs and appearance of a book, but also an infectious and distinctive sense of humour and zest for life. This editor-in-chief will always be in her debt for her contributions to his other writings as well as to this work, both of which are immeasurable.

On behalf of the authors, the editor-in-chief extends heartfelt thanks to the publishing team of Blackstone Press Ltd, in particular Alistair MacQueen, Heather Saward (who lent her name as well as her marvellous talent and energy to *Operation Heather*) and Jonathan Harris. Their vision, creativity, determination and patience are surely unrivalled in their profession. Despite sometimes almost unassailable logistical problems and the many human frailties of authors and editors, they have persevered purposefully, and have not wavered in their faith in us. We hope they feel that that faith has been justified.

On his own behalf, the editor-in-chief is greatly indebted to his administrative assistant, Lee McInnis, whom he believes to possess supernatural powers, and to the world's three greatest future lawyers, Marty Orozco, Edward 'Nick' Nicholas and Dara Bloom, who probably had no idea that the world contained paper in such quantity as was hurled at them to copy, organise, file and dispatch. Without their competence, cheerful good humour and often unspoken reminders of what is truly important in life, the thousands of pages of manuscript would have been literally overwhelming.

And so, after much time, dedication and effort, to which it sometimes seemed there would be no end, *Operation Heather* is complete. *Blackstone's Criminal Practice* is ready to begin its journey. There is no better way to launch it on its path than with words penned by Sir William Blackstone himself in his preface to the *Commentaries on the Laws of England:*

If, in the pursuit of these inquiries, the author hath been able to rectify any errors which either himself or others may have heretofore imbibed, his pains will be sufficiently answered: and, if in some points he is still mistaken, the candid and judicious reader will make due allowances for the difficulties of a search so new, so extensive, and so laborious.

Peter Murphy
Editor-in-Chief
March, 1991

Acknowledgements

Particular thanks are due to the editorial coordinator, Laurence Eastham. Thanks are also due to Moira Greenhalgh for the preparation of the index.

The Code for Crown Prosecutors in appendix 4 is reproduced with the kind permission of the Crown Prosecution Service.

Magistrates' Court Sentencing Guidelines 2004 are reproduced with the kind permission of the Magistrates' Association.

Judicial Studies Board Specimen Directions are reproduced with the kind permission of the Judicial Studies Board and are also available on their website (www.jsboard.co.uk).

The Sentencing Guidelines Council Guidelines in appendix 8 are reproduced with the kind permission of the Sentencing Guidelines Council.

The publishers would like to invite subscribers to email (blackstonescriminal@oup.com) with any feedback or comments so that the service can continue to be developed and improved.

Abbreviations

The following abbreviations have been used in this edition:

A-G	Attorney-General
A-G's Ref	Attorney-General's Reference
AJA 1999	Access to Justice Act 1999
ARA	Asset Recovery Agency
ASBA 2003	Anti-social Behaviour Act 2003
A-t, CSA 2001	Anti-terrorism, Crime and Security Act 2001
BA 1976	Bail Act 1976
CCRC	Criminal Cases Review Commission
CDA 1998	Crime and Disorder Act 1998
CDSA 2006	Criminal Defence Service Act 2006
CJA	Criminal Justice Act (dates vary)
CJCSA 2000	Criminal Justice and Court Services Act 2000
CJPA 2001	Criminal Justice and Police Act 2001
CJPO 1994	Criminal Justice and Public Order Act 1994
CPIA 1996	Criminal Procedure and Investigations Act 1996
CPS	Crown Prosecution Service
CrimPR	Criminal Procedure Rules 2005
C(S)A 1997	Crime (Sentences) Act 1997
CYPA	Children and Young Persons Act (dates vary)
DPP	Director of Public Prosecutions
DVCVA 2004	Domestic Violence, Crimes and Victims Act 2004
ECHR	European Convention on Human Rights
FA 1968	Firearms Act 1968
F(A)A	Firearms (Amendment) Act (dates vary)
FSMA 2000	Financial Services and Markets Act 2000
HRA 1998	Human Rights Act 1998
MCA 1980	Magistrates' Courts Act 1980
MDA 1971	Misuse of Drugs Act 1971
OAPA 1861	Offences Against the Person Act 1861
PACE 1984	Police and Criminal Evidence Act 1984
PCA 2002	Proceeds of Crime Act 2002
PCC(S)A 2000	Powers of Criminal Courts (Sentencing) Act 2000
POA	Public Order Act (dates vary)
PTA	Prevention of Terrorism Act (dates vary)
RIPA 2000	Regulation of Investigatory Powers Act 2000
RTA	Road Traffic Act (dates vary)
RTOA 1988	Road Traffic Offenders Act 1988
RTRA	Road Traffic Regulation Act (dates vary)
SGC	Sentencing Guidelines Council
SOA	Sexual Offences Act (dates vary)
SOCA	Serious Organised Crime Agency
SOCPA 2005	Serious Organised Crime and Police Act 2005
TA	Theft Act (dates vary)
TA 2000	Terrorism Act 2000
TA 2006	Terrorism Act 2006
VCRA 2006	Violent Crime Reduction Act 2006
YJCEA 1999	Youth Justice and Criminal Evidence Act 1999

Contributors

…n Atkinson, Barrister
…'s Bench Walk

…ailin, Barrister
… Chambers

…e Birch, LLB
…mith Professor of Law, University of Nottingham

…Cape, LLM, Solicitor
…fessor of Criminal Law and Practice, and Director of the Centre for Legal Research, …v Faculty, University of the West of England, Bristol

…lina Ezekiel, Barrister
… King's Bench Walk

…udi Fortson, LLB, Barrister
25 Bedford Row, London

Michael Hirst, LLB, LLM
Professor of Criminal Justice, De Montfort University, Leicester

Peter Hungerford-Welch, LLB, FHEA, Barrister
Associate Dean at The City Law School, City University, London

Adrian Keane, LLB, Barrister
Professor of Law and Dean, Inns of Court School of Law, The City Law School, City University, London

Andrew Keogh, LLB, LLM, Barrister, Solicitor
Partner, Tuckers Solicitors

Michael Lerego, QC, MA, BCL, FCIArb
Fountain Court Chambers

Richard McMahon, LLB, LLM, Barrister
Director of Civil Litigation, States of Guernsey, Crown Advocate of the Royal Court of Guernsey. Formerly Lecturer in Law, the University of Reading

Tim Moloney, Barrister
Tooks Chambers

Stephen Parkinson, LLB, Solicitor
Partner and Head of Kingsley Napley's Criminal Law Practice area

Edward Rees, QC, LLB
Doughty Street Chambers

His Honour Judge Peter Rook, QC
Central Criminal Court

Keir Starmer, QC
Doughty Street Chambers

Richard D. Taylor, MA, LLM, Barrister
Professor of English Law, Lancashire Law School, University of Central Lancashire

Contributors

Martin Wasik, LLB, MA, FRSA, Barrister
Recorder of the Crown Court, Professor of Criminal Justice, Keele University

Frances Webber, Barrister
Garden Court Chambers

Guide to Blackstone's Criminal Practice

COVERAGE

Blackstone's Criminal Practice is published annually and is available in paper and digital formats.

Set out in a single volume, the book covers all practice and procedure in the Crown Court and magistrates' courts. It has been designed to contain everything that a criminal law practitioner would need in their normal daily work.

The text consists of a clear, expert narrative that is regularly reviewed and updated. The strength and application of case precedent is assessed in detail and relevant extracts from judgments are reproduced. Relevant extracts from statutes, rules, and other legislative materials are also set out. In-depth guidance is provided on all complex matters of law.

ORGANISATION OF THE SUBJECT MATTER

Structured for clarity and ease of use, the book is divided into six substantive Parts (A to F), which largely follow the progress of a case, and nine Appendices (1 to 9). Each Part is further sub-divided into numbered Sections (e.g. **B1**, **B2**, **B3** etc.) where similarly themed information is grouped together for quick access. For a full list of Parts and Sections see the Contents List starting on page **xxi**.

There is a **Companion Web Site** to alert practitioners to key developments taking place during the life cycle of this edition. Please visit http://oup.com/blackstones/criminal

SUBJECT-FOCUSED PARTS

Part A Criminal Law A rigorous and detailed treatise of the general legal principles of criminal law including the essential elements of a crime, defences, liability, parties, and jurisdiction.

Part B Offences A systematic analysis of key substantive offences setting as necessary definitions, form of indictments, applicable procedural rules, sentencing guidelines, alternative verdicts, defences, elements and so forth.

Part C Road Traffic Offences In-depth coverage of all road traffic offences, set out in a separate Part for quick access.

Part D Procedure Step-by-step guidance covering the practice and procedure of a case from police investigation, through trial (both summary trial and trial on indictment), to final appeal.

Part E Sentencing Clear and authoritative guidance on every aspect of sentencing including custodial sentences, community sentences, orders, fines, disqualification and rehabilitation.

Part F Evidence Invaluable and detailed coverage of the principles and practice governing the complex area of evidence.

SOURCE-FOCUSED APPENDICES

The Appendices of *Blackstone's Criminal Practice* are source-focused and include the up-to-date text of the following:

Appendix 1 Criminal Procedure Rules 2005
Appendix 2 Codes of Practice under the Police and Criminal Evidence Act 1984
Appendix 3 Attorney-General's Guidelines
Appendix 4 The Code for Crown Prosecutors
Appendix 5 Codes, Guidelines and Protocols on Disclosure
Appendix 6 Materials on Human Rights
Appendix 7 The Consolidated Criminal Practice Direction
Appendix 8 Sentencing Guidelines Council Guidelines
Appendix 9 Protocol on Control and Management of Heavy Fraud and other Complex Criminal Cases

NAVIGATION

Research in *Blackstone's Criminal Practice* can be started either from a subject focus or a source focus because of its clear structure and its comprehensive indexing and referencing.

Tinted thumb tabs enable easy access to each of the Parts and are especially helpful when time is short, for instance whilst appearing in court. To facilitate navigation further the numbered Section headings also appear in the running heads at the top of each right-hand page and are reflected in the paragraph numbering. For instance, a cross-reference to **A4.4** refers to the fourth paragraph in Part A Section 4.

Cross-references to other useful paragraphs within the book appear throughout the text and these are set out in **bold**.

The book further benefits from a number of tables and indexes, as follows:

- **Useful References.** This is set out on the inside front cover and comprises of a list of important and useful paragraphs which often need to be accessed in a hurry.
- **Contents List** (p. **xxi**). This is a comprehensive listing of all the Parts and Sections in the book. There is also a Summary list of Contents (p. **xvii**), which gives a quick overview of the structure of the book.
- **Tables of Cases** (p. **xxxvii**), **Statutes** (p. **clx**), **Statutory Instruments** (p. **ccxxiii**) **and Codes of Practice, Practice Directions etc.** (p. **ccxxxi**). These are arranged alphabetically and provide an easy way of locating information on specific cases or sections of legislation. References to actual extracts (sections and sub-sections) are underlined.
- **Index** (p. **3139**). This is a fully comprehensive and much acclaimed subject index which it is beneficial to refer to when wishing to locate information on a specific topic across the whole book.
- **Calendar.** A three-year calendar is set out on the inside back cover.

ADDITIONAL FEATURES OF THE CD-ROM

The CD-ROM version of *Blackstone's Criminal Practice* contains the full text of the book and uses Folio functionality to enable searching, browsing, cutting and pasting and printing of information. The Contents List, Tables, Index and all cross references within the text are set out as live hypertext links so that clicking on a reference will take you directly to the relevant paragraph.

The CD-ROM includes the benefit of additional materials including: the full and updated texts of key statutes from 1996–2006, the Crown Prosecution Service Charging Standards and Casework Guidelines, and the Magistrates' Court Sentencing Guidelines 2004.

The CD-ROM is available to be purchased separately or as a special pack with the book. For further information on this service and ordering details please email: ep.info@oup.com

ADDITIONAL FEATURES OF ONLINE SERVICES

***Blackstone's Criminal Practice* Companion Web Site.** Free of charge to all *Blackstone's Criminal Practice* subscribers, this web site features key developments taking place during the lifecycle of this edition. Updates are organised by date and by Part, and are cross-referenced to the book for ease of use. Please visit www.oup.com/blackstones/criminal and bookmark the site.

***Blackstone's Criminal Practice Bulletin*:** A quarterly newsletter alerting readers to key developments in criminal law and sentencing. Bulletins published in October, January, April and July.

Summary of Contents

PART A CRIMINAL LAW

PART B OFFENCES

PART C ROAD TRAFFIC OFFENCES

PART D PROCEDURE

PART E SENTENCING

PART F EVIDENCE

APPENDICES

Contents

PART E SENTENCING

PART F EVIDENCE

APPENDICES

Table of Cases

Table of Cases

Table of Cases

Table of Cases

Table of Cases

Table of Cases

Table of Cases

Table of Cases

Table of Statutes

Where a reference is underlined, the relevant material is reproduced at that reference.

Table of Statutory Instruments

Where a reference is underlined, the relevant material is reproduced at that reference.

Adoption Rules 1984 (SI 1984 No. 265)
r. 6 . . . . **B3.93**
r. 18 . . . . **B3.93**
Air Navigation Order 2000 (SI 2000 No. 1562)
art. 65(1). **B11.229**
art. 65(2). **B11.229**
art. 67 . . . . **B11.76**
art. 122(5). **B11.76**
art. 122(6). **B11.229**
sch. 12, part A. **B11.76**
sch. 12, part B. **B11.229**
Aliens Order 1920. . . . . **A1.9**
Al-Qa'ida and Taliban (United Nations Measures) Order 2002 (SI 2002 No. 111) **B10.38**
Al-Qa'ida and Taliban (United Nations Measures) Order 2006 (SI 2006 No. 2952) **B10.38**
Asbestos Regulations 1969 (SI 1969 No. 690) **A5.17**
Assistants to Justices' Clerks Regulations 2006 (SI 2006 No. 3405) . . . **D3.28**
reg. 3 . . . . **D3.28**
reg. 4 . . . . **D3.28**
reg. 5 . . . . **D3.28**
Bail (Amendment) Act 1993 (Prescription of Prosecuting Authorities) Order 1994 (SI 1994 No. 1438) . . . **D7.67**
Breath Test (Approval) (No. 1) Order 1968 . . . . **F8.10**
Channel Tunnel (Security) Order 1994 (SI 1994 No. 570) **E5.3**
Child Support, Pensions and Social Security Act 2000 (Commencement No. 10) Order 2001 (SI 2001 No. 2619) **E10.23**
Children (Northern Ireland) Order 1995 (SI 1995 No. 755)
art. 4. . . . . **B3.93**
art. 21 . . . . **B3.93**
art. 23. **B3.93**
art. 27(2). **B3.93**
art. 34A(10) **B3.93**
art. 34C(2) **B3.93**
art. 60(1). **B3.93**
art. 75(1). **B3.93**
art. 159. . . . . **B3.93**
art. 160. . . . . **B3.93**
Children (Secure Accommodation) Regulations 1991 (SI 1991 No. 1505)
reg. 6 . . . . **D2.47**
reg. 10(1) **D2.47, D7.94**
Civil Partnership (Registration Provisions) Regulations 2005 (SI 2005 No. 3176)
reg. 13(4) **F8.16**
Civil Procedure Rules 1998 (SI 1998 No. 3132) **D4.4, D4.5, D7.96**
part 6 . . . . **B14.79**
r. 2.6(3). **F8.22**
r. 8.2 . . . . **D28.28**
r. 44.14. . . . . **D30.24**
r. 48.7 . . . . **D30.24**
part 52 . . . . **D28.14, D30.13**
Civil Procedure Rules 1998 (SI 1998 No. 3132) —*continued*
part 52 PD, para. 18.4 . . . . . . **D28.17**
part 52 PD, para. 18.6 . . . . . . **D28.17**
part 54 . . . . **D14.34, D28.28**
part 54 PD **D28.28**
part 54 PD, para. 5.2 . . . . **D28.28**
part 54 PD, para. 5.6 . . . . **D28.28**
part 54 PD, para. 5.7 . . . . **D28.28**
part 54 PD, para. 8.4 . . . . **D28.28**
part 54 PD, para. 8.5 . . . . **D28.28**
part 54 PD, para. 8.6 . . . . **D28.28**
part 54 PD, para. 15.1 . . . . . . **D28.28**
part 54 PD, para. 15.2 . . . . . . **D28.28**
r. 54.6 . . . . **D28.28**
r. 54.12. . . . . **D28.28**
r. 54.13. . . . . **D28.28**
r. 54.15. . . . . **D28.28**
r. 54.18. . . . . **D28.28**
sch. 1 . . . . **B14.79**
Collection of Fines (Final Scheme) Order 2006 (SI 2006 No. 1737) . . . **E17.7**
Community Drivers' Hours and Recording Equipment (Exemptions and Supplementary Provisions) Regulations 1986 (SI 1986 No. 1456) **C4.8**
Community Drivers' Hours and Recording Equipment Regulations 1986 (SI 1986 No. 1457) **C4.8**
Companies (Northern Ireland) Order 1986 (NI 6)
art. 427 . . . . **F19.1**
art. 440 . . . . **F19.1**
Companies (Northern Ireland) Order 1989 (NI 18)
art. 23 . . . . **F19.1**
Companies (Northern Ireland) Order 1986 (SI 1986 No. 1032)
art. 451 . . . . **B5.105**
Conditional Access (Unauthorised Decoders) Regulations 2000 (SI 2000 No. 1175). **B4.118**
Consumer Protection (Code of Practice for Traders on Price Indications) Approval Order 1988 (SI 1988 No. 2078) **B6.123**
Controlled Drugs (Substances Useful for Manufacture) Regulations 1991 (SI 1991 No. 1285) **B20.98, B20.99**
reg. 3 . . . . **B17.19, B20.99**
reg. 6(d) **B20.99**
reg. 7 . . . . **B20.98**
Controlled Drugs (Substances Useful for Manufacture) (Amendment) Regulations 1992 (SI 1992 No. 2914) **B20.98**
Controlled Drugs (Substances Useful for Manufacture) (Intra–Community Trade) Regulations 1993 (SI 1993 No. 2166) **B20.99**
Controlled Drugs (Substances Useful for Manufacture) (Intra-Community Trade) (Amendment) Regulations 2001 (SI 2001 No. 3683) . . **B20.99**
Controlled Drugs (Substances Useful for Manufacture) (Intra-Community Trade) (Amendment) Regulations 2004 (SI 2004 No. 850) . . . **B20.99**
Costs in Criminal Cases (General) Regulations 1986 (SI 1986 No. 1335) **D30.10, D30.21**
part I **D30.26**
reg. 1 . . . . **D30.26**
reg. 2 . . . . **D30.26**
part II. **D30.13**
reg. 3. . . . . . **D30.21, D30.23.D30.26**
reg. 3(1) **D30.26**
reg. 3(2) **D30.21, D30.26**
reg. 3(3) **D30.21, D30.26**
reg. 3(4) **D30.21, D30.26**
reg. 3(5) **D30.21, D30.26**
regs. 3A–3D. **D30.24**
part IIB **D30.25**
reg. 3A **D30.26**
reg. 3B **D30.26**
reg. 3B(1). **D30.26**
reg. 3B(2). **D30.26**
reg. 3B(3). **D30.26**
reg. 3B(4). **D30.26**
reg. 3C. **D30.26**
reg. 3C(1). **D30.26**
reg. 3C(2). **D30.26**
reg. 3C(3). **D30.26**
reg. 3C(4). **D30.26**
reg. 3C(5). **D30.26**
reg. 3C(6). **D30.26**
reg. 3D. **D30.26**
reg. 3E **D30.26**
reg. 3E(1) **D30.26**
reg. 3E(2) **D30.26**
reg. 3F(1) **D30.25**
reg. 3F(2) **D30.25**
reg. 3F(3) **D30.25**
reg. 3F(4) **D30.25**
reg. 3F(5) **D30.26**
reg. 3F(6) **D30.26**
reg. 3F(7) **D30.26**
reg. 3G **D30.25, D30.26**
reg. 3G(1). **D30.26**
reg. 3G(2). **D30.26**
reg. 3G(3). **D30.26**
reg. 3G(4). **D30.26**
reg. 3G(5) **D30.26**
reg. 3G(6). **D30.26**
reg. 3G(7). **D30.26**
reg. 3G(8) **D30.25, D30.26**
reg. 3H. **D30.25, D30.26**
reg. 3H(1) **D30.26**
reg. 3H(2) **D30.26**
reg. 3H(3) **D30.26**
reg. 3H(4) **D30.25, D30.26**
reg. 3H(5) **D30.26**
reg. 3H(6) **D30.25, D30.26**
reg. 3I. **D30.26**
regs. 4–13) . **D30.13, D30.16, D30.26**
reg. 5 . . . . **D30.13**
reg. 7 . . . . **D30.13**
reg. 9 . . . . **D30.13**
reg. 10 . . . . **D30.13**
reg. 11 . . . . **D30.13**

Table of Codes of Practice, Practice Directions etc.

Where a reference is underlined, the relevant material is reproduced at that reference.

Table of Codes of Practice, Practice Directions etc.

Section A1 *Actus Reus*: The External Elements of an Offence

A1.1 It is customary, for analytical purposes, to separate the essential elements of a crime into two main elements: (1) the prohibited act, omission, consequence or state-of-affairs (the *actus reus*); and (2) any fault element, such as intent or recklessness, required in respect of it (the *mens rea*). Smith & Hogan (*Criminal Law*, 11th ed., p. 37) define the *actus reus* as including 'all the elements in the definition of the crime except the accused's mental element'. It represents the external manifestation of the offence.

THE NATURE OF AN *ACTUS REUS*

Conduct Crimes and Result Crimes

A1.2 The *actus reus* of an offence may be defined in such a way that the accused's conduct must cause or result in specified consequences. Homicide offences, for example, require proof that D's conduct caused the death of another; and no assault can be committed if D's behaviour goes unnoticed by any victim. Such offences may be referred to as 'result crimes'. In contrast, many offences are defined in such a way that the consequences, if any, of D's behaviour are irrelevant to his liability. His behaviour may amount to the complete *actus reus* of the offence even if it fails to bring about the consequences he intends or indeed any consequences at all. The *actus reus* of blackmail, for example, is complete as soon as D makes an unwarranted demand with menaces. A demand is 'made' as soon as it is uttered, and does not require successful communication to the victim (or anyone else). The mere posting of a letter containing such a demand is sufficient (*Treacy v DPP* [1971] AC 537). Blackmail, therefore, is a 'conduct crime'.

The classification of offences into 'conduct crimes' and 'result crimes' may sometimes seem awkward and unhelpful. Nevertheless, it is always necessary to identify the constituent elements of an offence, and use of this classification sometimes highlights key differences between offences. Thus, the offence of indecent exposure formerly contained within the Town Police Clauses Act 1847, s. 28, was a result crime, because it required proof that D's conduct caused residents or 'passengers' to be 'annoyed, obstructed or endangered'. In contrast, the offence of genital exposure created by the SOA 2003, s. 66, is a conduct crime, because it requires proof only that D exposed himself and intended this to cause alarm or distress. Nobody need actually have suffered alarm or distress. In theory, nobody need even have seen the offending act.

The distinction between conduct crimes and result crimes may also be important in determining jurisdiction over cross-frontier offences. The general rule is that jurisdiction over a conduct crime depends on proof that some part of the relevant conduct occurred within England or Wales, whereas jurisdiction over a result crime ordinarily depends on at least some part of the proscribed result taking place there (see *Secretary of State for Trade v Markus* [1976] AC 35, per Lord Diplock at p. 61 and *Harden* [1963] 1 QB 8, but contrast *Smith (Wallace Duncan) (No. 4)* [2004] QB 1418). Cases involving international fraud may now fall within part I of the CJA 1993 (see **A8.4**). If so, jurisdiction may arise where any element of the offence occurs within England or Wales.

RELATIONSHIP BETWEEN *ACTUS REUS* AND *MENS REA*

A1.3 The general rule, expressed in the maxim, *actus non facit reum nisi mens sit rea*, is that an offence can be committed only where criminal conduct is accompanied by some element of fault, the precise fault element required depending upon the particular offence involved. There are nevertheless many offences of strict liability, in which no fault element need be proved (see A4). In such cases, one can therefore have an *actus reus* without any corresponding *mens rea*.

In theory, there can be no criminal liability based on *mens rea* alone, but if the *actus reus* element of a crime is defined very widely (as is sometimes the case) a 'guilty mind' may turn an objectively innocent act into the *actus reus* of that offence. Thus, a witness who tells the court something that he believes to be untrue is guilty of perjury, even if his evidence turns out, to his surprise, to be true after all (see **B14.9**); and a shopper who openly selects goods in a self-service store, whilst secretly nursing a dishonest intention to avoid paying for them, is regarded as committing theft at the moment he first selects them, even though he may have done nothing objectively wrong at that stage. The *actus reus* of perjury involves nothing more than giving material evidence in court; and the concept of appropriation, which lies at the heart of the *actus reus* of theft, has been defined so widely in cases such as *Gomez* [1993] AC 442 as to strip it of any special significance. Almost any form of dealing with another person's property, legitimate or otherwise, must now be regarded as an appropriation of it: the *actus reus* of theft (see generally **B4.25** ***et seq.***).

A person can meanwhile be guilty of a criminal attempt by doing an entirely lawful thing in the mistaken belief that he is doing something different, which would indeed have been criminal. If, for example, D imports a harmless vegetable powder mistakenly believing it to be heroin, he may be guilty of attempting to import a controlled drug, contrary to s. 1 of the Criminal Attempts Act 1981. The objectively lawful importation of the powder becomes the *actus reus* of the criminal attempt (*Shivpuri* [1987] AC 1; see **A6.40**).

A Mental Element in the *Actus Reus*?

A1.4 The usual distinction between the mental element and the external manifestation of a crime can be difficult to apply in cases where the crime is one of 'possessing', 'permitting', 'keeping', 'appropriating', etc, because these terms simultaneously import both mental and physical elements. A person may, for example, possess a controlled drug without realising what it is that he possesses, but he does not possess something which, unknown to him, has become stuck to the sole of his shoe or the blade of his penknife (*Warner v Metropolitan Police Commissioner* [1969] 2 AC 256; *Marriott* [1971] 1 WLR 187). It might therefore be argued that there is a mental element implicit in the *actus reus* of any offence of unlawful possession. From a strictly theoretical viewpoint, this cannot be correct. The correct analysis must be that the legal concept of possession involves both the *actus reus* element of physical possession and a state of mind, the *animus possidendi*, which can only be a part of the requisite *mens rea*. Nevertheless, it may be convenient in practice to treat the *animus possidendi* as if it were an *actus reus* element, because it must always be proved by the prosecution, even where, as in drug possession cases, the burden of proof in respect of other *mens rea* elements is placed on the defence (see **B20.11** ***et seq.***).

Contemporaneity of *Actus Reus* and *Mens Rea*

A1.5 The general rule is that, to be guilty of a criminal offence requiring *mens rea*, an accused must possess that *mens rea* when performing the act or omission in question, and it must relate to that particular act or omission. If, for example, D accidentally kills his wife in a car crash on Monday, the fact that he was planning to cut her throat on Tuesday does not make him guilty of her murder, even if he was thinking about the planned murder at the time of the accident, and even if he is subsequently delighted to find that his wife has died. The general rule as to contemporaneity must nevertheless be qualified in certain respects.

First, D's *mens rea* need not last beyond the moment at which he causes the *actus reus* to occur. He will not be excused merely because he abandons it before that *actus reus* is complete. After inflicting a fatal injury on V with murderous intent, D may repent of his actions and may even do his utmost to save V's life; but if V dies he will be guilty of murder (*Jakeman* (1983) 76 Cr App R 223, *per* Wood J at p. 228). In *Jakeman*, J booked suitcases containing drugs onto a series of flights terminating in London. She abandoned them in Paris, allegedly because she no longer intended to import them, but the cases were sent on to London where the drugs were discovered. The Court of Appeal held that J's loss of *mens rea* came too late to prevent her being guilty of an importation offence.

Secondly, the *actus reus* of a crime may consist of an extended or ongoing course of conduct, rather than one that occurs at one instant in time. The *actus reus* of rape, for example, extends from the moment of initial non-consensual penetration to the moment at which the penis is withdrawn. If D has no *mens rea* at the moment of penetration, but later becomes aware of the absence of consent, he may commit rape by not withdrawing immediately thereafter (*Kaitamaki v The Queen* [1985] AC 147). Consent may even be withdrawn after initial penetration, and rape may therefore be committed if, for example, D pays no heed when V protests that he should stop because he is hurting her.

A controversial example of the 'continuous act' principle can be found in *Fagan v Metropolitan Police Commissioner* [1969] 1 QB 439, where F was directed by a police officer to park his vehicle by the kerb, and drove it right onto the officer's foot. There was no proof that he did so deliberately, but it was clear that he deliberately left it there after the officer told him what he had done. His conviction for assaulting the officer was upheld by the Divisional Court on the basis that there was on ongoing act, which became a criminal assault once F became aware of it. James J said:

> It is not necessary that *mens rea* should be present at the inception of the *actus reus*; it can be superimposed on an existing act. On the other hand, the subsequent inception of *mens rea* cannot convert an act which has been completed without *mens rea* into an assault.

Thirdly, the courts may extend the above principle by treating a series of different actions culminating in the *actus reus* of a crime as if they were a single, extended or continuous course of conduct. It will then be sufficient if the accused possessed the requisite *mens rea* at any point during that course of conduct. If, for example, D attempts to murder V by beating him to death, and believes that he has done so, but actually kills V by burying or dismembering what he assumes to be his corpse, D will still be guilty of murder. As Lord Reid said in *Thabo Meli v The Queen* [1954] 1 WLR 228:

> It is much too refined a ground of judgment to say that, because the appellants were under a misapprehension at one stage and thought that their guilty purpose had been achieved before, in fact, it was achieved, therefore they are to escape the penalties of the law.

This principle has subsequently been applied, not only in cases where there was a prearranged plan, of which disposal of the body was a part (as in *Moore* [1975] Crim LR 229), but also in cases where there was no such plan. In *Church* [1966] 1 QB 59, C struck a woman and panicked because he mistakenly thought he had killed her. He threw her into a river, where she drowned. Edmund-Davies J, giving the judgment of the Court of Criminal Appeal, held that, '. . . if a killing by the first act would have been manslaughter, a later destruction of the supposed corpse should also be manslaughter'. *Church* was followed and extended in *Le Brun*

[1992] QB 61, where B struck his wife in the course of an argument outside their house, after she had refused to enter it with him. The blow left her unconscious. He then tried to drag her into the house. As he did so, her head struck the pavement, fracturing her skull and killing her. The case differed from *Church* in that the fatal impact was accidental, whereas Church's disposal of the 'body' was deliberate, but the Court of Appeal nevertheless upheld a conviction for manslaughter by identifying a continuous course of unlawful conduct. In attempting to drag his unconscious wife indoors, B was either trying to conceal his initial assault on her, or forcing her to enter the house against her wishes (this being the original reason for the assault). The trial judge had directed the jury to acquit if they concluded that B had been trying to aid or assist his wife when he attempted to move her, and the Court of Appeal agreed that this would have broken the essential nexus between the two halves of the incident.

A further difficulty arose in *A-G's Ref (No. 4 of 1980)* [1981] 1 WLR 705 where, in the course of a struggle, D pushed his girlfriend V over a landing rail onto the floor below and then, believing her dead, cut her throat and dismembered her in the bath so as to dispose of her body. It was impossible to establish whether V died in the original fall or whether he killed her (as in *Church*) by his subsequent actions. The Court of Appeal held that a manslaughter conviction was possible, despite uncertainty as to the actual cause of death, but only if it could be proved that each of D's acts was performed with the requisite *mens rea* for that offence. Since the initial fall may well have killed V, it would not suffice to establish *mens rea* (such as gross negligence) only in the subsequent act of disposal: the prosecution also had to disprove D's claim that he had merely pushed her away in a 'reflex action' when she dug her nails into him in the struggle on the upstairs landing.

VOLUNTARY AND INVOLUNTARY CONDUCT

A1.6 The vast majority of criminal offences require acts or omissions on the defendant's part, and these acts or omissions must ordinarily be willed or 'voluntary'. D does not therefore commit criminal damage if his enemies throw him from an upstairs window onto the roof of a car below. Nor is this merely because he lacks the requisite *mens rea* for that offence. It is because involuntary movements cannot ordinarily constitute the *actus reus* of any offence, not even one of strict liability. As Ashworth explains, 'It is not merely a denial of fault . . . It is more a denial of authorship . . . in these circumstances, it is fair to say that this was not D's act, but something which happened to D' (*Principles of Criminal Law*, 4th ed., pp. 99–100).

Physical compulsion is merely one possible cause of involuntary conduct. Such conduct may also be caused by uncontrollable reflex actions or by a physical collapse brought on by injury or illness. If, for example, D suffers a sudden and unforeseen stroke or blackout whilst driving his car, which then careers through a red traffic light and collides with another vehicle, no offence is committed by him. The same rule would apply if D loses control of his car when attacked by a swarm of bees (an example suggested by Devlin J in *Hill v Baxter* [1958] 1 QB 277).

'Involuntary' conduct in this context does not include acts done by reason of duress, necessity or coercion (as to which, see **A3.20** ***et seq.***) because such acts are still conscious, willed and rational; but it may include acts 'committed' by D when in a state of automatism: i.e. when not consciously in control of his own mind or body. A condition of automatism can arise where D is suffering from concussion, where he is a diabetic who suffers an attack of hypoglycaemia (very low blood sugar) after taking insulin (see *Quick* [1973] QB 910) or, arguably, where he commits the *actus reus* whilst in a somnambulistic trance induced by hypnotism.

Limitations on the Defence of Automatism

A1.7 Although involuntariness or automatism is ordinarily a complete defence to any criminal charge, the use of that defence is limited by a number of considerations. These are more fully explained at **A3.7** *et seq.* It must suffice to note at this point that the defence may be rendered invalid where D was culpable for falling into such a condition, as for example by driving whilst suffering from exhaustion (*Kay v Butterworth* (1945) 173 LT 191) or by abusing alcohol or drugs (*Lipman* [1970] 1 QB 152). It is also unavailable where the cause of the condition is a 'defect of reason arising from a disease of the mind', because this amounts in law to insanity. The term 'disease of the mind' embraces both organic and functional disorders of the mind, but excludes external causes, such as drugs, hypnosis or concussion. Epilepsy is in this sense a disease of the mind (*Sullivan* [1984] AC 156) as is a brain tumour (*Kemp* [1957] 1 QB 399) or even hyperglycaemia (excessive blood sugar) which may occur naturally in a diabetic (*Hennessy* [1989] 1 WLR 287). Sleepwalking was regarded in *Bratty v A-G for Northern Ireland* [1963] AC 386 as a classic example of non-insane automatism, but sleep-associated automatism may be caused by functional disorders of the mind and in *Burgess* [1991] 1 QB 92 the Court of Appeal held that any such condition which manifests itself in violence must be treated as one of insanity. Finally, the defence of automatism appears to be unavailable where D has some, albeit impaired, control over his actions (*Broome v Perkins* [1987] Crim LR 272; *A-G's Ref (No. 2 of 1992)* [1994] QB 91).

The Burden of Proof

Where the defence raise a defence of non-insane automatism, this must be disproved by the prosecution (in contrast to a defence of insanity, which must be proved by the defence) but there is always an evidential burden on the defence, who must produce some evidence of automatism before the prosecution can be required to address it (*Hill v Baxter* [1958] 1 QB 277; *Bratty v A-G for Northern Ireland* [1963] AC 386). See further, **F3.32**. **A1.8**

Situational Liability

It may be that voluntary conduct need not always be proved in cases where D is charged with a strict liability offence in which the *actus reus* takes the form not of a prohibited act or omission but of a prohibited state of affairs. Authority for this proposition can be found in *Larsonneur* (1933) 24 Cr App R 74 and *Winzar v Chief Constable of Kent* (1983) *The Times*, 28 March 1983. In the former case, L, a French citizen, visited the UK for the purpose of entering into a marriage of convenience. The police prevented this marriage and an order was served on her requiring her to leave and not re-enter the country. Instead of returning to France, L travelled to Ireland, whence she was deported in the custody of the Irish police, and handed over to the British police in Holyhead. They arrested her under the Aliens Order 1920 for 'being found in the United Kingdom' in breach of the original order excluding her. It was argued on L's behalf that she had returned to the UK only involuntarily, under physical compulsion, but the Court of Criminal Appeal held that the circumstances under which she was returned were 'perfectly immaterial'. All that mattered was that she was found in the UK on the occasion in question. Whether this reasoning would be followed today is open to question, and it is likely that any prosecution based on such facts would now be stayed as an abuse of process (see **D3.54**). **A1.9**

Somewhat different considerations arguably applied in *Winzar*, where the charge was one of being 'found drunk on a highway', contrary to the Licensing Act 1872, s. 12. W had originally been found drunk in a hospital and asked to leave. When he failed to do so, police officers removed him to their patrol car, which was parked on the highway outside, and then charged him with the offence in question. Upholding the conviction, Goff LJ pointed out that a distinction would otherwise have to be drawn between the drunk who leaves a restaurant when asked to do so and the drunk who is forcibly ejected after refusing to leave. If both are arrested in the street shortly afterwards, it would be wrong for the courts to regard the former as guilty and the latter as not. It is submitted, however, that the position must be different if the police were to drag a person from his own bed and into the street before charging him with being found drunk on a highway; that would undoubtedly involve an abuse of process.

OMISSION TO ACT

A1.10 Most criminal offences require the defendant to carry out some positive act before liability can be imposed. There can ordinarily be no liability for failure (or omission) to act, unless the law specifically imposes such a duty upon a particular person. The general rule is illustrated by this example from Stephen's *Digest of the Criminal Law* (3rd ed., 1887):

> A sees B drowning and is able to save him by holding out his hand. A abstains from doing so in order that B may be drowned, and B is drowned. A has committed no offence.

Although A may have failed to save B, he did no positive act to cause B's death. In some jurisdictions, A would always be under a duty to act in such a situation, at least where he does not have to put his own life in danger. Under English law, however, such a duty arises only in certain specific situations, and there are several offences (such as assaults or battery) which can be committed only through positive acts (see **A1.20**).

Where Statute Imposes a Specific Duty to Act

A1.11 There are many statutory provisions (mostly regulatory) which specifically impose duties on particular persons to act in particular ways and which impose criminal sanctions for failure or omission to act. A failure to keep proper accounts or business records, where these are required by law, may for example lead to criminal liability under the Companies Act 1985 or the Value Added Tax Act 1994. Road traffic law provides many further examples, including the offences of failing to stop after an accident and failing to provide a breath sample or a specimen for analysis.

Failure to Prevent or Report Criminal Conduct

A1.12 Failure to prevent or report the criminal activities of other persons is not ordinarily an offence. The offence of misprision of felony was abolished in 1967, but failure to report a known act of treason still amounts to misprision of treason and it also remains an offence at common law to refuse to assist a constable who calls for assistance in dealing with a breach of the peace (*Brown* (1841) Car & M 314; *Waugh* (1976) *The Times*, 1 October 1976). Modern legislation has added new offences of failure to disclose information relating to acts of terrorism or the funding of terrorism (see **B10.39** *et seq.*) and failure to disclose knowledge or suspicion of money laundering (see **B22.17**). As to the position of police officers who fail to act in accordance with their duty, see **A1.15**.

Duty Arising from Special Relationships

A1.13 **Care or Control of Children** If persons are in a close or special relationship to one another, the law may impose on one a duty to act on behalf of the other. Under the CYPA 1933, s. 1 (see **B2.114** *et seq.*), a parent or any other person over the age of 16 years who has responsibility for a child under that age may incur liability for any wilful neglect of that child that was likely to cause unnecessary suffering or injury to health. This specifically includes failure by a parent etc. to provide or obtain adequate food, clothing or medical care but could also include other forms of neglect, such as failure to rescue from drowning in circumstances of the kind described at **A1.10**. Neglect leading to death may lead to liability for manslaughter by gross negligence (*Downes* (1875) 13 Cox CC 111; *Lowe* [1973] QB 702). The wilful neglect of a child contrary to s. 1 of the 1933 Act does not automatically give rise to liability for manslaughter merely because death results (*Lowe*), but it may sometimes do so if, for example, there is proof of an intent to harm the child through such neglect. Indeed, a parent who deliberately starves a child to death may be guilty of murder (*Gibbins* (1918) 13 Cr App

R 134). As to the offence of causing or allowing the death of a child or vulnerable adult, see **B1.58**.

Assumption of Care for Another The CYPA 1933, s. 1, has no statutory counterpart in cases where the person in need of care or assistance is over the age of 16. In *Shepherd* (1862) 9 Cox CC 123 it was held that the parents of an 18-year-old and 'entirely emancipated' daughter were under no special duty to care for her. The common law nevertheless recognises that such a duty may arise in the context of a family relationship, as for example where a couple live together as husband and wife, or where a child continues to live with (and be dependent upon) his parents even after becoming an adult (see *Chattaway* (1922) 17 Cr App R 7). **A1.14**

If a person voluntarily undertakes to care for another who is unable to care for himself as a result of age, illness or other infirmity, he may thereby incur a duty to discharge that undertaking, at least until such time as he hands it over to someone else. In *Instan* [1893] 1 QB 450, D lived with her aunt, who was suddenly taken ill with gangrene in her leg and became unable either to feed herself or to call for help. D did not give her any food, nor did she call for medical help, even though she remained in the house and continued to eat her aunt's food. She was convicted of manslaughter. The principle laid down in *Instan* was applied and extended in *Stone* [1977] QB 354. Stone's sister, Fanny, came to live with him and his mistress, Dobinson. Fanny was suffering from anorexia, but was initially able to look after herself. Gradually, however, her condition deteriorated, until she became bed-ridden. She needed medical help, but none was summoned and she eventually died in squalor, covered in bed sores and filth. Stone and Dobinson were each convicted of her manslaughter and the Court of Appeal upheld their convictions. Because they had taken Fanny into their home, they had assumed a duty of care for her and had been grossly negligent in the performance of that duty. The fact that Fanny was Stone's sister was merely incidental to this.

Official, Contractual or Public Duties A person may in some cases incur criminal liability through failure to discharge his official duties or contractual obligations. A typical example is provided by *Pittwood* (1902) 19 TLR 37, in which P was employed to operate a level-crossing on a railway but omitted to close the crossing gates when a train was signalled. A cart was crossing the railway through the open gates when the train struck it and killed one of the carters. P was convicted of gross negligence manslaughter. In one sense this was based on his breach of contractual duty, but the victim was not, of course, a party to the contract, and P's liability can more accurately be based on the breach of a duty of care to users of the crossing, which his employers paid him to discharge, and on which the users of the crossing relied. In the absence of such a duty, it is doubtful whether any criminal liability could have arisen, whatever his contractual position with his employers (cf. *Smith* (1869) 11 Cox CC 210). **A1.15**

Neglect of duty by a police officer was examined by the Court of Appeal in *Dytham* [1979] QB 722. D, whilst on duty, stood aside and watched as a man was beaten to death outside a nightclub. He then left the scene, without calling for assistance or summoning an ambulance. For this, he was convicted of the common-law offence of wilful misconduct in public office. Lord Widgery CJ said (at p. 727):

> The allegation was not one of mere non-feasance, but of deliberate failure and wilful neglect. This involves an element of culpability which is not restricted to corruption or dishonesty, but which must be of such a degree that the misconduct impugned is calculated to injure the public interest so as to call for condemnation and punishment.

Although D was not charged with manslaughter, it is submitted that a conviction for manslaughter might be possible on such facts, if it were proved that the accused's inaction was a factor contributing to the death of the deceased. It was not clear in *Dytham* that D could have saved the deceased even if he had tried to do so.

See also *A-G's Ref (No. 3 of 2003)* [2005] 1 QB 73.

Duty to Avert a Danger of One's Own Making

A1.16 If a person creates a dangerous situation through his own fault, he may be under a duty to take reasonable steps to avert that danger, and may therefore incur criminal liability for failing to do so. In *Miller* [1983] 2 AC 161, M was 'sleeping rough' in a building, and fell asleep on his mattress while smoking a cigarette. When he awoke, he saw that his mattress was smouldering but, instead of calling for help, he simply moved into another room, thereby allowing the fire to flare up and spread. He was convicted of arson, not for starting the fire but for failing to do anything about it. Lord Diplock said (at p. 176):

> . . . I see no rational ground for excluding from conduct capable of giving rise to criminal liability, conduct which consists of failing to take measures that lie within one's power to counteract a danger that one has oneself created, if at the time of such conduct one's state of mind is such as constitutes a necessary ingredient of the offence.

In *Khan* [1998] Crim LR 830, the Court of Appeal considered the *Miller* principle in the context of manslaughter. The appellants had supplied a girl with heroin on which she accidentally overdosed, and then left her to die. It was held that the trial judge should first have ruled on whether there was evidence on which the jury could find that a duty of care (and thus a duty to act) had arisen. He should then have directed the jury to decide whether that duty had been breached. See also **B1.55**.

Failure to Provide Medical Treatment

A1.17 **Refusal of Consent to Treatment** Doctors and hospital authorities have a duty to provide medical care for their patients, and an omission to discharge that duty may sometimes involve criminal liability (e.g., for manslaughter or, in the case of a patient under 16, for wilful neglect under the CYPA 1933, s. 1), although this duty may be terminated if the patient refuses to accept medical treatment. If, for example, an adult hospital patient refuses his consent to a life-saving amputation, the medical staff, far from being under a duty to provide that treatment, would ordinarily be acting unlawfully if they ignored his wishes (*Re C (Adult: Refusal of Treatment)* [1994] 1 WLR 290; *Re W (Adult: Refusal of Treatment)* [2002] All ER (D) 223 (April).

Refusal of consent is not always decisive in such cases. Where minors are concerned, the High Court may exercise its wardship jurisdiction so as to override parental refusal of consent (*Re B (A Minor) (Wardship: Medical Treatment)* [1981] 1 WLR 1421) or refusal of consent by the minor himself (*Re W (A Minor) (Medical Treatment: Court's Jurisdiction)* [1993] Fam 64). Even in respect of adults, the court may sometimes hold that a refusal of consent to treatment is vitiated by lack of capacity or by undue influence (*Re T (Adult: Refusal of Treatment)* [1993] Fam 95) and doctors must then provide treatment, in accordance with that patient's best interests. In acute emergencies, where doctors have no time in which to appeal to the courts, they may sometimes need to act without consent. If, for example, Jehovah's Witnesses refuse to consent to the administration of an urgent blood transfusion to their child, doctors may need to act against their wishes, or risk prosecution (together with the parents) for manslaughter (cf. *Senior* [1899] 1 QB 283).

A1.18 **Withholding Treatment in the Best Interests of the Patient** If a patient is incapable of communicating his wishes, the doctor's normal duty is to do everything that he reasonably can to keep the patient alive. In certain circumstances, however, a doctor may be absolved of this duty, as the House of Lords recognised in *Airedale National Health Service Trust v Bland* [1993] AC 789. This case concerned a patient who had survived for three years in a 'persistent vegetative state' after suffering irreversible brain damage in the Hillsborough disaster. He continued to breathe normally, but was kept alive only by being fed through tubes. The NHS Trust sought a declaration from the courts that it might lawfully discontinue this artificial feeding and allow him to die with dignity and minimum distress. The House of Lords held that treatment could properly be withdrawn in such circumstances, because the best interests of the patient did not involve him being kept alive at all costs. Lord Goff nevertheless drew a fundamental distinction between acts and omissions in this context (at p. 865):

> . . . the law draws a crucial distinction between cases in which a doctor decides not to provide, or to continue to provide, for his patient treatment or care which could or might prolong his life, and those in which he decides, for example by administering a lethal drug, actively to bring his patient's life to an end . . . the former may be lawful, either because the doctor is giving effect to his patient's wishes . . . or even in certain circumstances in which . . . the patient is incapacitated from stating whether or not he gives his consent. But it is not lawful for a doctor to administer a drug to his patient to bring about his death, even though that course is prompted by a humanitarian desire to end his suffering, however great that suffering may be: see *Cox* (unreported) 18 September 1992 . . . So to act is to cross the Rubicon which runs between on the one hand the care of the living patient and on the other hand euthanasia.

See also *Frenchay Healthcare National Health Service Trust v S* [1994] 1 WLR 601. Similar issues can arise in respect of the very elderly or in respect of babies born with very severe mental or physical handicaps, especially where major (and possibly repeated) surgery would be needed to keep them alive (see *Re J* [1991] 2 WLR 140).

Practical and Financial Considerations Even apart from the question of whether treatment would be in the patient's best interests, it is recognised that financial or manpower constraints on the health service must come into consideration. It is clearly not practicable for the NHS to provide intensive forms of medical care (such as major surgery) to every patient, of whatever age, whose life might possibly be prolonged by it. **A1.19**

Offences for which Omissions cannot be the Basis of Liability

Some offences appear to be capable of commission only by positive acts. The offence of acting with intent to prevent the apprehension of an offender, contrary to the Criminal Law Act 1967, s. 4, is an example (see **B14.48** *et seq.*). Crimes of assault or battery arguably come into this category. This was at least the view of the Divisional Court in *Fagan v Metropolitan Police Commissioner* [1969] 1 QB 439 (see **A1.5**) although F's conviction was upheld on the basis that his conduct amounted to a continuing act, rather than an innocent act followed by a deliberate omission to rectify it. See further **B2.5**. **A1.20**

It has also been held that omissions cannot be the basis of liability for 'doing acts' likely to interfere with the peace and comfort of a residential occupier, contrary to the Protection from Eviction Act 1977 (*Ahmad* (1987) 84 Cr App R 64; and see **B13.15**) but the courts have not been consistent in interpreting references to 'acts' as necessarily excluding omissions. In *Speck* [1977] 2 All ER 859, for example, it was held that an omission could amount to an 'act' of gross indecency with a child, contrary to the Indecency with Children Act 1960, s. 1 (now repealed). See also *Yuthiwattana* (1984) 80 Cr App R 55, in which it was held that a landlord's omission to replace a lost key could be an 'act' of harassment against a tenant.

CAUSATION

Introduction

Causation issues appear to feature most frequently in homicide cases, but they can arise in respect of any 'result crime' (see, for example, **B5.10**, concerning causation issues in the context of deception offences under the Theft Acts). In order to establish whether a defendant can be guilty of a given result crime, one must first establish a factual link between his conduct and the result he is alleged to have caused. Once this has been established, a second and more difficult question must be considered, namely whether that conduct was a sufficient cause in law. This is sometimes called the question of 'imputability' or 'legal **A1.21** causation'. It involves issues of value-judgment and the allocation of responsibility for what has occurred.

Factual Causation

A1.22 The importance of proving factual causation is illustrated by *White* [1910] 2 KB 124. W put potassium cyanide in his mother's bedtime drink. When she was found dead the next morning, he was charged with her murder, but it was eventually established that his mother had consumed very little of the poison. She had died, coincidentally, of natural causes. W's conduct had not in any sense contributed to this. He was therefore guilty only of attempting to murder her.

It may also be necessary to prove a link between the proscribed result and a particular aspect of the defendant's conduct, such as his negligence. In *Dalloway* (1847) 2 Cox CC 273, D was charged with manslaughter after his cart had struck and killed a girl who ran out in front of him. D had not been holding the horse's reins at the time, but Erle J directed the jury that they could convict D of manslaughter only if they were satisfied that D could have avoided the accident had he been holding the reins correctly.

Factual causation is sometimes referred to as 'but for' (or *sine qua non*) causation, because it can be established only where the alleged result would not have occurred, or would not have occurred at the time or in the way it did, 'but for' the defendant's act or culpable omission. The only qualification to this basic rule involves cases of complicity or joint venture, under which a defendant may incur liability for encouraging or assisting the principal offender, even where it is proved that his conduct made no difference to the outcome. Procuring appears to be the only form of secondary participation that requires a causal link between the participation and the crime. See A5.1.

Legal or Imputable Causation

A1.23 Legal causation is a narrower and more subjective concept than factual causation. Not every cause in fact is a cause in law. To be so, it must be adjudged an 'operating and substantial' cause of the consequence in issue (*Smith* [1959] 2 QB 35) albeit that it does not have to be the only or even the principal such cause. The isolation of a legal cause from amongst a possible multitude of factual causes is a process involving subjective common sense rather than objectively measurable criteria, but when seeking to apportion possible criminal responsibility in this way, one must in practice look for some kind of abnormal and culpable behaviour. The logic behind such reasoning is explained by Hart and Honore, *Causation in the Law* (2nd ed., 1985):

> The notion that a cause is essentially something which interferes with or intervenes in the course of events which would normally take place, is central to our common-sense concept of cause . . . In distinguishing between causes and conditions, two contrasts are of prime importance. These are the contrasts between what is abnormal and what is normal in relation to any given thing or subject-matter, and between a free deliberate human action and all other conditions . . .
>
> In the case of a building destroyed by fire, 'mere conditions' will be factors such as the oxygen in the air, the presence of combustible material or the dryness of the building . . . which are present alike both . . . where such accidents occur and . . . where they do not . . . Such factors do not 'make the difference' between disaster and normal functioning, as . . . the dropping of a lighted cigarette does. . . .

Multiple Causes and Multiple Blame

A1.24 A defendant may be guilty of causing something to happen even if his conduct was not the only legal cause of it and even his conduct could not, on its own, have sufficed to make it happen (*Warburton* [2006] EWCA Crim 627). In *Hennigan* [1971] 3 All ER 133, H argued that he was not guilty of causing death by dangerous driving, because another driver was more to blame than him. The Court of Appeal replied that, as long as H's contribution was substantial, he could be held accountable. Without purporting to lay down any precise limits, the court suggested that, even if just 20 per cent of the blame could be attributed to H, that would suffice. *Hennigan* was followed in *Notman* [1994] Crim LR 518, where it was stated that anything more than a *de minimis* contribution could suffice. See also *Environment Agency v Empress Car Co. (Abertillery) Ltd* [1999] AC 22 (see **A1.28**).

Indirect Causation

Although legal causation must be 'operative and substantial', it need not necessarily be a direct cause of the proscribed result. In *McKechnie* (1992) 94 Cr App R 51, M inflicted serious head injuries on V. These were not in themselves fatal, but they prevented doctors from operating on V's duodenal ulcer, and V died when the ulcer burst. M was held to have caused his death. Not all indirect causes will be sufficiently proximate to the result; questions of fact and degree may be crucial, and it is therefore impossible to formulate any universal rule in such cases. Indirect causation may also be the basis of liability in cases involving crimes other than homicide. See for example *Roberts* (1971) 56 Cr App R 95 (see **A1.30**) and *Miller* (1992) 95 Cr App R 421 (see **B5.10**). **A1.25**

The 'Eggshell Skull' Rule

In criminal cases, as in tort, D must ordinarily take his victim as he finds him. If, for example, the victim of his assault is unusually vulnerable to physical injury as a result of an existing medical condition or old age, D must accept liability for any unusually serious consequences which result. In *Hayward* (1908) 21 Cox CC 692, H was seen to chase his wife into the road, threatening her with violence. She then collapsed and died as a result of a long-standing heart condition and H was held liable for her manslaughter. This principle was extended in *Blaue* [1975] 1 WLR 1411. B stabbed a woman. A blood transfusion would have saved her life, but she was a Jehovah's witness and refused to accept one. B was convicted of her manslaughter (on grounds of diminished responsibility) and this verdict was upheld by the Court of Appeal. Lawton LJ said at p. 1415): **A1.26**

> It has long been the policy of the law that those who use violence on other people must take their victims as they find them. This in our judgment means the whole man, not just the physical man. It does not lie in the mouth of the assailant to say that the victim's religious beliefs which inhibited him from accepting certain kinds of treatment were unreasonable.

One possible qualification to this general rule may need to be noted. Where the victim of a crime dies of heart failure etc., resulting from stress or fright, the charge is likely to be one of manslaughter, and it would then have to be proved that D's unlawful conduct was obviously dangerous, in the sense of being likely to cause some kind of injury. Where blows are struck, this is unlikely to be a problem, but what of cases in which the victim proved unusually vulnerable to injury caused by fear or stress? In *Dawson* (1985) 81 Cr App R 150 the Court of Appeal quashed D's conviction for the manslaughter of V, a 60-year-old petrol station attendant, who had died of a heart attack after being threatened with a replica gun. The court held that the trial judge had misdirected the jury by (*inter alia*) inviting them to take account of V's heart condition when deciding whether D's conduct had been obviously dangerous. D could not in fact have known of V's heart condition at the time. At first sight, *Dawson* may seem inconsistent with the eggshell skull rule, but it is probably wrong to regard it as a causation case at all. It merely decides that it was unfair to judge the dangerousness of D's conduct as if V's heart defect was already obvious to everyone concerned. It is submitted that the jury should instead have been directed to consider whether the act of threatening an elderly man (of unknown health) with a replica gun involved an obvious danger of shock-induced injury. The answer to that question would surely have been 'yes', and the eggshell skull rule could then have been applied. See also *Watson* [1989] 1 WLR 684, discussed at **B1.49**, and *Carey* [2006] EWCA Crim 604.

NOVUS ACTUS INTERVENIENS

Introduction

A1.27 A defendant will not be regarded as having caused the consequence for which it is sought to make him liable if there was a *novus actus interveniens* (or new intervening act) sufficient to break the chain of causation between his original action and the consequence in question. Although his original act may remain a factual cause, but for which the consequence would never have occurred, the intervening act may supplant it as the imputable or legal cause for the purpose of criminal liability. This intervening act may be the act of a third party, an act of the victim or an unforeseeable natural event, sometimes called an 'act of God'. These three variants will be considered in turn, but one general point may be made at the outset: no such intervening act can break the chain of causation if it merely complements or aggravates the ongoing effects of the defendant's initial conduct. Suppose, for example, that D attacks V, inflicting grave injuries, and that V later suffers further injuries, caused by his own foolishness, or by E's misconduct, or by some natural disaster. If V eventually dies of his *cumulative* injuries, there can be no question of the chain of causation being broken. The chain of causation can be broken only where the effect of the intervening act is so overwhelming that any initial injuries are relegated to the status of mere historical background. The detailed application of this principle will be explored in the specific contexts within which it may arise, but the basic principle is the same in each case.

If the aggravation of injuries cannot break the chain of causation, then *a fortiori* an omission to treat those initial injuries cannot do so, even if such neglect results in relatively minor injuries becoming fatal (*Holland* (1841) 2 Mood & R 351). As Lawton LJ said in *Blaue* [1975] 1 WLR 1411, where V refused a life-saving blood transfusion on religious grounds:

> The question for decision is what caused [V's] death. The answer is the stab wound. The fact that [V] refused to stop this end coming about did not break the causal connection between the act and death.

It can make no difference whether the omission is that of the victim (as in *Blaue*) or of a third party, such as a doctor. It may even be the result of an unforeseen natural event, such as a flood which prevents medical assistance from reaching the victim.

Acts of Third Parties

A1.28 **Deliberate and Informed Interventions** The subsequent intervention of a third party, other than one acting in concert with the accused (see *Kennedy (No. 2)* [2005] 1 WLR 2159) will ordinarily break the chain of causation if, but only if, it is free, deliberate and informed, and provides the immediate cause of the event in question (*Pagett* (1983) 76 Cr App R 279; *Latif* [1996] 1 WLR 104). Another way of stating this principle is that, 'voluntary conduct acts as a barrier in any causal enquiry in criminal law; by and large, D's voluntary conduct will usually be regarded as the cause of an act or omission if it was the last human conduct before the result' (Ashworth, *Principles of Criminal Law*, 4th ed., p. 127).

In *Latif*, L and S were involved in a plan to smuggle heroin into Britain. The heroin was delivered by S to a supposed accomplice in Pakistan, who was in fact an undercover operative of the U.S. Drug Enforcement Agency. It was then flown into Britain by a British customs officer, technically without lawful authority, whilst L and S were lured to a meeting in London, where they were arrested. It was held that the importation by the customs officer, whilst unlawful, was a deliberate third-party act for which S was not responsible, although S could still be convicted of being concerned in an *attempt* to import it, contrary to the Customs and Excise Management Act 1979, s. 170(2) (see **B17.21** *et seq.*). In contrast, the actions of an innocent agent, who is unaware of the true facts, cannot break the chain of causation. Had the case containing the heroin been forwarded by airline officials as lost luggage (as in *Jakeman* (1983) 76 Cr App R 223: see **A1.5**), S would have been held responsible for their actions.

In *Pagett*, P forcibly used his pregnant girlfriend, V, as a 'human shield' in a shoot-out with police officers. V was killed by bullets from officers returning his fire. He was convicted of her manslaughter. The Court of Appeal reasoned that the officers had acted 'involuntarily' in taking reasonable measures for the purpose of self-preservation and in the performance of their legal duty to apprehend P, and there was of course no suggestion that they shot V deliberately. Whether the police indeed acted 'reasonably' may be open to question; but this would make no difference to the outcome. Even if the police officers were at fault, their conduct was not free, deliberate and informed. P created a situation in which V's life was inevitably endangered, and what happened was a natural and foreseeable consequence of that behaviour.

In a controversial ruling that is difficult to reconcile with *Latif*, the House of Lords held in *Environment Agency v Empress Car Co. (Abertillery) Ltd* [1999] AC 22 that the operator of an installation from which diesel fuel escaped into a watercourse could be convicted of 'causing' that pollution, contrary to the Water Resources Act 1991, s. 85(1), even though the immediate cause of the disaster was an act of vandalism by an unknown third party, who had opened the tap on a fuel storage tank during the night. Significantly, the defendants had no measures in place to prevent such vandalism, or to restrict the subsequent escape of any fuel leaking from the tap. Lord Hoffmann reasoned that, 'there may be different answers to questions about causation when attributing responsibility to different people under different rules' or even 'when attributing responsibility to different people under the same rule'. Looking at the policy behind the provision in question, he continued:

> Strict liability is imposed in the interests of protecting controlled waters from pollution. . . . Clearly, therefore, the fact that a deliberate act of a third party, caused the pollution does not in itself mean that the defendants' creation of a situation in which the third party could so act did not also cause the pollution for the purposes of section 85(1).

Lord Hoffmann added that it remained necessary to consider whether the third party's act was a 'normal fact of life or something extraordinary':

> If it was in the general run of things a matter of ordinary occurrence, it will not negative the causal effect of the defendant's acts, even if it was not foreseeable that it would happen to that particular defendant or take that particular form. . . . The distinction between ordinary and extraordinary is one of fact and degree to which the [court] must apply common sense and knowledge of what happens in the area.

There is some authority to suggest that the *Empress* principle may be one of general application. In *Finlay* [2003] EWCA Crim 3868, it was applied by the Court of Appeal in the context of constructive manslaughter, when Buxton LJ held that a drug abuser who prepared a syringe of heroin for self-injection by a fellow abuser could be regarded as 'causing' the injection, which proved fatal. This, however, appears to have been doubted in *Kennedy (No. 2)* (see **A1.30**), in which Lord Woolf CJ preferred to view *Empress* as dependent on its own particular context. With respect, this may be the only way of reconciling *Empress* with *Latif*. The defendants in *Empress* had a duty to prevent pollution of the kind that occurred, and this arguably included (if only by implication) a duty to adopt reasonable safeguards against commonplace acts of vandalism. See also *National Rivers Authority v Yorkshire Water Services Ltd* [1995] 1 AC 444.

Medical Intervention It is foreseeable that the victim of an attack or accident may require medical treatment, but it is also foreseeable that his injuries may be misdiagnosed or that treatment may not be performed correctly. This is one reason why incorrect medical treatment is hardly ever categorised by the courts as amounting to a *novus actus interveniens*. An **A1.29**

equally valid reason, in many cases, is that failure to provide proper treatment for an initial injury rarely amounts to an independent cause of death or injury: it is far more likely that such failure will merely aggravate the original injury, or that it will allow the original injury to take its natural course. In particular, the 'switching off' of a life support system, even if wrongful, will never break the chain of causation flowing from the original injury (see *Malcherek* [1981] 1 WLR 690). Even where incorrect treatment leads to death or serious injury, it will only break the chain of causation if it is (a) unforeseeably bad, and (b) the sole significant cause of the death (or more serious injury) with which the accused is charged.

An exceptional case in which palpably wrong medical treatment was held to have broken the chain of causation was *Jordan* (1956) 40 Cr App R 152. J stabbed B, who was taken to hospital, where he died. J was initially convicted of his murder, but on appeal new evidence was admitted. This showed that at the time of B's death his wound had almost totally healed and that he had died as a result of a mix-up in which he was given antibiotics to which he had already proved highly allergic. The Court of Criminal Appeal concluded that, if the jury had heard this new evidence, they would have concluded that it was the medical treatment which had caused death and not the stab wound.

Smith [1959] 2 QB 35 is clearly distinguishable from *Jordan*. S stabbed his fellow soldier, C, with a bayonet during a barrack brawl. Other soldiers carried C to the camp medical centre, dropping him twice on the way. An overworked army doctor failed to notice that one of C's lungs had been pierced and the treatment given to him was described at the trial as 'thoroughly bad . . . it might well have affected his chances of recovery'. This did not however break the chain of causation. According to the Courts-Martial Appeals Court:

> If at the time of death the original wound is still an operating cause and a substantial cause, then the death can properly be said to be the result of the wound, albeit that some other cause of death is also operating. Only if it can be said that the original wounding is merely the setting in which another cause operates can it be said that the death did not result from the wound. Putting it another way, only if the second cause is so overwhelming as to make the original wound merely part of the history can it be said that the death does not flow from the wound.

C's death was therefore a case of death by multiple causes, and the stab wound was one of those causes. In contrast, the wound inflicted on B in *Jordan* had largely healed, and so the hospital treatment was in effect the sole cause of B's death. Furthermore, the mistreatment was so bizarre as to be unforeseeable. Had B died as a result of the first routine dose of antibiotics, J's murder conviction would almost certainly have been upheld. This is apparent from the later case of *Cheshire* [1991] 1 WLR 844, in which C shot V, who later died as a result of unfortunate medical complications arising from an tracheotomy he had undergone as part of his emergency treatment. The gunshot wounds had actually healed at the time of death, but the Court of Appeal upheld C's conviction on the grounds that the complications were still a natural consequence of his acts. After careful consideration of existing authorities, including *Jordan, Smith* and *Malcherek*, Beldam LJ concluded (at pp. 851–2):

> . . . when the victim of a criminal act is treated for wounds or injuries by a doctor or other medical staff attempting to repair the harm done, it will only be in the most extraordinary and unusual case that such treatment can be said to be so independent of the acts of the defendant that it could be regarded in law as a cause of the victim's death to the exclusion of the defendant's acts . . .
>
> Even though negligence in the treatment of the victim was the immediate cause of his death, the jury should not regard it as excluding the responsibility of the accused unless the negligent treatment was so independent of his acts, and in itself so potent in causing death, that they regard the contribution made by his acts as insignificant.

Cheshire was followed by the Court of Appeal in *Mellor* [1996] 2 Cr App R 245; see also *Gowans* [2003] EWCA Crim 3935.

Acts of the Victim

A1.30 In many cases, the *actus reus* of a crime is completed, not by an act of the offender, but by an act of his victim as where the victim of a criminal deception is tricked into making a payment into the deceiver's account. Another is where V injures himself in a fall whilst attempting to escape from an attack by D: the latter may be regarded as having caused that injury. In *Roberts* (1971) 56 Cr App R 95, R was convicted of an assault causing actual bodily harm to a young woman who was injured jumping from his moving car after he had assaulted her in that car. See also *DPP v Daley* [1980] AC 237, *Mackie* (1973) 57 Cr App R 453 and *Corbett* [1996] Crim LR 594. A clear direction on causation is essential in such cases. In *Williams* [1992] 1 WLR 380, it was held that the question is whether V's reaction was 'within a range of responses which might be anticipated from a victim in his situation', or whether it was 'so daft as to make it his own voluntary act which amounted to a *novus actus interveniens*'. The jury should not, in this context, be invited to make any allowance for D's youth or inexperience (*Marjoram* [2000] Crim LR 372). D's inability to foresee V's reaction may be relevant to the question of *mens rea*, but as far as causation is concerned, the only subjective element relates to V. As Stuart-Smith LJ pointed out in *Williams*, the jury must be directed 'to bear in mind any particular characteristic of the victim and the fact that, in the agony of the moment, a victim may act without thought and deliberation'.

Conversely, D cannot ordinarily be held responsible for 'causing' the voluntary and deliberate acts of V, merely because they were foreseeable responses to his own actions. The supplier of a controlled drug does not ordinarily 'cause' his client to take or ingest that drug, even if such conduct is entirely foreseeable and expected (see *Dalby* [1982] 1 WLR 425 and *Armstrong* [1989] Crim LR 149). The distinction between such cases and cases such as *Roberts* is that the drug supplier does not force his customers to do anything. They exercise informed free will and harm themselves by their own voluntary acts.

This is not to suggest that a drug dealer can never be guilty of manslaughter if his customer dies after taking the drugs supplied. There are at least two ways in which such liability might arise. The first is where D supplies contaminated drugs, or supplies a drug such as heroin to a child, who is unable to make an informed decision concerning the dangers involved. *Khan* [1998] Crim LR 830 should not be seen as authority to the contrary, even though the appellants' convictions were quashed in that particular case (because of a misdirection as to the duty of care).

More controversially the Court of Appeal ruled in *Rogers* [2003] 1 WLR 1374 and later in *Kennedy (No. 2)* [2005] 1 WLR 2159 that D may be guilty of manslaughter on the basis of joint enterprise if he and the deceased were 'jointly engaged' in the preparation and administration of the drug in question. As Lord Woolf CJ explained in *Kennedy:*

> To convict, the jury had to be satisfied that, when the heroin was handed to the deceased 'for immediate injection', he and the deceased were both engaged in the one activity of administering the heroin. These were not necessarily to be regarded as two separate activities; and the question that remains is whether the jury were satisfied that this was the situation. If the jury were satisfied of this then the appellant was responsible for taking the action in concert with the deceased to enable the deceased to inject himself with the syringe of heroin which had been made ready for his immediate use.

In *Rogers* the appellant had not merely procured the drugs or prepared the syringe: he had actively assisted his friend to inject the drugs by applying a tourniquet to bring up the vein at the crucial moment. On that basis, the court held that he was 'jointly responsible' for the act of injection, which was a criminal and dangerous act by virtue of the OAPA 1861, s. 23 (see **B2.66**). *Kennedy (No. 2)* extends this reasoning even to cases in which D takes no direct role in the acts of injecting, but merely prepares the drug for immediate injection by his fellow user. With respect, this obscures still further the already blurred distinction between a principal offender (who commits the crime and causes any relevant consequence) and the secondary party, who may assist, encourage or procure the commission of the offence, but does not himself commit it.

If, however, one accepts the joint venture argument, it is then relatively easy to support the court's approach to causation. In *Kennedy (No. 2)*, Lord Woolf CJ said (at [44]):

> The fact that a person who takes his own life does not commit an unlawful act by so doing, does not mean that a person who helps him to commit that act, if that helping act is contrary to section 23, does not commit an unlawful act. On the contrary, the helper does commit an unlawful act and could be charged under section 23 and convicted. He could also be convicted of manslaughter if the person he was helping dies in consequence. The requirement of an unlawful act is fulfilled. There should, in the appropriate case, be no difficulty in establishing foreseeability of risk. Nor should there be difficulty in establishing causation because the participants were acting in concert.

Acceptance of this joint venture argument does at least make it unnecessary in such cases to rely (as did the court in *Finlay* [2003] EWCA Crim 3868) on complex and unconvincing causation arguments derived from *Environment Agency v Empress Car Co. (Abertillery) Ltd* [1999] AC 22 (see **A1.28**). See further Ormerod and Forston, 'Drug Suppliers as Manslaughterers' [2005] Crim LR 819.

As explained at **A1.27**, a victim's aggravation or neglect of his injuries is unlikely to affect the chain of causation. Thus, in *Wall* (1802) 28 St Tr 51, W was found guilty of murdering a soldier, S, whom he had subjected to an illegal flogging, notwithstanding that S aggravated his condition by drinking spirits to ease the pain. A victim's subsequent suicide is (or at least should be) another matter. In *Dear* [1996] Crim LR 595, D appealed against his conviction for murder, arguing that V, whom he had repeatedly slashed with a knife, subsequently aggravated his own wounds so that they re-opened, with fatal results. D's conviction was nevertheless upheld.

More recently, the Court of Appeal in *Dhaliwal* [2006] 2 Cr App R 348 held that, where D inflicts physical and/or psychological abuse on V and thereby causes her some kind of recognised psychiatric illness (i.e. injury amounting in law to actual or grievous bodily harm for the purposes of the OAPA 1861, s. 47 or s. 20) his conduct may give rise to liability for manslaughter (i.e. constructive manslaughter) should this illness in turn cause V to commit suicide. Conditions such as post-traumatic stress disorder, battered wife syndrome, or reactive depression were identified as potential causes. In *Dhaliwal*, however, the prosecution could not prove that V had suffered any such pyschiatric injury. The infliction of mere psychological harm would not suffice.

The Court of Appeal left open the possibility that a manslaughter conviction might sometimes be supportable on a somewhat different basis, which had been suggested by the trial judge but disavowed by the prosecution, namely that: 'where a decision to commit suicide has been triggered by a physical assault which represents the culmination of a course of abusive conduct, it would be possible . . . to argue that the final assault played a significant part in causing the victim's death'.

Exceptional Natural Events

A1.31 An 'act of God' or other exceptional natural event may break the chain of causation leading from D's initial act, if it was the sole immediate cause of the consequence in question. Such an event must be 'of so powerful a nature that the conduct of the defendant was not a cause at all, but was merely a part of the surrounding circumstances' (*Southern Water Authority v Pegrum* [1989] Crim LR 442). If D attacks V and leaves him slowly dying of his injuries, the chain of causation may be broken if V is ultimately killed by a lightning bolt or a falling tree, rather than by the original injuries. In contrast, routine hazards, such as seasonal rain or cold winter nights, would not have such an effect (see *Alphacell Ltd v Woodward* [1972] AC 824). Such things are more readily foreseeable, but as Lord Hoffmann said in *Environment Agency v Empress Car Co. (Abertillery) Ltd* [1999] AC 22 (see **A1.28**):

> The true commonsense distinction is, in my view, between acts and events which, although not necessarily foreseeable in the particular case, are in the generality a normal and familiar fact of life, and acts or events which are abnormal and extraordinary. . . .
>
> . . . In the context of natural events, this distinction between normal and extraordinary events emerges in the decision of this House in *Alphacell Ltd v Woodward*.

Causation Issues and Alternative Explanations

The court or jury must of course be satisfied that D caused the event which is the subject of the charge against him. If possible innocent explanations cannot be disproved D must be acquitted. Difficulties may arise where the evidence suggests that D might have caused the *actus reus* in one of two or more different ways. The court or jury must be able to agree, not just on their verdict but on the basis for it, and must be directed accordingly. As Otton LJ explained in *Boreman* [2000] 1 All ER 307, 'where the two possible means by which the [offence] is effected comprise completely different acts, happening at different times . . . the jury ought to be unanimous on which act leads them to the decision to convict.' See also *Brown* (1983) 79 Cr App R 115 at **D17.44**. This does not mean, however, that a court or jury must always be able to agree on how exactly D committed the crime. It will suffice if they can agree that he must, one way or another, have committed it. Thus, if six jurors believe that D committed murder by killing V himself (or, if not, by hiring an assassin to kill for him) and the other six believe that he committed that same murder by hiring an assassin (or, if not, by killing V himself) they may still be able to convict D of that offence, because they can all agree that he was implicated in one way or another (*Giannetto* [1997] 1 Cr App R 1). Alternatively, the jury may have no idea as to how or when D committed the offence, and yet be able to agree that he must have done so, in one way or another *(A-G's Ref (No. 4 of 1980)* [1981] 1 WLR 705: see **A1.5**). In *Boreman*, however, V was beaten up by the appellants and later died in a fire at his home. There was some evidence that the beating had contributed to his death. There was also some evidence that the appellants had started the fire; but it did not follow that they must have killed V in one way or the other. It would not therefore suffice if some jurors thought they were guilty only on the first basis and some only on the second. **A1.32**

Section A2 *Mens Rea*

THE MENTAL ELEMENT GENERALLY

A2.1 In addition to proving that the accused satisfied the definition of the *actus reus* of the particular crime charged, the prosecution must also prove *mens rea*, i.e. that the accused had the necessary mental state or degree of fault at the relevant time. Lord Hailsham of St Marylebone said in *DPP v Morgan* [1976] AC 182 at p. 213: 'The beginning of wisdom in all the "*mens rea*" cases . . . is, as was pointed out by Stephen J in *Tolson* (1889) 23 QBD 168 at p. 185, that "*mens rea*" means a number of quite different things in relation to different crimes'. Thus one must turn to the definition of particular crimes to ascertain the precise *mens rea* required for specific offences. Nevertheless, there are a number of recurrent concepts (such as intention, recklessness etc.) which can usefully be examined here. There are some general points which can be made which ought to be borne in mind when looking at the definition of any individual crime. Some of these general points (such as the question of transferred *mens rea*) are best looked at after examining the meaning of particular concepts such as intention etc. but by way of introduction it is useful to point out the varied ways in which the individual concepts may be used.

Criminal offences vary in that some may require intention as the *mens rea*, some require only recklessness or some other state of mind and some are even satisfied by negligence. The variety in fact goes considerably further than this in that not only do different offences make use of different types of mental element, but also they utilise those elements in different ways. Compare, for example, assault occasioning actual bodily harm (OAPA 1861, s. 47) and criminal damage contrary to the Criminal Damage Act 1971, s. 1(1). Both are in one sense crimes of recklessness (see *Venna* [1976] QB 421 for assault, and the Criminal Damage Act 1971, s. 1(1), itself for criminal damage) but the *extent* to which they apply this concept is quite different. It has been confirmed that the mental element in assault occasioning actual bodily harm only extends to the element of 'assault' and not to the element of 'occasioning actual bodily harm'. In *Roberts* (1971) 56 Cr App Rep 95, the accused was liable even though he did not intend or foresee any actual bodily harm and this case was approved by the House of Lords in *Savage* [1992] 1 AC 699. In contrast, in relation to damaging any property belonging to another; the mental element applies not only to the elements of 'damaging' and 'property' but also to the element of 'belonging to another'. So in *Smith* [1974] QB 354, the accused was not guilty because he intended to damage only his own property, not property belonging to another. Thus the *range of application* of the concept of recklessness has been wider in relation to criminal damage than in relation to assault occasioning actual bodily harm.

This 'range of application' should be contrasted with the scope of meaning of recklessness which has recently undergone radical change. The House of Lords decision in *Metropolitan Police Commissioner v Caldwell* [1982] AC 341 *formerly* gave recklessness a so-called objective interpretation in relation to offences of criminal damage so as to include those who had failed to consider an obvious risk. In contrast, in relation to offences against the person, recklessness was understood in a more subjective sense to include only those who were actually aware of the relevant risk (see *Spratt* [1990] 1 WLR 1073). Thus recklessness differed in both its range (of application) and its scope (of meaning) as between assault and criminal damage. This led to further distinctions between the meaning of recklessness in the offence of criminal damage and its meaning in rape (see *S (Satnam)* (1983) 78 Cr App R 149), including the notion or attitude of 'couldn't care less', although the SOA 2003 has now redefined rape so as not to include recklessness as such.

Quite apart from the disappearance of recklessness from the definition of rape, much greater consistency of meaning as between criminal damage and offences against the person has now been restored (for the time being at least) by the decision of the House of Lords in *G* [2004] 1 AC 1034 which has overruled *Caldwell* and re-asserted a subjective test requiring actual awareness of risk in cases of criminal damage. However it is clear from both Lord Bingham's opinion at [28] and from Lord Rodger's at [69] that it is still perfectly *possible* that recklessness could have different meanings in relation to different offences.

Lord Rodger, in agreeing that the subjective meaning of recklessness was the correct one under the Criminal Damage Act 1971, nevertheless recognised that:

> . . . there is much to be said for the view that, if the law is to operate with the concept of recklessness, then it may properly treat as reckless the man who acts without even troubling to give his mind to a risk that would have been obvious to him if he had thought about it. This approach may be better suited to some offences than to others . . . the opposing view, that only advertent risk-taking should ever be included within the concept of recklessness in criminal law, seems to be based, at least in part, on the kind of thinking that the late Professor Hart demolished in his classic essay, 'Negligence, *Mens Rea* and Criminal Responsibility' (1961), reprinted in HLA Hart *Punishment and Responsibility* (1968), pp. 136–157.

It therefore remains true to say that, in considering the mental element of any particular crime one has to consider not only the *scope* (of meaning) of that element and its *range* (of application) but also the *context* of its use which may itself influence the scope of meaning to be adopted.

Finally, the position of the word expressly requiring the mental element may be significant as can be seen in the House of Lords decision in *Wings Ltd v Ellis* [1985] AC 272, which turned on the interpretation of the Trade Descriptions Act 1968, s. 14(1):

> It shall be an offence for any person in the course of any trade or business—
> (a) to make a statement which he knows to be false; or
> (b) recklessly to make a statement which is false.

The House was concerned with s. 14(1)(a) and held that the requirement of knowledge applied only to the element of the falsity of the statement and not to the act of making the statement in the first place. Thus Wings Ltd was convicted in relation to a statement in a brochure which was initially made innocently and which the company attempted to withdraw as soon as its falsity was realised. The statement was regarded as being made when a customer read it and booked a holiday and Wings Ltd was liable since by then the statement was known to the company to be false even though it was not known that the statement was being made. The decision is not beyond criticism but the contrast in wording between paras. (a) and (b) of s. 14(1) and the respective positioning of the words requiring *mens rea* help to explain the decision. The adverb 'recklessly' is right at the start of paragraph (b) so that it can naturally refer to both the act of making a statement and the requirement of its falsity whereas para. (a), instead of referring to 'knowingly making a false statement', which would be more consistent with para. (b), merely refers to making 'a statement which he knows to be false'. Thus the *range* of application of the concept of knowledge was restricted by the *position* of the word in the section.

Having made these preliminary remarks about the way in which *mens rea* concepts are utilised by Parliament and the courts, we can now turn to the more commonly found mental elements themselves and examine the scope of their meaning.

INTENTION

A2.2 'Intention' is a word that is usually used in relation to consequences. A person clearly intends a consequence if he wants that consequence to follow from his action. This is so whether the consequence is very likely or very unlikely to result. Thus an accused who shoots at another wanting to kill him, intends to kill whether the intended victim is 2 metres away and an easy target or whether he is 200 metres away and it would have taken an exceptionally good shot to hit him. In either case, even if the accused misses, he will be liable for a crime requiring intention to kill, such as attempted murder.

The meaning of 'intention' is not restricted to consequences which are wanted or desired (sometimes referred to as 'direct' intent) but includes consequences which an accused might not want to follow but which he knows are virtually certain to do so (sometimes referred to as 'oblique' or 'indirect' intent). At one point it seemed that there was support in the House of Lords for a very wide view of oblique intent, i.e. that it included a state of not wanting a consequence to occur while knowing that it was 'highly probable' or even just 'probable' or 'likely' (*Hyam v DPP* [1975] AC 55 and see also per Lord Diplock in *Lemon* [1979] AC 617 at p. 638). This was regarded as too wide by the Court of Appeal in *Mohan* [1976] QB 1 in relation to attempt and in *Belfon* [1976] 1 WLR 741 in relation to wounding with intent to cause grievous bodily harm under the OAPA 1861, s. 18. It seemed that intention might mean different things in different offences but much of the uncertainty appeared to have been resolved by the decisions of the House of Lords in *Moloney* [1985] AC 905 and *Hancock* [1986] AC 455, although further refinements have been added by another House of Lords case, *Woollin* [1999] AC 82.

The most important principles to emerge from *Moloney* were that (a) intention should have the same meaning throughout the criminal law (see per Lord Bridge of Harwich at p. 920F), although Lord Steyn appears to have cast doubt upon this in *Woollin*, and (b) the foresight of the probability of a consequence does not of itself amount to intention but may be evidence of it. Unfortunately the guidelines laid down in that case for directing a jury on this issue (essentially that the jury could, but would not be obliged to, infer that a person intended a consequence if he foresaw it as a 'natural' consequence of his action) were subsequently found by the House of Lords in *Hancock* to be 'unsafe and misleading'. Lord Scarman said ([1986] AC 455 at p. 473):

> [The guidelines] require a reference to probability. They also require an explanation that the greater the probability of a consequence the more likely it is that the consequence was foreseen and that if that consequence was foreseen the greater the probability is that that consequence was also intended. But juries also require to be reminded that the decision is theirs to be reached upon a consideration of all the evidence.

The result seemed to be that:

(a) Where there is clear evidence that the accused desired the consequence to occur, the question of whether the accused intended that consequence can be left to the jury without further elaboration.
(b) Where the accused may not have desired the consequence but may have foreseen it as a by-product of his action, a more detailed direction may be necessary.
(c) Such a direction would emphasise that 'the probability, however high, of a consequence is only a factor, though it may in some cases be a very significant factor, to be considered with all the other evidence in determining whether the accused intended to bring it about' (Lord Scarman in *Hancock* at p. 474).

The first two principles (paras. (a) and (b)) continue to apply following *Woollin*, whether the charge be murder or any other offence requiring intention. In the light of *Woollin*, para. (c) now seems potentially too broad, in relation to murder at least, since only foresight of a virtual certainty entitles a jury to find intention (in the absence of desire) on a murder charge (see further **B1.11** and **B1.12**). Given the statement of Lord Steyn in *Woollin* (at p. 96) that 'it does not follow that "intent" necessarily has precisely the same meaning in every context in the criminal law', it remains possible that lower levels of foresight could still be a sufficient basis for a legitimate inference in relation to other offences requiring intention. In either case, the effect of (c) seems to be that a discretion is conferred on the jury because the core notion of intention which they are inferring is left undefined (even after *Woollin*, in which Lord Steyn confirmed that 'the decision is for the jury upon a consideration of all the evidence in the case'). For more detail on intent in relation to murder, see **B1.11** and **B1.12**; in relation to wounding with intent to cause grievous bodily harm, see *Bowden* [1993] Crim LR 379, which reiterates that foresight of 'virtual certainty' or at least 'a very high degree of probability' is required.

RECKLESSNESS

Recklessness Generally

Essentially concerned with unjustified risk-taking, the precise meaning of the term 'recklessness' has been the subject of great controversy and will no doubt continue to be so. The reason for this is that recklessness has come to be the touchstone of criminal responsibility for a large number of criminal offences. For many offences, the precise boundaries of the concept of intention are not in themselves crucial as recklessness constitutes an alternative and sufficient *mens rea* and one which it is easier to prove. For example, under the Criminal Damage Act 1971, s. 1(1), a person has the requisite *mens rea* if he acts 'intending to destroy or damage any property or being reckless as to whether any property would be destroyed or damaged'. If an accused threw a stone which damaged X's window and is charged under s. 1(1), he may plausibly be able to say, for example, that he was aiming for the dog in front of the window and that he did not *intend* to damage the window. There would be little point here trying to argue that the accused realised that the probability was that he would miss the dog and break the window from which the jury should infer an intention to break the window. There would be a much greater chance of success in relying on recklessness which equally suffices for liability. The issue of foresight of probability as intention need only be explained in crimes such as murder or attempt where intention alone suffices for liability. **A2.3**

The relationship between intention and recklessness, and indeed the debate about the scope of recklessness itself, can be seen more clearly from the following list:

(a) Consequence desired: intention.
(b) Consequence foreseen as virtually certain: intention *may* be found.
(c) Consequence foreseen as probable: typically recklessness (subjective).
(d) Consequence foreseen as possible: typically recklessness (subjective).
(e) Consequence not foreseen but ought to have been: negligence (objective recklessness).
(f) Consequence even reasonable man would not foresee: strict liability.

The central case of intention is situation (a) although the jury may still find intention in situation (b) and possibly, although not in murder cases, even in (c). However, (b) and (c) are more appropriately and easily dealt with as recklessness where this will suffice for liability. Situation (d) is also capable of being within recklessness as is category (e). The difference between (d) and (e) essentially represents the distinction between the narrower subjective '*Cunningham*' recklessness (*Cunningham* [1957] 2 QB 396) and the wider objective '*Caldwell*' recklessness (*Metropolitan Police Commissioner v Caldwell* [1982] AC 341) favoured for two decades by the House of Lords but now rejected by them, for criminal damage at least, in *G* [2004] 1 AC 1034. Category (f), of course, is not a culpable state of mind and would not normally give rise to criminal responsibility except in relation to crimes of strict liability.

'Subjective' *Cunningham* Recklessness

A2.4 Following the decision of the House of Lords in *G* [2004] 1 AC 1034, this type of recklessness can perhaps now be referred to as 'standard' recklessness, but it has in the past often been referred to as *Cunningham* recklessness (*Cunningham* [1957] 2 QB 396).

It covers categories (b), (c) and (d) (most typically the latter two) in the list at **A2.3**. These states of mind, of course, equally qualified as recklessness under the *Caldwell* test (*Metropolitan Police Commissioner v Caldwell* [1982] AC 341), *Caldwell* merely adding category (e) to the scope of recklessness. The spread over categories (b), (c) and (d) emphasises the point that the degree of foresight of risk that constitutes subjective recklessness is not fixed but variable.

As Lord Bingham formulated it in *G* in relation to criminal damage, adopting the Law Commission's Draft Criminal Code (Law Com. No. 177):

> A person acts recklessly . . . with respect to—
> (i) a circumstance when he is aware of a risk that it exists or will exist;
> (ii) a result when he is aware of a risk that it will occur;
> and it is, in the circumstances known to him, unreasonable to take the risk.

The degree of foreseen risk which would make one reckless depends therefore on the reasonableness or otherwise of the risk. At one end of the scale, a surgeon operating on a critically ill patient may knowingly run a very high risk of his patient's death, but if the patient is even more likely to die if the operation is not attempted then it would be a reasonable risk to run and no one would describe the operation as reckless. There is a very strong justification which makes the operation reasonable. On the other hand, if one offers another a chocolate from a box containing 50, just one of which the offeror knows to contain arsenic, the offeror is clearly acting recklessly. The risk is a relatively low one (one in 50, or 2 per cent) but, since there is no justification for running the risk, it is an unreasonable one to take and the offeror is reckless. Thus in some circumstances, to run a very high risk may not be reckless and yet in others it may be reckless to run a relatively low risk. In the context of alleged criminal offences there will often be no plausible justification for running the risk (e.g., of wounding someone) and so often the foresight of *any* degree of risk, of the mere possibility of injury, may be sufficient. The greater the justification for running a risk, the higher the degree of *foreseen* risk which will be required to constitute recklessness.

Subjective Awareness of an Unreasonable Risk

A2.5 Following *G* [2004] 1 AC 1034, the emphasis is on the degree of risk that is actually foreseen by the accused or of which he is aware. It is to that extent that the test is subjective. The jury will perforce *normally* assess this by reference to what they themselves would have foreseen in the circumstances which is why in many cases there will be little difference in outcome whether they are directed to consider a test of what the accused actually appreciated or the alternative (under the previous test in *Metropolitan Police Commissioner v Caldwell* [1982] AC 341) of whether the risk would have been obvious to a reasonable person. Focussing on the actual awareness of the accused clearly may, however, make a difference where there is reason to suppose that the accused did not appreciate what the reasonable person would have appreciated. This is likely to be the case where the accused differs from the reasonable person in some relevant way, for example, because of age (the accused were 11 and 12 in *G*) or because of mental disorder (see *Stephenson* [1979] QB 695, one of a number of decisions which as a result of *G* must be regarded as rehabilitated, where the accused was incapable of appreciating the risk of lighting a small fire in a straw stack in order to keep warm). The list of situations where the jury will find a difference between the accused's appreciation of risk (or lack of it) and what the reasonable person would have realised is not closed. Any reason why the accused did not in fact appreciate the risk seems at first sight, in principle, to be admissible except for, it still seems clear, voluntary intoxication through drink or drugs — see Lord Bingham's reference in *G* at [32] to *Majewski* [1977] AC 443 (see **A3.10**).

On the other hand, as Lord Bingham stated in *G* at [39]:

> There is no reason to doubt the common sense which tribunals of fact bring to their task. In a contested case based on intention, the defendant rarely admits intending the injurious result in question, but the tribunal of fact will readily infer such an intention, in a proper case, from all the circumstances and probabilities and evidence of what the defendant did and said at the time. Similarly with recklessness: it is not to be supposed that the tribunal of fact will accept a defendant's assertion that he never thought of a certain risk when all the circumstances and probabilities and evidence of what he did and said at the time show that he did or must have done.

Whilst this may be true, the question of what the accused was actually aware of must be left to the jury and, if it is not, any conviction may be quashed as happened in *Briggs* [1977] 1 WLR 605, a pre-*Caldwell* case where the appellant claimed that it did not occur to him that he might damage the handle of another person's car which he was trying to forcibly open in order to move the car out of the way of his garage door. If the correct question is left to the jury, it may well be that a jury will not be sympathetic to a claim that an appellant, acting in bad temper or for some other unattractive motive, did not appreciate an obvious risk and will conclude that he was in fact aware of it. Furthermore, Lord Bingham in *G* seemed quite happy (at [14]) with the approach in *Parker* [1977] 1 WLR 600 whereby, when a defendant is fully aware of all the circumstances, including the degree of force he is using, closing one's mind to an obvious risk is regarded as equivalent to conscious awareness of the risk and:

> a man certainly cannot escape the consequences of his action in this particular set of circumstances by saying, 'I never directed my mind to the obvious consequences because I was in a self-induced state of temper.' (Geoffrey Lane LJ in *Parker* [1977] 1 WLR 600 at 604.)

One can explain this on the basis of the argument (referred to by Lord Bingham) that to close your mind to a risk you have first to realise that there is one (in which case it adds little to the requirement of awareness of risk) or alternatively on the basis that we all act in the light of a combination of explicit and implicit items of knowledge. I am aware in one sense (the implicit sense) that if I drive too fast I may cause an accident. I do not consciously think about this (at least most of the time) when driving as I am habituated to drive at a sensible speed. If I am late or angry or frustrated when driving, I may impulsively drive faster than is advisable. I may be aware of the risks in so doing but on occasions I may also truthfully be able to say I was so intent on getting to an appointment in time that the increased risk I ran did not consciously occur to me. But if I am aware of the speed I was doing, I do know (implicitly) of the increased risk even though my preoccupation with something else means I did not specifically think about it at the time. One can call this closing one's mind to the obvious or one can classify the case as one of implicit knowledge sufficient to satisfy a subjective test. In comparison, a child or mentally disordered person may lack even the implicit knowledge about the dangers of speed (or, as in *G*, about how fire can spread) and cannot in any sense be said to be aware of the risk. This was of no avail to the 'tipsy' defendant in *Booth v CPS* (2006) 170 JP 305, where the Divisional Court upheld a finding in effect that a pedestrian who steps out into the path of a car and is aware of the risk of a collision is implicitly aware of the risk of damaging the car. As Hallet LJ put it at [20] 'The magistrates were entitled to find . . . that if he was aware of the risk of a collision, inherent in that risk of a collision was not only the risk of personal injury but the risk of damage to property'.

Whatever the route to concluding that the accused is aware of a risk, which is the ultimate issue for the jury, even subjective recklessness then imposes an objective test of reasonableness as to whether it was reckless to run *that* risk (which is just one reason why labels of 'objective' or 'subjective' recklessness can be misleading or over simplistic). A very small risk may be unreasonable in many situations. For example, in *Chief Constable of Avon and Somerset Constabulary v Shimmen* (1986) 84 Cr App R 7 showing off one's martial arts skills to friends did not justify the small risk of which the accused was aware (despite his pride in his own skill) that he might misjudge matters and break the window he was shadow kicking. Nor would it avail the accused to say that personally he regarded the running of such a (low) risk to be justifiable or reasonable. The accused's awareness is only relevant as to the level of the risk, not as to its reasonableness. It is the court's assessment of reasonableness that counts (albeit looking at the level of risk perceived by the accused).

In many other situations however, running certain levels of risk are an inherent and accepted part of ordinary life. Driving a car carries a risk of damaging other vehicles but the degree of risk involved in driving with due care and attention is reasonable in the light of the overall balance as perceived in the current social consensus. Lighting a bonfire on Bonfire Night on one's own land inevitably carries *some* risk of fire spreading to adjoining land but, if reasonable precautions are taken so that the risk is sufficiently and suitably low, it would not be regarded as reckless to run that low risk of damage to another's property. But in the contexts in which many prosecutions are brought, there will be very little if any arguable justification for taking a risk (or for taking the degree of risk which was in fact taken) and the question will simply be whether the accused was aware of that risk.

'Objective' *Caldwell* Recklessness

A2.6 The *Caldwell* test of recklessness (*Metropolitan Police Commissioner v Caldwell* [1982] AC 341), now abandoned even for offences under the Criminal Damage Act 1971, was encapsulated in the following model direction given by Lord Diplock in *Caldwell* at p. 354:

> . . . a person charged with an offence under section 1(1) of the Criminal Damage Act 1971 is 'reckless as to whether any such property would be destroyed or damaged' if (1) he does an act which in fact creates an obvious risk that property will be destroyed or damaged and (2) when he does the act he either has not given any thought to the possibility of there being any such risk or has recognised that there was some risk involved and has nonetheless gone on to do it.

Although initially the same basic approach was simultaneously applied by the House of Lords decision in *Lawrence* [1982] AC 510 to the now defunct offence of causing death by reckless driving and thereafter for a time to manslaughter (see **B1.53**), the Criminal Damage Act 1971 was the last remaining arena in which the *Caldwell* test held any real sway. It is difficult to see now that there are any remaining offences of any significance to which this version of recklessness applies, whereby a person may be 'reckless' on the basis that he has failed to consider an obvious risk if he cannot be said to be aware of the risk (even in the sense explained above of closing his mind to a risk).

It would be dangerous however to write off entirely this 'objective' version of recklessness. In *G* [2004] 1 AC 1034 at [70], Lord Rodger recognised that the decision in *Caldwell* involved:

> [a] legitimate choice between two legal policies, I was initially doubtful whether it would be appropriate for the House to overrule it. . . . But, for the reasons that I have already indicated, I have come to share your lordships' view that we should indeed overrule *Caldwell* and set the law back on the track that Parliament originally intended it to follow. If Parliament now thinks it preferable for the 1971 Act to cover culpably inadvertent as well as advertent wrongdoers, it can so enact. The Law Commission recognised that, if codifying the law, Parliament might wish to adopt that approach: *A Criminal Code for England and Wales Vol 2 Commentary* (LC No. 177), paras. 8.21 and 17.6.

In *Caldwell* Lord Diplock took his wider view of recklessness encompassing both awareness of risk and failure to consider a risk because ([1982] AC 341 at p. 352):

> Neither state of mind seems to me to be less blameworthy than the other; but if the difference between the two constituted the distinction between what does and what does not in legal theory amount to a guilty state of mind for the purposes of a statutory offence of damage to property, it would not be a practicable distinction for use in a trial by jury.

The House of Lords in *G* has now taken the view that it is a practicable distinction. Questionable assertions by apparently culpable defendants that they were not aware of the risks inherent in their conduct will be left to the jury to resolve in the light of common sense inferences from the facts, aided perhaps by the response that closing one's mind to an obvious risk is equivalent to awareness of it. Judges will at least no longer have to tell juries to their own and the jury's obvious discomfort, as the trial judge was compelled to in *G*, that the accused can be guilty of an offence of recklessness where the risk is one that the accused would not have appreciated even if he had thought about it. This particular consequence of *Caldwell* was not explicitly spelled out in the decision itself but was, rightly or wrongly, regarded as implicit in it by the Divisional Court in *Elliot v C* [1983] 1 WLR 939. This was the aspect of *Caldwell* as interpreted that was most problematic — the rejection of the conditionally subjective test for determining whether a risk is obvious (i.e. the rejection of the idea that the risk had to be one which would have been obvious to the particular accused if he or she had actually stopped to think about it). Once that conditionally subjective test was rejected, it was not surprising that the law gradually withdrew from the *Caldwell* definition and that eventually the decision has been overruled in *G* even in relation to criminal damage. But, if the purely subjective approach to awareness of risk throws up its own problems (much will depend on how juries assess defences of 'it never occurred to me' and how problems of 'closing one's mind to the obvious' are dealt with), a modified form of *Caldwell* recklessness, where the risk must be one which the accused himself could have appreciated, may yet resurface at some time in the future, in relation to some offences at least. In truth there may be very little if any difference between a *Caldwell* test of recklessness moderated by a conditionally subjective test of 'obvious risk' and a 'subjective' awareness test of recklessness bolstered by a robust attitude to risks of which the accused is implicitly or subliminally aware or to which he may be regarded as having closed his mind. The idea that a purely subjective test of conscious awareness of risk at the time of acting can adequately deal with all the situations likely to arise has proved naïve in the past and a full reading of *G* reveals that the House of Lords is itself conscious of the risks of too simplistic an approach to complex issues.

MALICE

Many provisions of the OAPA 1861, notably ss. 18, 20, 23 and 24, define offences in terms of 'maliciously' performing an act and it is now well established that this word is not to be understood in the sense of 'wickedly' or 'with ill will' but as requiring either actual intention to cause the relevant harm or at least foresight of the risk of causing the particular type of harm. The classic formulation was given by the Court of Appeal in *Cunningham* [1957] 2 QB 396 where it was said: **A2.7**

> . . . malice must be taken . . . as requiring either (1) An actual intention to do the . . . harm . . .; or (2) recklessness as to whether such harm should occur or not (i.e., the accused has foreseen that the particular type of harm might be done and yet has gone on to take the risk of it).

The case of *W (A Minor) v Dolbey* (1983) 88 Cr App R 1 made it clear (as had Lord Diplock himself in *Metropolitan Police Commissioner v Caldwell* [1982] AC 341) that this meaning of malice 'as a term of art' was unaffected by the *Caldwell* definition of recklessness. In *W (A Minor) v Dolbey*, the magistrates had convicted, of malicious wounding, a juvenile who had fired at his friend an air rifle, which he believed not to be loaded. This was on the basis of

Caldwell recklessness (though arguably he was not even *Caldwell* reckless if he had consciously ruled out any risk of causing harm). The Divisional Court quashed the conviction since the juvenile did not foresee the risk of any harm to his friend. The Court of Appeal adopted a similar approach in quashing a conviction in *Morrison* (1988) 89 Cr App R 17, which was certainly not a case of ruling out the risk but of an accused not thinking about the risk to others in seeking to avoid arrest. The subjective meaning of malice was confirmed by the House of Lords in *Savage* [1992] 1 AC 699 (see **B2.28**). It is, however, sufficient for the accused to foresee that the harm 'might' or 'may' occur; it is not necessary that the accused foresees that it definitely would occur (*Rushworth* (1992) 95 Cr App R 252, and see more recently *DPP v A* [2001] Crim LR 140).

WILFULLY

A2.8 'Wilfully', which has some similarities with 'malice' since it dates from an earlier legislative vocabulary, should not be understood merely in its most obvious or literal sense of 'deliberately' or 'voluntarily'. It is now taken as a composite word to cover both intention and recklessness. Until recently, it arguably differed from malice in that it may not have been restricted to subjective recklessness but appeared to include *Caldwell* recklessness or something very similar to it. The leading case is *Sheppard* [1981] AC 394, which in many ways was the precursor of the decision in *Metropolitan Police Commissioner v Caldwell* [1982] AC 341. In *Sheppard*, Lord Diplock provided a model direction as follows:

> . . . on a charge of wilful neglect of a child under section 1 of the Children and Young Persons Act 1933 by failing to provide adequate medical aid, . . . the jury must be satisfied (1) that the child did in fact need medical aid at the time at which the parent is charged with failing to provide it (the *actus reus*) and (2) either that the parent was aware at that time that the child's health might be at risk if it were not provided with medical aid, or that the parent's unawareness of this fact was due to his not caring whether his child's health were at risk or not (the *mens rea*).

As Lord Diplock himself commented, this last state of mind 'imports the concept of recklessness which is a common concept in *mens rea* in the criminal law' and the model direction, though not identical, is remarkably similar in structure and effect to that subsequently laid down for recklessness in *Caldwell*.

It now seems likely however that the meaning of recklessness imported by the term wilful will be the same subjective one adopted in *G* [2004] 1 AC 1034 in preference to the *Caldwell* test. In *A-G's Ref (No. 3 of 2003)* [2005] QB 73, Pill LJ said in relation to the offence of misconduct in a public office (at [26] and [27]):

> Whether *Sheppard*, which was not cited in *Caldwell* and in which Lord Edmund-Davies did not, as in *Caldwell* a few months later, dissent, is consistent with *Cunningham* (not cited in *Sheppard*) and *G*, may be arguable, though, for present purposes, we greatly doubt whether there is any material difference. Lord Diplock is likely to have taken the view that the expression 'wilful neglect', in section 1 of the 1933 Act, required a subjective element not required in his view in *Caldwell* but, with the demise of *Caldwell*, the distinction is immaterial.
>
> . . . We do not accept the submission that *Sheppard* imposes a lower duty on the prosecution than does *G*. Indeed, we do not accept the submission that, in the present context, there is any material difference between them and, in our view, the approach to recklessness in *G* can be incorporated into a direction on wilfulness in relation to this offence.

Thus it would seem that wilfully now means intentionally or recklessly and the meaning of recklessness is the same subjective meaning which is discussed at **A2.4**. Any objective tendencies detectable in Lord Diplock's model direction in *Sheppard* can be regarded as having been discarded along with the rejection of his approach in *Caldwell*. The subjective aspect of the meaning of 'wilfully' can be seen to have been confirmed in *W* [2006] EWCA Crim 2723, although the case turned on knowledge rather than recklessness. Sir Igor Judge P (at [38]) quoted with approval Lord Keith's observation in *Sheppard* that '. . . a parent who has genuinely failed to appreciate that his child needs medical care, through personal inadequacy or stupidity or both, is not guilty'.

KNOWLEDGE

A2.9 'Knowledge' can be seen in many ways as playing the same role in relation to circumstances as intention plays in relation to consequences. One knows something if one is absolutely sure that it is so although, unlike intention, it is of no relevance whether one wants or desires the thing to be so. Since it is difficult ever to be absolutely certain of anything, it has to be accepted that a person who feels 'virtually certain' about something can equally be regarded as knowing it. See *Dunne* (1998) 162 JP 399 for confirmation of this approach. On the other hand, one may feel entirely sure and yet be proved wrong, in which case it is difficult to say that one 'knew'. For example, perjury involves making a statement in a judicial proceeding which, *inter alia*, one knows to be false. If the accused gave evidence which he felt absolutely sure was false but it turns out that he inadvertently told the truth, it cannot accurately be said that he 'knew' that his evidence was false. In fact, he can still be convicted of perjury since the offence also applies to statements which one does not believe to be true.

BELIEF

A2.10 The concept of belief could be interpreted as differing from knowledge merely in the respect adumbrated in A2.9, i.e. that beliefs can turn out to be mistaken whereas knowledge implies correctness of belief. The degree of certainty or conviction required to be experienced by the accused would on this view be the same for both belief and knowledge. This is almost, in effect, how belief has been interpreted in the context of handling stolen goods under the Theft Act 1968, s. 22, where the courts have stressed the need to distinguish belief from recklessness or suspicion and have held that it is not of itself sufficient that an accused believed it to be more probable than not that the goods were stolen. However, it has also been said that:

> Belief, of course, is something short of knowledge. It may be said to be the state of mind of a person who says to himself: 'I cannot say I know for certain that these goods are stolen, but there can be no other reasonable conclusion in the light of all the circumstances, in the light of all that I have heard and seen'. (Boreham J in *Hall* (1985) 81 Cr App R 260 at p. 264.)

The problem with this approach is that, even in the absence of the word 'belief', a court would no doubt hold that someone who felt that the only reasonable conclusion was that the goods were stolen, where the goods did indeed turn out to be stolen, could be said to know that fact. One is left therefore with the impression that the concept of belief adds little in this context to the requirement of knowledge.

Wilful blindness (deliberately shutting one's eyes to the truth) is sometimes said to be equivalent to knowledge (see per Lord Reid in *Warner v Metropolitan Police Commissioners* [1969] 2 AC 256 at p. 279G) but where an offence expressly requires knowledge or belief the better view seems to be that this may merely be regarded as evidence from which knowledge or belief may be inferred but should not be automatically equated with it (*Griffiths* (1974) 60 Cr App R 14).

NEGLIGENCE

A2.11 Some would exclude negligence from a discussion of *mens rea* on semantic grounds, i.e. on the basis that *mens rea* is concerned with states of mind and negligence is not a state of mind but is rather a failure to comply with the standards of the reasonable man. However, *mens rea* is here being used in the wider sense of the fault element required for liability, and although the required fault is, at least as regards the more serious offences, usually defined in terms of a state of mind, it is not exclusively so. Indeed, for the majority of criminal offences (the less serious ones), proof of *mens rea* in the sense of proof of a state of mind in relation to all the elements of the *actus reus* would be an unaffordable luxury. One alternative to requiring a mental state to be proved is to abandon the requirement of fault altogether and say that the only concern is whether the accused's conduct actually satisfies the *actus reus* of the offence charged. This is the solution of strict liability (see **A2.12**). To base liability on negligence is a less extreme and, to many, a more attractive solution which switches attention away from the accused's state of mind towards whether he has complied with the standards of the reasonable man.

Despite the potential appeal of the compromise of negligence, offences are rarely defined expressly in terms of negligence. Manslaughter is the one exception at common law but here the negligence has to be 'gross' (see **B1.52** to **B1.55**). Nor do statutory offences themselves normally expressly employ the words 'negligence' or 'negligently' but they do in effect often impose liability for negligence (i.e. for failure to comply with the standards of the reasonable man) through the following mechanisms.

(a) By express use of words equivalent to 'negligence' in the definition of the offence. The most obvious example is driving without due care and attention under the Road Traffic Act 1988, s. 3 (see **C6.1** to **C6.10**). Perhaps a less well known illustration is provided by the Intoxicating Substances (Supply) Act 1985, s. 1(1), which is as follows:

> It is an offence for a person to supply or offer to supply a substance other than a controlled drug—
> (a) to a person under the age of 18 whom he knows, or has reasonable cause to believe, to be under that age; or
> (b) to a person—
> (i) who is acting on behalf of a person under that age; and
> (ii) whom he knows, or has reasonable cause to believe, to be so acting,
> if he knows or has reasonable cause to believe that the substance is, or its fumes are, likely to be inhaled by the person under the age of 18 for the purpose of causing intoxication.

The minimum fault element running throughout this offence is 'reasonable cause to believe'. It matters not what the accused actually believes, it is what the reasonable man in the circumstances would have believed which counts and therefore the minimum basis of liability is negligence. The prosecution are not required to prove a state of mind, although the accused's knowledge of facts (e.g., that pupils from a particular school rather than others in the area are habitually involved in glue sniffing) may be a relevant circumstance in determining whether he had reasonable cause to believe that a particular purchaser was likely to inhale a substance for the purposes of intoxication.

(b) By judicial decision that the offence is still committed if the accused has made an unreasonable mistake of fact (see, e.g., *King* [1964] 1 QB 285, unreasonable mistake that first marriage void no defence to bigamy; *Phekoo* [1981] 1 WLR 1117, mistake under Protection from Eviction Act 1977 (harassment of residential occupiers) required to be reasonable). The accused is convicted despite his innocent state of mind because he is negligent in believing that the facts are such that he is committing no offence. The reasonable man would not have made the same mistake. Negligence is not here expressly made part of the definition of the offence but is introduced as a limit on what might otherwise be a defence with similar effect. Following the decision of the House of Lords in *B (A Minor) v DPP* [2000] 2 AC 428, it would appear that the courts will be much less ready to require mistakes to be reasonable (see further **A3.4**).

(c) By Parliament expressly requiring a belief to be reasonable as it has now done with an offence as serious as rape in the SOA 2003, s. 1(1). The offence remains one requiring intention as far as the act of penetration is concerned but given penetration by A and lack of consent by B, 'a person (A) commits an offence if— . . . (c) A does not reasonably believe that B consents'.

Other statutes provide 'no-negligence' defences of not dissimilar effect by means of different formulations, often putting the burden of proof on the accused, e.g., Trade Descriptions Act 1968, s. 24 ('took all reasonable precautions and exercised all due diligence') and Misuse of Drugs Act 1971, s. 28(2) ('. . . it shall be a defence for the accused to prove that he neither knew of nor suspected nor had reason to suspect the existence of some fact alleged by the prosecution which it is necessary for the prosecution to prove').

It is worth reiterating at this stage the point made earlier about the range of application of fault concepts to different elements of the *actus reus*. As has already been seen with the offence of rape, the fact that an offence is effectively satisfied by negligence as to one element does not mean that negligence will suffice for all the other elements. To return to the example of the Trade Descriptions Act 1968, s. 14(1), and *Wings Ltd v Ellis* [1985] AC 272 discussed in A2.1, that offence expressly requires knowledge as to the falsity of the statement but, as a result of the no-negligence defence in the Trade Descriptions Act 1968, s. 24 (on which the accused in *Wings Ltd v Ellis* chose not to rely), it is an offence satisfied by negligence in other respects, e.g., as to whether a particular statement is being made.

STRICT LIABILITY

The point just made is particularly important in connection with offences of so-called strict liability. The term 'strict liability' is sometimes loosely explained as meaning 'liability without fault' but this is misleading insofar as it suggests that no mental or fault element whatsoever is required. Strict-liability offences are normally those where no fault element is required in relation to one (perhaps crucial) element of the *actus reus* but where *mens rea* is required in relation to other aspects. The classic example is *Prince* (1875) LR 2 CCR 154 where the accused was convicted of taking a girl under the age of 16 out of the possession and against the will of her father. The accused's reasonable belief that she was over 16 was no defence, so even negligence was not required in relation to the element of her being over the age of 16. However, *mens rea* was required in relation to other elements of the offence, e.g., in relation to whether the taking was against the will of the father. As Bramwell B put it: 'If the taker believed he had the father's consent, though wrongly, he would have no *mens rea*'. (See Brooke LJ in *B (A Minor) v DPP* [2000] 2 AC 428 for a critical analysis of the influence of the decision in *Prince*, an influence which will henceforth be drastically reduced following the House of Lords decisions in that case and in *K* [2002] 1 AC 462.) The influence of these two House of Lords decisions has been illustrated in the Court of Appeal decision in *Kumar* [2005] 1 WLR 1352 in which it was held that the offence of buggery under the SOA 1956, s. 12 (as amended, but now replaced by the SOA 2003) was not a strict liability offence in respect of the other person's age. Thus an honest belief that the other person was under 16 was a valid defence (equivalent beliefs under the 2003 Act are now required to be reasonable). **A2.12**

Rather than talking of an offence as a whole being one of strict liability, it is more accurate to speak of it being an offence of strict liability with respect to a particular element or elements. Of course, the element in respect of which liability is strict may be the only element which has any possible criminal connotation, the remaining elements as to which some mental element is required being by contrast mundane and, in themselves, non-criminal in character. For example, in *Parker v Alder* [1899] 1 QB 20, the defendant was convicted of selling adulterated milk when the adulteration took place after the milk had left his control and was *en route* by rail to the purchaser. The offence was therefore of strict liability as regards the milk being adulterated and the only element left was the act of selling. To say that the offence requires *mens rea* in respect of this element, that it requires 'an intention to sell milk', has a hollow ring about it since that is not an intention which is in any way culpable. By contrast with *Prince* then, this is an example of an offence where the imposition of strict liability in relation to the one significant aspect of the *actus reus* effectively means that the offence can indeed give rise to liability without fault. At the other end of the scale, assault occasioning actual bodily harm could be regarded as an offence of strict liability as far as relates to the requirement of actual bodily harm since the only *mens rea* required relates to the assault and not to the element of actual bodily harm. However a person who intends to assault is clearly culpable and no one would describe this offence as giving rise to liability without fault.

On the other hand, a large number of regulatory offences are traditionally referred to as strict liability offences since, as with the case of *Parker v Alder* discussed above, no fault or mental element is required in respect of those features of the *actus reus* which give the offence its criminal character. The circumstances under which the courts will impose strict liability in respect of a particular statutory offence are difficult to predict and regard must be had to the authority (if any) on the individual statutory provision in question. The general approach of the courts is discussed in **A4.1** and **A4.2**.

TRANSFERRED *MENS REA*

A2.13 Transferred *mens rea* is often referred to as 'transferred malice' since the principal illustration is found in the case of *Latimer* (1886) 17 QBD 359 which was concerned with malicious wounding under the OAPA 1861, s. 20. The accused struck with his belt at C but missed and accidentally cut open the face of R. The Court for Crown Cases Reserved upheld the conviction. Lord Coleridge CJ pointed out that the section referred to wounding 'any other person'. This underlines the point that it is a question of interpreting the particular mental element required for the particular offence. The identity of the victim is not a material detail as far as most offences against the person are concerned, and therefore the accused's intention to injure A can be transferred so as to make the accused liable for an injury accidentally inflicted on B. The principle was applied more recently to the offence of manslaughter in *Mitchell* [1983] QB 741 where the accused assaulted A, aged 72, causing him to fall on to the even more elderly B (aged 89) ultimately causing her death. The Court of Appeal upheld the conviction for her manslaughter, Staughton J saying: 'We can see no reason of policy for holding that an act calculated to harm A cannot be manslaughter if it in fact kills B'. A more restrictive approach to the doctrine of transferred malice was taken by the House of Lords in *A-G's Ref (No. 3 of 1994)* [1998] AC 245. Lord Mustill (at p. 261) recognised the doctrine only as an ' "arbitrary exception to general principles" . . . useful enough to yield rough justice in particular cases . . . [which] could sensibly be retained not withstanding its lack of any sound intellectual basis'. However, it could not be extended to create liability for murder from an intentional infliction of grievous bodily harm on a pregnant woman which later resulted in the death of the child *in utero* subsequent to it having been born alive. Such a situation could give rise to liability for manslaughter, apparently without the need of the doctrine of transferred malice, but it was not murder. The decision seems to be influenced as much by the desire not to build any further on the grievous bodily harm/murder rule as by any deficiency in the transferred *mens rea* rule explained above. The logic of the decision would not necessarily preclude liability for murder of the child where the initial attack on the mother was with intent to *kill* her. More difficult would be the case where the attack was done with intent to destroy the foetus which resulted in a live birth followed by death. This would appear to be attempted child destruction (and possibly manslaughter) rather than murder.

This last point is further exemplified by the rule that the *mens rea* for one offence cannot be transferred so as to make an accused liable for a different offence even if the two offences happen to share similar terminology in their definition. This is illustrated by the case of

Pembliton (1874) LR 2 CCR 119 where the accused threw a stone at a crowd of people but missed and broke a glass window behind them. The jury found that he intended to hit the people but not the window. Although he could have been convicted of malicious wounding, had he injured someone, the Court for Crown Cases Reserved quashed his conviction for malicious damage since that was a separate offence with its own separate *mens rea* requiring foresight of damage to property rather than foresight of injury to a person. Lord Coleridge CJ observed that it would have been different if 'the jury had found that the prisoner had been guilty of throwing the stone recklessly, knowing that there was a window near which it might probably hit' for then he would have had the separate *mens rea* of the independent offence of malicious damage. If two separate offences have *precisely* the same *mens rea* then the problem disappears. Proof of the *mens rea* of one automatically involves proof of the *mens rea* of the other. This principle was applied in *Ellis* (1986) 84 Cr App R 235, in which it was held that an intention to import a prohibited substance is the *mens rea* sufficient both for importing a controlled drug of class A and also for the separate offence (cf. *Courtie* [1984] AC 463) of importing a controlled drug of class B. Thus if an accused believed he was importing a class B drug but was in fact importing a class A drug, he can be convicted of the latter offence since he had the necessary *mens rea* of an intention to import a prohibited substance. His mistake might be relevant in determining the sentence. Similarly, he could be convicted of importing a controlled drug even if he believed he was importing material prohibited under some other enactment, e.g., pornographic material.

The issue ultimately hinges on precisely what is required by the *mens rea* of the particular offence charged. This is an important point in relation to the liability of accessories (see A5.2) for an accessory must know or at least contemplate what it is the principal is going to do, and if the principal does something outside the scope of that contemplation, the accessory will not be liable. Thus if the accessory encourages violence against a *particular* victim and the principal deliberately chooses another victim not contemplated by the accessory, the accessory will not be liable (see *Saunders* (1573) 2 Plow 473). However, if the principal tries to carry out the agreed plan but it accidentally misfires and victim B rather than victim A is injured, then the doctrine of transferred intention applies to the accessory too and he will remain liable because the principal has at least tried to do what the accessory contemplated: the principal's acts, although perhaps not their consequences, are within the accessory's contemplation and *mens rea*.

PROOF OF *MENS REA*

The various mental states discussed in this section undeniably present courts and juries with difficult practical problems since even when one is clear about the precise meaning of the mental state to be proved, it is not easy to be sure whether that corresponds to what actually went on in the accused's mind. Even in apparently clear cases, the accused's denial may raise a doubt in the minds of the jury. If a man shoots at another at point-blank range with a revolver it may seem easy to infer that he intended to kill or at least injure that other but an accused may seek to deny this by asserting that he believed the revolver was not loaded or was merely a harmless imitation. In the absence of such an explanation, of course, a jury will doubtless infer that he intended the natural and probable result of his action, i.e. death or injury to the other. Apart from admissions from the accused, this is indeed the most obvious way to ascertain his state of mind. Thus juries will probably infer that the accused intended or at least foresaw the natural and probable consequences of his actions. This is unexceptionable as a purely factual inference. Problems have arisen, however, when courts have sought to elevate such an inference to the status of an irrebuttable presumption. In the light of one such decision, *DPP v Smith* [1961] AC 290, Parliament intervened to ensure that it remains open to the jury to find that the accused did not intend or foresee the consequences (see also *Frankland v The Queen* [1987] AC 576). The CJA 1967, s. 8, provides: A2.14

A court or jury, in determining whether a person has committed an offence,—
(a) shall not be bound in law to infer that he intended or foresaw a result of his actions by reason only of its being a natural and probable consequence of those actions; but
(b) shall decide whether he did intend or foresee that result by reference to all the evidence, drawing such inferences from the evidence as appear proper in the circumstances.

Although this section makes it clear that there is no irrebuttable presumption, the concluding words of para. (b) equally mean that a jury *may* infer that a person intended or foresaw the natural and probable consequences of his actions if this seems appropriate on all the evidence, for example, in the absence of any evidence explaining why the accused did not intend or foresee that consequence. (For further discussion of s. 8 and the relationship between foresight and intention in murder, see **B1.11** and **B1.12**.)

The CJA 1967, s. 8, can apply only where the prosecution are seeking to prove that the accused intended or foresaw something. Therefore whilst it can apply to the proof of intention in murder or to the proof of foresight in, for example, crimes of malice or subjective recklessness, it cannot apply where the definition of the offence does not require intention or foresight. Thus it is of no relevance to the element of manslaughter that requires the accused's act to be likely to cause bodily harm since that is a purely objective element which does not require any intent or foresight on the part of the accused (see *Lipman* [1970] 1 QB 152).

Section 8 is concerned with proof of intention and foresight in relation to consequences but a similar problem arises in relation to circumstances. Again, a reasonable prima facie rule is to assume that the accused was aware of facts of which the reasonable man would have been aware provided one is prepared to adjust that conclusion in the face of credible evidence from the accused as to why he was not actually aware of it. This will often take the form of a defence of mistake. The former requirement that such mistakes had always, as a matter of law, to be based on reasonable grounds was, in effect, an irrebuttable presumption that the accused was aware of facts of which the reasonable man would be aware. The House of Lords in *DPP v Morgan* [1976] AC 182, in abandoning this rule for crimes requiring subjective *mens rea*, performed a similar function in this area to that performed by the CJA 1967, s. 8, in relation to foresight of consequences. The reasonableness or otherwise of a mistake is certainly an important factor in deciding whether the accused actually made that mistake but the court must look at all the evidence in order to decide on the accused's actual state of mind.

The *Morgan* principle only applies to crimes for which a genuine mistake is inconsistent with the *mens rea* and does not apply to crimes which are in effect satisfied by negligence in this respect, for example, bigamy (see the comments of the Law Lords on *Tolson* (1889) 23 QBD 168 in *DPP v Morgan* itself but see also the approach now taken by the House of Lords in *B (A Minor) v DPP* [2000] 2 AC 428 and *K* [2002] 1 AC 462, which seems to make the *Tolson* approach much less likely). Paradoxically, the *Morgan* principle no longer applies to the offence of rape as the SOA 2003 now expressly requires a belief in consent to be reasonable.

Section A3 General Defences

CATEGORIES OF GENERAL DEFENCE

This section deals with defences which are available in relation to a range of offences rather than those which are only available in relation to a single crime. Particular defences to particular crimes (such as provocation in relation to murder) are dealt with in the section of this work dealing with the particular offence. The expression 'general defences' suggests something positive that must be put forward on behalf of the accused, but in truth it is more accurate to regard these defences as circumstances where the prosecution have been unable to prove all the requirements of liability beyond reasonable doubt. This is most obviously true of defences that consist of showing that the mental element of the offence charged may be missing (as with the defence of mistake) but it is also true of defences such as duress where the burden is not on the accused to show affirmatively that he was acting under duress but rather on the prosecution (once there is evidence before the court capable of supporting duress) to prove that the accused was not acting under duress. Nevertheless, it is still possible and helpful to divide general defences into two categories: **A3.1**

(a) those which involve a denial of the basic requirements of *mens rea* and voluntary conduct (the defences of mistake and automatism are best regarded in this way), and
(b) those which do not deny these basic requirements but which rely on other circumstances of excuse or justification, as in the defences of duress and self-defence.

These two categories will be examined in turn.

DEFENCES DENYING BASIC ELEMENTS OF LIABILITY

Mistake and Inadvertence: Offences Requiring Intention or Foresight

Because the defences of mistake and inadvertence consist of a denial of the *mens rea* of the particular crime charged, the nature and the availability of the defences will vary from offence to offence but it is possible to identify categories of offences for which consistent principles can be formulated. The first category consists of offences requiring subjective fault (e.g., crimes requiring intention or subjective recklessness). For this category of offences it is clear that either a mistake (i.e. a positive belief) that a particular ingredient of the offence charged is lacking or, alternatively, a simple failure to appreciate the presence of the same ingredient will operate as a defence. For example, A, out in open country, shoots V dead with a crossbow at a range of 200 metres. A has a defence if he thinks that V is a scarecrow (mistake) or, alternatively, if it has never occurred to him that V or anybody else might be so foolish as to traverse that part of the countryside selected by A to practise his archery (inadvertence). In either case A would lack the necessary *mens rea* for murder, the intention to kill or cause grievous bodily harm, although he may well be liable for other offences. Similarly, the offence of malicious wounding (OAPA 1861, s. 20) requires subjective awareness at least of the risk of wounding, and either mistake or inadvertence will suffice for a defence. See, for example, *W (A Minor) v Dolbey* (1983) 88 Cr App R 1, in which the Divisional Court held that the accused's belief that his air rifle was unloaded was a defence to a charge under s. 20. (This case also illustrates the artificiality and difficulty in many cases of distinguishing **A3.2** between mistake and inadvertence since the accused was also described as ignoring the risk that the gun might be unloaded. Fortunately, at least in this category of offences, it is not a distinction which needs to be made, a defence of lack of *mens rea* being present in either case.) See also *Morrison* (1988) Cr App R 17.

It should be stressed that because this category of offences requires subjective fault, the test of mistake (and of inadvertence) is also a subjective one; there is no requirement that the mistake be one which a reasonable man would have made (or that a reasonable man would have failed to appreciate that which the accused failed to appreciate). The previously traditional requirement that, as a matter of law, mistakes have to be reasonable was emphatically refuted by the House of Lords in *DPP v Morgan* [1976] AC 182, although it will naturally be more difficult to persuade a jury to accept that an accused genuinely made an unreasonable mistake. (The House of Lords upheld the convictions in *DPP v Morgan* itself on the basis that the accused had not actually held any mistaken belief.)

The important point is that the courts regard the rule that mistakes do not have to be reasonable in this context as a logical one which flows from the nature of the mental element required for this category of offences (see especially the speech of Lord Hailsham of St Marylebone in *DPP v Morgan*). Thus one can generalise that wherever an offence requires subjective awareness of a particular element, a genuine mistake that such an element is absent will be a defence.

The logic of this rule is unassailable as applied to proof of intention. If a man believes he is shooting at an inanimate object such as a scarecrow, he cannot at the same time by that very act intend to kill. The same is true where knowledge is required. A person who believes that the goods he buys are not stolen cannot at the same time know (or even believe) that the goods are stolen — the two states of mind are logically inconsistent with one another. However, with crimes satisfied by foresight or awareness of risk (i.e. crimes satisfied by malice or subjective recklessness) the logic is somewhat flawed. D can believe that his partner is consenting to sexual intercourse and yet at the same time be aware that there is a risk (an infinitesimally small one) that she is not consenting. Similarly, one can believe that the stone one throws in the open country is not going to injure someone whilst still recognising that there is a risk that someone lying out of sight might be injured. The point is that beliefs are not usually absolute and are not inconsistent with the recognition of the possibility of a contrary state of affairs (whereas a belief *is* inconsistent with *knowledge* of a contrary state of affairs). Of course, in most cases the belief will be sufficiently strong to leave only the faintest possibility (if any at all) in the believer's mind that he may be wrong and this small degree of possibility would not be sufficient to amount to recklessness or malice. It does, however, depend on what one means by 'belief' and also on what the jury understand by that term. Thus, even where it is wrong to require that a belief has to be based on reasonable grounds, it might be appropriate in some cases to direct them that the belief must be held reasonably strongly. This however is not the route taken by Parliament in reasserting the requirement of reasonableness of belief in consent in relation to rape in the SOA 2003.

Mistake and Inadvertence: Implications of the Demise of Objective Recklessness

A3.3 It is clear that inadvertence is no defence to an offence satisfied by objective recklessness even should that concept survive or re-surface anywhere in the criminal law following the overruling of *Metropolitan Police Commissioner v Caldwell* [1982] AC 341. It ought to be equally clear that a positive mistake can be a defence even to objective recklessness. The question of mistake in relation to consequences came to be considered under the heading of 'ruling out the risk' and the leading case was *Chief Constable of Avon and Somerset Constabulary v Shimmen* (1986) 84 Cr App R 7, where the accused claimed to have ruled out the risk of causing damage to a window when he aimed a martial-art-style kick in its direction, basing his view on his faith in his own prowess as an exponent of the Korean art of self-defence. In other words, he claimed to believe that no damage would result from his action (the subsequent shattering of the window revealing this belief to be a sadly mistaken one). The Divisional Court remitted the case to the magistrates with a direction to convict since the evidence did not show that the accused had ruled out all the risk (hence he was still reckless in consciously running a small risk). But the court also expressly left open the possibility that an accused whose mistake in his mind rules out any risk would not be objectively reckless (since he has neither failed to consider the risk nor consciously run it). The interesting point is the requirement that the risk has to be totally ruled out, which is akin to the court saying that mistaken beliefs have to be held with a degree of conviction equal to certainty and admitting of no doubts. Logically the same argument should apply in a case like *Shimmen* even following the reversal of *Caldwell* as *Shimmen* was not based on D's failure to consider a risk but on his appreciation that there remained a small but unjustified risk.

The overall point to note is that the treatment of mistakes should not vary as between subjective and objective recklessness since the latter merely extended the former to include failure to think and the person who acts under a mistaken belief has not failed to think — the only question can be whether he is subjectively reckless. His mistake is either inconsistent with the required awareness of an unreasonable risk, in which case he is not subjectively reckless, or, despite his mistake, he is still aware of an unreasonable level of risk — in which case, in principle, he may still be reckless. In general though, cases such as *Shimmen* apart, the courts seem to assume that where a person is treated as acting under a mistaken belief, that indicates that they are not at the same time conscious of any remaining risk that could be regarded as unreasonable.

Mistake and Inadvertence: Offences Satisfied by Negligence

A3.4 It is clear that inadvertence is no defence to a crime of negligence. (This assumes that the risk of which the accused was unaware was one of which a reasonable man would have been aware. Strictly speaking, of course, inadvertence is wide enough to cover failure to consider non-obvious risks but the normal context of the use of the word 'inadvertence' is one whereby it is assumed that the risk is one of which a reasonable man would have been aware.)

Equally clearly, mistake can be a defence to crimes of negligence subject to the important qualification that the mistake must be a reasonable one since an unreasonable mistake itself supplies the negligence which is the sufficient basis of liability. The House of Lords in *DPP v Morgan* [1976] AC 182 specifically stated that the old requirement of reasonableness still applies to offences not requiring full *mens rea*. The Law Lords deliberately refrained from overruling *Tolson* (1889) 23 QBD 168 which required a mistaken belief in the death of a spouse in the offence of bigamy to be based on reasonable grounds. As Lord Fraser of Tullybelton put it ([1976] AC 182 at p. 238):

> . . . bigamy was an absolute offence, except for one defence set out in a proviso, and it is clear that the mental element in bigamy is quite different from that in rape. In particular, bigamy does not involve any intention except the intention to go through a marriage ceremony, unlike rape in which I have already considered the mental element. So, if a defendant charged with bigamy believes that his spouse is dead, his belief does not involve the absence of any intent which forms an essential ingredient in the offence.

Thus, the logical argument that even an unreasonable mistake must deny the mental element, and so be a defence, does not apply to bigamy, and the offence is in effect interpreted as one satisfied by negligence as to whether the spouse is still alive. The courts sometimes adopt this approach in relation to other statutory offences as, for example, in *Phekoo* [1981] 1 WLR 1117 in relation to the offence of harassment of a residential occupier under the Protection from Eviction Act 1977, s. 1(3). The Court of Appeal held that a belief that a person was not a residential occupier had to be reasonable to afford a defence. This is entirely consistent with the House of Lords comments on *Tolson* in *DPP v Morgan*.

Treating the offence as one of negligence is at least a more sensitive approach than imposing strict liability (whereby even a reasonable mistake would be no defence) and again is in line with the sentiments expressed by Lord Diplock in *Sweet v Parsley* [1970] AC 132 where he said (at pp. 163–4):

> . . . had the significance of *Tolson* been appreciated here, as it was in the High Court of Australia, our courts, too, would have been less ready to infer an intention of Parliament to create offences for which an honest and reasonable mistake was no excuse.

When the Court of Appeal considered the case of *B (A Minor) v DPP* [2000] 2 AC 428, Brooke LJ clearly felt uneasy in holding that the offence under the Indecency with Children Act 1961, s. 1(1) (inciting a girl under 14 to commit an act of gross indecency), was one of strict liability in respect of the age of the girl. However, the House of Lords overturned the decision (also at [2000] 2 AC 428), holding not only that the offence was not one of strict liability but that the accused's honest belief that the girl was over 14 need not be based on reasonable grounds. Lord Nicholls indicated that 'as a matter of principle, the honest belief approach must be preferable' and that Lord Diplock's dictum in *Sweet v Parsley* referring to 'the absence of a belief, held honestly and upon reasonable grounds in the existence of facts which if true would make the act innocent' had in future to be read as though the reference to reasonable grounds were omitted. In *K* [2002] 1 AC 462, the House of Lords held K's honest belief that a girl was over 16 would be a defence to indecent assault under the Sexual Offences Act 1956, s. 14. Once again, as in *B (A Minor)*, their lordships held that the prosecution has to prove the absence of a belief in excusing circumstances and that such a defence of mistaken belief ought not to be tempered by a requirement that the belief be a reasonable one. Subjectivists welcomed these developments but it would be a pity if the courts regarded themselves as being confronted by a stark choice between full *mens rea* and strict liability and felt obliged to opt for strict liability in circumstances where the middle way of a defence of reasonable mistake and hence liability for negligence might better serve the social purposes of the legislation. The offences considered in these two House of Lords decisions have now been replaced by the SOA 2003 and the half-way house of a defence of reasonable belief in age has been preferred to a completely subjectivist solution.

The case of *Lamb* [1967] 2 QB 981 provides an unusual example of a defence of mistake succeeding in relation to an offence involving negligence (manslaughter). The accused had 'jokingly' pointed and fired a revolver containing two live bullets at his best friend, thereby killing him. His mistake was in believing that, because the bullets were not in the firing position, the gun could not fire when in fact, unknown to him, pulling the trigger caused the cylinder to rotate and, in this case, placed one of the bullets in the firing position. The trial judge in effect directed the jury that the accused's beliefs were irrelevant, as was the evidence called on his behalf to show that this was a mistake that the ordinary man might make. The Court of Appeal quashed the conviction commenting (at p. 990):

> . . . it would, of course, have been fully open to a jury, if properly directed, to find the defendant guilty because they considered his view as to there being no danger was formed in a criminally negligent way. But he was entitled to a direction that the jury should take into account the fact that he had undisputedly formed that view and that there was expert evidence as to this being an understandable view.

Thus an 'understandable' (reasonable) mistake could be a defence but a criminally negligent (unreasonable) one would not be.

Mistake and Inadvertence: Offences of Strict Liability

Even a reasonable mistake is no defence to an offence of strict liability, although many so-called offences of strict liability now have statutory defences available based on particular types of reasonable mistake, the burden of proof of such defences being put on the accused. See, for example, Misuse of Drugs Act 1971, s. 28 at **B20.20**. **A3.5**

Mistake of Law

Whilst the maxim 'Ignorance of the law is no excuse' generally holds good in English law, it is no more than a broad generalisation and is subject to exceptions. These exceptions are really no more than an illustration of the general theme already expounded — that where the accused lacks the *mens rea* required for the offence charged, he has a defence. Since *mens rea* generally relates to facts, it is mistake or ignorance of facts that is usually the basis of a denial of *mens rea*. However, in some offences the requirement of *mens rea* includes legal concepts and a mistake about that legal concept can mean that the accused lacks *mens rea*. Thus in *Smith* [1974] QB 354 the conviction of the accused for criminal damage was quashed on the basis of a mistaken belief that the property damaged was still his own property and was therefore not property 'belonging to another'. It was the accused's ignorance of the civil law on the question of when property belongs to another (in particular, the law relating to a landlord's fixtures) which caused him to mistakenly believe that the property did not belong to the landlord. He thus lacked the *mens rea* of the offence because of his ignorance of law, and this was relevant because the offence required *mens rea* in relation to the civil-law concept of ownership (belonging to another). **A3.6**

It should be stressed that the mistake must be one of civil law rather than about the ambit or meaning of a criminal provision. This precludes not only defences such as 'I didn't think burglary included breaking into houses during the day' but also, for example, a defence to theft of a wild creature based on a belief that a wild creature is not 'property'. The Theft Act 1968, s. 4(4), specifically states that wild creatures are property for the purpose of theft (although there are restrictions on the circumstances when they can be the subject of a charge of theft) and this is a matter of the criminal law rather than whether wild creatures are property in any other branch of the law. Similarly, on a charge of handling stolen goods, it would be no defence to say that one did not know that goods obtained by deception count as 'stolen' since this too is a matter of criminal rather than civil law (see Theft Act 1968, s. 24(4)). The point can be further illustrated by reference to *Johnson v Youden* [1950] 1 KB 544. It was an offence under the Building Materials and Housing Act 1945, s. 7, to sell a house in excess of the prescribed price. The defendant solicitor knew that an extra £250 was being paid to the builder in a separate account to be spent on possible future work which might be done to the house by the builder. Even if the solicitor genuinely believed that this was not part of the price under the Act his mistake was merely one of criminal law since s. 7(5) specifically stated that associated transactions had to be included in calculating the price.

Some offences expressly make the accused's beliefs about the legality of his action relevant and in these cases there can be no question that a mistake of law can be relevant. The most obvious example is the Theft Act 1968, s. 2(1), under which a person is not to be regarded as dishonest: '(a) if he appropriates the property in the belief that he has in law the right to deprive the other of it'. A less obvious example is provided by *Secretary of State for Trade and Industry v Hart* [1982] 1 WLR 481 which concerned the statutory offence of acting as auditor of a company 'at a time when he knows that he is disqualified'. As a director of the company Hart was disqualified but he did not know of the quite separate statutory provision which so provided. Thus, although he knew the facts (that he was a director of the company), he did not know that he was disqualified (as the offence specifically required). Contrast *A-G's Ref (No. 1 of 1995)* [1996] 1 WLR 970, where the offence did not require any specific knowledge that deposit-taking had to be licensed by the Bank of England. See also *Lee* [2001] 1 Cr App R 293 — mistake of law that arrest unlawful not capable of negating an intent to resist lawful arrest.

By the Statutory Instruments Act 1946, s. 3, it is a defence to prove that a relevant statutory instrument had not been issued at the time of the alleged offence although it is open to the Crown to prove that reasonable steps had been taken to bring it to the attention of relevant persons. However, it should be remembered that the *ultra vires* and unlawful nature of subordinate legislation or administrative decisions may be raised as a defence to a criminal charge (*Boddington v British Transport Police* [1999] 2 AC 143).

Automatism

A3.7 The defence of automatism arises where the accused's conduct lacks the basic requirement of being voluntary (see **A1.6** and **A1.7**).

The defence is limited to cases where there is a total destruction of voluntary control; impaired or reduced control is not enough (*A-G's Ref (No. 2 of 1992)* [1994] QB 91). Where the accused is conscious, automatism will be rare but possible (e.g., reflex actions when startled by a sudden loud noise or when stung by a swarm of bees while driving: see *Hill v Baxter* [1958] 1 QB 277 and *Burns v Bidder* [1967] 2 QB 227 at p. 240). Contrast the mistaken pressing of the accelerator rather than the brake in *A-G's Ref (No. 4 of 2000)* [2001] RTR 415, which was held not to be a case of automatism. Where the accused has acted in a state of unconsciousness, it is easier to conclude that he could not have acted otherwise, and in principle he should have the defence of automatism. The law imposes serious restrictions on such a defence, however, through the rules on voluntary intoxication and insanity to be discussed in **A3.9** to **A3.19**. The question which remains for discussion here is whether, even where the automatism is not caused by insanity or voluntary intoxication, there is some further restriction or requirement that the automatism should not be self-induced.

Such a requirement seemed to be suggested by the Court of Appeal in *Quick* [1973] QB 910 even though in that case it quashed the conviction of the appellant for assault. The alleged assault had taken place whilst the appellant (a diabetic) had been in a state of hypoglycaemia (low blood sugar) which the trial judge had (wrongly, in the view of the Court of Appeal) ruled amounted to insanity. The defence of (non-insane) automatism was thus never put to the jury, but Lawton LJ had the following to say (at pp. 922–3) about such a defence:

> A self-induced incapacity will not excuse . . . nor will one which could have been reasonably foreseen as a result of either doing, or omitting to do something, as, for example, taking alcohol against medical advice after using certain prescribed drugs, or failing to have regular meals while taking insulin . . .
>
> Had the defence of automatism been left to the jury, a number of questions of fact would have had to be answered . . . to what extent had he brought about his condition by not following his doctor's instructions about taking regular meals? Did he know that he was getting into a hypoglycaemic episode? If yes, why did he not use the antidote of eating a lump of sugar as he had been advised to do? On the evidence which was before the jury Quick might have had difficulty in answering these questions in a manner which would have relieved him of responsibility for his act.

It thus appeared after *Quick* that, even where automatism was not caught by the rules on insanity and intoxication, it was not available if it could be said to be self-induced. Thus in *Bailey* [1983] 1 WLR 760 a similar defence based on automatism caused by hypoglycaemia was held by the trial judge to be unavailable (on charges under the OAPA 1861, ss. 18 and 20) since it was self-induced. The Court of Appeal (whilst dismissing the appeal on the basis that no miscarriage of justice had actually occurred) held that this was too absolute a rule:

> In our judgment, self-induced automatism, other than that due to intoxication from alcohol or drugs, may provide a defence to crimes of basic intent. The question in each case will be whether

> the prosecution have provided the necessary element of recklessness. In cases of assault, if the accused knows that his actions or inaction are likely to make him aggressive, unpredictable or uncontrolled with the result that he may cause some injury to others and he persists in the action or takes no remedial action when he knows it is required, it will be open to the jury to find that he was reckless.

The result of these authorities would seem to be that the fact that automatism is self-induced is a bar to the defence only if the accused was at fault (to the degree required by the particular offence charged). A diabetic falling into a state of hypoglycaemia is not inevitably at fault since it is not common knowledge, even among diabetics, that a failure to take food after an insulin injection may lead to aggressive, unpredictable and uncontrolled conduct. What is more, the limitation on self-induced automatism as a defence could not apply at all to the offence under the OAPA 1861, s. 18, since even self-induced intoxication by drink or drugs would be a defence to such a charge, the offence being one, as will be seen, of specific intent. (Another way of looking at this would be to say that since *intent* to cause grievous bodily harm is required for this offence, the accused would have to *intend* to become violent through failure to take food in order to be deprived of the defence of automatism, cf. the Dutch courage rule in relation to intoxication discussed in **A3.12**.)

Intoxication: General Rule

Intoxication is not a defence as such. It is, for example, no defence to say (as is undoubtedly true in many cases) that the accused would not have acted as he did but for the fact that his inhibitions were reduced due to the effect of alcohol which he had consumed. On the contrary, intoxication operates so as to restrict what would otherwise be valid defences of mistake, inadvertence or automatism. However, intoxication provides very credible evidence of the fact that the accused did in fact make the mistake he alleges or that he did in fact fail to foresee the obvious risk he was running or that he was indeed in a state of automatism. The restrictions which the law imposes on defences caused by voluntary intoxication are a response to the evidential power of intoxication in supporting such defences and to the frequency and ease with which such defences could be put forward. **A3.8**

Intoxication: Voluntary and Involuntary

The restrictive rules apply only where the accused's intoxication is voluntary. This is satisfied if the accused knowingly takes alcohol or other intoxicating drugs (save under medical supervision or direction) and it is immaterial that the accused may have misjudged the degree to which he would become intoxicated (see *Allen* [1988] Crim LR 698). On the other hand, a person who thought he was drinking only orange juice but who was in fact drinking orange juice spiked with quantities of vodka would not be regarded as being voluntarily intoxicated and would have any defence that his resultant state of mind warranted on ordinary principles (e.g., lack of *mens rea*). However, just as with voluntary intoxication, if despite or because of his involuntary intoxication the accused forms the necessary *mens rea* for the crime, there is no separate defence of involuntary intoxication recognised by the law — see the fully reasoned decision of the House of Lords in *Kingston* [1995] 2 AC 355, which reversed the decision of the Court of Appeal and restored the trial judge's ruling that involuntary intoxication provided no defence where the accused (with the necessary *mens rea*) indecently assaulted a boy pursuant to an intent induced by the influence of drugs administered secretly to the accused by a third party. Thus, the only advantage of a finding that the intoxication was involuntary is that it avoids the application of the restrictive rules discussed at **A3.10**. **A3.9**

What counts as an intoxicating drug for the purposes of the restrictive rules governing voluntary intoxication has been discussed by the courts in two cases, *Bailey* [1983] 1 WLR 760 and *Hardie* [1985] 1 WLR 64. In *Bailey*, the Court of Appeal talked about the intoxication rules being applicable to 'dangerous drugs', i.e. those where it is 'common knowledge' that the taker 'may become aggressive or do dangerous or unpredictable things' (amphetamines and LSD being obvious examples). In the second case the court had to consider an accused, charged with an offence under the Criminal Damage Act 1971, s. 1(2), who had taken a number of Valium tablets (which were prescribed for someone else) and held that this did not necessarily amount to voluntary intoxication.

> [Valium is] wholly different in kind from drugs which are liable to cause unpredictability or aggressiveness . . . if the effect of a drug is merely soporific or sedative the taking of it, even in some excessive quantity, cannot in the ordinary way raise a *conclusive* presumption against the admission of proof of intoxication for the purpose of disproving *mens rea* . . .
>
> [The jury] should have been directed that if they came to the conclusion that, as a result of the Valium, the appellant was, at the time, unable to appreciate the risks to property and persons from his actions they should then consider whether the taking of the Valium was itself reckless.

Thus it would seem that there are two categories of drugs: 'dangerous' and 'non-dangerous', LSD being an obvious example of the former category and Valium being an example of the latter. Knowingly taking a 'dangerous' drug counts as voluntary intoxication whereas taking a 'non-dangerous' drug is governed by a similar rule to that discussed in relation to self-induced automatism (see A3.7) and depends on the actual knowledge of the offender as to the likely effects of the drug. Classification by the courts of various drugs into dangerous and non-dangerous is now awaited.

Intoxication: Specific and Basic Intent

A3.10 The principal restriction imposed on defences based on intoxication is that voluntary intoxication can only give rise to a defence to crimes of specific rather than basic intent. The precise nature of the distinction between these two categories of offence has been shrouded in obscurity ever since Lord Birkenhead used the phrase 'specific intent' in *DPP v Beard* [1920] AC 479. Matters are little clearer today, especially in the light of the *obiter* comments of the Court of Appeal in *Heard* [2007] 3 All ER 306. Prior to this decision, the view seemed to have emerged that any offence for which only intention will suffice as the mental element can be regarded as an offence of specific intent, whereas crimes satisfied by recklessness are to that extent crimes of basic intent. Thus murder, theft, robbery, wounding with intent, burglary under the Theft Act 1968, s. 9(1)(a), and any offence of attempt would all appear to be crimes requiring a specific intent and it is open to the accused to adduce evidence that he lacked the specific intent required by these offences due to voluntary intoxication. There is no doubt that these offences remain offences which require a specific intent.

However, the Court of Appeal in *Heard* took the view that the offence of sexual assault under the SOA 2003, s. 3, even though it required an intentional rather than reckless touching, was not in this respect an offence of specific intent, and evidence of intoxication could not be used to show that the touching was not intentional. (This was *obiter* since the Court of Appeal were clear that the appeal could be dismissed on the basis that on the facts the intoxication did not negate the accused's intent.) Rather than a distinction between intention and recklessness, Hughes LJ (at [31]) preferred the distinction referred to by Lord Simon in *DPP v Majewski* [1977] AC 443 (who was quoting from Fauteux J in the Canadian case of *George* (1960) 128 CCC 289 at p. 301) 'between (i) intention as applied to acts considered in relation to their purposes and (ii) intention as applied to acts apart from their purposes'. It is the first category which is regarded as specific intent and this appears to include not only cases of so-called ulterior intent, i.e. an intent to do something beyond the *actus reus*, as with wounding with intent to cause grievous bodily harm, but also intent to cause a consequence in result crimes such as murder, the consequence being death (or grievous bodily harm). Intention to touch seems to be regarded as an example of the second category i.e. intention as applied to acts apart from their purposes, and thus as not being a specific intent. The problem with this approach, however, is that it all depends how narrowly or broadly one describes the 'act'. If the act is described simply as moving one's hand with the result that it touches another, it would be an intentional act of moving with the specific intent (purpose) that it results in a touching. If, however, one describes it simply as an act of 'touching', as the Court of Appeal see it, it is simply an intentional act of touching, the purpose of causing a touching having been subsumed within the description of the act as a 'touching' which requires only a basic and not a specific intent. Conversely, murder which looks like doing an act (e.g., stabbing) with a purpose (e.g., of causing a consequence — death) could equally be described as a 'killing' which term subsumes the purpose and could therefore be regarded simply as an intentional act of killing without any express reference to purpose and thus as not involving a specific intent but only a basic intent to do the act of killing, which is clearly not the law.

Whatever the impact of the Court of Appeal's observations in *Heard* might turn out to be, certain other offences which do not specifically require intention but which require other special mental states, such as dishonesty, are clearly to be treated as offences of specific intent, e.g., handling stolen goods (*Durante* [1972] 1 WLR 1612). So too with criminal damage where the indictment restricts the allegation against the accused to intention as opposed to recklessness (see *Metropolitan Police Commissioner v Caldwell* [1982] AC 341 at p. 356). The view was previously taken in this work that aggravated criminal damage under s. 1(2) of the 1971 Act was not a crime requiring specific intent (unless restricted to an allegation of committing it intentionally) since it could be committed recklessly, but the Court of Appeal in *Heard* were of the view that the requirement of being reckless as to endangering life is a specific intent since it goes beyond the *actus reus* of causing damage and thus voluntary intoxication could be relevant to show that there was no recklessness as to the endangerment of life. This basis of specific intent is at least intelligible and does not depend on the narrowness or otherwise of the definition of the act, since it is based on the notion of ulterior intent, or rather ulterior *mens rea*, i.e. a *mens rea* going beyond the *actus reus* of the offence as defined. All offences other than those requiring specific intent can be regarded as crimes of basic intent and the accused will not be allowed to show that he lacked the *mens rea* or was in a state of automatism due to voluntary intoxication. Crimes requiring only basic intent clearly include manslaughter, malicious wounding, all forms of assault (except those requiring a specific intent such as assault with intent to rob), and taking a conveyance contrary to the Theft Act 1968, s. 12. Thus, in these cases, even the fact that the accused has 'completely blacked out', as was alleged in the leading House of Lords case of *DPP v Majewski*, will provide no defence, nor will the fact that he is hallucinating that he is fighting snakes at the centre of the earth, as was alleged in the Court of Appeal case of *Lipman* [1970] 1 QB 152. The rule applies not only to the person who is so intoxicated that he cannot remember anything of the offence (as in *Woods* (1981) 74 Cr App R 312) but also where the accused makes a mistake about a particular aspect of his actions as in *Fotheringham* (1988) 88 Cr App R 206.

However, where a defence of honest mistake is specifically provided in a statute, then it appears that even an intoxicated mistake may suffice despite the offence being one of basic intent. In *Jaggard v Dickinson* [1981] QB 527, the Divisional Court held that the defence of belief in the owner's consent under the Criminal Damage Act 1971, s. 5(2), was still available even though the defendant was drunk. The court seems to have been particularly impressed by the fact that s. 5(3) specifically provides that: 'For the purposes of this section it is immaterial whether a belief is justified or not if it is honestly held'. The decision must, regrettably, be regarded as confined to defences under the Criminal Damage Act 1971, s. 5, although the same sort of issue could arise, for example, in relation to the defence of mistaken belief under the Theft Act 1968, s. 12(6). Certainly the Court of Appeal was not prepared to allow, in relation to self-defence, a drunken mistake by the accused that he was being attacked (*O'Grady* [1987] QB 995 — see further **A3.37**).

Various justifications for the basic intent rule have been put forward, but none of them are particularly convincing, and the Australian courts have refused to adopt it (see *O'Connor*

(1980) 146 CLR 64). At root the rule seems to be one of legal policy — that an intoxicated offender should have a potential defence to the most serious offences such as murder or wounding with intent but should remain liable for an appropriate lesser offence of basic intent such as manslaughter or malicious wounding. The policy is embodied in both the Criminal Law Revision Committee's recommendations (14th Report, 1980, Cmnd 7844) and the Law Commission's Draft Criminal Code Bill (Law Commission No. 177), cl. 22. Although a Law Commission Consultation Paper (No. 127, 1993) proposed abolition of the basic intent rule, the final report (No. 229, 1995) reverted to recommending the retention of the rule in codified form. The Law Commission has recently returned to the issue in a report due to be published in Summer 2007.

A3.11 **Applying the Basic Intent Rule** Although the policy behind the basic intent rule is clear, the precise manner of its application is less so. Early editions of this work, in common with many other commentators, followed the words of Lord Elwyn Jones in *DPP v Majewski* [1977] AC 443, which stated that evidence of intoxication 'supplies the evidence of *mens rea*, of guilty mind, certainly sufficiently for crimes of basic intent' and therefore suggested that to proffer such evidence would seem to discharge the prosecution from the burden of showing that the accused had the *mens rea* or was acting voluntarily in relation to basic intent crimes.

The alternative view is that evidence of intoxication is simply irrelevant and has to be ignored on the question of whether the accused has the *mens rea* of a basic intent crime but that the jury have to answer the hypothetical question of whether the accused would have had the *mens rea* if, contrary to the facts, he had not been intoxicated. This was the approach favoured by the Court of Appeal in *Richardson* [1999] 1 Cr App R 392 but it is an approach not without difficulties, especially in cases where the intoxication has reduced the accused to a state of automatism or something close to it. In most cases of course, either approach will yield the same result since, in the absence of any other special factor apart from intoxication, the jury will assume that the accused would have foreseen the natural and probable consequence of his actions if not intoxicated. The actual decision to quash the convictions in *Richardson* is strange since the only other factor mentioned by the Court of Appeal was the fact that the appellants were university students (who are surely able to appreciate the natural and probable consequences of their actions, at least in their occasional sober moments, despite the fallibility sometimes revealed in their examination scripts) and the Court actually stated that the 'reason they did not [appreciate the risk] was the amount of drink they had consumed'. Despite this, *Richardson* usefully suggests an opportunity for the defence to raise the issue that there was some exculpatory or innocent cause of the accused's mistake or inadvertence, other than voluntary intoxication, even though it is difficult to discern such a cause on the facts of *Richardson* itself.

The degree of intoxication of which the accused has to adduce evidence has also been an issue as a result of the somewhat remarkable decision of the Court of Appeal in *McKnight* (2000) *The Times*, 5 May 2000. Here it was decided that the trial judge was correct not to have given the standard direction, based on *Sheehan* [1975] 1 WLR 739, telling the jury to take into account the evidence of intoxication in deciding whether the accused had formed the specific intent to kill or cause grievous bodily harm. This was despite the fact that the accused had approximately 300 microgrammes of alcohol per 100 millilitres of blood at the time of the killing. The Court of Appeal seems to have been unduly influenced by some dicta of the Privy Council in *Sooklal* [1999] 1 WLR 2011 where there was much weaker evidence of a much lower level of intoxication (see also *Porceddu* [2004] EWCA Crim 1043). Both the Privy Council and the Court of Appeal are in danger of reverting to the more demanding test of whether the accused was *incapable* of forming the intent as opposed to the question emphasised in *Sheehan* of whether the accused *actually* formed the intent. The decisions are very difficult to reconcile with a number of other Court of Appeal authorities, including *McKinley* [1994] Crim LR 944 and *Bennett* [1995] Crim LR 877.

Intoxication: the Dutch Courage Rule

The so-called Dutch courage rule is more important in principle than in practice. A person who deliberately makes himself intoxicated in order to commit a crime cannot raise a defence based on such intoxication, even to a crime of specific intent (*A-G for Northern Ireland v Gallagher* [1963] AC 349, per Lord Denning). The rule is eminently sensible but not necessarily applicable even to the facts of *A-G for Northern Ireland v Gallagher* itself and there seem to be no reported cases of it being applied since. The principle, however, is effectively the same as that laid down by the courts in relation to 'non-dangerous' drugs (see **A3.9**) — that if the accused has the fault element of the offence in becoming intoxicated, the lack of the fault element at the time of the offence due to such intoxication is irrelevant. **A3.12**

Insanity: General Principles: the M'Naghten Rules

The defence of insanity is still governed by the M'Naghten rules (*M'Naghten's Case* (1843) 10 Cl & F 200), which today operate largely as a restriction on what might otherwise be a complete defence based on lack of *mens rea* or automatism. Only where the accused falls under that limb of the rules which requires him not to know that his act is 'wrong' do the rules provide any defence additional to that which would be available under the above general principles. Until recently, even this possibility was a largely theoretical one since the consequences of an insanity verdict were so unattractive that seldom would an accused wish to seek one. The 'special verdict' of 'not guilty by reason of insanity' is provided for in the Trial of Lunatics Act 1883, s. 2, and is one that is required to be returned by a jury rather than simply as a result of the accused's plea (see *Crown Court at Maidstone, ex parte Harrow LBC* [1999] 3 All ER 542). Where a special verdict is returned, the Criminal Procedure (Insanity) Act 1964, s. 5, previously required a court to make an order that the accused be admitted to such hospital as may be specified by the Secretary of State but, since 1991 under the amended version of s. 5, the court now has a range of orders from which to choose (see **D12.27**). These now include an order for a hospital order (with or without a restriction order), a supervision order, and even an absolute discharge. The defence of insanity is therefore now much more attractive to an accused and is likely to be relied on more frequently (see Mackay and Kearns [1999] Crim LR 714 for an account of the relatively slow progress in this respect). However, the above flexibility does not apply where the offence to which the special verdict relates is murder or any other offence for which the sentence is fixed by law; in such a case the court must make a hospital order with a restriction order. Note the unsuccessful attempt in *Antoine* [2001] 1 AC 340, an unfitness to plead case, to reduce the charge to manslaughter on the grounds of diminished responsibility. In *Grant* [2002] QB 1030, the Court of Appeal adopted the same approach in relation to provocation. **A3.13**

Whilst the burden of proving insanity is on the accused on the balance of probabilities (see **A3.14**), for a special verdict to be returned the prosecution must prove that the accused 'did the act or made the omission charged' (Trial of Lunatics Act 1883, s. 2(1)), otherwise the defendant is entitled to a complete acquittal on the ground of lack of an *actus reus*, despite any insanity. It was confirmed in *A-G's Ref (No. 3 of 1998)* [2000] QB 401 that this does not involve proving *mens rea* (doubting *Egan* [1997] Crim LR 225, another unfitness to plead case, which has now been overruled in *Antoine*) but did require proof of 'the ingredients which constitute the *actus reus* of the crime' which seems to include the circumstances (other than *mens rea*) whose presence or absence render the act or omission criminally unlawful (such as, for example, on appropriate facts, the absence of legitimate grounds for self-defence).

Even before the disincentives to plead insanity were reduced, the scope of the M'Naghten rules had remained important. Once the defence put the accused's state of mind in issue, it was open to the prosecution to argue (see Lord Denning in *Bratty v A-G for Northern Ireland* [1963] AC 386) and to the trial judge to rule (see, for example, *Sullivan* [1984] AC 156) that the defence really amounted to insanity (see also the Criminal Procedure (Insanity) Act 1964, s. 6). The rules in effect marked out one boundary of the defences of automatism (as in *Sullivan*) or lack of *mens rea* (see, for example, *Clarke* [1972] 1 All ER 219 where, however, the accused was found on appeal not to be within the M'Naghten rules and thus had a complete defence of lack of *mens rea*). The rules still retain this definitional function but the consequences of having one's defence fall within the rules are no longer automatically so severe. The accused will now be able to put his state of mind in issue more readily with less fear (murder cases apart) of the court having to make an inappropriate order if it finds the accused to be within the rules.

It should be noted that the above discussion relates to trials on indictment and that s. 2 of the Trial of Lunatics Act 1883 is inapplicable to trial in magistrates' courts. That the defence of insanity is available in magistrates' courts and that it leads to a complete acquittal rather than the special verdict was fully explained by White in his article at [1991] Crim LR 501 and this has now been confirmed by the Divisional Court in *Horseferry Road Magistrates' Court, ex parte K* [1997] QB 23. Whilst magistrates have a power to make a hospital order under the Mental Health Act 1983, s. 37(3), even though the accused is not convicted, there is no power to commit to the Crown Court for a restriction order to be made under s. 41 of that Act. The significance of the availability of the defence of insanity in the magistrates' court will be considerably reduced if *DPP v H* [1997] 1 WLR 1406 is followed. In that case the Divisional Court followed the intimation given in *Ex parte K* that insanity could be a defence only in relation to crimes requiring *mens rea* or where *mens rea* was in issue. This decision may represent a pragmatic limitation on the availability of the insanity defence in summary trials (and in triable either way cases a plea of insanity is likely to result in the case being committed to the Crown Court as in *Ex parte K*). It is, however, open to criticism on the grounds that, as has already been pointed out, the defence of insanity can go beyond a mere denial of *mens rea*. This is true both in the sense that insanity may extend to automatism, i.e. a denial of voluntariness (which is normally a requirement even of crimes of strict liability) and also in that the defence may apply where the accused 'does not know that his act is wrong'. See also the commentary on *Ex parte K* at [1997] Crim LR 132 and the article by Ward at p. 796.

The status of the M'Naghten rules in terms of the doctrine of precedent is somewhat anomalous but they have long been treated as authoritative, a treatment confirmed by the House of Lords in *Sullivan* in 1983. In *M'Naghten's Case* (1843) 10 Cl & F 200, the crucial passage (at p. 210) in the response given by Tindal CJ (on behalf of all the other judges save Maule J) reads as follows (emphasis added):

> . . . the jurors ought to be told in all cases that *every man is to be presumed to be sane*, and to possess a sufficient degree of reason to be responsible for his crimes, *until the contrary be proved to their satisfaction*; and that to establish a defence on the ground of insanity, it must be clearly proved that, *at the time of the committing of the act*, the party accused was labouring under such *a defect of reason, from disease of the mind, as not to know the nature and quality of the act he was doing; or*, if he did know it, *that he did not know he was doing what was wrong*.

The emphases have been added and each emphasised phrase will now be explained in turn.

A3.14 **'. . . every man is to be presumed to be sane . . . until the contrary be proved to [the jury's] satisfaction'** This is the basis on which, exceptionally, the burden of proof in establishing the defence is placed on the accused but it is established that the proof need only be on the balance of probabilities (*Sodeman v The King* [1936] 2 All ER 1138, and see **F3.7**). This exception to the general rule on burden of proof is particularly problematical where the accused puts forward both insanity and non-insane automatism as in *Bratty v A-G for Northern Ireland* [1963] AC 386. The solution seems to lie in remembering that, just as with intoxication, the principal utility of evidence of insanity to an accused is that the insanity is itself explanatory evidence of why the accused was not conscious of his actions (or of their obvious results). Other evidence of automatism, such as, for example, a blow on the head causing concussion, need only raise a doubt in the minds of the jury as to whether the accused's act was involuntary, but insofar as the evidence consists of evidence of insanity, the jury must be convinced on a balance of probabilities that the act was involuntary. The result may be, as was possibly the case in *Bratty*, that a jury convicts even though they entertain some doubt as to whether the accused's act was voluntary because the only evidence causing that doubt is evidence of insanity and it is not sufficiently strong to convince them on a balance of probabilities. This may appear to be anomalous but it should be noted that in *Woolmington v DPP* [1935] AC 462, Lord Sankey said: '. . . it is the duty of the prosecution to prove the prisoner's guilt *subject to what I have already said as to the defence of insanity*' (emphasis added).

'. . . at the time of the committing of the act' The M'Naghten rules, in common with the other defences discussed in this section, are concerned with the accused's state of mind at the time of the alleged offence. The sanity or otherwise of the accused at other times may be relevant in other ways, not by way of defence but, for example, in relation to whether he is fit to plead (see **D12.22** *et seq.*) or in relation to the type of sentence or order to be passed. Such issues relating to the sanity of the accused at the time of the trial or the time of sentencing can arise whether or not the accused was sane or not at the time of the alleged offence. **A3.15**

'. . . a defect of reason' This is a central notion in the rules even though it is not the concept around which most of the case law turns. It is the basic reason why irresistible impulse and other emotional or volitional defects or disorders are not within the rules, since they are not defects of reason. Rationality is the litmus test of criminal responsibility, and defects of will are regarded either as non-existent or as irrelevant. In this respect, the defence of diminished responsibility is potentially much more liberal. However, given the way in which insanity can operate as a restriction on other defences, the requirement of a defect of reason may sometimes come to the defendant's aid. See *Clarke* [1972] 1 All ER 219 where the Court of Appeal held that even if the other elements of the rules were satisfied, there was no *defect* of reason but at most a mere absent-minded failure to use the powers of reasoning that the accused undoubtedly still possessed and thus the accused was entitled to have the simple defence of lack of *mens rea* considered by the jury rather than the defence of insanity. **A3.16**

'. . . from disease of the mind' The defect of reason must be caused by a disease of the mind (rather than by, for example, intoxication, which is probably the best explanation for the decision in *Thomas* [1995] Crim LR 314). It is the meaning of this concept around which most of the recent case law turns as it is this which primarily distinguishes insane automatism (a defence of insanity leading to the special verdict) from non-insane automatism (a defence of simple automatism leading to a complete acquittal). **A3.17**

The meaning of 'disease of the mind' is a legal question for the judge to decide rather than a medical one, even though the evidence of medical experts is required by the Criminal Procedure (Insanity and Unfitness to Plead) Act 1991, s. 1. In *Sullivan* [1984] AC 156, two medical experts in the course of their testimony stated that they would not regard something as a disease of the mind unless it produced a disorder of brain functions for a prolonged period — in the case of one witness for more than a day and in the case of the other for more than a month. It was therefore argued that the relatively short period over which an epileptic seizure takes place meant that epilepsy was not a disease of the mind. Lord Diplock emphatically rejected this argument noting (at p. 172) that:

> The nomenclature adopted by the medical profession may change from time to time. . . . But the meaning of the expression 'disease of the mind' as the cause of 'a defect of reason' remains unchanged for the purposes of the application of the M'Naghten rules. . . . 'mind' in the M'Naghten rules is used in the ordinary sense of the mental faculties of reason, memory and understanding. If the effect of a disease is to impair these faculties so severely as to have either of the consequences referred to in the latter part of the rules, it matters not whether the aetiology of the impairment is organic, as in epilepsy, or functional, or whether the impairment itself is

> permanent or is transient and intermittent, provided that it subsisted at the time of commission of the act.

The relevance of the medical evidence seems to be limited to showing that the impairment of the mental faculties did in fact take place and what in fact was the cause. The classification of that impairment and its cause (whether or not it is a defect of reason from disease of the mind), is then purely a matter of law for the judge. It can also be seen that to a large extent, whether something is a disease *of the mind* depends on the consequences it produces — impairment of the faculties of reason, memory and understanding. The disease certainly need not be one primarily located in the brain if it produces the relevant consequences there. Thus arteriosclerosis (hardening of the arteries) causing temporary loss of consciousness is a disease of the mind for these purposes even though it is of physical rather than mental origin (see per Devlin J in *Kemp* [1957] 1 QB 399 at p. 408).

However, not every cause of an impairment of these mental faculties is a *disease* of the mind. A disease is something *internal* to the accused and so:

> A malfunctioning of the mind of transitory effect caused by the application to the body of some *external* factor such as violence, drugs, including anaesthetics, alcohol and hypnotic influences cannot fairly be said to be due to disease (per Lawton LJ in *Quick* [1973] QB 910 at p. 922, emphasis added).

Quick's condition of hypoglycaemia was held not to have been due to a disease of the mind since it was attributable to an external factor — his use of insulin prescribed by his doctor:

> Such malfunctioning of his mind as there was, was caused by an external factor and not by a bodily disorder in the nature of a disease which disturbed the working of his mind (ibid. at pp. 922–3).

Treating the insulin, rather than the diabetes which necessitated the insulin, as the cause of the malfunctioning enabled the court in *Quick* to keep the case outside the M'Naghten rules. However, this course was not available in *Hennessy* [1989] 1 WLR 287, which again concerned a diabetic, this time suffering from the opposite condition of hyperglycaemia (excessive blood sugar) which is directly caused by the diabetes when uncorrected by the administration of insulin. It was thus the *absence* of an external factor which allowed the disease of diabetes to produce the malfunctioning and, given this effect of the disease, the Court of Appeal felt constrained to classify it as a disease of the mind. See also *Bingham* [1991] Crim LR 433.

The Court of Appeal in *Hennessy* also rejected the argument that the accused's anxiety and depression due to his marital problems constituted an external factor (even though there was medical evidence that anxiety and depression could contribute to an increased blood-sugar level). See also the Canadian case of *Rabey* (1977) 79 DLR (3d) 414, in which the Ontario Court of Appeal said (at p. 435) that 'the ordinary stresses and disappointments of life which are the common lot of mankind do not constitute an external cause'. This was subsequently approved by the English Court of Appeal in *Burgess* [1991] 1 QB 92. In this case, the court held that violence whilst sleepwalking or 'sleep associated automatism' was due to an internal factor and was therefore within the M'Naghten rules. Where there is a combination of internal and external factors, it would appear from *Roach* [2001] EWCA Crim 2698 that, if the jury might conclude that it is the external factors which are operative, a defence of non-insane automatism (which it is for the prosecution to disprove) should be left to them notwithstanding that the defence psychiatrists had described it as 'insane automatism' (where the burden is on the accused).

A3.18 **'. . . as not to know the nature and quality of the act he was doing'** This refers to the physical rather than moral quality of the act (per Lord Reading CJ in *Codere* (1916) 12 Cr App R 21) and according to Lord Diplock in *Sullivan* [1984] AC 156 at p. 173: 'Addressed to an audience of jurors in the 1980s it might more aptly be expressed as "He did not know what he was doing" '. Clearly this would be satisfied if the accused was unconscious at the time or, even if conscious, thought, to adopt an example quoted by Lord Denning in another context, that he was throwing a log rather than the baby on the fire. Equally clearly, the accused would have a defence of automatism or lack of *mens rea* respectively in these two situations, and this underlines the point previously made that the M'Naghten rules generally merely qualify what would otherwise be a complete defence.

'. . . or . . . that he did not know he was doing what was wrong' This is an alternative to not knowing the nature and quality of the act and is the only sense in which an insane person is given a defence where none would be available to the sane (knowledge of moral or legal wrongness, as opposed to knowledge of the facts which render it wrong, being generally irrelevant to criminal responsibility). The major question debated here is whether 'wrong' means legally wrong or morally wrong. It is suggested that the key to a proper understanding of this question is to recognise that the question is a negative one. If the accused *does* know *either* that his act is *morally* wrong (according to the ordinary standard adopted by reasonable men, per Lord Reading in *Codere* (1916) 12 Cr App R 21) *or* that it is *legally* wrong then it cannot be said that he does *not* know he was doing what was wrong. In the only two English decisions on the matter (*Codere* (1916) 12 Cr App R 21 and *Windle* [1952] 2 QB 826), it was only necessary to hold that it was correct to tell the jury that the accused could not rely on the defence if he knew that his act was legally wrong. Both were murder cases and it was not seriously suggested in either that the accused did not know his act was legally wrong and yet knew that it was morally wrong. (On the contrary, Windle thought he was morally right to kill his suicidal wife and yet knew it was legally wrong since he said, 'I suppose they will hang me for this'.) Despite the blunt *obiter dictum* in *Windle* (at p. 834) that ' "wrong" means contrary to law', it seems to be the better view that in the case of an accused who does not appreciate that his act is legally wrong but who does realise that it is morally wrong, the defence would not be made out. A3.19

DEFENCES INVOLVING OTHER EXCUSES AND JUSTIFICATIONS

Introduction

To treat certain defences as excuses or justifications and to deal with them separately from defences which deny the basic elements of liability is in one sense artificial since it can be pointed out, for example, that no one commits any offence unless he acts unlawfully and, if the accused has a defence of justification available, then he has not acted unlawfully and one of the basic elements of liability is missing. Equally, it can be pointed out that the defences treated here as a denial of the elements of liability, such as mistake of fact, may be also properly classified as excuses. In the end all classifications are somewhat artificial and are really made for convenience and ease of understanding and exposition. On these grounds it seems sensible to separate out defences where the accused admits that he has voluntarily committed what is prima facie a crime with the state of mind normally sufficient for that offence but at the same time asserts some *special* circumstances which he claims excuse or justify his actions. As Lord Wilberforce said of duress in *DPP for Northern Ireland v Lynch* [1975] AC 653 (at pp. 679–80): A3.20

> [It] is something which is superimposed upon the other ingredients which by themselves would make up an offence, i.e., upon act and intention. . . . the victim completes the act and knows that he is doing so; but the addition of the element of duress prevents the law from treating what he has done as a crime.

Duress by Threats: General Principles

There has been a great deal of development since the 1960s in the defence of duress by threats. Its basis seems to be excuse rather than justification; an analysis confirmed by the A3.21

House of Lords in *Hasan* [2005] 2 AC 467 at [18]. The details of the defence can conveniently be considered under three headings: the type of threat necessary, the required cogency of the threat, and the offences and persons excluded from the defence.

A3.22 **The Type of Threat Required** All the decisions recognising duress as a defence have concerned threats of death or grievous bodily harm although in *Steane* [1947] KB 997, Lord Goddard CJ, *obiter*, included fear of imprisonment which has not been ruled out by the plethora of more recent authorities — see, e.g., Lord Lane CJ in *Graham* [1982] 1 WLR 294 leaving open the question of whether false imprisonment could be relied on. It would seem from *Baker* [1997] Crim LR 497 that a threat of serious psychological injury will not suffice and in *Quayle* [2005] 1 WLR 3642 it was said that an 'imminent danger of physical injury was required. Another question is whether the threat has to be directed at the accused or whether threats to third parties, especially close relatives, can suffice. There seems to be more consensus on this point and certainly in principle threats to third parties should be *capable* of constituting duress since even the bravest man may be prepared to risk his own neck whilst flinching at subjecting his loved ones to serious peril. In *Ortiz* (1986) 83 Cr App R 173 threats to the accused's wife or family appear to have been considered to be sufficient and the suggestion in the 2003 Judicial Studies Board specimen direction that the threat can be directed to the accused or a member of his immediate family or alternatively 'to a person for whose safety the defendant would reasonably regard himself as responsible' commended itself to Lord Bingham in *Hasan* [2005] 2 AC 467 as being 'if strictly applied . . . consistent with the rationale of the duress exception'.

A3.23 **The Cogency of the Threat** The fact that the accused believes that a threat of death or grievous bodily harm will be carried out if he does not commit the offence is not of itself sufficient 'if a person of reasonable firmness sharing the characteristics of the defendant would not have given way to the threats' (third certified question in *Howe* [1987] AC 417). In other words, the threat is only sufficiently cogent, and the accused will only be excused, if a person of reasonable firmness might have done the same thing. This objective approach was most clearly articulated by Lord Lane CJ in *Graham* [1982] 1 WLR 294 in a suggested direction (at p. 300) later approved by the House of Lords in *Howe*:

> (1) Was the defendant, or may he have been, impelled to act as he did because, as a result of what he reasonably believed [the threatener] had said or done, he had good cause to fear that if he did not so act [the threatener] would kill him or . . . cause him serious physical injury? (2) If so, have the prosecution made the jury sure that a sober person of reasonable firmness, sharing the characteristics of the defendant, would not have responded to whatever he reasonably believed [the threatener] said or did by taking part [in the offence].

Although the requirement of reasonableness, in relation to the accused's belief as to the facts, has been questioned by, amongst others, the Law Commission (whose subjective approach in its 1993 Report on Legislating the Criminal Code continued to be preferred by Baroness Hale in *Hasan* [2005] 2 AC 467 and has been the subject of some vacillation in the Court of Appeal (see *DPP* v *Rogers* [1998] Crim LR 202, *Cairns* [1999] 2 Cr App R 137, *Martin* [2000] 2 Cr App R 42 and *Safi* [2004] 1 Cr App R 157), Lord Bingham, with whose speech the majority concurred in *Hasan*, was clear that 'there is no warrant for relaxing the requirement that the belief must be reasonable as well as genuine.'

Turning from reasonableness of belief to the reasonableness of the accused's response in committing the offence, the extent to which a person of reasonable firmness shares the characteristics of the accused is a moot point. In *Bowen* [1997] 1 WLR 372, Stuart-Smith LJ, in denying the relevance of low IQ, derived a number of principles from the case law of which the seventh and last was as follows (at p. 380):

> In the absence of some direction from the judge as to what characteristics are capable of being regarded as relevant, we think that the direction approved in [*Graham*] without more will not be

> as helpful as it might be, since the jury may be tempted, especially if there is evidence, as there was in this case, relating to suggestibility and vulnerability, to think that these are relevant. *In most cases it is probably only the age and sex of the defendant that is capable of being relevant. If so, the judge should . . . confine the characteristics in question to these.* (emphasis added)

For the majority of cases, this is, it is respectfully suggested, a useful working rule, and confirms earlier cases such as *Horne* [1994] Crim LR 584 and *Hegarty* [1994] Crim LR 353, which excluded psychiatric or medical evidence to the effect that the accused was unusually pliable or vulnerable to pressure or emotionally unstable or in a 'grossly elevated neurotic state'. There remains the difficult question of what characteristics other than age and sex can exceptionally be relevant. In *Bowen* Stuart-Smith LJ gave some examples in his second principle (at p. 379) whereby:

> the defendant may be in a category of persons who the jury may think less able to resist pressure than people not within that category. Obvious examples are age, where a young person may well not be so robust as a mature one; possibly sex, though many women would doubtless consider they had as much moral courage to resist pressure as men; pregnancy, where there is added fear for the unborn child; serious physical disability, which may inhibit self protection; recognised mental illness or psychiatric condition, such as post traumatic stress disorder leading to learned helplessness.

Putting aside age, the true relevance of most of these it is submitted lies in the fact that they increase the gravity of the threat rather than reducing the courage or steadfastness of the accused. A threat of physical violence to a pregnant woman is much more serious because of the vulnerability of the child in the womb. Similarly, physical violence to a physically disabled person is more serious and likely to result in more serious harm if there is reduced ability to defend oneself or ward off blows. On this basis, the mention of 'recognised mental illness or psychiatric condition, such as post traumatic stress disorder', which seems to refer to conditions rendering sufferers 'more susceptible to pressure and threats' (see the fifth principle described in the judgment of Stuart-Smith LJ at p. 379) may be thought problematic since it conflicts with the basic premise of the objective test of a person of reasonable firmness. However, it is clear that the courts will accept post-traumatic stress disorder as a relevant characteristic (see *Sewell* [2004] EWCA Crim 2322) and in *Antar* (2004) *The Times*, 4 November 2004 the evidence of a psychologist as to the appellant's level of suggestibility should, in the Court of Appeal's view, have been put before the jury since it was not merely put 'on the basis of the appellant's very low IQ, but on the basis of the psychologist's opinion that he functioned cognitively at a significantly impaired level; that he had a moderate (now a mild) learning disability; and importantly, that he had a level of suggestibility sufficiently higher than that of the general population.' The decision in *Antar* seems to be a fairly generous application of the fifth principle in *Bowen*, which is as follows.

> Psychiatric evidence may be admissible to show that the accused is suffering from some mental illness, mental impairment or recognised psychiatric condition provided persons generally suffering from such condition may be more susceptible to pressure and threats and thus to assist the jury in deciding whether a reasonable person suffering from such a condition might have been impelled to act as the defendant did. It is not admissible simply to show that in the doctor's opinion an accused, who is not suffering from such illness or condition, is especially timid, suggestible or vulnerable to pressure and threats. . . .

Vulnerability to pressure and threats is not of itself relevant unless, it seems, the accused belongs to a particular category of persons recognised as so vulnerable and this inevitably puts pressure on the criteria for recognising such a category, whether they be medical or otherwise.

The reference to a 'sober' person of reasonable firmness makes it plain that intoxication cannot be a relevant characteristic. Intoxication is of course normally self-induced (quaere whether involuntary intoxication might be relevant) and in *Flatt* [1996] Crim LR 576 it was held that other self-induced conditions, such as being a drug addict, are excluded.

The immediacy of the threat and the possibility of seeking official protection are matters which the Court of Appeal said, in *Hurst* [1995] 1 Cr App R 82, require more attention to be paid to them. These matters were considered in *Hudson* [1971] 2 QB 202 and the court there declined to lay down any hard and fast rules other than to say that:

> It is essential to the defence of duress that the threat shall be effective at the moment when the crime is committed. The threat must be a 'present' threat in the sense that it is effective to neutralise the will of the accused at that time.
>
> . . . the existence at that moment of threats sufficient to destroy his will ought to provide him with a defence even though the threatened injury may not follow instantly, but after an interval. . . .
>
> In the present case [of perjury] the threats . . . were likely to be no less compelling, because their execution could not be effected in the court room, if they could be carried out in the streets of Salford the same night.

Whether the accused could be expected to take any opportunity of rendering the threat ineffective in the meantime by, for example, seeking police protection was a matter for the jury and:

> In deciding whether such an opportunity was reasonably open to the accused the jury should have regard to his age and circumstances, and to any risks to him which may be involved.

In *Hasan* at [27], Lord Bingham attributed to the decision in *Hudson*:

> the unfortunate effect of weakening the requirement that execution of a threat must be reasonably believed to be imminent and immediate if it is to support a plea of duress . . . I can understand that the Court of Appeal [in *Hudson*] had sympathy with the predicament of the young appellants but I cannot, consistently with principle, accept that a witness testifying in the Crown Court at Manchester has no opportunity to avoid complying with a threat incapable of execution then or there.

For the future, Lord Bingham thought (at [28]) that it should:

> be made clear to juries that if the retribution threatened against the defendant or his family or a person for whom he reasonably feels responsible is not such as he reasonably expects to follow immediately or almost immediately on his failure to comply with the threat, there may be little if any room for doubt that he could have taken evasive action, whether by going to the police or in some other way, to avoid committing the crime with which he is charged.

Although, as matter of logic, both the question of the immediacy of the threat and the question of any opportunity to render it ineffective could be subsumed under the question of whether under the *Graham* test a person of reasonable firmness would have responded to the threat by committing the offence, Lord Bingham specifically warned (at [24]) against collapsing these questions together.

Duress by Threats: Excluded Offences and Persons

A3.24 Although duress has now been recognised as available on a wide range of charges, including strict liability offences (see *Eden DC v Braid* [1999] RTR 329), and is available in contempt proceedings (see *K* (1983) 78 Cr App R 82), and is to that extent a general defence, there have always been doubts about whether it extends to murder or certain types of treason.

A3.25 **Murder** In *Howe* [1987] AC 417, the House of Lords unequivocally held that the defence of duress is *not* available on a murder charge either to a principal offender or to a secondary party, and in so doing declined to follow its own previous decision in *DPP for Northern Ireland v Lynch* [1975] AC 653. Singling out murder in this way does itself raise some anomalies, particularly in that duress appears still to be a defence to wounding with intent under the OAPA 1861, whereas if the victim should die the intent to cause grievous bodily harm is sufficient to found a murder charge and the defence suddenly becomes unavailable. The exclusion of duress applies equally on a charge of attempted murder (see *Gotts* [1992] 2

AC 412). There is thus no defence in law on a charge of murder available, even to a 13-year-old complying with instructions from his father which he was too frightened to disobey (*Wilson* (2007) *The Times*, 6 June 2007).

The Law Commission has recommended in its Report 'Murder, Manslaughter and Infanticide' (Law Com No. 304, 2006) that duress should be a defence to murder but with the legal burden on the accused.

Treason Duress, or something akin to it, seems to have been recognised as a defence to certain forms of treason both as long ago as 1419 (*Oldcastle's Case* (1419) 1 Hale PC 50) and as relatively recently as 1945 in *Purdy* (1945) 10 JCL 182 (although see per Lord Goddard CJ in *Steane* [1947] KB 997 at p. 1005). Writers such as Hale and Stephen have doubted whether duress applies to the more serious forms of treason and the judges have traditionally reserved their opinion as to the extent to which duress is available (see, for example, Lord Brandon in *Howe* [1987] AC 417 at p. 438). Given the decision in *Howe*, the courts may well be unwilling to allow a plea of duress where the particular act of treason would inevitably lead to the deaths of identifiable individuals, even if it would be difficult or impossible to bring a murder charge in relation to those deaths. **A3.26**

Excluded Persons It is now clear that a person cannot rely on the defence of duress if he has voluntarily and knowingly exposed himself to the risk of such duress by joining a criminal organisation or gang. One of the earlier illustrations of this principle was in the Northern Ireland case of *Fitzpatrick* [1977] NI 20 where the accused had voluntarily joined the IRA and was therefore unable to plead duress based on threats from that organisation as a defence to, *inter alia*, armed robbery carried out on its behalf. The restriction on the defence was supported by dicta of members of the House of Lords in *DPP for Northern Ireland v Lynch* [1975] AC 653 and by provisions of various Commonwealth codes and has been applied by the English Court of Appeal in *Sharp* [1987] QB 853. Sharp was a member of a gang which had carried out a series of armed robberies. He sought to plead duress as a defence to manslaughter when a sub-postmaster was shot dead by the gang leader during the course of the last robbery. Sharp alleged that he had sought to withdraw from this robbery when he saw the guns being put into the car but that a gun had then been pointed at him and a threat made 'to blow his head off' if he did not participate. Lord Lane CJ said (at p. 861): **A3.27**

> . . . where a person has voluntarily, and with knowledge of its nature, joined a criminal organisation or gang which he knew might bring pressure on him to commit an offence and was an active member when he was put under such pressure, he cannot avail himself of the defence of duress.

It is clear from this statement that the organisation or gang must be one likely to exercise duress and the accused must be aware of this when he joins. In *Shepherd* (1987) 86 Cr App R 47, the accused, a member of a shoplifting gang, claimed that he found the experience unnerving and that he had only taken part in a subsequent burglary because of threats of violence to himself and his family. The Court of Appeal quashed the conviction for burglary as the trial judge had wrongly withdrawn the defence of duress from the jury purely on the basis that the accused had voluntarily joined a criminal organisation. Mustill LJ said (at p. 51):

> . . . the concerted shoplifting enterprise did not involve violence to the victim either in anticipation or in the way it was actually put into effect. The members of the jury have had to ask themselves whether the appellant could be said to have taken the risk of P's violence simply by joining a shoplifting gang.

The precise ambit of the accused's knowledge was at issue in a number of conflicting Court of Appeal cases between 1999 and 2003, most of them cases involving duress exercised in furtherance of debts run up for the illegal supply of drugs. The last of these cases, *Z* [2003] 1 WLR 1489 (although not in itself a drugs case) *appeared* to settle the conflict and held that the proper question relates to the risk of compulsion to commit 'offences of the type charged'. Thus on the facts of *Z*, the accused's participation in a prostitution racket may not have been thought by the jury to lay him open to an offence as serious as aggravated burglary. However *Z* went to the House of Lords under the name of *Hasan* [2005] 2 AC 467 and was reversed and the accused's conviction restored. The certified question was as follows:

> Whether the defence of duress is excluded when as a result of the accused's voluntary association with others:
> (i) he foresaw (or possibly should have foreseen) the risk of being subjected to any compulsion by threats of violence, or
> (ii) only when he foresaw (or should have foreseen) the risk of being subjected to compulsion to commit criminal offences, and, if the latter,
> (iii) only if the offences foreseen (or which should have been foreseen) were of the same type (or possibly of the same type and gravity) as that ultimately committed.

In a speech, which generally took a deliberately restrictive approach to the ambit of the defence of duress (see **A3.23**), Lord Bingham effectively selected option (i), which is of course the widest possible limitation on the defence. Not only that, it was the wider more objective form of option (i) which was approved, whereby it was enough that the risk of compulsion *ought* to have been foreseen rather than that it must have been *actually* foreseen by the accused. Option (i) means that not only do the foreseeable consequences of the compulsion not need to include offences of the same type as those with which the accused has actually been charged but there is not even any *requirement* that the foreseeable compulsion be related to the commission of any offences at all. The implications of this can be illustrated by reference to *Heath* [2000] Crim LR 109, where it seemed to be enough that the accused knew that in the drugs world violence is used to enforce debts and therefore, when his debt was enforced by means of requiring him to commit offences, he could not rely on duress.

Although it was Lord Bingham's speech with which the majority agreed, Baroness Hale, in agreeing with the decision to allow the Crown's appeal, answered the certified question in a slightly different fashion and chose option (ii) (again with, it would seem, the objective variant of 'should have foreseen'). Given that by definition in these cases a criminal offence has been committed following threats, it is difficult to see that there will be any significant cases (which ought to be covered) that would not be covered as being offences that 'should have been foreseen' under the objective variant of option (ii) favoured by Baroness Hale. This would suggest that the selection of option (i) by the majority is unnecessary and, arguably, unduly restrictive of the defence.

Baroness Hale also indicated a need to put a limitation on the exclusion of duress, by means of further explanation of the requirement of 'voluntary association' with the duressor, referring back also to the Law Commission's requirement that the exposure to the risk of duress should be 'without reasonable excuse', so as to cater for 'battered wives' or 'others in close personal or family relationships with their duressors and their associates, such as their mothers, brothers or children'. She prefaced this by saying (at [78]):

> It is one thing to deny the defence to people who choose to become members of illegal organisations, join criminal gangs, or engage with others in drug-related criminality. It is another thing to deny it to someone who has a quite different reason for becoming associated with the duressor and then finds it difficult to escape.

Necessity

A3.28 It has long been unclear whether a general defence of necessity exists in English law. The courts have now recognised a defence of duress of circumstances that achieves many of the same results. It is first necessary to examine the nature of, and the authorities concerning, necessity in order to appreciate the more recent cases on duress of circumstances.

Necessity differs from duress in that it is generally conceived of not as a concession to human frailty, i.e. as an excuse, but rather as a *justified* choice between two evils — the evil represented by committing the offence is outweighed by the greater evil which would ensue if the offence were not to be committed. This difference is often lost sight of because cases where necessity is raised also tend to be cases where there is an arguable case for excusing the accused.

The leading case of *Dudley* (1884) 14 QBD 273 is a good example which is complicated by the fact that it was a murder charge (and involved cannibalism). (As with duress, the courts are reluctant to widen the range of available defences in such cases.) The two accused had found themselves adrift in a small boat on the high seas with another man and the young cabin boy. They had had virtually no food or water for 20 days and had been reduced, for example, to drinking their own urine. Finally they killed and ate the cabin-boy who was likely anyway to have been the first to die and without this deed they would probably themselves not have survived the further four days which elapsed before they were rescued. In rejecting any defence of necessity on these facts, Lord Coleridge CJ constantly switched from the language of justification to that of excuse, but it was the notion of justification which appears to have been dominant. On that basis, the defence was probably doomed on the facts since the jury had found that there was no greater necessity for killing the boy than any of the others. Although *Dudley* was distinguished by Brooke LJ in *Re A (Children) (conjoined twins: surgical separation)* [2001] Fam 147, ruling to be lawful an operation which would save one conjoined twin but kill the other; the earlier case set the tone whereby English courts have generally rejected a defence of necessity even where the balance of evils points much more clearly in favour of committing the offence. Thus in *Buckoke v Greater London Council* [1971] Ch 655 (a civil case concerning the legality of instructions issued to drivers of fire-engines), Lord Denning MR (at p. 668) accepted as correct the proposition that a driver would have no defence if he proceeded through a red light to save a man in imminent peril in a blaze 200 yards away (regulations passed since would now permit this), '. . . nevertheless such a man should not be prosecuted. He should be congratulated.'

The defence is denied in law but the realities are recognised in practice by exercising discretion in prosecuting or sentencing. (The two accused in *Dudley* were sentenced to death but their sentences were later commuted to six months' imprisonment.)

So it seems that necessity as a justification is rarely recognised by English law (but see the dicta of Lord Brandon and Lord Goff in *F v West Berkshire Health Authority* [1990] 2 AC 1) as a general defence although *particular* offences may be defined in such a way as to make such a defence available. For example, the presence of the word 'unlawfully' in the OAPA 1861, s. 58, was used in *Bourne* [1939] 1 KB 687 to show that some abortions must be lawful and that that included one performed in good faith for the purpose of preserving the life of the mother (see now the Abortion Act 1967). Other statutes have more obvious specific defences such as that of lawful excuse in the Criminal Damage Act 1971 (see **B8.9**). The reluctance of the courts to recognise a *general* defence of necessity (as a justification) perhaps reflects sentiments similar to those expressed by Dickson J in the Supreme Court of Canada in *Perka* (1984) 13 DLR (4th) 1 where he said (at p. 14):

> It is still my opinion that, 'No system of positive law can recognise any principle which would entitle a person to violate the law because on his view the law conflicted with some higher social value' [*Morgentaler v The Queen* (1985) 53 DLR (3d) 161 at p. 209]. The Criminal Code has specified a number of identifiable situations in which an actor is justified in committing what would otherwise be a criminal offence. To go beyond that and hold that ostensibly illegal acts can be validated on the basis of their expediency, would import an undue subjectivity into the criminal law. It would invite the courts to second-guess the legislature and to assess the relative merits of social policies underlying criminal prohibitions.

Similar considerations influenced the Law Commission in once recommending (Law Com. No. 83 — but see now Law Com. No. 218, para. 35.7) that any general defence of necessity that might exist should be abolished. This proposal would have presented the apparent anomaly that a man who committed an offence in response to threats would have the defence of duress whereas if the pressure were created by some natural emergency or surrounding circumstances, no defence would be available. As will be seen in **A3.29**, the courts (and indeed the Law Commission — see Law Com. No. 218, para. 35.1) are now addressing this anomaly by recognising, as an excuse rather than as a justification, the defence of duress of circumstances which, again in the words of Dickson J in *Perka* is:

> much less open to criticism. It rests on a realistic assessment of human weakness, recognising that a liberal and humane criminal law cannot hold people to the strict obedience of laws in emergency situations where normal human instincts, whether of self-preservation or of altruism, overwhelmingly impel disobedience. The objectivity of the criminal law is preserved; such acts are still wrongful, but in the circumstances they are excusable. Praise is indeed not bestowed, but pardon is, when one does a wrongful act under pressure.

Duress of Circumstances

A3.29 The early authorities on the defence of duress of circumstances were a series of cases dealing with road traffic offences, but in *Pommell* [1995] 2 Cr App R 607 the Court of Appeal confirmed that the defence applies to all crimes except murder, attempted murder and some forms of treason. The first case was *Willer* (1986) 83 Cr App R 225 where the accused drove his car on to the pavement and into (and back out of) a shopping precinct to escape from a gang of youths bent on attacking himself and his passengers. At his trial for reckless driving, the judge refused to put the defence of necessity to the jury, but the Court of Appeal thought that 'a very different defence', that of duress, should have been available. According to Watkins LJ (at p. 227 emphasis added) the question then would be:

> whether or not upon the outward or the return journey, or both, the appellant was wholly driven *by force of circumstance* into doing what he did and did not drive the car otherwise than under that form of compulsion.

It should be noted that although there were, in a sense, threats to the accused in this case, it was not a case of duress *by threats* as traditionally understood since in such a case the accused commits in order to *comply* with the threatener's demands rather than merely to *escape* from the threats. On the distinction between the two types of duress, see *Cole* [1994] Crim LR 582. *Willer* was followed and applied in *Conway* [1989] QB 290, another reckless driving case, in which the Court of Appeal quashed the conviction, saying (at p. 297) 'it is still not clear whether there is a general defence of necessity' and 'necessity can only be a defence to a charge of reckless driving where the facts establish "duress of circumstances" '. See also *DPP v Harris* [1995] 1 Cr App R 170 for discussion of whether 'necessity of circumstances' can be a defence to a charge of driving without due care and attention for a police driver going through a red light. In *Backshall* [1998] 1 WLR 1506 the Court of Appeal confirmed that the defence is indeed available on a charge of driving without due care, a conclusion consistent with that in *Pommell* that the defence is of general application.

In *Martin* [1989] 1 All ER 652, duress of circumstances was recognised as a potential defence to driving while disqualified. According to Simon Brown J, it could arise from 'objective dangers threatening the accused or others' but 'the defence is available only if, from an objective standpoint, the accused can be said to be acting reasonably and proportionately in order to avoid a threat of death or serious injury'. The questions for the jury would then be virtually identical to that in relation to duress by threats (see **A3.21** to **A3.23**):

> . . . first, was the accused, or may he have been, impelled to act as he did because as a result of what he reasonably believed to be the situation he had good cause to fear that otherwise death or serious physical injury would result; second, if so, would a sober person of reasonable firmness, sharing the characteristics of the accused, have responded to that situation by acting as the accused acted?

The reference to the sober person of reasonable firmness shows that, as with duress by threats, the crucial question is not so much whether the accused was justified as whether he can be excused on the grounds that a reasonable person would have felt impelled to act in the same way.

The circumstances impelling the accused to act must be external to himself, so that the suicidal thoughts of life sentence prisoners could not of themselves amount to relevant circumstances excusing the offence of prison breaking according to the Court of Appeal in *Rodger* [1998] 1 Cr App R 143. The suicidal thoughts were 'a purely subjective element' as is the pain from which the cultivators of cannabis may wish to seek relief (*Quayle* [2005] 1 WLR 3642).

Duress of circumstances has also been allowed by the Divisional Court on a charge of driving with excess alcohol in *DPP v Bell* [1992] RTR 335, where the accused, because of his terror of his pursuers, ran back to his car and drove off some distance down the road. The fact he did not continue to drive all the way home supported the finding that he was driving because of his fear and not because of any prior intention to use his car to get home even if intoxicated. This contrasted with the earlier case of *DPP v Jones* [1990] RTR 33 where a similar defence failed because the accused drove the two miles home without even bothering to check whether he was still being pursued. *DPP v Davis* [1994] Crim LR 600 was to similar effect and reflected an increasingly restrictive attitude to both types of duress, which has since been explicitly articulated in *Hasan* [2005] 2 AC 467 (discussed at **A3.23** and **A3.27**) and applied in *Quayle* to deny the defence in relation to the production etc. of cannabis. *Quayle* was followed in *Altham* [2006] 1 WLR 3287, where the ECHR, Article 7 was unsuccessfully invoked by the appellant. *DPP v Mullally* [2006] EWHC 3448 (Admin) further illustrates the increasingly restrictive attitude to duress and its failure in a motoring case; the accused continued to drive despite having been informed that the police had arrived to deal with the threat of violence.

Marital Coercion

At common law there was a rebuttable presumption that a wife who committed an offence (except murder or treason) in the presence of her husband did so under coercion and that she should be acquitted. The presumption was abolished by the CJA 1925, s. 47, which nevertheless went on to provide that: **A3.30**

> on a charge against a wife for any offence other than treason or murder it shall be a good defence to prove that the offence was committed in the presence of, and under the coercion of, the husband.

Clearly this section imposes a legal burden of proof on the wife, but it has not been clear what exactly constitutes coercion and in what sense it differs from duress. Coercion is presumably wider than duress since otherwise the defence is otiose, the wife having to prove duress *plus* the actual presence of her husband. It seems that it is wider in that there is no need for threats of death or serious injury, it being sufficient that the wife acted because of the dominating influence of her husband, her will being 'overborne by the wishes of her husband' so that 'she was forced unwillingly to participate' (see *Shortland* [1996] 1 Cr App R 116, followed in *Cairns* [2003] 1 WLR 796 where a direction that 'coercion does not just mean physical force or the threat of physical force' was considered ambiguous and did not make clear that physical force or a threat of it was not actually required). The defence may be thought to be either an anachronism or a defence that, on the grounds of sexual equality, ought to be extended to husbands acting under the dominating influence of their wives. The Law Commission has recommended its abolition (Law Com. No. 83 and Law Com. No. 218, para. 32.6).

Self-defence, Prevention of Crime, and Related Defences Generally

These defences are generally regarded as matters of justification rather than excuse. It is **A3.31**
perhaps stretching matters a little to say that they are general defences since they are available

only as defences to crimes committed by the use of force (see *Renouf* [1986] 1 WLR 522, where reckless driving was regarded as involving force where the only relevant evidence of reckless driving was the 'forcing' of another car off the road). Nevertheless, they are undoubtedly available to a wide range of offences. Where there is evidence 'which if accepted could raise a prima facie case of self-defence, this should be left to the jury even if the accused has not formally relied upon self-defence' (*DPP (Jamaica) v Bailey* [1995] 1 Cr App R 257). Where self-defence is not available because the offence charged does not involve the use of force, duress of circumstances may equally be available (see *Symonds* [1998] Crim LR 280).

Self-defence, defence of property and defence of another (sometimes referred to collectively as 'private defence') are still governed by the common law whereas the law on prevention of crime is now contained in the Criminal Law Act 1967, s. 3(1), which provides that:

> A person may use such force as is reasonable in the circumstances in the prevention of crime, or in effecting or assisting in the lawful arrest of offenders or suspected offenders or of persons unlawfully at large.

The term 'crime' here means a crime in domestic law and this does not include a crime such as 'aggression', which is recognised only in customary international law (*Jones* [2007] 1 AC 136). More generally, in relation to 'direct action protesters' who claim 'to be justified in doing acts which would otherwise be criminal', Lord Hoffman had the following to say (at [94]):

> In a case in which the defence requires that the acts of the defendant should in all the circumstances have been reasonable, his acts must be considered in the context of a functioning state in which legal disputes can be peacefully submitted to the courts and disputes over what should be law or government policy can be submitted to the arbitrament of the democratic process. In such circumstances, the apprehension, however honest or reasonable, of acts which are thought to be unlawful or contrary to the public interest, cannot justify the commission of criminal acts and the issue of justification should be withdrawn from the jury. Evidence to support the opinions of the protesters as to the legality of the acts in question is irrelevant and inadmissible, disclosure going to this issue should not be ordered and the services of international lawyers are not required.

The criterion of 'such force as is reasonable in the circumstances' differs slightly from traditional formulations of the common-law rule for self-defence which usually also include some reference to necessity. See, for example, per Lord Lane CJ in *Williams* [1987] 3 All ER 411 at p. 414: 'the exercise of any necessary and reasonable force to protect himself'.

Some of the restrictive rules that applied at common law could be attributed to this reference to necessity but the modern trend seems to be to adopt a more flexible approach (as with the former so-called duty to retreat which, as will be seen, has now been abandoned). Given the fact that in most cases where the accused is acting in selfdefence he will also be acting to prevent a crime being committed by his aggressor, it would seem sensible for the tests for self-defence and prevention of crime to be identical. Even though the courts do not always formulate the test for self-defence in the exact words used in the Criminal Law Act 1967, s. 3, for prevention of crime, there is no evidence from any of the cases that any such differences are matters of substance. Indeed in *Beckford v The Queen* [1988] AC 130, Lord Griffiths said (at p. 145) that: 'the test to be applied for self-defence is that a person may use such force as is reasonable in the circumstances as he honestly believes them to be in the defence of himself or another'. Whilst his lordship was primarily concerned with the question of mistaken belief in this case, his dictum supports the view that the rules governing the use of force in self-defence and prevention of crime are now identical (see also *Clegg* [1995] 1 AC 482). If this is correct, the law can be formulated quite simply and neatly along the following lines:

A person may use such force as is reasonable in the circumstances for the purposes of:

(a) self-defence or
(b) defence of another or
(c) defence of property or
(d) prevention of crime or
(e) lawful arrest.

Although this formulation makes no express mention of any requirement that the use of force should be necessary (neither does the Criminal Law Act 1967, s. 3), it should be remembered that if the use of force is clearly unnecessary (e.g., because the initial aggressor has started to retreat — see *Priestnall v Cornish* [1979] Crim LR 310) it will not be 'reasonable in the circumstances' to use force.

Self-defence and Pre-emptive Strikes A person can use force to ward off an anticipated attack provided that it is anticipated as 'imminent' (*Chisam* (1963) 47 Cr App R 130). In *Beckford v The Queen* [1988] AC 130, Lord Griffiths said (at p. 144) 'a man about to be attacked does not have to wait for his assailant to strike the first blow or fire the first shot; circumstances may justify a pre-emptive strike'. However, if a threat of force may be expected to deter the attacker, it may be difficult to convince the jury that it was reasonable to use actual force (cf. *Cousins* [1982] QB 526). **A3.32**

Scope of Defence of Another Given the overlap already referred to between, e.g., self-defence and prevention of crime, the precise boundaries of the individual defences are not always clear. Thus it is unclear whether defence of another is restricted to defence of a relative (and if so, how close) or extends to anyone with a sufficient nexus with the defender (*Devlin v Armstrong* [1971] NI 13) or to anyone at all. In *Duffy* [1967] 1 QB 63 the Court of Appeal found it unnecessary to decide whether defence of another extended to defence of a sister since what was done could be justified on the alternative basis of prevention of crime. The only case where this might not be so would be where the defender knows that the attacker is, for example, insane or under age, so that it cannot be said that he is acting 'in the prevention of crime' (cf. the reasoning of Ward LJ in *Re A (Children) (conjoined twins: surgical separation)* [2001] Fam 147). In such a case one would need to determine whether the person being attacked has a sufficient nexus with the defender to be within the scope of defence of another. In order to prevent anomalies, the better view is surely that no such nexus should be required and that one can act in defence of any other person (as recommended by the Criminal Law Revision Committee (14th Report)) provided, as always, that the use of force is reasonable in the circumstances. **A3.33**

Scope of Defence of Property As with defence of another, it is unclear to what extent defending property of other persons is a justification for committing a crime, but the arguments in favour of having no restrictions are the same. In *DPP v Bayer* [2004] 1 WLR 2856, it was emphasised that the accused must be acting to ward off an 'unlawful or criminal act'. Therefore defence of property did not arise in relation to opposing the lawful sowing of GM seed. In relation to defence of one's own home, it should be noted that the statement approved in *Hussey* (1924) 18 Cr App R 160 that: 'In defence of a man's house, the owner or his family may kill a trespasser who would forcibly dispossess him of it' is of debatable authority today. Forceful resistance would no doubt be in order (which might unintentionally cause death) but deliberate killing would normally be hard to justify. **A3.34**

Following public controversy as to the degree of force permissible in one's own home in the aftermath of cases such as *Martin* [2002] 2 WLR 1 (see **A3.36**), a Joint Public Statement from the Crown Prosecution Service and the Association of Chief Police Officers was published and widely distributed in February 2005, giving guidance to householders faced with an intruder in their homes. It is available at www.cps.gov.uk/publications/prosecution/householders.html.

A3.35 **No Duty to Retreat per se** The statement approved in *Hussey* (1924) 18 Cr App R 160 and quoted in **A3.34** went on to say of the defender that '. . . in defending his home he need not retreat, as in other cases of self-defence, for that would be giving up his house to his adversary'. There is no longer any duty to retreat in any category of private defence. The duty was first watered down in *Julien* [1969] 1 WLR 839 where it was said (at p. 843) that 'what is necessary is that he should demonstrate by his actions that he does not want to fight'. Even this was subsequently held, in *Bird* [1985] 1 WLR 816, to be too restrictive. It is not 'necessary' to demonstrate by one's actions an unwillingness to fight. That is merely one way of negativing any suggestion that the defendant was the attacker or was acting out of motives of retaliation or revenge rather than self-defence, but it is by no means the only method of doing that. The denial of the duty to retreat underlines the shift away from formulating the defence as being the *necessary* use of force towards the use of force which is reasonable in the circumstances. If it is *possible* to retreat then the use of force is in one sense unnecessary but the real question is whether the accused acted reasonably in using force rather than retreating. As Edmund-Davies LJ said in *McInnes* [1971] 1 WLR 1600 at p. 1607: 'We prefer the view expressed by the Full Court of [South] Australia [in *Howe* [1958] SASR 95] that a failure to retreat is only an *element* in the consideration upon which the reasonableness of an accused's conduct is to be judged'. Similarly, there is no hard and fast rule that a person who initiates a confrontation cannot rely on self-defence (*Balogun* [1999] EWCA Crim 2120) nor that it cannot be used against an assailant who is known to be a police officer (*Burley* [2000] Crim LR 843). Although the appeal was dismissed on the facts, the Court of Appeal in *Rashford* [2005] EWCA Crim 3377 has re-emphasised that the fact that a person is the initial aggressor does not automatically mean that he cannot be acting in self-defence. Dyson LJ approved the Scottish decision in *Burns v HM Advocate* 1995 SLT 1090 as an important decision which should be more widely known wherein (at p. 1093H) it was said that the question:

> depends upon whether the violence offered by the victim was so out of proportion to the accused's own actings as to give rise to the reasonable apprehension that he was in an immediate danger from which he had no other means of escape, and whether the violence which he then used was no more than was necessary to preserve his own life or protect himself from serious injury.

A3.36 **The Degree of Force Permitted** The degree of force used by an accused will not be regarded as reasonable unless the accused believed that it was necessary to use that degree of force — it is unreasonable to use force that one knows to be unnecessary. However, necessity is not enough — fatal force may be the only way of stopping a starving man trying to steal a loaf of bread but that does not make killing in such circumstances justified: it is not reasonable in the circumstances.

The basic rule is that if the accused misjudges the degree of force permissible and uses excessive force, he is deprived of the defence. Although this may appear harsh on an accused who has genuinely tried to use only a reasonable degree of force but who has in fact over-reacted, the courts apply the rule in a manner which takes account of the motives of the accused and which is no longer wholly objective. Thus in *Palmer v The Queen* [1971] AC 814, Lord Morris of Borth-y-Gest said (at p. 832):

> . . . it will be recognised that a person defending himself cannot weigh to a nicety the exact measure of his necessary defensive action. If a jury thought that in a moment of unexpected anguish a person attacked had only done what he honestly and instinctively thought was necessary that would be most potent evidence that only reasonable defensive action had been taken. A jury will be told that the defence of self-defence, where the evidence makes its raising possible, will only fail if the prosecution show beyond doubt that what the accused did was not by way of self-defence.

This approach was described by Ormrod LJ in *Shannon* (1980) 71 Cr App R 192 at p. 194 as:

> a bridge between what is sometimes referred to as 'the objective test', that is what is reasonable judged from the viewpoint of an outsider looking at a situation quite dispassionately, and 'the subjective test', that is the viewpoint of the accused himself with the intellectual capabilities of which he may in fact be possessed and with all the emotional strains and stresses to which at the moment he may be subjected.

The Court of Appeal in this case quashed the conviction because the judge had ignored the subjective aspect of the question and put the question to the jury purely as: 'Did the appellant use more force than was necessary in the circumstances?' whereas the real question, according to Ormrod LJ (at p. 197), was:

> Was this stabbing within the conception of necessary self-defence judged by the standards of common sense, bearing in mind the position of the appellant at the moment of the stabbing, or was it a case of angry retaliation or pure aggression on his part?

It would seem that the reasonableness of the degree of force used is coming close to being treated as merely evidence of whether the accused was genuinely motivated by self-defence or whether he was in fact acting with some other illegitimate motive, excessive force being evidence that self-defence was not the accused's real purpose. In *Whyte* [1987] 3 All ER 416, the facts were said not to warrant a reference to the subjective aspect of the test as the accused had used an already open knife. However, in *Scarlett* [1993] 4 All ER 629, the failure of the trial judge to mention the subjective perspective caused the conviction to be quashed. Indeed the Court of Appeal in this case came very close to rendering the test a wholly subjective one by saying that provided the accused 'believed that the circumstances called for the degree of force used, he was not to be convicted even if his belief was unreasonable'. A restrictive interpretation of *Scarlett* was taken in *Owino* [1996] 2 Cr App R 128, but this was technically *obiter* as it was a case where the conviction was upheld on the grounds that the trial judge, in saying that the prosecution must prove that the accused did not believe that he was using reasonable force, went further in the defence's favour than the law required. The Court of Appeal took the view that it was certainly not incumbent on the judge to go further and state that the test of what force was reasonable was subjective. The move back towards the objective test has been further underlined by the Court of Appeal in *DPP v Armstrong-Braun* [1999] Crim LR 417. The circumstances of this case however seem to be a long way from the 'moment of unexpected anguish' envisaged in *Palmer* and referred to again approvingly by the Court of Appeal in the civil case *Cross v Kirkby* (2000) *The Times*, 5 April 2000. Even under the ECHR, Article 2 (which permits deadly force only where 'absolutely necessary'), some allowance appears to be made for 'heat of the moment' reactions (see *Andronicou v Cyprus* (1998) 25 EHRR 491). The troublesome borderline between subjective and objective considerations came up in a slightly different context in *Martin* [2002] 2 WLR 1. The defence tried to use the fact that, in relation to the objective condition in provocation, the House of Lords in *Smith* [2001] 1 AC 146 had allowed evidence of the accused's subjective psychiatric condition to be considered relevant. The Court of Appeal in *Martin* however said that self-defence was a distinct and complete defence and subject to different considerations. Whilst the physical characteristics of the defendant might be relevant (e.g., one presumes, to explain why a physically weaker individual used a weapon rather than physical force in self-defence) it would not be appropriate 'except in exceptional circumstances which would make the evidence especially probative, in deciding whether excessive force has been used to take into account whether the defendant is suffering from some psychiatric condition'. This of course immediately begs the question of what will count as 'exceptional circumstances' making such evidence 'especially probative'.

Where the charge is murder, there is no rule whereby, if the defence fails because of the use of excessive force, it can have the effect of reducing the conviction to manslaughter (*McInnes* [1971] 1 WLR 1600, confirmed in *Clegg* [1995] 1 AC 482). Such a rule was applied in Australia for some years (see *Howe* (1958) 100 CLR 448) but even there has been abrogated

(*Zecevic v DPP (Victoria)* (1987) 162 CLR 645). If excessive force were to be treated *purely* as an evidential factor in determining whether the accused intended to act in self-defence, there would be little or no scope for such a rule anyway but it should be noted that the Criminal Law Revision Committee (14th Report, para. 288) were in favour of the adoption of the Australian approach and this was embodied in the Draft Criminal Code Bill, cl. 59 (Law Com. No. 177). As things stand, however, the defence either succeeds, in which case the accused is acquitted, or it fails, in which case the accused will be convicted of murder (unless, as in *Martin*, the psychiatric evidence rejected as irrelevant to self-defence can be used as the basis for diminished responsibility (or provocation).

Mistakes of Fact and Self-defence

A3.37 An accused who mistakenly believes he is being attacked may still be able to rely on the defence of self-defence. Even where the main defence is that the accused was *actually* under attack, the judge may be under a duty to direct the jury on the defence of mistake if there is evidence capable of supporting such a defence (*Oatridge* (1991) 94 Cr App R 367).

Traditionally, the accused's belief had to be a reasonable one but the Court of Appeal relaxed this requirement in *Williams* [1987] 3 All ER 411, by analogy with the House of Lords decision in *DPP v Morgan* [1976] AC 182. The Criminal Law Revision Committee's recommendation that a person may use such force as is reasonable in the circumstances *as he believes them to be* was adopted by Lord Lane CJ as representing the law. This approach was approved and followed by the Privy Council in *Beckford v The Queen* [1988] AC 130, where the appeal was allowed because the trial judge had directed the jury that a reasonable belief was required. Under the ECHR, Article 2, a more demanding standard of honest belief 'for good reasons' may be required — certainly as far as trained law enforcement officers are concerned (see *Andronicou v Cyprus* (1998) 25 EHRR 491). The controversy as to how far the subjective belief rule will need amendment in the light of the HRA 1998 is discussed by Ashworth [2000] Crim LR 564 at 567 and by Leverick [2002] Crim LR 347. For the moment however, the subjective test certainly holds sway; in *Shaw v The Queen* [2001] 1 WLR 1519 even to the extent as to apply not only to the accused's belief as to the circumstances but also to his belief as to the danger involved.

The more subjective approach to mistake does not apply where the accused's mistake was due to voluntary intoxication (*O'Grady* [1987] QB 995). Although the actual conviction in this case was for manslaughter (a basic intent offence), the Court of Appeal seemed clear in the view that an intoxicated mistake could not be relied upon even in relation to a crime of specific intent such as murder. Lord Lane CJ said (at p. 999):

> We do not consider that any distinction should be drawn on this aspect of the matter between offences involving what is called specific intent, such as murder, and offences of so-called basic intent, such as manslaughter. . . . the question of mistake can and ought to be considered separately from the question of intent.

The last part of the above quotation from Lord Lane's judgment contrasts sharply with his lordship's own approach in *Williams,* where mistakes of fact were admitted even if unreasonable precisely because they can be said to negative the intent to act unlawfully. *O'Grady* has been criticised insofar as it applies to crimes of specific intent, but it was followed in *O'Connor* [1991] Crim LR 135 although in that case the conviction was reduced to manslaughter on the separate ground that the intoxication might have prevented the formation of the specific intention to cause grievous bodily harm. *O'Grady* and *O'Connor* have been re-affirmed by the Court of Appeal in *Hatton* [2006] 1 Cr App R 247. Whether the offence is one of specific intent or not is immaterial as far as the defence of self-defence is concerned and the accused cannot rely on a mistake about the existence or degree of an attack on himself which is due to self-induced intoxication. Lord Bingham regarded this position as having been settled as a matter of precedent by *O'Grady.* He also thought that the drunken mistake alleged in *Hatton* was 'pure conjecture' so that even if he had been minded to depart from *O'Grady*, that departure would have only been *obiter*. This perhaps explains his reluctance (at [26]) to enter into arguments as to whether the law was 'soundly based' which would have to be resolved 'elsewhere', although leave to appeal to the House of Lords was not granted. The facts of *Hatton*, where the accused had drunk over 20 pints of beer and could remember very little, were perhaps not the best on which to mount a challenge to *O'Grady*.

Unknown Circumstances Justifying Force in Self-defence etc.

The converse of mistaken belief in the need for self-defence is the use of force in circumstances where, unknown to the accused, the facts would in fact justify the use of force. The case of *Dadson* (1850) 2 Den CC 35 has long been thought to hold that no defence is available in these circumstances. Dadson shot and wounded a fleeing thief, but this degree of force was only permissible, even at that time, in the prevention of crime if the offence being committed amounted to a felony. The particular form of theft involved was only a felony if the thief had two previous convictions for the offence. Although this condition was in fact satisfied in this case, Dadson was unaware of this fact when he shot. His conviction was upheld. Although this case may be taken to lay down the general principle, it is modified in relation to force used to effect an arrest by the PACE 1984, s. 24. It may be argued that since, under s. 24, an arrest of a person is lawful if *in fact* he is, e.g., 'in the act of committing an offence' (s. 24(1)(b)), the use of force in such circumstances is also lawful under the Criminal Law Act 1967, s. 3. This argument appears to be compelling, though it would apply only to force used in effecting arrest, not self-defence or prevention of crime. However, s. 3 itself permits 'such force as is reasonable in the circumstances'. If the circumstances include the accused's state of mind (cf. *Williams* [1987] 3 All ER 411) it could be said that it is not *reasonable* to use force where the accused lacks any knowledge of the lawfulness of the arrest. Since an arrest can be effected without any force at all being used, the fact that the arrest itself is lawful under the PACE 1984 does not automatically validate the use of force, the reasonableness of which is a distinct question. **A3.38**

Infancy

Prior to the CDA 1998, s. 34, children fell into one of three age groups for the purposes of criminal responsibility. Once a child has reached the age of 14, no special defence based on his or her age was or is available. Children aged under 10 were (and still are) irrebuttably presumed to be incapable of criminal responsibility (*doli incapax*) by virtue of the CYPA 1933, s. 50, but in relation to children aged 10, 11, 12 or 13 there was formerly a rebuttable presumption of *doli incapax* which could be rebutted if the prosecution proved that the child had 'mischievous discretion', i.e. knew that what he or she did was 'seriously' wrong, not just naughty or mischievous (*JM v Runeckles* (1984) 79 Cr App R 255). In *C (A Minor) v DPP* [1996] AC 1 the Divisional Court had boldly decided that the rebuttable presumption no longer formed part of English law since it had become outdated in the changed conditions of society; this decision had however been promptly reversed in the House of Lords (also [1996] AC 1), where it was held that such a change could only be made by statute. Section 34 of the CDA 1998 effected that change by declaring that the 'rebuttable presumption of criminal law that a child aged 10 or over is incapable of committing an offence is hereby abolished'. It is only children under 10 therefore who are now specifically exempted from the criminal law on account of their age, the irrebuttable presumption in their case being unaffected, thus producing a clear line with responsibility commencing at the relatively young age of 10. **A3.39**

As far as children between 10 and 14 are concerned, the CDA 1998 would appear to leave them to be treated as equally responsible as adults since the *via media* of reversing rather than abolishing the presumption, which would have expressly permitted the defence to prove that the child did not understand that what he or she had done was seriously wrong, was argued for in Parliament but not accepted by the Government. The brief wording of s. 34 only expressly abolishes the rebuttable presumption in favour of the child, it does not expressly preclude the child from positively proving that he or she was incapable of committing an offence but, in view of the legislative history of s. 34, it would be a brave court that would interpret the section effectively to have merely reversed the burden of proof. Even so, in *CPS v P* (2007) 171 JP 349, Smith LJ thought that there was a potentially strong argument that the substantive defence survived.

However, in the light of the very young age of responsibility now created, the courts may well be receptive to exculpatory arguments on behalf of young children in appropriate cases. The age of the accused, whether over or under 14, is clearly a factor to be taken into account in assessing the reasonableness of the accused's conduct under the defences of provocation (see *DPP v Camplin* [1978] AC 705 at **B1.26**), duress (*Bowen* [1997] 1 WLR 372 at **A3.23**) and arguably self-defence (see **A3.36**). In crimes requiring subjective recklessness and *a fortiori* intention, the age of the accused may also be a relevant factor in assessing whether the accused did in fact foresee what might seem to be (to an adult) the obvious consequences of his actions or whether the accused was aware of the relevant circumstances. Such considerations were perhaps less acute under the old law since children who lacked an understanding of the likely consequences or full circumstances of their actions were likely to argue first that the prosecution had not discharged the burden of rebutting the presumption of *doli incapax* but, in the absence of the rebuttable presumption, arguments based on lack of *mens rea* may need to be pressed into service more often. Similarly, if a child can be shown by the defence not to be of normal development for his age (proving normal development was previously a common means for the prosecution to reverse the presumption of *doli incapax*), this could arguably be brought within the phrase 'retarded development of mind' in the Homicide Act 1957, s. 2, and thus open up the possibility of diminished responsibility on a murder charge. Arguments such as these will turn on the precise *mens rea* to be proved for the individual offence or the terms of a particular defence.

Section A4 Strict Liability and Vicarious Liability

STRICT LIABILITY GENERALLY

A4.1 Some offences do not require proof of *mens rea* in respect of one or more elements of *actus reus*. In respect of these elements, the offence is one of strict liability. Most such offences are statutory but some common-law offences, such as public nuisance (*Stephens* (1866) LR 1 QB 702), criminal libel and blasphemous libel (*Lemon* [1979] AC 617), are offences of strict liability, at least in part.

Strict liability usually arises under regulatory legislation, but it is also encountered in respect of offences where the principal statute is a rag-bag and where, accordingly, some offences to which particular defences apply none the less require full *mens rea* whereas in other offences to which such defences apply, the courts hold that the statutory defences exclude *mens rea*. Courts have regard to legislative policy as expressed in when and on what terms offences entered the law, whether they were brought forward into one consolidation despite their diverse origins, and whether one construction or another is likely to be most productive of anomalies (*K* [2002] 1 AC 642; *Kumar* [2005] 1 WLR 1352). Some statutes, of which the Trade Marks Act 1994, s. 92(1), affords an example, represent an intermediate form. These are treated as creating a prima facie liability involving certain limited mental elements as well as objective factual elements and transfer the onus of proof to a defendant to show that no offence had been committed because he believed on reasonable grounds in facts which the statute treats as exculpatory (*Johnstone* [2003] 1 WLR 1736; *Keane* [2001] FSR 7). If there is a common thread uniting cases of this sort, it is perhaps that strict liability is most likely to be applied where, from the acts performed, it would be difficult if not impossible for the court to infer that the accused acted with fault, be it intentionally or recklessly (advertently or inadvertently) (*Bradish* [1990] 1 QB 981).

Many of the enactments apply to particular trades, for example, the sale of food and drink, or medicines, or if of general application apply to few activities. Many presuppose the carrying on of a business where continuous attention to standards is important. Many of the enactments are new and represent an adaptation to an impersonal market economy. It is sometimes said that these are not 'real' crimes, but mere civil matters, prohibited under a penalty (*Sherras v De Rutzen* [1895] 1 QB 918). Such statements give no more than a rough indication of the sorts of activities to which strict liability is most likely to be applied. They do not serve as precise principles of demarcation, nor do they, as such, serve as tests for the imposition of strict liability. Strict liability within the range noted above is not incompatible with the HRA 1998 (*Muhamad* [2003] QB 1031; *Barnfather v Islington Education Authority* [2003] 1 WLR 2318).

TESTS FOR STRICT LIABILITY

A4.2 As Lord Reid noted in *Sweet v Parsley* [1970] AC 132, in cases where Parliament has not made it clear that strict liability is intended, the courts, in construing criminal legislation, start from the presumption that Parliament did not intend to punish a blameless individual and therefore that words importing *mens rea* must be read into the statute. Lord Reid also recognised, however, that strict liability is often applied to a class of quasi-criminal offences, those referred to by Wright J in *Sherras v De Rutzen* [1895] 1 QB 918 as acts which are not criminal in the real sense but which are prohibited, by a penalty, in the public interest. The question is, within this broad context, whether the danger to be guarded against is of such importance that strict liability is required (*Kirkland v Robinson* (1987) 151 JP 377). Within this broad category, courts must also inquire whether the imposition of strict liability would promote the objects of the legislation (*Lim Chin Aik v The Queen* [1963] AC 160). Whether a statutory offence falls within the category to which strict liability applies involves both a question of characterisation for courts, which are influenced by the sorts of generalisation noted above, and an inquiry into the likely efficacy of imposing strict liability. Thus, in *Gammon (Hong Kong) Ltd v A-G of Hong Kong* [1985] AC 1, a case involving breaches of building regulations, the Privy Council stressed that the matter was one of social concern, and that strict liability could be shown to promote the objects of the statute and, in particular, greater vigilance in the carrying out of works. In *Wings Ltd v Ellis* [1985] AC 272, the House of Lords relied upon the proposition that a requirement of full *mens rea* would stultify enforcement of the legislation. In *Matudi* [2003] EWCA Crim 697 the offence of importation of animal products contrary to the Products of Animal Origin (Import and Export) Regulations (SI 1996 No. 3124) was held to be one of strict liability, the court remarking that the unmonitored importation of animal products was of public concern because it posed hazards to human and animal health and possible economic consequences from an outbreak of, for example, foot and mouth disease. The social risk was great and the imposition of strict liability was likely to deter importers from acting improperly. Liability would also conduce to the use of reputable importers. The starting point is to determine how serious an offence the legislation creates and accordingly how much weight should be attached to the presumption of *mens rea* (*Muhamad* [2003] QB 1031).

Other criteria include the question of penalty. The circumstance that the likely penalty is pecuniary favours the imposition of strict liability (*Customs and Excise Commissioners, ex parte Claus* (1987) 86 Cr App R 189). This applies even though the maximum fine may be heavy (*Gammon (Hong Kong) Ltd v A-G of Hong Kong*). This is not an absolute principle: some offences bearing a heavy pecuniary penalty and even in theory a penalty of imprisonment attract strict liability (*Pharmaceutical Society of Great Britain v Storkwain Ltd* [1986] 1 WLR 903; *Blake* [1997] 1 WLR 1167; *Harrow LBC v Shah* [2000] 1 WLR 83). Allied to this is the mode of trial: where, as in *Ex parte Claus*, the offence is triable only summarily, strict liability will be more readily inferred than if the offence is triable either way or on indictment. Modern cases tend to stress the need for *mens rea* in serious offences (*Sheppard* [1981] AC 394). This is, however, a point of emphasis only and courts give considerable weight to the nature of the social danger involved, the context of the legislation as regulating a particular trade or business and, above all, the exigencies of successful enforcement.

The use of words importing *mens rea* elsewhere in a statute regulating a trade, profession or industry is often treated as an indication that an offence which uses no such words is intended to convey strict liability (*Pharmaceutical Society of Great Britain v Storkwain Ltd*; *Gammon (Hong Kong) Ltd v A-G of Hong Kong; Kirkland v Robinson* (1987) 151 JP 377; *Jackson* [2007] 1 WLR 1035). In this context, it should be noted that whilst some words such as 'intentionally' always convey *mens rea*, other words, referable to knowledge rather than to purpose, sometimes do not do so. In general, such words as 'permitting' convey the need to prove *mens rea* (*Sweet v Parsley* [1970] AC 132; *Reynolds v G.H. Austin & Sons Ltd* [1951] 2 KB 135). On some occasions they have been held not to do so (*Browning v J.W.H. Watson (Rochester) Ltd* [1953] 1 WLR 1172). The context in which a word is used may be significant and so too may be the use of the passive voice (*Cheshire County Council v Clegg* (1991) 89 LGR 600; *Cheshire County Council Trading Standards Dept, ex parte Alan Helliwell & Sons (Bolton) Ltd* [1991] Crim LR 210). 'Knowingly permitting' imports a requirement of *mens rea* into the statute (*Westminster City Council v Croyalgrange Ltd* [1986] 1 WLR 674; *Thomas* (1976) 63 Cr App R 65).

The position of the word 'knowingly' in a statutory offence may be crucial. In *Wings Ltd v Ellis* the offence of making a statement known to be false in a material particular contrary to the Trade Descriptions Act 1968, s. 14(1)(a) (see **B6.120**), was construed to require that the accused knew that the particular statement complained of was false, but not that the accused knowingly made a false statement. Wings Ltd was therefore convicted for unknowingly making a statement containing matter which was, to its knowledge, false. Apart from questions of effective enforcement, noted above, the House of Lords also relied on the literal and natural meaning of the words used and this of course was affected by their order in the subsection.

'Causing' poses difficulties both in respect of the necessary mental element and in respect of what may be regarded as having caused a prohibited phenomenon. 'Causing' is neutral as to whether *mens rea* is required (*Alphacell Ltd v Woodward* [1972] AC 824). As to what may be regarded as 'causing', regard must be had to the terms in which the statutory duty is imposed. In connection with the offence of causing polluting matter to enter controlled waters contrary to the Water Resources Act 1991, s. 15(1), the prosecution need not prove that the defendant person or entity did an affirmative act which caused the pollution. A person who, for example, stores polluting material on land which he occupies in a state where it may readily be released by a third party may be convicted of causing pollution where the act of such a party releases the substance provided that the act is not unnatural, extraordinary or unusual. If the event was a matter of ordinary occurrence it will not negative the causal effect of the defendant's acts even if it was not foreseeable that it could happen to that particular defendant or take that particular form (*Environment Agency v Empress Car Co. (Abertillery) Ltd* [1999] 2 AC 22).

Various meanings have been given to the term 'possession'. In *Warner v Metropolitan Police Commissioner* [1969] 2 AC 256, in connection with drug offences, the House of Lords held that a person may be said to 'possess' prohibited drugs if he knows that he possesses drugs, even though he is unaware of their precise characteristics. Yet in *Ashwell* (1885) 16 QBD 190 it was held that a man could not be said to 'possess' a sovereign when he thought he had received a shilling. In *Warner v Metropolitan Police Commissioner*, since rendered otiose by the Misuse of Drugs Act 1971, Lords Pearce, Wilberforce and Reid (dissenting) sought a construction which would require the prosecution to prove some element of knowledge of the thing in possession, but not so particular a degree of knowledge as to stultify enforcement of the legislation. The decision has been construed as meaning that one possesses an article of a dangerous sort provided that one has possession of a packet containing it (*Boyesen* [1982] AC 768). In the context of offensive weapons this means that it is not a defence for an accused person to show on a balance of probabilities that he did not know and could not be expected to know that the article was an offensive weapon (*Bradish* [1990] 1 QB 981; *Waller* [1991] Crim LR 381; *Steele* [1993] Crim LR 298).

Where a due-diligence or no-negligence defence applies to a prohibition apparently cast in absolute terms, the courts are likely to hold that the offence is one of strict liability (*Wings Ltd v Ellis; Kirkland v Robinson; Bradish; Harrow LBC v Shah*). Courts will ask whether strict liability promotes the purposes of the enactment and whether it is unduly burdensome to expose the accused to liability, leaving it to him to establish such a defence (*Davidson v Strong* (1997) *The Times*, 20 March 1997). The absence of such a defence does not, however, necessarily imply that *mens rea* is to be presumed (*Alphacell Ltd v Woodward*).

APPLICABILITY OF GENERAL DEFENCES TO OFFENCES OF STRICT LIABILITY

A4.3 Liability is in general strict, not absolute. General defences to crime therefore, with rare exceptions, apply to such offences.

In general, strict-liability offences involve proof that the accused voluntarily acted or omitted to act. This requirement may be displaced by the words of the statute. In *Larsonneur* (1933) 24 Cr App R 74, a French citizen who was deported from the Irish Free State to the UK against her will was convicted of being an alien 'found within' the UK in breach of immigration legislation. In *Winzar v Chief Constable of Kent* (1983) *The Times*, 28 March 1983, the accused was convicted of being found drunk on a highway even though his presence there was attributable to the police who took him from a hospital corridor to the highway and then drove him to the police station. It is, with respect, surprising that a requirement of voluntariness was not implied in the legislation in the above cases. Dicta in *Alphacell Ltd v Woodward* [1972] AC 824 at pp. 834, 845, 846 and 847 imply that this may properly be done.

It does, however, seem both from *Alphacell Ltd v Woodward* and from *Southern Water Authority v Pegrum* [1989] Crim LR 442 that act of God will amount to a defence. So too will automatism, provided that the degree of impairment is virtually absolute (*A-G's Ref (No. 2 of 1992)* [1994] QB 91). Insanity which does not amount to automatism is, however, a defence only to a crime requiring *mens rea* (*DPP v H* [1997] 1 WLR 1406). In *Burns v Bidder* [1967] 2 QB 227, the accused was acquitted of failing to accord precedence to a pedestrian when his brakes failed suddenly, but absence of fault is not a fully articulated defence in English law. Duress and duress of circumstances should apply to negate offences of strict liability since they represent independent circumstances of excuse. Mistake on the other hand will not serve as a defence to the extent that its effect is to negate *mens rea* which, *ex hypothesi*, is not applicable here (*DPP v Morgan* [1976] AC 182 per Lord Hailsham of St Marylebone). Even a mistake on reasonable grounds would not serve as a defence.

Many, perhaps most, statutory offences to which strict liability applies contain special defences, though this is not always the case. In pollution legislation particularly, because of the supposed ease of fabricating defences, no possibility is afforded to the accused to show that a matter arose without his fault. However, where a defence of 'without reasonable excuse' is provided, as with an anti-social behaviour order, it is not meaningful to characterise the offence as one of strict liability and the excuse put forward by the defence should be put to the jury notwithstanding the potential for fabricating defences (Nicholson [2006] 1 WLR 2857).

Statutory defences generally require that the infraction be the fault of another person and that the accused has exercised due diligence to prevent the infraction. They may well be expressed as a rigorous statutory code, the rigour being necessary to protect the public interest against, for example, trade in counterfeit goods (*McCrudden* [2005] EWCA Crim 466). There is considerable variation in the way in which such defences are drafted but the principles noted above generally apply. Variations in drafting can cause problems of interpretation, in particular in determining whether a corporation may defend itself by showing that it installed a system to prevent infraction or whether the relevant state of mind is that of an employee performing a function such as sale (*Tesco Stores Ltd v Brent London Borough Council* [1993] 1 WLR 1037). The leading modern examples of such defences are the Weights and Measures Act 1985, the Food Safety Act 1990 and the Trade Descriptions Act 1968. The onus of proving the defence lies on the accused (*Tesco Supermarkets Ltd v Nattrass* [1972] AC 153). The presence of such a defence is taken as an indication that liability is strict subject to making the defence out (*Bradish* [1990] 1 QB 981; *Waller* [1991] Crim LR 381).

The defendant must usually satisfy a persuasive burden only but in some cases an evidential burden may be imposed. An evidential burden makes inroads into the presumption of innocence protected by the ECHR, Article 6(2) and the HRA 1998. Such a provision will, however, be valid provided that it is objectively justified and proportionate (*Johnstone* [2003] 1 WLR 1736 at p. 1749 per Lord Nicholls; *Sheldrake v DPP* [2003] 2 WLR 1629; *Matthews* [2003] Crim LR 553). In some few cases, a legal burden of proof will be upheld where such a burden is necessary to the working of the legislation (*R (Grundy & Co Excavations Ltd) v Halton Division Magistrates' Court* (2003) 167 JP 387; *S* [2003] 1 Cr App R 602).

VICARIOUS LIABILITY

Certain offences are treated as imposing a regime of vicarious liability. Most vicarious-liability offences are in fact also offences of strict liability but there is no perfect coincidence between the two, partly because some few *mens rea* offences attract vicarious liability and partly because some strict-liability offences may be cast in terms which are not apt to impose vicarious liability. **A4.4**

The general rule is that criminal liability is personal, not vicarious (*Huggins* (1730) 2 Ld Raym 1574). A person may, of course, implicate himself in the crime of another through doctrines of complicity.

Care must be taken to distinguish between those situations which attract liability through doctrines of vicarious liability and those where the duty upon the employer is personal. In relation, for example, to an employer's duty to conduct his enterprise in such a way as to ensure the safety of his employee or not to expose to risk a person not employed by him (under the Health and Safety at Work etc. Act 1974, ss. 2(1) and 3(1)) the duty is personal to the employer. It follows that the employer's duty is defined, in the latter case, by reference to the undertaking and not the precise relationship between the entrepreneur and the employee or independent contractor as the case may be (*Associated Octel Co. Ltd* [1996] 1 WLR 1543). The effect, in the context of the Health and Safety at Work etc. Act 1974, s. 3, for example, is that if a person who is not an employee of the employer is exposed to health risks by the conduct of the employer's undertaking, the employer will be liable unless he can prove on the balance of probability that all that was reasonably practicable had been done by him or on his behalf to ensure against exposure to such risks. The question of what is reasonably practicable is one for the jury. The fact that an employee in carrying out work did so carelessly or omitted to take a necessary precaution does not of itself preclude the employer from establishing that he had done everything practicable to avoid risk. The employer need not be held liable even for an isolated act of negligence by the employee performing the work. The employer's duty to take all reasonably practicable steps includes ensuring that employees have the requisite level of skills and instruction, have had safe systems of work laid down for them, have been subjected to adequate supervision, and have been provided with safe plant and equipment (*Nelson Group Services (Maintenance) Ltd* [1999] 1 WLR 1526; *Gateway Foodmarkets Ltd* [1997] 3 All ER 78; *Hatton v Traffic Management Ltd* [2006] EWCA Crim 1156).

The accepted formula, which applies both to *mens rea* offences and to those of strict liability is the following dictum of Atkin J in *Mousell Brothers Ltd v London and North-Western Railway Co.* [1917] 2 KB 836 at p. 845):

> . . . while prima facie a principal is not to be made criminally responsible for the acts of his servants, yet the legislature may prohibit an act or enforce a duty in such words as to make the prohibition or the duty absolute; in which case the principal is liable if the act is in fact done by his servants. To ascertain whether a particular Act of Parliament has that effect or not regard must be had to the object of the statute, the words used, the nature of the duty laid down, the person upon whom it is imposed, the person by whom it would in ordinary circumstances be performed, and the person upon whom the penalty is imposed.

It is important to note that the duty is imposed in respect of a servant. Thus a licensee who is the joint proprietor of a shop cannot be held liable for the act of supplying liquor to a minor where the act of supply is that of an unlicensed co-proprietor because the latter is not her servant and, rather than serving her, is serving on her behalf (*Boucher v DPP* (1996) 160 JP 650).

While a duty imposed by a statute may appear to be imposed upon any person, an act such as sale or supply will often be done by an employee on behalf of an employer. Where a duty is imposed in terms of taking all steps to guard against harm which it is reasonable for an employer to take, the duty, and the liability in respect of any failure, will be personal (*Seaboard Offshore Ltd v Secretary of State for Transport* [1994] 1 WLR 541; *Associated Octel Co. Ltd* [1996] 1 WLR 1543; *Westminster City Council v Blenheim Leisure (Restaurants) Ltd* (1999) 163 JP 401). Similarly an owner of licensed premises may be held liable for selling drink not of the standard required, contrary to the Food and Safety Act 1990, s. 14(1), because the owner is a seller of the drink concerned and there is no reason to restrict the offence to the licensee (*Nottingham City Council v Wolverhampton and Dudley Breweries plc* [2004] QB 1274).

The test of whether a duty to regulate should be imposed on an employer is essentially whether the employer is best placed through discipline, training, supervision and maintenance standards to ensure compliance with legislation (*National Rivers Authority v Alfred McAlpine Homes (East) Ltd* [1994] 4 All ER 286). The nexus is essentially that of control, which will usually be satisfied by a course-of-employment formula but which sometimes, and in particular in relation to *mens rea* offences, is satisfied by the notion of delegation.

In respect of *mens rea* offences, vicarious liability may be imposed because the statutory command is addressed to a particular person such as a licensee, whilst the business may be carried on for periods of time by his delegate. In such a case, unless vicarious liability can be imposed, premises may well fall outside the ambit of a regulatory statute simply because the licensee, if not present, commits no offence, and his delegate is not made personally responsible under the statute.

The licensee cases ought to be considered anomalous. This was certainly the view of Lord Reid both in *Vane v Yiannopoullos* [1965] AC 486 and in *Tesco Supermarkets Ltd v Nattrass* [1972] AC 153 at p. 169. In the former case his lordship concluded that the existing ambit of vicarious liability ought to be upheld, but certainly not extended. According to Lords Reid and Evershed, the licensee could not be held vicariously liable when, he being on the premises, a *mens rea* offence was committed by his employee without his knowledge. Lords Donovan and Morris took a different view. The Court of Appeal in *Winson* [1969] 1 QB 371 concluded that such liability applied only where the statute was specifically addressed to the licensee and he had entirely delegated the management of his premises. Rather surprisingly, the Divisional Court in *Howker v Robinson* [1973] QB 178 concluded that vicarious liability for a *mens rea* offence was possible under the Licensing Act 1964, s. 169, which provides that the holder of a licence or his servant shall not knowingly sell intoxicating liquor to a person under 18. The effect of the altered wording was said not to exclude vicarious liability, but simply to add the servant as an additional target fit for prosecution. This is, of course, to ignore the entire basis in policy for vicarious responsibility in the licensee cases, though it can be brought within Atkin J's formulation in *Mousell Brothers Ltd v London and North-Western Railway Co.* [1917] 2 KB 836. It is submitted that *Howker v Robinson* ought to be regarded as wrongly decided; it is inconsistent with the tenor of their lordships' speeches in *Vane v Yiannopoullos* and it cannot be reconciled with *Winson.*

The fact that a person or organisation is empowered to undertake an activity under licence does not mean that he or it bears vicarious responsibility for the acts of employees. The legislation may impose the duty specifically upon a person within that body performing particular functions, such as for example keeping embryos (*A-G's Ref (No. 2 of 2003)* [2004] 1 WLR 2062).

The requisite nexus is sometimes course of employment and sometimes delegation. These formulations are properly regarded as overlapping, not conflicting. Delegation is, however, the appropriate test under the licensee cases for obvious reasons; the courts devised liability in such cases in order to ensure that an absentee licensee would not be able to insulate himself from liability in respect of the premises.

So far as the employment relationship is concerned, the liability of the employer extends, it is clear, to acts which he did not authorise and, indeed, forbade (*Ward v W.H. Smith* [1913] 3 KB 154; *Griffiths v Studebakers Ltd* [1924] 1 KB 102; *Anderton v Rodgers* [1981] Crim LR 404; *Piggly Wiggly Canadian Ltd* [1933] 4 DLR 491). Furthermore, vicarious liability applies to an act (e.g., a sale) by an employee even though the employer is on the premises (*Harrow LBC v Shah* [2000] 1 WLR 83).

Vicarious liability is usually but not always imposed in the case of strict liability offences. *Seaboard Offshore Ltd v Secretary of State for Transport* [1994] 1 WLR 541 illustrates the exceptional case. Section 100 of the Merchant Shipping Act 1995 imposes a duty on the owner of a ship to ensure that it is operated in a safe manner. The offence of failing to do so is a strict but not vicarious liability offence first because a wide range of omissions could constitute a failure to take reasonable steps, and secondly, because a wide range of persons might make an omission. This, together with other contextual evidence, led the court to conclude that the duty and the liability are personal to the owner.

Criminal liability is not to be imposed in every instance where an employer would be vicariously liable civilly. *Portsea Island Mutual Co-operative Society Ltd v Leyland* [1978] ICR 1195 illustrates the point. A milk roundsman hired a boy to assist him. The act was done by the roundsman for his employer's business and with intent to benefit the employer, but it was done contrary to the employer's instructions. The company did not employ the boy; it could only be held liable where it employed him either directly or through a properly authorised agent. The fact that a company might, on similar facts, be civilly liable to a lad who suffered injuries while accompanying the roundsman was irrelevant (*Rose v Plenty* [1976] 1 WLR 141). There is earlier authority to the same effect (*Star Cinema (Shepherd's Bush) Ltd v Baker* (1921) 126 LT 506).

The formulae of employment and delegation overlap (*Barker v Levinson* [1951] 1 KB 342). However, it has been said that delegation does not mean the same thing as employment. Thus Wrottesley LJ, in a civil action (*Gallagher v Dorman, Long and Co. Ltd* [1947] 2 All ER 38), stated (at p. 41): 'An employer does not, merely by employing his servant to work a crane, delegate to him the statutory duty of seeing that the crane is not overloaded'.

Delegation, surely, involves a bestowal of managerial functions. It is thus the right word to describe the licensee cases, but hardly the ordinary sale cases. The courts in the general run of cases have continued to use the notion of course of employment to describe the requisite nexus (e.g., *Winter v Hinckley and District Industrial Co-operative Society Ltd* [1959] 1 WLR 182; *Tesco Supermarkets Ltd v Nattrass* [1972] AC 153; *Winson* [1969] 1 QB 371; *Anderton v Rodgers* [1981] Crim LR 404). Furthermore, there is no reason to suppose that delegation and course of employment are the only nexuses available. A partner may be held liable for the acts of his fellow partner (*Clode v Barnes* [1974] 1 WLR 544). A licensee will be liable for an unlawful act of sale by his staff even though they are not his employees but those of the owner, since the licensee is alone responsible for ensuring adherence to licensing legislation (*Goodfellow v Johnson* [1966] 1 QB 83). The ultimate question ought to be whether the proprietor has control over the actions of the other, and there seems no reason to insist that such control be contractual in character.

The courts have interpreted the legislation in this sense, and they have not allowed themselves to be seduced by a nexus argument which would defeat enforcement of the legislation. Nor have they excused an employer whose servant intended to benefit himself. It has been suggested, it is submitted wrongly, that there ought not to be liability where the servant, in committing the infraction, acted in his own interests and not in the purported interests of the master (*Navarro v Moregrand Ltd* [1951] 2 TLR 674 at p. 681 per Denning LJ). The suggestion is clearly inconsistent with *ICR Haulage Ltd* [1944] KB 551 which, although on corporate liability, is permeated with vicarious liability concepts. Vicarious liability exists in order to ensure that employers and others to whom it applies will police their businesses. The question of whom the offender intended to benefit is irrelevant viewed from that perspective. This is even clearer when the positive defences discussed above are considered; whether a defence is available or not depends upon, and only upon, whether the particular steps outlined in the legislation are followed. The question of intent to benefit does not appear in the schemes.

Section A5 Parties to Offences

LIABILITY OF PRINCIPALS AND ACCESSORIES GENERALLY

Responsibility for a criminal offence may be incurred either as a principal offender or as an accessory. Liability as an accessory applies to all offences (including statutory ones) unless it is expressly excluded by statute (*Jefferson* [1994] 1 All ER 270). See the SOA 2003, s. 73, for an example of a partial exclusion. A principal offender is the actual perpetrator of the offence, the person whose individual conduct satisfied the definition of the particular offence in question, whilst an accessory is one who aids, abets, counsels or procures the commission of the offence. For indictable offences, the Accessories and Abettors Act 1861, s. 8, provides that such an accessory 'shall be liable to be tried, indicted, and punished as a principal offender'. The MCA 1980, s. 44(1), is of similar effect as far as summary offences are concerned. **A5.1**

The distinction between an accessory and a principal offender is thus in many cases of little importance. Indeed a person charged as a principal may be convicted even though the real case against him was that he was an accessory, although it is preferable that the particulars of the offence be drawn 'in such a way as to disclose with greater clarity the real nature of the case that the accused has to answer' (per Lord Hailsham of St Marylebone in *DPP for Northern Ireland v Maxwell* [1978] 1 WLR 1350 at p. 1357D). If this is not done and if the prosecution do not make plain in presenting the case to the jury that joint enterprise is one of the alleged bases of liability, it may be a misdirection for the judge to introduce it in summing up (see *Taylor* [1998] Crim LR 582). However, as *Giannetto* [1997] 1 Cr App R 1 demonstrates, if the jury are unsure as to whether D was an accessory or the principal, they can still convict (of murder) provided that they are all agreed that he was responsible on one basis or, if not, on the other (see also **A1.32** and *Morton* [2004] Crim LR 73).

The phrase 'aid, abet, counsel and procure' may be, and generally is, used as a whole even though the accused's conduct may be properly described only by one of the four constituent words (*Re Smith* (1858) 3 H & N 227). Partly for this reason, the precise meaning of each constituent word has not been authoritatively determined, but 'aid' and 'abet' are generally considered to cover, respectively, assistance and encouragement given at the time of the offence, whereas 'counsel' and 'procure' are more apt to describe advice and assistance given at an earlier stage. Individual words are occasionally the subject of judicial discussion, as in *A-G's Ref (No. 1 of 1975)* [1975] QB 773, where the accused had laced the drinks of a friend with alcohol knowing that he would soon be driving home. As a result the friend drove with an excess quantity of alcohol in his body and was convicted as principal. The accused was then charged with aiding, abetting, counselling and procuring that offence but the trial judge took the view that, since there was not the usual shared intention or meeting of minds between the principal and alleged accessory, the accused could not be said to be an accessory. The Court of Appeal took the view that — whilst that might be right for aiding, abetting and counselling — procuring did not require any sort of conspiracy or common purpose and therefore the accused could properly have been convicted. The court said (at p. 779F): 'To procure means to produce by endeavour'. And at p. 780B: 'You cannot procure an offence unless there is a causal link between what you do and the commission of the offence'.

By way of contrast, counselling does not require any causal link (see *Calhaem* [1985] QB 808), and as long as the advice or encouragement of the accessory comes to the attention of the principal offender, it does not matter that he would have committed the offence anyway, even if not encouraged by the accessory (see *A-G v Able* [1984] QB 795 at p. 812). The result of all the above seems to be that common purpose and causal link are alternative requirements for liability as an accessory. Where, as in the typical case, the accessory cannot be said to have caused the offence, a common purpose will be required (though not necessarily a prearranged plan, see *Mohan v The Queen* [1967] 2 AC 187 where the two accused, without prior arrangement, were jointly intent on inflicting grievous bodily harm). Where there is no such common purpose, procuring becomes the crucial concept and the establishment of a causal link is required.

Before leaving the question of terminology it is worth pointing out that much of the ancient nomenclature in this area has relatively recently become redundant. Before the abolition (by the Criminal Law Act 1967, s. 1) of the distinction between felonies and misdemeanours, it was necessary to distinguish, as far as felonies were concerned, between principals in the first degree (now simply principals), principals in the second degree (roughly corresponding to aiders and abettors, now simply accessories) and accessories before the fact (roughly counsellors and procurers, again now simply accessories). Such distinctions are today otiose and any last remaining significance was, it is hoped, removed by the House of Lords in *Howe* [1987] AC 147, disapproving the Court of Appeal decision in *Richards* [1974] QB 776, which had seemed to perpetuate these archaic distinctions for certain purposes (see **A5.12**). The only distinction which now needs to be made is between a principal offender and an accessory.

In the light of the Accessories and Abettors Act 1861, s. 8, even this distinction will not often be of significance, the accessory's liability being identical with that of the principal. The availability of duress on a murder charge used to depend on whether the accused was in truth a principal or merely an accessory, but that anomalous rule did not survive the House of Lords decision in *Howe* [1987] AC 417. The distinction between conduct constituting that of a principal and that of (at most) an accessory has however more recently resurfaced in another but somewhat different context in homicide. An example is where D assists a drug abuser to inject himself resulting in fatal (but unintended) consequences — see *Dias* [2002] 2 Cr App R 96 and *Rogers* [2003] 1 WLR 1374 (discussed further at the end of **B1.51**). If D's role (such as performing or taking part in the act of injection) can be classified as a cause of death, he is guilty of manslaughter as a principal but if he is merely assisting or encouraging (as most commentators would regard an act of supplying the drugs or even preparing and supplying a loaded syringe) he will not be guilty of manslaughter. In this latter situation, as far as the death is concerned, he is merely a putative aider and abettor and there is no offence known to law of self-manslaughter to which he can be accessory. However, in *Finlay* [2003] EWCA Crim 3868, the Court of Appeal has now found that, on the facts, supplying a loaded syringe to an addict who was determined to take it can give rise to liability as a principal for causing the death (via causing a noxious thing to be administered or taken contrary to the OAPA 1861, s. 23). One way of rationalising this controversial decision might have been to say that the deceased's act in this case was not truly voluntary given the level of her addiction. However, in *Kennedy* (*No. 2*) [2005] 1 WLR 2159, the Court of Appeal were not attracted to this type of explanation and, in following and applying *Finlay*, Lord Woolf CJ made it clear that the voluntary act of another does not necessarily break the chain of causation in this context.

Notwithstanding this latest decision, the fact that the voluntary act of another normally (or at least frequently) breaks the chain of causation and prevents a previous actor from being the principal is one of the main reasons that accessory liability is so important and significant in treating those who assisted or encouraged the offence as being equally guilty of it as the principal. Although it *often* does not matter whether a person is principal or accessory, it does matter where it is only an offence for D to do something to *another* (D negligently causes V's death, D guilty of manslaughter as principal) but not for that other to do it *to himself* (assisted or encouraged by D, V *independently* does an act which negligently causes his *own* death, V commits not even the *actus reus* of an offence and there is therefore no offence to which D can be accessory). Aside from relatively unusual situations such as that outlined above (and see *Ferguson v Weaving* [1951] 1 KB 814 for a difference between principals and accessories in the quite different context of vicarious liability), the most important general distinction which remains between accessories and principals lies in the mental element required of an accessory.

THE MENTAL ELEMENT FOR ACCESSORIES

The *actus reus* of an accessory involves two concepts: (a) aiding, abetting, counselling and procuring (b) an offence. The *mens rea* can also be expected to relate to these two concepts. The mental element for an accessory is generally considerably narrower and more demanding than that required for the principal offender in that intention or knowledge rather than recklessness or negligence or any other less culpable state of mind is required. The classic statement of the *mens rea* for an accessory is that of Lord Goddard CJ in *Johnson v Youden* [1950] 1 KB 544 at p. 546 that: 'Before a person can be convicted of aiding and abetting the commission of an offence, he must at least know the essential matters which constitute that offence'. **A5.2**

The Requirement of Knowledge

This applies even where the principal offence is one of strict liability as in *Callow v Tillstone* (1900) 83 LT 411 where a vet negligently certified meat as sound and fit for sale, and a butcher was convicted of the strict-liability offence of exposing for sale meat which was unsound and unfit for human consumption. The vet's conviction for aiding and abetting was quashed since negligence was not sufficient for this form of liability even though the butcher's liability as principal offender was not dependent on proof of any degree of fault whatsoever. **A5.3**

The importance of this principle can be further seen in *Smith v Mellors* (1987) 84 Cr App R 279 where Mellors and Soar were both charged under the Road Traffic Act 1972, s. 6(1)(a) (driving with excess alcohol, now Road Traffic Act 1988, s. 5(1)(a)). The prosecution were unable to prove who was the driver and who was the passenger. Nor could they prove that each defendant was aware that the other was over the limit. The magistrates ruled that there was no case to answer. The Divisional Court affirmed their decision whilst pointing out that, in the light of the MCA 1980, s. 44 (see **A5.1**), it was not always necessary to determine who was the accessory and who the principal. However, it was necessary where, as in this case, there was a material difference between the liability of the principal and the accessory. The Road Traffic Act 1972, s. 6(1)(a), created an offence of strict liability for the principal but the accessory could be liable only if he knew the facts. Only if both knew that the other was over the limit could both be convicted without proof of who was driving. Presumably, if it is proved that one party had the requisite knowledge, he, though not the other, could be convicted since in that case he would be liable whether or not he was the driver. Croom-Johnson LJ stated (at p. 284), 'It might be that an aider and abettor would be an aider and abettor if he was simply reckless as to whether or not the driver had the requisite amount of alcohol in his blood'. Whilst this statement might find some support in the earlier case of *Carter v Richardson* [1974] RTR 314, the better view seems to be that recklessness is not sufficient. In *Giorgianni v The Queen* (1985) 156 CLR 473, the Australian High Court, having discussed at length the English authorities, held that recklessness was not sufficient for an accessory to an offence of causing death by culpable (reckless) driving. The owner of a lorry involved in a fatal crash was not guilty as accessory unless he knew or was wilfully blind to the brake defect in the lorry. In *Blakely v DPP* [1991] Crim LR 763, which was more concerned with intention to aid (see A5.4) than with knowledge of circumstances, the Divisional Court was reluctant to countenance recklessness as sufficient *mens rea* for complicity, at least in relation to counselling or procuring.

Intention to Aid

A5.4 Lord Goddard's statement in *Johnson v Youden* [1950] 1 KB 544 (see A5.2) that the accessory 'must at least know the essential matters which constitute the offence' is not, and does not purport to be, a complete definition of the mental element because *inter alia*, it relates only to part (b) of the *actus reus* as set out in A5.2, i.e. the principal offence. It says nothing about the intention to 'aid, abet, counsel and procure'. As Devlin J put it in *National Coal Board v Gamble* [1959] 1 QB 11 (at p. 20):

> . . . aiding and abetting is a crime that requires proof of *mens rea*, that is to say, of intention to aid as well as of knowledge of the circumstances.

However, as Devlin J went on to point out, at p. 23, intention to aid does not require that the accused's purpose or motive must be that the principal offence should be committed:

> If one man deliberately sells to another a gun to be used for murdering a third, he may be indifferent about whether the third man lives or dies and interested only in the cash profit to be made out of the sale, but he can still be an aider and abettor. To hold otherwise would be to negative the rule that *mens rea* is a matter of intent only and does not depend on desire or motive.

Thus in *DPP for Northern Ireland v Lynch* [1975] AC 653 the accused's alleged opposition to the principal offence did not preclude a finding that he intended to aid. It is submitted that the question of intention to aid is now governed by the decisions in *Moloney* [1985] AC 905 and *Hancock* [1986] AC 455 discussed in A2.2 and that where the accused does not actually desire to assist or encourage the commission of an offence, but knows that his actions are extremely likely or virtually certain to have that result, then the question is one for the jury to infer whether or not he has the requisite intent. If *Woollin* [1999] AC 82 were to be applied beyond the context of the meaning of intention for murder, only foresight of a virtual certainty would entitle the jury to find intention. *Gillick v West Norfolk and Wisbech Area Health Authority* [1986] AC 112 is an example of a type of case where the uncertainties of the precise meaning of intention effectively confer a perhaps welcome discretion on whether to impose responsibility. That case concerned, *inter alia*, the question of whether a doctor giving contraceptive advice or treatment to a girl under the age of 16 could be liable as accessory to a subsequent offence of unlawful sexual intercourse committed by the girl's sexual partner. The House of Lords held that generally this would not be the case (the action was a civil one for a declaration) since the doctor would lack the necessary intention (even though he realised that his actions would facilitate such intercourse). One rationale for the decision would be that a jury would not infer intention in such circumstances if they thought that the doctor was acting in what he considered to be the girl's best interests (such situations are now expressly catered for in the SOA 2003, s. 73).

Similar reasoning could be applied to a troublesome group of cases involving the supply of articles for use in crime which the recipient already has some sort of civil right to receive. The general position seems to be that this is not aiding and abetting (see, for example, *Lomas* (1913) 9 Cr App R 220 concerning the return of a jemmy to its owner) because the alleged accessory does not intend to aid the offence but rather merely to comply with his supposed civil-law duties. Critics of this general position rightly point out that it can hardly apply to a person returning a revolver to its owner knowing that he is then going to use it to carry out a murder. But here a jury probably would infer intention to aid from the accused's knowledge of the effects of his action, and the flexibility of the notion of intention enables an appropriate solution to be found to situations for which it is difficult to formulate precise rules in advance.

It is particularly important to stress the need for an intention to aid where the accused may not personally appreciate the natural and probable consequences of his action as in *Clarkson* [1971] 1 WLR 1402 where there was 'at least the possibility that a drunken man with his self-discipline loosened by drink . . . might not intend that his presence should offer encouragement to rapers; . . . he might not realise that he was giving encouragement' (at p. 1406). The reference to intoxication underlines the fact that complicity normally requires intention rather than recklessness (*Blakely v DPP* [1991] Crim LR 763) and that, for the purposes of the *Majewski* rule (*DPP v Majewski* [1977] AC 443: see **A3.10**), complicity can be regarded as requiring specific intent.

The foregoing discussion was quoted approvingly in *Bryce* [2004] 2 Cr App R 592 at [63] where the Court of Appeal confirmed that an intention to assist (in the sense explained above) is required (although in many cases, as on the facts of *Bryce*, such an intention may be readily inferred from the voluntary performance of acts which obviously do in fact assist the principal offender, in the absence of a credible explanation from the accused as to why this was not his intention—see *Bryce* at [101]).

The Scope of the Joint Venture

The Contemplation Test The test of 'knowledge of the essential matters constituting the offence' needs some further elucidation since a strict requirement of knowledge is inappropriate or unworkable in certain situations, notably where the offence is to be committed in the future or by a person of whose precise intentions the accused cannot be certain in advance. A relatively simple case is where the accused knows that, for example, a burglary is to be committed and provides equipment to be used in the burglary. He is guilty even if he does not know of the precise time, date or place of the proposed offence. Provided that he knows the type of crime, i.e. that it will be a burglary, it does not matter that he does not know the details of the particular crime in the sense of a particular date at particular premises (see *Bainbridge* [1960] 1 QB 129 esp. at pp. 133–4). In some cases an accused may be convicted even though he is not sure whether the offence is to be burglary or some other type of crime such as handling or robbery. In *Maxwell* [1978] 1 WLR 1363, the accused had driven his car so as to guide a following car out to a remote public house into which a bomb was thrown from the second car. He argued that since he did not know exactly what type of offence was to be committed (it was obviously a terrorist attack of some sort but it was unclear whether it was to be a bombing or a shooting) he did not know the essential matters constituting the offences with which he was charged (under the Explosive Substances Act 1883). Nevertheless, Lowry CJ upheld the conviction of the accused in relation to the bombing saying (at pp. 1374–5): **A5.5**

> His guilt springs from the fact that he contemplates the commission of one (or more) of a number of crimes by the principal and he intentionally lends his assistance in order that such a crime will be committed. . . .
>
> The relevant crime must be within the contemplation of the accomplice and only exceptionally would evidence be found to support the allegation that the accomplice had given the principal a completely blank cheque.
>
> [He] must . . . have contemplated the bombing of the Crosskeys Inn as not the only possibility but one of the most obvious possibilities among the jobs which the principals were likely to be undertaking.

Thus the test in this sort of case is not so much knowledge (the accused cannot 'know' things in advance) as contemplation. It is capable of application in a wide range of situations including:

> that of two persons who agree to rob a bank on the understanding, either express or implied from conduct (such as the carrying of a loaded gun by one person with the knowledge of the other), that violence *may* be resorted to. The accomplice knows, not that the principal *will* shoot the

> cashier, but that he may do so; and if the principal does shoot him, the accomplice will be guilty of murder. (Ibid.)

This type of case has been the subject of a long line of authorities including the leading case of *Anderson* [1966] 2 QB 110, where the principal (Anderson) armed himself with a knife unknown to the accessory (Morris) who was nevertheless convicted of manslaughter (Anderson was convicted of murder). A five-judge Court of Criminal Appeal quashed Morris's conviction, Lord Parker CJ (at p. 118F–G) accepting as correct the following principles put forward on his behalf:

> where two persons embark on a joint enterprise, each is liable for the acts done in pursuance of that joint enterprise, . . . that includes liability for unusual consequences if they arise from the execution of the agreed joint enterprise.

Thus Morris would have been responsible for the sort of attack he had contemplated (i.e. one without a knife and without an intent to kill) and if death had happened to result he would have been liable for manslaughter: 'but . . . if one of the adventurers goes beyond what has been tacitly agreed as part of the common enterprise, his co-adventurer is not liable for the consequences of that unauthorised act' (p. 118G). See *Mahmood* [1995] RTR 48 for a case where the accessory contemplated reckless driving but not the unusual form of reckless driving concerned, and was therefore not responsible for that driving or the consequences.

A5.6 Contemplation of the *Mens Rea* of Murder The principles described at A5.5 have been further developed and applied in a series of decisions commencing with that of the Privy Council in *Chan Wing-Siu v The Queen* [1985] AC 168. In *Chan Wing-Siu*, the three appellants had broken into the victim's flat armed with knives to commit robbery. In the course of the robbery, the victim was stabbed to death. The trial judge directed the jury: 'You may convict . . . of murder if you come to the conclusion . . . that the accused contemplated that either of his companions might use a knife to cause serious bodily injury on any one or more of the occupants of that flat'. The Privy Council upheld the convictions for murder based upon this direction.

Although some difficulties were initially experienced (see *Barr* (1986) 88 Cr App R 362) in reconciling this approach (based on contemplation) with the test for intention laid down in *Moloney* [1985] AC 905 and *Hancock* [1986] AC 455 (see **A2.2**), the Court of Appeal in *Slack* [1989] QB 775 subsequently adopted a similar, though logically distinguishable, approach. The court (at p. 781E–G) made the important point that the *mens rea* required of the accessory is not necessarily the same as that of the principal offender:

> A [the principal offender] must be proved to have intended to kill or do serious harm at the time he killed. B [the accessory] may not be present at the killing; he may be a distance away, for example, waiting in the get-away car; he may be in another part of the house; he may not know that A has killed; he may have hoped, and probably did hope, that A would not kill or do serious injury. If however as part of their joint plan it was understood between them expressly or tacitly that if necessary one of them would kill or do serious harm as part of their common enterprise, then B is guilty of murder.

In *Hyde* [1991] 1 QB 134 it was made clear that foresight of what the principal may do is sufficient *mens rea* for the accessory even if there is not actual agreement between them. This point was confirmed by the Privy Council in *Hui Chi-ming* [1992] 1 AC 34 and has now been put beyond all doubt by the House of Lords in *Powell* [1997] 3 WLR 959 where the certified question was as follows (at p. 967):

> Is it sufficient to found a conviction for murder for a secondary party to a killing to have realised that the primary party might kill with intent to do so or must the secondary party have held such an intention himself?

The House answered, in accordance with previous Court of Appeal authorities, that the first part of the certified question was sufficient, i.e. the secondary party need only realise that the primary party might kill with intent to do so and the secondary party did not himself need to have the intention to kill; hence *Moloney* and *Hancock* did not apply directly to the *mens rea* of the secondary party. This substantive rule has, quite rightly, survived a challenge under the ECHR, Article 6 in *Concannon* [2002] Crim LR 213.

Departures from the Contemplated Method Reference must also be made to the House of Lords judgment in *English* [1997] 3 WLR 959, where the first certified question (at p. 968) was identical with that in *Powell* except that it expressly included, crucially as will be seen, an intention to cause grievous bodily harm. The House of Lords answer to the certified question, including this alternative state of mind on the part of the principal, was made subject to the qualification that, where the particular weapon used by the principal or the manner of its use was different from that contemplated by the accessory, that may take the killing outside the scope of the joint venture and the accessory may not be liable. In *English*, the accessory contemplated the intentional infliction of grievous bodily harm with a wooden post but the principal used a knife which on the evidence the jury could have found was unknown and unforeseen by the accessory. The trial judge had told the jury in effect that they could convict, even if the accessory did not know of the knife, if he nevertheless knew that there was a substantial risk that the principal might cause grievous bodily harm with the wooden post. This part of the direction was held to be defective and the conviction for murder quashed. **A5.7**

Lord Hutton was anxious to make it clear, however, that a difference in the weapon used would not always exempt the accessory 'if the weapon used by the principal is different to, but as dangerous as, the weapon which the secondary party contemplated he might use . . . for example, if he foresaw that the primary party might use a gun to kill and the latter used a knife to kill, or vice versa' (at p. 981). This observation is clearly correct although it is submitted that one aspect of the reason is that in such a case, as formulated, the accessory contemplates an act done with intent to kill and that is precisely what the principal does, the difference in weapon being relatively immaterial. The more difficult case is where the accessory contemplates merely an act done with intent to cause grievous bodily harm where the type of weapon may be highly material in determining the type of grievous bodily harm contemplated and in particular its propensity to cause death, a phrase also utilised in *Uddin* [1999] QB 431. It is clear now that in this situation the test is whether the act done by the principal (including the weapon used) is of a 'fundamentally different nature' to that contemplated by the accessory (*Rahman* [2007] 3 All ER 396). This test of 'fundamentally different' applies only where the accessory contemplates an intention to cause grievous bodily harm as opposed to an intention to kill. In the latter case, (point 1. below) the nature of the weapon used is immaterial since the contemplated intent is to kill and that is what is achieved. But, where the contemplated intent is only to cause grievous bodily harm but death is actually caused, the question of whether the method adopted is within D's contemplation or is 'fundamentally different' becomes important.

In *Rahman*, the following logical manner of putting the issues to a jury was suggested by Hooper LJ (at [69]):

1. Are you sure that D intended that one of the attackers would kill V intending to kill him or that D realised that one of the attackers might kill V with intent to kill him? If yes, guilty of murder. If no, go to 2.
2. Are you sure that either:
   (a) D realised that one of the attackers might kill V with intent to cause him really serious bodily harm; or
   (b) D intended that really serious bodily harm would be caused to V; or
   (c) D realised that one of the attackers might cause really serious bodily harm to V intending to cause him such harm?

   If no, not guilty of murder. If yes, go to question 3.

3. What was P's act which caused the death of V? (e.g., stabbing, shooting, kicking, beating). Go to question 4.
4. Did D realise that one of the attackers might do this act? If yes, guilty of murder. If no, go to the question 5.
5. What act or acts are you sure D realised that one of the attackers might do to cause V really serious harm? Go to question 6.
6. Are you sure that this act or these acts (which D realised one of the attackers might do) is/are not of a fundamentally different nature to P's act which caused the death of V? If yes, guilty of murder. If no, not guilty of murder.

The defence argument that in considering whether the principal's act (stabbing in this case) was fundamentally different from what was contemplated, the jury had to consider the possibility that the principal might actually have intended to kill rather than to cause grievous bodily harm was rejected by the Court of Appeal in *Rahman*. Although in one sense this might make the principal's act more dangerous than the one contemplated by the accessory, it would unduly complicate an already highly technical area of law and further enlarge, to an inappropriate extent, the escape route provided by the 'fundamentally different' test. It should be noted that the defence argument in *Rahman* was concerned only with the difference between the principal possibly having an intention to kill as opposed to the contemplated intention to cause grievous bodily harm, both of which suffice for murder. Slightly different considerations may apply where, as discussed at A5.8, the accessory only contemplates the principal having the *mens rea* for a separate and lesser offence and the principal is proven to have the *mens rea* for a more serious offence.

A5.8 **Divergence of *Mens Rea* — Residual Liability for Manslaughter (or lesser offence)** Difficult questions can arise where the difference between the two parties lies not so much in the act or weapon contemplated but more in the degree of *mens rea*, i.e. the accessory does not contemplate even the minimum degree of *mens rea* (e.g., intention to cause grievous bodily harm or to kill) with which the principal acts. The accessory is clearly not liable for the offence committed by the principal (e.g., murder), but does the accessory remain liable for the consequences of the principal's act by means of a lesser crime according to his own *mens rea* (e.g., manslaughter)? According to a line of authorities commencing with *Anderson* [1966] 2 QB 110 through *Lovesey* [1970] 1 QB 352, *Dunbar* [1988] Crim LR 693, *Wan* [1995] Crim LR 296 and *Perman* [1995] Crim LR 736 the answer appeared to be no. However another line of authorities (*Betty* (1963) 48 Cr App R 6, *Reid* (1975) 62 Cr App R 109 and *Stewart* [1995] 3 All ER 159), seemed to suggest that the answer may be yes. Aspects of the latter case were trenchantly and convincingly criticised by Sir John Smith at [1995] Crim LR 296 and [1995] Crim LR 422, but it is not the case that there is no room for reconciliation between the two approaches. As was concluded in *Stewart*, the fundamental question is whether what was done by the principal is within the scope of the joint venture contemplated by the accessory. The principal's *mens rea* will in some cases change the nature of his act and take it outside the joint venture just as much as if he had suddenly produced a weapon unforeseen by the accessory. However, in other cases, the fact that the principal does precisely the act contemplated by the accessory but with the *mens rea* for a more serious offence will not change the nature of the act nor take it outside the scope of the joint venture.

The above argument was accepted by the Court of Appeal in Northern Ireland in *Gilmour* [2000] 2 Cr App R 407, where the following hypothetical (posed in this work since the 1996 edition) was cited with approval by Sir Robert Carswell CJ:

> Suppose P and A agree that P will post a specific incendiary device to V, A contemplating only superficial injuries to V when he opens it but P foreseeing and hoping that the injuries will be serious or fatal. If V is killed as a result, P will clearly be guilty of murder, A is clearly not guilty of murder as an accessory but should be guilty of manslaughter because the act done by P is precisely what was envisaged. The fact that P happens also to have the *mens rea* of murder is

> irrelevant because it does not change the nature of the act that he does or the manner in which he does it.

The Court of Appeal decided that this was the correct principle to apply in *Gilmour*, where the accessory drove the principals to a housing estate where they threw a petrol bomb into a house causing a fierce fire in which three young boys died. Although the principals were guilty of murder as they had an intention to kill, unknown to the accessory who, in the view of the Court of Appeal, did not even contemplate an intention to cause grievous bodily harm, the accessory could nevertheless be guilty of manslaughter since he knew about the petrol bomb and the principals had 'carried out the very deed' contemplated by him.

Whilst the Court of Appeal's endorsement of the hypothetical posed above is welcome, the facts of *Gilmour* are not necessarily completely analogous with the example which is of the agreed use of a 'specific' incendiary device. In *Gilmour* the petrol bomb was of an unusually large size which is why the principals could be inferred to have intended to kill. The accessory was not specifically aware of its unusually large size which is why the Court of Appeal inferred he contemplated only a blaze causing damage, fear and intimidation rather than serious injury. If this was so, was the throwing of an unusually large bomb the 'very deed' contemplated by the accessory? Possibly not, but as against that the accessory did see the bomb glistening in the hand of the principal after they arrived at the estate and, at least at that stage, contemplated the throwing of that particular bomb. It does not appear to have been so large that it was beyond the range of his contemplation despite that the fact that his lack of specific or detailed knowledge of its size meant that one could not infer that he was aware of the principals' intention to kill.

Fundamentally Different Acts Suppose now, in contrast to the incendiary device hypothetical, that P and A agree that P shall assault V with an iron bar, A contemplating that P will act only with intent to cause actual bodily harm as opposed to grievous bodily harm. If P uses the bar with intent to kill or cause grievous bodily harm, there must come a point where P's intent changes the nature of the assault on V and the manner in which he does it (e.g, in the number or severity of the blows) so as to take what he does outside the scope of the joint venture. *Stewart* seems to be a case where the Court of Appeal, perhaps somewhat harshly, took the view that that particular line had not been crossed, that the accessory knew that an iron bar might be used and that the actual manner of its use was not beyond the scope of the joint venture. The point was not specifically put to the jury, but it is submitted that the best approach would be to ask the jury to consider whether the principal's act (causing death) *and the manner of its doing* was within the contemplation of the accessory and thus within the scope of the joint venture (cf. the reference to 'the manner in which a particular weapon is used' at the end of Lord Hutton's speech in *English*). Depending on the answer to this question, the accessory may or may not be liable for the consequences of the act even though the principal's *mens rea* makes him liable for a more serious offence such as murder. See *Roberts & Day* [2001] EWCA Crim 1594 for another example of the accessory being liable for manslaughter even though the principal did the act with sufficient *mens rea* for murder. *Roberts & Day* was discussed with approval in *A-G's Ref (No. 3 of 2004)* [2005] EWCA Crim 1882 (at [61]) as: A5.9

> authority for the proposition that the failure to 'foresee [that] a murderous state of mind would be harboured by his fellows' does not, of itself, mean that what the primary party did was outside the scope of the joint enterprise. However, as Laws LJ made clear, in his example, the participants all foresaw the same kind of violence being inflicted on their victim, let it be punching with the possibility of kicking to follow. One could put it another way. What happened was (so a jury would inevitably find) not fundamentally different from what [D] had foreseen might occur.

Gilmour [2000] 2 Cr App R 407 (see **A5.14**) was not cited or discussed either in *Roberts & Day* or *A-G's Ref (No. 3 of 2004)* but the principle is the same — see further the discussion in the commentary to *Roberts & Day* at [2001] Crim LR 984. The principle was applied in *D* [2005] EWCA 1981 where the Court of Appeal stated (at [38]):

> It is clear from the Court's decision in *Attorney General's Reference No. 3* that *the critical issue* on the question of whether the actions of the principal in causing the death of the victim were outwith the scope of the joint venture involving the secondary party, *is whether those actions were fundamentally different to what was contemplated.* (Emphasis added.)

Gage LJ went on to say (at [41]):

> we think it would have been better if the judge had given the jury a clear direction of the sort envisaged by the Court in *Uddin.* The jury would then have been properly alerted to the fact that they must concentrate on the issue of whether or not the evidence led to the inevitable conclusion that the actions of the co-accused which were contemplated were precisely the actions which caused death, namely punching, kicking and stamping. It seems to us that such a conclusion was almost inevitable and in all the circumstances we are not prepared to hold that the verdict of the jury was unsafe on that ground.

The manslaughter verdict was, however, quashed on the separate issue of withdrawal from the joint enterprise. The difficult factual issue in all these cases will be whether, in the words of Gage LJ, the 'actions . . . contemplated were precisely the actions which caused death' or, as the same idea was put by Carswell CJ in *Gilmour,* whether the principals had 'carried out the very deed' contemplated by the accessory, as opposed to doing an act which was fundamentally different.

As to what counts as contemplation, Lord Hutton in *English* [1997] 3 WLR 959 agreed with the Privy Council in *Chan Wing-Siu v The Queen* [1985] AC 168 that the realisation by the accessory of a fleeting risk which is then dismissed as altogether negligible is not sufficient, although the Court of Appeal in *Roberts* [1993] 1 All ER 583 said that to distinguish expressly between this and the continuing realisation of a real risk will, in most cases, be unnecessary, and would only serve to complicate directions and lead to confusion. Contemplation or foresight of a real or serious risk is clearly sufficient and it is immaterial whether the secondary party is present at the scene of the crime or lends assistance or encouragement in advance (*Rook* [1993] 1 WLR 1005).

Liability of Accessory where There is No Principal

A5.10 A person can be liable as an accessory even though the principal offender cannot be identified or has been acquitted in a previous trial (*Hui Chi-ming* [1992] 1 AC 34) or even earlier in the same trial (see *Hughes* (1860) Bell CC 242), although in this latter case such a result would only be justified where there was evidence admissible against the accessory but not against the alleged principal (see *Humphreys* [1965] 3 All ER 689). See also *Petch* [2005] 2 Cr App R 657, where the alleged principal was allowed to plead to a lesser offence in a subsequent trial. Where the same evidence is admissible against both it would normally be inconsistent for the same jury to acquit the principal and yet convict the accessory of a crime which it has already found has not been committed by the principal.

A5.11 **Liability where Principal has Complete Defence** In a number of cases the Court of Appeal has upheld convictions of accessories whilst recognising that the principal offender would have a valid defence. Thus in *Bourne* (1952) 36 Cr App R 125, a husband's conviction for aiding and abetting his wife to commit buggery with a dog was upheld even though it was recognised that the wife could not have been convicted as principal (she was not in fact charged) since she was acting under duress from her husband. In *Cogan* [1976] QB 217, Leak's terrified wife had intercourse with Cogan (who had allegedly been told by Leak that she would consent) because of her fear of her husband. Cogan's conviction for rape was quashed because the jury had been told, contrary to the law at the time, that his alleged belief that Mrs Leak was consenting had to be reasonable whereas it was possible that his belief was genuinely held, but Leak's conviction as accessory was upheld. The Court of Appeal pointed out (at p. 223) that:

> . . . one fact is clear — the wife had been raped. Cogan had had sexual intercourse with her without her consent. The fact that Cogan was innocent of rape because he believed that she was consenting does not affect the position that she was raped.

The court then pointed out (at pp. 223–4) that Leak could have been guilty as a principal acting through an innocent agent:

> Had Leak been indicted as a principal offender, the case against him would have been clear beyond argument. Should he be allowed to go free because he was charged with 'being aider and abettor to the same offence'? If we are right in our opinion that the wife had been raped (and no one outside a court of law would say that she had not been), then the particulars of offence accurately stated what Leak had done, namely, he had procured Cogan to commit the offence.

There has been some debate over the precise principle involved in these cases but everyone agrees that the result is just. To say that the liability is really that of a principal acting through an innocent agent can cause problems where the accused lacks some characteristic essential for liability as a principal, for example, if in *Cogan* it had been a woman, rather than Mrs Leak's husband, who had terrorised her into submitting to intercourse. The definition of rape, even in the SOA 2003, s. 1, still requires it in effect to be committed by a man, whereas there is no problem in convicting a person as accessory to an offence which he or she cannot commit as principal (see *Ram* (1893) 17 Cox CC 609, woman as accessory to rape). Thus it is probably preferable to adopt the principle that an accessory can be liable provided that there is the *actus reus* of the principal offence even if the principal offender is entitled to be acquitted because of some defence personal to himself.

It may well be, however, that this principle is limited to cases where the accessory has procured the *actus reus* (i.e. has caused it to be committed as was the case in both *Bourne* and *Cogan*). This would also be consistent with the position stated above (see **A5.1**) that procuring does not need a common intention between the accessory and the principal whereas other forms of aiding and abetting generally do. If the principal lacks the *mens rea* of the offence there can hardly be a common intention that it should be committed, but this is not required for procuring.

The above two paragraphs were specifically approved by the Court of Appeal in *Millward* [1994] Crim LR 527 as correctly stating the law. The accessory in that case was convicted on the basis of procuring the offence of causing death by reckless driving even though the actual driver (his employee) did not know of the defect in the vehicle and was not therefore personally reckless. The case is not an easy one in which to apply the current principles because of the peculiar difficulties in defining the *actus reus* of (causing death by) reckless driving which was nevertheless, in the view of the Court of Appeal, to be found in 'the taking of the vehicle in the defective condition on to the road so as to cause the death of the little boy'; the accessory, 'being aware of the defects, . . . had procured the offence by the giving of instructions to . . . his employee'. *Millward* was approved in *Wheelhouse* [1994] Crim LR 756 and was followed in *DPP v K and B* [1997] 1 Cr App R 36, where two girls were convicted of procuring the rape of another teenage girl by an unknown boy even though the boy may not have had the *mens rea* of rape and in any event had to be assumed not to be responsible under the rebuttable presumption of *doli incapax* (abolished by the CDA 1998, s. 34). It would apparently have been different if the boy had been shown to be under the age of 10, although the logic behind this last conclusion is not particularly compelling.

Of course, if not even the *actus reus* is committed there can be no liability. The situation in *Millward* would now be governed by the offence of dangerous rather than reckless driving, as is illustrated by *Loukes* [1996] 1 Cr App R 444. There is room for debate over how the *actus reus* of the old offence of reckless driving should be defined, but under the new offence the test of whether a person is driving dangerously is satisfied if 'it would be obvious to a competent and careful driver that driving the vehicle in its current state would be dangerous' (Road Traffic Act 1988, s. 2A(2)). If it would not be so obvious *to the driver*, and the driver is acquitted on that ground (as in *Loukes*) then, according to the Court of Appeal in that case, there is not even the *actus reus* as no-one has driven the vehicle dangerously. Therefore, in accordance with *Thornton v Mitchell* [1940] 1 All ER 339, the person responsible for maintaining the vehicle and sending it out on the road cannot be liable even as an accessory, a result described by the Court of Appeal as an 'injustice'. The same result was nevertheless reached in *Roberts* [1997] Crim LR 209.

The situation in *Thornton v Mitchell*, in which a bus driver was acquitted of driving without due care and attention, was somewhat simpler and clearer. The driver had had to rely on signals from his conductor in reversing the bus. Because of the conductor's negligence, two pedestrians were injured, one of them fatally. The conductor's conviction for aiding and abetting had to be quashed because clearly there was no principal offence of driving without due care to which he could be accessory. The driver had driven *with* due care rather than without it, so there was not even the *actus reus* of that offence. On the other hand, there was the *actus reus* of homicide (the causing of the death of the pedestrian). It may be that the conductor could have been liable for manslaughter (as might the employer in *Millward*), if his negligence were sufficiently gross, though only on the basis that the conductor was the principal (whose own conduct caused the death) since liability as an accessory requires intention or knowledge rather than negligence or recklessness (see **A5.3**).

A5.12 **Liability where Principal Liable Only for Lesser Offence** An analogous problem to that described in **A5.17** arises where there are two or more offences which share the same *actus reus*, for example, murder and manslaughter, or the offences under the OAPA 1861, ss. 18 and 20. If the principal offender commits the *actus reus* but with only the *mens rea* for the less serious of the two possible offences, can the accessory nonetheless be convicted of the more serious offence if he has sufficient *mens rea*? The Court of Appeal in *Richards* [1974] QB 776 appeared to make the answer depend on whether the accessory was present at the scene of the crime or not. However, this case almost certainly no longer represents the law following the House of Lords decision in *Howe* [1987] AC 417, where it was indicated that *Richards* should not be followed (see at pp. 436B and 457–8) and having regard to *Millward*, where it was immaterial that the procurer was not present. The issue cannot be regarded as finally settled as the question certified for the House in *Howe* was in the following terms:

> Can one who incites or procures by duress another to kill or to be a party to a killing be convicted of murder if that other is acquitted by reason of duress?

This differs from the *Richards* question in that (a) the alleged principal is not guilty of *any* crime and (b) his defence is duress rather than lack of *mens rea*. In fact the certified question in *Howe* really raises the same question as in *Bourne* (1952) 36 Cr App R 125 and the affirmative answer given by the House of Lords to the question can be regarded as confirmation of that decision. It would be extremely odd if an accessory could be convicted where the principal is acquitted altogether but could not be convicted if the principal happens to be guilty of some lesser offence. *Richards* can perhaps safely be regarded as no longer stating the law. However, just as with the principle following from *Bourne* and *Cogan*, it may be that the *mens rea* of the accessory can only be linked with the *actus reus* of the principal where the accessory can be said to have procured or caused the *actus reus*.

Such a limitation, however, would not apply to the Homicide Act 1957, s. 2(4), whereby 'The fact that one party to a killing is by virtue of this section [diminished responsibility] not liable to be convicted of murder shall not affect the question whether the killing amounted to murder in the case of any other party to it'. In other words an accessory with sufficient *mens rea* can be convicted of murder even though the principal offender is convicted only of manslaughter because of diminished responsibility.

Presence at the Scene of the Crime: Omissions

Neither mere presence at the scene of a crime nor a failure to prevent an offence will generally give rise to liability. However, presence at the scene of a crime is *capable* of constituting encouragement (see *Jefferson* [1994] 1 All ER 270 for a recent example and contrast *Coney* (1882) 8 QBD 534 — spectators at illegal prize fight, conviction quashed since jury directed that presence was *conclusive* evidence of encouragement). If the accused is present in pursuance of a prior agreement with the principal, that will normally amount to aiding and abetting, but if the accused is only accidentally present then he must know that his presence is actually encouraging the principal(s) (see *Allan* [1965] 1 QB 130, in which it was held that a secret intention to join in if required was not of itself sufficient); there must be both actual encouragement and also awareness of that fact (see *Allan* and *Tate* [1993] Crim LR 538). *Wilcox v Jeffery* [1951] 1 All ER 464 was a case where there was ample evidence to draw the inference of intentional encouragement from the presence of a spectator at an illegal saxophone performance (by an American forbidden to take employment in this country). The accused had not only paid for a ticket at the performance (thus his presence was not accidental) but had reported the arrival of the American at the airport in his magazine, *Jazz Illustrated*, and subsequently wrote a laudatory review of the concert. **A5.13**

Where the accused is present and has both the right and ability to control the principal offender, his failure to exercise that right of control may make him liable as an accomplice. Thus in *Rubie v Faulkner* [1940] 1 KB 571 a learner driver was convicted of driving without due care and attention in that he overtook on a bend, and the defendant who was supervising him was convicted of aiding and abetting him by failing to exercise his right of control. Similarly, in *Tuck v Robson* [1970] 1 WLR 741, a publican was held liable for aiding and abetting his customers to commit the offence of drinking after hours by failing to collect the customers' glasses or to eject them from the premises. See also *National Coal Board v Gamble* [1959] 1 QB 11, in which Slade J said: 'Mere passive acquiescence is sufficient only, I think, where the alleged aider and abettor has the power to control the offender *and is actually present when the offence is committed*' (emphasis added). Presence in this sort of case is arguably significant not only as evidence of encouragement but also as evidence that the accused has the knowledge that the offence is being committed and the opportunity to exercise control. In *J. F. Alford Transport Ltd* [1997] 2 Cr App R 326, the convictions of managers of a company for the offence of aiding and abetting the making of false tachograph records by the company's drivers were quashed because there was no evidence of knowledge in relation to any specific count. If such knowledge could have been proved, irrespective it was said of whether the accused was present when the offence was committed, the ability to control the action of the offender coupled with a decision to refrain from doing so would have been sufficient. Proof of encouragement and of knowledge of the facts may however be difficult to achieve where the accused is not present.

Withdrawal

There is often an interval between the act of the accessory and the completion of the offence by the principal offender. In some circumstances, a change of heart by the accessory coupled with steps to withdraw from participation in the offence can remove his responsibility for the completed offence (although he may remain liable for any completed offence of incitement or conspiracy). Precisely what is required for an effective withdrawal will vary from case to case. It may depend on how imminent the completed offence is at the time of the attempted withdrawal by the accomplice and also on the nature of assistance and encouragement already given by the accessory. Thus in *Becerra* (1975) 62 Cr App R 212, A1 gave A2 a knife to use if they were disturbed during the course of a burglary. When A1 heard the tenant coming he called to A2: 'There's a bloke coming. Let's go' and jumped out of a window and fled. A2, however, stabbed and killed the tenant. Both A1 and A2 were convicted of murder. A1's **A5.14** application for leave to appeal on the grounds that he should have been allowed the defence of withdrawal was refused since, according to Roskill LJ at p. 219 (emphasis added):

> if [he] wanted to withdraw *at that stage*, he would have to 'countermand', to use the word that is used in some of the cases or 'repent' to use another word so used, in some manner vastly different and vastly more effective than merely to say 'Come on, let's go' and go out through the window.

Similarly, leave to appeal against a conviction for murder was refused in *Baker* [1994] Crim LR 444, where the Court of Appeal was sceptical as to whether, even on D's version of events, he could be regarded as having effectively withdrawn from the joint enterprise. D inflicted three knife wounds, passed the knife to another, saying 'I'm not doing it', moved a few feet away and turned his back whilst others inflicted further wounds: the Court of Appeal considered that this constituted far from unequivocal notice that D was wholly disassociating himself from the entire enterprise. The words were quite capable of meaning no more than 'I will not myself strike any more blows'.

In *Becerra*, the court left open the question whether it was necessary to take all reasonable steps to prevent the commission of the crime which he had agreed the others should commit. As a minimum however, the accessory must communicate his intention to withdraw to the other parties; it is not sufficient merely to fail to turn up as arranged (*Rook* [1993] 1 WLR 1005). Such communication was found to be a sufficient withdrawal from a proposed burglary on the facts of *Whitefield* (1983) 79 Cr App R 36. The failure of the trial judge to put the defence of withdrawal to the jury was one of the grounds for the Court of Appeal quashing the conviction of Derek Bentley for murder, 45 years after he was hanged, following a reference by the Criminal Cases Review Commission (*Bentley* [1999] Crim LR 330).

In *Mitchell* (1999) 163 JP 75, the Court of Appeal drew a distinction between pre-planned and spontaneous violence. With the latter, the issue was not whether there had been communication of withdrawal but whether the original joint venture was still continuing at the time of the principal's act. *Mitchell* was followed in *O'Flaherty* [2004] 2 Cr App R 315, where the question was 'whether a particular defendant disengaged before the fatal injury or injuries were caused'.

Victims Not Regarded as Accessories

A5.15 Where an offence is designed to protect a particular class of persons, a member of that class, i.e. a 'victim' of the offence, cannot be convicted as accessory even though the offence takes place with his or her voluntary assistance. The principle is most likely to arise in the context of sexual offences where the offence takes place despite the victim's consent. The classic illustration is *Tyrrell* [1894] 1 QB 710, in which it was held that a girl under 16 could not be guilty of aiding and abetting an offence of unlawful carnal knowledge of her since the offence was created for the protection of the girl (see now SOA 2003, s. 9). The principle can sometimes rebound so that it results in the acquittal of some other party who is not a victim, as in *Whitehouse* [1977] QB 868 where a father was acquitted of inciting his 15-year-old daughter to commit incest with him. The girl was regarded as within the class of persons the offence was designed to protect and if the girl herself could not be liable, even as an accessory, her father could not be liable for inciting her to do something which was not a crime. A special offence of incitement in these particular circumstances was subsequently created by the Criminal Law Act 1977, s. 54 (see now SOA 2003, s. 26 at **B3.118**), but the general principle still remains. See *Pickford* [1995] QB 203 for a related problem.

VICARIOUS LIABILITY

A5.16 Other than where the accused has aided, abetted, counselled or procured the act of another, the general principle is that one cannot be held criminally responsible as a result of the act of another. Public nuisance and criminal libel were the only exceptions at common law. There are, however, two further exceptions to this principle in relation to statutory offences involving strict liability:

(a) where the words of the statute are apt to describe not only the physical perpetrator of an act but also some other person, typically his employer;
(b) where the statute casts some special duty on a person, typically a licensee of a public house, which he delegates to another (the delegation principle).

This aspect of vicarious liability is dealt with in A4.4.

CORPORATE LIABILITY

A5.17 An incorporated company is a legal person and can therefore be liable for strict-liability offences defined in such a way that the company satisfies the definition of the offence. Thus in *Alphacell Ltd v Woodward* [1972] AC 824 a company which owned a factory from which polluted matter entered a river had its conviction, for causing polluting matter to enter a stream contrary to the Rivers (Prevention of Pollution) Act 1951, upheld by the House of Lords. Similarly, in *Atkinson v Sir Alfred McAlpine & Son Ltd* (1974) 16 KIR 220, a company was held liable for failure to give written notice or provide protective clothing as required by the Asbestos Regulations 1969 (SI 1969 No. 690). Neither of these are cases of being held responsible for a particular act of an employee of the company but companies are also liable for acts done by individual employees to the same extent as are human employers (see **A4.4**), i.e. where the definition of the offence is equally capable of applying to the employer as well as to the employee. See *Green v Burnett* [1955] 1 QB 78 — employer (limited company) 'using' a vehicle through its employee.

The principles stated so far are only of any use in relation to offences that do not require proof of a state of mind. The personality of a company is a legal fiction and a company does not itself have a mind. However, a company can sometimes be guilty of an offence requiring a state of mind under a principle which identifies the acts and state of mind of a senior employee or officer of the company with the company itself. Under this principle a company can even be liable for a common-law offence, such as conspiracy to defraud, where the mental element is central to liability, as in *ICR Haulage Ltd* [1944] KB 551, where the agreement and intention of the managing director were regarded as those of the company. (There were ten other parties to the conspiracy in *ICR Haulage Ltd*, but a company cannot create a conspiracy with just a single director as at least two distinct minds are required for a conspiracy — see *McDonnell* [1966] 1 QB 233.) Precisely which employees or officers are identified with the company for these purposes is a matter of some debate. In the leading case of *Tesco Supermarkets Ltd v Nattrass* [1972] AC 153, a branch manager employed by the national chain of supermarkets was held not to be so identified. He was therefore another person so that the company could successfully rely on the defence under the Trade Descriptions Act 1968, s. 24(1). Contrast the result in *Tesco Stores Ltd v Brent London Borough Council* [1993] 1 WLR 1037, where the knowledge of, and information available to, a sales assistant was sufficient to prevent the company from being able to rely on the defence in the Video Recordings Act 1984, s. 11(2). Leaving such special defences aside, it seems that it will normally only be senior persons at or close to board level who will normally be identified with the company although in *DPP v Kent and Sussex Contractors Ltd* [1944] KB 146 the intention of the company's transport manager was treated as the company's intention. More typically, in *John Henshall (Quarries) Ltd v Harvey* [1965] 2 QB 233, a weighbridge operator was not identified with the company. In *National Coal Board v Gamble* [1959] 1 QB 11, the National Coal Board waived the point that their weighbridge operator was much too junior to be identified with the company but Slade J was dubious about the propriety of the court accepting jurisdiction on those terms.

However, hard and fast rules about which employees are identified cannot be laid down as, 'a board of directors can delegate part of their functions of management so as to make their delegate an embodiment of the company within the sphere of the delegation' (per Lord Reid in *Tesco Supermarkets Ltd v Nattrass* [1972] AC 53 at pp. 174–5). This is perhaps the best explanation of *DPP v Kent and Sussex Contractors Ltd* [1944] KB 146, whereas in *Tesco Supermarkets Ltd v Nattrass*, Lord Reid said (at p. 175) that:

> . . . the board never delegated any part of their functions. They set up a chain of command through regional and district supervisors, but they remained in control. The shop managers had to obey their general directions and also take orders from their superiors. The acts or omissions of shop managers were not acts of the company itself.

Lord Reid also said (at p. 170) that:

> It must be a question of law whether, once the facts have been ascertained, a person in doing particular things is to be regarded as the company or merely as the company's servant or agent.

Where the offence is a statutory one, the Privy Council has taken the view, in *Meridian Global Funds Management Asia Ltd v Securities Commission* [1995] 2 AC 500, that it is a question of construction of the particular statutory provisions. The decision illustrates that the employee identified with the company in respect of the commission of a statutory offence (although still quite senior on the facts) need not be classified as the 'directing mind and will' as is still required for the 'primary rule of attribution' applicable to common-law offences including manslaughter (as to which see the discussion of *A-G's Ref (No. 2 of 1999)* [2000] 3 WLR 195 below).

Although there seems to be no decision directly in point, it seems to be generally accepted that a company would only be identified with an act done by one of its officers within 'the scope of his office', to use the expression adopted in the Law Commission's Draft Criminal Code (Law Com. No. 177), cl. 30(2). For example, if a director driving to a board meeting causes death by his dangerous driving, the company would not be liable for the statutory offence, or for manslaughter, since the director was not exercising his managerial functions whilst driving, even though he was on his way to a place where he would exercise those functions. On the other hand, if the acts done are within the scope of his office, as with the false purchase tax returns made by the company secretary in *Moore v I. Bresler Ltd* [1944] 2 All ER 515, it does not matter that they are done to conceal a fraud on the company. (See the Law Commission's Draft Criminal Code Bill (Law Com. No. 177), cl. 30(6), for a proposal to reverse this case — the individual employee or director would, of course, remain liable.)

The only offences of which it appears a company cannot be convicted are murder and treason since these are not punishable by a fine which is the only possible strictly penal sanction against a company. There are many other offences for which it is difficult to see how a company could be convicted as principal, rape and bigamy being obvious examples where a company would lack a basic qualification for liability. However, there seems no reason in principle why a company should not, just like a human person, be liable as an accessory to offences such as these for which it could not be liable as a principal. *Mens rea* is, of course, required for liability as an accessory but a company was convicted of aiding and abetting causing death by dangerous driving in *Robert Millar (Contractors) Ltd* [1970] 2 QB 54 where a director knew the relevant facts. As to the possibility of a company being liable for perjury, see the Court of Appeal (Civil Division) decision in *Odyssey Re (London) Ltd v OIC Run-Off Ltd* (2000) *The Times*, 17 March 2000.

It has been clear for some time that a company can be convicted of manslaughter. On 8 December 1994 OLL Ltd, was convicted of manslaughter and fined £60,000 at Winchester Crown Court (Ognall J) following the deaths of four sixth-formers in the Lyme Bay canoe tragedy: the managing director was also convicted and sentenced to three years' imprisonment. However, in proceedings arising out of the Southall Rail Crash of 1997, it was confirmed in *A-G's Ref (No. 2 of 1999)* [2000] QB 796 that a company could be convicted of manslaughter only if an individual who could be identified with the company as its directing mind and could be shown (as in the OLL Ltd case) to have been guilty of the offence; his guilt could then be attributed to the company. The Court of Appeal held that with a common-law offence such as manslaughter there was no scope for a weaker rule of attribution based on the interpretation of the particular statute as in *Meridian* above. Nor, despite the fact that gross negligence manslaughter was held not to require proof of a state of mind, was there any principle of aggregation whereby the 'fault' of a number of individuals could be aggregated so as to establish gross negligence overall. Corporate liability for manslaughter at common law depended on the identification principle which meant that it was very difficult to prove against all but the smallest companies (as in OLL Ltd or, for a more recent illustration, see *Mark* [2004] EWCA Crim 2490). However, following a long gestation period, legislation creating a new statutory offence of corporate manslaughter and abolishing manslaughter by gross negligence in its application to corporations and other organisations covered by a new statutory offence, has now been enacted in the Corporate Manslaughter and Corporate Homicide Act 2007 (see **B1.128**), which received the Royal Assent on 26 July 2007. The Act's main provisions are expected to come into force in April 2008.

The liability of a company for an offence is, as has already been mentioned, additional to the liability of the individual employee, but the fact that the company is liable may also have the effect of casting the net of individual responsibility rather more widely. This is due to the fact that many statutes (see, e.g., Trade Descriptions Act 1968, s. 20) now contain a section imposing liability on any 'director, manager, secretary or other similar officer' with whose 'consent or connivance' the offence has been committed or to whose 'neglect' it is attributable. In many cases such a person would be liable on normal principles as an accessory. However, the reference to 'neglect' means the liability is wider than that for accessories for whom negligence is not normally sufficient (see **A5.3**). On the other hand, for an accused to be a manager within the meaning of provisions of the above kind requires that he has a position of real authority with both the power and responsibility to decide corporate policy. He must perform a governing role in respect of the affairs of the company rather than merely a day-to-day management function (see *Boal* [1992] 1 QB 591).

In some statutes, the reference to 'neglect' is omitted (see, e.g., Theft Act 1968, s. 18; Public Order Act 1986, s. 28; Copyright, Designs and Patents Act 1988, s. 110) and the prosecution have to rely on connivance or consent, both of which would appear to require the same degree of knowledge as aiding and abetting. Even here, though, the liability is potentially wider than that of an accessory since a positive act of aiding and abetting is not necessarily required. A conscious failure to prevent or report a fellow director committing an offence would seem to be enough, even though there is not a sufficiently clear or immediate right of control over the fellow director to give rise to liability as an accessory.

Section A6 Inchoate Offences

INCITEMENT

Definition

A6.1 Incitement is primarily a common-law offence, but there are also several statutory offences of incitement, notably under the OAPA 1861, s. 4 (solicitation of murder: see **B1.112**); the Official Secrets Act 1920, s. 7 (see **B9.17**, **B9.23**, **B9.29** and **B9.34**) and the Misuse of Drugs Act 1971, s. 19 (see **B20.76**). The following discussion primarily concerns incitement at common law, but the statutory offences are governed by similar principles. Incitement involves soliciting, encouraging or pressurising another person to commit an offence. The offence incited may be summary or indictable, but need not be committed by the person incited. Where it is committed, the inciter becomes a secondary party to that offence (see **A5.1**).

Indictment

A6.2 *Statement of Offence*

Incitement to theft contrary to common law

Particulars of Offence

A on or about the . . . day of . . . at . . . unlawfully incited P to steal a ruby ring belonging to V

Jurisdiction and Procedure

A6.3 The mode of trial for incitement is the same as for the offence incited. Thus, incitement to commit a summary offence is triable only summarily and incitement to commit an offence triable either way is triable either way (MCA 1980, s. 45 and sch. 1, para. 35).

Jurisdiction over common-law incitement in cases involving extra-territorial elements is largely governed by the same principles as apply to attempt (see **A6.38**). If the act incited would not itself be punishable under English law, no offence of incitement can be committed at common law; but if the act incited would be so punishable, it does not matter that some or all of its essential elements may occur abroad. See *Tompkins* [2006] EWCA Crim 2132.

Different principles apply to some statutory offences of incitement. The offence of solicitation to murder, for example, can be committed in England and Wales, even where the proposed murder is to be committed by a foreigner abroad in circumstances where English law cannot apply (*Abu Hamza* [2007] 2 WLR 226 (see **B1.116**)); and under the CJA 1993, s. 5(4), a person in England and Wales may be guilty of inciting the commission of a 'Group A offence' (see **A8.7**) even where this Group A offence is to be committed entirely abroad and would not itself be punishable under English law.

The Sexual Offences (Conspiracy and Incitement) Act 1996, s. 2, makes it an offence for a person in England and Wales to incite another person to commit a specified sexual act involving a child under the age of 16 outside the UK. The act incited must be an offence under local law, and one that would be a 'listed sexual offence' in the schedule to the Act, 'but for the fact that what he had in view would not be an offence triable in England and Wales' (i.e. but for the fact that it was to be committed outside the jurisdiction).

The enactment of the Sex Offenders Act 1997, s. 7, stripped the 1996 Act of much of its practical significance. That provision (later re-enacted as the SOA 2003, s. 72 (see **B3.268**)) extended English criminal jurisdiction over a wide range of sexual acts committed by British citizens or UK residents against children abroad. A person inciting a British citizen or resident to commit such an act abroad must accordingly be charged *not* under the 1996 Act, but with incitement at common law. A charge under the 1996 Act would now be appropriate only where the person incited is a foreigner who would not be subject to English law when abroad.

As to incitement to commit acts of terrorism abroad, see **B10.73**.

Sentence

The maximum penalty following conviction on indictment is at the discretion of the court, although judges must have regard to the penalties applicable in respect of the offence incited. The maximum penalty on summary conviction is the same as that for the offence incited (Criminal Law Act 1977, s. 28(1) and s. 30(4)). **A6.4**

Actus Reus

'A person may incite another to do an act by threatening or by pressure, as well as persuasion' (*Race Relations Board v Applin* [1973] QB 815, per Lord Denning MR at p. 825; *Evans* [1986] Crim LR 470). Incitement may also be implicit, as in *Invicta Plastics Ltd v Clare* [1976] RTR 251, where a 'Radatec' device was advertised in a motoring magazine, illustrated with a picture in which it was being used to detect police radar traps, contrary to the Wireless Telegraphy Act 1949. As Park J said, 'it is plain that readers were . . . incited to use the Radatec device.' A small printed warning, to the effect that such use was illegal, did not change the thrust of the advertisement. **A6.5**

Incitement can be committed even if the incitee refuses to act (a point apparently overlooked in *Goldman* [2001] Crim LR 822), and may even be committed by means of orders communicated via an automated computer system that has been programmed to operate the incitee's unlawful business (*R (O'Shea) v Coventry Magistrates' Court* [2004] Crim LR 948) but a total failure to communicate, as where written incitement is intercepted by the police, arguably amounts only to an attempt to incite (*Ransford* (1874) 13 Cox CC 9; *Krause* (1902) 66 JP 121).

Offences that Cannot be Incited

An accused cannot properly be charged with inciting X to aid, abet, counsel or procure an offence by Y which Y does not ultimately commit (*Bodin* [1979] Crim LR 176, a decision at first instance); nor is it an offence to incite another person to commit statutory or common-law conspiracy (Criminal Law Act 1977, s. 5(7)); but it may be an offence to incite X to incite Y to commit an offence, as long as this would not inevitably involve X conspiring with Y (*Sirat* (1986) 83 Cr App R 41; *Evans* [1986] Crim LR 470). **A6.6**

It is not an offence for a girl under 16 to incite or abet a man to have sexual intercourse with her, because the law prohibiting such intercourse exists for her protection (*Tyrrell* [1894] QB 710). The common-law offence of incitement cannot apply to a man who incites a child under 16 to engage in sexual activity, because she would commit no offence in so doing (*Whitehouse* [1977] QB 868); but see the SOA 2003, ss. 10 (see **B3.64**) and 26 (see **B3.118**).

Mens Rea

A6.7 To be guilty of incitement, one must ordinarily intend that the offence incited will be committed, although, as with attempt, recklessness as to circumstances may sometimes suffice (see **A6.36**). The accused must therefore intend or assume that the person he incites will act with the *mens rea* required for that offence. The terrorist who conceals a bomb in a postal packet does not incite postal workers to commit an offence under the Explosive Substances Acts, but uses them as his innocent agents. Insofar as *Curr* [1968] 2 QB 944 appears to require proof that persons incited actually possess such *mens rea*, it is manifestly erroneous; a person incited need not actually commit the offence at all, so it cannot be necessary to prove his *mens rea*. See *DPP v Armstrong* [2000] Crim LR 379 and *Claydon* [2006] 1 Cr App R 339.

The decision in *Shaw* [1994] Crim LR 365 must also be considered erroneous. S incited K to authorise payment by his employers on the basis of forged invoices. He was charged with inciting K to obtain property by deception, but argued that he was not dishonest because his purpose was to expose the laxity of his employers' security arrangements. The Court of Appeal accepted that, if true, this was a valid defence, but with respect it should not have done. S was guilty as long as he intended that K would dishonestly commit the offence incited (cf. *Smith* [1960] 2 QB 423 at **B15.9**).

Impossibility

A6.8 Impossibility in relation to incitement remains governed by the same principles that formerly applied to conspiracy and attempt (*Fitzmaurice* [1983] QB 1083). D cannot therefore be guilty of inciting another to commit a crime that it is, in the circumstances, impossible to commit. He cannot, for example, be convicted of inciting X to handle goods that are not proved to be stolen, nor can he be guilty of inciting Y to extract cocaine from a substance which contains none (cf. *DPP v Nock* [1978] AC 979). A child under the age of 10 is conclusively presumed incapable of committing an offence; inciting such a child to do so must accordingly be deemed impossible (see *Pickford* [1995] QB 203: a case involving the now-abandoned presumption that a boy under 14 was incapable of sexual intercourse).

The borderline between what is impossible and what is not may be difficult to draw. In *Fitzmaurice,* F was duped by his father into recruiting three other men for the supposed purpose of robbing a woman carrying wages from a bank in Bow. His father had meanwhile informed the police that a gang was lying in wait there for a raid on a security van, and the three men were arrested. It was argued that in the circumstances the proposed robbery was impossible, but the Court of Appeal disagreed. The offence incited by F was one of 'robbing a woman at Bow' and 'by no stretch of the imagination was that an impossible offence to carry out'. See also *DPP v Armstrong* [2000] Crim LR 379.

CONSPIRACY GENERALLY

A6.9 At common law, conspiracy was originally defined as an agreement between two or more persons to do an unlawful act, or to do a lawful act by unlawful means (*Mulcahy* (1868) LR 3 HL 306). The unlawful act did not have to be a criminal offence. The Criminal Law Act 1977, s. 5, abolished most (but not all) forms of common-law conspiracy, whilst s. 1 of the Act created a new statutory offence in their place.

Common Law and Statutory Conspiracies

A6.10 There are at least three distinct forms of conspiracy under English law, namely conspiracy to defraud at common law, conspiracy to commit a criminal offence contrary to the CLA 1977, s. 1, and conspiracy to commit abroad an offence under foreign law (contrary to the CLA

1977, s. 1A). The first two forms overlap because a conspiracy to defraud may also involve a statutory conspiracy, in which case the CJA 1987, s. 12, allows the prosecution to charge either offence (see **A6.25**). Two other forms of common-law conspiracy require brief consideration, namely conspiracy to corrupt public morals and conspiracy to outrage public decency; but their survival as separate forms of conspiracy is extremely doubtful. Section 5(3) of the 1977 Act purports to preserve such conspiracies as common-law offences, but only:

> if and in so far as [they] may be committed by entering into an agreement to engage in conduct which—
> (a) tends to corrupt public morals or outrages public decency; but
> (b) would not amount to or involve the commission of an offence if carried out by a single person otherwise than in pursuance of an agreement.

If, in other words, a conspiracy to outrage public decency involves an agreement to commit a substantive criminal offence, it can be charged *only* as a conspiracy under s. 1 of the Act. No overlap with the common-law offence is possible. When the 1977 Act was drafted, it was considered unclear whether any substantive offences of outraging public decency or corrupting public morals existed, and s. 5(3) was intended to preserve the effect of the notorious decisions of the House of Lords in *Shaw v DPP* [1962] AC 220 and *Knuller (Publishing, Printing and Promotions) Ltd v DPP* [1973] AC 435, lest statutory conspiracy failed to cover conduct of the kind dealt with in those cases. It is now clear that outraging public decency is indeed a substantive offence at common law (see **B3.280** ***et seq.***). Agreements to do acts amounting to that offence must accordingly be charged as statutory conspiracies. The only way in which the common-law form of conspiracy might survive would be if the concept of outraging public decency were deemed to be wider in the context of conspiracy than in the context of the substantive offence. There is no good reason why such a distinction should be made, and it therefore appears that this form of conspiracy has been subsumed within the statutory variant.

Authority in respect of corrupting public morals is sparse, but the Court of Criminal Appeal in *Shaw* held that it did indeed exist as a substantive common-law offence, and the House of Lords did not reject that view (although it did not form part of their *ratio decidendi*). It seems probable, therefore, that this form of common-law conspiracy has also been subsumed within the statutory offence, and that nothing at all has been preserved by s. 5(3). In any event, there has been no reported prosecution for this form of conspiracy since the 1977 Act came into force, and it does not warrant further discussion here.

STATUTORY CONSPIRACY

Definition

Criminal Law Act 1977, s. 1 **A6.11**

(1) Subject to the following provisions of this part of this Act, if a person agrees with any other person or persons that a course of conduct will be pursued which, if the agreement is carried out in accordance with their intentions, either—
  (a) will necessarily amount to or involve the commission of any offence or offences by one or more of the parties to the agreement; or
  (b) would do so but for the existence of facts which render the commission of the offence or any of the offences impossible,

  he is guilty of conspiracy to commit the offence or offences in question.

(2) Where liability for any offence may be incurred without knowledge on the part of the person committing it of any particular fact or circumstance necessary for the commission of the offence, a person shall nevertheless not be guilty of conspiracy to commit that offence by virtue of subsection (1) above unless he and at least one other party to the agreement intend

or know that the fact or circumstance shall or will exist at the time when the conduct constituting the offence is to take place.

(3) [Repealed.]

(4) In this part of this Act 'offence' means an offence triable in England and Wales.

Agreements relating to acts involving summary offences not punishable by imprisonment must be disregarded if the acts are to be done in contemplation or furtherance of a trade dispute (Trade Union and Labour Relations (Consolidation) Act 1992, s. 242).

Indictment

A6.12

Statement of Offence

Conspiracy to commit criminal damage contrary to section 1(1) of the Criminal Law Act 1977

Particulars of Offence

A [and B] on or about the . . . day of . . . conspired together [and/or with persons unknown] to damage the braking systems on two heavy goods vehicles belonging to V plc, with intent to endanger life, contrary to s. 1(2) of the Criminal Damage Act 1971

A single agreement (and a single count of conspiracy) may embrace conduct involving several offences, without being bad for duplicity (*Roberts* [1998] 1 Cr App R 441; *Greenfield* [1973] 1 WLR 1151; *Taylor* [2002] Crim LR 205 and **D11.26**). It was suggested in *Roberts* that, where a single count alleges an agreement to commit more than one offence, failure to prove the conspiracy in respect of any one of those offences would be fatal to the charge as a whole; but this must, with respect, be wrong (contrast *Fussell* [1997] Crim LR 812 and *Taylor* (above)). It may nevertheless be good practice to charge such a conspiracy by means of two or more separate counts. As Lord Bridge said in *Cooke* [1986] AC 909:

> A single agreement to pursue a course of conduct which involves the commission of two different specific offences could perfectly properly be charged in two counts alleging two different conspiracies, e.g. a conspiracy to steal a car and a conspiracy to obtain money by deception by selling the car with false registration plates and documents.

Whether an indictment for conspiracy alleges one ulterior offence or several, it is important that it properly identifies the individual offences in question, in accordance with the Indictments Act 1915, s. 3(1), and the Indictments Rules 1971, r. 6 (*Roberts* [1998] 1 Cr App R 441 at pp. 449–450). Where, for example, an indictment charges a conspiracy to commit criminal damage, it should make it clear whether this refers to the basic offence (contrary to the Criminal Damage Act 1971, s. 1(1)) or to the aggravated offence (contrary to s. 1(2)). See also *Booth* [1999] Crim LR 144 (arson). As to 'either/or' conspiracies, in which the parties agree to a course of conduct which will clearly involve the commission of some offence but cannot be certain which offence this will be, see *Hussain* [2002] Crim LR 407, *Singh* [2003] EWCA Crim 3712 (although *Singh* was overruled on other grounds in *Saik* [2007] 1 AC 18) and *Suchedina* [2007] 1 Cr App R 305.

An indictment for conspiracy must not be misleading. An indictment alleging that the defendants conspired to supply drugs to 'another' cannot sensibly apply to a case in which the intended recipient was one of the conspirators (*Jackson* (1999) *The Times*, 13 May 1999; *Drew* [2000] 1 Cr App R 91).

A conspiracy count may be joined to substantive counts in an indictment where the facts warrant it and the interests of justice demand it, but see the *Consolidated Criminal Practice Direction*, para. IV. 34.3 (see **appendix** 7) and **D11.83** generally.

Procedure and Sentencing

A6.13 Conspiracy is triable only on indictment, even where it relates to a summary offence; but under the Criminal Law Act 1977, s. 4(1), proceedings for conspiracy to commit summary offences may not be instituted except by or with the consent of the DPP. Where a prosecution for a substantive offence may only be brought by or with leave of the DPP or A-G, this is also required in respect of a charge of conspiracy to commit it (s. 4(2) and (3)). Where the time limit for prosecuting a summary offence has expired, s. 4(4) provides that a prosecution for conspiracy is also barred, but this rule applies only where the substantive offence has been committed. As to the power of local authorities to prosecute for conspiracy (e.g., in trade descriptions cases), see *Jarrett* [1987] Crim LR 517 and *Richards* [1999] Crim LR 598.

By the Criminal Law Act 1977, s. 3, a person guilty of conspiracy to commit murder, any offence for which the maximum penalty is life imprisonment, or any indictable offence punishable with imprisonment where no maximum term is specified is subject to a maximum penalty of life imprisonment. For the relevant principles relating to the sentencing of conspiracy to commit murder see *McNee* (2007) *The Times*, 31 May 2007 and *Barot* [2007] EWCA Crim 1119. The maximum for other statutory conspiracies is the same as the maximum provided for the completed offence.

Agreement

Agreement is the essence of conspiracy. There is no conspiracy if negotiations fail to result in firm agreement between the parties (*Walker* [1962] Crim LR 458) nor is there a conspiracy between A and B merely because each has conspired separately with C (*Griffiths* [1966] 1 QB 589). It is possible, however, to have conspiracies in which some parties never meet others. These include 'chain' and 'wheel' conspiracies. In a chain conspiracy, A agrees with B, B agrees with C, C agrees with D, etc. In a wheel conspiracy, A, at the 'hub', recruits B, C and D to his scheme (*Ardalan* [1972] 2 All ER 257). In either case, however, the alleged conspirators must each be shown to be party to a common design, and they must be aware that there is a larger scheme to which they are attaching themselves (*Meyrick* (1929) 21 Cr App R 94; *Chrastny* [1991] 1 WLR 1381; *Barratt* [1996] Crim LR 495). If B and C each believe they have their own individual agreements with A, there are two separate conspiracies, and a single count will not be valid, even if B and C are aware that A is making similar agreements with others (*Griffiths*). **A6.14**

Where a series of offences are committed by a group of persons over a period of months or years, the prosecution may be tempted to proceed on the basis of a single conspiracy count, in preference to several substantive counts; but this tactic may be misconceived, because such offences are more likely in practice to be the product of a series of different agreements, and a single count of conspiracy may be impossible to prove (see *Barratt*).

Parties to Conspiracies and Acquittal of Other Alleged Conspirators

At least two persons must agree in order for there to be a conspiracy, although a single accused may be charged and convicted, even if the identities of his fellow conspirators remain unknown. Furthermore, the Criminal Law Act 1977, s. 5(8), confirms the principle established in *DPP v Shannon* [1975] AC 717, namely that acquittal of the only other alleged parties to a conspiracy (whether in the current trial or at a previous trial) need not prevent the conviction of the remaining accused, 'unless under all the circumstances of the case his conviction is inconsistent with the acquittal of the other person or persons in question'. Conviction of A and acquittal of B would be inconsistent if B is acquitted on the basis of a defence which, if true, must exonerate both, or if the evidence against each is the same (*Longman* (1980) 72 Cr App R 121); but it may be permissible to convict A on the basis of a pre-trial confession or other evidence which is not admissible against B or which does not incriminate him (cf. *Roberts* (1983) 78 Cr App R 41; *Testouri* [2004] 2 Cr App R 26; *Elkins* [2005] EWCA Crim 2711). As to the position where only one conspirator actually intended the agreed crime to be committed, see **A6.20**. **A6.15**

A corporation may be a party to a conspiracy (*ICR Haulage Ltd* [1944] KB 551), but a company and one of its directors cannot be the only parties to it because there can be no meeting of minds in such circumstances (*McDonnell* [1966] 1 QB 233). Certain other combinations are excluded under the Criminal Law Act 1977, s. 2(2), which provides that a person cannot be convicted of statutory conspiracy if the only person(s) with whom he agrees (initially and during the currency of the agreement) are (a) his spouse; (b) children under the age of 10; and (c) intended victims of the relevant offences. If, however, a husband and wife conspire with a third person who does not fall within categories (b) or (c), all three may be liable to conviction (*Chrastny* [1991] 1 WLR 1381; cf. *Lovick* [1993] Crim LR 890).

Intended victims are exempt from liability for statutory conspiracy (s. 2(1)). This appears designed to apply the principle established in *Tyrell* [1894] QB 710 in respect of laws prohibiting intercourse with underaged girls, etc. (see **A6.6**), but might also apply to terminally ill persons who agree to their own mercy killing, or even to a man who pays a prostitute in return for her agreement to whip him. In contrast, the fact that A may be incapable of committing the substantive offence as a principal offender does not prevent him incurring liability for conspiracy with B, if they agree that B will commit that offence (*Duguid* (1906) 21 Cox CC 200; *Burns* (1984) 79 Cr App R 173; *Sherry* [1993] Crim LR 536).

Agreement to Engage in Criminal Conduct

A6.16 To amount to a conspiracy under the Criminal Law Act 1977, s. 1, an agreement must propose that a course of conduct be pursued which would necessarily involve the commission, by one or more of the parties, of a substantive offence which would itself be triable in England and Wales. A few substantive offences may be triable in England and Wales even if committed abroad, but conspiracies in England or Wales to commit acts abroad which are punishable *only* under the relevant foreign law must be dealt with under s. 1A. See further **A6.23**.

To be the subject of a conspiracy, the course of conduct proposed must be something that will be done by one or more of the parties to the agreement. An agreement to procure the commission of a murder by a third party (e.g., to contact and hire a professional 'hit man') is not, in itself, a conspiracy to murder, even though anyone hiring such an assassin would become a secondary party to murder once he does his job. In other words, a conspiracy to aid, abet or procure an offence is not indictable under the Criminal Law Act 1977. This at least was the view of the Court of Appeal in *Hollinshead* [1985] 1 All ER 850, approving a passage to such effect in *Smith and Hogan*. The appellants in *Hollinshead* conspired to market devices for use by third parties, which would falsify electricity meter readings and enable users to avoid paying for electricity used. The court held that this did not amount to a conspiracy to commit offences under the Theft Act 1978, s. 2, even though the users would commit such offences. The House of Lords in *Hollinshead* [1985] AC 975 did not dissent from this view, although they did not expressly decide the point. (Such conduct would now give rise to liability under the Fraud Act 2006, s. 7: see **B5.103**.)

Conditional Agreements and Contingencies

A6.17 Problems may also arise where agreements could be carried out without committing the alleged substantive offence, or where the parties recognise that it might not prove necessary to carry out the agreement itself. On the face of it, the first kind of agreement falls outside the definition of a conspiracy. In *Reed* [1982] Crim LR 819, the Court of Appeal stated that, if A and B agree to drive from London to Edinburgh in a time which might or might not be achievable without breaking speed limits, depending on the traffic conditions, they do not thereby agree that they will *necessarily* commit any offence and are not therefore guilty of conspiracy. The Court of Appeal subsequently approved this dictum in *Jackson* [1985] Crim LR 442, whilst purporting to distinguish it on the facts before them. The appellants in *Jackson* agreed with one W, who was on trial for burglary, that he would be shot in the leg so as to induce the court to treat him leniently, should he be convicted. They were charged with conspiracy to pervert the course of justice, but argued that, when the agreement was made, it was not known whether W would be convicted. Thus, the planned shooting would not necessarily have interfered with the course of justice. Rejecting this argument, the court replied that 'contingency planning' could amount to conspiracy:

> 'Necessarily' is not to be held to mean that there must inevitably be the carrying out of an offence, it means, if the agreement is carried out in accordance with the plan, there must be the commission of the offence referred to in the conspiracy count.

With respect, the agreed course of conduct (the shooting of W) was not contingent on the outcome of the trial: indeed, it was carried out before the trial ended. It was the effect of that conduct on the future course of justice that was uncertain. The convictions in *Jackson* can better be justified on the basis that the appellants conspired (unconditionally) to commit an act which was intended (conditionally on the outcome of the trial) to pervert the course of justice; and an act committed with such an intent is sufficient to amount to the substantive offence of perverting the course of justice (see **B14.30**). If, however, planning for a contingency may indeed amount to conspiracy (and *O'Hadhmaill* [1996] Crim LR 509 is clear authority that it may), motorists who agree to break speed limits, if necessary, in order to get to Edinburgh on time must after all be guilty, and robbers who agree to 'shoot to kill' if challenged must equally be guilty of conspiracy to murder. This was acknowledged by the House of Lords in *Saik* [2007] 1 AC 18; but their lordships distinguished such cases from that in which A and B agree to launder money or other property that they suspect may *possibly* represent the proceeds of crime. If they do not know or intend this to be the case (as is required by the Criminal Law Act 1977, s. 1(2) (see **A6.21**)), they are not guilty of conspiracy, even though it may transpire that their suspicions are well founded (in which case they may end up committing a substantive money laundering offence).

Agreement forms the basis of liability in conspiracy. Neither the abandonment of the agreement, nor failure to carry out its terms, can affect such liability once it has been incurred (see *Bolton* (1991) 94 Cr App R 74).

Agreement Without Real Intent

If the *actus reus* of conspiracy is agreement, the *mens rea* is harder to identify. The concept **A6.18**
of agreement does not necessarily import an intent by each party to carry out that agreement, but such an intent was (and still is) required in respect of conspiracy at common law (*Thomson* (1965) 50 Cr App R 1; *Yip Chieu-Chung v The Queen* [1995] 1 AC 111) whilst there are references in the Criminal Law Act 1977, s. 1(1) and 1(4), to agreements being carried out in accordance with the intentions of the parties. The issue of intent may become problematic where one or more of the parties does not intend to keep his part of the agreement, as where a hired assassin agrees to commit a murder for which he is engaged, but intends only to make off with his advance fee, or where the supposed assassin is working undercover for the police, and intends only to collect evidence against those who hired him. Is the dishonest assassin or undercover officer guilty of conspiracy to murder. If not, where does that leave the other parties to the supposed agreement?

The House of Lords considered such questions in a slightly different context in *Anderson* [1986] AC 27. The appellant was charged with conspiracy to effect a convicted prisoner's escape from jail. He had agreed to such a plan and had supplied the other conspirators with diamond cutting wire in furtherance of it, but claimed that he had never believed the jailbreak could succeed, and was concerned only to obtain the money he had been promised for the wire. One possible answer to this supposed defence was that it amounted to an admission of complicity in the conspiracy as a secondary party. This answer found favour with the Court of Appeal in *Anderson*, but the House of Lords left it unconsidered and preferred to categorise the appellant as a principal offender. Lord Bridge, with whom the other members of the appellate committee agreed, said:

> I . . . reject any construction of the statutory language which would require the prosecution to prove an intention on the part of each conspirator that the criminal offence or offences . . . should in fact be committed. . . .
>
> . . . [b]eyond the mere fact of agreement, the necessary *mens rea* of the crime is . . . established if, and only if . . . the accused . . . intended to play some part in the agreed course of conduct in furtherance of the criminal purpose which the agreed course of conduct was intended to achieve. Nothing less will suffice; nothing more is required.

Lord Bridge went on to emphasise that a person, such as an undercover agent, 'ostensibly agreeing [but] with the purpose of exposing and frustrating the purpose of the other parties' cannot be guilty of conspiracy. This must be correct, but the earlier excerpts from his speech are problematic in a number of respects, and much of what he said is now widely considered to have been wrong. To begin with, his ruling that a conspirator need not intend the offence in question to be committed does violence to the wording of the Criminal Law Act 1977, s. 1(1), is difficult to reconcile with s. 1(2) (see **A6.21**), and invokes bizarre visions of conspiracies in which *none* of the parties actually intends to carry out the supposed agreement. It is doubtful whether Lord Bridge could have meant this to be the law, however, because he refers to 'the criminal purpose which the agreed course of conduct was *intended* to achieve . . .'. Furthermore, earlier in his speech he had said, '[it] is, of course, necessary that any party to the agreement shall have assented to play his part . . . knowing that the part to be played by one or more of the others will amount to or involve the commission of an offence.'

On that basis, the fraudulent hit-man who intends only to make off with his advance fee cannot be guilty of conspiracy to murder, because he knows that without him the plan must fail. Similarly, fraudulent drug dealers who intend to supply their customers with harmless powder cannot be regarded as having conspired to supply drugs. Their plan is in fact to obtain property from the customers by deception. This interpretation makes far more sense and appears to have been accepted by the Court of Appeal in *Edwards* [1991] Crim LR 352 and by the Northern Ireland Court of Appeal in *McPhillips* (1990 unreported). See also *Yip Chieu-Chung v The Queen* [1995] 1 AC 111 (see **A6.20**).

Active and Passive Conspirators

A6.19 A second problem with Lord Bridge's ruling in *Anderson* [1986] AC 27 is that it appears to require each conspirator to intend playing some active part in furtherance of the conspiracy. If so, it is an astonishing proposition, for which there is no basis either in the Criminal Law Act 1977 or in any cases decided before or after it. In *Siracusa* (1989) 90 Cr App R 340, the Court of Appeal concluded that Lord Bridge could not have meant what he said. 'He cannot have been intending' said O'Connor LJ, 'that the organiser of a crime, who recruited others to carry it out, would not himself be guilty of conspiracy. . . . Participation in a conspiracy is infinitely variable: it can be active or passive'.

Where Only One Conspirator is Genuine

A6.20 A cannot be guilty of conspiracy if B (the only other party to the supposed agreement) intends to frustrate or sabotage it. This issue did not arise in *Anderson* [1986] AC 27, but the Privy Council were required to consider it in *Yip Chieu-Chung v The Queen* [1995] 1 AC 111, where N, the appellant's only fellow conspirator in a plan to smuggle heroin out of Hong Kong, was an undercover agent working with the knowledge of the authorities. In an opinion delivered by Lord Griffiths, the Privy Council held that, if N's purpose had been to prevent the heroin being smuggled, no indictable conspiracy would have existed:

> The crime of conspiracy requires an agreement between two or more persons to commit an unlawful act with the intention of carrying it out. It is the intention to carry out the crime that

> constitutes the necessary *mens rea* for the offence. As Lord Bridge pointed out [in *Anderson*] an undercover agent who has no intention of committing the crime lacks the necessary *mens rea* to be a conspirator.

Conspiracy under Hong Kong law remains a common-law offence, but Lord Griffiths did not seek to distinguish in this respect between common-law and statutory conspiracy. He was, however, able to uphold the appellant's conviction on the basis that N had intended to smuggle the heroin out of Hong Kong as agreed. The trap was to be sprung later, when the heroin arrived in Australia. The fact that the Hong Kong authorities acquiesced in this plan did not prevent it from being a criminal act. Both parties were therefore guilty, albeit that N would never be prosecuted.

Mens Rea as to Circumstances

At common law, a person could be guilty of conspiracy only if he and at least one other conspirator knew of any relevant circumstances necessary for the commission of the offence (*Churchill v Walton* [1967] 2 AC 224). The Criminal Law Act 1977, s. 1(2) (see **A6.11**), maintains this rule in relation to statutory conspiracies. Thus, it is a strict liability offence to sell or advertise goods which bear a false trade description, but there can be no conspiracy to commit this offence unless the parties to the alleged conspiracy know that the goods are falsely described or intend that they will be falsely described. This rule applies to all conspiracies, and not merely to those concerning strict liability offences. As the House of Lords noted in *Saik* [2007] 1 AC 18, any other interpretation would be absurd. On the other hand, knowledge of the relevant law which makes the proposed conduct illegal need not be proved, because ignorance of the law is no defence (*Broad* [1997] Crim LR 666). **A6.21**

Despite s. 1(2), an indictment may properly charge conspiracy to commit criminal damage or arson 'being reckless as to whether the life of another person would thereby be endangered', because actual endangerment is not 'a fact or circumstance necessary for the commission of the offence' under the Criminal Damage Act 1971 s. 1(2). It is necessary only that the conspirators realise that their plan *may*, if carried out, endanger life. See *Mir* (22 April 1994 unreported), *Browning* (6 November 1998 unreported), *Ryan* (1999) 163 JP 849, and *Saik*, per Lord Nicholls at [4].

Difficulties have arisen as to the application of the Criminal Law Act 1977, s. 1(2), to cases of conspiracy to commit money laundering offences under the 'old' law (i.e. in cases not governed by the PCA 2002 (see **B22**)). These difficulties arose largely because of uncertainty as to the proper interpretation of the substantive money laundering offences under the Drug Trafficking Act 1994 or the CJA 1988, but have now largely been resolved by decisions of the House of Lords in *Montila* [2005] 1 WLR 3141 and *Saik*, and by those of the Court of Appeal in *Harmer* [2005] 2 Cr App R 23, *Ali* [2006] QB 322 and *Suchedina* [2007] 1 Cr App R 305.

Reliance may no longer be placed on cases such as *Rizvi* [2003] EWCA Crim 3575, *Singh* [2003] EWCA Crim 3712 and *Sakavickas* [2005] 1 WLR 857 (examined in the 2006 edition of this work), because these were based on an interpretation of the substantive money laundering law that was later rejected by the House of Lords in *Montila*, and *Saik* confirms that none of those cases survives the ruling in *Montila*. See also El-Kurd [2007] EWCA Crim 1888.

The true position in respect of such conspiracies was summarised in *Harmer* [2005] 2 Cr App R 23, in which it was held that an agreement to convert or transfer property that is merely suspected of being the proceeds of criminal conduct cannot amount to a criminal conspiracy within the meaning of the Criminal Law Act 1977, s. 1. As May LJ explained:

> A defendant is not to be guilty of conspiracy [to commit a money laundering offence under the CJA 1988] unless he and at least one other party to the agreement intend or know that the money

> will be the proceeds of crime when the agreed conduct takes place. This intention or knowledge is precisely what the prosecution in the present case accepted they could not prove when the words 'knew or' were omitted from the particulars of count 2. If the prosecution cannot prove that the money was the proceeds of crime, they cannot prove that the appellant knew that it was. So section 1(2) of the 1977 Act applies and is not satisfied.

This dictum was later approved in *Saik* (per Lord Hope at [72]). A similar approach would seem to be called for in the context of conspiracies to commit offences under the PCA 2002, because, with the possible exception of offences under s. 328 (see **B22.9** ***et seq.***), the substantive money laundering offences can be committed only in respect of property that is in fact 'criminal property'. See also *R* [2007] 1 Cr App R 150. It follows that the Criminal Law Act 1977, s. 1(2), seriously compromises the Crown's ability to use a single 'umbrella' conspiracy count in preference to multiple charges alleging a series of substantive money laundering transactions. The price for using such a charge is the need to prove knowledge or intent as to the criminal character of the property in question, where proof of well-founded suspicion would generally suffice for the substantive offences. But *Saik* itself makes clear that where a conspiracy count looks to future transactions there can be no question of having to prove that the property in question is in fact of illicit origin, for *ex hypothesi* it is as yet unidentified. What matters is the intent of the conspirators. See *Suchedina* at [18] to [20].

Impossibility

A6.22 At common law it was a defence to a charge of conspiracy that the object of the conspiracy was impossible to achieve. One could not, for example, be guilty of a conspiracy to extract cocaine from a substance which proved not to contain any cocaine (*DPP v Nock* [1978] AC 979). The Criminal Law Act 1977, s. 1(1), was amended by the Criminal Attempts Act 1981, so as largely to eliminate defences based on impossibility. If A and B wrongly believe that cocaine can be extracted from a given substance, they may now commit an indictable conspiracy or attempt to do so. They may also enter into an indictable conspiracy to murder someone who turns out to be dead already or to handle goods which they wrongly believe to have been stolen. On the other hand, an agreement to pursue a course of conduct which the parties wrongly believe to be criminal, because they have misunderstood the law, cannot be indictable as a conspiracy (cf. *Taaffe* [1984] AC 539).

Jurisdiction Over Statutory Conspiracy

A6.23 Conspiracy under the Criminal Law Act 1977 must involve an agreement to commit an offence triable under English law (s. 1(4)) and this usually means an offence which is to be committed within England and Wales or aboard a British ship or aircraft. A number of offences can however be tried under English law even if committed abroad (e.g., offences under the Aviation Security Act 1982 (see **B10.198** ***et seq.***) or murder/ manslaughter committed by a British citizen on land outside the UK. Persons who conspire anywhere to commit such crimes abroad are therefore indictable under s. 1 (*Bow Street Metropolitan Stipendary Magistrate, ex parte Pinochet Ugarte (No. 3)* [2000] 1 AC 147).

Persons who conspire in England or Wales to commit acts outside the UK, which are criminal under the law of the foreign state concerned and would be crimes under English law if committed in England or Wales, may be indicted under the Criminal Law Act 1977, s. 1A. Note however that there is no overlap between s. 1 and s. 1A: if the proposed conduct would amount to an extraterritorial offence under English law, the conspiracy must be charged under s. 1, and not under s. 1A.

Conspiracy to commit a 'cross frontier' offence of fraud or dishonesty which would itself be triable in England or Wales as a Group A offence under part I of the CJA 1993 must likewise be indicted under the Criminal Law Act 1977, s. 1, rather than s. 1A. A person may be guilty of conspiracy to commit such an offence whether or not any act or omission in relation to that offence occurred in England or Wales (CJA 1993, s. 3(2); and see further **A8.4** ***et seq.***).

Even in cases not covered by the CJA 1993, conspirators who, whilst abroad, plot the commission of a crime within England or Wales, may be indicted under English law, even if none of them enter the jurisdiction or trigger any consequences here. See *Liangsiriprasert v United States* [1991] AC 225; *Sansom* (1991) 92 Cr App R 115; *Manning* [1998] 2 Cr App R 461; *R (Al-Fawwaz) v Governor of Brixton Prison* [2002] 1 AC 556 and **A8.4**.

Evidential Issues

There are no special evidential rules peculiar to conspiracy. In *Murphy* (1837) 8 C & P 297, **A6.24** proof of conspiracy was said to be generally 'a matter of inference deduced from certain criminal acts of the parties accused', but there is no actual need for any such acts, and conspiracies may also be proved, *inter alia*, by direct testimony, secret recordings or confessions, subject only to the proviso that A's pre-trial confession cannot ordinarily be evidence against B. The acts and statements of one conspirator may be given in evidence against both him and his fellow conspirators, provided they were done or said in furtherance of their common purpose, but that rule is not confined to conspiracies. See further **F16.40** ***et seq.***

CONSPIRACY TO DEFRAUD

Definition

The common-law offence of conspiracy to defraud was expressly preserved by the Criminal Law Act 1977, s. 5(2). There are two principal variants of this offence, although these are not mutually exclusive. The first is defined in the leading case of *Scott v Metropolitan Police Commissioner* [1975] AC 819, where Viscount Dilhorne said: **A6.25**

> . . . an agreement by two or more [persons] by dishonesty to deprive a person of something which is his or to which he is or would be or might be entitled [or] an agreement by two or more by dishonesty to injure some proprietary right of his suffices to constitute the offence . . .

There may or may not be an intent to deceive in such cases, and there may or may not be an intent to cause economic or financial loss to the proposed victim or victims, but it suffices if there is a dishonest agreement to expose the proposed victim to some form of economic risk or disadvantage to which he would not otherwise be exposed.

The second variant was also recognised in *Scott*, but has been more fully considered by the Privy Council in *Wai Yu-tsang v The Queen* [1992] AC 269. In this variant, there must be a dishonest agreement by two or more persons to 'defraud' another, by deceiving him into acting contrary to his duty. There is some doubt as to the exact scope of this offence. It was suggested (*obiter*) in *DPP v Withers* [1975] AC 842 that the person deceived must be a public official, and this was also the view of Lord Diplock in *Scott*, but the opinion of the Privy Council in *Wai Yu-tsang* was that it suffices if any person is deceived into acting contrary to the duty he owes to his clients or employers. The Privy Council approved and adopted the concept of 'intent to defraud' previously expounded by Lord Denning and Lord Radcliffe in *Welham v DPP* [1961] AC 103. *Welham* involved an alleged offence under the Forgery Act 1913, s. 6 (since repealed), rather than an alleged conspiracy, but the concept of 'intent to defraud' appears to be similar in each case. Lord Denning held in *Welham* that to defraud means 'to practise a fraud' and need not necessarily involve causing any form of economic loss or prejudice.

Either variant of conspiracy to defraud is capable of overlapping with the offence of statutory conspiracy under the Criminal Law Act 1977, s. 1 (see **A6.10** ***et seq.***). Such overlap will occur wherever the course of action agreed on would necessarily involve the commission of any offence or offences by one or more of the parties to the conspiracy if carried out in accordance with their intentions and would also involve a fraud being practised on another person. In such circumstances, the prosecution has a choice as to which kind of charge to prefer (CJA 1987, s. 12(1)). Under guidelines issued by the A-G in 2007, however, a charge of statutory conspiracy (or a charge alleging a substantive offence) should be brought in preference to a charge of conspiracy to defraud unless there are good reasons for doing otherwise. A charge of conspiracy to defraud may be appropriate where no charge of statutory conspiracy (or of a substantive offence) could properly reflect the gravity of the offence, and/or where such charges might require a large number of separate counts, severed trials, etc. There may also be cases in which the identification of specific target offences would be problematic.

A dishonest price-fixing or 'cartel' agreement may also amount to a conspiracy to defraud (see *Norris v Govt of the USA* [2007] WLR 1730) but such agreements may now be prosecuted as offences under the Enterprise Act 2002, s. 188.

Indictment, Sentence and Procedure

A6.26 Conspiracy to defraud is triable only on indictment. It is punishable by up to 10 years' imprisonment or a fine or both (CJA 1987, s. 12(3)). For trial purposes, it is a class 3 offence. An indictment for conspiracy to defraud should not lack particularity and should enable the defence and the judge to know precisely the nature of the prosecution's case (*Landy* [1981] 1 WLR 355). This prevents the prosecution from shifting their ground during the trial, unless they obtain leave of the judge and amend the indictment itself (*Landy*). A single count of conspiracy to defraud may be founded on evidence of several fraudulent transactions if it can be shown that those transactions were each effected pursuant to a single agreement (*Mba* [2006] EWCA Crim 624).

In *K* [2005] 1 Cr App 408, the Court of Appeal considered *Landy* and added this guidance as to the drafting of indictments for conspiracy to defraud:

> [The indictment] should identify the agreement alleged with the specificity necessary in the circumstances of each case; if the agreement alleged is complex, then details of that may be needed and those details will . . . form part of what must be proved. If this course is followed, it should then be clear what the prosecution must prove and the matters on which the jury must be unanimous: see *Bennett* [1999] EWCA Crim 1486. Further particulars should be given where it is necessary for the defendants to have further general information as to the nature of the charge and for the other purposes identified by Lawton LJ in *Landy*. Such further particulars form no part of the ingredients of the offence and on these the jury do not have to be unanimous, as this court correctly decided in *Hancock*.

Statement of Offence

Conspiracy to defraud contrary to common law

Particulars of Offence

A and B on divers days between . . . and . . . conspired together [and with . . .] to defraud the C Bank plc and its existing and potential shareholders, creditors and depositors

(i) by dishonestly concealing in the accounts of the C Bank the dishonouring of cheques in the sum of £50 million drawn on the account of D Ltd with the E Bank Inc, such cheques having been purchased by the C Bank

(ii) [etc.]

As to the power of local authorities to prosecute for conspiracy to defraud (e.g. in trade descriptions cases), see *Jarrett* [1997] Crim LR 517 and *Richards* [1999] Crim LR 598. As to the A-G's guidelines on prosecutions for conspiracy to defraud, see **A6.25** and **appendix 3**.

Actus Reus

As in cases of statutory conspiracy, there must always be an agreement (see **A6.14**). The agreement may however be wider in certain respects than that required in respect of the statutory offence. It need not be an agreement that would necessarily involve the commission of a substantive offence if carried out (*Scott v Metropolitan Police Commissioner* [1975] AC 819; *Cooke* [1986] AC 909) and it need not necessarily be envisaged that the fraud will be perpetrated by the conspirators themselves. In *Hollinshead* [1985] AC 975, the appellants agreed to market devices designed to falsify gas or electricity meters, which would enable customers (who were not themselves party to the conspiracy) to defraud their gas and electricity suppliers. The appellants had no intention of using the devices themselves, but they were nevertheless guilty of conspiracy to defraud. In such circumstances a charge under the Fraud Act 2006, s. 7 (see **B5.103**) would now be more appropriate (see **A6.25** and the A-G's guidelines on prosecutions for conspiracy to defraud at **appendix 3**). **A6.27**

Other reported illustrations of agreements amounting to conspiracy to defraud include: agreement to conceal a bank's losses or liabilities from its shareholders, creditors and depositors (*Wai Yu-tsang v The Queen* [1992] AC 269); agreement by company directors to conceal secret profits from the company, where the company would be entitled to demand that the profits be accounted for (*Adams v The Queen* [1995] 1 WLR 52); agreement by British Rail catering staff to sell their own refreshments to customers whilst on duty, thereby depriving British Rail of profits from legitimate sales (*Cooke* [1986] AC 909); agreement to falsify hire-purchase or credit applications, so as to induce credit companies or other lenders to make loans they might not otherwise be willing to make (*Allsop* (1976) 64 Cr App R 29); and agreement to make pirate copies of films, etc., thereby depriving the makers and distributors of legitimate profits (*Scott v Metropolitan Police Commissioner*). As in cases of statutory conspiracy (see **A6.15**), it may be possible in some cases for one of two alleged conspirators to be convicted while the other is acquitted; but this would only be possible where there is evidence admissible against one but not the other (see *Testouri* [2004] 2 Cr App R 26; *Elkins* [2005] EWCA Crim 2711).

As to the position where only one of the supposed conspirators really intends to proceed with or carry out the conduct agreed upon, see **A6.20**.

Mens Rea

To be guilty of conspiracy to defraud, D must be dishonest (in the *Ghosh* sense, as to which see **B4.37**) and must intend to defraud the proposed victim, in one or other of the senses explained at **A6.25**; but an intent to deceive is necessary only in respect of the second of the two variants of the offence. In *A-G's Ref (No. 1 of 1982)* [1983] QB 751, it was held that there can be no conspiracy to defraud where the defrauding would be a mere side-effect (rather than the 'true object') of the scheme agreed to, but this is now generally thought to be wrong, and has not been followed in subsequent cases. The correct position must be that D intends to defraud V wherever he is aware that the successful implementation of his plan will result in V being defrauded (cf. *McPherson* [1985] Crim LR 508). **A6.28**

Jurisdiction over Conspiracy to Defraud

In *Board of Trade v Owen* [1957] AC 602, the House of Lords held that jurisdiction over conspiracy to defraud was governed by the same principles as conspiracy to commit a crime. In other words, a conspiracy abroad to defraud a victim within England and Wales may be indictable here, but no indictment will lie where the victim is to be defrauded abroad. Lord Tucker said: **A6.29**

> A conspiracy to commit a crime abroad is not indictable in this country unless the contemplated crime is one for which an indictment would lie here . . . It necessarily follows that a conspiracy of the nature of that charged in count 3 [i.e. a conspiracy to defraud a West German government

department] — which in my view was a conspiracy to attain a lawful object by unlawful means, rather than to commit a crime — is not triable in this country, since the unlawful means and the ultimate object were both outside the jurisdiction.

See also *A-G's Ref (No. 1 of 1982)* [1983] QB 751 and *Naini* [1999] 2 Cr App R 398, and **A8**. The position is now different in respect of things done on or after 1 June 1999. Section 5(3) of the CJA 1993 provides that various acts done or omitted within England and Wales, whether by a conspirator or by someone acting as his agent, may bring all the conspirators within English jurisdiction, even if the defrauding was intended to occur abroad. Conspirators may even be liable on the basis of acts previously done in England and Wales, before the conspiracy was formed.

Impossibility

A6.30 The abolition of the defence of impossibility in respect of attempts and statutory conspiracies has not affected the operation of that defence in the context of conspiracy to defraud or the common law offence of incitement. See generally **A6.8** and **A6.22**.

ATTEMPT

Definition

A6.31 The law relating to attempts is primarily governed by the Criminal Attempts Act 1981.

Criminal Attempts Act 1981, s. 1

(1) If, with intent to commit an offence to which this section applies, a person does an act which is more than merely preparatory to the commission of the offence, he is guilty of attempting to commit the offence.

[(1A) and (1B) deal with attempts in England or Wales to commit acts abroad which would amount to offences of computer misuse (see **B18.20**) if committed in England and Wales.]

(2) A person may be guilty of attempting to commit an offence to which this section applies even though the facts are such that the commission of the offence is impossible.

(3) In any case where—

(a) apart from this subsection a person's intention would not be regarded as having amounted to an intent to commit an offence; but

(b) if the facts of the case had been as he believed them to be, his intention would be so regarded,

then for the purpose of subsection (1) above, he shall be regarded as having had an intent to commit that offence.

(4) This section applies to any offence which, if it were completed, would be triable in England and Wales as an indictable offence, other than—

(a) conspiracy (at common law or under section 1 of the Criminal Law Act 1977);

(b) aiding, abetting, counselling, procuring or suborning the commission of an offence;

(c) offences under section 4(1) (assisting offenders) or 5(1) (accepting or agreeing to accept consideration for not disclosing information about a relevant offence) of the Criminal Law Act 1967.

Where an offence is triable only summarily, it cannot be the object of a criminal attempt under s. 1, but provisions creating summary offences sometimes create matching offences of attempt: see for example the Road Traffic Act 1988, ss. 4 and 5, which create summary offences of driving *or attempting to drive* when unfit through drink or drugs or when over the prescribed limit for alcohol (see **C5.23** and **C5.37**). The Criminal Attempts Act 1981, s. 3, provides that 'attempts under special statutory provisions' shall be governed by rules which mirror those in s. 1(1)–(3).

Section 1(4)(b) does not preclude charges of attempt in relation to substantive offences of 'procuring' or charges of attempting to abet another person's suicide, contrary to the Suicide

Act 1961 (*McShane* (1977) 66 Cr App R 97); nor does anything in s. 1(4) preclude a charge of attempting to incite the commission of a criminal offence.

Indictment

Statement of Offence A6.32

Attempted murder contrary to section 1(1) of the Criminal Attempts Act 1981

Particulars of Offence

A on or about the . . . day of . . . attempted to murder V

A person charged on indictment with an attempt to commit an offence can be convicted on that charge, notwithstanding any evidence proving that he has actually committed the substantive offence (Criminal Law Act 1967, s. 6(4)). The same rule applies to summary trials. Thus, in *Webley v Buxton* [1977] QB 481, the Divisional Court held that justices had properly convicted the appellant of an attempt to take a conveyance contrary to the Theft Act 1968, s. 12 (which at that time was an offence triable either way) notwithstanding that the evidence proved him to have committed the full offence. This rule is unaltered by the Criminal Attempts Act 1981.

Evidence, Procedure and Sentencing

Criminal Attempts Act 1981, s. 2 A6.33

(1) Any provision to which this section applies shall have effect with respect to an offence under section 1 above of attempting to commit an offence as it has effect with respect to the offence attempted.

(2) This section applies to provisions of any of the following descriptions made by or under any enactment (whenever passed)—

(a) provisions whereby proceedings may not be instituted or carried on otherwise than by, or on behalf or with the consent of, any person (including any provisions which also make other exceptions to the prohibition);

(b) provisions conferring power to institute proceedings;

(c) provisions as to the venue of proceedings;

(d) provisions whereby proceedings may not be instituted after the expiration of a time limit;

(e) provisions conferring a power of arrest or search;

(f) provisions conferring a power of seizure and detention of property;

(g) provisions whereby a person may not be convicted or committed for trial on the uncorroborated evidence of one witness (including any provision requiring the evidence of not less than two credible witnesses);

(h) provisions conferring a power of forfeiture, including any power to deal with anything liable to be forfeited;

(i) provisions whereby, if an offence committed by a body corporate is proved to have been committed with the consent or connivance of another person, that person also is guilty of the offence.

An attempt to commit an offence which is triable only on indictment is itself triable only on indictment, whilst an attempt to commit an offence triable either way is triable either way (Criminal Attempts Act 1981, s. 4(1)).

By the Criminal Attempts Act 1981, s. 4, the maximum penalty for attempted murder is life imprisonment. Other indictable offences are subject to the same maximum as applies on conviction on indictment for the offence attempted, and if the offence is triable either way the maximum penalty on summary conviction is the same as the maximum penalty available for that offence tried summarily. The Court of Appeal in *Robson* (1974) CSP A1-4B01 indicated that it would be 'at least unusual that an attempt should be visited with punishment to the maximum extent that the law permits in respect of a completed offence'. It is submitted that the sentence for a given attempt should almost always be less than the sentence which would have been imposed if that offence been completed, but clearly much will depend on the stage at which the attempt failed, and the reason(s) for its non-completion. On the other hand, within an offence category, some examples of attempt may merit more severe punishment than some examples of the completed offence. For guidance as to the proper approach to sentencing for attempted murder in the light of the statutory scheme for murder sentencing under the CJA 2003, s. 269 and sch. 21, see *Ford* [2006] 1 Cr App R (S) 204.

Actus Reus

A6.34 Section 1(1) of the Criminal Attempts Act 1981 requires the accused to have committed an act which is 'more than merely preparatory' to the offence attempted. A mere omission cannot suffice, even where accompanied by the requisite *mens rea.* A refusal to call an ambulance for a person who is gravely ill cannot, for example, amount to attempted murder; but in *Nevard* [2006] EWCA Crim 2896 the Court of Appeal arguably erred in ruling that the same was true of N's attempt to deceive and put off the emergency services following a 999 call made by his victim. This surely was a positive act, and would, if successful, have resulted in the victim's death. Where trial is on indictment, it is for the judge to determine whether there is evidence on which a jury could properly find that the accused's actions did go beyond mere preparation, but it is then for the jury to decide that question as one of fact (s. 4(3); and see also *DPP v Stonehouse* [1978] AC 55).

At common law, acts amounting to attempts were distinguished from mere preparatory acts by the concept of 'proximity'. An example of the proximity test was provided in *Robinson* [1915] 2 KB 342, in which a jeweller clumsily faked a robbery at his premises with a view to making a fraudulent insurance claim in respect of his supposed loss. It was held that his conviction for attempting to obtain money from his insurers by false pretences could not stand, because he had been arrested before he could send any claim to his insurers. As it was not a decision under the 1981 Act, *Robinson* cannot be a binding authority on its interpretation, but it is unlikely that such a case would be decided differently under the Act. Indeed, a similar approach was adopted in *Campbell* [1991] Crim LR 268, where the appellant armed himself with an imitation gun, approached to within a yard of a post office which he intended to rob, but never drew his weapon; it was held that there was no evidence on which the jury could properly have concluded that his acts went beyond mere preparation. See also *Widdowson* (1985) 82 Cr App R 314. In *Gullefer* [1990] 1 WLR 1063, Lord Lane CJ stated that the crucial question was whether the accused had 'embarked upon the crime proper', but that it was not necessary, as some earlier cases had suggested, that the accused should have reached a 'point of no return' in respect of the full offence. This view was echoed in *A-G's Ref (No.1 of 1992)* [1993] Crim LR 274, in which it was held that attempted rape may be committed without the accused having physically attempted to penetrate his victim.

In *Jones* [1990] 1 WLR 1057, the appellant was charged with attempted murder. He climbed into his victim's car and drew a loaded gun with the intention of killing him, but was disarmed in a struggle that followed. The Court of Appeal held it was open to the jury to regard this as attempted murder and in his judgment Taylor LJ provided useful guidance as to the distinction between preparation and attempts:

> The question for the judge in the present case was whether there was evidence from which a reasonable jury, properly directed, could conclude that the appellant had done acts which were more than merely preparatory. Clearly his actions in obtaining the gun, in shortening it, in loading it, in putting on his disguise and going to the [ambush point] could only be regarded as preparatory acts. But . . . once he had got into the car, taken out the loaded gun and pointed it at the victim with the intention of killing him, there was sufficient evidence for the consideration of the jury on the charge of attempted murder. It was a matter for them to decide whether they were sure those acts were more than merely preparatory.

Similar reasoning was applied in *Geddes* [1996] Crim LR 894, in which G was found trespassing in the lavatory block of a school, armed with a large knife and lengths of rope and tape.

It appears that he had intended to kidnap a child, but his conviction for attempted false imprisonment was quashed on appeal. Citing *Campbell* with approval, Lord Bingham CJ held that no jury could properly have concluded that G's acts had gone beyond the stage of mere preparation. He may have equipped himself, and put himself in a position to commit the crime when the opportunity arose, but it could not be said that he had actually tried or started to commit it.

The question will often be one of fact and degree, and the answer may not always be obvious. In *Tosti* [1997] Crim LR 746 the appellants had provided themselves with cutting equipment, driven to the scene, concealed the cutting equipment nearby, and approached the door of the premises they intended to break into. They were disturbed as they examined the padlock, and were arrested shortly afterwards. On those facts, it was held that a jury *was* entitled to convict of attempted burglary. *Campbell* is perhaps distinguishable on those facts, but the contrast with *Geddes* is less obvious. See also *Toothill* [1998] Crim LR 876.

It may be necessary to identify the essential elements of the crime allegedly attempted, in order to determine whether D got beyond mere preparation. In *Nash* [1999] Crim LR 308, the Court of Appeal appears to have construed 'attempting to procure an act of gross indecency' as if it meant '*inciting* an act of gross indecency'; but procuring requires the commission of the offence procured (*Johnson* [1964] 2 QB 404) and it would seem, with respect, that the wrong test was applied.

Mens Rea

Intent is the essence of any crime of attempt under the 1981 Act, as it was at common law (*Pearman* (1984) 80 Cr App R 259). The prosecution must ordinarily prove that D acted with a specific intent to commit the particular crime attempted, even if the full offence is one of strict liability, or one in which the *mens rea* required falls short of the *actus reus* (*Boyton* [2005] EWCA Crim 2979). Thus, although murder may be committed by someone who intends only to cause grievous bodily harm, attempted murder requires nothing less than an intent to kill (*Whybrow* (1951) 35 Cr App R 141). Note, however, an important qualification to the general rule, explained at **A6.36**. **A6.35**

'Intent' in this context bears the meaning laid down in *Moloney* [1985] AC 905 (see **A2.2**) and *Nedrick* [1986] 1 WLR 1025. In most cases, however, a full *Nedrick* direction (see **B1.12**) would be unnecessary and potentially confusing. On a charge of attempted murder by shooting, for example, it may suffice to direct the jury to decide: (a) whether D shot V deliberately; and (b) if so, whether D was 'shooting to kill' (*Fallon* [1994] Crim LR 519).

In *Walker* (1989) 90 Cr App R 226, the defendants were convicted of attempted murder. They had hurled their victim from a third-floor balcony, but he had somehow survived the fall. After correctly directing the jury to decide whether the defendants were 'trying to kill him', the trial judge elaborated by suggesting that such an intent may sometimes be inferred in cases where there is a 'very high degree of probability' that death will result. The Court of Appeal upheld the convictions, but doubted whether any such elaboration was called for on the facts of the case. Although the judge's suggestion was perfectly correct, there was a danger of confusing the jury into thinking that foresight of high probability could be equated with intention.

Mens Rea as to Circumstances

Although the Criminal Attempts Act 1981, s. 1(1), specifies that the accused must act 'with intent to commit an offence to which this section applies', the Court of Appeal has qualified this principle by holding that, whilst intent is required as to any specified consequences of the accused's conduct, something less may suffice in respect of any relevant circumstances. In *Khan* [1990] 1 WLR 813, it was held that, since recklessness as to the victim's lack of consent **A6.36** sufficed in relation to the full offence of rape, the offence of attempted rape was committed where an accused intended (but failed) to have intercourse with a woman and was reckless as to her lack of consent. In *A-G's Ref (No. 3 of 1992)* [1994] 1 WLR 409, the court held that an accused is guilty of an attempt to commit a criminal offence if he is in one of the states of mind required for the full offence and he does his best, so far as he can, to supply what is missing from the completion of the full offence. A person who attempts to set fire to property, being reckless as to whether life would be endangered, may accordingly be convicted of an attempt to commit an offence under the Criminal Damage Act 1971, s. 1(2).

The rule as formulated in *A-G's Ref (No. 3 of 1992)* could arguably extend to offences in which liability as to circumstances is strict. If so, a person who attempts to take or make an indecent photograph of a girl he believes to be aged over 18, but who is in fact under 18, would thus be guilty of an attempt to commit an offence under the Protection of Children Act 1978, s. 1(1)(a) (see **B3.274**).

Conditional Intent

A6.37 Problems of conditional intent in attempts seldom arise otherwise than in relation to theft and related offences. A would-be thief may not know what he will find when searching through another person's property, and may not even be sure what he is hoping to find. In *Husseyn* (1978) 67 Cr App R 131, the accused dishonestly opened the door of a van, but were challenged just as they were about to examine a holdall lying inside the van. The holdall contained valuable scuba-diving equipment, but it was held that they could not be convicted on an indictment alleging that they attempted to steal that equipment. They did not even know what the holdall contained. Although much criticised, *Husseyn* remains good law under the 1981 Act, but it need not cause any real difficulties, provided care is taken in drafting the relevant information or indictment.

The Court of Appeal in *Husseyn* suggested that the accused could properly have been charged with an attempt to steal 'some or all of the contents' of the holdall but, following the abrogation of the rule in *Haughton v Smith* [1975] AC 476 (see **A6.40**), it would now be preferable simply to charge 'an attempt to steal from' the holdall or van. It would not then matter whether the holdall or van contained anything which the accused might want to steal, or indeed any property at all.

Attempts with a Foreign Element

A6.38 The Criminal Attempts Act 1981, s. 1(4) (see **A6.31**), restates the common-law rule that conduct cannot amount to a criminal attempt under English law unless it is directed towards the commission of a substantive offence which would itself be indictable under English law. An attempt in England and Wales to publish an obscene article in Scotland is not, for example, indictable under English law, because the ulterior offence would not be. Attempts to commit offences of fraud or dishonesty (if perpetrated on or after 1 June 1999) are now covered by part I of the CJA 1993 (see **A8.7**). An attempt in England and Wales to commit a 'Group A' offence (such as theft, forgery, etc.) abroad would be triable under the Criminal Attempts Act 1981, s. 1, because a Group A offence is triable under English law where any 'relevant event' concerning it takes place in England or Wales.

The CJA 1993 inserted s. 1A into the Criminal Attempts Act 1981, supposedly to cover cases where the accused in England and Wales attempts to commit abroad something which *would* be a Group A offence, but for the fact that it is not triable under English law. This provision is fundamentally at odds with itself. If a Group A offence is instigated by conduct within England and Wales, that offence will inevitably be triable under English law. Section 1A is merely a trap for unwary prosecutors, who may be tempted to use it instead of s. 1.

Where an attempt to commit an offence within England and Wales is instigated from abroad, the general rule is that such conduct does amount to an offence under s. 1. This has long been true where the attempt is furthered by consequences occurring within the jurisdiction (*Baxter* [1972] 1 QB 1; *DPP v Stonehouse* [1978] AC 55; but it is now clear that (as in conspiracy) such consequences are unnecessary (see *Latif* [1996] 1 WLR 104). As to attempts made abroad to commit Group A offences wholly or partly in England and Wales, see the CJA 1993, s. 3(3).

Withdrawal

There is no recognised defence of voluntary withdrawal in English law. If the accused has not progressed beyond the stage of mere preparatory acts (see **A6.34**) he can avoid incurring liability by refraining from further acts but, once he has gone beyond that stage, withdrawal will be irrelevant as far as his liability for attempt is concerned. **A6.39**

Impossibility

At common law, no offence of attempt could be committed where it would have been impossible (even in theory) for the accused to succeed in committing the substantive offence. Thus, the accused could not be guilty of attempting to steal from a bag or pocket which was empty, and he could not be guilty of attempting to handle stolen goods if the goods in question had been recovered by the police and had accordingly ceased to be stolen (*Haughton v Smith* [1975] AC 476). This rule was abrogated by the Criminal Attempts Act 1981, s. 1(2), but the precise effect of that provision was for a time uncertain. In *Anderton v Ryan* [1985] AC 560, the House of Lords held that a distinction had to be drawn between the person who attempts to commit a crime but fails because the crime is impossible (the 'empty pocket' kind of case) and the person who succeeds in doing an 'objectively innocent' act but labours under a mistaken view of the facts or circumstances, and wrongly believes that he is committing an offence. **A6.40**

Anderton v Ryan was thought to be an example of the latter type of case. R bought a video recorder in suspicious circumstances, firmly believing it to be stolen. There was, however, no evidence to prove that it was stolen, and the House of Lords held she could not be guilty even of an attempt to handle stolen goods. The decision was much criticised, and in *Shivpuri* [1987] AC 1 the House of Lords acknowledged that their earlier decision was wrong. Lord Bridge said:

> I am satisfied . . . that the concept of 'objective innocence' is incapable of sensible application in relation to the law of criminal attempts . . . Any attempt to commit an offence which . . . for any reason fails, so that in the event no offence is committed must, *ex hypothesi*, from the point of view of the criminal law, be objectively innocent. What turns what would otherwise . . . be an innocent act into a crime is the intent of the actor to commit an offence.

In *Shivpuri*, S was charged with an attempt to commit an offence under the Misuse of Drugs Act 1971, s. 3(1). He confessed to acting as a recipient and distributor of what he assumed to be an illegally imported drug. It transpired (to his surprise) that the substance was not a drug at all but he was still guilty of an attempt to commit the s. 3(1) offence. See also *Jones* [2007] EWCA Crim 1118.

If, however, the accused is not mistaken as to the facts, but wrongly believes that his actions amount to a criminal offence (i.e. as a result of his mistaken view of the law), this mistake cannot make him guilty of any criminal attempt. Section 1(2) does not apply in such cases (cf. *Taaffe* [1984] AC 539).

Interfering with Vehicles

Where the accused is seen interfering with a vehicle or trailer, it is often difficult to prove which of a number of possible offences he is trying to commit. A charge of attempt under the Criminal Attempts Act 1981, s. 1, may therefore be impossible to prove, but see the specific offence of interference with vehicles created by s. 9 (see **B4.108** ***et seq.***). **A6.41**

Section A7 Human Rights

A7.1 The European Convention for the Protection of Human Rights and Fundamental Freedoms (Cm. 8969) (the ECHR) is an international treaty of the Council of Europe. It was adopted in 1950, ratified by the UK in 1951 and entered into force in 1953. The unusual feature of the Convention, as an international human rights instrument, is that it provides a mechanism for individuals to enforce their Convention rights against state parties.

Since it was first drafted, the Convention has been amplified by a number of Protocols. One of the most important is Protocol 11, which abolished the European Commission of Human Rights. As a result, the Convention is now administered by two bodies: the European Court of Human Rights and the Committee of Ministers of the Council of Europe.

The Human Rights Act 1998 is designed 'to give further effect to the rights and freedoms guaranteed under the European Convention on Human Rights' (see the long title). It is intended to 'give people in the United Kingdom opportunities to enforce their rights under the European Convention in British courts rather than having to incur the cost and delay of taking a case to the European Human Rights ... Court in Strasbourg' (Prime Minister's preface to the White Paper, Bringing Rights Home, Cm. 3782).

Convention Rights

A7.2 The rights protected by the HRA 1998 are called 'Convention rights' (s. 1(1)). They are set out in sch. 1 to the HRA 1998.

In the HRA 1998, 'the Convention rights' means the rights and fundamental freedoms set out in: (a) Articles 2 to 12 of the ECHR, (b) Articles 1 to 3 of the First Protocol, and (c) Articles 1 and 2 of the Sixth Protocol (s. 1(1)).

The subject-matter of these rights is as follows:

Article 2:	The right to life
Article 3:	Prohibition on torture
Article 4:	Prohibition on slavery and forced labour
Article 5:	Right to liberty and security
Article 6:	Right to a fair trial
Article 7:	No punishment without law
Article 8:	Right to respect for private and family life
Article 9:	Freedom of thought, conscience and religion
Article 10:	Freedom of expression
Article 11:	Freedom of assembly and association
Article 12:	Right to marry
Article 14:	Prohibition on discrimination
Article 1, Protocol 1:	Protection of property
Article 2, Protocol 1:	Right to education
Article 3, Protocol 1:	Right to free elections

Article 1, Protocol 6: Abolition of the death penalty
Article 2, Protocol 6: Death penalty in times of war

These rights are to be read with Article 16 (restrictions on political activities of aliens), Article 17 (prohibition on abuse of rights) and Article 18 (limitation on use of restrictions on rights) (s. 1(1)).

Categories of Convention Rights

Convention rights are not all of equal status. The protection afforded under the ECHR and the HRA 1998 varies from right to right. Broadly speaking, the European Court of Human Rights recognises three categories of Convention rights: **A7.3**

Absolute Rights Absolute rights are those rights that are strongly protected and that cannot be restricted even in times of war or other public emergency: Article 2 (the right to life), Article 3 (prohibition on torture), Article 4(1) (prohibition on slavery) and Article 7 (no punishment without law). **A7.4**

Although there are special provisions dealing with the death penalty and death caused by the use of force, in all other respects the public interest cannot justify any interference with absolute rights.

Special Rights Special rights are those rights that are less strongly protected than absolute rights. They can be restricted even in times of war or other public emergency: Article 4(2) and (3) (prohibition on forced labour), Article 5 (right to liberty and security), Article 6 (fair trial), Article 9(1) (freedom of thought, conscience and religion — but not freedom to manifest religion or belief, which is a qualified right), Article 12 (right to marry), Protocol 1, Article 2 (the right to education), Protocol 1, Article 3 (right to free elections) and Protocol 6, Article 1 (abolition of the death penalty). **A7.5**

The practical difference between these rights and absolute rights is that restriction in the public interest can be justified, but only on the grounds expressly provided for within the text of the provision itself: e.g., Article 4(2) prohibits forced labour, but Article 4(3) then sets out a number of exceptions; similarly, the first sentence of Article 5(1) provides for the right to liberty and security of person; the second sentence then lists (exhaustively) all the circumstances in which that right can be restricted. Unless a restriction is expressly provided for in the text of the provision, the public interest cannot justify any interference with special rights.

Strictly speaking, Article 6 (fair trial) probably falls into a category of its own. That is because the European Court of Human Rights has read a number of implied restrictions into Article 6; including restrictions designed to ensure the protection of victims and vulnerable witnesses within the trial process. Such restrictions are limited and must be strictly necessary and proportionate. In all other respects, the public interest cannot justify any interference with Article 6 rights.

In *Brown v Stott* [2003] 1 AC 681, Lord Bingham said:

> The jurisprudence of the European Court very clearly establishes that while the overall fairness of a criminal trial cannot be compromised, the constituent rights comprised, whether expressly or implicitly, within Article 6 are not themselves absolute. Limited qualification of these rights is acceptable if reasonably directed by national authorities towards a clear and proper public objective and if representing no greater qualification than the situation calls for.

But, overall, the trial must be fair. If an accused has not had a fair trial, the verdict cannot stand and the conviction must be quashed (per Lord Hope in *Sinclair v HM Advocate* [2005] UKPC D2)

Qualified Rights Qualified rights are those rights that are to be balanced against the public interest and which can be restricted in times of war or other public emergency: **A7.6**

Article 8 (right to respect for private and family life), Article 9 (right to manifest religion or belief), Article 10 (freedom of expression), Article 11 (freedom of assembly and association), Article 14 (prohibition on discrimination) and Protocol 1, Article 1 (protection of property).

These rights are in positive form, but can be restricted where it can be shown that a restriction is (i) prescribed by law; (ii) legitimate; (iii) necessary and proportionate; and (iv) not discriminatory.

Protocol 1, Article 1 (protection of property) also probably falls into a category of its own because it is less well protected than the other qualified rights. Where property rights are interfered with, the question will be whether a 'fair balance' has been achieved between the individual's right to property and the general public interest.

The Legality of Restrictions on Convention Rights

A7.7 Any restriction on Convention rights must be lawful. In some places, such as Article 5, the word 'lawful' itself is used. In others, such as Articles 8 and 9, phrases such as 'in accordance with law' or 'prescribed by law' are used. Even where no express provision is made (e.g., in Protocol 1, Article 1), any restriction on Convention rights must nonetheless be 'lawful'.

Under the ECHR the term 'lawful' has a special meaning. A restriction on Convention rights will be 'lawful' only if: (i) there is an established legal basis in domestic law for the restriction — e.g., where it is provided for by legislation or special rules; (ii) the provision in question is 'accessible': i.e. those likely to be affected by it can find out what it says; and (iii) the provision in question is 'foreseeable': i.e. it is formulated with sufficient clarity to enable those likely to be affected by it to understand it and to regulate their conduct accordingly.

A7.8 **Established Legal Basis** Primary and subordinate legislation is a sufficient basis in domestic law for a restriction on Convention rights; so too is the common law (*Sunday Times v UK* (1979–80) 2 EHRR 245 at [47]). Home Office guidelines and internal police guidelines are unlikely to satisfy the requirement that provisions governing restrictions on Convention rights be accessible unless they are made publicly available (*Silver v UK* (1983) 5 EHRR 347; *Govell v UK* (1998) Appln. 27237/95 at [62]; *Khan v UK* (2001) 31 EHRR 1016). In *Christian v R* [2007] 2 WLR 120, the Privy Council held that the non-promulgation of a law may be good grounds for staying a prosecution.

A7.9 **Foreseeability** Absolute certainty is not required for a provision to be 'foreseeable'. In *Sunday Times v UK* (1979–80) 2 EHRR 245, the European Court said (at [49]):

> . . . whilst certainty is highly desirable, it may bring in its train excessive rigidity and the law must be able to keep pace with changing circumstances. Accordingly, many laws are inevitably couched in terms which, to a greater or lesser extent, are vague and whose interpretation and application are questions of practice.

The degree of certainty will depend on the circumstances. In some fields of application a fairly wide degree of flexibility is acceptable: e.g., general statutory provisions (*Rekvenyi v Hungary* (2000) 30 EHRR 519 at [34]; *Bronda v Italy* (2001) 33 EHRR 4 at [54]). In others, a relatively high level of certainty is required: e.g., where the deprivation of liberty is concerned (*Steel v UK* (1999) 28 EHRR 603; *Baranowski v Poland* (2000) Appln. 28358/95). In *Grigoriades v Greece* (1999) 27 EHRR 464, the European Court held that an offence of 'insulting' the army was sufficiently certain for Convention purposes (at [38]). But in *Hashman and Harrop v UK* (2000) 30 EHRR 241, the European Court held that the concept of a bind over to be of good behaviour was too vague and uncertain and thus a breach of the ECHR.

The Legitimacy of Restrictions on Convention Rights

Any restriction on Convention rights must be legitimate. For qualified rights, so long as a restriction genuinely pursues one of the aims set out in the article itself, it will be legitimate. The aims set out in Articles 8 to 11 include: national security, public safety, the prevention of disorder or crime and the protection of the rights and freedoms of others. A7.10

The Necessity and Proportionality of Restrictions on Convention Rights

Any restriction on Convention rights must be necessary and proportionate. For qualified rights, this requirement flows from the use of the phrase 'necessary in a democratic society' in Articles 8 to 11. A7.11

Necessary The word 'necessary' in the ECHR is not synonymous with 'reasonable'. In *Handyside v UK* (1976) 1 EHRR 737, the European Court said (at [48]): A7.12

> . . . whilst the adjective 'necessary', within the meaning of Article 10(2), is not synonymous with 'indispensable', neither has it the flexibility of such expressions as 'admissible', 'ordinary', 'useful', 'reasonable', or 'desirable'.

Nor will a restriction be necessary just because the majority are in favour of it (*Chassagnou v France* (2000) 29 EHRR 615 at [112]).

Proportionality A restriction will be proportionate only if the objective behind the restriction justifies interference with a Convention right, there is a rational connection between the objective and the restriction in question and the means employed are not more than is necessary to achieve the objective. A7.13

In making this assessment, the following factors are relevant: (i) whether relevant and sufficient reasons have been advanced for the restriction; (ii) whether there was a less restrictive, but equally effective, way of achieving the same objective; (iii) whether sufficient regard has been paid to the rights and interests of those affected (in some cases, e.g., in family cases, those affected should be consulted); (iv) whether safeguards exist to guard against error or abuse (e.g., in secret surveillance cases); and (v) whether the restriction in question destroys the very essence of the Convention right in issue.

Positive Obligations

The ECHR safeguards Convention rights by limiting the circumstances in which they can be restricted (if at all). Public authorities are under a duty to refrain from restricting Convention rights in any other circumstances. A7.14

The ECHR also safeguards Convention rights by imposing an obligation on public authorities to adopt positive measures to protect the Convention rights of individuals. In *Platform Artze für das Leben v Austria* (1991) 13 EHRR 204, the European Court said (at [32]):

> Genuine, effective freedom of peaceful assembly cannot . . . be reduced to a mere duty on the part of the state not to interfere; a purely negative conception would not be compatible with the object and purpose of Article 11. Like Article 8, Article 11 sometimes requires positive measures to be taken, even in the sphere of relations between individuals, if need be.

The extent of this obligation will vary according to such factors as the nature of the Convention right in issue, the importance of the right for the individual and the nature of the activities involved in the case.

The most onerous positive obligations arise where, by very definition, a Convention right requires the provision of resources: e.g., the right to free legal assistance in criminal cases under Article 6(3)(c). However, the doctrine of positive obligations under the ECHR is not restricted to the provision of resources in such circumstances. It includes a duty on the relevant authorities to put in place a legal framework which provides effective protection for Convention rights (*X and Y v Netherlands* (1986) 8 EHRR 235 at [27]). In *A v UK* (1999) 27 EHRR 611, the European Court held that the defence of 'reasonable chastisement' to an alleged offence of assaulting a child was so wide that the child's rights under Article 3 (the prohibition on ill-treatment) were not respected.

The ECHR can also impose a duty on the relevant authorities to take positive steps to prevent breaches of Convention rights. This duty is strictest where fundamental rights, such as the right to life or the prohibition on torture, are at stake (*Osman v UK* (2000) 29 EHRR 245 at [115]). However, such obligations must be interpreted in a way that does not impose an impossible or disproportionate burden on the authorities. Accordingly, not every claimed risk to life can entail for the authorities a Convention requirement to take operational measures to prevent that risk from materialising. It must be established that the authorities failed to do all that could reasonably be expected of them to avoid a 'real and immediate' risk to life which they knew or ought to have known about (*Osman v UK* (2000) 29 EHRR 245 at [116]). In *MC v Bulgaria* (2005) 40 EHRR 459, the European Court held that states have a positive obligation under Articles 3 and 8 to enact criminal law provisions effectively punishing rape and to apply them in practice through effective investigation and prosecution; to adopt a policy of only prosecuting rape where there was evidence of resistance on the part of the alleged victim violated this duty.

Prohibition on Abuse of Rights under Article 17

A7.15 **ECHR, Article 17**

> Nothing in this Convention may be interpreted as implying for any state, group or person any right to engage in any activity or perform any act aimed at the destruction of any of the rights and freedoms set forth herein or at their limitation to a greater extent than is provided for in this Convention.

The purpose of Article 17 is to prevent extremists using the ECHR to destroy the rights of others (*Lawless v Ireland (No. 3)* (1961) 1 EHRR 15 at [7]).

Article 17 can be applied only to those rights which are capable of being exercised so as to destroy the rights of others: it cannot be used to restrict rights designed to protect the individual such as those in Articles 5 and 6 (*Lawless v Ireland (No. 3)* at [7]; *Glimmerveen and Hagenbeek v Netherlands* (1979) 18 DR 187 at p. 195). Furthermore, any measure taken under Article 17 must be strictly proportionate to the threat to the rights of others (*De Becker v Belgium* (1961) Series B, No. 4, Appln. 214/56 at [279]; *Lehideux and Isorni v France* (2000) 30 EHRR 665).

The Interpretation of Convention Rights

A7.16 A number of general principles have emerged from the case law of the European Court of Justice and the Commission of Human Rights about the way in which Convention rights should be interpreted.

A7.17 **Object and Purpose** Convention rights should be interpreted in light of their object and purpose: i.e. to protect individual rights, maintain the rule of law and to uphold the ideas and values of a democratic society (*Golder v UK* (1979–80) 1 EHRR 524 at [34]; *Soering v UK* (1989) 11 EHRR 439 at [87]).

A7.18 **Practical and Effective** Convention rights should be interpreted in such a way as to make them 'practical and effective'. In *Soering v UK* (1989) 11 EHRR 439, the European Court held (at [87]):

> In interpreting the Convention regard must be had to its special character as a treaty for the collective enforcement of human rights and fundamental freedoms . . . Thus, the object and

purpose of the Convention as a living instrument for the protection of individual human beings require that its provisions be interpreted and applied so as to make its safeguards practical and effective.

Autonomous Meaning Words and phrases in the ECHR are to be given an autonomous meaning: i.e. the meaning ascribed by the European Court of Human Rights, not (necessarily) the meaning ascribed in the domestic law of the Contracting States. This is to prevent states undermining the efficacy of the ECHR (*Chassagnou v France* (2000) 29 EHRR 615 at [100]). A7.19

Living Instrument The ECHR is a 'living instrument' requiring a dynamic, evolving interpretation. For example, when considering what conduct might offend Article 3, the European Court held in the case of *Selmouni v France* (2000) 29 EHRR 365 (at [101]): A7.20

> The Court has previously examined cases in which it concluded that there had been treatment which could only be described as torture . . . However, having regard to the fact that the Convention is a 'living instrument' which must be interpreted in the light of present-day conditions . . . the Court considers that certain acts which were classified in the past as 'inhuman and degrading treatment' as opposed to 'torture' could be classified differently in future. It takes the view that the increasingly high standard being required in the area of the protection of human rights and fundamental liberties correspondingly and inevitably requires greater firmness in assessing breaches of the fundamental values of democratic societies.

Generous and Purposive Construction A generous and purposive construction is to be given to Convention rights under the HRA 1998 suitable to give to individuals the full measure of the fundamental rights and freedoms to which all persons in the state are to be entitled (*DPP ex parte Kebilene* [2000] 2 AC 326, Lord Hope at pp. 998E–F; for the general principle, see *Minister of Home Affairs v Fisher* [1980] AC 319 at p. 328). A7.21

Burden and Standard of Proving a Breach of Convention Rights

It is for the complainant to show that his Convention rights have been infringed, but for the relevant public authority to justify any infringement established (*Jersild v Denmark* (1995) 19 EHRR 1 at [31]; for the same approach under the Canadian Charter of Rights, see *Andrews v Law Society of British Columbia* (1989) 56 DLR (4th) 1, at p. 21). Where absolute rights are at stake, the standard of proof is high: beyond reasonable doubt. However, this can be established by the coexistence of sufficiently strong, clear and concordant inferences or similar unrebutted presumptions of fact. For example, in *Aksoy v Turkey* (1996) 23 EHRR 553, the European Court held (at [61]): A7.22

> . . . where an individual is taken into police custody in good health but is found to be injured at the time of release, it is incumbent on the State to provide a plausible explanation as to the causing of the injury, failing which a clear issue arises under Article 3 of the Convention.

Failure of the relevant authority to furnish information may also lead to adverse inferences being drawn (*Timurtas v Turkey* (2000) Appln. 23531/94 at [66]).

Waiver of Convention Rights

Convention rights can be waived only in limited circumstances and waiver must be established in an unequivocal manner (*Zana v Turkey* (1999) 27 EHRR 671 at [70]). In *Pfeifer and Plankl v Austria* (1992) 14 EHRR 692, the European Court held (at [37]): A7.23

> According to the Court's case law, the waiver of a right guaranteed by the Convention — in so far as it is permissible — must be established in an unequivocal manner. Moreover . . . in the case of procedural rights a waiver, in order to be effective for Convention purposes, requires minimum guarantees commensurate with its importance.

Failure to raise an issue cannot be automatically equated with waiver (*McGonnell v UK* (2000) 30 EHRR 289 at [44]–[46], in the context of a fair trial).

Certain Convention rights probably cannot be waived at all: e.g., absolute rights such as the right to life and the prohibition on torture and slavery, and perhaps also fair trial rights under Article 6 (*Pfeifer and Plankl v Austria* (1992) 14 EHRR 692 at [39]; a similar approach has been adopted under the Canadian Charter of Rights, see *Tran* (1994) 2 SCR 951). In *Jones* [2003] 1 AC 1, the House of Lords held that the appellant had waived his right to legal representation when he absconded at trial, both at common law and under the ECHR.

THE INTERPRETATION OF LEGISLATION

Primary Legislation

A7.24 **Human Rights Act 1998, s. 3**

(1) So far as it is possible to do so, primary legislation and subordinate legislation must be read and given affect in a way which is compatible with Convention rights.

The use of the word 'possible' is intended to convey a stronger interpretative requirement than 'reasonable' (Home Secretary, *Hansard*, vol. 313, col. 421).

The scope of the approach to interpretation authorised by s. 3 has been considered in a number of cases at the highest level. The leading case is now the decision of the House of Lords in *Ghaidan v Ghodin-Mendoza* [2004] 2 AC 557, where there was broad agreement that 'excessive concentration on the linguistic features of the [statute to be interpreted]', should be substituted in favour of a 'purposive' approach concentrating on 'the importance of the fundamental right involved'. As Lord Nicholls pointed out, if it is accepted that s. 3 was intended to supersede the pre-HRA principle that legislation had to be ambiguous before it was 'possible' to interpret it compatibly with the ECHR, Parliament cannot have intended the courts to 'depend critically upon the particular form of words adopted by the parliamentary draftsman' in the legislation in question without making the application of s. 3 'something of a semantic lottery' (*Ghaidan v Ghodin-Mendoza* at [31]).

In the earlier case of *R (Anderson) v Secretary of State for the Home Department* [2003] 1 AC 837, Lord Steyn indicated that a s. 3 interpretation 'is not available where the suggested interpretation is contrary to express statutory words or is by implication necessarily contradicted by the statute' (at [59]). The search to nail down the characteristics indicating such a 'contradiction' was considered in *Ghaidan v Ghodin-Mendoza* where Lord Rogers argued that 'however powerful the obligation in s. 3(1) it does not allow the courts to change the substance of a provision completely, to change a provision from one where Parliament says that x is to happen into one saying x is not to happen' (at [110]). For Lord Nicholls '[t]he meaning imported by application of s. 3 must be compatible with the underlying thrust of the legislation being construed' (at [31]).

Following this logic, interpreting the phrase in the Rent Act 1977, 'as his or her wife or husband' (Rent Act 1977, sch. 1, para. 2) to mean 'as if they were his wife or husband' in *Ghaidan* (at [51]) was fairly viewed as compatible with the thrust of the statute which was intended to include cohabiting as well as married couples but which, on its face, discriminated against homosexuals. However, to read s. 29 of the Crime (Sentences) Act 1997 in *Anderson* as precluding participation by the Home Secretary in setting the minimum period served by a mandatory life sentence prisoner was not deemed 'possible'.

Nothing in the HRA 1998 affects the validity, continuing operation or enforcement of primary legislation which is incompatible with Convention rights (s. 3(2)(b)). But in certain circumstances a 'declaration of incompatibility' can be made.

Declarations of Incompatibility

A7.25 Under the HRA 1998, certain courts are given the power to make declarations of incompatibility if they determine that a provision in primary legislation is incompatible with Convention rights (s. 4(2)). The relevant courts for England and Wales are the House of Lords, the Court of Appeal, the High Court and the Courts-Martial Appeal Court (s. 4(5)). A declaration of incompatibility is intended to operate as a signal to Parliament that an incompatibility has been found and to prompt remedial action. It does not affect the validity, continuing operation or enforcement of the provision in question (s. 4(6)(a)).

If a court is considering whether or not to make a declaration of incompatibility, the Crown has a right to be notified and can intervene (s. 5(1) and (2)). In criminal proceedings, if any application is to be made to the Court of Appeal for a declaration of incompatibility or any issue is to be raised which may have that effect, notice must be given in the notice of appeal and a copy of the notice served on the prosecutor (CrimPR, r. 68(3) and (4)). The Court of Appeal must then give notice to the Crown (r. 68.27).

Subordinate Legislation

A7.26 So far as it is possible to do so, subordinate legislation must be read and given effect in a way which is compatible with Convention rights (HRA 1998, s. 3(1)). As with primary legislation, this rule of interpretation applies whenever the subordinate legislation in question was enacted (s. 3(2)(a)). But, unlike the position in relation to primary legislation, where subordinate legislation cannot be read and given effect in a way which is compatible with Convention rights, this *does* affect its validity, continuing operation and enforcement (s. 3(2)(b) and (c)) and it can be quashed or declared invalid by reason of incompatibility (s. 10(4)). The only exception is where primary legislation prevents the removal of any incompatibility (s. 3(1)(c)). In such circumstances, a declaration of incompatibility can be made (s. 4(4)).

Statements of Compatibility

A7.27 For legislation passed after the HRA 1998 became law, s. 19 requires the minister of the Crown in charge of a Bill, before its Second Reading, to make a written, published statement that in his or her view the provisions of the Bill are compatible with Convention rights (a 'statement of compatibility'). If unable to do so, the minister must so state but add that the government nonetheless wishes to proceed with the Bill. A statement of compatibility does not bind a court (*A (No. 2)* [2002] 1 AC 45 per Lord Hope). The obligation to make a statement of compatibility applies only to government-sponsored Acts of Parliament.

The Relevance of Strasbourg Jurisprudence

A7.28 A court or tribunal determining a question which has arisen in connection with a Convention right must take into account judgments of the European Court and Commission of Human Rights and decisions of the ECmHR and Committee of Ministers (HRA 1998, s. 2(1)). But such judgments and decisions are not binding.

The approach to be taken to Strasbourg jurisprudence was considered by the House of Lords in *R (Ullah) v Special Adjudicator* [2004] 2 AC 323 where Lord Bingham made clear that since the ECHR is an international instrument, the correct interpretation of it can be authoritatively expounded only by the Strasbourg Court. From this, he concluded (at [20]):

> . . . it follows that a national court subject to a duty such as that imposed by section 2 should not without strong reason dilute or weaken the effect of the Strasbourg case law . . . It is of course open to member states to provide for rights more generous than those guaranteed by the Convention, but such provision should not be the product of interpretation of the Convention

> by national courts, since the meaning of the Convention should be uniform throughout the states party to it. The duty of national courts is to keep pace with the Strasbourg jurisprudence as it evolves over time: no more, but certainly no less.

But the UK's obligations under Article 46 do not automatically require domestic courts to quash the conviction in any case where the European Court finds a breach of the ECHR; see *Lyons* [2003] 1 AC 976.

PUBLIC AUTHORITIES

A7.29 The HRA 1998, s. 6, makes it unlawful for a public authority to act in a way which is incompatible with Convention rights, unless required to do so to give effect to primary legislation.

Human Rights Act 1998, s. 6

(1) It is unlawful for a public authority to act in a way which is incompatible with a Convention right.

(2) Subsection (1) does not apply to an act if—
  (a) as the result of one or more provisions of primary legislation, the authority could not have acted differently; or
  (b) in the case of one or more provisions of, or made under, primary legislation which cannot be read or given effect in a way which is compatible with the Convention rights, the authority was acting so as to give effect to or enforce those provisions.

In this context, 'act' includes a failure to act; but does not include a failure to legislate or make remedial orders (s. 6(6)).

The Definition of a Public Authority

A7.30 The HRA 1998 does not fully define a 'public authority'; but s. 6(3) does include within its meaning: (i) courts and tribunals; and (ii) any person certain of whose functions are functions of a public nature. The inclusion of 'any person certain of whose functions are functions of a public nature' is intended to expand, not restrict, the definition of public authority (Home Secretary, *Hansard*, HC 24 November 1997, col. 811).

Two kinds of public authority are thus recognised under the HRA 1998: 'pure' public authorities (such as government departments, local authorities or the police) and 'functional' public authorities (those bodies that are to be treated as public authorities when they are carrying out public functions). As the Parliamentary Joint Committee on Human Rights observed in its report, *The Meaning of Public Authority under the Human Rights Act* (Seventh Report (2003–04 HL 39; 2003–04 HC 382, March 3, 2004)), the intention of Parliament in enacting this scheme was that a wide range of bodies performing public functions would fall within the obligation under s. 6 to act in a manner compatible with the 'Convention rights' established under the Act (para. 3).

Identifying 'pure' public authorities is important because all of their acts are governed by s. 6(1). As the Lord Chancellor made clear when the Bill was being discussed in Parliament, 'there is no exemption for private acts' (*Hansard*, HL, col. 811 (24 November 1997)). In *Aston Cantlow and Wilmcote with Billesley Parochial Church Council v Wallbank* [2004] 1 AC 546, Lord Hope observed that although the test as to whether a person or body is, or is not, a 'pure' public authority is not capable of being defined precisely, a distinction should be drawn between those persons who, in Convention terms, are governmental organisations on the one hand and those who are non-governmental on the other. A person who would be regarded as a non-governmental organisation within the meaning of the ECHR, Article 34, ought not to be regarded as a 'pure' public authority for the purposes of the HRA 1998, s. 6. Drawing on the case of *Holy Monasteries v Greece* (1995) 20 EHRR 1, Lord Hope observed that the test of whether a person or body is a non-governmental organisation is whether it was established with a view to public administration as part of the process of government (at [50]). Adopting that test, the Parochial Church Council was not a 'pure' public authority.

Defining 'functional' public authorities has proved more difficult and controversial. In the early cases of *Poplar Housing and Regeneration Community Association Ltd v Donoghue* [2002] QB 48 and *R (Heather) v Leonard Cheshire Foundation* [2002] 2 All ER 936, the Court of Appeal treated the tests for a functional public authority under the HRA 1998 and for amenability to judicial review as, for practical purposes, the same. But the House of Lords in *Aston Cantlow and Wilmcote with Billesley Parochial Church Council v Wallbank* took a wider approach. Lord Nicholls considered that there should be a generous interpretation of a public function which would ensure the fullest protection of human rights while still allowing functional bodies to rely on their Convention rights when acting privately (at [11]). He accepted that there could be no single test of universal application, but indicated that factors to be taken into account include the extent to which, in carrying out the relevant function, the body is (i) publicly funded, (ii) is exercising statutory powers, (iii) is taking the place of central government or local authorities, or (iv) is providing a public service (at [12]). Thus the House of Lords has adopted a relatively narrow test for 'pure' public authorities, but balanced this against a correspondingly wide and flexible category of 'functional' public authority.

Remedies

A person who claims that a public authority has acted (or proposes to act) in a way that is incompatible with Convention rights may either bring proceedings against the authority in the appropriate court or tribunal; or rely on his Convention rights in any legal proceedings (HRA 1998, s. 7(1)). Legal proceedings in this context include proceedings brought by or at the instigation of a public authority, and any appeal against the decision of a court or tribunal (s. 7(6)). **A7.31**

Proceedings against a public authority can be brought only by an individual who is (or would be) a victim within the meaning of the ECHR, Article 34; likewise, only victims can rely on their Convention rights in legal proceedings (s. 6(1) and (7)).

In relation to any act (or proposed act) of a public authority which the court finds is (or would be) unlawful, it may grant such relief or remedy, or make such order, within its powers as it considers just and appropriate (s. 8(1)). But damages for breach of the HRA 1998 may be awarded only by a court which has power to award damages or to order the payment of compensation in civil proceedings (s. 8(2)). The level of damages will be assessed in accordance with the principles applied by the European Court of Human Rights (*R (Greenfield) v Secretary of State for the Home Department* [2005] 1 WLR 673).

Judicial Acts

Where individuals claim that their Convention rights have been infringed by a judicial act, they must bring their claim by way of an appeal or in such other forum as may be prescribed by rules (HRA 1998, s. 9(1): no rules have yet been made for England and Wales). But this does not expand the scope for judicial review of courts (s. 9(2)). The term 'judicial act' in this context includes the acts of members of tribunals, justices of the peace, clerks and other officers entitled to exercise the jurisdiction of the court (s. 9(5)). It also includes acts done on the instructions, or on behalf, of such individuals (HRA 1998, s. 9(5)). **A7.32**

In respect of a judicial act done in good faith, damages may not be awarded otherwise than to compensate a person to the extent required by the ECHR, Article 5(5) (s. 9(3)). An award of damages in respect of a judicial act done in good faith is to be made against the Crown, but only if the minister responsible for the court concerned, or nominated person or government department, is joined as a party (s. 9(4) and (5)).

Retrospectivity

A7.33 Proceedings against a public authority for breach of Convention rights can be brought only in relation to acts or omissions after 2 October 2000 (HRA 1998, s. 22(4)). The same applies where an individual otherwise seeks to rely on his Convention rights in legal proceedings, save where proceedings are brought by or at the instigation of a public authority — in which case a breach of Convention rights can be relied upon whenever the breach took place (s. 22(4)).

In *Kansal* [2002] 2 AC 69, the House of Lords held that the HRA 1998 did not apply to criminal trials before 2 October 2000 even if an appeal was heard after the relevant date. This was affirmed in *Benjafield* [2003] 1 AC 1099 (see also *Lambert* [2002] 2 AC 545).

Derogations and Reservations

A7.34 Convention rights under the HRA 1998 are subject to designated derogations (HRA 1998, s. 1(2)). Designated derogations cease to have effect after five years, unless renewed (s. 16). The designated derogation in place when the HRA came into force has now been repealed (Human Rights Act (Amendment) Order 2001 (SI 2001 No. 1216)). A further designated derogation came into force on 20 December 2001 (Human Rights Act (Amendment No. 2) Order 2001 (SI 2001 No. 4032)) but was repealed on 8 April 2005 (Human Rights Act 1998 (Amendment) Order 2005 (SI 2005 No. 1071)), following the decision of the House of Lords in *A v Secretary of State for the Home Department* [2005] 2 AC 68. The Prevention of Terrorism Act 2005 makes provision for derogating control orders, but no designated derogation has been brought into force.

Convention rights under the HRA 1998 are also subject to designated reservations (s. 1(2)). The UK has one reservation in place concerning the right to education under Protocol 1, Article 2. The terms of this derogation are set out in the HRA 1998, sch. 3, part II.

Substantive Challenges to the Criminal Law

A7.35 Subject to the ECHR, Article 7 and the procedural requirements of Articles 5 and 6, Parliament is free, in principle, to apply the criminal law to acts which are not carried out in the normal exercise of one of the rights protected under the Convention (see *Engel and others v Netherlands* (1976) 1 EHRR 647 and *Salabiaku v France* (1988) 13 EHRR 379 at [27]).

The position is different, however, where criminal offences overlap with Convention rights; particularly those contained in Articles 8 to 11. In such cases, the Strasbourg institutions will require any interference with a Convention right to be 'necessary in a democratic society' in pursuit of a legitimate aim. The tensions between sexual activity classified as criminal in Convention states and the Convention protected right of privacy provides a classic example.

In *Norris v Ireland* (1988) 13 EHRR 186 the European Court held that maintaining in force legislation prohibiting homosexual acts committed in private between consenting adult men constituted an interference with the applicant's right to respect for his private life under Article 8, following its judgment in *Dudgeon v UK* (1981) 4 EHRR 149. A similar result followed in *Sutherland v UK* (2001) Appln. 25186/94, where the applicant complained that fixing the minimum age for lawful homosexual activities at 18, rather than 16 (the minimum age for heterosexual activities), violated his right to respect for his private life under Article 8 and was discriminatory under Article 14.

Articles 9 and 10 have also been invoked to challenge substantive criminal law provisions. For example, in *Larissis v Greece* (1998) EHRR 329, the European Court found that the applicants' convictions for proselytising breached Article 9 insofar as they were directed towards civilians; in *Grigoriades v Greece* (1999) 27 EHRR 464, the European Court held that the applicant's conviction for insulting the army when he wrote a strong and intemperate letter to his commanding officer breached Article 10; in *Hertel v Switzerland* (1999) 28 EHRR 534, Article 10 was breached when the applicant was convicted for publishing his views on the hazardous effects of microwave ovens; and in *Gunduz v Turkey* (2005) 41 EHRR 59, the European Court found a breach of Article 10 when the applicant was convicted for inciting religious hatred because his speech was not an appeal to violence nor was it based on religious intolerance.

For examples going the other way, see *Laskey v UK* (1997) 24 EHRR 39, where the applicants' prosecution and conviction for assault and wounding in the course of consensual, sado-masochistic activities between adults was found not to breach Article 8; *APT v UK* (2001) 31 EHRR 203, where the European Court found no breach of Article 8 in the applicants' conviction for gross indecency in respect of consensual sexual acts involving violence; and *Zana v Turkey* (1999) 27 EHRR 2667, where the European Court held that prosecuting a member of a terrorist organisation for comments made to a journalist did not breach Article 10. In *Shayler* [2003] 1 AC 247, the House of Lords held that the provisions of the Official Secrets Act 1989 which created criminal offences of disclosure of certain material were not incompatible with Article 10.

THE INVESTIGATION OF CRIME

Duty to Investigate Crime Effectively

In certain circumstances, the ECHR obliges law enforcement bodies, such as the police, to carry out effective investigations where serious human rights issues arise, particularly where absolute rights such as the right to life or the prohibition on torture and inhuman or degrading treatment are concerned (see, for example, *Aydin v Turkey* (1997) 25 EHRR 251 at [103] and *Labita v Italy* (2000) Appln. 26772/95 at [131]). **A7.36**

Examples where the European Court has found that there has been a failure to conduct a thorough and effective investigation include: (i) failing to ascertain the identity of possible eye-witnesses; (ii) failing to question suspects at an early stage; (iii) failing to search for corroborating evidence; (iv) the adoption of an over-deferential attitude to those in authority; (v) failing to follow up proper complaints; (vi) ignoring obvious evidence; (vii) failing to carry out a proper autopsy; and (vii) failing to test gunpowder traces (see for example, *Aksoy v Turkey* (1996) 23 EHRR 553, *Aydin v Turkey* (1997) 25 EHRR 251, *Kurt v Turkey* (1998) 27 EHRR 373 and *Labita v Italy* (2000) Appln. 26772/95).

Surveillance

Secret surveillance amounts to a serious interference with an individual's private life under the ECHR, Article 8 (*Kopp v Switzerland* (1998) 27 EHRR 91). Therefore it must be 'prescribed by law': i.e. the applicable legal rules must be accessible and formulated with sufficient precision to enable citizens to foresee — if need be with appropriate advice — the consequences of their actions (see, for example, *Amann v Switzerland* (2000) 30 EHRR 843). Since intercepting telephone calls constitutes a serious interference with private life, particular precision in the law is required, including the rules applicable in prisons (*Doerga v Netherlands* (2004) 41 EHRR 45). **A7.37**

Surveillance must also be necessary and proportionate: police surveillance should be restricted to that which is strictly necessary to achieve the required objective. What is legitimate for the prevention and detection of serious crime may not be legitimate for less serious crime. Secret surveillance is tolerable under the Convention only insofar as it is strictly necessary for the protection of national security or the prevention of disorder or crime (*Klass v Germany* (1978) 2 EHRR 214).

Article 8 can be engaged where telephone calls (or other communications) are intercepted at work, even where they take place on private or internal telecommunications systems. In *Halford v UK* (1997) 24 EHRR 523, the European Court held (at [46]):

> ... telephone calls made from business premises as well as from the home may be covered by the notions of 'private life' and 'correspondence' within the meaning of Article 8(1).

The law on secret surveillance must be particularly precise and provide effective safeguards against abuse. Although there is no requirement that individuals be given prior notice of surveillance (because in most cases that would defeat its purpose), the law governing powers of secret surveillance must be clear enough to give citizens an adequate indication of the circumstances in which, and the conditions upon which, public authorities are entitled to resort to the use of such powers (*Halford v UK* (1997) 24 EHRR 523; *Malone v UK* (1984) 7 EHRR 14; *Khan v UK* (2001) 31 EHRR 1016; *Elahi v UK* (Appln. 30034/04)).

The RIPA 2000 was designed to ensure that surveillance carried out within the framework it provides is compatible with Article 8. In the vast majority of cases, that is likely to be so, but there remain examples where, for example, the interception of communications falls outside the strict definitions in RIPA 2000. In those cases Article 8 issues may arise (for intercepts abroad, see *X, Y and Z* (2000) *The Times*, 23 May 2000).

In *Perry v UK* (2004) 39 EHRR 3, a breach of Article 8 was found where the applicant was covertly videoed on his arrival at a police station and the resulting images were inserted in a montage of film for identification purposes. In *Segerstedt-Wiberg v Sweden* (2006) 44 EHRR 14, the European Court held that systematically collecting and storing information about individuals in a police file amounted to an interference with privacy under Article 8(1) and needed to be justified under Article 8(2), even where much of the information was available in the public domain.

Informers and Undercover Police Officers

A7.38 So long as informer and undercover officers do not actively instigate criminal offences, the fact that they carry out private surveillance does not *in itself* breach the ECHR, Article 8 because those who engage in serious crime cannot have any reasonable expectation that their activities will not be observed. As the European Court observed in *Ludi v Switzerland* (1992) 15 EHRR 173 (at [40]):

> ... the use of an undercover agent did not, either alone or in combination with the telephone interception, affect private life within the meaning of Article 8 ... [the applicant] must ... have been aware ... that he was engaged in a criminal act ... and that consequently he was running the risk of encountering an undercover police officer whose task would in fact be to expose him.

However, the law governing the use of undercover agents must be clear and precise; it must also provide safeguards against abuse (*Teixeira de Castro v Portugal* (1998) 28 EHRR 101). Where informers/undercover officers go beyond observation and actively incite the commission of an offence, issues of fairness under Article 6 will arise.

Entrapment

A7.39 It is unfair under the ECHR, Article 6 to prosecute an individual for a criminal offence incited by undercover agents, which, but for the incitement, would probably not have been committed. Even the public interest in the detection of serious crime cannot justify the instigation of criminal offences by undercover agents (*Teixeira de Castro v Portugal* (1999) 28 EHRR 101 at [39]). However, so long as informers and/or undercover officers keep within the reasonable limits of passive surveillance, no issue arises under Article 6 (fair trial); nor does any privacy issue arise under Article 8 (*Ludi v Switzerland* (1992) 15 EHRR 173). In *Looseley* [2001] 1 WLR 2060 (see **F2.26**), the House of Lords held that the approach of the domestic courts to entrapment was no different to the approach taken in *Teixeira de Castro v Portugal*.

Searching Individuals

In *R (Gillan) v Commissioner of Police for the Metropolis* [2006] 2 AC 307, the House of Lords held that the ECHR, Article 5 would usually not be engaged where a person was required to remain in one place during the course of a short stop and search (the case involved the wide powers available under ss. 44 and 45 of the Terrorism Act 2000). Lord Bingham reasoned that: **A7.40**

> . . . it will ordinarily be relatively brief. The person stopped will not be arrested, handcuffed,. . . confined or removed to a different place. I do not think, in the absence of special circumstances such a person could be regarded as being detained in the sense of confined or kept in custody, but more properly of being detained in the sense of kept from proceeding or kept waiting . . .

The House of Lords went on to hold that if a proper exercise of the power (i.e. in accordance with statute and PACE Code A) did amount to a deprivation of liberty then, provided it was lawful, Article 5(1)(b) would apply (lawful detention to secure an obligation prescribed by law). On the question of interference with Article 8 privacy rights, the House of Lords held that a superficial search of the individual and opening of bags, etc. would probably not engage Article 8 but, if it did (e.g., because personal papers were examined), Article 8(2) would usually justify the lawful exercise of stop and search powers.

Searching Premises and Vehicles

Search and seizure interfere with the right to private and family life, home and correspondence protected by the ECHR, Article 8. Therefore such measures must be justified in accordance with Article 8(2) of the Convention. Judicial authorisation is a highly relevant factor, but not determinative of the lawfulness of search and seizure under the ECHR. **A7.41**

Where there has been no judicial authorisation for a search, courts should be particularly vigilant to ensure that other safeguards exist to protect individuals from unnecessary intrusion into their privacy. At the very least, a proper legal framework with very strict limits on search powers will be required (*Camenzind v Switzerland* (1997) 28 EHRR 458 at [45]). Furthermore, where the police retain a discretion whether to enter premises, that discretion must be properly exercised (see *McLeod v UK* (1999) 27 EHRR 493 at [54]–[57]).

Any warrant authorising search and seizure must be clear, specific and contain safeguards against abuse. If a warrant is drawn in very broad terms or gives too much discretion to those executing it, it is likely to breach Article 8 (*Funke v France* (1993) 16 EHRR 297 at [56–57]). For example, the European Court has held that a warrant which authorised a search for 'documents' without any limitation is too broad for compliance with Article 8 (*Niemietz v Germany* (1992) 16 EHRR 97).

The notion of an individual's private life under Article 8 can be extended to his business and commercial premises (*Niemietz v Germany* (1992) 16 EHRR 97; *Sallinen v Finland* (2005) 44 EHRR 358). Therefore warrants to search business premises should comply with Article 8. Although lawyers' premises are not immune from search, professional confidentiality must be respected. In *Niemietz v Germany*, the European Court found a breach of Article 8 where a lawyer's offices were searched by the police acting on a court warrant in order to obtain information about the identity and whereabouts of a third party who was the subject of a criminal investigation.

Fingerprints and Other Samples

A7.42 Measures such as taking personal details, photographs and samples all engage the ECHR, Article 8 and must be justified (*Murray v UK* (1994) 19 EHRR 193). The prevention of crime can justify such measures, but only where they are prescribed by law, necessary and proportionate. In some cases, the collection of personal data from those who are not under suspicion can be justified, but only in very limited circumstances: e.g., where individuals are stopped crossing a national border and the purpose of the measures in question is the prevention of terrorism (*McVeigh, O'Neill and Evans v UK* (1981) 5 EHRR 71).

The retention of personal data is different from its collection and must be separately justified (*X v Germany* 9 Coll Dec 53; Appln. 1307/61). But in *R (S) v Chief Constable of South Yorkshire Police* [2004] 1 WLR 2196, the House of Lords held that the retention of fingerprints/samples following acquittal or discontinuance of a prosecution was not incompatible with Article 8(1). The prevention of terrorism (or other serious offences) can justify the retention of personal data, but only for so long as it serves that purpose (*McVeigh, O'Neill and Evans v UK*).

International Co-operation in the Investigation of Crime

A7.43 The ECHR is relevant to questions of international co-operation in the investigation of crime. Law enforcement officers from the UK, who carry out their functions in other countries remain subject to the ECHR. It will therefore be possible for a suspect arrested and detained abroad by UK law enforcement officers to claim a breach of Convention rights (*Reinette v France* (1989) 63 DR 189). The leading case on the extra-territorial application of the ECHR and the HRA 1998 is now *R (Al-Skeini) v Secretary of State for Defence* [2007] 3 WLR 33.

In addition, it would breach the ECHR if international co-operation in the investigation of crime exposed an individual to the risk of torture or ill-treatment contrary to Article 3, or interfered with his/her right to life under Article 2 (e.g., through extradition or deportation). However, there is no absolute rule that Contracting States to the ECHR should not co-operate with non-Contracting States merely because they do not comply with the standards set out in Article 6 (fair trial), unless there has been, or is likely to be, a flagrant denial of justice, co-operation should be refused (*Drozd and Janousek v France and Spain* (1992) 14 EHRR 745 at [110]).

ARREST AND PRE-TRIAL DETENTION

Reasonable Suspicion

A7.44 Article 5(1)(c) of the ECHR authorises arrest on 'reasonable suspicion' that an individual has committed an offence. Such suspicion requires objective justification. The honesty and good faith of a suspicion constitute indispensable elements of its reasonableness, but honest belief alone is not enough. There must be an objective basis justifying arrest and/or detention (*Fox, Campbell and Hartley v UK* (1990) 13 EHRR 157 at [32]). A reasonable suspicion can be based on information obtained from anonymous informers; but if challenged the authorities must furnish at least some evidence capable of satisfying a court under Article 5(3) (*O'Hara v UK* (2002) 34 EHRR 812). An arrest for failing to supply a name and address must be proportionate. In *Vasileva v Denmark* (2003) 40 EHRR 681, a breach of Article 5 was found where a 67-year-old woman was detained for 13 hours because she refused to give her name and address.

Preventative detention is not permitted under Article 5; to justify an arrest there must be a reasonable suspicion that the individual in question has committed a 'concrete and specific offence' (*Ireland v UK* (1978) 2 EHRR 25; *Guzzardi v Italy* (1980) 3 EHRR 333).

Reasons

Article 5(2) of the ECHR requires that anyone arrested 'be informed promptly, in a language which he understands, of the reasons for his arrest and of any charge against him'. The promptness of reasons is to be assessed in light of all the circumstances of the case. Giving reasons within a few hours might suffice where terrorist offences are suspected (*Fox, Campbell and Hartley v UK* (1990) 13 EHRR 157; *Murray v UK* (1994) 19 EHRR 193 at [40]). **A7.45**

The purpose of giving reasons for an arrest is to enable anyone arrested to challenge the lawfulness of his/her detention (*Fox, Campbell and Hartley v UK*; *Murray v UK*). But reasons need not be in writing (*X v Netherlands* (1966) 9 Yearbook 474; *X v Germany* (1974) 14 Yearbook 250). Merely informing an individual that he has been detained under emergency legislation is insufficient (*Ireland v UK* (1978) 2 EHRR 25).

Handcuffs and Restraints

The use of handcuffs and restraints is not prohibited by the ECHR, but unless justified on the facts of each case may raise issues under Articles 3 and 8. In *Raninan v Finland* (1997) 26 EHRR 563, the European Court held (at [56]): **A7.46**

> . . . handcuffing does not normally give rise to an issue under Article 3 . . . where the measure has been imposed with lawful arrest and detention and does not entail use of force, or public exposure, exceeding what is reasonably considered necessary in the circumstances. In this regard, it is of importance for instance whether there is reason to believe that the person concerned would resist arrest or abscond, cause injury or damage or suppress evidence.

In *Henaf v France* (2005) 40 EHRR 990, the European Court found a breach of Article 3 ECHR where the applicant was, for no good reason, handcuffed to a hospital bed while waiting for an operation.

Access to a Lawyer

The right to a fair trial under the ECHR, Article 6 normally requires that a suspect have access to a lawyer at the initial stages of a police investigation, particularly where steps may be taken which will impact on the defence (*Imbroscia v Switzerland* (1993) 17 EHRR 4411 at [36]; *John Murray v UK* (1996) 22 EHRR 29 at [63], [65] and [66]). However, the actual requirements of Article 6 at the pre-trial stage will vary according to the circumstances. In *Imbroscia v Switzerland* (1993) 17 EHRR 4411, the European Court held (at [36]): **A7.47**

> . . . the manner in which Article 6(1) and 3(c) is to be applied during the preliminary investigation depends on the special features of the proceedings involved and the circumstances of the case; in order to determine whether the aim of Article 6 — a fair trial — has been achieved, regard must be had to the entirety of the proceedings conducted in the case.

To deny access to a lawyer for a long period in a situation where the rights of the defence were irretrievably prejudiced is, whatever the justification, likely to be incompatible with Article 6 (*Magee v UK* (2001) 31 EHRR 822; *Averill v UK* (2001) 31 EHRR 839). But see *Brennan v UK* (2002) 34 EHRR 507, where no breach was found where denial of access to a lawyer was in good faith and on reasonable grounds.

Communications between a suspect and his lawyer should be confidential. In *S v Switzerland* (1991) 14 EHRR 667, the European Court held (at [48]):

> . . . an accused's right to communicate with his advocate out of hearing of a third person is one of the basic requirements of a fair trial in a democratic society and flows from Article 6(3)(c) of the Convention. If a lawyer were unable to confer with his client and receive

> confidential instructions from him without . . . surveillance, his assistance would lose much of its usefulness, whereas the Convention is intended to guarantee rights that are practical and effective.

But in rare cases, e.g. where serious crime is feared, it may be legitimate to intercept lawyer/client communications. However, the mere fact that a number of lawyers are co-ordinating their defence strategy cannot justify interference with lawyer/client confidentiality (*S v Switzerland*).

Access to Others

A7.48 Suspects in custody should normally be allowed access to their families. In *McVeigh, O'Neill and Evans v UK* (1981) 5 EHRR 71, the European Commission held (at [239]):

> Unless there is a danger of accomplices being warned, a failure to allow persons so detained to make contact with their families cannot be justified under Article 8(2) as being necessary for the prevention of crime etc.

Right to Silence

A7.49 The ECHR recognises a right to remain silent during police questioning. In *John Murray v UK* (1996) 22 EHRR 29, the European Court held (at [20]):

> . . . although not specifically mentioned in Article 6 of the Convention, there can be no doubt that the right to remain silent under police questioning and the privilege against self-incrimination are generally recognised international standards which lie at the heart of the notion of a fair procedure under Article 6.

That does not mean that adverse inference cannot be drawn from silence. The fairness of drawing such inferences is a matter to be determined at trial in light of all the evidence (see **F19**). But it does mean that the introduction into evidence in a criminal trial for the purpose of incriminating the accused of transcripts of statements made under compulsion (e.g., to non-prosecutorial inspectors) will breach Article 6 (*Saunders v UK* (1996) 23 EHRR 313; see also *Shannon v UK* (Appln. 6563/03)). The same applies where the authorities seek to compel a suspect to hand over incriminating documentation (*Funke v France* (1993) 16 EHRR 297). Incriminating answers obtained by the questioning of a suspect during incommunicado detention require very close scrutiny (*G v UK* (1984) 34 DR 75).

Right to be Brought Promptly before a Court

A7.50 Everyone arrested for a criminal offence has the right to be brought promptly before a judge or other officer authorised by law to exercise judicial power.

ECHR, Article 5

> (3) Everyone arrested or detained in accordance with the provisions of paragraph 1(c) of this Article shall be brought promptly before a judge or other officer authorised by law to exercise judicial power and shall be entitled to trial within a reasonable time or to release pending trial. Release may be conditioned by guarantees to appear for trial.

Article 5(3) does not depend on the detainee making an application for his case to be heard; it requires automatic consideration of the case by the court. It also requires provisional release once detention ceases to be reasonable (*TW v Malta; Aquilina v Malta* (2000) 29 EHRR 185). Although authorised by law to review detention, a commanding officer is not sufficiently independent and impartial to satisfy the requirements of Article 5(4) in court-martial cases (*Hood v UK* (2000) 29 EHRR 365; *Jordon v UK* (2001) 31 EHRR 6).

When determining whether an arrested person has been brought promptly before a judge or judicial officer, the scope for flexibility in interpreting and applying the notion of 'promptness' is very limited. In *Brogan and others v UK* (1988) 11 EHRR 117, the European Court held (at [62]) that a delay of four days and six hours was too long, even when an arrest is made under prevention of terrorism legislation.

Bail

A7.51 Despite its wording, the ECHR, Article 5(3) does not provide for trial within a reasonable period *or* release pending trial *as alternatives*: an accused person is entitled to trial within a reasonable period *and* release pending trial unless the prosecuting authorities advance relevant and sufficient reasons for refusing bail (*Wemhoff v Germany* (1968) 1 EHRR 55).

Grounds for refusing bail which have been approved by the European Court include: (i) fear of absconding (*Stogmuller v Austria* (1969) 1 EHRR 155; *Neumeister v Austria* (1968) 1 EHRR 91); (ii) interference with the course of justice (*Wemhoff v Germany*; *Letellier v France* (1991) 14 EHRR 83); (iii) prevention of further offences (*Matznetter v Austria* (1979–80) 1 EHRR 198; (iv) the preservation of public order (*Letellier v France*); and (v) the protection of the defendant (*IA v France* (1998) Appln. 28213/95). The mere fact that there are reasonable grounds for suspecting that a person has committed an offence is not enough (*Letellier v France*).

Conditional bail is permitted under the ECHR and should be granted as an alternative to pre-trial detention where objections to bail can be met with conditions (*Wemhoff v Germany*). Permissible conditions of bail include a requirement to surrender travel documents (*Stogmuller v Austria*), the imposition of a residence requirement (*Schmid v Austria* (1985) 44 DR 195) and the provision of a surety — which must be assessed by reference to the means of the accused (*Wemhoff v Germany*; *Neumeister v Austria*; *Schertenleib v Switzerland* (1980) 23 DR 137). The task of assessing appropriate bail conditions is as exacting as the task of deciding whether to grant bail at all (*Iwanczuk v Poland* (2004) 38 EHRR 148). Bail proceedings must be fair and there must be equality of arms between the prosecution and the defence. Although all of the fair trial requirements of Article 6(1) are not necessary in relation to a review by a court of the lawfulness of detention under Article 5(4), such review must have a judicial character and provide guarantees appropriate to the kind of deprivation in question. The proceedings should be adversarial and must ensure equality of arms between the prosecutor and the detained person, which will not be achieved if counsel for the detained person is denied access to those documents in the investigation file that are essential in order effectively to challenge the lawfulness of his or her client's detention (see, for *example, Garcia Alva v Germany* (2003) 37 EHRR 335 at [39]). In *R (Malik) v Central Criminal Court* [2006] 4 All ER 1141, the Divisional Court observed that Article 6 may apply at bail hearings and that bail hearings should normally take place in public. Legislation depriving courts of their ability to grant bail will breach Article 5 (see *Caballero v UK* (2000) 30 EHRR 643).

FAIR TRIAL IN CRIMINAL PROCEEDINGS

Meaning of 'criminal proceedings' under Article 6

A7.52 The fair trial requirements of the ECHR, Article 6 distinguish between criminal and civil proceedings. Whether proceedings are criminal or civil is to be determined according to three criteria: (i) the classification in domestic law — if classified as criminal, this is determinative; if classified as civil, this is a starting point, but not determinative; (ii) the nature of the conduct in question — sanctions which apply to the population as a whole, rather than to an identifiable sub-class, point toward a criminal classification; (iii) the severity of any possible penalty — severe penalties (including those with imprisonment in default) and penalties intended to deter are pointers towards a criminal classification of proceedings (*Engel v The Netherlands (No. 1)* (1976) 1 EHRR 647; *Benham v UK* (1996) 22 EHRR 293). The second and third criteria are alternative, not cumulative (see *Lauko v Slovakia* (2001) 33 EHRR 994 at [57]).

In *Steel and others v UK* (1999) 28 EHRR 603, the European Court held that although 'breach of the peace' is not classified as a criminal offence under English law, it is nonetheless to be considered an 'offence' within the meaning of Article 6(1) (at [54–55]). On the other hand, in *Escoubet v Belgium* (2001) 31 EHRR 46, the European Court found that a procedure whereby a driving licence could be withdrawn for 15 days on the direction of a Crown prosecutor where a driver was drunk did not amount to the determination of a criminal charge under Article 6. Similarly in *Benjafield* [2003] 1 AC 1099, the House of Lords held that confiscation proceedings were part of the sentencing process and did not involve a fresh criminal charge; accordingly Article 6(2) was not applicable to such proceedings. In *R (McCann) v Manchester Crown Court* [2003] 1 AC 787, the House of Lords held that the imposition of an ASBO under the CDA 1998 did not amount to the determination of a criminal charge. Such orders are preventative in character and thus no penalty is imposed.

A7.53 Right to be Informed of Charge

ECHR, Article 6

(3) Everyone charged with a criminal offence has the following minimum rights:

(a) to be informed promptly, in a language which he understands and in detail, of the nature and cause of the accusation against him;

The purpose of this provision is to enable the individual to begin preparing a defence (*GSM v Austria* (1983) 34 DR 119).

Where the offence is fairly specific, it may be enough to provide a brief description of the offence, the date, place and alleged victim (*Brozicek v Italy* (1990) 12 EHRR 371). Otherwise, the information provided should be detailed (*Pelisser and Sassi v France* (2000) 30 EHRR 715).

Right to Adequate Time and Facilities to Prepare a Defence

A7.54 **ECHR, Article 6**

(3) Everyone charged with a criminal offence has the following minimum rights:

. . .

(b) to have adequate time and facilities for the preparation of his defence.

The adequate time requirement inevitably depends on the nature and complexity of the case; it cannot be determined in the abstract but only by reference to the circumstances of each case (*X and Y v Austria* (1979) 15 DR 160). Where there is a late change of lawyer, an adjournment may be necessary. Where it is obvious that a lawyer has not had adequate time to prepare the defence properly, the court should consider adjourning the case on its own motion (*Goddi v Italy* (1984) 6 EHRR 457).

Disclosure

A7.55 Under the ECHR, a disclosure requirement is based on: (i) the requirement that there be equality of arms between prosecution and defence (*Jespers v Belgium* (1981) 27 DR 61); (ii) the accused's right to adequate time and facilities to prepare a defence under ECHR, Article 6(3)(b) (*Edwards v UK* (1992) 15 EHRR 417); and (iii) the requirement in Article 6(3)(d) that there be parity of conditions for the examination of witnesses (*Edwards v UK* (1992) 15 EHRR 417, Commission Report). In *Rowe and Davies v UK* (2000) 30 EHRR 1 (see **D9.30**), the European Court held (at [60]):

> It is a fundamental aspect of the right to a fair trial that criminal proceedings, including the elements of such proceedings which relate to procedure, should be adversarial and that there should be equality of arms between the prosecution and defence. The right to an adversarial trial means, in a criminal case, that both prosecution and defence must be given an opportunity to have knowledge of and comment on the observations filed and the evidence adduced by the other

> party . . . In addition Article 6(1) requires . . . that the prosecution authorities should disclose to the defence all material evidence in their possession for or against the accused . . . .

The requirement in Article 6(3)(d) that there be parity of conditions for the examination of witnesses requires disclosure of any material relevant to the testimony of the witnesses, including his/her credibility (*Edwards v UK* (1992) 15 EHRR 417, Commission Report).

The privacy rights of complainants may require notice to be given to them, along with an opportunity to make representations, when, for example, a witness summons is directed to a hospital to produce their medical records (*R (B) v Stafford Crown Court* [2007] 1 WLR 1524).

Public Interest Immunity

There may be circumstances under the ECHR in which material need not be disclosed to the defence on grounds of public interest immunity; but they must be subject to strict control by the courts. In *Rowe and Davies v UK* (2000) 30 EHRR 1, the European Court held (at [61]): **A7.56**

> . . . the entitlement to disclosure of relevant evidence is not an absolute right. In any criminal proceedings there may be competing interests, such as national security or the need to protect witnesses at risk of reprisals or keep secret police methods of investigation of crime, which must be weighed against the rights of the accused . . . In some cases it may be necessary to withhold certain evidence from the defence so as to preserve the fundamental rights of another individual or to safeguard an important public interest. However, only such measures restricting the rights of the defence which are strictly necessary are permissible under Article 6(1) . . . Moreover, in order to ensure that the accused receives a fair trial, any difficulties caused to the defence by a limitation on its rights must be sufficiently counterbalanced by the procedures followed by the judicial authorities.

Public interest immunity hearings on an *ex parte* basis do not necessarily breach Article 6 (*Jasper v UK* (2000) 30 EHRR 97; *Fitt v UK* (2000) 30 EHRR 223). However, where material should have been disclosed to the trial judge but was not, an *ex parte* hearing at the appeal stage is unlikely to be sufficient under Article 6 (see, for example, *Atlan v UK* (2002) 34 EHRR 833).

There is an important distinction between material that is, and material that is not, actually deployed against the accused. In *Edwards and Lewis v UK* (2005) 40 EHRR 893, the European Court found a breach of Article 6 where the material relevant to an issue to be decided by the judge rather than the jury (entrapment) was not disclosed on grounds of public interest immunity. The approach to be adopted by domestic courts was spelt out by the House of Lords in *H* [2004] 2 AC 134, where the earlier case of *Smith* [2001] 1 WLR 1031 was overruled as being incompatible with the ECHR. See also *Roberts v Parole Board* [2005] 2 AC 738, where the House of Lords considered the relationship between the right to equality of arms and the use of closed material in hearings before the Parole Board.

Right to an Independent and Impartial Tribunal

The ECHR, Article 6(1) provides that 'In the determination of . . . any criminal charge against him, everyone is entitled to a fair and public hearing by an independent and impartial tribunal established by law'. Independence must be institutional and functional; but does not require trial by jury (*X and Y v Ireland* (1981) 22 DR 51). **A7.57**

Relevant to the question of independence will be: (i) the manner of appointment and duration of office (*Le Compte, van Leuven and De Meyere v Belgium* (1981) 4 EHRR 1), but the mere fact that the executive appoint judges is not automatically a breach of Article 6, see *Campbell and Fell v UK* (1984) 7 EHRR 165); (ii) protection from external influences (*Piersack v Belgium* (1982) 5 EHRR 169); (iii) an appearance of independence (*Delcourt v*

Belgium (1969) 1 EHRR 355 at [31]; *Campbell and Fell v UK* at [78]). For a case on the use of clerks in the Scottish district courts, see *Clark (Procurator Fiscal) v Kelly* [2004] 1 AC 681.

On the question of impartiality, the European Court has adopted a dual test: (i) first assessing whether there is any evidence of actual bias; here impartiality is presumed unless there is proof to the contrary (ii) then assessing the circumstances alleged to give rise to a risk of bias; here the question is whether there are 'ascertainable facts which may raise doubts' about the court's impartiality (*Piersack v Belgium* (1982) 5 EHRR 169; *Hauschildt v Denmark* (1989) 12 EHRR 266). The behaviour of a judge towards counsel can raise issues of impartiality (e.g., where the judge frequently interrupts counsel) and there may be a breach of Article 6 where the behaviour in question prevents counsel from pursuing a line of argument or otherwise renders the trial unfair (*CG v UK* (2002) 34 EHRR 789). Judges are free to criticise developments in the law, but they should refrain from criticism (or praise) which by its nature and language gives rise to legitimate concerns about their impartiality (*Hoekstra v HM Advocate* (2000) HRLR 410, where the judge in question had criticised the ECHR in very strong terms).

Where a judge has taken key decisions before trial, issues of impartiality may arise. But the mere fact that a judge has previously decided a bail decision based on suspicion that the accused has committed an offence will not automatically preclude that judge's participation in the trial. In *Hauschildt v Denmark*, the European Court held (at [50]):

> . . . the questions which the judge has to answer when taking . . . pre-trial decisions are not the same as those which are decisive for his final judgment . . . Suspicion and a formal finding of guilt are not to be treated as being the same . . . therefore, the mere fact that a trial judge or an appeal judge . . . has also made pre-trial decisions in the case, including those concerning detention on remand, cannot be held as in itself justifying fears as to his impartiality.

Nor will the fact that a judge has dealt with the accused on a previous occasion; the key issue will be the nature and character of the previous decision (*Hauschildt v Denmark*, breach where trial judge previously refused bail on a high threshold test; cf. *Brown v UK* (1986) 8 EHRR 272, no breach where appeal court judge refusing leave had previously been involved in restraint proceedings, and *Depiets v France* (2004) 43 EHRR 1206, where one member of the court had conducted ancillary pre-trial hearings).

Allegations of impartiality must be properly investigated, unless they are manifestly devoid of merit (*Remli v France* (1996) 22 EHRR 253 at [48]; *Gregory v UK* (1997) 25 EHRR 577 at [44]). In some circumstances, the nature of the alleged bias or impartiality will require decisive action; directions to the jury to try the case on the evidence may not suffice (*Sander v UK* (2001) 31 EHRR 1003, where a juror had made racist jokes and comments and the judge declined to discharge the jury, but instead directed the jury to come to a verdict without prejudice). The limits of any inquiry about the deliberations of the jury were considered by the House of Lords in *Mirza* [2004] 1 AC 1118 (see **D18.16**).

Right to a Public Hearing

A7.58 ECHR, Article 6

> (1) In the determination of . . . any criminal charge against him, everyone is entitled to a fair and public hearing by an independent and impartial tribunal established by law. Judgment shall be pronounced publicly but the press and public may be excluded from all or part of the trial in the interest of morals, public order or national security in a democratic society, where the interests of juveniles or the protection of the private life of the parties so require, or to the extent strictly necessary in the opinion of the court in special circumstances where publicity would prejudice the interests of justice.

There is a presumption that ordinary criminal proceedings should be public, even where they involve dangerous individuals (*Campbell and Fell v UK* (1984) 7 EHRR 165 at [87]) (a less strict approach has, on occasion, be taken to the requirement that 'judgment shall be pronounced publicly', see *Pretto v Italy* (1984) 6 EHRR 182).

Legal Aid and Legal Representation

ECHR, Article 6 **A7.59**

(3) Everyone charged with a criminal offence has the following minimum rights:

...

(c) to defend himself in person or through legal assistance of his own choosing or, if he has not sufficient means to pay for legal assistance, to be given it free when the interests of justice so require.

Relevant to the 'interests of justice' test are: (i) the complexity of the case; (ii) the ability of the accused to understand and present the relevant arguments without assistance; (iii) the severity of the possible penalty (*Benham v UK* (1996) 22 EHRR 293; *Granger v UK* (1990) 12 EHRR 469; *Quaranta v Switzerland* (1991) Appln. 12744/87). Where deprivation of liberty is at stake, the interests of justice, in principle, call for legal aid and any refusal of legal aid should be kept under review (*Benham v UK*; *Granger v UK*; *Perks v UK* (2000) 30 EHRR 33). Rules that do not permit legal aid whatever the circumstances will invariably breach Article 6 (*Beet v UK* (Appln. 47676/99); *Lloyd v UK* (Appln. 29798/96)).

Merely allocating a lawyer to the accused is not enough under Article 6(3)(c) if that lawyer is manifestly unable to provide effective representation. In *Artico v Italy* (1981) 3 EHRR 1, where the applicant's nominated legal aid lawyer refused to represent him in an appeal against a fraud conviction and he was unable to secure the services of another lawyer, the European Court held (at [33] and [36]):

> Article 6(3) speaks of 'assistance' and not of 'nomination' . . . [M]ere nomination does not ensure effective assistance, since the lawyer appointed for legal aid purposes may die, fall seriously ill, be prevented for a protracted period from acting or shirk his duties. If they are notified of the situation, the authorities must either replace him or cause him to fulfil his obligations . . . Admittedly, a State cannot be held responsible for every shortcoming on the part of a lawyer appointed for legal aid purposes, but, in the particular circumstances, it was for the . . . authorities to take steps to ensure that the applicant enjoyed effectively the right to which they had recognised he was entitled.

In *Daud v Portugal* (2000) 30 EHRR 400, the European Court held that there had been a breach of Article 6 where defence counsel had not had sufficient time to prepare the case. Even though defence counsel made no application to adjourn the case, the court should have done so itself.

The right to be legally represented does not give an accused an absolute right to determine how his defence will be conducted: an accused cannot require counsel to disregard basic principles of his professional duty in the presentation of the accused's defence (*X v UK* (1980) 21 DR 126 at [6]).

In legal aid cases, an accused does not have an unqualified right to counsel of his choosing. In *Croissant v Germany* (1993) 16 EHRR 135, the European Court held (at [29]):

> [Article 6(3)(c)] is necessarily subject to certain limitations where free legal aid is concerned and . . . it is for the courts to decide whether the interests of justice require that the accused be defended by counsel appointed by them. When appointing defence counsel the national courts must certainly have regard to the defendant's wishes . . . However, they can override those wishes when there are relevant and sufficient grounds for holding that this is necessary in the interests of justice.

See also *Mayzit v Russia* (2005) 43 EHRR 805.

Rules requiring an accused to be represented by a lawyer where sexual offences are alleged will not necessarily breach Article 6(3)(c) (*Baegen v Netherlands* (Series A/327-B) (1995) at [77]).

Where a sanction such as the deprivation of liberty is at stake, the interests of justice require not only that a lawyer be appointed, but also that that lawyer be given an opportunity to make representations; see *Hooper v UK* (2005) 41 EHRR 1, where the applicant was bound over for 28 days for causing a disturbance in court without his lawyer having been heard on the matter (see also *Aerts v Belgium (*2000) 29 EHRR 50).

Right to be Present at Trial

A7.60 As a general rule, the accused has a right to be present at trial (*Ekbetani v Sweden* (1988) 13 EHRR 504 at [25]) and adducing important evidence in the absence of the accused will usually be unfair (*Barbera, Messegue and Jabardo v Spain* (1989) 11 EHRR 360 at [89]) Consequently the authorities are under a duty to notify all accused about the proceedings against them (*Goddi v Italy* (1984) 6 EHRR 457). However, the right to be present at trial is not an absolute right. For example, an accused can be excluded where he causes disruption to the proceedings, refuses to come to court, or makes himself too ill to attend, provided that his interests are protected, e.g., because his lawyer is present (*Ensslin and others v Germany* (1978) 14 DR 64, paras. 21 and 22, where the applicants were unable to attend trial because of ill-health induced by hunger strike). But special care is needed where the accused is ill (*Romanov v Russia* (2005) 44 EHRR 479).

An accused may waive his right to be present either expressly or impliedly by failing to attend the hearing having been given effective notice (*C v Italy* (1988) 56 DR 40 Appln. 10889/84). But waiver must be clear and unequivocal (*Colozza v Italy* (1985) 7 EHRR 516; *Brozicek v Italy* (1990) 12 EHRR 371; *Poitrimol v France* (1993) 18 EHRR 130; *Lala v Netherlands* (1994) 18 EHRR 856; *Pelladoah v Netherlands* (1995) 19 EHRR 81). There may be circumstances where an absent defendant is entitled to a rehearing when he subsequently emerges (*Colozza v Italy*). Moreover, where an accused chooses to be absent, counsel must nonetheless be permitted to attend the trial (*Poitrimol v France* (1993) 18 EHRR 130; *Geyseghem v Belgium* (2001) 32 EHRR 554). For consideration of the issue by the House of Lords, see *Jones* [2003] 1 AC 1 (see **D14.38**), where a trial in the absence of the accused was held not to have violated his Article 6 rights.

Right to Participate in the Trial

A7.61 All accused have a right to participate effectively in the proceedings. In *Stanford v UK* (1994) Series A, No. 282 (at [26]) and in *V v UK* (2000) 30 EHRR 121 (at [85]), the European Court held:

> . . . Article 6, read as a whole, guarantees the right of an accused to participate effectively in a criminal trial. In general this includes, inter alia, not only his right to be present, but also to hear and follow the proceedings.

Particular account must be taken of factors such as the accused's age and his ability to comprehend the proceedings. In respect of a young child charged with a grave offence attracting high levels of media and public interest, it is necessary to conduct the hearing in such a way as to reduce as far as possible his or her feelings of intimidation and inhibition (*V v UK* at [86] and [87]; *Practice Direction (Crown Court: Young Defendants)* [2000] 1 WLR 659 was made as a result). In *SC v UK* (2005) 40 EHRR 226, the European Court found a breach of Article 6(1) of the ECHR where the applicant, aged 11 and with limited intellectual ability, was unable to understand the criminal proceedings brought against him for robbery in the Crown Court. The European Court held that it was essential in such circumstances that the applicant be tried in a specialist tribunal.

Right to an Interpreter and Translation

A7.62 ECHR, Article 6

> (3) Everyone charged with a criminal offence has the following minimum rights:
> . . .

(e) to have the free assistance of an interpreter if he cannot understand or speak the language used in court.

This right is not subject to qualification, even if the accused is subsequently convicted; hence a convicted person cannot be ordered to pay the costs of an interpreter (*Luedicke, Delkasam and Koc v Germany* (1978) 2 EHRR 149 at [42] and [46]; *Ozturk v Germany* (1984) 6 EHRR 409).

The right to interpretation extends to all documentary material disclosed before trial; but this does not necessarily mean that all translations must be in written form; in limited circumstances, some oral translation is acceptable (*Luedicke, Delkasam and Koc v Germany*; *Kamasinski v Austria* (1989) 13 EHRR 36). The court has an obligation to ensure the quality of interpretation (*Kamasinski v Austria* at [74]). Responsibility for ensuring that a defendant who needs an interpreter gets appropriate assistance rests with the judge, not counsel. In *Cuscani v Italy* (2003) 36 EHRR 11, the European Court found a breach of Article 6 where the judge acceded to counsel's suggestion that the brother of the accused could translate for him at the sentencing phase.

Article 6(3)(e) applies only where the accused does not understand or speak the language used in court; it does not provide a right to conduct proceedings in the language of the accused's choice (*K v France* (1984) 35 DR 203 at [8] — applicant who understood French wanted to conduct his defence in the Breton language).

Pre-trial Publicity

Since pre-trial publicity can prejudice an accused's prospects of a fair trial, it can be restricted without necessarily breaching the ECHR, Article 10. In *Hodgson, Woolf Productions and the NUJ v UK* (1987) 10 EHRR 503, the European Commission held (at p. 509): **A7.63**

> . . . the need to ensure a fair trial and to protect members of the jury from exposure to prejudicial influences corresponds to a pressing social need . . . where there is a real risk of prejudice the appropriate response . . . is one which must lie, in principle, with the person responsible for ensuring the fairness of the trial, namely, the trial judge.

This was reinforced by the European Court in *Verlags GmbH & CoKG v Austria* (2002) Appln. 34315/96, which held (at [56]) that 'the limits of permissible comment on pending criminal proceedings may not extend to statements which are likely to prejudice, whether intentionally or not, the chances of a person receiving a fair trial or to undermine the confidence of the public in the role of the courts in the administration of justice'.

Prejudice will be harder to establish in a case tried by a judge than in a case tried by a jury (*Crociani v Italy* (1980) 22 DR 147 at [20]; see also *Ensslin and others v Germany* (1978) 14 DR 64 at [15]) and a proper balance between fair trial and press freedom must be maintained. In *Worm v Austria* (1997) 25 EHRR 454, the European Court held (at [50]):

> There is a general recognition of the fact that the courts cannot operate in a vacuum. Whilst the courts are the forum for the determination of a person's guilt or innocence on a criminal charge, this does not mean that there can be no prior or contemporaneous discussion of the subject-matter of criminal trials elsewhere, be it in specialised journals, in the general press or amongst the public at large . . . Provided that it does not overstep the bounds imposed in the interests of the proper administration of justice, reporting, including comment, on courts proceedings contributes to their publicity and is thus perfectly consonant with the requirement under Article 6(1) of the Convention that hearings be public. Not only do the media have the task of imparting such information and ideas; the public has a right to hear them.

Equality of Arms

The principle that there should be equality of arms between the parties before the court is fundamental to the notion of a fair trial under the ECHR, Article 6. In *Kaufman v Belgium* (1986) 50 DR 98, the European Commission held (at p. 115): **A7.64**

> ... [The Commission] recalls that it has repeatedly held that the right to a fair hearing, in both civil and criminal proceedings, entails that everyone who is a party to such proceedings shall have a reasonable opportunity of presenting his case to the court under conditions which do not place him at substantial disadvantage *vis-a-vis* his opponent ...

In particular, each party must know the case being made against him, have an effective opportunity to challenge it and an effective opportunity to advance his own case. See also *Roberts v Parole Board* [2005] 2 AC 736 and see further **A7.54**.

Right to an Adversarial Hearing

A7.65 All evidence and submissions should be made in the presence of the accused and in circumstances in which he has an opportunity to comment upon them. The right to an adversarial trial means the opportunity for the parties to have knowledge of and comment on the observations filed or evidence adduced by the other party (*Ruiz Mateos v Spain* (1993) 16 EHRR 505, at [63]; see also *Krcmar v Czech Republic* (2001) 31 EHRR 41 at [40]). This applies even where submissions are made by an independent party — such as an *amicus* lawyer — and are wholly objective (*Van Orshoven v Belgium* (1997) 26 EHRR 55, at [39]–[42]).

Reasons

A7.66 Article 6(1) of the ECHR obliges courts to give reasons for their judgments. In *Hiro Balani v Spain* (1995) 19 EHRR 566, the European Court held (at [27]):

> The Court reiterates that Article 6(1) obliges the courts to give reasons for their judgments, but cannot be understood as requiring a detailed answer to every argument. The extent to which this duty to give reasons applies may vary according to the nature of the decision. It is moreover necessary to take account, *inter alia*, of the diversity of the submissions that a litigant may bring before the courts and the differences existing in the Contracting States with regard to statutory provisions, customary rules, legal opinion and the presentation and drafting of judgments. That is why the question whether a court has failed to fulfil the obligation to state reasons, derived from Article 6 of the Convention, can only be determined in the light of the circumstances of the case.

In *Inner London Crown Court, ex parte London Borough of Lambeth* [2000]) Crim LR 303, the Divisional Court held that the Crown Court is as much under a duty to give reasons for its decision when it allows an appeal against conviction as when it dismisses one.

Trial within a Reasonable Period

A7.67 The right to trial within a reasonable period is guaranteed under the ECHR, Article 5(3) for those in pre-trial detention (see **A7.50**) and more generally for anyone facing criminal proceedings under Article 6(1). Since it is primarily concerned with those in pre-trial detention, the standards under Article 5(3) are more exacting than those under Article 6(1) (*Abdoella v Netherlands* (1995) 20 EHRR 585).

Time begins to run under both Article 5(3) and Article 6(1) when an individual is 'charged'. This may stretch back to arrest, rather than formal charge (*Eckle v Germany* (1983) 5 EHRR 1 at [73]; *Ewing v UK* (1988) 10 EHRR 141 at p. 143). However, in *A-G's Ref (No. 2 of 2001)* [2004] 2 AC 72, the House of Lords held that in England and Wales time will usually run from the time that an individual is formally charged or served with a summons.

Time ends for Article 5(3) purposes with the finding of guilt or innocence (*B v Austria* (1990) 13 EHRR 20); time ends for Article 6(1) purposes when the proceedings are over, including any appeal. Neither the court nor the prosecution is responsible for delays attributable to the applicant or his lawyers (*Konig v Germany* (1979–80) 2 EHRR 170). However, an accused is perfectly entitled to take legitimate points, if necessary, by way of appeal (*Ledonne (No. 1) v Italy* [1999] ECHR 25 at [25], where the applicant twice sought adjournment and twice challenged the validity of summons issued against him, but the prosecuting authorities could not provide good reason for two periods of delay totalling two years and ten months and on that basis breach of Article 6(1) was found).

Periods spent at large are discounted (*Girolami v Italy* (1991) A/196-E). The workload of the court is not a good reason for delay — and, in any event, should be supported with evidence of steps taken to alleviate the position (*Majaric v Slovenia* (2000) Appln. 28400/95 at [39]) — nor is a shortage of resources. Article 6(1) imposes on Contracting States the duty to organise their judicial system in such a way that their courts can meet their requirement to hear a case within a reasonable time (*Ledonne (No. 2) v Italy* (1999) Appln. 36719/97, 35742/97 and 38414/97 at [23]).

The remedy in domestic law for a breach of the requirement that there be trial within a reasonable period has been considered at the highest level on several occasions. In *Mills v HM Advocate* [2004] 1 AC 441, the Privy Council held that quashing a conviction was a possible, but exceptional, remedy. In the subsequent case of *A-G's Ref (No. 2 of 2001)*, a nine-judge House of Lords held that, where criminal proceedings are not dealt with in a reasonable period, there is necessarily a breach of Article 6(1), but the remedy to be afforded will depend on all the circumstances of the case.

Retroactive Offences

ECHR, Article 7 A7.68

(1) No one shall be held guilty of any criminal offence on account of any act or omission which did not constitute a criminal offence under national or international law at the time when it was committed. Nor shall a heavier penalty be imposed than the one that was applicable at the time the criminal offence was committed.

(2) This Article shall not prejudice the trial and punishment of any person for any act or omission which, at the time it was committed, was criminal according to the general principles of law recognised by civilised nations.

Article 7 prohibits not only the creation of retroactive offences by legislation, but also the retroactive application of existing criminal offences through the development of the common law (*X Ltd and Y v UK* (1982) 28 DR 77; *SW and CR v UK* (1996) 21 EHRR 363).

Double Jeopardy

Double jeopardy is dealt with in Protocol 7 of the ECHR. The UK has not ratified this yet. Limited protection from double jeopardy may also be provided for under Article 6 (*X v Austria* (1970) 35 EHRR CD 151; *S v Germany* (1983) 39 DR 43). A7.69

Costs

There is no right to costs for an accused under the ECHR (*Lutz v Germany* (1987) 10 EHRR 182 at [59], where a court refused to reimburse costs after proceedings against the applicant for road traffic offences were discontinued). However, where the court has a discretion to order costs, it must respect the presumption of innocence (*Minelli v Switzerland* (1983) 5 EHRR 554 at [37]). The presumption of innocence will not necessarily be infringed where costs are not awarded in a case where, by not disclosing his defence, the accused prolonged the proceedings against him (*Byrne v UK* [1998] EHRLR 626). A7.70

EVIDENCE

The Burden of Proof and the Presumption of Innocence

As a general rule the presumption of innocence imposes the burden of proving guilt on the prosecution. In *Barbera, Messegue and Jabardo* (1988) 11 EHRR 360, the European Court held (at [77]): A7.71

> [Article 6(2)] embodies the principle of the presumption of innocence. It requires, *inter alia*, that when carrying out their duties, the members of a court should not start with the preconceived idea that the accused has committed the offence charged; the burden of proof is on the prosecution . . .' (see also *Austria v Italy* (1963) 6 Yearbook 740, at p. 782).

However, where the prosecution has proved an offence, the burden of avoiding criminal liability can, within reasonable limits, pass to the defendant (*Lingens v Austria* (1981) 26 DR 171, at [4], which was a criminal prosecution of journalists for writing a defamatory article about a senior politician in which there was a burden on the accused to prove the truth of the statement which was the subject of the complaint as part of the defence).

Similarly, not all presumptions of law and/or fact will offend the presumption of innocence: the question is whether such presumptions remain within reasonable limits. In *Salabiaku v France* (1988) 13 EHRR 379, the European Court held (at [28]):

> Presumptions of fact or of law operate in every legal system. Clearly, the Convention does not prohibit such presumptions in principle. It does, however, require . . . States to remain within certain limits . . . Article 6(2) does not . . . regard presumptions of fact or of law provided for in the criminal law with indifference. It requires States to confine them within reasonable limits which take into account the importance of what is at stake and maintain the rights of the defence.

The relevant factors to be taken into account when assessing whether presumptions of fact or law are confined within reasonable limits were considered by the House of Lords in *Lambert* [2002] 2 AC 545 and *Johnstone* [2003] 1 WLR 1736 (see also *Sheldrake v DPP* [2005] 1 AC 264). The relevant principles are fully discussed at **F3.13** ***et seq.***

Standard of Proof

A7.72 Any doubt in criminal cases must be resolved in favour of the accused: see *Austria v Italy* (1963) 6 Yearbook 740, at p. 784 and *Barbera, Messegue and Jabardo* (1988) 11 EHRR 360.

Right to Call and Examine Witnesses

A7.73 **ECHR, Article 6**

> (3) Everyone charged with a criminal offence has the following minimum rights:
>
> . . .
>
> (d) to examine or have examined witnesses against him and to obtain the attendance and examination of witnesses on his behalf under the same conditions as witnesses against him.

This rule has not been applied inflexibly and there are certain circumstances in which hearsay evidence is permitted under the ECHR (see A7.74). Nonetheless, Article 6(3)(d) does embody the principle that there should be equality of arms between the parties before the court and this includes the right to advance and to challenge evidence in court. In *Krcmar v Czech Republic* (2001) 31 EHRR 41, the European Court held (at [40]):

> . . . the concept of a fair hearing also implies the right to adversarial proceedings, according to which the parties must have the opportunity not only to make known any evidence needed for their claims to succeed, but also to have knowledge of, and comment on, all evidence adduced or observations filed, with a view to influencing the courts' decision . . .

In addition Article 6 can require positive steps to be taken to ensure that the accused can confront and call witnesses (*Barbera, Messegue and Jabardo* (1988) 11 EHRR 360, at [78])

Steps legitimately taken to protect witnesses will not breach Article 6, for example, where special measures are taken to protect child witnesses (*R (D) v Camberwell Green Youth Court* [2005] 1 WLR 393).

Hearsay Evidence

As a general rule, under the ECHR, all the evidence should be produced in the presence of the accused at a public hearing. However, there are exceptions and reliance on hearsay evidence does not necessarily breach the ECHR: e.g., where there is some opportunity to challenge the evidence at an earlier committal hearing (*Kostovski v Netherlands* (1989) 12 EHRR 434 at [41]; *Trivedi v UK* (1997) EHRLR 521). But hearsay evidence must be kept within strict limits, 'having regard to the place that the right to a fair administration of justice holds in a democratic society, any measures restricting the rights of the defence should be strictly necessary. If a less restrictive measure can suffice then that measure should be applied' (*Van Mechelen and others v Netherlands* (1997) 25 EHRR 647 at [59]). The question in each case is whether there has been overall fairness (*Unterpertinger v Austria* (1968) 13 EHRR 175; *Kostovski v Netherlands*). Organising criminal proceedings in such a way as to protect the interests of child witnesses is legitimate, particularly where sexual offences are concerned, but clear and precise reasons are needed if the evidence of a child witness is to be admitted without any opportunity of challenge by the defence (*TS v Germany* (2005) 36 EHRR 1139). **A7.74**

Non-compellable Witnesses Hearsay evidence of non-compellable witnesses, such as close relatives or partners, can be relied upon (*Unterpertinger v Austria* (1968) 13 EHRR 175 at [30]; *Asch v Austria* (1991) 15 EHRR 597 at [28]). But this is subject to strict limits: such evidence should not be the sole or decisive evidence upon which conviction is based (*Asch v Austria* at [30]). **A7.75**

Illness and Death Hearsay evidence of witnesses who are too ill to attend court or who have died can be relied upon so long as there are counterbalancing factors to protect the defendant. Before resorting to such hearsay evidence, the court must conduct a careful inquiry to ensure that the trial will be fair despite the admission of hearsay evidence (*Ferrantelli and Santengelo v Italy* (1996) 23 EHRR 288; *Bricmont v Belgium* (1989) 12 EHRR 217; *Trivedi v UK* (1997) EHRLR 521; *MK v Austria* (1997) 24 EHRR CD 59). **A7.76**

Absconding Witnesses Hearsay evidence from witnesses who simply fail to appear at trial should rarely be relied upon (*Delta v France* (1990) 16 EHRR 574). However, the ECHR will not necessarily be breached where the relevant authorities can show that they have made extensive efforts to locate the witness and that his evidence is corroborated (*Doorson v Netherlands* (1996) 22 EHRR 330). **A7.77**

Fear of Reprisals Hearsay evidence of witnesses who genuinely fear reprisals if they attend court to give evidence can be relied upon, so long as there are counterbalancing factors to protect the defendant (*Saidi v France* (1993) 17 EHRR 251). **A7.78**

Anonymous Witnesses

Evidence from anonymous witnesses should be treated with caution under the ECHR, Article 6. In *Kostovski v The Netherlands* (1989) 12 EHRR 434, the European Court held (at [42] and [44]): **A7.79**

> If the defence is unaware of the identity of the person it seeks to question, it may be deprived of the very particulars enabling it to demonstrate that he or she is prejudiced, hostile or unreliable. Testimony or other declarations inculpating an accused may well be designedly untruthful or simply erroneous and the defence will scarcely be able to bring this to light if it lacks the information permitting it to test the author's reliability or cast doubt on his credibility . . . Although the growth in organised crime doubtless demands the introduction of appropriate measures, the Government's submissions appear . . . to lay insufficient weight on . . . 'the interest of everybody in a civilised society in a controllable and fair judicial procedure.' The right to a fair administration of justice holds so prominent a place in a democratic society that it cannot be sacrificed to expediency. The Convention does not preclude reliance at the investigation stage of criminal proceedings, on sources such as anonymous informants. However,

> the subsequent use of anonymous statements as sufficient evidence to found a conviction . . . is a different matter.

But evidence from anonymous witnesses can be relied upon, where justified, so long as there are counterbalancing factors to protect the defendant (*Doorson v The Netherlands* (1996) 22 EHRR 330). Cogent and specific evidence will be needed before anonymous evidence from law enforcement officers can be relied upon (*Van Mechelen and others v The Netherlands* (1997) 25 EHRR 647 at [61]).

Accomplice Evidence

A7.80 Reliance on the evidence of an accomplice is not prohibited under the ECHR (*X v Austria* (1962) Appln. No. 1599/62) but it may put in doubt the fairness of the proceedings if there are insufficient safeguards to protect the accused. Close scrutiny and control is called for. In *Baragiola v Switzerland* (1993) 75 DR 76; *X v UK* (1976) 7 DR 115, the European Commission held (at p. 118):

> . . . the sentences imposed on the co-defendants who had given evidence for the prosecution were considerably reduced and alleviated . . . As they ran the risk of losing the advantages they had been given if they went back on their previous statements or retracted their confessions, their statements were open to question. It was therefore necessary for the . . . courts to adopt a critical approach in assessing the statements.

Effective cross-examination is a minimum requirement: see *MH v UK* (1997) EHRLR 279 at pp. 279–80, the accused in that case had been unable to cross-examine a former accomplice witness on his guilty plea which had been admitted in evidence against him. The same result followed in *Luca v Italy* (2003) 36 EHRR 807, where the applicant was convicted of drug trafficking on the basis of statements from a co-accused whom he had never been given a chance to cross-examine.

Evidence of Informers and Undercover Officers

A7.81 Reliance on the evidence of informers and undercover officers is not prohibited under the ECHR, but safeguards are necessary to protect the rights of the defence (*Ludi v Switzerland* (1992) 15 EHRR 173, see also *X v Germany* (1989) 11 EHRR 84, where evidence was obtained by a ruse when an undercover officer posed as a remand prisoner). The defence must have the opportunity to challenge the evidence (*Ludi v Switzerland* at [49]). Moreover, the proceedings as a whole will be unfair if the informer or undercover officer incited the commission of an offence which would not otherwise have been committed (see **A7.39** and **F2.26**).

Unlawfully Obtained Evidence

A7.82 Evidence obtained in breach of absolute rights (such as rights under the ECHR, Article 3) should always be excluded from trial (*Ludi v Switzerland* (1992) 15 EHRR 173) (on the approach to be taken by domestic courts to evidence that may have been obtained by oppression, see the House of Lords decision in *Mushtaq* [2005] 1 WLR 1513). Evidence obtained by torture is inadmissible in any legal proceedings (*A v Secretary of State (No. 2)* [2006] 2 AC 221); for the approach of the European Court to such evidence, see *Jalloh v Germany* (Appln. 54810/00). Otherwise, the mere fact that evidence has been obtained in breach of qualified rights under the ECHR does not automatically lead to its exclusion. In *Khan v UK* (2001) 31 EHRR 1016, the European Court adopted the following approach (at [34]):

> The question which must be answered is whether the proceedings as a whole, including the way in which the evidence was obtained, were fair. This involves an examination of the 'unlawfulness' in question and, where violation of another Convention right is concerned, the nature of the violation found.

The central question under Article 6 is therefore overall fairness. Relevant to that assessment will be whether the breach of Convention rights was in good faith or not — and whether there was any element of entrapment or inducement. Whether the unlawfully obtained evidence is the only evidence against the accused will also be relevant, but not determinative (*Khan v UK* (2001) 31 EHRR 1016 at [36]).

The Protection against Self-incrimination

A7.83 The right to a fair trial includes 'the right of anyone charged with a criminal offence . . . to remain silent and not to contribute to incriminating himself' (*Funke v France* (1993) 16 EHRR 297). In *Saunders v UK* (1996) 23 EHRR 313, the European Court explained (at [68]) that:

> . . . although not specifically mentioned in Article 6 of the Convention, the right to silence and the right not to incriminate oneself, are generally recognised international standards which lie at the heart of the notion of a fair procedure under Article 6. Their rationale lies, *inter alia*, in the protection of the accused against improper compulsion by the authorities thereby contributing to the avoidance of miscarriages of justice and to the fulfilment of the aims of Article 6. The right not to incriminate oneself, in particular, presupposes that the prosecution in a criminal case seek to prove their case against the accused without resort to evidence obtained through methods of coercion or oppression in defiance of the will of the accused. In this sense the right is closely linked to the presumption of innocence contained in Article 6(2).

The protection against self-incrimination applies to criminal proceedings in respect of all types of criminal cases without distinction from the most simple to the most complex (*Saunders v UK* at [74]). It is not confined to statements of admission of wrongdoing or to remarks which are directly incriminating (*Saunders v UK*; see also *Heaney and McGuiness v Ireland* (2001) 33 EHRR 264, where failure by the applicants to account for their movements attracted adverse inferences). However, it does not protect individuals from taking the oath, which is designed to ensure that statements made are truthful (*Serves v France* (1999) 28 EHRR 267). The mere fact that the police place a police informant in a cell with an accused prisoner in the hope that he may say something to incriminate himself will not necessarily breach Article 6. But if that individual induces the accused person to incriminate himself by persistent questioning at the insistence of the police, Article 6 will be breached (see *Allan v UK* (2003) 36 EHRR 143).

However, the protection from self-incrimination is not absolute (see the comments of the European Court in *Saunders v UK* at [74]). A presumption that the owner of a car is responsible for speeding and parking offences does not necessarily breach the protection against self-incrimination (*Tora Tolmos v Spain* (17 May 1995) Appln. 23816/94; *D.N. v Netherlands* (26 May 1975) Appln. 6170/73; *J.P., K.R. and G.G. v Austria* (5 September 1989) Appln. 15135/89). In *Brown v Stott* [2003] 1 AC 681, the Privy Council found no violation of Article 6 where the statement made by an appellant under the RTA 1988, s. 172 was used by the prosecution against her (see **F9.25**). In *Weh v Austria* (2005) 40 EHRR 890, the European Court found no breach of Article 6 where the registered owner of a car was fined for failing to disclose the identity of the driver at the time of a speeding incident. Since no proceedings were contemplated against the registered owner, the European Court held that it was not a case that concerned compulsorily obtained information used in criminal proceedings.

Moreover, it is not the compulsory questioning as such that infringes the ECHR: it is the use in criminal proceedings of answers elicited as a result of criminal proceedings to incriminate a defendant (*Saunders v UK* at [67]; *Abas v Netherlands* (1997) Appln. 27943/95). Permitting the court to draw adverse inferences from silence does not equate with compulsory questioning and is permitted within limits (*John Murray v UK* (1996) 22 EHRR 29 at [46]–[52]; *Condron v UK* (2001) 31 EHRR 1). But where inferences can be drawn from an accused's silence during police interview, it is essential that he or she should have access to a lawyer before interview (*John Murray v UK* (1996) 22 EHRR 29 at [66]). Furthermore, where inferences can be drawn from an accused's silence during police interview, it is essential that the trial judge give due weight to the explanation advanced for that silence (see *Beckles v UK* (2003) 36 EHRR 162, where the trial judge failed to direct the jury properly when the accused remained silent on his solicitor's advice).

Intimate Samples

A7.84 The protection against self-incrimination does not prevent the use in criminal proceedings of intimate body samples obtained by compulsion. In *Saunders v UK* (1996) 23 EHRR 313, the European Court held (at [69]):

> . . . [the right not to incriminate oneself] does not extend to the use in criminal proceedings of material which may be obtained from the accused through the use of compulsory powers but which has an existence independent of the will of the suspect such as, inter alia, documents acquired pursuant to a warrant, breath, blood and urine samples and bodily tissues for the purpose of DNA testing.

Expert Evidence

A7.85 The principle that there must be equality between prosecution and defence applies in relation to expert witnesses (*Bonisch v Austria* (1985) 9 EHRR 191). But the mere fact that a court-appointed expert works at the same institute as the expert relied upon by the prosecution does not automatically breach the ECHR, Article 6 (*Brandstetter v Austria* (1991) 15 EHRR 378).

SENTENCE

Fair Trial Guarantees in Sentencing

A7.86 The fair trial requirements of the ECHR, Article 6 do not cease to apply at the sentencing stage, but the requirements do not apply in the same way. The presumption of innocence ceases to apply (*Engel v Netherlands* (1979–80) 1 EHRR 647 at [90]). For a similar approach under the Canadian Charter of Rights, see *R v Gardiner* (1982) 2 SCR 368.

Retroactive Penalties

A7.87 Article 7 of the ECHR, which protects individuals from being convicted of criminal offences which did not exist at the time the act was committed, also prohibits the imposition of a more severe penalty for an offence than that which applied at the time the offence was committed. The concept of a 'penalty' is autonomous: to render the protection offered by Article 7 effective, courts must be free to go behind appearances and assess for themselves whether a particular measure amounts in substance to a penalty (*Welch v UK* (1995) 20 EHRR 247). Factors relevant to this assessment are whether the measure in question was imposed following conviction for a criminal offence, the nature and purpose of the measure in question, its characterisation under national law, the procedure involved in the making and implementation of the measure and its severity.

A requirement to register under the Sexual Offences Act 2003 is not a penalty within the meaning of Article 7 (*Ibbotson v UK* [1999] Crim LR 153: see E25.1). Confiscation proceedings which permit courts to seize assets acquired before legislation came into force will not breach Article 7 so long as the legislation was in place before the offence giving rise to the confiscation proceedings was committed (*Welch v UK (*1995) 20 EHRR 247; *Taylor v UK* (1998) Appln. 31209/96). But where the definition of 'recidivist' is changed to include those convicted up to ten years before a second offence (and triggering extended sentence provisions), Article 7 may be breached (*Achour v France* (2005) 41 EHRR 751).

Proportionality in Sentencing

Where an individual is sentenced for conduct protected as a qualified right under the ECHR, any punishment must be proportionate (*Arrowsmith v UK* (1978) 19 DR 5). In *Price v UK* (2002) 34 EHRR 1285, the European Court held that to detain a severely disabled person in conditions where she was dangerously cold, ill and unable to use the toilet constituted degrading treatment under Article 3. See also *Mouisel v France* (2004) 38 EHRR 735, where the European Court found a breach of Article 3 where the relevant authorities failed to take sufficient care of the conditions in which the applicant, a prisoner suffering from leukaemia, was transferred to and from hospital. **A7.88**

Preventative Sentences

ECHR, Article 5 **A7.89**

> (4) Everyone who is deprived of his liberty by arrest or detention shall be entitled to take proceedings by which the lawfulness of his detention shall be decided speedily by a court and his release ordered if the detention is not lawful.

Where individuals are sentenced solely for the purposes of retribution, deterrence or protection of the public, Article 5(4) will be engaged as soon as the punitive part of the sentence is served and the preventative component begins. The key question at that stage is whether the prisoner's dangerousness continues to justify his detention.

APPEALS

Fair Trial Guarantees at the Appeal Stage

There is no requirement under the ECHR to set up an appeal procedure. Limitations can therefore be placed on the right to appeal, including time limits, so long as they are reasonable and proportionate (*Bricmont v Belgium* (1986) 48 DR 106, at p. 151). If time-limits for appealing are imposed, the relevant authorities are under a duty to inform the defendant of these limits (*Vacher v France* (1996) 24 EHRR 482, Appln. 20366/92, at [28]). **A7.90**

Although there is no requirement under the ECHR to set up an appeal procedure, where such an appeal procedure is set up, it must conform to Article 6 principles (*Delcourt v Belgium* (1970) 1 EHRR 335 at [25]). Inevitably, the way in which these principles are applied will not be the same as at trial and will depend upon the special features of appeal proceedings. In *Monnell & Morris v UK* (1987) 10 EHRR 205, the European Court held (at [56]):

> The manner in which paragraph 1, as well as paragraph 3(c), of Article 6 is to be applied in relation to appellate or cassation courts depends upon the special features of the proceedings involved. Account must be taken of the entirety of the proceedings conducted in the domestic legal order and of the role of the appellate or cassation court therein.

Where a court, including a court of appeal, has power to substitute a conviction for an offence other than that with which an individual is actually charged, the defence must be afforded an opportunity to deal with the alternative charge (*Pelissier v France* (2000) 30 EHRR 715, substitution of aiding and abetting for principal offence by the court of appeal). This is particularly so where it is conceivable that the defence would have been different.

Leave to Appeal

Article 6 of the ECHR applies to leave proceedings since these constitute part of the determination of the criminal charge (*Monnell & Morris v UK* (1987) 10 EHRR 205, at [54]). However, the limited nature of proceedings for leave to appeal may not require a full public hearing (*Monnell & Morris v UK* at [57] and [58]). Similarly, full reasons may not be needed at the leave stage (*Webb v UK* (1997) 24 EHRR CD 73 at p. 74). **A7.91**

Legal Aid and Legal Representation

A7.92 The interests of justice require that an appellant be granted legal aid where the case is a complex one and/or there are serious consequences at stake. The ability of the accused to understand the proceedings and effectively participate will be relevant in determining whether he requires legal assistance (*Granger v UK* (1990) 12 EHRR 469 at [46] and [47] — refusal of legal aid in appeal against conviction for perjury).

The more severe the potential penalty if the appeal is unsuccessful, the greater the need for representation *(Maxwell v UK* (1994) 19 EHRR 97 at [38]–[40]). But the prospects of success are important (*Monnell and Morris v UK* (1987) 10 EHRR 205 at [67]). Decisions about legal aid should be kept under review (*Granger v UK* at [46]).

Right to a Hearing

A7.93 The right to a public hearing does not automatically extend to every stage of the proceedings provided the process viewed as a whole has been fair. The nature of the appellate stage will determine whether a hearing is required. Where the appeal court is merely required to assess points of law which do not require oral argument, the need for a rehearing can be dispensed with (*Axen v Germany* (1983) 6 EHRR 195 at [28]). In contrast, where the court is having to determine the appellant's guilt or innocence based upon examination of law and the facts, there is a greater need for a full hearing (*Ekbatani v Sweden* (1988) 13 EHRR 504 at [32]).

Right to be Present

A7.94 There is no absolute rule that an appellant must be present during appellate proceedings: it depends what issues are being considered. Where on appeal the court is simply reviewing the findings of fact below, no new facts are adduced and there is no prospect of the sentence being increased, there is no duty on the authorities to ensure that the accused is present, particularly where he is represented (*Prinz v Austria* (2001) 31 EHRR 357 at [34]; see also *Belziuk v Poland* (2000) 30 EHRR 614). But where an assessment of the facts, or more particularly the appellant's mental state, are in issue, he should be present (*Cooke v Austria* (2001) 31 EHRR 338 at [42]; since the applicant's sentence could have been increased and the determination of this issue involved a fresh assessment of his mental state at the time of the killing, the presence of the applicant was essential; see also *Kamasinski v Austria* (1989) 13 EHRR 36 at [106]–[107]). Even where the sentence cannot be increased, the attendance of the accused may be required if the appeal court is likely to consider the motive for the offence and/or the accused's personality and character (*Pobornikoff v Austria* (2003) 36 EHRR 418).

Penalties for Appealing

A7.95 Loss of time as a penalty for appealing will not necessarily breach the ECHR (*Monnell & Morris v UK* (1987) 10 EHRR 205 at [46]). Nor will an increase in sentence which reflects an appeal court's re-assessment of the facts of the offence and any aggravating features necessarily breach the ECHR (*De Salvador Torres v Spain* (1996) 23 EHRR 601).

Extent to which Appeal Court may Remedy Trial Defects

A7.96 As a general rule, the whole of the proceedings, including any appeal, are relevant to an assessment of fairness under the ECHR, Article 6 (*Edwards v UK* (1992) 15 EHRR 417, non-disclosure at first instance). However, in some respects, an appeal court will not be able to rectify fairness problems that arose at trial: e.g., where a trial judge misdirects the jury on the question of adverse inferences (*Condron v UK* (2001) 31 EHRR 1 at [63]). Nor can an appeal court provide the required scrutiny in cases where material is not disclosed on grounds of pubic interest immunity (*Rowe and Davies v UK* (2000) 30 EHRR 1 at [65]).

Reasons in Appeal Cases

As a general rule, reasons should be given in an appeal hearing. However, full reasons need not necessarily be given at the leave stage (*Webb v UK* (1997) 24 EHRR CD 73; *X v Germany* (1981) 25 DR 240). A7.97

New Evidence

Once a person has been convicted and is therefore no longer 'charged with a criminal offence', establishing a duty on the relevant authorities to review the case in the light of new evidence is difficult (*X v Austria* (1962) 9 EHRR CD 17, at p. 21). However, where a procedure already exists for an appeal court to examine new evidence and determine whether it warrants a re-trial, the ECHR, Article 6 will apply (*Callaghan v UK* (1989) 60 DR 296). Failure to order a new trial will constitute a breach of the right to fair trial only if the appeal court declines to assess the new evidence (*Callaghan v UK* at pp. 300 to 302). A7.98

Section A8 Territorial and Extra-territorial Jurisdiction

INTRODUCTION

A8.1 A distinction must be drawn between the ambit of English criminal law, on the one hand, and 'venue', or the jurisdiction of particular courts, on the other. Things done beyond the ambit of English law cannot amount to offences under that law. Whether English law applies in a given case is therefore a question of substantive law, rather than one of procedure; but where English law does apply there are no longer any territorial restrictions on the jurisdiction of particular courts to try the alleged offence.

By the Supreme Court Act 1981, s. 46(1), the Crown Court has jurisdiction in proceedings on indictment for offences wherever committed, and in particular proceedings on indictment for offences within the jurisdiction of the Admiralty of England.

By the MCA 1980, s. 2(1), magistrates' courts are similarly free of territorial limitations on their criminal jurisdiction. Jurisdiction over summary offences was previously limited (with some exceptions) to offences committed within a court's own commission area, or within 500 yards of the boundary between that and another commission area, but this limitation was removed by the Courts Act 2003, s. 44.

TERRITORIAL JURISDICTION

The General Rule

A8.2 English criminal law applies throughout the realm of England and Wales and over all persons who come within the realm. Even though some such persons (e.g., foreign diplomats) may enjoy immunity from prosecution, they are nevertheless required to obey the law, and diplomatic immunity may in some cases be waived (see **A8.17**).

In contrast, English criminal law does not ordinarily extend to things done outside the realm, even when done by British citizens (see *Harden* [1963] 1 QB 8). Specific statutory provision is required before any part of English criminal law can apply to conduct abroad or indeed to things done in other parts of the UK, which have their own jurisdiction over crime. The common law had no extra-territorial ambit, and in the absence of such provision, a statutory offence is presumed subject to similar constraints. As Viscount Simonds said in *Cox v Army Council* [1963] AC 48, at p. 67:

> Apart from those exceptional cases in which specific provision is made in respect of acts committed abroad, the whole body of the criminal law of England deals only with acts committed in England.

Parliament may give an offence whatever extra-territorial application it thinks fit, but must do so expressly. Lord Morris of Borth-y-Gest explained the position in *Treacy v DPP* [1971] AC 537 (at pp. 552–3):

> In general, . . . acts committed out of England, even though they are committed by British subjects, are not punishable under the criminal law of this country. But, as Parliament is supreme, it is open to Parliament to pass an enactment in relation to such acts. It is, however, a

> general rule of construction that unless there is something which points to a contrary intention a statute will be taken to apply only to the UK. It would be open to Parliament to enact that if a British subject committed anywhere an act designated as blackmail he would commit an offence punishable in England. Such an enactment would, however, have to be in clear and express terms: specific provision would have to be made with regard to acts committed abroad . . .

Even where a statutory offence applies throughout the UK, the commission of an offence in Scotland or Northern Ireland does not ordinarily give rise to any liability under English law (or vice versa). Similarly, where the laws of British overseas territories (such as the Falkland Islands) incorporate elements of English criminal law, this does not make misconduct in such territories punishable in England and Wales.

The Territorial Limits

The realm (which marks the limit of criminal jurisdiction at common law) comprises the land territory of England and Wales and the airspace above it. It now includes the English section of the Channel Tunnel system (Channel Tunnel Act 1987, s. 10). The seaward boundary of the realm is in most cases the water's edge, but the realm includes such internal waters (bays, harbours, etc.) as lie within county boundaries. **A8.3**

By the Territorial Waters Jurisdiction Act 1878, ss. 2 and 7, English criminal law also applies (in respect of offences triable on indictment) to things done on the open sea within territorial limits. This ordinarily means within 12 nautical miles of the low water mark around the coast, or of a line drawn across the mouth of a designated bay or estuary (Territorial Waters Order in Council 1964; Territorial Sea Act 1987). A person who is not a British subject (as to which see **A8.12**) may not ordinarily be prosecuted under that Act for a crime committed aboard a foreign ship, unless a Principal Secretary of State certifies that the institution of such proceedings is expedient (see s. 3 of the 1878 Act), but note that this does not apply to prosecutions for drug trafficking offences under the Criminal Justice (International Co-operation) Act 1990, s. 19; and note also that territorial or internal waters adjacent to the coast of Scotland are now deemed to be part of Scotland (Scotland Act 1998, s. 126) and thus outwith English jurisdiction.

By the Criminal Jurisdiction (Offshore Activities) Order 1987 (SI 1987 No. 2198) and the Petroleum Act 1998, s. 10, English criminal law also extends to things done on (or within 500 metres of) platforms in designated areas of the continental shelf within which the UK claims rights to the seabed and natural resources. As to restrictions on prosecutions for certain offences, see the Petroleum Act 1998, s. 12.

CROSS-FRONTIER OFFENCES

The General Rule

An offence may be committed within England and Wales even where some elements or consequences occur abroad, at least in cases where the last essential constituent element of the offence takes place (i.e. the offence is completed) within England and Wales (*Harden* [1963] 1 QB 8; *Treacy v DPP* [1971] AC 537). In the case of a conduct crime, such as blackmail, the offence is complete upon the commission of the conduct in question, which in the case of blackmail is the making of the unwarranted demand. If this occurs within the jurisdiction, it matters not whether the intended consequences occur abroad, or indeed whether they occur at all (*Treacy*). In the case of a result crime, jurisdiction is established upon the occurrence of any specified result within England and Wales (*Secretary of State for Trade v Markus* [1976] AC 35). If the victim of an act of violence abroad subsequently dies in an English hospital, it seems odd to regard this as a case of murder or manslaughter 'committed in England', but the principle is firmly established in English law. **A8.4**

The position is less clear where some essential elements take place within the jurisdiction, but completion of the offence occurs elsewhere. As the Court of Appeal noted in *Manning* [1998] 2 Cr App R 461, a clear preponderance of authority suggests that, in the absence of specific statutory provision (such as may be found in the CJA 1993, part 1 (see **A8.7**), this does not suffice to establish jurisdiction. Under the 'terminatory' or 'last act' requirement, a crime is deemed to be committed only where it is completed. See, e.g., *Harden* [1963] 1 QB 8, *DPP v Stonehouse* [1978] AC 55 and *Nanayakkara* [1987] 1 WLR 265.

In *Smith (Wallace Duncan)* [1996] 2 Cr App R 1 and *Smith (Wallace Duncan) (No. 4)* [2004] QB 418, however, the Court of Appeal held that a crime may sometimes be committed within the jurisdiction, even where the last constituent element takes place abroad. Giving judgment in the latter case, Lord Woolf CJ justified this departure from precedent by reasoning that the terminatory requirement 'leads to a wholly unsatisfactory situation in contemporary circumstances' and that 'questions of jurisdiction, although they involve substantive law, have a strong procedural element and are less immutable than issues of pure substantive law'.

With respect, questions concerning the ambit of the criminal law are not in any real sense procedural, but concern the most fundamental of issues. Where (and to whom) does the criminal law apply? *Smith (Wallace Duncan) (No. 4)* is binding on trial courts, but in view of the conflict with *Manning* and earlier cases it may still be open to challenge on appeal. If *Smith* is correctly decided, the earlier enactment of the CJA 1993, part 1, which makes special provision for jurisdiction over acts of cross-frontier fraud and dishonesty, was ultimately proved unnecessary.

The terminatory approach to jurisdiction (and indeed the wider approach adopted in *Smith*) is capable of leading to the conviction under English law of a foreigner in respect of conduct abroad that has only indirectly produced a proscribed result within the jurisdiction. In *Perrin* [2002] EWCA Crim 747, for example, a French citizen was convicted in England of an offence under the Obscene Publications Act 1959, s. 2(1), merely because the contents of his foreign-based web site were accessed and downloaded (and thus 'published') by a police officer in England. No evidence was adduced as to whether this material was illegal under the law of the country from which it was uploaded.

Inchoate and Secondary Liability

A8.5 As to the rules governing inchoate offences of a cross-frontier kind, see **A6.3** (incitement at common law and under the Sexual Offences (Conspiracy and Incitement) Act 1996); **B1.112** (solicitation of murder); **B10.73** (incitement of terrorism abroad); **A6.23** (statutory conspiracy); **A6.29** (conspiracy to defraud) and **A6.38** (criminal attempts).

In respect of secondary offenders, the general rule is that if (but only if) D commits an offence in England, E may be liable as a secondary party to that offence, even if he has himself done nothing within the jurisdiction. In *Robert Millar (Contractors) Ltd* [1970] 2 QB 54, a fatal road accident occurred on a motorway in England when a visibly worn and defective front tyre on a lorry blew out at speed. The driver admitted causing death by dangerous driving, and the appellants, a Scottish haulage company and its managing director, were convicted as secondary parties, on the basis that they knew of the defect when they despatched the lorry from its Glasgow depot. The Court of Appeal rejected an argument that the appellants had done nothing in England. Fenton Atkinson LJ said:

> The offence of causing death by dangerous driving was committed in England . . . but the appellants are guilty of participating in that crime and not of some self-subsisting crime on their own account and, therefore, they are in the same position as the principal offender and they are liable to be tried in this country.

Statutory Provisions

A number of statutory provisions create special jurisdictional rules for specific offences or classes of offence. These include the OAPA 1861, s. 10 (see **B1.9**), which makes special provision for offences of murder or manslaughter in which an unlawful wound etc. in England leads to death abroad (or vice versa) and the Perjury Act 1911, s. 1(4) and (5) (see **B14.1** ***et seq.***), which deal with statements made abroad for the purpose of proceedings within the jurisdiction (and vice versa). **A8.6**

More recent provisions include the CJA 1993, part 1, which makes special provision for specified offences of cross-frontier fraud, blackmail or dishonesty, and the Computer Misuse Act 1990, ss. 4 to 7 (see **B18.4** and **B18.20**), which make special provision for offences involving unauthorised access to or modification of computer material.

Criminal Justice Act 1993

Faced with modern forms of international fraud and dishonesty, the traditional 'terminatory' approach to identifying the *locus* of a crime (see **A8.2**) was manifestly inadequate. As Buxton LJ pointed out in *Manning* [1998] 2 Cr App R 461, strict application of that principle would all too often mean that 'plainly dishonest conduct with a strong connection with this country [could not] be tried here'. The CJA 1993, part 1, which did not come into force until 1 June 1999, addresses this problem by introducing special rules in respect of designated offences, which are then divided into substantive 'Group A offences' and inchoate 'Group B offences'. **A8.7**

The Group A offences listed in s. 1 now comprise:

- offences under the TA 1968, ss. 1 (theft), 17 (false accounting), 19 (false statements by company directors, etc.), 21 (blackmail), 22 (handling stolen goods) and 24A (retaining credits from dishonest sources, etc.);
- offences under the Fraud Act 2006, ss. 1 (fraud), 6 (possession etc. of articles for use in frauds), 7 (making or supplying articles for use in frauds), 9 (participating in fraudulent business carried on by sole trader, etc.) and 11 (obtaining services dishonestly);
- offences under the Forgery and Counterfeiting Act 1981, ss. 1 (forgery), 2 (copying a false instrument), 3 (using a false instrument), 4 (using a copy of a false instrument), 5 (offences relating to money orders, share certificates, passports, etc.), 14 (counterfeiting notes and coins), 15 (passing etc. counterfeit notes and coins), 16 (custody or control of counterfeit notes and coins), 17 (making or custody or control of counterfeiting materials, etc.), 20 (importation of counterfeit notes and coins) and 21 (exportation of counterfeit notes and coins);
- offences under the Identity Cards Act 2006, s. 25; and
- cheating the public revenue.

The Group B offences are: conspiracy to commit a Group A offence (see **A6.23**); conspiracy to defraud (see **A6.29**); attempting to commit a Group A offence (see **A6.38**); and incitement to commit a Group A offence (see **A6.3**). The Secretary of State may by order add or remove any offence from either list (CJA 1993, s. 1(4)).

Prior to 15 January 2007, the Group A list included offences of deception under the TA 1968, ss. 15, 15A, 16, 17 and 20(2), and under the TA 1978, ss. 1 and 2. These offences were all repealed on that date by the Fraud Act 2006 but, under transitional provisions in that Act (see sch. 2, para. 3), this repeal 'does not affect any liability, investigation, legal proceeding or penalty for or in respect of any [deception] offence partly committed before commencement'.

No transitional arrangements have been made in respect of the jurisdiction provisions in the CJA 1993, however. This should not hinder prosecutions for alleged cases of cross-frontier deception dating entirely from before 15 January 2007, but may cause difficulty should the Crown seek to prosecute a defendant for a cross-frontier deception offence allegedly committed only partly before that date (e.g., where a deception before that date in England results after that date in the obtaining of property abroad).

This is unsatisfactory, but if *Smith (Wallace Duncan) (No. 4)* [2004] QB 418 is correctly decided (see **A8.4**), jurisdiction may be established over such cases even without recourse to the Act.

Relevant Events under the Criminal Justice Act 1993

A8.8 The key to establishing jurisdiction under the CJA 1993 is the occurrence of a 'relevant event' within England and Wales. Where such an event occurs, it is irrelevant whether the accused was a British citizen or whether he was at any material time in England and Wales (s. 3(1)). A relevant event is defined for most purposes as any event that is an essential element of the offence in question. It is not sufficient that some preparatory event occurred in England if that event is not itself a definitional element of the offence charged. Nor in a case such as *Atakpu* [1994] QB 69 (see **B4.27**), is there any relevant act of theft in England where D steals a car abroad and (having already completed that theft) brings the stolen car into England.

Special provision is made in s. 2(1A) for the new offence of fraud. Fraud is a conduct crime in which the actual making of a gain or the causing of a loss to another forms no part of the offence at all. But for s. 2(1A), a fraud successfully practised from abroad on a victim in England would not necessarily fall within English jurisdiction. See further **B5.100**.

Criminal Justice Act 1993, s. 2

(1) For the purposes of this Part, 'relevant event', in relation to any Group A offence, means (subject to subsection (1A)) any act or omission or other event (including any result of one or more acts or omissions) proof of which is required for conviction of the offence.

(1A) In relation to an offence under section 1 of the Fraud Act 2006 (fraud), 'relevant event' includes—

(a) if the fraud involved an intention to make a gain and the gain occurred, that occurrence;

(b) if the fraud involved an intention to cause a loss or to expose another to a risk of loss and the loss occurred, that occurrence.

(2) For the purpose of determining whether or not a particular event is a relevant event in relation to a Group A offence, any question as to where it occurred is to be disregarded.

(3) A person may be guilty of a Group A offence if any of the events which are relevant events in relation to the offence occurred in England and Wales.

The CJA 1993, s. 4, attempts to provide guidance as to what may constitute the occurrence of an event in England and Wales.

Criminal Justice Act 1993, s. 4

In relation to a Group A or Group B offence—

(a) there is an obtaining of property in England and Wales if the property is either despatched from or received at a place in England and Wales; and

(b) there is a communication in England and Wales of any information, instruction, request, demand or other matter if it is sent by any means:

(i) from a place in England and Wales to a place elsewhere; or

(ii) from a place elsewhere to a place in England and Wales.

The wording of this section is unfortunate, because in contrast to s. 2(1A) it does not provide that such events are necessarily 'relevant events'. 'Obtaining' was of course a 'relevant event' in respect of several deception offences under the Theft Acts, but these are now repealed. The 'communication' of a blackmail demand is not a 'relevant event' for the purposes of the offence of blackmail, because a blackmail demand can be 'made' under the TA 1968, s. 21, without ever being communicated (see *Treacy v DPP* [1971] AC 537 and **B5.87**).

OFFENCES ABOARD SHIPS OR AIRCRAFT

Offences Aboard British or UK ships

British ships (as defined in the Merchant Shipping Act 1995, s. 1) are not properly described as 'floating territory', but do sail under Admiralty jurisdiction when on the high seas (a term which in this context includes berths in foreign or Commonwealth ports (*Anderson* (1868) XI Cox CC 198; *Liverpool Justices, ex parte Molyneaux* [1972] 2 QB 384). Admiralty jurisdiction over indictable offences is now exercised by the ordinary criminal courts (see **A8.1**). **A8.9**

A British ship registered in the UK is a 'United Kingdom ship'. By the Merchant Shipping Act 1995, s. 281, English courts have jurisdiction over any person charged with committing an offence aboard a UK ship on the high seas, 'as if it had been committed on board a UK ship within the limits of its ordinary jurisdiction'. This includes jurisdiction over summary offences. Although s. 281 confusingly refers only to 'offences under this Act', the Magistrates' Courts Act 1980, s. 3A, and the Supreme Court Act 1981 s. 46A, ensure that it is in fact of general application.

Ships include small craft, but jet skis (or 'wet bikes') that are designed and used only for recreational purposes, rather than for navigation, are not considered to be ships at all, even if they have been registered as such in the UK (*Goodwin* [2005] EWCA Crim 3184).

Her Majesty's Ships and Vessels are not 'British ships' within the meaning of the Merchant Shipping Act 1995, but are subject to Admiralty jurisdiction (*Devon Justices, ex parte DPP* [1924] 1 KB 503). As to the position of civilians aboard Her Majesty's ships (or any other ships used for the purposes of any of Her Majesty's forces) see the Armed Forces Act 2006, sch. 15, para. 2, which will, when in force in November 2007, supplant equivalent provisions in the Naval Discipline Act 1957, s. 117.

As to the status of offshore oil and gas platforms, see **A8.3**. As to offences committed by a master or seaman from a UK ship (including offences committed after the loss of such a ship), see **A8.14**.

Offences aboard Foreign Ships, etc.

English criminal law does not ordinarily apply to things done on foreign ships outside English territorial limits but, by the Merchant Shipping Act 1995, s. 281 (see **A8.9**), a British citizen may be prosecuted under English law for an offence committed in a foreign port or harbour or aboard a foreign ship to which he does not belong, 'as if it had been committed on board a UK ship within the limits of its ordinary jurisdiction to try the offence . . .'. **A8.10**

In *Kelly* [1982] AC 665, the House of Lords held that the Merchant Shipping Act 1894, s. 686(1) (from which the current s. 281 is derived), was not merely a 'venue' provision, dealing with the jurisdiction of particular courts (see **A8.1**), but instead made the ordinary rules of English criminal law applicable to things done by British passengers on foreign ships. See also *Cumberworth* (1989) 89 Cr App R 187, in which what is now s. 282 was held to apply even where the foreign ship in question was docked (with its loading ramp lowered) in a foreign port.

A 'foreign ship' is defined by the Merchant Shipping Act 1995, s. 313, as one that is neither a UK ship nor a small unregistered British ship; but the term, 'foreign port or harbour' is narrower in that it excludes ports or harbours in the Republic of Ireland or in any Commonwealth country (*Liverpool Justices, ex parte Molyneux* [1972] 2 QB 384).

As to offences committed aboard ships of 'Convention countries' within the meaning of the Suppression of Terrorism Act 1978 (see **A8.15**), see s. 4(7) of that Act.

As to piracy *iure gentium* and offences under the Aviation and Maritime Security Act 1990, see **B10.196**, **B10.217** *et seq.* and **B10.221**.

Offences Committed in UK Airspace or on Board Aircraft in Flight Elsewhere

A8.11 At common law, land includes the airspace above it, and accordingly it is assumed that English criminal law automatically applies to things done in English airspace; but it does not apply to conduct in the skies over Scotland or Northern Ireland, even if it takes place aboard a British controlled aircraft. Jurisdiction over things done in flight elsewhere is governed by the Civil Aviation Act 1982, s. 92.

Civil Aviation Act 1982, s. 92

(1) Any act or omission taking place on board a British-controlled aircraft or (subject to subsection (1A) below) a foreign aircraft while in flight elsewhere than in or over the UK which, if taking place in, or in a part of, the United Kingdom, would constitute an offence under the law in force in, or in that part of, the United Kingdom shall constitute that offence; but this subsection shall not apply to any act or omission which is expressly or impliedly authorised by or under that law when taking place outside the United Kingdom.

(1A) Subsection (1) above shall only apply to an act or omission which takes place on board a foreign aircraft where—

(a) the next landing of the aircraft is in the United Kingdom, and

(b) in the case of an aircraft registered in a country other than the United Kingdom, the act or omission would, if taking place there, also constitute an offence under the law in force in that country.

(1B) Any act or omission punishable under the law in force in any country is an offence under that law for the purposes of subsection (1A) above, however it is described in that law.

'British-controlled aircraft' are defined in s. 92(5). The consent of the DPP is required in respect of any prosecutions brought in England under s. 92 (see s. 92(2)(a)).

No express provision has been made by legislation for criminal jurisdiction to extend to things done in the airspace above English territorial waters. Waters adjacent to England and Wales are not strictly part of England and Wales (in contrast to Scottish waters, which are now part of Scotland). By the Civil Aviation Act 1982, s. 106, references to the UK are deemed to include airspace above such waters; but this merely serves to *prevent* any possible reliance on s. 92 of the 1982 Act where aircraft are in flight above English waters. The only solution would be for the Territorial Waters Jurisdiction Act 1878 to be construed as extending by implication to such airspace.

As to offences committed in flight aboard aircraft of 'convention countries' within the meaning of the Suppression of Terrorism Act 1978 (see **A8.15**), see s. 4(7) of that Act.

As to terrorist offences and offences under the Aviation Security Act 1982, see **B10** and in particular **B10.198** *et seq.*

EXTRA-TERRITORIAL JURISDICTION

A8.12 Extra-territorial jurisdiction in English criminal law invariably has a statutory basis. Some statutory provisions extend the ambit of English criminal law generally (or substantial parts thereof) to specified classes of person. Persons subject to extra-territorial English criminal jurisdiction of this type include: Crown servants acting or purporting to act in the course of their employment (CJA 1948, s. 31(1)); masters or seamen from UK ships (Merchant Shipping Act 1995, s. 282); and members of the British armed forces or anyone else who is for the time being subject to service law. Such persons may be held liable under English law for extra-territorially committed crimes such as theft, assault or even dangerous driving (as in *Cox v Army Council* [1963] AC 48) which would otherwise have no extra-territorial ambit at all.

Legislation may alternatively provide an extra-territorial ambit to specific offences, as for example it has done in respect of murder or manslaughter on land outside the UK (see **B1.9**), sexual offences committed against children under the age of 16 (see **B3.268**) and a wide range of offences involving terrorism, hijacking or piracy (see generally **B10**).

Extra-territorial jurisdiction is ordinarily limited to things done or omitted by persons who hold some form of British nationality or domicile. There is little consistency in the exact form of British nationality required. Modern statutes typically restrict any extra-territorial application to British citizens (as does the Merchant Shipping Act 1995) or to UK nationals or residents (as does the International Criminal Court Act 2001). Some refer instead to 'United Kingdom persons', a term which includes Scottish partnerships and bodies incorporated in the UK. References in older statutes imposing criminal jurisdiction over 'British subjects', 'subjects of her Majesty' or 'citizens of the United Kingdom and colonies' for things done in foreign or Commonwealth countries or in Ireland must now be construed as references to British citizens, British overseas territories citizens, British overseas citizens, and British nationals (overseas): see the British Nationality Act 1948, s. 3(1), read in conjunction with the British Nationality Act 1981, s. 51.

There is a strong presumption that a provision creating extra-territorial criminal liability will not apply to things done or omitted by foreigners abroad (*Jameson* [1896] 2 QB 425; *Air India v Wiggins* [1980] 1 WLR 815).

In exceptional cases, however, a wider basis of jurisdiction may be specified in accordance with customary international law or specific treaty obligations. This may involve 'universal jurisdiction' over crimes (e.g., piracy, hijacking of aircraft and other offences against aviation security) that are recognised internationally as meriting or demanding such treatment, or it may involve (on a reciprocal convention basis) the assertion of jurisdiction over things done by persons in specified countries or things done elsewhere by nationals of specified countries. See, e.g., the Suppression of Terrorism Act 1978, s. 4 (**A8.15**).

Persons Subject to Armed Service Discipline

Where a British serviceman (or a civilian subject to service discipline) is guilty of conduct **A8.13** anywhere that would in England and Wales have amounted to an offence under English law, he may be charged with an offence under the Armed Forces Act 2006, s. 42. This provision (which should be read in conjunction with ss. 43 to 48) will when brought into force supplant three earlier provisions, namely the Army Act 1955, s. 70, the Air Force Act 1955, s. 70, and the Naval Discipline Act 1957, s. 42.

The relationship between an offence under s. 42 of the 2006 Act and a corresponding offence under the civilian law of England is essentially the same as that under the 1955 legislation and was explained in that context by Lord Rodger of Earlsferry in *Spear* [2002] 3 All ER 1074 (at p. 1088):

> Where anyone who is subject to military law is guilty of an act or omission in England that would be punishable by the law of England, he is also guilty of an offence under [the Army Act 1955] s. 70. Similarly, anyone who is guilty of an act or omission that would be punishable by the law of England if committed in England is guilty of an offence under s. 70 wherever he commits it, whether in some other part of the UK or elsewhere in the world: *Cox v Army Council*. So, for instance, a soldier or airman who possesses cocaine in England is guilty not only of an offence under s. 5(1) of the Misuse of Drugs Act 1971, but also of an offence against s. 70 of the Army Act or the Air Force Act, as the case may be, although he can, of course, be prosecuted for only one of them. If he possesses cocaine while on duty in Afghanistan, on the other hand, he does not commit an offence under s. 5(1) of the 1971 Act since the legislation does not apply there, but he is guilty of an offence under s. 70 of the relevant 1955 Act, because he would have been guilty of a contravention of s. 5(1) if he had been in possession of the drug in England. Offences of this kind, which mirror offences under English criminal law, are referred to as 'civil' offences (s. 70(2)). As s. 70(3) makes clear, these civil offences are triable by court-martial.

By the Armed Forces Act 2006, s. 51 (which will when brought into force supplant equivalent provisions in the Armed Forces Act 1976, s. 7) certain offences committed abroad by civilians subject to service discipline (including some offences under s. 42) may be tried by 'service civilian courts', but this does not extend to offences that would be triable only on indictment if committed within England and Wales.

Masters or Seamen from UK Ships

A8.14 **Merchant Shipping Act 1995, s. 282**

(1) Any act in relation to property or person done in or at any place (ashore or afloat) outside the United Kingdom by any master or seaman who at the time is employed in a United Kingdom ship, which, if done in any part of the United Kingdom, would be an offence under the law of any part of the United Kingdom, shall—
  (a) be an offence under that law, and
  (b) be treated for the purposes of jurisdiction and trial as if it had been done within the jurisdiction of the Admiralty of England.

(2) Subsection (1) above also applies in relation to a person who had been so employed within the period of three months expiring with the time when the act was done.

(3) Subsections (1) and (2) above apply to omissions as they apply to acts.

This provision is not expressly limited to British citizens or UK nationals, but such a limitation must arguably be inferred (see **A8.12**). Nor is it expressly limited to offences triable on indictment, but such a limitation is impliedly imposed by the fact that such offences are triable, 'as if committed within the jurisdiction of the Admiralty of England', because Admiralty jurisdiction does not extend over summary offences.

Section 282 is derived from the Merchant Shipping Act 1854, s. 267, which was the basis upon which jurisdiction was asserted over the shipwrecked cannibals in *Dudley and Stephens* (1884) 24 QBD 273. Note however that it has no application to things done by persons from British ships that are not registered in the UK, or to things done by passengers etc. from any ship. If a passenger from a sunken British vessel kills another in the sea in order to seize his lifejacket or raft, he will commit no offence under English law unless he is within territorial waters at the time.

Offences Committed in 'Convention Countries' or by Nationals of Convention Countries

A8.15 The Suppression of Terrorism Act 1978, s. 4, contains provisions which are little used (and are designed for use only where extradition is for some reason impracticable) but which in theory greatly enlarge the extra-territorial ambit of English criminal law. It must be emphasised that the offences affected need not, as a matter of law, have any connection with terrorism; but prosecutions relying upon s. 4 require the consent of the A-G (s. 4(4)) and, having regard to the overall purpose of the Act, it is doubtful whether such consent would ordinarily be given in the absence of a terrorist connection or some comparable consideration that might justify a prosecution in the public or national interest. In a case of kidnapping, however, the UK's obligations under the 1977 treaty might require the A-G to consent to prosecution, whether or not the offence had any possible link to terrorism.

Suppression of Terrorism Act 1978, s. 4

(1) If a person, whether a citizen of the United Kingdom and Colonies or not, does in a Convention country any act which, if he had done it in a part of the United Kingdom, would have made him guilty in that part of the United Kingdom of—
  (a) an offence mentioned in paragraph 1, 2, 4, 5, 10, 11, 11B, 12, 13, 14 or 15 of Schedule 1 to this Act; or
  (b) an offence of attempting to commit any offence so mentioned,
  he shall, in that part of the United Kingdom, be guilty of the offence or offences aforesaid of which the act would have made him guilty if he had done it there.

. . .

(3) If a person who is a national of a Convention country but not a citizen of the United Kingdom and Colonies does outside the United Kingdom and that Convention country any

> act which makes him in that Convention country guilty of an offence and which, if he had been a citizen of the United Kingdom and Colonies, would have made him in any part of the United Kingdom guilty of an offence mentioned in paragraph 1, 2 or 13 of Schedule 1 to this Act, he shall, in any part of the United Kingdom, be guilty of the offence or offences aforesaid of which the act would have made him guilty if he had been such a citizen.

As to offences committed aboard ships or aircraft of Convention countries, see s. 4(7).

Countries and Offences to which Section 4 Applies 'Convention countries' are those designated by the Secretary of State as Parties to the 1977 European Convention on the Suppression of Terrorism, namely: Albania, Austria, Belgium, Bulgaria, Croatia, Cyprus, Czech Republic, Denmark, Estonia, Finland, France, Georgia, Germany, Greece, Hungary, Iceland, Italy, Latvia, Liechtenstein, Lithuania, Luxembourg, Malta, Moldova, the Netherlands, Norway, Poland, Portugal, Republic of Ireland, Romania, Russian Federation, San Marino, Serbia and Montenegro, Slovakia, Slovenia, Spain, Sweden, Switzerland, Turkey and Ukraine. The UK, although a Party to the Convention, has not designated itself as a Convention country, which means that s. 4 gives English law no jurisdiction over things done in Scotland or Northern Ireland (or vice versa). An 'application of provisions order' made under s. 5 (see SI 1993 No. 2533) treats India for most purposes as if it were a Convention country; but an application of provisions order relating to the USA deals only with extradition, and excludes any jurisdiction under s. 4. **A8.16**

The offences to which s. 4(1) applies (excluding offences under Scots law or Northern Irish law) are murder, manslaughter, kidnapping and false imprisonment, together with offences under the Child Abduction Act 1984, s. 2, the OAPA 1861, ss. 28, 29 and 30, the Explosive Substances Act 1883, ss. 2 and 3, and the Firearms Act 1968, ss. 16 and 17(1).

The only offences in English law to which s. 4(3) of the 1978 Act applies are murder, manslaughter and offences under the Explosive Substances Act 1883, ss. 2 and 3.

JURISDICTIONAL IMMUNITIES

Diplomatic Immunity

Diplomatic immunity under English law is governed by the Diplomatic Privileges Act 1964, which incorporates certain provisions of the Vienna Convention on Diplomatic Relations 1961. These include Article 29, by which, 'the person of a diplomatic agent shall . . . not be liable to any form of arrest or detention', and Article 31(1), by which, 'a diplomatic agent shall enjoy immunity from the criminal jurisdiction of the receiving State'. By Article 37, the same privileges and immunities extend to 'the members of the family of a diplomatic agent forming part of his household . . ., if they are not nationals of the receiving State' and to 'members of the administrative and technical staff of the mission, together with members of their families forming part of their respective households . . ., if they are not nationals of or permanently resident in the receiving State'; but members of the service staff enjoy such immunity only in respect of acts performed in the course of their duties, and the private servants of members of the mission have no immunities from the criminal law other than those (if any) admitted by the receiving State. **A8.17**

By Article 39(2), the immunities of a diplomat 'shall normally cease when he leaves the country, or on expiry of a reasonable period in which to do so, but . . . with respect to acts performed . . . in the exercise of his functions as a member of the mission, immunity shall continue to subsist'. As to the rationale behind this rule, see *Bow Street Metropolitan Stipendiary Magistrate, ex parte Pinochet Ugarte (No. 3)* [2000] 1 AC 147, per Lord Browne-Wilkinson at p. 202.

Immunity from prosecution does not involve immunity from the duty to comply with the law. See, e.g., the Vienna Convention on Diplomatic Relations 1961, Article 41: 'It is the duty of all persons enjoying such privileges and immunities to respect the laws and regulations of the receiving state'. A foreign diplomat in England has no right or licence to ignore the rules of English law. If he commits an offence under English law he may be prosecuted for it, but only if his government waives diplomatic immunity. Even if immunity is not waived, other persons implicated as secondary parties to his offence may still face prosecution.

Consular Immunity

A8.18 Consular immunity is more limited than diplomatic immunity, and for most purposes excludes immunity from criminal prosecution, save in respect of acts performed in the course of consular duties. See generally the Consular Relations Act 1968.

Persons Connected with International Organisations

A8.19 In respect of an international organisation of which the UK is a member, the International Organisations Act 1968, s. 1, enables certain immunities to be granted to its officers or representatives. The exact terms of such immunities vary from one case to another. See, e.g., the United Nations and International Court of Justice (Immunities and Privileges) Order 1974 (SI 1974 No. 1261), the European Court of Human Rights (Immunities and Privileges) Order 2000 (SI 2000 No. 1817) and the International Maritime Organisation (Immunities and Privileges) Order 2002 (SI 2002 No. 1826). As with diplomatic immunities, these immunities may be waived by the organisation in question.

The Commonwealth Secretariat Act 1966 makes provision for immunities of officers of the Secretariat.

Foreign Heads of State and Government Ministers

A8.20 By the State Immunity Act 1978, s. 20, the Diplomatic Privileges Act 1964 applies (with appropriate modifications) to a foreign sovereign or head of State, his household and private servants, as it applies to the head of a diplomatic mission, to members of his family forming part of his household and to his private servants.

A former head of State, like a former diplomat, is entitled to immunity from prosecution only in respect of acts done by him (or on his orders) in connection with his former office; and there are certain offences (such as torture committed by agents of a State that is party to the 1984 Convention against Torture and other Cruel, Inhuman or Degrading Treatment or Punishment) to which even this immunity cannot attach (*Bow Street Metropolitan Stipendiary Magistrate, ex parte Pinochet Ugarte (No. 3)* [2000] 1 AC 147).

Visiting Forces

A8.21 When foreign or Commonwealth armed forces are stationed on British soil, criminal jurisdiction over their personnel and families etc. is ceded in some circumstances to their own authorities. See the Visiting Forces Act 1952, s. 3. Foreign naval vessels are immune from local jurisdiction, even in respect of offences committed within English ports or harbours.

Offences Committed on or within Diplomatic Premises

A8.22 The premises of diplomatic missions in England and Wales are not in any sense foreign territory, although such premises may not be entered by the police or by any other agents of the UK government except with the consent of the ambassador or head of the mission (Diplomatic Privileges Act 1964, s. 2(1) and sch. 3).

Subject to any individual claims to diplomatic immunity etc., offences committed on or within such premises are accordingly triable in England and Wales under the ordinary territorial principles of English law: see *Nejad* (1981 unreported) in which acts committed by terrorists who seized the Iranian embassy in London were held to be justiciable under English law; and see also *Radwan v Radwan* [1972] 3 All ER 967.

Section B1 Homicide and Related Offences

MURDER

Definition

Murder is when a [person] . . . unlawfully killeth . . . any reasonable creature *in rerum natura* under the Queen's peace, with malice aforethought . . . (Derived from *Coke's Institutes*, 3 Co Inst 47) **B1.1**

Procedure

Murder is triable only on indictment. It is a class 1 offence. **B1.2**

Indictment

Statement of Offence **B1.3**

Murder

Particulars of Offence

A on or about the . . . day of . . . murdered V

Alternative Verdicts

Criminal Law Act 1967, s. 6 **B1.4**

(2) On an indictment for murder a person found not guilty of murder may be found guilty—
(a) of manslaughter, or of causing grievous bodily harm with intent to do so; or
(b) of any offence of which he may be found guilty under an enactment specifically so providing, or under section 4(2) of this Act [assisting offenders]; or
(c) of an attempt to commit murder, or of an attempt to commit any other offence of which he might be found guilty;

but may not be found guilty of any offence not included above.

The major enactments specifically providing for an alternative verdict within s. 6(2)(b) are as follows:

(a) Suicide Act 1961, s. 2(2) (aiding and abetting suicide, see **B1.117**);
(b) Infant Life (Preservation) Act 1929, s. 2(2) (child destruction, see **B1.80** to **B1.88**);
(c) Infanticide Act 1938, s. 2(2) (infanticide, see **B1.70** to **B1.79**).

To these alternative verdicts must be added:

(d) manslaughter;
(e) wounding with intent (under the Criminal Law Act 1967, s. 6(2)(a));
(f) assisting (contrary to the Criminal Law Act 1967, s. 4(1)) anyone guilty of any of the above offences; and

(g) attempting to commit any of the above offences.

Murder is specifically excluded from the general rule on alternative verdicts laid down in the Criminal Law Act 1967, s. 6(3) (see **D18.50**).

Although s. 6(2)(a) refers to a person being 'found not guilty of murder', a person can still, under the common law, irrespective of s. 2, be found guilty of manslaughter as an alternative verdict where the jury are unable to agree and are discharged by the judge from returning a verdict on the charge of murder (*Saunders* [1988] AC 148). As to when it is necessary for a judge to leave an alternative verdict of manslaughter to a jury, see *Coutts* [2006] 1 WLR 2154, discussed at **D18.62**.

It is now permissible to include other counts in an indictment for murder (see *Connelly v DPP* [1964] AC 1254; as to joinder of counts generally, see **D11.56** ***et seq.***).

Sentence

B1.5 The penalty for murder is as follows:

> Murder: Life imprisonment (mandatory sentence) (Murder (Abolition of Death Penalty) Act 1965, s. 1(1)).
>
> Murder by a person aged 18 but under 21: Custody for life (mandatory sentence) (PCC(S)A 2000, s. 93).
>
> Murder by person aged under 18 at the time of the offence: Detention at Her Majesty's pleasure (mandatory sentence) (PCC(S)A 2000, s. 90).

See further **E4**.

Elements

B1.6 The definition set out at **B1.1** is often condensed to the form 'unlawful killing with malice aforethought', to be contrasted with those forms of manslaughter which consist of unlawful killing without malice aforethought. This contrast emphasises the point that the principal distinguishing feature of murder is malice aforethought, the *mens rea*, which can now be confidently stated to be an intention to kill or to cause grievous bodily harm. Since the *actus reus* of murder also governs both manslaughter and infanticide and affects certain other offences too, it is especially important to clarify the longer definition given by Coke.

B1.7 **Unlawful Killing** The word 'unlawfully' can be taken to exclude killings for which the accused has a complete and valid justification, such as killing (reasonably) in self-defence (see **A3.33** to **A3.38**). See also *Airedale NHS Trust v Bland* [1993] AC 789 for the distinction between (lawful) withdrawal of treatment supporting life and (unlawful) active termination of a patient's life. 'Killeth' or 'kills' means 'causes the death of', and reference should be made to the discussion of causation in **A1.22** to **A1.32** (most of the cases there discussed being homicide cases). It should also be noted that murder is a result crime for the purposes of the rule laid down by the House of Lords in *Miller* [1983] 2 AC 161 in relation to the duty to act in the face of a danger one has created oneself (see **A1.16**).

B1.8 **Any Reasonable Creature *in Rerum Natura*** This can be safely shortened to 'any human being' which includes a conjoined twin totally dependent on its twin for oxygenated blood (*Re A (Children) (Conjoined twins: surgical separation)* [2001] 2 WLR 480), provided that expression is understood as being limited to one who is born alive, i.e. when it is fully expelled from its mother's body (*Poulton* (1832) 5 C & P 329) with an existence independent of its mother. Although there are difficulties about identifying the precise time at which this occurs (Criminal Law Revision Committee, 14th Report, paras. 33–37), if death is caused before the child has an existence independent of its mother, the jury can convict of the offence of child destruction (see **B1.80** to **B1.89**). The accused's act may take place before the birth of the victim if it causes the victim to die after having been born alive but liability for murder or manslaughter will depend on the precise intention with which the act is done. The House of Lords decided in *A-G's Ref (No. 3 of 1994)* [1998] AC 245 that the child in utero is not simply a part of its mother as the Court of Appeal ([1996] QB 581) had held but that they are distinct organisms between which, however, the doctrine of transferred malice does not fully apply (see **A2.13**). An intention to inflict grievous bodily harm on the mother cannot ground liability for murder in respect of the subsequent live-birth-then-death of the child (although this can be manslaughter). It may however still be the case that there could be liability for the murder of the child if the intention was to kill the mother and certainly if it was intended to cause the child to die after having been born alive.

Under the Queen's Peace The original significance of this expression is somewhat unclear (see *Page* [1954] 1 QB 170), but the only killings it would now seem to exclude are those in the actual heat and exercise of war or in putting down a rebellion. Otherwise, the killing of aliens, whether within the jurisdiction or outside it, can amount to murder (or manslaughter) and is triable in England. Any doubts about the precise position in Coke's time in relation to killings taking place outside the jurisdiction (see *Page* [1954] 1 QB 170) are now resolved by the OAPA 1861, s. 9 (murder or manslaughter abroad), which provides as follows: **B1.9**

Offences against the Person Act 1861, s. 9

> Where any murder or manslaughter shall be committed on land out of the United Kingdom, whether within the Queen's dominions or without, and whether the person killed were a subject of Her Majesty or not, every offence committed by any subject of Her Majesty in respect of any such case, whether the same shall amount to the offence of murder or manslaughter, . . . may be dealt with, inquired of, tried, determined, and punished . . . in England or Ireland.

The section deals with the case where the whole of the *actus reus* takes place abroad, i.e. both the act causing death and the death itself. Section 10 of the 1861 Act is a similar provision which caters for cases where one of these two elements takes place inside, and the other outside, the jurisdiction.

Offences against the Person Act 1861, s. 10

> Where any person being criminally stricken, poisoned, or otherwise hurt upon the sea, or at any place out of England or Ireland, shall die of such stroke, poisoning, or hurt in England or Ireland, or, being criminally stricken, poisoned or otherwise hurt in any place in England or Ireland, shall die of such stroke, poisoning, or hurt upon the sea, or at any place out of England or Ireland, every offence committed in respect of any such case, whether the same shall amount to the offence of murder or of manslaughter, . . . may be dealt with, inquired of, tried, determined, and punished . . . in England or Ireland.

It will be noticed that under this section, as contrasted with s. 9, there is no express limitation on the offence requiring it to be committed 'by any subject of Her Majesty', since at least part of the *actus reus* has taken place within the jurisdiction. Nevertheless, in *Lewis* (1857) Dears & B 182, the Court for Crown Cases Reserved held that the predecessor of s. 10 (9 Geo. IV c. 34 s. 8) did not apply to a blow struck out of the jurisdiction by a foreigner which resulted in death within the jurisdiction. But it does not necessarily follow that in the case of a blow inflicted by a foreigner within the jurisdiction, but resulting in death outside it, there would not be an offence of murder triable here. Two of the points mentioned by the court in *Lewis* were that:

(a) it is impossible to say that the blow by a foreigner out of the jurisdiction was done 'feloniously' (now 'criminally' as a result of the Criminal Law Act 1967) as required by the section; and
(b) the killing should only be triable here if it could have been triable here had the death occurred at the place where the blow was given.

In our converse case of a blow inflicted within the jurisdiction causing death outside it, these objections are not applicable, since:

(a) the blow would be inflicted 'feloniously' or 'criminally' (even without an ensuing death it would constitute an assault or an unlawful wounding) since it was given within the jurisdiction; and
(b) if the death occurred here, the killing would clearly be triable here.

Thus it is submitted that, even accepting the authority of *Lewis*, s. 10 can apply to a foreigner inflicting injury in this country which results in death abroad.

The effect of all the above is that the killing of *anyone* by a British subject anywhere in the world (except, it would seem, in Scotland or Northern Ireland — see Hirst, M. at [1995] CLJ 488 and the words 'on land out of the United Kingdom' in s. 9) is triable here, and the killing of anyone by an alien is also triable here, if at least the accused's act, even if not the actual death, took place within the jurisdiction. By way of exception to all this, under the War Crimes Act 1991, certain killings in Germany or German Occupied Territory during the Second World War can be prosecuted in the United Kingdom irrespective of the nationality of the accused at the time of the alleged offence. (For offences committed on a British ship or aircraft, terrorist offences and jurisdictional questions generally, see **A8**.)

B1.10 **Abolition of Death within a Year and a Day Rule** The former limitation that death had to occur within a year and a day of the infliction of injury was abolished, in relation to acts or omissions on or after 17 June 1996, by s. 1 of the Law Reform (Year and a Day Rule) Act 1996. The abolition is 'for all purposes' and thus affects not only murder and manslaughter but also infanticide, aiding and abetting suicide, a coroner's verdict of suicide and any statutory offences of causing death such as causing death by dangerous driving.

However, by s. 2 of the 1996 Act, the A-G's consent is required before proceedings can be instituted for a 'fatal offence' where either:

(a) the injury alleged to have caused the death was sustained more than three years before the death occurred, or
(b) the person has previously been convicted of an offence committed in circumstances alleged to be connected with the death.

It may be noted that the three-year period is expressed to run from the date that the injury is sustained rather than the date of the accused's act or omission, which may in some cases be earlier.

B1.11 **Malice Aforethought** Malice aforethought, the *mens rea* for murder, is now considerably clearer and rather narrower than it has been in the past, the major remaining uncertainty relating to precisely how or when a jury should infer intention from foresight (see **A2.2**), a problem which is not confined to the offence of murder. Contrary to what may be suggested by the ancient term itself, neither ill will nor premeditation is *required*, and malice aforethought is satisfied by either:

(a) an intention to kill; or
(b) an intention to cause grievous bodily harm.

Care has to be taken when referring to any cases prior to 1957, since before s. 1 of the Homicide Act of that year, an intention to further any felony was also sufficient (the so-called felony-murder or constructive malice rule). Although it was clear that constructive malice was abolished by that Act, it has taken six House of Lords decisions, and further statutory intervention, to establish the following propositions:

(a) Murder requires intention, and nothing less (e.g., wicked recklessness as in Scotland) will suffice, i.e. it is a crime requiring specific intent, and, while foresight of virtual certainty may be evidence of intention, it is not to be equated with it (*Moloney* [1985] AC 905, explaining *Hyam v DPP* [1975] AC 55; see further A2.2).

(b) Grievous bodily harm should be given its ordinary and natural meaning, i.e. really serious bodily harm (*DPP v Smith* [1961] AC 290), and is not restricted to harm likely to endanger life (*Cunningham* [1982] AC 566). As Lord Edmund-Davies commented in that case (at pp. 582–3) 'I find it passing strange that a person can be convicted of murder if death results from, say, his intentional breaking of another's arm, an action, which, while calling for severe punishment, would in most cases be unlikely to kill.' His lordship went on to recognise, however, that any change in the law on this matter was a task for Parliament.

(c) Murder, like any other crime requiring proof of intention, involves proof of a subjective state of mind on the part of the accused.

Criminal Justice Act 1967, s. 8

A court or jury, in determining whether a person has committed an offence,—

(a) shall not be bound in law to infer that he intended or foresaw a result of his actions by reason only of its being a natural and probable consequence of those actions; but

(b) shall decide whether he did intend or foresee that result by reference to all the evidence, drawing such inferences from the evidence as appear proper in the circumstances.

(This reversed the effect of *DPP v Smith* [1961] AC 290, which had appeared to lay down an irrebuttable presumption that a man intends the natural and probable consequences of his actions, but had subsequently been said by the Privy Council in *Frankland v The Queen* [1987] AC 576 never to have accurately represented the common law of England.)

Thus, where an accused, as in *DPP v Smith* itself, does something of which the natural and probable result is death or grievous bodily harm, e.g., as in that case, driving at high speed in an erratic manner with a police officer clinging to the car, the logical processes available to the jury would appear to be as follows:

(a) They may, but do not have to, infer that death or grievous bodily harm was *intended* (CJA 1967, s. 8).

(b) They may, but do not have to, infer that death or grievous bodily harm was *foreseen* (CJA 1967, s. 8) *from which* they may, but do not have to, infer that death or grievous bodily harm was *intended* (*Moloney* [1985] AC 905, *Hancock* [1986] AC 455, and *Nedrick* [1986] 1 WLR 1025, and see A2.2).

(c) They may, in the light of all the evidence, decide not to draw the inferences in (a) or (b) above, and conclude that the accused lacked the *mens rea* for murder.

The difference between (a) and (b) is that in (a) the inference of intention is made directly, whereas in (b) it is made indirectly via foresight (of a virtual certainty, see *Nedrick* below). Process (a) seems to be where the jury conclude from all the evidence that the accused intended death etc., in the sense that he desired to cause it, and process (b) appears to be where a jury conclude that the accused intended death etc., even though he did not necessarily desire to cause it.

Direction on Foresight Rarely Needed Both the Court of Appeal and the House of Lords **B1.12**
have clearly indicated that, normally, there will be no necessity to refer expressly to the accused's foresight (see *Fallon* [1994] Crim LR 519 for an example of a direction being needlessly complicated). In the words of Lord Lane CJ in *Nedrick* [1986] 1 WLR 1025 at pp. 1027–8:

> [The jury] simply has to decide whether the defendant intended to kill or do serious bodily harm. In order to reach that decision the jury must pay regard to all the relevant circumstances, including what the defendant himself said and did.
>
> In the great majority of cases a direction to that effect will be enough, particularly where the defendant's actions amounted to a direct attack upon his victim, because in such cases the

> evidence relating to the defendant's desire or motive will be clear and his intent will have been the same as his desire or motive. But in some cases, of which this is one, the defendant does an act which is manifestly dangerous and as a result someone dies. The primary desire or motive of the defendant may not have been to harm that person, or indeed anyone. In that situation what further directions should a jury be given? . . .
>
> Where the charge is murder and in the rare cases where the simple direction is not enough, the jury should be directed that they are not entitled to infer the necessary intention, unless they feel sure that death or serious bodily harm was a virtual certainty (barring some unforeseen intervention) as a result of the defendant's actions and that the defendant appreciated that such was the case.

Lord Lane CJ used the words 'virtual certainty', but in *Walker* (1990) 90 Cr App R 226, the Court of Appeal, while obviously preferring this phrase, held that it was not a misdirection to instruct a jury in terms of 'a very high degree of probability'. This was permissible provided that the dividing line between intention and recklessness was not blurred as the House of Lords held had occurred in *Woollin* [1999] AC 82 through reference to foresight of 'a substantial risk'. Lord Steyn emphasised that the *Nedrick* direction was a 'tried and tested formula' which trial judges should continue to use. This was subject to, apparently for the purposes of clarity, the substitution of the words 'to find' for the words 'to infer'.

It is instructive to look at the actual facts of *Nedrick*, as these illustrate the narrowing of the scope of malice aforethought in recent years. The appellant poured paraffin through the front door of a house and set it alight, claiming that he wished to frighten the occupant but had no desire to kill or inflict grievous bodily harm. These facts are to all intents and purposes identical with those in *Hyam v DPP* [1975] AC 55, and in each case the death or deaths of child occupants were caused. Whereas the House of Lords in *Hyam v DPP* upheld a conviction for murder based on a direction that equated foresight of a high probability with intent, the same direction was held to be a misdirection in *Nedrick*. The conviction for murder was quashed and a verdict of manslaughter substituted.

It seems in such a case that the jury, if they accept the accused's evidence that he did not want to cause death or grievous bodily harm, would only be *entitled* to convict (and even then they would not be *compelled* to do so: see *Scalley* [1995] Crim LR 504 and the final observation of Lord Steyn in *Woollin*) if they felt sure that the accused foresaw death or grievous bodily harm as a 'virtual certainty'. See now the comments of the Court of Appeal in *Re A (Children) (Conjoined twins: surgical separation)* [2001] 2 WLR 480 where two of the judges (Ward and Brooke LJJ) seemed to assume that, if a doctor operates on conjoined twins knowing that the death of one of them is virtually certain to result, that in law amounts to an intention to kill. There was no reference to any discretion of the jury to find or not find intention. However, in *Mathews* [2003] 2 Cr App R 461, the Court of Appeal confirmed that it was still a matter for the jury and that 'the law has not yet reached a definition of intent in murder in terms of appreciation of virtual certainty'.

B1.13 **Law Commission Proposals on Intention in Murder** Further detailed analysis of the complexities of intention can be found in part 4 of the Law Commission Consultation Paper No. 177 (December 2005). The final report (Murder Manslaughter and Infanticide, Law Com No. 304, November 2006) clearly takes the view that the current law leaves some discretion with the jury as to when to infer intention from foresight of virtual certainty and that this is 'a strength and not a weakness'. It thus recommends (at paragraph 3.27):

> that the existing law governing the meaning of intention be codified as follows:
>
> (1) A person should be taken to intend a result if he or she acts in order to bring it about.
> (2) In cases where the judge believes that justice may not be done unless an expanded understanding of intention is given, the jury should be directed as follows: an intention to bring about a result may be found if it is shown that the defendant thought that the result was a virtually certain consequence of his or her action.

Special Defences Generally

There are three special defences to murder — diminished responsibility, provocation, and killing in pursuance of a suicide pact. All three are partial defences, reducing the offence from murder to manslaughter rather than leading to an outright acquittal, and all three are governed by the Homicide Act 1957. They are needed principally because the mandatory life sentence for murder does not leave any discretion to the judge in sentencing whereby he can take account of factors such as provocation, as he would normally be able to do on lesser charges where the sentence is not fixed by law. There is, however, a view that, even if the mandatory penalty were to be abolished, these defences should be retained as serving 'the valuable function of removing certain specific categories of acts from the stigma attaching to a conviction for murder and of ensuring that the facts were determined after a proper hearing before a jury' (House of Lords Select Committee on Murder and Life Imprisonment 1989, para. 82). **B1.14**

Before turning to the three special defences in more detail, it should also be noted that the offence of infanticide (see **B1.70** to **B1.79**) also reduces the stigma and introduces discretion as to sentence in relation to what would otherwise be murder. The difference is, however, that infanticide is an independent offence, which can be charged from the outset, whereas manslaughter on the basis of diminished responsibility or provocation arises only by way of defence. Infanticide is, however, an alternative verdict to murder (as, of course, is manslaughter) (see **B1.4**).

DIMINISHED RESPONSIBILITY

Basis of Defence

This defence is purely statutory, having been introduced for the first time into English law (it had long been known to the Scottish courts) by the Homicide Act 1957, s. 2. **B1.15**

Homicide Act 1957, s. 2

(1) Where a person kills or is party to the killing of another, he shall not be convicted of murder if he was suffering from such abnormality of mind (whether arising from a condition of arrested or retarded development of mind or any inherent causes or induced by disease or injury) as substantially impaired his mental responsibility for his acts or omissions in doing or being a party to the killing.

(2) On a charge of murder, it shall be for the defence to prove that the person charged is by virtue of this section not liable to be convicted of murder.

(3) A person who but for this section would be liable, whether as principal or as accessory, to be convicted of murder shall be liable instead to be convicted of manslaughter.

(4) The fact that one party to a killing is by virtue of this section not liable to be convicted of murder shall not affect the question whether the killing amounted to murder in the case of any other party to it.

Section 2(2) puts the burden of proof on the defence, although this burden is only required to be on the balance of probabilities rather than beyond reasonable doubt (*Dunbar* [1958] 1 QB 1, and see generally **F3.8** and **F3.40**). The placing of the burden on the defence does not breach the ECHR, Article 6 and is therefore unaffected by the HRA 1998 (*Lambert* [2001] 2 WLR 211, CA). Section 2 of the 1957 Act did not modify the ingredients of the offence of murder at common law but merely provided a benefit to defendants who were in a position to take advantage of it. The prosecution are themselves allowed to allege diminished responsibility where the accused puts forward a defence of insanity (Criminal Procedure (Insanity) Act 1964, s. 6), and in such a case (which it is difficult to imagine arising very often, but see *Nott* (1958) 43 Cr App R 8) the prosecution must satisfy the normal burden of proof beyond a reasonable doubt.

The defence of diminished responsibility has largely replaced the insanity defence in murder cases. However, it is not available on a charge of attempted murder (*Campbell* [1997] Crim LR 495) nor under the Criminal Procedure (Insanity) Act 1964, s. 4A(2), following a finding of unfitness to plead (*Antoine* [2001] 1 AC 340). The courts have interpreted and applied the defence in a fairly flexible manner to enable it to reduce a wide range of killings, where there are compelling mitigating circumstances, from murder to manslaughter. Nevertheless, some supporting medical evidence will invariably be required, and the court must formally be satisfied of the following ingredients.

B1.16 **Abnormality of Mind** It is clear from the leading case of *Byrne* [1960] 2 QB 396 that this is much wider than 'defect of reason' within the M'Naghten Rules (see **A3.16**). In the words of Lord Parker CJ (at p. 403), abnormality of mind means:

> a state of mind so different from that of ordinary human beings that the reasonable man would term it abnormal. It appears to us to be wide enough to cover the mind's activities in all its aspects, not only the perception of physical acts and matters, and the ability to form a rational judgment as to whether an act is right or wrong, but also the ability to exercise willpower to control physical acts in accordance with that rational judgment.

Thus, there was ample evidence that Byrne, as a sexual psychopath who found it difficult, if not impossible, to control his perverted sexual desires, and who had horrifyingly mutilated the body of a young woman after strangling her, came within s. 2, and his appeal was allowed.

The broad meaning of 'abnormality of mind' should be pointed out to the jury (*Brown* [1993] Crim LR 961) and then the matter is one for them. As to medical evidence, Lord Parker CJ in *Byrne* continued:

> medical evidence is no doubt of importance, but the jury are entitled to take into consideration all the evidence, including the acts or statements of the accused and his demeanour. They are not bound to accept the medical evidence if there is other material before them which, in their good judgment, conflicts with it and outweighs it.

In this case however, 'Properly directed, we do not think that the jury could have come to any other conclusion than that the defence . . . was made out' (ibid., at p. 405).

However, if the Court of Appeal feels that the jury have been properly directed and that they have perversely rejected the medical evidence 'with no facts and no circumstances shown before them which throw doubt upon the medical evidence', then it may itself substitute a verdict of manslaughter (see *Matheson* [1958] 1 WLR 474 and *Bailey* (1961) 66 Cr App R 31 n). On the other hand, the Privy Council in *Walton v The Queen* [1978] AC 788 refused to interfere with a verdict of murder, even though there was medical evidence from the defence supporting diminished responsibility and no contradictory medical evidence from the prosecution. The jury were entitled to consider the 'quantity and weight' of the medical evidence and 'to consider not only the medical evidence but the evidence on the whole facts and circumstances of the case', and to conclude that 'the defence on a balance of probabilities had not been established'. The approach in *Walton* was followed in *Sanders* (1991) 93 Cr App R 245.

B1.17 **Substantial Impairment of Mental Responsibility** Abnormality of mind is not in itself sufficient, it must be such as to 'substantially impair' the accused's 'mental responsibility'. Whether it does so:

> is a question of degree and essentially one for the jury. Medical evidence is, of course, relevant, but the question involves a decision not merely as to whether there was some impairment of the mental responsibility of the accused for his acts but whether such impairment can properly be called 'substantial', a matter upon which juries may quite legitimately differ from doctors. (*Byrne* [1960] 2 QB 396, per Lord Parker CJ at p. 404)

Lord Parker went on to refer with apparent approval to the practice (borrowed from Scotland) of referring to the requisite degree of impairment as established where there was in popular language 'partial or borderline insanity'. However, in *Seers* (1984) 79 Cr App 261 the Court of Appeal held that while this test may not have been inappropriate on the facts of *Byrne*, it was not helpful in a case such as *Seers*, where the accused was suffering from a depressive illness which the jury would clearly not regard as giving rise to partial or borderline insanity. Since the jury had been directed solely in terms of partial or borderline insanity, the conviction for murder was reduced to one of manslaughter, a verdict which, on the evidence, the jury would have been justified in returning. The Court of Appeal in *Egan* [1992] 4 All ER 470 said that explicit guidance should be given to the jury as to the meaning of 'substantial'. This should be done by adopting one of the two meanings approved in *Lloyd* [1967] 1 QB 175, namely that the jury should approach the word in a broad common-sense way, or 'that the word meant more than some trivial degree of impairment but less than total impairment'. However, in *Mitchell* [1995] Crim LR 506, the Court of Appeal declined to hold that such guidance was essential.

Although medical evidence is not conclusive on this issue, it is clearly desirable from the accused's point of view. Medical witnesses feel uneasy about testifying to a non-medical but rather legal or moral concept such as responsibility, but are generally prepared (and allowed by the court) to do so in order to make the defence workable. In *Campbell* (1986) 84 Cr App R 255 it was held that the judge rightly did not put the defence of diminished responsibility to the jury, where the medical witness's evidence (given primarily in support of a plea of provocation) was capable of showing an abnormality of mind but never addressed the question of substantial impairment. Even if the evidence had been relevant to that issue, it was said that since the burden of proof is on the defence, the judge's duty would merely be to draw the attention of defence counsel to the possible defence rather than raise it with the jury of his own accord.

Causes of Abnormality of Mind Under the Homicide Act 1957, s. 2, this may be due to 'a condition of arrested or retarded development of mind or any inherent causes or induced by disease or injury'. These possible causes have been fairly liberally interpreted. In *Vinagre* (1979) 69 Cr App R 104 the accused was said by the medical witnesses to be suffering from 'Othello syndrome', i.e. unfounded suspicion that his wife was having an affair, and successfully pleaded diminished responsibility, much to the apparent distaste of Lawton LJ in the Court of Appeal, who nevertheless felt unable to interfere with the verdict. It seems, however, that if the wife had *in fact* been having an affair, that would merely be a case of a jealous killing which the various causes in s. 2 were designed to exclude. It would then have been merely an abnormality of mind caused by jealousy rather than by the 'disease' of 'Othello syndrome'. Even then, evidence that the well-founded jealousy caused depression or some other condition that might be described as a disease would no doubt make a successful plea possible. Less controversially, post-natal depression and premenstrual tension can constitute a disease for these purposes and so give rise to diminished responsibility (see *Reynolds* [1988] Crim LR 679) as can battered woman's syndrome (*Ahluwalia* [1992] 4 All ER 889; *Hobson* [1998] 1 Cr App R 31). 'Mercy killing' can also be dealt with as manslaughter, where the dilemma which has caused the accused to kill can be said to have given rise to depression or some other medically recognised disorder which can be said to be the cause of an abnormality of mind. **B1.18**

Relevance of Intoxication

Voluntary Intoxication not a Permissible Cause Voluntary intoxication is not an acceptable cause of the abnormality. In *Tandy* [1989] 1 WLR 350, the accused was an alcoholic who strangled her 11-year-old daughter after drinking nine-tenths of a bottle of vodka and upon learning that her daughter had been sexually abused. She was clearly suffering from an abnormality of mind at the time of the killing, and the amount of alcohol in her bloodstream would have been lethal for most people. However, the Court of Appeal upheld the conviction **B1.19**

for murder based on the trial judge's direction that, for the defence to succeed, the abnormality had to be caused by the disease of alcoholism rather than by the voluntary ingestion of alcohol on the particular occasion. This would be the case 'If the alcoholism had reached the level at which her brain had been injured by the repeated insult from intoxicants so that there was gross impairment of her judgment and emotional responses' (per Watkins LJ, at p. 356). Even if this was not the case (as the jury must have found by their verdict), the alcoholism might still found a defence if it meant that the intoxication was not voluntary, i.e. if 'she was no longer able to resist the impulse to drink'. Although the defence medical witnesses testified to this effect, the prosecution witness was of the view that 'the appellant had control over whether she had the first drink of the day, but once she had had the first drink she was no longer in control' (ibid., at p. 354), and the Court of Appeal said (at p. 357) that 'the judge was correct in telling the jury that, if the taking of the first drink was not involuntary, then the whole of the drinking [on that day] was not involuntary'.

Tandy was followed in *Inseal* [1992] Crim LR 35, where the Court of Appeal approved of the trial judge's direction being given only in terms of this second issue of whether the drinking had become involuntary, since no medical evidence had been given on the first question of whether the brain had been 'injured by the repeated insults from intoxicants'.

The relevance in *Tandy* of the distinction between voluntary and involuntary intoxication is in answering the question of whether the abnormality of mind is caused by disease, i.e. alcoholism. If the intoxication is voluntary, then it constitutes a *novus actus interveniens* and breaks the causal link between the alcoholism and the abnormality of mind. If it is involuntary, in the sense that the accused's alcoholism meant she was no longer able to resist the impulse to take (even the first) drink, then the actual intoxication is not a *novus actus* but part of the causal chain between the alcoholism and the abnormality of mind. As Watkins LJ put it (ibid., at p. 356), 'if her drinking was involuntary then her abnormality of mind at the time of the act of strangulation was induced by her condition of alcoholism'.

If this is correct, then logically an alcoholic (or anybody else for that matter) whose orange juice, for example, is surreptitiously laced with vodka by another, might have difficulty relying on diminished responsibility. Even though his abnormality of mind is caused by involuntary intoxication, it would appear that it is not induced by disease. This seems rather harsh but a possible answer is that the abnormality might be said to be due to one of the other causes specified in s. 2(1), i.e. 'injury'. The spiker of the drinks could be said to be inflicting an injury via the alcohol on the accused's brain, just as much as if he clubbed him over the head, and thus the abnormality could be said to be induced by 'injury'. However, in *Di Duca* (1959) 43 Cr App R 167, the court was 'very doubtful' as to whether the transient effect of drink could amount to an injury and in *O'Connell* [1997] Crim LR 683 similar doubts were expressed in respect of the transient effects of voluntarily ingested Halcion (a sleeping drug). These doubts can be explained on the grounds that the courts were speaking of cases of *voluntary* intoxication. Rather than deny that the transient effect of drink or drugs can ever constitute an injury, it would be better merely to exclude voluntarily self-inflicted injuries (including the effects of voluntary intoxication) from the meaning of 'injury' within s. 2(1). Their exclusion can be justified on the grounds that, being voluntarily self-inflicted, they are not capable of substantially impairing responsibility within the meaning of the section. (See also Mackay, R.D. 'The Abnormality of Mind Factor in Diminished Responsibility' [1999] Crim LR 117.)

B1.20 **Intoxication Combined with Permissible Causes** A slightly different problem arises where there are two independent possible causes of the abnormality of mind, one of which *is* an allowable cause within s. 2(1) (e.g., a depressive illness) and the other of which is voluntary intoxication (which is clearly not allowable). This was essentially the situation in *Gittens* [1984] QB 698, where the judge told the jury to consider which was the substantial cause of the abnormality of mind, the accused's illness or the alcohol. The Court of Appeal held that this was a misdirection. The real question was not the relative strength of the contribution of the two causes but whether, whatever the contribution made by drink, there was an abnormality of mind: *due to causes specified in s. 2(1)*, which substantially impaired the accused's responsibility for the killing. An attempt to sum up the effect of this was made by Professor Smith in [1984] Crim LR 553–4 (in a passage approved by the Court of Appeal in *Atkinson* [1985] Crim LR 314 and again in *Egan* [1992] 4 All ER 470) as follows:

> the two questions for the jury, in logical sequence, would seem to be: 'Have the defence satisfied you on the balance of probabilities — that if the defendant had not taken drink — (i) he would have killed as he in fact did? And (ii) he would have been under diminished responsibility when he did so?'

This formulation has now been held to be erroneous by the House of Lords in *Dietschmann* [2003] 1 AC 1209. Question (i) is not appropriate or consistent with the true ratio of *Gittens*. An accused may thus succeed in the defence even if he may not have killed if he had not taken drink (although at para. 34 of *Dietschmann* it was recognised that in many such cases the jury will not in the event conclude that the accused's responsibility for his acts has in fact been substantially impaired). However, the real issue is not directly one of the causation of the killing but whether the abnormality of mind (apart from the drink) substantially impaired the accused's mental responsibility. Essentially it seems that the jury have to decide whether there is a *sufficient* abnormality of mind *caused by permissible factors* such as substantially to impair his responsibility, irrespective of the fact that the accused's abnormality may in fact have been accentuated even further by the ingestion of the alcohol and irrespective of whether or not the accused would still have killed if he had not taken drink.

It would appear from *Roberts* [2005] EWCA Crim 199 that, if the evidence of intoxication is not sufficiently significant to require a direction to consider whether the accused lacked the specific intent, neither is any direction to the jury needed to the effect that diminished responsibility can still be established even if the accused was drunk. Nothing need be said about intoxication in such a case. In contrast, in a case like *McNally* [2004] EWCA Crim 2501, where the appellant had consumed a (probably substantial) quantity of alcohol and had also consumed cannabis, guidance on the relationship between diminished responsibility and intoxication would be required so that the jury would understand that diminished responsibility could still be made out even if the accused was drunk at the time of the offence. *McNally* was a case in which the trial took place before *Dietschmann* and, the jury having been directed in accordance with *Atkinson* and *Egan*, the conviction for murder had to be quashed although a new trial was ordered to enable the jury to decide the issue of diminished responsibility independently of the evidence of intoxication. See also *Hendy* [2006] 2 Cr App R 489, where it was made clear that Lord Hutton in *Dietschmann* was simply clarifying what the law had always been under the 1957 Act. Convictions for murder from many years back have thus had to be quashed, as was also the case in *Robson* [2006] EWCA Crim 2749, where there was no transcript available of the summing-up ten years previously but it had to be assumed that the direction had been given in accordance with what was mistakenly thought to be the law pre-*Dietschmann*. A conviction for manslaughter was substituted.

Accepting Plea of Diminished Responsibility

It has already been noted that one cannot initially charge manslaughter on the basis of diminished responsibility, and so the accused has to be indicted for murder no matter how clearly he appears to come within the terms of the Homicide Act 1957, s. 2(1). In some cases the prosecution may be able to accept a plea of manslaughter to an indictment for murder. In *Cox* [1968] 1 WLR 308, Winn LJ said (at p. 310): **B1.21**

> that there are cases where, on an indictment for murder, it is perfectly proper, where the medical evidence is plainly to this effect, to treat the case as one of substantially diminished responsibility and accept, if it be tendered, a plea to manslaughter on that ground, and avoid a trial for murder.

However, the Court of Appeal in *Vinagre* (1979) 69 Cr App R 104 warned (in the context of the acceptance of a plea based on the 'Othello syndrome') that:

> it was never intended that pleas should be accepted on flimsy grounds [but only] when there is clear evidence of mental imbalance. We do not consider that in this case there was clear evidence of mental imbalance. There was clear evidence of killing by a jealous husband which, until modern times, no one would have thought was anything else but murder. (per Lawton LJ, at pp. 106–7)

Thus, in a novel or borderline sort of case, the plea ought not to be accepted but the evidence presented to a jury for their determination. The public interest may demand this in a notorious case such as that of the 'Yorkshire Ripper' (*The Times*, 23 May 1981). This was a striking case, in the sense that the prosecution were prepared to accept the plea in the light of unanimous psychiatric reports that the accused, Sutcliffe, was a paranoid schizophrenic, but the judge insisted that there should be a trial before a jury who convicted of murder. The nub of the problem is that, however unanimous the medical witnesses may be about there being an abnormality of mind, the question of whether that abnormality 'substantially impaired responsibility' is ultimately not a medical question but one for the jury. Thus, as a general rule, the prosecution should only accept a plea (and the judge should only approve that acceptance) where there is clear and convincing evidence of diminished responsibility. Of course, there may be exceptional cases where it is desirable to accept a plea on the basis of less convincing evidence because a trial is undesirable for other reasons, e.g., the accused is himself seriously and terminally ill.

PROVOCATION

Basis of Defence

B1.22 Unlike diminished responsibility, provocation was recognised at common law as a partial defence to murder long before the Homicide Act 1957, and is further distinguishable in that the burden of proof is not on the defence, i.e. the jury must clearly be told that, once there is evidence capable of supporting a finding that the accused was provoked, the burden is on the prosecution to prove beyond reasonable doubt that the case is not one of provocation. (See *Cascoe* [1970] 2 All ER 833.) Provocation is not available on a charge of attempted murder (*Bruzas* [1972] Crim LR 367) since it can be taken account of in sentencing, although to some it seems anomalous that a person can be convicted of attempted murder where he might only have been convicted of manslaughter had he succeeded. However, the position is the same for diminished responsibility (*Campbell* [1997] Crim LR 495).

The classic test of provocation at common law was that given by Devlin J in *Duffy* [1949] 1 All ER 932n and approved by the Court of Criminal Appeal in that case:

> Provocation is some act, or series of acts, done by the dead man to the accused which would cause in any reasonable person, and actually causes in the accused, a sudden and temporary loss of self-control, rendering the accused so subject to passion as to make him or her for the moment not master of his mind.

Although this passage has been approved again since 1957 in *Ibrams* (1981) 74 Cr App R 154, it has to be read in the light of the Homicide Act 1957, s. 3, which does not provide a complete definition of provocation, but provides as follows:

Homicide Act 1957, s. 3

> Where on a charge of murder there is evidence on which a jury can find that the person charged was provoked (whether by things done or by things said or by both together) to lose his self-control, the question whether the provocation was enough to make a reasonable man do as he did shall be left to be determined by the jury; and in determining that question the jury shall take

into account everything both done and said according to the effect which, in their opinion, it would have on a reasonable man.

Inherent in both Devlin J's definition at common law and the above statutory provision is the requirement of two conditions to be satisfied for the defence to be made out, namely:

(a) the 'subjective' condition that the accused was actually provoked so as to lose his self-control; and
(b) the 'objective' condition that the reasonable man would have done so.

Section 3 has effected significant changes to the way in which both these conditions operate.

The Subjective Condition

B1.23 The most obvious result of the Homicide Act 1957, s. 3, is that it is only on this issue that the judge can withdraw the defence of provocation from the jury on the ground that there is no evidence capable of supporting it. If there is any evidence capable of satisfying this subjective condition (whether from the accused or from the surrounding circumstances: see *Rossiter* (1992) 95 Cr App R 326 and *Cambridge* [1994] 1 WLR 971 and contrast *Wellington* [1993] Crim LR 616 and *Walch* [1993] Crim LR 714), the questions of whether the accused did in fact lose self control and whether the objective condition is satisfied have to be left to the jury. (Strictly speaking, the issue is whether the prosecution have proved beyond a reasonable doubt that the objective condition (or, alternatively, the subjective condition) is *not* satisfied.) As Lord Tucker put it in *Bullard v The Queen* [1957] AC 635 (at p. 642 emphasis added):

> It has long been settled law that if on the evidence, whether of the prosecution or of the defence, there is any evidence of provocation fit to be left to a jury, and whether or not this issue has been specifically raised at the trial by counsel for the defence and whether or not the accused has said in terms that he was provoked, it is the duty of the judge, after a proper direction, to leave it open to the jury to return verdict of manslaughter *if they are not satisfied beyond reasonable doubt that the killing was unprovoked.*

The above is true whatever the main defence run by the accused, whether it be one such as accident, self-defence, lack of intent or diminished responsibility which acknowledges that the accused caused the death or whether it be one such as alibi or act of another which denies even that the accused caused the death (see Lord Taylor CJ in *Cambridge* [1994] 1 WLR 971 at p. 976). It even appears to be true where counsel for the accused has indicated to the judge that provocation should not be put to the jury (*Burgess* [1995] Crim LR 425 and *Dhillon* [1997] 2 Cr App R 104). However, it was said in *Miao* (2003) *The Times*, 26 November 2003 that a mere speculative possibility that there was provoking conduct and loss of self-control is not enough. Although there was evidence from the accused that there had been provoking conduct, his evidence was that he did not lose self-control so the judge correctly did not leave provocation to the jury where the evidence of loss of self-control was 'minimal or fanciful'. Where the judge has, as a matter of law, to leave the issue of provocation to the jury, he should indicate to them, unless it is obvious (see *Scott* [1997] Crim LR 597), what evidence might support the conclusion that the accused had lost self-control. It is particularly important that the judge does so where counsel has not raised the issue at all (*Stewart* [1995] 4 All ER 999), and this includes identifying the evidence of what was specifically said or done to constitute the provocation. Otherwise the jury will find it impossible to assess, under the second objective question, whether the reasonable man would have reacted, to what was done or said, in the way that the accused did (see the Court of Appeal judgment in *Acott* [1996] 4 All ER 443). An issue of provocation could arise only if the judge considered that there was some evidence of a specific act or words of provocation resulting in a loss of selfcontrol. Loss of self-control caused by other factors such as fear, panic or circumstances was not enough nor was a mere speculative possibility of provocation in the absence of any actual evidence of acts or words of provocation (see the House of Lords' judgment in *Acott* [1997] 1 WLR 306).

B1.24 **Incidental Effects of s. 3** In addition to regulating the respective roles of judge and jury, s. 3 incidentally affects the question of what is capable of constituting provocation and what is capable of satisfying the subjective condition.

First, provocation is no longer restricted to 'some act, or series of acts', since s. 3, by its use of the phrase 'whether by things done or by things said or by both together', clearly envisages that words alone can constitute provocation (see *DPP v Camplin* [1978] AC 705 per Lord Diplock at p. 716). The acts, words, or indeed sounds, may even be perfectly lawful or commonplace ones as, for example, the crying of a young baby in *Doughty* (1986) 83 Cr App R 319 (see **B1.30**).

Secondly, it appears it no longer need be, although it generally will be, 'something done by the dead man to the accused'. It may be something done *by* a third person in some way connected with the victim (see *Davies* [1975] QB 691, conduct by wife's lover relevant to whether husband provoked to kill his wife). Alternatively it may be something done *to* a third person, such as the child, spouse or, as in *Pearson* [1992] Crim LR 193, the brother of the accused. Some people may retain self-control if attacked personally but understandably lose it in the face of an attack on a vulnerable loved one. On the other hand, provocation does seem to require conduct on the part of someone (things done or things said), and there is no such thing as provocation by circumstances, e.g., D in anguish at seeing his wife or children killed by a bolt of lightning runs wild in his car killing innocent pedestrians (see the example given by Steyn LJ in *Acott* [1997] 1 WLR 306 at p. 312 of a slowdown of traffic due to snow).

A third possible, but not yet fully accepted, candidate for modification is the rule that provocation must result in a 'sudden and temporary loss of self-control'. The practice of trial judges in domestic killings has sometimes been to allow the defence of provocation to go to the jury even where there has been an interval between the last act which might be relied upon as provocation and the actual killing (see for example *Pearson*). However, where the trial judge rules that the time gap is such that there is no evidence that the accused was in fact provoked to lose his self-control, and withdraws the defence from the jury, the Court of Appeal has at times shown itself not to be prepared to interfere and has applied the strict letter of the law. This is illustrated in *Ibrams* (1981) 74 Cr App R 154, where the last instance of provocation, consisting of 'gross bullying and terrorising', had taken place seven days before the accused's planned, pre-emptive and fatal attack. The Court of Appeal cited with approval the passage from the judgment of Devlin J (as he then was) in *Duffy* [1949] 1 All ER 932n, quoted at **B1.22**. The court also approved the following statement:

> circumstances which induce a desire for revenge are inconsistent with provocation, since the conscious formulation of a desire for revenge means that the person has had time to think, to reflect, and that would negative a sudden temporary loss of self-control, which is of the essence of provocation.

Subsequently in *Ahluwalia* [1992] 4 All ER 889, one of a number of cases of long term domestic violence and abuse where provocation has been in issue, the Court of Appeal regarded itself as still bound by this approach stating that 'important considerations of public policy would be involved should provocation be re-defined so as possibly to blur the distinction between sudden loss of self-control and deliberate retribution'. However, Lord Taylor CJ also made it clear that, provided there was a sudden loss of control, the interval between the provocation and that loss of control was a matter to be taken in account in assessing the evidence on the facts of the case and did not give rise to a rule of law:

> It is open to the judge, when deciding whether there is any evidence of provocation to be left to the jury, and open to the jury when considering such evidence, to take account of the interval between the provocative conduct and the reaction of the defendant to it. In some cases the interval between the provocative conduct and the defendant's reaction might wholly undermine the defence of provocation. However, that depends entirely on the facts of the individual case and was not a principle of law.

Their lordships accepted that the subjective element in that defence would not as a matter of law be negatived simply because of the delayed reaction in cases of women subjected frequently over a period to violent treatment, provided that there was at the time of the killing a sudden and temporary loss of self-control.

Thus the loss of self-control has to be sudden and temporary in that it comes over the accused quickly (whether or not it does so instantly after the provocation) and departs reasonably quickly as opposed to being a planned or premeditated killing. Such a killing will not give rise to a defence of provocation even if it follows a long history of serious abuse by the victim (although this might be relevant to a defence of diminished responsibility, as was eventually successful in *Ahluwalia* itself.)

Cases of planned killings after a long period of provocation should be distinguished from cases of cumulative provocation, where the last instance of provocation closest to the time of an unplanned killing is relatively minor but is 'the straw that breaks the camel's back' or, as in *Humphreys* [1995] 4 All ER 1008, 'the trigger which caused the appellant's self-control to snap'. Here there is no reason why the defence of provocation should not succeed, even though the last instance of provocation would not on its own have been sufficient to make the accused (or the reasonable man) lose self-control. The provocation adjacent to the time of the killing must obviously be viewed in the light of past history (see *Pearson* [1992] Crim LR 193). However, there must be evidence that the accused did actually lose self-control. This appeared to be lacking in *Thornton* [1992] 1 All ER 306 (but see the retrial ordered by the Court of Appeal following a reference by the Home Secretary: *Thornton (No. 2)* [1996] 1 WLR 1174 and also in *Cocker* [1989] Crim LR 740, in which the accused calmly and quietly killed his chronically ill wife after repeated entreaties by her to do so, and the Court of Appeal said that his evidence showed not that he had lost self-control but merely that he had finally acceded to his wife's wishes.

The Objective Condition

As a result of the Homicide Act 1957, s. 3, the judge can no longer withdraw the defence from the jury on the grounds that the reasonable man would not have done as the accused did. That is now solely an issue for the jury. The evidence of witnesses as to how the reasonable man would react is not admissible, but the extent to which the judge should direct the jury as to the meaning of the reasonable man test or how to answer the question left to them under s. 3 has become a vexed question. The latest 'definitive' answer to the question has now been given by the Privy Council in *A-G for Jersey v Holley* [2005] 2 AC 580, which effectively overrules the House of Lords decision in *Smith (Morgan)* [2001] 1 AC 146, which had itself only five years previously attempted to resolve a conflicting line of cases in the House of Lords, Privy Council and Court of Appeal. To make sense of *Holley* it is necessary to set out the chequered history of the objective component of the provocation defence. B1.25

DPP v Camplin Prior to the Homicide Act 1957, juries were told that the reasonable man shared none of the peculiarities of the accused. Thus, understandably, drunkenness, excitability, pugnacity or irascibility were not relevant characteristics. But neither, unfortunately, was a characteristic such as impotence, even where the provocation consisted, in part, of taunts about the accused's impotence, as in the much criticised decision of the House of Lords in *Bedder v DPP* [1954] 1 WLR 1119. However, *Bedder* did not survive s. 3 as interpreted by the House of Lords in *DPP v Camplin* [1978] AC 705. Given that words alone could now constitute provocation, it no longer made sense totally to exclude the characteristics of the accused, because: B1.26

> the gravity of verbal provocation may well depend upon the particular characteristics or circumstances of the person to whom a taunt or insult is addressed. To taunt a person because of his race, his physical infirmities or some shameful incident in his past may well be considered by the jury to be more offensive to the person addressed, however equable his temperament, if the

facts on which the taunt is founded are true than it would be if they were not. (*DPP v Camplin* [1978] AC 705 per Lord Diplock at p. 717)

Thus, Lord Diplock thought that:

> a proper direction to a jury on the question left to their exclusive determination by section 3 of the Act of 1957 would be on the following lines. The judge should state what the question is using the very terms of the section. He should then explain to them that the reasonable man referred to in the question is *a person having the power of self-control to be expected of an ordinary person of the sex and age of the accused, but in other respects sharing such of the accused's characteristics as they think would affect the gravity of the provocation to him*; and that the question is not merely whether such a person would in like circumstances be provoked to lose his self-control but also whether he would react to the provocation as the accused did. (ibid., per Lord Diplock at p. 718 emphasis added)

This direction became the model around which directions to juries were based for the next 20 years and, apart from the characteristics of age and sex, appeared to draw a clear distinction (see Ashworth, 'The Doctrine of Provocation', [1976] CLJ 292) between factors affecting the gravity of the provocation (deemed relevant) and factors merely affecting the power of self-control (deemed irrelevant). This distinction was also reflected in the House of Lords decision in *Morhall* [1996] AC 90, where the accused's addiction to glue sniffing was accepted as a relevant characteristic in assessing the gravity of provocation consisting of taunts about the addiction. On the other hand, the current state of being intoxicated due to glue or from some other cause, as opposed to the fact of one's addiction, would not be relevant since that would not affect the gravity of the provocation but rather the accused's powers of self-control, which are required to come up to the standard of the ordinary reasonable man.

B1.27 **Temporary Liberalisation of the *Camplin* Test** Despite the relative clarity of the *Camplin* test, a number of decisions of the Court of Appeal, in cases such as *Humphreys* [1995] 4 All ER 1008, *Dryden* [1995] 4 All ER 987 and *Thornton (No. 2)* [1996] 1 WLR 1174, were interpreted by some as liberalising the reasonable man test and to have weakened somewhat the distinction between characteristics or factors relevant to the gravity of the provocation and those relevant to powers of self-control. Nevertheless, the importance of the distinction was reiterated by the majority of the Privy Council in *Luc Thiet Thuan v The Queen* [1997] AC 131. Lord Goff, in giving the judgment of the majority, followed consistently the logic of his own judgment in *Morhall* [1996] AC 90, this time to deny the relevance to the objective test of a characteristic such as brain damage which, on the facts, merely affected powers of self-control rather than the gravity of the provocation. Lord Steyn, however, delivered a dissenting opinion which focused on the artificiality and apparent unfairness of, for example, allowing evidence of battered woman syndrome on the subjective question of whether the accused lost self-control but then telling the jury to ignore this factor on the second objective question of whether the reasonable woman would have lost self-control. Lord Steyn's approach was itself open to the criticism that it almost obliterated the distinction between the subjective and objective tests which s. 3 clearly, even if artificially, intended to preserve and that it gave insufficient acknowledgement to the role of the defence of diminished responsibility in giving recognition to factors such as brain damage reducing powers of self-control.

The Court of Appeal nevertheless took the view in *Campbell* [1997] 1 Cr App R 199 that it was not bound by the majority decision in *Luc Thiet Thuan* (nor constrained by anything in *Morhall*) and, fortified by Lord Steyn' s dissent, should follow instead the line apparently established in its own decisions referred to above whereby relevant factors appearing to affect the power of self-control were not limited just to age and sex. Thus in *Parker* [1997] Crim LR 760 the defence had sought to introduce evidence that D was a chronic alcoholic with some brain damage which rendered him more susceptible to provocation. The trial judge purported to follow *Luc Thiet Thuan* and refused to admit the evidence. The Court of Appeal quashed the conviction for murder since it regarded itself as bound to follow the Court of Appeal authorities in preference to *Luc Thiet Thuan*.

Parker was followed by the Court of Appeal in *Smith (Morgan)* [1999] QB 1079, in which the trial judge told the jury that, whilst the accused's severe depression was to be taken into account in assessing the gravity of the provocation, it was not to be taken into account in deciding whether an ordinary man sharing the accused's characteristics would have lost self-control, to which question it was 'neither here nor there'. The Court of Appeal quashed the conviction for murder and substituted a conviction for manslaughter but, exceptionally, itself granted leave to appeal to the House of Lords, certifying the following point of law:

> Are characteristics other than age and sex, attributable to the reasonable man, for the purpose of section 3 of the Homicide Act 1957 relevant not only to the gravity of the provocation to him but also to the standard of self-control to be expected.

The House of Lords in *Smith (Morgan)* [2001] 1 AC 146, by a three to two majority, dismissed the prosecution appeal and effectively answered 'Yes' to the certified question.

Lord Hoffmann took the view that (at p. 181):

> . . . the judge should not have directed the jury as a matter of law that the effect of Smith's depression on his powers of self-control was 'neither here nor there'. They should have been told that whether they took it into account in relation to the question of whether the behaviour of the accused had measured up to the standard of self-control which ought reasonably to have been expected of him was a matter for them to decide.

Although the House of Lords made it clear that there was no simple model direction or 'prescriptive formula' for the way in which the matter should be explained to the jury, in *Rowland* (2004) *The Times*, 12 January 2004, the Court of Appeal approved the Judicial Studies Board direction of April 2003 (which can be found in the 2005 edition of this work). This direction has now been radically revised (June 2007) in the light of the decision of the Privy Council in *Holley*.

The Decision in *Holley* and the Return to *Camplin* The significance and impact of *A-G for Jersey v Holley* [2005] 2 AC 580 on the law as stated in *Smith (Morgan)* [2001] 1 AC 146 can be seen from the first paragraph of Lord Nicholls' opinion on behalf of the majority of their lordships: **B1.28**

> This appeal from the Court of Appeal of Jersey calls for examination of the law relating to provocation as a defence or, more precisely, as a partial defence to a charge of murder. Jersey law on this subject is the same as English law. In July 2000 the House of Lords considered the ingredients of this defence in the Morgan Smith case (*R v Smith (Morgan)* [2001] 1 AC 146). The decision of the House in that case is in direct conflict with the decision of their Lordships' Board in *Luc Thiet Thuan v The Queen* [1997] AC 131. And the reasoning of the majority in the Morgan Smith case is not easy to reconcile with the reasoning of the House of Lords in *R v Camplin* [1978] AC 705 or *R v Morhall* [1996] AC 90. *This appeal, being heard by an enlarged Board of nine members, is concerned to resolve this conflict and clarify definitively the present state of English law, and hence Jersey law, on this important subject.* (emphasis added)

Lord Nicholls made it clear (at [22]–[23]) that the conflict was resolved in favour of *Luc Thiet Thuan v The Queen* [1997] AC 131 and that the majority view in *Smith (Morgan)* was erroneous since that majority view represents:

> a departure from the law as declared in section 3 of the Homicide Act 1957. It involves a significant relaxation of the uniform, objective standard adopted by Parliament. Under the statute the sufficiency of the provocation ('whether the provocation was enough to make a reasonable man do as [the defendant] did') is to be judged by one standard, not a standard which varies from defendant to defendant. Whether the provocative act or words and the defendant's response met the 'ordinary person' standard prescribed by the statute is the question the jury

> must consider, not the altogether looser question of whether, having regard to all the circumstances, the jury consider the loss of self-control was sufficiently excusable. The statute does not leave each jury free to set whatever standard they consider appropriate in the circumstances by which to judge whether the defendant's conduct is 'excusable'.

That *Holley* as a Privy Council decision does in fact, quite exceptionally, overrule *Smith (Morgan)* was confirmed by the Court of Appeal in *James* [2006] QB 588, where Lord Phillips CJ made it clear that trial judges were correct to follow *Holley* rather than *Smith (Morgan)*, as they had in fact already been doing. The result was that a conviction obtained as long ago as 1980 under the more restrictive *Camplin*-based law, which had been referred by the Criminal Cases Review Commission in the light of the more generous approach in *Smith* (*Morgan*), now became safe once more.

The decision of the majority in *Holley* effectively rehabilitates the two dissenting judgments in *Smith (Morgan)*. It has been previously contended in this work that there is a great deal to be said for those judgments, particularly that of Lord Hobhouse of Woodborough, who demonstrated that the earlier Court of Appeal judgments were not as inimical to the gravity/self-control dichotomy as had been supposed (see also the 2000 edition of this work at p. 120). There is an echo of this in Lord Nicholls' judgment in *Holley* where (at [25]) he rejects the view that, for example, in relation to a 'battered woman syndrome' case, evidence about battered women's syndrome can only be relevant to the subjective issue of actual loss of control and insists that it may still be relevant to the gravity of the provocation:

> . . . the evidence of the woman's condition may be relevant on two issues: whether she lost her self-control, and the gravity of the provocation for her. The jury will then decide whether in their opinion, having regard to the actual provocation and their view of its gravity for the defendant, a woman of her age having ordinary power of self-control might have done what the defendant did.

His lordship does not explain precisely or in detail exactly how it may be relevant but one obvious example would be where the provocation is about her status or condition of being a 'battered woman'. More broadly however, it would seem to be open to the defence to bring forward evidence that the defendant's syndrome and past history made the provocation appear more serious to her and thus affected the gravity of the provocation whilst accepting that the degree of self-control to be expected of her, in the face of the level of provocation as it appeared to her, was the degree of control that would be expected of an ordinary person of the age and sex of the accused.

The decision in *Holley* effectively returned the law to the state it was in following the earlier House of Lords decisions in *Camplin* and *Morhall* and rendered it consistent with the provisional recommendations of the Law Commission in its Consultation Paper No. 173 on Partial Defences to Murder (May 2004) where it stated 'that we prefer the minority position in *Smith (Morgan)*, which also accords broadly with the law in Australia, Canada and New Zealand, and with the recent provisional recommendations of the Irish Law Reform Commission'. The Law Commission's approach to this aspect of the provocation defence has not substantially changed and its latest thinking can be found in its Report 'Murder Manslaughter and Infanticide' (Law Com No. 304, November 2006).

Relationship between Provocation and Accused's Retaliation

B1.29 Although provocation can now clearly be constituted by words alone, more commonly and more cogently it will consist of a physical attack. In this context, too, the Homicide Act 1957, s. 3, effects a change. There is no longer any hard and fast rule that 'the mode of resentment must bear a reasonable relationship to the provocation', as had been laid down by the House of Lords in *Mancini v DPP* [1942] AC 1 at p. 9 in approving the trial judge's decision not to put the defence of provocation to the jury where the only acceptable evidence of provocation was an *unarmed* attack by the deceased to which the accused responded with a knife. (The jury in rejecting self-defence were regarded as having thereby rejected Mancini's story that the victim had himself attacked him with a knife.) Following the Homicide Act of 1957 (assuming there is some evidence that the accused actually was provoked to lose self-control) the judge is obliged to leave the question to the jury. The relationship between the provocation and what the accused did is certainly not an irrelevant factor for the jury but it is no longer 'a rule of law which they are bound to follow, but merely a consideration which may or may not commend itself to them' (*Phillips v The Queen* [1969] 2 AC 130 per Lord Diplock at p. 138).

Self-induced Provocation

An accused may be able to rely on provocation which he is partially responsible for bringing about. In *Edwards v The Queen* [1973] AC 648 the accused was blackmailing his victim, who had the temerity to swear at him and attack him with a knife. The accused then disarmed him and stabbed him 27 times. The Privy Council noted (at p. 658) that: B1.30

> the person sought to be blackmailed, did go to extreme lengths, in that he made a violent attack on the appellant with a knife, inflicting painful wounds and putting the appellant's life in danger. There was evidence of provocation and it was fit for consideration by the jury.

However, if the blackmail victim's reaction had not been so extreme, but had merely been a predictable, hostile reaction, such as 'vituperative words and even . . . blows from a fist,' then the blackmailer would not be able to 'rely on the predictable results of his own blackmailing conduct' (ibid., at p. 658).

To reconcile this approach with the words of the Homicide Act 1957, s. 3, one has to treat the Privy Council as merely laying down factors (such as the predictability of the victim's reaction) which the judge should take into account in deciding whether there is any real evidence that the subjective condition was satisfied and that the accused actually lost self-control. The reference to 'evidence fit for consideration by the jury' confirms that this was the Privy Council's intention. Certainly, to inflict 27 stab wounds was at least consistent with loss of control. This is preferable to saying that the reasonable man would not be provoked by the predictable results of his own wrongdoing, an approach which would be unsound, given the fact that the reaction of the reasonable man is now purely a matter for the jury. Thus in *Johnson* [1989] 1 WLR 740, the Court of Appeal substituted a verdict of manslaughter where the trial judge refused to leave provocation to the jury on the ground that the provocation was to some extent the result of the accused's own conduct. Since there was evidence that the accused was in fact provoked to lose his self-control, the defence had to be put to the jury.

The Court of Appeal does not now encourage artificial rules about what can or cannot constitute provocation in order to retain the control over the defence that used to be exercised prior to the Homicide Act 1957, under the guise of the former rules about the reactions of the reasonable man. The case of *Doughty* (1986) 83 Cr App R 319 is another example of their willingness to leave the issue to the jury as intended by the Act. The Court of Appeal rejected the trial judge's ruling that the perfectly natural crying of a 17-day-old baby could not constitute provocation even so as to satisfy the subjective condition, saying (at p. 326):

> We . . . feel that reliance can be placed upon the common sense of juries upon whom the task of deciding the issue is imposed by section 3 and that that common sense will ensure that only in cases where the facts fully justified it would their verdict be likely to be that they would hold that a defendant's act in killing a crying child would be the response of a reasonable man.

The same sentiments are no doubt appropriate to a jury's reaction to a case of self-induced provocation which is actually left to them.

KILLING IN PURSUANCE OF SUICIDE PACT

Homicide Act 1957, s. 4

B1.31 (1) It shall be manslaughter, and shall not be murder, for a person acting in pursuance of a suicide pact between him and another to kill the other or be a party to the other being killed by a third person.

The burden of proof that he was acting in pursuance of a suicide pact is placed on the accused by s. 4(2). This is a reverse legal burden on the balance of probabilities and is compatible with the ECHR, Article 6(2) (*A-G's Ref (No. 1 of 2004)* [2004] 1 WLR 2111 (at [130]–[132]).

'Suicide pact' is defined in s. 4(3) as:

> a common agreement between two or more persons having for its object the death of all of them, whether or not each is to take his own life, but nothing done by a person who enters into a suicide pact shall be treated as done by him in pursuance of the pact unless it is done while he has the settled intention of dying in pursuance of the pact.

Thus the burden of proof on the accused involves not only proof that there was in fact a suicide pact, but also that at the time of the killing the accused still had the intention of dying himself.

Killing in pursuance of a suicide pact is closely related to the offence of aiding and abetting suicide under the Suicide Act 1961, s. 2(1) (see **B1.117**). Section 2(2) provides that, if on an indictment for murder or manslaughter it is proved that the accused aided and abetted, counselled or procured the suicide of the person in question, the jury may find him guilty of that offence. If, on the other hand, the accused aided and abetted a killing by a third person, that is still potentially murder, but will be reduced to manslaughter under the Homicide Act 1957, s. 4, if it was done in pursuance of a suicide pact.

A useful discussion of the complexities and the merits (or otherwise) of the law in this area can be found in Law Commission Consultation Paper No. 177 (December 2005) at paras. 8.31–8.37. Their provisional proposal, noting how 'thin' a basis consent can be, would have subsumed killing in pursuance of a suicide pact within diminished responsibility. However, Law Com No. 304 (November 2006) now recommends (at para. 7.50) retaining s. 4 of the 1957 Act pending further public consultation on the broader issues relating to 'mercy' killing.

MANSLAUGHTER GENERALLY

Voluntary and Involuntary Manslaughter

B1.32 Manslaughter can be classified as either voluntary or involuntary. Voluntary manslaughter has in effect already been considered, since it consists of those killings which would be murder (because the accused has the relevant *mens rea* — hence the label *voluntary* manslaughter) but which are reduced to manslaughter because of one of the three special defences provided for by the Homicide Act 1957, discussed at **B1.15** to **B1.30**. Voluntary manslaughter is not an offence one can be indicted for, but rather is a verdict which can result from an initial indictment for murder. The actual verdict, however, will be simply 'manslaughter' without the label of 'voluntary'.

Involuntary manslaughter, on the other hand, refers to those types of manslaughter which can be charged in their own right and where the accused lacks the *mens rea* for murder, although equally they can result from an indictment for murder where the prosecution fail to prove the *mens rea*.

The fact that a verdict of manslaughter can reflect a number of different views of the facts taken by the jury (or by different members of the same jury) can lead to difficulties in sentencing and in relation to the normal rule requiring unanimity of verdicts (cf. **D17.44**). It was said by the Court of Criminal Appeal in *Larkin* [1943] KB 174 that it was 'most undesirable' that the jury should be asked to explain the basis of their verdict. However, in *Matheson* [1958] 1 WLR 474 the Court of Criminal Appeal said (at p. 480) that if diminished responsibility and some other ground such as provocation are left to the jury, the judge may, and generally should, ask the jury whether the verdict was based on diminished responsibility, or on the other ground or on both. This matter has been further considered in *Jones* (1999) *The Times*, 17 February 1999 (where neither of the above cases was referred to). The Court of Appeal made it clear that there is no obligation on the judge to ask any such question (of which advance warning should in any event be given), it being 'a matter entirely for him or her in the exercise of his or her discretion'. Neither is there any obligation on the jury to give an answer if asked, any such answer being merely additional information to help with sentence:

> . . . provided that the jury are agreed that the defendant is guilty of manslaughter, in the sense that they are sure that he perpetrated an unlawful act which caused the death of the accused, it is unnecessary that there be any unanimity by the jury as to the route by which that verdict is achieved.

This seems right on the facts of the case and for those cases (the majority) where the offence is at least manslaughter and may be murder if malice aforethought can be established and if provocation and diminished responsibility (if in issue) can be negatived. The prosecution has to prove causation and the unlawful act (such as an intentional assault), and negative complete defences such as self-defence if in issue, but the different possible reasons for an offence being manslaughter rather than murder are negative ones (reasonable doubt by the jury as to whether malice aforethought has been proved or whether diminished responsibility or provocation has been negatived). It is not a question of the prosecution having to prove any of these things for manslaughter; manslaughter is merely the residual verdict for any one of these reasons. It is submitted however that it would be different if manslaughter is alleged on two fundamentally separate grounds: unlawful act and gross negligence. It should not be sufficient that six jurors thought that the accused's act causing death was unlawful but not grossly negligent and the other six thought it was grossly negligent but not unlawful. Here the prosecution have not proved either of the two forms of manslaughter beyond reasonable doubt; it is quite different from a case where what would otherwise be murder has been proved and the jurors merely differ as to the reason for *reducing* the offence to manslaughter (see Taylor, 'Jury Unanimity in Homicide' [2001] Crim LR 283 and HH Judge Clarke 'Jury Unanimity — A Practitioner's Problem' [2001] Crim LR 301)

Definition of Involuntary Manslaughter

Superficially, this is the same as the definition for murder (see **B1.1**) without the requirement **B1.33** of malice aforethought. This is only helpful in that it emphasises that requirements such as that the victim be a fully born human being are equally part of the offence of manslaughter. It is more common to refer to manslaughter as 'unlawful killing without malice aforethought', but this is not particularly helpful, because it does not indicate which killings will be regarded as unlawful in the absence of malice aforethought. In fact there now appear to be two main categories of killing without malice aforethought which are regarded as unlawful and hence amount to manslaughter:

(a) killing by an unlawful act likely to cause bodily harm — often called 'unlawful act manslaughter' or 'constructive manslaughter'; and
(b) killing grossly negligently.

Procedure

B1.34 Manslaughter is triable only on indictment. It is a class 1 offence. It is a distinct offence from murder and attracts its own custody time-limit (*R (Wardle) v Crown Court at Leeds* [2002] 1 AC 754).

Indictment

B1.35

Statement of Offence

Manslaughter

Particulars of Offence

A on or about the . . . day of . . ., unlawfully killed V

Alternative Verdicts

B1.36 These include:

(a) child destruction (Infant Life (Preservation) Act 1929, s. 2(2)), see **B1.80** to **B1.88**);
(b) abortion (Infant Life (Preservation) Act 1929, s. 2(3)), see **B1.89** to **B1.98**);
(c) complicity in suicide (Suicide Act 1961, s. 2(2)), see **B1.117** to **B1.122**);
(d) assisting an offender (Criminal Law Act 1967, s. 4(2), see **B14.51**).

By way of exception to the general rule, there appears to be no such verdict as attempted manslaughter (see *Bruzas* [1972] Crim LR 367 and *Campbell* [1997] Crim LR 495).

Sentencing Guidelines: Diminished Responsibility

B1.37 The maximum penalty is life imprisonment (OAPA 1861, s. 5).

> In diminished responsibility cases there are various courses open to a judge. His choice of the right course will depend on the state of the evidence and the material before him. If the psychiatric reports recommend and justify it, and there are no contrary indications, he will make a hospital order. Where a hospital order is not recommended, or is not appropriate, and the defendant constitutes a danger to the public for an unpredictable period of time, the right sentence will, in all probabilities, be one of life imprisonment.
>
> In cases where the evidence indicates that the accused's responsibility for his acts was so grossly impaired that his degree of responsibility for them was minimal, then a lenient course will be open to the judge. Provided there is no danger of repetition of violence, it will usually be possible to make such an order as will give the accused his freedom, possibly with some supervision.
>
> There will however be cases in which there is no proper basis for a hospital order; but in which the accused's degree of responsibility is not minimal. In such cases the judge should pass a determinate sentence of imprisonment, the length of which will depend on two factors: his assessment of the degree of the accused's responsibility and his view as to the period of time, if any, for which the accused will continue to be a danger to the public. (*Chambers* (1983) 5 Cr App R (S) 190, per Leonard J at pp. 193–4)

An example of a case falling within the first category in *Chambers* is *Courtney* (1987) 9 Cr App R (S) 404. In that case the offender pleaded guilty to the manslaughter of his wife, whom he had strangled after a domestic argument. He immediately tried to revive her and to summon help. The offender had been undergoing treatment for depression and the medical witnesses agreed that the offender was suffering from depression to a degree which warranted his detention in hospital for treatment. The Court of Appeal, taking account of the medical advice that the offender did not represent a risk to other members of the public and that his depression could be cured within a year, varied a restriction order under the Mental Health Act 1983, s. 41, to a hospital order under s. 37 of that Act. See further the decision in *Birch* (1989) 11 Cr App R (S) 202, where the criteria for deciding between a hospital order, a life sentence and a determinate custodial sentence were discussed (see **E24.5**). A life sentence was upheld in *Sanderson* (1994) 15 Cr App R (S) 263, where the offender was a man with a long history of drug addiction and violence towards women. He had battered his girlfriend to death. The period specified under what is now the PCC(S)A 2000, s. 82A, was eight years.

In the second category of case is *Sangha* [1997] 1 Cr App R (S) 262, where the offender had suffered physical and mental cruelty and abuse from her husband over a period of 22 years. She had made several attempts at suicide. After she discovered that her husband had been having an affair, she took an overdose, but subsequently discharged herself from hospital and the following day stabbed her husband. He died four days later during which time the offender stabbed herself, causing minor injury. The medical evidence was that she was suffering from depressive illness and was subject to acute stress reaction. A sentence of 18 months' imprisonment was varied by the Court of Appeal to a probation order for three years, although by that time the offender had served five months of her sentence.

An example of the third type of case is *Derekis* [2005] 2 Cr App R (S) 1. After a long-running dispute between neighbours over levels of noise from the victim's home, the offender, a woman of 54, uttered threats after loud music came from the victim's home after 11p.m. The female victim went to the offender's home to remonstrate with her. The offender opened the door and stabbed the victim with a single blow to the heart, killing her. She pleaded guilty to manslaughter by reason of diminished responsibility. The Court of Appeal reduced the sentence of six years' imprisonment to three and a half years, on the basis that the offender was at the time of the offence suffering from a moderately severe depressive illness with associated anxiety and insomnia, she had no previous convictions, and the violence was completely out of character. See also *Hampson* [2001] 1 Cr App R (S) 288 and *Slater* [2006] 1 Cr App R (S) 8.

Sentencing Guidelines: Provocation

The SGC Guideline, *Manslaughter by Reason of Provocation* (November 2005) applies to offenders sentenced for this offence after 28 November 2005. For full text of this guideline, see **appendix 8**. **B1.38**

Sentencing Guidelines: Killing in Pursuance of Suicide Pact

The maximum penalty is life imprisonment (OAPA 1861, s. 5). **B1.39**

The offender in *Sweeney* (1986) 8 Cr App R (S) 419 pleaded guilty to the manslaughter of his wife. He was prone to depression and had married the deceased when she was suffering from advanced muscular dystrophy. They decided to commit suicide together by taking tablets and then setting fire to their car when they were inside it. Once the fire started both tried to escape, but the wife was killed. The offender suffered serious burns. The Court of Appeal reduced a four-year prison term to one of two years, that being 'sufficient, in our judgment, to mark the seriousness of this matter'. See also *England* (1990) 12 Cr App R (S) 98.

Sentencing Guidelines: Involuntary Manslaughter

The maximum penalty is life imprisonment (OAPA 1861, s. 5). **B1.40**

Fights In manslaughter arising from *fights*, 'the authorities demonstrate how widely the background facts vary in different cases' (*per* Bracewell J in *Cannon* [2001] 1 Cr App R (S) 286. In *Gratton* [2001] 2 Cr App R (S) 167 the offender and the deceased had been friends. They had been drinking together for some time when an argument developed over the offender's girlfriend. The offender struck the victim in the face, causing his chair to topple over. The victim's head struck some rocks and he died shortly afterwards from a brain haemorrhage. The offender had shown great remorse, at the time and subsequently, for what had happened. According to Tuckey LJ, for cases of this sort where death results from a single **B1.41**

blow causing the victim to strike his head on a hard object, the starting point on a plea of guilty is 12 months' imprisonment, although a non-custodial sentence is possible, and if there are features which amount to provocation it may be possible to suspend the prison sentence. Some general indications on sentencing in this type of case were given in *Coleman* (1991) 95 Cr App R 159, where Lord Lane CJ said that relevant mitigating factors would be lack of premeditation, where the injury had resulted from a single blow of moderate force, remorse, and an immediate admission of guilt, while aggravating factors would include a history of violent behaviour on the part of the offender, the fact that the assault was gratuitous or unprovoked and the fact that more than one blow had been struck. It is also clear from the authorities that cases where there was an accidental fall resulting in a fractured skull are to be distinguished from more serious cases where a victim on the ground has been kicked about the head or where a weapon has been used. According to Hutchinson LJ in *Harrison* [1996] 2 Cr App R (S) 250, 'cases of this sort which are superficially similar are often found on closer examination to differ in important details. A blow sufficient to fracture an egg-shell skull is very much less culpable than one which fractures a normal skull. An unlucky punch in the course of a spontaneous fight is very different from a wholly unprovoked blow to an innocent bystander'. In *Gunn* (1992) 13 Cr App R (S) 544, the offender, a man of good character, had known the victim for some years. After an evening spent drinking together they became involved in a fist-fight in the course of which the offender threw the victim into a garden where he struck his head on some concrete. The offender was convicted of manslaughter on an indictment for murder, and the Court of Appeal reduced a sentence of five years' imprisonment to one of three and a half years. In *Kime* [1999] 2 Cr App R (S) 3, the offender was convicted of manslaughter on an indictment for murder. He had been arguing in a car park with his girlfriend, when he took exception to an elderly man in a different group whom he took to have been laughing. The offender punched the man in the head, and the 80-year-old victim suffered a heart attack and collapsed. There was evidence that the victim had heart disease. Six years' imprisonment was regarded as 'severe but not manifestly excessive' by the Court of Appeal, Rose LJ noting that the men were of very different ages, the victim was vulnerable and had been minding his own business at the time of assault, and that the offender clearly had a propensity to behave violently when drunk. There are many appellate decisions on similar cases. Recent examples are *Lumsden* [2005] 2 Cr App R (S) 151, *Binstead* [2005] 2 Cr App R (S) 372 and *Roberts* [2006] 1 Cr App R (S) 183.

B1.42 **Firearms** In cases of manslaughter involving *firearms*, again much depends on the circumstances, particularly the degree of planning in the use of the firearm. In *O'Mahoney* (1980) 2 Cr App R (S) 57, a sentence of 15 years was upheld. The offender and two other men had set out to find a fourth man to give him a beating, having first obtained a pistol and some ammunition. Although they did not find the man they were looking for, a completely innocent man was shot in the chest at close range and killed after an argument at a club. In *Klair* (1995) 16 Cr App R (S) 660, following a dispute with his brother, the offender went to his brother's flat armed with a shotgun. The offender claimed that he intended only to frighten his brother, but the gun was fired and the brother was killed. On a conviction for manslaughter, the Court of Appeal upheld a sentence of seven years' imprisonment, Lord Lane CJ commenting that the case involved 'the greatest recklessness'. See also *Wesson* (1989) 11 Cr App R (S) 161, where a sentence of seven years was reduced to two years in a case where the offender had been cleaning his shotgun, waving it about but saying that it was unloaded, and it had discharged, killing his wife.

B1.43 **Course of Commission of Another Offence** In cases where manslaughter is committed in the *course of the commission of another offence*, such as burglary, robbery or arson, the Court of Appeal has held that the sentence should not be the same as would have been imposed for the lesser offence, and 'however unintended that killing may be, the sentence should reflect the gravity of the fact that death has been caused' (*Paget* (1982) 4 Cr App R (S) 399, per Robert Goff LJ). Again, a great deal depends on the precise circumstances of the killing. In *Cook*

(1982) 4 Cr App R (S) 237, where a manslaughter by stabbing in the course of a burglary was described as 'close to being accidental', a six-year sentence was appropriate, while a 10-year sentence was upheld in *Brophy* (1995) 16 Cr App R (S) 652, where two offenders broke into the house of an elderly lady who lived alone. When she was disturbed and ran out of the house the offender, described as 'a burglar with an appalling record, whose criminality arises from addiction to hard drugs', pushed her forcibly against a wall. The victim suffered a fractured pelvis, and died a few minutes later from shock and haemorrhage. A concurrent sentence of five years for the burglary was also upheld.

Manslaughter of Child Manslaughter of a *young child* normally attracts a custodial sentence between two and five years, depending on the degree of culpability, with sentences up to ten years being reserved for cases where there has been systematic physical assault or persistent ill-treatment of the child. In *Watts* [2002] 1 Cr App R (S) 228, described by Hooper J in the Court of Appeal as 'as bad a case of manslaughter by neglect as one could possibly come across', a life sentence was varied to one of ten years on a female offender who pleaded guilty. The child had been starved over a long period and there had been gross neglect. Seven years was reduced to five years in *Yates* [2001] 1 Cr App R (S) 428, where the offender pleaded guilty. He admitted shaking his three-month-old daughter on two occasions when she would not stop crying. A very exceptional case is *Turner* [2002] 1 Cr App R (S) 207, where a custodial sentence of 30 months was varied to a community rehabilitation order on a 'vulnerable' offender with severe learning difficulties, aged 17 at the time of the offence. **B1.44**

Gross Negligence Manslaughter Sentences for *gross negligence manslaughter* vary widely, reflecting the wide variety of situations in which the offence can be committed. At the top of the scale a sentence of 11 years' detention in a young offender institution was upheld in *Ballard* [2005] 2 Cr App R (S) 186, where the 18-year-old offender, after drinking heavily, drove his car over a prolonged period in a highly dangerous and erratic manner, at times accelerating towards groups of people who had to jump clear. His car then struck the victim, who was thrown into the air and died a short while later. In *Rodgers* [2005] 2 Cr App R (S) 105, a sentence of five years' imprisonment was upheld in the case of a landlord who installed a gas fire in a flat without adequate provision for ventilation, so that two tenants died from carbon monoxide poisoning. The Court of Appeal said that appropriate credit had been given for the guilty plea and other relevant factors. In *A-G's Ref (No. 16 of 2005)* [2006] 1 Cr App R (S) 161, the offender, a registered child-minder, had shaken a five-month-old baby in her charge, causing internal bleeding in his head which had led to death. The Court of Appeal said that the sentence of three years' imprisonment was lenient, but not outside the range which could be considered appropriate. In *Kite* [1996] 2 Cr App R (S) 295, the offender was the manager of a company organising leisure activities for young people, four of whom were drowned while taking part in a canoeing trip. He was convicted of gross negligence manslaughter on the basis that he had failed to establish adequate safety precautions. Two years' imprisonment was upheld. **B1.45**

CONSTRUCTIVE MANSLAUGHTER (KILLING BY AN UNLAWFUL ACT LIKELY TO CAUSE BODILY HARM)

The Unlawful Act

The accused's act must be unlawful, in that it constitutes a criminal offence in its own right (independently of the fact that it has caused death). See *Franklin* (1883) 15 Cox CC 163, where the fact that the accused had committed a tort did not make his act an unlawful one for the purposes of manslaughter, although it should be noted that the accused was nonetheless convicted on the ground of gross negligence. Typically the unlawful act will be an assault (see, e.g., *Larkin* [1943] KB 174) or some other offence against the person such as administering a noxious thing under the OAPA 1861, s. 23. **B1.46**

It now seems clear that the offence need not be directed against the person; an offence of arson or criminal damage can supply the required element of unlawfulness (*Goodfellow* (1986) 83 Cr App R 23). However, being a participant in the public order offence of affray will not suffice except insofar as the accused individually commits or is party to an assault perpetrated on the victim as part of the affray (*Carey* [2006] EWCA Crim 17).

The unlawful act must be an act which is unlawful in itself rather than one which is unlawful because of the negligent manner of its performance. Thus, driving without due care and attention does not count as an unlawful act for these purposes (see *Andrews v DPP* [1937] AC 576, per Lord Atkin at p. 585), otherwise unlawful act manslaughter would swallow up both the statutory offence of causing death by dangerous driving and also killing by gross negligence in the context of road traffic deaths. Perhaps a better way of excluding driving without due care and attention would be to say that the unlawful act must be an offence which requires the proof of full *mens rea* in the sense of intention or recklessness or some equally culpable state of mind. This would have the merit of also clearly excluding offences of strict liability (e.g., under health and safety legislation) which happen to result in death. Such situations should only be capable of amounting to manslaughter (and are only so treated) if they come within the gross negligence head discussed at **B1.52** to **B1.56**. Unfortunately, in *Andrews* [2003] Crim LR 477, the Court of Appeal treated the strict liability offence under the Medicines Act 1968 of administering a prescription only medicine (in this case insulin, in order to give someone a 'rush') as a sufficient unlawful act. The main point at issue was whether consent could be a defence by rendering the act lawful, which it clearly could not. However, the charge of administering a noxious thing contrary to the OAPA 1861, s. 23, (which had been left to lie on the file), would have been a much more appropriate offence on which to base the unlawful act.

The phrase 'unlawful act' connotes, an act as opposed to an omission, so that the fact that the accused has committed the offence of wilful neglect of a child under the CYPA 1933, s. 1, does not supply the unlawful act required (*Lowe* [1973] QB 702). The facts may, however, justify a verdict of manslaughter on some other ground such as gross negligence.

The *Mens Rea* of the Unlawful Act

B1.47 Although a person accused of manslaughter by definition lacks the *mens rea* for murder, the prosecution must normally prove that he has the *mens rea* appropriate to the unlawful act which caused the victim's death, a point well illustrated by the case of *Lamb* [1967] 2 QB 981, where the accused 'in jest' pointed a loaded revolver at his friend and pulled the trigger, believing that it was safe to do so because neither of the two bullets in the gun was in a chamber opposite the barrel. What neither the appellant nor his friend (who was similarly treating the incident as a joke) appreciated was that pulling the trigger rotated the cylinder so as to place one of the bullets opposite the barrel, and hence in the firing position. The Court of Appeal quashed the conviction for manslaughter on the ground that there was not proved 'the element of intent without which there can be no assault'. It would have been different had Lamb intended to frighten his friend (for then he would have had the *mens rea* of an unlawful act) — see *Ball* [1989] Crim LR 730. Since the decision in *Lamb* [1967] 2 QB 981, it has been confirmed that recklessness is sufficient *mens rea* for assault (*Venna* [1976] QB 421). However, it is subjective recklessness which applies (*Spratt* [1990] 1 WLR 1073) so Lamb would still lack the necessary *mens rea*. See also *Slingsby* [1995] Crim LR 570, where vigorous consensual sexual activity did not amount to a battery or other unlawful act since there was no intention to cause, or foresight of, harm.

The accused cannot, however, rely on his lack of *mens rea* induced by voluntary intoxication, as manslaughter is a crime of basic intent (see *Lipman* [1970] 1 QB 152). This was an extreme case in many ways, in which the accused killed his girlfriend whilst suffering LSD-induced hallucinations that he was at the centre of the earth being attacked by snakes. If the unlawful act alleged were to be a crime of specific intent, then the accused's intoxication *should* be relevant, but such situations are likely to be rare (see, however, *Watson* [1989] 1 WLR 684, burglary with intent to steal).

Likely to Cause Bodily Harm

The Objective Nature of the Test The classic formulation of this requirement, sometimes referred to as the requirement that the unlawful act be 'dangerous', is that of Edmund Davies J in *Church* [1966] 1 QB 59, where he said (at p. 70): **B1.48**

> the unlawful act must be such as all sober and reasonable people would inevitably recognise must subject the other person to, at least, the risk of some harm resulting therefrom, albeit not serious harm.

This formulation has the merit that it emphasises that the test is an objective one, which depends not on the accused's appreciation of likely harm but on what the sober and reasonable person would appreciate. The objective nature of the test was confirmed by the House of Lords in *DPP v Newbury* [1977] AC 500, where two youths pushed a paving stone off the parapet of a bridge into the path of an approaching train, thereby killing the guard. The House upheld the convictions for manslaughter and answered yes to the certified question, 'Can a defendant be properly convicted of manslaughter, when his mind is not affected by drink or drugs, if he did not foresee harm to another?'

On the other hand, the defendant's foresight of harm may be relevant to the separate question of whether he has the *mens rea* of the unlawful act if the unlawful act is an offence against the person. The House of Lords in *DPP v Newbury* [1977] AC 500 did not make it clear what the unlawful act was, and indeed appeared to be rather dismissive of the requirement of *mens rea* for the unlawful act. However, it now seems clear in the light of *Goodfellow* (1986) 83 Cr App R 23 (see **B1.46**) that criminal damage would be the obvious and sufficient unlawful act in *Newbury*, and that the two accused were probably reckless as to criminal damage, so that they did have the *mens rea* for an unlawful act even if they did not foresee harm to another. Even where the unlawful act is an assault, the *mens rea* need not relate to harm; an intention to put in fear is sufficient. Thus the following dictum of Lord Denning MR in *Gray v Barr* [1971] 2 QB 554, at p. 568, on which doubt was cast by Lord Salmon in *Newbury*, is perfectly sound in the context of a case where the unlawful act is an assault: 'the accused must do a dangerous act with the *intention* of frightening or harming someone, or with the *realisation* that it is likely to frighten or harm someone'. Lord Denning was not casting doubt on the requirement that the act be *objectively* likely to cause bodily harm (he refers to a 'dangerous' act), but was making the important and separate point that the accused must be shown to have the *mens rea* for whatever is alleged to be the unlawful act. See also *Jennings* [1990] Crim LR 588 and *Scarlett* [1993] 4 All ER 629.

Physical Harm Not Mere Emotional Disturbance The harm *likely* to result from the act must be physical harm. Emotional disturbance will not suffice, even though physical harm (and death) does in fact result from the foreseeable emotional disturbance: see *Dawson* (1985) 81 Cr App R 150, where the fact that a robbery of a petrol station was likely to cause emotional disturbance to the 60-year-old attendant was held not to be sufficient, even though the attendant, who had a weak heart, suffered a heart attack and died. The heart attack did constitute physical harm but the reasonable man would not have *foreseen* such physical harm as likely to result. The reasonable man is to be regarded as having the knowledge of facts that the accused has, and the accused in this case did not know that the attendant had a weak heart. A similar approach was taken in *Carey* [2006] EWCA Crim 17, where the Court of Appeal regarded it as an even clearer case than *Watson* in that the sober and reasonable bystander would not have recognised a risk of shock leading to a heart attack in the case of an apparently healthy 15-year-old girl. In *Watson* [1989] 1 WLR 684, however, the unlawful act was burglary under the Theft Act 1968, s. 9(1)(a), which allegedly caused the elderly occupier **B1.49**

(again with a weak heart) to suffer a heart attack and die. The Court of Appeal held (at p. 867) that, although the appellant did not know the age or physical condition of the occupier at the point of entry,

> the jury were entitled to ascribe to the bystander the knowledge which the appellant gained during the whole of his stay in the house . . . The unlawful act in the present circumstances comprised the whole of the burglarious intrusion and did not come to an end on the appellant's foot crossing the threshold . . .

The statement about the duration of the unlawful act seems, with respect, to stretch the definition of the offence under s. 9(1)(a) and can be regarded as *obiter*, since the conviction was quashed on another ground. However, the case is a useful illustration of the proposition that if the accused knows of the victim's susceptibility to physical harm, then that knowledge can be ascribed to the reasonable man and the accused's act can be regarded as 'likely to cause bodily harm'.

On the other hand, the reasonable man does not share the accused's mistaken beliefs. In *Ball* [1989] Crim LR 730, the accused mistakenly believed he had loaded his gun with blank cartridges but the reasonable bystander, not sharing that belief, would have considered the act of firing the gun dangerous.

B1.50 **The Nature of the Causal Link** A further limitation on the type of harm required was suggested in *Dalby* [1982] 1 WLR 425, where the Court of Appeal quashed a conviction for manslaughter based on the accused unlawfully supplying his friend with drugs, which his friend subsequently injected into himself with fatal consequences. Waller LJ said that the act had to be 'directed at the victim and likely to cause *immediate* injury, however slight' (emphasis added). The harm (or injury) in this case was caused by the deceased's own act of injecting the drugs. The mere supply of the drug was not dangerous in the sense that it was likely to cause *immediate* injury. The qualification suggested in *Dalby* is capable of restricting the scope of constructive manslaughter in a number of ways but it has been distinguished in subsequent cases.

In *Mitchell* [1983] QB 741 the accused assaulted X, causing him to fall on top of an elderly woman who died as a result. The Court of Appeal quite rightly had no difficulty in dismissing the argument that the accused's act was directed at X rather than at the deceased, saying that in *Dalby* [1982] 1 WLR 425 the court had been concerned with 'the quality of the act rather than the identity of the victim'. This is no real restriction on *Dalby* and is similar to the familiar transferred *mens rea* rule (see **A2.13**). In *Pagett* (1983) 76 Cr App R 279, the accused, at the end of a police siege, held the victim (a girl pregnant by him) in front of him as a shield while he fired at the police. The police fired back, in what the jury found to be a lawful manner, but unfortunately killed the girl. Pagett was convicted of manslaughter. The Court of Appeal was principally concerned with the question of whether the acts of the police in firing back constituted a *novus actus interveniens* (see **A1.27** to **A1.32**), which it held it was not because the police had been acting lawfully. However, the court briefly referred to the elements of unlawful act manslaughter and said (at p. 291):

> [the accused] committed not one but two unlawful acts, both of which were dangerous — the act of firing at the police, and the act of holding Gail Kinchen as a shield in front of him when the police might well fire shots in his direction in self-defence.

No mention was made of the *Dalby* requirement of 'directed at the victim' or 'likely to cause immediate injury'. However, the facts can be accommodated within the *Dalby* test, although with more difficulty than in *Mitchell* [1988] QB 741. Firing at the police certainly was directed at *a* victim and likely to cause immediate injury (at least to the police). Holding the girl as a shield was an act directed at her and in the circumstances likely to cause immediate harm to her, given that bullets were likely to be fired in the accused's direction as a result of the accused's own act.

The decision in *Goodfellow* (1986) 83 Cr App R 23 moves more clearly away from the limitation suggested in *Dalby*. The accused, wishing to be rehoused, set fire to his council house. The fire spread more rapidly than he had anticipated, and his wife and child, and another woman were killed in the blaze. The Court of Appeal upheld the conviction for manslaughter, even though the accused's acts were not directed at a victim but rather against property. Lord Lane CJ said (at p. 27) that all that had been intended to be said in *Dalby* was that 'there must be no fresh intervening cause between the act and the death'. His lordship went on:

> The questions which the jury have to decide on the charge of manslaughter of this nature are: (1) Was the act intentional? (2) Was it unlawful? (3) Was it an act which any reasonable person would realise was bound to subject some other human being to the risk of physical harm, albeit not necessarily serious harm? (4) Was that act the cause of death?

The *Dalby* limitation of 'likely to cause immediate injury' seems then to have been abandoned, regrettably perhaps, inasmuch as on facts such as *Goodfellow*, as Lord Lane CJ himself recognised, gross negligence manslaughter would appear to be available. Having said that, *Willoughby* [2005] 1 WLR 1880 shows that putting this sort of case on the basis of unlawful act manslaughter is preferable; it avoids the complications inherent in establishing the duty of care required for gross negligence manslaughter. It should also be noted that, in a case such as *Lamb* [1967] 2 QB 981 (see **B1.47**), Lord Lane's second question for the jury would need to be amplified in order to stress that an act is only unlawful if the accused has the *mens rea* for the particular unlawful act alleged. To ask, Was the act intentional? is not sufficient, since that can be interpreted merely as referring to voluntariness, e.g., on the facts of *Lamb*, as asking Did the accused intend to pull the trigger? rather than Did he intend to assault his friend? On the facts of *Goodfellow* (1986) 83 Cr App R 23, the problem does not really arise, because the accused clearly had the *mens rea* for criminal damage.

Drug-related Deaths, Causation and 'acting in concert' The essential requirement from *Dalby* [1982] 1 WLR 425 that 'there must be no intervening cause' between the accused's act and the victim's death has come into focus as a result of a number of decisions starting with *Kennedy* [1999] Crim LR 65, which was subsequently referred to the Court of Appeal by the Criminal Cases Review Commission, only for the conviction to be upheld a second time in the Court of Appeal in *Kennedy (No. 2)* [2005] 1 WLR 2159. The facts of *Kennedy* involved the accused supplying a prepared syringe of heroin with which the deceased voluntarily injected himself; that injection caused his death. The first time that the Court of Appeal upheld the conviction for manslaughter it was not entirely clear whether it was on the basis that the accused had *himself* committed an unlawful act of supply (plus encouragement to immediately inject) that constituted the unlawful act causing death or whether it was on the basis that the victim's own act of self-injection was, on some unspecified basis, an unlawful act for which the accused was responsible because he had encouraged it. Either way there were criticisms of the decision, including the argument that the deceased's own voluntary act should have broken the chain of causation (and of responsibility) between the accused's acts and the death. B1.51

In *Dias* [2002] 2 Cr App R 96, on similar facts to *Kennedy*, the Court of Appeal quashed the conviction for manslaughter, which in that case had been based on the act of self-injection *by the deceased* being unlawful, which it clearly was not in the requisite sense, and the Court noted that there being no offence of self-manslaughter, there could not be liability based on aiding and abetting such a non-existent offence. However, the Court did not actually overrule *Kennedy* and left open the possibility of manslaughter based on an unlawful act of supply as the dangerous act as 'there may possibly be situations where the chain of causation could be established. It is however important that that issue be left to the jury to determine, as happened at the trial in *Kennedy*'. Many commentators nevertheless found it difficult to see how 'the chain of causation could be established' in the face of the deceased's own voluntary act and *Kennedy* was at the time thought to remain ripe for overruling.

These cases were discussed further in *Rogers* [2003] 1 WLR 1374, where the deceased injected himself with heroin whilst the appellant held his belt round the deceased's arm as a tourniquet. The appellant's conviction for manslaughter was upheld because the application of the tourniquet was regarded as part and parcel of the act of injection causing death. The appellant was playing a part in the mechanics of the injection and thus committed the unlawful act as a principal, which this time was explicitly put as being under the OAPA 1861, s. 23 (administering a noxious thing rather than simply supply of a drug). Rose LJ referred approvingly to *Dias* as still supporting the proposition that 'even where a victim injects himself, the supplier of heroin may be guilty of manslaughter, provided causation is established . . . *A fortiori*, as it seems to us, a person who actively participates in the injection process commits the *actus reus*.' In *Finlay* [2003] EWCA Crim 3868, these comments were followed up when upholding a conviction for manslaughter in a case where there was no direct participation in the act of injection. This was on the basis that the appellant was nevertheless a principal participant in the offence of 'causing to be administered or taken' a noxious thing under the OAPA 1861, s. 23, by providing a loaded syringe to the deceased who injected herself with it – a consequence that was categorised as 'ordinary' rather than 'extraordinary'. The principles of causation seemed to be being stretched considerably here in saying that the supplier caused the injection and thus committed an unlawful act under s. 23, although it was arguable that the case could have been confined to its own facts where there was in reality only one possible likely outcome of giving the loaded syringe to the particularly vulnerable addict who had been asking for it.

However, when the case of *Kennedy* came back before the Court of Appeal following its referral by the CCRC, the conviction in that case too was upheld on the basis of a very similar analysis to that adopted in *Finlay*. If there was a difference, it was that Lord Woolf CJ in *Kennedy* seemed to make the causation issue turn less on whether the self-injection by the deceased could be regarded as an ordinary, rather than extraordinary, occurrence and consequence of the accused's acts but rather on whether the accused and the victim were acting 'in concert'. If they were so acting, the voluntary act of the deceased did not break the chain of causation. In summarising his conclusions as to why Kennedy's conviction could stand, Lord Woolf said:

> To convict, the jury had to be satisfied that, when the heroin was handed to the deceased 'for immediate injection', he and the deceased were both engaged in the one activity of administering the heroin. . . . If the jury were satisfied of this then the appellant was responsible for taking the action in concert with the deceased to enable the deceased to inject himself with the syringe of heroin which had been made ready for his immediate use. In our view, the jury would have been entitled to find (and indeed it is an appropriate finding) that in these circumstances the appellant and the deceased were jointly engaged in administering the heroin.
>
> The point in this case is that the appellant and the deceased were carrying out a 'combined operation' for which they were jointly responsible. Their actions were similar to what happens frequently when carrying out lawful injections: one nurse may carry out certain preparatory actions (including preparing the syringe) and hand it to a colleague who inserts the needle and administers the injection, after which the other nurse may apply a plaster. In such a situation, both nurses can be regarded as administering the drug. They are working as a team. Both their actions are necessary. They are interlinked but separate parts in the overall process of administering the drug. In these circumstances, as Waller LJ stated on the first appeal, they 'can be said to be jointly responsible for carrying out that act'.

The question will remain for critics of the decision whether it is appropriate to classify the non-injector as a principal in the above situation (as opposed to any responsibility being based on aiding and abetting the injection by the other, which, of course, is of no use where the other is injecting himself as that act is not unlawful). As far as the Court of Appeal is concerned, it appears that the matter is now settled and that manslaughter on the basis of an unlawful act under s. 23 can be left to the jury where the accused and the deceased were acting in concert (this would not of course be the case if the victim's act was a wholly extraordinary and unforeseeable one). Once the issue is left to the jury, juries appear to have no difficulty in finding the provider of the syringe to be responsible for manslaughter.

MANSLAUGHTER BY GROSS NEGLIGENCE

Basis of Liability

Manslaughter has traditionally been the one offence at common law in which negligence is expressly recognised as a sufficient basis of liability, but even here the negligence has to be 'gross'. Defining the precise degree of negligence required has always been problematical, and ultimately the question, being one of degree, has been one for the jury. This is evident from the following test laid down by Lord Hewart CJ in *Bateman* (1925) 19 Cr App R 8, at pp. 11–12: **B1.52**

> the facts must be such that, in the opinion of the jury, the negligence of the accused went beyond a mere matter of compensation between subjects and showed such disregard for the life and safety of others as to amount to a crime against the State and conduct deserving punishment.

In *Andrews v DPP* [1937] AC 576, at p. 583, Lord Atkin said that whilst this was:

> not . . . a precise definition of the crime . . . the substance of the judgment is most valuable, and in my opinion is correct. In practice it has generally been adopted by judges in charging juries in all cases of manslaughter by negligence.

Lord Atkin went on to say that in summarising the very high degree of negligence required:

> Probably of all the epithets that can be applied 'reckless' most nearly covers the case . . . but it is probably not all-embracing, for 'reckless' suggests an indifference to risk, whereas the accused may have appreciated the risk and intended to avoid it and yet shown such a high degree of negligence in the means adopted to avoid as would justify a conviction. (ibid., at p. 583)

Nevertheless, judges have often used the word 'reckless' to sum up to the jury the degree of fault required without making it clear how, if at all, this differs from the concept of gross negligence. This lack of clarity was perhaps inevitable while the meaning of 'reckless' in the criminal law generally was unclear. But after the apparently authoritative House of Lords decisions on the meaning of recklessness in *Metropolitan Police Commissioner v Caldwell* [1982] AC 341 and *Lawrence* [1982] AC 510, the issue became very difficult to ignore. In *Adomako* [1995] 1 AC 171 the House of Lords restored gross negligence rather than recklessness as the essential basis of liability, but to understand the current state of the law it is necessary to outline the somewhat chequered history of this variety of manslaughter over the decade prior to *Adomako.*

Despite the complex history, to be recounted at B1.53, the Court of Appeal, in *Misra* [2005] 1 Cr App R 328, has rejected the argument that gross negligence manslaughter offends against the principle of legal certainty inherent in the ECHR, Article. 7. In the Court of Appeal's view (Judge LJ at [48]):

> The decision of the House of Lords in *Adomako* clearly identified the ingredients of manslaughter by gross negligence. In very brief summary, confirming *Andrews v DPP* [1937] AC 576, the offence requires first, death resulting from a negligent breach of the duty of care owed by the defendant to the deceased, second, that in negligent breach of that duty, the victim was exposed by the defendant to the risk of death, and third, that the circumstances were so reprehensible as to amount to gross negligence.

His lordship reiterated later in his judgment at [64] that:

> ... the law is clear. The ingredients of the offence have been clearly defined, and the principles decided in the House of Lords in *Adomako*. They involve no uncertainty. The hypothetical citizen, seeking to know his position, would be advised that, assuming he owed a duty of care to the deceased which he had negligently broken, and that death resulted, he would be liable to conviction for manslaughter if, on the available evidence, the jury was satisfied that his negligence was gross. A doctor would be told that grossly negligent treatment of a patient which exposed him or her to the risk of death, and caused it, would constitute manslaughter.

When the Corporate Manslaughter and Corporate Homicide Act 2007, s. 20, is brought into force, the common-law offence of manslaughter by gross negligence will be abolished insofar as it concerns corporations or other organisations to which s. 1 of that Act applies (see **B1.128**).

Gross Negligence as Opposed to Objective Recklessness

The Incursion of a Test of Recklessness

B1.53 In *Seymour* [1983] 2 AC 493, the accused, having recently quarrelled with the woman with whom he lived, was involved in a minor collision between his 11-ton lorry and her car. The woman got out of the car, but was crushed between the lorry and her own car as the accused tried, allegedly, to shunt her car out of the way (moving it 10 to 20 feet and forcing a tyre off in the process). Rather than charge the statutory offence of causing death by reckless driving, the prosecution took the view (rightly in the view of the House of Lords) that this was such a bad case that the offence of common-law manslaughter was appropriate. Nevertheless, in referring to the fault element required, the judge directed the jury in terms of recklessness as then defined by the House of Lords in *Lawrence* [1982] AC 510 in relation to the statutory offence (see **A2.6**), save only that he omitted any reference to a risk of damage to property and limited the risk to 'an obvious and serious risk of causing physical harm'. Seymour appealed on the grounds that the *Lawrence* meaning of 'recklessness' was not applicable to common-law manslaughter, and that a more subjective meaning should be applied. The House of Lords dismissed the appeal and said that the *Lawrence* direction was appropriate (though without the reference to damage to property), the legal ingredients of the statutory offence and of common-law manslaughter being the same.

The decision raised many difficult issues including the question whether the *Lawrence* test of recklessness could be said to have completely supplanted the test of gross negligence in manslaughter. Clarification of this question appeared to come in the Privy Council decision in *Kong Cheuk Kwan v The Queen* (1985) 82 Cr App R 18. This case arose out of a collision in perfect weather between two hydrofoils in Hong Kong harbour, which resulted in the deaths of two passengers. Lord Roskill, in allowing the appeal, thought that here, too, a proper direction should have been based on *Lawrence*-type recklessness and appeared to confirm that the test is recklessness rather than gross negligence. Indeed Lord Roskill approved the comments of Watkins LJ in the Court of Appeal in *Seymour* (1983) 76 Cr App R 211, where he said (at p. 216): 'it is no longer necessary or helpful to make reference to compensation and negligence'.

The Restoration of the Gross Negligence Test

B1.54 The start of the return to the gross negligence test can be seen in *Prentice* [1994] QB 302, where the Court of Appeal made it clear that gross negligence had by no means been totally supplanted by recklessness. Indeed it was of the view that, 'leaving motor manslaughter aside, the proper test in manslaughter based on breach of duty was the gross negligence test and that the *Lawrence/Caldwell* recklessness test was . . . inappropriate in the present class of case'. One of the appellants (Adomako) appealed to the House of Lords which also considered these issues.

In *Adomako* [1995] 1 AC 171, the House was able to go further than the Court of Appeal and hold that the *Bateman/Andrews* gross negligence test was of general application and that there should be no separate test for motor manslaughter.

> . . . the law as stated in *Seymour* . . . should no longer apply since the underlying statutory provisions on which it rested have not been repealed by the Road Traffic Act 1991. It may be that cases of involuntary motor manslaughter will as a result become rare but I consider it unsatisfactory that there should be any exception to the generality of the statement which I have made . . . (per Lord Mackay LC at p. 187).

It is not immediately apparent why the reversion from *Lawrence* recklessness to gross negligence should make convictions for involuntary motor manslaughter any more rare (they had not exactly been common in the past). Part of the explanation may lie in the fact that in the Court of Appeal the convictions of Prentice and Sulman for manslaughter (not of the motorised variety) had been quashed because the direction in terms of *Lawrence* recklessness had failed to leave it open to the jury to take account of the excuses or mitigating circumstances that might have been relevant to the issue of gross negligence. Lord Mackay and the Court of Appeal may have regarded gross negligence as a narrower basis of liability than *Lawrence* recklessness; this is surprising in the light of Lord Atkin's comments in *Andrews v DPP* [1937] AC 576 (at p. 583) that 'reckless suggests an indifference to risk whereas the accused may have appreciated the risk and intended to avoid it and yet shown such a high degree of negligence in the means adopted to avoid the risk as would justify the conviction'. This seems more consistent with the view that gross negligence is *wider* than recklessness, particularly in the sense that negligently 'ruling out the risk' may negative recklessness but not necessarily gross negligence.

Whatever the explanation, Lord Mackay went on to answer the certified question before the House of Lords in *Adomako* (at p. 188):

> In cases of criminal negligence involving a breach of duty it is a sufficient direction to the jury to adopt the gross negligence test . . . it is not necessary to refer to the definition of recklessness in *Lawrence* [1982] AC 510, although it is perfectly open to the trial judge to use the word 'reckless' in its ordinary meaning as part of his exposition of the law if he deems it appropriate in the circumstances of the particular case.

His lordship emphasised that whilst a judge *may* feel it to be so appropriate to use the word reckless as indicating the extent to which a defendant's conduct must deviate from a proper standard of care, it would not be right 'to *require* that this should be done and certainly not right that it should incorporate the full detail required in *Lawrence*'. Furthermore, in *A-G's Ref (No. 2 of 1999)* [2000] QB 796, the Court of Appeal held that proof of gross negligence does not require proof of any particular state of mind and does not require evidence of the accused's state of mind. Although one can agree that a specific state of mind such as recklessness is not required, it is difficult to see how one can avoid looking into what facts the individual either knew (and failed to take adequate precautions for) or did not know about (but should have done). Either way, this surely requires evidence of the accused's state of mind. In *R (Rowley) v DPP* [2003] EWHC 693 (Admin), the absence of evidence of subjective recklessness was held to be an appropriate factor to take into account in a decision not to prosecute. However, it was confirmed in *Misra* [2005] 1 Cr App R 328 that the fault element that the prosecution have to prove remains gross negligence and, despite the rehabilitation of subjective recklessness in *G* [2004] 1 AC 1034 in relation to criminal damage, there is no warrant for replacing gross negligence in manslaughter with a requirement to prove subjective recklessness. Judge LJ noted (at [55]) of *Misra* that in his speech in *G*, Lord Bingham emphasised that 'he was not addressing the meaning of "reckless" in any other statutory or common law context than section 1(1) and (2) of the Criminal Damage Act 1971.' In *Mark* [2004] EWCA Crim 2490, Scott Baker LJ made the same point in coming to the same conclusion that it is gross negligence and not subjective recklessness that has to be proved. Thus the trial judge was correct in telling the jury in relation to the facts of that case that 'actual foresight or perception of the risk is not a prerequisite of the crime of gross negligence' and that an accused could be guilty of gross negligence simply on the basis of a complete failure to advert to what is an obvious and important matter, i.e. an obvious and serious risk of death.

Nature of Gross Negligence

B1.55 Running throughout Lord Mackay's judgment in *Adomako* [1995] 1 AC 171 is a concern that directions should be 'comprehensible to an ordinary member of the public who is called to sit on a jury' and he was therefore reluctant 'to state the law more elaborately' as had perhaps been attempted by the Court of Appeal. Nevertheless it is necessary to investigate a little more closely the essentials of gross negligence manslaughter. *Bateman* (1925) 19 Cr App R 8 and *Andrews v DPP* [1937] AC 576 are not necessarily all that helpful since they say little more than that the negligence must go beyond that required for civil liability, which is a question of degree for the jury; if matters had been entirely clear from those two cases, there would not have since been the many conflicting appellate pronouncements on the issue. Having expressed his approval of those two cases, Lord Mackay set out what he regarded as the essentials of gross negligence (at p. 187):

> . . . in my opinion the ordinary principles of the law of negligence apply to ascertain whether or not the defendant has been in breach of a duty of care towards the victim who has died. If such a breach of duty is established the next question is whether that breach of duty caused the death of the victim. If so, the jury must go on to consider whether that breach of duty should be characterised as gross negligence and therefore as a crime. This will depend on the seriousness of the breach of duty committed by the defendant in all the circumstances in which the defendant was placed when it occurred . . .
>
> . . . The essence of the matter which is supremely a jury question is whether, having regard to the risk of death involved, the conduct of the defendant was so bad in all the circumstances as to amount in their judgment to a criminal act or omission.

Two particular aspects of the above explanation are worthy of comment. The first is the re-introduction of the ordinary principles of negligence to decide whether there is a breach of a duty of care. This is not necessarily a simple matter especially if the factual situation is one where policy factors might impinge see, for example, *Ancell v McDermott* [1993] 4 All ER 355. Is it envisaged that the types of arguments raised by that sort of case could be relevant to whether a person is guilty of manslaughter and might need to be rehearsed in a criminal prosecution? Certainly the maxim '*ex turpi causa*' has no applicability in this context, as is illustrated by *Wacker* [2003] QB 1203 where the Court of Appeal confirmed that a duty of care could be owed by a lorry driver to illegal immigrants whom he had concealed in the back of his lorry. The policy factors here were clearly in favour of responsibility but in other situations they may point in the opposite direction. Assuming, however, that there are no relevant policy factors militating against a duty of care whether there *can be* a duty of care seems to be a question of law for the judge (*Khan* [1998] Crim LR 830 and *Singh* [1999] Crim LR 582 while whether there *actually is* a duty is a question of fact for the jury), one is still faced with the second issue, foreseeability of what type of risk? Various formulations have been used in the past including a risk to health and welfare, a risk of serious injury and a risk of death. *Singh* explicitly confined it to a risk of death whereby 'the circumstances must be such that a reasonably prudent person would have foreseen a serious and obvious risk not merely of injury, even serious injury, but of death' and in *Misra* [2005] 1 Cr App R 328, the Court of Appeal confirmed this approach as being in line with *Adomako* (and Lord Mackay's reference to 'having regard to the risk of death involved'). The court was emphatic, in the face of a challenge to the compatibility of gross negligence manslaughter with the principle of legal certainty inherent in the ECHR, Article 7, that it was now quite clear that a (foreseeable) risk of death was required and the point was also made that this was consistent with the offence being one designed to protect the right to life: 'In short, the offence requires gross negligence in circumstances where what is at risk is the life of an individual to whom the defendant owes a duty of care. As such it serves to protect his or her right to life' (Judge LJ at [52]). References to risks to 'safety', or indeed to any other consequence except death, are now superfluous and should be avoided (*Yaqoob* [2005] EWCA Crim 2169).

Sentencing Guidelines

See **B1.45**. **B1.56**

MOTOR MANSLAUGHTER AND ROAD TRAFFIC ACT OFFENCES

Until the coming into force of the Road Traffic Act 1991, s. 1, there appeared to be a complete overlap between (reckless) motor manslaughter and the statutory offence of causing death by reckless driving (see *Seymour* [1983] 2 AC 493). The 1991 Act replaced the offence of causing death by reckless driving in the Road Traffic Act 1988, s. 1, by the offence of causing death by dangerous driving and s. 2A of the 1988 Act defines the meaning of dangerous driving in a way which has echoes of the *Lawrence* definition of recklessness but is not identical with it; indeed it is somewhat wider in its scope. There thus ceased to be a complete overlap with motor manslaughter but it seems that manslaughter should still be reserved for the very worst cases. If a charge of manslaughter is being considered rather than the statutory offence, it should be borne in mind that causing death by dangerous driving is not an alternative verdict to manslaughter. Furthermore, Lord Roskill stated in *Seymour* (at p. 507) that it was not permissible to allow a trial to proceed on two separate counts, one statutory and the other at common law, and the same seems to be true in relation to the new offence. One should also bear in mind the comments of Lord Mackay LC in *Adomako* [1995] 1 AC 171 (see **B1.54**) that cases of involuntary motor manslaughter are likely to become rare following the re-establishment of gross negligence rather than recklessness. (See further **C3.3**.) **B1.57**

CAUSING OR ALLOWING THE DEATH OF A CHILD OR VULNERABLE ADULT

Definition

Domestic Violence, Crime and Victims Act 2004, s. 5 **B1.58**

(1) A person ('D') is guilty of an offence if—
 (a) a child or vulnerable adult ('V') dies as a result of the unlawful act of a person who—
  (i) was a member of the same household as V, and
  (ii) had frequent contact with him,
 (b) D was such a person at the time of that act,
 (c) at that time there was a significant risk of serious physical harm being caused to V by the unlawful act of such a person, and
 (d) either D was the person whose act caused V's death or—
  (i) D was, or ought to have been, aware of the risk mentioned in paragraph (c),
  (ii) D failed to take such steps as he could reasonably have been expected to take to protect V from the risk, and
  (iii) the act occurred in circumstances of the kind that D foresaw or ought to have foreseen.

(2) The prosecution does not have to prove whether it is the first alternative in subsection (1)(d) or the second (sub-paragraphs (i) to (iii)) that applies.

Procedure

The offence is triable only on indictment and is a class 3 offence. **B1.59**

The DVCVA 2004, s. 6(5), expressly provides for an offence under s. 6 to be treated as an offence of homicide for the purposes of:

(a) the MCA 1980, ss. 24 and 25, relating to mode of trial of a child or young person;
(b) the CDA 1998, s. 51A, relating to sending cases to the Crown Court in relation to children and young persons;
(c) the PCC(S)A 2000, s. 8, relating to the remittal of young offenders to youth courts for sentence.

It is a 'fatal offence' for the purposes of the Law Reform (Year and a Day Rule) Act 1996, s. 2, thereby requiring the A-G's consent to a prosecution in certain circumstances, including where the death occurs more than three years after the injury alleged to have caused it (DVCVA 2004, sch. 10, para. 33).

More controversially, under s. 6(1), 'where a person is charged in the same proceedings with an offence of murder or manslaughter and with an offence under section 5 in respect of the same death', s. 6(2), (3) and (4) affect the evidence and procedure applicable to the offence of murder or manslaughter in three different but related ways:

(a) under s. 6(2), where by virtue of the CJPO 1994, s. 35(3), inferences may be drawn in relation to the s. 5 offence from the accused's failure to give evidence or refusal to answer a question, the court or jury may also draw such inferences in determining whether he is guilty of murder or manslaughter (or any alternative verdict offence on those charges) even if there would otherwise be no case for him to answer in relation to murder or manslaughter (or the alternative verdict offence);
(b) under s. 6(3), unless the s. 5 offence is itself dismissed, the charge of murder or manslaughter is not to be dismissed on an application to the Crown Court under the CDA 1998, sch. 3, para. 2;
(c) under s. 6(4), the question of whether there is a case for the accused to answer on the charge of murder or manslaughter is not to be considered before the close of all the evidence (unless he has already ceased to be charged with the s. 5 offence).

Domestic Violence, Crime and Victims Act 2004, s. 6

(1) Subsections (2) to (4) apply where a person ('the defendant') is charged in the same proceedings with an offence of murder or manslaughter and with an offence under section 5 in respect of the same death ('the section 5 offence').
(2) Where by virtue of section 35(3) of the Criminal Justice and Public Order Act 1994 a court or jury is permitted, in relation to the section 5 offence, to draw such inferences as appear proper from the defendant's failure to give evidence or refusal to answer a question, the court or jury may also draw such inferences in determining whether he is guilty—
    (a) of murder or manslaughter, or
    (b) of any other offence of which he could lawfully be convicted on the charge of murder or manslaughter,

    even if there would otherwise be no case for him to answer in relation to that offence.
(3) The charge of murder or manslaughter is not to be dismissed under paragraph 2 of Schedule 3 to the Crime and Disorder Act 1998 (unless the section 5 offence is dismissed).
(4) At the defendant's trial the question whether there is a case for the defendant to answer on the charge of murder or manslaughter is not to be considered before the close of all the evidence (or, if at some earlier time he ceases to be charged with the section 5 offence, before that earlier time).

These provisions clearly contemplate proceedings for murder or manslaughter being brought where a child or vulnerable adult dies in A's (and often B's) household and there is evidence that A (and/or B) may have been guilty of an offence under s. 5 but there is not yet a *prima facie* case for murder or manslaughter against A or B (the problem in *Lane* (1986) 82 Cr App R 5). Proceedings for murder or manslaughter against A (and/or B), if instituted, cannot now be dismissed in advance by means of an application to dismiss in the Crown Court nor can the charges be dismissed at trial by a submission of no case to answer (the *Lane* problem) before the close of *all* the evidence, by when it will be known if and to what extent A has given evidence (and by when there may be other evidence incriminating him given by B in his or her own defence). In addition, A can actually be convicted of murder or manslaughter on the basis of inferences drawn from his failure to testify or his refusal to answer questions at his trial, even though without those inferences there would not be a case for him to answer in relation to murder or manslaughter. The fact that there would 'otherwise be no case for him to answer' does not necessarily mean that A is at risk of being convicted 'solely' on the basis of an inference from silence, since one would expect there to be other evidence, albeit not sufficient on its own to amount to a *prima facie* case, but there is a clear risk that it might amount to a conviction based 'mainly' on an inference from silence and, as such, it is highly likely to be subject to challenge under the ECHR, Article 6 (see **F19.24** and *Murray v UK* (1996) 22 EHRR 29). The government was of the view that the provision was compatible with the Convention (cf. Law Com No. 282, September 2003, paras 6.78–6.96 seeking to justify a similar but differently worded provision in their own draft Bill) because the trial judge would have the right and duty to prevent the case going to the jury at the conclusion of the evidence (rather than as normally at the half-way point) if the homicide conviction was likely to be based 'mainly' on the adverse inference from silence. This interpretation would, however, mean that there would be likely to be relatively few cases in which the judge could or would ultimately let the murder or manslaughter charge go to the jury on the basis of an adverse inference (where 'there would otherwise be no case for him to answer') and, if this is right, the phrase is of limited effect. It should be stressed that these provisions modify the evidential and procedural rules only in relation to offences of murder and manslaughter charged in the same proceedings as a s. 5 offence and do not affect the s. 5 offence itself, which is subject to the normal rules on no case to answer and adverse inferences and the like.

Indictment

Statement of Offence **B1.60**

Causing or allowing the death of a child [or vulnerable adult] contrary to section 5 of the Domestic Violence, Crime and Victims Act 2004.

Particulars of Offence

A, on or about the . . . day of . . . , being a member of the same household as a child [or vulnerable adult] V and having frequent contact with him, fell into one or other of the following alternatives, it being immaterial, and unnecessary to prove, which one it was, that is to say that *either* he caused the death of V as a result of his (A's) own unlawful act which carried a significant risk of serious physical harm being caused to V,

or, alternatively, he failed to take such steps as he could reasonably have been expected to take to protect V from the significant risk of serious physical harm from the unlawful act which caused V's death, the unlawful act having been committed in this alternative not by A but by another person who was a member of the same household as V and who had frequent contact with V, the significant risk in this alternative being one which A was aware of or ought to have been aware of and the other's unlawful act occurring in circumstances of the kind which A foresaw or ought to have foreseen.

Alternative Verdicts

There are no alternative verdicts specifically provided for and the offence is not itself an alternative verdict to murder or manslaughter, but note the procedural and evidential links to murder and manslaughter (see **B1.59**). The offence is in a sense, within itself, one self-contained alternative verdict in that the accused is guilty provided that it can be proved that he must have satisfied one or other of the two alternatives even though it cannot be proved which particular one. **B1.61**

Sentence

The maximum penalty is 14 years' imprisonment (DVCVA 2004, s. 5(7)). **B1.62**

Elements

B1.63 The offence is a response to the problems exemplified in *Lane* (1986) Cr App R 5 and discussed in Law Com No. 282 Children: Their Non-Accidental Death or Serious Injury (Criminal Trials). It implements some of the ideas inherent in the Law Commission proposals but does so in a substantially and significantly different manner. It goes beyond the Law Commission proposals by including vulnerable adults (defined in the DVCVA 2004, s. 5(6) as 'a person aged 16 or over whose ability to protect himself from violence, abuse or neglect is significantly impaired through physical or mental disability or illness, through old age or otherwise') as well as children (under 16), but it is limited to where such a person dies as a result of the unlawful act as opposed to being harmed in some other way. As can be seen from the draft indictment (see **B1.60**) there are two ways of committing the offence (it being unnecessary to prove which one it is). The first can be compared with unlawful act manslaughter and the second with gross negligence manslaughter, but there are significant differences in each case. Unlawful act manslaughter requires only that the unlawful act carry a risk of 'some harm resulting therefrom, albeit not serious harm' whereas under s. 5(1)(c) there has to be a 'significant risk of *serious* physical harm', which is defined in s. 5(6) as 'harm that amounts to grievous bodily harm for the purposes of the Offences Against the Person Act 1861'. The risk must also be a 'significant' one; 'significant' is an ordinary English word which should not be further defined for the jury and it is incorrect to tell the jury that it means 'more than minimal' (*Mujuru* [2007] EWCA Crim 1249). Comparing the second limb of the offence with gross negligence manslaughter reveals that there is no requirement under s. 5(1)(d)(ii) that the failure 'to take such steps as he reasonably could have been expected to take' has to be gross, but, on the other hand, it should be noted that as a result of s. 5(1)(a), the death must occur as a result of the unlawful act of *someone* (in the same household etc.), even if it is not the unlawful act of the accused. This introduces an element of unlawfulness that is not required for gross negligence manslaughter.

B1.64 **Unlawful Act** An unlawful act is defined in s. 5(5) as one that:

(a) constitutes an offence, or
(b) would constitute an offence but for being the act of—
  (i) a person under the age of ten, or
  (ii) a person entitled to rely on a defence of insanity.
Paragraph (b) does not apply to an act of D.

As with unlawful act manslaughter, it might frequently be an assault or some other offence against the person that is constituted by the unlawful act but it will only constitute an offence if the person who committed it had the *mens rea* required for that offence. This requirement is also implicit in subsection (5)(b) which specifically provides that an act is still unlawful for these purposes even if the person who committed it is under the age of 10 or can rely on the defence of insanity. There is no provision for the act to be unlawful even if the person who committed it lacks *mens rea.* Proving this when one is not sure whether it is the accused's act or the act of another person that caused death may cause problems, although it is enough to show that whoever committed the unlawful act must have done so with the relevant *mens rea* of that unlawful act. As far as the first limb of the offence is concerned, i.e. where it is the accused's unlawful act that has caused death, as opposed to it being the unlawful act of some other person, s. 5(5) is stated not to apply for the obvious reason that infancy or insanity would be defences available to the accused in any event.

B1.65 **Relationship of Offence with Child Cruelty** Where it is a child who has died, the unlawful act might constitute an offence of child cruelty under the CYPA 1933 (see **B2.114**). An aggravated offence of child cruelty where death occurs was part of the Law Commission's proposed mechanisms for dealing with the problems in this area (see Law Com No. 282, para. 6.2). Child cruelty can itself be committed in a large number of different ways (see **B2.115** and **B2.121**) and note that an 'act' for the purposes of the DVCVA 2004, s. 5, 'includes a course of conduct and also includes omission' (s. 5(6)). Provided the other requirements of s. 5 are satisfied, one can envisage a successful prosecution based on s. 5 where it can be proved that a child must have died as a result of child cruelty by one or the other of the two (or more) members of the child's household. Although the offence of child cruelty requires the accused to have 'responsibility' for the child, this is not required under s. 5, whereby it is enough that the accused was a member of the same household and had frequent contact with him.

Member of Same Household Section 5(4) explains further the concepts of 'member' and 'the same household as V'. B1.66

Domestic Violence, Crime and Victims Act 2004, s. 5

(4) For the purposes of this section—
 (a) a person is to be regarded as a 'member' of a particular household, even if he does not live in that household, if he visits it so often and for such periods of time that it is reasonable to regard him as a member of it;
 (b) where V lived in different households at different times, 'the same household as V' refers to the household in which V was living at the time of the act that caused V's death.

Section 5(4)(a) focuses on the *accused's* membership of a household and makes it clear that he does not have to live in it to be a member whereas s. 5(4)(b) focuses on V (the child or vulnerable adult) and makes it clear that it is the household that he 'lives in' at the time of the act causing death that is important. In focusing on the household V 'lives in' (as opposed to which households V is a member of), s. 5(4)(b) seems to ignore the possibility that V might be a member of different households during the period in which a course of conduct (see the definition of 'act' in s. 5(6)) took place.

Liability of Persons Aged under 16 Although in principle a sibling, or other person, who is himself under 16 could be guilty of an offence under s. 5 (as unlike child cruelty, the accused does not have to have responsibility for the child or vulnerable adult), s. 5(3) effectively excludes this possibility: B1.67

if D was not the mother or father of V—
 (a) D may not be charged with an offence under this section if he was under the age of 16 at the time of the act that caused V's death . . .

So a child sibling cannot be charged, but an under-age parent can be. Section 5(3)(b) goes on to provide that, other than for parents of V, a person cannot be held responsible for failures to take reasonable steps under s. 5(1)(d)(ii) prior to reaching the age of 16.

Failure to Take Steps In relation to the second alternative manner of commission of the offence, failing 'to take such steps as he could reasonably have been expected to take to protect V from the risk', whilst this is clearly an objective test, it is one that focuses on the steps that D could have been expected to take, not the steps that some paradigmatic reasonable person might have taken. This may be very important given that the potential accused may themselves have been at risk of abuse from other members of the household and focusing on the steps that the particular accused could have been reasonably expected to take was used in the Parliamentary debates to ward off suggestions that victims of domestic violence should be specifically exempted from the scope of the offence. Account can be taken of their situation through consideration of what steps they, in their situation, could reasonably be expected to take. B1.68

Directions on Offence The offence is designed to combat difficulties of proof, but it will be a challenging task to explain to juries precisely what it is that they must be satisfied of (see **B1.60**). Essentially, the jury must be satisfied that the accused (being a member of the same household etc.) *either* caused the victim's death by his own unlawful act (carrying a significant risk of serious physical harm) *or, if not,* that the accused failed to take steps that *he* could B1.69

reasonably have been expected to take to protect V from the risk of such harm from an unlawful act by another member of the same household and D ought to have both been aware of the significant risk and to have foreseen the circumstances in which the unlawful act occurred.

INFANTICIDE

Definition

B1.70 **Infanticide Act 1938, s. 1**

> (1) Where a woman by any wilful act or omission causes the death of her child being a child under the age of 12 months, but at the time of the act or omission the balance of her mind was disturbed by reason of her not having fully recovered from the effect of giving birth to the child or by reason of the effect of lactation consequent upon the birth of the child, then, notwithstanding that the circumstances were such that but for this Act the offence would have amounted to murder, she shall be guilty of [an offence], to wit of infanticide, and may for such offence be dealt with and punished as if she had been guilty of the offence of manslaughter of the child.

Procedure

B1.71 Infanticide is triable only on indictment. It is a class 1 offence.

Indictment

B1.72 *Statement of Offence*

Infanticide contrary to section 1(1) of the Infanticide Act 1938

Particulars of Offence

A on or about the . . . day of . . . did cause the death of her child V aged under 12 months by a wilful act [or omission], namely, smothering him with a pillow [failing to . . .], but at a time when the balance of her mind was disturbed by reason of the fact that she had not fully recovered from the effect of giving birth to V [and/or from the effect of lactation consequent on giving birth to V]

Alternative Verdicts

B1.73 Child destruction (Infant Life (Preservation) Act 1929, s. 2(2)), see **B1.80**.

Sentencing Guidelines

B1.74 The maximum sentence is life imprisonment (Infanticide Act 1938, s. 1).

The proper approach for sentencing in cases of infanticide was considered by the Court of Appeal in *Sainsbury* (1989) 11 Cr App R (S) 533. The offender had become pregnant at the age of 15. She did not tell anyone about this, and gave birth to the baby without medical assistance in the bathroom of her boyfriend's flat. The baby was then wrapped in a blanket, taken some distance away and drowned in a river. The sentencer accepted that the balance of the offender's mind was disturbed by the effect of giving birth and that she was very immature, but did not accept that her responsibility was removed altogether. He imposed a sentence of 12 months' detention in a young offender institution. The Court of Appeal, however, having regard to statistics which indicated that in 59 cases of infanticide dealt with between 1979 and 1988 there had been no custodial sentences, all offenders having been dealt with by way of probation, supervision or hospital orders, decided that although the offence was serious the mitigating factors were overwhelming, and varied the sentence to probation. See also *Lewis* (1989) 11 Cr App R (S) 457.

Elements Generally

The offence predates the introduction of the defence of diminished responsibility, and is designed to serve a similar role in relation to killings of very young children by their mothers in circumstances where the mothers are not fully responsible for their actions. It differs from diminished responsibility (and thus has survived the introduction of that defence) in that it can be charged from the outset and can be used to avoid charging a woman with the offence of murder in relation to her own child. Under s. 1(2), it can also be returned as an alternative verdict to murder, although s. (3) makes it clear that that is without prejudice to the jury's power on an indictment for murder to return a verdict of manslaughter or not guilty by reason of insanity. The offence covers a narrower range of circumstances than diminished responsibility, as the disturbance of the mother's mind must be due either to 'her not having fully recovered from the effect of giving birth' or to 'the effect of lactation consequent upon the birth of the child', criteria now regarded as outdated and unduly narrow. However, a legal burden of proof is placed on the defence in a case of diminished responsibility, where the prosecution are alleging the offence amounts to murder, the burden of proving that it is not a case of infanticide remains on the prosecution. Nevertheless the narrowness of the criteria for infanticide moved the Court of Appeal to conclude in *Kai-Whitewind*, [2005] 2 Cr App R 457, a case where a murder conviction was upheld and where there was no evidence to support infanticide as defined under the present law, that 'the law relating to infanticide is unsatisfactory and outdated. The appeal in this sad case demonstrates the need for a thorough re-examination.' See further Law Com No. 304 (November 2006), paras. 8.44 to 8.59 for a discussion of possible procedural reforms. **B1.75**

Meaning of 'Wilful'

As to the meaning of 'wilfully' generally, see **A2.8**. There appears to be no authority on the meaning of 'wilful' in this particular offence. It could be interpreted to mean merely 'voluntary', but that would raise the possibility that the offence could be committed even though the mother did not intend to cause death or serious bodily harm to the child. This could be avoided by reading the phrase 'notwithstanding that the circumstances were such that but for this Act the offence would have amounted to murder' as meaning 'notwithstanding *and provided that* etc.'. This reading seems unlikely, and would strictly mean that the elements of murder ought to be alleged in the indictment. Alternatively, 'wilful' could be given a similar interpretation to that adopted in relation to 'wilfully' in *Sheppard* [1981] AC 394, i.e., as requiring intention or recklessness in relation to the child's death. This would mean that the offence would cover a wider range of cases than just those where the offence would otherwise be murder, and would overlap with cases that would in any case only be manslaughter. This is probably not what was intended, but seems to be the result of how the offence is defined (murder was itself a wider offence in 1938 when the definition of infanticide was put on the statute book, and that definition has not changed even though the scope of the offence of murder has narrowed). The problem is not acute, since in practice it seems that the offence will only be charged where there is evidence that the mother did intend serious bodily harm or death, even though this is not necessarily an element of the offence which strictly has to be proved. **B1.76**

Act or Omission which Causes Death

See **A1.10** to **A1.20** for liability for omissions. See **A1.13** for the duty of parents to preserve the life of their children; essentially, parents have a duty to take any reasonable steps lying within their power to prevent harm to their child. See **A1.21** *et seq.* for the principles of causation. **B1.77**

'Of Her Child under the Age of 12 Months'

If the mother kills the child of another, even if it is in the course of killing her own child, then the killing of that other cannot amount to infanticide. If the mother intended to kill or cause **B1.78** grievous bodily harm, it would prima facie be murder but might be brought within the defence of diminished responsibility. Strictly speaking, the same principles apply if the mother kills, say, her own 11-month-old child as a result of giving birth to another child later in the same year, since the disturbance of her mind has to be due to the effects of the birth of the child which is killed.

The offence cannot apply once the child has reached the age of 12 months, but again, diminished responsibility would be the appropriate defence to consider. If, at the other end of the scale, the child has not been fully born before the mother kills it, the offence is not infanticide but child destruction (see **B1.80** to **B1.88**) and, by virtue of the Infant Life (Preservation) Act 1929, s. 2(2), child destruction is an alternative verdict to infanticide.

Complicity and Attempt

B1.79 Where a mother aids and abets the killing of her child by another (e.g., the father) but cannot be said to cause its death, it would appear that infanticide is inapplicable, and again, diminished responsibility would have to be relied on. If a third person (including, e.g., the father) aids and abets the mother to commit what is (for her) only infanticide, it would seem likely that, by analogy with the Homicide Act 1957, s. 2(4) (see **B1.15**), that third person should still be guilty of murder if he or she has the appropriate *mens rea.*

Some doubts have been expressed whether attempted infanticide is an offence known to the law, but such an indictment was approved in *Smith* [1983] Crim LR 789.

CHILD DESTRUCTION

Definition

B1.80 **Infant Life (Preservation) Act 1929, s. 1**

(1) Subject as hereinafter in this subsection provided, any person who, with intent to destroy the life of a child capable of being born alive, by any wilful act causes a child to die before it has an existence independent of its mother, shall be guilty of [an offence], to wit, of child destruction, and shall be liable on conviction thereof on indictment to life imprisonment:

Provided that no person shall be found guilty of an offence under this section unless it is proved that the act which caused the death of the child was not done in good faith for the purpose only of preserving the life of the mother.

Procedure

B1.81 Child destruction is triable only on indictment. It is a class 1 offence.

Indictment

B1.82 *Statement of Offence*

Child destruction contrary to section 1(1) of the Infant Life (Preservation) Act 1929

Particulars of Offence

A on or about the . . . day of . . ., with intent to destroy the life of a child capable of being born alive, did cause the death of the child of V, before it had an existence independent of the said V, by means of a wilful act, namely . . .

Alternative Verdict

B1.83 Abortion contrary to the OAPA 1861, s. 58 (Infant Life (Preservation) Act 1929, s. 2(3)).

Sentencing

B1.84 The maximum sentence is life imprisonment (Infant Life (Preservation) Act 1929, s. 1).

Relationship with Other Offences

B1.85 This offence was created to fill the gap between murder (which, as noted at **B1.1** and **B1.8**, requires a live birth) and abortion (which requires an attempt to procure a miscarriage, see **B1.89** to **B1.98**). A child killed in the process of being born would not be murdered, because there would be no live birth, and it would not be abortion since there was no miscarriage. The offence, however, overlaps with abortion, as it is not restricted to acts done while the child is in the process of being born and also covers the causing of miscarriage of a child 'capable of being born alive'. Abortion is an alternative verdict to child destruction (Infant Life (Preservation) Act 1929, s. 2(3)).

Meaning of 'Capable of Being Born Alive'

B1.86 **Infant Life (Preservation) Act 1929, s. 1**

(2) For the purposes of this Act, evidence that a woman had at any material time been pregnant for a period of 28 weeks or more shall be prima facie proof that she was at that time pregnant of a child capable of being born alive.

In addition to this statutory presumption, it is open to the prosecution to try to prove that a particular child was capable of being born alive even though it has not reached the relevant number of weeks gestation. In a civil case, *C v S* [1988] QB 135, the Court of Appeal held that a child between 18 and 21 weeks was not capable of being born alive, as it could not breathe. On the other hand, in *Rance v Mid-Downs Health Authority* [1991] 1 QB 587, Brooke J held that a child of 26 or 27 weeks gestation, who could have breathed unaided for two to three hours at least, was capable of being born alive.

Meaning of 'Wilful Act'

B1.87 In contrast to the offence of infanticide discussed at **B1.70** to **B1.79**, the definition requires a positive act and an omission will not suffice. 'Wilful' seems here to mean merely 'voluntary', as the *mens rea* of an 'intent to destroy the life of a child capable of being born alive' is separately stated. For the meaning of wilfulness generally, see **A2.8**. Recklessness is clearly insufficient.

Special Defences

B1.88 Under the proviso to the Infant Life (Preservation) Act 1929, s. 1(1), 'no person shall be found guilty . . . unless it is proved that the act which caused the death of the child was not done in good faith for the purpose only of preserving the life of the mother'.

Thus, the burden is on the prosecution to negate this defence, whether or not, it would seem, the accused adduces any evidence to raise the issue. The only cases relating to the scope of this defence are first instance rulings of trial judges, and even these were prosecutions for abortion under the OAPA 1861, s. 58, where the court implied a similar defence by analogy with the proviso currently under discussion. A fairly flexible view of the meaning of 'preserving the life of the mother' was taken in these cases. In *Bourne* [1939] 1 KB 687, at p. 694, Macnaghten J took the view that the jury could properly conclude that the accused was acting in good faith to preserve the life of the mother if he believed 'that the probable consequence of the continuance of the pregnancy will be to make the woman a physical or mental wreck'. In *Newton* [1958] Crim LR 469, Ashworth J referred to 'preserving the life or health of the woman . . . not only her physical health but also her mental health'.

The Abortion Act 1967, s. 5(1), provides a defence to a charge of child destruction as follows:

> No offence under the Infant Life (Preservation) Act 1929 shall be committed by a registered medical practitioner who terminates a pregnancy in accordance with the provisions of this Act.

The offence of child destruction and the presumption that a child is capable of being born alive at 28 weeks gestation no longer therefore represent one of the limits on the lawfulness of abortions under the 1967 Act. If the provisions of the 1967 Act (see below) are complied with, an act is neither abortion nor child destruction.

ABORTION

Definition

B1.89 **Offences against the Person Act 1861, s. 58**

> Every woman, being with child, who, with intent to procure her own miscarriage, shall unlawfully administer to herself any poison or other noxious thing, or shall unlawfully use any instrument or other means whatsoever with the like intent, and whosoever, with intent to procure the miscarriage of any woman, whether she be or be not with child, shall unlawfully administer to her or cause to be taken by her any poison or other noxious thing, or shall unlawfully use any instrument or other means whatsoever with the like intent, shall be guilty of [an offence], and being convicted thereof shall be liable to [imprisonment] for life.

Procedure

B1.90 Abortion is triable only on indictment. It is a class 1 offence.

Indictment

B1.91 *Statement of Offence (1)*

Administering poison with intent to procure miscarriage contrary to section 58 of the Offences against the Person Act 1861

Particulars of Offence

A on or about the . . . day of . . . did unlawfully administer [or cause to be administered] to V a poison or other noxious thing, namely . . ., with intent to procure her miscarriage

Statement of Offence (2)

Using an instrument or other means with intent to procure miscarriage contrary to section 58 of the Offences against the Person Act 1861

Particulars of Offence

A on or about the . . . day of . . . did unlawfully use the following means, namely . . ., with intent to procure the miscarriage of V

Sentencing Guidelines

B1.92 The maximum penalty is life imprisonment (OAPA 1861, s. 58).

Sentences of three years' imprisonment were upheld on offenders in *Scrimaglia* (1971) 55 Cr App R 280, who pleaded guilty to using an instrument to procure a miscarriage. Lord Parker CJ endorsed the trial judge's comment that 'Now that abortions can be performed legally either under the National Health Service or at the patient's own expense, operations such as yours, carried out at a cut price and in disgraceful, insanitary and even dangerous conditions, are totally unnecessary apart from being against the law'.

Elements Generally

B1.93 Given the large number of abortions now carried out legally under the provisions of the Abortion Act 1967 (see **B1.97**), the offence is comparatively rarely prosecuted. There are two peculiar features to note about the definition of the offence. First, it is in the nature of a statutory attempt. The *actus reus* does not require the actual procuring of a miscarriage, but rather an act done with the intention of procuring that result. Secondly, the requirements of the offence differ according to whether it is the (pregnant) woman herself or another person who is charged. In the case of the woman herself she must indeed be pregnant, whereas in the case of others, it is sufficient if she is believed to be pregnant and there is thus an intention to procure her miscarriage. This latter distinction is now almost redundant, because:

(a) if a non-pregnant woman is helped by another, she can be convicted either of aiding and abetting (*Sockett* (1908) 1 Cr App R 101) or conspiring with (*Whitchurch* (1890) 24 QBD 42) that other; and
(b) even if she is acting alone, she would appear to be guilty of an attempt to commit the offence under s. 58 as a result of the Criminal Attempts Act 1981, s. 1(2) (see **A6.31** ***et seq.***).

In practice, the woman herself is not prosecuted today, and the offence is aimed principally at third parties operating outside the terms of what is permitted under the Abortion Act 1967 and exploiting the woman's predicament for financial gain.

Intention to Procure Miscarriage

B1.94 For the meaning of 'intention', see **A2.2**. What stage of a pregnancy has to be reached before it is possible to 'miscarry' is a matter of some controversy. Is it as soon as the ovum is fertilised, or only when the fertilised ovum is implanted in the womb some 10 days later? If it were the former, then some types of so-called contraceptives, such as 'the morning-after' pill, would be technically illegal under the OAPA 1861, s. 58. However, in *R (Smeaton) v Secretary of State for Health* [2002] Crim LR 664, Munby J ruled that 'miscarriage' means the termination of an established pregnancy and that there is no established pregnancy prior to implantation. Hence the prescription of the morning-after pill is not a criminal offence.

'Poison or other Noxious Thing . . . Instrument or Other Means'

B1.95 If the indictment alleges the administration of a poison or noxious thing, it must either be a 'recognised poison' or, to be a noxious thing, some substance which is either harmful in itself or administered in such a quantity as to be harmful (*Cramp* (1880) 5 QBD 307) though not necessarily abortifacient (see *Marlow* (1964) 49 Cr App R 49). However, it may be that a practical way out of the difficulty, if there is any doubt about whether the substance administered constitutes a poison or noxious thing, would be to utilise that form of the offence that can be committed by 'any means whatsoever', and to frame the indictment accordingly as in Statement of Offence (2) at **B1.91**.

Special Defences

B1.96 It was held in *Bourne* [1939] 1 KB 687 that, by analogy to the proviso to the Infant Life (Preservation) Act 1929, s. 1(1), an act was not unlawful within s. 58 of the 1861 Act if it was done in good faith for the purpose only of preserving the life of the mother. This defence now seems to be entirely supplanted by the provision in the Abortion Act 1967, s. 5, that anything done with intent to procure a woman's miscarriage is unlawfully done unless authorised by s. 1 of the 1967 Act (see **B1.97**).

Abortion Act 1967, ss. 1 and 5

B1.97 **Abortion Act 1967, ss. 1 and 5**

1.—(1) Subject to the provisions of this section, a person shall not be guilty of an offence under the law relating to abortion when a pregnancy is terminated by a registered medical practitioner if two registered medical practitioners are of the opinion, formed in good faith—
(a) that the pregnancy has not exceeded its twenty-fourth week and that the continuance of the pregnancy would involve risk, greater than if the pregnancy were terminated, of injury to the physical or mental health of the pregnant woman or any existing children of her family; or
(b) that the termination is necessary to prevent grave permanent injury to the physical or mental health of the pregnant woman; or

(c) that the continuance of the pregnancy would involve risk to the life of the pregnant woman, greater than if the pregnancy were terminated; or

(d) that there is a substantial risk that if the child were born it would suffer from such physical or mental abnormalities as to be seriously handicapped.

(2) In determining whether the continuance of a pregnancy would involve such risk of injury to health as is mentioned in paragraph (a) or (b) of subsection (1) of this section, account may be taken of the pregnant woman's actual or reasonably foreseeable environment.

(3) Except as provided by subsection (4) of this section, any treatment for the termination of pregnancy must be carried out in a hospital vested in the Minister of Health or the Secretary of State under the National Health Service Acts, or in a place for the time being approved for the purposes of this section by the said Minister or the Secretary of State.

(3A) The power under subsection (3) of this section to approve a place includes power, in relation to treatment consisting primarily in the use of such medicines as may be specified in the approval and carried out in such manner as may be so specified, to approve a class of places.

(4) Subsection (3) of this section, and so much of subsection (1) as relates to the opinion of two registered medical practitioners, shall not apply to the termination of a pregnancy by a registered medical practitioner in a case where he is of the opinion, formed in good faith, that the termination is immediately necessary to save the life or to prevent grave permanent injury to the physical or mental health of the pregnant woman.

5.—(1) No offence under the Infant Life (Preservation) Act 1929 shall be committed by a registered medical practitioner who terminates a pregnancy in accordance with the provisions of this Act.

(2) For the purposes of the law relating to abortion, anything done with intent to procure a woman's miscarriage (or, in the case of a woman carrying more than one foetus, her miscarriage of any foetus) is unlawfully done unless authorised by section 1 of this Act and, in the case of a woman carrying more than one foetus, anything done with intent to procure her miscarriage of any foetus is authorised by that section if—

(a) the ground for termination of the pregnancy specified in subsection (1)(d) of that section applies in relation to any foetus and the thing is done for the purpose of procuring the miscarriage of the foetus, or

(b) any of the other grounds for termination of the pregnancy specified in that section applies.

One of the significant changes caused by the amendment of ss. 1 and 5 by the Human Fertilisation and Embryology Act 1990, s. 37, was that the legality of abortions ceased to be limited by the presumption in the Infant Life (Preservation) Act 1929 (see **B1.86**) that a child of 28 weeks' gestation is capable of being born alive; under the Abortion Act 1967, s. 5(1), compliance with the provisions of the Abortion Act is also a defence to a charge of child destruction. Instead there is now a fixed time-limit of 24 weeks for abortions under s. 1(1)(a) of the 1967 Act, but no time-limit at all (up to the point of a live birth) under s. 1(1)(b), (c) or (d). Section 1(3A) is intended to cater for drugs such as RU 486 (mifepristone) being used in places other than National Health Service hospitals or approved nursing homes. Section 5(2) makes it clear that selective reduction (procuring the miscarriage of one or more, but not all, of the foetuses in a multiple pregnancy) may in appropriate cases be authorised by s. 1.

Section 1 was considered by the House of Lords in *Royal College of Nursing of the United Kingdom v Department of Health and Social Security* [1981] AC 800, in which Lord Diplock said (at p. 828):

> Subsection 1 although it is expressed to apply only 'when a pregnancy is terminated by a registered medical practitioner' . . . also appears to contemplate treatment that is in the nature of a team effort and to extend its protection to all those who play a part in it.

Thus, methods of abortion, such as induction of premature delivery by means of prostaglandin drip, which involve nurses (or others) playing a substantial role, are covered, and all the participants are exempted provided that a registered medical practitioner accepts (loc. cit.):

responsibility for all stages of the treatment for the termination of the pregnancy. The particular method to be used should be decided by the doctor in charge of the treatment for termination of the pregnancy; he should carry out any physical acts, forming part of the treatment, that in accordance with accepted medical practice are done only by qualified medical practitioners, and should give specific instructions as to the carrying out of such parts of the treatment as in accordance with accepted medical practice are carried out by nurses or other members of the hospital staff without medical qualifications. To each of them, the doctor, or his substitute, should be available to be consulted or called on for assistance from beginning to end of the treatment.

Although s. 1 refers to when 'a pregnancy *is* terminated', its protection also extends to cases where the attempt to terminate is unsuccessful (see *Royal College of Nursing v DHSS* [1981] AC 800, per Lord Diplock at p. 828), a not insignificant point, since the offence under the Offences against the Person Act 1861, s. 58, is committed irrespective of whether a miscarriage is actually procured.

Medical Practitioners' Opinion The precise scope of the grounds for abortion enumerated in s. 1 are likely to continue to escape detailed interpretation by the courts, since the question is not whether these grounds actually exist but whether 'two registered medical practitioners are of the opinion, formed in good faith' that they exist. It was said in *Smith* [1973] 1 WLR 1510 that a conviction of a doctor without evidence as to professional practice and the medical probabilities was likely to be unsafe, but it was stressed that the question of good faith is a matter for the jury to be determined by reference to all the evidence (and the appeal in that case was dismissed). **B1.98**

Although under the Abortion Act 1967, s. 1(3), the termination must normally be carried out in a National Health Service hospital or an approved clinic, under s. 1(4) this requirement does not apply if just one registered medical practitioner 'is of the opinion, formed in good faith, that the termination is immediately necessary to save the life or to prevent grave permanent injury to the physical or mental health of the pregnant woman'. Although, as noted at **B1.96**, s. 5 makes compliance with the Act the sole test of unlawfulness for the purposes of the law of abortion, it is possible that this does not exclude a general defence such as duress of circumstances (see **A3.29** and also the Canadian case of *Morgentaler v The Queen* (1975) 53 DLR (3d) 161 discussed in L.H. Leigh, 'Necessity and the case of Dr Morgentaler' [1978] Crim LR 151), e.g., where a competent medical student finds himself, rather than a registered medical practitioner, in the sort of emergency situation outlined in s. 1(4).

Regulations have been made under s. 2(1) of the 1967 Act relating to the form of certificates of opinions, requiring notifications etc. of terminations and prohibiting disclosure of information in such notifications etc. Under s. 2(3) of the Act, contravention of the regulations is a summary offence, but would not appear to render an abortion illegal if the provisions of s. 1 of the Act are complied with. However, absence of the proper certificates may make it more difficult to show that the relevant opinion(s) had indeed been formed in good faith.

SUPPLYING OR PROCURING MEANS FOR ABORTION

Definition

Offences against the Person Act 1861, s. 59 **B1.99**

Whoever shall unlawfully supply or procure any poison or other noxious thing, or any instrument or thing whatsoever, knowing that the same is intended to be unlawfully used or employed with intent to procure the miscarriage of any woman, whether she be or be not with child, shall be guilty of [an offence], and being convicted thereof shall be liable . . . to imprisonment . . . for any term not exceeding five years.

Procedure

B1.100 Supplying or procuring means for abortion is triable only on indictment. It is a class 3 offence.

Indictment

B1.101 *Statement of Offence*

Supplying [or procuring] the means to procure a miscarriage contrary to section 59 of the Offences against the Person Act 1861

Particulars of Offence

A on or about the . . . day of . . . unlawfully supplied [or procured] a poison or other noxious thing, namely . . ., knowing that it was intended to be unlawfully used with intent to procure the miscarriage of V

Sentence

B1.102 The maximum sentence is five years (OAPA 1861, s. 59).

Elements

B1.103 'Supply' obviously means supply to another, and conversely 'procure' (any poison etc.) means procure *from* another, i.e. 'get possession of something of which you do not have possession already' (*Mills* [1963] 1 QB 522). Thus, the offence is not committed merely by producing the instrument or noxious thing etc. from one's cupboard (although the offence clearly is committed if it is then supplied, with the necessary knowledge, to another).

Although s. 59 refers to the accused's *knowledge* of the intentions of others, such old authorities as there are interpret this in effect as *belief* that the others intend unlawfully to use the poison etc. with intent to procure a miscarriage (*Hillman* (1863) Le & Ca 343; *Titley* (1880) 14 Cox CC 502) — i.e. the accused can be convicted even if in actual fact the other or others do not intend so to use it unlawfully. The effect of the Criminal Attempts Act 1981, s. 1(3) (see **A6.31** ***et seq.***), is probably that, quite apart from these decisions, the accused could now be convicted of attempt in these circumstances.

Special Defences

B1.104 The exemption from liability provided by the Abortion Act 1967, s. 1, is equally applicable to this offence, as s. 6 of the Act defines 'the law relating to abortion' as meaning, 'sections 58 and 59 of the OAPA 1861 and any rule of law relating to the procurement of abortion'.

CONCEALMENT OF BIRTH

Definition

B1.105 **Offences against the Person Act 1861, s. 60**

If any woman shall be delivered of a child, every person who shall, by any secret disposition of the dead body of the said child, whether such child died before, at, or after its birth, endeavour to conceal the birth thereof, shall be guilty of [an offence], and being convicted thereof shall be liable, at the discretion of the court, to be imprisoned for any term not exceeding two years.

Procedure

B1.106 Concealing the birth of a child is triable either way. When tried on indictment it is a class 3 offence.

Indictment

Statement of Offence B1.107

Endeavouring to conceal birth contrary to section 60 of the Offences against the Person Act 1861

Particulars of Offence

A on or about the . . . day of . . . endeavoured to conceal the birth of a child of which V had been delivered by a secret disposition of the dead body of that child

Alternative Verdicts

There are no alternative verdicts. It should also be noted that as a result of the Criminal Law Act 1967, sch. 2, it is no longer possible to convict of this offence on an indictment for murder, infanticide or child destruction. Other offences which should be borne in mind include the common-law misdemeanours of disposing of or destroying a dead body with intent to prevent an inquest being held (*Stephenson* (1884) 13 QBD 331) and preventing the burial of a body (see *Hunter* [1974] QB 95). See also **B14.47**. B1.108

Sentence

The maximum penalty is two years (OAPA 1861, s. 60). B1.109

Meaning of 'Child'

In *Berriman* (1854) 6 Cox CC 388, Erle J said (at p. 390) that the child must have: B1.110

> arrived at that stage of maturity at the time of birth, that it might have been a living child. . . . No specific limit can be assigned to the period when the chance of life begins, but it may, perhaps, be safely assumed that under seven months the great probability is that the child would not be born alive.

However, in *Colmer* (1864) 9 Cox CC 506, a child of just four or five months' gestational age, about the length of a man's finger, was said by Martin B at first instance to be within the definition. The decision has been doubted, and indeed the jury acquitted. The meaning given to 'child' in *Berriman* is probably preferable and would make the offence consistent with that of child destruction. The qualifying words 'capable of being born alive' in the Infant Life (Preservation) Act 1929 (see **B1.80**), although in one sense somewhat otiose if 'child' itself is given the more limited *Berriman* meaning, could be regarded as clarifying the ambiguity already demonstrated in these cases.

Secret Disposition

This is satisfied by putting the dead body in a place where it is unlikely to be found, even though the body is not concealed in the sense that it is completely hidden from view (see *Brown* (1870) LR 1 CCR 244). Conversely, hiding the body from view is not sufficient if it is in such a manner that the body is nevertheless likely to be found (see *George* (1868) 11 Cox CC 41). The accused's act must be done in relation to a dead body, so that the offence is not committed where the accused conceals a living child which later dies (*May* (1867) 10 Cox CC 448). However, there is almost certain to be liability for murder or manslaughter in this situation (or at least for attempt to commit an offence under the OAPA 1861, s. 60, where the accused believes the child is already dead). In *Hughes* (1850) 4 Cox CC 447, the accused concealed a living child, returned and found it dead, and replaced the covers which were concealing it. This was held to be an offence within a predecessor of s. 60 (9 Geo. 4 c. 31, s. 14), and to be a disposition of the dead body. An alternative and more appropriate charge would appear to be some form of homicide in relation to the initial act of concealing the living child which led to its death. B1.111

SOLICITATION OF MURDER

Definition

B1.112 **Offences against the Person Act 1861, s. 4**

Whosoever shall solicit, encourage, persuade or endeavour to persuade, or shall propose to any person, to murder any other person, whether he be a subject of Her Majesty or not, and whether he be within the Queen's dominions or not, shall be guilty of [an offence], and being convicted thereof shall be liable to imprisonment for life.

Procedure

B1.113 Solicitation of murder is triable only on indictment. It is a class 1 offence.

Indictment

B1.114 *Statement of Offence*

Soliciting to commit murder contrary to section 4 of the Offences against the Person Act 1861

Particulars of Offence

A on or about the . . . day of . . ., solicited [or encouraged etc.] X to murder V

Sentencing Guidelines

B1.115 The maximum penalty is life imprisonment (OAPA 1861, s. 4).

In *Kayani* [1997] 2 Cr App R (S) 313 a sentence of 12 years' imprisonment was upheld on an offender convicted for soliciting the murder of his niece and her husband. He was arrested by an undercover police officer posing as a contract killer, to whom payment of £20,000 was tendered partly in cash and partly in heroin. The offender received concurrent sentences for supplying heroin. In *Raw* (1983) 5 Cr App R (S) 229, where the offender attempted to contact someone who would murder his wife for a fee of £2,000, the Court of Appeal said that a prison sentence of seven years was 'the minimum sentence, regardless of the fact of the personality and circumstances of the appellant, that would constitute a proper deterrent'. This case was followed in *Peatfield* (1985) 7 Cr App R (S) 132, where a 10-year prison sentence was upheld on an offender who offered to pay a man £5,000 to murder his wife and 10-year-old daughter. In *Adamthwaite* (1994) 15 Cr App R (S) 241, however, where the offender had met with an undercover police officer and agreed to pay £5,000 for the murder of the offender's wife, the sentence of six years on a guilty plea was said to be 'on the high side' and was reduced to four years by the Court of Appeal. See also *A-G's Ref (No. 43 of 1996)* [1997] 1 Cr App R (S) 378.

Elements

B1.116 Although the soliciting must be done from within the jurisdiction, the phrase 'whether he be a subject of Her Majesty or not, and whether he be within the Queen's dominions or not' has now in effect been interpreted so that it applies not only to the person to be murdered but also to the person being solicited. Thus in *Abu Hamza* [2007] 2 WLR 226 it was no defence that the persons being solicited were of various nationalities and the murders were to take place abroad and that it was not proved that any of those solicited to murder were British nationals. The encouragement does not in any event have to be directed to a particular individual — see *Most* (1881) 7 QBD 244, where the offence was committed by means of a newspaper article. See also *El-Faisal* [2004] EWCA Crim 456, a case involving solicitation to indiscriminate killing which was recorded on tape, the defence of limitation to self-defence on the battlefield not being made out.

The offence is not complete until someone is in receipt of the solicitation, although the act of sending it can constitute an attempt (*Krause* (1902) 66 JP 121). It does not matter that the recipient is not in fact influenced, although in this case it might be prudent to allege an 'endeavour to persuade' in the particulars. Encouraging a pregnant woman to kill her child in the future, after it shall have been born alive, is an offence within the section (*Shephard* [1919] 2 KB 125). See *Tait* [1990] 1 QB 290 and **B1.127**. The principles relating to the inchoate offence of incitement (see **A6.1** to **A6.8**) will generally be applicable to this offence.

COMPLICITY IN SUICIDE

Definition

Suicide Act 1961, s. 2 **B1.117**

(1) A person who aids, abets, counsels or procures the suicide of another, or an attempt by another to commit suicide, shall be liable on conviction on indictment to imprisonment for a term not exceeding 14 years.

Procedure

Complicity in suicide is triable only on indictment. It is a class 3 offence. The consent of the DPP is required to initiate proceedings for this offence (Suicide Act 1961, s. 2(4)). The DPP cannot be required, nor does he have the power, to give an undertaking to withhold his consent to prosecution in advance of a contemplated assisted suicide, notwithstanding the compassionate factors of the particular case (*R (Pretty) v DPP* [2002] 1 AC 800). Nor does the offence contravene the ECHR, the House of Lords ruling on this point having been confirmed by the European Court of Human Rights in *Pretty v UK* (2002) 35 EHRR 1. **B1.118**

Indictment

Statement of Offence **B1.119**

Aiding, abetting, counselling or procuring suicide contrary to section 2(1) of the Suicide Act 1961

Particulars of Offence

A on or about the . . . day . . . did aid, abet, counsel or procure V to commit suicide

Alternative Verdicts

There are no alternative verdicts specifically provided for. The offence is itself an alternative verdict to murder or manslaughter (Suicide Act 1961, s. 2(2)). **B1.120**

Sentencing Guidelines

The maximum penalty is 14 years' imprisonment (Suicide Act 1961, s. 2). **B1.121**

In *Hough* (1984) 6 Cr App R (S) 406, Lord Lane CJ commented that this crime could vary 'from the borders of cold-blooded murder down to the shadowy area of mercy killing or common humanity'. In that case a nine-month prison term was upheld on a 60-year-old woman of unblemished character who had been a regular visitor to an 84-year-old woman who was partly blind, partly deaf, and suffered from arthritis. The old lady had persisted in various statements to the effect that she intended to take her own life, and the offender eventually supplied her with tablets. When she became unconscious, the offender placed a plastic bag over her head. In *Wallis* (1983) 5 Cr App R (S) 342, a sentence of 12 months' imprisonment was described by the Court of Appeal as 'at the extreme of leniency' in a case where the offender pleaded guilty to aiding the suicide of a 17-year-old flatmate by buying her tablets and alcohol, sitting with her while she took the tablets, and not calling an ambulance until she was dead. *Sweeney* (1986) 8 Cr App R (S) 419 and *England* (1990) 12 Cr App R (S) 98 were both cases involving suicide pacts. In the former, the facts of which were given at **B1.39**, a sentence of four years' imprisonment on the survivor was reduced to two years and, in the latter, a sentence of five years' imprisonment was reduced to three years.

Elements

B1.122 The offence would seem to be governed by the normal rules applicable to aiding and abetting crime (see **A5.1** to **A5.15**), this special statutory version having been created because the substantive offence of suicide was abolished by the Suicide Act 1961, s. 1. However, although aiding and abetting normally requires that the substantive offence be committed, or at least attempted, and there is usually no such thing as an attempt to aid and abet (see Criminal Attempts Act 1981, s. 1(4)), it is possible to convict of an attempt to commit the offence under s. 2(1). The person doing the aiding and abetting etc. is in this case the principal offender. This effectively extends the ambit of the offence to incitement to commit suicide, so that there can be liability even if the person encouraged does not in fact commit or attempt to commit suicide (see *McShane* (1977) 66 Cr App R 97). The accused must, of course, intend that someone commit or attempt to commit suicide (*A-G v Able* [1984] 1 QB 795) but it is unnecessary for the accused to know or believe that the person encouraged had been intending or contemplating suicide (*S* (2005) 149 SJ 390). Furthermore, the fact that the full offence was impossible to commit on the facts, because the person encouraged had no intention of committing suicide, was no bar to a successful prosecution for an attempt to aid and abet. Similarly, despite the confusion over whether there can generally be a conspiracy to aid and abet (see **A6.16**), there can be liability for conspiracy to aid and abet under s. 2(1) (*Reed* [1982] Crim LR 819).

It was suggested on behalf of the Criminal Cases Review Commission before the Court of Appeal in *Kennedy (No. 2)* [2005] 1 WLR 2159 that taking the reasoning in *Finlay* [2003] EWCA Crim 3868 (see **B1.51**) to its logical conclusion:

> the outcome would be that a person who assists another to commit suicide by providing a loaded syringe of heroin to another, in order that that person can take his own life, would now become a principal to murder . . . and that this 'would effectively drive a "coach and horses" through the offence of "assisted suicide" created by s. 2 of the Suicide Act 1961' and 'a direct and irreconcilable overlap between the s. 2 offence and the offence of murder'.

This argument was rejected as ignoring the role of the OAPA 1861, s. 23, in the manslaughter convictions of *Finlay* and *Kennedy* (where of course there is no statutory offence of aiding and abetting self-manslaughter to parallel s. 2 of the 1961 Act).

> In addition, Parliament, by enacting the Suicide Act 1961, must be taken to have provided a statutory code for offences, in situations involving an individual deliberately taking his own life. In view of s. 2 of the 1961 Act, it would be an abuse to prosecute someone assisting another to commit suicide for murder. Furthermore, in practice, it would not happen. (Lord Woolf CJ at [49]).

THREATS TO KILL

Definition

B1.123 **Offences against the Person Act 1861, s. 16**

> A person who without lawful excuse makes to another a threat, intending that that other would fear it would be carried out, to kill that other or a third person shall be guilty of an offence and liable on conviction on indictment to imprisonment for a term not exceeding 10 years.

Procedure

B1.124 Threatening to kill is triable either way. When tried on indictment it is a class 4 offence.

Indictment

Statement of Offence B1.125

Making a threat to kill contrary to section 16 of the Offences against the Person Act 1861

Particulars of Offence

A on or about the . . . day of . . ., without lawful excuse, threatened V that he would kill him [or that he would kill X] intending that V would fear that the said threat would be carried out

Sentencing Guidelines

The maximum penalty is 10 years' imprisonment (Criminal Law Act 1977, sch. 12, replacing OAPA 1861, s. 16). B1.126

Sentences approved by the Court of Appeal for this offence range downwards from the five years' imprisonment imposed in *Bowden* (1986) 8 Cr App R (S) 155, where the offender, under treatment for alcoholism, went to the home of a woman with whom he had formerly lived, and threatened her with a sword. The woman barricaded herself in the bedroom and the police had to force their way into the house to arrest the offender. In *Martin* (1993) 14 Cr App R (S) 645, four years' imprisonment was reduced to three years in a case where the offender sent two anonymous notes, stained with blood. In *Gaskin* (1996) *The Times*, 15 August 1996, Judge Allen in the Court of Appeal noted that cases of making threats to kill posed difficult sentencing problems, since they ranged from threats made in the heat of the moment to cases where the victim continued to fear for the future as well as having suffered short-term terror. In recognising that the instant appeal was a case of the latter type, the Court of Appeal upheld a prison sentence of four years. In *Choudhury* [1997] 2 Cr App R (S) 300 the offender, after being released on bail for a public order offence, made repeated threats to kill the police officer who had arrested him and also threatened the officer's family. The Court of Appeal reduced the prison sentence from three years to two years.

Elements

The words 'without lawful excuse' in the OAPA 1861, s. 16, would exempt, for example, a threat made reasonably in self-defence to deter an apprehended attack or to prevent crime (see *Cousins* [1982] QB 526). An implied threat will suffice (see the facts of *Solanke* [1970] 1 WLR 1), as will a threat that is only to be carried out at some time in the future, although it would seem that it has to be one that will be carried out by the accused, or at least under his instructions. It is the person to whom the threat is made, rather than the person to be killed, who must fear that the threat will be carried out, although often these two will be one and the same person. A threat to a pregnant woman in respect of her unborn child is not sufficient if the threat is to kill it before its birth. But if it is a threat to kill the child after its birth, then that would appear to be within the section (*Tait* [1990] 1 QB 290). B1.127

CORPORATE MANSLAUGHTER

The Corporate Manslaughter and Corporate Homicide Act 2007 received the Royal Assent on 26 July 2007. The Act is expected to come into force in April 2008. A commentary on aspects of the Act is to be found in the October Bulletin (distributed with this edition). B1.128

Definition

Corporate Manslaughter and Corporate Homicide Act 2007, s. 1 B1.129

(1) An organisation to which this section applies is guilty of an offence if the way in which its activities are managed or organised—
  (a) causes a person's death, and
  (b) amounts to a gross breach of a relevant duty of care owed by the organisation to the deceased.

(2) The organisations to which this section applies are—
(a) a corporation;
(b) a department or other body listed in Schedule 1;
(c) a police force;
(d) a partnership, or a trade union or employers' association, that is an employer.

(3) An organisation is guilty of an offence under this section only if the way in which its activities are managed or organised by its senior management is a substantial element in the breach referred to in subsection (1).

Procedure and Sentence

B1.130 The offence of corporate manslaughter is triable only on indictment. Proceedings may not be instituted without the consent of the DPP (Corporate Manslaughter and Corporate Homicide Act 2007, s. 17).

The maximum penalty available on conviction is a fine (s. 1(6)). On convicting an offender of corporate manslaughter, the court may, on the application of the prosecution, make a 'remedial order' under s. 9 and may make an order under s. 10 for the conviction and specified particulars to be publicised.

Relevant Duty of Care

B1.131 **Corporate Manslaughter and Corporate Homicide Act 2007, s. 2**

(1) A 'relevant duty of care', in relation to an organisation, means any of the following duties owed by it under the law of negligence—
(a) a duty owed to its employees or to other persons working for the organisation or performing services for it;
(b) a duty owed as occupier of premises;
(c) a duty owed in connection with—
(i) the supply by the organisation of goods or services (whether for consideration or not),
(ii) the carrying on by the organisation of any construction or maintenance operations,
(iii) the carrying on by the organisation of any other activity on a commercial basis, or
(iv) the use or keeping by the organisation of any plant, vehicle or other thing;
(d) a duty owed to a person who, by reason of being a person within subsection (2), is someone for whose safety the organisation is responsible.

(2) A person is within this subsection if—
(a) he is detained at a custodial institution or in a custody area at a court or police station;
(b) he is detained at a removal centre or short-term holding facility;
(c) he is being transported in a vehicle, or being held in any premises, in pursuance of prison escort arrangements or immigration escort arrangements;
(d) he is living in secure accommodation in which he has been placed;
(e) he is a detained patient.

(3) Subsection (1) is subject to sections 3 to 7.

(4) A reference in subsection (1) to a duty owed under the law of negligence includes a reference to a duty that would be owed under the law of negligence but for any statutory provision under which liability is imposed in place of liability under that law.

(5) For the purposes of this Act, whether a particular organisation owes a duty of care to a particular individual is a question of law. The judge must make any findings of fact necessary to decide that question.

(6) For the purposes of this Act there is to be disregarded—
(a) any rule of the common law that has the effect of preventing a duty of care from being owed by one person to another by reason of the fact that they are jointly engaged in unlawful conduct;
(b) any such rule that has the effect of preventing a duty of care from being owed to a person by reason of his acceptance of a risk of harm.

Sections 3 to 7 provide for the exclusion of certain duties of care from the definition of 'relevant duty of care'. In broad terms, the excluded duties are: duties arising from public policy decisions, exclusively public functions and statutory inspections (s. 3); duties owed by the Ministry of Defence in respect of military activities (s. 4); duties relating to policing and law enforcement (s. 5); duties relating to the way in which specified organisations (such as the fire service) respond to emergency circumstances (s. 6); and duties of any public authority relating to its child-protection or probation functions (s. 7).

Gross Breach

Corporate Manslaughter and Corporate Homicide Act 2007, s. 8 B1.132

(1) This section applies where—
  (a) it is established that an organisation owed a relevant duty of care to a person, and
  (b) it falls to the jury to decide whether there was a gross breach of that duty.
(2) The jury must consider whether the evidence shows that the organisation failed to comply with any health and safety legislation that relates to the alleged breach, and if so—
  (a) how serious that failure was;
  (b) how much of a risk of death it posed.
(3) The jury may also—
  (a) consider the extent to which the evidence shows that there were attitudes, policies, systems or accepted practices within the organisation that were likely to have encouraged any such failure as is mentioned in subsection (2), or to have produced tolerance of it;
  (b) have regard to any health and safety guidance that relates to the alleged breach.
(4) This section does not prevent the jury from having regard to any other matters they consider relevant.

Related Offences

An individual cannot be guilty of aiding, abetting, counselling or procuring the commission of an offence of corporate manslaughter (Corporate Manslaughter and Corporate Homicide Act 2007, s. 18(1)). B1.133

Section 19 makes provision as to the relationship between corporate manslaughter and health and safety offences.

Corporate Manslaughter and Corporate Homicide Act 2007, s. 19

(1) Where in the same proceedings there is—
  (a) a charge of corporate manslaughter or corporate homicide arising out of a particular set of circumstances, and
  (b) a charge against the same defendant of a health and safety offence arising out of some or all of those circumstances, the jury may, if the interests of justice so require, be invited to return a verdict on each charge.
(2) An organisation that has been convicted of corporate manslaughter or corporate homicide arising out of a particular set of circumstances may, if the interests of justice so require, be charged with a health and safety offence arising out of some or all of those circumstances.

Part B Offences

Section B2 Non-Fatal Offences Against the Person

ASSAULT AND BATTERY

Definition

B2.1 Strictly speaking, assault and battery are separate summary offences. An assault is committed when the accused intentionally or recklessly causes another to apprehend immediate and unlawful violence. A battery is committed when the accused intentionally or recklessly inflicts unlawful force. A battery may, but does not inevitably, follow an assault. Despite this technical difference, the term 'assault', or 'common assault', has been generally used, both in cases (*Fagan v Metropolitan Police Commissioner* [1969] 1 QB 439) and in statutes (OAPA 1861, ss. 38, 42, 47), to cover either an assault or a battery.

It is now necessary to be more specific when laying an information. The Divisional Court in *DPP v Taylor* [1992] QB 645 has held that all common assaults and batteries are now offences contrary to the CJA 1988, s. 39, and that the information must include a reference to that section. An information would be bad for duplicity if the phrase 'assault and battery' were used; the court suggested that 'assault by beating' was the appropriate wording. Despite this guidance, the point is not always picked up. In *Notman* [1994] Crim LR 518 the Court of Appeal made no comment on just such a duplicitous charge.

The CDA 1998, s. 29, creates a racially or religiously aggravated form of this offence which carries a higher maximum penalty. For the meaning of 'racially or religiously aggravated', see **B11.160** ***et seq.***

Procedure

B2.2 Common assault is generally triable only summarily (CJA 1988, s. 39), although the racially or religiously aggravated form of the offence created by CDA 1998, s. 29, is triable either way. However, a count for common assault may be included in an indictment in the circumstances prescribed by the CJA 1988, s. 40 (see **D10.15**). Common assault under s. 40 has the ordinary everyday meaning of that word, including battery (*Lynsey* [1995] 3 All ER 654). Furthermore, it is now possible for a jury to convict a defendant of common assault as an alternative verdict on an indictment for an offence such as racially or religiously aggravated assault or assault occasioning actual bodily harm, even if no count charging common assault has been included in the indictment (Criminal Law Act 1967, s. 6(3A), inserted by the DVCVA 2004, s. 11, with effect from 31 March 2005).

Sentencing Guidelines (Basic Offence)

The maximum penalties for common assault and battery other than in the racially or religiously aggravated form (see **B2.4**) are six months' imprisonment, a fine not exceeding level 5 on the standard scale, or both (CJA 1988, s. 39). **B2.3**

The Magistrates' Courts Guidelines (2004) indicate the following for a first-time offender pleading not guilty:

> **Aggravating Factors** For example, abuse of trust (domestic setting); on hospital/medical premises; group action; offender in position of authority; premeditated; injury; weapon; victim particularly vulnerable; victim serving the public; spitting; offence committed on bail; relevant previous convictions and any failures to respond to previous sentences.
>
> **Mitigating Factors** For example impulsive; minor injury; provocation; single blow.
>
> *Guideline*: Is it serious enough for a community penalty?

In *Fenton* (1994) 15 Cr App R (S) 682 the offender pleaded guilty to common assault (charges of assault occasioning actual bodily harm and dangerous driving were not proceeded with). In the course of an altercation between two motorists, the offender pushed the victim in the chest. The Court of Appeal said that almost all cases of violence between motorists would be so serious that only custody could be justified. The appropriate sentence was seven days' imprisonment. See also *Ross* (1994) 15 Cr App R (S) 384.

Racial or religious aggravation cannot be taken into account by the sentencer when sentencing for the basic offence of common assault. To do so would infringe the principle that the offender must not be sentenced for an offence for which he has not been charged and convicted (see *McGillivray* [2005] 2 Cr App R (S) 366; *Kentsch* [2006] 1 Cr App R (S) 737). Where there is evidence that racial or religious aggravation was present, the aggravated form of the offence should be charged.

Sentencing Guidelines (Racially or Religiously Aggravated Form of Offence)

The maximum penalty for the aggravated form of common assault is two years, a fine or both on indictment; six months, a fine not exceeding the statutory maximum or both summarily (CDA 1998, s. 29(3)). **B2.4**

The Magistrates' Courts Guidelines (2004) provide a higher guideline for this offence when tried summarily than for the basic offence, the guideline being whether the offence is so serious that only custody can be justified. The Court of Appeal in *Saunders* [2000] 1 Cr App R 458, as elaborated in *Kelly* [2001] 2 Cr App R (S) 341, has indicated that, when sentencing for the racially aggravated form of an offence, the sentencer should indicate what the appropriate sentence would have been in the absence of racial aggravation, and then add a further term to reflect the racial element. See further **B2.26**. In *Bell* [2001] 1 Cr App R (S) 376 a sentence of 12 months was appropriate for a 'gratuitously violent and woundingly offensive' physical and verbal assault by an intoxicated 30-year-old white offender on a 65-year-old black man in the street. See also *Foster* [2001] 1 Cr App R (S) 383.

Actus Reus of Assault

Actions and Words An assault requires conduct which causes the victim to apprehend the imminent application of unlawful force upon him (*Ireland* [1998] AC 147, per Lord Steyn at p. 161). A fear of *possible* violence may suffice (*Ireland*) and it may also suffice where the victim is unsure as to when exactly the threatened attack may occur; but as the Court of Appeal pointed out in *Constanza* [1997] 2 Cr App R 492, the conduct in question must at least provoke a fear of violence 'at some time not excluding the immediate future'. A threat of violence only in the more distant future cannot suffice. As to what may amount to unlawful **B2.5**

force, see **B2.8** and **B2.11** to **B2.16**. An omission to act arguably cannot amount to an assault, or indeed a battery, but see **B2.9**.

The relevant conduct in cases of assault may take the form of threatening acts or gestures, as for example where D brandishes a weapon at V or fires a shot in his direction; but it may also take the form of threatening words, or it may involve acts and words together. It may even involve a series of acts (*Cox* [1998] Crim LR 810). It was at one time thought that words alone, whether written or spoken, could never amount to an assault (*Meade and Belt* (1823) 1 Lew CC 184; *Russell on Crime*, 4th ed. 1865) but this view has now been rejected, both by the Court of Appeal in *Constanza* (a case involving the sending of threatening letters) and by the House of Lords in *Ireland* (a case involving telephone calls). Giving the judgment of the House of Lords in *Ireland*, Lord Steyn said:

> The proposition that a gesture may amount to an assault, but that words can never suffice, is unrealistic and indefensible. A thing said is also a thing done. There is no reason why something said should be incapable of causing an apprehension of immediate personal violence . . . I would, therefore, reject the proposition that an assault can never be committed by words.

The appellant in *Ireland* made 'silent' telephone calls to a number of women, and it was held that such conduct could amount to the *actus reus* of assault if it caused the victims to fear that physical violence might be used against them in the immediate future. It may suffice for this purpose if it causes the victim to fear the mere *possibility* of imminent violence, but it cannot suffice if the victim fears only the prospect of receiving further calls (*Ireland*, per Lord Hope at p. 166), nor can it suffice if it is clear to the victim that the accused or his friends can do nothing to harm her in the immediate future.

The concept of immediacy has nevertheless been interpreted with some flexibility, and there have been a number of recent cases in which 'stalkers' have been prosecuted for assault on that basis. In *Smith v Chief Superintendent, Woking Police Station* (1983) 76 Cr App R 234, the Divisional Court held that a threat of violence could be considered immediate, even though the accused was still outside the victim's home, looking in at her through a window, and would have needed to force an entry before he could attack her. In *Ireland*, the House of Lords adopted an even more flexible approach, stating (at p. 162) that 'there is no reason why a telephone caller who says to a woman in a menacing way, "I will be at your door in a minute or two" may not be guilty of an assault'. Such conduct may alternatively, and perhaps more appropriately, be prosecuted under the Protection from Harassment Act 1997 (see **B11.78** ***et seq.***).

B2.6 **Negated and Conditional Threats** Words used by the accused may indicate that no attack is threatened, even where the circumstances might otherwise suggest that one is. Thus, in *Tuberville v Savage* (1669) 1 Mod 3, T, in the course of a quarrel with S, placed his hand on the hilt of his sword (an act which might ordinarily have been construed as an assault) and exclaimed, 'If it were not assize time, I would not take such language from you'. This was held to be no assault, 'for the declaration of [T] was that he would not assault [S], the judges being in town'.

A 'conditional' threat of unlawful violence may amount to an assault, even though the victim is told that he may avoid such violence by complying with the defendant's conditions. Thus, in the civil case of *Read v Coker* (1853) 13 CB 850, the plaintiff successfully sued for assault on the basis that the defendant and his men had surrounded him and threatened to 'break his neck' if he refused to leave the defendant's premises. See also *Ansell v Thomas* [1974] Crim LR 31.

B2.7 **Result Crime** Although an assault may take the form of a 'failed battery', as where D's blow fails to connect with V, assault is always a result crime (see **A1.2**). No assault can be committed unless the threats are actually perceived by the victim. There is no assault if a stone thrown by D sails past V's head without him noticing (although D may have attempted to commit an offence under the OAPA 1861, s. 47). If, however, D threatens V with an imitation firearm, this will indeed amount to an assault, unless V knows that the weapon cannot fire (*Logdon v DPP* [1976] Crim LR 121). If V does apprehend the threat of imminent violence, it does not matter whether he is frightened by it. He may relish the opportunity to teach D a lesson, and yet still be regarded as the victim of D's assault.

Actus Reus of Battery

A battery requires the unlawful application of force upon the victim. It cannot include the circumstances of a telephone caller who thereby causes his victim's psychiatric injury (*Ireland* [1998] AC 147 at p. 161); but as to assault, see **B2.5**; as to liability under the Protection from Harassment Act 1997, see **B11.78** ***et seq.***). **B2.8**

Battery need not necessarily be preceded by any assault. A blow may, for example, be struck from behind, without warning. Nor need a battery involve any serious violence. Any unlawful touching of another may be classed as a battery. As Goff LJ stated in *Collins v Wilcock* [1984] 3 All ER 374 (at p. 378), 'everybody is protected, not only against physical injury, but against any form of physical molestation'.

Direct and Indirect Application of Force It is submitted that a battery must take the form of a positive act, rather than a mere omission, and that it must involve a *direct* application of force upon the victim. V might, for example, suffer pain or injury if he slips on a patch of oil which D has previously spilled and omitted to clear up, but it is very doubtful whether D can thereby be said to have battered him, even if the spillage of the oil was deliberate. The need for a positive act was emphasised by the Divisional Court in *Fagan v Metropolitan Police Commissioner* [1969] 1 QB 439 (as to which, see **A1.5**). If *Fagan* is correct, it would appear that there is no room in assault or battery cases for application of the *Miller* principle (see *Miller* [1983] 2 AC 161 explained at **A1.16**). Battery suggests some kind of attack, and it is submitted that one cannot attack another person through mere inaction. **B2.9**

The question whether a battery must involve a direct application of unlawful force to the victim is a matter of some controversy. In *Metropolitan Police Commissioner v Wilson* [1984] AC 242, the House of Lords held (albeit by implication) that *indirect* violence, such as the setting of a trap into which P falls, may not amount to a battery, although it may involve the unlawful 'infliction' of harm, for the purpose of liability under the OAPA 1861, s. 20, and that view has been reiterated by the House of Lords, both in *Savage* [1992] 1 AC 699 and in *Ireland* [1998] AC 147 at p. 160. *Martin* (1881) 8 QBD 54 is often said to be authority to the contrary, but that case merely decided that M's conduct in barring the doors to a theatre and putting out the lights could make him liable for the s. 20 'infliction' of grievous bodily harm upon a number of persons who were crushed in the ensuing panic. *Martin* is thus consistent with what was said in *Wilson* and has no bearing on the law of assault or battery.

Two cases do support the concept of indirect battery. In *DPP v K* [1990] 1 WLR 1067, the Divisional Court held that K, a schoolboy, was guilty of an offence under the OAPA 1861, s. 47, when he poured acid into a warm-air drier in his school cloakroom, causing injury to the next pupil who used it. This appears to have been a decision *per incuriam*, however, because no account was taken of *Wilson*. See Hirst, 'Assault, Battery and Indirect Violence' [1999] Crim LR 557. The point was expressly left undecided in *Haystead v Chief Constable of Derbyshire* [2000] 3 All ER 890, but *DPP v K* was recently followed in *DPP v Santa-Bermudez* (2004)168 JP 373 in which the defendant was held to have committed a battery against a police officer when he falsely assured her that he had no 'sharps' in his possession, and thus caused her to stab herself on a hypodermic needle as she searched him. However, none of the conflicting authorities or dicta was cited in that case.

The administering of a poison or noxious substance can only rarely involve a battery (e.g., where it is sprayed directly into the victim's face, as in *Gillard* (1988) 87 Cr App R 189: see **B2.66**). In contrast, setting one's dog on another person involves a direct use of force, because the dog is used as a weapon. The same may be said where A strikes B, causing her to drop and injure her child, C. In *Haystead v Chief Constable of Derbyshire*, this was held to be a battery against both B and C. By the same token, there must also be a battery where A attacks B by pushing over a ladder on which B is standing, or by striking B's horse, so that it rears and throws him.

Mens Rea of Assault or Battery

B2.10 An assault or battery must be committed intentionally or recklessly. Recklessness, in this context, means subjective or *Cunningham* recklessness. As explained at **A2.5**, the courts (notably in *Spratt* [1990] 1 WLR 1073 and *Savage* [1992] 1 AC 699) have held that objective (or *Caldwell*) recklessness is not a sufficient basis for liability in cases where assault or battery must be established. This is true both of common assault and of aggravated assaults under the OAPA 1861, s. 47, or the Police Act 1996, s. 89. Evidence of voluntary intoxication can never assist the defence in respect of such offences because they do not require 'specific intent' (see **A3.10**).

Lawful and Unlawful Force

B2.11 Assault or battery must involve the use or threat of unlawful force. The use or threat of force is not always unlawful. In particular, it may be justified on the basis of actual or implied consent; on the basis of self-defence, crime prevention or crowd control; or on the basis that it involved the lawful correction of a child.

The ordinary everyday jostling that one must expect on crowded pavements, corridors or trains cannot be considered unlawful unless it is excessive and unreasonable (*Wilson v Pringle* [1986] 2 All ER 440) and even where it is objected to, a mere technical battery is unlikely to be prosecuted; but difficulties have sometimes arisen where persons are touched by police officers against their will, because even a trivial technical assault or battery by a police officer takes that officer outside the scope of his duty, and prevents him from qualifying as the victim of any offence under the Police Act 1996, s. 89 (see **B2.31**).

Self-defence and related justifications for the use or threat of force are considered in section A3 and in particular at **A3.31**. The concepts of consent and lawful correction are considered below at **B2.12** and **B2.16**.

B2.12 **Consent** Where consent is in issue, the burden of disproving it is on the prosecution (*Donovan* [1934] 2 KB 498). The two principal questions that may arise in this context are: (1) Did the alleged victim in fact consent (expressly or by implication) to what was done; and (2) if so, do public policy considerations invalidate that consent?

Whether consent was given is usually a simple question of fact, but we are all 'deemed' to consent to various harmless or unavoidable everyday contacts with our fellow citizens, which for that reason cannot be unlawful. Participants in contact sports such as football are meanwhile deemed to consent to the risk of clumsy or mistimed tackles or challenges; but this does not include tackles that are deliberately late or intended to cause harm. As Lord Woolf CJ pointed out in *Barnes* [2005] 1 WLR 910, a jury should be told the importance of the distinction between D going for the ball, albeit late, and his 'going for' the victim.

The alleged victim must understand what he is consenting to, if his consent is to be effective (*Burrell v Harmer* [1967] Crim LR 169; *D* [1984] AC 778). This may require more than mere agreement to the physical act. In *Tabassum* [2000] 2 Cr App R 328, several women allowed T to examine their breasts on the basis of his false representation that he was medically qualified and conducting a survey into breast cancer. Upholding his conviction for indecent assault, Rose LJ said, 'There was consent to the nature of the act, but not its quality'. In *Richardson* [1999] QB 444, however, R, a dentist, was not guilty of assaulting her patients when she failed to tell them that she had been struck off the register. It may be that R's failure to disclose her disqualification did not alter the essential quality of the treatment she carried out; but clearly she would have been guilty had she drilled healthy teeth for fraudulent financial reasons.

The concept of 'informed consent' is crucial where it is alleged that D recklessly infected a partner with a sexually transmitted disease. *Clarence* (1888) 22 QBD 23 is no longer good law. *Dica* [2004] QB 1257 and *Konzani* [2005] 2 Cr App R 198 now establish that D commits no offence if there is informed consent by his sexual partner to the risk that he might infect her, but he may be guilty if he knows he has a serious infection (or symptoms thereof), and keeps his partner in the dark. As Judge LJ observed in *Konzani*:

> There is a critical distinction between taking a risk of the various, potentially adverse and possibly problematic consequences of sexual intercourse, and giving an informed consent to the risk of infection with a fatal disease.

Invalid Consent Where actual bodily harm (or worse) is deliberately inflicted, consent to it will ordinarily be deemed invalid on grounds of public policy, even if V knows exactly what he is consenting to. In *Brown* [1994] 1 AC 212, the House of Lords upheld convictions for offences under the OAPA 1861, ss. 20 and 47, in respect of a group of homosexual sado-masochists, who had engaged in acts of consensual torture with each other for the purpose of sexual gratification. Lord Templeman said (at pp. 231, 234 and 236): **B2.13**

> In some circumstances violence is not punishable under the criminal law. When no actual bodily harm is caused, the consent of the person affected precludes him from complaining. There can be no conviction for the summary offence of common assault if the victim has consented. . . . Even when violence is intentionally inflicted and results in . . . wounding or serious bodily harm the accused is entitled to be acquitted if the injury was a foreseeable incident of a lawful activity in which the person injured was participating. Surgery . . . is a lawful activity. . . . ritual [male] circumcision, tattooing, ear piercing and violent sports including boxing are lawful activities.
>
> . . . The question whether the defence of consent should be extended to the consequences of sado-masochistic encounters can only be decided by consideration of policy and public interest.
>
> . . . The violence of sado-masochistic encounters involves the indulgence of cruelty by sadists and the degradation of victims. Such violence is injurious to the participants and unpredictably dangerous. I am not prepared to invent a defence of consent for sado-masochistic encounters which breed and glorify cruelty and result in offences under sections 47 and 20 of the Act of 1861.

The defendants in *Brown* sought redress from the European Court of Human Rights (*Laskey v United Kingdom* (1997) 24 EHRR 39) but the court ruled that state interference in this aspect of their private lives could be justified on the basis of 'protection of health'.

The approach adopted in *Brown* is consistent with earlier decisions and dicta of the Court of Appeal and Court of Criminal Appeal. Thus, in *Donovan* [1934] 2 KB 498, it was stated that a 17-year-old girl could not give valid consent to a sado-masochistic caning; and in *A-G's Ref (No. 6 of 1980)* [1981] QB 715 Lord Lane CJ held that it would not be in the public interest to allow a defence of consent in the context of a fist-fight where actual bodily harm was intended and/or caused for no good reason ('minor struggles' being excepted).

A limitation on the *Brown* principle was subsequently asserted in *Wilson* [1996] 2 Cr App R 241, in which the Court of Appeal held that nothing said in *Brown* prevented a wife from permitting her husband to brand his initials on her buttocks using a hot knife. The branding was considered analogous to tattooing rather than to the acts of sado-masochism condemned in *Brown*. Furthermore, 'consensual activity between husband and wife in the privacy of the matrimonial home was not . . . normally a proper matter for criminal investigation, let alone criminal prosecution.'

Wilson must now be followed by trial courts, even if it appears to modify the law as stated in *Brown*, but it is not entirely clear how far its effects extend, especially since the view of the court was that the law should be left to develop on a case-by-case basis. Some clarification has been provided by *Emmett* (1999) *The Times*, 15 October 1999, in which the Court of Appeal held that dangerous and damaging sado-masochistic games (involving suffocation and burning) were not exempted by the *Wilson* principle, even where carried out consensually in what was effectively a husband and wife relationship.

B2.14 **Consensual Risk-taking** One must distinguish between consent to the deliberate infliction of injury and consent to a lawful (if dangerous) activity in which injury is accidentally caused (*Slingsby* [1995] Crim LR 571). It is clear that persons may ordinarily consent to sexual or other activities that involve a significant risk of injury, even where they could not validly consent to the deliberate infliction of such injury. In *Dica* Judge LJ explained (at [51]) why this is so:

> The problems of criminalising the consensual taking of risks . . . include the sheer impracticability of enforcement and the haphazard nature of its impact. The process would undermine the general understanding of the community that sexual relationships are pre-eminently private and essentially personal to the individuals involved in them. And if adults were to be liable to prosecution for the consequences of taking known risks with their health, it would seem odd that this should be confined to risks taken in the context of sexual intercourse, while they are nevertheless permitted to take the risks inherent in so many other aspects of everyday life . . .

See also *Meachen* [2006] EWCA Crim 2414. Another example of consensual risk-taking concerns 'rough and undisciplined horseplay'. In *Jones* (1986) 83 Cr App R 375, a group of youths tossed other youths into the air and let them fall to the ground. One of the victims suffered a ruptured spleen and another suffered a broken arm. The trial judge refused to allow the issue of consent to be raised, owing to the serious nature of the injuries, but the Court of Appeal held that the defence should (for what it was worth) have been left to the jury. This ruling was approved in *Brown* and followed in *Aitken* [1992] 1 WLR 1006, but its proper limits must be understood. Individuals may lawfully engage in rough horseplay only where there is at least a genuine belief that the 'victim' is consenting, and then only where no injury is intended. It is not a 'bully's charter'.

In *A-G's Ref (No. 6 of 1980)*, Lord Lane CJ also identified an exception covering 'dangerous exhibitions', although the extent of that exception has never been explored.

B2.15 **Medical Treatment** The law concerning the limits and effectiveness of consent to medical treatment is a highly specialised subject which cannot be covered in detail here; but the basic issues are examined at **A1.17**.

B2.16 **Lawful Correction or Chastisement** At common law, a parent or any other person acting *in loco parentis* may administer reasonable corporal punishment to control the behaviour of children in his care. Concepts of reasonableness have narrowed in recent years, as the Court of Appeal recognised in *H (Assault of child: Reasonable chastisement)* [2001] 2 FLR 431, and are strongly influenced by human rights issues. Caning, for example, was condemned by Strasbourg as 'inhuman and degrading treatment' (*A v United Kingdom* (1999) 27 EHRR 611) and must now be considered unlawful.

This is now reflected in the Children Act 2004, s. 58, which came into force on 15 January 2005 and clarifies the scope of reasonable correction or chastisement.

Children Act 2004, s. 58

(1) In relation to any offence specified in subsection (2), battery of a child cannot be justified on the ground that it constituted reasonable punishment.

(2) The offences referred to in subsection (1) are—
(a) an offence under section 18 or 20 of the Offences against the Person Act 1861 (wounding and causing grievous bodily harm);
(b) an offence under section 47 of that Act (assault occasioning actual bodily harm);
(c) an offence under section 1 of the Children and Young Persons Act 1933 (cruelty to persons under 16).

Section 58(5) repeals the CYPA 1933, s. 1(7), which provided that nothing in that section affected a parent or teacher's right to administer punishment. The effect of s. 58 is that smacking, spanking or any other physical punishment becomes an offence if it causes even minor harm or injury such as significant bruising (see **B2.27**) or if it can be characterised as cruelty under the CYPA 1933, s. 1 (see **B2.114**).

It does not follow that parental chastisement, which is neither cruel within the meaning of the CYPA 1933, s. 1, nor injurious within the meaning of the OAPA 1861, must necessarily be lawful. Smacking a small or handicapped child for failing to understand something he cannot be expected to understand might well be considered 'unreasonable' at common law, even if it causes no injury.

Under the Education Act 1996, s. 548, as substituted by the School Standards and Framework Act 1998, s. 131, teachers (even at private schools) no longer have any right to administer corporal punishment 'by virtue of their position'. It is also unlawful for a teacher to throw an object (such as a blackboard duster) at a pupil who is misbehaving (*Taylor* (1983) *The Times*, 28 December 1983), but staff may use reasonable force to restrain pupils who are violent or disruptive (Education Act 1996, s. 550A) or to avert an immediate danger of personal injury or damage to property (s. 548(5)).

ASSAULT WITH INTENT TO RESIST OR PREVENT ARREST

Definition

Offences against the Person Act 1861, s. 38 **B2.17**

Whosoever . . . shall assault any person with intent to resist or prevent the lawful apprehension or detainer of himself or of any other person for any offence, shall be guilty of [an offence], and being convicted thereof shall be liable, at the discretion of the court, to be imprisoned for any term not exceeding two years . . .

Procedure

Assault with intent to resist or prevent arrest is triable either way. When tried on indictment it is a class 3 offence. **B2.18**

Indictment

Statement of Offence **B2.19**

Assault with intent to resist arrest, contrary to section 38 of the Offences against the Person Act 1861

Particulars of Offence

A on or about the . . . day of . . . assaulted X with intent to resist or prevent the lawful apprehension of A [or another] for the commission of an offence

Sentence

The maximum penalty is two years (OAPA 1861, s. 38). As to sentencing considerations, see those applicable to assault occasioning actual bodily harm, at **B2.25**. **B2.20**

Elements

B2.21 On a literal reading of the OAPA 1861, s. 38, the only *actus reus* required is that of common assault (see **B2.5**), whereas the *mens rea* is that of common assault, coupled with an intent to resist or prevent one's own, or another person's, lawful arrest or detention, etc. Nevertheless, it is firmly established that the arrest or detention in question must in fact be lawful (*Self* [1992] 3 All ER 476; *Lee* [2001] 1 Cr App R 293) and this must accordingly be treated as a further essential *actus reus* element. The victim need not be a police officer. He may be a private citizen assisting such an officer, or a private citizen or store detective making a 'citizen's arrest'. In *Lee*, Rose LJ appears to have assumed that the victim must be the person seeking to make the lawful arrest; but this was *obiter* and (with respect) mistaken. There is no good reason why s. 38 should not extend to assaults on hapless citizens who unwittingly obstruct the accused's attempt to escape from pursuing officers. As to the contrast between the powers of arrest given to police officers and the more restricted powers given to private citizens, see *Self* and **D1.17**.

The *mens rea* requirement in s. 38 may be negatived by the accused's mistaken view of the facts, as for example where he mistakes CID officers for rival gangsters, and believes he is being abducted, rather than arrested. In such a case the accused would have no intent to resist lawful arrest. Indeed, he would not even have the *mens rea* of assault (*Kenlin v Gardiner* [1967] 2 QB 510; *Williams* [1987] 3 All ER 411; *Brightling* [1991] Crim LR 364). The mistake would not have to be a reasonable one (*Williams*; *Lee*; *Blackburn v Bowering* [1994] 1 WLR 1324). In contrast, the accused has no defence if his mistake is merely one of law, as for example where he does not appreciate that a citizen has a power of arrest, or where he assumes that an arrest is unlawful merely because he is (or believes himself to be) innocent of the offence in question. As Rose LJ said in *Lee*:

> Whether or not an offence has actually been committed or is believed by the defendant not to have been committed is irrelevant. We reach this conclusion without regret. Neither public order nor the clarity of the criminal law would be improved if juries were required to consider in relation to s. 38 offences the impact of a defendant's belief as to the lawfulness of his arrest in cases where a lawful arrest is being properly attempted on reasonable grounds.

ASSAULT OCCASIONING ACTUAL BODILY HARM

Definition

B2.22 **Offences against the Person Act 1861, s. 47**

> Whosoever shall be convicted upon an indictment of any assault occasioning actual bodily harm shall be liable . . . to [imprisonment for five years].

The CDA 1998, s. 29, creates a racially or religiously aggravated form of this offence which carries a higher maximum penalty. For the meaning of 'racially or religiously aggravated', see **B11.160** ***et seq.***

Procedure

B2.23 Assault occasioning actual bodily harm (whether in its aggravated form or not) is triable either way. When tried on indictment it is a class 3 offence. The *Consolidated Criminal Practice Direction*, para. V.51, *Mode of trial* (see **appendix** 7) states the following in relation to determining mode of trial for the basic offence:

> 51.10 Cases should be tried summarily unless the court considers that one or more of the following features is present in the case *and* that its sentencing powers are insufficient. Magistrates should take account of their powers under ss. 3 and 4 of the [PCC(S)A 2000] to commit for sentence, see para. 51.3(g): (a) the use of weapon of a kind likely to cause serious injury; (b) a weapon is used and serious injury is caused; (c) more than minor injury is caused by

kicking or head-butting; (d) serious violence is caused to those whose work has to be done in contact with the public or who are likely to face violence in the course of their work; (e) violence to vulnerable people (e.g. the elderly and infirm); (f) the offence has clear motivation.

The same considerations apply to cases of domestic violence.

Indictment

B2.24

Statement of Offence

Assault occasioning actual bodily harm, contrary to section 47 of the Offences against the Person Act 1861

Particulars of Offence

A on or about the . . . day of . . . assaulted V thereby causing him actual bodily harm

Sentencing Guidelines (Basic Offence)

The maximum penalty for the offence other than in the racially or religiously aggravated form (see **B2.26**) is five years (OAPA 1861, s. 47) on indictment; six months, or a fine not exceeding level 5, or both, summarily. B2.25

The Magistrates' Courts Guidelines (2004) indicate the following for a first-time offender pleading not guilty:

Aggravating Factors For example, abuse of trust (domestic setting); deliberate kicking or biting; extensive injuries (may be psychological); headbutting; group action; offender in position of authority; on hospital, medical or school premises; premeditated; victim particularly vulnerable; victim serving public; weapon; offence committed on bail; relevant previous convictions and any failures to respond to previous sentences.

Mitigating Factors For example minor injury; provocation; single blow.

Guideline: Is it so serious that only custody is appropriate?

In *Audit* (1994) 15 Cr App R (S) 36 the offender, after drinking heavily, assaulted another man by punching him in the face, causing a cut to the eyebrow which needed stitches and bruising to the face and jaw. The Court of Appeal said that a custodial sentence of three months was appropriate. In *Graham* [1993] Crim LR 628, the female offender, after an argument in a restaurant, assaulted a woman who had called her names, by hitting her in the face. She suffered black eyes and a swollen nose. Six months' imprisonment was reduced to 28 days. Four months' imprisonment was the appropriate sentence in *Marples* [1998] 1 Cr App R (S) 335 where, in the course of an altercation in a taxi queue, the defendant struck the victim in the face, breaking his nose.

Heavier sentences will be imposed where the assault was committed against a police officer or involved a vulnerable victim. Nine months' imprisonment was upheld on a guilty plea in *Broyd* [2002] 1 Cr App R (S) 197, where the offender head-butted an officer who was trying to arrest him causing a split lip and a chipped tooth. See also *Casey* [2000] 1 Cr App R (S) 221. If it is not proved that the offender knew that the victim was a police officer, then the heavier sentence will not be appropriate (*Stosiek* (1982) 4 Cr App R (S) 205). In *Glover* (1993) 14 Cr App R (S) 261 a sentence of four months' detention in a young offender institution was varied to a probation order where a 20-year-old woman, described as immature and of limited intelligence, had slapped her three-year-old son in the face, causing a swollen and bruised cheek and a bruise inside the mouth, but in *Barnes* (1993) 14 Cr App R (S) 547 a custodial sentence was upheld, though reduced from 6 months to 28 days, where a man left in charge of the 10-month-old daughter of the woman with whom he was living, slapped the child in the face causing bruising.

Longer sentences will also be proper, *inter alia*, where a weapon is used by the offender, or the assault is committed upon a public servant. Six months' imprisonment was appropriate in *McNally* [2000] 1 Cr App R (S) 535, where a relative of a hospital patient became abusive with medical staff and struck a doctor in the face. The victim suffered bruising and bleeding in the ear which caused a hearing loss. In *McDermott* [2007] 1 Cr App R (S) 145, a sentence of 15 months' imprisonment was upheld on a man who, while under the influence of drink, had punched an ambulance attendant to the head. Although the offender pleaded guilty he had relevant previous convictions and the offence fell into a pattern of alcohol-related violence. In *Byrne* [2000] 1 Cr App R (S) 282, where a schoolteacher was assaulted by a parent who forced his way into the staff room, 15 months' imprisonment was reduced to nine months. There is no reason to treat an assault committed by one motorist upon another after a road accident or dispute as any less serious than an assault committed in other circumstances (*Arnold* [1996] 1 Cr App R (S) 115, where six months imprisonment was upheld for headbutting the victim, causing a broken nose). *Arnold* was followed and applied in *Maben* [1997] 2 Cr App R (S) 341 and *Sharpe* [2000] 1 Cr App R (S) 1. Nor should assaults between spouses receive more lenient treatment than other assaults (*Nicholas* (1994) 15 Cr App R (S) 381, where three years' imprisonment was appropriate for serious and repeated assaults by a man on his wife, even after she had obtained a non-molestation injunction against him). An offender convicted of assault committed by 'stalking' the victim over a four-year period received a sentence of 21 months' imprisonment in *Smith* [1998] 1 Cr App R (S) 138.

Racial or religious aggravation cannot be taken into account by the sentencer when sentencing for the basic offence of assault occasioning actual bodily harm (see **B2.3**).

Sentencing Guidelines (Racially or Religiously Aggravated Form of Offence)

B2.26 The maximum penalty for the aggravated form of the offence is seven years, a fine or both on indictment; six months, a fine not exceeding the statutory maximum or both summarily (CDA 1998, s. 29(2)).

The Magistrates' Courts Guidelines (2004) provide a higher guideline for this offence when tried summarily than for the basic offence, the guideline being whether magistrates' sentencing powers are sufficient.

The relevance of racial aggravation as a factor in sentencing has been the subject of guidance from the Court of Appeal in *Saunders* [2000] 1 Cr App R 458 and in *Kelly* [2001] 2 Cr App R (S) 341, both cases of assault occasioning actual bodily harm. The Court established that the sentencer should indicate what the appropriate sentence would have been for the offence in the absence of racial aggravation and then add a further term to reflect the racial element, so that the total sentence would reflect the overall criminality. Even if the basic offence would not have crossed the custody threshold, the aggravation may mean that it did so. In *Pells* (2004) *The Times*, 21 April 2004, the Court of Appeal stated that, when determining the degree of sentencing uplift appropriate to a racially aggravated offence, the differential maximum penalties under the CDA 1998 scheme carried no special significance. In *Saunders*, Rose LJ referred to a number of relevant features of such cases, such as the nature of the racial hostility, its duration and locality. In *Kelly*, matters said to aggravate the racial element were: where the racist element was a planned part of the offence; the offence was part of a pattern of racist offending; the offender was part of a group promoting racist activities; and the deliberate setting up of the victim to humiliate or offend. The impact on the victim was also important, such as where the offence took place in or near the victim's home; where the victim was particularly vulnerable, or was providing a service to the public; where the timing or location of the offence was such as to maximise the harm or distress it caused; if expressions of racial hostility were repeated or prolonged; if fear and distress throughout a particular community resulted from the offence; or if particular distress was caused to the victim or the victim's family.

Actus Reus

An offence under the OAPA 1861, s. 47, must involve an assault or battery (as to which see **B2.5** *et seq.*) and it must be established that this assault or battery occasioned (i.e. caused) the victim actual bodily harm. Such injury cannot ordinarily be consented to (see **B2.12**). As to the position where bodily harm results from the cumulative effect of a series of separate incidents, see *Cox* [1998] Crim LR 810. As long as there was a direct assault or battery, it does not matter if the bodily harm was suffered indirectly. In *Roberts* (1971) 56 Cr App R 95, R assaulted a young woman in his car, and frightened her to the extent that she leaped from it to escape whilst it was still in motion; she suffered injuries as a result. R was convicted of a s. 47 offence. Stephenson LJ said: **B2.27**

> The test is: was [her injury] the natural result of what [R] said and did, in the sense that it was something that could reasonably have been foreseen as the consequence of what he was saying or doing.

'Actual bodily harm' has been defined as any injury which is 'calculated to interfere with the health or comfort of the [victim]' (*Miller* [1954] 2 QB 282, per Lynskey J at p. 292). Minor cuts and bruises may satisfy this test; in *R (T) v DPP* [2003] Crim LR 622, it was held that a momentary loss of consciousness by the victim, following a kick to the head, could properly be regarded as actual bodily harm even where there was no other discernible evidence of injury. The CPS Charging Standards do not, however, encourage the bringing of s. 47 charges in the absence of more serious injuries, such as broken teeth, extensive bruising or cuts etc., which require medical treatment.

It was held in *DPP v Smith* [2006] 1 WLR 157 that the cutting of a substantial part of the victim's hair in the course of an assault may involve actual bodily harm, even though no pain or other injury may be involved, as may putting paint on it or some unpleasant substance which marks or damages it. Sir Igor Judge P said (at [18]):

> Even if, medically and scientifically speaking, the hair above the surface of the scalp is no more than dead tissue, it remains part of the body and is attached to it. While it is so attached . . . it falls within the meaning of 'bodily' in the phrase 'actual bodily harm'. It is concerned with the body of the individual victim.

If this is correct, a haircut represents one more exception to the general rule that actual bodily harm cannot validly be consented to.

A recognisable psychiatric illness may amount to actual or grievous bodily harm (*Chan-Fook* [1994] 1 WLR 689; *Ireland* [1998] AC 147). Where such illness or injury is alleged, it must be proved by expert psychiatric evidence (*Chan-Fook*) and there must also be expert evidence to prove that the defendant's conduct was the cause of that injury. For the purposes of s. 47, this conduct must involve an assault or battery. In the absence of expert evidence, there may be no case to leave to the jury (*Morris* [1998] 1 Cr App R 386). Distress, grief, anxiety or other psychological harm, not amounting to any recognisable psychiatric illness, is not bodily harm for the purposes of the 1861 Act (*Dhaliwal* [2006] 2 Cr App R 348).

Mens Rea

The *mens rea* of a s. 47 offence is no different from that required in respect of a common assault or battery (see **B2.10**). Although the causing of actual bodily harm is an additional *actus reus* element, no *mens rea* as to it is required. If injury is caused, it need not even be proved that the injury was foreseeable, because this element of the offence is one of strict liability. This is now clear from the decision of the House of Lords in *Savage* [1992] 1 AC 699, in which S aimed to throw the contents of a beer glass over B, but inadvertently allowed the glass to slip from her hand and break, with the result that B was injured by it. It was held that a conviction for malicious wounding could not be sustained in the absence of proof that S had at least foreseen the possibility of injury to B, but a conviction for an offence under s. **B2.28**

47 could be substituted, because throwing beer over B was an intentional assault (indeed a battery) and that same assault had resulted in B's injury. Similarly, in a case such as *Ireland* [1998] AC 147, where threats are made by letter or by telephone etc., *mens rea* for a s. 47 offence can be established if D intends or foresees that V may be frightened into apprehending immediate violence. He need not intend or foresee (nor even have any reason to foresee) that V will suffer psychiatric injury.

ASSAULT ON CONSTABLE IN EXECUTION OF DUTY

Definition

B2.29 **Police Act 1996, s. 89**

(1) Any person who assaults a constable in the execution of his duty, or a person assisting a constable in the execution of his duty, shall be guilty of an offence and liable on summary conviction to imprisonment for a term not exceeding six months or to a fine not exceeding level 5 on the standard scale, or to both.

Procedure and Sentencing

B2.30 This offence is triable only summarily.

The maximum penalties are six months' imprisonment, a fine not exceeding level 5, or both (Police Act 1996, s. 89(1)). The Magistrates' Courts Guidelines (2004) indicate the following for a first-time offender pleading not guilty:

Aggravating Factors For example any injuries caused; gross disregard for police authority; group action; premeditated; spitting; racial or religious aggravation; offence committed on bail; relevant previous convictions and any failures to respond to previous sentences.

Mitigating Factors For example impulsive; unaware that the person was a police officer.

Guideline: Is it so serious that only custody is appropriate?

See also the sentencing considerations for assault occasioning actual bodily harm, at **B2.25**.

Actus Reus

B2.31 An offence under the Police Act 1996, s. 89, must involve an assault or battery (as defined in **B2.5** *et seq.*) and it must be proved that the victim was a police or prison officer (of any rank) acting in the execution of his duty, or a person assisting such an officer. As to assaults on members of international joint investigation teams, see the Police Act 1996, s. 89(4) and SOCPA 2005, s. 57. As to assaults on persons carrying out surveillance in England and Wales under the Regulation of Investigatory Powers Act 2000, s. 76A, see the Crime (International Co-operation) Act 2003, s. 84. As to assaults on traffic officers, see the Traffic Management Act 2004, s. 10(1); as to assaults on revenue and customs officers, see the Commissioners for Revenue and Customs Act 2005, s. 32; as to assaults on designated Serious Organised Crime Agency staff, see SOCPA 2005, s. 51. An off-duty police officer may act in the course of duty if a breach of the peace or other incident occurs which justifies immediate action on his part (see *Albert v Lavin* [1982] AC 546) but it is essential in all cases that the officer is shown to have been acting lawfully, because even a minor, technical and inadvertent act of unlawfulness on his part will mean that he cannot have been acting in the execution of his duty (*Riley v DPP* (1989) 91 Cr App R 14; *Kerr v DPP* [1995] Crim LR 394). A violent assault in response to a trivial act of unlawfulness on the part of a police officer may be punishable on some other basis (e.g., as a common assault or battery, or as assault occasioning actual bodily harm), but although common assault is necessarily included within any s. 89 assault, courts of summary jurisdiction have no power to convict of included offences, and it may therefore be desirable to draft alternative charges in cases where the legality of the officer's conduct is in doubt (*Kerr v DPP; Bentley v Brudzinski* (1982) 75 Cr App R 217).

The precise limits of a constable's duty remain undefined. It is clear, however, that a police officer may be acting in the execution of his duty, even where he is doing more than the minimum which the law requires of him (*Waterfield* [1964] 1 QB 164; *Coffin v Smith* (1980) 71 Cr App R 221). It is also clear that any action amounting to assault, battery, unlawful arrest or trespass to property takes the officer outside the course of his duty (*Davis v Lisle* [1936] 2 KB 434) but even where an officer has no legal right to remain on private property when required to leave, offensive remarks telling him to 'go away' will not necessarily suffice to withdraw any implied permission he may have had to enter or remain, and the officer must in any event be given a reasonable opportunity to leave once such permission has effectively been withdrawn (see *R (Fullard) v Woking Magistrates' Court* [2005] EWHC 2922 (Admin)). Some of the most difficult cases in this area concern the power of a police officer to touch or take hold of an individual (without arresting him) in order to speak with or restrain him. As the Divisional Court held in *Donnelly v Jackman* [1970] 1 WLR 562, it is not every interference with a citizen's liberty that will amount to a course of conduct sufficient to take the officer out of the execution of his duty; but how far an officer may go in attracting or retaining the citizen's attention appears to be largely a question of fact. In *Collins v Wilcock* [1984] 1 WLR 1172, a police officer was held to have committed a battery when, without purporting to exercise any lawful power of arrest, she held a woman by the arm in order to question her, whereas in *Mepstead v DPP* (1996) 160 JP 475, it was held to be lawful for a police officer to take hold of a person's arm in order to attract his attention and calm him down. Police powers are more fully examined in **D1**.

Mens Rea

The *mens rea* required in respect of this offence is no different from that required in respect of common assault or battery. The defendant need not know, or even have reason to suspect, that his victim is a police officer or that the officer is acting in the execution of his duty (*Forbes* (1865) 10 Cox CC 362; *Blackburn v Bowering* [1994] 1 WLR 1324). In this respect, the offence is one of strict liability. In *Albert v Lavin* [1982] AC 546, D unlawfully assaulted a man who attempted to prevent him from causing a breach of the peace. He claimed not to know that this man was a police officer, but the House of Lords held that his alleged mistake was irrelevant. He would have been guilty of an assault or battery even if the man had not been a police officer, because the officer had been doing only what any citizen would have had the right to do in the circumstances. In contrast, if D honestly believes that he is being attacked or kidnapped by criminals, and uses force to resist them, he will not be guilty of a s. 89 offence, even though the 'criminals' prove to be police officers who were acting lawfully at the time. D's honest belief in his need to act in self-defence would negative any *mens rea* for assault (*Kenlin v Gardiner* [1967] 2 QB 510; *Blackburn v Bowering*; and see generally A3.37). **B2.32**

RESISTING OR WILFULLY OBSTRUCTING CONSTABLE

Definition

Police Act 1996, s. 89 **B2.33**

(2) Any person who resists or wilfully obstructs a constable in the execution of his duty, or a person assisting a constable in the execution of his duty, shall be guilty of an offence and liable on summary conviction to imprisonment for a term not exceeding one month or to a fine not exceeding level 3 on the standard scale, or to both.

Procedure

This offence is triable only summarily (Police Act 1996, s. 89(2)). As to powers of arrest, see D1.8 *et seq.* **B2.34**

Sentencing Guidelines

B2.35 The maximum penalties are 1 month's imprisonment, a fine not exceeding level 3, or both (Police Act 1996, s. 89(2)). The Magistrates' Courts Guidelines (2004) indicate the following for a first-time offender pleading not guilty:

> **Aggravating Factors** For example attempt to impede arrest; group action; premeditated; racial or religious aggravation; offence committed on bail; relevant previous convictions and any failures to respond to previous sentences.
>
> **Mitigating Factors** For example genuine misjudgment; impulsive action; minor obstruction.
>
> *Guideline*: Is discharge or fine appropriate?

The guideline fine is Starting Point A, see **E17.5**.

Elements

B2.36 A defendant obstructs a police constable if he makes it more difficult for him to carry out his duty (*Hinchcliffe v Sheldon* [1955] 1 WLR 1207, *obiter*). While 'resisting' implies some physical action, no physical act is necessary to constitute obstruction. Simple refusal to answer questions does not constitute an obstruction (*Rice v Connolly* [1966] 2 QB 414), neither does advising another person not to answer (*Green v DPP* (1991) 155 JP 816). Answering questions incorrectly may, however, amount to obstruction, although the distinction is not always clear (see *Ledger v DPP* [1991] Crim LR 439).

A person may obstruct by omission, provided that such a person is under an initial duty to act (*Lunt v DPP* [1993] Crim LR 534). There is also a common-law offence of refusing to aid a constable who is attempting to prevent or to quell a breach of the peace and who calls for assistance (*Waugh* (1986) *The Times*, 1 October 1986).

In *Green v Moore* [1982] QB 1044 the court held that a tip-off to persons who were preparing to commit an offence, and who as a result of the tip-off decided not to commit such an offence, could amount to an obstruction. Police could still be said to be acting in execution of their duty even if only making general inquiries before an offence was committed. The court admitted that this was a difficult situation, since the result of the tip-off was in fact the prevention of crime. Liability would turn, however, on the *mens rea* and the question of whether the defendant's intent was to assist the potential criminal or to assist the police. If D's intention is simply to stop or prevent the commission of the crime, no offence is committed where he warns off the potential offender by pointing out the danger of detection and arrest. If, however, D's intention is to enable the potential offender to commit his crime (or a similar crime) at a more opportune moment, he may be guilty of obstruction.

In *R (DPP) v Glendinning* (2005) 169 JP 649, the Administrative Court held (following *Bastable v Little* [1907] 1 KB 59) that no offence of wilful obstruction is committed where D warns motorists of a police speed trap ahead, unless it is established that those warned were either already speeding or were likely to do so at the location of the speed trap.

A constable is not acting in the course of his duty, and a person cannot therefore be liable for obstructing him in the course of such action, if what he is doing is carrying out an arrest which is in fact unlawful (*Edwards v DPP* (1993) 97 Cr App R 301).

If obstruction (rather than resistance) is alleged, it must be proved to have been wilful. The defendant does not commit wilful obstruction if he tries to help the police, even if he actually makes their job more difficult (*Wilmott v Atack* [1977] QB 498) nor can he be guilty if he is unaware that he is obstructing police officers at all (*Ostler v Elliott* [1980] Crim LR 584), but if the defendant deliberately obstructs the police, it will be no defence to argue that he was merely trying to prevent the arrest of a person he believed to be innocent (*Lewis v Cox* [1985] QB 509). As to the obstruction of international joint investigation teams, see the Police Act 1996, s. 89(4) and SOCPA 2005, s. 57. As to the obstruction of traffic officers, see the Traffic

Management Act 2004, s. 10(2); as to the obstruction of revenue and customs officers, see the Commissioners for Revenue and Customs Act 2005, s. 31; as to the obstruction of designated Serious Organised Crime Agency staff, see SOCPA 2005, s. 51; as to the obstruction or hindrance of emergency workers or persons assisting such workers, see the Emergency Workers (Obstruction) Act 2006, ss. 1 to 4.

WOUNDING OR INFLICTING GRIEVOUS BODILY HARM

Definition

Offences against the Person Act 1861, s. 20 **B2.37**

> Whosoever shall unlawfully and maliciously wound or inflict any grievous bodily harm upon any other person, either with or without any weapon or instrument, shall be guilty of [an offence], and being convicted thereof shall be liable to [imprisonment for not more than five years].

The CDA 1998, s. 29, creates a racially or religiously aggravated form of this offence which carries a higher maximum penalty. For the meaning of 'racially or religiously aggravated', see **B11.160**.

Procedure

Both forms of the offence are triable either way. When tried on indictment it is a class 3 offence. The considerations relevant to determining mode of trial for the basic offence given in the *Consolidated Criminal Practice Direction*, para. V. 51, *Mode of trial* (see **appendix** 7) are the same as for assault occasioning actual bodily harm (see **B2.23**). **B2.38**

Indictment

Statement of Offence **B2.39**

> Unlawful wounding, contrary to section 20 of the Offences against the Person Act 1861

Particulars of Offence

> A on or about the . . . day of . . . unlawfully and maliciously wounded [or inflicted grievous bodily harm on] V

Alternative Verdicts

A verdict of assault occasioning actual bodily harm under the OAPA 1861, s. 47, can be returned. (See Criminal Law Act 1967, s. 6(3).) **B2.40**

Sentencing Guidelines (Basic Offence)

The maximum penalty for the offence other than in the racially or religiously aggravated form (see **B2.46**) is five years (OAPA 1861, s. 20) on indictment; six months, a fine not exceeding level 5, or both, summarily (MCA 1980, s. 32(1)). **B2.41**

When dealt with summarily, the Magistrates' Courts Guidelines (2004) indicate the following for a first-time offender pleading not guilty:

> **Aggravating Factors** For example abuse of trust (domestic setting); deliberate kicking/biting; extensive injuries; group action; prolonged assault; offender in position of authority; on hospital, medical or school premises; premeditated; victim particularly vulnerable; victim serving public; weapon; offence committed on bail; relevant previous convictions and any failures to respond to previous sentences.
>
> **Mitigating Factors** For example minor wound; provocation.
>
> *Guideline*: Are magistrates' sentencing powers sufficient?

Sentences of up to three years for this offence have been upheld by the Court of Appeal where aggravating factors have been present, or where the offence has been close to the borderline with the offence of wounding with intent; such sentences will be imposed where the assault was committed against a police officer or other public servant or against a child.

A sentence of three years' imprisonment was upheld in *Brown* [2001] 1 Cr App R (S) 83, where a father inflicted grievous bodily harm on his six-week-old son by shaking him violently, causing injury which would affect the child's development. The offender was convicted of the offence at trial, but found not guilty of causing grievous bodily harm with intent. A sentence of 12 months concurrent for cruelty to a child was upheld, that matter referring to a period after the injuries had been inflicted when the child was in distress and the offender failed to summon medical help. The Court of Appeal stated that the sentence was at the upper end of the acceptable bracket but was consistent with the jury's verdict and reflected available mitigation. In *Ambrose* [1997] 1 Cr App R (S) 404, the 22-year-old offender came across the victim, a man who had molested him some years before. After a degree of further provocation from the victim, the offender punched him in the face, causing him to fall and strike his head. The victim suffered multiple cerebral haemorrhage, and was in a confusional state from which it was uncertain whether he would recover. The Court of Appeal reduced a sentence of three and a half years' imprisonment to one of 18 months. Rougier J commented that the original sentence was out of line with other cases and that, given the decision in *Coleman* (1991) 95 Cr App R 159 (see **B1.41**), if the victim had died it was unlikely that the sentence would have been as long as three and a half years. See also *McCarthy* (1995) 16 Cr App R (S) 1038. In *Jane* [1998] 2 Cr App R (S) 363 the offender took some cans of lager from a shop without paying for them and, when the shopkeeper tried to prevent him from leaving, the offender wrestled the shopkeeper to the floor and then kicked him in the face, causing the loss of one eye. The Court of Appeal reduced a sentence of three and a half years to one of two and half years, Sullivan J commenting that, although the consequences for the victim were dreadful, no weapon was used, there was no premeditation and the attack was not sustained. It was a lashing out in panic to escape from the shop. The offence in *Moss* [2000] 1 Cr App R (S) 307 took place during a rugby match, in the course of which the offender punched an opposing player in the face, fracturing his eye-socket. The offender was convicted after a trial, and the Court of Appeal upheld the sentence of eight months' imprisonment imposed by the trial judge.

B2.42 **Use of Weapon** The use of a weapon is an important aggravating feature. A sentence of four years was reduced to 30 months on appeal in *Simpson* [1998] 1 Cr App R (S) 197, where the offender had made an unprovoked attack on a stranger, stabbing him in the arm with a chisel. A plea of guilty to unlawful wounding had been accepted on the basis that the offender had at the time been too drunk to form the necessary intent for an offence of wounding with intent. In *Bayes* (1994) 16 Cr App R (S) 290, after a driving incident, the offender attacked the driver of the other vehicle, punching him in the face and striking him on the back with a hammer, causing superficial bruising and cuts. Fifteen months' imprisonment was reduced to nine months to take account of personal mitigation and remorse.

B2.43 **Glassing** Reported cases involving 'glassing' include *Jones* (1984) 6 Cr App R (S) 55, where the offender hit the victim on the side of the head with a glass and then pushed the edge of the glass into the victim's face, causing probable loss of sight in one eye. A sentence of two years' imprisonment was upheld. More recently, in *Robertson* [1998] 1 Cr App R (S) 21, the Court of Appeal noted that, in the light of earlier authorities, any sentence of more than two years' imprisonment for unlawful wounding required careful scrutiny to see if it was justified on the facts. In that case the offender had been drinking in a public house and had thrust a beer glass into another man's face, causing wounds to his face. A sentence of 30 months was reduced to two years. Two years was also appropriate in *Singleton* [1998] 1 Cr App R (S) 199, a very similar case but where the injuries were more severe, the victim remaining at risk of visual loss or possible blindness. In *Marsden* (1993) 15 Cr App R (S) 177, the offender became involved in an argument in a public house and, after having been asked to leave, threw a glass across the room. It hit the victim and caused a cut to the head which required hospital treatment. A sentence of 12 months' imprisonment was upheld. See also **B2.57**.

Malicious Transmission of Venereal Disease In *P (SJ)* [2006] EWCA Crim 2599, the offender had unprotected sexual relations with a man, without informing him that she had been diagnosed as HIV positive. When he became infected, she led him to believe, to his great distress, that he had infected her. She eventually pleaded guilty to the malicious infliction of grievous bodily harm, and a sentence of 32 months' imprisonment was upheld on appeal. The court heard representations from the Terrence Higgins Trust to the effect that deterrent sentences in cases such as this had adverse effects on the willingness of suspected HIV sufferers to seek treatment or to undergo testing, but concluded that the courts had a duty to deter those who knew that they were HIV positive from recklessly transmitting the virus. **B2.44**

Racial or Religious Aggravation in Basic Offence Racial or religious aggravation cannot be taken into account by the sentencer when sentencing for the basic offence of wounding or inflicting grievous bodily harm (see **B2.3**). **B2.45**

Sentencing Guidelines (Racially or Religiously Aggravated Form of Offence)

The maximum penalty for the aggravated form of wounding or inflicting grievous bodily harm is seven years, a fine or both on indictment; six months, a fine not exceeding the statutory maximum or both summarily (CDA 1998, s. 29(2)). **B2.46**

The Magistrates' Courts Guidelines (2004) provide the same guideline for this offence when tried summarily as for the basic offence, while stressing the importance of the aggravation in assessing the seriousness of the offence.

The Court of Appeal indicated in *Saunders* [2000] 1 Cr App R 458 that, when sentencing for the racially aggravated form of an offence, the sentencer may usefully consider the appropriate sentence for the offence in the absence of racial aggravation and then add a further term for the racial element. See further **B2.26**. What was described as a 'disgraceful and unprovoked incident of racial violence' attracted a sentence of 18 months' detention in a young offender institution in *Bray* (1992) 13 Cr App R (S) 5, notwithstanding the offender's previous good character.

Elements

The *actus reus* of an offence under the OAPA 1861, s. 20, may involve either unlawful wounding or the infliction of grievous bodily harm. Wounding requires the breaking of the continuity of the whole of the skin (dermis and epidermis) or the breaking of the inner skin within the cheek, lip or urethra (*Smith* (1837) 8 C & P 173; *Waltham* (1849) 3 Cox 442). It does not include the rupturing of internal blood vessels (*J.J.C. (A Minor) v Eisenhower* [1983] 3 All ER 230). In theory, even trivial wounds may qualify, but the Charging Standards agreed between the police and the CPS urge that minor wounds should not in practice be charged under s. 20. Where, however, there is evidence of a serious wound, this ought generally to be charged as wounding, rather than as inflicting grievous bodily harm (*McReady* [1978] 1 WLR 1376). **B2.47**

Grievous bodily harm is not defined in the 1861 Act, but has been interpreted as meaning no more and no less than really serious harm (*DPP v Smith* [1961] AC 290; *Cunningham* [1982] AC 566; cf. *Saunders* [1985] Crim LR 230). There is no definitive list of the kind of injuries that may be considered really serious, but it is clear that a number of individually minor injuries may collectively become grievous (see *Birmingham* [2002] EWCA Crim 2608, in which a large number of minor wounds were found capable of amounting to GBH on a charge of aggravated burglary). Where the seriousness of an injury is questionable, a trial judge may withdraw a charge of grievous bodily harm from the jury. The CPS Charging

Standards list examples of injuries which may be considered sufficiently serious, but this list can at best be of persuasive value in court. Psychiatric injury or illness may involve really serious harm (*Ireland* [1998] AC 147; *Dhaliwal* [2006] 2 Cr App R 348) but its cause and effect will need to be proved by expert psychiatric evidence, as in cases of alleged psychiatric injury brought under s. 47 (see **B2.27**).

B2.48 **Infliction** Section 20 refers to the 'infliction' of grievous bodily harm. The meaning of this term was once a matter of some uncertainty and debate, but appears to have been largely resolved by the recent decision of the House of Lords in *Ireland* [1998] AC 147, where Lord Steyn, in giving the majority judgment, held (at p. 160) that harm could be inflicted without the need for an assault, and that in the context of the 1861 Act, there was no radical divergence between the meanings of the words 'cause' and 'inflict' (see also *Salisbury* [1976] VR 452; *Wilson* [1984] AC 242). Grievous bodily harm within the meaning of s. 20 could thus be inflicted by means of menacing telephone calls which gave rise to serious psychiatric injury, whether or not the injury was caused by fear of imminent physical attack.

On the other hand, Lord Steyn later denied that the words 'cause' and 'inflict' were exactly synonymous, and this point was developed by Lord Hope, who said that, although there was no real practical difference between the two words, the word 'inflict' invariably implies detriment to the victim of some kind. Lord Steyn and Lord Hope both appear to have stopped just short of overruling the authority of *Clarence* (1888) 22 QBD 23, in which it was held that grievous bodily harm was caused, *but not inflicted*, where C enjoyed consensual sexual intercourse with his wife, without warning her that he was infected with a venereal disease, which she then contracted. The authority and rationale of *Clarence* was nevertheless gravely damaged by what was said and decided in *Ireland* and in *Dica* [2004] QB 1257 (see **B2.12**), the Court of Appeal concluded that it should no longer be followed. Judge LJ said:

> The effect of this judgment in relation to s. 20 is to remove some of the outdated restrictions against the successful prosecution of those who, knowing that they are suffering HIV or some other serious sexual disease, recklessly transmit it through consensual sexual intercourse, and inflict grievous bodily harm on a person from whom the risk is concealed and who is not consenting to it. In this context, *Clarence* has no continuing relevance. Moreover, to the extent that *Clarence* suggested that consensual sexual intercourse of itself was to be regarded as consent to the risk of consequent disease, again, it is no longer authoritative. If however, the victim consents to the risk, this continues to provide a defence under s 20 . . .

The injury in question must it seems be inflicted (directly or indirectly) by some deliberate, non-accidental conduct on the part of the accused. In *Brady* [2006] EWCA Crim 2413, D had consumed a significant quantity of alcohol at a nightclub. As he sat down on a low railing on the first-floor gallery above the dance floor, he lost his balance and fell, landing on V and crippling her. The Court of Appeal opined (*obiter*) that although the fall may have been accidental, the act of perching drunkenly on the rail was not. Hallett LJ said (at [25]):

> This deliberate act, on any view, led almost immediately and directly to the fall over the railing and to the infliction of grievous bodily harm. It was a substantial cause of the infliction of those injuries. We would not be inclined to accept, therefore, [counsel's] submission that, because it was the unintentional fall rather than the deliberate act which, in fact, caused [the victim's] injuries, this broke the chain of causation. The one led inevitably to the other.

D's apparent lack of mens rea could then be addressed under the *Majewski* rule (as to which see **A3.10**). His appeal against his conviction was however allowed on other grounds.

B2.49 **Maliciously** A s. 20 offence must be committed 'maliciously'. Maliciousness requires *either* an intent to do some kind of bodily harm to another person *or* recklessness (in the subjective or *Cunningham* sense) as to whether any such harm might be caused. The harm intended or foreseen by the defendant need not amount to a wound or grievous bodily harm: an intent to cause minor injury, which inadvertently results in the infliction of a wound or serious injury, is sufficient to found liability under s. 20 (*Mowatt* [1968] 1 QB 421; *Sullivan* [1981] Crim

LR 46; *DPP v W* [2006] EWHC 92 (Admin)). On the other hand, there cannot ordinarily be liability under s. 20 if the defendant was unaware that his conduct might cause any injury at all (*Savage* [1992] 1 AC 699; *Meachen* [2006] EWCA Crim 2414). The only qualification to this rule concerns cases of voluntary intoxication: such intoxication cannot be relied upon by a defendant in order to negative *mens rea* under s. 20, because it is not a crime of 'specific intent' (see *Brady* [2006] EWCA Crim 2413 at **B2.48** and **A3.10**).

In *Barnes* [2005] 1 WLR 910, Lord Woolf CJ suggested that recklessness in this context, 'means no more than the defendant foresaw the risk that some bodily harm (however slight) might result from what he was going to do and yet, ignoring that risk, he went on to commit the offending act'. If that were indeed so, most tackles committed in contact sports such as football would (as Lord Woolf concedes) be deemed 'malicious'. With respect, however, such conduct is not reckless at all unless the risk taking in question can be described as unreasonable or unjustified in the circumstances.

The Court of Appeal held in *Beeson* [1994] Crim LR 190 that it was unnecessary to direct the jury on the meaning of the word 'maliciously'; but whilst such an omission may have been unimportant on the facts of that particular case (where the only real issue was self-defence), there will be many cases in which careful guidance on its meaning must be vital. The concept of maliciousness is further explained at **A2.7**.

WOUNDING OR CAUSING GRIEVOUS BODILY HARM WITH INTENT

Definition

Offences against the Person Act 1861, s. 18 **B2.50**

Whosoever shall unlawfully and maliciously by any means whatsoever wound or cause any grievous bodily harm to any person with intent to do some grievous bodily harm to any person, or with intent to resist or prevent the lawful apprehension or detainer of any person, shall be guilty of [an offence], and being convicted thereof shall be liable to [imprisonment] for life.

Procedure

Wounding or causing grievous bodily harm with intent is triable on indictment only. It is a class 3 offence. **B2.51**

Indictment

Statement of Offence **B2.52**

Wounding [or causing grievous bodily harm] with intent, contrary to section 18 of the Offences against the Person Act 1861

Particulars of Offence

A on or about the . . . day of . . . unlawfully and maliciously wounded [or caused grievous bodily harm to] V with intent to do him grievous bodily harm [or to prevent the lawful apprehension of X]

As to the proper form of indictment in a 'transferred malice' case, where it is alleged that the accused wounded the victim whilst intending to do grievous bodily harm to another, see *Monger* [1973] Crim LR 301, *Slimmings* [1999] Crim LR 69.

Alternative Verdicts

This subject is complex, and is dealt with in detail at **D18.41** *et seq.* and **D18.58**. Where wounding is alleged in a count under the OAPA 1861, s. 18, then wounding under s. 20 and s. 47 assault are possible alternative verdicts. *Lahaye* [2006] 1 Cr App R 205, confirms that on a charge of wounding with intent to do grievous bodily harm, a conviction for malicious **B2.53** wounding (under the OAPA, s. 20) is available even if not expressly charged on the indictment, and even if the prosecution have presented the case as one of deliberate and premeditated stabbing. The Court of Appeal nevertheless recommended that it would be preferable, in such cases, for the lesser offence to be included on the face of the indictment. If, however, the s. 18 count alleges the causing of grievous bodily harm only, the situation is more complex. Problems have arisen in recent cases where an alternative count of inflicting grievous bodily harm under s. 20 has not been specified, and the alternative verdict of *causing* grievous bodily harm under s. 20 has been accepted. Strictly speaking, this is an offence unknown to law, given the use of the term 'inflicting' in the offence created by s. 20.

The House of Lords in *Mandair* [1995] 1 AC 208, overruling the previous decision on the point by the Court of Appeal in *Field* (1993) 97 Cr App R 357, has held that a judge is entitled under the Criminal Law Act 1967, s. 6(3), to leave to a jury a conviction under s. 20 as an alternative to s. 18 because the term 'causing' is wide enough to include 'inflicting' (see *Metropolitan Police Commissioner v Wilson* [1984] AC 242). Even though in *Mandair* the word 'inflicting' was not used, the meaning is clear given the context of the direction in the case and the wording of the verdict. A verdict of 'causing grievous bodily harm contrary to s. 20' can only mean causing grievous bodily harm by inflicting it, as that is the particular method referred to in s. 20. Therefore the jury had not returned a verdict unknown to law. The case was remitted to the Court of Appeal for a decision on a further point it had not considered. *Mandair* was applied in *White* [1995] Crim LR 393.

Although it is now clear that an alternative verdict can be considered following an oral direction, the House of Lords in *Mandair* re-affirmed the point that it is preferable to add an alternative specific count using the correct wording of the statute. Normally, if the accused is acquitted under s. 18 without an alternative indictment under s. 20, a later prosecution under s. 20 cannot be brought, but in circumstances where the accused was for some reason not in jeopardy of a s. 20 conviction in the first trial, a later prosecution can arguably be brought. See *Old Street Magistrates' Court, ex parte Davies* [1995] Crim LR 629, and *Brookes* [1995] Crim LR 630, where the initial charge was under s. 20, and the subsequent charge was under s. 18.

Sentencing Guidelines

B2.54 The maximum penalties for this offence and related offences are:

Wounding or causing grievous bodily harm with intent to do grievous bodily harm: life imprisonment (OAPA 1861, s. 18);

Wounding or causing grievous bodily harm with intent to resist arrest: life imprisonment (OAPA 1861, s. 18);

Attempting to choke, suffocate or strangle with intent: life imprisonment (OAPA 1861, s. 21);

Throwing corrosive fluid: life imprisonment (OAPA 1861, s. 29).

A custodial sentence will almost always be required for this offence (*A-G's Ref (No. 33 of 1997)* [1998] 1 Cr App R (S) 352). The normal sentencing bracket is in the range of three to eight years, although sentences over eight years are upheld in particularly grave cases. Relevant aggravating factors include the extent of the injuries, the degree of premeditation, racial motivation, use of a weapon, and kicking or stamping on the victim. Mitigating factors such as a plea of guilty and the previous good character of the offender may be of little weight in very serious cases, but significant provocation is to be taken into account.

B2.55 **Knives** Numerous appellate authorities involve the infliction of very serious injuries by the use of a knife. A sentence of nine years was upheld in *Pollin* [1997] 2 Cr App R (S) 356, where the offender, after a disagreement over rent, drove to the victim's home and stabbed him 21 times with a kitchen knife in a 'ferocious and totally unprovoked attack', leaving the victim with some permanent disability. The Court of Appeal held that on the facts the sentence was not excessive, even on a guilty plea. In *A-G's Ref (No. 4 of 1998)* [1998] 2 Cr App R (S) 388 the offender, under the influence of drink, stabbed a man in a pub. The victim suffered injuries requiring the removal of his spleen. The offender pleaded guilty. In the Court of Appeal Lord Bingham CJ said that the sentence of three and a half years 'fell very well below the appropriate range'. In a contested case, the proper sentence would have been seven or eight years and, on a guilty plea, five to six years. In *Samuels-Furness* [2005] 2 Cr App R (S) 521, the offender stabbed the victim in the side with a kitchen knife, causing serious damage to the victim's liver and one kidney, which had to be removed. The offender and victim were known to each other, and both were addicted to heroin. The attack was unprovoked, but the offender apparently believed that the victim had been responsible for an earlier attack in which the offender had been stabbed in the head. The Court of Appeal said that the appropriate sentence, on a guilty plea entered at a late stage, was seven years' imprisonment.

Other Weapons The use of other weapons will attract comparable sentences, depending upon the extent of the injuries, taken together with relevant mitigating and aggravating factors. In *Chesterman* (1984) 6 Cr App R (S) 151, a 12-year sentence was upheld on an offender who fired a shotgun twice at a police officer. The officer was permanently blinded and suffered other injuries. The offender was acquitted of attempted murder, but the case was described as 'at the very top of the scale for offences of causing grievous bodily harm with intent'. In *Craney* [1996] 2 Cr App R (S) 336 sentences of 11 years were proper in a case where an unprovoked and racially motivated attack by two youths using a torch and an iron bar left the victim with severe head injuries inducing a coma, requiring him to be placed on a life-support machine, and a badly broken leg resulting from the victim's attempts to flee from his attackers. In *A-G's Ref (No. 3 of 2000)* [2001] 1 Cr App R (S) 92, the offender was convicted of causing grievous bodily harm with intent after pouring boiling water over the victim's back and shoulders, causing severe mixed depth burns. The act was premeditated and calculated to cause severe pain and injury. Rose LJ said that the sentence of three years was unduly lenient and that the proper sentence following a trial was at least six years. B2.56

Glassing The Court of Appeal has considered many cases where a broken bottle or glass has been used as a weapon, and on a number of occasions in recent years has corrected unduly lenient sentences. In *A-G's Ref (No. 14 of 2000)* [2001] 1 Cr App R (S) 55, the offender was convicted of wounding with intent. He had struck the victim in the face with a beer glass causing deep lacerations which required 44 stitches and would result in permanent scarring. Roch LJ said that the tariff after a contested case of this sort was between four and six years. On the facts, where the injuries were severe and the offender had no effective mitigation, two years was unduly lenient and a sentence in the order of five years should have been passed. In *A-G's Ref (No. 15 of 1998)* [1999] 1 Cr App R (S) 209 the offender and the victim had been drinking together when an argument arose between them. The offender struck the victim in the face with a pint glass, causing multiple lacerations and requiring surgery. He pleaded guilty to wounding with intent and received a sentence of six months. The Court of Appeal said that the lowest possible sentence was two and a half years, with an unspecified allowance for the fact that the offender had been sentenced twice. Finally, in *A-G's Ref (No. 24 of 1998)* [1999] 1 Cr App R (S) 278, where the facts were almost identical to the last case but where the offender was convicted after a trial, Rose LJ in the Court of Appeal found that a sentence of two years' imprisonment was unduly lenient. A sentence in the order of five years should have been passed. B2.57

Kicking or Stamping It is clear that where an offender causes grievous bodily harm by kicking or stamping on the victim's head while the latter is on the ground, he should receive a substantial custodial term. In *Ivey* (1981) 3 Cr App R (S) 185 a man of previous good character became caught up in a fracas at a club, during the course of which he knocked a man to the ground and stamped on his head, inflicting grave injuries to his face and skull. A B2.58

four-year sentence was upheld, Griffiths LJ explaining (at p. 186) that, 'The degree of injury likely to be caused by kicking a man in the head when he is down is of a wholly different degree to that which is likely to be suffered in the course of a fist fight. . . . The injuries thereby inflicted are often appalling.' *Ivey* has been followed and applied in several cases, including *A-G's Ref (No. 59 of 1996)* [1997] 2 Cr App R (S) 250. Another example is *Richards* [1998] 1 Cr App R (S) 87, where the offender attacked a man outside a pub and, when the victim was on the ground, kicked him in the face, throat and head. The victim suffered various injuries including fractures to the skull and the left eye socket. In the Court of Appeal, Ognall J stated that, had the case been contested, a sentence of seven years would have been appropriate and that, on a guilty plea by a man of previous good character, as in this case, the sentence of five years was not excessive. The Court of Appeal said that five years' imprisonment was appropriate in *Clarke* [2006] 1 Cr App R (S) 80, where the offender, a man with no previous convictions, had, in the course of a road rage incident, pulled the victim from his car and kicked him in the head when he was on the ground. The offender was wearing steel toe-capped boots, and the Court said that the boots should be treated as equivalent to a weapon.

B2.59 **Corrosive Fluid** In cases where corrosive fluid is thrown, lengthy terms will be appropriate. In *Radford* (1986) 8 Cr App R (S) 60, five years was upheld where the offender squirted a corrosive substance into the victim's face, causing substantial loss of vision in one eye. The offender in *Carrington* [1999] 2 Cr App R (S) 206 threw some liquid containing sulphuric acid into the face of his former girlfriend. The victim received prompt first aid treatment, and fortunately suffered no long-term damage. In light of the fact that the attack was premeditated and that the offender had contested the case and had shown no remorse, a sentence of six years' imprisonment was upheld.

Elements

B2.60 An offence under the OAPA 1861, s. 18, may take one of four different forms, namely:

(a) wounding with intent to do grievous bodily harm;
(b) causing grievous bodily harm with intent to do so;
(c) maliciously wounding with intent to resist or prevent the lawful apprehension etc. of any person; or
(d) maliciously causing grievous bodily harm with intent to resist or prevent lawful apprehension etc. of any person.

As to the meaning of the terms 'wound' and 'grievous bodily harm', see **B2.47**. Following the decision of the House of Lords in *Ireland* [1998] AC 147, it now seems unlikely that anything of significance turns on the supposed difference between 'causing' injury in cases under s. 18 and 'inflicting' injury in cases under s. 20. This means that the *actus reus* elements of the two offences are for most purposes the same. The difference lies in the specific intent required under s. 18. Where it is alleged that the accused acted with intent to cause grievous bodily harm, the jury should be directed along the following or similar lines: 'You must feel sure that [D] intended to cause serious bodily harm to [V]. You can only decide what his intention was by considering all the relevant circumstances and in particular what he did and what he said about it' (*Purcell* (1986) 83 Cr App R 45).

If the accused is alleged to have acted with intent to do grievous bodily harm, the concept of maliciousness is rendered otiose and need not be examined (*Mowatt* [1968] 1 QB 421). Where, in contrast, it is alleged that the defendant merely intended to resist arrest etc., maliciousness becomes an important further element to be proved. If, for example, D tries to pull free from the officer arresting him and quite unforeseeably injures the officer in the process, he could not be considered to have acted maliciously and could not therefore be convicted of an offence under s. 18. If, however, he intended or foresaw that he would cause some minor injury, he could indeed be adjudged malicious.

Where it is alleged that the accused acted with intent to avoid or resist the lawful apprehension of any person, it may be his own arrest or that of another that he resisted, but the lawfulness of that arrest or detention must in either event be proved by the prosecution (*Howarth* (1828) 1 Mood 207). It does not follow that the accused must be proved to have known that the arrest etc. was lawful, but in a case such as *Kenlin v Gardiner* [1967] 2 QB 510, where the accused mistook arresting officers for kidnappers, mistaken self-defence may be raised by the defence in accordance with the principles established in *Williams* [1987] 3 All ER 411. See generally **A3.31**.

ADMINISTERING POISON ETC. SO AS TO ENDANGER LIFE ETC.

Definition

Offences against the Person Act 1861, s. 23 **B2.61**

Whosoever shall unlawfully and maliciously administer to or cause to be administered to or taken by any other person any poison or other destructive or noxious thing, so as thereby to endanger the life of such person, or so as thereby to inflict upon such person any grievous bodily harm, shall be guilty of [an offence], and being convicted thereof shall be liable . . . to [imprisonment] for any term not exceeding 10 years.

Note also the Anti-terrorism, Crime and Security Act 2001, s. 113 (see **B10.124**).

Procedure

An offence under the OAPA 1861, s. 23, is triable only on indictment. It is a class 3 offence. **B2.62**

Indictment

Statement of Offence **B2.63**

Administering poison so as to endanger life [or so as to cause grievous bodily harm], contrary to section 23 of the Offences against the Person Act 1861

Particulars of Offence

A on or about the . . . day of . . . unlawfully and maliciously administered to V a poison, namely . . ., so as thereby to endanger the life of the said V [or so as to inflict on the said V grievous bodily harm]

Alternative Verdicts

Under the OAPA 1861, s. 25, if a jury are not satisfied that a person charged under s. 23 is guilty of that offence but they are satisfied that he is guilty of an offence under s. 24 (see **B2.68** to **B2.73**), then they can acquit under s. 23 and return a verdict of guilty under s. 24, and the accused will be sentenced as if he had been tried on indictment under s. 24. **B2.64**

Sentence

The maximum penalty for administering any poison or noxious thing, so as to endanger life or inflict grievous bodily harm is 10 years (OAPA 1861, s. 23). **B2.65**

Actus Reus

According to the Court of Appeal in *Kennedy (No. 2)* [2005] 1 WLR 2159, the OAPA 1861, s. 23, creates two distinct offences: the first involves actually administering a noxious substance and the second causing a noxious substance to be administered. In either case, the administration must endanger life or inflict grievous bodily harm. **B2.66**

In *Gillard* (1988) 87 Cr App R 189, it was held that 'administration' includes any conduct that directly or indirectly brings the noxious thing into contact with the victim's body, including cases in which a noxious substance such as CS gas or ammonia is sprayed at the victim. The Court held that the meaning of the word 'administer' was a matter of law and that it was not limited to cases involving the ingestion of a substance. *Dones* [1987] Crim LR 682, in which it was held that 'administering' had a quasi-medical meaning, was not followed in *Gillard*.

If the poison etc. is not consumed by the victim and does not come into contact with his body in a way that may harm him, there can, at most, be an attempt to administer it (see *Dale* (1852) 6 Cox CC 14).

The administering must be unlawful. Consent will normally negate unlawfulness, but not where it is procured by deception or where considerations of public policy invalidate that consent. A person cannot, for example, validly consent to being injected with a dangerous drug, such as heroin, unless this is done for *bona fide* medical reasons (*Cato* [1976] 1 WLR 110).

In *Rogers* [2003] 1 WLR 1374, the Court of Appeal held that R was guilty of administering heroin to V (as a principal offender) when he applied a tourniquet to V's arm as the latter injected himself. It was held that by applying and holding the tourniquet, R had played an active part in the mechanics of the injection that caused V's death. *Kennedy* follows this approach and takes it even further, by applying it to cases in which the accused merely prepared the syringe and its contents, for the deceased to use. The Court reasoned that they could each be regarded as involved in a 'joint venture'. (See also **A1.30**.) Lord Woolf CJ said:

> The fact that a person who self injects does not commit an unlawful act by so doing, does not mean that a person who helps him . . . does not commit an unlawful act. On the contrary, the helper . . . could be charged under s. 23 and convicted. He could also be convicted of manslaughter if the person he was helping dies in consequence.

This wide interpretation of 'administering' appears to include conduct that might previously have been labelled as 'causing administration' (as in *Finlay* [2003] EWCA Crim 3868), but conduct that causes the victim unwittingly to administer the substance to himself (see *Harley* (1830) 4 C & P 369) may still be classed as an offence of 'causing'.

Whether a substance is a poison, etc. is largely a question of fact, but the meaning of the term 'noxious' was examined in *Marcus* [1981] 1 WLR 774, where M put sleeping pills into her neighbour's milk. Were sleeping pills a noxious substance? The question was held to be one of both quantity and quality. Something which is harmless in small doses may be noxious in larger doses or when taken at the wrong time. Its effect on the victim is what is important. The Court referred to the dictionary definition of 'noxious' as 'injurious, hurtful, harmful, unwholesome' and held that it could also apply to objectionable or obnoxious substances, although the potential of such a wide definition is greater in s. 24, where no dangerous or harmful consequence is required. See also *Hill* (1986) 83 Cr App R 386 and *Gantz* [2004] EWCA Crim 2862 (see **B2.73**).

Mens Rea

B2.67 The *mens rea* required under the OAPA 1861, s. 23, is maliciousness, which has the same meaning as it does under s. 20 (see **B2.49**). This means that D must act either with intent or with subjective recklessness; but this *mens rea* requirement applies only to the act of administering or causing the administration of the noxious substance. It does not extend to the consequences of that administration, which are governed by strict or constructive liability. D may therefore be guilty even if he did not intend or foresee that his action would cause grievous bodily harm or endanger life. See *Cato* [1976] 1 WLR 110 and *Kennedy (No. 2)* [2005] 1 WLR 2159 at [20].

ADMINISTERING POISON ETC. WITH INTENT

Definition

Offences against the Person Act 1861, s. 24 B2.68

Whosoever shall unlawfully and maliciously administer to or cause to be administered to or taken by any other person any poison or other destructive or noxious thing, with intent to injure, aggrieve, or annoy such person, shall be guilty of [an offence] and being . . . convicted thereof shall be liable to [imprisonment for a term not exceeding five years].

Procedure

Administering poison etc. with intent is triable only on indictment. It is a class 3 offence. B2.69

Indictment

Statement of Offence B2.70

Administering poison with intent, contrary to section 24 of the Offences against the Person Act 1861

Particulars of Offence

D on or about the . . . day of . . . unlawfully and maliciously administered to V a poison, namely . . . with intent to injure, aggrieve or annoy the said V

Alternative Verdicts

See **B2.64**. B2.71

Sentence

The maximum penalty is five years (OAPA 1861, s. 24). In *Jones* (1990) 12 Cr App R (S) 233, Glidewell LJ accepted that the appropriate sentencing bracket for this offence was equivalent to that for an offence of wounding or inflicting grievous bodily harm under the OAPA 1861, s. 20 (see **B2.41**), or a serious example of an offence of assault occasioning actual bodily harm under the OAPA 1861, s. 47 (see **B2.25**), on the basis that the maximum penalty available for each of the three offences is five years. Nine months was said to be the correct sentence in *Hogan* (1994) 15 Cr App R (S) 834, where the offender gave to a woman a drink which contained a large quantity of a Class C drug. It caused her to fall into a deep sleep for a day. Two years' imprisonment was appropriate in *Liles* [2000] 1 Cr App R (S) 31, where the offender allowed two young boys to inhale isobutyle nitrate so that they became dizzy and unwell. B2.72

Elements

The *actus reus* of the OAPA 1861, s. 24, is similar to that of s. 23, save that no consequential harm or endangerment is required. It is a conduct crime. B2.73

As with s. 23, D must act maliciously in administering the noxious thing, but there is a further or ulterior intent, namely to injure, aggrieve or annoy, which must additionally be proved. This means that s. 24 – the lesser offence – is one of specific intent for the purposes of the *Majewski* rule (see **A3.10**), whereas the more serious s. 23 offence is one of basic intent.

Section 24 has been used successfully to prosecute defendants who 'spike' their victims' drinks with drugs such as ecstasy (*Gantz* [2005] 1 Cr App R (S) 587) or who ply children with such drugs for improper purposes. The 'overstimulation' of a victim's metabolism that such action is intended to cause can be viewed as a type of injury. In *Hill* (1986) 83 Cr App R 386, H administered slimming pills to young boys in order to keep them awake. The House of Lords held that he had been properly convicted under s. 24. Lord Griffiths said:

> The defence conceded that the tablets were a noxious thing and that the respondent had unlawfully administered them to the boys. In these circumstances the only issue that the jury had to determine was whether he did so with the intent to injure them. . . . Here was a man who admitted being sexually attracted to young boys plying them with a drug which he knew would overstimulate and excite them and doing so with a reckless disregard for what might be the safe dosage and, in fact, giving them a gross overdose. The only reasonable inference to draw from such conduct was an intention that the drug should injure the boys in the sense of causing harm to the metabolism of their bodies by overstimulation with the motive of either ingratiating himself with them or, more probably, rendering them susceptible to homosexual advances.

FALSE IMPRISONMENT

Definition

B2.74 False imprisonment is a common-law offence, but is not often charged. It is much more common as a civil action in tort. The overlap with kidnapping (see **B2.80**) and child abduction (see **B2.86**) means that those offences are more likely to be charged than a simple false imprisonment.

The case of *Rahman* (1985) 81 Cr App R 349 provides the following definition (at p. 353): 'False imprisonment consists in the unlawful and intentional or reckless restraint of a victim's freedom of movement from a particular place.'

Procedure

B2.75 False imprisonment is triable only on indictment. It is a class 3 offence.

Indictment

B2.76 *Statement of Offence*

False imprisonment

Particulars of Offence

D on divers days between the . . . day of . . . and the . . . day of . . . falsely imprisoned V and detained the said V against his will

Sentencing Guidelines

B2.77 The maximum penalty is at large (common-law offence). For indications of appropriate sentencing, see those applicable to kidnapping at **B2.83**.

Actus Reus

B2.78 This consists of preventing the victim's freedom of movement. The victim may be restrained physically or by deliberate intimidation (*James* (1997) *The Times*, 2 October 1997). A victim might be detained in a building or vehicle, or simply prevented from going on his way. In *Bird v Jones* (1845) 7 QB 742, a civil case, the victim was prevented from going in one particular direction in which he wished to go, but there was an alternative route available to him; this did not constitute a false imprisonment.

The *actus reus* is the imprisoning without lawful excuse, and there seems no logical reason for requiring that the victim realise this is the case. No such realisation is necessary in the tort of false imprisonment (*Meering v Grahame White Aviation Co. Ltd* (1919) 122 LT 44).

The imprisonment must be unlawful. Two main situations arise where this can be problematic. One is in respect of a parent restraining a child. In *Rahman* (1985) 81 Cr App R 349 the question arose of the limits of a parent's right to lawfully restrain a child. The defendant had taken his 15-year-old daughter from her foster parents against her will. He was convicted and appealed. The court held that it was a question of fact in each case whether a parent had overstepped the limits of lawful correction and restraint. Whether the child's lack of consent was relevant must also be a question of fact depending on the circumstances of a particular case. In this case the appellant's appeal was dismissed. He had overstepped his right as a parent to exercise normal parental control. (See also kidnapping at **B2.80** and child abduction at **B2.86**.)

The other main situation in the context of which false imprisonment can arise is where an arrest is carried out by either a constable or a private citizen, which turns out to be unlawful. The lawfulness of an arrest is to be decided by reference to the general law, including the PACE 1984, s. 24. See, as to lawful and unlawful arrests, **D1.8** *et seq.* If the arrest is unlawful, the *actus reus* of the offence will have been committed.

Mens Rea

Rahman (1985) 81 Cr App R 349 states that the *mens rea* for false imprisonment is intention or recklessness. Recklessness here means subjective or *Cunningham* recklessness (*James* (1997) *The Times*, 2 October 1997). **B2.79**

The offence is one of basic intent, and therefore evidence of the accused's voluntary intoxication is irrelevant. This was recently confirmed in *Hutchins* [1988] Crim LR 379, which case also emphasised the overlap and analogy with kidnapping.

In that case the accused, having taken drugs at a party, took a neighbour hostage. He was charged with both kidnapping and false imprisonment. It was confirmed that his intoxication was irrelevant, and the court took the opportunity to define both 'false imprisonment' and 'kidnapping'. It emphasised that in kidnapping the taking must be by force or fraud, and that the definition was in terms of 'taking or carrying away' rather than a mere detaining, which would suffice for false imprisonment.

KIDNAPPING

Definition

Kidnapping is a common-law offence. It overlaps partly with false imprisonment (see **B2.74**) and partly with child abduction (see **B2.86**). **B2.80**

The offence consists of the taking or carrying away of one person by another by force or fraud, without the consent of that person and without lawful excuse. It is no longer necessary for the victim to be 'secreted', nor is it necessary for him to be removed from the jurisdiction, although these were once considered to be essential elements of the offence; but it is still necessary that the victim is deprived of his liberty: (*D* [1984] AC 778; *Hendy-Freegard* [2007] EWCA Crim 1236 (see **B2.84**).

Procedure

Kidnapping is triable only on indictment. It is a class 3 offence. **B2.81**

Indictment

Statement of Offence **B2.82**

Kidnapping

Particulars of Offence

A on or about the . . . day of . . . unlawfully took and carried away V against his will

Despite the acknowledged overlap between the offences of kidnapping and statutory abduction, an indictment should not contain counts for both offences (*C* (1990) *The Times*, 9 November 1990).

Sentencing Guidelines

B2.83 The maximum penalty is at large (common-law offence).

Some general observations on sentencing for this offence were provided in *Spence* (1983) 5 Cr App R (S) 413, where Lord Lane CJ said (at p. 416):

> there is a wide possible variation in seriousness between one instance of the crime and another. At the top of the scale of course, come the carefully planned abductions where the victim is used as a hostage or where ransom money is demanded. Such offences will seldom be met with less than eight years' imprisonment or thereabouts. Where violence or firearms are used, or there are other exacerbating features such as detention of the victim over a long period of time, then the proper sentence will be very much longer than that. At the other end of the scale are those offences which can perhaps scarcely be classed as kidnapping at all. They very often arise as a sequel to family tiffs or lovers' disputes, and they seldom require anything more than 18 months' imprisonment, and sometimes a great deal less.

In *Brown* (1985) 7 Cr App R (S) 15, a case of unpremeditated kidnapping and false imprisonment of a young woman by forcing her into her car and causing her minor injuries in an ensuing struggle, sentences of five years concurrent were imposed on the kidnapping and false imprisonment counts. See also *Lucas* [2000] 1 Cr App R (S) 5. In *A-G's Ref (No. 77 of 1998)* [1999] 2 Cr App R (S) 336 the offender was convicted of kidnapping and indecently assaulting a seven-year-old girl whom he enticed into his car. After assaulting the girl he returned her to the street where he had found her. In the Court of Appeal, Rose LJ indicated that a sentence in the order of eight or nine years would have been appropriate. Kidnapping was employed for political ends in *Barak* (1985) 7 Cr App R (S) 404, where sentences varying between 10 and 14 years were imposed on the offenders involved. See also *Bond* (1994) 15 Cr App R (S) 196.

Actus Reus

B2.84 The *actus reus* of kidnapping (as defined at **B2.80**) is similar to that of false imprisonment (see **B2.74**) insofar as it involves the unlawful deprivation of V's liberty; but it differs from false imprisonment in that it also requires V to be taken or carried away, either by force or by fraud. He need not be carried far: in *Wellard* [1978] 3 All ER 161, D impersonated a constable and thereby tricked or coerced V into walking a few yards to his car in order to submit to a 'drugs search'. This was held to be a sufficient 'taking'.

In *D* [1984] AC 778, the House of Lords held that a parent who took custody of his own child in contravention of a court order could be guilty of kidnapping, and a majority held that the rule was more general, and that parents could be acting without lawful excuse in some circumstances by taking their children even where there was no court order. It will be a question of fact whether or not a parent has a lawful excuse to exercise such physical control over the whereabouts of the child.

Kidnapping must be committed without the valid consent of the victim. Consent or compliance procured by force or fear is not true consent (*Greenhalgh* [2001] EWCA Crim 1367).

Very young children may be incapable of giving such consent (see *D* [1984] AC 778); but it may sometimes prove difficult to show force or fraud if a child is simply picked up and taken. In such circumstances, a charge under the Child Abduction Act 1984 may be more appropriate. If a person initially consents to being taken away, the offence will nevertheless be committed if that consent is later withdrawn and force is used to maintain a kidnapping (*Lewis* (22 March 1993 unreported)).

As to the need for a deprivation of liberty, this appears to have been overlooked in *Cort* [2004] QB 388, in which D tricked his 'victims' into riding in his car by deceiving them into thinking that their bus had broken down. This was held to be sufficient for an offence of kidnapping, even though there was no evidence to suggest that D made any attempt to detain them against their will. But *Cort* is inconsistent with *Wellard* and was doubted in *Hendy-Freegard* [2007] EWCA Crim 1236, where Lord Phillips CJ said (at [55]):

> We cannot see that there was justification for extending the offence of kidnapping to cover the situation in which the driver of the car has no intention of detaining his passenger against her will nor of doing other than taking her to the destination to which she wishes to go, simply because in some such circumstances the driver may have an objectionable ulterior motive. The consequence of the decision in *Cort* would seem to be that the mini-cab driver, who obtains a fare by falsely pretending to be an authorised taxi, will be guilty of kidnapping.

In *Hendy-Freegard,* D tricked his victims into making certain journeys they would not otherwise have made; but these journeys were made independently, and D did not even accompany them. The Court of Appeal held that this could not amount to kidnapping, for otherwise, as Lord Phillips CJ pointed out at [57]:

> . . . the bigamist who induces a woman to travel to the church for a wedding ceremony might be guilty not merely of bigamy but also of kidnapping. Such a submission transforms the offence of kidnapping in a manner that cannot be justified, even on the basis of the decision in *Cort.*

Mens Rea

The *mens rea* is not specifically discussed in *D* [1984] AC 778, but the Court of Appeal in *Hutchins* [1988] Crim LR 379 pointed out the close analogy between false imprisonment and kidnapping, the differences being in the *actus reus.* This indicates that the *mens rea* is likely to be the same as that for false imprisonment (see B2.79). **B2.85**

CHILD ABDUCTION

Abduction by Person Connected with Child: Definition

Child Abduction Act 1984, s. 1 **B2.86**

(1) Subject to subsections (5) and (8) below, a person connected with a child under the age of 16 commits an offence if he takes or sends the child out of the United Kingdom without the appropriate consent.

(2) A person is connected with a child for the purposes of this section if—
 (a) he is a parent of the child; or
 (b) in the case of a child whose parents were not married to each other at the time of his birth, there are reasonable grounds for believing that he is the father of the child; or
 (c) he is a guardian of the child; or
 (d) he is a person in whose favour a residence order is in force with respect to the child; or
 (e) he has custody of the child.

(3) In this section 'the appropriate consent', in relation to a child, means—
 (a) the consent of each of the following—
  (i) the child's mother;
  (ii) the child's father, if he has parental responsibility for him;
  (iii) any guardian of the child;
  (iv) any person in whose favour a residence order is in force with respect to the child;
  (v) any person who has custody of the child; or
 (b) the leave of the court granted under or by virtue of any provision of part II of the Children Act 1989; or
 (c) if any person has custody of the child, the leave of the court which awarded custody to him.

(4) A person does not commit an offence under this section by taking or sending a child out of the United Kingdom without obtaining the appropriate consent if—
 (a) he is a person in whose favour there is a residence order in force with respect to the child, and
 (b) he takes or sends him out of the United Kingdom for a period of less than one month.

(4A) Subsection (4) above does not apply if the person taking or sending the child out of the United Kingdom does so in breach of an order under part II of the Children Act 1989.

(5) A person does not commit an offence under this section by doing anything without the consent of another person whose consent is required under the foregoing provisions if—
  (a) he does it in the belief that the other person—
    (i) has consented; or
    (ii) would consent if he was aware of all the relevant circumstances; or
  (b) he has taken all reasonable steps to communicate with the other person but has been unable to communicate with him; or
  (c) the other person has unreasonably refused to consent.

(5A) Subsection (5)(c) above does not apply if—
  (a) the person who refused to consent is a person—
    (i) in whose favour there is a residence order in force with respect to the child; or
    (ii) who has custody of the child; or
  (b) the person taking or sending the child out of the United Kingdom is, by so acting, in breach of an order made by a court in the United Kingdom.

(6) Where, in proceedings for an offence under this section, there is sufficient evidence to raise an issue as to the application of subsection (5) above, it shall be for the prosecution to prove that that subsection does not apply.

(7) For the purposes of this section—
  (a) 'guardian of a child', 'residence order' and 'parental responsibility' have the same meaning as in the Children Act 1989; and
  (b) a person shall be treated as having custody of a child if there is in force an order of a court in the United Kingdom awarding him (whether solely or jointly with another person) custody, legal custody or care and control of the child.

(8) This section shall have effect subject to the provisions of the schedule to this Act in relation to a child who is in the care of a local authority, detained in a place of safety, remanded to local authority accommodation or the subject of proceedings or an order relating to adoption.

Abduction by Person Connected with Child: Procedure

B2.87 The consent of the DPP is required before a prosecution under s. 1 of the Act can be brought (Child Abduction Act 1984, s. 4(2)). The offence is triable either way (s. 4(1)). When tried on indictment it is a class 3 offence.

Abduction by Person Connected with Child: Indictment

B2.88

Statement of Offence

Child abduction by person connected with child contrary to section 1 of the Child Abduction Act 1984

Particulars of Offence

A on or about the . . . day of . . ., being a parent of V, a child under the age of 16 years, unlawfully took the said V out of the United Kingdom, to wit to Dallas, Texas, in the United States of America, without the consent of . . .

Abduction by Person Connected with Child: Sentence

B2.89 The maximum penalty is seven years (Child Abduction Act 1984, s. 4(1)) on indictment; six months, a fine not exceeding level 5 or both, summarily. In *Downes* (1994) 15 Cr App R (S) 435 three years' imprisonment was upheld on a father who abducted his two-yearold daughter in defiance of a court order denying him access to the child, and took her abroad. In *Holland* [1996] 1 Cr App R (S) 368, 18 months' imprisonment was upheld for the abduction by a father of his daughter who was in the care of foster parents by order of a court. See also *Taylor* [1997] 1 Cr App R (S) 329.

Abduction by Person Connected with Child: *Actus Reus*

B2.90 The offence can only be committed by a person 'connected with' the child, and this is defined in the Child Abduction Act 1984, s. 1(2) (see **B2.86**).

Such a person must either take, or be responsible for sending, the child out of the UK himself. This offence is not committed by holding the child within the jurisdiction. The meanings of 'taking' and of 'sending' are set out in s. 3 of the Act, and include causing a child to be taken, inducing a child to accompany the accused or any other person, and causing a child to be sent.

Lack of appropriate consent is a necessary circumstance which must be established. Consent of each of the persons mentioned in s. 1(3)(a) is required, or if there is a custody order in force the court's permission must be sought. Alternatively, the leave of the court under part II of the Children Act 1989 will suffice.

Abduction by Person Connected with Child: *Mens Rea*

No *mens rea* is specified in the definition of the offence, but it can be deduced from the 'defences' available under the Child Abduction Act 1984, s. 1(5), at least in respect of the circumstance of lack of appropriate consent (see **B2.92**). **B2.91**

Abduction by Person Connected with Child: Defences

Under the Child Abduction Act 1984, s. (5), an accused will not be liable if he acts in the belief that the appropriate person has consented, or would have done so if he had known the relevant circumstances. There is no requirement that such belief be reasonable, and the test is therefore subjective. **B2.92**

There is an additional objectively based defence if either the accused has taken all reasonable steps to communicate with the appropriate person, or if the consent has been unreasonably withheld. Magistrates, or on indictment the jury, would decide the issue of reasonableness as one of fact. If the consent needed is that of the court, then, under s. 1(5A), the provision concerning unreasonably withheld consent does not apply.

Once the accused provides prima facie evidence of any such defence, then the burden is on the prosecution to disprove it.

Abduction of Child by Other Persons: Definition

The Child Abduction Act 1984, s. 2(1), creates two further offences covering cases in which someone other than a parent or other person connected to the child takes or detains a child under the age of 16. They may apply to the child's father where he was not married to the mother at the time of the child's birth, but note the defence provided by s. 2(3), discussed at **B2.98**. **B2.93**

Child Abduction Act 1984, s. 2

(1) Subject to subsection (3) below, a person, other than one mentioned in subsection (2) below, commits an offence if, without lawful authority or reasonable excuse, he takes or detains a child under the age of 16—
  (a) so as to remove him from the lawful control of any person having lawful control of the child; or
  (b) so as to keep him out of the lawful control of any person entitled to lawful control of the child.

(2) The persons are—
  (a) where the father and mother of the child in question were married to each other at the time of his birth, the child's father and mother;
  (b) where the father and mother of the child in question were not married to each other at the time of his birth, the child's mother; and
  (c) any other person mentioned in section 1(2)(c) to (e) above.

(3) In proceedings against any person for an offence under this section, it shall be a defence for that person to prove—
  (a) where the father and mother of the child in question were not married to each other at the time of his birth—

(i) that he is the child's father; or

(ii) that, at the time of the alleged offence, he believed, on reasonable grounds, that he was the child's father; or

(b) that, at the time of the alleged offence, he believed that the child had attained the age of sixteen.

Abduction by Other Persons: Procedure

B2.94 Offences under s. 2(1) are triable either way. When tried on indictment they are class 3 offences. In contrast to alleged s. 1 offences committed by persons connected with the child, prosecutions under the Child Abduction Act 1984, s. 2, do not require the consent of the DPP.

Abduction by Other Persons: Indictment

B2.95 *Statement of Offence*

Child abduction contrary to section 2(1)(b) of the Child Abduction Act 1984

Particulars of Offence

A on or about the . . . day of . . . without lawful authority or reasonable excuse detained V, a child under the age of 16 years, so as to keep him out of the lawful control of X, a person entitled to lawful control of V

Abduction by Other Persons: Sentence

B2.96 As for s. 1, see **B2.89**. In *Cooper* (1994) 15 Cr App R (S) 470 a sentence of 18 months was upheld where the offender had taken a baby from a pram outside a shop and kept it for four hours. In *Whitlock* (1994) 15 Cr App R (S) 146 the offender had induced a 13-year-old boy to get off the school bus and spend the morning with him. Three years' imprisonment was reduced to two years. Four years' imprisonment was upheld in *Parsons* [1996] 1 Cr App R (S) 36, where a man with a record of sexual offences attempted to abduct a 13-year-old child by offering her a lift in his car.

Abduction by Other Persons: Elements

B2.97 Section 2(1) requires an intentional or reckless taking or detention of a child under the age of 16, the effect or objective consequence of which is to remove or to keep that child within the meaning of s. 2(1)(a) or (b) – each of which creates a separate and distinct offence (*Foster v DPP* [2005] 1 WLR 1400). 'Detaining' is defined in the Child Abduction Act 1984, s. 3, so as to include causing the child to be detained or inducing the child to remain with the accused or another person. 'Taking' is defined in s. 3 so as to include causing or inducing the child to accompany the accused or any other person or causing the child to be taken. A child can be removed from lawful control without necessarily being taken to another place. It may suffice if the child is deflected into some unauthorised activity induced by the accused (see *Leather* (1993) 98 Cr App R 179, where children were persuaded by D to go with him to look for a 'missing bicycle'). Nor need D's conduct be the sole cause of the abduction, as long as it was more than merely peripheral. It is no defence that another cause may be the child's own decision or state of mind (*A* [2000] 2 All ER 177).

The words, 'so as to' do not import any further *mens rea*; an offence may therefore be committed whether or not the accused intends to interfere with another person's lawful control or entitlement (*Foster v DPP*). Insofar as *Re Owens* [2000] 1 Cr App R 195 suggests otherwise, it is inconsistent with *Leather* and was not followed in *Foster v DPP*. The consent of that other person would amount to 'lawful authority', but the consent of the child is irrelevant. This distinguishes the offence from that of kidnapping, as does the absence of any requirement of force or fraud (see **B2.80**).

Abduction by Other Persons: Defences

Section 2(3)(a) provides a defence only if the parents of the child were not married at the time the child was born and the accused is, or reasonably believes himself to be, the father of that particular child. It does not apply where D mistakenly takes the wrong child from a nursery, thinking it to be his daughter, although it is just possible that D may in such circumstances be able to advance a defence of reasonable excuse under s. 2(1) (*Berry* [1996] 2 Cr App R 226). The burden of proving that such a taking or detention was committed without lawful authority or reasonable excuse rests with the Crown (*ibid*). B2.98

TAKING OF HOSTAGES

Definition

Taking of Hostages Act 1982, s. 1 B2.99

(1) A person, whatever his nationality, who, in the United Kingdom or elsewhere—
  (a) detains any other person ('the hostage'), and
  (b) in order to compel a State, international governmental organisation, or person to do or abstain from doing any act, threatens to kill, injure or continue to detain the hostage,

commits an offence.

Procedure

The consent of the A-G is required before a prosecution can be brought under the Taking of Hostages Act 1982, s. 1. Taking hostages is triable only on indictment. It is a class 1 offence. B2.100

Indictment

Statement of Offence B2.101

Hostage taking contrary to section 1 of the Taking of Hostages Act 1982

Particulars of Offence

A on divers days between the . . . day of . . . and the . . . day of . . ., detained V, and in order to compel the Government of the United Kingdom to release from prison certain convicted offenders, threatened to kill the said V

Sentence

The maximum penalty is life imprisonment (Taking of Hostages Act 1982, s. 1(2)). B2.102

Elements

The *actus reus* consists of detaining any person, and making threats to kill, injure or continue to detain that person. B2.103

The *mens rea* defined is in terms of the purpose for which the act and threat take place, and in that respect the accused's motive is relevant. The offence could therefore be seen as one of further or ulterior intent to cause the doing or abstaining from any act, and such intent or purpose must be proved, although it does not have to be achieved.

BIGAMY

Definition

Offences against the Person Act 1861, s. 57 B2.104

Whosoever, being married, shall marry any other person during the life of the former husband or wife, whether the second marriage shall have taken place in England or Ireland or elsewhere, shall be guilty of [an offence], and being convicted thereof shall be liable to [imprisonment] for any term not exceeding seven years . . .: Provided, that nothing in this section contained shall extend to any second marriage contracted elsewhere than in England and Ireland by any other than a subject of Her Majesty, or to any person marrying a second time whose husband or wife shall have been continually absent from such person for the space of seven years then last past, and shall not have been known by such person to be living within that time, or shall extend to any person who, at the time of such second marriage, shall have been divorced from the bond of the first marriage, or to any person whose former marriage shall have been declared void by the sentence of any court of competent jurisdiction.

Procedure

B2.105 Bigamy is triable either way (MCA 1980, s. 17 and sch. 1). When tried on indictment it is a class 3 offence.

Indictment

B2.106 *Statement of Offence*

Bigamy contrary to section 57 of the Offences against the Person Act 1861

Particulars of Offence

A on or about the . . . day of . . . married V during the life of his wife, W

Sentencing Guidelines

B2.107 The maximum penalty is seven years, a fine, or both, on indictment (OAPA 1861, s. 57); six months, a fine not exceeding the statutory maximum, or both, summarily.

There are very few Court of Appeal decisions on the proper approach to sentencing for this offence. According to Waller LJ in *Crowhurst* (1978) CSP B9-43A01:

> It appears to this court that the sentence for bigamy must vary very much with the particular circumstances of the case. In many cases of bigamy it is possible to deal with the case by some sentence which does not involve deprivation of liberty. In other cases there may be a clear deception which has resulted in some injury to the woman concerned; in which an immediate custodial sentence must be passed, and the length of that sentence must depend greatly on the seriousness of the injury that has been done.

On the facts of the particular case, where the marriage was not consummated and lasted only a week, but where the woman's evidence was that she would not have married the offender had she known that he was still married, a short custodial sentence was held to be proper. The Court of Appeal reduced an 18-month sentence, which was 'wholly out of proportion to the gravity of this offence', to one of four months. *Crowhurst* was followed and applied in *Smith* (1994) 15 Cr App R (S) 407. In more recent cases, this offence has arisen in the context of bogus marriages designed to avoid immigration controls. In *Khan* [2005] 2 Cr App R (S) 273, the offender, who was lawfully married and of previous good character, went through two further marriage ceremonies with Bangladeshi nationals with intent to assist them in avoiding immigration controls. The Court of Appeal upheld sentences totalling 27 months on the offender, who pleaded guilty, and 18 months on her co-defendant, for aiding and abetting one of the offences. See also *Cairns* [1997] 1 Cr App R (S) 118.

Actus Reus

B2.108 The *actus reus* of bigamy is committed where D 'marries' another person whilst still lawfully married to a surviving spouse. No offence is committed, however, where D's original spouse has been missing for seven years or more (see **B2.113**); nor is any offence committed under English law where a foreigner commits bigamy abroad, even if his original marriage was registered in England. If, however, D is a British (or British overseas, etc.) citizen, it is irrelevant where the bigamous marriage takes place, because bigamy is punishable in England and Wales (or in Northern Ireland) if committed by such a person anywhere in the world (*Earl Russell* [1901] AC 446). This includes bigamy committed in Scotland, even though s. 57 is not applicable under Scots law (*Topping* (1856) Dears 647).

The Act of 'Marrying' Although the OAPA 1861, s. 57, uses the term 'marry', a bigamous marriage must inevitably be void under English law. Section 57 is accordingly construed as criminalising the act of bigamously *purporting* to marry (*Allen* (1872) LR 1 CCR 367). B2.109

The existence of other reasons for invalidity of the second 'marriage', such as the second spouse's lack of age or capacity, is no defence on a charge of bigamy (*Allen*). D must, however, go through a ceremony of marriage that purports to be legally binding. D does not commit bigamy where, for example, he contracts an unregistered Islamic marriage in England without disclosing the existence of a subsisting marriage (*Al-Mudaris v Al-Mudaris* [2001] All ER (D) 288 (Feb)).

'Being Married' The burden is on the prosecution to prove both that D was validly married on an earlier occasion *and* that this marriage was still subsisting at the time of the second ceremony. The validity of the original marriage cannot be presumed, as it might be presumed in civil cases, but may be proved by adducing a certified copy of the relevant entry in the Register of Marriages (see **F8.15** ***et seq.*** and **F16.26**) together with evidence of the identity of the parties to the marriage. See *Tolson* (1864) 4 F & F 103; *Birtles* (1911) 6 Cr App R 177. In the case of a marriage celebrated abroad, expert evidence of local marriage law may be required (*Sussex Peerage Case* (1844) 11 Cl & F 85; and see **F10.16** ***et seq.***). B2.110

If D alleges that his earlier marriage is invalid for a particular reason, he need do no more than raise the issue, and the burden will then be on the prosecution to establish its validity (*Kay* (1887) 16 Cox CC 292). An admission by D as to the validity of his earlier marriage may suffice, but not where the marriage was celebrated abroad (*Naguib* [1917] 1 KB 359; *Flaherty* (1847) 2 Car & Kir 782).

Polygamous Marriages A British citizen who practises polygamy abroad in accordance with local law commits no offence under s. 57. This is not because his conduct is lawful where it takes place. It is because, as far as the English law of bigamy is concerned, polygamous or even potentially polygamous marriages have never been considered to be marriages at all, even though they may be recognised as valid by the civil courts in accordance with the rules of private international law. B2.111

Nevertheless, a marriage registered in the UK is necessarily monogamous, and precludes any subsequent polygamy by either part to it; and if D is domiciled in England and Wales (or in any other country that prohibits polygamy), he cannot lawfully practice polygamy abroad. An overseas marriage contracted by someone with English domicile must accordingly be considered monogamous.

A potentially polygamous foreign marriage may become monogamous in certain circumstances, notably where the party who might otherwise have been entitled to take a second spouse subsequently acquires a domicile of choice in a country that does not permit polygamy. This may happen, for example, where D settles permanently in England and Wales, thereby acquiring an English domicile. If D were than to contract a further marriage in England and Wales, he would thereby commit bigamy (*Sagoo* [1975] QB 885). If D also acquires British citizenship, s. 57 would equally apply to any second marriage he might later enter into abroad.

Mens Rea

There is no specific mention of the requisite *mens rea* for the offence in the OAPA 1861, s. 57. This is unlikely to cause any problems in respect of the intent to go through a ceremony of marriage, but what if the accused mistakenly believes his first spouse to be dead or mistakenly believes himself to be lawfully divorced? In other sections of the 1861 Act strict liability was once applied to certain circumstances of an offence (see *Prince* (1875) LR 2 CCR 154), and the absence of the word 'malicious' from s. 57, in contrast to its presence in other sections, was at one time taken to suggest that strict liability applied under s. 57. B2.112

The leading case on the *mens rea* for bigamy has for many years been *Tolson* (1889) 23 QBD 168. The accused had remarried, reasonably, but mistakenly, believing that her first husband was dead. It was held that a mistake of this kind was a good defence to the charge, as long as it was a reasonable one. The same argument would also apply where the accused believed that she was divorced, or that her first marriage was void, etc. The situation has always been different as regards the proviso in s. 57, relating to seven years' absence of the first spouse, because this may provide a defence, even where the accused suspects that his spouse is still alive (see **B2.113**).

Tolson was followed by the Court of Appeal in *Gould* [1968] 2 QB 65, and confirmed, *obiter*, by the House of Lords in *DPP v Morgan* [1976] AC 182, but its authority has been undermined by the House of Lords in *B (a minor) v DPP* [2000] 2 AC 428 in which it was held that, where *mens rea* may be ousted by an honest but mistaken belief, it is as well ousted by an unreasonable belief as by a reasonable one. It is accordingly submitted that the same principles must apply to mistake in bigamy cases as to mistake in other crimes. The reasonableness or otherwise of any alleged mistake should now be considered irrelevant, except when assessing its credibility.

Continual Absence of First Spouse for Seven Years

B2.113 Under the proviso to the OAPA 1861, s. 57, the accused has a defence to a charge of bigamy if his husband or wife 'shall have been continually absent . . . for the space of seven years then last past, and shall not have been known [by the accused] to have been living within that time'. The scope and limitations of this proviso must be noted. First, it does nothing to relieve the prosecution from its duty to prove that the first spouse was indeed alive at the time of the second ceremony. Even if the accused remarried just a few months after his first spouse's disappearance, a prosecution for bigamy would still fail in the absence of such proof. Secondly, if the accused honestly believed his spouse to be dead after a shorter period than seven years (see **B2.112**) the proviso defence is not necessary. On the other hand, if the conditions of the proviso are satisfied, it does not matter whether the accused really believed his first spouse to be dead at all. The spouse's continuous absence (combined with the absence of any news of his being alive) is a sufficient defence in itself.

To establish the defence, the accused must adduce evidence of continual absence for the requisite seven-year period. The prosecution must then prove either that there was no such continual absence, or that the accused knew the spouse to be alive at some time during that period (*Curgerwen* (1865) LR 1 CCR 1). Actual knowledge would have to be proved. The accused need not even have attempted to contact his spouse or ascertain whether his spouse was alive (*Jones* (1842) C & Mar 614; *Briggs* (1856) Dears & B 98). If s. 57 had been intended to impose any such duty on the accused, it would surely have stipulated this expressly.

CHILD CRUELTY

Definition

B2.114 **Children and Young Persons Act 1933, s. 1**

(1) If any person who has attained the age of sixteen years and has responsibility for any child or young person under that age, wilfully assaults, ill-treats, neglects, abandons, or exposes him, or causes or procures him to be assaulted, ill-treated, neglected, abandoned, or exposed, in a manner likely to cause him unnecessary suffering or injury to health (including injury to or loss of sight, or hearing, or limb, or organ of the body, and any mental derangement), that person shall be guilty of [an offence], and shall be liable—

(a) on conviction on indictment, to a fine or alternatively, or in addition thereto, to imprisonment for any term not exceeding ten years;

(b) on summary conviction, to a fine not exceeding the prescribed sum, or alternatively or in addition thereto, to imprisonment for any term not exceeding six months.

(2) For the purposes of this section—
(a) a parent or other person legally liable to maintain a child or young person or the legal guardian of a child or young person shall be deemed to have neglected him in a manner likely to cause injury to his health if he has failed to provide adequate food, clothing, medical aid or lodging for him, or if, having been unable otherwise to provide such food, clothing, medical aid or lodging, he has failed to take steps to procure it to be provided under the enactments applicable in that behalf;
(b) where it is proved that the death of an infant under three years of age was caused by suffocation (not being suffocation caused by disease or the presence of any foreign body in the throat or air passages of the infant) while the infant was in bed with some other person who has attained the age of sixteen years, that other person shall, if he was, when he went to bed, under the influence of drink, be deemed to have neglected the infant in a manner likely to cause injury to its health.

(3) A person may be convicted of an offence under this section—
(a) notwithstanding that actual suffering or injury to health, or the likelihood of actual suffering or injury to health, was obviated by the action of another person;
(b) notwithstanding the death of the child or young person in question.

Indictment

Statement of Offence **B2.115**

Cruelty to a person under the age of 16, contrary to s. 1(1) of the Children and Young Persons Act 1933

Particulars of Offence

A, between the . . . day of . . . and the . . . day of . . ., being a person who had attained the age of 16 and having responsibility for V, a child under that age, wilfully neglected the said V in a manner likely to cause her unnecessary suffering or injury to her health by failing to provide medical aid for her

The drafting of indictments for offences under this section may be complicated by the fact that the offence can be committed in several different ways. As to the importance of identifying the appropriate form of allegation in a given case, see *Hayles* [1969] 1 QB 364 and *Beard* (1987) 85 Cr App R 395.

Procedure

An offence under this provision is triable either way. When tried on indictment, it is a class 3 offence. Where an alleged offence is tried summarily, the CYPA 1933, s. 14, has effect. **B2.116**

Children and Young Persons Act 1933, s. 14

(1) Where a person is charged with committing any of the offences mentioned in the first Schedule to this Act in respect of two or more children or young persons, the same information or summons may charge the offence in respect of all or any of them, but the person charged shall not, if he is summarily convicted, be liable to a separate penalty in respect of each child or young person except upon separate informations.

(2) The same information or summons may charge him with the offence of assault, ill-treatment, neglect, abandonment, or exposure, together or separately, and may charge him with committing all or any of those offences in a manner likely to cause unnecessary suffering or injury to health, alternatively or together, but when those offences are charged together, the person charged shall not, if he is summarily convicted, be liable to a separate penalty for each.

Sentencing Guidelines

The maximum penalty on conviction on indictment is 10 years' imprisonment. The maximum penalty on summary conviction is six months' imprisonment, or a fine not exceeding the prescribed sum, or both. **B2.117**

A distinction is drawn in the cases between instances of violent assault, where the victim is a child, and cases of cruelty or neglect.

B2.118 **Infliction of Injury** In the former cases, a more usual charge is assault occasioning actual bodily harm or, where appropriate, a more serious offence against the person, but sometimes a prosecution under the CYPA 1933, s. 1 will be brought instead. In *J and M* [2005] 1 Cr App R (S) 284 the Court of Appeal emphasised the importance of establishing the basis on which an offender is being sentenced, and noted that this was particularly important where two defendants blamed each other. In such a case the sentencer must either resolve the conflict by hearing evidence, or accept the mitigation, sentencing each defendant on the basis of his or her plea. A second distinction which is generally drawn is between those cases where there has been deliberate infliction of injury, of a serious nature, perhaps on more than one occasion, where a lengthy custodial sentence will be upheld, and one-off cases of less serious injury which have taken place in a context of very considerable economic or domestic pressure, where a rather lower custodial sentence is the norm.

In *Bacon* [1997] 1 Cr App R (S) 335, parents had disciplined their 15-year-old son for misbehaviour in a cruel and brutal manner, which involved pouring paint thinners over the victim, forcing him to eat cigarettes and chaining him up in the garage. A sentence of three years' imprisonment imposed on the father was reduced to 18 months on appeal, in the light of personal mitigation. A community rehabilitation order with a programme in parenting skills was held not to be unduly lenient in *A-G's Ref (No. 105 of 2004)* [2005] 2 Cr App R (S) 250, a case where the 41-year-old offender pleaded guilty to using excessive chastisement on three of his children, aged 8, 10 and 13. The Court of Appeal said the offences arose from a distorted view of what was appropriate, rather than from cruelty for its own sake.

In *Smith* (1984) 6 Cr App R (S) 174, a father pleaded guilty to the offence of cruelty to his four-month-old mentally handicapped baby, whose arm he had broken by biting it. A sentence of 18 months' imprisonment was reduced on appeal to nine months. May LJ commented that a distinction had to be drawn between cases of 'deliberate wickedness' and cases 'which can really be described as disasters, which have come not only upon the child, but also upon the child's parents, largely due to the latter's inability to cope with an infant, sometimes in circumstances of unemployment, sometimes in circumstances of inadequate housing'. Whilst holding that the instant case was of the latter type, the court nevertheless felt that a custodial sentence was inevitable, given the injury which had been inflicted. In *Oates* (1991) 12 Cr App R (S) 742, the offender pleaded guilty to cruelty to the 11-month-old child of the woman with whom he was cohabiting. He smacked the child in the chest and grabbed it at the back of the ears causing a fingernail injury. The child was found to be suffering from a number of bruises when taken to hospital. The Court of Appeal reduced the sentence of nine months' imprisonment to four months, on the basis that the injury had been caused by a 'momentary reaction to exasperation', the injuries were not serious and that the offender had desisted from his attack very quickly, had shown remorse and had pleaded guilty at the first opportunity.

B2.119 **Cruelty or Neglect** Most of the reported cases on cruelty or neglect (as opposed to infliction of an injury) arise from the offender's culpable failure to summon medical assistance for a child. In *Taggart* [1999] 2 Cr App R (S) 68 the offender's child aged three and a half suffered severe scalding while in the bath. It was accepted that the scalding had been accidental, but the offender pleaded guilty to cruelty on the basis of his failure to summon medical attention until more than 24 hours later. The appropriate sentence was 30 months' imprisonment.

A case of more general neglect is *Harvey* (1987) 9 Cr App R (S) 524. A mother was convicted of four counts of cruelty to her four children aged between four and eight years. The mother was frequently drunk, the living accommodation was dirty, pornographic material was left lying about and the children were not kept clean and were denied affection; there was one instance of a failure to arrange medical attention when it was needed. A sentence of nine months' imprisonment was upheld. See also *Crank* [1996] 2 Cr App R (S) 363 and *Weaver* [1998] 2 Cr App R (S) 56.

In *Colwell* (1994) 15 Cr App R (S) 323 the offender admitted that over a period of about a year she had left her daughter, aged three, at home on her own all day while she went out to work. The Court of Appeal said that a custodial sentence was appropriate in such a case but, in light of the financial problems the mother faced in bringing up her child alone, the adverse impact on the child of the mother's imprisonment and the fact that Colwell had served one month in custody prior to the appeal, the sentence was varied from six months' imprisonment to a probation order. In *A-G's Ref (No. 57 of 1995)* [1996] 2 Cr App R (S) 159 a conditional discharge was held to have been an unduly lenient sentence where an eight-year-old child who was already ill suffered hypothermia as a result of being left alone in a car in cold weather for half an hour.

Another category of neglect is where injury has been inflicted upon the offender's child by another person with the offender's knowledge. Sentences totalling five years' imprisonment were upheld in *Creed* [2000] 1 Cr App R (S) 304, where a woman had failed to protect her child from sustained violence over a period of seven months from the man with whom she was living, and had delayed calling for medical attention following the infliction of grave injuries by him which had caused the child's death. The man had been convicted of murder. See also *Rawlinson* (1992) 14 Cr App R (S) 30.

Actus Reus: Age and Responsibility

To be guilty of an offence under the CYPA 1933, s. 1, an accused must have been over the age of 16 at the time of the offence, and must have 'had responsibility' for the child or young person in question. If proof of the defendant's or victim's ages is an issue, reference may be made to the CYPA 1933, s. 99, which provides (s. 99(2)) that, where in such a case the person by or in respect of whom the offence was allegedly committed 'appears to the court to have been at the date of the alleged offence a child or young person or to have been under or to have attained a particular age, as the case may be, he shall . . . be presumed to have been under or to have attained that age, as the case may be, unless the contrary is proved'. Where this presumption applies, the defence may have the burden of proving that the young person in question was in fact over the age of 16 (s. 99(4)). **B2.120**

'Responsibility' in this context may be shared by more than one person, and it may involve questions both of fact and law (*Liverpool Society for the Prevention of Cruelty to Children v Jones* [1914] 3 KB 813). Any person who has parental responsibility or who has any other legal liability to maintain a child or young person will be 'presumed' to have responsibility for him under the Act and 'shall not be taken to have ceased to be responsible for him by reason of the fact that he does not have care of him' (CYPA 1933, s. 17(1)(a) and (2)); but other persons, such as baby-sitters or teachers, may also have responsibility whilst a child or young person is in their care (s. 17(1)(b)).

Actus Reus: Conduct

Although the CYPA 1933, s. 1, creates just one offence, it may take a number of different forms (*Hayles* [1969] 1 QB 364; *Harding* [1997] Crim LR 815). It may take the form of positive abuse (assault, ill-treatment, abandonment or exposure) or of mere neglect, or it may take the form of causing or procuring abuse or neglect. The abuse or neglect in question must be committed 'in a manner likely to cause unnecessary suffering or injury to health' (as to which see s. 1(1)); but the offence is essentially a conduct crime rather than a result crime. It need not therefore be shown that any such injury was caused, and indeed it is no defence to show that any suffering of or danger to the victim was obviated by the action of another person (s. 1(3)(a)). **B2.121**

'Assault' in this context will usually mean a battery, as to which see **B2.8** ***et seq.*** Ill-treatment is self-explanatory in the context of the requirement that it must be likely to cause unnecessary suffering or injury (see below). In *Boulden* (1957) 41 Cr App R 105, the Court of Appeal considered a case of abandonment in which a father of five children had left them and travelled to Scotland. Although the evidence was somewhat contradictory, the court found sufficient evidence to show that he had 'washed his hands' of his children, and had 'left them to their fate'; this was sufficient proof of abandonment.

The offence of exposing a child in a manner likely to cause unnecessary suffering or injury has had little consideration in case law. Exposure to bad weather in itself would not be enough, given the second limb of the *actus reus* (*Williams* (1910) 4 Cr App R 89, a case concerning the Children Act 1908).

B2.122 **Neglect** Cases of neglect have received frequent attention in the courts. The requisite neglect will be deemed to have occurred, and therefore need not be proved, in the circumstances set out in s. 1(2)(a) and (b), although the Court of Appeal in *Wills* [1990] Crim LR 714 stressed that even where neglect is deemed the *mens rea* element of the offence must be proved (see below). Where s. 1(2)(a) applies, it may be the basis for proving neglect; in any event, it gives a general indication of what constitutes neglect. For example, a relative who was not the legal guardian of, or legally liable to maintain, a child, but who was looking after him for several weeks, might be under a duty to act (see **A1.13** ***et seq.***). Such a person would then be expected to provide care of the kind mentioned in s. 2(1)(a).

The Court of Appeal in *S and M* [1995] Crim LR 486 explained 'neglecting' in the context of failing to obtain medical help. Either S the parent or M the boyfriend assaulted the child, who had bruising to the spine and buttocks. There was then further neglect in the failure to get medical help. The argument that there was no neglect because there was nothing a doctor could have done, was rejected. The Court of Appeal held that S or M had neglected the child within the meaning of the statute by refraining from seeking medical help, being reckless as to whether the child might need such help. There are difficulties not addressed in this case concerning the burden of proof, given that it was clear that one party had committed the assault but it was not clear which. However, there is clearly an argument that both were liable for neglect, both being under a duty to act.

The Court of Appeal in *Wills* were concerned with the meaning of the phrase 'in a manner likely to cause unnecessary suffering or injury to health' and more particularly the exact meaning of the word 'likely'. The trial judge had relied on remarks of Lord Diplock in *Sheppard* [1981] AC 394, that 'likely' was simply meant to exclude what was highly unlikely. Although the Court of Appeal agreed that these remarks were *obiter dicta*, it found that Lord Diplock had properly construed the word in the context of this statute, given the difficulties for parents in deciding how serious an injury is, and the possible grave consequences of lack of treatment. The court went on to point out however that, because of the 'deeming' provision under s. 1(2)(a) of the Act, it was unnecessary for the court to come to a decision about the meaning of the word, and these remarks too were *obiter*. In the context of interpreting s. 1(2)(a), it was held that medical aid included medical supervision or medical care in the sense of observation to discover the gravity of any particular injury. The deeming provision was also relevant in *Sheppard* and was explained by Lord Diplock as follows:

> Did the parents fail to provide . . . in the period before [the child's] death medical aid that was in fact adequate in view of his actual state of health at the relevant time? This, as it seems to me, is a pure question of objective fact to be determined in the light of what has become known by *the date of the trial* to have been the child's actual state of health at the relevant time. It does not depend upon whether a reasonably careful parent, with knowledge of those facts only which such a parent might reasonably be expected to observe for himself, would have thought it prudent to have recourse to medical aid.

The requisite *mens rea* must still be proved, even when the deeming provisions apply.

Mens Rea

The *mens rea* of this offence is defined as 'wilfully' carrying out any of the various modes of the *actus reus. Sheppard* [1981] AC 394 is the leading case on the interpretation of the word in this context, and although it was decided only in the context of the neglect provision, there is no reason why it should not apply equally to all the positive modes of committing the offence. **B2.123**

In *Sheppard*, a child aged 16 months died of hypothermia following severe gastroenteritis. The parents were poor and of low intelligence, and had not appreciated the seriousness of his condition. They were convicted under s. 1 on the basis of an objective test. The House of Lords in *Sheppard* allowed the defendants' appeal, and Lord Diplock explained the *mens rea* requirement as follows:

> The proper direction to be given to a jury on a charge of wilful neglect of a child under section 1 of the Children and Young Persons Act 1933 by failing to provide adequate medical aid, is that the jury must be satisfied (1) that the child did in fact need medical aid at the time at which the parent is charged with failing to provide it (the actus reus) and (2) either that the parent was aware at the time that the child's health might be at risk if it were not provided with medical aid, or that the parent's unawareness of this fact was due to his not caring whether the child's health was at risk or not (the *mens rea*).

This passage was formerly interpreted by some commentators as conveying *Caldwell* recklessness; but this was always difficult to reconcile with the concept of 'not caring', or with Lord Diplock's observation in *Sheppard* that the concept of what the reasonable parent would observe and understand has no part to play in the *mens rea* of this offence. In *W (Emma)* [2006] EWCA Crim 2723 it was held that a parent may be guilty of wilful neglect where he knows that his child needs medical care, but deliberately refrains from obtaining it, or fails to obtain it because he does not care whether it is needed or not. But if a parent, whether through personal inadequacy or stupidity or both, genuinely fails to appreciate that his child needs medical care, then the parent does not act wilfully and is not guilty of the offence.

General

A defendant can be charged under the CYPA 1933, s. 1, even if death occurs (s. 1(3)(b)) and in such circumstances the charge is often coupled with a charge of murder or manslaughter brought against that defendant and/or a co-defendant. Note also the DVCVA 2004, s. 5 (see B1.58). **B2.124**

The Children Act 2004, s. 58(5), repeals the CYPA 1933, s. 1(7), which formerly provided that nothing in that section affected a parent or teacher's right to administer punishment (see B2.16).

FEMALE GENITAL MUTILATION

Definition **B2.125**

Female Genital Mutilation Act 2003, ss. 1 to 4

1.—(1) A person is guilty of an offence if he excises, infibulates or otherwise mutilates the whole or any part of a girl's labia majora, labia minora or clitoris.

(2) But no offence is committed by an approved person who performs—

(a) a surgical operation on a girl which is necessary for her physical or mental health, or

(b) a surgical operation on a girl who is in any stage of labour, or has just given birth, for purposes connected with the labour or birth.

(3) The following are approved persons—

(a) in relation to an operation falling within subsection (2)(a), a registered medical practitioner,

(b) in relation to an operation falling within subsection (2)(b), a registered medical

Part B Offences

practitioner, a registered midwife or a person undergoing a course of training with a view to becoming such a practitioner or midwife.
(4) There is also no offence committed by a person who—
(a) performs a surgical operation falling within subsection (2)(a) or (b) outside the United Kingdom, and
(b) in relation to such an operation exercises functions corresponding to those of an approved person.
(5) For the purpose of determining whether an operation is necessary for the mental health of a girl it is immaterial whether she or any other person believes that the operation is required as a matter of custom or ritual.
2. A person is guilty of an offence if he aids, abets, counsels or procures a girl to excise, infibulate or otherwise mutilate the whole or any part of her own labia majora, labia minora or clitoris.
3.—(1) A person is guilty of an offence if he aids, abets, counsels or procures a person who is not a United Kingdom national or permanent United Kingdom resident to do a relevant act of female genital mutilation outside the United Kingdom.
(2) An act is a relevant act of female genital mutilation if—
(a) it is done in relation to a United Kingdom national or permanent United Kingdom resident, and
(b) it would, if done by such a person, constitute an offence under section 1.
(3) But no offence is committed if the relevant act of female genital mutilation—
(a) is a surgical operation falling within section 1(2)(a) or (b), and
(b) is performed by a person who, in relation to such an operation, is an approved person or exercises functions corresponding to those of an approved person.
4.—(1) Sections 1 to 3 extend to any act done outside the United Kingdom by a United Kingdom national or permanent United Kingdom resident.
(2) If an offence under this Act is committed outside the United Kingdom—
(a) proceedings may be taken, and
(b) the offence may for incidental purposes be treated as having been committed,
in any place in England and Wales or Northern Ireland.

This Act came into force on 3 March 2004 and supplants the little-used Prohibition of Female Circumcision Act 1985. The most obvious difference is that the principal provisions of the 2003 Act extend to acts done outside the UK by UK nationals or permanent UK residents (s. 4); and this will include (by s. 3) aiding, abetting, counselling or procuring a person who is not a UK national or permanent UK resident to do a relevant act of female genital mutilation outside the UK; and (by s. 2) aiding, abetting, counselling or procuring a girl or woman to mutilate herself.

Procedure and Sentence

B2.126 Offences under the Act are triable either way. By s. 5, the maximum penalty following conviction on indictment is imprisonment for 14 years or a fine (or both); and on summary conviction imprisonment for up to six months or a fine not exceeding the statutory maximum (or both).

Section B3 Sexual Offences

The SOA 2003 represents the most important overhaul of the law governing sexual offences since at least Victorian times. Some offences have been swept away, others have been redefined, whilst the SOA 2003 introduced a great number of new ones. Part 1 of the Act created over 50 offences. Some carry different sentences depending upon the precise factual ingredients proved, which in accordance with the decision in *Courtie* [1984] AC 463 means they actually create even more offences. Section 140 repeals or revokes much of the previous legislation as listed in sch. 7. The Sexual Offences Act 2003 (Commencement Order) 2004 (SI 2004 No. 874) brought the Act fully into force on 1 May 2004. **B3.1**

Section 141 empowered the Secretary of State to make transitional provisions, but no such provisions have been enacted. It followed that, where there was doubt as to whether an offence of rape occurred before or after the coming into force of the SOA 2003, the prosecution failed because it could not be proved whether a statutory offence was committed under the old or the new law (*A (Prosecutor's Appeal)* [2006] 1 Cr App R 433; *Newbon* [2005] Crim LR 738). The lacuna has been addressed in s. 55 of the Violent Crime Reduction Act 2006, which came into effect on 12 February 2007. This deeming provision covers the situation where an accused is charged in respect of the same conduct both with an offence under the SOA 2003 and an offence under the old law, and the only thing preventing him being found guilty of the 2003 Act offence or the offence under the old law is the fact that it has not been proved beyond a reasonable doubt that the time when the conduct took place was either after the coming into force of the enactment providing for the offence or before the repeal of the old law. In such circumstances, for the purpose of determining guilt, it will be conclusively presumed that the time when the conduct took place was when the old law applied if the offence attracted a lesser maximum penalty; otherwise it will be presumed the conduct took place after the implementation of the new law.

The key objectives of the Act are to modernise the law governing sexual offences and to protect children and other vulnerable individuals from sexual abuse. The principles underpinning the new legislation include non-discrimination between men and women and non-discrimination between those of different sexual orientation. All offences are gender neutral in that they can be committed by either sex, apart from rape as a principal. The Act also aims to refocus the law on critical issues such as consent and protection of sexual autonomy.

For the old law, which will continue to apply to offences committed before 1 May 2004, reference may be made to the 2004 edition of this work. Certain offences have been retained, with some amendments, rather than included within the SOA 2003; for example, the soliciting offences become gender neutral, whilst in respect of indecent photographs of children the Act redefines the term 'child' for the purposes of the Protection of Children Act 1978 as a person under 18 years, rather than 16 (see **B3.278**).

For further discussion of the policy underlying the new legislation and some trenchant criticism of the complexity and density of drafting, the extensive overlapping between offences, and the breadth of the offences, reference may be made to *Rook and Ward on Sexual Offences* (3rd edn, Sweet & Maxwell, 2004), *Blackstone's Guide to the Sexual Offences Act 2003* (OUP, 2004) and to articles by J. Temkin and A. Ashworth and by J. Spencer in [2004] Crim LR at pp. 328 and 347 respectively.

For sentencing of offenders convicted of offences under the SOA 2003 on or after 14 May 2007, see the SGC definitive guideline reproduced in part 8 of **appendix 8**.

Presumptions and Alternative Verdicts

B3.2 In relation to rape (SOA 2003, s. 1), assault by penetration (s. 2), sexual assault (s. 3) and causing a person to engage in sexual activity without consent (s. 4), presumptions as to consent and/or reasonable belief as to consent may apply. They do not apply to inchoate offences. However, the evidential presumptions about consent (s. 75) arise very rarely in practice as in most cases it is likely that sufficient evidence will be adduced, from whatever source, to raise an issue as to consent and reasonable belief as to consent. In contrast to the rebuttable presumptions of s. 75, s. 76 creates conclusive presumptions. However, essentially they replicate the previous common law (with some limited extension) as to deception as to the nature or purpose of the act, and impersonation, and so will rarely be triggered (see *Jheeta* [2007] EWCA Crim 1699 at **B3.12**). These are dealt with fully in relation to rape and cross-referenced in respect of the other offences to which they apply. Beyond the limited type of case where s. 76 arises, and assuming that s. 75 has no application, the issue has to be addressed in the context of s. 74 (see **B3.8**).

One characteristic of the new legislation is that there is considerable overlap, or potential overlap, between offences. This leads to considerable dependence upon prosecutorial discretion. The exercise of discretion is now vital in many areas, including in respect of the young, the mentally disordered and adult relatives. The CPS is alive to the need for consistency in the proper exercise of its discretion and has published guidelines (Sexual Offences Act 2003: Legal Guidance (July 2004)). The issue of alternative offences and included offences is covered at **B3.285** and referred to throughout the text.

RAPE

B3.3 Rape is a statutory offence which can be committed by a man upon a woman or another man. It consists of non-consensual vaginal, anal or oral intercourse.

Sexual Offences Act 2003, s. 1

(1) A person (A) commits an offence if—
  (a) he intentionally penetrates the vagina, anus or mouth of another person (B) with his penis,
  (b) B does not consent to the penetration, and
  (c) A does not reasonably believe that B consents.
(2) Whether a belief is reasonable is to be determined having regard to all the circumstances, including any steps A has taken to ascertain whether B consents.
(3) Sections 75 and 76 apply to an offence under this section.

Sections 75 and 76 deal with presumptions as to consent.

Procedure

Rape is triable only on indictment. It is a class 2 offence. Formerly it was presumed that a boy under the age of 14 was incapable of sexual intercourse. This rule was abolished by the SOA 1993, s. 1, and does not apply where penetration occurred after 20 September 1993. Where the victim of the offence was under 16 at the time of the offence, the extended jurisdiction provisions of s. 72 apply. **B3.4**

For the special protections relating to complainants in sexual cases, see **F7.13**.

See **B3.285** for alternative verdicts.

Indictment

Statement of Offence **B3.5**

Rape, contrary to section 1 of the Sexual Offences Act 2003.

Particulars of Offence

A, on or about the . . . day of . . . penetrated the [vagina][anus][mouth] of V with his penis without her consent and not reasonably believing that V did consent.

Sentencing Guidelines

The maximum penalty for rape is life imprisonment and the maximum penalty for attempted rape is life imprisonment (SOA 2003, s. 1(4)). The SGC Guideline, *Sexual Offences Act 2003* (April 2007), applies to offenders sentenced for this offence on or after 14 May 2007. For the full text of this guideline, see **appendix 8** at part 8. The SGC has determined that the sentencing starting points established in *Millberry* [2003] 1 WLR 546 should apply to all non-consensual offences involving penetration of the anus or vagina, or penile penetration of the mouth. The starting point for a case involving an adult victim raped by a single offender in a case that involves no aggravating features at all is five years, and where any of the particular aggravating factors identified in the offence guidelines are involved the starting point is eight years. In addition, where identified aggravating factors exist and the victim is a child aged 13 or over but under 16, the recommended starting point is 10 years; for the rape of a child under 13 where there are no aggravating factors, a starting point of 10 years is recommended, rising to 13 years for cases involving any of the particular aggravating factors identified in the guideline. Aggravating and mitigating factors are set out in the guideline, but these are additional to those set out in the SGC Guideline on *Seriousness* (December 2004), paras. 1.20 to 1.24 (see **appendix 8** at part 3). The sentences for public protection (see **E5**) must be considered in all cases of rape. In every case the court should consider a disqualification from working with children (see **E23.11**) and a sexual offences prevention order (SOPO) (see **E23.12**). There is a notification requirement under the CJA 2003, s. 80 and sch. 3 (see **E25**). **B3.6**

Guidance on sentencing in respect of the offences of rape, following the change of definition of that offence in the SOA 2003, was provided by the Court of Appeal in *A-G's Ref (No. 104 of 2004) (Garvey)* [2005] 1 Cr App R (S) 666. The Court stated that the starting point for an adult for rape should be five years, whether the penetration was of the vagina, anus or mouth, and whether the victim was male or female. It should be varied upwards or downwards in accordance with the aggravating and mitigating features and higher starting points identified in *Millberry* [2003] 1 WLR 546 (see now the SGC Guideline). In *Ismail* [2005] 2 Cr App R (S) 542, a case of forcible oral sex, the Court stressed that for the purposes of sentencing offences of rape under the new Act no distinction is to be drawn between oral rape and other forms of the offence. It said that, although there is no risk of pregnancy associated with oral rape, there remains a danger of infection from sexually transmitted diseases and that amounts itself to an aggravating feature. A sentence of six years' detention in a young offender institution was upheld on the 18-year-old offender who committed the offence on a 16-year-old girl in a public place at night. The offender had no previous convictions, and pleaded guilty at the plea and directions hearing.

For young offenders, the sentence for rape should normally be significantly shorter than that for an adult. However, this approach admits of exceptions and is not meant to be of invariable and inevitable application; where the facts of the case are particularly serious, the youth of the offender will not necessarily mitigate the appropriate sentence (see *Asi-Akram* [2006] 1 Cr App R (S) 260 and *Patrick M* [2005] 1 Cr App R (S) 218). See *Corran* [2005] 2 Cr App R (S) 453 for non-prescriptive guidance to sentencers in respect of young offenders and child victims. See also *B* [2006] EWCA Crim 330 for an example of where the Court of Appeal upheld an indeterminate sentence detaining the 15-year-old offender for life where, as a pupil, he had forced a teacher to perform oral sex twice, having dragged her from the classroom and told her he would kill her. The sentencing judge fixed a notional sentence of nine years with a specific term of three years and eight months. The Court of Appeal held that the case was unique and exceptional violence had been used and that the offender's young age had to be balanced against the seriousness of the offence. While the age of the offender was something a court had to take strongly into account, it could not be a matter that prevented an appropriate sentence on particular facts.

Millberry, based on advice submitted to the Court of Appeal by the Sentencing Advisory Panel was the leading guideline case for the offence.

Lord Woolf CJ said in *Millberry* that there were three dimensions to consider in assessing the gravity of an individual offence of rape. These were (i) the degree of harm to the victim, (ii) the level of culpability of the offender, and (iii) the level of risk posed by the offender to society. While rape will always be a most serious offence, its gravity will depend very much upon the circumstances of the particular case, and it will always be necessary to consider an individual case as a whole, taking into account the three dimensions referred to. His lordship agreed with the Panel's advice that the same starting points for sentencing were applicable whether the rape was perpetrated on a female victim or a male victim, and whether the offence was a vaginal rape or an anal rape. His lordship also expressed general agreement with the Panel that cases of 'relationship rape' and 'acquaintance rape' should be treated as being of equal seriousness to cases of 'stranger rape', with the sentence being increased or reduced, in each case, by the presence of specific aggravating or mitigating factors.

Lord Woolf CJ stated that while 'the maximum credit should only be given for a timely guilty plea', courts should reduce sentence in a case of rape in which the offender pleads guilty. This is because 'victims of rape can find it an extremely distressing experience to give evidence' and also because the guilty plea 'demonstrates that the offender appreciates how wrong his conduct was and regrets it'. These were more important reasons for taking account of the guilty plea in rape cases than the avoidance of taking up the time of the court and incurring expense unnecessarily.

If an offender has previous convictions for sexual or violent offences, this can be a significant aggravating feature. The offender's good character, although it should not be ignored, does not justify a substantial reduction of what would otherwise be the appropriate sentence. The fact that the offences were committed some years ago can be taken into account, but only to a limited extent.

In *A-G's Refs (Nos. 14 and 15 of 2006)* [2007] 1 All ER 718, the first offender, Webster, pleaded guilty to four counts of rape and five counts of indecent assault committed on a baby, and three counts of taking or permitting to be taken indecent photographs of a child. He pleaded guilty to a further count of indecent assault on a girl aged 14. The second offender, French, who was aged 17 or 18 when the offences were committed, pleaded guilty to one count of rape, four counts of indecent assault and three counts of making or permitting to be taken indecent photographs of a child. There was photographic evidence to show that the baby had been abused by the offenders on five separate occasions. The Court of Appeal upheld the sentence of life imprisonment on Webster and observed that it was questionable whether he would ever be released. In commenting that the aggravating features of this appalling case went beyond those envisaged in the guideline cases, the Court of Appeal increased the appropriate minimum term from 6 years (based on a national determinate sentence of 18 years and reduced by one third to reflect the plea of guilty) to one of 8 years (based on a notional determinate sentence of 24 years adjusted in the same way). French received an extended sentence of ten years with a custodial term of five years and an extension period of five years, and that sentence was upheld on appeal. For other recent cases where life imprisonment was upheld for offences of rape, see *Henry* [2006] EWCA Crim 2394, *Frost* [2006] EWCA Crim 830. See also *B (Samuel)* [2006] 2 Cr App R (S) 472, where the Court of Appeal substituted imprisonment for public protection for life imprisonment.

Actus Reus

Rape, as a principle, can only be committed by a man. A woman who encourages or assists a man to penetrate another person, not reasonably believing the other person is consenting, may be convicted of aiding and abetting rape (*Cogan* [1976] QB 217). **B3.7**

Section 1 of the SOA 2003 makes clear that the vital ingredients of the *actus reus* consist of penetration by the penis of the vagina, anus or mouth of the complainant, together with the absence of consent of the complainant. 'Vagina' is to be taken as including the vulva (s. 79(9)). The slightest penetration is sufficient. In respect of penetration of the vagina, it is not necessary to show the hymen was ruptured. Whether the defendant ejaculates or not is irrelevant.

References to the parts of the body specified above include references to a part surgically constructed (in particular through gender reassignment surgery) (s. 79(3)). The offence thus protects transsexuals. It also, however, means that a person who benefits from a surgically constructed penis can commit the offence of rape.

Penile penetration of the mouth without consent now constitutes rape whereas formerly it amounted only to indecent assault.

Penetration is a continuing act from entry to withdrawal (s. 79(2)). It follows that if there is no longer consent to penetration, the man must withdraw (*Kaitamaki v The Queen* [1985] AC 147; *Tarmohammed* [1997] Crim LR 458). If the man is aware that a person has ceased to consent to penetration, he cannot claim that there was a consent to its continuation (*Cooper* [1994] Crim LR 531). In the event of a claim of a mistaken belief that consent persisted, an accused will be guilty of rape if he did not reasonably believe, having regard to all the circumstances, that the person continued to consent (s. 1(2)).

Absence of Consent

Section 74 of the 2003 Act defines consent to the extent that it provides: 'For the purposes of this part, a person consents if he or she agrees by choice and has the freedom and capacity to make that choice'. The definition, with its emphasis on free agreement, is designed to focus upon the complainant's autonomy. It highlights the fact that a complainant who simply freezes with no protest or resistance may nevertheless not be consenting. To have the freedom to make a choice a person must be free from physical pressure, but it remains a matter of fact for a jury as to what degree of coercion has to be exercised upon a person's mind before he or she is not agreeing by choice with the freedom to make that choice. **B3.8**

'Capacity' is an integral part of the definition of consent. A valid consent can only be given by a person who has the capacity to give it. The SOA 2003 does not define capacity. Common law principles that developed under the old law suggest that a complainant will not have had capacity to agree by choice where her understanding and knowledge were so limited that she was not in a position to decide whether or not to agree (*Howard* (1965) 50 Cr App R 56). This may arise in a variety of different circumstances; for instance, when a complainant is suffering from some forms of mental disorder, very young or intoxicated by alcohol or drugs. These principles still apply under the SOA 2003. When summing up the judge should give the jury some assistance with the meaning of 'capacity' in circumstances where a complainant was affected by voluntarily induced intoxication. He should also assist the jury on the issue of whether, and to what extent, they could take that voluntary intoxication into account in deciding whether the complainant had consented. See *Bree* [2007] 2 All ER 676 and *Contes* [2007] EWCA Crim 1471 at [44].

If through drink a complainant has temporarily lost the capacity to choose whether to have intercourse on the relevant occasion, he or she is not consenting. However, where the complainant has voluntarily consumed even substantial quantities of alcohol, but nevertheless remains capable of choosing whether or not to have intercourse and, in drink, agrees to do so, this would not be rape. A drunken consent is still a consent. A complainant's consumption of alcohol may lead to him or her to behave differently from the way he or she would have behaved if entirely sober. However, in *Bree* it was pointed out that as a matter of practical reality, capacity to consent may evaporate well before a complainant becomes unconscious. Whether this is so depends on the actual state of mind of the complainant on the particular occasion.

The anachronism that a woman could not in law refuse sexual intercourse with her husband had been brought to a timely end by a unanimous House of Lords in *R* [1992] 1 AC 599. The Court of Appeal have since held that a man may properly be convicted of raping his wife even though the offence was committed over 20 years before the final demise of the marital exemption (*Barry C* [2004] EWCA Crim 292).

Mens Rea

B3.9 First, the prosecution must prove that the accused intended to penetrate the vagina, anus or mouth of another. Following the reasoning in *Heard* [2007] 3 All ER 306 in respect of sexual assault, this would seem to be no more than a requirement that the penetration be deliberate (meaning simply voluntarily willed movement), and self-induced intoxication does not provide a defence. In any event, in the vast majority of cases, if penetration is proved there will be no issue as to whether it was intentional. Secondly, by virtue of s. 1(1)(c), the prosecution must also prove that the accused did not reasonably believe that the complainant was consenting at the time of penetration. Whilst this section reverses the decision in *DPP v Morgan* [1976] AC 182 and abolishes the wholly subjective test for the mental element, the Act does not adopt a test based on what a reasonable man would have believed. The provision focuses upon the belief of the particular accused. Since s. 1(2) provides that regard is to be had to 'all the circumstances, including any steps A has taken to ascertain whether B consents' in determining whether an accused had a reasonable belief, it is clear that a jury may take into account relevant characteristics of the accused, such as extreme youth, a learning disability and any mental disorder that might affect a person's capacity to understand the true nature of a situation. Section 1(2) does not positively require an accused to have taken steps to ascertain whether the complainant consents. However, this is something the jury will consider when considering the reasonableness of his belief. More steps are likely to be expected where there is no established relationship. Under the old law, rape was held to be a crime of basic intent and self-induced intoxication could not be used as the basis of a denial of *mens rea*. In *Woods* (1982) 74 Cr App R 312, the Court of Appeal held that 'reasonable grounds' under the Sexual Offences (Amendment) Act 1976, s. 1(2), were grounds that would have been reasonable had the accused been sober. See also *Fotheringham* (1989) 88 Cr App R 206. Whilst the SOA 2003, s. 1(2), does stipulate that whether a person's belief is reasonable is to be determined having regard to all the circumstances, given that the new test has become more objective it is likely that the Court of Appeal's reasoning under the old law will continue to apply. Whilst self-induced intoxication may be relevant as to whether a defendant may have had a genuine belief that the complainant was consenting, it is not a relevant factor when considering whether such a belief may have been reasonable.

In *A-G's Ref (No. 79 of 2006)* [2007] 1 Cr App R(S) 752, the Court of Appeal, when dealing with an application to make a reference, expressed the view that it had doubts about the ruling of the trial judge that it is not a defence to a charge under ss. 1 or 2 of the SOA 2003 if the accused has made a mistake, however reasonable, as to the identity of the person to whom the sexual activity is directed. The judge had felt that he must adopt the narrow view in that the offences related to a named complainant (B), and the requirement in s. 1(2) cannot widen the scope of such consideration so as to allow for the accused's state of mind in relation to any third party. The Court observed that a possible alternative way of dealing with such a very rare set of circumstances would be to hold that the offence is committed if a reasonable (therefore sober) person would have realised that the person being penetrated or sexually touched was not the person whom the accused thought he was consensually penetrating.

A direction upon absence of reasonable belief falls to be given by the judge when, but only when, there is material on which a jury might come to the conclusion that (a) the complainant did not in fact consent, but (b) the accused thought she was consenting. Such a direction is not necessary where prosecution and defence cases on consent are diametrically opposed and there is simply no scope, in the case of either party, for any misunderstanding by the accused as to presence of consent (*Taran* [2006] EWCA Crim 1498).

Evidential Presumptions about Consent

The SOA 2003 creates evidential presumptions and conclusive presumptions as to consent and reasonable belief in consent. **B3.10**

Evidential presumptions Section 75 of the SOA 2003 lists circumstances in which the complainant is taken not to have consented to the relevant act *unless* sufficient evidence is adduced to raise an issue as to whether the complainant consented. Also the accused is to be taken not to have reasonably believed that the complainant consented *unless* sufficient evidence is adduced to raise an issue as to whether he reasonably believed it (s. 75(1)). **B3.11**

There must be some foundation in the evidence, and it must not be merely speculative or fanciful for there to be sufficient evidence. However, it is vital to understand that if the trial judge decides (presumably at the close of the evidence) that there is sufficient evidence (from whatever admissible source) to raise an issue as to whether the complainant consented and/or the accused reasonably believed the complainant was consenting, then the judge will put the issues to the jury in accordance with the key sections (i.e. ss. 74 and 1(2)), and the s. 75 route is barred. In the relatively rare cases where the judge decides that there is not sufficient evidence on one or both of the issues, a s. 75 direction must be given on that issue. To find absence of consent and/or absence of reasonable belief, the jury have to be sure of three matters: (i) that the accused did the relevant act (in the case of rape, it is the intentional penile penetration of the complainant's vagina, anus or mouth: s. 77) (s. 75(1)(a)); (ii) any of the s. 75(2) circumstances existed; and (iii) the accused knew those circumstances existed (s. 75(1)(c)). It should be noted that where a s. 75 evidential presumption arises there is no question of the issue being removed from the jury.

The circumstances in which evidential presumptions about consent apply are set out in s. 75(2)(a) to (f).

Sexual Offences Act 2003, s. 75

(2) The circumstances are that—
  (a) any person was, at the time of the relevant act or immediately before it began, using

violence against the complainant or causing the complainant to fear that immediate violence would be used against him;
(b) any person was, at the time of the relevant act or immediately before it began, causing the complainant to fear that violence was being used, or that immediate violence would be used, against another person;
(c) the complainant was, and the defendant was not, unlawfully detained at the time of the relevant act;
(d) the complainant was asleep or otherwise unconscious at the time of the relevant act;
(e) because of the complainant's physical disability, the complainant would not have been able at the time of the relevant act to communicate to the defendant whether the complainant consented;
(f) any person had administered to or caused to be taken by the complainant, without the complainant's consent, a substance which, having regard to when it was administered or taken, was capable of causing or enabling the complainant to be stupefied or overpowered at the time of the relevant act.

The circumstances set out in s. 75(2) are not exhaustive of the cases where consent will be absent. The categories of threats and behaviour capable of negating consent are wider than the categories to which the presumptions apply. For example, the evidential presumptions under (a) and (b) do not deal with the situation where a complainant fears future as opposed to 'immediate violence' although in such circumstances the complainant may well not be consenting.

Section 75(3) provides that in s. 75(2)(a) and (b) the reference to the time immediately before the relevant act began is, in the case of an act which is one of a continuous series of sexual activities, a reference to the time immediately before the first sexual activity began.

B3.12 **Conclusive Presumptions about Consent** In contrast to the rebuttable presumptions of the SOA 2003, s. 75, s. 76 creates conclusive presumptions.

Sexual Offences Act 2003, s. 76

(1) If in proceedings for an offence to which this section applies it is proved that the defendant did the relevant act and that any of the circumstances specified in subsection (2) existed, it is to be conclusively presumed—
(a) that the complainant did not consent to the relevant act, and
(b) that the defendant did not believe that the complainant consented to the relevant act.
(2) The circumstances are that—
(a) the defendant intentionally deceived the complainant as to the nature or purpose of the relevant act;
(b) the defendant intentionally induced the complainant to consent to the relevant act by impersonating a person known personally to the complainant.

Section 76 essentially replicates the common law, although both limbs of s. 76(2) in some respects go further. Where the prosecution is able to prove that the accused did the relevant act (in the case of rape, the intentional penile penetration of the complainant's vagina, anus or mouth: s. 77), and either of the circumstances set out in s. 76(2) existed, it is conclusively presumed that the complainant did not consent to the relevant act and that the accused did not believe that the complainant consented to the relevant act. The jury should be directed to convict if they find either of these matters proved. For the presumption to arise, the deception or impersonation must be shown to have operated upon the mind of the complainant so as to induce consent (see Temkin and Ashworth at [2004] Crim LR 328 at p. 335).

Section 76(2)(a) follows the common law, which established that in the comparatively rare cases where the complainant has been induced to consent on the basis of fraudulent misrepresentations as to the nature of the act there was no consent (see *Williams* [1923] 1 KB 340 and *Flattery* [1877] 2 QB 410). Arguably the inclusion of the word 'purpose' extends the pre-existing law which had evolved to the extent that deceptions as to the purpose of the physical act were sufficient to vitiate consent (see *Tabassum* [2000] 2 Cr App R 328 and *Green* [2002]

EWCA Crim 1501). However, as was stressed by the Court of Appeal in *Jheeta* [2007] EWCA Crim 1699, s. 76(2)(a) does not address the 'quality' of the act, but confines itself to its 'purpose'. It follows that deception by representing a false medical purpose may be sufficient to trigger s. 76, but not if consent is induced by a bogus ceremony of marriage or false promise of payment (see facts of *Linekar* [1995] 2 Cr App R 49 as considered in *Jheeta* at [25]).

In *Jheeta* the Court of Appeal held that no conclusive presumptions arose merely because the complainant had been deceived in some way by disingenuous blandishments from or the lies of the accused. The creation of a bizarre fantasy which had pressurised the complainant into having sexual intercourse with the accused more frequently than she otherwise would have done was not a deception as to the nature or purpose of sexual intercourse. Such conduct might be deceptive or persuasive, but would rarely go to the nature or purpose of intercourse.

Section 76(2)(b) extends the law by widening the categories of impersonation sufficient to vitiate consent beyond the complainant's husband or regular sexual partner to 'a person known personally to the complainant'.

Consent in Absence of Presumption In most cases neither the evidential nor conclusive presumptions will arise, and the jury must determine whether the prosecution have established absence of consent and/or absence of reasonable belief in accordance with the key definitions in ss. 74 and 1(2). **B3.13**

The approach recommended in *Olugboja* [1982] QB 320 had left juries with very little guidance as to the parameters of consent apart from the standard direction that submission is not necessarily consent. Whilst the new law represents a significant improvement, it leaves juries to grapple with such concepts as freedom, choice and capacity. It remains for the jury to resolve such questions as whether the degree of coercion and/or abuse of power or authority exercised upon a complainant's mind was such that she did not agree by choice with the freedom to make that choice. It may well be, for example, that a threat to expose a woman's previous sexual conduct to her family in order to persuade her to have sex with another person will negate consent, particularly if the woman comes from a milieu in which such a revelation might pose the danger of physical harm or even death to her (*Sharif* [2004] EWCA Crim 3386). Such questions are left for juries to resolve.

Non-disclosure of STDs and Consent At common law a man who had consensual intercourse with another person, knowing but not disclosing that he suffers from a sexually transmitted illness, could not be convicted of rape. In *Mohammed Dica* [2004] QB 1257, the Court of Appeal, referring to the old law, stated that consent to sexual intercourse defeated liability for rape. Clearly, deceptions by the accused as to purely marginal matters which do not relate to the nature and purpose of the act did not vitiate consent at common law. Nor would they do so under the SOA 2003. However, consent in the SOA 2003, s. 74, requires agreement by choice and a person must have the freedom and capacity to make that choice. Sections 75 and 76 are illustrations of this principle but are not exhaustive of it. As yet the parameters of consent under s. 74 are not entirely clear. What if the deception is something of fundamental importance to the complainant? On any view, a failure to disclose any sexually transmitted disease (STD) is not a deception as to the nature or purpose of the act, and accordingly the conclusive presumption under s. 76(2)(a) does not arise. In *B* [2007] 1 WLR 1567, it was held that an accused's failure to disclose his HIV status did not affect the issue of consent in rape where there had been no allegations that the accused had deceived the complainant. Latham LJ stated (at [17]): **B3.14**

> Where one party to sexual activity has a sexually transmissible disease which is not disclosed to the other party any consent that may have been given to that activity by the other party is not thereby vitiated. The act remains a consensual act. However, the party suffering from the sexual transmissible disease will not have any defence to any charge which may result from harm

> created by that sexual activity, merely by virtue of that consent, because such consent did not include consent to infection by the disease.

Ignorance defeats consent under the OAPA 1861, s. 20, where the illness is life-threatening (*Konzani* [2005] 2 Cr App R 198: see **B2.12**). The position may well be different as to positive misrepresentations as to HIV status. Even following *B*, there is an argument that a jury would be entitled to decide that a person who agrees to unprotected sex, having been deceived by his or her partner in respect of the fact that he was, say, HIV-positive, does not have the freedom to make that choice as defined in s. 74 which was intended to mark a change in the previous law. At the very least, a lie about HIV status would be relevant to a complainant's state of mind unless he or she was willing to run the risk of contracting the disease. Relevance to choice is not limited to an appreciation of the barest physical nature of the act and the willingness to perform it. For strident criticism of the decision in *B*, see L. H. Leigh 'Two cases on consent in rape' in (2007) Archbold News 5.

Attempted Rape

B3.15 Attempted rape is governed by the principles of the law of attempts generally (see **A6.31**). Attempted rape may be charged as such, or may be an alternative verdict on a charge of rape where the evidence does not disclose that the accused achieved sexual intercourse with the victim.

The mental element in attempted rape is the same as that required for the full offence, namely an intent to penetrate and the absence of reasonable belief in consent. (The courts are likely to follow the reasoning under the old law in *Khan* [1990] 1 WLR 813.) It is not necessary to prove that the accused had gone so far as to attempt physical penetration of the vagina, anus or mouth. It suffices if acts be proved which the jury could regard as more than merely preparatory (*A-G's Ref (No.1 of 1992)* [1993] 1 WLR 274).

ASSAULT BY PENETRATION

B3.16 This is a new statutory offence created in response to the recommendation by the Sexual Offences Review, which recognised that non-consensual penetration by objects or parts of the body other than the penis can be as serious in their impact on the victim as rape. It also recommended that the offence should be defined in a way that would enable it to be used where there was doubt as to the nature of the penetration (e.g., where a child knows it was penetrated but cannot say whether it was by a penis, finger or another object).

Sexual Offences Act 2003, s. 2

(1) A person (A) commits an offence if—
 (a) he intentionally penetrates the vagina or anus of another person with a part of his body or anything else,
 (b) the penetration is sexual,
 (c) B does not consent to the penetration, and
 (d) A does not reasonably believe that B consents.
(2) Whether a belief is reasonable is to be determined having regard to all the circumstances, including any steps A has taken to ascertain whether B consents.
(3) Sections 75 and 76 apply to an offence under this section.

Procedure

B3.17 Assault by penetration is triable only on indictment. It is a class 2 offence. The extended jurisdiction provisions of s. 72 (see **B3.268**) apply where the victim was under 16 at the time of the offence.

See **B3.285** for alternative verdicts.

Sentencing

The maximum penalty for assault by penetration is life imprisonment (SOA 2003, s. 2(4)). The SGC Guideline, *Sexual Offences Act 2003* (April 2007), applies to offenders sentenced for this offence on or after 14 May 2007. For the full text of this guideline, see **appendix 8** at part 8. The SGC has indicated sentencing ranges and starting points for the offence of assault by penetration, distinguishing between cases of penetration involving a part of the offender's body, penetration with an object, and cases where penetration is accompanied by other factors such as abduction of the victim, abuse of trust, etc. Aggravating and mitigating factors are set out in the guideline, but these are additional to those set out in the SGC Guideline on *Seriousness* (December 2004), paras. 1.20–1.24 (see **appendix 8**). The sentences for public protection (see **E5**) must be considered in all cases of assault by penetration. In every case the court should consider a disqualification from working with children (see **E23.11**) and a SOPO (see **E23.12**). There is a notification requirement under the CJA 2003, s. 80 and sch. 3 (see **E25**). **B3.18**

Guidance on sentencing in respect of the offences of assault by penetration was provided by the Court of Appeal in *A-G's Ref (No. 104 of 2004) (Garvey)* [2005] 1 Cr App R (S) 666. The Court stated that the redefinition of the offence of rape and the introduction of the offence of assault by penetration, both with a maximum of life imprisonment, must mean that the sentences to be passed for digital penetration are now at a higher level than would have been appropriate when they were dealt with as indecent assault (which carries a maximum of ten years' imprisonment). A plea of guilty must always be taken into account. For young offenders, the sentence for assault by penetration should be significantly shorter than that for an adult. See also *Corran* [2005] 2 Cr App R (S) 453. *Garvey* was followed and applied in *Child* [2006] 1 Cr App R (S) 720, where a sentence of 30 months' imprisonment was appropriate for brief penetration with the fingers and the tongue of the vagina of the 18-year-old victim while she was asleep. The offender had been trusted to share a room with the victim and her partner and baby. The offender had previous convictions, but none for sexual offences. He pleaded guilty to assault by penetration but claimed that he had been drinking and had little recollection of the incident.

Indictment

Statement of Offence **B3.19**

Assault by penetration contrary to section 2(1) of the Sexual Offences Act 2003.

Particulars of Offence

A, on or about the . . . day of . . . penetrated the [vagina] [anus] of V with [ ] without [her][his] consent and did not reasonably believe that V was consenting.

Actus Reus

The essence of the offence is penetration of the vagina or anus of another person. The penetration may be penetration with a part of the offender's body, for example, a finger or a fist, or with anything else, for example, a dildo or a sharp object. The term 'anything else' will include an animal or other living organism. As with rape, references to a vagina include a surgically constructed vagina (SOA 2003, s. 79(3)). The penetration is a continuing act from entry to withdrawal (s. 79(2)). **B3.20**

Penetration must be 'sexual' in character. The requirement that conduct (penetration, touching etc.) is 'sexual' recurs in a number of offences. Section 78 of the SOA 2003 seeks to explain the approach to be adopted when considering whether particular conduct is 'sexual' for the purposes of the Act.

Sexual Offences Act 2003, s. 78

For the purposes of this part (except section 71) penetration, touching or any other activity is sexual if a reasonable person would consider that—

(a) whatever its circumstances or any person's purpose in relation to it, it is because of its nature sexual, or
(b) because of its nature it may be sexual and because of its circumstances or the purpose of any person in relation to it (or both) it is sexual.

Section 78(a) covers conduct where the nature of the activity is unambiguously sexual. To determine whether the conduct is 'sexual' it should be considered without reference to its circumstances or the purpose of the accused. For example, in respect of penile penetration or oral sex, the activity is sexual whatever the accused's purpose. It follows that it will not be a defence to a charge under s. 2 to claim that penetration was performed not for sexual gratification but as an assertion of dominance.

The correct approach to the application of s. 78(b) where the nature of the activity is ambiguous and 'may' be sexual, was set out by the Court of Appeal in *H* [2005] 1 WLR 2005. The Court said that the provision contains two distinct questions for the jury: first, whether they, as 12 reasonable people, considered that, because of its nature, the touching *might* be sexual: and, if so, secondly, whether, in view of the circumstances and/or the purpose of any person in relation to it, the touching *was* in fact sexual. These are two distinct questions which must be considered separately. The nature of the touching refers to the actual touching that took place and, therefore, in considering whether the touching, because of its nature, might be sexual, the jury is not concerned with the circumstances before or after the touching or the purpose of the accused in relation to it. In *H*, there was evidence that before pulling the complainant's tracksuit bottoms, the accused had said to her 'Do you fancy a shag?' At trial, it was submitted on behalf of the accused that the touching that had occurred could not be regarded by a reasonable person as 'sexual' within the meaning of the Act. The trial judge took the view that there were clearly circumstances, including the words allegedly spoken beforehand, which could make what had occurred sexual. The Court of Appeal said that the judge had not adopted the required two-stage approach to s. 78(b) but had looked at the matter as a whole. The problem with that was that, in a borderline case, a person's intention could make a touching sexual, even though the nature of the touching could not be sexual. That, said the Court, is not an appropriate approach, even though in the great majority of cases the result will be the same.

The Court in *H* disapproved the decision in *George* [1956] Crim LR 52, an allegation of indecent assault in which it was held that a shoe fetishist's act in removing a woman's shoe was not capable of being indecent. *George* was expressly approved in *Court* [1989] AC 28, where the House of Lords set out the meaning of 'indecency' in the offence of indecent assault and the reasoning in *Court* is essentially reproduced in the definition of 'sexual' in s. 78. The potentially wide scope of the application of s. 78(b) is highlighted by the Court's discussion of *George* in *H*. A wide variety of conduct is capable of being regarded by a reasonable person as possibly being 'sexual', albeit the vast majority of people would regard it as objectively innocuous.

Section 78(b) will have the effect of making an intimate medical examination involving digital examination of the vagina or anus 'sexual' where the examination is not a bona fide examination and the doctor's purpose is sexual gratification. Arguably, even where a doctor conducts a properly required intimate medical examination, if it was conducted in an inappropriate manner, it may be concluded that the activity was 'sexual' if it can be established that the doctor had an ulterior purpose of sexual gratification. See the facts of *Bolduc and Bird* (1967) 63 DLR (2d) 82, where a doctor carried out a necessary examination but allowed a friend to be present for his sexual gratification.

It is instructive to consider examples of activities which are not unambiguously 'sexual' but may be 'sexual' following the approach outlined in s. 78(b) as interpreted in *H*. For example, a slap on an athlete's buttocks by her coach is capable of being considered 'sexual' but may not be so where the occasion, filing off a field after a game, is not obviously sexual and where no words or gestures connote a sexual purpose (*Gauthier* Can Cr L. Digest 42887 and see also *J (BJ)* (1996) 193 AR 151 (Alta SC)). Stroking the legs of another is certainly capable of being sexual (*Price (David)* [2004] 1 Cr App R 145). The accused's admission in that case that he had done it because he was a shoe fetishist would be admissible under the second question in s. 78(b).

As with all the non-consensual sexual offences, it is a fundamental requirement of the offence that the prosecution can establish the complainant's absence of consent.

For consent and public policy, and, in particular, where an accused deliberately inflicts injury upon a complainant, see *Meachen* [2006] EWCA Crim 2414 and see **B2.12**.

In appropriate circumstances the presumptions in ss. 75 and 76 will apply. See **B3.10** ***et seq.***

Mens Rea

The accused must intend to penetrate the vagina or anus of another person. On a natural reading of the section, the prosecution need not prove that the accused intended the penetration should be 'sexual'. **B3.21**

As with rape, the prosecution must prove that the accused did not reasonably believe that the complainant was consenting (see **B3.11**). In appropriate circumstances, the presumptions in ss. 75 and 76 as to consent and/or reasonable belief as to consent will apply. The 'relevant act' under s. 77 is 'the defendant intentionally penetrating, with a part of his body or anything else, the vagina or anus of another person, where the penetration is sexual'.

SEXUAL ASSAULT

Sexual Offences Act 2003, s. 3 **B3.22**

(1) A person (A) commits an offence if—
 (a) he intentionally touches another person (B),
 (b) the touching is sexual,
 (c) B does not consent to the touching, and
 (d) A does not reasonably believe that B consents.
(2) Whether a belief is reasonable is to be determined having regard to all the circumstances, including any steps A has taken to ascertain whether B consents.
(3) Sections 75 and 76 apply to an offence under this section.

Sections 75 and 76 relate to the presumptions as to consent (see **B3.10** ***et seq.***).

Procedure

Sexual assault when tried on indictment is a class 3 offence. The extended jurisdiction provisions of s. 72 (see **B3.268**) apply to this offence where the victim was under 16 at the time of the offence. **B3.23**

See **B3.285** for alternative verdicts.

Indictment

Statement of Offence **B3.24**

Sexual assault contrary to section 3(1) of the Sexual Offences Act 2003.

Particulars of Offence

A on or about the . . . day of . . . sexually touched V without [his] [her] consent not reasonably believing that V was consenting.

Sentencing

The maximum sentence for an offence under the SOA 2003, s. 3, on conviction on indictment is ten years' imprisonment. On summary conviction, the maximum sentence is **B3.25** imprisonment for a term not exceeding six months or the statutory maximum fine, or both (s. 3(4)).

The SGC Guideline, *Sexual Offences Act 2003* (April 2007), applies to offenders sentenced for this offence on or after 14 May 2007. For the full text of this guideline, see **appendix 8** at part 8. Aggravating and mitigating factors are set out in the guideline, but these are additional to those set out in the SGC Guideline on *Seriousness* (December 2004), paras. 1.20 – 1.24 (see **appendix 8** at part 3). The sentences for public protection (see **E5**) must be considered in all cases of sexual assault. In every case the court should consider a disqualification from working with children (see **E23.11**) and a SOPO (see **E23.12**). There is a notification requirement under the CJA 2003, s. 80 and sch. 3, subject to the age of the offender and the sentence imposed (see **E25**).

B3.26 **Range of Sexual Assaults** The offence of sexual assault covers many activities formerly within the offence of indecent assault, although the most serious offences within that former category will now be prosecuted as rape, assault by penetration or a child sex offence. Sexual assault covers all forms of non-consensual sexual touching, but mainly applies to the lesser forms of assault.

It should be noted that, where the contact was between part of the offender's body (other than genitalia) and part of the victim's body (other than genitalia), the recommended starting point is a community order if the victim is aged 13 or over. This starting point applies to an offender of previous good character in a contested case. Different considerations apply where there is an element of persistence.

B3.27 **Nature of Sexual Touching** The exact nature of the sexual touching will be the key factor in assessing the seriousness of a sexual assault. For the purposes of the guideline, therefore, types of sexual touching are broadly grouped in terms of seriousness. In all cases, the fact that the offender has ejaculated or has caused the victim to ejaculate will increase the seriousness of the offence.

Elements

B3.28 The *actus reus* may simply be defined as touching where the touching is 'sexual' in character. There is no requirement of force or violence: the lightest touching will suffice. Nor is any element of 'hostility' required as was held to be the case in one line of indecent assault authorities. Section 79(8) provides that touching includes touching with any part of the body, with anything else, and through anything. In particular, it includes touching amounting to penetration. Touching a person through that person's clothing clearly amounts to a touching for the purposes of this offence, so too does touching the victim's clothing even though the person of the victim is not touched through clothing (*H* [2005] 1 WLR 2005 at [26]). In one area, sexual assault is narrower than indecent assault which could be committed if the accused caused the complainant to apprehend that she was about to be touched indecently (cf. *Rolfe* (1952) 36 Cr App R 4). If touching does not occur, the offence is not completed, although the circumstances may amount to an attempt.

Section 78, which provides when a touching or other activity is 'sexual', is considered at **B3.20**. If the act itself is objectively equivocal, the purpose of the defendant may be a relevant consideration as provided by s. 78(b), and that must be a reference to his own (subjective) purpose.

The prosecution must establish that the complainant did not consent to the touching (see **B3.8**).

The mental element for this offence consists of an intentional touching coupled with an absence of reasonable belief that the complainant was consenting. In *Heard* [2007] 3 All ER 306, the Court of Appeal confirmed that the prosecution must prove that the touching was deliberate, and a reckless touching is not sufficient. Voluntary intoxication cannot be relied upon as defeating intentional touching. However, if the touching is an unintended accident, such as a consequence of impairment of control of the limbs, no offence under s. 3 is committed. A drunken accident is still an accident. See **B3.8**.

In appropriate circumstances, the evidential and conclusive presumptions about consent in ss. 75 and 76 (see **B3.10** *et seq.*) may apply to this offence (s. 77).

CAUSING A PERSON TO ENGAGE IN SEXUAL ACTIVITY WITHOUT CONSENT

Sexual Offences Act 2003, s. 4 **B3.29**

(1) A person (A) commits an offence if—
  (a) he intentionally causes another person (B) to engage in an activity,
  (b) the activity is sexual,
  (c) B does not consent to engaging in the activity, and
  (d) A does not reasonably believe that B consents.
(2) Whether a belief is reasonable is to be determined having regard to all the circumstances, including any steps A has taken to ascertain whether B consents.
(3) Sections 75 and 76 apply to an offence under this section.

Procedure

Causing a person to engage in sexual activity, when tried on indictment, is a class 3 offence. It is, however, a class 2 offence where penetration is involved. The extended jurisdiction provisions of the SOA 2003, s. 72 (see **B3.268**), apply to this offence where the victim was under 16. **B3.30**

See **B3.285** for alternative verdicts.

Indictment

Statement of Offence **B3.31**

Causing a person to engage in sexual activity without consent contrary to section 4(1) of the Sexual Offences Act 2003.

Particulars of Offence

A, on or about the . . . day of . . . caused V to engage in a sexual activity without her [his] consent [namely, to allow her vagina [anus] [mouth] to be penetrated by [the penis of] another [or—to penetrate the anus or vagina of another by [V's body][an object] or—to penetrate the mouth of another by V's penis] not reasonably believing that V was consenting.

Sentencing

The maximum punishment varies according to the activity concerned and is set out in the SOA 2003, s. 4(4) and (5). **B3.32**

Sexual Offences Act 2003, s. 4

(4) A person guilty of an offence under this section, if the activity caused involved—
  (a) penetration of B's anus or vagina,
  (b) penetration of B's mouth with a person's penis,
  (c) penetration of a person's anus or vagina with a part of B's body or by B with anything else, or
  (d) penetration of a person's mouth with B's penis,
is liable, on conviction on indictment, to imprisonment for life.
(5) Unless subsection (4) applies, a person guilty of an offence under this section is liable—
  (a) on summary conviction, to imprisonment for a term not exceeding six months or to a fine not exceeding the statutory maximum or both;
  (b) on conviction on indictment, for a term not exceeding 10 years.

The SGC Guideline, *Sexual Offences Act 2003* (April 2007), applies to offenders sentenced for this offence on or after 14 May 2007. For the full text of this guideline, see **appendix 8** at part 8. The SGC has indicated sentencing ranges and starting points for the offence of causing a person to engage in sexual activity without consent. The guideline states that the same degree of seriousness applies whether an offender causes an act to take place, incites an act that actually takes place, or incites an act that does not take place only because it is prevented by factors beyond the control of the offender. The same sentencing starting points apply whether the activity was caused or incited, or actually took place, but some reduction will generally be appropriate when the incited activity does not, in fact, take place. Aggravating and mitigating factors are set out in the guideline, but these are additional to those set out in the SGC Guideline on *Seriousness* (December 2004), paras. 1.20 – 1.24 (see **appendix 8** at part 3). The sentences for public protection (see **E5**) must be considered in all cases of assault by penetration. In every case the court should consider a disqualification from working with children (see **E23.11**) and a SOPO (see **E23.12**). There is a notification requirement under the CJA 2003, s. 80 and sch. 3 (see **E25**).

Elements

B3.33 *Actus Reus* The offence covers the situation where A causes B to engage in sexual activity without B's consent, whether or not A also engages in it and whether or not A is present. The term 'activity' is not defined, and is capable of being given a wide interpretation, although it must have actually taken place. The activity which B is caused to engage in may involve B alone such as where A forces B to masturbate himself or herself, or it may be with A, or with a third person (whether or not the third person consents) or even an animal. It would include causing a person to act as a prostitute. The activity must be 'sexual' in accordance with s. 78 (see **B3.20**). The word 'causes' is not defined and so any causative conduct may suffice, including threats of violence, inducements or persuasion. The prosecution must establish that B did not consent to engaging in the activity (see **B3.8**).

This complicated new offence overlaps partly with rape which is also cast in terms of vaginal, anal or oral penetration. The offence is wider than rape, in that rape can be committed only by a man, as a principal and does not involve penetration with an object. This offence can be committed by and against persons of either sex and includes cases of 'female rape', i.e. where A causes B to penetrate her vagina with his penis. Furthermore, the offence makes A criminally liable for causing B to engage in sexual activity where B cannot himself be convicted of any offence because he has a defence such as duress or is under the age of criminal responsibility (see the discussion at [2004] Crim LR 328 at p. 330).

The aggravated form of the offence covers all the activities mentioned in s. 4(4). All involve some form of penetration, either penetration of the anus or vagina with a penis or with anything else *or* the penetration of the mouth with a penis. This attracts a maximum penalty of life imprisonment. There is a residual category of sexual activities, which do not involve any of the above penetrations, which attract the lower penalty. This category is wider than sexual assault, not least because it covers the case where A forces B to take an active role in touching a third party such as coercing the victim to masturbate another or coercing B to masturbate himself. Following the principle in *Courtie* [1984] AC 463, since different factual ingredients attract different punishments, separate offences are created and this must be reflected in the indictment.

B3.34 *Mens Rea* The accused must *intend* to cause another person to enter into the activity in the sense that it must have been deliberate. However, following the reasoning in *Heard* [2007] 3 All ER 306, an accused's state of voluntary intoxication at the time of the causing is not a relevant factor when deciding whether he had this intent. Furthermore, the prosecution does not have to prove that the accused intended the activity to be 'sexual'.

As with all non-consensual offences, the prosecution must prove that the defendant did not reasonably believe the complainant (B) was consenting (see **B3.8**). This would appear to apply to the time when the complainant engaged in the activity.

Presumptions In appropriate circumstances, the SOA 2003, ss. 75 and 76 (evidential presumptions and conclusive presumptions about consent), will apply to this offence (see **B3.10** ***et seq.***). Under s. 77, the 'relevant act' is 'the defendant intentionally penetrating, with a part of his body or anything else, the vagina or anus of another person, where the penetration is sexual'. **B3.35**

RAPE AND OTHER OFFENCES AGAINST CHILDREN UNDER 13

Sections 5 to 8 of the SOA 2003 mirror the non-consensual offences in ss. 1 to 4 of the Act but apply specifically to cases where the child is under 13. In respect of each section, any apparent consent is irrelevant for the purposes of proving the offence as is any mistake as to the child's age. The offences are gender neutral. **B3.36**

Exceptions to Aiding, Abetting and Counselling

Sexual Offences Act 2003, s. 73 **B3.37**

(1) A person is not guilty of aiding, abetting or counselling the commission against a child of an offence to which this section applies if he acts for the purpose of—
  (a) protecting the child from sexually transmitted infection,
  (b) protecting the physical safety of the child,
  (c) preventing the child from becoming pregnant, or
  (d) promoting the child's emotional well-being by the giving of advice,
and not for the purpose of obtaining sexual gratification or for the purpose of causing or encouraging the activity constituting the offence or the child's participation in it.

(2) This section applies to—
  (a) an offence under any of sections 5 to 7 (offences against children under 13);
  (b) an offence under section 9 (sexual activity with a child);
  (c) an offence under section 13 which would be an offence under section 9 if the offender were aged 18;
  (d) an offence under any of sections 16, 25, 30, 34 and 38 (sexual activity) against a person under 16.

(3) This section does not affect any other enactment or any rule of law restricting the circumstances in which a person is guilty of aiding, abetting or counselling an offence under this part.

Section 73 exempts a person from liability for aiding, abetting, or counselling the commission of an offence against a child in circumstances where the person acts for the purposes specified in the section and not for sexual gratification. Section 73 applies to a number of offences dealt with in the remainder of this section.

Rape of a Child under 13

Sexual Offences Act 2003, s. 5 **B3.38**

(1) A person commits an offence if—
  (a) he intentionally penetrates the vagina, anus or mouth of another person with his penis, and
  (b) the other person is under 13.

Procedure

An allegation of an offence contrary to s. 5 is triable only on indictment and is a class 2 offence. It is also an offence to which the extra-territorial jurisdiction provisions of s. 72 apply (see **B3.268**). **B3.39**

See **B3.285** for alternative verdicts.

Indictment

B3.40 *Statement of Offence*

Rape of a child under 13 contrary to section 5 of the Sexual Offences Act 2003

Particulars of Offence

A, on or about the . . . day of . . . penetrated the [vagina][anus][mouth] of V a child then under the age of 13 years with his penis.

Sentencing

B3.41 The maximum sentence is imprisonment for life (s. 5(2)).

The SGC Guideline, *Sexual Offences Act 2003* (April 2007), applies to offenders sentenced on or after 14 May 2007 for rape of a child under 13. For the full text of this guideline, see **appendix 8**, at part 8. The SGC has determined that the sentencing starting points established in *Millberry* [2003] 1 WLR 546 should apply to all non-consensual offences involving penetration of the anus or vagina, or penile penetration of the mouth. The starting point for rape of a child under 13 where there are no aggravating factors is 10 years, rising to 13 years for cases involving any of the particular aggravating factors identified in the guideline. The aggravating and mitigating factors in the guideline are additional to those set out in the SGC Guideline on *Seriousness* (December 2004), paras. 1.20 – 1.24 (see **appendix 8** at part 3). The sentences for public protection (see **E5**) must be considered in all cases of rape. In every case the court should consider a disqualification from working with children (see **E23.11**) and a SOPO (see **E23.12**). There is a notification requirement under the CJA 2003, s. 80 and sch. 3 (see **E25**).

Elements

B3.42 The elements of the offence are the same as those for rape and reference should therefore be made to **B3.7** to **B3.15**.

In contrast to rape of an adult, consent to sexual intercourse is no defence and so there is no requirement on the prosecution to prove that the accused did not reasonably believe that the victim was consenting. The position in respect of a child close to her 13th birthday where the accused maintains that the sex was consensual has caused some difficulties in practice. Strictly speaking, so far as it is relevant, the issue of consent is for the trial judge in a *Newton* hearing and CPS policy is simply to charge an accused with the s. 5 offence. But some judges have resisted depriving a jury of the opportunity of deciding such an important issue and encouraged the prosecution to charge rape under s. 1 with the s. 5 offence as an alternative. Plainly, this does not appear to have been the Parliamentary intention.

In respect of ss. 5 to 8, it is necessary to prove that the victim was under the age of 13 at the time of the offence but the sections do not require the prosecution to prove that the accused knew or suspected that the child was under that age. In *Corran* [2005] 2 Cr App R (S) 253 the Court of Appeal stated that a mistaken belief as to the child's age will only amount to mitigation. In *G (Secretary of State for the Home Department intervening)* [2006] 1 WLR 2052, the 15-year-old accused had pleaded guilty to an offence under s. 5 committed with a 12-year-old. The plea was entered on an accepted basis that the complainant consented and the offender thought she was 15 years old. His appeal was on the grounds that s. 5 was incompatible with the ECHR, Articles 6 and 8. The Court rejected the Article 6 argument, holding that there was no incompatibility between that Article and s. 5. But the prosecution of a child under s. 5 rather than s. 13 could, on the particular facts, produce consequences that infringed the child's Article 8(1) rights in ways that could not be justified under Article 8(2). For example, the child could theoretically be sentenced to detention for life and be made subject to the notification requirements for sex offenders. But if no criticism could be made of the initial decision to charge under s. 5 then it was not necessary for a judge to substitute a charge under s. 13 simply because it later transpired that the sexual intercourse was consensual. The judge could ensure that there was no breach of Article 8 by adjusting the sentence appropriately. The House of Lords has since granted leave to appeal the decision of the Court of Appeal.

The provisions of s. 73 apply to this offence (see **B3.37**).

Assault of a Child under 13 by Penetration

Sexual Offences Act 2003, s. 6 **B3.43**

(1) A person commits an offence if—
  (a) he intentionally penetrates the vagina or anus of another person with a part of his body or anything else,
  (b) the penetration is sexual, and
  (c) the other person is under 13.

Procedure

B3.44 An allegation of an offence contrary to s. 6 is triable only on indictment and is a class 2 offence. It is an offence to which the extra-territorial jurisdiction provisions of s. 72 apply (see B3.268).

See **B3.285** for alternative verdicts.

Indictment

Statement of Offence **B3.45**

Assault of a child under 13 by penetration contrary to section 6 of the Sexual Offences Act 2003

Particulars of Offence

A, on or about the . . . day of . . . penetrated the vagina [anus] of V a child then under the age of 13 years.

Sentencing

B3.46 The maximum sentence is imprisonment for life (s. 6(2)).

The SGC Guideline, *Sexual Offences Act 2003* (April 2007), applies to offenders sentenced on or after 14 May 2007 for assault of a child under 13 by penetration. For the full text of this guideline, see **appendix 8** at part 8. The SGC has indicated sentencing ranges and starting points for the offence of assault by penetration, distinguishing between cases of penetration involving a part of the offender's body, penetration with an object and cases where penetration is accompanied by other factors such as abduction of the victim, abuse of trust, etc. Aggravating and mitigating factors in the Guideline are additional to those set out in the SGC Guideline on *Seriousness* (December 2004), paras. 1.20 – 1.24 (see **appendix 8** at part 3). The sentences for public protection (see **E5**) must be considered in all cases of assault by penetration. In every case the court should consider a disqualification from working with children (see **E23.11**) and a SOPO (see **E23.12**). There is a notification requirement under the CJA 2003, s. 80 and sch. 3 (see **E25**).

Initial indications on sentencing in respect of the offence of assault of a child under 13 by penetration were given by the Court of Appeal in *Corran* [2005] 2 Cr App R (S) 453. The Court said that although life imprisonment was the maximum sentence, the punishment level would depend on the particular circumstances. No precise guidance could be given. Where young offenders were involved, factors relating to sentence would include presence of consent; the offender's age compared to the victim's age (so for a teenager, where the other party consented, a short custodial period would suffice); the relationship between the offender and the victim; their respective characters and maturity; the number of occasions of penetration and its circumstances, such as contraception being used; the emotional and physical consequences for the victim; the degree of remorse of the offender. A mitigating factor for a young offender would be a reasonable belief that the victim was 16, and a plea of guilty would be pertinent.

Elements

B3.47 The basic elements of the offence are the same as those governing such an assault on an adult and reference should therefore be made to **B3.16** to **B3.21**. However, consent is no defence and so there is no requirement on the prosecution to prove that the accused did not reasonably believe that the victim was consenting. It is necessary to prove that the victim was under the age of 13 at the time of the offence, but as with s. 5, it is not necessary to show that the accused knew or suspected that to be the case (see **B3.42**).

Section 73 applies to this offence (see **B3.37**).

Sexual Assault of a Child under 13

B3.48 Sexual Offences Act 2003, s. 7

(1) A person commits an offence if—
 (a) he intentionally touches another person,
 (b) the touching is sexual, and
 (c) the other person is under 13.

Procedure

B3.49 An allegation of an offence contrary to s. 7 is triable either way; when tried on indictment, it is a class 3 offence upon trial. The extra-territorial jurisdiction provisions of s. 72 apply (see **B3.268**)

See **B3.285** for alternative verdicts.

Indictment

B3.50 *Statement of Offence*

Sexual assault of a child under 13 contrary to section 7 of the Sexual Offences Act 2003

Particulars of Offence

A, on or about the . . . day of . . . sexually touched V, then a child under the age of 13 years.

Sentencing

B3.51 The maximum sentence for an offence under the SOA 2003, s. 7, on conviction on indictment is 14 years' imprisonment. On summary conviction, the maximum sentence is imprisonment for a term not exceeding six months or the statutory maximum fine, or both.

The SGC Guideline, *Sexual Offences Act 2003* (April 2007), applies to offenders sentenced on or after 14 May 2007 for sexual assault of a child under 13. For the full text of this guideline, see **appendix 8** at part 8. Aggravating and mitigating factors in the guideline are additional to those set out in the SGC Guideline on *Seriousness* (December 2004), paras. 1.20 – 1.24 (see **appendix 8** at part 3). The sentences for public protection (see **E5**) must be considered in all cases of sexual assault. In every case the court should consider a disqualification from working with children (see **E23.11**) and a SOPO (see **E23.12**). There is a notification requirement under the CJA 2003, s. 80 and sch. 3, if the offender was aged 18 or over or was sentenced to at least 12 months' imprisonment (see **E25**).

Elements

B3.52 The elements of this offence are the same as for the adult offence (see **B3.28**) save that consent is not a defence. It is submitted that there is a necessary implication that this offence is one of strict liability as to age: see by analogy *K* [2002] 1 AC 642.

In respect of aiding, abetting and counselling, s. 73 applies to this offence (see **B3.37**).

Causing or Inciting a Child under 13 to Engage in Sexual Activity

Sexual Offences Act 2003, s. 8 B3.53

(1) A person commits an offence if—
- (a) he intentionally causes or incites another person (B) to engage in an activity,
- (b) the activity is sexual, and
- (c) B is under 13.

Procedure

An allegation of an offence contrary to s. 8 is triable either way, except where the activity involved is penetrative when the allegation is triable on indictment only. It is ordinarily a class 3 offence when tried on indictment, but if the activity involves penetration then it is a class 2 offence. The extra-territorial jurisdiction provisions of s. 72 apply (see **B3.268**). B3.54

See **B3.285** for alternative verdicts.

Indictment

Statement of Offence B3.55

Causing or inciting a child under 13 to engage in sexual activity contrary to section 8 of the Sexual Offences Act 2003

Particulars of Offence

A, on or about the . . . day of . . . caused V, then a child under the age of 13 years, to engage in sexual activity consisting of the penetration of V's [anus] [vagina] [mouth] with a part of V's body [an object].

Sentencing

The maximum sentence for an offence under the SOA 2003, s. 8, varies according to the type of activity involved. B3.56

Sexual Offences Act 2003, s. 8

(2) A person guilty of an offence under this section, if the activity caused or incited involved—
- (a) penetration of B's anus or vagina,
- (b) penetration of B's mouth with a person's penis,
- (c) penetration of a person's anus or vagina with a part of B's body or by B with anything else, or
- (d) penetration of a person's mouth with B's penis

is liable, on conviction on indictment, to imprisonment for life.

(3) Unless subsection (2) applies, a person guilty of an offence under this section is liable—
- (a) on summary conviction, to imprisonment for a term not exceeding 6 months or to a fine not exceeding the statutory maximum or both;
- (b) on conviction on indictment, to imprisonment for a term not exceeding 14 years.

The SGC Guideline, *Sexual Offences Act 2003* (April 2007), applies to offenders sentenced for this offence on or after 14 May 2007. For the full text of this guideline, see **appendix 8** at part 8. Aggravating and mitigating factors in the guideline are additional to those set out in the SGC Guideline on *Seriousness* (December 2004), paras. 1.20 – 1.24 (see **appendix 8** at part 3). The sentences for public protection (see E5) must be considered in all cases of causing or inciting a child under 13 to engage in sexual activity. In every case the court should consider a disqualification from working with children (see **E23.11**) and a SOPO (see **E23.12**). There is a notification requirement under the CJA 2003, s. 80 and sch. 3 (see E25).

Elements

The basic elements of the offence of causing a child to engage in sexual activity are the same as those relating to the corresponding offence in relation to an adult and reference should therefore be made to **B3.29** to **B3.35**. In contrast to a similar offence against an adult, B3.57

consent is no defence and so there is no requirement on the prosecution to prove that the accused did not reasonably believe that the victim was consenting. It is necessary to prove that the victim was under the age of 13 at the time of the offence.

In *Walker* [2006] EWCA Crim 1907, the Court of Appeal held that the essence of the offence of incitement was the encouragement of a person under the age of 13 to engage in the activity. It is that encouragement that has to be intentional or deliberate. It is not necessary to prove that the accused intended that the encouraged sexual activity should actually happen. On the face of it, that is at odds with the general position in relation to incitement that a person must intend that the activity incited actually take place (see **A6.7**). In *Jones* [2007] EWCA Crim 1118, the Court of Appeal held that the gravamen of the offence is the incitement of children under the age of 13 to engage in sexual activity; it is not concerned with the effect on a particular child. In *Jones*, graffiti had been written on the walls of toilets on trains and in railway stations. The graffiti offered payment for sex to girls between the ages of 8 and 13 and a contact number was given. A police officer pretending to be a 12-year-old girl made contact with J. J and the officer exchanged text messages clarifying her pretended age and the sex acts he wished to perform. They arranged to meet and J was arrested. He was convicted of an offence contrary to s. 8. He appealed contending, *inter alia*, that he did not have the requisite intent because it was an essential element of the offence that he intended to cause an actual child under the age of 13 to engage in sexual activity. The Court of Appeal held that the criminality at which the offence is aimed is the incitement and it matters not if this is directed at a particular child or a very large group of children, or whether the child or children can be identified.

For the meaning of 'sexual', see **B3.20**.

CHILD SEX OFFENCES

B3.58 The child sex offences under the SOA 2003 Act which protect children under the age of 16 are contained in ss. 9 to 15 of the Act. In contrast to ss. 5 to 8, a reasonable mistaken belief as to the child's age will be capable of founding a defence but only if the child is 13 years of age or older. The offences are all gender neutral.

Sexual Activity with a Child

B3.59 **Sexual Offences Act 2003, s. 9**

(1) A person aged 18 or over (A) commits an offence if—
 (a) he intentionally touches another person (B),
 (b) the touching is sexual, and
 (c) either—
  (i) B is under 16 and A does not reasonably believe that B is 16 or over, or
  (ii) B is under 13.

Procedure

B3.60 An allegation of an offence contrary to s. 9 is triable either way unless the sexual activity involves penetration, in which case it is triable only on indictment. It is a class 3 offence when tried on indictment. The extra-territorial jurisdiction provisions of s. 72 apply (see **B3.268**). See **B3.285** for alternative verdicts.

Indictment

B3.61 *Statement of Offence*

Sexual activity with a child contrary to section 9(1) of the Sexual Offences Act 2003.

Particulars of Offence

A, on or about the . . . day of . . ., being then a person aged 18 or over, intentionally sexually touched V, then a child under the age of [16] [13] years
or

A, on or about the . . . day of . . ., being then a person aged 18 or over, intentionally sexually touched V, then a child under the age of [16] [13] years, by penetrating V's [anus] [vagina] with a part of A's body, namely . . . [an object]

Sentencing

B3.62 The maximum sentence for an offence under the SOA 2003, s. 9, varies according to the activity involved.

Sexual Offences Act 2003, s. 9

(2) A person guilty of an offence under this section, if the touching involved—
  (a) penetration of B's anus or vagina with a part of A's body or anything else,
  (b) penetration of B's mouth with A's penis,
  (c) penetration of A's anus or vagina with a part of B's body, or
  (d) penetration of A's mouth with B's penis,
is liable, on conviction on indictment, to imprisonment for a term not exceeding 14 years.

(3) Unless subsection (2) applies, a person guilty of an offence under this section is liable—
  (a) on summary conviction, to imprisonment for a term not exceeding 6 months or to a fine not exceeding the statutory maximum or both;
  (b) on conviction on indictment, to imprisonment for a term not exceeding 14 years.

The maximum penalty also varies with the age of the offender. If the offender is aged under 18, the maximum penalty is five years (see **B3.81**).

The SGC Guideline, *Sexual Offences Act 2003* (April 2007), applies to offenders sentenced for sexual activity with a child on or after 14 May 2007. For the full text of this guideline, see **appendix 8** at part 8. There are separate guidelines for offenders aged 18 and over (guideline 3A) and offenders aged under 18 (guideline 7). Aggravating and mitigating factors in the guideline are additional to those set out in the SGC Guideline on *Seriousness* (December 2004), paras. 1.20 – 1.24 (see **appendix 8** at part 3). The sentences for public protection (see **E5**) must be considered in all cases of causing or inciting a child under 13 to engage in sexual activity. In every case the court should consider a disqualification from working with children (see **E23.11**) and a SOPO (see **E23.12**). There is a notification requirement under the CJA 2003, s. 80 and sch. 3 (see **E25**).

Where penetration has occurred, the appropriate sentence will depend upon a range of factors, including the respective ages of the parties, especially where there is a significant gap in their ages, the degree of breach of trust, planning or corruption involved. In *Davies* [2006] 1 Cr App R (S) 213, the offender was 19 and the victim 13. The offender said that sexual intercourse had been consensual and the victim had told him she was 15. The offender had numerous previous convictions, but none for sexual offences. The Court of Appeal said that a sentence of nine months' detention in a young offender institution was appropriate on a guilty plea. In *Chadwick* [2006] 1 Cr App R (S) 641, the respective ages of the parties were also 19 and 13, and sexual intercourse took place at a social event when both parties were drunk, the offender having given the victim alcohol. A sentence of six months' detention in a young offender institution was appropriate on a plea for an offender with no previous convictions. A more serious case is *Wingrove* [2006] 1 Cr App R (S) 232, where the offender was 22 and the victim was 13. The offender had sexual intercourse with her on three occasions and although he pleaded guilty at the first opportunity, reports indicated that he failed to appreciate the seriousness of what he had done. An extended sentence of four years, with a custodial term of two years, was appropriate.

A different category of the offence is represented by *Lister* [2006] 1 Cr App R (S) 369, where the offender was a 31-year-old physical education teacher in a school who admitted sexual activity with a 15-year-old girl at the school. The sexual activity amounted to passionate embracing and kissing. The Court of Appeal said that the appropriate sentence was one of nine months' imprisonment. In *Held* [2007] 1 Cr App R (S) 118, the offender was a

41-year-old woman with no previous convictions who assisted in coaching a girls' football team. She pleaded guilty to sexual activity in the course of a relationship lasting several months with a 14-year-old girl, who was a member of the team. The offender admitting kissing her breasts and partially penetrating the girl's vagina with her fingers. A sentence of 12 months' imprisonment was upheld by the Court of Appeal, on the basis that the offence involved a considerable abuse of trust, and despite hardship occasioned to the offender's family.

Elements

B3.63 The basic elements of the offence are the same as those in respect of such an assault on an adult and reference should therefore be made to **B3.22** to **B3.28**.

As to 'sexual', see **B3.20**. For 'touching', see **B3.28**.

In addition, it is a defence if, even though the complainant was under 16, the accused reasonably believed the complainant to be 16 years old or older. The defence is not available if the child is under 13.

The provisions of s. 73 apply to this offence (see **B3.37**).

Causing or Inciting a Child to Engage in Sexual Activity

B3.64 Sexual Offences Act 2003, s. 10

(1) A person aged 18 or over (A) commits an offence if—
(a) he intentionally causes or incites another person (B) to engage in an activity,
(b) the activity is sexual, and
(c) either—
(i) B is under 16 and A does not reasonably believe that B is 16 or over, or
(ii) B is under 13.

Procedure

B3.65 An allegation of an offence contrary to s. 10 is ordinarily triable either way but, where the activity involves penetration, it is indictable only. Upon trial on indictment, it is a class 3 offence but where penetration is involved it is a class 2 offence. The extra-territorial jurisdiction provisions of s. 72 apply (see **B3.268**).

See **B3.285** for alternative verdicts.

Indictment

B3.66 *Statement of Offence*

Intentionally causing or inciting a child to engage in a sexual activity contrary to section 10(1) of the Sexual Offences Act 2003.

Particulars of Offence

A, on or about the . . . day of . . . [being then a person aged 18 or over] intentionally caused or incited V, then a child under [16] [13] years of age, to engage in a sexual activity, namely . . .

or

A, on or about the . . . day of . . . [being then a person aged 18 years or over] intentionally caused or incited V, then a child under the age of [16] [13] years, to engage in sexual activity, namely the penetration of V's [anus] [vagina] by another

Sentencing

B3.67 The maximum sentence for an offence under the SOA 2003, s. 10, varies according to the activity concerned. Section 10(2) and (3) indicate the maximum sentence which applies and in terms almost identical to s. 9(2) and (3) (see **B3.62**).

The maximum penalty also varies with the age of the offender. If the offender is aged under 18, the maximum penalty is five years (see **B3.81**).

The SGC Guideline, *Sexual Offences Act 2003* (April 2007), applies to offenders sentenced for causing or inciting a child to engage in sexual activity on or after 14 May 2007. For the full text of this guideline, see **appendix 8** at part 8. There are separate guidelines for offenders aged 18 and over (guideline 3A) and offenders aged under 18 (guideline 7). Aggravating and mitigating factors in the guideline are additional to those set out in the SGC Guideline on *Seriousness* (December 2004), paras. 1.20 – 1.24 (see **appendix 8** at part 3). The sentences for public protection (see **E5**) must be considered in all cases of causing or inciting a child under 13 to engage in sexual activity. In every case the court should consider a disqualification from working with children (see **E23.11**) and a SOPO (see **E23.12**). There is a notification requirement under the CJA 2003, s. 80 and sch. 3 (see **E25**).

Elements

The offender must be at least 18 years of age. Plainly, when the victim is under the age of 13, then the offence will be covered by s. 8. A reasonable belief that the victim was over 16 years of age affords a defence unless the victim was under 13. **B3.68**

For the meaning of 'sexual' see **B3.20**.

Engaging in Sexual Activity in the Presence of a Child

Sexual Offences Act 2003, s. 11 **B3.69**

(1) A person aged 18 or over (A) commits an offence if—
- (a) he intentionally engages in an activity,
- (b) the activity is sexual,
- (c) for the purpose of obtaining sexual gratification, he engages in it—
  - (i) when another person (B) is present or is in a place from which A can be observed, and
  - (ii) knowing or believing that B is aware, or intending that B should be aware, that he is engaging in it, and
- (d) either—
  - (i) B is under 16 and A does not reasonably believe that B is 16 or over, or
  - (ii) B is under 13.

Procedure

An allegation of an offence contrary to s. 11 is triable either way; when tried on indictment it is a class 3 offence. The extra-territorial jurisdiction provisions of s. 72 apply (see **B3.268**). **B3.70**

See **B3.285** for alternative verdicts.

Indictment

Statement of Offence **B3.71**

Intentionally engaging in sexual activity in the presence of a child contrary to section 11(1) of the Sexual Offences Act 2003.

Particulars of Offence

A, on or about the . . . day of . . . [being then a person aged 18 years or over] intentionally engaged in a sexual activity for the purpose of obtaining sexual gratification from knowing that V, then a child under the age of [16][13] years was present or was in a place from which he could observe A and knew [believed] that V was aware that he was engaging in it [intending that V should be aware that he was engaging in it]

Sentencing

The maximum sentence for an offence under the SOA 2003, s. 11 on indictment is ten years' imprisonment. On summary conviction, the maximum sentence is six months or a fine not exceeding the statutory maximum, or both (s. 11(2)). **B3.72**

The maximum penalty also varies with the age of the offender. If the offender is aged under 18, the maximum penalty is five years (see **B3.81**).

The SGC Guideline, *Sexual Offences Act 2003* (April 2007), applies to offenders sentenced for engaging in sexual activity in the presence of a child on or after 14 May 2007. For the full text of this guideline, see **appendix 8** at part 8. There are separate guidelines for offenders aged 18 and over (guideline 3A) and offenders aged under 18 (guideline 7). Aggravating and mitigating factors in the guideline are additional to those set out in the SGC Guideline on *Seriousness* (December 2004), paras. 1.20 – 1.24 (see **appendix 8** at part 3). The sentences for public protection (see **E5**) must be considered in all cases of causing or inciting a child under 13 to engage in sexual activity. In every case the court should consider a disqualification from working with children (see **E23.11**) and a SOPO (see **E23.12**). There is a notification requirement under the CJA 2003, s. 80 and sch. 3 (see **E25**).

Elements

B3.73 The offender must be aged 18 or over and must intentionally engage in sexual activity with a person other than the victim.

It is a defence that the alleged offender reasonably believed the victim to be aged 16 or over unless the victim is under 13.

For 'sexual gratification', see **B3.78**. For the meaning of 'sexual', see **B3.20**.

Causing a Child to Watch a Sex Act

B3.74 **Sexual Offences Act 2003, s. 12**

(1) A person aged 18 or over (A) commits an offence if—
  (a) for the purpose of obtaining sexual gratification, he intentionally causes another person (B) to watch a third person engaging in an activity, or to look at an image of any person engaging in an activity,
  (b) the activity is sexual, and
  (c) either—
    (i) B is under 16 and A does not reasonably believe that B is 16 or over, or
    (ii) B is under 13.

Procedure

B3.75 An allegation of an offence contrary to s. 12 is triable either way; when tried on indictment it is a class 3 offence. The extra-territorial jurisdiction provisions of s. 72 apply (see **B3.268**).

See **B3.285** for alternative verdicts.

Indictment

B3.76 *Statement of Offence*

Causing a child to watch a sexual act contrary to section 12(1) of the Sexual Offences Act 2003

Particulars of Offence

A, on or about the . . . day of . . . [being then a person aged 18 years or over] for the purpose of obtaining sexual gratification for himself intentionally caused V a child under the age of [16][13] years to watch a third person engaging in [or][look at an image of another person engaging in], a sexual activity, the said A not reasonably believing that V was aged 16 or over.

Sentencing

B3.77 The maximum sentence for an offence under the SOA 2003, s. 12 on conviction on indictment is ten years' imprisonment. On summary conviction the maximum sentence is six months or a fine not exceeding the statutory maximum, or both (s. 12(2)).

The maximum penalty also varies with the age of the offender. If the offender is aged under 18, the maximum penalty is five years (see **B3.81**).

The SGC Guideline, *Sexual Offences Act 2003* (April 2007), applies to offenders sentenced for causing a child to watch a sexual act on or after 14 May 2007. For the full text of this guideline, see **appendix 8** at part 8. There are separate guidelines for offenders aged 18 and over (guideline 3A) and offenders aged under 18 (guideline 7). Aggravating and mitigating factors in the guideline are additional to those set out in the SGC Guideline on *Seriousness* (December 2004), paras. 1.20 – 1.24 (see **appendix 8** at part 3). The sentences for public protection (see **E5**) must be considered in all cases of causing or inciting a child under 13 to engage in sexual activity. In every case the court should consider a disqualification from working with children (see **E23.11**) and a SOPO (see **E23.12**). There is a notification requirement under the CJA 2003, s. 80 and sch. 3 (see **E25**).

Elements

The offender must be aged 18 or over and must intentionally engage in sexual activity with a person other than the victim. **B3.78**

It is a defence that the alleged offender reasonably believed the victim to be aged 16 or over unless the victim was under 13.

For the meaning of 'sexual', see **B3.20**.

In *Abdullahi* [2007] 1 WLR 225, the Court of Appeal considered whether it was necessary for the purposes of s. 12 for the sexual gratification to be simultaneous or contemporaneous or synchronised with the watching of the sexual activity or image. The court ruled that there was nothing in the language of s. 12 to suggest that that was the case and consequently the gratification could be deferred until much later. (For commentary on this case by Professor David Ormerod, see [2007] Crim LR 184.)

The offence has a 'bolted on intent' in that the intentional act must be 'for the purpose of obtaining sexual gratification'. It is therefore an offence of specific intent and, consequently, voluntary intoxication may negate the intent required for the offence (*Heard* [2007] 3 All ER 306).

Child Sex Offences Committed by Children or Young Persons

Sexual Offences Act 2003, s. 13 **B3.79**

(1) A person under 18 commits an offence if he does anything which would be an offence under any of sections 9 to 12 if he were aged 18.
(2) A person guilty of an offence under this section is liable—
   (a) on summary conviction, to imprisonment for a term not exceeding 6 months or a fine not exceeding the statutory maximum or both;
   (b) on conviction on indictment, to imprisonment for a term not exceeding 5 years.

Procedure

An allegation of an offence contrary to s. 13 is triable either way; when tried on indictment it is a class 3 offence. The extra-territorial jurisdiction provisions of s. 72 apply (see **B3.268**). **B3.80**

See **B3.285** for alternative verdicts.

Sentencing

The maximum sentence for an offence under s. 13 on conviction on indictment is five years' imprisonment. On summary conviction, the maximum is six months or a fine not exceeding the statutory maximum, or both (s. 13(2)). **B3.81**

The SGC Guideline, *Sexual Offences Act 2003* (April 2007), applies to offenders under 18 sentenced for these offences on or after 14 May 2007. For the full text of the relevant guidelines, see **appendix** 8 at part 8. There is in each case a notification requirement under the CJA 2003, s. 80 and sch. 3 if the offender was sentenced to at least 12 months' imprisonment (see E25).

Elements

B3.82 For the elements of the offences contrary to ss. 9 to 12, see **B3.63**, **B3.68**, **B3.73** and **B3.78**.

If the offence charged under s. 13 would amount to an offence under s. 9 if the offender was aged 18, then the provisions of s. 73 apply (see **B3.37**).

Arranging or Facilitating Commission of a Child Sex Offence

B3.83 Sexual Offences Act 2003, s. 14

(1) A person commits an offence if—
   (a) he intentionally arranges or facilitates something that he intends to do, intends another person to do, or believes that another person will do, in any part of the world, and
   (b) doing it will involve the commission of an offence under any of sections 9 to 13.
(2) A person does not commit an offence under this section if—
   (a) he arranges or facilitates something that he believes another person will do, but that he does not intend to do or intend another person to do, and
   (b) any offence within subsection (1)(b) would be an offence against a child for whose protection he acts.
(3) For the purposes of subsection (2), a person acts for the protection of a child if he acts for the purpose of—
   (a) protecting the child from sexually transmitted infection,
   (b) protecting the physical safety of the child,
   (c) preventing the child from becoming pregnant, or
   (d) promoting the child's emotional well-being by the giving of advice,
   and not for the purpose of obtaining sexual gratification or for the purpose of causing or encouraging the activity constituting the offence within subsection (1)(b) or the child's participation in it.

Procedure

B3.84 An allegation of an offence contrary to s. 14 is triable either way; when tried on indictment it is a class 3 offence. The extra-territorial jurisdiction provisions of s. 72 apply (see **B3.268**).

See **B3.285** for alternative verdicts.

Indictment

B3.85 *Statement of Offence*

Arranging or facilitating commission of a child sex offence contrary to section 14(1) of the Sexual Offences Act 2003.

Particulars of Offence

A, on [or about] the . . . day of . . . intentionally arranged the doing or facilitating of an act [intending that it be done] [by himself] [by another] [believing that it would be done by another] [in any part of the world] and knowing that the doing of it will involve [sexual activity with a child under 16 years of age] [causing or inciting a child under the age of 16 to engage in sexual activity][causing or inciting a child under 16 years of age to engage in sexual activity][engaging in sexual activity in the presence of a child under 16 years of age][causing a child under 16 years of age to watch a sexual act].

Sentencing

The maximum sentence for an offence under the SOA 2003, s. 14, on conviction on indictment is 14 years' imprisonment. On summary conviction, the maximum sentence is six months or a fine not exceeding the statutory maximum, or both (s. 14(4)). B3.86

The SGC Guideline, *Sexual Offences Act 2003* (April 2007), applies to offenders sentenced on or after 14 May 2007 for arranging or facilitating a child sex offence. For the full text of this guideline, see **appendix 8** at part 8. Aggravating and mitigating factors in the guideline are additional to those set out in the SGC Guideline on *Seriousness* (December 2004), paras. 1.20 – 1.24 (see **appendix 8** at part 3). The sentences for public protection (see E5) must be considered in all cases of sexual assault. In every case the court should consider a disqualification from working with children (see **E23.11**) and a SOPO (see **E23.12**). There is a notification requirement under the CJA 2003, s. 80 and sch. 3, if the offender was aged 18 or over or was sentenced to at least 12 months' imprisonment (see **E25**).

Elements

The elements of offences under ss. 9 to 13 are set out in **B3.63, B3.68, B3.73, B3.78** and **B3.80.** B3.87

The defence set out in s. 14(2) would cover such acts for the physical and emotional well-being of a child as the provision of contraceptives and the giving of advice as an 'agony aunt'.

Meeting a Child following Sexual Grooming

Sexual Offences Act 2003, s. 15 B3.88

(1) A person aged 18 or over (A) commits an offence if—
- (a) having met or communicated with another person (B) on at least two earlier occasions, he—
  - (i) intentionally meets B, or
  - (ii) travels with the intention of meeting B in any part of the world,
- (b) at the time, he intends to do anything to or in respect of B, during or after the meeting and in any part of the world, which if done will involve the commission by A of a relevant offence,
- (c) B is under 16, and
- (d) A does not reasonably believe that B is 16 or over.

(2) In subsection (1)—
- (a) the reference to A having met or communicated with B is a reference to A having met B in any part of the world or having communicated with B by any means from, to or in any part of the world;
- (b) 'relevant offence' means—
  - (i) an offence under this part,
  - (ii) an offence within any of paragraphs 61 to 92 of schedule 3, or
  - (iii) anything done outside England and Wales and Northern Ireland which is not an offence within sub-paragraph (i) or (ii) but would be an offence within sub-paragraph (i) if done in England and Wales.

Procedure

An allegation of an offence contrary to s. 15 is triable either way; when tried on indictment it is a class 3 offence. The extra-territorial jurisdiction provisions of s. 72 apply (see **B3.268**). See **B3.285** for alternative verdicts. B3.89

Indictment

Statement of Offence B3.90

Meeting a child following sexual grooming contrary to section 15(1) of the Sexual Offences Act 2003

Particulars of Offence

A, on or about the . . . day of . . . having met or communicated with V a child under the age of 16 years on two earlier occasions intentionally met V [travelled with the intention of meeting V] and with intent to [specify facts constituting relevant offence].

Sentencing

B3.91 The maximum sentence for an offence under the SOA 2003, s. 15, on conviction on indictment is ten years' imprisonment. On summary conviction, the maximum is six months or a fine not exceeding the statutory maximum, or both (s. 15(4)).

The SGC Guideline, *Sexual Offences Act 2003* (April 2007), applies to offenders sentenced on or after 14 May 2007 for meeting a child following sexual grooming. For the full text of this guideline, see **appendix 8** at part 8. Aggravating and mitigating factors in the guideline are additional to those set out in the SGC Guideline on *Seriousness* (December 2004), paras. 1.20 – 1.24 (see **appendix 8** at part 3). The sentences for public protection (see **E5**) must be considered in all cases of sexual grooming. In every case the court should consider a disqualification from working with children (see **E23.11**) and a SOPO (see **E23.12**). There is a notification requirement under the CJA 2003, s. 80 and sch. 3 (see **E25**).

In *Raza* [2007] 1 Cr App R (S) 79, the 55-year-old offender was convicted after a trial of abducting a child from the care of her foster parents for a short period of time, and meeting a child following sexual grooming contrary to s. 15. The victim was aged 13 and had severe learning difficulties and significant behavioural problems. A sentence of imprisonment of three and a half years was upheld. See also *Mansfield* [2005] EWCA Crim 927.

Elements

B3.92 The offender must be aged 18 or over and a reasonable belief that the victim was 16 or over constitutes a defence.

A relevant offence is defined under s. 15(2) as being any offence under part 1 or paras. 61 to 92 of sch. 3 to the Act. Part 1 is comprised of ss. 1 to 79 and the sch. 3 paragraphs referred to identify sexual offences under the law of Northern Ireland.

ABUSE OF A POSITION OF TRUST

B3.93 Offences involving abuse of a position of trust are contained in ss. 16 to 19 of the SOA 2003. The conditions giving rise to a position of trust between A and B are set out in s. 21.

The offences set out in ss. 16 to 19 essentially correspond to the offences under ss. 9 to 12 but with the added element of the breach of trust and some other minor differences.

Section 22 provides further definitions relevant to the operation of ss. 16 to 19.

Sections 23 and 24 make specific provision for defences to charges under ss. 16 to 19. Section 23 provides a defence to such a charge if B is aged 16 or over and A and B are either lawfully married or civil partners of each other. Section 24 provides a defence if a lawful sexual relationship existed between A and B before the formation of a relationship between them of the type referred to in s. 21.

The defences provided for by ss. 23 and 24 must be proved by the accused. It is submitted that the burden is evidential.

Sexual Offences Act 2003, s. 21 to 24

21.—(1) For the purposes of sections 16 to 19, a person (A) is in a position of trust in relation to another person (B) if—

(a) any of the following subsections applies, or
(b) any condition specified in an order made by the Secretary of State is met.

(2) This subsection applies if A looks after persons under 18 who are detained in an institution by virtue of a court order or under an enactment, and B is so detained in that institution.

(3) This subsection applies if A looks after persons under 18 who are resident in a home or other place in which—
(a) accommodation and maintenance are provided by an authority under section 23(2) of the Children Act 1989 or Article 27(2) of the Children (Northern Ireland) Order 1995 (SI 1995/755), or
(b) accommodation is provided by a voluntary organisation under section 59(1) of that Act or Article 75(1) of that Order,

and B is resident, and is so provided with accommodation and maintenance or accommodation, in that place.

(4) This subsection applies if A looks after persons under 18 who are accommodated and cared for in one of the following institutions—
(a) a hospital,
(b) an independent clinic,
(c) a care home, residential care home or private hospital,
(d) a community home, voluntary home or children's home,
(e) a home provided under section 82(5) of the Children Act 1989, or
(f) a residential family centre,

and B is accommodated and cared for in that institution.

(5) This subsection applies if A looks after persons under 18 who are receiving education at an educational institution and B is receiving, and A is not receiving, education at that institution.

(6) This subsection applies if A is appointed to be the guardian of B under Article 159 or 160 of the Children (Northern Ireland) Order 1995 (SI 1995/755).

(7) This subsection applies if A is engaged in the provision of services under, or pursuant to anything done under—
(a) sections 8 to 10 of the Employment and Training Act 1973, or
(b) section 114 of the Learning and Skills Act 2000,

and, in that capacity, looks after B on an individual basis.

(8) This subsection applies if A regularly has unsupervised contact with B (whether face to face or by any other means)—
(a) in the exercise of functions of a local authority under section 20 or 21 of the Children Act 1989, or
(b) in the exercise of functions of an authority under article 21 or 23 of the Children (Northern Ireland) Order 1995.

(9) This subsection applies if A, as a person who is to report to the court under section 7 of the Children Act 1989 or article 4 of the Children (Northern Ireland) Order 1995 on matters relating to the welfare of B, regularly has unsupervised contact with B (whether face to face or by any other means).

(10) This subsection applies if A is a personal adviser appointed for B under—
(a) section 23B(2) of, or paragraph 19C of schedule 2 to, the Children Act 1989, or
(b) article 34A(10) or 34C(2) of the Children (Northern Ireland) Order 1995,

and, in that capacity, looks after B on an individual basis.

(11) This subsection applies if—
(a) B is subject to a care order, a supervision order or an education supervision order, and
(b) in the exercise of functions conferred by virtue of the order on an authorised person or the authority designated by the order, A looks after B on an individual basis.

(12) This subsection applies if A—
(a) is an officer of the Service appointed for B under section 41(1) of the Children Act 1989,
(b) is appointed a children's guardian of B under rule 6 or rule 18 of the Adoption Rules 1984 (SI 1984/265), or
(c) is appointed to be the guardian ad litem of B under rule 9.5 of the Family Proceedings Rules 1991 (SI 1991/1247) or under article 60(1) of the Children (Northern Ireland) Order 1995,

and, in that capacity, regularly has unsupervised contact with B (whether face to face or by any other means).

(13) This subsection applies if—

(a) B is subject to requirements imposed by or under an enactment on his release from detention for a criminal offence, or is subject to requirements imposed by a court order made in criminal proceedings, and

(b) A looks after B on an individual basis in pursuance of the requirements.

22.—(1) The following provisions apply for the purposes of section 21.

(2) Subject to subsection (3), a person looks after persons under 18 if he is regularly involved in caring for, training, supervising or being in sole charge of such persons.

(3) A person (A) looks after another person (B) on an individual basis if—

(a) A is regularly involved in caring for, training or supervising B, and

(b) in the course of his involvement, A regularly has unsupervised contact with B (whether face to face or by any other means).

(4) A person receives education at an educational institution if—

(a) he is registered or otherwise enrolled as a pupil or student at the institution, or

(b) he receives education at the institution under arrangements with another educational institution at which he is so registered or otherwise enrolled.

(5) [Contains various definitions: see below.]

23.—(1) Conduct by a person (A) which would otherwise be an offence under any of sections 16 to 19 against another person (B) is not an offence under that section if at the time—

(a) B is 16 or over, and

(b) A and B are lawfully married.

(2) In proceedings for such an offence it is for the defendant to prove that A and B were lawfully married at the time.

24.—(1) Conduct by a person (A) which would otherwise be an offence under any of sections 16 to 19 against another person (B) is not an offence under that section if, immediately before the position of trust arose, a sexual relationship existed between A and B.

(2) Subsection (1) does not apply if at that time sexual intercourse between A and B would have been unlawful.

(3) In proceedings for an offence under any of sections 16 to 19 it is for the defendant to prove that such a relationship existed at that time.

Section 22(5) provides that 'authority' in relation to England and Wales means a local authority and contains definitions of a wide range of other terms used in s. 21.

Abuse of Position of Trust: Sexual Activity with a Child

B3.94 Sexual Offences Act 2003, s. 16

(1) A person aged 18 or over (A) commits an offence if—

(a) he intentionally touches another person (B),

(b) the touching is sexual,

(c) A is in a position of trust in relation to B,

(d) where subsection (2) applies, A knows or could reasonably be expected to know of the circumstances by virtue of which he is in a position of trust in relation to B, and

(e) either—

(i) B is under 18 and A does not reasonably believe that B is 18 or over, or

(ii) B is under 13.

(2) This subsection applies where A—

(a) is in a position of trust in relation to B by virtue of circumstances within section 21(2), (3), (4) or (5), and

(b) is not in such a position of trust by virtue of other circumstances.

(3) Where in proceedings for an offence under this section it is proved that the other person was under 18, the defendant is to be taken not to have reasonably believed that that person was 18 or over unless sufficient evidence is adduced to raise an issue as to whether he reasonably believed it.

(4) Where in proceedings for an offence under this section—

(a) it is proved that the defendant was in a position of trust in relation to the other person by virtue of circumstances within section 21(2), (3), (4) or (5), and

(b) it is not proved that he was in such a position of trust by virtue of other circumstances, it is to be taken that the defendant knew or could reasonably have been expected to know of the circumstances by virtue of which he was in such a position of trust unless sufficient evidence is adduced to raise an issue as to whether he knew or could reasonably have been expected to know of those circumstances.

Procedure

B3.95 An allegation of an offence contrary to s. 16 is triable either way; when tried on indictment it is a class 3 offence. The extra-territorial jurisdiction provisions of s. 72 apply (see **B3.268**).

See **B3.285** for alternative verdicts.

Indictment

B3.96 *Statement of Offence*

Sexual activity with a child by a person in a position of trust contrary to section 16(1) of the Sexual Offences Act 2003

Particulars of Offence

A, on or about the . . . day of . . . being then a person in a position of trust towards V a child under the age of [18][13] sexually touched V.

Sentencing

B3.97 The maximum sentence for an offence under the SOA 2003, s. 16, on conviction on indictment is five years' imprisonment. On summary conviction, the maximum sentence is six months or a fine not exceeding the statutory maximum, or both (s. 16(5)).

The SGC Guideline, *Sexual Offences Act 2003* (April 2007), applies to offenders sentenced on or after 14 May 2007 for abuse of a position of trust: sexual activity with a child. For the full text of this guideline, see **appendix 8** at part 8. Aggravating and mitigating factors in the guideline are additional to those set out in the SGC Guideline on *Seriousness* (December 2004), paras. 1.20 – 1.24 (see **appendix 8** at part 3). The sentences for public protection (see E5) must be considered in all such cases. In every case the court should consider a disqualification from working with children (see **E23.11**) and a SOPO (see **E23.12**). There is a notification requirement under the CJA 2003, s. 80 and sch. 3 if the offender is imprisoned, detained in a hospital or receives a community sentence of at least 12 months (see **E25**).

Elements

B3.98 The basic elements of the offence are the same as required in s. 9 (see **B3.63**). In addition, the offender must be in a position of trust and the victim may be as old as 17 and not 15 as in s. 9.

It is a defence if the accused reasonably believes that the victim is 18 or over when in fact she is not, unless the child is under 13 in which case that defence is not available.

There are two rebuttable presumptions under this section which impose an evidential burden on the accused. Under s. 16(3), if it is proved that the victim was under the age of 18, the accused is taken to have not reasonably believed the victim to be over 18 unless sufficient evidence is adduced to raise an issue as to whether the accused did in fact have that reasonable belief. It is then for the prosecution to prove to the criminal standard that he did not have that reasonable belief.

Under s. 16(4), if it is proved that the accused is in a position of trust in relation to the alleged victim by virtue of circumstances within s. 21(2), (3), (4) or (5) and it is not proved that the position of trust arose because of other circumstances, then it is taken that the accused either knew or could reasonably have been expected to know of the circumstances placing him in a position of trust unless sufficient evidence is adduced to raise an issue as to whether he did in fact know or could have reasonably been expected to know of the circumstances founding the position of trust. Once sufficient evidence has been adduced then, as with s. 16(3), it is for the prosecution to prove the contrary to the criminal standard.

The provisions of s. 73 apply to this offence (see **B3.37**).

Abuse of Position of Trust: Causing or Inciting a Child to Engage in Sexual Activity

B3.99 **Sexual Offences Act 2003, s. 17**

(1) A person aged 18 or over (A) commits an offence if—
- (a) he intentionally causes or incites another person (B) to engage in an activity,
- (b) the activity is sexual,
- (c) A is in a position of trust in relation to B,
- (d) where subsection (2) applies, A knows or could reasonably be expected to know of the circumstances by virtue of which he is in a position of trust in relation to B, and
- (e) either—
  - (i) B is under 18 and A does not reasonably believe that B is 18 or over, or
  - (ii) B is under 13.

Procedure

B3.100 An allegation of an offence contrary to s. 17 is triable either way. When it is tried on indictment it is ordinarily a class 3 offence, but if the activity involves penetration, it is a class 2 offence. The extra-territorial provisions of s. 72 apply (see **B3.268**).

See **B3.285** for alternative verdicts.

Indictment

B3.101 *Statement of Offence*

Causing or inciting a child by a person in a position of trust to engage in sexual activity contrary to section 17(1) of the Sexual Offences Act 2003.

Particulars of Offence

A, on or about the . . . day of . . . being then in a position of trust towards V a child under the age of [18][13] caused or incited V to engage in a sexual activity.

Sentencing

B3.102 The maximum sentence for an offence under the SOA 2003, s. 17, is the same as that for a s. 16 offence (see **B3.97**).

The SGC Guideline, *Sexual Offences Act 2003* (April 2007), applies to offenders sentenced on or after 14 May 2007 for abuse of a position of trust: causing or inciting a child to engage in sexual activity. For the full text of this guideline, see **appendix 8** at part 8. Aggravating and mitigating factors in the guideline are additional to those set out in the SGC Guideline on *Seriousness* (December 2004), paras. 1.20 – 1.24 (see **appendix 8** at part 3). The sentences for public protection (see **E5**) must be considered in all such cases. In every case the court should consider a disqualification from working with children (see **E23.11**) and a SOPO (see **E23.12**). There is a notification requirement under the CJA 2003, s. 80 and sch. 3 if the offender is imprisoned, detained in a hospital or receives a community sentence of at least 12 months (see **E25**).

Elements

B3.103 The basic elements of an offence contrary to s. 17 are the same as those under s. 10 (see **B3.68**) but there are some differences: the offender must be in a position of trust and the victim may be as old as 17. The same assumptions apply as under s. 16 (see **B3.98**).

Abuse of Position of Trust: Sexual Activity in Presence of Child

Sexual Offences Act 2003, s. 18 B3.104

(1) A person aged 18 or over (A) commits an offence if—
(a) he intentionally engages in an activity,
(b) the activity is sexual,
(c) for the purpose of obtaining sexual gratification, he engages in it—
(i) when another person (B) is present or is in a place from which A can be observed, and
(ii) knowing or believing that B is aware, or intending that B should be aware, that he is engaging in it,
(d) A is in a position of trust in relation to B,
(e) where subsection (2) applies, A knows or could reasonably be expected to know of the circumstances by virtue of which he is in a position of trust in relation to B, and
(f) either—
(i) B is under 18 and A does not reasonably believe that B is 18 or over, or
(ii) B is under 13.

Procedure

An allegation of an offence contrary to s. 18 is triable either way; when tried on indictment it is a class 3 offence. The extra-territorial jurisdiction provisions of s. 72 apply (see **B3.268**). B3.105

See **B3.285** for alternative verdicts.

Sentencing

The maximum sentence for an offence under the SOA 2003, s. 18, is the same as that for a s. 16 offence (see **B3.97**). B3.106

The SGC Guideline, *Sexual Offences Act 2003* (April 2007), applies to offenders sentenced on or after 14 May 2007 for abuse of a position of trust: sexual activity in presence of a child. For the full text of this guideline, see **appendix 8** at part 8. Aggravating and mitigating factors in the guideline are additional to those set out in the SGC Guideline on *Seriousness* (December 2004), paras 1.20 – 1.24 (see **appendix 8** at part 3). The sentences for public protection (see **E5**) must be considered in all such cases. In every case the court should consider a disqualification from working with children (see **E23.11**) and a SOPO (see **E23.12**). There is a notification requirement under the CJA 2003, s. 80 and sch. 3 if the offender is imprisoned, detained in a hospital or receives a community sentence of at least 12 months (see **E25**).

Elements

The basic elements of an offence contrary to s. 18 are the same as those under s. 11 (see **B3.73**) but there are some differences. The differences are that the offender must be in a position of trust and the victim may be as old as 17. The same assumptions apply as under s. 16 (see **B3.98**). B3.107

For 'gratification', see **B3.78**.

Abuse of Position of Trust: Causing a Child to Watch a Sexual Act

Sexual Offences Act 2003, s. 19 B3.108

(1) A person aged 18 or over (A) commits an offence if—
(a) for the purpose of obtaining sexual gratification, he intentionally causes another person (B) to watch a third person engaging in an activity, or to look at an image of any person engaging in an activity,
(b) the activity is sexual,
(c) A is in a position of trust in relation to B,
(d) where subsection (2) applies, A knows or could reasonably be expected to know of the circumstances by virtue of which he is in a position of trust in relation to B, and

(e) either—
(i) B is under 18 and A does not reasonably believe that B is 18 or over, or
(ii) B is under 13.

Procedure

B3.109 An allegation of an offence contrary to s. 19 is triable either way; when tried on indictment it is a class 3 offence. The extra-territorial jurisdiction provisions of s. 72 apply (see **B3.268**). See **B3.285** for alternative verdicts.

Sentencing

B3.110 The maximum sentence for an offence under the SOA 2003, s. 19, is the same as that for an offence under s. 16 (see **B3.97**).

The SGC Guideline, *Sexual Offences Act 2003* (April 2007), applies to offenders sentenced on or after 14 May 2007 for abuse of a position of trust: causing a child to watch a sexual act. For the full text of this guideline, see **appendix 8** at part 8. Aggravating and mitigating factors in the guideline are additional to those set out in the SGC Guideline on *Seriousness* (December 2004), paras. 1.20 – 1.24 (see **appendix 8** at part 3). The sentences for public protection (see E5) must be considered in all such cases. In every case the court should consider a disqualification from working with children (see **E23.11**) and a SOPO (see **E23.12**). There is a notification requirement under the CJA 2003, s. 80 and sch. 3 if the offender is imprisoned, detained in a hospital or receives a community sentence of at least 12 months (see **E25**).

Elements

B3.111 The basic elements of an offence contrary to s. 19 are the same as those under s. 12 (see B3.78) but there are some differences. The differences are that the offender must be in a position of trust and the victim may be as old as 17. The same assumptions apply as under s. 16 (see **B3.98**).

For 'gratification', see **B3.78**

FAMILIAL CHILD SEX OFFENCES

B3.112 Incest was not prohibited by the criminal law of England and Wales until the Punishment of Incest Act 1908. Until then it was punishable only by the ecclesiastical courts.

In ss. 25 and 26, the SOA 2003 creates two gender-neutral offences which are designed to counter the sexual abuse and exploitation of children within the 'family unit'. Section 25 creates an offence of sexual activity with a child family member and s. 26 creates an offence of inciting a child family member to engage in sexual activity. There are common features of each offence governed by ss. 27, 28 and 29. Section 27 defines which relationships between A and B are relevant for the purposes of those sections. Sections 28 and 29 make specific provision for defences to charges under s. 25 or s. 26. Section 28 provides a defence to such a charge if B is aged 16 or over and A and B are either lawfully married or civil partners of each other. Section 29 provides a defence if a lawful sexual relationship existed between A and B before the formation of a relationship between them of the type referred to in s. 27(3), (4) or (5). If the relationship is one referred to in s. 27(2) (see below), or would fall within that subsection if B had not been adopted by another, then the defence is not available.

The defences provided for by ss. 28 and 29 must be proved by the accused. It is submitted that the burden is evidential.

Sexual Offences Act 2003, ss. 27 to 29

27.—(1) The relation of one person (A) to another (B) is within this section if—
(a) it is within any of subsections (2) to (4), or

(b) it would be within one of those subsections but for section 67 of the Adoption and Children Act 2002 (status conferred by adoption).

(2) The relation of A to B is within this subsection if—

(a) one of them is the other's parent, grandparent, brother, sister, half-brother, half-sister, aunt or uncle, or

(b) A is or has been B's foster parent.

(3) The relation of A to B is within this subsection if A and B live or have lived in the same household, or A is or has been regularly involved in caring for, training, supervising or being in sole charge of B, and—

(a) one of them is or has been the other's step-parent,

(b) A and B are cousins,

(c) one of them is or has been the other's stepbrother or stepsister, or

(d) the parent or present or former foster parent of one of them is or has been the other's foster parent.

(4) The relation of A to B is within this subsection if—

(a) A and B live in the same household, and

(b) A is regularly involved in caring for, training, supervising or being in sole charge of B.

(5) For the purposes of this section—

(a) 'aunt' means the sister or half-sister of a person's parent, and 'uncle' has a corresponding meaning;

(b) 'cousin' means the child of an aunt or uncle;

(c) a person is a child's foster parent if—

(i) he is a person with whom the child has been placed under section 23(2)(a) or 59(1)(a) of the Children Act 1989 (fostering for local authority or voluntary organisation), or

(ii) he fosters the child privately, within the meaning given by section 66(1)(b) of that Act;

(d) a person is another's partner (whether they are of different sexes or the same sex) if they live together as partners in an enduring family relationship;

(e) 'step-parent' includes a parent's partner and 'stepbrother' and 'stepsister' include the child of a parent's partner.

28.—(1) Conduct by a person (A) which would otherwise be an offence under section 25 or 26 against another person (B) is not an offence under that section if at the time—

(a) B is 16 or over, and

(b) A and B are lawfully married.

(2) In proceedings for such an offence it is for the defendant to prove that A and B were lawfully married at the time.

29.—(1) Conduct by a person (A) which would otherwise be an offence under section 25 or 26 against another person (B) is not an offence under that section if—

(a) the relation of A to B is not within subsection (2) of section 27,

(b) it would not be within that subsection if section 67 of the Adoption and Children Act 2002 did not apply, and

(c) immediately before the relation of A to B first became such as to fall within section 27, a sexual relationship existed between A and B.

(2) Subsection (1) does not apply if at the time referred to in subsection (1)(c) sexual intercourse between A and B would have been unlawful.

(3) In proceedings for an offence under section 25 or 26 it is for the defendant to prove the matters mentioned in subsection (1)(a) to (c).

Sexual Activity with a Child Family Member

Sexual Offences Act 2003, s. 25 B3.113

(1) A person (A) commits an offence if—

(a) he intentionally touches another person (B),

(b) the touching is sexual,

(c) the relation of A to B is within section 27,

(d) A knows or could reasonably be expected to know that his relation to B is of a description falling within that section, and

(e) either—
(i) B is under 18 and A does not reasonably believe that B is 18 or over, or
(ii) B is under 13.

(2) Where in proceedings for an offence under this section it is proved that the other person was under 18, the defendant is to be taken not to have reasonably believed that that person was 18 or over unless sufficient evidence is adduced to raise an issue as to whether he reasonably believed it.

(3) Where in proceedings for an offence under this section it is proved that the relation of the defendant to the other person was of a description falling within section 27, it is to be taken that the defendant knew or could reasonably have been expected to know that his relation to the other person was of that description unless sufficient evidence is adduced to raise an issue as to whether he knew or could reasonably have been expected to know that it was.

Procedure

B3.114 An allegation of an offence contrary to s. 25 is triable either way unless the alleged offender is 18 or over at the time of the offence and penetration is involved, in which case the allegation is triable on indictment only. It is a class 3 offence when tried on indictment. The extra-territoriality provisions of s. 72 apply (see **B3.268**).

See **B3.285** for alternative verdicts.

Indictment

B3.115 *Statement of Offence*

Sexual activity with a child family member contrary to section 25(1) of the Sexual Offences Act 2003

Particulars of Offence

A on or about the . . . day of . . . being then in a family relationship to V, a child then under the age of [18][13] years sexually touched V

or

A, on or about the . . . day of . . . being then in a family relationship to V, a child then under the age of [18] [13] years, sexually touched V by penetrating V's [anus] [vagina] with a part of his body [an object] or [by penetrating V's mouth with his penis]

or

A, on or about the . . . day of . . . being then in a family relationship to V, a child then under the age of [18] [13] years, sexually touched V by allowing V to penetrate A's [anus] [vagina] with a part of V's body [an object] or [by allowing V to penetrate A's mouth with his penis].

Sentencing

B3.116 Where the accused is over 18 and the activity involved penetration, the maximum penalty for an offence under the SOA 2003, s. 25, is 14 years' imprisonment. Otherwise, in the case of an offender aged 18 or over, the maximum penalty where the offence is tried on indictment is 14 years. In any other case, on conviction on indictment, the maximum penalty is five years and, on summary conviction, it is six months or a fine not exceeding the statutory maximum, or both (s. 25(4) to (6)).

The maximum penalty also varies with the age of the offender. If the offender is under 18 the maximum penalty is five years (see **B3.81**).

The SGC Guideline, *Sexual Offences Act 2003* (April 2007), applies to offenders sentenced for sexual activity with a child family member on or after 14 May 2007. For the full text of this guideline, see **appendix 8** at part 8. There are separate guidelines for offenders aged 18 and over (guideline 3A) and offenders aged under 18 (guideline 7). Aggravating and mitigating factors in the guideline are additional to those set out in the SGC Guideline on *Seriousness* (December 2004), paras. 1.20 – 1.24 (see **appendix 8** at part 3). The sentences for public protection (see E5) must be considered in all such cases. In every case the court should consider a disqualification from working with children (see **E23.11**) and a SOPO (see **E23.12**).

There is a notification requirement under the CJA 2003, s. 80 and sch. 3 if the offender is aged 18 or over or was sentenced to at least 12 months' imprisonment (see **E25**).

In *Thomas* [2006] 1 Cr App R (S) 602, the offender admitted to having sexual intercourse with the 17-year-old victim. She had been in care since the age of 11 and had been placed in the foster care of the offender and his wife in 2002. The offences took place after the victim had moved away to semi-independent accommodation. The Court of Appeal reduced the sentence of four years' imprisonment to one of 30 months. The important factors when sentencing for this offence, it was said, were the age of the parties, the nature of the sexual activity and the number of occasions on which it had taken place.

Elements

The basic elements of the offence are the same as those in s. 9 (see **B3.63**) but with the additional necessity of the existence of a relationship between the parties of the kind encompassed by s. 27. **B3.117**

For 'sexual', see **B3.20**. As to 'touching', see **B3.28**.

The provisions of s. 73 apply (see **B3.37**) where the alleged victim is less than 16 years old.

Inciting a Child Family Member to Engage in Sexual Activity

Sexual Offences Act 2003, s. 26 **B3.118**

(1) A person (A) commits an offence if—
  (a) he intentionally incites another person (B) to touch, or allow himself to be touched by, A,
  (b) the touching is sexual,
  (c) the relation of A to B is within section 27,
  (d) A knows or could reasonably be expected to know that his relation to B is of a description falling within that section, and
  (e) either—
    (i) B is under 18 and A does not reasonably believe that B is 18 or over, or
    (ii) B is under 13.

Procedure

An allegation of an offence contrary to s. 26 is triable either way unless the alleged offender is 18 or over at the time of the offence and penetration is involved, in which case the allegation is triable on indictment only. It is a class 3 offence when tried on indictment. The extra-territorial jurisdiction provisions of s. 72 apply (see **B3.268**). **B3.119**

See **B3.285** for alternative verdicts.

Indictment

Statement of Offence **B3.120**

Inciting a child family member to engage in sexual activity contrary to section 26 of the Sexual Offences Act 2003.

Particulars of Offence

A, on or about the . . . day of . . . being then in a family relationship to V, a child under the age of [18][13] years incited V [to touch A sexually] [to allow himself to be touched by A sexually]

Sentencing

The provisions as to penalties for an offence under the SOA 2003, s. 26, are contained in s. 26(4) to (6) and are in identical terms to s. 25(4) to (6) (see **B3.116**). **B3.121**

The maximum penalty also varies with the age of the offender. If the offender is under 18 the maximum penalty is five years (see **B3.81**).

The SGC Guideline, *Sexual Offences Act 2003* (April 2007) applies to offenders sentenced for intentionally inciting sexual touching by a child family member on or after 14 May 2007. For the full text of this guideline, see **appendix 8** at part 8. There are separate guidelines for offenders aged 18 and over (guideline 3A) and offenders aged under 18 (guideline 7). Aggravating and mitigating factors in the guideline are additional to those set out in the SGC Guideline on *Seriousness* (December 2004), paras. 1.20 – 1.24 (see **appendix 8** at part 3). The sentences for public protection (see **E5**) must be considered in all such cases. In every case the court should consider a disqualification from working with children (see **E23.11**) and a SOPO (see **E23.12**). There is a notification requirement under the CJA 2003, s. 80 and sch. 3 if the offender is aged 18 or over or was sentenced to at least 12 months' imprisonment (see **E25**).

Elements

B3.122 The elements of this offence are similar to those in respect of a s. 10 offence (see **B3.68**) but the offence is much more limited in scope, being restricted to incitement and applying only to sexual touching.

For 'incitement', see **B3.57**. For 'sexual', see **B3.20**. For 'touching', see **B3.28**.

OFFENCES AGAINST PERSONS WITH A MENTAL DISORDER IMPEDING CHOICE

B3.123 Sections 30 to 41 of the SOA 2003 cover a wide range of offences designed to protect persons of either gender who suffer from a mental disorder. The legislation is wider than any previous enactments to protect people vulnerable as a result of their mental state. By virtue of s. 79(6), 'mental disorder' is as defined in s. 1 of the Mental Health Act 1983, and so a person with a learning difficulty finds protection in the Act. In addition, activities prohibited by the Act extend beyond sexual intercourse and indecent assault to sexual touching of a mentally disordered person, the causing or inciting of sexual activity by a mentally disordered person, engaging in sexual activity in the presence of a mentally disordered person and causing a mentally disordered person to watch sexual activity.

Sections 30 to 33 govern offences arising out of sexual activity with persons with a mental disorder which impedes their capacity for choice.

Sexual Activity with a Person with a Mental Disorder Impeding Choice

B3.124 **Sexual Offences Act 2003, s. 30**

(1) A person (A) commits an offence if—
 (a) he intentionally touches another person (B),
 (b) the touching is sexual,
 (c) B is unable to refuse because of or for a reason related to a mental disorder, and
 (d) A knows or could reasonably be expected to know that B has a mental disorder and that because of it or for a reason related to it B is likely to be unable to refuse.

(2) B is unable to refuse if—
 (a) he lacks the capacity to choose whether to agree to the touching (whether because he lacks sufficient understanding of the nature or reasonably foreseeable consequences of what is being done, or for any other reason), or
 (b) he is unable to communicate such a choice to A.

Procedure

B3.125 An allegation of an offence contrary to s. 30 is triable either way unless the conduct involves penetration, in which case it is triable only on indictment. Upon trial on indictment, it is ordinarily a class 3 offence but, where the activity involves penetration, it is a class 2 offence. The extra-territorial jurisdiction provisions of s. 72 apply (see **B3.268**).

See **B3.285** for alternative verdicts.

Indictment

Statement of Offence B3.126

Sexual touching of a person who was then unable to refuse because of a reason relating to a mental disorder contrary to section 30(1) of the Sexual Offences Act 2003.

Particulars of Offence

A, on or about the . . . day of . . . intentionally sexually touched V a person who he knew [ought reasonably to have known] was unable to refuse to be touched by reason of a mental disorder

or

A, on or about the . . . day of . . . sexually touched V, a person who he knew [ought reasonably to have known] was unable to refuse to be touched by reason of a mental disorder by penetrating V's [anus] [vagina] with a part of his, A's, body [an object]

or

A, on or about the . . . day of . . . sexually touched V, a person who he knew [ought reasonably to have known] was unable to refuse to be touched by reason of a mental disorder by allowing V to penetrate A's [anus] [vagina] with a part of his, V's, body [to penetrate A's mouth with his, V's, penis].

Sentencing

The maximum penalty applicable is determined by the nature of the activity. B3.127

Sexual Offences Act 2003, s. 30

(3) A person guilty of an offence under this section, if the touching involved—
 (a) penetration of B's anus or vagina with a part of A's body or anything else,
 (b) penetration of B's mouth with A's penis,
 (c) penetration of A's anus or vagina with a part of B's body, or
 (d) penetration of A's mouth with B's penis,
 is liable, on conviction on indictment, to imprisonment for life.

(4) Unless subsection (3) applies, a person guilty of an offence under this section is liable—
 (a) on summary conviction, to imprisonment for a term not exceeding 6 months or to a fine not exceeding the statutory maximum or both;
 (b) on conviction on indictment, to imprisonment for a term not exceeding 14 years.

It is a curiosity of the section that in the case of penetration by touching, the maximum penalty is enhanced where A commits the offence by penetration by a part of the body or by an object, but where the essence of the offence is allowing B to penetrate A's anus or vagina, penetration by an object is not comprehended. Penetration enhances the maximum penalty where it is with a part of B's body.

The SGC Guideline, *Sexual Offences Act 2003* (April 2007), applies to offenders sentenced on or after 14 May 2007 for sexual activity with a person with a mental disorder impeding choice. For the full text of this guideline, see **appendix 8** at part 8. Aggravating and mitigating factors in the guideline are additional to those set out in the SGC Guideline on *Seriousness* (December 2004), paras. 1.20 – 1.24 (see **appendix 8** at part 3). The sentences for public protection (see E5) must be considered in all such cases. In every case the court should consider a disqualification from working with children (see **E23.11**) and a SOPO (see **E23.12**). There is a notification requirement under the CJA 2003, s. 80 and sch. 3 (see E25).

In *A-G's Ref (No. 106 of 2005)* [2006] 2 Cr App R (S) 521, a community rehabilitation order was imposed on a man of 45 for sexual activity with a young woman of 17 who had an IQ of 65 and whose vocabulary skills were those of a child of about eight years. Sexual intercourse took place on three occasions. Rose LJ commented (at [19] to [21]) that one would normally expect a custodial sentence in the order of at least 12 to 18 months in such a case but, although the sentence was lenient, it was not, in all the circumstances, unduly lenient.

Elements

B3.128 The elements of the offence are essentially the same as those required for an offence under s. 9 (see **B3.63**) but with the additional elements concerning the victim's mental disorder(see s. 30(1)(c)) and the *mens rea* of the accused (see s. 30(1)(d)).

In *Hulme v DPP* (2006) 170 JP 598, a woman with cerebral palsy and a mental age well below her actual age of 27 could not communicate her feelings as to sexual acts in a way that a person of her age without her disabilities would be able to. The evidence was that when *H* touched her private parts she did not know what to do or say but it made her sad, hurt and upset. She was therefore unable to communicate her choice within the meaning of s. 30 because of or for a reason related to a mental disorder and she was therefore unable to refuse within the meaning of the section.

The provisions of s. 73 apply to this offence (see **B3.37**) when the alleged victim is less than 16 years old.

Causing or Inciting a Person with a Mental Disorder Impeding Choice to Engage in Sexual Activity

B3.129 **Sexual Offences Act 2003, s. 31**

(1) A person (A) commits an offence if—
 (a) he intentionally causes or incites another person (B) to engage in an activity,
 (b) the activity is sexual,
 (c) B is unable to refuse because of or for a reason related to a mental disorder, and
 (d) A knows or could reasonably be expected to know that B has a mental disorder and that because of it or for a reason related to it B is likely to be unable to refuse.

(2) B is unable to refuse if—
 (a) he lacks the capacity to choose whether to agree to engaging in the activity caused or incited (whether because he lacks sufficient understanding of the nature or reasonably foreseeable consequences of the activity, or for any other reason), or
 (b) he is unable to communicate such a choice to A.

Procedure

B3.130 An allegation of an offence contrary to s. 31 is triable either way unless the conduct involves penetration, in which case it is triable only on indictment. Upon trial on indictment, it is a class 3 offence. The extra-territorial jurisdiction provisions of s. 72 apply (see **B3.268**).

See **B3.285** for alternative verdicts.

Indictment

B3.131 *Statement of Offence*

Causing or inciting a person who was then unable to refuse because of a mental disorder impeding choice to engage in sexual activity contrary to section 31(1) of the Sexual Offences Act 2003.

Particulars of Offence

A, on or about the . . . day of . . . intentionally caused or incited V a person who he knew [ought reasonably to have known] was unable to refuse consent to the said activity by reason of mental disorder to engage in a sexual activity

or

A, on or about the . . . day of . . . intentionally caused or incited V, a person who he knew [ought reasonably to have known] was unable to refuse consent to the said activity by reason of mental disorder, to engage in a sexual activity, namely, causing or inciting the penetration of V's [anus] [vagina] or [V's mouth with the penis of another]

Sentencing

The provisions as to the maximum sentence for an offence under s. 31 are the same as those which apply in respect of an offence under s. 30 (see **B3.127**). Note that where penetration by A is involved, the section speaks simply of penetration but does not specify whether it must be with a part of the body alone or whether it may be with an object. On the other hand, where it is B who penetrates the body of another, provision is explicitly made for penetration by an object. It may therefore be arguable that penetration by A must be with a part of the body only. **B3.132**

The SGC Guideline, *Sexual Offences Act 2003* (April 2007), applies to offenders sentenced on or after 14 May 2007 for this offence. For the full text of this guideline, see **appendix 8**, at part 8. Aggravating and mitigating factors in the guideline are additional to those set out in the SGC Guideline on *Seriousness* (December 2004), paras. 1.20 – 1.24 (see **appendix 8** at part 3). The sentences for public protection (see **E5**) must be considered in all such cases. In every case the court should consider a disqualification from working with children (see **E23.11**) and a SOPO (see **E23.12**). There is a notification requirement under the CJA 2003, s. 80 and sch. 3 (see **E25**).

A sentence of three years' imprisonment was reduced on appeal to 15 months in *Jones* [2006] 2 Cr App R (S) 117, a case where the offender was convicted after a trial of an offence under s. 31. The victim was a 19-year-old man who suffered from Down's syndrome and had a mental age of five. The Court of Appeal said the general sentencing consideration set out in *Millberry* [2003] 1 WLR 546 (see **B3.6**) applied, but that offences of this type were comparable in seriousness with sexual offences against children. The victim was vulnerable and suggestible. The offender's drunkenness at the time of the offence provided no mitigation.

Elements

The elements of the offence are essentially the same as those required for an offence under s. 10 (see **B3.68**), but with the additional elements concerning the victim's mental disorder (see s. 31(1)(c)) and the accused's *mens rea* (see s. 31(1)(d)). **B3.133**

Engaging in Sexual Activity in the Presence of a Person with a Mental Disorder

Sexual Offences Act 2003, s. 32 **B3.134**

(1) A person (A) commits an offence if—
- (a) he intentionally engages in an activity,
- (b) the activity is sexual,
- (c) for the purpose of obtaining sexual gratification, he engages in it—
  - (i) when another person (B) is present or is in a place from which A can be observed, and
  - (ii) knowing or believing that B is aware, or intending that B should be aware, that he is engaging in it,
- (d) B is unable to refuse because of or for a reason related to a mental disorder, and
- (e) A knows or could reasonably be expected to know that B has a mental disorder and that because of it or for a reason related to it B is likely to be unable to refuse.

(2) B is unable to refuse if—
- (a) he lacks the capacity to choose whether to agree to being present (whether because he lacks sufficient understanding of the nature of the activity, or for any other reason), or
- (b) he is unable to communicate such a choice to A.

Procedure

An allegation of an offence contrary to s. 32 is triable either way. It is a class 3 offence when tried on indictment. The extra-territorial jurisdiction provisions of s. 72 apply (see **B3.268**). **B3.135**

See **B3.285** for alternative verdicts.

Sentencing

B3.136 The maximum sentence for an offence under the SOA 2003, s. 32, on conviction on indictment is ten years' imprisonment. On summary conviction, the maximum sentence is six months or a fine not exceeding the statutory maximum, or both (s. 32(3)).

The SGC Guideline, *Sexual Offences Act 2003* (April 2007), applies to offenders sentenced on or after 14 May 2007 for this offence. For the full text of this guideline, see **appendix 8** at part 8. Aggravating and mitigating factors in the guideline are additional to those set out in the SGC Guideline on *Seriousness* (December 2004), paras. 1.20 – 1.24 (see **appendix 8** at part 3). The sentences for public protection (see **E5**) must be considered in all such cases. In every case the court should consider a disqualification from working with children (see **E23.11**) and a SOPO (see **E23.12**). There is a notification requirement under the CJA 2003, s. 80 and sch. 3 (see **E25**).

Elements

B3.137 The elements of the offence are essentially the same as those required for an offence under s. 11 (see **B3.73**) but with the additional elements concerning the victim's mental disorder (see s. 3(1)(c)) and the accused's *mens rea* (see s. 32(1)(d)).

For 'gratification', see **B3.78**.

Causing a Person with a Mental Disorder Impeding Choice to Watch a Sexual Act

B3.138 Sexual Offences Act 2003, s. 33

(1) A person (A) commits an offence if—
- (a) for the purpose of obtaining sexual gratification, he intentionally causes another person (B) to watch a third person engaging in an activity, or to look at an image of any person engaging in an activity,
- (b) the activity is sexual,
- (c) B is unable to refuse because of or for a reason related to a mental disorder, and
- (d) A knows or could reasonably be expected to know that B has a mental disorder and that because of it or for a reason related to it B is likely to be unable to refuse.

(2) B is unable to refuse if—
- (a) he lacks the capacity to choose whether to agree to watching or looking (whether because he lacks sufficient understanding of the nature of the activity, or for any other reason), or
- (b) he is unable to communicate such a choice to A.

Procedure

B3.139 An allegation of an offence contrary to s. 33 is triable either way. It is a class 3 offence when tried on indictment. The extra-territorial jurisdiction provisions of s. 72 apply (see **B3.268**).

See **B3.285** for alternative verdicts.

Sentencing

B3.140 The maximum sentence for an offence under the SOA 2003, s. 33, on conviction on indictment is ten years' imprisonment. On summary conviction, the maximum is six months or a fine not exceeding the statutory maximum, or both (s. 33(3)).

The SGC Guideline, *Sexual Offences Act 2003* (April 2007) applies to offenders sentenced on or after 14 May 2007 for this offence. For the full text of this guideline, see **appendix 8** at part 8. Aggravating and mitigating factors in the guideline are additional to those set out in the SGC Guideline on *Seriousness* (December 2004), paras. 1.20 – 1.24 (see **appendix 8** at part 3). The sentences for public protection (see **E5**) must be considered in all such cases. In every case the court should consider a disqualification from working with children (see **E23.11**) and a SOPO (see **E23.12**). There is a notification requirement under the CJA 2003, s. 80 and sch. 3 (see **E25**).

Elements

The elements of the offence are essentially the same as those required for an offence under s. 12 (see **B3.78**) but with the additional elements concerning the victim's mental disorder (see s. 33(1)(c)) and the accused's *mens rea* (see s. 33(1)(d)). **B3.141**

For 'gratification', see **B3.78**.

INDUCEMENTS TO PERSONS WITH A MENTAL DISORDER

Sections 34 to 37 cover sexual activity in relation to a mentally disordered victim where agreement is obtained by inducement, threat or deception. **B3.142**

Inducement, Threat or Deception to Procure Sexual Activity with a Person

Sexual Offences Act 2003, s. 34 **B3.143**

(1) A person (A) commits an offence if—
- (a) with the agreement of another person (B) he intentionally touches that person,
- (b) the touching is sexual,
- (c) A obtains B's agreement by means of an inducement offered or given, a threat made or a deception practised by A for that purpose,
- (d) B has a mental disorder, and
- (e) A knows or could reasonably be expected to know that B has a mental disorder.

Procedure

An allegation of an offence contrary to s. 34 is triable either way unless the conduct involves penetration, in which case it is triable only on indictment. Upon trial on indictment it is ordinarily a class 3 offence, but where the activity includes penetration then it is a class 2 offence. The extra-territorial jurisdiction provisions of s. 72 apply (see **B3.268**). **B3.144**

See **B3.285** for alternative verdicts.

Indictment

Statement of Offence **B3.145**

Intentionally sexually touching a person suffering from mental disorder by agreement procured by inducement, threat or deception contrary to section 34(1) of the Sexual Offences Act 2003.

Particulars of Offence

A, on or about the . . . day of . . . sexually touched V *[by penetration . . . by procuring penetration]* a person who he then knew or ought reasonably to have known suffered from a mental disorder by agreement procured by an inducement offered or given, a threat made or a deception practised on V.

Sentencing

The maximum sentence varies according to the nature of the activity involved. **B3.146**

Sexual Offences Act 2003, s. 34

(2) A person guilty of an offence under this section, if the touching involved—
- (a) penetration of B's anus or vagina with a part of A's body or anything else,
- (b) penetration of B's mouth with A's penis,
- (c) penetration of A's anus or vagina with a part of B's body, or
- (d) penetration of A's mouth with B's penis,

is liable, on conviction on indictment, to imprisonment for life.

(3) Unless subsection (2) applies, a person guilty of an offence under this section is liable—

(a) on summary conviction, to imprisonment for a term not exceeding 6 months or a fine not exceeding the statutory maximum or both;
(b) on conviction on indictment, to imprisonment for a term not exceeding 14 years.

Note that where B penetrates A, the penalty is only enhanced where penetration is by part of B's body.

The SGC Guideline, *Sexual Offences Act 2003* (April 2007), applies to offenders sentenced on or after 14 May 2007 for this offence. For the full text of this guideline, see **appendix 8**, at part 8. Aggravating and mitigating factors in the guideline are additional to those set out in the SGC Guideline on *Seriousness* (December 2004), paras. 1.20 – 1.24 (see **appendix 8** at part 3). The sentences for public protection (see **E5**) must be considered in all such cases. In every case the court should consider a disqualification from working with children (see **E23.11**) and a SOPO (see **E23.12**). There is a notification requirement under the CJA 2003, s. 80 and sch. 3 (see **E25**).

Elements

B3.147 The elements of the offence are essentially the same as those under s. 9 (see **B3.63**) but also include additional features relating to the agreement obtained by means of an inducement, threat or deception, the mental disorder of the victim and the *mens rea* of the accused. The Home Office Explanatory Notes to the 2003 Act give examples of what might be sufficient to constitute an inducement, threat or deception. An inducement might be the promise of anything from sweets to a holiday; a threat might be a statement by the offender that he would hurt a member of the victim's family; and a deception might be a statement by the offender that the victim will get into trouble if he does not engage in sexual activity.

The provisions of s. 73 apply (see **B3.37**) when the alleged victim is under 16 years of age.

Causing a Person with a Mental Disorder to Engage in or Agree to Engage in Sexual Activity by Inducement, Threat or Deception

B3.148 Sexual Offences Act 2003, s. 35

(1) A person (A) commits an offence if—
(a) by means of an inducement offered or given, a threat made or a deception practised by him for this purpose, he intentionally causes another person (B) to engage in, or to agree to engage in, an activity,
(b) the activity is sexual,
(c) B has a mental disorder, and
(d) A knows or could reasonably be expected to know that B has a mental disorder.

Procedure

B3.149 An allegation of an offence contrary to s. 35 is triable either way unless the conduct involves penetration, in which case it is triable only on indictment. Upon trial on indictment, it is a class 3 offence. The extra-territorial jurisdiction provisions of s. 72 apply (see **B3.268**).

See **B3.285** for alternative verdicts.

Sentencing

B3.150 Where the activity concerned consists of anal, vaginal or oral penetration, the maximum penalty is life imprisonment. Otherwise, on indictment, it is 14 years' imprisonment or, on summary conviction, six months or a fine not exceeding the statutory maximum, or both (s. 35(2) and (3)).

The SGC Guideline, *Sexual Offences Act 2003* (April 2007), applies to offenders sentenced on or after 14 May 2007 for this offence. For the full text of this guideline, see **appendix 8**, at part 8. Aggravating and mitigating factors in the guideline are additional to those set out in the SGC Guideline on *Seriousness* (December 2004), paras. 1.20 – 1.24 (see **appendix 8** at part 3). The sentences for public protection (see E5) must be considered in all such cases. In every case the court should consider a disqualification from working with children (see **E23.11**) and a SOPO (see **E23.12**). There is a notification requirement under the CJA 2003, s. 80 and sch. 3 (see **E25**).

Elements

The elements of the offence are essentially the same as those under s. 10 (see **B3.68**) but also include the additional features relating to the agreement obtained by means of an inducement, threat or deception, the mental disorder of the victim and the *mens rea* of the accused. It should also be noted that the scope of s. 35 is limited to causing sexual activity and unlike s. 10 does not include inciting. For examples of inducement, threat and deception, see **B3.147**. **B3.151**

Engaging in Sexual Activity in the Presence, Procured by Inducement, Threat or Deception, of a Person with a Mental Disorder

Sexual Offences Act 2003, s. 36 **B3.152**

(1) A person (A) commits an offence if—
 (a) he intentionally engages in an activity,
 (b) the activity is sexual,
 (c) for the purpose of obtaining sexual gratification, he engages in it—
  (i) when another person (B) is present or is in a place from which A can be observed, and
  (ii) knowing or believing that B is aware, or intending that B should be aware, that he is engaging in it,
 (d) B agrees to be present or in the place referred to in paragraph (c)(i) because of an inducement offered or given, a threat made or a deception practised by A for the purpose of obtaining that agreement,
 (e) B has a mental disorder, and
 (f) A knows or could reasonably be expected to know that B has a mental disorder.

Procedure

An allegation of an offence contrary to s. 36 is triable either way. If tried on indictment, it is a class 3 offence. The extra-territorial jurisdiction provisions of s. 72 apply (see **B3.268**). **B3.153**

See **B3.285** for alternative verdicts.

Sentencing

The maximum sentence for an offence under the SOA 2003, s. 36, on conviction on indictment is ten years' imprisonment. On summary conviction, the maximum penalty is six months or a fine not exceeding the statutory maximum, or both (s. 36(2)). **B3.154**

The SGC Guideline, *Sexual Offences Act 2003* (April 2007), applies to offenders sentenced on or after 14 May 2007 for this offence. For the full text of this guideline, see **appendix 8** at part 8. Aggravating and mitigating factors in the guideline are additional to those set out in the SGC Guideline on *Seriousness* (December 2004), paras. 1.20 – 1.24 (see **appendix 8** at part 3). The sentences for public protection (see E5) must be considered in all such cases. In every case the court should consider a disqualification from working with children (see **E23.11**) and a SOPO (see **E23.12**). There is a notification requirement under the CJA 2003, s. 80 and sch. 3 (see **E25**).

Elements

B3.155 The elements of the offence are essentially the same as those under s. 11 (see **B3.73**) but also include the additional features relating to the agreement obtained by means of an inducement, threat or deception, the mental disorder of the victim and the *mens rea* of the accused. For examples of inducement, threat and deception, see **B3.147**.

For 'gratification', see **B3.78**.

Causing a Person with a Mental Disorder to Watch a Sexual Act by Inducement, Threat or Deception

B3.156 **Sexual Offences Act 2003, s. 37**

(1) A person (A) commits an offence if—
   (a) for the purpose of obtaining sexual gratification, he intentionally causes another person (B) to watch a third person engaging in an activity, or to look at an image of any person engaging in an activity,
   (b) the activity is sexual,
   (c) B agrees to watch or look because of an inducement offered or given, a threat made or a deception practised by A for the purpose of obtaining that agreement,
   (d) B has a mental disorder, and
   (e) A knows or could reasonably be expected to know that B has a mental disorder.

Procedure

B3.157 An allegation of an offence contrary to s. 37 is triable either way. If tried on indictment, it is a class 4 offence. The extra-territorial jurisdiction provisions of s. 72 apply (see **B3.268**).

See **B3.285** for alternative verdicts.

Sentencing

B3.158 The maximum sentence for an offence under the SOA 2003, s. 37, on conviction on indictment is ten years' imprisonment. On summary conviction, the maximum penalty is six months or a fine not exceeding the statutory maximum, or both (s. 37(2))

The SGC Guideline, *Sexual Offences Act 2003* (April 2007), applies to offenders sentenced on or after 14 May 2007 for this offence. For the full text of this guideline, see **appendix 8** at part 8. Aggravating and mitigating factors in the guideline are additional to those set out in the SGC Guideline on *Seriousness* (December 2004), paras. 1.20 – 1.24 (see **appendix 8** at part 3). The sentences for public protection (see **E5**) must be considered in all such cases. In every case the court should consider a disqualification from working with children (see **E23.11**) and a SOPO (see **E23.12**). There is a notification requirement under the CJA 2003, s. 80 and sch. 3 (see **E25**).

Elements

B3.159 The elements of the offence are essentially the same as those under s. 12 (see **B3.78**) but also include the additional features relating to the agreement obtained by means of an inducement, threat or deception, the mental disorder of the victim and the *mens rea* of the accused. For examples of inducement, threat and deception, see **B3.147**.

For 'gratification', see **B3.78**.

CARE WORKERS FOR PERSONS WITH A MENTAL DISORDER

Sections 38 to 41 govern offences committed by care workers against people with a mental disorder in their care. **B3.160**

Section 42 defines a care worker for the purposes of these sections.

Sections 43 and 44 provide for defences analogous to those set out in ss. 23 and 24 (see B3.93).

Sexual Offences Act 2003, ss. 42 to 44

42.—(1) For the purposes of sections 38 to 41, a person (A) is involved in the care of another person (B) in a way that falls within this section if any of subsections (2) to (4) applies.

(2) This subsection applies if—

(a) B is accommodated and cared for in a care home, community home, voluntary home or children's home, and

(b) A has functions to perform in the home in the course of employment which have brought him or are likely to bring him into regular face to face contact with B.

(3) This subsection applies if B is a patient for whom services are provided—

(a) by a National Health Service body or an independent medical agency, or

(b) in an independent clinic or an independent hospital,

and A has functions to perform for the body or agency or in the clinic or hospital in the course of employment which have brought him or are likely to bring him into regular face to face contact with B.

(4) This subsection applies if A—

(a) is, whether or not in the course of employment, a provider of care, assistance or services to B in connection with B's mental disorder, and

(b) as such, has had or is likely to have regular face to face contact with B.

(5) In this section—

'care home' means an establishment which is a care home for the purposes of the Care Standards Act 2000;

'children's home' has the meaning given by section 1 of that Act;

'community home' has the meaning given by section 53 of the Children Act 1989;

'employment' means any employment, whether paid or unpaid and whether under a contract of service or apprenticeship, under a contract for services, or otherwise than under a contract;

'independent clinic', 'independent hospital' and 'independent medical agency' have the meaning given by section 2 of the Care Standards Act 2000;

'National Health Service body' means—

(a) a Health Authority,

(b) a National Health Service trust,

(c) a Primary Care Trust, or

(d) a Special Health Authority;

'voluntary home' has the meaning given by section 60(3) of the Children Act 1989.

43.—(1) Conduct by a person (A) which would otherwise be an offence under any of sections 38 to 41 against another person (B) is not an offence under that section if at the time—

(a) B is 16 or over, and

(b) A and B are lawfully married.

(2) In proceedings for such an offence it is for the defendant to prove that A and B were lawfully married at the time.

44.—(1) Conduct by a person (A) which would otherwise be an offence under any of sections 38 to 41 against another person (B) is not an offence under that section if, immediately before A became involved in B's care in a way that falls within section 42, a sexual relationship existed between A and B.

(2) Subsection (1) does not apply if at that time sexual intercourse between A and B would have been unlawful.

(3) In proceedings for an offence under any of sections 38 to 41 it is for the defendant to prove that such a relationship existed at that time.

Care Workers: Sexual Activity with a Person with a Mental Disorder

B3.161 **Sexual Offences Act 2003, s. 38**

(1) A person (A) commits an offence if—
(a) he intentionally touches another person (B),
(b) the touching is sexual,
(c) B has a mental disorder,
(d) A knows or could reasonably be expected to know that B has a mental disorder, and
(e) A is involved in B's care in a way that falls within section 42.

(2) Where in proceedings for an offence under this section it is proved that the other person had a mental disorder, it is to be taken that the defendant knew or could reasonably have been expected to know that that person had a mental disorder unless sufficient evidence is adduced to raise an issue as to whether he knew or could reasonably have been expected to know it.

Procedure

B3.162 An allegation of an offence contrary to s. 38 is triable either way unless the conduct involves penetration, in which case it is triable only on indictment. Upon trial on indictment, it is a class 3 offence. The extra-territorial jurisdiction provisions of s. 72 apply (see **B3.268**).

See **B3.285** for alternative verdicts.

Indictment

B3.163 *Statement of Offence*

Sexual touching of a mentally disordered person by a person involved in the care of that person contrary to section 38(1) of the Sexual Offences Act 2003.

Particulars of Offence

A, on or about the . . . day of . . . being then involved in V's care, knowing that V had a mental disorder or in circumstances where he could reasonably be expected to know that V had a mental disorder, intentionally sexually touched V *[namely, by penetration . . .]*

Sentencing

B3.164 The maximum sentence for an offence under the SOA 2003, s. 38, varies depending on the sexual activity concerned. Where the touching amounts to penetration the maximum penalty on indictment is 14 years. For these purposes penetration of B's anus or vagina may be with a part of A's body or anything else. Where B penetrates A, the higher penalty allies to bodily penetration of A's anus or vagina or mouth with B's penis. It does not extend to penetration of A's sexual organs or mouth with anything else. Where touching does not amount to penetration, the maximum penalty on indictment is ten years, and on summary conviction is six months or a fine not exceeding the statutory maximum, or both (s. 38(3) and (4)).

The SGC Guideline, *Sexual Offences Act 2003* (April 2007), applies to offenders sentenced on or after 14 May 2007 for this offence. For the full text of this guideline, see **appendix 8** at part 8. Aggravating and mitigating factors in the guideline are additional to those set out in the SGC Guideline on *Seriousness* (December 2004), paras. 1.20 – 1.24 (see **appendix 8** at part 3). The sentences for public protection (see **E5**) must be considered in all such cases. In every case the court should consider a disqualification from working with children (see **E23.11**) and a SOPO (see **E23.12**). There is a notification requirement under the CJA 2003, s. 80 and sch. 3 subject to the age of offender and the sentence imposed (see **E25**).

Elements

B3.165 The elements of the offence are essentially the same as those under s. 9 (see **B3.63**) but also include the additional features relating to the position of the accused as a care worker, the mental disorder of the victim and the *mens rea* of the accused. As a good illustration of the way in which the SOA 2003 has widened protection for persons who are vulnerable because of their mental state, proceedings have been brought successfully under s. 38 where the complainant was suffering from post-natal depression when her social worker had sexual intercourse with her (*Bradford* [2006] EWCA Crim 2629).

The provisions of s. 73 apply (see **B3.37**) when the alleged victim is less than 16 years old.

Care Workers: Causing or Inciting Sexual Activity

Sexual Offences Act 2003, s. 39 **B3.166**

(1) A person (A) commits an offence if—
 (a) he intentionally causes or incites another person (B) to engage in an activity,
 (b) the activity is sexual,
 (c) B has a mental disorder,
 (d) A knows or could reasonably be expected to know that B has a mental disorder, and
 (e) A is involved in B's care in a way that falls within section 42.

(2) Where in proceedings for an offence under this section it is proved that the other person had a mental disorder, it is to be taken that the defendant knew or could reasonably have been expected to know that that person had a mental disorder unless sufficient evidence is adduced to raise an issue as to whether he knew or could reasonably have been expected to know it.

Procedure

An allegation of an offence contrary to s. 39 is triable either way unless the conduct involves penetration, in which case it is triable only on indictment. Upon trial on indictment, it is a class 3 offence. The extra-territorial jurisdiction provisions of s. 72 apply (see **B3.268**). **B3.167**

See **B3.285** for alternative verdicts.

Indictment

Statement of Offence **B3.168**

Causing or inciting a mentally disordered person to engage in a sexual activity by a care worker for whose care he was responsible contrary to section 39(1) of the Sexual Offences Act 2003.

Particulars of Offence

A, on or about the . . . day of . . . being then involved in V's care knowing that V had a mental disorder or in circumstances where he could reasonably be expected to have known that V had a mental disorder intentionally caused or incited V, to engage in a sexual activity *[namely, by penetration . . .]*.

Sentencing

Where penetration is concerned, the maximum penalty on indictment is 14 years' imprisonment. Otherwise it is ten years on conviction on indictment or, on summary conviction, six months or a fine not exceeding the statutory maximum, or both (s. 39(3) and (4)). Note that for these purposes penetration attracting the higher penalty may be of B's anus or vagina seemingly by any part of the body or an object, or B's mouth with a person's penis. Where, however, it is B who penetrates another's anus or vagina such penetration may be by any part of B's body or anything else or by penetration of another's mouth by B's penis. **B3.169**

The SGC Guideline, *Sexual Offences Act 2003* (April 2007), applies to offenders sentenced on or after 14 May 2007 for this offence. For the full text of this guideline, see **appendix 8** at part 8. Aggravating and mitigating factors in the guideline are additional to those set out in the SGC Guideline on *Seriousness* (December 2004), paras. 1.20 – 1.24 (see **appendix 8** at part 3). The sentences for public protection (see **E5**) must be considered in all such cases. In every case the court should consider a disqualification from working with children (see **E23.11**) and a SOPO (see **E23.12**). There is a notification requirement under the CJA 2003, s. 80 and sch. 3 subject to the age of the offender and the sentence imposed (see **E25**).

Elements

B3.170 The elements of the offence are essentially the same as those under s. 10 (see **B3.68**) but also include the additional features relating to the position of the accused as a care worker, the mental disorder of the victim and the *mens rea* of the accused.

Care Workers: Sexual Activity in the Presence of a Person with a Mental Disorder

B3.171 **Sexual Offences Act 2003, s. 40**

(1) A person (A) commits an offence if—
  (a) he intentionally engages in an activity,
  (b) the activity is sexual,
  (c) for the purpose of obtaining sexual gratification, he engages in it—
    (i) when another person (B) is present or is in a place from which A can be observed, and
    (ii) knowing or believing that B is aware, or intending that B should be aware, that he is engaging in it,
  (d) B has a mental disorder,
  (e) A knows or could reasonably be expected to know that B has a mental disorder, and
  (f) A is involved in B's care in a way that falls within section 42.

(2) Where in proceedings for an offence under this section it is proved that the other person had a mental disorder, it is to be taken that the defendant knew or could reasonably have been expected to know that that person had a mental disorder unless sufficient evidence is adduced to raise an issue as to whether he knew or could reasonably have been expected to know it.

Procedure

B3.172 An allegation of an offence contrary to s. 40 is triable either way. If tried on indictment, it is a class 3 offence. The extra-territorial jurisdiction provisions of s. 72 apply (see **B3.268**).

See **B3.285** for alternative verdicts.

Sentencing

B3.173 The maximum sentence for an offence under the SOA 2003, s. 40, on conviction on indictment is seven years' imprisonment. On summary conviction, the maximum is six months or a fine not exceeding the statutory maximum, or both.

The SGC Guideline, *Sexual Offences Act 2003* (April 2007), applies to offenders sentenced on or after 14 May 2007 for this offence. For the full text of this guideline, see **appendix 8** at part 8. Aggravating and mitigating factors in the guideline are additional to those set out in the SGC Guideline on *Seriousness* (December 2004), paras. 1.20 – 1.24 (see **appendix 8** at part 3). The sentences for public protection (see **E5**) must be considered in all such cases. In every case the court should consider a disqualification from working with children (see **E23.11**) and a SOPO (see **E23.12**). There is a notification requirement under the CJA 2003, s. 80 and sch. 3 subject to the age of the offender and the sentence imposed (see **E25**).

Elements

B3.174 The elements of the offence are essentially the same as those under s. 11 (see **B3.73**) but also include the additional features relating to the position of the accused as a care worker, the mental disorder of the victim and the *mens rea* of the accused.

For 'gratification', see **B3.78**.

Care Workers: Causing a Person with a Mental Disorder to Watch a Sexual Act

Sexual Offences Act 2003, s. 41 B3.175

(1) A person (A) commits an offence if—
  (a) for the purpose of obtaining sexual gratification, he intentionally causes another person (B) to watch a third person engaging in an activity, or to look at an image of any person engaging in an activity,
  (b) the activity is sexual,
  (c) B has a mental disorder,
  (d) A knows or could reasonably be expected to know that B has a mental disorder, and
  (e) A is involved in B's care in a way that falls within section 42.

(2) Where in proceedings for an offence under this section it is proved that the other person had a mental disorder, it is to be taken that the defendant knew or could reasonably have been expected to know that that person had a mental disorder unless sufficient evidence is adduced to raise an issue as to whether he knew or could reasonably have been expected to know it.

Procedure

An allegation of an offence contrary to s. 41 is triable either way. If tried on indictment, it is a class 3 offence. The extra-territorial jurisdiction provisions of s. 72 apply (see **B3.268**). B3.176

See **B3.285** for alternative verdicts.

Sentencing

The maximum penalties for an offence under the SOA 2003, s. 41, are the same as for an offence under s. 40 (see **B3.173**). B3.177

The SGC Guideline, *Sexual Offences Act 2003* (April 2007), applies to offenders sentenced on or after 14 May 2007 for this offence. For the full text of this guideline, see **appendix 8** at part 8. Aggravating and mitigating factors in the guideline are additional to those set out in the SGC Guideline on *Seriousness* (December 2004), paras. 1.20 – 1.24 (see **appendix 8** at part 3). The sentences for public protection (see **E5**) must be considered in all such cases. In every case the court should consider a disqualification from working with children (see **E23.11**) and a SOPO (see **E23.12**). There is a notification requirement under the CJA 2003, s. 80 and sch. 3 subject to the age of the offender and the sentence imposed (see **E25**).

Elements

The elements of the offence are essentially the same as those under s. 12 (see **B3.78**) but also include the additional features relating to the position of the accused as a care worker, the mental disorder of the victim and the *mens rea* of the accused. The offence under s. 41 is also limited to 'causing' whilst s. 12 prohibits both causing and incitement. B3.178

For 'gratification', see **B3.78**.

ABUSE OF CHILDREN THROUGH PROSTITUTION AND PORNOGRAPHY

Sections 47 to 50 govern offences against children that are committed in relation to prostitution or pornography. Section 51 is a definitional section of common application to each of ss. 47 to 50. B3.179

Sexual Offences Act 2003, s. 51

(1) For the purposes of sections 48 to 50, a person is involved in pornography if an indecent image of that person is recorded; and similar expressions, and 'pornography', are to be interpreted accordingly.

(2) In those sections 'prostitute' means a person (A) who, on at least one occasion and whether or not compelled to do so, offers or provides sexual services to another person in return for payment or a promise of payment to A or a third person; and 'prostitution' is to be interpreted accordingly.
(3) In subsection (2), 'payment' means any financial advantage, including the discharge of an obligation to pay or the provision of goods or services (including sexual services) gratuitously or at a discount.

Paying for Sexual Services of a Child

B3.180 **Sexual Offences Act 2003, s. 47**

(1) A person (A) commits an offence if—
(a) he intentionally obtains for himself the sexual services of another person (B),
(b) before obtaining those services, he has made or promised payment for those services to B or a third person, or knows that another person has made or promised such a payment, and
(c) either—
(i) B is under 18, and A does not reasonably believe that B is 18 or over, or
(ii) B is under 13.
(2) In this section, 'payment' means any financial advantage, including the discharge of an obligation to pay or the provision of goods or services (including sexual services) gratuitously or at a discount.

Procedure

B3.181 An allegation of an offence contrary to s. 47 is triable either way unless the conduct involves penetration, in which case it is triable only on indictment. Upon trial on indictment, it is ordinarily a class 3 offence but where penetration is alleged then it is a class 2 offence. The extra-territorial jurisdiction provisions of s. 72 apply (see **B3.268**).

See **B3.285** for alternative verdicts.

Indictment

B3.182 *Statement of Offence*

Intentionally obtaining the sexual services of a person under the age of 18 years by prior payment or promise of payment to that person or another person contrary to section 47(1) of the Sexual Offences Act 2003.

Particulars of Offence

A, on or about the . . . day of . . . intentionally obtained the sexual services of V then a child under the age of 18 [13] years then knowing that V was under the age of 18 years or not believing on reasonable grounds that V was over the age of 18 years by making or promising payment for such services to V or to another person before obtaining those services.

Sentencing

B3.183 The maximum penalty for an offence under the SOA 2003, s. 47, varies according to the age of the child and whether or not the offence involved penetration.

Sexual Offences Act 2003, s. 47

(3) A person guilty of an offence under this section against a person under 13, where subsection (6) applies, is liable on conviction on indictment to imprisonment for life.
(4) Unless subsection (3) applies, a person guilty of an offence under this section against a person under 16 is liable—
(a) where subsection (6) applies, on conviction on indictment, to imprisonment for a term not exceeding 14 years;
(b) in any other case—
(i) on summary conviction, to imprisonment for a term not exceeding 6 months or a fine not exceeding the statutory maximum or both;
(ii) on conviction on indictment, to imprisonment for a term not exceeding 14 years.

(5) Unless subsection (3) or (4) applies, a person guilty of an offence under this section is liable—
  (a) on summary conviction, to imprisonment for a term not exceeding 6 months or a fine not exceeding the statutory maximum or both;
  (b) on conviction on indictment, to imprisonment for a term not exceeding 7 years.

(6) This subsection applies where the offence involved—
  (a) penetration of B's anus or vagina with a part of A's body or anything else,
  (b) penetration of B's mouth with A's penis,
  (c) penetration of A's anus or vagina with a part of B's body or by B with anything else, or
  (d) penetration of A's mouth with B's penis.

The SGC Guideline, *Sexual Offences Act 2003* (April 2007), applies to offenders sentenced on or after 14 May 2007 for this offence. For the full text of this guideline, see **appendix 8** at part 8. Aggravating and mitigating factors in the guideline are additional to those set out in the SGC Guideline on *Seriousness* (December 2004), paras. 1.20 – 1.24 (see **appendix 8** at part 3). The sentences for public protection (see **E5**) must be considered in all such cases. In every case the court should consider a disqualification from working with children (see **E23.11**) and a SOPO (see **E23.12**). There is a notification requirement under the CJA 2003, s. 80 and sch. 3 where the victim was under 16 and the offender was aged 18 or over or was sentenced to at least 12 months' imprisonment (see **E25**).

Elements

The offender (A) must intentionally obtain the sexual services of a person under the age of 18 (B). Before he does so he must have either made or promised payment to the child or a third party or must be aware that such a payment has been made or promised. **B3.184**

Section 47(2) contains a very broad definition of payment.

It is a defence for A that he reasonably believed that B was not under 18 years of age even though B was actually under 18. However, if B was under 13 at the material time then no such defence is available.

Causing or Inciting Child Prostitution or Pornography

Sexual Offences Act 2003, s. 48 **B3.185**

(1) A person (A) commits an offence if—
  (a) he intentionally causes or incites another person (B) to become a prostitute, or to be involved in pornography, in any part of the world, and
  (b) either—
    (i) B is under 18, and A does not reasonably believe that B is 18 or over, or
    (ii) B is under 13.

Procedure

An allegation of an offence contrary to s. 48 is triable either way. If tried on indictment, it is a class 3 offence. The extra-territorial jurisdiction provisions of s. 72 apply (see **B3.268**). **B3.186**

See **B3.285** for alternative verdicts.

Indictment

Statement of Offence **B3.187**

Intentionally causing or inciting a child under the age of 18 years to become a prostitute in any part of the world contrary so section 48(1) of the Sexual Offences Act 2003

or

Intentionally causing or inciting a child under the age of 18 years to be involved in pornography in any part of the world contrary to section 48(1) of the Sexual Offences Act 2003.

Particulars of Offence

A, on or about the . . . day of . . . intentionally caused [incited] V then a child under the age of 18 years to engage in prostitution in any part of the world [to engage in pornography in any part of the world]

Sentencing

B3.188 The maximum sentence for an offence under the SOA 2003, s. 48, on conviction on indictment is 14 years' imprisonment. On summary conviction, the maximum sentence is six months or a fine of the statutory maximum, or both (s. 48(2)).

The SGC Guideline, *Sexual Offences Act 2003* (April 2007), applies to offenders sentenced on or after 14 May 2007 for this offence. For the full text of this guideline, see **appendix 8** at part 8. Aggravating and mitigating factors in the guideline are additional to those set out in the SGC Guideline on *Seriousness* (December 2004), paras. 1.20 – 1.24 (see **appendix 8** at part 3). The sentences for public protection (see **E5**) must be considered in all such cases. In every case the court should consider a disqualification from working with children (see **E23.11**) and a SOPO (see **E23.12**).

Elements

B3.189 The offender (A) must intentionally cause or incite a person under the age of 18 (B) to become a prostitute or become involved in pornography. Plainly, for an accused to be guilty of the incitement offence it is not necessary that B actually becomes a prostitute or involves himself in pornography.

It is a defence for A that he reasonably believed that B was not under 18 years of age even though B was actually under 18. However, if B was under 13 at the material time then no such defence is available.

Controlling a Child Prostitute or a Child Involved in Pornography

B3.190 **Sexual Offences Act 2003, s. 49**

(1) A person (A) commits an offence if—
  (a) he intentionally controls any of the activities of another person (B) relating to B's prostitution or involvement in pornography in any part of the world, and
  (b) either—
    (i) B is under 18, and A does not reasonably believe that B is 18 or over, or
    (ii) B is under 13.

Procedure

B3.191 An allegation of an offence contrary to s. 49 is triable either way. If tried on indictment, it is a class 3 offence. The extra-territorial jurisdiction provisions of s. 72 apply (see **B3.268**).

See **B3.285** for alternative verdicts.

Indictment

B3.192 *Statement of Offence*

Intentionally controlling the activities of another person under the age of 18 years relating to that person's prostitution or involvement in prostitution or pornography in any part of the world contrary to section 49 of the Sexual Offences Act 2003.

Particulars of Offence

A, on or about the . . . day of . . . intentionally controlled activities of V, then a child under the age of 18 years or over relating to V's involvement in any part of the world in prostitution [pornography].

Sentencing

B3.193 The maximum sentence for an offence under the SOA 2003, s. 49, on conviction on indictment is 14 years' imprisonment. On summary conviction, the maximum sentence is six months or a fine of the statutory maximum, or both (s. 49(2)).

The SGC Guideline, *Sexual Offences Act 2003* (April 2007), applies to offenders sentenced on or after 14 May 2007 for this offence. For the full text of this guideline, see **appendix 8** at part 8. Aggravating and mitigating factors in the guideline are additional to those set out in the SGC Guideline on *Seriousness* (December 2004), paras. 1.20 – 1.24 (see **appendix 8** at part 3). The sentences for public protection (see **E5**) must be considered in all such cases. In every case the court should consider a disqualification from working with children (see **E23.11**) and a SOPO (see **E23.12**).

Elements

The essence of the offence is that A must intentionally control the prostitution or pornography-related activities of B. For 'control' see **B3.208**. **B3.194**

It is a defence for A that he reasonably believed that B was not under 18 years of age even though B was actually under 18. However, if B was under 13 at the material time then no such defence is available.

B Part B Offences

Arranging or Facilitating Child Prostitution or Pornography

Sexual Offences Act 2003, s. 50 **B3.195**

(1) A person (A) commits an offence if—
  (a) he intentionally arranges or facilitates the prostitution or involvement in pornography in any part of the world of another person (B), and
  (b) either—
    (i) B is under 18, and A does not reasonably believe that B is 18 or over, or
    (ii) B is under 13.

Procedure

An allegation of an offence contrary to s. 50 is triable either way. If tried on indictment, it is a class 3 offence. The extra-territorial jurisdiction provisions of s. 72 apply (see **B3.268**). See **B3.285** for alternative verdicts. **B3.196**

Sentencing

The maximum sentence for an offence under the SOA 2003, s. 50, on conviction on indictment is 14 years' imprisonment. On summary conviction, the maximum sentence is six months or a fine of the statutory maximum, or both (s. 50(2)). **B3.197**

The SGC Guideline, *Sexual Offences Act 2003* (April 2007), applies to offenders sentenced on or after 14 May 2007 for this offence. For the full text of this guideline, see **appendix 8** at part 8. Aggravating and mitigating factors in the guideline are additional to those set out in the SGC Guideline on *Seriousness* (December 2004), paras. 1.20 – 1.24 (see **appendix 8** at part 3). The sentences for public protection (see **E5**) must be considered in all such cases. In every case the court should consider a disqualification from working with children (see **E23.11**) and a SOPO (see **E23.12**).

Elements

The offender (A) must intentionally arrange or facilitate the involvement in prostitution or pornography of a person under the age of 18 (B). **B3.198**

It is a defence for A that he reasonably believed that B was not under 18 years of age even though B was actually under 18. However, if B was under 13 at the material time then no such defence is available.

EXPLOITATION OF PROSTITUTION

Offences concerning Exploitation of Prostitution

B3.199 Sections 52 and 53 of the SOA 2003 concern the exploitation of prostitution. Common interpretation provisions in s. 54 apply to them.

Sexual Offences Act 2003, s. 54

(1) In sections 52 and 53, 'gain' means—
  (a) any financial advantage, including the discharge of an obligation to pay or the provision of goods or services (including sexual services) gratuitously or at a discount; or
  (b) the goodwill of any person which is or appears likely, in time, to bring financial advantage.

(2) In those sections 'prostitute' and 'prostitution' have the meaning given by section 51(2).

Gain is expressed in terms of either financial advantage or good will which appears likely to bring financial advantage in the future. Financial advantage is widely defined by s. 54(1).

The extra-territorial jurisdiction provisions of s. 72 do not apply to these offences and therefore the accused's acts constituting the offence must be committed in England and Wales.

Causing or Inciting Prostitution for Gain

B3.200 **Sexual Offences Act 2003, s. 52**

(1) A person commits an offence if—
  (a) he intentionally causes or incites another person to become a prostitute in any part of the world, and
  (b) he does so for or in the expectation of gain for himself or a third person.

Procedure

B3.201 An allegation of an offence contrary to s. 52 is triable either way. If tried on indictment, it is a class 3 offence.

See **B3.285** for alternative verdicts.

Indictment

B3.202 *Statement of Offence*

Intentionally causing or inciting a person to become a prostitute in any part of the world in the expectation of gain contrary to section 52(1) of the Sexual Offences Act 2003.

Particulars of Offence

A, on or about the . . . day of . . . intentionally and in the expectation of gain to himself or another caused [incited] V to become a prostitute in any part of the world.

Sentencing

B3.203 The maximum penalty for an offence under the SOA 2003, s. 52, on conviction on indictment is seven years' imprisonment. On summary conviction, the maximum is six months or a fine not exceeding the statutory maximum, or both (s. 52(2)).

The SGC Guideline, *Sexual Offences Act 2003* (April 2007), applies to offenders sentenced on or after 14 May 2007 for this offence. For the full text of this guideline, see **appendix 8** at part 8. Aggravating and mitigating factors in the guideline are additional to those set out in the SGC Guideline on *Seriousness* (December 2004), paras. 1.20 – 1.24 (see **appendix 8** at part 3). The sentences for public protection (see E5) must be considered in all such cases. In every case the court should consider a disqualification from working with children (see **E23.11**) and a SOPO (see **E23.12**).

Elements

The essence of the offence is that the accused must intentionally cause or incite another person to become a prostitute in any part of the world. The person's acts must, however, have been done in England and Wales as the extra-territorial jurisdiction provisions of s. 72 do not apply. Plainly, the person incited need not in fact have engaged in an act of prostitution. The accused must act in the expectation of gain for himself or a third person. **B3.204**

The wide definition of 'prostitute' contained in s. 51(2) applies to this offence by virtue of s. 54(2) (see **B3.179**).

Controlling Prostitution for Gain

Sexual Offences Act 2003, s. 53 **B3.205**

(1) A person commits an offence if—
 (a) he intentionally controls any of the activities of another person relating to that person's prostitution in any part of the world, and
 (b) he does so for or in the expectation of gain for himself or a third person.

Procedure

An allegation of an offence contrary to s. 53 is triable either way. If tried on indictment, it is a class 3 offence. **B3.206**

See **B3.285** for alternative verdicts.

Sentencing

The maximum penalty for an offence under the SOA 2003, s. 53, on conviction on indictment is seven years' imprisonment. On summary conviction, the maximum is six months or a fine not exceeding the statutory maximum, or both (s. 53(2)). **B3.207**

The SGC Guideline, *Sexual Offences Act 2003* (April 2007), applies to offenders sentenced on or after 14 May 2007 for this offence. For the full text of this guideline, see **appendix 8** at part 8. Aggravating and mitigating factors in the guideline are additional to those set out in the SGC Guideline on *Seriousness* (December 2004), paras. 1.20 – 1.24 (see **appendix 8** at part 3). The sentences for public protection (see **E5**) must be considered in all such cases. In every case the court should consider a disqualification from working with children (see **E23.11**) and a SOPO (see **E23.12**).

Elements

The essence of the offence is that the accused must intentionally control any of the activities of another person relating to that person's prostitution in any part of the world. Such control may be direct or through an intermediary. In *Drew* (December 2006 unreported), a first instance decision by HHJ Rivlin in the Crown Court at Southwark, it was held that 'control' is a simple everyday word which may embrace 'compulsion' as one of its more extreme manifestations but, equally, it may also embrace any one of a number of situations involving the power to exert influence over another person's behaviour in connection with a particular activity. Thus 'control' could well include a person 'ordering', 'directing', 'instructing' or 'requiring' a prostitute either to do or not to do something in connection with any of her activities in that capacity. The judge adopted the suggestion in *Rook and Ward on Sexual Offences* (3rd edn, Sweet & Maxwell, 2004), pp. 309–11, that the provision may include: controlling the prostitute's days of employment, her hours of employment, where she should work, the price to be charged by her and the commission to be paid to the agency, the services which she shall or shall not render or the clothing she should not wear in the course of her work. The judge held that the fact that a prostitute may be willing to work on these terms, **B3.208** and be subject to one kind of control or another, may possibly amount to a mitigating circumstance, but cannot affect the issue of criminal responsibility.

Because the extra-territorial jurisdiction provisions of s. 72 do not apply, the accused's acts must, however, be done in or from England and Wales. Here too 'prostitution' bears the wide protective meaning in s. 51(2) (see **B3.179**). Thus, controlling an activity relating to a single act of prostitution is sufficient to bring an offender within the section.

The accused must act with an expectation of gain. Such an expectation may be for himself or a third party. 'Gain' is defined in terms of financial advantage (see s. 54(1) at **B3.199**).

TRAFFICKING

B3.209 Sections 57 to 59 provide for offences which were formerly governed by nationality and immigration legislation. The sections speak of 'relevant offences', a term defined in s. 60(1). Extended jurisdiction provisions are contained in s. 60(2) and (3).

Sexual Offences Act 2003, s. 60

(1) In sections 57 to 59, 'relevant offence' means—
  (a) an offence under this Part,
  (b) an offence under section 1(1)(a) of the Protection of Children Act 1978 (c 37),
  (c) an offence listed in schedule 1 to the Criminal Justice (Children) (Northern Ireland) Order 1998 (SI 1998/1504),
  (d) an offence under article 3(1)(a) of the Protection of Children (Northern Ireland) Order 1978 (SI 1978/1047), or
  (e) anything done outside England and Wales and Northern Ireland which is not an offence within any of paragraphs (a) to (d) but would be if done in England and Wales or Northern Ireland.

(2) Sections 57 to 59 apply to anything done—
  (a) in the United Kingdom, or
  (b) outside the United Kingdom, by a body incorporated under the law of a part of the United Kingdom or by an individual to whom subsection (3) applies.

(3) This subsection applies to—
  (a) a British citizen,
  (b) a British overseas territories citizen,
  (c) a British National (Overseas),
  (d) a British Overseas citizen,
  (e) a person who is a British subject under the British Nationality Act 1981,
  (f) a British protected person within the meaning given by section 50(1) of that Act.

The reference at s. 60(1)(b) to the Protection of Children Act 1978, s. 1(1)(a), relates to photographs and pseudo-photographs (see **B3.274**). The effect of the jurisdiction provisions is that any offence under part 1 of the SOA 2003 or the 1978 Act is encompassed by ss. 57 to 59. In addition, any behaviour abroad by any of the persons mentioned in s. 60(2) or a corporation which, if committed within England, Wales or Northern Ireland would be caught by s. 60(1), becomes triable in England and Wales.

The ambit of s. 60 is in one way narrower than s. 72 (see **B3.268**) in that the status of British resident is not sufficient to bring a person within the section. However, s. 60 applies beyond citizenship and covers the circumstances set out in s. 60(3) which are not within the compass of s. 72.

Trafficking into the UK for Sexual Exploitation

B3.210 **Sexual Offences Act 2003, s. 57**

(1) A person commits an offence if he intentionally arranges or facilitates the arrival in the United Kingdom of another person (B) and either—

(a) he intends to do anything to or in respect of B, after B's arrival but in any part of the world, which if done will involve the commission of a relevant offence, or
(b) he believes that another person is likely to do something to or in respect of B, after B's arrival but in any part of the world, which if done will involve the commission of a relevant offence.

Procedure

An allegation of an offence contrary to s. 57 is triable either way and is a class 3 offence when tried on indictment. The extra-territorial jurisdiction provisions of s. 60 apply (see **B3.209**). **B3.211**

See **B3.285** for alternative verdicts.

Indictment

Statement of Offence **B3.212**

Intentionally arranging or facilitating the arrival in the United Kingdom of another person for the purposes of sexual exploitation contrary to section 57(1) of the Sexual Offences Act 2003

Particulars of Offence

A, on or about the . . . day of . . . intentionally arranged or facilitated the arrival in the United Kingdom of V intending to do acts to or in respect of V, after V's arrival but in any part of the world which will involve the commission of a relevant offence namely [here set out the acts constituting the relevant offence]

or

A, on or about the . . . day of . . . intentionally arranged or facilitated the arrival in the United Kingdom of V believing that another person was likely to do an act to or in respect of V after V's arrival but in any part of the world, which would involve the commission of a relevant offence, namely [here set out the relevant offence]

Sentencing

The maximum penalty on conviction on indictment is 14 years' imprisonment. On summary conviction, the maximum penalty is six months or a fine not exceeding the statutory maximum, or both (s. 57(2)). **B3.213**

The SGC Guideline, *Sexual Offences Act 2003* (April 2007), applies to offenders sentenced on or after 14 May 2007 for this offence. For the full text of this guideline, see **appendix 8** at part 8. Aggravating and mitigating factors in the guideline are additional to those set out in the SGC Guideline on *Seriousness* (December 2004), paras. 1.20 – 1.24 (see **appendix 8** at part 3). The sentences for public protection (see **E5**) must be considered in all such cases. In every case the court should consider a disqualification from working with children (see **E23.11**) and a SOPO (see **E23.12**). For powers of forfeiture relating to land, vehicles, ships and aircraft used in commission of an offence under the SOA 2003, ss. 57 to 59, see the VCRA 2006, s. 54 and sch. 4.

In *Maka* [2006] 2 Cr App R (S) 101, sentences totalling 18 years were upheld in the case of an offender who trafficked a 15-year-old Lithuanian girl into the country and repeatedly sold her to others for the purposes of prostitution. The Court of Appeal derived some assistance from the reasoning in the earlier case of *A-G's Ref (No. 6 of 2004) (Plakici)* [2005] 1 Cr App R (S) 83 (see **B23.18**) in which a sentence of ten years had been increased on appeal to 23 years in relation to a variety of offences, some of which were similar to the trafficking offence in the present case. In that case, however, a higher sentence was justified by the considerable number of women involved, the greater sums of money, and the offender's involvement over a longer period of time. Both the above cases were considered in *Roci* [2006] 2 Cr App R (S) 106, where a sentence of nine years' imprisonment was appropriate where the offender had arranged for the immigration of a number of adult women who were willing to work as prostitutes into the country. The women had been coerced by threats and by reason of the conditions in which they were required to work, but the coercion and corruption was much less than that in *Maka*. In *Ramaj* [2006] 2 Cr App R (S) 557, a sentence of five years' detention in a young offender institution was appropriate where the offender facilitated the arrival of an 18-year-old girl into the country with a view to prostitution, but where there was no clear evidence of coercion. The Court of Appeal was referred to both *Roci* and *Maka*, and was of the view that the facts of those cases were very much more serious. In *Kizlaite* [2007] 1 Cr App R (S) 156, however, sentences totalling 11 years and 21 years' detention in a young offender institution were upheld in the case of two offenders who were described by the Court of Appeal as 'sexual slave traders'.

Elements

B3.214 It is plainly not necessary that any relevant offence occurs.

Whilst the relevant offence may take place anywhere in the world, the conduct which amounts to facilitating or arranging the arrival in the UK must take place in the UK unless the perpetrator is an individual falling within the ambit of s. 60(3) or a body incorporated within the UK.

'Arrangement' and 'facilitation' are questions of fact.

Trafficking within the UK for Sexual Exploitation

B3.215 **Sexual Offences Act 2003, s. 58**

(1) A person commits an offence if he intentionally arranges or facilitates travel within the United Kingdom by another person (B) and either—
   (a) he intends to do anything to or in respect of B, during or after the journey and in any part of the world, which if done will involve the commission of a relevant offence, or
   (b) he believes that another person is likely to do something to or in respect of B, during or after the journey and in any part of the world, which if done will involve the commission of a relevant offence.

Procedure

B3.216 An allegation of an offence contrary to s. 58 is triable either way and is a class 3 offence when tried on indictment. The extra-territorial jurisdiction provisions of s. 60 apply (see B3.209).

See B3.285 for alternative verdicts.

Indictment

B3.217 *Statement of Offence*

Intentionally arranging or facilitating travel within the United Kingdom of another person for the purposes of sexual exploitation contrary to section 58(1) of the Sexual Offences Act 2003.

Particulars of Offence

A, on or about the . . . day of . . . intentionally arranged or facilitated travel within the United Kingdom by V intending to do an act to or in respect of B during or after the journey and in any part of the world which, if done, would involve the commission of a relevant offence, namely [here specify the relevant offence].

or

A, on or about the . . . day of . . . intentionally arranged or facilitated travel within the United Kingdom by V believing that another person would be likely to do something to or in respect of V during or after the journey which if done would involve the commission of a relevant offence, namely [here specify the relevant offence].

Sentencing

The maximum penalty on conviction on indictment is 14 years' imprisonment. On summary conviction, the maximum penalty is six months or a fine not exceeding the statutory maximum, or both (s. 58(2)). B3.218

The approach to sentencing of offences under s. 57 is applicable to offences under s. 58 (see B3.213).

Elements

It is plainly not necessary that any relevant offence occurs. B3.219

Whilst the relevant offence may take place anywhere in the world, the conduct which amounts to facilitating or arranging the arrival in the UK must take place in the UK unless the perpetrator is an individual falling within the ambit of s. 60(3) or a body incorporated within the UK.

'Arrangement' and 'facilitation' are matters of fact.

Trafficking out of the UK for Sexual Exploitation

Sexual Offences Act 2003, s. 59 B3.220

(1) A person commits an offence if he intentionally arranges or facilitates the departure from the United Kingdom of another person (B) and either—
   (a) he intends to do anything to or in respect of B, after B's departure but in any part of the world, which if done will involve the commission of a relevant offence, or
   (b) he believes that another person is likely to do something to or in respect of B, after B's departure but in any part of the world, which if done will involve the commission of a relevant offence.

Procedure

An allegation of an offence contrary to s. 59 is triable either way and is a class 3 offence when tried on indictment. The extra-territorial jurisdiction provisions of s. 60 apply (see B3.209). B3.221

See B3.285 for alternative verdicts.

Sentencing

The maximum penalty on conviction on indictment is 14 years' imprisonment. On summary conviction, the maximum penalty is six months or a fine not exceeding the statutory maximum, or both (s. 59(2)). See also **B3.213**. B3.222

Elements

It is plainly not necessary that any relevant offence occurs. B3.223

Whilst the relevant offence may take place anywhere in the world, the conduct which amounts to facilitating or arranging the arrival in the UK must take place in the UK unless the perpetrator is an individual falling within the ambit of s. 60(3) or a body incorporated within the UK.

'Arrangement' and 'facilitation' are matters of fact.

PREPARATORY OFFENCES

Administering a Substance with Intent

B3.224 **Sexual Offences Act 2003, s. 61**

(1) A person commits an offence if he intentionally administers a substance to, or causes a substance to be taken by, another person (B)—
   (a) knowing that B does not consent, and
   (b) with the intention of stupefying or overpowering B, so as to enable any person to engage in a sexual activity that involves B.

Procedure

B3.225 An allegation of an offence contrary to s. 61 is triable either way; when tried on indictment, it is a class 3 offence. The extra-territorial jurisdiction provisions of s. 72 apply (see **B3.268**) if the victim was under the age of 16 at the time of the alleged offence.

See **B3.285** for alternative verdicts.

Indictment

B3.226 *Statement of Offence*

Intentionally administering a substance to or causing a substance to be taken by another with the intention of stupefying or overpowering that other in order to enable another person to engage in sexual activity with that person contrary to section 61(1) of the Sexual Offences Act 2003.

Particulars of Offence

A, on or about the . . . day of . . . intentionally administered a substance to [caused a substance to be taken by] V knowing that V did not consent and with the intention of stupefying or overpowering V so as to enable himself or another to engage in a sexual activity involving V.

Sentencing

B3.227 The maximum penalty for an offence under the SOA 2003, s. 61, on conviction on indictment is ten years' imprisonment. On summary conviction, the maximum is six months or a fine not exceeding the statutory maximum, or both.

The SGC Guideline, *Sexual Offences Act 2003* (April 2007), applies to offenders sentenced on or after 14 May 2007 for this offence. For the full text of this guideline, see **appendix 8** at part 8. Aggravating and mitigating factors in the guideline are additional to those set out in the SGC Guideline on *Seriousness* (December 2004), paras. 1.20 – 1.24 (see **appendix 8** at part 3). The sentences for public protection (see **E5**) must be considered in all such cases. In every case the court should consider a disqualification from working with children (see **E23.11**) and a SOPO (see **E23.12**). There is a notification requirement under the CJA 2003, s. 80 and sch. 3 (see **E25**).

Elements

B3.228 The Home Office Explanatory notes to the 2003 Act suggest that the substance may be administered to the victim in any way, e.g., in a drink, by injection or by covering the victim's face with a cloth impregnated with the substance. The offence is made out both where A administers the substance to the victim, B, or he persuades a third party, C, to administer the substance because C knows B and so is more easily able to do so. The intended sexual activity need not involve A but instead it may be planned that a third party have sex with B.

For the meaning of consent, see **B3.8**.

For 'sexual', see **B3.20**.

Committing an Offence with Intent to Commit a Sexual Offence

Sexual Offences Act 2003, s. 62 **B3.229**

(1) A person commits an offence under this section if he commits any offence with the intention of committing a relevant sexual offence.
(2) In this section, 'relevant sexual offence' means any offence under this Part (including an offence of aiding, abetting, counselling or procuring such an offence).

Procedure

An allegation of an offence contrary to s. 62 is triable either way unless the offence alleged is one of either kidnapping or false imprisonment. In such a case, the alleged offence is triable on indictment only. If tried on indictment, it is ordinarily a class 3 offence, but if the alleged offence is one of kidnapping or false imprisonment then it is a class 2 offence. If the victim was under 16 years of age at the time of the offence, the extra-territorial jurisdiction provisions of s. 72 apply (see **B3.268**). **B3.230**

See **B3.285** for alternative verdicts.

Indictment

Statement of Offence **B3.231**

Committing an offence with intent to commit a sexual offence contrary to section 62(1) of the Sexual Offences Act 2003.

Particulars of Offence

A, on or about the . . . day of . . . [e.g., unlawfully had in his possession a controlled drug of class B with intent to administer the same] with the intention of committing a relevant sexual offence, namely [specify relevant sexual offence e.g., under s. 61(1) of the Sexual Offences Act 2003].

Sentencing

The maximum penalty on conviction on indictment is ten years' imprisonment. However, where the offence is committed by kidnapping or false imprisonment, the maximum penalty is imprisonment for life. On summary conviction, the maximum penalty is six months or a fine not exceeding the statutory maximum, or both (s. 62(3) and (4)). **B3.232**

The SGC Guideline, *Sexual Offences Act 2003* (April 2007), applies to offenders sentenced on or after 14 May 2007 for this offence. For the full text of this guideline, see **appendix 8** at part 8. Aggravating and mitigating factors in the guideline are additional to those set out in the SGC Guideline on *Seriousness* (December 2004), paras. 1.20 – 1.24 (see **appendix 8** at part 3). The sentences for public protection (see **E5**) must be considered in all such cases. In every case the court should consider a disqualification from working with children (see **E23.11**) and a SOPO (see **E23.12**). There is a notification requirement under the CJA 2003, s. 80 and sch. 3, subject to the age of the offender and the sentence passed and subject to the age of the victim (see **E25**).

In *Wisniewski* [2005] 2 Cr App R (S) 236, the Court of Appeal dealt with a case of battery with intent to commit a sexual offence, where the offender had attacked two women, both of whom had sustained injuries but had managed to escape. Consecutive sentences of 18 months and three-and-a-half years were appropriate, giving full allowance for an early guilty plea. Rose LJ said that the offence was new but the nature of the conduct was not, and sentencers should be guided by the pre-existing authorities. Matters relevant to sentencing in such a case were the method and degree of force used, the nature and extent of the indecency intended, the degree of vulnerability of, and harm to, the victim, the circumstances of the attack, including the time of day and the place, and the level of risk posed by the offender. The offender's good character would afford only limited mitigation. Except where a good deal of violence was inflicted, the level of sentence was generally to be lower than was appropriate for offences of rape or attempted rape in similar circumstances.

Elements

B3.233 An offence 'under this part' means any within the SOA 2003, ss. 1 to 79.

It is submitted that it is not necessary for the prosecution to prove that a specific sexual offence was intended by the offender. Instead it will be sufficient that jurors are sure that an offence under part 1 was intended even though they may disagree as to the nature of the offence that the accused intended.

Trespass with Intent to Commit a Sexual Offence

B3.234

Sexual Offences Act 2003, s. 63

(1) A person commits an offence if—
  (a) he is a trespasser on any premises,
  (b) he intends to commit a relevant sexual offence on the premises, and
  (c) he knows that, or is reckless as to whether, he is a trespasser.

(2) In this section—
  'premises' includes a structure or part of a structure;
  'relevant sexual offence' has the same meaning as in section 62;
  'structure' includes a tent, vehicle or vessel or other temporary or movable structure.

Procedure

B3.235 An allegation of an offence contrary to s. 63 is triable either way; when tried on indictment, it is a class 3 offence. The extra-territorial jurisdiction provisions of s. 72 apply (see **B3.268**) if the victim was under the age of 16 at the time of the alleged offence.

See **B3.285** for alternative verdicts.

Indictment

B3.236

Statement of Offence

Trespass with intent to commit a sexual offence contrary to section 63(1) of the Sexual Offences Act 2003

Particulars of Offence

A, on or about the . . . day of . . . being a trespasser on premises and knowing that, or being reckless as to whether he was, a trespasser, intended to commit a relevant sexual offence on the premises, namely [here specify the relevant offence].

Sentencing

B3.237 The maximum penalty for an offence under the SOA 2003, s. 63, on conviction on indictment is ten years' imprisonment. On summary conviction, the maximum is six months or a fine not exceeding the statutory maximum, or both.

The SGC Guideline, *Sexual Offences Act 2003* (April 2007), applies to offenders sentenced on or after 14 May 2007 for this offence. For the full text of this guideline, see **appendix 8** at part 8. Aggravating and mitigating factors in the guideline are additional to those set out in the SGC Guideline on *Seriousness* (December 2004), paras. 1.20 – 1.24 (see **appendix 8** at part 3). The sentences for public protection (see **E5**) must be considered in all such cases. In every case the court should consider a disqualification from working with children (see **E23.11**) and a SOPO (see **E23.12**). There is a notification requirement under the CJA 2003, s. 80 and sch. 3, subject to the age of the offender and the sentence passed and subject to the age of the victim (see **E25**).

Elements

The offender must be at least reckless as to whether he is trespassing. As to the necessity for the prosecution to prove the nature of the relevant offence intended, see **B3.233**. **B3.238**

SEX WITH AN ADULT RELATIVE

Sex with an Adult Relative: Penetration

Sexual Offences Act 2003, s. 64 **B3.239**

(1) A person aged 16 or over (A) commits an offence if—
  (a) he intentionally penetrates another person's vagina or anus with a part of his body or anything else, or penetrates another person's mouth with his penis,
  (b) the penetration is sexual,
  (c) the other person (B) is aged 18 or over,
  (d) A is related to B in a way mentioned in subsection (2), and
  (e) A knows or could reasonably be expected to know that he is related to B in that way.
(2) The ways that A may be related to B are as parent, grandparent, child, grandchild, brother, sister, half-brother, half-sister, uncle, aunt, nephew or niece.
(3) In subsection (2)—
  (a) 'uncle' means the brother of a person's parent, and 'aunt' has a corresponding meaning;
  (b) 'nephew' means the child of a person's brother or sister, and 'niece' has a corresponding meaning.
(4) Where in proceedings for an offence under this section it is proved that the defendant was related to the other person in any of those ways, it is to be taken that the defendant knew or could reasonably have been expected to know that he was related in that way unless sufficient evidence is adduced to raise an issue as to whether he knew or could reasonably have been expected to know that he was.

Procedure

An allegation of an offence contrary to s. 64 is triable either way; when tried on indictment, it is a class 3 offence. **B3.240**

See **B3.285** for alternative verdicts.

Sentencing

The maximum penalty for an offence under the SOA 2003, s. 64, on conviction on indictment is two years' imprisonment. On summary conviction, the maximum is six months or a fine not exceeding the statutory maximum, or both (s. 64(5)). **B3.241**

The SGC Guideline, *Sexual Offences Act 2003* (April 2007), applies to offenders sentenced on or after 14 May 2007 for this offence. For the full text of this guideline, see **appendix 8** at part 8. Aggravating and mitigating factors in the guideline are additional to those set out in the SGC Guideline on *Seriousness* (December 2004), paras. 1.20 – 1.24 (see **appendix 8** at part 3). The sentences for public protection (see **E5**) must be considered in all such cases. In every case the court should consider a disqualification from working with children (see **E23.11**) and a SOPO (see **E23.12**). There is a notification requirement under the CJA 2003, s. 80 and sch. 3, subject to the age of the offender and the sentence imposed (see **E25**).

The age of the victim and the degree of coercion and corruption present will be especially relevant (*A-G's Ref (No. 1 of 1989)* [1989] 1 WLR 1117). According to Lord Lane CJ in *A-G's Ref (No. 1 of 1989)*:

> . . . it is stating the obvious to say that the gravity of the offence of incest varies greatly according, primarily, to the age of the victim and the related matter, namely, the degree of coercion or corruption.

> ... we venture to make the following suggestions as a broad guide to the level of sentence for various categories of the crime of incest. All are on the assumption that there has been no plea of guilty.
>
> *(1) Where the girl is over 16*
>
> Generally speaking a range from three years' imprisonment down to a nominal penalty will be appropriate depending in particular on the one hand on whether force was used, and upon the degree of harm, if any, to the girl, and on the other the desirability where it exists of keeping family disruption to a minimum. The older the girl, the greater the possibility that she may have been willing or even the instigating party to the liaison, a factor which will be reflected in the sentence. In other words, the lower the degree of corruption, the lower the penalty.

Elements

B3.242 Section 64 of the SOA 2003 contains a rebuttable presumption as to the accused's *mens rea* in respect of the relationship between him and the person he penetrates. If the prosecution prove that the relationship is a relevant one for the purposes of s. 64 then the accused is taken to have either known of that relationship, or could reasonably have been expected to know of it, unless he adduces sufficient evidence so as to raise an issue as to whether he knew or could reasonably have known of that relationship. The burden is evidential and once sufficient evidence is raised then the prosecution has the usual burden of proving the contrary to the criminal standard.

Sex with an Adult Relative: Consenting to Penetration

B3.243 Sexual Offences Act 2003, s. 65

(1) A person aged 16 or over (A) commits an offence if—
 (a) another person (B) penetrates A's vagina or anus with a part of B's body or anything else, or penetrates A's mouth with B's penis,
 (b) A consents to the penetration,
 (c) the penetration is sexual,
 (d) B is aged 18 or over,
 (e) A is related to B in a way mentioned in subsection (2), and
 (f) A knows or could reasonably be expected to know that he is related to B in that way.

Procedure

B3.244 An allegation of an offence contrary to s. 65 is triable either way; when tried on indictment, it is a class 3 offence.

See **B3.285** for alternative verdicts.

Indictment

B3.245 *Statement of Offence*

Consenting to the penetration of his body by a related person contrary to section 65(1) of the Sexual Offences Act 2003

Particulars of Offence

A on or about the ... day of ... being then a person aged 16 years or over permitted V a person related to her and over the age of 18 years sexually to penetrate [her vagina or anus][his anus] [with his penis, fingers,] [with a part of her body, namely her fingers].

Sentencing

B3.246 The maximum sentence for an offence under the SOA 2003, s. 65, on conviction on indictment is two years. On summary conviction, the maximum is six months or a fine not exceeding the statutory maximum, or both (s. 65(5)). See also **B3.241**.

Elements

Section 65 contains a rebuttable presumption as to the accused's *mens rea* in respect of the relationship between him and the person he penetrates. The provision is identical to that contained within s. 64 and reference should therefore be had to **B3.242** for its nature and effect. **B3.247**

OTHER OFFENCES

Exposure

Sexual Offences Act 2003, s. 66 **B3.248**

(1) A person commits an offence if—
 (a) he intentionally exposes his genitals, and
 (b) he intends that someone will see them and be caused alarm or distress.

Procedure

An allegation of an offence contrary to s. 66 is triable either way; when tried on indictment, it is a class 3 offence. **B3.249**

See **B3.285** for alternative verdicts.

Sentencing

The maximum penalty for an offence under the SOA 2003, s. 66, on conviction on indictment is two years' imprisonment. On summary conviction, the maximum is six months or a fine not exceeding the statutory maximum, or both. **B3.250**

The SGC Guideline, *Sexual Offences Act 2003* (April 2007), applies to offenders sentenced on or after 14 May 2007 for exposure. For the full text of this guideline, see **appendix 8** at part 8. Aggravating and mitigating factors in the guideline are additional to those set out in the SGC Guideline on *Seriousness* (December 2004), paras. 1.20 – 1.24 (see **appendix 8** at part 3). The sentences for public protection (see **E5**) must be considered in all such cases. In every case the court should consider a disqualification from working with children (see **E23.11**) and a SOPO (see **E23.12**). There is a notification requirement under the CJA 2003, s. 80 and sch. 3, subject to the age of the offender, the age of the victim, and the sentence imposed (see **E25**).

In *Mailer* [2006] 2 Cr App R (S) 563, a sentence of six months' imprisonment was upheld on a 26-year-old offender who exposed himself on two separate occasions to the same young woman while travelling on a bus. The offender indicated a plea of guilty in the magistrates' court but was committed for sentence. He had eight previous offences of indecent exposure on his record. See also *Cosco* [2005] 2 Cr App R (S) 405 at **B3.283**.

Elements

The essence of the offence is that the accused intentionally exposes his genitals and intends that another person see them and is thereby caused alarm or distress. The offence thus has a 'bolted on intent' and is therefore one of specific intent. Consequently, voluntary intoxication may negate the intent required for the offence (see *Heard* [2007] 3 All ER 306). **B3.251**

Voyeurism

Sexual Offences Act 2003, ss. 67 and 68 **B3.252**

67.—(1) A person commits an offence if—
 (a) for the purpose of obtaining sexual gratification, he observes another person doing a private act, and

(b) he knows that the other person does not consent to being observed for his sexual gratification.

(2) A person commits an offence if—

(a) he operates equipment with the intention of enabling another person to observe, for the purpose of obtaining sexual gratification, a third person (B) doing a private act, and

(b) he knows that B does not consent to his operating equipment with that intention.

(3) A person commits an offence if—

(a) he records another person (B) doing a private act,

(b) he does so with the intention that he or a third person will, for the purpose of obtaining sexual gratification, look at an image of B doing the act, and

(c) he knows that B does not consent to his recording the act with that intention.

(4) A person commits an offence if he instals equipment, or constructs or adapts a structure or part of a structure, with the intention of enabling himself or another person to commit an offence under subsection (1).

68.—(1) For the purposes of section 67, a person is doing a private act if the person is in a place which, in the circumstances, would reasonably be expected to provide privacy, and—

(a) the person's genitals, buttocks or breasts are exposed or covered only with underwear,

(b) the person is using a lavatory, or

(c) the person is doing a sexual act that is not of a kind ordinarily done in public.

(2) In section 67, 'structure' includes a tent, vehicle or vessel or other temporary or movable structure.

Procedure

B3.253 An allegation of an offence contrary to s. 67 is triable either way; when tried on indictment, it is a class 3 offence.

See **B3.285** for alternative verdicts.

Indictment

B3.254 *Statement of Offence*

Operating equipment with the intention of enabling another person to observe a private act for the purposes of sexual gratification contrary to section 67(2) of the Sexual Offences Act 2003

Particulars of Offence

A, on or about the . . . day of . . . knowing that V did not consent thereto operated equipment with the intention of enabling another person to observe V doing a private act.

Sentencing

B3.255 The maximum penalty for an offence under the SOA 2003, s. 67, on conviction on indictment is two years' imprisonment. On summary conviction, the maximum is six months or a fine not exceeding the statutory maximum, or both (s. 67(5)).

The SGC Guideline, *Sexual Offences Act 2003* (April 2007), applies to offenders sentenced on or after 14 May 2007 for voyeurism. For the full text of this guideline, see **appendix 8** at part 85. Aggravating and mitigating factors in the guideline are additional to those set out in the SGC Guideline on *Seriousness* (December 2004), paras. 1.20 – 1.24 (see **appendix 8** at part 3). The sentences for public protection (see **E5**) must be considered in all such cases. In every case the court should consider a disqualification from working with children (see **E23.11**) and a SOPO (see **E23.12**). There is a notification requirement under the CJA 2003, s. 80 and sch. 3, subject to the age of the offender and the sentence imposed (see **E25**).

A sentence of nine months' imprisonment on a plea of guilty was appropriate for this offence in *Turner* [2006] 2 Cr App R (S) 327. The offender, the manager of a health centre, had installed a video camera above the showers at the centre and had filmed women taking showers. He had retained the images on video cassettes, but had not shown them to anyone else. The Court of Appeal said that custody was appropriate because of the offender's breach of his position as manager and because of the psychological impact on the four women concerned. In *IP* [2005] 1 Cr App R (S) 578, the offender pleaded guilty to voyeurism. He had installed a video camera in the loft above the bathroom, so that he could view his stepdaughter, aged 24, in the shower. A sentence of eight months' imprisonment was varied by the Court of Appeal to a community rehabilitation order with a condition that the offender must participate in a sex-offender group programme. The offender was of previous good character, had made early admissions of guilt and had now moved out of the family home.

Elements

As to 'gratification', see **B3.78**. For 'consent', see **B3.8**. 'Private act' is defined in s. 68 (see B3.252). **B3.256**

Intercourse with an Animal

Sexual Offences Act 2003, s. 69 **B3.257**

(1) A person commits an offence if—
  (a) he intentionally performs an act of penetration with his penis,
  (b) what is penetrated is the vagina or anus of a living animal, and
  (c) he knows that, or is reckless as to whether, that is what is penetrated.
(2) A person (A) commits an offence if—
  (a) A intentionally causes, or allows, A's vagina or anus to be penetrated,
  (b) the penetration is by the penis of a living animal, and
  (c) A knows that, or is reckless as to whether, that is what A is being penetrated by.

Procedure

An allegation of an offence contrary to s. 69 is triable either way; when tried on indictment, it is a class 3 offence. **B3.258**

See **B3.285** for alternative verdicts.

Sentencing

The maximum penalty for an offence under the SOA 2003, s. 69, on conviction on indictment is two years' imprisonment. On summary conviction, the maximum is six months or a fine not exceeding the statutory maximum, or both (s. 69(3)). **B3.259**

The SGC Guideline, *Sexual Offences Act 2003* (April 2007), applies to offenders sentenced on or after 14 May 2007 for intercourse with an animal. For the full text of this guideline, see **appendix 8** at part 8. Aggravating and mitigating factors in the guideline are additional to those set out in the SGC Guideline on *Seriousness* (December 2004), paras. 1.20 – 1.24 (see **appendix 8** at part 3). The sentences for public protection (see **E5**) must be considered in all such cases. In every case the court should consider a disqualification from working with children (see **E23.11**) and a SOPO (see **E23.12**). There is a notification requirement under the CJA 2003, s. 80 and sch. 3, subject to the age of the offender and the sentence imposed (see E25).

In respect of buggery with an animal (now superseded), in one case involving buggery with a dog, *Higson* (1984) 6 Cr App R (S) 20, the Court of Appeal substituted a probation order for a two-year term of imprisonment on the footing that it was the offender and his wife who needed help, and not the dog. In *Tierney* (1991) 12 Cr App R (S) 216, a custodial sentence of three months was imposed where the defendant persuaded his wife to commit sexual acts with their dog. Photographs of the incident were later seen by staff at a laboratory. In *P* (1992) 13 Cr App R (S) 369, the offender pleaded guilty to attempted buggery with a dog, a video recording of the incident later being sent to the woman's employer by the man she was living with who had persuaded her to commit the offence. Three months' imprisonment was varied to allow the woman's immediate release from prison.

Elements

B3.260 The essence of the offence is an intentional act of penetration by the penis and so it can be committed only by a male person. Penetration must be of the vagina or anus of a living animal. 'Vagina' or 'anus' is defined in s. 79(10) to include references to any similar part. The accused must know or be reckless as to whether that is what is penetrated.

By contrast, the offence under s. 69(2) can be committed by a male or female person as the essence of it is that the offender intentionally allows his or her anus or her vagina to be penetrated by the penis of a living animal. The accused must know or be reckless that it is the anus or vagina that is being penetrated.

Sexual Penetration of a Corpse

B3.261 **Sexual Offences Act 2003, s. 70**

(1) A person commits an offence if—
  (a) he intentionally performs an act of penetration with a part of his body or anything else,
  (b) what is penetrated is a part of the body of a dead person,
  (c) he knows that, or is reckless as to whether, that is what is penetrated, and
  (d) the penetration is sexual.

Procedure

B3.262 An allegation of an offence contrary to s. 67 is triable either way and if tried on indictment, it is a class 4 offence.

See **B3.285** for alternative verdicts.

Sentencing

B3.263 The maximum penalty for an offence under the SOA 2003, s. 70, on conviction on indictment is two years' imprisonment. On summary conviction, the maximum is six months or a fine not exceeding the statutory maximum, or both (s. 70(2)).

The SGC Guideline, *Sexual Offences Act 2003* (April 2007), applies to offenders sentenced on or after 14 May 2007 for sexual penetration of a corpse. For the full text of this guideline, see **appendix 8** at part 8. Aggravating and mitigating factors in the guideline are additional to those set out in the SGC Guideline on *Seriousness* (December 2004), paras. 1.20 – 1.24 (see **appendix 8** at part 3). In every case the court should consider a disqualification from working with children (see **E23.11**) and a SOPO (see **E23.12**).

Elements

B3.264 The essence of the offence is the intentional penetration of the body of a dead person. That penetration can be by means of either a part of the body or an object. The accused must know that or be reckless as to whether he is penetrating a part of the body of a dead person and the penetration must be sexual. For 'sexual', see **B3.20**.

Sexual Activity in a Public Lavatory

B3.265 **Sexual Offences Act 2003, s. 71**

(1) A person commits an offence if—
  (a) he is in a lavatory to which the public or a section of the public has or is permitted to have access, whether on payment or otherwise,
  (b) he intentionally engages in an activity, and,
  (c) the activity is sexual.

(2) For the purposes of this section, an activity is sexual if a reasonable person would, in all the circumstances but regardless of any person's purpose, consider it to be sexual.

Procedure and Sentencing

An allegation of an offence contrary to s. 71 is triable summarily only. **B3.266**

The maximum penalty upon conviction is six months' imprisonment or a fine not exceeding level 5, or both (s. 71(3)).

The SGC Guideline, *Sexual Offences Act 2003* (April 2007), applies to offenders sentenced on or after 14 May 2007 for sexual activity in a public lavatory. For the full text of this guideline, see **appendix 8** at part 8. Aggravating and mitigating factors in the guideline are additional to those set out in the SGC Guideline on *Seriousness* (December 2004), paras. 1.20 – 1.24 (see **appendix 8** at part 3). In every case the court should consider a disqualification from working with children (see **E23.11**) and a SOPO (see **E23.12**).

Elements

An offender must intentionally engage in sexual activity in a lavatory to which the public, or a section of the public, is permitted access either by payment or otherwise. The definition of 'sexual' is objective for the purposes of s. 71. **B3.267**

TERRITORIAL AND EXTRA-TERRITORIAL JURISDICTION

Extra-territorial jurisdiction is provided for in respect of many offences under the Act by s. 72. **B3.268**

Sexual Offences Act 2003, s. 72

(1) Subject to subsection (2), any act done by a person in a country or territory outside the United Kingdom which—
 (a) constituted an offence under the law in force in that country or territory, and
 (b) would constitute a sexual offence to which this section applies if it had been done in England and Wales or in Northern Ireland,
constitutes that sexual offence under the law of that part of the United Kingdom.
(2) Proceedings by virtue of this section may be brought only against a person who was on 1st September 1997, or has since become, a British citizen or resident in the United Kingdom.
(3) An act punishable under the law in force in any country or territory constitutes an offence under that law for the purposes of this section, however it is described in that law.
(4) Subject to subsection (5), the condition in subsection (1)(a) is to be taken to be met unless, not later than rules of court may provide, the defendant serves on the prosecution a notice—
 (a) stating that, on the facts as alleged with respect to the act in question, the condition is not in his opinion met,
 (b) showing his grounds for that opinion, and
 (c) requiring the prosecution to prove that it is met.
(5) The court, if it thinks fit, may permit the defendant to require the prosecution to prove that the condition is met without service of a notice under subsection (4).
(6) In the Crown Court the question whether the condition is met is to be decided by the judge alone.
(7) Schedule 2 lists the sexual offences to which this section applies.

Schedule 2, para. 1 applies to England and Wales.

Sexual Offences Act 2003, sch. 2, para. 1

In relation to England and Wales, the following are sexual offences to which section 72 applies—
 (a) an offence under any of sections 5 to 15 (offences against children under 13 or under 16);

(b) an offence under any of sections 1 to 4, 16 to 41, 47 to 50 and 61 where the victim of the offence was under 16 at the time of the offence;
(c) an offence under section 62 or 63 where the intended offence was an offence against a person under 16;
(d) an offence under—
  (i) section 1 of the Protection of Children Act 1978 (indecent photographs of children), or
  (ii) section 160 of the Criminal Justice Act 1988 (possession of indecent photograph of child),

in relation to a photograph or pseudo-photograph showing a child under 16.

SOLICITING

B3.269 **Street Offences Act 1959, s. 1**

(1) It shall be an offence for a common prostitute (whether male or female) to loiter or solicit in a street or public place for the purpose of prostitution.
(2) A person guilty of an offence under this section shall be liable on summary conviction to a fine of an amount not exceeding level 2 on the standard scale, as defined in section 75 of the Criminal Justice Act 1982, or, for an offence committed after a previous conviction, to a fine of an amount not exceeding level 3 on that scale.
(3) [Repealed by SOCPA 2005, schs. 7 and 17.]
(4) For the purposes of this section 'street' includes any bridge, road, lane, footway, subway, square, court, alley or passage, whether a thoroughfare or not, which is for the time being open to the public; and the doorways and entrances of premises abutting on a street (as hereinbefore defined), and any ground adjoining and open to a street, shall be treated as forming part of the street.

Sexual Offences Act 1985, ss. 1, 2, and 4

1.—(1) A person commits an offence if he solicits another person (or different persons) for the purpose of prostitution—
(a) from a motor vehicle while it is in a street or public place; or
(b) in a street or public place while in the immediate vicinity of a motor vehicle that he has just got out of or off,

persistently or in such manner or in such circumstances as to be likely to cause annoyance to the person (or any of the persons) solicited, or nuisance to other persons in the neighbourhood.

(2) A person guilty of an offence under this section shall be liable on summary conviction to a fine not exceeding level 3 on the standard scale.
(3) In this section 'motor vehicle' has the same meaning as in the Road Traffic Act 1988.

2.—(1) A person commits an offence if in a street or public place he persistently solicits another person (or different persons) for the purpose of prostitution.
(2) A person guilty of an offence under this section shall be liable on summary conviction to a fine not exceeding level 3 on the standard scale.

4.—(1) References in this Act to a person soliciting another person for the purpose of prostitution are references to his soliciting that person for the purpose of obtaining that person's services as a prostitute.
(2) and (3) [Repealed.]
(4) For the purposes of this Act 'street' includes any bridge, road, lane, footway, subway, square, court, alley or passage, whether a thoroughfare or not, which is for the time being open to the public; and the doorways and entrances of premises abutting on a street (as hereinbefore defined), and any ground adjoining and open to a street, shall be treated as forming part of the street.

Procedure

B3.270 An allegation of an offence contrary to s. 1 of the Street Offences Act 1959 or the Sexual Offences Act 1985 is triable summarily only.

Sentencing

The maximum penalties are as follows: B3.271

Loitering for the purposes of prostitution under the Street Offences Act 1959: A fine not exceeding level 2 on the standard scale, or for an offence committed after a previous conviction, a fine not exceeding level 3 (Street Offences Act 1959, s. 1(2)).

Persistent soliciting of persons under the SOA 1985, s. 1 or s. 2: A fine not exceeding level 3 on the standard scale (SOA 1985, s. 1(2), s. 2(2)).

Elements of Loitering or Soliciting for Purposes of Prostitution

Soliciting can be carried out by either a male or female, the essence of the offence being the solicitation of another to engage in prostitution (*DPP v Bull* [1995] QB 88). The person soliciting need not be in a public place provided the solicitation extends into a public place (*Behrendt v Burridge* [1977] 1 WLR 29). 'Loitering' is simply lingering with no intent to move on either on foot or in a vehicle (*Bridge v Campbell* (1947) 177 LT 444). There is no definition of public place and any issue will be resolved as a matter of fact and degree (*Glynn v Simmonds* [1952] 2 All ER 57; *Elkins v Cartlidge* [1947] 1 All ER 829). B3.272

Elements of Kerb-crawling and Persistent Soliciting

The offence of kerb-crawling under s. 1 requires that there must be a likelihood of causing annoyance to the person solicited or nuisance to the neighbourhood. The magistrates are entitled to use local knowledge in the determination of the latter issue (*Paul v DPP* (1989) 90 Cr App R 173). B3.273

For 'public place', see **B3.272**. For 'street', see **B3.269**.

INDECENT PHOTOGRAPHS OF CHILDREN

Protection of Children Act 1978, ss. 1 and 1A B3.274

1.—(1) It is an offence for a person—

(a) to take, or permit to be taken or to make, any indecent photograph or pseudo-photograph of a child; or

(b) to distribute or show such indecent photographs or pseudo-photographs; or

(c) to have in his possession such indecent photographs or pseudo-photographs, with a view to their being distributed or shown by himself or others; or

(d) to publish or cause to be published any advertisement likely to be understood as conveying that the advertiser distributes or shows such indecent photographs or pseudo-photographs, or intends to do so.

1A.—(1) This section applies where, in proceedings for an offence under section 1(1)(a) of taking or making an indecent photograph of a child, or for an offence under section 1(1)(b) or (c) relating to an indecent photograph of a child, the defendant proves that the photograph was of the child aged 16 or over, and that at the time of the offence charged the child and he—

(a) were married, or

(b) lived together as partners in an enduring family relationship.

(2) Subsections (5) and (6) also apply where, in proceedings for an offence under section 1(1)(b) or (c) relating to an indecent photograph of a child, the defendant proves that the photograph was of the child aged 16 or over, and that at the time when he obtained it the child and he—

(a) were married, or

(b) lived together as partners in an enduring family relationship.

(3) This section applies whether the photograph showed the child alone or with the defendant, but not if it showed any other person.

(4) In the case of an offence under section 1(1)(a), if sufficient evidence is adduced to raise an issue as to whether the child consented to the photograph being taken or made, or as to whether the defendant reasonably believed that the child so consented, the defendant is not guilty of the offence unless it is proved that the child did not so consent and that the defendant did not reasonably believe that the child so consented.

(5) In the case of an offence under section 1(1)(b), the defendant is not guilty of the offence unless it is proved that the showing or distributing was to a person other than the child.

(6) In the case of an offence under section 1(1)(c), if sufficient evidence is adduced to raise an issue both—

(a) as to whether the child consented to the photograph being in the defendant's possession, or as to whether the defendant reasonably believed that the child so consented, and

(b) as to whether the defendant had the photograph in his possession with a view to its being distributed or shown to anyone other than the child,

the defendant is not guilty of the offence unless it is proved either that the child did not so consent and that the defendant did not reasonably believe that the child so consented, or that the defendant had the photograph in his possession with a view to its being distributed or shown to a person other than the child.

Criminal Justice Act 1988, ss. 160 and 160A

160.—(1) It is an offence for a person to have any indecent photograph or pseudo-photograph of a child in his possession.

(2) Where a person is charged with an offence under subsection (1) above, it shall be a defence for him to prove—

(a) that he had a legitimate reason for having the photograph or pseudo-photograph in his possession; or

(b) that he had not himself seen the photograph or pseudo-photograph and did not know, nor had any cause to suspect, it to be indecent; or

(c) that the photograph or pseudo-photograph was sent to him without any prior request made by him or on his behalf and that he did not keep it for an unreasonable time.

160A.—(1) This section applies where, in proceedings for an offence under section 160 relating to an indecent photograph of a child, the defendant proves that the photograph was of the child aged 16 or over, and that at the time of the offence charged the child and he—

(a) were married, or

(b) lived together as partners in an enduring family relationship.

(2) This section also applies where, in proceedings for an offence under section 160 relating to an indecent photograph of a child, the defendant proves that the photograph was of the child aged 16 or over, and that at the time when he obtained it the child and he—

(a) were married, or

(b) lived together as partners in an enduring family relationship.

(3) This section applies whether the photograph showed the child alone or with the defendant, but not if it showed any other person.

(4) If sufficient evidence is adduced to raise an issue as to whether the child consented to the photograph being in the defendant's possession, or as to whether the defendant reasonably believed that the child so consented, the defendant is not guilty of the offence unless it is proved that the child did not so consent and that the defendant did not reasonably believe that the child so consented.

Procedure

B3.275 An allegation of an offence contrary to s. 1 of the Protection of Children Act 1978 is triable either way; when tried on indictment, it is a class 3 offence. An allegation of an offence contrary to s. 160(1) of the CJA 1988 is similarly triable either way and upon trial on indictment is a class 3 offence. Proceedings in relation to either offence may not be instituted without the consent of the DPP. The extra-territorial jurisdiction provisions of the SOA 2003, s. 72 (see **B3.268**) apply in respect of a photograph or pseudo-photograph of a child under the age of 16.

Indictment

In *Thompson* [2004] 2 Cr App R 262, the Court of Appeal gave guidance as to the drafting of an indictment where a case involves possession of a large number of photographs under the CJA 1988, s. 160. It is submitted that the same guidance will apply to prosecutions under the 1978 Act. The following principles were set out in *Thompson*: **B3.276**

(1) In addition to the specific counts, a comprehensive count should be included to cover the remainder.

(2) The photographs used in the specific counts should, if practicable, be selected so as to be broadly representative of the images in the comprehensive count. If agreement can be reached as to the number of photographs to be included at each level (see *Oliver* [2003] 1 Cr App R 463 at **B3.277**), the need for the judge to view the entirety of the offending material may be avoided.

(3) Where it is impracticable to present the court with specific counts that are agreed to be representative of the comprehensive count, there must be available to the court an approximate breakdown of the number of images at each of the five levels (see *Oliver* at **B3.277**). That may best be achieved by the prosecution providing the defence with a schedule setting out the information and ensuring that the defence has an opportunity, well in advance of the sentencing hearing, of viewing the images and checking the accuracy of the schedule.

(4) The specific counts should make it clear whether the image in question is a real image or a pseudo-image: the same count should not charge both. There might be a significant difference between the two and, where there was a dispute, there should be alternative counts.

(5) Each image charged in a specific count should be identified by its 'jpg' or other reference so that it is clear with which image the specific count is dealing.

(6) The estimated age range of the child shown in each of the images should, where possible, be provided to the court.

In practice judges will usually view a selection of the material in order to establish the seriousness of the contents.

Sentencing

The maximum penalty for an offence under the Protection of Children Act 1978, s. 1, is ten years on indictment if committed on or after 11 January 2001 (otherwise three years); six months and/or a fine to the statutory maximum on summary conviction (Protection of Children Act 1978, s. 8; MCA 1980, s. 32; CJCSA 2000, s. 41). The maximum penalty for an offence under the CJA 1988, s. 160, is, if committed on or after 11 January 2001, five years on indictment, six months and/or a fine not exceeding the statutory maximum on summary conviction (CJCSA 2000, s. 41). If committed before that date, the offence is summary only, punishable with six months' imprisonment or a fine not exceeding level 5 on the standard scale, or both. **B3.277**

The SGC Guideline, *Sexual Offences Act 2003* (April 2007), applies to offenders sentenced on or after 14 May 2007 for these offences. For the full text of this guideline, see **appendix 8** at part 8. Aggravating and mitigating factors in the guideline are additional to those set out in the SGC Guideline on *Seriousness* (December 2004), paras. 1.20 – 1.24 (see **appendix 8** at part 3). The sentences for public protection (see **E5**) must be considered in all such cases. In every case the court should consider a disqualification from working with children (see **E23.11**) and a SOPO (see **E23.12**). There is a notification requirement under the CJA 2003, s. 80 and sch. 3 if the photographs showed persons under the age of 16; this is also subject to the age of the offender and the sentence imposed (see **E25**).

Sentencing guidelines for these offences were issued by the Court of Appeal in *Oliver* [2003] 1 Cr App R 463. Rose LJ, giving the judgment of the court in *Oliver*, observed that it was likely that the number of child pornography cases detected and prosecuted was only a small proportion of the real total, and that increased access to the internet has greatly exacerbated the problem by making pornographic images more easily accessible. His lordship said that the Court of Appeal agreed with the advice of the Sentencing Advisory Panel, that the two primary factors determinative of the seriousness of a particular offence are the nature of the indecent material and the extent of the offender's involvement with it.

The Court of Appeal identified five categories of indecent image, described as Level 1 (least serious) to Level 5 (most serious): (1) images depicting erotic posing with no sexual activity, (2) sexual activity between children, or solo masturbation by a child, (3) non-penetrative sexual activity between adults and children, (4) penetrative sexual activity between adults and children, (5) sadism or bestiality. It will usually be necessary for sentencers to view for themselves the images involved, unless there is an agreed description of what those images depict. The SGC Guidelines (April 2007) now state that Level 2 images should be defined as 'non-penetrative sexual activity between children or solo masturbation by a child', and that Level 4 images should be defined as 'penetrative sexual activity involving a child or children, or both children and adults'. This means that offences involving any form of sexual penetration of the vagina or anus or penile penetration of the mouth (except where they involve sadism or intercourse with an animal, which fall within Level 5) should be classified as activity at Level 4.

The seriousness of an individual offence increases with the offender's proximity to, and responsibility for, the original abuse. Any element of commercial gain will place an offence at a high level of seriousness. In the court's judgment, swapping of images can properly be regarded as a commercial activity, albeit without financial gain, because it fuels demand for such material. Wide-scale distribution, even without financial profit, is intrinsically more harmful than a transaction limited to two or three individuals, both by reference to the potential use of the images by active paedophiles, and by reference to the shame and degradation to the original victims. Merely locating an image on the internet will generally be less serious than downloading it. Downloading it will generally be less serious than taking an original film or photograph of indecent posing or activity.

The Court of Appeal specified a number of different sentencing starting points, from fines through community sentences to custodial terms, which were to be applied in accordance with the nature of the material, the number of images, and whether the case involved possession, distribution, or production. The custody threshold will usually be passed where any of the material has been shown or distributed to others, or, in cases of possession, where there is a large amount of material at Level 2, or a small amount at Level 3 or above. Specific factors identified as aggravating the seriousness of an offence of this kind are: (i) if the images have been shown or distributed to a child, (ii) if there are a large number of images (sentencers must make their own assessment of whether the numbers are small or large, bearing in mind the principles applying by virtue of *Canavan* [1998] 1 Cr App R 79, and see **D19.58**), (iii) the manner in which a collection of images is stored on a computer, which may indicate a more or less sophisticated approach (an offence will be less serious if images have been viewed by the offender but not stored), (iv) images posted on a public area of the internet or distributed in a way that makes it more likely that they will be found accidentally by others, (v) if the offender was responsible for the original production of the images, especially if the child or children were members of the offender's family or were drawn from vulnerable groups, or if the offender has abused a position of trust, (vi) the age of the children may be an aggravating feature in some cases, such as where there has been an assault on a baby or very young child.

When dealt with summarily, the Magistrates' Courts Guidelines (2004) indicate the following, for a first-time offender pleading not guilty:

Aggravating Factors For example abuse of trust; commercial gain; involvement in production; large number of images; particularly young or vulnerable children; offence committed on bail; relevant previous convictions and any failures to respond to previous sentences

Mitigating Factors For example images at the lowest categories of COPINE; one photograph only; possession for own use; pseudo images

Guideline: Are magistrates' sentencing powers sufficient?

Elements of the 1978 Act Offence

For the puposes of the Protection of Children Act 1978, a child is a person under the age of 18 (s. 7(6)).

A person's intention in making photographs of children may be relevant to his *mens rea* but it is not relevant to the question of whether they are indecent for the purposes of s. 1(1)(a) (*Smethurst* [2002] 1 Cr App R 50). 'Making' can be comprised of simply copying an indecent photograph (*Atkins v DPP* [2000] 1 WLR 1427). If a person opens an attachment to an e-mail which contains an indecent photograph of a child, he makes a photograph for the purposes of the Act. If he intentionally opens the attachment and he knows that it contains an indecent photograph of a child or is likely to contain such a photograph, then he is guilty of making a photograph for the purposes of the Act (*Smith* [2003] 1 Cr App R 212). Section 2(3) provides that a person is to be taken as having been a child at any material time if it appears, from the evidence as a whole, that he was then under the age of 18. **B3.278**

The offence is not incompatible with the ECHR, Article10 (*Graham-Kerr* (1989) 88 Cr App R 302).

The offence of showing an indecent photograph of a child is not made out where the accused proposes to show it only to himself. Nor can he be convicted of possession with intent to show such a photograph where he possesses the photograph only with intent to show it to himself (*ET* (1999) 163 JP 349). Similarly, the phrase 'with a view to' distribution of indecent photographs or pseudo-photographs in the Protection of Children Act 1978, s. 1(1)(c), requires that the distribution or showing must be at least one of the accused's purposes, but not necessarily his primary purpose. Thus in *Dooley* [2006] 1 WLR 775, the accused did not intend to show or distribute indecent images when he downloaded pornography with a view to placing it in a secure file but did not have time to remove it from a shared file before others could look at it. If an offender provides another person with a password to access a computer in order to view relevant images, that is sufficient to amount to 'showing' (*Fellows and Arnold* [1997] 1 Cr App R 244). In *Price* [2006] EWCA Crim 3363, the Court of Appeal held that the offence under s. 1(1)(b) is one of strict liability, subject only to the defence in s. 1(4).

Under s. 1(4), it is a defence to a charge of distribution or possession if the accused proves that he had a legitimate reason for either possessing, showing or distributing such photographs or he had not seen the photographs and did not know or have reason to suspect that they were indecent.

If the photograph or pseudo-photograph is made pursuant to an appropriate authorisation given by a relevant authority for the purposes of the prevention, detection or investigation of crime or criminal proceedings, then the making is exempt from criminal proceedings under s. 1B.

Elements of the 1988 Act Offence

Under the CJA 1988, s. 160, simple possession of a relevant photograph or pseudo-photograph may constitute an offence. **B3.279**

In *Porter* [2006] 1 WLR 2633, it was held that the offence of possession required that the accused had possession or control of the images. If the images had been deleted from his computer then it would be a question of fact as to whether he had control of them. That question could be answered by reference to whether he had the expertise and equipment to retrieve the images. In *Steele* [1993] Crim LR 298, the Court of Appeal held that an accused was not in possession of an image if his computer cached an indecent image of a child without his knowledge.

The defence set out in s. 160(2) is available if the accused did not have cause to suspect that the photograph was an indecent photograph of a child (*Collier* [2005] 1 WLR 843), albeit he suspected that the image was of an indecent nature.

OUTRAGING PUBLIC DECENCY

B3.280 At common law it is an offence to outrage public decency, to expose the person or to engage in or simulate a sexual act in public. As to the offence of outraging public decency by way of obscene publication, see **B19.18**.

Procedure

B3.281 The offence is triable either way; and if tried on indictment, it is a class 3 offence.

See **B3.285** for alternative verdicts.

Indictment

B3.282 *Statement of Offence*

Outraging public decency

Particulars of Offence

A on or about the . . . day of . . . outraged public decency, namely by publicly, to wit in the street at . . ., having sexual intercourse with X, within the sight and to the outrage of other persons then present

Sentencing

B3.283 The maximum penalty for the common-law offence on conviction on indictment is imprisonment and/or a fine at large. On summary conviction, the maximum is six months or a fine not exceeding scale 5 on the standard scale, or both. The maximum penalty for the summary offence under the Vagrancy Act 1824, s. 4, is three months' imprisonment, or a fine not exceeding level 3 on the standard scale or both; on a second conviction and commitment to the Crown Court for sentence, it is 12 months. See further **B3.250**.

In *Cosco* [2005] 2 Cr App R (S) 405, a case decided shortly before the SOA 2003 came into force, the offender was convicted on three counts of outraging public decency by exposing himself on a beach where he could be seen by children. He had 13 previous convictions for similar behaviour. The Court of Appeal said that, bearing in mind that under the 2003 Act the maximum sentence would be two years, the appropriate sentence in this case was 18 months' imprisonment. See also *Miah* [2006] 2 Cr App R (S) 304.

Elements

B3.284 In *Rose v DPP* [2006] 1 WLR 2626, the accused had been filmed by CCTV cameras whilst a woman performed oral sex upon him in the foyer of a bank at just before 1 a.m. The manageress of the bank had seen the footage of the act upon reviewing the tapes in the normal course of her job. The Court of Appeal held that the District Judge had been wrong to convict as the act was seen only by those who participated in it and therefore there was insufficient public element.

ALTERNATIVE VERDICTS

Plainly, there is a degree of overlap between many of the offences contained within the SOA 2003 and thus an offender may sometimes be found guilty of a lesser charge than that upon which he is indicted (see **D18.41** *et seq.* for the applicable general principles). In the case of an allegation of rape, it is possible that the accused could be alternatively found guilty of attempted rape, assault by penetration, sexual assault, sexual activity with a child, sexual activity with a child family member, sexual activity with a person having a mental disorder impeding choice, sexual activity by a care worker or sex with an adult relative. In respect of rape of a child, an accused may alternatively be found guilty of attempted rape, assault by penetration, sexual assault of a child contrary to s. 7 or sexual assault of a child contrary to s. 9. **B3.285**

KEEPING A BROTHEL AND RELATED OFFENCES

Sexual Offences Act 1956, ss. 33 to 36 **B3.286**

33. It is an offence for a person to keep a brothel, or to manage, or act or assist in the management of, a brothel.

33A.—(1) It is an offence for a person to keep, or to manage, or act or assist in the management of a brothel to which people resort for practices involving prostitution (whether or not also for other practices).

(2) In this section 'prostitution' has the meaning given by section 51(2) of the Sexual Offences Act 2003.

34. It is an offence for the lessor or landlord of any premises or his agent to let the whole or part of the premises with the knowledge that it is to be used, in whole or in part, as a brothel, or, where the whole or part of the premises is used as a brothel, to be wilfully a party to that use continuing.

35.—(1) It is an offence for the tenant or occupier, or person in charge, of any premises knowingly to permit the whole or part of the premises to be used as a brothel.

(2) Where the tenant or occupier of any premises is convicted . . . of knowingly permitting the whole or part of the premises to be used as a brothel, the first schedule to this Act shall apply to enlarge the rights of the lessor or landlord with respect to the assignment or determination of the lease or other contract under which the premises are held by the person convicted.

(3) Where the tenant or occupier of any premises is so convicted . . . and either—

(a) the lessor or landlord, after having the conviction brought to his notice, fails or failed to exercise his statutory rights in relation to the lease or contract under which the premises are or were held by the person convicted; or

(b) the lessor or landlord, after exercising his statutory rights so as to determine that lease or contract, grants or granted a new lease or enters or entered into a new contract of tenancy of the premises to, with or for the benefit of the same person, without having all reasonable provisions to prevent the recurrence of the offence inserted in the new lease or contract;

then, if subsequently an offence under this section is committed in respect of the premises during the subsistence of the lease or contract referred to in paragraph (a) of this subsection or (where paragraph (b) applies) during the subsistence of the new lease or contract, the lessor or landlord shall be deemed to be a party to that offence unless he shows that he took all reasonable steps to prevent the recurrence of the offence.

References in this subsection to the statutory rights of a lessor or landlord refer to his rights under the First Schedule to this Act . . .

36. It is an offence for the tenant or occupier of any premises knowingly to permit the whole or part of the premises to be used for the purposes of habitual prostitution (whether any prostitute involved is male or female).

Sexual Offences Act 1967, s. 6

Premises shall be treated for purposes of sections 33 to 35 of the Act of 1956 as a brothel if people resort to it for the purpose of lewd homosexual practices in circumstances in which resort thereto for lewd heterosexual practices would have led to its being treated as a brothel for the purposes of those sections.

Procedure

B3.287 An allegation of an offence contrary to ss. 33 to 36 of the SOA 1956 or s. 6 of the SOA 1967 is triable summarily only with the exception of an allegation of an offence contrary to s. 33A. That offence is triable either way.

Sentence

B3.288 Under each section bar s. 33A, for an offence committed after a previous conviction for the same or a related offence, the maximum penalty is six months or a fine not exceeding level 4 on the standard scale, or both; otherwise three months or a fine not exceeding level 3 on the standard scale, or both (SOA 1956, s. 37 and sch. 2). For an offence under s. 33A, the maximum penalty is seven years' imprisonment; on summary conviction, it is six months or the statutory maximum fine, or both.

The SGC Guideline, *Sexual Offences Act 2003* (April 2007), applies to offenders sentenced on or after 14 May 2007 for these offences. For the full text of this guideline, see **appendix 8** at part 8. Aggravating and mitigating factors in the guideline are additional to those set out in the SGC Guideline on *Seriousness* (December 2004), paras. 1.20 – 1.24 (see **appendix 8** at part 3). The sentences for public protection (see E5) must be considered in all such cases. In every case the court should consider a disqualification from working with children (see E23.11) and a SOPO (see E23.12).

Meaning of 'Brothel' and 'Prostitution'

B3.289 A brothel is essentially a place where people are allowed to engage in unlawful sexual intercourse. For refinements of that definition see *Kelly v Purvis* [1983] AC 663, *Stevens v Christy* (1987) 85 Cr App R 249, *Donovan v Gavin* [1965] 2 QB 648, and *Korie* [1966] 1 All ER 50. By virtue of s. 6 of the SOA 1967, homosexual activity is as capable as heterosexual activity of founding the existence of a brothel.

Keeping a Brothel

B3.290 This offence can be committed under ss. 34, 35(1) or 36.

Managing etc. a Brothel

B3.291 The nature and extent of the activities which comprise management or assisting in the management of a brothel have been considered in a number of cases, including *Stevens v Christy* (1987) 85 Cr App R 249, *DPP v Curley* [1991] COD 186, *Abbott v Smith* [1965] 2 QB 662 and *Jones v DPP* (1992) 96 Cr App R 130.

Keeping a Brothel: Requirement of Knowledge

B3.292 A person does not keep a brothel unless he is aware that the premises are to be used by more than one prostitute for the purposes of prostitution.

Landlord Letting Premises as a Brothel

B3.293 The offence under the SOA 1956, s. 34, requires the landlord to know that the premises are to be used as a brothel or are being used as a brothel.

Tenant Permitting Premises to be Used as a Brothel

B3.294 Plainly, this offence applies to tenants who sublet their premises or simply allow the premises to be used as a brothel. If a tenant or occupier is convicted of allowing premises to be used as a brothel then the landlord of those premises has increased powers of eviction in relation to that tenancy under the SOA 1956, s. 35. If the landlord fails to exercise those powers or grants a new lease or licence to the offender, and the tenant or occupier repeats the offence, then the landlord will be liable as a party to the offence unless he shows that he took all reasonable steps to prevent the recurrence of the offence.

Tenant Permitting Premises to be Used for Prostitution

Section 36 of the SOA 1956 creates an offence of permitting premises to be used for prostitution. In contrast to those sections dealing with brothels, the offence can be committed if only one prostitute engages in prostitution in the premises. **B3.295**

Keeping a Disorderly House

It is an offence at common law for a person to keep a disorderly house. **B3.296**

Procedure

This common-law offence is triable either way and when tried on indictment is a class 3 offence. **B3.297**

Sentencing

As a common-law offence, punishment is at large by imprisonment or fine, or both. **B3.298**

Elements

The elements of the common-law offence of keeping a disorderly house were set out in *Tan* [1983] QB 1053: **B3.299**

(a) there must be some element of keeping open house;
(b) the house must not be regulated by the restraints of morality, or must be unchaste or of bad repute;
(c) it must be so conducted as to violate law and good order.

In *Moores v DPP* [1992] QB 125, it was held that the accused must also be aware that the house was used in that way. The requisite disorderliness of the house is not confined to sexual behaviour (*Berg* (1927) 20 Cr App R 38).

Section B4 Theft, Handling Stolen Goods and Related Offences

THEFT

Definition

B4.1 **Theft Act 1968, s. 1**

(1) A person is guilty of theft if he dishonestly appropriates property belonging to another with the intention of permanently depriving the other of it; and 'thief' and 'steal' shall be construed accordingly.

Procedure

B4.2 Theft is triable either way (MCA 1980, s. 17 and sch. 1, para. 28). When tried on indictment it is a class 3 offence. It is a Group A offence for jurisdiction purposes under the CJA 1993, part I (see **A8.7**). The *Consolidated Criminal Practice Direction*, para. V.51, *Mode of trial* (see **D6.21**) states (para. 51.7) that theft should be tried summarily unless the court considers that one or more of the following features is present in the case *and* that its sentencing powers are insufficient:

(a) Breach of trust by a person in a position of substantial authority, or in whom a high degree of trust is placed.
(b) Theft which has been committed or disguised in a sophisticated manner.
(c) Theft committed by an organised gang.
(d) The victim is particularly vulnerable to theft (e.g., the elderly or infirm).
(e) The unrecovered property is of high value (at least £10,000).

Indictment

B4.3 *Statement of Offence*

Theft contrary to section 1(1) of the Theft Act 1968

Particulars of Offence

A on or about the . . . day of . . . stole a pearl necklace belonging to V

It is proper to allege in a single count the theft of an aggregate sum of money or items of property where the evidence does not disclose the precise dates and amounts of each individual transaction, provided that D's conduct amounted to a continuous offence over a period of time. Such an allegation is usually referred to as theft of a 'general deficiency'. Thus it would be proper to indict for theft of the total sum missing on a day on which D was bound to account for it, even though he clearly took it in instalments (*Balls* (1871) LR 1 CCR 328) or theft of all items stolen from a department store on one day, even though the various articles emanated from different departments of the store (*Wilson* (1979) 69 Cr App R 83; *Heaton v Costello* (1984) 148 JP 688). A count drafted in this way is not bad for duplicity. This principle also applies where 'money' was in different forms and it could not be said whether what was stolen was a debt, cash drawn from a bank account or cash disposed of otherwise and representing funds provided by clients of financial advisers (*Hallam* [1995] Crim LR 323). The elements of the offence must exist throughout, otherwise there would be a lack of coincidence (see **B4.27**). As to indictments for continuous offences generally, see *DPP v Merriman* [1973] AC 584 and **D11.26** *et seq.*

Not all the items mentioned in an information or count do have to be proved to have been stolen (*Machent v Quinn* [1970] 2 All ER 255), provided it is proved that D stole one of the articles. However, there will be cases where the prosecution should not include in a single count more than one allegation of theft, for example where several items are alleged to have been stolen from an employer on different days (*Jackson* (1991) *The Guardian*, 20 November 1991). Some property must be specified in the indictment or information.

As to the relevance of conditional intention in drafting an indictment, see **B4.44**. As to the relationship between theft and handling, see **B4.140**.

Alternative Verdicts

In addition to the general power under the Criminal Law Act 1967, s. 6(3), the TA 1968, **B4.4**
s. 12(4), provides that, as an alternative to a conviction of theft, the jury may on a trial on indictment for theft find D guilty of an offence under s. 12(1) (taking a motor vehicle or other conveyance without authority etc.; see **B4.91** to **B4.99**). He is liable then as he would have been liable under s. 12(2) on summary conviction (s. 12(4): see **B4.93**).

Sentencing Guidelines: Offences of Theft Generally

The maximum penalty is seven years (TA 1968, s. 1(7)) on indictment; six months or a **B4.5**
fine not exceeding the statutory maximum, or both, summarily. Under the Penalties for Disorderly Behaviour (Amount of Penalty) Order 2002 (SI 2002 No. 1837), as amended by the Penalties for Disorderly Behaviour (Amount of Penalty) (Amendment No. 2) Order 2004 (SI 2004 No. 2468), this offence is a penalty offence and the amount payable is £80.

Theft is such a wide offence that no general sentencing guideline can be given. In *Upton* (1980) 2 Cr App R (S) 132, in which the offender was convicted of theft of goods worth £5 from the supermarket of which he was deputy manager, Lord Lane CJ said:

> This was petty theft and in ordinary circumstances it would, and should, not have attracted any immediate sentence of imprisonment.
>
> . . . non-violent petty offenders should not be allowed to take up what has become valuable space in prison. If there really is no alternative . . . to an immediate prison sentence, then it should be as short as possible . . . a prison sentence, however short, is a very unpleasant experience indeed for the inmates.

When dealt with summarily, the Magistrates' Courts Guidelines (2004) indicate the following for a first-time offender pleading not guilty:

> **Aggravating Factors** For example high value; planned; sophisticated; racial or religious aggravation; adult involving children; organised team; related damage; vulnerable victim; offence committed on bail; relevant previous convictions and any failures to respond to previous sentences.
>
> **Mitigating Factors** For example impulsive action; low value.
>
> *Guideline*: Is it serious enough for a community penalty?

Sentencing Guidelines: Shoplifting

B4.6 In *Page* [2005] 2 Cr App R (S) 221, the Court of Appeal set out a number of principles appropriate when dealing with isolated adult shoplifters. Lord Justice Rose said that shoplifting was a classic offence for which custody would be the sentence of last resort and would almost never be appropriate for a first offence. Insofar as older authorities including *Keogh* (1994) 15 Cr App R (S) 279 suggested the contrary, they were no longer to be regarded as authoritative. A community sentence might in some cases be appropriate on a plea by a first-time offender even when other adults were involved and the offence was organised (see *Howells* [1999] 1 Cr App R (S) 335). Where the offence or offences were attributable to drug addiction, a drug treatment and testing order would often be appropriate. A short custodial term, not more than one month, might be appropriate for an offender who persistently offended on a minor scale. If that persistence also involved preparation of equipment by the offender to facilitate the offence, two months might be called for. Even where an offender was to be sentenced for a large number of such offences or where he had a history of persistent similar offending on a significant scale, the comparative lack of seriousness of the offence and the need for proportionality between the sentence and the particular offence would, on a plea of guilty, rarely require a total sentence of more than two years and would often merit no more than 12 to 18 months. Young offenders would usually be dealt with appropriately by a non-custodial penalty.

The guidance in *Page* is not intended to affect the level of the sentence appropriate for shoplifting by organised gangs. When that occurred repeatedly, or on a large scale, sentences of the order of four years might well be appropriate, even on a plea of guilty. If violence was used against a shopkeeper after theft, so that a charge of robbery was inapt, a sentence in excess of four years was likely to be appropriate. Taking young children along when shoplifting is regarded by the courts as a serious aggravating feature (*Moss* (1986) 8 Cr App R (S) 276).

When dealt with summarily, the relevant Magistrates' Association Guidelines (2004) are those set out at **B4.5**.

Sentencing Guidelines: Theft from the Person

B4.7 This category covers the taking of articles from handbags, shopping bags and the activities of pickpockets. While the majority of such cases are dealt with by non-custodial sentences, particularly fines, custodial sentences have been upheld by the Court of Appeal, particularly in cases where the offender has a record of similar offending (e.g., *Mullins* [2000] 2 Cr App R (S) 372: three years upheld where stealing women's handbags had become the offender's speciality), and cases of 'professional' pickpocketing (e.g., *Wilson* (1981) 3 Cr App R (S) 102: three years upheld on offenders who worked as a team, one distracting the victim while the other stole from the victim's bag, and who had numerous previous convictions for similar offending). In *Dhunay* (1986) 8 Cr App R (S) 107, where airport baggage handlers were guilty of persistently stealing from luggage, the Court of Appeal said that deterrent sentences were appropriate and the starting point was three years' imprisonment. In *Masagh* (1990) 12 Cr App R (S) 568, Lloyd LJ stressed that while heavy custodial sentences were appropriate for systematic pickpocketing, particularly by offenders with records, they were quite wrong for isolated offences committed by an individual.

When dealt with summarily, the relevant Magistrates' Courts Guidelines (2004) are those set out at **B4.5**.

Sentencing Guidelines: Theft in Breach of Trust

B4.8 When dealt with summarily, the Magistrates' Courts Guidelines (2004) for 'theft in breach of trust' indicate the following for a first-time offender pleading not guilty:

Aggravating Factors For example casting suspicion on others; racial or religious aggravation; committed over a period; high value; organised team; planned; senior employee; sophisticated; vulnerable victim; offence committed on bail; relevant previous convictions and any failures to respond to previous sentences.

Mitigating Factors For example impulsive action; low value; previous inconsistent attitude by employer; single item; unsupported junior.

Guideline: Is it so serious that only custody is appropriate?

The guideline cases of *Barrick* (1985) 81 Cr App R 78 and *Clark* [1998] 2 Cr App R 137 are concerned with serious cases where:

> a person in a position of trust, for example, an accountant, solicitor, bank employee or postman, has used that privileged and trusted position to defraud his partners or clients or employers or the general public of sizeable sums of money. He will usually, as in this case, be a person of hitherto impeccable character. It is practically certain, again as in this case, that he will never offend again and, in the nature of things, he will never again in his life be able to secure similar employment with all that that means in the shape of disgrace for himself and hardship for himself and also his family.

The guidelines indicate that such a case will attract immediate custody, save in very exceptional circumstances or where the sum involved is small. Matters to be taken into account by the court, apart from the size of the sum involved, are (a) the quality and degree of trust reposed in the offender, (b) the period over which the thefts were committed, (c) the use to which the money was put, (d) the effect upon the victim, (e) the impact on the public and public confidence, (f) effect upon fellow employees or business partners, (g) effect on the offender, (h) his own history, (i) matters of mitigation special to himself, (j) any help given by him to the police.

The Court of Appeal in *Clark* found that the sentencing guidelines in *Barrick* required revision because of the impact of inflation and the reduction in the maximum sentence for theft from ten years to seven years. In the light of these changes, their lordships made the following suggestions, stressing that they were guidelines only and that many factors other than the amount involved might affect the sentence:

> Where the amount stolen was not small but was less than £17,500, terms of imprisonment from the very short up to 21 months would be appropriate; cases involving sums between £17,500 and £100,000 would merit two to three years; cases involving sums between £100,000 and £250,000 would merit between three to four years; cases involving £250,000 to £1 million would merit between five and nine years; cases involving £1 million or more would merit ten years or more. Those terms were appropriate for contested cases. Pleas of guilty would attract an appropriate discount. Where the sums involved were exceptionally large and not stolen on a single occasion, or the dishonesty was directed at more than one victim or group of victims, consecutive sentences might be called for.

The following cases were decided after revision of the guidelines in *Clark*. Decisions prior to that case need to be treated with caution and appropriate adjustments made.

Sentences totalling five years' imprisonment were upheld in *Neary* [1999] 1 Cr App R (S) 431. The offender was a solicitor who stole £288,000 from companies for whose affairs he was responsible. Despite the offender's guilty plea and considerable personal mitigation, May LJ in the Court of Appeal said that this was a very serious continuing breach of trust and the sentence was within the guidelines. In *Whitehouse* [1999] 2 Cr App R (S) 259, a sentence of two years' imprisonment in the case of an employee of a haulage company who pleaded guilty to the theft of property worth £17,700 was approved. The offence was a clear breach of trust, committed when he was disappointed and bitter at having been released by his employers after a trial period. The Court of Appeal noted that the revenge motive for the offence was an aggravating factor additional to those referred to in the guideline cases. Two years was also upheld on a guilty plea in *Hale* [2002] 1 Cr App R (S) 205 where the offender, the manager of a care home, used the pension books of elderly residents to obtain £13,000, in part to fund his own drug addiction. Although the sentence was something of a departure from the guideline in *Clark*, the Court of Appeal approved the trial judge's comment that 'there could hardly be a more culpable case of breach of trust than this'. Twelve months' imprisonment was appropriate in *Griffiths* [2000] 1 Cr App R (S) 240, where a club treasurer, a 44-year-old man of previous good character, stole a total of £7,300 over a seven-year period and attempted to conceal the thefts by falsifying documents. The offender pleaded guilty to theft and false accounting. Fourteen months was reduced to nine months in *James* [2000] 1 Cr App R (S) 285, where a post office counter clerk pleaded guilty to two counts of theft. She stole a total of £5,318 from her till and altered stock records to conceal the offences. The offender pleaded guilty only on the day when the trial was due to start and she had one previous conviction, for deception. The Court of Appeal took into account the fact that the offender was a single parent with financial problems who was under severe threat from creditors. In *Roberts* [1999] 1 Cr App R (S) 381, the offender, a serving police officer, was convicted of the theft of a watch worth about £90 from a police property store in a 'moment of madness'. As a result of the offence he had lost his job, after 19 years in the police service. The Court of Appeal reduced the term of imprisonment from four months to two months, Mitchell J observing that, had the offender not been a police officer, a custodial sentence would probably not have been necessary.

Elements

B4.9 It has been said that theft consists of four elements: '(i) a dishonest (ii) appropriation (iii) of property belonging to another (iv) with the intention of permanently depriving the owner of it' (*Lawrence* [1971] 1 QB 373 at p. 376 per Megaw LJ, approved, in the House of Lords (sub nom. *Lawrence v Metropolitan Police Commissioner*) [1972] AC 626 at p. 632, per Viscount Dilhorne). A more accurate description is that theft consists of five elements, since it may be important to separate consideration of the meaning of 'property' from consideration of whether that property 'belongs to another'. Further, theft can sometimes be committed against persons other than the 'owner'.

Meaning of 'Property'

B4.10 It cannot be said that theft has been committed unless some form of property has been dealt with in such a way as to comply with the other elements of the offence. 'Property' is partially defined in the TA 1968, s. 4, as follows:

(1) 'Property' includes money and all other property, real or personal, including things in action and other intangible property.

(2) A person cannot steal land, or things forming part of land and severed from it by him or by his directions, except in the following cases, that is to say—

(a) when he is a trustee or personal representative, or is authorised by power of attorney, or as liquidator of a company, or otherwise, to sell or dispose of land belonging to another, and he appropriates the land or anything forming part of it by dealing with it in breach of the confidence reposed in him; or

(b) when he is not in possession of the land and appropriates anything forming part of the land by severing it or causing it to be severed, or after it has been severed; or

(c) when, being in possession of the land under a tenancy, he appropriates the whole or part of any fixture or structure let to be used with the land.

For purposes of this subsection 'land' does not include incorporeal hereditaments; 'tenancy' means a tenancy for years or any less period and includes an agreement for such a tenancy, but a person who after the end of a tenancy remains in possession as statutory tenant or otherwise is to be treated as having possession under the tenancy, and 'let' shall be construed accordingly.

(3) A person who picks mushrooms growing wild on any land, or who picks flowers, fruit or foliage from a plant growing wild on any land, does not (although not in possession of the land) steal what he picks, unless he does it for reward or for sale or other commercial purpose.

For purposes of this subsection 'mushroom' includes any fungus, and 'plant' includes any shrub or tree.

(4) Wild creatures, tamed or untamed, shall be regarded as property; but a person cannot steal a wild creature not tamed nor ordinarily kept in captivity, or the carcase of any such creature, unless either it has been reduced into possession by or on behalf of another person and possession of it has not since been lost or abandoned, or another person is in course of reducing it into possession.

Money Coins and banknotes are property (see, for example, *Davis* (1988) 88 Cr App R 347). 'Money' does not include cheques or funds held in banks and building societies, but see **B4.13** and **B4.14**. **B4.11**

Real Property Land is property, but under the TA 1968, s. 4(2), it can be stolen only in very limited circumstances. There is, however, a theft of land when a person who is a trustee or personal representative, or who is authorised by power of attorney, or as liquidator of a company, or otherwise, to sell or dispose of land *belonging to another* appropriates the land or anything forming part of it by dealing with it in breach of the confidence reposed in him (s. 4(2)(a)). **B4.12**

A person who is not in possession of land (which includes a person occupying the land under a licence as opposed to a tenancy) can commit theft by appropriating something forming part of the land, by severing it or causing it to be severed, or after it has been severed (s. 4(2)(b)), but picking wild mushrooms or the flowers, fruit or foliage of wild plants cannot be theft unless it is done (dishonestly) for reward or sale or other commercial purpose (s. 4(3)). 'Mushroom' includes any fungus and 'plant' includes any shrub or tree (ibid.). See, however, the Wildlife and Countryside Act 1981, s. 13 and sch. 8.

It is not theft for someone in possession of land to appropriate something forming part of the land, by severing it or causing it to be severed or after it has been severed, unless the occupation is under a tenancy and the thing appropriated is the whole or part of a fixture or structure let to be used with the land (s. 4(2)(c)). 'Tenancy' is defined in s. 4(2) to mean a tenancy for years or any less period and includes an agreement for such a tenancy. A person in possession as a statutory tenant or otherwise in possession after the end of a tenancy is to be treated as in possession under the tenancy.

The restrictions imposed by s. 4(2) do not apply to incorporeal hereditaments (or intangible real property) such as easements, profits à prendre and rentcharges.

Although a prosecution for theft can rarely be brought in respect of land, the dishonest obtaining of land may in some cases be prosecuted as an offence under the TA 1968, s. 15, or (where it occurs on or after 15 January 2007) as fraud, contrary to the Fraud Act 2006, s. 1 (see **B5.1**).

Personal Property Personal property includes tangible personal property, which might also be described as 'things (or choses) in possession', 'chattels' or 'goods'. In addition to such things as cars, televisions and handbags, personal property includes paper upon which an examination or other confidential information is written. A cheque, bill of exchange or other valuable security (or even an uncompleted cheque form or cheque book) has a value and is property capable of being appropriated (see *Arnold* [1997] 4 All ER 1, *Clark* [2002] 1 Cr App R 141), but following *Preddy* [1996] AC 815 a charge of theft in respect of such an appropriation is likely to be problematic. See **B5.17**. **B4.13**

Personal property also includes things in action and other intangible property; 'things in action' are otherwise known as 'choses in action'.

'Chose in action' is a known legal expression used to describe all personal rights of property which can only be claimed or enforced by action, and not by taking physical possession.

(*Torkington v Magee* [1902] 2 KB 427 at p. 430, per Channell J quoted in *Kohn* (1979) 69 Cr App R 395 at p. 404)

A debt for a liquidated, or known, sum is a common form of thing in action. The term also includes shares in a company. In *Marshall* [1998] 2 Cr App R 282, the Court of Appeal, stated, *obiter*, that, because the issuing of a ticket resulted in the creation of a contract between the customer and London Underground, the contractual rights arising were enforceable by action:

> Therefore it is arguable, we suppose, that by the transaction each party has acquired a chose in action. On the side of the purchaser it is represented by a right to use the ticket to the extent which it allows travel on the underground system. On the side of London Underground Limited it encompasses the right to insist that the ticket is used by no one other than the purchaser. It is that right which is disregarded when the ticket is acquired by the appellant and sold on.

'Other intangible property' includes patents (Patents Act 1977, s. 30), copyright (Copyright, Designs and Patents Act 1988, s. 1) and design rights (Copyright, Designs and Patents Act 1988, s. 213). The Privy Council held in *A-G of Hong Kong v Nai-Keung* [1987] 1 WLR 1339 that export quotas for textiles in Hong Kong are a form of 'other intangible property', on the basis that such quotas may be freely bought and sold. However, confidential information is not a form of intangible property (see *Oxford v Moss* (1978) 68 Cr App R 183). Thus a student was not guilty of theft for copying the questions from an examination paper and then returning the paper. If the student had intended to keep the paper itself, he could have been charged with theft of the piece of paper. It might have been theft even if the examination paper had been returned if it was no longer the same thing, by analogy with *Downes* (1983) 77 Cr App R 260 (see **B4.38**). The tax vouchers belonging to the Inland Revenue which were stolen in *Downes* are best described as 'other intangible property', since the Court of Appeal was not interested in the vouchers as pieces of paper, and they could not be a thing in action since no one could sue on them.

B4.14 **Bank Accounts** An account held at a bank or a building society provides the account holder with a thing in action. Provided the account is in credit, the relationship of debtor and creditor exists between the bank and the customer. The debt cannot be physically handled or possessed, but it can be enforced by action and is a thing in action which may be stolen (*Kohn* (1979) 69 Cr App Rep 395 at p. 404; see also, e.g., *Chan Man-sin v The Queen* [1988] 1 WLR 196; *Wille* (1987) 86 Cr App R 296; *Preddy* [1996] AC 815 at p. 825).

The Court of Appeal went further in *Kohn* in saying that if the account is within the agreed limits of an overdraft facility, there is an obligation on the bank to meet cheques drawn on that account. This is an obligation which may be enforced by action and so constitutes a right of property which may properly be described as a thing in action (*Kohn* (1979) 69 Cr App R 395 at p. 407 and *Chan Man-sin v The Queen* [1988] 1 WLR 196 at p. 198E).

There is not even a notional relationship of debtor and creditor when the account is overdrawn and not within the limit of an overdraft facility. The bank may decline to honour a cheque drawn on an account in that state. If it does honour such a cheque, it does so only as a matter of honour and not as the consequence of an obligation. Thus where the account is overdrawn without authority, there is no thing in action capable of being stolen (*Kohn* (1979) 69 Cr App R 395 at p. 408).

It is important to be aware that what really matters in these cases is whether the property belongs to another (*Preddy* [1996] AC 815 (at p. 834) and see **B4.19** to **B4.21**).

B4.15 **Wild Creatures** Wild creatures are property but, where a wild creature is neither tamed nor ordinarily kept in captivity, it (or the carcase of such a creature) can be stolen only if it has either (a) been reduced into possession by or on behalf of another person and possession has not since been lost or abandoned, or (b) another person is in the course of reducing it into possession (TA 1968, s. 4(4)).

Things that Cannot Be Stolen

Electricity cannot be stolen (see *Low v Blease* [1975] Crim LR 513) but it is an offence to abstract electricity contrary to the TA 1968, s. 13 (see **B4.112** ***et seq.***). **B4.16**

The Court of Appeal has affirmed the view that human bodies (or parts thereof) cannot be stolen as, without more, they are not capable of being property protected by rights (*Kelly* [1999] QB 621, following *Sharpe* (1857) Dears & B 160). Parts of a corpse are capable of being property 'if they have acquired different attributes by virtue of the application of skill, such as dissection or preservation techniques, for exhibition or teaching purposes' (*Kelly* at p. 632, following *Doodeward v Spence* (1907) 6 CLR 406 and *Dobson v North Tyneside Health Authority* [1997] 1 WLR 596 at p. 601). It follows that, e.g., Egyptian mummies in museums can be stolen in view of the preservation techniques used to ensure that they can be displayed. In *Kelly* the court indicated potential future developments in the law when it said, at p. 632:

> It may be that if . . . the question arises, the courts will hold that human body parts are capable of being property for the purposes of [TA 1968, s. 4], even without the acquisition of different attributes, if they have a use or significance beyond their mere existence. This may be so if, for example, they are intended for use in an organ transplant operation, for the extraction of DNA or, for that matter, as an exhibit in a trial.

Whether human gametes or embryos can be protected by the law of theft remains to be seen, but there is a natural reluctance to engage in property based discussions when discussing material that has the potential for human life. There are offences in relation to human corpses created by the Human Tissue Act 1961 and the Anatomy Act 1984, and the Human Fertilisation and Embryology Act 1990, s. 41 makes breach of various provisions of the Act an offence. It remains to be considered whether certain items, less controversial, can be stolen even if they are simply removed from the body, but it is submitted that it is clear that they should be regarded as property. Examples include hair (in particular, hair of a loved one offered as a present even if not displayed in a casket or brooch) and toenails and fingernails (for those keen to collect them, so the artist who retained a collection of such nails and of her own pubic hair should be regarded as having property rights in them even before she used them in some of her work for the Edinburgh Festival 1998). Some indication that there is no doubt that these items would be property is provided by the Court of Appeal's failure to comment on the conviction when reducing the sentence (on an appeal against sentence) of a driver for theft when he poured a sample of urine away (see *Welsh* [1974] RTR 478).

Meaning of 'Belonging to Another'

The TA 1968, s. 5, provides assistance in determining to whom property belongs: **B4.17**

Theft Act 1968, s. 5

(1) Property shall be regarded as belonging to any person having possession or control of it, or having in it any proprietary right or interest (not being an equitable interest arising only from an agreement to transfer or grant an interest).

(2) Where property is subject to a trust, the persons to whom it belongs shall be regarded as including any person having a right to enforce the trust, and an intention to defeat the trust shall be regarded accordingly as an intention to deprive of the property any person having that right.

(3) Where a person receives property from or on account of another, and is under an obligation to the other to retain and deal with that property or its proceeds in a particular way, the property or proceeds shall be regarded (as against him) as belonging to the other.

(4) Where a person gets property by another's mistake, and is under an obligation to make restoration (in whole or in part) of the property or its proceeds or of the value thereof, then to the extent of that obligation the property or proceeds shall be regarded (as against him) as belonging to the person entitled to restoration, and an intention not to make restoration

shall be regarded accordingly as an intention to deprive that person of the property or proceeds.

(5) Property of a corporation sole shall be regarded as belonging to the corporation notwithstanding a vacancy in the corporation.

The identity of the 'other' is generally irrelevant. All that is required is that the property belongs to someone other than D. In *Sullivan* [2002] Crim LR 758, the trial judge decided that property did not belong to another when it, money, had belonged to a drug dealer but he was dead. With respect, however, the property must have belonged to someone when it was appropriated. It may have belonged to the drug dealer's principal (if he had one), or to his estate or (failing that) to the Crown.

Ownership, Possession or Control

B4.18 In the classic case, theft is perpetrated against the owner of property, who need not be in possession, whether actual or constructive (*Hancock* [1990] 2 QB 242). However, it can be perpetrated against people with lesser interests in the property, as the TA 1968, s. 5(1), makes clear. A person may be in control of property, even though unaware of its presence, since the general principle is that control of a site by excluding others from it is prima facie control of articles on the site (see *Woodman* [1974] QB 754 at p. 758, where the site owner was in control of scrap metal which, unknown to him, had been left after the site's clearance, and see *Waverley BC v Fletcher* [1996] QB 334).

If the interest of a person satisfies s. 5(1), the property belongs to that person for the purposes of the TA 1968. In *Turner (No. 2)* [1971] 1 WLR 901, the Court of Appeal held that an owner of property can steal that property from someone else with a sufficient interest, including mere possession through a bailment. On that basis, they upheld D's conviction for stealing his own car from V who had been undertaking repairs on it. D had dishonestly removed the car from V's premises during the night, apparently with the intention of evading his duty to pay for the repairs. The trial judge had directed the jury to decide the case without reference to any repairer's lien that V might have had over the car, and the Court of Appeal therefore had to decide whether the conviction could be upheld even if there was no lien. They did uphold the conviction, although in reality it is hard to see how; but for the lien (which gave V the right to retain the car until paid) D's removal of the car could ever have been categorised as dishonest under the TA 1968, s. 2(1). *Meredith* [1973] Crim LR 253, a first instance case, is not easy to reconcile with *Turner*, but arguably is right in principle; the judge ruled that D could not be guilty of stealing his own car from a police pound if the police had no right to retain it.

The other to whom the property belongs need not be an individual, but may be a corporation. It can own money, things in action and other property which may be stolen from it by persons who are in total control of it by reason of shareholding and directorships (*A-G's Ref (No. 2 of 1982)* [1984] QB 624; *Philippou* (1989) 89 Cr App R 290). In cases where persons in control of a company are accused of theft of the company's property, issues may arise relating to other aspects of the offence of theft, including appropriation (see **B4.25**), dishonesty (see **B4.34** to B4.37) and intention permanently to deprive (see **B4.38** to **B4.44**).

Under the Treasure Act 1996, s. 4(1), when treasure is found, it vests, subject to prior interests and rights, in the franchisee (if there is one) and otherwise in the Crown. 'Treasure' is defined in s. 1 of that Act; 'prior interests or rights' is defined in s. 2; and 'franchisee' is defined in s. 5.

Proprietary Right or Interest

B4.19 For the purposes of the TA 1968, property 'belongs' to any person who has any proprietary right or interest in it other than an equitable interest arising only from an agreement to transfer or grant an interest (s. 5(1)). A partner, who has a proprietary interest in partnership property, may steal it, as his co-partners also have such an interest (*Bonner* [1970] 1 WLR 838). In *Marshall* [1998] 2 Cr App R 282, the accused acquired London Underground tickets and travel cards that had not been fully used up and sold them to other travellers. The Court of Appeal held that the tickets 'belonged to London Underground'. Although the tickets had previously been issued to travellers, London Underground retained a sufficient proprietary right or interest in the tickets for the purposes of s. 5(1).

If it is established that one person has handed to another property under a trust, the giver retains a beneficial interest in that property, which is a proprietary interest for the purposes of s. 5(1) and (2) (see *Clowes (No. 2)* [1994] 2 All ER 316 and *Wain* [1995] 2 Cr App R 660). It is, therefore, not necessary to use s. 5(3) in such cases. In practice, it is most likely that s. 5(3) will continue to be used to avoid intricate discussions of the law of trusts, although the requirement that the obligation be a legal one under s. 5(3) may give rise to the necessity to deal with exactly the same issues. One view is that s. 5(3) is, in fact, more difficult to satisfy, see the discussion of *Wain* at (1994) 1 Arch News 5.

A bank account (i.e. the debt owed by the bank to the account holder) belongs to the customer (*Kohn* (1979) 69 Cr App R 395). When a thing in action is created by the writing of a cheque, the only person to whom it can belong is the payee. Thus he cannot steal a thing in action when a cheque is written in his favour (*Davies* (1988) 88 Cr App R 347 at p. 351).

Trust property 'belongs' to the trustee who has legal title to it and also to 'any person having a right to enforce the trust' (s. 5(2)), that is, any beneficiary or, in the case of a charitable trust, the A-G (Charities Act 1993, s. 33). A trustee who appropriates trust property with the intention of defeating the trust is to be regarded as intending to deprive the person who has the right to enforce the trust of property (TA 1968, s. 5(2)). A solicitor is required to hold client money in a separate bank account. Any money paid in, and the thing in action representing that money, is held by the solicitor satisfying s. 5(2), so that transferring funds to a business account is theft (see *Hedworth* (1998 unreported)).

However, secret profits which become subject to a constructive trust do not thereby 'belong', for the purposes of the TA 1968, to the person for whose benefit the trust was imposed. In *A-G's Ref (No. 1 of 1985)* [1986] QB 491, a publican sold his own beer in a tied house, keeping the profit for himself. A constructive trust arose in respect of the profits; but the Court of Appeal took the view that s. 5(2) does not result in this profit 'belonging' to the brewery for the purposes of the law of theft. Behaviour which had previously not been considered to be criminal would otherwise have been criminalised and clearer words were needed to make such a major change. There was in any event no identifiable trust property which could form the subject-matter of a theft charge. The obligation of the publican was only to account for the profit being made, until, if ever, that profit was identified as a separate piece of property, which then could provide the basis for a theft charge. See also *Governor of Pentonville Prison, ex parte Tarling* (1978) 70 Cr App R 77.

Similarly, a bribe received by an employee does not 'belong' to the employer and the employee does not commit theft when he keeps it (*Powell v MacRae* [1977] Crim LR 571).

The limitation arising from *A-G's Ref (No. 1 of 1985)* does not apply to all property that is subject to a constructive trust. Where property is fraudulently obtained from another person, the proceeds of that fraud (e.g., funds credited to a bank account) may become subject to a constructive trust in favour of that person and will then 'belong' to him for the purposes of s. 5(2) (*Re Holmes* [2005] 1 WLR 1857 at [23]).

Property Belonging to Another: Equitable Proprietary Interests

The TA 1968 deals with two instances where property has been transferred but is nevertheless to be regarded as belonging to another so that the recipient may be guilty of theft: s. 5(3) (see **B4.20**

B4.23) and s. 5(4) (see B4.24). These provisions need not be relied upon where the transferor retains an equitable proprietary interest in the property because that interest is sufficient to satisfy s. 5(1). Indeed, there is a view that s. 5(1) ought to be used more often so as to avoid the complexities of s. 5(3) (see *Wakeman v Farrar* [1974] Crim LR 136). Nevertheless, it is clear that some overlap exists. In *Hallam* [1995] Crim LR 323, the Court of Appeal held that the clients of financial advisers, having paid cheques in the expectation that investments would be made on their behalf, retained an equitable interest in the cheques, their proceeds and any balance in accounts operated by D or the company through which they operated to which the payment could be traced. It was immaterial whether the property was regarded as belonging to another through s. 5(1) or (3). See also *Governor of Brixton Prison, ex parte Levin* [1997] AC 741.

An equitable proprietary interest may be retained by the transferor where the criteria for the application of s. 5(4) are satisfied, i.e. where property is got on the basis of another's mistake (see *Chase Manhattan Bank NA v Israel-British Bank (London) Ltd* [1981] Ch 105). Where this is the case, reliance on s 5(4) will not strictly be necessary. In *Shadrokh-Cigari* [1988] Crim LR 465, a child's bank account in England was mistakenly credited by an American bank with £286,000 instead of £286. Realising the error, S, the child's guardian, dishonestly appropriated all but £21,000 of this for his own use. It was held (applying *Chase Manhattan*) that the American bank retained an equitable interest in the transferred funds, although the court accepted that an argument based on s. 5(4) would also succeed. *Chase Manhatten* has been criticised in subsequent civil cases (see *Re Goldcorp Exchange Ltd* [1995] 1 AC 74 and *Westdeutsche Landesbank Girozentrale v Islington LBC* [1996] AC 669), but *Shadrokh-Cigari* was followed in *Webster* [2006] EWCA Crim 2894. In *Webster* D, a soldier, was charged with stealing a medal 'belonging to the Secretary of State' by selling it on the Internet. His captain had been issued with two of these medals by mistake, and had passed one of them to D. The court held that the Secretary of State had 'clearly' retained a proprietary interest in the medal for the purposes of s. 5(1), and it was not therefore open to the captain to permit its sale (as D alleged he had done).

Property must Belong to Another when Appropriated

B4.21 At the time of the appropriation, there must be property belonging to another in existence. There can be no theft where a person decides not to pay for a meal after he has eaten it (*Corcoran v Whent* [1977] Crim LR 52; see also *Stuart* (1982) *The Times*, 14 December 1982). It is particularly important when considering charges related to intangible property that, first, the type of property be identified, and, then, that those to whom it belongs be identified, as is exemplified by *Preddy* [1996] AC 815 (see B5.16).

A chose, or thing, in action is, for example, created by a cheque. This chose in action can only ever belong to the payee. He cannot steal it because he is the only person to whom it ever belongs. Another chose in action exists, which is the debt owed by the bank to the account holder who wrote the cheque. However, this thing in action (or part of it, assuming that the cheque would not extinguish the account) is never acquired by the payee. For the purposes of theft, there are a number of ways around this '*Preddy*' problem. First, D need not acquire anything for theft. Rather, he must appropriate it, which includes destruction or, presumably, reduction of the property (see B4.28). Secondly, TA 1968, s. 5(3), may apply to make the property apparently belonging to D actually, for the purposes only of theft, belong to another (see B4.23). Finally, the person for whom a thing in action is created (D, the payee) may hold it as a trustee for its creator; whether this argument is viable remains to be determined (see *Nathan* [1997] Crim LR 835).

The act of appropriation may coincide with the transfer of ownership in that property. For example the alleged act of appropriation may be the pouring of petrol into the car's tank at a self-service station. This is also the moment of transfer of ownership (Sale of Goods Act

1979, s. 18). It was originally assumed that there could not be theft in this instance. However, *Gomez* [1993] AC 442 decided that consent of the owner is irrelevant in deciding whether there has been an appropriation (see **B4.29**). Therefore, the only question in the example is whether the property belonged to another. It appears to be consistent with the decision in *Gomez* that theft has been committed in this example, provided the *mens rea* is present.

In *Morris* [1984] AC 320 Lord Roskill argued that difficult questions of whether contracts were void or voidable on the ground of mistake or fraud or whether any mistake is sufficiently fundamental to vitiate a contract should, so far as possible, be confined to those fields of law to which they are immediately relevant and should not be dragged into the law of theft. This view was quoted with approval by Parker LJ in *Dobson v General Accident Fire and Life Assurance Corporation plc* [1990] 1 QB 274 and this portion of the judgment of Parker LJ was later approved by Lord Keith in *Gomez*.

The intricacies of the civil law cannot, however, be ignored where they determine ownership or proprietary rights. In *Walker* [1984] Crim LR 112, D sold a video cassette recorder to a customer who then returned it as faulty. D resold it to a third party and was charged with stealing it from the customer. D's defence was that under the law on sale of goods, the customer had rejected the recorder (so that ownership of it had reverted to him). Dunn LJ, giving the judgment of the Court of Appeal, stated that 'a careful direction as to the law relating to the passing of property and rejection of goods under the provisions of the Sale of Goods Act was plainly required' and that on this issue 'there is no distinction between the civil law and the criminal law'.

In *Edwards v Ddin* [1976] 1 WLR 942, the Divisional Court applied rule 5(1) of what is now the Sale of Goods Act 1979, s. 18, to hold that D became the owner of petrol when it was poured into his car by a garage attendant. Driving off later without paying could not be theft. It is unlikely that there was an appropriation at an earlier time. (In such a situation it may be that a deception or fraud offence or the offence of making off without payment is committed: see **B5.69**.)

The Court of Appeal in *Wheeler* (1991) 92 Cr App R 279 was obliged to examine the intricacies of the Sale of Goods Act 1979, s. 22, in determining D's liability not only for theft, but also for obtaining property by deception (see **B5.23**) and in *Davies v Leighton* (1978) 68 Cr App R 4 the civil law had to be applied to determine when ownership in goods was transferred at a supermarket.

An example of the peculiarities produced by a failure to pay due regard to the state of the civil law is presented by the House of Lords decision in *Hinks* [2001] 2 AC 241 (see **B4.29**) in which their lordships contrived to hold that a person who acquires an indefeasible title to property under the civil law may still, if considered dishonest, be convicted of stealing that property as a consequence of one and the same set of events. On the facts of *Hinks*, D's title to the property might perhaps have been challenged on the basis of undue influence, but that was not the basis for the ruling.

Abandoned Goods

In *Small* (1988) 86 Cr App R 170 the Court of Appeal, in considering whether a person is dishonest if he has a belief that property has been abandoned, referred to *White* (1912) 7 Cr App R 266 and *Ellerman's Wilson Line Ltd v Webster* [1952] 1 Lloyd's Rep 179 and implicitly assumed that the proposition from those cases that one cannot steal abandoned property remains correct. In *Rostron* [2003] EWCA Crim 2206, the Court of Appeal confirmed the decision in *Hibbert v McKiernan* [1948] 2 KN 162 that the issue is whether there was evidence that the property (in this case golf balls that had been hit into a lake on a course) was property belonging to another. If there is, it is then a matter for the jury to determine whether **B4.22** they did so belong (in this case to the golf club as the players had abandoned them) or had been abandoned. Convictions for theft were upheld.

Obligation to Retain and Deal with Property or Proceeds

B4.23 Section 5(3) of the TA 1968 provides:

> Where a person receives property from or on account of another, and is under an obligation to the other to retain and deal with that property or its proceeds in a particular way, the property or proceeds shall be regarded (as against him) as belonging to the other.

See **B4.20** for consideration of the circumstances in which the retention of an equitable proprietary interest means that a sufficient interest is maintained in the property for it to belong to another, and thus there may be no need for recourse to s. 5(3).

Section 5(3) becomes crucial to the prosecution only where no other person has any true legal or equitable interest in the property. It operates as a 'deeming' provision so that, where D is under the specified obligation, the property may for the purposes of the law of theft be treated as if it belonged to another. See *Adams* [2003] EWCA Crim 3620, where s. 5(3) was applied to ensure that cheques made payable to D and creating a chose in action belonging only to him nevertheless could be regarded as property belonging to another because their creation was a part of a process whereby D was managing an investment account for another.

The obligation in s. 5(3) must be a legal one. A moral or social obligation is not sufficient (*Hall* [1973] QB 126; *Wakeman v Farrar* [1974] Crim LR 136; *Meech* [1974] QB 549; *Mainwaring* (1981) 74 Cr App R 99; *Davidge v Bunnett* [1984] Crim LR 297; *DPP v Huskinson* (1988) 152 JP 582; *Breaks* [1998] Crim LR 349; *Smith* (1997 unreported); *Klineberg* [1999] 1 Cr App R 427; *Re Kumar* [2000] Crim LR 504: cf. *Hayes* [1977] 1 WLR 234).

The Court of Appeal in *Arnold* [1997] 4 All ER 1 held that what needs to be identified is an obligation 'which clearly requires the recipient of the property to retain and deal with that property or its proceeds in a particular way for the benefit of the transferor' and 'no words of limitation in relation to the interest of the transferor's interest' should be introduced over and above those demanded by s. 5(3).

D need not have been under an obligation to deal with the particular monies or property handed over: 'It is sufficient that he is under an obligation to keep in existence a fund equivalent to that which he has received' (J. C. Smith, *The Law of Theft*, 8th ed., para. 2–74; *Lewis v Lethbridge* [1987] Crim LR 59). The courts' approach in identifying whether there is a legal obligation is consistent with civil law principles. Whether an agent is obliged to keep his principal's money or property separate from his own or whether the relationship is merely that of creditor and debtor will depend upon their intentions. In *Williams* [1995] Crim LR 77 D acted as a solicitor in a client's property transaction. After completion of the transaction, he retained £3,000 which should have been used to pay the mortgagee. D was held to be under a separate obligation to the bank, which was more than merely a commercial undertaking, even though the client was the owner and legal recipient of the money to whom D also owed an obligation.

An obligation will normally arise where a person receives money for onward transmission to a charity (for example, from sponsors), either because the charity imposes such an obligation as a condition of involvement or because the sponsors impose such an obligation, at least implicitly, in handing over the money (*Wain* [1995] 2 Cr App R 660). See also *Dyke* [2002] 1 Cr App R 404, where it was held that the 'collector of money from the public receives that money subject to the charitable trust and shall treat the money as belonging to the beneficiaries of that charity' (this may be an overly general statement in that its truth depends on the facts, but usually they will give rise to such an obligation); it was made clear in *Dyke* that it was important not to charge the theft as against the donors but as against the beneficiaries of the charity. Thus where the money, or its equivalent, is not handed over to the charity, that money belongs to another, and provided the other elements of the offence are satisfied (in particular dishonesty), a conviction for theft may follow (see *Wain*, overruling any suggestions to the contrary in *Lewis v Lethbridge*). Indeed, in such a situation, D may have had a trust imposed upon him sufficient to satisfy s. 5(2) (which seems to be the explanation for the sentence in *Wain* at p. 665f).

The express contractual duty to deal with investors' money in a particular way in *Smith* (1997 unreported) meant that the necessary obligation existed. As theft was alleged to be from the resulting company rather than the investors, the allegation of theft was upheld. In *Klineberg*, the allegation was that the money was stolen from intending purchasers of timeshares rather than from the company established to sell the timeshares. This meant that the necessary obligation had to be established with regard to each of the intending purchasers. This could be established on the facts (taking particular account of the element of the scheme whereby investors' money would be safeguarded by a trusteeship pending completion of the purchase) and, since it was established that the money had not been used properly, theft convictions were upheld.

The general proposition, therefore, is that there must be an obligation imposed on D, arising independently of s. 5(3) (which does not create such obligations), and that must be a legal obligation. A difficult example is to be found in *Floyd v DPP* [2000] Crim LR 411, in which it was held that there was an obligation upon D satisfying s. 5(3) where she had accepted money from her work colleagues that they expected would be forwarded to a company from which her colleagues had ordered goods. She did not forward the money. Following the cases above, it would not be surprising if there were an obligation to forward, which is recognised by the court, perhaps in the form of a trust (compare the approach in the charities cases where an obligation was imposed to forward the money collected to the charity: see *Wain* [1995] 2 Cr App R 660). Whether such an obligation arises is a question of fact; no such decision was made in this case as is shown by the statement that 'it is not necessary in order to demonstrate that property is received on account of another that that other has a legal or equitable interest in the property'. But what then is the ground for the obligation? Sir John Smith suggests in his commentary on *Wain* that it could only have been a contract, but, whilst there was a contract between the company and the colleagues (as purchasers of its goods) and between the colleagues and D, there was no contract between D and the company (she was not the company's agent, but was simply collecting the money for onward transmission). The position might now be different if the Contract (Rights of Third Parties) Act 1999 were held to apply to such a contract; the contract between F and her colleagues would require her to retain and deal with the money in a particular way and this would apparently 'confer a benefit' on the company, thus satisfying s. 1(1)(b) of that Act. The company would therefore be able to enforce that term and the money could be regarded as belonging to it under s. 5(3).

It is not sufficient that a duty to account arises (*Powell v MacRae* [1977] Crim LR 571). Section 5(3) does not therefore apply to the secret profit scenario illustrated by *A-G's Ref (No. 1 of 1985)* [1986] QB 491 (see **B4.19**). As Lord Lane CJ explained in that case:

> [D] received the money on his own account as a result of his private venture. No doubt . . . he is under an obligation to account to the employers at least for the profit he has made out of his venture, but that is a different matter. The fact that A may have to account to B for money he has received from X does not mean necessarily that he received the money on account of B.

Nor is it sufficient to establish the relationship of debtor and creditor. In *Hall* [1973] QB 126, a travel agent received money from customers as deposits and payments for air flights which were never provided nor was any of the money refunded. However, D's only obligation in relation to the money was as a debtor to the customers; he was not obliged to retain and deal with the money in a particular way. It might have been possible to make special arrangements which would have satisfied s. 5(3), but this would have required the creation of something akin to a separate fund out of which only the flight tickets for these particular customers could have been purchased. It is unlikely that such an arrangement will exist in such circumstances.

It would seem to be implicit, at least in the requirement that the obligation be a legal one, that it must also be one which is legally enforceable. Two cases cause some problems with regard to this requirement. To the extent that these cases run contrary to the clear requirement that the obligation must be a legal one, they must each be regarded as highly questionable. In *Cullen* (1974 unreported) the Court of Appeal held that theft was committed when V gave D, his mistress, £20 to buy food and pay certain domestic debts but she spent it on herself. The problem is that it is usually thought that the parties to 'domestic arrangements' about housekeeping do not intend to create legally enforceable obligations (*Balfour v Balfour* [1919] 2 KB 571) and yet Roskill LJ (giving the judgment of the court) stated that D had a legal obligation to deal with the money as V directed and it did not cease to be such an obligation simply because D was his mistress at the time.

Meech [1974] QB 549 is even harder to reconcile with the above principles. V fraudulently obtained a cheque from a finance company and D undertook to cash it for him. Having discovered V's fraud, D then arranged for some accomplices to stage a fake robbery in which the proceeds of the cheque (withdrawn by D from his own account) were taken. Because of his own fraud, V could not have enforced D's undertaking to pay him the proceeds, but D was nevertheless convicted on the basis of s. 5(3).

The courts have made clear that whether an obligation sufficient to satisfy s. 5(3) arises depends upon the particular facts of the case (see *Hall* and *McHugh* (1993) 97 Cr App R 335). The functions of judge and jury were described as follows in *Mainwaring* at p. 107 (approved in *Dubar* [1994] 1 WLR 1484 and *Breaks* [1998] Crim LR 349):

> Whether or not an obligation arises is a matter of law, because an obligation must be a legal obligation. But a legal obligation arises only in certain circumstances, and in many cases the circumstances cannot be known until the facts have been established. It is for the jury, not the judge, to establish the facts, if they are in dispute.
>
> What, in our judgment, a judge ought to do is this: if the facts relied upon by the prosecution are in dispute he should direct the jury to make their findings on the facts, and then say to them: 'If you find the facts to be such-and-such, then I direct you as a matter of law that a legal obligation arose to which section 5(3) applies.

If the facts are not in dispute, it may be appropriate for the judge to direct the jury that an obligation had been undertaken by the person receiving the property.

According to *McHugh*, the obligation must be understood by both parties. However, it is submitted that the crucial factor is only that D be aware of it. There might be circumstances where D knows that an obligation is imposed upon him, but the other person concerned is ignorant of this obligation. This should be sufficient for liability. D must know of the obligation (*Wills* (1991) 92 Cr App R 297), but for such knowledge it is not necessary that he understand that an obligation existed, rather he must appreciate the necessary facts which, as a matter of law, amount to an obligation (*Dubar*).

Obligation to Make Restoration of Property as Property Belonging to Another

B4.24 The TA 1968, s. 5(4), deals with the case where ownership in property is passed by mistake to another who is under an obligation to return the property or its proceeds. Section 5(4) covers both tangible and intangible property. The property is regarded, as against the recipient, as belonging to the person entitled to restoration:

> Where a person gets property by another's mistake, and is under an obligation to make

restoration (in whole or in part) of the property or its proceeds or of the value thereof, then to the extent of that obligation the property or proceeds shall be regarded (as against him) as belonging to the person entitled to restoration, and an intention not to make restoration shall be regarded accordingly as an intention to deprive that person of the property or proceeds.

As the Court of Appeal recognised in *Gilks* [1972] 1 WLR 1341, s. 5(4) was enacted to deal with the mischief of the decision in *Moynes v Cooper* [1956] 1 QB 439, in which D was overpaid in his weekly wages, having received an advance payment which was not then deducted from his pay packet at the end of the week. D committed no offence under the Larceny Act 1916 by keeping this money because, *inter alia*, he was held to be the only person with a legal interest in it. The TA 1968, s. 5(4), would now apply to such a case: D clearly 'got' property in the form of coins and notes, and this would be deemed (as against him) to belong to his employer.

In *A-G's Ref (No. 1 of 1983)* [1985] QB 182, s. 5(4) was applied to intangible property. A policewoman had been mistakenly credited with wages and overtime for a day which she had not worked. Her bank account was credited by credit transfer with £74.74. The Court of Appeal was satisfied that she had got property, since she had acquired a thing in action against her bank. This is clearly a form of property (see **B4.14**). See also *Stalham* [1993] Crim LR 310.

Not only does 'property' have a wide meaning, but so also does the word 'got'. It is about as wide a word as could possibly have been adopted (*A-G's Ref (No. 1 of 1983)*). Consequently, it would not only cover the handing over of coins and notes as in *Moynes v Cooper*, but also the crediting of a bank account by credit transfer.

Section 5(4) applies only where some error has been made by the giver of the property which amounts to a mistake. In *Moynes v Cooper* the mistake was the error of the wages clerk in believing that M was entitled to his full wages, whereas he should have deducted the money received in advance. In *A-G's Ref (No. 1 of 1983)* the mistake was the belief that the policewoman had worked on a particular day and was entitled to wages and overtime, when in fact she had not so worked.

Section 5(4) does not apply unless the obligation to make restoration is a legal obligation (*Gilks* [1972] 1 WLR 1341). In *Gilks* D placed a bet on a horse called Flying Scot. The race was won by Flying Taff. The relief manager paid out to D as if he had backed the winning horse and so D was overpaid by £106.63. D knew that a mistake had been made, but decided to keep the money. The Court of Appeal held that D did not owe a legal obligation to return the money because the bookmaker could not have sued on a gaming transaction (*Morgan v Ashcroft* [1938] 1 KB 490). The court held further that s. 5(4) did not apply to D's moral or social obligation to return the money.

In *A-G's Ref (No. 1 of 1983)* [1985] QB 182 the Court of Appeal decided that 'restoration' has the same meaning as 'restitution'. Consequently, it has to be established that the recipient of the property is under an obligation within the general principles of restitution. The Court of Appeal went on to say that a recipient of property is obliged to pay for a benefit received when it has been given under a mistake on the part of the giver about a material fact. The mistake has to be about a fundamental or essential fact and the payment must have been induced by the mistaken fact (*Norwich Union Fire Insurance Society Ltd v Wm H. Price Ltd* [1934] AC 455). Consequently, not everyone who receives property under a mistake sufficient to satisfy the first element of s. 5(4) will, as a result of that mistake, be under an obligation to make restoration.

In *Davis* (1988) 88 Cr App R 347 the court indicated that the 'language of quasi-contract and of other parts of the civil law' are 'unwelcome visitors to a statute which is supposed to furnish lay juries with tests which they can readily grasp and apply'. It is submitted that the solution must be not a refusal to make use of the law of quasi-contract or restitution, but rather that care should be taken in directions given to juries such that the jury are clear that if they find certain facts then an obligation to restore has been established. This approach is consistent with that to be used when directing juries with regard to s. 5(3) as laid down in *Mainwaring* (1981) 74 Cr App R 99 (see **B4.23**).

'Appropriation'

B4.25 By the TA 1968, s. 3:

> (1) Any assumption by a person of the right of an owner amounts to an appropriation, and this includes, where he has come by the property (innocently or not) without stealing it, any later assumption of a right to it by keeping or dealing with it as owner.
>
> (2) Where property or a right or interest in property is or purports to be transferred for value to a person acting in good faith, no later assumption by him of rights which he believed himself to be acquiring shall, by reason of any defect in the transferor's title, amount to theft of the property.

The meaning of 'appropriation' has been considered in four House of Lords cases: *Lawrence v Metropolitan Police Commissioner* [1972] AC 626; *Morris* [1984] AC 320; *Gomez* [1993] AC 442 and *Hinks* [2001] 2 AC 24 (see **B4.29**). In *Gomez* three members of the House of Lords (Lords Jauncey, Browne-Wilkinson and Slynn) agreed with the speech of Lord Keith. Lord Lowry dissented. Lord Browne-Wilkinson also delivered a speech which considered some of the ramifications of Lord Keith's speech.

In *Gomez* the House of Lords approved the decision in *Morris* that it is unnecessary to prove that an accused assumed all of another's rights over the property alleged to have been stolen. It is sufficient to prove the assumption of *any* of the rights of an owner, see **B4.26** and **B4.28**. 'Appropriation' does not require a 'taking'; and the decision of the Court of Appeal in *Gallasso* (1993) 98 Cr App R 284 is accordingly wrong. Contrary to the view expressed by the Court of Appeal in *Ngan* [1998] 1 Cr App R 331, the owner need not be deprived of property; see **B4.31**).

The main issue in *Gomez* concerned the role of consent in appropriation. Their lordships here followed *Lawrence* in holding that the consent or authorisation of the owner does not prevent an act being an appropriation. There is still an apparent tendency in some decisions to look for something that seems similar to the requirement in *Morris* of an adverse interference or usurpation of the rights of the owner (see, e.g., *Ngan*, where the court talks of the need for the 'assertion of a right adverse to' the owner; and *Marshall* [1998] 2 Cr App R 282). *Morris*, however, is no longer good law on this point.

It should be noted that appropriation can occur through an innocent agent's acts, as where D, by signing false invoices, sets in motion a chain of events which will result in the company's account being debited (*Stringer* (1992) 94 Cr App R 13).

Assumption of One or More of the Rights of an Owner

B4.26 In *Gomez* [1993] AC 442, Lord Keith stated, approving *Morris* [1984] AC 320 on this point, that on a charge of theft it is sufficient (despite the contrary wording of the TA 1968, s. 3) for the prosecution to prove the assumption by D of any of the rights of the owner. It followed that 'the removal of an article from the shelf [of a supermarket] and the changing of the price label on it constituted an assumption of one of the rights of the owner and hence an appropriation'. Lord Keith further stated that 'the switching of price labels on the article is in itself an assumption of one of the rights of the owner, whether or not it is accompanied by some other act such as removing the article from the shelf and placing it in a basket or trolley' because 'no one but the owner has the right to remove a price label from an article or to place a price label upon it'.

A dishonest appropriation of another person's property need not necessarily be theft. Arguably the label switcher should not be regarded as stealing by that act alone because, if his intent is to purchase the item in question a few minutes later, it would be by this later purchase (and not by the label switching) that he would eventually deprive the owner of his property. This argument, however, is impliedly rejected both in *Morris* and in *Gomez*.

Careful consideration must be given to cases in which D is charged with theft on the basis that he dishonestly drew cheques on another person's account. A director may, for example, have drawn cheques on his company's account. In *Ngan* [1998] 1 Cr App R 331, Leggatt LJ said (at pp. 335–6):

> [The] act of theft itself was the presentation of the cheque. Until then no right as against the Bank had been exercised . . . In [*Governor of Pentonville Prison, ex parte Osman* [1990] 1 WLR 277] the Divisional Court held that appropriation occurs when a cheque is presented. We agree; but it does not follow that it cannot occur earlier . . . In one sense the very act of signing each cheque might be regarded as an assumption of a right. But it must be remembered that the right assumed is not to the cheque, but to the property or chose in action, that is, to the debt mistakenly due from the Bank. . . . [*Gomez*] has no application here, because until on each occasion a cheque was presented for payment there was no dealing with any of [the other's] rights to the balance mistakenly standing to the credit of the appellant. Her acts of signing the cheques and sending them to her sister were preparatory acts, and more needed to be done by or on behalf of the appellant before [the other] could be deprived of their property.

Whether any 'dealing' with the property is required under *Gomez* is (with respect) open to doubt. Furthermore, *Osman* actually holds that the mere issuing of a cheque (the first delivery of a cheque, complete in form, to a person who takes it as holder: Bills of Exchange Act 1882, s. 2) can be a sufficient act of appropriation. In *Osman*, the court observed that there is a difference between when theft was complete in law (upon issuing of the cheque) and when it was complete in fact (upon actual debiting of the account).

It may be argued that if an accused has forged a cheque on another person's bank account there has been no appropriation of the other person's rights against the bank because a bank is not entitled to debit a customer with the amount of a forged cheque. In *Chan Man-sin v The Queen* [1988] 1 WLR 196, Lord Oliver of Aylmerton (delivering the advice of the Privy Council) said (at p. 199):

> . . . it is, in their lordship's view, beyond argument that one who draws, presents and negotiates a cheque on a particular bank account is assuming the rights of the owner of the credit in the account or (as the case may be) of the pre-negotiated right to draw on the account up to the agreed figure. Ownership, of course, consists of a bundle of rights and it may well be that there are other rights which an owner could exert over the chose in action in question which are not trespassed upon by the particular dealing which the thief chooses to assume. In [*Morris*] [1984] AC 320, however, the House of Lords decisively rejected a submission that it was necessary, in order to constitute an appropriation as defined by section 3(1) of the [TA 1968], to demonstrate an assumption by the accused of all the rights of an owner.

In *Wille* (1987) 86 Cr App R 296, W, a director of a company had issued numerous cheques on the company's bank account (which was at all times in credit) for his own benefit. Each cheque was signed by himself alone and had been honoured by the bank despite the fact that the mandate from the company authorised it to honour only cheques bearing two signatures. Accordingly the bank was not entitled to debit the amounts of the cheques to the company's account. Nevertheless, W was rightly convicted of stealing the debts owed by the bank to the company. Woolf LJ said (at p. 302):

> When what the appellant did in this case is considered, it is hard to see what more he could do to assume the rights of the owner in respect of the account at Barclays Bank to the extent of the amount for which the cheques were drawn, than to draw a cheque, issue the cheque, and then take steps which were designed to achieve that the account of the company at the bank was debited with the amount of the cheque. . . . The fact that the company may still have rights

against the bank for the amounts of those cheques is . . . irrelevant to the issues with which the jury were concerned.

In both *Wille* and *Chan Man-sin v The Queen*, the cheques were honoured by the banks (see also **B4.28**). If the cheques had not been honoured, there might still have been an appropriation following the principles outlined in the discussion above (see *Wheatley* v *Commissioner of Police of the British Virgin Islands* [2006] 1 WLR 1683).

More Than One Appropriation of the Same Property

B4.27 It appears to follow from *Gomez* [1993] AC 442 that one item may be appropriated on a number of occasions (see also **B4.28**). If this were right it would be for the prosecution to choose which act of appropriation it was going to concentrate upon, choosing the act in relation to which it was easiest to prove the other elements of theft. Alternatively, it might be that only the first act of appropriation may be considered, on the basis that a person may not steal an item which he has already stolen. The relevance of the second part of the TA 1968, s. 3(1), to this issue remains to be clarified. It provides that a person who has 'come by the property (innocently or not) *without stealing it*' (emphasis supplied) may appropriate it by a specified later act (see **B4.32**). This might mean that the label switcher in a supermarket cannot be guilty of theft if charged for his actions at the cash desk (trying to pay less than he should), because he will already have stolen the item by the switching of a label. The Court of Appeal in *Atakpu* [1994] QB 69 has confirmed that 'if goods have once been stolen . . . they cannot be stolen again by the same thief'. It is submitted that the best point to consider whether theft has been committed is at the cash desk, taking account of what has gone before as evidence of the crime. So the solution is to consider what is the complete activity, which may be spread over a period of time. In *Atakpu*, the Court of Appeal decided that *Gomez* should not be interpreted so as to rule out appropriation as a continuous course of action; it preferred 'to leave it for the commonsense of the jury to decide that the appropriation can continue for so long as the thief can sensibly be regarded as in the act of stealing or, in more understandable words, so long as he is "on the job" as the editors of Smith and Hogan . . . suggest the test should be'. This *obiter* statement appears to support the position prior to the decision in *Gomez* when careful thought had to be given to three Court of Appeal decisions (*Hale* (1978) 68 Cr App R 415, *Gregory* (1981) 77 Cr App R 41 and *Pitham* (1977) 65 Cr App R 45). *Hale* and *Gregory* support the proposition that appropriation is a continuing act.

In *Hale*, a decision which remains good law (*Lockley* [1995] Crim LR 656), the Court of Appeal stated that the 'act of appropriation does not suddenly cease. It is a continuous act and it is a matter for the jury to decide whether or not the act of appropriation has finished'. Consequently, Hale's conviction for robbery could be upheld, because the view was taken that the act of appropriation was continuing so as to coincide with the use of force after the jewellery box had been seized. A similar approach was taken in *Gregory*, thus enabling a burglary conviction to be upheld, because the view was taken that the act of appropriation was a 'continuing process'. In *Pitham*, it was decided that the act of appropriation was complete upon an offer to sell furniture, so that handling convictions could be upheld.

In *Hallam* [1995] Crim LR 323, it was not possible to identify whether the defendants stole a chose in action or the proceeds of it, but they had failed to account for the sums received. It was held that, provided the other elements of theft are present, a conviction is possible in such circumstances without identifying which form of property was stolen, since there was property throughout which did always belong to another (see **B4.20**; cf. *Caresana* [1996] Crim LR 667).

It is important to note that an item may be stolen, whether once or more than once, only if all the elements of theft are present. In particular, it may be essential to determine whether the property concerned does still belong to another, see **B4.21**.

Identifying the Act of Appropriation

A thief may appropriate property belonging to another without ever obtaining that property. B4.28
There was, for example, an appropriation in *Corcoran v Anderton* (1980) 71 Cr App R 104 where D tugged at a lady's handbag, causing her to drop it, even though he never obtained control over the bag.

Dishonestly causing the destruction of property can itself be theft (*Kohn* (1979) 69 Cr App R 395). This was confirmed in *Graham* [1997] 1 Cr App R 302, where Lord Bingham CJ said:

> We wish to make it clear that nothing we said was intended to cast doubt upon the principle that theft of a chose in action may be committed when a chose in action belonging to another is destroyed by the defendant's act of appropriation as defined by section 3(1) of the Act.

See also *Williams* [2001] 1 Cr App R 362. It should be remembered that, where the property is destroyed or extinguished but there is an obligation on the bank to restore so that the transaction may be a legal nullity, there can still be an appropriation and an intention permanently to deprive, as decided in *Chan Man-sin v R* [1988] 1 WLR 196, which was confirmed in *Wille* (1989) 86 Cr App R 296 (see also **B4.26**, **B4.31** and **B4.39**).

There must be an act which can be regarded as an appropriation that takes place when the identified property exists and belongs to another (*Preddy* [1996] AC 815 (see **B5.17** ***et seq.***); *Forsyth* [1997] 2 Cr App R 299 and *Briggs* [2004] 1 Cr App R 451). For the position where cheques are involved, see **B4.26**. Where the property is a bank account, but the activity controlling it is not a cheque, great care must be taken to determine whether there is an act of appropriation. So in *Naviede* [1997] Crim LR 662, the Court of Appeal said:

> We are not satisfied that a misrepresentation which persuades the account holder to direct payment out of his account is an assumption of the rights of the account holder as owner such as to amount to an appropriation of his rights within section 3(1) of the 1968 Act.

It is important to emphasise that identifying what amounts to an act of appropriation is a separate and subsequent issue to that of assessing what is the property that might be appropriated. The Court of Appeal in *Hilton* appear to have grasped the point, since they endeavoured to determine what was the property, and whether it was appropriated by D. Where D signs a cheque for an improper purpose, or forges a cheque or issues instructions to a bank, an appropriation may be identified, because those acts are 'the key' to the property. Where D's act is more remote or where it induces the victim to do an act which acts as the key to the property, it may be impossible to identify an act that can be termed an appropriation.

There will be difficulties if an act of appropriation is not carefully identified. It is not sufficient that the thing in action has been reduced or destroyed. It must also be the case that D did that act himself or through innocent agents. There was an act of appropriation in *Hilton*, because, as Sir John Smith explains in his commentary on *Naviede*,

> There, D had direct control of a bank account belonging to a charity. He caused payments to be made from that account to settle his personal debts. That was a completely straightforward case of theft of the thing in action belonging to another.

This, he goes on to say, is a very different scenario from that appertaining in cases such as *Carasena* [1996] Crim LR 67, *Preddy* [1996] AC 815, *Graham* [1997] 1 Cr App R 302, *Cooke* [1997] Crim LR 436 and *Naviede* which 'were all concerned with the situation where D by deception induces V to initiate a transaction whereby V's bank account is debited and D's is credited' (commentary to *Naviede* at p. 666). See also *Briggs* [2004] 1 Cr App R 451, in which D deceived elderly relatives into authorising a transfer of £49,500 from the proceeds of their house sale into a bank account controlled by D. As in *Naviede*, the Court of Appeal held that the transfer was not an act of appropriation by D, even though her dishonest intent was not in doubt. Giving the judgment of the court, Silber J said (at [13]):

> We are fortified in coming to that view by three further factors. First, no case has been cited to us where it has been held that an appropriation occurs where the relevant act is committed by the victim albeit as a result of deception. Second, . . . there would [otherwise] be little need for many deception offences as many acts of deceptive conduct would be covered by theft, but it is noteworthy that the Theft Act 1968 (as amended) contains deception offences to deal with the case where a defendant by deception induces a person to take a step which leads to the wrongdoing of gaining property by deception (section 15) or obtaining a money transfer by deception (section 15A) or obtaining a pecuniary advantage (section 16). Third, we have already referred to the explanation of the word 'appropriation' in section 3(1) of the Theft Act 1968 and it is a word which connotes a physical act rather than a more remote action triggering the payment which gives rise to the charge. The Oxford English Dictionary defines 'appropriation' as 'to take possession for one's own, to take to oneself'. It is not easy to see why an act of deceiving an owner to do something would fall within the meaning of 'appropriation'.

(As to the replacement of the old deception offences by the new offence of fraud, see **B5.1**.)

Despite *Briggs,* the difficulties associated with identifying the act of appropriation would suggest that this remains a matter worthy of further consideration. The difficulties encountered are exacerbated by the wide range of activities that may be identified as an appropriation after the interpretation of that phrase by the House of Lords in *Morris* [1984] AC 320 and *Gomez* [1993] AC 442 (see **B4.26**). These problems are exacerbated by the decision of the House of Lords in *Hinks* [2001] 2 AC 241, since it is difficult to see what act of appropriation is committed by the recipient of a gift and there is little, if any, limit to what may amount to such an act if it is possible to be a thief when receiving an indefeasible gift of property (see also A. T. H. Smith (1999) 58 CLJ 10 and J. Beatson and A. P. Simester (1999) 115 LQR 372).

Consent or Authority of Owner

B4.29 It is now clear that 'consent to or authorisation by the owner of the taking by the rogue is irrelevant' per Lord Keith in *Gomez* [1993] AC 442 at p. 464. In reaching this conclusion, the House of Lords in *Gomez* approved the decision of *Lawrence v Metropolitan Police Commissioner* [1972] AC 626 and decided that, on this point, the decision of the House of Lords in *Morris* [1984] AC 320 was erroneous. See also *Hinks* [2001] 2 AC 241.

In *Lawrence* the House of Lords held that on a charge of theft it is unnecessary to prove that the appropriation was without the consent of the owner. The House rejected an argument that s. 1(1) must be construed as though it contained the words, 'without the consent of the owner'. Viscount Dilhorne said (at pp. 631–2):

> I see no ground for concluding that the omission of the words 'without the consent of the owner' was inadvertent and not deliberate, and to read the subsection as if they were included is, in my opinion, wholly unwarranted. Parliament by the omission of these words has relieved the prosecution of the burden of establishing that the taking was without the owner's consent. That is no longer an ingredient of the offence.

In *Lawrence* D was a taxi-driver who picked up V, an Italian, at an airport. The proper fare for the journey was 10*s.* 6*d.* (52.5p). V offered a £1 note, but this was rejected by D. V then offered his wallet, and D took from it another £6. The House of Lords held that D dishonestly appropriated property belonging to V and so upheld the theft conviction. Whilst they were asked to consider the issue of consent and provided the answer already alluded to, Viscount Dilhorne, stated (at p. 631) that '. . . the facts of this case . . . fall far short of establishing that [V] had so consented'.

The House of Lords in *Gomez* also decided (at p. 460) that no 'sensible distinction can be made in this context between consent and authorisation'; thus, whilst an act by way of adverse interference with or usurpation of the rights of an owner (see Lord Roskill in *Morris* at p. 332) does amount to an appropriation, the concept is not limited to such acts. In arriving at this view, their lordships accepted that the decision of the Court of Appeal (Civil Division) in *Dobson v General Accident Fire and Life Assurance Corporation plc* [1990] 1 QB 274 was correct, and Lord Keith found himself in full agreement with the judgment of Parker LJ in that case.

In *Gomez* D, an assistant manager of an electrical shop, obtained the consent or authorisation of the manager for goods to be delivered to others against two building society cheques which D knew to be stolen. The manager consented to this because D told him that the bank had indicated that the cheques were acceptable; despite this consent, D's conviction for theft was upheld.

The House of Lords held that *Lawrence* was correctly decided, contrary dicta in *Morris* were *obiter* and erroneous and that the cases of *Skipp* [1975] Crim LR 114 and *Fritschy* [1985] Crim LR 745 were wrongly decided. It now appears that in *Skipp* there was an appropriation each time a load was put onto D's lorry, and not only when he deviated from his authorised route. In *Fritschy* there was an appropriation as soon as D took possession of V's Kruggerrands in England, and not only when he deviated from V's instructions to deliver them to a bank in Switzerland. Whether theft is committed in a similar case depends upon whether the other elements of the offence are present. In addition to *Skipp* and *Fritschy*, which were specifically referred to in *Gomez*, it would seem, as a matter of logic, that the following cases were also wrongly decided: *Meech* [1974] QB 549 (where it might now be decided that an appropriation took place when M resolved to deprive another of the proceeds of a cheque the other had obtained as a result of forgery and not only at the later time of the fake robbery); *Hircock* (1978) 67 Cr App R 278 (where it would now be decided that there was an appropriation when H got the car on a hire-purchase agreement and not only later when he sold it); *Eddy v Niman* (1981) 73 Cr App R 237 (where it would now be decided that an appropriation was committed when a shopper put goods into a wire basket provided by the supermarket); *McPherson* [1973] Crim LR 191 (where it would now be decided that M appropriated the whisky bottles when she removed them from the shelves). Whether theft was committed in cases similar to these depends upon the existence of the other elements of theft. In particular, having regard to Lord Roskill's concern about the honest customer in a supermarket, the honest customer does appropriate the goods he removes from the shelves, but does not commit theft because he is not dishonest. As Lord Browne-Wilkinson puts it in *Gomez* (at p. 495), appropriation is an 'objective description of the act done irrespective of the mental state of either the owner or the accused'. The mental state of the owner is irrelevant, and D's own mental state need be considered only in relation to the questions of dishonesty and intention permanently to deprive.

It follows from *Gomez* that there will be considerable overlap between the offence of theft and the offence of obtaining property by deception contrary to the TA 1968, s. 15 (see **B5.14** *et seq.*) which, despite its repeal under the Fraud Act 2006 (see **B5.1**), remains applicable to things done before 15 January 2007 (when the Fraud Act was brought fully into force). Lord Browne-Wilkinson expressed little concern as to the overlap, but pointed out that land can rarely be stolen but can always be obtained by deception. Only Lord Lowry (who dissented) was prepared to consider the Eighth Report of the Criminal Law Revision Committee (1966) Cmnd. 2977, which preceded the TA 1968 and which clearly shows that such an extensive overlap was not intended by those who drafted the Act.

The House of Lords has confirmed the line of authority in *Lawrence* and *Gomez* in its most recent statement (*Hinks* [2001] 2 AC 241). This takes the apparent logic of these decisions to a conclusion that is little short of absurd, as it concludes that a person may be guilty of theft when he is the recipient of an indefeasible gift of property, liability for theft depending upon the presence or absence of dishonesty. The House rejected the argument, deriving from the decision of the Court of Appeal in *Mazo* [1997] 2 Cr App R 518, that the decision in *Gomez* should be limited to those circumstances where the act was done with the victim's consent but that consent was obtained by fraud, deception or a false representation (see also *Briggs* [2004] 1 Cr App R 451). Whilst this approach did not clearly form part of the decision of the House in *Gomez*, it did form a part of the question asked of the House and would allow more ready consistency between the civil and the criminal law. This is because consent obtained by deception would be voidable and so it would not offend the civil law to hold the person guilty of theft. The House has determined that the recipient of a gift may be guilty of theft, even where there is no challenge to the civil law legality of the transaction, provided that he is dishonest. Even if dishonesty can be proved, however, it remains necessary to prove that the property in question still belonged to another at the moment of appropriation (see **B4.21**).

In *Ascroft* [2004] 1 Cr App R (S) 326, D, who ran a road haulage firm, challenged a confiscation order imposed following his conviction for conspiracy to steal goods from containers carried on his lorries. The prosecution proved that sealed containers were regularly opened by his accomplices, without breaking the seals, and that parts of each consignment (typically cases of spirits) were then removed before the containers were closed up again. This appears to have occurred in each case near the company's depot, in Lancashire. Counsel for D nevertheless argued that in 17 of the 25 acts of theft to which this count of conspiracy related, the goods in question had already been stolen even before the containers were opened. They had been stolen, he argued, when the sealed containers were loaded onto the lorries in Scotland, and thus beyond the ambit of the English law of theft. See **A8.2**.

The Court of Appeal acknowledged that a charge of conspiracy to steal under English law cannot be based on an agreement to steal goods in Scotland. The question, therefore, was whether the contents of the containers in question were dishonestly appropriated when first collected in Scotland, or whether the appropriation occurred in England, when the containers were improperly opened and the selected goods removed. The Court of Appeal preferred the latter view. Scott Baker LJ said:

> We do not believe that *Gomez* was ever intended to apply to the sort of situation that obtains in this case. The reality seems to us to be that there was a conspiracy to steal goods being conveyed in the appellant's company's lorries as and when appropriate opportunities occurred, with the actual operation to achieve their removal from the lorries (which, we would add, requires some effort and subtlety) taking place at or near the appellant's premises. If the appellant's argument is correct, the theft involves not only those goods that the conspirators subsequently stole but also those that they left in the lorry.
>
> . . . In our judgment there never was in any ordinary sense of the word an appropriation of the stolen goods until the conspirators removed them from the containers.

Appropriation and Companies

B4.30 In *R (A) v Snaresbrook Crown Court* [2001] EWHC Admin 456, the Divisional Court stated that it was 'prepared to accept as being obvious that a company cannot steal from itself'. Companies can commit crimes, including theft, only by the agency of individuals, thus confirming the application of the identification principle (see **A5.17**). Where the charge is one of theft by someone from the company, those principles do not, of course, apply.

In *Gomez* [1993] AC 442 Lord Browne-Wilkinson (at p. 496) considered the position of persons charged with theft from a company:

> the whole question of consent by the company [is] irrelevant. Whether or not those controlling the company consented or purported to consent to the abstraction of the company's property by the accused, he will have appropriated the property of the company. The question will be whether the other necessary elements are present, viz. was such appropriation dishonest and was it done with the intention of permanently depriving the company of such property?

Lord Browne-Wilkinson disapproved *McHugh* (1988) 88 Cr App R 385, and approved *A-G's Ref (No. 2 of 1982)* [1984] QB 624 and *Phillippou* (1989) 89 Cr App R 290. As the Divisional Court in *R (A) v Snaresbrook Crown Court* makes clear: 'whatever was [D's] objective, and whether he was authorised to do this by the company or not,' the question is whether he assumed the rights of the owner.

Where the authorised signatory is the sole proprietor of the company, the Court of Appeal in *A-G's Ref (No. 2 of 1982)* took the view that an appropriation is committed, though the case is mainly concerned with the question of dishonesty. This approach was followed in *Philippou*. Indeed, the Court of Appeal said (at pp. 299–300):

> [Lord Roskill] cannot be understood as saying that the prosecution must prove that the appropriation alleged was without the authority of the owner, or that would be directly contrary to what was said in *Lawrence v Metropolitan Police Commissioner*. We think it obvious that the House of Lords in *Morris* was not inserting into the definition of theft in section 1(1) after the word 'appropriates' the words 'without the authority of the owner'.

There has been debate as to whether it is possible for the appropriation to be dishonest where D is the company controller. However, the Divisional Court in *R (A) v Snaresbrook Crown Court* took the view that there are circumstances of theft from a company, including the facts of the instant case, where it was possible to identify dishonesty. Much, it is submitted, will depend upon the number of people identified with the company and how many of them approved D's act.

Appropriation without Loss to the Owner

Since an appropriation may occur even though not all the rights of an owner are assumed, it follows that the owner need not necessarily lose his property. In *Chan Man-sin v The Queen* [1988] 1 WLR 196, C, an accountant, forged company cheques to his own benefit. The company would lose nothing, since it would be entitled to have the initial debit in its account reversed, but it was held that C had appropriated property belonging to another and since he had the requisite *mens rea* his conviction for theft was upheld. **B4.31**

Appropriation after Innocent Acquisition by Later Assumption of Rights

By the TA 1968, s. 3(1), where D has come by the property (innocently or not) without stealing it, any later assumption of a right to it by keeping it or dealing with it as owner amounts to an appropriation. If committed with the requisite *mens rea*, such an appropriation may be theft. **B4.32**

For this rule to operate, D must originally have 'come by the property . . . without stealing it'. The obvious interpretation is that, if D has got the property by stealing it, whatever he later does with it cannot constitute an appropriation and, therefore, theft. Since *Gomez* [1993] AC 442 this interpretation may present particular problems which are considered at B4.27.

In order to have appropriated property of which he already has possession, an alleged thief must have later assumed a right of an owner, but only by keeping the property or dealing with it as owner. The latter may cause no problems. However, it may not always be easy to establish that a person has kept property as owner. In *Broom v Crowther* (1984) 148 JP 592, D had come into possession of a theodolite. Once he became aware that it was stolen, he kept it in his possession, but he had not come to any decision as to what to do with it. This finding of fact by the magistrates was inconsistent with an inference that he was keeping the theodolite as owner. The Divisional Court decided that he had not assumed a right to the theodolite by keeping it as owner and quashed the conviction for theft. The Court indicated that the factors relevant in determining the matter were that he had not kept the theodolite for a long time (he had had it for between four and five months), he had not attempted to dispose of it and had not even used it. It simply remained in his bedroom.

Appropriation: Purchaser in Good Faith of Stolen Goods

B4.33 **Theft Act 1968, s. 3(2)**

> Where property or a right or interest in property is or purports to be transferred for value to a person acting in good faith, no later assumption by him of rights which he believed himself to be acquiring shall, by reason of any defect in the transferor's title, amount to theft of the property.

Ordinarily a person who has gained possession of property appropriates that property if he then keeps or deals with it as owner (TA 1968, s. 3(1); see **B4.32**). However, s. 3(2) provides an exception, which is fairly limited. D must, first, have given value for property in which he consequently appears to gain an interest. It is irrelevant that the civil law would say, on the facts of a particular instance, that he does not actually gain any such interest. Secondly, D must have initially acted in good faith. In *Broom v Crowther* (1984) 148 JP 592 (see **B4.32**) D seems not to have acquired the theodolite in good faith. His conviction was quashed, however, because it was not shown that D had subsequently kept or dealt with it as owner.

As to the position of persons who unwittingly buy stolen goods, but sell or dispose of them once they become aware of the truth, see also *Bloxham* [1983] 1 AC 109, which is examined at **B4.137** and **B4.139**. See also *Wheeler* (1991) 92 Cr App R 279. As regards the words 'rights which he believed himself to be acquiring', the relevant time at which the belief must be held is the moment when the receiver purchased for value (*Adams* [1993] Crim LR 72).

Meaning of 'Dishonesty'

B4.34 The concept of 'dishonesty', like the concept of 'intention permanently to deprive', is a question of the state of D's mind, part of the *mens rea* of theft. Consequently, inferences may be drawn from his conduct, even though conduct is not determinative of *mens rea*, see *Ingram* [1975] Crim LR 457 and *Boggeln v Williams* [1978] 1 WLR 873.

The TA 1968 provides a partial definition of 'dishonesty'. A general definition has been provided by the Court of Appeal in *Ghosh* [1982] QB 1053. The decision whether somebody is 'dishonest' is one for either the jury or the magistrates.

Circumstances in which Appropriation is Not to Be Regarded as Dishonest

B4.35 **Theft Act 1968, s. 2**

> (1) A person's appropriation of property belonging to another is not to be regarded as dishonest—
> (a) if he appropriates the property in the belief that he has in law the right to deprive the other of it, on behalf of himself or a third person; or
> (b) if he appropriates the property in the belief that he would have the other's consent if the other knew of the appropriation and the circumstances of it; or
> (c) (except where the property came to him as trustee or personal representative) if he appropriates the property in the belief that the person to whom the property belongs cannot be discovered by taking reasonable steps.
>
> (2) A person's appropriation of property belonging to another may be dishonest notwithstanding that he is willing to pay for the property.

The TA 1968, s. 2(1)(a), requires only that it be shown that D had an honest belief that he was entitled to take the property. It is not necessary to show that he had an honest belief that he was entitled to take it in the way that he did (*Robinson* [1977] Crim LR 173, following the decision on the earlier law in *Skivington* [1968] 1 QB 166). However, D's method of taking property may render him liable for some other offence. The issue of the reasonableness of the belief is relevant only in considering whether D had an honest belief (*Holden* [1991] Crim LR 478).

The importance of drawing the jury's attention to the provisions of s. 2(1)(a) was emphasised by the Court of Appeal in *Falconer-Atlee* (1973) 58 Cr App R 348. The Court of Appeal held in *Wootton* [1990] Crim LR 201 that a trial judge should direct the jury on s. 2(1)(a) whenever a claim of right is raised, even though a direction in accordance with *Ghosh* [1982] QB 1053 (see **B4.34**) is likely to cover all the occasions when s. 2(1)(a) might be applicable. See also *Forrester* [1992] Crim LR 793.

The Court of Appeal considered s. 2(1)(a) and (b) in *A-G's Ref (No. 2 of 1982)* [1984] QB 624. It was held that persons who between them represent the directing mind and will of a company cannot rely on s. 2(1)(b) to negate the dishonesty of their appropriation of the company's property if the only consent they can allege is the consent of themselves which they say should be deemed to be the company's consent by virtue of the doctrine that their minds are the minds of the company (the identification theory) for in those circumstances there is no consent by an 'other', only their own consent. Whether such persons could establish a defence under s. 2(1)(a) would depend on whether the prosecution could prove that they did not honestly believe that they were entitled to do what they did. The court firmly rejected arguments that, when all the members and directors of a company act in concert in appropriating the property of their company, they cannot be held to have acted dishonestly. The appropriation of corporate funds may well prejudice the interests of the company's creditors, even if its own members are not harmed.

Dishonesty Notwithstanding Willingness to Pay

Although D's appropriation of V's property may sometimes be considered dishonest even though he is willing to pay for it (notably where he knows that V is not willing to sell it to him), his willingness to pay a fair price may in other circumstances be indicative of his honesty. See *Boggeln v Williams* [1978] 1 WLR 873. To put it another way, it is often D's evident intent to *avoid* paying that most clearly demonstrates his dishonesty. **B4.36**

Meaning of 'Dishonesty' According to *Ghosh*

The Court of Appeal in *Ghosh* [1982] QB 1053 established a dishonesty test that applies both to theft and to other offences of dishonesty. It is subordinate to the TA 1968, s. 2(1), so where in a theft case D's conduct is deemed *not* to be dishonest under that provision the *Ghosh* test need not even be considered; but where s. 2(1) is not applicable or does not provide the answer (and it never positively defines dishonesty), the *Ghosh* test becomes paramount. **B4.37**

According to *Ghosh* (at p. 1064D–E) a two-part test must be applied:

> [1.] . . . a jury must first of all decide whether according to the ordinary standards of reasonable and honest people what was done was dishonest. If it was not dishonest by those standards, that is the end of the matter and the prosecution fails.
>
> If it was dishonest by those standards, then the jury must consider [the second question].
>
> [2] . . . the jury must consider whether the defendant himself must have realised that what he was doing was by [the standards of reasonable and honest people] dishonest.

Where a *Ghosh* direction is necessary, the exact words in *Ghosh* should be used (*Hyam* [1997] Crim LR 439). The questions must be asked in the indicated order; to reverse them is confusing (*Green* [1992] Crim LR 292). The Court of Appeal in *Ghosh* gave further explanation of the second question when it said (at p. 1064E–G):

> In most cases, where the actions are obviously dishonest by ordinary standards, there will be no doubt about it. It will be obvious that the defendant himself knew that he was acting dishonestly. It is dishonest for a defendant to act in a way which he knows ordinary people consider to be dishonest, even if he asserts or genuinely believes that he is morally justified in acting as he did. For example, Robin Hood or those ardent anti-vivisectionists who remove animals from vivisection laboratories are acting dishonestly, even though they may consider themselves to be morally justified in doing what they do, because they know that ordinary people would consider these actions to be dishonest.

With respect, the question of what an anti-vivisectionist believes may well be a question of fact that has to be left to the jury. In many other cases, however, dishonesty will not be in issue. Bank robbery, for example, is so obviously dishonest that a *Ghosh* direction will not be required. In *Roberts* (1985) 84 Cr App R 117, a decision concerned with handling stolen goods, the Court of Appeal indicated that a full *Ghosh* direction would not be necessary unless D raised the issue by, for example, suggesting that he did not know that anybody would regard his actions as dishonest. Further, in *Price* (1989) 90 Cr App R 409, a decision concerned with the TA 1978, ss. 1 and 2, the Court of Appeal, following *Roberts*, said (at p. 411):

> . . . it is by no means in every case involving dishonesty that a *Ghosh* direction is necessary. Indeed in the majority of such cases, of which this was one, it is unnecessary and potentially misleading to give such a direction. It need only be given in cases where the defendant might have believed that what he is alleged to have done was in accordance with the ordinary person's idea of honesty.

In consequence D's convictions were upheld when the judge had not given a *Ghosh* direction, since the only question relevant to dishonesty was whether D honestly believed that he was the beneficiary of a trust fund or not (see also *Buzalek* [1991] Crim LR 130 (a fraudulent trading case), *Brennen* [1990] Crim LR 118 (a handling case) and *Green* [1992] Crim LR 292 (a s. 20 case)). But in other cases failure to direct on *Ghosh* could be fatal to a conviction: see *Clarke* [1996] Crim LR 824.

In *Rostron* [2003] EWCA Crim 2206, the Court of Appeal upheld D's conviction for the theft of golf balls from a lake on a private golf course, even though no *Ghosh* direction had been provided. The view of the trial judge and of the Court of Appeal appears to have been that there could be no doubting D's dishonesty if he knew he had no right to go onto the golf course (at night) in order to take the balls. With respect, his knowledge that he had no 'right' (and no permission) to act in this way merely meant that he had no possible defence under s. 2(1)(a) or (b). But D also argued that he saw no harm in fishing for the balls, given that nobody else seemed interested in recovering them, and this surely entitled him to a *Ghosh* direction, especially since his case appears to have elicited considerable public sympathy at the time.

Rostron may be contrasted with *Clowes (No. 2)* [1994] 2 All ER 316 and *Lightfoot* (1992) 97 Cr App R 24 in which it was held that, for the purposes of the *Ghosh* test (which is the sole test of dishonesty in the context of fraud or deception offences), D's knowledge of the civil or criminal law is irrelevant. With respect, this surely overstates the point. It is more likely that D will be considered dishonest if he realises that his actions are unlawful.

It is clear that the meaning of dishonesty provided by the Court of Appeal in *Ghosh* [1982] QB 1053 also applies to obtaining property by deception (*Ghosh* and *Woolven* (1983) 77 Cr App R 231), to procuring the execution of a valuable security by deception (*Ghosh*), to handling stolen goods (*Roberts* (1985) 84 Cr App R 117), to obtaining services by deception (*Price* (1989) 90 Cr App R 410), and to evasion of liability by deception (*Price*). It is also clear that the same test must apply to dishonesty in the context of offences under the Fraud Act 2006 (see **B5.97**).

Intention Permanently to Deprive

B4.38 On a charge of theft the prosecution must prove that D had an intention permanently to deprive another of property at the time that property was appropriated. The fact that D later returns the property does not negate the intention present at the time of the appropriation (*McHugh* (1993) 97 Cr App R 335). Nothing less than an intention permanently to deprive will do (*Warner* (1970) 55 Cr App R 93 at p. 96; *Cocks* (1976) 63 Cr App R 79 at p. 81). The TA 1968, s. 6, may assist in establishing whether or not there is such an intention. In most cases, though, s. 6 will not need to be referred to because there will be no factors in the case which demand consideration of the special circumstances covered by that section. Section 6 should be referred to 'in exceptional cases only' (*Lloyd* [1985] QB 829; *Coffey* [1987] Crim LR 498).

In *Duru* [1974] 1 WLR 2 it was held that there was an intention permanently to deprive where a stolen cheque is inevitably returned to the bank on which it is drawn as a paid cheque is not the same thing as that which was stolen. However, this has been overruled by the decision of the House of Lords in *Preddy* [1996] AC 815, where it was said that 'there can have been no intention on the part of the payee permanently to deprive the drawer of the cheque form, which would on presentation of the cheque for payment be returned to the drawer via his bank'. Their lordships then said that *Duru* had 'to this extent been wrongly decided'. This then must create doubt about the decision in *Downes* (1983) 77 Cr App R 260 in which the stolen property was vouchers which self-employed individuals could present to persons for whom they worked to establish their right to receive payments without deduction of PAYE income tax. The vouchers when used were returned to the Inland Revenue. The fact that they had been used and could not be reused made them different things from the stolen vouchers. The argument relied upon *Duru*, and so the case must be regarded as wrong. However, in neither case did the court rely upon s. 6 (although some consideration was given to it in *Downes*). In *Marshall* [1998] 2 Cr App R 282, the Court of Appeal relied upon s. 6 in a similar type of case to uphold a conviction for theft (see **B4.39**).

Intention to Treat Property as One's Own to Dispose of

Theft Act 1968, s. 6 **B4.39**

(1) A person appropriating property belonging to another without meaning the other permanently to lose the thing itself is nevertheless to be regarded as having the intention of permanently depriving the other of it if his intention is to treat the thing as his own to dispose of regardless of the other's rights; and a borrowing or lending of it may amount to so treating it if, but only if, the borrowing or lending is for a period and in circumstances making it equivalent to an outright taking or disposal.

(2) Without prejudice to the generality of subsection (1) above, where a person, having possession or control (lawfully or not) of property belonging to another, parts with the property under a condition as to its return which he may not be able to perform, this (if done for purposes of his own and without the other's authority) amounts to treating the property as his own to dispose of regardless of the other's rights.

The Court of Appeal in *Lloyd* [1985] QB 829 observed (at p. 834B) that s. 6 of the TA 1968 means that there are circumstances where D is 'deemed to have the intention permanently to deprive, even though he may intend the owner eventually to get back the object which has been taken'.

Different approaches have been taken to the interpretation of s. 6. In *Lloyd* [1985] QB 829 the Court of Appeal, relying on the judgment of Edmund-Davies LJ in *Warner* (1970) 55 Cr App R 93, indicated that it would try to interpret s. 6 'in such a way as to ensure that nothing is construed as an intention permanently to deprive which would not prior to the 1968 Act have been so construed'. On the other hand, the Court of Appeal in *Downes* (1983) 77 Cr App R 260 was desirous of giving the words of s. 6 their normal meaning.

The latter view, meaning that it is not essential to consider the law prior to the TA 1968, appears to be the view more likely to be accepted by future courts. Acceptance of that view is supported by the approaches taken to s. 6 by the Court of Appeal in *Duru* [1974] 1 WLR 2, the Privy Council in *Chan Man-sin v The Queen* [1988] 1 WLR 196 and the Divisional Court in *Governor of Pentonville Prison, ex parte Osman* [1990] 1 WLR 277. Further, Edmund-Davies LJ in *Warner* (1970) 55 Cr App R 93 did not say that the pre-existing law should determine the meaning of s. 6, but that its aim was to prevent specious pleas which might have succeeded previously. The Court of Appeal in *Bagshaw* [1988] Crim LR 321 said that the observations of the Court of Appeal in *Lloyd* were *obiter* 'and that there may be other occasions on which the section applies'. Finally, the Court of Appeal in *Fernandes* [1996] 1 Cr App R 175 made clear that s. 6(1) is not limited to the illustrations given in *Lloyd*.

That s. 6 generally and s. 6(1) specifically should not be interpreted narrowly is supported by the decision in *Chan Man-sin v The Queen* [1988] 1 WLR 196. The Privy Council briefly referred to the Hong Kong equivalent of s. 6(1) and said that even if it were possible that the fraud practised by D would be discovered there would be an intention permanently to deprive, since D was 'purporting to deal with the companies' property without regard to their rights'. D had forged cheques belonging to a company for which he was the accountant. He may well have known that once the fraud was discovered these cheques would have no effect and thus the companies would lose nothing. The critical notion in s. 6(1) is the 'intention to treat the thing as his own to dispose of regardless of the other's rights' and so s. 6(1) should not be artificially limited in its scope (*Fernandes* [1996] 1 Cr App R 175).

In *Marshall* [1998] 2 Cr App R 282) unexpired London Underground tickets and travel cards were acquired by the accused from travellers who no longer needed them and these tickets and cards were then dishonestly resold to other travellers. It was assumed that many of these tickets would (when expired) have been returned to or retained by London Underground, but the Court of Appeal held that the accused were in any case guilty of theft by virtue of s. 6(1). This approach may permit the upholding of convictions in cases such as *Downes* (1983) 77 Cr App R 260 (for the problem presented by *Preddy* [1996] AC 815, see **B4.38**). In *Downes*, the Court of Appeal took the view, *obiter*, that the first part of s. 6(1) would clearly cover the facts of the case. The court was not impressed by a submission that the first part of s. 6(1) applied only to cases in which property is taken from its owner and then sold back to him. In *Coffey* [1987] Crim LR 498 the court was satisfied that a situation in which property was held to ransom would be a clear case for the application of s. 6(1). Where the judge must direct the jury on the first part of s. 6(1), it is important for him to draw the jury's attention to all the requisite elements. It is a material misdirection to fail to give adequate guidance as to the effect of the words 'to dispose of' (*Cahill* [1993] Crim LR 141), but a narrow dictionary definition should not be taken to that phrase *DPP v Lavender* [1994] Crim LR 297).

B4.40 **Borrowing or Lending** In *Velumyl* [1989] Crim LR 299, the Court of Appeal rejected an argument that a person who borrowed money from his employer expecting to return an equivalent sum had no intention permanently to deprive the employer of that money. There was such an intention because 'the borrower' had no intention of returning the objects that he had taken.

In *Bagshaw* [1988] Crim LR 321, the Court of Appeal said, *obiter*, 'that it would be open to the judge to leave to the jury . . . the question whether it was Bagshaw's intention to keep the "borrowed" cylinders until there was no more gas in them, by which time all their "virtue" would have gone, before returning them in one way or another to BOC'. In *Coffey* [1987] Crim LR 498, Coffey had been convicted of obtaining property by deception. He had been in dispute with Hodkinson and decided to exert pressure on him by obtaining from him baking equipment and keeping it until the dispute was resolved. It was not entirely clear what Coffey would do if he did not achieve his purpose. The Court of Appeal said that if the jury might have thought that D 'intended to return the goods even if Hodkinson did not do what he wanted, they would not convict unless they were sure that he intended that the period of detention should be so long as to amount to an outright taking'. These cases appear to be suggesting that an intention to borrow or lend property can amount to an intention permanently to deprive only when almost all, if not all, the 'virtue' in the property has gone. See also *Clinton v Cahill* [1998] NI 200. In *Coffey* the court also said that 'the reference in section 6(1) to "borrowing" (plainly used in a loose sense to denote non-consensual assumption of possession coupled with an intention ultimately to restore the object taken) shows that the "deprivation" can be "permanent" even if it is meant to be temporary'. Further, the court pointed out that 'the reference to "the thing itself" in s. 6(1) indicates that the question of deprivation will not always be confined to the tangible object itself'. The object may be returned after 'its useful qualities have been exhausted' and there may nevertheless be an intention permanently to deprive, as in *Downes* (1983) 77 Cr App 260 and *Duru* [1974] 1 WLR 2.

Parting with Property on a Condition which D may not be Able to Perform The TA 1968, s. 6(2) clearly covers such instances as a person pawning the property of another, hoping that he will be able to redeem the property at the appropriate time. **B4.41**

Trust Property In relation to trust property, the TA 1968, s. 5(2) provides that 'an intention to defeat the trust shall be regarded as an intention to deprive of the property any person having that right'. The right referred to is the right to enforce the trust and 'that person' is the person to whom the trust property belongs (see **B4.20**). Section 5(2) states only that an intention to defeat the trust is an intention to deprive. An intention to deprive permanently must still be established. **B4.42**

Property Got by Another's Mistake Section 5(4) of the TA 1968 provides that 'an intention not to make restoration shall be regarded accordingly as an intention to deprive that person of the property or proceeds'. 'That person' is the person who is entitled to restoration (see **B4.25**). Section 5(4) states only that the intention not to make restoration is an intention to deprive. It must still be established whether there was an intention to deprive permanently. **B4.43**

Conditional Intention There has been a problem of 'conditional intention' in relation to attempted theft when nothing has been taken and it is argued for D that he had not decided to take anything but was simply ascertaining whether there was something worth taking. In *Easom* [1971] 2 QB 315 the Court of Appeal said that 'a conditional appropriation will not do'. So rummaging through a handbag with that intention was not sufficient. In *Husseyn* (1977) 67 Cr App R 131, the Court of Appeal followed *Easom* and so held that D was not guilty of attempted theft of some sub-aqua equipment from a holdall, because he had not yet looked into the bag and decided whether there was anything worth stealing. The solution to this problem is the same as in burglary (see **B4.68**). If the indictment is drafted generally (e.g., an attempt to steal some or all of the contents of the handbag or the holdall) the prosecution do not have to prove that D intended to steal the specific item present, but simply that he did intend to steal anything worth stealing (*A-G's Ref (Nos. 1 and 2 of 1979*) [1980] QB 180). **B4.44**

Theft of Mails within the British Postal Area

For most purposes, the Theft Acts apply only to things done within England and Wales or (notably where the CJA 1993, part 1, applies) to things done partly in England and partly abroad (see generally **A8**); but the TA 1968, s. 14, creates a special rule in respect of mail in transit within any part of the British Postal Area. **B4.45**

Theft Act 1968, s. 14

(1) Where a person—
 (a) steals or attempts to steal any mailbag or postal packet in the course of transmission as such between places in different jurisdictions in the British postal area, or any of the contents of such a mailbag or postal packet, or
 (b) in stealing or with intent to steal any such mailbag or postal packet or any of its contents, commits any robbery, attempted robbery or assault with intent to rob;

 then, notwithstanding that he does so outside England and Wales, he shall be guilty of committing or attempting to commit the offence against this Act as if he had done so in England or Wales, and he shall accordingly be liable to be prosecuted, tried and punished in England and Wales without proof that the offence was committed there.

(2) In subsection (1) above the reference to different jurisdictions in the British postal area is to

be construed as referring to the several jurisdictions of England and Wales, of Scotland, of Northern Ireland, of the Isle of Man and of the Channel Islands.

There are specific offences concerned with mail thefts: it is an offence, contrary to the Postal Services Act 2000, s. 83, for a postal operator to interfere with the mail; and it is an offence, contrary to s. 84, for any person to interfere with the mail. For other offences, see ss. 85 to 88. Section 125 of that Act defines 'mail bag' and 'postal packet'.

ROBBERY AND ASSAULT WITH INTENT TO ROB

Definition

B4.46 **Theft Act 1968, s. 8**

(1) A person is guilty of robbery if he steals, and immediately before or at the time of doing so, and in order to do so, he uses force on any person or puts or seeks to put any person in fear of being then and there subjected to force.

(2) A person guilty of robbery, or of an assault with intent to rob, shall on conviction on indictment be liable to imprisonment for life.

Procedure

B4.47 Robbery and assault with intent to rob are triable only on indictment and are class 3 offences.

Indictment

B4.48 *Statement of Offence*

Robbery contrary to section 8(1) of the Theft Act 1968

Particulars of Offence

A on the . . . day of . . . robbed V of a gold watch

As to the practice of including a count for an offence contrary to the Firearms Act 1968, see *French* (1982) 75 Cr App R 1 per Lord Lane CJ.

Alternative Verdicts

B4.49 Theft is the obvious alternative verdict by the application of the Criminal Law Act 1967, s. 6(3). The House of Lords in *Maxwell* [1990] 1 WLR 401 has held that the trial judge is only obliged to leave such a lesser alternative verdict to the jury if necessary in the interests of justice, for example, if the question of force was in doubt but there was substantial evidence of theft.

The decision in *Tennant* [1976] Crim LR 133, that it is not possible under the Criminal Law Act 1967, s. 6(3), to convict a person of an assault on a charge of robbery, needs to be reconsidered in the light of *Metropolitan Police Commissioner v Wilson* [1984] AC 242. An allegation of robbery may in many cases impliedly include an allegation of an assault, because most uses of force will involve an assault, even though it is not possible exactly to assimilate 'force' as required for robbery with 'assault'.

Sentencing Guidelines

B4.50 The maximum penalty for robbery is life imprisonment (TA 1968, s. 8(2)). The maximum penalty for assault with intent to rob is life imprisonment (TA 1968, s. 8(2)). The combination of violence and theft makes robbery the most serious of the common offences of dishonesty. The great majority of offenders convicted of robbery receive custodial sentences.

The SGC has issued a Guideline on sentencing for three important categories of this offence: (i) street robbery or 'mugging', (ii) robberies of small businesses and (iii) the less sophisticated commercial robberies. Separate sentencing ranges and starting points are indicated for adults and for young offenders. For the text of the Guideline, see **appendix 9**. The Guideline applies to the sentencing of offenders convicted of robbery who are sentenced on or after 1 August 2006.

The Guideline does *not* include two other categories of robbery: (iv) professionally planned commercial robberies and (v) violent personal robberies in the home. In the former category the case of *O'Driscoll* (1986) 8 Cr App R (S) 121 indicates that the appropriate sentencing range is 13-16 years for a first-time offender pleading not guilty. Longer terms may be appropriate where extreme violence is used. This category overlaps with some cases of aggravated burglary where comparable sentences are passed (see **B4.75**). In the latter category, the guideline cases are *Turner* (1975) 61 Cr App R 67, *Daly* (1981) 3 Cr App R (S) 340 and *Gould* (1983) 5 Cr App R (S) 72.

In *Turner* there were 19 appellants, members of a gang which, over a four-year period had carried out 20 armed robberies on banks and security vans, netting over £1 million at 1975 values. Firearms and ammonia were carried, but used only to frighten, and injuries inflicted were slight. Lawton LJ said (at p. 91) that the normal starting-point for sentence for anyone taking part in a bank robbery or in the hold-up of a security or a Post Office van should be 15 years, if firearms were carried and no serious injury done. The lack of a previous criminal record is not, he said, to be regarded as a powerful mitigating matter. In *Daly*, Lord Lane CJ indicated that in a bank-robbery type of case, the most serious features calling for heavy sentences are:

> . . . detailed planning, use of loaded firearms or ammonia, where a number of men execute a planned attack on a bank or a similar target in the hope of stealing substantial sums of money, where the participants are masked and armed either with guns, handguns or sawnoff shotguns, or sometimes with ammonia, and squirt ammonia into the faces of clients or staff of the bank in order to overpower resistance. In such cases, as Lawton LJ in *Turner* (of which everyone is aware) has rightly said that a starting-point of 15 years is correct. It may be, and no doubt will in nearly every case where there has been a plea of guilty, possible to reduce that term in the light of the plea and in the light of the assistance given to the police and other mitigating factors. It may be necessary on the other hand in some cases to increase the starting number of years because of the number of offences which the particular defendant has committed during the course of his depredation.

In *Gould* Lord Lane CJ confirmed that the *Turner* guidelines remained the basis for sentencing in armed robbery offences. He also added:

> Some of the features likely to mitigate an offence are, a plea of guilty, the youth of the offender, a previously clean record, the fact that the defendant had no companion when committing the offence and the fact that no one was injured. On the other hand the fact that a real rather than imitation weapon was used, that it was discharged, that violence was used upon the victim, that a number of men took part in the attack, that careful reconnaissance and planning were involved, that there was more than one offence committed by the offender, are all matters which the court must put into the balance on the other side of the scale when determining the correct sentence for any particular offender. These considerations are of course not exhaustive and are not intended so to be.

For robberies in the so-called 'first division', which are the subject of the guideline cases of *Turner, Daly* and *Gould*, the normal starting-point is 15 years. Sentences of 18 years and 17 years were imposed in *Knight* (1981) 3 Cr App R (S) 211 and *Reed* (1988) 10 Cr App R (S) 243 respectively. Wholly abnormal crimes, such as the Great Train Robbery, will attract sentence in excess of 18 years (*Wilson* [1965] 1 QB 408). The 'irreducible minimum' in such cases is said to be 11 years (*Davis* (1980) 2 Cr App R (S) 168).

Actus Reus: Requirement of Theft

B4.51 'Steal' in the TA 1968, s. 8(1), must mean theft contrary to s. 1 (although the Court of Appeal surprisingly treated this matter as open in *Forrester* [1992] Crim LR 793). In *Robinson* [1977] Crim LR 173 it was held that where D uses or threatens force in order to appropriate property to which he believes he is entitled, then he cannot be guilty of either theft (see the TA 1968, s. 2(1)(a)) or robbery, even if he knows the force to be unlawful. If theft is intended but not committed (e.g., because V has nothing for D to steal) a charge of assault with intent to rob under s. 8(2) or a charge of attempted robbery under the Criminal Attempts Act 1981, s. 1 (see **A6.31**) may still be possible.

Actus Reus: Use of Force or Fear of Subjection to Force in Order to Steal

B4.52 To be guilty of robbery, D must either use force or put another person in fear of being then and there subjected to force, and he must do this in order to steal. In *Shendley* [1970] Crim LR 49 the trial judge clearly erred by directing the jury that: '. . . if the violence was unconnected with the stealing but you are satisfied there was a stealing it . . . would be open to you to find [D] guilty of robbery . . . without violence'. The Court of Appeal quashed D's conviction for robbery and substituted a conviction for theft. It would not matter, however, if D also had some additional motive for using or threatening force.

In *Dawson* (1976) 64 Cr App R 170 the Court of Appeal held that 'force' is a word in ordinary use, which juries understand. The jury in that case were entitled to find that force was used where the defendants stood around the victim, one of them nudged him and his wallet was stolen. In such cases, an implicit threat of force may suffice, as where a gang surround the victim in order to steal from him. It does not then matter whether the victim is actually put in fear or not: it is the intention of the perpetrator that matters (*B and R v DPP* (2007) 171 JP 404).

Whether the force has been used on a person (or someone has been put in fear of the use of force) is a question for the jury to consider, and it appears that they may conclude that force has been used when it is used indirectly. In *Clouden* [1987] Crim LR 56 the Court of Appeal dismissed an appeal against a conviction for robbery when D had wrenched the victim's shopping basket from her hand and run off with it. This also appears to have been the view of the Divisional Court in *Corcoran v Anderton* (1980) 71 Cr App R 104. Indeed, it should not matter in such a case that V's grip on her bag is too strong for D to break: by grabbing the bag with intent, D has appropriated it and the theft (and robbery) is complete.

Force must be used immediately before or at the time of stealing. Consequently, it is important to know whether D had already finished committing the theft when the force or threat was used (see **B4.27** and *James* [1997] Crim LR 598).

Mens Rea

B4.53 Clearly the *mens rea* for theft is required. This indicates dishonesty (see **B4.34** to **B4.37**) and intention permanently to deprive (see **B4.38** to **B4.44**) as well as the intention to appropriate the property in question. There must also be intention or at least recklessness as to the use of force. The accidental use of force during the course of an ordinary theft would not suffice since D must use the force in order to steal. Similarly, D does not commit robbery merely because he is interrupted by V in the course of a theft or burglary and V momentarily fears that D will attack her.

BURGLARY

Definition

Theft Act 1968, s. 9 B4.54

(1) A person is guilty of burglary if—
 (a) he enters any building or part of a building as a trespasser and with intent to commit any such offence as is mentioned in subsection (2) below; or
 (b) having entered any building or part of a building as a trespasser he steals or attempts to steal anything in the building or that part of it or inflicts or attempts to inflict on any person therein any grievous bodily harm.

(2) The offences referred to in subsection (1)(a) above are offences of stealing anything in the building or part of a building in question, of inflicting on any person therein any grievous bodily harm, and of doing unlawful damage to the building or anything therein.

Section 9 creates two groups of offences: one of entering a building (or part of a building) as a trespasser with the requisite intent, contrary to s. 9(1)(a); the other of having entered a building (or part of a building) as a trespasser and committing a specified offence, contrary to s. 9(1)(b). In each case there are now (by s. 9(4) as amended) two offences dependent upon whether the building is or is not a dwelling. The different sentence provisions applicable (see **B4.58**) mean that, under *Courtie* [1984] AC 463, burglary of a dwelling is now a distinct offence from burglary of any other type of building.

Procedure

By virtue of the MCA 1980, s. 17 and sch. 1, para. 28, most forms of burglary are triable either way. When tried on indictment, burglary is a class 3 offence. However: B4.55

(a) if the burglary comprises the commission of, or an intention to commit, an offence which is triable only on indictment, then the burglary is also triable only on indictment (sch. 1, para. 28(b));
(b) if the burglary is in a dwelling-house and any person in the dwelling was subjected to violence or the threat of violence, the offence is triable only on indictment (sch. 1, para. 28(c)) (the violence need not have been used as part of effecting the burglary: *McGrath* [2004] 1 Cr App R 173);
(c) if the burglary is a domestic burglary and the accused, who is now aged 18 or over, has two previous separate convictions for domestic burglary in respect of offences committed after 30 November 1999, the offence is triable only on indictment (PCC(S)A 2000, s. 111(4)).

Burglary triable only on indictment is a class 3 offence.

In the *Consolidated Criminal Practice Direction*, para. V.51, *Mode of trial* (see **appendix** 7), separate guidelines are given for burglary at a dwelling-house and burglary at non-dwellings. The guidelines for burglary from a dwelling-house state (para. V.51.5) that cases should be tried summarily unless the court considers that one or more of the following features is present *and* that its sentencing powers are insufficient:

(a) Entry in the daytime when the occupier (or another) is present.
(b) Entry at night of a house which is normally occupied, whether or not the occupier (or another) is present.
(c) The offence is alleged to be one of a series of similar offences.
(d) When soiling, ransacking, damage or vandalism occurs.
(e) The offence has professional hallmarks.
(f) The unrecovered property is of high value (at least £10,000).
(g) The offence is racially motivated.

The guidelines for burglary from non-dwellings state (para. 51.6) that cases should be tried summarily unless the court considers that one or more of the following features is present *and* that its sentencing powers are insufficient:

(a) Entry of a pharmacy or doctor's surgery.
(b) Fear is caused or violence is done to anyone lawfully on the premises (e.g., nightwatchman; security guard).
(c) The offence has professional hallmarks.
(d) Vandalism on a substantial scale.
(e) The unrecovered property is of high value (at least £10,000).

Indictment

B4.56 *Statement of Offence*

Burglary with intent contrary to section 9(1)(a) of the TA 1968

Particulars of Offence

A, on or about the . . . day of . . . entered a dwelling [or part of a dwelling, or a building or part of a building], namely . . ., as a trespasser with intent to steal therein [or inflict grievous bodily harm upon a person therein, or to do unlawful damage to the building or anything therein]

Statement of Offence

Burglary contrary to section 9(1)(b) of the TA 1968

Particulars of Offence

A on or about the . . . day of . . ., having entered a dwelling [or part of a dwelling, or a building or part of a building], namely . . ., as a trespasser, stole therein [or attempted to steal therein, or inflicted grievous bodily harm upon . . . therein]

In *Machent v Quinn* [1970] 2 All ER 255 the Divisional Court decided that it is unnecessary for the prosecution to prove that all the articles mentioned in an information or an indictment have been stolen. Proof that D stole any one of those articles is sufficient.

Alternative Verdicts

B4.57 By virtue of the Criminal Law Act 1967, s. 6(3), on a charge of burglary contrary to the TA 1968, s. 9(1)(b), D may be convicted of the underlying offence that the court alleges he committed in the building (*Lillis* [1972] 2 QB 236). There is no express provision separate from the Criminal Law Act 1967, s. 6(3), but that section has been applied with important consequences in the offence of burglary. The House of Lords in *Metropolitan Police Commissioner v Wilson* [1984] AC 242 considered the meaning of 'inflicts grievous bodily harm' and also considered what alternative verdicts might generally be available and, specifically, whether a conviction under the OAPA 1861, s. 47, could be an alternative verdict to burglary under the TA 1968, s. 9(1)(b). The House decided that that was possible, having ruled on the meaning of the Criminal Law Act 1967, s. 6(3). Whether a conviction under the OAPA 1861, s. 47, is an alternative verdict depends upon whether one of the four options envisaged by the Criminal Law Act 1967, s. 6(3), is satisfied:

> First, the allegation in the indictment expressly amounts to an allegation of another offence. Secondly, the allegation in the indictment impliedly amounts to an allegation of another offence. Fourthly, the allegation in the indictment impliedly includes an allegation of another offence. (per Lord Roskill at p. 258)

A charge of burglary with intent to inflict grievous bodily harm impliedly includes an allegation of an offence contrary to the OAPA 1861, s. 47, since an assault may be alleged by the charge, although it is not an essential element to that offence. Consequently, there will be some cases where an assault offence is possible as an alternative verdict to burglary.

The approach in *Wilson* has been applied in *Whiting* (1987) 85 Cr App R 78. The Court of Appeal decided that it is possible that a person may be found guilty of burglary under the TA 1968, s. 9(1)(a) on a charge of burglary under s. 9(1)(b), because s. 9(1)(b) impliedly includes an allegation of an offence contrary to s. 9(1)(a). Of course, such an alternative verdict can be arrived at in some, but not all cases, since these two offences are essentially quite different in certain respects (see below).

Sentencing Guidelines

The maximum penalty which may be imposed for burglary, and the penalty likely to be imposed in a particular case, varies according to whether the burglary is in respect of a dwelling or in respect of premises other than a dwelling. **B4.58**

The maximum penalty for burglary of a building or part of a building which is a dwelling is 14 years' imprisonment on indictment, six months or a fine not exceeding the statutory maximum, or both, summarily (TA 1968, s. 9(3)).

A minimum custodial sentence of three years must be imposed by the court where an offender aged 18 or over is convicted of a third 'domestic burglary', where all three of the offences were committed after 30 November 1999, and where there are no particular circumstances relating to any of the offences, or the offender, such that the imposition of a custodial sentence of at least three years would be unjust in all the circumstances (PCC(S)A 2000, s. 111, and see **E6.3**).

When dealt with summarily, the Magistrates' Courts Guidelines (2004) indicate the following for a first-time offender pleading not guilty:

> **Aggravating Factors** For example force used or threatened; group enterprise; high value (in economic or sentimental terms) of property stolen; more than minor trauma caused; professional planning/organisation/execution; significant damage or vandalism; victim injured; victim present at the time; vulnerable victim (if ANY of these factors are present, magistrates should commit for sentence); racial or religious aggravation; offence committed on bail; relevant previous convictions and any failures to respond to previous sentences
>
> **Mitigating Factors** For example first offence of its type AND low value property stolen AND no significant damage or disturbance AND no injury or violence; minor part played; theft from attached garage; vacant property (ONLY if one or more of the above factors are present AND none of the aggravating factors listed are present should you consider NOT committing for sentence).
>
> *Guideline*: Are magistrates' sentencing powers sufficient?

In respect of burglaries from dwellings, the Court of Appeal issued sentencing guidelines in *McInerney* [2003] 1 All ER 1089, following a proposal from the Sentencing Advisory Panel. The guidelines have direct application only to cases of domestic burglary, and where the trespass is accompanied by theft or an intention to steal. In his judgment in *McInerney* Lord Woolf CJ re-stated a number of the observations of Lord Bingham CJ in the earlier guideline case of *Brewster* [1998] 1 Cr App R (S) 220. These include the fact that domestic burglary is, and always has been, regarded as a very serious offence. It may cause considerable loss to the victim, but the loss of material possessions is only part of the reason why domestic burglary is so regarded. Victims of burglary are left with a sense of violation and insecurity. In general it is more frightening for the victim if they are present in the house when the burglary takes place, and if the intrusion takes place at night, but that does not mean that the offence is not serious if the victim returns to an empty house during the daytime to find that it has been burgled. The seriousness of the offence can vary almost infinitely from case to case. It may involve an impulsive act involving an item of little value (reaching through a window to take a bottle of milk, or stealing a can of petrol from an outhouse). At the other end of the spectrum it may involve a professional, planned operation, directed at objects of high value. The record of the offender is of more significance in the case of domestic burglary than in the case of some other crimes. It is common knowledge that many domestic burglars are drug addicts who burgle and steal in order to raise money to satisfy their cravings for drugs.

The guidelines in *McInerney* recommend starting points which are applicable to sentencing after a trial; they do not take account of personal mitigation, or the discount for a guilty plea. It should also be borne in mind that where an offence of domestic burglary is committed by an offender aged 18 or over, who has two or more previous convictions for domestic burglary committed after 30 November 1999, the presumptive minimum sentence prescribed by PCC(S)A 2000, s. 111, is a custodial sentence of three years, unless there are specific circumstances which relate to any of the offences, or to the offender, which would make that sentence unjust in all the circumstances (see **E6.3**). Lord Woolf CJ indicated (at para 16) that s. 111 'gives the sentencer a fairly substantial degree of discretion as to the categories of situations where the presumption can be rebutted'.

(a) The Court of Appeal stated that for a low-level burglary committed by a first-time domestic burglar (and for some second-time domestic burglars), where there is no damage to property and no property (or only property of very low value) is stolen, the starting point should be a community sentence. Other types of cases at this level would include thefts (provided they are of items of low value) from attached garages or from vacant property.

(b) The Panel described a 'standard domestic burglary' as one which displays most of the following features: (i) theft of electrical goods such as a television or video, (ii) theft of personal items such as jewellery, (iii) damage is caused by the break-in itself, (iv) some turmoil in the home, such as drawers upturned or damage to some items, (v) no injury or violence, but some trauma caused to the victim. The Court of Appeal stated that the starting point when sentencing for a standard domestic burglary, committed by a first-time domestic burglar, and some second-time domestic burglars, should be a community sentence subject to conditions to ensure that the sentence is both an effective punishment and one which offers action by the probation service to tackle the offender's criminal behaviour and any underlying problems such as drug addiction. Only if the sentencing court is satisfied that the offender has demonstrated by his or her behaviour that punishment in the community is not practicable should the courts resort to a custodial sentence. Factors that will indicate that a community sentence is not a practical option may relate to the effect of the offence on the victim, the nature of the offence, or the offender's record.

(c) In the case of a 'standard domestic burglary' which additionally displays any one of the 'medium relevance' aggravating factors listed below, and committed by a first-time offender, the starting point is a community sentence subject to similar conditions as those referred to in (b) above.

(d) In the case of a 'standard domestic burglary' which additionally displays any one of the 'high relevance' aggravating factors listed below, and committed by a first-time offender, the starting point is a custodial sentence of 18 months. The starting point for a second-time domestic burglar committing such an offence should be a custodial sentence of three years. When committed by a burglar with two or more previous convictions for domestic burglary, the starting point is a custodial sentence of four and a half years. The presence of more than one 'high relevance' factor could bring the sentence for an offence at this level significantly above the suggested starting points.

In its advice the Panel divided aggravating factors into two categories. Lord Woolf CJ said that courts should now apply these factors, but that there is no clear line between the two categories and that they can overlap.

Medium level aggravating features are: (i) a vulnerable victim, although not targeted as such, (ii) the victim was at home (whether day-time or night-time burglary), (iii) goods of high value were taken (economic or sentimental), (iv) the burglars worked in a group.

High level aggravating features are: (i) force used or threatened against the victim, (ii) victim injured (as a result of force used or threatened), (iii) the especially traumatic effect on the victim, in excess of the trauma generally associated with a standard burglary, (iv) professional planning, organisation or execution, (v) vandalism of the premises, in excess of the damage generally associated with a standard burglary, (vi) the offence was racially aggravated, (vii) a vulnerable victim deliberately targeted (including cases of 'deception' or 'distraction' of the elderly).

Lord Woolf CJ added that the number of offences in relation to which the offender is to be sentenced may indicate that he or she is a professional burglar, which is a high level aggravating feature, but that even if they do not fall within that category the number of offences could still constitute a mid-level aggravating feature. The fact that the offender is on bail or on licence at the time of the offence can be an aggravating feature, as can the fact that the offence was committed out of spite. His lordship also referred to confrontation between the householder and the burglar as being an aggravating feature.

Mitigating factors include (i) a first offence, (ii) nothing, or only property of very low value, is stolen, (iii) the offender played only a minor part in the burglary, (iv) there is no damage or disturbance to the property, (v) the fact that the crime was committed on impulse, (vi) the offender's age or state of health, physical or mental, (vii) evidence of genuine remorse, response to previous sentences, and ready co-operation with the police.

It is also necessary to take into account a timely plea of guilty. If PCC(S)A 2000, s. 111 applies, the discount for a guilty plea is limited to 20 per cent of the determinate sentence of at least three years (see **E6.3**).

Burglary committed in relation to premises other than a dwelling is regarded as somewhat less serious than the previous category. The maximum penalty for burglary other than from a dwelling is ten years' imprisonment on indictment, six months or a fine not exceeding the statutory maximum, or both, summarily (TA 1968, s. 9(3)). When an offence of 'non-dwelling' burglary is committed, and the offence is dealt with summarily, the Magistrates' Courts Guidelines (2004) indicate the following for a first-time offender pleading not guilty:

Aggravating Factors For example forcible entry; group offence; harm to business; occupants frightened; professional operation; repeat victimisation; school or medical premises; soiling, ransacking, damage; racial or religious aggravation; offence committed on bail; relevant previous convictions and any failures to respond to previous sentences.

Mitigating Factors For example low value; nobody frightened; no damage or disturbance.

Guideline: Is it serious enough for a community penalty?

Decisions of the Court of Appeal indicate that some cases of 'non-dwelling' burglary will be regarded as so serious that only a custodial sentence can be justified.

An example is *Dorries* (1993) 14 Cr App R (S) 608, where the offenders pleaded guilty to burglary of a shop. They had been seen in the vicinity of the shop and, when the police arrived, they drove away. Entry had been effected by removing bricks from a wall, and property worth £600 had been taken. A hammer, crowbar and radio scanner were found in their car. The Court of Appeal agreed with the sentencer that only a custodial sentence could be justified, but reduced the sentence from ten months to six months. In contrast to *Dorries*, the Court of Appeal held in *Tetteh* (1994) 15 Cr App R (S) 46 that the offence did not pass the threshold of seriousness. The offender had forced open the spirits store at a YMCA club and the drayman's entry cover had been opened to give access to the street. Nothing had been taken however, and it was an opportunistic rather than a planned offence. The Court of Appeal said that a community sentence would have been the proper sentence. See also *Carlton* (1994) 15 Cr App R (S) 335.

Where the offence is an isolated one committed by a younger offender with a good record, a community order is the preferred sentence. In *Lawrence* (1982) 4 Cr App R (S) 69 the offender, aged 23, together with three others had taken a conveyance, driven to another

B

Part B Offences

town, broken the window of a shop and stolen television sets, video recorders and tape recorders. A sentence of 18 months was varied to 150 hours' community service (this took account of a period in custody; otherwise 190 hours would have been proper). Lord Lane CJ said that the offender 'has all the marks of someone who, at this stage in his life, is capable of settling down'. Lawrence had two previous convictions for dishonesty but none since 1976.

Some other specific types of burglary have been the subject of comment by the Court of Appeal. In *Hunter* (1994) 15 Cr App R (S) 530, a case involving 'ram-raiding', the Court of Appeal upheld sentences of five years in respect of two offenders and four years in respect of a third. The first two offenders had, on separate occasions, reversed a van through the door of an electrical shop and driven a car into the window of a clothing shop. Goods had been stolen and damage caused totalling nearly £12,000. The third offender had been involved only in the second incident, at the scene of which all three had been arrested. In *Larcher* (1979) 1 Cr App R (S) 137 the offender admitted a series of burglaries of doctors' premises and chemists' shops in order to obtain drugs. Although he had not served a custodial sentence before, five years was imposed by the Court of Appeal. Sentences of five years were also approved in two cases of burglary with intent to rape. In *Staunton* (1981) 3 Cr App R (S) 375 the offender went to a house occupied by a widow and her 15-year-old daughter, forced entry to the house and ripped out the telephone wires. He subsequently fled after waking some dogs and being seen by the widow. In *Bolland* (1988) 10 Cr App R (S) 129 the offender entered at night the house of a woman known to him, assaulted her and threatened her with a knife.

Elements Common to Both s. 9(1)(a) and s. 9(1)(b)

B4.59 Despite the fact that s. 9(1)(a) and s. 9(1)(b) of the TA 1968 create separate offences, there are a number of elements which are common to both and which can, therefore, be examined together. A 'building or part of a building' must be or have been 'entered' as 'a trespasser' in order for burglary to have been committed. The trespassory entry requirement demands a consideration not only of whether the entry was trespassory, but also whether D knew that it was trespassory, or was reckless. The difference lies in s. 9(1)(a) with the need for an intention to commit certain offences and in s. 9(1)(b) with the need to do certain things in the building (see, e.g., *O'Leary* (1986) 82 Cr App R 341 at p. 343).

B4.60 **Meaning of 'Building' and 'Dwelling'** The TA 1968 does not define a 'building', other than by providing that inhabited vehicles or vessels are deemed to be buildings. Whether a given thing can be called a building is not always straightforward and may be context-dependent. The best known judicial definition is that provided by Byles J in *Stevens v Gourley* (1859) CBNS 99 at p. 112: 'a structure of considerable size and intended to be permanent or at least to endure for a considerable period'. Such structures need not be inhabited, nor need they have doors, windows or foundations. A garden shed, a multi-storey car park and a portakabin office might each be regarded as a building, although the status of a tent is doubtful. In *B v Leathley* [1979] Crim LR 314, it was held that a freezer container in a farmyard was a building. The freezer was 25 feet long with 7 feet square cross-section, weighing about three tons and had been in place for two or three years.. In *Norfolk Constabulary v Seekings* [1986] Crim LR 167, however, a disconnected freezer trailer was held not to be a building. In *Manning* (1871) LR 1 CCR 338 it was decided that a building does not have to be complete. In that case the building was a house which was very nearly complete, but the court was satisfied that less complete structures could also be 'buildings'.

Section 9(4) provides:

> References in subsections (1) and (2) above to a building, and the reference in subsection (3) above to a dwelling, shall apply also to an inhabited vehicle or vessel, and shall apply to any such vehicle or vessel at times when the person having a habitation in it is not there as well as at times when he is.

'Inhabited vehicles' include caravans and motor homes (or even derelict vehicles) that are used for habitation at the relevant time. It is submitted that a caravan is not 'inhabited' when laid up unoccupied for the winter, even if it is fully stocked and furnished. Some HGVs now provide a sleeping area in the cab for long-distance drivers to rest in; but it seems unlikely that a sleeping HGV driver could properly be said to 'inhabit' his lorry, unless he has nowhere else to live at the time.

Inhabited vessels include occupied houseboats and ships on which at least some members of the crew can be said to 'live', rather than merely work. A person who, in order to steal etc., boards such a ship or enters a cabin or compartment on a ship knowing he is not permitted to do so will accordingly commit burglary, provided that he is at the time subject to English law (as to which see **A8.9** *et seq.*).

Since a person need enter only a part of a building as a trespasser to be a burglar, it is possible for a person lawfully on premises to become a burglar by entering another part of the building to which he is not entitled to enter. In *Walkington* [1979] 1 WLR 1169, the Court of Appeal decided that it is for the jury to decide whether an area physically marked out is sufficiently segregated to amount to a 'part of a building'. In this case, D had gone behind the sales counter in a large store. The counter was movable, but occupied a clearly identified area. In the circumstances, the court took the view that there was evidence on which the jury could conclude that there was a separate part of the building identified by the counter area, since there was a physical partition and the management impliedly prohibited customers from entering the area.

For the reasons given at **B4.58**, it may be important to determine whether the building in question was a 'dwelling', but there is surprisingly little authority on that question. See *Lees* [2007] EWCA Crim 94. In many cases, the facts will be plain. An inhabited building or vehicle, etc. must be a dwelling, whereas a shop or factory will not be. Difficulties may however arise in the case of a building (or part of a building) that has been constructed or adapted to serve as a dwelling but has not been (is not currently) used as such. In the absence of authority, it is submitted that the reasons for distinguishing between dwellings and other premises must be considered. If (as in *Lees*) the new house that is burgled is still unoccupied and is still owned by the building contractors, no resident occupier will be distressed, violated or endangered by that burglary, which is in effect no different from a burglary of commercial premises. The position is less clear where a house has been purchased and furnished as a home, but is burgled shortly before the new owners move in. Arguably, this should be treated as burglary of a dwelling; but cf. the Public Order Act 1986, s. 8 (see **B11.53**) and the Terrorism Act 2000, s. 121, each of which define a dwelling as a building, etc. that is currently occupied or used as a dwelling.

Meaning of 'Entry' In *Collins* [1973] QB 100, the Court of Appeal decided (at p. 106) that D has to make 'an effective and substantial entry into' a building or part of a building. This phrase was considered by the Court of Appeal in *Brown* [1985] Crim LR 212 and it took the view that the important point was whether the entry was 'effective'. A person could, therefore, enter a building when only part of the body is actually within it, so B had entered where the top half of his body was leaning into a shop window. The prosecution does not have to prove that the person was capable of stealing when only partially in a building. The issue is whether the partial entry was capable of constituting entry, as it was where D was stuck in an open window; the matter is then for the tribunal of fact to decide (*Ryan* (1996) 160 JP 610). **B4.61**

It was said in *Collins* that entry must be 'deliberate'. Consequently, it cannot be shown that this element of the crime has been satisfied if the entry is accidental, which it might be, for example, if boundaries of private land are unclear or obstructed by snow.

It is not clear whether a person who boards an inhabited vessel, but fails to get inside, can be said to have 'entered' the vessel. Arguably he has not, and is in the same position as someone who climbs onto the roof of a building. There may be an attempted burglary on such facts, but nothing more.

B4.62 **Meaning of 'as a Trespasser'** It is important that at the time D entered the building, his entry was as a trespasser (see *Laing* [1995] Crim LR 395). A trespasser is someone who does not have permission, express or implied, to be on the premises. Since this is an aspect of the criminal law, it must be shown that there was a trespassory entry, and also that the person entered with *mens rea* (i.e. he knew that he was entering as a trespasser or was reckless as to whether this was so).

Adequate permission can be given by someone other than the householder. In *Collins* [1973] QB 100, D went past a house where he knew a young lady lived. He climbed a ladder up to her window and peered in. She was lying naked on the bed, which was near the window. Collins descended the ladder, took off all his clothes, except his socks, and climbed back up the ladder. As he reached the window, the young lady woke up and, thinking he was her boyfriend, invited him in; they then had sexual intercourse. She then realised that it was not her boyfriend. Collins was convicted of burglary. His appeal against that conviction succeeded because the jury had not been asked to consider the vital question whether he had entered the building as a trespasser and whether he knew or was reckless as to whether he was entering as a trespasser. It was accepted by the Court of Appeal that an invitation from the young lady would have been sufficient to make Collins's entry not trespassory and so consideration should have been given to when her invitation was made, i.e. whether he was outside the building at that time or not. Presumably such permission could be overridden by someone with a greater interest in the building in question.

The court expressed its view on *mens rea* as follows (at p. 105E):

> . . . there cannot be a conviction for entering premises 'as a trespasser' within the meaning of section 9 of the TA [1968] unless the person entering does so knowing that he is a trespasser and nevertheless deliberately enters, or, at the very least, is reckless as to whether or not he is entering the premises of another without the other party's consent.

The matter will not always be a simple one of deciding whether at the time D entered, permission had been granted. Permission, specific or general, may be exceeded. It is then to be determined whether that makes the entry trespassory. In *Jones* [1976] 1 WLR 672 D and E dishonestly entered a house belonging to D's father and there stole two television sets. The question for the court was whether they had entered as trespassers for the purposes of s. 9. The court said:

> a person is a trespasser for the purpose of section 9(1)(b) of the TA 1968 if he enters premises of another knowing that he is entering in excess of the permission that has been given to him, or being reckless as to whether he is entering in excess of the permission that has been given to him to enter. Provided the facts are known to the accused which enable him to realise that he is acting in excess of the permission given or that he is acting recklessly as to whether he exceeds that permission, then that is sufficient for the jury to decide that he is in fact a trespasser.

Since the jury were satisfied that the accused acted outside the scope of any permission they might otherwise have had to visit, their conviction for burglary was upheld.

It is essential, therefore, for the person entering to know that entry is prohibited, or at least be advertently reckless as to the prohibition. In *Walkington* [1979] 1 WLR 1169 (see **B4.60**) the Court of Appeal emphasised that it was necessary in order for a conviction to be sustained that D knew he was not supposed to enter the counter area.

The common-law doctrine of trespass *ab initio* has no application to burglary under the TA 1968. (*Collins* [1973] QB 100 at p. 107.) If D enters a building, etc. otherwise than as a trespasser, he does not become a burglar merely by committing a theft inside that building.

Burglary with Intent (s. 9(1)(a)): Proof of Intent

On a charge of burglary with intent contrary to the TA 1968, s. 9(1)(a), it must be shown that, at the time of the entry (not before and not after), D intended to commit the offences listed in s. 9(2). As to intention generally, see **A2.2**. **B4.63**

Intent to Commit an Offence of Stealing 'Stealing' is defined in the TA 1968, s. 1, see **B4.1**. It is not burglary to enter a building with intent to abstract electricity because abstracting electricity is not stealing (*Low v Blease* [1975] Crim LR 513). In *Gregory* (1981) 77 Cr App R 41, the Court of Appeal said (at p. 46): **B4.64**

> In a case of burglary of a dwelling-house and before any property is removed from it, it may consist of a continuing process and involve either a single appropriation by one or more persons or a number of appropriations of the property in the house by several persons at different times during the same incident. . . . Thus a person who may have more the appearance of a handler than the thief can nevertheless still be convicted of theft, and thus of burglary, if the jury are satisfied that with the requisite dishonest intent he appropriated, or took part in the appropriation, of another person's goods.

As to the question whether, in theft and therefore burglary, an appropriation is instantaneous or continuing, see **B4.28**.

Intent to Commit an Offence of Inflicting Grievous Bodily Harm In order to prove an intention to commit grievous bodily harm on a charge of burglary with intent it is unnecessary to prove an assault (*Metropolitan Police Commissioner v Wilson* [1984] AC 242). As to the meaning of 'grievous bodily harm', see generally **B2.47**. **B4.65**

In *O'Neill* (1986) *The Times*, 17 October 1986 the Court of Appeal appears to have decided, presumably on the facts of the particular case in question, that charges of burglary by entering a building with intent to inflict grievous bodily harm should not have been left to the jury because there was no specific express evidence of such intent. No weapons had been carried and no grievous bodily harm had been committed, even though two persons on the premises had been assaulted. The offence is committed by intending, at the time of entering premises as a trespasser, to inflict grievous bodily harm, and the fact that no grievous bodily harm is actually inflicted does not affect liability, though it may make it very difficult to prove the intent.

Intent to Commit an Offence of Doing Unlawful Damage It is to be presumed that this phrase refers to what is now criminal damage, see **B8.1** to **B8.25**. **B4.66**

Intent to Commit an Offence of Rape The SOA 2003, s. 140 and sch. 7 removed the form of burglary, under the Theft Act 1968, s. 9(1)(a), where the person entered as a trespasser with intent of raping any person therein. A new offence of trespass with intent to commit a sexual offence has been created by the SOA 2003, s. 63 (see **B3.234**). **B4.67**

Conditional Intent At one stage it was thought that a 'burglar's charter' had been created by the case of *Husseyn* (1977) 67 Cr App R 131. The argument was that if a person only intended to steal that which he found worth stealing then there was no intention to steal, since it was conditional on his finding something worth stealing, which might not be the case. The solution to this problem was found by the Court of Appeal in *Walkington* [1979] 1 WLR 1169 and adopted by the Court of Appeal in *A-G's Refs (Nos. 1 and 2 of 1979)* [1980] QB 180. If a person is charged with burglary, contrary to s. 9(1)(a) of the TA 1968, by entering a building as a trespasser with intent to steal therein, and there is no reference to the stealing of specific items, that person is guilty if he has an intention to steal anything in the building and the fact that there was nothing in the building worth his stealing is immaterial. The problem is identical to that which may arise on a charge of theft: see **B4.44**. **B4.68**

Burglary (s. 9(1)(b)): Proof of Stealing or Grievous Bodily Harm

B4.69 On a charge of burglary contrary to the Theft Act 1968, s. 9(1)(b), the prosecution must establish that D either stole or attempted to steal in the building or part of a building, or inflicted or attempted to inflict on any person in the building or part of a building any grievous bodily harm. For the meaning of 'steal' and 'inflict grievous bodily harm', see **B4.1** and **B2.47**. For the law of attempts, see **A6.31** *et seq.* It is not burglary under s. 9(1)(b) to cause unlawful damage, though intent to cause such damage is relevant to burglary with intent contrary to s. 9(1)(a).

Related Offence

B4.70 An offence that might be considered as an alternative to burglary is that contrary to the Vagrancy Act 1824, s. 4(1), which, after amendment by the CJA 2003 (amongst other statutes) provides, *inter alia*, that (i) every person wandering abroad and lodging in any barn or outhouse, or in any deserted or unoccupied building, or in the open air, or under a tent, or in any cart or waggon, and not giving a good account of himself or herself; (ii) every person being found in or upon any dwelling house, warehouse, coach-house, stable, or outhouse, or in any enclosed yard, garden, or area, for any unlawful purpose; commits an offence. An offence in category (i) has a maximum penalty of a fine on level 1 of the standard scale; an offence in category (ii) has a maximum penalty of a level 3 fine. 'For an unlawful purpose' means for the purpose of committing an offence, such as burglary. Hiding from the police is not such a purpose (*L v CPS* [2007] EWHC 1843 (Admin)).

AGGRAVATED BURGLARY

Definition

B4.71 Theft Act 1968, s. 10

(1) A person is guilty of aggravated burglary if he commits any burglary and at the time has with him any firearm or imitation firearm, any weapon of offence, or any explosive.

Procedure

B4.72 Aggravated burglary is triable only on indictment. It is a class 3 offence.

Indictment

B4.73 *Statement of Offence*

Aggravated burglary contrary to section 10(1) of the Theft Act 1968

Particulars of Offence

A on or about the . . . day of . . . having entered a dwelling [or part of a dwelling, or a building or part of a building], namely . . ., as a trespasser stole therein [or attempted to steal therein, or inflicted grievous bodily harm upon . . . therein] and at the time had with him a firearm [or an imitation firearm, or a weapon of offence or an explosive], namely . . .

See also **B4.56**.

Alternative Verdicts

B4.74 Burglary contrary to either s. 9(1)(a) or s. 9(1)(b) of the Theft Act 1968 (by virtue of the Criminal Law Act 1967, s. 6(3)). See also **B4.57**.

Sentencing Guidelines

B4.75 The maximum penalty is: life imprisonment (Theft Act 1968, s. 10(2)).

Towards the top of the scale of seriousness is *O'Driscoll* (1986) 8 Cr App R (S) 121, where the offender gained access to the home of an elderly man and struck him a number of blows with a hammer. The victim was also threatened with a lighted gas poker, tied up with wire and gagged. A sentence of 15 years was upheld. Subsequent decisions which treat *O'Driscoll* as a guideline case include *A-G's Refs (Nos. 32 and 33 of 1995)* [1996] 2 Cr App R (S) 345 and *Eastap* [1997] 2 Cr App R (S) 55. Seven years' imprisonment was upheld in *Brady* [2000] 1 Cr App R (S) 410 where the offender, a man with numerous previous convictions including three for robbery, entered a bungalow occupied by a woman aged 70, threatened her with a chisel and demanded money. He left taking £50 and a radio. In *A-G's Ref (No. 10 of 1996)* [1997] 1 Cr App R (S) 76 the offender, a man with a long criminal record, together with three friends all armed with baseball bats, staged a revenge attack at the home of a man the offender believed to have stolen property from him. The offender beat the victim with a bat, causing a depressed fracture of the skull and other injuries. A sentence of 15 months' imprisonment was increased to four years on appeal, with an unspecified allowance for the element of double jeopardy.In *A-G's Ref (No. 16 of 1994)* (1995) 16 Cr App R (S) 629, the offender, who had a record of violent offences and was armed with a baseball bat, went to the flat of a man he knew. He used the bat to smash property in the flat, thereby frightening the female occupant. A sentence of 18 months' imprisonment was increased to three years.

Meaning of 'Firearm', 'Imitation Firearm', 'Weapon of Offence', 'Explosive'

Theft Act 1968, s. 10 **B4.76**

(1) . . . and for this purpose—
- (a) 'firearm' includes an airgun or air pistol, and 'imitation firearm' means anything which has the appearance of being a firearm, whether capable of being discharged or not, and
- (b) 'weapon of offence' means any article made or adapted for use for causing injury to or incapacitating a person, or intended by the person having it with him for such use; and
- (c) 'explosive' means any article manufactured for the purpose of producing a practical effect by explosion, or intended by the person having it with him for that purpose.

Paragraph (a) Whilst a definition of 'imitation firearm' is provided, there is no definition of 'firearm', except to make clear that it includes airguns and air pistols. It may be that the general definition of 'firearm' in the Firearms Act 1968 is appropriate (see **B12.4**). **B4.77**

Paragraph (b) In *Stones* [1989] 1 WLR 156, approved in *Kelly* (1992) 97 Cr App R 245, the Court of Appeal said (at p. 160): **B4.78**

> It is not necessary to prove the intention to use the [weapon] to cause injury etc. during the course of the burglary.
>
> . . . The mischief at which the section is clearly aimed is that if a burglar has a weapon which he intends to use to injure some person unconnected with the premises burgled [as in the instant case], he may nevertheless be tempted to use it if challenged during the course of the burglary and put under sufficient pressure.

The court also drew attention to the similarity between this paragraph and the provisions of the Prevention of Crime Act 1953, s. 1, concerned with the possession of offensive weapons. Whilst the two provisions are not identical since the phrase 'incapacitating a person' does not appear in s. 1 of the 1953 Act, some assistance may be obtained from the cases concerned with possession of offensive weapons. The defence of lawful authority or reasonable excuse for the possession of an offensive weapon (see **B12.128** to **B12.130**) does not appear to apply to aggravated burglary.

Paragraph (c) The definition of 'explosive' for the purposes of aggravated burglary is narrower than that to be found in the Explosive Substances Act 1883, but that Act may be of assistance in determining the meaning of the TA 1968, s. 10(1)(c). **B4.79**

Relevant Time

The gravamen of the aggravated offence of burglary with intent is entry into a building with a weapon. Therefore, at least one of the entrants to the building must have a weapon with him **B4.80** at that time (*Klass* [1998] 1 Cr App R 453). If, however, D is charged, as in *O'Leary* (1986) 82 Cr App R 341, with aggravated burglary by stealing *after* entry, under the TA 1968, s. 10 and s. 9(1)(b), it follows that, according to the Court of Appeal in that case (at p. 343):

> . . . the time at which [D] must be proved to have had with him a weapon of offence to make him guilty of aggravated burglary was the time at which he actually stole . . .

In *O'Leary* D entered a building as a trespasser, armed himself with a knife from the kitchen and confronted the occupiers to demand their cash and jewellery. This was an act of theft, and since D at that point had the kitchen knife in his hand it became aggravated burglary, even though he may have entered the building unarmed. See also *Kelly* (1992) 97 Cr App R 245.

A conviction under s. 9(1)(a) and s. 10 could not have been upheld in *O'Leary* because it would have been necessary to prove an intention to steal at the time of entry and possession of the weapon of offence at that time. See also *Francis* [1982] Crim LR 363.

Meaning of 'Has with Him'

B4.81 There is a requirement for a degree of immediate control of the weapon of offence or other article (*Kelt* [1977] 1 WLR 1365 and *Pawlicki* [1992] 1 WLR 827). Indeed, 'the word will normally mean "carrying" ' (*Kelt* and *Klass* [1998] 1 Cr App R 453). The cases decided on the Prevention of Crime Act 1953, s. 1 (possession of offensive weapons) are of no assistance because of the different purposes of the two offencecreating sections (*Kelly* (1992) 97 Cr App R 245). Since a dictum in *Stones* [1989] 1 WLR 156 at p. 160, it has been unclear whether the prosecution must prove that D knew he had a weapon of offence with him or knew he had something with him which was, in fact, a weapon of offence. It is submitted that the latter is to be preferred. It is more consistent with the general approach to this type of offence. For the comparable offence contrary to the Firearms Act 1968, s. 19, see **B12.84**. For the related offence contrary to the Firearms Act 1968, s. 1, see **B12.19**. For the decision on the drugs legislation that lies at the heart of many of these decisions, see **B20.13**. This issue has also recently arisen for decision under the Prevention of Crime Act 1953, s. 1 where the matter is controversial (see **B12.126**). The offence contrary to the Firearms Act 1968, s. 18, explicitly requires knowledge (see **B12.83**).

REMOVAL OF ARTICLES FROM PLACES OPEN TO THE PUBLIC

Definition

B4.82 **Theft Act 1968, s. 11**

(1) Subject to subsections (2) and (3) below, where the public have access to a building in order to view the building or part of it, or a collection or part of a collection housed in it, any person who without lawful authority removes from the building or its grounds the whole or part of any article displayed or kept for display to the public in the building or that part of it or in its grounds shall be guilty of an offence.

Procedure

B4.83 Removal of an article from a place open to the public is triable either way (MCA 1980, s. 17 and sch. 1, para. 28). When tried on indictment it is a class 3 offence.

Indictment

B4.84 *Statement of Offence*

Removing an article from a place open to the public contrary to section 11 of the Theft Act 1968

Particulars of Offence

A on or about the . . . day of . . . without lawful authority removed from the V art gallery, being a place to which the public then had access in order to view an art collection therein, a painting, namely *Portrait of the Madonna* by von Klomp

Sentence

The maximum penalty is five years on indictment (TA 1968, s. 11(4)); six months and/or a fine not exceeding the statutory maximum summarily. No sentencing guidelines are reported for this offence. **B4.85**

Purpose for which the Public Have Access

An offence under the TA 1968, s. 11(1), can be committed only in relation to a building to which the public have access for the purpose of viewing the building (or a part of it) or a collection (or part of a collection). It is the purpose of the inviter in granting access that matters (*Barr* [1978] Crim LR 244). **B4.86**

Meaning of 'Collection'

Theft Act 1968, s. 11 **B4.87**

(1) For this purpose, 'collection' includes a collection got together for a temporary purpose, but references in this section to a collection do not apply to a collection made or exhibited for the purpose of effecting sales or other commercial dealings.

Time of Public Access

Theft Act 1968, s. 11 **B4.88**

(2) It is immaterial for purposes of subsection (1) above, that the public's access to a building is limited to a particular period or particular occasion; but where anything removed from a building or its grounds is there otherwise than as forming part of, or being on loan for exhibition with, a collection intended for permanent exhibition to the public, the person removing it does not thereby commit an offence under this section unless he removes it on a day when the public have access to the building as mentioned in subsection (1) above.

If an art gallery, for example, is usually open it is possible for an offence under s. 11(1) to be committed on a day when the gallery is closed by removing an item which is part of a collection intended for permanent exhibition, whether it is actually on display or kept in store and exhibited on a rota basis (*Durkin* [1973] QB 786).

Meaning of 'Displayed or Kept for Display'

Whether an article is displayed, or kept for display, depends upon the intention of the person setting out the articles. For example, in *Barr* [1978] Crim LR 244 it was found that a cross and ewer in a church were not on display but were intended to be aids to worship and devotion. **B4.89**

Belief in Lawful Authority

Theft Act 1968, s. 11 **B4.90**

(3) A person does not commit an offence under this section if he believes that he has lawful authority for the removal of the thing in question or that he would have it if the person entitled to give it knew of the removal and the circumstances of it.

It is submitted that, if an accused raises the issue of his belief, it is then for the prosecution to prove beyond reasonable doubt that he had no such belief (compare the position under s. 12 of the Act, see **B4.97**). As to the defence of mistake generally, see **A3.2** to **A3.6**.

TAKING CONVEYANCE WITHOUT AUTHORITY

Definition

Theft Act 1968, s. 12 **B4.91**

(1) Subject to subsections (5) and (6) below, a person shall be guilty of an offence if, without having the consent of the owner or other lawful authority, he takes any conveyance for his own or another's use or, knowing that any conveyance has been taken without such authority, drives it or allows himself to be carried in or on it.

Procedure

B4.92 An offence under the TA 1968, s. 12(1), is triable only summarily. However, a count for such an offence may be included in an indictment for another offence in the circumstances set out in the CJA 1988, s. 40 (see **D11.15**). On the trial of an indictment for theft, the jury may find the accused guilty of an offence under s. 12(1) as an alternative verdict (TA 1968, s. 12(4)).

Proceedings for the offence (unless they fall within s. 12(4)) in relation to a mechanically propelled vehicle (a) shall not be commenced after the end of the period of three years beginning with the day on which the offence was committed, but (b) subject to that, may be commenced at any time within the period of six months beginning with the relevant day (s. 12(4A)). 'The relevant day' means (a) in the case of a prosecution for an offence under s. 12(1) by a public prosecutor, the day on which sufficient evidence to justify the proceedings came to the knowledge of any person responsible for deciding whether to commence any such proceedings; (b) in the case of a prosecution for an offence under s. 12(1), which is commenced by a person other than a public prosecutor after the discontinuance of a prosecution falling within s. 12(4B)(a) and relates to the same facts, the day on which sufficient evidence to justify the proceedings came to the knowledge of the person who has decided to commence the prosecution or (if later) the discontinuance of the other prosecution; (c) in the case of any other prosecution for an offence under s. 12(1), the day on which sufficient evidence to justify the proceedings came to the knowledge of the person who has decided to commence the prosecution (s. 12(4B)). For the purposes of s. 12(4A)(b), a certificate of a person responsible for deciding whether to commence a prosecution of a kind mentioned in s. 12(4B)(a) as to the date on which such evidence as is mentioned in the certificate came to the knowledge of any person responsible for deciding whether to commence any such prosecution shall be conclusive evidence of that fact (s. 12(4C)).

Sentencing Guidelines

B4.93 The maximum penalty for taking a conveyance without authority is six months and/or a fine not exceeding level 5 (TA 1968, s. 12(2)). Additionally, for the offence or an attempt to commit it in respect of a motor vehicle, there is discretionary disqualification (Road Traffic Offenders Act 1988, sch. 2). The same maximum penalty and liability for disqualification applies in relation to the offence of driving or allowing oneself to be carried in or on a conveyance taken without authority.

The Magistrates' Courts Guidelines (2004) indicate the following for a first-time offender pleading not guilty:

> **Aggravating Factors** For example group action; premeditated; related damage; professional hallmarks; vulnerable victim; offence committed on bail; relevant previous convictions and any failures to respond to previous sentences.
>
> **Mitigating Factors** For example misunderstanding with owner; soon returned; vehicle belonging to family or friend.
>
> *Guideline*: Is it serious enough for a community penalty?

In *Bushell* (1987) 9 Cr App R (S) 537 the offender, aged 17 and with no previous convictions, took a friend's car without permission and crashed it, damaging it beyond repair. A sentence of 180 hours' community service, together with a disqualification for one year, was upheld by the Court of Appeal. Where the offence is combined with other offences arising out of the same circumstances, an immediate custodial sentence may be appropriate. Thus in *Jeary* (1986) 8 Cr App R (S) 491 the offender, aged 18, and with one previous finding of guilt for assault occasioning actual bodily harm, pleaded guilty to two counts of taking a conveyance, two counts of theft, and asked for two other offences to be taken into consideration. He was involved with others in taking several cars in the course of an evening and driving them at high speed in a city centre 'just as a bit of fun'. Three cars were damaged, one beyond repair.

The offender also admitted taking property from the cars, though most of that was recovered. The Court of Appeal agreed with the sentencer's view that the offences were so serious that a non-custodial sentence could not be justified because, in addition to the unlawful taking, the cars had been deliberately damaged. Four months' detention was upheld.

Meaning of 'Conveyance'

Whilst the marginal note to the TA 1968, s. 12, uses the phrase 'motor vehicle or other conveyance', the section itself refers only to a 'conveyance'. A definition of 'conveyance' is to be found in s. 12(7)(a): **B4.94**

> 'conveyance' means any conveyance constructed or adapted for the carriage of a person or persons whether by land, water or air, except that it does not include a conveyance constructed or adapted for use only under the control of a person not carried in or on it, and 'drive' shall be construed accordingly.

This definition would ordinarily include a pedal cycle, but s. 12(5), which creates a separate offence (see **B4.107**), makes clear that the offence under s. 12(1) does not apply in relation to pedal cycles. Otherwise, it is a very wide definition. In *Neal v Gribble* (1978) 68 Cr App R 9, the Divisional Court had to consider whether a horse was a conveyance within the meaning of s. 12. The court was of the view that it was not such a conveyance, since the definition in s. 12(7)(a) 'seems to be directed towards artefacts rather than towards animals'.

Taking for his Own or Another's Use

It is essential that a conveyance be moved in order for it to be taken, however small that movement may be. Merely trying to start the engine of a motor vehicle without moving the vehicle does not amount to taking it (*Bogacki* [1973] QB 832). Attempt is not available as an alternative offence (Criminal Attempts Act 1981, s. 1(1) and (4)). On a charge of taking it is not necessary that D used the conveyance to convey himself, merely that he 'took' it. In *Pearce* [1973] Crim LR 321 an appeal against conviction was dismissed where D had placed the conveyance, an inflatable rubber dinghy, on a trailer and drove away with it. **B4.95**

On a charge of taking, the prosecution must prove that D took the conveyance 'for his own or another's use'. In *Bow* (1976) 64 Cr App R 54, it was argued that D had not taken the conveyance 'for his own use' when he got into a Land Rover which was obstructing his way and released its handbrake and let it coast for about 200 yards. The Court of Appeal said (at p. 58):

> The short answer . . . is that where as here, a conveyance is taken and moved in a way which necessarily involves its use as a conveyance, the taker cannot be heard to say that the taking was not for that use. If he has in fact taken the conveyance and used it as such, his motive in so doing is . . . quite immaterial.

In *Stokes* [1983] RTR 59, D pushed a car round a corner as a practical joke. The conviction could not be upheld because the judge failed specifically to emphasise the importance of establishing that someone was being conveyed inside the car or riding on it, i.e. failed clearly to require a finding that the car was being taken for use as a conveyance, rather than merely that it was 'taken'.

Pearce, Bow and *Stokes* were further explained by the Court of Appeal in *Marchant* (1984) 80 Cr App R 361. Robert Goff LJ, giving the judgment of the court, stated that 'to be guilty of the offence, D must have both taken the vehicle, i.e. have taken control of it and caused it to be moved, and he must have done so for his own or another's use'. That phrase requires that it be taken *for use as* a conveyance, which is satisfied provided that is why the conveyance was taken, rather than that it must have been taken *as* a conveyance. For example, if a person takes a car by pushing it around a corner and leaving it, he satisfies the first element of this requirement. If, at the time he moves it, he intends to get it going after he has returned to it, his purpose is plain: it was for use as a conveyance and the offence has been committed. In *Pearce* the dinghy was clearly taken and D's purpose was to use it as a dinghy, that is, as a conveyance. In *Bow* D actually used the Land Rover as a conveyance whilst taking it. In *Stokes* D did take the conveyance, but his purpose was not to use it as a conveyance and so the offence was not committed.

Once a vehicle has been taken, it cannot be taken again by the same accused, but, where a first taker abandons a vehicle, that same vehicle may be taken by another (*DPP v Spriggs* [1994] RTR 1).

Without the Consent of the Owner or Other Lawful Authority

B4.96 On a charge of taking a conveyance without authority, the prosecution must prove that the taking was actually without the owner's consent or other lawful authority (*Ambler* [1979] RTR 217 and *Sturrock v DPP* [1996] RTR 216). 'Owner' is defined by the TA 1968, s. 12(7)(b), in relation to a conveyance which is the subject of a hiring agreement or hire-purchase agreement, as meaning the person in possession of the conveyance under that agreement.

In *Whittaker v Campbell* [1984] QB 318 the two defendants, neither of whom had a driving licence, had come by Dunn's licence. They hired a van, using that acquired licence by pretending that one of them was Dunn. They paid the appropriate hire charge and drove the van away. The Divisional Court was asked to consider the effect of the false representation on the consent that was obtained as a consequence. It stated that there is no general principle of law that fraud vitiates consent. The court took the view that where force is used, it is possible to distinguish between consent and mere submission, but that when the factor being exercised was fraud and not force, no such sensible distinction can be drawn. In common-sense terms, the owner has consented and, despite the fraud, that means that no offence is committed.

In *Peart* [1970] 2 QB 672, the Court of Appeal quashed a conviction where D had falsely represented to the owner of a car that he needed it to drive from Bedlington to Alnwick to sign a contract. The owner let him have the vehicle, provided he returned it that day. As he all along intended he drove the car instead to Burnley in the evening. The court reserved the question whether a fundamental misrepresentation can vitiate consent (according to *Whittaker v Campbell* it would appear that it does not), but decided that the sort of false pretence in the particular case did not vitiate the consent, and the activity involved was not the type of activity with which the TA 1968, s. 12, was concerned.

In *Phipps* (1970) 54 Cr App R 300 the Court of Appeal approved a direction by the trial judge that if, after a lawful purpose had been fulfilled, D then did not return the car but drove it off on his own business, the offence was committed. It is not clear whether a deception was practised upon the owner, and the decision of the Court of Appeal does not raise the issue of such a deception. It may, therefore, be that this case can be regarded as consistent with *Peart* and *Whittaker v Campbell* since in *Phipps* there may well have been no question of consent obtained by fraud or a false representation. Rather it seems that it was a case of D going beyond the limits of the consent that had been given by the owner of the car (see also *McKnight v Davies* [1974] RTR 4).

Mens Rea of Offence of Taking

B4.97 There are two aspects to the mental element of the offence.

First, the taking must be intentional. In *Blayney v Knight* (1974) 60 Cr App R 269, Lord Widgery CJ, giving the judgment of the court, stated, 'I do not see how anybody could be charged with taking a motor car because of the fact that the car accidentally moves forward'.

Secondly, the TA 1968, s. 12(6), provides:

> A person does not commit an offence under this section by anything done in the belief that he

has lawful authority to do it or that he would have the owner's consent if the owner knew of his doing it and the circumstances of it.

It is essential that this belief exist at the time of the taking. It is not enough if the owner says, later, that he would have consented had he known (*Ambler* [1979] RTR 217). This question is one for the magistrates to decide and they may well take into account a factor such as the likelihood of a person genuinely believing that an owner would authorise another to drive a car when uninsured. Clearly an owner could provide such an authorisation (*Clotworthy* [1981] RTR 477). An example of what might amount to 'unlawful authority' is given by *Briggs* [1987] Crim LR 708, where D claimed that he was repairing the motor cycle for a friend. Since the judge had not focused the attention of the jury on this matter, the conviction was quashed by the Court of Appeal.

The onus of proof of this matter lies on the prosecution (*MacPherson* [1973] RTR 157; *Gannon* (1987) 87 Cr App R 254) but before that stage is reached, it is for D to raise the issue. He must call evidence or point to some evidence which tends to show that he held the necessary belief (*Gannon*).

The offence is one of basic intent for the purposes of any defence involving voluntary intoxication (*Gannon, MacPherson*). As to basic and specific intent generally, see **A3.8** to **A3.12**.

Driving or Allowing himself to be Carried

B4.98 Section 12(7)(a) of the TA 1968 indicates that 'drive' is to be construed in accordance with the meaning of 'conveyance' (see **B4.94**) and therefore includes 'driving' not only motor vehicles, but any land, water or air conveyance. The meaning of 'drives' is considered generally at **C1.8**.

On a charge of allowing himself to be carried in or on a conveyance taken without authority, it is not enough for the prosecution to prove that D was in or on the conveyance, there must have been some movement of the conveyance (*Miller* [1976] Crim LR 417; *Diggin* (1980) 72 Cr App R 204). If a taker of a motor vehicle offers a person a lift and he gets into the seat next to the driver, the person is not allowing himself to be driven before the driver turns on the ignition switch (*Diggin*).

Mens Rea of Offence of Driving or Allowing himself to be Carried

B4.99 On a charge of driving or allowing himself to be carried in or on a conveyance taken without authority, it must be proved that D knew that the conveyance had been taken without lawful authority (*Diggin* (1980) 72 Cr App R 204 and *Boldizsar v Knight* [1980] Crim LR 653). As to the meaning of these terms, see **B4.94** to **B4.97**. It seems that D need not be aware that the taker took the conveyance for his own or another's use, though no doubt ordinarily he will know this. As to knowledge generally, see **A2.9**.

The TA 1968, s. 12(6), applies to the offence of driving or allowing oneself to be carried in or on a conveyance taken without consent (see **B4.98**).

AGGRAVATED VEHICLE-TAKING

B4.100 The Aggravated Vehicle-Taking Act 1992 created aggravated forms of the offence contrary to the TA 1968, s. 12(1) (see **B4.91** to **B4.99**), through the TA 1968, s. 12A.

Theft Act 1968, s. 12A

(1) Subject to subsection (3) below, a person is guilty of aggravated taking of a vehicle if—
 (a) he commits an offence under section 12(1) above (in this section referred to as a 'basic offence') in relation to a mechanically propelled vehicle; and

(b) it is proved that, at any time after the vehicle was unlawfully taken (whether by him or another) and before it was recovered, the vehicle was driven, or injury or damage was caused, in one or more of the circumstances set out in paragraphs (a) to (d) of subsection (2) below.

(2) The circumstances referred to in subsection (1)(b) above are—

(a) that the vehicle was driven dangerously on a road or other public place;

(b) that, owing to the driving of the vehicle, an accident occurred by which injury was caused to any person;

(c) that, owing to the driving of the vehicle, an accident occurred by which damage was caused to any property, other than the vehicle;

(d) that damage was caused to the vehicle.

Since the maximum penalty is greater where death is caused (see **B4.103**), s. 12A creates two offences (see *Sherwood* [1995] RTR 60, following *Courtie* [1984] AC 403).

Procedure

B4.101 The offences are triable either way. When tried on indictment they are class 3 offence.

D has no right to elect trial on indictment where the only allegation is of damage to the vehicle or other property or both and the total value of the damage alleged to have been caused is less than the 'relevant sum' (i.e. £5,000) (MCA 1980, ss. 22 and 33 and sch. 2: see **D6.31**).

Alternative Verdict

B4.102 Under the TA 1968, s. 12A(5), where D is charged with either of these offences but found not guilty, he may be convicted of the basic offence, contrary to the TA 1968, s. 12(1) (see **B4.91** ***et seq.*** and **D21.48**). If convicted of the basic offence at the Crown Court, that court has the same powers and duties as a magistrates' court would have had on convicting him of such an offence (s. 12A(6)) (see **B4.93**).

Sentence

B4.103 The maximum penalty is, on indictment, two years or a fine or both. The maximum penalty, on indictment, is increased to 14 years (five years where the offence was committed before 27 February 2004) where it is proved that, in circumstances falling within the TA 1968, s. 12A(2)(b), the accident caused the death of the person concerned (TA 1968, s. 12A(4)).

The maximum penalty on summary conviction is a term of imprisonment not exceeding six months or a fine not exceeding the statutory maximum or both. The limit on penalties imposed by the MCA 1980, s. 33(1), with regard to an offence tried summarily in pursuance of the MCA 1980, s. 22, does not apply where the offence is aggravated vehicle-taking (MCA 1980, s. 33(3)).

By virtue of the Road Traffic Offenders Act 1988, ss. 28, 96 and 97 and sch. 2, part II, where a person is convicted of aggravated vehicle-taking, disqualification from driving is obligatory, endorsement of licence is obligatory and the penalty points which may be imposed for the offence are 3 to 11. As to disqualification, endorsement of licence and penalty points, see **C8**. The fact that D did not drive the vehicle at any particular time or at all is not a special reason to avoid obligatory disqualification (Road Traffic Offenders Act 1988, s. 34).

When tried summarily, the Magistrates' Courts Guidelines (2004) indicate the following for a first-time offender pleading not guilty:

Aggravating Factors For example trying to avoid detection or arrest; competitive driving, racing, showing off; disregard of warnings e.g. from passengers or others in the vicinity; group action; police pursuit; premeditated; serious injury/damage; serious risk; offence committed on bail; relevant previous convictions and any failures to respond to previous sentences.

Mitigating Factors For example passenger only; single incident of bad driving; speed not excessive; very minor injury/damage.

Guideline: Is it so serious that only custody is appropriate?

In *Bird* (1993) 14 Cr App R (S) 343, the Court of Appeal said that, when sentencing for this offence, relevant aggravating features would be related to the overall culpability of the driver: how bad the driving was and for how long it had lasted and, to a lesser extent, how much injury or damage had been caused. Drink would affect the assessment of culpability, but where drink was a major factor in the case it would be the subject of a separate charge. Mitigation might be found in a guilty plea showing contrition, but the youth of the offender would be of less significance in this type of case than in others, since the offence was aimed primarily at young offenders. See also *Evans* (1994) 15 Cr App R (S) 137, *Sealey* (1994) 15 Cr App R (S) 189, *Robinson* (1994) 15 Cr App R (S) 452 and *Frostick* [1998] 1 Cr App R (S) 257.

Actus Reus

The offences of aggravated vehicle-taking are committed only if, first, an offence under the TA 1968, s. 12(1) (see **B4.91 to B4.99**), is committed in relation to a mechanically propelled vehicle (s. 12A(1)(a)). In the Road Traffic Act 1988, s. 185, the following are defined and are all mechanically propelled vehicles: heavy locomotive, heavy motor car, invalid carriage, light locomotive, motor car, motor cycle, motor tractor, and motor vehicle. Secondly, the prosecution must prove that, at any time after the vehicle was taken and before it was recovered, one or more of the circumstances in s. 12A(2)(a) to (d) occurred (s. 12A(1)(b)). All that the prosecution has to prove is that the circumstances occurred, it does not have to prove that D was the cause of them (see *Dawes v DPP* [1995] 1 Cr App R 65); it is for D to prove one of the specific defences if he is to avoid conviction (see **B4.106**). **B4.104**

The circumstances of aggravation in s. 12A(2) are listed at **B4.100**. The phrase 'driven dangerously', which occurs in s. 12A(2)(a), is defined in s. 12A(7) in identical terms to the definition which applies to the offence of dangerous driving (see **C3.9**). Whilst the vehicle must be driven dangerously for s. 12A(2)(a) to apply, there is no such requirement in s. 12A(2)(b) or (c), so the simple fact that the vehicle is being driven, without fault, is sufficient (*Marsh* [1997] 1 Cr App R 67, in which M was guilty under s. 12A(2)(b) when he drove a vehicle without permission and knocked a pedestrian down despite driving apparently carefully). The question is whether the driving was the cause of the accident. It is unnecessary for D to be the driver or even for him to be in or near the car when the incident occurs. None of the other phrases used in s. 12A(2) are specifically defined. For 'damage', see **B8.5**; for 'driving', see **C1.8**; for 'accident', see **C1.1** and *Branchflower* [2005] 1 Cr App R 140, where it was decided that 'accident' in this offence is perfectly capable of applying to an untoward occurrence that has adverse physical results, notwithstanding that one event in the chain of events which led to the untoward occurrence was a deliberate act on the part of some mischievous person.

An offence under s. 12A may be committed only in the period after the vehicle is taken and before it is recovered. A vehicle is recovered when it is restored to its owner or other lawful possession or custody (s. 12A(8)); a similar concept is used in the offence of handling stolen goods, see **B4.135**. 'Owner' has the same meaning as in s. 12 (s. 12A(8)) (see **B4.96**).

Mens Rea

Mens rea has to be established with regard to the first element of an offence of aggravated vehicle-taking, that is the *mens rea* of the basic offence (see **B4.97** and **B4.99**). No *mens rea* need be shown with regard to the second element, the circumstances of aggravation: the offences are offences of strict liability in that regard. **B4.105**

Specific Defence

B4.106 **Theft Act 1968, s. 12A**

(3) A person is not guilty of an offence under this section if he proves that, as regards any such proven driving, injury or damage as is referred to in subsection (1)(b) above, either—
  (a) the driving, accident or damage referred to in subsection (2) above occurred before he committed the basic offence; or
  (b) he was neither in nor in the immediate vicinity of the vehicle when that driving, accident or damage occurred.

TAKING OR RIDING A PEDAL CYCLE WITHOUT AUTHORITY

B4.107 It is an offence, contrary to the TA 1968, s. 12(5), and subject to s. 12(6) (see B4.97), for a person, without having the consent of the owner or other lawful authority, to take a pedal cycle for his own or another's use, or ride a pedal cycle knowing it to have been taken without such authority. In *Sturrock v DPP* [1996] RTR 216, it was held that it is not necessary to have a formal statement of ownership from the owner of a cycle where the primary facts permit the inference that the cycle had not been abandoned and had an owner. The offence is punishable on summary conviction with a fine not exceeding level 3 on the standard scale.

INTERFERENCE WITH VEHICLES

Definition

B4.108 **Criminal Attempts Act 1981, s. 9**

(1) A person is guilty of the offence of vehicle interference if he interferes with a motor vehicle or trailer or with anything carried in or on a motor vehicle or trailer with the intention that an offence specified in subsection (2) below shall be committed by himself or some other person.
(2) The offences mentioned in subsection (1) above are—
  (a) theft of the motor vehicle or trailer or part of it;
  (b) theft of anything carried in or on the motor vehicle or trailer; and
  (c) an offence under section 12(1) of the Theft Act 1968 (taking and driving away without consent);

  and, if it is shown that a person accused of an offence under this section intended that one of those offences should be committed, it is immaterial that it cannot be shown which it was.

Procedure

B4.109 The offence is triable summarily only (Criminal Attempts Act 1981, s. 9(3)).

Sentence

B4.110 The maximum penalty is imprisonment for a term not exceeding three months or a fine not exceeding level 4 on the standard scale or both (Criminal Attempts Act 1981, s. 9(3)).

The Magistrates' Courts Guidelines (2004) indicate the following for a first-time offender pleading not guilty:

Aggravating Factors For example disabled passenger vehicle; emergency service vehicle; racial or religious aggravation; group action; planned; related damage; offence committed on bail; relevant previous convictions and any failures to respond to previous sentences.

Mitigating Factors For example impulsive action.

Guideline: Is it serious enough for a community penalty?

Elements

As to theft, see B4.1 *et seq.* As to offences under the TA 1968, s. 12(1), see B4.91 *et seq.* **B4.111**

There is no definition of 'interference'. Clearly there has to be interference as well as intention. Merely looking into cars is probably not an act of interference whereas opening doors and putting pressure on the door handles is an act of interference. However, whether placing a hand on a door handle is an act of interference is not clear, nor was it clarified in the Crown Court case of *Reynolds and Warren v Metropolitan Police* [1982] Crim LR 831.

'Motor vehicle' and 'trailer', by virtue of s. 9(5), have the same meaning as in the Road Traffic Act 1988, s. 185(1):

> 'motor vehicle' means, subject to section 20 of the Chronically Sick and Disabled Persons Act 1970 (which makes special provision about invalid carriages, within the meaning of that Act), a mechanically propelled vehicle intended or adapted for use on roads, and 'trailer' means a vehicle drawn by a motor vehicle.

ABSTRACTING ELECTRICITY

Definition

Theft Act 1968, s. 13 **B4.112**

> A person who dishonestly uses without due authority, or dishonestly causes to be wasted or diverted, any electricity shall [be guilty of an offence].

Procedure

Abstracting electricity is triable either way (MCA 1980, s. 17 and sch. 1, para. 28). When tried on indictment it is a class 3 offence. **B4.113**

Indictment

Statement of Offence **B4.114**

Abstracting electricity contrary to section 13 of the Theft Act 1968

Particulars of Offence

A on or about the . . . day of . . . dishonestly and without due authority used [or dishonestly caused to be wasted or diverted] a quantity of electricity

Sentencing Guidelines

The maximum penalty is five years (TA 1968, s. 13) on indictment; six months or a fine not exceeding the statutory maximum, or both, summarily. **B4.115**

In *Hodkinson* (1980) 2 Cr App R (S) 331, the offender pleaded guilty to abstracting electricity, in that he had fitted a device to the electricity meter at his home, which caused the meter to give a false reading. Bristow J commented that:

> In the judgment of this court deliberately stealing electricity in this way is an offence which calls for deterrent treatment when caught. In the circumstances of this case this court has come to the conclusion that the necessary deterrent element would be sufficiently dealt with by a sentence of one month's immediate imprisonment, accompanied by a fine of £750.

See also *Western* (1987) 9 Cr App R (S) 6.

Actus Reus

Electricity cannot be property and so when electricity is 'obtained' the only available offence is the present one (*Low v Blease* [1975] Crim LR 513). Any use, waste or diversion of electricity will suffice (*Low v Blease*), so a meter does not have to be tampered with (*McCreadie* **B4.116**

(1992) 96 Cr App R 143). Electricity is abstracted where the electricity supply to a house is reconnected without the consent of the electricity supplier (*Boggeln v Williams* [1978] 1 WLR 873). It is also abstracted where the electricity supply to a house is caused not to be registered by the meter (*Collins v DPP* (1987) *The Times*, 20 October 1987). It may well be an abstraction of electricity to make a call from a telephone belonging to another person (*Low v Blease*).

Mens Rea

B4.117 Abstracting electricity is an offence of dishonesty to which the definition provided by the Court of Appeal in *Ghosh* [1982] QB 1053 applies (see **B4.37**). This is so even though the Court of Appeal in *Boggeln v Williams* [1978] 1 WLR 873 took the view that 'dishonesty' was to be approached as a subjective concept in s. 13.

FRAUDULENT USE OF TELECOMMUNICATION SYSTEMS AND FRAUDULENT RECEIPT OF PROGRAMMES

B4.118 It is an offence, contrary to the Communications Act 2003, s. 125(1), for a person dishonestly to obtain an electronic communications service where he does so with intent to avoid payment of a charge applicable to the provision of that service. Section 125(2) makes it clear that it is not an offence under s. 125 to obtain a service mentioned in the Copyright, Designs and Patents Act 1988, s. 297(1) (see below). The offence is triable either way, and the maximum penalty is, on conviction on indictment, imprisonment for a term not exceeding five years or a fine or both and, on summary conviction, imprisonment for a term not exceeding six months or a fine not exceeding the statutory maximum or both (s. 125(3)). It is also an offence, contrary to s. 126(1) for a person to have in his possession or under his control anything which may be used for obtaining an electronic communications service, provided he has the requisite intention (which is defined in s. 126(3)). It is also an offence, contrary to s. 126(2), for a person to supply or offer to supply anything which may be so used, where he knows or believes that the intentions of the person supplied or offered fall within s. 126(3). Both offences under s. 126 are triable either way and the maximum penalty, on conviction on indictment, is a term of imprisonment not exceeding five years, a fine or both and, on summary conviction, a term of imprisonment not exceeding six months, a fine not exceeding the statutory maximum or both (s. 126(5)). For neither of these offences will an intention fall within s. 126(3) if it relates exclusively to the obtaining of a service mentioned in the Copyright, Designs and Patents Act 1988, s. 297(1) (s. 126(4)). For the definition of relevant terms, see s. 126(6) and s. 151.

It is a summary offence, contrary to the Copyright, Designs and Patents Act 1988, s. 297(1), dishonestly to receive a programme included in a broadcasting or cable programme service provided from a place in the UK with intent to avoid payment of any charge applicable to the reception of the programme. Section 297A of the 1988 Act (inserted by the Conditional Access (Unauthorised Decoders) Regulations 2000 (SI 2000 No. 1175) creates an offence triable either way concerned with certain commercial activities in relation to unauthorised decoders (that is apparatus to enable receipt of encrypted transmissions).

The Mobile Telephones (Re-programming) Act 2002 (as amended by the VCRA 2006) creates four offences concerned with the re-programming of mobile telephones: changing a unique device identifier (s. 1(1)(a)); interfering with a unique device identifier's operation (s. 1(1)(b)); offering or agreeing to change, or interfere with the operation of, a unique device identifier (s. 1(1)(c)); and offering or agreeing to arrange for another person to do so (s. 1(1)(d)). The last two offences were added by the 2006 Act with effect from 6 April 2007.

A unique device identifier is an electronic equipment identifier which is unique to a mobile wireless communications device (s. 1(2) and s. 2(4)); a SIM card is an obvious example. A person does not commit an offence if he is the device manufacturer or he does the act with the written consent of the manufacturer (s. 1(2)). The maximum penalty is, on indictment, five years' imprisonment or a fine or both, and summarily, six months' imprisonment or a fine not exceeding the statutory maximum or both (s. 1(4)). The Act also creates three offences concerned with the possession or supply of things for such programming. A person commits an offence by: (1) having in his custody or under his control anything which may be used for the purpose of changing or interfering with a unique device identifier's operation where he has the intention to use the thing unlawfully for that purpose or to allow it to be used unlawfully for that purpose (s. 2(1)); (2) supplying anything which may be used for the purpose of changing or interfering with a unique device identifier's operation where he knows or believes that the person to whom it is supplied intends to use it unlawfully for that purpose or to allow it to be used unlawfully for that purpose (s. 2(2)); (3) offering to supply anything which may be used for the purpose of changing or interfering with a unique device identifier's operation where he knows or believes that the person to whom it is offered intends, if it is supplied to him, to use it unlawfully for that purpose or to allow it to be used unlawfully for that purpose (s. 2(3)). The maximum penalty, on indictment, is five years' imprisonment or a fine or both and, summarily, is six months' imprisonment or a fine not exceeding the statutory maximum or both (s. 2(6)).

In *Nadig* (1993) 14 Cr App R (S) 49 the offender was convicted of fraudulent use of a telecommunications system. He used a tone-dialling device to make calls from a telephone box without paying. A suspended sentence was held to be wrong in principle for an isolated offence. Auld J, in the Court of Appeal, said that the preferred sentence was a fine, and that comparison between sentencing for this offence and sentencing for abstracting electricity (see **B4.115**) would be helpful only where the fraudulent use of the telephone had taken place over a period of time. See also *Adewale* (1994) 15 Cr App R (S) 790 and *Aslam* [1996] 2 Cr App R 377.

GOING EQUIPPED

Definition

Theft Act 1968, s. 25 **B4.119**

(1) A person shall be guilty of an offence if, when not at his place of abode, he has with him any article for use in the course of or in connection with any burglary or theft.
(2) A person guilty of an offence under this section shall on conviction on indictment be liable to imprisonment for a term not exceeding three years.
(3) Where a person is charged with an offence under this section, proof that he had with him any article made or adapted for use in committing a burglary or theft shall be evidence that he had it with him for such use.
(4) [Repealed.]
(5) For purposes of this section an offence under section 12(1) of this Act of taking a conveyance shall be treated as theft.

As of 15 January 2006, this provision no longer contains any reference to going equipped for a 'cheat', which was defined as an offence under the TA 1968, s. 15, but the Fraud Act 2006, ss. 6 and 7, create (as of that date) new offences of possessing, making or supplying articles for use in frauds (see **B5.101** ***et seq***).

Procedure

Going equipped for stealing is triable either way (MCA 1980, s. 17 sch. 1, para. 28). When tried on indictment it is a class 3 offence. **B4.120**

Indictment

B4.121 *Statement of Offence*

Going equipped for burglary contrary to section 25 of the Theft Act 1968

Particulars of Offence

A on or about the . . . day of . . ., not being at his place of abode, had with him articles, namely a jemmy and a kitchen knife, for use in the course of or in connection with burglary

Sentence

B4.122 The maximum penalty is three years (TA 1968, s. 25(2)) on indictment; six months or a fine not exceeding the statutory maximum, or both, summarily. If committed with reference to the theft or taking of motor vehicles, disqualification is discretionary (Road Traffic Offenders Act 1988, sch. 2). There are no reported sentencing guidelines for this offence, but in *Ferry* [1997] 2 Cr App R (S) 42 a sentence of 12 months' imprisonment was upheld where the offenders, found in possession of a cordless drill, screwdrivers, surgical gloves and a map, were targeting a series of telephone boxes in a rural area.

When dealt with summarily, the Magistrates' Courts Guidelines (2004) indicate the following for a first-time offender pleading not guilty.

Aggravating Factors For example group action; sophisticated; specialised equipment; number of items; people put in fear; offence committed on bail; relevant previous convictions and any failures to respond to previous sentences.

Mitigating Factors None.

Guideline: Is it serious enough for a community penalty? Consider forfeiture and destruction.

Relation to Other Offences

B4.123 It is not an offence under the TA 1968, s. 25, to keep or possess articles intended for use in theft, burglary etc. as long as those articles are kept at home. An individual who has been found to possess a jemmy or similar implement at his place of abode may, however, be charged under the Criminal Damage Act 1971, s. 3, if it appears that the thing in question might be used to damage windows, locks etc. in the course of forcing an entry for the purpose of theft or burglary. Firearms or imitation firearms kept for the purpose of a robbery or aggravated burglary come within the scope of the TA 1968, s. 25, but more obviously come within the provisions of the Firearms Act 1968.

When not at his Place of Abode

B4.124 'Place of abode' is not defined in the TA 1968. It could include a caravan or motor vehicle, but in *Bundy* [1977] 1 WLR 914, the Court of Appeal held that a vehicle is not to be regarded as a place of abode unless parked at a site where D abides or intends to abide. If a traveller keeps housebreaking tools in his vehicle, he will therefore commit an offence under the TA 1968, s. 25, whenever he drives his vehicle away from that site.

Meaning of 'Has with Him'

B4.125 This phrase in the TA 1968, s. 25, must bear the same meaning as in s. 10 of the Act (see **B4.80**) and implies a degree of immediate control (*Kelt* [1977] 1 WLR 1365). It would suffice if D had the article in his car or bag, at his place of work, or on his person. In *Re McAngus* [1994] Crim LR 602 the Divisional Court held, in relation to extradition proceedings, that a s. 25 offence could be made out where the applicant showed undercover agents counterfeit shirts stored in a bonded warehouse.

Any Article for Use in the Course of or in Connection with any Burglary or Theft

B4.126 The connection between the articles and the proposed theft etc. must not be too remote. In *Mansfield* [1975] Crim LR 101, D was charged under the TA 1968, s. 25, with possessing another person's driving licence, with intent to use this to obtain employment, in the course of which he would have an opportunity to steal. Not surprisingly, the Court of Appeal quashed his conviction.

As to the offences which may be intended, see the TA 1968, s. 25(5). Although the taking of pedal cycles contrary to s. 12(5) of the Act is not one of those offences, the possession of bolt-cutters etc. for cutting cycle locks could readily be interpreted as intended for use in theft. Burglary includes burglary with intent to inflict grevious bodily harm etc. under s. 9(1)(a) and theft includes theft with force which would amount to robbery.

The most ordinary of articles, including footwear and clothing, could be used in the course of such crimes, but in practice s. 25 is used only in connection with articles which seem intended to play a prominent or obvious role: something which D would not have with him if he was not intending to commit such a crime. Coshes, masks, jemmies, glass-cutters and skeleton keys are obvious examples; less obvious perhaps are credit cards stolen or illicitly borrowed from their real owners (see also *Re McAngus* [1994] Crim LR 602: counterfeit clothing). This does not mean that apparently innocuous articles cannot be within the scope of the section. Bottles of wine were found to constitute such articles in *Doukas* [1978] 1 WLR 372, where D had apparently brought the wine to the hotel where he worked as a waiter in order dishonestly to sell it to his employer's customers, who would be deceived (contrary to s. 15 of the Act) into thinking that they were buying wine from the employer. A charge under the Fraud Act 2006, s. 6, would now be more appropriate on such facts.

The article need not be intended for use that day, nor for use by D himself, but it must be intended for *future* use. The possession of articles that *have been used* in theft etc. with a view to disposing of them is not an offence under s. 25, although a charge under the Criminal Law Act 1967, s. 4, may be appropriate (*Ellames* [1974] 1 WLR 1391).

In the absence of a confession or other self-incriminating behaviour by D, it may sometimes be difficult to prove that the article was indeed intended for use in the course of or in connection with burglary or theft, and proof of intent is needed: it is not sufficient to show that D merely contemplated possible use (*Hargreaves* [1985] Crim LR 243). Section 25(3) is of very limited use in this respect, since it only states the obvious. If D was found to be carrying a jemmy or a bunch of skeleton keys, a court or jury would in any case consider this to be evidence (and possibly sufficient proof) of intent to commit burglary. Possession of a torch or screwdriver would be less likely to be considered evidence of such intent, and here s. 25(3) is of no help at all (*Harrison* [1970] Crim LR 415).

HANDLING STOLEN GOODS

Definition

B4.127 **Theft Act 1968, s. 22**

(1) A person handles stolen goods if (otherwise than in the course of the stealing) knowing or believing them to be stolen goods he dishonestly receives the goods, or dishonestly undertakes or assists in their retention, removal, disposal or realisation by or for the benefit of another person, or if he arranges to do so.
(2) A person guilty of handling stolen goods shall on conviction on indictment be liable to imprisonment for a term not exceeding 14 years.

Procedure

B4.128 Handling stolen goods is triable either way (MCA 1980, s. 17 and sch. 1, para. 28). When tried on indictment it is a class 3 offence. It is a Group A offence for jurisdiction purposes under the CJA 1993, part I (see **A8.4**).

According to the *Consolidated Criminal Practice Direction*, para. V.51, *Mode of trial* (see **appendix** 7), cases of handling should be tried summarily unless the court considers that one or more of the following features is present in the case *and* that its sentencing powers are insufficient:

(a) Dishonest handling of stolen property by a receiver who has commissioned the theft.
(b) The offence has professional hallmarks.
(c) The property is of high value (at least £10,000).

Indictment

B4.129 **First Count**

Statement of Offence

Handling stolen goods contrary to section 22(1) of the TA 1968

Particulars of Offence

A on or about the . . . day of . . . dishonestly received stolen goods, namely a pearl necklace belonging to V, knowing or believing the same to be stolen goods

Second Count

Statement of Offence

Handling stolen goods contrary to section 22(1) of the TA 1968

Particulars of Offence

A on or about the . . . day of . . . dishonestly undertook or assisted in the retention, removal, disposal or realisation of stolen goods, namely a pearl necklace belonging to V, by or for the benefit of B, or dishonestly arranged to do so, knowing or believing the same to be stolen goods

It may be prudent to include both counts unless there is clear evidence of one particular form of handling and the prosecution intend to present the case exclusively in those terms. See further *Deakin* [1972] 1 WLR 1618.

The general deficiency principle applies to counts for handling stolen goods (for the application of this principle to theft, see **B4.3**, and for the drafting of counts for continuous offences generally, see **D11.29**). It is, therefore, proper to indict for the handling of a total amount of money if the evidence does not precisely disclose the date or amount of each dishonest transaction but the transactions are so closely linked as to be, in effect, a continuous transaction (*Cain* [1983] Crim LR 802). However, if D is charged with handling items of property which are clearly the proceeds of different thefts, burglaries or robberies, and which are received or dealt with on separate occasions, there should be a separate count of handling for each occasion (*Smythe* (1980) 72 Cr App R 8).

Theft Act 1968, s. 27

(1) Any number of persons may be charged in one indictment, with reference to the same theft, with having at different times or at the same time handled all or any of the stolen goods, and the persons so charged may be tried together.
(2) On the trial of two or more persons indicted for jointly handling any stolen goods the jury may find any of the accused guilty if the jury are satisfied that he handled all or any of the stolen goods, whether or not he did so jointly with the other accused or any of them.

The TA 1968, s. 27(2), arguably goes further than the general rule, established in *DPP v Merriman* [1973] AC 584, that a person jointly indicted for an offence may be convicted of committing it independently of the others. The TA 1968, s. 27(2), also covers cases in which two co-accused handle goods on separate occasions (*French* [1973] Crim LR 632).

Sentencing Guidelines

B4.130 The maximum penalty is 14 years (TA 1968, s. 22(2)) on indictment; six months or a fine not exceeding the statutory maximum, or both, summarily.

When dealt with summarily, the Magistrates' Courts Guidelines (2004) indicate the following for a first-time offender pleading not guilty:

> **Aggravating Factors** For example high level of profit accruing to handler; high value (including sentimental) of goods; provision by handler of regular outlet for stolen goods; proximity of the handler to the primary offence; seriousness of the primary offence; sophistication; the particular facts, e.g., the goods handled were the proceeds of a domestic burglary; threats of violence or abuse of power by handler in order to obtain goods; offence committed on bail; relevant previous convictions and any failures to respond to previous sentences
>
> **Mitigating Factors** For example isolated offence; little or no benefit accruing to handler; low monetary value of goods
>
> *Guideline*: Is it serious enough for a community penalty?

In *Webbe* [2002] 1 Cr App R (S) 82, the Court of Appeal issued sentencing guidelines for this offence, based upon a proposal submitted by the Sentencing Advisory Panel. According to Rose LJ in that case, the relative seriousness of a particular case of handling depends upon the interplay of a number of different factors. One important issue is whether the handler has had advance knowledge of the original offence (or has directly or indirectly made known his willingness to receive the proceeds of the original offence), as compared with a handler who has had no connection with the original offence but who has dishonestly accepted the stolen goods at an undervalue. Where the handler has had knowledge of the original offence, the seriousness of the handling is inevitably linked to the seriousness of the original offence. The replacement value of the goods is often a helpful indication of the seriousness of the offence, but monetary value in itself should not be regarded as the determining factor. Features to be taken as aggravating the offence of handling are (i) the physical or temporal closeness of the handler to the primary offence; (ii) particular seriousness in the primary offence; (iii) high value of the goods to the loser, including sentimental value; (iv) the fact that the goods were the proceeds of a domestic burglary; (v) sophistication in relation to the handling; (vi) a high level of profit made or expected by the handler; (vii) the provision by the handler of a regular outlet for stolen goods; (viii) threats of violence or abuse of power by the handler over others (for example an adult commissioning criminal activity by children or a drug dealer pressurising addicts to steal in order to pay for their habit); and (ix) the commission of the offence while on bail. Relevant mitigating factors include (i) low monetary value of the goods; (ii) the fact that the offence was a one-off offence, committed by an otherwise honest offender; (iii) the fact that there is little or no benefit to the offender; and (iv) voluntary restitution to the victim.

Where the property handled is of low monetary value (less than £1,000) and was acquired for the receiver's own use, the starting point should generally be a moderate fine or, in some cases (particularly if a fine cannot be paid by a particular defendant), a discharge. Such an outcome would be appropriate in relation to someone of previous good character handling low value domestic goods for his own use. Irrespective of value, the presence of any one of the aggravating features referred to above is likely to result in a community sentence. A community sentence may be appropriate where property worth less than £1,000 is acquired for resale or where more valuable goods are acquired for the handler's own use. Such a sentence may well be appropriate in relation to a young offender with little criminal experience, playing a peripheral role. But adult offenders with a record of dishonesty are likely to attract a custodial sentence. An offender with either a record of offences for dishonesty or who engages in sophisticated law-breaking will attract a custodial sentence. When fixing the length of that sentence, the aggravating and mitigating features referred to above will come into play, as will the personal mitigation of the offender, who may (in accordance with *Ollerenshaw* [1999] 1

Cr App R (S) 65) be dealt with by a somewhat shorter sentence than might, at first blush, otherwise have seemed appropriate.

In more serious cases of handling, factors to be taken into consideration will include whether an offence is committed in the context of a business, whether the offender is acting as an organiser or distributor of the proceeds of crime and whether the offender has made himself available to other criminals as willing to handle the proceeds of thefts or burglaries. According to these and other circumstances, sentences in the range of 12 months to four years are likely to be appropriate if the value of the goods involved is up to around £100,000. Where the value of the goods is in excess of that figure, or where the offence is highly organised and bears the hallmarks of a professional commercial operation, a sentence of four years and upwards is likely to be appropriate, and it will be higher where the source of the handled property is known by the handler to be a serious violent offence such as armed robbery.

Meaning of 'Goods', 'Stolen Goods', 'Theft' etc.

B4.131 Sections 22 to 24 of the TA 1968 deal with what are referred to therein as 'stolen goods' but the combined effect of ss. 24 and 34(2)(b) ensures that the provisions apply to a wider range of property than the ordinary meaning of that term might suggest.

Theft Act 1968, s. 34(2)(b)

'goods', except insofar as the context otherwise requires, includes money and every other description of property except land, and includes things severed from the land by stealing.

A credit balance in a bank account might be regarded as stolen goods if it directly or indirectly represents the proceeds of theft etc. (s. 24(2); *Forsyth* [1997] 2 Cr App R 299: but see **B4.148**). As to things severed from land, see **B4.12**.

The concept of stolen goods has an extended meaning by statute.

Theft Act 1968, ss. 24 and 24A

24.—(1) The provisions of this Act relating to goods which have been stolen shall apply whether the stealing occurred in England or Wales or elsewhere, and whether it occurred before or after the commencement of this Act, provided that the stealing (if not an offence under this Act) amounted to an offence where and at the time when the goods were stolen; and references to stolen goods shall be construed accordingly.

(2) For purposes of those provisions references to stolen goods shall include, in addition to the goods originally stolen and parts of them (whether in their original state or not),—

(a) any other goods which directly or indirectly represent or have at any time represented the stolen goods in the hands of the thief as being the proceeds of any disposal or realisation of the whole or part of the goods stolen or of goods so representing the stolen goods; and

(b) any other goods which directly or indirectly represent or have at any time represented the stolen goods in the hands of a handler of the stolen goods or any part of them as being the proceeds of any disposal or realisation of the whole or part of the stolen goods handled by him or of goods so representing them.

(3) But no goods shall be regarded as having continued to be stolen goods after they have been restored to the person from whom they were stolen or to other lawful possession or custody, or after that person and any other person claiming through him have otherwise ceased as regards those goods to have any right to restitution in respect of the theft.

(4) For purposes of the provisions of this Act relating to goods which have been stolen (including subsections (1) to (3) above) goods obtained in England or Wales or elsewhere either by blackmail or, subject to subsection (5) below, by fraud (within the meaning of the Fraud Act 2006) shall be regarded as stolen; and 'steal', 'theft' and 'thief' shall be construed accordingly.

(5) Subsection (1) above applies in relation to goods obtained by fraud as if—

(a) the reference to the commencement of this Act were a reference to the commencement of the Fraud Act 2006, and

(b) the reference to an offence under this Act were a reference to an offence under section 1 of that Act.

24A.—(8) References to stolen goods include money which is dishonestly withdrawn from an account to which a wrongful credit has been made, but only to the extent that the money derives from the credit.

Section 24 is printed here as amended by the Fraud Act 2006, but the amendments (which include substituting in s. 24(4) a reference to fraud in place of the original reference to the TA 1968, s. 15) does not affect the operation of s. 24 in relation to goods obtained in the circumstances described in s. 15(1) where the obtaining is the result of a deception made before 15 January 2007 (Fraud Act 2006, sch. 2, para. 4).

If the property in question appears to represent the proceeds of an offence that falls outside the scope of the TA 1968, s. 24 or s. 24A(8) it may be possible to consider charges under the 'money laundering' provisions (as to which, see **B22**). These provisions overlap significantly with the offence of handling, and, even where the goods concerned are stolen, the prosecution may in some cases find it easier to charge one or more of the offences they create in preference to handling. As to the handling of dishonestly obtained money transfers, see the TA 1968, s. 24A, discussed at **B4.145** ***et seq.***

Goods Obtained by Blackmail or Fraud The TA 1968, s. 24(4) governs s. 24(1) to (3) and extends the meaning of 'stolen goods' to cover the fruits or proceeds of fraud offences and offences under s. 21 (blackmail). No mention of burglary or robbery is needed, because any property obtained by such means must necessarily have been obtained by theft. **B4.132**

Goods Stolen outside England and Wales TA 1968 offences (other than theft of mails under s. 14 and offences on British ships etc.) do not ordinarily apply to conduct taking place outside England or Wales (see generally **B4.45** and **A8**) but s. 24(1), read in conjunction with s. 24(4), ensures that property obtained outside the jurisdiction, by what would in England have been regarded as theft, blackmail or fraud, will be regarded as stolen property within the jurisdiction if either: **B4.133**

(a) the stealing etc. was (exceptionally) punishable as an extraterritorial offence under English law (for example, where the thief was a British citizen aboard a foreign ship to which he did not belong: Merchant Shipping Act 1995, s. 281); or
(b) the stealing was punishable under the law then in force where it took place.

Thus, if a thief stole property in Spain, and D received it (or its proceeds) in England, knowing of the circumstances, D may be guilty of handling under s. 22, but it must be proved that the conduct of the thief was, at the time of the theft, punishable under Spanish law. It is not possible to rely on any presumption that foreign law will be similar to English law, nor can judicial notice be taken of foreign law for such a purpose (*Ofori* (1994) 99 Cr App R 223). See also **F10.16** for the general rules on evidence of foreign law.

Fruits and Proceeds of Stolen Goods Although wide-ranging, the TA 1968, s. 24(2), is significantly narrower than the corresponding provision in the Larceny Act 1916, which it replaced. The old law failed to distinguish between the proceeds of stolen goods in the hands of a thief or receiver of stolen goods, and such proceeds in the hands of an innocent person. Thus, anything purchased with, or exchanged for, stolen goods or the proceeds thereof would itself become categorised as stolen goods, even if it had never itself been possessed by either the thief or a receiver. In theory, the potential spread of the contagion was almost limitless. **B4.134**

The present position is that property is categorised as stolen only if it is the original property stolen, or something that has at some time represented the proceeds thereof in the hands of the original thief or of a dishonest handler. For example, if a person innocently acquires a stolen bicycle and then (still innocently) part-exchanges it for a new one, the new cycle cannot be categorised as stolen goods; but it would be otherwise if he knew the original one was stolen.

It may be difficult to determine whether property subsequently acquired by the thief or by an alleged handler represents the proceeds of a disposal of the original stolen goods. Classification may be particularly problematic where bank accounts are involved. A thief (A) may for example pay into his account both legitimately obtained moneys (such as his salary) and the proceeds of his thefts. He may then buy goods with funds drawn from that account, or arrange for funds to be transferred to other accounts. In *A-G's Ref (No. 4 of 1979)* [1981] 1 WLR 667, the Court of Appeal held in such a case that any credit balance in A's account constitutes, in part, stolen goods and that funds withdrawn from that account by A may also constitute stolen goods, to the extent that they derive from the original theft, etc. If the withdrawal involves a sum greater than the amount covered by 'legitimate' funds in the account, it must necessarily represent (at least in part) the proceeds of theft; but in other cases, it must be proved that A intended the withdrawal to represent such proceeds, as where his intention is to settle up with an accomplice to whom he 'owes' part of the proceeds. Note that it is A's intention which matters. The recipient's belief that this is what the withdrawal represents cannot suffice (*ibid.*).

If A withdraws money (i.e. cash) from his account, and hands this to B as B's share of the proceeds of theft, B undoubtedly receives stolen goods (TA 1968, s. 24A(8): see **B4.131**). If, however, A arranges for funds to be transferred from his account to an account operated by B, then, for reasons which are explained in **B4.148**, B cannot be guilty of handling the chose in action thereby created in his favour. The proper charge would be one of dishonestly retaining a wrongful credit, contrary to the TA 1968, s. 24A (see **B4.145** ***et seq.***) or one of knowingly acquiring or possessing the proceeds of criminal conduct, contrary to the PCA 2002, s. 329 (see **B4.150** and **B22.12**).

B4.135 **Goods Restored to Owner etc.** As to what amounts to restoration to lawful possession, see *Haughton v Smith* [1975] AC 476 and *A-G's Ref (No. 1 of 1974)* [1974] QB 744. In the latter case, a police officer immobilised a parked car he suspected to contain stolen goods, and apprehended D when he attempted to start it. The question arose whether D could be guilty of handling at the time of his arrest, or whether the goods had already been taken into lawful police custody. It was held by the Court of Appeal that, if the police officer had already resolved to prevent the removal of the goods under any circumstances, they would indeed have ceased to be stolen; but if he had remained in doubt, and had resolved only to seek a satisfactory explanation before deciding whether or not to take charge of them, then they would remain stolen.

On somewhat different facts, it was held in *Metropolitan Police Commissioner v Streeter* (1980) 71 Cr App R 113 that stolen goods were not taken into lawful custody merely because they had been marked for later identification and followed in the thief's possession to a rendezvous with the handler.

If there is any doubt about the status of such property when received, it may sometimes be desirable to charge theft (since receiving will usually amount to appropriation of property belonging to another), or it may be easier to prove that D arranged to receive the goods before they ceased to be stolen. Other possibilities are attempt (now that *Haughton v Smith* is no longer good law) and conspiracy.

'Loss of right to restitution' is a matter determined by the civil law. Briefly, this right will be lost where a stolen cheque or other negotiable instrument is acquired by a person who can establish title to it as a holder in due course (see Bills of Exchange Act 1882, s. 29). See also the Factors Act 1889, s. 2 (theft by mercantile agent and sale to bona fide purchaser) and the Hire Purchase Act 1964, s. 27.

Goods which are 'stolen' in the sense of being the proceeds of deception, rather than theft, may have become in law the property of the obtainer, albeit subject to the victim's right to rescind for fraud. In such a case, any bona fide purchaser may acquire good title to them (Sale of Goods Act 1979, s. 23). Property obtained by blackmail will sometimes give the blackmailer voidable title (as with deception); but since some kinds of blackmail are analogous to robbery, there will be cases in which no title passes, because the victim never 'consented' to parting with it. Loss to right to restitution of the original property need not usually prevent any proceeds from continuing to be classed as stolen goods.

Actus Reus: Goods must be Stolen

However dishonest D may be, there can be no offence of handling stolen goods unless the goods in question were in fact stolen goods at the time of the alleged handling. See **B4.140**. However, a person who has done an act which would be a sufficient act of handling, intended to handle, was dishonest and believed the goods to be stolen will be liable for an attempt to handle if the goods were not stolen (Criminal Attempts Act 1981, s. 1(2) and (3); *Shivpuri* [1987] AC 1; see generally **A6.40**). The cases of *Haughton v Smith* [1975] AC 476 and *Anderton v Ryan* [1985] AC 560, which were formerly authority for the contrary proposition, are no longer good law. **B4.136**

Proof that handled goods were stolen may be facilitated by the TA 1968, s. 27(4), which provides for the use, in theft or handling cases, of statutory declarations by witnesses to loss of goods in transit where D is notified and does not require personal attendance of the witnesses.

Theft Act 1968, s. 27

(4) In any proceedings for the theft of anything in the course of transmission (whether by post or otherwise), or for handling stolen goods from such a theft, a statutory declaration made by any person that he dispatched or received or failed to receive any goods or postal packet, or that any goods or postal packet when dispatched or received by him were in a particular state or condition, shall be admissible as evidence of the facts stated in the declaration, subject to the following conditions:—

(a) a statutory declaration shall only be admissible where and to the extent to which oral evidence to the like effect would have been admissible in the proceedings; and

(b) a statutory declaration shall only be admissible if at least seven days before the hearing or trial a copy of it has been given to the person charged, and he has not, at least three days before the hearing or trial or within such further time as the court may in special circumstances allow, given the prosecutor written notice requiring the attendance at the hearing or trial of the person making the declaration.

(4A) Where the proceedings mentioned in subsection (4) above are proceedings before a magistrates' court inquiring into an offence as examining justices that subsection shall have effect with the omission of the words from 'subject to the following conditions' to the end of the subsection.

(5) This section is to be construed in accordance with section 24 of this Act; and in subsection (3)(b) above the reference to handling stolen goods shall include any corresponding offence committed before the commencement of this Act.

Actus Reus: The Forms of Handling

The TA 1968, s. 22, must be read in conjunction with s. 24 (see **B4.131**). The term 'handling' is a form of shorthand embracing the several forms of dealing in the property specified in s. 22(1). In *Bloxham* [1983] 1 AC 109, Lord Bridge of Harwich stated, *obiter*, that s. 22 creates two distinct offences: receiving (or arranging to receive) being one and the various other forms being different variants of the other; but as most commentators have been quick to point out, this is, strictly speaking, incorrect. There is only one offence (*Griffiths v Freeman* [1970] 1 WLR 659), and an indictment alleging 'handling' without specifying the form is not therefore bad for duplicity (*Nicklin* [1977] 1 WLR 403). On the other hand, Lord Bridge's dictum has been accepted as a good indication of proper practice. An indictment **B4.137** should indicate which of the two main forms of handling is alleged, and if both are alleged there should be separate counts. A person cannot be accused of one and convicted on the basis of the other (*Nicklin*).

Except in cases of receiving or arranging to receive, it must be both alleged and proved that D assisted, or acted for the benefit of, another person: this is the main difference between receiving etc. and the other variants of the offence.

Receiving and Arranging to Receive

B4.138 The TA 1968 does not define 'receiving', but cases on receiving decided under the Larceny Act 1916, s. 33, defined it as involving the taking of possession or control of property, either jointly, or exclusively (*Frost* (1964) 48 Cr App R 284). Possession does not necessarily require physical handling, nor indeed would such handling suffice in the absence of any intent to possess or control the goods (*Hobson v Impett* (1957) 41 Cr App R 138). It is sufficient that the goods were handled by D's agents on his behalf (*Miller* (1854) 6 Cox CC 353). Things in action, which are not capable of physical handling, can certainly be received, as where the proceeds of a stolen cheque are credited to a bank account.

Arranging to receive is a substantive offence which may consist of the kind of preparatory arrangements that would fall short of constituting an attempt to receive, or of arrangements with an innocent party, so that there would be no conspiracy. It is not enough, however, for arrangements to be made for receipt of goods that have yet to be stolen. This might be conspiracy to steal and to handle stolen goods, but cannot be a full s. 22 offence (*Park* (1987) 87 Cr App R 164).

Undertaking or Assisting in Retention, Removal, Disposal or Realisation by or for the Benefit of Another Person

B4.139 In *Bloxham* [1983] 1 AC 109, D innocently purchased a car which he later came to realise must have been stolen. He sold it to an unidentified person at a knockdown price, and it was alleged that this amounted to realisation for the benefit of that unidentified purchaser. The House of Lords disagreed, on the basis that the sale (realisation) was for the benefit of D himself, and Lord Bridge of Harwich added (at pp. 113–14):

> The offence can be committed in relation to any one of [four named] activities in one or other of two ways. First, the offender may himself undertake the activity *for the benefit of* another person. Secondly, the activity may be undertaken *by* another person and the offender may assist him . . . the category of other persons contemplated by the subsection is subject to the same limitations in whichever way the offence is committed. Accordingly, a purchaser, as such, of stolen goods, cannot . . . be 'another person' within the subsection, since his act of purchase could not sensibly be described as a disposal or realisation of the stolen goods *by* him . . . therefore, even if the sale to him could be described as a disposal or realisation for his benefit, the transaction is not . . . within the ambit of the subsection.

See also *Gingell* (1999) 163 JP 648 and *Tokeley-Parry* [1999] Crim LR 578.

Assisting in the retention of stolen goods requires active assistance to be given to the other person. Accommodating or banking the stolen property would suffice (*Pitchley* (1972) 57 Cr App R 30); but mere failure to cooperate with the police during a search for stolen goods would not (*Brown* [1970] 1 QB 105). It is not necessary that the assistance should be successful; an attempt to deceive the police during such a search will amount to the complete offence under the TA 1968, s. 22 (*Kanwar* [1982] 1 WLR 845).

Disposing of or assisting in the disposal or realisation of stolen goods typically means moving the property from one place to another or converting it from one form into another (*Forsyth* [1997] 2 Cr App R 299 at p. 317). This may be a continuing offence and may be committed in England even where much of the relevant conduct occurs abroad (*Forsyth*). Because handling is a group A offence for the purposes of the CJA 1993, part III, it would now suffice for any 'relevant event' to occur within the jurisdiction. Cases of 'money laundering', in which arrangements are made for the transfer, concealment or investment, etc., of criminal property (including stolen goods) may also involve offences under the Proceeds of Crime Act 2002, ss. 327 to 329. Such offences will in many cases be easier to prove than handling, and carry the same maximum penalties: see **B22.15**.

Relationship between Handling and other Offences

The TA 1968, s. 22, stipulates that the offence of handling may only be committed 'otherwise than in the course of the stealing'. The stealing referred to is the crime whereby the goods become 'stolen' in the first place. (This may, under s. 24(4), take the form of blackmail or fraud: see **B4.132**). The stipulation prevents thieves or blackmailers etc. becoming handlers whilst still participating in the original offence, which may take the form of a continuous or on-going series of acts (see **B4.128**). Where, for example, burglar A passes the items he steals to his accomplice, burglar B, who carries them to the get-away car, B might otherwise become a handler through 'receiving' stolen goods. It may therefore be necessary for the prosecution to prove, in appropriate cases, that the stealing had been completed prior to the alleged act of handling and was not still in progress at the time. This was the issue in *Pitham* (1976) 65 Cr App R 45, where the appellants were invited by one M to pay him for furniture belonging to another man, who was in prison at the time. They agreed a price with M and removed the furniture, and were indicted on those facts with alternative counts of burglary and handling. (As to the joinder of 'mutually destructive' counts within a single indictment, see *Bellman* [1989] AC 836 and **D11.59**.) They were convicted of handling and their convictions were upheld on appeal; Lawton LJ took the view that the jury were fully justified in finding that the appellants had dealt with the furniture only after M had stolen it by assuming the right to dispose of it. They had either helped M to steal the goods or M had stolen them and got rid of them by sale to the appellants; but the jury had, by their verdict, rejected the former possibility. **B4.140**

The prosecution need not affirmatively prove every alleged handler to be innocent of the original theft, blackmail or deception. The courts have refused to place such a burden on the prosecution where there is no evidence to suggest that D was anything other than a handler (*Cash* [1985] QB 801). Problems may however arise where the evidence is ambiguous, as where property that has been stolen in a burglary is discovered a day later, hidden in D's attic. Under the doctrine of recent possession (see **F3.50**), the court or jury may legitimately infer, in the absence of any alternative explanation, that D must either have been the burglar or have dishonestly received the property knowing it to be stolen; but unless there is some further evidence to indicate which of the two offences D committed, it would appear to be impossible for them to draw one inference rather than the other.

The problem in such cases would not be solved merely by treating the words 'otherwise than in the course of the stealing' as a proviso or qualification to the general words of s. 22, and thus as a matter to be raised and proved by the defence under the rule as to the burden of proof which was affirmed by the House of Lords in *Hunt* [1987] AC 352 (see **F3.12**). The prosecution would still have to prove that D 'received the goods, knowing or believing them to be stolen', D would not have done so if he had appropriated them as the original burglar. Nor is it permissible for the court or jury to convict D of whichever offence appears, on balance, to be the more likely possibility. They must be sure that D is guilty of the specific offence of which they convict him (*A-G of Hong Kong v Yip Kai-foon* [1988] AC 642; cf. *Bellman* [1989] AC 836, per Lord Griffiths at p. 838).

It does not follow that D must be acquitted in such circumstances. The courts have recognised two possible solutions to the problem, each of which enables a conviction to be recorded. The first, and preferable, solution is for the prosecution to compromise by seeking

B

Part B Offences

a conviction for theft. Although a thief or burglar cannot become guilty of handling in the course of the original stealing, the offences of theft and handling are not mutually exclusive. Receiving property stolen or obtained in an earlier, completed theft must invariably involve a further appropriation of it, and it follows that a dishonest receiver of such goods must be a thief as well (*Stapylton v O'Callaghan* [1973] 2 All ER 782). It is accordingly open to the prosecution to include within the indictment a count for theft, drawn sufficiently widely to cover an appropriation of the property on any date between that of the original theft or burglary etc. and the date on which the property was found in D's possession (*More* [1987] 1 WLR 1578). This count may be additional to more specific counts, such as for handling or burglary, or it may stand alone; but the prosecution should in either case be able to prove that D stole the property at some point, and it need not matter if they cannot prove whether it was theft by burglary or theft by receiving (*Shelton* (1986) 83 Cr App R 379).

In *Shelton* the Court of Appeal offered the following advice (at pp. 384–5).

> As we have been asked by counsel to do so, for the guidance of judges and counsel we make the following comments. First that the long established practice of charging theft and handling as alternatives should continue whenever there is a real possibility, not a fanciful one, that at trial the evidence might support one rather than the other. Secondly, that there is a danger that juries may be confused by reference to second or later appropriations since the issue in every case is whether the defendant has in fact appropriated property belonging to another. If he has done so, it is irrelevant how he came to make the appropriation provided it was in the course of theft. Thirdly, that a jury should be told that a handler can be a thief, but he cannot be convicted of being both a thief and a handler. Fourthly, that handling is the more serious offence, carrying a heavier penalty because those who knowingly have dealings with thieves encourage stealing. Fifthly, in the unlikely event of the jury not agreeing amongst themselves whether theft or handling has been proved, they should be discharged. Finally, and perhaps most importantly, both judges and counsel when directing and addressing juries should avoid intellectual subtleties which some jurors may have difficulty in grasping; the golden rule should be 'Keep it short and simple'.

The second possible solution to the problem has the support of the Privy Council in *A-G of Hong Kong v Yip Kai-foon* [1988] AC 642 and that of the Court of Appeal in *Foreman* [1991] Crim LR 702, but is, with respect, based on doubtful logic. In *Yip Kai-foon*, the Privy Council took the view that, where the evidence was equally consistent with robbery or handling, and the jury was accordingly unable to convict D of robbery, it would then be open to them to rely upon his 'innocence' of that offence as proof that he must have committed handling. This is objectionable, in that it can lead to a conviction for handling being recorded when the jury think it more likely that D committed robbery, burglary or simple theft (see Sir John Smith's commentary on *Ryan v DPP* [1994] Crim LR 457). It is accordingly submitted that a widely drawn count for theft offers a more logical solution to cases in which it is unclear how D acquired the stolen property.

A third possible solution would be for charges to be laid instead under part 7 of the Proceeds of Crime Act 2002. Section 327 of that Act (see **B22.5**) creates offences of concealing, disguising, converting or transferring abroad 'criminal property' (as defined in s. 340). Section 329 (see **B22.12**) creates offences of acquiring, using or possessing such property. This includes property that directly or indirectly represents any person's benefit from criminal conduct (including D's own conduct). Dishonesty need not be proved, and mere suspicion as to the provenance of the property may suffice. If misused, charges of this kind could enable lazy prosecutors to sidestep the basic *mens rea* requirements of the TA 1968, and it is submitted that the courts should discourage any such practice. As to the overlap between these offences and handling stolen goods, see *Wilkinson v DPP* [2006] EWHC 3012 (Admin) and **B22.15**.

Mens Rea: Dishonesty

Dishonesty must bear the same meaning as it does in fraud or deception cases and (save for the fact that the TA 1968, s. 2, is not directly applicable) in theft. In other words, it is dishonesty in the *Ghosh* sense (*Ghosh* [1982] QB 1053, see **B4.37**). As to the possible relationship between knowledge and dishonesty, see **B4.142**. **B4.141**

Mens Rea: Knowledge or Belief that the Goods are Stolen

On a charge of handling stolen goods, it must be proved that D actually knew that the goods were stolen, or correctly believed that they were. This knowledge or belief must correspond in time with the *actus reus* (*Williams* [1994] Crim LR 934). In cases of handling by receiving, this means the moment of receipt or acquisition. If D only later becomes aware that the goods are stolen, this will not suffice, even if his retention of them is clearly dishonest (*Brook* [1993] Crim LR 455). On the other hand, dishonest retention in such circumstances may sometimes amount to theft (subject to the TA 1968, s. 3(2), which precludes such liability in cases where the property was acquired bona fide and for value); or it may amount to an offence under the Proceeds of Crime Act 2002, s. 329 (see **B22.12**). **B4.142**

Knowledge of the circumstances which make the goods stolen will generally suffice for liability in cases of alleged handling whether or not D appreciated the legal consequences of those circumstances. An accused's belief that the proceeds of blackmail are something different from stolen goods will accordingly be no defence. Nor should it be any defence for an accused to argue that he believed the goods to be the proceeds of theft, when they are in fact the proceeds of blackmail or deception. In either event, the goods are stolen, and his belief is not incorrect in any material sense.

Another immaterial error would be one about the precise identity of the goods. It would be no defence for an accused to argue that he thought a container held stolen whisky, when in fact it contained stolen cigars (*McCullum* (1973) 57 Cr App R 645).

An accused's ignorance of the law may prevent him from being considered dishonest. For example, a person may know that certain property indirectly represents the proceeds of the sale, by a thief or handler, of the original stolen goods, but may not realise that these proceeds are accordingly 'stolen goods' within the meaning of the TA 1968, s. 24. Not realising the legal position, he is perhaps unlikely to realise that his handling of them would be considered dishonest according to the standards of reasonable and honest people.

Belief that goods are stolen is an alternative *mens rea* to knowledge of that fact. It is not of course an alternative to the goods actually *being* stolen (*Haughton v Smith* [1975] AC 485 at p. 503). If the goods are not in fact stolen, there may be an attempt to handle stolen goods (see **B4.136**) or he may actually steal them himself, but he cannot be guilty of handling.

The distinction between knowledge and belief is not crucial in this context, since either state of mind may suffice for liability. In *Hall* (1985) 81 Cr App R 260, the Court of Appeal nevertheless attempted to distinguish between the two concepts. The court suggested that a person 'knows' that goods are stolen if someone with first-hand knowledge (such as the thief) has told him so; whereas he 'believes' that fact if he does not know it for certain, but realises that there is no other reasonable conclusion to be drawn in the light of all the circumstances. With respect, however, a person cannot properly be said to 'know' a fact merely because someone else has told him about it. He can only know a fact (or indeed testify as to such a fact at a criminal trial) if he himself has first-hand knowledge of it, as for example where he personally witnesses the theft taking place or where he positively identifies property which he knows to have been stolen (cf. *Overington* [1978] Crim LR 692; *Hulbert* (1979) 69 Cr App R 243). Failing this, he can at most 'believe' the goods to be stolen.

The critical distinction in handling cases is that between knowledge or belief, on the one hand, and suspicion, on the other, because it has been held on many occasions that suspicion, even grave suspicion accompanied by dishonesty and a wilful failure to make reasonable enquiries, cannot suffice for liability (*Griffiths* (1974) 60 Cr App R 14; *Pethick* [1980] Crim LR 242; *Moys* (1984) 79 Cr App R 72; *Forsyth* [1997] 2 Cr App R 299). The Court of Appeal in *Hall* suggested that a person may believe goods to be stolen where he 'refuses to believe what his brain tells him is obvious', but this suggestion has rightly been rejected as potentially confusing (*Forsyth*). A person cannot sensibly be said to believe what he refuses to believe, and the test must be a subjective one, rather than an objective test based on what D ought to have realised. In *Forsyth*, the Court of Appeal defined belief as 'the mental acceptance of a fact as true or existing', and suggested that juries might be directed in the following terms, as previously suggested by Lord Lane CJ in *Moys*:

> . . . it must be proved that the defendant was aware of the theft or that he believed the goods to be stolen. Suspicion that they were stolen, even coupled with the fact that he shut his eyes to the circumstances, is not enough, although these matters may be taken into account . . . in deciding whether or not the necessary knowledge or belief existed.

This is certainly preferable to the definition attempted in *Hall*, but the definition of belief remains imprecise. Does belief on balance of probabilities suffice, or must D have felt sure of it, beyond reasonable doubt? In *Forsyth*, the Court of Appeal merely observed, rather unhelpfully, that 'between suspicion and belief there may be a range of awareness' and it would therefore be safer to assume that the stricter concept of belief applies. In other words, a person believes that goods are stolen only if he harbours no serious or substantial doubt as to that fact.

A person who deals with goods that he suspects *may* be stolen and who deliberately 'asks no questions' might perhaps be considered dishonest, but is not guilty of handling. Dealers in second-hand goods know that from time to time they may be offered goods which turn out to be stolen, but cannot cross-examine their suppliers every time they buy. On the other hand, a person who has already concluded that the goods he is being offered *must* be stolen (for example, because he notices that the serial number has been removed from the car stereo he is being offered for a knock-down price) cannot set up his failure to ask questions as a defence. He is in fact only pretending to be blind to the truth. See *Griffiths* (1974) 60 Cr App R 14. See also **F3.50**.

Previous Convictions as Evidence of *Mens Rea*

B4.143 On a charge of handling, the TA 1968, s. 27(3) (which remains in force despite the enactment of the 'bad character' provisions of the CJA 2003), makes evidence of D's previous convictions for theft or handling, or of D's previous dealings in stolen goods, admissible in certain circumstances for the limited purpose of proving his knowledge or belief that the goods were stolen on the present occasion. Section 27(3), and its relationship to the regime laid down by the CJA 2003, is examined at **F12.48** ***et seq***.

Effect of Conviction or Acquittal of the Alleged Thief

B4.144 A conviction for handling stolen goods does not depend on the conviction of the alleged thief (or blackmailer etc.), nor is it even necessary to identify him in every case. It follows that there is nothing necessarily inconsistent in the acquittal of the alleged thief and the conviction at the same trial of the alleged handler. It may be, for example, that the handler is convicted on the basis of a confession that is not admissible against his co-accused. On the other hand, acquittal of the alleged thief could sometimes be inconsistent with conviction of the handler at the same trial. The tribunal of fact must be satisfied that the goods are stolen, and this would not, for example, be consistent with acquittal of a child who is alleged to have been the thief, but who is found to be under the age of criminal responsibility (cf. *Walters v Lunt* [1951] 2 All ER 645).

At the trial of a person for handling stolen goods, conviction by a court in, or by a Service court outside, the UK of another person for stealing those goods is admissible evidence that that person did commit the theft. If the alleged handler wishes to argue that the goods were not stolen, he will have to prove it on balance of probabilities (PACE 1984, s. 74; see *Barnes* [1991] Crim LR 132 and **F11.3**). Conviction of the alleged thief by a foreign court is not, however, admissible as evidence that he committed the theft. This may hamper the use of the TA 1968, s. 24(1) (see **B4.131**), somewhat, although it does not preclude expert evidence that an act would have been an offence under foreign law.

DISHONESTLY RETAINING A WRONGFUL CREDIT

Definition

Theft Act 1968, s. 24A **B4.145**

(1) A person is guilty of an offence if—
 (a) a wrongful credit has been made to an account kept by him or in respect of which he has any right or interest;
 (b) he knows or believes that the credit is wrongful; and
 (c) he dishonestly fails to take such steps as are reasonable in the circumstances to secure that the credit is cancelled.

(2) References to a credit are to a credit of an amount of money.

(2A) A credit to an account is wrongful to the extent that it derives from—
 (a) theft;
 (b) blackmail; or
 (c) fraud (contrary to the Fraud Act 2006); or
 (d) stolen goods.

(3) and (4) [Repealed.]

(5) In determining whether a credit to an account is wrongful, it is immaterial (in particular) whether the account is overdrawn before or after the credit is made.

(6) A person guilty of an offence under this section shall be liable on conviction on indictment to imprisonment for a term not exceeding ten years.

(7) Subsection (8) below applies for purposes of provisions of this Act relating to stolen goods (including subsection (2A) above).

(8) References to stolen goods include money which is dishonestly withdrawn from an account to which a wrongful credit has been made, but only to the extent that the money derives from the credit.

(9) 'Account' means an account kept with—
 (a) a bank;
 (b) a person carrying on a business which falls within subsection (10) below; or
 (c) an issuer of electronic money (as defined for the purposes of Part 2 of the Financial Services and Markets Act 2000).

(10) A business falls within this subsection if—
 (a) in the course of the business money received by way of deposit is lent to others; or
 (b) any other activity of the business is financed, wholly or to any material extent, out of the capital of or the interest on money received by way of deposit.

(11) References in subsection (10) above to a deposit must be read with—
 (a) section 22 of the Financial Services and Markets Act 2000;
 (b) any relevant order under that section; and
 (c) Schedule 2 to that Act;

but any restriction on the meaning of deposit which arises from the identity of the person making it is to be disregarded.

(12) For the purposes of subsection (10) above—
 (a) all the activities which a person carries on by way of business shall be regarded as a single business carried on by him; and
 (b) 'money' includes money expressed in a currency other than sterling

Section 24A is shown as amended by the Fraud Act 2006, sch. 1, para. 7; but these amendments do not affect the operation of the TA 1968, s. 24A in relation to credits falling within s. 24A(3) or (4) and made before 15 January 2007 (see the Fraud Act 2006, sch. 2, para. 5). This means that s. 24A will continue to apply where a credit represents or is derived from a money transfer obtained before that date, contrary to the TA 1968, s. 15A. See **B4.148**.

Procedure and Sentence

B4.146 An offence under s. 24A is triable either way (MCA 1980, s. 17 and sch. 1, para. 28). When tried on indictment, it is a class 3 offence. It is a Group A offence for jurisdiction purposes under the CJA 1993, part I (see **A8.4**).

The maximum penalty is 10 years (TA 1968, s. 24A(6)) on indictment; six months and/or a fine not exceeding the statutory maximum on summary conviction. There are no reported sentencing guidelines for this offence.

Indictment

B4.147

Statement of Offence

Dishonestly retaining a wrongful credit, contrary to section 24A(1) of the Theft Act 1968

Particulars of Offence

A between the . . . day of . . . and the . . . day of . . . knowing or believing that a wrongful credit, namely a transfer of £20,000 obtained by B from Abbey National plc, contrary to section 1 of the Fraud Act 2006, had been made to a current account (no. . . .) kept jointly by A and B at Barclays Bank plc, dishonestly failed to take such steps as were reasonable in the circumstances to secure that the credit was cancelled

Wrongful Credits and Stolen Goods

B4.148 One (at least arguable) side-effect of the decision of the House of Lords in *Preddy* [1996] AC 815 (see **B5.17**) was that, where D dishonestly obtained a money transfer from V, the sum thereby credited to D's account could no longer be categorised as stolen goods. This indeed was the view of the Law Commission when reviewing the impact of *Preddy*. To some extent, this is now addressed by the enactment of the Fraud Act 2006 and the consequential amendment of the Theft Act 1968, s. 24, so as to classify the proceeds of fraud as stolen goods; but this assists only in respect of frauds committed on or after 15 January 2007. Furthermore, even where A pays stolen bank notes directly into his account, the proceeds of a subsequent transfer from that account to an account held by B cannot be classed as stolen goods, because any credit balance thereby created in B's account is an entirely different chose in action from the credit balance which previously represented the stolen money in A's account. B's credit balance admittedly represents the proceeds of A's original crime, but it has never done so in the hands of the original thief, and any argument that it does so in the hands of a handler of the stolen property (i.e. B) is circular, because that presupposes the very point it seeks to establish, namely that the funds in B's account are stolen goods. In *A-G's Ref (No. 4 of 1979)* [1981] 1 WLR 667, it was held that B may be guilty of handling in such circumstances; but this cannot stand with *Preddy* on that particular issue.

The TA 1968, s. 24A, addresses the problem by ensuring (originally through subss. (3) and (4) and now through subs. (2A)) that D commits an offence where he dishonestly retains a credit which he knows or correctly believes represents or is derived from theft, blackmail, s. 15A deception (prior to 15 January 2007), fraud (contrary to the Fraud Act 2006, s. 1) or stolen goods. If, for example, A pays stolen money into his account and transfers the funds from that account to an account owned by B, a wrongful credit has been made to B's account, and B may commit a s. 24A offence if he dishonestly retains it, knowing or believing it to be derived from one or other of those offences. Section 24A(8), meanwhile, provides that any *money* dishonestly withdrawn from an account to which a wrongful credit has been made can be classed as stolen goods, subject to the principles explained in **B4.134** in respect of withdrawals from accounts into which both 'clean' and 'dirty' money has been paid. It may seem strange that the proceeds of A's original theft can be classed as stolen goods when paid into A's own bank account, cease to be so classified when effectively 'transferred' to B's account, and yet revert to being stolen goods when dishonestly withdrawn as cash by B; but such is now the law.

Dishonesty, Omissions and Bona Fide Purchasers

The offence created by s. 24A(1) is one of dishonest omission. Dishonesty must bear the same meaning as in offences of handling or deception (i.e. the test set out in *Ghosh* [1982] QB 1053: see **B4.37**, **B4.141** and **B4.142**), but knowledge cannot always be equated with dishonesty. A may discover that B has caused the payment of a wrongful credit into their joint account. It may be difficult for her to insist on the cancellation of this credit, unless she is prepared to inform on B, but would a court or jury necessarily categorise her inactivity as dishonest? Similarly, although the bona fide purchaser of a credit is not exempted from liability under s. 24A where he retains the credit after belatedly discovering it to have been a wrongful one (contrast the TA 1968, s. 3(2)) it may be very difficult to persuade a jury that such a person acted dishonestly. **B4.149**

The word 'cancelled' as used in s. 24A(1)(c) means cancelling the original credit so as to achieve the same effect as if it had not been made in the first place. In many cases that will be achieved by a corresponding debit reversing the original entry in the account (*Lee* [2006] EWCA Crim 156, per Moore-Bick LJ at [24]).

Wrongful Credits and the Proceeds of Criminal Conduct

The Proceeds of Crime Act 2002, s. 327 (see **B22.5**), creates offences of concealing, disguising, converting or transferring abroad 'criminal property' (as defined in s. 340 of the Act). Section 329 (see **B22.12**) creates offences of acquiring, using or possessing such property. This includes property that directly or indirectly represents any person's benefit from criminal conduct. Dishonesty need not be proved, and mere suspicion as to the provenance of the property may suffice. These offences nevertheless carry higher maximum penalties than offences under the TA 1968, s. 24A. **B4.150**

Where a money transfer is made, e.g., from a thief's account to an account held by D, what is credited to D's account represents the benefit to the thief of his original crime, and (in contrast to the position under the TA 1968, s. 22) it does not matter for this purpose that it was never held by the thief himself. *Preddy* [1996] AC 815 does not apply to or affect the operation of money laundering offences. Since the TA 1968, s. 24A, applies only to wrongful credits made on or after 18 December 1996 (Theft (Amendment) Act 1996, s. 2(2)), whereas criminal property may, for the purposes of the 2002 Act, derive from ancient crimes, this may occasionally also be a reason for prosecutors to prefer a charge under the 2002 Act.

ADVERTISING REWARDS FOR RETURN OF GOODS STOLEN OR LOST

Definition

Theft Act 1968, s. 23 **B4.151**

> Where any public advertisement of a reward for the return of any goods which have been stolen or lost uses any words to the effect that no questions will be asked, or that the person producing the goods will be safe from apprehension or inquiry, or that any money paid for the purchase of the goods or advanced by way of loan on them will be repaid, the person advertising the reward

and any person who prints or publishes the advertisement shall on summary conviction be liable to a fine not exceeding level 3 on the standard scale.

Elements

B4.152 The TA 1968, s. 23, does not necessarily forbid the offering of rewards for the return of stolen goods, nor does it necessarily prohibit advertisements promising that 'no questions will be asked'. What it prohibits are public advertisements which *combine* an offer of a reward with a promise that no questions will be asked or that immunity will be granted. It does not matter if the advertiser is uncertain whether the goods were lost or stolen; he may even be confident that they were only lost.

The printing or publishing of an offending advertisement is an offence of strict liability (*Denham v Scott* (1984) 77 Cr App R 210).

For the meaning of 'goods', 'stolen goods', 'theft' etc., see **B4.131**.

UNLAWFUL DEALING IN CULTURAL OBJECTS

B4.153 The Dealing in Cultural Objects (Offences) Act 2003, s. 1, creates an offence of acquiring, disposing of, importing or exporting tainted cultural objects, or agreeing or arranging to do so.

By ss. 1 and 2 of the Act, a 'tainted cultural object' is one that has been criminally removed from a building or structure of historical, architectural or archaeological interest where the object has at any time formed part of the building or structure, or from a monument of such interest. This removal may have been criminal under UK law or 'under the law of any other country or territory', but the offence of dealing itself (extensively defined in s. 3) has not been given any extraterritorial ambit.

By s. 4, proceedings for an offence relating to the dealing in a tainted cultural object may be instituted by order of the Commissioners of Customs and Excise if it appears to them that the offence has involved the importation or exportation of such an object.

Section B5 Deception, Fraud and Blackmail

DECEPTION AND FRAUD: OLD AND NEW LAW

The Theft Acts 1968 and 1978 created a number of deception offences, which dealt with situations in which something was obtained, secured or procured, or in which some liability was evaded, as a result of the successful and dishonest deception of another person. **B5.1**

The relevant offences in the 1968 Act were those created by s. 15 (obtaining property), s. 15A (obtaining a money transfer), s. 16 (obtaining a pecuniary advantage) and s. 20(2) (procuring the execution of a valuable security). The 1978 Act, in replacing one troublesome provision of the 1968 Act (namely, s. 16(2)(a)), added the offences of obtaining services (TA 1978, s. 1), securing remission of an existing liability (TA 1978, s. 2(1)(a)), inducing a creditor to wait for or forgo payment (s. 2(1)(b)) and obtaining exemption from, or abatement of, liability to make a payment (s. 2(1)(c)). These offences were repealed by the Fraud Act 2006, sch. 1, para. 1, with effect from 15 January 2007 (Fraud Act 2006 (Commencement) Order 2006 (SI 2006 No. 3200)); but the repeal does not affect any liability, investigation, legal proceeding or penalty for or in respect of any offence 'partly committed' before that date. An offence will be deemed to have been partly committed before commencement of the new law if (a) a 'relevant event' (defined as any act, omission or other event, including any result of one or more acts or omissions, proof of which is required for conviction of the offence) occurs before commencement and (b) another event occurs after commencement (sch. 2, para. 3).

The repealed provisions were replaced on 15 January 2007:

(1) by a general offence of fraud (Fraud Act 2006, s. 1) that may be committed:
   (a) by dishonestly making a false (i.e. untrue or misleading) representation with a view to gain or with intent to cause loss (s. 2);
   (b) by dishonestly (and with a view to gain or with intent to cause loss) failing to disclose information when under a legal duty to disclose it (s. 3);
   (c) by dishonest abuse of a position — arising when one person was expected to safeguard, or not to act against, the financial interests of another, but he acts (or omits to act) with a view to gain or with intent to cause loss (s. 4); and
(2) by an offence of obtaining services dishonestly (which in many ways corresponds to the offence under s 1 of the 1978 Act, but is broader in that it does not require any deception, or indeed any fraudulent representation).

See further **B5.93** ***et seq.***

The Fraud Act 2006 also creates (*inter alia*) offences of making or possessing articles for use in such crimes (e.g., false identity documents, counterfeit goods or stolen credit cards) (see **B5.101** ***et seq.***) but does not (as was once proposed) abrogate the common-law offence of conspiracy to defraud.

Where frauds are committed over a long period of time, and involve false representations etc. committed prior to commencement of the new law, it seems likely that the old law will continue to be relied upon, even where any gain or obtaining takes place long after commencement. This is because, although the old law is given transitional application under sch. 2, para. 3, the new offence of fraud has no retrospective effect, and creates a conduct crime rather than a result crime. The obtaining of property in 2008 as a result of a fraudulent representation made in 2005 would not form any part of the *actus reus* of the new fraud offence. If, however, the fraudulent representation was deemed to be ongoing, prosecutors might be in a position to choose between proceeding under the old law and proceeding under the new; and the new offence of obtaining services dishonestly (s. 11), being a result crime, may involve an earlier dishonest act, such as a deception. If so, old and new offences may again overlap.

No transitional arrangements have been made in respect of the jurisdiction provisions in the CJA 1993, part 1 (see **A8.7**). As of 15 January 2007, the deception offences abruptly ceased to be Group A offences under that part and were replaced by the new offences (Fraud Act 2006, sch. 1, para. 24) but this makes no express allowance for deception offences partly committed before commencement.

DECEPTION GENERALLY

Definition

B5.2 The TA 1968, s. 15(4), provides a partial definition of the concept of deception. It applies to the offences under ss. 15, 15A, 16 and 20(2) of the 1968 Act and also, by virtue of the TA 1978, s. 5(1), to offences under the 1978 Act.

Theft Act 1968, s. 15

(4) . . . 'deception' means any deception (whether deliberate or reckless) by words or conduct as to fact or as to law, including a deception as to the present intentions of the person using the deception or any other person.

This does not really attempt to explain what a deception is; it merely indicates that a deception under the Theft Acts 1968 and 1978 may possess certain characteristics which might have precluded convictions for offences involving false representation under the Larceny Act 1916. (For example, it was not previously an offence to deceive another by making a false statement as to one's present intentions, or as to a point of law.)

The best known judicial definition of deception is that of Buckley J in *Re London and Globe Finance Corporation Ltd* [1903] 1 Ch 728 at p. 732:

To deceive is . . . to induce a man to believe that a thing is true which is false.

This was quoted with approval in *DPP v Ray* [1974] AC 370 and is consistent with the normal dictionary meaning of the term, but does not quite tell the full story, because more recent cases, notably *Metropolitan Police Commissioner v Charles* [1977] AC 177 and *Lambie* [1982] AC 449, appear to establish that it is deception falsely to persuade someone that something only *may* be true. See **B5.9**.

Reckless Deception

Even if it survives in some contexts, which is doubtful, *Caldwell* recklessness (see A2.5) cannot be applicable to cases of deception under the Theft Acts, because all the deception offences require proof of dishonesty, and a person can hardly be considered dishonest if it has never occurred to him that he may be deceiving someone. *Cunningham* recklessness (see A2.4) is therefore the relevant concept. See *Large v Mainprize* [1989] Crim LR 213, *Feeny* (1991) 94 Cr App R 1 and *Goldman* [1997] Crim LR 894. **B5.3**

Deception and Machines

In the absence of firm authority (the point being left open in *Davies v Flackett* [1973] RTR 8), it is generally assumed that offences of actual or intended deception can be practised only against a living person. This seems to have been accepted (*obiter*) in *Re Holmes* [2005] 1 WLR 1857, in which it was suggested that the Computer Misuse Act 1990, s. 2 (see **B18.8**), might be used in cases where attempts are made to hack into computers for fraudulent purposes. **B5.4**

A person who obtains and uses another's personal identification number or password to withdraw funds from a computerised bank account or to withdraw cash from a bank's automatic service till could not therefore be regarded as obtaining anything 'by deception'. In the latter case, he could nevertheless be guilty of theft, as if he had used that other's key to open a safe, and a deception (or theft) charge may be possible if bank staff are later induced to act on falsified instructions relayed by the computer (see further **B5.34**).

Deception of a Person Other than the Victim

A deception need not necessarily be practised against the ultimate victim of the offence concerned. Where, for example, a retailer is deceived into accepting payment by a cheque supported by a guarantee card that is used in excess of authority, a conviction for obtaining a pecuniary advantage (namely borrowing by way of overdraft from the bank) by deception (TA 1968, s. 16(1)(b)) may still be imposed, even though the bank itself has not been deceived (*Kovacks* [1974] 1 WLR 370; *Smith v Koumourou* [1979] Crim LR 116; *Metropolitan Police Commissioner v Charles* [1977] AC 177). **B5.5**

On the other hand, it was held in *Rozeik* [1996] 1 WLR 159 that, where D was charged with obtaining cheques from finance companies by deception, convictions could not be justified unless it was proved that branch managers or employees who had signed the relevant cheques had been deceived, rather than having acted as parties to the fraud. If two such persons had signed a relevant cheque, it would have to be proved that at least one of them had been deceived. It would not be enough to prove that other employees, such as those who had prepared the blank cheque forms, had been deceived.

A further qualification must be added in respect of offences under the TA 1978, ss. 1 and 2. The s. 2(1)(b) offence in particular cannot be committed without the deception operating on the mind of the creditor or his agent (see *Gee* [1999] Crim LR 397).

Deception and False Representations

Because the relevant offences under the Theft Acts 1968 and 1978 are not expressed in terms of making false statements or representations, there is arguably no reason why a deception offence need involve the making of any such things. The courts sometimes go to great lengths to find 'implied representations' when the better view is that none are necessary. It is submitted that it suffices if the accused 'by words or conduct' induces a false belief in the other person's mind. If, on the other hand, it is alleged that the accused deceived his victim (or another) with a number of false representations, a court or jury should convict only if collectively satisfied as to the falsity of at least one of those representations. It will not suffice if half the jury are satisfied as to the falsity of one and half as to the falsity of another (*Brown* **B5.6**

(1983) 79 Cr App R 115), unless they can agree that *some* at least of the representations must have been false, or that their cumulative effect was misleading, and that the other person was thereby deceived (*Agbim* [1979] Crim LR 171). See also *Price* [1991] Crim LR 465.

Deception by Conduct

B5.7 Examples of deception by conduct are provided by *DPP v Stonehouse* [1978] AC 55, and *Williams* [1980] Crim LR 589. In *Williams*, the accused dishonestly presented obsolete Yugoslavian banknotes at a bureau de change, and asked for them to be exchanged for sterling. The counter staff assumed, as he had hoped, that the notes were current, and he made a handsome profit. He never said that the notes were current, but his conduct certainly implied it, and the Court of Appeal therefore opined that a charge of obtaining property by deception should have been put to the jury. This must surely be correct: if a false representation is needed, then one was implicit in his conduct; but a better way of explaining it is that he deliberately deceived the counter staff into making the false assumption.

In *DPP v Stonehouse*, the accused left his clothes on a beach in Miami, and slipped out of the USA under a false name, in the hope that insurance companies in England would be deceived into thinking him drowned, and thus into paying out on life assurance policies in favour of his wife. The scheme failed, but he was found guilty of an attempt to commit offences under the TA 1968, s. 15. See also *Hamilton* (1990) 92 Cr App R 54.

Dishonest overcharging for goods or services in situations where the purchaser trusts or relies upon the provider to charge a fair and reasonable price has been held to be capable of giving rise to liability for obtaining property by deception (see *Silverman* (1988) 86 Cr App R 214 and *Jones* (1993) *The Times*, 15 February 1993).

Deception by Omission

B5.8 It is clear that the courts are prepared to construe misleading omissions as deceptions in appropriate cases. A good illustration of this approach is provided by *Firth* (1989) 91 Cr App R 217, in which a consultant obstetrician omitted to inform his hospital that certain of his patients were being treated privately, with the result that no charge was made to him or to them for use of National Health Service beds and facilities. It could no doubt have been argued that he had impliedly represented the women in question to have been National Health Service patients, but the Court of Appeal held instead that 'it mattered not whether it was an act of commission or omission'. See also *Rai* [2000] 1 Cr App R 233.

Deception, Uncertainty and Indifference

B5.9 There has been difficulty in deciding whether there is a deception where the accused made a false representation to a person who remained unconvinced of its truth, or who was not particularly concerned to verify it, but who was prepared to give the accused the property or advantage sought as long as he did not know for a fact that the representation was false.

This problem might arise where a person tells a false 'hard luck' story, and is given money on the basis that the story might be true and that he should have the benefit of the doubt. More significantly, it will arise where a cheque guarantee card or credit card is used to make a payment. Tendering the card is a representation that the person tendering it is authorised to use it, but the person taking the payment need not concern himself whether that is so. As long as the card is current, certain formalities are correctly attended to, and the signature corresponds with that on the card, then the bank or card company can be relied upon to pay, even if the tenderer has exceeded his authority, and even (depending on the exact conditions of use relating to the particular card) if he has stolen the card. The person taking the payment may, therefore, take the view that the correctness of the representation is of no concern to him. A third type of situation is a tender of a forged or invalid ticket, which the person to whom it is tendered, although both concerned and suspicious, accepts because he does not feel that he can prove what he suspects.

The leading cases on this question were concerned with cheque cards and credit cards but indicate that a deception would be committed in all three situations. In *Metropolitan Police Commissioner v Charles* [1977] AC 177, a gaming club accepted the accused's cheques because they were backed by a valid guarantee card. The club took the view that if the accused was exceeding his authority from his bank (as indeed he was), this was no concern of theirs, but the manager added in the course of his testimony that the position would have been different had the club possessed actual knowledge of the accused's lack of authority. On these facts, the House of Lords found that there had been a deception for the purposes of the TA 1968, s. 16(2)(b).

Metropolitan Police Commissioner v Charles was followed in *Lambie* [1982] AC 449, where goods had been purchased with a credit card which the accused knew she had no right to use. Both cases have attracted hostile academic comment, but it is submitted that the practical consequences would have been most unfortunate had their lordships reached any other interpretation. In contrast, a sales assistant or shopkeeper is unlikely to be concerned with matters such as the customer's ability to pay off his credit card account, or whether the customer was entirely honest when applying for the card in the first place. If the customer is currently authorised to use the card, that is probably all that concerns him.

Lambie and *Charles* were distinguished on the basis of authorised use in *Nabina* [1999] All ER (D) 733. N obtained credit cards by providing banks with false information about his financial and personal details, and used these cards in retail outlets to purchase goods he could not afford. The prosecution argued that N was not then entitled to put himself forward as being entitled to use the cards and every use of them, in whatever outlet he went into and presented those cards on behalf of the relevant bank, was a dishonest deception. The Court of Appeal disagreed. N was dishonest, but remained at the relevant times the lawful holder of the cards, whereas in *Lambie* L's contractual right to use the card had already been rescinded. As Lord Bingham CJ explained, it was doubtful whether N by his conduct could be said to have represented anything more than that he had authority to bind the bank and that the transaction would be honoured; but there was no evidence to suggest that any transaction had been dishonoured, or that the issuer had regarded the accused, in using the card, as acting outside the authorisation that had mistakenly been given to him. It is submitted that N should instead have been charged with obtaining possession of the cards themselves by deception, when he deceived the banks into issuing them.

A person who persuades someone to draw a cheque in his favour and use a cheque card to guarantee it, even though both know that this would be in excess of authority, may also be guilty of a deception of the bank, which would presumably honour the cheque in the mistaken belief that the payee had relied on the card in good faith. Alternatively, both could be charged with conspiracy to defraud the bank.

Relationship of Deception to Consequences

To constitute one of the offences dealt with in this section the obtaining, procuring, evasion etc. must be a consequence (albeit perhaps not solely a consequence) of the deception. If a person tells a false 'hard luck' story to someone who gives him money despite being completely uninterested in the truth or otherwise of the story (a different situation from that where he considers that it might not be true but gives the deceiver the benefit of the doubt), there is only an attempt to deceive (*Hensler* (1870) 22 LT 691). A motorist who had already filled his car's tank with petrol before practising a deception on the attendant cannot be guilty of obtaining that petrol by deception (*Collis-Smith* [1971] Crim LR 716; *Coady* [1996] Crim LR 518). Furthermore, the deception must not be too remote from the obtaining. If a person deceives someone into allowing him to bet on a horse, and the horse wins, then the deceiver **B5.10** may be guilty of an offence under the TA 1968, s. 16(2)(c) (see **B5.36** to **B5.43**), but is probably not guilty of obtaining the winnings by that deception, because the immediate cause of his obtaining those winnings is not the deception, but is the fact that his horse has won (*Clucas* [1949] 2 KB 226).

Clucas was distinguished by the Court of Appeal in *Miller* (1992) 95 Cr App R 421, where M, posing as a taxi driver, picked up foreign visitors at London airports and then charged them up to ten times the proper fare. He was convicted of obtaining property by deception, and appealed on the ground that all his victims had realised that they were being cheated by the time they came to hand over the excessive fares demanded. It appeared that they paid so as to avoid trouble or because they were afraid of losing their luggage. The Court of Appeal nevertheless upheld his conviction as there was ample evidence on which a jury could conclude that the initial deception of his victims was the effective cause of the losses they suffered.

Evidence from the alleged victim of the deception may sometimes be the only satisfactory way of proving that he was indeed deceived and that it was because of the deception that he let the accused obtain the property etc. There will be few circumstances in which the prosecution can safely dispense with such evidence (*Tirado* (1974) 59 Cr App R 80); but see *Etim v Hatfield* [1975] Crim LR 234, where the Divisional Court was satisfied that the defendant could not possibly have obtained a social security payment to which he was not entitled, had the unidentified Post Office employee responsible not been deceived by his falsified order book. See also *Doukas* [1978] 1 WLR 372; *Hamilton* (1990) 92 Cr App R 54; and *Modupe* [1991] Crim LR 530.

Deception as to the Future: Worthless Cheques

B5.11 For a deception to be an offence under the Theft Acts 1968 or 1978, it must be a deception as to existing facts, or as to law. A representation that something will happen in the future will not suffice. It therefore will not do to argue that, when one person issues a worthless cheque to another, he has deceived the other into thinking that it will be honoured. For similar reasons, if a person falsely promises to perform a service for someone in the future, it cannot be argued that the person to whom the promise was made has been deceived into thinking that the service will be performed. There may indeed have been a criminal deception, but in either case, the deception must be expressed in terms of present fact.

The key to the problem is to be found in the TA 1968, s. 15(4), itself. As this makes clear, a deception may relate to the present intentions of the deceiver or of anyone else. These are 'as much a fact as the state of his digestion' (*Edgington v Fitzmaurice* (1885) 29 ChD 459). The person who was promised the service may have been deceived into thinking that the promisor intended to perform the promised service. The person who received the worthless cheque may have been deceived into thinking that the issuer of the cheque intended or believed it would be honoured.

In *Gilmartin* [1983] QB 953, the Court of Appeal held that a person who issues a cheque impliedly represents that the existing circumstances are such that in the ordinary course of events one would expect the cheque to be honoured. He does not necessarily represent that there are already sufficient funds in the account: there will not ordinarily be any deception if the issuer of a cheque is expecting sufficient funds to be credited to the account in time to meet the cheque on presentation; but see *Greenstein* [1975] 1 WLR 1353 (see **B5.12**).

Other Deceptions Involving Cheques

B5.12 The express or implied representations associated with issuing a cheque may be somewhat different from those envisaged in *Gilmartin* [1983] QB 953 (see **B5.11**). The issuer may, for example, indicate that he is unsure about the adequacy of his current account, but that he will indemnify the holder in the event of dishonour. *Gilmartin* would not then be applicable.

There may also be special circumstances in which a person might be guilty of a dishonest deception even where he expects the cheque to be honoured on presentation as where a cheque guarantee card is used (see **B5.9**). A further example is provided by *Greenstein* [1975] 1 WLR 1353, where the appellants drew cheques for sums vastly exceeding their credit limits in order to subscribe for the largest possible number of shares in oversubscribed company flotations. They relied on being allocated only a small percentage of the shares applied for, and on the issuing houses' refund cheques arriving in time to ensure their own cheques would be honoured. They had been warned that such tactics were considered improper, and in some cases had given an express undertaking that their cheques would be honoured on first presentation (something of which they could not in fact be sure and which did not always happen). In those circumstances they were held to have deceived the issuing houses, and to have committed offences under the TA 1968, s. 15.

Dishonesty

Relatively little need be added here to what has been said about dishonesty in theft (see **B4.35** *et seq.*); indeed it should be remembered that *Ghosh* [1982] QB 1053 is itself a deception case. Certain distinctions must, however, be noted. **B5.13**

The most important distinction is that the TA 1968, s. 2 is not directly applicable to any of the deception offences. This means, for example, that it is not necessarily impossible for a person to be guilty of an offence of obtaining a thing by deception when he believes himself to have a legal right to the thing in question (cf. s. 2(1)(a)). In practice, however, this distinction is probably of limited significance, because the *Ghosh* test of dishonesty, although less precise on this point, is likely to be more generous to an accused than s. 2 itself. Belief in a moral claim of right might suffice under *Ghosh*, but it would not suffice under s. 2 alone. See also *Woolven* (1983) 77 Cr App R 231, *Melwani* [1989] Crim LR 565 and *Lightfoot* (1993) 97 Cr App R 24.

When considering the issue of dishonesty, it would be wrong to assume that proof of an intention to deceive must *ipso facto* prove dishonesty (*Potger* (1970) 55 Cr App R 42; *O'Connell* (1991) 94 Cr App R 39; *Clarke* [1996] Crim LR 824). The jury should be warned against any such assumption.

Selection of Charges Generally

The deception offences overlap extensively. If a person deceives someone into accepting a cheque backed by a cheque guarantee card he has no right to use, he may thereby obtain property or services contrary to the TA 1968, s. 15, or the TA 1978, s. 1. He may also force his bank to honour the cheque, and to grant him an increased overdraft contrary to the TA 1968, s. 16(2)(b). (It matters not that only the payee of the cheque was deceived: see **B5.5**.) The position is complicated by the fact that, in many deception offences, false instruments are made or used, contrary to the Forgery and Counterfeiting Act 1981, s. 1 or s. 3. **B5.14**

In some respects, this kind of overlap can work to the advantage of the prosecution, since they may be able to succeed on one count of an indictment even if they fail on others; but there is at the same time added scope for error and confusion, and multiple counts may not always be advisable. Considerable care should therefore be taken in selecting the most suitable charges. It is not practicable to provide guidance here on the most appropriate charge in every possible situation, but the following general points may assist.

What has been Obtained? If goods, cash or other kinds of property (within the meaning of the TA 1968, s. 4(1)) appear to have been acquired as a result of the alleged deception, then a charge under the TA 1968, s. 15 (see **B5.23** *et seq.*), should ordinarily be brought in **B5.15**

Part B Offences

preference to other possible deception charges arising from the same facts. Where, however, D deceives V into drawing a cheque or draft in D's favour, or into transferring funds into D's account, a charge brought under s. 15 may be impossible to establish and alternative charges must be considered. See generally **B5.17**.

B5.16 **Deception and Theft** Following the decision of the House of Lords in *Gomez* [1993] AC 442 (see **B4.25** ***et seq.***), most cases in which property has been acquired by deception will now be chargeable as theft, which may be easier to prove. Conviction in a s. 15 prosecution requires proof not only that the property in question was obtained dishonestly and with intent to permanently deprive the person to whom it belonged, but also that it was obtained as a result of a successful deception of the victim or some other person. In contrast, a charge of theft merely requires proof of a dishonest appropriation coupled with an intent to permanently deprive. If for example D dishonestly selects goods in a self-service shop, intending to pay for them with a stolen credit card or cheque, his selection of the goods will in itself have amounted to theft, without the need for proof that the intended deception was successful. Nor need theft involve any obtaining of another's property. Destruction of that property may suffice, as where D empties V's bank account, thereby extinguishing the chose in action it represented. *Preddy* [1996] AC 815 (see **B5.17**) does not affect a charge of theft brought on that basis (see *Williams* [2001] 1 Cr App R 362 and **B4.28**).

B5.17 **Loans, Cheques and Money Transfers** Where D deceives V into making a loan or advance, whether by way of mortgage or otherwise, this will rarely involve the direct provision of cash. More commonly, V will issue D with a cheque or draft for the sum agreed, or arrange for that sum to be credited electronically to D's account. Where a cheque or draft is issued, D acquires both the piece of paper on which it is printed and the chose in action it represents, namely the payee's right to enforce it. Where funds are credited to D's account, any credit balance thereby created is again a chose in action (although if the account remains overdrawn, D acquires no chose in action at all). A chose in action is property within the meaning of the TA 1968, s. 4, but in such cases D acquires a brand new chose in action rather than one which ever belonged to V; and this appears to preclude any charge of obtaining 'property belonging to another' (see *Preddy* [1996] AC 815, overruling *Duru* [1974] 1 WLR 2; and see also **B4.14**). The position is not significantly altered where the initial transfer is made to a firm of solicitors acting in the transaction (*Preddy* per Lord Goff at pp. 837–8 and see also *Nathan* [1997] Crim LR 835).

If a loan or advance is provided in the form of a cheque or banker's draft, a charge of obtaining the completed instrument by deception ought in principle to be viable, since this is tangible property, a valuable security; but in *Preddy* Lord Goff assumed (*obiter*) that D could not intend to permanently deprive the drawer of the instrument, because 'a cheque on presentation for payment is returned to the drawer via his bank'. With respect, banks no longer routinely return cheques to drawers after payment; and where exceptionally they do so, the thing returned is a mere piece of paper. It has ceased to be a valuable security (see *Duru*, which surely remains correct on that point). Nevertheless, in *Clark* [2001] Crim LR 572 the Court of Appeal held that it would be 'wholly inappropriate' for them to reject Lord Goff's approach on that point, and the issue must probably be considered closed.

A number of other charges may, however, be considered. Where the alleged offence was committed on or after 18 December 1996 (and before 15 January 2007), the obvious charge is one of obtaining a money transfer by deception, contrary to the TA 1968, s. 15A (see **B5.31** ***et seq.***). In other cases, the prosecution may be able to prove theft (see **B5.16**) or conspiracy to defraud (see **A6.17** ***et seq.***). Where a cheque or draft is issued to D, either by V or by an innocent solicitor to whom funds have been transferred electronically, D may be guilty of procuring the execution of a valuable security by deception contrary to the TA 1968, s. 20(2) (see *Cooke* [1997] Crim LR 436, *Aston* [1998] Crim LR 498 and **B5.44** ***et seq.***). Such a charge may (at least arguably) be brought in respect of the authorisation of a CHAPS order, for the reasons given by the Court of Appeal in *King* [1992] QB 20 (see **B5.49**). The Court of Appeal in *Bolton* (1991) 94 Cr App R 74 suggested that an alternative charge would be one of procuring the execution of the mortgage deed by deception, but this will not work where the mortgage deed is executed by the borrower himself, nor will charges of conspiracy or attempt to procure execution of a cheque or CHAPS authorisation succeed unless it can be proved that the accused intended his deception would result in the execution of such a security (see *Mensah-Lartey* [1996] 1 Cr App R 143).

A charge of obtaining services by deception was for many years precluded by the decision of the Court of Appeal in *Halai* [1983] Crim LR 624, in which it was held that the provision of a mortgage advance was not a service for the purposes of the TA 1978, s. 1 (see **B5.58**). *Halai* has been widely condemned. It was not overruled in *Preddy*, but the Court of Appeal has repeatedly declared it to have been decided *per incuriam* on that point (see *Graham* [1997] 1 Cr App R 302; *Cooke* [1997] Crim LR 436 and *Cummings-John* [1997] Crim LR 660). In respect of offences committed on or after 18 December 1996, the Theft (Amendment) Act 1996 inserted a new s. 1(3) into the TA 1978, so as to make it clear that the obtaining of a loan is indeed an obtaining of services.

Jurisdictional Issues The selection of charges in cases with a foreign or 'cross-frontier' element may be influenced by jurisdictional considerations, especially where the alleged acts or events took place before 1 June 1999, which is the date on which the CJA 1993, part I was brought into force. The deception offences are all 'Group A' offences for the purpose of jurisdiction under part I. This means that they can be tried in England and Wales if any 'relevant event' (i.e. any essential element of the offence) takes place there on or after that date (see **A8.5**). Where, however, the acts or events in question occurred prior to that date, the better view is that jurisdiction generally depends on where the actual obtaining took place. A deception practised from England would not be an offence if the obtaining took place abroad (see *Harden* [1963] 1 QB 8, *Tirado* (1974) 59 Cr App R 80 and *Manning* [1998] 2 Cr App R 461). A contrary view adopted by the Court of Appeal in *Smith* [1996] 2 Cr App R 1 was disapproved in *Manning* but reasserted in *Smith (Wallace Duncan) (No. 4)* [2004] QB 1418 (see **A8.2**). **B5.18**

Purpose and Effect The prosecution must carefully consider what exactly the deception in question has achieved, and what it was intended to achieve. If for example the accused has paid a hotelier with a stolen cheque for services already provided, this cannot in itself amount to an offence under the TA 1978, s. 1, because the services have already been obtained (*Collis-Smith* [1971] Crim LR 716; *Coady* [1996] Crim LR 518). If an offence under s. 1 has been committed, it can only be on the basis of some deception practised before the services were provided, and that might depend on whether the accused intended to practise this trick from the start. **B5.19**

The TA 1978, s. 2(1)(b), might be more appropriate in such a case; but a charge under this provision would fail if the accused misused his own cheque card or credit card, knowing that the bank concerned would have to pay. The accused could not then be regarded as intending to make permanent default on his liability to pay. A charge under the TA 1968, s. 16(2)(b) might be the only effective one on such facts.

Forgery and Deception Charges of making or using a false instrument may have considerable advantages over deception offences where such instruments have been made or used for fraud. The complete offence may be committed without any successful deception, and without the obtaining or procuring of any benefit by the accused. He must of course intend to deceive ('induce somebody to accept [the falsified instrument] as genuine'), and thereby induce the person deceived to act to his own or another's prejudice, but the accused need not have succeeded in this object, and it is not necessary to prove he has been dishonest (*Campbell* (1984) 80 Cr App R 47). On the other hand, an instrument may be deceptive for the purpose **B5.20**

of offences under the TA 1968 without being 'false' within the meaning of the Forgery and Counterfeiting Act 1981 (*More* [1987] 1 WLR 1578). See further **B6.2**.

B5.21 **Going Equipped** Another possible charge in cases where a successful deception cannot be proved is one under the TA 1968, s. 25 (going equipped for a cheat); but it must be proved that the accused 'had with him' something which he intended should be used for an offence under s. 15: an intent to misuse a credit card in order to obtain services would not suffice. See further **B4.119** ***et seq.***

B5.22 **Specialised Legislation** Deception offences under the Theft Acts 1968 and 1978 may sometimes be less appropriate and harder to prove than offences under the Companies Acts or other specialised enactments. See generally **B7**.

OBTAINING PROPERTY BY DECEPTION

B5.23 **Theft Act 1968, s. 15**

(1) A person who by any deception dishonestly obtains property belonging to another, with the intention of permanently depriving the other of it, shall on conviction on indictment be liable to imprisonment for a term not exceeding 10 years.
(2) For purposes of this section a person is to be treated as obtaining property if he obtains ownership, possession or control of it, and 'obtain' includes obtaining for another or enabling another to obtain or to retain.
(3) Section 6 above shall apply for purposes of this section, with the necessary adaptation of the reference to appropriating, as it applies for purposes of section 1.
(4) For purposes of this section 'deception' means any deception (whether deliberate or reckless) by words or conduct as to fact or as to law, including a deception as to the present intentions of the person using the deception or any other person.

Note that as regards acts prior to 15 January 2007, this offence is repealed and replaced by the offence under the Fraud Act 2006 (see **B5.1**).

Procedure and Jurisdiction

B5.24 Obtaining property by deception is triable either way (MCA 1980, s. 17 and sch. 1, para. 28). When tried on indictment it is a class 3 offence. It is a Group A offence for jurisdiction purposes under the CJA 1993, part I (see **A8.4**).

The *Consolidated Criminal Practice Direction*, para. V.51, *Mode of trial* (see **appendix** 7) states (at para. V.51.7) that fraud should be tried summarily unless the court considers that one or more of the following features is present in the case *and* that its sentencing powers are insufficient:

(a) Breach of trust by a person in a position of substantial authority, or in whom a high degree of trust is placed.
(b) Fraud which has been committed or disguised in a sophisticated manner.
(c) Fraud committed by an organised gang.
(d) The victim is particularly vulnerable to fraud (e.g., the elderly or infirm).
(e) The unrecovered property is of high value (at least £10,000).

In addition, the practice direction states (para. 51.9) that social security fraud should be tried summarily unless the court considers that one or more of the following features is present in the case *and* that its sentencing powers are insufficient:

(a) Organised fraud on a large scale.
(b) The frauds are substantial and carried out over a long period of time.

For the liability of officers of a company for an offence committed by the company, see the TA 1968, s. 18, and **B5.68**.

Indictment

Statement of Offence B5.25

Obtaining property by deception contrary to section 15(1) of the Theft Act 1968

Particulars of Offence

A on or about the . . . day of . . . dishonestly obtained from V a pearl necklace, with intent to deprive the said V of it permanently, by deception, namely by falsely representing that he was an employee of a jewellery restorer who had sent him to collect the said necklace for restoration

Sentencing Guidelines

The maximum penalty is 10 years (TA 1968, s. 15(1)) on indictment; six months, or a fine not exceeding the statutory maximum, or both, summarily. B5.26

When dealt with summarily, the Magistrates' Courts Guidelines (2004) indicate the following for a first-time offender pleading not guilty:

Aggravating Factors For example committed over a lengthy period; large sums or valuable goods; two or more involved; victim particularly vulnerable; use of stolen credit/debit card, cheque books, or giros; offence committed on bail; relevant previous convictions and any failures to respond to previous sentences.

Mitigating Factors For example impulsive action; short period; small sum.

Guideline: Is it serious enough for a community penalty?

The sentencing pattern for this and related offences of deception overlaps substantially with that for theft (see **B4.5** to **B4.8**). Since the offence varies so widely, there is no guideline judgment. There are however the general comments of Lord Lane CJ in *Bibi* [1980] 1 WLR 1193, where it was said that shorter sentences would be appropriate for the more petty frauds where small amounts of money are involved and the remarks of Lord Woolf CJ in *Mills* [2002] 2 Cr App R (S) 229, that where an offence of dishonesty has been committed by a first offender, particularly a woman who is the sole carer of children, the sentencer should always consider carefully whether a custodial sentence is really necessary and that, even if it is, a sentence for the minimum appropriate period should be passed (see further **E2.7**). The appropriate sentencing bracket for frauds committed by professional persons was reconsidered in *Clark* [1998] 2 Cr App R 137, which is discussed at **B4.8**. Large-scale commercial frauds will attract lengthy custodial sentences. In *Copeland* (1982) 4 Cr App R (S) 110 the offender was involved in a well organised scheme by which cheque-books and cheque cards were stolen in Britain, passports were obtained in the names of the losers, and teams of two went to the Continent, using the passports, and obtained money by means of the stolen cheque-books and cards. Each trip netted about £15,000 and the scheme had been in operation for a considerable time. The offender had several previous convictions for dishonesty resulting in prison terms of up to three years. The Court of Appeal reduced the sentence for the present offences from six years to four years. In *Griffiths* (1989) 11 Cr App R (S) 216 the offender, an 'intelligent and resourceful man', pleaded guilty to 23 counts of deception relating to a total of 93 multiple applications for shares. He made a profit of £5,000, but if all the applications had been successful he would have made £64,000. The Court of Appeal said that an immediate custodial sentence was appropriate, varying the original sentence of 12 months, with six to serve and six suspended, to an immediate term of six months. A striking case illustrating what the Court of Appeal described as 'a classic sentencing problem' is *Jackson* (1992) 13 Cr App R (S) 22. The offenders were husband and wife. They each pleaded guilty to three counts of obtaining property by deception and asked for similar offences, 31 and 47 respectively, to be taken into consideration. The offenders, who found themselves in severe financial difficulties, had bought a number of stolen store credit cards and had used them to obtain clothing and other items from various shops to the value of about £4,000, of which £1,000 was recovered. Sentences of 15 months' imprisonment in each case were reduced by the Court of Appeal to community service orders in the light of the offenders' previous good records and other strong personal mitigation. In *Stevens* (1993) 14 Cr App R (S) 372, the Court of Appeal noted that various forms of mortgage fraud had become more prevalent in recent years. Relevant factors in sentencing such offences were the degree of involvement of the individual offender, the duration of the fraud, the personal benefit derived and whether the offender was a professional person. A sentence of three years on an offender who was involved in 14 transactions and had recruited others to the fraud was upheld.

In contrast to these frauds are what may be described as the activities of 'con men'. Non-custodial sentences will often be appropriate but, once again, much turns on the sum involved. Also relevant is the method of deception ('callous' deception of the elderly, for example, will attract a more severe sentence) and the previous record of the offender. In *Ball* [2001] 1 Cr App R (S) 171, where a father and son defrauded a widow of 81 of almost £5,000 by three deceptions relating to the need for repairs to her house and a further attempted deception, sentences of three years and four years were said by the Court of Appeal to be 'severe but not excessive'. In *Hafeez* [1998] 1 Cr App R (S) 276, the offender pleaded guilty to conspiring to obtain by deception, by carrying out repair work on cars which was not needed, or by charging customers for repair work which had not been done. A sentence of three years' imprisonment on the defendant, who had organised the 'cynical and deeply dishonest' deception, was upheld, while a second defendant who was more peripherally involved, received 12 months.

B5.27 **Benefit Fraud etc.** Most cases involving the dishonest obtaining of social security benefits or payments are dealt with summarily under the Social Security Administration Act 1992, s. 111A (see **B16.15**). More serious cases will be prosecuted under the TA 1968, s. 15. A number of social security and other benefit frauds have reached the Court of Appeal. In *Stewart* (1987) 9 Cr App R (S) 135, as updated in *Graham* [2005] 1 Cr App R (S) 640, the Court of Appeal provided the following guidance for Crown Court sentencers:

> . . . only a small proportion of offences of this nature . . . are dealt with in the Crown Court. . . . If prosecuted at all, the run of the mill offence is almost certain to be before the magistrates.
>
> . . . These offences involve the dishonest abstraction of honest taxpayers' money, and are not to be treated lightly. They are easy to commit and difficult and expensive to track down. However it must be remembered that they are non-violent, non-sexual and non-frightening crimes.
>
> In some cases immediate [custody] is unavoidable. At the top of the range, requiring substantial sentences, perhaps of two and a half years' imprisonment and upwards, are the carefully organised frauds on a large scale in which considerable sums of money are obtained . . . These offenders are in effect professional fraudsmen, as is often apparent from their previous records. . . .
>
> As to the remainder, who form the great majority of those appearing in the Crown Court, the sentence will depend on an almost infinite variety of factors, only some of which it is possible to forecast. It may well be advisable as a first precaution for the court to enquire what steps the department proposes to take to recover their loss from the offender. Counsel for the Crown should be equipped to assist the court on this aspect of the matter . . .
>
> Other considerations which may affect the decision of the court are: (i) a guilty plea; (ii) the amount involved and the length of time over which the defalcations were persisted in (bearing in mind that a large total may in fact represent a very small amount weekly), (iii) the circumstances in which the offence began (e.g. there is a plain difference between a legitimate claim which becomes false owing to a change of situation and on the other hand a claim which is false from the very beginning); (iv) the use to which the money is put (the provision of household necessities is more venial than spending the money on unnecessary luxury); (v) previous character; (vi) matters special to the offender, such as illness, disability, family difficulties, etc.; (vii) any voluntary repayment of the amounts overpaid.
>
> If immediate imprisonment is necessary, a short term of up to about 9 or 12 months will usually be sufficient in a contested case where the overpayment is less than, say, £20,000 . . .

> Where no immediate custodial sentence is imposed, and the amount of overpayment is below, say, £1,000 or thereabouts, a compensation order is often of value. This will usually only be the case where the defendant is in work.

The guidelines in *Stewart* (1987) 9 Cr App R (S) 135 were applied to bring sentences within the 'normal' nine to 12-month range in *Graham* (1988) 10 Cr App R (S) 352 and *Miah* (1989) 11 Cr App R (S) 163. In *McDonagh* (1989) 11 Cr App R (S) 94, however, two years was upheld in respect of a 'deliberate, ingenious and calculated course of conduct' and three years was upheld in *Perry* (1989) 11 Cr App R (S) 58 where there was 'persistent deliberation' and a total of more than £44,000 obtained by deception. More than £100,000 was obtained in *Adewuyi* [1997] 1 Cr App R (S) 254, a case of 'exceptional seriousness', where a sentence of four years' imprisonment was approved by the Court of Appeal.

Actus Reus: Property Belonging to Another

B5.28 'Property', in the TA 1968, s. 15(1), bears the same meaning as it does in theft cases. The definition provided in s. 4(1) (see **B4.10** to **B4.15**) applies by virtue of s. 34(1). Subsections (2) to (4) of s. 4 are not mentioned in s. 34, and do not therefore apply to any offences other than theft (see s. 1(3)). This means that there are no special rules precluding or restricting charges of obtaining land by deception.

The term 'belonging to another' likewise bears the same basic meaning as it does in relation to theft (see **B4.17**), s. 5(1) also being of general application by virtue of s. 34(1). However, as with s. 4, it is only s. 5(1) that applies in respect of offences other than theft, and subsections (2) to (5) cannot be relied upon for these purposes.

Cheques involve special considerations. If one person tricks another into negotiating to him a cheque of which the other is presently the payee or holder, he may be regarded as obtaining both the cheque itself and the chose in action it represents (i.e. the right to enforce it against the drawer and endorsers in the event of it being dishonoured). Both are forms of property belonging to the other person within the TA 1968, ss. 4(1) and 5(1). However, deceiving someone into *issuing* a cheque involves no obtaining of another person's chose in action, because there was no right to enforce the cheque before it was issued. The prosecution may be able to charge the accused with an offence under s. 15A (see **B5.31**) or with procuring the execution of a valuable security contrary to the TA 1968, s. 20(2) (see **B5.44**).

Actus Reus: The Obtaining

B5.29 As to the need to prove a causative connection between the deception and the obtaining, see **B5.10**. 'Obtaining' is defined widely in the TA 1968, s. 15(2), so that an offence under s. 15(1) may be committed when and where the deceiver obtains possession or control of the property in question, even if he does not obtain ownership (and vice versa). This raises the question of whether the deceiver can be guilty of obtaining the same property more than once. Can an offence involving only the obtaining of ownership be followed by a further offence involving the obtaining of physical possession or control? Since property can be regarded as 'belonging to another' in any of these three senses, the logical answer would appear to be 'yes', and it would also appear to be possible for a thief to follow up his initial appropriation of physical possession with a deceptive obtaining of legal title. The position is complicated, however, by *Atakpu* [1994] QB 69, in which the Court of Appeal held that there cannot ordinarily be successive thefts of the same property by the same thief. Most cases of obtaining property by deception also amount to theft (see *Gomez* [1993] AC 442 at **B4.21** ***et seq.***), and it could be argued that much of the reasoning adopted in *Atakpu* is applicable to both offences, but *Atakpu* was not concerned with cases in which ownership and possession are obtained or appropriated in separate transactions, and does not necessarily apply to them. *Atakpu* is considered, insofar as it deals with theft, at **B4.27**.

If the property obtained by a deception was obtained for a person other than the deceiver then that other person may be a party to the offence, but need not be (*Duru* [1974] 1 WLR 2; *DPP v Stonehouse* [1978] AC 55).

Curiously, enabling another person to *retain* property can be an offence under the TA 1968, s. 15, whereas enabling oneself to retain property cannot be.

Mens Rea

B5.30 On a charge of obtaining property by deception contrary to the TA 1968, s. 15(1), the prosecution must prove that the accused acted dishonestly and with the intention of permanently depriving of the property. As to dishonesty, see **B5.13**. As to intention permanently to deprive, the whole of the definition of this concept in the TA 1968, s. 6, is applicable to s. 15 by virtue of s. 15(3). Section 6 is discussed at **B4.39** to **B4.41**.

OBTAINING A MONEY TRANSFER BY DECEPTION

B5.31 Theft Act 1968, s. 15A

(1) A person is guilty of an offence if by any deception he dishonestly obtains a money transfer for himself or another.

(2) A money transfer occurs when—
  (a) a debit is made to one account,
  (b) a credit is made to another, and
  (c) the credit results from the debit or the debit results from the credit.

(3) References to a credit and to a debit are to a credit of an amount of money and to a debit of an amount of money.

(4) It is immaterial (in particular)—
  (a) whether the amount credited is the same as the amount debited;
  (b) whether the money transfer is effected on presentation of a cheque or by another method;
  (c) whether any delay occurs in the process by which the money transfer is effected;
  (d) whether any intermediate credits or debits are made in the course of the money transfer;
  (e) whether either of the accounts is overdrawn before or after the money transfer is effected.

(5) A person guilty of an offence under this section shall be liable on conviction on indictment to imprisonment for a term not exceeding ten years.

Note that as regards acts prior to 15 January 2007, this offence is repealed and replaced by the offence under the Fraud Act 2006 (see **B5.1**).

Procedure, Jurisdiction and Sentence

B5.32 An offence under the TA 1968, s. 15A, is triable either way (MCA 1980, s. 17 and sch. 1, para. 28). When tried on indictment, it is a class 3 offence. It is a Group A offence for jurisdiction purposes under the CJA 1993, part I (see **A8.4**). As to the circumstances in which summary trial of fraud cases may be inappropriate, see **B5.24**.

The maximum penalty is 10 years on indictment (TA 1968, s. 15A(5)); six months and/or a fine not exceeding the statutory maximum on summary conviction. This is the same as for offences under s. 15. For sentencing guidelines in s. 15 cases, see **B5.26**. In *Roach* [2002] 1 Cr App R (S) 43, however, the Court of Appeal said that the guidelines in *Clark* [1998] 2 Cr App R 127 (see **B4.8**) were restricted to theft or deception committed in breach of trust from employers, and were not applicable to a case where the offender, a carer looking after an elderly woman, had received signed blank cheques from the woman and than cashed them for herself, obtaining £2,875. A sentence of 18 months' imprisonment was upheld on a guilty plea.

Indictment

B5.33

Statement of Offence

Obtaining a money transfer by deception, contrary to section 15A(1) of the Theft Act 1968

Particulars of Offence

A on the . . . day of . . . dishonestly obtained from Abbey National plc a money transfer, namely the crediting of an unsecured loan of £5,000 to his current account at Abbey National plc, by deception, namely by falsely representing that he was in paid employment at that time.

Elements

In a typical mortgage or loan transaction, an account held by the borrower or by someone acting on his behalf is credited with a sum of money, and an account held by the lending institution is debited as a result. The ambit of the TA 1968, s. 15A, is confined to such cases (s. 15A(2) and (3)). An account for the purpose of s. 15A must be kept with a bank or with a person carrying on business in which money received by way of deposit is lent to others or in which any other activity of the business is financed, to any material extent, out of the capital of or out of the interest on money received by way of deposit (s. 15B(3) and (4)). B5.34

A bank account is not credited, for the purposes of s. 15A, while the bank with which the account is kept maintains a reservation that precludes the account holder from dealing with the funds in question. 'Credited', in this context, means credited unconditionally (*Re Holmes* [2005] 1 WLR 1857, per Stanley Burnton J). This rule may in fact assist prosecutors in cases where an initial electronic transfer requires subsequent confirmation by an officer of the bank before it becomes available to the account holder, because the initial transfer may not have involved any human mind that could be deceived (see **B5.4**). If confirmation is not forthcoming, there may still be an attempt to commit a s. 15A offence.

Deception has the same meaning in s. 15A as in s. 15 (s. 15B(2)). As to this meaning, see **B5.2** *et seq.* Dishonesty is not defined, but clearly bears the same meaning as in other deception offences (see **B5.13**). An intent permanently to deprive need not be proved.

Relationship to Other Offences

Although *Preddy* [1996] AC 815 decided that fraudulently obtained money transfers are not obtained from the lender in contravention of the TA 1968, s. 15, a number of other offences may be committed in the course of such frauds (see **B5.17**). These may have to be relied upon in cases where the conduct in question occurred before s. 15A became law. B5.35

OBTAINING A PECUNIARY ADVANTAGE BY DECEPTION

Theft Act 1968, s. 16 B5.36

(1) A person who by any deception dishonestly obtains for himself or another any pecuniary advantage shall on conviction on indictment be liable to imprisonment for a term not exceeding five years.

(2) The cases in which a pecuniary advantage within the meaning of this section is to be regarded as obtained for a person are cases where—

(a) [repealed]

(b) he is allowed to borrow by way of overdraft, or to take out any policy of insurance or annuity contract, or obtains an improvement of the terms on which he is allowed to do so; or

(c) he is given the opportunity to earn remuneration or greater remuneration in an office or employment, or to win money by betting.

(3) For purposes of this section 'deception' has the same meaning as in section 15 of this Act.

Note that as regards acts prior to 15 January 2007, this offence is repealed and replaced by the offence under the Fraud Act 2006 (see **B5.1**).

Procedure and Jurisdiction

B5.37 An offence under the Theft Act 1968, s. 16, is triable either way (MCA 1980, s. 17 and sch. 1, para. 28). When tried on indictment it is a class 3 offence. It is a Group A offence for jurisdiction purposes under the CJA 1993, part I (see **A8.4**). For the provisions of the *Consolidated Criminal Practice Direction*, para. V.51, *Mode of trial* relating to fraud generally, see **B5.24**.

For the liability of officers of a company for an offence committed by the company, see the TA 1968, s. 18, and **B5.68**.

Indictment

B5.38

Statement of Offence

Obtaining a pecuniary advantage by deception contrary to section 16(1) of the Theft Act 1968

Particulars of Offence

A on or about the . . . day of . . . dishonestly obtained for himself a pecuniary advantage, namely being allowed to borrow by way of overdraft from the V Bank, by deception, namely by falsely representing that he was then entitled to use a cheque guarantee card when issuing a cheque numbered . . . drawn on account number . . . at the said V Bank

Sentence

B5.39 The maximum penalty is five years (TA 1968, s. 16(1)) on indictment; six months, a fine not exceeding the statutory maximum, or both, summarily. There is no guideline judgment reported for an offence under the TA 1968, s. 16(1). For sentencing guidelines for offences of deception generally, see **B5.26**. For sentencing guidelines for theft offences, see **B4.5** to **B4.8**.

Elements

B5.40 Some of the terms used in the TA 1968, s. 16(1), have already been explained. 'Deception' and 'dishonestly' bear the same meanings as in s. 15 (see **B5.2** to **B5.13**) but 'obtaining a pecuniary advantage' is a mere term of art, which has no meaning save that given to it in s. 16. As the House of Lords held in *DPP v Turner* [1974] AC 537, if the accused's deception has produced any of the consequences specified in s. 16(2) then a pecuniary advantage 'is to be regarded as obtained'. There cannot then be any room for argument about whether the accused (or another) actually derived any real profit from the transaction. Conversely, if the accused has profited in some way *not* covered by s. 16(2), there can be no question of liability under s. 16(1): some other charge would have to be considered (e.g., under the TA 1978).

Pecuniary Advantage: Being Allowed to Borrow by Way of Overdraft etc.

B5.41 As well as being an offence under the TA 1968, s. 16(1), borrowing cash could involve a more serious offence under s. 15, as could the use of a cheque-book and cheque guarantee card to buy goods in circumstances where the bank has no choice but to honour cheques on an overdrawn account. To this extent, the two provisions overlap, since the bank does (albeit unwillingly) 'allow' the overdraft, and the offences are committed even though it was not the bank that was deceived but someone else (*Waites* [1982] Crim LR 369 and see **B5.5**). The offence created by s. 16(2)(b) has the advantage from the prosecution viewpoint of being complete as soon as overdraft facilities have been granted, even if they have not been used (*Watkins* [1976] 1 All ER 578) but it has a limited ambit: a bank loan is not the same as an overdraft, nor can an overdraft be incurred by misuse of a credit card. Section 16(2)(b) is equally inapt where the accused has misused cheques stolen from another person. See further *Metropolitan Police Commissioner v Charles* [1977] AC 177; *Bevan* (1986) 84 Cr App R 143; *Kovacs* [1974] 1 WLR 370.

Pecuniary Advantage: Opportunity to Earn Remuneration etc.

The essence of the offence defined in the TA 1968, s. 16(2)(c), is the obtaining of the opportunity: it does not matter whether the accused (or anyone else for whom he has acted) has earned any remuneration or won his bet. In respect of betting, this provision filled the gap in the old law apparently revealed in *Clucas* [1949] 2 KB 226: see **B5.10**. **B5.42**

As to the meaning of 'opportunity to earn remuneration in an office or employment', see *McNiff* [1986] Crim LR 57, and *Callender* [1993] QB 303, where it was held that s. 16(2)(c) covered the case of a self-employed accountant who obtained work from clients by falsely claiming to hold CIMA qualifications.

Relationship between s. 16(2)(b) and s. 16(2)(c)

The TA 1968, s. 16, apparently creates only one offence, but a conviction on an indictment alleging an offence under s. 16(2)(b) cannot be supported when the evidence points only to an offence under s. 16(2)(c) (cf. *Aston* (1970) 55 Cr App R 48). **B5.43**

PROCURING EXECUTION OF A VALUABLE SECURITY BY DECEPTION

Theft Act 1968, s. 20 **B5.44**

(2) A person who dishonestly, with a view to gain for himself or another or with intent to cause loss to another, by any deception procures the execution of a valuable security shall on conviction on indictment be liable to imprisonment for a term not exceeding seven years; and this subsection shall apply in relation to the making, acceptance, endorsement, alteration, cancellation or destruction in whole or in part of a valuable security, and in relation to the signing or sealing of any paper or other material in order that it may be made or converted into, or used or dealt with as, a valuable security, as if that were the execution of a valuable security.

(3) For purposes of this section 'deception' has the same meaning as in section 15 of this Act, and 'valuable security' means any document creating, transferring, surrendering or releasing any right to, in or over property, or authorising the payment of money or delivery of any property, or evidencing the creation, transfer, surrender or release of any such right, or the payment of money or delivery of any property, or the satisfaction of any obligation.

Note that as regards acts prior to 15 January 2007, this offence is repealed and replaced by the offence under the Fraud Act 2006 (see **B5.1**).

This offence is frequently of significance in deception cases where cheques and similar instruments are involved, and not only where they have been executed in favour of the accused.

The concepts of dishonesty and deception bear the same meanings as in s. 15 of the Act (see **B5.2** to **B5.13**).

Procedure and Jurisdiction

An offence under the Theft Act 1968, s. 20, is triable either way (MCA 1980, s. 17 and sch. 1, para. 28). When tried on indictment it is a class 3 offence. It is a Group A offence for jurisdiction purposes under the CJA 1993, part I (see **A8.4**). For the provisions of the *Consolidated Criminal Practice Direction*, para. V.51, *Mode of trial* relating to fraud generally, see **B5.24**. **B5.45**

For the liability of officers of a company for an offence committed by the company, see the TA 1968, s. 18, and **B5.68**.

Indictment

B5.46

Statement of Offence

Procuring the execution of a valuable security by deception contrary to section 20(2) of the Theft Act 1968

Particulars of Offence

A on or about the . . . day of . . ., with a view to gain for himself, dishonestly procured V to execute a valuable security, namely a cheque for £10,000, by deception, namely by falsely representing to the said V that goods of that value had been supplied to V's account

Sentence

B5.47 The maximum penalty is seven years (TA 1968, s. 20(2)) on indictment; six months, a fine not exceeding the statutory maximum, or both, summarily. There is no guideline judgment reported for an offence under the TA 1968, s. 20(2). For sentencing guidelines for offences of deception generally, see **B5.26**. For sentencing guidelines for theft offences, see **B4.5** to **B4.8**.

Actus Reus: Meaning of 'Valuable Security'

B5.48 The definition of the term 'valuable security' provided by the TA 1968, s. 20(3), clearly embraces cheques, bills of exchange and banker's drafts, all of which authorise the payment of money. Share certificates, irrevocable letters of credit (*Benstead* (1982) 75 Cr App R 276), bills of lading and vouchers evidencing credit card sales also come within the definition (*Beck* [1985] 1 WLR 22). It was held in *Manjdadria* [1993] Crim LR 73 that a telegraphic or electronic transfer of funds cannot in itself be a valuable security. A similar conclusion was reached in *Johl* [1994] Crim LR 522. *Manjdadria* does not, however, prevent a document authorising a money transfer from being classified as a valuable security. It merely decides that the transfer itself cannot be one (*Peter Weiss v Government of Germany* [2000] Crim LR 484). In *King* [1992] 1 QB 20, the Court of Appeal held that a Clearing House Automated Payment System (CHAPS) order, which must be signed by bank officials as well as by the customer, was a valuable security and was executed within the extended meaning of s. 20(2) (see **B5.49**). *King* was approved by the House of Lords in *Kassim* [1992] 1 AC 9.

Meaning of 'Execution'

B5.49 Execution is partly defined within the TA 1968, s. 20(2) itself, but the definition has proved capable of differing interpretations. Should terms such as 'acceptance' be construed in their technical sense (as where the bank on which a bill is drawn signs its acceptance of liability on that instrument) or should they be construed in a wider sense, as they are used in ordinary language?

In a number of Court of Appeal decisions on the meaning of 'execution', notably *Beck* [1985] 1 WLR 22, it was formerly held that 'execution' for the purposes of s. 20(2) bore the wider meaning, and extended to any act giving effect to or carrying out the terms of the security in question. Payment of a cheque was thus regarded as a form of execution; but doubts were raised as to the correctness of this non-technical interpretation and in *Kassim* [1992] 1 AC 9, the House of Lords concluded that *Beck* was wrongly decided. Lord Ackner said that s. 20(2) contemplates acts being done to or in connection with bills of exchange and other such instruments but does not contemplate, and accordingly is not concerned with, giving effect to the documents by the carrying out of the instructions which they may contain, such as the delivery of goods or the payment of money. Section 20(2) nevertheless provides that some actions which do not amount to execution in the strict sense shall be treated as if they were acts of execution. Thus, the signing of any paper 'in order that it may be . . . dealt with as a valuable security' will be treated as equivalent to execution, and this extension of the concept of execution was relied upon by the Court of Appeal in *King* [1992] 1 QB 20 (see **B5.17**).

'Procuring'

In *Beck* [1985] 1 WLR 22, Watkins LJ stated that 'procuring' is a word in common usage, meaning 'to cause or bring about'. This interpretation has more recently been followed in *Aston* [1998] Crim LR 498, in which the Court of Appeal also approved a passage from Professor Sir John Smith's *Law of Theft* (8th ed at para. 6–18), to the effect that D must be proved to have at least been reckless as to the possibility that his deception would lead to the execution of some type of valuable security. D need not specifically have intended that he would receive a valuable security rather than (say) cash, although a specific intent of this kind may have to be proved if the charge is one of conspiracy or attempt to procure one (see *Mensah-Lartey* [1996] 1 Cr App R 143). A further qualification has been added by the House of Lords in *Kassim* [1992] 1 AC 9, in which it was held that D cannot be regarded as procuring any form of execution (such as the cancellation of the security) which takes place only after his fraudulent plans have already succeeded. To hold otherwise would involve 'confusing consequences with intention'. **B5.50**

Mens Rea: With a View to Gain or with Intent to Cause Loss

The TA 1968, s. 20(2) specifies an ulterior intent, and the full offence may be committed without either consequence actually occurring. 'Gain' and 'loss' are defined (as for blackmail and false accounting) in s. 34(2)(a) of the 1968 Act: **B5.51**

> 'gain' and 'loss' are to be construed as extending only to gain or loss in money or other property, but as extending to any such gain or loss whether temporary or permanent; and—
> (i) 'gain' includes a gain by keeping what one has, as well as a gain by getting what one has not; and
> (ii) 'loss' includes a loss by not getting what one might get, as well as a loss by parting with what one has.

There may be an 'intent to gain' even where the accused merely seeks to acquire property that is owing to him (*A-G's Ref No. 1 of 2001*) [2002] 3 All ER 849). In a false-accounting case (*Eden* (1971) 55 Cr App R 193) it was emphasised that an intent to gain or lose on a temporary basis may suffice under s. 34(2)(a); but contrast *Golechha* [1989] 1 WLR 1050, where the Court of Appeal adopted a very restrictive view of s. 34(2) and held that falsification made with intent to postpone the enforcement of a debt by the creditor was not made with a view to gain by keeping money or other property. See also *Lee Cheung Wing v The Queen* [1992] Crim LR 440 at **B6.13**.

OBTAINING SERVICES BY DECEPTION

Theft Act 1978, s. 1 **B5.52**

> (1) A person who by any deception dishonestly obtains services from another shall be guilty of an offence.
> (2) It is an obtaining of services where the other is induced to confer a benefit by doing some act, or causing or permitting some act to be done, on the understanding that the benefit has been or will be paid for.
> (3) Without prejudice to the generality of subsection (2) above, it is an obtaining of services where the other is induced to make a loan, or to cause or permit a loan to be made, on the understanding that any payment (whether by way of interest or otherwise) will be or has been made in respect of the loan.

Note that as regards acts prior to 15 January 2007, this offence is repealed and replaced by the offence under the Fraud Act 2006 (see **B5.1**).

Procedure and Jurisdiction

Obtaining services by deception is triable either way (TA 1978, s. 4(1)). When tried on indictment it is a class 3 offence. It is a Group A offence for jurisdiction purposes under **B5.53** the CJA 1993, part I (see **A8.4**). For the provisions of the *Consolidated Criminal Practice Direction*, para. V.51, *Mode of trial* relating to fraud generally, see **B5.24**.

For the liability of officers of a company for an offence committed by the company, see the TA 1968, s. 18 (which is applied to the TA 1978, s. 1, by s. 5(1) of the 1978 Act), and **B5.68**.

Indictment

B5.54 *Statement of Offence*

Obtaining services by deception contrary to section 1(1) of the TA 1978

Particulars of Offence

A on or about the . . . day of . . . dishonestly obtained from V services, namely the preparation of A's will, by deception, namely by falsely representing to the said V that a cheque in the sum of . . . numbered . . . and drawn on the X Bank, was a good and valid payment for V's professional fees

Sentence

B5.55 The maximum penalty is five years (TA 1978, s. 4(2)(a)) on indictment; six months, a fine not exceeding the statutory maximum, or both, summarily. There is no guideline judgment reported for an offence under the TA 1978, s. 1. In *Takyi* [1998] 1 Cr App R (S) 372, the offender attempted to board an international flight using a passport which belonged to someone else. He pleaded guilty to attempting to obtain services by deception, the Court of Appeal reducing his prison sentence from nine months to three months on appeal. For sentencing guidelines for offences of deception generally, see **B5.26**. For sentencing guidelines for theft offences, see **B4.5** to **B4.8**.

Relationship with Other Offences

B5.56 The TA 1978, s. 1, together with s. 2 and (less directly) s. 3 of the 1978 Act, replaced s. 16(2)(a) of the TA 1968, which had been described as 'a judicial nightmare' (*Royle* [1971] 1 WLR 1764 per Edmund-Davies LJ).

There is some overlap between this provision and other deception offences. In particular, an obtaining of services might also result in the execution of a valuable security or the obtaining of an unauthorised overdraft, and the same deception could be responsible for both. There will be circumstances in which an obtaining of property might also be described as an obtaining of services, as where goods are obtained on hire-purchase or some kind of leasing arrangement (*Widdowson* (1985) 82 Cr App R 314).

Deception, Dishonesty and Obtaining

B5.57 'Deception' in the TA 1978, s. 1, bears the same meaning as in the TA 1968, s. 15, and other deception offences (TA 1978, s. 5(1)), and the concept of dishonesty is likewise identical. For discussion of these concepts, see **B5.2** to **B5.13**. It would seem from the TA 1978, s. 1(2), that, in contrast to the offences under the 1968 Act, the person from whom the services are obtained must himself be a victim of the deception; he must be 'induced' to provide them, and this presumably means induced by the deception. As far as the obtaining is concerned, there is no mention in s. 1(2) of 'obtaining for another or enabling another to obtain' (contrast s. 15(2) of the 1968 Act and s. 2(4) of the 1978 Act) but in *Nathan* [1997] Crim LR 835 the Court of Appeal could see no justification for restricting the ambit of the offence so as to exclude such conduct. Nor need the deception relate to the prospect of payment (*Naviede* [1997] Crim LR 662).

Meaning of 'Services'

The TA 1978, s. 1(2), defines 'services' in terms of benefits (which would include accommodation, travel, education, medical care etc.), but excludes benefits which are provided gratuitously. In *Halai* [1983] Crim LR 624, the Court of Appeal held that a building society had not provided services merely by allowing the accused to open a savings account because building societies do not charge any fees for such accounts. The position would be different if the accused practices his deception in order to open a current account with a bank which charges for services provided to such accounts (*Shortland* [1995] Crim LR 893; *Sofroniou* [2004] QB 1218). It was also held in *Halai* that a mortgage advance falls outside the definition of 'services', but this ruling was widely criticised and has been abrogated (in respect of matters occurring on or after 18 December 1996) by the TA 1978, s. 1(3), which was inserted by the Theft (Amendment) Act 1996, s. 4, in response to such criticism. Even in respect of matters occurring before that date, it has been held on several occasions that *Halai* should no longer be followed (see *Graham* [1997] 1 Cr App R 302, *Cooke* [1997] Crim LR 436, *Cummings-John* [1997] Crim LR 660 and *Smith (Wallace Duncan) (No. 4)* [2004] QB 1418). B5.58

If one person deceives another into providing free benefits which the other would normally have charged for then there can be no offence under the TA 1978, s. 1, though there may be an offence under s. 2(1)(c).

A typical offence under the TA 1978, s. 1, will involve the accused deceiving someone into thinking that the accused would pay him for the benefit provided, when the accused had no intention of so paying. However, an offence may be committed under this section involving a deception that has nothing to do with intent to pay. If the service is only available to qualified persons, or is available to some at a lower price than others, then a deception as to status may be sufficient. (See *Adams* [1993] Crim LR 525.) If a person claims to be a paid-up member of a club, and thus entitled to use club facilities free of further charge, the club may thereby be deceived into providing a benefit on the understanding that it *has been* paid for (via the membership fee).

EVASION OF LIABILITY BY DECEPTION

Theft Act 1978, s. 2 B5.59

(1) Subject to subsection (2) below, where a person by any deception—
  (a) dishonestly secures the remission of the whole or part of any existing liability to make a payment, whether his own liability or another's; or
  (b) with intent to make permanent default in whole or in part on any existing liability to make a payment, or with intent to let another do so, dishonestly induces the creditor or any person claiming payment on behalf of the creditor to wait for payment (whether or not the due date for payment is deferred) or to forgo payment; or
  (c) dishonestly obtains any exemption from or abatement of liability to make a payment;

  he shall be guilty of an offence.

(2) For purposes of this section 'liability' means legally enforceable liability; and subsection (1) shall not apply in relation to a liability that has not been accepted or established to pay compensation for a wrongful act or omission.

(3) For purposes of subsection (1)(b) a person induced to take in payment a cheque or other security for money by way of conditional satisfaction of a pre-existing liability is to be treated not as being paid but as being induced to wait for payment.

(4) For purposes of subsection (1)(c) 'obtains' includes obtaining for another or enabling another to obtain.

Note that as regards acts prior to 15 January 2007, this offence is repealed and replaced by the offence under the Fraud Act 2006 (see **B5.1**).

'Deception' in the TA 1978, s. 2, bears the same meaning as in the TA 1968, s. 15, and other deception offences (TA 1978, s. 5(1)), and the concept of dishonesty is likewise identical. For discussion of these concepts, see **B5.2** to **B5.13**.

Procedure and Jurisdiction

B5.60 Offences under the Theft Act 1978, s. 2, are triable either way (TA 1978, s. 4(1)). When tried on indictment they are class 3 offences. These are Group A offences for jurisdiction purposes of the CJA 1993, part I (see **A8.4**). For the provisions of the *Consolidated Criminal Practice Direction*, para. V.51, *Mode of trial* relating to fraud generally, see **B5.24**.

For the liability of officers of a company for an offence committed by the company, see the TA 1968, s. 18 (which is applied to the TA 1978, s. 2, by s. 5(1) of the 1978 Act), and **B5.68**.

Indictment

B5.61

Statement of Offence

Evasion of liability by deception contrary to section 2(1)(a) of the Theft Act 1978

Particulars of Offence

A on or about the . . . day of . . . dishonestly secured the remission of the whole of an existing liability to make a payment to V for a quantity of petrol, by deception, namely by falsely representing to the said V that he (A) was then entitled to use a credit card issued by the X Oil Company and that V would receive payment for the said petrol from the X Oil Company

Sentence

B5.62 The maximum penalty is five years (TA 1978, s. 4(2)(a)) on indictment; six months, a fine not exceeding the statutory maximum, or both, summarily. There is no guideline judgment reported for an offence under the TA 1978, s. 2. For sentencing guidelines for offences of deception generally, see **B5.26**. For sentencing guidelines for theft offences, see **B4.5** to **B4.8**.

Relationship with Other Offences

B5.63 Whereas the TA 1978, s. 1, penalises the dishonest obtaining of services, this provision generally confines itself to the dishonest evasion of a pre-existing liability to pay for something. There is nevertheless some degree of overlap between s. 1 and s. 2(1)(c), either or both of which could apply where a person dishonestly deceives another into providing him with some benefit at a reduced price. Further overlaps exist between the three distinct offences created by paragraphs (a) to (c) of s. 2(1). See *Sibartie* [1983] Crim LR 470.

There may also be some overlap between s. 2 offences and the offence of making off without payment under s. 3 (see **B5.69**) as for example where D tricks V into waiting for him to 'fetch his wallet from the car' and then makes off (cf. *DPP v Ray* [1974] AC 370). If, however, D deceives V into accepting a worthless cheque in payment, or into allowing him to 'put a cheque in the post' the following day, then s. 2(1)(b) clearly provides the more appropriate charge, because D now leaves with V's consent and V no longer expects payment on the spot when D 'makes off' (see *Hammond* [1982] Crim LR 611; *Vincent* [2001] 1 WLR 1172).

Liability to Make a Payment

B5.64 The concept of a liability to make a payment is common to all three offences under the TA 1978, s. 2(1), and is explained in s. 2(2). It must in every case be a liability which is legally enforceable. It is possible to commit an offence under the TA 1978, s. 1, or the TA 1968, s. 16(2)(c), by deceiving someone into providing a service or accepting a bet under an unlawful or unenforceable contract, but one cannot commit an offence under the TA 1978, s. 2, by practising a deception in order to avoid paying an unenforceable debt, nor can it be an offence under s. 2(1)(c) to obtain an unlawful service free of the usual charge. In contrast, the fact that liability may be enforceable only when a court order has been obtained does not prevent it from being an existing liability for the purposes of s. 2(1) (*Modupe* [1991] Crim LR 530).

Special provision is made in the TA 1978, s. 2(2), for liabilities arising out of allegedly wrongful acts or omissions. The subsection provides that it can be an offence to evade such a liability only if the liability has been accepted or established. There are doubtless good policy reasons for excluding cases in which the existence of liability is still disputed, but the effect of this rule may be surprising. Thus, a person would commit no offence under the TA 1978 by brazenly denying responsibility for damage he knows he has caused to another's property, but he will risk prosecution if he admits causing the damage but gives a false name and address 'to which the bill may be sent'. It is submitted that if there is an informal admission of liability which is later retracted then liability can no longer be treated as having been accepted or established.

Securing Remission of an Existing Liability

'Remission' means release. The offence under the TA 1978, s. 2(1)(a), is therefore committed where a person has deceived another into releasing him (or a third party) from all or part of an existing liability to pay. It is not committed where another is deceived into thinking that no liability exists, nor where he is deceived into extending the deadline for payment (though there may then be an offence under s. 2(1)(b)). B5.65

The Court of Appeal held in *Jackson* [1983] Crim LR 617 that the accused was properly convicted of an offence under s. 2(1)(a) where he had induced another to accept a stolen credit card in payment for petrol previously supplied. The other's acceptance of the card meant that he would henceforward look to the card issuer for payment.

The position is arguably similar where a person, by deception, dishonestly induces another person to accept a cheque in payment of a liability, even if the cheque is not backed by a guarantee card. The TA 1978, s. 2(3), which provides that, for the purposes of s. 2(1)(b), inducing someone to accept payment by cheque constitutes an inducement to wait for payment, is not applicable to the offence under s. 2(1)(a), and a person who takes a cheque in such circumstances takes it in substitution (albeit conditional substitution) for payment in cash. Having accepted it, he cannot ordinarily sue for the debt without making any effort to present the cheque for payment. In the event of dishonour, he could choose to sue either on the cheque or for the original debt; but even though the remission of the debt is thus conditional (*Gunn v Bolckow, Vaughan & Co.* (1875) LR 10 Ch App 491), it could still be within the scope of s. 2(1)(a), which says nothing about remission having to be unconditional.

Nevertheless, it would be better to rely on s. 2(1)(b) in any case where it can be proved that the accused passed a worthless cheque with intent to make permanent default in payment. It is in cases where the accused was only stalling for time that the point becomes significant.

Inducement of a creditor to accept less than the full amount of a debt in full satisfaction of the debt may be more problematic because, unless the creditor gives a deed of release or joins with other creditors in agreeing to a compromise, the balance of the debt may still be sued for, there being no valid consideration for the release (*D & C Builders Ltd v Rees* [1966] 2 QB 617). So it would seem there has not been a remission of liability within s. 2(1)(a). A better charge would be one brought under s. 2(1)(b), assuming that an intent to make permanent default can be proved.

Inducing a Creditor to Wait For or Forgo Payment

The TA 1978, s. 2(3), applies to the offence under s. 2(1)(b). The need to prove an intent to make permanent default distinguishes s. 2(1)(b) from the other two s. 2 offences, but in other respects it is wider than the others, since the creditor or his agents need not grant either exemption from or remission of any liability to pay. It will suffice if they are deceived into B5.66

doing without payment, either permanently or (as they imagine) temporarily (for example, if a person falsely tells a creditor that he has no money on him, and the creditor has no choice but to wait). If the deceiver is indeed granted remission of or exemption from an existing liability, this may also involve the creditor forgoing payment, and the deceiver may also be guilty of an offence under s. 2(1)(b) (*Holt* [1981] 1 WLR 1000). Note that the deception must be practised against the creditor or some person claiming payment on his behalf (*Gee* [1999] Crim LR 397).

As to the meaning of the words, 'or with intent to let another do so; see *Attewell-Hughes* [1991] 1 WLR 955.

Obtaining Exemption from or Abatement of Liability

B5.67 Exemption from liability under the TA 1978, s. 2(1)(c), includes exemption from either an existing or a freshly created liability (*Firth* (1989) 91 Cr App R 217). In this respect its scope is wider than that of the other s. 2 offences. In *Sibartie* [1983] Crim LR 470 it was held that the offence could be committed through use of an invalid season ticket. Most commentators have taken the view that this was overextending the meaning of s. 2(1)(c) and that a better charge would have been one under s. 2(1)(b), but *Sibartie* perhaps indicates that the judges prefer not to draw too rigid a distinction between the different s. 2 offences.

LIABILITY OF COMPANY OFFICERS FOR OFFENCES COMMITTED BY THE COMPANY

B5.68 **Theft Act 1968, s. 18**

(1) Where an offence committed by a body corporate under section 17 of this Act is proved to have been committed with the consent or connivance of any director, manager, secretary or other similar officer of the body corporate, or any person who was purporting to act in any such capacity, he as well as the body corporate shall be guilty of that offence, and shall be liable to be proceeded against and punished accordingly.

(2) Where the affairs of a body corporate are managed by its members, this section shall apply in relation to the acts and defaults of a member in connection with his functions of management as if he were a director of the body corporate.

In respect of things done wholly or partly prior to 15 January 2007, s. 18 also applies to offences under the TA 1968 ss. 15 and 16 and to offences under the TA 1978 ss. 1 and 2 (see TA 1978, s. 5(1) and the Fraud Act 2006, sch. 2, para. 3).

As to the limitations on the scope of s. 18, see the discussion of *Boal* [1992] 1 QB 591 at A5.17. As to the limitations on the importance of s. 18, offences to which it applies can only be committed by corporations if the persons who control them possess the requisite *mens rea*, which can then be imputed to the corporation. Such persons will necessarily be guilty as joint perpetrators or as accessories under the general law governing complicity in offences, without any need for reference to s. 18. Any junior manager or officer who knowingly assists in the commission of such an offence by his company will similarly incur secondary liability.

This leaves s. 18 with one significant function. It may apply to senior officers or directors who knowingly consent to the commission of relevant offences, without themselves doing any acts that could result in liability as accessories under the general law (see further A5.17).

MAKING OFF WITHOUT PAYMENT

Theft Act 1978, s. 3 **B5.69**

(1) Subject to subsection (3) below, a person who, knowing that payment on the spot for any goods supplied or service done is required or expected from him, dishonestly makes off without having paid as required or expected and with intent to avoid payment of the amount due shall be guilty of an offence.

(2) For purposes of this section 'payment on the spot' includes payment at the time of collecting goods on which work has been done or in respect of which service has been provided.

(3) Subsection (1) above shall not apply where the supply of the goods or the doing of the service is contrary to law, or where the service done is such that payment is not legally enforceable.

Procedure

Making off without payment is triable either way (TA 1978, s. 4(1)). When tried on indictment it is a class 3 offence. For the provisions of the *Consolidated Criminal Practice Direction*, para. V.51, *Mode of trial* relating to fraud generally, see B5.24. **B5.70**

Indictment

Statement of Offence **B5.71**

Making off without payment contrary to section 3(1) of the Theft Act 1978

Particulars of Offence

A on or about the . . . day of . . ., knowing that payment on the spot of £ . . . was required of him for petrol supplied to him by V, dishonestly made off without having paid the amount due as so required and with intent to avoid payment thereof

Sentence

The maximum penalty is two years (TA 1978, s. 4(2)(b)) on indictment; six months, a fine not exceeding the statutory maximum, or both, summarily. There is no guideline judgment reported for an offence under the TA 1978, s. 3, when tried on indictment. For sentencing guidelines for offences of deception generally, see **B5.26**. For sentencing guidelines for theft offences, see **B4.5** to **B4.8**. **B5.72**

When dealt with summarily, the Magistrates' Courts Guidelines (2004) indicate the following for a first-time offender pleading not guilty:

Aggravating Factors For example deliberate plan; high value, two or more involved; racial or religious aggravation; victim particularly vulnerable; offence committed on bail; relevant previous convictions and any failures to respond to previous sentences.

Mitigating Factors For example impulsive action; low value.

Guideline: Is discharge or fine appropriate?

The guideline fine is Starting Point B (see E17.5).

In *Foster* (1994) 15 Cr App R (S) 340 the Court of Appeal upheld a sentence of three months' imprisonment on an offender convicted of four counts of making off without payment. He had engaged taxis to take him on trips resulting in fares between £37 and £63 and had disappeared without paying. The offences were planned, and the offender was at the time subject to a suspended sentence of nine months imposed for offences of conspiracy to burgle and theft. That sentence was activated consecutively, making 12 months' imprisonment in all.

Overlap with Other Offences under the Theft Acts 1968 and 1978

B5.73 A possible overlap between making off without payment and evasion of a liability by deception is considered at **B5.63**. Because of the relative ease with which the offence of making off without payment can be proved, it may be charged in circumstances where a more serious charge of theft or of obtaining etc. might otherwise have been pressed. If, for example, it is clear that the accused dishonestly made off without paying for his meal, or for the petrol which has been put into his car's tank, the TA 1978, s. 3, provides the obvious charge. It may be that the accused never intended to pay, and therefore committed theft or an offence under the TA 1968, s. 15, but this will be far harder to prove in the absence of a confession or other evidence of the accused's state of mind at the time of the original obtaining.

Payment on the Spot for Goods Supplied or Service Done

B5.74 The phrase 'payment on the spot' used in the TA 1978, s. 3(1), is partially explained in s. 3(2). The 'spot' in question is the place where payment is required, and this will usually be the premises where the transaction takes place, but it may sometimes mean something narrower (see **B5.75**).

Under the TA 1978, s. 5(2), 'goods' in s. 3(1) is to be interpreted in accordance with the TA 1968, s. 34(2)(b), and it can be assumed that 'service' bears the same meaning as in s. 1 of the 1978 Act (see **B5.58**).

The required payment must be one which is legally enforceable (TA 1978, s. 3(3)). It is possible to commit an offence of obtaining property or services by deception by tricking another person into entering into a legally unenforceable transaction; but the evasion of an unenforceable obligation, whether by deception or by making off, cannot be an offence.

Meaning of 'Making Off'

B5.75 In *Brooks* (1982) 76 Cr App R 66, it was held that the words 'dishonestly makes off' are easily understandable by a jury, and ordinarily require no elaboration in a summing-up; but such elaboration may be needed in some cases. If D practices a deception, as a result of which V *allows* him to leave without paying, this cannot be an offence under s. 3, and a jury must be directed accordingly. As Pill LJ explained in *Vincent* [2001] 1 WLR 1172, 'If the expectation [of payment on the spot] is defeated by an agreement, it cannot be said to exist. The fact that the agreement is obtained dishonestly does not re-instate the expectation.' A charge of evading liability by deception may be more appropriate here. See *Hammond* [1982] Crim LR 611.

'Making off' ordinarily means leaving the premises concerned, and if D is stopped at the exit he will usually have committed only an attempt (*McDavitt* [1981] Crim LR 843), but this must be a question of fact. If, for example, D slips away from the top-floor restaurant in a department store, without paying for his meal at the counter, and is caught on the ground floor before leaving the building, there can be little doubt that he has made off within the meaning of the s. 3 (cf. *Brooks* (1982) 76 Cr App R 66). If D hires a taxi but then makes off without paying, the relevant 'spot' is in the place where the taxi is standing. If D travels on a public transport system without a ticket and dishonestly makes off when required to produce one, it will be no defence to argue that payment should have been made before the journey began (*Moberley v Alsop* (1991) 156 JP 514). An honest passenger inadvertently travelling without a ticket would of course be expected to pay during or after the journey. See also *Aziz* [1993] Crim LR 708.

Mens Rea: Dishonesty and Intent to Avoid Payment

On a charge of making off without payment the prosecution must prove that the accused intended to make permanent default (*Allen* [1985] AC 1029). If the accused made off, but intended to pay later, or knew he would have to do so (because the person to whom payment was due knew his address), he will not be guilty. **B5.76**

As to the meaning of 'dishonesty', see *Ghosh* [1982] QB 1053 and **B4.37**. The issue of dishonesty may arise where the accused walked out of a restaurant in protest at poor service or poor food. If he considered himself to be acting reasonably, and thought that ordinary honest people would agree, then he should not be considered dishonest.

SUPPRESSION OF DOCUMENTS

Theft Act 1968, s. 20 **B5.77**

(1) A person who dishonestly, with a view to gain for himself or another or with intent to cause loss to another, destroys, defaces or conceals any valuable security, any will or other testamentary document or any original document of or belonging to, or filed or deposited in, any court of justice or any government department shall on conviction on indictment be liable to imprisonment for a term not exceeding seven years.

Procedure

Suppression of documents is triable either way (TA 1978, s. 4(1)). When tried on indictment it is a class 3 offence. For the provisions of the *Consolidated Criminal Practice Direction*, para. V.51, *Mode of trial* relating to fraud generally, see **B5.24**. **B5.78**

Indictment

Statement of Offence **B5.79**

Destroying a valuable security contrary to section 20(1) of the Theft Act 1968

Particulars of Offence

A on or about the . . . day of . . ., dishonestly and with a view to gain for himself, destroyed a deed of trust executed by V

Sentence

The maximum penalty is seven years (TA 1968, s. 20(1)) on indictment; six months, a fine not exceeding the statutory maximum, or both, summarily. There is no guideline judgment reported for an offence under the TA 1968, s. 20(1). For sentencing guidelines for offences of deception generally, see **B5.26**. For sentencing guidelines for theft offences, see **B4.5** to **B4.8**. **B5.80**

Elements

The TA 1968, s. 20(1), is little used, perhaps because offences involving the destruction or concealment of wills etc. are difficult to detect. The defacing of such instruments may sometimes amount to forgery if intended to deceive, and destruction etc. might in many cases be charged as theft or criminal damage. **B5.81**

Most of the terms used in this provision have been discussed elsewhere. The meaning of 'dishonesty' is discussed in **B4.34** ***et seq.*** and **B5.13**. The definition of 'view to gain' etc. in s. 34(2)(a) is discussed at **B5.51**. 'Valuable security' is defined in s. 20(3) (see **B5.44** and **B5.50**).

BLACKMAIL

Definition

B5.82 **Theft Act 1968, s. 21**

(1) A person is guilty of blackmail if, with a view to gain for himself or another or with intent to cause loss to another, he makes any unwarranted demand with menaces; and for this purpose a demand with menaces is unwarranted unless the person making it does so in the belief—
(a) that he has reasonable grounds for making the demand; and
(b) that the use of the menaces is a proper means of reinforcing the demand.

(2) The nature of the act or omission demanded is immaterial, and it is also immaterial whether the menaces relate to action to be taken by the person making the demand.

(3) A person guilty of blackmail shall on conviction on indictment be liable to imprisonment for a term not exceeding 14 years.

Procedure and Jurisdiction

B5.83 Blackmail is triable only on indictment (TA 1968, s. 21(3); MCA 1980, s. 17 and sch. 1, para. 28). It is a class 3 offence. It is a Group A offence for jurisdiction purposes under the CJA 1993, part I (see **A8.4**).

Indictment

B5.84 *Statement of Offence*

Blackmail contrary to section 21(1) of the Theft Act 1968

Particulars of Offence

A on or about the . . . day of . . ., with a view to gain for himself, made an unwarranted demand for £1,000 from V with menaces

Sentencing Guidelines

B5.85 The maximum penalty is 14 years (TA 1968, s. 21(3)).

In *Witchelo* (1992) 13 Cr App R (S) 371 the offender received a sentence of 13 years after conviction of six offences of blackmail. He had written to food producers and threatened to contaminate their products. Some food was contaminated, and the offender obtained £32,000. He received a further four years for related offences. See also *Telford* (1992) 13 Cr App R (S) 676, where eight years was appropriate and *Riolfo* [1997] 1 Cr App R (S) 57, where a sentence of six years was substituted.

Sentences of six years and five years were reduced to four years and three years in *Cox* (1979) 1 Cr App R (S) 190, where the offenders removed discs and tapes from their employer and demanded £275,000 as the price for returning them. Three years was said to be appropriate in *Stone* (1989) 11 Cr App R (S) 176, where the offender took part in homosexual activities with the victim and then demanded sums of money under the threat of disclosing the victim's behaviour to the police. See also *Hadjou* (1989) 11 Cr App R (S) 29 and *Hollingworth* (1994) 15 Cr App R (S) 258. In *Havell* [2006] 2 Cr App R (S) 633 sentences of three years' and two years' imprisonment were appropriate for offenders convicted of seven counts of blackmail. They ran an illicit wheel-clamping business. Motorists who stopped their cars on land for a short period found that they were clamped and prevented from driving away until they had paid a sum of money between £45 and £95. The offenders behaved in a hostile manner.

View to Gain or Intent to Cause Loss

B5.86 Demands reinforced by improper threats do not necessarily constitute blackmail, which can only be committed 'with a view to gain . . . or intent to cause loss' (TA 1968, s. 21(1)). The concepts of gain and loss are defined in s. 34(2)(a) of the Act (see **B5.51**) as extending only to gain or loss, temporary or permanent, in money or other property. 'Gain' includes keeping what one has; 'loss' includes not getting what one might have got; and it is certainly possible to commit blackmail by using improper menaces in the course of demanding money or other property to which one is legally entitled (*Lawrence* (1971) 57 Cr App R 64); but merely seeking sexual favours or political advantage is not blackmail, though procuring sexual intercourse by threats etc. may amount to rape if the woman concerned is found to have submitted without genuinely consenting (see *Olugboja* [1982] QB 320 and **B3.10** *et seq.*).

A blackmailer need not be seeking any kind of material profit. In *Bevans* (1987) 87 Cr App R 64, the accused used menaces in order to obtain a pain-killing injection from a doctor; this was held to be blackmail as the drug involved was a form of property.

Meaning of 'Making a Demand'

The definition of the offence of blackmail in the TA 1968, s. 21, is deliberately drafted in such a way as to penalise the making of the demand, rather than the obtaining of property or the intimidation of the victim. In other words, it is a 'conduct crime', in which the effectiveness of the accused's behaviour is irrelevant (whether for jurisdictional or any other purpose), and in which the results thereof form no constituent part of the offence. **B5.87**

'Demands' are not defined in the Act. A demand need not be expressed openly. As was pointed out in *Studer* (1915) 85 LJ KB 1017, 'it may be in language only a request'; and indeed it need not even be that, if the context makes the blackmailer's meaning clear.

The kidnapper who writes to the child's parents, asking them whether they regard the child as being worth £10,000, would clearly be regarded as having 'demanded' that sum. Similarly, there would be a demand where a man offers to sell a victim his 'protection' whilst his friends demonstrate their willingness to wreck the victim's premises in the event of the offer being declined (*Colister* (1955) 39 Cr App R 100).

The earlier authorities did not provide any definite answer to the question whether a demand could be 'made' without successful communication to the intended recipient; but the question came before the House of Lords in *Treacy v DPP* [1971] AC 537, where the accused had posted his blackmail demand from England to a victim in West Germany. If receipt of the demand was regarded as an essential part of its 'making' then the blackmail would have been completed (and thus committed, for jurisdictional purposes) in West Germany, beyond the territorial ambit of the TA 1968; but it was held that the demand was made earlier, and within the jurisdiction, when the letter was posted.

Following *Treacy*, the successful communication of the demand cannot properly be described as an element of the offence of blackmail, and it was accordingly doubtful whether the receipt of a demand by a victim in England could render a 'cross-frontier' blackmailer liable for any offence under English law. The point was left open in *Treacy*, although it was suggested (*obiter*) that the concept of a 'continuing demand' might constitute a basis for jurisdiction. The CJA 1988, part I (see **A8.7**) was intended to clarify the position. By s. 4(b) of that Act, there is now deemed to be a 'communication' of a demand within the jurisdiction if it is sent from England and Wales to a place elsewhere, or sent from elsewhere to a place in England and Wales. The wording is unfortunate, because communication is not a 'relevant event' for the purposes of that Act. What s. 4(b) ought to have said is that there is a '*making*' of a demand in England and Wales in either of those circumstances, but it seems likely that a court would construe section 4(b) so as to give effect to its intended meaning.

Attempted Blackmail

It follows from the way blackmail is defined that offences of attempted blackmail must be unlikely occurrences. One could perhaps have such an offence where a telephone call is cut off just as the caller is starting to present his demand, or where a letter containing demands is **B5.88** seized just as the demander is about to post it; but in other circumstances it would seem that either the full offence is committed or only preparatory acts, which would not suffice for liability under the Criminal Attempts Act 1981.

Meaning of 'Menaces'

B5.89 In drafting the proposals which later became incorporated into the TA 1968, s. 21, the Criminal Law Revision Committee adopted the term 'menaces' in preference to 'threats', on the basis that the latter term might possibly be too wide. As the Court of Appeal later said in *Clear* [1968] 1 QB 670:

> Words or conduct which would not intimidate or influence anyone to respond to the demand would not be menaces . . ., but threats and conduct of such a nature and extent that the mind of an ordinary person of normal stability and courage might be influenced or made apprehensive so as to accede unwillingly to the demand would be sufficient for a jury's consideration.

Menaces are therefore serious or significant threats; but since blackmail cases rarely involve any dispute about whether the alleged threats, if proved, were serious, there is generally no need for a trial judge to define the term for the jury. (See *Lawrence* (1971) 57 Cr App R 64; and *Garwood* [1987] 1 WLR 319, in which it was said, somewhat questionably, that the term 'menaces' is an ordinary English word which any jury can be expected to understand.)

Nevertheless, there are at least two situations in which it is recognised that the jury may need guidance:

(a) A threat which one person would find trivial may be one which another would find terrifying. Some people are more timid than others, and fear is not always rational, even in people who may otherwise be very brave. If a demander knows that his victim suffers from arachnophobia, his threat to drop a large spider down the victim's back would obviously be calculated to have at least the same impact as a threat of serious violence. In *Garwood* [1987] 1 WLR 319, it was recognised that the victim's 'unusual timidity' could be taken into account, provided the accused knew of it; and it is submitted that it should suffice if the accused merely hoped to discover such weakness (for example, where he mistakenly believed the victim suffers from such a phobia).

(b) In the converse situation, where an apparently serious threat failed to intimidate the victim at all (perhaps because he knew something the blackmailer did not), the jury should be told that liability may still be incurred (*Clear* [1968] 1 QB 670).

Meaning of 'Unwarranted Demands'

B5.90 A demand with menaces will be unwarranted unless the demander genuinely believes both that he has reasonable grounds for making the demand, and that it is proper to reinforce it with those particular menaces. Note that he need not have reasonable grounds for his belief: it is a subjective test of what he thinks is reasonable and proper. Once the issue is raised, the prosecution will have the burden of proving that the accused had no such belief.

A menace may be considered improper without necessarily being a threat to do anything improper. Publicising a person's scandalous behaviour may in itself be perfectly legitimate: threatening him with such publicity in order to extract money from him would clearly be a classic case of blackmail.

In *Harvey* (1980) 72 Cr App R 139, the Court of Appeal stated that one cannot believe a threat to be proper if one knows it would be unlawful (i.e. criminal) to carry it out. This seemingly conflicts with the later pronouncement of the Court of Appeal in *Cousins* [1982] QB 526 that a threat to kill might sometimes be lawful where the killing threatened would not be; but the dicta in *Harvey* clearly indicate a link between legality and propriety. A fanatic might believe that he would be *justified* in killing or threatening to kill for the sake of his cause, but it seems that he cannot argue that he believes such threats to be *proper* when he knows that what he threatens would be criminal (*Harvey* (1980) 72 Cr App R 139 at p. 142).

In this respect, blackmail can be contrasted with robbery. A person who takes back property borrowed from him by another, believing that he is entitled to recover the property, cannot be guilty of stealing it, and thus cannot be guilty of robbery if he threatens violence in order to recover it; but since he can hardly believe his threats of violence are proper, he will almost certainly be guilty of blackmail (*Lawrence* (1971) 57 Cr App R 64; *Harvey* (1980) 72 Cr App R 139).

HARASSMENT OF DEBTORS

Administration of Justice Act 1970, s. 40 **B5.91**

(1) A person commits an offence if, with the object of coercing another person to pay money claimed from the other as a debt due under a contract, he—
   (a) harasses the other with demands for payment which, in respect of their frequency or the manner or occasion of making any such demand, or of any threat or publicity by which any demand is accompanied, are calculated to subject him or members of his family or household to alarm, distress or humiliation;
   (b) falsely represents, in relation to the money claimed, that criminal proceedings lie for failure to pay it;
   (c) falsely represents himself to be authorised in some official capacity to claim or enforce payment; or
   (d) utters a document falsely represented by him to have some official character or purporting to have some official character which he knows it has not.

(2) A person may be guilty of an offence by virtue of subsection (1)(a) above if he concerts with others in the taking of such action as is described in that paragraph, notwithstanding that his own course of conduct does not by itself amount to harassment.

(3) Subsection (1)(a) above does not apply to anything done by a person which is reasonable (and otherwise permissible in law) for the purpose—
   (a) of securing the discharge of an obligation due, or believed by him to be due, to himself or to persons for whom he acts, or protecting himself or them from future loss; or
   (b) of the enforcement of any liability by legal process.

(4) A person guilty of an offence under this section shall be liable on summary conviction to a fine of not more than level 5 on the standard scale.

The overlap between this summary offence and blackmail is clearly significant. If a person acts for the purpose of coercing another person into paying money, he necessarily acts 'with a view to gain', and some at least of the tactics proscribed by paras. (a) to (d) of the Administration of Justice Act 1970, s. 40(1), could well amount to the use of menaces. The most significant distinction between the two offences (insofar as they both apply to debt-collection) is that a threatener's beliefs about the propriety of his threats may be crucial in a blackmail prosecution, but largely irrelevant on a charge of harassment.

OTHER OFFENCES INVOLVING THREATS OR DEMANDS

B5.92 Threats to kill, whether or not amounting to blackmail, may be punishable under the OAPA 1861, s. 16 (see **B1.123** to **B1.127**). Threats of immediate violence may be punished as assault (see **B2.5**) or under the Public Order Act 1986 (see **B11**); and if done for the purposes of theft may amount to robbery or assault with intent to rob (see **B4.46** ***et seq.***). Threats to damage property may be covered by the Criminal Damage Act 1971, s. 2 (see **B8.26** to **B8.30**). Threats of violence for the purpose of securing entry to premises may be covered by the Criminal Law Act 1977, s. 6(1) (see **B13.22**). The Criminal Law Act 1977, s. 51, deals with bomb hoaxes (see **B11.115**), which may or may not be made with a view to gain etc.

Contamination of goods (often connected with blackmail of the manufacturers or suppliers) is punishable under the Public Order Act 1986, s. 38 (see **B11.121**).

The demanding of payment for unsolicited goods may be an offence under the Unsolicited Goods and Services Act 1972, s. 2(1), and if supported by threats, it may be a more serious (but still only summary) offence under s. 2(2) of that Act.

Sending threatening letters is covered by the Malicious Communications Act 1988, s. 1 (see **B19.41**). As to the offences under the Protection from Harassment Act 1997, see **B11.78** ***et seq.***

FRAUD ACT 2006: GENERAL

B5.93 The Fraud Act 2006 was brought fully into force on 15 January 2007 (Fraud Act 2006 (Commencement) Order 2006 (SI 2006 No. 3200). It has no retrospective effect. Transitional provisions are considered at **B5.1**. Much of the Act is based on proposals made by the Law Commission in its 2002 Report on Fraud (LC 276, Cm. 5560) but the Commission's proposed abolition of the offence of conspiracy to defraud has not been enacted.

THE OFFENCE OF FRAUD

B5.94 **Fraud Act 2006, s. 1**

(1) A person is guilty of fraud if he is in breach of any of the sections listed in subsection (2) (which provide for different ways of committing the offence).
(2) The sections are—
 (a) section 2 (fraud by false representation),
 (b) section 3 (fraud by failing to disclose information), and
 (c) section 4 (fraud by abuse of position).

Sections 2 to 4 of the Act are reproduced and examined at **B5.97** ***et seq.*** Section 5, which specifies the *mens rea* required, is reproduced and examined at **B5.100**. In all three variants of the offence, the focus is on proscribed conduct and ulterior intent, whereas the consequences of that conduct are not legally significant. Fraud is, in other words, a conduct crime, in which causation issues cannot arise and in which unsuccessful 'attempts' to defraud may in law amount to a complete or substantive offence. Indeed, it is hard to imagine conduct that could give rise to liability for attempted fraud under the Criminal Attempts Act 1981, other than cases analagous to *Anderton v Ryan* [1985] AC 560, in which D tries to defraud V but unwittingly tells the truth.

Procedure, Sentence and Jurisdiction

B5.95 **Fraud Act 2006, s. 1**

(3) A person who is guilty of fraud is liable—
 (a) on summary conviction, to imprisonment for a term not exceeding 12 months or to a fine not exceeding the statutory maximum (or to both);
 (b) on conviction on indictment, to imprisonment for a term not exceeding 10 years or to a fine (or to both).

In relation to an offence committed before the implementation of the CJA 2003, s. 154(1) (which increases the sentencing powers of magistrates' courts), the reference to 12 months in s. 1(3) is to be read as a reference to 6 months.

When tried on indictment, fraud is a class 3 offence. It is a Group A offence for jurisdiction purposes under the CJA 1993, part 1 (see **A8.4**). Company officers may be proceeded against and punished for any such offence committed by the company with their consent or connivance, see the Fraud Act 2006, s. 12(2). As to the position where a body corporate is managed by its members, see s. 12(3).

Indictment

Statement of Offence B5.96

Fraud, contrary to the Fraud Act 2006, section 1.

Particulars of Offence

A on or about the . . . day of . . . 2007, dishonestly made a false representation to B, namely, . . . knowing this to be untrue [or misleading] and intending thereby to make a gain for himself [or to expose B to a risk of loss].

Fraud by False Representation

Fraud Act 2006, s. 2 B5.97

(1) A person is in breach of this section if he—
 (a) dishonestly makes a false representation, and
 (b) intends, by making the representation—
  (i) to make a gain for himself or another, or
  (ii) to cause loss to another or to expose another to a risk of loss.
(2) A representation is false if—
 (a) it is untrue or misleading, and
 (b) the person making it knows that it is, or might be, untrue or misleading.
(3) 'Representation' means any representation as to fact or law, including a representation as to the state of mind of—
 (a) the person making the representation, or
 (b) any other person.
(4) A representation may be express or implied.
(5) For the purposes of this section a representation may be regarded as made if it (or anything implying it) is submitted in any form to any system or device designed to receive, convey or respond to communications (with or without human intervention).

Intent to gain and intent to cause loss are examined in **B5.100**. Dishonesty is not defined in the Act, but clearly is intended to have the same meaning as that formerly applicable in deception cases, namely the *Ghosh* test (*Ghosh* [1982] QB 1053, discussed at **B5.13**).

Much of what has already been said about false representations in the context of deception offences (see **B5.2 *et seq.***) applies equally to the new law, but when a false representation is made mere knowledge of (or recklessness as to) the falsity will suffice, whereas the old law required a successful deception and obtaining to result before the offence was complete. Section 2(3) states that any allegedly false representation must concern matters of fact or law, so a broken promise is not in itself a false representation; but (as was the case under the TA 1968, s. 15(4)) a statement or representation may be false if it misrepresents the current intentions or state of mind of the person making it or anyone else, so a promise involves a false representation if D never intended to keep that promise.

As with a blackmail demand, a false representation is 'made' as soon as it is uttered. There is no need for such a representation to be communicated to the intended recipient or anyone else. An offence under s. 1 may thus be complete even if, say, the letter containing the offending representation is lost or intercepted in the post: cf. *Treacy v DPP* [1971] AC 537 (see **B5.87**).

Where D dishonestly tenders a stolen credit or debit card to pay for goods or services, it is clear that he makes a false representation. Even if he says nothing, he impliedly represents that he is the authorised user of that card and believes himself to be entitled to use it; but where D tenders a cheque that his bank refuses to honour, the position would appear to be much the same as that discussed in **B5.11**. As in *Gilmartin* [1983] QB 953, one must identify a false representation as to the existing state of the account (although this may take account of existing expectations, such as salaries due to be credited or standing orders due to be debited).

An important difference between the old and new laws concerns false representations that are intended to 'deceive' ATMs, 'chip and pin' card readers, or other machines. Section 2(5) enables the offence of fraud to apply in such cases. In contrast the old law on deception excluded them on the basis that 'a machine cannot be deceived' (see **B5.4**).

Fraud by Failing to Disclose Information

B5.98 Fraud Act 2006, s. 3

A person is in breach of this section if he—
- (a) dishonestly fails to disclose to another person information which he is under a legal duty to disclose, and
- (b) intends, by failing to disclose the information—
  - (i) to make a gain for himself or another, or
  - (ii) to cause loss to another or to expose another to a risk of loss.

Under the Theft Acts, liability for deception offences could be incurred in some cases through dishonest omissions to provide correct information (see *Firth* (1989) 91 Cr App R 217 and **B5.8**). The Fraud Act 2006, s. 3, introduces a potentially broader concept of fraud through non-disclosure in cases where there is a legal duty to disclose. 'Legal duty' is not defined in the Act, but the Law Commission provided this explanation in its Report (LC 276 (2002)) at paras 7.28 and 7.29:

> Such a duty may derive from statute (such as the provisions governing company prospectuses), from the fact that the transaction in question is one of the utmost good faith (such as a contract of insurance), from the express or implied terms of a contract, from the custom of a particular trade or market, or from the existence of a fiduciary relationship between the parties (such as that of agent and principal).
>
> For this purpose there is a legal duty to disclose information not only if the defendant's failure to disclose it gives the victim a cause of action for damages, but also if the law gives the victim a right to set aside any change in his or her legal position to which he or she may consent as a result of the non-disclosure. For example, a person in a fiduciary position has a duty to disclose material information when entering into a contract with his or her beneficiary, in the sense that a failure to make such disclosure will entitle the beneficiary to rescind the contract and to reclaim any property transferred under it.

Fraud by Abuse of Position

B5.99 Fraud Act 2006, s. 4

(1) A person is in breach of this section if he—
- (a) occupies a position in which he is expected to safeguard, or not to act against, the financial interests of another person,
- (b) dishonestly abuses that position, and
- (c) intends, by means of the abuse of that position—
  - (i) to make a gain for himself or another, or
  - (ii) to cause loss to another or to expose another to a risk of loss.

(2) A person may be regarded as having abused his position even though his conduct consisted of an omission rather than an act.

This offence is in theory broader than the Law Commission's proposed offence of 'dishonest *and secret* abuse of position', but in practice nothing is likely to turn on this, because such abuse is most unlikely to take place openly.

The clear intention of the provision is to cover the dishonest abuse of any position of financial trust or responsibility, including that of a trustee, company director or executor, but it is not confined to fiduciary relationships and would extend to frauds committed by employees, including those that could not be prosecuted as theft; as, for example, where a cinema projectionist copies newly released films for private profit (cf. *Scott v Metropolitan Police Commissioner* [1975] AC 819) or where hotel or catering staff supply (and retain the profits from) their own food or drink, thereby depriving their employer of profits that would otherwise have been made from such sales (cf. *Cooke* [1986] AC 909).

Liability for omission might arise where, for example, a company director or employee dishonestly fails to secure or negotiate for a contract, lease or other business opportunity for the company, with the object of later securing it for himself. Whether given behaviour amounts to an abuse of an accused's position must largely be a question of fact for a jury, but it would be proper in many cases for a judge to make rulings or give directions as to the existence of fiduciary duties or other relationships.

Where D has abused his position by dishonestly appropriating V's property for himself, a charge of theft may well be easier to establish than a charge of fraud. In *Hinks* [2001] 2 AC 241, for example, D's liability for theft did not depend on whether her position as V's carer was one in which she was 'expected to safeguard or not to act against' V's financial interests; and indeed it seems doubtful whether it was such a position.

Intent to Gain or Cause Loss

Fraud Act 2006, s. 5 **B5.100**

(1) The references to gain and loss in sections 2 to 4 are to be read in accordance with this section.
(2) 'Gain' and 'loss'—
  (a) extend only to gain or loss in money or other property;
  (b) include any such gain or loss whether temporary or permanent;
  and 'property' means any property whether real or personal (including things in action and other intangible property).
(3) 'Gain' includes a gain by keeping what one has, as well as a gain by getting what one does not have.
(4) 'Loss' includes a loss by not getting what one might get, as well as a loss by parting with what one has.

Section 5 is closely based on the TA 1968, s. 34(2)(a), which governed offences under the TA 1968, s. 20(2) (procuring the execution of a valuable security) and will continue to govern offences under s. 21 of that Act (blackmail) (see **B5.51** and **B5.86**). The specified intent is 'ulterior', in that no gain or loss need actually result. This might have created jurisdictional limitations in respect of transnational or 'cross-frontier' offences: not in cases where any false representations, etc., are made within England and Wales (because in such cases the offence is wholly committed in England as soon as the false representation is made) but only in the converse case where the representation etc. is made abroad, with intent to deceive a victim within the jurisdiction, or with intent to gain or cause loss, etc., there. This is because the CJA 1993, part 1, applies English criminal law to transnational offences of fraud or dishonesty if, but only if, a 'relevant event' takes place within the jurisdiction — and the fraudulent obtaining of property etc. following a false representation or abuse of position etc. is not itself a 'relevant event' (see **A8.8**).

Schedule 1, para. 25, partly addresses this issue by inserting a new subsection (1A) into the CJA 1993, s. 2. This provides that, in relation to an offence of fraud under s. 1 of the 2006 Act, a 'relevant event' includes —

(a) if the fraud involved an intention to make a gain and the gain occurred, that occurrence; and
(b) if the fraud involved an intention to cause a loss or to expose another to a risk of loss and the loss occurred, that occurrence.

Clearly, however, this will not assist the prosecution in cases where a person intended by his conduct abroad to make a gain or cause a loss within England and Wales, but failed to do so. This deliberate omission is curious, because it conflicts with a strong trend towards the assumption of jurisdiction over acts such as conspiracies abroad that are intended to cause, but fail to cause, harm within the jurisdiction. See *Liangsiriprasert v United States* [1991] 1 AC 255 and **A6.23**.

POSSESSION OR CONTROL OF ARTICLES FOR USE IN FRAUDS

B5.101 **Fraud Act 2006, s. 6**

(1) A person is guilty of an offence if he has in his possession or under his control any article for use in the course of or in connection with any fraud.

An 'article' includes for this purpose (or for the purposes of the PACE 1984, s. 1(7)(b)) any program or data held in electronic form (Fraud Act 2006, s. 8(1)). This addresses the importance of computer technology in the perpetration of frauds. This offence complements the offence of having custody or control of a false instrument with intent (Forgery and Counterfeiting Act 1981, s. 5 — see **B6.43**) and to some extent supplants the offence of 'going equipped' under the TA 1968, s. 25 (see **B4.119**). The latter provision is amended by the Fraud Act 2006 so that it no longer applies to the possession of articles intended for use in a 'cheat'. In its application to offences of fraud, the new offence has a much wider ambit than s. 25, which did not (and in its application to burglary or theft still does not) apply to articles possessed by an accused at his place of abode. Moreover, the only kind of 'cheat' to which it related was an offence under the TA 1968, s. 15, whereas the new offence may apply to the possession, anywhere, of articles of any description that are intended for use in respect of any fraud offences under the Fraud Act 2006.

Procedure, Sentence and Jurisdiction

B5.102 **Fraud Act 2006, s. 6**

(2) A person guilty of an offence under this section is liable—
   (a) on summary conviction, to imprisonment for a term not exceeding 12 months or to a fine not exceeding the statutory maximum (or to both);
   (b) on conviction on indictment, to imprisonment for a term not exceeding 5 years or to a fine (or to both).

In relation to an offence committed before the implementation of the CJA 2003, s. 154(1) (which increases the sentencing powers of magistrates' courts), the reference to 12 months in s. 6(2) is to be read as a reference to 6 months.

When tried on indictment, this is a class 3 offence. It is a Group A offence for jurisdiction purposes under the CJA 1993, part 1 (see **A8.7**). Company officers may be proceeded against and punished for any such offence committed by the company with their consent or connivance, see the Fraud Act 2006, s. 12(2). As to the position where a body corporate is managed by its members, see s. 12(3).

MAKING OR SUPPLYING ARTICLES FOR USE IN FRAUDS

B5.103 **Fraud Act 2006, s. 7**

(1) A person is guilty of an offence if he makes, adapts, supplies or offers to supply any article—
   (a) knowing that it is designed or adapted for use in the course of or in connection with fraud, or
   (b) intending it to be used to commit, or assist in the commission of, fraud.

As to the meaning of the term, 'article', see s. 8(1), at **B5.101**. The offence created by s. 7(1) overlaps substantially with offences such as forgery or copying a false instrument (see **B6.28** and **B6.33**) but could also be used to prosecute persons who make, adapt, advertise or supply devices such as 'black boxes' for the purpose of falsifying readings on electricity meters.

Procedure, Sentence and Jurisdiction

Fraud Act 2006, s. 7 **B5.104**

(2) A person guilty of an offence under this section is liable—
(a) on summary conviction, to imprisonment for a term not exceeding 12 months or to a fine not exceeding the statutory maximum (or to both);
(b) on conviction on indictment, to imprisonment for a term not exceeding 10 years or to a fine (or to both).

In relation to an offence committed before the implementation of the CJA 2003, s. 154(1) (which increases the sentencing powers of magistrates' courts), the reference to 12 months in s. 7(2) is to be read as a reference to 6 months.

When tried on indictment, this is a class 3 offence. It is a Group A offence for jurisdiction purposes under the CJA 1993, part 1 (see **A8.7**). Company officers may be proceeded against and punished for any such offence committed by the company with their consent or connivance, see the Fraud Act 2006, s. 12(2). As to the position where a body corporate is managed by its members, see s. 12(3).

PARTICIPATING IN FRAUDULENT BUSINESS CARRIED ON BY SOLE TRADER ETC.

Fraud Act 2006, s. 9 **B5.105**

(1) A person is guilty of an offence if he is knowingly a party to the carrying on of a business to which this section applies.
(2) This section applies to a business which is carried on—
(a) by a person who is outside the reach of section 458 of the Companies Act 1985 or Article 451 of the Companies (Northern Ireland) Order 1986 (S.I. 1986/1032) (offence of fraudulent trading), and
(b) with intent to defraud creditors of any person or for any other fraudulent purpose.
(3) The following are within the reach of section 458 of the 1985 Act—
(a) a company (within the meaning of that Act);
(b) a person to whom that section applies (with or without adaptations or modifications) as if the person were a company;
(c) a person exempted from the application of that section.
(4) [Applies to Northern Ireland.]
(5) 'Fraudulent purpose' has the same meaning as in section 458 of the 1985 Act or Article 451 of the 1986 Order.

The offence of fraudulent trading by registered companies or by other legal persons to which the Companies Act 1985, s. 458, or its Northern Ireland equivalent apply (and these now include limited liability partnerships) is dealt with at **B7.11** *et seq.*

The Fraud Act 2006, s. 9, gives effect to a recommendation of the Law Commission in its Report on Multiple Offending (Law Com. No. 277, Cm. 5609 (2002)) by adopting the s. 458 offence and applying it to fraudulent trading committed by unincorporated businesses such as those operated by sole traders or partnership firms, or by persons (such as employees) connected with such businesses.

As to the carrying on of a business, see **B7.13**. As to intent to defraud creditors and other fraudulent purposes, see **B7.15**.

Procedure, Sentence and Jurisdiction

Fraud Act 2006, s. 9 **B5.106**

(6) A person guilty of an offence under this section is liable—
(a) on summary conviction, to imprisonment for a term not exceeding 12 months or to a fine not exceeding the statutory maximum (or to both);

(b) on conviction on indictment, to imprisonment for a term not exceeding 10 years or to a fine (or to both).

In relation to an offence committed before the implementation of the CJA 2003, s. 154(1) (which increases the sentencing powers of magistrates' courts), the reference to 12 months in s. 9(6) is to be read as a reference to 6 months.

When tried on indictment, this is a class 3 offence. It is a Group A offence for jurisdiction purposes under the CJA 1993, part 1 (see **A8.7**), whereas fraudulent trading under the Companies Act is not. The maximum penalty of ten years' imprisonment is higher than that formerly applicable to fraudulent trading by companies, but the Fraud Act 2006, s. 10, increases the penalty for that offence, so the two offences now carry identical penalties.

OBTAINING SERVICES DISHONESTLY

B5.107 **Fraud Act 2006, s. 11**

(1) A person is guilty of an offence under this section if he obtains services for himself or another—
   (a) by a dishonest act, and
   (b) in breach of subsection (2).
(2) A person obtains services in breach of this subsection if—
   (a) they are made available on the basis that payment has been, is being or will be made for or in respect of them,
   (b) he obtains them without any payment having been made for or in respect of them or without payment having been made in full, and
   (c) when he obtains them, he knows—
      (i) that they are being made available on the basis described in paragraph (a), or
      (ii) that they might be,
   but intends that payment will not be made, or will not be made in full.

This offence is in part derived from the offence of obtaining services by deception contrary to the TA 1978, s. 1 (see **B5.52** ***et seq.***), which it replaces. It resembles that offence in that it requires the dishonest obtaining of services, and is therefore a 'result crime', in contrast to the new offence of fraud itself, which has been made into a conduct crime. It also resembles the old offence in that it has no application to the obtaining of services other than those that are provided in return for payment.

In other respects, however, the new offence is significantly broader than the old. It does not require any deception, nor indeed does it require any fraudulent representation. If a person (D) merely sneaks into a cinema to watch a film without paying, he will be guilty of the offence, assuming that he is dishonest and that he does succeed in obtaining some service as a result.

The terms 'service' and 'obtaining' are not properly defined in the Fraud Act 2006 (contrast the TA 1978, s. 1(2), in which the obtaining of services was defined as the conferring of a benefit by doing an act or permitting an act to be done). If, in the above example, D were to be caught and ejected from the cinema before the film began, there might be room for argument as to whether he obtained a service merely by going into the theatre or by passing the ticket collection point, although the better view appears to be that he would at that stage be guilty only of an attempt to commit the offence. In contrast, the new offence can be committed only where D intends to avoid payment or payment in full, whereas the old offence could potentially be committed where D did intend to pay, but knew that he was not qualified for or entitled to use the service (see **B5.58**).

Where D resorts to false representations in order to obtain (or attempt to obtain) a service, it might sometimes be more appropriate to consider a charge of fraud. According to the explanatory notes accompanying the Fraud Act 2006, the offence of obtaining services dishonestly may be committed where D uses false credit card details or other false personal information in order to obtain data or software that is available on the Internet to persons who have paid for access rights to that service. With respect, reliance on such a charge might enable arguments to be raised as to whether D 'intended that payment would not be made, or would not be made in full'. D might plausibly argue that he intended that someone else would pay for the service, such as the lawful holder of the credit card or the bank which issued the card. In contrast, he would appear to have no possible defence to a charge of fraud on the basis of a false representation (namely the implied representation that he was entitled to use the credit card).

Indictment

Statement of Offence B5.108

Obtaining services dishonestly, contrary to the Fraud Act 2006, section 11.

Particulars of Offence

A on or about the . . . day of . . . 2007, dishonestly entered the . . . Cinema in . . . without paying the required entrance fee, and viewed [a part of] the film then being screened, knowing that payment was required and intending that such payment would not be made.

Procedure, Sentence and Jurisdiction

Fraud Act 2006, s. 11 B5.109

(3) A person guilty of an offence under this section is liable—
- (a) on summary conviction, to imprisonment for a term not exceeding 12 months or to a fine not exceeding the statutory maximum (or to both);
- (b) on conviction on indictment, to imprisonment for a term not exceeding 5 years or to a fine (or to both).

In relation to an offence committed before the implementation of the CJA 2003, s. 154(1) (which increases the sentencing powers of magistrates' courts), the reference to 12 months in s. 11(3) is to be read as a reference to 6 months.

When tried on indictment, this is a class 3 offence. It is a Group A offence for jurisdiction purposes under the CJA 1993, part 1 (see **A8.7**). Company officers may be proceeded against and punished for any such offence committed by the company with their consent or connivance, see the Fraud Act, s. 12(2). As to the position where a body corporate is managed by its members, see s. 12(3).

Section B6 Falsification, Forgery and Counterfeiting

COMPARISON WITH FRAUD AND DECEPTION OFFENCES

B6.1 There is a significant overlap between the offences covered in this section and the offences of fraud and deception covered in **B5**. Offences of falsification, false accounting or forgery committed on or after 15 January 2007 will often involve conduct amounting equally to fraud within the meaning of the Fraud Act 2006, s. 1 (see **B5.93** ***et seq.***), although dishonesty, which is an essential element of any fraud or false accounting offence, need not be proved in cases charged under the Forgery and Counterfeiting Act 1981, the Trade Marks Act 1994 or the Trade Descriptions Act 1968.

Conduct pre-dating 15 January 2007 may alternatively give rise to liability for deception offences under the Theft Acts 1968 or 1978, but the differences between those offences and the offences considered in this section are more pronounced. Not only do the deception offences require proof of dishonesty, but in addition they are 'result crimes' that are committed only if the accused succeeds in deceiving another person and in securing some profit, gain or advantage for himself or another. If all that can be proved is that the accused forged an instrument or made a false statement, a deception offence cannot be established.

FALSIFICATION

Falsification, False Statements and False Instruments

B6.2 The concept of falsity, as applied to documents or instruments, is not always the same as that of falsity in statements. A lie is a false statement, but documents containing lies or false statements are not always regarded as false instruments.

As far as offences under the Forgery and Counterfeiting Act 1981 are concerned, an instrument is only false if it purports to be something it is not, or if it 'tells a lie' about its own authorship, origins or history. Conversely, such an instrument might be false in one or more of those respects, despite being a true and accurate statement of the matters with which it deals (as where an exact copy of a genuine document purports to be the original). See further, s. 9 of the Act (see **B6.23** to **B6.26**), which provides an exhaustive definition of falsity for those purposes.

For most purposes a document is not regarded as 'falsified' unless it has been fraudulently altered or interfered with. Such a document will usually be rendered 'false' for the purposes of the Forgery and Counterfeiting Act 1981, even if falsified by the same person who made it in the first place (see s. 9(1)(g) of the Act); but the concept of falsification would not necessarily extend to the inclusion of false statements in an original document or record. For example, the offence of falsification by a bankrupt of his papers (Insolvency Act 1986, s. 355(2)(b)) would not be committed where the bankrupt merely enters incorrect details when drawing up his accounts; the correct charge would be one of making false entries, contrary to s. 355(2)(c) (see **B7.45**).

There are few decided cases on the meaning of 'falsification', but the issue arose in *Edwards v Toombs* [1983] Crim LR 43, where it was held that an act which interferes with a mechanical (or presumably electronic) recording device (in that case a turnstile meter at a soccer stadium) can amount to falsification of the record, for the purpose of liability under the TA 1968, s. 17(1)(a).

Falsification is 'deemed' to bear a further meaning in the TA 1968, s. 17, by virtue of s. 17(2), but this has no wider application, and is therefore dealt with in the analysis of that provision at **B6.10** and **B6.11**.

Part B Offences

FALSE ACCOUNTING

Theft Act 1968, s. 17 **B6.3**

(1) Where a person dishonestly, with a view to gain for himself or another or with intent to cause loss to another,—
  (a) destroys, defaces, conceals or falsifies any account or any record or document made or required for any accounting purpose; or
  (b) in furnishing information for any purpose produces or makes use of any account, or any such record or document as aforesaid, which to his knowledge is or may be misleading, false or deceptive in a material particular; he shall, on conviction on indictment, be liable to imprisonment for a term not exceeding seven years.

(2) For purposes of this section a person who makes or concurs in making in an account or other document an entry which is or may be misleading, false or deceptive in a material particular, or who omits or concurs in omitting a material particular from an account or other document, is to be treated as falsifying the account or document.

Procedure and Jurisdiction

False accounting is triable either way (MCA 1980, s. 17 and sch. 1, para. 28). When tried on indictment it is a class 3 offence. It is a Group A offence for jurisdiction purposes under the CJA 1993, part I (see **A8.7**). For the provisions of the *Consolidated Criminal Practice Direction*, para. V.51, *Mode of trial* relating to fraud generally, see **B5.24**. **B6.4**

For the liability of officers of a company for an offence committed by the company, see the TA 1968, s. 18, **B5.68** and **A5.17**.

Indictment

Statement of Offence **B6.5**

False accounting contrary to section 17(1)(a) of the Theft Act 1968

Particulars of Offence

A on or about the . . . day of . . . dishonestly and with a view to gain for himself [or for X] [or with intent to cause loss to Y] falsified a document required for an accounting purpose, namely a ledger, by making therein an entry which was misleading, false or deceptive in a material particular in that it falsely purported to show that A had received the sum of £10,000 from Z in payment for services rendered

Statement of Offence

Furnishing false information contrary to section 17(1)(b) of the Theft Act 1968

Particulars of Offence

A on or about the . . . day of . . . dishonestly and with a view to gain for himself, in furnishing information to Q for accounting purposes, produced to the said Q a ledger, knowing that an entry therein, namely an entry purporting to show that A had received the sum of £10,000 from Z in payment for services rendered, was misleading, false or deceptive in a material particular, namely in falsely purporting to show that A had received the said sum from Z

Sentence

B6.6 The maximum penalty is seven years (TA 1968, s. 17(1)) on indictment; six months, a fine not exceeding the statutory maximum, or both, summarily. There is no guideline judgment reported for an offence under the TA 1968, s. 17(1), but in *Smith* (1994) 15 Cr App R (S) 145 30 months' imprisonment was upheld for false accounting, where the offender had obtained a book of Inland Revenue vouchers, and used them falsely so as to cause a loss to the Revenue of £50,000. For sentencing guidelines for offences of deception generally, see **B5.26**. For sentencing guidelines for theft offences, see **B4.5** to **B4.8**.

Scope of Offence

B6.7 The TA 1968, s. 17, creates two distinct offences: destruction, concealment or falsification etc. (s. 17(1)(a)) and using false or misleading documents etc. in furnishing information (s. 17(1)(b)). The user of falsified accounts may well be the person who falsified them, but this is not necessarily so. A person does not, however, commit an offence under s. 17(1)(b) unless he knows of the misleading, false or deceptive nature of the documents in question. Section 17(2) seems incapable of applying to s. 17(1)(b) because it deals only with falsification — the subject-matter of s. 17(1)(a).

Relationship to Other Offences

B6.8 There is clearly a potential overlap between the falsification of accounts or records under the TA 1968, s. 17(1)(a), and the offence of forgery under the Forgery and Counterfeiting Act 1981, s. 1, and a similar overlap may occur between the TA 1968, s. 17(1)(b), and the offence of using a false instrument under s. 3 of the 1981 Act. Nevertheless it would be quite wrong to suggest that any case of false accounting must necessarily involve forgery (*Dodge* [1972] 1 QB 416). As explained in **B6.2**, the concept of falsity in the 1981 Act is a narrow one, and does not generally extend to the making of false or misleading entries when compiling a document, or to the destruction (as opposed to the falsification) of documents or records.

A further area of significant overlap involves documents relating to the affairs of companies or bankrupts. See the Companies Act 1985, s. 450 and the Insolvency Act 1986, ss. 209 and 355(2) (see **B7.10**, **B7.35** and **B7.45**).

Cases of false accounting are often closely associated with various other offences under the TA 1968. The falsification or concealment may be a cover for past, contemporaneous or future offences under ss. 1 or 15 of the 1968 Act, and it is not unusual for an indictment to include counts for both false accounting and theft. In *Eden* (1971) 55 Cr App R 193, the Court of Appeal expressed the view that the inclusion of parallel counts of this kind should be discouraged if they would both stand or fall by the same evidence; but the inclusion of both counts was at the same time recognised as prudent in a situation where (as in *Eden* itself) theft might be harder to prove.

False accounting and theft are not always clearly distinguishable from each other. The courts appear prone at times to confuse the appropriation of money or things in action (such as debts) with the falsification or misuse of documents or records relating to them. *Monaghan* [1979] Crim LR 673 is an example of this. The accused's dishonest failure to record a payment of £3.99 on the supermarket till she was operating, with a view to taking an equivalent sum from the till later in the day, was held to amount to theft, even though the cash was properly placed in the till, where it belonged, and even though the accused would no doubt have taken different notes and coins anyway. Even after *Gomez* [1993] AC 442 (see **B4.25** ***et seq.***), the better view must be that she had done nothing more than falsify the till roll; but if *Monaghan* is indeed correct, the overlap between the TA 1968, s. 17, and theft must be very substantial.

Accounts, Records and Documents

The word 'account' must be given the meaning it bears in normal English usage (*Scot-Simmonds* [1994] Crim LR 933). A record or account need not necessarily be a document. In *Edwards v Toombs* [1983] Crim LR 43 it was held that a turnstile meter at a soccer stadium was a record, and thus within the scope of the section. See also *Solomons* [1909] 2 KB 980 (taximeter). Conversely, a document or record need not be an account, as long as it is made or required for an accounting purpose, either by the accused or by another person. This purpose need not be anything more than a secondary or incidental one; thus in *A-G's Ref (No. 1 of 1980)* [1981] 1 WLR 34 it was held that loan proposal forms, which would eventually be used by the loan company for an accounting purpose, could be the subject of an offence under the TA 1968, s. 17 (see also *Cummings-John* [1997] Crim LR 660). Whether a document is one required for an accounting purpose is a question of fact and will ordinarily need to be proved by the prosecution. See *Okanta* [1997] Crim LR 451, *Osinuga v DPP* [1998] Crim LR 216, *Sundhers* [1998] Crim LR 497 and *Manning* [1998] 2 Cr App R 461. **B6.9**

Extended Meaning of Falsification under Theft Act 1968, s. 17(2)

The TA 1968, s. 17(2), gives 'falsification' a specially extended meaning for the purposes of s. 17(1)(a). It clearly embraces the preparation of false accounts as well as the falsification of existing ones (*Scot-Simmonds* [1994] Crim LR 933). It does not, however, purport to provide an exhaustive definition of the concept, and it was held in *Edwards v Toombs* [1983] Crim LR 43 that anything amounting to falsification within the ordinary meaning of the term (see **B6.2**) would equally amount to falsification for s. 17 purposes. **B6.10**

Falsification by Omission

The TA 1968, s. 17(2), expressly provides that the omission of material information from a document etc. can have the effect of falsifying it. In *Shama* [1990] 1 WLR 661 the Court of Appeal upheld the conviction of a telephone operator who had failed even to start filling out standard forms provided by his employer for the recording of international calls. He was held to have falsified the forms by leaving them unmarked. A statement or record with material omissions may be misleading for purposes of s. 17(1)(b) even if it contains no outright lies; there is authority to the effect that such statements may also be regarded as being 'false in a material particular' (*Lord Kylsant* [1932] 1 KB 442) but it would not be necessary to rely thereon. **B6.11**

Meaning of 'Material'

Falsity etc. is not a basis of liability under the TA 1968, s. 17, unless it is falsity 'in a material particular'. The meaning of this concept was examined in *Mallett* [1978] 1 WLR 820, where the Court of Appeal rejected the argument that the falsity etc. must be material in the sense of being directly connected with the accuracy etc. of an accounting process. In *Mallett* the accused had furnished false information to a finance company concerning the status of a potential customer. The falsity was material to the company's decision to finance the **B6.12** transaction, and the form containing the false information was required for accounting purposes. It was held that the accused had been rightly convicted even though no accounts had been rendered inaccurate by his supply of false information.

Mens Rea

B6.13 In false accounting there need be no proof of any intent to permanently deprive another person of his property. What is needed is dishonesty (in the *Ghosh* [1982] QB 1053 sense, see **B4.37**) coupled with a 'view to gain' or 'intent to cause loss'; and in *Eden* (1971) 55 Cr App R 193 it was said that this might involve nothing more than an intent to gain or avoid loss on a temporary basis, perhaps in order to play for time, whilst losses caused by honest incompetence are made good. In *Lee Cheung Wing v The Queen* [1992] Crim LR 440, falsified documents were used by securities dealers to mask withdrawals of unauthorised profits from accounts they had kept secret from their employers. The Privy Council held that the falsification of these documents had been made with a view to gain and constituted an offence under equivalent legislation in Hong Kong.

As to the meaning of 'gain' and 'loss', see the TA 1968, s. 34(2)(a), *Golechha* [1989] 1 WLR 1050 and *A-G's Ref (No. 1 of 2001)* [2002] 3 All ER 840 (see **B5.51**).

FALSE STATEMENTS BY OFFICERS OF COMPANY OR ASSOCIATION

B6.14 **Theft Act 1968, s. 19**

(1) Where an officer of a body corporate or unincorporated association (or person purporting to act as such), with intent to deceive members or creditors of the body corporate or association about its affairs, publishes or concurs in publishing a written statement or account which to his knowledge is or may be misleading, false or deceptive in a material particular, he shall on conviction on indictment be liable to imprisonment for a term not exceeding seven years.

(2) For purposes of this section a person who has entered into a security for the benefit of a body corporate or association is to be treated as a creditor of it.

(3) Where the affairs of a body corporate or association are managed by its members, this section shall apply to any statement which a member publishes or concurs in publishing in connection with his functions of management as if he were an officer of the body corporate or association.

Procedure and Jurisdiction

B6.15 An offence under the Theft Act 1968, s. 19, is triable either way (MCA 1980, s. 17 and sch. 1, para. 28). When tried on indictment it is a class 3 offence. It is a Group A offence for jurisdiction purposes under the CJA 1993, part I (see **A8.7**). For the provisions of the *Consolidated Criminal Practice Direction*, para. V.51, *Mode of trial* relating to fraud generally, see **B5.24**.

Indictment

B6.16 *Statement of Offence*

Publishing a false statement contrary to section 19(1) of the Theft Act 1968

Particulars of Offence

A on or about the . . . day of . . ., being a director of a body corporate, namely X plc, with intent to deceive the members or creditors or the said X plc, published a written statement about the affairs of the said X plc which to his knowledge was misleading, false or deceptive in a material particular in that it falsely stated that X plc then had no contingent liabilities

Sentence

B6.17 The maximum penalty is seven years (TA 1968, s. 19(1)) on indictment; six months, a fine not exceeding the statutory maximum, or both, summarily. There is no guideline judgment reported for an offence under the TA 1968, s. 19(1). For sentencing guidelines for offences of deception generally, see **B5.26**. For sentencing guidelines for theft offences, see **B4.5** to **B4.8**.

Relationship to Other Offences

B6.18 The commission of an offence under the TA 1968, s. 19(1), by a company director may be in circumstances in which the company itself commits an offence under s. 17 or possibly ss. 15 or 16 for which the director may be liable under s. 18. There is clearly some overlap between such liability and possible liability under s. 19(1), subject to the consideration that under s. 19(1) there need be no successful deception, no proof of dishonesty and no need for the statement to be made or required for any accounting purpose, but, insofar as the s. 19 offence can be committed by officers of an unincorporated association, its scope is nevertheless wider than that of s. 18.

Meaning of 'Officer of a Body Corporate or Unincorporated Association'

B6.19 In relation to registered companies, the term 'officer' includes a director, manager or secretary (Companies Act 1985, s. 744), and an auditor may also be considered to be an officer (*Shacter* [1960] 2 QB 252). As to the meaning of manager, see the discussion of *Boal* [1992] 1 QB 591 at **A5.17**.

In relation to unincorporated associations, treasurers, secretaries and chairmen would be considered to be officers; as would any partner publishing or concurring in the publication of an offending statement in connection with his firm's affairs. Where the affairs of a company or association are managed by its members, a member may commit this offence (TA 1968, s. 19(3)).

Intent to Deceive Members or Creditors

B6.20 A statement published with intent to deceive only prospective members or creditors would not appear to come within the ambit of this offence, but would be likely to fall within the Financial Services and Markets Act 2000, s. 397 (see **B7.17**). The TA 1968, s. 19(2), provides that for the purposes of s. 19, a person who has entered into a security for the benefit of a body corporate or association is to be treated as a creditor of it. This seems to refer to a guarantor, though the precise scope of the subsection is unclear.

FORGERY AND KINDRED OFFENCES: GENERAL CONSIDERATIONS

Offences and Penalties under Part I of the Forgery and Counterfeiting Act 1981

B6.21 The Forgery and Counterfeiting Act 1981, s. 30, together with the schedule to that Act, repealed a number of older statutory offences of forgery, and s. 13 abolished the offence of forgery at common law. In their place, part I (ss. 1 to 13) of the Act created the following offences:

(a) making a false instrument (s. 1);
(b) copying a false instrument (s. 2);
(c) using a false instrument (s. 3);
(d) using a copy of a false instrument (s. 4);
(e) having custody or control of specified kinds of false instrument (s. 5(1)); and
(f) making or having custody etc. of machines, paper etc. for making false instruments of that kind (s. 5(3)).

These offences all require proof of an 'intention to induce somebody to accept the instrument as genuine' (or as a copy of a genuine instrument) and 'by reason of so accepting it to do or not to do some act to his own or any other person's prejudice'. They are punishable following conviction on indictment with up to 10 years' imprisonment under s. 6(2) and (3) of the Act.

In addition, subsections (2) and (4) of s. 5 create two further, less serious, offences, which do not require proof of this ulterior intent, but which are otherwise comparable to the offences created by s. 5(1) and (3) respectively. These are punishable with up to two years' imprisonment under s. 6(4).

On summary conviction, all eight offences attract up to six months' imprisonment and/or a fine not exceeding the statutory maximum (s. 6(1)).

The above offences all use certain key terms, the meanings of which are defined in ss. 8 to 10 of the Act.

Meaning of 'Instrument'

B6.22 **Forgery and Counterfeiting Act 1981, s. 8**

(1) Subject to subsection (2) below, in this part of this Act 'instrument' means—
  (a) any document, whether of a formal or informal character;
  (b) any stamp issued or sold by the Post Office;
  (c) any Inland Revenue stamp; and
  (d) any disc, tape, soundtrack or other device on or in which information is recorded or stored by mechanical, electronic or other means.

(2) A currency note within the meaning of part II of this Act is not an instrument for the purposes of this part of this Act.

(3) A mark denoting payment of postage which the Post Office authorise to be used instead of an adhesive stamp is to be treated for the purposes of this part of this Act as if it were a stamp issued by the Post Office.

It had been recognised that one of the many difficulties surrounding the old Forgery Act 1913 was uncertainty about what kinds of article fell within the scope of the offences it created. The fact that it referred to 'documents', without providing any definition of that term, meant, *inter alia*, that doubts surrounded things such as wrappers on goods or the signatures on paintings or other works of art (*Closs* (1857) Dears & B 460; *Smith* (1858) Dears & B 566; *Douce* [1972] Crim LR 105). In proposing the new legislation, the Law Commission advocated the adoption of the term 'instrument' instead, on the basis that forgery and its kindred offences should apply only to those documents, such as cheques, which create rights and duties, or which give directions that are to be accepted and acted upon. This proposal was seemingly rejected; the term 'instrument' has indeed been adopted in the Act, but it has been defined in such a way that it includes any document (still without defining that term!) and several things that might not otherwise have been thought of as documents at all. The only documents excluded are currency notes, which are covered by the counterfeiting offences in part II of the Act.

Electronic impulses representing passwords for accessing computers are too ephemeral to be instruments (*Gold* [1988] AC 1063) though the misuse of such a password may be an offence under the Computer Misuse Act 1990 (see **B18**).

Meaning of 'False' and 'Making'

B6.23 **Forgery and Counterfeiting Act 1981, s. 9**

(1) An instrument is false for the purposes of this part of this Act—
  (a) if it purports to have been made in the form in which it is made by a person who did not in fact make it in that form; or
  (b) if it purports to have been made in the form in which it is made on the authority of a person who did not in fact authorise its making in that form; or
  (c) if it purports to have been made in the terms in which it is made by a person who did not in fact make it in those terms; or

(d) if it purports to have been made in the terms in which it is made on the authority of a person who did not in fact authorise its making in those terms; or
(e) if it purports to have been altered in any respect by a person who did not in fact alter it in that respect; or
(f) if it purports to have been altered in any respect on the authority of a person who did not in fact authorise the alteration in that respect; or
(g) if it purports to have been made or altered on a date on which, or at a place at which, or otherwise in circumstances in which, it was not in fact made or altered; or
(h) if it purports to have been made or altered by an existing person but he did not in fact exist.

(2) A person is to be treated for the purposes of this part of this Act as making a false instrument if he alters an instrument so as to make it false in any respect (whether or not it is false in some other respect apart from that alteration).

As was the position at common law and under the earlier legislation, a false statement in a document or instrument does not ordinarily make that instrument a forgery; a false instrument is one which purports to be something which it is not (*Re Windsor* (1865) 10 Cox CC 118; *Warneford* [1994] Crim LR 753).

The Forgery and Counterfeiting Act 1981, s. 9(1), lists the ways in which an instrument may be false. It is an exhaustive list: an instrument cannot be regarded as false on any alternative basis. On the other hand, an indictment does not need to specify the exact ground on which an instrument is alleged to be false.

Falsity as to Authorship or Authority (s. 9(1)(a), (c), (d) or (h)) An instrument will be false if the supposed maker did not make it at all, or if it has been altered since he made it. The obvious example of such falsity would be where one person forges another's signature on a cheque (*Lack* (1986) 84 Cr App R 342). **B6.24**

The concept might appear to be a simple one, but is not always so. In *Macer* [1979] Crim LR 659, decided under earlier, but essentially similar, provisions, it was held *not* to be forgery for a person to sign his own name on a cheque, but with a different signature from his normal one, with a view to later denying its authenticity. It was said that the cheque did not 'purport' to have been signed by any other person. On such facts, it would be better to charge an offence, or attempted offence, of evading a liability by deception under the TA 1978, s. 2.

Another difficulty concerns the use of assumed names. There is generally no law against the use of assumed names. An instrument signed in a false name is not necessarily a forgery, even if the false name has been used for dishonest purposes (*More* [1987] 1 WLR 1578). However, assuming the name of another person in the pretence of being that other person may constitute forgery. In *More*, the accused stole a cheque and paid it into a building society account opened in the same name as the payee. He later withdrew the proceeds, using withdrawal forms signed in that same name, and was charged, *inter alia*, with forgery of those forms. The House of Lords held that the forms were not forgeries: they purported to have been signed by the person who had opened the account, as indeed they had been, and (crucially) did not refer back to the original cheque.

More was distinguished in *Atunwa* [2006] EWCA Crim 673, in which the accused was found in possession of cheques purporting to have been signed on behalf of registered companies, but bearing the signatures of unknown individuals who (if they existed at all) had no connection with those companies. His convictions for possessing false instruments with intent (see **B6.43**) were upheld. Dyson LJ said (at [8]):

> If A signs a cheque on behalf of X Limited in the name of B, and B is authorised to sign cheques on behalf of X Limited, A commits the offence; he purports to make an instrument 'in the terms in which it is made on the authority of a person who did not in fact authorise its making in those terms' . . . But the offence may also be committed if A purports to sign a cheque on behalf of X

Limited in his own name where he is not an authorised signatory. In this situation too, A purports to make an instrument in the terms in which it is made on the authority of a person who did not in fact authorise its making in those terms. In both cases the cheque tells a lie about itself, namely that it is a cheque duly signed by a person authorised to sign the cheque on behalf of the company.

B6.25 **Falsification by Alteration (s. 9(1)(e))** Alteration of an instrument so as to change its value or terms would come within paragraph (c) of the Forgery and Counterfeiting Act 1981, s. 9(1), if the alteration is intended to pass undetected. Paragraph (e) of s. 9(1) covers alterations which purport to be those of someone other than the person who made, or authorised the making of, the instrument, even an alteration which purports to be unauthorised (done, for example, for the purpose of falsely accusing someone else of forgery). If the person purportedly responsible for the alteration did not really exist then the instrument would be false by virtue of s. 9(1)(h).

B6.26 **Falsity as to Date, Place or Circumstances (s. 9(1)(g))** An instrument which is dated otherwise than with the date on which it is made is not necessarily false, because in some cases it is recognised that the date indicates, not the date of making, but the date at which the instrument becomes enforceable (as with a postdated cheque).

The final part of s. 9(1)(g) is a 'sweeping-up' provision, which is potentially very wide ranging. In some circumstances, the concept of falsity can be hard to distinguish from that of mere false statements which fall outside the scope of the Act (see **B6.2**).

In *Donnelly* [1984] 1 WLR 1017, the Court of Appeal held that a jeweller's certificate purporting to value jewellery that did not really exist was a forgery. Had the certificate merely lied about the value of real items inspected, it could not have been a forgery, and *Donnelly* has been criticised on the basis that there is no difference between a certificate which lies about real items and one which lies about fictional items. Some commentators argue that *Donnelly* cannot stand with *More* [1987] 1 WLR 1578 (see **B6.24**) but, with respect, the certificate did not merely tell lies; it was not merely an inflated valuation; it purported to be something it was not: a valuation based on an inspection of real jewellery.

Donnelly was followed in *Jeraj* [1994] Crim LR 595 but disapproved in *Warneford* [1994] Crim LR 753. The issue now appears to have been settled by *A-G's Ref (No. 1 of 2000)* [2001] 1 WLR 331, in which Lord Woolf CJ followed *Donnelly* and clearly identified the principle to be applied in cases brought under s. 9(1)(g): namely that a document which tells lies about the circumstances under which it is made becomes a forgery if, but only if, those circumstances need to exist before the document can properly be made. One cannot, for example, produce a valuation of jewellery (even an inaccurate one) unless the jewellery in question exists; nor can one issue a genuine receipt for a security that has not in fact been received (see *Jeraj*).

Meaning of 'Prejudice' and 'Induce'

B6.27 **Forgery and Counterfeiting Act 1981, s. 10**

(1) Subject to subsections (2) and (4) below, for the purposes of this part of this Act an act or omission intended to be induced is to a person's prejudice if, and only if, it is one which if it occurs—
- (a) will result—
  - (i) in his temporary or permanent loss of property; or
  - (ii) in his being deprived of an opportunity to earn remuneration or greater remuneration; or
  - (iii) in his being deprived of an opportunity to gain a financial advantage otherwise than by way of remuneration; or
- (b) will result in somebody being given an opportunity—
  - (i) to earn remuneration or greater remuneration from him; or
  - (ii) to gain a financial advantage from him otherwise than by way of remuneration; or

(c) will be the result of his having accepted a false instrument as genuine, or a copy of a false instrument as a copy of a genuine one, in connection with his performance of any duty.

(2) An act which a person has an enforceable duty to do and an omission to do an act which a person is not entitled to do shall be disregarded for the purposes of this part of this Act.

(3) In this part of this Act references to inducing somebody to accept a false instrument as genuine, or a copy of a false instrument as a copy of a genuine one, include references to inducing a machine to respond to the instrument or copy as if it were a genuine instrument or, as the case may be, a copy of a genuine one.

(4) Where subsection (3) above applies, the act or omission intended to be induced by the machine responding to the instrument or copy shall be treated as an act or omission to a person's prejudice.

(5) In this section 'loss' includes not getting what one might get as well as parting with what one has.

The Forgery and Counterfeiting Act 1981, s. 10, provides an exhaustive definition of the concept of 'prejudice' for the purposes of the six offences which require an intent to induce another person to act or omit to act to his own or another's prejudice (see **B6.21**). 'Inducing' is only defined to the extent that it applies to machines.

To be guilty of one of these offences, an accused need not have induced any reaction at all: it is a matter of ulterior intent, rather than of *actus reus* (*Ondhia* [1998] 2 Cr App R 150). It would not however suffice that the accused was merely aware that prejudice might result (*Garcia* [1988] Crim LR 115).

Section 10(1)(a) covers situations in which acceptance of a false instrument would result in loss, or loss of potential profit; s. 10(1)(b) covers situations where actual loss might be difficult to identify, but where someone might be able to obtain a pecuniary advantage from the person induced; and the broad scope of s. 10(1)(c) is illustrated by *Campbell* (1984) 80 Cr App R 47, in which it was held that a bank would be prejudiced if it was induced to pay or collect payment on a forged cheque, whether or not it suffered financially by so doing, and whether or not anyone profited thereby. Another illustration is provided by *Utting* [1987] 1 WLR 1375, where, but for a defective indictment, the accused might have been convicted of forging an instrument in order to induce the police to act to their prejudice by not prosecuting him. See also *A-G's Ref (No. 1 of 2001)* [2002] 3 All ER 840.

The effect of s. 10(2) is that it cannot be an offence under the Act to make or use a false instrument in order to secure or protect one's lawful rights against anyone it is intended to deceive; but in the case of cheques and other instruments covered by s. 5, s. 10(2) and (4) might still apply.

Subsections (3) and (4) of s. 10 ensure, *inter alia*, that the use of a forged card in an automatic service till could be an offence under s. 3, and making such a forged card could be an offence under s. 1. In contrast, the obtaining of cash using such a device would not be regarded as a deception offence under the TA 1968 or TA 1978, both of which lack any provisions akin to these (see **B5**). The correct charge in such a case would be theft. Subsections (3) and (4) would also apply where forged identification cards are used in computers etc., but not where hackers merely transmit or key in false user identification numbers, these being too ephemeral to constitute 'instruments' under s. 8 (*Gold* [1988] AC 1063). Similar considerations would apply to the misuse of another person's card and personal identification number in a bank automatic service till. Misuse of a user identification may, however, be an offence under the Computer Misuse Act 1990 (see **B18**).

FORGERY

B6.28 **Forgery and Counterfeiting Act 1981, s. 1**

A person is guilty of forgery if he makes a false instrument, with the intention that he or another shall use it to induce somebody to accept it as genuine, and by reason of so accepting it to do or not to do some act to his own or any other person's prejudice.

Procedure and Jurisdiction

B6.29 Forgery is triable either way (Forgery and Counterfeiting Act 1981, s. 6). When tried on indictment it is a class 3 offence. It is a Group A offence for jurisdiction purposes under the CJA 1993, part I (see **A8.7**).

Indictment

B6.30 *Statement of Offence*

Forgery contrary to section 1 of the Forgery and Counterfeiting Act 1981

Particulars of Offence

A on or about the . . . day of . . . made a false instrument, namely a document purporting to be the will of X, with the intention of using it to induce Y to accept it as genuine and by reason of so accepting to give A a Ming vase forming part of the estate of X to the prejudice of the beneficiaries under the true will of X

Sentence

B6.31 The maximum sentence is 10 years on indictment; six months or a fine not exceeding the statutory maximum or both summarily (Forgery and Counterfeiting Act 1981, s. 6). There is no guideline judgment reported for this offence but in *Lincoln* (1994) 15 Cr App R 333, where the offender forged the signature of his estranged wife on a contract for sale of a house and a Land Registry transfer, it was held that the proper sentence was six months' imprisonment.

Elements

B6.32 Most of the key terms used in the Forgery and Counterfeiting Act 1981, s. 1, are considered in **B6.22** to **B6.27**. By virtue of s. 9(2), 'making' a false instrument includes falsifying an existing one; but however it is made, it must be proved that it was made with the specified 'double intention': it must be proved that the accused intended both that the instrument would be accepted as genuine and that someone would therefore act to his own or another's prejudice. It is a specific intent; recklessness or foresight will not suffice (*Garcia* [1988] Crim LR 115). In *Ondhia* [1998] 2 Cr App R 150, O created a false 'copy bill of lading', not for the purpose of using it directly to deceive any other person, but for the purpose of feeding it into his fax machine, so that the recipient of his call would receive the facsimile copy thereby created. This was held to amount to an offence of forgery under s. 1. No doubt O would also have been guilty of copying a false instrument, contrary to s. 2 of the Act, but overlapping offences are common in English law, and there is nothing artificial or unnatural in the argument that a person who faxes a forged document to another 'uses' that document for the purpose of inducing that other (or indeed a third party) to accept it as genuine. A person who relies upon a facsimile of a bill of lading will recognise it to be a facsimile; and if he is deceived by the facsimile, he is deceived by the original from which it was made.

On the other hand, dishonesty is not an essential ingredient in this or any other offences under the Act (*Campbell* (1984) 80 Cr App R 47; *Winston* [1999] 1 Cr App R 337), and the intent is ulterior, so that actual inducement or prejudice need not be proved, and need not even be intended to take place within the jurisdiction (cf. *Treacy v DPP* [1971] AC 537; *Berry* [1985] AC 246).

COPYING A FALSE INSTRUMENT

Definition

Forgery and Counterfeiting Act 1981, s. 2 B6.33

It is an offence for a person to make a copy of an instrument which is, and which he knows or believes to be, a false instrument, with the intention that he or another shall use it to induce somebody to accept it as a copy of a genuine instrument, and by reason of so accepting it to do or not to do some act to his own or any other person's prejudice.

Procedure and Jurisdiction

The offence is triable either way (Forgery and Counterfeiting Act 1981, s. 6). When tried on indictment it is a class 3 offence. It is a Group A offence for jurisdiction purposes under the CJA 1993, part I (see A8.7). B6.34

Indictment

Statement of Offence B6.35

Copying a false instrument contrary to section 2 of the Forgery and Counterfeiting Act 1981

Particulars of Offence

A on or about the . . . day of . . . made a copy of an instrument, namely a document purporting to be the will of X, which was and which he knew to be a false instrument, with the intention of using it to induce Y to accept it as genuine and by reason of so accepting to give A a Ming vase forming part of the estate of X to the prejudice of the beneficiaries under the true will of X

Sentence

The maximum sentence is 10 years on indictment; six months or a fine not exceeding the statutory maximum or both summarily (Forgery and Counterfeiting Act 1981, s. 6). B6.36

Elements

The Forgery and Counterfeiting Act 1981, s. 2, does not deal with copies which are intended to be passed off as originals, even if they are themselves copies of copies, nor does it deal with instruments which purport to be copies of originals which do not in fact exist. (The correct charge for making such copies is one of forgery under s. 1.) This provision aims instead at copies (particularly photocopies) which purport to be true copies of original instruments, but which are not, either because the original has been falsified prior to photocopying etc., or because the original was a complete forgery from the start. B6.37

It might be argued that there is really no need for such a provision, since a document which purports to be a photocopy of a genuine instrument, but which is in fact a copy of a forgery, would *ipso facto* be false under s. 9(1)(g) (and see *Utting* [1987] 1 WLR 1375). This might be true where the original is a total forgery; but difficulties could arise in other circumstances. If, for example, an individual is required to send to some person a copy of his birth certificate, and takes a photocopy for that purpose, knowing that the original was falsified in some way by his father 10 years before, it could be argued that the photocopy is a true copy of the certificate, and thus not false within s. 9 at all. Section 2, however, would clearly apply in such circumstances.

USING A FALSE INSTRUMENT: USING COPY OF FALSE INSTRUMENT

B6.38 **Forgery and Counterfeiting Act 1981, ss. 3 and 4**

3. It is an offence for a person to use an instrument which is, and which he knows or believes to be, false, with the intention of inducing somebody to accept it as genuine, and by reason of so accepting it to do or not to do some act to his own or any other person's prejudice.
4. It is an offence for a person to use a copy of an instrument which is, and which he knows or believes to be, a false instrument, with the intention of inducing somebody to accept it as a copy of a genuine instrument, and by reason of so accepting it to do or not to do some act to his own or any other person's prejudice.

Procedure and Jurisdiction

B6.39 Both offences are triable either way (Forgery and Counterfeiting Act 1981, s. 6). When tried on indictment they are class 3 offences. It is a Group A offence for jurisdiction purposes under the CJA 1993, part I (see **A8.7**).

Indictment

B6.40 *Statement of Offence*

Using a false instrument contrary to section 3 of the Forgery and Counterfeiting Act 1981

Particulars of Offence

A on or about the . . . day of . . . used an instrument, namely a document purporting to be the will of X, which was and which he knew to be false, with the intention of inducing Y to accept it as genuine and by reason of so accepting to give A a Ming vase forming part of the estate of X to the prejudice of the beneficiaries under the true will of X

This form may easily be adapted for a charge under s. 4.

Sentence

B6.41 The maximum sentence is 10 years on indictment; six months or a fine not exceeding the statutory maximum or both summarily (Forgery and Counterfeiting Act 1981, s. 6). There are no guideline judgments reported for these offences.

In *Singh* [1999] 1 Cr App R (S) 490, the Court of Appeal upheld a sentence of eight months' imprisonment on an offender who had pleaded guilty to an offence under s. 3, in that he had attempted to use a false British passport at Gatwick Airport in order to travel to Canada. After reviewing a number of authorities involving the misuse of passports, Rose LJ explained that a deterrent custodial sentence within the range of six to nine months would usually be merited. A guilty plea would always attract an appropriate discount, but previous good character and personal mitigation were of very limited value. *Singh* was, however, revisited by the Court of Appeal in *Kolawole* [2005] 2 Cr App R (S) 71, where Rose LJ said that in light of international events in recent years and the increase in public concern that they had generated, sentences at a higher level were now appropriate, and that in such a case as *Singh* the appropriate sentence, even on a guilty plea by a person of good character, should usually be in the range of 12 to 18 months.

Elements

B6.42 Whereas the Forgery and Counterfeiting Act 1981, s. 1, penalises the making of a false instrument, even if it is never used for its intended purpose or intended for use outside the jurisdiction, s. 3 strikes at the use of such an instrument, even if it was not originally made to be used in a way prohibited by s. 3, or made outside the jurisdiction. The same 'double intention' is required as in s. 1: see **B6.32** and *Tobierre* [1986] 1 WLR 125.

Section 4 relates to s. 2 as s. 3 relates to s. 1. Like s. 2 it does not apply to copies which purport to be originals; and like s. 3 it does not matter who made the copy, or for what purpose it was made.

'Using' is not defined in the Act. Previous legislation used the term 'uttering', and using was the principal form of uttering (*Harris* [1966] 1 QB 184). 'Use' must presumably bear its ordinary meaning: 'to put into action or service: avail oneself of: . . . to carry out a purpose or action by means of' (*Webster's Ninth New Collegiate Dictionary*). However, the use need not be successful: the full offence may be committed even if the instrument is at once recognised as a forgery.

OFFENCES RELATING TO STAMPS, SHARE CERTIFICATES, IDENTITY DOCUMENTS ETC.

Forgery and Counterfeiting Act 1981, s. 5 **B6.43**

(1) It is an offence for a person to have in his custody or under his control an instrument to which this section applies which is, and which he knows or believes to be, false, with the intention that he or another shall use it to induce somebody to accept it as genuine, and by reason of so accepting it to do or not to do some act to his own or any other person's prejudice.
(2) It is an offence for a person to have in his custody or under his control, without lawful authority or excuse, an instrument to which this section applies which is, and which he knows or believes to be, false.
(3) It is an offence for a person to make or to have in his custody or under his control a machine or implement, or paper or any other material, which to his knowledge is or has been specially designed or adapted for the making of an instrument to which this section applies, with the intention that he or another shall make an instrument to which this section applies which is false and that he or another shall use the instrument to induce somebody to accept it as genuine, and by reason of so accepting it to do or not to do some act to his own or any other person's prejudice.
(4) It is an offence for a person to make or to have in his custody or under his control any such machine, implement, paper or material, without lawful authority or excuse.
(5) The instruments to which this section applies are—
 (a) money orders;
 (b) postal orders;
 (c) United Kingdom postage stamps;
 (d) Inland Revenue stamps;
 (e) share certificates;
 (f) passports and documents which can be used instead of passports;
 (fa) [repealed];
 (g) [repealed];
 (h) travellers' cheques;
 (ha) bankers' drafts;
 (hb) promissory notes;
 (j) cheque cards;
 (ja) debit cards;
 (k) credit cards;
 (l) certified copies relating to an entry in a register of births, adoptions, marriages or deaths and issued by the Registrar-General, the Registrar-General for Northern Ireland, a registration officer or person lawfully authorised to register marriages; and
 (m) certificates relating to entries in such registers.
(6) In subsection (5)(e) above 'share certificate' means an instrument entitling or evidencing the title of a person to a share or interest—
 (a) in any public stock, annuity, fund or debt of any government or State, including a State which forms part of another State; or
 (b) in any stock, fund or debt of a body (whether corporate or unincorporated) established in the United Kingdom or elsewhere.
(7) An instrument is also an instrument to which this section applies if it is a monetary

instrument specified for the purposes of this section by an order made by the Secretary of State.

(8) The power under subsection (7) above is exercisable by statutory instrument subject to annulment in pursuance of a resolution of either House of Parliament.

Identity Cards Act 2006, ss. 25 and 26

25.—(1) It is an offence for a person with the requisite intention to have in his possession or under his control—

(a) an identity document that is false and that he knows or believes to be false;

(b) an identity document that was improperly obtained and that he knows or believes to have been improperly obtained; or

(c) an identity document that relates to someone else.

(2) The requisite intention for the purposes of subsection (1) is—

(a) the intention of using the document for establishing registrable facts about himself; or

(b) the intention of allowing or inducing another to use it for establishing, ascertaining or verifying registrable facts about himself or about any other person (with the exception, in the case of a document within paragraph (c) of that subsection, of the individual to whom it relates).

(3) It is an offence for a person with the requisite intention to make, or to have in his possession or under his control—

(a) any apparatus which, to his knowledge, is or has been specially designed or adapted for the making of false identity documents; or

(b) any article or material which, to his knowledge, is or has been specially designed or adapted to be used in the making of false identity documents.

(4) The requisite intention for the purposes of subsection (3) is the intention—

(a) that he or another will make a false identity document; and

(b) that the document will be used by somebody for establishing, ascertaining or verifying registrable facts about a person.

(5) It is an offence for a person to have in his possession or under his control, without reasonable excuse—

(a) an identity document that is false;

(b) an identity document that was improperly obtained;

(c) an identity document that relates to someone else; or

(d) any apparatus, article or material which, to his knowledge, is or has been specially designed or adapted for the making of false identity documents or to be used in the making of such documents.

(6) A person guilty of an offence under subsection (1) or (3) shall be liable, on conviction on indictment, to imprisonment for a term not exceeding ten years or to a fine, or to both.

(7) A person guilty of an offence under subsection (5) shall be liable—

(a) on conviction on indictment, to imprisonment for a term not exceeding two years or to a fine, or to both;

(b) on summary conviction in England and Wales, to imprisonment for a term not exceeding twelve months or to a fine not exceeding the statutory maximum, or to both;

(c) [Scotland and Northern Ireland];

but, in relation to an offence committed before the commencement of section 154(1) of the Criminal Justice Act 2003, the reference in paragraph (b) to twelve months is to be read as a reference to six months.

(8) For the purposes of this section—

(a) an identity document is false only if it is false within the meaning of part 1 of the Forgery and Counterfeiting Act 1981 (see section 9(1) of that Act); and

(b) an identity document was improperly obtained if false information was provided, in or in connection with the application for its issue or an application for its modification, to the person who issued it or (as the case may be) to a person entitled to modify it;

and references to the making of a false identity document include references to the modification of an identity document so that it becomes false.

(9) Subsection (8)(a) does not apply in the application of this section to Scotland.

(10) In this section 'identity document' has the meaning given by section 26.

26.—(1)In section 25 'identity document' means any document that is, or purports to be—

(a) an ID card;
(b) a designated document;
(c) an immigration document;
(d) a United Kingdom passport (within the meaning of the Immigration Act 1971);
(e) a passport issued by or on behalf of the authorities of a country or territory outside the United Kingdom or by or on behalf of an international organisation;
(f) a document that can be used (in some or all circumstances) instead of a passport;
(g) a UK driving licence; or
(h) a driving licence issued by or on behalf of the authorities of a country or territory outside the United Kingdom.

(2) In subsection (1) 'immigration document' means—
(a) a document used for confirming the right of a person under the Community Treaties in respect of entry or residence in the United Kingdom;
(b) a document which is given in exercise of immigration functions and records information about leave granted to a person to enter or to remain in the United Kingdom; or
(c) a registration card (within the meaning of section 26A of the Immigration Act 1971);
and in paragraph (b) 'immigration functions' means functions under the Immigration Acts (within the meaning of the Asylum and Immigration (Treatment of Claimants, etc.) Act 2004).

(3) In that subsection 'UK driving licence' means—
(a) a licence to drive a motor vehicle granted under Part 3 of the Road Traffic Act 1988 (c. 52); or
(b) a licence to drive a motor vehicle granted under Part 2 of the Road Traffic (Northern Ireland) Order 1981 (S.I. 1981/154 (N.I. 1)).

The Forgery and Counterfeiting Act 1981, s. 5(5)(f) (knowingly and with intent etc having custody or control etc of false passports or documents which can be used instead of passports) and (fa) (knowingly and with intent etc having custody or control etc of false immigration documents) were repealed (along with the accompanying definitions in s. 5(9) to (11)) by the Identity Cards Act 2006, s. 44 and sch. 2. On a literal reading of the 2006 Act, these repeals came into force at Royal Assent (i.e. on 30 March 2006), whereas the replacement offences under the Identity Cards Act 2006, s. 25, did not come into force until 7 June 2006 (Identity Cards Act 2006 (Commencement No. 1) Order (SI 2006 No. 1439)), but in *R (CPS)* v *Bow Street Magistrates' Court* [2007] 1 WLR 291 it was held that this was obviously a draftsman's error and did not reflect the true intention of Parliament. In order to give effect to that intention, the repeals would therefore be regarded as coming into force on 7 June.

A further challenge to the effectiveness of ss. 25 and 26 was rejected in *Soule Ali* [2007] 1 WLR 1599. It was argued in that case that attempts to use false or stolen French or Belgian identity cards at French border controls in Dover could not amount to offences under s. 25 because (i) no register has yet been created; (ii) the offence could not be committed by someone who was not on the register; and (iii) the person to whom false documentation is handed must for this purpose be a person who is able to access the register. The Court of Appeal rejected each of these arguments, reasoning that s. 25 was clearly intended to punish any conduct that would previously have been punishable under the Forgery and Counterfeiting Act 1981, s. 5(f) or (fa).

Procedure and Jurisdiction

Offences under the Forgery and Counterfeiting Act 1981, s. 5(1) and (3) are triable either way (Forgery and Counterfeiting Act 1981, s. 6) as are offences under the Identity Cards Act 2006, s. 25(5). When tried on indictment they are class 3 offences. Offences under the Identity Cards Act 2006, s. 25(1) and (3) are triable only on indictment. All are Group A offences for jurisdiction purposes under the CJA 1993, part I (see **A8.7**). **B6.44**

Indictment

B6.45 *Statement of Offence*

Having custody or control of a false instrument contrary to section 5(1) of the Forgery and Counterfeiting Act 1981

Particulars of Offence

A on or about . . . day of . . . had in his custody or under his control an instrument, namely a purported United Kingdom 'penny black' postage stamp, knowing the same to be false, with the intention of using it to induce V to accept it as genuine and by reason of so accepting to act to his prejudice by purchasing it from A as if genuine

This form may easily be adapted for a charge under s. 5(2), (3) or (4).

Alternative Verdicts

B6.46 Based on the usual principles of law governing alternative verdicts (Criminal Law Act 1967, s. 6(3): see **D18.41** *et seq.*), it is submitted that on an indictment for an offence under the Forgery and Counterfeiting Act 1981, s. 5(1), the jury may return a verdict of guilty of an offence under s. 5(2); and that on an indictment for an offence under s. 5(3) the jury may return a verdict of guilty under s. 5(4). It may, nevertheless, be prudent to add alternative counts.

Sentence

B6.47 The maximum sentence for an offence under s. 5(1) or 5(3) of the Forgery and Counterfeiting Act 1981 is 10 years on indictment; six months or a fine not exceeding the statutory maximum or both summarily (Forgery and Counterfeiting Act 1981, s. 6).

In *Cheema* [2002] Cr App R (S) 356, the offender was convicted of having custody or control of 12 false passports, intending that they would be used as genuine passports, contrary to s. 5(1). A sentence of four years' imprisonment was reduced to three years. The Court of Appeal in *Kolawole* [2005] 2 Cr App R (S) 71 approved the sentence in *Cheema*, but disapproved *Siliavski* [2000] 1 Cr App R (S) 23 and *Balasubramaniam* [2002] Cr App R (S) 17. Five years' imprisonment for possessing 250 counterfeit passports with intent was upheld in *Kuosmanen* [2005] 1 Cr App R (S) 354. See also **B6.41**.

The maximum sentence for an offence under s. 5(2) or 5(4) of the Forgery and Counterfeiting Act 1981 is two years on indictment; six months or a fine not exceeding the statutory maximum or both summarily (Forgery and Counterfeiting Act 1981, s. 6). The same maximum penalties apply to offences under the Identity Cards Act 2006, s. 25 (see s. 25(6) and (7)).

Elements

B6.48 It is not generally an offence merely to have custody or control of false instruments, or materials etc. for making them, even if the instruments or materials are intended for some unlawful purpose (though having such items with one when not at one's place of abode and for use in the course of or in connection with any cheat may be an offence under the Theft Act 1968, s. 25: see **B4.119** to **B4.126**). The instruments listed in the Forgery and Counterfeiting Act 1981, s. 5(5), and in the Identity Cards Act 2006, s. 25 have been singled out for protection, as have those to which the Mental Health Act 1983, s. 126, applies (specified documents relating to mental health). The Identity Cards Act 2006 also makes it an offence to possess or have control of genuine identity documents in the circumstances specified in s. 25(1)(b) and (c).

Most of the terms used in the Forgery and Counterfeiting Act 1981, s. 5, are considered in **B6.22** to **B6.27**, but the concepts of 'custody or control' and 'lawful authority or excuse' require some comment.

Custody or Control The offences in the Forgery and Counterfeiting Act 1981, s. 5, are not limited to having the offending items on one's person, or even 'with' one in the sense required for liability under comparable legislation dealing with offensive weapons or theft etc. (e.g., TA 1968, ss. 10 and 25; see **B4.81** and **B4.125**). It will suffice if they are kept in one's home, garage, car or workplace. Problems of liability based on 'innocent possession', such as sometimes arise in other offences (e.g., possession of drugs or firearms) should not be a problem, because the prosecution must prove the accused's knowledge of the falsity and, in cases under s. 5(1) or 5(3), his ulterior intent. One might perhaps know of the falsity etc. without knowing one had custody or control (cf. *Wings Ltd v Ellis* [1985] AC 272), but such a case would be most unusual, and it is doubtful whether strict liability would be imposed even then. **B6.49**

Lawful Authority or Excuse In the absence of any definition in the Forgery and Counterfeiting Act 1981 itself, the concept of lawful excuse must presumably extend to any recognised general defences, and would also cover possession with intent to hand the relevant items to the police or other authorities at the first reasonable opportunity (*Wuyts* [1969] 2 QB 474; *Sunman* [1995] Crim LR 569). It would seem that the burden of proving lawful authority or excuse must only be evidential: contrast s. 17(4) of the Act (making or having implements etc. for counterfeiting protected coins), where the legal burden of proof is expressly placed on the accused. If this is correct, then once the accused raises the issue of lawful authority or excuse, the prosecution must disprove it beyond reasonable doubt. (As to the legal and evidential burdens of proof in relation to the accused generally, see **F3.1** *et seq.* and **F3.40**.) **B6.50**

FORGERY, FALSIFICATION ETC. OF REGISTERS, CERTIFICATES OR CERTIFIED COPIES

Forgery Act 1861

Under the Forgery Act 1861, ss. 36 and 37, it is an offence, punishable with a maximum penalty of life imprisonment, unlawfully to destroy, deface, injure etc. any register of births, baptisms, marriages, deaths or burials; to cause or permit such damage; or knowingly to make, sign or permit the making of false entries or insertions in such registers or in copies thereof, or knowingly to issue false certificates or copies. These provisions overlap with those of the Forgery and Counterfeiting Act 1981, but deal with acts of damage and destruction as well as with falsification. **B6.51**

Other Provisions Relating to Registers and Certificates

As to the falsification of birth or death certificates, see the Births and Deaths Registration Act 1953, s. 37. As to the making of false statements and the use of false certificates in connection with births and deaths, see the Perjury Act 1911, s. 4 (see **B14.21**). Various non-parochial registers deposited with the Registrar-General are protected under the Non-parochial Registers Act 1840, s. 8. **B6.52**

As to dishonestly inducing another to alter entries under the Land Registration Act 2002, see s. 124 of that Act. See also s. 123 of that Act (suppression of information).

The falsification of any pedigree upon which title to land (or some interest therein) depends, with intent to defraud a purchaser who might thereby be induced to accept the title offered, is punishable with up to two years' imprisonment and/or a fine under the Law of Property Act 1925, s. 183. The A-G must give leave before any prosecution is commenced.

As to falsification of entries in the register of trade marks, see the Trade Marks Act 1994, s. 94. As to forgery of a county court summons or other process of a county court, see the County Courts Act 1984, s. 135.

COUNTERFEITING AND KINDRED OFFENCES

Introduction

B6.53 The counterfeiting of currency notes and 'protected coins' is dealt with in part II (ss. 14 to 28) of the Forgery and Counterfeiting Act 1981; the counterfeiting of hallmarks and dies etc. is protected under the Hallmarking Act 1973, s. 6; as to 'counterfeit goods' to which false trade marks are applied, so as to imitate the products of leading manufacturers, see the Trade Marks Act 1994, ss. 92 and 97 (see **B6.87** to **B6.93**).

Scope of Offences under Part II of the Forgery and Counterfeiting Act 1981

B6.54 Part II of the Forgery and Counterfeiting Act 1981 applies only in respect of currency notes and protected coins, as defined in s. 27.

Forgery and Counterfeiting Act 1981, s. 27

(1) In this part of this Act—
'currency note' means—
 (a) any note which—
  (i) has been lawfully issued in England and Wales, Scotland, Northern Ireland, any of the Channel Islands, the Isle of Man or the Republic of Ireland: and
  (ii) is or has been customarily used as money in the country where it was issued: and
  (iii) is payable on demand: or
 (b) any note which—
  (i) has been lawfully issued in some country other than those mentioned in paragraph (a)(i) above: and
  (ii) is customarily used as money in that country: and
'protected coin' means any coin which—
 (a) is customarily used as money in any country: or
 (b) is specified in an order made by the Treasury for the purposes of this part of this Act.
(2) The power to make an order conferred on the Treasury by subsection (1) above shall be exercisable by statutory instrument.
(3) A statutory instrument containing such an order shall be laid before Parliament after being made.

British or Irish notes come within the Act even if no longer customarily used as money (s. 27(1)(a)); but foreign or Commonwealth notes must be in current use (s. 27(1)(b)). Neither kind need ever have been legal tender: Scottish notes, for example, are not legal tender even in Scotland (and see also s. 28(3)).

Coins must either be in current use or be specified by the Treasury for the purpose of this Act. The following coins have been so specified: sovereigns, half-sovereigns, krugerrands, coins which are denominated in fractions of krugerrands, Maria-Theresia thalers dated 1780 and euro-coins (Forgery and Counterfeiting (Protected Coins) Orders 1981 and 1999 (SI 1981 No. 1505 and 1999 No. 2095)). The counterfeiting of ancient coins *not* specified for these purposes cannot be an offence under this Act, however dishonest the motives.

Meaning of 'Counterfeit'

B6.55 **Forgery and Counterfeiting Act 1981, s. 28**

(1) For the purposes of this part of this Act a thing is a counterfeit of a currency note or of a protected coin—
 (a) if it is not a currency note or a protected coin but resembles a currency note or protected coin (whether on one side only or on both) to such an extent that it is reasonably capable of passing for a currency note or protected coin of that description: or
 (b) if it is a currency note or protected coin which has been so altered that it is reasonably capable of passing for a currency note or protected coin of some other description.

(2) For the purposes of this part of this Act—
(a) a thing consisting of one side only of a currency note, with or without the addition of other material, is a counterfeit of such a note:
(b) a thing consisting—
(i) of parts of two or more currency notes: or
(ii) of parts of a currency note, or of parts of two or more currency notes, with the addition of other material,

is capable of being a counterfeit of a currency note.

(3) References in this part of this Act to passing or tendering a counterfeit of a currency note or a protected coin are not to be construed as confined to passing or tendering it as legal tender.

It is not possible to argue that a one-sided note or coin is *ipso facto* incapable of passing for a genuine one, but in other respects the question of what kind of imitation can amount to a counterfeit is one of fact. An incompetent counterfeiter whose notes would fool nobody can be guilty of an attempt to counterfeit or of an offence under s. 17 of the Act (making or having custody of materials etc. for counterfeiting; see **B6.79 to B6.84**).

Section 19 of the Act (imitation coins produced for promotional purposes) appears to assume that a coin may imitate a British coin in size, shape and substance, without necessarily being a counterfeit. Since any such coins could, in some circumstances, be confused with the real thing (e.g., when mixed in a handful of change in poor light), it would seem that a counterfeit must be 'reasonably capable' of bearing some direct scrutiny, if not perhaps close or careful scrutiny.

Sentencing Guidelines

The maximum penalties for the various offences are set out in the sections dealing with them below. The following notes refer to counterfeiting generally. **B6.56**

In *Crick* (1981) 3 Cr App R (S) 275, a case where the offender pleaded guilty to possessing a press for making silver coins, and to making counterfeit 50 pence coins, which he had used to obtain goods from vending machines, Mustill J made the following general remarks about the offences of counterfeiting notes or coinage:

> Coining is a serious offence. It was rightly treated as such by the learned judge, who correctly took the view that it called for an immediate custodial sentence. It must, however, be recognised that not all such offences are of the same gravity. At one extreme is the professional forger, with carefully prepared plates, and elaborate machinery, who manufactures large quantities of banknotes and puts them into circulation. A long sentence of imprisonment is appropriate in such a case. Here the offence is at the other end of the scale. The tools used to make the blanks were primitive, and were not acquired specially for the purpose; the techniques used were amateurish, and there was little real attempt to make the blanks a facsimile of a 50 pence piece. The coins were not, and could not have been, put into general circulation.

A three-year sentence was, accordingly, reduced to one of nine months.

Longer sentences will be upheld for production of banknotes, but much depends on the sophistication of the enterprise and the success of the offenders. Sentences of nine years were reduced to seven years in *Barry* (1983) 5 Cr App R (S) 11, where the offenders had obtained printing machinery and counterfeited £5 notes. See also *Allyson* (1989) 11 Cr App R (S) 60 and *Britton* (1994) 15 Cr App R (S) 482.

In *Howard* (1985) 82 Cr App R 262, the Court of Appeal laid down guidelines for sentencing in cases involving counterfeit notes. It was said that a custodial sentence would be required in nearly all cases where counterfeit notes have been passed, and that possession of large quantities of notes, indicating proximity to the counterfeiters, would be a most important consideration in determining the severity of the sentence.

In *Everett* (1983) 5 Cr App R (S) 207 the offender had bought two counterfeit £20 notes for £4 each and changed them at a club. Whilst the offence was a 'one-off', the offender had previous convictions for dishonesty, and a sentence of 12 months was upheld. In *Shah* (1987) 9 Cr App R (S) 167 the offender, while on bail in relation to unrelated charges, attempted to purchase a record using a counterfeit £50 note. The offender had previous convictions, but of a nature different to the current offence. There was no evidence of dealing in counterfeit currency, and the offender contested the case on the ground that he had not realised the note to be counterfeit. Steyn J said that while this case was at the lower end of the spectrum of seriousness, 'in the absence of exceptional circumstances an immediate custodial sentence is necessary in all cases involving the tendering or passing of forged banknotes'. A 12-month prison sentence, suspended for two years, together with a supervision order, was upheld.

COUNTERFEITING NOTES OR COINS

B6.57 Forgery and Counterfeiting Act 1981, s. 14

(1) It is an offence for a person to make a counterfeit of a currency note or of a protected coin, intending that he or another shall pass or tender it as genuine.
(2) It is an offence for a person to make a counterfeit of a currency note or of a protected coin without lawful authority or excuse.

Procedure

B6.58 Offences under the Forgery and Counterfeiting Act 1981, s. 14(1), are by s. 22 of the Act, triable either way. When tried on indictment they are class 3 offences. If committed on or after 1 August 2000, they are Group A offences for jurisdiction purposes under the CJA 1993, part I (SI 2000 No. 1878); see **A8.7**.

Indictment

B6.59 *Statement of Offence*

Counterfeiting contrary to section 14(1) of the Forgery and Counterfeiting Act 1981

Particulars of Offence

A on or about the . . . day of . . . made a counterfeit of a currency note, namely a Bank of England £5 note, intending to pass or tender the same as genuine

Alternative Verdicts

B6.60 It is submitted that, on an indictment for an offence under the Forgery and Counterfeiting Act 1981, s. 14(1), it is open to the jury to return a verdict of guilty of the offence under s. 14(2) (see generally the Criminal Law Act 1967, s. 3, and **D18.34** ***et seq.***). It may, however, be prudent to add an alternative count.

Sentence

B6.61 The Forgery and Counterfeiting Act 1981, s. 22, prescribes the maximum penalties: for an offence under s. 14(1), the maximum penalty is 10 years and/or a fine on indictment; six months and/or a fine not exceeding the statutory maximum summarily; for an offence under s. 14(2), it is two years and/or a fine on indictment; six months and/or a fine not exceeding the statutory maximum summarily. For sentencing guidelines, see **B6.56**.

Elements

B6.62 In the Forgery and Counterfeiting Act 1981, s. 14, a distinction is drawn (as in s. 5 of the Act: see **B6.43** to **B6.50**) between cases in which there is proof of an intent that the fake item shall be passed as genuine (s. 14(1)) and cases in which there is not (s. 14(2)). In the latter kind of case counterfeiting is still an offence (albeit a less serious one), unless the maker has lawful authority or excuse. The reason for this is that even the honest manufacture of realistic fakes carries risks of confusion or subsequent misuse. See *Heron* [1982] 1 WLR 451, decided under the Coinage Offences Act 1936, in which the making of counterfeit coins was held to be an offence without proof of any intent to deceive; see also *Selby v DPP* [1972] AC 515.

The intent specified in the Forgery and Counterfeiting Act 1981, s. 14(1), is ulterior. The actual passing of the counterfeit need never happen, and it would suffice even if it was intended to happen outside the jurisdiction, as long as the counterfeiting itself was committed within it. In contrast to ss. 1 to 4 and s. 5(1) of the Act, there is no need to prove an intent to induce someone to act to his own or another's prejudice.

PASSING, TENDERING OR DELIVERING COUNTERFEIT NOTES OR COINS

Forgery and Counterfeiting Act 1981, s. 15 **B6.63**

(1) It is an offence for a person—
  (a) to pass or tender as genuine any thing which is, and which he knows or believes to be, a counterfeit of a currency note or of a protected coin; or
  (b) to deliver to another any thing which is, and which he knows or believes to be, such a counterfeit, intending that the person to whom it is delivered or another shall pass or tender it as genuine.

(2) It is an offence for a person to deliver to another, without lawful authority or excuse, any thing which is, and which he knows or believes to be, a counterfeit of a currency note or of a protected coin.

Procedure

Offences under the Forgery and Counterfeiting Act 1981, s. 15, are, by s. 22 of the Act, triable either way. When tried on indictment they are class 3 offences. If committed on or after 1 August 2000, they are Group A offences for jurisdiction purposes under the CJA 1993, part I (SI 2000 No. 1878); see **A8.7**. **B6.64**

Indictment

Statement of Offence **B6.65**

Passing a counterfeit note contrary to section 15(1) of the Forgery and Counterfeiting Act 1981

Particulars of Offence

A on or about the . . . day of . . . passed to V a counterfeit of a currency note, namely a Bank of England £5 note, knowing or believing the same to be counterfeit

Alternative Verdicts

It is submitted that, on an indictment for an offence under the Forgery and Counterfeiting Act 1981, s. 15(1)(b), it is open to the jury to return a verdict of guilty of the offence under s. 15(2) (see generally the Criminal Law Act 1967, s. 3, and **D18.41** *et seq.*). It may, however, be prudent to add an alternative count. **B6.66**

Sentence

The Forgery and Counterfeiting Act 1981, s. 22, prescribes the maximum penalties: for an offence under s. 15(1)(a) or (b), the maximum penalty is 10 years and/or a fine on indictment; six months and/or a fine not exceeding the statutory maximum summarily; for an offence under s. 15(2), it is two years and/or a fine on indictment; six months and/or a fine not exceeding the statutory maximum summarily. For sentencing guidelines, see **B6.56**. **B6.67**

Scope of Offence

B6.68 The Forgery and Counterfeiting Act 1981, s. 15, follows the same pattern as s. 14 (see **B6.57** to **B6.62**), in that it distinguishes between cases in which a counterfeit is passed as genuine or delivered to another with intent that he should so pass it, and cases in which it is merely 'delivered', perhaps expressly described as a reproduction (see *Selby v DPP* [1972] AC 515). The latter kind of case attracts less serious penalties, but is still regarded as dangerous and undesirable.

Meaning of 'Passing' and 'Tendering'

B6.69 'Passing' suggests acceptance by the person to whom the thing is given, but a counterfeit may be *tendered* as genuine, even if it is at once rejected, and an offence may be committed even where the item in question is not passed or tendered as legal tender (Forgery and Counterfeiting Act 1981, s. 28(3)). Many forms of notes etc. used as money are not legal tender (e.g., Scottish notes), and many protected coins have a collectors' value exceeding any nominal value as currency.

Knowledge and Belief

B6.70 It would not be an offence under the Forgery and Counterfeiting Act 1981, s. 15, to pass or tender a note etc. which one suspects *may* be a counterfeit, even if the suspicion is a strong one. The section requires knowledge or belief, as in handling stolen goods under the Theft Act 1968, s. 22 (see **B4.142**), and those terms must presumably bear the same meanings as under that provision.

Meaning of 'Delivering'

B6.71 'Delivering', in the Forgery and Counterfeiting Act 1981, s. 15(1)(b) and (2), need not involve any intent to deceive as to the nature of the thing delivered, but the more serious offence under s. 15(1)(b) may be committed if it is intended that the counterfeits should eventually be tendered as genuine, by the recipient or some other person.

Lawful Authority or Excuse

B6.72 An obvious example of lawful delivery, which would not be an offence under the Forgery and Counterfeiting Act 1981, s. 15(2), would be where the counterfeits are handed over to the police; but lawful excuse could extend to general defences, such as mistake or duress. In view of the contrast with s. 17(4) (see **B6.84**), in which the legal burden of proof is expressly placed on the accused, it seems clear that the defence have only an evidential burden to discharge under s. 15(2). If the issue is raised by evidence, the prosecution must disprove the existence of lawful authority or excuse (see generally **F3.1** ***et seq.*** and **F3.13** ***et seq.***), but if there is no evidence capable of supporting such a defence, the judge need not leave it to the jury (*Sunman* [1995] Crim LR 569).

CUSTODY OR CONTROL OF COUNTERFEIT NOTES OR COINS

B6.73 **Forgery and Counterfeiting Act 1981, s. 16**

(1) It is an offence for a person to have in his custody or under his control any thing which is, and which he knows or believes to be, a counterfeit of a currency note or of a protected coin, intending either to pass or tender it as genuine or to deliver it to another with the intention that he or another shall pass or tender it as genuine.

(2) It is an offence for a person to have in his custody or under his control, without lawful authority or excuse, any thing which is, and which he knows or believes to be, a counterfeit of a currency note or of a protected coin.

(3) It is immaterial for the purposes of subsections (1) and (2) above that a coin or note is not in

a fit state to be passed or tendered or that the making or counterfeiting of a coin or note has not been finished or perfected.

Procedure

Offences under the Forgery and Counterfeiting Act 1981, s. 16(1), are, by s. 22 of the Act, triable either way. When tried on indictment they are class 3 offences. If committed on or after 1 August 2000, they are Group A offences for jurisdiction purposes under the CJA 1993, part I (SI 2000 No. 1878); see **A8.7**. **B6.74**

Indictment

Statement of Offence **B6.75**

Having custody or control of a counterfeit note contrary to section 16(1) of the Forgery and Counterfeiting Act 1981

Particulars of Offence

A on or about the . . . day of . . . had in his custody or under his control a counterfeit of a currency note, namely a Bank of England £5 note, knowing or believing the same to be counterfeit and intending to pass or tender it as genuine [or to deliver it to X with the intention that X should pass or tender it as genuine]

Alternative Verdicts

It is submitted that on an indictment for an offence under the Forgery and Counterfeiting Act 1981, s. 16(1), it is open to the jury to return a verdict of guilty of the offence under s. 16(2) (see generally the Criminal Law Act 1967, s. 3, and **D18.41** ***et seq.***). It may, however, be prudent to add an alternative count. **B6.76**

Sentence

The Forgery and Counterfeiting Act 1981, s. 22, prescribes the maximum penalties: for an offence under s. 16(1), the maximum penalty is 10 years and/or a fine on indictment; six months and/or a fine not exceeding the statutory maximum summarily; for an offence under s. 16(2), it is two years and/or a fine on indictment; six months and/or a fine not exceeding the statutory maximum summarily. For sentencing guidelines, see **B6.56**. **B6.77**

Elements

Section 16 of the Forgery and Counterfeiting Act 1981 follows the same format as ss. 14 and 15 (see **B6.57** to **B6.72**). Section 16 serves the same kind of function as that served by s. 5(1) and (2) in relation to forgery offences (see **B6.43** to **B6.50**). As to the meaning of 'custody and control' in this context, see the discussion of s. 5 at **B6.49**. **B6.78**

OFFENCES RELATING TO MATERIALS AND IMPLEMENTS FOR COUNTERFEITING

Definitions

Forgery and Counterfeiting Act 1981, s. 17 **B6.79**

(1) It is an offence for a person to make, or to have in his custody or under his control, any thing which he intends to use, or permit any other person to use, for the purpose of making a counterfeit of a currency note or of a protected coin with the intention that it be passed or tendered as genuine.

(2) It is an offence for a person without lawful authority or excuse—
(a) to make; or
(b) to have in his custody or under his control,
any thing which, to his knowledge, is or has been specially designed or adapted for the making of a counterfeit of a currency note.

(3) Subject to subsection (4) below, it is an offence for a person to make, or to have in his custody or under his control, any implement which, to his knowledge, is capable of imparting to any thing a resemblance—
(a) to the whole or part of either side of a protected coin: or
(b) to the whole or part of the reverse of the image on either side of a protected coin.

(4) It shall be a defence for a person charged with an offence under subsection (3) above to show—
(a) that he made the implement or, as the case may be, had it in his custody or under his control, with the written consent of the Treasury; or
(b) that he had lawful authority otherwise than by virtue of paragraph (a) above, or a lawful excuse, for making it or having it in his custody or under his control.

Procedure

B6.80 Both offences under the Forgery and Counterfeiting Act 1981, s. 17, are, by s. 22 of the Act, triable either way. When tried on indictment they are class 3 offences. If committed on or after 1 August 2000, they are Group A offences for jurisdiction purposes under the CJA 1993, part I (SI 2000 No. 1878); see **A8.7**.

Indictment

B6.81

Statement of Offence

Having custody or control of thing intended for use in making a counterfeit, with intent, contrary to section 17(1) of the Forgery and Counterfeiting Act 1981

Particulars of Offence

A on or about the . . . day of . . . had in his custody or under his control a press and a quantity of inks intending to use the same to make a counterfeit of a currency note, namely a Bank of England £5 note, with the intention that such note be passed or tendered as genuine

Sentence

B6.82 The Forgery and Counterfeiting Act 1981, s. 22, prescribes the maximum penalties: for an offence under s. 17(1), the maximum penalty is 10 years and/or a fine on indictment; six months and/or a fine not exceeding the statutory maximum summarily; for an offence under s. 17(2) or (3), it is two years and/or a fine on indictment; six months and/or a fine not exceeding the statutory maximum summarily. For sentencing guidelines, see **B6.56**.

Scope of Offence

B6.83 The Forgery and Counterfeiting Act 1981, s. 17, serves the same kind of function as that served by s. 5(3) and (4) in relation to forgery offences (see **B6.43 to B6.50**), and it follows s. 5 in distinguishing between cases where there is proof of an intent to pass false items as genuine and cases where there is not. Subsection (1) of s. 17 deals with the more serious kind of case; subsections (2) and (3) deal with the less serious kind. Either subsection may apply, not only to essential counterfeiting materials such as inks, but also to optional 'quality-control' devices such as chromolins (*Maltman* [1995] 1 Cr App R 239).

Lawful Authority or Excuse

B6.84 Subsection (3) of the Forgery and Counterfeiting Act 1981, s. 17 is subject to subsection (4), which expressly places the burden of proving lawful authority or excuse on the defence. However, subsection (2) is not subject to subsection (4). This indicates that the legal burden lies on the prosecution to disprove beyond reasonable doubt defences of lawful excuse etc. under s. 17(2), and indeed under all other provisions in the Act except s. 17(3). See generally **F3.1** ***et seq.*** and **F3.13** ***et seq.***

IMPORTATION AND EXPORTATION OF COUNTERFEIT NOTES OR COINS

Forgery and Counterfeiting Act 1981, ss. 20 and 21 **B6.85**

20. The importation, landing or unloading of a counterfeit of a currency note or of a protected coin without the consent of the Treasury is hereby prohibited.

21.—(1) The exportation of a counterfeit of a currency note or of a protected coin without the consent of the Treasury is hereby prohibited.

(2) A counterfeit of a currency note or of a protected coin which is removed to the Isle of Man from the United Kingdom shall be deemed to be exported from the United Kingdom—
(a) for the purposes of this section: and
(b) for the purposes of the customs and excise Acts, in their application to the prohibition imposed by this section.

Sections 20 and 21 impose prohibitions, but are not themselves offence-creating provisions. The relevant offences are those created under the Customs and Excise Management Act 1979, ss. 50 and 68 (see **B17.11** and **B17.18**). If committed on or after 1 August 2000, any such offences involving breaches of ss. 20 or 21 are Group A offences for jurisdiction purposes under the CJA 1993, part I (see **A8.7**).

POWERS OF SEARCH, SEIZURE AND FORFEITURE

B6.86 Powers of search and seizure in relation to false instruments and the means of their production are contained in the Forgery and Counterfeiting Act 1981, s. 7(1). Broadly similar powers in relation to counterfeiting are contained in s. 24(1) of that Act.

An order for the forfeiture, destruction or disposal of such objects may be obtained from a magistrates' court, if it is satisfied that the order is conducive to the public interest; but anyone claiming a proprietary right or other interest in the objects concerned must be given the opportunity to 'show cause why the order should not be made' (ss. 7(4) and 24(4)). Where convictions are imposed under the Act, the court concerned may order the destruction or forfeiture of any object which has been shown to relate to the offence, or it may order it to be dealt with in such other manner as it thinks fit (ss. 7(3) and 24(3)). Any applicant claiming an interest in the object concerned must be given the opportunity to oppose the order under ss. 7(4) or 24(4).

FALSE APPLICATION OR USE OF TRADE MARKS

Trade Marks Act 1994, s. 92 **B6.87**

(1) A person commits an offence who with a view to gain for himself or another, or with intent to cause loss to another, and without the consent of the proprietor—
(a) applies to goods or their packaging a sign identical to, or likely to be mistaken for, a registered trade mark, or
(b) sells or lets for hire, offers or exposes for sale or hire or distributes goods which bear, or the packaging of which bears, such a sign, or
(c) has in his possession, custody or control in the course of a business any such goods with a view to the doing of anything, by himself or another, which would be an offence under paragraph (b).

(2) A person commits an offence who with a view to gain for himself or another, or with intent to cause loss to another, and without the consent of the proprietor—
(a) applies a sign identical to, or likely to be mistaken for, a registered trade mark to material intended to be used—
(i) for labelling or packaging goods,
(ii) as a business paper in relation to goods, or
(iii) for advertising goods, or

(b) uses in the course of a business material bearing such a sign for labelling or packaging goods, as a business paper in relation to goods, or for advertising goods, or

(c) has in his possession, custody or control in the course of a business any such material with a view to the doing of anything, by himself or another, which would be an offence under paragraph (b).

(3) A person commits an offence who with a view to gain for himself or another, or with intent to cause loss to another, and without the consent of the proprietor—

(a) makes an article specifically designed or adapted for making copies of a sign identical to, or likely to be mistaken for, a registered trade mark, or

(b) has such an article in his possession, custody or control in the course of a business, knowing or having reason to believe that it has been, or is to be, used to produce goods, or material for labelling or packaging goods, as a business paper in relation to goods, or for advertising goods.

Sentence and Procedure

B6.88 Offences under the Trade Marks Act 1994, s. 92, are punishable on indictment with a fine and/or a maximum of 10 years' imprisonment; on summary conviction with imprisonment for six months and/or a fine not exceeding the statutory maximum (s. 92(6)). When tried on indictment they are class 3 offences. Relevant sentencing decisions are *Ansari* [2000] 1 Cr App R (S) 94, *Burns* [2001] 1 Cr App R (S) 220, *Gleeson* [2002] 1 Cr App R (S) 485, *Woolridge* [2006] 1 Cr App R (S) 72 and *Kirkwood* [2006] 2 Cr App R (S) 263. Proceedings for offences committed by partnerships must be brought against the partnership in the name of the firm, and not that of the partners (s. 101(1)). As to the liability of individual partners, see **B6.91**.

Local weights and measures authorities are responsible for the enforcement of s. 92, and for this purpose are vested with the same powers to make test purchases, enter premises, seize goods and documents, etc., as under the Trade Descriptions Act 1968, ss. 27 to 29 and 33 (Trade Marks Act 1994, s. 93).

Requirement for Specific Offence

B6.89 Although commercial activities involving trade in counterfeit goods will often involve the commission of offences under the Trade Descriptions Act 1968 (see **B6.94** *et seq.*), and in some cases offences under the TA 1968, it was felt that a set of specific offences should exist to combat this trade. Such offences were originally introduced by s. 58A of the Trade Marks Act 1938, inserted by s. 300 of the Copyright, Designs and Patents Act 1988. The Trade Marks Act 1994, s. 92, repeals and replaces these offences with broadly similar, but not identical, provisions.

Scope of Offences under Trade Marks Act 1994, s. 92

B6.90 The offences created by the Trade Marks Act 1994, s. 92(1) to (3), deal only with the infringement, etc., of registered trade marks in respect of goods. A trade mark is defined in s. 1 of the 1994 Act as any sign capable of being represented graphically which is capable of distinguishing goods or services of one undertaking from those of other undertakings. It may consist of words, names, designs, letters, numerals or the shape of goods or their packaging. Registration gives the owner a property right in it, which is protected under the 1994 Act (s. 2). Section 92 does not, however, apply to infringement of trade marks in respect of services. Furthermore, s. 92(4) provides that no offence can be committed under s. 92 unless the goods involved are goods in respect of which the trade mark has been registered, or the use of the counterfeit mark, etc., would take unfair advantage of, or be detrimental to the distinctive character or reputation of, a trade mark that has a reputation in the UK.

An offence under s. 92(1), (2) or (3), can be committed only when the offending sign is used as an indication or badge of trade origin. This involves a question of fact in each case, namely whether the sign would be so perceived by the average customer of the type of goods in question. See *Johnstone* [2003] 1 WLR 1736 and *Thompson* [2006] EWCA Crim 3058. A 'bootleg' compact disc of music by artists such as the Rolling Stones, if it does not purport to be anything *other* than a bootleg recording, does not offend under s. 92, even though the name, 'Rolling Stones' is a registered trademark. It would be otherwise if the disc purported to be (or would be perceived by customers as) a work released *by* the Rolling Stones, because the use of the trade mark under those circumstances would indeed purport to indicate the trade origin of the disc itself, and not merely serve to identify the artists.

Mens Rea and Defences

The accused must in all cases be shown to have acted with a view to gain or with an intent to cause loss to another. This is the same ulterior intent that is required under the TA 1968, ss. 17 and 21, and it must have the same meaning as it bears there (see **B5.51**). This may not necessarily mean, however, that the accused acted dishonestly, knowingly or fraudulently. **B6.91**

Under s. 92(5), it is a defence for the accused to prove that he believed on reasonable grounds that the use or proposed use of the offending sign concerned was not an infringement of the registered trademark. This applies both to cases in which the accused reasonably believes there is no such registered trademark and to cases in which he is aware of the trademark but unaware that it is being infringed (*Johnstone* [2003] 1 WLR 1736). The burdens imposed here are persuasive and not merely evidential (*ibid*).

It does not follow that someone who is simply ignorant of the existence of a registered trademark, or who has not paid any attention to it, still less someone who has been reckless of its existence, has a defence under s. 92(5) (*McCrudden* [2005] EWCA Crim 466).

By s. 101(4), 'Where a partnership is guilty of an offence under this Act, every partner, other than a partner who is proved to have been ignorant of or to have attempted to prevent the commission of the offence, is also guilty of the offence and liable to be proceeded against and punished accordingly'. This does not require the prior conviction of the firm. It merely requires the court to be satisfied that the firm (which may no longer exist) is or was guilty of such an offence (*Wakefield* (2004) 168 JP 505).

Offences Committed by Bodies Corporate

Directors, managers or other officers of a body corporate who connive at or consent to the commission of an offence by that body will be guilty of the same offence (s. 101(5)). As to the meaning of the term 'manager', see *Boal* [1992] 1 QB 591 and **A5.17**. **B6.92**

Forfeiture Provisions

The Trade Marks Act 1994, s. 97, provides for the making of forfeiture orders in relation to counterfeit goods or packaging (or articles used in their production, etc.) seized in connection with the investigation or prosecution of an offence under s. 92, an offence under the Trade Descriptions Act 1968, or an offence of dishonesty or deception. Such orders may be sought either from the court before which relevant criminal proceedings have been brought or, where no such application has been made, by way of complaint to a magistrates' court (s. 97(2)). **B6.93**

If satisfied that a relevant offence has been committed in relation to the goods, etc. (or other goods which are representative of them), the court may order that they be destroyed in accordance with its directions, or that they be released to a specified person, on condition (a) that he causes offending signs to be removed or obliterated and (b) that any order against him to pay costs in those proceedings is complied with (s. 97(7)).

FALSE TRADE DESCRIPTIONS IN RESPECT OF GOODS

B6.94 **Trade Descriptions Act 1968, s. 1**

(1) Any person who, in the course of a trade or business—
 (a) applies a false trade description to any goods; or
 (b) supplies or offers to supply any goods to which a false trade description is applied; shall, subject to the provisions of this Act, be guilty of an offence.

(2) Sections 2 to 6 of this Act shall have effect for the purposes of this section and for the interpretation of expressions used in this section, wherever they appear in this Act.

Procedure and Enforcement

B6.95 Except where otherwise specified, all offences under the Trade Descriptions Act 1968 are triable either way. When tried on indictment, they are class 3 offences. Enforcement of the Act is primarily the responsibility of local weights and measures authorities. In practice, this means the trading standards department of the relevant local authority. Authorised officers have the power to make test purchases, and may in certain circumstances enter premises to inspect and seize goods and documents for the purpose of determining whether offences are being committed (Trade Descriptions Act 1968, ss. 27 to 28). As to offences involving the obstruction of trading standards officers or the provision of false information, see s. 29 (see **B6.112**).

No prosecution for an offence under the Act may be commenced after the expiration of three years from its commission, or one year from its discovery by the prosecutor, whichever is the earlier (s. 19(1)). In *Beaconsfield Justices, ex parte Johnston & Sons Ltd* (1985) 149 JP 535, it was held that a prosecuting authority 'discovers' an offence as soon as it becomes aware of it, even if it does not collect enough admissible evidence to bring a prosecution until a later date. The time limits set under s. 19 also apply to charges of conspiracy to contravene the Act (*Pain* [1986] BTCL 142). Section 19(2) and (4) contain further provisions concerning time-limits for summary prosecutions under the Act, but these are negated, as far as either way offences are concerned, by the MCA 1980, s. 127(2). Summary trials for s. 1 offences are therefore governed by the time-limits imposed by s. 19(1).

Indictment

B6.96 *Statement of Offence*

Applying a false trade description to goods, contrary to section 1(1)(a) of the Trade Descriptions Act 1968

Particulars of Offence

A on a day unknown between . . . and . . . in the course of a trade or business, namely . . . falsified the odometer reading on a Ford Fiesta motor car, registration no. . . . , so as to indicate that the said car had covered 12,050 miles, whereas the true figure was in excess of 35,000 miles.

Sentence

B6.97 The penalty on summary conviction is a fine not exceeding £5,000; on conviction on indictment, the penalty is a fine and/or imprisonment for up to two years (Trade Descriptions Act 1968, s. 18). There are a number of reported decisions of the Court of Appeal which provide guidance on sentencing for the offences under s. 1. No material difference appears to have been drawn between s. 1(1)(a) and s. 1(1)(b) for sentencing purposes. It should always be borne in mind when sentencing for offences involving strict liability that, if the offender denies knowledge of material matters, the prosecution is required to establish fault at the sentencing stage beyond reasonable doubt, even after a guilty plea (see *Lester* (1975) 63 Cr App R 144). For observations on sentencing under this Act, as compared to the Trade Marks Act 1994, see *Bhad* [1999] 2 Cr App R (S) 139.

In *Gupta* (1985) 7 Cr App R (S) 172 Lawton LJ observed that 'clocking' of motor cars was 'all too prevalent from one end of England and Wales to the other'. He noted that very often dishonest second-hand car dealers were punished by way of fine, but said that the proper sentence in many such cases was a custodial sentence together with a fine to remove the profit which had been made. Subsequent cases involving 'clocking' of cars are *Davies* (1992) 13 Cr App R (S) 459, where the offender (a man 'who had dabbled in criminal activities in motor cars on previous occasions') was convicted of 28 offences and a sentence of nine months' imprisonment was upheld, and *Waring* (1994) 15 Cr App R (S) 371, where four offences were admitted and a sentence of six months' imprisonment together with compensation orders of £990 were upheld. Examples of sentencing in respect of goods other than cars are provided by *Ahmadi* (1994) 15 Cr App R (S) 254, where the offender had been re-cycling toner cartridges for photocopying machines and passing them off as new ones, six months' imprisonment being upheld on appeal, and *Foster* (1992) 12 Cr App R (S) 394 where the offender marketed a slimming diet in respect of which false claims were made. The Court of Appeal accepted that, although the offender had contested the case, imposition of the maximum sentence of two years' imprisonment was inappropriate in light of mitigation, and reduced the term to one of 18 months.

Elements

Section 1 of the Trade Descriptions Act 1968 creates two distinct offences, the offence under s. 1(1)(a) and the offence under s. 1(1)(b). They are each offences of strict liability, subject to possible 'no fault' defences under s. 24 or s. 25 of the Act (see **B6.106** ***et seq.***). No intent to deceive need be proved, nor need the defendant be proved to know the falsity of the description (*Swithland Motors Ltd v Peck* [1991] RTR 322 at p. 328). There is some tentative authority to the effect that the defendant must at least know that the trade description has been applied to the goods (*Cottee v Douglas Seaton (Used Cars)* [1972] 1 WLR 1408) but this cannot be correct, because it is clear from s. 24(3) of the Act that the prosecution do not have to prove the existence of such knowledge. On the contrary, it is for the defence to prove that the defendant did not know (*and* could not with reasonable diligence have ascertained) that the description had been applied to the goods. As to other fundamental distinctions between trade description offences and fraud offences or deception offences under the Theft Acts, see **B6.1**. **B6.98**

The Course of Trade or Business

It is essential for the prosecution to prove either that a false trade description was applied in the course of a trade or business (Trade Descriptions Act 1968, s. 1(1)(a)), or that goods to which such a description had been applied were supplied or offered for supply in the course of a trade or business (s. 1(1)(b)). No immediate offence is committed under the Act where a private individual falsely describes goods he is selling, either to another private individual or to someone acting in the course of a trade or business (cf. *John v Matthews* [1970] 2 QB 443). It is possible, however, for a private individual to be held responsible for the falsity of a subsequent trade description, as for example where a private car owner falsifies the mileage recorded on his car's odometer before selling it to a dealer, who then offers it for sale in the course of his business, without realising that the odometer has been falsified. Section 23 of the Act enables prosecutions to be brought against both persons in cases such as this, or (using the 'bypass procedure') against the private car owner alone (see **B6.110**). **B6.99**

Persons working in professional practice (lawyers, veterinary surgeons, etc.) act in the course of a trade or business (*Roberts v Leonard* (1995) 94 LGR 284), and although the Trade Descriptions Act 1968 is usually considered to be a 'consumer protection' statute, it is clear that transactions between traders, businessmen or professionals also fall within its scope. A business may be a sideline (*Fletcher v Sledmore* [1973] RTR 371) but must be more than a self-financing hobby (cf. *Blakemore v Bellamy* [1983] RTR 303).

Problems can arise in respect of activities which are peripheral or incidental to the accused's trade, business or profession. In *Havering LBC v Stevenson* [1970] 1 WLR 1375, S operated a car-hire business. He regularly traded in his cars for new models once they had been used for two years. He sold one such car on which the odometer reading had been falsified. This was held to be an offence under s. 1(1)(b), even though his business was not one of dealing in cars. He had sold the car 'in the course of business', because such sales were a regular, if peripheral, part of his business and the proceeds were used by him as a regular source of business finance.

Stevenson must be contrasted with *Davies v Sumner* [1984] 1 WLR 1301, in which D was a self-employed courier who used his car to transport films, videos and other material throughout Wales. He eventually traded it to a dealer in part exchange for a new one, but the odometer reading of 18,000 miles was found to be false. The true mileage covered was over 100,000. The House of Lords distinguished this case from *Stevenson* on the basis, *inter alia*, that D's sale of his car could only be classed as being made in the course of his business if he conducted such transactions with some regularity. He had not, however, carried out any previous transactions of that kind, nor was it clear that he had planned to carry out more in future.

Trade Descriptions in Respect of Goods

B6.100 **Trade Descriptions Act 1968, s. 2**

(1) A trade description is an indication, direct or indirect, and by whatever means given, of any of the following matters with respect to any goods or parts of goods, that is to say—
 (a) quantity, size or gauge;
 (b) method of manufacture, production, processing or reconditioning;
 (c) composition;
 (d) fitness for purpose, strength, performance, behaviour or accuracy;
 (e) any physical characteristics not included in the preceding paragraphs;
 (f) testing by any person and results thereof;
 (g) approval by any person or conformity to a type approved by any person;
 (h) place or date of manufacture, production, processing or reconditioning;
 (i) person by whom manufactured, produced, processed or reconditioned;
 (j) other history, including previous ownership or use.

(2) The matters specified in subsection (1) of this section shall be taken—
 (a) in relation to any animal, to include sex, breed or cross, fertility and soundness;
 (b) in relation to any semen, to include the identity and characteristics of the animal from which it was taken and measure of dilution.

(3) In this section, 'quantity' includes length, width, height, area, volume, capacity, weight and number.

(4) and (5) [Detailed provisions as to agricultural produce, seeds, food and drugs.]

'Goods' are defined in s. 39 as including ships, aircraft, things attached to land and growing crops. The country of origin of goods is deemed to be that in which they last underwent a treatment or process resulting in a substantial change (s. 36).

Section 2 is definitive, rather than merely illustrative, and some descriptions (e.g., concerning the availability of after-sales service) may fall through the net it casts. The list is also confined to matters of fact. Statements of opinion cannot therefore be trade descriptions within the meaning of s. 2, but the dividing line between fact and opinion is not always clear. For example, to describe a television as having 'superb' picture quality would ordinarily be seen as mere opinion; but such a description must at least indicate (as a fact) that a reasonable picture can be obtained from the set. Similarly, a car cannot be in 'good condition' if it is not even in working order (cf. *Robertson v Dicicco* [1972] RTR 431 and *Furniss v Scholes* [1974] RTR 133). See also s. 3(3) to (4) of the Act (see **B6.102**) as to matters which are not strictly trade descriptions, but which may be may be deemed to be false trade descriptions under that section.

An odometer reading is a trade description within s. 2(1)(j) (*Hammertons Cars Ltd* [1976] 1

WLR 1243). A dealer's statement that a car has a valid MOT certificate is clearly a trade description within s. 2(1)(f), but the mileage etc. recorded on such a certificate is deemed not to be (*Corfield v Sevenways Garage Ltd* [1985] RTR 109; cf. *Coventry Justices, ex parte Farrand* [1988] RTR 273).

A representation to the effect that particular goods are of a type tested or approved by a particular person (such as a famous sportsman) may come within s. 2(1)(f) or (g), but offences created by the Trade Descriptions Act 1968, ss. 12 and 13 may in some cases be more apposite. The s. 12(1) offence is one of falsely representing that a person supplies goods or services to members of the Royal Family; the s. 12(2) offence is one of using, without authorisation, an emblem or device suggesting receipt of the Queen's Award to Industry; and the s. 13 offence is one of representing that goods or services are of a kind supplied to any person. These offences are subject to the same procedures and penalties as offences under s. 1. See *Wall v Rose and Sargent* (1998) 162 JP 38.

Falsity in Trade Descriptions

Trade Descriptions Act 1968, s. 3 **B6.101**

(1) A false trade description is a trade description which is false to a material degree.
(2) A trade description which, though not false, is misleading, that is to say, likely to be taken for an indication of any of those matters specified in section 2 of this Act as would be false to a material degree, shall be deemed to be a false trade description.
(3) Anything which, though not a trade description, is likely to be taken for an indication of any of those matters and, as such an indication, would be false to a material degree, shall be deemed to be a false trade description.
(4) A false indication, or anything which is likely to be taken as an indication which would be false, that any goods comply with a standard specified or recognised by any person or implied by the approval of any person shall be deemed to be a false trade description, if there is no such person or no standard so specified, recognised or implied.

The question whether a trade description is false to a material degree is largely one of fact. Some cases suggest that a description should not be considered materially false if it could not be expected to mislead anyone. In *Donnelly v Rowlands* [1970] 1 WLR 1600, a dairyman sold milk in a bottle embossed with the name of another dairy, but sealed with his own silver cap. It was held that there was no false trade description, because the correctly labelled cap made it clear that the milk was his produce, and that only the bottle containing it belonged to the other dairy. It has also been held that the *de minimis* rule applies, so that insignificant or purely technical inaccuracies do not make a trade description false to a material degree (*Ford Motor Co. Ltd* [1974] 1 WLR 1220).

A trade description may be literally correct, but misleading because of what it omits. Under s. 3(2), it may then be treated as if it were a false trade description. An example is provided by *Inner London Justices, ex parte Wandsworth Borough Council* [1983] RTR 425, in which a dealer described a car as having had 'one previous owner', whilst omitting to point out that this owner was a car leasing company. This was deemed to be a false trade description by virtue of s. 3(2).

Section 3(3) deals with things which are likely to be taken for trade descriptions, but which do not strictly speaking fall within any of the categories listed in s. 2(1). Its possible effect was illustrated in *Holloway v Cross* [1981] 1 All ER 1012, in which a dealer acquired a car which had obviously exceeded the very low mileage shown on its odometer. He described it to a customer as having covered an 'estimated' 45,000 miles, but it was proved that the car must have covered some 70,000 miles, and he was prosecuted under s. 1(1)(b). The justices who heard his case held that his estimate was a mere opinion, and thus not an 'indication of . . . history or use' within s. 2(1)(j); but they nevertheless convicted him on the basis that it would be taken by the non-expert customer to be just such an indication. The Divisional Court upheld his conviction, their only doubt being whether it was absolutely necessary to rely on s. 3(3) rather than on s. 2(1) itself.

The unauthorised use of a trade mark does not necessarily involve the application of a false trade description, unless it is thereby implied that the goods were manufactured, distributed, processed or approved of by the owner of that trade mark, which is a question of fact that depends upon all the circumstances of the case. It may, for example, be clear that the goods are being supplied as cheap imitations, rather than being passed off as the genuine article (see *Veys* (1992) 157 JP 567 and *Kent County Council v Price* (1993) 157 JP 1161). The sale or supply of counterfeit goods may be more appropriately dealt with under the Trade Marks Act 1994, s. 92 (see **B6.87** *et seq.*).

Application of Description to Goods

B6.102 **Trade Descriptions Act 1968, s. 4**

(1) A person applies a trade description to goods if he—
  (a) affixes or annexes it to or in any manner marks it on or incorporates it with—
    (i) the goods themselves, or
    (ii) anything in, on or with which, the goods are supplied; or
  (b) places the goods in, on or with anything which the trade description has been affixed or annexed to, marked on or incorporated with, or places any such thing with the goods; or
  (c) uses the trade description in any manner likely to be taken as referring to the goods.
(2) An oral statement may amount to the use of a trade description.
(3) Where goods are supplied in pursuance of a request in which a trade description is used and circumstances are such as to make it reasonable to infer that the goods are supplied as goods conforming to that trade description, the person supplying the goods shall be deemed to have applied the trade description to the goods.

The methods of application listed in s. 4 are definitive, rather than merely illustrative, but nothing in s. 4 (or in s. 1) requires that a trade description must be applied by a person selling or supplying the goods. It may accordingly be applied by a trade buyer, as for example where a used car dealer falsely states that the vehicle offered to him is good only for scrap (*Fletcher v Budgen* [1974] 1 WLR 1056) or where an antique dealer falsely states that a Chippendale chair offered for sale to him is a modern reproduction. On the other hand, although s. 4 is silent on the point, it has been held that a description first applied by a dealer only after the completion of a sale cannot come within the proper scope of the Act, since it cannot influence the transaction in question (*Hall v Wickens Motors (Gloucester) Ltd* [1972] 1 WLR 1418).

A trade description may be applied by mere implication, and may even be applied secretly. In *Cottee v Douglas Seaton (Used Cars)* [1972] 1 WLR 1408, it was held that a false trade description was secretly applied to a car when serious rust defects in its bodywork (and previous amateur repairs) were concealed with paint.

One effect of s. 4(3) is that the delivery of goods which fail to meet a previously agreed contractual specification may involve an offence under s. 1(1)(b) (see *Shropshire County Council v Simon Dudley Ltd* (1997) 161 JP 224).

Advertisements

B6.103 **Trade Descriptions Act 1968, s. 5**

(1) The following provisions of this section shall have effect where in an advertisement a trade description is used in relation to any class of goods.
(2) The trade description shall be taken as referring to all goods of the class, whether or not in existence at the time the advertisement is published—
  (a) for the purpose of determining whether an offence has been committed under paragraph (a) of section 1(1) of this Act; and
  (b) where goods of the class are supplied or offered to be supplied by a person publishing or displaying the advertisement, also for the purpose of determining whether an offence has been committed under paragraph (b) of the said section 1(1).

(3) In determining for the purposes of this section whether any goods are of a class to which a trade description used in an advertisement relates regard shall be had not only to the form and content of the advertisement but also to the time, place, manner and frequency of its publication and all other matters making it likely or unlikely that a person to whom the goods are supplied would think of the goods as belonging to the class in relation to which the trade description is used in the advertisement.

This provision supplements s. 4 (see **B6.102**) by clarifying the circumstances in which an advertisement shall be taken to apply to particular goods. A manufacturer or distributor who falsely describes goods in an advertisement to potential customers commits an offence under s. 1(1)(a), even if the goods have already been supplied to the retailers. Furthermore, the retailers may themselves be guilty of supplying goods to which the false trade description has been applied, subject however to a possible defence under s. 24 (see **B6.106**). Section 39 of the Act provides that 'advertisements' include catalogues, circulars and price lists, but the section does not purport to give an exhaustive definition.

Offers to Supply

Trade Descriptions Act 1968, s. 6 **B6.104**

A person exposing goods for supply or having goods in his possession for supply shall be deemed to offer to supply them.

Section 6 ensures that traders who display falsely described goods in their shops or showrooms are covered by s. 1(1)(b). From a strict contractual position, such displays are mere invitations to treat (*Fisher v Bell* [1961] 1 QB 394). In *Stainthorpe v Bailey* [1980] RTR 7, a motor dealer was held to have offered to supply a vehicle with a falsified odometer even though it was kept at his home rather than his business premises. It had been advertised for sale and a trading standards officer posing as a prospective purchaser was invited to inspect it.

The term, 'supply' is not defined in the Act, but must include dispositions by way of sale, leasing, hire-purchase or even promotional gift (see *Cahalne v Croydon London Borough Council* (1985) 149 JP 561 at p. 565). In *Formula One Autocentres v Birmingham City Council* [1999] RTR 195, it was held that the return of a car to a customer after a service constitutes a 'supply' of that car to the customer. Since the supposed service had not been carried out as specified in that case, it amounted to an offence under s. 1. This saved the respondent authority from having to prove *mens rea* under s. 14 (see **B6.113** *et seq.*) but the decision seems, with respect, to impose strict liability where Parliament did not intend it.

Disclaimers

The Trade Descriptions Act 1968 makes no express reference to disclaimers, but in some areas of trade and business the practice has developed of relying on disclaimers wherever it is feared that trade descriptions may not be accurate. The purpose of such disclaimers is to displace or negate any false impression that a doubtful trade description might otherwise create (*Hammertons Cars* [1976] 1 WLR 1243; *Wandsworth London Borough Council v Bentley* [1980] RTR 429). Disclaimer cases can therefore be distinguished from defences under s. 24 of the Act (see **B6.106**) which operate on the basis that the *actus reus* of the offence has indeed been committed. It has been held that in order to be effective disclaimers must be 'as bold, precise and compelling as the trade description itself' (*Norman v Bennett* [1974] 1 WLR 229, per Lord Widgery CJ at p. 232). Disclaimers in small print or on obscure notices cannot therefore suffice (*Waltham Forest London Borough Council v TG Wheatley (Central Garage) Ltd* [1978] RTR 157), nor may a disclaimer itself be phrased misleadingly or ambiguously (as in *Corfield v Starr* [1981] RTR 380, where a notice next to a car's odometer stated that the 'Customer's Protection Act' (*sic*) precluded the dealers from verifying the accuracy of the mileage recorded — this might have given the impression that, but for this fictitious statute, the dealers would have been able to verify the recorded mileage, whereas the dealers knew it to be incorrect). Oral disclaimers may in theory be effective, but in practice are unlikely to **B6.105** provide full protection, if only because the offence may be complete before the oral disclaimer is made (*Lewin v Fuell* (1991) 155 JP 206).

Used car dealers may be unable to verify the recorded mileages on vehicles acquired by them. A prominent disclaimer placed next to or across the suspect odometer display will usually suffice to avoid liability under s. 1(1)(b) (*Ealing London Borough Council v Taylor* (1995) 159 JP 460), but not where the dealer knows more about the vehicle's true history than he reveals (*Farrand v Lazarus* [2002] 3 All ER 175).

It has been stated in a number of cases (including *Southwood* [1987] 1 WLR 1361, *Southend Borough Council v White* (1991) 156 JP 463 and (*obiter*) in *Shrewsbury Crown Court, ex parte Venables* [1994] Crim LR 61) that disclaimers cannot be relied upon in cases where false trade descriptions have been applied by the defendant himself, contrary to s. 1(1)(a). Where a disclaimer is added only after the application of a false trade description, it will come too late to avoid liability that has already been incurred (*Newman v Hackney London Borough Council* [1982] RTR 296); and the courts are rightly unwilling to assist dishonest dealers who deliberately falsify odometers etc., but it is clear that cases can arise in which the application of a false trade description is not dishonest and is accompanied by a contemporaneous disclaimer. *Bull* [1997] RTR 123 was such a case. B, a car dealer, displayed for sale a car bearing an odometer reading he rightly regarded as suspect. He placed a clearly worded disclaimer over the odometer itself, thereby avoiding any liability under s. 1(1)(b), but at the moment of sale he entered the false odometer reading on the invoice, subject again to a clear disclaimer, which stated that the mileage could not be verified and 'must be considered incorrect'. This led to a conviction under s. 1(1)(a), but his conviction was quashed by the Court of Appeal, on the basis that the disclaimer was attached to the invoice in such a way as to prevent it from ever being false. *Newman* was distinguished on that basis and *Southwood* was not discussed, but it is submitted that *Bull* is rightly decided on its facts and that disclaimers may, in appropriate cases, prevent liability from being incurred under s. 1(1)(a).

Defence of Mistake, Accident, etc.

B6.106 **Trade Descriptions Act 1968, s. 24**

(1) In any proceedings for an offence under this Act it shall, subject to subsection (2) of this section, be a defence for the person charged to prove—
  (a) that the commission of the offence was due to a mistake or to reliance on information supplied to him or to the act or default of another person, an accident or some other cause beyond his control; and
  (b) that he took all reasonable precautions and exercised all due diligence to avoid the commission of such an offence by himself or any person under his control.

(2) If in any case the defence provided by the last foregoing subsection involves the allegation that the commission of the offence was due to the act or default of another person or to reliance on information supplied by another person, the person charged shall not, without leave of the court, be entitled to rely on that defence unless, within a period ending seven clear days before the hearing, he has served on the prosecutor a notice in writing giving such information identifying or assisting in the identification of that other person as was then in his possession.

(3) In any proceedings for an offence under this Act of supplying or offering to supply goods to which a false trade description is applied it shall be a defence for the person charged to prove that he did not know, and could not with reasonable diligence have ascertained, that the goods did not conform to the description or that the description had been applied to the goods.

The prosecution must prove the essential elements of the relevant offence before s. 24 becomes a consideration (*Hotel Plan Ltd v Tameside Metropolitan Borough Council* [2001] EWHC Admin 154). To rely on s. 24, an accused must establish at least one of the five elements in s. 24(1)(a) *and* satisfy the reasonable precautions/due diligence test in s. 24(1)(b) (see *Wings Ltd v Ellis* [1985] AC 272). 'Reasonable diligence' is also central to defences under

s. 24(3). On traditional principles of statutory interpretation, the accused appears to bear a legal burden of proof under s. 24 but, in order to avoid incompatibility with the ECHR, Article 6(2), it may now be necessary to reinterpret s. 24 as imposing only an evidential burden. If so, the prosecution would be required to disprove any defence raised under s. 24 (see HRA 1998, s. 3, and **F3.6**).

Where mistake is pleaded, this must be the accused's own mistake and not, for example, that of an employee (*Birkenhead and District Co-operative Society Ltd v Roberts* [1970] 1 WLR 1497). A mistake by an employee may be pleaded as the act or default of another person (*Tesco Supermarkets Ltd v Nattrass* [1972] AC 153) but must then be notified in advance of the trial (s. 24(2)). Where a company is charged, the acts or defaults of its directors, etc., must be treated as its own, but the acts of mere branch managers may be treated as acts of third parties (*Tesco Supermarkets Ltd v Nattrass*). Any such third parties must be identified, where possible, under s. 24(2).

Due (or Reasonable) Diligence under s. 24 What amounts to 'due diligence' or 'reasonable **B6.107** diligence' is largely be a question of fact. The two expressions mean much the same thing (*Texas Homecare v Stockport Metropolitan Borough Council* (1988) 152 JP 83). In the case of used motor vehicles, it has been held that dealers should be careful to disclaim the accuracy of an odometer reading, unless they can verify it from the vehicle's log book or service record, from previous owners (*Simmons v Potter* [1975] RTR 347) or from a careful examination of the vehicle's age and condition (*Naish v Gore* [1971] 3 All ER 737). In practice it will not be enough for a dealer to rely on information as to mileage or roadworthiness provided by an MOT certificate (*Barker v Hargreaves* [1981] RTR 197) but there is no rule of law governing the precautions that must be taken in particular cases (*Ealing London Borough Council v Taylor* (1995) 159 JP 460).

Where it is alleged that employees were to blame, the accused must be able to show that a satisfactory system of training, supervision and inspection was provided (*Tesco Supermarkets v Nattrass* [1972] AC 153). Where goods are sold in large quantities, samples should be examined to ensure that they conform to any trade description applied to them. The adequacy of any system of sampling is a question of fact. In *Rotherham Metropolitan Borough Council v Raysun (UK) Ltd* (1988) *The Times*, 27 April 1988, 100,000 packets of 'poisonless' crayons were imported from Hong Kong, but only one packet was tested for toxicity by the defendants and it was not clear whether any tests had been carried out in Hong Kong. It was held that the due diligence test under s. 24(1) had not been satisfied.

Defences to Charges under s. 1(1)(a) The Court of Appeal held in *Southwood* [1987] 1 **B6.108** WLR 1361 that a person who deliberately falsifies a car odometer cannot rely on any s. 24 defence. As Lord Lane CJ explained, 'by falsifying the instrument, he has disqualified himself from asserting that he has taken any precautions, let alone reasonable precautions'. This does not, however, preclude reliance on s. 24(1) where the accused has mistakenly, despite taking all reasonable precautions, applied a false trade description (*Bull* [1997] RTR 123).

Innocent Publication of Advertisement

Trade Descriptions Act 1968, s. 25 **B6.109**

In proceedings for an offence under this Act committed by the publication of an advertisement it shall be a defence for the person charged to prove that he is the person whose business it is to publish or arrange for the publication of advertisements and that he received the advertisement for publication in the ordinary course of business and did not know and had no reason to suspect that its publication would amount to an offence under this Act.

This defence is additional to the ones provided in s. 24 (see **B6.106**). A shopkeeper who places an advertisement in his window may argue that such advertising is an ordinary (if only a peripheral) part of his business (see the cases discussed at **B6.99**).

Offences Due to the Act or Default of Another Person

B6.110 **Trade Descriptions Act 1968, s. 23**

Where the commission by any person of an offence under this Act is due to the act or default of some other person that other person shall be guilty of the offence, and a person may be charged with and convicted of the offence by virtue of this section whether or not proceedings are taken against the first-mentioned person.

Section 23 is usually referred to as the 'by-pass' provision, although it does not always operate in that way. It may equally operate so as to enable the 'other person' to be joined as a co-defendant. The drafting of the provision is faulty, since it suggests that proof of the guilt of the first person is an essential pre-requisite for the conviction of the 'other person'; and yet the first person may well be able to escape liability under s. 24(1) for the very reason that the offence was caused by the act or default of the other person. In *Coupe v Guyett* [1973] 1 WLR 669, the Divisional Court resolved this problem by holding that a s. 23 prosecution may succeed in cases where it is proved that the 'first person' *would* have been guilty, but for the fact that he has a s. 24 defence. This interpretation is in fact consistent with the wording of s. 24(1)(a). This also refers to the 'commission of the offence', even though it actually provides defendants with a complete defence.

In cases where the 'other person' was himself acting in the course of a trade or business, it is unlikely that resort to s. 23 would ever be strictly necessary. If, for example, Dealer 1 falsifies the mileage recorded on the odometer of a car, and sells it through the trade to Dealer 2, who is prosecuted for an offence under s. 1(1)(b), it would be possible to prosecute Dealer 1 under s. 23, but it would usually be easier to prosecute him under s. 1(1)(a), for applying the false trade description in the first place. Section 23 may, however, be useful where it is desired to prosecute a private individual, who has 'clocked' his car before selling it to the trade, but who cannot be prosecuted directly under s. 1 (see *Olgeirsson v Kitching* [1986] 1 WLR 304).

Directors and Officers of Corporations

B6.111 Where offences committed by corporations are proved to have been committed with the consent and connivance of a director or other officer of the corporation, or any person acting in that capacity (or to have been attributable to neglect on the part of any such person), he may also be convicted of the offence (Trade Descriptions Act 1968, s. 20). See *T* (2006) 170 JP 313.

Obstruction of Authorised Officers

B6.112 **Trade Descriptions Act 1968, s. 29**

(1) Any person who—
(a) wilfully obstructs an officer of a local weights and measures authority or of a government department acting in pursuance of this Act; or
(b) wilfully fails to comply with any requirement properly made to him by such an officer under section 28 of this Act; or
(c) without reasonable cause fails to give such an officer so acting any other assistance or information which he may reasonably require of him for the purpose of the performance of his functions under this Act,

shall be guilty of an offence and liable on conviction to a fine not exceeding level 3 on the standard scale.

(2) If any person, in giving any such information as is mentioned in the preceding subsection, makes any statement which he knows to be false, he shall be guilty of an offence.

(3) Nothing in this section shall be construed as requiring a person to answer any question or give any information if to do so might incriminate him.

Section 28 gives authorised officers the power, in specified circumstances, to enter premises and inspect and seize goods and documents, but no solicitor can be compelled to produce privileged documents etc. under that section (s. 28(7)). An offence under s. 29(2), which is triable either way and subject to the same penalties as an offence under s. 1, can be committed even during an interview under caution, in which the suspect has the right to remain silent (*Page* [1996] Crim LR 439). It follows that a s. 29(2) offence may also be committed where D has the right to remain silent under s. 29(3).

FALSE TRADE DESCRIPTIONS IN RESPECT OF SERVICES, ACCOMMODATION OR FACILITIES

Trade Descriptions Act 1968, s. 14 **B6.113**

(1) It shall be an offence for any person in the course of any trade or business—
(a) to make a statement which he knows to be false; or
(b) recklessly to make a statement which is false;
as to any of the following matters, that is to say,—
(i) the provision in the course of any trade or business of any services, accommodation or facilities;
(ii) the nature of any services, accommodation or facilities provided in the course of any trade or business;
(iii) the time at which, manner in which or persons by whom any services, accommodation or facilities are so provided;
(iv) the examination, approval or evaluation by any person of any services, accommodation or facilities so provided; or
(v) the location or amenities of any accommodation so provided.

(2) For the purposes of this section—
(a) anything (whether or not a statement as to any of the matters specified in the preceding subsection) likely to be taken as a statement as to any of those matters as would be false shall be deemed to be a false statement as to that matter; and
(b) a statement made regardless of whether it is true or false shall be deemed to be made recklessly, whether or not the person making it had reasons for believing that it might be false.

(3) In relation to any services consisting of or including the application of any treatment or process or the carrying out of any repair, the matters specified in subsection (1) of this section shall be taken to include the effect of the treatment, process or repair.

(4) In this section, 'false' means false to a material degree and 'services' does not include anything done under a contract of service.

Procedure and Enforcement

The position is the same as for offences under the Trade Descriptions Act 1968, s. 1 (see **B6.95**). **B6.114**

Indictment

Statement of Offence **B6.115**

Recklessly making a false statement, contrary to section 14(1)(b) of the Trade Descriptions Act 1968

Particulars of Offence

A Ltd on or about the . . . day of . . . in the course of their trade or business, recklessly stated that the Hotel . . . in . . . provided air conditioned accommodation in all rooms, whereas the said hotel was not equipped with air-conditioning.

In *Piper* (1996) 160 JP 116 the Court of Appeal offered guidance on the framing of charges for offences contrary to the Trade Descriptions Act 1968, s. 14(1). Subparagraphs (i) to (v) of section 14(1)(b) overlap, and there may be cases in which the facts potentially fall within more than one of them. It is therefore inadvisable to specify any of these sub-paragraphs. The particulars of the offence should be limited to identifying the offending statement and the way in which it is alleged to have been false. Further particulars may be provided, by order if appropriate, if the defence are embarrassed by insufficient knowledge of the allegation they have to meet.

Sentence

B6.116 The penalty on summary conviction is a fine not exceeding £5,000; on conviction on indictment, the penalty is a fine and/or imprisonment for up to two years (Trade Descriptions Act 1968, s. 18). In *Burridge* (1985) 7 Cr App (S) 125 the offender pleaded guilty to four offences of making false statements as to the nature of services provided. He was the director of a small company which repaired washing machines, and on the occasions in question invoices had been submitted to customers even though the specified work had not been carried out. A sentence of nine months' imprisonment was imposed, with three months to serve and the balance suspended. Lord Lane CJ said that the sentence was, 'if anything, on the light side'.

Elements

B6.117 The two offences created by the Trade Descriptions Act 1968, s. 14(1), have some elements in common with offences under s. 1, but differ in a number of important respects, notably in that the s. 14 offences each require proof of *mens rea*: knowledge of the falsity of the statement, in the case of offences under s. 14(1)(a); and recklessness as to its falsity, in the case of offences under s. 14(1)(b). This does not mean that strict liability has no role to play in respect of offences under s. 14(1) (see *Wings Ltd v Ellis* [1985] AC 272 at **B6.120**).

The Course of Trade or Business

B6.118 The concept of a trade or business must have broadly the same meaning as it has in respect of offences under the Trade Descriptions Act 1968, s. 1 (see **B6.99**); and see also *Breeze* [1973] 1 WLR 994, in which it was held to be an offence under s. 14 for a person who was not a qualified architect to offer his services, commercially, on the basis that he was so qualified. *Breeze* was decided before *Roberts v Leonard* (1995) 94 LGR 284, in which it was finally decided that the business activities of professional men are performed in the course of a trade or business.

Where A, in the course of a trade or business, makes a false statement as to the provision of services, etc. by B, this must mean services, etc. provided (or supposedly provided) by B in the course of a trade or business.

False Statements under s. 14

B6.119 As is the case under the Trade Descriptions Act 1968, s. 1, a false statement under s. 14 must be false to a material degree (s. 14(4)). Section 14(2)(a) serves the same function in respect of s. 14(1) as s. 3(2) and (3) serve in relation to s. 1 (see **B6.101**). This means that misleading statements or indications, even if technically correct, may involve offences under s. 14.

In contrast to the position under s. 1, it has been held that offences under s. 14 can be committed, even where the offending statement is made after the transaction to which it relates has been completed. In *Breed v Cluett* [1970] 2 QB 459, a s. 14 offence was committed by a builder who falsely stated, after completing the sale of a bungalow, that the building was covered by a ten-year NHBRC guarantee. It has also been held that s. 14 can apply to statements concerning services which have already been provided. In *Bevelectric Ltd* (1992) 157 JP 323, the defendants, who carried on a washing machine repair business, always told customers that their machines needed new motors, regardless of whether this was the case. They were charged with offences under s. 14(1)(b), on the basis that their statements falsely indicated that genuine assessments had been made of the condition of the machines. Upholding their convictions, Staughton LJ stated that 'a false statement about services already provided is within the section if it is connected or associated with the supply of the services in question'.

A statement which is not false at the time it is made does not become so, merely because the defendant or a third party subsequently fails to provide services, etc. in accordance with that statement (*Sunair Holidays Ltd v Dodd* [1970] 1 WLR 1037; *Sunair Holidays Ltd* [1973] 1 WLR 1105). It does not, for example, criminalise a failure to fulfil a contractual obligation which the defendant entered into in good faith; but a promise as to the future may involve representations of present fact (e.g., as to the maker's present intentions or policies) and may thus come within the scope of s. 14 (cf. *British Airways Board v Taylor* [1976] 1 WLR 13).

Mens Rea

The offence created by the Trade Descriptions Act 1968, s. 14(1)(a), was surely meant to be a full *mens rea* offence. To commit it, the defendant must 'make a statement which he knows to be false' and the draftsman no doubt assumed that this meant the same thing as 'knowingly making a false statement'. In *Wings Ltd v Ellis* [1985] AC 272, however, the House of Lords held that the offence was one of 'partially strict' liability, because the defendant need not know he is making the statement, as long as he knows that some part of it is false. In that case, W published a holiday brochure which they found to contain inaccurate information concerning accommodation provided at a hotel in Sri Lanka. They tried to ensure that this faulty information was not communicated to potential customers, but unknown to them a travel agent subsequently provided a customer with an uncorrected copy of the brochure, which he read. W argued that they did not know of the error in the brochure when it was printed, and did not know that the customer would be shown an uncorrected copy once the error had been discovered. They did not therefore knowingly make a false statement concerning the hotel. The House of Lords held that this did not matter. When the brochure was read by the customer, W already knew the statement was false, and the offence was therefore made out. **B6.120**

B

'Recklessness' under s. 14(1)(b) must be construed in accordance with s. 14(2)(b), and is a wider concept than recklessness in Theft Act deception cases (see **B5.2** and **B5.3**). It is sufficient if the defendant 'did not have regard to the truth or falsity of his, advertisement, even though it cannot be shown that he was deliberately closing his eyes to the truth or that he had any kind of dishonest mind' (*MFI Warehouses Ltd v Nattrass* [1973] 1 WLR 307 per Lord Widgery CJ at p. 313). See also *Dixons Ltd v Roberts* (1984) 148 JP 513.

Part B Offences

As to circumstances in which *mens rea* can be attributed to a corporation, see **A5.17**. As to the liability of directors or officers, see the Trade Descriptions Act 1968, s. 20 at **B6.111**.

Services, Accommodation and Facilities

The provision of services, accommodation or facilities for the purposes of the Trade Descriptions Act 1968, s. 14, must ordinarily involve something different from the supply of goods (*Newell v Hicks* [1984] RTR 135; *Westminster City Council v Ray Alan (Manshops) Ltd* [1982] 1 WLR 383), but a guarantee relating to goods may involve the promise of a service (*Ashley v Sutton London Borough Council* (1994) 159 JP 631; cf. *Breed v Cluett* [1970] 2 QB 459 — NHBRC guarantee on bungalow). Repair, servicing, insurance, parking or credit arrangements for purchasers or prospective purchasers of goods may be classed as services or facilities, but may also involve the supply of goods (see *Formula One Autocentres v Birmingham City Council* [1999] RTR 195 at **B6.104**). **B6.121**

'Accommodation' clearly includes hotel rooms and holiday lettings, and 'services' include house builders' guarantees and the professional services of architects, etc., but s. 14 does not appear to cover false or misleading statements concerning residential or commercial property sales or lettings. These are covered by the Property Misdescriptions Act 1991, s. 1 (see **B6.124**).

It is not necessary for an information or indictment to specify whether an allegedly false trade description refers to services, facilities or accommodation, as long as it identifies the offending statement and the sense in which it is alleged to be false (see *Piper* (1996) 160 JP 116 at B6.115).

Defences, Disclaimers and By-pass Procedures

B6.122 The rules governing the use of disclaimers for the purpose of nullifying potential misdescriptions under the Trade Descriptions Act 1968, s. 1, would appear to be equally applicable to cases under s. 14 (see for example *Clarksons Holidays Ltd* (1972) 57 Cr App R 38). The same is true of third-party or by-pass prosecutions under s. 23 (see **B6.110**). The s. 24(1) defence (see **B6.106**) can be pleaded in s. 14 cases (*Wings Ltd v Ellis* [1985] AC 272) but the *mens rea* elements required for offences under s. 14 make it less likely that defendants will need to have recourse to that defence.

MISLEADING PRICES AND PROPERTY MISDESCRIPTIONS

Misleading Price Indications

B6.123 Misleading price indications as to goods (but not services, etc.) were once covered, somewhat unsatisfactorily, by the Trade Descriptions Act 1968, s. 11. The Consumer Protection Act 1987, part III, now deals more comprehensively with misleading price indications as to goods, services, accommodation or facilities. It is supplemented by the Code of Practice for Traders on Price Indications, issued and approved by the Secretary of State under s. 25 of the Act (see SI 1988/2078) and by regulations which make specific provision for price indications in respect of methods of payment (credit cards, etc.), bureaux de change and ticket resales. The Code of Practice does not have direct legal effect, but conformity to it (or contraventions of it) may be relied upon evidentially in determining whether an offence has been committed under s. 20 (s. 25(2)). For an example of the effect of the Code of Practice, see *Mirror Group Newspapers v Northants County Council* [1997] Crim LR 882.

In brief, the Consumer Protection Act 1987, s. 20, makes it an offence:

(a) for a person acting in the course of any business of his to give any consumers a misleading indication as to the price at which goods, services, accommodation or facilities are available (see, for example, *D.S.G. Retail Ltd v Oxfordshire County Council* [2001] 1 WLR 1765 and *Suffolk County Council v Hillarys Blinds Ltd* (2002) 166 JP 380); or
(b) for such a person to fail to take all reasonable steps to prevent consumers from relying on an indication which was correct when first given, but which has become incorrect thereafter.

The scope of these offences is in some respects narrower than that of Trade Descriptions Act offences, in that the indication must be given to consumers (defined in s. 20(6) of the 1987 Act) and must be made by someone acting in the course of his own business, thus excluding the acts of mere employees (see *Warwickshire County Council, ex parte Johnson* [1993] AC 583). Senior officers of a corporation may however incur liability for acts committed through their default etc. under s. 40(2).

A number of specific defences are provided by s. 24 of the 1987 Act, and s. 39 provides a more general 'due diligence' defence. Where this defence is applicable, s. 40(1) permits prosecutions to be brought against responsible third parties. In contrast to the position under the Trade Descriptions Act 1968, s. 23 (see **B6.110**), a third party can be prosecuted under s. 40(1) only if he was acting in the course of any business of his at the relevant time. Private individuals cannot be prosecuted under the 1987 Act.

In all other respects, the rules governing procedures, time limits, enforcement, modes of trial and penalties are the same as for 'either way' offences under the Trade Descriptions Act 1968 (see **B6.95** and **B6.97**).

Property Misdescriptions

As previously explained (see **B6.121**), the Trade Descriptions Act 1968 does not appear to cover false or misleading statements concerning residential or commercial property sales or lettings. These may, however, be covered by the Property Misdescriptions Act 1991, s. 1, which applies to false or misleading statements concerning 'prescribed matters' and made in the course of an estate agency business or property development business (otherwise than in the course of providing conveyancing services). The Property Misdescriptions (Prescribed Matters) Order 1992 (SI 1992/2834) provides a list of 'prescribed matters'. The list includes: physical or structural characteristics, location, aspect, view, proximity to facilities, accommodation, measurements, survey reports, guarantees, history, length of time for sale, price, tenure/estate, council tax classification and planning permission status. **B6.124**

Liability is strict, subject to proof of a due diligence defence under s. 2 (see *Enfield London Borough Council v Castles Estate Agents Ltd* (1996) 160 JP 618). Employees of estate agents etc. can be convicted where the misdescription results from their acts or defaults, whether or not proceedings are taken against the employer (s. 1(2)). Offences are triable either way and punishable on summary conviction with a fine not exceeding £5,000 or by an unlimited fine following conviction on indictment. They are not punishable by imprisonment.

In other respects, the rules governing procedures, time limits and enforcement (set out in s. 5 and in the schedule to the Act) are the same as for 'either way' offences under the Trade Descriptions Act 1968 (see **B6.95** and **B6.97**).

Section B7 Company, Investment and Insolvency Offences

OFFENCES UNDER THE COMPANIES ACT 1985: GENERAL

Scope of the Companies Act 1985

B7.1 The Companies Act 1985 contains nearly 200 offence-creating provisions, many of which must be read in conjunction with various other provisions which do not themselves create offences. Some provisions relate to relatively minor, regulatory, defaults or irregularities; others may involve serious acts of fraud. The distinction is not, however, clear-cut, because minor defaults and irregularities will often be associated with more serious crime, e.g., where improperly maintained accounts or records are used to conceal fraudulent trading or unlawful loans to directors. In such cases, an indictment may include counts alleging fraud offences and counts alleging lesser defaults and irregularities, many of which are triable either way.

A general work on criminal law cannot attempt to cover all possible offences under the Companies Act 1985 or to investigate the relationship between the offence-creating provisions and the rest of the Act. Readers requiring fuller coverage must therefore refer to specialist works on company law.

Extensive changes to company law have been made by the Companies Act 2006. On 28 February 2007 the government announced that the main changes made by the 2006 Act would be brought into force in three parts, some on 1 October 2007, others on 6 April 2008 and the remainder on 1 October 2008.

This section concentrates on the principal fraud-related offences under the companies legislation. A complete table of offences, together with provisions relating to mode of trial and penalties under the 1985 Act, is contained in sch. 24 to that Act. Those offences which are punishable with imprisonment or discussed further in this chapter are listed at **B7.2**.The table will be repealed by s. 1295 of and sch. 16 to the 2006 Act. Provisions relating to mode of trial and penalties under the 2006 Act are contained in the sections creating the offences.

Schedule of Offences and Punishments under the Companies Act 1985

Companies Act 1985, sch. 24, Abridged B7.2

Section of Act creating offence	General nature of offence	Mode of prosecution	Punishment
12(3B), 30(5C), 43(3B), 49(8B), 117(7A), 403(2A), 419(5A), 685(6A), 686(3A) and 691(4A).	Person making false statement under section 12(3A), 30(5A), 43(3A), 49(8A), 117(3A), 403(1A) 419(1A) or (1B), 685(4A), 686(2A) or 691(3A) which he knows to be false or does not believe to be true.	1. On indictment. 2. Summary.	Two years or a fine; or both. Six months or the statutory maximum; or both.
95(6)	Knowingly or recklessly authorising or permitting misleading, false or deceptive material in statement by directors under section 95(5).	1. On indictment. 2. Summary.	Two years or a fine; or both. Six months or the statutory maximum; or both.
110(2)	Making misleading, false or deceptive statement in connection with valuation under section 103 or 104.	1. On indictment. 2. Summary.	Two years or a fine; or both. Six months or the statutory maximum; or both.
117(7)	Company doing business or exercising borrowing powers contrary to section 117.	1. On indictment. 2. Summary.	A fine. The statutory maximum.
143(2)	Company acquiring its own shares in breach of section 143.	1. On indictment. 2. Summary.	In the case of the company, a fine. In the case of an officer of the company who is in default, two years or a fine; or both. In the case of the company, the statutory maximum. In the case of an officer of the company who is in default, six months or the statutory maximum; or both.
151(3)	Company giving financial assistance towards acquisition of its own shares.	1. On indictment. 2. Summary	Where the company is convicted, a fine. Where an officer of the company is convicted, two years or a fine; or both. Where the company is convicted, the statutory maximum. Where an officer of the company is convicted, six months or the statutory maximum; or both.
173(6)	Director making statutory declaration under section 155 or 173, without having reasonable grounds for opinion expressed in it.	1. On indictment. 2. Summary.	Two years or a fine; or both. Six months or the statutory maximum; or both.
210(3)	Failure to discharge obligation of disclosure under part VI; other forms of non-compliance with that part.	1. On indictment. 2. Summary.	Two years or a fine; or both. Six months or the statutory maximum; or both.

B

Part B Offences

Section of Act creating offence	General nature of offence	Mode of prosecution	Punishment
216(3)	Failure to comply with company notice under section 212; making false statement in response, etc.	1. On indictment. 2. Summary.	Two years or a fine; or both. Six months or the statutory maximum; or both.
221(5) or 222(4)	Company failing to keep accounting records (liability of officers).	1. On indictment. 2. Summary.	Two years or a fine; or both. Six months or the statutory maximum; or both.
222(6)	Officer of company failing to secure compliance with, or intentionally causing default under section 222(5) (preservation of accounting records for requisite number of years).	1. On indictment. 2. Summary.	Two years or a fine; or both. Six months or the statutory maximum; or both.
234ZA(6)	Making a statement in a directors' report as mentioned in section 234ZA(2) which is false.	1. On indictment 2. Summary	Two years or a fine; or both. 12 months or the statutory maximum; or both.
245E(3) & 245G(7)	Using or disclosing tax information in contravention of section 245E(1) or (2) or disclosing information in contravention of 245G(2) or (3).	1. On indictment 2. Summary	Two years or a fine; or both. 12 months or the statutory maximum.
323(2)	Director dealing in options to buy or sell company's listed shares or debentures.	1. On indictment. 2. Summary.	Two years or a fine; or both. Six months or the statutory maximum; or both.
324(7)	Director failing to notify interest in company's shares; making false statement in purported notification.	1. On indictment. 2. Summary.	Two years or a fine; or both. Six months or the statutory maximum; or both.
326(2), (3), (4), (5)	Various defaults in connection with company register of directors' interests.	Summary.	One-fifth of the statutory maximum. [Daily default fine: Except in the case of s. 326(5), one-fiftieth of the statutory maximum.]
328(6)	Director failing to notify company that members of his family have, or have exercised, options to buy shares or debentures; making false statement in purported notification.	1. On indictment. 2. Summary.	Two years or a fine; or both. Six months or the statutory maximum; or both.
329(3)	Company failing to notify investment exchange of acquisition of its securities by a director.	Summary.	One-fifth of the statutory maximum. [Daily default fine: one-fiftieth of the statutory maximum.]
342(1)	Director of relevant company authorising or permitting company to enter into transaction or arrangement, knowing or suspecting it to contravene section 330.	1. On indictment. 2. Summary.	Two years or a fine; or both. Six months or the statutory maximum; or both.
342(2)	Relevant company entering into transaction or arrangement for a director in contravention of section 330.	1. On indictment. 2. Summary.	Two years or a fine; or both. Six months or the statutory maximum; or both.

Section of Act creating offence	General nature of offence	Mode of prosecution	Punishment
342(3)	Procuring a relevant company to enter into transaction or arrangement known to be contrary to section 330.	1. On indictment. 2. Summary.	Two years or a fine; or both. Six months or the statutory maximum; or both.
389B(1)	Person making false, misleading or deceptive statement to auditor.	1. On indictment. 2. Summary.	Two years or a fine; or both. Six months or the statutory maximum; or both.
429(6)	Offeror failing to send copy of notice or making statutory declaration knowing it to be false, etc.	1. On indictment. 2. Summary.	Two years or a fine; or both. Six months or the statutory maximum; or both. [Daily default fine: one-fiftieth of the statutory maximum.]
444(3)	Failing to give Secretary of State, when required to do so, information about interests in shares, etc.; giving false information.	1. On indictment. 2. Summary.	Two years or a fine; or both. Six months or the statutory maximum; or both.
449(6)	Wrongful disclosure of information to which section 449 applies.	1. On indictment. 2. Summary.	Two years or a fine; or both. Six months or the statutory maximum; or both.
450	Destroying or mutilating company documents; falsifying such documents or making false entries; parting with such documents or altering them or making omissions.	1. On indictment. 2. Summary.	Seven years or a fine; or both. Six months or the statutory maximum; or both.
451	Providing false information in purported compliance with section 447.	1. On indictment. 2. Summary.	Seven years or a fine; or both. Six months or the statutory maximum; or both.
458	Being a party to carrying on company's business with intent to defraud creditors, or for any fraudulent purpose.	1. On indictment. 2. Summary.	Ten years or a fine; or both. Six months or the statutory maximum; or both.
652E(2)	Person failing to perform duty imposed by section 652B(6) or 652C(2) with intent to conceal the making of application under section 652A.	1.On indictment 2 Summary	Seven years or a fine or both Six months or the statutory maximum or both.

Scope of Offences under the Companies Act 1985

The Companies Act 1985 is primarily concerned with registered companies as defined in s. 735 (i.e. those registered under this and former Companies Acts), but some of the provisions have a wider ambit. Unregistered companies are relatively uncommon; the provisions in sch. 22 to the Act are applied to some such companies by s. 718. More importantly, many provisions of part XIV (ss. 431–457: company investigations) apply also to companies incorporated outside Great Britain which are or have been carrying on business in Great Britain (s. 453). **B7.3**

Procedural Provisions in Respect of Summary Proceedings

Companies Act 1985, s. 731 **B7.4**

(1) Summary proceedings for any offence under the Companies Acts may (without prejudice to any jurisdiction exercisable apart from this subsection) be taken against a body corporate at

any place at which the body has a place of business, and against any other person at any place at which he is for the time being.

(2) Notwithstanding anything in section 127(1) of the Magistrates' Courts Act 1980, an information relating to an offence under the Companies Acts which is triable by a magistrates' court in England and Wales may be so tried if it is laid at any time within three years after the commission of the offence and within 12 months after the date on which evidence sufficient in the opinion of the Director of Public Prosecutions or the Secretary of State (as the case may be) to justify the proceedings comes to his knowledge.

(3) [Applies only to Scotland.]

(4) For purposes of this section, a certificate of the Director of Public Prosecutions . . . or the Secretary of State (as the case may be) as to the date on which such evidence as is referred to above came to his knowledge is conclusive evidence.

Section 731(2) has no effect in relation to the summary trial of offences triable either way (*Thames Metropolitan Stipendiary Magistrate, ex parte Horgan* [1998] QB 719). These provisions are repealed and repeated, with minor changes of layout, in ss. 1127(1) and 1128(1) and (4) of the Companies Act 2006.

PROHIBITED TRANSACTIONS INVOLVING LOANS ETC. TO DIRECTORS AND CONNECTED PERSONS

B7.5 A loan or other credit transaction between a company and one or more of its directors may be entered into on terms or in circumstances which are not in the company's best interests; in extreme cases the transaction will merely be a cover for the fraudulent abstraction of company money or the means of funding an illegal share support operation. The Companies Act 1985, s. 330, accordingly prohibits various kinds of loans and credit transactions, subject to exceptions contained in ss. 332 to 338, and provides (in s. 341) civil remedies for breach (avoidance of the transaction, account of profits and indemnity against loss). From 1 October 2008, these provisions will be repealed and replaced by ss. 197 to 214 of the Companies Act 2006.

The 1985 Act distinguishes between 'relevant companies' and other companies. The term 'relevant company' is defined in s. 331(6) so as to comprise public companies and companies which are in the same group as a public company, e.g., subsidiaries of a public company. The wider prohibitions in s. 330(3) and (4) apply only to relevant companies. In addition, it is only contraventions of s. 330 by relevant companies or their directors that may lead to criminal penalties under s. 342. There are no criminal penalties for breach of the equivalent provisions under the 2006 Act.

A company is a public company if its memorandum of association states that it is to be a public company and the requirements as to registration have been complied with (s. 1(3)). Its name must end with the words 'public limited company' (or the abbreviation 'p.l.c.') or, if its registered office is in Wales, their Welsh equivalents (ss. 25(1) and 27). A certificate of incorporation given by the Registrar of Companies stating that the company is a public company is conclusive evidence that it is a public company and that the requirements of the Act as to registration have been complied with (s. 13(7)).

Companies Act 1985, ss. 330 and 342

General restriction on loans etc. to directors and persons connected with them

330.—(1) The prohibitions listed below in this section are subject to the exceptions in sections 332 to 338.

(2) A company shall not—

(a) make a loan to a director of the company or of its holding company;

(b) enter into any guarantee or provide any security in connection with a loan made by any person to such a director.

(3) A relevant company shall not—
   (a) make a quasi-loan to a director of the company or of its holding company;
   (b) make a loan or a quasi-loan to a person connected with such a director;
   (c) enter into a guarantee or provide any security in connection with a loan or quasi-loan made by any other person for such a director or a person so connected.

(4) A relevant company shall not—
   (a) enter into a credit transaction as creditor for such a director or a person so connected;
   (b) enter into any guarantee or provide any security in connection with a credit transaction made by any other person for such a director or a person so connected.

(5) For purposes of sections 330 to 346, a shadow director is treated as a director.

(6) A company shall not arrange for the assignment to it, or the assumption by it, of any rights, obligations or liabilities under a transaction which, if it had been entered into by the company, would have contravened subsection (2), (3) or (4); but for the purposes of sections 330 to 347 the transaction is to be treated as having been entered into on the date of the arrangement.

(7) A company shall not take part in any arrangement whereby—
   (a) another person enters into a transaction which, if it had been entered into by the company, would have contravened any of subsections (2), (3), (4) or (6); and
   (b) that other person, in pursuance of the arrangement, has obtained or is to obtain any benefit from the company or its holding company or a subsidiary of the company or its holding company.

Criminal penalties for breach of s. 330

342.—(1) A director of a relevant company who authorises or permits the company to enter into a transaction or arrangement knowing or having reasonable cause to believe that the company was thereby contravening section 330 is guilty of an offence.

(2) A relevant company which enters into a transaction or arrangement for one of its directors or for a director of its holding company in contravention of section 330 is guilty of an offence.

(3) A person who procures a relevant company to enter into a transaction or arrangement knowing or having reasonable cause to believe that the company was thereby contravening section 330 is guilty of an offence.

(4) A person guilty of an offence under this section is liable to imprisonment or a fine, or both.

(5) A relevant company is not guilty of an offence under subsection (2) if it shows that, at the time the transaction or arrangement was entered into, it did not know the relevant circumstances.

For procedural and sentencing provisions, see **B7.2** and **B7.4**.

Definitions and Significant Terms

Shadow director in s. 330(5) means a person in accordance with whose directions or instructions the directors of a company are accustomed to act (s. 741(2)). A company is a subsidiary of a holding company if the holding company (i) owns a majority of the shares in the subsidiary; or (ii) is a member of the subsidiary and has the right to appoint or remove a majority of the board of directors; or (iii) is a member of the subsidiary and pursuant to an agreement with the other shareholders controls alone a majority of the voting rights (s. 736, supplemented by s. 736A). Section 330 is further supplemented by definitions in ss. 331 and 346. The definitions are widely drawn so as to render avoidance difficult. **B7.6**

(a) Payment by a company to a third party for the benefit of a director is not a loan (*Champagne Perrier-Jouet SA v HH Finch Ltd* [1982] 1 WLR 1359). Section 330(3) extends the general restriction to quasi-loans to catch transactions under which a relevant company pays money to a third party for the benefit of the director rather than to the director himself. 'Quasi-loan' is defined in s. 331(3), (4) and (9).

(b) Section 346 defines 'connected persons' so as to include certain relatives of, trustees for, and partners of a director (s. 346(2)). The word 'partner' in s. 346(2)(d) refers to a person with whom the director carries on a business with a view to profit (see the Partnership Act 1890, ss. 1 and 2), rather than the modern use of the word 'partner' to describe a person with whom the director lives; domestic relationships are the subject of s. 346(2)(a) and in s. 346(2)(e), which relates to Scottish firms, the word 'partner' is clearly used in the business sense. Because of the words in brackets at the beginning of s. 346(2) '(not himself being a director)', a director cannot be connected with himself as a trustee within s. 346(2)(c) (*Clydebank Football Club Ltd v Steedman* [2002] SLT 109).

(c) The definition of 'connected persons' also includes companies in which the director and persons connected with him have an interest in at least one-fifth of the equity share capital or are entitled to exercise or control at least one-fifth of the voting power in general meeting (s. 326(2)(b) and (4)–(8)).

(d) The distinction between a guarantee and an indemnity is important in civil law, because a guarantee has to be in writing or evidenced by writing in order to be enforceable, whereas an indemnity does not. The distinction is often difficult to draw, so s. 331(2) provides an extended definition of 'guarantee' for the purposes of s. 330 so as to include an indemnity.

(e) By s. 337 a credit transaction is defined as a transaction under which one party ('the creditor') supplies any goods or sells any land under a hire-purchase agreement or a conditional sale agreement; leases or hires any land or goods in return for periodical payments; otherwise disposes of land or supplies goods or services on the understanding that payment (whether in a lump sum or instalments or by way of periodical payments or otherwise) is to be deferred. The terms 'hire-purchase agreement' and 'conditional sale agreement' in s. 331(7)(a) have the same meanings as in the Consumer Credit Act 1974 (ss. 774 and 331(10)).

Permitted Transactions

B7.7 The following transactions are not prohibited by the Companies Act 1985, ss. 330(1) and 332 and 338:

(a) Short-term quasi-loans which have to be reimbursed within two months may be permitted up to a total value of £5,000 (s. 332). This permits, *inter alia*, use of company credit cards etc. (but only by directors personally, not by connected persons).

(b) Intercompany loans, quasi-loans within the same group and guarantees of loans or quasi-loans may be permitted under s. 333, if they would otherwise be prohibited *only* by the fact that a director of one company is associated with another. See also s. 336, below.

(c) Small loans totalling no more than £5,000, which would otherwise come within s. 330(2)(a), are permitted (s. 334).

(d) Credit transactions (otherwise caught by s. 330(4)) may be permitted under s. 335 if they do not total more than £10,000 or if made in the ordinary course of the company's business and on ordinary credit terms, as might reasonably be given to unconnected persons.

(e) Loans or quasi-loans by a company to its holding company or guarantees of loans or quasi-loans to its holding company are permitted by s. 336(1). A company can also enter into a credit transaction (s. 331(7)) with its holding company or can guarantee a credit transaction with its holding company (s. 336(2)).

(f) Loans etc. made to fund a director's expenditure on behalf of the company, or to enable him to perform his duties, may be permitted under s. 337, up to a limit of £20,000, subject to a requirement that they are either approved in advance by a general meeting of the company (after full disclosure), or made conditional on approval at or before the next annual general meeting. Failing such approval, they must be repaid within six months of that meeting.

(g) Under s. 338, loans, quasi-loans and guarantees totalling up to £100,000 may be made to any director or connected person by a money-lending company on normal terms and in the ordinary course of its business; and for these purposes loans etc. to a company 'associated' with a director are not counted towards that aggregate, unless he 'controls' that company within the meaning of s. 346(5). If the money-lending company is a banking company, there is no restriction on the amounts involved; if the loan is made for the purpose of facilitating the purchase or improvement of a director's main residence, a director of a money-lending company may be given the same favourable terms as company employees, up to a limit of £100,000.

Complicated provisions for calculating the totals of relevant amounts and the value of transactions are contained in ss. 339 and 340. Section 232 provides for the disclosure in the company's annual accounts of loans, quasi-loans and other dealings in favour of directors and connected persons.

FINANCIAL ASSISTANCE PROVIDED BY COMPANIES IN CONNECTION WITH THE ACQUISITION OF THEIR OWN SHARES

The provision by a company of financial assistance in connection with the acquisition of its **B7.8**
own shares may in some circumstances be unobjectionable, but in other instances company funds may be improperly depleted by loans for the purchase of its own shares and the loans never repaid. Following particularly scandalous instances of asset-stripping of companies with cash or other liquid assets (described in *Re VGM Holdings Ltd* [1942] Ch 235 at p. 239), widely drawn legislation was enacted in 1929; but this rendered criminal many harmless transactions, while providing wholly inadequate penalties for serious fraud. Accordingly, the legislation was recast in a more complex form in 1981 and is now to be found in ss. 151 to 158 of the Companies Act 1985. The mischief to which it is directed is that the resources of the company and its subsidiaries should not be used directly or indirectly to assist the purchaser financially to make the acquisition, because this may prejudice the interests of creditors of the company or group and the interests of shareholders other than those whose shares are bought (*Chaston v SWP Group plc* [2002] EWCA Civ 1999 at [31]).

Section 151 contains a general prohibition, s. 152 contains definitions and ss. 153 and 154 identify transactions not prohibited by s. 151. Sections 155 to 158, which contain a procedure which may be followed by private companies, are outside the scope of this book. Sections 151 to 158 are replaced by ss. 677 to 683 of the Companies Act 2006. The new provisions, which the government intends to bring into force on 1 October 2008, will apply only to public companies.

Companies Act 1985, s. 151

(1) Subject to the following provisions of this chapter [i.e. ss. 151 to 158] where a person is acquiring or is proposing to acquire shares in a company, it is not lawful for the company or any of its subsidiaries to give financial assistance directly or indirectly for the purpose of that acquisition before or at the same time as the acquisition takes place.

(2) Subject to those provisions, where a person has acquired shares in a company and any liability has been incurred (by that or any other person), for the purpose of that acquisition, it is not lawful for the company or any of its subsidiaries to give financial assistance directly or indirectly for the purpose of reducing or discharging the liability so incurred.

(3) If a company acts in contravention of this section, it is liable to a fine, and every officer of it who is in default is liable to imprisonment or a fine, or both.

For procedural and sentencing provisions, see **B7.2** and **B7.4**. Although the only penalty expressly provided for breach of s. 151 (and its predecessors) is criminal, the civil courts held, after initial hesitation, that breaches of the prohibition also give rise to civil remedies. There is now a substantial body of case law in civil litigation on the interpretation of ss. 151 to 153.

Financial assistance is defined in s. 152(1) as meaning assistance given by way of gift, guarantee, security, release, waiver loan or indemnity (other than indemnity in respect of the indemnifier's own neglect or default); or by way of certain transactions analogous to loans; or by way of the assignment of rights under loans or analogous transactions; or in any other way which materially reduces the net assets of the company; or financial assistance given by a company without net assets. Assistance given to the acquirer for the purpose of discharging his liabilities includes assistance given for the purpose of restoring him to his previous financial position (s. 152(3)).

The words 'acquire' and 'acquiring' are apt to cover both a subscription for shares newly issued by the company and a purchase of shares already issued from an existing shareholder. The word 'purchase' in the original 1929 Act was replaced by 'acquire' in the Companies Act 1948, thereby reversing the decision in *Re VGM Holdings Ltd* [1942] Ch 235.

Transactions for the acquisition of shares can be complex, but the legislation requires an examination of the substance and reality of the transaction. The words 'directly or indirectly' make it necessary to see what has happened to the company's money and who has acquired the shares and then determine whether the company's money has been used to finance the acquisition (*Wallersteiner v Moir* [1974] 1 WLR 991 at p. 1014D). The term 'financial assistance' has no technical meaning and has to be construed in a commercial context, involving an inquiry into the commercial realities of the transaction (*Chaston v SWP Group plc* [2002] EWCA Civ 1999 at [32]). In that case payment of accountants' fees by a subsidiary company for the purpose of preparing a report to facilitate the accused's acquisition of shares in the payer's holding company was held to constitute financial assistance. But financial assistance involves something by way of aid or help; in *M T Realisations Ltd v Digital Equipment Co Ltd* [2003] EWCA Civ 494, a rescheduling of instalments of the purchase price, which included the re-routing of payments due to the company to the vendor rather than to the purchaser (to which the company was by now indebted), did not amount to financial assistance, because the company did not give the purchaser anything that the purchaser did not already have as a secured creditor of the company.

It is the company's purpose that determines whether there has been a breach of s. 151 (i.e. the purpose of the person(s) acting on the company's behalf), not the purpose of the transferor(s) of shares (*Dyment v Boyden* [2004] EWCA Civ 1586 at [29] to [35]).

The question whether the company's net assets have been reduced 'to a material extent' is one of degree depending on the facts of the case (*Partlett v Guppys (Bridport) Ltd* [1996] BCC 299 at p. 308). The Institute of Chartered Accountants in England and Wales has issued recommendations in 'The Interpretation of Materiality in Financial Reporting' (revised November 1996) and the Auditing Practices Board has issued an International Standard on Auditing (UK and Ireland) No. 320 'Audit Materiality' (December 2004).

Permitted Transactions

B7.9 Certain transactions that would otherwise be prohibited by s. 151 are permitted under s. 153. These include (i) assistance which is unintended or incidental to some larger purpose and given in good faith in the interests of the company (s. 153(1) and (2)); (ii) lawful dividend or bonus share issues (s. 153(3)); (iii) money loaned in the course of a money lending company's ordinary business (s. 153(4)(a)); and (iv) assistance provided as part of a bona fide share-owning scheme or arrangement for employees, former employees or their families (s. 153(4)(b) and (c)). Public companies may take advantage of s. 153(4) only if they have net assets which are not thereby reduced or if the assistance is provided out of distributable profits (s. 154(1)).

The 'larger purpose' provision in s. 153(1)(a) and (2)(a) was given a narrow construction in *Brady v Brady* [1989] AC 755. Family disagreements had resulted in management deadlock, bringing a flourishing business to the brink of liquidation, which was avoided only by a complex restructuring to split the business between the rival factions. Part of the transaction by which this was achieved involved financial assistance by a company to reduce a liability incurred in the acquisition of shares in that company (p. 777D). The House of Lords held that it was necessary to distinguish between a purpose and the reason why the purpose was formed, otherwise s. 151 would be easily avoided, that a 'larger purpose' could not be found in the benefits likely to flow from the transaction and that a desire to end management deadlock did not constitute a 'larger purpose' within s. 153 (p. 778F–780H).

The phrase 'in good faith in the interests of the company' is a composite expression which postulates that those responsible for procuring the company to provide the assistance act in the genuine belief that it is being done in the company's interest (*Brady v Brady* [1989] AC 755 at p. 777G–778F).

Where an agreement can be performed in a lawful or an unlawful manner, it is to be construed as requiring the parties to perform the agreement in a lawful manner (*Partlett v Guppys (Bridport) Ltd* [1996] BCC 299; *Brady v Brady* [1989] AC 755 at p. 783C–H).

The prohibition in s. 151 is directed to the assisting company and does not extend to companies registered outside Great Britain. It therefore does not prohibit a subsidiary registered abroad from giving financial assistance for the acquisition of shares in its English holding company (*Arab Bank plc v Mercantile Holdings Ltd* [1994] Ch 71).

B Part B Offences

DESTRUCTION, MUTILATION OR FALSIFICATION OF COMPANY DOCUMENTS

Companies Act 1985, s. 450 B7.10

(1) An officer of a company, who—
   (a) destroys, mutilates or falsifies, or is privy to the destruction, mutilation or falsification of a document affecting or relating to the company's property or affairs, or
   (b) makes, or is privy to the making of, a false entry in such a document, is guilty of an offence, unless he proves that he had no intention to conceal the state of affairs of the company or to defeat the law.

(1A) Subsection (1) applies to an officer of an authorised insurance company which is not a body corporate as it applies to an officer of a company.

(2) Such a person as above mentioned who fraudulently either parts with, alters or makes an omission in any such document or is privy to fraudulent parting with, fraudulent altering or fraudulent making of an omission in, any such document, is guilty of an offence.

(3) A person guilty of an offence under this section is liable to imprisonment or a fine, or both.

(4) Sections 732 (restriction on prosecutions), 733 (liability of individuals for corporate default) and 734 (criminal proceedings against unincorporated bodies) apply to an offence under this section.

(5) In this section 'document' includes information recorded in any form.

For procedural and sentencing provisions, see **B7.2** and **B7.4**. Section 1124 of and sch. 3, para. 4 to the 2006 Act replace sub-s. (3) with provisions equivalent to the provisions relating to this offence in sch. 24 to the 1985 Act (schedule of offences and punishments); s. 450(4) is repealed by s. 1295 of and sch. 16 to the 2006 Act, but equivalent provisions to ss. 732 to 734 of the 1985 Act are applied to s. 450 by ss. 1121 to 1123 and 1126(1) of the Act.

This is one of the most serious offences under the Companies Act 1985, punishable by up to seven years' imprisonment in addition to any fine. Such conduct (which might take the form of deleting computer files as well as interference with physical documents) may be designed to remove evidence of serious fraud. It may be designed to frustrate or hinder an investigation into the company's affairs under part XIV (ss. 431 to 453) of the Act; but the offence may be committed whether or not any such investigation is in prospect.

The wording of the offence is similar to Insolvency Act 1986, s. 206(1)(c) and (d) and (4)(b). It follows from *A-G's Ref (No. 1 of 2004)* [2004] 1 WLR 2111 (at [80] to [84]) and *Sheldrake v DPP* [2005] 1 AC 264 (at [32]) that the imposition of the full persuasive burden on the defendant is compatible with the ECHR, Article 6.

FRAUDULENT TRADING

B7.11 **Companies Act 1985, s. 458**

> If any business of a company is carried on with intent to defraud creditors of the company or creditors of any other person, or for any fraudulent purpose, every person who was knowingly a party to the carrying on of the business in that manner is liable to imprisonment or a fine, or both.
>
> This applies whether or not the company has been, or is in the course of being, wound up.

This section is repealed by s 1295 of, and sch 16 to, the Companies Act 2006 and replaced by s 993 of the 2006 Act. Section 993(1) and (2) is to the same effect as s. 458, but with minor drafting alterations. The government intends to bring the change into effect on 1 October 2007.

Companies Act 2006, s. 993

> (1) If any business of a company is carried on with intent to defraud creditors of the company or creditors of any other person, or for any fraudulent purpose, every person who is knowingly a party to the carrying on of the business in that manner commits an offence.
> (2) This applies whether or not the company has been, or is in the course of being, wound up.
> (3) A person guilty of an offence under this section is liable—
> (a) on conviction on indictment, to imprisonment for a term not exceeding ten years or a fine (or both);
> (b) on summary conviction—
> (i) in England and Wales, to imprisonment for a term not exceeding twelve months or a fine not exceeding the statutory maximum (or both);
> (ii) [applies to Scotland and Northern Ireland].

For procedural and sentencing provisions under the 1985 Act, see **B7.2** and **B7.4**. For disqualification orders, see **E23.8**. The Court of Appeal provided guidance on sentencing in cases of fraudulent trading in *Smith* [1997] 2 Cr App R (S) 167, where the offenders had admitted using misleading accounts and false invoices to maintain the credit of a marketing company which had eventually failed, with losses of £520,000. Neither offender had previous convictions, the offence had taken place six years ago, and the offenders and their families had suffered considerably as a result of the offence. Sentences of three years' imprisonment were reduced to 18 months. Disqualifications for five years under the Company Directors Disqualification Act 1986 were upheld. In the Court of Appeal, Potter LJ observed that this case lay towards the lower end of a wide spectrum of offences covered by the offence of fraudulent trading. At one extreme there may have been deliberate reckless trading on a large scale aimed at a rapid return, with no genuine intention to discharge the company's debts but simply to milk creditors and line the directors' pockets. At the other end of the scale there may have been a properly funded business which has run into financial problems, where the directors have attempted to trade in order to save their own and their employees' jobs, but come to a point where they should have faced up to reality and ceased to trade. His lordship observed that the amount of loss involved and the level of criminality of the offender were important considerations in sentencing but that, broadly speaking, a charge of fraudulent trading resulting in loss to creditors is somewhat less seriously regarded than a charge of theft or fraud of the same amount. Credit should be given for personal mitigation, including a timely guilty plea and the tendering of full assistance to the receiver. See also *Thobani* [1998] 1 Cr App R (S) 227, *Ward* [2001] 2 Cr App R (S) 146 and *Furr* [2007] EWCA Crim 191.

Fraudulent trading by companies has featured for a long time both in criminal law and civil law. The Insolvency Act 1986, s. 213, provides that persons who were knowingly parties to such conduct may be required to contribute to the assets of the company concerned in the course of its winding-up; but, unlike the criminal provision in the Companies Act 1985, s. 458, the civil provision has no application unless the company goes into liquidation. The Fraud Act 2006, s. 9, now makes fraudulent trading by sole traders and other non-corporate entities a criminal offence (see **B5.105**).

Indictment

Statement of Offence **B7.12**

Fraudulent trading contrary to section 458 [993] of the Companies Act 1985 [2006]

Particulars of Offence

A between the . . . day of . . . and the . . . day of . . . was knowingly a party to the carrying on of certain business of a company called . . . with intent to defraud creditors of the said company [or with intent to defraud creditors of . . .] [or for a fraudulent purpose, namely . . .]

Carrying on the Business of the Company

The company in question may be registered or (by virtue of the Companies Act 1985, sch. 22: see **B7.3**) unregistered. The meaning of the words 'any business of the company has been carried on with intent to defraud creditors' has been considered in cases under the Insolvency Act 1986, s. 213. In *Morphitis v Bernasconi* [2003] Ch 552 (at [42] to [49]) the Court of Appeal considered that s. 458 is aimed at the carrying on of a business and not the execution of individual transactions in the course of carrying on that business. Thus not every fraud perpetrated on a customer amounts to fraudulent trading. But circumstances can arise, as in *Re Gerald Cooper Chemicals Ltd* [1978] Ch 262, in which a single transaction in which only one creditor is defrauded will suffice (see also *Lockwood* [1986] Crim LR 244). In *Philippou* (1989) 89 Cr App R 290, it was held that the fraudulent obtaining of an air travel organiser's licence from the Civil Aviation Authority involved carrying on a business for a fraudulent purpose, as the licence was essential to that business. **B7.13**

Intent to Defraud and Knowledge

Although the concept of intent to defraud was defined in *Welham v DPP* [1961] AC 103 in a way which appeared to include no specific requirement of dishonesty, it is now clear that dishonesty is an essential element both in fraudulent trading and in other fraud offences involving similar terminology. See *Cox* (1982) 75 Cr App R 291. The extent to which a jury need be directed on the meaning of dishonesty varies from case to case. A full *Ghosh* direction (see **B4.37**) would not be appropriate in a case where the accused denies any knowledge of the allegedly fraudulent activities, whereas such a direction might be essential where he admits the facts and claims that he regarded them as normal business practice. See *Miles* [1992] Crim LR 657 and **B4.37**; and see also *Goldman* [1997] Crim LR 894. **B7.14**

Welham v DPP remains significant insofar as it establishes that there need not be any intent to cause financial loss to another person. Deliberately and dishonestly putting another person's property or financial interests in jeopardy may suffice (*Allsop* (1977) 64 Cr App R 29; *Wai Yu-Tsang v The Queen* [1992] 1 AC 269), whether or not there is any deception (*Scott v Metropolitan Police Commissioner* [1975] AC 819), and it may be fraud to deceive public officers into failing to perform their duty (*Welham v DPP*; cf. *Philippou* (1989) 89 Cr App R 290 at **B7.13**).

In *Bank of India v Morris* [2005] BCC 739 at [14] the Court of Appeal held (albeit on a concession) that knowledge includes 'blind-eye' knowledge, namely a firmly grounded suspicion of specific facts and a deliberate decision to avoid confirming that they exist.

Frauds on Creditors and Other Fraudulent Purposes

B7.15 A typical example of fraudulent trading involves a company which has lapsed into insolvency, but which continues to obtain credit in circumstances where its directors know that there can be little if any chance of the creditors being paid. It would probably not be considered dishonest for debts to be incurred in the expectation that they could be repaid shortly after they fall due, because many debts are paid at least a few days or weeks late; but a jury may well consider it dishonest for debts to be incurred when they could at best be repaid months late (*Grantham* [1984] QB 675).

The argument that the words 'any fraudulent purpose' should be construed *eiusdem generis* with defrauding creditors, and that defrauding customers etc. should not be regarded as falling within the scope of this provision, was rejected in *Kemp* [1988] QB 645 where the Court of Appeal held that the mischief aimed at is fraudulent trading generally, and not just insofar as it affects creditors. In *Philippou* (1989) 89 Cr App R 290, the fraudulent obtaining of an air travel organiser's licence was held to have involved fraudulent trading. This latter case perhaps stretches the meaning of 'purpose', because the licence was obtained as a means to an end, rather than as an end in itself; but it signals a clear rejection of any attempt to restrict the offence to frauds on creditors or potential creditors. As to the meaning of 'creditors' under s. 458, see *Smith* [1996] 2 Cr App R 1.

It is not necessarily fraudulent trading for a holding company to issue letters of comfort in respect of a subsidiary which it later allows to go into insolvent liquidation, though it would largely depend on whether the holding company was sincere at the time the letters were issued (*Re Augustus Barnett & Son Ltd* [1986] BCLC 170). Preference of one creditor over another may be open to attack in the civil courts under the Insolvency Act 1986, but is unlikely to be deemed fraudulent trading (*Re Sarflax Ltd* [1979] Ch 592).

Persons who May be Liable for Fraudulent Trading

B7.16 The Court of Appeal held in *Miles* [1992] Crim LR 657 that the offence of fraudulent trading can be committed only by persons who exercise some kind of controlling or managerial function within the company. But employees who exercise no such function (including junior managers and managers of local branches) might, despite this narrow interpretation of the Companies Act 1985, s. 458, incur liability as secondary parties to offences committed by the company's directors or senior managers. And persons holding no formal position within the company, such as shadow directors, could meanwhile incur liability for fraudulent trading if they exercise de facto managerial powers.

In *Maidstone Buildings Provisions Ltd* [1971] 1 WLR 1085, it was said that some positive action on the part of a company secretary, rather than inertia, was required to make him liable under s. 458. Passivity on the part of an executive director might be different, but *mens rea* would be needed in any event.

OFFENCES UNDER THE FINANCIAL SERVICES AND MARKETS ACT 2000

Introduction

B7.17 The Financial Services and Markets Act 2000 makes provision for the regulation of financial services and markets. Section 19 contains a 'general prohibition' against carrying on a regulated activity in the UK, unless authorised or exempt. Regulated activities are specified in the Financial Services and Markets Act (Regulated Activities) Order 2001 (SI 2001 No. 544).

The regulator, the Financial Services Authority, has the functions of making rules, preparing and issuing codes, giving general guidance and determining general policy and principles

(s. 2(4)). In discharging those functions it must, so far as is reasonably possible, act in a way which is compatible with four regulatory objectives, (i) market confidence, (ii) public awareness, (iii) the protection of consumers and (iv) the reduction of financial crime (s. 2(1) and (2)). The objective of reducing financial crime is reducing the extent to which it is possible for a business carried on by a regulated person or carried on in contravention of the general prohibition to be used for a purpose connected with financial crime (s. 6(1)). Financial crime includes any offence involving fraud or dishonesty, misconduct in, or misuse of information relating to, a financial market, or handling the proceeds of crime (s. 6(3)).

The Financial Services and Markets Act 2000 itself creates a relatively small number of criminal offences. Breaches of the Financial Services and Markets Act and rules are mainly enforced by remedies in civil courts or disciplinary procedures. Where the Act creates offences, proceedings can be instituted only by the Financial Services Authority or the Secretary of State or the DPP or with the consent of the DPP (s. 401). Summary proceedings may be taken against a company or unincorporated association at any place where it has a place of business (s. 403(5)). Where an offence committed by a body corporate is proved to have been committed with the consent or connivance of a director or other officer, or is attributable to his neglect, he may also be prosecuted for that offence (s. 400(1)).

Contravention of the General Prohibition

By the Financial Services and Markets Act 2000, s. 23(1), contravention of the general prohibition is punishable, on indictment, with a maximum penalty of two years' imprisonment or a fine, or both; on summary conviction, the maximum penalty is six months' imprisonment or a fine of the statutory maximum, or both. By s. 23 (3), it is a defence for the accused to show that he took all reasonable precautions and exercised all due diligence to avoid committing the offence. **B7.18**

False Claims to be Authorised or Exempt

Section 24 of the Financial Services and Markets Act 2000 creates a summary offence of making false claims to be authorised or exempt, punishable by a maximum of six months' imprisonment or a fine not exceeding level 5 on the standard scale, or both. Where the offence involves or includes the public display of any material, the maximum fine is multiplied by the number of days of any public display. Again it is a defence for the accused to show that he took all reasonable precautions and exercised all due diligence to avoid committing the offence. **B7.19**

Breach of Restrictions on Financial Promotion

Section 25 of the Financial Services and Markets Act 2000 and the Financial Services and Markets Act 2000 (Financial Promotion) Order 2005 (SI 2005 No. 1529) impose restrictions on financial promotion (communication of an invitation or inducement to engage in investment activity) in the course of business. By s. 25, breach of the restrictions on financial promotion is an offence. It is punishable on indictment with a maximum penalty of two years' imprisonment or a fine, or both; on summary conviction, the maximum penalty is six months' imprisonment or a fine of the statutory maximum, or both (s. 25(1)). It is a defence for the accused to show that he believed on reasonable grounds that the content of the communication was prepared, or approved for the purposes of s. 21, by an authorised person or that he took all reasonable precautions and exercised all due diligence to avoid committing the offence (s. 25(2)). **B7.20**

Information Gathering and Investigations

Part XI of the Act (ss. 165 to 177) gives the Financial Services Authority power to require authorised persons to provide information or produce documents and gives the Authority or **B7.21** the Secretary of State power to appoint investigators. Section 177 creates offences in relation to information gathering and investigations.

Financial Services and Markets Act 2000, s. 177

(3) A person who knows or suspects that an investigation is being or is likely to be conducted under this part is guilty of an offence if—
  (a) he falsifies, conceals, destroys or otherwise disposes of a document which he knows or suspects is or would be relevant to such an investigation, or
  (b) he causes or permits the falsification concealment destruction or disposal of such a document, unless he shows that he had no intention of concealing the facts disclosed by the documents from the investigator.

(4) A person who, in purported compliance with a requirement imposed on him under [part XI of the Financial Services and Markets Act 2000]—
  (a) provides information which he knows to be false or misleading in a material particular, or
  (b) recklessly provides information which is false or misleading in a material particular,

is guilty of an offence.

An offence under s. 177(3) or (4) is punishable on indictment with a maximum penalty of two years' imprisonment or a fine, or both; on summary conviction, the maximum penalty is six months' imprisonment or a fine of the statutory maximum, or both.

A person who, without reasonable excuse, fails to comply with a requirement under part XI can be dealt with by the High Court as if in contempt (s. 177(1) and (2)). By s. 177(6), intentional obstruction of the exercise of any rights conferred by an entry and search warrant issued by a justice of the peace under s. 176 is a summary offence punishable with a maximum of three months' imprisonment or a fine not exceeding level 5 on the standard scale, or both.

Changes of Control over Authorised Persons

B7.22 Steps which would result in a change of control of an authorised person (usually a company) must be notified to the Financial Services Authority, and a person who fails to comply with the duty to notify the Authority commits a summary offence (Financial Services and Markets Act 2000, s. 191(1) and (2)). If the Financial Services Authority is not satisfied that approval requirements are met, it can issue a notice of objection after first giving a warning notice. It is also a criminal offence to carry out the proposal within three months unless the Financial Services Authority has given approval or served a warning notice (s. 191(3)) or to carry out the proposal once a warning notice has been given (s. 191(4)). Each of these offences is triable summarily and carries a maximum penalty of a fine not exceeding level 5 on the standard scale (s. 191(6)). If a person acquires control after a notice of objection has been given, he commits a more serious offence, triable on indictment and punishable with a maximum of two years' imprisonment or a fine, or both; on summary conviction, the maximum penalty is a fine not exceeding the statutory maximum (s. 191(5) and (7)).

Auditors and Actuaries

B7.23 By virtue of part XXII of the Financial Services and Markets Act 2000, rules can require an authorised person to appoint an auditor or actuary. An authorised person who knowingly or recklessly gives an appointed auditor or actuary information which is false or misleading in a material particular commits an offence under s. 346. The maximum penalty on conviction on indictment is two years' imprisonment or a fine, or both; on summary conviction, it is three months' imprisonment or a fine not exceeding the statutory maximum, or both.

Misleading Statements and Practices

B7.24 The Financial Services and Markets Act 2000, s. 397, supplanted the Financial Services Act 1986, s. 47, and is mostly similar in form. Offences under s. 397 are punishable on indictment by a maximum of seven years' imprisonment and/or a fine; on summary conviction by up to six months' imprisonment and/or a fine not exceeding the statutory maximum (s. 397(8)). In *Feld* [1999] 1 Cr App R (S) 1, sentences totalling six years were approved after a trial for raising in excess of £20 million by false statements relating to the financial position of a company under the Financial Services Act 1986, s. 47. Sentences totalling two years for nine counts of making a false instrument were ordered to run concurrently. According to the Court of Appeal, factors relevant to sentence include the amount of the fraud, the manner in which it was carried out, the period over which it took place, the persistence with which it was carried out, the position of the offender in the company, abuse of trust, the consequences of the fraud, the effect on public confidence in the City and the integrity of commercial life, the loss to small investors, the personal benefit to the offender, and the plea, age and character of the offender.

Financial Services and Markets Act 2000, s. 397

(1) This subsection applies to a person who—
  (a) makes a statement, promise or forecast which he knows to be misleading, false or deceptive in a material particular;
  (b) dishonestly conceals any material facts whether in connection with a statement, promise or forecast made by him or otherwise; or
  (c) recklessly makes (dishonestly or otherwise) a statement, promise or forecast which is misleading, false or deceptive in a material particular.

(2) A person to whom subsection (1) applies is guilty of an offence if he makes the statement, promise or forecast or conceals the facts for the purpose of inducing, or is reckless as to whether it may induce, another person (whether or not the person to whom the statement, promise or forecast is made)—
  (a) to enter or offer to enter into, or to refrain from entering or offering to enter into, a relevant agreement; or
  (b) to exercise, or refrain from exercising, any rights conferred by a relevant investment.

Section 397 must be read in conjunction with the Financial Services and Markets Act 2000 (Misleading Statements and Practices) Order 2001 (SI 2001 No. 3645) and with sch. 2 to the Act. The territorial ambit of the provision is prescribed by s. 397(6). It is a defence for a person to whom s. 397(1)(a) applies to show that his statement, promise or forecast was made in conformity with price stabilising rules or control of information rules under the Act or Commission Regulation (EC) no. 2273/2003 (s. 397(4)).

The gist of the offence created by s. 397(1) and (2) lies in the making of the statements or the concealment of the facts. There is a different mental element in each of the three matters dealt with in s. 397(1); only (b), concealment of material facts, requires dishonesty. Dishonesty must here bear the same meaning as in deception offences (see *Ghosh* [1982] QB 1053 and **B4.37**). Where an offence under s. 397(1)(c) is charged, the accused may be guilty even if he neither misleads, nor intends to mislead, anyone. The comment of Lord Bingham in *G* [2004] 1 AC 1034 (at [28]) (see **A2.5**) that he is not in that case addressing the meaning of 'reckless' in other statutory contexts leaves open the meaning of 'recklessly' and 'reckless' in s. 397(1) and (2).

A false or misleading promise must be one which is false or misleading when made (e.g., because the speaker never has any intention or expectation that it will ever be kept). It is not enough to prove that a promise was broken (cf. *Re Augustus Barnett & Son Ltd* [1986] BCLC 170, discussed at **B7.15**).

Where several false or misleading statements are alleged, they may be included in a single count (*Linnell* [1969] 1 WLR 1514), but the judge must warn the jury that they cannot convict merely because some jurors are satisfied as to the falsity of one statement and the others are satisfied as to the falsity of another (*Brown* (1983) 79 Cr App R 115: see **D17.44**).

Financial Services and Markets Act 2000, s. 397

(3) Any person who does any act or engages in any course of conduct which creates a false or misleading impression as to the market in or the price or value of any relevant investments is guilty of an offence if he does so for the purpose of creating that impression and of thereby inducing another person to acquire, dispose of, subscribe for or underwrite those investments or to refrain from doing so or to exercise, or refrain from exercising, any rights conferred by those investments.

. . .

(5) In proceedings brought against any person for an offence under subsection (3) it is a defence for him to show—

(a) that he reasonably believed that his act or conduct would not create an impression that was false or misleading as to the matters mentioned in that subsection;

(b) that he acted or engaged in the conduct—

(i) for the purpose of stabilising the price of investments; and

(ii) in conformity with price stabilising rules; or

(c) that he acted or engaged in the conduct in conformity with control of information rules; or

(d) that he acted or engaged in the conduct in conformity with the relevant provisions of Commission Regulation (EC) No. 2273/2003 of 22 December 2003 implementing Directive 2003/6/EC of the European Parliament and of the Council as regards exemptions for buy-back programmes and stabilisation of financial instruments.

. . .

(7) Subsection (3) does not apply unless—

(a) the act is done, or the course of conduct is engaged in, in the United Kingdom; or the false or misleading impression is created there.

Section 397(3) is not confined to the rigging of investment markets. False information concerning the value (for example) of any public or private company, if circulated with intent to persuade any person to invest in such a company, would be covered. It could also apply to improper 'share support' operations, as where a company bidding to take over another engages in practices designed to falsify or distort the market value of its own shares, making these appear more attractive to shareholders in the target company, to whom they would be offered in exchange.

Market rigging schemes will often involve conspiracies (conspiracy to defraud or statutory conspiracy). In *A-G's Ref (Nos. 14, 15 and 16 of 1995)* (1997) *The Times*, 10 April 1997, the Court of Appeal stated that offenders who took part in conspiracy to defraud involving the creation of false share markets to influence the fate of takeovers would ordinarily receive custodial sentences. Deterrent sentences were appropriate since creating false share markets could lead both to a fraud on shareholders and to considerable damage to the City. See also *Chauhan* [2000] 2 Cr App R (S) 230.

Offences under s. 397 involving publication of a trading statement which gave a false and misleading account of a company's revenue and profit, were considered in *Bailey* [2006] 2 Cr App R (S) 250. The offenders were convicted, after a trial, of recklessly (rather than knowingly) making the relevant statement. In light of personal mitigation sentences were reduced to nine months and 18 months' imprisonment. Confiscation and compensation orders were also made. See also *Hipwell* [2006] 2 Cr App R (S) 636 (financial journalist tipping companies in which he had bought shares).

INSOLVENCY OFFENCES: GENERAL

B7.25 The law relating to personal and corporate insolvency was consolidated in the Insolvency Act 1986. The principal offences under the Act are contained in part IV, chapter X (in relation to company insolvency), and part IX, chapter VI (in respect of bankruptcy of individuals). Some serious offences are created by the Insolvency Rules 1986 (SI 1986 No. 1925).

The scale, complexity and specialised subject-matter of this legislation again precludes comprehensive coverage of its offences within a general work on criminal law. This section accordingly covers only the principal offences; for information concerning minor and regulatory offences, a specialist work on insolvency must be consulted.

Penalties

Penalties for offences under the Insolvency Act 1986, together with brief descriptions of the offences and details of modes of trial, are set out in sch. 10. This is reproduced in abridged form at B7.58. B7.26

OFFENCES CONCERNING COMPANY INSOLVENCY AND LIQUIDATION

Procedure in Summary Proceedings

Insolvency Act 1986, s. 431 B7.27

(1) Summary proceedings for any offence under any of parts I to VII of this Act may (without prejudice to any jurisdiction exercisable apart from this subsection) be taken against a body corporate at any place at which the body has a place of business, and against any other person at any place at which he is for the time being.
(2) Notwithstanding anything in section 127(1) of the Magistrates' Courts Act 1980, an information relating to such an offence which is triable by a magistrates' court in England and Wales may be so tried if it is laid at any time within 3 years after the commission of the offence and within 12 months after the date on which evidence sufficient in the opinion of the Director of Public Prosecutions or the Secretary of State (as the case may be) to justify the proceedings comes to his knowledge.
(3) [Applies only to Scotland.]
(4) For purposes of this section, a certificate of the Director of Public Prosecutions, the Lord Advocate or the Secretary of State (as the case may be) as to the date on which such evidence as is referred to above came to his knowledge is conclusive evidence.

Insolvency and Winding Up

A company can be wound up by an order of the High Court or (if its paid up share capital does not exceed £120,000) by an order of the county court with winding-up jurisdiction for the district in which the company's registered office is situated (Insolvency Act 1986, s. 117). This is called a compulsory winding up. A company can also be wound up voluntarily if the company passes a resolution for voluntary winding up under s. 84. A company that is being wound up is referred to as being in liquidation. Companies in liquidation are not always insolvent, and the offences contained within the Insolvency Act 1986 are often capable of applying to the winding up of solvent companies. In practice, however, prosecutions under the Act usually concern the winding up of insolvent companies. B7.28

The date at which winding up commences can be crucial to the application of the relevant law. A voluntary winding up commences when the resolution for winding up is passed by the company (s. 86) and, under s. 129, this remains the relevant date even when a winding-up order is later made in respect of that company. In compulsory winding up, the relevant date is the date on which the winding-up petition was presented (s. 129(2)).

As to the application of the Insolvency Act 1986 to limited liability partnerships, see the Limited Liability Partnerships Regulations 2001 (SI 2001 No. 1090), reg. 5.

False Declarations of Solvency in Voluntary Liquidations

Insolvency Act 1986, s. 89 B7.29

(1) Where it is proposed to wind up a company voluntarily, the directors (or, in the case of a company having more than two directors, the majority of them) may at a directors' meeting

make a statutory declaration to the effect that they have made a full inquiry into the company's affairs and that, having done so, they have formed the opinion that the company will be able to pay its debts in full, together with interest at the official rate (as defined in section 251), within such period, not exceeding 12 months from the commencement of the winding up, as may be specified in the declaration.

. . .

(4) A director making a declaration under this section without having reasonable grounds for the opinion that the company will be able to pay its debts in full, together with interest at the official rate, within the period specified is liable to imprisonment or a fine, or both.

(5) If the company is wound up in pursuance of a resolution passed within 5 weeks after the making of the declaration, and its debts (together with interest at the official rate) are not paid or provided for in full within the period specified, it is to be presumed (unless the contrary is shown) that the director did not have reasonable grounds for his opinion.

This section now applies, subject to modifications, to friendly societies (Friendly Societies Act 1992, s. 23 and sch. 10).

For procedural provisions, see **B7.27**; for sentencing provisions, see **B7.58** and **B7.59**.

The importance of the declaration is that it determines whether the winding up will be a members' or a creditors' winding up (s. 90). In the latter, the company has to call a creditors' meeting (s. 98) and the creditors' nomination of the liquidator takes precedence over the members' nomination (s. 100). In a creditors' winding up it is an offence under s. 166 for any liquidator nominated by the members to dispose of company property (except perishables and other goods likely to diminish in value) unless and until his status is confirmed by a creditors' meeting. This prohibits the once prevalent practice of selling assets of insolvent companies to directors or others associated with the company at knock-down prices without the creditors being warned or consulted (see *Re Centrebind Ltd* [1967] 1 WLR 377).

Fraud etc. in Anticipation of Winding Up

B7.30 Insolvency Act 1986, s. 206

(1) When a company is ordered to be wound up by the court, or passes a resolution for voluntary winding up, any person, being a past or present officer of the company, is deemed to have committed an offence if, within the 12 months immediately preceding the commencement of the winding up, he has—
   (a) concealed any part of the company's property to the value of £500 or more, or concealed any debt due to or from the company, or
   (b) fraudulently removed any part of the company's property to the value of £500 or more, or
   (c) concealed, destroyed, mutilated or falsified any book or paper affecting or relating to the company's property or affairs, or
   (d) made any false entry in any book or paper affecting or relating to the company's property or affairs, or
   (e) fraudulently parted with, altered or made any omission in any document affecting or relating to the company's property or affairs, or
   (f) pawned, pledged or disposed of any property of the company which has been obtained on credit and has not been paid for (unless the pawning, pledging or disposal was in the ordinary way of the company's business).

(2) Such a person is deemed to have committed an offence if within the period above mentioned he has been privy to the doing by others of any of the things mentioned in paragraphs (c), (d) and (e) of subsection (1); and he commits an offence if, at any time after the commencement of the winding up, he does any of the things mentioned in paragraph (a) to (f) of that subsection, or is privy to the doing by others of any of the things mentioned in paragraphs (c) to (e) of it.

(3) For purposes of this section, 'officer' includes a shadow director.

(4) It is a defence—
   (a) for a person charged under paragraph (a) or (f) of subsection (1) (or under subsection (2) in respect of the things mentioned in either of those two paragraphs) to prove that he had no intent to defraud, and

(b) for a person charged under paragraph (c) or (d) of subsection (1) (or under subsection (2) in respect of the things mentioned in either of those two paragraphs) to prove that he had no intent to conceal the state of affairs of the company or to defeat the law.

(5) Where a person pawns, pledges or disposes of any property in circumstances which amount to an offence under subsection (1)(f), every person who takes in pawn or pledge, or otherwise receives, the property knowing it to be pawned, pledged or disposed of in such circumstances, is guilty of an offence.

For procedural provisions, see **B7.27**; for sentencing provisions, see **B7.58** and **B7.59**.

Fraud is a definitional element in the offences under s. 206(1)(b) and (e), and must therefore be proved by the prosecution. In the case of other offences under s. 206(1), liability is strict, unless an accused is able to rely on the defence provided by s. 206(4). The burden placed on the accused under this provision is the full persuasive burden. This does not infringe the ECHR, Article 6 (see *A-G's Ref (No. 1 of 2004)* [2004] 1 WLR 2111 and *Sheldrake v DPP* [2005] 1 AC 624, holding that *Carass* [2002] 1 WLR 1714 was wrongly decided: see **F3.19**). The combined effect of s. 206(1) and (2) is that offences can be committed before or after commencement of winding up. Offences under s. 206(1)(c) to (e) can be committed by officers who are 'privy' to the acts of others; these others need not themselves be officers nor need they be guilty of any offence.

Subsections (1) and (2) create separate offences; a charge cannot be brought under s. 206(1) in respect of things done after the commencement of the winding up.

Fraudulent Conduct and Intent to Defraud References to fraudulent conduct in the Insolvency Act 1986, s. 206(1), and to 'intent to defraud' in s. 206(4)(a), must be concerned with the same concept (for further discussion of this in the context of fraudulent trading, see **B7.14**). It must, in other words, involve dishonesty, but need not involve deceit. **B7.31**

Receipt of Property Disposed of Contrary to s. 206(1)(f) etc. The wording of the Insolvency Act 1986, s. 206(5), seems open to two possible interpretations. One possibility is that the recipient need know only of the circumstances specified in s. 206(1)(f), and that knowledge of whether the person disposing of the property could establish a defence under s. 206(4) is irrelevant; fraud is not, after all, a definitional element in an offence under s. 206(1)(f). The other possibility is that the prosecution must prove the recipient's knowledge of the disposer's guilt, and that that guilt arises only where the disposer is unable to prove a defence under s. 206(4); the recipient would therefore need to know that no such defence could be established (in other words, he must be shown to know that the disposer is acting fraudulently). It is submitted that the latter interpretation is the correct one; the former could lead to cases in which the recipient is convicted despite the acquittal of the disposer and would be in marked contrast to the position under the corresponding bankruptcy provision (Insolvency Act 1986, s. 359 — see **B7.49**). In contrast, there is nothing illogical in a rule under which conviction of the disposer is made easier than conviction of the recipient. **B7.32**

For the approach to disposal otherwise than in the ordinary course of business, see *Countrywide Banking Corporation Ltd v Dean* [1998] AC 338 and the older cases of *Bolus* (1870) 23 LT 339 and *Thomas* (1870) 22 LT 138.

Transactions in Fraud of Creditors

Insolvency Act 1986, s. 207 **B7.33**

(1) When a company is ordered to be wound up by the court or passes a resolution for voluntary winding up, a person is deemed to have committed an offence if he, being at the time an officer of the company—

(a) has made or caused to be made any gift or transfer of, or charge on, or has caused or connived at the levying of any execution against, the company's property, or

(b) has concealed or removed any part of the company's property since, or within 2 months before, the date of any unsatisfied judgment or order for the payment of money obtained against the company.

(2) A person is not guilty of an offence under this section—

(a) by reason of conduct constituting an offence under subsection (1)(a) which occurred more than 5 years before the commencement of the winding up, or

(b) if he proves that, at the time of the conduct constituting the offence, he had no intent to defraud the company's creditors.

For procedural provisions, see **B7.27**; for sentencing provisions, see **B7.58** and **B7.59**.

Although s. 207(1)(a) is widely expressed, its effect is heavily curtailed by s. 207(2). The burden placed on the accused under s. 207(2)(b) would appear to be the full persuasive burden (see *A-G's Ref (No. 1 of 2004)* [2004] 1 WLR 2111, *Sheldrake v DPP* [2005] 1 AC 624 and **F3.13** *et seq.*).

There is old authority to the effect that any intent to defraud creditors must refer to creditors at the time of the action concerned (*Hopkins* [1896] 1 QB 652), but this seems doubtful on principle, and would produce very unsatisfactory results where the company has a long-term debt problem, but a series of short-term creditors (see *Seillon* [1982] Crim LR 676).

A person 'causes' a thing to be done when he orders or directs it to be done (*Houston v Buchanan* [1940] 2 All ER 179).

Misconduct in the Course of Winding Up

B7.34 **Insolvency Act 1986, s. 208**

(1) When a company is being wound up, whether by the court or voluntarily, any person, being a past or present officer of the company, commits an offence if he—

(a) does not to the best of his knowledge and belief fully and truly discover to the liquidator all the company's property, and how and to whom and for what consideration and when the company disposed of any part of that property (except such part as has been disposed of in the ordinary way of the company's business), or

(b) does not deliver up to the liquidator (or as he directs) all such part of the company's property as is in his custody or under his control, and which he is required by law to deliver up, or

(c) does not deliver up to the liquidator (or as he directs) all books and papers in his custody or under his control belonging to the company and which he is required by law to deliver up, or

(d) knowing or believing that a false debt has been proved by any person in the winding up, fails to inform the liquidator as soon as practicable, or

(e) after the commencement of the winding up, prevents the production of any book or paper affecting or relating to the company's property or affairs.

(2) Such a person commits an offence if after the commencement of the winding up he attempts to account for any part of the company's property by fictitious losses or expenses; and he is deemed to have committed that offence if he has so attempted at any meeting of the company's creditors within the 12 months immediately preceding the commencement of the winding up.

(3) For the purposes of this section, 'officer' includes a shadow director.

(4) It is a defence—

(a) for a person charged under paragraph (a), (b) or (c) of subsection (1) to prove that he had no intent to defraud, and

(b) for a person charged under paragraph (e) of that subsection to prove that he had no intent to conceal the state of affairs of the company or to defeat the law.

For procedural provisions, see **B7.27**; for sentencing provisions, see **B7.58** and **B7.59**.

This is an important section, because the reason for appointing the liquidator is to ensure that the winding up is conducted by an independent person. That purpose would be defeated if the liquidator was unable to obtain access to and control of the company's property and records. The burden imposed on the defence by s. 208(4) would appear to be the full persuasive burden of proof (see *A-G's Ref (No. 1 of 2004)* [2004] 1 WLR 2111, *Sheldrake v DPP* [2005] 1 AC 624 and **F3.13** ***et seq.***).

It is not necessary for the liquidator to have demanded the specific property in question. There is accordingly a continuing duty to disclose and deliver any valuable items of which the liquidator may be unaware (*McCredie* [2000] BCC 617).

The offences contained within s. 208(1)(d) and s. 208(2) do not allow for the proving of any special defences. Under s. 208(2), full and frank disclosure to the liquidator does not excuse previous lies told to creditors, and under s. 208(1)(d) mere hesitation in disclosing a false claim may be sufficient.

Falsification of Company Books

B7.35

Insolvency Act 1986, s. 209

(1) When a company is being wound up, an officer or contributory of the company commits an offence if he destroys, mutilates, alters or falsifies any books, papers or securities, or makes or is privy to the making of any false or fraudulent entry in any register, book of account or document belonging to the company with intent to defraud or deceive any person.

For procedural provisions, see **B7.27**; for sentencing provisions, see **B7.58** and **B7.59**.

Section 209(1) appears to divide into two distinct halves. Destroying, mutilating altering or falsifying books, papers or securities forms the first half, and making false or fraudulent entries in company documents etc. forms the second. If this interpretation is correct, certain important consequences follow.

First, the phrase 'belonging to the company' appears to govern only the latter half of s. 209(1), as does the phrase 'with intent to defraud or deceive'. This means that the destruction or falsification of papers or securities belonging to another person would suffice (as where D destroys P's bill of exchange or debenture certificate, on which the company would be liable), and it also follows that fraud or deceit need not be proved by the prosecution in such cases.

Secondly, 'documents' are defined in s. 436 as including computer records and other non-documentary records. This means, for example, that the fraudulent insertion of false entries on a company computer record would be an offence under s. 209(1) if the insertion is made with intent to defraud or deceive. On the other hand, it would seem that the destruction or mutilation of such records could not be an offence within s. 209(1) (i.e. the first part thereof), unless the records could be regarded as 'books, papers or securities'. It might be better to consider charges under the Companies Act 1985, s. 450, in such cases (see **B7.10**).

Material Omissions from Statements Relating to the Company's Affairs

B7.36

Insolvency Act 1986, s. 210

(1) When a company is being wound up, whether by the court or voluntarily, any person, being a past or present officer of the company, commits an offence if he makes any material omission in any statement relating to the company's affairs.
(2) When a company has been ordered to be wound up by the court, or has passed a resolution for voluntary winding up, any such person is deemed to have committed that offence if, prior to the winding up, he has made any material omission in any such statement.
(3) For the purposes of this section, 'officer' includes a shadow director.
(4) It is a defence for a person charged under this section to prove that he had no intent to defraud.

For procedural provisions, see **B7.27**; for sentencing provisions, see **B7.58** and **B7.59**.

The scope of this provision is of enormous width, but the defence in s. 210(4) keeps it within reasonable bounds. Unlike the equivalent provision in respect of bankruptcy (s. 356(1); see

B7.46), it is not necessary that the material omission be made in a statement under any provision of the Act, such as the statutory statement of affairs under s. 131 in compulsory winding up; any statement, oral or written, would seem to be within its scope, whether made during winding up or prior to it. If a material omission was understandable in the circumstances (as where the statement was informal and unrehearsed), it would be difficult to conclude that there was any intent to defraud.

False Representations to Creditors

B7.37 **Insolvency Act 1986, s. 211**

(1) When a company is being wound up, whether by the court or voluntarily, any person, being a past or present officer of the company—
   (a) commits an offence if he makes any false representation or commits any other fraud for the purpose of obtaining the consent of the company's creditors or any of them to an agreement with reference to the company's affairs or to the winding up, and
   (b) is deemed to have committed that offence if, prior to the winding up, he has made any false representation, or committed any other fraud, for that purpose.
(2) For purposes of this section, 'officer' includes a shadow director.

For procedural provisions, see B7.27; for sentencing provisions, see B7.58 and B7.59.

In view of the fact that s. 211 makes no provision for an accused to prove that he acted without fraudulent intent, and in view of the references to false representations 'or any other fraud', it is submitted that the offence of making false representations should be construed as requiring the prosecution to prove fraud. This interpretation gains some support from *Cherry* (1871) 12 Cox 32, in which it was said (in relation to bankruptcy provisions) that, in this context, 'false' means 'fraudulent'.

Re-use of Company Names

B7.38 **Insolvency Act 1986, s. 216**

(1) This section applies to a person where a company ('the liquidating company') has gone into insolvent liquidation on or after the appointed day and he was a director or shadow director of the company at any time in the period of 12 months ending with the day before it went into liquidation.
(2) For the purposes of this section, a name is a prohibited name in relation to such a person if—
   (a) it is a name by which the liquidating company was known at any time in that period of 12 months, or
   (b) it is a name which is so similar to a name falling within paragraph (a) as to suggest an association with that company.
(3) Except with leave of the court or in such circumstances as may be prescribed, a person to whom this section applies shall not at any time in the period of 5 years beginning with the day on which the liquidating company went into liquidation—
   (a) be a director of any other company that is known by a prohibited name, or
   (b) in any way, whether directly or indirectly, be concerned or take part in the promotion, formation or management of any such company, or
   (c) in any way, whether directly or indirectly, be concerned or take part in the carrying on of a business carried on (otherwise than by a company) under a prohibited name.

For procedural provisions, see B7.27; for sentencing provisions, see B7.58 and B7.59.

Section 216 deals with one aspect of 'Phoenix companies', where companies in insolvent liquidation would re-appear, with almost identical names, businesses and directors, a few months later. The re-born companies would in law be new enterprises, unfettered by the unpaid debts of the previous ones, but would, to outside appearances, be the same as before, and they often acquired assets cheaply from the liquidator of the previous company. The prohibition of 'Centrebinding' (see B7.29) and the tighter regulation of insolvency practitioners has done much to eliminate such practices, but re-use of a familiar name was considered worthy of proscription in its own right. The court which may give leave under

s. 216(3) is the court having jurisdiction to wind up companies, and a company is regarded as going into insolvent liquidation if its assets are insufficient to meet its liabilities and the expenses of the winding up (s. 216(5) and (7)). References, in relation to a time, to a name by which a company is known, are to the name of the company at that time or to any name under which the company carries on business at that time (s. 216(6)).

Contravention of s. 216 may involve civil liability under s. 217 as well as the criminal penalties prescribed in sch. 10. The offence created by s. 216 is one of strict liability (*Cole* [1998] BCC 87).

BANKRUPTCY OFFENCES

The provisions of the Insolvency Act 1986, part IX, chapter VI, which deal with the principal bankruptcy offences, are in many respects similar, but by no means identical, to the provisions dealing with offences concerning company insolvency and liquidation. In individual insolvency the trustee in bankruptcy performs a role similar to that of a liquidator in company liquidation. **B7.39**

Scheme of Chapter VI

Insolvency Act 1986, s. 350 **B7.40**

(1) Subject to section 360(3) below, this chapter applies where the court has made a bankruptcy order on a bankruptcy petition.
(2) This chapter applies whether or not the bankruptcy order is annulled, but proceedings for an offence under this chapter shall not be instituted after the annulment.
(3) Without prejudice to his liability in respect of a subsequent bankruptcy, the bankrupt is not guilty of an offence under this chapter in respect of anything done after his discharge; but nothing in this group of parts prevents the institution of proceedings against a discharged bankrupt for an offence committed before his discharge.
(3A) Subsection (3) is without prejudice to any provision of this chapter which applies to a person in respect of whom a bankruptcy restrictions order is in force.
(4) It is not a defence in proceedings for an offence under this chapter that anything relied on, in whole or in part, as constituting that offence was done outside England and Wales.
(5) Proceedings for an offence under this chapter or under the rules shall not be instituted except by the Secretary of State or by or with the consent of the Director of Public Prosecutions.
(6) A person guilty of any offence under this chapter is liable to imprisonment or a fine, or both.

Penalties for offences under chapter VI (ss. 353 to 362) are prescribed by sch. 10, the relevant parts of which are printed at **B7.58**.

Definitions

Insolvency Act 1986, ss. 351 and 381 **B7.41**

351. In the following provisions of this chapter—
(a) references to property comprised in the bankrupt's estate or to property possession of which is required to be delivered up to the official receiver or the trustee of the bankrupt's estate include any property which would be such property if a notice in respect of it were given under section 307 (after-acquired property), section 308 (personal property and effects of bankrupt having more than replacement value) or section 308A (vesting in trustee of certain tenancies);
(b) 'the initial period' means the period between the presentation of the bankruptcy petition and the commencement of the bankruptcy; and
(c) a reference to a number of months or years before petition is to that period ending with the presentation of the bankruptcy petition.

381.—(1) 'Bankrupt' means an individual who has been adjudged bankrupt, and, in relation to a bankruptcy order, it means the individual adjudged bankrupt by that order.
(2) 'Bankruptcy order' means an order adjudging an individual bankrupt.
(3) 'Bankruptcy petition' means a petition to the court for a bankruptcy order.

Under s. 306 the bankrupt's estate vests in his trustee in bankruptcy. Under s. 307, the bankrupt's trustee may by notice in writing claim for his estate property acquired or devolved upon the bankrupt since commencement of his bankruptcy; and under s. 308 he may similarly claim tools of trade, household effects etc., which would not ordinarily be claimed, but which appear to have a realisable value exceeding the cost of reasonable replacements.

Further definitions (not printed in this work) are to be found in ss. 382 to 385.

Defence of Innocent Intention

B7.42 **Insolvency Act 1986, s. 352**

Where in the case of an offence under any provision of this chapter it is stated that this section applies, a person is not guilty of the offence if he proves that, at the time of the conduct constituting the offence, he had no intent to defraud or to conceal the state of his affairs.

In *A-G's Ref (No. 1 of 2004)* [2004] 1 WLR 2111, Lord Woolf CJ said (at [92]):

In the light of *Lambert* [[2002] 2 AC 740], we accept that in appropriate cases [s. 352] may be read down as imposing no more than an evidential burden of proof. Its effect within chapter VI depends on the context of its application. In section 357(1), it has to be so read.

Offences of Non-disclosure

B7.43 **Insolvency Act 1986, s. 353**

(1) The bankrupt is guilty of an offence if—
(a) he does not to the best of his knowledge and belief disclose all the property comprised in his estate to the official receiver or the trustee, or
(b) he does not inform the official receiver or the trustee of any disposal of any property which but for the disposal would be so comprised, stating how, when, to whom and for what consideration the property was disposed of.
(2) Subsection (1)(b) does not apply to any disposal in the ordinary course of a business carried on by the bankrupt or to any payment of the ordinary expenses of the bankrupt or his family.
(3) Section 352 applies to this offence.

For procedural provisions, see **B7.40**; for sentencing provisions, see **B7.58** and **B7.59**. As to the meaning of 'property' see **B7.41**. Section 353(1)(b) is primarily concerned with property which the bankrupt has had at some time and which the trustee might be able to trace and reclaim through exercise of his powers under the Act.

As to what might or might not amount to disposal 'in the ordinary course of business', see B7.32 and *Countrywide Banking Corporation Ltd v Dean* [1998] AC 338.

Concealment of Property and Failure to Account for Losses

B7.44 **Insolvency Act 1986, s. 354**

(1) The bankrupt is guilty of an offence, if—
(a) he does not deliver up possession to the official receiver or trustee, or as the official receiver or trustee may direct, of such part of the property comprised in his estate as is in his possession or under his control, and possession of which he is required by law so to deliver up,
(b) he conceals any debt due to or from him or conceals any property the value of which is not less than the prescribed amount and possession of which he is required to deliver up to the official receiver or trustee, or
(c) in the 12 months before petition, or in the initial period, he did anything which would have been an offence under paragraph (b) above if the bankruptcy order had been made immediately before he did it.
Section 352 applies to this offence.
(2) The bankrupt is guilty of an offence if he removes, or in the initial period removed, any property the value of which was not less than the prescribed amount and possession of which he has or would have been required to deliver up to the official receiver or the trustee.
Section 352 applies to this offence.

(3) The bankrupt is guilty of an offence if he without reasonable excuse fails, on being required to do so by the official receiver, the trustee or the court—
  (a) to account for the loss of any substantial part of his property incurred in the 12 months before petition or in the initial period, or
  (b) to give a satisfactory explanation of the manner in which such a loss was incurred.

For procedural provisions, see B7.40; for sentencing provisions, see B7.58 and B7.59. For the defence under s. 352 (defence of innocent intention), see B7.42. The 'prescribed amount' for the purposes of s. 354 is fixed by the Insolvency Proceedings (Monetary Limits) Order 1986 (SI 1986 No. 1996, as amended by SI 2004 No. 547) at £1,000.

The offence contained within s. 354(3) differs from those contained within the preceding subsections in that it is absolute, and does not allow for any possible defence under s. 352. As Sachs LJ said in *Salter* [1968] 2 QB 793 (in relation to a similarly worded offence under the Bankruptcy Act 1914) at p. 798:

> A jury should be directed that if they are satisfied as regards the total sum of money constituting 'the loss of any substantial part of his estate' the bankrupt had not at the time of the alleged failure given with such reasonable detail as was appropriate in the circumstances an explanation which is both reasonably clear and true of how such sum was made up (for the loss may be composed of more than one component), of how it came to be lost, and of where the money has gone, then the offence has been committed. The degree of particularity required of the bankrupt may vary greatly according to the facts of the case: sums which are really small in relation to 'the substantial part of the estate' need not of course be traced, but an explanation unsupported by sufficient detail can be very unsatisfactory indeed. [The provision] intends to and does, in the interests of the business community as a whole, put in peril the man who goes bankrupt without having so conducted his affairs as to be able satisfactorily to explain why some substantial loss has been incurred. It is as well to make it plain that, as the offence is absolute, it follows that, once a prosecution has been initiated, no issue arises before verdict as to the reasons why the failure has occurred or as to any motive which led to that failure.

An explanation, if clear and true, need not also be 'satisfactory' in the sense of clearing the bankrupt of blame. If, for example, the explanation reveals heavy gambling losses, this may still be satisfactory for the purposes of s. 354.

The offence under s. 354(3)(a) is compatible with the accused's right to silence and not to incriminate himself (*Kearns* [2002] 1 WLR 2815).

Concealment or Falsification of Books and Papers

Insolvency Act 1986, s. 355 **B7.45**

(1) The bankrupt is guilty of an offence if he does not deliver up possession to the official receiver or the trustee, or as the official receiver or trustee may direct, of all books, papers and other records of which he has possession or control and which relate to his estate or his affairs.
Section 352 applies to this offence.
(2) The bankrupt is guilty of an offence if—
  (a) he prevents, or in the initial period prevented, the production of any books, papers or records relating to his estate or affairs;
  (b) he conceals, destroys, mutilates or falsifies, or causes or permits the concealment, destruction, mutilation or falsification of, any books, papers or other records relating to his estate or affairs;
  (c) he makes or causes or permits the making of, any false entries in any book, document or record relating to his estate or affairs; or
  (d) in the 12 months before petition, or in the initial period, he did anything which would have been an offence, under paragraph (b) or (c) above if the bankruptcy order had been made before he did it.
Section 352 applies to this offence.
(3) The bankrupt is guilty of an offence if—
  (a) he disposes of, or alters or makes any omission in, or causes or permits the disposal,

altering or making of any omission in, any book, document or record relating to his estate or affairs, or

(b) in the 12 months before petition, or in the initial period, he did anything which would have been an offence under paragraph (a) if the bankruptcy order had been made before he did it.

(4) In their application to a trading record subsections (2)(d) and (3)(b) shall have effect as if the reference to 12 months were a reference to two years.

(5) In subsection (4) 'trading record' means a book, document or record which shows or explains the transactions or financial position of a person's business, including—
(a) a periodic record of cash paid and received,
(b) a statement of periodic stock-taking, and
(c) except in the case of goods sold by way of retail trade, a record of goods sold and purchased which identifies the buyer and seller or enables them to be identified.

Section 352 applies to this offence.

For procedural provisions, see **B7.40**; for sentencing provisions, see **B7.58** and **B7.59**. For the meaning of 'the initial period', see **B7.41**. For the defence under s. 352 (lack of fraudulent intent), see **B7.42**.

'Causing' an act means ordering or directing it, and 'permitting' it means allowing it to happen (*Houston v Buchanan* [1940] 2 All ER 179). It is not always clear whether an accused must be proved to know the circumstances which make the act criminal, although, in this context, it is unlikely that such proof would be required. Where an accused has, for example, permitted an assistant to clear out old files in his office, and it transpires that these included papers relating to his estate or affairs, it is submitted that his only possible defence to a charge under s. 355(2)(b) would be that provided by s. 352.

The offences under s. 355(2) and (3) overlap with the Theft Act 1968, s. 17 (see **B6.3**), and the Forgery and Counterfeiting Act 1981, s. 1 (see **B6.28**).

False Statements

B7.46 **Insolvency Act 1986, s. 356**

(1) The bankrupt is guilty of an offence if he makes or has made any material omission in any statement made under any provision in this group of parts and relating to his affairs.

Section 352 applies to this offence.

(2) The bankrupt is guilty of an offence if—
(a) knowing or believing that a false debt has been proved by any person under the bankruptcy, he fails to inform the trustee as soon as practicable; or
(b) he attempts to account for any part of his property by fictitious losses or expenses; or
(c) at any meeting of his creditors in the 12 months before petition or (whether or not at such a meeting) at any time in the initial period, he did anything which would have been an offence under paragraph (b) if the bankruptcy order had been made before he did it; or
(d) he is, or at any time has been, guilty of any false representation or other fraud for the purpose of obtaining the consent of his creditors, or any of them, to an agreement with reference to his affairs or to his bankruptcy.

For procedural provisions, see **B7.40**; for sentencing provisions, see **B7.58** and **B7.59**. For the defence under s. 352 (lack of fraudulent intent), see **B7.42**.

Section 356(1) differs from the equivalent company liquidation offence (s. 210) in that the statement concerned must be one made under relevant provisions of the Act. This might be a 'statement of affairs' under s. 288 or a statement made in purported compliance with s. 333 or any other relevant provision.

The defence under s. 352 applies only to s. 356(1); the offences under s. 356(2) require proof of knowledge or belief. Thus, proof of the inaccuracy of a bankrupt's account would not suffice to prove an offence under s. 366(2)(b): it must also be proved to be fictitious (i.e. that the inaccuracy is deliberate). In respect of s. 356(2)(d), fraud must be proved (see the analysis of the equivalent provision in s. 211 at **B7.37**). In respect of the other offences under s. 356(2), the requisite *mens rea* need not necessarily involve fraud, which thus becomes wholly irrelevant to the issue of guilt: the prosecution need not prove it, and it will not avail the defence to prove its absence.

Fraudulent Disposal or Concealment of Property

Insolvency Act 1986, s. 357 **B7.47**

(1) The bankrupt is guilty of an offence if he makes or causes to be made, or has in the period of 5 years ending with the commencement of the bankruptcy made or caused to be made, any gift or transfer of, or any charge on, his property.
Section 352 applies to this offence.

(2) The reference to making a transfer of or charge on any property includes causing or conniving at the levying of any execution against the property.

(3) The bankrupt is guilty of an offence if he conceals or removes, or has at any time before the commencement of the bankruptcy concealed or removed, any part of his property after, or within 2 months before, the date on which a judgment or order for the payment of money has been obtained against him, being a judgment or order which was not satisfied before the commencement of the bankruptcy.
Section 352 applies to this offence.

For procedural provisions, see **B7.40**; for sentencing provisions, see **B7.58** and **B7.59**; for definitions, see **B7.41**. Section 357(1) is similar to the companies offence contained within s. 207 (see **B7.33**) and, like s. 207, would be of very wide application but for the defence provided under s. 352 (see **B7.42**). A bankrupt who commits an offence under s. 357 can expect to receive a custodial sentence, even if of previous good character (*Mungroo* [1998] BPIR 784).

The Debtors Act 1869, s. 13(3), creates an offence similar in form to the Insolvency Act 1986, s. 357(3), but it does not require there to be a bankruptcy, and places the burden of proving fraud on the prosecution. The Debtors Act 1869, s. 13(2), creates an offence of making gifts etc. with intent to defraud creditors; again this is not dependent on bankruptcy.

Absconding with Property

Insolvency Act 1986, s. 358 **B7.48**

The bankrupt is guilty of an offence if—

(a) he leaves, or attempts or makes preparations to leave, England and Wales with any property the value of which is not less than the prescribed amount and possession of which he is required to deliver up to the official receiver or the trustee, or

(b) in the 6 months before the petition, or in the initial period, he did anything which would have been an offence under paragraph (a) if the bankruptcy order had been made immediately before he did it.

Section 352 applies to this offence.

For procedural provisions, see **B7.40**; for sentencing provisions, see **B7.58** and **B7.59**; for definitions, see **B7.41**. The 'prescribed amount' is fixed by the Insolvency Proceedings (Monetary Limits) Order 1986 (SI 1986 No. 1996, as amended by SI 2004 No. 547) at £1,000.

If the bankrupt has done nothing worse than travel abroad with property (e.g., his car) with which he has later returned, it may well be easy for him to show that he had no intent to defraud and thus take advantage of the defence under s. 352 (see **B7.42**).

Fraudulent Dealing with Property Obtained on Credit

Insolvency Act 1986, s. 359 **B7.49**

(1) The bankrupt is guilty of an offence if, in the 12 months before petition, or in the initial

period, he disposed of any property which he had obtained on credit and, at the time he disposed of it, had not paid for.
Section 352 applies to this offence.

(2) A person is guilty of an offence if, in the 12 months before petition or in the initial period, he acquired or received property from the bankrupt knowing or believing—
   (a) that the bankrupt owed money in respect of the property, and
   (b) that the bankrupt did not intend, or was unlikely to be able, to pay the money he so owed.

(3) A person is not guilty of an offence under subsection (1) or (2) if the disposal, acquisition or receipt of the property was in the ordinary course of a business carried on by the bankrupt at the time of the disposal, acquisition or receipt.

(4) In determining for the purposes of this section whether any property is disposed of, acquired or received in the ordinary course of a business carried on by the bankrupt, regard may be had, in particular, to the price paid for the property.

(5) In this section references to disposing of property include pawning or pledging it; and references to acquiring or receiving property shall be read accordingly.

For procedural provisions, see **B7.40**; for sentencing provisions, see **B7.58** and **B7.59**. For definitions, see **B7.41**. For the defence of no intent under s. 352, see **B7.42**.

The mischief against which s. 359 strikes is that of obtaining goods on credit, and then selling or otherwise disposing of them, often on disadvantageous terms or for inadequate consideration, as a method of raising cash which may be unobtainable by more conventional means. Such methods are generally resorted to only by persons who are already in serious financial difficulties, and prejudice the interests of the unpaid suppliers.

As to what may amount to disposal 'otherwise than in the ordinary course of business', see B7.32.

Obtaining Credit: Engaging in Business

B7.50 **Insolvency Act 1986, s. 360**

(1) The bankrupt is guilty of an offence if—
   (a) either alone or jointly with any other person, he obtains credit to the extent of the prescribed amount or more without giving the person from whom he obtains it the relevant information about his status; or
   (b) he engages (whether directly or indirectly) in any business under a name other than that in which he was adjudged bankrupt without disclosing to all persons with whom he enters into any business transaction the name in which he was so adjudged.

(2) The reference to the bankrupt obtaining credit includes the following cases—
   (a) where goods are bailed to him under a hire-purchase agreement, or agreed to be sold to him under a conditional sale agreement, and
   (b) where he is paid in advance (whether in money or otherwise) for the supply of goods or services.

(3) A person whose estate has been sequestrated in Scotland, or who has been adjudged bankrupt in Northern Ireland, is guilty of an offence if, before his discharge, he does anything in England and Wales which would be an offence under subsection (1) if he were an undischarged bankrupt and the sequestration of his estate or the adjudication in Northern Ireland were an adjudication under this part.

(4) For the purposes of subsection (1)(a), the relevant information about the status of the person in question is the information that he is an undischarged bankrupt or, as the case may be, that his estate has been sequestrated in Scotland and that he has not been discharged.

(5) This section applies to the bankrupt after discharge while a bankruptcy restrictions order is in force in respect of him.

(6) For the purposes of subsection (1)(a) as it applies by virtue of subsection (5), the relevant information about the status of the person in question is the information that a bankruptcy restrictions order is in force in respect of him.

For procedural provisions, see **B7.40**; for sentencing provisions, see **B7.58** and **B7.59**.

Section 360 is not subject to the defence of innocent intention under s. 352. The offences re-enacted in s. 360 have always been regarded as absolute. Thus, in *Duke of Leinster* [1924] 1 KB 311, it was held that D committed the offence even though his agent had been instructed to inform the creditor of D's status and had failed to do so. See also *Dyson* [1894] 2 QB 176.

Credit to the Extent of the Prescribed Amount The amount prescribed by the Insolvency Proceedings (Monetary Limits) Order 1986 (SI 1986 No. 1996, as amended by SI 2004 No. 547) for the purposes of the Insolvency Act 1986, s. 360, is £500. This limit governs the aggregate of the credit obtained, and it cannot be circumvented merely by ensuring that no one transaction exceeds the limit (*Juby* (1886) 16 Cox 160; *Hartley* [1972] 2 QB 1). It seems to have been assumed in *Hartley* that the prescribed amount nevertheless refers to the aggregate obtained from any one creditor. If this is correct, it would be no offence for a bankrupt to obtain £499 worth of credit from each of four different persons without admitting to being a bankrupt. This proposition is of doubtful validity, for, although the section refers in the singular to 'the person' from whom credit is obtained, there would not seem to be any obvious rejection therein of the general principle that the singular includes the plural (Interpretation Act 1978, s. 6(c)). On the other hand, it might be argued that the purpose of the provision is to protect unwary creditors from the risk of substantial losses, and that as long as no one creditor is unknowingly exposed to a potential loss of £500 or more, the bankrupt's conduct is unobjectionable. It is far from obvious that this is the sole purpose of the provision and, in any event, the risk of loss to each is increased by the increase in the aggregate of the bankrupt's debt. **B7.51**

Obtaining Any obtaining must be of credit given to the bankrupt himself. Credit given to him jointly with another is expressly included, but cases where credit is obtained by the bankrupt as agent for another person to whom the creditor looks for payment would not be covered (*Godwin* (1980) 71 Cr App R 97). 'Obtaining' has a narrower meaning for the purposes of s. 360 than it has, for example, in respect of insider dealing; it must involve 'some conduct, either by words or otherwise. . . which amounts to an obtaining' (*Hayat* (1976) 63 Cr App R 181). There may not necessarily have been any 'obtaining' in this sense where the bankrupt's bank account becomes overdrawn as a result of the dishonouring of certain incoming cheques and the honouring of certain cheques drawn by him on that account; it will be a question of fact for the jury (*Hayat*). There is no obtaining of credit where the bankrupt defaults on an existing hire-purchase obligation and thereby becomes liable to pay the arrears (*Miller* [1977] 1 WLR 1129) nor where funds are received from a business partner in the course of a joint venture. It makes no difference if the bankrupt intends to default on his side of the bargain: 'It is the nature of the agreement which determines whether or not credit has been obtained, not the intention of the defendant' (*Ramzan* [1998] 2 Cr App R 328, per Ebsworth J at p. 334). **B7.52**

Credit is 'obtained' where any goods or monies concerned are received (*Ellis* [1899] 1 QB 230), but the Insolvency Act 1986, s. 350(4) (see **B7.40**), ensures that the provisions of chapter VI have extraterritorial effect, and so it will be no defence to argue that credit was obtained abroad.

Engaging in Business A bankrupt may engage in business without necessarily disclosing his status, although he cannot become a company director, manager or promoter without leave of the court (see the Company Directors Disqualification Act 1986, ss. 11 and 13 at **B7.56**). He must not hide his bankruptcy by using a different name. The reference in the Insolvency Act 1986, s. 360(1)(b), to indirectly engaging in business is designed to deal with bankrupts who procure some other persons to 'front' businesses effectively controlled by themselves. **B7.53**

FRAUD IN RESPECT OF VOLUNTARY ARRANGEMENTS

B7.54 Parts I and VIII of the Insolvency Act 1986 make provision for voluntary arrangements by agreement with creditors for the satisfaction of debts or a scheme of arrangement.

Insolvency Act 1986, s. 6A

(1) If, for the purpose of obtaining the approval of the members or creditors of a company to a proposal for a voluntary arrangement, a person who is an officer of the company—
 (a) makes any false representation, or
 (b) fraudulently does, or omits to do, anything,
 he commits an offence.
(2) Subsection (1) applies even if the proposal is not approved.
(3) For purposes of this section 'officer' includes a shadow director.

This section was inserted by the Insolvency Act 2000, s. 3 and sch. 3. A new s. 262A, which makes similar provision for fraud etc. by individual debtors, is also inserted. For sentencing provisions, see B7.58 and B7.59.

FALSE CLAIM OF STATUS AS CREDITOR

B7.55 The Insolvency Rules 1986 (SI 1986 No. 1925) generally fall outside the scope of this work, but the following provision should be noted.

Insolvency Rules 1986, r. 12.18

(1) Where the rules provide for creditors, members of a company or contributories in a company's winding up a right to inspect any documents, whether on the court's file or in the hands of a responsible insolvency practitioner or other person, it is an offence for a person, with the intention of obtaining a sight of documents which he has not under the rules any right to inspect, falsely to claim a status which would entitle him to inspect them.

This offence is triable either way. On conviction on indictment for an offence contrary to r. 12.18, the maximum penalty is two years' imprisonment and/or a fine; on summary conviction, it is six months' imprisonment and/or a fine of the statutory maximum.

OFFENCES RELATING TO DISQUALIFICATION

Disqualification from Company Management etc.

B7.56 **Company Directors Disqualification Act 1986, s. 11**

(1) It is an offence for a person to act as director of a company or directly or indirectly to take part in or be concerned in the promotion, formation or management of a company, without the leave of the court, at a time when—
 (a) he is an undischarged bankrupt, or
 (b) a bankruptcy restrictions order is in force in respect of him.
(2) 'The court' for this purpose is the court by which the person was adjudged bankrupt or, in Scotland, sequestration of his estates was awarded.
(3) In England and Wales, the leave of the court shall not be given unless notice of intention to apply for it has been served on the official receiver; and it is the latter's duty, if he is of opinion that it is contrary to the public interest that the application should be granted, to attend on the hearing of the application and oppose it.

Subsection (1) is printed as substituted by the Enterprise Act 2002, s. 257 and sch. 21.

This offence is triable either way. On conviction on indictment, the maximum penalty is two years' imprisonment and/or a fine; on summary conviction, it is six months' imprisonment and/or a fine of the statutory maximum (Company Directors Disqualification Act 1986, s. 13). Liability is strict; it is no defence that the accused honestly believed that his bankruptcy had been discharged at the relevant time (*Brockley* [1994] Crim LR 671).

Note that the directors of companies which have been wound up as insolvent, unlike bankrupts, will not be disqualified in this way unless a court order is made to that effect.

The scope of the prohibition is illustrated by *Campbell* (1983) 78 Cr App R 95, where it was held that a disqualified person could commit the offence by advising on financial matters and on company restructuring as a 'management consultant'.

Disqualification is clearly to be taken seriously and enforced strictly. Deliberate or reckless infringement will accordingly merit a custodial sentence in the absence of mitigating circumstances (*Theivendran* (1992) 13 Cr App R (S) 601).

Disqualification under the Insolvency Act 1986

It is an offence under the Insolvency Act 1986, s. 31, for a bankrupt who is undischarged or subject to a bankruptcy restrictions order to act as a receiver or manager on behalf of debenture holders, unless appointed by the court, and since such a person is also disqualified from acting as an insolvency practitioner (Insolvency Act 1986, s. 390(4) and (5)), it follows that he commits an offence under s. 389 if he acts as a liquidator, administrator, or trustee in bankruptcy. **B7.57**

SCHEDULE OF OFFENCES UNDER THE INSOLVENCY ACT 1986

Insolvency Act 1986, sch. 10, Abridged **B7.58**

Section	General nature of offence	Mode of prosecution	Punishment
6A(1)	False representation or fraud for purpose of obtaining members' or creditors' approval of proposed voluntary arrangement.	1. On indictment. 2. Summary.	Seven years or a fine; or both. Six months or the statutory maximum; or both.
31	Bankrupt acting as receiver or manager.	1. On indictment. 2. Summary.	Two years or a fine; or both. Six months or the statutory maximum; or both.
89(4)	Director making statutory declaration of company's solvency without reasonable grounds for his opinion.	1. On indictment. 2. Summary.	Two years or a fine; or both. Six months or the statutory maximum; or both.
206(1)	Fraud, etc. in anticipation of winding up.	1. On indictment. 2. Summary	Seven years or a fine; or both. Six months or the statutory maximum; or both.
206(2)	Privity to fraud in anticipation of winding up; fraud, or privity to fraud, after commencement of winding up.	1. On indictment. 2. Summary	Seven years or a fine; or both. Six months or the statutory maximum; or both.
206(5)	Knowingly taking in pawn or pledge, or otherwise receiving, company property.	1. On indictment. 2. Summary.	Seven years or a fine; or both. Six months or the statutory maximum; or both.
207	Officer of company entering into transaction in fraud of company's creditors.	1. On indictment. 2. Summary.	Two years or a fine; or both. Six months or the statutory maximum; or both.

Section	General nature of offence	Mode of prosecution	Punishment
208	Officer of company misconducting himself in course of winding up.	1. On indictment. 2. Summary.	Seven years or a fine; or both. Six months or the statutory maximum; or both.
209	Officer or contributory destroying, falsifying, etc. company's books.	1. On indictment. 2. Summary	Seven years or a fine; or both. Six months or the statutory maximum; or both.
210	Officer of company making material omission from statement relating to company's affairs.	1. On indictment. 2. Summary	Seven years or a fine; or both. Six months or the statutory maximum; or both.
211	False representation or fraud for purposes of obtaining creditors' consent to an agreement in connection with winding up.	1. On indictment. 2. Summary	Seven years or a fine; or both. Six months or the statutory maximum; or both.
216(4)	Contravening restrictions on re-use of name of company in insolvent liquidation.	1. On indictment. 2. Summary	Two years or a fine; or both. Six months or the statutory maximum; or both.
262A(1)	False representation or fraud for purposes of obtaining creditors' approval of proposed voluntary arrangement.	1. On indictment. 2. Summary	Seven years or a fine; or both. Six months or the statutory maximum; or both.
353(1)	Bankrupt failing to disclose property or disposals to official receiver or trustee.	1. On indictment. 2. Summary	Seven years or a fine; or both. Six months or the statutory maximum; or both.
354(1)	Bankrupt failing to deliver property to, or concealing property from, official receiver or trustee.	1. On indictment. 2. Summary	Seven years or a fine; or both. Six months or the statutory maximum; or both.
354(2)	Bankrupt removing property which he is required to deliver to official receiver or trustee.	1. On indictment. 2. Summary	Seven years or a fine; or both. Six months or the statutory maximum; or both.
354(3)	Bankrupt failing to account for loss of substantial part of property.	1. On indictment. 2. Summary	Two years or a fine; or both. Six months or the statutory maximum; or both.
355(1)	Bankrupt failing to deliver books, papers and records to official receiver or trustee.	1. On indictment. 2. Summary	Seven years or a fine; or both. Six months or the statutory maximum; or both.
355(2)	Bankrupt concealing, destroying etc. books, papers or records, or making false entries in them.	1. On indictment. 2. Summary	Seven years or a fine; or both. Six months or the statutory maximum; or both.
355(3)	Bankrupt disposing of, or altering, books papers or records relating to his estate or affairs.	1. On indictment. 2. Summary	Seven years or a fine; or both. Six months or the statutory maximum; or both.
356(1)	Bankrupt making material omission in statement relating to his affairs.	1. On indictment. 2. Summary	Seven years or a fine; or both. Six months or the statutory maximum; or both.
356(2)	Bankrupt making false statement, of failing to inform trustee, where false debt proved.	1. On indictment. 2. Summary	Seven years or a fine; or both. Six months or the statutory maximum; or both.
357	Bankrupt fraudulently disposing of property.	1. On indictment. 2. Summary	Two years or a fine; or both. Six months or the statutory maximum; or both.

Section	General nature of offence	Mode of prosecution	Punishment
358	Bankrupt absconding with property he is required to deliver to official receiver or trustee.	1. On indictment. 2. Summary	Two years or a fine; or both. Six months or the statutory maximum; or both.
359(1)	Bankrupt disposing of property obtained on credit and not paid for.	1. On indictment. 2. Summary	Seven years or a fine; or both. Six months or the statutory maximum; or both.
359(2)	Obtaining property in respect of which money is owed by a bankrupt	1. On indictment. 2. Summary	Seven years or a fine; or both. Six months or the statutory maximum; or both.
360(1)	Bankrupt obtaining credit or engaging in business without disclosing his status or name in which he was made bankrupt.	1. On indictment. 2. Summary	Two years or a fine; or both. Six months or the statutory maximum; or both.
360(3)	Person made bankrupt in Scotland or Northern Ireland obtaining credit, etc. in England and Wales.	1. On indictment. 2. Summary	Two years or a fine; or both. Six months or the statutory maximum; or both.
389	Acting as insolvency practitioner when not qualified.	1. On indictment. 2. Summary	Two years or a fine; or both. Six months or the statutory maximum; or both.
429(5)	Contravening s. 429 in respect of disabilities imposed by county court on revocation of administration.	1. On indictment. 2. Summary	Two years or a fine; or both. Six months or the statutory maximum; or both.

SENTENCING: INSOLVENCY AND BANKRUPTCY OFFENCES

There are relatively few reported sentencing decisions on insolvency and bankruptcy offences. **B7.59** In *Thievendran* (1992) 13 Cr App R (S) 601, the offender pleaded guilty to eight offences contrary to s. 360(1) of the Insolvency Act 1986. Although he had been made bankrupt in 1980, the offender for several years continued to act as a director of a group of companies which he had set up. The companies traded honestly, but were later wound up. The offender was sentenced to nine months' imprisonment and was disqualified from acting as a company director for ten years. The Court of Appeal found that while there had been a 'plain flouting of the order' in this case, no dishonesty had been established. The prison term was accordingly reduced to six months and suspended for two years; the disqualification period was halved. In contrast, in *Vanderwell* [1998] 1 Cr App R (S) 439, the offender pleaded guilty to two counts of being concerned in the management of a company while an undischarged bankrupt, one count of obtaining credit as a bankrupt, one of obtaining by deception, one of failing to keep proper business accounts and one of concealment of debts. The offender had been made bankrupt in 1978 and again in 1986. He was sentenced to imprisonment in 1990 and disqualified from acting as a company director. On his release he again started trading and accumulated debts of £25,000. The Court of Appeal accepted that the offender was 'thoroughly dishonest', and upheld a total prison sentence of four years and three months, together with a company director disqualification for 15 years. See also *Thompson* (1992) 14 Cr App R (S) 89, *Teece* (1993) 15 Cr App R (S) 302, *Dawes* [1997] 1 Cr App R (S) 149 and *Ashby* [1998] 2 Cr App R (S) 37. In *Mungroo* [1998] BPIR 784, the Court of Appeal stated that a bankrupt offender, against whom a judgment debt had been entered, who concealed assets and used them to pay personal debts, could expect to receive a custodial sentence, even if of previous exemplary character.

Section B8 Damage to Property

SIMPLE CRIMINAL DAMAGE

B8.1 **Criminal Damage Act 1971, s. 1**

(1) A person who without lawful excuse destroys or damages any property belonging to another intending to destroy or damage any such property or being reckless as to whether any such property would be destroyed or damaged shall be guilty of an offence.

The CDA 1998, s. 30, creates a racially or religiously aggravated form of this offence which carries a higher maximum penalty (see **B8.38**). For the meaning of racially or religiously aggravated, see **B11.160** *et seq.*

Procedure

B8.2 Criminal damage is generally triable either way (MCA 1980, s. 17 and sch. 1, para. 29). When tried on indictment it is a class 3 offence. However, where the value of the property alleged to have been destroyed or the value of the alleged damage is not more than £5,000 (unless the destruction or damage was by fire and thus constitutes arson, see **B8.20** to **B8.25**), criminal damage (unless charged in the racially aggravated form) is treated as if it were triable only summarily (MCA 1980, s. 22 and sch. 2). This does not convert it into a summary offence for all purposes and thus there can still be an attempt to commit low value criminal damage even though only an attempt to commit an indictable offence is caught by the Criminal Attempts Act 1981, s. 1(4) (*Bristol Justices, ex parte E* [1999] 1 WLR 390). For consideration of the mode of trial for criminal damage, including the method of determining the value involved, see **D6**. Even if the value involved is not more than £5,000, a count for criminal damage may be included in an indictment for another offence in the circumstances set out in the CJA 1988, s. 40 (see **D11**).

The guidelines in the *Consolidated Criminal Practice Direction*, para. V.51.18, *Mode of trial* (see **appendix** 7), which apply where the value involved is more than £5,000, state that, in general, cases should be tried summarily unless the court considers that one or more of the following features is present in the case *and* that its sentencing powers are insufficient:

(a) Deliberate fire-raising (an offence under the Criminal Damage Act, s. 1(1), committed by destroying or damaging property by fire is charged as arson — see **B8.20** to **B8.25**).
(b) Committed by a group.
(c) Damage of a high value.
(d) The offence has clear racial motivation.

The aggravated form of the offence is triable either way, irrespective of the value of the damage. Even if the value is not more than £5,000, simple criminal damage is available on indictment as an alternative verdict if the aggravated element is not made out (*Fennell* [2000] 1 WLR 2011).

Indictment

Statement of Offence B8.3

Criminal damage contrary to section 1(1) of the Criminal Damage Act 1971

Particulars of Offence

A on or about the . . . day of . . . did without lawful excuse damage [or destroy] a glass window, having a value of £120, belonging to V intending to damage [or destroy] such property or being reckless as to whether such property would be damaged [or destroyed]

Sentence

For the maximum penalty and for sentencing guidelines, see **B8.36** to **B8.40**. B8.4

Meaning of 'Damage'

'Damage' is left undefined in the Criminal Damage Act 1971. The courts have construed the term liberally. Criminal damage is not limited to permanent damage, so smearing mud on the walls of a police cell may be criminal damage. See *Roe v Kingerlee* [1986] Crim LR 735, where it was also said that: 'What constitutes criminal damage is a matter of fact and degree and it is for the justices, applying their common sense, to decide whether what occurred was damage or not'. In *Fiak* [2005] EWCA Crim 2381, where a blanket was soaked (but not soiled) with water from a toilet in a police cell and three cell floors were flooded, a conclusion that the blanket and floor were not damaged (even though the damage was remediable) 'would have been incomprehensible'. B8.5

Older (persuasive) authorities under pre-1971 enactments further illustrate the breadth of the notion of damage: see, for example, *Roper v Knott* [1898] 1 QB 868 (milk damaged by adulteration with water) and *Tacey* (1821) Russ & Ry 452 (machine damaged by removal of essential part, although if the constituent part or parts are not themselves damaged it is important to charge damage to the machine, i.e., to the whole rather than to the parts — see *Woolcock* [1977] Crim LR 104 and 161). *Hardman v Chief Constable of Avon and Somerset* [1986] Crim LR 330 is a more modern illustration of the scope of the meaning of 'damage', in which water-soluble pavement paintings were held to constitute damage to the pavement.

The damage need not be tangible or visible if it affects the value or performance of the property: see *Cox v Riley* (1986) 83 Cr App R 54, where a plastic circuit card for controlling a computerised saw was held to have been damaged by the erasure of the programs electronically written on it. Nor did it matter that the damage was not permanent in that it could be remedied, as restoring the programs necessitated 'time, labour and expense'. See now *Whiteley* (1991) 93 Cr App R 25, where a computer disk was held to be damaged by the addition and deletion of files. The interference with the disk amounted to an 'impairment of the value or usefulness of the disk to the owner'. These two decisions remain significant for the general meaning of damage but are overtaken as regards their own particular facts by the Computer Misuse Act 1990, s. 3(6), which restricts the meaning of damage for the purposes of the Criminal Damage Act 1971 where it is done by 'the modification of the contents of a computer' (see further **B18.12**).

Meaning of 'Property'

Criminal Damage Act 1971, s. 10 B8.6

(1) In this Act 'property' means property of a tangible nature, whether real or personal, including money and—
  (a) including wild creatures which have been tamed or are ordinarily kept in captivity . . .; but
  (b) not including mushrooms growing wild on any land or flowers, fruit or foliage or a plant growing wild on any land.

This definition of property is wider than that in the Theft Act 1968, s. 4 (see **B4.10** to

B4.16), in that it lacks the restrictions on stealing land in that section, but, on the other hand, is narrower in that it does not include 'things in action and other intangible property'. Thus, land can be damaged by, e.g., dumping on it, even though it cannot be stolen (see discussion in *Cox v Riley* (1986) 83 Cr App 54 and **B8.5**). However, a copyright cannot be damaged by infringing it (contrast the offences under the Copyright, Designs and Patents Act 1988, s. 107), even though it can in theory be stolen. In *Cox v Riley*, even though the erased program might be said to be 'intangible property', the property alleged to be damaged was the circuit card and not the erased program itself. See also *Whiteley* (1991) 93 Cr App R 25, discussed in **B8.5**. (Note that both *Whiteley* and *Cox v Riley* have now to be read in the light of the Computer Misuse Act 1990, s. 3(6); see **B18.11**).

Meaning of 'Belonging to Another'

B8.7 **Criminal Damage Act 1971, s. 10**

(2) Property shall be treated for the purposes of this Act as belonging to any person—
(a) having the custody or control of it;
(b) having in it any proprietary right or interest (not being an equitable interest arising only from an agreement to transfer or grant an interest); or
(c) having a charge on it.

The effect of this provision (as with theft, see **B4.17** to **B4.23**) is that an owner can be guilty of criminal damage to his own property if at the same time it belongs to someone else within the extended meaning of s. 10.

Mens Rea

B8.8 This is satisfied by either intention or recklessness, and it is the latter, wider concept which has proved crucial. It seemed clear for 20 years following *Metropolitan Police Commissioner v Caldwell* [1982] AC 341 that recklessness in this context did not require subjective appreciation of the risk of causing damage, but was also satisfied by a failure to consider an obvious risk. In *Metropolitan Police Commissioner v Caldwell* Lord Diplock gave the following model direction (at p. 354):

> . . . a person charged with an offence under section 1(1) of the Criminal Damage Act 1971 is 'reckless as to whether any such property would be destroyed or damaged' if (1) he does an act which in fact creates an obvious risk that property will be destroyed or damaged and (2) when he does the act he either has not given any thought to the possibility of there being any such risk or has recognised that there was some risk involved and has nonetheless gone on to do it.

The risk needed only be obvious in the sense that it would have been obvious to the reasonable man, not to the accused if he or she had stopped to think (*Elliott v C* [1983] 1 WLR 939), nor to a person of the age of the accused or sharing the accused's characteristics (*R (Stephen Malcolm)* (1984) 79 Cr App R 334; *Miller* [1983] 2 AC 161). However in *G* [2004] 1 AC 1034, the House of Lords has overruled its own previous decision in *Caldwell* and restored a subjective test to the meaning of recklessness for the purposes of the Criminal Damage Act 1971 as it ruled that this had always been Parliament's intention.

Lord Bingham adopted the meaning of recklessness given in the Law Commission's Draft Criminal Code (Law Com. No. 177) to the effect that

> A person acts recklessly . . . . with respect to—
> (i) a circumstance when he is aware of a risk that it exists or will exist;
> (ii) a result when he is aware of a risk that it will occur;
> (iii) and it is, in the circumstances known to him, unreasonable to take the risk.

For a more detailed analysis of the implications of this return to a subjective test of recklessness, see **A2.4** to **A2.6**. Suffice to say here that in many cases the change may not make all that much practical difference; the jury will normally conclude in relation to most if not all obvious risks that the accused was actually aware of the risk and thus liable even under a subjective test. The notion of closing one's mind to an obvious risk is also likely to be pressed into service where, as in the case of *Parker* [1977] 1 WLR 600, referred to seemingly approvingly by Lord Bingham as a case of conscious awareness of risk, the accused claims not to have been aware of a risk because of his anger or other unsympathetic emotion. The concept of closing one's mind was referred to in the quite remarkable case of *Booth v CPS* (2006) 170 JP 305, which concerned the damage caused by a pedestrian to the bonnet of a vehicle into the path of which he suddenly stepped out. The Divisional Court upheld the findings of magistrates that the accused pedestrian was aware:

> of the risks associated with running into the road, namely the risk of a collision and the damage to property. Aware of those risks, he then deliberately put them out of his mind and, for reasons of his own, ran out into the path of a car.

One might have thought that the more obvious risk in such a case, as argued by the defence, is one of risk of injury to the pedestrian but the Court was not sympathetic to arguments which they regarded as, in effect, inviting them to characterise the particular findings of the magistrates as perverse.

Where the accused lacks the ability to appreciate an obvious risk (e.g., as in *G* itself, because of youth, or as in *Stephenson* [1979] QB 695, because of mental illness), the subjective test will clearly make a major difference and the courts will no longer be compelled to convict because of what the accused ought to have been aware of had he had the degree of awareness of the standard reasonable man (see *Elliott v C* and *R (Stephen Malcolm)*, both of which can now be regarded as overruled along with *Caldwell*).

It will be noted that the test of recklessness refers to both circumstances and consequences. In criminal damage cases it will normally be the awareness of risk of a consequence — damage to property — which will be relevant. In this connection it appears from *G* that it is the awareness of the risk of damage to the property named in the charge that is relevant, in that case damage to the building rather than simply to the wheelie bins (given that Lord Bingham said (at [33]) that 'they would have had little defence' to a charge of recklessly damaging the wheelie-bins). On the other hand it would not be necessary to foresee the extent of the damage (i.e. in *G*, £1 million worth of damage to the building).

Awareness of risk of circumstances can also be relevant however, the circumstance being that the property was 'belonging to another'. If A decides to destroy all his papers in his filing cabinet but is aware of the risk that some of his flat-mate's valuable papers may also be in the cabinet and may also be destroyed, he is aware of the risk of a circumstance, that some of the property belongs to another. However, if he is not aware of any such risk and believes he is simply destroying his own property, he is not guilty under a subjective test (see *Smith* [1974] QB 354 for an analogous example where the mistake was one of law).

Meaning of 'Without Lawful Excuse'

The meaning of 'lawful excuse' is specially provided for in relation to this offence in the Criminal Damage Act 1971, s. 5 (which, however, is not applicable to the aggravated offence of criminal damage under s. 1(2) — see **B8.11** to **B8.19**). **B8.9**

Criminal Damage Act 1971, s. 5

(2) A person charged with an offence to which this section applies shall, whether or not he would be treated for the purposes of this Act as having a lawful excuse apart from this subsection, be treated for those purposes as having a lawful excuse—

(a) if at the time of the act or acts alleged to constitute the offence he believed that the person or persons whom he believed to be entitled to consent to the destruction of or damage to the property in question had so consented, or would have so consented to it if he or they had known of the destruction or damage and its circumstances; or

(b) if he destroyed or damaged or threatened to destroy or damage the property in question or, in the case of a charge of an offence under section 3 above, intended to use or cause or permit the use of something to destroy or damage it, in order to protect property belonging to himself or another or a right or interest in property which was or which he believed to be vested in himself or another, and at the time of the act or acts alleged to constitute the offence he believed—

(i) that the property, right or interest was in immediate need of protection; and
(ii) that the means of protection adopted or proposed to be adopted were or would be reasonable having regard to all the circumstances.

(3) For the purposes of this section it is immaterial whether a belief is justified or not if it is honestly held.
(4) For the purposes of subsection (2) above a right or interest in property includes any right or privilege in or over land, whether created by grant, licence or otherwise.
(5) This section shall not be construed as casting doubt on any defence recognised by law as a defence to criminal charges.

The words in s. 5(2) 'whether or not he would be treated for the purposes of this Act as having a lawful excuse apart from this subsection' together with s. 5(5), indicate that the section is not intended to be an exhaustive account of the circumstances of lawful excuse. Thus, general defences such as duress or prevention of crime are not excluded (cf. *Baker* [1997] Crim LR 497) but they do require the accused to be acting reasonably and damaging perimeter fencing in order to challenge the lawful storage of nuclear weapons was held not be reasonable by the Divisional Court in *Hutchinson v DPP* (2000) *Independent*, 20 November 2000). A motorist who damages a wheel clamp to free his car, having parked on another's property knowing of the risk of being clamped, does not have a lawful excuse (*Lloyd v DPP* [1992] 1 All ER 982: contrast the entirely different approach to wheel clamping in the Scottish case *Black v Carmichael* (1992) *The Times*, 25 June 1992).

Section 5 specifically covers two alternative types of belief which are outlined in more detail in s. 5(2):

(a) belief in consent; or
(b) belief in the immediate necessity to protect property.

B8.10 **Subjective Nature of Belief** Section 5(3) emphasises that the question is the purely subjective one of whether the belief is honestly held, not whether it is justified or reasonable. In *Jaggard v Dickinson* [1981] QB 527, the accused, due to intoxication, mistakenly believed she would have had the owner's consent to breaking a window in order to gain access to a house (unfortunately she tried to break into the wrong house). The Divisional Court quashed her conviction, saying (per Mustill J, at pp. 531–2): '. . . the court is required by section 5(3) to focus on the existence of the belief, not its intellectual soundness; and a belief can be just as much honestly held if it is induced by intoxication, as if it stems from stupidity, forgetfulness or inattention'.

Although the test under s. 5(2)(b)(ii) is clearly *subjective* and the question is not whether the accused's action is *in fact* reasonable (contrast *Hutchinson v DPP* above) but whether the accused *believed* it to be reasonable, whether an accused is acting 'in order to protect property' under s. 5(2)(b) does seem to have an objective aspect. In *Hunt* (1977) 66 Cr App R 105, the accused set fire to bedding to draw attention to a defective fire alarm in old people's accommodation which the court ruled was not 'in order to protect property', despite the accused's belief that it would ultimately have that effect. See further *Hill* (1988) 89 Cr App R 74, where the accused's beliefs about the ultimate effects of damaging perimeter fencing at a United States naval base were held not to amount to a purpose of protecting property, or to a belief that property was in *imminent* need of protection under s. 5(2)(b)(i). See however *Chamberlain v Lindon* [1998] 1 WLR 1252 for a case where these two requirements were satisfied. There is no requirement that the threat to property believed to be in need of protection is a threat of *unlawful* damage (*Jones* [2005] QB 259).

If the accused does hold a belief provided for in s. 5, it is immaterial as far as his liability for criminal damage is concerned that he has some ulterior fraudulent or criminal purpose. Thus, in *Denton* [1981] 1 WLR 1446, the accused set fire to the cotton mill where he worked, because he believed he had been asked to do so by his employer with a view to gaining the insurance money on the property. The Court of Appeal quashed his conviction for criminal damage, pointing out that if the owner himself had caused the damage he would have committed no offence (under s. 1(1), though other charges might be possible), since he was not damaging property 'belonging to another', and hence the accused, who believed he was acting on behalf of the owner and with his consent, should be in no worse position. In fact, the 'employer' (an individual) in this case was not strictly the owner of the property, which legally belonged to the company, a separate legal entity. This did not particularly matter on the facts, since it was conceded that the accused honestly believed that his 'employer' was the person 'entitled to consent' within s. 5(2)(a). Contrast *Appleyard* (1985) 81 Cr App R 319, where a managing director was convicted of destroying the company's store, and was not allowed to claim that he himself was the person entitled to consent to the damage. It would seem, therefore, that the belief under s. 5(2)(a) must relate to some other person having the right to consent and not to the accused himself. If a person mistakenly believes he is the actual owner (as opposed to being merely the person entitled to consent), then he has a defence, not under s. 5(2) but because he lacks *mens rea* (see *Smith* [1974] QB 354).

AGGRAVATED CRIMINAL DAMAGE

Criminal Damage Act 1971, s. 1 **B8.11**

(2) A person who without lawful excuse destroys or damages any property, whether belonging to himself or another—
   (a) intending to destroy or damage any property or being reckless as to whether any property would be destroyed or damaged; and
   (b) intending by the destruction or damage to endanger the life of another or being reckless as to whether the life of another would be thereby endangered;

shall be guilty of an offence.

Procedure

Aggravated criminal damage is triable only on indictment. It is a class 3 offence. **B8.12**

Indictment

Statement of Offence **B8.13**

Destroying [or damaging] property with intent to endanger life [or being reckless as to whether life would be endangered] contrary to section 1(2) of the Criminal Damage Act 1971

Particulars of Offence

A on or about the . . . day of . . . did without lawful excuse damage [or destroy] a motor vehicle belonging to V, intending to damage [or destroy] such vehicle or being reckless as to whether such vehicle would be damaged [or destroyed] and intending by such damage [or destruction] to endanger the life of V or being reckless as to whether the life of V would be thereby endangered

Alternative Verdicts

It is submitted that in some cases, on an indictment for aggravated criminal damage, it may be possible for the jury to return an alternative verdict of simple criminal damage, pursuant to the Criminal Law Act 1967, s. 3 (**D18.41** ***et seq.***). However, this is problematic in that it will be possible only where: **B8.14**

(a) it is specifically alleged that the property in question belonged not to the accused but to another (which is not an essential averment under the Criminal Damage Act 1971, s. 1(2), but is under s. 1(1)); and

(b) there is no issue as to lawful excuse (the meaning of which differs as between the two offences, inasmuch as the provisions of the Criminal Damage Act 1971, s. 5, do not apply to offences under s. 1(2)).

It is therefore always appropriate to add an alternative count (which may be done even where the value of the property is less than £5,000 — see CJA 1988, s. 40, and **D11.15**). In the absence of such an alternative count, trial judges may be reluctant to leave the alternative to the jury (see generally **D18.58** ***et seq***).

Sentence

B8.15 For the maximum penalty and for sentencing guidelines, see **B8.36** to **B8.39**.

Relationship to Simple Criminal Damage

B8.16 Aggravated criminal damage is identical with the offence under the Criminal Damage Act 1971, s. 1(1), as far as relates to the meaning of damage and property (see **B8.5** and **B8.6**), but differs in three main respects:

(a) The presence of the aggravating ulterior *mens rea* of intention to endanger life or recklessness as to whether life would be endangered.

(b) The fact that the offence can be committed irrespective of whether the property 'belongs to another'.

(c) The inapplicability of s. 5 of the Act to the meaning of 'lawful excuse'.

B8.17 *Mens Rea* The overruling of *Metropolitan Police Commissioner v Caldwell* [1982] AC 341 (see **B8.8**) applies equally to this offence and therefore it must be shown in accordance with *G* [2004] 1 AC 1034 that the accused must be subjectively aware of the risk of endangering the life of another. Again, the more obvious the risk of endangering life, the more likely that the jury will conclude that the accused was aware of the risk unless he gives some plausible explanation of why he would not have appreciated the obvious. According to the Court of Appeal in *Heard* [2007] 3 All ER 306 (see **A3.10**), recklessness as to endangering life is not a basic intent but is a specific (ulterior) intent and it would thus seem that voluntary intoxication can be admitted in order to show that the accused did not appreciate the risk of endangering life.

In the case of attempt to commit an offence under the Criminal Damage Act 1971, s. 1(2), recklessness as to life being endangered will suffice even though a specific intent to cause damage is also required (*A-G's Ref (No. 3 of 1992)* [1994] 1 WLR 409).

B8.18 **Requirement that Danger to Life Result from Damage Intended** The accused must be at least reckless as to causing damage, as to endangering life and also as to whether life would be endangered *as a result of the damage.* The offence was thus not made out in *Steer* [1988] AC 111, where the accused shot through a window behind which two people were standing. Although the accused was reckless as to whether life would be endangered, the danger to life was not caused by the damage to the window but by the firing of the bullet. Compare *Webster* [1995] 2 All ER 168, where damaging the windscreen of a moving car or ramming the car was held to be capable of endangering life as a result of the damage. Furthermore, it is the damage which the accused intended, or as to which he was reckless, which is relevant, rather than the actual damage which happens to be caused. See *Dudley* [1989] Crim LR 57, where only trivial damage, not likely to endanger life, was *actually* caused, but the appellant's conviction was upheld since he created a *risk* of much more serious damage which was capable of endangering life.

B8.19 **Meaning of 'Without Lawful Excuse'** The partial definition of 'lawful excuse' in the Criminal Damage Act 1971, s. 5, is not applicable, because belief in the owner's consent or of the immediate need to protect *property* cannot justify the endangering of human life. However, 'without lawful excuse' in any other sense remains part of the definition of the offence so that, e.g., damaging property in lawful self-defence would not be criminal even if it endangers the aggressor's (or possibly even a third party's) life, provided that it was reasonable to do so.

ARSON

Criminal Damage Act 1971, s. 1 **B8.20**

(3) An offence committed under this section by destroying or damaging property by fire shall be charged as arson.

Procedure

Simple arson contrary to the Criminal Damage Act 1971, s. 1(1) and (3), is triable either way (MCA 1980, s. 17 and sch. 1, para. 29). When tried on indictment it is a class 4 offence. For the guidelines for determining mode of trial see **B8.2**. The value involved in simple arson does not cause the MCA 1980, s. 22, to restrict the mode of trial because arson is, by sch. 2 to the MCA 1980, not an offence to which s. 22 applies. **B8.21**

Aggravated arson contrary to the Criminal Damage Act 1971, s. 1(2) and (3), is triable only on indictment. It is a class 3 offence.

Indictment

The wording of the Criminal Damage Act 1971, s. 1(3) (see **B8.20**), has been held to be mandatory in the Crown Court and a charge of criminal damage 'contrary to s. 1(1) plus (3) of the Act' was held to be a nullity in *Booth* [1999] Crim LR 144. However, *Booth* was distinguished in *Drayton* (2005) 169 JP 593 in the context of a charge in a magistrates' court. The charge of damage by fire under s. 1(1), (3) and (4) was held to be a valid one to which the accused could lawfully plead guilty and on which he could be lawfully committed for sentence. The important issue was that the allegation was at least identified as 'damage *by fire*' rather than by the use of the specific word 'arson' with which it was synonymous, although it would be preferable to use the word 'arson'. Hedley J said (at [11]) that: **B8.22**

> the essence of section 1(3), the mischief which it is designed to address, is that the defendant shall know that he is facing an allegation of damage by fire, because by section 1(4) the penalties in relation to damage by fire are different and significantly potentially more severe than those of simple criminal damage by other means.

In *Booth*, the charge in the Crown Court was conspiracy to incite a variety of forms of criminal damage including damage by fire but it appears that the indictment whilst mentioning s. 1(3) did not specifically mention either 'arson' or 'damage *by fire*'. The focus in *Drayton* was on damage by fire and nothing else and, in describing the offence alleged in ordinary language avoiding technical terms like arson and giving reasonable information as to the nature of the charge, it complied with the requirements of the CrimPR, r. 7.2. Hedley J left open the position in the Crown Court saying (at [10]):

> Clearly on indictment where the rules require both a statement of offence and particulars of offence it is desirable that the word arson should continue to be used in the statement of offence. Whether the absence of that word arson from a count that plainly alleges damage by fire and nothing else invalidates the count must await decision as and when that point arises.

Statement of Offence

Arson contrary to section 1(1) and (3) of the Criminal Damage Act 1971

Particulars of Offence

A on or about the . . . day of . . . did without lawful excuse damage by fire a motor vehicle, having a value of £3,500, belonging to V intending to damage such vehicle by fire or being reckless as to whether such vehicle would be damaged by fire

An offence under s. 1(2) by fire must also be charged as arson. In such a case there should be separate counts of arson with intent to endanger life and arson being reckless as to whether life would be endangered (see *Hoof* (1980) 72 Cr App 126; *sed quaere*, the two forms of *mens rea* do not mean that the section creates two offences, and, of course, the maximum penalty is the same).

First Count

Statement of Offence

Arson contrary to section 1(2) and (3) of the Criminal Damage Act 1971

Particulars of Offence

A on or about the . . . day of . . . did without lawful excuse damage by fire a motor vehicle, having a value of £3,500, belonging to V intending to damage such vehicle by fire and intending by such damage to endanger the life of V

Second Count

As above, but alleging instead of the intent to endanger life: '. . . and being reckless as to whether the life of V would thereby be endangered'

Alternative Verdicts

B8.23 See **B8.14**. On indictment for arson under the Criminal Damage Act 1971, s. 1(1) and (3) or s. 1(2) and (3), it is submitted that the jury should not be invited to return an alternative verdict of guilty of criminal damage other than by fire, even under the corresponding subsection of s. 1, because of the different nature of the *actus reus*. In the unlikely event of doubt as to the method of causing the damage, an alternative count should be added.

Sentence

B8.24 For the maximum penalty and for sentencing guidelines, see **B8.36** to **B8.40**.

Elements

B8.25 Arson differs from simple or aggravated criminal damage only in that the destruction or damage to the property must be 'by fire'. *Quaere* whether this might extend to damage caused, for example, by water in saving the property from imminent destruction by the fire, or by a fall resulting from the collapse due to fire of a structure on which the property had stood.

THREATS TO DESTROY OR DAMAGE PROPERTY

B8.26 **Criminal Damage Act 1971, s. 2**

A person who without lawful excuse makes to another a threat, intending that that other would fear it would be carried out,—

(a) to destroy or damage any property belonging to that other or a third person; or

(b) to destroy or damage his own property in a way which he knows is likely to endanger the life of that other or a third person;

shall be guilty of an offence.

Procedure

B8.27 A threat to destroy or damage property is triable either way (MCA 1980, s. 17 and sch. 1, para. 29). When tried on indictment it is a class 3 offence.

Indictment

Statement of Offence B8.28

Threatening to destroy property contrary to section 2(a) of the Criminal Damage Act 1971

Particulars of Offence

A on or about the . . . day of . . . did without lawful excuse make a threat to V to destroy a motor vehicle belonging to V [or X] intending that V would fear that the threat would be carried out

Sentence

For the maximum penalty see **B8.36**. B8.29

Elements

For the meaning of 'without lawful excuse', see **B8.9**, but note that by virtue of the Criminal Damage Act 1971, s. 5(1), the partial definition of 'lawful excuse' does not apply where the accused knows that the threatened damage is likely to endanger life. This is no doubt for the same sorts of reasons that s. 5 does not apply to aggravated criminal damage under s. 1(2). B8.30

There is no requirement that the threat be carried out or be capable of being carried out immediately, or that the accused intended to carry it out or that the person threatened *actually* fears that it will be carried out, provided that the accused *intends* that there should be such fear.

A threat to set oneself on fire may come within s. 2(a) if, objectively considered, it constitutes a threat that another's property may be destroyed or damaged as a consequence (*Cakmak* [2002] 2 Cr App R 158).

POSSESSION WITH INTENT TO DESTROY OR DAMAGE PROPERTY

Criminal Damage Act 1971, s. 3 B8.31

A person who has anything in his custody or under his control intending without lawful excuse to use it or cause or permit another to use it—
(a) to destroy or damage any property belonging to some other person; or
(b) to destroy or damage his own or the user's property in a way which he knows is likely to endanger the life of some other person;
shall be guilty of an offence.

Procedure

Possession of an article with intent to destroy or damage property is triable either way (MCA 1980, s. 17 and sch. 1, para. 29). When tried on indictment it is a class 3 offence. B8.32

Indictment

Statement of Offence B8.33

Possession of an article with intent to destroy [or damage] property contrary to section 3 of the Criminal Damage Act 1971

Particulars of Offence

A on or about the . . . day of . . . did have in his custody [or under his control] a can of spray paint intending without lawful excuse to use it [or cause or permit X to use it] to damage a motor vehicle belonging to V

Sentence

B8.34 For the maximum penalty, see **B8.36**.

Elements

B8.35 The essence of the offence is the intention to use the article, *any article*, or to cause or permit it to be used, to cause damage. A conditional intention to so use it if given circumstances arise will suffice (*Buckingham* (1976) 63 Cr App R 159).

The partial definition of 'lawful excuse' in the Criminal Damage Act 1971, s. 5, is applicable only to the form of the offence in s. 3(a) and not to that in s. 3(b), although it is still open to the accused to put forward a lawful excuse independently of s. 5.

The Criminal Damage Act 1971, s. 6, enables the police to search for articles used, or intended to be used, to cause criminal damage.

Criminal Damage Act 1971, s. 6

(1) If it is made to appear by information on oath before a justice of the peace that there is reasonable cause to believe that any person has in his custody or under his control or on his premises anything which there is reasonable cause to believe has been used or is intended for use without lawful excuse—
 (a) to destroy or damage property belonging to another; or
 (b) to destroy or damage any property in a way likely to endanger the life of another,
 the justice may grant a warrant authorising any constable to search for and seize that thing.

(2) A constable who is authorised under this section to search premises for anything, may enter (if need be by force) and search the premises accordingly and may seize anything which he believes to have been used or to be intended to be used as aforesaid.

(3) The Police (Property) Act 1897 (disposal of property in the possession of the police) shall apply to property which has come into the possession of the police under this section as it applies to property which has come into the possession of the police in the circumstances mentioned in that Act.

SENTENCING: OFFENCES INVOLVING DAMAGE TO PROPERTY

Maximum Penalties

B8.36 Criminal damage, with intent to endanger life or recklessness whether life is endangered: Life imprisonment (Criminal Damage Act 1971, s. 4(1)).

Criminal damage: 10 years (Criminal Damage Act 1971, s. 4(2)) on indictment; six months or a fine not exceeding the statutory maximum, or both, summarily. If, however, damage is quantified at less than £5,000, so that the offence is treated as triable summarily only: three months, a fine not exceeding level 4 on the standard scale, or both.

Racially or religiously aggravated criminal damage: 14 years on indictment (CDA 1998, s. 30(2)); six months or a fine not exceeding the statutory maximum, or both, summarily.

Arson (where either of the above offences is committed by fire): Life imprisonment (Criminal Damage Act 1971, s. 4(1)) on indictment; where criminal damage by fire, but not criminal damage with intent or recklessness whether life is endangered, six months or a fine not exceeding the statutory maximum, or both, summarily.

Threat to destroy or damage property: 10 years (Criminal Damage Act 1971, s. 4(2)) on indictment; six months or a fine not exceeding the statutory maximum, or both, summarily.

Possessing article with intent to destroy or damage property: 10 years (Criminal Damage Act 1971, s. 4(2)) on indictment; six months or a fine not exceeding the statutory maximum, or both, summarily.

Sentencing Guidelines (Basic Offence)

Where tried summarily, the Magistrates' Courts Guidelines (2004) indicate the following for a first-time offender pleading not guilty: B8.37

Aggravating Factors For example deliberate; group offence; serious damage; targeting; vulnerable victim; offence committed on bail; relevant previous convictions and any failures to respond to previous sentences.

Mitigating Factors For example impulsive action; minor damage; provocation.

Guideline: Is discharge or fine appropriate?

The guideline fine is Starting Point C (see **E17.5**).

There are few Court of Appeal decisions relating to simple criminal damage. In *Bowles* (1988) 10 Cr App R (S) 146, a sentence of 14 days' imprisonment was upheld in a case where the offender daubed paint over the door and surrounding walls of South Africa House, as a political protest. In *Toomey* (1993) 14 Cr App R (S) 42, the offender smashed the windows and door of a restaurant after an argument with the owner. Customers were in the restaurant at the time and over £2,000 worth of damage was done. Eighteen months' imprisonment was reduced to 12 months on appeal. Racial or religious aggravation cannot be taken into account by the sentencer when sentencing for the basic offence of criminal damage. To do so would infringe the principle that the offender must not be sentenced for an offence for which he has not been charged and convicted (see *McGillivray* [2005] Crim LR 484). Where there is evidence that racial or religious aggravation was present, the aggravated form of the offence should be charged.

B Part B Offences

Sentencing Guidelines (Racially or Religiously Aggravated Form of Offence)

The Magistrates' Courts Guidelines (2004) provide a higher guideline for this offence when tried summarily than for the basic offence, the guideline being whether the offence is serious enough for a community penalty. B8.38

The Court of Appeal indicated in *Saunders* [2000] 1 Cr App R 458 that, when sentencing for the racially aggravated form of an offence the sentencer may usefully consider the appropriate sentence for the offence in the absence of racial aggravation and then add a further term for the racial element. See further **B2.26**. In *Johnston* [2006] 1 Cr App R (S) 665, a sentence of six years' detention in a young offender institution was upheld for racially aggravated criminal damage in the form of damaging headstones in a Jewish cemetery, combined with other racially aggravated offences. Sixty-two headstones had been smashed or pushed over, with damage estimated at £100,000. The judge indicated that the sentence for the basic offence would have been three years, with a further three years to reflect the racial element. The Court of Appeal noted that the case contained a number of high-level aggravating features, and had clearly been calculated to cause maximum distress to the families of those whose graves had been targeted.

Sentencing Guidelines: Criminal Damage with Intent to Endanger Life etc.

In *Dodd* [1997] 1 Cr App R (S) 127, the offender pleaded guilty to damaging property being reckless whether life was endangered, and to driving while disqualified. He had driven his car, at between 35 and 40 mph through the glass-fronted doors of Plymouth Magistrates' Court and through inner doors, the car coming to rest against the rear wall of the building, causing £34,000 worth of damage. Nobody was injured. A sentence of four years' imprisonment for the criminal damage offence was upheld by the Court of Appeal. In *Kavanagh* [1998] 1 Cr App R (S) 241 the offender, after an argument with his partner, released gas from a gas fire and threatened to blow up their flat. The police were called and the threat was not carried out. A sentence of four years' imprisonment was reduced to three years on appeal. See also *McCann* [2000] 1 Cr App R (S) 495. B8.39

Sentencing Guidelines: Arson

B8.40 The Court of Appeal cases taken together indicate that there should be a psychiatric report available on the offender in cases of arson, and that where there is appropriate psychiatric evidence, a medical disposal, such as probation order with a condition of psychiatric treatment or a hospital order, may be passed. Minor cases can be dealt with by non-custodial sentences. Otherwise, in the absence of mitigation, a custodial sentence will generally be appropriate. Longer custodial sentences are appropriate where substantial damage has been caused, or where death or serious injury has been risked by the offender.

In *A-G's Ref (No. 66 of 1997)* [2000] 1 Cr App R (S) 149, a case of arson with intent to endanger life, the Court of Appeal said that a sentence within the range of eight to ten years following a trial would have been appropriate in a case where the offender set fires in a bungalow in which several members of his family were asleep. The fire was extinguished before much damage had been done. Rose LJ said that the offence showed clear evidence of intention and planning. See also *A-G's Ref (Nos. 78, 79 and 85 of 1998)* [2000] 1 Cr App R (S) 371, where a sentence of eight years was said by the Court of Appeal to be at the lower end of the sentencing bracket for an offence of arson with intent to endanger life. The offender threw petrol bombs at a house, causing grave injuries to two small children who lived there. The injuries were likely to lead to extensive and permanent scarring.

Four years' imprisonment for an offence of arson being reckless whether life was endangered was upheld in *Harding* [2000] 1 Cr App R (S) 327. The offender set fire to a semi-detached house when drunk and following a violent argument with his wife. The wife left, taking the children with her, and the offender then started fires in different rooms of the house, causing extensive fire and smoke damage. The adjoining house, occupied by an elderly lady, was also damaged. Four years was appropriate for an offence of arson in *Elliott* (1989) 11 Cr App R (S) 67, where the offender set fire to a depot where he had formerly been employed, causing damage to the extent of £1,811,000. Two years' detention in a young offender institution was upheld in *Letham* [2000] 1 Cr App R (S) 185, where the 16-year-old offender pleaded guilty to arson. He had started a fire at a school where he had formerly been a pupil, causing damage to the extent of £400,000. Sullivan J in the Court of Appeal said that if the offender had not been young and of good character a significantly longer sentence would have been justified.

A combination order was held to have been an unduly lenient sentence in *A-G's Ref (No. 35 of 1996)* [1997] 1 Cr App R (S) 350, where the offender, who had fallen into rent arrears, started a fire in his flat which caused £2,000 worth of damage. The Court of Appeal stated that a sentence of three years' imprisonment would normally be appropriate for such an offence. A probation order was held to have been an unduly lenient sentence for arson being reckless whether life was endangered in *A-G's Ref (No. 61 of 1996)* [1997] 2 Cr App R (S) 316. The offender, in a jealous rage, set light to some of his girlfriend's clothes in the bedroom of their terraced house. He then maimed her dog with a sledgehammer, locked the door and left the fire burning. The fire was seen by police officers and extinguished before it spread to the next-door house. A sentence of two years' imprisonment was substituted by the Court of Appeal, the sentence being discounted for an unspecified period by virtue of the offender being sentenced twice for the offence.

Section B9 Offences Affecting Security

ACTS PREJUDICIAL TO SAFETY OR INTERESTS OF STATE ('SPYING')

Official Secrets Act 1911, s. 1 **B9.1**

(1) If any person for any purpose prejudicial to the safety or interests of the State—
- (a) approaches, inspects, passes over or is in the neighbourhood of, or enters any prohibited place within the meaning of this Act, or
- (b) makes any sketch, plan, model, or note which is calculated to be or might be or is intended to be directly or indirectly useful to an enemy; or
- (c) obtains, collects, records, or publishes, or communicates to any other person any secret official code word or pass word, or any sketch, plan, model, article, or note, or other document or information which is calculated to be or might be or is intended to be directly or indirectly useful to an enemy;

he shall be guilty of [an offence].

Procedure

B9.2 This offence is triable only on indictment. It is a class 1 offence.

Official Secrets Act 1911, s. 8

A prosecution for an offence under this Act shall not be instituted except by or with the consent of the Attorney-General.

By virtue of the Official Secrets Act 1911, s. 10(1) and (2), and the Official Secrets Act 1920, s. 8(3), a competent British court in the place where the offence was committed has jurisdiction to try a person, and a court in England has jurisdiction to try a person alleged to have committed the instant offence, even though the offence was committed elsewhere. The Official Secrets Act 1911 contains the basic provisions, the 1920 Act amplifies them by making clear that a person commits the offence, for the purposes of trial, either where it was committed, or, if that is outside the jurisdiction of the English courts, where he was found. As to territorial jurisdiction generally, see **A8**.

In addition to general powers (see **D3.78** *et seq.*), the Official Secrets Act 1920, s. 8(4), permits the court, on the application of the prosecution, on grounds of national safety to exclude all or some of the public from a trial, except for the sentencing of the person once found guilty. This power not only applies to the offences under the 1911 and 1920 Acts, but also to the offences under the Official Secrets Act 1989, except those created by s. 8. The ambit of s. 8(4) was considered by the House of Lords in *A-G v Leveller Magazine Ltd* [1979]

AC 440, in relation to the granting of anonymity to a prosecution witness. The judge's wide discretion in this area was upheld. Likewise, the restrictive trial arrangements in *Shayler* [2003] ACD 79 (which included screens and anonymity for security services witnesses and a requirement of prior notice by the accused in relation to any questions or evidence relating to security or intelligence on penalty of contempt) were upheld, albeit in circumstances where the accused refused to give any assurance that he would not attempt to raise a 'public interest' defence (which the House of Lords had already ruled was unavailable to him).

The Official Secrets Act 1911, s. 10(3), limits the courts outside the UK which may try such offences to those which may impose the greatest punishment allowed by law. It also provides that a sheriff court in Scotland cannot try such offences.

Indictment

B9.3 *Statement of Offence*

Entering a prohibited place contrary to section 1(1)(a) of the Official Secrets Act 1911.

Particulars of Offence

A on or about the . . . day of . . ., for a purpose prejudicial to the safety or interests of the State, namely . . ., entered a prohibited place, namely . . .

Sentencing Guidelines

B9.4 A person guilty of an offence under the Official Secrets Act 1911, s. 1, is liable to imprisonment for a term not exceeding 14 years (Official Secrets Act 1920, s. 8(1)).

Offences committed under the Official Secrets Act 1911, s. 1, will inevitably attract a lengthy custodial sentence. In *Prime* (1983) 5 Cr App R (S) 127, the offender pleaded guilty to seven offences against the Official Secrets Acts. The offender had been employed for nine years in the Government Communications Service, where he had access to highly sensitive intelligence information of importance to national security. During that period he passed on information to the Soviet Union. For the espionage offences, he received consecutive terms of 14, 14, and seven years' imprisonment. These sentences were upheld on appeal. In *Schulze* (1986) 8 Cr App R (S) 463, the offenders' home was found to contain spying equipment, forged documents and radio receiving equipment. They were convicted of doing acts preparatory to the commission of an offence under s. 1 of the Act. Sentences of ten years were upheld in each case.

Offence Not Limited to 'Spying'

B9.5 The Official Secrets Act 1911, s. 1, is stated in the marginal note as being concerned with 'penalties for spying', but it is not limited to 'spying' and extends to sabotage and temporary sabotage (*Chandler v DPP* [1964] AC 763).

Mens Rea: Purpose Prejudicial to the Safety or Interests of the State

B9.6 An offence under the Official Secrets Act 1911, s. 1(1), may be committed in a number of ways, which must be considered separately. However, the *mens rea* requirement that a person act with a 'purpose prejudicial to the safety or interests of the State' is common to each paragraph of s. 1(1). The House of Lords in *Chandler v DPP* [1964] AC 763, held that it is not necessary to establish an overt act on the part of the accused which would show the requisite purpose — circumstantial evidence will suffice. It is to be presumed that a sketch, plan, model etc. made, obtained, collected, recorded, published or communicated by a person not acting under lawful authority is made etc. for a purpose prejudicial to the interests of the State until the contrary is proved. Furthermore, as regards the phrase 'prejudicial to the safety or interests of the State': 'State' does not mean the government or the executive, or UK residents. The country or the realm are good synonyms as is 'the organised community' or 'the organs of government of a national community'. Whether a person's purpose is prejudicial to the safety or interests of the State is a matter for the jury to decide on the basis that it is for the Crown to decide what is for the safety or interests of the State and that decision of the Crown is not challengeable. Thus, the opinion of the accused as to what is in the safety or interests of the State is irrelevant (see *Bettaney* [1985] Crim LR 104). Similarly, in a prosecution under related regulations in *M* (1916) 11 Cr App R 207, it was held that the information provided to the enemy need not be correct provided that the accused intended to inform the enemy. See further **B9.65**.

Approaching, etc. Prohibited Place

'Prohibited place' is defined by the Official Secrets Act 1911, s. 3. **B9.7**

Official Secrets Act 1911, ss. 3 and 12

3. For the purposes of this Act, the expression 'prohibited place' means—
   (a) any work of a defence, arsenal, naval or air force establishment or station, factory, dockyard, mine, minefield, camp, ship, or aircraft belonging to or occupied by or on behalf of His Majesty, or any telegraph, telephone, wireless or signal station, or office so belonging or occupied, and any place belonging to or occupied by or on behalf of His Majesty and used for the purpose of building, repairing, making, or storing any munitions of war, or any sketches, plans, models, or documents relating thereto, or for the purpose of getting any metals, oil, or minerals of use in time of war;
   (b) any place not belonging to His Majesty where any munitions of war, or any sketches, models, plans or documents relating thereto, are being made, repaired, gotten or stored under contract with, or with any person on behalf of, His Majesty, or otherwise on behalf of His Majesty; and
   (c) any place belonging to or used for the purposes of His Majesty which is for the time being declared by order of a Secretary of State to be a prohibited place for the purposes of this section on the ground that information with respect thereto, or damage thereto, would be useful to an enemy; and
   (d) any railway, road, way, or channel, or other means of communication by land or water (including any works or structures being part thereof or connected therewith), or any place used for gas, water, or electricity works or other works for purposes of a public character, or any place where any munitions of war, or any sketches, models, plans or documents relating thereto, are being made, repaired, or stored otherwise than on behalf of His Majesty, which is for the time being declared by order of a Secretary of State to be a prohibited place for the purposes of this section, on the ground that information with respect thereto, or the destruction or obstruction thereof, or interference therewith, would be useful to an enemy.

12. In this Act, unless the context otherwise requires,—
   Any reference to a place belonging to His Majesty includes a place belonging to any department of the Government . . . whether the place is or is not actually vested in His Majesty; . . .
   The expression 'document' includes part of a document;
   The expression 'model' includes design, pattern and specimen;
   The expression 'sketch' includes any photograph or other mode of representing any place or thing;
   The expression 'munitions of war' includes the whole or any part of any ship, submarine, aircraft, tank or similar engine, arms and ammunition, torpedo, or mine, intended or adapted for use in war, and any other article, material, or device, whether actual or proposed, intended for such use; . . .

The Official Secrets (Prohibited Places) Order 1994 (SI 1994 No. 968), made under s. 3(c), provide that the works and offices of the UKAEA at Dounreay, the BNF sites at Sellafield and Capenhurst, the Urenco site at Capenhurst and the UKAEA sites at Harwell and Windscale are prohibited places. Further, any place used by the Civil Aviation Authority is a place belonging to Her Majesty under s. 3(c) (Civil Aviation Act 1982, s. 18(2) to (4)); and any electronic communications station or office belonging to, or occupied by, the provider of a public electronic communications service is a prohibited place (Communications Act 2003, sch. 17, para. 2).

Making Sketches etc. Useful to Enemy

B9.8 For the definitions of 'sketch' and 'model' in the Official Secrets Act 1911, s. 12, see **B9.7**.

As to the meaning of the word 'enemy', the Court of Appeal in *Parrott* (1913) 8 Cr App R 186, held that 'it does not mean necessarily someone with whom this country is at war, but a potential enemy with whom we might some day be at war'.

Obtaining or Communicating Sketches etc. Useful to Enemy

B9.9 A partial definition of the words 'obtains' and 'communicates' is provided by the Official Secrets Act 1911, s. 12:

Official Secrets Act 1911, s. 12

Expressions referring to communicating include any communicating, whether in whole or in part, and whether the sketch, plan, model, article, note, document, or information itself or the substance, effect, or description thereof only be communicated; expressions referring to obtaining or retaining any sketch, plan, model, article, note, or document, include the copying or causing to be copied the whole or any part of any sketch, plan, model, article, note, or document, and expressions referring to the communication of any sketch, plan, model, article, note or document include the transfer or transmissions of the sketch, plan, model, article, note or document.

For the definitions of 'sketch', 'model' and 'enemy', see **B9.7** and **B9.8**.

The Official Secrets Act 1920, s. 2(1), provides that communication with a foreign agent is to be evidence that the accused has obtained or communicated information useful to an enemy with a purpose prejudicial to the safety or interests of the State. Section 2(2)(a) lays down the circumstances in which a person is deemed to have been in communication with a foreign agent, unless he proves the contrary. They are:

(a) he has, either within or without the UK, visited the address of a foreign agent or consorted or associated with a foreign agent; or
(b) either within or without the UK, the name or address of, or any other information regarding a foreign agent has been found in his possession, or has been supplied by him to any other person, or has been obtained by him from any other person.

'Foreign agent' is defined by s. 2(2)(b) as including any person who is, or has been, or is reasonably suspected of being or having been employed by a foreign power either directly or indirectly for the purpose of committing an act, either within or without the UK, prejudicial to the safety or interests of the State, or who has, or is reasonably suspected of having, either within or without the UK, committed, or attempted to commit, such an act in the interests of a foreign power.

Finally, s. 2(2)(c) provides that an address, whether or not in the UK, is deemed to be the address of a foreign agent, and communications to that address deemed to be communications with a foreign agent, if the address is reasonably suspected of being an address for the receipt of communications or where he resides, or resorts for giving or receiving communications or carries on a business. The relevance of the activities of a foreign agent in proving the above requirements was considered in *Kent* (1943) 28 Cr App R 23.

Related Offences

B9.10 (a) A duty to give information about the commission of an offence under the Official Secrets Act 1911, s. 1(1), may be imposed by a chief officer of police acting under the Official Secrets Act 1920, s. 6. It is an offence to fail to provide such information. A person guilty of this offence is liable, on conviction on indictment, to imprisonment for a term not exceeding two years or a fine, or both or, on summary conviction, to a term of imprisonment not exceeding three months or a fine not exceeding the prescribed sum or both (Official Secrets Act 1920, s. 8(2)).

(b) The Official Secrets Act 1920, s. 7, makes it an offence to attempt, solicit or endeavour to persuade, or to aid and abet or do an act preparatory to, an offence under the Official Secrets Act 1911, s. 1(1) or the Official Secrets Act 1920, s. 6. The penalty for this offence is the same as for the substantive offence.

(c) It is an offence, contrary to the Official Secrets Act 1989, s. 5(6), for a person to disclose any information, document or other article which he knows, or has reasonable cause to believe, to have come into his possession as a result of a contravention of the Official Secrets Act 1911, s. 1.

(d) The European Communities Act 1972, s. 11(2), protects Euratom secrets. It creates an offence which is to be regarded as an offence under the 1911 Act, and thus the provision in relation to restriction on prosecution (see **B9.2**) applies.

European Communities Act 1972, s. 11

(2) Where a person (whether a British subject or not) owing either—
(a) to his duties as a member of any Euratom institution or committee, or as an officer or servant of Euratom; or
(b) to his dealings in any capacity (official or unofficial) with any Euratom institution or installation or with any Euratom joint enterprise;
has occasion to acquire, or obtain cognisance of, any classified information, he shall be guilty of [an offence] if, knowing or having reason to believe that it is classified information, he communicates it to any unauthorised person or makes any public disclosure of it, whether in the United Kingdom or elsewhere and whether before or after the termination of those duties or dealings.

Sections 10 and 11 of the 1911 Act, dealing with the extent of the Act and the place of trial of the offence, and saving for laws of British possessions, do not apply to this offence.

This offence is triable either way; it may be dealt with summarily only with the consent of the A-G. A person guilty of the offence is liable on conviction on indictment to imprisonment for a term not exceeding two years or a fine or both, or, on summary conviction, to a term of imprisonment not exceeding three months or a fine not exceeding the prescribed sum or both.

'Classified information' means any facts, information, knowledge, documents or objects that are subject to the security rules of a Member State or any Euratom institution (European Communities Act 1972, s. 11(2)).

HARBOURING 'SPIES'

Official Secrets Act 1911, s. 7 **B9.11**

If any person knowingly harbours any person whom he knows, or has reasonable grounds for supposing, to be a person who is about to commit or who has committed an offence under this Act, or knowingly permits to meet or assemble in any premises in his occupation or under his control any such persons, or if any person having harboured any such person, or permitted to meet or assemble in any premises in his occupation or under his control any such persons, wilfully omits or refuses to disclose to a superintendent of police any information which it is in his power to give in relation to any such person he shall be guilty of [an offence].

Procedure

As to prosecutions requiring the consent of the A-G, see **B9.2**. **B9.12**

The offence is triable either way, subject to the proviso to the Official Secrets Act 1920,

s. 8(2), which provides that the offence may be dealt with summarily only with the consent of the A-G. When tried on indictment it is a class 1 offence.

As to the special provisions relating to place of trial, territorial jurisdiction, excluding the public from the trial and offences tried outside the UK, see **B9.2**.

Indictment

B9.13 *Statement of Offence*

Harbouring an offender contrary to section 7 of the Official Secrets Act 1911.

Particulars of Offence

A on or about the . . . day of . . . harboured O whom he knew or had reasonable grounds for supposing was about to commit [or had committed] an offence under the Official Secrets Act 1911, namely [state the offence].

Sentence

B9.14 The maximum penalty is: on conviction on indictment, imprisonment for a term not exceeding two years or a fine or both; on summary conviction, a term of imprisonment not exceeding three months or a fine not exceeding the prescribed sum or both (Official Secrets Act 1920, s. 8(2)).

Offence not Limited to Harbouring 'Spies'

B9.15 The offence is not limited to harbouring 'spies', since the person being harboured must simply have committed an 'offence under this Act', which means any act, omission, or other thing which is punishable under the 1911 Act (Official Secrets Act 1911, s. 12).

Meaning of 'Superintendent of Police'

B9.16 **Official Secrets Act 1911, s. 12**

In this Act, unless the context otherwise requires,—

. . .

The expression 'superintendent of police' includes any police officer of a like or superior rank and any person upon whom the powers of a superintendent of police are for the purposes of this Act conferred by a Secretary of State.

Related Offences

B9.17 The Official Secrets Act 1920, s. 7, makes it an offence to attempt, solicit or endeavour to persuade, or to aid and abet or do an act preparatory to, an offence under the Official Secrets Act 1911, s. 7.

GAINING ACCESS TO PROHIBITED PLACES

B9.18 **Official Secrets Act 1920, s. 1**

(1) If any person for the purpose of gaining admission, or of assisting, any other person to gain admission, to a prohibited place, within the meaning of the Official Secrets Act 1911 . . ., or for any other purpose prejudicial to the safety or interests of the State within the meaning of the said Act—

(a) uses or wears, without lawful authority, any naval, military, air-force, police, or other official uniform, or any uniform so nearly resembling the same as to be calculated to deceive, or falsely represents himself to be a person who is or has been entitled to use or wear any such uniform; or

(b) orally, or in writing in any declaration or application, or in any document signed by him or on his behalf, knowingly makes or connives at the making of any false statement or any omission; or

(c) tampers with any passport or naval, military, air-force, police, or other official pass, permit, certificate, licence, or other document of a similar character (hereinafter in this section referred to as an official document), or has in his possession any forged, altered, or irregular official document; or

(d) personates, or falsely represents himself to be a person holding, or in the employment of a person holding office under His Majesty, or to be or not to be a person to whom an official document or secret official code word or pass word has been duly issued or communicated, or with intent to obtain an official document, secret official code word or pass word, whether for himself or any other person, knowingly makes any false statement; or

(e) uses, or has in his possession or under his control, without the authority of the Government Department or the authority concerned, any die, seal, or stamp of or belonging to, or used, made or provided by any Government Department, or by any diplomatic, naval, military, or air force authority appointed by or acting under the authority of His Majesty, or any die, seal or stamp so nearly resembling any such die, seal or stamp as to be calculated to deceive, or counterfeits any such die, seal or stamp, or uses, or has in his possession, or under his control, any such counterfeited die, seal or stamp;

he shall be guilty of [an offence].

Procedure

As to prosecutions requiring the consent of the A-G, see **B9.2**. **B9.19**

The offence is triable either way, subject to the proviso to the Official Secrets Act 1920, s. 8(2), which provides that the offence may be dealt with summarily only with the consent of the A-G. When tried on indictment it is a class 1 offence.

As to the special provisions relating to place of trial, territorial jurisdiction, excluding the public from the trial and offences tried outside the UK, see **B9.2**.

Indictment

Statement of Offence **B9.20**

Unlawfully wearing a uniform for the purpose of gaining access to a prohibited place contrary to section 1(1) of the Official Secrets Act 1920.

Particulars of Offence

A on or about the . . . day of . . ., for the purpose of gaining admission to a prohibited place, namely . . ., wore a naval [or military etc.] uniform without lawful authority.

Sentence

The maximum penalty is: on conviction on indictment, imprisonment for a term not exceeding two years or a fine or both; on summary conviction, a term of imprisonment not exceeding three months or a fine not exceeding the prescribed sum or both (Official Secrets Act 1920, s. 8(2)). **B9.21**

Elements

For the meaning of 'prohibited place', see **B9.7**. For the meaning of 'purpose prejudicial to the safety or interests of the State', see **B9.6**. **B9.22**

By virtue of the Official Secrets Act 1911, s. 12, 'office under His Majesty' includes any office or employment in or under any department of the government of the UK or of any British possession. A police officer is in employment under Her Majesty (see *Lewis v Cattle* [1938] 2 KB 454).

Related Offences

The Official Secrets Act 1920, s. 7, makes it an offence to attempt, solicit or endeavour to persuade, or to aid and abet or do an act preparatory to, an offence under the Official Secrets Act 1920, s. 1(1). The mental element for the s. 7 offence was considered in *Bingham* [1973] QB 870. **B9.23**

RETENTION AND POSSESSION OF OFFICIAL DOCUMENTS ETC.

B9.24 **Official Secrets Act 1920, s. 1**

(2) If any person—

(a) retains for any purpose prejudicial to the safety or interests of the State any official document, whether or not completed or issued for use, when he has no right to retain it, or when it is contrary to his duty to retain it, or fails to comply with any directions issued by any government department or any person authorised by such department with regard to the return or disposal thereof, or

(b) allows any other person to have possession of any official document issued for his use alone, or communicates any secret official code word or pass word so issued, or, without lawful authority or excuse, has in his possession any official document or secret official code word or pass word issued for the use of some person other than himself, or on obtaining possession of any official document by finding or otherwise, neglects or fails to restore it to the person or authority by whom or for whose use it was issued, or to a police constable; or

(c) without lawful authority or excuse, manufactures or sells, or has in his possession for sale any such die, seal or stamp as aforesaid;

he shall be guilty of [an offence].

Procedure

B9.25 As to prosecutions requiring the consent of the A-G, see **B9.2**.

The offence is triable either way, subject to the proviso to the Official Secrets Act 1920, s. 8(2), which provides that the offence may be dealt with summarily only with the consent of the A-G. When tried on indictment it is a class 1 offence.

As to the special provisions relating to place of trial, territorial jurisdiction, excluding the public from the trial and offences tried outside the UK, see **B9.2**.

Indictment

B9.26 *Statement of Offence*

Retaining an official document contrary to section 1(2) of the Official Secrets Act 1920.

Particulars of Offence

A on or about the . . . day of . . ., for a purpose prejudicial to the safety or interests of the State, namely . . ., retained an official document, namely. . ., when he had no right to retain it [or when it was contrary to his duty to retain it].

Sentence

B9.27 The maximum penalty is: on conviction on indictment, imprisonment for a term not exceeding two years or a fine or both; on summary conviction, a term of imprisonment not exceeding three months or a fine not exceeding the prescribed sum or both (Official Secrets Act 1920, s. 8(2)).

Elements

B9.28 For the meaning of 'official document', see the Official Secrets Act 1920, s. 1(1)(c) at **B9.18**. For the meaning of 'die, seal or stamp', see s. 1(1)(e) of that Act. For the meaning of 'communicate', see **B9.9**.

For the meaning of 'purpose prejudicial to the safety or interests of the State', see **B9.6**.

Related Offences

B9.29 The Official Secrets Act 1920, s. 7, makes it an offence to attempt, solicit or endeavour to persuade, or to aid and abet or do an act preparatory to, an offence under the Official Secrets Act 1920, s. 1(2).

INTERFERING WITH OFFICERS OF POLICE OR MEMBERS OF ARMED FORCES IN VICINITY OF PROHIBITED PLACE

Official Secrets Act 1920, s. 3 **B9.30**

No person in the vicinity of any prohibited place shall obstruct, knowingly mislead or otherwise interfere with or impede, the chief officer or a superintendent or other officer of police, or any member of His Majesty's forces engaged on guard, sentry, patrol, or other similar duty in relation to the prohibited place, and, if any person acts in contravention of, or fails to comply with, this provision, he shall be guilty of [an offence].

Procedure

As to the restriction on prosecutions requiring the consent of the A-G, see **B9.2**. **B9.31**

This offence is triable either way, subject to the proviso to the Official Secrets Act 1920, s. 8(2), which provides that the offence may be dealt with summarily only with the consent of the A-G. When tried on indictment it is a class 1 offence.

As to the special provisions relating to territorial jurisdiction, excluding the public from the trial and offences tried outside the UK, see **B9.2**.

Sentence

The maximum penalty is: on conviction on indictment, imprisonment for a term not exceeding two years or a fine or both; on summary conviction, a term of imprisonment not exceeding three months or a fine not exceeding the prescribed sum or both (Official Secrets Act 1920, s. 8(2)). **B9.32**

Elements

For the meaning of 'prohibited place', see **B9.7**. **B9.33**

In *Adler v George* [1964] 2 QB 7, it was held that the phrase 'in the vicinity of' in the Official Secrets Act 1920, s. 3, is to be interpreted as 'in or in the vicinity of' so that obstruction of someone at an airbase could constitute an offence under the section.

The word 'obstruct' presumably has the same meaning as in the offence of obstruction of a police officer in the execution of his duty (see **B2.29** to **B2.32**). The meaning of 'superintendent' is considered at **B9.16**.

Related Offences

The Official Secrets Act 1920, s. 7, makes it an offence to attempt, solicit or endeavour to persuade, or to aid and abet or do an act preparatory to, an offence under the Official Secrets Act 1920, s. 3. As to the offences of assaulting and obstructing a police officer in the execution of his duty, see **B2.29** to **B2.32**. **B9.34**

DISCLOSURE OF SECURITY AND INTELLIGENCE INFORMATION

Official Secrets Act 1989, s. 1 **B9.35**

(1) A person who is or has been—
(a) a member of the security and intelligence services; or
(b) a person notified that he is subject to the provisions of this subsection,
shall be guilty of an offence if without lawful authority he discloses any information, document or other article relating to security or intelligence which is or has been in his

possession by virtue of his position as a member of any of those services or in the course of his work while the notification is or was in force.

Procedure and Extra-territoriality

B9.36 **Official Secrets Act 1989, ss. 9, 11, and 15**

9.—(1) Subject to subsection (2) below, no prosecution for an offence under this Act shall be instituted in England and Wales or in Northern Ireland except by or with the consent of the Attorney-General or, as the case may be, the Attorney-General for Northern Ireland.

(2) Subsection (1) above does not apply to an offence in respect of any such information, document or article as is mentioned in section 4(2) above but no prosecution for such an offence shall be instituted in England and Wales or in Northern Ireland except by or with the consent of the Director of Public Prosecutions or, as the case may be, the Director of Public Prosecutions for Northern Ireland.

11.—(5) Proceedings for an offence under this Act may be taken in any place in the United Kingdom.

15.—(1) Any act—

(a) done by a British citizen or Crown servant; or

(b) done by any person in any of the Channel Islands or the Isle of Man or any colony,

shall, if it would be an offence by that person under any provision of this Act other than section 8(1), (4) or (5) when done by him in the United Kingdom, be an offence under that provision.

This offence is triable either way (Official Secrets Act 1989, s. 10(1)). When tried on indictment it is a class 1 offence.

The power to exclude the public under the Official Secrets Act 1920, s. 8(4), applies to the instant offence by virtue of the Official Secrets Act 1989, s. 11(4) (see **B9.2**).

Indictment

B9.37 *Statement of Offence*

Unlawful disclosure of information contrary to section 1(1) of the Official Secrets Act 1989.

Particulars of Offence

A on or about the . . . day of . . ., being a person notified that he was subject to the provisions of section 1 of the Official Secrets Act 1989, without lawful authority disclosed to P a document, namely . . ., which related to security or intelligence and which the said A had in his possession in the course of his work while the said notification was in force.

Sentence

B9.38 The maximum penalty is: on conviction on indictment, imprisonment for a term not exceeding two years or a fine or both; on summary conviction, imprisonment for a term not exceeding six months or a fine not exceeding the statutory maximum or both (Official Secrets Act 1989, s. 10(1)).

Persons who Can Commit Offence

B9.39 An offence under the Official Secrets Act 1989, s. 1(1), can be committed by either a person who is or has been a member of the security and intelligence services, or someone who is or has been a notified person (i.e. notified that he is subject to s. 1 of the Act).

Official Secrets Act 1989, s. 1

(6) Notification that a person is subject to subsection (1) above shall be effected by a notice in writing served on him by a Minister of the Crown; and such a notice may be served if, in the Minister's opinion, the work undertaken by the person in question is or includes work connected with the security and intelligence services and its nature is such that the interests of national security require that he should be subject to the provisions of that subsection.

(7) Subject to subsection (8) below, a notification for the purposes of subsection (1) above shall be in force for the period of five years beginning with the day on which it is served but may be renewed by further notices under subsection (6) above for periods of five years at a time.

(8) A notification for the purposes of subsection (1) above may at any time be revoked by a further notice in writing served by the Minister on the person concerned; and the Minister shall serve such a further notice as soon as, in his opinion, the work undertaken by that person ceases to be such as is mentioned in subsection (6) above.

Meaning of 'Security' and 'Intelligence'

Official Secrets Act 1989, s. 1 **B9.40**

(9) In this section 'security or intelligence' means the work of, or in support of, the security and intelligence services or any part of them, and references to information relating to security or intelligence include references to information held or transmitted by those services or by persons in support of, or of any part of, them.

The security service has now been placed on a statutory basis (see the Security Service Act 1989), as has the Secret Intelligence Service (Intelligence Services Act 1994).

Disclosure of Information

Official Secrets Act 1989, ss. 1 and 13 **B9.41**

1.—(2) The reference in subsection (1) above to disclosing information relating to security or intelligence includes a reference to making any statement which purports to be a disclosure of such information or is intended to be taken by those to whom it is addressed as being such a disclosure.

13.—(1) In this Act—

'disclose' and 'disclosure', in relation to a document or other article, include parting with possession of it.

'Disclose' is not defined merely as 'make public', for example. This is capable of causing difficulties in relation to the absolute right of an accused to provide his legal advisers with instructions relating to his defence. It is possible to do so only if the provision of his instructions would not involve the commission of a further offence by such disclosure to his lawyers. In cases where, for example, the alleged disclosure was not widely publicised, the accused's lawyers may need to seek authorisation under s. 7 before they can even view the subject-matter of the indictment. Undoubtedly there is likely to be an application for such trials to be held in camera. Although Lord Bingham in *Shayler* [2003] 1 AC 247, suggested a special advocate solution (at [34]), this related only to a judicial review of a refusal to authorise disclosure, not criminal proceedings in which the accused seeks to provide his lawyers with instructions/material relevant to his defence.

The issue of prior publication is relevant to whether the disclosure in question is damaging but not decisive of it: see the White Paper *Reform of Section 2 of the Official Secrets Act 1911* (1988) Cm. 408 at paras. 62–63. The White Paper recommendations 'bear directly on the interpretation of the Act' (*Shayler* [2003] 1 AC 247 at [11]).

Meaning of 'Without Lawful Authority'

The Official Secrets Act 1989, s. 1(1), applies only to unauthorised disclosures. Section 7 provides for the only circumstances in which a disclosure may be made 'with lawful authority'. Only s. 7(1) applies to s. 1(1), since the offence applies only to the limited range of Crown servants who work for the security and intelligence services, or who are notified as being covered by the provisions of s. 1(1). **B9.42**

Official Secrets Act 1989, s. 7

(1) For the purposes of this Act a disclosure by—

(a) a Crown servant; or

(b) a person, not being a Crown servant or government contractor, in whose case a notification for the purposes of section 1(1) above is in force,

is made with lawful authority if, and only if, it is made in accordance with his official duty.

As to the broader provisions relating, generally, to authorised disclosures, see **B9.52**; as to defences, see **B9.43**.

Defences

B9.43 **Official Secrets Act 1989, ss. 1 and 7**

1.—(5) It is a defence for a person charged with an offence under this section to prove that at the time of the alleged offence he did not know, and had no reasonable cause to believe, that the information, document or article in question related to security or intelligence.

7.—(4) It is a defence for a person charged with an offence under any of the foregoing provisions of this Act to prove that at the time of the alleged offence he believed that he had lawful authority to make the disclosure in question and had no reasonable cause to believe otherwise.

Although the legal burden appears to lie upon the accused, it is likely that only an evidential burden would be compatible with the ECHR, Article 6 (see *Keogh* [2007] 1 WLR 1500 and **F3.13** *et seq*).

According to the House of Lords in *Shayler* [2003] 1 AC 247, there is no additional defence of a disclosure being in the national or public interest, the offence contrary to the Official Secrets Act 1989, s. 1(1), or the offence contrary to s. 4(1). The House held that the blanket ban on disclosures by members of the security services nevertheless satisfied the requirements of the ECHR, Article 10(2). The intention to counter terrorism, criminal activity, hostile activity and subversion was a sufficient purpose to satisfy Article 10(2), and the restrictions were clear, and so prescribed by law. The restrictions were also necessary in a democratic society because of the defences that existed (which vary from offence to offence): the two means of gaining authorisation for a disclosure under s. 7 and the possibility of challenging an adverse decision under judicial review (with a suitably rigorous and intensive form of review for the alleged breach of a Convention right). Moreover, no prosecution would take place without the consent of the A-G.

'Public interest', however, remains relevant to whether any particular disclosure is damaging (i.e. for *all* offences except those under s. 1(1) and s. 4 of the Act): see White Paper *Reform of Section 2 of the Official Secrets Act 1911* (1988) Cm. 408, para. 61. For offences requiring damaging disclosure, it is necessary for the prosecution to prove not only that the disclosure is damaging but also that the person making the disclosure knows or has reasonable grounds to believe that it would be damaging (in the sense that it is likely to have that effect). It is insufficient for the prosecution to prove that there were reasonable grounds to believe that the disclosure might be damaging, or that this was merely a possibility.

Although the House held that Shayler himself was not 'within striking distance' of the defence of necessity (as to which, see further **A3.28** to **A3.29**), necessity remains available as a defence to *all* offences under the 1989 Act. The potential width of the defence is illustrated by one of the prosecution's stated reasons for not proceeding with the case against Katharine Gun, namely that it could not rebut her defence of necessity. She was a GCHQ employee who, in 2004, was charged with s. 1 disclosure of the US request for the UK to spy on the UN in the run-up to the Iraq war. Her publicly stated defence was a desire to prevent a war without a lawfully obtained second UN resolution.

Related Offences

B9.44 It is an offence, contrary to the Official Secrets Act 1989, s. 1(3), for a Crown servant or government contractor to make a damaging disclosure of security or intelligence information (see **B9.45** to **B9.54**).

DAMAGING DISCLOSURE OF SECURITY AND INTELLIGENCE INFORMATION

Official Secrets Act 1989, s. 1 **B9.45**

(3) A person who is or has been a Crown servant or government contractor shall be guilty of an offence if without lawful authority he makes a damaging disclosure of any information, document or other article relating to security or intelligence which is or has been in his possession by virtue of his position as such but otherwise than as mentioned in subsection (1) above.

Procedure

As to the requirement of consent of the A-G, see the Official Secrets Act 1989, s. 9(1), and **B9.36**. **B9.46**

The offence is triable either way (s. 10(1)). When tried on indictment it is a class 1 offence.

As to provisions relating to place of trial, territorial jurisdiction and excluding the public from the trial, see **B9.36**.

Indictment

Statement of Offence **B9.47**

Unlawfully making a damaging disclosure of information relating to security [or intelligence] contrary to section 1(3) of the Official Secrets Act 1989.

Particulars of Offence

A on or about the . . . day of . . ., being then [or having been] a Crown servant [or government contractor], without lawful authority disclosed to P information relating to security [or intelligence], namely . . ., which was in his possession by virtue of his position as a Crown servant [or government contractor], which disclosure caused [or disclosure of which would have been likely to cause] damage to the work of the security and intelligence services [or the work of . . ., being part of the security and intelligence services].

Sentence

The maximum penalty is: on conviction on indictment, imprisonment for a term not exceeding two years or a fine or both; on summary conviction, imprisonment for a term not exceeding six months or a fine not exceeding the statutory maximum or both (Official Secrets Act 1989, s. 10(1)). **B9.48**

Meaning of 'Security', 'Intelligence', 'Disclosure', 'Damaging Disclosure'

For the meaning of 'security' and 'intelligence', see **B9.40**. For the meaning of 'disclosure', see **B9.41**. The words 'damaging disclosure' are defined by the Official Secrets Act 1989, s. 1(4). **B9.49**

Official Secrets Act 1989, s. 1

(4) For the purposes of subsection (3) above a disclosure is damaging if—
(a) it causes damage to the work of, or of any part of, the security and intelligence services; or
(b) it is of information or a document or other article which is such that its unauthorised disclosure would be likely to cause such damage or which falls within a class or description of information, documents or articles the unauthorised disclosure of which would be likely to have that effect.

This offence is committed whether or not the information disclosed was secret or confidential, and whether or not the disclosure was damaging to national interests (*A-G v Blake* [1997] Ch 84 (per Sir Richard Scott (*obiter*)). 'Public interest' is relevant to whether the disclosure is damaging, see **B9.43**.

Meaning of 'Crown Servant'

B9.50 **Official Secrets Act 1989, s. 12**

12.—(1) In this Act 'Crown servant' means—

(a) a Minister of the Crown;

(aa) a member of the Scottish Executive or a junior Scottish minister;

(ab) the First Minister of Wales, a Welsh Minister appointed under section 48 of the Government of Wales Act 2006, the Counsel General to the Welsh Assembly Government or a Deputy Welsh Minister;

(b) [repealed]

(c) any person employed in the civil service of the Crown, including Her Majesty's Diplomatic Service, Her Majesty's Overseas Civil Service, the civil service of Northern Ireland and the Northern Ireland Court Service;

(d) any member of the naval, military or air forces of the Crown, including any person employed by an association established for the purposes of part XI of the Reserve Forces Act 1996;

(e) any constable and any other person employed or appointed in or for the purposes of any police force (including the Police Service of Northern Ireland and the Police Service of Northern Ireland Reserve) or of the Serious Organised Crime Agency;

(f) any person who is a member or employee of a prescribed body or a body of a prescribed class and either is prescribed for the purposes of this paragraph or belongs to a prescribed class of members or employees of any such body;

(g) any person who is the holder of a prescribed office or who is an employee of such a holder and either is prescribed for the purposes of this paragraph or belongs to a prescribed class of such employees.

The Official Secrets Act 1989 (Prescription) Order 1990 (SI 1990 No. 200), art. 2 and sch. 1, prescribes classes of members or employees of certain bodies as 'Crown servants' for the purpose of s. 12(1)(f); art. 3 prescribes classes of members or employees as 'Crown servants' for the purposes of s. 12(1)(g).

The 1989 Act applies to the First Minister and deputy First Minister in Northern Ireland and Northern Ireland Ministers and junior Ministers in the same way as it applies to Crown servants (Official Secrets Act 1989, s. 12(5)).

Meaning of 'Government Contractor'

B9.51 **Official Secrets Act 1989, ss. 12 and 13**

12.—(2) In this Act 'government contractor' means, subject to subsection (3) below, any person who is not a Crown servant but who provides, or is employed in the provision of, goods or services—

(a) for the purposes of any Minister of the Crown or person mentioned in paragraph (a), (ab) or (b) of subsection (1) above, of any of the services, forces or bodies mentioned in that subsection or of the holder of any office prescribed under that subsection; or

(b) under an agreement or arrangement certified by the Secretary of State as being one to which the government of a State other than the United Kingdom or an international organisation is a party or which is subordinate to, or made for the purposes of implementing, any such agreement or arrangement.

(3) Where an employee or class of employees of any body, or of any holder of an office, is prescribed by an order made for the purposes of subsection (1) above—

(a) any employee of that body, or the holder of that office who is not prescribed or is not within the prescribed class; and

(b) any person who does not provide, or is not employed in the provision of, goods or services for the purposes of the performance of those functions of the body or the holder of the office in connection with which the employee or prescribed class of employees is engaged,

shall not be a government contractor for the purposes of this Act.

13.—(1) In this Act—

. . .

'international organisation' means, subject to subsections (2) and (3) below, an organisation of which only States are members and includes a reference to any organ of such an organisation;

. . .

'State' includes the government of a State and any organ of its government and references to a State other than the United Kingdom include references to any territory outside the United Kingdom.

(2) In section 12(2)(b) above the reference to an international organisation includes a reference to any such organisation whether or not one of which only States are members and includes a commercial organisation.

(3) In determining for the purposes of subsection (1) above whether only States are members of an organisation, any member which is itself an organisation of which only States are members, or which is an organ of such an organisation, shall be treated as a State.

'Without Lawful Authority'

An offence under the Official Secrets Act 1989, s. 1(3), is committed only if the disclosure is 'without lawful authority'. The only circumstances in which a disclosure is made with lawful authority are to be found in s. 7. **B9.52**

Official Secrets Act 1989, s. 7

(1) For the purposes of this Act a disclosure by—
 (a) a Crown servant; or
 (b) a person, not being a Crown servant or government contractor, in whose case a notification for the purposes of section 1(1) above is in force,

is made with lawful authority if, and only if, it is made in accordance with his official duty.

(2) For the purposes of this Act a disclosure by a government contractor is made with lawful authority if, and only if, it is made—
 (a) in accordance with an official authorisation; or
 (b) for the purposes of the functions by virtue of which he is a government contractor and without contravening an official restriction.

(3) For the purposes of this Act a disclosure made by any other person is made with lawful authority if, and only if, it is made—
 (a) to a Crown servant for the purposes of his functions as such; or
 (b) in accordance with an official authorisation.

. . .

(5) In this section 'official authorisation' and 'official restriction' mean, subject to subsection (6) below, an authorisation or restriction duly given or imposed by a Crown servant or government contractor or by or on behalf of a prescribed body or a body of a prescribed class.

Certain bodies have been prescribed by the Official Secrets Act 1989 (Prescription) Order 1990 (SI 1990 No. 200), art. 4 and sch. 3, for the purpose of s. 7(5) so as to enable them to give official authorisations or restrictions.

Official Secrets Act 1989 (Prescription) Order 1990, sch. 3

PRESCRIPTIONS: SECTIONS 7(5) AND 8(9)

The Civil Aviation Authority	Sections 7(5) and 8(9)
The Investigatory Powers Tribunal established under section 65 of the Regulation of Investigatory Powers Act 2000	Section 7(5)

Specific Defences

The defence of having no knowledge or reasonable cause to believe that information related to security or intelligence, created by the Official Secrets Act 1989, s. 1(5), and the defence that the accused believed that he had lawful authority for disclosure, apply to this offence. There is no defence of disclosure in the public or national interest for an offence under s. 1(1) (*Shayler* [2003] 1 AC 247), but 'public interest' is relevant to whether the disclosure is damaging. The defences are considered at **B9.43**. **B9.53**

Related Offences

B9.54 It is an offence, contrary to the Official Secrets Act 1989, s. 1(1), for a present or past member of the security and intelligence services or a notified person to make a disclosure of security or intelligence information (see **B9.35** to **B9.44**).

DAMAGING DISCLOSURE OF DEFENCE INFORMATION

B9.55 **Official Secrets Act 1989, s. 2**

(1) A person who is or has been a Crown servant or government contractor shall be guilty of an offence if without lawful authority he makes a damaging disclosure of any information, document or other article relating to defence which is or has been in his possession by virtue of his position as such.

Procedure

B9.56 As to the requirement of consent of the A-G, see **B9.36**. The offence is triable either way (Official Secrets Act 1989, s. 10(1)). When tried on indictment it is a class 1 offence.

As to provisions relating to place of trial, territorial jurisdiction and excluding the public from the trial, see **B9.36**.

Indictment

B9.57 *Statement of Offence*

Unlawfully making a damaging disclosure of information relating to defence contrary to section 2(1) of the Official Secrets Act 1989.

Particulars of Offence

A on or about the . . . day of . . ., being then [or having been] a Crown servant [or government contractor], without lawful authority disclosed to P information relating to defence, namely . . ., which was in his possession by virtue of his position as a Crown servant [or government contractor], which disclosure prejudiced [or disclosure of which would have been likely to prejudice] the capability of the armed forces of the Crown to carry out their tasks [or other form of damage specified in s. 2(2): see **B9.59**].

Sentence

B9.58 The maximum penalty is: on conviction on indictment, imprisonment for a term not exceeding two years or a fine or both; on summary conviction, imprisonment for a term not exceeding six months or a fine not exceeding the statutory maximum or both.

Elements

B9.59 The meaning of 'disclosure' is considered at **B9.41**.

Official Secrets Act 1989, s. 2

(2) For the purposes of subsection (1) above a disclosure is damaging if—

(a) it prejudices the capability of, or any part of, the armed forces of the Crown to carry out their tasks or leads to loss of life or injury to members of those forces or serious damage to the equipment or installations of those forces; or

(b) otherwise than in paragraph (a) above, it endangers the interests of the United Kingdom abroad, seriously obstructs the promotion or protection by the United Kingdom of those interests or endangers the safety of British citizens abroad; or

(c) it is of information or of a document or article which is such that its unauthorised disclosure would be likely to have any of those effects.

. . .

(4) In this section 'defence' means—

(a) the size, shape, organisation, logistics, order of battle, deployment, operations, state of readiness and training of the armed forces of the Crown;

(b) the weapons, stores or other equipment of those forces and the invention, development, production and operation of such equipment and research relating to it;
(c) defence policy and strategy and military planning and intelligence;
(d) plans and measures for the maintenance of essential supplies and services that are or would be needed in time of war.

The meanings of 'Crown servant' and 'government contractor' are considered at **B9.50** and **B9.51**. As to the meaning of 'without lawful authority', see s. 7 of the Act, at **B9.52**. As to the only circumstances in which a disclosure is made with lawful authority, see **B9.52**.

Specific Defences

Official Secrets Act 1989, s. 2 **B9.60**

(3) It is a defence for a person charged with an offence under this section to prove that at the time of the alleged offence he did not know, and had no reasonable cause to believe, that the information, document or article in question related to defence or that its disclosure would be damaging within the meaning of subsection (1) above.

To ensure compliance with the ECHR, Article 6, the accused has only an evidential burden as regards proving this defence (*Keogh* [2007] 1 WLR 1500: cf. the Terrorism Act 2000, s. 118 and see further **F3.13** ***et seq***).

The defence that the accused believed that he had lawful authority for disclosure, created by the Official Secrets Act 1989, s. 7(4), also applies to this offence, and is considered at **B9.43** together with other defences.

DAMAGING DISCLOSURE OF INTERNATIONAL RELATIONS INFORMATION

Official Secrets Act 1989, s. 3 **B9.61**

(1) A person who is or has been a Crown servant or government contractor shall be guilty of an offence if without lawful authority he makes a damaging disclosure of—
(a) any information, document or other article relating to international relations; or
(b) any confidential information, document or other article which was obtained from a State other than the United Kingdom or an international organisation,

being information or a document or article which is or has been in his possession by virtue of his position as a Crown servant or government contractor.

Procedure

As to the requirement of the A-G's consent, see **B9.36**. The offence is triable either way (Official Secrets Act 1989, s. 10(1)). When tried on indictment it is a class 1 offence. **B9.62**

As to provisions relating to place of trial, territorial jurisdiction and excluding the public from the trial, see **B9.36**.

Indictment

Statement of Offence **B9.63**

Unlawfully making a damaging disclosure of information relating to international relations contrary to section 3(1) of the Official Secrets Act 1989.

Particulars of Offence

A on or about the . . . day of . . ., being then [or having been] a Crown servant [or government contractor], without lawful authority disclosed to P information relating to international relations, namely . . ., which was in his possession by virtue of his position as a Crown servant [or government contractor], which disclosure endangered [or disclosure of which would have been likely to endanger] the interests of the United Kingdom abroad [or other form of damage specified in s. 3(2): see **B9.65**].

Sentence

B9.64 The maximum penalty is: on conviction on indictment, imprisonment for a term not exceeding two years or a fine or both; on summary conviction, imprisonment for a term not exceeding six months or a fine not exceeding the statutory maximum or both (Official Secrets Act 1989, s. 10(1)).

Elements

B9.65 The meaning of 'disclosure' is considered at **B9.41**. The phrases 'damaging disclosure', 'international relations' and 'confidential information' are defined by the Official Secrets Act 1989, s. 3.

Official Secrets Act 1989, s. 3

(2) For the purposes of subsection (1) above a disclosure is damaging if—
  (a) it endangers the interests of the United Kingdom abroad, seriously obstructs the promotion or protection by the United Kingdom of those interests or endangers the safety of British citizens abroad; or
  (b) it is of information or of a document or article which is such that its unauthorised disclosure would be likely to have any of those effects.

(3) In the case of information or a document or article within subsection (1) above—
  (a) the fact that it is confidential, or
  (b) its nature or contents,
may be sufficient to establish for the purposes of subsection (2)(b) above that the information, document or article is such that its unauthorised disclosure would be likely to have any of the effects there mentioned.

(5) In this section 'international relations' means the relations between States, between international organisations or between one or more States and one or more such organisations and includes any matter relating to a State other than the United Kingdom or to an international organisation which is capable of affecting the relations of the United Kingdom with another State or with an international organisation.

(6) For the purposes of this section any information, document or article obtained from a State or organisation is confidential at any time while the terms on which it was obtained require it to be held in confidence or while the circumstances in which it was obtained make it reasonable for the State or organisation to expect that it would be so held.

Section 13 of the Act defines 'State and international organisation' (see **B9.51**). The meanings of 'Crown servant' and 'government contractor' are considered at **B9.50** and **B9.51**. The phrase 'without lawful authority' is defined by s. 7 of the Act (see **B9.52**). The Act does not define the 'interests of the United Kingdom abroad'. This is an inchoate concept which raises important and difficult issues of interpretation. There is some first instance authority for the proposition that the concept of the national interest is to be treated as synonymous with the interests of the government of the day. On the other hand, it is axiomatic that the interests of any particular political party, or of any individual public official, are not to be equated with the interests of the UK as a whole. A good indication of the kind of harm contemplated by s. 3 is set out in the White Paper *Reform of Section 2 of the Official Secrets Act 1911* (1988) Cm. 408 at para. 27.

Specific Defences

B9.66 **Official Secrets Act 1989, s. 3**

(4) It is a defence for a person charged with an offence under this section to prove that at the time of the alleged offence he did not know, and had no reasonable cause to believe, that the information, document or article in question was such as is mentioned in subsection (1) above or that its disclosure would be damaging within the meaning of that subsection.

To ensure compliance with the ECHR, Article 6, the accused has only an evidential burden as regards proving this defence (*Keogh* [2007] 1 WLR 1500: cf. the Terrorism Act 2000, s. 118 and see further **F3.13** ***et seq***).

The defence that the accused believed that he had lawful authority for disclosure also applies to this offence. For defences generally, see **B9.43**.

DISCLOSURE OF INFORMATION RELEVANT TO CRIMINAL INVESTIGATIONS

Official Secrets Act 1989, s. 4 **B9.67**

(1) A person who is or has been a Crown servant or government contractor is guilty of an offence if without lawful authority he discloses any information, document or other article to which this section applies and which is or has been in his possession by virtue of his position as such.

(As to the materials referred to, see s. 4(2) and (3) at **B9.71**.)

Procedure

As to the requirement of the consent of the A-G, see **B9.36**. This offence is triable either way (Official Secrets Act 1989, s. 10(1)). When tried on indictment it is a class 1 offence. **B9.68**

As to provisions relating to the place of trial, territorial jurisdiction and excluding the public from the trial, see **B9.36**.

Indictment

Statement of Offence **B9.69**

Unlawful disclosure of information resulting in the commission of an offence contrary to section 4(1) of the Official Secrets Act 1989.

Particulars of Offence

A on or about the . . . day of . . ., being then [or having been] a Crown servant [or government contractor], without lawful authority disclosed to P information, which was such that its unauthorised disclosure resulted in the commission of an offence, namely . . .

Sentence

The maximum penalty is: on conviction on indictment, imprisonment for a term not exceeding two years or a fine or both; on summary conviction, imprisonment for a term not exceeding six months or a fine not exceeding the statutory maximum or both (Official Secrets Act 1989, s. 10(1)). **B9.70**

Elements

Official Secrets Act 1989, s. 4 **B9.71**

(2) This section applies to any information, document or other article—
  (a) the disclosure of which—
    (i) results in the commission of an offence; or
    (ii) facilitates an escape from legal custody or the doing of any other act prejudicial to the safekeeping of persons in legal custody; or
    (iii) impedes the prevention or detection of offences or the apprehension or prosecution of suspected offenders; or
  (b) which is such that its unauthorised disclosure would be likely to have any of those effects.

(3) This section also applies to—
  (a) any information obtained by reason of the interception of any communication in obedience to a warrant issued under section 2 of the Interception of Communications Act 1985 or under the authority of an interception warrant under section 5 of the Regulation of Investigatory Powers Act 2000, any information relating to the obtaining of information by reason of any such interception and any document or other article which is or has been used or held for use in, or has been obtained by reason of, any such interception; and

(b) any information obtained by reason of action authorised by a warrant issued under section 3 of the Security Service Act 1989, any information relating to the obtaining of information by reason of any such action and any document or other article which is or has been used or held for use in, or has been obtained by reason of, any such action.

. . .

(6) In this section 'legal custody' includes detention in pursuance of any enactment or any instrument made under an enactment.

The meaning of 'discloses' has been considered at **B9.41**. With regard to the meaning of 'without lawful authority', see s. 7 of the Act, at **B9.52**.

Specific Defences

B9.72 Official Secrets Act 1989, s. 4

(4) It is a defence for a person charged with an offence under this section in respect of a disclosure falling within subsection (2)(a) above to prove that at the time of the alleged offence he did not know, and had no reasonable cause to believe, that the disclosure would have any of the effects there mentioned.

(5) It is a defence for a person charged with an offence under this section in respect of any other disclosure to prove that at the time of the alleged offence he did not know, and had no reasonable cause to believe, that the information, document or article in question was information or a document or article to which this section applies.

Although the accused appears to have the legal burden of proving these defences, it is likely that only an evidential burden would be compatible with the ECHR, Article 6 (see *Keogh* [2007] 1 WLR 1500 and **F3.13** ***et seq***).

The defence that the accused believed that he had lawful authority for disclosure also applies to this offence (see **B9.43** for all defences). There is no defence of disclosure in the public or national interest (*Shayler* [2003] 1 AC 247; see **B9.43**).

OTHER OFFENCES RELATING TO UNAUTHORISED DISCLOSURE OF INFORMATION

B9.73 Other offences dealing with the unauthorised disclosure of information are listed below. They are subject to the same procedural rules governing consent for commencement of proceedings, mode of trial, place of trial, territorial jurisdiction and exclusion of the public from the trial as the offence under s. 1(1) of the Act (see Official Secrets Act 1989, ss. 9, 11 and 15, and **B9.36**). As to sentence, see s. 10 of the Act.

The terms 'disclose', 'Crown servant', 'government contractor', 'State', 'international organisation' and 'without lawful authority' have the same meanings as elsewhere in the Act (see **B9.41, B9.50, B9.51** and **B9.52**).

The other offences created by the Official Secrets Act 1989 are:

(a) Disclosure of information resulting from unauthorised disclosures or entrusted in confidence (s. 5(1) and (2)). This offence provides additional protection for information 'protected against disclosure' (for the meaning of which, see s. 5(5)). Under the 1989 Act, it is not an offence merely to be the recipient of unsolicited information where the disclosure of that information involves the commission of an offence under the Act by the person who provides the information. However, the effect of s. 5 is that, where a third party comes into possession of information either directly or indirectly as a result of an unauthorised disclosure, that third party may be guilty of an offence if he further discloses it. Section 5 applies to any information, document or other article which is protected against disclosure by ss. 1 to 4.

(b) Disclosure of information possessed in contravention of the Official Secrets Act 1911,

s. 1 (Official Secrets Act 1989, s. 5(6)). For s. 1 of the 1911 Act, see **B9.1** to **B9.10**.

(c) Disclosure of information entrusted in confidence to other states or an international organisation (Official Secrets Act 1989, s. 6(1) and (2)). Under this provision, a disclosure is to be regarded as 'damaging' if it would be so regarded in relation to an offence under ss. 1(3), 2(1) or 3(1) (s. 6(4)). For the meaning of 'damaging disclosure' under those provisions, see **B9.49, B9.59** and **B9.65** and the White Paper *Reform of Section 2 of the Official Secrets Act 1911* (1988) Cm. 408 at para. 28.

(d) Disclosure of official information which can be used for gaining access to protected information (Official Secrets Act 1989, s. 8(6)). For the meaning of 'disclosure of official information', see s. 8(7).

The CJA 1991, s. 91, creates an offence of wrongful disclosure of information by a person employed in pursuance of prison escort arrangements. The offence is triable either way. On conviction on indictment, the maximum penalty is imprisonment for a term not exceeding two years or a fine, or both; on summary conviction, the maximum penalty is imprisonment for a term not exceeding six months or a fine not exceeding the statutory maximum, or both. The CJPO 1994, s. 14, creates a similar offence in respect of the wrongful disclosure of information relating to offenders detained at secure training centres.

FAILURE TO SAFEGUARD INFORMATION

The Official Secrets Act 1989, s. 8, creates three offences concerned with failure to safeguard information: **B9.74**

(a) Section 8(1) makes it an offence for a Crown servant or government contractor to fail to safeguard certain information.

(b) Section 8(4) makes it an offence for a person with information as a consequence of an unauthorised disclosure or entrusted in confidence to fail to safeguard it.

(c) Section 8(5) makes it an offence for a person with information entrusted in confidence to States or international organisations to fail to comply with official directions for its return or disposal.

Official Secrets Act 1989, s. 8

(1) Where a Crown servant or government contractor, by virtue of his position as such, has in his possession or under his control any document or other article which it would be an offence under any of the foregoing provisions of this Act for him to disclose without lawful authority he shall be guilty of an offence if—

(a) being a Crown servant, he retains the document or article contrary to his official duty; or

(b) being a government contractor, he fails to comply with an official direction for the return or disposal of the document or article,

or if he fails to take such care to prevent the unauthorised disclosure of the document or article as a person in his position may reasonably be expected to take.

. . .

(4) Where a person has in his possession or under his control any document or other article which it would be an offence under section 5 above for him to disclose without lawful authority, he shall be guilty of an offence if—

(a) he fails to comply with an official direction for its return or disposal; or

(b) where he obtained it from a Crown servant or government contractor on terms requiring it to be held in confidence or in circumstances in which that servant or contractor could reasonably expect that it would be so held, he fails to take such care to prevent its unauthorised disclosure as a person in his position may reasonably be expected to take.

(5) Where a person has in his possession or under his control any document or other article which it would be an offence under section 6 above for him to disclose without lawful authority, he shall be guilty of an offence if he fails to comply with an official direction for its return or disposal.

Procedure

B9.75 As to the requirement of consent of the A-G, see **B9.36**. These offences are triable summarily only (Official Secrets Act 1989, s. 10(2)). Section 11(5) (place of trial) applies to these offences (see **B9.36**).

Sentence

B9.76 The maximum penalty on summary conviction is imprisonment for a term not exceeding three months or a fine not exceeding level 5 on the standard scale or both (Official Secrets Act 1989, s. 10(2)).

Common Elements

B9.77 Certain elements are common to all three offences:

The terms 'possession' and 'control' are not defined by the Act, but 'possession' appears as an essential requirement in a number of criminal offences, and, it is submitted, should be interpreted in the same way as in relation to, e.g., dangerous drugs (see **B20.7** ***et seq.***). The meaning of the word 'disclose' is considered at **B9.41**.

As to the meaning of 'official direction', the Official Secrets Act 1989, s. 8(9), provides that 'official direction' means a direction duly given by a Crown servant or government contractor or by or on behalf of a prescribed body or a body of a prescribed class. The Official Secrets Act 1989 (Prescription) Order (SI 1990 No. 200), art. 4 (as amended by SI 2003 No. 1918 art. 2, sch. 2), specifies the bodies which have the power to impose official restrictions for the purpose of s. 8(9); the Civil Aviation Authority and certain security-related tribunals have such power.

As to the only circumstances in which a disclosure is made with lawful authority, see s. 7 of the Act and **B9.52**.

Elements Specific to s. 8(1) and (4)

B9.78 The meanings of 'Crown servant' and 'government contractor' are considered at **B9.50** and **B9.51**. However, for the purposes of this offence, the Official Secrets Act 1989, s. 8(3), provides that 'Crown servant' includes a person notified within the meaning of s. 1(1), who is not otherwise either a Crown servant or a government contractor (see **B9.39**).

Elements Specific to s. 8(5)

B9.79 The information protected by this offence is that which it would be an offence to disclose under s. 6 of the Act (see **B9.73**). As to such information, see s. 6(1).

Specific Defences

B9.80 The accused's belief that he had lawful authority for the disclosure is a defence to all three charges under the Official Secrets Act 1989, s. 8. As to this and other defences, see **B9.43**.

In relation to the offence under s. 8(1) only, the Official Secrets Act 1989, s. 8(2), provides that it is a defence for a Crown servant to prove that at the time of the alleged offence he believed that he was acting in accordance with his official duty and had no reasonable cause to believe otherwise. Although the legal burden of proving this defence appears to lie on the accused, it is likely that only an evidential burden would be compatible with the ECHR, Article 6 (see *Keogh* [2007] 1 WLR 1500 and **F3.13** ***et seq.***).

UNLAWFUL INTERCEPTION OF COMMUNICATIONS BY PUBLIC AND PRIVATE SYSTEMS

The Regulation of Investigatory Powers Act 2000 (RIPA 2000), s. 1, creates two interception offences. One (s. 1(1)) is concerned with the interception of communications transmitted by either public postal or public telecommunications systems; the other offence (s. 1(2)) is concerned with the interception of communications transmitted by private telecommunications systems. **B9.81**

Definition

Regulation of Investigatory Powers Act 2000, s. 1 **B9.82**

(1) It shall be an offence for a person intentionally and without lawful authority to intercept, at any place in the United Kingdom, any communication in the course of its transmission by means of—
   (a) a public postal service; or
   (b) a public telecommunication system.

(2) It shall be an offence for a person—
   (a) intentionally and without lawful authority, and
   (b) otherwise than in circumstances in which his conduct is excluded by subsection (6) from criminal liability under this subsection,

   to intercept, at any place in the United Kingdom, any communication in the course of its transmission by means of a private telecommunication system.

Procedure

The offences are triable either way (RIPA 2000, s. 1(7)). When tried on indictment, an offence under s. 1 is a class 3 offence. Proceedings for an offence cannot be instituted except, in England and Wales, with the consent of the DPP (RIPA 2000, s. 1(8)(a)). **B9.83**

Sentence

The maximum punishment is: on conviction on indictment, imprisonment for a term not exceeding two years, or a fine, or both; and, on summary conviction, a fine not exceeding the statutory maximum (RIPA 2000, s. 1(7)). **B9.84**

Elements of the Offence: Postal Service and Telecommunications Systems

Section 2(1) of the RIPA 2000 defines various terms. **B9.85**

'Public postal service' means any postal service which is offered to or provided to, or to a substantial section of, the public in one or more parts of the UK. 'Postal service' means any service which (a) consists in the following, or in any one or more of them, namely, the collection, sorting, conveyance, distribution and delivery (whether in the UK or elsewhere) of postal items; and (b) is offered or provided as a service the main purpose of which, or one of the main purposes of which, is to make available, or to facilitate, a means of transmission from place to place of postal items containing communications.

'Public telecommunication system' means any such parts of a telecommunication system by means of which any public telecommunications service is provided as are located in the UK. 'Telecommunication system' means any system (including the apparatus comprised in it) which exists (whether wholly or partly in the UK or elsewhere) for the purpose of facilitating the transmission of communications by any means involving the use of electrical or electro-magnetic energy.

'Public telecommunications service' means any telecommunications service which is offered or provided to, or to a substantial section of, the public in any one or more parts of the UK.

'Telecommunications service' means any service that consists in the provision of access to, and of facilities for making use of, any telecommunication system (whether or not one provided by the person providing the service).

'Private telecommunication system' means any telecommunication system which, not being a public telecommunication system, is a system which satisfies certain conditions: (a) it is attached, directly or indirectly and whether or not for the purpose of the communication in question, to a public telecommunication system; and (b) there is apparatus comprised in the system which is both located in the UK and used (with or without other apparatus) for making the attachment to the public telecommunication system.

General terms are defined in the RIPA 2000, s. 81: 'apparatus' includes any equipment, machinery or device and any wire or cable; 'communication' includes (a) (except in the definition of 'postal service' in s. 2(1)) anything transmitted by means of a postal service; (b) anything comprising speech, music, sounds, visual images or data of any description; and (c) signals serving either for the impartation of anything between persons, between a person and a thing or between things or for the actuation or control of any apparatus; a 'person' includes any organisation and any association or combination of persons.

Interception

B9.86 Section 2(2) of the RIPA 2000 defines 'interception' for the purposes of the Act. A person intercepts a communication in the course of its transmission by means of a telecommunication system if, and only if, he (a) so modifies or interferes with the system or its operation, (b) so monitors transmissions made by means of the system, or (c) so monitors transmissions made by wireless telegraphy to or from apparatus comprised in the system, as to make some or all of the contents of the communication available, while being transmitted, to a person other than the sender or intended recipient of the communication.

References to the interception of a communication do not include reference to the interception of any communication broadcast for general reception (s. 2(3)).

Modification of a telecommunication system includes references to the attachment of any apparatus to, or other modification of or interference with (a) any part of the system, or (b) any wireless telegraphy apparatus used for making transmissions to or from apparatus comprised in the system (s. 2(6)).

An interception takes place in the UK if, and only if, the modification, interference or monitoring or, in the case of a postal item, the interception is effected by conduct within the UK and the communication is either (a) intercepted in the course of its transmission by means of a public telecommunication system; or (b) intercepted in the course of its transmission by means of a private telecommunication system in a case in which the sender or intended recipient of the communication is in the UK (s. 2(4)).

The period during which a communication is being transmitted by a telecommunication system includes any time when the system by means of which the communication is being, or has been, transmitted is used for storing it in a manner that enables the intended recipient to collect it or otherwise to have access to it (s. 2(7)). Section 2(7) has the effect of extending the time of communication until the intended recipient has collected it (and therefore includes 'mirrored' e-mails) (*R (NTL) v Ipswich Crown Court* [2003] QB 131). The contents of a communication made available to a person while being transmitted includes any case in which any of the contents of the communication, while being transmitted, are diverted or recorded so as to be available to a person subsequently (s. 2(8)). The tape recording of a telephone call by one party to it, without the knowledge of the other party, does not amount to interception of a communication within this section (*Hardy* [2003] 1 Cr App R 494). Nor does a recording of what one person said on the telephone, picked up by a surveillance device placed in his car which did not record any speech by the other party (*E* [2004] 1 WLR 3279).

'Postal item' means any letter, postcard or other such thing in writing as may be used by the sender for imparting information to the recipient, or any packet or parcel (s. 2(11)).

The exception in relation to traffic data provides that references to the interception of a communication in the course of its transmission by means of a postal service or telecommunication system do not include reference to (a) any conduct that takes place in relation only to so much of the communication as consists in any traffic data comprised in or attached to a communication (whether by the sender or otherwise) for the purposes of any postal service or telecommunication system by means of which it is being or may be transmitted; or (b) any such conduct, in connection with conduct falling within paragraph (a), as gives a person who is neither the sender nor the intended recipient only so much access to a communication as is necessary for the purpose of identifying traffic data so comprised or attached (s. 2(5)). 'Traffic data' means (a) any data identifying, or purporting to identify, apparatus or location to or from which the communication is or may be transmitted; (b) any data identifying or selecting, or purporting to identify or select, apparatus through which, or by means of which, the communication is or may be transmitted; (c) any data comprising signals for the actuation of apparatus used for the purpose of a telecommunication system for effecting (in whole or in part) the transmission of any communication; and (d) any data identifying the data or other data as data comprised in or attached to a particular communication. The expression 'traffic data' includes data identifying a computer file or computer program, access to which is obtained, or which is run, by means of the communication to the extent only that the file or program is identified by reference to the apparatus in which it is stored (s. 2(9)).

References, in relation to traffic data comprising signals for the actuation of apparatus, to a telecommunication system by means of which a communication is being or may be transmitted include references to any telecommunication system in which that apparatus is comprised, and references to traffic data being attached to a communication include references to the data and the communication being logically associated with each other (s. 2(10)). 'Data' in relation to a postal item means anything written on the outside of the item (s. 2(10)).

Lawful Authority

Regulation of Investigatory Powers Act 2000, ss. 1, 3 and 4 **B9.87**

1.—(5) Conduct has lawful authority for the purposes of this section if, and only if—
(a) it is authorised by or under section 3 or 4;
(b) it takes place in accordance with a warrant under section 5 ('an interception warrant'); or
(c) it is in exercise, in relation to any stored communication, of any statutory power that is exercised (apart from this section) for the purpose of obtaining information or of taking possession of any document or other property;

and conduct (whether or not prohibited by this section) which has lawful authority for the purpose of this section by virtue of paragraph (a) or (b) shall also be taken to be lawful for all other purposes.

3.—(1) Conduct by any person consisting in the interception of a communication is authorised by this section if the communication is one which, or which that person has reasonable grounds for believing, is both—
(a) a communication sent by a person who has consented to the interception; and
(b) a communication the intended recipient of which has so consented.

(2) Conduct by any person consisting in the interception of a communication is authorised by this section if—
(a) the communication is one sent by, or intended for, a person who has consented to the interception; and

(b) surveillance by means of that interception has been authorised under part II.

(3) Conduct consisting in the interception of a communication is authorised by this section if—

(a) it is conduct by or on behalf of a person who provides a postal service or a telecommunications service; and

(b) it takes place for purposes connected with the provision or operation of that service or with the enforcement, in relation to that service, of any enactment relating to the use of postal services or telecommunications services.

(4) Conduct by any person consisting in the interception of a communication in the course of its transmission by means of wireless telegraphy is authorised by this section if it takes place—

(a) with the authority of a designated person under section 48 of the Wireless Telegraphy Act 2006 (interception and disclosure of wireless telegraphy messages); and

(b) for purposes connected with anything falling within subsection (5).

(5) Each of the following falls within this subsection—

(a) the grant of wireless telegraphy licences under the Wireless Telegraphy Act 2006;

(b) the prevention or detection of anything which constitutes interference with wireless telegraphy; and

(c) the enforcement of—

(i) any provision of part 2 (other than chapter 2 and sections 27 to 31) or part 3 of that Act, or

(ii) any enactment not falling within sub-paragraph (i),

that relates to such interference.

4.—(1) Conduct by any person ('the interceptor') consisting in the interception of a communication in the course of its transmission by means of a telecommunication system is authorised by this section if—

(a) the interception is carried out for the purpose of obtaining information about the communications of a person who, or who the interceptor has reasonable grounds for believing, is in a country or territory outside the United Kingdom;

(b) the interception relates to the use of a telecommunications service provided to persons in that country or territory which is either—

(i) a public telecommunications service; or

(ii) a telecommunications service that would be a public telecommunications service if the persons to whom it is offered or provided were members of the public in a part of the United Kingdom;

(c) the person who provides that service (whether the interceptor or another person) is required by the law of that country or territory to carry out, secure or facilitate the interception in question;

(d) the situation is one in relation to which such further conditions as may be prescribed by regulations made by the Secretary of State are required to be satisfied before conduct may be treated as authorised by virtue of this subsection; and

(e) the conditions so prescribed are satisfied in relation to that situation.

The Telecommunications (Lawful Business Practice) (Interception of Communications) Regulations 2000 (SI 2000 No. 2699) have been passed under s. 4(2) of the RIPA 2000, authorising certain lawful business practices. These authorisations do not exceed those permitted by Articles 5.2 and 14.1 of Directive 97/66/EC. In particular, the Regulations specify that interceptions can only be authorised if the system controller has made all reasonable efforts to inform the users of the system that communications may be intercepted. The Information Commissioner's Office has issued guidance to businesses on employment practices which includes information on the circumstances in which interceptions may be permitted within the workplace and the precautions which must be taken by employers to protect the privacy of the workforce.

The Regulation of Investigatory Powers (Conditions for the Lawful Interception of Persons outside the United Kingdom) Regulations 2004 (SI 2004 No. 157) prescribe the following conditions under s. 4(1)(d): (a) the interception is carried out for the purposes of a criminal investigation; and (b) the criminal investigation is being carried out in a country or territory that is party to an international agreement designated for the purposes of s. 1(4).

Probably the most important means of making an interception lawful will be through action taken under an interception warrant. There are extensive statutory procedures in relation to the issuing, exercising and oversight of such warrants (RIPA 2000, ss. 5 to 11).

It should be noted that providers of relevant services have an obligation to maintain an interception capability if required by the Secretary of State under the RIPA 2000, s. 12.

Further, there is a provision providing a general saving for lawful conduct:

Regulation of Investigatory Powers Act 2000, s. 80

Nothing in any of the provisions of this Act by virtue of which conduct of any description is or may be authorised by any warrant, authorisation or notice, or by virtue of which information may be obtained in any manner, shall be construed—

(a) as making it unlawful to engage in any conduct of that description which is not otherwise unlawful under this Act and would not be unlawful apart from this Act;

(b) as otherwise requiring—

(i) the issue, grant or giving of such a warrant, authorisation or notice, or

(ii) the taking of any step for or towards obtaining the authority of such a warrant, authorisation or notice,

before any such conduct of that description is engaged in; or

(c) as prejudicing any power to obtain information by any means not involving conduct that may be authorised under this Act.

As to the continuing validity of a warrant issued under the Interception of Communications Act 1985, see the RIPA 2000, s. 82(4).

Private Telecommunications Interceptions: Defence

A person's conduct is excluded from criminal liability for the offence contrary to the RIPA 2000, s. 1(2), if he is a person with a right to control the operation or the use of the system; or he has the express or implied consent of such a person to make the interception (s. 1(6)). In *Stanford* [2006] 1 WLR 1554, it was held that 'control' means 'authorise and forbid' and not the unrestricted ability physically to use and operate the system. Any other approach would contravene the purposes of the legislation. **B9.88**

INCITEMENT TO DISAFFECTION

Incitement to Disaffection Act 1934, ss. 1 and 2 **B9.89**

1. If any person maliciously and advisedly endeavours to seduce any member of His Majesty's forces from his duty or allegiance to His Majesty, he shall be guilty of an offence under this Act.

2.—(1) If any person, with intent to commit or to aid, abet, counsel, or procure the commission of an offence under section 1 of this Act, has in his possession or under his control any document of such a nature that the dissemination of copies thereof among members of His Majesty's forces would constitute such an offence, he shall be guilty of an offence under this Act.

As to armed forces discipline, see the Armed Forces Act 2006 (when in force) and the Army Act 1955, the Air Force Act 1955 and the Naval Discipline Act 1957 (which continue to apply until the 2006 Act is implemented).

Police Act 1996, s. 91

(1) Any person who causes, or attempts to cause, or does any act calculated to cause, disaffection amongst the members of any police force, or induces or attempts to induce, or does any act calculated to induce, any member of a police force to withhold his services, shall be guilty of an offence . . .

(2) This section applies to special constables appointed for a police area as it applies to members of a police force.

There are like offences in relation to Ministry of Defence police (see the Ministry of Defence Police Act 1997, s. 6).

Procedure

B9.90 **Incitement to Disaffection Act 1934, s. 3**

(2) No prosecution in England under this Act shall take place without the consent of the Director of Public Prosecutions.

(3) Where a prosecution under this Act is being carried on by the Director of Public Prosecutions, a court of summary jurisdiction shall not deal with the case summarily without the consent of the Director.

The offences under the Incitement to Disaffection Act 1934 and the Police Act 1996 are triable either way. When tried on indictment they are class 3 offences.

Sentence

B9.91 The maximum penalties are:

Incitement to Disaffection Act 1934, s. 1: on indictment, two years and/or a fine; summarily, four months and/or a fine not exceeding the statutory maximum (Incitement to Disaffection Act 1934, s. 3(1)). The court also has power to order the destruction or other disposal of any documents connected with the offence after conviction of the accused and after expiration of the time during which an appeal may be lodged (Incitement to Disaffection Act 1934, s. 3(4)).

Police Act 1996, s. 91: on indictment, two years and/or a fine; summarily, six months and/or a fine not exceeding the statutory maximum.

Elements

B9.92 It is not necessary to show that any particular individual was the object of the attempted seduction. It suffices if the attempt was directed to members of the armed forces, or a police force generally (*Bowman* (1912) 76 JP 271). However, if the allegation is that the attempt was to seduce particular individuals, the status of any such particular individual as a serving member of the force at the time of the offence must be proved. It also appears necessary that the accused had the *mens rea* of knowing that the person concerned was such a serving member, though this may be proved circumstantially, for example by evidence that the offence was committed at a military establishment or police station, or that the person concerned was in uniform (see *Fuller* (1797) 2 Leach 790). 'Allegiance' was considered in *Joyce v DPP* [1946] AC 347, and the correct form of the indictment was considered in *Arrowsmith* [1975] QB 678.

The method of attempted seduction, whether by written or oral communication, is irrelevant, though circumstances such as the offering of an inducement or the use of threats or blackmail will no doubt affect sentence.

Section B10 Terrorism, Piracy and Hijacking

TERRORISM: OVERVIEW

Until the Terrorism Act 2000 (TA 2000), anti-terrorist powers were provided by means of temporary provisions which were renewed on an annual basis by Parliament. The TA 2000 gave permanent effect to anti-terrorist powers for the first time. Those powers have since been supplemented by the Anti-terrorism, Crime and Security Act 2001 (A-tCSA 2001) and the Terrorism Act 2006 (TA 2006). This section deals with the substantive offences and investigative and other powers provided for by each of those Acts, along with other relevant miscellaneous provisions contained within additional legislation. Offences related to piracy and hijacking, which might be perpetrated in a terrorist context, are also set out in this section. Finally, the breach of control orders designed to limit the activities of suspected terrorists and imposed under the Prevention of Terrorism Act 2005 is dealt with. **B10.1**

OFFENCES UNDER THE TERRORISM ACT 2000: GENERAL

The TA 2000 created a number of offences which were designed to fill perceived gaps in available legislative provision aimed at countering acts of terrorism. In addition it developed the system of proscribing organisations, first introduced in response to Irish terrorism in 1974, and created new powers in respect of the investigation of offences and the arrest and detention of suspects. **B10.2**

Definition of Terrorism

Terrorism Act 2000, s. 1 **B10.3**

(1) In this Act 'terrorism' means the use or threat of action where—
  (a) the action falls within subsection (2),
  (b) the use or threat is designed to influence the government or an international governmental organisation or to intimidate the public or a section of the public, and
  (c) the use or threat is made for the purpose of advancing a political, religious or ideological cause.

(2) Action falls within this subsection if it—
   (a) involves serious violence against a person,
   (b) involves serious damage to property,
   (c) endangers a person's life, other than that of the person committing the action,
   (d) creates a serious risk to the health or safety of the public or a section of the public, or
   (e) is designed seriously to interfere with or seriously to disrupt an electronic system.

The definition of terrorism is widely drawn and, in essence, involves the use or threat of violence for political, religious or ideological reasons. Terms used in s. 1(1) and (2) are defined in s. 1(4) and 1(5). The references to action, person, public, property and government apply equally whether the action, person, public property or government is inside or outside the UK (s. 1(4)(a) to (d) and (5)). In *F* [2007] 3 WLR 164 it was held that the meaning of the phrase 'a country other than the United Kingdom' in s. 1(4)(d) is plain and the terrorist legislation applies equally in respect of undemocratic countries as it does in relation to democratic governments.

Special Evidence Provisions

B10.4 **Terrorism Act 2000, s. 118**

(1) Subsection (2) applies where in accordance with a provision mentioned in subsection (5) it is a defence for a person charged with an offence to prove a particular matter.
(2) If the person adduces evidence which is sufficient to raise an issue with respect to the matter the court or jury shall assume that the defence is satisfied unless the prosecution proves beyond reasonable doubt that it is not.
(3) Subsection (4) applies where in accordance with a provision mentioned in subsection (5) a court—
   (a) may make an assumption in relation to a person charged with an offence unless a particular matter is proved, or
   (b) may accept a fact as sufficient evidence unless a particular matter is proved.
(4) If evidence is adduced which is sufficient to raise an issue with respect to the matter mentioned in subsection (3)(a) or (b) the court shall treat it as proved unless the prosecution disproves it beyond reasonable doubt.
(5) The provisions in respect of which subsections (2) and (4) apply are—
   (a) sections 12(4), 39(5)(a), 54, 57, 58, 77 and 103 of this Act, and
   (b) sections 13, 32 and 33 of the Northern Ireland (Emergency Provisions) Act 1996 (possession and information offences) as they have effect by virtue of schedule 1 to this Act.

Special evidence provisions, as set out in the TA 2000, s. 118, apply in relation to a number of the offences contained within the legislation. They are specified in s. 118(5). Those provisions are concerned with many of the offences which impose a reverse burden on the defendant and are designed to ensure that the legislation is not incompatible with the ECHR. (For analysis of the effect of reverse burdens, see **F3.13**.) In addition, there are special rules relating to documentary evidence set out in s. 120.

Terrorism Act 2000, s. 120

(1) A document which purports to be—
   (a) a notice or direction given or order made by the Secretary of State for the purposes of a provision of this Act, and
   (b) signed by him or on his behalf,
   shall be received in evidence and shall, until the contrary is proved, be deemed to have been given or made by the Secretary of State.
(2) A document bearing a certificate which—
   (a) purports to be signed by or on behalf of the Secretary of State, and
   (b) states that the document is a true copy of a notice or direction given or order made by the Secretary of State for the purposes of a provision of this Act,
   shall be evidence (or, in Scotland, sufficient evidence) of the document in legal proceedings.
(3) In subsections (1) and (2) a reference to an order does not include a reference to an order made by statutory instrument.

(4) The Documentary Evidence Act 1868 shall apply to an authorisation given in writing by the Secretary of State for the purposes of this Act as it applies to an order made by him.

MEMBERSHIP OF A PROSCRIBED ORGANISATION

Terrorism Act 2000, s. 11 **B10.5**

(1) A person commits an offence if he belongs or professes to belong to a proscribed organisation.

Procedure

The offence of belonging to a proscribed organisation is triable either way and when tried on indictment is a class 3 offence. Under the TA 2000, s. 117(2), the consent of the DPP is required for proceedings to be instituted but, if it appears to him that the offence is committed for a purpose wholly or partly connected with the affairs of a country other than the UK, then the A-G must consent to the prosecution (s. 117(2A)). **B10.6**

The procedure set out in the Proscribed Organisations (Applications for Deproscription) Regulations 2001 (SI 2001 No. 107) enables an application to be made for an organisation to be removed from the list of organisations contained in sch. 2. An appeal against a refusal to remove an organisation from the list may be made to the Proscribed Organisations Appeal Committee under the TA 2000, s. 5(1) and (2).

Sentencing

The maximum penalty is: on conviction on indictment, imprisonment for a term not exceeding ten years, a fine, or both; on summary conviction, imprisonment for a term not exceeding six months, a fine not exceeding the statutory maximum, or both (TA 2000, s. 11(3)). **B10.7**

In *Hundal* [2004] 2 Cr App R (S) 355, the offenders were convicted of offences under s. 11, as belonging to the International Sikh Youth Federation. It was accepted that the offenders did not know that the organisation was proscribed in the UK. Sentences of 30 months' imprisonment were reduced to 12 months in each case.

Elements

Proscribed organisations are listed in the TA 2000, sch. 2. It is an offence to be a member of an organisation listed in sch. 2 or an organisation operating under the name of an organisation listed in sch. 2. Under s. 3(3), the Secretary of State may add an organisation to the list contained in sch. 2 if he is of the belief that the organisation is involved in terrorism (s. 3(3)). He may also remove or otherwise amend the schedule (s. 3(4)). **B10.8**

Under s. 3(6), if the Secretary of State is of the belief that a proscribed organisation is operating under a different name than one listed in sch. 2 or is operating under a name that does not appear in sch. 2 but is to all intents and purposes the same organisation as one listed in sch. 2, he may direct that the name not specified shall be treated as the same as one listed in sch. 2. By way of example, the Proscribed Organisations (Name Changes) Order 2006 (SI 2006 No. 1919) ensures that 'Kongra Gele Kurdistan' and 'Kadek', whilst they are names not listed in sch. 2, are to be treated as further names for the Kurdistan Workers Party (the PKK) which does appear there.

If a person joins an organisation in a country where the organisation is not proscribed, he nonetheless commits the offence if he remains a member of the organisation and travels to this jurisdiction (*Hundal* [2004] 2 Cr App R 307).

Under the TA 2006, s. 17 (see **B10.137**), if a person does anything outside the UK which would amount to an offence under s. 11(1) if done in any part of it, he will be liable for the offence in that part of the UK.

Under the TA 2000, s. 10(1), the following evidence may not be called by the prosecution in proceedings for this offence:

(a) evidence of anything done in relation to an application under s. 4 to deproscribe the organisation;
(b) evidence of anything done in relation to proceedings before the Proscribed Organisations Appeal Commission under the TA 2000, s. 5, or the HRA 1998, s. 7(1);
(c) evidence of anything done in relation to a further appeal on a matter of law under the TA 2000, s. 6; and
(d) any document submitted for any of the above purposes.

However, s. 10(2) allows such evidence to be called by the defence.

A person convicted of an offence contrary to s. 11 has a potential appeal available to him under s. 7 of the Act. The first two requirements of s. 7 are that an appeal to the Proscribed Organisations Appeal Commission under s. 5 must have been allowed and that an order has been made to deproscribe the organisation under s. 3(3)(b) in accordance with an order of the Commission under s. 5(4) (s. 7(1)(a) and (b)). Then, if the person was convicted of an offence under any of ss. 11 to 13, 15 to 19 and 56 and the activity to which the charge referred took place on or after the date of the refusal to deproscribe against which the appeal under s. 5 was brought, the right of appeal arises (s. 7(1)(c) and (d)). See also the Court of Appeal (Appeals from Proscribed Organisations Appeal Commission) Rules 2002 (SI 2002 No. 1843).

Specific Defence

B10.9 **Terrorism Act 2000, s. 11**

(2) It is a defence for a person charged with an offence under subsection (1) above to prove—
(a) that the organisation was not proscribed on the last (or only) occasion on which he became a member or began to profess to be a member, and
(b) that he has not taken part in the activities of the organisation at any time while it was proscribed.

In *Sheldrake v DPP* [2005] 1 AC 264, the House of Lords read down s. 11(2) so as to interpret it as imposing only an evidential burden on the accused. Even though the intention of Parliament had been to impose a legal burden, that burden was not a proportionate and legitimate response to the threat posed by terrorism, and illegitimately infringed the presumption of innocence.

SUPPORTING A PROSCRIBED ORGANISATION

B10.10 **Terrorism Act 2000, s. 12**

(1) A person commits an offence if—
(a) he invites support for a proscribed organisation, and
(b) the support is not, or is not restricted to, the provision of money or other property (within the meaning of section 15).

(2) A person commits an offence if he arranges, manages or assists in arranging or managing a meeting which he knows is—
(a) to support a proscribed organisation,
(b) to further the activities of a proscribed organisation, or
(c) to be addressed by a person who belongs or professes to belong to a proscribed organisation.

(3) A person commits an offence if he addresses a meeting and the purpose of his address is to encourage support for a proscribed organisation or to further its activities.

Procedure

An allegation of an offence contrary to the TA 2000, s. 12, is triable either way; when tried on indictment it is a class 3 offence. Under s. 117(2), the consent of the DPP is required for proceedings to be instituted but, if it appears to the DPP that the offence is committed for a purpose wholly or partly connected with the affairs of a country other than the UK, then the A-G must consent to the prosecution (s. 117(2A)). B10.11

The appeal available in respect of a conviction under s. 11 is also available in respect of a conviction under s. 12 (see **B10.8**)

Sentencing

The maximum penalty is: on conviction on indictment, imprisonment for a term not exceeding ten years, a fine, or both; on summary conviction, imprisonment for a term not exceeding six months, a fine not exceeding the statutory maximum, or both (TA 2000, s. 12(6)). B10.12

Elements

For 'proscribed organisation', see **B10.6** B10.13

A 'meeting' consists of a gathering of three or more people (TA 2000, s. 12(5)(a)).

Specific Defence

Terrorism Act 2000, s. 12 B10.14

(4) Where a person is charged with an offence under subsection (2)(c) in respect of a private meeting it is a defence for him to prove that he had no reasonable cause to believe that the address mentioned in subsection (2)(c) would support a proscribed organisation or further its activities.

The defence under s. 12(4) is subject to the provisions of s. 118 of the 2000 Act and thus an evidential burden is imposed on the accused. He is therefore required to adduce sufficient evidence to raise the issue as a defence. The defence is satisfied unless the Crown disproves it to the criminal standard (see **B10.4**).

WEARING A UNIFORM

Terrorism Act 2000, s. 13 B10.15

(1) A person in a public place commits an offence if he—
 (a) wears an item of clothing, or
 (b) wears, carries or displays an article,
 in such a way or in such circumstances as to arouse reasonable suspicion that he is a member or supporter of a proscribed organisation.

Procedure

An allegation of an offence contrary to the TA 2000, s. 13, is triable summarily only. Under s. 117(2), the consent of the DPP is required for proceedings to be instituted but, if it appears to him that the offence is committed for a purpose wholly or partly connected with the affairs of a country other than the UK, then the A-G must consent to the prosecution (s. 117(2A)). B10.16

The appeal available in respect of a conviction under s. 11 is also available in respect of a conviction under s. 13 (see **B10.8**).

Sentencing

The maximum penalty is imprisonment for a term not exceeding six months, a fine not exceeding level 5 on the standard scale, or both (TA 2000, s. 13(3)). B10.17

Elements

B10.18 By virtue of the TA 2000, s. 121, an 'article' includes a substance or any other thing and a 'public place' is one to which the public have access, whether for payment or not.

In *Rankin v Murray* 2004 SLT 1164, the offender had worn jewellery which bore the initials 'UVF'. The Scottish High Court of Justiciary held that the wearing of a ring in which prominent initials could readily be seen was sufficient to arouse in the mind of an objective observer reasonable suspicion that R was a supporter, if not a member, of a proscribed organisation. Even on the assumption it was established that R had received the ring as a gift, regularly visited Northern Ireland, and was not a member or supporter of the said organisation, those facts did not negate the actual suspicion of the officers nor the objectively reasonable basis for that suspicion.

For 'proscribed organisation' and deproscription, see **B10.6**.

For the related public order offence, see **B11.11**.

TERRORIST FUND-RAISING

B10.19 **Terrorism Act 2000, s. 15**

(1) A person commits an offence if he—
   (a) invites another to provide money or other property, and
   (b) intends that it should be used, or has reasonable cause to suspect that it may be used, for the purposes of terrorism.

(2) A person commits an offence if he—
   (a) receives money or other property, and
   (b) intends that it should be used, or has reasonable cause to suspect that it may be used, for the purposes of terrorism.

(3) A person commits an offence if he—
   (a) provides money or other property, and
   (b) knows or has reasonable cause to suspect that it will or may be used for the purposes of terrorism.

Procedure

B10.20 An allegation of an offence contrary to the TA 2000, s. 15 is triable either way and when tried on indictment is a class 3 offence. Under s. 117(2), the consent of the DPP is required for proceedings to be instituted but, if it appears to him that the offence is committed for a purpose wholly or partly connected with the affairs of a country other than the UK, then the A-G must consent to the prosecution (s. 117(2A)).

See **B10.77** for extended jurisdiction provisions in relation to this offence.

Sentencing

B10.21 The maximum penalty is: on conviction on indictment, imprisonment for a term not exceeding 14 years, a fine, or both; on summary conviction, imprisonment for a term not exceeding six months, a fine not exceeding the statutory maximum, or both (TA 2000, s. 22). A court may also make a forfeiture order (s. 23(1)). For further details, in relation to the offences under s. 15(1) and (2), see s. 23(2), (6), (7) and (9) and sch. 4. For further details in relation to the offence under s. 15(3), see s. 23(3), (6), (7) and (9) and sch. 4.

Elements

B10.22 By virtue of the TA 2000, s. 121, 'property' includes property wherever situated and whether real or personal, heritable or moveable, things in action and other intangible or incorporeal property.

Specific Defences

Section 21 of the TA 2000 provides a number of specific defences to an allegation of an offence contrary to s. 15. Each of the defences involves co-operation with police officers. **B10.23**

(1) Under s. 21(1), no offence is committed if a person who is involved in any of the actions covered by s. 15 is acting with the express consent of a constable.
(2) By virtue of s. 21(2), if a person is involved in a transaction or arrangement relating to money or other property, no offence is committed if he discloses to a constable (a) his suspicion or belief that the money or other property is terrorist property, and (b) the information on which his suspicion or belief is based. This defence applies only where a person makes a disclosure as soon as is reasonably practicable and on his own initiative after he becomes concerned in the relevant transaction (s. 21(3)). By virtue of s. 21(4), if a constable forbids a person from continuing his involvement in the transaction or arrangement in relation to which the disclosure was made but he nevertheless continues, the defence does not apply. For 'terrorist property', see **B10.27**.
(3) For any person charged with an offence under s. 15(2) or (3), but not s. 15(1), the defence is open to him to prove that he intended to make a disclosure of the kind mentioned in s. 21(2) and (3), but there is a reasonable excuse for his failure to do so (s. 21(5)).

The TA 2000 makes special provision for employees where their employer has established a procedure for making any required disclosure. Under s. 21(6), in relation to all these defences, where a person is in employment and his employer has established a procedure for making disclosures, the duty of disclosure on the employee is to make disclosure in accordance with the procedure. 'Transaction or arrangement relating to money or other property' includes a reference to use or possession (s. 21(7)).

For the compatibility of the reverse burden with the ECHR, Article 6, see **F3.13** *et seq.*

POSSESSION OF PROPERTY

Terrorism Act 2000, s. 16 **B10.24**

(1) A person commits an offence if he uses money or other property for the purposes of terrorism.
(2) A person commits an offence if he—
  (a) possesses money or other property, and
  (b) intends that it should be used, or has reasonable cause to suspect that it may be used, for the purposes of terrorism.

Procedure

An allegation of an offence contrary to the TA 2000, s. 16 is triable either way and when tried on indictment is a class 3 offence. Under s. 117(2), the consent of the DPP is required for proceedings to be instituted but, if it appears to him that the offence is committed for a purpose wholly or partly connected with the affairs of a country other than the UK, then the A-G must consent to the prosecution (s. 117(2A)). **B10.25**

See **B10.77** for extended jurisdiction provisions in relation to this offence.

Sentencing

The maximum penalty is: on conviction on indictment, imprisonment for a term not exceeding 14 years, a fine, or both; on summary conviction, imprisonment for a term not exceeding six months, a fine not exceeding the statutory maximum, or both (TA 2000, s. 22). A court may also make a forfeiture order (s. 23(1)); for further details, see s. 23(2), (6), (7) and (9) and sch. 4. **B10.26**

Elements

B10.27 For 'terrorism', see **B10.3**. By virtue of s. 14(1) of the 2000 Act, 'terrorist property' means (a) money or other property which is likely to be used for the purposes of terrorism (including any resources of a proscribed organisation), (b) proceeds of the commission of acts of terrorism, and (c) proceeds of acts carried out for the purposes of terrorism. The 'proceeds' of an act include any property which wholly or partly, and directly or indirectly, represents the proceeds of the act (including payments or other regards in connection with its commission). An organisation's resources include any money or other property which is applied or made available, or is to be applied or made available, for use by the organisation (s. 14(2)). For 'property', see **B10.22**.

The offence is one of specific intent and is concerned with knowingly providing money or other property in support of a proscribed organisation. If the organisation has been properly proscribed, the offence cannot be seen as disproportionate (*O'Driscoll v Secretary of State for the Home Department* [2003] ACD 35).

Specific Defences

B10.28 The defences available to a person charged with an offence contrary to the TA 2000, s. 16, are the same as those available to a person charged with an offence contrary to s. 15 (see **B10.23**).

For the compatibility of the reverse burden with the ECHR, Article 6, see **F3.13** ***et seq.***

FUNDING ARRANGEMENTS

B10.29 **Terrorism Act 2000, s. 17**

A person commits an offence if—

(a) he enters into or becomes concerned in an arrangement as a result of which money or other property is made available or is to be made available to another, and

(b) he knows or has reasonable cause to suspect that it will or may be used for the purposes of terrorism.

Procedure

B10.30 An allegation of an offence contrary to the TA 2000, s. 17, is triable either way and when tried on indictment is a class 3 offence. Under s. 117(2), the consent of the DPP is required for proceedings to be instituted but, if it appears to him that the offence is committed for a purpose wholly or partly connected with the affairs of a country other than the UK, then the A-G must consent to the prosecution (s. 117(2A)).

See **B10.77** for extended jurisdiction provisions in relation to this offence.

Sentencing

B10.31 The maximum penalty is: on conviction on indictment, imprisonment for a term not exceeding 14 years, a fine, or both; on summary conviction, imprisonment for a term not exceeding six months, a fine not exceeding the statutory maximum, or both (TA 2000, s. 22). A court may also make a forfeiture order (s. 23(1)); for further details, see s. 23(4), (6), (7) and (9) and sch. 4.

Elements

B10.32 For 'terrorism', see **B10.3**.

Specific Defences

The defences available to a person charged with an offence contrary to the TA 2000, s. 17, are the same as those available to a person charged with an offence contrary to s. 15 (see **B10.23**). **B10.33**

For the compatibility of the reverse burden with the ECHR, Article 6, see **F3.13** *et seq.*

MONEY LAUNDERING

Terrorism Act 2000, s. 18 **B10.34**

(1) A person commits an offence if he enters into or becomes concerned in an arrangement which facilitates the retention or control by or on behalf of another person of terrorist property—
- (a) by concealment,
- (b) by removal from the jurisdiction,
- (c) by transfer to nominees, or
- (d) in any other way.

Procedure

An allegation of an offence contrary to s. 18 is triable either way and when tried on indictment is a class 3 offence. Under s. 117(2), the consent of the DPP is required for proceedings to be instituted, but if it appears to him that the offence is committed for a purpose wholly or partly connected with the affairs of a country other than the UK, then the A-G must consent to the prosecution (s. 117(2A)). **B10.35**

See **B10.77** for extended jurisdiction provisions in relation to this offence.

Sentencing

The maximum penalty is: on conviction on indictment, imprisonment for a term not exceeding 14 years, a fine, or both; on summary conviction, imprisonment for a term not exceeding six months, a fine not exceeding the statutory maximum, or both (TA 2000, s. 22). A court may also make a forfeiture order (s. 23(1)); for further details, see s. 23(5), (6), (7) and (9) and sch. 4. **B10.36**

Elements

For terrorism, see **B10.3**. For terrorist property, see **B10.22**. **B10.37**

Specific Defence

Terrorism Act 2000, s. 18 **B10.38**

(2) It is a defence for a person charged with an offence under subsection (1) to prove that he did not know and had no reasonable cause to suspect that the arrangement related to terrorist property.

In addition to the defence set out in s. 18(2), the same defences available to a person charged with an offence contrary to s. 15 (see **B10.23**) are available to a person charged with an offence contrary to s. 18.

For the compatibility of the reverse burden with the ECHR, Article 6, see **F3.13** *et seq.*

There are related measures issuing from the United Nations Security Council. The Terrorism (United Nations Measures) Order 2006 (SI 2006 No. 2657), the Al-Qa'ida and Taliban (United Nations Measures) Order 2002 (SI 2002 No. 111), the Al-Qa'ida and Taliban (United Nations Measures) Order 2006 (SI 2006 No. 2952) and the North Korea (United Nations Measures) Order 2006 (SI 2006 No. 2958) are designed to restrict the availability of funds and financial services to terrorists and create powers to freeze the accounts of suspected terrorists. The orders create offences concerned with dealing in the funds of persons designated under orders, making funds available to such designated persons or circumventing prohibitions imposed under the orders. The offences are all punishable by imprisonment.

FAILURE TO COMPLY WITH A DUTY OF DISCLOSURE

B10.39 **Terrorism Act 2000, s. 19**

(1) This section applies where a person—
  (a) believes or suspects that another person has committed an offence under any of sections 15 to 18, and
  (b) bases his belief or suspicion on information which comes to his attention in the course of a trade, profession, business or employment.

(1A) But this section does not apply if the information came to the person in the course of a business in the regulated sector.

(2) The person commits an offence if he does not disclose to a constable as soon as is reasonably practicable—
  (a) his belief or suspicion, and
  (b) the information on which it is based.

Procedure

B10.40 An allegation of an offence contrary to the TA 2000, s. 19, is triable either way and when tried on indictment is a class 3 offence. Under s. 117(2), the consent of the DPP is required for proceedings to be instituted but, if it appears to him that the offence is committed for a purpose wholly or partly connected with the affairs of a country other than the UK, then the A-G must consent to the prosecution (s. 117(2A)).

Sentencing

B10.41 The maximum penalty is: on conviction on indictment, imprisonment for a term not exceeding five years, a fine or both; on summary conviction, imprisonment for a term not exceeding six months, a fine not exceeding the statutory maximum, or both (TA 2000, s. 19(8)).

Elements

B10.42 For the offences under the TA 2000, ss. 15 to 18, see **B10.19** ***et seq.***

By virtue of s. 19(7), a person is treated as having committed one of the offences in ss. 15 to 18 if (a) he has taken an action or been in possession of a thing, and (b) he would have committed an offence under one of those sections if he had been in the UK at the time when he took the action or was in possession of the thing.

The term 'a business in the regulated sector' must be construed in accordance with sch. 3A (s. 19(7A)).

'A constable' includes a member of staff of the Serious Organised Crime Agency authorised for the purpose by its Director General (s. 19(7B)).

Specific Defence

B10.43 **Terrorism Act 2000, s. 19**

(3) It is a defence for a person charged with an offence under subsection (2) to prove that he had a reasonable excuse for not making the disclosure.

(4) Where—
  (a) a person is in employment,
  (b) his employer has established a procedure for the making of disclosures of the matters specified in subsection (2), and
  (c) he is charged with an offence under that subsection,

it is a defence for him to prove that he had disclosed the matters specified in that subsection in accordance with the procedure.

(5) Subsection (2) does not require disclosure by a professional legal adviser of—
 (a) information which he obtains in privileged circumstances, or
 (b) a belief or suspicion based on information which he obtains in privileged circumstances.

For the compatibility of the reverse burden with the ECHR, Article 6, see **F3.13** *et seq.*

Failure to Disclose: Regulated Sector

Terrorism Act 2000, s. 21A **B10.44**

(1) A person commits an offence if each of the following three conditions is satisfied.
(2) The first condition is that he—
 (a) knows or suspects, or
 (b) has reasonable grounds for knowing or suspecting,
 that another person has committed an offence under any of sections 15 to 18.
(3) The second condition is that the information or other matter—
 (a) on which his knowledge or suspicion is based, or
 (b) which gives reasonable grounds for such knowledge or suspicion,
 came to him in the course of a business in the regulated sector.
(4) The third condition is that he does not disclose the information or other matter to a constable or nominated officer as soon as is practicable after it comes to him.

Procedure

An allegation of an offence contrary to the TA 2000, s. 21A, is triable either way and when tried on indictment is a class 3 offence. The offence was inserted into the 2000 Act by the A-tCSA 2001. **B10.45**

Sentencing

The maximum penalty is, on conviction on indictment, imprisonment for a term not exceeding five years or a fine or both; and, on summary conviction, imprisonment for a term not exceeding six months or a fine not exceeding the statutory maximum or both (TA 2000, s. 21A(12)). **B10.46**

Elements

Section 21A(6) of the TA 2000 provides that, when a court is deciding whether a person has committed an offence under this section, the court must decide whether he followed any relevant guidance issued by a supervisory authority or any other appropriate body approved by the Treasury and published in a manner that the Treasury thought appropriate in order to bring it to the attention of persons likely to be affected by it. **B10.47**

For the purposes of s. 21A(4), s. 21A(7) requires that a disclosure to a nominated officer is made to a person nominated by the accused's employer to receive disclosures under the section in the course of the accused's employment and in the manner prescribed by the employer for those purposes.

By virtue of s. 21A(11), a person is taken to have committed an offence under s. 21A(2) if he has taken action or been in possession of a thing and when he did that he would have committed an offence if he had done it in the UK.

The meanings of 'supervisory authority' and 'regulated sector' are to be found in sch. 3A to the 2000 Act (s. 21A(10)).

Specific Defences Section 21A(5) of the TA 2000 provides that a person does not commit an offence under the section if he has a reasonable excuse for not disclosing the information or other matter or he is a professional legal adviser and the information or matter came to him in legally privileged circumstances. Legally privileged circumstances are defined in s. 21A(8) as **B10.48**

being when information is given to a legal adviser by a client (or his representative) in connection with legal advice, by a person (or his representative) seeking legal advice or by any other person in connection with proceedings which are in progress or contemplated. Information or other material which is provided in furtherance of a criminal purpose is not covered by s. 21A(8) (s. 21A(9)).

Under s. 21B (inserted by the A-tCSA 2001), a disclosure is not to be taken to breach any restriction on the disclosure of information, however imposed, if it fulfils three conditions. The first is that the information or other matter disclosed came to the person in the course of a business in the regulated sector. The second is that the information or other matter causes the person to know or suspect, or gives him reasonable grounds for knowing or suspecting, that another person has committed an offence under ss. 15 to 18 of the 2000 Act. Third, the person to whom the information or other matter has been given must inform a constable or nominated officer as soon as practicable after receiving it.

Information about Acts of Terrorism

B10.49 **Terrorism Act 2000, s. 38B**

(1) This section applies where a person has information which he knows or believes might be of material assistance—
(a) in preventing the commission by another person of an act of terrorism, or
(b) in securing the apprehension, prosecution or conviction of another person,
in the United Kingdom, for an offence involving the commission, preparation or instigation of an act of terrorism.
(2) The person commits an offence if he does not disclose the information as soon as reasonably practicable in accordance with subsection (3).
(3) Disclosure is in accordance with this subsection if it is made—
(a) in England and Wales, to a constable . . .

B10.50 **Procedure** Section 38B was inserted into the TA 2000 by s. 117(2) of the A-tCSA 2001. An offence under s. 38B is triable either way; when tried on indictment it is a class 3 offence.

B10.51 **Sentencing** The maximum penalty is, on conviction on indictment, imprisonment for a term not exceeding five years, a fine or both; on summary conviction, imprisonment for a term not exceeding six months, a fine not exceeding the statutory maximum or both (TA 2000, s. 38B(5)).

B10.52 **Elements** Under the TA 2000, s. 38B(6), the offence may, for the purposes of the proceedings, be taken to have occurred in any place where the accused is or has been since he first knew or believed that the information might be of material assistance in the way referred to in s. 38B(1). The proceedings may also be taken in any such place.

B10.53 **Specific Defence** Section 38B(4) of the TA 2000 provides that it is a defence for the accused to prove that he had a reasonable excuse for failing to make the required disclosure.

For the compatibility of the reverse burden with the ECHR, Article 6, see **F3.13** *et seq.*

WEAPONS TRAINING

B10.54 **Terrorism Act 2000, s. 54**

(1) A person commits an offence if he provides instruction or training in the making or use of—
(a) firearms,
(aa) radioactive material or weapons designed or adapted for the discharge of any radioactive material,
(b) explosives, or
(c) chemical, biological or nuclear weapons.
(2) A person commits an offence if he receives instruction or training in the making or use of—

(a) firearms,
(aa) radioactive material or weapons designed or adapted for the discharge of any radioactive material,
(b) explosives, or
(c) chemical, biological or nuclear weapons.

(3) A person commits an offence if he invites another to receive instruction or training and the receipt—
(a) would constitute an offence under subsection (2), or
(b) would constitute an offence under subsection (2) but for the fact that it is to take place outside the United Kingdom.

. . .

Procedure

An allegation of an offence contrary to the TA 2000, s. 54, is triable either way and if tried on indictment is a class 3 offence. Under s. 117(2), the consent of the DPP is required for proceedings to be instituted, but if it appears to him that the offence is committed for a purpose wholly or partly connected with the affairs of a country other than the UK, then the A-G must consent to the prosecution (s. 117(2A)). **B10.55**

Sentencing

The maximum penalty is: on conviction on indictment, a sentence of imprisonment not exceeding ten years, a fine or both; on summary conviction, a sentence of imprisonment not exceeding six months, a fine not exceeding the statutory maximum or both (TA 2000, s. 54(6)). The court may order forfeiture of anything which the court considers to have been in the person's possession for purposes connected with the offence (s. 54(7)). Before making a forfeiture order, the court must give an opportunity to be heard to any person, other than the offender, who claims to be the owner of or otherwise interested in anything which can be forfeited (s. 54(8)). A forfeiture order does not come into force until there is no further possibility of it being varied, or set aside, on appeal (disregarding any power of a court to grant leave to appeal out of time) (s. 54(9)). **B10.56**

Elements

By virtue of the TA 2000, s. 54(4), the provision of, or invitation to, training referred to in s. 54(1) and (3) can be to specific persons or generally. **B10.57**

Section 55 of the Act provides definitions of most of the items referred to in s. 54(1). Thus:

- 'biological weapon' means a biological agent or toxin (within the meaning of the Biological Weapons Act 1974) in a form capable of use for hostile purposes or anything to which s. 1(1)(b) of that Act applies;
- 'chemical weapon' has the meaning given by s. 1 of the Chemical Weapons Act 1996;
- 'radioactive material' means radioactive material capable of endangering life or causing harm to human health;
- a 'firearm' is defined in s. 121 as including an air gun or air pistol.

Under s. 17 of the TA 2006 (see **B10.137**) if a person does anything outside the UK which would amount to an offence under s. 54 if done in any part of the UK, he will be liable for the offence in that part of the UK.

Specific Defence

Terrorism Act 2000, s. 54 **B10.58**

(5) It is a defence for a person charged with an offence under this section in relation to instruction or training to prove that his action or involvement was wholly for a purpose other than assisting, preparing for or participating in terrorism.

The defence under s. 54(4) is subject to the provisions of s. 118 of the 2000 Act and thus imposes an evidential burden on the accused. He is therefore required to adduce sufficient evidence to raise the issue as a defence. It will be assumed that the defence is satisfied unless the Crown disproves it to the criminal standard. (see **B10.4**).

DIRECTING A TERRORIST ORGANISATION

B10.59 **Terrorism Act 2000, s. 56**

(1) A person commits an offence if he directs, at any level, the activities of an organisation which is concerned in the commission of acts of terrorism.

Procedure

B10.60 An allegation of an offence contrary to the TA 2000, s. 56, is triable on indictment only and is a class 3 offence. Under s. 117(2), the consent of the DPP is required for proceedings to be instituted but, if it appears to him that the offence is committed for a purpose wholly or partly connected with the affairs of a country other than the UK, then the A-G must consent to the prosecution (s. 117(2A)).

For the extended jurisdiction provisions in relation to this offence, see **B10.78**.

The Terrorism Protocol issued by the President of the Queen's Bench Division on 30 January 2007 applies to this offence. The Protocol provides for administrative arrangements specific to terrorist cases and is available at http://www.hmcourts-service.gov.uk/cms/files/management_of _terrorism_cases.pdf.

Sentencing

B10.61 A person convicted of this offence is liable to imprisonment for life (TA 2000, s. 56(2)).

Elements

B10.62 For 'terrorism', see **B10.3**.

POSSESSION OF AN ARTICLE FOR TERRORIST PURPOSES

B10.63 **Terrorism Act 2000, s. 57**

(1) A person commits an offence if he possesses an article in circumstances which give rise to a reasonable suspicion that his possession is for a purpose connected with the commission, preparation or instigation of an act of terrorism.

Procedure

B10.64 An allegation of an offence contrary to the TA 2000, s. 57, is triable either way; if tried on indictment it is a class 3 offence. Under s. 117(2), the consent of the DPP is required for proceedings to be instituted but, if it appears to him that the offence is committed for a purpose wholly or partly connected with the affairs of a country other than the UK, then the A-G must consent to the prosecution (s. 117(2A)).

For the extended jurisdiction provisions in relation to this offence, see **B10.78**.

Sentence

B10.65 The maximum penalty is: on conviction on indictment, imprisonment for a term not exceeding 15 years, a fine, or both; on summary conviction, imprisonment for a term not exceeding six months, a fine not exceeding the statutory maximum, or both (TA 2000, s. 57(4)). The maximum penalty was increased from ten years to 15 years on 13 April 2006 by the TA 2006,

s. 13(1), but that does not have effect in relation to offences committed before that date (s. 13(2)).

Elements

Under the TA 2000, s. 57(3), if it is proved that an article was on any premises at the same time as the accused, or was on premises of which the accused was the occupier or which he habitually used otherwise than as a member of the public, the court may assume that he possessed the article unless the accused proves that he did not know of the presence of the article on the premises or had no control over it. By virtue of s. 118, the burden on the accused is evidential (see **B10.4**). **B10.66**

In *Rowe* [2007] EWCA Crim 635, a five-judge court of the Court of Appeal presided over by Phillips CJ held that a document or record was capable of constituting an article for the purposes of s. 57. The court observed that ss. 57 and 58 (see **B10.68**) deal with different aspects of activities relating to terrorism. Section 57 deals with possession of articles *for the purpose* of terrorist acts. Section 58 is concerned with the collecting or holding of information that *is of a kind likely to be useful* to those involved in acts of terrorism. Section 57 also includes a specific intention whilst s. 58 does not. Those differences between the two sections were said to be rational features of a statute whose aims included the prohibition of different types of support for, and involvement in, terrorism. There is thus no basis for any conclusion that Parliament intended to have a completely separate regime for documents and records from that which applies to other articles. In so holding, the court found that the decision to the opposite effect in *M* [2007] EWCA Crim 218 was reached *per incuriam. Rowe* has since been followed in *M(No. 2)* [2007] EWCA Crim 970.

Specific Defence

Terrorism Act 2000, s. 57 **B10.67**

(2) It is a defence for a person charged with an offence under this section to prove that his possession of the article was not for a purpose connected with the commission, preparation or instigation of an act of terrorism.

The defence under s. 57(2) is subject to the provisions of s. 118 and thus imposes an evidential burden on the accused. He is therefore required to adduce sufficient evidence to raise the issue as a defence. It will be assumed that the defence is satisfied unless the Crown disproves it to the criminal standard (see **B10.4**).

COLLECTION OF INFORMATION

Terrorism Act 2000, s. 58 **B10.68**

(1) A person commits an offence if—
- (a) he collects or makes a record of information of a kind likely to be useful to a person committing or preparing an act of terrorism, or
- (b) he possesses a document or record containing information of that kind.

Procedure

An allegation of an offence contrary to the TA 2000, s. 58, is triable either way; if tried on indictment it is a class 3 offence. Under s. 117(2), the consent of the DPP is required for proceedings to be instituted but, if it appears to him that the offence is committed for a purpose wholly or partly connected with the affairs of a country other than the UK, then the A-G must consent to the prosecution (s. 117(2A)). **B10.69**

For the extended jurisdiction provisions in relation to this offence, see **B10.78**.

Sentencing

B10.70 The maximum penalty is: on conviction on indictment, a term of imprisonment not exceeding 15 years, a fine, or both; on summary conviction, a term of imprisonment not exceeding six months, a fine not exceeding the statutory maximum, or both (TA 2000, s. 58(4)). A court may make a forfeiture order of any document or record containing information of the kind mentioned in s. 58(1)(a) (s. 58(5)); for further details, see s. 58(6) and (7).

In *Mansha* [2007] 1 Cr App R (S) 410, sentence of six years' imprisonment was upheld for possessing information likely to be useful to a terrorist, where the offender was in possession of detailed information relating to a soldier who had been decorated for bravery in Iraq. The Court of Appeal said that a substantial sentence was necessary to act as a deterrent and to mark the extreme seriousness of terrorist offences.

Elements

B10.71 Section 58(2) provides that a 'record' includes a photographic or electronic record.

Specific Defence

B10.72 **Terrorism Act 2000, s. 58**

(3) It is a defence for a person charged with an offence under this section to prove that he had a reasonable excuse for his action or possession.

The defence under s. 58(3) is subject to the provisions of s. 118 and thus imposes an evidential burden on the accused. The accused is therefore required to adduce sufficient evidence to raise the issue as a defence. It will be assumed that the defence is satisfied unless the Crown disproves it to the criminal standard (see **B10.4**).

In *F* [2007] 2 All ER 193 it was held by the Court of Appeal that possession of documents as part of an effort to change an illegal or undemocratic regime could not constitute a reasonable excuse under s. 58(3).

TERRORISM OVERSEAS

Inciting Terrorism Overseas

B10.73 **Terrorism Act 2000, s. 59**

(1) A person commits an offence if—
- (a) he incites another person to commit an act of terrorism wholly or partly outside the United Kingdom, and
- (b) the act would, if committed in England and Wales, constitute one of the offences listed in subsection (2).

(2) Those offences are—
- (a) murder,
- (b) an offence under section 18 of the Offences against the Person Act 1861 (wounding with intent),
- (c) an offence under section 23 or 24 of that Act (poison),
- (d) an offence under section 28 or 29 of that Act (explosions), and
- (e) an offence under section 1(2) of the Criminal Damage Act 1971 (endangering life by damaging property).

(3) A person guilty of an offence under this section shall be liable to any penalty to which he would be liable on conviction of the offence listed in subsection (2) which corresponds to the act which he incites.

(4) For the purposes of subsection (1) it is immaterial whether or not the person incited is in the United Kingdom at the time of the incitement.

(5) Nothing in this section imposes criminal liability on any person acting on behalf of, or holding office under, the Crown.

Procedure By virtue of the TA 2000, s. 59(3), an allegation of an offence contrary to s. 59 is triable in the same way that the substantive offence listed in s. 59(2) would be tried. As all of those offences are triable only on indictment, s. 59 is effectively indictable only. It is a class 3 offence. Under s. 117(2), the consent of the DPP is required for proceedings to be instituted but, if it appears to him that the offence is committed for a purpose wholly or partly connected with the affairs of a country other than the UK, then the A-G must consent to the prosecution (s. 117(2A)). **B10.74**

The Terrorism Protocol (see **B10.60**) applies to this offence.

For the extended jurisdiction provisions in relation to this offence, see **B10.78**.

Sentencing The maximum penalty is that which would be available on conviction of the substantive offence (TA 2000, s. 59(3)). **B10.75**

Elements For 'incitement', see **A6.1.** For murder, see **B1.1**; for the OAPA 1861, ss. 18, 23, 24, 28 and 29, see **B2.50, B2.61** and **B2.68, B12.174** and **B12.178** respectively; for the CDA 1971, s. 1(2), see **B8.11.** **B10.76**

Terrorist Bombing Committed Abroad and Terrorist Financing Abroad

Terrorism Act 2000, ss. 62 and 63 **B10.77**

62.—(1) If—

(a) a person does anything outside the United Kingdom as an act of terrorism or for the purposes of terrorism, and

(b) his action would have constituted the commission of one of the offences listed in subsection (2) if it had been done in the United Kingdom,

he shall be guilty of the offence.

(2) The offences referred to in subsection (1)(b) are—

(a) an offence under section 2, 3 or 5 of the Explosive Substances Act 1883 (causing explosions, &c),

(b) an offence under section 1 of the Biological Weapons Act 1974 (biological weapons), and

(c) an offence under section 2 of the Chemical Weapons Act 1996 (chemical weapons).

63.—(1) If—

(a) a person does anything outside the United Kingdom, and

(b) his action would have constituted the commission of an offence under any of sections 15 to 18 if it had been done in the United Kingdom,

he shall be guilty of the offence.

(2) For the purposes of subsection (1)(b), section 18(1)(b) shall be read as if for 'the jurisdiction' there were substituted 'a jurisdiction'.

The 2000 Act provides for extended jurisdiction in relation to offences of terrorist bombing and terrorism finance committed outside the UK.

Extended Jurisdiction for Offences Committed Abroad For Terrorist Purposes

Terrorism Act 2000, ss. 63A to 63E **B10.78**

63A.—(1) If—

(a) a United Kingdom national or a United Kingdom resident does anything outside the United Kingdom, and

(b) his action, if done in any part of the United Kingdom, would have constituted an offence under any of sections 56 to 61

he shall be guilty in that part of the United Kingdom of the offence.

(2) For the purposes of this section and sections 63B and 63C a 'United Kingdom national' means an individual who is—

(a) a British citizen, a British overseas territories citizen, a British National (Overseas) or a British Overseas citizen,

(b) a person who under the British Nationality Act 1981 is a British subject, or

(c) a British protected person within the meaning of that Act.

(3) For the purposes of this section and sections 63B and 63C a 'United Kingdom resident' means an individual who is resident in the United Kingdom.

63B.—(1) If—

(a) a United Kingdom national or a United Kingdom resident does anything outside the United Kingdom as an act of terrorism or for the purposes of terrorism, and

(b) his action, if done in any part of the United Kingdom, would have constituted an offence listed in subsection (2),

he shall be guilty in that part of the United Kingdom of the offence.

(2) These are the offences—

(a) murder, manslaughter, culpable homicide, rape, assault causing injury, assault to injury, kidnapping, abduction or false imprisonment,

(b) an offence under section 4, 16, 18, 20, 21, 22, 23, 24, 28, 29, 30 or 64 of the Offences against the Person Act 1861,

(c) an offence under any of sections 1 to 5 of the Forgery and Counterfeiting Act 1981,

(d) the uttering of a forged document or an offence under section 46A of the Criminal Law (Consolidation) (Scotland) Act 1995,

(e) an offence under section 1 or 2 of the Criminal Damage Act 1971,

(f) an offence under article 3 or 4 of the Criminal Damage (Northern Ireland) Order 1977,

(g) malicious mischief,

(h) wilful fire-raising.

63C.—(1) If—

(a) a person does anything outside the United Kingdom as an act of terrorism or for the purposes of terrorism,

(b) his action is done to, or in relation to, a United Kingdom national, a United Kingdom resident or a protected person, and

(c) his action, if done in any part of the United Kingdom, would have constituted an offence listed in subsection (2),

he shall be guilty in that part of the United Kingdom of the offence.

(2) These are the offences—

(a) murder, manslaughter, culpable homicide, rape, assault causing injury, assault to injury, kidnapping, abduction or false imprisonment,

(b) an offence under section 4, 16, 18, 20, 21, 22, 23, 24, 28, 29, 30 or 64 of the Offences against the Person Act 1861,

(c) an offence under section 1, 2, 3, 4 or 5(1) or (3) of the Forgery and Counterfeiting Act 1981,

(d) the uttering of a forged document or an offence under section 46A(1) of the Criminal Law (Consolidation) (Scotland) Act 1995.

(3) For the purposes of this section and section 63D a person is a protected person if—

(a) he is a member of a United Kingdom diplomatic mission within the meaning of Article 1(b) of the Vienna Convention on Diplomatic Relations signed in 1961 (as that Article has effect in the United Kingdom by virtue of section 2 of and schedule 1 to the Diplomatic Privileges Act 1964),

(b) he is a member of a United Kingdom consular post within the meaning of Article 1(g) of the Vienna Convention on Consular Relations signed in 1963 (as that Article has effect in the United Kingdom by virtue of section 1 of and schedule 1 to the Consular Relations Act 1968),

(c) he carries out any functions for the purposes of the European Medicines Agency, or

(d) he carries out any functions for the purposes of a body specified in an order made by the Secretary of State.

(4) The Secretary of State may specify a body under subsection (3)(d) only if—

(a) it is established by or under the Treaty establishing the European Community or the Treaty on European Union, and

(b) the principal place in which its functions are carried out is a place in the United Kingdom.

(5) If in any proceedings a question arises as to whether a person is or was a protected person, a certificate-

(a) issued by or under the authority of the Secretary of State, and

(b) stating any fact relating to the question,

is to be conclusive evidence of that fact.

63D.—(1) If—

(a) a person does anything outside the United Kingdom as an act of terrorism or for the purposes of terrorism,

(b) his action is done in connection with an attack on relevant premises or on a vehicle ordinarily used by a protected person,

(c) the attack is made when a protected person is on or in the premises or vehicle, and

(d) his action, if done in any part of the United Kingdom, would have constituted an offence listed in subsection (2),

he shall be guilty in that part of the United Kingdom of the offence.

(2) These are the offences—

(a) an offence under section 1 of the Criminal Damage Act 1971,

(b) an offence under article 3 of the Criminal Damage (Northern Ireland) Order 1977,

(c) malicious mischief,

(d) wilful fire-raising.

(3) If—

(a) a person does anything outside the United Kingdom as an act of terrorism or for the purposes of terrorism,

(b) his action consists of a threat of an attack on relevant premises or on a vehicle ordinarily used by a protected person,

(c) the attack is threatened to be made when a protected person is, or is likely to be, on or in the premises or vehicle, and

(d) his action, if done in any part of the United Kingdom, would have constituted an offence listed in subsection (4),

he shall be guilty in that part of the United Kingdom of the offence.

(4) These are the offences—

(a) an offence under section 2 of the Criminal Damage Act 1971,

(b) an offence under article 4 of the Criminal Damage (Northern Ireland) Order 1977,

(c) breach of the peace (in relation to Scotland only).

(5) 'Relevant premises' means—

(a) premises at which a protected person resides or is staying, or

(b) premises which a protected person uses for the purpose of carrying out his functions as such a person.

63E.—(1) Proceedings for an offence which (disregarding the Acts listed in subsection (2)) would not be an offence apart from section 63B, 63C or 63D are not to be started—

(a) in England and Wales, except by or with the consent of the Attorney General,

(b) in Northern Ireland, except by or with the consent of the Advocate General for Northern Ireland.

(2) These are the Acts—

(a) the Internationally Protected Persons Act 1978,

(b) the Suppression of Terrorism Act 1978,

(c) the Nuclear Material (Offences) Act 1983,

(d) the United Nations Personnel Act 1997.

(3) For the purposes of sections 63C and 63D it is immaterial whether a person knows that another person is a United Kingdom national, a United Kingdom resident or a protected person.

(4) In relation to any time before the coming into force of section 27(1) of the Justice (Northern Ireland) Act 2002, the reference in subsection (1)(b) to the Advocate General for Northern Ireland is to be read as a reference to the Attorney General for Northern Ireland.

Sections 63A to 63E represent important provisions extending the jurisdiction of the courts of the UK to deal with offences committed outside it by and against persons associated with the UK.

INVESTIGATIVE AND COUNTER-TERRORISM POWERS: GENERAL

B10.79 The TA 2000 instituted a number of investigative and counter-terrorist powers relating, *inter alia*, to matters such as information held by persons that could be of value to a terrorist investigation as well as the arrest and detention of suspects.

INVESTIGATIVE POWERS UNDER THE TERRORISM ACT 2000

B10.80 Sections 32 to 39 of, and schs. 5 and 6 to, the TA 2000 provide a plethora of powers to be deployed in terrorist investigations. They are dealt with below. The definition of a terrorist investigation is contained in s. 32.

Terrorism Act 2000 s. 32

In this Act, 'terrorist investigation' means an investigation of—

(a) the commission, preparation or instigation of acts of terrorism,
(b) an act which appears to have been done for the purposes of terrorism,
(c) the resources of a proscribed organisation,
(d) the possibility of making an order under s. 3(3), or
(e) the commission, preparation or instigation of an offence under this Act or under part 1 of the Terrorism Act 2006 other than an offence under section 1 or 2 of that Act.

Cordons

B10.81 Police officers, usually of the rank of superintendent or higher, are empowered under ss. 33 and 34 of the TA 2000 to designate an area as a cordoned area for the purposes of a terrorist investigation. An order may be made only when it is considered expedient for the purposes of a terrorist investigation. The cordoned area must be demarcated by tape or in any other manner that the officer considers appropriate. Sections 35 and 36 provide for the duration of a cordon and the powers of a constable in relation to that cordon respectively. A failure to comply with the requirements of a constable in relation to the cordoned area is a summary offence punishable by up to three months' imprisonment.

Information and Evidence

B10.82 Section 37 of the TA 2000 gives effect to sch. 5, which contains a number of provisions relating to the securing of information for the purposes of terrorist investigations. Insofar as it is relevant to England and Wales, it is reproduced below.

Terrorism Act 2000, sch. 5

Para 1

(1) A constable may apply to a justice of the peace for the issue of a warrant under this paragraph for the purposes of a terrorist investigation.
(2) A warrant under this paragraph shall authorise any constable—
  (a) to enter premises mentioned in sub-paragraph (2A),
  (b) to search the premises and any person found there, and
  (c) to seize and retain any relevant material which is found on a search under paragraph (b).
(2A) The premises referred to in sub-paragraph (2)(a) are—
  (a) one or more sets of premises specified in the application (in which case the application is for a 'specific premises warrant'); or
  (b) any premises occupied or controlled by a person specified in the application, including such sets of premises as are so specified (in which case the application is for an 'all premises warrant').
(3) For the purpose of sub-paragraph (2)(c) material is relevant if the constable has reasonable grounds for believing that—

(a) it is likely to be of substantial value, whether by itself or together with other material, to a terrorist investigation, and
(b) it must be seized in order to prevent it from being concealed, lost, damaged, altered or destroyed.

(4) A warrant under this paragraph shall not authorise—
(a) the seizure and retention of items subject to legal privilege, or
(b) a constable to require a person to remove any clothing in public except for headgear, footwear, an outer coat, a jacket or gloves.

(5) Subject to paragraph 2, a justice may grant an application under this paragraph if satisfied—
(a) that the warrant is sought for the purposes of a terrorist investigation,
(b) that there are reasonable grounds for believing that there is material on premises to which the application relates which is likely to be of substantial value, whether by itself or together with other material, to a terrorist investigation and which does not consist of or include excepted material (within the meaning of paragraph 4 below),
(c) that the issue of a warrant is likely to be necessary in the circumstances of the case; and
(d) in the case of an application for an all premises warrant, that it is not reasonably practicable to specify in the application all the premises which the person so specified occupies or controls and which might need to be searched.

Para 2

(1) This paragraph applies where an application for a specific premises warrant is made under paragraph 1 and—
(a) the application is made by a police officer of at least the rank of superintendent,
(b) the application does not relate to residential premises, and
(c) the justice to whom the application is made is not satisfied of the matter referred to in paragraph 1(5)(c).

(2) The justice may grant the application if satisfied of the matters referred to in paragraph 1(5)(a) and (b).

(3) Where a warrant under paragraph 1 is issued by virtue of this paragraph, the powers under paragraph 1(2)(a) and (b) are exercisable only within the period of 24 hours beginning with the time when the warrant is issued.

(4) For the purpose of sub-paragraph (1) 'residential premises' means any premises which the officer making the application has reasonable grounds for believing are used wholly or mainly as a dwelling.

Para 3

(1) Subject to sub-paragraph (2), a police officer of at least the rank of superintendent may by a written authority signed by him authorise a search of specified premises which are wholly or partly within a cordoned area.

(2) A constable who is not of the rank required by sub-paragraph (1) may give an authorisation under this paragraph if he considers it necessary by reason of urgency.

(3) An authorisation under this paragraph shall authorise any constable—
(a) to enter the premises specified in the authority,
(b) to search the premises and any person found there, and
(c) to seize and retain any relevant material (within the meaning of paragraph 1(3)) which is found on a search under paragraph (b).

(4) The powers under sub-paragraph (3)(a) and (b) may be exercised—
(a) on one or more occasions, and
(b) at any time during the period when the designation of the cordoned area under section 33 has effect.

(5) An authorisation under this paragraph shall not authorise—
(a) the seizure and retention of items subject to legal privilege;
(b) a constable to require a person to remove any clothing in public except for headgear, footwear, an outer coat, a jacket or gloves.

(6) An authorisation under this paragraph shall not be given unless the person giving it has reasonable grounds for believing that there is material to be found on the premises which—
(a) is likely to be of substantial value, whether by itself or together with other material, to a terrorist investigation, and
(b) does not consist of or include excepted material.

(7) A person commits an offence if he wilfully obstructs a search under this paragraph.

(8) A person guilty of an offence under sub-paragraph (7) shall be liable on summary conviction to—
 (a) imprisonment for a term not exceeding three months,
 (b) a fine not exceeding level 4 on the standard scale, or
 (c) both.

Para 4

In this Part—
 (a) 'excluded material' has the meaning given by section 11 of the Police and Criminal Evidence Act 1984,
 (b) 'items subject to legal privilege' has the meaning given by section 10 of that Act, and
 (c) 'special procedure material' has the meaning given by section 14 of that Act;

and material is 'excepted material' if it falls within any of paragraphs (a) to (c).

Para 5

(1) A constable may apply to a circuit judge for an order under this paragraph for the purposes of a terrorist investigation.
(2) An application for an order shall relate to particular material, or material of a particular description, which consists of or includes excluded material or special procedure material.
(3) An order under this paragraph may require a specified person—
 (a) to produce to a constable within a specified period for seizure and retention any material which he has in his possession, custody or power and to which the application relates;
 (b) to give a constable access to any material of the kind mentioned in paragraph (a) within a specified period;
 (c) to state to the best of his knowledge and belief the location of material to which the application relates if it is not in, and it will not come into, his possession, custody or power within the period specified under paragraph (a) or (b).
(4) For the purposes of this paragraph—
 (a) an order may specify a person only if he appears to the Circuit judge to have in his possession, custody or power any of the material to which the application relates, and
 (b) a period specified in an order shall be the period of seven days beginning with the date of the order unless it appears to the judge that a different period would be appropriate in the particular circumstances of the application.
(5) Where a circuit judge makes an order under sub-paragraph (3)(b) in relation to material on any premises, he may, on the application of a constable, order any person who appears to the judge to be entitled to grant entry to the premises to allow any constable to enter the premises to obtain access to the material.

Para 6

(1) A circuit judge may grant an application under paragraph 5 if satisfied—
 (a) that the material to which the application relates consists of or includes excluded material or special procedure material,
 (b) that it does not include items subject to legal privilege, and
 (c) that the conditions in sub-paragraphs (2) and (3) are satisfied in respect of that material.
(2) The first condition is that—
 (a) the order is sought for the purposes of a terrorist investigation, and
 (b) there are reasonable grounds for believing that the material is likely to be of substantial value, whether by itself or together with other material, to a terrorist investigation.
(3) The second condition is that there are reasonable grounds for believing that it is in the public interest that the material should be produced or that access to it should be given having regard—
 (a) to the benefit likely to accrue to a terrorist investigation if the material is obtained, and
 (b) to the circumstances under which the person concerned has any of the material in his possession, custody or power.

Para 7

(1) An order under paragraph 5 may be made in relation to—
 (a) material consisting of or including excluded or special procedure material which is expected to come into existence within the period of 28 days beginning with the date of the order;

(b) a person who the circuit judge thinks is likely to have any of the material to which the application relates in his possession, custody or power within that period.

(2) Where an order is made under paragraph 5 by virtue of this paragraph, paragraph 5(3) shall apply with the following modifications—

(a) the order shall require the specified person to notify a named constable as soon as is reasonably practicable after any material to which the application relates comes into his possession, custody or power,

(b) the reference in paragraph 5(3)(a) to material which the specified person has in his possession, custody or power shall be taken as a reference to the material referred to in paragraph (a) above which comes into his possession, custody or power, and

(c) the reference in paragraph 5(3)(c) to the specified period shall be taken as a reference to the period of 28 days beginning with the date of the order.

(3) Where an order is made under paragraph 5 by virtue of this paragraph, paragraph 5(4) shall not apply and the order—

(a) may only specify a person falling within sub-paragraph (1)(b), and

(b) shall specify the period of seven days beginning with the date of notification required under sub-paragraph (2)(a) unless it appears to the judge that a different period would be appropriate in the particular circumstances of the application.

Para 8

(1) An order under paragraph 5—

(a) shall not confer any right to production of, or access to, items subject to legal privilege, and

(b) shall have effect notwithstanding any restriction on the disclosure of information imposed by statute or otherwise.

(2) Where the material to which an application under paragraph 5 relates consists of information contained in a computer—

(a) an order under paragraph 5(3)(a) shall have effect as an order to produce the material in a form in which it can be taken away and in which it is visible and legible, and

(b) an order under paragraph 5(3)(b) shall have effect as an order to give access to the material in a form in which it is visible and legible.

Para 9

(1) An order under paragraph 5 may be made in relation to material in the possession, custody or power of a government department.

(2) Where an order is made by virtue of sub-paragraph (1)—

(a) it shall be served as if the proceedings were civil proceedings against the department, and

(b) it may require any officer of the department, whether named in the order or not, who may for the time being have in his possession, custody or power the material concerned, to comply with the order.

(3) In this paragraph 'government department' means an authorised government department for the purposes of the Crown Proceedings Act 1947.

Para 10

(1) An order of a Circuit judge under paragraph 5 shall have effect as if it were an order of the Crown Court.

(2) Criminal Procedure Rules may make provision about proceedings relating to an order under paragraph 5.

(3) In particular, the rules may make provision about the variation or discharge of an order.

Para 11

(1) A constable may apply to a Circuit judge for the issue of a warrant under this paragraph for the purposes of a terrorist investigation.

(2) A warrant under this paragraph shall authorise any constable—

(a) to enter premises mentioned in sub-paragraph (3A),

(b) to search the premises and any person found there, and

(c) to seize and retain any relevant material which is found on a search under paragraph (b).

(3) A warrant under this paragraph shall not authorise—

(a) the seizure and retention of items subject to legal privilege;

(b) a constable to require a person to remove any clothing in public except for headgear, footwear, an outer coat, a jacket or gloves.

(3A) The premises referred to in sub-paragraph (2)(a) are—

(a) one or more sets of premises specified in the application (in which case the application is for a 'specific premises warrant'); or

(b) any premises occupied or controlled by a person specified in the application, including such sets of premises as are so specified (in which case the application is for an 'all premises warrant').

(4) For the purpose of sub-paragraph (2)(c) material is relevant if the constable has reasonable grounds for believing that it is likely to be of substantial value, whether by itself or together with other material, to a terrorist investigation.

Para 12

(1) A circuit judge may grant an application for a specific premises warrant under paragraph 11 if satisfied that an order made under paragraph 5 in relation to material on the premises specified in the application has not been complied with.

(2) A circuit judge may also grant an application for a specific premises warrant under paragraph 11 if satisfied that there are reasonable grounds for believing that—

(a) there is material on premises specified in the application which consists of or includes excluded material or special procedure material but does not include items subject to legal privilege, and

(b) the conditions in sub-paragraphs (3) and (4) are satisfied.

(2A) A circuit judge or a District Judge (Magistrates' Courts) may grant an application for an all premises warrant under paragraph 11 if satisfied—

(a) that an order made under paragraph 5 has not been complied with, and

(b) that the person specified in the application is also specified in the order.

(2B) A Circuit judge or a District Judge (Magistrates' Courts) may also grant an application for an all premises warrant under paragraph 11 if satisfied that there are reasonable grounds for believing—

(a) that there is material on premises to which the application relates which consists of or includes excluded material or special procedure material but does not include items subject to legal privilege, and

(b) that the conditions in sub-paragraphs (3) and (4) are met.

(3) The first condition is that—

(a) the warrant is sought for the purposes of a terrorist investigation, and

(b) the material is likely to be of substantial value, whether by itself or together with other material, to a terrorist investigation.

(4) The second condition is that it is not appropriate to make an order under paragraph 5 in relation to the material because—

(a) it is not practicable to communicate with any person entitled to produce the material,

(b) it is not practicable to communicate with any person entitled to grant access to the material or entitled to grant entry to premises to which the application for the warrant relates, or

(c) a terrorist investigation may be seriously prejudiced unless a constable can secure immediate access to the material.

Para 13

(1) A constable may apply to a Circuit judge for an order under this paragraph requiring any person specified in the order to provide an explanation of any material—

(a) seized in pursuance of a warrant under paragraph 1 or 11, or

(b) produced or made available to a constable under paragraph 5.

(2) An order under this paragraph shall not require any person to disclose any information which he would be entitled to refuse to disclose on grounds of legal professional privilege in proceedings in the High Court.

(3) But a lawyer may be required to provide the name and address of his client.

(4) A statement by a person in response to a requirement imposed by an order under this paragraph—

(a) may be made orally or in writing, and

(b) may be used in evidence against him only on a prosecution for an offence under paragraph 14.

(5) Paragraph 10 shall apply to orders under this paragraph as it applies to orders under paragraph 5.

Para 14

(1) A person commits an offence if, in purported compliance with an order under paragraph 13, he—

(a) makes a statement which he knows to be false or misleading in a material particular, or

(b) recklessly makes a statement which is false or misleading in a material particular.

(2) A person guilty of an offence under sub-paragraph (1) shall be liable—

(a) on conviction on indictment, to imprisonment for a term not exceeding two years, to a fine or to both, or

(b) on summary conviction, to imprisonment for a term not exceeding six months, to a fine not exceeding the statutory maximum or to both

Para 15

(1) A police officer of at least the rank of superintendent may by a written order signed by him give to any constable the authority which may be given by a search warrant under paragraph 1 or 11.

(2) An order shall not be made under this paragraph unless the officer has reasonable grounds for believing—

(a) that the case is one of great emergency, and

(b) that immediate action is necessary.

(3) Where an order is made under this paragraph particulars of the case shall be notified as soon as is reasonably practicable to the Secretary of State.

(4) A person commits an offence if he wilfully obstructs a search under this paragraph.

(5) A person guilty of an offence under sub-paragraph (4) shall be liable on summary conviction to—

(a) imprisonment for a term not exceeding three months,

(b) a fine not exceeding level 4 on the standard scale, or

(c) both.

Para 16

(1) If a police officer of at least the rank of superintendent has reasonable grounds for believing that the case is one of great emergency he may by a written notice signed by him require any person specified in the notice to provide an explanation of any material seized in pursuance of an order under paragraph 15.

(2) Sub-paragraphs (2) to (4) of paragraph 13 and paragraph 14 shall apply to a notice under this paragraph as they apply to an order under paragraph 13.

(3) A person commits an offence if he fails to comply with a notice under this paragraph.

(4) It is a defence for a person charged with an offence under sub-paragraph (3) to show that he had a reasonable excuse for his failure.

(5) A person guilty of an offence under sub-paragraph (3) shall be liable on summary conviction to—

(a) imprisonment for a term not exceeding six months,

(b) a fine not exceeding level 5 on the standard scale, or

(c) both.

Para 17

For the purposes of sections 21 and 22 of the Police and Criminal Evidence Act 1984 (seized material: access, copying and retention)—

(a) a terrorist investigation shall be treated as an investigation of or in connection with an offence, and

(b) material produced in pursuance of an order under paragraph 5 shall be treated as if it were material seized by a constable.

Financial Information

B10.83 Section 38 of the TA 2000 gives effect to sch. 6. Where a circuit judge has made the relevant supporting order, a named constable may require a financial institution to provide customer information for the purposes of a terrorist investigation (sch. 6, para. 1(1)). That information must be supplied in such a way and within such time as the constable specifies and notwithstanding any restriction on the disclosure of information imposed by statute or otherwise (para. 1(2)). It is a summary offence for the institution to fail to comply with the requirement (para. 1(3)), but it is a defence for the institution to prove that the information required was not in the institution's possession, or that it was not reasonably practicable for the institution to comply with the requirement (para. 1(4)). The penalty for the offence is a fine not exceeding level 5 on the standard scale (para. 1(5)). If the offence was committed with the consent or connivance of an officer of the institution, or was attributable to neglect on the part of an officer of the institution, that officer, as well as the institution, is guilty of the offence (para. 8(1) and (2)). The maximum penalty is imprisonment for a term not exceeding six months, a fine not exceeding level 5 on the standard scale, or both (para. 8(3)).

An application for an order under sch. 6 must be made by a police officer of at least the rank of superintendent. A circuit judge should make the order only if satisfied that the order is sought for the purposes of a terrorist investigation, the tracing of terrorist property is desirable for the purposes of the investigation, and the order will enhance the effectiveness of the investigation (paras. 2, 3 and 5).

'Customer information' is defined in para. 7(1):

(a) information whether a business relationship exists or existed between a financial institution and a particular person ('a customer');
(b) a customer's account number;
(c) a customer's full name;
(d) a customer's date of birth;
(e) a customer's address or former address;
(f) the date on which a business relationship between a financial institution and a customer begins or ends;
(g) any evidence of a customer's identity obtained by a financial institution in pursuance of or for the purposes of any legislation relating to money laundering; and
(h) the identity of a person sharing an account with a customer.

A 'business relationship' exists between a financial institution and a person if (and only if) (a) there is an arrangement between them designed to facilitate the carrying out of frequent or regular transactions between them, and (b) the total amount of payments to be made in the course of the arrangement is neither known nor capable of being ascertained when the arrangement is made (para. 7(2)).

If a financial institution provides 'customer information', it is not admissible in evidence in criminal proceedings against the institution or any of its officers or employees (para. 9(1)), except in relation to proceedings for an offence contrary to para. 1(3) or para. 8.

Account Monitoring Orders

B10.84 Account monitoring orders can be imposed on financial institutions in relation to accounts (whether all or particular) held by any person specified in an application by virtue of s. 38A of and sch. 6A to the TA 2000. During a specified period the institution is required to provide information of a specified description to an appropriate officer (para. 2(4) and (5)). The order must be complied with irrespective of any legislative or other restriction on the disclosure of information (para. 6(2)). Ordinarily, a statement made by a financial institution in response to an account monitoring order may not be used in evidence against it in criminal proceedings. However, there are certain exceptions to that rule. The statement may be used:

(a) in the case of proceedings for contempt of court;
(b) in the case of proceedings under s. 23 (forfeiture) where the financial institution has been convicted of an offence under any of ss. 15 to 18 (terrorist property offences: see **B10.19** to **B10.38**); or
(c) on a prosecution for an offence where, in giving evidence, the financial institution makes a statement inconsistent with the first statement (but the statement may not be used against a financial institution unless evidence relating to it is adduced or a question relating to it is asked by or on behalf of the financial institution in the proceedings arising out of the prosecution (para. 7(1) to (3)).

Disclosure of and Interference with Information Offences

Terrorism Act 2000 s. 39 **B10.85**

(1) Subsection (2) applies where a person knows or has reasonable cause to suspect that a constable is conducting or proposes to conduct a terrorist investigation.
(2) The person commits an offence if he—
 (a) discloses to another anything which is likely to prejudice the investigation, or
 (b) interferes with material which is likely to be relevant to the investigation.
(3) Subsection (4) applies where a person knows or has reasonable cause to suspect that a disclosure has been or will be made under any of sections 19 to 21 or 38B.
(4) The person commits an offence if he—
 (a) discloses to another anything which is likely to prejudice an investigation resulting from the disclosure under that section, or
 (b) interferes with material which is likely to be relevant to an investigation resulting from the disclosure under that section.
(5) It is a defence for a person charged with an offence under subsection (2) or (4) to prove—
 (a) that he did not know and had no reasonable cause to suspect that the disclosure or interference was likely to affect a terrorist investigation, or
 (b) that he had a reasonable excuse for the disclosure or interference.
(6) Subsections (2) and (4) do not apply to a disclosure which is made by a professional legal adviser—
 (a) to his client or to his client's representative in connection with the provision of legal advice by the adviser to the client and not with a view to furthering a criminal purpose, or
 (b) to any person for the purpose of actual or contemplated legal proceedings and not with a view to furthering a criminal purpose.
(7) A person guilty of an offence under this section shall be liable—
 (a) on conviction on indictment, to imprisonment for a term not exceeding five years, to a fine or to both, or
 (b) on summary conviction, to imprisonment for a term not exceeding six months, to a fine not exceeding the statutory maximum or to both.
(8) For the purposes of this section—
 (a) a reference to conducting a terrorist investigation includes a reference to taking part in the conduct of, or assisting, a terrorist investigation, and
 (b) a person interferes with material if he falsifies it, conceals it, destroys it or disposes of it, or if he causes or permits another to do any of those things.

There are two offences concerned with the disclosure of or interference with information linked to a terrorist investigation created by s. 39.

The defence provided for under s. 39(5)(a) is subject to the provisions of s. 118 of the TA 2000 (see **B10.4**), but the defence under s. 39(5)(b) is not. For the significance of the reverse burden, see **F3.13** *et seq.*

COUNTER-TERRORIST POWERS UNDER THE TERRORISM ACT 2000

Arrest without Warrant

B10.86 Section 41(1) of the TA 2000 provides that a constable may arrest without warrant any person whom he reasonably suspects to be a terrorist. When a person is arrested under s. 41, he must be taken as soon as is reasonably practicable to the police station which the constable who arrests him considers the most appropriate (sch. 8, para. 1(4)). PACE Code H, issued in July 2006, applies to such detainees (see **appendix 2** for a summary of the provisions of Code H).

Detention

B10.87 Where a person is arrested under the power provided by the TA 2000, s. 41, the provisions of sch. 8 apply to his detention, treatment, review of detention and extension of detention (s. 41(2)). A person detained under s. 41 may be detained (unless detained under any other power) for no longer than the period of 48 hours beginning (a) with the time of his arrest, or (b) if he was being detained under sch. 7 when he was arrested under s. 41, with the time when his examination under sch. 7 began (s. 41(3)). If a reviewing officer reviewing the person's detention under sch. 8, part II, does not authorise continued detention, the person must (unless detained in accordance with s. 41(5) or (6) or under any other power) be released (s. 41(4)). Where a police officer intends to make an application for a warrant of further detention under sch. 8, para. 29, the person may be detained pending the making of the application (s. 41(5)). Where an application has been made under sch. 8, para. 29 or 36, he may be detained until the proceedings in relation to the application are concluded (s. 41(6)). If an application under sch. 8, para. 29 or 36, is refused, that does not prevent his continued detention under s. 41, although he must be released at the end of the relevant period.

Identification

B10.88 An authorised person may take any steps which are reasonably necessary for (a) photographing the detained person, (b) measuring him, or (c) identifying him (TA 2000, sch. 8, para. 2(1)).

Detained Person's Rights

Informing a Named Person

B10.89 **Terrorism Act 2000, sch. 8, para. 6**

(1) Subject to paragraph 8, a person detained under schedule 7 or section 41 at a police station in England, Wales or Northern Ireland shall be entitled, if he so requests, to have one named person informed as soon as is reasonably practicable that he is being detained there.

(2) The person named must be—

(a) a friend of the detained person,

(b) a relative, or

(c) a person who is known to the detained person or who is likely to take an interest in his welfare.

(3) Where a detained person is transferred from one police station to another, he shall be entitled to exercise the right under this paragraph in respect of the police station to which he is transferred.

The exercise of this right may be delayed by an officer of at least the rank of superintendent if he believes that there will be interference with the investigation, evidence or a person, or that persons will be alerted and the prevention of crime or the recovery of a criminal benefit will be made more difficult (sch. 8, para. 8(1)(a), (4) and (5)). If authorisation for delay is given orally, it must be recorded in writing as soon as reasonably practicable (para. 8(6)). The reason for the delay must be communicated to the detained person and recorded as soon as reasonably practicable (para. 8(7)) and if the reason for the delay ceases to exist the detained person must be allowed to exercise his right without further delay (para. 8(8)). The detained person must be allowed to exercise the right to inform a named person of his whereabouts before the end of his period of detention under the TA 2000 (para. 8(2)).

Informing a Solicitor

Terrorism Act 2000, sch. 8, para. 7 **B10.90**

(1) Subject to paragraphs 8 and 9, a person detained under schedule 7 or section 41 at a police station in England, Wales or Northern Ireland shall be entitled, if he so requests, to consult a solicitor as soon as is reasonably practicable, privately and at any time.

(2) Where a request is made under sub-paragraph (1), the request and the time at which it was made shall be recorded.

Delay in the exercise of the right to consult a solicitor may be authorised on similar grounds to those justifying delay in contacting a named person (see **B10.89**).

Schedule 8, para. 9 provides for a consultation with a solicitor to be in the sight and hearing of a police officer.

Fingerprints and Intimate and Non-intimate Samples

Terrorism Act 2000, sch. 8, para. 10 **B10.91**

(1) This paragraph applies where a person is detained in England, Wales or Northern Ireland under schedule 7 or section 41.

(2) Fingerprints may be taken from the detained person only if they are taken by a constable—
- (a) with the appropriate consent given in writing, or
- (b) without that consent under sub-paragraph (4).

(3) A non-intimate sample may be taken from the detained person only if it is taken by a constable—
- (a) with the appropriate consent given in writing, or
- (b) without that consent under sub-paragraph (4).

(4) Fingerprints or a non-intimate sample may be taken from the detained person without the appropriate consent only if—
- (a) he is detained at a police station and a police officer of at least the rank of superintendent authorises the fingerprints or sample to be taken, or
- (b) he has been convicted of a recordable offence and, where a non-intimate sample is to be taken, he was convicted of the offence on or after 10th April 1995 (or 29th July 1996 where the non-intimate sample is to be taken in Northern Ireland).

(5) An intimate sample may be taken from the detained person only if—
- (a) he is detained at a police station,
- (b) the appropriate consent is given in writing,
- (c) a police officer of at least the rank of superintendent authorises the sample to be taken, and
- (d) subject to paragraph 13(2) and (3), the sample is taken by a constable.

(6) Subject to sub-paragraph (6A) an officer may give an authorisation under sub-paragraph (4)(a) or (5)(c) only if—
- (a) in the case of a person detained under section 41, the officer reasonably suspects that the person has been involved in an offence under any of the provisions mentioned in section 40(1)(a), and the officer reasonably believes that the fingerprints or sample will tend to confirm or disprove his involvement, or
- (b) in any case, the officer is satisfied that the taking of the fingerprints or sample from the person is necessary in order to assist in determining whether he falls within section 40(1)(b).

(6A) An officer may also give an authorisation under sub-paragraph (4)(a) for the taking of fingerprints if—
- (a) he is satisfied that the fingerprints of the detained person will facilitate the ascertainment of that person's identity; and

(b) that person has refused to identify himself or the officer has reasonable grounds for suspecting that that person is not who he claims to be.

(6B) In this paragraph references to ascertaining a person's identity include references to showing that he is not a particular person.

(7) If an authorisation under sub-paragraph (4)(a) or (5)(c) is given orally, the person giving it shall confirm it in writing as soon as is reasonably practicable.

Paragraph 10 sets out the circumstances in which fingerprints and non-intimate samples may be taken from the detained person. Under para. 13(4), a sample of hair, other than pubic hair, may be taken by cutting hairs or by plucking hairs with their roots so long as no more are plucked than the person taking the sample reasonably considers to be necessary for a sufficient sample.

Paragraph 10(5) provides for the taking of intimate samples when (a) a person is detained at a police station, (b) the appropriate consent is given in writing, (c) a police officer of at least the rank of superintendent authorises the sample to be taken, and (d) the sample is taken by a constable. A doctor must take any intimate sample other than a urine sample or a dental impression (para. 13(2)). A dental impression must be taken by a dentist (para. 13(3)).

Authorisation for the taking of such samples may be given only if the following conditions are satisfied:

(a) in the case of a person detained under the TA 2000, s. 41, the officer reasonably suspects that the person has been involved in an offence under the provisions mentioned in s. 40(1)(a), and the officer reasonably believes that the fingerprints or sample will tend to confirm or disprove his involvement, or

(b) in any case, the officer is satisfied that the taking of the fingerprints or a sample from the person is necessary in order to assist in determining whether he falls within s. 40(1)(b) (i.e. whether he has been involved in the commission, preparation or instigation of an act of terrorism) (sch. 8, para. 10(6)).

Whilst such authorisation may be given orally, it must then be confirmed in writing as soon as is reasonably practicable (para. 10(7)).

If the detained person refuses to consent to the giving of a sample, a court may be entitled to draw appropriate adverse inferences against him (see **F19**).

Any fingerprints or samples or information provided may be used only for the purpose of a terrorist investigation. A check cannot be made against such samples under the PACE 1984, s. 63A(1), except for the purpose of a terrorist investigation (TA 2000, sch. 8, para. 14(3)).

Review and Extension of Detention

B10.92 The TA 2006 has extended the maximum period of detention without charge to 28 days. Parts II and III of sch. 8 to the TA 2000 contain detailed provisions on review and extension of detention.

Section 41 of the TA 2000 requires periodical review of the detention of a suspect. The first review must be carried out as soon as is reasonably practicable after the time of the person's arrest and any subsequent reviews must be carried out at intervals of not more than 12 hours (sch. 8, para. 21(1) to (3)). A review may be postponed if at the latest time when it should be carried out (a) the detained person is being questioned by a police officer and an officer is satisfied that an interruption of the questioning would prejudice the investigation, (b) no review officer is readily available, or (c) it is not practicable for any other reason to carry it out (sch. 8, para. 22(1)). If a review is postponed, a review must be carried out as soon as is reasonably practicable after the postponement (sch. 8, para. 22(2)). The authorisation of continued detention is governed by sch. 8, para. 23.

Terrorism Act 2000, sch. 8, para 23

(1) A review officer may authorise a person's continued detention only if satisfied that it is necessary—
  (a) to obtain relevant evidence whether by questioning him or otherwise,
  (b) to preserve relevant evidence,
  (ba) pending the result of an examination or analysis of any relevant evidence or of anything the examination or analysis of which is to be or is being carried out with a view to obtaining relevant evidence,
  (c) pending a decision whether to apply to the Secretary of State for a deportation notice to be served on the detained person,
  (d) pending the making of an application for the Secretary of State for a deportation notice to be served on the detained person, or
  (e) pending consideration by the Secretary of State whether to serve a deportation notice on the detained person, or
  (f) pending a decision whether the detained person should be charged with an offence.

The review officer must not authorise continued detention unless the investigation or process for deportation is being conducted diligently and expeditiously (sch. 8, para. 23(2) and (3)). The detained person or a solicitor representing him who is available at the time of the review must be given an opportunity to make oral or written representations about the detention before the review officer decides whether to authorise detention (para. 26(1) and (2)). The review officer may refuse oral representations by the person detained if he considers that he is unfit because of his condition or behaviour (para. 26(3)). The detained person has the right to have a named person informed and to consult a solicitor (paras. 6 and 7: see **B10.89** and **B10.90**); when authorising continued detention, the review officer must inform the detained person of those rights where he has not exercised them or inform him that they have been delayed. Under para. 27(1) and (2), the review officer must also review the reasons for the delay under para. 8 (see **B10.89**).

A warrant of further detention may be sought by a Crown Prosecutor or a police officer of at least the rank of superintendent. The application is made to a judicial authority (a specially designated District Judge) (para. 29(1) and (4)). If a warrant is granted it authorises further detention of the person under s. 41 for a specified period. Information on which the applicant for extension intends to rely may be withheld from the detained person or anyone representing him upon application to the District Judge (para. 34(1)).

There may be extension or further extension of the specified period upon further application by an officer of at least the rank of superintendent (para. 36(1)). Where the application would extend the period to a time that is no more than 14 days after (in effect) arrival at the police station and no application has previously been made to a senior judge, the application is heard by the judicial authority; in any other case, the application must be heard by a senior judge (i.e. a judge of the High Court) (para. 36(1A), (1B) and (7)). The decision of the judge of the High Court is not amenable to judicial review.

If at any time it appears to the police officer or other person in charge that any of the conditions under which the warrant was issued no longer apply, he must (a) if he has custody of the detained person, release him immediately, and (b) if he does not, immediately inform the person who does have custody that those matters no longer apply and that person must release him immediately (para. 37(1) to (3)).

Search of Premises for a Person

Powers of search are provided for under s. 42 of the TA 2000. Upon application by a constable, a magistrate may issue a warrant in relation to specified premises if he is satisfied that there are reasonable grounds for suspecting that a person whom the constable reasonably suspects to be a person falling within s. 40(1)(b) (i.e. a person who is or has been concerned in the commission, preparation or instigation of acts of terrorism) is to be found there (s. 42(1)). **B10.93**

Any constable is thereby authorised to enter and search the specified premises for the purpose of arresting the person under s. 41 (s. 42(2)).

Search of Person

B10.94 A constable may stop and search a person whom he reasonably suspects to be a terrorist to discover whether he has in his possession anything which may constitute evidence that he is a terrorist (TA 2000, s. 43(1)). In addition a constable may search a person arrested under s. 41 to discover whether he has in his possession anything which may constitute evidence that he is a terrorist (s. 43(2)).

Stop and Search Power

B10.95 Section 44 of the TA 2000 provides a power of stop and search, the exercise of which is governed by s. 45.

When an authorisation is given under s. 44, any constable in uniform is authorised:

(a) to stop a vehicle in an area or at a specified place and to search (i) the vehicle, (ii) the driver of the vehicle, (iii) a passenger in the vehicle, and (iv) anything in or on the vehicle or carried by the driver or a passenger; and
(b) to stop a pedestrian in an area or at a specified place and to search (i) the pedestrian, and (ii) anything carried by him.

For the authorisation to be given, the person giving it must consider it expedient for the prevention of acts of terrorism (s. 44(3)).

The powers under s. 44 may be exercised only for the purpose of searching for articles of a kind which could be used in connection with terrorism, and may be exercised whether or not the constable has grounds for suspecting the presence of articles of that kind (s. 45(1)). A constable may seize and retain an article which he discovers in the course of a s. 44 search and which he reasonably suspects is intended to be used in connection with terrorism (s. 45(2)). A constable exercising this power may not require a person to remove any clothing in public except for headgear, footwear, an outer coat, a jacket or gloves (s. 45(3)).

If a constable proposes to search a person or vehicle under s. 44, he may detain the person or vehicle for such time as is reasonably required to permit the search to be carried out at or near the place where the person or vehicle is stopped. If a person or vehicle is stopped under s. 44, a written statement is to be provided. In addition, the vehicle driver or the pedestrian may request a written statement that it or they were stopped by virtue of s. 44. Such an application must be made within 12 months of the stop (s. 45(4) to (6)). Under s. 47, any person who fails to stop a vehicle when required to do so by a constable acting under a s. 44 authorisation, or who wilfully obstructs a constable exercising such a power, commits a summary offence. It is punishable by up to six months' imprisonment or a fine up to level 5, or both.

In *R (Gillan) v Metropolitan Police Commissioner* [2006] 2 AC 307, it was held, as a matter of construction, that ss. 44 and 45 did not require that, in order for an authorisation to be given under s. 44, there had to be reasonable grounds for considering that the powers were necessary and suitable for the prevention of terrorism. Moreover, the powers did not conflict with the ECHR. So far as Article 5 rights are concerned, a stop and search did not involve a deprivation of liberty as the stop would be for a very short period of time and the action was one of being detained in the sense of being kept from proceeding or being kept waiting. If it did amount to a detention, it could be justified as being 'in order to secure the fulfilment of any obligation prescribed by law' as set out in Article 5(1)(b). So far as Article 8 is concerned, the intrusion would normally be insufficiently serious to engage the ECHR. If it did, a proper exercise of the power could be justified as being in pursuit of a legitimate aim and proportionate under Article 8(2). If the power was properly exercised it was difficult to see how it could infringe Articles 10 and 11, but if it was misused then they could be infringed. If either were engaged then, provided that the exercise of the power was lawful, it would be expected that the justifications in para. 2 of those articles would also apply. In each case the provision had to be 'lawful' for the purposes of the ECHR in that the exercise of the power to stop and search had to be governed by rules of law which were not arbitrary but were clear and accessible. The law was held to be sufficiently clear and free from arbitrariness.

Prohibiting or Restricting Parking

Under s. 48 of the TA 2000 authorisation may be given to prohibit or restrict the parking of vehicles on a specified road if the person giving it considers it expedient for the prevention of acts of terrorism (s. 48(1) and (2)). The power may then be exercised by a constable placing a traffic sign on the road concerned (s. 49(1)). A constable exercising the power may suspend a parking place (s. 49(2)). **B10.96**

The period of authorisation must not exceed 28 days (s. 50(1) and (2)). An authorisation may be renewed in writing by the authoriser or by a person who could have authorised it and s. 50 applies as if it were a new authorisation (s. 50(3)). Section 51 penalises any person who contravenes any relevant restriction or prohibition. A person charged under s. 51 will be found not guilty if he proves that he had a reasonable excuse for the act or omission in question (s. 51(3)). Under s. 51(4), possession of a current disabled person's badge does not of itself constitute a reasonable excuse.

The offences under s. 51 are triable summarily only. For an offence contrary to s. 51(1), a person is liable to a fine not exceeding level 4 (s. 51(5)). For the offence contrary to s. 51(2), a person is liable to imprisonment for a term not exceeding three months, a fine not exceeding level 4 on the standard scale, or both (s. 51(6))

Terrorism Act 2000, s. 51

(1) A person commits an offence if he parks a vehicle in contravention of a prohibition or restriction imposed by virtue of section 48.

(2) A person commits an offence if—

(a) he is the driver or other person in charge of a vehicle which has been permitted to remain at rest in contravention of any prohibition or restriction imposed by virtue of section 48, and

(b) he fails to move the vehicle when ordered to do so by a constable in uniform.

Port and Border Controls

A number of port and border controls are made available by s. 53(1) of, and sch. 7 to, the TA 2000. The exercise of the powers created in sch. 7 is not affected by any of the rights conferred by s. 1 of the Immigration Act 1971 (general principles regulating entry into and stay in the UK). These border controls operate in respect of Northern Ireland (TA 2000, sch. 7, para. 4). **B10.97**

An examining officer may stop and detain a person in order to question him for the purpose of determining whether he appears to be a person falling within the TA 2000, s. 40(1)(b): i.e. a person who is or has been concerned in the commission, preparation or instigation of acts of terrorism. An examining officer may exercise his powers whether or not he has grounds for suspecting that a person falls within s. 40(1)(b) (sch. 7, para. 2(4)).

An examining officer may also undertake searches in relation to the power to question. It should be noted that PACE Code A does not apply to searches carried out under sch. 7, but there is a specific Code, made under the TA 2000, sch. 14, para. 6.

The examining officer may board a ship or aircraft to enter a vehicle for the purpose of determining whether to exercise the power to search and question (sch. 7, para. 9(4)). In addition, he may detain an item (a) for the purpose of examination, for a period not exceeding seven days beginning with the day on which detention commences, (b) while he believes that it may be needed for use as evidence in criminal proceedings, or (c) while he believes that it may be needed in connection with a decision by the Secretary of State whether to make a deportation order under the Immigration Act 1971 (sch. 7, para. 11(2)). The power under sch. 7, para.11(2) is exercisable in respect of any item which is given to an examining officer in accordance with para. 5(d), is searched or found on a search under para. 8, or is examined under para. 9 (sch. 7, para. 11(1)).

Ports Designation

B10.98 The owners or agents of a ship or aircraft which is employed to carry passengers for reward on a journey to which the TA 2000, sch. 7, para. 12 applies, must not arrange for it to call at a port in Great Britain or Northern Ireland for the purpose of embarking or disembarking passengers unless (a) the port is a designated port, or (b) an examining officer approves the arrangement (para. 12(2)). If an aircraft is making such a journey but not for the purpose of carrying passengers for reward, the aircraft's captain must not permit it to call at or leave Great Britain or Northern Ireland unless (a) the port is a designated port, or (b) he gives at least 12 hours' notice in writing to a constable for the police area in which the port is situated (para. 12(3)). The journeys to which the schedule applies are those between Great Britain, Northern Ireland and the Republic of Ireland. Designated ports are listed in the Table to the TA 2000, sch. 7.

Controls on Embarkation and Disembarkation

B10.99 The Secretary of State has a number of powers to control the embarkation or disembarkation of passengers to and from ships and aircraft and so underpin the other powers under the TA 2000, sch. 7. He may, *inter alia*, give notice designating control areas within ports and specifying conditions for the embarkation and disembarkation of passengers.

Carding

B10.100 Paragraph 16(1) of sch. 7 to the TA 2000 applies to persons travelling between Great Britain, Northern Ireland and the Republic of Ireland. Any such persons, if required to do so by an examining officer, must complete and produce to the officer a card containing such information as is specified in an order. The Terrorism Act 2000 (Carding) Order 2001 (SI 2001 No. 426) lists the information that a card must contain.

Provision of Passenger Information

B10.101 Paragraph 17 of sch. 7 to the TA 2000 applies to a ship or aircraft travelling between Great Britain, Northern Ireland and the Republic of Ireland. The owners or agents of a ship or aircraft to which para. 17 applies must comply with any written request to provide specified information by an examining officer as soon as reasonably practicable. Schedule 7 to the Terrorism Act 2000 (Information) Order 2002 (SI 2002 No. 1945) specifies the relevant information.

Offences

B10.102 **Terrorism Act 2000, sch. 7, para. 18**

(1) A person commits an offence if he—
  (a) wilfully fails to comply with a duty imposed under or by virtue of this Schedule,
  (b) wilfully contravenes a prohibition imposed under or by virtue of this Schedule, or
  (c) wilfully obstructs, or seeks to frustrate, a search of examination under or by virtue of this Schedule.

The maximum penalty for this summary offence is imprisonment for a term not exceeding three months, a fine not exceeding level 4 on the standard scale, or both (para. 18(2)).

ANTI-TERRORISM, CRIME AND SECURITY ACT 2001: GENERAL

In the wake of the attack on the World Trade Center in New York on 11 September 2001, the A-tCSA 2001 introduced a number of new offences designed to combat the potential use by terrorists of poisons and chemical, biological and nuclear weapons. In addition, new powers were introduced to allow for the forfeiture of assets available to terrorists and the disclosure of information by public bodies. **B10.103**

OFFENCES UNDER THE ANTI-TERRORISM, CRIME AND SECURITY ACT 2001

The A-tCSA 2001 creates a number of offences to deal with weapons of mass destruction. **B10.104**

Security of Pathogens and Toxins

Anti-terrorism, Crime and Security Act 2001, s. 67 **B10.105**

(1) An occupier who fails without reasonable excuse to comply with any duty or direction imposed on him by or under this part [which is concerned with the security of pathogens and toxins] is guilty of an offence.

(2) A person who, in giving information to a person exercising functions under this part, knowingly or recklessly makes a statement which is false or misleading in a material particular is guilty of an offence.

Procedure An allegation of an offence contrary to the TA 2000, s. 67, is triable either way (A-tCSA 2001, s. 67(3)); when tried on indictment it is a class 3 offence. **B10.106**

Offences by corporate bodies are dealt with in the A-tCSA 2001, s. 68 and those by partnerships and unincorporated associations in s. 69.

Sentence The maximum penalties are, on conviction on indictment, imprisonment for a term not exceeding five years or a fine or both; and, on summary conviction, imprisonment for a term not exceeding six months or a fine not exceeding the statutory maximum or both (A-tCSA 2001, s. 67(3)). **B10.107**

Elements Schedule 5 to the A-tCSA 2001 lists the range of powers in relation to the security of pathogens and toxins set out in part 7 of the Act. Under s. 58(2), that list can be amended subject to the requirement that no pathogen or toxin should be added unless the Secretary of State is satisfied that it could be used in an act of terrorism to endanger life or cause serious harm to human health (s. 58(3)). By s. 74(1), 'act of terrorism' has the same meaning as in the TA 2000 (see **B10.3**). **B10.108**

Use of Nuclear Weapons

Anti-terrorism, Crime and Security Act 2001, s. 47 **B10.109**

(1) A person who—
- (a) knowingly causes a nuclear weapon explosion;
- (b) develops or produces, or participates in the development or production of, a nuclear weapon;
- (c) has a nuclear weapon in his possession;
- (d) participates in the transfer of a nuclear weapon; or
- (e) engages in military preparations, or in preparations of a military nature, intending to use, or threaten to use, a nuclear weapon,

is guilty of an offence.

Procedure An allegation of an offence contrary to the A-tCSA 2001, s. 47, is triable on indictment only (s. 47(5)) and is a class 3 offence. The Terrorism Protocol (see **B10.60**) applies to proceedings taken under s. 67. **B10.110**

The acts founding culpability can be committed outside the UK but only by a 'United Kingdom person' (s. 47(7)) and proceedings may be instituted for an offence committed outside the UK (s. 51(1)). A 'United Kingdom person' is defined by s. 56(1) as a UK national, a Scottish partnership, or a body incorporated under the law of a part of the UK. A UK national is a British citizen, a British Overseas Territories citizen, a British National (Overseas) or a British Overseas citizen, or a British subject or British protected person within the meaning of the British Nationality Act 1981 (s. 56(2)).

Proceedings under s. 47 may be commenced only by or with the consent of the A-G (s. 55).

B10.111 **Sentence** The maximum penalty is imprisonment for life (A-tCSA 2001, s. 47(5)).

B10.112 **Elements** Participating in the development or production of a nuclear weapon is defined in the A-tCSA 2001, s. 47(3), as (a) facilitating the development by another of the capability to produce or use a nuclear weapon, or (b) facilitating the making by another of a nuclear weapon. In each case, the person participating must know or have reason to believe that his act has or will have the effect in (a) or (b).

Participating in the transfer of a nuclear weapon is defined in s. 47(4) as (a) buying it or otherwise acquiring it or agreeing with another to do so, or (b) selling or otherwise disposing of it or agreeing with another to do so, or (c) making arrangements whereby another person acquires or disposes of it or agreeing with a third person to do so.

Exceptions

B10.113 **Anti-terrorism, Crime and Security Act 2001, s. 48**

(1) Nothing in section 47 applies—
   (a) to an act which is authorised under subsection (2); or
   (b) to an act done in the course of an armed conflict.
(2) The Secretary of State may—
   (a) authorise any act which would otherwise contravene section 47 in such manner and on such terms as he thinks fit; and
   (b) withdraw or vary any authorisation given under this subsection.
(3) Any question arising in proceedings for an offence under section 47 as to whether anything was done in the course of an armed conflict shall be determined by the Secretary of State.
(4) A certificate purporting to set out any such determination and to be signed by the Secretary of State shall be received in evidence in any such proceedings and shall be presumed to be so signed unless the contrary is shown.

Specific Defences

B10.114 **Anti-terrorism, Crime and Security Act 2001, s. 49**

(1) In proceedings for an offence under section 47(1)(c) or (d) relating to an object it is a defence for the accused to show that he did not know and had no reason to believe that the object was a nuclear weapon.
(2) But he shall be taken to have shown that fact if—
   (a) sufficient evidence is adduced to raise an issue with respect to it; and
   (b) the contrary is not proved by the prosecution beyond reasonable doubt.
(3) In proceedings for such an offence it is also a defence for the accused to show that he knew or believed that the object was a nuclear weapon but, as soon as reasonably practicable after he first knew or believed that fact, he took all reasonable steps to inform the Secretary of State or a constable of his knowledge or belief.

B10.115 **Related Offence** Under s. 54 of the A-tCSA 2001, it is an offence for a person to knowingly or recklessly make a false or misleading statement in order to obtain (or oppose the variation or withdrawal of) authorisation for the purposes of s. 47. The provision also applies in relation to an authorisation under s. 50 (see **B10.116**).

Secondary Parties to Chemical, Biological and Nuclear Weapons Offences

Anti-terrorism, Crime and Security Act 2001, s. 50 **B10.116**

(1) A person who aids, abets, counsels or procures, or incites, a person who is not a United Kingdom person to do a relevant act outside the United Kingdom is guilty of an offence.

(2) For this purpose a relevant act is an act that, if done by a United Kingdom person, would contravene any of the following provisions—

(a) section 1 of the Biological Weapons Act 1974 (offences relating to biological agents and toxins);

(b) section 2 of the Chemical Weapons Act 1996 (offences relating to chemical weapons); or

(c) section 47 above (offences relating to nuclear weapons).

Procedure An allegation of an offence contrary to the A-tCSA 2001, s. 50, is triable on indictment only (s. 50(5)) and is a class 3 offence. The Terrorism Protocol (see **B10.60**) applies to proceedings taken under s. 50. **B10.117**

The acts founding culpability can be committed outside the UK but only by a 'United Kingdom person' (s. 50(6)) and proceedings may be instituted for an offence committed outside the UK (s. 51(1)). See further **B10.110**.

Proceedings may be commenced only by or with the consent of the A-G (s. 55).

Sentence The maximum penalty is imprisonment for life (s. 50(5)). **B10.118**

Specific Defence

Anti-terrorism, Crime and Security Act 2001, s. 50 **B10.119**

(3) Nothing in this section applies to an act mentioned in subsection (1) which—

(a) relates to a relevant act which would contravene section 47; and

(b) is authorised by the Secretary of State;

and section 48(2) applies for the purpose of authorising acts that would otherwise constitute an offence under this section.

(4) A person accused of an offence under this section in relation to a relevant act which would contravene a provision mentioned in subsection (2) may raise any defence which would be open to a person accused of the corresponding offence ancillary to an offence under that provision.

Disclosures Prejudicing Nuclear Security

Anti-terrorism, Crime and Security Act 2001, s. 79 **B10.120**

(1) A person is guilty of an offence if he discloses any information or thing the disclosure of which might prejudice the security of any nuclear site or of any nuclear material—

(a) with the intention of prejudicing that security; or

(b) being reckless as to whether the disclosure might prejudice that security.

Procedure An allegation of an offence contrary to the A-tCSA 2001, s. 79, is triable either way (s. 79(3)); when tried on indictment it is a class 3 offence. **B10.121**

The acts founding culpability can be committed outside the UK but only by a 'United Kingdom person' (see **B10.110**) and proceedings may be instituted for an offence committed outside the UK (s. 79(6)).

Proceedings may be commenced only by or with the consent of the A-G (s. 81(1)).

Sentence The maximum penalties are, on conviction on indictment, imprisonment for a term not exceeding seven years, a fine or both and, on summary conviction, imprisonment for a term not exceeding six months or a fine not exceeding the statutory maximum or both (A-tCSA 2001, s. 79(3)). **B10.122**

Related Offence Section 80 of the A-tCSA 2001 prohibits disclosures relating to uranium enrichment technology. **B10.123**

Use or Threat of Use of Noxious Substances or Things to Cause Harm and Intimidate

B10.124 **Anti-terrorism, Crime and Security Act 2001, s. 113**

(1) A person who takes any action which—
(a) involves the use of a noxious substance or other noxious thing;
(b) has or is likely to have an effect falling within subsection (2); and
(c) is designed to influence the government or an international governmental organisation or to intimidate the public or a section of the public,
is guilty of an offence.
(2) Action has an effect falling within this subsection if it—
(a) causes serious violence against a person anywhere in the world;
(b) causes serious damages to real or personal property anywhere in the world;
(c) endangers human life or creates a serious risk to the health or safety of the public or a section of the public; or
(d) induces in members of the public the fear that the action is likely to endanger their lives or create a serious risk to their health or safety;
but any effect on the person taking the action is to be disregarded.
(3) A person who—
(a) makes a threat that he or another will take any action which constitutes an offence under subsection (i); and
(b) intends thereby to induce in a person anywhere in the world the fear that the threat is likely to be carried out,
is guilty of an offence.

B10.125 **Procedure** An allegation of an offence contrary to the A-tCSA 2001, s. 113, is triable either way (s. 113(4)); when tried on indictment it is a class 3 offence.

Conduct which occurs outside the UK will be covered by s. 113 provided two conditions are met (s. 113A). The first is that the conduct is done for the purpose of advancing a political, religious or ideological cause. The second is that the conduct is (a) by a UK national or a UK resident, (b) by any person done to, or in relation to, a UK national, a UK resident or a protected person, or (c) by any person done in the circumstances which fall within the TA 2000, s. 63D(1)(b) and (c) or (3)(b) and (c) (s. 113A(2) and (3)). As to the TA 2000, s. 63D, see **B10.78**. 'United Kingdom national', 'United Kingdom resident', and 'protected person' have the same meaning as in the TA 2000, ss. 63C and 63D (s. 113A(4)). By virtue of s. 113A(5), it is immaterial whether a person knows that another is a UK national, UK resident or a protected person.

Section 113B(1) provides that the consent of the A-G is necessary for the institution of proceedings under s. 113, and s. 113B(2) provides for such proceedings to be taken, and the offence for incidental purposes to be treated as having been committed, in any part of the UK.

B10.126 **Sentence** The maximum penalty is, on indictment, 14 years' imprisonment, a fine or both; on summary conviction, six months' imprisonment, a fine not exceeding the statutory maximum or both (A-tCSA 2001, s. 113(4)).

B10.127 **Elements** For the meaning of 'noxious thing' in the OAPA 1861, see **B2.66**.

Under the A-tCSA 2001, s. 113(5), 'government' means the government of the UK or a part of the UK or of a country other than the UK. Under the same section, 'public' includes the public of a country other than the UK.

'Substance' includes any biological agent and any other natural or artificial substance (whatever its form, origin or method of production) (s. 115(1)).

For a person to be guilty of an offence under s. 113(3), it is not necessary for him to have any particular person in mind as the person in whom he intends to induce the belief in question (s. 115(2)).

Hoaxes Involving Noxious Substances or Things

Anti-terrorism, Crime and Security Act 2001, s. 114 **B10.128**

(1) A person is guilty of an offence if he—
  (a) places any substance or other thing in any place; or
  (b) sends any substance or other thing from one place to another (by post, rail or any other means whatever);
  with the intention of inducing in a person anywhere in the world a belief that it is likely to be (or contain) a noxious substance or other noxious thing and thereby endanger human life or create a serious risk to human health.

(2) A person is guilty of an offence if he communicates any information which he knows or believes to be false with the intention of inducing in a person anywhere in the world a belief that a noxious substance or other noxious thing is likely to be present (whether at the time the information is communicated or later) in any place and thereby endanger human life or create a serious risk to human health.

Procedure The offence is triable either way (A-tCSA 2001, s. 114(3)); when tried on indictment it is a class 3 offence. **B10.129**

Sentence The maximum penalty is, on indictment, 14 years' imprisonment, a fine or both; on summary conviction, six months' imprisonment, a fine not exceeding the statutory maximum or both (A-tCSA 2001, s. 113(4)). **B10.130**

Elements See **B10.127** for definitions of the elements of the offence. **B10.131**

For a person to be guilty of an offence under s. 114 it is not necessary for him to have any particular person in mind as the person in whom he intends to induce the belief in question (s. 115(2)).

OTHER POWERS UNDER THE ANTI-TERRORISM, CRIME AND SECURITY ACT 2001

Forfeiture of Cash

Powers to seize and forfeit cash which is either intended to be used for terrorist purposes, or represents the resources of a proscribed organisation or represents property obtained through terrorist activities are contained in sch. 1 to the A-tCSA 2001. Under s. 1(1), the powers are exercisable through civil proceedings in the magistrates' courts and, under s. 1(2), that is whether or not criminal proceedings have been instituted. **B10.132**

Freezing Orders

Detailed provisions in relation to the making of freezing orders are set out in the A-tCSA 2001, ss. 4 to 8 and sch. 3. The procedure for making an order is set out in ss. 10 to 14. **B10.133**

Under s. 4, the Treasury may make such a freezing order, prohibiting any person from making funds available to a specified person or persons, if the Treasury reasonably believes:

(a) either (i) action to the detriment of the UK's economy (or part of it) has been or is likely to be taken by a person or persons, or (ii) action constituting a threat to the life or property of one or more nationals of the UK or residents of the UK has been or is likely to be taken by a person or persons; and
(b) if one person is believed to have taken or be likely to take the action, that the person is (i) the government of a country or territory outside the UK, or (ii) a resident of a country or territory outside the UK or, where two or more persons are believed to be involved, each of them falls within category (i) or (ii)).

'National' and 'resident' are defined in s. 9.

Disclosure by Public Authorities

B10.134 **Anti-Terrorism, Crime and Security Act 2001, s. 17**

(1) This section applies to the provisions listed in schedule 4, so far as they authorise the disclosure of information.

(2) Each of the provisions to which this section applies shall have effect, in relation to the disclosure of information by or on behalf of a public authority, as if the purposes for which the disclosure of information is authorised by that provision included each of the following—

(a) the purposes of any criminal investigation whatever which is being or may be carried out, whether in the United Kingdom or elsewhere;

(b) the purposes of any criminal proceedings whatever which have been or may be initiated, whether in the United Kingdom or elsewhere;

(c) the purposes of the initiation or bringing to an end of any such investigation or proceedings;

(d) the purpose of facilitating a determination of whether any such investigation or proceedings should be initiated or brought to an end.

(3) The Treasury may by order made by statutory instrument add any provision contained in any subordinate legislation to the provisions to which this section applies.

(4) The Treasury shall not make an order under subsection (3) unless a draft of it has been laid before Parliament and approved by a resolution of each House.

(5) No disclosure of information shall be made by virtue of this section unless the public authority by which the disclosure is made is satisfied that the making of the disclosure is proportionate to what is sought to be achieved by it.

(6) Nothing in this section shall be taken to prejudice any power to disclose information which exists apart from this section.

(7) The information that may be disclosed by virtue of this section includes information obtained before the commencement of this section.

The duties of disclosure of information by public bodies to investigators were significantly widened by s. 17. The provisions to which the extended disclosure duties relate are set out in sch. 4. Under s. 17(5), the public body must be satisfied that the disclosure is proportionate to the objectives of the request. Section 18 places limitations on disclosure of information for the purposes of proceedings overseas.

OFFENCES UNDER THE TERRORISM ACT 2006

B10.135 The TA 2006 was passed in the wake of the bombings and attempted bombings of the London Underground system in July 2005. The statute creates a number of new offences designed to counter the activities of terrorists which had not been previously addressed by legislation.

Encouragement of Terrorism

B10.136 **Terrorism Act 2006, s. 1**

(1) This section applies to a statement that is likely to be understood by some or all of the members of the public to whom it is published as a direct or indirect encouragement or other inducement to them to the commission, preparation or instigation of acts of terrorism or Convention offences.

(2) A person commits an offence if—

(a) he publishes a statement to which this section applies or causes another to publish such a statement; and

(b) at the time he publishes it or causes it to be published, he—

(i) intends members of the public to be directly or indirectly encouraged or otherwise induced by the statement to commit, prepare or instigate acts of terrorism or Convention offences; or

(ii) is reckless as to whether members of the public will be directly or indirectly encouraged or otherwise induced by the statement to commit, prepare or instigate such acts or offences.

Procedure An allegation of an offence contrary to the TA 2006, s. 1, is triable either way (s. 1(7)); when tried on indictment it is a class 3 offence. The consent of the DPP is necessary for the institution of proceedings (s. 19(1)) unless the offence is committed wholly or partly in connection with the affairs of a country outside the UK, in which case the consent of the A-G is required (s. 19(2)). **B10.137**

By virtue of s. 17, the offence under s. 1 may be committed by any person of any nationality anywhere in the world. The courts of the UK therefore have universal jurisdiction in relation to the offence. If a person does anything outside the UK which would constitute an offence in any part of the UK, he will be guilty of the offence in that part of the UK. Proceedings in respect of the offence may be taken anywhere in the UK and the offence may be treated for incidental purposes as having been committed in any such place (s. 17(4)).

Sentence The maximum penalty is, on conviction on indictment, imprisonment for a term not exceeding seven years or a fine, or both, and, on summary conviction, imprisonment for a term not exceeding six months or a fine not exceeding the statutory maximum, or both (TA 2006, s. 1(7) and (8)). **B10.138**

Elements By virtue of s. 1(3), the statements that are likely to be understood by members of the public as indirectly encouraging the commission or preparation of acts of terrorism or Convention offences include every statement which (a) glorifies the commission or preparation (whether in the past, in the future or generally) of such acts or offences; and (b) is a statement from which those members of the public could reasonably be expected to infer that what is being glorified is being glorified as conduct that should be emulated by them in existing circumstances. **B10.139**

'Terrorism' has the same definition as applies under the TA 2000 (see **B10.3**).

'Convention offence' means an offence listed in the TA 2006, sch. 1 or an equivalent offence under the law of a country or territory outside the UK. The Convention offences in sch. 2 are as follows:

Explosives offences: an offence under the OAPA 1861, ss. 28 to 30 (causing injury by explosions, causing explosions and handling or placing explosives) or under the Explosive Substances Act 1883, ss. 2 to 5 (see **B12.151** ***et seq.***).

Biological weapons: an offence under the Biological Weapons Act 1974, s. 1 (see **B10.173**).

Offences against internationally protected persons: an offence under the Internationally Protected Persons Act 1978, s. 1(3) (threats etc. in relation to protected persons), or an offence mentioned in s. 1(1)(a) of that Act (attacks against protected persons committed outside the UK) which is committed (whether in the UK or elsewhere) in relation to a protected person or an offence mentioned in s. 1(1)(b) of that Act (attacks on relevant premises etc.) which is committed (whether in the UK or elsewhere) in connection with an attack—

(a) on relevant premises or on a vehicle ordinarily used by a protected person, and

(b) at a time when a protected person is in or on the premises or vehicle.

Hostage-taking: an offence under the Taking of Hostages Act 1982, s. 1 (hostage-taking: see **B2.99**).

Hijacking and other offences against aircraft: offences under the Aviation Security Act 1982, ss. 1 to 3 and 6(2) (see **B10.199** ***et seq.***).

Offences involving nuclear material: an offence mentioned in the Nuclear Material (Offences) Act 1983, s. 1(1) which is committed (whether in the UK or elsewhere) in relation to or by means of nuclear material and an offence under s. 2 of that Act (see **B10.191**).

Offences under the Aviation and Maritime Security Act 1990: offences under the Aviation and Maritime Security Act 1990, ss. 1 and 9 to 14 (see **B10.216** ***et seq.***).

Offences involving chemical weapons: an offence under the Chemical Weapons Act 1996, s. 2 (see **B10.177**).

Terrorist funds: an offence under the TA 2000, ss. 15 to 18 (see **B10.19** to **B10.30**).
Directing terrorist organisation: an offence under the TA 2000, s. 56 (see **B10.59**).
Offences involving nuclear weapons: an offence under the A-tCSA 2001, s. 47 (see **B10.109**).
Conspiracy etc.: conspiracy to commit a Convention offence or inciting, attempting, aiding, abetting, counselling or procuring the commission of a Convention offence.

The questions of how a statement is likely to be understood and what members of the public could reasonably be expected to infer from it must be determined having regard both (a) to the contents of the statement as a whole, and (b) to the circumstances and manner of its publication (s. 1(4)).

'Glorification' is defined in s. 20(2) as including any form of praise or celebration, and cognate expressions are to be construed accordingly.

'Conduct that should be emulated in existing circumstances' includes conduct that is illustrative of a type of conduct that should be so emulated (s. 20(7)).

By virtue of s. 20(3), references to 'the public' (a) are references to the public of any part of the UK or of a country or territory outside the UK, or any section of the public, and (b) except in s. 9(4), also include references to a meeting or other group of persons which is open to the public (whether unconditionally or on the making of a payment or the satisfaction of other conditions).

References to a person's publishing a statement are references to (a) his publishing it in any manner to the public, (b) his providing electronically any service by means of which the public have access to the statement, or (c) his using a service provided to him electronically by another so as to enable or to facilitate access by the public to his statement (s. 20(4)). This subsection does not apply to the references to a publication in s. 2 (see **B10.141**).
Under s. 20(5), 'providing a service' includes making a facility available.

References to a statement are references to a communication of any description, including a communication without words consisting of sounds or images or both (s. 20(6)).

For the purposes of s. 1(1) to (3), it is irrelevant (a) whether anything mentioned in those subsections relates to the commission, instigation or preparation of one or more particular acts of terrorism or Convention offences, of acts of terrorism or Convention offences of a particular description, or of acts of terrorism or Convention offences generally, and (b) whether any person is in fact encouraged or induced by the statement to commit, prepare or instigate any such act or offence (s. 1(5)).
Section 18 provides that, where an offence under part 1 of the Act is committed by a body corporate and is proved to have been committed with the consent or connivance of a director, manager, secretary or other similar officer of the body corporate (or a person purporting to act in that capacity), he (as well as the body corporate) is guilty of that offence and is liable to be proceeded against and punished accordingly. For the purposes of the section, where a body corporate is managed by its members, a member is a director.

For extended jurisdiction in respect of suppliers of information society services who are established in the UK where a relevant act occurs in the EEA, see the Electronic Commerce Directive (Terrorism Act 2006) Regulations 2007 (SI 2007 No. 1550). The Regulations also provide for special defences and limited liability where they apply.

B10.140 **Defence** Section 1(6) of the TA 2006 provides that, where it is not proved that the accused intended the statement directly or indirectly to encourage or otherwise induce the commission, preparation or instigation of acts of terrorism or Convention offences, it is a defence for him to show (a) that the statement neither expressed his views nor had his endorsement (whether by virtue of s. 3 or otherwise); and (b) that it was clear, in all the circumstances of the statement's publication, that it did not express his views and (apart from the possibility of his having been given and failed to comply with a notice under s. 3(3); see **B10.146**) did not have his endorsement).

Dissemination of Terrorist Publications

Terrorism Act 2006, s. 2 **B10.141**

(1) A person commits an offence if he engages in conduct falling within subsection (2) and, at the time he does so—
- (a) he intends an effect of his conduct to be a direct or indirect encouragement or other inducement to the commission, preparation or instigation of acts of terrorism;
- (b) he intends an effect of his conduct to be the provision of assistance in the commission or preparation of such acts; or
- (c) he is reckless as to whether his conduct has an effect mentioned in paragraph (a) or (b).

(2) For the purposes of this section a person engages in conduct falling within this subsection if he—
- (a) distributes or circulates a terrorist publication;
- (b) gives, sells or lends such a publication;
- (c) offers such a publication for sale or loan;
- (d) provides a service to others that enables them to obtain, reward, listen to or look at such a publication, or to acquire it by means of a gift, sale or loan;
- (e) transmits the contents of such a publication electronically; or
- (f) has such a publication in his possession with a view to its becoming the subject of conduct falling within any of paragraphs (a) to (e).

Procedure An allegation of an offence contrary to s. 2 of the TA 2006 is triable either way (s. 2(11)); when tried on indictment it is a class 3 offence. The consent of the DPP is necessary for the institution of proceedings (s. 19(1)) unless the offence is committed wholly or partly in connection with the affairs of a country outside the UK, in which case the consent of the A-G is required (s. 19(2)). **B10.142**

The provisions of s. 17 apply to this offence (see **B10.137**). For the liability of company directors, see **B10.139**.

Sentence The maximum penalty is, on conviction on indictment, imprisonment for a term not exceeding seven years or a fine, or both, and, on summary conviction, imprisonment for a term not exceeding six months or a fine not exceeding the statutory maximum, or both (TA 2006, s. 2(11) and (12)). **B10.143**

Elements A publication is a terrorist publication, in relation to the conduct mentioned in the TA 2006, s. 2(2), if matter contained in it is likely (a) to be understood, by some or all of the persons to whom it is or may become available as a consequence of that conduct, as a direct or indirect encouragement or other inducement to them to the commission, preparation or instigation of acts of terrorism; or (b) to be useful in the commission or preparation of such acts and to be understood, by some or all of those persons, as contained in the publication, or made available to them, wholly or mainly for the purpose of being so useful to them (s. 2(3)). **B10.144**

Matter that is likely to be understood by a person as indirectly encouraging the commission or preparation of acts of terrorism includes any matter which (a) glorifies the commission or preparation (whether in the past, in the future or generally) of such acts, and (b) is matter from which that person could reasonably be expected to infer that what is being glorified is being glorified as conduct that should be emulated by him in existing circumstances (s. 2(4)).

Whether a publication is a terrorist publication must be determined (a) as at the time of the conduct, and (b) having regard both to the contents of the publication as a whole and to the circumstances in which the conduct occurs (s. 2(5)).

References to the effect of a person's conduct in relation to a terrorist publication include references to an effect of the publication on one or more persons to whom it is or may become available as a consequence of that conduct (s. 2(6)).

It is irrelevant whether anything in s. 2(1) to (4) is in relation to the commission, preparation or instigation of one or more particular acts of terrorism, of acts of terrorism of a particular description or of acts of terrorism generally (s. 2(7)). It is also irrelevant whether any person is in fact encouraged or induced by the matter contained in any articles to commit, prepare or instigate acts of terrorism, or in fact makes use of it in the commission or preparation of such acts (s. 2(8)).

'Article' includes anything for storing data (s. 20(2)). 'Publication' means any article or record of any description that contains any of the following, or a combination of them: matter to be read, matter to be listened to, matter to be looked at or watched (s. 2(13)).

B10.145 **Specific Defences** The Act provides for two special defences to an allegation under s. 2. The first defence concerns the defendant establishing that the views were not his nor did he endorse them.

Terrorism Act 2006, s. 2

(9) In proceedings for an offence under this section against a person in respect of conduct to which subsection (10) applies, it is a defence for him to show—
(a) that the matter by reference to which the publication in question was a terrorist publication neither expressed his views nor had his endorsement (whether by virtue of section 3 or otherwise); and
(b) that it was clear, in all the circumstances of the conduct, that that matter did not express his views and (apart from the possibility of his having been given and failed to comply with a notice under [s. 3(3): see **B10.146**]) did not have his endorsement.

(10) This subsection applies to the conduct of a person to the extent that—
(a) the publication to which his conduct related contained matter by reference to which it was a terrorist publication by virtue of [s. 2(3)(a)]; and
(b) that person is not proved to have engaged in that conduct with the intention specified in [s. 2(1)(a)].

The second defence relates to Internet activity and repeat statements.

Terrorism Act 2006, s. 3

(5) In proceedings against a person for an offence under section 1 or 2 the requirements of subsection (2)(a) to (c) are not, in his case, to be regarded as satisfied in relation to any time by virtue of subsection (4) if he shows that he—
(a) has, before that time, taken every step he reasonably could to prevent a repeat statement from becoming available to the public and to ascertain whether it does; and
(b) was, at that time, a person to whom subsection (6) applied.

(6) This subsection applies to a person at any time when he—
(a) is not aware of the publication of the repeat statement; or
(b) having become aware of its publication, has taken every step that he reasonably could to secure that it either ceased to be available to the public or was modified as mentioned in subsection (3)(b).

B10.146 **Internet Activity** In relation to the TA 2006, ss. 1 and 2, where a statement is published or caused to be published in the course of, or in connection with, the provision or use of a service provided electronically, or conduct falling within s. 2(2) was in the course of, or in connection with, the provision or use of such a service, the provisions of s. 3 apply (s. 3(1)). The statement or article or record to which the conduct relates is to be regarded as having the endorsement of a person at any time more than two working days after a constable has given him notice under s. 3(3) and the relevant person has failed, without reasonable excuse, to comply with the notice (s. 3(2)). A notice under s. 3(3) is one which (a) declares that, in the opinion of the constable giving it, the statement or the article or record is unlawfully terrorism-related; (b) requires the relevant person to secure that the statement or the article or record, so far as it is so related, is not available to the public or is modified so as no longer to be so related; (c) warns the relevant person that a failure to comply with the notice within two working days will result in the statement, or the article or record, being regarded as having his endorsement; and (d) explains how, under s. 3(4), he may become liable by virtue of the notice if the statement, or the article or record, becomes available to the public after he has complied with the notice. Where a person is given the notice and complies with it, but subsequently publishes or causes to be published a repeat statement (i.e. a statement which is, or is for all practical purposes, the same or to the same effect as the statement to which the notice related, or to matter contained in the article or record to which it related), the requirements of s. 3(2) are to be regarded as satisfied in relation to the times of that subsequent publication by the relevant person (s. 3(4)).

Section 3(7) sets out when a statement or an article or record is unlawfully terrorism-related.

A notice under s. 3(3) must be given to a person only (a) by delivering it to him in person, or (b) by sending it to him, by means of a postal address providing for delivery to be recorded, at his last known address (s. 4(1)). As to the giving of a notice to a corporate body or a firm or an unincorporated body or association, see s. 4(2) to (6) and (8). The time when a notice is to be regarded as given is (a) where it is delivered to a person, the time at which it is so delivered, and (b) where it is sent by a recorded delivery postal service, the time recorded as the time of its delivery (s. 4(7)).

For extended jurisdiction in respect of suppliers of information society services who are established in the UK where a relevant act occurs in the EEA, see the Electronic Commerce Directive (Terrorism Act 2006) Regulations 2007 (SI 2007 No. 1550). The Regulations also provide for special defences and limited liability where they apply.

Search Power If a magistrate is satisfied that there are reasonable grounds for suspecting that articles likely to be the subject of conduct falling within s. 2(2)(a) to (e) and to be treated as a terrorist publication are likely to be found on any premises, he may issue a warrant authorising a constable (a) to enter and search the premises, and (b) to seize anything found there which the constable has reason to believe is such an article (TA 2006, s. 28(1) and (2)). The person searching may use such force as is reasonable in the circumstances for exercising the power (s. 28(3)). **B10.147**

Preparation of Terrorist Acts

Terrorism Act 2006, s. 5 **B10.148**

(1) A person commits an offence if, with the intention of—
- (a) committing acts of terrorism, or
- (b) assisting another to commit such acts,

he engages in any conduct in preparation for giving effect to his intention.

Procedure The offence is indictable only (TA 2006, s. 5(1)) and is a class 3 offence. The consent of the DPP is necessary for the institution of proceedings (s. 19(1)) unless the offence is committed wholly or partly in connection with the affairs of a country outside the UK, in which case the consent of the A-G is required (s. 19(2)). **B10.149**

The Terrorism Protocol (see **B10.60**) applies to this offence.
The provisions of s. 17 apply to this offence (see **B10.137**)

For the liability of company directors, see **B10.139**.

Sentence The maximum penalty is life imprisonment (TA 2006, s. 5(3)). **B10.150**

Elements By virtue of the TA 2006, s. 5(2), it is irrelevant whether the intention and preparation referred to in s. 5(1) relate to one or more particular acts of terrorism, acts of terrorism of a particular description, or acts of terrorism generally. **B10.151**

Training for Terrorism

B10.152 **Terrorism Act 2006, s. 6**

(1) A person commits an offence if—
(a) he provides instruction or training in any of the skills mentioned in subsection (3); and
(b) at the time he provides the instruction or training, he knows that a person receiving it intends to use the skills on which he is being instructed or trained—
(i) for or in connection with the commission or preparation of acts of terrorism or Convention offences; or
(ii) for assisting the commission or preparation by others of such acts or offences.

(2) A person commits an offence if—
(a) he receives instruction or training in any of the skills mentioned in subsection (3); and
(b) at the time of the instruction or training, he intends to use the skills which he is being instructed or trained—
(i) for or in connection with the commission or preparation of acts of terrorism or Convention offences; or
(ii) for assisting the commission or preparation by others of such acts or offences.

(3) The skills are—
(a) the making, handling or use of a noxious substance, or of substances of a description of such substances;
(b) the use of any method or technique for doing anything else that is capable of being done for the purposes of terrorism, in connection with the commission or preparation of an act of terrorism or Convention offence or in connection with assisting the commission or preparation by another of such an act or offence; and
(c) the design or adaptation for the purposes of terrorism, or in connection with the commission or preparation of acts of terrorism or Convention offences, of any method or technique for doing anything.

B10.153 **Procedure** An allegation of an offence contrary to s. 6 of the TA 2006 is triable either way (s. 6(5)); when tried on indictment it is a class 3 offence. The consent of the DPP is necessary for the institution of proceedings (s. 19(1)) unless the offence is committed wholly or partly in connection with the affairs of a country outside the UK, in which case the consent of the A-G is required (s. 19(2)).

The provisions of s. 17 apply to this offence (see **B10.137**). For the liability of company directors, see **B10.139**.

B10.154 **Sentence** The maximum penalty is, on conviction on indictment, imprisonment for a term not exceeding ten years or a fine, or both, and, on summary conviction, imprisonment for a term not exceeding six months or a fine not exceeding the statutory maximum, or both (TA 2006, s. 6(5) and (6)).

On conviction, the court may order the forfeiture of anything the court considers to have been in the person's possession for purposes connected with the offence (s. 7(1)).

B10.155 **Elements** It is irrelevant (a) whether any instruction or training that is provided is provided to one or more particular persons or generally; (b) whether the acts or offences in relation to which a person intends to use such skills consist of one or more particular acts of terrorism or Convention offences, acts of terrorism or Convention offences of a particular description, or acts of terrorism or Convention offences generally; and (c) whether assistance that a person intends to provide to others is intended to be provided to one or more particular persons or to one or more persons whose identities are not yet known (TA 2006, s. 6(4)).

'Noxious substance' means (a) a dangerous substance within the meaning of the A-tCSA 2001, part 7, or (b) any other substance which is hazardous or noxious or which may be or become hazardous or noxious only in certain circumstances. 'Substance' includes any natural or artificial substance (whatever its origin or method of production and whether in solid or liquid form or in the form of a gas or vapour) and any mixture of substances (s. 6(7)).

Attendance at a Place for Terrorist Training

Terrorism Act 2006, s. 8 **B10.156**

(1) A person commits an offence if—
(a) he attends at any place, whether in the United Kingdom or elsewhere;
(b) while he is at that place, instruction or training of the type mentioned in section 6(1) of this Act or section 54(1) of the Terrorism Act 2000 is provided there;
(c) that instruction or training is provided there wholly or partly for purposes connected with the commission or preparation of acts of terrorism or Convention offences; and
(d) the requirements of subsection (2) are satisfied in relation to that person.

(2) The requirements of this subsection are satisfied in relation to a person if—
(a) he knows or believes that instruction or training is being provided there wholly or partly for purposes connected with the commission or preparation of acts of terrorism or Convention offences; or
(b) a person attending at that place throughout the period of that person's attendance could not reasonably have failed to understand that instruction or training was being provided there wholly or partly for such purposes.

Procedure An allegation of an offence contrary to s. 8 of the TA 2006 is triable either way (s. 8(4)); when tried on indictment it is a class 3 offence. The consent of the DPP is necessary for the institution of proceedings (s. 19(1)) unless the offence is committed wholly or partly in connection with the affairs of a country outside the UK, in which case the consent of the A-G is required (s. 19(2)). **B10.157**

The provisions of s. 17 apply to this offence (see **B10.137**). For the liability of company directors, see **B10.139**.

Sentence The maximum penalty is, on conviction on indictment, imprisonment for a term not exceeding ten years or a fine, or both, and, on summary conviction, imprisonment for a term not exceeding six months or a fine not exceeding the statutory maximum, or both (TA 2006, s. 8(4) and (5)). **B10.158**

Elements It is immaterial (a) whether the person concerned receives the instruction or training himself; and (b) whether the instruction or training is provided for purposes connected with one or more particular acts of terrorism or Convention offences, acts of terrorism or Convention offences of a particular description, or acts of terrorism or Convention offences generally (TA 2006, s. 8(3)). **B10.159**

Making and Possession of Radioactive Devices or Materials

Terrorism Act 2006, s. 9 **B10.160**

(1) A person commits an offence if—
(a) he makes or has in his possession a radioactive device, or
(b) he has in his possession radioactive material,

with the intention of using the device or material in the course of or in connection with the commission or preparation of an act of terrorism or for the purposes of terrorism, or of making it available to be so used.

Procedure An allegation of an offence contrary to s. 9 of the TA 2006 is triable on indictment only (s. 9(3)) and is a class 3 offence. The consent of the DPP is necessary for the institution of proceedings (s. 19(1)) unless the offence is committed wholly or partly in connection with the affairs of a country outside the UK, in which case the consent of the A-G is required (s. 19(2)). **B10.161**

The Terrorism Protocol (see **B10.60**) will of necessity apply to this offence even though it is not explicitly identified in the protocol.

The provisions of s. 17 apply to this offence (see **B10.137**). For the liability of company directors, see **B10.139**.

B10.162 **Sentence** The maximum penalty is imprisonment for life (TA 2006, s. 9(3)).

B10.163 **Elements** 'Radioactive device' means (a) a nuclear weapon or other nuclear explosive device; (b) a radioactive material dispersal device; (c) a radiation-emitting device (TA 2006, s. 9(4)). 'Device' includes any of the following, whether or not fixed to land, namely, machinery, equipment, appliances, tanks, containers, pipes and conduits (s. 9(5)). 'Nuclear material' has the same meaning as in the Nuclear Material (Offences) Act 1983, s. 6. 'Radioactive material' is defined in s. 9(4).

Misuse of Radioactive Devices or Material and Misuse and Damage of Nuclear Facilities

B10.164 **Terrorism Act 2006, s. 10**

(1) A person commits an offence if he uses—
- (a) a radioactive device, or
- (b) radioactive material,

in the course of or in connection with the commission of an act of terrorism or for the purposes of terrorism.

(2) A person commits an offence if, in the course of or in connection with the commission of an act of terrorism or for the purposes of terrorism, he uses or damages a nuclear facility in a manner which—
- (a) causes a release of radioactive material; or
- (b) creates or increases a risk that such material will be released.

B10.165 **Procedure** An allegation of an offence contrary to s. 10 of the TA 2006 is triable on indictment only (s. 10(3)) and is a class 3 offence. The consent of the DPP is necessary for the institution of proceedings (s. 19(1)) unless the offence is committed wholly or partly in connection with the affairs of a country outside the UK, in which case the consent of the A-G is required (s. 19(2)).

The Terrorism Protocol (see **B10.60**) will of necessity apply to this offence even though it is not explicitly identified in the protocol.

The provisions of s. 17 apply to this offence (see **B10.137**). For the liability of company directors, see **B10.139**.

B10.166 **Sentence** On conviction on indictment, the maximum penalty is life imprisonment (TA 2006, s. 10(3)).

B10.167 **Elements** 'Nuclear facility' means (a) a nuclear reactor, including a reactor installed in or on any transportation device for use as an energy source in order to propel it or for any other purposes; or (b) a plant or conveyance being used for the production, storage, processing or transport of radioactive material (TA 2006, s. 10(4)). 'Nuclear reactor' has the same meaning as in the Nuclear Installations Act 1965, s. 26 (TA 2006, s. 10(5)). 'Transportation device' means any vehicle or any space object (within the meaning of the Outer Space Act 1986) (TA 2006, s. 10(5)). 'Radioactive device' and 'radioactive material' have the same meaning as in s. 9.

Terrorist Threats Relating to Radioactive Devices and Material and Nuclear Facilities

B10.168 **Terrorism Act 2006, s. 11**

(1) A person commits an offence if, in the course of or in connection with the commission of an act of terrorism or for the purposes of terrorism—
- (a) he makes a demand—
  - (i) for the supply to himself or to another of a radioactive device or of radioactive material;
  - (ii) for a nuclear facility to be made available to himself or to another; or
  - (iii) for access to such a facility to be given to himself or to another;
- (b) he supports the demand with a threat that he or another will take action if the demand is not met; and
- (c) the circumstances and manner of the threat are such that it is reasonable for the person

to whom it is made to assume that there is real risk that the threat will be carried out if the demand is not met.

(2) A person also commits an offence if—

(a) he makes a threat falling within subsection (3) in the course of or in connection with the commission of an act of terrorism or for the purposes of terrorism; and

(b) the circumstances and manner of the threats are such that it is reasonable for the person to whom it is made to assume that there is real risk that the threat will be carried out, or would be carried out if demands made in association with the threat are not met.

(3) A threat falls within this subsection if it is—

(a) a threat to use radioactive material;

(b) a threat to use a radioactive device; or

(c) a threat to use or damage a nuclear facility in a manner that releases radioactive material or creates or increases a risk that such material will be released.

Procedure An allegation of an offence contrary to s. 11 of the TA 2006 is triable on indictment only (s. 11(4)) and is a class 3 offence. The consent of the DPP is necessary for the institution of proceedings (s. 19(1)) unless the offence is committed wholly or partly in connection with the affairs of a country outside the UK, in which case the consent of the A-G is required (s. 19(2)). **B10.169**

The Terrorism Protocol (see **B10.60**) will of necessity apply to this offence even though it is not explicitly specified in the protocol.

The provisions of s. 17 apply to this offence (see **B10.137**). For the liability of company directors, see **B10.139**.

Sentence On conviction on indictment, the maximum penalty is life imprisonment (TA 2006, s. 11(4)). **B10.170**

Elements For 'nuclear facility', see **B10.167**. For 'radioactive device' and 'radioactive material', see **B10.163**. **B10.171**

MISCELLANEOUS OFFENCES RELATING TO CHEMICAL AND NUCLEAR WEAPONS

In addition to those offences provided for under the TA 2000, the A-tCSA 2001 and the TA 2006, there are a number of miscellaneous operative legislative provisions relating to chemical, biological and nuclear weapons deriving from the Biological Weapons Act 1974, the Chemical Weapons Act 1996 and the Nuclear Material (Offences) Act 1983. **B10.172**

Developing, Producing etc. Biological Agents, Toxins and Weapons

Biological Weapons Act 1974, s. 1 **B10.173**

(1) No person shall develop, produce, stockpile, acquire or retain—

(a) any biological agent or toxin of a type and in quantity that has no justification for prophylactic, protective or other peaceful purposes; or

(b) any weapon, equipment or means of delivery designed to use biological agents or toxins for hostile purposes or in armed conflict.

(1A) A person shall not—

(a) transfer any biological agent or toxin to another person or enter into an agreement to do so, or

(b) make arrangements under which another person transfers any biological agent or toxin or enters into an agreement with a third party to do so,

if the biological agent is likely to be kept or used (whether by the transferee or any other person) otherwise than for prophylactic, protective or other peaceful purposes and he knows or has reason to believe that that is the case.

Procedure An allegation of an offence contrary to the Biological Weapons Act 1974, s. 1, is **B10.174**

triable on indictment only (s. 1(3)) and is a class 3 offence. The Terrorism Protocol (see **B10.60**) applies to proceedings taken under this section.

The acts founding culpability can be committed outside the UK but only by a 'United Kingdom person' (s. 1A(1)); proceedings may be instituted, and for incidental purposes taken as having been committed, anywhere in the UK (s. 1A(2)). A 'United Kingdom person' is defined by s. 1A(4) in terms identical to those used by the A-tCSA 2001, s. 56 (see **B10.110**).

If the requirements of s. 1B are met, then proceedings for the offence may be instituted by the Director of Revenue and Customs Prosecutions or by order of the Commissioners of Revenue and Customs.

B10.175 **Sentence** The maximum penalty is imprisonment for life (Biological Weapons Act 1974, s. 1(3)).

B10.176 **Elements** Under the Biological Weapons Act 1974, s. 1(2), 'biological agent' means any microbial or other biological agent and 'toxin' means any toxin, whatever its origin or method of production.

Use etc. of Chemical Weapons

B10.177 **Chemical Weapons Act 1996, s. 2**

(1) No person shall—
- (a) use a chemical weapon;
- (b) develop or produce a chemical weapon;
- (c) have a chemical weapon in his possession;
- (d) participate in the transfer of a chemical weapon;
- (e) engage in military preparations, or in preparations of a military nature, intending to use a chemical weapon.

. . .

(8) A person contravening this section is guilty of an offence. . . .

B10.178 **Procedure** An allegation of an offence contrary to the Chemical Weapons Act 1996, s. 2, is triable on indictment only (s. 2(8)) and is a class 3 offence. The Terrorism Protocol (see **B10.60**) applies to this offence. The consent of the A-G is required for the institution of proceedings under this section (s. 31(1)).

The acts founding culpability can be committed outside the UK but only by a 'United Kingdom person' (s. 3(1)) and proceedings may be instituted, and for incidental purposes taken as having been committed, anywhere in the UK (s. 3(5)). A 'United Kingdom person' is defined by s. 3(2) in terms identical to those used by the A-tCSA 2001, s. 56 (see **B10.110**).

B10.179 **Sentence** The maximum penalty is imprisonment for life (Chemical Weapons Act 1996, s. 2(8)). As to the power of forfeiture, see s. 30.

Elements

B10.180 **Chemical Weapons Act 1996, ss. 1 and 10**

1.—(1) Chemical weapons are—
- (a) toxic chemicals and their precursors;
- (b) munitions and other devices designed to cause death or harm through the toxic properties of toxic chemicals released by them;
- (c) equipment designed for use in connection with munitions and devices falling with in paragraph (b).

(2) Subsection (1) is subject to sections 2(2) and (3), 10(1) and 11(2) (by virtue of which an object is not a chemical weapon if the use or intended use is only for permitted purposes).

(3) Permitted purposes are—
- (a) peaceful purposes;
- (b) purposes related to protection against toxic chemicals;
- (c) legitimate military purposes;
- (d) purposes of enforcing the law.

(4) Legitimate military purposes are all military purposes except those which depend on the use of the toxic properties of chemicals as a method of warfare in circumstances where the main object is to cause death, permanent harm or temporary incapacity to humans or animals.
(5) A toxic chemical is a chemical which through its chemical action on life processes can cause death, permanent harm or temporary incapacity to humans or animals; and the origin, method of production and place of production are immaterial.
(6) A precursor is a chemical reactant which takes part at any stage in the production (by whatever method) of a toxic chemical.
(7) References to an object include references to a substance.
10.—(1) If an object is in the possession of a person who intends that it will be used only for permitted purposes, it is not a chemical weapon for the purposes of sections 4(1) and (3) and 5(1) and (2); and in deciding whether permitted purposes are intended the types and quantities of objects shall be taken into account.

It should be noted that 's. 11(2)', referred to in s. 1(2), above does not apply to this offence.

The specific provisions are as follows:

Chemical Weapons Act 1996, s. 2

(2) For the purposes of subsection (1)(a) an object is not a chemical weapon if the person uses the object only for permitted purposes; and in deciding whether permitted purposes are intended the types and quantities of objects shall be taken into account.
(3) For the purposes of subsection (1)(b), (c), (d) or (e) an object is not a chemical weapon if the person does the act there mentioned with the intention that the object will be used only for permitted purposes; and in deciding whether permitted purposes are intended the types and quantities of objects shall be taken into account.

Specific Defence Under the Chemical Weapons Act 1996, s. 2(6), it is a defence for the accused to prove (a) that he neither knew nor suspected nor had reason to suspect that the object was a chemical weapon, or (b) that he knew or suspected it to be a chemical weapon and as soon as reasonably practicable after he first so knew or suspected he took all reasonable steps to inform the Secretary of State or a constable of his knowledge or suspicion. By virtue of s. 2(7), the s. 2(6) defence does not prejudice any other defence which it is open to a person charged with this offence to raise. **B10.181**

Restrictive and Enforcement Powers under the Chemical Weapons Act 1996

Issuing of Notices in Relation to Suspicious Objects By virtue of s. 4 of the Chemical Weapons Act 1996, if the Secretary of State has grounds to suspect that an object is a chemical weapon and someone appears to be in possession of it or has a sufficient interest in it, a notice may be issued to that person which will state, *inter alia*, that destruction of the object is being considered and that the object must not be relinquished before a specified date. **B10.182**

Powers of Entry, Search and Seizure Section 5 of the Chemical Weapons Act 1996 gives powers of entry, search and seizure in relation to suspected involvement with chemical weapons. If the Secretary of State has reasonable cause to believe that, on premises to which the public has access or where the occupier consents to access, an object is on such premises and it is a chemical weapon, he may authorise entry and search of the premises (s. 5(1)). A magistrate may issue a warrant to enter premises of whatever nature if there is reasonable cause to believe that an object, which is a chemical weapon, is on the premises (s. 5(2)). The person issued with the warrant may take such people and equipment with him as are necessary, and objects found on the relevant premises may be seized and removed or immobilised and made safe (s. 5(3) to (7)). **B10.183**

Power to destroy removed objects Section 6 of the Chemical Weapons Act 1996 provides for the destruction of objects removed under the power provided by virtue of s. 5. **B10.184**

Chemical Weapons Premises

B10.185 Chemical Weapons Act 1996, s. 11

(1) No person shall—
  (a) construct premises he intends to be used to produce chemical weapons;
  (b) alter premises in circumstances where he intends that they will be used to produce chemical weapons;
  (c) instal or construct equipment he intends to be used to produce chemical weapons;
  (d) alter equipment in circumstances where he intends that it will be used to produce chemical weapons;
  (e) permit the construction on land he occupies of premises he intends to be used to produce chemical weapons;
  (f) permit premises on land he occupies to be altered in circumstances where he intends that they will be used to produce chemical weapons;
  (g) permit the installation or construction on land he occupies of equipment he intends to be used to produce chemical weapons;
  (h) permit equipment on land he occupies to be altered in circumstances where he intends that it will be used to produce chemical weapons.

(2) For the purposes of subsection (1) an object is not a chemical weapon if the person intends that the object will be used only for permitted purposes; and in deciding whether permitted purposes are intended the types and quantities of objects shall be taken into account.

(3) A person contravening this section is guilty of an offence and liable on conviction on indictment to imprisonment for life.

B10.186 **Procedure** An allegation of an offence contrary to the Chemical Weapons Act 1996, s. 11, is triable on indictment only (s. 11(3)).

B10.187 **Sentence** The maximum sentence is one of imprisonment for life.

Chemicals Used for Permitted Purposes

B10.188 Chemical Weapons Act 1996, s. 19

(1) Subject to section 20 (which relates to licences) no person shall—
  (a) use a schedule 1 toxic chemical or precursor for a permitted purpose, or
  (b) produce or have in his possession a Schedule 1 toxic chemical or precursor with the intention that it will be used for a permitted purpose.

(2) A schedule 1 toxic chemical or precursor is a toxic chemical or precursor listed in schedule 1 to the annex on chemicals to the Convention; and for ease of reference that schedule is set out in the schedule to this Act.

(3) A person contravening this section is guilty of an offence . . ..

B10.189 **Procedure** An allegation of an offence contrary to the Chemical Weapons Act 1996, s. 19, is triable either way (s. 19(3)); when tried on indictment it is a class 3 offence.

The consent of the Secretary of State is necessary for the institution of proceedings under the section (s. 31(2)).

B10.190 **Sentence** The maximum penalty, whether on summary conviction or indictment, is a fine (Chemical Weapons Act 1996, s. 19(3)).

Holding or Dealing with Nuclear Material

B10.191 Nuclear Material (Offences) Act 1983, s. 2

(1) If a person, whatever his nationality, in the United Kingdom or elsewhere contravenes subsections (2), (3) or (4) below he shall be guilty of an offence.

(2) A person contravenes this subsection if he receives, holds or deals with nuclear material—
  (a) intending, or for the purpose of enabling another, to do by means of that material an act which is an offence mentioned in [s. 1(1)(a) or (b), i.e. murder, manslaughter, or an offence contrary to the OAPA 1861, ss. 18 or 20]; or
  (b) being reckless as to whether another would do such an act.

(3) A person contravenes this subsection if he—

(a) makes to another person a threat that he or any other person will do by means of nuclear material such an acts as is mentioned in [s. 2(2)(a)] above; and
(b) intends that the person to whom the threat is made shall fear that it will be carried out.
(4) A person contravenes this subsection if, in order to compel a State, international governmental organisation or person to do, or abstain from doing, any act he threatens that he or any other person will obtain nuclear material by an act which is an offence mentioned in [s. 1(1)(c), i.e. theft, robbery, assault with intent to rob, burglary or aggravated burglary].

Procedure An allegation of an offence contrary to the Nuclear Material (Offences) Act 1983, s. 2, is triable on indictment only (s. 2(5)). Proceedings for an offence which (disregarding the Internationally Protected Persons Act 1978, the Suppression of Terrorism Act 1978, the United Nations Personnel Act 1997 and the TA 2000) would not be an offence but for the Nuclear Materials (Offences) Act 1983, must have the consent of the A-G if they are to be instituted. **B10.192**

The provisions of the Terrorism Protocol (see **B10.60**) will apply if the offence is committed for terrorist purposes as defined under the TA 2000 (see **B10.3**).

Sentence The maximum penalty is imprisonment for a term not exceeding 14 years and also not exceeding the term to which a person would be liable for the offence constituted by doing the contemplated act at the place where the conviction occurs and at the time of the offence to which the conviction relates (Nuclear Materials (Offences) Act 1983, s. 2(5)). **B10.193**

Elements By virtue of the Nuclear Material (Offences) Act 1983, s. 6(1) and (5), references to 'nuclear material' relate to 'nuclear material used for peaceful purposes' within the meaning of the Convention on the Physical Protection of Nuclear Material 1980. Under s. 6(2), any statement by the Secretary of State to the effect that the nuclear material either was or was not for peaceful purposes will be conclusive as to the issue. For the implications of such a provision reversing the burden of proof in the light of the ECHR, Article 6, see **F3.13** ***et seq.*** **B10.194**

PIRACY

Merchant Shipping and Maritime Security Act 1997, sch. 5 **B10.195**

Article 101 Piracy consists of any of the following acts:
(a) any illegal acts of violence or detention, or any act of depredation, committed for private ends by the crew or the passengers of a private ship or a private aircraft, and directed—
(i) on the high seas, against another ship or aircraft, or against persons or property on board such ship or aircraft;
(ii) against a ship, aircraft, persons or property in a place outside the jurisdiction of any State;
(b) any act of voluntary participation in the operation of a ship or of an aircraft with knowledge of facts making it a pirate ship or aircraft;
(c) any act of inciting or of intentionally facilitating an act described in subparagraph (a) or (b).

Article 102 The acts of piracy, as defined in article 101, committed by a warship, government ship or government aircraft whose crew has mutinied and taken control of the ship or aircraft are assimilated to acts committed by a private ship or aircraft.

Article 103 A ship or aircraft is considered a pirate ship or aircraft if it is intended by the persons in dominant control to be used for the purpose of committing one of the acts referred to in article 101. The same applies if the ship or aircraft has been used to commit any such act, so long as it remains under the control of the persons guilty of that act.

Procedure

Aviation Security Act 1982, s. 5 **B10.196**

(1) Any court in the United Kingdom having jurisdiction in respect of piracy committed on the high seas shall have jurisdiction in respect of piracy committed by or against an aircraft, wherever that piracy is committed.

Piracy *iure gentium* is a class 1 offence and triable only on indictment.

The Aviation Security Act 1982, s. 5, gives any court in the UK with jurisdiction to try an offence of piracy jurisdiction over such an offence in respect of an aircraft wherever it is committed. The fact that the accused is a foreign national does not affect the jurisdiction of a court. However, the English courts will be slow to assume jurisdiction when the offence of piracy alleged has no real connection with England and Wales (*Republic of Bolivia v Indemnity Mutual Marine Assurance Co. Ltd.* [1909] 1 KB 785).

Sentence

B10.197 **Piracy Act 1837, s. 2**

> Whosoever, with intent to commit or at the time of or immediately before or immediately after committing the crime of piracy in respect of any ship or vessel, shall assault, with intent to murder, any person being on board of or belonging to such ship or vessel, or shall stab, cut or wound any such person, or unlawfully do any act, by which the life of such person may be endangered, shall be guilty of [an offence], and being convicted thereof shall be liable to imprisonment for life.

An act of piracy *iure gentium* committed without the aggravating acts described within s. 2 is punishable by imprisonment and a fine at large at common law. Any specific offences committed during the piracy are punishable as if committed on land (Offences at Sea Act 1799).

HIJACKING OF AIRCRAFT AND SHIPS AND RELATED OFFENCES

B10.198 A number of offences relating to the safety of aircraft are provided for by the Aviation Security Act 1982. In addition, in giving effect to the Rome Convention 1988 and the Fixed Platforms Protocol 1988, the Aviation and Maritime Security Act 1990 creates a number of offences concerned with the safety of ships and fixed platforms. The Acts also provide for the safety of aircraft, aerodromes and air navigation installations against acts of violence (Aviation Security Act 1982, part II); with regard to the policing of airports (Aviation Security Act 1982, part III); and in relation to the protection of ships and harbour areas against acts of violence (Aviation and Maritime Security Act 1990, part II).

Hijacking of Aircraft

B10.199 **Aviation Security Act 1982, s. 1**

> (1) A person on board an aircraft in flight who unlawfully, by the use of force or by threats of any kind, seizes the aircraft or exercises control of it commits the offence of hijacking, whatever his nationality, whatever the State in which the aircraft is registered and whether the aircraft is in the United Kingdom or elsewhere but subject to subsection (2) below.

B10.200 **Procedure** Under s. 1(1) of the Aviation Security Act 1982, the general rule is that a person can be found guilty of an offence contrary to s. 1 whatever his nationality, wherever the aircraft is registered and wherever the aircraft is at the time of the offence. But, under s. 1(2), if the aircraft is used in military, police or customs service or both the place of take-off and landing are in the territory of the state where the plane is registered, s. 1(1) will not apply unless the alleged hijacker is a UK national or his act is committed in the UK or the aircraft is registered in the UK or is used in the military or customs service of the UK or the service of any police force in the UK.

An allegation of an offence contrary to s. 1 is triable on indictment only and is a class 3 offence.

Proceedings for an offence under s. 1 can be instituted only with the consent of the A-G (s. 8(1)).

Section 37 of the Act makes similar provision for the liability of bodies corporate to that contained in s. 18 of the TA 2006 (see **B10.139**).

Aviation Security Act 1982, s. 37

(1) Where an offence under this Act . . . has been committed by a body corporate and is proved to have been committed with the consent or connivance of, or to be attributable to any neglect on the part of, any director, manager, secretary or other similar officer of the body corporate, or any person who was purporting to act in any such capacity, he as well as the body corporate shall be guilty of that offence and shall be liable to be proceeded against and punished accordingly.

(2) Where the affairs of a body corporate are managed by its members, subsection (1) above shall apply in relation to the acts and defaults of a member in connection with his functions of management as if he were a director of the body corporate.

Sentence The maximum penalty is life imprisonment (Aviation Security Act 1982, s. 1(3)). **B10.201**

Elements 'In flight' is defined in s. 38(3)(a) of the Aviation Security Act 1982 as being from the point when all an aircraft's external doors are closed following embarkation until the point when one of those doors is opened for disembarkation. When a plane is forced to land, it is 'in flight' until the competent authorities take responsibility for the plane and its occupants and any property on board. **B10.202**

'Military service' is defined so as to include naval and air force service (s. 38).

'United Kingdom national' is a person who is (a) a British citizen, a British Dependent Territories citizen or a British overseas citizen, (b) a British subject under the British Nationality Act 1981, or (c) a British protected person (s. 38).

Destroying, Damaging or Endangering the Safety of an Aircraft

Aviation Security Act 1982, s. 2 **B10.203**

(1) It shall, subject to subsection (4) below, be an offence for any person unlawfully and intentionally—
   (a) to destroy an aircraft in service or so to damage such an aircraft as to render it incapable of flight or as to be likely to endanger its safety in flight; or
   (b) to commit on board an aircraft in flight any act of violence which is likely to endanger the safety of the aircraft.

(2) It shall also, subject to subsection (4) below, be an offence for any person unlawfully and intentionally to place, or cause to be placed, on an aircraft in service any device or substance which is likely to destroy the aircraft, or is likely so to damage it, as to render it incapable of flight or as to be likely to endanger its safety in flight; but nothing in this subsection shall be construed as limiting the circumstances in which the commission of any act—
   (a) may constitute an offence under subsection (1) above, or
   (b) may constitute attempting or conspiring to commit, or aiding, abetting, counselling or procuring, or being art and part in, the commission of such an offence.

Procedure Under the Aviation Security Act 1982, s. 2(3), the general rule is that a person can be found guilty of an offence contrary to s. 2 whatever his nationality, wherever the aircraft is registered and wherever the aircraft is at the time of the offence. But under s. 2(4), if the aircraft is used in military, police or customs service, s. 2(1) and (2) will not apply unless the alleged act is committed in the UK or, if the act is committed outside the UK, it is committed by a UK national. **B10.204**

An allegation of an offence contrary to s. 2 is triable on indictment only and is a class 3 offence.

Proceedings for an offence under s. 2 can be instituted only with the consent of the A-G (s. 8(1)).

Sentence The maximum penalty is life imprisonment (Aviation Security Act 1982, s. 2(5)). **B10.205**

Elements 'Unlawful' in relation to an act in the UK means that it constitutes an offence under the law of the part of the UK in which it is committed. In relation to an act outside the **B10.206**

UK, 'unlawful' means that it would constitute an offence if committed in England, Scotland or Wales if it had been committed there (Aviation Security Act 1982, s. 2(6)).

'Act of violence' is any act in the UK which constitutes the offence of murder, manslaughter, culpable homicide or assault, an offence under any of ss. 18, 20, 21, 22, 23, 24, 28 or 29 of the OAPA 1861, or an offence under s. 2 of the Explosive Substances Act 1883. Outside the UK, it is any act which would constitute any of the offences mentioned above if it occurred in the UK (s. 2(7)).

'In service' is defined as the period from pre-flight preparation of the aircraft to a time 24 hours after it has landed following completion of the flight (s. 38(3)(b)). For 'in flight', see **B10.202**. For 'United Kingdom national', see **B10.202**.

Other Acts Endangering or Likely to Endanger the Safety of an Aircraft

B10.207 **Aviation Security Act 1982, s. 3**

(1) It shall, subject to subsections (5) and (6) below, be an offence for any person unlawfully and intentionally to destroy or damage any property to which this subsection applies, or to interfere with the operation of any such property, where the destruction, damage or interference is likely to endanger the safety of the aircraft in flight.

(2) Subsection (1) above applies to any property used for the provision of air navigation facilities, including any land, building or ship so used, and including any apparatus or equipment so used, whether it is on board an aircraft or elsewhere.

(3) It shall also, subject to subsections (4) and (5) below, be an offence for any person intentionally to communicate any information which is false, misleading or deceptive in a material particular, where the communication of the information endangers the safety of an aircraft in flight or is likely to endanger the safety of aircraft in flight.

B10.208 **Procedure** Provisions concerning jurisdiction are contained within s. 3(5) and (6).

Aviation Security Act 1982, s. 3

(5) Subsections (1) and (3) above shall not apply to the commission of any act unless either the act is committed in the United Kingdom or, where it is committed outside the United Kingdom—
(a) the person committing it is a United Kingdom national; or
(b) the commission of the act endangers or is likely to endanger the safety in flight of civil aircraft registered in the United Kingdom or chartered by demise to a lessee whose principal place of business, or (if he has no place of business) whose permanent residence, is in the United Kingdom; or
(c) the act is committed on board a civil aircraft which is so registered or so chartered; or
(d) the act is committed on board a civil aircraft which lands in the United Kingdom with the person who committed the act still on board.

(6) Subsection (1) above shall also not apply to any act committed outside the United Kingdom and so committed in relation to property which is situated outside the United Kingdom and is not used for the provision of air navigation facilities in connection with international air navigation, unless the person committing the act is a United Kingdom national.

An allegation of an offence contrary to s. 3 is triable on indictment only (s. 3(5)) and is a class 3 offence.

Proceedings for an offence under s. 3 can be instituted only with the consent of the A-G (s. 8(1)).

B10.209 **Sentence** The maximum penalty is life imprisonment (Aviation Security Act 1982, s. 3(7)).

B10.210 **Elements** 'Property' includes any land, buildings or work, any aircraft or vehicle and any baggage, cargo or any other article of any description (s. 38(1)).

'Civil aircraft' constitutes any aircraft other than an aircraft used in military, customs or police service (s. 3(8)).

For 'unlawful', see **B10.206**. For 'United Kingdom national', see **B10.202**. For 'in flight', see **B10.202**.

Specific Defence

Aviation Security Act 1982, s. 3 **B10.211**

(4) It shall be a defence for a person charged with an offence under subsection (3) above to prove—

(a) that he believed, and had reasonable grounds for believing, that the information was true; or

(b) that, when he communicated the information, he was lawfully employed to perform duties which consisted of or included the communication of information and that he communicated the information in good faith in the performance of those duties.

See **F3.13** ***et seq.*** for the significance of the reverse burden within this defence.

Dangerous Articles

Aviation Security Act 1982, s. 4 **B10.212**

(1) It shall be an offence for any person without lawful authority or reasonable excuse (the proof of which shall lie on him) to have with him—

(a) in any aircraft registered in the United Kingdom, whether at a time when the aircraft is in the United Kingdom or not, or

(b) in any other aircraft at a time when it is in, or in flight over, the United Kingdom or

(c) in any part of an aerodrome in the United Kingdom, or

(d) in any air navigation installation in the United Kingdom which does not form part of an aerodrome,

any article to which this section applies.

Procedure An allegation of an offence contrary to the Aviation and Maritime Security Act 1990, s. 4, is triable either way (s. 4(4)); when tried on indictment it is a class 3 offence. **B10.213**

Sentence The maximum penalty on conviction on indictment is imprisonment for a term not exceeding five years or a fine or both; on summary conviction, it is imprisonment for a term not exceeding three months, a fine not exceeding the statutory maximum or both (Aviation Security Act 1982, s. 4(4)). **B10.214**

Elements

Aviation Security Act 1982, s. 4 **B10.215**

(3) For the purposes of this section a person who is for the time being in an aircraft, or in part of an aerodrome, shall be treated as having with him in an aircraft, or in that part of the aerodrome, as the case may be, an article to which this section applies if—

(a) where he is in an aircraft, the article, or an article in which it is contained, is in the aircraft and has been caused (whether by him or by any other person) to be brought there as being, or as forming part of, his baggage on a flight in the aircraft, or has been caused by him to be brought there as being, or as forming part of, any other property to be carried on such a flight, or

(b) where he is in part of an aerodrome (otherwise than in an aircraft), the article, or an article in which it is contained, is in that or any other part of the aerodrome and has been caused (whether by him or by any other person) to be brought into the aerodrome as being, or as forming part of, his baggage on a flight from that aerodrome or has been caused by him to be brought there as being, or as forming part of, any other property to be carried on such a flight on which he is also to be carried,

notwithstanding that the circumstance may be such that (apart from this subsection) he would not be regarded as having the article with him in the aircraft or in a part of the aerodrome, as the case may be.

Section 4(2) sets out the articles to which s. 4 is relevant:

(a) any firearm, or any article having the appearance of being a firearm, whether capable of being discharged or not;

(b) any explosive, any article manufactured or adapted (whether in the form of a bomb, grenade or otherwise) so as to have the appearance of being an explosive, whether it is capable of producing a practical effect by explosion or not, or any article marked or labelled so as to indicate that it is or contains an explosive; and

(c) any article (not falling within either of the preceding paragraphs) made or adapted for use for causing injury to or incapacitating a person or for destroying or damaging property, or intended by the person having it with him for such use, whether by him or by any other person.

'Explosive' means any article manufactured for the purpose of producing a practical effect by explosion, or intended for that purpose by a person having the article with him. Firearm includes an airgun or air pistol (s. 38(1)).

'Have with him' receives some explanation in s. 4(3) but s. 4(5) provides that nothing in s. 4(3) shall be taken to limit the circumstances in which a person could be regarded as having an article with him.

For 'in flight', see **B10.202**. For 'United Kingdom national', see **B10.202**. For 'unlawfully', see **B10.206**.

'Air navigation installation' means any building, works, apparatus or equipment used wholly or mainly for the purpose of assisting air traffic control or as an aid to air navigation, together with any land contiguous or adjacent to any such building, works, apparatus or equipment and used wholly or mainly for purposes connected therewith (s. 38(1)).

Endangering Safety at Aerodromes

B10.216 **Aviation and Maritime Security Act 1990, s. 1**

(1) It is an offence for any person by means of any device, substance or weapon intentionally to commit at an aerodrome serving international civil aviation any act of violence which—

(a) causes or is likely to cause death or serious personal injury, and

(b) endangers or is likely to endanger the safe operation of the aerodrome or the safety of persons at the aerodrome.

(2) It is also, subject to subsection (4) below, an offence for any person by means of any device, substance or weapon unlawfully and intentionally—

(a) to destroy or seriously to damage—

(i) property used for the provision of any facilities at an aerodrome serving international civil aviation (including any apparatus or equipment so used), or

(ii) any aircraft which is at such aerodrome but is not in service, or

(b) to disrupt the services of such an aerodrome,

in such a way as to endanger or be likely to endanger the safe operation of the aerodrome or the safety of persons at the aerodrome.

B10.217 **Procedure** Under s. 1(3) of the Aviation Security Act 1982, the general rule is that a person can be found guilty of an offence contrary to s. 2 whatever his nationality and wherever the aircraft is at the time of the offence. But, under s. 1(4), if the aircraft is used in military, police or customs service, s. 1(1) and (2) will not apply unless the alleged act is committed in the UK or, if the act is committed outside the UK, it is committed by a UK national.

An allegation of an offence contrary to s. 1 is triable on indictment only (s. 1(5)) and is a class 3 offence.

Proceedings for an offence under s. 1 can be instituted only with the consent of the A-G (s. 1(7)).

B10.218 **Sentence** The maximum penalty is life imprisonment (Aviation and Maritime Security Act 1990, s. 1(5)).

B10.219 **Elements** 'Act of violence' is defined by the Aviation and Maritime Security Act 1990,

s. 1(9), in terms identical to those used under the Aviation Security Act 1982, s. 2(7) (see B10.206).

'Aerodrome' means any area of land or water designed, equipped, set apart or commonly used for affording facilities for the landing and departure of aircraft. It includes any area or space, whether on the ground, on the roof of a building or elsewhere, which is designed, equipped or set apart for affording facilities for the landing and departure of aircraft capable of descending or climbing vertically (Civil Aviation Act 1982, s. 105(1)).

For 'United Kingdom national', see **B10.202**. For 'unlawfully', see **B10.206.** For 'in service', see **B10.206.**

Hijacking of Ships

Aviation and Maritime Security Act 1990, s. 9 **B10.220**

(1) A person who unlawfully, by the use of force or threats of any kind, seizes a ship or exercises control of it, commits the offence of hijacking a ship, whatever his nationality and whether the ship is in the United Kingdom or elsewhere, but subject to subsection (2) below.

Procedure Under the Aviation and Maritime Security Act 1990, s. 9(1), the general rule is that a person can be found guilty of an offence contrary to s. 9 whatever his nationality and wherever the ship is at the time of the offence. But under s. 9(2), if the ship is a warship or any other ship used as a naval auxiliary or in police or customs service, s. 9(1) will not apply unless the person seizing or exercising control of the ship is a UK national or his act is committed in the UK or, finally, the ship is used in the naval or customs service of the UK or the service of any police force in the UK. **B10.221**

An allegation of an offence contrary to s. 9 is triable on indictment only and is a class 3 offence.

Proceedings for an offence under s. 9 can be instituted only with the consent of the A-G (s. 16(1)).

Sentence The maximum penalty is life imprisonment (Aviation and Maritime Security Act 1990, s. 9(3)). **B10.222**

Elements For 'United Kingdom national', see **B10.202.** **B10.223**

In s. 17(1) of the Aviation and Maritime Security Act 1990, 'ship' is defined as meaning any vessel (including hovercraft, submersible craft and other floating craft) other than one which permanently rests on, or is permanently attached to, the seabed, or has been withdrawn from navigation or laid up.

'Naval service' includes military and air force service (s. 17(1)).

Other Aviation Security Offences

Further offences dealing with the safety of ships and fixed platforms are provided for under ss. 10 to 13 of the Aviation and Maritime Security Act 1990. **B10.224**

Aviation and Maritime Security Act 1990, ss. 10, 11, 12, and 13

10.—(1) A person who unlawfully, by the use of force or by threats of any kind, seizes a fixed platform or exercises control of it, commits an offence, whatever his nationality and whether the fixed platform is in the United Kingdom or elsewhere.

(2) A person guilty of an offence under this section is liable on conviction on indictment to imprisonment for life.

11.—(1) Subject to subsection (5) below, a person commits an offence if he unlawfully and intentionally—

(a) destroys a ship or a fixed platform,

(b) damages a ship, its cargo or a fixed platform so as to endanger, or to be likely to endanger, the safe navigation of the ship, or as the case may be, the safety of the platform, or

(c) commits on board a ship or on a fixed platform an act of violence which is likely to endanger the safe navigation of the ship, or as the case may be, the safety of the platform.

(2) Subject to subsection (5) below, a person commits an offence if he unlawfully and intentionally places, or causes to be placed, on a ship or fixed platform any device or substance which—

(a) in the case of a ship, is likely to destroy the ship or is likely so to damage it or its cargo as to endanger its safe navigation, or

(b) in the case of a fixed platform, is likely to destroy the fixed platform or so to damage it as to endanger its safety.

(3) Nothing in subsection (2) above is to be construed as limiting the circumstances in which the commission of any act—

(a) may constitute an offence under subsection (1) above, or

(b) may constitute attempting or conspiring to commit, or aiding, abetting, counselling, procuring or inciting, or being art and part in, the commission of such an offence.

(4) Except as provided by subsection (5) below, subsections (1) and (2) above apply whether any such act as is mentioned in those subsections is committed in the United Kingdom or elsewhere and whatever the nationality of the person committing the act.

(5) Subsections (1) and (2) above do not apply in relation to any act committed in relation to a warship or any other ship used as a naval auxiliary or in customs or police service unless—

(a) the person committing the act is a United Kingdom national, or

(b) his act is committed in the United Kingdom, or

(c) the ship is used in the naval or customs service of the United Kingdom or in the service of any police force in the United Kingdom.

(6) A person guilty of an offence under this section is liable on conviction on indictment to imprisonment for life.

12.—(1) Subject to subsection (6) below, it is an offence for any person unlawfully and intentionally—

(a) to destroy or damage any property to which this subsection applies, or

(b) seriously to interfere with the operation of any such property,

where the destruction, damage or interference is likely to endanger the safe navigation of any ship.

(2) Subsection (1) above applies to any property used for the provision of maritime navigation facilities, including any land, building or ship so used, and including any apparatus or equipment so used, whether it is on board a ship or elsewhere.

(3) Subject to subsection (6) below, it is also an offence for any person intentionally to communicate any information which he knows to be false in a material particular, where the communication of the information endangers the safe navigation of any ship.

(4) It is a defence for a person charged with an offence under subsection (3) above to prove that, when he communicated the information, he was lawfully employed to perform duties which consisted of or included the communication of information and that he communicated the information in good faith in performance of those duties.

(5) Except as provided by subsection (6) below, subsections (1) and (3) above apply whether any such act as is mentioned in those subsections is committed in the United Kingdom or elsewhere and whatever the nationality of the person committing the act.

(6) For the purposes of subsections (1) and (3) above any danger, or likelihood of danger, to the safe navigation of a warship or any other ship used as a naval auxiliary or in customs or police service is to be disregarded unless—

(a) the person committing the act is a United Kingdom national, or

(b) his act is committed in the United Kingdom, or

(c) the ship is used in the naval or customs service of the United Kingdom or in the service of any police force in the United Kingdom.

(7) A person guilty of an offence under this section is liable on conviction on indictment to imprisonment for life.

13.—(1) A person commits an offence if—

(a) in order to compel any other person to do or abstain from doing any act, he threatens that he or some other person will do in relation to any ship or fixed platform an act which is an offence by virtue of section 11(1) of this Act, and

(b) the making of that threat is likely to endanger the safe navigation of the ship or, as the case may be, the safety of the fixed platform.

(2) Subject to subsection (4) below, a person commits an offence if—

(a) in order to compel any other person to do or abstain from doing any act, he threatens that he or some other person will do an act which is an offence by virtue of section 12(1) of this Act, and

(b) the making of that threat is likely to endanger the safe navigation of any ship.

(3) Except as provided by subsection (4) below, subsections (1) and (2) above apply whether any such act as is mentioned in those subsections is committed in the United Kingdom or elsewhere and whatever the nationality of the person committing the act.

(4) Section 12(6) of this Act applies for the purposes of subsection (2)(b) above as it applies for the purposes of section 12(1) and (3) of this Act.

(5) A person guilty of an offence under this section is liable on conviction on indictment to imprisonment for life.

Procedure Each of the offences is triable only on indictment. Proceedings may be instituted only with the consent of the A-G. **B10.225**

Sentence The maximum sentence for each offence is one of life imprisonment. **B10.226**

Elements For 'act of violence', see **B10.206**. For 'unlawful', see **B10.206**. **B10.227**

Related Offences and Powers

There are two ancillary offences relevant to provisions within the Aviation and Maritime Security Act 1990 along with a power of delivery to a ship's master: **B10.228**

Ancillary Offences under s. 14(1): Sections 14(1) and 14(2) of the Act provide that, where a person (of whatever nationality) does any act outside the UK which, if done in the UK, would constitute an offence of murder, attempted murder, manslaughter, culpable homicide or assault, or an offence under the OAPA 1861, ss. 18, 20, 21, 22, 23, 28 and 29, or an offence contrary to s. 2 of the Explosive Substances Act 1883, his act constitutes that offence if it is done in connection with an offence under the Aviation and Maritime Security Act 1990, ss. 9, 10, 11, or 12 committed or attempted by him. These provisions are without prejudice to the jurisdiction clauses of the Merchant Shipping Act 1995, ss. 281 and 282 or the Petroleum Act 1998, s. 10 (Aviation and Maritime Security Act 1990, s. 14(3)).

Inducing or Assisting in Commission of Offences under s. 14(4): It is an offence for any person in the UK to induce or assist the commission outside the UK of any act which would, but for the Aviation and Maritime Security Act 1990, s. 9(2), be an offence under s. 9 (s. 14(4)(a)); but for s. 11(5) would be an offence under s. 11 (s. 14(4)(b)); but for s. 12(6) would be an offence under s. 12 (s. 14(4)(c)); or but for s. 13(4) would be an offence under s. 13 (s. 14(4)(d)). The offences are triable on indictment only and the maximum penalty is life imprisonment (s. 14(5)).

Master's Power of Delivery: Section 15 of the Act provides the master of a ship with the power to deliver a person to an appropriate officer in the UK or any other Rome Convention country where he has reasonable grounds to believe that that person has (a) committed an offence under ss. 9, 11, 12 or 13, (b) attempted to commit such an offence, or (c) aided, abetted, counselled, procured or incited, been art and part in, the commission of such an offence.

BREACH OF CONTROL ORDERS

Control orders are designed so as to impose necessary obligations on a person to protect members of the public from a risk of terrorism (Prevention of Terrorism Act 2005, s. 1(1)). Control orders may be either derogating or non-derogating. **B10.229**

Breach of a Control Order

B10.230 **Prevention of Terrorism Act 2005, s. 9**

(1) A person who, without reasonable excuse, contravenes an obligation imposed on him by a control order is guilty of an offence.

(2) A person is guilty of an offence if—

(a) a control order by which he is bound at a time when he leaves the United Kingdom requires him, whenever he enters the United Kingdom, to report to a specified person that he is or has been the subject of such an order;

(b) he re-enters the United Kingdom after the order has ceased to have effect;

(c) the occasion on which he re-enters the United Kingdom is the first occasion on which he does so after leaving while the order was in force; and

(d) on that occasion he fails, without reasonable excuse, to report to the specified person in the manner that was required by the order.

(3) A person is guilty of an offence if he intentionally obstructs the exercise by any person of a power conferred by section 7(9).

B10.231 **Procedure** An allegation of an offence contrary to s. 9(1) or (2) of the Prevention of Terrorism Act 2005 is triable either way and upon trial on indictment is a class 3 offence. The offence under s. 9(3) is summary only.

B10.232 **Sentence** The maximum penalty for an offence under the Prevention of Terrorism Act 2005, s. 9(1) and (2), is, on summary conviction, six months' imprisonment or a fine to the statutory maximum, or both. On conviction on indictment, the maximum sentence is five years' imprisonment or a fine, or both. The court may not conditionally discharge the offender. The maximum penalty on conviction for an offence under s. 9(3) is six months' imprisonment or a fine to level 5, or both.

Section B11 Offences Affecting Public Order

INTRODUCTION

The POA 1986 abolished a number of common-law offences, including riot, unlawful assembly and affray, replacing them with statutory offences of riot, violent disorder, affray, threatening behaviour etc. and disorderly conduct. It extended controls over processions and created controls over open-air assemblies. It expanded the law relating to incitement to racial hatred and provided for exclusion of certain offenders from sporting events, notably association football matches. This section also deals with surviving offences under the POA 1936 and the Unlawful Drilling Act 1819 and the common-law offence of public nuisance. **B11.1**

PROHIBITION OF QUASI-MILITARY ORGANISATIONS

Public Order Act 1936, s. 2 **B11.2**

(1) If the members or adherents of any association of persons, whether incorporated or not, are—

(a) organised or trained or equipped for the purpose of enabling them to be employed in usurping the functions of the police or of the armed forces of the Crown; or

(b) organised and trained or organised and equipped either for the purpose of enabling them to be employed for the use or display of physical force in promoting any political object, or in such manner as to arouse reasonable apprehension that they are organised and either trained or equipped for that purpose;

then any person who takes part in the control or management of the association, or in so organising or training as aforesaid any members or adherents thereof, shall be guilty of an offence under this section.

Procedure

B11.3 Offences under the POA 1936, s. 2, are triable either way (POA 1936, s. 7(1)). When tried on indictment they are class 3 offences. By virtue of s. 2(2), no prosecution shall be instituted without the consent of the A-G.

Public Order Act 1936, s. 2

(4) In any criminal or civil proceedings under this section proof of things done or of words written, spoken or published (whether or not in the presence of any party to the proceedings) by any person taking part in the control or management of an association or in organising, training or equipping members or adherents of an association shall be admissible as evidence of the purposes for which, or the manner in which, members or adherents of the association (whether those persons or others) were organised, or trained, or equipped.

Indictment

B11.4

Statement of Offence

Taking part in the control or management [or organising or training members or adherents] of an association contrary to section 2(1)(a) of the Public Order Act 1936

Particulars of Offence

A between the . . . day of . . . and the . . . day of . . . took part in the management or control [or organising or training members or adherents] of an association, namely . . ., whose members or adherents were organised, trained or equipped for the purpose of enabling them to be employed in usurping the functions of the police or the armed forces of the Crown

Sentence

B11.5 The maximum penalty is two years or a fine or both on indictment; six months or a fine not exceeding the prescribed sum or both summarily (POA 1936, s. 7(1)).

Specific Defences

B11.6

Public Order Act 1936, s. 2

Provided that in any proceedings against a person charged with the offence of taking part in the control or management of such an association as aforesaid it shall be a defence to that charge to prove that he neither consented to nor connived at the organisation, training, or equipment of members or adherents of the association in contravention of the provisions of this section.

Furthermore, s. 2(6) provides that s. 2 does not prohibit the employment of a reasonable number of people as stewards to assist in the preservation of order at a public meeting held on private premises, or the making of arrangements for that purpose or the instruction of people to be so employed in their lawful duties as such stewards, or their being furnished with badges or other distinguishing signs.

The imposition of a legal burden upon the accused is open to challenge in the light of the human rights cases on the 'reverse burden' (see **F3.13** ***et seq.***).

Powers of High Court in Relation to Quasi-military Organisations

B11.7

Public Order Act 1936, s. 2

(3) If upon application being made by the Attorney-General it appears to the High Court that any association is an association of which members or adherents are organised, trained, or equipped in contravention of the provisions of this section, the court may make such order as appears necessary to prevent any disposition without the leave of the court of property held by or for the association and in accordance with rules of court may direct an inquiry and report to be made as to any such property as aforesaid and as to the affairs of the association

and make such further orders as appear to the court to be just and equitable for the application of such property in or towards the discharge of the liabilities of the association lawfully incurred before the date of the application or since that date with the approval of the court, in or towards the repayment of moneys to persons who became subscribers or contributors to the association in good faith and without knowledge of any such contravention as aforesaid, and in or towards any costs incurred in connection with any such inquiry and report as aforesaid or in winding-up or dissolving the association, and may order that any property which is not directed by the court to be so applied as aforesaid shall be forfeited to the Crown.

Under s. 2(5) a High Court judge may grant a search warrant with a view to seizing evidence of the commission of an offence under s. 2. The judge must be satisfied on information under oath that there is reasonable ground for believing that an offence under s. 2 has been committed, and that evidence of it may be found at the place specified in the information. Application must be made by a police officer of a rank not lower than inspector.

PROHIBITION OF UNLAWFUL DRILLING

Unlawful Drilling Act 1819, s. 1 **B11.8**

All meetings and assemblies of persons for the purpose of training or drilling themselves, or of being trained or drilled, to the use of arms of for the purpose of practising military exercise, movements or evolutions, without any lawful authority from Her Majesty or a Secretary of State . . . shall be and the same are hereby prohibited and every person who shall be present at or attend any such meeting or assembly for the purpose of training or drilling any other person or persons to the use of arms or the practice of military exercise, movements or evolutions or who shall train or drill any other person or persons to the use of arms or the practice of military exercise, movements or evolutions, or who shall aid and assist therein, being legally convicted thereof, shall be liable to be imprisoned for any term not exceeding seven years . . . and every person who shall attend or be present at any such meeting or assembly as aforesaid, for the purpose of being, or who shall at any such meeting or assembly be trained or drilled to the use of arms, or the practice of military exercise, movements or evolutions, being legally convicted thereof, shall be liable to be punished by fine and imprisonment not exceeding two years.

Procedure

Offences under the Unlawful Drilling Act 1819, s. 1, are triable only on indictment. They are class 3 offences. Proceedings must be commenced within six calendar months after commission of the offence (Unlawful Drilling Act 1819, s. 7). **B11.9**

Sentence

The maximum penalties prescribed by the Unlawful Drilling Act 1819, s. 1, for offences under the section are: **B11.10**

(a) for persons who have attended or been present for the purpose of training or drilling any other person or persons, or who have trained or drilled any other person or persons, or who have aided or assisted in the training or drilling of others: seven years;
(b) for persons who have attended or been present for the purpose of being trained or drilled, or who have been trained or drilled: two years.

PROHIBITION OF UNIFORMS IN CONNECTION WITH POLITICAL OBJECTS

B11.11 **Public Order Act 1936, s. 1**

(1) Subject as hereinafter provided, any person who in any public place or at any public meeting wears uniform signifying his association with any political organisation or with the promotion of any political object is guilty of an offence:

Provided that, if the chief officer of police is satisfied that the wearing of any such uniform as aforesaid on any ceremonial, anniversary, or other special occasion will not be likely to involve risk of public disorder, he may, with the consent of a Secretary of State, by order permit the wearing of such uniform on that occasion either absolutely or subject to such conditions as may be specified in the order.

Procedure

B11.12 An offence under the POA 1936, s. 1(1), is triable only summarily (POA 1936, s. 7(2)).

Public Order Act 1936, s. 1

(2) Where any person is charged before any court with an offence under this section, no further proceedings in respect thereof shall be taken against him without the consent of the Attorney-General except such as are authorised by [section 25 of the Prosecution of Offences Act 1985], so, however, that if that person is remanded in custody he shall, after the expiration of a period of eight days from the date on which he was so remanded, be entitled to be released on bail without sureties unless within that period the Attorney-General has consented to such further proceedings as aforesaid.

Sentence

B11.13 The maximum penalty is imprisonment for a term not exceeding three months or a fine not exceeding level 4 on the standard scale, or both (POA 1936, s. 7(2)).

Uniform Signifying Association with a Political Organisation etc.

B11.14 In *O'Moran v DPP* [1975] QB 864 the Divisional Court held that the defendant was wearing a uniform when wearing a black beret, because that beret was worn by each member of the group to signify that he was a member of a group in association with others. The court took the view that the wearing of a uniform signifying the requisite association may be proved either by evidence showing that that uniform has been used in the past as that of a political organisation, in which case it is sufficient to show that it is associated with an organisation even if it is not possible to show exactly which organisation that uniform is to be identified with, or by evidence showing that the group in question assembled together wearing the uniform so as to indicate an association with each other and that, further, by their conduct it was indicated that the uniform associated them with political activity.

Meaning of 'Public Place' and 'Public Meeting'

B11.15 The concept of 'public place' in the POA 1936 was frequently litigated. All that litigation is relevant to the instant offence and also to the POA 1986, and probably also all other legislation in which a similar concept plays an important part.

Public Order Act 1936, s. 9

(1) In this Act the following expressions have the meanings hereby respectively assigned to them, that is to say:—

. . .

'Public place' includes any highway and any other premises or place to which at the material time the public have or are permitted to have access, whether on payment or otherwise.

This is an incomplete definition. The question of whether a particular place is a 'public place' depends upon a number of factors as decided by a series of cases on the since repealed s. 5 of the POA 1936. (See also **B12.127**.)

Whether a place is a public place depends upon an assessment of the factual position at 'the material time'. Consequently, the Divisional Court decided in *Marsh v Arscott* (1982) 75 Cr App Rep 211 that a shop car park could not be a public place at 11.30 p.m. when the shop was shut. If at the material time, the public do have access as members of the public rather than under any other provision of law, s. 9 means that that place is a public place even if entry may be refused to certain people. Accordingly a public house was held to be a public place by the Divisional Court in *Lawrenson v Oxford* [1982] Crim LR 185. On the other hand the Court of Appeal in *Edwards* (1978) 67 Cr App R 228 held that the front garden of a house was not a public place because people have access only on an individual basis as lawful visitors. The Divisional Court in *Cawley v Frost* [1976] 1 WLR 1207 held that a place is a 'public place' even if the public are denied access to parts of it. Consequently, a football ground is a public place, even though members of the public are permitted only to go to certain areas and are denied access to other private areas.

Public Order Act 1936, s. 9

(1) In this Act the following expressions have the meanings hereby respectively assigned to them, that is to say:—

'Meeting' means a meeting held for the purpose of the discussion of matters of public interest or for the purpose of the expression of views on such matters; . . .

'Public meeting' includes any meeting in a public place and any meeting which the public or any section thereof are permitted to attend, whether on payment or otherwise.

Related Offences

It is an offence, contrary to the Uniforms Act 1894, s. 3, to wear or to employ someone to wear, without permission, the uniform or other dress bearing any of the regimental or other distinctive marks of such uniform of Her Majesty's naval or military forces or the Air Force. The offence is punishable on summary conviction with imprisonment for a term not exceeding one month or a fine not exceeding level 3. **B11.16**

It is an offence, contrary to the Merchant Shipping Act 1970, s. 87(3), to wear the merchant navy uniform or any part of it or something resembling such uniform. The offence is punishable on summary conviction with a fine not exceeding level 3. There are, however, no regulations prescribing what the merchant navy uniform is.

It is an offence, contrary to the Police Act 1996, s. 90(2), for someone who is not a police officer to wear any article of police uniform, which includes distinctive badges, marks and documents, where it gives that person an appearance so resembling a member of a police force that it is calculated to deceive. The offence is punishable on summary conviction with a fine not exceeding level 3.

For offences relating to the use of uniforms to gain access to prohibited places (Official Secrets Act 1920, s. 1(1)), see **B9.18** to **B9.23**.

RIOT

Public Order Act 1986, s. 1 **B11.17**

(1) Where 12 or more persons who are present together use or threaten unlawful violence for a common purpose and the conduct of them (taken together) is such as would cause a person of reasonable firmness present at the scene to fear for his personal safety, each of the persons using unlawful violence for the common purpose is guilty of riot.

(2) It is immaterial whether or not the 12 or more use or threaten unlawful violence simultaneously.
(3) The common purpose may be inferred from conduct.
(4) No person of reasonable firmness need actually be, or be likely to be, present at the scene.
(5) Riot may be committed in private as well as in public places.

Procedure

B11.18 Riot is triable only on indictment (POA 1986, s. 1(6)). It is a class 3 offence. A prosecution for riot or incitement to riot may be commenced only by, or with the consent of, the DPP (POA 1986, s. 7(1)).

Indictment

B11.19 *Statement of Offence*

Riot contrary to section 1 of the Public Order Act 1986

Particulars of Offence

A on or about the . . . day of . . ., being one of 12 or more persons present together at . . . and using [or threatening] unlawful violence for a common purpose, namely . . ., used unlawful violence for the said common purpose by assaulting members of the public, the conduct of the 12 or more persons aforesaid, taken together, being such as would cause a person of reasonable firmness present at the scene to fear for his personal safety.

This form of indictment was approved by the Court of Appeal in *Tyler* (1992) 96 Cr App R 332 and *Jefferson* [1994] 1 All ER 270.

As to the importance of alleging the presence of the required 12 persons, see by analogy *Mahroof* (1989) 88 Cr App R 317 (a case concerned with violent disorder: see **B11.31** and **B11.34**). See also *Fleming* (1989) 153 JP 517; *Worton* (1989) 154 JP 201.

The POA 1986, s. 7(2), declares that for the purposes of the rules against charging more than one offence in the same count, each of sections 1 to 5 of the Act creates one offence.

Alternative Verdicts

B11.20 The POA 1986, s. 7(3), provides for alternative verdicts on charges under the Act without mentioning s. 1. However, the Criminal Law Act 1967, s. 6(3) (see **D18.42** *et seq.*), would allow the jury on an indictment for riot to return an alternative verdict of guilty of violent disorder under the POA 1986, s. 2, or of affray under s. 3 (see also **B11.32**). It may, however, be prudent to add alternative counts.

Sentencing Guidelines

B11.21 The maximum penalty is 10 years or a fine or both (POA 1986, s. 1(6)).

Some general guidance on the gravity of public order offences, including riot, is to be found in *Caird* (1970) 54 Cr App R 499, a case, like several others cited below, decided in respect of common-law offences of public order which have been replaced by the statutory scheme in the POA 1986. In *Caird*, Sachs LJ said (at pp. 506–8) that:

> When there is wanton and vicious violence of gross degree the court is not concerned with whether it originates from gang rivalry or from political motives. It is the degree of mob violence that matters and the extent to which the public peace is being broken . . .
>
> In the view of this court, it is a wholly wrong approach to take the acts of any individual participator in isolation. They were not committed in isolation and, as already indicated, it is that very fact that constitutes the gravity of the offence.

In *Muranyi* (1986) 8 Cr App R (S) 176, the offender pleaded guilty to riot. He had been concerned in planning and instigating a number of attacks on football supporters. Between

30 and 150 people attacked visiting football supporters, a number of whom suffered serious injuries, including one who was stabbed in the neck with a bottle which severed an artery. Five years' imprisonment was upheld on appeal. Leggatt J, in the Court of Appeal, dealt with the argument that Muranyi had not been seen with a weapon on these occasions by saying that: 'He plainly was leading others who to his knowledge were equipped with the assortment of weapons to which we have referred'. In *Pilgrim* (1983) 5 Cr App R (S) 140, three offenders had been involved in a riot in which 100 youths, equipped with various weapons, had attacked a public house frequented by members of an opposing group, and subsequently attacked a number of people who were unconnected with the event, one of whom was killed. The first offender was convicted of manslaughter in respect of that, and received sentences totalling eight years. The other two received sentences of five years and three years respectively. The Court of Appeal upheld the sentences, Lord Lane CJ saying that:

> What the court has to pay regard to is the level of violence used, the scale of the riot or affray as described by the witnesses, the extent to which it is premeditated, or on the other hand spontaneously arises, and finally the number of people who are engaged in its execution . . .
>
> This case . . . is as good an example as any of how mob violence feeds upon itself, and how it is apt to, and very frequently does, end in catastrophic events, as the death of May indicates in the present case.

In *Najeeb* [2003] 2 Cr App R (S) 408 the offenders had been involved in a riot involving clashes between hundreds of white and Asian males, following a speech made by a leader of the British National Party. Police officers were attacked with stones and petrol bombs, and two officers were stabbed. Stolen cars were set alight and many premises were severely damage estimated at £27 million was caused. Over 100 defendants pleaded guilty to riot before different judges and were sentenced to terms of imprisonment between four and six and a half years. Defendants under 18 were sentenced to terms of between 6 and 18 months. Rose LJ in the Court of Appeal said that, in a case of riot on this scale, the sentence for a ringleader, after a trial, should be around the maximum of 10 years. In a contested case, for an active and persistent participant who used petrol bombs a sentence of eight to nine years was appropriate. Those who were present for a significant period, throwing stones, could expect five years. Where the evidence was overwhelming, because a defendant's activity had been caught on camera, little discount was to be expected for a guilty plea. In cases of serious riot deterrent sentences were required so that good character and personal mitigation would carry comparatively little weight.

Twelve or More Persons Present Using or Threatening Violence for a Common Purpose

It is immaterial whether or not the 12 or more use or threaten unlawful violence simultaneously (POA 1986, s. 1(2)). It is also immaterial (by s. 6(7)) whether all of the 12 or more intend to use violence or are aware that their conduct may be violent (the mental element in the offence of riot: see **B11.27**). In other words, a person may be guilty of riot even if some of the 12 or more co-rioters are not guilty of riot (or of violent disorder or affray) because of lack of *mens rea* (see **B11.34**). Common purpose may be inferred from the conduct of the rioters (POA 1986, s. 1(3)) together with such circumstances as the carrying of banners, shouting of slogans, threats and the like. **B11.22**

Accused Must Use Violence

Each accused must use, rather than merely threaten, unlawful violence to be guilty (see *Jefferson* [1994] 1 All ER 270). **B11.23**

Meaning of 'Unlawful Violence'

Public Order Act 1986, s. 8 **B11.24**

In this part—

. . .

'violence' means any violent conduct, so that—
(a) except in the context of affray, it includes violent conduct towards property as well as violent conduct towards persons, and
(b) it is not restricted to conduct causing or intended to cause injury or damage but includes any other violent conduct (for example, throwing at or towards a person a missile of a kind capable of causing injury which does not hit or falls short).

As to the meaning of 'unlawful', see **B11.42**.

Consequences of the Use or Threat of Violence

B11.25 Under the POA 1986, s. 1(1), riot occurs where a person of reasonable firmness present at the scene *would* be caused, not *was* caused, to fear for his personal safety. Further, s. 1(4) provides that: 'No person of reasonable firmness need actually be, or be likely to be, present at the scene' (see **B11.43**).

Place of Commission

B11.26 Riot may occur in private as well as in public places (POA 1986, s. 1(5)).

Mens Rea

B11.27 A person is guilty of riot only if he intends to use violence or is aware that his conduct may be violent (POA 1986, s. 6(1)). A direction as to *mens* rea must normally be given (*Blackwood* [2002] EWCA Crim 3102), and care must be taken to distinguish between principal offenders and aiders and abettors in that direction (see also **A5**).

Effect of Voluntary, Self-induced Intoxication on *Mens Rea*

B11.28 The POA 1986, s. 6, deals with the problem of whether a person's intoxication should be taken into account when determining that of which an accused was aware. Consequently, the problems encountered with the defence of self-induced intoxication (see **A3.9** to **A3.12**) and the effect of intoxication on mistakes which a person makes are of no direct concern in the offence of riot.

Public Order Act 1986, s. 6

(5) For the purposes of this section a person whose awareness is impaired by intoxication shall be taken to be aware of that of which he would be aware if not intoxicated, unless he shows either that his intoxication was not self-induced or that it was caused solely by the taking or administration of a substance in the course of medical treatment.
(6) In subsection (5) 'intoxication' means any intoxication, whether caused by drink, drugs or other means, or by a combination of means.

VIOLENT DISORDER

B11.29 **Public Order Act 1986, s. 2**

(1) Where three or more persons who are present together use or threaten unlawful violence and the conduct of them (taken together) is such as would cause a person of reasonable firmness present at the scene to fear for his personal safety, each of the persons using or threatening unlawful violence is guilty of violent disorder.
(2) It is immaterial whether or not the three or more use or threaten unlawful violence simultaneously.
(3) No person of reasonable firmness need actually be, or be likely to be, present at the scene.
(4) Violent disorder may be committed in private as well as in public places.

Procedure

B11.30 Violent disorder is triable either way (POA 1986, s. 2(5)). However, according to the *Consolidated Criminal Practice Direction*, para. V.51, *Mode of trial* (see **appendix** 7), 'Cases of violent disorder should generally be committed for trial'. When tried on indictment, violent disorder is a class 3 offence.

Indictment

Statement of Offence B11.31

Violent disorder contrary to section 2(1) of the Public Order Act 1986

Particulars of Offence

A on or about the . . . day of . . ., being one of three or more persons present together at . . . and using [or threatening] unlawful violence used [or threatened to use] unlawful violence by assaulting members of the public, the conduct of the three or more persons aforesaid, taken together, being such as would cause a person of reasonable firmness present at the scene to fear for his personal safety.

The POA 1986, s. 7(2), declares that for the purposes of the rules against charging more than one offence in the same count, each of ss. 1 to 5 of the Act creates one offence.

Violent disorder is not committed unless there are three or more persons together. In *Mahroof* (1988) 88 Cr App R 317, the jury had acquitted two of the accused named in the indictment, but had convicted Mahroof. The Court of Appeal decided that there was a sufficient allegation in the indictment, even though no other persons were named, 'subject to two *very important* qualifications':

(a) 'that there is evidence before the jury that there were three people involved in the criminal behaviour, though not necessarily those named in the indictment' (see also *Lemon* [2002] EWCA Crim 1661), and
(b) 'that the defence are apprised of what it is they have to meet'.

The court made clear that the best way, and generally the only way, of satisfying the second qualification is by putting it in the indictment. This could be done by adding the phrase, after naming certain individuals, 'and others', which could have been pursued in this case by the defence seeking particulars, which would have led to the provision of information about two other people who were known about. In *Mahroof*, qualification (b) was not satisfied. This decision was followed in *Fleming* (1989) 153 JP 517 and was followed and applied by the Court of Appeal in *Worton* (1989) 154 JP 201, although the court seems to have been satisfied, perhaps too easily, that the defence was sufficiently apprised of the matter. It seems unsatisfactory that qualification (b) should be satisfied by the evidence given by the prosecution at the trial, rather than information provided in advance of the trial.

If one or more of the defendants may lack the *mens rea* for the offence, the determination of numbers is not affected (see **B11.34**). See also *Mechen* [2004] EWCA Crim 388, confirming that acquittal of a person on the grounds of self-defence removes them from inclusion in the minimum number required for the offence.

Alternative Verdicts

Public Order Act 1986, s. 7 B11.32

(3) If on the trial on indictment of a person charged with violent disorder . . . the jury find him not guilty of the offence charged, they may (without prejudice to section 6(3) of the Criminal Law Act 1967) find him guilty of an offence under section 4.
(4) The Crown Court has the same powers and duties in relation to a person who is by virtue of subsection (3) convicted before it of an offence under section 4 as a magistrates' court would have on convicting him of the offence.

As to the operation of the POA 1986, s. 7(3), see *Mahroof* (1988) 88 Cr App R 317 and *Worton* (1989) 154 JP 201. Section 7(3) applies only where the jury has found the defendant not guilty, whether as a result of its own deliberations or as a result of following the judge's proper direction (*Carson* (1990) 92 Cr App R 236). The Criminal Law Act 1967, s. 6(3) (see

D18.42 *et seq.*), may be resorted to where the defendant on arraignment pleads not guilty to an offence contrary to the POA 1986, s. 2 or 3, but wishes to plead guilty to an offence contrary to s. 4 (*O'Brien* (1992) 156 JP 925). The operation of the 1967 Act is unaffected by the POA 1986, so, on a charge of violent disorder, it is possible, provided the elements of the offence are established, to substitute a conviction, for example, of affray under s. 3 (see *Fleming* (1989) 153 JP 517). Particular attention must be paid to matters such as the different meanings of 'violence' in the offences (see *McGuigan* [1991] Crim LR 719 and see **B11.34** and **B11.43**). The same principles apply to finding a person guilty of an offence contrary to s. 4 in the alternative.

Sentencing Guidelines

B11.33 The maximum penalty is five years, a fine or both, on indictment (POA 1986, s. 2(5)); six months, a fine not exceeding the statutory maximum, or both, summarily.

When dealt with summarily, the Magistrates' Courts Guidelines (2004) indicate the following for a first-time offender pleading not guilty:

> **Aggravating Factors** For example busy public place; fighting between rival groups; large group; people put in fear; planned; vulnerable victims; weapon; racial or religious aggravation; offence committed on bail; relevant previous convictions and any failures to respond to previous sentences.
>
> **Mitigating Factors** For example impulsive; provocation.
> *Guideline*: Are magistrates' sentencing powers sufficient?

In *Greenall* [2005] 2 Cr App R (S) 276, sentences of four years' imprisonment were upheld for the organisers of a conspiracy to cause violent disorder, and sentences of two years were upheld for those who took part, when rival football supporters arranged to fight each other at a railway station. Some of the gang were armed with bottles, fighting continued for several minutes and three participants were knocked unconscious. See also *Alderson* (1989) 11 Cr App R (S) 301, where a sentence of 30 months was upheld in respect of a racially motivated attack by the offender (who had seven previous convictions, mainly for dishonesty) and three other men, upon a group of Jordanian students, who were punched, kicked, butted and struck with a chair. Eighteen months' imprisonment was upheld on three offenders of previous good character in *Watson* (1990) 12 Cr App R (S) 477. One of the offenders, who had witnessed the stabbing of a workmate, who eventually died from his wound, met co-defendants and went to the scene of the stabbing, the premises of a taxi firm, to exact revenge. They broke in and attacked a taxi driver and a 17-year-old female controller, who were unconnected with the stabbing incident. See also *Sturton* (1992) 13 Cr App R (S) 116, *Betts* (1995) 16 Cr App R (S) 436 and *Green* [1997] 2 Cr App R (S) 191.

Actus Reus

B11.34 **Three or More People Present Together Using or Threatening Violence** It is immaterial whether or not the three or more use or threaten unlawful violence simultaneously (POA 1986, s. 2(2)).

As stated at **B11.31**, it is essential to establish that three or more people were together using or threatening violence. The Court of Appeal in *Church* (12 November 1999 unreported) felt that assistance can be derived from the decision of the Divisional Court in *Allen v Ireland* [1984] 1 WLR 903 where Kerr LJ stated (at p. 212) that voluntary presence at an affray 'is capable of raising a prima facie case of participation . . ., but that mere voluntary presence is not sufficient . . . unless the court is satisfied that he at least also gave some overt encouragement to the others who were directly involved in the affray or threatening behaviour'. Whether any particular defendant is involved is, then, a question of fact. In *Fleming* (1989) 153 JP 517, the Court of Appeal made it clear that a jury should be directed that 'if it cannot be sure that three or more of the defendants were using or threatening violence, then it should acquit every defendant, even if satisfied that one or more particular defendants were unlawfully fighting'. See also *McGuigan* [1991] Crim LR 719. Usually, therefore, when only three are named in the indictment, the jury must acquit all three if they acquit one. This is not the case where the jury is satisfied that others not charged were taking part in the violent disorder in which case the jury may convict (*Worton* (1989) 154 JP 201). Account can be taken of such others only if the requirements established in *Mahroof* (1988) 88 Cr App R 317 (see **B11.31**) are satisfied. Further, where one (or more) defendant is acquitted as a result of lack of *mens rea* (see **B11.36**), the determination of the number of persons is unaffected (POA 1986, s. 6(7)). Thus if one (or more) of the named defendants is found not guilty because he lacks *mens rea*, the remaining defendants may be found guilty, even if there are only two of them.

Other Elements Unlike the offence of riot, it is not part of the definition of violent disorder that those present have a common purpose. **B11.35**

For the elements of unlawful violence, producing fear in a person of reasonable firmness, and place of commission, see the discussion of those elements in the offence of riot at **B11.24** to **B11.26**.

Mens Rea

Public Order Act 1986, s. 6 **B11.36**

(2) A person is guilty of violent disorder . . . only if he intends to use or threaten violence or is aware that his conduct may be violent or threaten violence.

The *mens rea* is subjective, see **B11.73**. For the effect of voluntary, self-induced intoxication on *mens rea*, see the discussion in relation to the offence of riot at **B11.28**.

AFFRAY

Public Order Act 1986, s. 3 **B11.37**

(1) A person is guilty of affray if he uses or threatens unlawful violence towards another and his conduct is such as would cause a person of reasonable firmness present at the scene to fear for his personal safety.
(2) Where two or more persons use or threaten the unlawful violence, it is the conduct of them taken together that must be considered for the purposes of subsection (1).
(3) For the purposes of this section a threat cannot be made by the use of words alone.
(4) No person of reasonable firmness need actually be, or be likely to be, present at the scene.
(5) Affray may be committed in private as well as in public places.

Procedure

Affray is triable either way (POA 1986, s. 3(7)). According to the *Consolidated Criminal Practice Direction*, para. V.51, *Mode of trial* (see **appendix** 7), cases of affray should be tried summarily unless the court considers that one or more of the following features is present in the case *and* that its sentencing powers are insufficient: **B11.38**

(a) Organised violence or use of weapons.
(b) Significant injury or substantial damage.
(c) The offence has clear racial motivation.
(d) An attack on police officers, ambulance staff, firefighters and the like.

When tried on indictment, affray is a class 3 offence.

Prosecutions for affray should be instituted only where the incident gives rise to serious disturbance to public order (Law Commission Report No. 123, para. 3.38, referred to in

Davison [1992] Crim LR 31); it is thoroughly bad practice to charge what are straightforward assaults as public order offences (*Connor* (13 March 2000 unreported)).

Indictment

B11.39 *Statement of Offence*

Affray contrary to section 3(1) of the Public Order Act 1986

Particulars of Offence

A on or about the . . . day of . . . used [or threatened] violence towards one V, the conduct of A being such as to cause a person of reasonable firmness present at the scene to fear for his personal safety

The POA 1986, s. 7(2), declares that for the purpose of the rules against charging more than one offence in the same count, each of sections 1 to 5 of the Act creates one offence.

Alternative Verdicts

B11.40 **Public Order Act 1986, s. 7**

(3) If on the trial on indictment of a person charged with . . . affray the jury find him not guilty of the offence charged, they may (without prejudice to section 6(3) of the Criminal Law Act 1967) find him guilty of an offence under section 4.

(4) The Crown Court has the same powers and duties in relation to a person who is by virtue of subsection (3) convicted before it of an offence under section 4 as a magistrates' court would have on convicting him of the offence.

It is important that the jury be properly directed as to the lesser offence, which it should consider only if it is unsure that affray has been committed (*Stanley* [1993] Crim LR 618). The differences between the offences may be crucial (see *Va Kun Hau* [1990] Crim LR 518, where s. 4 was not available because the act took place in a dwelling house).

As to the interrelationship between s. 7(3) and the Criminal Law Act 1967, s. 6(3), see **B11.32**.

Sentencing Guidelines

B11.41 The maximum penalty is three years, a fine, or both, on indictment (POA 1986, s. 3(7)); six months, a fine not exceeding the statutory maximum, or both, summarily.

When dealt with summarily, the Magistrates' Courts Guidelines (2004) indicate the following for a first-time offender pleading not guilty:

Aggravating Factors For example busy public place; football related; group action; injuries caused; people actually put in fear; vulnerable victim(s); racial or religious aggravation; offence committed on bail; relevant previous convictions and any failures to respond to previous sentences.

Mitigating Factors For example provocation; did not start the trouble; stopped as soon as the police arrived.

Guideline: Is it so serious that only custody is appropriate?

In *Holmes* [1999] 2 Cr App R (S) 100 two offenders, after an evening of heavy drinking, started a fight with another customer in a fish and chip shop, in which the victim was punched and kicked. They pleaded guilty in the magistrates' court to affray, and were committed for sentence. In light of personal mitigation, custodial sentences were reduced from 15 months to nine months by the Court of Appeal. In *Oliver* [1999] 1 Cr App R (S) 394, 12 months was appropriate for a man who admitted creating a disturbance on a transatlantic flight. He assaulted his wife, was abusive to a steward and behaved in a threatening manner. It was accepted that the offender had been under stress at the time, but the sentencer was right to take account of concern over the prevalence of such incidents. See also *McCallum* [2002] 1

Cr App R (S) 488. In *Williams* [1997] 2 Cr App R (S) 97, the affray took the form of a racially motivated disturbance involving a large number of men who had been drinking heavily after the Cup Final. There was a lot of shouting and bottles were thrown in the vicinity of a shop owned by an Asian family. Abusive racist remarks were made, but no physical injury was caused. A sentence of 12 months' imprisonment was appropriate. See also *Fox* [2006] 1 Cr App R (S) 97.

Meaning of 'Threat' and 'Unlawful Violence'

The essential elements of affray, according to the Court of Appeal, are '(a) the use or threat of violence by the defendant; (b) to another person; which (c) would cause a third person to fear for his or her own safety' (*Thind* [1999] Crim LR 842). For (a) and (b), see below. For (c), see **B11.43**. Lord Bingham CJ has described affray in *Smith* [1997] 1 Cr App R 14 at p. 16: **B11.42**

> It typically involves a group of people who may well be shouting, struggling, threatening, waving weapons, throwing objects, exchanging and threatening blows and so on. Again, typically, it involves a continuous course of conduct, the criminal character of which depends on the general nature and effect of the conduct as a whole and not on particular incidents and events which may take place in the course of it. Where reliance is placed on such a continuous course of conduct, it is not necessary for the Crown to identify and prove particular incidents.

These 'typical activities' must amount to the use or threat of unlawful violence (POA 1986, s. 3(1)). The definition of 'violence' in affray is different from its definition for other purposes in POA 1986. By s. 8, violence, for affray, does not include violent conduct towards property. It is, therefore, limited to violent conduct towards persons. Otherwise, s. 8 provides:

> 'violence' means any violent conduct, so that—
>
> . . .
>
> (b) it is not restricted to conduct causing or intended to cause injury or damage but includes any other violent conduct (for example, throwing at or towards a person a missile of a kind capable of causing injury which does not hit or falls short).

In *Rothwell* [1993] Crim LR 626, it was held that the word 'unlawful' is intended to ensure that defences such as self-defence apply to offences under the POA 1986 (see also *Key* (24 November 1992 unreported), *Afzal* [1993] Crim LR 791 and *Pulham* [1995] Crim LR 296).

Since a threat cannot be made by words alone (POA 1986, s. 3(3)), there must be conduct on the part of the accused; the fact that the experience was frightening does not make aggressive words sufficient (*Robinson* [1993] Crim LR 581). However, in *Dixon* [1993] Crim LR 579, ordering a dog to attack was sufficient to constitute a threat, because there was conduct, the dog being used as a weapon. Since the dog did attack, it is arguable that there was conduct but, had the dog not attacked, what would have been the conduct sufficient to satisfy s. 3(3)? See also *Dackers* [2000] All ER (D) 1958.

The words 'threatens unlawful violence' carry their ordinary and natural meaning so that the carrying of dangerous weapons, such as petrol bombs by a group of persons can, in some circumstances, constitute the threat of violence, without those weapons being waved or brandished (*I v DPP* [2001] 2 WLR 765). Lord Hutton supported this view by reference to applicable cases on the common-law offence of affray: see *Sharp* [1957] 1 QB 552 and *Taylor* [1973] AC 964 (where it was said that mere words are not sufficient, but that brandishing weapons is not always required). Whether the carrying of weapons is sufficient in any given case is a matter for the tribunal of fact to decide having regard to the facts of the case.

Unlawful violence must be used or threatened to another. That other must be present at the scene (*I v DPP*). As the only people proved to be present in *I v DPP* were the members of the gang possessing and brandishing petrol bombs, there was no 'another' to whom violence was used or threatened and so there was no affray.

The Test for Conduct Causing Fear

B11.43 The test, as for riot and violent disorder, is whether a person of reasonable firmness present at the scene *would* be caused, not *was* caused, to fear for his personal safety. No person of reasonable firmness need actually be, or be likely to be, present at the scene (POA 1986, s. 3(4)).

In *Davison* [1992] Crim LR 31, the Court of Appeal, taking account of Law Commission Report No. 123, decided that the conduct to be considered is that of the accused. Its consequences are judged by an objective standard, i.e. whether the hypothetical bystander of reasonable firmness (not the person assaulted) would be put in fear of his personal safety if he was there. Account may be taken of the nature of the premises and scene where the incident actually took place, and of the fact that the violence was limited to those involved and that others present were not afraid (*DPP v Cotcher* (1992) *The Times*, 29 December 1992). In *Sanchez* (1996) 160 JP 321, the Divisional Court approved the commentary of Professor Sir John Smith to *Davison* as being the correct approach: 'the question in the present case was not whether a person of reasonable firmness in [the victim's] shoes would have feared for his personal safety but whether [the] hypothetical person, present in the room and seeing [the accused's] conduct towards [the victim] would have so feared . . . [The offence] is designed for the protection of the bystander. It is a public order offence. There are other offences for the protection of persons at whom the violence is aimed'. The court commented that it thought that, even though the instant case might fit s. 3 (where S had lunged at V with a knife in a car parked in a car park in the middle of the night), it was not the most appropriate charge. See also *Rafferty* (2004) *The Times*, 21 April 2004.

In *Carey* [2006] EWCA Crim 17, the Court of Appeal decided that affray was to be defined without reference to the Law Commission report which preceded the POA 1986 and that the words used in the legislation were to be given their ordinary unglossed meaning. Thus, it was improper to require a person of reasonable firmness to be 'terrified' (as was required under the common-law offence of affray). The incident in question was short-lived and the injuries actually inflicted were comparatively slight; but the defendants were apparently fit teenagers acting in a very aggressive manner. It was open to the jury to conclude that a person of reasonable firmness present at the time would have feared for his personal safety.

Mens Rea

B11.44 **Public Order Act 1986, s. 6**

(2) A person is guilty of . . . affray only if he intends to use or threaten violence or is aware that his conduct may be violent or threaten violence.

The *mens rea* is subjective, see **B11.73**. A direction about *mens rea* should normally be given (*Mann* [2002] EWCA Crim 3045). For the effect of voluntary, self-induced intoxication on *mens rea*, see the discussion in relation to the offence of riot at **B11.28**.

FEAR OR PROVOCATION OF VIOLENCE

B11.45 **Public Order Act 1986, s. 4**

(1) A person is guilty of an offence if he—
  (a) uses towards another person threatening, abusive or insulting words or behaviour, or
  (b) distributes or displays to another person any writing, sign or other visible representation which is threatening, abusive or insulting,

with intent to cause that person to believe that immediate unlawful violence will be used against him or another by any person, or to provoke the immediate use of unlawful violence by that person or another, or whereby that person is likely to believe that such violence will be used or it is likely that such violence will be provoked.

(2) An offence under this section may be committed in a public or a private place, except that no offence is committed where the words or behaviour are used, or the writing, sign or other visible representation is distributed or displayed, by a person inside a dwelling and the other person is also inside that or another dwelling.

The CDA 1998, s. 31, created a racially or religiously aggravated form of this offence. For the meaning of racially or religiously aggravated, see **B11.160**.

Procedure

B11.46 An offence under the POA 1986, s. 4(1), is, by s. 4(4) of the Act, triable summarily only. The racially aggravated form of the offence is triable either way (CDA 1998, s. 31(4)). If, on trial on indictment, the jury find the accused not guilty of the racially aggravated form of the offence, they may find him guilty of the basic offence (s. 31(6)).

The POA 1986, s. 7(2), declares that for the purposes of the rules against charging more than one offence in the same information, each of ss. 1 to 5 of the Act creates one offence. The offence under s. 4 may be committed in one of four ways (*Winn v DPP* (1992) 156 JP 881, and see **B11.49**). Care must be taken in formulating the charge so that the way of committing the offence reflects the facts of the case, otherwise there may be unjustifiable variance between the charge and the particulars alleged. More than one way of committing the offence may be included and amendment is possible if necessary (*Winn v DPP; Loade v DPP* [1990] 1 QB 1052: for amendment, see **D20.9**).

The person towards whom threatening, abusive or insulting words or behaviour are used can be held to perceive the threatening words or behaviour when he does not give evidence at the trial (*Swanston v DPP* (1997) 161 JP 203). Of course, there must be other evidence, as there was in *Swanston* in view of the small area in which the incidents took place, and the evidence of the police constable.

Sentencing Guidelines (Basic Offence)

B11.47 The maximum penalty is six months or a fine not exceeding level 5 or both (POA 1986, s. 4(4)).

The Magistrates' Courts Guidelines (2004) indicate the following for a first-time offender pleading not guilty:

> **Aggravating Factors** For example football related; group action; people put in fear; vulnerable victim; on hospital/medical or school premises; victim serving the public; offence committed on bail; relevant previous convictions and any failures to respond to previous sentences.
>
> **Mitigating Factors** For example minor matter; short duration.
>
> *Guideline*: Is it serious enough for a community penalty?

Racial or religious aggravation cannot be taken into account by the sentencer when sentencing for the basic offence of fear or provocation of violence. To do so would infringe the principle that the offender must not be sentenced for an offence for which he has not been charged and convicted (see *McGillivray* [2005] 2 Cr App R (S) 366). Where there is evidence that racial aggravation was present, the aggravated form of the offence should be charged. See **E1.9** for increase in sentence, under the CJA 2003, s. 146, for aggravation relating to disability or sexual orientation.

Sentencing Guidelines (Racially or Religiously Aggravated Form of Offence)

B11.48 The maximum penalty for the aggravated form of the offence is two years, a fine or both on indictment; six months, a fine not exceeding the statutory maximum or both summarily (CDA 1998, s. 31(4)).

The Magistrates' Courts Guidelines (2004) provide a higher guideline for this offence when tried summarily than for the basic offence, the guideline being whether the offence is so serious that only custody is appropriate.

The Court of Appeal stated in *Saunders* [2000] 1 Cr App R 458 and in *Kelly* [2001] 2 Cr App R (S) 341, that when sentencing for the racially aggravated form of an offence the sentencer should indicate the appropriate sentence for the offence in the absence of racial aggravation and then add a further term for the racial element. See further **B2.26**. In *Miller* [1999] 2 Cr App R (S) 392, the Court of Appeal upheld a sentence of 18 months' imprisonment where the offender, who had been travelling on a train without a ticket, used verbal racial abuse towards the train conductor. The conductor feared that he was about to be struck. The offender pleaded guilty before the magistrates to an offence under CDA 1998, s. 31, but was committed to Crown Court for sentence. In the Court of Appeal, Judge Colston QC said that it was plain from the CDA 1998 that racial aggravation was a 'very significant factor' in sentencing. The offender had an 'appalling record' for public order and allied offences and in the circumstances had no option but to plead guilty.

The Four Ways of Committing an Offence under s. 4

B11.49 Common to all four ways of committing an offence under the POA 1986, s. 4, are (i) the use of threatening words or behaviour or the distribution or display of threatening, abusive or insulting writing etc. (see **B11.51** to **B11.53**) and (ii) the requirement as to *mens rea* in s. 6(3) (see **B11.54**). The four ways, as indicated in *Winn v DPP* (1992) 156 JP 881, are:

(a) the accused must 'intend the person against whom the conduct is directed to believe that immediate unlawful violence will be used against him or another by [any] person' — as McCowan LJ put it in *Swanston v DPP* (1997) 161 JP 203, 'It is a vital component of the offence that it does not have to be shown that the other person believed: it has to be shown that the [accused] had the intention to cause that person to believe' that immediate unlawful violence would be used against him;

(b) the accused must 'intend to provoke the immediate use of unlawful violence by that person or another';

(c) 'the person against whom [the words, behaviour, distribution or display] are directed is likely to believe that such violence will be used' (note that the person who must be caused to believe that violence will be used or threatened is the person to whom the words, behaviour, distribution or display are directed, see *Loade v DPP* [1990] 1 QB 1052);

(d) 'it is likely that such violence will be provoked'.

In paragraphs (c) and (d) above, 'such violence' means 'immediate unlawful violence' (see *Horseferry Road Metropolitan Stipendiary Magistrate, ex parte Siadatan* [1991] 1 QB 260).

Uses Towards

B11.50 The Divisional Court in *Atkin v DPP* (1989) 89 Cr App R 199 held that the phrase 'uses towards' in the POA 1986, s. 4(1)(a), connotes the physical presence of the person to whom the words were used. That other person must perceive with his own senses the threatening words or behaviour (see also **B11.43**). In *Atkin* the conviction had to be quashed, since the person outside the dwelling was only aware of the threat because it was relayed to him by a Customs and Excise officer.

Threatening, Abusive or Insulting

B11.51 The phrase 'threatening, abusive or insulting words or behaviour' used in the POA 1986, s. 4(1)(a), is not defined in the Act. However, 'threatening, abusive or insulting' was used with reference to words or behaviour in the POA 1936, s. 5, and the Metropolitan Police Act 1839, s. 54(13).

The House of Lords in *Brutus v Cozens* [1973] AC 854 decided that 'insulting' is to be given its ordinary meaning and the question whether words or behaviour are insulting is a question of fact. The same approach is adopted with regard to the words 'threatening' and 'abusive' and the courts have adopted this approach in interpretation of the 1986 Act (*DPP v Clarke* (1991) 94 Cr App R 359, a decision on s. 5). In *Ambrose* (1973) 57 Cr App R 538, the Court of Appeal said that rude or offensive words were not necessarily insulting. The Divisional Court in *Masterson v Holden* [1986] 1 WLR 101 seems to have thought that conduct was insulting if it was unacceptable in public, so that it was able to uphold the conviction of two men for an offence under the Metropolitan Police Act 1839, s. 54(13), who had been kissing and cuddling each other at a bus stop on Oxford Street. Many people may find such conduct objectionable and even offensive, but it must be doubted whether, on its ordinary meaning, it can be described as insulting (or threatening or abusive). The Divisional Court in *Parkin v Norman* [1983] QB 92 held that masturbating in a public lavatory in the sight of a stranger, in this case a police officer, is conduct capable of being insulting because the stranger might be a heterosexual who would be insulted by such homosexual conduct. It must again be questioned whether such conduct is accurately described as insulting (or threatening or abusive) or whether the most accurate description might be that it is offensive, which is not sufficient to found a conviction under s. 4. However, the *Concise Oxford Dictionary* includes in its definition of 'insult', 'offend the self-respect or modesty of', and it may be that it is the affront to modesty which constituted the insult in *Masterson v Holden* and *Parkin v Norman*. In *Vigon v DPP* (1998) 162 JP 115, it was held that secretly filming people in a changing area where they tried on swimwear could amount to insulting behaviour. Whether such behaviour can properly be described as 'insulting' must again be questioned — it would seem better to have described it as a nuisance (although such behaviour falls outside the Act; it is an offence under the SOA 2003, s. 67: see **B3.252**). Describing an Asian as a 'fucking Islam' is almost undeniably abusive, if not insulting (*R (DPP) v Humphrey* [2005] EWHC 822 (Admin)).

For relevant ECHR issues, see **B11.68**.

Meaning of 'Writing' and 'Display'

'Writing' includes typing, printing, lithography, photography and other modes of representing or reproducing words in a visible form (Interpretation Act 1978, s. 5 and sch. 1). As to 'display', see **B11.70**. **B11.52**

Place of Commission

Public Order Act 1986, ss. 4 and 8 **B11.53**

4.—(2) An offence under this section may be committed in a public or a private place, except that no offence is committed where the words or behaviour are used, or the writing, sign or other visible representation is distributed or displayed, by a person inside a dwelling and the other person is also inside that or another dwelling.

8. In this part—

'dwelling' means any structure or part of a structure occupied as a person's home or as other living accommodation (whether the occupation is separate or shared with others) but does not include any part not so occupied, and for this purpose 'structure' includes a tent, caravan, vehicle, vessel or other temporary or movable structure.

'The other person' referred to in s. 4(2) is the same person as is referred to as 'another person' in s. 4(1)(a). Thus the offence is not committed in a dwelling if the only person to whom the words or behaviour are used, etc. (see **B11.50**) is also in that or another dwelling (*Atkin v DPP* (1989) 89 Cr App R 199). It appears to follow that the offence can be committed by the use of telephones and fax machines.

Where common parts (a communal landing) were the means of access to living accommodation, they were not part of a dwelling, even though access was via an entry phone system, and were not part of the living area or home (*Rukwira v DPP* [1993] Crim LR 882). See also *Francis* [2007] 1 WLR 1021 in which it was held that a police cell is not living accommodation.

Mens Rea

B11.54 The intention with which the defendant must act is to be found in s. 4(1) (see **B11.45**) as explained further at **B11.49**. Thus, the *mens rea* that must be proved is dependent upon which form of the offence is charged.

For all four forms of the offence, the following applies.

Public Order Act 1986, s. 6

(3) A person is guilty of an offence under section 4 only if he intends his words or behaviour, or the writing, sign or other visible representation, to be threatening, abusive or insulting, or is aware that it may be threatening, abusive or insulting.

Whichever *mens rea* applies, the question of whether immediate unlawful violence was intended arises. In *DPP v Ramos* [2000] Crim LR 768 it was decided that it is the victim's state of mind that 'is crucial rather than the statistical risk of violence actually occurring within a very short space of time'. Thus, there was evidence on the basis of which the magistrate could infer the requisite intention as to the belief of the victims since the letters that were sent contained a very serious threat, of a bombing campaign, and there was nothing to exclude the immediate future from the period when that violence would be used. This case demonstrates the importance of identifying whether there will be immediate violence. The Divisional Court in *Horseferry Road Metropolitan Stipendiary Magistrate, ex parte Siadatan* [1991] 1 QB 260 decided that it is not sufficient that the conduct was likely to lead to violence at some unspecified time in the future. However, it decided also that 'immediate' does not mean 'instantaneous', so a relatively short time interval may elapse between the act and the violence. The court also decided that 'immediate' connotes proximity in both time and causation, i.e. the violence must result within a relatively short period of time and without any intervening occurrence. Thus, as it was not contended that immediate unlawful violence would be provoked as a result of the publication of *The Satanic Verses*, the failure to issue a summons against Penguin Viking Books Ltd was not open to challenge. The Divisional Court held in *Valentine v DPP* [1997] COD 339 that the justices were entitled to find the accused guilty where his threats caused a woman to fear 'immediate' violence the next time she went to work, but only because she might have gone to work the same night that the threat was made. Assistance on this matter may also be found in the concept of immediacy in assault (see **B2.5**), referred to by the Divisional Court in *DPP v Ramos*. As to the definition of 'violence' in the POA 1986, s. 8, see **B11.24**.

Since the POA 1986, s. 6, deals with intoxication when determining that of which an accused was aware, the general problems encountered with self-induced intoxication (see **A3.9** to **A3.12**), and the effect of intoxication on mistakes, are of no direct concern in this offence.

INTENTIONALLY CAUSING HARASSMENT, ALARM OR DISTRESS

B11.55 **Public Order Act 1986, s. 4A**

(1) A person is guilty of an offence if, with intent to cause a person harassment, alarm or distress, he—
  (a) uses threatening, abusive or insulting words or behaviour, or disorderly behaviour, or
  (b) displays any writing, sign or other visible representation which is threatening, abusive or insulting,

thereby causing that or another person harassment, alarm or distress.

The CDA 1998, s. 31, created a racially or religiously aggravated form of this offence. For the meaning of racially or religiously aggravated, see **B11.160** ***et seq.***

Procedure and Sentencing Guidelines (Basic Offence)

The basic offence is triable summarily only (POA 1986, s. 4A(5)). The maximum penalty is a term of imprisonment not exceeding six months or a fine not exceeding level 5 on the standard scale or both (s. 4A(5)). For the power of arrest, see **B11.62**. **B11.56**

The Magistrates' Courts Guidelines (2004) indicate the following for a first-time offender pleading not guilty:

> **Aggravating Factors** For example football related; group action; victims specially targeted; high degree of planning; night time offence; weapon; offence committed on bail; relevant previous convictions and any failures to respond to previous sentences.
>
> **Mitigating Factors** For example short duration.
>
> *Guideline*: Is it serious enough for a community penalty?

Racial or religious aggravation cannot be taken into account by the sentencer when sentencing for the basic offence. See **B11.47**.

Procedure and Sentencing Guidelines (Racially or Religiously Aggravated Form of Offence)

The aggravated form of the offence is triable either way (CDA 1998, s. 31(4)). If, on trial on indictment, the jury find the accused not guilty of the racially aggravated form of the offence, they may find him guilty of the basic offence (s. 31(6)). The maximum penalty on indictment is a term of imprisonment for two years, a fine or both and, on summary trial, a term of imprisonment for six months, or a fine not exceeding the statutory maximum, or both (s. 31(4)). **B11.57**

The Magistrates' Courts Guidelines (2004) provide a higher guideline for this offence when tried summarily than for the basic offence, the guideline being whether the offence is so serious that only custody is appropriate.

The Court of Appeal stated in *Saunders* [2000] 1 Cr App R 458 and in *Kelly* [2001] 2 Cr App R (S) 341, that when sentencing for the racially aggravated form of an offence the sentencer should indicate the appropriate sentence for the offence in the absence of racial aggravation and then add a further term for the racial element. See further **B2.26**. Three months' imprisonment was appropriate in *Jacobs* [2001] 2 Cr App R (S) 174, where the victim was a female police officer subjected to repeated verbal racial abuse by a female suspect who had been arrested and taken to the police station. Bennett J commented that 'police officers are entitled to be protected, just as any other members of the public, from racial abuse'. See also *Jesson* [2000] 2 Cr App R (S) 200 and *Shand* [2002] 1 Cr App R (S) 291.

Meaning of 'Harassment, Alarm or Distress' etc.

Harassment, alarm or distress have not been defined, but it is assumed that they are ordinary words of the English language unless and until a definition is provided. The guidance on these words under the POA 1986, s. 5, supports this approach, see **B11.71**. **B11.58**

For the meaning of the phrase 'threatening, abusive or insulting', see **B11.51**. For the meaning of 'disorderly behaviour', see **B11.69**. For the meaning of 'writing', see **B11.52**. For the meaning of 'display' in the POA 1986, s. 5, see **B11.70**.

No prosecution should be brought unless it can be established that prosecution is necessary in order to prevent public disorder, thereby avoiding breach of the ECHR, Article 10 (*Dehal v CPS* (2005) 169 JP 581).

The statute requires that there be a causal connection between what the accused does and the other person's harassment, alarm or distress, as was emphasised in *Rogers v DPP* (22 July 1999 unreported). It was held that the causal connection was not broken where a cat breeder heard the noise of the crowd and was concerned by it and its cumulative increase, but watched the incident on his security close circuit television.

Place of Commission of Offence

B11.59 **Public Order Act 1986, s. 4A**

(2) An offence under this section may be committed in a public or a private place, except that no offence is committed where the words or behaviour are used, or the writing, sign or other visible representation is displayed, by a person inside a dwelling and the person who is harassed, alarmed or distressed is also inside that or another dwelling.

As to the consideration of the similar provision in s. 5(2), see **B11.72**.

A police cell is not a place which a person occupies as living accommodation, and cannot be classified as a dwelling or living accommodation for the purposes of s. 4A (*Francis* [2007] 1 WLR 1021).

Mens Rea

B11.60 This is an offence requiring proof of an intention to cause harassment, alarm or distress (POA 1986, s. 4A(1)). This is the fundamental question and it may be inferred where the accused's 'activities are committed in the context of a large crowd there to express disapproval of [the other's] activities and in the context of fence removal and penetration of the police line' even though there is no evidence that the accused knew that the other was present at the scene or could directly experience the disorderly behaviour (*Rogers v DPP* (22 July 1999 unreported)). It may also be inferred from the words used, though it does not necessarily follow that the requisite intention is established by the use of words such as 'black bastard' (*DPP v Weeks* (2000) *Independent*, 17 July 2000). As to the meaning of 'intention', see **A2.2**. For the effect of voluntary, self-induced intoxication on *mens rea*, see the discussion in relation to the offence of riot at **B11.28**.

Specific Defence

B11.61 **Public Order Act 1986, s. 4A**

(3) It is a defence for the accused to prove—
  (a) that he was inside a dwelling and had no reason to believe that the words or behaviour used, or the writing, sign or other visible representation displayed, would be heard or seen by a person outside that or any other dwelling; or
  (b) that his conduct was reasonable.

The imposition of a legal burden upon the accused is open to challenge in the light of the human rights cases on the 'reverse burden' (see **F3.13** ***et seq.***).

Police Powers

B11.62 Under the CJPA 2001, s. 42(1), a constable at the scene may give a direction to any person if (a) that person is present outside or in the vicinity of any premises that are used by any individual ('the resident') as his dwelling; (b) that constable believes, on reasonable grounds, that that person is present there for the purpose (by his presence or otherwise) of representing to the resident or another individual (whether or not one who uses the premises as his dwelling), or of persuading the resident or such another individual (i) that he should not do something that he is entitled or required to do, or (ii) that he should do something that he is not under an obligation to do, and (c) that constable also believes, on reasonable grounds, that the presence of that person (either alone or together with that of any other persons who are also present) (i) amounts to, or is likely to result in, the harassment of the resident, or (ii) is likely to cause alarm or distress to the resident. Further detail on the power to issue directions is contained in s. 42(2) to (6). A person who knowingly contravenes such a direction is guilty of an offence and is liable, on summary conviction, to imprisonment for a term not exceeding three months (or six months where the contravention is of a direction under s. 42(4)(b)) or a fine not exceeding level 4 on the standard scale or both (CJPA, s. 42(7) to (7C)).

Constables in uniform and, in certain areas, community support officers have powers to disperse groups and to remove persons under 16 to their place of residence under the ASBA 2003, ss. 30 to 36. For the power to be available, an officer of at least the rank of superintendent must create an authorisation for a period of up to six months on the basis that he has reasonable grounds for believing (a) that any members of the public have been intimidated, harassed, alarmed or distressed as a result of the presence or behaviour of groups of two or more persons in public places in any locality in his police area, and (b) that anti-social behaviour is a significant and persistent problem in the relevant locality (ss. 30(1) and (2), 31, 32 and 36). If a constable in uniform (or community support officer where s. 33 is satisfied) has reasonable grounds for believing that the presence or behaviour of a group of two or more persons in any public place in the relevant locality has resulted, or is likely to result, in any members of the public being intimidated, harassed, alarmed or distressed (s. 30(3)), he has the power to give one or more of the following directions: (a) requiring the persons in the group to disperse (either immediately or by such time as he may specify and in such way as he may specify), (b) requiring any of those persons whose place of residence is not within the relevant locality to leave it or any part of it (either immediately or by such time as he may specify and in such way as he may specify), (c) prohibiting any of those persons whose place of residence is not within the relevant locality from returning to it or any part of it for such period (not exceeding 24 hours) from the giving of the direction as he may specify (s. 30(4)). This power does not apply where a group of persons is (a) engaged in lawful conduct under the Trade Union and Labour Relations (Consolidation) Act 1992, s. 220, or (b) taking part in a public procession within the meaning of the POA 1986, s. 11 (s. 30(5)). Any such direction must be proportionate in the circumstances (see *MB v DPP* (2007) 171 JP 10). A constable in uniform also has power, between the hours of 9 p.m. and 6 a.m., to remove someone who he finds in any public place in the relevant locality, and who he has reasonable grounds to believe is under 16 and who is not under the effective control of a parent or responsible person aged at least 18 to their place of residence unless he has reasonable grounds for believing that the person would, if removed there, be likely to suffer significant harm (s. 30(6)).

A person who knowingly contravenes a s. 30(4) direction commits an offence and is liable on summary conviction to a fine not exceeding level 4 on the standard scale or imprisonment for a term not exceeding three months or both (s. 32(2)).

Alternative Offence

It is a summary offence, contrary to the CJA 1967, s. 91, where a person in any public place is, while drunk, of disorderly behaviour (see **B11.218**). **B11.63**

HARASSMENT, ALARM OR DISTRESS

Public Order Act 1986, s. 5 **B11.64**

(1) A person is guilty of an offence if he—
  (a) uses threatening, abusive or insulting words or behaviour, or disorderly behaviour, or
  (b) displays any writing, sign or other visible representation which is threatening, abusive or insulting,

  within the hearing or sight of a person likely to be caused harassment, alarm or distress thereby.

[(2) and (3) concern the place of commission of the offence and a specific defence: see **B11.72** and **B11.74**.]

The CDA 1998, s. 31, created a racially or religiously aggravated form of this offence. For the meaning of racially or religiously aggravated, see **B11.160** *et seq.*; the definition has effect as if the person likely to be caused harassment, alarm or distress were the victim of the offence (s. 31(7)).

Procedure

B11.65 It is, by s. 5(6) of the Act, triable summarily only. The racially or religiously aggravated form of the offence is also triable only summarily.

The POA 1986, s. 7(2), declares that, for the purposes of the rules against charging more than one offence in the same information, each of ss. 1 to 5 of the Act creates one offence.

Sentencing Guidelines (Basic Offence)

B11.66 The maximum penalty is a fine not exceeding level 3 (POA 1986, s. 5(6)). Under the Penalties for Disorderly Behaviour (Amount of Penalty) Order 2002 (SI 2002 No. 1837), as amended by the Penalties for Disorderly Behaviour (Amount of Penalty) (Amendment No. 2) Order 2004 (SI 2004 No. 2468), this offence is a penalty offence and the amount payable is £80.

The Magistrates' Courts Guidelines (2004) indicate the following for a first-time offender pleading not guilty:

> **Aggravating Factors** For example football related; group action; vulnerable victim; offence committed on bail; relevant previous convictions and any failures to respond to previous sentences.
>
> **Mitigating Factors** For example stopped as soon as police arrived; trivial incident.
>
> *Guideline*: Is discharge or fine appropriate?

The guideline fine is Starting Point B (see **E17.5**).

Racial or religious aggravation cannot be taken into account by the sentencer when sentencing for the basic offence (see **B11.47**); see **E1.9** for increase in sentence, under the CJA 2003, s. 146, for aggravation relating to disability or sexual orientation.

Sentencing Guidelines (Racially or Religiously Aggravated Form of Offence)

B11.67 The maximum penalty is a fine not exceeding level 4 (CDA 1998, s. 31(5)).

The Magistrates' Courts Guidelines (2004) provide a higher guideline for this offence than for the basic offence, the guideline being whether the offence is serious enough for a community sentence. It should be noted that, since the offence is non-imprisonable, certain community sentences are unavailable.

The Court of Appeal indicated in *Saunders* [2000] 1 Cr App R 458, that when sentencing for the racially aggravated form of an offence the sentencer may usefully consider the appropriate sentence for the offence in the absence of racial aggravation and then add a further term for the racial element. See further **B2.26**.

Compliance with the European Convention on Human Rights

B11.68 In *Percy v DPP* (2002) 166 JP 93, the Divisional Court rejected an argument that the existence of the POA 1986, s. 5, was in itself a breach of Article 10. Section 5 satisfies the necessary balance between the right to the freedom of expression and the right of others not to be insulted and distressed that is required by Article 10(2). However, the conviction was quashed on the particular application of s. 5 to the facts and the consequent failure to comply with Article 10. This was because, although there could be sufficient reason for a prosecution where it was necessary to limit freedom of expression (in this case, the denigration of an object of veneration or symbolic importance for one cultural group, namely the American flag), the response had to be proportionate. Since the District Judge had simply stated that it was proportionate, it was not clear that the proper test had been applied and so compliance with Article 10 was not established. See also *Norwood v DPP* [2003] Crim LR 888, where the Court decided that the mechanics of Article 10's operation on a prosecution under s. 5 are confined to the objective defence of reasonableness in s. 5(3). In assessing that reasonableness, regard must be had to all the circumstances, including those for which Article 10(2) provides. See also *Dehal v CPS* (2005) 169 JP 581. Further, in *Hammond v DPP* (2004) 168 JP 601 (a case on POA 1986, s. 5), the Divisional Court decided that, in determining whether words or behaviour are insulting (or threatening or abusive), the traditional approach under *Brutus v Cozens* [1973] AC 854 (see **B11.51**) is to be followed, and also that full account must be taken of the provisions under the ECHR that are concerned with the freedom of expression. In the context of a prosecution under the POA, s. 5, the ECHR issues may also arise in considering whether the defendant's conduct was reasonable (s. 5(3)(c)). The relevant provisions of the ECHR were Articles 10 (freedom of expression) and 9 (freedom of religion) and the justices had appropriately structured the questions (along the lines indicated above in *Percy*) in deciding that H's banner (which bore the words: 'Stop Immorality', 'Stop Homosexuality', and 'Stop Lesbianism' and, in the corners, the words 'Jesus is Lord') did involve a breach of s. 5.

Threatening, Abusive or Insulting Words or Behaviour; Disorderly Behaviour; Writing

For the meaning of the phrase 'threatening, abusive or insulting', see **B11.51**. This element of the offence and that of causing harassment, alarm or distress are separate and different; the two must not be equated. The approach in *Brutus v Cozens* [1973] AC 854 (i.e. that words should be given their ordinary meaning: see **B11.51**) should be adopted in considering the meaning of disorderly behaviour. The disorderly behaviour need not be threatening, abusive or insulting nor is it necessary to prove any feeling of insecurity in an apprehensive sense (*Chambers v DPP* [1995] Crim LR 896). For the meaning of 'writing', see **B11.52**. **B11.69**

Display

The Divisional Court in *Chappell v DPP* (1988) 89 Cr App R 82 held that magistrates were correct to decide that the posting of an envelope, with writing containing abusive or insulting words concealed inside it, through a letter box could not amount to a 'display'. This approach might apply to envelopes containing threatening, abusive or insulting material even in public. **B11.70**

Within the Hearing or Sight of a Person Likely to be Caused Harassment, Alarm or Distress

Harassment, alarm and distress are alternatives. Distress, by its very nature, involves an element of emotional disturbance or upset, but harrassment does not (*Southard v DPP* [2006] EWHC 3449 (Admin)). 'Harassment' does not demand any element of apprehension about personal safety (*Chambers v DPP* [1995] Crim LR 896). **B11.71**

In *Taylor v DPP* (2006) 170 JP 485, it was held that there must be evidence that there was someone *able* to hear or see the accused's conduct, and that the prosecution does not have to call evidence that he or she did *actually* hear the words spoken or see the behaviour. To the extent that there was a difference of approach between Collins J and Silber J in *Holloway v DPP* [2004] EWHC 2621 (Admin), the preference was for the approach of the former.

In *Lodge v DPP* (1988) *The Times*, 26 October 1988, the Divisional Court decided that whether a person was likely to be caused harassment, alarm or distress is a matter of fact to be determined by the magistrates. The court indicated that it is sufficient if the other person in question, in that case a police officer, feels alarm (or harassment or distress) for someone else, for example a child.

In *DPP v Orum* [1989] 1 WLR 88, the Divisional Court decided that, where the only people present were the defendant, his girlfriend with whom he was having an argument and two police officers, a police officer can be a person likely to be caused harassment, alarm or distress. However, if an officer is the only other person present and he is not likely to be caused harassment, alarm or distress, no offence is committed, because the element of causation is lacking. However, the Court of Appeal in *Ball* (1989) 90 Cr App R 378, without reference to *Orum*, was of the opinion that in such circumstances a police officer could arrest the person because he could have reasonable cause to suspect that an offence had been committed, since the conduct in s. 5 does not have to be directed towards another person. As to the 'harassment' of police officers, see also *R v DPP* [2006] EWHC 1375 (Admin) and *Southard v DPP*.

Place of Commission of Offence

B11.72 **Public Order Act 1986, s. 5**

(2) An offence under this section may be committed in a public or a private place, except that no offence is committed where the words or behaviour are used, or the writing, sign or other visible representation is displayed, by a person inside a dwelling and the other person is also inside that or another dwelling.

The Divisional Court in *Chappell v DPP* (1988) 89 Cr App R 82 held that the delivery of a letter to a person within his or her own home, where he or she reads it and is alarmed or distressed by its contents, cannot be an offence under s. 5. Such conduct would constitute an offence contrary to the Malicious Communications Act 1988, s. 1(1). See also **B11.59**.

Mens Rea

B11.73 **Public Order Act 1986, s. 6**

(4) A person is guilty of an offence under section 5 only if he intends his words or behaviour, or the writing, sign or other visible representation, to be threatening, abusive or insulting, or is aware that it may be threatening, abusive or insulting or (as the case may be) he intends his behaviour to be or is aware that it may be disorderly.

Whether the accused had the intention or awareness is to be tested subjectively in the light of the whole evidence, the burden of proof beyond a reasonable doubt lying upon the prosecution (*DPP v Clarke* (1991) 94 Cr App R 359). The accused must intend the behaviour to be disorderly or be aware that it might be disorderly (*Chambers v DPP* [1995] Crim LR 896).

For the effect of voluntary, self-induced intoxication on *mens rea*, see the discussion in relation to the offence of riot at **B11.28**.

Specific Defence

B11.74 **Public Order Act 1986, s. 5**

(3) It is a defence for the accused to prove—
(a) that he had no reason to believe that there was any person within hearing or sight who was likely to be caused harassment, alarm or distress, or
(b) that he was inside a dwelling and had no reason to believe that the words or behaviour used, or the writing, sign or other visible representation displayed, would be heard or seen by a person outside that or any other dwelling, or
(c) that his conduct was reasonable.

The burden of proving this defence lies on the accused on the balance of probabilities (see **F3.5** and **F3.40**), but the imposition of a legal burden upon the accused is open to challenge in the light of the human rights cases on the 'reverse burden' (see **F3.13 *et seq.***). An objective test must be used to assess the conduct referred to in s. 5(3)(c) (*DPP v Clarke* (1991) 94 Cr App R 359; *Kwasi Poku v DPP* [1993] Crim LR 705; *Morrow v DPP* [1994] Crim LR 58; *Lewis v DPP* (1996 unreported).

Police Powers

As to a constable's power to issue directions to stop the harassment of a person at his home, see B11.62. **B11.75**

Related Offence

It is an offence, contrary to the Air Navigation Order 2000 (SI 2000 No. 1562) art. 67, (a) to use any threatening, abusive or insulting words towards an aircraft crew member, (b) to behave in a threatening, abusive, insulting or disorderly manner towards an aircraft crew member, or (c) to interfere intentionally with the performance by an aircraft crew member of his duties. The offences mentioned in (a) and (b) are triable summarily only. On conviction the maximum penalty is a fine not exceeding level 4 on the standard scale (art. 122(5) and sch. 12, part A). The offence mentioned in (c) is triable either way. The maximum penalty on conviction on indictment is a term of imprisonment not exceeding two years, a fine, or both; on summary conviction, the maximum penalty is a fine not exceeding the statutory maximum. **B11.76**

Alternative Offence

The summary offence of being drunk and disorderly (see **B11.218**) may be an appropriate alternative offence. **B11.77**

Part B Offences

PUTTING PEOPLE IN FEAR OF VIOLENCE

Protection from Harassment Act 1997, s. 4 **B11.78**

(1) A person whose course of conduct causes another to fear, on at least two occasions, that violence will be used against him is guilty of an offence if he knows or ought to know that his course of conduct will cause the other so to fear on each of those occasions.

The CDA 1998, s. 32 created a racially or religiously aggravated form of this offence. For the meaning of 'racially or religiously aggravated', see **B11.160** ***et seq.***

Procedure

The offence is triable either way (Protection from Harassment Act 1997, s. 4(4)) and, when tried on indictment, is a class 3 offence. The racially aggravated form of the offence is also triable either way (CDA 1998, s. 32(4)). If, on trial on indictment, the jury find the accused not guilty of racially aggravated harassment, they may find him guilty of the basic offence (s. 32(6)). **B11.79**

Section 4(5) provides that if, on trial on indictment for this offence, a person is found not guilty, the jury may find him guilty of the offence under s. 2 (see **B11.87** ***et seq.***). If convicted of the offence under s. 2, the Crown Court has the same powers and duties in relation to that person as a magistrates' court would have on convicting him of the offence (s. 4(6)).

A judge who rules that there is no case to answer on an indictment alleging an offence under s. 4 may nevertheless allow the jury to consider an alternative verdict of harassment, contrary to s. 2 (*Livesey* [2006] EWCA Crim 3344, applying *Carson* (1990) 92 Cr App R 236).

Sentencing Guidelines (Basic Offence)

The maximum penalty is five years, a fine or both on indictment; six months, a fine not exceeding the statutory maximum, or both, summarily (Protection from Harassment Act 1997, s. 4(4)). The court has power on conviction for the offence under s. 4 to impose a restraining order on the offender under s. 5 of the Act. See **E23.13**. **B11.80**

When tried summarily, the Magistrates' Courts Guidelines (2004) provide for a first-time offender pleading not guilty:

Aggravating Factors For example disregard of warning; excessive persistence; interference with employment/business; invasion of victim's home; involvement of others; threat to use weapon or substance (including realistic imitations); use of violence or grossly offensive material; where photographs or images of a personal nature are involved; offence committed on bail; relevant previous convictions and any failures to respond to previous sentences.

Mitigating Factors For example initial provocation; short duration.

Guideline: Is it so serious that only custody is appropriate?

A restraining order should be considered. Racial or religious aggravation cannot be taken into account by the sentencer when sentencing for the basic offence (see **B11.47**); see **E1.9** for increase in sentence, under the CJA 2003, s. 146, for aggravation relating to disability or sexual orientation.

In *Hill* [2000] 1 Cr App R (S) 8, a sentence of 12 months was appropriate for an offender who pleaded guilty to an offence under s. 4. He had persistently telephoned a girl aged 13 and made sexual threats to her. A similar sentence was upheld in *Onabanjo* [2001] 2 Cr App R (S) 27. See also *Jones* [2002] 1 Cr App R (S) 536.

Sentencing Guidelines (Racially or Religiously Aggravated Form of Offence)

B11.81 The maximum penalty is seven years, a fine or both on indictment; six months, a fine not exceeding the statutory maximum, or both, summarily (CDA 1998, s. 32(4)). A restraining order may be made (s. 37(7)).

The Magistrates' Courts Guidelines (2004) provide a higher guideline for this offence when tried summarily than for the basic offence, the guideline being whether magistrates' sentencing powers are appropriate. A restraining order should be considered.

The Court of Appeal stated in *Saunders* [2000] 1 Cr App R 458 and in *Kelly* [2001] 2 Cr App R (S) 341, that when sentencing for the racially aggravated form of an offence the sentencer should indicate the appropriate sentence for the offence in the absence of racial aggravation and then add a further term for the racial element. See further **B2.26**.

Course of Conduct

B11.82 **Protection from Harassment Act 1997, s. 7**

(3) A 'course of conduct' must involve—
  (a) in the case of conduct in relation to a single person (see section 1(1)), conduct on at least two occasions in relation to that person, or
  (b) in the case of conduct in relation to two or more persons (see section 1(1A)), conduct on at least one occasion in relation to each of those persons.

(3A) A person's conduct on any occasion shall be taken, if aided, abetted, counselled or procured by another—
  (a) to be conduct on that occasion of the other (as well as conduct of the person whose conduct it is); and
  (b) to be conduct in relation to which the other's knowledge and purpose, and what he ought to have known, are the same as they were in relation to what was contemplated or reasonably foreseeable at the time of the aiding, abetting, counselling or procuring.

(4) 'Conduct' includes speech.

(5) References to a person, in the context of the harassment of a person, are references to a person who is an individual.

Section 7(3) was amended, and s. 7(5) was added, by the SOCPA 2005, s. 125(7), in consequence of the introduction of the offence (contrary to s. 1(1A)) where two or more persons are harassed (see **B11.87**).

How separate the two occasions must be remains to be seen. The nature of stalking, the activity which primarily created the need for the new offences, might mean that the occasions are likely to be on separate days, although it may be possible to differentiate activities on one day where they can be viewed as not being continuous. The further apart the incidents, the less likely it is that they will be regarded as a course of conduct. See *Lau v DPP* [2000] Crim LR 580. It was recognised, however, that circumstances can be conceived 'where incidents, as far apart as a year, could constitute a course of conduct'. The type of incidents would be those intended to occur on an annual event such as a religious festival or a birthday. Further, the fewer the number of incidents, the less likely that there would be a course of conduct. In *R (A) v DPP* [2004] EWHC 2454 (Admin), it was confirmed that there must be at least two occasions where the threats or other conduct giving rise to the fear of violence have been made or carried out by the accused.

'Conduct' would appear to allow different events to occur, but nevertheless may be regarded as contributing to a course of conduct. In *R (Taffurelli) v DPP* [2004] EWHC 2791 (Admin), it was accepted that the deliberate failure to control dogs following a number of complaints could constitute conduct.

As to the general approach to interpretation of this statute, see **B11.91** *et seq.*

Other Elements of the Offence

B11.83 'Violence' is not defined in the Protection from Harassment Act 1997. As to the similar, though not identical, concept defined for the purposes of the POA 1986, see **B11.24** and **B11.42**.

The accused's conduct must cause the complainant to fear that violence will be used against him; it is not sufficient if it seriously frightened the complainant as to what might happen (*Henley* [2000] Crim LR 582; *Caurti v DPP* [2002] Crim LR 131). It is always a question of fact (*Caurti* and *R (Simon Howard) v DPP* [2001] EWHC Admin 17) and, whilst it can be inferred from the evidence, there should, if possible, be direct evidence from the complainant (*R v DPP* [2001] Crim LR 396 and *Caurti*).

Mens Rea

B11.84 **Protection from Harassment Act 1997, s. 4**

(2) For the purposes of this section, the person whose course of conduct is in question ought to know that it will cause another to fear that violence will be used against him on any occasion if a reasonable person in possession of the same information would think the course of conduct would cause the other so to fear on that occasion.

In expanding upon what the accused ought to know, *Kelly v DPP* (2002) 166 JP 621 held that the effect of s. 4(2) is that fear must have been caused on each occasion within the course of conduct, but this is not a requirement for the offence under ss. 1 and 2 (see **B11.87** *et seq.*). A direction under s. 4(2) should be routinely given (*Henley* [2000] Crim LR 582).

Defences

B11.85 **Protection from Harassment Act 1997, ss. 4 and 12**

4.—(3) It is a defence for a person charged with an offence under this section to show that—
(a) his course of conduct was pursued for the purpose of preventing or detecting crime,
(b) his course of conduct was pursued under any enactment or rule of law or to comply with any condition or requirement imposed by any person under any enactment, or
(c) the pursuit of his course of conduct was reasonable for the protection of himself or another or for the protection of his or another's property.

12.—(1) If the Secretary of State certifies that in his opinion anything done by a specified person on a specified occasion related to—
(a) national security,
(b) the economic well-being of the United Kingdom, or
(c) the prevention or detection of serious crime,
and was done on behalf of the Crown, the certificate is conclusive evidence that this Act does not apply to any conduct of that person on that occasion.

In s. 12, 'specified' means specified in the certificate in question (s. 12(2)). A document purporting to be such a certificate is to be received in evidence and, unless the contrary is proved, treated as being such a certificate (s. 12(3)). For consideration of when the course of conduct may be reasonable, see **B11.97**.

As the burden of proof appears to lie upon the accused, it could be open to challenge under the HRA 1998, see **F3.13**.

In *Kellett v DPP* [2001] EWHC Admin 107, the Divisional Court held that the accused goes well beyond conduct that is reasonable if, rather than simply reporting that a person was at home when the accused contended she should be working, the accused alleged fraud and an extortionate salary on the part of the other person.

Police Powers

B11.86 As to a constable's power to issue directions to stop the harassment of a person at his home, see **B11.62**.

OFFENCE OF HARASSMENT

B11.87

Protection from Harassment Act 1997, ss. 1, 1A and 2

1.—(1) A person must not pursue a course of conduct—
(a) which amounts to harassment of another, and
(b) which he knows or ought to know amounts to harassment of the other.

(1A) A person must not pursue a course of conduct—
(a) which involves harassment of two or more persons, and
(b) which he knows or ought to know involves harassment of those persons, and
(c) by which he intends to persuade any person (whether or not one of those mentioned above)—
(i) not to do something that he is entitled or required to do, or
(ii) to do something that he is not under any obligation to do.

2.—(1) A person who pursues a course of conduct in breach of section 1(1) or (1A) is guilty of an offence.

Section 1(1A) was inserted by SOCPA 2005, s. 125(2).

The CDA 1998, s. 32, created a racially or religiously aggravated form of this offence. For the meaning of 'racially or religiously aggravated, see **B11.160** ***et seq.***

See **B11.82** for the definition of 'course of conduct'.

Procedure

B11.88 The basic offence is triable summarily only (Protection from Harassment Act 1997, s. 2(2)). The aggravated form of the offence is triable either way. A judge who rules that there is no case to answer on an indictment alleging an offence under s. 4 of the Act may nevertheless allow the jury to consider an alternative verdict of harassment, contrary to s. 2 (*Livesey* [2006] EWCA Crim 3344, applying *Carson* (1990) 92 Cr App R 236).

Sentencing Guidelines (Basic Offence)

B11.89 The maximum penalty is imprisonment for six months, a fine not exceeding the statutory maximum, or both (Protection from Harassment Act 1997, s. 2(2)). The court has power on conviction for the offence under s. 2 to impose a restraining order on the offender under s. 5 of the Act. See E23.13.

The Magistrates' Courts Guidelines (2004) refer to the same aggravating and mitigating factors as apply to the offence under s. 4 (see **B11.81**), except for 'threat to use weapon or substance' which does not appear in the guidelines for s. 2. The Guideline is lower than that for the s. 4 offence. Magistrates should consider whether the offence is serious enough for a community penalty. A restraining order should be considered.

Racial or religious aggravation cannot be taken into account by the sentencer when sentencing for the basic offence of harassment. See **B11.47**.

Sentencing Guidelines (Racially or Religiously Aggravated Form of Offence)

The maximum penalty is two years, a fine or both on indictment; six months, a fine not exceeding the statutory maximum, or both, summarily (CDA 1998, s. 32(3)). A restraining order may be made (s. 32(7)). **B11.90**

The Magistrates' Courts Guidelines (2004) provide a higher guideline for this offence when tried summarily than for the basic offence, the guideline being whether the offence is so serious that only custody is appropriate. A restraining order should be considered.

The Court of Appeal stated in *Saunders* [2000] 1 Cr App R 458 and in *Kelly* [2001] 2 Cr App R (S) 341, that when sentencing for the racially aggravated form of an offence the sentencer should indicate the appropriate sentence for the offence in the absence of racial aggravation and then add a further term for the racial element. See further **B2.26**.

Elements of the Offence

Course of Conduct There must be a course of conduct (see **B11.82**), which must amount to harassment. Thus, not all courses of conduct will satisfy this offence. In *Lau v DPP* [2000] Crim LR 580, the Divisional Court held that, although only two incidents are necessary, the fewer the number of incidents and the further apart they are, the less likely that there will be a finding of harassment. See also *Woolford v DPP* (9 May 2000 unreported). See also *Hills* [2001] 1 FLR 580 and *Pratt v DPP* (2001) *The Times*, 22 August 2001. Following *Pratt*, the Court of Appeal in *Patel* [2005] 1 Cr App R 440 decided that the incidents must be so connected in type and in context as to justify the conclusion that they can amount to a course of conduct. In *Baron v Crown Prosecution Service* (13 June 2000 unreported), the court accepted that the more spread out and limited in number the incidents and the more indirect their means of delivery (in this case by letter), the less likely that there was a course of conduct which amounted to harassment. However, there is no rule and it will depend upon the facts of each individual case. In this case two letters sent some four and a half months apart could be a course of conduct amounting to harassment. In *Kelly v DPP* (2002) 166 JP 621, it was decided that it is possible for a number of calls made over a short space of time (three calls in five minutes) to amount to a course of conduct, taking into account the separate and distinct nature of the calls. The space of time between them was only one relevant factor. Listening to the messages at the same time did not prevent them from amounting to a course of conduct. Some incidents will not amount to harassment, such as the presentation of an unwanted gift, but they can be the background against which further events are viewed and, if repeated, they may become harassment (*King v DPP* (2000) *Independent*, 31 July 2000). So, the fact that an accused performs a number of acts, more than two, does not mean that there is harassment, though there may be a course of conduct. Where there is a continuing offence, it is possible to take into account events occurring outside the six-month limitation period imposed by the Magistrates' Courts Act 1980, s. 127, provided that at least one of the incidents occurred within that time period (*DPP v Baker* (2005) 169 JP 140). **B11.91**

Two or More Persons Harassed The problems caused where there are two or more persons being harassed (see *DPP v Dunn* [2001] 1 Cr App R 352, *Caurti v DPP* [2002] Crim LR 131 and *DPP v Dziurzynski* (2002) 166 JP 545) are resolved by the introduction of a specific statutory solution in the Protection from Harassment Act 1997, s. 1(1A) (see **B11.87**). **B11.92**

Publication by Press as Harassment It has been held by the Court of Appeal, Civil Division, in *Thomas v News Group Newspapers Ltd* (2001) *The Times*, 25 July 2001, that the **B11.93**

publication of press articles is, in law, capable of amounting to harassment, although only in very rare circumstances. Whether conduct is reasonable depends upon the circumstances of the particular case. It was common ground between the parties that, before press publications are capable of constituting harassment, they must be attended by some exceptional circumstances which justifies sanctions and the restriction on the freedom of expression (under the ECHR, Article 10) that they involve. An example of such conduct amounting to harassment which was agreed by the parties to that case was the publication of press articles calculated to incite racial hatred of an individual.

B11.94 **Indirect Awareness** A person may be aware of a course of conduct, or parts of it, indirectly. So, the offence was complete when the victim knew of the relevant telephone calls made by the defendant, even though that knowledge came from being informed by a third party, provided there was evidence on the basis of which the court can properly conclude that the defendant was pursuing a course of conduct with the necessary *mens rea* (*Kellett v DPP* [2001] EWHC Admin 107).

Definition of Harassment

Protection from Harassment Act 1997, s. 7

B11.95 (2) References to harassing a person include alarming the person or causing the person distress.

In *DPP v Ramsdale* (2001) *Independent*, 19 March 2001, the Divisional Court took the view that the definition of harassment in s. 7 is inclusive and not exhaustive. Harassment includes negative emotion by repeated molestation, annoyance or worry. The words 'alarm, and distress' are to be taken disjunctively and not conjunctively. There is a minimum level of alarm or distress which must be suffered in order to constitute harassment.

References to a person, in the context of the harassment of a person, are references to a person who is an individual (Protection from Harassment Act 1997, s. 1(5)).

For concepts similar to, if not identical with, 'harassment', 'alarm' and 'distress' in the 1997 Act, see the POA 1986, ss. 4A and 5, and **B11.58** and **B11.71**. The courts, in view of the individual's right to protest and demonstrate about issues of public interest, will resist any attempts to interpret the statute widely (*Huntingdon Life Sciences Ltd v Curtin* (1997) *The Times*, 11 December 1997). However, 'whatever may have been the purpose behind [the Act], its words are clear, and it can cover harassment of any sort' (*DPP v Selvanayagam* (1999) *The Times*, 23 June 1999, per Collins J). This is subject to the defences mentioned at **B11.97**, one of which was the issue in *Selvanayagam*.

Mens Rea

B11.96 The *mens rea* for this offence, as defined in the Protection from Harassment Act 1997, s. 1(1)(b), is that the accused knows or ought to know that the course of conduct amounts to harassment of the other. Assistance in understanding, and thus determining, when a defendant ought so to know is provided by s. 1(2).

Protection from Harassment Act 1997, s. 1

(2) For the purposes of this section, the person whose course of conduct is in question ought to know that it amounts to or involves harassment of another if a reasonable person in possession of the same information would think the course of conduct amounted to or involved harassment of the other.

In *Colohan* [2001] EWCA Crim 1251, it was decided that s. 1(2) contains an objective test of what a reasonable person would think and in that case the submission that the relevant characteristics of the accused (schizophrenia) should be attributed to the reasonable person was rejected. If an accused intends to cause alarm or distress and actually does so, that is likely to meet the requirements of s. 1(1)(b) (*Baron v Crown Prosecution Service* (13 June 2000 unreported)).

Lawful Courses of Conduct

Protection from Harassment Act 1997, s. 1 **B11.97**

(3) Subsection (1) or (1A) does not apply to a course of conduct if the person who pursued it shows—
(a) that it was pursued for the purpose of preventing or detecting crime;
(b) that it was pursued under any enactment or rule of law or to comply with any condition or requirement imposed by any person under any enactment, or
(c) that in the particular circumstances the pursuit of the course of conduct was reasonable.

It would appear not to be sufficient for the accused to show that it was either his opinion that one of these conditions was satisfied or that it was reasonable to believe that one of these conditions was satisfied, although reasonableness may enter the calculation through the requirements needed to satisfy s. 1(3)(a) and (b) (see, e.g., the Criminal Law Act 1967, s. 3(1), and the PACE 1984, s. 24). The requirement in s. 1(3)(c) poses an objective test, namely whether the conduct of the accused is, in the judgment of the jury or magistrates, reasonable; there is no warrant for attaching to the word 'reasonable' or via the words 'particular circumstances' the standards or characteristics of the accused himself (*Colohan* [2001] EWCA Crim 1251). The imposition of a legal burden upon the accused is open to challenge in the light of the human rights cases on the 'reverse burden' (see **F3.13** ***et seq.***).

In *DPP v Selvanayagam* (1999) *The Times*, 23 June 1999, the Divisional Court considered the relevance of an injunction to the question of whether the course of conduct being pursued by M and S was reasonable. The injunction was in force against S (and others), but not against M. The terms of the injunction were crucial. It endeavoured to prevent harassment (defined as in the 1997 Act) of H and his family. Thus it was difficult to see how the course of conduct in contravention of the injunction and being harassment could be reasonable. There might be circumstances in which it was necessary for those covered by the injunction to go on to the other's land, but to make this of relevance they would have to explain away a course of conduct and not merely one emergency entry on to that land. In the case of M, it was not sufficient to be aware of the existence of the injunction. M would have to be aware of its specific terms. M was not sufficiently aware, and so the defence of reasonableness of the course of conduct was open for consideration. In the balancing exercise to determine reasonableness, the existence, in general terms, of the injunction would be relevant, though it would have little impact. On a more general level, when engaging in the balancing of different interests (such as the right of peaceful protest and the right to quiet enjoyment of property) the courts may have to get involved in the same sort of exercise as occurs when considering the exercise of the police powers to prevent a breach of the peace. It does not follow that it is always the first party's rights that are protected (e.g., to process). They may, in effect, be held responsible for the reaction of the other party. Priority will, however, always be given, where possible, to lawful activity that is not (deliberately) provocative. For consideration of this problem, see *Redmond-Bate v DPP* (1999) 163 JP 789.

For the special defence relating to national security etc., see s. 12 at **B11.85**.

Police Powers

As to a constable's power to issue directions to stop the harassment of a person at his home, see **B11.62**. **B11.98**

Related Offence

The Protection from Harassment Act 1997, s. 3(6), makes it an offence, where the High Court or a county court has granted an injunction under s. 3(3)(a) (which may be imposed to restrain the defendant in a claim in civil proceedings by a person who is the victim of harassment within s. 1 from pursuing any conduct which amounts to harassment), for a person, without reasonable excuse, to do anything which he is prohibited from doing by **B11.99**

B Part B Offences

such an injunction. Such conduct is not punishable as a contempt of court (s. 3(7)) nor can a person be convicted of this offence for any conduct which has been punished as a contempt of court (s. 3(8)). A person guilty of this offence is liable, on conviction on indictment, to imprisonment for a term not exceeding five years or a fine or both; and, on summary conviction, to imprisonment for a term not exceeding six months or a fine not exceeding the statutory maximum or both (s. 3(9)).

HARASSMENT OF A PERSON IN HIS HOME

Definition

B11.100 Criminal Justice and Police Act 2001, s. 42A

(1) A person commits an offence if—

(a) that person is present outside or in the vicinity of any premises that are used by any individual ('the resident') as his dwelling;

(b) that person is present there for the purpose (by his presence or otherwise) of representing to the resident or another individual (whether or not one who uses the premises as his dwelling), or of persuading the resident or such another individual—

(i) that he should not do something that he is entitled or required to do; or

(ii) that he should do something that he is not under any obligation to do;

(c) that person—

(i) intends his presence to amount to the harassment of, or to cause alarm or distress to, the resident; or

(ii) knows or ought to know that his presence is likely to result in the harassment of, or to cause alarm or distress to, the resident; and

(d) the presence of that person—

(i) amounts to the harassment of, or causes alarm or distress to, any person falling within subsection (2); or

(ii) is likely to result in the harassment of, or to cause alarm or distress to, any such person.

Section 42A was inserted by SOCPA 2005, s. 126.

Procedure and Sentence

B11.101 The offence is triable summarily only (CJPA 2001, s. 42A(4)).

The maximum penalty is imprisonment for a term not exceeding six months, or a fine not exceeding level 4 on the standard scale, or both.

Elements of the Offence

B11.102 Criminal Justice and Police Act 2001, s. 42A

(2) A person falls within this subsection if he is—

(a) the resident,

(b) a person in the resident's dwelling, or

(c) a person in another dwelling in the vicinity of the resident's dwelling.

(3) The references in subsection (1)(c) and (d) to a person's presence are references to his presence either alone or together with that of any other persons who are also present.

'Dwelling' has the same meaning as in the POA 1986, part 1 (s. 42A(7)).

In addition to s. 42A(1)(c), above, a person (A) ought to know that his presence is likely to result in the harassment of, or to cause alarm or distress to, a resident if a reasonable person in possession of the same information would think that A's presence was likely to have that effect (s. 42A(4)).

Police Powers

B11.103 As to a constable's powers to issue directions to stop the harassment of a person in his home, see B11.62.

PUBLIC NUISANCE

Definition

In recent times, the Court of Appeal has expressed approval of the following definitions of public nuisance: B11.104

> Public nuisance is an offence at common law. A person is guilty of a public nuisance (also known as a common nuisance) who (a) does an act not warranted by law, or (b) omits to discharge a legal duty, if the effect of the act or omission is to endanger the life, health, property, morals, or comfort of the public, or to obstruct the public in the exercise or enjoyment of rights common to all Her Majesty's subjects. (*Goldstein* [2004] 2 All ER 589 at [3].)

> A common nuisance is an act not warranted by law or an omission to discharge a legal duty, which act or omission obstructs or causes inconvenience or damage to the public in the exercise of rights common to all of His Majesty's subjects. (*Stephen's Digest of Criminal Law*, confirmed in *A-G v PYA Quarries Ltd* [1957] 2 QB 169, per Romer LJ, *Madden* [1975] 1 WLR 1379 and *Shorrock* [1994] QB 279.)

> Nuisance, nocumentum, or annoyance, signifies anything that worketh hurt, inconvenience, or damage. And nuisances are of two kinds; public or common nuisances, which affect the public, and are an annoyance to all the King's subjects; for which reason we must refer them to the class of public wrongs, or crimes and misdemeanours; and private nuisances, which are the objects of our present consideration, and may be defined, anything done to the hurt or annoyance of the lands, tenements or hereditaments of another. (*Blackstone's Commentaries*, confirmed in *A-G v PYA Quarries Ltd* [1957] 2 QB 169 and quoted, with apparent approval, in *Shorrock* [1994] QB 279.)

The courts do not have power to abolish the offence (*Rimmington* [2006] 1 AC 459 at [31]).

Procedure and Limit on Prosecution

It is a common-law offence, triable either way, for a person to cause a public nuisance. When tried on indictment, it is a class 3 offence. B11.105

The House of Lords in *Rimmington* [2006] 1 AC 459 has made clear that this offence should not ordinarily be prosecuted where there is a statutory offence covering the relevant mischief. Lord Bingham said (at [30]):

> It cannot in the ordinary way be a reason for resorting to the common law offence that the prosecutor is freed from mandatory time limits or restrictions on penalty. It must rather be assumed that Parliament imposed the restrictions which it did having considered and weighed up what the protection of the public reasonably demanded. I would not go to the length of holding that conduct may never be lawfully prosecuted as a generally expressed common law crime where it falls within the terms of a specific statutory provision, but good practice and respect for the primacy of statute do in my judgment require that conduct falling within the terms of a specific statutory provision should be prosecuted under that provision unless there is good reason for doing otherwise.

The statutory offences that may be prosecuted include the following (as identified by Lord Bingham in *Rimmington* at [29]): statutory nuisance under the Environmental Protection Act 1990, s. 79(1); dumping of waste under the Environmental Protection Act 1990, s. 33; polluting controlled waters under the Water Resources Act 1991, s. 85; wilfully obstructing the highway under the Highways Act 1980, s. 137; harassment under the Protection from Harassment Act 1997, ss. 1 and 4; racially or religiously aggravated offences under the CDA 1998, s. 32; dealing with raves, etc. under the CJPO 1994, s. 63; bomb hoaxes under the Criminal Law Act 1977, s. 51; sending substances inducing someone to believe they are noxious under the Anti-terrorism, Crime and Security Act 2001, s. 114; sending by post matter that is obscene or indecent or is likely to injure a postal worker under the Postal Services Act 2000, s. 85; sending malicious etc. communications under the Malicious

Communications Act 1988, s. 1; and improperly using a public electronic communications network under the Communications Act 2003, s. 127.

Sentence

B11.106 On conviction on indictment, the maximum sentence is at the discretion of the court. On summary conviction, the statutory maxima apply. In *Ruffell* (1992) 13 Cr App R (S) 204, the offender organised an 'acid house' party in unsuitable premises which was attended by a large number of people. A road leading to the site was blocked by traffic, local residents were disturbed by noise throughout the night, and litter and excrement were deposited in adjoining woodlands. He pleaded guilty to causing a public nuisance. A 12-month suspended prison sentence was upheld by the Court of Appeal but a fine imposed in addition was quashed because of the offender's lack of means. A sentence of four years for conspiracy to cause a public nuisance was upheld in *Ong* [2001] 1 Cr App R (S) 404, where the offenders arranged with others to cause the abandoning of a Premiership football match by switching off the floodlights. Had the scheme succeeded the offenders stood to make a substantial sum from betting on the outcome of the match.

Private and Public Nuisance

B11.107 The torts and the crime are closely connected: 'public nuisance is defined by reference to private nuisance and as differing from private nuisance only in the range of its effect' (*Shorrock* [1994] QB 279). The idea that public nuisance could be committed by isolated acts or isolated acts in a series (which originated from Denning LJ's judgment in *A-G v PYA Quarries Ltd* [1957] 2 QB 169) was firmly rejected by the House of Lords in *Rimmington* [2006] 1 AC 459 (at [37]):

> to permit a conviction of causing a public nuisance to rest on an injury caused to separate individuals rather than on an injury suffered by the community or a significant section of it as a whole was to contradict the rationale of the offence and pervert its nature

See further **B11.110**.

Where someone suffers particular damage as a result of a public nuisance they may sue in tort for public nuisance.

Nuisance

B11.108 There must be conduct by the accused which 'renders the enjoyment of life and property uncomfortable' (*White* (1775) 1 Burr 333, per Lord Mansfield) or 'materially affects the reasonable comfort and convenience of a class of Her Majesty's subjects' (*A-G v PYA Quarries Ltd* [1957] 2 QB 169, approved by the Court of Appeal in *Johnson* [1996] 2 Cr App R 434).

Professor Sir John Smith has stated that 'the interference with the public's rights must be substantial and unreasonable' (*Smith and Hogan on Criminal Law* (9th ed., 1999) at p. 755). Thus, as he points out, not all obstructions of the highway amount to a public nuisance (see, e.g., *Dwyer v Mansfield* [1946] KB 437 and *DPP v Jones* [1999] 2 AC 240).

Criminal convictions have for example been successful in the following circumstances:

(a) the accused was responsible for a house which was ruinous and likely to fall down thus endangering people using the highway (*Watts* (1757) 1 Salkeld 357);
(b) the accused carried her child whilst infected with smallpox along the public highway, thus incurring the risk of infecting others (*Vantandillo* (1815) 4 M & S 73);
(c) the accused took a horse infected with a contagious disease along the highway thus risking infecting others (*Henson* (1852) Dears 24);
(d) the accused sold meat unfit for human consumption (*Stephens* (1866) LR 1 QB 702);

(e) the accused caused 30 houses and the highway to be affected by dust and noise from its quarry (*A-G v PYA Quarries Ltd* [1957] 2 QB 169);
(f) the accused sniffed glue in a school playground when staff and pupils were absent (*Sykes v Homes* [1985] Crim LR 791, holding that it was a nuisance within the Local Government (Miscellaneous Provisions) Act 1982, s. 40 — whether it would be a public nuisance would depend upon the public nature of the nuisance);
(g) the accused allowed a rave to take place in his field (*Shorrock* [1994] QB 279).

Act or Omission

It is clear that a public nuisance may be caused by either an act (see, e.g., *Vantandillo* (1815) 4 M & S 73 and *A-G v PYA Quarries Ltd* [1957] 2 QB 169) or an omission (see, e.g., *Watts* (1757) 1 Salkeld 357 and *Shorrock* [1994] QB 279; see also *A-G v Tod Heatley* [1897] 1 Ch 560, where it was held that it was the duty of the owner of land to prevent it from being used as a dumping ground which caused a public nuisance). **B11.109**

The Public Nature of the Nuisance

In order to establish that a crime has been committed, it is necessary to establish the essential public nature of the nuisance. It is clear that not all the public need be affected. But it must be established that the act or omission was sufficiently widespread or indiscriminate as to amount to a public rather than a private nuisance. In *A-G v PYA Quarries Ltd* [1957] 2 QB 169, Romer LJ stated: **B11.110**

> any nuisance is 'public' which materially affects the reasonable comfort and convenience of life of a class of Her Majesty's subjects. The sphere of the nuisance may be described generally as 'the neighbourhood'; but the question whether the local community within that sphere comprises sufficient number of persons to constitute a class of the public is a question of fact in every case. It is not necessary, in my judgment, to prove that every member of the class has been injuriously affected; it is sufficient to show that a representative cross-section of the class has been so affected for an injunction to issue.

In the same case, Denning LJ said, 'a public nuisance is a nuisance which is so widespread in its range or so indiscriminate in its effect that it would not be reasonable to expect one person to take proceedings on his own responsibility to put a stop to it, but that it should be taken on the responsibility of the community at large'. In that case, there was a public nuisance where 30 houses and the highway were affected by dust and noise from the workings of a quarry (see also *Mutters* (1864) Le & Ca 491).

In *Rimmington* [2006] 1 AC 459, the House of Lords held (at [12]) that 'a common injury is a, perhaps the, distinguishing feature of this offence.' Further (at [36]) that what must be looked for is whether the act of omission contemplated by the accused 'was likely to inflict significant injury on a substantial section of the public exercising their ordinary rights as such'. In consequence, the House overruled the decision in *Johnson* [1996] 2 Cr App R 434, where the conviction had been upheld after the accused had made hundreds of telephone calls to at least 13 women in South Cumbria. The error was that this was a series of acts involving individual members of the public and could not constitute the necessary effect on the public or a significant section of the public for there to be a public nuisance. So, per Lord Nicholls at [42], a telephone hoax call might involve a public nuisance if it was a call that an explosive device had been left at a railway station as opposed to a call which would only inconvenience the recipient. So R's conviction was quashed as he had sent offensive and racist messages to a series of individuals. G's conviction was quashed because of the lack of *mens rea*, but it was stated that, if the *mens rea* had been present, sending salt through the post anticipating that, if it leaked, it could be thought to be anthrax and its effect would be sufficiently serious to affect a section of the public could have been a public nuisance.

Mens Rea

B11.111 The 'requirement as to the accused's state of mind is the same whether the proceedings brought be civil or criminal. Actual knowledge of the nuisance need not be established'. The *mens rea*, therefore, is that the defendant is 'guilty of the offence charged if either he knew or he ought to have known, in the sense that the means of knowledge were available to him, that there was a real risk that the consequences of the licence granted by [the accused] in respect of his field [on which a rave took place] would be to create the sort of nuisance that in fact occurred' (*Shorrock* [1994] QB 279, approved in *Rimmington* [2006] 1 AC 459).

Vicarious Liability

B11.112 For the ordinary rules relating to vicarious liability, see A4.4. However, a master may be liable for a public nuisance even if the act of the servant is contrary to the master's orders (see *Stephens* (1866) LR 1 QB 702 and *Smith and Hogan on Criminal Law* (9th ed., 1999), p. 757). The decision in *Stephens* was doubted in *Chisholm v Doulton* (1889) 22 QBD 736. It remains to be seen whether such a rule will continue to apply and, if so, if it will apply consistently to all forms of public nuisance (a view the decision in *Shorrock* [1994] QB 279 may be interpreted as implicitly supporting, see *Smith and Hogan on Criminal Law*, p. 757).

Defences

B11.113 Statutory authorisation is a defence to public nuisance, provided that the statute covers that which is done (see *Hammersmith and City Railway Company v Brand and Louisa* (1868) LR 4 QB 171, *Managers of the Metropolitan Asylum District v Hill* (1881) LR 6 AC 193, *London, Brighton and South Coast Railway v Truman* (1885) LR 11 AC 45 and *Saunders v Holborn District Board of Works* [1895] 1 QB 64).

Compliance with the European Convention on Human Rights

B11.114 The House of Lords in *Rimmington* [2006] 1 AC 459 took the view that the offence of public nuisance did not breach ECHR, Article 7. It should be noted, first, that the House decided that it should be prosecuted rarely as it should be used only where there was no statutory nuisance that ordinarily ought to be prosecuted (see **B11.105**); secondly, the House emphasised the requirement of a sufficiently serious effect on the public or a section of it (see **B11.110**); finally, it confirmed the *mens rea* requirement (see **B11.111**). The standards that the House identified were, per Lord Bingham (at [35]) that the:

> offence must be clearly defined in law . . . and a norm cannot be regarded as a law unless it is formulated with sufficient precision to enable the citizen to foresee, if need be with appropriate advice, the consequences which a given course of conduct may entail. . . . It is accepted that absolute certainty is unattainable, and might entail excessive rigidity since the law must be able to keep pace with changing circumstances, some degree of vagueness is inevitable and development of the law is a recognised feature of common law courts . . . But the law-making function of the courts must remain within reasonable limits . . . existing offences may not be extended to cover facts which did not previously constitute a criminal offence. The law may be clarified and adapted to new circumstances which can reasonably be brought under the original concept of the offence. . . . But any development must be consistent with the essence of the offence and be reasonably foreseeable . . . and the criminal law must not be extensively construed to the detriment of an accused, for instance by analogy.

Lord Bingham took the view (at [36] and [37]) that these requirements would not have been met had the recent development moving the law away from the requirement for an effect on the public or a significant section of it not been re-emphasised.

BOMB HOAXES

Criminal Law Act 1977, s. 51 **B11.115**

(1) A person who—
  (a) places any article in any place whatever; or
  (b) dispatches any article by post, rail or any other means whatever of sending things from one place to another,

with the intention (in either case) of inducing in some other person a belief that it is likely to explode or ignite and thereby cause personal injury or damage to property is guilty of an offence.

In this subsection 'article' includes substance.

(2) A person who communicates any information which he knows or believes to be false to another person with the intention of inducing in him or any other person a false belief that a bomb or other thing liable to explode or ignite is present in any place or location whatever is guilty of an offence.

Procedure

Offences under the Criminal Law Act 1977, s. 51, are triable either way. When tried on indictment they are class 3 offences. **B11.116**

Indictment

First Count **B11.117**

Statement of Offence

Perpetrating bomb hoax contrary to section 51(1) of the Criminal Law Act 1977

Particulars of Offence

A on or about the . . . day of . . . placed an article, namely a parcel, in [or: dispatched by post (or rail etc.) an article, namely a parcel, to] the Dead Parrot Public House at . . . with the intention of inducing in V, the manager of the said house, a belief that the said parcel was likely to explode or ignite and thereby cause personal injury or damage to property therein

Second Count

Statement of Offence

Perpetrating bomb hoax contrary to section 51(2) of the Criminal Law Act 1977

Particulars of Offence

A on or about the . . . day of . . . communicated to V the information that a parcel containing a bomb liable to explode or ignite was present on the premises of the Dead Parrot Public House at . . ., knowing or believing the said information to be false and with the intention of inducing in V the false belief that it was true

Sentencing Guidelines

The maximum penalty is seven years on indictment; six months, a fine not exceeding the statutory maximum, or both, summarily (Criminal Law Act 1977, s. 51(4)). **B11.118**

In *Harrison* [1997] 2 Cr App R (S) 174, a sentence of four years' imprisonment was upheld on an offender who made a series of telephone calls to a theatre saying that a bomb had been planted. The offender had previous convictions for similar offences and was said to be suffering from a personality disorder but not mental illness. In *Dunbar* (1987) 9 Cr App R (S) 393, the offenders pleaded guilty to communicating a bomb hoax. They telephoned the police to say that incendiary devices had been placed in various stores, apparently in order to cause financial loss to the stores. Sentences of 12 months' imprisonment were upheld by the Court of Appeal, Leggatt J commenting that:

> A bomb hoax of this kind, as this court has had occasion to say in the past, is a public nuisance, and it is important not to underrate the anxiety and apprehension that this kind of behaviour

engenders. The public rightly expect judges to pass severe sentences as a mark of public disapprobation of this kind of offence.

In *Harris* [2005] 2 Cr App R (S) 649, the offender manufactured two devices designed to look like bombs. He took one to a police station and one to a restaurant. The premises and surrounding area had to be evacuated. There was no evidence that the offender suffered from a treatable mental disorder. Bearing in mind that his conduct had been more than a nuisance and had caused fear and disruption, a total sentence of three years' imprisonment was appropriate on a guilty plea.

Elements

B11.119 A call stating 'there is a bomb' is sufficient to comprise the offence, even though there is no reference to a place or location (*Webb* (1995) *The Times*, 19 June 1995).

By the Criminal Law Act 1977, s. 51(3), for a person to be guilty of an offence under s. 51(1) or (2), it is not necessary for him to have any particular person in mind as the person in whom he intends to induce the belief mentioned in the relevant subsection.

Related Offence

B11.120 It is an offence, contrary to the Fire and Rescue Services Act 2004, s. 49(1), if a person knowingly gives or causes to be given a false alarm of fire to a person acting on behalf of a fire and rescue authority. A person guilty of such an offence is liable, on summary conviction, to a fine not exceeding level 4 on the standard scale, or a term of imprisonment not exceeding three months, or to both (Fire and Rescue Services Act 2004, s. 49(2) and (3)).

CONTAMINATION OF OR INTERFERENCE WITH GOODS

B11.121 **Public Order Act 1986, s. 38**

(1) It is an offence for a person, with the intention—
 (a) of causing public alarm or anxiety, or
 (b) of causing injury to members of the public consuming or using the goods, or
 (c) of causing economic loss to any person by reason of the goods being shunned by members of the public, or
 (d) of causing economic loss to any person by reason of steps taken to avoid such alarm or anxiety, injury or loss,

to contaminate or interfere with goods, or make it appear that goods have been contaminated or interfered with, or to place goods which have been contaminated or interfered with, or which appear to have been contaminated or interfered with, in a place where goods of that description are consumed, used, sold or otherwise supplied.

(2) It is also an offence for a person, with any such intention as is mentioned in paragraph (a), (c) or (d) of subsection (1), to threaten that he or another will do, or claim that he or another has done, any of the acts mentioned in that subsection.

(3) It is an offence for a person to be in possession of any of the following articles with a view to the commission of an offence under subsection (1)—
 (a) materials to be used for contaminating or interfering with goods or making it appear that goods have been contaminated or interfered with, or
 (b) goods which have been contaminated or interfered with, or which appear to have been contaminated or interfered with.

Procedure

B11.122 Offences under the POA 1986, s. 38, are triable either way (POA 1986, s. 38(4)). When tried on indictment they are class 3 offences.

Indictment (for an Offence Contrary to s. 38(1)(a))

Statement of Offence B11.123

Contamination of goods contrary to section 38(1)(a) of the Public Order Act 1986

Particulars of Offence

A on or about the . . . day of . . . with the intention of causing public alarm or anxiety, placed certain goods, namely 100 jars of . . . brand honey which had been contaminated by the insertion of fragments of broken glass therein, in a place where goods of that description are sold to the public, namely V's department store, . . .

Sentence

The maximum penalty is 10 years, a fine or both, on indictment (POA 1986, s. 38(4)); six months, a fine not exceeding the statutory maximum, or both, summarily. In *Cruickshank* [2001] 2 Cr App R (S) 278, the offender pleaded guilty to contaminating food in a supermarket by inserting pins, needles or nails into various items. He persisted in this behaviour for three months, and some minor injuries were incurred by customers who bought the contaminated products. There was no logical explanation for the offender's behaviour, and no financial motive, but a medical disposal was not recommended. Three years' imprisonment was upheld by the Court of Appeal. Examples of cases involving *threats* to contaminate goods are *Witchelo* (1992) 13 Cr App R (S) 371 (see **B5.85**) and *Smith* (1994) 15 Cr App R (S) 106. B11.124

Meaning of 'Goods'

In the POA 1986, s. 38 'goods' includes substances whether natural or manufactured and whether or not incorporated in or mixed with other goods (s. 38(5)). B11.125

Meaning of 'Claim' that Acts Have Been Committed

The reference in the POA 1986, s. 38(2), to a person claiming that certain acts have been committed does not include a person who in good faith reports or warns that such acts have been, or appear to have been, committed (s. 38(6)). B11.126

PRISON MUTINY

The Prison Security Act 1992 created the offence of prison mutiny. For offences relating to the escape of prisoners, see **B14.64** ***et seq.*** B11.127

Prison Security Act 1992, s. 1

(1) Any prisoner who takes part in a prison mutiny shall be guilty of an offence and liable, on conviction on indictment, to imprisonment for a term not exceeding ten years or to a fine or to both.

(2) For the purposes of this section there is a prison mutiny where two or more prisoners, while on the premises of any prison, engage in conduct which is intended to further a common purpose of overthrowing lawful authority in that prison.

(3) For the purposes of this section the intentions and common purpose of prisoners may be inferred from the form and circumstances of their conduct and it shall be immaterial that conduct falling within subsection (2) above takes a different form in the case of different prisoners.

(4) Where there is a prison mutiny, a prisoner who has or is given a reasonable opportunity of submitting to lawful authority and fails, without reasonable excuse, to do so shall be regarded for the purposes of this section as taking part in the mutiny.

(5) Proceedings for an offence under this section shall not be brought except by or with the consent of the Director of Public Prosecutions.

(6) In this section—
'conduct' includes acts and omissions;

'prison' means any prison, young offender institution or remand centre which is under the general superintendence of, or is provided by, the Secretary of State under the Prison Act 1952, including a contracted out prison within the meaning of part IV of the Criminal Justice Act 1991;

'prisoner' means any person for the time being in a prison as a result of any requirement imposed by a court or otherwise that he be detained in legal custody.

Sentences of up to nine years' imprisonment were upheld in *Lambert* [2006] 2 Cr App R (S) 107 for the instigators of a prison mutiny at Lincoln prison. During the riot, which lasted for several hours and spread to all parts of the prison, a prison officer was attacked and knocked unconscious, there were numerous other instances of violence, and damage in excess of £2 million was caused. The offenders were convicted after a trial which lasted for 13 weeks. In *Mitchell* (1995) 16 Cr App R (S) 924, custodial sentences of five years were upheld in respect of two offenders convicted of prison mutiny. They had taken a leading part in an incident involving 120 remand prisoners which had caused extensive damage at Reading prison.

The offence may be committed in one of two ways as found in s. 1(2) and (4). Section 1(2) is committed where there is a common purpose and that is aimed at overthrowing lawful authority in the prison. This latter requirement is a stronger word than 'subversion' and is not synonymous with 'widespread failure to follow lawful orders'; it is limited to serious disturbances and does not cover a mere defiance of, or challenge to, that lawful authority. The offence in s. 1(4) is committed on a deemed basis and is parasitic to the commission of the s. 1(2) offence. An indictment should make clear on which basis the offence is charged (*Mason* [2005] 1 Cr App R 145). Where the s. 1(4) offence is charged, the prosecution must prove that there was a prison mutiny and that the defendant participated in it at some stage (*Griffin* (17 August 1999 unreported)).

CONTROL OF PROCESSIONS, ASSEMBLIES AND MEETINGS

Advance Notice of Public Procession

B11.128 It is an offence, contrary to the POA 1986, s. 11(7), for a person organising a public procession to fail to satisfy the requirements in s. 11 concerning the giving of notice of the procession to the police. Having given notice, an organiser commits an offence if the date when the procession is held, the time when it starts or its route differ from the date, time or route specified in the notice. The offence is triable only summarily and is punishable with a fine not exceeding level 3.

It is a defence, under s. 11(8), for the accused to prove that he did not know of, and neither suspected nor had reason to suspect, the failure to satisfy the requirements or (as the case may be) the difference of date, time or route. It is also a defence, under s. 11(9), when the offence turns on a difference of date, time or route, for the accused to prove that the difference arose from circumstances beyond his control or from something done with the agreement of a police officer or by his direction.

Failure to Comply with Conditions Imposed on Public Procession

B11.129 Under the POA 1986, s. 12, conditions may be imposed on public processions. Conditions may be imposed either in advance or at the time of the procession by the senior police officer acting under s. 12(1) to (3). It is an offence, triable only summarily:

(a) for a person who organises a public procession knowingly to fail to comply with a condition (s. 12(4)) (see *DPP v Baillie* [1995] Crim LR 426);

(b) for a person who takes part in such a procession knowingly to fail to comply with a condition (s. 12(5));

(c) for a person to incite another to commit an offence under s. 12(5) (s. 12(6)).

In the case of the organiser's offence and the offence committed by a person taking part, it is a defence to prove that the failure to comply with a condition arose from circumstances beyond the accused's control.

The maximum penalty for the organiser's offence and the inciter's offence is imprisonment for a term not exceeding three months or a fine not exceeding level 4 or both. A person who commits an offence by taking part in a procession is liable to a fine not exceeding level 3.

Contravening Prohibition of Public Procession

Under the POA 1986, s. 13, a public procession may be prohibited. Where the procession is to take place outside the City of London or the metropolitan police district, it is the district council, on application from the chief officer of police and with the approval of the Secretary of State, which may make a procession prohibition order (s. 13(1) to (3)). In the City of London or the metropolitan police district, it is the relevant Commissioner, with the approval of the Secretary of State, who may make a procession prohibition order (s. 13(4)). **B11.130**

It is an offence, triable only summarily:

(a) for a person to organise a public procession the holding of which he knows to be prohibited (s. 13(7));
(b) for a person to take part in a public procession the holding of which he knows to be prohibited (s. 13(8));
(c) for a person to incite another to commit an offence under s. 13(8) (s. 13(9)).

The maximum penalty for the organiser's offence and the inciter's offence is imprisonment for a term not exceeding three months or a fine not exceeding level 4 or both. A person who commits an offence by taking part in a procession is liable to a fine not exceeding level 3.

Failure to Comply with Conditions Imposed on Public Assembly

Under the POA 1986, s. 14, conditions may be imposed on public assemblies. Conditions may be imposed either in advance or at the time of the assembly by the senior police officer acting under s. 14(1) to (3). It is an offence, triable only summarily: **B11.131**

(a) for a person who organises a public assembly knowingly to fail to comply with a condition (s. 14(4)) (see *DPP v Baillie* [1995] Crim LR 426);
(b) for a person who takes part in such an assembly knowingly to fail to comply with a condition (s. 14(5)) (see *Broadwith v DPP* [2000] All ER (D) 225;
(c) for a person to incite another to commit an offence under s. 14(5) (s. 14(6)).

The term 'public assembly' means an assembly of 2 or more persons in a public place which is wholly or partly open to the air (s. 16).

In the case of the organiser's offence and the offence committed by a person taking part, it is a defence to prove that the failure to comply with a condition arose from circumstances beyond the defendant's control.

The maximum penalty for the organiser's offence and the inciter's offence is imprisonment for a term not exceeding three months or a fine not exceeding level 4 or both. A person who commits an offence by taking part in an assembly is liable to a fine not exceeding level 3.

Contravention of Prohibition of Trespassory Assembly

Under the POA 1986, s. 14A, the chief officer of police has the power, if he reasonably believes that it is intended to hold a trespassory assembly which may result in serious disruption to the life of the community or significant damage to the land, building or monument which is of historical, archaeological or scientific importance, to apply to the district council **B11.132** for an order prohibiting for a specified period the holding of all trespassory assemblies in the district or part of it, but the order must not last for more than four days and must not apply to an area greater than that represented by a circle of five miles radius from a specified centre. The council must receive the consent of the Secretary of State for the making of such an order. The Metropolitan Police Commissioner or the Commissioner of the City of London Police may make such an order with the consent of the Secretary of State.

It is an offence, triable only summarily:

(a) for a person to organise an assembly which he knows is prohibited by an order under s. 14A (s. 14B(1));
(b) for a person to take part in an assembly which he knows is prohibited by such an order (s. 14B(2));
(c) for a person to incite another to commit an offence under s. 14B(2) (s. 14B(3)).

An assembly is not trespassory where the user of the highway is reasonable. This is determined by the ordinary law. Use of the highway is not restricted to the right of passage and matters incidental or ancillary to it. The public has the right to use the public highway for any reasonable and usual mode, including peaceful assembly on the highway, as is consistent with and does not obstruct the general public's primary right of passage. Further the use of the highway must not amount to a public or private nuisance (*DPP v Jones* [1999] 2 AC 240).

The maximum penalty for the organiser's offence and the inciter's offence (notwithstanding the MCA 1980, s. 45(3), which sets the offence for incitement as the same as for the substantive offence) is imprisonment for a term not exceeding three months or a fine not exceeding level 4 on the standard scale or both (s. 14B(5) and (7)). A person who commits an offence by taking part is liable to a fine not exceeding level 3 on the standard scale (s. 14B(6)).

A constable in uniform has power, which may be exercised only within the area to which an order under s. 14A applies, to stop someone he reasonably believes to be on his way to an assembly prohibited by an order under s. 14A and to direct him not to proceed in the direction of the assembly (s. 14C(1) and (2)). A person who fails to comply with such a direction which he knows has been given commits a summary offence punishable with a fine not exceeding level 3 on the standard scale (s. 14C(3) and (5)).

Dispersal of Groups and Removal of Persons under 16 to Their Place of Residence

B11.133 Where a relevant officer has reasonable grounds for believing (a) that any members of the public have been intimidated, harassed, alarmed or distressed as a result of the presence or behaviour of groups of two or more persons in public places in any locality in his police area (the 'relevant locality'), and (b) that anti-social behaviour is a significant and persistent problem in the relevant locality, that officer may give an authorisation that the powers conferred on a constable under the ASBA 2003, s. 30(3) to (6) are to be exercisable for a period specified in the authorisation which does not exceed six months (ASBA 2003, s. 30(1) and (2)). Any reference to the presence or behaviour of a group of persons is to be read as including a reference to the presence or behaviour of any one or more of the persons in the group (s. 30(7)).

A constable's powers to give directions are subject to the requirement in s. 30(3) that the constable in uniform must have reasonable grounds for believing that the presence or behaviour of a group of two or more persons in any public place in the relevant locality has resulted, or is likely to result, in any members of the public being intimidated, harassed, alarmed or distressed. If so, the constable may, under s. 30(4), give one or more of the following directions: (a) a direction requiring the persons in the group to disperse (either immediately or by such time as he may specify and in such was as he may specify), (b) a direction requiring any of those persons whose place of residence is not within the relevant locality to leave it or any part of it (either immediately or by such time as he may specify and in such way as he may specify), and (c) a direction prohibiting any of those persons whose place of residence is not within the relevant locality from returning to it or any part of it for such period (not exceeding 24 hours) from the beginning of the direction as he may specify. The direction may be given orally, to any person individually or to two or more persons together, and may be withdrawn or varied by the person who gave it: s. 32(1). Mere presence in a designated dispersal area, whilst capable of being the basis for the forming of a belief under s. 30(3), was not normally sufficient for giving a direction under s. 30(4). Unless there were exceptional circumstances, a reasonable belief under s. 30(4) had normally to depend, in part at least, on some behaviour by the group indicating that harassment, alarm, intimidation or distress had resulted or would result (*MB v DPP* (2007) 171 JP 10).

Such a direction may not be given in respect of a group of persons (a) who are engaged in conduct which is lawful under the Trade Union and Labour Relations (Consolidation) Act 1992, s. 220, or (b) who are taking part in a public procession within the meaning of the POA 1986, s. 11(1) in respect of which (i) written notice has been given in accordance with s. 11, or (ii) such notice is not required as provided by s. 11(1) and (2) ASBA 2003, s. 30(5)). If, between the hours of 9 pm and 6 am, a constable in uniform finds a person in any public place in the relevant locality who he has reasonable grounds for believing (a) is under the age of 16, and (b) is not under the effective control of a parent or a responsible person aged 18 or over, he may remove the person to their place of residence unless he has reasonable grounds for believing that the person would, if removed to that place, be likely to suffer significant harm (s. 30(6)). There are supplemental provisions with regard to the issuing of an authorisation by the relevant officer to be found in ss. 31 and 32(4). A person who knowingly contravenes a s. 30(4) direction commits an offence and, on summary conviction, is liable to imprisonment for not more than three months, a fine not exceeding level 4 on the standard scale, or both (s. 32(2)).

Meaning of 'Removal' In *R (W) v Metropolitan Police Commissioner* [2006] 3 WLR 1098 it was held that the word 'remove' in s. 30(6) naturally and compellingly means 'take away using reasonable force if necessary'. It was also held that s. 30(6) does not have an illegitimate curfew effect. The constable is not free to act arbitarily, he must act for the purpose for which the power was conferred. There are two purposes: (a) to protect children under 16 within a designated dispersal area at night from the physical and social risks of anti-social behaviour by others; (b) to prevent children from themselves participating in anti-social behaviour within a designated dispersal area at night. There is no power to remove a child simply because he is in the designated dispersal area. Further, the power should be exercised only if it is reasonable to do so and in so deciding constables must have regard to circumstances such as how young the child is, how late at night it is, whether the child is vulnerable or in distress, the child's explanation for his conduct and presence in the area, and the nature of the actual or imminently anticipated anti-social behaviour. **B11.134**

Protests In *R (Singh) v Chief Constable of West Midlands Police* [2007] 2 All ER 297 the appellant challenged the use of a s. 30 authorisation which had been created to deal with New Year revelries when used to deal with disturbances outside a theatre which was showing a play to which many Sikhs objected. First, the Court of Appeal held that s. 30 can be applied to protests. Secondly, it held that its usage was not a breach of Articles 9, 10 or 11 of the ECHR as, on the critical issue of proportionality, the evidence demonstrated that the police had considered the correct questions; these involved a recognition of the particular importance of the right to protest and the need to determine whether some alternative, less intrusive means could have been used. Thirdly, it held that there was no reason to restrict the use of the authorisation and bar its use in relation to matters that were not anticipated when it was originally made as that would be absurd and unworkable. **B11.135**

Miscellaneous Community support officers may also have the dispersal powers (s. 33). **B11.136**

For the meaning of 'anti-social behaviour', 'local authority', 'public place', 'relevant locality' and 'relevant officer', see s. 36.

Demonstrations without Authorisation in Designated Area

B11.137 Under the SOCPA 2005, s. 132(1), any person who (a) organises a demonstration in a public place in the designated area, or (b) takes part in a demonstration in a public place in the designated area, or (c) carries on a demonstration by himself in a public place in the designated area, is guilty of an offence if, when the demonstration starts, authorisation for the demonstration has not been given under s. 134(2). Sections 132 to 138 apply to demonstrations whenever they started, thus the provisions applied to a demonstration in Parliament Square that commenced in 2001 (*R (Haw) v Home Secretary* [2006] QB 780). It is a defence for a person accused of such an offence to show that he reasonably believed that authorisation had been given (s. 132(2)). Whether this offence, in imposing a burden on the accused, will survive challenge under the ECHR awaits a judicial decision, but the restrictions imposed by s. 132 on the right to demonstrate do not infringe the right to freedom of peaceful assembly provided in the ECHR, Article 11(1) because they can be justified under Article 11(2) (*Blum v DPP* [2006] EWHC 3209 (Admin)).

The offence does not apply where the demonstration is a public procession under the POA 1986, ss. 11(1), 11(2), 12 or 13 (s. 132(3)). Nor is it an offence if the Trade Union and Labour Relations (Consolidation) Act 1992, s. 220 applies (s. 132(4)). The POA 1986, s. 14, does not apply to such demonstrations (s. 132(6)). 'The designated area' means the area specified in an order under s. 138 (s. 132(7)(a)). 'Public place' means any highway or any place to which at the material time the public or any section of the public has access, on payment or otherwise, as of right or by virtue of express or implied permission (s. 132(7)(b)). References to any person organising a demonstration include a person participating in its organisation; references to any person organising a demonstration do not include a person carrying on a demonstration by himself, and references to any person or persons taking part in a demonstration (except in s. 132(1)) include a person carrying on a demonstration by himself: SOCPA 2005, s. 132(7)(c), (d) and (e). A person guilty of the offence contrary to s. 132(1)(a) is liable on summary conviction to imprisonment for a term not exceeding three months, a fine not exceeding level 4 on the standard scale or both (s. 136(1)). A person guilty of the offence contrary to s. 132(1)(b) or (c) is liable on summary conviction to a fine not exceeding level 3 on the standard scale.

A person may seek authorisation for a demonstration in a designated area (for the details, see ss. 133 to 135). Each person who takes part in or organises a demonstration in the designated area is guilty of an offence if (a) he knowingly fails to comply with a condition imposed under s. 134(3), which is applicable to him (except where it is varied under s. 135); or (b) he knows or should have known that the demonstration is carried on otherwise than in accordance with the particulars set out in the authorisation. It is a defence to show (in a paragraph (a) case) that the failure to comply, or (in a paragraph (b) case) that the divergence from the particulars, arose from circumstances beyond his control, or from something done with the agreement, or by the direction, of a police officer (s. 134(8)). Whether this burden survives a challenge under the ECHR awaits judicial decision. A person found guilty of this offence is liable on summary conviction (a) if the offence was in relation to his capacity as organiser of the demonstration, to imprisonment for a term not exceeding three months, a fine not exceeding level 4 on the standard scale, or both, (b) otherwise, to a fine not exceeding level 3 on the standard scale (s. 136(3)).

A person who takes part in or organises a demonstration and who knowingly fails to comply with a condition that is applicable to him and that is imposed or varied by a direction under s. 135 is guilty of an offence (s. 135(3)). For the ability to add or vary conditions to the authorisation given under s. 134, see s. 135(1) and (2). It is a defence for such a person to show that the failure to comply arose from circumstances beyond his control (s. 135(4)). A person found guilty of this offence is liable on summary conviction (a) if the offence was in relation to his capacity as organiser of the demonstration, to imprisonment for a term not exceeding three months, a fine not exceeding level 4 on the standard scale, or both, (b) otherwise, to a fine not exceeding level 3 on the standard scale (s. 136(3)).

Endeavouring to Break up a Public Meeting

It is an offence, contrary to the Public Meeting Act 1908, s. 1(1), for a person at a lawful public meeting to act in a disorderly manner for the purpose of preventing the transaction of the business for which the meeting was called together. The offence is triable summarily only. A person guilty of the offence is liable to imprisonment for a term not exceeding six months or to a fine not exceeding level 5 or to both. **B11.138**

There is no definition of either 'meeting' or 'public meeting' in the Public Meeting Act 1908 though there is in the POA 1936, s. 9. The case law that exists is concerned with whether the public meeting is lawful or not and indicates that a lawful meeting may be held on a highway, even if it might amount to an obstruction of that highway (*Burden v Rigler* [1911] 1 KB 337). Further, a public meeting does not cease to be lawful just because there is disorderly opposition from other persons (*Beatty v Gillbanks* (1882) 9 QBD 308, the authority of which does not, on this point, seem to be doubted by the Divisional Court in *Duncan v Jones* [1936] 1 KB 218). As to 'lawful' in the context of lawful courses of conduct, see **B11.97**.

It is an offence, contrary to the Public Meeting Act 1908, s. 1(2), to incite another person to commit an offence under s. 1; the offence is subject to similar punishment.

Failure to Comply with Constable's Request with Regard to Public Meeting

It is an offence, contrary to the Public Meeting Act 1908, s. 1(3), for a person to refuse or fail to declare his name and address when asked to do so by a constable who reasonably suspects the person of committing an offence under the Public Meeting Act 1908, s. 1(1) or s. 1(2) (see **B11.138**) if the constable has been requested to ask for them by the chairman of the meeting. It is an offence to give a false name and address in such circumstances. A person guilty of the offence is liable to a fine not exceeding level 1. **B11.139**

Illegal Electoral Practice with Regard to Public Meeting

It is one of the illegal electoral practices, contrary to the Representation of the People Act 1983, s. 97(1), for a person at a lawful public meeting to act, or incite others to act, in a disorderly manner for the purpose of preventing the transaction of the business for which the meeting was called together. The offence is triable summarily only. It is punishable on summary conviction with a fine not exceeding level 5. **B11.140**

'Lawful public meeting' in this offence means a political meeting held in any constituency between the date of the issue of the writ for the return of a Member of Parliament for the constituency and the date at which a return to the writ is made, or a meeting held with reference to a local government election in the electoral area for that election in the period beginning with the last date on which notice of the election may be published in accordance with the local government election rules and ending with the day of the election (Representation of the People Act 1983, s. 97(2)).

OFFENCES UNDER THE FOOTBALL (OFFENCES) ACT 1991

B11.141 The Football (Offences) Act 1991 creates three offences: throwing of missiles (s. 2), indecent or racialist chanting (s. 3) and going onto the playing area (s. 4).

Football (Offences) Act 1991, ss. 2, 3, and 4

2. It is an offence for a person at a designated football match to throw anything at or towards—
   (a) the playing area, or any area adjacent to the playing area to which spectators are not generally admitted, or
   (b) any area in which spectators or other persons are or may be present, without lawful authority or lawful excuse (which shall be for him to prove).

3.—(1) It is an offence to engage or take part in chanting of an indecent or racialist nature at a designated football match.

(2) For this purpose—
   (a) 'chanting' means the repeated uttering of any words or sounds (whether alone or in concert with one or more others); and
   (b) 'of racialist nature' means consisting of or including matter which is threatening, abusive or insulting to a person by reason of his colour, race, nationality (including citizenship) or ethnic or national origins.

4. It is an offence for a person at a designated football match to go onto the playing area, or any area adjacent to the playing area to which spectators are not generally admitted, without lawful authority of lawful excuse (which shall be for him to prove).

Sentence and Procedure

B11.142 The offences are all triable summarily only.

The maximum penalty is a fine not exceeding level 3 on the standard scale (s. 5(2)).

The Magistrates' Courts Guidelines (2004) indicate the following for a first-time offender pleading not guilty to an offence under s. 2 (throwing missiles):

Aggravating Factors For example object likely to cause injury (e.g., coin, glass, bottle, stone); racial or religious aggravation; offence committed on bail; relevant previous convictions and any failures to respond to previous sentences

Mitigating Factors None

Guideline: Is discharge or fine appropriate?

The guideline fine is Starting Point B (see **E17.5**).

The Magistrates' Courts Guidelines (2004) indicate the following for a first-time offender pleading not guilty to an offence under s. 4 (going on to the playing area):

Aggravating Factors For example being drunk; deliberate provocative act; inciting others; offence committed on bail; relevant previous convictions and any failures to respond to previous sentences

Mitigating Factors None

Guideline: Is discharge or fine appropriate?

The guideline fine is Starting Point A (see **E17.5**).

In relation to both offences under s. 2 and s. 4, the court must consider imposing a banning order. If no banning order is made, the court must give reasons. Community rehabilitation orders and curfew orders are the only available community sentences for these offences.

Elements

B11.143 A 'designated football match' is an association football match designated, or of a description designated, for the purposes of the Act by the Secretary of State. The Football (Offences)

(Designation of Football Matches) Order 2004 (SI 2004 No. 2410) designates football matches for this purpose.

References to things done at a designated football match include anything done at the ground:

(a) within the period beginning two hours before the start of the match or (if earlier) two hours before the time at which it is advertised to start and ending one hour after the end of the match,
(b) where the match is advertised to start at a particular time on a particular day but does not take place, within the period beginning two hours before and ending one hour after the advertised starting time (s. 1(2)).

When the phrase 'you're just a town of Pakis' was used at a football match, that was a chant of a racialist nature. The term 'Paki' was being used in a racially derogatory or insulting sense. It is possible that the context could make it non-racialist, so each use would have to be considered on a case-by-case basis (*DPP v Stoke on Trent Magistrates' Court* [2003] 3 All ER 1096).

OFFENCES UNDER THE FOOTBALL SPECTATORS ACT 1989

The Football Spectators Act 1989 was designed to control the admission of spectators at designated football matches and provided for the making of restriction orders on persons convicted of offences of violence or disorder at, or in connection with, such matches. In the light of the Taylor Report on the deaths which occurred at Hillsborough, many of its provisions, particularly those relating to a national football membership scheme, have not been, and are not likely to be, brought into force. However, the majority of the provisions relating to the grant of licences to admit spectators and the whole of part II (which concerns football matches taking place outside England and Wales) are in force. **B11.144**

Under s. 9, it is an offence to admit spectators to watch a designated football match unless it is played at licensed premises. By virtue of s. 10(13), it is a summary offence for any responsible person to contravene any term or condition of a licence granted to admit spectators to any premises for the purpose of watching any designated football match played there. It is a defence, in accordance with s. 10(14), for an accused to prove that the contravention took place without his consent and that he took all reasonable precautions and exercised all due diligence to avoid the commission of such an offence. The relevant licences are those issued by the Football Licensing Authority under the Football Spectators (Seating) Order 2006 (SI 2006 No. 1661). The Football Spectators (Prescription) Order 2004 (SI 2004 No. 2409) (as amended by SI 2006 No. 761) designates matches for the purposes of the Act.

As to banning orders and other powers to exclude persons from football matches, see E23.3.

TICKET TOUTS

Criminal Justice and Public Order Act 1994, s. 166 **B11.145**

(1) It is an offence for an unauthorised person to—
  (a) sell a ticket for a designated football match, or
  (b) otherwise to dispose of such a ticket to another person.

Sentence and Procedure

The offence is triable summarily (CJPO 1994, s. 166(3)). **B11.146**

The maximum sentence is a fine not exceeding level 5 on the standard scale (CJPO 1994, s. 166(3)).

The Magistrates' Courts Guidelines (2004) indicate the following for a first-time offender pleading not guilty to an offence under s. 166:

> **Aggravating Factors** For example commercial operation; counterfeit tickets; in possession of a large number of tickets/potential high value; sophisticated operation; offence committed on bail; relevant previous convictions and any failures to respond to previous sentences
>
> **Mitigating Factors** For example single ticket
>
> *Guideline*: Is discharge or fine appropriate?

The guideline fine is Starting Point B (see E17.5). The court must consider imposing a banning order. If no banning order is made, the court must give reasons. Community rehabilitation orders and curfew orders are the only available community sentences for this offence.

Elements

B11.147 A person is 'an unauthorised person' unless he is authorised in writing to sell tickets for the match by the organisers of the match; 'ticket' means anything which purports to be a ticket; and 'selling' a ticket includes offering to sell it, exposing it for sale, making it available for sale by another; advertising that it is available for purchase; and giving it to a person who pays or agrees to pay for some other goods or services or offers to do so (CJPO 1994, s. 166(2)). For the meaning of 'designated football match', see the Ticket Touting (Designation of Football Matches) Order 2007 (SI 2007 No. 790).

Search of Person and Premises

B11.148 The PACE 1984, s. 32, has effect in relation to an offence under the CJPO 1994, s. 166, as if the power conferred on a constable to enter and search any vehicle extended to any vehicle which the constable has reasonable grounds for believing was being used for any purpose connected with the offence (s. 166(5)).

INTIMIDATION OR ANNOYANCE BY VIOLENCE OR OTHERWISE

B11.149 **Trade Union and Labour Relations (Consolidation) Act 1992, s. 241**

(1) A person commits an offence who, with a view to compelling another person to abstain from doing or to do any act which that person has a legal right to do or abstain from doing, wrongfully and without legal authority—
   (a) uses violence to or intimidates that person or his wife or children, or injures his property,
   (b) persistently follows that person about from place to place,
   (c) hides any tools, clothes or other property owned or used by that person, or deprives him of or hinders him in the use thereof,
   (d) watches or besets the house or other place where that person resides, works, carries on business or happens to be, or the approach to any such house or place, or
   (e) follows that person with two or more other persons in a disorderly manner in or through any street or road.

(2) A person guilty of an offence under this section is liable on summary conviction to imprisonment for a term not exceeding six months or a fine not exceeding level 5 on the standard scale, or both.

Sentence and Procedure

B11.150 An offence under the Trade Union and Labour Relations (Consolidation) Act 1992, s. 241, is triable summarily only.

The maximum penalty is six months and/or a fine not exceeding level 5 (Trade Union and Labour Relations (Consolidation) Act 1992, s. 241(2)).

Elements

It was made clear by the Divisional Court in *Todd v DPP* [1996] Crim LR 344 that the offence is not limited to trade disputes. It can, therefore, apply to someone engaged in an anti-roads protest (as in *Todd*) and might apply, for example, to stalking (see also Professor Sir John Smith at [1996] Crim LR 345). The general elements of the offence are, first, the *mens rea*, which is dealt with below and, secondly, the requirements that the act be done 'wrongfully' and 'without lawful authority'. No special consideration has been given to the phrase 'without lawful authority' apart from the creation of a defence for trade unions acting in contemplation or furtherance of a dispute, which is treated as a defence, below. **B11.151**

Meaning of 'Wrongfully' Scott J in *Thomas v National Union of Mineworkers (South Wales Area)* [1986] Ch 20 decided that the authorities established that conduct must, in order to be an offence under what was, prior to consolidation, the Conspiracy, and Protection of Property Act 1875, s. 7, be tortious (at p. 61). This approach to the question of whether there is a wrongful act does indeed seem to be consistent with the existing case law. The Court of Appeal in *Ward, Lock & Co. Ltd v Operative Printers' Assistants' Society* (1906) 22 TLR 327 clearly took the view that s. 7 (now the Trade Union and Labour Relations (Consolidation) Act 1992, s. 241) was concerned only to provide a criminal remedy to what was already recognised as being a civil wrong. Thus in order for the criminal remedy to be available, it had to be established that what was done was a civil wrong, without reference to the provisions of the Act. **B11.152**

Intimidates The Court of Appeal in *Jones* (1974) 59 Cr App R 120, whilst not wishing to define 'intimidation' exhaustively, said that: **B11.153**

> . . . 'intimidate' in this section includes putting persons in fear by the exhibition of force or violence or the threat of force or violence, and there is no limitation restricting the meaning to cases of violence or threats of violence to the person.

In *Connor v Kent* [1891] 2 QB 545, the court also did not want to attempt an exhaustive definition of the word, preferring instead to make clear (at p. 559) that 'intimidate' is 'a word of common speech and everyday use; and it must receive, therefore, a reasonable and sensible interpretation according to the circumstances of the cases as they arise from time to time'. Further assistance may be gleaned from the decision of Stuart-Smith J in *News Group Newspapers Ltd v SOGAT 82 (No. 2)* [1987] ICR 181, at pp. 204–5, considering the related tort of intimidation.

Persistently Follows In *Smith v Thomasson* (1890) 62 LT 68, Hawkins J stated that: 'It is impossible to define generally what is "persistently following"'. However, it was held dogging of a workman's footsteps could amount to 'persistently following' him. See also *Elsey v Smith* 1982 SCCR 218. **B11.154**

Deprivation of Property The Court of Appeal in *Fowler v Kibble* [1922] 1 Ch 487 made clear the significance of the requirement that the activity must be wrongful separately from a consideration of the section creating the offence. Thus there could be no offence where a workman did not let miners who were not members of a particular union have safety lamps because such an act of deprivation was not unlawful. **B11.155**

Watches or Besets In general, it would seem that the words 'watch' and 'beset' are viewed as words of the ordinary English language, see, e.g., *J. Lyons & Sons v Wilkins* [1899] 1 Ch 811 and *Ward, Lock & Co. Ltd v Operative Printers' Assistants' Society* (1906) 22 TLR 327. The High Court of Justiciary in *Gatt v Philp* 1983 JC 51 took the view that the essence of the offence comprised preventing access to and egress from somewhere. Thus a sit-in satisfied this element of the offence. **B11.156**

The watching and besetting must be 'wrongful', that is, unlawful without reference to s. 241. Thus, e.g., in *J. Lyons & Sons v Wilkins* [1899] 1 Ch 811, careful consideration was given to the question of whether the activity amounted to a nuisance and was therefore 'wrongful' and within the ambit of the section. The length of time the people were present was relevant, since that would help determine whether there was a nuisance. Consequently, lawful picketing is not 'watching and besetting' unless it amounts to a nuisance, or some other tort or other wrong such as obstruction of the highway (see, e.g., *News Group Newspapers Ltd v SOGAT 82 (No. 2)* [1987] ICR 181 and *Walters v Green* [1899] 2 Ch 696; see also *Bonsall* [1985] Crim LR 150).

In *Charnock v Court* [1899] 2 Ch 35 and *Farmer v Wilson* (1900) 69 LJ QB 496, it was made clear that the offence is committed when any place where the person happens to be is watched and beset, whether or not such persons are in the service or employment of any person. This latter point in *Farmer v Wilson* makes clear that the offence is not solely concerned with employment disputes.

B11.157 **Following in a Disorderly Manner** Whether the following is in a disorderly manner is a question of fact in each case, and therefore will depend upon the conduct of the defendant and all the circumstances of the particular case, see *McKenzie* [1892] 2 QB 519 and *Elsey v Smith* 1982 SCCR 218.

Mens Rea: With a View to Compel Any Other Person

B11.158 This is a *mens rea* requirement importing not motive but purpose according to the Divisional Court in *DPP v Fidler* [1992] 1 WLR 91, explaining *J. Lyons & Sons v Wilkins* [1899] 1 Ch 255. The Divisional Court stated that purpose is a more objective concept not concerned with the different motives with which members of the group might have joined, for example, a demonstration. The court also decided that the accused's purpose must be one to compel and not merely to persuade (see also *Bonsall* [1985] Crim LR 150 and *McKenzie* [1892] 2 QB 519). It is not necessary to show that the compulsion was in any way effective (*Agnew v Munro* (1891) 18 R (J) 22). The phrase 'such other person' refers back to the person whom the defendant has a view to compel to abstain from doing or to do something (*J. Lyons & Sons v Wilkins* [1899] 1 Ch 811).

Application to Trade or Employment Disputes

B11.159 **Trade Union and Labour Relations (Consolidation) Act 1992, s. 220**

(1) It shall be lawful for a person in contemplation or furtherance of a trade dispute to attend—
  (a) at or near his own place of work, or
  (b) if he is an official of a trade union, at or near the place of work of a member of that union whom he is accompanying and whom he represents,

  for the purpose only of peacefully obtaining or communicating information, or peacefully persuading any person to work or abstain from working.

(2) If a person works or normally works—
  (a) otherwise than at any one place, or
  (b) at a place the location of which is such that attendance there for a purpose mentioned in subsection (1) above is impracticable,

  his place of work for the purposes of that subsection shall be any premises of his employer from which he works or from which his work is administered.

(3) In the case of a worker who is not in employment where—
  (a) his last employment was terminated in connection with a trade dispute, or
  (b) the termination of his employment was one of the circumstances giving rise to a trade dispute,

  in relation to that dispute his former place of work shall be treated for the purposes of subsection (1) as being his place of work.

(4) A person who is an official of a trade union by virtue only of having been elected or appointed to be a representative of some of the members of the union shall be regarded for the purposes of subsection (1) above as representing only those members; but otherwise an official of a trade union shall be regarded for those purposes as representing all its members.

RACIALLY OR RELIGIOUSLY AGGRAVATED OFFENCES

The CDA 1998 introduced a series of racially aggravated offences, i.e. existing offences which are racially aggravated according to the definition in s. 28. These provisions have been extended by the Anti-terrorism, Crime and Security Act 2001, s. 39, so as to include religiously aggravated offences. **B11.160**

Crime and Disorder Act 1998, s. 28

(1) An offence is racially or religiously aggravated for the purposes of sections 29 to 32 below if—

(a) at the time of committing the offence, or immediately before or after doing so, the offender demonstrates towards the victim of the offence hostility based on the victim's membership (or presumed membership) of a racial or religious group; or

(b) the offence is motivated (wholly or partly) by hostility towards members of a racial or religious group based on their membership of that group.

(2) In subsection (1)(a) above—

'membership', in relation to a racial or religious group, includes association with members of that group;

'presumed' means presumed by the offender.

(3) It is immaterial for the purposes of paragraph (a) or (b) of subsection (1) above whether or not the offender's hostility is also based, to any extent, on any other factor not mentioned in that paragraph.

(4) In this section 'racial group' means a group of persons defined by reference to race, colour, nationality (including citizenship) or ethnic or national origins.

(5) In this section 'religious group' means a group of persons defined by reference to religious belief or lack of religious belief.

The offences which may be racially or religiously aggravated are an offence contrary to the OAPA 1861, ss. 20 and 47 and common assault (CDA 1998, s. 29: see **B2.1**, **B2.22** and **B2.37**), criminal damage (CDA 1998, s. 30: see **B8.1**), offences contrary to the POA 1986, ss. 4, 4A and 5 (CDA 1998, s. 31: see **B11.45**, **B11.55** and **B11.64**) and harassment contrary to the Protection from Harassment Act 1997, ss. 2 and 4 (CDA 1998, s. 32: see **B11.78** and **B11.87**). In each case, the court must first establish that the basic offence has been committed and then consider whether it was racially or religiously aggravated within the meaning of s. 28. The racially or religiously aggravated form of each offence carries a higher maximum penalty than the ordinary form of the offence and this is reflected by significantly higher sentences in practice (see *Kelly* [2001] 1 Cr App R (S) 341; *Bridger* [2006] EWCA Crim 3169 and **E1.9**).

If the offence is not one of those to which s. 28 applies, it is for the sentencer to decide whether it was racially aggravated and, if it was, to treat this as an aggravating factor in sentencing (CJA 2003, s. 145). See generally *Rogers* [2007] 2 WLR 280.

Racial or Religious Groups By the CDA 1998, s. 28(4), a 'racial group' means a group of persons defined by reference to race, colour, nationality (including citizenship) or ethnic or national origins. This definition is derived from that used in the Race Relations Act 1976 and is also used in the POA 1986, s. 17 (see **B11.169**). A broad and non-technical approach to this definition has been adopted in the context of s. 28. In *Rogers* [2007] 2 WLR 280, the House of Lords was asked, 'Do those who are not of British origin constitute a racial group within s. 28(4)?' The unanimous answer was 'yes'. 'Foreigners' likewise constitute such a group; and of course it follows that those who are of British origin must enjoy the same legal protection as those who are not: each forms for these purposes a 'racial group', even though many more racial groups exist within them. See also *DPP v M* [2004] 1 WLR 2758 and *A-G's Ref (No. 4 of 2004)* [2005] 1 WLR 2810. **B11.161**

Jews, Sikhs and Romany gypsies are recognised ethnic racial groups (see *Mandla v Dowell Lee*

[1983] 2 AC 548, *Commission for Racial Equality v Dutton* [1989] QB 783 and **B11.169**) but travellers and Rastafarians are not. The latter nevertheless share beliefs that identify them as members of a religious group (*Crown Suppliers (Property Services Agency) v Dawkins* [1993] ICR 517).

Although in other contexts 'religion' has been interpreted as involving a belief in some kind of god or supernatural being (*R v Registrar General, ex parte Segerdal* [1970] 2 QB 697), a much broader approach is clearly required in the context of s. 28. It is clear from s. 28(5) that a 'religious group' may for these purposes include a group defined by its lack of religious beliefs. If, for example, D assaults V because V is an atheist or humanist who rejects religious beliefs, D must be guilty of a religiously aggravated offence.

B11.162 **Proof of Hostility** A racially or religiously aggravated offence may but need not have been committed for racial or religious motives. It suffices if the accused formed the view that the victim was a member of a racial or religious group and then said or did something that demonstrated hostility towards him based on membership of that group. This will usually involve racist words or gestures, but may in some cases be manifested in other ways (see *Rogers* [2007] 2 WLR 280 per Baroness Hale at [13]).

To be guilty of an offence that is racially or religiously aggravated, it is not necessary that the accused be of a different racial, national or ethnic (or religious) group from the victim (*White* [2001] 1 WLR 1352). Section 28(2) specifically addresses the possibility that D's attack on V may be aggravated as a result of D's hostility to V's actual or supposed association with other groups. D may also be mistaken as to V's own race or religion.

In *DPP v Pal* [2000] Crim LR 756, Simon Brown LJ stated that, for the purposes of s. 28(1)(a), it will always be necessary for the prosecution to prove the demonstration of racial hostility, although the use of racially abusive insults will ordinarily be found sufficient. Following this, the Divisional Court in *DPP v McFarlane* [2002] EWHC 485 (Admin) decided that, where the expressions 'jungle bunny', 'black bastard' and 'wog' were used, the offence was properly made out as the words were used immediately before and at the time of the commission of the offence contrary to the POA 1986, s. 4 (see **B11.45** ***et seq.***), those words were of a racial nature, and they were racial, threatening and abusive towards the victim. The decision in *Pal*, where the words 'white man's arse licker' and 'brown Englishman' were used, was to be limited to its own particular facts, notably that both parties were Asian. Even so, *DPP v Pal* appears hard to reconcile with s. 28(2), as Baroness Hale noted in *Rogers* at [15].

The fact that the accused may have had some additional reason for his choice of words is immaterial (*McFarlane*; *DPP v Woods* [2002] EWHC 85 (Admin); *DPP v Green* (2004) *The Times*, 7 July 2004; *DPP v M*). Also irrelevant is the victim's perception of the incident and the fact that the accused's frame of mind was such that he would have abused any person standing where the complainant was by reference to an obvious physical characteristic, such as obesity or baldness (*Woods*). The accused need not act for any racial or religious motive (*DPP v Green*). It would nevertheless be wrong for charges of aggravated offences to be brought where vulgar abuse has included racial epithets that did not, when all the relevant circumstances are considered, indicate hostility to the victim on account of his race or religion (*Rogers* per Baroness Hale at [17]).

In *G and T v DPP* (2004) 168 JP 313, the Divisional Court considered the two routes to establishing racial aggravation of an offence. Section 28(1)(a) requires the prosecution to prove facts that indicate that the defendant had demonstrated racial hostility at the time of the committing the offence or immediately before or after doing so. This is not to prove the accused's state of mind, but what he did or said so as to demonstrate racial hostility towards the victim. The demonstration will often be by way of words, shouting, holding up a banner, etc. or by adherence to a group that is demonstrating racial hostility. Section 28(1)(b) is concerned with the accused's motivation, which does concern his state of mind. Often the evidence establishing this will involve the kind of demonstration referred to in relation to s. 28(1)(a). The prosecution may base its case on both of s. 28(1)(a) and (b) and cases may arise where it is legitimate to require the prosecution to make clear the basis upon which it is proceeding. In *Taylor v DPP* (2006) 170 JP 485, it was decided that use of phrases such as 'fucking nigger' and 'fucking coon bitch', patently not used in a jesting manner, must, in the circumstance of the case, have led any judge to find that the offence (in this case, the POA 1986, s. 5(1)(a)) was motivated, at least in part, by racial hostility as described in s. 28(1)(b). It is also clear that it is better that this matter be dealt with more explicitly, in particular that the two possible approaches in s. 28 be clearly identified and separated for the benefit of the jury.

Timing of Demonstration of Hostility The word 'immediately' in s. 28(1) qualifies both 'before' and 'after', and this means that the subsection deals with words uttered or acts done in the immediate context of the substantive offence, so it was not possible that the section was satisfied where the accused had quit the scene and used the relevant words when sitting in his own house (which was the next door house) some 20 minutes after the criminal damage had been caused (*Parry v DPP* [2004] EWHC 3112 (Admin)). **B11.163**

USING WORDS OR BEHAVIOUR OR DISPLAYING WRITTEN MATERIAL STIRRING UP RACIAL HATRED

Public Order Act 1986, s. 18 **B11.164**

(1) A person who uses threatening, abusive or insulting words or behaviour, or displays any written material which is threatening, abusive or insulting, is guilty of an offence if—
(a) he intends thereby to stir up racial hatred, or
(b) having regard to all the circumstances racial hatred is likely to be stirred up thereby.

Procedure

An offence under the POA 1986, s. 18, is triable either way. When tried on indictment it is a class 3 offence. No proceeding may be instituted except by, or with the consent of, the A-G (POA 1986, s. 27(3)). **B11.165**

For the liability of corporate officers, see **B11.175**.

Indictment

Statement of Offence **B11.166**

Displaying threatening, abusive or insulting material with intent to stir up racial hatred contrary to section 18 of the Public Order Act 1986

Particulars of Offence

A on or about the . . . day of . . . at . . . displayed certain threatening, abusive or insulting materials, namely a quantity of pamphlets entitled . . . with intent thereby to stir up racial hatred

The POA 1986, s. 27(2), declares that for the purposes of the rules against charging more than one offence in the same count, each of sections 18 to 23 of the Act creates one offence.

Sentencing Guidelines

The maximum penalty is seven years' imprisonment, a fine, or both, on indictment (POA 1986, s. 27(3)); six months, a fine not exceeding the statutory maximum, or both, summarily. **B11.167**

Relevant sentencing decisions are *Relf* (1979) 1 Cr App R (S) 111 and *Edwards* (1983) 5 Cr App R (S) 145. See, however, *Gray* [1999] 1 Cr App R (S) 50 at **B11.186**.

The court also has a power to order forfeiture where the accused is convicted of displaying written material.

Public Order Act 1986, s. 25

(1) A court by or before which a person is convicted of—
  (a) an offence under section 18 relating to the display of written material, or
  (b) an offence under section 19, 21 or 23,
  shall order to be forfeited any written material . . . produced to the court and shown to its satisfaction to be written material . . . to which the offence relates.
(2) An order made under this section shall not take effect—
  (a) in the case of an order made in proceedings in England and Wales, until the expiry of the ordinary time within which an appeal may be instituted or, where an appeal is duly instituted, until it is finally decided or abandoned . . .
(3) For the purposes of subsection (2)(a)—
  (a) an application for a case stated or for leave to appeal shall be treated as the institution of an appeal, and
  (b) where a decision on appeal is subject to a further appeal, the appeal is not finally determined until the expiry of the ordinary time within which a further appeal may be instituted or, where a further appeal is duly instituted, until the further appeal is finally decided or abandoned.

Meaning of 'Racial Hatred'

B11.168 The essence of the offence under the POA 1986, s. 18, lies in the use of words or behaviour or the display of material either when the accused intends to stir up racial hatred (s. 18(1)(a)) or where racial hatred is, in the circumstances, likely to be stirred up (s. 18(1)(b)). The concept of 'racial hatred' is therefore central to the offence.

Public Order Act 1986, s. 17

In this part [i.e. ss. 17 to 29] 'racial hatred' means hatred against a group of persons defined by reference to colour, race, nationality (including citizenship) or ethnic or national origins.

B11.169 **What is a Racial Group?** In the Race Relations Act 1976, 'racial group' is defined as meaning 'a group of persons defined by reference to colour, race, nationality or ethnic or national origins'. In *Mandla v Dowell Lee* [1983] 2 AC 548, it was necessary to determine whether the Sikhs are a 'racial group' for the purposes of the 1976 Act. The House of Lords was satisfied that it was necessary to determine whether Sikhs are a group defined by ethnic origins, since none of the other descriptions would distinguish them from at least some other groups of people. In holding that Sikhs are an ethnic group, Lord Fraser of Tullybelton said (at pp. 562D–563A):

> For a group to constitute an ethnic group in the sense of the Act of 1976, it must, in my opinion, regard itself, and be regarded by others, as a distinct community by virtue of certain characteristics. Some of these characteristics are essential; others are not essential but one or more of them will commonly be found and will help to distinguish the group from the surrounding community. The conditions which appear to me to be essential are these: (1) a long shared history, of which the group is conscious as distinguishing it from other groups, and the memory of which it keeps alive; (2) a cultural tradition of its own, including family and social customs and manners, often but not necessarily associated with religious observance. In addition to those two essential characteristics the following characteristics are, in my opinion, relevant; (3) either a common geographical origin, or descent from a small number of common ancestors; (4) a common language, not necessarily peculiar to the group; (5) a common literature peculiar to the group; (6) a common religion different from that of neighbouring groups or from the general community surrounding it; (7) being a minority or being an oppressed or a dominant group within a larger community, for example a conquered people (say the inhabitants shortly after the Norman conquest) and their conquerors might both be ethnic groups.
>
> A group defined by reference to enough of these characteristics would be capable of including converts, for example, people who marry into the group, and of excluding apostates. Provided a person who joins the group feels himself or herself to be a member of it, and is accepted by other members, then he is, for the purposes of the Act, a member. . . . In my opinion, it is possible for a person to fall into a particular racial group either by birth or by adherence, and it makes no difference, so far as the Act of 1976 is concerned, by which route he finds his way into the group.

Lord Templeman, taking a similar approach to that of Lord Fraser, said (at p. 569E):

> In my opinion, for the purposes of the Race Relations Act a group of persons defined by reference to ethnic origins must possess some of the characteristics of a race, namely group descent, a group of geographical origin and a group history.

Lord Fraser also approved the decision of the New Zealand Court of Appeal in *King-Ansell v Police* [1979] 2 NZLR 531 that Jews form a group with common ethnic origins within the New Zealand Race Relations Act 1971. In the course of his judgment, Richardson J said (at p. 543):

> . . . a group is identifiable in terms of its ethnic origins if it is a segment of the population distinguished from others by a sufficient combination of shared customs, beliefs, traditions and characteristics derived from a common or presumed common past, even if not drawn from what in biological terms is a common racial stock. It is that combination which gives them an historically determined social identity in their own eyes and in the eyes of those outside the group. They have a distinct social identity based not simply on group cohesion and solidarity but also on their belief as to their historical antecedents.

Gypsies properly so called, rather than 'travellers', are capable of being a racial group on the basis of their ethnic origin (*Commission for Racial Equality v Dutton* [1989] QB 783). Following the test in *Mandla v Dowell Lee*, the Court of Appeal held that Rastafarians are not members of an ethnic group separate from the rest of the Afro-Caribbean community (*Dawkins v Crown Suppliers (Property Services Agency)* (1993) *The Times*, 4 February 1993).

In *White* [2001] 1 WLR 1352, the Court of Appeal, following *Mandla* and *Ealing LBC*, noted that the statutory language is to be given a broad, non-technical meaning and that words are to be construed as generally used in England and Wales. In its judgment, 'the word "African" does describe a "racial group" defined by reference to race. In ordinary speech, the word "African" denotes a limited group of people regarded as of common stock and regarded as one of the major divisions of humankind having in common distinct physical features. It denotes a personal characteristic of the blacks of Africa'. On the other hand, the Court of Appeal took the view that the expression 'South American', in England and Wales, probably does not have a racial connotation: 'The range of physical characteristics in the populations of that continent, and in the absence of prominence of any one group, is such that the use of the expression "South American" does not bring to mind particular racial characteristics. We would not expect there to be a common perception in England and Wales of a South American racial group'.

Threatening, Abusive or Insulting

For discussion of the phrase 'threatening, abusive or insulting', see **B11.51**. **B11.170**

Meaning of 'Written Material'

In the POA 1986, ss. 17 to 29, 'written material' includes any sign or other visible representation (s. 29). For the meaning of 'writing', see **B11.52**. **B11.171**

Mens Rea

For the offence under the POA 1986, s. 18(1)(a), an intention to stir up racial hatred is required. The *mens rea* of the offence under s. 18(1)(b) is established by reference to s. 18(5): **B11.172**

> A person who is not shown to have intended to stir up racial hatred is not guilty of an offence under this section if he did not intend his words or behaviour, or the written material, to be, and was not aware that it might be, threatening, abusive or insulting.

Place of Commission

B11.173 **Public Order Act 1986, s. 18**

(2) An offence under this section may be committed in a public or a private place, except that no offence is committed where the words or behaviour are used, or the written material is displayed, by a person inside a dwelling and are not heard or seen except by other persons in that or another dwelling.

(4) In proceedings for an offence under this section it is a defence for the accused to prove that he was inside a dwelling and had no reason to believe that the words or behaviour used, or the written material displayed, would be heard or seen by a person outside that or any other dwelling.

Section 29 provides that, in ss. 17 to 29:

'dwelling' means any structure or part of a structure occupied as a person's home or other living accommodation (whether the occupation is separate or shared with others) but does not include any part not so occupied; and for this purpose 'structure' includes a tent, caravan, vehicle, vessel or other temporary or movable structure.

Offence Does Not Apply to Broadcasts or Cable Programme Services

B11.174 The POA 1986, s. 18, does not (by s. 18(6)) apply to words or behaviour used, or written material displayed, solely for the purpose of being included in a programme service. Such activity is controlled by s. 22 of the Act, see **B11.185**.

Liability of Corporate Officers

B11.175 **Public Order Act 1986, s. 28**

(1) Where a body corporate is guilty of an offence under this part and it is shown that the offence was committed with the consent or connivance of a director, manager, secretary or other similar officer of the body, or a person purporting to act in any such capacity, he as well as the body corporate is guilty of the offence and liable to be proceeded against and punished accordingly.

(2) Where the affairs of a body corporate are managed by its members, subsection (1) applies in relation to the acts and defaults of a member in connection with his functions of management as it applies to a director.

As to corporate liability generally, and the liability of corporate officers in the light of the case of *Boal* [1992] QB 591, see **A5.17**.

Defence for Reports of Parliamentary and Judicial Proceedings

B11.176 **Public Order Act 1986, s. 26**

(1) Nothing in this part applies to a fair and accurate report of proceedings in Parliament.

(2) Nothing in this part applies to a fair and accurate report of proceedings publicly heard before a court or tribunal exercising judicial authority where the report is published contemporaneously with the proceedings or, if it is not reasonably practicable or would be unlawful to publish a report of them contemporaneously, as soon as publication is reasonably practicable and lawful.

This and the general defences (see A3) are the only defences available to an accused. The truth of material, or belief in its truth, is not a defence (*Birdwood* (11 April 1995 unreported)).

PUBLISHING OR DISTRIBUTING WRITTEN MATERIAL STIRRING UP RACIAL HATRED

B11.177 **Public Order Act 1986, s. 19**

(1) A person who publishes or distributes written material which is threatening, abusive or insulting is guilty of an offence if—

(a) he intends thereby to stir up racial hatred, or
(b) having regard to all the circumstances racial hatred is likely to be stirred up thereby.

Procedure

An offence under the POA 1986, s. 19, is triable either way (POA 1986, s. 27(3)). When tried on indictment it is a class 3 offence. No proceeding may be instituted except by, or with the consent of, the A-G (POA 1986, s. 27(3)). **B11.178**

The POA 1986, s. 27(2), declares that for the purposes of the rules against charging more than one offence in the same count or information, each of ss. 18 to 23 of the Act creates one offence.

For the liability of corporate officers, see **B11.175**.

Sentence

The maximum penalty for an offence under the POA 1986, s. 19, is, by s. 27(3) of the Act, two years' imprisonment or a fine or both, on indictment; six months, a fine not exceeding the statutory maximum or both, summarily. The court also has a power under s. 25 to order forfeiture where the offender has been convicted of displaying written material (see **B11.167**). **B11.179**

Meaning of Terms Used in Defining the Offence

For the meaning of 'racial hatred' see **B11.168**. For the meaning of 'threatening, abusive or insulting', see **B11.51**. For the meaning of 'written material', see **B11.171**. **B11.180**

References in the POA 1986, ss. 17 to 29, to the publication or distribution of written material are, by s. 19(3) of the Act, to the publication or distribution of that material to the public or a section of the public.

Defences

In proceedings for an offence under the POA 1986, s. 19, it is, by virtue of s. 19(2), a defence for an accused who is not shown to have intended to stir up racial hatred to prove that he was not aware of the content of the material and did not suspect, and had no reason to suspect, that it was threatening, abusive or insulting. The burden of proof of this defence lies on the accused on the balance of probabilities (see generally **F3.5** and **F3.40**). The imposition of a legal burden upon the accused is open to challenge in the light of the human rights cases on the 'reverse burden' (see **F3.13** *et seq.*). The defence in the POA 1986, s. 26 (savings for reports of parliamentary and judicial proceedings: see **B11.176**), applies to s. 19. **B11.181**

These and the general defences (see **A3**) are the only offences available to an accused. The truth of the material, or a belief in its truth, is not a defence (*Birdwood* (11 April 1995 unreported)).

PUBLIC PERFORMANCE, BROADCASTING AND POSSESSION OF MATERIALS STIRRING UP RACIAL HATRED

General Provisions

Sections 20 to 23 of the POA 1986 deal with the public performance, broadcasting and possession of materials intended to, or likely to, stir up racial hatred. The offences are triable either way, and the following general provisions of part III of the Act apply: **B11.182**

(a) Prosecution may only be by, or with the consent of, the A-G (s. 27(1)).
(b) Each section creates one offence (s. 27(2)).

(c) The maximum penalty is two years and/or a fine, on indictment; six months and/or a fine not exceeding the statutory maximum, summarily (s. 27(3)).
(d) There is a saving for fair and accurate reports of parliamentary or judicial proceedings (see **B11.176**).
(e) For the liability of corporate officers, see **B11.175**.

For the meaning of 'racial hatred' see **B11.168**. For the meaning of 'threatening, abusive or insulting', see **B11.51**. For the meaning of 'written material', see **B11.171**.

References in the POA 1986, ss. 17 to 29, to the publication or distribution of written material are, by s. 19(3) of the Act, to the publication or distribution of that material to the public or a section of the public. References to the distribution, showing or playing of a recording are, by s. 21(2), to the distribution, showing or playing of the recording to the public or a section of the public. 'Recording' means any record from which visual images or sounds may, by any means, be reproduced (s. 21(2)).

As to the limited defences available and that the truth of material, or a belief in its truth, is not a defence, see *Birdwood* (11 April 1995 unreported).

Public Performance of Play Stirring up Racial Hatred

B11.183 **Public Order Act 1986, s. 20**

(1) If a public performance of a play is given which involves the use of threatening, abusive or insulting words or behaviour, any person who presents or directs the performance is guilty of an offence if—
(a) he intends thereby to stir up racial hatred, or
(b) having regard to all the circumstances (and, in particular, taking the performance as a whole) racial hatred is likely to be stirred up thereby.

Section 20(5) of the POA 1986 provides that the words 'play' and 'public performance' in s. 20 have the same meaning as in the Theatres Act 1968.

Theatres Act 1968, s. 18

In this Act—

. . .

'play' means—
(a) any dramatic piece, whether involving improvisation or not, which is given wholly or in part by one or more persons actually present and performing and in which the whole or a major proportion of what is done by the person or persons performing, whether by way of speech, singing or acting, involves the playing of a role; and
(b) any ballet given wholly or in part by one or more persons actually present and performing, whether or not it falls within paragraph (a) of this definition;

. . .

'public performance' includes any performance in a public place within the meaning of the Public Order Act 1936 and any performance which the public or any section thereof are permitted to attend, whether on payment or otherwise.

The meaning of 'public place' in the POA 1936 is considered at **B11.15**.

Public Order Act 1986, s. 20

(2) If a person presenting or directing the performance is not shown to have intended to stir up racial hatred, it is a defence for him to prove—
(a) that he did not know and had no reason to suspect that the performance would involve the use of the offending words or behaviour, or
(b) that he did not know and had no reason to suspect that the offending words or behaviour were threatening, abusive or insulting, or
(c) that he did not know and had no reason to suspect that the circumstances in which the performance would be given would be such that racial hatred would be likely to be stirred up.

(3) This section does not apply to a performance given solely or primarily for one or more of the following purposes—
(a) rehearsal,
(b) making a recording of the performance, or
(c) enabling the performance to be included in a programme service,
but if it is proved that the performance was attended by persons other than those directly concerned with the giving of the performance or the doing in relation to it of the things mentioned in paragraph (b) or (c), the performance shall, unless the contrary is shown, be taken not to have been given solely for the purposes mentioned above.
(4) For the purposes of this section—
(a) a person shall not be treated as presenting a performance of a play by reason only of his taking part in it as a performer,
(b) a person taking part as a performer in a performance directed by another shall be treated as a person who directed the performance if without reasonable excuse he performs otherwise than in accordance with that person's direction, and
(c) a person shall be taken to have directed a performance of a play given under his direction notwithstanding that he was not present during the performance;
and a person shall not be treated as aiding or abetting the commission of an offence under this section by reason only of his taking part in a performance as a performer.

Distributing, Showing or Playing a Recording Stirring up Racial Hatred

Public Order Act 1986, s. 21 **B11.184**

(1) A person who distributes, or shows or plays, a recording of visual images or sounds which are threatening, abusive or insulting is guilty of an offence if—
(a) he intends thereby to stir up racial hatred, or
(b) having regard to all the circumstances racial hatred is likely to be stirred up thereby.
(2) [See **B11.182**]
(3) In proceedings for an offence under this section it is a defence for an accused who is not shown to have intended to stir up racial hatred to prove that he was not aware of the content of the recording and did not suspect, and had no reason to suspect, that it was threatening, abusive or insulting.
(4) This section does not apply to the showing or playing of a recording solely for the purpose of enabling the recording to be included in a programme service.

Broadcasting Programme Stirring up Racial Hatred

Public Order Act 1986, s. 22 **B11.185**

(1) If a programme involving threatening, abusive or insulting visual images or sounds is included in a programme service, each of the persons mentioned in subsection (2) is guilty of an offence if—
(a) he intends to stir up racial hatred, or
(b) having regard to all the circumstances racial hatred is likely to be stirred up thereby.
(2) The persons are—
(a) the person providing the programme service,
(b) any person by whom the programme is produced or directed, and
(c) any person by whom offending words or behaviour are used.
(3) If the person providing the service, or a person by whom the programme was produced or directed, is not shown to have intended to stir up racial hatred, it is a defence for him to prove that—
(a) he did not know and had no reason to suspect that the programme would involve the offending material, and
(b) having regard to the circumstances in which the programme was included in a programme service, it was not reasonably practicable for him to secure the removal of the material.
(4) It is a defence for a person by whom the programme was produced or directed who is not shown to have intended to stir up racial hatred to prove that he did not know and had no reason to suspect—
(a) that the programme would be included in a programme service, or
(b) that the circumstances in which the programme would be so included woud be such that racial hatred would be likely to be stirred up.

(5) It is a defence for a person by whom offending words or behaviour were used and who is not shown to have intended to stir up racial hatred to prove that he did not know and had no reason to suspect—
 (a) that a programme involving the use of the offending material would be included in a programme service, or
 (b) that the circumstances in which a programme involving the use of the offending material would be so included, or in which a programme so included would involve the use of the offending material, would be such that racial hatred would be likely to be stirred up.

(6) A person who is not shown to have intended to stir up racial hatred is not guilty of an offence under this section if he did not know, and had no reason to suspect, that the offending material was threatening, abusive or insulting.

Possession of Written Material or Recording Stirring up Racial Hatred

B11.186 **Public Order Act 1986, s. 23**

(1) A person who has in his possession written material which is threatening, abusive or insulting, or a recording of visual images or sounds which are threatening, abusive or insulting, with a view to—
 (a) in the case of written material, its being displayed, published, distributed, or included in a programme service, whether by himself or another, or
 (b) in the case of a recording, its being distributed, shown, played, or included in a programme service, whether by himself or another, is guilty of an offence if he intends racial hatred to be stirred up thereby or, having regard to all the circumstances, racial hatred is likely to be stirred up thereby.

(2) For this purpose regard is to be had to such display, publication, distribution, showing, playing, or inclusion in a programme service as he has, or it may reasonably be inferred that he has, in view.

(3) In proceedings for an offence under this section it is a defence for an accused who is not shown to have intended to stir up racial hatred to prove that he was not aware of the content of the written material or recording and did not suspect, and had no reason to suspect, that it was threatening, abusive or insulting.

In *Gray* [1999] 1 Cr App R (S) 50, the offender was found in possession of a quantity of magazines containing racist material, and he was involved in their distribution. A prison sentence of 12 months following a plea of guilty to the offence under s. 23(1) was upheld on appeal. The Court of Appeal commented that reported decisions dating from the 1970s and 1980s for similar offences might no longer be an adequate guide to current sentencing practice, since 'the grave social damage done by offences and remarks of a racist nature is now perhaps better known than it was then'. See **B11.167**.

USING WORDS OR BEHAVIOUR OR DISPLAYING WRITTEN MATERIAL STIRRING UP RELIGIOUS HATRED

Note: The provisions of the Public Order Act 1986, ss. 29A to 29L have not been brought into force.

B11.187 **Public Order Act 1986, s. 29B**

(1) A person who uses threatening words or behaviour, or displays any written material which is threatening, is guilty of an offence if he intends thereby to stir up religious hatred.

Procedure

B11.188 An offence under the POA 1986, s. 29B(1), is triable either way (s. 29L(3)). When tried on indictment, it is a class 3 offence. No proceedings may be instituted except by or with the consent of the A-G (s. 29L(1)). For the purposes of rules against charging more than one offence in the same count or information, this section creates one offence (s. 29L(2)). For the liability of corporate offenders, see s. 29M, which is worded in the standard format.

Sentence

B11.189 The maximum penalty is, on conviction on indictment, imprisonment for a term not exceeding seven years, a fine, or both; on summary conviction, the maximum is a term of imprisonment not exceeding six months, a fine not exceeding the statutory maximum, or both (POA 1986, s. 29L(3)).

In relation to the offence relating to the display of written material, the court has the following forfeiture power.

Public Order Act 1986, s. 29I

(1) A court by or before which a person is convicted of—
   (a) an offence under section 29B relating to the display of written material, or
   (b) an offence under section 29C, 29E or 29G,
   shall order to be forfeited any written material or recording produced to the court and shown to its satisfaction to be written material or a recording to which the offence relates.
(2) An order made under this section shall not take effect—
   (a) in the case of an order made in proceedings in England and Wales, until the expiry of the ordinary time within which an appeal may be instituted or, where an appeal is duly instituted, until it is finally decided or abandoned.
   (b) [Scotland]
(3) For the purposes of subsection (2)(a)—
   (a) an application for a case stated or for leave to appeal shall be treated as the institution of an appeal, and
   (b) where a decision on appeal is subject to a further appeal, the appeal is not finally determined until the expiry of the ordinary time within which a further appeal may be instituted or, where a further appeal is duly instituted, until the further appeal is finally decided or abandoned.

Elements

B11.190 A key concept is the meaning of 'religious hatred'.

Public Order Act 1986, s. 29A

In this Part 'religious hatred' means hatred against a group of persons defined by reference to religious belief or lack of religious belief.

It is possible that the meaning of 'religion' will play a part in considering this offence. It is a notoriously difficult concept to define. For a consideration of this issue in the context of religiously aggravated offences, see **B11.161**. It is submitted that, utilising the jurisprudence under the ECHR, Article 9, regarding these words as ordinary words of the English language is the approach that will be adopted. The Government, in the *Explanatory Memorandum*, provides a list of 'religions widely recognised in this country' and lists: Christianity, Islam, Hinduism, Judaism, Buddhism, Sikhism, Rastafarianism, Baha'ism, Zoroastrianism and Jainism. For those who lack a religious belief, the Government lists groups such as atheists and humanists. These offences are, according to the Government, 'based on the fact that the group do not share the particular religious beliefs of the perpetrator'.

In order to meet many of the deep concerns that this legislation would prevent what has been acceptable behaviour, particularly that of those wishing to convert people to their own religion or of comedians, entertainers and social commentators, and a feeling that the existence of the ECHR, Articles 9, 10 and 11 would not provide sufficient protection, the Act provides as follows.

Public Order Act 1986, s. 29J

Nothing in this Part shall be read or given effect in a way which prohibits or restricts discussion, criticism or expressions of antipathy, dislike, ridicule, insult or abuse of particular religions or the beliefs or practices of their adherents, or of any other belief system or the beliefs or practices of its adherents, or proselytising or urging adherents of a different religion or belief system to cease practising their religion or belief system.

The offence may be committed in a public or a private place, but no offence is committed where the words or behaviour are used or the written material is displayed by a person inside a dwelling and are not heard or seen except by other persons in that or another dwelling (s. 29B(2)). The offence does not apply to words or behaviour used or written material displayed solely for the purpose of being included in a programme service (s. 29B(5)). For the relevant offence that may be committed, see **B11.207**. 'Dwelling' means any structure or part of a structure occupied as a person's home or other living accommodation (whether the occupation is separate or shared with others) but does not include any part not so occupied, and 'structure' includes a tent, caravan, vehicle, vessel or other temporary or movable structure (s. 29N).

For a discussion of 'threatening, abusive or insulting', see **B11.51**. 'Written material' includes any sign or other visible representation (s. 29N).

The accused must have the relevant intention (s. 29B(1)).

There is a special saving for reports of parliamentary and judicial proceedings.

Public Order Act 1986, s. 29K

(1) Nothing in this part applies to a fair and accurate report of proceedings in Parliament or in the Scottish Parliament.

(2) Nothing in this part applies to a fair and accurate report of proceedings publicly heard before a court or tribunal exercising judicial authority where the report is published contemporaneously with the proceedings or, if it is not reasonably practicable or would be unlawful to publish a report of them contemporaneously, as soon as publication is reasonably practicable and lawful.

Defence

B11.191 It is a defence for the accused to prove that he was inside the dwelling and had no reason to believe that the words or behaviour used or the written material displayed would be heard or seen by a person outside that or any other dwelling (POA 1986, s. 29B(4)).

Powers of Arrest

B11.192 A constable may arrest anyone he reasonably suspects is committing this offence (POA 1986, s. 29B(3)). The citizen's power of arrest in the PACE 1984, s. 24A, does not apply to this offence (PACE 1984, s. 24A(5)).

PUBLISHING OR DISTRIBUTING WRITTEN MATERIAL STIRRING UP RELIGIOUS HATRED

Note: The provisions of the Public Order Act 1986, ss. 29A to 29L have not been brought into force.

B11.193 **Public Order Act 1986, s. 29C**

(1) A person who publishes or distributes written material which is threatening is guilty of an offence if he intends thereby to stir up religious hatred.

Procedure

B11.194 An offence under the POA 1986, s. 29C(1), is triable either way (s. 29L(3)). When tried on indictment, it is a class 3 offence. No proceedings may be instituted except by or with the consent of the A-G (s. 29L(1)). For the purposes of rules against charging more than one offence in the same count or information, this section creates one offence (s. 29L(2)). For the liability of corporate offenders, see s. 29M, which is worded in the standard format.

Sentence

The maximum penalty is, on conviction on indictment, imprisonment for a term not exceeding seven years, a fine, or both; on summary conviction, the maximum is a term of imprisonment not exceeding six months, a fine not exceeding the statutory maximum, or both (POA 1986, s. 29L(3)). **B11.195**

In relation to the offence relating to the display of written material, the court has a forfeiture power, see **B11.189**.

Elements

As to the meaning of 'religious hatred' and the special provision on the protection of freedom of expression (POA 1986, s. 29J), see **B11.190**. As to the meaning of 'threatening', see **B11.51**, but note that it is only material that is threatening which forms this offence. **B11.196**

References to the publication or distribution of written material are to its publication or distribution to the public or a section of the public (s. 29C(2)).

The accused must have the relevant intention (s. 29C(1)).

For savings for reports of parliamentary and judicial proceedings under POA 1986, s. 29K, see **B11.190**.

PUBLIC PERFORMANCE OF PLAY STIRRING UP RELIGIOUS HATRED

Note: The provisions of the Public Order Act 1986, ss. 29A to 29L have not been brought into force.

Public Order Act 1986, s. 29D **B11.197**

(1) If a public performance of a play is given which involves the use of threatening words or behaviour, any person who presents or directs the performance is guilty of an offence if he intends thereby to stir up religious hatred.

Procedure

An offence under the POA 1986, s. 29D(1), is triable either way (s. 29L(3)). When tried on indictment, it is a class 3 offence. No proceedings may be instituted except by or with the consent of the A-G (s. 29L(1)). For the purposes of rules against charging more than one offence in the same count or information, this section creates one offence (s. 29L(2)). For the liability of corporate offenders, see s. 29M, which is worded in the standard format. **B11.198**

Sentence

The maximum penalty is, on conviction on indictment, imprisonment for a term not exceeding seven years, a fine, or both; on summary conviction, the maximum is a term of imprisonment not exceeding six months, a fine not exceeding the statutory maximum, or both (POA 1986, s. 29L(3)). **B11.199**

Elements

As to the meaning of 'religious hatred' and the special provision on the protection of freedom of expression (POA 1986, s. 29J), see **B11.190**. As to the meaning of 'threatening', see **B11.51**, but note that it is only material that is threatening which forms this offence. **B11.200**

The offence does not apply to certain performances.

Public Order Act 1986, s. 29D

(2) This section does not apply to a performance given solely or primarily for one or more of the following purposes—
(a) rehearsal,
(b) making a recording of the performance, or
(c) enabling the performance to be included in a programme service;
but if it is proved that the performance was attended by persons other than those directly connected with the giving of the performance or the doing in relation to it of the things mentioned in paragraph (b) or (c), the performance shall, unless the contrary is shown, be taken not to have been given solely or primarily for the purpose mentioned above.

As regards those who may or may not be directing a performance, the following provision applies.

Public Order Act 1986, s. 29D

(3) For the purposes of this section—
(a) a person shall not be treated as presenting a performance of a play by reason only of his taking part in it as a performer,
(b) a person taking part as a performer in a performance directed by another shall be treated as a person who directed the performance if without reasonable excuse he performs otherwise than in accordance with that person's direction, and
(c) a person shall be taken to have directed a performance of a play given under his direction notwithstanding that he was not present during the performance;
and a person shall not be treated as aiding or abetting the commission of an offence under this section by reason only of his taking part in a performance as a performer.

The accused must have the relevant intention (POA 1986, s. 29D(1)).

'Play' and 'public performance' have the same meaning as in the Theatres Act 1968 (s. 29D(4)). Further, the Theatres Act 1968, ss. 9 (script as evidence of what was performed), 10 (power to make copies of script) and 15 (powers of entry and inspection) apply to this offence (s. 29D(5)).

For savings for reports of parliamentary and judicial proceedings under s. 29K, see **B11.190**.

Power of Arrest

B11.201 The citizen's power of arrest in the PACE 1984, s. 24A, does not apply to this offence (PACE 1984, s. 24A(5)).

DISTRIBUTING, SHOWING OR PLAYING A RECORDING STIRRING UP RELIGIOUS HATRED

Note: The provisions of the Public Order Act 1986, ss. 29A to 29L have not been brought into force.

B11.202 **Public Order Act 1986, s. 29E**

(1) A person who distributes, or shows or plays, a recording of visual images or sounds which are threatening is guilty of an offence if he intends thereby to stir up religious hatred.

Procedure

B11.203 An offence under the POA 1986, s. 29E(1), is triable either way (s. 29L(3)). When tried on indictment, it is a class 3 offence. No proceedings may be instituted except by or with the consent of the A-G (s. 29L(1)). For the purposes of rules against charging more than one offence in the same count or information, this section creates one offence (s. 29L(2)). For the liability of corporate offenders, see s. 29M, which is worded in the standard format.

Sentence

The maximum penalty is, on conviction on indictment, imprisonment for a term not exceeding seven years, a fine, or both; on summary conviction, the maximum is a term of imprisonment not exceeding six months, a fine not exceeding the statutory maximum, or both (POA 1986, s. 29L(3)). **B11.204**

In relation to the offence relating to the display of written material, the court has a forfeiture power, see **B11.189**.

Elements

As to the meaning of 'religious hatred', and the special provision on the protection of freedom of expression (POA 1986, s. 29J), see **B11.190**. As to the meaning of 'threatening', see **B11.51**, but note that it is only material that is threatening which forms this offence.Section 29E defines 'recording'. **B11.205**

Section 29E defines 'recording'.

Public Order Act 1986, s. 29E

(2) In this Part 'recording' means any record from which visual images or sounds may, by any means, be reproduced; and references to the distribution, showing or playing of a recording are to its distribution, showing or playing to the public or a section of the public.

The accused must have the relevant intention (s. 29E(1)).

This offence does not apply to the showing or playing of a recording solely for the purpose of enabling it to be included in a programme service (s. 29E(3)). For the relevant offence, see. **B11.207**.

For savings for reports of parliamentary and judicial proceedings under s. 29K, see **B11.190**.

Power of Arrest

The citizen's power of arrest in the PACE 1984, s. 24A, does not apply to this offence (PACE 1984, s. 24A(5)). **B11.206**

BROADCASTING OR INCLUDING PROGRAMME IN PROGRAMME SERVICE STIRRING UP RELIGIOUS HATRED

Note: The provisions of the Public Order Act 1986, ss. 29A to 29L have not been brought into force.

Public Order Act 1986, s. 29F **B11.207**

(1) If a programme involving threatening visual images or sounds is included in a programme service, each of the persons mentioned in subsection (2) is guilty of an offence if he intends thereby to stir up religious hatred.

(2) The persons are—
- (a) the person providing the programme service,
- (b) any person by whom the programme is produced or directed, and
- (c) any person by whom offending words or behaviour are used.

Procedure

An offence under the POA 1986, s. 29F(1), is triable either way (s. 29L(3)). When tried on indictment, it is a class 3 offence. No proceedings may be instituted except by or with the consent of the A-G (s. 29L(1)). For the purposes of rules against charging more than one offence in the same count or information, this section creates one offence (s. 29L(2)). For the liability of corporate offenders, see s. 29M, which is worded in the standard format. **B11.208**

Sentence

B11.209 The maximum penalty is, on conviction on indictment, imprisonment for a term not exceeding seven years, a fine, or both; on summary conviction, the maximum is a term of imprisonment not exceeding six months, a fine not exceeding the statutory maximum, or both (POA 1986, s. 29L(3)).

Elements

B11.210 As to the meaning of 'religious hatred', and the special provision on the protection of freedom of expression (POA 1986, s. 29J), see **B11.190**. As to the meaning of 'threatening', see **B11.51**, but note that it is only material that is threatening which forms this offence. 'Programme service' has the same meaning as in the Broadcasting Act 1990 (s. 29N). 'Programme' means any item which is included in a programme service (s. 29N).

The accused must have the relevant intention (s. 29F(1)).

For savings for reports of parliamentary and judicial proceedings under s. 29K, see **B11.190**.

Power of Arrest

B11.211 The citizen's power of arrest in the PACE 1984, s. 24A, does not apply to this offence (PACE 1984, s. 24A(5)).

POSSESSION OF INFLAMMATORY MATERIAL

Note: The provisions of the Public Order Act 1986, ss. 29A to 29L have not been brought into force.

B11.212

Public Order Act 1986, s. 29G

(1) A person who has in his possession written material which is threatening, or a recording of visual images or sounds which are threatening, with a view to—
   (a) in the case of written material, its being displayed, published, distributed, or included in a programme service whether by himself or another, or
   (b) in the case of a recording, its being distributed, shown, played, or included in a programme service, whether by himself or another,

is guilty of an offence if he intends religious hatred to be stirred up thereby.

Procedure

B11.213 An offence under the POA 1986, s. 29G(1), is triable either way (s. 29L(3)). When tried on indictment, it is a class 3 offence. No proceedings may be instituted except by or with the consent of the A-G (s. 29L(1)). For the purposes of rules against charging more than one offence in the same count or information, this section creates one offence (s. 29L(2)). For the liability of corporate offenders, see s. 29M, which is worded in the standard format.

Sentence

B11.214 The maximum penalty is, on conviction on indictment, imprisonment for a term not exceeding seven years, a fine, or both; on summary conviction, the maximum is a term of imprisonment not exceeding six months, a fine not exceeding the statutory maximum, or both (POA 1986, s. 29L(3)).

In relation to the offence relating to the display of written material, the court has a forfeiture power, see **B11.189**.

Elements

As to the meaning of 'religious hatred', and the special provision on the protection of freedom of expression (POA 1986, s. 29J), see **B11.190**. As to the meaning of 'threatening', see **B11.51**, but note that it is only material that is threatening which forms this offence. **B11.215**

For this offence regard is had to such display, publication, distribution, showing, playing, or inclusion in a programme service as the accused has, or it may be reasonably be inferred that he has, in view (s. 29G(2)).

The accused must have the relevant intention (s. 29G(1)).

For savings for reports of parliamentary and judicial proceedings under s. 29K, see **B11.190**.

Power of Arrest

The citizen's power of arrest in the PACE 1984, s. 24A, does not apply to this offence (PACE 1984, s. 24A(5)). **B11.216**

Entry and Search

Public Order Act 1986, s. 29H **B11.217**

(1) If in England and Wales a justice of the peace is satisfied by information on oath laid by a constable that there are reasonable grounds for suspecting that a person has possession of written material or a recording in contravention of section 29G, the justice may issue a warrant under his hand authorising any constable to enter and search the premises where it is suspected the material or recording is situated.
(2) [Scotland]
(3) A constable entering or searching premises in pursuance of a warrant issued under this section may use reasonable force if necessary.
(4) In this section 'premises' means any place and, in particular, includes—
(a) any vehicle, vessel, aircraft or hovercraft,
(b) any offshore installation as defined in section 12 of the Mineral Workings (Offshore Installations) Act 1971, and
(c) any tent or movable structure.

DRUNK AND DISORDERLY

Offence, Procedure and Sentence

It is a summary offence, contrary to the CJA 1967, s. 91(1), where 'Any person who in any public place is guilty, while drunk, of disorderly behaviour . . .'. The maximum penalty for the offence is a fine not exceeding level 3 on the standard scale. The Magistrates' Courts Guidelines (2004) indicate the following for a first-time offender pleading not guilty: **B11.218**

Aggravating Factors For example offensive language or behaviour; with group; on hospital/medical or school premises; on public transport; racial or religious aggravation; offence committed on bail; relevant previous convictions and any failures to respond to previous sentences.

Mitigating Factors For example induced by others; no significant disturbance; not threatening.
Guideline: Is discharge or fine appropriate?

The guideline fine is Starting Point A (see **E17.5**). Community rehabilitation orders and curfew orders are the only available community sentences for this offence.

Under the Penalties for Disorderly Behaviour (Amount of Penalty) Order 2002 (SI 2002 No. 1837), as amended, this offence is a penalty offence and the amount payable is £80.

Drunk

B11.219 It was held by the Divisional Court in *Neale v R.M.J.E. (a minor)* (1984) 80 Cr App R 20 that the natural and ordinary meaning of the word 'drunk' in this statutory context is that it is limited to cases of drunkenness induced by alcohol. It is not, therefore, committed where the state of the accused is a product of glue-sniffing. The Divisional Court took into account, first, the statutory context, and its history in deriving from the Licensing Act 1872, s. 12, which was clearly concerned with the regulation of the sales of intoxicating liquor, and secondly the primary dictionary meanings which were limited to alcohol-induced states. This decision was followed by the Divisional Court in *Lanham v Rickwood* (1984) 148 JP 737, a decision on the meaning of the word 'drunk' in the Licensing Act 1872, s. 12, which states: 'Every person found drunk in any highway or other public place, whether building or not, or on any licensed premises, shall be liable to a penalty'. In both of these decisions, the different approach of the Divisional Court in *Bradford v Wilson* (1983) 147 JP 573 was rejected because it was, clearly, of no assistance. In that case it had been held that the offence of driving whilst unfit through drink or drugs contrary to the Road Traffic Act 1972, s. 5(2), was committed where someone was unfit through glue-sniffing.

In *Lanham v Rickwood* it was also decided that the condition in which the accused was found does not have to be solely attributable to alcohol:

> In each case, the magistrates have to ask themselves, no doubt as a matter of simple common sense, whether a person's loss of self-control is attributable to his having indulged in an excessive consumption of intoxicating liquor. If the evidence before them is that he has indulged both in an excessive consumption of intoxicating liquor and also in some other form of activity, such as glue-sniffing, which may also have affected his self-control, they have to decide, as a matter of common sense, whether they are satisfied that, apart from the glue-sniffing, he has consumed intoxicating liquor to an extent which affects his steady self-control.

This decision is important not only on multiple causes of a condition, but also because it gives an indication of what is meant by 'drunk'. In *Neale v R.J.M.E. (a minor)* Robert Goff LJ made the same point about the meaning of drunkenness: 'the word "drunk", in ordinary common speech, . . . refers to someone who has taken intoxicating liquor to an extent which affects his steady self control'. Note that a person may be in a condition which can be described as 'drunk' but that need not be the same condition as that necessary to raise the defence of intoxication.

Disorderly Behaviour

B11.220 It is to be assumed that the words will be regarded as words of the ordinary English language having no special meaning. Thus reliance may be placed upon a dictionary meaning and the understanding of the magistrates. The disorderly conduct, though, must occur before the person is arrested as the gravamen of the offence is disorderly conduct whilst being drunk (*R (H) v CPS* (2006) 170 JP 4).

Public Place

B11.221 The CJA 1967, s. 91(4), provides that, in s. 91, ' "public place" includes any highway and any other premises or place to which at the material time the public have or are permitted to have access, whether on payment or otherwise'.

Power to Take to Treatment Centre

B11.222 Under the CJA 1972, s. 34(1), where a constable arrests a person for an offence contrary to either the Licensing Act 1872, s. 12, or the CJA 1967, s. 91(1), he may, if he thinks fit, take that person to any place approved for the purposes as a treatment centre for alcoholics; while a person is being so taken he shall be deemed to be in lawful custody'. It is to be presumed that this provision is an exception to the generally applicable obligation in the PACE 1984, s. 30, to take an arrested person to a police station 'as soon as practicable after the arrest' (see **D1.12**). It is further to be presumed that this power continues to exist, although the specific powers of arrest under the Licensing Act 1872, s. 12, and the CJA 1967, s. 91, have been removed, consequent upon the changes to the PACE 1984, s. 24 (see **D1.14**). A person taken to an approved centre under the CJA 1972, s. 34(1), is not thereby liable to be detained in such a centre (s. 34(2)). The exercise of the power under s. 34 does not preclude the person being charged with any offence (s. 34(2)).

Related Offences

Found Drunk in Public It is an offence, contrary to the Licensing Act 1872, s. 12, where a person is 'found drunk in any highway or other public place, whether a building or not, or on any licensed premises'. An offender is liable to a fine not exceeding level 1 on the standard scale. Under the Penalties for Disorderly Behaviour (Amount of Penalty) Order 2002 (SI 2002 No. 1837), as amended, this offence is a penalty offence and the amount payable is £50. Where the person, whilst drunk, is guilty of disorderly behaviour, the CJA 1967, s. 91 (see **B11.218**), has replaced this offence. **B11.223**

The fact that the person's presence in the highway (or public place) is momentary and/or involuntary is irrelevant (*Winzar v Chief Constable of Kent* (1983) *The Times*, 28 March 1983). In that case, W, when found to be drunk, was told to leave hospital, having been taken there on a stretcher. The police were called when he was found slumped on a chair in a corridor. The police took him to a police car on the highway outside the hospital. He was 'found to be drunk' because he was 'perceived to be drunk', which meant 'to become aware of'. Although the police were aware that he was drunk in the hospital, he was found to be drunk in the highway, even though the only reason he was in the highway was because the police had taken him there. The Licensing Act 1902, s. 8, defines 'public place' as including 'any place to which the public have access, whether on payment or otherwise'. A person 'found drunk in any highway or other public place, whether a building or not, or on any licensed premises' may be dealt with according to law (Licensing Act 1902, s. 1).

Alcohol Consumption in Designated Public Places It is an offence, contrary to the CJPA 2001, s. 12(4), for a person to fail without reasonable excuse to comply with a requirement imposed upon him under s. 12(2). Under s. 12(2), a constable who reasonably believes that a person is or has been consuming intoxicating liquor in a designated public place or intends to consume intoxicating liquor in such a place may require the person concerned (a) not to consume in that place anything which is, or which the constable reasonably believes to be, intoxicating liquor, (b) to surrender anything in his possession which is, or which the constable reasonably believes to be, intoxicating liquor or a container for such liquor (other than a sealed container). The maximum penalty is a fine not exceeding level 2 on the standard scale (s. 12(4)). Under the Penalties for Disorderly Behaviour (Amount of Penalty) Order 2002 (SI 2002 No. 1837), as amended, this offence is a penalty offence and the amount payable is £50. The offence under s. 12 replaces byelaws having similar effect (s. 15). **B11.224**

Drunk while in Charge of a Child It is a summary offence, contrary to the Licensing Act 1902, s. 2(1), where a 'person is found drunk in any highway or other public place, whether a building or not, or on any licensed premises, while having the charge of a child apparently under the age of seven years'. He is liable, on conviction, to a fine not exceeding level 2 on the standard scale or to a term of imprisonment not exceeding one month. If the child appears to the court to be under the age of seven, the child is deemed to be under that age unless the contrary is proved (s. 2(2)). The person so found may be apprehended (s. 2(1)). **B11.225**

Drunk and in Charge of a Carriage, etc. It is an offence, contrary to the Licensing Act 1872, s. 12, where a person is drunk 'while in charge on any highway or other public place of any carriage, horse, cattle, or steam engine'. An offender is liable to a fine not **B11.226**

exceeding level 1 on the standard scale or to a term of imprisonment not exceeding one month. There is power to apprehend an offender. The term 'carriage' includes a motor vehicle or trailer (Road Traffic Act 1988, s. 191) and a bicycle, whether ridden or pushed (*Corkery v Carpenter* [1951] 1 KB 102). 'Cattle' includes pigs and sheep (*Child v Hearns* (1874) LR 9 Exch 176).

A person liable to be charged with an offence under s. 3A, 4, 5, 7 or 30 of the Road Traffic Act 1988 is not liable to be charged under s. 12 of the Licensing Act 1872 (Road Traffic Act 1988, s. 5). As to the relevant road traffic offences, see **C5**.

It is an offence, contrary to the Town Police Clauses Act 1847, s. 61, to be intoxicated while driving a hackney carriage; a person found guilty is liable to a penalty not exceeding level 1 on the standard scale. It is also an offence, contrary to the London Hackney Carriages Act 1843, s. 28, to be drunk during employment as a driver of a hackney carriage, or as a driver or conductor of a stage carriage in the Metropolitan Police District.

B11.227 **Drunk and in Possession of Loaded Firearm** It is an offence, contrary to the Licensing Act 1872, s. 12, where a person is drunk when in possession of any loaded firearms. An offender is liable to a fine not exceeding level 1 on the standard scale or to a term of imprisonment not exceeding one month. As to firearms offences, see **B12**.

B11.228 **Drunk on Board Ship** It is an offence, contrary to the Merchant Shipping Act 1995, s. 101, to be drunk and persisting, after being refused admission on that account, in attempting to enter a passenger ship and also to be drunk on board a passenger ship, and refusing to leave ship when requested.

The Railways and Transport Safety Act 2003 creates a series of offences concerned with the effects of alcohol (and drugs) on board ships. Each offence is triable either way and is punishable, on conviction on indictment, with imprisonment for a term not exceeding two years, a fine or both; and, on summary conviction, with a fine not exceeding the statutory maximum (s. 82). A power of arrest is created by s. 85. The offences are as follows. (a) It is an offence, contrary to s. 78, when the ability of professional staff (masters and pilots at all times, and seamen when on duty) to carry out their duties is impaired because of drink or drugs. (b) It is an offence, contrary to s. 79, for professional seamen not on duty where their ability to take action to protect the safety of passengers in the event of an emergency is impaired because of drink or drugs. (c) It is an offence, contrary to s. 80, where the ability of non-professionals concerned in the navigation of a ship is impaired because of drink or drugs.

B11.229 **Drunk on an Aircraft** It is an offence, contrary to the Air Navigation Order 2000 (SI 2000 No. 1562), art. 65(1), for a person to enter any aircraft when drunk or to be drunk in any aircraft. It is also an offence, contrary to art. 65(2), for a person, when acting as an aircraft crew member or being carried in any aircraft for the purpose of so acting, to be under the influence of drink or drugs to such an extent as to impair his capacity to act. Both offences are triable either way. The maximum penalty is: on conviction on indictment, a term of imprisonment not exceeding five years, a fine, or both; and, on summary conviction, a fine not exceeding the statutory maximum (art. 122(6) and sch. 12, part B). A sentence of eight months for this offence was upheld in *Ayodeji* [2001] 1 Cr App R (S) 370. A person commits an offence, contrary to the Railways and Transport Safety Act 2003, s. 92, if (a) he performs an aviation function at a time when his ability to perform the function is impaired because of drink or drugs, or (b) he carries out an activity which is ancillary to an aviation function at a time when his ability to perform the function is impaired because of drink or drugs. The offence is triable either way and is punishable, on conviction on indictment, with imprisonment for a term not exceeding two years, a fine or both and, on summary conviction, with a fine not exceeding the statutory maximum (s. 95). A power of arrest is created by s. 97.

B11.230 **Purchasing Liquor for Drunkard** Where a person is convicted of one of the offences mentioned in the Inebriates Act 1898, sch. 1, and that person in the previous 12 months has been convicted on three occasions of one of those offences, the court may order that notice of the conviction be sent to the police authority for the police area where the court is situated (Licensing Act 1902, s. 6(1)). The offences mentioned in the Inebriates Act 1898, sch. 1 are: offences contrary to the Licensing Act 1872, ss. 12 and 18, the Town Police Clauses Act 1847, s. 61, the London Hackney Carriages Act 1843, s. 28 and the Merchant Shipping Act 1995, s. 101. Such an habitual drunkard commits a summary offence if, within three years of the conviction, he 'purchases or obtains, or attempts to purchase or obtain, any intoxicating liquor at any premises licensed for the sale of intoxicating liquor by retail, or at the premises of any club registered' under the Licensing Act 1902, part III. An offender is liable to a fine not exceeding level 1 on the standard scale.

Under the Licensing Act 2003, s. 142, it is a summary offence for a person, on relevant premises, to knowingly obtain or attempt to obtain alcohol for consumption on those premises by a person who is drunk (s. 142(1)). The maximum penalty is a fine not exceeding level 3 on the standard scale (s. 142(2)).

Drunk and disorderly person failing to leave or entering after request not do so Under the Licensing Act 2003, s. 143, a person who is drunk and disorderly commits an offence if, without reasonable excuse he fails to leave relevant premises when requested to do so by a constable or by a person to whom s. 143(2) applies, or he enters or attempts to enter relevant premises after a constable or a person to whom s. 143(2) applies has requested him not to enter (s. 143(1)). Section 143(2) applies: (a) to any person who works at the premises in a capacity, whether paid or unpaid, which gives him authority to make such a request, (b) in the case of licensed premises, to (i) the holder of a premises licence in respect of the premises, and (ii) the designated premises supervisor (if any) under such a licence, (c) in the case of premises in respect of which a club premises certificate has effect, to any member or officer of the club which holds the certificate who is present on the premises in a capacity which enables him to make such a request, and (d) in the case of premises which may be used for a permitted temporary activity by virtue of part 5, to the premises user in relation to the temporary event notice in question. The maximum penalty, on summary conviction, is a fine not exceeding level 1 on the standard scale (s. 143(3)). A constable is obliged, on request by a person to whom s. 143(2) applies, to help to expel from relevant premises a person who is drunk or disorderly and to help to prevent such a person from entering relevant premises (s. 143(4)). B11.231

Children and Alcohol It is a summary offence, contrary to the Children and Young Persons Act 1933, s. 5, for anyone to give, or to cause to be given, to any child under five intoxicating liquor, except on a doctor's order or in cases of sickness, apprehended sickness or other urgent cause. An offender is liable to a fine not exceeding level 1 on the standard scale. The Licensing Act 2003 has introduced a number of new offences concerned with children and alcohol including allowing an unaccompanied child to be on premises used for the supply or consumption of alcohol (s. 145), selling alcohol to children under 18 (s. 146), allowing the sale of alcohol to children under 18 (s. 147), persistently selling alcohol to children (s. 147A, inserted by the VCRA 2006, s. 23 with effect from 6 April 2007), selling or supplying liqueur confectionery to children under 16 (s. 148), individuals under 18 buying or attempting to buy alcohol or being supplied where he is a club member (s. 149(1)), buying or attempting to buy alcohol on behalf of an individual under 18 or making arrangements for supply where he is a club member (s. 149(3)), individuals under 18 knowingly consuming alcohol on relevant premises (s. 150), delivering alcohol to children under 18 (s. 151), sending a child under 18 to obtain alcohol (s. 152), knowingly allowing an individual under 18 to make a sale or supply (where in a club) of alcohol, where the accused is a responsible person (s. 153). B11.232

Sale to Habitual Drunkard A licensee may commit an offence by selling to an habitual drunkard (Licensing Act 1902, s. 6(2)(b)). B11.233

B11.234 **Drunkenness and disorderly conduct** It is an offence for certain persons knowingly to allow disorderly conduct on relevant premises (Licensing Act 2003, s. 140(1)). The offence applies (a) to any person who works at the premises in a capacity, whether paid or unpaid, which authorises him to prevent the conduct, (b) in the case of licensed premises, to (i) the holder of a premises licence in respect of the premises, and (ii) the designated premises supervisor (if any) under such a licence, (c) in the case of premises in respect of which a club premises certificate has effect, to any member or officer of the club which holds the certificate who at the time the conduct takes place is present on the premises in a capacity which enables him to prevent it, and (d) in the case of premises which may be used for a permitted temporary activity by virtue of part 5, to the premises user in relation to the temporary event notice in question (s. 140(2)). 'Relevant premises' is defined in s. 159. The maximum penalty, on summary conviction, is a fine not exceeding level 3 on the standard scale (s. 140(3)).

B11.235 **Selling alcohol to a person who is drunk** It is an offence for a person within the Licensing Act 2003, s. 141(2), if, on relevant premises, he knowingly sells or attempts to sell alcohol to a person who is drunk or allows alcohol to be sold to such a person (s. 141(1)). Section 141(2) applies to (a) any person who works at the premises in a capacity, whether paid or unpaid, which gives him authority to sell the alcohol concerned, (b) in the case of licensed premises, (i) the holder of a premises licence in respect of the premises, and (ii) the designated premises supervisor (if any) under such a licence, (c) in the case of premises in respect of which a club premises certificate has effect, any member or officer of the club which holds the certificate who at the time the sale (or attempted sale) takes place is present on the premises in a capacity which enables him to prevent it, and (d) in the case of premises which may be used for a permitted temporary activity by virtue of part 5, the premises user in relation to the temporary event notice in question (s. 141(2)). Section 141 applies in relation to the supply of alcohol by or on behalf of a club to or to the order of a member of the club as it applies in relation to the sale of alcohol (s. 141(3)). The maximum penalty, on summary conviction, is a fine not exceeding level 3 on the standard scale (s. 141(4)).

B11.236 **Offences in relation to unauthorised licensable activities and alcohol** A person commits an offence if, on any premises, he exposes for sale by retail any alcohol in circumstances were the sale by retail of that alcohol on those premises would be an unauthorised licensable activity (Licensing Act 2003, s. 137(1)). 'Unauthorised licensable activity' is defined in ss. 137(2) and 136. For other definitions, see ss. 159, 191 (alcohol), 192 (sale by retail), and 193. There is a due diligence defence, see s. 139. For provisions in relation to institution of proceedings, jurisdiction and procedure, see ss. 186 and 188. For the application of the Act to vessels, vehicles and moveable structures, see s. 189. The maximum penalty, on summary conviction, is imprisonment not exceeding six months or a fine not exceeding £20,000 or both (s. 137(3)). As to forfeiture and destruction or other dealing with alcohol, see s. 137(4).

A person commits an offence if he has in his possession or under his control alcohol which he intends to sell by retail or supply in circumstances where that activity would be an unauthorised licensable activity (s. 138(1)). 'Unauthorised licensable activity' is defined in ss. 138(2) and 136. The reference to the supply of alcohol is a reference to the supply of alcohol by or on behalf of a club to, or to the order of, a member of the club (s. 138(3)). For other definitions and procedural matters, see above. There is a due diligence defence, see s. 139. The maximum penalty, on summary conviction, is a fine not exceeding level 2 on the standard scale (s. 138(4)). As to forfeiture and destruction or other dealing with alcohol, see s. 138(5).

B11.237 **Selling alcohol on or from moving vehicles** It is an offence, contrary to the Licensing Act 2003, s. 156(1), for a person to sell by retail alcohol on or from a vehicle at a time when the vehicle is not permanently or temporarily parked. The maximum penalty, on summary conviction, is imprisonment not exceeding three months, or a fine not exceeding

£20,000, or both (s. 156(2)). A reasonable precautions and due diligence defence is provided (s.156(3)).

Selling alcohol on trains Where, under the Licensing Act 2003, s. 157(1) to (4), a magistrates' court has prohibited the sale of alcohol on a railway vehicle, it is an offence, contrary to s. 157(5), where a person knowingly (a) sells or attempts to sell alcohol in contravention of such an order, or (b) allows the sale of alcohol in contravention of such an order. The maximum penalty, on summary conviction, is imprisonment not exceeding three months, or a fine not exceeding £20,000, or both (s. 157(6)). **B11.238**

OFFENCES IN CONNECTION WITH SPORTING EVENTS

Alcohol on Coaches and Trains

Sporting Events (Control of Alcohol etc.) Act 1985, s. 1 **B11.239**

(2) A person who knowingly causes or permits alcohol to be carried on a vehicle to which this section applies is guilty of an offence—
 (a) if the vehicle is a public service vehicle and he is the operator of the vehicle or the servant or agent of the operator, or
 (b) if the vehicle is a hired vehicle and he is the person to whom it is hired or the servant or agent of that person.

(3) A person who has alcohol in his possession while on a vehicle to which this section applies is guilty of an offence.

(4) A person who is drunk on a vehicle to which this section applies is guilty of an offence.

Sentence and Procedure Offences under the Sporting Events (Control of Alcohol etc.) Act 1985, s. 1, are, by s. 8 of the Act, triable summarily only and punishable: **B11.240**

(i) in the case of an offence under s. 1(2), a fine not exceeding level 4 on the standard scale;
(ii) in the case of an offence under s. 1(3), a fine not exceeding level 3 on the standard scale or imprisonment for a term not exceeding three months, or both;
(iii) in the case of an offence under s. 1(4), a fine not exceeding level 2 on the standard scale.

Meaning of 'Vehicle'

Sporting Events (Control of Alcohol etc.) Act 1985, s. 1 **B11.241**

(1) This section applies to a vehicle which—
 (a) is a public service vehicle or railway passenger vehicle, and
 (b) is being used for the principal purpose of carrying passengers for the whole or part of a journey to or from a designated sporting event.

(2) to (4) [see 11.239]

(5) In this section 'public service vehicle' and 'operator' have the same meaning as in the Public Passenger Vehicles Act 1981.

Meaning of 'Designated Sporting Event'

Sporting Events (Control of Alcohol etc.) Act 1985, s. 9 **B11.242**

(3) 'Designated sporting event'—
 (a) means a sporting event or proposed sporting event for the time being designated, or of a class designated, by order made by the Secretary of State, and
 (b) includes a designated sporting event within the meaning of part II of the Criminal Law (Consolidation) (Scotland) Act 1995;

and an order under this subsection may apply to events or proposed events outside Great Britain as well as those in England and Wales.

See the Sports Grounds and Sporting Events (Designation Order) 1985 (SI 1985 No. 1151), as amended.

Alcohol on Other Vehicles

B11.243 **Sporting Events (Control of Alcohol etc.) Act 1985, s. 1A**

(2) A person who knowingly causes or permits alcohol to be carried on a motor vehicle to which this section applies is guilty of an offence—
(a) if he is its driver, or
(b) if he is not its driver but is its keeper, the servant or agent of its keeper, a person to whom it is made available (by hire, loan or otherwise) by its keeper or the keeper's servant or agent, or the servant or agent of a person to whom it is so made available.

(3) A person who has alcohol in his possession while on a motor vehicle to which this section applies is guilty of an offence.

(4) A person who is drunk on a motor vehicle to which this section applies is guilty of an offence.

B11.244 **Sentence and Procedure** Offences under the Sporting Events (Control of Alcohol etc.) Act 1985, s. 1A are, by s. 8, triable summarily only and punishable.

(i) in the case of an offence under s. 1A(2), a fine not exceeding level 4 on the standard scale;
(ii) in the case of an offence under s. 1A(3), a fine not exceeding level 3 on the standard scale or imprisonment for a terms not exceeding three months, or both;
(iii) in the case of an offence under s. 1A(4), a fine not exceeding level 2 on the standard scale.

Meaning of Terms

B11.245 **Sporting Events (Control of Alcohol etc.) Act 1985, s. 1A**

(1) This section applies to a motor vehicle which—
(a) is not a public service vehicle but is adapted to carry more than 8 passengers, and
(b) is being used for the principal purpose of carrying two or more passengers for the whole or part of a journey to or from a designated sporting event.

. . .

(5) In this section—
'keeper', in relation to a vehicle, means the person having the duty to take out a licence for it under the Vehicle Excise and Registration Act 1994,
'motor vehicle' means a mechanically propelled vehicle intended or adapted for use on roads, and
'public service vehicle' has the same meaning as in the Public Passenger Vehicles Act 1981.

Containers etc. at Sports Grounds

B11.246 **Sporting Events (Control of Alcohol etc.) Act 1985, s. 2**

(1) A person who has alcohol or an article to which this section applies in his possession—
(a) at any time during the period of a designated sporting event when he is in any area of a designated sports ground from which the event may be directly viewed, or
(b) while entering or trying to enter a designated sports ground at any time during the period of a designated sporting event at that ground, is guilty of an offence.

(1A) Subsection (1)(a) above has effect subject to section 5A(1) of this Act.

(2) A person who is drunk in a designated sports ground at any time during the period of a designated sporting event at that ground or is drunk while entering or trying to enter such a ground at any time during the period of a designated sporting event at that ground is guilty of an offence.

Special provision is made by s. 5A(1) for private rooms from which the sporting event can be viewed; although prospectively repealed by the Licensing Act 2003, s. 198 and sch. 6, this provision remains in force.

B11.247 **Sentence and Procedure** Offences under the Sporting Events (Control of Alcohol etc.) Act 1985, s. 2, are, by s. 8 of the Act, triable summarily only and punishable.

(i) in the case of an offence under s. 2(1), a fine not exceeding level 3 on the standard scale or imprisonment for a term not exceeding three months, or both;
(ii) in the case of an offence under s. 2(2), a fine not exceeding level 2 on the standard scale.

The Magistrates' Courts Guidelines (2004) indicate the following for a first-time offender pleading not guilty to an offence under s. 2(1):

Aggravating Factors For example concealed; group action; high alcoholic content liquor; large amount of alcohol; offensive language/behaviour used; offence committed on bail; relevant previous convictions and any failures to respond to previous sentences

Mitigating Factors For example low alcoholic content liquor; small amount of alcohol

Guideline: Is discharge or fine appropriate?

The guideline fine is Starting Point B (see **E17.5**).

The Magistrates' Courts Guidelines (2004) indicate the following for a first-time offender pleading not guilty to an offence under s. 2(2):

Aggravating Factors For example group action; offensive language/behaviour used; offence committed on bail; relevant previous convictions and any failures to respond to previous sentences

Mitigating Factors For example no significant disturbance; not threatening

Guideline: Is discharge or fine appropriate?

The guideline fine is Starting Point A (see **E17.5**).

Both for the s. 2(1) and s. 2(2) offence, the court must consider imposing a banning order. If no banning order is made, the court must give reasons. Community rehabilitation orders and curfew orders are the only available community penalties for these offences.

Meaning of Terms For the meaning of 'designated sporting event', see **B11.242**. **B11.248**

Sporting Events (Control of Alcohol etc.) Act 1985, s. 9

(2) 'Designated sports ground' means any place—
  (a) used (wholly or partly) for sporting events where accommodation is provided for spectators, and
  (b) for the time being designated, or of a class designated, by order made by the Secretary of State;

and an order under this subsection may include provision for determining for the purposes of this Act the outer limit of any designated sports ground.

. . .

(4) The period of a designated sporting event is the period beginning two hours before the start of the event or (if earlier) two hours before the time at which it is advertised to start and ending one hour after the end of the event, but—
  (a) where an event advertised to start at a particular time on a particular day is postponed to a later day, the period includes the period in the day on which it is advertised to take place beginning two hours before and ending one hour after that time, and
  (b) where an event advertised to start at a particular time on a particular day does not take place, the period is the period referred to in paragraph (a) above.

The articles to which s. 2 applies are defined in s. 2(3):

This section applies to any article capable of causing injury to a person struck by it, being—
  (a) a bottle, can or other portable container (including such an article when crushed or broken) which—
    (i) is for holding any drink, and
    (ii) is of a kind which, when empty, is normally discarded or returned to, or left to be recovered by, the supplier, or
  (b) part of an article falling within paragraph (a) above;

but does not apply to anything that is for holding any medicinal product (within the meaning of the Medicines Act 1968).

Possession of Flares, Fireworks, etc. at Sports Grounds

Sporting Events (Control of Alcohol etc.) Act 1985, s. 2A

(1) A person is guilty of an offence if he has an article or substance to which this section applies in his possession— **B11.249**

(a) at any time during the period of a designated sporting event when he is in any area of a designated sports ground from which the event may be directly viewed, or
(b) while entering or trying to enter a designated sports ground at any time during the period of a designated sporting event at the ground.
(2) It is a defence for the accused to prove that he had possession with lawful authority.
(3) This section applies to any article or substance whose main purpose is the emission of a flare for purposes of illuminating or signalling (as opposed to igniting or heating) or the emission of smoke or a visible gas; and in particular it applies to distress flares, fog signals, and pellets and capsules intended to be used as fumigators or for testing pipes, but not to matches, cigarette lighters or heaters.
(4) This section also applies to any article which is a firework.

For the meaning of 'designated sporting event', see **B11.242**; for the meaning of 'designated sports ground', see **B11.248**.

B11.250 **Sentence and Procedure** Offences under the Sporting Events (Control of Alcohol etc.) Act 1985, s. 2A are, by s. 8, triable summarily only, and punishable:

(i) in the case of an offence under s. 1A(2), a fine not exceeding level 4 on the standard scale;
(ii) in the case of an offence under s. 1A(3), a fine not exceeding level 3 on the standard scale or imprisonment for a terms not exceeding three months, or both;
(iii) in the case of an offence under s. 1A(4), a fine not exceeding level 2 on the standard scale.

Section B12 Offences Relating to Weapons

FIREARMS OFFENCES GENERALLY

The Firearms Acts 1968 to 1997 control the possession etc. of firearms by dividing such weapons into a number of different categories, namely (i) firearms, (ii) firearms within s. 1 of the FA 1968, (iii) prohibited weapons, (iv) shotguns and (v) air weapons. The F(A)A 1988, s. 8, introduced a provision relating to the deactivation of a weapon thus taking it out of a category into which it would otherwise have fallen (see **B12.8**). Many of the offences control ammunition as well as firearms. The two important concepts are ammunition generally, and ammunition to which s. 1 of the FA 1968 applies. Care needs to be taken where the item is an 'imitation firearm' because some offences expressly make reference to imitation firearms (see **B12.11**), while the reach of other offences extends to imitation firearms by operation of the FA 1982, ss. 1 and 2 (**B12.14**). **B12.1**

General Procedural Provisions

Section 51(1) to (3) of the FA 1968 provides that the mode of trial, maximum punishments and powers of convicting courts with respect to offences created by that Act shall be as set out in sch. 6 to that Act, which is reproduced at **B12.3**. **B12.2**

Firearms Act 1968, s. 51

(4) Notwithstanding section 127(1) of the Magistrates' Courts Act 1980 or section 136 of the Criminal Procedure (Scotland) Act 1995 (limitation of time for taking proceedings) summary proceedings for an offence under this Act, other than an offence under section

22(3) or an offence relating specifically to air weapons, may be instituted at any time within four years after the commission of the offence:
Provided that no such proceedings shall be instituted in England after the expiration of six months after the commission of the offence unless they are instituted by, or by the direction of, the Director of Public Prosecutions.

Sections 46 to 49 of the FA 1968 provide for powers of search, demand by a constable for production of certificates, and police powers in relation to arms traffic.

Powers of forfeiture exercisable by a convicting court may be found in two places. Part II of sch. 6 to the FA 1968 (**B12.3**) provides certain specific powers. Section 52 provides generally for forfeiture and disposal of firearms and for cancellation of certificates. As from 6 April 2007, s. 50(3) of the VCRA 2006 applies insofar as it makes provision for ss. 46, 51(4), 52 and 58 of the FA 1968 to apply as if ss. 28, 29 and 35 of the 2006 Act were contained in that Act (see the Violent Crime Reduction Act 2006 (Commencement No. 2) Order 2007 (SI 2007 No. 858)). The following provisions of the VCRA 2006 came into force on 31 May 2007: (a) s. 45 (power of members of staff to search school pupils for weapons) insofar as it extends to England; (b) s. 46 (power to search further education students for weapons) insofar as it extends to England; (c) s. 48 (amendment of police power to search schools etc. for weapons).

Firearms Act 1968, s. 52

(1) Where a person—
- (a) is convicted of an offence under this Act (other than an offence under section 22(3) or an offence relating specifically to air weapons) or is convicted of a crime for which he is sentenced to imprisonment, or detention in a young offender institution or in a young offenders' institution in Scotland or is subject to a detention and training order; or
- (b) has been ordered into a recognizance to keep the peace or to be of good behaviour, a condition of which is that he shall not possess, use or carry a firearm; or
- (c) is subject to a community order containing a requirement that he shall not possess, use or carry a firearm; or
- (d) [applies to Scotland only]

the court by or before which he is convicted, or by which the order is made, may make such order as to the forfeiture or disposal of any firearm or ammunition found in his possession as the court thinks fit and may cancel any firearm certificate or shot gun certificate held by him.

(1A) In subsection (1)(c) 'community order' means—
- (a) a community order within the meaning of part 12 of the Criminal Justice Act 2003 made in England and Wales, or
- (b) a probation order made in Scotland.

(2) Where the court cancels a certificate under this section—
- (a) the court shall cause notice to be sent to the chief officer of police by whom the certificate was granted; and
- (b) the chief officer of police shall by notice in writing require the holder of the certificate to surrender it; and
- (c) it is an offence for the holder to fail to surrender the certificate within 21 days from the date of the notice given him by the chief officer of police.

(3) A constable may seize and detain any firearm or ammunition which may be the subject of an order for forfeiture under this section.

(4) A court of summary jurisdiction or, in Scotland, the sheriff may, on the application of the chief officer of police, order any firearm or ammunition seized and detained by a constable under this Act to be destroyed or otherwise disposed of.

(5) In this section references to ammunition include references to a primer to which section 35 of the Violent Crime Reduction Act 2006 applies and to an empty cartridge case incorporating such a primer.

B12.3

Firearms Act 1968, sch. 6

Part I Table of Punishment

Section of this Act creating offence	General nature of offence	Mode of prosecution	Punishment	Additional provisions
Section 1(1)	Possessing etc. firearm or ammunition without certificate.	(a) Summary (b) On indictment	6 months or a fine of the prescribed sum; or both. (i) where the offence is committed in an aggravated form within the meaning of section 4(4) of this Act, 7 years, or a fine; or both. (ii) in any other case, 5 years or a fine; or both.	[*Applies to Scotland only.*]
Section 1(2)	Non-compliance with condition of firearm certificate	Summary	6 months or a fine of level 5 on the standard scale; or both.	
Section 2(1)	Possessing, etc. shot gun without shot gun certificate	(a) Summary (b) On indictment	6 months or the statutory maximum or both. 5 years or a fine or both.	[*Applies to Scotland only.*]
Section 2(2)	Non-compliance with condition of shot gun certificate.	Summary	6 months or a fine of level 5 on the standard scale; or both.	[*Applies to Scotland only.*]
Section 3(1)	Trading in firearms without being registered as firearms dealer.	(a) Summary (b) On indictment	6 months or a fine of the prescribed sum; or both. 5 years or a fine; or both.	
Section 3(2)	Selling firearm to person without a certificate.	(a) Summary (b) On indictment.	6 months or a fine of the prescribed sum, or both. 5 years or a fine; or both.	
Section 3(3)	Repairing, testing etc. firearm for person without a certificate.	(a) Summary (b) On indictment	6 months or a fine of the prescribed sum; or both. 5 years of a fine; or both.	
Section 3(5)	Falsifying certificate, etc. with view to acquisition of firearm.	(a) Summary (b) On indictment	6 months or a fine of the prescribed sum; or both. 5 years or a fine; or both.	

Section of this Act creating offence	General nature of offence	Mode of prosecution	Punishment	Additional provisions
Section 3(6)	Pawnbroker taking firearm in pawn.	Summary	3 months or a fine of level 3 on the standard scale; or both.	
Section 4(1), (3)	Shortening a shot gun; conversion of firearms.	(a) Summary (b) On indictment	6 months or a fine of the prescribed sum; or both. 7 years or a fine; or both.	
Section 5(1)(a), (ab), (aba), (ac), (ad), (ae), (af) or (c)	Possessing or distributing prohibited weapons or ammunition.	On indictment	10 years or a fine, or both.	
Section 5(1)(b)	Possessing or distributing prohibited weapons designed for discharge of noxious liquid etc.	(a) Summary (b) On indictment	6 months or a fine of the statutory maximum, or both. 10 years or a fine, or both.	
Section 5(1A)(a)	Possessing or distributing firearm disguised as other object.	On indictment	10 years or a fine, or both.	
Section 5(1A)(b), (c), (d), (e), (f), or (g)	Possessing or distributing other prohibited weapons.	(a) Summary (b) On indictment	6 months or a fine of the statutory maximum, or both. 10 years or a fine, or both.	
Section 5(5)	Non-compliance with condition of Defence Council authority.	Summary	6 months or a fine of level 5 on the standard scale; or both.	
Section 5(6)	Non-compliance with requirement to surrender authority to possess, etc. prohibited weapon or ammunition.	Summary	A fine of level 3 on the standard scale.	
Section 6(3)	Contravention of order under s. 6 (or corresponding Northern Irish order) restricting removal of arms.	Summary	3 months or, for each firearm or parcel of ammunition in respect of which the offence is committed, a fine of level 3 on the standard scale; or both.	Para. 2 of part II of this schedule applies.
Section 7(2)	Making false statement in order to obtain police permit.	Summary	6 months or a fine of level 5 on the standard scale; or both.	
Section 9(3)	Making false statement in order to obtain permit for auction of firearms etc.	Summary	6 months or a fine not exceeding level 5 on the standard scale; or both.	

Section 13(2)	Making false statement in order to obtain permit for removal of signalling apparatus.	Summary	6 months or a fine of level 5 on the standard scale; or both.	
Section 16	Possession of firearm with intent to endanger life or injure property.	On indictment	Life imprisonment or a fine; or both.	
Section 16A	Possession of firearm or imitation firearm with intent to cause fear of violence.	On indictment	10 years or a fine, or both.	
Section 17(1)	Use of firearm or imitation firearm to resist arrest.	On indictment	Life imprisonment or a fine; or both.	Paras. 3 to 5 of Part II of this schedule apply.
Section 17(2)	Possessing firearm or imitation firearm while committing an offence in schedule 1 or, in Scotland, an offence specified in schedule 2.	On indictment	Life imprisonment or a fine; or both.	Paras. 3 and 6 of part II of this schedule apply.
Section 18(1)	Carrying firearm or imitation firearm with intent to commit indictable offence (or, in Scotland, an offence specified in schedule 2) or to resist arrest.	On indictment	Life imprisonment or a fine; or both.	
Section 19	Carrying firearm or imitation firearm in public place.	(a) Summary except if the firearm is a firearm specified in section 5(1)(a), (ab), (aba), (ac), (ad), (ae) or (af) or section 5(1A)(a) of this Act. (b) On indictment (but not *in the case of imitation firearm or* if the firearm is an air weapon).	6 months or a fine of the prescribed sum; or both. *7 years or a fine; or both.* [(i) if the weapon is an imitation firearm, 12 months or a fine, or both; (ii) in any other case, 7 years or a fine, or both.]	

Section of this Act creating offence	General nature of offence	Mode of prosecution	Punishment	Additional provisions
Section 20(1)	Trespassing with firearm or imitation firearm in a building	(a) Summary except if the firearm is a firearm specified in section 5(1)(a), (ab), (aba), (ac), (ad), (ae) or (af) or section 5(1A)(a) of this Act. (b) On indictment (but not in the case of an imitation firearm or if the firearm is an air weapon).	6 months or a fine of the prescribed sum; or both. 7 years or a fine; or both.	
Section 20(2)	Trespassing with firearm or imitation firearm on land.	Summary	3 months or a fine of level 4 on the standard scale; or both.	
Section 21(4)	Contravention of provisions denying firearms to ex-prisoners and the like.	(a) Summary (b) On indictment	6 months or a fine of the prescribed sum; or both. 5 years or a fine; or both.	
Section 21(5)	Supplying firearms to person denied them under section 21.	(a) Summary (b) On indictment	6 months or a fine of the prescribed sum; or both. 5 years or a fine; or both.	
Section 21A	Person making improper use of air weapon.	Summary	A fine of level 3 on the standard scale.	Paras. 7 and 8 of part II of this schedule apply
Section 22(1)	Person under 17 acquiring firearm [or person under 18 acquiring air weapon].	Summary	6 months or a fine of level 5 on the standard scale; or both.	
Section 22(1A)	Person under 18 using certified firearm for unauthorised purpose.	Summary	3 months or a fine of level 5 on the standard scale or both.	
Section 22(2)	Person under 14 having firearm in his possession without lawful authority.	Summary	6 months or a fine of level 5 on the standard scale; or both.	

Section 22(3)	Person under 15 having with him a shot gun without adult supervision.	Summary	A fine of level 3 on the standard scale.	Para. 8 of part II of this schedule applies.
Section 22(4)	Person under *17* [18] having with him an air weapon or ammunition therefore.	Summary	A fine of level 3 on the standard scale.	Paras. 7 and 8 of part II of this schedule apply.
Section 23(1)	*Person under 17 making improper use of air weapon when under supervision; person supervising him permitting such use.* [Person supervising a person under 18 and allowing him to make improper use of air weapon.]	Summary	A fine of level 3 on the standard scale.	Paras. 7 and 8 of part II of this schedule apply.
Section 23(4)	*Person under 17 making improper use of air weapon on private premises.*	*Summary*	*A fine of level 3 on the standard scale.*	*Paras. 7 and 8 of part II of this schedule apply.*
Section 24(1)	Selling or letting on hire a firearm to person under 17 [or an air weapon to a person under 18]	Summary	6 months or a fine of level 5 on the standard scale; or both.	
Section 24(2)	Supplying firearm or ammunition (being of a kind to which section 1 of this Act applies) to person under *17* [18].	Summary	6 months or a fine of level 5 on the standard scale; or both.	
Section 24(3)	Making gift of shot gun to person under 15.	Summary	A fine of level 3 on the standard scale.	schedule applies.
Section 24(4)	Supplying air weapon to person under 14.	Summary	A fine of level 3 on the standard scale.	Paras. 7 and 8 of part II of this schedule apply.
Section 24A(1) or (2)	Acquisition by a minor of an imitation firearm and supplying him.	Summary	In England and Wales, 6 months or a fine of level 5 on the standard scale, or both. [Further provision re Scotland.]	

Section of this Act creating offence	General nature of offence	Mode of prosecution	Punishment	Additional provisions
Section 25	Supplying firearm to person drunk or insane.	Summary	3 months or a fine of level 3 on the standard scale; or both.	
Section 26(5)	Making false statement in order to procure grant or renewal of a firearm or shot gun certificate.	Summary	6 months or a fine of level 5 on the standard scale; or both.	
Section 29(3)	Making false statement in order to procure variation of a firearm certificate.	Summary	6 months or a fine of level 5 on the standard scale; or both.	
Section 30D(3)	Failing to surrender certificate on revocation.	Summary	A fine of level 3 on the standard scale.	
Section 32B(5)	Failure to surrender expired European firearms pass.	Summary	A fine of level 3 on the standard scale.	
Section 32C(6)	Failure to produce European firearms pass or Article 7 authority for variation or cancellation etc.; failure to notify loss or theft of firearm identified in pass or to produce pass for endorsement.	Summary	3 months or a fine of level 5 on the standard scale; or both.	
Section 38(8)	Failure to surrender certificate of registration [or register of transactions] on removal of firearms dealer's name from register.	Summary	A fine of level 3 on the standard scale.	
Section 39(1)	Making false statement in order to secure registration or entry in register of a place of business.	Summary	6 months or a fine of level 5 on the standard scale; or both.	
Section 39(2)	Registered firearms dealer having place of business not entered in the register.	Summary	6 months or a fine of level 5 on the standard scale; or both.	

Section 39(3)	Non-compliance with condition of registration.	Summary	6 months or a fine of level 5 on the standard scale; or both.	
Section 40(5)	Non-compliance by firearms dealer with provisions as to register of transactions; making false entry in register.	Summary	6 months or a fine of level 5 on the standard scale; or both.	
Section 42A	Failure to report transaction authorised by visitor's shot gun permit.	Summary	3 months or a fine of level 5 on the standard scale or both.	
Section 46	Obstructing constable or civilian officer in exercise of search powers.	Summary	6 months or a fine of level 5 on the standard scale; or both.	
Section 47(2)	Failure to hand over firearm or ammunition on demand by constable.	Summary	3 months, or a fine of level 4 on the standard scale; or both.	
Section 48(3)	Failure to comply with requirement of a constable that a person shall declare his name and address.	Summary	A fine of level 3 on the standard scale.	
Section 48A(4)	Failure to produce firearms pass issued in another Member State.	Summary	A fine of level 3 on the standard scale.	
Section 49(3)	Failure to give constable facilities for examination of firearms in transit, or to produce papers.	Summary	3 months or, for each firearm or parcel of ammunition in respect of which the offence is committed, a fine of level 3 on the standard scale; or both.	Para. 2 of part II of this schedule applies.
Section 52(2)(c)	Failure to surrender firearm or shot gun certificate cancelled by court on conviction.	Summary	A fine of level 3 on the standard scale.	

Note: Schedule 6, part 1 is amended by the VCRA 2006. Prospective amendments are shown above in square brackets; prospective repeals are shown in italics; most take effect from 1 October 2007 (see SI 2007 No. 2180).

PART II

1. [Applies to Scotland only.]
2. In the case of an offence against section 6(3) or 49(3) of this Act, the court before which the offender is convicted may, if the offender is the owner of the firearms or ammunition, make such order as to the forfeiture of the firearms or ammunition as the court thinks fit.
3.—(1) Where in England or Wales a person who has attained the age of seventeen is charged before a magistrates' court with an offence triable either way listed in schedule 1 to the Magistrates' Courts Act 1980 ('the listed offence') and is also charged before that court with an offence under section 17(1) or (2) of this Act, the following provisions of this paragraph shall apply.
(2) Subject to the following subparagraph the court shall proceed as if the listed offence were triable only on indictment and sections 18 to 23 of the said Act of 1980 (procedure for determining mode of trial of offences triable either way) shall not apply in relation to that offence.
(3) If the court determines not to commit the accused for trial in respect of the offence under section 17(1) or (2), or if proceedings before the court for that offence are otherwise discontinued, the preceding subparagraph shall cease to apply as from the time when this occurs and—
 (a) if at that time the court has not yet begun to inquire into the listed offence as examining justices, the court shall, in the case of the listed offence, proceed in the ordinary way in accordance with the said sections 18 to 23, but
 (b) if at that time the court has begun so to inquire into the listed offence, those sections shall continue not to apply and the court shall proceed with its inquiry into that offence as examining justices, but shall have power in accordance with section 25(3) and (4) of the said Act of 1980 to change to summary trial with the accused's consent.
4. Where a person commits an offence under section 17(1) of this Act in respect of the lawful arrest or detention of himself for any other offence committed by him, he shall be liable to the penalty provided by part I of this schedule in addition to any penalty to which he may be sentenced for the other offence.
5. If on the trial of a person for an offence under section 17(1) of this Act the jury are not satisfied that he is guilty of that offence but are satisfied that he is guilty of an offence under section 17(2), the jury may find him guilty of the offence under section 17(2) and he shall then be punishable accordingly.
6. The punishment to which a person is liable for an offence under section 17(2) of this Act shall be in addition to any punishment to which he may be liable for the offence first referred to in section 17(2).
7. The court by which a person is convicted of an offence under section 21A, 22(4), 23(1) or (4) or 24(4) of this Act may make such order as it thinks fit as to the forfeiture or disposal of the air weapon or ammunition in respect of which the offence was committed.
8. The court by which a person is convicted of an offence under section 21A, 22(3) or (4), 23(1) or (4) or 24(4) may make such order as it thinks fit as to the forfeiture or disposal of any firearm or ammunition found in his possession.
9. The court by which a person is convicted of an offence under section 24(3) of this Act may make such order is it thinks fit as to the forfeiture or disposal of the shotgun or ammunition in respect of which the offence was committed.

Meaning of 'Firearm'

B12.4 **Firearms Act 1968, s. 57**

(1) In this Act, the expression 'firearm' means a lethal barrelled weapon of any description from which any shot, bullet or other missile can be discharged, and includes—
 (a) any prohibited weapon, whether it is such a lethal weapon as aforesaid or not; and
 (b) any component part of such a lethal or prohibited weapon; and
 (c) any accessory to any such weapon designed or adapted to diminish the noise or flash caused by firing the weapon.

The meaning of 'prohibited weapon' is considered at **B12.50** ***et seq.*** There is no statutory definition of a 'lethal barrelled weapon'. The Divisional Court in *Grace v DPP* (1989) 153 JP 491, held that the prosecution has the obligation to prove the following in order to satisfy the definition:

(a) whether the weapon was one from which any shot, bullet or other missile could be discharged or whether it could be adapted so as to be made capable of discharging such a missile, and
(b) if so satisfied, whether it was a lethal barrelled weapon.

As to the first question, see *Freeman* [1970] 1 WLR 788, where a starting pistol was capable of discharging bullets since the barrel had been partially drilled, and *Anderson* [2006] EWCA Crim 738, where it was confirmed that an unloaded or ineffectively loaded gun could be a firearm.

In determining the second question, the Divisional Court, in *Read v Donovan* [1947] KB 326 (a case under the predecessor to s. 57), established an enduring test, namely that a weapon is lethal if it is capable of causing injury from which death might result, regardless of the maker's intentions.

Whether a device is a 'lethal barrelled weapon' is ultimately a question of fact (see *Grace v DPP*). The correct approach, according to the Court of Appeal in *Singh* [1989] Crim LR 724, is for a judge to determine whether the device is capable of amounting to a firearm. Then he should leave to the jury the question of whether it actually is a lethal weapon. In *Singh*, the judge had correctly left the jury to decide the matter where there was a dispute between expert witnesses as to whether the device (a hand-held signalling discharger) had a barrel.

The following devices were found, on the facts of the particular case, to be 'lethal barrelled' weapons: (i) a signal pistol, capable of killing at short range (*Paul* [1999] Crim LR 79); (ii) a dummy revolver which could be converted into a weapon capable of killing a man at a range of five feet (*Cafferata v Wilson* [1936] 3 All ER 149); (iii) an airgun which was capable of causing injury from which death might result if it was misused (*Moore v Gooderham* [1960] 1 WLR 1308); (iv) an air pellet revolver capable of causing injury from which death could result if misused (*Thorpe* [1987] 1 WLR 383 (applying *Read v Donovan* and *Moore v Gooderham*)); (v) two air rifles suitable for shooting small vermin, and two air rifles suitable for target practice, which 'could cause injury from which death might result if fired at point blank range at a vulnerable part of the body' (*Castle v DPP* (1998) *The Times* 3 April 1998). In *Castle v DPP*, the magistrates were entitled to draw the inference that the guns were lethal barrelled weapons, having regard to assertions made by a salesman that the guns were working and for what purpose they would be suitable.

Meaning of 'Prohibited Weapon'

The FA 1968, s. 57(4), makes it clear that 'prohibited weapon' has the meaning assigned to it by s. 5(2): see **B12.50** ***et seq.*** By virtue of the F(A)A 1988, s. 7(1), the conversion of a weapon does not affect its classification as a prohibited weapon (see **B12.54**). **B12.5**

Meaning of 'Shotgun'

'Shotgun' has the meaning assigned to it by the FA 1968, s. 1(3)(a) (see s. 57(4)). **B12.6**

Firearms Act 1968, s. 1

(3) This section applies to every firearm except—
  (a) a shotgun within the meaning of this Act, that is to say a smooth-bore gun (not being an airgun) which—
    (i) has a barrel not less than 24 inches in length and does not have any barrel with a bore exceeding 2 inches in diameter;
    (ii) either has no magazine or has a non-detachable magazine incapable of holding more than two cartridges; and
    (iii) is not a revolver gun. . . .

(3A) A gun which has been adapted to have such a magazine as is mentioned in subsection (3)(a)(ii) above shall not be regarded as falling within that provision unless the magazine bears a mark approved by the Secretary of State for denoting that fact and that mark has been

> made, and the adaptation has been certified in writing as having been carried out in a manner approved by him, either by one of the two companies mentioned in section 58(1) of this Act or by such other person as may be approved by him for that purpose.

The companies mentioned in s. 58(1) are the Society of the Mystery of Gunmakers of the City of London and the Birmingham Proof House.

The length of the barrel of a firearm shall be measured from the muzzle to the point at which the charge is exploded on firing (s. 57(6)(a)). 'Revolver', in relation to a smoothbore gun, means a gun containing a series of chambers, which revolve when the gun is fired (s. 57(2B)).

Meaning of 'Air Weapon'

B12.7 Section 57(4) of the FA 1968 states that an 'air weapon' has the meaning assigned to it by s. 1(3)(b) of that Act, 'that is to say, *an air rifle, air gun or air pistol* which does not fall within section 5(1) and which is not of a type declared by rules made by the Secretary of State under section 53 of this Act to be specially dangerous'.

As the Court of Appeal stated in *Thorpe* [1987] 1 WLR 383, carbon dioxide is not air, and therefore s. 48 of the FA(A)A 1997 was enacted to provide that the words 'an air rifle, airgun or air pistol' as they appear both in s. 1(3)(b) and in the Firearms (Dangerous Air Weapons) Rules 1969 (SI 1969 No. 47) include 'a rifle, pistol or gun powered by compressed carbon dioxide'.

An air weapon may also be a 'firearm' for the purposes of s. 1 FA, 1968, but only (i) where it has been designated as being 'specially dangerous' (see **B12.21**), or (ii) it falls within the FA 1968, s. 5(1) (see **B12.50**).

De-activated Weapons

B12.8 Any firearm may be de-activated and so cease to be a firearm.

Firearms (Amendment) Act 1988, s. 8

> For the purposes of the principal Act and this Act it shall be presumed, unless the contrary is shown, that a firearm has been rendered incapable of discharging any shot, bullet or other missile, and has consequently ceased to be a firearm within the meaning of those Acts, if—
> (a) it bears a mark which has been approved by the Secretary of State for denoting that fact and which has been made either by one of the two companies mentioned in section 58(1) of the principal Act or by such other person as may be approved by the Secretary of State for the purposes of this section; and
> (b) that company or person has certified in writing that work has been carried out on the firearm in a manner approved by the Secretary of State for rendering it incapable of discharging any shot, bullet or other missile.

The 'two companies' are identified at **B12.6**.

Note the judgment of the Courts-Martial Appeal Court concerning de-activated weapons, and the component parts of a weapon (whether de-activated or not) in *Ashton* [2007] EWCA Crim 234:

> So long as a de-activated weapon remains in its complete state, there is therefore a justification in permitting it to be possessed or indeed traded on the open market. But it is clear from the exception that it is not intended to apply to any component part of such a weapon and that must be for the good public policy reason that once a weapon, de-activated or not, is disassembled then the parts which are then made available are capable of being re-assembled into a working weapon.

Meaning of 'Ammunition'

B12.9 The FA 1968, s. 57(2), provides a general definition of 'ammunition'.

Firearms Act 1968, s. 57(2)

> (2) In this Act, the expression 'ammunition' means ammunition for any firearm and includes

grenades, bombs and other like missiles, whether capable of use with a firearm or not, and also includes prohibited ammunition.

Section 58(3) makes clear that control over ammunition is in addition to, and not in derogation of, any enactment relating to the keeping and sale of explosives.

Cap-type Primers

Section 35 of the VCRA 2006, which came into force on 6 April 2007, creates summary offences in connection with cap-type primers designed for use in metallic ammunition for a firearm. By s. 35(2), it is an offence for a person to sell to another either (a) a primer to which s. 35 applies, or (b) an empty cartridge case incorporating such a primer, unless that other person falls within s. 35(3). Persons falling within s. 35(3) include (a) a registered firearms dealer; (b) a person who sells by way of any trade or business either primers or empty cartridge cases incorporating primers, or both; (c) the holder of a certificate authorising him to possess a firearm of a relevant kind; (d) the holder of a certificate authorising him to possess ammunition of a relevant kind. **B12.10**

Section 35(4) of the VCRA 2006 makes it an offence for a person to buy or to attempt to buy (a) a primer to which s. 35 applies, or (b) an empty cartridge case incorporating such a primer, unless he falls within s. 35(5). Although slightly different in phrasing, s. 35(5) covers the same persons as are covered by s. 35(3). Section 35 binds persons in the service of Her Majesty but such a person is expressly exempted from its restrictions if he is authorised as specified under s. 35(6). By s. 50(4) 'a person is in the service of Her Majesty if he is deemed to be in such service (or to be in the naval, military or air service of Her Majesty) for the purposes of and under section 54 of the 1968 Act (Crown application)' but s. 50(4) is not yet in force insofar as it applies to s. 35.

OFFENCES RELATING TO IMITATION FIREARMS

Offences Applying to Imitation Firearms by virtue of the Wording of the Section

Some offences, by their definition, apply to 'imitation firearms', see, for example, the offence contrary to the FA 1968, s. 17(1). If this is the case, 'imitation firearm' has the following definition, according to s. 57(4). **B12.11**

Firearms Act 1968, s. 57

(4) . . . 'imitation firearms' means any thing which has the appearance of being a firearm (other than such a weapon as is mentioned in section 5(1)(b) of this Act) whether or not it is capable of discharging any shot, bullet or other missile.

Weapons in s. 5(1)(b) are one category of prohibited weapons, that is, a weapon designed or adapted for the discharge of any noxious liquid, gas or other thing, see **B12.50**.

'Appearance of Being a Firearm' Whether an item is an 'imitation firearm' is a matter for the tribunal of fact to decide, taking an objective view (*K v DPP* [2006] EWHC 2183 (Admin)): 'In a case where there may be some doubt as to whether the thing was an imitation firearm, the authorities show that the tribunal of fact may take into account the views of witnesses who saw the thing, see *R v Morris and King* 79 Cr App R 104. In this case, the justices, having seen the BB gun, were in our judgment quite entitled to hold that it was an imitation firearm' (per Gage LJ at [13]). In *K v DPP*, the Divisional Court appears to have accepted as being correct the submission of the respondent that once the tribunal of fact had found the thing to be an imitation firearm, its character cannot change depending on the knowledge and perception of the person against whom it is used; in that case, the victim knew that a BB gun was an imitation firearm but he also knew that it was capable of firing a pellet which could cause him injury. In *Morris and King*, the accused was in possession of two **B12.12**

metal pipes bound together, giving the appearance of being a double-barrelled shotgun that could be regarded as an imitation firearm.

B12.13 **The Device Must Be a 'Thing' that is Distinct From the Holder of It** In *Bentham* [2005] 1 WLR 1057, the House of Lords held that, for a person to be in possession of an imitation firearm (FA 1968, s. 17(2); see **B12.80**), that person must be in possession of a 'thing' that is separate or distinct from himself. A person's hands or fingers are not a thing. Therefore, the conviction for possession of an imitation firearm, where the accused put his hand inside a zipped-up jacket forcing the material out so as to give the impression that he had a gun, was quashed. The accused might well have been pretending to have a firearm, but that was not the offence. This case does not affect the decision in *Morris* (1984) 79 Cr App R 104, because there the accused was clearly in possession of a thing (two metal pipes bound together). In *Williams* [2006] EWCA Crim 1650, it was held that, in the context of having a firearm with intention to commit an indictable offence contrary to the FA 1968, s. 18 (see **B12.83**), the relevant question was whether the thing had the appearance of a firearm at the relevant time.

Offences Applying to Imitation Firearms by virtue of the Firearms Act 1982

B12.14 Offences which do not fall within **B12.11** may nevertheless extend to imitation firearms if the FA 1982 covers the offence in question. In brief, the following matters have to be considered to determine whether an offence falls within the FA 1982, and thus extends to an imitation firearm:

(a) The FA 1982 applies to any firearm which has the appearance of being a firearm to which the FA 1968, s. 1, applies and is readily convertible into such a firearm (FA 1982, s. 1(1)). For the purpose of an imitation firearm all air weapons are covered, whether or not they are specially dangerous (s. 1(4)(a)). However, the definition does not apply to component parts and accessories (s. 1(4)(b)).

(b) This definition of imitation firearm applies to all offences which are concerned with a firearm to which the FA 1968, s. 1, applies (FA 1982, s. 1(2)), except ss. 4(3) and (4), 16 to 20 and 47 of the FA 1968 (FA 1982, s. 2(2)(a) and (b) and (3)).

Firearms Act 1982, ss. 1 and 2

1.—(1) This Act applies to an imitation firearm if—

(a) it has the appearance of being a firearm to which section 1 of the 1968 Act (firearms requiring a firearm certificate) applies; and

(b) it is so constructed or adapted as to be readily convertible into a firearm to which that section applies.

(2) Subject to section 2(2) of this Act and the following provisions of this section, the 1968 Act shall apply in relation to an imitation firearm to which this Act applies as it applies in relation to a firearm to which section 1 of that Act applies.

(3) Subject to the modifications in subsection (4) below, any expression given a meaning for the purposes of the 1968 Act has the same meaning in this Act.

(4) For the purposes of this section and the 1968 Act, as it applies by virtue of this section—

(a) the definition of air weapon in section 1(3)(b) of that Act (air weapons excepted from requirement of firearm certificate) shall have effect without the exclusion of any type declared by rules made by the Secretary of State under section 53 of that Act to be specially dangerous; and

(b) the definition of firearm in section 57(1) of that Act shall have effect without paragraphs (b) and (c) of that subsection (component parts and accessories).

...

(6) For the purposes of this section an imitation firearm shall be regarded as readily convertible into a firearm to which section 1 of the 1968 Act applies if—

(a) it can be so converted without any special skill on the part of the person converting it in the construction or adaptation of firearms of any description; and

(b) the work involved in converting it does not require equipment or tools other than such as are in common use by persons carrying out works of construction and maintenance in their own homes.

...

2.—(2) The following provisions of the 1968 Act do not apply by virtue of this Act to an imitation firearm to which this Act applies, that is to say—
(a) section 4(3) and (4) . . .; and
(b) the provisions of that Act which relate to, or to the enforcement of control over, the manner in which a firearm is used or the circumstances in which it is carried;

but without prejudice, in the case of the provisions mentioned in paragraph (b) above, to the application to such an imitation firearm of such of those provisions as apply to imitation firearms apart from this Act.

(3) The provisions referred to in subsection (2)(b) are sections 16 to 20 and section 47.

If the FA 1982 does apply, a special defence is introduced by s. 1:

Firearms Act 1982, s. 1

(5) In any proceedings brought by virtue of this section for an offence under the 1968 Act involving an imitation firearm to which this Act applies, it shall be a defence for the accused to show that he did not know and had no reason to suspect that the imitation firearm was so constructed or adapted as to be readily convertible into a firearm to which section 1 of that Act applies.

Section Creating the Offence Not Applying to Imitation Firearm

If any section of the FA 1968 does not fall into either B12.11 or B12.14, it is a section which does not apply to an imitation firearm, however that phrase is defined. **B12.15**

Offences Concerning 'Realistic Imitation Firearms'

From 1 October 2007, a person commits a summary offence contrary to s. 36 of the VCRA 2006 if he (a) manufactures a realistic imitation firearm; or (b) modifies an imitation firearm so that it becomes a realistic imitation firearm; or (c) sells a realistic imitation firearm; or (d) brings a realistic imitation firearm into Great Britain or causes one to be brought into Great Britain. Specific defences are set out in s. 37 of the 2006 Act. A 'realistic imitation firearm' is defined by s. 38. **B12.16**

Violent Crime Reduction Act 2006, s. 38

(1) In sections 36 and 37 'realistic imitation firearm' means an imitation firearm which—
(a) has an appearance that is so realistic as to make it indistinguishable, for all practical purposes, from a real firearm; and
(b) is neither a de-activated firearm nor itself an antique.

(2) For the purposes of this section, an imitation firearm is not (except by virtue of subsection (3)(b)) to be regarded as distinguishable from a real firearm for any practical purpose if it could be so distinguished only—
(a) by an expert;
(b) on a close examination; or
(c) as a result of an attempt to load or to fire it.

(3) In determining for the purposes of this section whether an imitation firearm is distinguishable from a real firearm—
(a) the matters that must be taken into account include any differences between the size, shape and principal colour of the imitation firearm and the size, shape and colour in which the real firearm is manufactured; and
(b) the imitation is to be regarded as distinguishable if its size, shape or principal colour is unrealistic for a real firearm.

Offences: Not Conforming to Specifications for Imitation Firearms

From 1 October 2007, and pursuant to s. 39(1) of the VCRA 2006, the Secretary of State may by regulations make provision requiring imitation firearms to conform to specifications which are (a) set out in the regulations; or (b) approved by such persons and in such manner as may be so set out. By virtue of s. 39(2), a person commits a summary offence if '(a) he manufactures an imitation firearm which does not conform to the specifications required of it **B12.17** by regulations under this section; (b) he modifies an imitation firearm so that it ceases to conform to the specifications so required of it; (c) he modifies a firearm to create an imitation firearm that does not conform to the specifications so required of it; or (d) he brings an imitation firearm which does not conform to the specifications so required of it into Great Britain or causes such an imitation firearm to be brought into Great Britain'.

Supplying Imitation Firearms to Persons under 18

B12.18 See **B12.100**.

POSSESSING ETC. FIREARM OR AMMUNITION WITHOUT FIREARM CERTIFICATE

B12.19 **Firearms Act 1968, s. 1**

(1) Subject to any exemption under this Act, it is an offence for a person—
  (a) to have in his possession, or to purchase or acquire, a firearm to which this section applies without holding a firearm certificate in force at the time, or otherwise than as authorised by such a certificate;
  (b) to have in his possession, or to purchase or acquire, any ammunition to which this section applies without holding a firearm certificate in force at the time, or otherwise than as authorised by such a certificate, or in quantities in excess of those so authorised.

The aggravated form of the offence (shortened shotguns and converted firearms) is to be found in the FA 1968, s. 4(4):

Firearms Act 1968, s. 4

(4) A person who commits an offence under section 1 of this Act by having in his possession, or purchasing or acquiring, a shotgun which has been shortened contrary to subsection (1) [of section 4] or a firearm which has been converted as mentioned in subsection (3) [of section 4] (whether by a registered firearms dealer or not), without holding a firearm certificate authorising him to have it in his possession, or to purchase or acquire it, shall be treated for the purposes of provisions of this Act relating to the punishment of offences as committing that offence in an aggravated form.

Indictment (for Offence under the Firearms Act 1968, s. 1(1)(a))

B12.20 *Statement of Offence*

Possessing a firearm without holding a current firearm certificate contrary to section 1(1)(a) of the Firearms Act 1968

Particulars of Offence

A on or about the . . . day of . . . was in possession of [or: purchased (or acquired)] a firearm to which section 1 of the Firearms Act 1968 applies, namely a . . ., without holding a firearm certificate in force at that time

As to procedure and sentence, see the FA 1968, ss. 51 and 52 at **B12.2** and sch. 6 at **B12.3**. As to those firearms and ammunition to which the FA 1968, s. 1, applies, see **B12.21** and **B12.23**.

Exemptions relating to Shotguns and some Air Weapons

B12.21 Section 1 of the FA 1968 applies to all firearms except shotguns and certain air weapons (the meaning of which is considered at **B12.6** and **B12.7**). However, sawn-off shotguns and air weapons declared by the Secretary of State to be 'specially dangerous', are firearms to which s. 1 applies. Certain air weapons have been declared to be 'specially dangerous' by statutory instrument.

Firearms (Dangerous Air Weapons) Rules 1969 (SI 1969 No. 47), rr. 2 and 3

2.—(1) Subject to paragraph (2) below, rule 3 of these rules applies to an air weapon (that is to say, an air rifle, airgun or air pistol)—

(a) which is capable of discharging a missile so that the missile has, on being discharged from the muzzle of the weapon, kinetic energy in excess, in the case of an air pistol of 6ft lb or, in the case of an air weapon other than an air pistol, of 12 ft lb.
(b) which is disguised as another object.

(2) Rule 3 of these rules does not apply to a weapon which only falls within paragraph (1)(a) above and which is designed for use only when submerged in water.

3. An air weapon to which this rule applies is hereby declared to be specially dangerous.

Given that the expression 'firearm' in s. 57(1) includes the components of, and accessories to lethal barrelled weapons, it follows that the components of, and accessories to, shotguns (other than those with a shortened barrel), and air weapons (other than those declared to be specially dangerous), are also not included in the phrase 'firearms to which s. 1 of the FA 1968 applies'.

By virtue of s. 7(2) of the F(A)A 1988, the conversion of a weapon into a shotgun or air weapon does not affect its classification as a firearm to which s. 1 applies. Section 7(2) and (3) provide:

Firearms (Amendment) Act 1988, s. 7

(2) Any weapon which—
(a) has at any time since the coming into force of section 2 above been a weapon to which section 1 of the principal Act applies; or
(b) would at any previous time have been such a weapon if those sections had then been in force, shall if it has, or at any time has had, a rifled barrel less than 24 inches in length, be treated as a weapon to which section 1 of the principal Act applies notwithstanding anything done for the purpose of converting it into a shotgun or an air weapon.

(3) For the purposes of subsection (2) above there shall be disregarded the shortening of a barrel by a registered firearms dealer for the sole purpose of replacing part of it so as to produce a barrel not less than 24 inches in length.

Extension to Imitation Firearms

By s. 1 of the FA 1982, that Act applies to the FA 1968, s. 1, thus extending it to imitation firearms, as defined in the FA 1982 (see **B12.14**). **B12.22**

Ammunition to which the Firearms Act 1968, s. 1, Applies

Section 1 applies to all ammunition except that excluded by s. 1(4). **B12.23**

Firearms Act 1968, s. 1

(4) This section applies to any ammunition for a firearm, except the following articles, namely—
(a) cartridges containing five or more shot, none of which exceeds 0.36 inch in diameter;
(b) ammunition for an airgun, air rifle or air pistol; and
(c) blank cartridges not more than one inch in diameter measures immediately in front of the rim or cannelure of the base of the cartridge.

Primed cartridges (ones without gunpowder) are not excluded under s. 1(4)(c) because such a cartridge is capable of producing an explosive effect and it is therefore ammunition (*Stubbings* [1990] Crim LR 811, and see *Burfitt v A & E Kille* [1939] 2 KB 743).

Firearm Certificate

A person does not commit the offence if he has a firearm certificate granted by a chief officer of police under s. 26 of the FA 1968 (see s. 57(4)). A firearm certificate is a public document. In *Paul* [1999] Crim LR 79, the Court of Appeal rejected the possibility of allowing the jury to approach the words in a firearm certificate as those of the ordinary English language (as in *Brutus v Cozens* [1973] AC 854): **B12.24**

> If [a firearm certificate] is to fulfil the clear statutory objective of providing a certain and effective system of control of particular firearms it is obvious and a matter of common sense that it should have a certain and consistent meaning. That can only be achieved by trial judges determining the

> meaning as a matter of law, leaving it to the jury in each case to determine . . . whether the physical attributes of the firearm in question bring it within that meaning.

The trial judge in *Paul* had to decide what the words 'humane killer' in the certificate meant, and it would be for the jury to decide whether they covered the revolver in question, a Ruger 357. In doing this, it is not the intention of the possessor/transferor or transferee that matters, but the physical characteristics of the weapon. The trial judge correctly drew on the definition of 'slaughtering instrument' in s. 57(4) in defining 'humane killer' as meaning 'a firearm specially designed or adapted for instantaneous slaughter of animals . . .'.

Firearm certificates are issued in accordance with the provisions of the Firearms Acts 1968 to 1997, provisions which have been significantly amended by the F(A)A 1997 (see the Firearms Rules 1998 (SI 1998 No. 1941, as amended by SI 2005 No. 3344)). Conditions may be imposed by the grant of a certificate on the use of a firearm, and certain conditions are statutorily imposed, for example, that any rifle or muzzle-loading pistol, which is not a prohibited weapon (see **B12.50** ***et seq.***) and is covered by a certificate, may be used only for target shooting and that the certificate holder must be a member of an approved rifle or muzzle-loading pistol club (F(A)A 1997, s. 44(1)).

It is an offence to fail to comply with the conditions of a certificate (s. 1(2)). For rules relating to procedure and sentence, see **B12.2** and **B12.3**. As to possession authorised in accordance with a European firearms pass or other documents for European purposes, see the FA 1968, ss. 32A to 32C.

Meaning of 'Acquire'

B12.25 The FA 1968, s. 57(4), provides that 'acquire' means 'hire, accept as a gift or borrow': the word 'acquisition' is to be construed accordingly.

Possession Generally

B12.26 In *Sullivan v Earl of Caithness* [1976] QB 966, the Divisional Court held that an owner of firearms is in possession of them even if they are kept in another's custody. Physical custody of a firearm need not be established in order to prove that the accused was in possession of it. Furthermore, a person does not have to be present in the place where the firearms are kept in order to be in possession of them (*Hall v Cotton* [1987] QB 504). Whether a person is in possession of firearms is a question of fact (*Hall v Cotton*). Custodial possession, and the physical possession of firearms, can reside in different people. In *Woodage v Moss* [1974] 1 WLR 411, the accused was held to be in possession of a firearm when he was handed it by an unknown person to deliver it to a dealer as a surrendered weapon. In *Uddin* [2005] EWCA Crim 2653, the Court of Appeal held that the accused was not in possession of the firearm (contrary to the FA 1968, s. 16; see **B12.69**) because, although he appeared to have intended to purchase the firearm, he never had his hands on the bag or the firearm within it. In different circumstances, the accused might have been considered to have acquired control of the firearm if the purchase had gone through, even though he did not yet physically possess it.

Possession and *Mens Rea*

B12.27 The offences contrary to the FA 1968, ss. 1 and 19 (see **B12.19** and **B12.84**), are both absolute offences, a principle drawn from a line of cases commencing with the possession of drugs case, *Warner v Metropolitan Police Commissioner* [1969] 2 AC 256 (see **B20.14**). In *Hussain* [1981] 1 WLR 416, the Court of Appeal held that although s. 1 creates an absolute offence, the accused must know that he is in possession of something which is, in fact, a firearm (or ammunition, as the case may be: *Amos* (29 September 1999 unreported)). *Hussain* was followed in *Vann* [1996] Crim LR 52, a case on s. 19, where the Court of Appeal held that a person does not have to know that the item which he has with him is a firearm, so no *mens rea* is required except insofar as is necessary to establish that the accused has the article with him. See also *Howells* [1977] QB 614 (also on s. 1). An offence contrary to s. 1 is committed, even where the accused does not know there is a firearm in the container which he possesses (*Waller* [1991] Crim LR 381; cf. the position with regard to drugs at **B20.16**). In *Harrison* [1996] 1 Cr App R 138, a case concerned with s. 19, the Court of Appeal, following *Waller*, held that, if a person claims that he was mistaken as to whether what he possessed was a loaded shotgun or loaded air weapon, his argument will not avail, provided he knowingly had possession of the item. Although H knowingly had possession of a shotgun, but claimed that he was not aware that it was loaded, his argument failed and his conviction was upheld. In *Price v DPP* (1996 unreported), the Divisional Court held (following *Bradish* [1990] 1 QB 981 (see **B12.51**), *Waller*, *Steele* [1993] Crim LR 298, and *Harrison*) that a person was in possession of the contents of a rucksack (ammunition) when he had knowledge of possession of the rucksack, but had no idea of its contents (and was indeed mistaken as to whom it belonged, and as to its nature and quality). See also *Cremin* [2007] EWCA Crim 666.

In *Amos* it was held to be no defence for a person to say that he had forgotten about his possession of an item or that he erroneously believed that it had been destroyed or disposed of, even if the original acquisition had been lawful under a firearm certificate.

EXEMPTIONS AND DEFENCES FOR THE PURPOSES OF THE FIREARMS ACT 1968, s. 1

The FA 1968, s. 1(1), indicates that the offence is 'subject to any exemption under this Act'. The relevant exemptions are listed in **B12.29** to **B12.42**. **B12.28**

Holders of Police Permits

A person may have a permit from the chief officer of police, under the FA 1968, s. 7(1) (and see the Firearms Rules 1998 (SI 1998 No. 1941)), which allows him to have in his possession, without a certificate, a firearm and/or ammunition in accordance with the terms of the permit. It is a summary offence, contrary to s. 7(2), for a person knowingly or recklessly to make a statement which is false in any material particular for the purpose of procuring, whether for himself or another, the grant of a permit under s. 7(1). **B12.29**

As to procedure and sentence, see **B12.2** and **B12.3**.

Authorised Dealers

The FA 1968, s. 8(1), allows a registered firearms dealer, or a servant, to have in his possession, or purchase or acquire, without a certificate, a firearm or ammunition in the ordinary course of that business. This exemption applies even if the firearm or ammunition is in the possession of, or acquired by, the dealer or his servant at a place which is not his place of business (s. 8(1A)). A firearms dealer is defined by s. 57(4) as a person who, by way of trade or business (a) manufactures, sells, transfers, repairs, tests or proves firearms or ammunition to which s. 1 applies or shotguns; or (b) sells or transfers air weapons. The significant change to this definition is the inclusion of air weapons by the VCRA 2006, s. 31(3), which came into force on 6 April 2007 (see the Violent Crime Reduction Act 2006 (Commencement No. 2) Order 2007 (SI 2007 No. 858)), insofar as the definition of 'registered' in s. 57(4) applies to (i) the FA 1968, ss. 33 to 39 and 45; (ii) the FA 1968, s. 56, insofar as that provision applies to a notice required or authorised by s. 36 or s. 38 of that Act; and (iii) FA 1968, sch. 5. A person is a registered firearms dealer in Great Britain under s. 33 (see the Firearms Rules 1998 (SI 1998 No. 1941)). **B12.30**

Auctioneers, Carriers and Warehousemen

An auctioneer, carrier or warehouseman, or a servant, may, under the FA 1968, s. 9(1), have in his possession, without a certificate, a firearm or ammunition in the ordinary course of **B12.31** business. It is a summary offence, contrary to the F(A)A 1988, s. 14(1), for an auctioneer, carrier or warehouseman (a) to fail to take reasonable precautions for the safe custody of any firearm or ammunition which, by virtue of the FA 1968, s. 9(1), he or any servant of his has in his possession without holding a certificate; or (b) to fail to report forthwith to the police the loss or theft of any such firearm or ammunition. The offence is punishable with a term of imprisonment not exceeding six months, or a fine not exceeding level 5 on the standard scale, or both.

Licensed Slaughterers

B12.32 A licensed slaughterer may, under the FA 1968, s. 10, have in his possession, without a certificate, a slaughtering instrument (see *Paul* [1999] Crim LR 79) or ammunition in any slaughterhouse or knacker's yard in which he is employed. Further, the person in charge of storing such instruments at the slaughterhouse or knacker's yard may have them in his possession, without a certificate, for that purpose. (As to the European Weapons Directive, see **B12.58**.)

Possession etc. in Connection with Rifle or Pistol Clubs, Sports, Athletics and other Approved Activities

B12.33 The FA 1968, s. 11, and the F(A)A 1988, s. 15, provide a number of exemptions:

(a) a person carrying a firearm or ammunition belonging to someone who has a certificate may have the same in his possession under instructions from and for the use of the certificate holder for sporting purposes only (FA 1968, s. 11(1));
(b) a person, without a certificate, may have a firearm in his possession at an athletic meeting to start races (s. 11(2));
(c) a person in charge of a miniature rifle range may have in his possession, or purchase or acquire without a certificate, miniature rifles and ammunition suitable for the range; a person may use these at such a range without a certificate (s. 11(4));
(d) a member of an approved rifle club, miniature rifle club or pistol club may have in his possession without a certificate, a firearm or ammunition when engaged as a club member in target practice (F(A)A 1988, s. 15(1)).

Approval is granted by the Secretary of State (see s. 15). As to the European Weapons Directive, see **B12.58**.

Possession etc. in Connection with the Theatre or Films

B12.34 A person taking part in a theatrical performance or rehearsal or the production of a film may have a firearm in his possession without a certificate, but only during and for the purpose of the performance, rehearsal or production (FA 1968, s. 12).

Possession etc. as Equipment for Ship, Aircraft or Aerodrome

B12.35 A person may, under the FA 1968, s. 13(1), without holding a certificate:

(a) have in his possession a firearm, signalling apparatus or ammunition on board a ship or aircraft or at an aerodrome, provided it is equipment for same;
(b) remove signalling apparatus or ammunition, if it is aircraft equipment, from one aircraft to another at an aerodrome or into or from storage and keep such equipment in storage at an aerodrome;
(c) if he has a permit from a constable, remove a firearm, signalling apparatus or ammunition to or from a ship or aircraft at an aerodrome to or from a place specified in the permit.

It is an offence, contrary to s. 13(2), for a person knowingly or recklessly to make a statement which is false in any material particular for the purpose of procuring, either for himself or another person, the grant of a permit under s. 13(1)(c). As to procedure and sentence, see **B12.2** and **B12.3**.

Persons in the Service of the Crown

By virtue of the FA 1968, s. 54(1), the possession of firearms by persons in the service of the Crown is not covered by the FA 1968. Section 54 applies only to a person in possession of a firearm when in his capacity as a servant of Her Majesty or a police officer, otherwise a firearm certificate is necessary. See *Heritage v Claxon* (1941) 85 SJ 323 and *Tarttelin v Bowen* [1947] 2 All ER 837. **B12.36**

The offence under the FA 1968, s. 1, does apply insofar as it relates to the purchase and acquisition of firearms subject to s. 54(2), which provides a person in the service of the Crown with a defence if he is duly authorised in writing to purchase or acquire firearms and ammunition for public service without a certificate, and a person in the naval, military or air services, provided the chief officer of police is satisfied that he must purchase a firearm or ammunition, is entitled to a certificate without any payment.

For the purposes of s. 54, certain persons are deemed to be in Her Majesty's naval, military or air service, insofar as they are not otherwise in, or treated as being in, any such service (s. 54(4)). Such persons are:

(a) the members of any foreign force when they are serving with any of Her Majesty's naval, military or air forces;
(b) members of any cadet corps approved by the Secretary of State when:
  (i) they are engaged as members of the corps, or in connection with, drill or target shooting; and
  (ii) in the case of possession of prohibited weapons or prohibited ammunition when engaged in target shooting, they are on service premises; and
(c) persons providing instruction to any members of such a cadet corps (s. 54(5)).

'Foreign force' and 'service premises' are defined in s. 54(6).

A person under the supervision of a member of the armed forces may, without holding a certificate or obtaining the Secretary of State's authority under s. 5, have in his possession a firearm and ammunition on service premises (F(A)A 1988, s. 16A(1)). This provision does not apply to persons engaged in providing security protection of service premises, e.g., civilian guards (F(A)A 1988, s. 16A(2)).

'Armed forces' and 'service premises' are defined in s. 16A(3). A similar exception applies in respect of persons trained or assessed under the supervision of the Ministry of Defence Police (s. 16B).

Proof Houses of the Societies and Small Heath Rifle Range

By virtue of the FA 1968, s. 58(1), the proof houses of the Master, Wardens and Society of the Mystery of Gunmakers of the City of London and the guardians of the Birmingham Proof House or the rifle range at Small Heath in Birmingham are exempt from the Act's provisions. This protection extends to people carrying firearms to or from such places. **B12.37**

Antique Firearm Sold or Purchased as a Curiosity or Ornament

Section 1 of the FA 1968 does not apply to an antique firearm which is sold, transferred, purchased, acquired or possessed as a curiosity or ornament (s. 58(2)). Whether a firearm is an antique firearm is a question of fact and degree (*Richards v Curwen* [1977] 1 WLR 747; *Bennett v Brown* (1980) 71 Cr App R 109), and is therefore a matter for a jury (*Burke* (1978) 67 Cr App R 220). It is not sufficient for the accused honestly and reasonably to believe that the firearm is an antique firearm; it must actually be so (see *Howells* [1977] QB 614). **B12.38**

Borrowed Rifle on Private Premises

B12.39 By virtue of the F(A)A 1988, s. 16, a person who is at least 17 may, without holding a certificate, borrow a rifle from the occupier of private premises and use it on those premises in the presence of either the occupier or a servant, provided the occupier holds a certificate and the borrower's possession and use of it comply with any conditions in the certificate. In addition the borrower may purchase or acquire ammunition for the rifle, if the certificate authorises the purchase of ammunition and the borrower's possession and use of the ammunition complies with any conditions in the certificate.

Holders of Visitors' Permits

B12.40 By virtue of the F(A)A 1988, s. 17(1), the holder of a visitor's permit, granted by a chief officer of police under s. 17(2) to (9), may have in his possession, without a certificate, a firearm or ammunition to which the FA 1968, s. 1, and the Firearms Rules 1998 (SI 1998 No. 1941) apply. A visitor's shotgun permit does not authorise the purchase or acquisition of any shotgun with a magazine, except where s. 17(1A)(a) to (d) applies (s. 17(1A)). No visitor's permit will be issued unless the visitor produces a European firearms pass (see **B12.24**) and satisfies other criteria (s. 17(3A)). It is an offence, for a person (a) to make any statement which he knows to be false for the purpose of procuring the grant of a permit under this section; or (b) to fail to comply with a condition subject to which such a permit is held by him (s. 17(10)). The offence is punishable on summary conviction with imprisonment for a term not exceeding six months, or a fine not exceeding level 5 on the standard scale, or both. As to the extension of the usual time period within which summary proceedings must be instituted, see **B12.2**.

Firearms Acquired for Export

B12.41 See **B12.111** *et seq.* This defence is primarily concerned with the acquisition of firearms for export, but must also cover their possession for that purpose.

Possession of a Museums Firearms Licence

B12.42 By virtue of the F(A)A 1988, s. 19 and its schedule, a person involved with the management of certain museums may, if he has a museums firearms licence, without a certificate, have in his possession, and purchase or acquire, for the purposes of the museum, firearms and ammunition which are or are to be normally exhibited or kept on its premises or on such of them as are specified in the licence. Certain specific museums are listed in para. 5 of the schedule, which also provides that similar museums, maintained wholly or mainly out of money provided by Parliament or a local authority, are also covered. Further, any museum or similar institution, which is for the time being fully registered with the Museums and Galleries Commission, is also covered (Firearms (Museums) Order 1997 (SI 1997 No. 1692)).

The following two summary offences exist in relation to museums firearms licences. See **B12.2** concerning the extension of the usual period within which summary proceedings must be instituted. Express provision is made in connection with each offence committed by bodies corporate (F(A)A 1988, sch., paras. 5 and 6).

(a) It is an offence, contrary to para. 4(1) of the schedule,
  - (i) for a person to make any statement which he knows to be false for the purpose of procuring the grant, renewal or variation of a licence;
  - (ii) for the person or any of the persons responsible for the management of a museum to fail to comply or to cause or permit another person to fail to comply with any condition specified in the licence held in respect of that museum.

The offence is punishable with imprisonment for a term not exceeding six months or a fine not exceeding level 5 on the standard scale, or both. It is a defence for a person proceeded against under para. 4(1)(b) to prove that he took all reasonable precautions and exercised all due diligence to avoid the commission of the offence (para. 4(4)).

(b) It is an offence, contrary to para. 4(3) of the schedule, for a person to fail to comply with a notice under para. 2(4) from the Secretary of State requiring the surrender of a revoked licence. The offence is triable summarily and is punishable with a fine not exceeding level 3 on the standard scale.

Where the firearm is an imitation firearm there is a special defence under the FA 1982, s. 1(5); see **B12.14** above.

OFFENCES RELATING TO SHOTGUNS

Possessing etc. Shotgun without Shotgun Certificate

Firearms Act 1968, s. 2 **B12.43**

(1) Subject to any exemption under this Act, it is an offence for a person to have in his possession, or to purchase or acquire, a shotgun without holding a certificate under this Act authorising him to possess shotguns.

As to procedure and sentence, see **B12.2**. The meaning of 'shotgun' is considered at **B12.6**. This section does not extend to imitation firearms, see **B12.11**.

The term 'shotgun certificate' is defined by the FA 1968, s. 57(4) as 'a certificate granted by a chief officer of police . . . authorising a person to possess shotguns'. Such certificates are issued by chief officers of police under the FA 1968, s. 26, the related provisions in part II, and the Firearms Rules 1998 (SI 1998 No. 1941).

For the meaning of 'acquire', see **B12.25**. For the meaning of 'possession', see **B12.26**.

The exemptions applicable in the case of firearms from liability under the FA 1968, s. 1, also apply to this offence (see **B12.29** to **B12.42**). In addition, holders of certificates granted in Northern Ireland are exempt (FA 1968, s. 15).

Failure to Comply with Condition of Shotgun Certificate

Firearms Act 1968, s. 2 **B12.44**

(2) It is an offence for a person to fail to comply with a condition subject to which a shotgun certificate is held by him.

This is a summary offence. For procedure and sentence, see **B12.2** and **B12.3**. The meaning of 'shotgun certificate' is considered at **B12.43**. For the meaning of 'shotgun', see **B12.6**.

SPECIFIC OFFENCES RELATING TO AIR WEAPONS

Prohibition on Sale or Transfer of Air Weapons except by Registered Dealers

From a date to be announced, it will be an offence if a person (other than a registered firearms dealer) 'sells or transfers an air weapon, exposes such a weapon for sale or transfer or has such a weapon in his possession for sale or transfer' (FA 1968, s. 3(1)(c), inserted by the VCRA 2006, s. 31(1)). Section 57(4) of the FA 1968 is amended so that a 'firearms dealer' includes a person who sells or transfers air weapons (VCRA 2006, s. 31(3)). **B12.45**

Sales of Air Weapons by way of Trade or Business to be Face to Face

Section 32 of the VCRA 2006, which came into force on 1 October 2007, makes it an offence for a person to transfer possession of an air weapon, by way of trade or business, to an individual in Great Britain (who is not registered as a firearms dealer) other than when the buyer and seller are in the presence of each other. **B12.46**

Violent Crime Reduction Act 2006, s. 32

(1) This section applies where a person sells an air weapon by way of trade or business to an individual in Great Britain who is not registered as a firearms dealer.
(2) A person is guilty of an offence if, for the purposes of the sale, he transfers possession of the air weapon to the buyer otherwise than at a time when both—
  (a) the buyer, and
  (b) either the seller or a representative of his,
  are present in person.
(3) The reference in subsection (2) to a representative of the seller is a reference to—
  (a) a person who is employed by the seller in his business as a registered firearms dealer;
  (b) a registered firearms dealer who has been authorised by the seller to act on his behalf in relation to the sale; or
  (c) a person who is employed by a person falling within paragraph (b) in his business as a registered firearms dealer.

This is a summary offence. The maximum penalty is imprisonment for six months, a fine not exceeding level 5, or both.

Age Limits on Purchasing and Selling Air Weapons

B12.47 The following measures enacted by the VCRA 2006 came into force on 1 October 2007.

It is an offence for a person under the age of 18 to purchase or hire an air weapon or ammunition for an air weapon (FA 1968, s. 22(1)(a), as amended by the VCRA 2006, s. 33(2)).

It is an offence for any person to sell, or let on hire, such a weapon or ammunition to a person under the age of 18 (FA 1968, s. 24(1)(a), as amended by the VCRA 2006, s. 33(4)).

Persons Firing an Air Weapon beyond Premises

B12.48 A person (of any age) who fires an air weapon beyond premises commits an offence (whether he is supervised or not) unless he has the consent of the occupier of any premises he fired into or across (FA 1968, s. 21A, inserted by the VCRA 2006, s. 34(2) in force from 1 October 2007).

Firearms Act 1968, s. 21A

(1) A person commits an offence if—
  (a) he has with him an air weapon on any premises; and
  (b) he uses it for firing a missile beyond those premises.
(2) In proceedings against a person for an offence under this section it shall be a defence for him to show that the only premises into or across which the missile was fired were premises the occupier of which had consented to the firing of the missile (whether specifically or by way of a general consent).

Meaning of 'Premises', Further Defences, Penalties

B12.49 'Premises' is defined by the FA 1968, s. 57(4) to include any land. Section 23 provides that no offence is committed where a person has with him an air weapon or ammunition at a time when being a member of a rifle club or miniature rifle club for the time being approved by the Secretary of State for the purposes of s. 23, or of s.15 of the F(A)A 1988 (see **B12.33**), he is engaged as such a member or in connection with target practice or he is using the weapon or ammunition at a shooting gallery where the only firearms used are either air weapons or miniature rifles not exceeding 0.23 inch calibre (s. 23(2)).

The offence contrary to s. 23(4) carries the same penalty as the offence under s. 22(4) as well as the same forfeiture and disposal powers (see sch. 6). The offence contrary to s. 23(1) carries the same penalty as the offence under s. 22(4) as well as the same forfeiture and disposal provisions (see sch. 6).

POSSESSING OR DISTRIBUTING PROHIBITED WEAPONS OR AMMUNITION

Firearms Act 1968, s. 5 **B12.50**

(1) A person commits an offence if, without the authority of the Secretary of State . . . , he has in his possession, or purchases, or acquires, or manufactures, sells or transfers—

(a) any firearm which is so designed or adapted that two or more missiles can be successively discharged without repeated pressure on the trigger;

(ab) any self-loading or pump-action rifled gun other than one which is chambered for 0.22 rim-fire cartridges;

(aba) any firearm which either has a barrel less than 30 centimetres in length or is less than 60 centimetres in length overall, other than an air weapon, a muzzle-loading gun or a firearm designed as signalling apparatus;

(ac) any self-loading or pump-action smooth-bore gun which is not an air weapon or chambered for 0.22 rim-fire cartridges and either has a barrel less than 24 inches in length or is less than 40 inches in length overall;

(ad) any smooth-bore revolver gun other than one which is chambered for 9 mm rim-fire cartridges or a muzzle-loading gun;

(ae) any rocket launcher, or any mortar, for projecting a stabilised missile, other than a launcher or mortar designed for line-throwing or pyrotechnic purposes or as signalling apparatus;

(af) any air rifle, air gun or air pistol which uses, or is designed or adapted for use with, a self-contained gas cartridge system;

(b) any weapon of whatever description designed or adapted for the discharge of any noxious liquid, gas or other thing;

(c) any cartridge with a bullet designed to explode on or immediately before impact, any ammunition containing or designed or adapted to contain any such noxious thing as is mentioned in paragraph (b) above and, if capable of being used with a firearm of any description, any grenade, bomb (or other like missile), or rocket or shell designed to explode as aforesaid.

(1A) Subject to section 5A of this Act, a person commits an offence if, without the authority of the Secretary of State, he has in his possession, or purchases or acquires, or sells or transfers—

(a) any firearm which is disguised as another object;

(b) any rocket or ammunition not falling within paragraph (c) of subsection (1) of this section which consists in or incorporates a missile designed to explode on or immediately before impact and is for military use;

(c) any launcher or other projecting apparatus not falling within paragraph (ae) of that subsection which is designed to be used with any rocket or ammunition falling within paragraph (b) above or with ammunition which would fall within that paragraph but for its being ammunition falling within paragraph (c) of that subsection;

(d) any ammunition for military use which consists in or incorporates a missile designed so that a substance contained in the missile will ignite on or immediately before impact;

(e) any ammunition for military use which consists in or incorporates a missile designed, on account of its having a jacket and hard-core, to penetrate armour plating, armour screening or body armour;

(f) any ammunition which incorporates a missile designed or adapted to expand on impact;

(g) anything which is designed to be projected as a missile from any weapon and is designed to be, or has been, incorporated in—

(i) any ammunition falling within any of the preceding paragraphs; or

(ii) any ammunition which would fall within any of those paragraphs but for its being specified in subsection (1) of this section.

(2) The weapons and ammunition specified in subsections (1) and (1A) of this section (including, in the case of ammunition, any missiles falling within subsection (1A)(g) of this section) are referred to in this Act as 'prohibited weapons' and 'prohibited ammunition' respectively.

Section 5(1)(af) was added by the ASBA 2003, s. 39(1) and (3). If a person has in his possession an air rifle, air gun or air pistol of the kind described in the FA 1968, s. 5(1)(af), then (a) s. 5(1) shall not prevent the person's continued possession of the air rifle, air gun or air pistol; (b) s. 1 shall apply; and (c) a chief officer of police may not refuse to grant or renew, and may not revoke or partially revoke, a firearm certificate on the ground that the person does not have a good reason for having the air rifle, air gun or air pistol in his possession (ASBA 2003, s. 39(4)). But these provisions do not apply to possession in the circumstances described in the FA 1968, s. 8, which is concerned with authorised dealing (ASBA 2003, s. 39(5)); see **B12.30** for authorised dealing.

Mens Rea

B12.51 The offence is one of strict liability (*Bradish* [1990] 1 QB 981, following *Howells* [1977] QB 614 and *Hussain* [1981] 1 WLR 416 (see **B12.27**), and distinguishing *Warner v Metropolitan Police Commissioner* [1969] 2 AC 256).

All that the prosecution need prove, in addition to actual possession, is that the accused knowingly had in his possession an article which was in fact a prohibited weapon. The court distinguished *Warner v Metropolitan Police Commissioner* [1969] 2 AC 256, insofar as it dealt with the 'container' cases. It was submitted that the weapon of which the defendant was in possession was a spray canister containing CS gas and, therefore, he was not in possession of the contents of the container if he could show that he neither knew, nor could reasonably have been expected to know, that it was a prohibited weapon. The court rejected this submission (for the reasoning, see *Bradish* [1990] 1 QB 981 at pp. 991–3). The court thought that *Bradish* was not a 'container' case. This was a prohibited weapon because of the combination of the canister itself and its contents. The 'container' was an essential part of the weapon.

In *Law* [1999] Crim LR 837, the Court of Appeal held that s. 5(1)(a) of the FA 1968 (as amended) 'does not import either explicitly or implicitly any intention on the part of the designer or the adaptor'. The vital words are 'can be successfully discharged'. Note that the transcript wrongly refers to 's. 5(1A)'. The case concerns s. 5(1)(a).

As to procedure and sentence, see ss. 51, 52 and sch. 6 at **B12.2** and **B12.3**, and also **B12.101**.

Meaning of 'Prohibited Weapon' and 'Prohibited Ammunition'

B12.52 These phrases are defined in the FA 1968, s. 5(2), see **B12.50**. The amendments introduced by the F(A)A 1988 have not overruled all decisions under the unamended section.

A weapon satisfies s. 5(1)(a) if it is capable of burst fire, making it a weapon from which 'two or more missiles can be successively discharged'. This will be the case even if a weapon has been adapted and only experts would be able to make it operate as an automatic weapon (*Law* [1999] Crim LR 837).

A 'Lightning Strike', a hand-held device from which electricity is emitted, was a prohibited weapon within s. 5(1)(b), because electricity is a noxious thing in view of the stunning effect it has on its victims and it is discharged from the device (*Flack v Baldry* [1988] 1 WLR 393). An empty bottle of washing-up liquid is not a weapon, and therefore filling it with hydrochloric acid does not make it a prohibited weapon, and merely filling a bottle does not 'adapt' it within s. 5(1)(b) (*Formosa* [1991] 2 QB 1). The court approved *Titus* [1971] Crim LR 279, where it was held that a water pistol is not a prohibited weapon even when used to discharge a noxious liquid.

A person is in possession of a prohibited weapon even when it is in parts (*Pannell* (1982) 76 Cr App R 53, where the accused had possession of all the parts). A weapon may be a prohibited weapon even if one essential element is missing, such as the trigger (*Clarke* [1986] 1 WLR 209, and see *Brown* (1992) *The Times*, 27 March 1992, where it was held that a stun gun which did not work because of some unknown fault, and was not proved ever to have worked, was a prohibited weapon). A 'firearm', for the purposes of s. 5(1)(a), is defined by s. 57(1) so as to include the component parts of a firearm (*Clarke*).

Statutory Definition of Terms

Firearms Act 1968, ss. 5 and 57 **B12.53**

5.—(7) For the purposes of this section and section 5A of this Act—
 (a) any rocket or ammunition which is designed to be capable of being used with a military weapon shall be taken to be for military use;
 (b) references to a missile designed so that a substance contained in the missile will ignite on or immediately before impact include references to any missile containing a substance that ignites on exposure to air; and
 (c) references to a missile's expanding on impact include references to its deforming in any predictable manner on or immediately after impact.

(8) For the purposes of subsection (1)(aba) and (ac) above, any detachable, folding, retractable or other movable butt-stock shall be disregarded in measuring the length of any firearm.

(9) Any reference in this section 5 to a muzzle-loading gun is a reference to a gun which is designed to be loaded at the muzzle end of the barrel or chamber with a loose charge and a separate ball (or other missile).

57.—(2A) In this Act 'self-loading' and 'pump-action' in relation to any weapon mean respectively that it is designed or adapted (otherwise than as mentioned in section 5(1)(a)) so that it is automatically reloaded or that it is so designed or adapted that it is reloaded by the manual operation of the fore-end or forestock of the weapon.

(2B) In this Act 'revolver', in relation to a smooth-bore gun, means a gun containing a series of chambers which revolve when the gun is fired.

. . .

(6) For purposes of this Act—
 (a) the length of the barrel of a firearm is measured from the muzzle to the point at which the charge is exploded on firing.

. . .

Conversion Not to Affect Classification as Prohibited Weapon

The F(A)A 1988 introduced an important change into the law as regards the conversion of weapons. Consequently, care needs to be taken in reading cases on the unamended s. 5 of the FA 1968, insofar as they are concerned with the conversion of weapons. **B12.54**

Firearms (Amendment) Act 1988, s. 7(1)

(1) Any weapon which—
 (a) has at any time (whether before or after the passing of this Act) been a weapon of a kind described in section 5(1) of the principal Act as amended by or under section 1 . . .; and
 (b) is not a self-loading or pump-action smooth-bore gun which has at any such time been such a weapon by reason only of having had a barrel of less than 24 inches in length,

shall be treated as a prohibited weapon notwithstanding anything done for the purpose of converting it into a weapon of a different kind.

As to the de-activation of firearms, see **B12.8**.

Imitation Firearms for the Purposes of the Firearms Act 1968, s. 5

A prohibited weapon is a form of 'firearm to which s. 1 of the FA 1968, applies', and therefore s. 5 of the FA 1968 may apply to imitation firearms (see **B12.11**). In any event, possession (etc.) of an imitation prohibited weapon would be an offence contrary to s. 1. **B12.55**

Authority of the Secretary of State and the Defence Council

The Secretary of State may grant an authority permitting possession of a prohibited weapon or ammunition. **B12.56**

Firearms Act 1968, s. 5(3), (4)

(3) An authority given to a person by the Defence Council under this section shall be in writing and be subject to conditions specified therein.

(4) The conditions on the authority shall include such as the Defence Council, having regard to the circumstances of each particular case, think fit to impose for the purpose of securing that the prohibited weapon or ammunition to which the authority relates shall not endanger the public safety or the peace.

The functions of the Defence Council are performed by the Secretary of State (Transfer of Functions (Prohibited Weapons) Order 1968 (SI 1968 No. 1200)). It is an offence to fail to comply with a condition of an authority (s. 5(5)). An authority may be revoked at any time by notice (s. 5(6)). As to procedure and sentence, see **B12.2** and **B12.3**.

Authority of the Secretary of State for Theatrical Performances

B12.57 The Secretary of State may, under s. 12(2):

(a) authorise a person in charge of a theatrical performance or rehearsal or the production of a cinematograph film to have possession of a prohibited weapon if it is required for the purpose of the performance, rehearsal or production; and

(b) authorise such other person as he may select to have possession of it while taking part in the performance, rehearsal or production.

Various Exemptions arising under the European Weapons Directive

B12.58 Section 5A(1) provides six exemptions to the obligation to have the authority of the Secretary of State under s. 5(1A), which arise from the European Weapons Directive and are concerned with possession or dealing with weapons in different situations.

The six exemptions apply to:

(a) persons who are authorised by a certificate under the Act to possess, purchase or acquire a prohibited weapon or ammunition (s. 5A(1) and (2));

(b) persons recognised by the law of another Member State as collectors of firearms, or a body concerned in the cultural or historical aspects of weapons (s. 5A(3));

(c) persons authorised by a firearm certificate or a visitor's firearm permit, to possess, purchase or acquire expanding ammunition or the missile for such ammunition, in order lawfully to shoot deer, to shoot vermin or (in the course of estate management activities) other wildlife, to kill animals humanely, or to shoot in order to protect other animals or humans (s. 5A(4));

(d) persons who are entitled under the FA 1968, s. 10, to have a slaughtering instrument in their possession are also entitled to have expanding ammunition, or the missile for any such ammunition, in their possession if it is designed to be capable of being used with a slaughtering instrument (s. 5A(5));

(e) persons who sell or transfer expanding ammunition or the missile for such ammunition to persons who hold a certificate by virtue of the FA 1968, s. 5A(4) (s. 5A(6));

(f) persons who carry on the business of a firearms dealer, and who may deal in expanding ammunition or the missile for any such ammunition in the ordinary course of that business (s. 5A(7)).

Firearms Act 1968, s. 5A

(1) Subject to subsection (2) below, the authority of the Secretary of State shall not be required by virtue of subsection (1A) of section 5 of this Act for any person to have in his possession, or to purchase, acquire, sell or transfer, any prohibited weapon or ammunition if he is authorised by a certificate under this Act to possess, purchase or acquire that weapon or ammunition subject to a condition that he does so only for the purpose of it being kept or exhibited as part of a collection.

(2) No sale or transfer may be made under subsection (1) above except to a person who—

(a) produces the authority of the Secretary of State under section 5 of this Act for his purchase or acquisition; or
(b) shows that he is, under this section or a licence under the schedule to the Firearms (Amendment) Act 1988 (museums etc.) entitled to make the purchase or acquisition without the authority of the Secretary of State.

(3) The authority of the Secretary of State shall not be required by virtue of subsection (1A) of section 5 of this Act for any person to have in his possession, or to purchase or acquire, any prohibited weapon or ammunition if his possession, purchase or acquisition is exclusively in connection with the carrying on of activities in respect of which—
(a) that person; or
(b) the person on whose behalf he has possession, or makes the purchase or acquisition, is recognised, for the purposes of the law of another member State relating to firearms, as a collector of firearms or a body concerned in the cultural or historical aspects of weapons.

(4) The authority of the Secretary of State shall not be required by virtue of subsection (1A) of section 5 of this Act for any person to have in his possession, or to purchase or acquire, or to sell or transfer, any expanding ammunition or the missile for any such ammunition if—
(a) he is authorised by a firearm certificate or a visitor's firearm permit to possess, purchase or acquire, any expanding ammunition; and
(b) the certificate or permit is subject to a condition restricting the use of any expanding ammunition to use in connection with any one or more of the following, namely—
(i) the lawful shooting of deer;
(ii) the shooting of vermin or, in the course of carrying on activities in connection with the management of any estate, other wildlife;
(iii) the humane killing of animals;
(iv) the shooting of animals for the protection of other animals or humans.

(5) The authority of the Secretary of State shall not be required by virtue of subsection (1A) of section 5 of this Act for any person to have in his possession any expanding ammunition or the missile for any such ammunition if—
(a) he is entitled, under section 10 of this Act, to have a slaughtering instrument and the ammunition for it in his possession; and
(b) the ammunition or missile in question is designed to be capable of being used with a slaughtering instrument.

(6) The authority of the Secretary of State shall not be required by virtue of subsection (1A) of section 5 of this Act for the sale or transfer of any expanding ammunition or the missile for any such ammunition to any person who produces a certificate by virtue of which he is authorised under subsection (4) above to purchase or acquire it without the authority of the Secretary of State.

(7) The authority of the Secretary of State shall not be required by virtue of subsection (1A) of section 5 of this Act for a person carrying on the business of a firearms dealer, or any servant of his, to have in his possession, or to purchase, acquire, sell or transfer, any expanding ammunition or the missile for any such ammunition in the ordinary course of that business.

(8) In this section—
(a) references to expanding ammunition are references to any ammunition which incorporates a missile which is designed to expand on impact; and
(b) references to the missile for any such ammunition are references to anything which, in relation to any such ammunition, falls within section 5(1A)(g) of this Act.

Section 5A provides defences in relation to activity in Great Britain, so where the weapon is for 'the management of any estate' (s. 5A(4)(b)) that meant an estate in Great Britain (*Lacey v Commissioner of Police for the Metropolitan Police Service* [2000] Crim LR 853).

Section 57(4A) provides that the European Weapons Directive is to be taken as authorising the use of a firearm or ammunition as or with a slaughtering instrument and the use of a firearm and ammunition (a) for sporting purposes, (b) for the shooting of vermin or, in the course of carrying on activities in connection with the management of any estate, of other wildlife, and (c) for competition purposes and target shooting outside competitions.

Small Firearms and the Firearms Act 1968, s. 5

The firearms legislation was amended twice in 1997. The F(A)A 1997 extended the **B12.59** limitations on firearms ownership, but exempted small calibre pistols. That exemption was removed by the Firearms (Amendment) (No. 2) Act 1997. The central provision is to be found in the FA 1968, s. 5(1)(aba) (as amended) (see **B12.50**) to which special exemptions have been provided as listed at **B12.60**.

Small Firearms: Special Exemptions

B12.60 The special exemptions created by the F(A)A 1997 and the Firearms (Amendment) (No. 2) Act 1997 provide that, in the following situations, the authority of the Secretary of State is not required in order to avoid liability for the offence contrary to s. 5(1)(aba) of the FA 1968 (see **B12.50**).

B12.61 **Slaughtering Instruments** A person may have in his possession, purchase or acquire, or sell or transfer 'a slaughtering instrument if he is authorised by a firearm certificate to have the instrument in his possession, or to purchase or acquire it' (F(A)A 1997, s. 2(a)). A person may have in his possession 'a slaughtering instrument if he is entitled, under section 10 of the 1968 Act, to have it in his possession without a firearm certificate' (s. 2(b)). As to s. 10 of the 1968 Act, see **B12.32**.

B12.62 **Firearms Used for the Humane Killing of Animals** A person may have in his possession, purchase or acquire, or sell or transfer 'a firearm if he is authorised by a firearm certificate to have the firearm in his possession, or to purchase or acquire it, subject to a condition that it is only for use in connection with the humane killing of animals' (F(A)A 1997, s. 3).

B12.63 **Shot Pistols used for Shooting Vermin** A person may have in his possession, purchase or acquire, or sell or transfer 'a shot pistol if he is authorised by a firearm certificate to have the shot pistol in his possession, or to purchase or acquire it, subject to a condition that it is only for use in connection with the shooting of vermin' (F(A)A 1997, s. 4(1)). 'Shot pistol' means a smooth-bored gun which is chambered for 410 cartridges or 9mm rim-fire cartridges (s. 4(2)).

B12.64 **Races at Athletic Meetings** A person may 'have a firearm in his possession at an athletic meeting for the purpose of starting races at that meeting' (F(A)A 1997, s. 5(1)). A person may have in his possession, purchase or acquire, or sell or transfer 'a firearm if he is authorised by a firearm certificate to have the firearm in his possession, or to purchase or acquire it, subject to a condition that it is only for use in connection with starting races at athletic meetings' (F(A)A 1997, s. 5(2)).

B12.65 **Trophies of War** A person may have in his possession 'a firearm which was acquired as a trophy of war before 1st January 1946 if he is authorised by a firearm certificate to have it in his possession' (F(A)A 1997, s. 6).

B12.66 **Firearms of Historic Interest** The following provisions have effect without prejudice to s. 58(2) of the 1968 Act which is concerned with antique firearms, and which is an additional exception (F(A)A 1997, s. 7(4)). For s. 58(2) of the 1968 Act, see **B12.38**.

(a) A person may have in his possession, purchase or acquire, or sell or transfer, a firearm which was (i) manufactured before 1 January 1919; and (ii) is of a specified description 'if he is authorised by a firearm certificate to have the firearm in his possession, or to purchase or acquire it, subject to a condition that he does so only for the purpose of its being kept or exhibited as part of a collection' (s. 7(1)). The Secretary of State may specify descriptions of firearms for the purposes of s. 7(1) if it appears to him that firearms of that description were manufactured before 1 January 1919 and ammunition for firearms of that type is not readily available (s. 7(2)). The Firearms (Amendment) Act 1997 (Firearms of Historic Interest) Order 1997 (SI 1997 No. 1537) has been made in exercise of that power.

(b) A person may have in his possession, or may purchase or acquire, or sell or transfer 'a firearm which is of particular rarity, aesthetic quality or technical interest, or is of historical importance, if he is authorised by a firearm certificate to have the firearm in his possession subject to a condition requiring it to be kept and used only at a designated place (s. 7(3)). Places will be designated by the Secretary of State (s. 7(3)).

Weapons and Ammunition used for Treating Animals This special exception applies not only to the offence contrary to s. 5(1)(aba) but also any offence contrary to s. 5(1)(b) or (c) (see **B12.50**). A person may have in his possession, purchase or acquire, or sell or transfer 'any firearm, weapon or ammunition designed or adapted for the purpose of tranquillising or otherwise treating any animal, if he is authorised by a firearm certificate to possess, or to purchase or acquire, the firearm, weapon or ammunition subject to a condition restricting its use in connection with the treatment of animals' (F(A)A 1997, s. 8). B12.67

Disabled Persons The authority of the Secretary of State is not required under the FA 1968, s. 5(1)(aba), for a registered disabled person with a physical disability approved by the Secretary of State to 'have in his possession or to purchase, acquire, sell or transfer a pistol chambered for 0.22 or smaller rim-fire cartridges if he is authorised under the Act to possess, purchase or acquire that weapon subject to a [relevant] condition' (Firearms (Amendment) (No. 2) Act 1997, s. 2(1) and (2)). The certificate granted for that purpose must be subject to the condition that the weapon is stored and used only at designated premises and possession of the weapon outside such designated premises is permitted only for transfer to and use at premises at which a shooting competition is taking place on specified conditions (s. 2(3)). B12.68

POSSESSION OF FIREARM WITH INTENT TO ENDANGER LIFE

Firearms Act 1968, s. 16 B12.69

> It is an offence for a person to have in his possession any firearm or ammunition with intent by means thereof to endanger life or to enable another person by means thereof to endanger life whether any injury has been caused or not.

As to procedure and sentence, see ss. 51, 52 and sch. 6; **B12.2** and **B12.3**.

Indictment

Statement of Offence B12.70

> Having a firearm in possession with intent to endanger life, contrary to section 16 of the Firearms Act 1968

Particulars of Offence

> A on or about the . . . day of . . . at . . . had in his possession a firearm, namely . . ., with intent by means thereof to endanger life

No Extension to Imitation Firearms

'Firearm' carries the general meaning provided by the FA 1968, s. 57(1), see **B12.4**. The section does not extend to imitation firearms, because there is no express reference to such firearms, and because the FA 1982, s. 2(2) and (3), makes clear that that Act does not extend to this section. B12.71

Intent to Endanger Life

The test is proof of intention to behave in such a way as will in fact, to the accused's knowledge, endanger life (*Brown* [1995] Crim LR 328 and *Anderson* [2006] EWCA Crim 833, disapproving the dictum in *East* [1990] Crim LR 413). A specific intent to endanger life has to be established (*Bathh* 28 May 1999 unreported, CA). The person whose life it is intended to endanger need not be in the UK (*El-Hakkoui* [1975] 1 WLR 396) and the intent need not be an immediate or unconditional one, although it is necessary that the accused have B12.72

possession of a firearm or ammunition with a view to using them if and when the occasion arises (*Bentham* [1973] QB 357 and *Jones* [1997] QB 798). An intention to endanger life is not defined by the physical capabilities of any bullet at the time when the trigger comes to be pulled, so the intention could be present where the bullet or cartridge was a misfire. If the accused knew that the ammunition could not work, that would be relevant to intention (*Anderson*). The life that the accused intends to endanger must be someone else's and not his own (*Norton* [1977] Crim LR 478). Where the charge is of possessing a firearm or ammunition with intent to enable another to endanger life, it must be proved that the possessor had an intention that life be endangered by the firearm or ammunition (*Jones*).

The Court of Appeal in *Georgiades* [1989] 1 WLR 759, held that it is possible for an accused to intend to endanger life for a lawful purpose, as when raising the defence of self-defence. Cases where such a defence could be successfully raised must be very rare. However, in the instant case, the conviction under the FA 1968, s. 16, had to be quashed because the question of whether the intention to endanger life might have been a lawful one was not left to the jury.

POSSESSION OF FIREARM OR IMITATION FIREARM WITH INTENT TO CAUSE FEAR OF VIOLENCE

B12.73 **Firearms Act 1968, s. 16A**

It is an offence for a person to have in his possession any firearm or imitation firearm with intent—

(a) by means thereof to cause, or

(b) to enable another person by means thereof to cause,

any person to believe that unlawful violence will be used against him or another person.

As to procedure and sentence, see **B12.2** and **B12.3**.

Indictment

B12.74 *Statement of Offence*

Having a firearm in possession with intent to cause a person to believe that unlawful violence will be used against him or another, contrary to section 16A of the Firearms Act 1968

Particulars of Offence

A on or about the . . . day of . . . had in his possession a firearm, namely . . ., with intent by means thereof to cause V, to believe that unlawful violence would be used against him or another

Elements

B12.75 For the meaning of 'firearm', see **B12.4**; for the meaning of 'imitation firearm', see **B12.11**. The concept of 'possession' is considered at **B12.26**. For the meaning of 'unlawful violence', see **B11.42**.

In *K v DPP* [2006] EWHC 2183 (Admin), the Divisional Court rejected the appellant's submission that the knowledge of all those present, and in particular the complainant, that the gun was an imitation firearm and not a real one, was such as to make the commission of the offence impossible. K's purpose or intention was to make the complainant fear violence and it was not fatal to the conviction that the complainant was aware that it was an imitation firearm (that fact might be relevant to sentence).

It is not appropriate to attempt to draw parallels with the provisions of the Prevention of Crime Act 1953: 'the plain language of section 16A embraces the situation where an offender forms an intention to cause fear of violence at or immediately before his actions which are designed to cause such fear' (*Goluchowski* [2006] EWCA Crim 1972). See also **B12.125**.

USE OF FIREARM TO RESIST ARREST

Firearms Act 1968, s. 17 **B12.76**

(1) It is an offence for a person to make or attempt to make any use whatsoever of a firearm or imitation firearm with intent to resist or prevent the lawful arrest or detention of himself or another person.

As to sentence, see ss. 51 and 52 and sch. 6, and **B12.3**.

Indictment

Statement of Offence **B12.77**

Using firearm with intent to resist [or: prevent] arrest, contrary to section 17(1) of the Firearms Act 1968

Particulars of Offence

A on or about the . . . day of . . . at . . . used a firearm, namely . . . with intent to resist his lawful arrest or detention [or: to prevent the lawful arrest or detention of X]

Alternative Verdicts

Firearms Act 1968, sch. 6, part II, para. 5 **B12.78**

If on the trial of a person for an offence under section 17(1) of this Act the jury are not satisfied that he is guilty of that offence but are satisfied that he is guilty of an offence under section 17(2), the jury may find him guilty of the offence under section 17(2) and he shall then be punishable accordingly.

As to the offence under s. 17(2), see **B12.80** to **B12.82**.

Firearms and Imitation Firearms

By virtue of the FA 1968, s. 17(4), a restricted definition of 'firearm', as provided by s. 57(1) applies (see **B12.4** above), except that component parts of and accessories to such firearms are not part of the definition for the purposes of the s. 17 offence (i.e. the definition in s. 57(1), except for paras. (b) and (c)). **B12.79**

Section 17 expressly refers to 'imitation firearm', and therefore it is the definition in s. 57(1), as applied by s. 17(4), that is relevant (see **B12.11**). The FA 1982 is not relevant to this offence.

POSSESSING FIREARM WHILE COMMITTING AN OFFENCE IN THE FIREARMS ACT 1968, sch. 1

Firearms Act 1968, s. 17(2) **B12.80**

(2) If a person, at the time of his committing or being arrested for an offence specified in schedule 1 to this Act, has in his possession a firearm or imitation firearm, he shall be guilty of an offence under this subsection unless he shows that he had it in his possession for a lawful object.

As to procedure and sentence, see ss. 51, 52 and sch. 6, and **B12.2** and **B12.3**. See also **B12.77** and **B12.78**.

Elements

As to the meaning of 'firearm' and 'imitation firearm' in the FA 1968, s. 17, generally, see B12.79. **B12.81**

An offence under s. 17(1) is committed where the accused has possession of the firearm. He need not 'have it with him' (see **B12.83**). There is a consistent use of these two different terms in the FA 1968. Therefore, the same meaning of possession was applied in *North* [2001] EWCA Crim 544, as is applied to the offence contrary to the FA 1968, s. 1 (see **B12.19**).

Offences Specified in the Firearms Act 1968, sch. 1

B12.82 The offences specified in sch. 1 are:

offences under the Criminal Damage Act 1971, s. 1 (damage to property);
offences under the OAPA 1861, ss. 20 to 22 (inciting bodily injury, garrotting, criminal use of stupefying drugs), 30 (laying explosive to building), 32 (endangering railway passengers by tampering with track), 38 (assault with intent to commit offence or resist arrest) and 47 (assault);
offences under the Child Abduction Act 1984, part I (abduction of children);
theft, robbery, burglary, blackmail and any offence under the TA 1968, s. 12(1);
offences under the Police Act 1996, s. 89(1) or the Police (Scotland) Act 1967, s. 41 (assaulting constable in execution of his duty);
offences under the CJA 1991, s. 90(1) (assaulting prisoner custody officer);
offences under the CJPO 1994, s. 13(1) (assaulting secure training centre custody officer);
offences under the Immigration and Asylum Act 1999, sch. 11, para. 4 (assaulting a detainee custody officer);
offences under the SOA 2003, ss. 1 (rape), 2 (assault by penetration), 4 (causing a person to engage in sexual activity involving penetration without consent), 5 (rape of a child under 13), 6 (assault by penetration of a child under 13), 8 (causing or inciting a child under 13 to engage in sexual activity involving penetration), 30 (sexual activity involving penetration with a person with a mental disorder impeding choice) and 31 (causing or inciting a person with a mental disorder impeding choice to engage in sexual activity involving penetration);
aiding or abetting the commission of any such offence;
attempting to commit any such offence.

In *Nelson* [2001] 1 QB 55, the Court of Appeal confirmed that the statute is clear that a specified offence need not have been committed, but the accused must have been lawfully arrested for one.

OFFENCES INVOLVING CARRYING OF FIREARMS

Carrying Firearm or Imitation Firearm with Intent to Commit an Indictable Offence or to Resist Arrest

B12.83 **Firearms Act 1968, s. 18**

(1) It is an offence for a person to have with him a firearm or imitation firearm with intent to commit an indictable offence, or to resist arrest or prevent the arrest of another, in either case while he has a firearm or imitation firearm with him.

As to procedure and sentence, see ss. 51, 52, sch. 6, and **B12.2** and **B12.3**.

The Court of Appeal in *Stoddart* [1998] 2 Cr App R 25, has made clear that there are three elements to this offence:

(a) that the accused had with him a firearm;
(b) that he intended to have it with him; and
(c) that at the same time he had the intention to commit an indictable offence or to resist or prevent arrest.

The general definition of 'firearm' in the FA 1968, s. 57(1), applies, see **B12.4**. Since there is an express reference to 'imitation firearm', the definition in s. 57(4) applies, and the FA 1982 has no application, see **B12.14**.

Possession is not enough: the law requires the evidence to establish that the accused had the weapon with him. The classic case is carrying it, or a person may have it with him if it is immediately available to him, but 'if all that can be shown is possession in the sense that it is in your house or in a shed or somewhere where you have ultimate control, that is not enough' (per Scarman LJ in *Kelt* [1977] 1 WLR 1365; for the meaning of 'possession', see **B12.26**). In *Pawlicki* [1992] 1 WLR 827, the Court of Appeal explained *Kelt* on the basis that the court had been trying to highlight the importance of propinquity as a necessary ingredient distinguishing this offence from those relating to possession. Whilst rejecting the possibility of a statutory definition, the court, taking into account a purposive approach, relied upon a concept of 'ready accessibility' and decided that the defendants in an auction room had firearms with them which were in a car some 50 yards away. In *Bradish* [2004] EWCA Crim 1340, the Court of Appeal decided that to suggest that someone has with them a gun when it is at home some miles away and it is available to them defeats the object of the legislation. The defendants had made no arrangements that would have enabled them quickly to acquire the gun in the course of a robbery if they had needed it for their purposes. On a common-sense basis, they did not have the gun with them.

The accused must also have intended to have the firearm with him. Section 18(2) renders proof that the accused had the firearm with him and that he intended to commit an indictable offence or to resist or prevent arrest probative of his intention to have the firearm with him (*Stoddart*). Section 18(2) provides:

Firearms Act 1968, s. 18(2)

(2) In proceedings for an offence under this section proof that the accused had a firearm or imitation firearm with him and intended to commit an offence, or to resist or prevent arrest, is evidence that he intended to have it with him while doing so.

The Court of Appeal in *Houghton* [1982] Crim LR 112, held that it is necessary to establish the intent only at the moment to which the charge relates, which in this case was when the imitation firearm was pulled out of a holster by the accused. The intent may be formed at the same time as the accused begins to have the gun with him. It need not be formed at any earlier stage. It is not necessary to show an intention to use the firearm in the furtherance of the indictable offence (*Stoddart*). The intent must be free from duress (*Fisher* [2004] Crim LR 938).

By virtue of the Interpretation Act 1978, s. 5 and sch. 1, 'indictable offence' means an offence which, if committed by an adult, is triable on indictment, whether it is exclusively so triable or triable either way.

Carrying Loaded Firearm in Public Place

Firearms Act 1968, s. 19 **B12.84**

A person commits an offence if, without lawful authority or reasonable excuse (the proof whereof lies on him), he has with him in a public place—

(a) a loaded shot gun,
(b) an air weapon (whether loaded or not),
(c) any other firearm (whether loaded or not) together with ammunition suitable for use in that firearm, or
(d) an imitation firearm.

As to procedure and sentence, see ss. 51, 52, sch. 6, and **B12.2** and **B12.3**. Note that the offence is summary only in relation to imitation firearms or where the firearm is an air weapon (see *Weeks* [2006] EWCA Crim 1412, but note that the judgment wrongly refers to s. 19 of the ASBA 2003; the correct amending provision is s. 37 of that Act).

By s. 57(4) a 'public place' includes 'any highway and any other premises or place to which at the material time the public have or are permitted to have access whether on payment or otherwise' (*Anderson v Miller* (1976) 64 Cr App R 178, where it was held that the space behind a shop counter is a public place).

Section 19 applies to imitation firearms (see **B12.11**). For the definition of 'shotgun' see **B12.6**.

The term 'loaded' has an extended meaning in the circumstances set out in s. 57(6).

Firearms Act 1968, s. 57

(6) For purposes of this Act—

. . .

(b) a shotgun or an air weapon shall be deemed to be loaded if there is ammunition in the chamber or barrel or in any magazine or other device which is in such a position that the ammunition can be fed into the chamber or barrel by the manual or automatic operation of some part of the gun or weapon.

The offence under s. 19 is absolute: see **B12.27**. In *Vann* [1996] Crim LR 52, V had a loaded weapon with her because 'she had the gun with her in the present case, physically in her possession, and . . . was aware that she had it, even if she was ignorant of the fact that it was a gun'. In *Jones* [1995] QB 235, the Court of Appeal held, following the Divisional Court in *Ross v Collins* [1982] Crim LR 368, that possession of a firearm or ammunition certificate was not in itself lawful authority to have a firearm and ammunition in a public place.

Whereas an honest, mistaken belief in facts, which if true would provide a lawful authority, is capable of being a reasonable excuse, there can be no reasonable excuse where the belief is in something which could not be lawful authority even if true, such as the accused's belief that he held a valid certificate when the certificate was, in fact, invalid (see also *Taylor v Mucklow* (1973) 117 SJ 792).

Reasonable excuse is unlikely to include a plea that the accused was unaware of the nature of the item that he had with him, or that the firearm was in a container and he did not know its contents nor had a reasonable opportunity to inspect, but the point was left undecided in *Vann*. Whether the imposition of the burden on the defendant is compliant with the ECHR, Article 6 remains to be determined, see **F3.13**. Arguments against the reverse burden include the fact that the offence is triable either way and, on indictment, carries a high maximum penalty. On the other hand, the definitional elements of the offence have to be proved by the prosecution and the offence deals with a serious problem.

PROHIBITION ON POSSESSION OR ACQUISITION OF FIREARMS BY CONVICTED PERSONS

B12.85 Section 21 of the FA 1968 imposes certain restrictions on the possession and acquisition of firearms by convicted persons. By s. 21(4), it is an offence for a person to contravene any of the 'foregoing provisions' of the section. The 'foregoing provisions' are the provisions of s. 21(1) to (3A), which provide as follows.

A person who has been sentenced to custody for life or to preventive detention, or to imprisonment, or to corrective training, youth custody or detention in a young offender institution (or Scottish equivalent) for three years or more, must not at any time have a firearm or ammunition in his possession (s. 21(1)).

A person who has been sentenced to imprisonment, youth custody, detention in a young offender institution (or Scottish equivalent), a secure training order, or a detention and training order for three months or more, but less than three years, must not at any time before the expiration of the period of five years from the date of his release have a firearm or ammunition in his possession (s. 21(2)). (By virtue of s. 21(2A), 'date of release' means: for a sentence partly served and partly suspended, the date on which the offender completes the part to be served in prison and, in the case of a person subject to a secure training order or detention and training order, the date on which he is released from detention (under the order or under the CJPO 1994, s. 4 or under the PCC(S)A 2000, s. 104, as the case may be) or the date halfway through the total period specified by the court in making the order, whichever is the latest; in the case of a person who has been subject to an intermittent custody order under the CJA 2003, s. 183(1)(b), the date of his final release.)

A person who is serving a sentence of imprisonment to which an intermittent custody order under the CJA 2003, s. 183, relates must not during any specified licence period have a firearm or ammunition in his possession (FA 1968, s. 21(2B)).

A person who holds a licence issued under the CYPA 1933, s. 53 (or Scottish equivalent), or is subject to a recognisance to keep the peace or be of good behaviour with a condition relating to the possession of firearms (or Scottish equivalent), must not, at any time during which he holds the licence, or is so subject, have a firearm or ammunition in his possession (s. 21(3)).

As to procedure and sentence, see ss. 51, 52 and sch. 6, and **B12.2** and **B12.3**. If a person is prohibited in Northern Ireland from having a firearm or ammunition in his possession, he is also so prohibited in Great Britain (s. 21(3A)).

A person may apply to the Crown Court for the removal of such prohibitions (FA 1968, s. 21(6); *Gordon v Northampton Crown Court* (20 December 1999 unreported)). For the procedure, see s. 21(7) and sch. 3.

Section 21 does not extend to imitation firearms, because there is no express reference to such firearms and because the FA 1982 only extends to firearms to which s. 1 of the FA 1968 applies, whereas this section applies to firearms generally.

Firearms Act 1968, s. 21(5)

(5) It is an offence for a person to sell or transfer a firearm or ammunition to, or to repair, test or prove a firearm or ammunition for, a person whom he knows or has reasonable ground for believing to be prohibited by this section from having a firearm or ammunition in his possession.

The offence carries the same range of sentence as the offence contrary to s. 21(4) above (see sch. 6 at **B12.3**) and is triable either way.

PROHIBITION ON POSSESSION OR ACQUISITION OF FIREARMS BY PERSONS UNDER SPECIFIED AGES

A series of summary offences created by the FA 1968, ss. 22 to 24, deals with the acquiring, having in possession, use, sale or letting to, supply to and making a gift to a young person of a variety of firearms. The requisite age of the young person is not the same in each case. As to procedure and sentence, see ss. 51, 52 and sch. 6 at **B12.2** and **B12.3**. The following relevant definitions have been given above: 'firearm' (**B12.4**); 'shotgun' (**B12.6**); 'air weapon' (**B12.7**); 'ammunition' (**B12.9**); firearm to which the Firearm Act 1968, s. 1, applies (**B12.21**); ammunition to which the FA 1968, s. 1, applies (**B12.23**). **B12.86**

Person under 17 Acquiring Firearm

It is an offence, contrary to the FA 1968, s. 22(1), for a person under the age of 17 to purchase or hire any firearm or ammunition. This section does not extend to imitation firearms. **B12.87**

Persons under 18 Acquiring an Air Weapon

B12.88 From 1 October 2007, the wording of s. 22(1) of the FA 1968 will read: 'It is an offence (a) for a person under the age of eighteen to purchase or hire an air weapon or ammunition for an air weapon; (b) for a person under the age of seventeen to purchase or hire a firearm or ammunition of any other description' (VCRA 2006, s. 33(2)).

Person under 18 Possessing Firearm

B12.89 A person under 18 may, as the holder of a certificate, have a firearm in his possession, but it is an offence to use that firearm for a purpose not authorised by the European Weapons Directive (FA 1968, s. 22(1A); see also **B12.58**).

Person under 14 Having Firearm in his Possession Without Lawful Authority

B12.90 It is an offence, contrary to the FA 1968, s. 22(2), for a person under the age of 14 to have in his possession any firearm or ammunition to which s. 1 of the 1968 Act or s. 15 of the F(A)A 1988 applies, except in circumstances where under s. 11(1), (3) or (4) of the 1968 Act, or s. 15 of the F(A)A 1988, he is entitled to have possession of it without holding a firearm certificate (see **B12.33**). Since this offence refers to firearms to which s. 1 of the FA 1968 applies, the FA 1982 applies and so this section extends to imitation firearms within that Act, see **B12.14**.

Person under 15 Having with him a Shotgun without Adult Supervision

B12.91 It is an offence, contrary to the FA 1968, s. 22(3), for a person under the age of 15 to have with him an assembled shotgun except while under the supervision of a person over the age of 21, or while the shotgun is so covered with a securely fastened gun cover that it cannot be fired. This section does not extend to imitation firearms because there is no express reference to such firearms and the FA 1982 does not apply. The offence consists in a person 'having with him' such a weapon, see **B12.83**.

Person under 17 [18] Having with him an Air Weapon or Ammunition

B12.92 It is an offence, contrary to the FA 1968, s. 22(4), and subject to s. 23, for a person under the age of 17 to have with him an air weapon or ammunition for an air weapon. This section does not extend to imitation firearms, because there is no express reference to such firearms and the FA 1982 does not apply. As with the previous offence, this offence is concerned with a person having such a weapon with him. As to this, see **B12.83**. The offence is subject to s. 23, which introduces certain defences and (prior to amendments made to s. 23 by the VCRA 2006, s. 34) two further offences. Note that the age limit specified in s. 22(4) was increased from 14 to 17 by the ASBA 2003, s. 38(2)(a), and (from 1 October 2007) the age limit is further increased to 18 years of age, by the VCRA 2006, s. 33(3). Situations that arise before and after the coming into force of s. 34 of the VCRA 2006, insofar as that section amends the FA 1968, s. 23, are summarised below.

Firearms Act 1968, s. 23 (prior to implementation of the VCRA 2006, s. 34)

(1) It is not an offence under section 22(4) of this Act for a person to have with him an air weapon or ammunition while he is under the supervision of a person of or over the age of twenty-one; but where a person has with him an air weapon on any premises in circumstances where he would be prohibited from having it with him but for this subsection, it is an offence—

(a) for him to use it for firing any missile beyond those premises; or

(b) for the person under whose supervision he is to allow him so to use it.

(2) . . .

(3) It is not an offence under section 22(4) of this Act for a person of or over the age of fourteen to have with him an air weapon or ammunition on private premises with the consent of the occupier.

(4) But where a person has with him an air weapon on premises in circumstances where he would be prohibited from having it with him but for subsection (3), it is an offence for him to use it for firing any missile beyond those premises.

Person under 17 [18] Having with him an Air Weapon or Ammunition and who is Acting under Supervision Prior to the implementation of the VCRA 2006, s. 34 (i.e. 1 October 2007), a person who would be prohibited from having the weapon with him, but for s. 23, commits an offence (contrary to s. 23(1) if he uses it for firing any missile beyond those premises or for the person under whose supervision he is to allow him so to use it. **B12.93**

Person aged 14 or over Having with him an Air Weapon or Ammunition and who is Acting with the Consent of the Occupier of Private Premises It is not an offence for a person of 14 or over to have with him an air weapon or ammunition on private premises with the consent of the occupier (s. 23(3), as inserted by the ASBA 2003, s. 38(3)(b)). But in those circumstances, it is an offence for him to use the air weapon for firing any missile beyond those premises (s. 23(4), as inserted by the ASBA 2003, s. 38(3)(b)). **B12.94**

Firearms Act 1968, s. 23 (post VCRA 2006, s. 34: i.e. 1 October 2007)

23.—(1) It is not an offence under section 22(4) of this Act for a person to have with him an air weapon or ammunition while he is under the supervision of a person of or over the age of twenty-one; but where a person has with him an air weapon on any premises in circumstances where he would be prohibited from having it with him but for this subsection, it is an offence—

(a) . . . [deleted]

(b) . . . [deleted]

for the person under whose supervision he is to allow him to use it for firing any missile beyond those premises.

(1A) In proceedings against a person for an offence under subsection (1) it shall be a defence for him to show that the only premises into or across which the missile was fired were premises the occupier of which had consented to the firing of the missile (whether specifically or by way of a general consent).

(2) . . .

(3) It is not an offence under section 22(4) of this Act for a person of or over the age of fourteen to have with him an air weapon or ammunition on private premises with the consent of the occupier.

(4) [deleted by the VCRA 2006, s. 34(3)(c)]

Person under 17[18] Having with him an Air Weapon or Ammunition and who is Acting under Supervision From 1 October 2007 (when the VCRA 2006, s. 34 came into force), by virtue of s. 23(1), no offence is committed while the person is under the supervision of a person of or over the age of 21 but, where the person has with him an air weapon on any premises in circumstances where he would be prohibited from having it with him but for s. 23, it is an offence for the person *supervising him* to allow him to use it for firing any missile beyond those premises (VCRA 2006, s. 34(3)(a)). However, 'it shall be a defence for him to show that the only premises into or across which the missile was fired were premises the occupier of which had consented to the firing of the missile (whether specifically or by way of a general consent)' (s. 23(1A), as inserted by the VCRA 2006, s. 34(3)(b)). **B12.95**

Selling or Letting on Hire a Firearm to Person under 17, or an Air Weapon to a Person under 18 It is an offence, contrary to the FA 1968, s. 24(1), to sell or let on hire any firearm or ammunition to a person under the age of 17. This section does not extend to imitation firearms, because there is no express reference to such firearms and the FA 1982 does not apply. It is a defence, according to s. 24(5), to prove that the person charged with the offence believed the other person to be of or over the age mentioned in that provision and had reasonable ground for that belief. Since 1 October 2007 (when the VCRA 2006, s. 33 came into force), s. 24(1) of the FA 1968 is extended to air weapons or ammunition for an air weapon. Thus s. 24(1) reads: 'It is an offence (a) to sell or let on hire an air weapon or ammunition for an air weapon to a person under the age of eighteen; (b) to sell or let on **B12.96**

hire a firearm or ammunition of any other description to a person under the age of seventeen' (VCRA 2006, s. 33(4)).

B12.97 **Supplying Certain Firearms or Ammunition to Person under 14** It is an offence, contrary to the FA 1968, s. 24(2):

(a) to make a gift of or lend any firearm or ammunition to which s. 1 applies to a person under the age of 14; or
(b) to part with the possession of any such firearm or ammunition to a person under that age, except in circumstances where that person is entitled under s. 11(1), (3) or (4), or under the F(A)A 1988, s. 15, to have possession thereof without holding a firearm certificate.

Since this offence refers to firearms to which s. 1 of the FA 1968, applies, the FA 1982 applies and so this section extends to imitation firearms within that Act (see **B12.14**). As with the previous offence it is a defence to make a reasonable mistake as to age (see the defence under the FA 1968, s. 24(1)). It is also a defence if possession is permitted under s. 11(1), (3) or (4); or under the F(A)A 1988, s. 15 (sports, athletics and other approved activities; rifle and pistol clubs; see **B12.33**).

B12.98 **Making Gift of Shotgun to Person under 15** It is an offence, contrary to the FA 1968, s. 24(3), to make a gift of a shotgun or ammunition for a shotgun to a person under the age of 15. This section does not extend to imitation firearms because there is no express reference to such firearms and the FA 1982 does not apply. As with the offence contrary to the FA 1968, s. 24(1), it is a defence to make a reasonable mistake as to age (see the defence under s. 24(1)).

B12.99 **Supplying Air Weapon to Person under 17 [18]** It is an offence, contrary to the FA 1968, s. 24(4):

(a) to make a gift of an air weapon or ammunition for an air weapon to a person under the age of 17 [18]; or
(b) to part with the possession of an air weapon or ammunition for an air weapon to a person under the age of 17 [18] except where by virtue of s. 23 (see above) the person is not prohibited from having it with him.

Note that the age limit was increased from 14 to 17 by the ASBA 2003, s. 38, and from 1 October 2007 the age limit is further increased to 18 years of age, by the VCRA 2006, s. 33(5).

There are the following defences to this offence:

(i) As with the offence contrary to the FA 1968, s. 24(1), it is a defence to make a reasonable mistake as to age; see the defence under s. 24(5).
(ii) A person may be entitled to have the weapon or ammunition with him under s. 23, see the offence under s. 22(4).

B12.100 **Supplying Imitation Firearms to Persons under 18** From 1 October 2007, a new s. 24A of the FA 1968 makes it an offence for a person under the age of 18 to purchase an imitation firearm (VCRA 2006, s. 40).

It is also be an offence by for a person to sell an imitation firearm to a person under the age of 18 (s. 24A(2)). It is a defence to show that the person charged with the offence (a) believed the other person to be aged 18 or over; and (b) had reasonable ground for that belief (s. 24A(3)). A person shall be taken to have shown the matters specified in s. 24A(3) if (a) sufficient evidence of those matters is adduced to raise an issue with respect to them; and (b) the contrary is not proved beyond a reasonable doubt. For the definition of 'imitation firearm', see **B12.11**.

SHORTENING AND CONVERSION OF FIREARMS

Definitions

Section 4(1) of the FA 1968 makes it an offence to shorten the barrel of a shotgun to a length less than 24 inches. Section 4(3) makes it an offence for a person other than a registered firearms dealer to convert into a firearm anything which, though having the appearance of being a firearm, is so constructed as to be incapable of discharging any missile through its barrel. **B12.101**

Section 6(1) of the F(A)A 1988 makes it an offence to shorten to a length less than 24 inches the barrel of any smooth-bore gun to which the FA 1968, s. 1, applies, other than one which has a barrel with a bore exceeding two inches in diameter.

Procedure and Sentence

All three offences are triable either way. **B12.102**

The range of sentence for all three offences is the same, that is, the guilty person is liable, on summary conviction, to a term of imprisonment not exceeding six months, or a fine not exceeding the prescribed sum, or both, and, on conviction on indictment, to a term of imprisonment not exceeding five years or a fine or both.

As to the courts' power to order forfeiture or disposal of firearms and ammunition, see the FA 1968, ss. 51, 52 and sch. 6 at **B12.2** and **B12.3**.

Elements and Defences

As to the meaning of: 'shotgun', see **B12.6**; 'smooth-bore gun to which s. 1 of the FA 1968 applies'; 'registered firearms dealer', see **B12.30**; 'firearm' see **B12.4**. **B12.103**

The length to which the barrel may be shortened is crucial for the first two offences, and this is to be measured, by virtue of s. 57(6)(a), from the muzzle to the point at which the charge is exploded on firing.

By virtue of the FA 1968, s. 4(2), a registered firearms dealer does not commit the offence contrary to s. 4(1) if the barrel is shortened for the sole purpose of replacing a defective part of the barrel so as to produce a barrel not less than 24 inches in length. The F(A)A 1988, s. 6(2), provides the same defence to the offence under s. 6(1).

TRANSFER OF FIREARMS AND AMMUNITION TO BE IN PERSON

The F(A)A 1997 introduces measures concerned with the transfer etc. of firearms and ammunition. In all cases it is an offence to breach the provisions provided for in ss. 32 to 35. For transfers relating to air weapons, see **B12.45**. **B12.104**

Punishment and Mode of Trial

The punishment and mode of trial of the offences depends upon the weaponry involved (F(A)A 1997, s. 36): **B12.105**

(a) where the offence is committed 'in relation to a transfer or other event involving a firearm or ammunition to which section 1 of the 1968 Act applies' it is punishable, on summary conviction, with a term of imprisonment not exceeding six months, or a fine not exceeding the statutory maximum or both and, on conviction on indictment, with a term of imprisonment not exceeding five years, or a fine, or both (s. 36(a));

(b) where the offence is committed 'in relation to a transfer or other event involving a shot gun' it is punishable, on summary conviction only, with a term of imprisonment not exceeding six months, or a fine not exceeding level 5 on the standard scale, or both (s. 36(b)).

The Offences

B12.106 The offences to which these sentence and mode of trial provisions apply are set out in the detailed provisions of ss. 32 to 35 and are summarised below.

B12.107 **Failure to Comply with s. 32(2)** It is an offence for a transferor or transferee to fail to comply with s. 32(2). There must be a transfer to which s. 32 applies. Under s. 32(1), such a transfer is where, in Great Britain:

> (a) a firearm or ammunition to which section 1 of the 1968 Act applies is sold, let on hire, lent or given by any person, or
> (b) a shot gun is sold, let on hire or given, or lent for a period of more than 72 hours by any person,
>
> to another person who is neither a registered firearms dealer nor a person who is entitled to purchase or acquire the firearm or ammunition without holding a firearm or shot gun certificate or a visitor's firearm or shot gun permit.

The obligations on the transferor or transferee are that 'the transferee must produce to the transferor the certificate or permit entitling him to purchase or acquire the firearm or ammunition being transferred' (s. 32(2)(a)); 'the transferor must comply with any instructions contained in the certificate or permit produced by the transferee' (s. 32(2)(b)), and 'the transferor must hand the firearm or ammunition to the transferee, and the transferee must receive it, in person' (s. 32(2)(c)).

B12.108 **Failure to Give Notice under s. 33** The failure by a party to a transaction to which the F(A)A 1997, s. 33, applies to give the notice required by that section is an offence (s. 33(4)). The relevant transaction occurs where, in Great Britain, any firearm to which s. 1 of the 1968 Act applies is sold, let on hire, lent or given or any shot gun is sold, let on hire or given, or lent for a period of more than 72 hours (s. 33(1)). Any party to a transfer to which s. 33 applies who is the holder of a firearm or shotgun certificate or, as the case may be, a visitor's firearm or shotgun permit which relates to the firearm in question must within seven days of the transfer give notice to the chief officer of police who granted his certificate or permit (s. 33(2)). The notice must contain a description of the firearm in question (giving its identification number if any) and state the nature of the transaction and the name and address of the other party; any such notice must be sent by registered post or by recorded delivery (s. 33(3)).

B12.109 **Failure to Give Notice under s. 34** The failure, without reasonable excuse, to give the notice required by s. 34 is an offence (s. 34(4)). There is an obligation to give a notice in two sets of circumstances. First, the firearm or shotgun certificate holder who was last in possession of the firearm before it was de-activated, destroyed or lost (whether by theft or otherwise) must, within seven days of that event, give notice of it to the chief officer of police who granted the certificate or permit (s. 34(1)). This requirement applies to firearms to which a firearm or shotgun certificate relates, and firearms to which a visitor's firearm or shotgun permit relates (s. 34(1)). Secondly, where there is ammunition to which s. 1 of the 1968 Act applies and to which a firearm certificate or a visitor's firearm permit relates and that ammunition has been lost (whether by theft or otherwise), the certificate or permit holder who was last in possession of the ammunition before the loss must, within seven days of that event, give notice of it to the chief officer of police who granted the certificate or permit (s. 34(2)). A notice must describe the firearm or ammunition in question (giving the identification number of the firearm if any), must state the nature of the event and must be sent by registered post or the recorded delivery service (s. 34(3)). A firearm is deactivated 'if it would, by virtue of section 8 of the 1988 Act be presumed to be rendered incapable of discharging any shot, bullet or other missile' (s. 34(5)). For s. 8 of the 1988 Act, see **B12.8**).

Breach of s. 35 Section 35 creates two offences. First, failure to give a notice required by s. 35(1) (s. 35(2)) and, secondly, the failure, without reasonable excuse, to give a notice required by s. 35(3) (s. 35(4)). Under s. 35(1), a transferor must, within 14 days of any disposal, give notice of it to the chief officer of police who granted his certificate where, outside Great Britain, 'any firearm or shot gun is sold or otherwise disposed of by a transferor whose acquisition or purchase of the firearm or shot gun was authorised by a firearm certificate or shot gun certificate'. Under s. 35(3), a firearm or shot gun certificate holder 'who was last in possession of the firearm or ammunition before [the] event [must] within 14 days of the event give notice of it to the chief officer of police who granted the certificate'. The 'event' in question is where, outside Great Britain, a firearm to which a firearm or shot gun certificate relates is de-activated, destroyed or lost (whether by theft or otherwise) or any ammunition to which s. 1 of the 1968 Act applies, and a firearm certificate relates, is lost (whether by theft or otherwise) (s. 35(3)). To comply with s. 35, the notice must contain a description of the firearm or ammunition in question (including any identification number), state the nature of the event and, in the case of a disposal, the name and address of the other party (s. 35(5)). 'De-activated' is defined in the same way as for s. 34, see **B12.109**. Such a notice must be sent within 14 days of the disposal or other event if it is sent from a place in the UK, by registered post or by the recorded delivery service and, in any other case, in such manner as most closely corresponds to the use of registered post or the recorded delivery service (s. 35(6)). **B12.110**

BUSINESS, EXPORT AND OTHER TRANSACTIONS INVOLVING FIREARMS AND AMMUNITION

Scope of Offences

There are 15 firearms offences concerned with business and other transactions. These can be considered in four separate groups reflecting the varying modes of trial and penalties. **B12.111**

Either-way offences:

(a) trading in firearms without being registered as a firearms dealer (FA 1968, s. 3(1));
(b) selling firearms to person without a certificate (s. 3(2));
(c) repairing, testing etc. firearms for person without a certificate (s. 3(3));
(d) falsifying a certificate etc. with a view to the acquisition of a firearm (s. 3(5));
(e) transactions with person not a registered firearms dealer (s. 42(2));
(f) supplying firearms to person denied them under s. 21(5) (this offence is dealt with at **B12.85**).

Summary offences with maximum penalty three months' imprisonment or level 5 fine:

(a) failure to report transaction authorised by visitor's shotgun permit (FA 1968, s. 42A(3));
(b) failure by person who resides in Great Britain to report purchase or acquisition of firearms in other Member States (FA 1968, s. 18A(6));
(c) failure of firearms dealer to include particulars of agreement as required by the European Weapons Directive and FA 1968, s. 18(1A) (s. 18(6)).

Summary offences with maximum penalty six months' imprisonment or level 5 fine:

(a) failure of registered firearms dealer to notify police of export transaction (F(A)A 1988, s. 18(5));
(b) transfer of shotguns (s. 4(5));
(c) restriction on sale of ammunition for smooth-bore guns (s. 5(2)).

Summary offences with maximum penalty six months' imprisonment or level 3 fine:

(a) pawnbroker taking firearm in pawn (FA 1968, s. 3(6));

(b) supplying firearm to person drunk or insane (s. 25);
(c) contravention of order prohibiting movement of arms and ammunition (s. 6(3)).

Either-way Offences

B12.112 **Firearms Act 1968, s. 3**

(1) A person commits an offence if, by way of trade or business, he—
   (a) manufactures, sells, transfers, repairs, tests or proves any firearm or ammunition to which section 1 of this Act applies, or a shotgun; or
   (b) exposes for sale or transfer, or has in his possession for sale, transfer, test or proof any such firearm or ammunition, or a shotgun, [*or*
   (c) sells or transfers an air weapon, exposes such a weapon for sale or transfer or has such a weapon in his possession for sale or transfer,]
without being registered under this Act as a firearms dealer.

(2) It is an offence for a person to sell or transfer to any other person in the United Kingdom, other than a registered firearms dealer, any firearm or ammunition to which section 1 of this Act applies, or a shotgun, unless that other produces a firearm certificate authorising him to purchase or acquire it, or as the case may be, his shotgun certificate, or shows that he is by virtue of this Act entitled to purchase or acquire it without holding a certificate.

(3) It is an offence for a person to undertake the repair, test or proof of a firearm or ammunition to which section 1 of this Act applies, or of a shotgun, for any other person in the United Kingdom other than a registered firearms dealer as such, unless that other produces or causes to be produced a firearm certificate authorising him to have possession of the firearm or ammunition or, as the case may be, his shotgun certificate, or shows that he is by virtue of this Act entitled to have possession of it without holding a certificate.

. . .

(5) A person commits an offence if, with a view to purchasing or acquiring, or procuring the repair, test or proof of, any firearm or ammunition to which section 1 of this Act applies, or a shotgun, he produces a false certificate or a certificate in which any false entry has been made or personates a person to whom a certificate has been granted or makes any false statement.

The italicised words in square brackets were added by the VCRA 2006, s. 31, and will come into force on a day to be announced.

As to procedure and sentence, see ss.51, 52 and sch. 6, and **B12.2** and **B12.3**.

The FA 1982, on imitation firearms, applies to these offences (see **B12.14**).

For the meaning of: 'firearm or ammunition to which the FA 1968, s. 1, applies', see **B12.21**; 'shotgun', see **B12.6**; 'firearm certificate', see **B12.24**; 'shotgun certificate', see **B12.43**; 'registered firearms dealer', see **B12.30**. 'Transfer' is defined by the FA 1968, s. 57(4), as including let on hire, give, lend and part with possession, and 'transferee' and 'transferor' are construed accordingly.

The offence in s. 3(2) is an absolute one (*Paul* [1999] Crim LR 79). This must be true of the similar offences. The test is an objective one: 'whether the firearm in question corresponds with the description relied on in a certificate produced by the transferee'. The intentions of the transferee as to use are irrelevant (*Paul*).

In the offence contrary to s. 3(5), the offence requires consideration of what is a 'false certificate', a 'false entry' or a 'false statement'. The consideration of the analogous phrases in the Forgery and Counterfeiting Act 1981 (see **B6.23** to **B6.26**) may be of assistance in ascertaining the meaning of these terms.

With respect to s. 3(1), relevant exemptions include exemption where the accused is authorised to deal with firearms, for persons in the service of the Crown, for proof houses, and where the firearm is an antique firearm sold or purchased as a curiosity or ornament, although all of the exemptions in ss. 7 to 13, 15, 54 and 58(1) and (2) of the FA 1968, and ss. 15 to 19 of the F(A)A 1988 (see **B12.29** to **B12.42**) apply.

By s. 9(2) it is not an offence for an auctioneer to sell by auction, expose for sale by auction or have in his possession for sale by auction, a firearm or ammunition when he is not a registered firearms dealer, provided he has a permit from the chief officer of police and he complies with the terms of that permit. It is a summary offence for a person knowingly or recklessly to make a statement false in any material particular for the purpose of procuring for himself or another the grant of such a permit (s. 9(3)).

The same exemptions apply to offences under the FA 1968, s. 3(2) and (3). In addition, by virtue of s. 8(2), a person does not commit an offence under s. 3(2) if he (a) parts with possession of any firearm or ammunition, otherwise than in pursuance of a contract of sale or hire by way of gift or loan, to a person who shows that he is by virtue of this Act entitled to have possession of the firearm or ammunition without holding a certificate, or (b) returns to another person a shotgun which he has lawfully undertaken to repair, test or prove for another. By virtue of s. 9(4) it is not an offence under s. 3(2) for a carrier or warehouseman, or a servant, to deliver any firearm or ammunition in the ordinary course of his business or employment as such.

Summary Offences with Maximum Penalty Six or Three Months' Imprisonment and/or Level 5 Fine

Five offences which are only triable summarily are to be found in the F(A)A 1988. **B12.113**

The two offences introduced in compliance with the European Weapons Directive (breach of s. 18(6) or s. 18A(6) of the 1988 Act) are punishable with a maximum penalty of three months' imprisonment, or a fine not exceeding level 5 on the standard scale, or both.

The penalty in respect of the remaining three offences is that a guilty person is liable to a term of imprisonment not exceeding six months, or a fine not exceeding level 5 on the standard scale, or both. The provision extending the usual time within which proceedings must be instituted applies to these offences, see **B12.2**. The first offence, contrary to s. 18(5), is designed to ensure that a registered firearms dealer, who sells a firearm or shotgun to a person entitled to purchase the same under s. 18(1) without a certificate, sends a notice of the transaction within 48 hours to the chief officer of police. The required details of such a notice are laid down by s. 18(3). The second offence, contrary to s. 4(5), is designed to enable the police to be aware of who has possession of a shotgun when it is transferred without the intervention of a registered firearms dealer. Section 4 requires the police to be given notice of such a transfer and it is an offence to fail to comply with the provisions of s. 4. The third offence, contrary to s. 5(2), makes it an offence to sell certain ammunition to a person who is not a registered firearms dealer and is not permitted by a certificate or otherwise to have the gun for which certain ammunition is required. The ammunition covered is that to which the FA 1968, s. 1, does not apply and which can be used in a shotgun or smooth-bore gun to which that section applies.

Summary Offences with Maximum Penalty Six Months' Imprisonment and/or Level 3 Fine

It is a summary offence, contrary to the FA 1968, s. 3(6), for a pawnbroker to take in pawn any firearm or ammunition to which s. 1 applies. **B12.114**

It is a summary offence, contrary to s. 25, for a person to sell or transfer any firearm or ammunition to, or to repair, prove or test any firearm or ammunition for, another person whom he knows to be, or has reasonable cause for believing to be, drunk or of unsound mind.

It is a summary offence, contrary to s. 6(3), to contravene any order prohibiting the movement of arms and ammunition made under s. 6, any earlier corresponding legislation or any corresponding Northern Ireland legislation. This offence is supported by the power of the police, under s. 49, to search for and seize any firearms or ammunition which they have reason to believe are being removed in contravention of such an order. A person having custody or control of the firearms or ammunition must allow the police reasonable facilities to examine and inspect such articles and any documentation. Failure to comply with this power is a summary offence punishable in the same way as the offence contrary to s. 6(3).

Failure to Comply with Instructions by Police Officers

B12.115 It is an offence, contrary to the FA 1968, s. 47(2), for a person having a firearm or ammunition with him to fail to hand it over when required to do so by a constable acting under s. 47(1). This provision enables a constable to require a person whom he has reasonable cause to suspect of having a firearm, with or without ammunition, with him in a public place, or (b) to be committing, or about to commit, elsewhere than in a public place, an offence contrary to ss. 18(1), (2) and 20, to hand over the firearm or any ammunition for examination by the constable. Section 47 also provides a power of search of person and vehicle (s. 47(3) and (4)).

It is also an offence, contrary to s. 48(3), for a person to refuse to declare to a constable his name and address or to fail to give his true name and address when required to do so by a constable acting under s. 48. This enables a constable to require the production of a relevant certificate when he believes a person to be in possession of a firearm to which s. 1 applies, or a shotgun.

As to procedure and sentence, see ss. 51, 52 and sch. 6 at **B12.2** and **B12.3**.

Miscellaneous Offences Relating to Permits, Certificates and Authorisations

B12.116 Permits, certificates and authorisations perform an important function under the Firearms Acts 1968 to 1992 since, when relevant, they authorise what would otherwise be an offence. Since they are so important a number of offences are created which relate to their obtaining and use. Reference has already been made to some of these offences under specific offences in the preceding parts of this section.

In addition, the following summary offences have been created:

(a) To make a false statement in order to procure the grant or renewal of a firearm or shotgun certificate (FA 1968, s. 26(5)). It is punishable with a term of imprisonment not exceeding six months, or a fine not exceeding level 5 on the standard scale, or both.
(b) To make a false statement in order to procure the variation of a firearm certificate (s. 29(3)). It is punishable with a term of imprisonment not exceeding six months, or a fine not exceeding level 5 on the standard scale, or both.
(c) To fail to surrender a certificate on revocation (s. 30(4)). It is punishable with a fine not exceeding level 3 on the standard scale.
(d) On removal of a firearms dealer's name from the register, to fail to surrender a certificate of registration or register of transactions (s. 38(8)). It is punishable with a fine not exceeding level 3 on the standard scale.
(e) To make a false statement in order to secure firearms dealer registration or entry in the register of a place of business (s. 39(1)). It is punishable with a term of imprisonment not exceeding six months, or a fine not exceeding level 5 on the standard scale, or both.
(f) For a registered firearms dealer to have a place of business not entered on the register (s. 39(2)). It is punishable with a term of imprisonment not exceeding six months, or a fine not exceeding level 5 on the standard scale, or both.
(g) Not to comply with a condition of firearms dealer registration (s. 39(3)). It is punishable with a term of imprisonment not exceeding six months, or a fine not exceeding level 5 on the standard scale, or both.
(h) For a firearms dealer not to comply with provisions as to the register of transactions and to make a false entry in the register (s. 40(5)). These offences are punishable with a term of imprisonment not exceeding six months, or a fine not exceeding level 5 on the standard scale, or both.

(i) To fail to surrender a firearm or shotgun certificate cancelled by a court on conviction (s. 52(2)(c)). It is punishable with a fine not exceeding level 3 on the standard scale.
(j) To fail to comply with a notice from a chief officer of police who has revoked a certificate requiring the holder of the certificate to surrender forthwith the certificate and any firearms and ammunition which are in the holder's possession by virtue of the certificate (s. 12(2)). The offence is punishable with imprisonment for a term not exceeding three months, or a fine not exceeding level 4 on the standard scale, or both.

Further summary offences (under the FA 1968, ss. 32B(5), 32C(6), 42A(3) and 48A(4)) have been created to ensure compliance with the European Weapons Directive.

SENTENCING GUIDELINES FOR FIREARMS OFFENCES

Section 51A of the FA 1968 (as inserted by the CJA 2003, s. 287) provides for minimum custodial sentences for certain firearms offences, where such offence was committed on or after 22 January 2004. For details, see E6.3. **B12.117**

Several Court of Appeal decisions provide guidance on the appropriate sentencing bracket for the most serious firearms offences.

The Court of Appeal in *Avis* [1998] 1 Cr App R 420, reviewed sentencing levels for a number of such offences. These offences had been coming before the courts more frequently in recent years, and on some occasions sentencing levels had failed properly to reflect public concern. Lord Bingham CJ said that, given the clear public need to discourage unlawful possession and use of firearms (both real and imitation) and Parliament's intention expressed by the continuing increase in maximum penalties, the courts should treat offences under the FA 1968 as serious. Save for minor infringements which might be and were properly dealt with summarily, offences committed under ss. 1(1), 2(1), 3, 4, 5(1A), 16, 16A, 17(1) and (2), 18(1), 19 and 21(4) would generally merit custodial sentences, even on a plea of guilty and where the offender had no previous record. On breaches of ss. 4, 5, 16, 16A, 17(1) and (2), 18(1), 19 or 21, the custodial term was likely to be considerable, and where the four questions suggested by the court (set out below) yielded answers adverse to the offender, terms at or approaching the maximum might in a contested case be appropriate. An indeterminate sentence should, however, be imposed only where the established criteria for imposing such a sentence were met.

His lordship said that the appropriate level of sentence for firearms offences would, as for any other offence, depend on all the particular facts relevant to the offence and the offender, and it would be wrong for the Court of Appeal to prescribe unduly restrictive sentencing guidelines. However, it would usually be appropriate for the sentencing court to ask itself four questions:

(a) What sort of weapon was involved? Genuine weapons were more dangerous than imitation firearms, loaded firearms more dangerous than unloaded, unloaded for which ammunition was available more dangerous than where none was available. Possession of a firearm which had no lawful use, such as a sawn-off shotgun, would be viewed even more seriously than possession of a firearm capable of unlawful use.
(b) What, if any, use had been made of the firearm? The court had to take account of all the circumstances surrounding any use made of the firearm; the more prolonged and premeditated and violent, the more serious the offence was likely to be.
(c) With what intention, if any, did the defendant possess or use the firearm? Generally the more serious offences under the Act were those requiring proof of a specific criminal intent to endanger life, cause fear of violence, resist arrest, or commit an indictable offence. The more serious the act intended, the more serious the offence.
(d) What was the defendant's record? The seriousness of any firearm offence was inevitably

increased if the offender had an established record of committing firearms offences or crimes of violence.

In *Clarke* [1997] 1 Cr App R (S) 323, the Court of Appeal confirmed that it was not appropriate to follow sentencing levels prescribed in cases decided before the increases in maximum penalties brought about by the CJPOA 1994.

In *Gourley* [1999] 2 Cr App R (S) 148, a sentence of four years' imprisonment for possessing a sawn-off shotgun without a certificate was reduced on appeal to three years. Although the offender had pleaded guilty, the offence was aggravated because live ammunition had been found along with the gun, the barrel had been shortened, and the offender had a previous conviction for violence. In *Hudson* [1998] 1 Cr App R (S) 124, the gun was of the same type but, in addition, was loaded and ready for use. The correct sentence, according to the Court of Appeal, was four years on a guilty plea. The Court of Appeal noted in *Ashman* [1997] 1 Cr App R (S) 241, that the maximum sentence for this offence had been increased to seven years by the CJPOA 1994 and that a general increase in sentencing levels was in accordance with Parliament's intentions, even where possession was by a 'caretaker or minder' of the weapon. The Court of Appeal in *Higgins* [1998] 1 Cr App R (S) 333, confirmed that a distinction should be maintained when sentencing for possession of firearms other than shortened shotguns, but that sentences should nonetheless reflect public concerns about firearms generally. Fifteen months' imprisonment was appropriate in that case, where the offender was found to have a semi-automatic pistol and 55 rounds of ammunition at his home. It was accepted that the offender, who pleaded guilty, had taken the pistol from a nephew who had threatened to harm himself, but the offender had retained the weapon for six months, even after the nephew's death.

Possession of a firearm with intent to cause fear of violence merited a sentence of two years' imprisonment on conviction in *Carey* [2000] 1 Cr App R (S) 179, where the offender threatened police officers with an air pistol. In *A-G's Ref (No. 49 of 1999)* [2000] 1 Cr App R (S) 436, the Court of Appeal said that any sentence less than two years' imprisonment was inappropriate in a case where the offender had threatened a taxi driver with a replica handgun. The community service order which had been imposed by the trial judge after a guilty plea was, accordingly, an unduly lenient sentence. In *Thompson* [1999] 2 Cr App R (S) 292, where the offender was described as eccentric but representing no public danger, four months' imprisonment was appropriate on a guilty plea for threatening a man in a pub with an unloaded air pistol.

OFFENSIVE WEAPONS

B12.118 **Prevention of Crime Act 1953, s. 1**

(1) Any person who without lawful authority or reasonable excuse, the proof whereof shall lie on him, has with him in any public place any offensive weapon shall be guilty of an offence.

Procedure

B12.119 This offence is triable either way (Prevention of Crime Act 1953, s. 1(1)).

Indictment

B12.120 *Statement of Offence*

Having an offensive weapon in a public place contrary to section 1 of the Prevention of Crime Act 1953

Particulars of Offence

A on the . . . day of . . . had with him in a public place, namely . . . an offensive weapon, namely . . . without lawful authority or reasonable excuse

'Time' and 'place' are material elements of the instant offence which must, therefore, be stated with accuracy in the particulars of the offence (*Allamby* [1974] 1 WLR 1494).

Where the weapon may be offensive under two of the categories of offensive weapons, the indictment need not contain two counts (*Flynn* (1985) 82 Cr App R 319).

Sentencing Guidelines

The maximum penalty is: on conviction on indictment, imprisonment for a term not exceeding four years or a fine or both; on summary conviction, a term of imprisonment not exceeding six months, or a fine not exceeding £5,000 or both (Prevention of Crime Act 1953, s. 1(1)). **B12.121**

When dealt with summarily, the Magistrates' Courts Guidelines (2004) indicate the following for a first-time offender pleading not guilty:

> **Aggravating Factors** For example location of offence; group action or joint possession; offender under influence of drink or drugs; racial or religious aggravation; people put in fear/weapon brandished; planned use; very dangerous weapon; offence committed on bail; relevant previous convictions and any failures to respond to previous sentences.
>
> **Mitigating Factors** For example acting out of genuine fear; carried only on a temporary basis; no attempt to use; not premeditated.
>
> *Guideline*: Is it so serious that only custody is appropriate?

The Court of Appeal issued sentencing guidelines for this offence in *Celaire* [2003] 1 Cr App R (S) 610, based on advice from the Sentencing Advisory Panel. Rose LJ, giving the judgment of the court, said that the task of issuing guidelines was not made easier by the fact that the maximum penalty for this offence was four years, but the maximum penalty for possessing an article with a blade or point in a public place (see **B12.131**) was two years. For avoidance of doubt, the judgment related to offences of possessing an offensive weapon with a four-year maximum. In determining the appropriate sentence it was necessary to consider three interlinking factors: (a) the offender's intention in committing the offence, (b) the circumstances of the offence, and (c) the nature of the weapon involved. As to intention, specific factors that would aggravate the offence are: planned use of the weapon to commit or threaten violence or to intimidate, if the offence was motivated by hostility to a minority individual or group, commission of the offence while the offender was under the influence of drink or drugs, and commission of the offence in the course of carrying out another crime. As to the circumstances of the offence, specific factors that would aggravate the offence are: its commission on school premises, or in a hospital or other place where vulnerable people are likely to be found, or at public gatherings, or on public transport (or at an airport: *Charles* [2005] 1 Cr App R (S) 253), or in licensed premises. By itself the nature of the weapon would not be a prime determinant of sentence, since the use of a relatively less dangerous weapon to threaten or create fear would be at least as serious as possession of a more dangerous weapon where no attempt had been made to use it. The nature of the weapon could, however, assist the court in drawing inferences as to the offender's intention, such as where a weapon which is offensive *per se* has been carried, or a weapon has been designed or adapted to cause serious injury. Mitigation might be found if the weapon was being carried on a temporary basis, and might also arise from personal factors, co-operation with the police, and a timely guilty plea. In relation to an adult offender of previous good character, the custody threshold would almost invariably be passed where there was a combination of dangerous circumstances and use of the weapon to threaten or cause fear. Alternatively, there would be cases (no threat had been made and the weapon was not particularly dangerous), where the custody threshold might not be passed and a community sentence towards the upper end of the range might be appropriate. Where the weapons offence was ancillary to another more serious offence, concurrent sentences would normally be appropriate; if the weapons offence was distinct and independent from the other offence, a consecutive sentence was usually called for, subject to the usual considerations of totality.

Meaning of 'Offensive Weapon'

B12.122 **Prevention of Crime Act 1953, s. 1**

(4) In this section 'offensive weapon' means any article made or adapted for use for causing injury to the person, or intended by the person having it with him for such use by him or by some other person.

It is not always easy to establish whether a particular article is an offensive weapon. According to the Court of Appeal in *Simpson* [1983] 1 WLR 1494, there are three possible categories of offensive weapon:

(a) an article made for use for causing injury to the person, commonly known as a weapon that is offensive *per se*;
(b) an article adapted for use for causing injury to the person;
(c) an article which the person carrying it intends to use for the purpose of causing injury to the person.

Frequently there is little or no distinction between the first two categories, but there is a very clear distinction between the first two and the third categories. In the third category, the prosecution must prove the intent to injure in cases involving weapons in the third category.

Weapons Offensive *Per Se*

B12.123 A flick-knife is an offensive weapon *per se* (*Lawrence* (1971) 57 Cr App R 64, *Allamby* [1974] 1 WLR 1494, and *Gibson v Wales* [1983] 1 WLR 393). Trial judges are entitled to take judicial notice of the fact that a flick-knife is an offensive weapon *per se* (*Simpson* [1983] 1 WLR 1494). See also the Restriction of Offensive Weapons Act 1959, s. 1 at **B12.140**.Whilst it is clear that a flick-knife is an offensive weapon, this will not be the case with all articles. Not all knives are offensive weapons *per se* (*Simpson*). Not all sheath knives are offensive weapons (*Simpson*). In *Patterson v PC 108D PK* (1984) *The Times*, 21 June 1984, it was held that a lock knife is not an offensive weapon *per se*. In a decision on the Aviation Security Act 1982, s. 4(2)(c), it was held that a butterfly knife is necessarily an article for use for causing injury to the person and judicial notice can be taken of that fact (*DPP v Hynde* [1998] 1 WLR 1222, where the court referred to both the definition in the CJA 1988 and the decision in *Simpson*).

It remains to be seen whether trial judges may now regard it as determined that items are offensive weapons *per se*, either by regarding the matter as one of which they may take judicial notice, or by being bound by previous decisions. However, against this must be weighed the consideration that the decision whether a weapon is offensive *per se* is one for a jury to take (see, in particular, the decision of the Court of Appeal in *Williamson* (1977) 67 Cr App R 35). It was held in *Butler* [1988] Crim LR 695, that a sword stick is a weapon, offensive *per se*. The trial judge had left the matter to the jury, but the Court of Appeal regarded this as, if anything, over generous. In *Houghton v Chief Constable of Greater Manchester* (1986) 84 Cr App R 319, it was held that a truncheon is an offensive weapon *per se*, in part because it does not possess *per se* any innocent quality.

Where an article has no readily apparent use except to cause injury to the person, it is submitted that judicial notice may well be appropriate.

Where there is doubt whether an article is an offensive weapon *per se*, the deciders of fact must have their attention drawn to the statutory definition, but determining whether any particular article is such a weapon is a matter of fact (*Williamson* (1977) 67 Cr App R 35; *Simpson* [1983] 1 WLR 1494; *Humphries* (1987) *Independent*, 13 April 1987). The conclusion by magistrates that a rice flail was an offensive weapon *per se* could not successfully be challenged, because it was legitimately reached in accordance with the evidence (*Copus v DPP* [1989] Crim LR 577). In *Dhindsa* [2005] EWCA Crim 1198, the Court of Appeal decided, following *Williamson,* that it was for the jury to decide whether a knuckle-duster was an offensive weapon *per se*.

If an article has an innocent purpose, which may have to be the main purpose for which it is produced, it will not be an offensive weapon *per se*. This follows from, for example, the cases on knives (see above), from *Houghton v Chief Constable of Greater Manchester* and from *Petrie* [1961] 1 WLR 358, where it was held that an ordinary razor is not an offensive weapon *per se*, and from *Humphreys* [1977] Crim LR 225, where it was held that an ordinary penknife is not an offensive weapon *per se*.

Where the article is a weapon, offensive *per se*, there is no requirement on the prosecution that it be proved that the possessor also had an intention to use it to cause injury (*Davis v Alexander* (1970) 54 Cr App R 398, and *Southwell v Chadwick* (1986) 85 Cr App R 235). While the prosecution must prove that the accused had possession of the offensive weapon, they need not prove a specific intent to injure (see **B12.126**).

It may be relevant, though the courts have not referred to the provision, that there is a list of offensive weapons created by statutory instrument for the purposes of the offence contrary to the CJA 1988, s. 141 (manufacture, sale or hire of offensive weapons), see **B12.141**.

B Part B Offences

Weapons Adapted to Cause Injury

Whether an article falls into this category is a decision of fact to be answered by the jury or magistrates (*Williamson* (1977) 67 Cr App R 35) and see *Warne v DPP* (3 June 1997 unreported), where the Divisional Court also made clear that the fact that the item was later used for a violent purpose was not necessarily determinative of the issue whether it had been adapted to cause injury. It was not possible, in this case, to sustain the conclusion that a pick-axe handle, when it had lost its head, had, on the evidence available, been adapted for use for causing injury to the person. Experimentation with the article may assist the jury in determining whether it is an offensive weapon. If such experimentation is permitted, the Court of Appeal decided in *Higgins* (1989) *The Times*, 16 February 1989, that the experiment must take place in open court, when, of course, it is possible for counsel to address the issue. Clear examples of articles falling within this category are a bottle which is deliberately broken so that the jagged end can be pushed into the victim's face (*Simpson* [1983] 1 WLR 1494) and a potato with a razor blade inserted into it (*Williamson*). In *Sills* [2006] EWHC 3383 (Admin) an unscrewed pool cue was held to be capable of being treated as 'adapted'. **B12.124**

It is not settled whether 'injury to the person' includes self-inflicted injury: a proposition that it does do so was not challenged in the Divisional Court in *Bryan v Mott* (1975) 62 Cr App R 71. Notwithstanding that the expressed intention of the accused (to commit suicide) was not unlawful, he had no reasonable excuse for having the article in a public place for that purpose. On the other hand, a judge of the Crown Court (sitting at Beverley) ruled that an element in the offence was injury to a person other than the possessor of the weapon (*Fleming* [1989] Crim LR 71).

Weapons Intended to be Used to Cause Injury

The accused must form the intention to cause injury at the time and place which should be specified with accuracy in the charge. It is not sufficient that he had the necessary intention at some earlier stage (*Allamby* [1974] 1 WLR 1494). But an intention to use the object or article as a weapon if the occasion were to arise may be sufficient. Recklessness as to how it might be used in the future is not sufficient (*Byrne* [2004] Crim LR 582, following *Patterson v Block* (12 September 1984 unreported)). A judge will need to give carefully crafted directions regarding the meaning of 'intention' (see **A2.2**). **B12.125**

The intention to cause injury to the person may apparently be satisfied by the intention to inflict injury on one's self, but the authorities, weak as they are, conflict. An intention to frighten or to intimidate is not an intention to cause injury unless his intention was to cause injury by shock (*Rapier* (1979) 70 Cr App R 17, following *Edmonds* [1963] 2 QB 142, and explaining *Woodward v Koessler* [1958] 1 WLR 1255). It follows that the trial judge must give a careful direction in cases where it is appropriate to make the distinction: see also *Snooks* [1997] Crim LR 230.

The prosecution must prove the element of specific intention (see *Petrie* [1961] 1 WLR 358, making the comparative point that, if the article is an offensive weapon *per se*, there is no need to prove such intention). Each case must depend upon its own facts based on all the circumstances of the case. The use to which the weapon is put might assist in determining what the intention of the possessor was. Indeed in some cases it may of itself be sufficient to establish the necessary intent (see *Harrison v Thornton* (1966) 68 Cr App R 28, *Dayle* [1974] 1 WLR 181 and *Ohlson v Hylton* [1975] 1 WLR 724).

It is important to note that '[the] Act of 1953 is meant to deal with a person who goes out with an offensive weapon, it may be a cosh or a knife, without any reasonable excuse' (per Lord Goddard CJ in *Jura* [1954] 1 QB 503).

Actual use can be dealt with by charging appropriate offences against the person. This was made clear by the Court of Criminal Appeal in *Jura*, where a conviction for this offence was quashed where the appellant had possession of an air rifle at a shooting gallery, which he then used to fire at a woman companion. It was his use of the rifle which was unlawful, not his carrying of it, for which he had a reasonable excuse. The point is confirmed by the Court of Appeal in *Dayle* [1974] 1 WLR 181. The trial judge, following *Jura*, held that it was open to a jury to find that there was no possession of an offensive weapon when an inoffensive article lawfully carried was offensively used. The Court of Appeal agreed with this approach. The appellant would not have been in possession of an offensive weapon when he took the car jack and brace in the heat of the moment.

The cases of *Jura*, and *Dayle* were applied in *Ohlson v Hylton* [1975] 1 WLR 724, where a workman was held not to be guilty of the offence where he took a hammer from his work bag and struck a fellow traveller at an Underground station. The hammer was properly in his possession. Lord Widgery CJ delivering the judgment of the court, said at pp. 728–9:

> . . . I would hold that an offence under section 1 is not committed where a person arms himself with a weapon for *instant* attack on his victim. It seems to me that the section is concerned only with a man who, possessed of a weapon, forms the necessary intent before an occasion to use actual violence has arisen. In other words, it is not the actual use of the weapon with which the section is concerned, but the carrying of a weapon with intent to use it if occasion arises . . .
>
> I accept that it is unnecessary for the prosecution to prove that the relevant intent was formed from the moment when the defendant set out on his expedition. An innocent carrying of say, a hammer can be converted into an unlawful carrying when the defendant forms the guilty intent, provided, in my view, that the intent is formed before the actual occasion to use violence has arisen.

Ohlson v Hylton was applied in *Humphreys* [1977] Crim LR 225, and by the Divisional Court in *Bates v Bulman* [1979] 1 WLR 1190. In *Humphreys*, the Court of Appeal held that no offence was committed where a person had a penknife on him, and then used it in desperation: it had not been carried in a public place with the necessary intent. In *Bates v Bulman* [1979] 1 WLR 1190, the Divisional Court held that the accused, who acquired an unopened clasp knife with the immediate intention of using it as an offensive weapon, did not commit the instant offence, because 'the purport of the [1953] Act . . . is to cover the situation where an accused person . . . has with him and is carrying an offensive weapon intending that it shall be used, if necessary, for offensive purposes' (per Stocker J). Stocker J also said that it:

> would be a rather academic and over-analytical approach [to make] a distinction between an innocent weapon subsequently used with the intention of an assault and which is being carried innocently . . ., and a similar article which is acquired either by borrowing from somebody else or fortuitously by being picked up in the street.

The above casts doubts upon the accuracy of an earlier decision of the Divisional Court where it was held that an offence was committed when the accused, in the course of a fight between others, picked up a stone, thus arming himself, and threw it at one of the fighters, but missed him (*Harrison v Thornton* (1966) 68 Cr App R 28). See also **B12.83**.

In *Veasey* [1999] Crim LR 158, the Court of Appeal confirmed that in cases where the real issue is the use of an offensive weapon, a charge of assault is 'quite adequate'. The instant offence is concerned with the carrying of any offensive weapon and not with its use (a distinction drawn by Professor Sir John Smith and approved by the Court (see now *Smith and Hogan: Criminal Law* (11th edn, OUP, 2005) at p. 585)). See also *C v DPP* [2002] Crim LR 322.

In *Edmonds* [1963] 2 QB 142, the Court of Appeal held (at pp. 149–50) that in a case of joint possession, the appropriate direction is:

> . . . consider the nature of each article and the case of each man individually and separately, and have regard to the circumstances as a whole and the time of day. Are you sure that each man intended to use the article he carried to injure someone? Alternatively, are you satisfied that he was party to a common purpose, with one or more of the others, of using one or more of the articles for inflicting injury upon someone? And, when you consider this alternative, you must first be sure that he knew that one or both of the others had the article which each of them was shown to be carrying.

Meaning of 'Has with Him'

In *Densu* [1998] 1 Cr App R 400, counsel had contemplated arguing that the trial judge was wrong when he ruled that the phrase 'has with him' was satisfied 'if the prosecution proved that the appellant merely knew that he had the baton with him but did not know that it was a weapon'. But counsel abandoned the point when shown two unreported cases by the Registrar of the Court of Appeal Criminal Division (namely, *Vann* [1996] Crim LR 52, and *Matrix* [1997] Crim LR 901). The Court of Appeal makes no comment on the abandonment of the argument but it is arguable that the point remains open. The cases referred to above are not ones concerned with the Prevention of Crime Act 1953. *Vann* [1996] Crim LR 52 is concerned with a 'have with him' offence, contrary to the FA 1968, s. 19 (and which followed *Hussain* [1981] 1 WLR 416, a possession offence under the FA 1968, s. 1: see **B12.84** and **B12.27**). *Matrix* [1997] Crim LR 901 is concerned with a possession offence contrary to the Protection of Children Act 1978. In both cases, the drugs decision of *Warner v Metropolitan Police Commissioner* [1969] 2 AC 256 (see **B20.12**), is relevant. In *Cugullere* [1961] 1 WLR 858, the Court of Criminal Appeal held that the phrase under consideration 'must mean "knowingly has with him in any public place"'. The accused must knowingly have possession of the article in question. A person who forgets that he has the offensive weapon in his possession, nevertheless has it with him (*McCalla* (1988) 87 Cr App R 372). But in *Russell* (1984) 81 Cr App R 315, the Court of Appeal stated that the court in *Cugullere* had been applying 'the general principle of criminal responsibility which makes it incumbent on the prosecution to prove full *mens rea*'. *Russell* is at odds with *McCalla*. Professor Sir John Smith pointed out ([1998] Crim LR 347) that, in *Densu*, the Court of Appeal made no reference to *Russell* (or indeed to *Cugullere*) and he did not accept that *Russell* was decided *per incuriam*. It is submitted that the point is open for further consideration. In *R (Bayliss) v DPP* [2003] EWHC 245 (Admin), the Divisional Court examined *Cugullere, McCalla*, and subsequent decisions. It reached the conclusion that forgetfulness does not change the fact that a person had an offensive weapon with him. In *Amos* (29 September 1999 unreported) it was held that it is no defence for a person who acquires a firearm or ammunition under a firearm certificate **B12.126** but whose firearm certificate ceases to cover his continuing possession to say that he has forgotten about his possession of this item or erroneously believed it had been destroyed or disposed of (see **B12.27** and consider the discussion in *Nicholson* [2006] 1 WLR 2857). Forgetfulness might be relevant to the issue of whether the accused had good reason for being in possession of the article, (see **B12.130**). In considering the offence contrary to the CJA 1988, s. 139(1) (see **B12.131**), the court in *Daubney* (2000) 164 JP 519, held that, as a general principle, a person only has something with him or in his possession if he knows that he has with him or is in possession of the object in question. Thus the judge's summing up, which may have made the jury think that a mere belief that a knife was somewhere in the accused's van would be sufficient, was incorrect.

Meaning of 'Public Place'

B12.127 **Prevention of Crime Act 1953, s. 1**

(4) In this section 'public place' includes any highway and any other premises or place to which at the material time the public have or are permitted to have access, whether on payment or otherwise.

Whether somewhere is a 'public place' is a question of fact; but whether it is capable of being such a place is a question of law (*Hanrahan* [2004] EWCA Crim 2943). 'Public place' was considered in *Knox v Anderton* (1982) 76 Cr App R 156. The Divisional Court, in part relying on decisions on other pieces of legislation such as the Public Order Act 1936 (see **B11.15**), concluded that a reasonable bench of justices could decide that the upper landing of a block of flats which could be reached without hindrance was a 'public place', as there were no barriers or notices restricting access. In *Williams v DPP* (1992) 95 Cr App R 415, the landing of a block of flats, to which access could be gained only by way of key, security code, tenants' intercom or caretaker, was not a 'public place' for the purposes of the Criminal Law Act 1967, s. 91 (being drunk and disorderly, see **B11.218**), because only those admitted by or with the implied consent of the occupiers of the block of flats had access. People with access were not present as members of the public. The justices had misread *Knox v Anderton*, believing that the mere absence of notices restricting access had been sufficient in that case to determine that the area was a public place.

Lawful Authority or Reasonable Excuse: the Burden of Proof

B12.128 The Prevention of Crime Act 1953, s. 1(1) (see **B12.118**), clearly lays the burden of proving either lawful authority or reasonable excuse upon the accused, but only once the possession of an offensive weapon has been established (*Petrie* [1961] 1 WLR 358). Thus, if the weapon is either made or adapted to be offensive, the prosecution has to prove no more than possession of the article, whereas with the third category of offensive weapons the prosecution has to prove the requisite intent before the burden passes to the defendant to prove either lawful authority or reasonable excuse.

It is for the accused to satisfy the jury as to either a lawful authority or reasonable excuse on a balance of probability and not beyond a reasonable doubt (*Brown* (1971) 55 Cr App R 478). See generally **F3.8** and **F3.40**. The imposition of a legal burden upon the accused might be open to challenge in the light of the human rights cases on the 'reverse burden', but see *Lynch v Dpp* [2003] QB 137 (see **F3.13**).

Note that the s. 1(1) offence and the element of reasonable excuse (or lawful authority), relates to the carrying of the weapon, and not with its use, as is made clear by Lord Goddard CJ giving the judgment of the Court of Criminal Appeal in *Jura* [1954] 1 QB 503 (see also *Dayle* [1974] 1 WLR 181 and *Bryan v Mott* (1975) 62 Cr App R 71) and see **B12.126**.

Lawful Authority

B12.129 The Divisional Court said in *Bryan v Mott* (1975) 62 Cr App R 71 at p. 73:

> The reference to lawful authority in the section is a reference to those people who from time to time carry an offensive weapon as a matter of duty — the soldier and his rifle and the police officer with his truncheon.

See also *Houghton v Chief Constable of Greater Manchester* (1986) 84 Cr App R 319.

Private security guards do not have explicit lawful authority to carry, for example, a truncheon. They have neither a statutory power, nor a duty, to do so (see *Bryan v Mott* (1975) 62 Cr App R 71). Any contractual duty would be irrelevant (see *Spanner* [1973] Crim LR 704). Such a person may have a reasonable excuse, see *Malnik v DPP* [1989] Crim LR 451 (see **B12.130**).

Reasonable Excuse

In *Densu* [1998] 1 Cr App R 400, the Court of Appeal held that the defence of reasonable excuse arises only once it is established that the accused was in possession of an offensive weapon. A reasonable excuse does not arise if the argument is that the accused did not know that what he was carrying was, by definition, an offensive weapon. Any other approach would defeat the statutory purpose. This is not to be confused with cases where a person forgets that he had an offensive weapon with him. Forgetfulness may be relevant to the issue whether he had a reasonable excuse: see *Glidewell* (1999) 163 JP 557 (below). The court in *Densu* held that 'the cases where the defence of reasonable excuse will be available are restricted'. A number of reasonable excuses have been recognised. The obvious form is where a person has an article properly in his possession for a legitimate purpose, such as the penknife in *Humphreys* [1977] Crim LR 225, and the workman's hammer in *Ohlson v Hylton* [1975] 1 WLR 724 (see **B12.126**). **B12.130**

An argument, frequently heard, is that a person has a reasonable excuse to carry a weapon for the purposes of self-defence should the carrier be attacked. The problem with this argument is that the carrier is likely to be routinely carrying the weapon by reason of an actual or perceived threat of harm to the carrier. The carrying of a weapon as a general precaution is insufficient to establish a reasonable excuse (see *Evans v Hughes* [1972] 1 WLR 1452, following *Evans v Wright* [1964] Crim LR 466 and *Grieve v Macleod* [1967] Crim LR 424), and this view has been confirmed by the Court of Appeal in *Densu* (see also *Peacock* [1973] Crim LR 639, *Bradley v Moss* [1974] Crim LR 430 and *Bryan v Mott* (1975) 62 Cr App R 71). But where a person anticipated imminent attack and carried the weapon for his own personal defence against a specific danger, the circumstances might constitute a reasonable excuse.

Ordinarily, one cannot legitimately arm oneself with an offensive weapon with which to repel unlawful violence when one has deliberately and knowingly brought about the situation in which such violence was liable to be inflicted (*Malnik v DPP* [1989] Crim LR 451, per Bingham LJ). Bingham LJ went on to state that the position was quite different in the case of those to whom society has entrusted the responsibility for enforcing the law, and indeed there is a difference in the case of those such as security guards who are handling valuable property in the course of their ordinary occupation and have reason to fear attack.

There must be 'good' reason for the possession of the offensive weapon. In *Southwell v Chadwick* (1986) 85 Cr App R 235, the Court of Appeal accepted that it was a reasonable excuse for a person to have in his possession a machete knife in its scabbard and a catapult for use for killing grey squirrels, so that he could obtain food for his wild birds which he kept under licence. In *Callaghan* (30 October 1987 unreported), the Court of Appeal held that the jury should have been left to consider whether the accused had a reasonable excuse for being in possession of a machete, which he used in a fight, when his claim was that he had bought it for domestic use and was taking it back to his home after having lent it to a friend.

Where a weapon offensive *per se* was carried, but merely as a theatrical property as part and parcel of fancy dress worn by a person going to or from a fancy dress party, the Court of

Appeal accepted that the innocent motive could amount to a reasonable excuse (*Houghton v Chief Constable of Greater Manchester* (1987) 84 Cr App R 319). The accused was dressed in a police uniform and was carrying a truncheon and was held, on the facts, to have a reasonable excuse.

In *Densu* the Court of Appeal referred to an example provided by May LJ in *McCalla* (1988) 87 Cr App R 372, that might amount to a reasonable excuse:

> if someone driving along a road where earlier there had been a demonstration were to see and pick up a police truncheon which had obviously been dropped there and were to put it into the boot of his car, intending to take it to the nearest police station, and then were to be stopped within a few minutes, he would have a reasonable excuse for having the truncheon with him in the boot of the car.

In *Glidewell* (1999) 163 JP 557, the Court of Appeal held that 'depending on the circumstances of the particular case, forgetfulness may be relevant to whether or not a defendant has a reasonable excuse for possession of an offensive weapon'. Factors that might be relevant are (in relation to the facts of the instant case): the accused did not introduce the weapons into his car; the weapons had been in the car for a relatively short period of time; the accused was very busy on the night in question. As these all bore on the question of forgetfulness, they were matters for the jury. See also *Ivey* (15 August 2000 unreported), where forgetfulness was relevant to the reasonable excuse that D had put the knife in his pocket as part of moving his possessions from one house to another (the knife having been bought as an ornament) and he had had his possessions in his car for two weeks and had forgotten about the knife). See also *Lorimer* [2003] EWCA Crim 721. In *R (Bayliss) v DPP* [2003] EWHC 245 (Admin), the Divisional Court accepted that there may be circumstances where forgetfulness is relevant to the defence of good reason, but it is not relevant to having the weapon with him (as to which see **B12.126**). Simple forgetfulness would not be sufficient to amount to a reasonable excuse, as is made clear in *Glidewell* (and see *DPP v Gregson* (1993) 96 Cr App R 240 at **B12.133** and *Hargreaves* [2000] 1 Arch News 2, disapproved in *Jolie* (2003) 167 JP 313), but factors causing forgetfulness such as an illness or the taking of medication would be relevant.

OTHER OFFENCES INVOLVING POSSESSION OF WEAPONS

Having Article with Blade or Point in a Public Place

B12.131 It is an offence triable either way, contrary to the CJA 1988, s. 139(1), for a person to have with him in a public place an article to which the section applies.

Criminal Justice Act 1988, s. 139

(1) Subject to subsections (4) and (5) below, any person who has an article to which this section applies with him in a public place shall be guilty of an offence.
(2) Subject to subsection (3) below, this section applies to any article which has a blade or is sharply pointed except a folding pocket knife.
(3) This section applies to a folding pocket knife if the cutting edge of its blade exceeds 3 inches.
(4) It shall be a defence for a person charged with an offence under this section to prove that he had good reason or lawful authority for having the article with him in a public place.
(5) Without prejudice to the generality of subsection (4) above, it shall be a defence for a person charged with an offence under this section to prove that he had the article with him—
  (a) for use at work;
  (b) for religious reasons; or
  (c) as part of any national costume.

...

(7) In this section 'public place' includes any place to which at the material time the public have or are permitted access, whether on payment or otherwise.
(8) This section shall not have effect in relation to anything done before it comes into force.

Section 139 covers any article which has a blade or is sharply pointed except a folding pocket knife. A folding pocket knife is covered if the cutting edge of its blade exceeds three inches.

If a knife is secured in the open position by a locking device, it is not a folding pocket knife because it is not immediately foldable at all times by virtue of the folding process (*Harris v DPP* (1992) 96 Cr App R 235). *Harris* was followed in *Deegan* [1998] 2 Cr App R 121, where a challenge to the established meaning on the basis of what Ministers said in *Hansard* was rejected on the basis that what they said was not sufficiently clear. Determining whether an article fell within the CJA 1988, s. 139, is a matter of law for the judge to decide (*Davis* [1998] Crim LR 564). There is no room for applying the decision in *Brutus v Cozens* [1973] AC 854, because the 'issue was not the simple etymological meaning of the word "blade"'. The test is not whether the article is capable of causing injury, because the offence is limited to articles which 'happen to have something that could be described as a blade', so a common-sense test is to be applied that the article must be 'within the same broad category as a knife or a sharply pointed instrument'. Thus the court allowed the appeal on the basis that a screw-driver does not fall within s. 139, but cf. *Manning* [1998] Crim LR 198. The decision in *Davis* does not require the item to be sharp. What is required is that the item must have a blade, so a blunt butter knife was an item within s. 139 (*Brooker v DPP* [2005] EWHC 1132).

As a general principle, a person has something with him or it is in his possession if he knows that he has it with him, or is in possession of the object in question. A judge erred in his charge to the jury when he used words that might have made the jury think that a mere belief that a knife was somewhere in the accused's van would be sufficient (*Daubney* (2000) 164 JP 519). In *Jolie* (2003) 167 JP 313, the court ruled that relevant to the element of possession was proof that the accused was either aware of the presence of the knife in the vehicle (when he made the journey in the course of which he was stopped) or that he was responsible for putting the knife in the place where it was later found.

Public Place

'Public place' includes any place to which, at the material time, the public have or are permitted access, whether on payment or otherwise (s. 139(7)). In *Roberts* [2004] 1 WLR 181, the Court of Appeal held that it did not include land adjacent to that to which the public had access. Unimpeded access to a place does not necessarily make it a public place, it must be determined whether public access was implied or tolerated (*Harriott v DPP* [2005] EWHC 965 (Admin)). **B12.132**

'Good Reason': Lawful Authority

Whilst forgetfulness is not in itself a good reason, an accused who has what might be a good reason for possession of the item (e.g., a knife used regularly at work in a restaurant) should have that left to the deciders of fact, and the fact that he has forgotten about possession of the item is a factor in deciding whether he did, indeed, have good reason for possession (*Bird* [2004] EWCA Crim 964). See also **B12.126**. **B12.133**

Two defences are created by s. 139(4) and (5). First, it is a defence for the accused to prove that he had good reason or lawful authority for having the article with him in a public place. It was held in *Godwin v DPP* (1992) 96 Cr App R 244, that the accused had to prove his good reason on a balance of probabilities so that merely providing an uncontradicted explanation is not necessarily sufficient (in the instant case, it was held that magistrates were entitled to disbelieve such a defence). Having considered the effect of *Lambert* [2002] 2 AC 545 (see **F3.8**), the Divisional Court in *L v DPP* [2003] QB 137, held that the reverse onus provision in relation to a good reason for having the article in s. 139 did not breach the ECHR, Article 6. The court took the view that a fair balance had been achieved in s. 139, which is readily distinguishable from that in the Misuse of Drugs Act 1971, s. 28 (see **B20.20**), as the prosecution has to prove that the accused knows that he had the relevant article in his possession. Further, there is a strong public interest in bladed articles not being carried in public without good reason and, taking into account Parliament's decision, this requirement was not an improper rights infringement. The accused has to prove something within his own knowledge and the court can be expected to scrutinise the evidence with a view to deciding if a good reason existed. Usually the question will be whether the reason was a good one or not. And the limited sentence available was also relevant. See also *Mathews* [2004] QB 690.

In *Bown* [2004] 1 Cr App R 151, it was held that there are some limits, as a matter of law, on the defence of good reason. It is for the judge to determine whether the explanation is capable of amounting to a good reason and, if so, it is for the jury to determine whether it did so amount. Since the words in s. 139(4) are ordinary words of the English language, it is only in the clearest of cases that the matter can be withdrawn from the jury. Further, the good reason must be related to both having the bladed article and having it with him in a public place. It could not, in this case, be a good reason to have a knife in public in the evening because the accused might want to harm himself with it some time the next day. That is simply too detached a set of facts and too detached a link to come within the statute. Whether wanting to inflict self-harm could ever be a good reason was not determined. Forgetfulness alone does not amount to a good reason (*DPP v Gregson* (1992) 96 Cr App R 240, confirmed in *Manning* and *Hargreaves* [2000] 1 Arch News 2; see also *Jolie* (2003) 167 JP 313, at **B12.130**, disapproving *DPP v Gregson* and *Hargreaves*; and see *Bird* [2004] EWCA Crim 964).

For assistance on the meaning of 'good reason', the Court of Appeal in *Emmanuel* [1998] Crim LR 347, looked to the concept of 'reasonable excuse' under the Prevention of Crime Act 1953 (see **B12.130**). Professor Sir John Smith pointed out ([1998] Crim LR 347) that the defence in the 1996 Act was intended to be a narrower one than that of reasonable excuse in the 1953 Act. In *Emmanuel* the Court of Appeal held that 'good reason' includes self-defence.

Secondly, and without prejudice to the generality of the first, it is a defence for the accused to prove that he had the article with him for use at work, or for religious reasons, or as part of any national costume. Whether an article was for use for work (and therefore the other purposes also) is a matter to be determined in accordance with the approach in *Brutus v Cozens*, as the statute uses words of the ordinary English language. It is a matter for the jury to determine having been so directed by the judge (*Manning*). See also *Mohammed v Chief Constable of South Yorkshire Police* [2002] EWHC 406 (Admin), where it was held that it cannot be a good reason that a person ultimately is going to use an article for a lawful purpose or that he requires ultimately something to be done to that article for a lawful purpose; there must be a sufficient connection in time between the possession and the carrying out of that purpose (M had the meat cleaver in his van for too long for the purpose of having it sharpened, which could otherwise have been a good reason). The court followed the approach in *Brutus v Cozens*, probably on the basis that there is no special meaning required for the terms of the defence, whereas whether the article falls within the offence in the first place does not warrant application of that approach (see *Deegan*) or perhaps out of fear that juries might apply the offence too widely to such items as screwdrivers. In *Giles* [2003] EWCA Crim 1287, it was held that a person must have a specific good reason for having the item in his possession. It is not enough, where the item has a blade satisfying s. 139, that he might think of using part of it, say the corkscrew.

Religious Reasons

B12.134 The second defence in the CJA 1988, s. 139(5), is that the person has the article with him for religious reasons. In *Wang* [2005] 1 WLR 661, the House of Lords decided that there were no circumstances in which the judge could direct a conviction. In this case, the accused carried a bag in which he had a curved martial arts sword, in its sheath. He claimed that he was a Buddhist and that he practised Shaolin, a traditional martial art and that the knife was a willow leaf knife, which was one of the 18 weapons in which a Shaolin follower must become expert. The House of Lords held that had the trial judge directed the jury in the ordinary way, it seemed very likely that they would have convicted. However, the nature and extent of the accused's religious motivation had been the subject of evidence and his claim that he did not want to leave the weapon at home, with no one looking after it, were pre-eminently matters for the jury.

Procedure and Sentence

The offence is punishable, on summary conviction, with a term of imprisonment not exceeding six months or a fine not exceeding the statutory maximum or both and, on conviction on indictment, to a term of imprisonment not exceeding four years or a fine or both (CJA 1988, s. 139(6)). Where the offence of possession of an article was committed prior to 15 January 2007 (when the VCRA 2006, s. 42 came into force), the maximum penalty on indictment is two years' imprisonment. **B12.135**

When dealt with summarily, the Magistrates' Courts Guidelines (2004) are the same as those for possession of an offensive weapon (see **B12.106**).

In *Datson* [1999] 1 Cr App R (S) 84, the offender was in a pub when he was seen to transfer a knife from his bag and put it inside his jacket. The police were called. The offender claimed that he had found the knife when removing belongings from his former matrimonial home. The Court of Appeal said that, in light of the guilty plea and the offender's relatively good record, the appropriate sentence was probably a community service order. Since the offender had served three weeks of his two-month prison sentence, a conditional discharge was substituted. In *Baldwin* [2000] 1 Cr App R (S) 81, the offender was arrested by a store detective on suspicion of shoplifting. When the police were called, the offender handed over a kitchen knife with a five-inch blade, which had been concealed in his sock. The offender pleaded guilty to an offence under s. 139, but claimed that he was carrying the knife for his own protection. He was addicted to drugs, had a bad record for offences of dishonesty, but no previous convictions for carrying a weapon. The Court of Appeal reduced the prison sentence of 18 months to one of six months. See further **B12.105**.

Having Article with Blade or Point on School Premises

It is an offence triable either way, contrary to the CJA 1988, s. 139A(1), for a person to have an article to which s. 139 applies (see **B12.131**) with him on school premises. **B12.136**

Criminal Justice Act 1988, 139A

(1) Any person who has an article to which section 139 of this Act applies with him on school premises shall be guilty of an offence.
(2) Any person who has an offensive weapon within the meaning of section 1 of the Prevention of Crime Act 1953 with him on school premises shall be guilty of an offence.
(3) It shall be a defence for a person charged with an offence under subsection (1) or (2) above to prove that he had good reason or lawful authority for having the article or weapon with him on the premises in question.
(4) Without prejudice to the generality of subsection (3) above, it shall be a defence for a person charged with an offence under subsection (1) or(2) above to prove that he had the article or weapon in question with him—
(a) for use at work;
(b) for educational purposes,
(c) for religious reasons; or
(d) as part of any national costume.

. . .

(6) In this section and section 139B, 'school premises' means land used for the purposes of a school excluding any land occupied solely as a dwelling by a person employed at the school; and 'school' has the meaning given by section 4 of the Education Act 1996.

'Has with him' will be understood in the same way as under the Prevention of Crime Act 1953 (see **B12.126**).

The Education Act 1996, s. 4(1) defines 'school' to mean:

> an educational institution which is outside the further education sector and the higher education sector and is an institution for providing—
> (a) primary education,
> (b) secondary education, or
> (c) both primary and secondary education,
> whether or not the institution also provides . . . further education.

The offence is punishable, on summary conviction, with a term of imprisonment not exceeding six months or a fine not exceeding the statutory maximum or both and, on conviction on indictment, to a term of imprisonment not exceeding four years or a fine or both (CJA 1988, s. 139A(5)). Where the offence of possession of an article was committed prior to 15 January 2007 (when the VCRA 2006, s. 42 came into force), the maximum penalty on indictment is two years' imprisonment.

It is a defence for a person charged with the offence to prove that he had good reason or lawful authority for having the article with him on the premises in question (s. 139A(3)); as to lawful authority, see **B12.129** and **B12.130**. It is also a defence for an accused to prove that he had the article with him for use at work, for educational purposes, for religious reasons, or as part of any national costume (s. 139A(4)). The imposition of a legal burden upon the accused is open to challenge in the light of the human rights cases on the 'reverse burden' (see **F3.13**).

Under the CJA 1988, s. 139B, a constable has a power of entry to school premises to search the premises and any person on them for any article to which s. 139 applies or for any offensive weapon within the meaning of the Prevention of Crime Act 1953, s. 1, if he has reasonable grounds for suspecting that an offence under the CJA 1988, s. 139A, is being or has been committed. If the constable finds any article which he has reasonable grounds for suspecting is such an article, he may seize and retain it. Reasonable force may be used, if necessary.

Note that the following provisions of the VCRA 2006 came into force on 31 May 2007: (a) s. 45 (power of members of staff to search school pupils for weapons) insofar as it extends to England; (b) s. 46 (power to search further education students for weapons) insofar as it extends to England; (c) s. 48 (amendment of police power to search schools etc. for weapons).

Having Offensive Weapon on School Premises

B12.137 It is an offence triable either way, contrary to the CJA 1988, s. 139A(2), for a person to have an offensive weapon as defined in the Prevention of Crime Act 1953 (see **B12.122** to **B12.126**) with him on school premises. 'Has with him' will be understood in the same way as under the Prevention of Crime Act 1953 (see **B12.126**). As to the meaning of 'school premises' and 'school', see **B12.136**. It is punishable, on summary conviction, with a term of imprisonment not exceeding six months or a fine not exceeding the statutory maximum or both and, on conviction on indictment, to a term of imprisonment not exceeding four years or a fine or both (CJA 1988, s. 139A(5)(b)). The same defences as for the offence contrary to s. 139A(1) apply to this offence, see **B12.136**. For the power of entry and search, see **B12.136**.

Possession of Crossbow by Person under 17

B12.138 It is a summary offence, contrary to the Crossbows Act 1987, s. 3, for a person under the age of 17 (with effect from 1 October 2007, when the VCRA 2007, s. 44 came into force, the relevant age is 18) to have with him: (a) a crossbow which is capable of discharging a missile;

or (b) parts of a crossbow which together (and without any other parts) can be assembled to form a crossbow capable of discharging a missile, unless he is under the supervision of a person who is 21 years of age or older. The offence does not apply to crossbows with a draw weight of less than 1.4 kilograms. A person guilty of the offence is liable to a fine not exceeding level 3 on the standard scale. The court may also make such order as it thinks fit as to the forfeiture or disposal of any crossbow or part of a crossbow in respect of which the offence was committed.

For offences by trespassers on premises carrying weapons, see **B13.76** and **B13.77**.

MANUFACTURE, SALE, HIRE AND PURCHASE OF WEAPONS

There are four summary offences concerned with the manufacture etc. of various types of weapons generally: **B12.139**

(a) manufacture, sale or hire etc. of dangerous weapons, contrary to the Restriction of Offensive Weapons Act 1959, s. 1(1);
(b) manufacture, sale and hire of offensive weapons, contrary to the CJA 1988, s. 141(1);
(c) sale and letting on hire of a crossbow to a person under 17, contrary to the Crossbows Act 1987, s. 1;
(d) purchase and hiring of a crossbow by a person under 17, contrary to the Crossbows Act 1987, s. 2.

In addition to these offences, there are certain offences of a similar nature which relate only to knives (see **B12.144** *et seq.*).

Manufacture, Sale or Hire etc. of Dangerous Weapons

Restriction of Offensive Weapons Act 1959, s. 1 **B12.140**

(1) Any person who manufactures, sells or hires or offers for sale or hire or exposes or has in his possession for the purposes of sale or hire, or lends or gives to any other person—
  (a) any knife which has a blade which opens automatically by hand pressure applied to a button, spring or other device in or attached to the handle of the knife, sometimes known as a 'flick-knife' or 'flick gun'; or
  (b) any knife which has a blade which is released from the handle or sheath thereof by the force of gravity or the application of centrifugal force and which, when released, is locked in place by means of a button, spring, lever, or other device, sometimes known as a 'gravity knife',

shall be guilty of an offence and shall be liable on summary conviction to imprisonment for a term not exceeding six months or to a fine not exceeding level 5 on the standard scale or to both such imprisonment and fine.

In addition, the Restriction of Offensive Weapons Act 1959, s. 1(2), prohibits the importation of any such knife described in s. 1(1).

Manufacture, Sale and Hire of Offensive Weapons

Criminal Justice Act 1988, s. 141 **B12.141**

(1) Any person who manufactures, sells or hires or offers for sale or hire, exposes or has in his possession for the purpose of sale or hire, or lends or gives to any other person, a weapon to which this section applies shall be guilty of an offence.

Subsection (4) also prohibits the importation of a weapon to which this section applies.

By virtue of the CJA 1988, s. 141(1), a person guilty of the offence is liable to imprisonment for a term not exceeding six months, or to a fine not exceeding level 5 on the standard scale, or both.

The weapons to which s. 141 applies are those listed in the schedule to the Criminal Justice Act 1988 (Offensive Weapons) Order 1988 (SI 1988 No. 2019). This makes the following offensive weapons for the purpose of the instant offence, other than weapons which are antiques.

Criminal Justice Act 1988 (Offensive Weapons) Order 1988 (SI 1988 No. 2019), Sch.

. . .

(a) a knuckleduster, that is, a band of metal or other hard material worn on one or more fingers, and designed to cause injury, and any weapon incorporating a knuckleduster;
(b) a swordstick, that is, a hollow walking-stick or cane containing a blade which may be used as a sword;
(c) the weapon sometimes known as a 'handclaw', being a band of metal or other hard material from which a number of sharp spikes protrude, and worn around the hand;
(d) the weapon sometimes known as a 'belt buckle knife', being a buckle which incorporates or conceals a knife;
(e) the weapon sometimes known as a 'push dagger', being a knife the handle of which fits within a clenched fist and the blade of which protrudes from between two fingers;
(f) the weapon sometimes known as a 'hollow kubotan', being a cylindrical container containing a number of sharp spikes;
(g) the weapon sometimes known as a 'footclaw', being a bar of metal or other hard material from which a number of sharp spikes protrude, and worn strapped to the foot;
(h) the weapon sometimes known as a 'shuriken', 'shaken' or 'death star', being a hard non-flexible plate having three or more sharp radiating points and designed to be thrown;
(i) the weapon sometimes known as a 'balisong' or 'butterfly knife', being a blade enclosed by its handle, which is designed to split down the middle, without the operation of a spring or other mechanical means, to reveal the blade;
(j) the weapon sometimes known as a 'telescopic truncheon', being a truncheon which extends automatically by hand pressure applied to a button, spring or other device in or attached to its handle;
(k) the weapon sometimes known as a 'blowpipe' or 'blow gun' being a hollow tube out of which hard pellets or darts are shot by the use of breath;
(l) the weapon sometimes known as a 'kusari gama', being a length of rope, cord, wire or chain fastened at one end to a sickle;
(m) the weapon sometimes known as a 'kyoketsu shoge', being a length of rope, cord, wire or chain fastened at one end to a hooked knife;
(n) the weapon sometimes known as a 'manrikigusari' or 'kusari', being a length of rope, cord, wire or chain fastened at each end to a hard weight or hand grip;
(o) a disguised knife, that is any knife which has a concealed blade or concealed sharp point and is designed to appear to be an everyday object of a kind commonly carried on the person or in a handbag, briefcase, or other hand luggage (such as a comb, brush, writing instrument, cigarette lighter, key, lipstick or telephone); [inserted by the Criminal Justice Act 1988 (Offensive Weapons) Order 2002]
(p) a stealth knife, that is a knife or spike, which has a blade, or sharp point, made from a material that is not readily detectable by apparatus used for detecting metal and which is not designed for domestic use or for use in the processing, preparation or consumption of food or as a toy;
(q) a straight, side-handled or friction-lock truncheon (sometimes known as a baton). [(p) and (q) inserted by the Criminal Justice Act 1988 (Offensive Weapons) (Amendment) Order 2004]

For the purposes of the schedule, a weapon is an antique if it was manufactured more than 100 years before the date of any offence alleged to have been committed in respect of the weapon.

It is a defence for the accused to prove (note that from a date to be announced, the word 'show' is substituted by s. 43(3) of the VCRA 2006) that he is:

(i) carrying out functions on behalf of the Crown or a visiting force (see the CJA 1988, s. 141(5) to (7)); or
(ii) making a weapon available to a museum or gallery (s. 141(8), (10) and (11)); or

(iii) a person acting on behalf of a museum or gallery loaning or hiring a weapon for proper purposes (see s. 141(9)).

Previous editions of this work have suggested that the imposition of a legal burden upon the accused is open to challenge in the light of the human rights jurisprudence regarding 'reverse burdens' (see **F3.13**), but consider s. 43(3) of the VCRA 2006 (not yet in force). Note also the 'theatre defence' in s. 14(11A) to (11E), inserted by s. 43(4) of the VCRA 2006 (not yet in force).

Sale or Letting on Hire of a Crossbow to a Person under 17

Crossbows Act 1987, s. 1 **B12.142**

> A person who sells or lets on hire a crossbow or a part of a crossbow to a person under the age of 17 [18] is guilty of an offence, unless he believes him to be 17 [18] years of age or older and has reasonable ground for the belief.

Note the increased age limit (as from a date to be announced) introduced by s. 44 of the VCRA 2006. A person guilty of the offence is liable to imprisonment for a term not exceeding six months, to a fine not exceeding level 5 on the standard scale, or to both. The court also has power to order the forfeiture or disposal of any crossbow or part of a crossbow in respect of which the offence was committed (s. 6(1) and (3)).

Purchase or Hiring of a Crossbow by a Person under 17

Crossbows Act 1987, s. 2 **B12.143**

> A person under the age of 17 [18] who buys or hires a crossbow or part of a crossbow is guilty of an offence.

Note that (from a date to be announced) the age limit is increased to 18 years (VCRA 2006, s. 44). A person guilty of the offence is liable to a fine not exceeding level 3 on the standard scale. The court has power to order the forfeiture or disposal of any crossbow or part of a crossbow in respect of which the offence was committed (s. 6(2) and (3)).

MANUFACTURE, MARKETING, SALE, HIRE AND PURCHASE OF KNIVES

The Offensive Weapons Act 1996, s. 6, created an offence relating to the sale of knives to persons under 16. The Knives Act 1997 has created two either-way offences (unlawful marketing of knives and publications in connection with the marketing of knives). All these offences are in addition to the existing summary offences mentioned at **B12.139**. **B12.144**

Sale of Knives and Certain Articles with Blade or Point to Persons under 16

Criminal Justice Act 1988, s. 141A **B12.145**

> (1) Any person who sells to a person under the age of 16 [18] years an article to which this section applies shall be guilty of an offence and liable on summary conviction to imprisonment for a term not exceeding six months, or a fine not exceeding level 5 on the standard scale, or both.

Note the increased age limit (effective from 1 October 2007) introduced by s. 43(2) of the VCRA 2006.

By the CJA 1988, s. 141A(2), the offence applies to:

(a) any knife, knife blade or razor blade,
(b) any axe, and
(c) any other article which has a blade or which is sharply pointed and which is made or adapted for use for causing injury to the person.

Section 141A(1) does not apply to:

(a) a folding knife if the cutting edge of its blade does not exceed 7.62 centimetres (3 inches);
(b) razor blades permanently enclosed in a cartridge or housing where less than 2 millimetres of any blade is exposed beyond the place which intersects the highest point of the surfaces preceding and following such blades (Criminal Justice Act 1988 (Offensive Weapons) (Exemptions) Order 1996 (SI 1996 No. 3064), art. 2).

As to articles made or adapted to cause injury under the Prevention of Crime Act 1953, see **B12.124** and **B12.125**. Section 141A does not apply to any article described in the Restriction of Offensive Weapons Act 1959, s. 1 (see **B12.140**), an order made under the CJA 1988, s. 141(2) (see **B12.141**), or any order made under s. 141A itself (s. 141A(3)). It is a defence for a person charged with the offence to prove that he took all reasonable precautions and exercised due diligence to avoid the commission of the offence (s. 141A(4)); the imposition of a legal burden upon the accused is open to challenge in the light of the human rights jurisprudence regarding 'reverse burdens' (see **F3.13**).

Unlawful Marketing of Knives

B12.146 **Knives Act 1997, s. 1**

(1) A person is guilty of an offence if he markets a knife in a way which—
 (a) indicates, or suggests, that it is suitable for combat; or
 (b) is otherwise likely to stimulate or encourage violent behaviour involving the use of the knife as a weapon.

The offence is triable either way s. 1(5)). The maximum penalty is: on conviction on indictment, imprisonment for a term not exceeding two years or a fine, or both; on summary conviction, imprisonment for a term not exceeding six months or a fine not exceeding the statutory maximum, or both (s. 1(5)).

Elements

B12.147 'Knife' means an instrument which has a blade or is sharply pointed (s. 10). A person markets a knife if he sells or hires it, he offers, or exposes, it for sale or hire or has it in his possession for the purpose of sale or hire (s. 1(4)). A knife is suitable for combat if it is suitable for use as a weapon for inflicting injury on a person or causing a person to fear injury (s. 10). 'Violent behaviour' means an unlawful act inflicting injury on a person or causing a person to fear injury (s. 10).

An indication or suggestion that a knife is suitable for combat may, in particular, be given or made by a name or description which is applied to the knife, which is on the knife or any packaging in which it is contained or which is included in any advertisement which, expressly or by implication, relates to the knife (s. 1(3)).

Defences

B12.148 **Knives Act 1997, ss. 3 and 4**

3.—(1) It is a defence for a person charged with an offence under section 1 to prove that—
 (a) the knife was marketed—
  (i) for use by the armed forces of any country;
  (ii) as an antique or curio; or
  (iii) as falling within such other category (if any) as may be prescribed;
 (b) it was reasonable for the knife to be marketed in that way; and
 (c) there were no reasonable grounds for suspecting that a person into whose possession the knife might come in consequence of the way in which it was marketed would use it for an unlawful purpose.

4.—(1) It is a defence for a person charged with an offence under section 1 to prove that he did not know or suspect, and had no reasonable grounds for suspecting, that the way in which the knife was marketed—

(a) amounted to an indication or suggestion that the knife was suitable for combat; or
(b) was likely to stimulate or encourage violent behaviour involving the use of the knife as a weapon.

(2) It is a defence for a person charged with an offence under section 2 to prove that he did not know or suspect, and had no reasonable grounds for suspecting, that the way in which the knife was marketed—
(a) amounted to an indication or suggestion that the knife was suitable for combat; or
(b) was likely to stimulate or encourage violent behaviour involving the use of the knife as a weapon.

(3) It is a defence for a person charged with an offence under section 1 or 2 to prove that he took all reasonable precautions and exercised all due diligence to avoid committing the offence.

The imposition of a legal burden upon the accused is open to challenge in the light of the human rights cases on the 'reverse burden' (see **F3.13**).

Publications relating to Knives

Knives Act 1997, s. 2 **B12.149**

(1) A person is guilty of an offence if he publishes any written, pictorial or other material in connection with the marketing of any knife and that material—
(a) indicates or suggests that the knife is suitable for combat; or
(b) is otherwise likely to stimulate or encourage violent behaviour involving the use of the knife as a weapon.

The maximum penalty is: on conviction on indictment, imprisonment for a term not exceeding two years or a fine, or both; on summary conviction, imprisonment for a term not exceeding six months or a fine not exceeding the statutory maximum, or both.

For definition of the terms used in s. 2, see **B12.147**.

Specific defences are provided by s. 4(2) and (3) (see **B12.148**).

MINDING A 'DANGEROUS WEAPON'

Section 28 of the VCRA 2006 creates a new offence of using a person to mind a 'dangerous weapon', being a weapon intended to be made available for an unlawful purpose. By s. 28(3), 'dangerous weapon' means (a) a firearm other than an air weapon or a component part of, or accessory to, an air weapon; or (b) a weapon to which the CJA 1988, s. 141 applies (see **B12.141**). The penalties are set out in s. 29. Sections 28 and 29 of the VCRA 2006 came into force on 26 April 2007 (see the Violent Crime Reduction Act 2006 (Commencement No. 2) Order (SI 2007 No. 858)). **B12.150**

Violent Crime Reduction Act 2006, ss. 28 and 29

28.— (1) A person is guilty of an offence if—
(a) he uses another to look after, hide or transport a dangerous weapon for him; and
(b) he does so under arrangements or in circumstances that facilitate, or are intended to facilitate, the weapon's being available to him for an unlawful purpose.

(2) For the purposes of this section the cases in which a dangerous weapon is to be regarded as available to a person for an unlawful purpose include any case where—
(a) the weapon is available for him to take possession of it at a time and place; and
(b) his possession of the weapon at that time and place would constitute, or be likely to involve or to lead to, the commission by him of an offence.

(3) In this section 'dangerous weapon' means—
(a) a firearm other than an air weapon or a component part of, or accessory to, an air weapon; or
(b) a weapon to which section 141 or 141A of the Criminal Justice Act 1988 applies (specified offensive weapons, knives and bladed weapons).

(4) [Scotland.]

29.—(1) This section applies where a person ('the offender') is guilty of an offence under section 28.

(2) Where the dangerous weapon in respect of which the offence was committed is a weapon to which section 141 or 141A of the Criminal Justice Act 1988 (specified offensive weapons, knives and bladed weapons) applies, the offender shall be liable, on conviction on indictment, to imprisonment for a term not exceeding 4 years or to a fine, or to both.

(3) Where—

(a) at the time of the offence, the offender was aged 16 or over, and

(b) the dangerous weapon in respect of which the offence was committed was a firearm mentioned in section 5(1)(a) to (af) or (c) or section 5(1A)(a) of the 1968 Act (firearms possession of which attracts a minimum sentence),

the offender shall be liable, on conviction on indictment, to imprisonment for a term not exceeding 10 years or to a fine, or to both.

(4) On a conviction in England and Wales, where—

(a) subsection (3) applies, and

(b) the offender is aged 18 or over at the time of conviction,

the court must impose (with or without a fine) a term of imprisonment of not less than 5 years, unless it is of the opinion that there are exceptional circumstances relating to the offence or to the offender which justify its not doing so.

(5) In relation to times before the commencement of paragraph 180 of schedule 7 to the Criminal Justice and Court Services Act 2000, the reference in subsection (4) to a sentence of imprisonment, in relation to an offender aged under 21 at the time of conviction, is to be read as a reference to a sentence of detention in a young offender institution.

(6) On a conviction in England and Wales, where—

(a) subsection (3) applies, and

(b) the offender is aged under 18 at the time of conviction,

the court must impose (with or without a fine) a term of detention under section 91 of the Powers of Criminal Courts (Sentencing) Act 2000 of not less than 3 years, unless it is of the opinion that there are exceptional circumstances relating to the offence or to the offender which justify its not doing so.

CAUSING EXPLOSION LIKELY TO ENDANGER LIFE OR PROPERTY

B12.151 **Explosive Substances Act 1883, s. 2**

A person who in the United Kingdom or (being a citizen of the United Kingdom and Colonies) in the Republic of Ireland unlawfully and maliciously causes by any explosive substance an explosion of a nature likely to endanger life or to cause serious injury to property shall, whether any injury to person or property has actually been caused or not, be guilty of an offence. . . .

Indictment

B12.152 *Statement of Offence*

Causing an explosion contrary to section 2 of the Explosive Substances Act 1883.

Particulars of Offence

A on or about the . . . day of . . . maliciously caused by an explosive substance an explosion of a nature likely to endanger life or to cause serious injury to property, namely the explosion at . . . Town Hall on the . . . day of . . .

Procedure

B12.153 The offence is triable on indictment only (Explosive Substances Act 1883, s. 2) and is a class 3 offence.

Proceedings for a crime under this Act shall not be instituted except by or with the consent of the A-G (s. 7(1)); proceedings are not instituted until following remands in custody or bail since such remands are expressly excluded from the operation of s. 7(1) by the Prosecution of Offences Act 1985, s. 25(2) (*Wale* (1991) *The Times*, 9 May 1991, in which the proceedings for the offence contrary to s. 4 were held not to be effectively instituted until the committal proceedings). Further, in *Elliott* (1984) 81 Cr App R 115 at p. 121, the Court of Appeal concluded that the Explosive Substances Act 1883, s. 7 'should be interpreted as meaning that instituting proceedings relates to the time when a person comes to court to answer the charge' so the relevant time is 'when he attends at the magistrates' court to answer the charge'; it held that any other interpretation would 'overlook and ignore' the provisions of the Prosecution of Offences Act 1985, s. 6.

Sentence

The maximum penalty is imprisonment for life (Explosive Substances Act 1883, s. 2). Relevant sentencing cases are *McDonald* [2002] 2 Cr App R (S) 113 and *Jones* (1995) 16 Cr App R (S) 107. Powers of forfeiture and disposal of matter are provided by the Explosives Act 1875, ss. 89 and 96; these apply to this offence (1983 Act, s. 8(1)). See also **B12.142**. **B12.154**

Explosive Substance and Explosion

'Explosive substance' is 'deemed to include any materials for making any explosive substance; also any apparatus, machine, implement or materials used, or intended to be used, or adapted for causing, or aiding in causing, any explosion in or with any explosive substance; also any part of any such apparatus, machine or implement' (Explosive Substances Act 1883, s. 9(1)). **B12.155**

The Court of Appeal decided in *Wheatley* [1979] 1 WLR 144, that the definition of 'explosive' in the Explosives Act 1875, s. 3, applies to the 1883 Act.

Explosives Act 1875, s. 3

> The term 'explosive' in this Act — (1) Means gunpowder, nitro-glycerine, dynamite, guncotton, blasting powders, fulminate of mercury or of other metals, coloured fires and every other substance, whether similar to those above mentioned or not, used or manufactured with a view to producing a practical effect by explosion or a pyrotechnic effect; and (2) includes fog-signals, fireworks, fuses, rockets, percussion caps, detonators, cartridges, ammunition of all description, and every adaptation or preparation of an explosive as above defined.

In *Wheatley*, fire-dampened sodium chlorate mixture, used in a pipe bomb, was an explosive substance, even if it had only a pyrotechnic effect. In *Bouch* [1983] QB 246, the Court of Appeal held that 'pyrotechnic effect' has a broad meaning and is not limited to, e.g., fireworks. A flare is a pyrotechnic device. There does not have to be an explosion. A fireball produced by a petrol bomb has a pyrotechnic effect.

The meaning of 'explosion' was considered by the Court of Appeal in *Bouch*, where the definition used in the 1886 edition of the *Encyclopaedia Britannica* was approved:

> 'explosion' may for our purpose be defined as the sudden or extremely rapid conversion of a solid or liquid body of small bulk into gas or vapour, occupying very many times the volume of the original substance, and, in addition, highly expanded by the heat generated during the transformation. This sudden or very rapid expansion of volume is attained by an exhibition of force, more or less violent according to the constitution of the original substance and the circumstances of explosion. Any substance capable of undergoing such a change upon the application of heat, or other disturbing cause, is called 'explosive'.

The inevitable concomitant of a successful petrol bomb is an explosion because it produces a fireball, though it does not always have a blast effect. A petrol bomb will produce a blast effect where it does not ignite immediately upon impact but ignites after a pause. See also *Elliott* (1984) 81 Cr App R 115 adopting this approach.

Explosive substances have included a shot gun (*Downey* [1971] NI 224), a firearm (*Fegan* (1971) 78 Cr App R 189), part of a vessel filled with an explosive substance (*Charles* (1892) 17 Cox CC 499) and electronic timers (*Berry (No.* 3) [1994] 2 All ER 913), as well as the more obvious substances, such as dynamite or gunpowder (*Hallam* [1957] 1 QB 569), plaster gelatine and detonators (*Stewart and Harris* (1959) 44 Cr App R 29), and a stick of gelignite, a length of fuse and a detonator (*McCarthy* [1964] 1 WLR 196). The petrol in a petrol bomb combines with the air to create an explosive substance, so the petrol, bottle and wick are materials for making that explosive substance (*Bouch*).

Who in the United Kingdom

B12.156 In *Ellis* (1991) 95 Cr App R 52, Swinton Thomas J held, on a motion to quash two counts in an indictment, that 'the words "who in the United Kingdom" do not govern the person but govern the acts'. In reaching this conclusion the judge had pointed out that 'to construe section 3 . . . so as to limit the offence to a person who is physically present in the United Kingdom when he causes explosions runs not only wholly contrary to common sense but wholly contrary to the whole tenor of the law as it has developed over the last century and particularly over the last two decades'.

Mens Rea

B12.157 The *mens rea is* that the act must be done 'maliciously' (see **B2.49** and **A2.7**). It is often said that there is no need for foresight by the defendant of (a) endangerment of life or (b) serious injury to property. The jury assesses the likelihood of either objectively. Without asserting that this proposition is incorrect, or overstated, consider *R v G* [2004] 1 AC 1034 and *Cunningham* [1957] 2 QB 396.

Punishment of Accessories

B12.158 See **B12.172**.

Power of Search etc.

B12.159 Section 8(1) of the Explosive Substances Act 1883 extends certain powers in the Explosives Act 1875 to this offence. The powers are: to search for explosives (s. 73); to seize and detain explosives liable to forfeiture (s. 74); and to inspect wharves, carriages, boats etc. with explosives in transit (s. 75).

ATTEMPT TO CAUSE EXPLOSION OR MAKING OR KEEPING EXPLOSIVE WITH INTENT TO ENDANGER LIFE OR PROPERTY

B12.160 **Explosive Substances Act 1883, s. 3**

(1) A person who in the United Kingdom or a dependency or (being a citizen of the United Kingdom and Colonies) elsewhere unlawfully and maliciously—
  (a) does any act with intent to cause, or conspires to cause, by an explosive substance an explosion of a nature likely to endanger life, or cause serious injury to property, whether in the United Kingdom or the Republic of Ireland, or
  (b) makes or has in his possession or under his control an explosive substance with intent by means thereof to endanger life, or cause serious injury to property, whether in the United Kingdom or the Republic of Ireland, or to enable any other person so to do,

shall, whether any explosion does or does not take place, and whether any injury to person or property is actually caused or not, be guilty of an offence . . .

Procedure

B12.161 The offence is triable on indictment only (Explosive Substances Act 1883, s. 3(1)) and is a class 3 offence. As to the need for the A-G's consent, see **B12.153**.

Sentence

B12.162 The maximum penalty is imprisonment for life (Explosive Substances Act 1883, s. 3(1)). The explosive substance is forfeited. The related provisions of the Explosives Act 1875 (ss. 89 and 96) apply (s. 8(1)).

In *Martin* [1999] 1 Cr App R (S) 477, the Court of Appeal issued guidelines for the sentencing of this offence. Lord Bingham CJ said that the appropriate sentence would depend upon a number of factors, including the nature, size and likely effect of the explosive device, the nature and extent of any death, injury or damage caused, together with the role and motivation of the individual offenders.

In cases of conspiracy to cause an explosion, key factors would be the target of that conspiracy, and the likely result of any explosion. A conspiracy whose primary object was to endanger life should attract a higher sentence than one primarily directed to damaging property. On the facts of the case before the court, the offenders were members of the IRA who had planned to cause explosions, using 37 bombs at electricity substations. They had been arrested before the plan could be implemented. The political, economic and social threat in this case had been grave, and death or personal injury, though not the primary intention, had been an obvious risk. The sentence was reduced from 35 years' imprisonment to 28 years, a term designed to correlate with the period typically served by the perpetrator of a murder with severely aggravating features. In *A-G's Ref (No. 13 of 2002)* [2003] 1 Cr App R (S) 48, the offender built a number of sophisticated explosive devices with lethal potential. A sentence of five years' imprisonment for the offence under s. 3 was increased to nine years on appeal. The Court of Appeal said that 12 years would have been appropriate without the element of double jeopardy.

Elements

For the meaning of 'in the United Kingdom', see **B12.156**; 'dependency' means the Channel Islands, the Isle of Man and any colony, other than a colony for whose external relations a country other than the UK is responsible (Explosive Substances Act 1883, s. 3(2)). *Abedin* [2004] EWCA Crim 2232 confirms that a jury is bound to acquit if it thinks that the intention of the accused was to cause an explosion to endanger life or damage property abroad and not in the UK. **B12.163**

For the meaning of 'explosive substance' and 'explosive', see **B12.155**. For the meaning of 'making explosives', see **B12.166**.

Mens Rea

The *mens rea* is that the act, whatever it might be, must be done 'maliciously' (see **B2.49** and **A2.7**). It would appear not to be possible to possess a substance maliciously if it is not known what the substance is. Thus the approach in the cases decided on the Explosive Substances Act 1883, s. 4, by the Court of Criminal Appeal in *Hallam* [1957] 1 QB 569 and *Stewart* (1959) 44 Cr App R 29 (see **B12.166**), may be applicable to this offence also, rather than the rules relating to possession developed in relation to controlled drugs (see **B20.7**). **B12.164**

Punishment of Accessories and Powers of Search

See **B12.172** for punishment of accessories. See **B12.159** for powers of search. **B12.165**

MAKING OR POSSESSION OF EXPLOSIVE UNDER SUSPICIOUS CIRCUMSTANCES

Explosive Substances Act 1883, s. 4 **B12.166**

(1) Any person who makes or knowingly has in his possession or under his control any explosive substance, under such circumstances as to give rise to a reasonable suspicion that he is not making it or does not have it in his possession or under his control for a lawful object, shall,

> unless he can show that he made it or had it in his possession or under his control for a lawful object, be guilty of [an offence] . . .

Procedure

B12.167 The offence is triable on indictment only (Explosive Substances Act 1883, s. 4(1)) and is a class 3 offence. As to the need for the A-G's consent, see **B12.153**. Note *McVitie* [1960] 2 QB 483 regarding particulars of the offence.

Sentence

B12.168 On conviction on indictment, the maximum penalty is 14 years' imprisonment, and the explosive substance must be forfeited (Explosive Substances Act 1883, s. 4(1)). A sentence of 42 months was upheld in *Lloyd* [2001] 2 Cr App R (S) 493, where the offender, who had 14 previous convictions for weapons-related offences, pleaded guilty to making four explosive devices, but not intending to use them to cause harm.

Possession, Control or Making and *Mens Rea*

B12.169 The accused must know that he has the substance in his possession or control (*Berry (No. 3)* [1994] 2 All ER 913, at p. 918h). In *Hallam* [1957] 1 QB 569, the Court of Criminal Appeal decided the meaning of the section was clear and that 'the person must not only knowingly have in his possession the substance but must know that it is an explosive substance', but he does not have to have 'any particular chemical knowledge'. The Court of Criminal Appeal followed this decision in *Stewart* (1959) 44 Cr App R 29. The word 'knowingly' prefaces 'possession' and 'control' and not 'making', but, nevertheless, 'all three categories of person must be shown to have known that the substance was an explosive substance' (*Berry (No.3)*, at p. 918g). It was said in *Berry* that 'no person who makes a substance can be unaware that he had done so' although this must be read as being subject to the general defences (see A3).

The Court of Appeal in *Hallam* also said that 'if evidence is given that the person had the substance in his possession, and some evidence of circumstances which give rise to a reasonable suspicion that he had not got it for a lawful purpose is given, the jury are then entitled to infer that he knew it was an explosive substance'. However, there is nothing in this approach which should be interpreted as suggesting that the burden of proof is not on the prosecution to prove *mens rea*, and that is particularly so where the substance is not so obviously an explosive substance, e.g., a timer as opposed to gunpowder or gelignite. The jury must be sure that the maker intended the timer to be used to cause explosions (*Berry (No.3)*, at p. 919).

Reasonable Suspicion

B12.170 'Reasonable suspicion' is an objective requirement, which must be proved by the prosecution (see *Fegan* (1971) 78 Cr App R 189).

Lawful Object

B12.171 In *Fegan* (1971) 78 Cr App R 189, the Court of Criminal Appeal, Northern Ireland, held that 'the expression "lawful object" cannot be defined exhaustively or with precision'. The court decided that possession and purpose must not be confused, so, 'possession of a firearm for the purpose of protecting the possessor, his wife or family from acts of violence may be possession for a lawful object'. That purpose 'cannot be founded on a mere fancy, or some aggressive motive' and the 'threatened danger must be reasonably and genuinely anticipated, must appear reasonably imminent, and must be of a nature which could not reasonably be met by more pacific means' (*Fegan*). The Court of Appeal in *A-G's Ref (No. 2 of 1983)* [1984] QB 456, agreed with this approach. The House of Lords appears to have adopted the same approach in *Berry* [1985] AC 246. The court, in *Fegan*, held that a person cannot possess an item for a lawful object if he also has it for an unlawful object. The Court of Appeal in *Campbell* [2004] EWCA Crim 2309, refused to grant leave to appeal against conviction where the trial judge had ruled that the defendant never had a lawful reason for possession of the explosive substances, even if it was the case that they were made by him when he was young in order to put into hollow trees and down rabbit holes and had simply been retained as part of the detritus of childhood. It is necessary for people not to store explosive items without good reasons and this defendant was irresponsible in doing what he had done.

As the statute makes clear, the burden of proof of this defence lies upon the defence (see *Berry (No. 3)* [1994] 2 All ER 913 at p. 920f and *Fegan*) and it must be proved on a balance of probabilities (*Fegan*). That view must be open to challenge in the light of the human rights cases on the 'reverse burden' (see **F3.6**).

Punishment of Accessories

Explosive Substances Act 1883, s. 5 **B12.172**

> Any person who within or (being a subject of Her Majesty) without Her Majesty's dominions by the supply of or solicitation for money, the providing of premises, the supply of materials, or in any manner whatsoever, procures, counsels, aids, abets, or is accessory to, the commission of any crime under this Act, shall be guilty of [an offence], and shall be liable to be tried and punished for that crime, as if he had been guilty as a principal.

Notwithstanding s. 5, the commission of an offence contrary to s. 4 may be aided and abetted (*McCarthy* [1964] 1 WLR 196). For a general consideration of participation in crime, see **A5**, and, in particular, **A5.11**.

Powers of Search

See **B12.159** for powers of search. **B12.173**

CAUSING BODILY INJURY BY GUNPOWDER

Offences Against the Person Act 1861, s. 28 **B12.174**

> Whosoever shall unlawfully and maliciously, by the explosion of gunpowder or other explosive substance, burn, maim, disfigure, disable, or do any grievous bodily harm to any person, shall be guilty of [an offence].

Procedure and Sentence

The offence is triable on indictment (OAPA 1861, s. 28) and is a class 3 offence. **B12.175**
The maximum penalty is imprisonment for life (s. 28).

Elements

In *Howard* [1993] Crim LR 213, the Court of Appeal decided that a petrol bomb is an explosive substance. The definition of 'explosive substance' under the Explosive Substances Act 1883 (see **B12.155**) was used by the trial judge and noted by the Court of Appeal. It clearly is of assistance, but may not be determinative of the concept as it appears in the OAPA 1861. It is submitted that the term should mean the same in both pieces of legislation. The Court of Appeal wondered if the trial judge should not have asked the jury to determine whether the petrol bomb was an explosive substance. This can be correct only if the jury were being asked to determine whether the facts about a petrol bomb satisfied the definition of explosive substance given to them by the judge. **B12.176**

It is to be assumed that the words 'burn, maim, disfigure, disable, or do any grievous bodily harm' will carry their ordinary meaning, unless a decision suggests otherwise. Indeed this was the approach of the Court of Appeal in interpreting the meaning of 'disable' in *James* (1979) 70 Cr App R 215. 'Maim' has a technical legal meaning which is injury of any part of a man's body which may make him less able to defend himself (12 *Halsbury's Statutes*, at p. 109), so there was no proof of an intent to maim or disable in *Sullivan* (1841) Car & M 209, where the blow was aimed at the head of the victim, but it would have been otherwise had it been aimed at his arm to prevent his being able to use it. 'Disfigure' means to do an external injury which may detract from the personal appearance (12 *Halsbury's Statutes*, at p. 109). 'Disable' covers both permanent and temporary disablement (*James*, a decision on s. 29, and not applying *Boyce* (1824) 1 Mood CC 29). As to 'grievous bodily harm', see B2.37.

Mens Rea

B12.177 The *mens rea* is 'maliciously', which, it is submitted, refers both to the consequence as well as the explosion. As to the meaning of 'maliciously', see **B2.49** and **A2.7**.

CAUSING GUNPOWDER TO EXPLODE, SENDING AN EXPLOSIVE SUBSTANCE OR THROWING CORROSIVE FLUID WITH INTENT

B12.178 **Offences Against the Person Act 1861, s. 29**

> Whosoever shall unlawfully and maliciously cause any gunpowder or other explosive substance to explode, or send or deliver or to cause to be taken or received by any person any explosive substance or any other dangerous or noxious thing, or put or lay at any place, or cast or throw at or upon or otherwise apply to any person, any corrosive fluid or any destructive or explosive substance, with intent in any of the cases aforesaid to burn, maim, disfigure, or disable any person, or to do some grievous bodily harm to any person, shall, whether any bodily injury be effected or not, be guilty of [an offence].

Procedure and Sentence

B12.179 This offence is triable on indictment (OAPA 1861, s. 29) and is a class 3 offence.

On conviction on indictment, the maximum penalty is life imprisonment.

Elements

B12.180 For the meaning of 'explosive substance' and 'burn, maim, disfigure, or disable', see **B12.155**. For 'grievous bodily harm', see **B2.37**.

In *Crawford* (1845) 2 Car & Kir 129, the Court for Crown Cases Reserved upheld a conviction on the basis that boiling water was 'destructive matter'. For the meaning of noxious thing, see **B2.66**.

Mens Rea

B12.181 The *mens rea* of the offence consists of 'maliciously' doing one of the prohibited acts and with intent to produce one of the prohibited consequences. As to the meaning of 'maliciously', see **B2.49** and **A2.7**. As to 'intention', see **A2.2**.

PLACING GUNPOWDER NEAR A BUILDING ETC. WITH INTENT TO DO BODILY INJURY TO ANY PERSON

B12.182 **Offences Against the Person Act 1861, s. 30**

> Whosoever shall unlawfully and maliciously place or throw in, into, upon, against, or near any building, ship or vessel any gunpowder or other explosive substance, with intent to do any bodily injury to any person, shall, whether or not any explosion take place, and whether or not any bodily injury be effected, be guilty of [an offence].

Procedure and Sentence

The offence is triable on indictment (OAPA 1861, s. 30) and is a class 3 offence. B12.183

The maximum penalty is 14 years' imprisonment.

Elements

For the meaning of 'explosive substance', see **B12.155**. Although the substance need not explode, it must be capable of exploding, so to throw a bottle containing only gunpowder and an unlit fuse would not constitute the offence, because the act would merely be that of throwing a bottle (*Shephard* (1868) 19 LT 19 at p. 20). B12.184

Mens Rea

The placing or throwing must be done 'maliciously' (as to which see **B2.49** and **A2.7**), and it must be done with intent to do bodily injury (as to 'intent', see **A2.2**). It is to be noted that the phrase is bodily injury and not grievous bodily harm. It appears to be a wider term in the sense that it need not be serious, but it may be more limited if it applies only to physical injury. B12.185

MAKING OR HAVING GUNPOWDER ETC. WITH INTENT TO COMMIT OR ENABLE ANY PERSON TO COMMIT A FELONY

Offences Against the Person Act 1861, s. 64 B12.186

Whosoever shall knowingly have in his possession, or make or manufacture, any gunpowder, explosive substance, or any dangerous or noxious thing, or any machine, engine, instrument, or thing, with intent by means thereof to commit, or for the purpose of enabling any other person to commit, any of the felonies in this Act mentioned shall be guilty of an [offence].

Procedure and Sentence

The offence is triable on indictment and is a class 3 offence. B12.187

The maximum penalty is two years' imprisonment.

Elements

For the meaning of 'possession', see, by analogy, the drug possession cases at **B20.7**, but note that the possession in this offence must be 'knowingly', see **B12.189**. B12.188

For the meaning of 'explosive substance', see **B12.155**. For the meaning of 'noxious thing', see **B2.66**.

Mens Rea

The *mens rea* requires that there be an act (possession, making or manufacturing) which is done 'knowingly'. As to the meaning of 'knowingly', see **A2.9**. There must also be an intent to commit a felony within the OAPA 1861. As to the meaning of 'intent', see **A2.2**. The reference to 'felonies' is to any offence within the 1861 Act for which a person (not previously convicted) may be tried on indictment otherwise than at his own instance (Criminal Law Act 1967, s. 10 and sch. 2, para. 8). B12.189

FIREWORKS OFFENCES

There are a number of offences concerned with fireworks, which include the following. B12.190

(a) It is an offence, contrary to the Explosives Act 1875, s. 80, for a person to throw, cast, or fire any firework in or into any highway, street, thoroughfare or public place. On summary conviction, the maximum penalty is a fine not exceeding level 5 on the standard scale. Under the Penalties for Disorderly Behaviour (Amount of Penalty) Order 2002 (SI 2002 No. 1837), this offence is a penalty offence and the amount payable is £80.

(b) The Fireworks Act 2003, s. 11(1), provides that any person who contravenes a prohibition imposed by fireworks regulations is guilty of an offence. The relevant regulations are the Fireworks Regulations 2004 (SI 2004 No. 1836). Any person guilty of such an offence is liable, on summary conviction, to imprisonment for a term not exceeding six months or a fine not exceeding level 5 on the standard scale or both (Fireworks Act 2003, s. 11(3)). The defence of due diligence, in the Consumer Protection Act 1987, s. 39, applies to this offence (Fireworks Act 2003, s. 11(7)). The offence under s. 11 is also a penalty offence with £80 as the amount payable.

Section B13 Offences Affecting Enjoyment of Premises

UNLAWFUL EVICTION AND HARASSMENT OF OCCUPIER

Definition

The Protection from Eviction Act 1977, s. 1, creates three offences which may be considered together. The first offence, contrary to s. 1(2), is concerned with unlawful eviction (the statute using the words 'deprives'); the other two offences, contrary to s. 1(3) and (3A), are concerned with harassment of a residential occupier. The main differences between the two harassment offences is that the one contrary to s. 1(3) can be committed by any person and it is necessary to prove intention, whereas the offence contrary to s. 1(3A) can be committed only by the landlord or agent and no intention need be proved. Section 1(3) does not create two offences (*Schon v Camden London Borough Council* (1986) 84 LGR 830, per Glidewell LJ). **B13.1**

Protection from Eviction Act 1977, s. 1

(2) If any person unlawfully deprives the residential occupier of any premises of his occupation of the premises or any part thereof, or attempts to do so, he is guilty of an offence unless he proves that he believed, and had reasonable cause to believe, that the residential occupier had ceased to reside in the premises.

(3) If any person with intent to cause the residential occupier of any premises—
(a) to give up the occupation of the premises or any part thereof; or
(b) to refrain from exercising any right or pursuing any remedy in respect of the premises or part thereof;
does acts likely to interfere with the peace or comfort of the residential occupier or members of his household, or persistently withdraws or withholds services reasonably required for the occupation of the premises as a residence, he shall be guilty of an offence.

(3A) Subject to subsection (3B) below the landlord of a residential occupier or an agent of the landlord shall be guilty of an offence if—
(a) he does acts likely to interfere with the peace or comfort of the residential occupier or members of his household, or
(b) he persistently withdraws or withholds services reasonably required for the occupation of the premises in question as a residence,
and (in either case) he knows, or has reasonable cause to believe, that that conduct is likely to cause the residential occupier to give up the occupation of the whole or part of the premises or to refrain from exercising any right or pursuing any remedy in respect of the whole or part of the premises.

Procedure

B13.2 The Protection from Eviction Act 1977, s. 6, provides that proceedings may be instituted by councils of districts and London boroughs, the Common Council of the City of London, councils of Welsh counties and county boroughs and the Council of the Scilly Isles.

The offence is triable either way. When tried on indictment it is a class 3 offence.

Indictment

B13.3

First Count

Statement of Offence

Unlawful eviction contrary to section 1(2) of the Protection from Eviction Act 1977

Particulars of Offence

A on the . . . day of . . . unlawfully deprived V, the residential occupier, of his occupation of premises, namely . . ., by changing the locks of the said premises during the absence of V and the members of his household

Second Count

Statement of Offence

Unlawful harassment contrary to section 1(3) of the Protection from Eviction Act 1977

Particulars of Offence

A on divers dates between . . . and . . . did acts likely to interfere with the peace and comfort of [or: withdrew (or withheld) services reasonably required for occupation, namely . . ., from] V, the residential occupier of premises at . . ., namely . . ., with intent to cause V to give up his occupation of the said premises [or: to refrain from exercising the right to . . .] [or: to refrain from pursuing a remedy of . . .], without reasonable cause to believe that he had ceased to reside in the premises

Although strictly speaking in an indictment for the offence contrary to s. 1(3) there need be no reference to a 'persistent' withdrawing or withholding of services, as a matter of practice it is desirable that it should be included (*Abrol* [1972] Crim LR 318). It would not appear that s. 1(3) is a possible alternative offence to s. 1(2), although Glidewell LJ, giving the judgment of the Divisional Court in *Costelloe v London Borough of Camden* [1986] Crim LR 249, stated that charging the two offences in the alternative would not be objectionable.

Sentence

B13.4 The maximum penalty is: on summary conviction, a fine not exceeding the prescribed sum or imprisonment for a term not exceeding six months or both; on conviction on indictment, a fine or imprisonment for a term not exceeding two years or both (Protection from Eviction Act 1977, s. 1(4)).

In *Khan* [2001] 2 Cr App R (S) 553, a sentence of 15 months' imprisonment was upheld on conviction after a trial where the offender and four associates kicked down the door to the victim's flat when she was out, caused wanton damage to the victim's possessions and made threats of violence against her. See also *Pittard* (1994) 15 Cr App R (S) 108.

Persons who can Commit Offence

B13.5 The offences contrary to the Protection from Eviction Act 1977, s. 1(2) and (3), may be committed by 'any person', whereas the offence contrary to s. 1(3A) may be committed only by 'the landlord of a residential occupier or an agent of the landlord'. It may be that if the eviction is 'unlawful' within s. 1(2) only by virtue of the provisions of s. 3(1), the offence can be committed only by a landlord or agent (see **B13.11**).

Liability of Corporate Officers

B13.6 The Protection from Eviction Act 1977, s. 1(6), makes provision for the liability of officers of a body corporate which is guilty of one of the two offences:

Protection from Eviction Act 1977, s. 1

(6) Where an offence under this section committed by a body corporate is proved to have been committed with the consent or connivance of, or to be attributable to any neglect on the part of, any director, manager or secretary or other similar officer of the body corporate or any person who was purporting to act in any such capacity, he as well as the body corporate shall be guilty of that offence and shall be liable to be proceeded against and punished accordingly.

Meaning of 'Residential Occupier'

Protection from Eviction Act 1977, s. 1 B13.7

(1) In this section 'residential occupier', in relation to any premises, means a person occupying the premises as a residence, whether under a contract or by virtue of any enactment or rule of law giving him the right to remain in occupation or restricting the right of any other person to recover possession of the premises.

Provided an occupier has a right to remain in occupation, or the right of any other person to recover possession of the premises is restricted, he is a 'residential occupier'. It has to be ascertained whether a given occupier has sufficient residential protection to qualify under this statute. In *Blankley* [1979] Crim LR 166, Judge Clover in the Knightsbridge Crown Court held, considering the earlier offence contrary to the Rent Act 1965, s. 30, that there was no case to answer since the occupier was not a tenant but merely a contractual licensee. With respect, this decision cannot be correct, since the Protection from Eviction Act 1977 is not concerned with whether the occupier is a tenant, but whether the occupation that he has, granted by whatever means, satisfies the statutory requirements. Those requirements may be satisfied under a contractual licence. Lord Widgery CJ, giving the judgment of the Divisional Court, accepted in *Thurrock Urban District Council v Shina* (1972) 70 LGR 301 that a licensee could be a residential occupier, whilst recognising that a licence may more easily be terminated than a tenancy. This case is also a decision on the Rent Act 1965, s. 30. Of course, once a licence is ended, the person is usually no longer a residential occupier and falls outside the protection provided by these offences (see *Portsmouth City Council, ex parte Knight* (1983) 82 LGR 184; *Surrey Heath Borough Council, ex parte Li* (1984) 16 HLR 79).

The wider approach being advocated also follows from the decision of the Divisional Court in *Norton v Knowles* [1969] 1 QB 572 (a decision on the Rent Act 1965, s. 30) that a person living in a caravan which was not attached to the land was a residential occupier. Although the caravan was connected to the drains, water pipes and electricity supply and had a telephone, it does not appear that these factors were necessarily essential to the decision. What was essential was the relationship between the landlord and the caravan dweller.

Belief that Person not Residential Occupier

In relation to the harassment offence contrary to the Protection from Eviction Act 1977, s. 1(3), the Court of Appeal in *Phekoo* [1981] 1 WLR 1117 held, on the basis that conviction for the offence is conviction for a truly criminal offence and attaches serious social stigma to the offender, that, where the issue is raised that the accused reasonably believed that the person who was harassed was not a residential occupier, it is for the Crown to prove that that belief was not honest. Although this decision directly applies only to the offence contrary to s. 1(3), there appears to be no good reason why it does not also apply to the offence contrary to s. 1(2) and 1(3A). Whether it is still good law that there must be a reasonable basis for the belief, or whether the belief has only to be an honest one, is a question which is open. See the discussion of 'mistake' at **A3.2** to **A3.6**. For reasons of compliance with the ECHR, Article 6(2), it is anticipated that the burden will be confirmed as lying on the prosecution, see *A-G's Ref (No. 1 of 2004)* [2004] 1 WLR 2111 and **F3.13** ***et seq.*** B13.8

Meaning of 'Premises'

B13.9 Lord Widgery CJ, giving the judgment of the Divisional Court in *Thurrock Urban District Council v Shina* (1972) 70 LGR 301, decided that the word 'premises' in the Rent Act 1965, s. 30, the precursor to the Protection from Eviction Act 1977, should be given its normal wide meaning. He had no doubt that a single room, together with shared use of a bathroom and kitchen, did fall within the meaning of 'premises'. 'Premises' may include a caravan, together with the land upon which it stands (see *Norton v Knowles* [1969] 1 QB 572).

Meaning of 'Occupying Premises as a Residence'

B13.10 'Occupying premises as a residence' has the same meaning as it had in the Rent Act 1977 (*Schon v Camden London Borough Council* (1986) 84 LGR 830). Thus, a person may occupy premises as his residence although he is physically absent from them, provided that the absence is not, and is not intended to be, permanent, and either his spouse or some other member of the family is physically in occupation or, at the very least, his furniture and belongings remain in the premises.

Elements Specific to s. 1(2)

B13.11 **Unlawfully Depriving Occupier** The Protection from Eviction Act 1977, s. 3(1), makes it unlawful for the owner to enforce against the occupier, otherwise than by court proceedings, his right to recover possession of the premises where those premises have been let as a dwelling under a tenancy (which is not a statutorily protected tenancy or an excluded tenancy) and the tenancy has come to an end but the occupier continues to reside in the premises. In *Patel v Pirabakaran* [2006] EWCA Civ 685, a case under s. 2 of the 1977 Act on the meaning of 'let as a dwelling', Wilson LJ said (at [34]): 'the phrase "let as a dwelling" in s. 2 of the Act of 1977 means "let wholly or partly as a dwelling" and so applies to premises which are let for mixed residential and business purposes'.

The Court of Appeal in *Yuthiwattana* (1984) 80 Cr App R 55 was satisfied that s. 1(2) is concerned with eviction, and so an unlawful deprivation must have the character of an eviction. Kerr LJ, giving the judgment of the Court, held that it was going too far to require an eviction to be of a permanent character. He said (at p. 63):

> For instance, if the owner of the premises unlawfully tells the occupier that he must leave the premises from some period, it may be months or weeks, and then excludes him from the premises, or does anything else with the result that the occupier effectively has to leave the premises and find other accommodation, then it would in our view be open to a jury to convict the owner under subsection (2) on the ground that he had unlawfully deprived the occupier of his occupation. On the other hand, cases which are more properly described as 'locking out' or not admitting an occupier on one or even more isolated occasions, so that in effect he continues to be allowed to occupy the premises but is then unable to enter, seem to us to fall appropriately under subsection (3)(a) or (b), which deal with acts of harassment.

Consequently the conviction under a count charging the offence contrary to s. 1(2) had to be quashed because the occupier was excluded for only one night. This decision was followed by the Divisional Court in *Costelloe v London Borough of Camden* [1986] Crim LR 249, where Glidewell LJ held that there is an offence under s. 1(2) where the landlord intends to exclude the occupier permanently and the occupier thinks he has been excluded permanently, even if the landlord then changes his mind and the occupier is later admitted. What matters is whether the exclusion appears to be permanent. Woolf J put the point slightly differently saying:

> The proper test is: What was the nature of the exclusion? Was it, whether it be short or long, an exclusion designed to evict the tenant from the premises? If it was, then it falls within section 1(2). If on the other hand all that occurred was the deprivation of the occupation of the premises

for a short period of time and that was the object of the exercise, then it would not fall within section 1(2).

Belief that Occupier had Ceased to Reside in Premises No offence is committed if the accused believes, on reasonable grounds, that a residential occupier has ceased to reside in the premises. This is a matter for the jury to determine. Thus the trial judge erred in *Davidson-Acres* [1980] Crim LR 50, when he himself decided questions as to the time and existence of the accused's belief. **B13.12**

Elements Specific to s. 1(3)

Harassment with Intent It is essential under this offence to establish the necessary intent. If it is not present, it may be that an offence contrary to the Protection from Eviction Act 1977, s. 1(3A), has been committed. It has been held that the meaning of the word 'intent' must be approached in the same way as in the law of murder (see **B1.6** and **B1.11**, as indicated in *AMK (Property Management) Ltd* [1985] Crim LR 600). On the other hand, the House of Lords in *Burke* [1991] AC 135 held that 'intention' in this context means with the purpose or motive of causing the occupier to give up occupation of the premises. This would appear to be a more limited understanding of the word 'intent' than usually applies in criminal law, and might not, therefore, be followed in a case to which the usual understanding actually applied on the facts. See generally, **A2.2**. The intention must be either to cause the occupier to give up the premises (s. 1(3)(a)), or to refrain from exercising any right or pursuing any remedy in respect of the premises (s. 1(3)(b)). **B13.13**

With regard to s. 1(3)(a), the Court of Appeal allowed the appeals in part in *AMK* (*Property Management*) *Ltd* [1985] Crim LR 600 because the trial judge had not made clear to the jury that the consequences of the building work designed to refurbish a block of flats were not simply to be equated with an intention to evict. An intention to evict must be established and, whilst the works could have been carried out without an intention to evict, the company's acts were reasonable and not of the kind covered by s. 1(3)(a). Ormrod LJ, giving the judgment of the Court of Appeal in *McCall v Abelesz* [1976] QB 585 (a decision on the Rent Act 1965, s. 30), held that it is not sufficient to establish that the accused was completely indifferent as to cutting off the gas supply to the occupier, nor would it be sufficient for the accused simply to allow things to happen which might have the effect of causing the occupier to leave, since these could not be equated with an intent to cause the occupier to give up the occupation of the premises. If the accused realised that there was a real likelihood that these activities would result in the occupier leaving, the general approach to the meaning of 'intent' might result in a decision that the accused did intend to cause the occupier to give up occupation of the premises. Applying the orthodox interpretation of intent, the requirement should be that the accused at least foresaw the occupier leaving as a virtually certain result of his conduct (as to the general approach to 'intent', see **A2.2**).

With regard to s. 1(3)(b), the Divisional Court in *Schon v Camden London Borough Council* (1986) 84 LGR 830 held that 'an intention to persuade [the occupier] to leave for a limited period of time in order to enable work to be done and thereafter to allow her to return, was not an intent to cause her to give up her occupation of the premises. Notwithstanding that, it would be an intent which fell within the second intention within s. 1(3) because it would be an intention to cause her to refrain from exercising her right to live in the premises and to be physically present in the premises.' Since the charge was specifically worded to refer to s. 1(3)(b), the necessary intent was not established and the appeal against conviction was allowed.

Belief that Person Harassed not Residential Occupier The decision of the Court of Appeal on this matter in *Phekoo* [1981] 1 WLR 1117 applies to this offence, and is considered at **B13.8**. **B13.14**

B13.15 **Acts Likely to Interfere with Peace or Comfort** The Protection from Eviction Act 1977, uses the phrase 'does acts', which requires that there be conduct on the part of the accused, but that phrase does not require that there be more than one act (*Polycarpou* (1978) 9 HLR 129). Consequently, removing the sole source of heat of a tenant would satisfy this requirement of the offence.

It may be that the Court of Appeal in *McCall v Abelesz* [1976] 1 QB 585 had in mind the need to establish personal conduct, as distinct from merely taking advantage of the consequences of the acts of others with the accused actually doing nothing. In *Ahmad* (1987) 84 Cr App R 64, the Court of Appeal held that the phrase 'does acts' does not impose a responsibility to rectify damage which the accused has already caused by an act done innocently. Thus, a later failure to take steps to rectify what he has caused, even if with the requisite intent, is not the doing of an act or acts for the purposes of s. 1(3). Clearly an act and not an omission is required, and the doctrine established by the House of Lords in *Miller* [1983] 2 AC 161 (see **A1.16**) does not apply. In *Yuthiwattana* (1984) 80 Cr App R 55, in addition to *the failure* to provide a front door key, which would not of itself have sufficed, there was proof of other sufficient acts which included entering the occupier's room without permission, removing his record player and records, and shouting at him.

Kerr LJ, delivering the judgment of the Court of Appeal in *Yuthiwattana* (1984) 80 Cr App R 55, and explaining the *obiter dictum* of Ormrod LJ in *McCall v Abelesz* [1976] 1 QB 585, held that it is not necessary that the acts in question should constitute a breach of the civil law, but simply that the accused's act be one calculated to interfere with the occupier's peace and comfort which was intended to cause him to give up his occupation of the premises. *Yuthiwattana* was approved by the House of Lords in *Burke* [1991] AC 135.

The relevant acts must be ones 'likely to' interfere with peace or comfort. It should be noted that until the amendment introduced by the Housing Act 1988, s. 29(1), this phrase read 'calculated to', which caused uncertainty. The phrase 'likely to' is a matter of objective analysis, not of realisation or calculation on the part of the accused.

B13.16 **Persistently Withdrawing or Withholding Services** The Divisional Court in *Westminster City Council v Peart* (1968) 66 LGR 561, a decision on the Rent Act 1965, s. 30, held that 'persistently' in the identically worded precursor of the present provision, refers to the withholding of as well as the withdrawing of services. Withdrawal of a service on one day was not sufficient to satisfy the element of persistency. Lord Parker CJ, giving the judgment of the court, left open the question of whether failing to pay for a gas or electricity supply, as a result of which a gas or electricity company disconnects the service, can properly be described as the landlord withholding a service. Clearly, where the accused permanently cuts off the electricity supply, there is a persistent withholding (see *Boaks* (1967) 205 EG 103, a decision on the Rent Act 1965, s. 30).

Elements Specific to s. 1(3A)

B13.17 **Landlord Harassing Residential Occupier** The points made in relation to the offence contrary to s. 1(3) regarding the meaning of 'does acts likely to interfere with the peace or comfort of the residential occupier or members of his household' and 'persistently withdraws or withholds services reasonably required for the occupation of the premises in question as a residence', apply in full to the s. 1(3A) offence. However, the offence contrary to s. 1(3A) differs in that it can be committed only by a landlord (or agent) and it is not necessary to establish intention, although knowledge or belief must be established.

B13.18 **Meaning of 'Landlord'**

Protection from Eviction Act 1977, s. 1

(3C) In subsection (3A) above 'landlord', in relation to a residential occupier of any premises, means the person who, but for—

(a) the residential occupier's right to remain in occupation of the premises, or
(b) a restriction on the person's right to recover possession of the premises,
would be entitled to occupation of the premises and any superior landlord under whom that person derives title.

If it is necessary to discover the identity of the landlord, a notice may be served on his agent or other person under s. 7 of the Act, requiring the disclosure of the landlord's full name and address. If such is not forthcoming, the person on whom the notice is served is guilty of a summary offence and liable to a fine not exceeding level 4 on the standard scale.

Knowledge or Belief The landlord, though not requiring an intention, must know or have reasonable cause to believe that the residential occupier is likely to be caused to give up occupation of the premises (see *R (McGowan) v Brent Justices* (2002) 166 JP 29). B13.19

Specific Defences

The Protection from Eviction Act 1977, s. 1(2), provides that a person is not guilty of the eviction offence if 'he proves that he believed, and had reasonable cause to believe, that the residential occupier had ceased to reside in the premises'. The accused must prove the belief and its reasonable foundation on a balance of probabilities (*Desai* (1992) *The Times*, 3 February 1992). B13.20

Protection from Eviction Act 1977, s. 1

(3B) A person shall not be guilty of an offence under subsection (3A) above if he proves that he had reasonable grounds for doing the acts or withdrawing or withholding the services in question.

The imposition of a legal burden upon the accused is open to challenge in the light of *A-G's Ref (No.1 of 2004)* [2004] 1 WLR 2111 (see **F3.13** *et seq.*). The likely success of such a challenge is questionable since this defence is almost in the form of a due diligence defence.

Related Offences

The offences contrary to the Criminal Law Act 1977, part I (see **B13.22** to **B13.32**), may be relevant. In particular, even if a person's activity does not fall within the Protection from Eviction Act 1977 offence because, for example, the 'victim' is not a residential occupier, the offence contrary to the Criminal Law Act 1977, s. 6, using or threatening violence to secure entry, may nevertheless cover the relevant activity. B13.21

USE OR THREAT OF VIOLENCE FOR PURPOSE OF SECURING ENTRY TO PREMISES

Definition

It is a summary offence, by virtue of the Criminal Law Act 1977, s. 6(1), for any person, without lawful authority, to use or threaten violence for the purpose of securing entry into any premises for himself or for any other person, provided that: B13.22

(a) there is someone present on those premises at the time who is opposed to the entry which the violence is intended to secure; and
(b) the person using or threatening the violence knows that that is the case.

Procedure and Sentence

The Criminal Law Act 1977, s. 12(8), provides that 'no rule of law ousting the jurisdiction of magistrates' courts to try offences where a dispute of title to property is involved shall preclude magistrates' courts from trying offences under this part of this Act'. By virtue of B13.23

s. 6(5), a person found guilty of this offence is liable to imprisonment for a term not exceeding six months or to a fine not exceeding level 5 on the standard scale or to both.

Elements

B13.24 Some of the elements of this offence are further defined by the Criminal Law Act 1977:

(a) *Uses or threatens violence*: according to s. 6(4)(a), it is immaterial whether the violence in question is directed against the person or against property.

(b) *Entry*: according to s. 6(4)(b), it is immaterial whether the entry which the violence is intended to secure is for the purpose of acquiring possession of the premises in question or for any other purpose. As to the meaning of entry in the analogous offence of burglary, see **B4.61**.

(c) *Premises*: according to s. 12, this means any building, any part of a building under separate occupation, any land ancillary to a building, the site comprising any building or buildings together with any land ancillary thereto. By s. 12(2) the references to a building apply to any structure other than a moveable one, and to any moveable structure, vehicle or vessel designed or adapted for residential purposes; and further that (i) part of a building is under separate occupation if anyone is in occupation or entitled to occupation of that part as distinct from the whole, and (ii) land is ancillary to a building if it is adjacent to it and used (or intended for use) in connection with the occupation of that building or any part of it.

(d) *Lawful authority* is considered in s. 6(2), which provides that the fact that a person has any interest in or right to possession or occupation of any premises shall not constitute lawful authority for the use or threat of violence by him or anyone else for the purpose of securing his entry into those premises.

Specific Defence

B13.25 No offence is committed if the person is a displaced residential occupier or a protected intending occupier of the premises in question or is acting on behalf of such an occupier. If the accused adduces sufficient evidence that he was, or was acting on behalf of, such an occupier he is presumed to be, or to be acting on behalf of, such an occupier unless the contrary is proved by the prosecution (Criminal Law Act 1977, s. 6(1A)). The imposition of a legal burden upon the accused is open to challenge in the light of the human rights cases on the 'reverse burden' (see **F3.13**).

B13.26 **Displaced Residential Occupier** Section 6(7) of the Criminal Law Act 1977 makes clear that it is s. 12 which determines when a person is to be regarded as a 'displaced residential occupier' of any premises or of any access to any premises, which involves also considering the meaning of 'trespasser' (the meaning of 'premises' has been considered at **B13.24**).

Section 12(3) defines 'displaced residential occupier' by providing that any person who was occupying any premises as a residence immediately before being excluded from occupation by anyone who entered those premises, or any access to those premises, as a trespasser, is a displaced residential occupier of the premises for the purposes of this part of the Act, so long as he continues to be excluded from occupation of the premises by the original trespasser or any subsequent trespasser. Such a person is also regarded, by s. 12(5), as a displaced residential occupier of any access to those premises.

Section 12(4) provides that a person, who was himself occupying the premises in question as a trespasser immediately before being excluded from occupation, is not a displaced residential occupier of the premises. Section 12(6) provides an extended meaning of 'trespasser' so that anyone who enters or is on or in occupation of any premises by virtue of (a) any title derived from a trespasser, or (b) any licence or consent given by a trespasser or by a person deriving title from a trespasser, is himself treated as a trespasser for present purposes alone, and phrases involving a reference to a trespasser will be construed accordingly. Further s. 12(7) provides that anyone who is on any premises as a trespasser does not cease to be a trespasser by virtue of being allowed time to leave the premises, nor does anyone cease to be a displaced residential occupier of any premises by virtue of any such allowance of time to a trespasser.

It is also important to consider the meaning of 'access' which is provided by s. 12. It means, in relation to any premises, any part of any site or building within which those premises are situated which constitutes an ordinary means of access to those premises (whether or not that is its sole or primary use).

Protected Intending Occupier Section 6(7) of the Criminal Law Act 1977 also indicates that s. 12A has effect for determining when any person is to be regarded as a protected intending occupier of any premises (or any access to those premises: s. 12A(11)). **B13.27**

Criminal Law Act 1977, s. 12A

(1) For the purposes of this part of this Act [part II] an individual is a protected intending occupier of any premises at any time if at that time he falls within subsection (2), (4) or (6) below.

(2) An individual is a protected intending occupier of any premises if—
  (a) he has in those premises a freehold interest or a leasehold interest with not less than two years still to run;
  (b) he requires the premises for his own occupation as a residence;
  (c) he is excluded from occupation of the premises by a person who entered them, or any access to them, as a trespasser; and
  (d) he or a person acting on his behalf holds a written statement—
    (i) which specifies his interest in the premises;
    (ii) which states that he requires the premises for occupation as a residence for himself; and
    (iii) with respect to which the requirements in subsection (3) below are fulfilled.

(3) The requirements referred to in subsection (2)(d)(iii) above are—
  (a) that the statement is signed by the person whose interest is specified in it in the presence of a justice of the peace or commissioner for oaths; and
  (b) that the justice of the peace or commissioner for oaths has subscribed his name as a witness to the signature.

(4) An individual is also a protected intending occupier of any premises if—
  (a) he has a tenancy of those premises (other than a tenancy falling within subsection (2)(a) above or (6)(a) below) or a licence to occupy those premises granted by a person with a freehold interest or a leasehold interest with not less than two years still to run in the premises;
  (b) he requires the premises for his own occupation as a residence;
  (c) he is excluded from occupation of the premises by a person who entered them, or any access to them, as a trespasser; and
  (d) he or a person acting on his behalf holds a written statement—
    (i) which states that he has been granted a tenancy of those premises or a licence to occupy those premises;
    (ii) which specifies the interest in the premises of the person who granted that tenancy or licence to occupy ('the landlord');
    (iii) which states that he requires the premises for occupation as a residence for himself; and
    (iv) with respect to which the requirements in subsection (5) below are fulfilled.

(5) The requirements referred to in subsection (4)(d)(iv) above are—
  (a) that the statement is signed by the landlord and by the tenant or licensee in the presence of a justice of the peace or commissioner for oaths;
  (b) that the justice of the peace or commissioner for oaths has subscribed his name as a witness to the signatures.

(6) An individual is also a protected intending occupier of any premises if—
  (a) he has a tenancy of those premises (other than a tenancy falling within subsection (2)(a) or (4)(a) above) or a licence to occupy those premises granted by an authority to which this subsection applies;

(b) he requires the premises for his own occupation as a residence;
(c) he is excluded from occupation of the premises by a person who entered the premises, or any access to them, as a trespasser; and
(d) there has been issued to him by or on behalf of the authority referred to in paragraph (a) above a certificate stating that—
(i) he has been granted a tenancy of those premises or a licence to occupy those premises as a residence by the authority; and
(ii) the authority which granted that tenancy or licence to occupy is one to which this subsection applies, being of a description specified in the certificate.

(7) Subsection (6) above applies to the following authorities—
(a) any body mentioned in section 14 of the Rent Act 1977 (landlord's interest belonging to local authority etc.);
(b) the Housing Corporation;
(c) [repealed]; and
(d) a registered social landlord within the meaning of the Housing Act 1985 . . .

(7A) Subsection (6) also applies to the Secretary of State if the tenancy or licence is granted by him under Part III of the Housing Associations Act 1985.

If a person makes a statement for the purposes of s. 12A(2)(d) or (4) which he knows to be false in a material particular (see **B6.12** for meaning), or if he recklessly makes such a statement which is false in a material particular, he commits an offence (s. 12A(8)) and is liable on summary conviction to imprisonment for a term not exceeding six months or a fine not exceeding level 5 on the standard scale or both (s. 12A(10)).

ADVERSE OCCUPATION OF RESIDENTIAL PREMISES

Definition

B13.28 **Criminal Law Act 1977, s. 7**

(1) . . . any person who is on any premises as a trespasser after having entered as such is guilty of an offence if he fails to leave those premises on being required to do so by or on behalf of—
(a) a displaced residential occupier of the premises; or
(b) an individual who is a protected intending occupier of the premises.

Procedure and Sentence

B13.29 The offence is triable summarily (Criminal Law Act 1977, s. 7(5)). Where the offence relates to a protected intending occupier, a document purporting to be a certificate under the Criminal Law Act 1977, s. 12A(6)(d) (see **B13.27**) is to be received in evidence and, unless the contrary is proved, is deemed to have been issued by or on behalf of the authority stated in the certificate (s. 12A(9)(b)).

The maximum penalty is imprisonment for a term not exceeding six months or a fine not exceeding level 5 on the standard scale or both (s. 7(5)).

Elements

B13.30 Premises includes a reference to any access to them, whether or not such access itself constitutes premises within the meaning of the Criminal Law Act 1977, part II (s. 7(4)).

For the meaning of 'displaced residential occupier' and 'protected intending occupier', see **B13.26** and **B13.27**.

Specific Defences

B13.31 Section 7(3) provides that it is a defence for the accused to prove that:

(a) he believed that the person requiring him to leave the premises was not a displaced residential occupier or protected intending occupier of the premises or a person acting on behalf of a displaced residential occupier or protected intending occupier (Criminal Law Act 1977, s. 7(2));

(b) the premises in question are or form part of premises used mainly for non-residential purposes, and that he was not on any part of the premises used wholly or mainly for residential purposes.

The imposition of a legal burden upon the accused is open to challenge in the light of the human rights cases on the 'reverse burden' (see **F3.13** *et seq.*).

Where the accused was requested to leave the premises by a person claiming to be or to act on behalf of a protected intending occupier of the premises, it is a defence for the accused to prove that, although asked to do so by the accused at the time the accused was requested to leave, that person failed at that time to produce to the accused a s. 12A statement or certificate (s. 12A(9)(a)) (see **B13.27**).

TRESPASSING DURING THE CURRENCY OF AN INTERIM POSSESSION ORDER

Definition

Criminal Justice and Public Order Act 1994, s. 76 **B13.32**

(2) . . . a person who is present on premises as a trespasser at any time during the currency of the order commits an offence.

. . .

(4) A person who was in occupation of the premises at the time of service of the order but leaves them commits an offence if he re-enters the premises as a trespasser or attempts to do so after the expiry of the order but within the period of one year beginning with the day on which it was served.

Procedure and Sentence

The offences are triable summarily only (CJPOA 1994, s. 76(5)). **B13.33**

The maximum penalty is a term of imprisonment not exceeding six months or a fine not exceeding level 5 on the standard scale or both (s. 76(5)).

Elements

References to 'the order' are to be construed as referring to an interim possession order which has been made in respect of any premises and served in accordance with rules of court (CJPOA 1994, s. 76(1)); references to 'the premises' are to the premises covered by the order (s. 76(1)). For the meaning of 'premises', which has the same meaning as in the Criminal Law Act 1977, part II, see **B13.24**. An interim possession order means an interim possession order (so entitled) made under rules of court for the bringing of summary proceedings for possession of premises which are occupied by trespassers (CJPOA 1994 (s. 75(4)). **B13.34**

A person who is in occupation of the premises at the time of service of the order is to be treated for the purposes of s. 76 as being present as a trespasser (s. 76(6)).

Specific Defence

Section 76(3) of the CJPOA 1994 provides a specific defence to a charge under s. 76(2). No offence is committed by a person if he leaves the premises within 24 hours of the time of service of the order and does not return, or a copy of the order was not fixed to the premises in accordance with rules of court. The legal burden of proving the defence is imposed upon the accused; this burden is open to challenge in the light of the human rights cases on the 'reverse burden' (see **F3.13**). **B13.35**

B

Part B Offences

INTERIM POSSESSION ORDERS: FALSE OR MISLEADING STATEMENTS

Definition

B13.36 **Criminal Justice and Public Order Act 1994, s. 75**

(1) A person commits an offence if, for the purpose of obtaining an interim possession order, he—
  (a) makes a statement which he knows to be false or misleading in a material particular; or
  (b) recklessly makes a statement which is false or misleading in a material particular.

(2) A person commits an offence if, for the purpose of resisting the making of an interim possession order, he—
  (a) makes a statement which he knows to be false or misleading in a material particular, or
  (b) recklessly makes a statement which is false or misleading in a material particular.

Procedure and Sentence

B13.37 This offence is triable either way (CJPOA 1994, s. 75(3)).

The maximum penalty is, on indictment, imprisonment for a term not exceeding two years or a fine or both, and, summarily, imprisonment for a term not exceeding six months or a fine not exceeding the statutory maximum or both (s. 75(3)).

Elements

B13.38 'Statement' in relation to an interim possession order, means any statement, in writing or oral and whether as to fact or belief, made in or for the purposes of the proceedings (CJPOA 1994, s. 75(4)). For the meaning of 'interim possession order', see **B13.36**; for the meaning of 'premises', see **B13.24**.

AGGRAVATED TRESPASS

Definition

B13.39 **Criminal Justice and Public Order Act 1994, s. 68**

(1) A person commits the offence of aggravated trespass if he trespasses on land and, in relation to any lawful activity which persons are engaging in or are about to engage in on that or adjoining land, does there anything which is intended by him to have the effect—
  (a) of intimidating those persons or any of them so as to deter them or any of them from engaging in that activity,
  (b) of obstructing that activity, or
  (c) of disrupting that activity.

Procedure and Sentence

B13.40 The offence is triable summarily (CJPOA 1994, s. 68(3)). A charge is not void for duplicity where it states that the accused intended to 'deter, disrupt or obstruct' a hunt because these elements overlap. Therefore, there is no need for each element to be the subject of a separate charge (*Nelder v DPP* (1998) *The Times*, 11 June 1998).

The maximum penalty is imprisonment for a term not exceeding three months or a fine not exceeding level 4 on the standard scale or both (s. 68(3)).

Elements

B13.41 There are three elements to the offence: trespass on land in the open air; an intention to have one of three effects stated in subsections (a), (b) and (c) (despite the lack of the word 'or' after (a), Rafferty J in *Tilly v DPP* (2001) 166 JP 22 confirmed that this is the correct interpretation); and an act done towards that end (*Winder v DPP* (1996) 160 JP 713 and *Barnard v DPP* (1999) *The Times*, 9 November 1999). Whether the activity is lawful is defined by the CJPOA 1994, s. 68(2).

Criminal Justice and Public Order Act 1994, s. 68

(2) Activity on any occasion on the part of a person or persons on land is 'lawful' for the purpose of this section if he or they may engage in the activity on the land on that occasion without committing an offence or trespassing on the land.

This requires that the activity or task be lawful. It does not require that the way it is to be done must be lawful. Clearing land and felling trees was the activity in question in *Hibberd v Muddle* (1996 unreported); it was held to be a lawful activity, even though the means used may have been in breach of the Health and Safety at Work etc. Act 1974. There is an 'activity' only where someone is present on the land who could be intimidated or not allowed to get on with what they are entitled to (*Tilly v DPP*). By the CJPOA 1994, s. 68(5), 'land' does not include those highways and roads excluded for the purposes of s. 61(9) (see **B13.49**). Where the charge is under s. 68(1)(c), an intention to disrupt must be proved, but actual disruption need not be established (*Winder v DPP* (1996) 160 JP 713). Further, the Divisional Court was satisfied that the decision of the magistrate that the requisite intention was present was justified, as the trespassers ran towards a hunt, that being an act that was not merely preparatory to actual disruption, although that running was not itself intended to disrupt the hunt. As to the possible application of the defence of property as an answer to the charge, see *DPP v Bayer* [2004] 1 WLR 2856.

In *Ayliffe v DPP* [2006] QB 227, the Divisional Court was concerned with whether the offence was committed where protesters trespassed on sites and interfered with activity there that was in preparation for action in the Gulf and Iraq and held that (1) that, following *Jones* [2007] 1 AC 136, in the absence of express provision to the contrary, the term 'offence' in a domestic statute was ordinarily treated as referring to an offence committed in the domestic sphere against a common law or statutory rule, and, since the 1994 Act did not define the word 'offence', that term, as used in s. 68(2), was to be understood as referring to an offence under domestic criminal law and not to the crime of aggression in international law. The crime of aggression in international law had not been assimilated into domestic law.

Power to Remove Persons

Under the CJPOA 1994, s. 69(1), the senior police officer present at the scene has the power to direct a person or persons to leave land if he reasonably believes: **B13.42**

(a) that a person is committing, has committed or intends to commit the offence of aggravated trespass on land; or
(b) that two or more persons are trespassing on land and are present there with the common purpose of intimidating persons so as to deter them from engaging in a lawful activity or of obstructing or disrupting a lawful activity.

If a person knowing that a direction under s. 69(1) has been given which applies to him fails to leave the land as soon as practicable or, having left, again enters the land as a trespasser within the period of three months beginning with the day on which the direction was given, he commits an offence and is liable on summary conviction to imprisonment for a term not exceeding three months or a fine not exceeding level 4 on the standard scale or both (s. 69(3)). If the police officer giving the direction does not communicate it, any constable at the scene may communicate it (s. 69(2)).

It is a defence for the accused to show (i) that he was not trespassing on land, or (ii) that he has a reasonable excuse for failing to leave the land as soon as practicable or, as the case may be, for again entering the land as a trespasser (s. 69(4)).

FAILURE TO LEAVE OR RE-ENTRY TO LAND AFTER POLICE DIRECTION TO LEAVE

Definition

B13.43 **Criminal Justice and Public Order Act 1994, s. 61**

(4) If a person knowing that a direction under subsection (1) above has been given which applies to him—
(a) fails to leave the land as soon as reasonably practicable, or
(b) having left again enters the land as a trespasser within the period of three months beginning with the day on which the direction was given,
he commits an offence . . .

Procedure and Sentence

B13.44 The offence is triable summarily (CJPOA 1994, s. 61(4)).

The maximum penalty is imprisonment for a term not exceeding three months or a fine not exceeding level 4 on the standard scale or both (s. 61(4)).

Elements

B13.45 **Criminal Justice and Public Order Act 1994, s. 61**

(1) If the senior police officer present at the scene reasonably believes that two or more persons are trespassing on land and are present there with the common purpose of residing there for any period, that reasonable steps have been taken by or on behalf of the occupier to ask them to leave and—
(a) that any of those persons has caused damage to the land or to property on the land or used threatening, abusive or insulting words or behaviour towards the occupier, a member of his family or an employee or agent of his, or
(b) that those persons have between them six or more vehicles on the land, he may direct those persons, or any of them, to leave the land and to remove any vehicles or other property they have with them on the land.

In *R (Fuller) v Chief Constable of Dorset Police* [2002] 3 All ER 57, the court decided that s. 61 did not breach the ECHR, Article 6, because, although the police procedure applied without recourse to a court, it did not prevent a challenge through the courts to the power of arrest or prosecution or to the decision of the landowner (the local authority). Nor was s. 61 in breach of Article 8; whilst a measure that prevents a traveller or gypsy from residing in his vehicle on land may breach Article 8, it does not necessarily do so, following *South Buckinghamshire DC v Porter* [2002] 1 All ER 425, as it may be justifiable under Article 8(2)) or, for similar reasons as applied to Article 8 under Article 1 of the First Protocol. Even more clearly, there was no breach of Article 3. (As to Article 8 rights and trespassers, see also *Kay v London Borough of Lambeth* [2006] UKHL 10.)

The offence is committed only where a direction to leave has been given. The court in *Fuller* decided that it followed from construing s. 61 narrowly that, as a direction could be given to leave at some time in the future, the offence could not be committed before the time permitted in the direction had expired. Further, if the trespassers had not had an opportunity to comply with the landowner's request to leave, a direction under s. 61 was not lawful or valid.

Where the senior police officer reasonably believes that the person was not originally a trespasser on the land, a direction may still be made if the person has become a trespasser and the senior police officer reasonably believes that the conditions in s. 61(1) are satisfied after the person became a trespasser (s. 61(2)).

B13.46 **Definitions** Section 61(9) of the CJPOA 1994 defines certain terms used in the section.

(a) 'Land' does not include:
  (i) buildings other than agricultural buildings (within the meaning of the Local Government Finance Act 1988, sch. 5, paras. 3 to 8) or scheduled monuments (within the meaning of the Ancient Monuments and Archaeological Areas Act 1979);
  (ii) land forming part of a highway unless it is a footpath, bridleway or byway open to all traffic within the meaning of the Wildlife and Countryside Act 1981, part III, is a restricted byway within the meaning of the Countryside and Rights of Way Act 2000, part II or is a cycle track under the Highways Act 1980 or the Cycle Tracks Act 1984.

(b) 'Occupier' means the person entitled to possession of the land by virtue of an estate or interest held by him.

(c) Subject to the extension of its meaning with regard to common land (see below), 'trespass' means trespass as against the occupier of the land.

(d) In relation to damage to property on land, 'property' has the meaning in the Criminal Damage Act 1971, s. 10(1) (see **B8.6**), and 'damage' includes the deposit of any substance capable of polluting the land.

(e) 'Vehicle' includes:
  (i) any vehicle, whether or not it is in a fit state for use on roads, and includes any chassis or body, with or without wheels, appearing to have formed part of such a vehicle, and any load carried by, and anything attached to, such a vehicle; and
  (ii) a caravan as defined in the Caravan Sites and Control of Development Act 1960, s. 29(1).

(f) A person may be regarded as having a purpose of residing in a place notwithstanding that he has a home elsewhere.

Where the persons are on common land (as defined in the Commons Registration Act 1965, s. 22), the references to trespassing or trespassers are references to acts and persons doing acts which constitute either a trespass as against the occupier or an infringement of the commoners' rights; references to 'the occupier' include the commoners or any of them or, in the case of common land to which the public has access, the local authority as well as any commoner (s. 61(7)). Persons are not trespassers as against any commoner or the local authority if they are permitted to be there by the other occupier (s. 61(8)(b)).

The person must know of the direction and, it would appear, that it applies to him (s. 61(4)). If the police officer giving the direction does not communicate it to the persons to be removed, any constable may do so (s. 61(3)).

Specific Defence

It is a defence for the accused to show that he was not trespassing on the land, or that he had a reasonable excuse for failing to leave the land as soon as reasonably practicable or, as the case may be, for again entering the land as a trespasser (CJPOA 1994, s. 61(6)). The imposition of a legal burden upon the accused is open to challenge in the light of the human rights cases on the 'reverse burden' (see **F3.13** ***et seq.***). **B13.47**

Powers of Seizure

A constable may seize and remove vehicles after a direction under the CJPOA 1994, s. 61, has been given, provided the criteria in s. 62 are satisfied. **B13.48**

B

Part B Offences

TRESPASSER'S FAILURE TO LEAVE LAND ON POLICE DIRECTION AFTER OCCUPIER'S REQUEST

Definition

Criminal Justice and Public Order Act 1994, s. 62B

B13.49 (1) A person commits an offence if he knows that a direction under section 62A(1) has been given which applies to him and—
(a) he fails to leave the relevant land as soon as reasonably practicable, or
(b) he enters any land in the area of the relevant local authority as a trespasser before the end of the relevant period with the intention of residing there.

The CJPOA 1994, ss. 62A to 62E, create complementary offences and provide powers to remove trespassers where an alternative site is available.

Procedure and Sentence

B13.50 The offence is triable summarily (CJPOA 1994, s. 62B(3)).

The maximum penalty is imprisonment for a term not exceeding three months, a fine not exceeding level 4 on the standard scale, or both (s. 62B(3)).

Elements

The power of the police to require someone to leave is provided by s. 62A:

B13.51 **Criminal Justice and Public Order Act 1994, s. 62A**

(1) If the senior police officer present at a scene reasonably believes that the conditions in subsection (2) are satisfied in relation to a person and land, he may direct the person—
(a) to leave the land:
(b) to remove any vehicle and other property he has with him on the land.
(2) The conditions are—
(a) that the person and one or more others ('the trespassers') are trespassing on the land;
(b) that the trespassers have between them at least one vehicle on the land;
(c) that the trespassers are present on the land with the common purpose of residing there for any period;
(d) if it appears to the officer that the person has one or more caravans in his possession or under his control on the land, that there is a suitable pitch on a relevant caravan site for that caravan or for each of those caravans;
(e) that the occupier of the land or a person acting on his behalf has asked the police to remove the trespassers from the land.
(3) A direction under subsection (1) may be communicated to the person to whom it applies by any constable at the scene.
(4) Subsection (5) applies if—
(a) a police officer proposes to give a direction under subsection (1) in relation to a person and land, and
(b) it appears to him that the person has one or more caravans in his possession or under his control on the land.
(5) The officer must consult every local authority within whose area the land is situated as to whether there is a suitable pitch for the caravan or each of the caravans on a relevant caravan site which is situated in the local authority's area.

B13.52 **Definitions** The following terms are defined by the CJPOA 1994, s. 62A(6). 'Caravan' and 'caravan site' have the same meaning as in the Caravan Sites and Control of Development Act 1960, part 1. 'Relevant caravan site' means a caravan site which is (a) situated in the area of a local authority within whose area the land is situated; and (b) managed by a relevant site manager. 'Relevant site manager' means (a) a local authority within whose area the land is situated; (b) a registered social landlord (which definition may be amended by the Secretary of

State: s. 62A(7) and (8)). 'Registered social landlord' means a body registered as a social landlord under the Housing Act 1996, chapter 1.

The 'relevant period' in s. 62B(1) is the period of three months starting with the day on which the direction is given (s. 62B(2)).

'Land' does not include buildings other than (a) agricultural buildings within the meaning of the Local Government Finance Act 1988, sch. 5, paras. 3 to 8 or (b) scheduled monuments within the meaning of the Ancient Monuments and Archaeological Areas Act 1979 (s. 62E(2)). 'Local authority' means (a) in Greater London, a London borough or the Common Council of the City of London, (b) in England outside Greater London, a county council, a district council or the Council of the Isles of Scilly, (c) in Wales, a county council or a county borough council (s. 62E(3)). 'Occupier', 'trespass', 'trespassing' and 'trespasser' have the meanings given by s. 61 in relation to England and Wales (see **B13.45**) (s. 62E(4)). 'The relevant land' means the land in respect of which a direction under s. 62A(1) is given (s. 62E(5)). 'The relevant local authority' means (a) if the relevant land is situated in the area of more than one local authority (but is not in the Isles of Scilly), the district council or county borough council within whose area the relevant land is situated, (b) if the relevant land is situated in the Isles of Scilly, the Council of the Isles of Scilly, (c) in any other case, the local authority within whose area the relevant land is situated (s. 62E(6)). 'Vehicle' has the meaning given by s. 61 (see **B13.45**) (s. 62E(7)). A person may be regarded as having a purpose of residing in a place even if he has a home elsewhere (s. 62E(8)).

Common Land Modifications The CJPOA 1994, ss. 62A to 62C have effect in relation to common land with the modifications in s. 62D (s. 62D(1)). In that context, references to trespassing and trespassers have effect as if they were reference to acts, and persons doing acts, which constitute (a) a trespass as against the occupier, or (b) an infringement of the commoners' rights (s. 62D(2)). References to the occupier (a) in the case of land to which the public has access, include the local authority and any commoner, (b) in any other case, include the commoners or any of them (s. 62D(3)). Section 62D(1) does not (a) require action by more than one occupier, or (b) constitute persons trespassers as against any commoner or other local authority if they are permitted to be there by the other occupier (s. 62D(4)). 'Common land', 'commoner' and 'the local authority' have the meanings given by s. 61 (see **B13.45**). **B13.53**

Defences

Criminal Justice and Public Order Act 1994, s. 62B **B13.54**

(5) In proceedings for an offence under this section it is a defence for the accused to show—
- (a) that he was not trespassing on the land in respect of which he is alleged to have committed the offence, or
- (b) that he had a reasonable excuse—
  - (i) for failing to leave the relevant land as soon as reasonably practicable, or
  - (ii) for entering land in the area of the relevant local authority as a trespasser with the intention of residing there, or
- (c) that, at the time the direction was given, he was under the age of 18 years and was residing with his parent or guardian.

It is possible that there might be a challenge to this provision as being in breach of the ECHR, Article 6(2), see **F3.13** *et seq.*

Power of Seizure

A constable may seize and remove vehicles after a direction under the CJPOA 1994, s. 62A(1), has been given, provided the criteria in s. 62C are satisfied. **B13.55**

FAILURE TO LEAVE AN EXCLUSION ZONE AFTER BEING ORDERED TO DO SO

Definition

B13.56 **Serious Organised Crime and Police Act 2005, s. 112**

(5) Any person who knowingly contravenes a direction given to him under this section is guilty of an offence . . .

Procedure and Sentence

B13.57 The offence is triable summarily (SOCPA 2005, s. 112(5)).

The maximum penalty is imprisonment for a term not exceeding four months or a fine not exceeding level 4 on the standard scale or both (s. 112(5)).

Elements

B13.58 **Serious Organised Crime and Police Act 2005, s. 112**

(1) A constable may direct a person to leave a place if he believes, on reasonable grounds, that the person is in the place at a time when he would be prohibited from entering it by virtue of—
- (a) an order to which subsection (2) applies, or
- (b) a condition to which subsection (3) applies.

(2) This subsection applies to an order which—
- (a) was made, by virtue of any enactment, following the person's conviction of an offence, and
- (b) prohibits the person from entering the place or from doing so during a period specified in the order.

(3) This subsection applies to a condition which—
- (a) was imposed, by virtue of any enactment, as a condition of the person's release from a prison in which he was serving a sentence of imprisonment following his conviction of an offence, and
- (b) prohibits the person from entering the place or from doing so during a period specified in the condition.

(4) A direction under this section may be given orally.

'Sentence of imprisonment' and 'prison' are to be construed in accordance with the CJCSA 2000, s. 62(5) (s. 112(8)(a)). The reference to a release from prison includes a reference to a temporary release (s. 112(8)(b)). 'Place' includes an area (s. 112(9)).

Section 112 applies whether or not the order or condition in s. 112(1) was made or imposed before or after the commencement of s. 112 (s. 112(10)).

A person may be excluded from an area following a conviction (i) under the PCC(S)A 2000, s. 40A (see **E11.47**); (ii) (until the relevant repeal is fully implemented) where an exclusion requirement applies under the PCC(S)A 2000, sch. 2; or (iii) by virtue of a condition attached to an ASBO (see **D24.2** and **D24.11**) but note that the SOCPA 2005, s. 112 cannot have any application where the ASBO is made in civil proceedings. Exclusions may also arise under the Licensed Premises (Exclusion of Certain Persons) Act 1980 (see **E23.1**) and by virtue of a football banning order (see **E23.3**).

FAILURE TO LEAVE LAND OR RE-ENTRY TO LAND: RAVES

Definition

B13.59 **Criminal Justice and Public Order Act 1994, s. 63**

(6) If a person knowing that a direction has been given which applies to him—
- (a) fails to leave the land as soon as reasonably practicable, or

(b) having left again enters the land within the period of 7 days beginning with the day on which the direction was given,

he commits an offence . . .

Procedure and Sentence

The offence is triable summarily (CJPOA 1994, s. 63(6)). B13.60

The maximum penalty is imprisonment for a term not exceeding three months or a fine not exceeding level 4 on the standard scale or both (CJPOA 1994, s. 63(6)). Where a person has been convicted of this offence and the court is satisfied that sound equipment which has been seized from him under s. 64(4), or which was in his possession or under his control at the relevant time, has been used at the gathering, it may make an order for forfeiture in respect of that property in compliance with the provisions of s. 66 (s. 66(1)).

Elements

The section applies only to gatherings of the kind specified in the CJPOA 1994, s. 63(1); in the marginal note to s. 63, and in common parlance, such gatherings are called raves. The offence is committed only where a direction to leave has been given. B13.61

Criminal Justice and Public Order Act 1994, s. 63

(1) This section applies to a gathering on land in the open air of 20 or more persons (whether or not trespassers) at which amplified music is played during the night (with or without intermissions) and is such as, by reason of its loudness and duration and the time at which it is played, is likely to cause serious distress to the inhabitants of the locality; and for this purpose—

(a) such a gathering continues during intermissions in the music and, where the gathering extends over several days, throughout the period during which the amplified music is played at night (with or without intermissions); and

(b) 'music' includes sounds wholly or predominantly characterised by the emission of a succession of repetitive beats.

(1A) This section also applies to a gathering if—

(a) it is a gathering of 20 or more persons who are trespassing on the land; and

(b) it would be a gathering of a kind mentioned in subsection (1) above if it took place on land in the open air.

(2) If, as respects any land, a police officer of at least the rank of superintendent reasonably believes that—

(a) two or more persons are making preparations for the holding there of a gathering to which this section applies,

(b) ten or more persons are waiting for such a gathering to begin there, or

(c) ten or more persons are attending such a gathering which is in progress, he may give a direction that those persons and any other persons who come to prepare or wait for or to attend the gathering are to leave the land and remove any vehicles or other property they have with them on the land.

The terms 'trespasser' and 'vehicle' have the same meaning as in s. 61 of the 1994 Act (see **B13.45**). 'Land in the open air' includes a place partly open to the air (s. 63(10)).

The person must know of the direction and, it would appear, that it applies to him (s. 63(6)). If the police officer giving the direction does not communicate it to the persons to be removed, any constable at the scene may do so (s. 63(3)). Persons shall be treated as having had a direction communicated to them if reasonable steps have been taken to bring it to their attention (s. 63(4)).

Exempt Persons and Gatherings

Directions do not apply to 'exempt persons' (CJPOA 1994, s. 63(5)). An 'exempt person', in relation to land (or any gathering on land), means the occupier, any member of his family and B13.62

any employee or agent of his and any person whose home is situated on the land (s. 63(10)). As to the meaning of 'occupier', see **B13.45**.

Directions do not apply, in England and Wales, to a gathering licensed by an entertainment licence (s. 63(9)(a)).

Specific Defence

B13.63 It is a defence to a charge under the CJPOA 1994, s. 63(6), for the accused to show that he had a reasonable excuse for failing to leave the land as soon as reasonably practicable or, as the case may be, for again entering the land (s. 63(7)). The imposition of a legal burden upon the accused is open to challenge in the light of the human rights cases on the 'reverse burden' (see **F3.13** ***et seq.***).

The offence does not apply to a gathering in relation to a licensable activity within the meaning of the Licensing Act 2003, s. 1(1)(c) (provision of certain forms of entertainment) which is carried on under and in accordance with an authorisation within the meaning of s. 136 of that Act (s. 63(9)).

Further Offence

B13.64 A person commits an offence, contrary to the CJPOA 1994, s. 63(7A) if (a) he knows that a direction under s. 63(2) has been given which applies to him, and (b) he makes preparations for or attends a gathering to which s. 63 applies within the period of 24 hours starting when the direction was given. A person guilty of this offence is liable, on summary conviction, to imprisonment for a term not exceeding three months or a fine not exceeding level 4 on the standard scale, or both (s. 63(7B)).

Police Powers

B13.65 Sections 63 to 65 and 67 of the CJPOA 1994 provide certain additional police powers for the purpose of controlling or prohibiting gatherings of the kind specified in s. 63(1) (see **B13.61**).

(a) A constable authorised to enter land for any purpose in accordance with s. 64(1) and (2) by a police officer of at least the rank of superintendent may enter the land without a warrant (s. 64(3)).

(b) A constable may seize and remove vehicles or sound equipment (as defined in s. 64(6)) after a s. 63 direction provided the criteria in s. 64(4) and (5) are satisfied. Any vehicles so seized and removed may be retained in accordance with regulations made by the Secretary of State (s. 67(1)). Any sound equipment so seized and removed may be retained until the conclusion of proceedings against the person from whom it was seized for an offence under s. 63 (s. 67(2)). Any authority is entitled to recover from a person from whom a vehicle has been seized such charges as may be prescribed in respect of the removal, retention, disposal and destruction of the vehicle by the authority (s. 67(4)).

(c) A constable in uniform has power, at a place within five miles of the boundary of the site of the rave, to stop a person, except an exempt person, whom the constable reasonably believes to be on his way to a rave and direct him not to proceed in the direction of the rave (s. 65(1), (2) and (3)). It is a summary offence for a person, knowing that such a direction has been given to him, to fail to comply with that direction, and such a person is liable on conviction to a fine not exceeding level 3 on the standard scale (s. 65(4)).

UNAUTHORISED CAMPERS: FAILURE TO LEAVE OR RETURNING TO THE LAND

Definition

Criminal Justice and Public Order Act 1994, s. 77 **B13.66**

(3) If a person knowing that a direction under subsection (1) has been given which applied to him—
(a) fails, as soon as practicable, to leave the land or remove from the land any vehicle or other property which is the subject of the direction, or
(b) having removed any such vehicle or property again enters the land with a vehicle within the period of three months beginning with the day on which the direction was given,
he commits an offence . . .

Procedure and Sentence

The offence is triable summarily only (CJPOA 1994, s. 77(3)). **B13.67**

The maximum penalty is a fine not exceeding level 3 on the standard scale (s. 77(3)).

Direction

Criminal Justice and Public Order Act 1994, s. 77 **B13.68**

(1) If it appears to a local authority that persons are for the time being residing in a vehicle or vehicles within that authority's area—
(a) on any land forming part of a highway;
(b) on any other unoccupied land; or
(c) on any occupied land without the consent of the occupier,
the authority may give a direction that those persons and any others with them are to leave the land and remove the vehicle or vehicles and any other property they have with them on the land.

Notice of a direction must be served on the persons to whom the direction applies, but it is sufficient for the direction to specify the land and (except where it applies to only one person) to be addressed to all occupants of the vehicles on the land, without naming them (s. 77(2)). Where it is impracticable to serve a direction on a person named in it, it is treated as duly served on him if a copy is fixed in a prominent place to the vehicle concerned; and where the direction is directed to unnamed occupants of vehicles, it is treated as duly served on those occupants if it is fixed in a prominent place to every vehicle on the land in question at the time when service is thus effected (s. 79(2)). The local authority must take such steps as are reasonably practicable to ensure that a copy of the direction is displayed on the land in question (otherwise than by being fixed to a vehicle) in a manner designed to ensure that it is likely to be seen by any person camping on the land (s. 79(3)). Notice of a direction is to be given by the local authority to the owner of the land and to any occupier of that land unless, after reasonable inquiries, it is unable to ascertain their names and addresses (s. 79(4)).

A direction operates to require persons who re-enter the land within the period of three months with vehicles or other property to leave and remove the vehicles or other property as it operates in relation to the persons and vehicles or other property on the land when the direction was given (s. 77(4)).

Definitions

Section 77(6) of the CJPOA 1994 provides definitions for certain terms used in the section. A person may be regarded as residing on any land notwithstanding that he has a home elsewhere. 'Land' means land in the open air. 'Vehicle' and 'occupier' are defined in the same terms as in s. 61 (see **B13.45**). **B13.69**

Specific Defence

B13.70 It is a defence for the accused to show that his failure to leave or to remove the vehicle or other property as soon as practicable, or his re-entry with a vehicle, was due to illness, mechanical breakdown or other immediate emergency (CJPOA 1994, s. 77(5)). The imposition of a legal burden upon the accused is open to challenge in the light of the human rights cases on the 'reverse burden' (see **F3.13 *et seq.***).

Magistrates' Removal Order

B13.71 On a complaint made by a local authority, a magistrates' court, if satisfied that persons and vehicles in which they are residing are present on land within that authority's area in contravention of such a direction, may make an order requiring the removal of any vehicle or other property and any person residing in it (CJPOA 1994, s. 78(1)). Such an order may authorise the local authority to take such steps as are reasonably necessary to ensure that the order is complied with and, in particular, may authorise the authority, by its officers and servants, to enter upon the land specified in the order, and to take, in relation to any vehicle or property to be removed in pursuance of the order, such steps for securing entry and rendering it suitable for removal as may be specified in the order (s. 78(2)). The local authority must give to the owner and occupier at least 24 hours' notice of its intention to enter any occupied land unless after reasonable inquiries it is unable to ascertain their names and addresses (s. 78(3)). A person who wilfully obstructs any person in the exercise of any power conferred on him by an order under s. 78 commits an offence and is liable, on summary conviction, to a fine not exceeding level 3 on the standard scale (s. 78(4)). Where a complaint is made, a summons issued by the court requiring the person(s) to whom it is directed to appear before it to answer to the complaint may be directed either to the occupant of a particular vehicle on the land in question or to all occupants of vehicles on the land in question, without naming him or them (s. 78(5)). There is no power to issue a warrant for arrest upon failure to appear (s. 78(6)). The owner and occupier of the land are entitled to appear and be heard at any proceedings (s. 79(4)).

TRESPASS ON A PROTECTED SITE

Definition

B13.72 **Serious Organised Crime and Police Act 2005, s. 128**

(1) A person commits an offence if he enters, or is on, any protected site in England and Wales or Northern Ireland as a trespasser.

Procedure and Sentence

B13.73 The offence is triable summarily only (SOCPA 2005, s. 128(5)).

The maximum penalty is imprisonment for a term not exceeding six months, a fine not exceeding level 5 on the standard scale, or both (s. 128(5)).

No proceedings for the offence may be instituted against any person in England and Wales except by or with the consent of the A-G (s. 128(6)(a)).

Elements

B13.74 A 'protected site' means a nuclear site or a designated site (SOCPA 2005, s. 128(1A)). 'Nuclear site' means (a) so much of any premises in respect of which a nuclear site licence (within the meaning of the Nuclear Installations Act 1965) is for the time being in force as lies within the outer perimeter of the protection provided for those premises; and (b) so much of any other premises of which premises falling within paragraph (a) form a part as lies within that outer perimeter (s. 128(1B)). For this purpose (a) the outer perimeter of the protection provided for any premises is the line of the outermost fences, walls or other obstacles provided or relied on for protecting those premises from intruders; and (b) that line shall be determined on the assumption that every gate, door or other barrier across a way through a fence, wall or other obstacle is closed (s. 128(1C)). A 'designated site' means a site (a) specified or described (in any way) in an order made by the Secretary of State, and (b) designated for the purposes of s. 128 by the order (SOCPA 2005, s. 128(2)). The land that the Secretary of State may designate must be comprised in Crown land, or comprised in land belonging to Her Majesty in her private capacity or to the immediate heir to the Throne in his private capacity, or it must appear to the Secretary of State that it is appropriate to designate the site in the interests of national security (s. 128(3)). 'Site' means the whole or part of any building or buildings, or any land, or both (s. 128(8)(a)). 'Crown land' means land in which there is a Crown interest or a Duchy interest (s. 128(8)(b)). 'Crown interest' means an interest belonging to Her Majesty in right of the Crown and 'Duchy interest' means an interest belonging to Her Majesty in right of the Duchy of Lancaster or belonging to the Duchy of Cornwall (s. 128(9)). Sites have been designated by the Serious Organised Crime and Police Act 2005 (Designated Sites) Order 2005 (SI 2005 No. 3447) and the Serious Organised Crime and Police Act 2005 (Designated Sites under Section 128) Order 2007 (SI 2007 No. 930); the former designates 13 sites of military significance and the latter designates 16 sites associated with the government, the security services and the Royal family.

A person who is on any protected site as a trespasser does not cease to be a trespasser by virtue of being allowed time to leave the site (s. 128(7)).

A person cannot claim not to be a trespasser by virtue of the rights of the public in relation to access to land under the Countryside and Rights of Way Act 2000, s. 2(1), since that provision does not apply in respect of land in respect of which a designation order is in force (s. 131(1)).

Defence

Serious Organised Crime and Police Act 2005, s. 128

(4) It is a defence for a person charged with an offence under this section to prove that he did not know, and had no reasonable cause to suspect, that the site in relation to which the offence is alleged to have been committed was a protected site. **B13.75**

OTHER OFFENCES BY TRESPASSERS

Trespassing with Firearm in a Building or on Land

Firearms Act 1968, s. 20 **B13.76**

(1) A person commits an offence if, while he has a firearm or imitation firearm with him, he enters or is in any building or part of a building as a trespasser and without reasonable excuse (the proof whereof lies on him).

(2) A person commits an offence if, while he has a firearm or imitation firearm with him, he enters or is on any land as a trespasser and without reasonable excuse (the proof whereof lies on him).

The mode of trial for trespassing with firearm in a building is either way, although if the weapon is an air weapon or an imitation firearm, the offence is triable summarily only. The mode of trial for trespassing with a firearm on any land is summary only. As to the extension of the usual time-limit within which summary proceedings must be instituted, see **B12.2**.

The offence of trespassing with a firearm in a building is punishable, on summary conviction, with a term of imprisonment not exceeding six months or a fine not exceeding the prescribed sum or both; and, on conviction on indictment, with a term of imprisonment not exceeding five years or a fine or both. The offence of trespassing with a firearm on any land is punishable, on summary conviction, with a term of imprisonment not exceeding three months or a fine not exceeding level 4 on the standard scale or both. As to the courts' power to order forfeiture or disposal of firearms and ammunition, see **B12.3**.

The meaning of 'firearm' is considered at **B12.4**. Imitation firearms (see **B12.12**) fall within this section. The Firearms Act 1968, s. 20(3), defines 'land' as including land covered by water.

Trespassing with Weapon of Offence

B13.77 It is a summary offence, contrary to the Criminal Law Act 1977, s. 8(1), for a person who is on any premises as a trespasser, after having entered as such, without lawful authority or reasonable excuse to have with him on the premises any weapon of offence. As to disputes as to title to property on summary trial, see **B13.23**.

By virtue of s. 8(3), a person guilty of this offence is liable to imprisonment for a term not exceeding six months or to a fine not exceeding level 5 on the standard scale or to both.

The meanings of the words 'premises' and 'trespasser' have been considered at **B13.24** and **B13.25**. The phrase, 'weapon of offence' is defined by s. 8(2) as meaning any article made or adapted for causing injury to or incapacitating a person, or intended by the person having it with him for such use. The same definition of 'weapon of offence' is used in the offence of aggravated burglary contrary to the Theft Act 1968, s. 10. For further discussion of this subject, see **B4.76**.

Trespassing on Premises of Foreign Missions, etc.

B13.78 It is a summary offence, contrary to the Criminal Law Act 1977, s. 9(1), for a person to enter or be on any premises to which s. 9 applies as a trespasser. As to disputes as to title to property on summary trial, see **B13.23**.

By virtue of s. 9(6), proceedings for this offence may not be instituted against any person except by or with the consent of the A-G.

By virtue of s. 9(5), a person guilty of this offence is liable to imprisonment for a term not exceeding six months or to a fine not exceeding level 5 on the standard scale or to both.

The phrase 'enters as a trespasser', is partly defined by the 1977 Act, since meanings are given for 'entry' and 'trespasser' (see **B13.24** and **B13.25** respectively). Similar terms also appear in the offence of burglary (see **B4.61** and **B4.62**).

The premises to which s. 9 applies are listed in s. 9(2):

Criminal Law Act 1977, s. 9

(2) This section applies to any premises which are or form part of—

- (a) the premises of a diplomatic mission within the meaning of the definition in Article 1(i) of the Vienna Convention on Diplomatic Relations signed in 1961 as that Article has effect in the United Kingdom by virtue of section 2 of and schedule 1 to the Diplomatic Privileges Act 1964;
- (aa) the premises of a closed diplomatic mission;
- (b) consular premises within the meaning of the definition in paragraph 1(j) of Article 1 of the Vienna Convention on Consular Relations signed in 1963 as that Article has effect in the United Kingdom by virtue of section 1 of and schedule 1 to the Consular Relations Act 1968;
- (bb) the premises of a closed consular post;
- (c) any other premises in respect of which any organisation or body is entitled to inviolability by or under any enactment; and
- (d) any premises which are the private residence of a diplomatic agent (within the meaning of Article 1(e) of the Convention mentioned in paragraph (a) above) or of any other person who is entitled to inviolability of residence by or under any enactment.

(2A) In subsection (2) above—

'the premises of a closed diplomatic mission' means premises which fall within Article 45 of the Convention mentioned in subsection (2)(a) above (as that Article has effect in the United Kingdom by virtue of the section and schedule mentioned in that paragraph); and

'the premises of a closed consular post' means premises which fall within Article 27 of the Convention mentioned in subsection (2)(b) above (as that Article has effect in the United Kingdom by virtue of the section and schedule mentioned in that paragraph).

Insofar as the general meaning of 'premises' is relevant, see **B13.24**. Section 9(4) creates an important evidential provision in relation to establishing whether given premises are covered by s. 9 or not, since in any proceedings for this offence 'a certificate issued by or under the authority of the Secretary of State stating that any premises were or formed part of premises of any description mentioned in paragraphs (a) to (d) of subsection (2) above at the time of the alleged offence shall be conclusive evidence that the premises were or formed part of premises of that description at that time'.

By virtue of s. 9(3), it is a defence for the accused to prove that he believed that the premises in question were not premises to which s. 9 applies. The imposition of a legal burden upon the accused by s. 9(3) is open to challenge in the light of the human rights cases on the 'reverse burden' (see **F3.13** *et seq.*).

Obstruction of Court Officers Executing Process against Unauthorised Occupiers

It is a summary offence, contrary to the Criminal Law Act 1977, s. 10(1), and without prejudice to the Sheriffs Act 1887, s. 8(2), if a person resists or intentionally obstructs any **B13.79**
person who is in fact an officer of a court engaged in executing any process issued by the High Court or any county court for the purpose of enforcing any judgment or order for the recovery of any premises or for the delivery of possession of any premises. As to disputes as to title to property on summary trial, see **B13.23**.

By virtue of s. 6(5), a person guilty of this offence is liable to imprisonment for a term not exceeding six months or to a fine not exceeding level 5 on the standard scale or to both.

A similar phrase to 'resists or intentionally obstructs' appears in the offence involving the obstruction of a constable contrary to the Police Act 1996, s. 89(2) (see **B2.33**).

'Officer of a court' according to s. 10(6) means any sheriff, under sheriff, deputy sheriff, bailiff or officer of a sheriff, and any bailiff or other person who is an officer of a county court within the meaning of the County Courts Act 1984, s. 147.

The offence does not apply unless the judgment or order in question was given or made in proceedings brought under any provisions of rules of court applicable only in circumstances where the person claiming possession of any premises alleges that the premises in question are occupied solely by a person or persons (not being a tenant or tenants holding over after the termination of the tenancy) who entered into or remained in occupation of the premises without the licence or consent of the person claiming possession or any predecessor in title of his.

'Premises' in this section has a slightly wider meaning than in the other offences in part II of the Criminal Law Act 1977. Section 12 states that 'premises' means any building, any part of a building under separate occupation, any land ancillary to a building, the site comprising any building or buildings together with any land ancillary thereto, and (for the purposes only of ss. 10 and 11) any other place. The references to a building apply also to any structure other than a moveable one, and to any moveable structure, vehicle or vessel designed or adapted for residential purposes; and:

(a) part of a building is under separate occupation if anyone is in occupation or entitled to occupation of that part as distinct from the whole; and

(b) land is ancillary to a building if it is adjacent to it and used (or intended for use) in connection with the occupation of that building or any part of it.

Note that the PACE 1984, s. 17(1)(c)(ii) (see **D1.94**) provides the police with a power of entry to premises to arrest a person for this offence.

By virtue of s. 10(3), it is a defence for the accused to prove that he believed that the person he was resisting or obstructing was not an officer of a court. The imposition of a legal burden upon the accused by s. 10(3) is open to challenge in the light of the human rights cases on the 'reverse burden' (see **F3.13** ***et seq.***).

There is a related offence under s. 10(A1) of resisting or intentionally obstructing any person who is an enforcement officer, or is acting under the authority of an enforcement officer and is engaged in executing a writ issued from the High Court.

Trespassing on Licensed Aerodromes

B13.80 It is an offence, contrary to the Civil Aviation Act 1982, s. 39, for a person to trespass on any land forming part of an aerodrome licensed in pursuit of an Air Navigation Order. The maximum punishment is, on summary conviction, a fine not exceeding level 3 on the standard scale (s. 39(1)). No one may be convicted unless it is proved that, at the material time, notices warning trespassers of their liability under s. 39 were posted so as to be readily seen and read by members of the public, in such positions on or near the boundary of the aerodrome as appear to the court to be proper (s. 39(2)).

Trespassing on a Railway

B13.81 It is an offence, contrary to the British Transport Commission Act 1949, s. 55(1), to trespass on any railway lines, sidings, embankments, tunnels, cuttings or similar railway works. On summary conviction, the maximum penalty is a fine not exceeding level 3 on the standard scale. Under the Penalties for Disorderly Behaviour (Amount of Penalty) Order 2002 (SI 2002 No. 1837), as amended, this offence is a penalty offence and the amount payable is £50.

Poaching Offences

B13.82 There are five poaching offences, the primary focus of which is the protection of game rights, but which involve trespass to land, see Game Act 1831, s. 30 (poaching by day and poaching by day in company), Night Poaching Act 1828, s. 1 (night poaching by unlawfully entering land and night poaching by unlawfully being on land) and the Deer Act 1991, s. 1 (poaching of deer). Further, it is an offence to take or destroy fish from water which is private property or in which there is a private right of fishery (Theft Act 1968, sch. 1, para. 2(1)).

Trespass with Intent to Commit a Sexual Offence

B13.83 It is no longer burglary to enter a building as a trespasser with the intention of raping someone (see **B4.54** ***et seq.***), but it is an offence, contrary to the SOA 2003, s. 63, knowingly or recklessly to trespass on any premises intending to commit a relevant sexual offence (see **B3.234**).

Section B14 Offences Against the Administration of Justice

PERJURY IN A JUDICIAL PROCEEDING

Perjury Act 1911, s. 1 B14.1

(1) If any person lawfully sworn as a witness or as an interpreter in a judicial proceeding wilfully makes a statement material in that proceeding, which he knows to be false or does not believe to be true, he shall be guilty of perjury, and shall, on conviction thereof on indictment, be liable to imprisonment for a term not exceeding seven years, or to a fine or to both imprisonment and fine.

(2) The expression 'judicial proceeding' includes a proceeding before any court, tribunal, or person having by law power to hear, receive, and examine evidence on oath.

(3) Where a statement made for the purposes of a judicial proceeding is not made before the tribunal itself, but is made on oath before a person authorised by law to administer an oath to the person who makes the statement, and to record or authenticate the statement, it shall, for the purposes of this section, be treated as having been made in a judicial proceeding.

(4) A statement made by a person lawfully sworn in England for the purposes of a judicial proceeding:
(a) in another part of His Majesty's dominions; or
(b) in a British tribunal lawfully constituted in any place by sea or land outside His Majesty's dominions; or
(c) in a tribunal of any foreign state,
shall, for the purposes of this section, be treated as a statement made in a judicial proceeding in England.

(5) Where, for the purposes of a judicial proceeding in England, a person is lawfully sworn under the authority of an Act of Parliament:
(a) in any other part of His Majesty's dominions; or
(b) before a British tribunal or a British officer in a foreign country, or within the jurisdiction of the Admiralty of England;
a statement made by such person so sworn as aforesaid (unless the Act of Parliament under which it was made otherwise specifically provides) shall be treated for the purposes of this section as having been made in the judicial proceeding in England for the purposes whereof it was made.

(6) The question whether a statement on which perjury is assigned was material is a question of law to be determined by the court of trial.

The Perjury Act 1911, s. 1, applies to intermediaries appointed under the YJCEA 1999, s. 29, as it applies to interpreters (s. 29(7)). This includes intermediaries who assist in the examination of a witness otherwise than in the course of judicial proceedings: the examination shall be taken to be part of the judicial proceeding in which that witness's evidence is given.

Procedure

Perjury in a judicial proceeding is triable only on indictment. It is a class 3 offence. B14.2

The Perjury Act 1911, provides:

Perjury Act 1911, s. 8

Where an offence against this Act or any offence punishable as perjury or as subornation of perjury under any other Act of Parliament is committed in any place either on sea or land outside the United Kingdom, the offender may be proceeded against, indicted, tried, and punished . . . in England.

It is not altogether clear whether this provision was intended to extend the ambit of the Act in any way, or whether it was, as the marginal note ('venue') suggests, intended merely to provide for the trial of any extraterritorial offences created under the preceding sections. On balance, the latter interpretation is to be preferred. The extraterritorial scope of s. 1, for example, is precisely governed by subsections (4) and (5), and these provisions would not have been necessary if s. 8 had any wider meaning. As to territorial jurisdiction generally, see **A8**.

Indictment

B14.3 *Statement of Offence*

Perjury contrary to section 1(1) of the Perjury Act 1911

Particulars of Offence

A on the . . . day of . . ., having been lawfully sworn as a witness in a judicial proceeding, namely the trial of a criminal cause at the Central Criminal Court entitled The Queen v B.C., wilfully made a statement material in that proceeding which he knew to be false, namely that the accused B.C. had been in the City of Leicester on the . . . day of . . .

As to the drafting of indictments for perjury and related offences under the Perjury Act 1911, s. 12 provides as follows:

Perjury Act 1911, s. 12

(1) In an indictment—
   (a) for making any false statement or false representation punishable under this Act; or
   (b) for unlawfully, wilfully, falsely, fraudulently, deceitfully, maliciously, or corruptly taking, making, signing, or subscribing any oath, affirmation, solemn declaration, statutory declaration, affidavit, deposition, notice, certificate, or other writing,

   it is sufficient to set forth the substance of the offence charged, and before which court or person (if any) the offence was committed without setting forth the proceedings or any part of the proceedings in the course of which the offence was committed, and without setting forth the authority of any court or person before whom the offence was committed.

(2) In an indictment for aiding, abetting, counselling, suborning, or procuring any other person to commit any offence hereinbefore in this section mentioned, or for conspiring with any other person, or with attempting to suborn or procure any other person, to commit any such offence, it is sufficient—
   (a) where such offence has been committed, to allege that offence, and then to allege that the defendant procured the commission of the offence; and
   (b) where such offence has not been committed, to set forth the substance of the offence charged against the defendant without setting forth any matter or thing which it is unnecessary to aver in the case of an indictment for a false statement or false representation punishable under this Act.

Sentencing Guidelines

B14.4 The maximum penalty for perjury in judicial proceedings is seven years (Perjury Act 1911, s. 1).

There are numerous Court of Appeal decisions dealing with sentencing for this offence. They indicate that a custodial sentence is almost always necessary since, as Roskill LJ said in *Davies* (1974) 59 Cr App R 311 at p. 313:

It is often said there is too much perjury committed in courts, and it is regrettably true as everyone sitting in court knows. But it is one thing to suspect that perjury has been committed

> and another thing to prove it. Perjury is not always easy to prove. Perjurers are not easily brought to justice. When they are they must be punished.

It seems that where the original charge in relation to which the perjury was committed was one of very serious crime, the penalty for the perjury should be proportionately higher. A sentence of six years for perjury was upheld in *Dunlop* [2001] 2 Cr App R (S) 133. The offender gave false evidence in his own defence in a murder trial, and repeated it at a retrial with the result that he was discharged after a second jury disagreement. He later admitted both the murder and the perjury. The six-year sentence was ordered to run consecutively to a sentence of seven years which he was already serving. In *Archer* [2003] 1 Cr App R (S) 446, a sentence of four years was upheld in respect of an offender who was convicted of two counts of perjury and two counts of perverting the course of justice, in respect of civil proceedings for libel which he had brought against a newspaper. The Court of Appeal held that there was no inherent difference in seriousness between perjury in civil as against criminal proceedings. Other factors were more relevant, including the number of offences committed, the time scale over which they had taken place, whether the lies were planned and persisted in, whether the defendant had implicated others, and whether the perjury had affected the outcome of the original proceedings.

In *Hall* (1982) 4 Cr App R (S) 153 Talbot J (at p. 155) said that '. . . it is almost inconceivable that a sentence of less than three months would be given for a deliberate perjury in the face of the court', since 'such false evidence strikes at the whole basis of the administration of the law'. In that case a three-month sentence was upheld on a 62-year-old woman who had given false alibi evidence at a magistrates' court in respect of a man charged with assault occasioning actual bodily harm. A sentence of six months' imprisonment was upheld in *Healey* (1990) 12 Cr App R (S) 297, in respect of perjury committed in the course of a means inquiry in a magistrates' court. The offender appeared in court for failure to pay a fine of £200. He then gave evidence on oath that he was employed, and that the fine could be recovered by an attachment of earnings order. This evidence was untrue.

Meaning of 'Statements in Judicial Proceedings'

The effect of the Perjury Act 1911, s. 1 (2) and (3), is that perjury need not take the form of false evidence in court. A false affidavit sworn in connection with a judicial proceeding may amount to perjury, as may false evidence given on oath before a tribunal. **B14.5**

The position is slightly different in the case of false written evidence tendered in criminal proceedings under the CJA 1967, s. 9, and of false written evidence admitted in committal proceedings under the MCA 1980, s. 5A. Wilful falsity in such cases attracts a maximum penalty of two years and/or a fine, as opposed to the seven year maximum for perjury itself, but in all other respects the principles contained within the Perjury Act 1911 are applicable. These offences are dealt with at **B14.18**.

The CJA 1988, s. 32, enables a person outside the UK to give evidence at a criminal trial in England or Wales through a live television link. As with evidence to which the Perjury Act 1911, s. 1(5), applies, any such evidence is treated for the purposes of the Perjury Act 1911, s. 1, as given in the trial concerned (CJA 1988, s. 32(3)).

By the European Communities Act 1972, s. 11(1)(a), all relevant provisions of the Perjury Act 1911 are applicable to statements made on oath before the European Court of Justice, or any court attached thereto, whether or not the person responsible is a British citizen. See also the Evidence (European Court) Order 1976 (SI 1976 No. 428).

Meaning of 'Lawfully Sworn'

Evidence Act 1851, s. 16 **B14.6**

> Every court, judge, justice, officer, commissioner, arbitrator, or other person, now or hereafter having by law or by consent of parties authority to hear, receive, and examine evidence, is hereby

empowered to administer an oath to all such witnesses as are legally called before them respectively.

A conviction for perjury is impossible if the accused was incompetent to testify in the proceedings in which his perjury is alleged to have been committed (*Clegg* (1868) 19 LT 47).

It is possible for a witness or interpreter to make a solemn affirmation in place of the oath, whether or not the taking of an oath would be contrary to his religious beliefs, and the Perjury Act 1911, s. 15(2), provides that references therein to 'oaths' and 'swearing' embrace affirmations. The affirming witness is thus equally subject to the Perjury Act 1911. Furthermore, s. 15(1) provides that:

Perjury Act 1911, s. 15

(1) For the purposes of this Act, the forms and ceremonies used in administering an oath are immaterial, if the court or person before whom the oath is taken has power to administer an oath for the purpose of verifying the statement in question, and if the oath has been administered in a form and with ceremonies which the person taking the oath has accepted without objection, or has declared to be binding on him.

As to oaths and affirmations generally, see **F4.26** to **F4.31**.

Wilfulness

B14.7 It might seem at first sight that the requirement of wilfulness in the Perjury Act 1911, s. 1, is otiose, since an offence under the section can be committed only by someone who does not believe it to be true; but conduct is wilful only if it is deliberate or intentional (*Senior* [1899] 1 QB 283), and it must therefore be proved that any alleged perjury was not the result of a misunderstanding or a slip of the tongue, whereby the accused might perhaps have said something he did not mean (*Millward* [1985] QB 519). As to wilfulness generally, see **A2.8**.

Materiality

B14.8 'Material' means important or significant: something which matters. See *Mallett* [1978] 1 WLR 820, in which the Court of Appeal so construed the phrase 'false in a material particular', in a prosecution under the Theft Act 1968, s. 17(1). Under the Perjury Act 1911, s. 1(6), the question of what is material is one of law (i.e. for the judge to decide). Although A must know of the falsity of his statement (or not believe in its truth) he need not know or believe it to be material (*Millward* [1985] QB 519).

The truth or falsity of the accused's statement need not be crucial to the outcome of the case. It would suffice, for example, if the accused's lies prevented the other side from pursuing a certain line of questioning which might have been material to the question of his credibility (*Millward* [1985] QB 519; and see also *Baker* [1895] 1 QB 797). A statement may also be material even though it ought strictly to have been excluded by the court or judge before whom it was made (*Gibbon* (1862) Le & Ca 109; cf. *Philpotts* (1851) 2 Den CC 302).

Clear examples of immaterial statements are hard to find amongst the reported cases. It was held in *Tate* (1871) 12 Cox CC 7 that it was not perjury for the accused to swear at X's trial for assault that he had seen X's wife commit adultery, because that would have been irrelevant to the question whether X had indeed committed the assault; but this decision has been doubted (*Hewitt* (1913) 9 Cr App R 192) and it has since been held that evidence is material if it may affect the likely penalty in criminal proceedings, even if it is immaterial to the question of liability (*Wheeler* [1917] 1 KB 283). A rare reported example of lies that were held to be immaterial is *Sweet-Escott* (1971) 55 Cr App R 316, where in committal proceedings D had denied having any previous convictions. He did have some; but these dated from over 20 years before, and it was held that they could not have made any difference to the outcome of the proceedings.

Truth or Falsity of the Statement

On a literal interpretation of the Perjury Act 1911, s. 1, it would seem that a person could be convicted of perjury as a result of a statement which he did not believe to be true, but which was in fact true after all. Prosecutions are hardly likely to be brought in respect of manifestly true statements, but if this literal interpretation is correct, it would ease the prosecution's task in cases where the accused's state of mind is easier to prove than the truth or falsity of his evidence. If, for example, the accused had testified that event X took place on 5 July, and the prosecution can prove that the accused had no idea whether that event took place or not, this should suffice as proof of his perjury, even if there is no evidence that it did not take place on 5 July. See *Rider* (1986) 83 Cr App R 207. **B14.9**

This was indeed the position at common law (*Allen v Westley* (1629) Het 97) and although the Court of Appeal appears to have assumed in *Millward* [1985] QB 519 that proof of falsity is required under the Perjury Act 1911, this was unconsidered and strictly *obiter*. Most commentators support the literal interpretation, which also found some favour with the Court of Appeal in *Rider* (1986) Cr App R 207, although the point was ultimately left open in that case.

It may at first seem rather difficult to reconcile the 'literal' interpretation of the Perjury Act 1911, s. 1, with s. 13, which effectively requires corroboration of any allegation of falsity before a conviction for perjury can be obtained, but the wording of s. 13 is not in fact inconsistent with that interpretation, as the Court of Appeal noted in *Rider* (1986) 83 Cr App R 207. As to s. 13, see **B14.14**.

False Statements of Opinion

An expression of opinion, not genuinely held by the witness making it, may amount to perjury (*Schlesinger* (1847) 10 QB 670). **B14.10**

Perjury Based on Inconsistent Statements

Where A has on separate occasions made two or more inconsistent statements on oath, and must have been guilty of deliberate perjury on at least one of those occasions, a conviction will not be possible unless the prosecution can prove which of the statements were perjured. **B14.11**

Prosecution for Perjury where Accused's Evidence Secured his Acquittal in Previous Trial

Problems may arise where a person has been acquitted of a criminal charge after giving evidence of his own innocence, but further evidence has come to light which tends to prove, not just that he lied in the course of his testimony, but that he must have been wrongly acquitted. If a person is tried for perjury, can the prosecution adduce evidence which is flatly inconsistent with his acquittal at the earlier trial? **B14.12**

The House of Lords in *DPP v Humphrys* [1977] AC 1 denied that the doctrine of issue estoppel has any place in criminal proceedings, but declined to abolish the closely related doctrine laid down in *Sambasivam v Public Prosecutor of Malaya Federation* [1950] AC 458 and *G (an infant) v Coltart* [1967] 1 QB 432, under which it was said that the prosecution must accept the accused's innocence of any alleged crimes of which he has previously been acquitted. The *Sambasivam* rule was nevertheless rejected by the House of Lords in *Z* [2000] 2 AC 483. The accused's previous acquittal is therefore no longer an obstacle to his prosecution for perjury.

On the other hand, it would be oppressive and unfair for an accused to be prosecuted for perjury after successfully defending himself on the original charge, unless significant new prosecution evidence has become available to contradict his original evidence. If the prosecution are merely hoping that a different jury might believe their original witnesses rather than the accused, the prosecution should be stopped as an abuse of process. This was recognised, both in *Humphrys* and in *Z*.

As to the effect of previous verdicts in criminal cases generally, see **F11**.

Proof of Previous Judicial Proceeding

B14.13 If the fact of the proceeding at which the perjury is alleged to have taken place is not admitted, this may be proved by production of the record of the trial (or a copy thereof: CJA 1988, s. 27) or, in the case of trials on indictment, in accordance with the Perjury Act 1911, s. 14.

Perjury Act 1911, s. 14

On a prosecution—
(a) for perjury alleged to have been committed on the trial of an indictment . . .; or
(b) for procuring or suborning the commission of perjury on any such trial,
the fact of the former trial shall be sufficiently proved by the production of a certificate containing the substance and effect (omitting the formal parts) of the indictment and trial purporting to be signed by the clerk of the court, or other person having the custody of the records of the court where the indictment was tried, or by the deputy of that clerk or other person, without proof of the signature or official character of the clerk or person appearing to have signed the certificate.

A's allegedly perjured statements, if not admitted, may be proved by the testimony of persons who were present at the trial. One such witness would suffice, since s. 13 (see **B14.14**) applies only to evidence of falsity. Alternatively, the shorthand writer's record may be admissible under the CJA 1988, s. 24.

Requirement of Corroboration as to Falsity

B14.14 **Perjury Act 1911, s. 13**

A person shall not be liable to be convicted of any offence against this Act, or of any offence declared by any other Act to be perjury or subornation of perjury, or to be punishable as perjury or subornation of perjury, solely upon the evidence of one witness as to the falsity of any statement alleged to be false.

This provision does not lay down any corroboration requirement as to the fact that the accused made the alleged statement, or as to his knowledge or belief at the time (*O'Connor* [1980] Crim LR 43). If it is not being alleged that the statement was false (e.g., where it is alleged that neither the accused nor anyone else could have known whether it was true or not), then s. 13 has no application.

Where s. 13 does apply, its interpretation is troublesome. It does not expressly refer to 'corroboration' at all, and it was accordingly argued in *Hamid* (1979) 69 Cr App R 324 that, provided the prosecution case does not depend on a single witness as to falsity, the technicalities of the law relating to corroboration do not apply; but the Court of Appeal disagreed. It follows that a jury will need to be directed as to what other evidence might be capable of providing that corroboration, and the absence of any such direction will amount to a material irregularity. See also *Rider* (1986) 83 Cr App R 207 and *Carroll* [1993] Crim LR 613.

Although a single witness to falsity must be corroborated, this corroboration may take the form of documentary evidence, and may originate from the accused himself, as in *Threlfall* (1914) 10 Cr App R 112, where the accused had written a letter, parts of which appeared to be self-incriminating.

Where the accused is alleged to have confessed prior to the trial, the evidence of two witnesses to the confession has been held to be sufficient for the purposes of s. 13. It is not necessary that they should have witnessed confessions on separate occasions (*Peach* [1990] 2 All ER 966).

Aiding and Abetting etc.

Perjury Act 1911, s. 7 B14.15

(1) Every person who aids, abets, counsels, procures, or suborns another person to commit an offence against this Act shall be liable to be proceeded against, indicted, tried and punished as if he were a principal offender.
(2) Every person who incites another person to commit an offence against this Act shall be guilty of an offence, and, on conviction thereof on indictment, shall be liable to imprisonment, or to a fine, or to both such imprisonment and fine.

'Suborning' is merely another term, in this context, for procuring, and s. 7(1) thus adds nothing of significance to the general law of secondary participation in crime, as governed by the Accessories and Abettors Act 1861 (see generally **A5.1** *et seq.*).

The Perjury Act 1911, s. 7(2), similarly adds nothing of substance to the common-law rules governing incitement; but the maximum term of imprisonment for an offence under s. 7(2) is limited by the Powers of the Criminal Courts Act 1973, s. 18, to two years, a restriction which does not apply to the common-law offence.
The Perjury Act 1911, s. 13 (see **B14.14**), applies to offences under this provision. All complicity offences are triable either way except complicity in an offence under the Perjury Act 1911, s.1 (perjury in judicial proceedings).

OFFENCES AKIN TO PERJURY

False Testimony of Unsworn Child Witnesses in Criminal Proceedings

The Perjury Act 1911, s. 16(2), provides that nothing in that Act applies to the unsworn evidence of children (see **F4.21**) but under the YJCEA 1999, s. 57, which came into force on 24 July 2002, children or other persons who wilfully give false evidence in criminal proceedings when testifying unsworn (by virtue of s. 56 of that Act: see **F4.23**), and who would be guilty of perjury if testifying on oath, will be guilty of a summary offence, which supplants that previously applying under the CYPA 1933, s. 38. The penalty for children (aged under 14) is a fine not exceeding £250; others may face a fine not exceeding £1,000 and/or imprisonment for a term not exceeding six months (YJCEA 1999, s. 57(2) and (3)). B14.16

False Unsworn Evidence under the Evidence (Proceedings in Other Jurisdictions) Act 1975

Perjury Act 1911, s. 1A B14.17

If any person, in giving any testimony (either orally or in writing) otherwise than on oath, where required to do so by an order under section 2 of the Evidence (Proceedings in Other Jurisdictions) Act 1975, makes a statement:
(a) which he knows to be false in a material particular, or
(b) which is false in a material particular and which he does not believe to be true,
he shall be guilty of [an offence] and shall be liable on conviction on indictment to imprisonment for a term not exceeding two years or a fine or both.

This section serves a function similar to that served in respect of sworn evidence by the Perjury Act 1911, s. 1(4) (see **B14.1**). In contrast to the uncertainty concerning the need for proof of actual falsity in prosecutions under s. 1, it is clear in this case that such proof is indeed required. As to the meaning of the phrase 'false in a material particular', see the discussion at **B14.8**.

Section 13 applies (see **B14.14**); and offences under this provision are triable either way (MCA 1980, s. 17 and sch. 1, para. 14).

False Written Statements Tendered in Criminal Proceedings

B14.18 **Criminal Justice Act 1967, s. 89**

(1) If any person in a written statement tendered in evidence in criminal proceedings by virtue of section 9 of this Act, or in proceedings before a court-martial by virtue of the said section 9 as extended by section 12 . . . or by section 99A of the Army Act 1955 or section 99A of the Air Force Act 1955, wilfully makes a statement material in those proceedings which he knows to be false or does not believe to be true, he shall be liable on conviction on indictment to imprisonment for a term not exceeding two years or a fine or both.

(2) The Perjury Act 1911 shall have effect as if this section were contained in that Act.

Magistrates' Courts Act 1980, s. 106

(1) If any person in a written statement admitted in evidence in criminal proceedings by virtue of section 5B above wilfully makes a statement material in those proceedings which he knows to be false or does not believe to be true, he shall be liable on conviction on indictment to imprisonment for a term not exceeding two years or a fine or both.

(2) The Perjury Act 1911 shall have effect as if this section were contained in that Act.

The only obvious distinction between these offences and perjury itself lies in the maximum penalties, which stand at two years compared with the maximum of seven under the Perjury Act 1911, s. 1. Although there is no specific provision, it would seem that these offences are triable either way, since, in each of the two sections set out above, subsection (2) assimilates them into the Perjury Act 1911 and, by virtue of the MCA 1980, s. 17 and sch. 1, para. 14, all offences under the Perjury Act 1911, except those under ss. 1, 3 and 4, are so triable. (Sections 3 and 4 of the Perjury Act 1911 expressly made offences under those sections triable either way.)

Section 13 of the Perjury Act 1911 is applicable to both offences: see **B14.14**.

False Statements Made on Oath outside Judicial Proceedings

B14.19 **Perjury Act 1911, s. 2**

If any person:

(1) being required or authorised by law to make any statement on oath for any purpose, and being lawfully sworn (otherwise than in a judicial proceeding) wilfully makes a statement which is material for that purpose and which he knows to be false or does not believe to be true; or

(2) wilfully uses any false affidavit for the purposes of the Bills of Sale Act 1878, as amended by any subsequent enactment,

he shall be guilty of [an offence], and, on conviction thereof on indictment, shall be liable to imprisonment for a term not exceeding seven years or to a fine or to both such imprisonment and fine.

The offence created by this section is of limited application. Affidavits sworn in connection with judicial proceedings must be dealt with under the Perjury Act 1911, s. 1(3). As to statutory declarations, see s. 5, discussed in **B14.22**.

Section 13 applies (see **B14.14**), and offences under this provision are triable either way (MCA 1980, sch. 1, para. 14).

False Statements with Reference to Marriage

B14.20 **Perjury Act 1911, s. 3**

(1) If any person:

(a) for the purpose of procuring a marriage, or a certificate or licence for marriage, knowingly and wilfully makes a false oath, or makes or signs a false declaration, notice or certificate required under any Act of Parliament for the time being in force relating to marriage; or

(b) knowingly and wilfully makes, or knowingly and wilfully causes to be made, for the purpose of being inserted in any register of marriage, a false statement as to any particular required by law to be known and registered relating to any marriage; or

(c) forbids the issue of any certificate or licence for marriage by falsely representing himself to be a person whose consent to the marriage is required by law knowing such representation to be false; or

(d) with respect to a declaration made under section 16(1A) or 27B(2) of the Marriage Act 1949:

(i) enters a caveat under subsection (2) of the said section 16, or

(ii) makes a statement mentioned in subsection (4) of the said section 27B, which he knows to be false in a material particular,

he shall be guilty of [an offence,] and, on conviction thereof on indictment, shall be liable to imprisonment for a term not exceeding seven years or to a fine or to both imprisonment and fine [and on summary conviction thereof shall be liable to a penalty not exceeding the prescribed sum].

(2) No prosecution for knowingly and wilfully making a false declaration for the purpose of procuring any marriage out of the district in which the parties or one of them dwell shall take place after the expiration of eighteen months from the solemnization of the marriage to which the declaration refers.

An offence under the Perjury Act 1911, s. 3, is committed only by a person who acts for the purpose of procuring a marriage or licence etc. but whether or not he succeeds in this purpose is irrelevant. A false statement cannot, however, give rise to liability under the Perjury Act 1911, s. 3(1)(a) or (b), unless it concerns something which must by law be stated correctly (*Frickey* [1956] Crim LR 421).

See also the Civil Partnership Act 2004, s. 80 (false statements etc. with reference to civil partnerships).

The Perjury Act 1911, s. 13 (see **B14.14**) applies both to s. 3 and to s. 80 of the 2004 Act (by virtue of s. 80(4)).

False Statements about Births and Deaths

Perjury Act 1911, s. 4 **B14.21**

(1) If any person:

(a) wilfully makes any false answer to any question put to him by any registrar of births or deaths relating to the particulars required to be registered concerning any birth or death, or, wilfully gives to any such registrar any false information concerning any birth or death or the cause of any death; or

(b) wilfully makes any false certificate or declaration under or for the purposes of any Act relating to the registration of births or deaths, or, knowing any such certificate or declaration to be false, uses the same as true or gives or sends the same as true to any person; or

(c) wilfully makes, gives or uses any false statement or declaration as to a child born alive as having been still-born, or as to the body of a deceased person or still-born child in any coffin, or falsely pretends that any child born alive was still-born; or

(d) makes any false statement with intent to have the same inserted in any register of births or deaths:

he shall be guilty of [an offence] and shall be liable:

(i) on conviction thereof on indictment, to imprisonment for a term not exceeding seven years, or to a fine instead of the said punishments; and

(ii) on summary conviction thereof, to a penalty not exceeding [the prescribed sum].

(2) A prosecution on indictment for an offence against this section shall not be commenced more than three years after the commission of the offence.

As to the particulars requiring registration in relation to births or deaths, see the Births and Deaths Registration Act 1953, s. 39, and orders made thereunder. In contrast to the position under the Perjury Act 1911, s. 3, the wilful provision of any false information concerning a birth or death may involve liability, whether or not its provision was a strict legal requirement.

False statements as to the paternity of a child are obvious examples of the s. 4 offence, but cases of artificial insemination by donor (AID) can give rise to problems. The Family Law

Reform Act 1987, s. 27, provides that, where a married couple agree to such a scheme, the child 'shall be treated as the child of the parties to the marriage', and this probably means that the husband can lawfully be registered as the father; but some doubts have been expressed as to this, especially since s. 27(3) precludes the inheritance of titles of honour by such children.

Section 13 of the Perjury Act 1911, applies: see **B14.14** above.

False Statutory Declarations etc.

B14.22 **Perjury Act 1911, s. 5**

If any person knowingly and wilfully makes (otherwise than on oath) a statement false in a material particular, and the statement is made:
(a) in a statutory declaration; or
(b) in an abstract, account, balance sheet, book, certificate, declaration, entry, estimate, inventory, notice, report, return, or other document which he is authorised or required to make, attest, or verify, by any public general Act of Parliament for the time being in force; or
(c) in any oral declaration or oral answer which he is required to make by, under, or in pursuance of any public general Act of Parliament for the time being in force,
he shall be guilty of [an offence] and shall be liable on conviction thereof on indictment to imprisonment for any term not exceeding two years, or to a fine or to both such imprisonment and fine.

Perjury Act 1911, s. 15(2)

. . . The expression 'statutory declaration' means a declaration made by virtue of the Statutory Declarations Act 1835, or of any Act, order in council, rule or regulation applying or extending the provisions thereof;

As to the meaning of the phrase 'knowingly and wilfully' in this context, see *Sood* [1998] 2 Cr App R 355. The principal limitation on the scope of s. 5 (b) and (c) is the need to prove that A was statutorily authorised or required to make the declaration etc. which is alleged to be false. It would not appear to suffice that the declaration was made in connection with, or for the purpose of procuring, some benefit which is the subject of legislative control; but false statements in such circumstances are frequently penalised under other legislation. See, for example, the CJA 1925, s. 36, which creates an offence of making a statement which one knows to be untrue for the purpose of procuring a passport.

Section 13 applies to offences under s. 5 (see **B14.14**), and offences under s. 5 are triable either way (MCA 1980, s. 17 and sch. 1, para. 14).

False Declarations etc. to Obtain Registration for Carrying on a Vocation

B14.23 **Perjury Act 1911, s. 6**

If any person:
(a) procures or attempts to procure himself to be registered on any register or roll kept under or in pursuance of any public general Act of Parliament for the time being in force of persons qualified by law to practise any vocation or calling; or
(b) procures or attempts to procure a certificate of the registration of any person on any such register or roll as aforesaid,
by wilfully making or producing or causing to be made or produced either verbally or in writing, any declaration, certificate, or representation which he knows to be false or fraudulent, he shall be guilty of [an offence] and shall be liable on conviction thereof on indictment to imprisonment for any term not exceeding 12 months, or to a fine, or to both such imprisonment and fine.

A person should be charged with 'procuring' only where he has succeeded in his purpose under s. 6 (a) or (b). Where he fails in this, the charge should be one of attempting to procure, and this would be construed in accordance with the Criminal Attempts Act 1981, s. 3: see generally **A6.31 *et seq.***

Section 13 applies (see B14.14); and offences under this section are triable either way (MCA 1980, s. 17 and sch. 1, para. 14).

Offences under the Land Registration Act 2002

The offences shown below supplanted offences previously created by the Land Registration Act 1925, ss. 115 to 117, on 13 October 2003. **B14.24**

Land Registration Act 2002, ss. 123 and 124

123.—(1) A person commits an offence if in the course of proceedings relating to registration under this Act he suppresses information with the intention of—
(a) concealing a person's right or claim, or
(b) substantiating a false claim.
(2) A person guilty of an offence under this section is liable—
(a) on conviction on indictment, to imprisonment for a term not exceeding two years or to a fine;
(b) on summary conviction, to imprisonment for a term not exceeding six months or to a fine not exceeding the statutory maximum, or to both.

124.—(1) A person commits an offence if he dishonestly induces another—
(a) to change the register of title or cautions register, or
(b) to authorise the making of such a change.
(2) A person commits an offence if he intentionally or recklessly makes an unauthorised change in the register of title or cautions register.
(3) A person guilty of an offence under this section is liable—
(a) on conviction on indictment, to imprisonment for a term not exceeding 2 years or to a fine;
(b) on summary conviction, to imprisonment for a term not exceeding six months or to a fine not exceeding the statutory maximum, or to both.
(4) In this section, references to changing the register of title include changing a document referred to in it.

As to restrictions on the privilege against self-incrimination, see the Land Registration Act 2002, s. 125.

Relationship of Perjury Act 1911 to Other Enactments

Perjury Act 1911, s. 16 **B14.25**

(1) Where the making of a false statement is not only an offence under this Act, but also by virtue of some other Act is a corrupt practice or subjects the offender to any forfeiture or disqualification or to any penalty other than imprisonment, or fine, the liability of the offender under this Act shall be in addition to and not in substitution for his liability under such other Act.
(2) Nothing in this Act shall apply to a statement made without oath by a child under the provisions of the Prevention of Cruelty to Children Act 1904 and the Children Act 1908.
(3) Where the making of a false statement is by any other Act, whether passed before or after the commencement of this Act, made punishable on summary conviction, proceedings may be taken either under such other Act or under this Act:
Provided that where such an offence is by any Act passed before the commencement of this Act, as originally enacted, made punishable only on summary conviction, it shall remain only so punishable.

The provisions referred to in s. 16(2) have long been repealed. As to the position where a child gives false unsworn evidence in criminal proceedings, see B14.16.

PERVERTING THE COURSE OF JUSTICE

Definition

It is an offence at common law to do an act tending and intended to pervert the course of public justice (including criminal investigations and proceedings before tribunals). **B14.26**

Procedure

B14.27 This offence is triable only on indictment. It is a class 3 offence.

Indictment

B14.28 *Statement of Offence*

Perverting the course of justice

Particulars of Offence

A on or about the ... day of ... did an act tending to pervert the course of justice, namely falsifying a number of documents, namely ..., intended to be used as evidence in the prosecution of one X on indictment number ... preferred against the said X according to law in the Central Criminal Court, intending that the course of justice should thereby be perverted

Sentencing Guidelines

B14.29 The maximum penalty is life imprisonment and/or a fine.

The cases reflect the wide range of circumstances in which this offence may be committed. Those involving interference with, or threats to, witnesses or jurors are considered at **B14.41** below. Other cases involve the concealing of evidence, the giving of false or misleading information to the police and false allegations of crime. According to the Court of Appeal in *Walsh* (1993) 14 Cr App R (S) 671, sentencers must take care that the sentence reflects the actions taken by the offender which were intended to pervert the course of justice, rather than the substantive offence itself.

In *A-G's Ref (No. 19 of 1993)* (1994) 15 Cr App R (S) 760, the offender had killed a woman, dismembered her body, and placed the parts in plastic bags which he had disposed of in various places. Five years later he surrendered to the police and admitted what had happened. He was sentenced to three years' imprisonment for manslaughter and one year, concurrent, for doing an act tending to pervert the course of justice. The Court of Appeal said that the latter offence had been committed with persistence in a manner which any right-thinking member of the public would regard as grossly offensive. The proper sentence should have been two, or even three, years.

In *Johnson* [1998] 1 Cr App R (S) 169, the offender was seen by police officers indecently exposing himself and, when interviewed, he gave his brother's name and address. A summons was issued to the brother, at which point the deception was discovered. The Court of Appeal reduced a sentence of six months' imprisonment for doing an act tending to pervert the course of justice to two months on appeal. See also *Saxon* [1999] 1 Cr App R (S) 385 and *Hurst* (1990) 12 Cr App R (S) 373. *Hurst* was a more serious case, where the offender gave another man's name, and presented that other man's driving licence, when he was stopped by the police and arrested for having excess blood alcohol. The offender was convicted and disqualified in the other man's name before the deception came to light. A sentence of three and a half years' imprisonment following a guilty plea was reduced to 18 months on appeal.

Comparable sentences would appear to be appropriate where the offence takes the form of a false allegation of crime. In *Goodwin* (1989) 11 Cr App R (S) 194 a 20-year-old woman made a false complaint of rape, naming a particular man. The man was arrested and held in custody for 14 days, being released when the woman admitted what she had done. A sentence of three years' detention in a young offender institution was reduced on appeal to 18 months. Lord Lane CJ said that: 'It is necessary to make people understand that this sort of lie will be met by severe punishment. But we have to balance against that the age of this young woman and the circumstances in which she saw fit to tell these lies.' See also *Gregson* (1993) 14 Cr App R (S) 85 and *Sadiq* [1999] 2 Cr App R (S) 325.

Substantive Offences, Conspiracy and Attempt

B14.30 Indictments tended to allege attempts or conspiracies to pervert the course of justice, because it was thought that actual perversion of the course of justice would often be difficult to prove. Indeed, this form of indictment was used even in some cases where the course of justice had been wholly frustrated: see *Britton* [1973] RTR 502. It is now recognised, however, that an act which is intended to have this effect, and is capable of succeeding, may constitute the substantive offence, and should be charged accordingly. The Criminal Attempts Act 1981 does not generally have any application in such cases (unless perhaps A has failed to perform the act he intended) and references to 'attempts' to pervert the course of justice are accordingly misleading (*Rowell* [1978] 1 WLR 132; *Machin* [1980] 1 WLR 763; *Williams* (1991) 92 Cr App R 158).

Where there appears to have been a conspiracy, there may sometimes be certain advantages in charging the statutory offence under the Criminal Law Act 1977, s. 1; but see the *Consolidated Criminal Practice Direction*, para. 34.3 on the use of conspiracy charges.

Acts which May Amount to Perverting the Course of Justice

B14.31 The following acts have been held capable of amounting to this offence. It will be noted that some of them are equally capable, in certain circumstances, of amounting to contempt of court, offences under the Criminal Law Act 1967, s. 4 or s. 5, or subornation etc. of perjury; but in many cases the present offence has a wider scope, and may be easier to establish. In every case, however, there must be some positive act; mere failure to point out an error, as where the wrong person is prosecuted, cannot suffice (*Headley* [1995] Crim LR 737), nor is the offence committed by a motorist who fails to report an accident until any alcohol in his body has been eliminated (*Clark* [2003] 2 Cr App R 363). In *Sookoo* (2002) *The Times*, 10 April 2002, the court warned that charges of perverting the course of justice should not without good reason be added to cases in which a suspect has merely told lies when questioned. In many cases such charges 'only serve to complicate the sentencing process'. See also *Hamshaw* [2003] EWCA Crim 2435.

B14.32 **Deliberately Assisting a Person to Evade Arrest** *Thomas* [1979] QB 326 is an example of such a case. In contrast to the offence under the Criminal Law Act 1967, s. 4, it does not matter whether the offence was arrestable, and it is not strictly necessary to prove the guilt of the person assisted. Cf. *Spinks* [1982] 1 All ER 587.

B14.33 **Destroying, Falsifying or Concealing Potential Evidence** This form of the offence can occur whether or not legal proceedings have already been instigated (*Vreones* [1891] 1 QB 360; *Murray* [1982] 2 All ER 225; *Firetto* [1991] Crim LR 208; *Rafique* [1993] 3 WLR 617; *Kiffin* [1994] Crim LR 449). It was said in *Selvage* [1982] QB 372 that, if proceedings have not been instigated at that time, an investigation must have been in progress; but this would fail to deal with measures designed to prevent an offence ever being discovered, and cannot be reconciled with *Vreones*. In *Selvage*, the accused attempted to falsify details on X's driving licence, so as to obscure the fact he had endorsements; but this was with a view to protecting him if he should ever commit, and be charged with, a future road traffic offence. Insofar as the dicta in that case seem to refer to evidence in actual but undiscovered crimes or potential civil disputes, it is submitted that they are *obiter* and wrong. See also *Sharpe* [1938] 1 All ER 48 and *Sinha* [1995] Crim LR 68. An offence of perverting the course of justice may be committed by falsifying or procuring false evidence, even where the defendant's motive was to procure what he believed would be a true and fair verdict; although this is ultimately a matter for the consideration of the jury *(A-G's Ref (No. 1 of 2002)* [2003] Crim LR 410).

B14.34 **Interfering with Jurors or Witnesses** Successful prosecutions have been brought in cases involving interfering with jurors (*Mickleburgh* [1995] 1 Cr App R 297) or interfering with potential witnesses, so as to prevent or dissuade them from testifying (*Kellett* [1976] QB 372;

Panayiotou [1973] 1 WLR 1032) or so as to persuade them to change their evidence. There must be an intent to influence the course or outcome of the case in some way (*Lalani* [1999] 1 Cr App R 481). If the accused knowingly sought to prevent true evidence being given, or to procure false evidence, then his guilt is clear, even if no bribe, threat, undue pressure or other unlawful means were used (*Toney* [1993] 1 WLR 364). Problems may, however, arise where the accused claims that his object was to prevent a witness giving false evidence. Mere persuasion will not necessarily be an offence in such a case, even if the accused was wrong in believing that the witness's proposed evidence was false; but if the accused resorted to improper measures, he may be guilty. What is improper is generally a question of fact, but a jury should be directed that any threats, or any use of force, amounts to perversion of the course of justice, even where the threat is to take legal action for defamation or to exercise some other legal right, as long as the prosecution can prove necessary intent to influence the witness's evidence (*Toney*). One kind of threat should however be distinguished from the rest: a mere warning to a witness that he may be prosecuted for perjury if he gives false evidence should be insufficient to constitute an offence of perverting the course of justice. The new offences of witness or jury intimidation, which are created by the CJPO 1994, s. 51, operate in addition to, rather than in derogation of, the common law: see **B14.41**.

B14.35 **Offer or Agreement by Potential Witness** An offer or agreement by a potential witness to withhold (or, presumably, to change) his evidence in return for payment etc. may amount to perverting the course of justice (*Bassi* [1985] Crim LR 671). *Bassi* has been criticised as being inconsistent with *Murray* [1982] 2 All ER 225, where it was said that the offence would only be complete where a person has done something which might, without further action on his part, lead to potential injustice; but it could be argued that the course of justice is jeopardised as soon as any such offer or agreement is made, even if the witness could eventually decide to tell the truth after all, and if *Bassi* is inconsistent with *Murray*, it is to be preferred. See also the Criminal Law Act 1967, s. 5(1), discussed in **B14.59** to **B14.63**.

B14.36 **Confession to Another's Crime** Confessing to, or pleading guilty to, another person's crime, in order to shield him may amount to an offence (*Devito* [1975] Crim LR 175 but cf. *Headley* [1995] Crim LR 737).

B14.37 **Abuse of Police Discretion** Knowingly acting outside the limits of one's discretion as a police officer, so as to shield or excuse another person (e.g., a friend) from criminal charges may amount to perverting the course of justice (*Coxhead* [1986] RTR 411). It is for the jury to decide whether A had any discretion to act as he did, and, if not, whether he might mistakenly have believed he had (*Coxhead*). See also *Ward* [1995] Crim LR 398.

B14.38 **False Allegations** Making false allegations against another person, intending that he should be prosecuted or knowing that he might be may be an offence (*Rowell* [1978] 1 WLR 132). Where false stories merely waste police time, a charge under the Criminal Law Act 1967, s. 5(2), may be more appropriate (see **B14.68**) but even where no alleged offender is named, there may be a risk that an innocent person could be arrested and/or prosecuted, and this may accordingly amount to perverting the course of justice (see *Cotter* [2003] QB 951). It makes no difference if, unknown to the accused, the subject of these allegations has died, because the vice of the offence lies in the intent (*Brown* [2004] EWCA Crim 744). Where it can be proved that D acted with intent to pervert the course of justice (e.g., by falsely reporting a crime), it is not necessary to prove whether he intended to pervert the course of criminal or civil justice (*Iaquaniello* [2005] EWCA Crim 2029).

Compensation of Victims and Settlement of Disputes

B14.39 No offence is committed where one person merely offers to settle his civil dispute with another by offering (or asking for) payment, or where a third party offers such a settlement on behalf of one or other litigant (*Panayiotou* [1973] 1 WLR 1032 at p. 1038).

The position becomes more complicated and uncertain where the offer is made to the victim of a crime, who is a potential prosecution witness; but the Criminal Law Act 1967, s. 5(1) (see **B14.59**), appears to recognise that the victim would commit no offence merely by accepting an offer of 'reasonable compensation for loss or injury' in return for not disclosing the crime, and it may be inferred that the offeror would equally commit no offence. An agreement to accept more than such compensation (i.e. a bribe) would appear to be an offence under s. 5(1) (assuming the offence to have been arrestable) and the offeror would be a party to this, whether or not he is also guilty of perverting the course of justice (see *Ali* [1993] Crim LR 396). And see, with regard to advertisements offering rewards for the return of stolen goods, the Theft Act 1968, s. 23.

OFFENCES AKIN TO PERVERSION OF COURSE OF JUSTICE

Certain other kinds of conduct might be regarded as amounting to the perversion of public justice, but are more commonly charged under other heads. In addition to those dealt with below, certain forms of advertisement offering rewards for the return of stolen goods contravene the Theft Act 1968, s. 23 (see **B4.151** and **B4.152**). Concealing or transferring the proceeds of criminal conduct for the purpose of avoiding prosecution may be punishable under the Proceeds of Crime Act 2002, s. 327, and 'tipping off' another person as to a proposed money laundering investigation may be punishable under s. 333 of that Act (see **B22** for the offences). **B14.40**

Intimidation of, or Retaliation against, Witnesses, Jurors and Others

The intimidation of witnesses, jurors or other persons involved in legal proceedings or investigations may be punishable at common law, not only as tending to the perversion of the course of justice (see **B14.34**), but also as contempt of court. Retaliation against former witnesses etc. is also punishable as contempt (see **B14.83**). Indeed, any improper interference with or approach to a witness or juror (present, past or future), whether based on intimidation, bribery or persuasion, will almost invariably be punishable under one or other of those heads. See, for example, *Mickleburgh* [1995] 1 Cr App R 297 and *A-G v Judd* [1995] COD 15 at **B14.83**. **B14.41**

Acts of intimidation or retaliation may, alternatively, be dealt with under the CJPO 1994, s. 51, or (where the victim is a witness or potential witness in a civil case) under the CJPA 2001, ss. 39 to 41.

Criminal Justice and Public Order Act 1994, s. 51

(1) A person commits an offence if—
  (a) he does an act which intimidates, and is intended to intimidate, another person ('the victim'),
  (b) he does the act knowing or believing that the victim is assisting in the investigation of an offence or is a witness or potential witness or a juror or potential juror in proceedings for an offence, and
  (c) he does it intending thereby to cause the investigation or the course of justice to be obstructed, perverted or interfered with.

(2) A person commits an offence if—
  (a) he does an act which harms, and is intended to harm, another person or, intending to cause another person to fear harm, he threatens to do an act which would harm that other person,
  (b) he does or threatens to do the act knowing or believing that the person harmed or threatened to be harmed ('the victim'), or some other person, has assisted in an investigation into an offence or has given evidence or particular evidence in proceedings for an offence, or has acted as a juror or concurred in a particular verdict in proceedings for an offence, and
  (c) he does or threatens to do it because of that knowledge or belief.

(3) For the purposes of subsections (1) and (2) it is immaterial that the act is or would be done, or that the threat is made—
(a) otherwise than in the presence of the victim, or
(b) to a person other than the victim.
(4) The harm that may be done or threatened may be financial as well as physical (whether to the person or a person's property) and similarly as respects an intimidatory act which consists of threats.
(5) The intention required by subsection (1)(c) and the motive required by subsection (2)(c) above need not be the only or the predominating intention or motive with which the act is done or, in the case of subsection (2), threatened.
(6) A person guilty of an offence under this section shall be liable—
(a) on conviction on indictment, to imprisonment for a term not exceeding five years or a fine or both;
(b) on summary conviction, to imprisonment for a term not exceeding six months or a fine not exceeding the statutory maximum or both.
(7) If, in proceedings against a person for an offence under subsection (1) above, it is proved that he did an act falling within paragraph (a) with the knowledge or belief required by paragraph (b), he shall be presumed, unless the contrary is proved, to have done the act with the intention required by paragraph (c) of that subsection.
(8) If, in proceedings against a person for an offence under subsection (2) above, it is proved that within the relevant period—
(a) he did an act which harmed, and was intended to harm, another person, or
(b) intending to cause another person fear of harm, he threatened to do an act which would harm that other person,
and that he did the act, or (as the case may be) threatened to do the act with the knowledge or belief required by paragraph (b), he shall be presumed, unless the contrary is proved, to have done the act or (as the case may be) threatened to do the act with the motive required by paragraph (c) of that subsection.
(9) In this section—
'investigation into an offence' means such an investigation by the police or other person charged with the duty of investigating offences or charging offenders;
'offence' includes an alleged or suspected offence;
'potential', in relation to a juror, means a person who has been summoned for jury service at the court at which proceedings for the offence are pending; and
'the relevant period'—
(a) in relation to a witness or juror in any proceedings for an offence, means the period beginning with the institution of the proceedings and ending with the first anniversary of the conclusion of the trial or, if there is an appeal or reference under section 17 of the Criminal Appeal Act 1968, of the conclusion of the appeal;
(b) in relation to a person who has or is believed by the accused to have, assisted in an investigation into an offence, but was not also a witness in proceedings for an offence, means the period of one year beginning with any act of his, or any act believed by the accused to be an act of his, assisting in the investigation; and
(c) in relation to a person who both has or is believed by the accused to have, assisted in the investigation into an offence and was a witness in proceedings for the offence, means the period beginning with any act of his, or any act believed by the accused to be an act of his, assisting in the investigation and ending with the anniversary mentioned in paragraph (a) above.

An offence of intimidation under s. 51(1) may be committed even where the victim refuses to be intimidated (*Patrascu* [2004] 4 All ER 1066) but cannot be committed on the basis of a mistaken belief that an investigation is in progress. See *Singh* [1999] Crim LR 681. It follows that 'belief for the purposes of s. 51(2) must also mean a correct or justified belief. A criminal attempt may however be committed on the basis of a mistaken belief (see **A6.40**).

B14.42 **Relationship with Common-law Offence** Apart from being triable either way, the offence created by s. 51(1) appears to offer few advantages over the common-law offence of perverting the course of justice (which is preserved under s. 51(11)). The latter would indeed be committed even if bribery or persuasion were used in place of intimidation. As to the burden of proof, the Court of Appeal in *A-G's Ref (No. 1 of 2004)* [2004] 1 WLR 2111 had 'no hesitation in concluding' that for this offence the legal burden of proof imposed on a defendant by s. 51(7) is both justified and proportional under the ECHR, Article 6.

In contrast, the offence created by s. 51(2) covers conduct that would not ordinarily amount to perverting the course of justice, and carries heavier penalties than those available for contempt of court (as to which, see **B14.79**). Committal for contempt may not, in any case, be a wholly satisfactory method of dealing with conduct of this type, especially where it occurs after the original trial has ended.

Sentence In *Williams* [1997] 2 Cr App R (S) 221 the offender, after having been convicted of false imprisonment and unlawful wounding, wrote to the victim of those offences from prison, threatening her with violence. For this offence under s. 51(2), to which the offender pleaded guilty, a further sentence of two years' imprisonment, consecutive to the three-year term being served, was upheld by the Court of Appeal. Harrison J noted that the offence under s. 51(2) carried a maximum of five years, as compared with two years for contempt of court, and said that such intimidation must be viewed extremely seriously. The Court of Appeal in *Watmore* [1998] 2 Cr App R (S) 46 upheld a sentence of four years' imprisonment where the offender was convicted of an offence under s. 51. The offender had encountered a man who had earlier given evidence against him in a magistrates' court, and had punched and butted the victim, causing severe cuts and bruises. The court noted that incidents of witness intimidation were now endemic, and becoming worse. See also *Edmonds* [1999] 1 Cr App R (S) 475. **B14.43**

Witnesses in Civil Proceedings The CJPA 2001 makes similar provision (in ss. 39 to 41) to protect witnesses and potential witnesses in civil cases. Section 39 corresponds to the CJPO 1994, s. 51(1); the CJPA 2001, s. 40 corresponds to s. 51(2) of the 1994 Act. The CJPA 2001, ss. 39 to 41, came into force on 1 August 2001, but apply only in respect of 'relevant' proceedings that were commenced after that time (s. 41). **B14.44**

Embracery and Bribery

The bribery of a juror, or other attempts to influence jurors out of court, may in theory be charged as the common law offence of embracery, but are more likely in practice to be dealt with as perverting the course of justice or as contempt of court (*Owen* [1976] 1 WLR 840). **B14.45**

Improper payments to judges, magistrates, or other judicial officers may be punished as contempt or as bribery at common law (*Harrison* (1800) 1 East PC 382). Receipt of the bribe could also be charged as the common-law offence of misconduct in a public office (as to which see *Llewellyn-Jones* [1968] 1 QB 429).

As to contempt of court, see **B14.69** to **B14.110**.

Personating a Juror

It is an offence at common law, punishable with a fine and imprisonment at large, to impersonate someone summoned for jury service, so as to sit in his place. The motive is irrelevant (*Clark* (1918) 82 JP 295). **B14.46**

Disposing of a Body with Intent to Prevent an Inquest

The concealment, disposal or destruction of a corpse is a common-law offence, punishable with a fine and imprisonment at large, if done to prevent the holding of a lawful inquest as to the death (*Stephenson* (1884) 13 QBD 331). There is a separate common-law offence of preventing the decent and lawful burial of a body. This may be committed by anyone who unlawfully conceals or destroys a body (see *Hunter* [1974] QB 95). **B14.47**

In *Godward* [1998] 1 Cr App R (S) 385 the offender pleaded guilty to obstructing the coroner by concealing a body. The police found the decomposed body of a man in the offender's flat. Godward had failed to disclose the whereabouts of the body, despite being twice asked by the police to assist them in tracing him. Lord Bingham CJ, in the Court of Appeal, said that the most important factor was the intention of the perpetrator. If the purpose was to obstruct the course of justice and to make it difficult to bring home a charge against the offender or another person, the offence would merit punishment towards the top of the appropriate bracket. If such intention was lacking, a lesser sentence was appropriate. On the present facts, a prison sentence of four years was reduced to three years. See also *Blakemore* [1997] 2 Cr App R (S) 255.

On sentencing for the latter offence, Ousley J commented in *Whiteley* [2001] 2 Cr App R (S) 119 that this was a serious matter, capable of interfering with the administration of justice and causing grief for the bereaved. It deprived the deceased of a proper burial and sometimes raised anxieties in the minds of relatives as to whether the person had been dead when the attempts at concealment had been made. On the facts, where the offender had not been in any way responsible for the death but had assisted in removing the body of a man who was a drug addict from the flat where he had died to conceal it in a ditch, a sentence of 30 months was reduced to 18 months, with a further three months consecutive for failing to answer bail upheld. See also *Parry* (1986) 8 Cr App R (S) 476.

ASSISTING OFFENDERS

Definition

B14.48 **Criminal Law Act 1967, s. 4**

(1) Where a person has committed a relevant offence, any other person who, knowing or believing him to be guilty of the offence or of some other relevant offence, does without lawful authority or reasonable excuse any act with intent to impede his apprehension or prosecution shall be guilty of an offence.

(1A) In this section and section 5 below, 'relevant offence' means—

(a) an offence for which the sentence is fixed by law,

(b) an offence for which a person of 18 years or over (not previously convicted) may be sentenced to imprisonment for a term of five years (or might be so sentenced but for the restrictions imposed by section 33 of the Magistrates' Courts Acts 1980).

At common law, a person knowingly rendering assistance to a person who had committed a felony became an accessory after the fact, and thus guilty of that felony. This provision created a specific offence to replace that principle.

Procedure

B14.49 **Criminal Law Act 1967, s. 4**

(4) No proceedings shall be instituted for an offence under subsection (1) . . . except by or with the consent of the Director of Public Prosecutions.

Indictment

B14.50 *Statement of Offence*

Assisting an offender contrary to section 4(1) of the Criminal Law Act 1967

Particulars of Offence

A on the . . . day of . . ., X having committed a relevant offence, namely robbery, knowing or believing that X had committed the said offence or some other relevant offence, without lawful authority or reasonable excuse harboured X in his house, with intent to impede the apprehension or prosecution of X

Alternative Verdicts

Criminal Law Act 1967, s. 4 B14.51

(2) If on the trial of an indictment for a relevant offence the jury are satisfied that the offence charged (or some other offence of which the accused might on that charge be found guilty) was committed, but find the accused not guilty of it, they may find him guilty of any offence under subsection (1) . . . of which they are satisfied that he is guilty in relation to the offence charged (or that other offence).

If A is not initially charged with a s. 4 offence, but with a substantive relevant offence, and the possibility of an alternative verdict under subsection (2) manifests itself in the course of the trial, the defence should be given sufficient opportunity to meet such a possibility. The possibility should not be raised after the court has finished hearing evidence (*Cross* [1971] 3 All ER 641; *Vincent* (1972) 56 Cr App R 281).

Sentencing Guidelines

Where the principal offence is subject to a sentence fixed by law the maximum penalty is ten years, a fine, or both, on indictment (Criminal Law Act 1967, s. 4(3)(a)); and six months, a fine not exceeding the statutory maximum, or both, summarily. Where the principal offence is subject to a sentence of 14 years, the maximum penalty is seven years, a fine, or both, on indictment (Criminal Law Act 1967, s. 4(3)(b)); and six months, a fine not exceeding the statutory maximum, or both, summarily. Where the principal offence is subject to a sentence of 10 years, the maximum penalty is five years, a fine, or both, on indictment (Criminal Law Act 1967, s. 4(3)(c)); and six months, a fine not exceeding the statutory maximum, or both, summarily. In other cases: the maximum penalty is three years, a fine, or both, on indictment (Criminal Law Act 1967, s. 4(3)(d)); and six months, a fine not exceeding the statutory maximum, or both, summarily. B14.52

In *Matthews* (1982) 4 Cr App R (S) 233 the offender had allowed another man, wanted by the police in connection with an armed robbery, to stay in his flat for 3 to 4 weeks; a sentence of 12 months' imprisonment was upheld. In *Hunter* (1984) 6 Cr App R (S) 54 the offender harboured a man wanted for the shooting of another man and, when the police came to his flat, told them he was not there; a sentence of 12 months' imprisonment was held to be appropriate. By contrast, in *Mosely* (1988) 10 Cr App R (S) 55 the offender hid two men away from the police without knowing what crimes they were wanted for. The men were subsequently sentenced to lengthy custodial terms for robbery and burglary. A sentence of eight months imposed on the offender was reduced on appeal to three months. See also *Urwin* [1996] 2 Cr App R (S) 281.

Offence Cannot be Committed by Omission

This offence is not capable of taking the form of an omission. Shielding another person by silence etc. is rarely a crime, but see the Criminal Law Act 1967, s. 5, and **B14.59**. B14.53

Requirement that Relevant Offence has been Committed

An offence under the Criminal Law Act 1967, s. 4, can be committed only where a relevant offence has previously been committed by the person assisted, and proof of that person's guilt is accordingly an essential element in proof of this offence. B14.54

It is not necessary for the person allegedly assisted to be convicted of his offence before someone can be convicted of assisting (*Donald* (1986) Cr App R 49), nor is the person assisted's conviction conclusive proof of his guilt at the subsequent trial of a person accused of assisting; but the prior conviction of the person assisted will raise a presumption that he was guilty, and this will simplify the task of the prosecution at the trial. It would be for the defence to prove, on balance of probabilities, that the conviction of the person assisted was wrong. See the PACE 1984, s. 74, and **F11.5**.

Evidence of the acquittal of the person assisted at a previous trial is not admissible at the assister's trial, however; and even where the assister and the person allegedly assisted are tried together, confession evidence admissible against one might not be admissible against the other. In *Spinks* [1982] 1 All ER 587 an admission by the person allegedly assisted that he had committed the relevant offence was held to be inadmissible against the accused on a charge of assisting him, but contrast *Hayter* [2003] 1 WLR 1910, in which the court held that the reasoning behind the ruling in *Spinks* has been undermined by the enactment of the PACE 1984, s. 74.

It may even be possible for the same court or jury to acquit Dl of committing the alleged offence, but convict D2 of assisting him to evade apprehension. Such a verdict would however be justifiable only where evidence admissible against D2 is inadmissible against Dl. If the court or jury has any real doubts as to the guilt of Dl, D2 must also be acquitted. Cf. *Shannon* [1975] AC 717 (conviction of single conspirator).

Many of the problems arising from use of s. 4 can be avoided by charging an assister with perverting the course of justice: see **B14.26** to **B14.39**. In some cases there may be an overlap between s. 4 and the money laundering offences in the Proceeds of Crime Act 2002, part 7 (see B22).

Knowledge of or Belief in the Guilt of the Person Assisted

B14.55 By analogy with decisions concerning the offence of handling stolen goods (where knowledge or belief is similarly a *mens rea* element), it is clear that the accused must either know or positively believe in the guilt of the person assisted. Mere suspicion, however strong and well founded, would not suffice. On the other hand, the Criminal Law Act 1967, s. 4(1), expressly provides that an accused may be guilty even if he is mistaken about what offence the person assisted has committed; and the language used is wide enough to embrace cases where the accused knew that the person assisted must have committed a serious offence, but had no idea what offence it may have been (*Morgan* [1972] 1 QB 436).

Intent to Impede Apprehension or Prosecution

B14.56 The intent to impede the apprehension etc. of the person assisted is an ulterior intent. It is not necessary that the person assisted should have benefited from the accused's actions; indeed, they may be wholly unsuccessful and lead unwittingly to his immediate arrest.

Lawful Authority or Reasonable Excuse

B14.57 The legal burden of proving the accused's absence of lawful authority etc. appears to rest on the prosecution (*Brindley* [1971] 2 QB 300). In contrast to certain other offences in which lawful authority or reasonable excuse may be raised, the Criminal Law Act 1967, s. 4, does not impose the burden of proof on the accused; see, e.g., the Prevention of Crime Act 1953, s. 1 (**B12.118**). However, the accused must raise the issue by some admissible evidence, before this burden arises. As to evidential burdens on the defence, see generally **F3.5** *et seq.* It is difficult to imagine what might amount to lawful authority or reasonable excuse in any normal circumstances.

No Offence of Attempting to Assist

B14.58 There can be no offence of attempting to commit an offence under the Criminal Law Act 1967, s. 4 (Criminal Attempts Act 1981, s. 1(4)).

CONCEALING OFFENCES

Definition

Criminal Law Act 1967, s. 5 **B14.59**

(1) Where a person has committed a relevant offence, any other person who, knowing or believing that the offence or some other relevant offence has been committed, and that he has information which might be of material assistance in securing the prosecution or conviction of an offender for it, accepts or agrees to accept for not disclosing that information any consideration other than the making good of loss or injury caused by the offence, or the making of reasonable compensation for that loss or injury, shall be liable on conviction on indictment to imprisonment for not more than two years. . . .

(5) The compounding of an offence other than treason shall not be an offence otherwise than under this section.

The term 'relevant offence' is defined by s. 4(1A) (see **B14.48**).

Procedure

No proceedings shall be instituted for an offence under this section except by or with the consent of the DPP (s. 5(3)). **B14.60**

Concealing a relevant offence is triable either way where the underlying offence is so triable (MCA 1980, s. 17 and sch. 1, para. 26). As in the case of assisting offenders, contrary to the Criminal Law Act 1967, s. 4, an anomalous position arises with respect to the purely summary offence of taking a conveyance without authority (see **B14.49**).

Indictment

Statement of Offence **B14.61**

Concealing a relevant offence contrary to section 5(1) of the Criminal Law Act 1967

Particulars of Offence

A on the . . . day of . . ., X having committed a relevant offence, namely robbery, knowing or believing that the said or some other relevant offence had been committed and that he had information which might be of material assistance in securing the prosecution or conviction of X for it, accepted (or agreed to accept) consideration, namely a payment of £1,000, which was neither a making good of loss or injury caused by the said offence nor the making of reasonable compensation therefor, for not disclosing the said information

Sentencing Guidelines

The maximum penalty on indictment is two years (Criminal Law Act 1967, s. 5(1)). Summarily, the maximum penalty is six months and/or a fine not exceeding the statutory maximum. As to sentencing, see the cases considered in respect of assisting offenders in B14.52. **B14.62**

Elements

The common-law offences of misprision of felony and compounding a felony were both abolished by the Criminal Law Act 1967. Misprision of treason remains an offence and there are now statutory offences of non-disclosure in relation to certain terrorist offences (see **B10.39** ***et seq.***) and money laundering (see **B22**). With these exceptions, the non-disclosure of offences cannot ordinarily be punishable. Compounding an offence other than treason cannot now be an offence other than under the Criminal Law Act 1967, s. 5(1) (s. 5(5)). **B14.63**

The striking of a bargain, in which a promise of silence or non-disclosure is exchanged for consideration going beyond reasonable compensation to the victim, is another matter, and is punishable under s. 5(1). It is the agreement which constitutes the gist of the offence. The accused will remain guilty, even if he later breaks the agreement and informs the police.

As with the Criminal Law Act 1967, s. 4 (see **B14.48** to **B14.58**), the prosecution must prove that the other person did indeed commit a relevant offence (see **B14.54**); and where this might be difficult there may similarly be advantages in charging a person who has agreed to conceal a crime with perverting the course of justice. A person who demands money for his silence might also be guilty of blackmail (see **B14.92** to **B14.100**).

As with assisting offenders there can be no offence of attempting to commit an offence under this section (Criminal Attempts Act 1981, s. 1(4)).

OTHER OFFENCES RELATING TO OFFENDERS

Escape

B14.64 It is a common-law offence, punishable on indictment by a fine and imprisonment at large, to escape from legal custody. The escape may be from police custody following arrest (*Timmis* [1976] Crim LR 129) or from custody or imprisonment etc. following remand or conviction (*Moss* (1985) 82 Cr App R 116).

In a case of alleged escape, the prosecution must prove that the D was in custody; that he knew this (or was reckless as to whether he was or not); that the custody was lawful; and that he intentionally escaped from it (*Dhillon* [2006] 1 WLR 1535; see also *Dillon v The Queen* [1982] AC 484). But it is irrelevant whether he was guilty of the crime for which he was arrested or imprisoned (*Waters* (1873) 12 Cox CC 390).

A partial definition of 'legal custody' is provided by s. 13(2) of the Prison Act 1952:

Prison Act 1952, s. 13

(2) A prisoner shall be deemed to be in legal custody while he is confined in, or is being taken to or from, any prison and while he is working, or is for any other reason, outside the prison in the custody or under the control of an officer of the prison and while he is being taken to any place to which he is required or authorised by or under this Act or the CJA 1982 to be taken, or is kept in custody in pursuance of any such requirement or authorisation.

The references to 'prison' apply equally to remand centres and young offender institutions (Prison Act 1952, s. 43(5)). The reference to 'an officer of the prison' is to be construed as a reference to a prisoner custody officer performing custodial duties at the prison (CJA 1991, s. 87(6)).

A person may be in lawful custody even though he is not physically restrained or guarded (e.g., where he is left unguarded in court). The question of whether D was in custody at the relevant time is primarily a question of fact, to be decided on a case-by-case basis (see *Rumble* (2003) 167 JP 205). A juvenile who is remanded into the custody of the local authority under the CYPA 1969, s. 23, without a security requirement, and who has been told by a member of the youth offending team to remain where he is, may be guilty of escaping from lawful custody if he makes off when left unsupervised (see *H v DPP* [2003] Crim LR 560).

In *Page* (1987) 9 Cr App R (S) 348 the offender pleaded guilty to escaping from lawful custody. There was no pre-planning involved. The offender took the opportunity to escape from custody in the cells of a magistrates' court by taking advantage of a disturbance in the cells, pushing the officer behind a gate and tying it with a belt. A sentence of 21 months' imprisonment was upheld on appeal. Eighteen months was said to be proper in respect of each count in *Williams* (1987) 9 Cr App R (S) 531, where the offender escaped twice, once from a police station and once from a remand centre. According to the Court of Appeal in *Clarke* (1994) 15 Cr App R (S) 825, in most cases of escape from custody it is necessary to impose a custodial sentence to run consecutively to the sentence being served. See also *Hammond* (1995) 16 Cr App R (S) 142.

Breach of Prison

This offence is similar to escape, but must involve some breaking, cutting, or forcing in the course of the escape. It need not involve escape from an actual prison (forcing open a police station window would suffice) and need not involve any deliberate damage (see *Haswell* (1821) Russ & Ry 458, where accidental dislodging of loose bricks while scaling the prison wall was held to suffice). **B14.65**

The case of *Coughtrey* [1997] 2 Cr App R (S) 269 provides sentencing guidelines for this offence. The offender was serving a life sentence for murder and escaped after two years by burning through the perimeter fence with cutting equipment and then scaling the outer wall. He gave himself up a week later. A sentence of seven years' imprisonment for prison breach was reduced on appeal to four years. McCowan LJ in the Court of Appeal noted that breaking prison is a very serious offence for which a substantial sentence of imprisonment is always to be expected because of the fear and apprehension it generates, the disruption to prison life, the violence and disorder that it may lead to, and the need to deter the culprit and others. Factors to be taken into account in fixing the length of the sentence will include (i) the nature and circumstances of the original offence, (ii) the offender's conduct while in prison, (iii) the methods employed in effecting escape and, in particular, whether any violence was used and whether there was extensive planning and outside assistance, (iv) whether he surrendered himself and how soon, and (v) a plea of guilty. If the original sentence is a determinate one, the sentence for prison breach should almost always be ordered to run consecutively. If the original sentence is a life sentence, the sentence for prison breach should usually be the same as if he had been serving a determinate sentence, but it will have to be served concurrently.

Remaining at Large after Temporary Release

Under the Prisoners (Return to Custody) Act 1995, s. 1(1), a person who has been temporarily released in pursuance of rules made under the Prison Act 1952, s. 47(5), will be guilty of a summary offence, punishable by imprisonment for a term not exceeding six months and/or a fine not exceeding level 5 on the standard scale if: **B14.66**

(a) without reasonable excuse he remains unlawfully at large at any time after the expiry of the period for which he was temporarily released; or
(b) knowing or believing an order recalling him to have been made, and while unlawfully at large by virtue of such an order, he fails, without reasonable excuse, to take all necessary steps for complying as soon as reasonably practicable with that order.

The offence does not apply to persons temporarily released from secure training centres (s. 1(2)).

Assisting Escape and Harbouring Escapees

The following offences have been created by statute: **B14.67**

Prison Act 1952, s. 39

Any person who aids any prisoner in escaping or attempting to escape from a prison or who, with intent to facilitate the escape of any prisoner, conveys any thing into a prison or to a prisoner sends anything (by post or otherwise) into a prison or to a prisoner or places any thing anywhere outside a prison with a view to its coming into the possession of a prisoner, shall be guilty of [an offence] and liable to imprisonment for a term not exceeding ten years.

Criminal Justice Act 1961, s. 22

(2) If any person knowingly harbours a person who has escaped from a prison or other institution to which . . . section 39 [of this Act] applies, or who, having been sentenced in

Part B Offences

> any part of the United Kingdom or in any of the Channel Islands or the Isle of Man to imprisonment or detention, is otherwise unlawfully at large, or who gives to any such person any assistance with intent to prevent, hinder or interfere with his being taken into custody, he shall be liable—
> (a) on summary conviction, to imprisonment for a term not exceeding six months, or to a fine not exceeding [£5,000] or to both;
> (b) on conviction on indictment, to imprisonment for a term not exceeding ten years, or to a fine, or to both.

These offences apply where the escape is from a prison, remand centre or young offender institution; but the Prison Act 1952, s. 13, does not apply to, and neither statutory offence can therefore be committed in respect of, a person who escapes from custody whilst in transit to or from prison, or from court etc. (*Nicoll v Catron* (1985) 81 Cr App R 339; *Moss* (1985) 82 Cr App R 116). In both *Nicoll v Catron*, and *Moss*, it was stated (*obiter*) that common-law offences had been committed, even though the statutory offences under the Prison Act 1952, s. 39, and the CJA 1961, s. 22, had not. These offences were not identified in *Moss*, and *Nicoll v Catron* contains only a reference to perverting the course of justice; but there is also a common-law offence of forcible rescue from lawful custody (see 2 Hawk PC, ch. 21).

The most serious reported sentencing case is *Bowman* [1997] 1 Cr App R (S) 282, where a sentence of seven years' imprisonment was upheld in respect of a conspiracy to assist prisoners to escape by smuggling a pistol into Durham Prison. The pistol was found after a search by prison officers. In *Walker* (1990) 12 Cr App R (S) 65, a sentence of nine months' imprisonment was upheld on an offender who pleaded guilty to aiding a prisoner to escape from an open prison by meeting him outside the prison and giving him a lift in his car. In *Williams* (1992) 13 Cr App R (S) 236, the appropriate sentence was said to be 15 months where the offender had changed places with a prisoner in an open prison for one night to allow the prisoner to spend a night at home. Twelve months' imprisonment was reduced to nine months in *Taylor* (1994) 15 Cr App R (S) 893 where the offender pleaded guilty to harbouring an escaped prisoner, his brother.

Mental Health Act 1983, s. 128

> (1) Where any person induces or knowingly assists another person who is liable to be detained in a hospital within the meaning of part II of this Act or is subject to guardianship under this Act to absent himself without leave he shall be guilty of an offence.
> (2) Where any person induces or knowingly assists another person who is in legal custody by virtue of section 137 [of this Act] to escape from such custody he shall be guilty of an offence.
> (3) Where any person knowingly harbours a patient who is absent without leave or is otherwise at large and liable to be retaken under this Act or gives him any assistance with intent to prevent, hinder or interfere with his being taken into custody or returned to the hospital or other place where he ought to be he shall be guilty of an offence.
> (4) Any person guilty of an offence under this section shall be liable—
> (a) on summary conviction, to imprisonment for a term not exceeding six months or to a fine not exceeding the statutory maximum, or to both;
> (b) on conviction on indictment, to imprisonment for a term not exceeding two years or to a fine of any amount, or to both.

Wasting Police Time

B14.68 **Criminal Law Act 1967, s. 5**

> (2) Where a person causes any wasteful employment of the police by knowingly making to any person a false report tending to show that an offence has been committed, or to give rise to apprehension for the safety of any persons or property, or tending to show that he has information material to any police inquiry, he shall be liable on summary conviction to imprisonment for not more than six months or to a fine of not more than level 4 on the standard scale or to both.

No proceedings for this offence may be instituted except by or with the consent of the DPP (Criminal Law Act 1967, s. 5(3)). By virtue of the Penalties for Disorderly Behaviour

(Amount of Penalty) Order 2002 (SI 2002 No. 1837), as amended, the offence under s. 5(2) is a penalty offence and the amount payable is £80.

As to the relationship between the s. 5(2) offence and the more serious offence of perverting the course of justice, see *Cotter* [2003] QB 951.

As to false (hoax) fire alarms, see the Fire and Rescue Services Act 2004, s. 49, discussed at **B11.115**.

CONTEMPT OF COURT

The last part of this section is primarily concerned with criminal contempt of court, and more particularly with that offence in so far as it affects the criminal courts. Some reference is necessarily made to civil contempt and to the jurisdiction of the civil courts in respect of criminal contempt, but those topics are not covered in any detail.

Nature of Contempt

Criminal contempt of court is a broadly based offence, and can take a number of different forms. At common law, it has been defined as behaviour 'involving an interference with the due administration of justice, either in a particular case or more generally as a continuing process' (*A-G v Leveller Magazine Ltd* [1979] AC 440, per Lord Diplock at p. 449). It is not possible to provide an exhaustive list of the ways in which the offence can be committed, although a substantial number of typical examples are given at **B14.82** to **B14.99**. As Donaldson MR said in *A-G v Newspaper Publishing plc* [1988] Ch 333 at p. 368: **B14.69**

> The law of contempt is based on the broadest of principles, namely that the courts cannot and will not permit interference with the due administration of justice. Its application is universal. The fact that it is applied in novel circumstances . . . is not a case of widening its application. It is merely a new example of its application.

Broadly based though it is, criminal contempt can nevertheless be categorised according to whether it is committed 'in the face of the court' or committed indirectly (i.e. a 'constructive' contempt, such as the publication of a book or article prejudicing a forthcoming trial in a way which may influence potential jurors or witnesses). Only the superior courts have jurisdiction to punish for constructive contempts (*Lefroy* (1873) LR 8 QB 134), whereas any court of record (including county courts and coroners' courts) may punish contempt in the face of the court. (As to the position of magistrates' courts, see **B14.73**.) It does not follow that constructive contempt of an inferior court must go unpunished; jurisdiction to commit for such contempt may be exercised by the Divisional Court of the Queen's Bench Division under the Rules of the Supreme Court 1965, ord. 52 (see **B14.77**).

Criminal contempt of court has traditionally been distinguished from civil contempt, which takes the form of non-compliance with a court order (or an undertaking in lieu of an order) favouring another party. This distinction has always been problematic, particularly since quasi-criminal sanctions are applicable to both categories. It has also been held that the appropriate standard of proof is that beyond reasonable doubt, even in cases of civil contempt (see e.g., *Re Bramblevale Ltd* [1970] Ch 128), and even though the proceedings may remain civil proceedings to which the Civil Evidence Acts apply (see e.g., *Savings & Investment Bank Ltd v Gasco Investments (Netherlands) BV (No. 2)* [1988] Ch 422). The distinction has been criticised both by the Phillimore Committee (Cmnd 5794), which advocated its abolition, and by the Court of Appeal (Civil Division) in *A-G v Newspaper Publishing plc* [1988] Ch 333, which suggested a reclassification under which the misleading terms 'civil' and 'criminal' would no longer be used.

Few real points of distinction remain; but in cases of civil contempt it is usually up to the opposing party to instigate proceedings, and he generally retains the right to waive the contempt. In contrast, cases of criminal contempt are generally prosecuted by the A-G or by the court acting of its own motion, and opposing parties have no say in the matter (*Home Office v Harman* [1983] 1 AC 280 per Lord Scarman at p. 310); and see s. 7 (**B14.107**) and s. 10 (**B14.96**) of the Contempt of Court Act 1981, which limit the right to prosecute for some forms of criminal contempt. A minor point of distinction is that certain persons, notably peers and Members of Parliament, are generally immune from arrest for civil contempt (*Stourton v Stourton* [1963] P 302), but not for criminal contempt.

Parties

B14.70 In *Balogh v St Albans Crown Court* [1975] QB 73, Lord Denning MR held that criminal contempt of court is governed by the ordinary principles of criminal liability. If this is correct, it follows that complicity in the offence, as a secondary party, would require *mens rea*, even where liability of the principal offender is strict under the Contempt of Court Act 1981 (see **B14.100** to **B14.107**). Where a corporation publishes material amounting to contempt, the corporation itself is the obvious principal offender, but a newspaper editor (or his counterpart in television etc.) would usually be regarded as a joint principal, because of his special responsibility for the content of the publication, and, where *mens rea* is required, his *mens rea* could arguably be imputed to the company on the basis that he manages that part at least of the company's business.

The dictum of Lord Goddard CJ in *Evening Standard Co. Ltd* [1954] 1 QB 578, that the liability of the editor and company is vicarious, is contrary to principle and has generally been doubted. Employees (e.g., reporters) are not publishers, but might be liable as secondary parties if they act with *mens rea*. See *Griffiths, ex parte A-G* [1957] 2 QB 192.

Courts and Tribunals Protected by the Law of Contempt

B14.71 One must distinguish between the protection of the law of contempt, which is afforded to all courts and tribunals exercising the judicial power of the State, and the jurisdiction to punish for contempt, which is possessed at common law only by courts of record, and to differing extent according to whether the court is superior or inferior. (As to the position of magistrates' courts, which are not courts of record, but which have statutory powers to deal with some contempts, see **B14.73**).

There appears to be no definitive list of the bodies which qualify for protection. Some do not qualify, even though they are called 'courts', e.g., local valuation courts. Others do qualify, even though they lack that title, e.g., industrial tribunals (*Peach Grey & Co. v Sommers* [1995] 2 All ER 513) and mental health review tribunals (*P v Liverpool Daily Post and Echo Newspapers plc* [1991] 2 AC 370). The ones which lack protection are those which exercise administrative, rather than judicial functions. It is not enough that they act judicially in discharging such functions (*A-G v British Broadcasting Corporation* [1981] AC 303; *General Medical Council v British Broadcasting Corporation* [1998] 1 WLR 1573). Even magistrates lose the protection of the law of contempt when sitting as licensing justices, because this is an administrative function (*A-G v British Broadcasting Corporation* [1981] AC 303 at p. 348).

Mode of Trial

B14.72 Cases of alleged contempt are tried by procedures which are peculiar to that offence. It remains theoretically possible to prosecute criminal contempt on indictment, but this is hardly ever done, and in the last reported case in which it was, the Court of Appeal condemned the procedure as inappropriate, and quashed the convictions which had been imposed (*D* [1984] AC 778 at p. 792). In practice, therefore, criminal contempt is dealt with summarily, either by the court acting of its own motion (as it will usually do in respect of contempt in the face of the court) or by a more formal process in which an application for committal is made to the Divisional Court of the Queen's Bench Division under the Rules of the Supreme Court 1965, ord. 52 (**B14.88**).

Jurisdiction and Procedure: Magistrates' Courts

Magistrates' courts have no inherent jurisdiction over contempt, but possess statutory powers. In addition to the power to imprison fine defaulters, s. 63(3) of the MCA 1980 empowers magistrates to deal with defaults in respect of other orders. This power is exercisable either of the court's own motion or by order on complaint (Contempt of Court Act 1981, s. 17). The maximum fine is £50 per day or £5,000; the maximum period of custody is two months. Contempt in the face of the court is dealt with under the Contempt of Court Act 1981, s. 12, and MCA 1980, s. 97(4). **B14.73**

Magistrates' Courts Act 1980, s. 97

(4) If any person attending or brought before a magistrates' court refuses without just excuse to be sworn or give evidence, or to produce any document or thing, the court may commit him to custody until the expiration of such period not exceeding one month as may be specified in the warrant or until he sooner gives evidence or produces the document or thing or impose on him a fine not exceeding £2,500 or both.

Contempt of Court Act 1981, s. 12

(1) A magistrates' court has jurisdiction under this section to deal with any person who—
   (a) wilfully insults the justice or justices, any witness before or officer of the court or any solicitor or counsel having business in the court, during his or their sitting or attendance in court or in going to or returning from the court; or
   (b) wilfully interrupts the proceedings of the court or otherwise misbehaves in court.

(2) In any such case the court may order any officer of the court, or any constable, to take the offender into custody and detain him until the rising of the court; and the court may, if it thinks fit, commit the offender to custody for a specified period not exceeding one month or impose on him a fine not exceeding £2,500, or both.

(2A) A fine imposed under subsection (2) above shall be deemed, for the purposes of any enactment, to be a sum adjudged to be paid by a conviction.

(3) [Repealed.]

(4) A magistrates' court may at any time revoke an order of committal made under subsection (2) and, if the offender is in custody, order his discharge.

(5) Section 135 of the Powers of Criminal Courts (Sentencing) Act 2000 (limit on fines in respect of young persons) and the following provisions of the Magistrates' Courts Act 1980 apply in relation to an order under this section as they apply in relation to a sentence on conviction or finding of guilty of an offence, and those provisions of the Magistrates' Courts Act 1980 are sections 75 to 91 (enforcement); section 108 (appeal to Crown Court); section 136 (overnight detention in default of payment); and section 142(1) (power to rectify mistakes).

The principles to be applied in exercising jurisdiction under these sections are set out by the *Consolidated Criminal Practice Direction*, para. V.54, *Contempt in the face of the magistrates' court.* Most insults or interruptions should ordinarily be dealt with by securing an apology and undertaking as to future conduct; but if it is necessary to detain the alleged offender, he should ordinarily be granted public funding, given access to legal advice, and brought back before the court before the end of the day's business. If he admits contempt, he should ordinarily be dealt with that day if possible; but if he contests the issue or objects to being sentenced by the original panel, or if his conduct was directed towards that panel, another panel should deal with his case at the earliest opportunity, taking account of the need to ensure a fair trial under ECHR, Article 6. Bail should ordinarily be offered pending any later hearing. Any period of committal imposed should take account of any period on remand and be for the shortest period commensurate with the need to preserve good order in the courts.

Section 12(1)(a) is not applicable where D has uttered threats rather than insults (*Havant Justices, ex parte Palmer* (1985) 149 JP 609, although uttering threats might involve 'misbehaviour' in court under s. 12(1)(b)). Magistrates have no jurisdiction over constructive contempts. These must be dealt with by a Divisional Court under the RSC 1965, ord. 52 (see **B14.90**).

Jurisdiction and Procedure: the Crown Court

B14.74 Although the Crown Court is a superior court of record, the Rules of the Supreme Court 1965, ord. 52, r. 1(2), provides that the Divisional Court of the Queen's Bench Division has exclusive jurisdiction over contempts committed in the course of criminal proceedings, 'except where the contempt is committed in the face of the court, or where it consists of disobedience to an order of the court or a breach of an undertaking to the court'. This would appear at first sight to limit the Crown Court's inherent jurisdiction over contempt to those exceptions, but it does not, because the Supreme Court Act 1981, s. 45(4), provides that the Crown Court has, in relation to contempt, 'the like powers, rights, privileges and authority as the High Court'. The power of the High Court to make an order of its own initiative against a person guilty of contempt is expressly preserved intact by the Rules of the Supreme Court 1965, ord. 52, r. 5, and the Crown Court's power is preserved with it (see **B14.79**).

B14.75 **Contempt Requiring Immediate Action** In some cases, it may be proper for the Crown Court to act of its own motion, without the institution of formal committal proceedings under ord. 52. The question was considered *obiter*, but at length, by the Court of Appeal (Civil Division) in *Balogh v St Albans Crown Court* [1975] QB 73. Lord Denning MR and Stephenson LJ rejected suggestions that the Crown Court could properly so act only in respect of contempt committed *in* court, but at the same time stressed that judges should be slow to invoke their powers. As Stephenson LJ said (at pp. 89–90):

> Procedure for contempt by motion under the Rules of the Supreme Court 1965, ord. 52, rr. 1 and 2, might be described as summary, but when a judge of the High Court or Crown Court proceeds of his own motion, the procedure is more summary still. It must never be invoked unless the ends of justice really require such drastic means: it appears to be rough justice; it is contrary to natural justice; and it can only be justified if nothing else will do.

Further guidance has been provided by the Divisional Court in *DPP v Channel Four Television Co. Ltd* [1993] 2 All ER 517, in which it was stated that 'sensitive' contempt cases, involving such issues as the duty of a journalist to disclose the source of his information, should invariably be determined by the Divisional Court. Even in less sensitive cases, a trial judge should act of his own motion only where the contempt is clear and affects a trial already in progress or one just about to start. He should satisfy himself that no other procedure would suffice to prevent the obstruction of justice or the integrity of the trial, and he should avoid appearing to be the prosecutor in his own cause; the CPS may take over this role and may in some cases bring proceedings before another judge of the Crown Court. The suggestion that judges should where possible avoid determining contempts against themselves is supported by *Balogh* and by the House of Lords in *Re Lonrho plc* [1990] 2 AC 154 but, even where the affected trial is over, it may sometimes remain appropriate for the judge to deal summarily with an obvious contempt involving undisputed facts (see *Santiago* [2005] 2 Cr App R 366, in which the Court of Appeal supported a trial judge's decision to deal with such a contempt instead of referring it to the CPS).

An example of contempt calling for immediate action is conduct which deliberately disrupts the trial, whether committed inside the courtroom or outside it. In *Morris v Crown Office* [1970] 2 QB 114, Welsh language campaigners who physically disrupted a sitting of the High Court were summarily committed to prison for three months. Less serious disruptions may still merit summary punishment, but there may be times when it would be wiser for the judge to rise, leaving those wishing to behave badly to do so in his absence (*Lewis* (1999) *The Times*, 4 November 1999).

The intimidation of witnesses or jurors during the course of a trial, or other forms of interference with them, has also been held to warrant an immediate judicial response. In *Goult* (1982) 76 Cr App R 140, the offender was summarily committed to prison by a Crown Court judge for 18 months (reduced on appeal to nine months) for intimidating jurors, both in and out of court. Lord Lane CJ said (at p. 144):

> . . . there is every reason . . . for the judge to take the sort of steps which the judge took here . . . not only for the question of the dignity of the court, but also for the reassurance of other jurors who would be awaiting their call to duty in the court.

See also *Giscombe* (1983) 79 Cr App R 79 and *McLeod* [2001] Crim LR 589.

Various other contempts in the face of the court may require immediate action. These include contempts by witnesses who refuse to be sworn, or who refuse to answer questions, and contempts by jurors.

Procedural Safeguards Where a judge considers summarily punishing the alleged contemnor, certain procedures should ordinarily be followed. These are particularly important when the contemnor is at risk of committal to prison, and may in appropriate cases include: B14.76

(1) the immediate arrest and detention of the offender;
(2) telling the offender directly what the contempt is stated to have been;
(3) giving a chance to apologise;
(4) affording the opportunity of being advised and represented by counsel and making any necessary order for legal aid for that purpose;
(5) granting any adjournment that may be required;
(6) entertaining counsel's submission; and
(7) if satisfied that punishment is merited, imposing it within the limits fixed by statute (*Hill* [1986] Crim LR 457; *Wilkinson v S* [2003] 1 WLR 1254).

In *Moran* (1985) 81 Cr App R 51, Lawton LJ offered the following guidance (at p. 53):

> First, a decision to imprison the man for contempt of court should never be taken too quickly. The judge should give himself time for reflection as to what is the best course to take. Secondly, he should consider whether that time for reflection should not extend to a different day because overnight thoughts are sometimes better than thoughts on the spur of the moment. Thirdly, the judge should consider whether the seeming contemnor should have some advice. We do not accept the proposition which was tentatively put forward on this appeal that this contemnor had a right to legal advice. Sometimes situations arise in court when the judge has to act quickly and to pass such sentence as he thinks appropriate at once; so there cannot be any right to legal advice. Justice does not require a contemnor in the face of the court to have a right to legal advice. But if the circumstances are such that it is possible for the contemnor to have advice, he should be given an opportunity of having it. In practice what usually happens is that somebody gives the contemnor advice. He takes it, apologises to the court and that is the end of the matter. Giving a contemnor an opportunity to apologise is one of the most important aspects of this summary procedure, which in many ways is draconian. If there is a member of the Bar in court who could give advice, a wise judge would ask that member of the Bar if he would be willing to do so. The member of the Bar is entitled to say no, but in practice never does.

See also *Bromell* (1995) *The Times*, 9 February 1995 and *Huggins* [2007] 2 Cr App R 107.

Although not fully recognised in *Moran*, a right to legal representation is in fact guaranteed under the ECHR, Article 6(3)(c) (and not only in cases where imprisonment is likely).

Jurisdiction and Procedure: the Divisional Court of the Queen's Bench Division

The Divisional Court inherently possesses all the powers of a superior court and may act of its own motion in respect of contempts committed against it; but its more important jurisdiction is under the Rules of the Supreme Court 1965, ord. 52, r. 1(2), in respect of contempts which are committed against lower courts, and which either cannot be dealt with by the court in question (e.g., constructive contempt of an inferior court) or are not suitable for summary punishment by a court acting of its own motion (see *Balogh v St Albans Crown* B14.77

Court [1975] QB 73 and **B14.74** to **B14.76**). In particular, contempts in the form of publications prejudicial to current or forthcoming Crown Court trials would ordinarily be dealt with by the Divisional Court: see for example *A-G v English* [1983] 1 AC 116. The Rules of the Supreme Court 1965, ord. 52, insofar as it is relevant to contempt of criminal courts, is set out at **B14.79**.

Jurisdiction and Procedure: The Court of Appeal and the House of Lords

B14.78 Contempt of the Court of Appeal may be dealt with either by the court acting of its own motion or by application for committal under the Rules of the Supreme Court 1965, ord. 52. Such an application may be made to the Court of Appeal itself. Order 52, r. 1(2), does not apply. An alleged contempt of the House of Lords is determinable by the House alone (see *Re Lonrho plc* [1990] 2 AC 154).

Rules of Court Governing Committal for Contempt

B14.79 **Rules of the Supreme Court 1965, ord. 52**

(contained in the Civil Procedure Rules 1998 (SI 1998 No. 3132), sch. 1)

Committal for contempt of court

1.—(1) The power of the High Court or Court of Appeal to punish for contempt of court may be exercised by an order of committal.

(2) Where contempt of court—
  (a) is committed in connection with—
    (i) any proceedings before a Divisional Court of the Queen's Bench Division, or
    (ii) criminal proceedings, except where the contempt is committed in the face of the court or consists of disobedience to an order of the court or a breach of an undertaking to the court, or
    (iii) proceedings in an inferior court,
  (b) is committed otherwise than in connection with any proceedings, then . . . an order of committal may be made only by a Divisional Court of the Queen's Bench Division.

This paragraph shall not apply in relation to contempt of the Court of Appeal.

(3) and (4) [Omitted as they deal with the powers of the civil courts.]

Application to Divisional Court

2.—(1) No application to a Divisional Court for an order of committal against any person may be made unless permission to make such an application has been granted in accordance with this rule.

(2) An application for such permission must be made without notice to a Divisional Court, except in vacation when it may be made to a judge in chambers, and must be supported by a statement setting out the name and description of the applicant, the name, description and address of the person sought to be committed and the grounds on which his committal is sought, and by an affidavit, to be filed before the application is made, verifying the facts relied on.

(3) The applicant must give notice of the application for permission not later than the preceding day to the Crown Office and must at the same time lodge in that office copies of the statement and affidavit.

(4) Where an application for permission under this rule is refused by a judge in chambers, the applicant may make a fresh application for such permission to a Divisional Court.

(5) An application made to a Divisional Court by virtue of paragraph (4) must be made within eight days after the judge's refusal to give permission or, if a Divisional Court does not sit within that period, on the first day on which it sits thereafter.

Application for order after leave to apply granted

3.—(1) When permission has been granted under rule 2 to apply for an order of committal, the application for the order must be made by motion to a Divisional Court and, unless the court or judge granting permission has otherwise directed, there must be at least eight clear days between the service of the notice of motion and the day named therein for the hearing.

(2) Unless within 14 days after such permission was granted the claim form is issued the permission shall lapse.

(3) Subject to paragraph (4), the claim form, accompanied by a copy of the statement and

affidavit in support of the application for permission, must be served personally on the person sought to be committed.

(4) Without prejudice to the powers of the court or judge under part 6 of the CPR, the court or judge may dispense with service under this rule if it or he thinks it just to do so.

Application to court other than Divisional Court

4.—(1) Where an application for an order of committal may be made to a court other than a Divisional Court, the application must be made by motion and be supported by an affidavit.

(2) Subject to paragraph (3), the notice of motion, stating the grounds of the application and accompanied by a copy of the affidavit in support of the application, must be served personally on the person sought to be committed.

(3) Without prejudice to its powers under part 6 of the CPR, the court may dispense with service under this rule if it thinks it just to do so.

(4) This rules does not apply to committal applications which under rules 1(2) and 3(1) should be made to a Divisional Court but which, in vacation, have been properly made to a single judge in accordance with RSC Order 64, rule 4.

Saving for power to commit without application for purpose

5. Nothing in the foregoing provisions of this order shall be taken as affecting the power of the High Court or Court of Appeal to make an order of committal of its own initiative against a person guilty of contempt of court.

Provisions as to hearing

6.—(1) Subject to paragraph (2), the court hearing an application for an order of committal may sit in private in the following cases, that is to say—

(a) where the application arises out of proceedings relating to the wardship or adoption of an infant or wholly or mainly to the guardianship, custody, maintenance or upbringing of an infant, or rights of access to an infant;

(b) where the application arises out of proceedings relating to a person suffering or appearing to be suffering from mental disorder within the meaning of the Mental Health Act 1983;

(c) where the application arises out of proceedings in which a secret process, discovery or invention was in issue;

(d) where it appears to the court that in the interests of the administration of justice or for reasons of national security the application should be heard in private; but, except as aforesaid, the application shall be heard in public.

(2) If the court hearing an application in private by virtue of paragraph (1) decides to make an order of committal against the person sought to be committed, it shall in public state—

(a) the name of that person,

(b) in general terms the nature of the contempt of court in respect of which the order of committal is being made, and

(c) the length of the period for which he is being committed.

(3) Except with the leave of the court hearing an application for an order of committal, no grounds shall be relied upon at the hearing except the grounds set out in the statement under rule 2 or, as the case may be, in the claim form or application notice under rule 4.

(4) If on the hearing of the application the person sought to be committed expresses a wish to give oral evidence on his own behalf, he shall be entitled to do so.

Power to suspend execution of committal order

7.—(1) The court by whom an order of committal is made may by order direct that the execution of the order of committal shall be suspended for such period or on such terms or conditions as it may specify.

(2) Where execution of an order of committal is suspended by an order under paragraph (1), the applicant for the order of committal must, unless the court otherwise directs, serve on the person against whom it was made a notice informing him of the making and terms of the order under that paragraph.

Warrant for arrest

7A. A warrant for the arrest of a person against whom an order of committal has been made shall not, without further order of the court, be enforced more than 2 years after the date on which the warrant is issued.

Discharge of person committed

8.—(1) The court may, on the application of any person committed to prison for any contempt of court, discharge him.

(2) [Deals with sequestration.]

Saving for other powers

9. Nothing in the foregoing provisions of this order shall be taken as affecting the power of the court to make an order requiring a person guilty of contempt of court, or a person punishable by virtue of any enactment in like manner as if he had been guilty of contempt of the High Court, to pay a fine or to give security for his good behaviour, and those provisions, so far as applicable, and with the necessary modifications, shall apply in relation to an application for such an order as they apply in relation to an application for an order of committal.

Penalties for Contempt

B14.80 The maximum penalties which may be imposed for contempt of court are now governed by the Contempt of Court Act 1981, s. 14.

Contempt of Court Act 1981, s. 14

(1) In any case where a court has power to commit a person to prison for contempt of court and (apart from this provision) no limitation applies to the period of committal, the committal shall (without prejudice to the power of the court to order his earlier discharge) be for a fixed term, and that term shall not on any occasion exceed two years in the case of committal by a superior court, or one month in the case of committal by an inferior court.

(2) In any case where an inferior court has power to fine a person for contempt of court and (apart from this provision) no limit applies to the amount of the fine, the fine shall not on any occasion exceed £2,500.

(2A) In the exercise of jurisdiction to commit for contempt of court or any kindred offence the court shall not deal with the offender by making an order under section 60 of the Powers of Criminal Courts (Sentencing) Act 2000 (an attendance centre order) if it appears to the court, after considering any available evidence, that he is under 17 years of age.

(2A) A fine imposed under subsection (2) above shall be deemed, for the purposes of any enactment, to be a sum adjudged to be paid by a conviction.

(3) [Repealed.]

(4) Each of the superior courts shall have the like power to make a hospital order or guardianship order under section 37 of the Mental Health Act 1983 or an interim hospital order under section 38 of that Act in the case of a person suffering from mental illness or severe mental impairment who could otherwise be committed to prison for contempt of court as the Crown Court has under that section in the case of a person convicted of an offence.

(4A) Each of the superior courts shall have the like power to make an order under section 35 of the said Act of 1983 (remand for report on accused's mental condition) where there is reason to suspect that a person who could be committed to prison for contempt of court is suffering from mental illness or severe mental impairment as the Crown Court has under that section in the case of an accused person within the meaning of the section.

(4A) For the purposes of the preceding provisions of this section a county court shall be treated as a superior court and not as an inferior court.

(By oversight there are now *two* subsections numbered (2A) and *two* numbered (4A).)

As to the maximum penalties which may be imposed by magistrates' courts, see **B14.73**.

There is no power to impose a custodial sentence on an offender under the age of 21 for contempt of court (PCC(S)A 2000, s. 89); *Byas* (1995) 16 Cr App R (S) 869). For offenders aged between 18 and 20 inclusive, detention may be ordered where appropriate under the PCC(S)A 2000, s. 108 (see further **E17.2**). Courts dealing with persons who are found guilty of criminal contempt have no power to make community rehabilitation orders (*Palmer* [1992] 1 WLR 568).

Sentencing Guidelines: Contempts Amounting to Other Offences

Where the same conduct can amount both to contempt of court and to a more specific statutory offence (as is the case with deliberate non-attendance by a person summoned as a witness), the courts must have some regard to the maximum penalty in respect of the statutory offence when considering a possible penalty for contempt, but they are not bound by any such maximum if there are aggravating features (*Montgomery* [1995] 2 Cr App R 23). **B14.81**

Imprisonment without Legal Representation

The PCCA 1973, s. 21, which generally prohibits the imprisonment of legally unrepresented persons, does not apply in cases of committal for contempt (*Newbury Justices, ex parte Pont* (1984) 78 Cr App R 255); but see the observation of the court in *Moran* (1985) 81 Cr App R 51 as to the wisdom of making advice available (**B14.76**). **B14.82**

Forms of Contempt: Intimidation of or Interference with or Retaliation against Witnesses or Jurors

An attempt to interfere with jurors or witnesses, whether by way of intimidation, bribery or persuasion, may be punished as contempt at common law. This principle extends not only to litigants and members of the public but also to court officials and jury bailiffs, who should avoid any discussion of cases with jurors (*Mickleburgh* [1995] 1 Cr App R 297). In practice, such cases will ordinarily require police investigation, and may then more appropriately be dealt with under the CJPO 1994, s. 51 (see **B14.41**) or as conduct tending to pervert the course of justice. **B14.83**

Intimidation or harassment of former witnesses or jurors, or retaliation against them, is an equally serious matter (*A-G v Judd* [1995] COD 15). Although the original trial may be over, it is essential that former witnesses or jurors are protected, so that they will not be afraid to do their duty (*A-G v Butterworth* [1963] 1 QB 696).

In *Connolly v Dale* [1996] QB 120, a police inspector was found to be in contempt for obstructing attempts by an accused person's enquiry agent to obtain alibi evidence on behalf of his client, and for threatening him with prosecution under what is now the Police Act 1996, s. 89(2). This was despite the fact that the officer had acted in good faith, for the purpose, as he saw it, of preventing the contamination of identification evidence.

Sentencing Guidelines

In *Wedlock* [1996] 1 Cr App R (S) 391 the offender had been on trial in the Crown Court for theft. After the principal prosecution witness had finished giving her evidence in chief the case was adjourned overnight. That evening the offender drove past the witness, threw something at her, and made an abusive remark. The Court of Appeal upheld the sentence of six months' imprisonment for the contempt. Six months' imprisonment was upheld in *Bryan* [1998] 2 Cr App R (S) 109, where the offender, the brother of a man on trial for murder, mouthed threatening words from the public gallery at a witness giving evidence in the case. See also *Stredder* [1997] 1 Cr App R (S) 209, where 12 months' imprisonment was upheld in a case where the offender, who was about to stand trial for theft, approached the sole prosecution witness in the court building, referred to damage which had been done to the witness's car, and said 'that was just a warning'. **B14.84**

Comparable sentences have been upheld by the Court of Appeal in respect of attempts to influence jurors. A sentence of 18 months was reduced to nine months in *Goult* (1982) 4 Cr App R (S) 355 where the offender intimidated women jurors by staring at them in a threatening manner and driving past them slowly in his car so that they felt frightened. See also *Palache* (1993) 14 Cr App R (S) 294. In *Sparks* (1995) 16 Cr App R (S) 480, the offenders had sat in the public gallery in the Crown Court and, for their own amusement, made threatening gestures towards a juror. The jury had to be discharged as a result. Nine months' imprisonment was reduced to six months on appeal. In *Mitchell-Crinkley* [1998] 1 Cr App R (S) 368, the offender attended the trial of a friend and recognised one of the jurors. He telephoned the juror and told him that a previous jury in the case had failed to agree. Imprisonment for 12 months was upheld. See also **B14.41** *et seq.*

Forms of Contempt: Disruption of Proceedings and Misbehaviour in Court

B14.85 A deliberate disruption of proceedings in court, whether staged by persons involved in those proceedings, or by demonstrators etc. may be punished as contempt, and in most cases will be dealt with by the court acting of its own motion. See *Morris v Crown Office* [1970] 2 QB 114. The same is true of misconduct, such as wolf-whistling at female jurors or witnesses (see *Powell* (1993) 98 Cr App R 224), and of assaults on court officials whilst they are engaged in the administration of justice (*Re de Court* (1997) *The Times*, 27 November 1997). Whether noisy protests from the public gallery following conviction or sentence are so serious as to amount to contempt is a matter which the trial court or judge is usually best placed to decide, but in many cases the best way of dealing with it may be for the judge to rise, and let the disturbance subside (*Lewis* (1999) *The Times*, 4 November 1999). Outbursts in court may, however, be contempts, even in the absence of an intent to disrupt the proceedings (*Huggins* [2007] 2 Cr App R 107).

Sentencing Guidelines

B14.86 In *Morris v Crown Office* [1970] 2 QB 114, Welsh language campaigners who physically disrupted a sitting of the High Court were summarily committed to prison for three months, and on appeal Salmon LJ warned that judges might consider sentences of up to six months to be appropriate in any future cases. In *McDaniel* (1990) 12 Cr App R (S) 44, the offender was aged 31 and had minor previous convictions. He attended the trial of his brother at the Crown Court where he and others had been warned about noisy conversations during the proceedings. When his brother was convicted and sentenced there was a general commotion during which the offender called the judge 'a dog'. A sentence of three months' imprisonment for addressing such personal abuse to the judge was reduced on appeal to 14 days. See also *Lewis* (1999) *The Times*, 4 November 1999.

Forms of Contempt: Committed by Witnesses, Jurors or Defendants

B14.87 A juror who fails to attend court when duly summoned commits a summary offence under the Juries Act 1974, s. 20(1), but may alternatively be punished 'as if it were criminal contempt . . . in the face of the court' (s. 20(2)). Jurors may likewise be punished for contempt if they refuse or fail to discharge their obligations in accordance with the jury oath (*Schot* [1997] 2 Cr App R 383).

A witness who refuses to be sworn, or refuses to produce documents or answer questions properly put to him, will be in contempt. In *Wicks* (31 January 1995 unreported), the Court of Appeal emphasised that witnesses who have been threatened are not thereby excused from giving evidence. As to the liability of witnesses who fail to obey witness summonses, see **D14.90**. As to the position of journalists who wish to protect their sources of information, special provision is made by the Contempt of Court Act 1981, s. 10 (see **B14.96**).

As to contempt by a convicted defendant who refuses to appear in court for sentencing, see *Santiago* [2005] 2 Cr App R 366.

Sentencing Guidelines

Guidance on sentencing for contempt where a witness refuses to give evidence has been provided by the Court of Appeal in *Montgomery* [1995] 2 Cr App R 23 and in *Robinson* [2006] 2 Cr App R (S) 587. In the former case a sentence of 12 months' imprisonment for failure to attend court and persistent refusal to testify or explain the refusal was reduced to three months. In the latter case, where a defence witness gave evidence in chief but refused to answer any question in cross-examination, a sentence of four months' imprisonment was upheld on appeal. It emerges from these decisions that, in the absence of wholly exceptional circumstances, an immediate custodial sentence is appropriate for a refusal to testify, but that the sentence will often be shorter than that imposed in a case of interference with a witness or juror. The principal matters affecting sentence are the gravity of the offence being tried, the extent to which the failure to testify affected the course of the trial, whether the refusal was aggravated by defiance or impertinence to the judge, the antecedents and personal circumstances of the contemnor, and whether a special deterrent is needed (such as where it becomes clear that there has been systematic intimidation of witnesses to prevent their giving evidence). The contemnor should normally be sentenced at the end of the trial, or at least at the end of the prosecution case, to allow him time to reconsider his position. See also *Cole* [1997] 1 Cr App R (S) 228. **B14.88**

Forms of Contempt: Contempt by Advocates

An advocate who deliberately fails to attend a hearing with intent to hinder or delay the course of justice would be guilty of contempt (*Weston v Central Criminal Court Courts Administrator* [1977] QB 32). It could also be a contempt to persist in adducing inadmissible evidence, or in a forbidden line of questioning, or generally to disobey or disregard orders of the court or to treat the court with gross disrespect. It is not, however, contempt to do whatever is ethically and professionally appropriate to provide a client with zealous representation, even if this brings the advocate into conflict with the court for such is his duty. **B14.89**

A person who conducts litigation or purports to exercise a right of audience when not entitled to do so is guilty of an offence under the Courts and Legal Services Act 1990, s. 70, and may also be punished for contempt (see s. 70(6)).

Forms of Contempt: Conduct or Publication Scandalising the Court

The courts must be slow to hold that criticism of judges or of the court system itself can amount to contempt, however outspoken or intemperate it may be (*Editor of the New Statesman, ex parte DPP* (1928) 44 TLR 301; *Metropolitan Police Commissioner, ex parte Blackburn (No. 2)* [1968] 2 QB 150); but it may be contempt if it uses scurrilous abuse to discredit the judge or the judicial system (*Gray* [1900] 2 QB 36). **B14.90**

Forms of Contempt: Publication Prejudicial to the Administration of Justice

This is one of the most important and complex varieties of contempt. Prejudice may be caused, *inter alia*, by revealing matters which might be inadmissible in evidence, and which may influence jurors etc. (as in *Clarke, ex parte Crippen* (1910) 103 LT 636 and *Parke* [1903] 2 KB 432); by sensational and misleading coverage of a trial (see the comments of McCowan LJ in *Taylor* (1993) 98 Cr App R 361); by commenting on the merits of the case or prejudging it (see *Hutchison, ex parte McMahon* [1936] 2 All ER 1514); or by publicly disclosing sensitive material that was subject to a court order restricting such disclosure, even where the order was addressed to another (*A-G v Newspaper Publishing plc* [1997] 1 WLR 926). Newspapers and other publishers may also commit contempt where they make payments to witnesses on terms which may encourage perjured evidence, or seek to pressurise litigants into **B14.91** abandoning their actions (see *A-G v Hislop* [1991] 1 QB 514). Publication of material by one person, when another person has already been served with an injunction prohibiting disclosure of that material pending trial of the issue of its confidentiality, may be a criminal contempt by the publisher because it destroys the subject-matter of the dispute (*A-G v Times Newspapers Ltd* [1992] 1 AC 191; *A-G v Punch Ltd* [2003] 1 AC 1046). It is not necessary that the publisher in such a case should intend to cause the harm that the third party injunction was ultimately designed to prevent. It is not for editors or broadcasters to decide (for example) whether publication of material which a third party has been ordered not to disclose would or would not harm the national interest. An honest belief on their part that no such harm would be caused is accordingly no defence (ibid).

Publication of material capable of prejudicing or impeding forthcoming legal proceedings does not necessarily amount to contempt. If the proceedings in question are not 'active' within the meaning of the Contempt of Court Act 1981 (see **B14.103**) or if there is no substantial risk of serious prejudice at the time of publication, then publication amounts to contempt only if there is proof of an intent to interfere with the course of justice in those proceedings. Recklessness or negligence will not suffice (*A-G v News Group Newspapers plc* [1989] QB 110; *A-G v Newspaper Publishing plc*). Where there is a substantial risk of serious prejudice to active proceedings, liability may be strict, but subject to certain defences (see generally **B14.102** to **B14.109**).

According to the Divisional Court in *A-G v News Group Newspapers plc*, publications which deliberately set out to prejudice possible future legal proceedings, and which do in fact create a real risk of such prejudice, may constitute contempt, even where those proceedings were not even imminent at the time of publication (e.g., where nothing had yet been done to instigate them). The case involved a highly prejudicial campaign run by the *Sun* newspaper with a view to ensuring that a doctor accused of raping a child would in due course be prosecuted. Watkins LJ acknowledged that this decision represented an extension of the law, but argued that the common law was 'a living body of law capable of adaption and expansion to meet fresh needs'. Doubts have subsequently been expressed as to the correctness of this view, which could be seen as a threat to investigative journalism. In *A-G v Sport Newspapers Ltd* [1991] 1 WLR 1194, a differently constituted Divisional Court held that material published by the *Sport* concerning a suspect in a murder inquiry did not amount to intentional interference in the course of justice, but Hodgson J went on to state (*obiter*) that *News Group Newspapers* was wrongly decided, and it seems that Bingham LJ would have been prepared to follow it only on the basis that he considered it wrong to depart from such a recent precedent.

Sentencing Guidelines

B14.92 In *A-G v News Group Newspapers Ltd* (1984) 6 Cr App R (S) 418 the Divisional Court dealt with a case where a newspaper had published, during the course of a trial, a picture of one of two defendants on trial for causing injury to their baby, with the headline: 'Baby was blinded by dad'. This statement was wholly misleading. The newspaper subsequently apologised and the court accepted that the contempt was not deliberate. According to Stephen Brown LJ (at p. 420):

> We are bound to say that this newspaper headline and photograph greatly surprised us and gravely disturbed us. It is fortunate indeed that the trial was not interrupted but it has to be made plain that there is a strict duty of care placed upon those who publish news items relating to trials to see that they do not run the risk of interfering with the course of justice. There was a clear and grave risk of that in this case.
>
> Taking into account all the facts, bearing in mind the nature of the apology, and bearing in mind the fact that it was not intentional but nevertheless a serious contempt, the order of this court is that the respondents be fined the sum of £5,000.

Forms of Contempt: Disclosures Relating to Jury Deliberations

Contempt of Court Act 1981, s. 8 **B14.93**

(1) Subject to subsection (2) below, it is a contempt of court to obtain, disclose or solicit any particulars of statements made, opinions expressed, arguments advanced or votes cast by members of a jury in the course of their deliberations in any legal proceedings.

(2) This section does not apply to any disclosure of any particulars—

(a) in the proceedings in question for the purpose of enabling the jury to arrive at their verdict, or in connection with the delivery of that verdict, or

(b) in evidence in any subsequent proceedings for an offence alleged to have been committed in relation to the jury in the first mentioned proceedings,

or to the publication of any particulars so disclosed.

(3) Proceedings for a contempt of court under this section (other than Scottish proceedings) shall not be instituted except by or with the consent of the Attorney-General or on the motion of a court having jurisdiction to deal with it.

This provision was enacted following the failure of the prosecution in *A-G v New Statesman and Nation Publishing Co. Ltd* [1981] QB 1. The contempt may be committed both by jurors and by a person who further discloses or publishes the information he has been given (see *A-G v Associated Newspapers Ltd* [1994] 2 AC 238). In *Mickleburgh* [1995] 1 Cr App R 297, Lord Taylor CJ warned that defence solicitors who take statements from former jurors, or make enquiries of former jurors, run a grave risk of being in contempt of court under s. 8, unless they first obtain leave from the Court of Appeal. Similar advice was given by Henry J in *McGlusky* (1993) 98 Cr App R 223.

If a juror genuinely believes that there had been a miscarriage of justice due to failings on the part of his fellow jurors, he would not, merely by expressing such concerns to the trial judge or the Court of Appeal, commit any contempt of court under s. 8(1) (*Mirza* [2004] 1 AC 1118). A letter detailing such concerns may even be passed to counsel, with instructions to forward it unopened to the court. But the position is different where the juror communicates with a defendant or third party who had no authority to receive disclosures on behalf of the court; this will be punishable under s. 8(1) (*A-G v Scotcher* [2005] 1 WLR 1867).

Forms of Contempt: Misuse of Tape Recorders In Court

Contempt of Court Act 1981, s. 9 **B14.94**

(1) Subject to subsection (4) below, it is a contempt of court—

(a) to use in court, or bring into court for use, any tape recorder or other instrument for recording sound, except with the leave of the court;

(b) to publish a recording of legal proceedings made by means of any such instrument, or any recording derived directly or indirectly from it, by playing it in the hearing of the public or any section of the public, or to dispose of it or any recording so derived, with a view to such publication;

(c) to use any such recording in contravention of any conditions of leave granted under paragraph (a).

(2) Leave under paragraph (a) of subsection (1) may be granted or refused at the discretion of the court, and if granted may be granted subject to such conditions as the court thinks proper with respect to the use of any recording made pursuant to the leave; and where leave has been granted the court may at the like discretion withdraw or amend it either generally or in relation to any particular part of the proceedings.

(3) Without prejudice to any other power to deal with an act of contempt under paragraph (a) of subsection (1), the court may order the instrument, or any recording made with it, or both, to be forfeited; and any object so forfeited shall (unless the court otherwise determines on application by a person appearing to be the owner) be sold or otherwise disposed of in such manner as the court may direct.

(4) This section does not apply to the making or use of sound recordings for purposes of official transcripts of proceedings.

The *Consolidated Criminal Practice Direction*, para. I.2, *Unofficial tape recording of proceedings* notes s. 9 and provides the following guidance on the granting of leave to make recordings:

I.2.2 The discretion given to the court to grant, withhold or withdraw leave to use tape recorders or to impose conditions as to the use of the recording is unlimited, but the following factors may be relevant to its exercise: (a) the existence of any reasonable need on the part of the applicant for leave, whether a litigant or a person connected with the press or broadcasting, for the recording to be made; (b) the risk that the recording could be used for the purpose of briefing witnesses out of court; (c) any possibility that the use of the recorder would disturb the proceedings or distract or worry any witnesses or other participants.

I.2.3 Consideration should always be given whether conditions as to the use of a recording made pursuant to leave should be imposed. The identity and role of the applicant for leave and the nature of the subject-matter of the proceedings may be relevant to this.

I.2.4 The particular restriction imposed by section 9(1)(b) applies in every case, but may not be present to the mind of every applicant to whom leave is given. It may therefore be desirable on occasion for this provision to be drawn to the attention of those to whom leave is given.

I.2.5 The transcript of a permitted recording is intended for the use of the person given leave to make it and is not intended to be used as, or to compete with, the official transcript mentioned in section 9(4).

Forms of Contempt: Photography and Sketching etc. in Court

B14.95 The taking of photographs in court, or the publication of such photographs, is sometimes punished as contempt (see *The Times*, 15 July 1986), but may also be punished as a summary offence (carrying a level 3 fine) under the CJA 1925, s. 41, which also deals with sketches. It is an offence under s. 41(1) to:

(a) take or attempt to take in any court any photograph, or with a view to publication make or attempt to make in any court any portrait or sketch of any person, being a judge of the court or a juror or a witness in or a party to any proceedings before the court, whether civil or criminal; or
(b) publish any photograph, portrait or sketch taken or made in contravention of the foregoing provisions of this section or any reproduction thereof.

'Judge' includes a registrar, magistrate, justice and coroner (s. 41(2)(a)). Photography includes video-tape; and the police are not exempt from the prohibition (*Loveridge* [2001] 2 Cr App R 591). Photography in the precincts of the court building is also covered (s. 41(2)(c)). The publication of sketches drawn from memory once outside the court is not prohibited.

Forms of Contempt: Refusal to Disclose Sources of Published Information

B14.96 A journalist or other person who refuses to disclose the source of information he has published may be in contempt of court, but regard must be had to the Contempt of Court Act 1981, s. 10, which provides:

> No court may require a person to disclose, nor is any person guilty of contempt of court for refusing to disclose, the source of information contained in a publication for which he is responsible, unless it be established to the satisfaction of the court that disclosure is necessary in the interests of justice or national security or for the prevention of disorder or crime.

In order to satisfy the court of the necessity of disclosure, proof is required, on balance of probabilities; it is not enough merely to assert the need (see *Secretary of State for Defence v Guardian Newspapers Ltd* [1985] AC 339). Nor is convenience the same thing as necessity; but necessity is a relative concept, and may be something less than absolute indispensability (*Re an Inquiry under the Company Securities (Insider Dealing) Act 1985* [1988] AC 660). 'Prevention of crime' includes the general control of crime and not just the prevention of specific acts (*Re an Inquiry under the Company Securities (Insider Dealing) Act 1985*). See generally **F9.13**.

Forms of Contempt: Breaches of Reporting Restrictions on Cases Heard in Public

Deliberate (or perhaps reckless) breach of reporting restrictions imposed under the Contempt of Court Act 1981, s. 4 (see **D3.84**) would appear to be a form of statutory contempt, whether or not any real risk of prejudice is involved. See generally *Horsham Justices, ex parte Farquharson* [1982] QB 762. **B14.97**

The *Consolidated Criminal Practice Direction*, para. I.3, *Restrictions on reporting proceedings* provides as follows:

> I.3.3 It is necessary to keep a permanent record of such orders for later reference. For this purpose all orders made under s. 4(2) must be formulated in precise terms, having regard to the decision of *Horsham Justices, ex parte Farquharson* [1982] QB 762, and orders under both sections [i.e. s. 4(2) and s. 11 of the 1981 Act] must be committed to writing either by the judge personally or by the clerk of the court under the judge's directions. An order must state (a) its precise scope, (b) the time at which it shall cease to have effect, if appropriate, and (c) the specific purpose of making the order. Courts will normally give notice to the press in some form that an order has been made under either section of the 1981 Act and the court staff should be prepared to answer any inquiry about a specific case, but it is and will remain, the responsibility of those reporting cases, and their editors, to ensure that no breach of any orders occurs and the onus rests with them to make inquiry in any case of doubt.

As to reporting restrictions generally, see **D3.82**; for reporting restrictions when a case is sent to the Crown Court, see the CDA 1998, s. 52B at **D10.10**.

Forms of Contempt: Publication of Matter Exempted from Disclosure in Court

Contempt of Court Act 1981, s. 11 **B14.98**

> In any case where a court (having power to do so) allows a name or other matter to be withheld from the public in proceedings before the court, the court may give such directions prohibiting the publication of that name or matter in connection with the proceedings as appear to the court to be necessary for the purpose for which it was so withheld.

The *Consolidated Criminal Practice Direction*, para. I.3, *Restrictions on reporting proceedings* (at **B14.97**). Breach of the order could (as with breaches of orders under the Contempt of Court Act 1981, s. 4), constitute a statutory contempt. As to the principles of 'open justice', see **D3.82** *et seq.*

The power to make such an order must not be used merely 'for the benefit of the comfort and feelings of defendants' as by safeguarding them from unwanted publicity or molestation (*Evesham Justices, ex parte McDonagh* [1988] QB 553). It is properly employed to safeguard the identity of children and young persons, complainants in rape cases, witnesses who might later be exposed to violence or blackmail, or revelation of whose identity might prejudice national security.

It may be necessary for a court to sit in camera when hearing evidence in support of an application under the Contempt of Court Act 1981, s. 11 (*Tower Bridge Magistrates' Court, ex parte Osbourne* (1989) 88 Cr App R 28).

Forms of Contempt: Publications Relating to Proceedings in Camera

Administration of Justice Act 1960, s. 12 **B14.99**

> (1) The publication of information relating to proceedings before any court sitting in private shall not of itself be contempt of court except in the following cases, that is to say—
> (a) where the proceedings—
> (i) relate to the exercise of the inherent jurisdiction of the High Court with respect to minors;
> (ii) are brought under the Children Act 1989; or
> (iii) otherwise relate wholly or mainly to the maintenance or upbringing of a minor;

(b) where the proceedings are brought under part VIII of the Mental Health Act 1959, or under any provision of that Act authorising an application or reference to be made to a Mental Health Review Tribunal or to a county court;
(c) where the court sits in private for reasons of national security during that part of the proceedings about which the information in question is published;
(d) where the information relates to a secret process, discovery or invention which is in issue in the proceedings;
(e) where the court (having power to do so) expressly prohibits the publication of all information relating to the proceedings or of information of the description which is published.

(2) Without prejudice to the foregoing subsection, the publication of the text or a summary of the whole or part of an order made by a court sitting in private shall not of itself be contempt of court except where the court (having power to do so) expressly prohibits the publication.
(3) In this section references to a court include references to a judge and to a tribunal and to any person exercising the functions of a court, a judge or a tribunal; and references to a court sitting in private include references to a court sitting in camera or in chambers.
(4) Nothing in this section shall be construed as implying that any publication is punishable as contempt of court which would not be so punishable apart from this section (and in particular where the publication is not so punishable by reason of being authorised by rules of court).

In *P v Liverpool Daily Post and Echo Newspapers plc* [1991] 2 AC 370, the House of Lords held that nothing in s. 12(1) prohibits publication of the fact that a court or tribunal is to sit etc., nor does it prohibit the naming of a person involved (but see **B14.98**).

Attempted Contempt

B14.100 Criminal contempt can take the form either of conduct which is intended to interfere with the course of justice, or of conduct which tends to have that effect. It is not therefore essential that any real harm is done. If the intent is proved, the measures adopted may be hopelessly ineffective (*Castro, Skipworth's and the Defendant's Case* (1873) LR 9 QB 230), and if the tendency is proved, there may sometimes be an element of strict liability, although this is now largely confined to certain publications (see **B14.102**).

This leaves little scope for offences of attempted contempt, but one could have a case in which a person fails, not only to interfere with the proceedings, but to perform the act by which he intends so to do. An example of such a case is *Balogh v St Albans Crown Court* [1975] QB 73, where Balogh intended to disrupt a trial by pumping laughing-gas into the court-room, but was arrested before he could do so. Doubts were expressed by Stephenson LJ about the very existence of any crime of attempted contempt, but Balogh had not in any case got beyond the stage of mere preparation, and the doubts were left unresolved. It is submitted that there are no compelling reasons for denying the existence of that offence (see the judgment of Lord Denning MR), but the problem will seldom arise in practice.

Mens Rea

B14.101 It has been recognised that *mens rea* in criminal contempt cases is something of a minefield, owing to the piecemeal development of the common-law offence, and the lack of codification (see the observations of Lord Donaldson MR in *A-G v Newspaper Publishing plc* [1988] Ch 333 at p. 373).

At common law, some forms of contempt carried strict liability. Thus, in *Odhams Press Ltd, ex parte A-G* [1957] 1 QB 73, Odhams Press was held to be guilty of contempt for publishing an article which tended to prejudice the course of justice in a forthcoming trial, even though it was not informed that the trial was forthcoming, and was not even proved to have been reckless as to the possibility. This rule seems to have been confined in practice to publication cases (see *A-G v English* [1983] 1 AC 116 per Lord Diplock at p. 141), and insofar as interference with the course of justice in 'particular proceedings' is concerned, it is now expressly so confined by ss. 1 and 2 of the Contempt of Court Act 1981, which indeed limit its application more tightly still (see **B14.103**).

This leaves two further issues to be considered. First, whether strict liability can still apply in any areas not covered by the Contempt of Court Act 1981; and secondly, whether anything less than a specific intent may suffice where strict liability is excluded under the Act. These issues are considered at **B14.108** and **B14.109** respectively.

Strict Liability: the Contempt of Court Act 1981

Contempt of Court Act 1981, ss. 1 and 2 and sch. 1 B14.102

The strict liability rule

1. In this Act 'the strict liability rule' means the rule of law whereby conduct may be treated as a contempt of court as tending to interfere with the course of justice in particular legal proceedings regardless of intent to do so.

Limitation of scope of strict liability

2.—(1) The strict liability rule applies only in relation to publications, and for this purpose 'publication' includes any speech, writing, broadcast cable programme or other communication in whatever form, which is addressed to the public at large or any section of the public.

(2) The strict liability rule applies only to a publication which creates a substantial risk that the course of justice in the proceedings in question will be seriously impeded or prejudiced.

(3) The strict liability rule applies to a publication only if the proceedings in question are active within the meaning of this section at the time of the publication.

(4) Schedule 1 applies for determining the times at which proceedings are to be treated as active within the meaning of this section.

SCHEDULE 1

TIMES WHEN PROCEEDINGS ARE ACTIVE FOR PURPOSES OF SECTION 2

Preliminary

1. In this schedule 'criminal proceedings' means proceedings against a person in respect of an offence, not being appellate proceedings or proceedings commenced by motion for committal or attachment in England and Wales or Northern Ireland; and 'appellate proceedings' means proceedings on appeal from or for the review of the decision of a court in any proceedings.
2. Criminal, appellate and other proceedings are active within the meaning of section 2 at the times respectively prescribed by the following paragraphs of this schedule; and in relation to proceedings in which more than one of the steps described in any of those paragraphs is taken, the reference in that paragraph is a reference to the first of those steps.

Criminal proceedings

3. Subject to the following provisions of this schedule, criminal proceedings are active from the relevant initial step specified in paragraph 4 until concluded as described in paragraph 5.
4. The initial steps of criminal proceedings are:—
   (a) arrest without warrant;
   (b) the issue, or in Scotland the grant, of a warrant for arrest;
   (c) the issue of a summons to appear; [or in Scotland the grant of a warrant to cite;]
   (d) the service of an indictment or other document specifying the charge;
   (e) except in Scotland, oral charge.
5. Criminal proceedings are concluded—
   (a) by acquittal or, as the case may be, by sentence;
   (b) by any other verdict, finding, order or decision which puts an end to the proceedings;
   (c) by discontinuance or by operation of law.
6. The reference in paragraph 5(a) to sentence includes any order or decision consequent on conviction or finding of guilt which disposes of the case, either absolutely or subject to future events, and a deferment of sentence under section 1 of the Powers of Criminal Courts (Sentencing) Act 2000, section 202 of the Criminal Procedure (Scotland) Act 1995 or Article 14 of the Treatment of Offenders (Northern Ireland) Order 1976.

7. Proceedings are discontinued within the meaning of paragraph 5(c)—
   (a) in England and Wales or Northern Ireland, if the charge or summons is withdrawn or a *nolle prosequi* entered;
   (aa) in England and Wales, if they are discontinued by virtue of section 23 of the Prosecution of Offences Act 1985;
   (b) in Scotland, if the proceedings are expressly abandoned by the prosecutor or are deserted *simpliciter*;
   (c) in the case of proceedings in England and Wales or Northern Ireland commenced by arrest without warrant, if the person arrested is released, otherwise than on bail, without having been charged.
8. Criminal proceedings before a court-martial or standing civilian court are not concluded until the completion of any review of finding or sentence.
9. Criminal proceedings in England and Wales or Northern Ireland cease to be active if an order is made for the charge to lie on the file, but become active again if leave is later given for the proceedings to continue.
9A. Where proceedings in England and Wales have been discontinued by virtue of section 23 of the Prosecution of Offences Act 1985, but notice is given by the accused under subsection (7) of that section to the effect that he wants the proceedings to continue, they become active again with the giving of that notice.
10. Without prejudice to paragraph 5(b) above, criminal proceedings against a person cease to be active—
   (a) if the accused is found to be under a disability such as to render him unfit to be tried or unfit to plead or, in Scotland, is found to be insane in bar of trial; or
   (b) if a hospital order is made in his case under section 51(5) of the Mental Health Act 1983 or Article 57(5) of the Mental Health (Northern Ireland) Order 1986 or, in Scotland, where a transfer order ceases to have effect by virtue of section 73(1) of the Mental Health (Scotland) Act 1984, but become active again if they are later resumed.
11. Criminal proceedings against a person which become active on the issue or the grant of a warrant for his arrest cease to be active at the end of the period of 12 months beginning with the date of the warrant unless he has been arrested within that period, but become active again if he is subsequently arrested.

Other proceedings at first instance

12. Proceedings other than criminal proceedings and appellate proceedings are active from the time when arrangements for the hearing are made or, if no such arrangements are previously made, from the time the hearing begins, until the proceedings are disposed of or discontinued or withdrawn; and for the purposes of this paragraph any motion or application made in or for the purposes of any proceedings, and any pre-trial review in the county court, is to be treated as a distinct proceeding.
13. In England and Wales or Northern Ireland arrangements for the hearing of proceedings to which paragraph 12 applies are made within the meaning of that paragraph—
   (a) in the case of proceedings in the High Court for which provision is made by rules of court for setting down for trial, when the case is set down;
   (b) in the case of any proceedings, when a date for the trial or hearing is fixed.
14. In Scotland arrangements for the hearing of proceedings to which paragraph 12 applies are made within the meaning of that paragraph—
   (a) in the case of an ordinary action in the Court of Session or in the sheriff court, when the record is closed;
   (b) in the case of a motion or application, when it is enrolled or made;
   (c) in any other case, when the date for a hearing is fixed or a hearing is allowed.

Appellate proceedings

15. Appellate proceedings are active from the time when they are commenced—
   (a) by application for leave to appeal or apply for review, or by notice of such an application;
   (b) by notice of appeal or of application for review;
   (c) by other originating process,

   until disposed of or abandoned, discontinued or withdrawn.
16. Where, in appellate proceedings relating to criminal proceedings, the court—
   (a) remits the case to the court below; or

(b) orders a new trial or a *venire de novo*, or in Scotland grants authority to bring a new prosecution,

any further or new proceedings which result shall be treated as active from the conclusion of the appellate proceedings.

Prior to the enactment of these provisions, it had been held that the prejudging of court proceedings was necessarily contempt (see e.g., *A-G v Times Newspapers Ltd* [1974] AC 273), and this is still true of publications which create a real risk of prejudicing a fair trial and which are intended to influence jurors, to dissuade one of the parties from contesting the case, or otherwise to interfere with the proceedings (*A-G v Hislop* [1991] 1 QB 514); but in the absence of proof of such intent, it would have to be proved that the prejudgment or other comment created a substantial risk of serious prejudice etc. in respect of active proceedings (as defined in sch. 1). Strict liability will then apply, subject to qualifications and defences contained or preserved within the Contempt of Court Act 981, ss. 3 to 5 (**B14.103**).

Substantial Risk of Prejudice The question whether a publication creates a substantial risk of serious prejudice etc. is ultimately one of fact (*Re Lonrho plc* [1990] 2 AC 154, per Lord Bridge at p. 208). The creation of such a risk must accordingly be proved beyond reasonable doubt (*A-G v Unger* [1998] 1 Cr App R 308). 'Substantial' in this context does not mean 'weighty', but rather 'not insubstantial' or 'not minimal' (*A-G v News Group Newspapers Ltd* [1987] QB 1). Account may be taken of the likely effect of the publication on the parties, witnesses or court. Whilst it may sometimes be material, in assessing the risk of prejudice to any proceedings, that the defendant has already confessed or has intimated an intention to plead guilty, it would be most dangerous for publishers to rely on such considerations, because pleas may be changed and confessions retracted or excluded from evidence (*A-G v Unger*). Still less should a publisher assume that the weight of evidence against a defendant would place the outcome of any contested trial beyond doubt (*ibid.*). The courts do however recognise that the proximity of the publication to any future trial may be an important consideration. The longer the interval between publication and trial, the less likely it is that any serious prejudice will be caused, especially if the publication contains nothing that could amount to inadmissible evidence (*A-G v News Group Newspapers Ltd; A-G v Independent Television News Ltd* [1995] 1 Cr App R 204; *A-G v Unger*). In contrast, the risk of prejudicing the court (and especially a jury) may be heightened by the vulnerability of the defendant, the high profile of the case or any inaccuracy in the reporting (*A-G v Unger*). **B14.103**

In recent cases (notably *A-G v Unger* (above), *A-G v Birmingham Post and Mail* [1999] 1 WLR 361 and *A-G v Guardian Newspapers Ltd* (1999) *Independent*, 30 July 1999) the courts have sought to ensure that the test applied in contempt cases is consistent with the test applied in appeals against conviction, where it is alleged that a jury may have been prejudiced by improper media coverage. The courts should not reason, on the one hand, that any jurors who read or viewed the publication would have ignored the offending publication when reaching their verdict, and yet reason, on the other hand, that the publication in question created a substantial risk of serious prejudice. How this consistency should be achieved is more problematic, given that the risk in contempt cases must be judged prospectively, and without regard to the actual outcome of the trial, but in *A-G v Guardian Newspapers* Sedley LJ argued that a publication should be found in contempt only if of such a nature that it would be asking too much of any juror to put it out of his mind when directed to do so by the trial judge. Sedley LJ was also influenced by considerations of human rights issues; in particular by the consideration that any restrictions on media freedom should be necessary and proportionate to any risk of prejudice that such publications might involve.

Innocent Publication or Distribution

Contempt of Court Act 1981, s. 3 **B14.104**

(1) A person is not guilty of contempt of court under the strict liability rule as the publisher of

any matter to which that rule applies if at the time of publication (having taken all reasonable care) he does not know and has no reason to suspect that relevant proceedings are active.

(2) A person is not guilty of contempt of court under the strict liability rule as the distributor of a publication containing any such matter if at the time of distribution (having taken all reasonable care) he does not know that it contains such matter and has no reason to suspect that it is likely to do so.

(3) The burden of proof of any fact tending to establish a defence a afforded by this section to any person lies upon that person.

This section falls short of providing a general 'no fault' defence. In particular it does not protect publishers who are aware of the proceedings, but blamelessly unaware of the prejudicial effect of the publication (see *Evening Standard Co. Ltd* [1954] 1 QB 578).

Fair and Accurate Reports of Proceedings

B14.105 **Contempt of Court Act 1981, s. 4**

(1) Subject to this section a person is not guilty of contempt of court under the strict liability rule in respect of a fair and accurate report of legal proceedings held in public, published contemporaneously and in good faith.

(2) [See **D3.84** and **B14.97**.]

(3) [If publication of a report is postponed as a result of an order under subsection (2), a report published as soon as practicable after the order expires is to be treated as contemporaneous and therefore entitled under subsection (1) to protection from contempt proceedings.]

Discussion of Public Affairs

B14.106 **Contempt of Court Act 1981, s. 5**

A publication made as or as part of a discussion in good faith of public affairs or other matters of general public interest is not to be treated as a contempt of court under the strict liability rule if the risk of impediment or prejudice to particular legal proceedings is merely incidental to the discussion

Whereas the Contempt of Court Act 1981, s. 3, creates defences to charges of contempt, s. 5 follows ss. 2 and 4(1) in restricting the scope of the strict liability rule itself, and the burden of proof does not lie on the alleged contemnor. If the publication is part of a wider discussion, the publisher is guilty of contempt under the strict liability rule only if it is proved that there is a substantial risk of prejudice to active proceedings (s. 2) and that this is not merely incidental to the wider discussion. See generally *A-G v English* [1983] 1 AC 116.

If, in the course of a wider discussion, the publisher intends to influence the outcome of proceedings, then (even apart from the good faith issue) he may be guilty of contempt independently of the Act (see s. 6(c) at **B14.107**).

Contempt of Court Act 1981: General Provisions

B14.107 **Contempt of Court Act 1981, ss. 6 and 7**

6. Nothing in the foregoing provisions of this Act—
   (a) prejudices any defence available at common law to a charge of contempt of court under the strict liability rule;
   (b) implies that any publication is punishable as contempt of court under that rule which would not be so punishable apart from those provisions;
   (c) restricts liability for contempt of court in respect of conduct intended to impede or prejudice the administration of justice.
7. Proceedings for a contempt of court under the strict liability rule (other than Scottish proceedings) shall not be instituted except by or with the consent of the A-G or on the motion of a court having jurisdiction to deal with it.

Strict Liability: Where the Act Does Not Apply

It is possible (but, it is submitted, unlikely) that strict liability may apply in certain circumstances not covered by the Contempt of Court Act 1981. This is because the Act only defines the scope of the strict liability rule insofar as it applies to conduct tending to interfere with particular proceedings. In *A-G v Newspaper Publishing plc* [1988] Ch 333, Sir John Donaldson MR suggested that examples of possible strict liability outside the scope of the Contempt of Court Act 1981 could include retaliation against a person who has given evidence in previous proceedings (which could themselves no longer be affected) and marrying a ward of court without the court's consent. The better view, however, would seem to be that such contempts do not carry strict liability. A person who punishes another for giving evidence or serving on a jury must at the very least be reckless as to the implications of his conduct on the due administration of justice, and this recklessness is the more probable basis of his liability. As for the wardship example (or other cases of interference with a court order), there is clear authority to the effect that recklessness as to the existence of the order is the minimum *mens rea* that will suffice (*Re F (A Minor) (Publication of Information)* [1977] Fam 58). **B14.108**

Cases in which Intent is Required by the Contempt of Court Act 1981

Where the Contempt of Court Act 1981 expressly rules out any question of strict liability (e.g., in respect of publications tending to prejudice proceedings which may be forthcoming but which are not active), it is clear that a specific intent must be present. In *A-G v Newspaper Publishing plc* [1988] Ch 333, Lloyd LJ said: **B14.109**

> In cases covered by the Act to which the strict liability rule does not apply, there is no room for a state of mind which falls short of intention. There is no middle way.
>
> I would therefore hold that the *mens rea* required in the present case is an intent to interfere with the course of justice. As in other branches of the criminal law, that intent may exist, even though there is no desire to interfere with the course of justice. Nor need it be the sole intent. It may be inferred, even though there is no overt proof. The more obvious the interference with the course of justice, the more readily will the requisite intent be inferred.

See also *A-G v Newspaper Publishing plc* [1997] 1 WLR 926 per Lord Bingham CJ at p. 936.

Appeals

Appeals in contempt cases are governed by the Administration of Justice Act 1960, s. 13. An appeal against a finding of criminal contempt lies as of right. Leave is not required (*Hourigan* [2003] EWCA Crim 2306). **B14.110**

Administration of Justice Act 1960, s. 13

(1) Subject to the provisions of this section, an appeal shall lie under this section from any order or decision of a court in the exercise of jurisdiction to punish for contempt of court (including criminal contempt); and in relation to any such order or decision the provisions of this section shall have effect in substitution for any other enactment relating to appeals in civil or criminal proceedings.

(2) An appeal under this section shall lie in any case at the instance of the defendant and, in the case of an application for committal or attachment, at the instance of the applicant; and the appeal shall lie—

(a) from an order or decision of any inferior court not referred to in the next following paragraph, to a divisional court of the High Court;

(b) from an order or decision of a county court or any other inferior court from which appeals generally lie to the Court of Appeal, and from an order or decision of a single judge of the High Court or of a judge of that court, to the Court of Appeal;

(bb) from an order or decision of the Crown Court to the Court of Appeal;

(c) from an order or decision of a divisional court or the Court of Appeal (including a decision of either of those courts on an appeal under this section), and from an order or decision of the . . . Courts-Martial Appeal Court, to the House of Lords.

(3) The court to which an appeal is brought under this section may reverse or vary the order or decision of the court below and make such other order as may be just; and without prejudice to the inherent powers of any court referred to in subsection (2) of this section, provision may be made by rules of court for authorising the release on bail of an appellant under this section.

(4) Subsections (2) to (4) of section 1 and section 2 of this Act shall apply to an appeal to the House of Lords under this section as they apply to an appeal to that House under the said section 1, except that so much of the said subsection (2) as restricts the grant of leave to appeal shall apply only where the decision of the court below is a decision on appeal to that court under this section.

(5) In this section 'court' includes any tribunal or person having power to punish for contempt; and references in this section to an order or decision of a court in the exercise of jurisdiction to punish for contempt of court include references—

(a) to an order or decision of the High Court, the Crown Court or a county court under any enactment enabling that court to deal with an offence as if it were contempt of court;

(b) to an order or decision of a county court, or of any court having the powers of a county court, under section 14, 92 or 118 of the County Courts Act 1984;

(c) to an order or decision of a magistrates' court under subsection (3) of section 63 of the Magistrates' Courts Act 1980,

but do not include references to orders under section 5 of the Debtors Act 1869, or under any provision of the Magistrates' Courts Act 1980, or the County Courts Act 1984, except those referred to in paragraphs (b) and (c) of this subsection and except section 38 and 142 of the last mentioned Act so far as those sections confer jurisdiction in respect of contempt of court.

(6) This section does not apply to a conviction or sentence in respect of which an appeal lies under part I of the Criminal Appeal Act 1968, or to a decision of the Criminal Division of the Court of Appeal under that part of that Act.

Section 13(1) and (2)(bb) give the Court of Appeal jurisdiction to hear an appeal against a refusal of bail by the Crown Court pending the determination of contempt proceedings against him (*Serumaga* [2005] 1 WLR 3366).

Section 13(2) was considered by the Court of Appeal in *A-G v Hislop* [1991] 1 QB 514. It was held that the words 'application for committal or attachment' refer to the original application, rather than to the appeal itself: in other words, it gives a right of appeal to an unsuccessful applicant for a committal or attachment order. It does not matter if the applicant is actually seeking to have the alleged contemnor fined rather than committed to prison (this in any case being a matter for the court), nor if the alleged contemnor is a corporation which could not be committed or attached.

Appeals from the Crown Court were originally heard by the Civil Division of the Court of Appeal, but are now, more appropriately, heard by the Criminal Division; see the Supreme Court Act 1981, s. 53(2)(b).

BREACH OF NON-MOLESTATION OR RESTRAINING ORDERS

B14.111 The DVCVA 2004, s. 1, inserts a new s. 42A into the Family Law Act 1996. This makes breach of a non-molestation order (defined in s. 42 of the 1996 Act) a criminal offence, but only if committed on or after 1 July 2007 (see the DVCVA 2004, sch. 12, para. 1) and not where a power of arrest under the Family Law Act 1996, s. 47, has been attached to a non-molestation order before that date, unless that power of arrest no longer has effect (Domestic Violence, Crime and Victims Act (Commencement No. 9 and Transitional Provisions) Order 2007 (SI 2007 No. 1845), art 3). It will remain possible for breach of a non-molestation order to be dealt with as a civil contempt of court, but s. 42A(3) and (4) prevent a defendant being punished twice for the same breach.

Family Law Act 1996, s. 42A

(1) A person who without reasonable excuse does anything that he is prohibited from doing by a non-molestation order is guilty of an offence.

(2) In the case of a non-molestation order made by virtue of section 45(1), a person can be guilty of an offence under this section only in respect of conduct engaged in at a time when he was aware of the existence of the order.

(3) Where a person is convicted of an offence under this section in respect of any conduct, that conduct is not punishable as a contempt of court.

(4) A person cannot be convicted of an offence under this section in respect of any conduct which has been punished as a contempt of court.

(5) A person guilty of an offence under this section is liable—

(a) on conviction on indictment, to imprisonment for a term not exceeding five years, or a fine, or both;

(b) on summary conviction, to imprisonment for a term not exceeding 12 months, or a fine not exceeding the statutory maximum, or both.

(6) A reference in any enactment to proceedings under this Part, or to an order under this Part, does not include a reference to proceedings for an offence under this section or to an order made in such proceedings.

'Enactment' includes an enactment contained in subordinate legislation within the meaning of the Interpretation Act 1978.

The penalties that may be imposed for an offence under s. 42A are identical to those that may be imposed under the Protection from Harassment Act 1997, s. 5(5), for breach of restraining orders made under ss. 5 or 5A of that Act, as to which see the SGC Guideline on Breach of a Protective Order, considered at E23.13 and set out in **appendix 8**.

Section B15 Corruption

COMMON-LAW OFFENCES

Misconduct in Public Office

B15.1 In *Bembridge* (1783) 3 Doug 327, Lord Mansfield set out two basic principles which underpin the offence of misconduct in public office. The first is that 'a man accepting an office of trust concerning the public, especially if attended with profit, is answerable criminally to the King for misbehaviour in his office'. The second is that, 'where there is a breach of trust, fraud, or imposition, in a matter concerning the public, though as between individuals it would only be actionable, yet as between the King and the subject it is indictable'. The offence was subsequently examined by the Court of Appeal in *Dytham* (1979) 69 Cr App R 387 and *A-G's Ref (No. 3 of 2003)* [2005] 1 QB 73. An extensive exploration of both English and Commonwealth authorities can also be found in the judgment of the Supreme Court of Canada in *Boulanger* [2006] 2 SCR 49.

These cases establish that the offence may take many forms, and may involve either an improper act or an omission, but the misconduct must be wilful, and the offender must be a public officer acting as such. Magistrates, judges, registrars, council officials, ministers, civil servants and police officers are all public officers. Wilful misconduct involves 'deliberately doing something which is wrong, knowing it to be wrong or with reckless indifference as to whether it is wrong or not' (*A-G's Ref (No. 3 of 2003)* at [28]). There must be, 'an element of culpability which is not restricted to corruption or dishonesty but . . . must be of such a degree that the misconduct impugned is calculated to injure the public interest so as to call for condemnation and punishment' (*Dytham,* per Lord Widgery CJ at p. 394). 'The threshold is a high one requiring conduct so far below acceptable standards as to amount to an abuse of the public's trust in the office holder. A mistake, even a serious one, will not suffice' (*A-G's Ref (No. 3 of 2003)* at [56]).

In *Dytham* (see **A1.15**), a police officer was convicted of this offence for ignoring a serious and violent offence that was being committed in front of his eyes. In *A-G's Ref (No. 1 of 2007)* [2007] EWCA Crim 760 a police officer was convicted of it for misusing the Police National Computer in order to supply confidential information to a known criminal. In *Bowden* [1996] 1 WLR 98 a local authority manager was convicted of it for improperly arranging for his men to carry out work at his girlfriend's house. See also *Borron* (1820) 3 B & Ald 432 and *Llewellyn-Jones* [1968] 1 QB 429.

Misconduct in public office is triable only on indictment and is a class 3 offence. The penalty is imprisonment and/or a fine, at the discretion of the court.

Bribery at Common Law

B15.2 It is an offence at common law to bribe the holder of a public office, or for any such office holder to accept such a bribe (*Whitaker* [1914] 3 KB 1283; *Lancaster* (1890) 16 Cox CC 737). There is considerable overlap in this respect with the offence of misconduct in public office (see **B15.1**). It is immaterial for the purposes of the common-law offence if the functions of the person who receives or is offered the bribe have no connection with the UK and are performed abroad (Anti-terrorism, Crime and Security Act 2001, s. 108(1)). Where the offer of a bribe is not accepted, the offeror may still be guilty of attempting to commit the offence.

Bribery at common law is triable only on indictment and is a class 3 offence. The penalty is imprisonment and/or a fine, at the discretion of the court. In practice, prosecutions are generally brought under one of the relevant statutory provisions, which are considered below.

STATUTORY OFFENCES

The principal legislation dealing with corruption is to be found in the Public Bodies Corrupt Practices Act 1889 and the Prevention of Corruption Act 1906, which are supplemented by the Prevention of Corruption Act 1916 and the Anti-terrorism, Crime and Security Act 2001, part 12. The 1889 Act deals with corruption in local government and in other public bodies; the 1906 Act deals with the corruption of agents, whether the agents of public bodies or not. There is a degree of overlap between the two principal Acts where the agents of public bodies are involved, but it should be noted that councillors in local government are not agents, and corruption of such councillors cannot therefore be dealt with under the 1906 Act. Conversely, the Crown is not a public body, and therefore the corruption of Crown servants cannot be dealt with under the 1889 Act (*Natji* [2002] 1 WLR 2337). **B15.3**

CORRUPTION IN PUBLIC OFFICE

Definition

Public Bodies Corrupt Practices Act 1889, s. 1 **B15.4**

(1) Every person who shall by himself or by or in conjunction with any other person, corruptly solicit or receive, or agree to receive, for himself, or for any other person, any gift, loan, fee, reward, or advantage whatever as an inducement to, or reward for, or otherwise on account of any member, officer, or servant of a public body as in this Act defined, doing or forbearing to do anything in respect of any matter or transaction whatsoever, actual or proposed, in which the said public body is concerned, shall be guilty of [an offence].

(2) Every person who shall by himself or by or in conjunction with any other person corruptly give, promise, or offer any gift, loan, fee, reward, or advantage whatsoever to any person, whether for the benefit of that person or of another person, as an inducement to or reward for or otherwise on account of any member, officer, or servant of any public body as in this Act defined, doing or forbearing to do anything in respect of any matter or transaction whatsoever, actual or proposed, in which such public body as aforesaid is concerned, shall be guilty of [an offence].

Procedure

No prosecution for this offence may be instituted except by or with the consent of the A-G (Public Bodies Corrupt Practices Act 1889, s. 4). The offence is triable either way (Public Bodies Corrupt Practices Act 1889, s. 2(a)). When tried on indictment it is a class 3 offence. **B15.5**

Indictment

Statement of Offence **B15.6**

Corruption contrary to section 1(2) of the Public Bodies Corrupt Practices Act 1889

Particulars of Offence

A on or about the . . . day of . . . corruptly offered as a gift to X, a member of a public body, namely . . ., the sum of £5,000, as an inducement to the said X to cast his vote at a meeting of the said public body held on . . . in favour of the award to A & Co. Ltd of a contract with the said public body for the construction of new municipal swimming-baths

Penalties

B15.7 **Public Bodies Corrupt Practices Act 1889, s. 2**

Any person on conviction for offending as aforesaid shall, at the discretion of the court before which he is convicted,—

(a) be liable—

(i) on summary conviction, to imprisonment for a term not exceeding six months or to a fine not exceeding the statutory maximum, or to both; and

(ii) on conviction on indictment, to imprisonment for a term not exceeding seven years or to a fine, or to both; and

(b) in addition be liable to be ordered to pay to such body, and in such manner as the court directs, the amount or value of any gift, loan, fee, or reward received by him or any part thereof; and

(c) be liable to be adjudged incapable of being elected or appointed to any public office for five years from the date of his conviction, and to forfeit any such office held by him at the time of his conviction; and

(d) in the event of a second conviction for a like offence he shall, in addition to the foregoing penalties, be liable to be adjudged to be for ever incapable of holding any public office, and to be incapable for five years of being registered as an elector, or voting at an election either of members to serve in Parliament or of members of any public body, and the enactments for preventing the voting and registration of persons declared by reason of corrupt practices to be incapable of voting shall apply to a person adjudged in pursuance of this section to be incapable of voting; and

(e) if such person is an officer or servant in the employ of any public body upon such conviction he shall, at the discretion of the court, be liable to forfeit his right and claim to any compensation or pension to which he would otherwise have been entitled.

For sentencing guidelines, see **B15.20**.

Definition of Relevant Terms

B15.8 **Public Bodies Corrupt Practices Act 1889, s. 7**

The expression 'public body' means any council of a county or council of a city or town, any council of a municipal borough, also any board, commissioners, select vestry, or other body which has power to act under and for the purposes of any Act relating to local government, or the public health, or to poor law or otherwise to administer money raised by rates in pursuance of any public general Act, and includes any body which exists in a country or territory outside the United Kingdom and is equivalent to any body described above:

The expression 'public office' means any office or employment of a person as a member, officer, or servant of such public body:

The expression 'person' includes a body of persons, corporate or unincorporate:

The expression 'advantage' includes any office or dignity, and any forbearance to demand any money or money's worth or valuable thing, and includes any aid, vote, consent, or influence, or pretended aid, vote, consent, or influence, and also includes any promise or procurement of or agreement or endeavour to procure, or the holding out of any expectation of any gift, loan, fee, reward, or advantage, as before defined.

The definition of a public body in s. 7 is supplemented by the Prevention of Corruption Act 1916, s. 4(2), which provides that it includes 'local and public authorities of all descriptions'. The Public Bodies Corrupt Practices Act 1889 is not therefore confined to corruption in local government. Any body with public or statutory duties to perform, other than one run for private profit, comes within its scope (*DPP v Holly* [1978] AC 43). Some, such as the Civil Aviation Authority, are expressly described as such in the legislation creating them, but this is not essential. The Crown is not a public body. The corruption of Crown servants must therefore be dealt with under the 1906 Act (*Natji* [2002] 1 WLR 2337.

Meaning of 'Corruptly'

'Corruptly' means purposefully doing an act which the law forbids as tending to corrupt (*Wellburn* (1979) 69 Cr App R 254). Any improper and unauthorised gift, payment or other inducement offered to a councillor or other such officer is likely to be considered corrupt. D need not be proved to have acted dishonestly, as long as he knew that the gift or bribe was connected with the performance of public duties, whether by way of reward for past performance, or of inducement to secure future performance. No bargain need be struck between the parties involved (*Andrews-Weatherfoil Ltd* [1972] 1 WLR 118), and it is no defence for the recipient to prove that his acceptance of a corrupt gift failed to influence him in the performance of his duties (see *Parker* (1985) 82 Cr App R 69). Nor is it necessary to prove that any person serving under the state or other public body, or holding a public office, was aware of the improper offer having been made, or the bribe having been passed, provided that the apparent purpose of the transaction was to affect the conduct of such a person corruptly (*Jagdeo Singh v The State of Trinidad and Tobago* [2006] 1 WLR 146). **B15.9**

In *Smith* [1960] 2 QB 423, S's offer of a bribe to a mayor was held to amount to an offence under the Public Bodies Corrupt Practices Act 1889, s. 1, even though his motive was supposedly to expose the mayor as corrupt. S intended that the mayor should accept the bribe and that in so doing the mayor would be acting corruptly. S's own conduct was accordingly corrupt within the meaning of the Act. This must be contrasted with the position where D is offered a bribe by E and purports to accept it for the purpose of exposing E or of procuring evidence against him; the Court of Appeal has said that this 'would plainly not be corrupt' (*Mills* (1978) 68 Cr App R 154 at p. 159). On such facts, D would neither be acting corruptly himself, nor inducing another person to so act.

It is possible that a payment intended as a corrupt gift could be received innocently by the recipient, i.e. without him understanding it to be a reward or inducement. In such a case, only the giver would be guilty of corruption (*Millray Window Cleaning Co. Ltd* [1962] Crim LR 99).

Under the Local Government Act 1972, ss. 94 and 95, any member of a local authority who has a direct pecuniary interest in a contract or a proposed contract involving that authority must disclose it and refrain from taking part in consideration of the matter. Failure to comply with this requirement is punishable on summary conviction by a fine.

The Presumption of Corruption

Prevention of Corruption Act 1916, s. 2 **B15.10**

> Where in any proceedings against a person for an offence under the Prevention of Corruption Act 1906, or the Public Bodies Corrupt Practices Act 1889, it is proved that any money, gift, or other consideration has been paid or given to or received by a person in the employment of His Majesty or any government department or a public body by or from a person, or agent of a person, holding or seeking to obtain a contract from His Majesty or any government department or public body, the money, gift, or consideration shall be deemed to have been paid or given and received corruptly as such inducement or reward as is mentioned in such Act unless the contrary is proved.

This presumption applies only to gifts etc. given to or received by employees (thus excluding payments to councillors) and only to cases in which a contract is being sought or has been obtained. It would not apply where D seeks only the granting of planning permission (*Dickinson* (1948) 33 Cr App R 5). In relevant cases, it will remain necessary for the prosecution to prove that the payment etc. was made or offered, and that the person offering or giving it was holding or seeking a relevant contract. Only then will any burden be placed on the defence. The burden in question was originally a full legal burden (see *Braithwaite* [1983] 1 WLR 385; *Evans-Jones* (1923) 17 Cr App R 121) but the imposition of such a burden arguably infringes the ECHR, Article 6(2) (see **A7** and **appendix 6**). The problem may be side-stepped by charging conspiracy or attempt instead of the full offence (*A-G, ex parte Rockall* [2000] 1 WLR 882). Alternatively, a court may re-interpret the burden as evidential only, in accordance with the HRA 1998, s. 3 (see **F3.13** ***et seq.***). The presumption does not apply to cases that fall within English criminal jurisdiction only by virtue of the Anti-terrorism, Crime and Security Act 2001 (see s. 110 of that Act).

Corrupt Intent and Companies

B15.11 Corruption cases often involve improper gifts etc. made by directors on behalf of their companies. In such cases, the company may itself be liable on the basis that the *mens rea* of such directors is that of the company's own mind. See generally **A5.17**.

Invalid Appointment or Election

B15.12 **Public Bodies Corrupt Practices Act 1889, s. 3**

(2) A person shall not be exempt from punishment under this Act by reason of the invalidity of the appointment or election of a person to a public office.

CORRUPTION OF AGENTS

Definition and Penalty

B15.13 **Prevention of Corruption Act 1906, s. 1**

(1) If any agent corruptly accepts or obtains, or agrees to accept or attempts to obtain, from any person, for himself or for any other person, any gift or consideration as an inducement or reward for doing or forbearing to do, or for having after the passing of this Act done or forborne to do, any act in relation to his principal's affairs or business, or for showing or forbearing to show favour or disfavour to any person in relation to his principal's affairs or business; or

If any person corruptly gives or agrees to give or offers any gift or consideration to any agent as an inducement or reward for doing or forbearing to do, or for having after the passing of this Act done or forborne to do, any act in relation to his principal's affairs or business, or for showing or forbearing to show favour or disfavour to any person in relation to his principal's affairs or business; or

If any person knowingly gives to any agent, or if any agent knowingly uses with intent to deceive his principal, any receipt, account, or other document in respect of which the principal is interested, and which contains any statement which is false or erroneous or defective in any material particular, and which to his knowledge is intended to mislead the principal;

he shall be guilty of [an offence] and shall be liable:

(a) on summary conviction, to imprisonment for a term not exceeding 6 months or to a fine not exceeding the statutory maximum, or to both; and

(b) on conviction on indictment, to imprisonment for a term not exceeding seven years or to a fine, or to both.

(2) For the purposes of this Act the expression 'consideration' includes valuable consideration of any kind; the expression 'agent' includes any person employed by or acting for another; and the expression 'principal' includes an employer.

(3) A person serving under the Crown or under any corporation or any . . . borough, county, or district council, or any board of guardians, is an agent within the meaning of this Act.

(4) For the purposes of this Act it is immaterial if—

(a) the principal's affairs or business have no connection with the United Kingdom and are conducted in a country or territory outside the United Kingdom;

(b) the agent's functions have no connection with the United Kingdom and are carried out in a country or territory outside the United Kingdom.

For sentencing guidelines, see **B15.20**.

Procedure

No prosecution for this offence may be instituted except by or with the consent of the A-G (Prevention of Corruption Act 1906, s. 2). The offence is triable either way (Prevention of Corruption Act 1906, s. 1). When tried on indictment it is a class 3 offence. **B15.14**

Meaning of 'Agent'

The definition of an agent in the Prevention of Corruption Act 1906, s. 1(2) and (3), is supplemented by the Prevention of Corruption Act 1916, s. 4(3), which provides that a person serving under any other public body within the meaning of that Act is an agent for the purposes of the 1906 Act. (As to the meaning of the term 'public body', see **B15.8**.) This does not appear to embrace local authority councillors, who should be dealt with under the Public Bodies Corrupt Practices Act 1889, but the definition is otherwise extremely wide, and applies to both the public and the private or commercial fields. An agent may be an employee, and any person serving under the Crown or under any public body comes within the Prevention of Corruption Act 1916, s. 4(3), whether or not an agent or employee within the ordinary meaning of the term. In *Barrett* [1976] 1 WLR 946 it was held that a superintendent registrar is accordingly an agent, serving under the Crown. **B15.15**

Outside the public domain, the term 'agent' must probably be more narrowly construed, so as to apply only to employees and agents in the strict sense (i.e. those who act on behalf of others). A retailer who is described as an 'agent' for particular manufacturers, but who is in fact an independent dealer or stockist, would not appear to be an agent for the purposes of this Act. A bribe offered direct to such a retailer, with a view to securing preferential allocation of products or services, would not therefore appear to be proscribed under the Prevention of Corruption Acts, or for that matter at common law. A bribe offered to his agent or employee would be another matter.

An agent need not be acting as an agent of his principal at the relevant time, as long as the Act in question is done 'in relation to his principal's affairs' (*Morgan v DPP* [1970] 3 All ER 1053).

Comparison with the Public Bodies Corrupt Practices Act 1889

In most respects the offences created by the Prevention of Corruption Act 1906 correspond with those in the Public Bodies Corrupt Practices Act 1889. The concept of corruption is the same (see *Harvey* [1999] Crim LR 70), as is the scope of the 'presumption of corruption' in the Prevention of Corruption Act 1916, s. 2 (see **B15.10**); and although the 1906 Act uses the words, 'gift or consideration' instead of the 1889 formula, 'gift, loan, fee, reward or advantage', this would not seem to be of any real significance. The 1906 Act also refers to *attempts* to obtain gifts etc., whereas the 1889 Act refers to the *soliciting* of such gifts, and this may be more significant in that the solicitation of a gift may not necessarily be regarded by a jury as anything more than 'merely preparatory' to the obtaining of such a gift. It would be a question of fact in every case. **B15.16**

False Statements under the Prevention of Corruption Act 1906

The Prevention of Corruption Act 1906, s. 1(1), creates one offence which has no equivalent in the 1889 legislation: that of knowingly giving to an agent, or knowing use by an agent, of documents etc. which are false, erroneous or defective, and which are intended to mislead the agent's principal. It was held in *Sage v Eicholz* [1919] 2 KB 171 that this offence does not require any bribery or corruption of the agent; the agent may himself be deceived by it. More recently, however, it was held in *Tweedie* [1984] QB 729 that such liability can arise only where the document in question originates from outside any business or organisation in which both principal and agent are involved. Were it otherwise, 'an employee who put a false entry on his timesheet would be guilty of an offence under the Act' (per Lawton LJ at p. 734). **B15.17**

'Knowingly' must here mean knowledge of the falsity etc. as well as of the giving, but proof of wilful blindness will suffice. See *Westminster City Council v Croyalgrange Ltd* [1986] 1 WLR 674.

BRIBERY AND CORRUPTION COMMITTED ABROAD

B15.18 **Anti-terrorism, Crime and Security Act 2001, s. 109**

(1) This section applies if—
 (a) a national of the United Kingdom or a body incorporated under the law of any part of the United Kingdom does anything in a country or territory outside the United Kingdom, and
 (b) the act would, if done in the United Kingdom, constitute a corruption offence (as defined below).
(2) In such a case—
 (a) the act constitutes the offence concerned, and
 (b) proceedings for the offence may be taken in the United Kingdom.
(3) These are corruption offences—
 (a) any common law offence of bribery;
 (b) the offences under section 1 of the Public Bodies Corrupt Practices Act 1889 (corruption in office);
 (c) the first two offences under section 1 of the Prevention of Corruption Act 1906 (bribes obtained by or given to agents).
(4) A national of the United Kingdom is an individual who is—
 (a) a British citizen, a British Overseas Territories citizen, a British National (Overseas) or a British Overseas citizen,
 (b) a person who under the British Nationality Act 1981 is a British subject, or
 (c) a British protected person within the meaning of that Act.

This provision was enacted 'to demonstrate the UK's commitment to join forces with the international community in the fight against corruption'. Note however that it does not give English courts jurisdiction over corruption committed in other parts of the UK (which may give rise to difficulties in cross-frontier corruption cases) and whilst it criminalises corruption by UK companies abroad, it does not appear to cover the acts of their wholly owned foreign subsidiaries. The so-called 'presumption of corruption' has no application in cases to which s. 109 applies (see s. 110).

ABUSES IN RESPECT OF HONOURS

B15.19 Under the Honours (Prevention of Abuses) Act 1925, s. 1, a person who accepts, obtains, gives or offers gifts or other valuable consideration, or who agrees to do so, as an inducement or reward for procuring, assisting or endeavouring to procure the grant of a dignity or title of honour to any person, is liable on conviction on indictment to imprisonment for a term not exceeding two years, and/or to a fine, or on summary conviction to three months' imprisonment and/or a fine not exceeding £5,000.

SENTENCING GUIDELINES FOR CORRUPTION OFFENCES

B15.20 At the top end of the scale of seriousness is *Donald* [1997] 2 Cr App R (S) 272, where sentences totalling 11 years were upheld in respect of a detective-constable in a regional crime squad who pleaded guilty, at a late stage of his trial, to four counts of corruption. He had accepted various sums of money from a man against whom criminal proceedings were being brought to disclose confidential information about the inquiry and to destroy surveillance logs. The officer had agreed to accept about £50,000 and actually received about £18,500. The sentencing judge commented that the case was 'almost unique' in its seriousness. The

Court of Appeal said the sentence was severe, but not manifestly excessive. In *Foxley* (1995) 16 Cr App R (S) 879, the offender was convicted of 12 counts of corruption contrary to the Prevention of Corruption Act 1906. While employed by the Ministry of Defence he had received payments in excess of £2 million in relation to the placing of government contracts. Four years' imprisonment was upheld, the Court of Appeal observing that six years would have been appropriate for a younger man (the offender was aged 71).

In *Wilson* (1982) 4 Cr App R (S) 337 the offender, a man of previous good character, was convicted of conspiracy to commit corruption and three counts of corruption. He was a purchasing agent and chief buyer with a manufacturing concern, and he accepted gifts of £2,500 in return for showing favour to a company supplying parts to his employer. A sentence of three and a half years was reduced to 18 months, taking into account personal mitigation, including the break-up of his family, the loss of his home and his business. In *Dearnley* [2001] 2 Cr App R (S) 201, a council employee and a supplier of security services to the council pleaded guilty to corruption in the form of supplying a car worth £5,445 and misrepresenting a loan in order to pay off a personal debt. A sentence of 18 months was reduced to 12 months by the Court of Appeal, Rafferty J noting that custody was required as a deterrent and was inevitable, but that there had been no lack of value for the security services paid for by the council, the car was a modest one, and that both defendants, previously of good character, were now 'broken men'.

The offenders in *Garner* (1988) 10 Cr App R (S) 445 pleaded guilty to conspiracy to corrupt. They were concerned in bribing a prison officer to take various items, including luxury foods, alcohol and cigars to one of the offenders who was serving a prison sentence: sentences of 18 months, 12 months, and 12 months suspended were upheld. Offering a bribe to a police officer was the nature of the corruption in *McGovern* (1980) 2 Cr App R (S) 389. The offender was arrested in connection with a burglary, and offered a bribe of £2,000 to the police involved in the case. Fifteen months was reduced to nine months' imprisonment for the corruption offence. In *Oxdemir* (1985) 7 Cr App R (S) 382 the offender tried to bribe a police officer with £50 or a free meal at the offender's restaurant if he did not report a driving offence by the offender's son. The appropriate sentence was said by the Court of Appeal to be three months' imprisonment.

Section B16 Revenue and Social Security Offences

PROSECUTIONS, PENALTIES AND MONEY SETTLEMENTS

B16.1 Frauds committed against the Public Revenue often involve Theft Act offences, such as false accounting (see **B6.3**) or offences under the Perjury Act 1911, s. 5(b) (see **B14.22**), but may instead be prosecuted as offences under revenue legislation, or as the common-law offence of cheating the public revenue. In many cases, tax frauds are not prosecuted at all. HM Revenue and Customs are often content to impose financial penalties and accept a money settlement, once full disclosure has been made. Taxpayers under investigation are nevertheless warned that the Revenue gives no undertaking that it will refrain from prosecuting, even if the taxpayer fully co-operates (see *Allen (No. 2)* [2001] 4 All ER 768). As to the need for interviews with suspected tax offenders to be conducted in accordance with PACE Code C, even in cases where the Revenue would ordinarily seek to reach a monetary settlement and avoid any criminal prosecution, see *Gill* [2004] 1 WLR 469.

CHEATING THE PUBLIC REVENUE

B16.2 The common-law offence of cheating the public revenue is triable only on indictment and punishable by a fine and/or imprisonment at large. It is a Group A offence for jurisdiction purposes under the CJA 1993, part I (see **A8.7**).

The parameters of the offence are not entirely clear, but it may be committed by dishonestly making false statements with intent to deceive or prejudice HM Revenue and Customs or the Department of Social Security (*Hudson* [1956] 2 QB 252). Dishonest failure to declare a tax or national insurance liability may also suffice. In *Mavji* (1987) 84 Cr App R 34, Michael Davies J said (at p. 37): 'This appellant . . . had a statutory duty to make VAT returns and pay over to the Crown the VAT due. He dishonestly failed to do either. Accordingly, he was guilty of cheating . . . the public revenue. No further act or omission is required.' See also *Redford* (1988) 89 Cr App R 1 and *Allen (No. 2)* [2001] 4 All ER 768.

FRAUDULENT EVASION OF INCOME TAX

B16.3 **Finance Act 2000, s. 144**

(1) A person commits an offence if he is knowingly concerned in the fraudulent evasion of income tax by him or any other person.
(2) A person guilty of an offence under this section is liable—
   (a) on summary conviction, to imprisonment for a term not exceeding six months or a fine not exceeding the statutory maximum, or both;
   (b) on conviction on indictment, to imprisonment for a term not exceeding seven years or a fine, or both.
(3) This section applies to things done or omitted on or after 1st January 2001.

In many respects, this offence mirrors the common-law offence of cheating, but only in respect of income tax evasion. The words 'knowingly concerned' and 'fraudulent evasion' appear in the Customs and Excise Management Act 1979, s. 170(2) (see **B17.21**), and reference should be made to the case law under that section (see **B17.28** and **B17.29**). Any dishonest attempt to evade or conceal one's income tax liabilities would appear to amount to an offence under s. 144; as would conduct that is intended to facilitate fraudulent evasion by another taxpayer. Dishonest financial advisers, or clients who provide the taxpayer with false invoices etc. may also be 'knowingly concerned' in the act of evasion. Paying a taxpayer a specially reduced fee in cash might also suffice, but only if the person making this payment knows that he is thereby facilitating the dishonest non-disclosure of this payment by the taxpayer. See D Ormerod, 'Fraudulent Evasion of Income Tax' [2002] Crim LR 3.

FRAUD IN RELATION TO TAX CREDITS

The Tax Credits Act 2002 and regulations made thereunder make provision for means-tested awards of tax credits, primarily for working families with dependent children. **B16.4**

Tax Credits Act 2002, s. 35

(1) A person commits an offence if he is knowingly concerned in any fraudulent activity undertaken with a view to obtaining payments of a tax credit by him or any other person.
(2) A person who commits an offence under subsection (1) is liable—
  (a) on summary conviction, to imprisonment for a term not exceeding six months, or a fine not exceeding the statutory maximum, or both, or
  (b) on conviction on indictment, to imprisonment for a term not exceeding seven years, or a fine, or both.

For the words 'knowingly concerned' see **B17.20**, **B17.28** and **B17.29**. The words 'fraudulent activity undertaken with a view to obtaining payments of a tax credit' would clearly cover the dishonest completion of an application form for tax credits.

FALSIFICATION ETC. OF DOCUMENTS CALLED FOR INSPECTION

Falsification of documents with a view to deceiving tax inspectors may be charged as offences under various general provisions (e.g., false accounting, cheating or fraudulent evasion of income tax), but s. 20BB deals specifically with such behaviour. **B16.5**

Taxes Management Act 1970, s. 20BB

(1) Subject to subsections (2) to (4) below, a person shall be guilty of an offence if he intentionally falsifies, conceals, destroys or otherwise disposes of, or causes or permits the falsification, concealment, destruction or disposal of, a document which—
  (a) he has been required by a notice under section 20 or 20A above or an order under section 20BA above, or
  (b) he has been given an opportunity in accordance with section 20B(1) above, to deliver, or to deliver or make available for inspection.
(2) A person does not commit an offence under subsection (1) above if he acts—
  (a) with the written permission of a General or Special Commissioner, the inspector or an officer of the board,
  (b) after the document has been delivered or, in a case within section 20(3) or (8A) above, inspected, or
  (c) after a copy has been delivered in accordance with section 20B(4) or (14) above and the original has been inspected.
(3) A person does not commit an offence under subsection (1)(a) above if he acts after the end of the period of two years beginning with the date on which the notice is given or the order is made, unless before the end of that period the inspector or an officer of the Board has

notified the person in writing that the notice or order has not been complied with to his satisfaction.

(4) A person does not commit an offence under subsection (1)(b) above if he acts—

(a) after the end of the period of six months beginning with the date on which an opportunity to deliver the document was given, or

(b) after an application for consent to a notice being given in relation to the document has been refused.

(5) A person guilty of an offence under subsection (1) above shall be liable—

(a) on summary conviction, to a fine not exceeding the statutory maximum;

(b) on conviction on indictment, to imprisonment for a term not exceeding two years or to a fine or to both.

VAT FRAUDS

B16.6 **Value Added Tax Act 1994, s. 72**

(1) If any person is knowingly concerned in, or in the taking of steps with a view to, the fraudulent evasion of VAT by him or any other person, he shall be liable—

(a) on summary conviction, to a penalty of the statutory maximum or of three times the amount of the VAT, whichever is the greater, or to imprisonment for a term not exceeding 6 months or to both; or

(b) on conviction on indictment, to a penalty of any amount or to imprisonment for a term not exceeding 7 years or to both.

(2) Any reference in subsection (1) above or subsection (8) below to the evasion of VAT includes a reference to the obtaining of—

(a) the payment of a VAT credit; or

(b) a refund under section 35, 36 or 40 of this Act or section 22 of the [Value Added Tax Act 1983]; or

(c) a refund under any regulations made by virtue of section 13(5); or

(d) a repayment under section 39;

and any reference in those subsections to the amount of the VAT shall be construed—

(i) in relation to VAT itself or a VAT credit, as a reference to the aggregate of the amount (if any) falsely claimed by way of credit for input tax and the amount (if any) by which output was falsely understated, and

(ii) in relation to a refund or repayment falling within paragraph (b), (c) or (d) above, as a reference to the amount falsely claimed by way of refund or repayment.

(3) If any person—

(a) with intent to deceive produces, furnishes or sends for the purposes of this Act or otherwise makes use for those purposes of any document which is false in a material particular; or

(b) in furnishing any information for the purposes of this Act makes any statement which he knows to be false in a material particular or recklessly makes a statement which is false in a material particular,

he shall be liable—

(i) on summary conviction, to a penalty of the statutory maximum or, where subsection (4) or (5) below applies, to the alternative penalty specified in that subsection if it is greater, or to imprisonment for a term not exceeding 6 months or to both; or

(ii) on conviction on indictment, to a penalty of any amount or to imprisonment for a term not exceeding 7 years or to both.

(4) In any case where—

(a) the document referred to in subsection (3)(a) above is a return required under this Act, or

(b) the information referred to in subsection (3)(b) above is contained in or otherwise relevant to such a return,

the alternative penalty referred to in subsection (3)(i) above is a penalty equal to three times the aggregate of the amount (if any) falsely claimed by way of credit for input tax and the amount (if any) by which output tax was falsely understated.

(5) In any case where—

(a) the document referred to in subsection (3)(a) above is a claim for a refund under section

35, 36 or 40 of this Act or section 22 of the [Value Added Tax Act 1983] for a refund under any regulations made by virtue of section 13(5) or for a repayment under section 39, or

(b) the information referred to in subsection (3)(b) above is contained in or otherwise relevant to such a claim,

the alternative penalty referred to in subsection (3)(i) above is a penalty equal to three times the amount falsely claimed.

(6) The reference in subsection (3)(a) above to furnishing, sending or otherwise making use of a document which is false in a material particular, with intent to deceive, includes a reference to furnishing, sending or otherwise making use of such a document, with intent to secure that a machine will respond to the document as if it were a true document.

(7) Any reference in subsection (3)(a) or subsection (6) above to producing, furnishing or sending a document includes a reference to causing a document to be produced, furnished or sent.

(8) Where a person's conduct during any specified period must have involved the commission by him of one or more offences under the preceding provisions of this section, then, whether or not the particulars of that offence or those offences are known, he shall, by virtue of this subsection, be guilty of an offence and liable—

(a) on summary conviction, to a penalty of the statutory maximum or, if greater, three times the amount of any VAT that was or was intended to be evaded by his conduct, or to imprisonment for a term not exceeding 6 months or to both; or

(b) on conviction on indictment to a penalty of any amount or to imprisonment for a term not exceeding 7 years or to both.

(9) Where an authorised person has reasonable grounds for suspecting that an offence has been committed under the preceding provisions of this section, he may arrest anyone whom he has reasonable grounds for suspecting to be guilty of the offence.

(10) If any person acquires possession of or deals with any goods, or accepts the supply of any services, having reason to believe that VAT on the supply of the goods or services, on the acquisition of the goods from another member State or on the importation of the goods from a place outside the member States has been or will be evaded, he shall be liable on summary conviction to a penalty of level 5 on the standard scale or three times the amount of the VAT, whichever is the greater.

(11) If any person supplies or is supplied with goods or services in contravention of paragraph 4(2) of Schedule 11, he shall be liable on summary conviction to a penalty of level 5 on the standard scale.

(12) Subject to subsection (13) below, sections 145 to 155 of the [Customs and Excise Management Act 1979] (proceedings for offences, mitigation of penalties and certain other matters) shall apply in relation to offences under this Act (which include any act or omission in respect of which a penalty is imposed) and penalties imposed under this Act as they apply in relation to offences and penalties under the customs and excise Acts as defined in that Act; and accordingly in section 154(2) as it applies by virtue of this subsection the reference to duty shall be construed as a reference to VAT.

(13) In subsection (12) above the references to penalties do not include references to penalties under sections 60 to 70.

For the Customs and Excise Management Act 1979, ss. 145 to 154, see **B17.2** to **B17.7**. For case law on 'knowingly concerned' and 'fraudulent evasion', see **B17.20**, **B17.28** and **B17.29.** The Court of Appeal held in *McCarthy* [1981] STC 298, that a dishonest omission to register for VAT may constitute an offence of taking steps to evade that tax under what is now s. 72(1). In *Hashash* [2006] EWCA Crim 2518 the Court of Appeal held that liability for payment of VAT may arise in respect of fraudulent transactions involving non-existent goods.

Section 72(8) enables a charge to be brought on the basis of a general deficiency. As to the circumstances in which this should be resorted to, see *Rasool* [1997] 1 WLR 1092. As to the wording of indictments generally, see *Ike* [1996] Crim LR 515.

TAXATION ETC. IN THE EUROPEAN COMMUNITY

B16.7 The CJA 1993, s. 71, creates an offence of involvement, within the UK, in specified EC fraud offences committed against the laws of other Member States. Despite this international dimension, the offence is not an extraterritorial one. The courts of England and Wales are not concerned with acts committed in other parts of the UK, nor does s. 71 penalise frauds in other Member States.

Definition

B16.8 **Criminal Justice Act 1993, s. 71**

(1) A person who, in the United Kingdom, assists in or induces any conduct outside the United Kingdom which involves the commission of a serious offence against the law of another Member State is guilty of an offence under this section if—
   (a) the offence involved is one consisting in or including the contravention of provisions of the law of that Member State which relate to any of the matters specified in subsection (2);
   (b) the offence involved is one consisting in or including the contravention of other provisions of that law so far as they have effect in relation to any of those matters; or
   (c) the conduct is such as to be calculated to have an effect in that Member State in relation to any of those matters.

(2) The matters mentioned in subsection (1) are—
   (a) the determination, discharge or enforcement of any liability for a Community duty or tax;
   (b) the operation of arrangements under which reliefs or exemptions from any such duty or tax are provided or sums in respect of any such duty or tax are repaid or refunded;
   (c) the making of payments in pursuance of Community arrangements made in connection with the regulation of the market for agricultural products and the enforcement of the conditions of any such payments;
   (d) the movement into or out of any Member State of anything in relation to the movement of which any Community instrument imposes, or requires the imposition of, any prohibition or restriction; and
   (e) such other matters in relation to which provision is made by any Community instrument as the Secretary of State may by order specify.

(3) For the purposes of this section—
   (a) an offence against the law of a Member State is a serious offence if provision is in force in that Member State authorising the sentencing, in some or all cases, of a person convicted of that offence to imprisonment for a maximum term of twelve months or more; and
   (b) the question whether any conduct involves the commission of such an offence shall be determined according to the law in force in the Member State in question at the time of the assistance or inducement.

. . .

(9) In this section—

'another Member State' means a Member State other than the United Kingdom;

'Community duty or tax' means any of the following, that is to say—
   (a) any Community customs duty;
   (b) an agricultural levy of the Economic Community;
   (c) value added tax under the law of another Member State;
   (d) any duty or tax on tobacco products, alcoholic liquors or hydrocarbon oils which, in another Member State, corresponds to any excise duty;
   (e) any duty, tax or other charge not falling within paragraphs (a) to (d) of this definition which is imposed by or in pursuance of any Community instrument on the movement of goods into or out of any Member State;

'conduct' includes acts, omissions and statements;

'contravention' includes a failure to comply; and

'the customs and excise Acts' has the same meaning as in the Customs and Excise Management Act 1979.

(10) References in this section, in relation to a Community instrument, to the movement of

anything into or out of a Member State include references to the movement of anything between Member States and to the doing of anything which falls to be treated for the purposes of that instrument as involving the entry into, or departure from, the territory of the Community of any goods (within the meaning of that Act of 1979).

Procedure and Sentence

An offence under the CJA 1993, s. 71, is triable either way, and is punishable following conviction on indictment by imprisonment for up to seven years or by a fine or both; six months and/or a fine not exceeding the statutory maximum following summary conviction (CJA 1993, s. 71(6)). When tried on indictment, it is a class 3 offence. **B16.9**

Elements

The term 'induce' in the CJA 1993, s. 71(1) is an ordinary English word meaning 'to prevail upon, persuade, bring about or give rise to'. This suggests that an offence against the laws of another Member State must actually be committed before liability can arise under s. 71. The conduct giving rise to that offence may involve or may merely be 'calculated' (i.e. likely) to have an effect in relation to the matters listed in s. 71(2). **B16.10**

Evidence of Foreign Law

Proof of the relevant law in the Member State concerned is facilitated by the CJA 1993, s. 71(5), although other methods of proving foreign law may still be used (see **F10.16**). Section 71(5) enables English courts to ascertain whether specified conduct would, if proved, amount to a specified offence under foreign law. It does not, however, allow English courts to assume that persons convicted of such offences by foreign courts were in fact guilty as charged; and convictions imposed by foreign courts are not admissible for that purpose. The PACE 1984, s. 74 (see **F11.5**), does not apply to the judgments of foreign courts, and the rule in *Hollington v Hewthorn* [1943] KB 587, still applies in that context. The obtaining of evidence may, however, be facilitated by procedures established under the Crime (International Cooperation) Act 2003. **B16.11**

Defences

Criminal Justice Act 1993, s. 71 **B16.12**

(4) In any proceedings against any person for an offence under this section it shall be a defence for that person to show—
 (a) that the conduct in question would not have involved the commission of an offence against the law of the Member State in question but for circumstances of which he had no knowledge; and
 (b) that he did not suspect or anticipate the existence of those circumstances and did not have reasonable grounds for doing so.

The burden of proving any such matter is ostensibly placed on the defence, but this burden may need to be construed as evidential only, following the views expressed by the House of Lords in *Sheldrake v DPP* [2005] 1 AC 204 (see **F3.13** ***et seq.***).

SENTENCING GUIDELINES FOR REVENUE OFFENCES

The maximum penalty for cheating or making false statements to the prejudice of the public revenue is at large (common-law offence). The maximum penalty for evasion of duty is seven years (Customs and Excise Management Act 1979, s. 170). **B16.13**

In respect of revenue offences, charges may be brought under a range of statutory provisions. The sentencing decisions listed below relate to cases where the offenders were found guilty of theft, conspiracy to defraud, false accounting, and VAT offences, as well as cheating or making a false statement to the Public Revenue. Sentencing principles appear to be similar, whichever offence is established.

General guidance on sentencing for revenue offences was provided by the Court of Appeal in *A-G's Ref (Nos. 87 and 86 of 1999)* [2001] 1 Cr App R (S) 505. In summary, Kennedy LJ said that, where over a period of time an offender has evaded tax, he must not only pay the tax and a financial penalty but a custodial sentence should be imposed as well. The length of the sentence will depend on the amount of tax evaded, the period of time involved, the effort made to conceal the evasion, whether others were drawn in and corrupted, the character of the offender, the extent (if known) of his personal gain, whether there was a guilty plea, and the amount of money recovered.

In *Milbern Investments Ltd* (1981) 3 Cr App R (S) 107, it was suggested in argument that the majority of people in the offender's position would, in the discretion of the tax authorities, not have been prosecuted. Watkins LJ, however, said (at p. 110):

> Courts are not to be hamstrung by the practice of some other arbitrary body in coming to its conclusions within the different powers given to it by Parliament, in the way it should exercise those powers in respect of people who do not deal with the Revenue honestly. That is not to say that a court is not permitted to look at what the Revenue would or might have done in any given case. It might be helpful to do so at times. However, it would be wholly improper for the court to regard itself as in any way governed by the practice of the Revenue.

Several groups of cases may be identified under the general heading of Revenue offences. The first group concerns employers or business people who fail to deduct tax from wages. In *Thornhill* (1980) 2 Cr App R (S) 310, the loss to the Revenue was £3,278. Six months' imprisonment, for conspiracy to defraud, was reduced to two months, since, in this type of case 'it is the effect of imprisonment rather than perhaps its length which is of importance'. In *Hayes* (1981) 3 Cr App R (S) 205, a case referred to as a 'guideline' in several later cases, the loss was £19,424, the offender had a clean record and pleaded guilty to theft. The prison sentence of two and a half years was reduced to nine months. In *Ball* (1987) 9 Cr App R (S) 94, the loss was between £60,000 and £70,000. The Court of Appeal noted that the loss was substantially greater than in the last cited case, and that the offender in this case had served custodial sentences in the past. Three and a half years' imprisonment was reduced to two years. The case of *Sivyer* (1987) 9 Cr App R (S) 428 was on a different scale, with losses of £400,000. Sentences varying from four years for conspiracy to defraud in respect of the main actors, with lesser terms for those playing minor roles or who pleaded guilty to the charges, were upheld on appeal.

A second group of cases concerns failure to disclose income to the Revenue and making false claims for allowances. In *Trevithick* (1986) 8 Cr App R (S) 31, a two-year prison sentence was upheld on an offender who pleaded guilty to seven counts of making a false statement with intent to defraud the Revenue, in the event evading payment of £48,000 in income tax. The offender had previous convictions for dishonesty. In *Rogers* (1995) 16 Cr App R (S) 720, the offender pleaded guilty to two counts of cheating the public revenue, by concealing £112,000 of income from his business. In the Court of Appeal, Hobhouse LJ observed that the normal sentencing bracket for such offences would be somewhere between six months and 18 months. Eighteen months was upheld in this case, because the dishonesty was systematic and persistent. In *James* [1997] 2 Cr App R (S) 294, however, a sentence of nine months' imprisonment was reduced to five months, where the sum involved was £35,000, the offender had co-operated with the tax authorities, and had been 'unfortunate to find himself in the hands of a dishonest accountant'.

A third group of cases is VAT frauds. Examples are *Richardson* (1992) 13 Cr App R (S) 51, where the offender registered for VAT as a haulage business and made three fraudulent claims for repayment to a total sum of £7,900, and a custodial sentence of 18 months was reduced to

12 months on appeal, and *Lal* (1993) 15 Cr App R (S) 143, where the offender made a series of fraudulent claims in respect of VAT, with a total loss to the Revenue of £41,000, and a sentence of two and a half years' imprisonment was upheld. In *Aziz* [1996] 1 Cr App R (S) 265, where the offender misdescribed adult footwear as children's footwear, which was zero-rated, with an estimated loss to the Revenue of £400,000, a sentence of four and a half years' imprisonment was upheld. About £1.5 million was obtained by means of fraudulent claims for repayment in *Alibhai* (1992) 13 Cr App R (S) 682. A term of seven years, for the offence of conspiring to obtain by deception, was said by the Court of Appeal to be right in principle and not excessive. In *A-G's Refs (Nos. 88, 89, 90 and 91 of 2006); Meehan* [2006] EWCA Crim 3254 the Court of Appeal stated that the organisers of multi-million pound frauds should expect sentences of imprisonment well into double figures.

SOCIAL SECURITY FRAUDS

The dishonest obtaining and/or retention of benefits may well involve the commission of offences under the Theft Act 1968, but the Social Security Administration Act 1992, s. 111A, creates further offences carrying comparable penalties and requiring similar proof of dishonesty. **B16.14**

Social Security Administration Act 1992, s. 111A

(1) If a person dishonestly—
   (a) makes a false statement or representation; or
   (b) produces or furnishes, or causes or allows to be produced or furnished, any document or information which is false in a material particular,

   with a view to obtaining any benefit or other payment or advantage under the relevant social security legislation (whether for himself or for some other person), he shall be guilty of an offence.

(1A) A person shall be guilty of an offence if—
   (a) there has been a change of circumstances affecting any entitlement of his to any benefit or other payment or advantage under any provision of the relevant social security legislation;
   (b) the change is not a change that is excluded by regulations from the changes that are required to be notified;
   (c) he knows that the change affects an entitlement of his to such a benefit or other payment or advantage; and
   (d) he dishonestly fails to give a prompt notification of that change in the prescribed manner to the prescribed person.

(1B) A person shall be guilty of an offence if—
   (a) there has been a change of circumstances affecting any entitlement of another person to any benefit or other payment or advantage under any provision of the relevant social security legislation;
   (b) the change is not a change that is excluded by regulations from the changes that are required to be notified;
   (c) he knows that the change affects an entitlement of that other person to such a benefit or other payment or advantage; and
   (d) he dishonestly causes or allows that other person to fail to give a prompt notification of that change in the prescribed manner to the prescribed person.

(1C) This subsection applies where—
   (a) there has been a change of circumstances affecting any entitlement of a person ('the claimant') to any benefit or other payment or advantage under any provision of the relevant social security legislation;
   (b) the benefit, payment or advantage is one in respect of which there is another person ('the recipient') who for the time being has a right to receive payments to which the claimant has, or (but for the arrangements under which they are payable to the recipient) would have, an entitlement; and
   (c) the change is not a change that is excluded by regulations from the changes that are required to be notified.

(1D) In a case where subsection (1C) above applies, the recipient is guilty of an offence if—
 (a) he knows that the change affects an entitlement of the claimant to a benefit or other payment or advantage under a provision of the relevant social security legislation;
 (b) the entitlement is one in respect of which he has a right to receive payments to which the claimant has, or (but for the arrangements under which they are payable to the recipient) would have, an entitlement; and
 (c) he dishonestly fails to give a prompt notification of that change in the prescribed manner to the prescribed person.

(1E) In a case where that subsection applies, a person other than the recipient is guilty of an offence if—
 (a) he knows that the change affects an entitlement of the claimant to a benefit or other payment or advantage under a provision of the relevant social security legislation;
 (b) the entitlement is one in respect of which the recipient has a right to receive payments to which the claimant has, or (but for the arrangements under which they are payable to the recipient) would have, an entitlement; and
 (c) he dishonestly causes or allows the recipient to fail to give a prompt notification of that change in the prescribed manner to the prescribed person.

(1F) In any case where subsection (1C) above applies but the right of the recipient is confined to a right, by reason of his being a person to whom the claimant is required to make payments in respect of a dwelling, to receive payments of housing benefit—
 (a) a person shall not be guilty of an offence under subsection (1D) or (1E) above unless the change is one relating to one or both of the following—
  (i) the claimant's occupation of that dwelling;
  (ii) the claimant's liability to make payments in respect of that dwelling; but
 (b) subsections (1D)(a) and (1E)(a) above shall each have effect as if after 'knows' there were inserted 'or could reasonably be expected to know'.

(1G) For the purposes of subsections (1A) to (1E) above a notification of a change is prompt if, and only if, it is given as soon as reasonably practicable after the change occurs.

(2) [repealed]

(3) A person guilty of an offence under this section shall be liable—
 (a) on summary conviction, to imprisonment for a term not exceeding six months, or to a fine not exceeding the statutory maximum, or to both; or
 (b) on conviction on indictment, to imprisonment for a term not exceeding seven years, or to a fine, or to both.

Section 112 complements s. 111A with a range of purely summary offences. These largely mirror the offences created by s. 111A and require similar knowledge of relevant matters, but do not require proof of dishonesty. Under s. 112(2), such offences are punishable by fines not exceeding level 5 on the standard scale, and/or by imprisonment for a term not exceeding three months.

In respect of any charge brought under s. 111A or s. 112, the prosecution must prove that any 'change of circumstances' which a person failed to report would (and not merely could or might) have affected an entitlement to benefit etc. (*King v Kerrier District Council* [2006] EWHC 500 (Admin)). See also *Passmore* [2007] All ER (D) 178 (Jun), where it was held that the defendant committed no offence by failing to disclose that he had formed a company from which he had received no income. For the running of time within which a prosecution must be brought under s. 116(2), see *Eyeson v Milton Keynes Council* [2005] EWHC 1160 (Admin).

The fraudulent evasion of an obligation to make social security contributions is dealt with under s. 114 of the Act. Any person 'knowingly concerned in the fraudulent evasion of any contributions which he or any other person is liable to pay' may be sentenced on indictment to imprisonment for up to seven years; or on summary conviction to a fine not exceeding the statutory maximum.

Procedural provisions relating to the prosecution of offences under the Social Security Administration Act 1992 are contained in s. 116.

Social Security Administration Act 1992, s. 116

(1) Any person authorised by the Secretary of State in that behalf may conduct any proceedings under any provision of this Act other than section 114 or under any provision of the Jobseekers Act 1995 before a magistrates' court although not a barrister or solicitor.

(2) Notwithstanding anything in any Act—

(a) proceedings for an offence under this Act other than an offence relating to housing benefit or council tax benefit or for an offence under the Jobseekers Act 1995 may be begun at any time within the period of 3 months from the date on which evidence, sufficient in the opinion of the Secretary of State to justify a prosecution for the offence, comes to his knowledge or within a period of 12 months from the commission of the offence, whichever period last expires; and

(b) proceedings for an offence under this Act relating to housing benefit or council tax benefit may be begun at any time within the period of 3 months from the date on which evidence, sufficient in the opinion of the appropriate authority to justify a prosecution for the offence, comes to the authority's knowledge or within a period of 12 months from the commission of the offence, whichever period last expires.

(2A) Subsection 2 above shall not be taken to impose any restriction on the time when proceedings may be begun for an offence under section 111A above.

(3) For the purposes of subsection (2) above—

(a) a certificate purporting to be signed by or on behalf of the Secretary of State as to the date on which such evidence as is mentioned in paragraph (a) of that subsection came to his knowledge shall be conclusive evidence of that date; and

(b) a certificate of the appropriate authority as to the date on which such evidence as is mentioned in paragraph (b) of that subsection came to the authority's knowledge shall be conclusive evidence of that date.

Sentencing Guidelines for Social Security Fraud

Sentencing guidelines for social security fraud cases which reach the Crown Court were laid down by the Court of Appeal in *Stewart* (1987) 9 Cr App R (S) 135 and *Graham* [2005] 1 Cr App R (S) 640 (see **B5.27**). For sentencing for the summary offence under the Social Security Administration Act 1992, s. 112, the Magistrates' Courts Guidelines (2004) indicate the following for a first-time offender pleading not guilty: **B16.15**

Aggravating Factors For example claim fraudulent from the start; fraudulent claims over a long period; large amount; organised group offence; planned deception; offence committed on bail; relevant previous convictions and any failures to respond to previous sentences.

Mitigating Factors For example misunderstanding of regulations; pressurised by others; small amount.

Guideline: Is it serious enough for a community penalty?

Section B17 Offences under Customs and Excise Legislation

B17.1 This section deals with the most important offences under the Customs and Excise Management Act 1979 ('the Act') and the Commissioners for Revenue and Customs Act 2005. A number of specific procedural provisions apply to prosecutions for any offence under the Acts, and it will be convenient to consider these before turning to the offences themselves.

PROCEDURAL PROVISIONS

Institution of Proceedings

B17.2 With limited exceptions, prosecutions under the Acts may be commenced by the Commissioners and in the name of an officer of the Customs and Excise Service. By ss. 34 and 35 of the Commissioners for Revenue and Customs Act 2005, the Director of Revenue and Customs Prosecutions is empowered to institute and conduct criminal proceedings in England and Wales relating to a criminal investigation by the Revenue and Customs and must take over the conduct of criminal proceedings instituted by the Revenue and Customs in England and Wales.

Customs and Excise Management Act 1979, s. 145

(1) Subject to the following provisions of this section, no proceedings for an offence under the customs and excise Acts or for condemnation under schedule 3 to this Act shall be instituted except—
(a) by or with the consent of the Director of Revenue and Customs Prosecutions, or
(b) by order of, or with the consent of, the Commissioners for Her Majesty's Revenue and Customs.
(2) Subject to the following provisions of this section, any proceedings under the customs and excise Acts instituted by order of the Commissioners in a magistrates court . . . shall be commenced in the name of an officer of Revenue and Customs.
(3) [Applies to Scotland only.]
(4) [Repealed by the Commissioners for Revenue and Customs Act 2005, sch. 5.]
(5) Nothing in the foregoing provisions of this section, shall prevent the institution of proceedings for an offence under the customs and excise Acts by order and in any case in which he thinks it proper that proceedings should be so instituted.
(6) Notwithstanding anything in the foregoing provisions of this section, where any person has been detained for any offence for which he is liable to be detained under the customs and excise Acts, any court before which he is brought may proceed to deal with the case although the proceedings have not been instituted in accordance with this section.

This provision applies also to conspiracy to commit an offence under the Act (*Whitehead* [1982] QB 1272).

Time-limits

B17.3 Section 146A of the Act provides the following time-limits for instituting proceedings, which override the general limitation provisions of the MCA 1980, s. 127.

Customs and Excise Management Act 1979, s. 146A

(1) Except as otherwise provided in the customs and excise Acts, and notwithstanding anything in any other enactment, the following provisions shall apply in relation to proceedings for an offence under those Acts.

(2) Proceedings for an indictable offence shall not be commenced after the end of the period of 20 years beginning with the day on which the offence was committed.
(3) Proceedings for a summary offence shall not be commenced after the end of the period of three years beginning with that day but, subject to that, may be commenced at any time within six months from that date on which sufficient evidence to warrant the proceedings came to the knowledge of the prosecuting authority.
(4) For the purposes of subsection (3) above, a certificate of the prosecuting authority as to the date on which such evidence as is there mentioned came to that authority's knowledge shall be conclusive evidence of that fact.

Proceedings in Magistrates' Courts

Customs and Excise Management Act 1979, s. 147 **B17.4**

(2) Where, in England or Wales, a magistrates court has begun to inquire into an information charging a person with an offence under the customs and excise Acts as examining justices the court shall not proceed under section 25(3) of the Magistrates' Courts Act 1980 to try the information summarily without the consent of—
(a) the Attorney-General, in a case where the proceedings were instituted by his order and in his name; or
(b) the Commissioners, in any other case.
(3) In the case of proceedings in England or Wales, without prejudice to any right to require the statement of a case for the opinion of the High Court, the prosecutor may appeal to the Crown Court against any decision of a magistrates' court in proceedings for an offence under the customs and excise Acts.

Place of Trial

Customs and Excise Management Act 1979, s. 148 **B17.5**

(1) Proceedings for an offence under the customs and excise Acts may be commenced—
(a) in any court having jurisdiction in the place where the person charged with the offence resides or is found; or
(b) if any thing was detained or seized in connection with the offence, in any court having jurisdiction in the place where that thing was so detained or seized or was found or condemned as forfeited; or
(c) in any court having jurisdiction anywhere in that part of the United Kingdom, namely—
(i) England and Wales,
(ii) Scotland, or
(iii) Northern Ireland,
in which the place where the offence was committed is situated.
(2) Where any such offence was committed at some place outside the area of any commission of the peace, the place of the commission of the offence shall, for the purposes of the jurisdiction of any court, be deemed to be any place in the United Kingdom where the offender is found or to which he is first brought after the commission of the offence.
(3) The jurisdiction under subsection (2) above shall be in addition to and not in derogation of any jurisdiction or power of any court under any other enactment.

Powers of Court and Commissioners in Relation to Penalties

Customs and Excise Management Act 1979, ss. 149 to 152 **B17.6**

149.—(1) Where, in any proceedings for an offence under the customs and excise Acts, a magistrates court in England or Wales or a court of summary jurisdiction in Scotland, in addition to ordering the person convicted to pay a penalty for the offence—
(a) orders him to be imprisoned for a term in respect of the same offence; and
(b) further (whether at the same time or subsequently) orders him to be imprisoned for a term in respect of non-payment of that penalty or default of a sufficient distress to satisfy the amount of that penalty,
the aggregate of the terms for which he is so ordered to be imprisoned shall not exceed 15 months.

(2) [Repealed.]

(3) [Applies to Northern Ireland only.]

150.—(1) Where liability for any offence under the customs and excise Acts is incurred by two or more persons jointly, those persons shall each be liable for the full amount of any pecuniary penalty and may be proceeded against jointly or severally as the Director of Revenue and Customs Prosecutions (in relation to proceedings instituted in England and Wales) or the Commissioners (in relation to proceedings instituted in Scotland or Northern Ireland) may see fit.

(2) In any proceedings for an offence under the customs and excise Acts instituted in England, Wales or Northern Ireland, any court by whom the matter is considered may mitigate any pecuniary penalty as they see fit.

(3) In any proceedings for an offence or for the condemnation of any thing as being forfeited under the customs and excise Acts, the fact that security has been given by bond or otherwise for the payment of any duty or for compliance with any condition in respect of the non-payment of which or non-compliance with which the proceedings are instituted shall not be a defence.

151. The balance of any sum paid or recovered on account of any penalty imposed under the customs and excise Acts, after paying any such compensation or costs as are mentioned in section 139 of the Magistrates Courts Act 1980 to persons other than the Commissioners, shall, notwithstanding any local or other special right or privilege of whatever origin, be accounted for and paid to the Commissioners or as they direct.

152. The Commissioners may, as they see fit—

(a) compound an offence (whether or not proceedings have been instituted in respect of it) and compound proceedings or for the condemnation of any thing as being forfeited under the customs and excise Acts; or

(b) restore, subject to such conditions (if any) as they think proper, any thing forfeited or seized under those Acts; or

(c) and (d) [repealed];

but paragraph (a) above shall not apply to proceedings on indictment in Scotland.

Evidential Provisions

B17.7 The Acts make the following important provisions regarding the burden of proof as to certain documents and certain frequently recurring facts.

Customs and Excise Management Act 1979, s. 154

(1) An averment in any process in proceedings under the customs and excise Acts—

(a) that those proceedings were instituted by the order of the Commissioners; or

(b) that any person is or was a Commissioner, officer or constable, or a member of Her Majesty's armed forces or coastguard; or

(c) that any person is or was appointed or authorised by the Commissioners to discharge, or was engaged by the orders or with the concurrence of the Commissioners in the discharge of, any duty; or

(d) that the Commissioners have or have not been satisfied as to any matter as to which they are required by any provision of those Acts to be satisfied; or

(e) that any ship is a British ship; or

(f) that any goods thrown overboard, staved or destroyed were so dealt with in order to prevent or avoid the seizure of those goods,

shall, until the contrary is proved, be sufficient evidence of the matter in question.

(2) Where in any proceedings relating to customs or excise any question arises as to the place from which any goods have been brought or as to whether or not—

(a) any duty has been paid or secured in respect of any goods; or

(b) any goods or other things whatsoever are of the description or nature alleged in the information, writ or other process; or

(c) any goods have been lawfully imported or lawfully unloaded from any ship or aircraft; or

(d) any goods have been lawfully loaded into any ship or aircraft or lawfully exported or were lawfully water-borne; or

(e) any goods were lawfully brought to any place for the purpose of being loaded into any ship or aircraft or exported; or

(f) any goods are or were subject to any prohibition of or restriction on their importation or exportation,

then where those proceedings are brought by or against the Commissioners, a law officer of the Crown or an officer, or against any other person in respect of anything purporting to have been done in pursuance of any power or duty conferred or imposed on him by or under the custom and excise Acts, the burden of proof shall be upon the other party to the proceedings.

Commissioners for Revenue and Customs Act 2005, s. 24

(1) A document that purports to have been issued or signed by or with the authority of the Commissioners—
(a) shall be treated as having been so issued or signed unless the contrary is proved, and
(b) shall be admissible in any legal proceedings.

(2) A document that purports to have been issued by the Commissioners and which certifies any of the matters specified in subsection (3) shall (in addition to the matters provided for by subsection (1)(a) and (b)) be treated as accurate unless the contrary is proved.

(3) The matters mentioned in subsection (2) are—
(a) that a specified person was appointed as a commissioner on a specified date,
(b) that a specified person was appointed as an officer of Revenue and Customs on a specified date,
(c) that at a specified time or for a specified purpose (or both) a function was delegated to a specified Commissioner,
(d) that at a specified time or for a specified purpose (or both) a function was delegated to a specified committee, and
(e) that at a specified time or for a specified purpose (or both) a function was delegated to another specified person.

(4) A photographic or other copy of a document acquired by the Commissioners shall, if certified by them to be an accurate copy, be admissible in any legal proceedings to the same extent as the document itself.

(5) Section 2 of the Documentary Evidence Act 1868 (proof of documents) shall apply to a Revenue and Customs document as it applies in relation to the documents mentioned in that section.

(6) In the application of that section to a Revenue and Customs document the schedule to that Act shall be treated as if—
(a) the first column contained a reference to the Commissioners, and
(b) the second column contained a reference to a Commissioner or a person acting on his authority.

(7) In this section—
(a) 'Revenue and Customs document' means a document issued by or on behalf of the Commissioners, and
(b) a reference to the Commissioners includes a reference to the Commissioners of Inland Revenue and to the Commissioners of Customs and Excise.

OFFENCES IN CONNECTION WITH COMMISSIONERS AND OFFICERS

Section 33 of the Commissioners for Revenue and Customs Act 2005 confers a power of arrest on an authorised officer of the Revenue and Customs if the officer reasonably suspects that a person has committed, is committing or is about to commit an offence under any of ss. 30 to 32. **B17.8**

Unlawful Assumption of Character of Commissioner or Officer

Commissioners for Revenue and Customs Act 2005, s. 30 **B17.9**

(1) A person commits an offence if he pretends to be a Commissioner or an officer of Revenue and Customs with a view to obtaining—
(a) admission to premises,
(b) information, or
(c) any other benefit.

This is a summary offence with a maximum penalty of six months' imprisonment and a fine at level 5 on the standard scale, or both.

Obstruction of Officers etc.

B17.10 **Commissioners for Revenue and Customs Act 2005, s. 31**

(1) A person commits an offence if without reasonable excuse he obstructs—
  (a) an officer of Revenue and Customs,
  (b) a person acting on behalf of the Commissioners or an officer of Revenue and Customs, or
  (c) a person assisting an officer of Revenue and Customs.

This is a summary offence with a maximum penalty of one month's imprisonment and a fine at level 3 on the standard scale, or both. The general principles concerning obstruction of a police officer (see **B2.33** to **B2.36**) apply. Thus a person who gives false information to officers of the Revenue and Customs, so making it harder for officers to perform their duty, is guilty of obstruction (*George* [1981] Crim LR 185).

IMPROPER IMPORTATION AND EXPORTATION OF GOODS

Improper Importation of Goods

B17.11 **Customs and Excise Management Act 1979, s. 50**

(1) Subsection (2) below applies to goods of the following descriptions, that is to say—
  (a) goods chargeable with a duty which has not been paid; and
  (b) goods the importation, landing or unloading of which is for the time being prohibited or restricted by or under any enactment.

(2) If any person with intent to defraud Her Majesty of any such duty or to evade any such prohibition or restriction as is mentioned in subsection (1) above—
  (a) unships or lands in any port or unloads from any aircraft in the United Kingdom or from any vehicle in Northern Ireland any goods to which this subsection applies, or assists or is otherwise concerned in such unshipping, landing or unloading; or
  (b) removes from their place of importation or from any approved wharf, examination station, transit shed or customs and excise station any goods to which this subsection applies or assists or is otherwise concerned in such removal,

he shall be guilty of an offence under this subsection and may be arrested.

(3) If any person imports or is concerned in importing any goods contrary to any prohibition or restriction for the time being in force under or by virtue of any enactment with respect to those goods, whether or not the goods are unloaded, and does so with intent to evade the prohibition or restriction, he shall be guilty of an offence under this subsection and may be arrested.

B17.12 **Procedure and Penalties** This offence is triable either way. When tried on indictment it is a class 3 offence. As to the power of arrest, see *Smith* [1973] QB 924.

Penalties are provided by the Customs and Excise Management Act 1979, s. 50(4): on indictment, a penalty of any amount, or imprisonment for a term not exceeding seven years or both; on summary conviction, a penalty of the prescribed sum or of three times the value of the goods, whichever is the greater, or imprisonment for a term not exceeding six months, or both. Enhanced penalties are provided for by s. 50(5) and sch. 1 and are imposed in the following types of cases.

(i) Where the goods in respect of which the offence is committed are drugs, the importation of which is prohibited by the Misuse of Drugs Act 1971, s. 3 (see **B17.15**). If the drug is a Class A or Class B drug (as to the meaning of which, see **B20.1**), on summary conviction, the penalty is six months and/or a penalty not exceeding the prescribed amount, or three times the value of the goods, whichever is the greater; on indictment, there is a penalty of unlimited amount and, in the case of a Class A drug, life imprisonment, or, in the case of a Class B drug,

14 years' imprisonment. If the drug is a Class C drug (see **B20.1**), the penalty is, on summary conviction, three months and/or a penalty of £500, or three times the value of the goods, whichever is the greater. On indictment there is a penalty of unlimited amount and 14 years' imprisonment.

(ii) Where the importation is of any weapon or ammunition of a kind mentioned in the Firearms Act 1968, s. 5(1)(a), (ab), (aba), (ac), (ad), (ae), (af) or (c) or (1A)(a) (see **B12.50**) or of a counterfeit of a currency note or of a protected coin without the Treasury's consent (Forgery and Counterfeiting Act 1981, s. 20: see **B6.85**), the maximum penalty on indictment is enhanced to ten years by s. 50(5A) of, and sch. 1 to, the Act.

Elements As to prohibition or restriction, see *Superheater Co. Ltd v Commissioners of Customs and Excise* [1969] 1 WLR 858. **B17.13**

Goods entering the country by air are imported before they are unloaded, and goods brought in by sea are imported before they are landed. By the Customs and Excise Management Act 1979, s. 5(2), the time of importation of goods brought in by sea is the time when the ship comes within the limits of the port. Goods which are unloaded at an airport and held in a customs area pending trans-shipment to a foreign destination are nonetheless regarded as having been imported into the UK (*Smith* [1973] QB 924, applying dicta in *DPP v Doot* [1973] AC 807).

A person who brings in items under a 'duty free' arrangement for others, for example a bus driver bringing in goods for his passengers, is an importer of the goods and if they are beneficially his he can be convicted of being knowingly concerned in the fraudulent evasion of duty payable on them (*Collins* [1987] Crim LR 256).

Duplication of Offences Section 50(7) of the Customs and Excise Management Act 1979 prevents duplication of offences and possible double jeopardy problems. **B17.14**

Customs and Excise Management Act 1979, s. 50

(7) In any case where a person would, apart from this subsection, be guilty of—

(a) an offence under this section in connection with the importation of goods contrary to a prohibition or restriction; and

(b) a corresponding offence under the enactment or other instrument imposing the prohibition or restriction, being an offence for which a fine or other penalty is expressly provided by that enactment or other instrument,

he shall not be guilty of the offence mentioned in paragraph (a) of this subsection.

Prohibition on Importation and Exportation of Controlled Drugs

Misuse of Drugs Act 1971, s. 3 **B17.15**

(1) Subject to subsection (2) below—

(a) the importation of a controlled drug; and

(b) the exportation of a controlled drug,

are hereby prohibited.

(2) Subsection (1) above does not apply—

(a) to the importation or exportation of a controlled drug which is for the time being excepted from paragraph (a) or, as the case may be, paragraph (b) of subsection (1) above by regulations under section 7 of this Act; or

(b) to the importation or exportation of a controlled drug under and in accordance with the terms of a licence issued by the Secretary of State and in compliance with any conditions attached thereto.

Section 18(2) of the Misuse of Drugs Act 1971 makes it an offence to contravene any conditions imposed on a licence under s. 3. As to controlled drugs generally, see **B20.1**.

Section 3 of the Misuse of Drugs Act 1971 creates a prohibition, but does not expressly create an offence. Consequently, evasion of this prohibition should be charged as an offence of fraudulent evasion of duty (under the Customs Management Act 1979, s. 170) or as improper importation or exportation of goods (under ss. 50 and 68). It is also possible, where appropriate, to charge a conspiracy to evade the prohibition imposed by the Misuse of Drugs Act 1971, s. 3.

For sentencing guidelines relating to controlled drugs, including importation of drugs, see **B20.105** ***et seq.***

Misdescription of Imported Goods

B17.16 **Customs and Excise Management Act 1979, s. 50**

(6) If any person—

(a) imports or causes to be imported any goods concealed in a container holding goods of a different description; or

(b) directly or indirectly imports or causes to be imported or entered any goods found, whether before or after delivery, not to correspond with the entry made thereof,

he shall be liable on summary conviction to a penalty of three times the value of the goods or level 3 on the standard scale, whichever is the greater.

This offence appears clearly to be a strict liability offence. It meets the criteria for strict liability and in particular it emphasises the need to take care in the furnishing of information, packaging of imports, etc. (*Gammon (Hong Kong) Ltd v A-G of Hong Kong* [1985] AC 1; and see generally A4).

Improper Unloading of Goods Loaded etc. for Exportation

B17.17 **Customs and Excise Management Act 1979, s. 67**

(1) If any goods which have been loaded or retained on board any ship or aircraft for exportation are not exported to and discharged at a place outside the United Kingdom but are unloaded in the United Kingdom, then, unless—

(a) the unloading was authorised by the proper officer; and

(b) except where the officer otherwise permits, any duty chargeable and unpaid on the goods is paid and any drawback or allowance paid in respect thereof is repaid,

the master of the ship or the commander of the aircraft and any person concerned in the unshipping, relanding, landing, unloading or carrying of the goods from the ship or aircraft without such authority, payment or repayment shall each be guilty of an offence under this section.

(2) The Commissioners may impose such conditions as they see fit with respect to any goods loaded or retained as mentioned in subsection (1) above which are permitted to be unloaded in the United Kingdom.

(3) If any person contravenes or fails to comply with, or is concerned in any contravention of or failure to comply with, any condition imposed under subsection (2) above he shall be guilty of an offence under this section.

(4) Where any goods loaded or retained as mentioned in subsection (1) above or brought to a customs and excise station for exportation by land are—

(a) goods from a warehouse, other than goods which have been kept, without being warehoused, in a warehouse by virtue of section 92(4) . . .;

(b) transit goods;

(c) other goods chargeable with a duty which has not been paid; or

(d) drawback goods,

then if any container in which the goods are held is without the authority of the proper officer opened, or any mark, letter or device on any such container or on any lot of the goods is without that authority cancelled, obliterated or altered, every person concerned in the opening, cancellation, obliteration or alteration shall be guilty of an offence under this section.

The offence is triable only summarily. The penalty is forfeiture of goods and a penalty of three times the value of the goods or level 3 on the standard scale, whichever is the greater (s. 67(5)).

Offences in Relation to Exportation of Prohibited or Restricted Goods

Customs and Excise Management Act 1979, s. 68 **B17.18**

(1) If any goods are—
   (a) exported or shipped as stores; or
   (b) brought to any place in the United Kingdom for the purpose of being exported or shipped as stores,

and the exportation or shipment is or would be contrary to any prohibition or restriction for the time being in force with respect to those goods under or by virtue of any enactment, the goods shall be liable to forfeiture and the exporter or intending exporter of the goods and any agent of his concerned in the exportation or shipment or intended exportation or shipment shall each be liable on summary conviction to a penalty of three times the value of the goods or level three on the standard scale, whichever is the greater.

(2) Any person knowingly concerned in the exportation or shipment as stores, or in the attempted exportation or shipment as stores, of any goods with intent to evade any such prohibition or restriction as is mentioned in subsection (1) above shall be guilty of an offence under this subsection and may be arrested

. . .

(5) If by virtue of any such restriction as is mentioned in subsection (1) above any goods may be exported only when consigned to a particular place or person and any goods so consigned are delivered to some other place or person, the ship, aircraft or vehicle in which they were exported shall be liable to forfeiture unless it is proved to the satisfaction of the Commissioners that both the owner of the ship, aircraft or vehicle and the master of the ship, commander of the aircraft or person in charge of the vehicle—
   (a) took all reasonable steps to secure that the goods were delivered to the particular place to which or person to whom they were consigned; and
   (b) did not connive at or, except under duress, consent to the delivery of the goods to that other place or person.

(6) In any case where a person would, apart from this subsection be guilty of—
   (a) an offence under subsection (1) or (2) above; and
   (b) a corresponding offence under the enactment or instrument imposing the prohibition or restriction in question, being an offence for which a fine or other penalty is expressly provided by that enactment or other instrument,

he shall not be guilty of the offence mentioned in paragraph (a) of this subsection.

Procedure and Penalties The offence is triable either way. When tried on indictment it is a class 3 offence. As to the power of arrest, see *Smith* [1973] QB 924. **B17.19**

The Customs and Excise Management Act 1979, s. 68(3), (4) and (4A) and sch. 1, prescribe penalties. On summary conviction there may be imposed a penalty of the prescribed sum or of three times the value of the goods whichever is the greater, or imprisonment for a term not exceeding six months or both. On conviction on indictment there may be imposed a penalty of any amount, or imprisonment for a term not exceeding two years, or both. Provision is made for enhancement of penalties for dealing respectively with drugs, firearms and counterfeit notes and currency; the enhanced penalties which apply are the same as those under s. 50 (see **B17.12**).

The penalties are also modified where a person is convicted of an offence contrary to s. 68 by virtue of the application of reg. 3 of the Controlled Drugs (Substances Useful for Manufacture) Regulations 1991 (SI 1991 No. 1285), which makes provision in relation to the breach of certain EC legislation designed to enable the authorities to obtain information on any orders for, or operations involving, substances used for the manufacture of controlled drugs. In these cases, the maximum penalty under s. 68(1)(b) is a fine not exceeding the statutory maximum, and, under s. 68(3)(a), the maximum penalty is a fine not exceeding the statutory maximum or imprisonment for a term not exceeding three months.

Provision for forfeiture is made, subject to defences, by s. 68(5) above.

Elements Under similar defence legislation, it was held that a person may be convicted of **B17.20**

an offence of unlawful exportation even though he intends to bring the goods back to the UK (*Berner* (1953) 37 Cr App R 113).

A person can be concerned with the exportation of goods even if the acts which he performs take place at a time other than that which constitutes exportation. A person can be so concerned, for example, at a time prior to the departure of an aircraft (*Garrett v Arthur Churchill (Glass) Ltd* [1970] 1 QB 92).

The prosecution must show both that the export of the goods was prohibited (e.g., by the Export Control (Security and Para-military Goods) Order 2006 (SI 2006 No. 1696)), and that the accused knew that the goods fell into a prohibited category (*Daghir* [1994] Crim LR 945). The Customs and Excise Management Act 1979, s. 68(2), is cast in terms of evasion. This does not require an element of fraud or dishonesty, but is, rather, given its ordinary English meaning, i.e. 'to get around or avoid' (*Hurford-Jones* (1977) 65 Cr App R 263).

In *Garrett v Arthur Churchill (Glass) Ltd* [1970] 1 QB 92, it was held that a person who hands over goods belonging to another, knowing that the other proposes to export them unlawfully, is knowingly concerned in the unlawful importation. The duty to hand over goods to their owner yields to the public interest in preventing such exportation.

Under the Export of Goods (Control) Order 1994 (SI 1994 No. 1191), an export which would otherwise be forbidden may be licensed by the Department of Trade and Industry. Such a licence will not bar a prosecution under s. 68(2) where a shipment is in fact to a destination other than that specified in the licence. Even if it cannot be proved that a licence was obtained by misrepresentation, a prosecution may still be brought if the actor seeks to evade the prohibition by specifying a sham consignee (*Redfern and Dunlop Ltd (Aircraft Division)* [1993] Crim LR 43).

An order prohibiting exportation is no less valid where its substance falls within a matter governed by the common commercial policy of the EU, provided that the order and any EEC Regulation are not incompatible (*Searle and KCS Products* [1996] Crim LR 58).

FRAUDULENT EVASION OF DUTY ('SMUGGLING')

B17.21 **Customs and Excise Management Act 1979, s. 170**

(1) Without prejudice to any other provision of the Customs and Excise Acts 1979, if any person—
(a) knowingly acquires possession of any of the following goods, that is to say—
(i) goods which have been unlawfully removed from a warehouse or Queens warehouse;
(ii) goods which are chargeable with a duty which has not been paid;
(iii) goods with respect to the importation or exportation of which any prohibition or restriction is for the time being in force under or by virtue of any enactment; or
(b) is in any way knowingly concerned in carrying, removing, depositing, harbouring, keeping or concealing or in any manner dealing with any such goods,
and does so with intent to defraud Her Majesty of any duty payable on the goods or to evade any such prohibition or restriction with respect to the goods he shall be guilty of an offence under this section and may be arrested.

(2) Without prejudice to any other provision of the Customs and Excise Acts 1979, if any person is, in relation to any goods, in any way knowingly concerned in any fraudulent evasion or attempt at evasion—
(a) of any duty chargeable on the goods;
(b) of any prohibition or restriction for the time being in force with respect to the goods under or by virtue of any enactment; or
(c) of any provision of the Customs and Excise Acts 1979 applicable to the goods,
he shall be guilty of an offence under this section and may be arrested

. . .

(5) In any case where a person would, apart from this subsection, be guilty of—
(a) an offence under this section in connection with a prohibition or restriction; and
(b) a corresponding offence under the enactment or other instrument imposing the prohibition or restriction, being an offence for which a fine or other penalty is expressly provided by that enactment or other instrument,

he shall not be guilty of the offence mentioned in paragraph (a) of this subsection.

For the offence of 'people smuggling' under the Immigration Act 1971, s. 25, see **B23.15**.

Procedure

The offence is triable either way. When tried on indictment it is a class 3 offence. The Customs and Excise Management Act 1979, s. 170(5), operates to prevent duplication of proceedings and possible double jeopardy problems. **B17.22**

Indictment (for Offences under s. 170(1)(b))

Statement of Offence **B17.23**

Being knowingly concerned in concealing goods with intent to avoid prohibition on importation contrary to section 170(1)(b) of the Customs and Excise Management Act 1979.

Particulars of Offence

A on the . . . day of . . . was knowingly concerned in concealing goods, that is to say a quantity of a controlled drug, namely . . . valued at £ . . ., with intent to evade the prohibition on importation of the said goods then in force pursuant to section 3 of the Misuse of Drugs Act 1971.

As to the Misuse of Drugs Act 1971, s. 3, see **B17.15** and as to controlled drugs generally, see **B20.1**.

Sentencing Guidelines

The maximum penalty on summary conviction is a penalty of the prescribed sum or of three times the value of the goods, whichever is the greater, and/or to imprisonment for a term not exceeding six months. The maximum penalty on indictment is a penalty of any amount and/or imprisonment for a term not exceeding seven years (Customs and Excise Management Act 1979, s.170(3)). **B17.24**

When dealt with summarily, the Magistrates' Courts Guidelines (2004) indicate the following for evasion of duty under s. 170, for a first-time offender pleading not guilty, with duty evaded in the region of £1,000 to £10,000:

Aggravating Factors For example abuse of power (e.g., use of children/vulnerable adults); offender is a customs/police officer; playing an organisational role; professional operation; repeated imports over a period of time; substantial amount of duty evaded; threats of violence; two or more types of goods; warning previously given; offence committed on bail; relevant previous convictions and any failures to respond to previous sentences

Mitigating Factors For example co-operation with authorities; no evidence of pre-planning; small amounts of duty evaded; under pressure from others to commit offence

Guideline: Is it so serious enough for a community penalty? Restitution should be made. Consider forfeiture.

In cases involving drugs, firearms and counterfeiting, penalties may be enhanced (s. 170(4) and (4A) and sch. 1). The enhancement is identical to that provided for in the case of s. 50 of the Act (see **B17.12**). For sentencing guidelines in drugs cases, see **B20.105** ***et seq.*** In cases involving seal skins the maximum penalty is two years' imprisonment (s. 170(4B)).

Guideline Cases on Fraudulently Evading Duty Sentencing guidelines for fraudulently evading duty on alcohol or cigarettes were issued by the Court of Appeal in *Czyzewski* [2004] 1 Cr App R (S) 289, superseding earlier guidance given by that court in *Dosanjh* [1998] 3 All ER 603. The Court had regard to its comment in *Kefford* [2002] 2 Cr App R (S) 495 (see **B17.25**

E2.5) that, 'in the case of economic crimes . . . prison is not necessarily the only appropriate form of punishment', particularly for those who have no record of previous offending. Rose LJ stated that the principal factors in gauging the seriousness of such an offence are the level of duty evaded, the complexity and sophistication of the organisation involved, the function of the offender within that organisation, and the amount of personal profit to the particular defendant. An offence will be aggravated if the offender (1) played an organisational role, (2) made repeated importations, particularly in the face of a warning from the authorities, (3) was a professional smuggler (as further elaborated in the judgment), (4) used a legitimate business as a front, (5) abused a position of privilege, (6) used children or vulnerable adults, (7) threatened violence to those seeking to enforce the law, (8) dealt in goods with an additional health risk because of possible contamination, or (9) disposed of goods to under-age purchasers. In addition, there are the statutory aggravating factors of offending while on bail or having previous convictions. Mitigating factors will include a prompt plea of guilty, co-operation with the authorities and, to a limited extent, previous good character. Pressure from others to commit the offence may, depending on the circumstances, afford mitigation.

Following trial, for an offender with no relevant previous convictions and disregarding personal mitigation, the following starting points are appropriate:

(a) Where the duty evaded is less than £1,000, and the level of personal profit is small, the starting point is a moderate fine.

(b) Where the duty evaded by a first-time offender is not more than £10,000 (which approximately equates to 65,000 cigarettes), or the offending is at a low level within an organisation, a community sentence, or a higher level of fine is appropriate. The custody threshold is likely to be passed if any of the aggravating features identified above is present.

(c) Where the duty evaded is between £10,000 and £100,000, whether the offender is operating individually or at a low level in an organisation, up to nine months' custody is the starting point. Some of these cases can appropriately be dealt with by magistrates.

(d) Where the duty evaded is in excess of £100,000, the length of the custodial sentence will be determined, principally, by the degree of professionalism of the offender and the presence or absence of other aggravating factors. Subject to that, the duty evaded will indicate starting points as follows: £100,000 to £500,000 — nine months to three years; £500,000 to £1 million — three to five years; in excess of £1 million — five to seven years.

If many millions of pounds of duty have been evaded, it may be appropriate to impose consecutive sentences or, alternatively, to charge an offence of cheating the public revenue (see **B16.2**), for which the maximum sentence is life imprisonment, rather than charging the offence under s. 170.

In all cases sentencers should consider their powers to order confiscation of assets under the PCA 2002 (see **E21**), compensation orders in clear cases under the PCC(S)A 2000, s.130, deprivation orders (especially of vehicles) under s. 143 of that Act (see **E20.1**), and disqualification from driving where a motor vehicle has been used under s. 147 of that Act (see **E23.10**). If any of these additional orders is contemplated, the court should warn the defence, so that argument may be heard. If licensed premises have been used for the sale of smuggled goods, the court should notify the licensing authority.

B17.26 **Sentencing Cases on Evading Prohibitions** In *Sperr* (1992) 13 Cr App R (S) 8, a sentence of nine months' imprisonment was imposed on an offender who pleaded guilty to being knowingly involved in fraudulently evading the prohibition on the importation of a prohibited species of endangered falcon. He was stopped when entering the country and found to have four young birds concealed in his car. The material imported by the offender in *Payne* (1995) 16 Cr App R (S) 782 was 1,796 canisters of CS gas, found concealed within the bodywork of his car. The possession of CS gas is prohibited by the Firearms Act 1968. The

Court of Appeal said that importation of CS gas in anything other than a modest quantity should be dealt with by a custodial sentence, notwithstanding that its possession for personal protection is lawful in other countries, although the offender's sentence was reduced from three years' to two years' imprisonment.

Scope of Offence

These are wide prohibitions. Section 170 of the Customs and Excise Management Act 1979 covers importing, exporting, those concerned in actual import and export, and even persons who cannot be proved to be implicated in an actual import or export; it is hard to think of anything in s. 170(2) which does not in fact come within s. 170(1) (*Neal* [1984] 3 All ER 156). One possibility may be, however, that a person could knowingly come into possession of unlawfully imported goods contrary to s. 170(1)(a)(iii) without himself being concerned in their importation contrary to s. 170(2)(b). **B17.27**

Actus Reus

The words 'fraudulent evasion', in the Customs and Excise Management Act 1979, s. 170(2), are not limited to entering the UK with goods concealed and with no intention of declaring them before a customs officer, (see *A-G's Ref (No. 1 of 1981)* [1982] QB 848). It does not require an actual fraudulent importation or the deceiving of anyone; the offence can be committed by evasion or attempted evasion even if the accused's acts took place abroad (*Latif* [1996] 1 WLR 104). The offence in s. 170(2) could relate to a single incident or a series of incidents forming an activity, any of which could be charged in a single count (*Martin* [1998] 2 Cr App R 385). Neither s. 170(1) nor (2) is restricted to those who form part of an original smuggling team (*Neal* [1984] 3 All ER 156). A person may be liable for acts done abroad prior to the actual smuggling, as well as for participation in the act of entry itself, and for acts subsequent to entry relating, for example, to disposal of the goods (*Jakeman* (1983) 76 Cr App R 223; *Wall* [1974] 1 WLR 930 where the accused took part in Afghanistan in the loading of cannabis for the purpose of exporting it to the UK). **B17.28**

The section has been construed very widely. In *Green* [1976] QB 985, the accused and another arranged customs clearance for a crate which, at the moment of importation, contained cannabis. Customs officials substituted a harmless substance before the crate left the warehouse. The accused, who assisted in the operation by renting a garage and unloading a crate, was held liable on the footing that the evasion of the prohibition continues until the goods cease to be prohibited goods or, possibly, are exported. Renting a garage is an act concerned in the evasion of the prohibition. A narrower and, it is submitted, less difficult ground for decision might be that the making of such arrangements constituted being concerned in the evasion, at least if it was done before substitution of the contents, though such an approach could encounter difficulties of proof. Evasion of the relevant prohibition is a continuing process; thus a person who, even after goods have been innocently imported by a carrier, falsely declares that his possessions contain no prohibited material, commits the offence (*Coughlan* (12 May 1997 unreported)).

The same principles as to when the offence begins and ends appear in cases of conspiracy to evade a prohibition, etc. There can, it is said, be no abstract limit to the time when or place at which the crime is committed, provided always that the goods, the subject-matter of the charge, are goods which are the subject of a prohibition on importation and the acquisition is done knowingly and with intent to evade that prohibition or restriction (*Ardalan* [1972] 1 WLR 463). In *Caippara* (1987) 87 Cr App R 316, in the context of importation of drugs, the Court of Appeal held that a person may be guilty if it be proved that he was willing to participate in a chain of activities which would result in drugs being imported into the UK, notwithstanding that the Customs has substituted a harmless substance for them before delivery to the recipient. Acts done after importation can be done in furtherance of a conspiracy since the conspiracy is not to import but to evade a restriction (*Borro* [1973] Crim LR 513).

EC Council regulations are enactments the evasion of which is an offence under s. 170(2)(b). For the purpose of prohibiting trade in endangered species, the offence is committed under English law by a person concerned in importation notwithstanding that the initial country of entry is not the UK (*Sissen* [2001] 1 WLR 902).

No defence of necessity at common law in the interests of pain relief, whether for the person importing or others, can be raised to an unauthorised importation of a prohibited drug (*Quayle* [2005] 2 Cr App R 527).

The fact of importation, where relevant, must be proved. It is then incumbent on the accused to prove factors in justification mentioned in s. 154 of the Act (see **B17.7**), such as that the goods were made here or that duty has been paid (*Watts* (1979) 70 Cr App R 187; *Mizel v Warren* [1973] 1 WLR 899).

Mens Rea

B17.29 Under the Customs and Excise Management Act 1979, s. 170(1), it must be shown that the accused knowingly performed certain acts with intent to defraud Her Majesty or with intent to evade a relevant prohibition or restriction. In relation to knowingly harbouring goods, it is usually enough to show that goods which were subject to duty were found in the possession of the accused. This will establish a prima facie case of knowingly harbouring subject to the accused's ability to rebut this by evidence casting doubt upon his knowledge. Once the Crown has adduced a case of knowing possession, the accused must prove that the goods were in fact customed; see s. 154 (at **B17.7**) and *Cohen* [1951] 1 KB 505. In respect of the importation of indecent material, it is enough if the person knows the material to be indecent; he need not know the precise nature of the indecency portrayed (*Forbes* [2002] 2 AC 512).

It was held in *Latif* [1996] 1 WLR 104, that the guilty mind need not subsist at the time of the importation: thus one who is recruited to pick up a package which has already arrived has a sufficient *mens rea* because he is then concerned with bringing about the importation.

A person who presents goods for an assessment of duty does not act fraudulently by not disclosing his assessment of their worth, or by failing to alert a customs officer that the officer's valuation is wrong. In the absence of a false statement or concealment, the payment of duty demanded by a customs officer discharges the person's liability (*Customs and Excise Commissioners v Tan* [1977] AC 650).

The prosecution must under s. 170(2) prove both an intent to evade a prohibition and knowledge on the part of the accused of the relevant circumstances, for example in a case of smuggling by sea that he had in fact entered territorial waters. Mere knowledge by the accused that he was at the relevant time running the risk of entering territorial waters is not enough (*Panayi (No. 2)* [1989] 1 WLR 187).

The accused may have formed a guilty intent outside the UK. If the intent is formed abroad and acts constituting the offence are done there, liability will be complete. Subsequent repentance will not found a defence (*Jakeman* (1983) 76 Cr App R 223).

It need not be proved that the accused was aware of the exact nature of the articles to which a restriction applies. If a person believes himself to be engaged in the importation of goods which are not subject to a restriction or prohibition, he cannot be convicted (*Taaffe* [1984] AC 539). He is to be judged on the facts as he believed them to be. If he believes himself to be importing narcotics whereas the substance is snuff, he may be convicted of attempting to evade a prohibition or restriction (*Shivpuri* [1987] AC 1). If on the other hand he imports drugs believing them to be pornography, he will be liable for the offence (*Ellis* (1986) 84 Cr App R 235; *Hennessey* (1978) 68 Cr App R 419). A person who knows the nature of the material imported and who believes it to be obscene will be liable for the offence even though no jury trying a case under the Obscene Publications Act 1959 has determined the article to be so: knowledge and belief suffice for guilt (*Dunne* (1998) 162 JP 399).

Particular problems concern drugs where importation and exportation offences vary in severity according to whether the drug is a Class A, B, or C drug. Lord Bridge intimated in *Shivpuri* [1987] AC 1 that the legislative history of the Misuse of Drugs Act 1971 makes clear that, while possession of class A, B, or C drugs are distinct offences, the offence of being concerned in importation requires proof only that the accused knew that he was engaged in evading restrictions on the importation of a prohibited article. Lord Bridge's dictum was followed in *Siracusa* (1989) 90 Cr App R 340. The prosecution must prove that the accused knew that the goods in question were prohibited goods, but need not prove that the accused knew (precisely) what they were. But the same case holds that, on a charge of conspiracy to contravene s. 170(2) by the importation of heroin for example, the prosecution must prove that the agreed course of conduct was to import heroin, because the agreement is the essence of conspiracy and one cannot prove an agreement to import heroin by proving an agreement to import cannabis.

Offences under other provisions, for example regulations relating to the importation of animal products intended for human consumption, carry strict liability (see *Matudi* [2003] EWCA Crim 697 and **A4.2**).

Untrue Declarations

Customs and Excise Management Act 1979, s. 167 **B17.30**

(1) If any person either knowingly or recklessly—
- (a) makes or signs, or causes to be made or signed, or delivers or causes to be delivered to the Commissioners or an officer, any declaration, notice, certificate or other document whatsoever; or
- (b) makes any statement in answer to any question put to him by an officer which he is required by or under any enactment to answer,

being a document or statement produced or made for any purpose or any assigned matter, which is untrue in any material particular, he shall be guilty of an offence under this subsection and may be arrested; and any goods in relation to which the document or statement was made shall be liable to forfeiture.

(2) Without prejudice to subsection (4) below, a person who commits an offence under subsection (1) above shall be liable—
- (a) on summary conviction, to a penalty of the prescribed sum, or to imprisonment for a term not exceeding six months, or to both; or
- (b) on conviction on indictment, to a penalty of any amount, or to imprisonment for a term not exceeding two years, or to both.

(3) If any person—
- (a) makes or signs, or causes to be made or signed, or delivers or causes to be delivered to the Commissioners or an officer, any declaration, notice, certificate or other document whatsoever; or
- (b) makes any statement in answer to any question put to him by an officer which he is required by or under any enactment to answer,

being a document or statement produced or made for any purpose of any assigned matter, which is untrue in any material particular, then, without prejudice to subsection (4) below, he shall be liable on summary conviction to a penalty of level 4 on the standard scale.

In *Cross* [1987] Crim LR 43, it was held that the construction of documents is for the judge and not the jury.

It may be that inadvertent *Caldwell* recklessness is applicable to the offence, under s. 167(1), notwithstanding *G* [2004] 1 AC 1034, because it does not require dishonesty. See generally

A2.5 *et seq.* The offence under s. 167(3) would seem to be an offence of strict liability (*Patel v Comptroller of Customs* [1966] AC 356).

Counterfeiting Documents

B17.31 **Customs and Excise Management Act 1979, s. 168**

(1) If any person—
  (a) counterfeits or falsifies any document which is required by or under any enactment relating to an assigned matter or which is used in the transaction of any business relating to an assigned matter; or
  (b) knowingly accepts, receives or uses any such document so counterfeited or falsified; or
  (c) alters any such document after it is officially issued; or
  (d) counterfeits any seal, signature, initials or other mark of, or used by, any officer for the verification of such a document or for the security of goods or for any other purpose relating to an assigned matter,

he shall be guilty of an offence under this section and may be arrested.

Offences under s. 168(1) are triable either way. Under s. 168(2) the penalty, on indictment, is a penalty of any amount and/or imprisonment for a term not exceeding two years. The penalty on summary conviction, is a penalty of the prescribed sum and/or imprisonment for a term not exceeding six months.

In *Patel v Comptroller of Customs* [1966] AC 356, it was held that falsification and counterfeiting require *mens rea.* It may be helpful to refer to the law on these subjects under the Forgery and Counterfeiting Act 1981. See generally **B6.23** to **B6.26** and **B6.55**.

Section B18 Offences Involving Misuse of Computers

In many instances involving the use of a computer to commit an offence, such as theft or fraud, the means of commission creates no special difficulty in achieving a conviction. This section is concerned with a limited range of situations involving unauthorised access by a person to data or programs held in a computer, whether for a further criminal purpose or not, and with the improper processing of personal data. For offences involving possession or distribution of indecent pseudo-photographs of children downloaded from the Internet, see B3.274. **B18.1**

UNAUTHORISED ACCESS OFFENCE ('HACKING')

Computer Misuse Act 1990, s. 1 **B18.2**

(as prospectively amended by the Police and Justice Act 2006)

(1) A person is guilty of an offence if—
- (a) he causes a computer to perform any function with intent to secure access to any program or data held in any computer, or to enable any such access to be secured;
- (b) the access he intends to secure, or to enable to be secured, is unauthorised; and
- (c) he knows at the time when he causes the computer to perform the function that that is the case.

(2) The intent a person has to have to commit an offence under this section need not be directed at—
- (a) any particular program or data;
- (b) a program or data of any particular kind; or
- (c) a program or data held in any particular computer.

The Police and Justice Act 2006, s. 35 amends s. 1(a) of the 1990 Act by adding the words 'or to enable any such access to be secured' and amends s.1(b) above by inserting the words ', or to enable to be secured,'. These amendments apply only where every act and other event proof of which is required for conviction of the offence takes place after s. 35(2) of the 2006 Act comes into force.

Procedure and Sentence

Section 1 of the Computer Misuse Act 1990 originally created a summary offence, but when the Police and Justice Act 2006, s. 35(3) is brought into force the offence will become triable either way. Normally prosecutions for summary offences must be brought within six months of the commission of the offence (MCA 1980, s. 127). A prosecution for the offence under s. 1 may, however, be brought within six months of the date on which evidence sufficient in the opinion of the prosecutor to warrant the proceedings came to his knowledge, but, in any event, no proceedings can be brought more than three years after the commission of the **B18.3** offence (Computer Misuse Act 1990, s. 11). This provision was construed against the prosecutor in *Morgans v DPP* [1999] 1 WLR 968, where it was held that the relevant date is when the prosecutor (or other officer in charge of the case) acquires the evidence, not when he decides that proceedings are warranted. When the Police and Justice Act 2006, sch. 14, para. 23 is brought into force, s. 11 will be repealed as a consequence of the offence being reclassified as an either-way offence.

Once the Police and Justice Act 2006, s. 35(3) is brought into force, on conviction on indictment the maximum penalty is two years' imprisonment or a fine or both. On summary conviction, the maximum sentence is imprisonment for a term not exceeding six months, or a fine not exceeding level 5 or both; once s. 35(3) is brought into force, the maximum fine on summary conviction will be increased to the statutory maximum. For cases giving some guidance on sentencing for offences under the Computer Misuse Act 1990, see **B18.18**.

Actus Reus

B18.4 The *actus reus* of the offence requires the accused to 'cause a computer to perform any function'. This is meant to exclude mere physical contact with a computer and the scrutiny of data without any interaction with a computer (thus the reading of confidential computer output, the reading of data displayed on the screen, or 'computer eavesdropping', are not covered). On the other hand there is no requirement that the defendant should succeed in obtaining access to the program or data, or be successful in subverting computer security measures in place. A remote hacker would, thus, 'cause a computer to perform any function' if he accessed it remotely and the computer responded, e.g., by activating a computer security device or by offering a log-on menu. The substantive offence is thus drafted in such a way as to include conduct which might usually be thought to fall within the scope of the law of attempt. The words 'any computer' in s. 1(1)(a) entail that the offence is not restricted to a case where the accused uses one computer to gain unauthorised access to the target computer. Direct access to the target computer is also covered (see *A-G's Ref (No. 1 of 1991)* [1993] QB 94 and *Bow Street Metropolitan Stipendiary Magistrate, ex parte Government of the United States* [2000] 1 Cr App R 61, per Lord Hobhouse at p. 72).

The access to the program or data which the defendant intends to secure must be 'unauthorised' access (s. 1(1)(b)). In *DPP v Bignell* [1998] 1 Cr App R 1, the Divisional Court held that an offence under s. 1 of the Computer Misuse Act 1990 was not committed where police officers, for private purposes, instructed a computer operator to extract details of two cars from a police computer. This was because the officers were entitled to access the computer, albeit only for legitimate police purposes. In the case Astill J commented that the Act was designed to criminalise 'breaking into computer systems', and noted that misuse of the data once obtained was not covered by the Act but might constitute an offence under the Data Protection Act 1984, s. 5(2)(b) (which was then in force), and this clearly influenced the Divisional Court in holding that the conduct lay outside the 1990 Act. The decision in *Bignell* is open to criticism on the ground that, on an ordinary construction of language, authorising a person's access for one (legitimate) purpose ought not to be regarded as authorising his access for another (non-legitimate) purpose (see, by analogy, the burglary case of *Jones* [1976] 1 WLR 672 at **B4.62**). The authority of *Bignell* is to some extent undermined by the decision of the House of Lords in *Bow Street Metropolitan Stipendiary Magistrate, ex parte Government of the United States.* In that case one Allison, an employee of American Express, was authorised to access certain client accounts to check matters relating to credit. It was alleged that she in fact obtained access to other accounts and passed on confidential details to accomplices who were able to forge credit cards and obtain large sums of money. The issue was whether Allison could be extradited from England to the United States and the House of Lords, reversing the decision of the Divisional Court, held that she could. Lord Hobhouse had no difficulty in finding that the alleged conduct of Allison fell within the provisions of s. 1. His lordship then considered the decision in *Bignell*, and pointed out that the Divisional

Court in that case had fallen into error in asking itself whether the accused had authority to access data of that general kind, a mistake also made by the same court in the instant case. The correct question (applying the wording of s. 1 and s. 17(5)(a)) was whether the officers had authority to access the *actual data* involved. Even so, Lord Hobhouse thought that the outcome in *Bignell* was 'probably right'. It was distinguishable from the instant case because the police officers in *Bignell* had instructed the (innocent) computer operator to access the data. The access had been made by that person, and he had not exceeded his authority in doing so. It seems that in the circumstances there had been no 'unauthorised access', and hence an essential element of the *actus reus* was missing.

Mens Rea

There are two limbs to the *mens rea* of the offence. The first limb is the 'intent to secure access to any program or data held in any computer'. The word 'any' makes it clear that the intent need not relate to the computer which the accused is at that time operating. The Computer Misuse Act 1990, s. 1(2), explains that the intent of the accused need not be directed at any particular program or data, so as to include the hacker who accesses a computer without any clear idea of what he will find there. Recklessness is insufficient; still less would careless or inattentive accessing of the computer suffice for liability. The second limb is that the accused must know at the time when he causes the computer to perform the function that the access which he intends to secure is unauthorised. The prosecution must prove both limbs. The amendment to s. 1 by the Police and Justice Act 2006 is designed to extend the offence to cases where the accused's intention is to enable someone else to secure unauthorised access, or to enable the accused to secure unauthorised access at some later time. B18.5

Attempts

Until the amendments in the Police and Justice Act 2006 come into effect this offence is summary only and thus there can be no charge of an attempt in respect of it. There is, however, the possibility of secondary liability arising under the MCA 1980, s. 44(1), where, for example, a person supplies a hacker with information which would assist him, such as a confidential computer password. The operator of a computer hacker 'bulletin board' might, therefore, come within the reach of the offence. B18.6

Definitions

A number of terms are defined in the Computer Misuse Act 1990, s. 17. B18.7

Computer Misuse Act 1990, s. 17

(1) The following provisions of this section apply for the interpretation of this Act.
(2) A person secures access to any program or data held in a computer if by causing a computer to perform any function he—
(a) alters or erases the program or data;
(b) copies or moves it to any storage medium other than that in which it is held or to a different location in the storage medium in which it is held;
(c) uses it; or
(d) has it output from the computer in which it is held (whether by having it displayed or in any other manner);
and references to access to a program or data (and to an intent to secure such access) shall be read accordingly.
(3) For the purposes of subsection (2)(c) above a person uses a program if the function he causes the computer to perform—
(a) causes the program to be executed; or
(b) is itself a function of the program.
(4) For the purposes of subsection (2)(d) above—
(a) program is output if the instructions of which it consists are output; and
(b) the form in which any such instructions or any other data is output (and in particular whether or not it represents a form in which, in the case of instructions, they are capable

of being executed or, in the case of data, it is capable of being processed by a computer) is immaterial.

(5) Access of any kind by any person to any program or data held in a computer is unauthorised if—

(a) he is not himself entitled to control access of the kind in question to the program or data; and

(b) he does not have consent to access by him of the kind in question to the program or data from any person who is so entitled,

but this subsection is subject to section 10.

(6) References to any program or data held in a computer include references to any program or data held in any removable storage medium which is for the time being in the computer; and a computer is to be regarded as containing any program or data held in any such medium.

(7) A modification of the contents of any computer takes place if, by the operation of any function of the computer concerned or any other computer—

(a) any program or data held in the computer concerned is altered or erased; or

(b) any program or data is added to its contents;

and any act which contributes towards causing such a modification shall be regarded as causing it.

(8) Such a modification is unauthorised if—

(a) the person whose act causes it is not himself entitled to determine whether the modification should be made; and

(b) he does not have consent to the modification from any person who is so entitled.

(9) References to the home country concerned shall be read in accordance with section 4(6) above.

(10) References to a program include references to part of a program.

When the Police and Justice Act 2006, sch. 14, para. 29 is brought into force, s. 17 will be amended. In s. 17(2), after 'such access' there is inserted 'or to enable such access to be secured', s. 17(7) is omitted and for s. 17(8) there is substituted:

(8) An act done in relation to a computer is unauthorised if the person doing the act (or causing it to be done)—

(a) is not himself a person who has responsibility for the computer and is entitled to determine whether the act may be done; and

(b) does not have consent to the act from any such person

In this subsection 'act'includes a series of acts.

The terms 'computer', 'data' and 'program' are not defined in the Computer Misuse Act 1990 and should, therefore, be given their ordinary meaning by the courts. Section 10 of the Act deals with access to computer material for law enforcement purposes.

UNAUTHORISED ACCESS OFFENCE WITH INTENT TO COMMIT FURTHER OFFENCES

B18.8 **Computer Misuse Act 1990, s. 2**

(1) A person is guilty of an offence under this section if he commits an offence under section 1 above ('the unauthorised access offence') with intent—

(a) to commit an offence to which this section applies; or

(b) to facilitate the commission of such an offence (whether by himself or by any other person);

and the offence he intends to commit or facilitate is referred to below in this section as the further offence.

(2) This section applies to offences—

(a) for which the sentence is fixed by law; or

(b) for which a person of 21 years of age or over (not previously convicted) may be sentenced to imprisonment for a term of five years (or, in England and Wales, might be so sentenced but for the restrictions imposed by section 33 of the Magistrates' Courts Act 1980).

(3) It is immaterial for the purposes of this section whether the further offence is to be committed on the same occasion as the unauthorised access offence or on any future occasion.
(4) A person may be guilty of an offence under this section even though the facts are such that the commission of the further offence is impossible.

Procedure and Sentence

Section 2 of the Computer Misuse Act 1990 creates an offence, triable either way. Where a charge is brought under s. 2, a conviction for the lesser offence under s. 1 is possible if the further intention is not proved (s. 12). When the Police and Justice Act 2006, sch. 14, para. 24 is brought into force, s. 12 will be repealed. **B18.9**

The maximum penalty on conviction on indictment is five years' imprisonment, or a fine or both; on summary conviction, the maximum is six months or a fine of the statutory maximum or both (s. 2(5)). For cases giving some guidance on sentencing for offences under the Computer Misuse Act 1990, see **B18.18**.

Elements

The offence under s. 2 of the Computer Misuse Act 1990 is committing the unauthorised access offence under s. 1 (see **B18.2**) with intent to commit or facilitate the commission of a more serious 'further' offence. It is not necessary to prove that the intended further offence has actually been committed. **B18.10**

A person will be guilty of an offence under s. 2 in a range of situations. Obtaining the unauthorised access may, for example, be done with the intention of committing theft, such as by diverting funds, which are in the course of an electronic funds transfer, to the accused's own bank account, or to the bank account of an accomplice. It would also cover the case where the accused gained unauthorised access to sensitive information held on computer with a view to blackmailing the person to whom that information related.

Section 2(2) explains what qualifies as a further offence for the purposes of the s. 2 offence. Section 2(3) makes clear that the accused may intend to commit the further offence on the same occasion as the unauthorised access offence (as in the theft example just given) or on a future occasion (as in the blackmail example). Section 2(4) makes it possible to convict a person who intended to commit the further offence even if, on the facts, that would be impossible (e.g., where the intended blackmail victim was, unknown to the accused, dead). This rule is analogous to that in the Criminal Attempts Act 1981, s. 1(2), as applied in *Shivpuri* [1987] AC 1. See **A6.40**.

UNAUTHORISED MODIFICATION OF COMPUTER MATERIAL

The following provision applies only in respect of acts committed prior to the coming into force of the Police and Justice Act 2006, s. 36, which substitutes s. 3 (see **B18.16**). **B18.11**

Computer Misuse Act 1990, s. 3 **B18.12**

(1) A person is guilty of an offence if—
(a) he does an act which causes an unauthorised modification of the contents of any computer; and
(b) at the time when he does the act he has the requisite intent and the requisite knowledge.
(2) For the purposes of subsection (1)(b) above the requisite intent is an intent to cause a modification of the contents of any computer and by so doing—
(a) to impair the operation of any computer;
(b) to prevent or hinder access to any program or data held in any computer; or
(c) to impair the operation of any such program or the reliability of any such data.
(3) The intent need not be directed at—
(a) any particular computer;

(b) any particular program or data or a program or data of any particular kind; or
(c) any particular modification or a modification of any particular kind.

(4) For the purposes of subsection (1)(b) above the requisite knowledge is knowledge that any modification he intends to cause is unauthorised.

(5) It is immaterial for the purposes of this section whether an unauthorised modification or any intended effect of it of a kind mentioned in subsection (2) above is, or is intended to be, permanent or merely temporary.

(6) For the purposes of the Criminal Damage Act 1971 a modification of the contents of a computer shall not be regarded as damaging any computer or computer storage medium unless its effect on that computer or computer storage medium impairs its physical condition.

Procedure and Sentence

B18.13 Section 3 of the Computer Misuse Act 1990 creates an offence triable either way. Where a charge is brought under s. 3, a conviction for an offence under s. 1 is possible (s. 12). When the Police and Justice Act 2006, sch. 14, para. 24 is brought into force, s. 12 will be repealed.

The maximum penalty on conviction on indictment is five years' imprisonment, or a fine or both; on summary conviction, the maximum is six months or a fine of the statutory maximum or both (s. 3(7)). For cases giving some guidance on sentencing for offences under the Computer Misuse Act 1990, see **B18.18**.

Elements

B18.14 When read in the context of the Computer Misuse Act 1990, s. 17 (see **B18.7**), it is clear that a wide range of different forms of conduct are included by s. 3. It covers all cases involving deliberate (recklessness is insufficient) alteration or erasure of any program or data held on a computer (s. 17(7)(a)), where the accused intended thereby to impair a computer's operation, hinder access to computer material by a legitimate user or impair the operation or reliability of computer held material, and where he knew that the intended modification was unauthorised. In *DPP v Lennon* (2006) 170 JP 532 the Divisional Court held that an offence under s. 3 was committed where a former employee of a company, acting on a grudge, impaired the operation of the company's computer by using a program to generate and send 5 million e-mails to the company. The court rejected a defence argument under s. 17(8)(b) that the owner of a computer set up to receive e-mails must be taken to have consented to the sending of e-mails, holding that such implied consent was not without limits and that the owner could not be taken to consent to multiple e-mails being sent for the purposes of swamping his computer system. In *Zezev and Yarimaka v Governor of HM Prison Brixton* [2002] 2 Cr App R 515, it was held that an offence was committed under s. 3 where the accused placed on the files of another person's computer a bogus e-mail which purported to come from a person who had not sent it. It does not have to be proved that the defendant had any specific target computer, program or data in mind.

Section 3 would also extend to a case where the accused intentionally introduced a computer 'worm' program into a computer system, where such a program uses up all the spare capacity on the computer by adding programs or data to the computer's contents (s. 17(7)(b)), thereby impairing its operation (s. 3(2)(a)). A likely effect of the introduction of a 'worm' is to prevent or hinder access to a legitimate user (s. 3(2)(b)).

Also within the section is the intentional introduction of a computer 'virus' into a computer system. Where X deliberately introduces into circulation material contaminated with a computer virus and Y, an innocent party, uses that material on his computer, impairing its operation, it seems that X would be guilty of the offence at the time he introduced the material into circulation, since s. 17(7) states that any act which contributes towards causing such a modification shall be regarded as causing it. The liability of X would be unaffected by Y passing the material on, without using it or opening it, to another innocent party, Z, who uses it and thus impairs the operation of his computer since X's intent need not be directed at any particular computer, program or data (s. 3(3)).

The s. 3 offence would also cater for a case where the accused intentionally causes an unauthorised modification of the contents of a computer, intending thereby to prevent or hinder access by legitimate users to any data or program held on the computer (see, e.g., *Turner* (1984) 13 CCC (3d) 430, where a hacker placed a 'locking device' on computer-held data, rendering the data inaccessible). By s. 3(5) it is immaterial whether this modification or its intended effect is, or is intended to be, permanent or temporary.

Relationship with Other Offences

B18.15 Section 3(6) of the Computer Misuse Act 1990 deals with the relationship between the offence under s. 3 and the offence of criminal damage under the Criminal Damage Act 1971. In *Cox v Riley* (1986) 83 Cr App R 54 the accused deliberately erased computer programs which were held on a physical storage medium, a 'printed circuit card', by pressing the 'delete' button repeatedly. His conviction for criminal damage was approved by the Divisional Court on the basis that the erasure of programs from the card damaged the *card* (the programs themselves, being intangible property, fall outside the scope of the 1971 Act, by virtue of s. 10(1) of that Act). See also *Whiteley* (1991) 93 Cr App R 25, decided prior to the coming into force of the Computer Misuse Act 1990. Section 3(6) of the 1990 Act states that the scope of the 1971 Act in computer cases is confined to circumstances where the physical condition of the computer, or computer storage medium, has been impaired. The intended effect of this is that were the facts of *Cox v Riley* to recur, the accused would be guilty not of criminal damage, but of the offence under s. 3 of the 1990 Act. This result will follow so long as the card, or disk, is at the relevant time in the computer, since it will then form part of the 'contents of any computer' (s. 3(1)(a) and 17(6)), but would not apply where the accused removes the disk first and then wipes it with a magnet. In such a case, it would still seem to be necessary to rely upon the Criminal Damage Act 1971.

UNAUTHORISED ACTS WITH INTENT TO IMPAIR OPERATION OF COMPUTER ETC.

B18.16 When the Police and Justice Act 2006, s. 36, is brought into force the following provisions will be substituted for s. 3 of the 1990 Act.

Computer Misuse Act 1990, s. 3

(as prospectively substituted by the Police and Justice Act 2006, s. 36)

(1) A person is guilty of an offence if—
 (a) he does any unauthorised act in relation to a computer;
 (b) at the time when he does the act he knows that it is unauthorised; and
 (c) either subsection (2) or subsection (3) below applies.
(2) This subsection applies if the person intends by doing the act—
 (a) to impair the operation of any computer;
 (b) to prevent or hinder access to any program or data held in any computer;
 (c) to impair the operation of any such program or the reliability of any such data; or
 (d) to enable any of the things mentioned in paragraphs (a) to (c) above to be done
(3) This subsection applies if the person is reckless as to whether the act will do any of the things mentioned in paragraphs (a) to (d) of subsection (2) above.
(4) The intention referred to in subsection (2) above, or the recklessness referred to in subsection (3) above, need not relate to—
 (a) any particular computer;
 (b) any particular program or data; or
 (c) a program or data of any particular kind.
(5) In this section—

(a) a reference to doing an act includes a reference to causing an act to be done;
(b) 'act' includes a series of acts;
(c) a reference to impairing, preventing or hindering something includes a reference to doing so temporarily.

When the substituted s. 3 is brought into force, it will create an offence triable either way, punishable, on conviction on indictment, to imprisonment for a term not exceeding ten years or to a fine or both and, on summary conviction, with six months or a fine up to the statutory maximum or both (s. 3(6)).

An offence is not committed under the new s. 3 unless every act or other event proof of which is required for conviction of the offence takes place after the Police and Justice Act 2006, s. 36, comes into force (s. 38(3)). Where this is not the case the prosecution may continue to rely on the old version of s. 3 (s. 38(4)). The effect of the new section will be that a person commits an offence if he performs any unauthorised act in relation to a computer, knowing it to be unauthorised, if he intends by doing the act to do one of the things set out in s. 3(2), or if he is reckless as to whether by doing the act he will do one of the things set out in s. 3(2). The inclusion of liability for recklessness under the new section is a significant extension of liability.

MAKING, SUPPLYING OR OBTAINING ARTICLES FOR USE IN OFFENCES UNDER SECTIONS 1 OR 3

B18.17 When the Police and Justice Act 2006, s. 37, is brought into force, a new s. 3A will be inserted into the 1990 Act.

Computer Misuse Act 1990, s. 3A

(1) A person is guilty of an offence if he makes, adapts, supplies or offers to supply any article intending it to be used to commit, or to assist in the commission of, an offence under section 1 or 3.
(2) A person is guilty of an offence if he supplies or offers to supply any article believing that it is likely to be used to commit, or to assist in the commission of, an offence under section 1 or 3.
(3) A person is guilty of an offence if he obtains any article with a view to its being supplied for use to commit, or to assist in the commission of, an offence under section 1 or 3.
(4) In this section 'article' includes any program or data held in electronic form.

When the new section 3A is brought into force, it will create three new offences triable either way, each punishable, on conviction on indictment, with imprisonment for a term not exceeding two years or to a fine or both and, on summary conviction, with six months or a fine up to the statutory maximum or both (s. 3A(5)).

An offence is not committed under the new s. 3A unless every act or other event proof of which is required for conviction of the offence takes place after the Police and Justice Act 2006, s. 37, comes into force (s. 38(5)). It is clear that the reason for the creation of this offence is the growing market in electronic 'hacker tools'; which can be used for breaking into, or compromising, computer systems. According to guidance notes published together with the 2006 Act, if the accused is charged with an offence under s. 3A(2) in relation to a quantity of articles, the prosecution would need to prove its case in relation to any particular one or more of those articles, but it would not be enough to prove that the accused believed that a certain proportion of the articles was likely to be used in connection with an offence under s. 1 or 3. In the offence under s. 3A(2) the relevant *mens rea* is 'belief' — by analogy with the offence of handling stolen goods it is submitted that mere suspicion would not be enough.

SENTENCING FOR OFFENCES UNDER THE COMPUTER MISUSE ACT 1990

There are no guideline cases on sentencing for offences under the Computer Misuse Act 1990. In *Delamare* [2003] 2 Cr App R (S) 474 four months' detention was appropriate for a bank employee who sold confidential details of two bank account holders. In *Lindesay* [2002] 1 Cr App R (S) 370, nine months' imprisonment was upheld on a computer consultant who corrupted the Web sites of clients of a company which had dismissed him. He pleaded guilty to three charges under s. 3 of the 1990 Act. See also *Maxwell-King* [2001] 2 Cr App R (S) 136, *Parr-Moore* [2003] 1 Cr App R (S) 425 and *Debnath* [2006] 2 Cr App R (S) 169. In *Vallor* [2004] 1 Cr App R (S) 319, two years' imprisonment was upheld on an offender who pleaded guilty to three offences of releasing computer viruses on the Internet, contrary to s. 3. For sentencing for offences involving possession or distribution of indecent pseudo-photographs of children downloaded from the Internet, see **B3.277**. **B18.18**

B

Part B Offences

JURISDICTIONAL PROVISIONS

Liability for offences under the Computer Misuse Act 1990, s. 1 or s. 3, requires proof of at least one 'significant link' with the 'home country concerned' which for the purposes of English law means England and Wales. By ss. 4 and 5, this link is satisfied where the accused was in England and Wales when he committed the act in question. Alternatively, it is satisfied where the targeted computer was situated in England and Wales. **B18.19**

In contrast, s. 4(3) enables a s. 2 offence to be committed entirely abroad, provided that the 'further offence' would itself fall within English jurisdiction. If that offence is itself an extra-territorial offence, there need be no connection with England and Wales at all.

Section 4(4), read in conjunction with s. 8(1), applies s. 2 to cases in which the 'further offence' is an offence only under a foreign system of law, but would have qualified as a further offence within the meaning of s. 2(2) if committed within England and Wales. This applies only where the underlying s. 1 offence *does* have a significant link with England and Wales. It would, for example, cover a case in which D, in England, gains unauthorised access to a computer in France, with a view to committing a crime under French law that would have been punishable with imprisonment for five years or more if committed by an adult in England and Wales.

Computer Misuse Act 1990, ss. 4 and 5

(as prospectively amended by the Police and Justice Act 2006)

4.—(1) Except as provided below in this section, it is immaterial for the purposes of any offence under section 1 or 3 above—
- (a) whether any act or other event proof of which is required for conviction of the offence occurred in [England and Wales]; or
- (b) whether the accused was in [England and Wales] at the time of any such act or event.

(2) Subject to subsection (3) below, in the case of such an offence at least one significant link with domestic jurisdiction must exist in the circumstances of the case for the offence to be committed.

(3) There is no need for any such link to exist for the commission of an offence under section 1 above to be established in proof of an allegation to that effect in proceedings for an offence under section 2 above.

(4) Subject to section 8 below, where—
- (a) any such link does in fact exist in the case of an offence under section 1 above; and
- (b) commission of that offence is alleged in proceedings for an offence under section 2 above;

section 2 above shall apply as if anything the accused intended to do or facilitate in any place outside [England and Wales] which would be an offence to which section 2 applies if it took place in [England and Wales] were the offence in question.

5.—(1) The following provisions of this section apply for the interpretation of section 4 above.

(2) In relation to an offence under section 1, either of the following is a significant link with domestic jurisdiction—
(a) that the accused was in [England and Wales] at the time when he did the act which caused the computer to perform the function; or
(b) that any computer containing any program or data to which the accused by doing that act secured or intended to secure unauthorised access, or enabled or intended to enable unauthorised access to be secured, was in [England and Wales] at that time.

(3) In relation to an offence under section 3, either of the following is a significant link with domestic jurisdiction—
(a) that the accused was in [England and Wales] at the time when he did the unauthorised act (or caused it to be done); or
(b) that the unauthorised act was done in relation to a computer in [England and Wales].

JURISDICTION OVER INCHOATE OFFENCES

B18.20 Sections 6 and 7 of the Computer Misuse Act 1990 make special provision for jurisdiction over inchoate offences under the Act, as does the Criminal Attempts Act 1981, s. 1(1A) and (1B); but in practice, s. 1(1A) and (1B) are of no conceivable use to prosecutors, for the same reason that s. 1A of that Act is of no use: see **A6.38**.

Computer Misuse Act 1990, ss. 6 and 7

(as prospectively amended by the Police and Justice Act 2006)

6.—(1) On a charge of conspiracy to commit an offence under section 1, 2 or 3 above, the following questions are immaterial to the accused's guilt—
(a) the question where any person became a party to the conspiracy; and
(b) the question whether any act, omission or other event occurred in the home country concerned.

(2) On a charge of attempting to commit an offence under section 3 above the following questions are immaterial to the accused's guilt—
(a) the question where the attempt was made; and
(b) the question whether it had an effect in the home country concerned.

(3) On a charge of incitement to commit an offence under section 1, 2 or 3 above, the question where the incitement took place is immaterial to the accused's guilt.

7.—(4) Subject to section 8 below, if any act done by a person in England and Wales would amount to the offence of incitement to commit an offence under section 1, 2 or 3 above but for the fact that what he had in view would not be an offence triable in England and Wales—
(a) what he had in view shall be treated as an offence under this Act for the purposes of any charge of incitement brought in respect of that act; and
(b) any such charge shall accordingly be triable in England and Wales.

EVIDENCE OF FOREIGN LAW

B18.21 **Computer Misuse Act 1990, s. 8**

(1) A person is guilty of an offence triable by virtue of section 4(4) above only if what he intended to do or facilitate would involve the commission of an offence under the law in force where the whole or any part of it was intended to take place.

(2) [Repealed.]

(3) A person is guilty of an offence triable by virtue of section 1(1A) of the Criminal Attempts Act 1981 or by virtue of section 7(4) above only if what he had in view would involve the commission of an offence under the law in force where the whole or any part of it was intended to take place.

(4) Conduct punishable under the law in force in any place is an offence under that law for the purposes of this section, however it is described in that law.

(5) Subject to subsection (7) below, a condition specified in [subsection (1) or (3)] above shall be taken to be satisfied unless not later than rules of court may provide the defence serve on the prosecution a notice—
  (a) stating that, on the facts as alleged with respect to the relevant conduct, the condition is not in their opinion satisfied;
  (b) showing their grounds for that opinion; and
  (c) requiring the prosecution to show that it is satisfied.

(6) In subsection (5) above 'the relevant conduct' means—
  (a) where the condition in subsection (1) above is in question, what the accused intended to do or facilitate
  (c) where the condition in subsection (3) above is in question, what the accused had in view.

(7) The court, if it thinks fit, may permit the defence to require the prosecution to show that the condition is satisfied without the prior service of a notice under subsection (5) above.

(8) [Scotland.]

(9) In the Crown Court the question whether the condition is satisfied shall be decided by the judge alone.

OFFENCES UNDER THE DATA PROTECTION ACT 1998

The Data Protection 1998 Act repeals and replaces the Data Protection Act 1984. The offence-creating provisions of the 1998 Act came into force on 1 March 2000, and they apply to offences committed after that date. Proceedings for any criminal offence under the 1998 Act may be brought only by the Information Commissioner (formerly the Data Protection Commissioner), or by or with the consent of the DPP (s. 60(1)). The maximum penalties for the offences created are, in summary proceedings, a fine not exceeding the statutory maximum and, on indictment, an unlimited fine (s. 60(2)). Whenever a person is convicted of an offence under the Act, the court may in addition order that data material appearing to the court to be connected with the offence be forfeited or erased (s. 60(4)). An order under s. 60(4) must not be made before any person (other than the offender) claiming to be the owner or otherwise interested in the data material who has applied to the court is given an opportunity to show cause why the order should not be made. For liability of directors, see s. 61. **B18.22**

Section 17(1) requires that personal data within the meaning of the Act must not be processed unless an entry in respect of the data controller is included in the register maintained by the Commissioner under s. 19, although by s. 17(3) regulations may provide that s. 17(1) does not apply in respect of processing of a particular description, where that processing is unlikely to prejudice the rights and freedoms of data subjects. Contravention of s. 17(1) by a data controller is an offence under s. 21(1). Section 20 imposes a duty on every data controller included in the register to notify the Commissioner, as and when required by regulations, of details of the registrable particulars and of measures taken by the data controller to ensure compliance with the seventh data protection principle (that appropriate technical and organisational measures shall be taken against unauthorised or unlawful processing of personal data and against accidental loss or destruction of, or damage to, personal data). Failure by a data controller to comply with this duty is an offence (s. 21(2)). This is an offence of strict liability, although s. 21(3) provides for a due diligence defence.

It is an offence for a person to fail to comply with an enforcement notice issued under s. 40 where the Commissioner is satisfied that a data controller has contravened or is contravening any of the data protection principles, or an information notice issued under s. 43 or a special information notice issued under s. 44 (s. 47(1)). This is an offence of strict liability, although s. 47(3) provides for a due diligence defence. It is also an offence under s. 47(2), for a person to make a statement in purported compliance with an information notice or a special information notice which he knows to be false in a material particular, or where he recklessly makes such a statement which is false.

Data Protection Act 1998, s. 55

(1) A person must not knowingly or recklessly, without the consent of the data controller—
   (a) obtain or disclose personal data or the information contained in personal data, or
   (b) procure the disclosure to another person of the information contained in personal data.

(2) Subsection (1) does not apply to a person who shows—
   (a) that the obtaining, disclosing or procuring—
      (i) was necessary for the purpose of preventing or detecting crime, or
      (ii) was required or authorised by or under any enactment, by any rule of law or by the order of a court.
   (b) that he acted in the reasonable belief that he had in law the right to obtain or disclose the data or information or, as the case may be, to procure the disclosure of the information to the other person,
   (c) that he acted in the reasonable belief that he would have had the consent of the data controller if the data controller had known of the obtaining, disclosing or procuring, and the circumstances of it, or
   (d) that in the particular circumstance the obtaining, disclosing or procuring was justified as being in the public interest.

(3) A person who contravenes subsection (1) is guilty of an offence.

(4) A person who sells personal data is guilty of an offence if he has obtained the data in contravention of subsection (1).

(5) A person who offers to sell personal data is guilty of an offence if—
   (a) he has obtained the data in contravention of subsection (1), or
   (b) he subsequently obtains the data in contravention of that subsection.

(6) For the purposes of subsection (5) an advertisement indicating that personal data are or may be for sale is an offer to sell the data.

Further it is made an offence under s. 56 for a person, in connection with the recruitment of another person as an employee, or the continued employment of another person, or any contract for the provision of services to him by another person, to require that other person to supply or produce certain records which, by s. 56(6), includes records of that other person's previous convictions and cautions.

Section B19 Offences Involving Writing, Speech or Publication

CRIMINAL LIBEL

Definition

It is an offence at common law to publish a defamatory libel whether false or not (*Boaler v The Queen* (1888) 21 QBD 284 per Field J at pp. 286–7). A defamatory libel is a libel which tends to vilify a person and bring that person into hatred, contempt and ridicule (see *Thorley v Lord Kerry* (1812) 4 Taunt 355 per Mansfield CJ at p. 364; *Goldsmith v Pressdram Ltd* [1977] QB 83 at p. 87; *Wells Street Stipendiary Magistrate, ex parte Deakin* [1980] AC 477 at p. 487). **B19.1**

By virtue of the Libel Act 1843 (Lord Campbell's Act), ss. 4 and 5, the maximum sentence for criminal libel depends on whether the offender knew the libel to be false. Arguments that either s. 4 or s. 5 or both created one or more statutory offences in addition to or substitution for the common-law offence were rejected in *Boaler v The Queen* (1888) 21 QBD 284 and *Munslow* [1895] 1 QB 758.

Procedure

Criminal libel is triable only on indictment. It is a class 3 offence. By the Law of Libel Amendment Act 1888, s. 8: **B19.2**

> No criminal prosecution shall be commenced against any proprietor, publisher, editor, or any person responsible for the publication of a newspaper for any libel published therein without the order of a judge at chambers being first had and obtained.
> Such application shall be made on notice to the person accused, who shall have an opportunity of being heard against such application.

No appeal lies against the judge's decision (*Ex parte Pulbrook* [1892] 1 QB 86). As to the criteria to be considered, see *Goldsmith v Pressdram Ltd* [1977] QB 83 at **B19.6**.

Indictment and Subsequent Pleadings

Indictment

Statement of Offence **B19.3**

Unlawfully publishing a defamatory libel [knowing the same to be false]

Particulars of Offence

A on or about the . . . day of . . . published a defamatory libel concerning V in the form of an article published in the . . . newspaper entitled 'Crooked Politician Exposed', [knowing the same to be false], which article contained the following defamatory statements concerning V:

1 'V has not exactly suffered financially from public office because of his power to influence the placing of contracts for municipal works' (meaning thereby that V had corruptly solicited or received money or other consideration for influencing the award of such contracts in his capacity as . . .)

2 etc.

Additional explanation of meaning may have to be given where the statements consist of innuendo (*Yates* (1872) 12 Cox CC 233).

B19.4 **Plea of Justification and Public Benefit etc.**

A says he is not guilty and for a further plea, says that all the defamatory matters alleged in the indictment are true.

Particulars

1 In reply to the statement numbered 1 set out in the indictment, A says that the statement is true, in that V did on or about . . . corruptly solicit payment from X in return for voting to award a contract to X for the construction of . . . at a meeting of . . . to be held on . . .
2 etc.

A further says that it was for the public benefit that the defamatory matters charged in the indictment should be published because V is an elected public official of . . . and because the said corruption should be exposed.

The prosecution may simply join issue with this plea by replication. These forms are based on those suggested in the now superseded Indictment Rules 1915 and 1916. Because of the terms of the Libel Act 1843, s. 6 (see **B19.6**), this is one of the rare cases in which the defence must submit a written plea if the plea of justification and public benefit is to be considered. This does not, of course, affect the right of the accused to plead not guilty.

Alternative Verdicts and Sentence

B19.5 **Libel Act 1843, ss. 4 and 5**

4. If any person shall maliciously publish any defamatory libel, knowing the same to be false, every such person, being convicted thereof, shall be liable to be imprisoned . . . for any term not exceeding two years, and to pay such fine as the court shall award.
5. If any person shall maliciously publish any defamatory libel, every such person being convicted thereof, shall be liable to fine or imprisonment, or both, as the court may award, such imprisonment not to exceed the term of one year.

Sections 4 and 5 of the Libel Act 1843 are not definitional, offence-creating provisions, they merely prescribe maximum penalties for the common-law offence (*Boaler v The Queen* (1888) 21 QBD 284; *Munslow* [1895] 1 QB 758). On a count alleging that the accused unlawfully published a defamatory libel knowing it to be false it is open to the jury to convict the accused of publishing a defamatory libel without knowing it to be false (*Boaler v The Queen*). A finding that the accused published a defamatory libel unlawfully is a finding that he published it maliciously (*Munslow*).

Elements and Defences

B19.6 The *mens rea* of criminal libel is an intention to publish the statement actually found to be a defamatory libel, and probably nothing more (*Munslow* [1895] 1 QB 758 at p. 765 — there is a similar rule for blasphemous libel: *Whitehouse v Lemon* [1979] AC 617, see **B19.11**). In order to render the accused liable to the heavier penalty provided for in the Libel Act 1843, s. 4, it is necessary to prove that the accused knew that the libel was false.

Publication to the person defamed is sufficient, at least if it is likely to result in a breach of the peace (*Adams* (1888) 22 QBD 66), even though civil liability for libel is not incurred without publication to a third party. The publication must be in permanent form in order to constitute a libel rather than a slander. Writing is the principal form of libel; the spoken word is the principal form of slander. Which other forms of publication are libel and which are slander is a question of some difficulty. The publication of words in the course of a public performance of a play is deemed by the Theatres Act 1968, ss. 4 and 7, to be publication in a permanent form, but a prosecution arising from such publication would require the consent of the A-G (Theatres Act 1968, s. 8). The publication of words in the course of any programme included in a programme service, as defined in the Broadcasting Act 1990, is deemed by s. 166(1) of that Act to be publication in permanent form.

Where the prosecution is of a 'proprietor, publisher, editor or any person responsible for the publication of a newspaper for any libel published therein', the leave of a judge in chambers is required (Law of Libel Amendment Act 1888, s. 8). The proper criteria for exercising this discretion were discussed and found to be satisfied in *Goldsmith v Pressdram Ltd* [1977] QB 83 and include the showing of a clear prima facie case and that the public interest requires the institution of criminal proceedings. The likelihood of the libel provoking a serious breach of the peace would be a relevant but not necessary factor. See also *Desmond v Thorne* [1983] 1 WLR 163. Although it would appear that employers can be vicariously liable for criminal libels published by their employees in the course of their employment, it is a defence under the Libel Act 1843, s. 7, for any such defendant 'to prove that such publication was made without his authority, consent, or knowledge, and that the said publication did not arise from want of due care or caution on his part'.

The prosecution need not prove that the alleged libel was untrue, and it is not even a defence in itself for the defendant to show that his statement was true (though this would be sufficient to avoid civil liability) unless it was for the public benefit that the matters charged should be published (Libel Act 1843, s. 6).

Libel Act 1843, s. 6

> On the trial of any indictment or information for a defamatory libel, the defendant having pleaded such plea as hereinafter mentioned, the truth of the matters charged may be inquired into, but shall not amount to a defence, unless it was for the public benefit that the said matters charged should be published; and to entitle the defendant to give evidence of the truth of such matters charged as a defence to such indictment or information it shall be necessary for the defendant, in pleading to the said indictment or information, to allege the truth of the said matters charged in the manner now required in pleading a justification to an action for defamation, and further to allege that it was for the public benefit that the said matters charged should be published, and the particular fact or facts by reason whereof it was for the public benefit that the said matters charged should be published, to which plea the prosecutor shall be at liberty to reply generally, denying the whole thereof; and if after such plea the defendant shall be convicted on such indictment or information it shall be competent to the court, in pronouncing sentence, to consider whether the guilt of the defendant is aggravated or mitigated by the said plea, and by the evidence given to prove or to disprove the same:
>
> Provided always, that the truth of the matters charged in the alleged libel complained of by such indictment or information shall in no case be inquired into without such plea of justification: Provided also, that in addition to such plea it shall be competent to the defendant to plead a plea of not guilty: Provided also, that nothing in this Act contained shall take away or prejudice any defence under the plea of not guilty which it is now competent to the defendant to make under such plea to any action or indictment or information for defamatory words or libel.

The defence of privilege applies to criminal libel as it does in tort (*Rule* [1937] 2 KB 375) and the defence of fair comment on a matter of public interest probably also applies although the point was left open in *Goldsmith v Pressdram Ltd* [1977] QB 83 at p. 90.

BLASPHEMY AND BLASPHEMOUS LIBEL

Definition

At common law, blasphemy is defined as the publication (orally or, for libel, in writing) of matter which vilifies or is contemptuous of or which denies the truth of the Christian religion or the Bible or the Book of Common Prayer and which is couched in indecent, scurrilous or offensive terms likely to shock and outrage the feelings of the general body of Christian believers. **B19.7**

Procedure

B19.8 Blasphemy and blasphemous libel are triable only on indictment. They are class 3 offences. For the restriction provided by the Law of Libel Amendment Act 1888, s. 8, on prosecution for a libel contained in a newspaper, see **B19.2**.

Indictment

B19.9 The following form of indictment is based on that used in *Whitehouse v Lemon* [1979] AC 671 (see at p. 620), which was a private prosecution.

Statement of Offence

Blasphemous libel contrary to common law

Particulars of Offence

A on or about the . . . day of . . . published or caused to be published in a newspaper called . . . a blasphemous libel concerning the Christian religion, namely . . ., vilifying Christ in his life and in his crucifixion, which libel was likely to shock and outrage the feelings of the general body of Christian believers

Sentence

B19.10 The maximum penalty is imprisonment for life and/or a fine.

Elements

B19.11 The two most significant cases are *Whitehouse v Lemon* [1979] AC 617 and *Chief Metropolitan Stipendiary Magistrate, ex parte Choudhury* [1991] 1 QB 429.

In *Whitehouse v Lemon*, it was held by the House of Lords that the *mens rea* of blasphemy requires only an intention to publish the words found to be blasphemous. There is no requirement that the accused should have recognised or intended that his words would be blasphemous or be taken by others to be blasphemous.

The defence under the Libel Act 1843, s. 7 (see **B19.6**), would appear to apply to blasphemous libel (*Bradlaugh* (1883) 15 Cox CC 217). Section 6 of the Libel Act 1843 (plea of justification), however, is clearly expressed to apply to defamatory libel and hence not to blasphemous libel.

In *Chief Metropolitan Stipendiary Magistrate, ex parte Choudhury*, it was decided that blasphemy is only concerned with the Christian religion and does not extend to attacks on other religions such as the Islamic religion. The Court of Appeal was not prepared to extend an offence for which there had only been two prosecutions in 70 years and which the Law Commission had recommended in 1985 should be abolished (Law Com. No. 145). There was also the danger that: 'Since the only mental element in the offence is the intention to publish the words complained of, there would be a serious risk that the words might, unknown to the author, scandalise and outrage some sect or religion' (p. 448). See the Racial and Religious Hatred Act 2006 for the offences under the Public Order Act 1986 requiring an intention to stir up religious hatred where religion is not limited to Christianity (see in particular the Explanatory memorandum to the Bill). Even where the Christian religion is concerned, since the middle of the nineteenth century, it has been no longer blasphemous to make a sober reasoned attack; a libel is not blasphemous unless it is a scurrilous vilification (at p. 442). In *Wingrove v UK* (1996) 24 EHRR 1 the refusal of a classification certificate for a video recording on the grounds that it infringed the criminal law of blasphemy did not amount to a violation of the right to freedom of expression under the ECHR, Article 10.

SEDITION AND SEDITIOUS LIBEL

Definition

Sedition is any act done, or words spoken (or, for seditious libel, written and published), with a seditious intention and having a seditious tendency (Stephen's Digest, 9th ed, 1950). The meaning of 'seditious' is considered at **B19.15** and **B19.16**. **B19.12**

Procedure and Indictment

Sedition and seditious libel are triable only on indictment. They are class 1 offences. **B19.13**

The words alleged to be seditious must be specified in the indictment (see *Bradlaugh v The Queen* (1878) 3 QBD 607 at p. 619).

Sentence

The maximum penalty is imprisonment for life and/or a fine. **B19.14**

Seditious Tendency

According to Stephen's Digest the tendency of an act or words is seditious if it is a tendency: **B19.15**

(a) to bring into hatred or contempt, or to excite disaffection against, the sovereign or the government and constitution of the United Kingdom or either House of Parliament or the administration of justice; or
(b) to excite the sovereign's subjects to attempt, otherwise than by lawful means, the alteration of any matter in Church or State by law established; or
(c) to incite persons to any crime in disturbance of the peace; or
(d) to raise discontent or disaffection amongst the sovereign's subjects; or
(e) to promote feelings of ill will and hostility between different classes of those subjects.

Seditious Intention

Given the potentially broad scope of the categories of seditious tendency, the requirement of the *mens rea* of seditious intention is an important limitation on the scope of the offence. Although it is possible to find older cases belittling this requirement of intention (e.g., *Grant* (1848) 7 St Tr NS 507) later cases such as *Burns* (1886) 16 Cox CC 355 emphasise that the intention must be proved subjectively to exist and in the light of the CJA 1967, s. 8, this is surely right. In *Chief Metropolitan Stipendiary Magistrate, ex parte Choudhury* [1991] 1 QB 429, the seditious intention required was said (at p. 453) to be: **B19.16**

> an intention to incite to violence or to create public disturbance or disorder against [Her] Majesty or the institutions of government. Proof of an intention to promote feelings of ill will and hostility between different classes of subjects does not alone establish a seditious intention. Not only must there be proof of an incitement to violence in this connection, but it must be violence or resistance or defiance for the purpose of disturbing constituted authority.

As to intention generally, see A2.2.

OBSCENE LIBEL AND OUTRAGING PUBLIC DECENCY

It is an offence at common law to publish an obscene libel, but the Obscene Publications Act 1959, s. 2(4), provides that: **B19.17**

> A person publishing an article shall not be proceeded against for an offence at common law consisting of the publication of any matter contained or embodied in the article where it is of the essence of the offence that the matter is obscene.

Subsection (4A) makes similar provision in respect of a film exhibition as defined in the Cinemas Act 1985.

The rationale for these provisions is to prevent evasion by the prosecution of the defences available under the 1959 Act by charging the common-law offence. Section 2(4) does not apply to the common-law offence of conspiracy to corrupt public morals since such a conspiracy does not consist of publication within s. 2(4) but rather of the *agreement* to corrupt public morals by publishing (*Shaw v DPP* [1962] AC 220). The law officers, however, gave undertakings to Parliament in 1964 (*Parliamentary Debates (Hansard), House of Commons*, 3 June 1964, col. 1212) that conspiracy to corrupt public morals would not be used so as to circumvent the defences available under s. 4. On the other hand, there is a separate offence at common law of outraging public decency (see **B3.280**), and conspiracy to do so, and this, it was held in *Gibson* [1990] 2 QB 619, is not barred by s. 2(4), even though in that case the offence involved the publication of an article (a human foetus earring) which was, in a loose sense, obscene. The article was not likely to deprave or corrupt and was therefore not obscene within the meaning of the Obscene Publications Act 1959 and was not therefore covered by s. 2(4). The Court of Appeal therefore upheld the convictions for outraging public decency, holding also that, by analogy with *Whitehouse v Lemon* [1979] AC 617 (see **B19.11**), the only intention required was an intention to do an act that in fact outraged public decency. An intention to outrage public decency or an appreciation of the risk of such outrage was not required; if it were otherwise, it was said, an accused might escape liability by the very baseness of his own standards. Conversely, in *Rowley* [1991] 1 WLR 1020, it was held that, if the accused's acts are not in themselves likely to outrage public decency, evidence of his lewd or disgusting intention or motive could not so render them and was irrelevant.

For conspiracy to outrage public decency and conspiracy to corrupt public morals, see **A6.10**.

PUBLISHING, OR HAVING FOR PUBLICATION FOR GAIN, AN OBSCENE ARTICLE

Definition

B19.18 Obscene Publications Act 1959, s. 2

(1) Subject as hereinafter provided, any person who, whether for gain or not, publishes an obscene article or who has an obscene article for publication for gain (whether gain to himself or gain to another) shall be liable . . .

Procedure

B19.19 Offences under the Obscene Publications Act 1959, s. 2(1), are triable either way. When tried on indictment they are class 3 offences. A prosecution must not be commenced more than two years after the commission of the offence (s. 2(3)).

Where the article in question is a moving picture film of width 16 mm or more, and the publication in question is by a film exhibition as defined in the Cinemas Act 1985, then proceeding may not be instituted except by, or with the consent of, the DPP (Obscene Publications Act 1959, s. 2(3A)). For restrictions on prosecuting for common-law offences in cases involving obscenity, see the Obscene Publications Act 1959, s. 2(4) and (4A), at **B19.17**.

Indictment (for Offence of Having for Gain)

B19.20 *Statement of Offence*

Having an obscene article for publication for gain, contrary to section 2(1) of the Obscene Publications Act 1959

Particulars of Offence

A on or about the . . . day of . . . had an obscene article, namely . . . for publication for gain to himself or another

Sentencing Guidelines

B19.21 The maximum penalty is three years' imprisonment, a fine, or both, on indictment (Obscene Publications Act 1959, s. 2(1)); six months' imprisonment, a fine not exceeding the statutory maximum, or both, summarily.

A number of Court of Appeal decisions deal with sentencing for offences in relation to obscene publications. In *Holloway* (1982) 4 Cr App R (S) 128, where the offender had been selling pornographic books, films and tapes on a commercial scale, Lawton LJ said:

> Experience has shown . . . that fining these pornographers does not discourage them. Fines merely become an expense of the trade and are passed on to purchasers of the pornographic matter, so that prices go up and sales go on.
>
> In the judgment of this court, the only way of stamping out this filthy trade is by imposing sentences of imprisonment on first offenders and all connected with the commercial exploitation of pornography: otherwise front men will be put up and the real villains will hide behind them. It follows, in our judgment, that the salesmen, projectionists, owners and suppliers behind the owners should on conviction lose their liberty. For first offenders sentences need only be comparatively short, but persistent offenders should get the full rigour of the law. In addition, the courts should take the profit out of this illegal filthy trade by imposing very substantial fines.
>
> . . . We wish to make it clear that the guidelines we have indicated apply to those who commercially exploit pornography. We do not suggest that sentences of imprisonment would be appropriate for a newsagent who is carrying on a legitimate trade in selling newspapers and magazines and who has the odd pornographic magazine in his possession, probably because he has been careless in not looking to see what he is selling . . . he can be discouraged, and usually should be, by a substantial fine from repeating his carelessness. Nor do we suggest that a young man who comes into possession of a pornographic videotape and who takes it along to his rugby or cricket club to amuse his friends by showing it should be sentenced to imprisonment. On conviction he too can be dealt with by the imposition of a fine. The matter might be very different if owners or managers of clubs were to make a weekly practice of showing 'blue' films to attract custom. Like the pornographers of Soho they would be engaging in the commercial exploitation of pornography.

A case towards the top end of the scale is *Lamb* [1998] 1 Cr App R (S) 77, where a sentence of 30 months' imprisonment was appropriate for an offender who pleaded guilty to five offences of possessing an obscene article for publication for gain. The offender had three previous convictions for similar offences and earned his living by supplying pornographic videos by mail order. Sentences totalling 18 months were upheld in *Ibrahim* [1998] 1 Cr App R (S) 157, where the offender was employed in a shop which supplied obscene videos, the offences being aggravated by his continuing to do so after having been warned by the police. Custodial sentences of six months were approved in *Doorgashurn* (1988) 10 Cr App R (S) 195 and *Knight* (1990) 12 Cr App R (S) 319 where, in both cases, shopkeepers kept obscene books and video tapes for sale as part of their general trade. A fine of £2,000 was also imposed in the latter case; in the former case the shopkeeper was bankrupt by the time of sentence. In *Knight*, Wright J regarded it as a significant aggravating factor that children's comics were for sale in the shop and that children could and sometimes did see the obscene material which was on display. In *Ibrahim*, Lord Bingham CJ referred to the comments of Maurice Kay J in *Mather* (10 June 1997 unreported) to the effect that there is now a greater awareness of the link between the supply of pornographic material and the commission of serious sexual offences, and that sentences in this area are likely to increase rather than remain at the level indicated in *Knight*. Three months' imprisonment was appropriate in *Pace* [1998] 1 Cr App R (S) 121 for an offender who worked as a 'front man' in a shop selling pornographic videos, who was convicted in respect of possession of one tape. The Court of Appeal indicated the continuing relevance of the guidelines in *Holloway*.

Meaning of 'Obscenity'

B19.22 **Obscene Publications Act 1959, s. 1**

(1) For the purposes of this Act an article shall be deemed to be obscene if its effect or (where the article comprises two or more distinct items) the effect of any one of its items is, if taken as a whole, such as to tend to deprave and corrupt persons who are likely, having regard to all relevant circumstances, to read, see or hear the matter contained or embodied in it.

Although this does not purport to be an exhaustive definition of obscenity it is the only definition which counts for the purposes of the Act and the judge must not leave the jury with the impression that it is sufficient if the article is obscene in the ordinary sense of being 'filthy', 'loathsome' or 'lewd' (*Anderson* [1972] 1 QB 304 [1971] 3 All ER 1152). It is the tendency to deprave and corrupt which is important. This can refer merely to the effect on the mind in terms of stimulating fantasies and it is not necessary that physical or overt sexual activity should result (*DPP v Whyte* [1972] AC 849). Indeed obscenity is not necessarily concerned with sexual depravity but has included in the past material advocating drug taking or violence (*John Calder (Publications) Ltd v Powell* [1965] 1 QB 509; *Calder and Boyars Ltd* [1969] 1 QB 151).

The persons likely to be depraved or corrupted need not be wholly innocent to begin with: the further corruption of the less innocent is also included. Nor is it necessary that all those likely to read, see or hear the article should be corrupted. It is sufficient that the article should tend to deprave or corrupt a significant proportion of them. This may be much less than 50 per cent but must not be numerically negligible (*DPP v Whyte* [1972] AC 849).

It is the effect of the publication by the accused that counts (that is, the effect on persons likely to read, see or hear the article as a result of *that* publication) rather than the effect of publication by anyone else, 'unless it could reasonably have been expected that the publication by the other person would follow from publication by the person charged' (Obscene Publications Act 1959, s. 2(6)).

The fact that there are other materials in circulation which are as obscene as, or which are not materially different from, the articles in question is not of itself relevant nor does it render the articles in question acceptable. The jury should apply the standards of 'ordinary, decent right-minded people' to the actual articles before them (*Elliott* [1996] 1 Cr App R 432).

Admittedly shocking, disgusting and outrageous material may not be obscene if 'instead of tending to encourage anyone to homosexuality, drug taking or senseless brutal violence, it would have precisely the opposite effect' (per Salmon LJ in *Calder and Boyars Ltd* [1969] 1 QB 151 at p. 169) — a limitation on the meaning of obscenity approved by the Court of Appeal in *Anderson* [1972] 1 QB 304 as the 'aversion argument'.

Meaning of 'Article'

B19.23 The term 'article' is defined in the Obscene Publications Act 1959, s. 1(2), as 'any description of article containing or embodying matter to be read or looked at or both, any sound record, and any film or other record of a picture or pictures'. A video cassette is within s. 1(2) (*A-G's Ref (No. 5 of 1980)* [1981] 1 WLR 88).

Articles which are not themselves to be read or looked at or listened to are still treated as within s. 1(2) if they are 'intended to be used . . . for the reproduction or manufacture therefrom of articles containing or embodying matter to be read, looked at or listened to' (Obscene Publications Act 1964, s. 2(1), which thus now makes it clear that, e.g., a photographic negative would be an article within the Obscene Publications Act 1959, s. 1(2), even if it was not itself to be looked at but merely used for producing prints). See also *Fellows* [1997] 1 Cr App R 244 (images held on computer disk in digitised form).

An 'article' may be regarded as a single item (e.g., a novel as in *Penguin Books* [1961] Crim LR 176), in which case, in assessing whether it has a tendency to deprave and corrupt, the jury should look at the effect of the article as a whole rather than at the effect in isolation of specific passages within it. However, an article may comprise a number of items (as in the case of the magazine in *Anderson* [1972] 1 QB 304); each item must then be judged individually and it is sufficient if the effect of any one of the items, taken as a whole, is to tend to deprave and corrupt. In *Anderson* [1972] 1 QB 304, Lord Widgery CJ said (at p. 312):

> A novelist who writes a complete novel and who cannot cut out particular passages without destroying the theme of the novel is entitled to have his work judged as a whole, but a magazine publisher who has a far wider discretion as to what he will and will not insert by way of items is to be judged under the 1959 Act on what we call the item to item basis.

In *Goring* [1999] Crim LR 670, one film was treated as containing a number of distinct items, and whether a particular film is to be judged as a whole or on an item by item basis is a question of law for the judge.

Role of Expert Evidence

Expert evidence is not admissible on the question whether an article is obscene since that is a matter for the jury. However, where the subject-matter of an article is beyond the experience of the ordinary person, such as the characteristics and effects of cocaine and the methods of ingesting it, expert evidence is admissible to inform the jury about that subject-matter. It then remains a matter entirely for the jury, armed with this information, whether an article advocating the taking of cocaine has a tendency to deprave or corrupt (*Skirving* [1985] QB 819). In contrast, where an article is concerned with sexual activity, the jury need no special information to assess that activity before proceeding to the question of whether the article itself is obscene. **B19.24**

Where the persons likely to be depraved or corrupted are members of a special class, such as primary schoolchildren, there may be a special rule allowing expert evidence on the likely effect of unusual material on them if a jury cannot be expected to understand the likely impact of the material without assistance (*DPP v A & BC Chewing Gum Ltd* [1968] 1 QB 159). However, it still remains, even in this 'highly exceptional' (*Anderson* [1972] 1 QB 304 at p. 313) type of case, for the jury to decide whether the factual effect should be classified as depraving or corrupting, and expert evidence would not be admissible on that issue.

As to expert evidence generally, see **F10**, especially **F10.15**.

Meaning of 'Publication'

Obscene Publications Act 1959, s. 1 **B19.25**

(3) For the purposes of this Act a person publishes an article who—
  (a) distributes, circulates, sells, lets on hire, gives, or lends it, or who offers it for sale or for letting for hire; or
  (b) in the case of an article containing or embodying matter to be looked at or a record, shows, plays or projects it, or, where the matter is data stored electronically, transmits that data.

(4) For the purposes of this Act a person also publishes an article to the extent that any matter recorded on it is included by him in a programme included in a programme service.

(5) Where the inclusion of any matter in a programme so included would, if that matter were recorded matter, constitute the publication of an obscene article for the purposes of this Act by virtue of subsection (4) above, this Act shall have effect in relation to the inclusion of that matter in that programme as if it were recorded matter.

(6) In this section 'programme' and 'programme service' have the same meaning as in the Broadcasting Act 1990.

In *Taylor* [1995] 1 Cr App R 131, the Court of Appeal held that a photographic developer, who develops a film sent to him by customers depicting obscene acts and who makes prints as requested and sends the prints back to those customers, publishes the prints by way of selling or distributing them.

The concluding words of s. 1(3)(b) relating to the transmission of electronically stored data were added by the CJPO 1994, sch. 9, para. 3, and were applied in *Waddon* [2000] All ER (D) 502 to the transmission of obscene images to a web site in the United States and then back again to a subscriber in the UK, which constituted publication within the jurisdiction. It seems from *Perrin* [2002] EWCA Crim 747 that it is immaterial where the major steps to set up a web site are taken; it is access to the web pages within the jurisdiction which constitutes evidence of publication within s. 1(3)(b).

Having an Obscene Article for Publication for Gain

B19.26 This form of the offence was added by the Obscene Publications Act 1964, s. 1(1), to deal with limitations on the publication form of the offence, notably that displaying an obscene article in a shop window does not amount to offering it for sale (*Mella v Monahan* [1961] Crim LR 175) and that supplying to a supposedly non-corruptible person (e.g., a police officer) may not be a publication tending to deprave or corrupt anyone (*Clayton* [1963] 1 QB 163).

By s. 1(2) of the 1964 Act '. . . a person shall be deemed to have an article for publication for gain if with a view to such publication he has the article in his ownership, possession or control'. Thus a person having obscene articles for sale in sex shops (cf. *O'Sullivan* [1995] 1 Cr App R 455) 'has' them *for* publication for gain' even though he may not yet have technically offered them for sale and actually published them in that sense. Since the provision deals with prospective publication rather than actual publication, s. 1(3)(b) of the 1964 Act provides that:

> the question whether the article is obscene shall be determined by reference to such publication for gain of the article as in the circumstances it may reasonably be inferred he had in contemplation and to any further publication that could reasonably be expected to follow from it, but not to any other publication.

In a case such as *O'Sullivan*, the original prospective publication which it may reasonably be inferred D had in contemplation would be the sale in a sex shop, and the further publication that may reasonably be expected to follow from it (note the absence here of any reference to reasonably inferring *D's contemplation*) might (or might not, depending on the circumstances) include such matters as further circulation, lending, selling or showing the article by the original purchaser from the sex shop. The jury then has to consider the tendency to deprave and corrupt as a result of those prospective publications. The Court of Appeal in *O'Sullivan* thought that the complexity of the direction to the jury necessitated by this provision and its relationship with the provisions of the Obscene Publications Act 1959 was such that the judge would be best advised to follow the order of the statutory provisions without attempting to improve upon them or to redefine the wording of the Acts. If a judge had any doubts about his proposed direction, he ought to commit it to writing and invite comment from counsel before they made their final speeches.

Things (such as negatives) from which obscene articles are to be made for publication but which things are not themselves to be published are deemed by s. 2(2) of the 1964 Act to be had for publication.

Defence of Having No Reasonable Cause to Suspect

B19.27 Under the Obscene Publications Act 1959, s. 2(5), it is a defence for the accused to prove that 'he had not examined the article in respect of which he is charged' and that he 'had no reasonable cause to suspect that it was such that his publication of it would make him liable to be convicted of an offence under this section'.

This defence applies where the form of the alleged offence is publishing. Where the alleged offence is having for publication for gain, the Obscene Publications Act 1964, s. 1(3)(a), provides a similar defence except that it refers to 'no reasonable cause to suspect that it was such that his having it would make him liable'.

Defence of Public Good

Obscene Publications Act 1959, s. 4 **B19.28**

(1) Subject to subsection (1A) of this section a person shall not be convicted of an offence against section 2 of this Act . . . if it is proved that publication of the article in question is justified as being for the public good on the ground that it is in the interests of science, literature, art or learning, or of other objects of general concern.

Under s. 4(1A) the defence of public good does not apply to moving picture films or soundtracks but in relation to such articles there is instead a defence of public good 'on the ground that it is in the interests of drama, opera, ballet or any other art, or of literature or learning'. Section 4(2) declares: 'that the opinion of experts as to the literary, artistic, scientific or other merits of an article may be admitted in any proceedings under this Act either to establish or to negative the said ground'. The issue of public good arises only if the article is first shown to be obscene and the expert evidence authorised by s. 4(2) is only admissible in relation to whether the article is in the interests of science, literature, art etc. and not in relation to whether the article is obscene in the first place. This should be pointed out to the jury (*A-G's Ref (No. 3 of 1977)* [1978] 1 WLR 1123). In *DPP v Jordan* [1978] AC 699, Lord Wilberforce said (at p. 719):

> The judgment to be reached under section 4(1) and the evidence to be given under section 4(2) must be in order to show that publication should be permitted in spite of obscenity — not to negative obscenity.

The jury need some explanation of their task under s. 4, and should not be left, as was said in *Calder and Boyars Ltd* [1969] 1 QB 151 at p. 172, 'to sink or swim in its dark waters'. The Court of Appeal went on to say that the jury should consider:

> on the one hand, the number of readers they believe would tend to be depraved and corrupted by the book, the strength of the tendency to deprave and corrupt and the nature of the depravity or corruption. On the other hand they should assess the strength of the literary, sociological or ethical merit which they consider the book to possess. They should then weigh up all these factors and decide whether on balance the publication is proved to be justified as being for the public good.

It is for the jury to decide the issue of public good, the evidence of the experts going merely to the literary merits etc. which the jury then have to balance against the admitted obscenity of the article (see *Penguin Books* [1961] Crim LR 176).

The phrase 'other objects of general concern' in s. 4(1), refers to objects falling within the same area as those specifically mentioned there, namely science, literature, art or learning, and thus expert evidence that obscene material is psychologically beneficial to persons with certain sexual tendencies in that it would relieve their sexual tensions and might divert them from antisocial activities is inadmissible (*DPP v Jordan* [1977] AC 699). On the other hand, the ethical merits of a book do come within 'other merits' in s. 4(2) and expert evidence on that issue is admissible (*Penguin Books*).

The word 'learning' in s. 4(1) is a noun and means the product of scholarship, rather than being a verb encompassing teaching. Expert evidence that obscene articles have merit for the purposes of sex education, or value in teaching or providing information about sexual matters, is not admissible because such matters are not in the interests of 'learning' as that word is used in s. 4(1) (*A-G's Ref (No. 3 of 1977)* [1978] 1 WLR 1123).

Search, Seizure and Forfeiture

B19.29 Section 3 of the Obscene Publications Act 1959 empowers a justice of the peace to issue a warrant for the search and seizure of obscene articles kept for publication for gain. A warrant which authorised a search for 'any other material of a sexually explicit nature' is on the face of it bad since such articles are not necessarily obscene (*Darbo v DPP* [1991] Crim LR 56).

The CJA 1967, s. 25, requires that the information must be laid by, or on behalf of, the DPP, or by a constable. The articles must then be brought before a justice of the peace who may issue a summons to the occupier of the premises from where the articles were seized to show cause why the articles should not be forfeited. See *Olympia Press Ltd v Hollis* [1973] 1 WLR 1520 and R.T.H. Stone, 'Obscene Publications: the problems persist' [1986] Crim LR 139 for discussion of the procedure. The defence of public good under s. 4(1) applies to the procedure under s. 3. So also does s. 2(2) of the Obscene Publications Act 1964 deeming negatives etc. to be had or kept for publication even though not themselves to be published. By virtue of the Prosecution of Offences Act 1985, s. 3(2)(d) it is the duty of the DPP to take over the conduct of any proceedings commenced by summons under the Obscene Publications Act 1959, s. 3. Section 3 (and, no doubt, the offence of having for publication for gain) applies equally to articles kept for publication abroad as it does to articles kept for publication in England and Wales (*Gold Star Publications Ltd v DPP* [1981] 1 WLR 732).

OBSCENE PERFORMANCES OF PLAYS

B19.30 The obscene *performance* of a play, being unlike the written script of the play a transient thing, cannot amount to an article within the Obscene Publication Act 1959. Nor, it seems does the performance of an obscene play amount to the publication of its script. However, the Theatres Act 1968, s. 2(2), makes it an offence 'if an obscene performance of a play is given, whether in public or private'. The offence is committed by 'anyone who (whether for gain or not) presented or directed' the performance and the penalties are the same as under the Obscene Publications Act 1959 (see **B19.21**), which is also echoed in the definition of obscenity (Theatres Act 1968, s. 2(1); cf. **B19.22**), in the time-limit of two years for prosecution (s. 2(3); cf. **B19.19**), the exclusion of proceedings at common law in respect of the performance of a play (s. 2(4); cf. **B19.17**) and the defence of public good (s. 3, cf. **B19.28**). Section 7 of the Theatres Act 1968 contains a number of exceptions to the offence under s. 2 including the performance of a play given on a domestic occasion in a private dwelling, and s. 18 contains interpretation provisions explaining, *inter alia*, what is a play and who is, and who is not, to be treated as a presenter or director.

INDECENT DISPLAYS

Definition

B19.31 **Indecent Displays (Control) Act 1981, s. 1**

(1) If any indecent matter is publicly displayed the person making the display and any person causing or permitting the display to be made shall be guilty of an offence.

Procedure

B19.32 Offences under the Indecent Displays (Control) Act 1981, s. 1(1), are, by s. 4(1) of the Act, triable either way. When tried on indictment they are class 3 offences.

Sentence

The maximum penalty is two years or a fine or both, on indictment; a fine not exceeding the statutory maximum, summarily (Indecent Displays (Control) Act 1981, s. 4(1)). B19.33

Meaning of 'Indecent'

It seems clear that something can be indecent for the purposes of the Indecent Displays (Control) Act 1981 without being obscene for the purposes of the Obscene Publications Act 1959 (see *Stanley* [1965] 2 QB 327, decided under the Post Office Act 1953, s. 11 — posting obscene or indecent matter). There is no defence of public good to a charge under the Indecent Displays (Control) Act 1981, s. 1(1). Section 1(5) provides that, in determining whether any displayed matter is indecent, '(a) there shall be disregarded any part of that matter which is not exposed to view'. This underlines the fact that the offence is only concerned with that which is publicly displayed, so this is one occasion where one can judge a book (or magazine or any other article) by its cover. On the other hand, in assessing indecency, 'account may be taken of the effect of juxtaposing one thing with another' (s. 1(5)(b)). B19.34

Meaning of 'Matter'

'Matter' includes 'anything capable of being displayed, except that it does not include an actual human body or any part thereof' (Indecent Displays (Control) Act 1981, s. 1(5)). By s. 1(2), 'Any matter which is displayed in or so as to be visible from any public place shall, for the purposes of this section, be deemed to be publicly displayed'. B19.35

Meaning of 'Public Place'

Indecent Displays (Control) Act 1981, s. 1 B19.36

(3) In subsection (2) above, 'public place', in relation to the display of any matter, means any place to which the public have or are permitted to have access (whether on payment or otherwise) while that matter is displayed except—
   (a) a place to which the public are permitted to have access only on payment which is or includes payment for that display; or
   (b) a shop or any part of a shop to which the public can only gain access by passing beyond an adequate warning notice;

   but the exclusions contained in paragraphs (a) and (b) above shall only apply where persons under the age of 18 years are not permitted to enter while the display in question is continuing.

Section 1(6) sets out minimum requirements with which an adequate warning notice must comply.

Exclusions

Section 1(4) of the Indecent Displays (Control) Act 1981 contains a number of exclusions for matter: B19.37

(a) included in a television broadcasting service or other television programme service (as defined in the Broadcasting Act 1990), or
(b) displayed in an art gallery or museum and only visible from within the gallery or museum, or
(c) displayed by or with the authority of, and visible only from within a building occupied by, the Crown or a local authority, or
(d) included in a performance of a play (as defined in the Theatres Act 1968) or a film exhibition (as defined in the Cinemas Act 1985).

OTHER OFFENCES

Sending Indecent etc. Articles through Post

B19.38 **Postal Services Act 2000, s. 85**

(3) A person commits an offence if he sends by post a postal packet which encloses—
(a) any indecent or obscene print, painting, photograph, lithograph, engraving, cinematograph film or other record of a picture or pictures, book, card or written communication, or
(b) any other indecent or obscene article (whether or not of a similar kind to those mentioned in paragraph (a)).

(4) A person commits an offence if he sends by post a postal packet which has on the packet, or on the cover of the packet, any words, marks or designs which are of an indecent or obscene character.

This offence is triable either way. The maximum penalty is 12 months, on indictment; a fine not exceeding the statutory maximum, summarily.

Whether something is 'obscene' under this section does not depend on the person or persons to whom the packet is addressed, but is to be determined using an objective test, regardless of the addressees (*Kosmos Publications Ltd v DPP* [1975] Crim LR 345; see also *Stanley* [1965] 2 QB 327; *Stamford* [1972] 2 QB 391).

Unsolicited Publications

B19.39 **Unsolicited Goods and Services Act 1971, s. 4**

(1) A person shall be guilty of an offence if he sends or causes to be sent to another person any book, magazine or leaflet (or advertising material for any such publication) which he knows or ought reasonably to know is unsolicited and which describes or illustrates human sexual techniques.

(2) A person found guilty of an offence under this section shall be liable on summary conviction to a fine not exceeding level 5 on the standard scale.

(3) A prosecution for an offence under this section shall not in England and Wales be instituted except by, or with the consent of, the DPP.

The sending of advertising material may be an offence even if that material does not itself describe or illustrate human sexual techniques (*DPP v Beate Uhse Ltd* [1974] QB 158).

Improper Use of Public Electronic Communications Network

B19.40 **Communications Act 2003, s. 127**

(1) A person is guilty of an offence if he—
(a) sends by means of a public electronic communications network a message or other matter that is grossly offensive or of an indecent, obscene or menacing character; or
(b) causes any such message or matter to be so sent.

(2) A person is guilty of an offence if, for the purpose of causing annoyance, inconvenience or needless anxiety to another, he—
(a) sends by means of a public electronic communications network, a message that he knows to be false,
(b) causes such a message to be sent; or
(c) persistently makes use of a public electronic communications network.

(3) A person guilty of an offence under this section shall be liable, on summary conviction, to imprisonment for a term not exceeding six months or to a fine not exceeding level 5 on the standard scale, or to both.

(4) Subsections (1) and (2) do not apply to anything done in the course of providing a programme service (within the meaning of the Broadcasting Act 1990.

The term 'public electronic communications network' is defined in chapter 1 of part 2 of the 2003 Act. Programme services are covered by the Obscene Publications Act 1959 (see **B19.25**). As to the meaning of *grossly* offensive under s. 127(1), see *DPP v Collins* [2006]

1 WLR 2223, where it was held by the House of Lords, contrary to the findings of the magistrates, that telephone messages sent to an MP about immigration and asylum issues (referring to 'Wogs', 'Pakis', 'Black bastards' and 'Niggers') were grossly offensive, irrespective of the actual reaction of the particular recipients. The offence is complete as soon as the message is sent and the test was said to be (at [10]) whether the message is 'couched in terms liable to cause gross offence to those to whom it relates' (not necessarily the recipients). Although intention or awareness of the grossly offensive nature of the message was required, Lord Bingham said (at [12]) that:

> a culpable state of mind will ordinarily be found where a message is couched in terms showing an intention to insult those to whom the message relates or giving rise to the inference that a risk of doing so must have been recognised by the sender.

Lord Carswell (at [22]) concluded that:

> the messages would be regarded as grossly offensive by reasonable persons in general, judged by the standards of an open and just multiracial society. The terms used were opprobrious and insulting, and not accidentally so. I am satisfied that reasonable citizens, not only members of the ethnic minorities referred to by the terms, would find them grossly offensive.

Lord Brown of Eaton-under-Heywood recognised (at [26-27]) that a conversation in these terms between two racists, neither of whom were offended, would be caught since the speakers would certainly know that the grossly offensive terms used were insulting to those to whom they applied and the section was intended to protect the integrity of the public communication system. The possible implications for certain types of telephone chat lines, given that the section also refers to messages of an obscene or indecent character, were expressly left open for another day.

Under the Penalties for Disorderly Behaviour (Amount of Penalty) Order 2002 (SI 2002 No. 1837), an offence under s. 127 is a fixed penalty offence and the amount payable is £80.

Indecent or Offensive or Threatening Letters etc.

Malicious Communications Act 1988, s. 1 **B19.41**

(1) Any person who sends to another person—
 (a) a letter, electronic communication or article of any description which conveys—
  (i) a message which is indecent or grossly offensive;
  (ii) a threat; or
  (iii) information which is false and known or believed to be false by the sender; or
 (b) any article or electronic communication which is, in whole or part, of an indecent or grossly offensive nature,

is guilty of an offence if his purpose, or one of his purposes, in sending it is that it should, so far as falling within paragraph (a) or (b) above, cause distress or anxiety to the recipient or to any other person to whom he intends that it or its contents or nature should be communicated.

(2) A person is not guilty of an offence by virtue of subsection (1)(a)(ii) above if he shows—
 (a) that the threat was used to reinforce a demand made by him on reasonable grounds; and
 (b) that he believed, and had reasonable grounds for believing, that the use of the threat was a proper means of reinforcing the demand.

(2A) In this section 'electronic communication' includes—
 (a) any oral or other communication by means of an electronic communications network; and
 (b) any communication (however sent) that is in electronic form.

(3) In this section references to sending include references to delivering or transmitting and to causing to be sent, delivered or transmitted or delivered and 'sender' shall be construed accordingly.

(4) A person guilty of an offence under this section shall be liable on summary conviction to imprisonment for a term not exceeding six months or to a fine not exceeding level 5 on the standard scale.

The terms of s. 1 were considered in *Connolly v DPP* [2007] 2 All ER 1012. 'Indecent or grossly offensive' were said to be ordinary English words and thus it was impossible to say that the court below was not entitled to conclude that 'shocking and disturbing' close-up photographs of aborted foetuses and of an abortion were grossly offensive. They were intended to cause distress and anxiety to those who received them and the fact that there was also a political or educational motive behind the accused's actions was of no avail. Furthermore, to the extent that the accused was exercising her rights under the ECHR, Articles 9 and 10 to freedom of speech or religion in sending the material, the restriction on those rights effected by the criminal prosecution was justified under Articles 9(2) and 10(2) as being necessary for the protection of the rights of others, namely the rights of the employees of the three pharmacies who were in receipt of the photographs.

Publications Harmful to Children and Young Persons

B19.42 **Children and Young Persons (Harmful Publications) Act 1955, s. 2**

(1) A person who prints, publishes, sells or lets on hire a work to which this Act applies, or has any such work in his possession for the purpose of selling it or letting it on hire, shall be guilty of an offence and liable, on summary conviction, to imprisonment for a term not exceeding four months or to a fine not exceeding level 3 on the standard scale or to both.

Provided that, in any proceedings taken under this subsection against a person in respect of selling or letting on hire a work or of having it in his possession for the purpose of selling it or letting it on hire, it shall be a defence for him to prove that he had not examined the contents of the work and had no reasonable cause to suspect that it was one to which this Act applies.

(2) A prosecution for an offence under this section shall not, in England and Wales, be instituted except by, or with the consent of, the Attorney-General.

By s. 1, the works to which the Act applies are:

> . . . any book, magazine or other like work which is of a kind likely to fall into the hands of children or young persons and consists wholly or mainly of stories told in pictures (with or without the addition of written matter) being stories portraying—
> (a) the commission of crimes; or
> (b) acts of violence or cruelty; or
> (c) incidents of a repulsive or horrible nature;
> in such a way that the work as a whole would tend to corrupt a child or young person into whose hands it might fall.

Section 3 provides powers of entry, search, seizure and, on conviction, forfeiture.

Indecent Photographs of Children

B19.43 The offences under the Protection of Children Act 1978 dealing with indecent photographs of children are dealt with at **B3.274** ***et seq.***

Video Recordings Act 1984 Offences

B19.44 The Video Recordings Act 1984 established a system for the classification by the British Board of Film Classification of video recordings supplied to the public through video rental and other outlets. Sections 9 to 14 of the 1984 Act create various offences, all originally summary and punishable only by fines, relating to the supply, or possession for supply, of video recordings which have not been classified or with a false indication as to their classification etc. However, the CJPO 1994, s. 88, made the two most serious offences (under ss. 9 and 10 of the 1984 Act) indictable and punishable by a maximum of two years' imprisonment or six months on summary conviction. The other offences under the 1984 Act remain summary but the offences under ss. 11, 12 and 14 of the Act have been made imprisonable with a maximum sentence of six months.

In brief, the offences under the 1984 Act are as follows.

(a) supplying a video recording of an unclassified work (s. 9);
(b) possessing a video recording of an unclassified work for the purposes of supply (s. 10);
(c) supplying a video recording of a classified work to a person who has not attained the age specified in the classification certificate (s. 11);
(d) supplying a video recording with a restricted classification from a place other than a licensed sex shop (s. 12) (see *Interfact Ltd v Liverpool City Council* (2005) 169 JP 353: it is the place of delivery rather than each despatch which counts, and mail order catalogues constitute 'offers' to supply illegally);
(e) supplying a video recording which does not comply with the requirements as to labelling (s. 13);
(f) supplying a video recording containing a false indication as to classification (s. 14).

Section 10 is set out below as an example of the provision made. An offence under the section is punishable, on indictment, with two years' imprisonment or a fine or both and, on summary conviction, with six months or a fine not exceeding £20,000 or both.

Video Recordings Act 1984, s. 10

(1) Where a video recording contains a video work in respect of which no classification certificate has been issued, a person who has the recording in his possession for the purpose of supplying it is guilty of an offence unless—
  (a) he has it in his possession for the purpose only of a supply which, if it took place, would be an exempted supply, or
  (b) the video work is an exempted work.
(2) It is a defence to a charge of committing an offence under this section to prove—
  (a) that the accused believed on reasonable grounds that the video work concerned or, if the video recording contained more than one work to which the charge relates, each of those works was either an exempted work or a work in respect of which a classification certificate had been issued,
  (b) that the accused had the video recording in his possession for the purpose only of a supply which he believed on reasonable grounds would, if it took place, be an exempted supply by virtue of section 3(4) or (5) of this Act, or
  (c) that the accused did not intend to supply the video recording until a classification certificate had been issued in respect of the video work concerned.

Certain video works are exempted from the provisions of the 1984 Act. The meaning of an exempted work is set out in s. 2 of the Act. Broadly, a work is exempted if it is designed to inform, educate or instruct, it is concerned with sport, religion or music or it is a video game. However, there are restrictions on these exemptions where, for example, the video work depicts, to any significant extent, human sexual activity, gross violence, human excretory functions or techniques likely to be useful in the commission of offences. For a minimalist view of what is required for such depictions, see *Kent County Council v Multi Media Marketing (Canterbury) Ltd* (1995) *The Times*, 9 May 1995. 'Human sexual activity' does not require material that would be regarded as hard pornography or as offensive. A video work is also not exempted if to any significant extent it depicts criminal activity which is likely to any significant extent to stimulate or encourage the commission of offences. Section 3 of the 1984 Act provides for the meaning of exempted supply, which includes a supply which is neither for reward nor in the course or furtherance of a business.

Section B20 Offences Related to Drugs

CONTROLLED DRUGS

Meaning of 'Controlled Drug'

B20.1 **Misuse of Drugs Act 1971, s. 2**

(1) In this Act—

(a) the expression 'controlled drug' means any substance or product for the time being specified in part I, II, or III of schedule 2 to this Act; and

(b) the expressions 'Class A drug', 'Class B drug' and 'Class C drug' mean any of the substances and products for the time being specified respectively in part I, part II and part III of that schedule;

and the provisions of part IV of that schedule shall have effect with respect to the meanings of expressions used in that schedule.

The schedule may be, and frequently has been, amended by regulations made in accordance with s. 2 of the 1971 Act. Note that methylamphetamine (commonly known as 'crystal meth') was reclassified from Class B to Class A with effect from 18 January 2007 (Misuse of Drugs Act 1971 (Amendment) Order 2006 (SI 2006 No. 3331)).

Misuse of Drugs Act 1971, sch. 2

CONTROLLED DRUGS

PART I CLASS A DRUGS

1. The following substances and products, namely:—

(a) Acetorphine.
Alfentanil.
Allylprodine.
Alphacetylmethadol.
Alphameprodine.
Alphamethadol.
Alphaprodine.
Anileridine.
Benzethidine.
Benzylmorphine (3-benzylmorphine).
Betacetylmethadol.
Betameprodine.
Betamethadol.
Betaprodine.
Bezitramide.
Bufotenine.
Carfentanil.
Clonitazene.

Coca leaf.
Cocaine.
Desomorphine.
Dextromoramide.
Diamorphine.
Diampromide.
Diethylthiambutene.
Difenoxin (1-(3-cyano-3, 3-diphenylpropyl)-4- phenylpiperidine-4-carboxylic acid).
Dihydrocodeinone *O*-carboxymethyloxime.
Dihydroetorphine.
Dihydromorphine.
Dimenoxadole.
Dimepheptanol.
Dimethylthiambutene.
Dioxaphetyl butyrate.
Diphenoxylate.
Dipipanone.
Drotebanol (3,4-dimethoxy-17-methylmorphinan-6 β, 14-diol).
Ecgonine, and any derivative of ecgonine which is convertible to ecgonine or to cocaine.
Ethylmethylthiambutene.
Eticyclidine.
Etonitazene.
Etorphine.
Etoxeridine.
Etryptamine.
Fentanyl.
Fungus (of any kind) which contains psilocin or an ester of psilocin.
Furethidine.
Hydrocodone.
Hydromorphinol.
Hydromorphone.
Hydroxypethidine.
Isomethadone.
Ketobemidone.
Levomethorphan.
Levomoramide.
Levophenacylmorphan.
Levorphanol.
Lofentanil.
Lysergamide.
Lysergide and other *N*-alkyl derivatives of lysergamide.
Mescaline.
Metazocine.
Methadone.
Methadyl acetate.
Methylamphetamine
Methyldesorphine.
Methyldihydromorphine (6-methyldihydromorphine).
Metopon.
Morpheridine.
Morphine.
Morphine methoromide, morphine *N*-oxide and other pentavalent nitrogen morphine derivatives.
Myrophine.
Nicomorphine (3,6-dinicotinoyl-morphine).
Noracymethadol.
Norlevorphanol.
Normethadone.
Normorphine.
Norpipanone.
Opium, whether raw, prepared or medicinal.
Oxycodone.
Oxymorphone.
Pethidine.
Phenadoxone.
Phenampromide.
Phenazocine.
Phencyclidine.
Phenomorphan.
Phenoperidine.
Piminodine.
Piritramide.
Poppy-straw and concentrate of poppy-straw.
Proheptazine.
Properidine (1-methyl-4-phenyl- piperidine-4-carboxylic acid isopropyl ester).
Psilocin.
Racemethorphan.
Racemoramide.
Racemorphan.
Remifentanil.
Rolicyclidine.
Sufentanil.
Tenocylidine.
Thebacon.
Thebaine.
Tilidate.
Trimeperidine.
4-Bromo-2,5-dimethoxy-a-methylphenethylamine.
4-Cyano-2-dimethylamino-4, 4-diphenylbutane.
4-Cyano-1-methyl-4-phenyl- piperidine.
N,N-Diethyltryptamine.
N,N-Dimethyltryptamine.
2,5-Dimethoxy-a, 4-dimethylphenethylamine.
N-Hydroxy-tenamphetamine
1-Methyl-4-phenylpiperidine-4- carboxylic acid.
2-Methyl-3-morpholino-1, 1-diphenylpropanecarboxylic acid.
4-Methyl-aminorex
4-Phenylpiperidine-4-carboxylic acid ethyl ester.

(b) any compound (not being a compound for the time being specified in subparagraph (a) above) structurally derived from tryptamine or from a ring-hydroxy tryptamine by substitution at the nitrogen atom of the sidechain with one or more alkyl substituents but no other substituent;

(ba) Allyl(a-methyl-3,4-methylenedioxyphenethyl)amine
2-Amino- 1-(2,5-dimethoxy-4-methylphenyl)ethanol
2-Amino- 1-(3,4-dimethoxyphenyl)ethanol
Benzyl(a-methyl-3,4-methylenedioxyphenethyl)amine
4-Bromo-b,2,5-trimethoxyphenethylamine
N-(4-sec-Butylthio-2,5-dimethoxyphenethyl)hydroxylamine
CycIopropylmethyI(a-methyl-3,4-methylenedioxyphenethyl)amine
2-(4,7-Dimethoxy-2,3-dihydro-1H-indan-5-yl)ethylamine
2-(4,7-Dimethoxy-2,3-dihydro-1H-indan-5-yl)-1-methylethylamine
2-(2,5-Dimethoxy-4-methylphenyl)cyclopropylamine
2-(1,4-Dimethoxy-2-naphthyl)ethylamine
2-(1,4-Dimethoxy-2-naphthyl)-1-methylethylamine
N-(2,5-Dimethoxy-4-propylthiophenethyl)hydroxylamine
2-(1,4-Dimethoxy-5, 6, 7,8-tetrahydro-2-naphthyl)ethylamine
2-(1,4-Dimethoxy-5,6,7,8-tetrahydro-2-naphthy1)-1-methylethylamine
a,a-Dimethyl-3,4-methylenedioxyphenethylamine
a,a-Dimethyl-3,4-methylenedioxyphenethyl(methyl)amine
Dimethyl(a-methyl-3,4-methylenedioxyphenethyl)amine
N-(4-Ethylthio-2,5-dimethoxyphenethyl)hydroxylamine
4-lodo-2,5-dimethoxy-a-methylphenethyl(dimethyl)amine
2-(1,4-Methano-5,8-dimethoxy-1,2,3,4-tetrahydro-6-naphthyl)ethylamine
2-(1,4-Methano-5,8-dimethoxy-1,2,3,4-tetrahydro-6-naphthyl)1-methylethylamine
2-(5-Methoxy-2,2-dimethyl-2,3-dihydrobenzo[b] furan-6-yl)-1 methylethylamine
2-Methoxyethyl(a-methyl-3,4-methylenedioxyphenethyl)amine
2-(5-Methoxy-2-methyl-2,3-dihydrobenzo[b]furan-6-yl)-1methylethylamine
b-Methoxy-3,4-methylenedioxyphenethylamine
1-(3,4-Methylenedioxybenzyl)butyl(ethyl)amine
1-(3,4-Methylenedioxybenzyl)butyl(methyl)amine
2-(a-Methyl-3,4-methylenedioxyphenethylamino)ethanol
a-Methyl-3,4-methylenedioxyphenethyl(prop-2-ynyl)amine
N-Methyl -N-(a-methyl -3,4-methylenedioxyphenethyl)hydroxylamine
O-Methyl -N-(a-methyl-3,4methylenedioxyphenethyl)hydroxylamine
a-Methyl-4-(methylthio)phenethylamine
b,3,4,5-Tetramethoxyphenethylamine
b,2,5-Trimethoxy-4-methylphenethylamine.

(c) any compound (not being methoxyphenamine or a compound for the time being specified in subparagraph (a) above) structurally derived from phenethylamine, an *N*-alkylphenethylamine, a-methylphenethylamine, an *N*-alkyl-a-methylphenethylamine, a-ethylphenethylamine, or an *N*-alkyl-a-ethylphenethylamine by substitution in the ring to any extent with alkyl, alkoxy, alkylenedioxy or halide substituents, whether or not further substituted in the ring by one or more other univalent substituents.

(d) any compound (not being a compound for the time being specified in subparagraph (a) above) structurally derived from fentanyl by modification in any of the following ways, that is to say,
  (i) by replacement of the phenyl portion of the phenethyl group by any heteromonocycle whether or not further substituted in the heterocycle;
  (ii) by substitution in the phenethyl group with alkyl, alkenyl, alkoxy, hydoxy, halogeno, haloalkyl, amino or nitro groups;
  (iii) by substitution in the piperidine ring with alkyl or alkenyl groups;
  (iv) by substitution in the aniline ring with alkyl, alkoxy, alkylenedioxy, halogeno or haloalkyl groups;
  (v) by substitution at the 4-position of the piperidine ring with any alkoxycarbonyl or alkoxyalkyl or acyloxy group;
  (vi) by replacement of the *N*-propionyl group by another acyl group;

(e) any compound (not being a compound for the time being specified in subparagraph (a) above) structurally derived from pethidine by modification in any of the following ways, that is to say,

(i) by replacement of the 1-methyl group by an acyl, alkyl whether or not unsaturated, benzyl or phenethyl group, whether or not further substituted;
(ii) by substitution in the piperidine ring with alkyl or alkenyl groups or with a propano bridge, whether or not further substituted;
(iii) by substitution in the 4-phenyl ring with alkyl, alkoxy, aryloxy, halogeno or haloalkyl groups;
(iv) by replacement of the 4-ethoxycarbonyl by any other alkoxycarbonyl or any alkoxyalkyl or acyloxy group;
(v) by formation of an *N*-oxide or of a quaternary base.

2. Any stereoisomeric form of a substance for the time being specified in paragraph 1 above not being dextromethorphan or dextrorphan.
3. Any ester or ether of a substance for the time being specified in paragraph 1 or 2 above not being a substance for the time being specified in part II of this schedule.
4. Any salt of a substance for the time being specified in any of paragraphs 1 to 3 above.
5. Any preparation or other product containing a substance or product for the time being specified in any of paragraphs 1 to 4 above.
6. Any preparation designed for administration by injection which includes a substance or product for the time being specified in any of paragraphs 1 to 3 of part II of this schedule.

Part II Class B Drugs

1. The following substances and products, namely:—

(a) Acetyldihydrocodeine.
Amphetamine.
Codeine.
Dihydrocodeine.
Ethylmorphine (3-ethylmorphine).
Glutethimide.
Lefetamine.
Mecloqualone.
Methaqualone.
Methcathinone.
Methylphenidate.
a-Methylphenethylthydroxylamine
Methylphenobarbitone.
Nicodine.
Nicodicodine (6- nicotinoyldihydrocodeine).
Norcodeine.
Pentazocine.
Phenmetrazine.
Pholcodine.
Propiram.
Zipeprol.

(b) Any 5,5 disubstituted barbituric acid.

2. Any stereoisomeric form of a substance for the time being specified in paragraph 1 of this part of this schedule.
3. Any salt of a substance for the time being specified in paragraph 1 or 2 of this part of this schedule.
4. Any preparation or other product containing a substance or product for the time being specified in any of paragraphs 1 to 3 of this part of this schedule, not being a preparation falling within paragraph 6 of part I of this schedule.

Part III Class C Drugs

1. The following substances, namely:—

(a) Alprazolam.
Aminorex.
Benzphetamine.
Bromazepam.
Brotizolam.
Buprenorphine.
Camazepam.
Cannabinol
Cannabinol derivatives
Cannabis and cannabis resin
Cathine.
Cathinone.
Chlordiazepoxide.
Chlorphentermine.
Clobazam.
Clonazepam.
Clorazepic acid.
Clotiazepam.
Cloxazolam.
Delorazepam.
Dextropropoxyphene.
Diazepam.
Diethylpropion.
Estazolam.
Ethchlorvynol.
Ethinamate.

(a) (*contd*) Ethyl loflazepate.
Fencamfamin.
Fenethylline.
Fenproporex.
Fludiazepam.
Flunitrazepam.
Flurazepam.
Halazepam.
Haloxazolam.
4-Hydroxy-n-butyric acid.
Ketamine
Ketazolam.
Loprazolam.
Lorazepam.
Lormetazepam.
Mazindol.
Medazepam.
Mefenorex.
Mephentermine.
Meprobamate.
Mesocarb.
Methyprylone.
Midazolam.
Nimetazepam.
Nitrazepam.
Nordazepam.
Oxazepam.
Oxazolam.
Pemoline.
Phendimetrazine.
Phentermine.
Pinazepam.
Pipradrol.
Prazepam.
Pyrovalerone.
Temazepam.
Tetrazepam.
Triazolam.
N-Ethylamphetamine.
Zolpidem.

(b) 4-Androstene-3, 17-dione.
5-Androstene-3, 17-diol.
Atamestane.
Bolandiol.
Bolasterone.
Bolazine.
Boldenone.
Bolenol.
Bolmantalate.
Calusterone.
4-Chloromethandienone.
Clostebol.
Drostanolone.
Enestebol.
Epitiostanol.
Ethyloestrenol.
Fluoxymesterone.
Formebolone.
Furazabol.
Mebolazine.
Mepitiostane.
Mesabolone.
Mestanolone.
Mesterolone.
Methandienone.
Methandriol.
Methenolone.
Methyltestosterone.
Metribolone.
Mibolerone.
Nandrolone.
19-Nor-4-Androstene-3, 17-dione.
19-Nor-5-Androstene-3, 17-diol.
Norboletone.
Norclostebol.
Norethandrolone.
Ovandrotone.
Oxabolone.
Oxandrolone.
Oxymesterone.
Oxymetholone.
Prasterone.
Propetandrol.
Quinbolone.
Roxibolone.
Silandrone.
Stanolone.
Stanozolol.
Stenbolone.
Testosterone.
Thiomesterone.
Trenbolone.

(c) any compound (not being Trilostane or a compound for the time being specified in sub-paragraph (b) above) structurally derived from 17-hydroxyandrostan-3-one or from 17-hydroxyestran-3-one by modification in any of the following ways, that is to say,
(i) by further substitution at position 17 by a methyl or ethyl group;
(ii) by substitution to any extent at one or more of positions 1, 2, 4, 6, 7, 9, 11 or 16, but at no other position;
(iii) by unsaturation in the carbocyclic ring system to any extent, provided that there are no more than two ethylenic bonds in any one carbocyclic ring;
(iv) by fusion of ring A with a heterocyclic system;

(d) any substance which is an ester or ether (or, where more than one hydroxyl function is available, both an ester and an ether) of a substance specified in sub-paragraph (b) or described in sub-paragraph (c) above or of cannabinol, or a cannabinol derivative;

(e) Chorionic Gonadotrophin (HCG). Somatotropin.
Clenbuterol. Somatrem.
Non-human chorionic gonadotrophin. Somatropin.

2. Any stereoisomeric form of a substance for the time being specified in paragraph 1 of this part of this schedule not being phenylpropanolamine.
3. Any salt of a substance for the time being specified in paragraph 1 or 2 of this part of this schedule.
4. Any preparation or other product containing a substance for the time being specified in any of paragraphs 1 to 3 of this part of this schedule.

Part IV Meaning of Certain Expressions Used in this Schedule

For the purposes of this schedule the following expressions (which are not among those defined in section 37(1) of this Act) have the meanings hereby assigned to them respectively, that is to say—

'cannabinol derivatives' means the following substances, except where contained in cannabis or cannabis resin, namely tetrahydro derivatives of cannabinol and 3-alkyl homologues of cannabinol or of its tetrahydro derivatives;

'coca leaf' means the leaf of any plant of the genus *Erythroxylon* from whose leaves cocaine can be extracted either directly or by chemical transformation;

'concentrate of poppy-straw' means the material produced when poppy-straw has entered into a process for the concentration of its alkaloids;

'medicinal opium' means raw opium which has undergone the process necessary to adapt it for medicinal use in accordance with the requirements of the British Pharmacopoeia, whether it is in the form of powder or is granulated or is in any other form, and whether it is or is not mixed with neutral substances;

'opium poppy' means the plant of the species *Papaver somniferum* L;

'poppy straw' means all parts, except the seeds, of the opium poppy after mowing;

'raw opium' includes powdered or granulated opium but does not include medicinal opium.

Unnecessary to Distinguish between Drugs in Usual Form and Stereoisomeric Forms, Salts or Esters The MDA 1971, sch. 2, lists drugs in their basic and stereoisomeric forms, and their esters or salts are also included. The Court of Appeal in *Greensmith* [1983] 1 WLR 1124, held that it is not necessary to distinguish between the natural substance or a substance resulting from chemical transformation, and that both substances (in that case cocaine) are controlled. **B20.2**

The word 'cocaine' in para. 1 of sch. 2, part I (Class A drugs), is the generic word, including not only the direct extracts of the coca leaf, but also whatever results from a chemical transformation, listed in paras. 2 to 5. The Court of Appeal in *Watts* [1984] 1 WLR 757, without referring to *Greensmith*, arrived at the same conclusion: 'amphetamine' in sch. 2, part II, para. 1 (Class B drugs), is a generic word including all of its stereoisomers. Pure dexamphetamine (even though this was also mentioned in para. 1) and pure levoamphetamine are included in the word 'amphetamine'. A person, who possesses a racemic mixture of dexamphetamine and levoamphetamine, possesses 'amphetamine'.

Heroin (diamorphine) is usually available in the form of a salt (typically diamorphine hydrochloride). It is arguable that prosecutions would have failed if possession of 'heroin' were charged rather than one of its salts: the Court of Appeal decisions of *Greensmith* and *Watts* prevent that result.

Material Occurring Naturally Controlled drugs are defined by their scientific name (for example, 'diamorphine' (heroin)). But 'any controlled drug described in schedule 2 by its scientific name is not established by proof of possession of naturally occurring material of which the described drug is one of the constituents unseparated from the others. This is so whether or not the naturally occurring material is also included as another item in the list of controlled drugs' (*DPP v Goodchild* [1978] 1 WLR 578, per Lord Diplock, at p. 583). In the case of the latter possibility, the offence would allude to the naturally occurring material, and **B20.3**

not its constituent elements. Thus, cannabis, and fungus that contains psilocin, are described as such in sch. 2.

B20.4 **'Preparations' and 'products' which contain a controlled drug are controlled** The word 'preparation' is not a technical word but 'a word to be addressed in its ordinary English meaning' (*Thomson* [2003] EWCA Crim 3477). The fact that there were dried-up psilocybin mushrooms in a bag was evidence from which it was possible for the jury to infer that the substance was a preparation. Thus, psilocybin mushrooms which had been picked, packed and frozen were not 'a preparation' within the MDA 1971, sch. 2, part I, para. 5, because 'prepare' means 'to make ready or fit; to bring into a suitable state; to subject to a process of bringing it to a required state' (*Hodder v DPP* [1989] Crim LR 261). Freezing is not an act of preparation but of preservation. In order to prepare something it is not necessary to undertake a chemical or technical process (see *Stevens* [1981] Crim LR 568, where the acts of drying and then powdering mushrooms was to prepare them; and see *Martin* [2006] EWCA Crim 109). A 'preparation' requires the substance to be altered by human action to put it into a condition in which it can be used, as in *Cunliffe* [1986] Crim LR 547, where mushrooms were dried.

In *Walker* [1987] Crim LR 565, the Court of Appeal declined to express any view as to whether merely picking psilocybin mushrooms is an act of preparation. However, such mushrooms did fall within sch. 2, because they constituted a 'product' (and 'products' containing a controlled drug also fall within sch. 2). Bear in mind that all these cases predate the specific inclusion of 'fungus (of any kind) which contains psilocin or an ester of psilocin' as a Class A drug in sch. 2 by the Drugs Act 2005, s. 21. Note that recently, courts at first instance have been reluctant to rule that the altered condition of a plant, in which a controlled substance naturally subsists, falls within sch. 2 to the MDA 1971 (*Mardle* (14 December 2004 unreported, Gloucester Crown Court), *Francis* (20 April 2005 unreported, Canterbury Crown Court) and *Sette* (13 March 2006 unreported, Kingston Crown Court). *Sette* was concerned with a quantity of dried *echinopsis peruviana* (cacti), which contains mescaline. The learned recorder stayed the case on the basis that the law was uncertain, and that Her Majesty's Revenue and Customs has levied VAT on some vendors of this species of cactus. None of these first decision rulings has been the subject of scrutiny by a higher court. It is submitted that the real ambiguity tends to be on the facts rather than on the law, namely, whether it can be proved that someone had prepared the plant for consumption (in the *Hodder* sense), or had merely preserved it.

Meaning of 'Cannabis' and 'Cannabis Resin'

B20.5 **Misuse of Drugs Act 1971, s. 37**

'cannabis' (except in the expression 'cannabis resin') means any plant of the genus *Cannabis* or any part of any such plant (by whatever name designated) except that it does not include cannabis resin or any of the following products after separation from the rest of the plant, namely—

(a) mature stalk of any such plant,
(b) fibre produced from mature stalk of any such plant, and
(c) seed of any such plant,

'cannabis resin' means the separated resin, whether crude or purified, obtained from any plant of the genus *Cannabis*.

'Cannabinol', 'Cannabinol derivatives' and 'Cannabis and cannabis resin' became Class C drugs on 29 January 2004 (Misuse of Drugs Act 1971 (Modification) (No. 2) Order 2003 (SI 2003 No. 3201)). The definition of 'cannabis' has, over the years, been widened to bring more of the plant under control (*Harris* [1996] 1 Cr App R 369). In *Thomas* [1981] Crim LR 496, the Court of Appeal held that the substance was cannabis resin, even though on microscopic examination it was shown to contain elements of the natural form from which the resin had not been extracted. There was sufficient separated material, and *DPP v Goodchild* [1978]

1 WLR 578 did not lead to the conclusion that the wrong charge had been laid. In *Hill* (1993) 96 Cr App R 456, the Court of Appeal held that where the charge specifies the supply of 'cannabis resin' it is not enough to prove that the accused supplied either 'cannabis' or 'cannabis resin'. The court distinguished *Best* (1979) 70 Cr App R 21 (see **B20.9**) where the charge particularised the drug as either cannabis or cannabis resin.

Proof of Substance as Controlled Drug

Expert evidence (such as an analyst's certificate) is not required in all cases, but the prosecution must establish the identity of the drug referred to in the charge with sufficient certainty (*Hill* (1993) 96 Cr App R 456). In *Chatwood* [1980] 1 WLR 874, it was held that the admissions of an accused as to his knowledge of the substance may constitute sufficient evidence to identify what it is. The court approved the statement of the law made by Lord Widgery CJ in *Bird v Adams* [1972] Crim LR 174: **B20.6**

> If a man admits possession of a substance which he says is a dangerous drug, if he admits it in circumstances like the present where he also admits that he has been peddling the drug, it is of course possible that the item in question was not a specified drug at all but the admission in those circumstances is not an admission of some fact about which the admitter knows nothing. This is the kind of case in which the appellant had certainly sufficient knowledge of the circumstances of his conduct to make his admission at least prima facie evidence of its truth and that was all that was required at the stage of the proceedings at which the submission to the justices was made.

The statements of the accused in *Chatwood* were sufficient to provide prima facie evidence of the nature of the substance in their possession. Only one of the accused gave evidence claiming that the substance was flour; the jury disbelieved him and convicted. The appeal against conviction was dismissed.

The opinion of the accused as to the nature of the substance he possessed must be such that his opinion is reliable. The usefulness of such statements by the accused may be limited to committal proceedings. As to admissions by the accused generally, see **F17**.

POSSESSION OF CONTROLLED DRUGS

Misuse of Drugs Act 1971, s. 5 **B20.7**

(1) Subject to any regulations under section 7 of this Act for the time being in force, it shall not be lawful for a person to have a controlled drug in his possession.
(2) Subject to section 28 of this Act and to subsection (4) below, it is an offence for a person to have a controlled drug in his possession in contravention of subsection (1) above.

'Contravention' includes a failure to comply (MDA 1971, s. 37(1)).

Since the range of sentence for this offence depends upon the class of drug involved (see **B20.105**), the House of Lords decision in *Courtie* [1984] AC 463, establishes that s. 5(2) creates not one but three offences. See also *Ellis* (1986) 84 Cr App R 235.

Procedure

For powers of entry, search and seizure under the MDA 1971, see **B20.77**. **B20.8**

Offences under the MDA 1971, s. 5(2), are (by s. 25 of and sch. 4 to the Act) triable either way. When tried on indictment they are class 3 offences. According to the *Consolidated Criminal Practice Direction*, para.V.51, *Mode of trial* (see **appendix** 7), cases of possession of Class A drugs should be committed for trial unless the amount is small and consistent only with personal use; cases of possession of Class B drugs should be committed for trial when the quantity is substantial, and not consistent only with personal use.

Summary trial may be instituted by an information laid 12, rather than the usual six, months from the date of commission of the offence (MDA 1971, s. 25(4)).

For the liability of corporate officers, see **B20.24**.

Indictment

B20.9 *Statement of Offence*

Possession of controlled drug contrary to section 5(1) of the Misuse of Drugs Act 1971

Particulars of Offence

A on the . . . day of . . . unlawfully had in his possession a controlled drug of Class [A, B, or C] namely . . .

Where a count specifies more than one drug in the same class, the count does not offend the rules against duplicity (*Best* (1979) 70 Cr App R 21). But if the count specifies a particular controlled drug then the existence of that substance must be established (see *Muir v Smith* [1978] Crim LR 293). Where a charge specifies a quantity of drugs, it is sufficient to prove that the accused acted in relation to part of that quantity and no question of a 'partial verdict' arises (*Peevey* (1973) 57 Cr App R 554).

It is not necessary to distinguish between a controlled drug and its stereoisomeric form, or a salt or ester in a count (see **B20.2**).

Sentencing Guidelines

B20.10 See **B20.105** to **B20.109**.

Meaning of 'Possession'

B20.11 Lord Hope in the House of Lords in *Lambert* [2002] 2 AC 545, stated that 'there are two elements to possession. There is the physical element, and there is the mental element'. The approach of Lord Hope is reflected in the other judgments delivered in that case. It confirms the approach taken by the Court of Appeal in *McNamara* (1988) 87 Cr App R 246, and is settled law.

B20.12 **Custody or control** 'The physical element involves proof that the thing is in the custody of the defendant or subject to his control', per Lord Hope in *Lambert* [2002] 2 AC 545 (see also Lord Scarman in *Boyesen* [1982] AC 768). This is enlarged by the MDA 1971, s. 37(3): 'For the purposes of this Act the things which a person has in his possession shall be taken to include any thing subject to his control which is in the custody of another'.

The description of possession given by Lord Wilberforce in *Warner v Metropolitan Police Commissioner* [1969] 2 AC 256, at pp. 310–11, remains relevant:

> The question, to which an answer is required, and in the end a jury must answer it, is whether in the circumstances the accused should be held to have possession of the substance, rather than mere control. In order to decide between these two, the jury should, in my opinion, be invited to consider all the circumstances — to use again the words of *Pollock and Wright* — the 'Modes or events' — by which the custody commences and the legal incident in which it is held. By these I mean relating them to typical situations, that they must consider the manner and circumstances in which the substance, or something which contains it, has been received, what knowledge or means of knowledge or guilty knowledge as to the presence of the substance, or as to the nature of what has been received, he had at the time of receipt or thereafter up to the moment when he is found with it; his legal relation to the substance or package (including his right of access to it). On such matters as these (not exhaustively stated) they must make the decision whether, in addition to physical control, he has, or ought to have imputed to him the intention to possess, or knowledge that he does possess, what is in fact a prohibited substance. If he has this intention or knowledge, it is not additionally necessary that he should know the nature of the substance.

The aspect of knowledge as a component of possession is dealt with at **B20.13**.

If a person orders a controlled drug, directing that it be sent by post to his address, he is in possession of that drug from the time it arrives through the letter box (*Peaston* (1978) 69 Cr App R 203). A person smoking cannabis resin has that drug in his possession at the time of the smoking (*Chief Constable of Cheshire Constabulary v Hunt* (1983) 147 JP 567).

Knowledge of Possession A person must know that he is in possession of something which is, in fact, a controlled drug: see *Warner v Metropolitan Police Commissioner* [1969] 2 AC 256, *Boyesen* [1982] AC 768, *McNamara* (1988) 87 Cr App R 246, and *Lambert* [2002] 2 AC 545, where, for example, Lord Clyde states, 'The second element involves that the defendant knows that the thing in question is under his control. He need not know what its nature is, but so long as he knows that the thing, whatever it is, is under his control, it is in his possession'. An accused's lack of knowledge of the quality of the thing might be a defence under the MDA 1971, s. 28. It is important to keep this often neglected provision in mind (see **B20.20**). Ignorance of, or mistake as to the quality of the substance in question does not prevent the accused being in possession of it, provided that the substance turns out to be a controlled drug. Thus, the accused was in possession of the amphetamine tablets in a bottle in her holdall, even if she was mistaken as to their quality (see *Lockyer v Gibb* [1967] 2 QB 243 and consider *Irving* [1970] Crim LR 642). In *Searle v Randolph* [1972] Crim LR 779, the accused knew that he had cigarettes; he simply made a mistake about the quality of the tobacco, and so was in possession of a controlled drug since one of the cigarettes contained cannabis. **B20.13**

A person does not possess something of which he is completely unaware. If a drug is put into someone's pocket without his knowledge, he is not in possession of it (*Warner v Metropolitan Police Commissioner* and *McNamara*). The accused was not in possession in *Marriott* [1971] 1 All ER 595, where the cannabis resin on the knife could only be detected by a forensic scientist and the accused had no knowledge of any substance. A person remains in possession of something even if he has forgotten about it (*Martindale* [1986] 1 WLR 1042, following *Buswell* [1972] 1 WLR 64; cf. *Russell* (1984) 81 Cr App R 315).

Joint Possession One or more co-accused may be jointly charged with possession, but mere knowledge of the presence of a drug in the hands of a confederate is not enough: joint possession must be established (*Searle* [1971] Crim LR 592). Lord Widgery CJ, giving the judgment of the court, said, 'The sort of direction to which the deputy recorder should have opened the jury's mind was to ask them to consider whether these drugs formed a common pool from which all had the right to draw'. See also *Wright* (1975) 119 SJ 825. In *Strong* (1989) *The Times*, 26 January 1990, the prosecution put the case on the basis that there was joint possession, that is, that each of the co-accused had control of one or more of the packages of cannabis. The Court of Appeal followed *Searle*, and said that what was being looked for was whether each person had the right to say what should be done with the cannabis. Mere presence in the same vehicle as the drugs, and knowing they were there, was not sufficient. It is unclear whether a person can aid and abet another to possess a controlled drug, but consider *Bland* [1988] Crim LR 41, *Conway* [1994] Crim LR 826, *McNamara* [1998] Crim LR 278, *Arshad* [2002] EWCA Crim 1549, *Jacobs* [2002] EWCA Crim 610, and *Bailey* [2004] EWCA Crim 2169. There must be some *actual* control in order to be in joint possession of an item. An item can be used by a number of different people and if there is evidence that they have some active involvement in the use of the items, they will all be in possession, It is not sufficient that someone is capable of taking control of the item in question. **B20.14**

Cases Involving Small Quantities of Controlled Drug

There are two points. First, the quantity of drug might be so slight as to amount, in reality, to nothing. Secondly, the fact that the quantity of drug is miniscule might be evidence of an accused's lack of knowledge of the existence of the thing. **B20.15**

(i) Whether a drug is visible or measurable Lord Widgery CJ, giving the majority judgment of the Divisional Court in *Bocking v Roberts* [1974] QB 307, said (at pp. 309–10):

> . . . it is quite clear that the prosecution have to prove that there was some of the drug in the possession of the defendant to justify the charge, and the distinction which has to be drawn in cases of this kind is whether the quantity of the drug was enough to justify the conclusion that he was possessed of a quantity of the drug or whether, on the other hand, the traces were so slight that they really indicated no more than that at some previous time he had been in possession of the drug. It seems to me that that is the distinction that has to be drawn, although its application to individual cases is by no means easy.

This test was approved by the House of Lords in *Boyesen* [1982] AC 768. Lord Scarman said 'if it is visible, tangible, and measurable, it is certainly something'. See also *Worsell* [1970] 1 WLR 111, *Graham* [1970] 1 WLR 113, and *Searle v Randolph* [1972] Crim LR 779. The House of Lords rejected a 'usability' test requiring that there be an amount of a drug sufficient to be used (or misused) for there to be something present. *Carver* [1978] QB 472 was overruled.

(ii) Minute amount as evidence of lack of knowledge Lord Scarman, in *Boyesen*, drew attention to the statement of Lord Diplock delivering the judgment of the Privy Council in *DPP v Brooks* [1974] AC 862, where he said: 'In the ordinary use of the word "possession", one has in one's possession whatever is, to one's own knowledge, physically in one's custody or under one's physical control'. Lord Scarman added, 'If the quantity in custody or control is so minute, the question arises: was it so minute that it cannot be proved that the accused knew he had it?' A good illustration, said Lord Scarman, is the New Zealand case of *Police v Emirali* [1976] 1 NZLR 286. Small quantities of drug were found in a vacuum cleaner which others had used, as well as a burned deposit on a metal clip of the type used for smoking marijuana cigarettes. The amount of the drug on the clip was only just measurable. On such facts an accused might properly argue that he was not in possession of the substance at all; and see the approach taken by Stinson J in *Colyer* [1974] Crim LR 243.

Drugs in Containers

B20.16 Two leading cases are *McNamara* (1988) 87 Cr App R 270, and *Lambert* [2002] 2 AC 545 at [126]. In *Lambert*, Lord Clyde said:

> if the defendant is in possession of the container and knows that there is something in it, he will be taken to be in possession of the contents of the container. . . . Where the drug is in a container, it is sufficient for the prosecution to prove that the defendant had control of the container, that he knew of its existence and that there was something in it, and that the something was in fact the controlled drug which the prosecution alleges it to be. The prosecution does not require to prove that the accused knew that the thing was a controlled drug.

If the accused had no right to open the container and ascertain its contents, it is arguable that the accused was not in possession of the contents (see *Warner v Metropolitan Police Commissioner* [1969] 2 AC 256, per Lord Morris at pp. 287 and 296, Lord Pearce at p. 306 and Lord Wilberforce at p. 312; *McNamara*; and *Wright* (1975) 62 Cr App R 169).

Subject to s. 28 of the MDA 1971, a mistake as to the nature of the contents will not avail the accused (cf. some of the statements in the House of Lords in *Warner v Metropolitan Police Commissioner* [1969] 2 AC 256, per Lord Reid at p. 281, Lord Morris at pp. 285, 290 and 296, Lord Guest at p. 302, Lord Pearce at p. 305 and Lord Wilberforce at p. 311).

Evidence Establishing Earlier Possession

B20.17 The existence of drug traces, or a minute quantity of a controlled drug, might be evidence that the accused had been in possession of a measurable/usable quantity of the substance: see *Worsell* [1970] 1 WLR 111 and *Graham* [1970] 1 WLR 113 (and consider *Hambleton v*

Callinan [1968] 2 QB 427). However, it is important that care is taken in bringing charges on this basis. In *Pragliola* [1977] Crim LR 612, the Court of Appeal held that the charge of unlawful possession was oppressive and not justifiable where the accused was charged solely on the basis that a pipe, which contained a drug trace, was returned to him.

A related situation is that in which a trace of a controlled drug, e.g., amphetamine powder, is found in a urine sample (see *Hambleton v Callinan*).

Mens Rea

Warner v Metropolitan Police Commissioner [1969] 2 AC 256 established that the offence of unlawful possession of a controlled drug under the Drugs (Prevention of Misuse) Act 1964, s. 1(1), was an absolute offence. In *Lewis* (1988) 87 Cr App R 270, the Court of Appeal remarked that 'it is clear that if a defendant is proved to have knowledge of this control of prohibited articles, it is generally immaterial that he is in ignorance or under a mistake as to their extent or qualities'. This is the basic rule, but it is essential to read *Warner* and *Lewis* with s. 28 of the MDA 1971 in mind (see *Lambert* [2002] 2 AC 545 at **B20.20**, and note the commentary to *Lewis* by the late Professor Sir John Smith QC [1988] Crim LR 517. See also *Public Prosecutor v Tan Kiam Peng* [2006] SGHC 207). **B20.18**

Defence under s. 5(4)

The MDA 1971, s. 5(4), provides a defence to simple possession (s. 5(2)) but the existence of that defence does not preclude any other defences being raised. **B20.19**

Misuse of Drugs Act 1971, s. 5

(4) In any proceedings for an offence under subsection (2) above in which it is proved that the accused had a controlled drug in his possession, it shall be a defence for him to prove—
  (a) that, knowing or suspecting it to be a controlled drug, he took possession of it for the purpose of preventing another from committing or continuing to commit an offence in connection with that drug and that as soon as possible after taking possession of it he took all such steps as were reasonably open to him to destroy the drug or to deliver it into the custody of a person lawfully entitled to take custody of it; or
  (b) that, knowing or suspecting it to be a controlled drug, he took possession of it for the purpose of delivering it into the custody of a person lawfully entitled to take custody of it and that as soon as possible after taking possession of it he took all such steps as were reasonably open to him to deliver it into the custody of such a person.

. . .

(6) Nothing in subsection (4) above shall prejudice any defence which it is open to a person charged with an offence under this section to raise apart from that subsection.

Where the accused buried drugs (e.g., cannabis) it was not sufficient to satisfy the defence in s. 5(4)(a) that the forces of nature might or would destroy the drugs eventually: rather it was for the accused to show that he took all such steps as were reasonably open to him to destroy them and the acts of destruction must be his (*Murphy* [2003] 1 WLR 422). The Court of Appeal in *Dempsey* (1985) 82 Cr App R 291, made clear that the defence in s. 5(4)(b) is available only if the accused's purpose is to act in accordance with that subsection.

The decision in *Lambert* [2002] 2 AC 545 (see **B20.20** and **F3.13**) means that the imposition of the persuasive burden in s. 5(4) is open to challenge: and consider *Keogh* [2007] 1 WLR 1500.

DEFENCE UNDER THE MISUSE OF DRUGS ACT 1971, s. 28

Misuse of Drugs Act 1971, s. 28 **B20.20**

(1) This section applies to offences under any of the following provisions of this Act, that is to say section 4(2) and (3), section 5(2) and (3), section 6(2) and section 9.

(2) Subject to subsection (3) below, in any proceedings for an offence to which this section applies it shall be a defence for the accused to prove that he neither knew of nor suspected nor had reason to suspect the existence of some fact alleged by the prosecution which it is necessary for the prosecution to prove if he is to be convicted of the offence charged.

(3) Where in any proceedings for an offence to which this section applies it is necessary, if the accused is to be convicted of the offence charged, for the prosecution to prove that some substance or product involved in the alleged offence was the controlled drug which the prosecution alleges it to have been, and it is proved that the substance or product in question was that controlled drug, the accused—

(a) shall not be acquitted of the offence charged by reason only of proving that he neither knew nor suspected nor had reason to suspect that the substance or product in question was the particular controlled drug alleged; but

(b) shall be acquitted thereof—

(i) if he proves that he neither believed nor suspected nor had reason to suspect that the substance or product in question was a controlled drug; or

(ii) if he proves that he believed the substance or product in question to be a controlled drug, or a controlled drug of a description, such that, if it had in fact been that controlled drug or a controlled drug of that description, he would not at the material time have been committing any offence to which this section applies.

(4) Nothing in this section shall prejudice any defence which it is open to a person charged with an offence to which this section applies to raise apart from this section.

In *Lambert* [2002] 2 AC 545, the House of Lords decided that the placing of a legal burden on the defence was contrary to the ECHR, Article 6. It did not issue a declaration of incompatibility, but, using the HRA 1998, s. 3, their lordships interpreted the MDA 1971, s. 28, so as to avoid incompatibility. The effect of *Lambert* seems to be that s. 28 imposes only an evidential burden upon the accused (but see further **F3.13**; and see *Carrera* [2002] EWCA Crim 2527, and consider *Keogh* [2007] 1 WLR 1500).

If the defence asserts 'that he did not know that the bag or other container which he was carrying contained a controlled drug and believed it contained a different type of article such as a video film, this defence arises under section 28(2) and not under section 28(3)' (per Lord Hutton in *Lambert* at [181], applying *Salmon v HM Advocate* [1998] Scot HC 12). The cases of *Lambert* and *Salmon* are essential reading as they lucidly explain the operation of s. 28 — a section which is often misunderstood: see *Barr* [2005] EWCA Crim 1764 (where *Lambert* was followed), and note *Carrera* [2002] EWCA Crim 2527, where the Court of Appeal said that 'following *Lambert* there may well be further debate as to the extent of the burden on the prosecution given the wording of section 28(2) and (3), but it is not necessary or appropriate to conduct that debate in order to resolve this appeal'.

Self-induced intoxication is not a relevant consideration in the exercise of the statutory defence under s. 28(2)(3)(b) (*Young* [1984] 2 All ER 164).

Section 28 does not apply to conspiracies to commit an MDA offence as they are not statutory offences created under the 1971 Act (*McGowan* [1990] Crim LR 399).

REGULATIONS AUTHORISING POSSESSION OF CONTROLLED DRUGS

B20.21 Section 7(1) of the MDA 1971 provides a general power for the Secretary of State to make regulations to except from s. 5(1) (and ss. 3(1)(a) or (b) and 4(1)(a)) controlled drugs that are specified in the regulations, and to make such other provision as he thinks fit to make lawful activity which under ss. 4(1), 5(1), and 6(1) would otherwise be unlawful (and criminal): see the Misuse of Drugs Regulations 2001 (SI 2001 No. 3998, as amended) at **B20.22**. The Secretary of State is required to exercise this power to ensure that it is not unlawful under s. 5(1) for a doctor, dentist, veterinary practitioner, veterinary surgeon, pharmacist or person lawfully conducting a retail pharmacy business to have a controlled drug in his possession for the purpose of his acting in such a capacity; similar provision is made with regard to the offence in s. 4(1) (s. 7(3)). However, that power is subject to s. 7(4), whereby the production, supply and possession of a drug may be made wholly unlawful or unlawful except for research or other special purposes or whereby the activities of practitioners, pharmacists and person lawfully conducting retail pharmacy businesses may be made unlawful except where they act under a licence or other authority from the Secretary of State. The relevant regulations are the Misuse of Drugs (Designation) Order 2001 (SI 2001 No. 3997).

Whether the accused was acting in his capacity as a medical practitioner is a matter for the jury to decide (*Abraham* [2002] EWCA Crim 2870).

The regulations contain provisions which make lawful certain acts which, otherwise, would be offences under the MDA 1971. The regulations have been heavily amended. Regulations 2 to 10 have been reproduced here (as amended). Regulations 15 to 17 provide for exemptions in relation to prescriptions. Other regulations deal with requirements as to the marking of bottles and other containers, keeping of registers and records, furnishing of information and destruction of controlled drugs. There are eight schedules.

Burden of Proof re Exceptions under Regulations The leading case is *Hunt* [1987] AC 352. A statute may place a burden of proof on the accused by implication, although it does not do so expressly (as to the significance of *Hunt* on issues of burden of proof generally, see **F3.9**). Lord Griffiths said that the MDA 1971, s. 7(1), gives the Secretary of State power to make two kinds of exceptions: **B20.22**

(a) exceptions under s. 7(1)(a), whereby the power is given to provide that it is not an offence to possess certain drugs;
(b) exceptions under s. 7(1)(b), where the power is given to clothe certain persons with immunity from what would otherwise be unlawful acts, which is achieved by the remainder of the regulations.

Lord Griffiths said (at pp. 376–7):

> These latter regulations provide special defences to what would otherwise be unlawful acts and would, I accept, place a burden upon defendants to bring themselves within the exceptions if it were necessary to do so. I say 'if it were necessary to do so' because of the extreme improbability that an exempted person would be charged with an offence.

This *obiter dictum* appears to mean that establishing the protection of any of regs. 5 to 13 places a burden of proof on the accused. Where, however, reg. 4 defines the essential ingredient of an offence, the prosecution must prove possession of the drug alleged beyond reasonable doubt. In *Hunt*, preparations of morphine containing not more than 0.2 per cent of morphine were exempted from the offence under s. 5(2), and the prosecution adduced no evidence of the composition of the preparation in question. It was held that the prosecution had failed to prove its case, and that the accused was entitled to an acquittal.

It follows that the incidence of proof may vary, depending upon which regulation is engaged. Where the accused shoulders a burden of proving a particular fact or matter, regard should be had to the decision of the House of Lords in *Lambert* [2002] 2 AC 545 (see **B20.20** and **F3.13**; and consider *Keogh* [2007] 1 WLR 1500).

Misuse of Drugs Regulations 2001, regs. 2 to 10 and schs. 1 to 5 and 8

Interpretation

2.—(1) In these Regulations, unless the context otherwise requires—
'the Act' means the Misuse of Drugs Act 1971;
'accountable officer' has the same meaning as in the Health Act 2006;
'authorised as a member of a group' means authorised by virtue of being a member of a class as respects which the Secretary of State has granted an authority under and for the

purposes of regulation 8(3), 9(3) or 10(3) which is in force, and 'his group authority', in relation to a person who is a member of such a class, means the authority so granted to that class;

'care home' in relation to—

(a) England and Wales has the same meaning as in the Care Standards Act 2000; and

(b) Scotland means the accommodation provided by a care home service;

'care home service' has the same meaning as in the Regulation of Care (Scotland) Act 2001;

'clinical management plan' has the same meaning as in the Prescription Only Medicines (Human Use) Order 1997;

'the Common Services Agency for the health service' means the body established under section 10 of the National Health Service (Scotland) Act 1978;

'document' means anything in which information of any description is recorded (within the meaning of the Civil Evidence Act 1995);

'equivalent body' means a Local Health Board in Wales, a Health Board in Scotland or the Northern Ireland Central Services Agency for the Health and Social Services in Northern Ireland;

'exempt product' means a preparation or other product consisting of one or more component parts, any of which contains a controlled drug, where—

(a) the preparation or other product is not designed for administration of the controlled drug to a human being or animal;

(b) the controlled drug in any component part is packaged in such a form, or in combination with other active or inert substances in such a manner, that it cannot be recovered by readily applicable means or in a yield which constitutes a risk to health; and

(c) no one component part of the product or preparation contains more than one milligram of the controlled drug or one microgram in the case of lysergide or any other N-alkyl derivative of lysergamide;

'Health Board' means a board constituted under section 2 of the National Health Service (Scotland) Act 1978;

'health prescription' means a prescription issued by a doctor or a dentist under the National Health Service Act 1977, the National Health Service (Scotland) Act 1978, the Health and Personal Social Services (Northern Ireland) Order 1972 or the National Health Service (Isle of Man) Acts 1948 to 1979 (Acts of Tynwald) or upon a form issued by a local authority for use in connection with the health service of that authority;

'installation manager' and 'offshore installation' have the same meanings as in the Mineral Workings (Offshore Installations) Act 1971;

'Local Health Board' means a Local Health Board established in accordance with section 16BA of the National Health Service Act 1977;

'master' and 'seamen' have the same meanings as in the Merchant Shipping Act 1995;

'medicinal product' has the same meaning as in the Medicines Act 1968;

'NHS Business Services Authority' means the special health authority established under Article 2 of the NHS Business Services Authority (Awdurdod Gwasanaethau Busnes-y-GIG) (Establishment and Constitution) Order 2005;

'the Northern Ireland Central Services Agency for the Health and Social Services' means the body established under Article 26 of the Health and Personal Social Services (Northern Ireland) Order 1972;

'nurse independent prescriber' has the same meaning as in the Prescription Only Medicines (Human Use) Order 1997, and such a person may only prescribe controlled drugs in accordance with regulation 6B;

'officer of customs and excise' means an officer within the meaning of the Customs and Excise Management Act 1979;

'operating department practitioner' means a person who is registered under the Health Professions Order 2001 as an operating department practitioner;

'patient group direction' has the same meaning as in the Prescription Only Medicines (Human Use) Order 1997;

'pharmacist' has the same meaning as in the Medicines Act 1968;

'prescriber identification number' means the number recorded against a person's name by the relevant National Health Service agency for the purposes of that person's private prescribing;

'prescription' means a prescription issued by a doctor for the medical treatment of a single individual, by a supplementary prescriber for the medical treatment of a single individual; by a nurse independent prescriber for the medical treatment of a single individual, by a dentist for the dental treatment of a single individual or by a veterinary surgeon or veterinary practitioner for the purposes of animal treatment;

'Primary Care Trust' means a Primary Care Trust established under section 16A of the National Health Service Act 1977;

'private prescribing' means issuing prescriptions other than health prescriptions, {or veterinary prescriptions};

'professional register' means the register maintained by the Nursing and Midwifery Council under article 5 of the Nursing and Midwifery Order 2001;

'professional registration number' means the number recorded against a person's name in the register of any body that licenses or regulates any profession of which that person is a member;

'register' means either a bound book, which does not include any form of loose leaf register or card index, or a computerised system which is in accordance with best practice guidance endorsed by the Secretary of State under section 2 of the National Health Service Act 1977;

'registered chiropodist' has the same meaning as in the Prescription Only Medicines (Human Use) Order 1997;

'registered midwife' has the same meaning as in the Prescription Only Medicines (Human Use) Order 1997;

'registered nurse' has the same meaning as in the Prescription Only Medicines (Human Use) Order 1997;

'registered occupational therapist' has the same meaning as in the Prescription Only Medicines (Human Use) Order 1997;

'registered optometrist' has the same meaning as in the Prescription Only Medicines (Human Use) Order 1997;

'registered orthoptist' has the same meaning as in the Prescription Only Medicines (Human Use) Order 1997;

'registered orthotist and prosthetist' has the same meaning as in the Prescription Only Medicines (Human Use) Order 1997;

'registered paramedic' has the same meaning as in the Prescription Only Medicines (Human Use) Order 1997;

'registered pharmacy' has the same meaning as in the Medicines Act 1968;

'registered physiotherapist' has the same meaning as in the Prescription Only Medicines (Human Use) Order 1997;

'registered radiographer' has the same meaning as in the Prescription Only Medicines (Human Use) Order 1997;

'relevant National Health Service agency' means, for England and Wales, the NHS Business Services Authority; for Scotland, the Common Services Agency for the health service; and for Northern Ireland, the Northern Ireland Central Services Agency for the Health and Social Services;

'retail dealer' means a person lawfully conducting a retail pharmacy business or a pharmacist engaged in supplying drugs to the public at a health centre within the meaning of the Medicines Act 1968;

'supplementary prescriber' has the same meaning as in the Prescription Only Medicines (Human Use) Order 1997;

'veterinary prescription' means a prescription issued by a veterinary surgeon or veterinary practitioner for the purposes of animal treatment;

'wholesale dealer' means a person who carries on the business of selling drugs to persons who buy to sell again.

(2) In these Regulations any reference to a regulation or schedule shall be construed as a reference to a regulation contained in these Regulations or, as the case may be, to a schedule to these Regulations, and any reference in a regulation or schedule to a paragraph shall be construed as a reference to a paragraph of that regulation or schedule.

(3) Nothing in these Regulations shall be construed as derogating from any power or immunity of the Crown, its servants or agents.

Specification of controlled drugs for purposes of Regulations

3. Schedules 1 to 5 shall have effect for the purpose of specifying the controlled drugs to which certain provisions of these Regulations apply.

Exceptions for drugs in Schedules 4 and 5 and poppy-straw

4.—(1) Section 3(1) of the Act (which prohibits the importation and exportation of controlled drugs) shall not have effect in relation to the drugs specified in Schedule 5.

(2) The application of section 3(1) of the Act, in so far as it creates an offence, and the application of sections 50(1) to (4), 68(2) and (3) or 170 of the Customs and Excise Management Act 1979, in so far as they apply in relation to a prohibition or restriction on importation or exportation having effect by virtue of section 3 of the Act, are hereby excluded in the case of importation or exportation by any person for administration to himself of any drug specified in Part II of Schedule 4 which is contained in a medicinal product.

(3) Section 5(1) of the Act (which prohibits the possession of controlled drugs) shall not have effect in relation to—

(a) any drug specified in Part II of Schedule 4 which is contained in a medicinal product;

(b) the drugs specified in Schedule 5.

(4) Sections 4(1)(which prohibits the production and supply of controlled drugs) and 5(1) of the Act shall not have effect in relation to poppy-straw.

(5) Sections 3(1), 4(1) and 5(1) of the Act shall not have effect in relation to any exempt product.

Exceptions for drugs in Schedule 1

4A.—(1) Section 5(1) of the Act (which prohibits the possession of controlled drugs) shall not have effect in relation to a fungus (of any kind) which contains psilocin or an ester of psilocin where that fungus—

(a) is growing uncultivated;

(b) is picked by a person already in lawful possession of it for the purpose of delivering it as soon as is reasonably practicable into the custody of a person lawfully entitled to take custody of it and it remains in that person's possession for and in accordance with that purpose;

(c) is picked for either of the purposes specified in paragraph (2) and is held for and in accordance with the purpose specified in paragraph (2)(b), either by the person who picked it or by another person; or

(d) is picked for the purpose specified in paragraph (2)(b) and is held for and in accordance with the purpose in paragraph (2)(a), either by the person who picked it or by another person.

(2) The purposes specified for the purposes of this paragraph are—

(a) the purpose of delivering the fungus as soon as is reasonably practicable into the custody of a person lawfully entitled to take custody of it; and

(b) the purpose of destroying the fungus as soon as is reasonably practicable.

Licences to produce etc. controlled drugs

5. Where any person is authorised by a licence of the Secretary of State issued under this regulation and for the time being in force to produce, supply, offer to supply or have in his possession any controlled drug, it shall not by virtue of section 4(1) or 5(1) of the Act be unlawful for that person to produce, supply, offer to supply or have in his possession that drug in accordance with the terms of the licence and in compliance with any conditions attached to the licence.

General authority to supply and possess

6.—(1) Notwithstanding the provisions of section 4(1)(b) of the Act, any person who is lawfully in possession of a controlled drug may supply that drug to the person from whom he obtained it.

(2) Notwithstanding the provisions of section 4(1)(b) of the Act, any person who has in his possession a drug specified in Schedule 2, 3, 4 or 5 which has been supplied by or on the prescription of a practitioner, a registered nurse, a supplementary prescriber or a person specified in Schedule 8 for the treatment of that person, or of a person whom he represents, may supply that drug to any doctor, dentist or pharmacist for the purpose of destruction.

(3) Notwithstanding the provisions of section 4(1)(b) of the Act, any person who is lawfully in possession of a drug specified in Schedule 2, 3, 4 or 5 which has been supplied by or on the prescription of a veterinary practitioner or veterinary surgeon for the treatment of animals may supply that drug to any veterinary practitioner, veterinary surgeon or pharmacist for the purpose of destruction.

(4) It shall not by virtue of section 4(1)(b) or 5(1) of the Act be unlawful for any person in respect of whom a licence has been granted and is in force under section 16(1) of the Wildlife and Countryside Act 1981 to supply, offer to supply or have in his possession any drug specified in Schedule 2 or 3 for the purposes for which that licence was granted.

(5) Notwithstanding the provisions of section 4(1)(b) of the Act, any of the persons specified in paragraph (7) may supply any controlled drug to any person who may lawfully have that drug in his possession.

(6) Notwithstanding the provisions of section 5(1) of the Act, any of the persons so specified may have any controlled drug in his possession.

(7) The persons referred to in paragraphs (5) and (6) are
- (a) a constable when acting in the course of his duty as such;
- (b) a person engaged in the business of a carrier when acting in the course of that business;
- (c) a person engaged in the business of a postal operator (within the meaning of the Postal Services Act 2000) when acting in the course of that business;
- (d) an officer of customs and excise when acting in the course of his duty as such;
- (e) a person engaged in the work of any laboratory to which the drug has been sent for forensic examination when acting in the course of his duty as a person so engaged;
- (f) a person engaged in conveying the drug to a person who may lawfully have that drug in his possession.

Supply of articles for administering or preparing controlled drugs

6A.—(1) Notwithstanding the provisions of section 9A(1) and (3) of the Act, any of the persons specified in paragraph (2) may, when acting in their capacity as such, supply or offer to supply the following articles—
- (a) a swab;
- (b) utensils for the preparation of a controlled drug;
- (c) citric acid;
- (d) a filter;
- (e) ampoules of water for injection, only when supplied or offered for supply in accordance with the Medicines Act 1968 and of any instrument which is in force thereunder.
- (f) ascorbic acid

(2) The persons referred to in paragraph (1) are—
- (a) a practitioner;
- (b) a pharmacist;
- (c) a person employed or engaged in the lawful provision of drug treatment services.
- (d) a supplementary prescriber acting under and in accordance with the terms of a clinical management plan.

Authority for Nurse Independent Prescribers

6B. A nurse independent prescriber may only prescribe—
- (a) diamorphine, morphine or oxycodone for use in palliative care;
- (b) buprenorphine or fentanyl for transdermal use in palliative care;
- (c) diamorphine or morphine for pain relief in respect of suspected myocardial infarction or for relief of acute or severe pain after trauma including in either case post-operative pain relief;
- (d) chlordiazepoxide hydrochloride or diazepam for treatment of initial or acute withdrawal symptoms caused by the withdrawal of alcohol from persons habituated to it;
- (e) codeine phosphate, dihydrocodeine tartrate or co-phenotrope; and
- (f) diazepam, lorazepam or midazolam for use in palliative care or treatment of tonic-clonic seizures.

Administration of drugs in Schedules 2, 3, 4 and 5

7.—(1) Any person may administer to another any drug specified in Schedule 5.

(2) A doctor or dentist may administer to a patient any drug specified in Schedule 2, 3 or 4.

(3) Any person other than a doctor or dentist may administer to a patient, in accordance with the directions of a doctor or dentist, any drug specified in Schedule 2, 3 or 4.

(4) Notwithstanding the provisions of paragraph (3), a nurse independent prescriber may administer to a patient, without the directions of a doctor or dentist, any controlled drug which she may prescribe under regulation 6B provided it is administered for a purpose for which it may be prescribed under that regulation.

(5) Notwithstanding the provisions of paragraph (3), any person may administer to a patient in accordance with the specific directions of an a nurse independent prescriber any controlled drug which the nurse independent prescriber may prescribe under regulation 6B provided it is administered for a purpose for which it may be prescribed under that regulation.

(6) Notwithstanding the provisions of paragraph (3), a supplementary prescriber acting under and in accordance with the terms of a clinical management plan may administer to a patient, without the directions of a doctor or dentist, any drug specified in Schedule 2, 3 or 4.

(7) Notwithstanding the provisions of paragraph (3), any person may administer to a patient, in accordance with the directions of a supplementary prescriber acting under and in accordance with the terms of a clinical management plan, any drug specified in Schedule 2, 3 or 4.

Production and supply of drugs in Schedules 2 and 5

8.—(1) Notwithstanding the provisions of section 4(1)(a) of the Act—

(a) a practitioner or pharmacist, acting in his capacity as such, may manufacture or compound any drug specified in Schedule 2 or 5;

(b) a person lawfully conducting a retail pharmacy business and acting in his capacity as such may, at the registered pharmacy at which he carries on that business, manufacture or compound any drug specified in Schedule 2 or 5.

(2) Notwithstanding the provisions of section 4(1)(b) of the Act, any of the following persons, that is to say—

(a) a practitioner;

(b) a pharmacist;

(c) a person lawfully conducting a retail pharmacy business;

(d) the person in charge or acting person in charge of a hospital or care home which is wholly or mainly maintained by a public authority out of public funds or by a charity or by voluntary subscriptions;

(e) in the case of such a drug supplied to her by a person responsible for the dispensing and supply of medicines at the hospital or care home, the senior registered nurse or acting senior registered nurse for the time being in charge of a ward, theatre or other department in such a hospital or care home as aforesaid;

(ea) in the case of such a drug supplied to him by a person responsible for the dispensing and supply of medicines at a hospital, an operating department practitioner practising in that hospital;

(f) a person who is in charge of a laboratory the recognised activities of which consist in, or include, the conduct of scientific education or research and which is attached to a university, university college or such a hospital as aforesaid or to any other institution approved for the purpose under this sub-paragraph by the Secretary of State;

(g) a public analyst appointed under section 27 of the Food Safety Act 1990;

(h) a sampling officer within the meaning of Schedule 3 to the Medicines Act 1968;

(i) a person employed or engaged in connection with a scheme for testing the quality or amount of the drugs, preparations and appliances supplied under the National Health Service Act 1977 or the National Health Service (Scotland) Act 1978 and the regulations made thereunder;

(j) a person authorised by the Pharmaceutical Society of Great Britain for the purposes of section 108 or 109 of the Medicines Act 1968,

(k) a supplementary prescriber acting under and in accordance with the terms of a clinical management plan,

may, when acting in his capacity as such, supply or offer to supply any drug specified in Schedule 2 or 5 to any person who may lawfully have that drug in his possession, except that nothing in this paragraph authorises—

(i) the person in charge or acting person in charge of a hospital or care home, having a pharmacist responsible for the dispensing and supply of medicines, to supply or offer to supply any drug;

(ii) a senior registered nurse or acting senior registered nurse for the time being in charge of a ward, theatre or other department to supply any drug otherwise than for administration to a patient in that ward, theatre or department in accordance with the directions of a doctor, dentist, supplementary prescriber acting under and in accordance with the terms of a clinical management plan or, subject to paragraph (2A), a nurse independent prescriber; or

(iii) an operating department practitioner to supply any drug otherwise than for administration to a patient in a ward, theatre or other department in accordance with the directions of a doctor, dentist, supplementary prescriber acting under and in accordance with the terms of a clinical management plan or, subject to paragraph (2A), a nurse independent prescriber.

(2A) The directions given by a nurse independent prescriber referred to in paragraph (2)(ii) and (iii) shall relate only to a controlled drug which she may prescribe under regulation 6B and a purpose for which it may be prescribed under that regulation.

(3) Notwithstanding the provisions of section 4(1)(b) of the Act, a person who is authorised as a member of a group may, under and in accordance with the terms of his group authority and in compliance with any conditions attached thereto, supply or offer to supply any drug specified in Schedule 2 or 5 to any person who may lawfully have that drug in his possession.

(4) Notwithstanding the provisions of section 4(1)(b) of the Act, a person who is authorised by a written authority issued by the Secretary of State under and for the purposes of this paragraph and for the time being in force may, at the premises specified in that authority and in compliance with any conditions so specified, supply or offer to supply any drug specified in Schedule 5 to any person who may lawfully have that drug in his possession.

(5) Notwithstanding the provisions of section 4(1)(b) of the Act—

(a) the owner of a ship, or the master of a ship which does not carry a doctor among the seamen employed in it; or

(b) the installation manager of an offshore installation,

may supply or offer to supply any drug specified in Schedule 2 or 5—

(i) for the purpose of compliance with any of the provisions specified in paragraph (6), to any person on that ship or installation;

(ii) to any person who may lawfully supply that drug to him;

(iii) to any constable for the purpose of the destruction of that drug.

(6) The provisions referred to in paragraph (5) are any provision of, or of any instrument which is in force under—

(a) the Mineral Workings (Offshore Installations) Act 1971;

(b the Health and Safety at Work etc. Act 1974 or

(c) the Merchant Shipping Act 1995.

(7) Notwithstanding the provisions of section 4(1)(b) of the Act, a nurse independent prescriber may, when acting in her capacity as such, supply or offer to supply—

(a) codeine phosphate, dihydrocodeine tartrate and co-phenotrope;

(b) diamorphine and morphine for pain relief in respect of suspected myocardial infarction or for relief of acute or severe pain after trauma including in either case post-operative pain relief;

(c) diamorphine, morphine and oxycodone for use in palliative care; and

(d) fentanyl for transdermal use in palliative care,

to any person who may lawfully have any of these drugs in his possession.

(8) Notwithstanding the provisions of section 4(1)(b) of the Act—

(a) a registered nurse, when acting in her capacity as such, may supply or offer to supply, under and in accordance with the terms of a patient group direction, diamorphine for the treatment of cardiac pain to a person admitted as a patient to a coronary care unit or an accident and emergency department of a hospital;

(b) a registered nurse or a person specified in Schedule 8 may, when acting in their capacity as such, supply or offer to supply, under and in accordance with the terms of a patient group direction, any drug specified in Schedule 5 to any person who may lawfully have that drug in his possession.

Production and supply of drugs in Schedules 3 and 4

9.—(1) Notwithstanding the provisions of section 4(1)(a) of the Act—

(a) a practitioner or pharmacist, acting in his capacity as such, may manufacture or compound any drug specified in Schedule 3 or 4;

(b) a person lawfully conducting a retail pharmacy business and acting in his capacity as such may, at the registered pharmacy at which he carries on that business, manufacture or compound any drug specified in Schedule 3 or 4;

(c) a person who is authorised by a written authority issued by the Secretary of State under and for the purposes of this sub-paragraph and for the time being in force may, at the premises specified in that authority and in compliance with any conditions so specified, produce any drug specified in Schedule 3 or 4.

(2) Notwithstanding the provisions of section 4(1)(b) of the Act, any of the following persons, that is to say—

(a) a practitioner;

(b) a pharmacist;

(c) a person lawfully conducting a retail pharmacy business;

(d) a person in charge of a laboratory the recognised activities of which consist in, or include, the conduct of scientific education or research;

(e) a public analyst appointed under section 27 of the Food Safety Act 1990;

(f) a sampling officer within the meaning of Schedule 3 to the Medicines Act 1968;

(g) a person employed or engaged in connection with a scheme for testing the quality or amount of the drugs, preparations and appliances supplied under the National Health Service Act 1977 or the National Health Service (Scotland) Act 1978 and the regulations made thereunder;

(h) a person authorised by the Pharmaceutical Society of Great Britain for the purposes of section 108 or 109 of the Medicines Act 1968,

(i) a supplementary prescriber acting under and in accordance with the terms of a clinical management plan,

may, when acting in his capacity as such, supply or offer to supply any drug specified in Schedule 3 or 4 to any person who may lawfully have that drug in his possession.

(3) Notwithstanding the provisions of section 4(1)(b) of the Act—

(a) a person who is authorised as a member of a group, under and in accordance with the terms of his group authority and in compliance with any conditions attached thereto;

(b) the person in charge or acting person in charge of a hospital or care home;

(c) in the case of such a drug supplied to her by a person responsible for the dispensing and supply of medicines at that hospital or care home, the senior registered nurse or acting senior registered nurse for the time being in charge of a ward, theatre or other department in a hospital or care home,

(d) in the case of such a drug supplied to him by a person responsible for the dispensing and supply of medicines at a hospital, an operating department practitioner practising in that hospital;

may, when acting in his capacity as such, supply or offer to supply any drug specified in Schedule 3, or any drug specified in Schedule 4 which is contained in a medicinal product, to any person who may lawfully have that drug in his possession, except that nothing in this paragraph authorises—

(i) the person in charge or acting person in charge of a hospital or care home, having a pharmacist responsible for the dispensing and supply of medicines, to supply or offer to supply any drug;

(ii) a senior registered nurse or acting senior registered nurse for the time being in charge of a ward, theatre or other department to supply any drug otherwise than for administration to a patient in that ward, theatre or department in accordance with the directions of a doctor, dentist, supplementary prescriber acting under and in accordance with the terms of a clinical management plan or, subject to paragraph (2A), a nurse independent prescriber; or

(iii) an operating department practitioner to supply any drug otherwise than for administration to a patient in a ward, theatre or other department in accordance with the directions of a doctor, dentist, supplementary prescriber acting under and in accordance with the terms of a clinical management plan or, subject to paragraph (2A), a nurse independent prescriber.

(3A) The directions given by a nurse independent prescriber referred to in paragraph (2)(ii) and (iii) shall relate only to a controlled drug which she may prescribe under regulation 6B and a purpose for which it may be prescribed under that regulation.

(4) Notwithstanding the provisions of section 4(1)(b) of the Act—

(a) a person who is authorised by a written authority issued by the Secretary of State under and for the purposes of this sub-paragraph and for the time being in force may, at the premises specified in that authority and in compliance with any conditions so specified, supply or offer to supply any drug specified in Schedule 3 or 4 to any person who may lawfully have that drug in his possession;

(b) a person who is authorised under paragraph (1)(c) may supply or offer to supply any drug which he may, by virtue of being so authorised, lawfully produce to any person who may lawfully have that drug in his possession.

(5) Notwithstanding the provisions of section 4(1)(b) of the Act—

(a) the owner of a ship, or the master of a ship which does not carry a doctor among the seamen employed in it;

(b) the installation manager of an offshore installation,

may supply or offer to supply any drug specified in Schedule 3, or any drug specified in Schedule 4 which is contained in a medicinal product—

(i) for the purpose of compliance with any of the provisions specified in regulation 8(6), to any person on that ship or installation; or

(ii) to any person who may lawfully supply that drug to him.

(6) Notwithstanding the provisions of section 4(1)(b) of the Act, a person in charge of a laboratory may, when acting in his capacity as such, supply or offer to supply any drug specified in Schedule 3 which is required for use as a buffering agent in chemical analysis to any person who may lawfully have that drug in his possession.

(7) Notwithstanding the provisions of section 4(1)(b) of the Act, a nurse independent prescriber may, when acting in her capacity as such, supply or offer to supply—

(a) diazepam, lorazepam and midazolam for use in palliative care or treatment of tonic-clonic seizures;

(b) buprenorphine for transdermal use in palliative care; and

(c) chlordiazepoxide hydrochloride and diazepam for treatment of initial or acute withdrawal symptoms caused by the withdrawal of alcohol from persons habituated to it,

to any person who may lawfully have any of these drugs in his possession.

(8) Notwithstanding the provisions of section 4(1)(b) of the Act, a registered nurse or a person specified in Schedule 8, when acting in their capacity as such, may supply or offer to supply, under and in accordance with the terms of a patient group direction, any drug specified in Schedule 4 [or, with effect from 1 January 2008, Midazolam] to any person who may lawfully have that drug in his possession, except that this paragraph shall not have effect in the case of—

(a) the supply or offer to supply of any of the anabolic steroid drugs specified in Part II of Schedule 4; and

(b) any drug or preparation which is designed for administration by injection and which is to be used for the purpose of treating a person who is addicted to a drug;

(c) for the purposes of paragraph (b) above, a person shall be regarded as being addicted to a drug if, and only if, he has as a result of repeated administration become so dependent upon the drug that he has an overpowering desire for the administration of it to be continued.

Possession of drugs in Schedules 2, 3 and 4

10.—(1) Notwithstanding the provisions of section 5(1) of the Act—

(a) a person specified in one of sub-paragraphs (a) to (k) of regulation 8(2) may have in his possession any drug specified in Schedule 2;

(b) a person specified in one of sub-paragraphs (a) to (i) of regulation 9(2) may have in his possession any drug specified in Schedule 3 or 4;

(c) a person specified in regulation 9(3)(b) to (d) or (6) may have in his possession any drug specified in Schedule 3;

(d) a person specified in regulation 9(3)(b) to (d) may have in his possession any drug specified in Part I of Schedule 4 which is contained in a medicinal product;

(e) a person specified in regulation 9(7) may have in her possession any drug specified in that regulation in accordance with the conditions specified in that regulation;

for the purpose of acting in his capacity as such a person, except that nothing in this paragraph authorises—

(i) a person specified in sub-paragraph (e) or (ea) of regulation 8(2);

(ii) a person specified in sub-paragraph (c) or (d) of regulation 9(3); or

(iii) a person specified in regulation 9(6),

to have in his possession any drug other than such a drug as is mentioned in the paragraph or sub-paragraph in question specifying him.

(2) Notwithstanding the provisions of section 5(1) of the Act, a person may have in his

possession any drug specified in Schedule 2, 3 or Part I of Schedule 4 for administration for medical, dental or veterinary purposes in accordance with the directions of a practitioner, a supplementary prescriber acting under and in accordance with the terms of a clinical management plan or a nurse independent prescriber, except that this paragraph shall not have effect in the case of a person to whom the drug has been supplied by or on the prescription of a doctor, a supplementary prescriber or a nurse independent prescriber, if—

(a) that person was then being supplied with any controlled drug by or on the prescription of another doctor, another supplementary prescriber or another nurse independent prescriber and failed to disclose that fact to the first mentioned doctor, supplementary prescriber or nurse independent prescriber before the supply by him or on his prescription; or

(b) that or any other person on his behalf made a declaration or statement, which was false in any particular, for the purpose of obtaining the supply or prescription.

(3) Notwithstanding the provisions of section 5(1) of the Act, a person who is authorised as a member of a group may, under and in accordance with the terms of his group authority and in compliance with any conditions attached thereto, have any drug specified in Schedule 2, 3 or Part I of Schedule 4 in his possession.

(4) Notwithstanding the provisions of section 5(1) of the Act—

(a) a person who is authorised by a written authority issued by the Secretary of State under and for the purposes of this sub-paragraph and for the time being in force may, at the premises specified in that authority and in compliance with any conditions so specified, have in his possession any drug specified in Schedule 3 or 4;

(b) a person who is authorised under regulation 9(1)(c) may have in his possession any drug which he may, by virtue of being so authorised, lawfully produce;

(c) a person who is authorised under regulation 9(4)(a) may have in his possession any drug which he may, by virtue of being so authorised, lawfully supply or offer to supply.

(5) Notwithstanding the provisions of section 5(1) of the Act—

(a) any person may have in his possession any drug specified in Schedule 2, 3 or Part I of Schedule 4 for the purpose of compliance with any of the provisions specified in regulation 8(6);

(b) the master of a foreign ship which is in a port in Great Britain may have in his possession any drug specified in Schedule 2, 3 or Part I of Schedule 4 so far as necessary for the equipment of the ship.

(6) The foregoing provisions of this regulation are without prejudice to the provisions of regulation 4(3)(a).

Schedule 1

Controlled Drugs Subject to the Requirements of Regulations 14, 15, 16, 18, 19, 20, 23, 26 and 27

1. The following substances and products, namely:—

(a) Bufotenine
Cannabinol
Cannabinol derivatives not being dronabinol or its stereoisomers
Cannabis and cannabis resin
Cathinone
Coca leaf
Concentrate of poppy-straw
Eticyclidine
Etryptamine
Fungus (of any kind) which contains psilocin or an ester of psilocin
Lysergamide
Lysergide and otherN-alkyl derivatives of lysergamide
Mescaline
Methcathinone
Psilocin
Raw opium
Rolicyclidine
Tenocyclidine
4-Bromo-2,5-dimethoxy-a-methylphenethylamine

N,N-Diethyltryptamine
N,N-Dimethyltryptamine
2,5-Dimethoxy-a,4-dimethylphenethylamine
N-Hydroxy-tenamphetamine
4-Methyl-aminorex

(b) any compound (not being a compound for the time being specified in sub-paragraph (a) above) structurally derived from tryptamine or from a ring-hydroxy tryptamine by substitution at the nitrogen atom of the sidechain with one or more alkyl substituents but no other substituent;

(c) the following phenethylamine derivatives, namely—
Allyl (a-methyl-3,4-methylenedioxyphenethyl) amine
2-Amino-1-(2,5-dimethoxy-4-methylphenyl) ethanol
2-Amino-1-(3,4-dimethoxyphenyl) ethanol
Benzyl(a-methyl-3,4-methylenedioxyphenethyl) amine
4-Bromo-b,2,5-trimethoxyphenethylamine
N-(4-sec-Butylthio-2,5-dimethoxyphenethyl) hydroxylamine
Cyclopropylmethyl(a-methyl-3,4-methylenedioxyphenethyl) amine
2-(4,7-Dimethoxy-2,3-dihydro-1H-indan-5-yl) ethylamine
2-(4,7-Dimethoxy-2,3-dihydro-1H-indan-5-yl)-1-methylethylamine
2-(2,5-Dimethoxy-4-methylphenyl) cyclopropylamine
2-(1,4-Dimethoxy-2-naphthyl) ethylamine
2-(1,4-Dimethoxy-2-naphthyl)-1-methylethylamine
N-(2,5-Dimethoxy-4-propylthiophenethyl)hydroxylamine
2-(1,4-Dimethoxy-5,6,7,8-tetrahydro-2-naphthyl) ethylamine
2-(1,4-Dimethoxy-5,6,7,8-tetrahydro-2-naphthyl)-1-methylethylamine
a,a-Dimethyl-3,4-methylenedioxyphenethylamine
a,a-Dimethyl-3,4-methylenedioxyphenethyl(methyl) amine
Dimethyl (a-methyl-3,4-methylenedioxyphenethyl) amine
N-(4-Ethylthio-2,5-dimethoxyphenethyl) hydroxylamine
4-Iodo-2,5-dimethoxy-a-methylphenethyl (dimethyl) amine
2-(1,4-Methano-5,8-dimethoxy-1,2,3,4-tetrahydro-6-naphthyl) ethylamine
2-(1,4-Methano-5,8-dimethoxy-1,2,3,4-tetrahydro-6-naphthyl)-1-methylethylamine
2-(5-Methoxy-2,2-dimethyl-2,3-dihydrobenzo[b]furan-6-yl)-1-methylethylamine
2-Methoxyethyl (a-methyl-3,4-methylenedioxyphenethyl) amine
2-(5-Methoxy-2-methyl-2,3-dihydrobenzo[b]furan-6-yl)-1-methylethylamine
b-Methoxy-3,4-methylenedioxyphenethylamine
1-(3,4-Methylenedioxybenzyl) butyl (ethyl) amine
1-(3,4-Methylenedioxybenzyl) butyl(methyl) amine
2-(a-Methyl-3,4-methylenedioxyphenethylamino) ethanol
a-Methyl-3,4-methylenedioxyphenethyl(prop-2-ynyl) amine
N-Methyl-N-(a-methyl-3,4-methylenedioxyphenethyl) hydroxylamine
O-Methyl-N-(a-methyl-3,4-methylenedioxyphenethyl) hydroxylamine
a-Methyl-4-(methylthio) phenethylamine
b,3,4,5-Tetramethoxyphenethylamine
b,2,5-Trimethoxy-4-methylphenethylamine

(d) any compound (not being methoxyphenamine or a compound for the time being specified in sub-paragraph (a) above) structurally derived from phenethylamine, an N-alkylphenethylamine, a-methylphenethylamine, an N-alkyl-a-methylphenethylamine, a-ethylphenethylamine, or an N-alkyl-a-ethylphenethylamine by substitution in the ring to any extent with alkyl, alkoxy, alkylenedioxy or halide substitutents, whether or not further substituted in the ring by one or more other univalent substituents;

(e) any compound (not being a compound for the time being specified in Schedule 2) structurally derived from fentanyl by modification in any of the following ways, that is to say —
(i) by replacement of the phenyl portion of the phenethyl group by any heteromonocycle whether or not further substituted in the heterocycle;
(ii) by substitution in the phenethyl group with alkyl, alkenyl, alkoxy, hydroxy, halogeno, haloalkyl, amino or nitro groups;
(iii) by substitution in the piperidine ring with alkyl or alkenyl groups;

(iv) by substitution in the aniline ring with alkyl, alkoxy, alkylenedioxy, halogeno or haloalkyl groups;
(v) by substitution at the 4-position of the piperidine ring with any alkoxycarbonyl or alkoxyalkyl or acyloxy group;
(vi) by replacement of the N-propionyl group by another acyl group;

(f) any compound (not being a compound for the time being specified in Schedule 2) structurally derived from pethidine by modification in any of the following ways, that is to say—
(i) by replacement of the l-methyl group by an acyl, alkyl whether or not unsaturated, benzyl or phenethyl group, whether or not further substituted;
(ii) by substitution in the piperidine ring with alkyl or alkenyl groups or with a propano bridge, whether or not further substituted;
(iii) by substitution in the 4-phenyl ring with alkyl, alkoxy, aryloxy, halogeno or haloalkyl groups;
(iv) by replacement of the 4-ethoxycarbonyl by any other alkoxycarbonyl or any alkoxyalkyl or acyloxy group;
(v) by formation of an N-oxide or of a quaternary base.

2. Any stereoisomeric form of a substance specified in paragraph 1.
3. Any ester or ether of a substance specified in paragraph 1 or 2.
4. Any salt of a substance specified in any of paragraphs 1 to 3.
5. Any preparation or other product containing a substance or product specified in any of paragraphs 1 to 4, not being a preparation specified in Schedule 5.

Schedule 2

Controlled Drugs Subject to the Requirements of Regulations 14, 15, 16, 18, 19, 20, 21, 23, 26 and 27

1. The following substances and products, namely:

Acetorphine
Alfentanil
Allylprodine
Alphacetylmethadol
Alphameprodine
Alphamethadol
Alphaprodine
a-Methylphenethylhydroxylamine
Anileridine
Benzethidine
Benzylmorphine (3-benzylmorphine)
Betacetylmethadol
Betameprodine
Betamethadol
Betaprodine
Bezitramide
Carfentanil
Clonitazene
Cocaine
Desomorphine
Dextromoramide
Diamorphine
Diampromide
Diethylthiambutene
Difenoxin
Dihydrocodeinone O-carboxymethyl-oxime
Dihydroetorphine
Dihydromorphine
Dimenoxadole
Dimepheptanol
Dimethylthiambutene
Dioxaphetyl butyrate
Diphenoxylate
Dipipanone
Dronabinol
Drotebanol
Ecgonine, and any derivative of ecgonine which is convertible to ecgonine or to cocaine
Ethylmethylthiambutene
Etonitazene
Etorphine
Etoxeridine
Fentanyl
Furethidine
Hydrocodone
Hydromorphinol
Hydromorphone
Hydroxypethidine
Isomethadone
Ketobemidone
Levomethorphan
Levomoramide
Levophenacylmorphan
Levorphanol
Lofentanil
Medicinal opium
Metazocine
Methadone
Methadyl acetate
methobromide, morphine N-oxide and other pentavalent nitrogen morphine derivatives

Methyldesorphine
Methyldihydromorphine (6-methyldihydromorphine)
Metopon
Morpheridine
Morphine
Morphine methobromide, morphine N-oxide and other pentavalent nitrogen morphine derivatives
Myrophine
Nicomorphine
Noracymethadol
Norlevorphanol
Normethadone
Normorphine
Norpipanone
Oxycodone
Oxymorphone
Pethidine
Phenadoxone
Phenampromide
Phenazocine
Phencyclidine
Phenomorphan
Phenoperidine
Piminodine
Piritramide
Proheptazine
Properidine
Racemethorphan
Racemoramide
Racemorphan
Remifentanil
Sufentanil
Thebacon
Thebaine
Tilidate
Trimeperidine
Zipeprol
4-Cyano-2-dimethylamino-4,4-diphenylbutane
4-Cyano-1-methyl-4- phenylpiperidine
1-Methyl-4-phenylpiperidine-4-carboxylic acid
2-Methyl-3-morpholino-1,1-diphenyl-propane- carboxylic acid α-Methylphenethylhydroxlamine
4-Phenylpiperidine-4-carboxylic acid ethyl ester

2. Any stereoisomeric form of a substance specified in paragraph 1 not being dextromethorphan or dextrorphan.
3. Any ester or ether of a substance specified in paragraph 1 or 2, not being a substance specified in paragraph 6.
4. Any salt of a substance specified in any of paragraphs 1 to 3.
5. Any preparation or other product containing a substance or product specified in any of paragraphs 1 to 4, not being a preparation specified in Schedule 5.
6. The following substances and products, namely—

Acetyldihydrocodeine
Amphetamine
Codeine
Dextropropoxyphene
Dihydrocodeine
Ethylmorphine (3-ethylmorphine)
Fenethylline
Glutethimide
Lefetamine
Mecloqualone
Methaqualone
Methylamphetamine
Methylphenidate
Nicocodine
Nicodicodine (6-nicotinoyldihydrocodeine)
Norcodeine
Phenmetrazine
Pholcodine
Propiram
Quinalbarbitone

7. Any stereoisomeric form of a substance specified in paragraph 6.
8. Any salt of a substance specified in paragraph 6 or 7.
9. Any preparation or other product containing a substance or product specified in any of paragraphs 6 to 8, not being a preparation specified in Schedule 5.

Schedule 3

Controlled Drugs Subject to the Requirements of Regulations 14, 15 (except temazepam), 16, 18, 22, 23, 24, 26 and 27

1. The following substances, namely:—

(a) Benzphetamine
Buprenorphine
Cathine
Chlorphentermine
Diethylpropion
Ethchlorvynol
Ethinamate
Flunitrazepam
Mazindol
Mephentermine
Meprobamate
Methylphenobarbitone

Methyprylone
[after 1 January 2008,
Midazolam]
Pentazocine
Phendimetrazine
Phentermine
Pipradrol
Temazepam

(b) any 5, 5 disubstituted barbituric acid not being quinalbarbitone.

2. Any stereoisomeric form of a substance specified in paragraph 1 not being phenylpropanolamine.
3. Any salt of a substance specified in paragraph 1 or 2.
4. Any preparation or other product containing a substance specified in any of paragraphs 1 to 3, not being a preparation specified in Schedule 5.

Schedule 4

Part I Controlled Drugs Subject to the Requirements of Regulations 22, 23 26 and 27

1. The following substances and products, namely:—

Alprazolam
Aminorex
Bromazepam
Brotizolam
Camazepam
Chlordiazepoxide
Clobazam
Clonazepam
Clorazepic acid
Clotiazepam
Cloxazolam
Delorazepam
Diazepam
Estazolam
Ethyl loflazepate
Fencamfamin
Fenproporex
Fludiazepam
Flurazepam
Halazepam
Haloxazolam
4-Hydroxy-n-butyric acid
Ketamine
Ketazolam
Loprazolam
Lorazepam
Lormetazepam
Medazepam
Mefenorex
Mesocarb
[until 1 January 2008,
Midazolam]
Nimetazepam
Nitrazepam
Nordazepam
Oxazepam
Oxazolam
Pemoline
Pinazepam
Prazepam
Pyrovalerone
Tetrazepam
Triazolam
N-Ethylamphetamine
Zolpidem

2. Any stereoisomeric form of a substance specified in paragraph 1.
3. Any salt of a substance specified in paragraph 1 or 2.
4. Any preparation or other product containing a substance or product specified in any of paragraphs 1 to 3, not being a preparation specified in Schedule 5.

Part II Controlled Drugs Excepted from the Prohibition on Possession When in the Form of a Medicinal Product; Excluded from the Application of Offences arising from the Prohibition on Importation and Exportation When Imported or Exported in the Form of a Medicinal Product by any Person for Administration to Himself; and Subject to the Requirements of Regulations 22, 23, 26 and 27

1. The following substances, namely—

4-Androstene-3, 17-dione
5-Androstene-3, 17 diol
Atamestane
Bolandiol
Bolasterone
Bolazine
Boldenone
Bolenol
Bolmantalate
Calusterone
4-Chloromethandienone
Clostebol
Drostanolone
Enestebol
Epitiostanol
Ethyloestrenol

Fluoxymesterone
Formebolone
Furazabol
Mebolazine
Mepitiostane
Mesabolone
Mestanolone
Mesterolone
Methandienone
Methandriol
Methenolone
Methyltestosterone
Metribolone
Mibolerone
Nandrolone
19-Nor-4-Androstene-3, 17-dione
19-Nor-5-Androstene-3, 17 diol
Norboletone
Norclostebol
Norethandrolone
Ovandrotone
Oxabolone
Oxandrolone
Oxymesterone
Oxymetholone
Prasterone
Propetandrol
Quinbolone
Roxibolone
Silandrone
Stanolone
Stanozolol
Stenbolone
Testosterone
Thiomesterone
Trenbolone

2. Any compound (not being Trilostane or a compound for the time being specified in paragraph 1 of this Part of this Schedule) structurally derived from 17-hydroxyandrostan-3-one or from 17-hydroxyestran-3-one by modification in any of the following ways, that is to say —
   (a) by further substitution at position 17 by a methyl or ethyl group;
   (b) by substitution to any extent at one or more of positions 1, 2, 4, 6, 7, 9, 11 or 16, but at no other position;
   (c) by unsaturation in the carbocyclic ring system to any extent, provided that there are no more than two ethylenic bonds in any one carbocyclic ring;
   (d) by fusion of ring A with a heterocyclic system.
3. Any substance which is an ester or ether (or, where more than one hydroxyl function is available, both an ester and an ether) of a substance specified in paragraph 1 or described in paragraph 2 of this Part of this Schedule.
4. The following substances, namely—
   Chorionic Gonadotrophin (HCG)
   Clenbuterol
   Non-human chorionic gonadotrophin
   Somatotropin
   Somatrem
   Somatropin
5. Any stereoisomeric form of a substance specified or described in any of paragraphs 1 to 4 of this Part of this Schedule.
6. Any salt of a substance specified or described in any of paragraphs 1 to 5 of this Part of this Schedule.
7. Any preparation or other product containing a substance or product specified or described in any of paragraphs 1 to 6 of this Part of this Schedule, not being a preparation specified in Schedule 5.

SCHEDULE 5

CONTROLLED DRUGS EXCEPTED FROM THE PROHIBITION ON IMPORTATION, EXPORTATION AND POSSESSION AND SUBJECT TO THE REQUIREMENTS OF REGULATIONS 24 AND 26

1. (1) Any preparation of one or more of the substances to which this paragraph applies, not being a preparation designed for administration by injection, when compounded with one or more other active or inert ingredients and containing a total of not more than 100 milligrams of the substance or substances (calculated as base) per dosage unit or with a total concentration of not more than 2.5% (calculated as base) in undivided preparations.
   (2) The substances to which this paragraph applies are acetyldihydrocodeine, codeine, dihydrocodeine, ethylmorphine, nicocodine, nicodicodine (6-nicotinoyldihydrocodeine), norcodeine and pholcodine and their respective salts.
2. [Revoked.]

3. Any preparation of medicinal opium or of morphine containing (in either case) not more than 0.2% of morphine calculated as anhydrous morphine base, being a preparation compounded with one or more other active or inert ingredients in such a way that the opium or, as the case may be, the morphine cannot be recovered by readily applicable means or in a yield which would constitute a risk to health.
4. Any preparation of dextropropoxyphene, being a preparation designed for oral administration, containing not more than 135 milligrams of dextropropoxyphene (calculated as base) per dosage unit or with a total concentration of not more than 2.5% (calculated as base) in undivided preparations.
5. Any preparation of difenoxin containing, per dosage unit, not more than 0.5 milligrams of difenoxin and a quantity of atropine sulphate equivalent to at least 5% of the dose of difenoxin.
6. Any preparation of diphenoxylate containing, per dosage unit, not more than 2.5 milligrams of diphenoxylate calculated as base, and a quantity of atropine sulphate equivalent to at least 1% of the dose of diphenoxylate.
7. Any preparation of propiram containing, per dosage unit, not more than 100 milligrams of propiram calculated as base and compounded with at least the same amount (by weight) of methylcellulose.
8. Any powder of ipecacuanha and opium comprising—
   10% opium, in powder,
   10% ipecacuanha root, in powder, well mixed with
   80% of any other powdered ingredient containing no controlled drug.
9. Any mixture containing one or more of the preparations specified in paragraphs 1 to 8, being a mixture of which none of the other ingredients is a controlled drug.

Schedule 8

(1) Any of the following persons may supply or administer a specified controlled drug under a patient group direction, namely—
  (a) a person who holds a certificate of proficiency in ambulance paramedic skills issued by, or with the approval of, the Secretary of State, or a person who is a registered paramedic;
  (b) [revoked];
  (c) a registered midwife;
  (d) a registered optometrist;
  (e) a registered chiropodist;
  (f) a registered orthoptist;
  (g) a registered physiotherapist;
  (h) a registered radiographer;
  (i) a registered occupational therapist;
  (j) a registered orthotist and prosthetist.

The MDA 1971, s. 30, provides that a licence or other authority issued by the Secretary of State may be general or specific, and it may be issued on such terms and subject to such conditions (including, in the case of a licence, the payment of a prescribed fee) as the Secretary of State thinks proper, and may be modified or revoked by him at any time.

In *Dunbar* [1981] 1 WLR 1536, the Court of Appeal had to consider the meaning of the Misuse of Drugs Regulations 1973 (SI 1973 No. 797), reg. 10(2), in determining whether or not a doctor was unlawfully in possession of drugs. This case is applicable to reg. 10(2) of the 2001 Regulations and probably states a principle applicable to licences and authorisations generally. It was held that, for the purposes of reg. 10(2), it is not necessary for the doctor to have patients, since self-administration may well be appropriate. What matters is whether the doctor was acting bona fide in his capacity as a medical practitioner. This is a matter for the jury to decide. In *Dunbar*, the jury had not been given the opportunity to consider whether the doctor wanted the drugs for self-treatment or to commit suicide, and his conviction of unlawful possession was quashed. The mere fact that a person holds a licence, or authorisation, will not afford a defence where the possession of the drug is clearly outside the terms or conditions of the licence or authorisation, or is for an improper purpose. The issue must be left to the tribunal of fact to determine (see *Abraham* [2002] EWCA Crim 2870).

Defence of Necessity Unavailable

Quayle [2005] 1 WLR 3642 and *Altham* [2006] 1 WLR 3287 decide that necessity is not a defence to any of the offences under the MDA 1971 where someone has possession of, is cultivating or is supplying cannabis in order to relieve pain. In *Quayle*, the Court of Appeal pointed out that cannabis, cannabis resin and most cannabinoids are designated as drugs which may be used only for medical or scientific research (and they are drugs to which s. 7(4) of the MDA 1971 applies). Mance LJ said (at [54]): **B20.23**

> The effect of that designation is that, whatever benefits might be perceived or suggested for any individual patients, if these particular drugs were available for medical prescription and use (other than research), such individual benefits were and are in the legislator's view outweighed by disbenefits of strength sufficient in the national interest to require a general prohibition.

For further consideration of necessity, see **A3.27** and especially **A3.28**.

Liability of Corporate Officers

Misuse of Drugs Act 1971, s. 21 **B20.24**

> Where any offence under this Act or part II of the Criminal Justice (International Cooperation) Act 1990 committed by a body corporate is proved to have been committed with the consent or connivance of, or to be attributable to any neglect on the part of, any director, manager, secretary or other similar officer of the body corporate, or any person purporting to act in such capacity, he as well as the body corporate shall be guilty of that offence and liable to be proceeded against accordingly.

As to corporate liability generally, see **A5.17**.

SUPPLYING OR OFFERING TO SUPPLY ETC. CONTROLLED DRUG

Misuse of Drugs Act 1971, s. 4 **B20.25**

> (1) Subject to any regulations under section 7 of this Act for the time being in force, it shall not be lawful for a person—
> (a) to produce a controlled drug; or
> (b) to supply or offer to supply a controlled drug to another.
> (2) . . .
> (3) Subject to section 28 of this Act, it is an offence for a person—
> (a) to supply or offer to supply, a controlled drug to another in contravention of subsection 1 above; or
> (b) to be concerned in the supplying of such a drug to another in contravention of that subsection; or
> (c) to be concerned in the making to another in contravention of that subsection of an offer to supply such a drug.

Given that s. 4(3) attracts different maximum penalties determined by the class of drug involved, *Courtie* [1984] AC 463 establishes that s. 4(3) creates more than one offence. Notwithstanding that there is more than one offence created, there are a number of elements common to each of these offences (save for offers to supply), namely, (i) that there must be a 'controlled drug'; (ii) that the activity with regard to that drug must involve a 'supply' in some form; and (iii) that the activity must be in contravention of s. 4(1). The question of what substances are controlled drugs is dealt with at **B20.2** to **B20.6**.

Procedure

B20.26 Offences under the MDA 1971, s. 4(3), are (by s. 25 of and sch. 4 of the Act) triable either way. When tried on indictment they are class 3 offences. According to the *Consolidated Criminal Practice Direction*, para. V.51, *Mode of trial* (see **appendix** 7), cases of supplying Class A drugs should be committed for trial; cases of supplying Class B drugs should be committed for trial unless there is only small-scale supply for no payment. No guidelines are given in relation to Class C drugs.

Summary trial may be instituted by an information laid 12, rather than the usual six, months from the date of commission of the offence (MDA 1971, s. 25(4)).

For the liability of corporate officers, see **B20.24**. For possible problems which may arise with identifying the person to whom the supply is made, see **B20.28**.

Sentencing Guidelines

B20.27 See **B20.105** to **B20.109**. The Drugs Act 2005 inserts a new s. 4A into the MDA 1971, which specifies for sentencing purposes an aggravating feature of supply of a controlled drug. If the offender convicted of an offence under s. 4(3) is aged 18 or over and the offence was committed on or in the vicinity of school premises, or the offence involved commission by the offender of a courier who at the relevant time was under 18, the sentencing court must treat such fact as an aggravating feature of the offence and must state in open court that the offence is so aggravated. An offence under s. 4(3) is a drug trafficking offence within the meaning of the Proceeds of Crime Act 2002, sch. 2 (see **E21.11**). A minimum custodial sentence of seven years applies for the third Class A drug trafficking offence (see **E6.1**). A forfeiture order (see **E20.4**) or a confiscation order (see **E21**) may be imposed.

Meaning of 'Supply'

B20.28 The words 'supply' and 'supplying' mean the same whenever those words appear in the MDA 1971, as well as for the purposes of the Regulations and orders made under the Act (see **B20.21**): see *Maginnis* [1987] AC 303. By s. 37(1) of the 1971 Act, 'supplying' includes distributing. There is a 'supply' where the accused purchases drugs on behalf of a third party, and then transfers the drug to that party (or where a drug is distributed within a small social group) (see *Buckley* (1979) 69 Cr App R 371 and *Denslow* [1998] Crim LR 566).

In *Maginnis*, Lord Keith, in a speech with which three other members of the House of Lords concurred, held that the word 'supply' is to be ascertained 'by reference to the ordinary natural meaning of the word together with any assistance which may be afforded by the context' (see also *Holmes v Chief Constable Merseyside Police* [1976] Crim LR 125).

Lord Keith said (at p. 309):

> The word 'supply', in its ordinary natural meaning, conveys the idea of furnishing or providing to another something which is wanted or required in order to meet the wants or requirements of that other. It connotes more than the mere transfer of physical control of some chattel or object from one person to another. No one would ordinarily say that to hand over something to a mere custodier was to supply him with it. The additional concept is that of enabling the recipient to apply the thing handed over to purposes for which he desires or has a duty to apply it. In my opinion it is not a necessary element in the conception of supply that the provision should be made out of the personal resources of the person who does the supplying. Thus if an employee draws from his employer's store materials or equipment which he requires for purposes of his work, it involves no straining of language to say that the storekeeper supplies him with those materials or that equipment, notwithstanding that they do not form part of the storekeeper's own resources and that he is merely the custodier of them. I think the same is true if it is the owner of the business who is drawing from his own storekeeper tools or materials which form part of his own resources. The storekeeper can be said to be supplying him with what he needs. If a trafficker in controlled drugs sets up a store of these in the custody of a friend whom he thinks unlikely to attract the suspicions of the police, and later draws on the store for the purposes of his

trade, or for his own use, the custodier is in my opinion rightly to be regarded as supplying him with drugs.

Maginnis has been applied in cases other than under the MDA 1971: see *Devon County Council v DB Cars Ltd* [2001] EWHC Admin 521, and *Formula One Autocentre Ltd v Birmingham City Council* [1999] RTR 195.

The *Maginnis* approach provides little difficulty in a typical case where a person transfers both the custody and control of a controlled drug to another (see *Mills* [1963] 1 QB 522).

Maginnis also deals with cases where D1 transfers drugs to D2 for 'safekeeping'. In *Dempsey* (1985) 82 Cr App R 291, Michael, who was a registered drug addict, and in lawful possession of a controlled drug, asked Maureen to hold some of the drug for him while he went to the toilet to inject himself with the rest of it. The police then arrested both of them. The Court of Appeal held that whether or not Michael had supplied the drug to Maureen was a question of fact, and since the matter was not left to the jury to decide, his conviction for an offence contrary to the MDA 1971, s. 4(3)(a), had to be quashed. The court proceeded on the basis that Michael had transferred the drug to Maureen either for her own use, or to hand on to someone else (in which case there would have been a supply), or he may simply have given it to her for safekeeping (in which case there was no supply by Michael). A supply occurs only where there is a transfer for the benefit of the transferee (Maureen) rather than for the transferor (Michael).

Dempsey appeared to conflict with *Delgado* [1984] 1 WLR 89 (a case of possession with intent to supply). The trial judge directed the jury that Delgado's intention to return cannabis, which had been given to him for 'safekeeping', was an intention to supply contrary to s. 5(3). The Court of Appeal dismissed the appeal on the grounds that 'supply' covers a wide range of transactions, and that a 'feature common to all those transactions is a transfer of physical control of a drug from one person to another'.

In *Maginnis*, the House of Lords reconciled the cases by holding that 'supply' involves more than a mere transfer of physical control of the item from one person to another but includes a further concept, namely, that of 'enabling the recipient to apply the thing handed over to purposes for which he desires or has a duty to apply it'. The result appears to be that if A gives drugs to B for safekeeping, A has not supplied B with them for the purposes of s. 4. But, were B to return the drugs to A (or where he intends to do so), B would be guilty of supplying the drugs to A (or possessing them with that intention) (see *Panton* [2001] EWCA Crim 611, following *Maginnis*, where P, acting as a custodian of drugs, intended to return them to the depositor — he had therefore committed an offence contrary to s. 5(3)). In *Pentecost* (10 March 1998 unreported), the Court of Appeal held that the trial judge had not erred when he directed the jury that '. . . supply does not require a physical handing over as such by the custodian. It would be sufficient if, with the intention that the trafficker retakes the drugs, the custodian did something to enable the trafficker to achieve that object'.

It is important not to confuse purpose, or intention, with motive (which is irrelevant) (see *X* [1994] Crim LR 827, where X was a registered police informer; his motive of causing a drugs dealer to be caught did not affect whether there was a supply).

In *Harris* [1968] 1 WLR 769, it was held that injecting another with a drug in the recipient's possession is not 'supplying' that drug to the recipient, particularly since physical control was not transferred to the recipient. This case must be read with care (having regard to the fact that it pre-dates the MDA 1971).

When Supply etc. Lawful

Conduct otherwise proscribed by the MDA 1971, s. 4(1), may be licensed or authorised by the Misuse of Drugs Regulations 2001 (see generally, **B20.21**). Regulation 4(3) provides in **B20.29** effect that it shall not be unlawful to supply or offer to supply poppy-straw. Subsequent regulations provide various exemptions for medical personnel, pharmacists and midwives, and for research activities.

Section 4(1)(b) and (3)(a): Offering to Supply

B20.30 An offer may be by words or conduct. If it is by words, it must be ascertained whether an offer to supply a controlled drug was made. It does not matter whether or not the accused had a controlled drug in his possession or had access to controlled drugs, or whether or not the substance in his possession was a controlled drug at all. The position might be different where the offer is made by conduct (*Mitchell* [1992] Crim LR 723; *Haggard v Mason* [1976] 1 WLR 187). Whether the accused intends to carry the offer into effect is irrelevant; the offence is complete upon the making of an offer to supply (*Goodard* [1992] Crim LR 588, see also *Gill* (1993) 97 Cr App R 215, *Showers* [1995] Crim LR 400, and *Haslock* [2001] EWCA Crim 1321). The offence is committed whether or not the offer is genuine. Once made, an offer cannot be withdrawn (*Prior* [2004] Crim LR 849). It is not helpful to refer to principles of contract law in determining whether there is an offer (*Dhillon* [2000] Crim LR 760 and see *Prior*).

Section 4(3)(b): Being Concerned in Supply to Another

B20.31 The three ingredients of this offence were set out by the Court of Appeal in *Hughes* (1985) Cr App R 344, p. 348:

(a) the supply of a drug to another, or, as the case may be, the making of an offer to supply the drug to another in contravention of s. 4(1) of the MDA 1971;
(b) participation by the accused in an enterprise involving such supply or, as the case may be, such an offer to supply; and
(c) knowledge by the accused of the nature of the enterprise, i.e. that it involved supply of a drug or, as the case may be, offering to supply a drug.

It is the duty of the judge to assist the jury as to the meaning of the phrase 'concerned in' (*Hughes*). A person may be concerned by being involved at a distance in making an offer to supply a controlled drug (*Blake* (1978) 68 Cr App R 1).

For the purposes of ss. 4 and 5(3), the 'another' cannot be someone charged in the same count, but it can be someone charged in other counts in the same indictment (*Smith* (14 February 1983 unreported), *Ferrera* (1984 unreported), *Adepoju* [1988] Crim LR 378, *Connelly* (1991) 156 JP 406, *Reeves* [2001] EWCA Crim 91, and note *Gingell* (1999) 163 JP 648, which makes the same point in the context of a charge of handling stolen goods; see **B4.139**). For cases of conspiracy to supply to 'another' where that other is a co-conspirator, see *Drew* [2000] 1 Cr App R 91 and *Jackson* (1999) *The Times*, 13 May 1999; in neither judgment was the effect of *Adepoju* discussed.

Defence under s. 28

B20.32 The defence under the MDA 1971, s. 28, is discussed at **B20.20.** Note that s. 28 does not apply to *an offer* to supply a controlled drug (*Mitchell* [1992] Crim LR 723). This is because the offence is rooted in the making of the offer, and not in the quality of the substance offered (which, if it existed at all, might be innocuous).

POSSESSION OF CONTROLLED DRUG WITH INTENT TO SUPPLY

Misuse of Drugs Act 1971, s. 5 **B20.33**

(3) Subject to section 28 of this Act, it is an offence for a person to have a controlled drug in his possession, whether lawfully or not, with intent to supply it to another in contravention of section 4(1) of this Act.

Given that s. 5(3) attracts different maximum penalties determined by the class of drug involved, *Courtie* [1984] AC 463 establishes that s. 5(3) creates more than one offence.

For the meaning of 'controlled drug', see **B20.1**; as to the meaning of 'possession', see **B20.11** *et seq.* For circumstances in which possession may be lawful by virtue of the Misuse of Drugs Regulations 2001, see **B20.21**.

Procedure

Offences under the MDA 1971, s. 5(3), are (by s. 25 of and sch. 4 to the Act) triable either way. When tried on indictment they are class 3 offences. According to the *Consolidated Criminal Practice Direction*, para. V.51, *Mode of trial* (see **appendix** 7), cases of possessing Class A drugs with intent to supply should be committed for trial; cases of possessing Class B drugs with intent to supply should be committed for trial unless there is only small-scale supply for no payment. No guidelines are given in relation to Class C drugs. **B20.34**

Summary trial may be instituted by an information laid 12, rather than the usual six, months from the date of commission of the offence (MDA 1971, s. 25(4)).

For the liability of corporate officers, see **B20.24**.

Indictment

The form of indictment provided at **B20.9** may be adapted by addition of the specific intent to the particulars of the offence. **B20.35**

Alternative Verdicts

In *Blackford* (1989) 89 Cr App R 239, the Court of Appeal, exercising its general power under the Criminal Law Act 1967, substituted a conviction of possession under the MDA 1971, s. 5(2), for that under s. 5(3). **B20.36**

Sentencing Guidelines

See **B20.105** to **B20.109**. This is a drug trafficking offence within the meaning of the Proceeds of Crime Act 2002, sch. 2 (see **E21.11**). A minimum custodial sentence of seven years applies for the third Class A drug trafficking offence (see **E6.1**). A forfeiture order (see **E20.4**) or a confiscation order (see **E21**) may be imposed. **B20.37**

Intent to Supply

Section 5 of the MDA 1971 has been amended by the Drugs Act 2005, s. 2, so as to add s. 5(4A) to (4C); however, it is unlikely that these amendments will be brought into force. **B20.38**

Misuse of Drugs Act 1971, s. 5

(4A) In any proceedings for an offence under subsection 3(a) above, if it is proved that the accused had an amount of a controlled drug in his possession which is not less than the prescribed amount, the court or jury must assume that he had the drug in his possession with the intent to supply it as mentioned in subsection (3).

(4B) Subsection (4A) above does not apply if evidence is adduced which is sufficient to raise an issue that the accused may not have had the drug in his possession with that intent.

(4C) Regulations under subsection (4A) above have effect only in relation to proceedings for an offence committed after the regulations come into force.

'Supply' is an element in the offences created by ss. 4(3) and 5(3), and the expression means the same in each context (see *Maginnis* [1987] AC 303). For the meaning of 'supply', see **B20.28**.

For the purposes of s. 5(3), the prosecution need only establish that the accused had the drug in his possession with the intention of supplying it to another. A mistake as to the drug in question is irrelevant (*Leeson* [2000] 1 Cr App R 233).

'Intent to supply' means an intent on the part of the possessor of the drugs to supply, and not an intention that the drug should be supplied by another person (*Greenfield* (1983) 78 Cr App R 179). As to proving an intent to supply, and the admissibility of evidence of large amounts of money, an extravagant lifestyle or drug equipment, see **F1.13**.

In *Downes* [1984] Crim LR 552, the Court of Appeal decided that where two people were in joint possession (for the meaning of this phrase, see **B20.14**) they were not both involved in a joint venture to supply unless both had an intention to supply. Mere knowledge on the part of one that the other intended to supply is not sufficient.

For the purposes of ss. 4 and 5(3), the 'another' cannot be someone charged in the same count, but it can be someone charged in other counts in the same indictment (see **B20.31**).

Defences

B20.39 The defence under s. 28 is dealt with at **B20.20**.

In *Taylor* [2002] 1 Cr App R 519, D, a Rastafarian, argued that, as the prosecution had conceded that his possession with intent to supply cannabis was purely for religious purposes (see also **B11.161**), convicting him would be a breach of the ECHR, Article 9. The Court of Appeal held that there was no breach of Article 9. Article 9(2) was satisfied as there was a pressing social need to combat the public health, and public safety dangers, arising from drugs such as cannabis. This was evidenced, in part, by the Single Convention on Narcotic Drugs 1971; and see *Andrews* [2004] EWCA Crim 947 (a case under the Customs and Excise Management Act 1979, s. 170).

PRODUCTION OF CONTROLLED DRUG

B20.40 **Misuse of Drugs Act 1971, s. 4**

(2) Subject to section 28 of this Act, it is an offence for a person—
(a) to produce a controlled drug in contravention of subsection (1) [of section 4]; or
(b) to be concerned in the production of such a drug in contravention of that subsection by another.

For the meaning of 'controlled drug', see **B20.1**. As to the circumstances in which production may be lawful pursuant to the Misuse of Drugs Regulations 1985 (SI 1985 No. 2066), see **B.20.21**.

Each of paras. (a) and (b) creates separate offences. Since the range of sentence for this offence depends upon the class of drug involved (see **B20.105**), the House of Lords decision in *Courtie* [1984] AC 463, establishes that each paragraph to s. 4(2) creates more than one offence.

Procedure

B20.41 Offences under the MDA 1971, s. 4(2), are (by s. 25 of and sch. 4 to the Act) triable either way. When tried on indictment they are class 3 offences.

Summary trial may be instituted by an information laid 12, rather than the usual six, months from the date of commission of the offence (MDA 1971, s. 25(4)).

For the liability of corporate officers, see **B20.24**.

Sentencing Guidelines

See **B20.105** to **B20.109**. This is a drug trafficking offence within the meaning of the Proceeds of Crime Act 2002, sch. 2 (see **E21.11**). A minimum custodial sentence of seven years applies for the third Class A drug trafficking offence (see **E6.1**). A forfeiture order (see **E20.4**) or a confiscation order (see **E21**) may be imposed for a drug trafficking offence. **B20.42**

Meaning of 'Produce', 'Concerned in Production'

Misuse of Drugs Act 1971, s. 37 **B20.43**

(1) . . . 'produce', where the reference is to producing a controlled drug, means producing it by manufacture, cultivation or any other method, and 'production' has a corresponding meaning; . . .

The Court of Appeal in *Russell* (1991) 94 Cr App R 351, held that the conversion of one form of Class A drug into another form of the same genus may be production and that the conversion of the salt cocaine hydrochloride to free base cocaine, i.e. from a substance described in the MDA 1971, sch. 2, para. 4 to a substance described in para. 5 of that schedule, was a production. This was because it was 'the production of a substance (not by manufacture or cultivation but by "other means" [referring to the definition in s. 37(1)]) with physical and chemical features different from the cocaine hydrochloride from which it springs, albeit sharing the same generic term, cocaine'.

Stripping a cannabis plant, which had been cut and harvested, is producing a controlled drug because the action, by 'other means', produces a part of the plant which is a controlled drug (*Harris* [1996] 1 Cr App R 369).

Being 'concerned in the production' requires evidence that the accused played an identifiable role in the production of the drug in question. This was not satisfied where the accused simply permitted two others who were producing drugs to use his kitchen (*Farr* [1982] Crim LR 745).

Defence under s. 28

As to the defence under the MDA 1971, s. 28, see **B20.20**. **B20.44**

PROHIBITION ON IMPORTATION AND EXPORTATION OF CONTROLLED DRUGS

Misuse of Drugs Act 1971, s. 3 **B20.45**

(1) Subject to subsection (2) below—
  (a) the importation of a controlled drug: and
  (b) the exportation of a controlled drug,
  are hereby prohibited.
(2) Subsection (1) above does not apply—
  (a) to the importation or exportation of a controlled drug which is for the time being excepted from paragraph (a) or, as the case may be, paragraph (b) of subsection (1) above by regulations under section 7 of this Act; or
  (b) to the importation or exportation of a controlled drug under and in accordance with the terms of a licence issued by the Secretary of State and in compliance with any conditions attached thereto.

This section, which is of considerable importance, imposes a prohibition, but it does not create an offence. It is generally enforced by the use of charges of improper importation or exportation of goods, fraudulent evasion of duty or, where appropriate, conspiracy to evade the prohibition contained in the section. As to these offences, see **B17.12** ***et seq.*** For the relationship between s. 3 offences and offences under the Customs and Excise Acts, see *Whitehead* [1982] QB 1272.

The meaning of the term 'controlled drug' and the circumstances in which exemptions may be permitted by regulation are discussed in **B20.1** to **B20.6** and **B20.21** to **B20.22**.

CULTIVATING PLANT OF THE GENUS CANNABIS

B20.46 **Misuse of Drugs Act 1971, s. 6**

(1) Subject to any regulations under section 7 of this Act for the time being in force, it shall not be lawful for a person to cultivate any plant of the genus Cannabis.

(2) Subject to section 28 of this Act, it is an offence to cultivate any such plant in contravention of subsection (1) above.

Procedure

B20.47 Offences under the MDA 1971, s. 6, are (by s. 25 of and sch. 4 to the Act) triable either way. When tried on indictment they are class 3 offences.

Summary trial may be instituted by an information laid 12, rather than the usual six, months from the date of commission of the offence (MDA 1971, s. 25(4)).

For the liability of corporate officers, see **B20.24**.

Sentencing Guidelines

B20.48 See **B20.105** to **B20.109**.

Meaning of 'Cannabis'

B20.49 The definition of 'cannabis' provided in the MDA 1971, s. 37(1) (see **B20.5**), does not apply to the use of the word 'cannabis' in s. 6 of the Act, since the context of the instant offence clearly requires that the plant itself be cultivated.

Meaning of 'Cultivate'

B20.50 This term is not defined in the Act. *Quaere*, whether it would be sufficient for a person who did not introduce it but passively permitted a plant of the genus *Cannabis* to continue in a place over which he has control without tending it, or whether some active steps to keep the plant alive or to cause it to grow must be taken. It may be more appropriate to charge possession in such a case.

Mens Rea

B20.51 The prosecution is not required to prove that the accused knew that the plant he cultivated was in fact cannabis (*Champ* (1981) 73 Cr App R 367), but note that an accused may have a defence under the MDA 1971, s. 28 (see **B20.20**).

When Cultivation may be Lawful

B20.52 The Misuse of Drugs Regulations 2001 (**B20.22**) contain various exemptions from this prohibition. See, in particular, reg. 12, by virtue of which a person licensed by the Secretary of State may cultivate a plant of the genus *Cannabis* in accordance with the terms of the licence and in compliance with any conditions attached to it.

OFFENCES RELATING TO OPIUM

B20.53 **Misuse of Drugs Act 1971, s. 9**

Subject to section 28 of this Act, it is an offence for a person—

(a) to smoke or otherwise use prepared opium; or

(b) to frequent a place used for the purpose of opium smoking; or

(c) to have in his possession
  (i) any pipes or other utensils made or adapted for use in connection with the smoking of opium, being pipes or utensils which have been used by him or with his knowledge and permission in that connection or which he intends to use or permit others to use in that connection; or
  (ii) any utensils which have been used by him or with his knowledge and permission in connection with the preparation of opium for smoking.

Section 9 creates three discrete offences, rather than three methods of committing the same offence, in paragraphs (a), (b), and (c).

Procedure

Offences under the MDA 1971, s. 9, are (by s. 25 of and sch. 4 to the Act) triable either way. When tried on indictment they are class 3 offences. **B20.54**

Summary trial may be instituted by an information laid 12, rather than the usual six, months from the date of commission of the offence (MDA 1971, s. 25(4)).
For the liability of corporate officers, see **B20.24**.

Sentence

See **B20.108** *et seq.* **B20.55**

Elements and Defence

By the MDA 1971, s. 37(1), 'prepared opium' means opium prepared for smoking and includes dross and any other residues remaining after opium has been smoked. **B20.56**

For the meaning of 'possession' in relation to the offence of the unlawful possession of a controlled drug, see **B20.11** to **B20.18**.

The defence under s. 28 of the Act also applies to these offences (see **B20.20**).

PROHIBITION OF SUPPLY ETC. OF ARTICLES FOR ADMINISTERING OR PREPARING CONTROLLED DRUGS

Misuse of Drugs Act 1971, s. 9A **B20.57**

(1) A person who supplies or offers to supply any article which may be used or adapted to be used (whether by itself or in combination with another article or other articles) in the administration by any person of a controlled drug to himself or another, believing that the article (or the article as adapted) is to be so used in circumstances where the administration is unlawful, is guilty of an offence.
(2) It is not an offence under subsection (1) above to supply or offer to supply a hypodermic syringe, or any part of one.
(3) A person who supplies or offers to supply any article which may be used to prepare a controlled drug for administration by any person to himself or another believing that the article is to be so used in circumstances where the administration is unlawful is guilty of an offence.
(4) [See **B20.61**.]
(5) In this section, references to administration by any person of a controlled drug to himself include a reference to his administering it to himself with the assistance of another.

Given that the penalty does not vary with the controlled drug in question, there are only two offences, one under s. 9A(1), and the other under s. 9A(3).

Procedure

Offences under the MDA 1971, s. 9A, are (by s. 25 of and sch. 4 to the Act) triable only **B20.58** summarily. Summary trial may be instituted by an information laid 12, rather than the usual six, months from the date of commission of the offence (MDA 1971, s. 25(4)).

For the liability of corporate officers, see **B20.24**.

Sentence

B20.59 See **B20.105** and **B20.109**.

Elements

B20.60 This offence deals with articles which enable people to administer controlled drugs to themselves or others. The section was intended to outlaw 'drug kits', but the offence has rarely been invoked. It is subject to the Misuse of Drugs Regulations 2001, reg. 6A (permitting the supply of articles for administering or preparing controlled drugs by certain persons; see B20.22).

As to the meaning of 'controlled drug', see **B20.1**.

It is not clear whether the definition given in *Maginnis* [1987] AC 303, of 'supply' applies to this offence (see **B20.28**).

Defences

B20.61 To fall within the MDA 1971, s. 9A, the articles must be for the unlawful administration of a controlled drug.

Misuse of Drugs Act 1971, s. 9A

(4) For the purposes of this section, any administration of a controlled drug is unlawful except—
  (a) the administration by any person of a controlled drug to another in circumstances where the administration of the drug is not unlawful under section 4(1) of this Act, or
  (b) the administration by any person of a controlled drug to himself in circumstances where having the controlled drug in his possession is not unlawful under section 5(1) of this Act.

Notwithstanding s. 9A(1) and (3), certain persons may supply or offer to supply certain articles as laid down in the Misuse of Drugs Regulations 2001, reg. 6A, see **B20.22**.

OCCUPIERS AND THOSE CONCERNED IN MANAGEMENT OF PREMISES KNOWINGLY PERMITTING OR SUFFERING DRUG-RELATED ACTIVITIES

B20.62 **Misuse of Drugs Act 1971, s. 8**

A person commits an offence if, being the occupier or concerned in the management of any premises, he knowingly permits or suffers any of the following activities to take place on those premises, that is to say—
  (a) producing or attempting to produce a controlled drug in contravention of section 4(1) of this Act;
  (b) supplying or attempting to supply a controlled drug to another in contravention of section 4(1) of this Act, or offering to supply a controlled drug to another in contravention of section 4(1);
  (c) preparing opium for smoking;
  (d) smoking cannabis, cannabis resin or prepared opium.

Note that s. 38 of the CJPA 2001 has been repealed by the Drugs Act 2005, s. 23, sch. 1, para. 6. Had s. 38 come into force, it would have amended s. 8(d) of the 1971 Act, by adding the words 'administering or using a controlled drug which is unlawfully in any person's possession at or immediately before the time when it is administered or used'.

As to the meaning of 'controlled drug', see **B20.1**; 'producing', see **B20.43**; 'supplying', see **B20.28**.

Procedure

Offences under the MDA 1971, s. 9, are (by s. 25 of and sch. 4 to the Act) triable either way. When tried on indictment they are class 3 offences. **B20.63**

Summary trial may be instituted by an information laid 12, rather than the usual six, months from the date of commission of the offence (MDA 1971, s. 25(4)).

For the liability of corporate officers, see **B20.24**.

Indictment

Statement of Offence **B20.64**

Being the occupier [or: concerned in the management] of premises knowingly permitting or suffering production of a controlled drug, contrary to section 8 of the Misuse of Drugs Act 1971.

Particulars of Offence

A on or about the . . . day of . . ., being the occupier [or: being concerned in the management] of certain premises situated at and known as . . ., knowingly permitted or suffered on the said premises the production of a controlled drug of Class B, namely . . ., such production being contrary to section 4(1) of the Misuse of Drugs Act 1971.

Sentence

See **B20.105** to **B20.109**. **B20.65**

Meaning of 'Occupier'

Section 8 of the MDA 1971 is aimed at the occupiers or the managers of premises because it is they who may exercise immediate supervision over the activities carried on within them. A person does not have to be a tenant, or to have an estate in land, in order to be an 'occupier' for the purposes of s. 8. The term 'occupier' should be given a commonsense interpretation (*Tao* [1977] QB 141). What should not be involved is an overly narrow or legalistic definition of that term. For the purposes of s. 8, a person is in occupation of premises, whatever his legal status, if the prosecution can show that the accused exercised control, or had the authority of another, to exclude persons from premises or to prohibit any of the activities referred to in s. 8. **B20.66**

In *Tao*, the Court of Appeal dismissed an appeal against conviction by an undergraduate who had an exclusive contractual licence from college of a room, which gave him not merely a right to use the room, but also sufficient exclusivity of possession to ensure that he was an occupier. It was held to be enough that the accused had a contractual licence to use the room. He may not have been able to exclude college staff from entering his room but he could exclude cannabis smokers or, for that matter, any smoker. He was in a position to exercise control over the activities that took place there. Although the Court of Appeal approved the result in *Mogford* (1970) 63 Cr App R 168, the court did not approve of the reasoning. It was not entirely clear what Neild J, in *Mogford*, meant by 'legal possession', given that an individual can be in legal possession of premises without being a tenant or having any estate in land (see *Errington v Errington* [1952] 1 KB 290 and cf. *Heslop v Burns* [1974] 1 WLR 1241). Furthermore, it is not entirely clear from the report what the facts in *Mogford* really were; it may be that a jury would not have been able to say exactly what the nature of the arrangement was, and so whether it amounted to occupation of those premises (a matter, which evidently troubled the court in *Campbell* [1982] Crim LR 595).

There are two further cases that usefully illustrate the meaning of 'occupier' for the purposes of s. 8. In *Read v DPP* [1997] 10 CL 120, the Divisional Court dismissed an appeal by way of case stated against R's conviction of being the occupier of premises in which he knowingly permitted or suffered the smoking of cannabis to take place contrary to s. 8(d). R contended that he was not the occupier of the premises because the tenancy of the council house was in the name of his girlfriend with whom he had been cohabiting for some nine years. The court held that R was clearly an occupier and his claim to the contrary was unrealistic. In *Coid* [1998] Crim LR 199, C was charged under s. 8. C was the boyfriend of Miss M: he cohabited with her at the premises although she was the tenant. When she was away, C would look after the premises. Drugs paraphernalia were found in the premises. When interviewed, C gave the address as being his. C's defence was in part that he was not an occupier for the purpose of the MDA 1971. The Court of Appeal held that Miss M's tenancy did not preclude C from being an occupier, which was a question of fact for the jury, and the judge gave a proper direction.

Meaning of 'Concerned in the Management of Premises'

B20.67 To be a manager, the accused must run, organise and plan the use of the premises (see *Josephs* (1977) 65 Cr App R 253), and so must be involved in more than menial or routine duties (see *Abbott v Smith* [1964] 2 QB 662). A person satisfies the requirement of a manager even if he has no lawful right or title to be on the premises.

There is no definition of 'premises' in the MDA 1971, although it appears in other legislation where it is provided with a wide definition, e.g., under the Protection from Eviction Act 1977 (see **B13.9**).

'Knowingly Permits or Suffers'

B20.68 The Court of Appeal in *Thomas* (1976) 63 Cr App R 65, held that 'knowingly' adds nothing to the words 'permits or suffers'. The word was probably included in the MDA 1971, s. 8, to put beyond doubt that proof of knowledge is required. This explains why the offence is not made subject to s. 28. Note that in *Sweet v Parsley* [1970] AC 132, the House of Lords decided that the word 'permits' in the forerunner to s. 8, imported *mens rea*. Wilful blindness as to forbidden activity taking place on premises may be sufficient, but mere suspicion is not (*Thomas*). For the purposes of s. 8(a) and (b), even where the particular drug is specified, it is not necessary for the Crown to prove more than knowledge of the production or supply of a controlled drug (*Bett* [1999] 1 All ER 600). The accused need not know the identity of the drug or its class.

In *Brock* [2001] 1 WLR 1159, a drop-in centre operated a policy that protected the confidentiality of clients in that no information was to be passed on without the express permission of the individual, unless there was an element of danger, safety or personal harm involved. Whilst relevant, such policies are not determinative of the matter. It was for that reason that the trial judge directed the jury that 'the law does not permit you to write or operate a private policy so as to exempt you from the law's requirements'. The Court of Appeal rejected the submission that 'reasonable' has a subjective element: 'A belief by a defendant that he has taken reasonable steps does not afford any defence. . . . It is not for the defendant to judge his own conduct', per Rose LJ. The court added that, 'What the prosecution must prove to establish the offence of permitting under section 8(b) is (i) knowledge, actual or by closing eyes to the obvious, that heroin dealing is taking place; and (ii) unwillingness to prevent it, which can be inferred from failure to take reasonable steps readily available to prevent it'.

In *Souter* [1971] 1 WLR 1187 (decided under s. 5 of the Dangerous Drugs Act 1965), Edmund Davies LJ said, 'The best indication of such unwillingness is proof of failure to take reasonable steps readily available to prevent the prohibited activity. Conversely, all steps taken by the accused to prevent it have a direct bearing on the charge and should be brought to the attention of the jury'.

It is submitted that a further factor for the court to consider is whether the accused allowed the activity to go on 'not caring whether an offence was committed or not'. In *Souter*, Edmund Davies LJ adopted the test of 'permitting' as expressed by Lord Parker CJ in *Gray's Haulage v Arnold* [1966] 1 WLR 534:

> Actual knowledge or knowledge of circumstances so that it could be said that they had shut their eyes to the obvious, or had allowed something to go on, not caring whether an offence was committed or not.

Not caring whether a contravention of the prohibited activity takes place or not was held to be a relevant feature of 'permitting' in *James v Smee* [1955] 1 QB 89. Mere acquiescence in what is taking place on premises is unlikely to amount to permitting that activity (see *Bradbury* [1996] Crim LR 808).

In *Auguste* [2004] 1 WLR 917 the Court of Appeal considered s. 8(d), and held that Parliament was seeking to deal with the situation where a person might discover, by reason of the smell, that activity was taking place, thus the requisite activity had to be taking place for the offence to be committed.

The Divisional Court stated in *Taylor v Chief Constable of Kent* [1981] 1 WLR 606, that an occupier who permits another to cultivate cannabis plants (cannabis was then a Class B drug) permits or suffers their production (i.e. there is an overlap between the offences contrary to the MDA 1971, ss. 4 and 6, see **B20.40** and **B20.46**), and so commits an offence contrary to s. 8.

ASSISTING IN OR INDUCING COMMISSION OUTSIDE UK OF OFFENCE PUNISHABLE UNDER CORRESPONDING LAW

Misuse of Drugs Act 1971, s. 20 **B20.69**

> A person commits an offence if in the United Kingdom he assists in or induces the commission in any place outside the United Kingdom of an offence punishable under the provisions of a corresponding law in force in that place.

Procedure

The offence under the MDA 1971, s. 20, is (by s. 25 of and sch. 4 to the Act) triable either way. When tried on indictment it is a class 3 offence. **B20.70**

Summary trial may be instituted by an information laid 12, rather than the usual six, months from the date of commission of the offence (MDA 1971, s. 25(4)).

For the liability of corporate officers, see **B20.24**.

Sentence

See **B20.105** to **B20.109**. This is a drug trafficking offence within the meaning of the Proceeds of Crime Act 2002, sch. 2 (see **E21.11**). A minimum custodial sentence of seven years applies for the third Class A drug trafficking offence (see **E6.1**). A forfeiture order (see E20.4) or a confiscation order (see E21) may be imposed for a drug trafficking offence. **B20.71**

Meaning of 'Assisting'

Assisting is not to be narrowly construed but must be construed as an ordinary English word (*Vickers* [1975] 1 WLR 811; *Evans* (1977) 64 Cr App R 237; and *Panayi* (1987) 86 Cr App R 261). In *Vickers* the accused was guilty when, as he had agreed, he took speaker cabinets to Italy, knowing that cannabis would then be loaded into them and shipped to the US. In *Evans* the accused had assisted in the UK in the importation of cannabis into Canada from Brussels by the making of arrangements to provide for a human carrier and by carrying those arrangements through. **B20.72**

Commission of Offence outside UK

The offence outside the UK must have been committed (*Panayi* (1987) 86 Cr App R 261). It is only if such an offence is committed that there is something which can be assisted, so the **B20.73** convictions of the accused in *Panayi* were quashed when they had been arrested in British territorial waters having sailed from Spain in a yacht with a quantity of cannabis (then a Class B drug) destined for Holland. If an offence is committed and the accused did an act of assistance, the offence under s. 20 of the MDA 1971 is committed even if it is not possible to identify the principal offender and the final act of importation was effected by an innocent third party (*Ahmed* [1990] Crim LR 648).

Meaning of 'Corresponding Law'

B20.74 **Misuse of Drugs Act 1971, s. 36**

(1) In this Act the expression 'corresponding law' means a law stated in a certificate purporting to be issued by or on behalf of the government of a country outside the United Kingdom to be a law providing for the control and regulation in that country of the production, supply, use, export and import of drugs and other substances in accordance with the provisions of the Single Convention on Narcotic Drugs signed at New York on 30 March 1961 or a law providing for the control and regulation in that country of the production, supply, use, export and import of dangerous or otherwise harmful drugs in pursuance of any treaty, convention or other agreement or arrangement to which the government of that country and Her Majesty's Government in the United Kingdom are for the time being parties.

(2) A statement in any such certificate as aforesaid to the effect that any facts constitute an offence against the law mentioned in the certificate shall be evidence, and in Scotland sufficient evidence, of the matters stated.

Mens Rea

B20.75 The offence is not one of strict liability (*Vickers* [1975] 1 WLR 811), but it is required that (a) the accused intended to assist, i.e. he must know what he is doing and the purpose with which it is done (*Vickers*, at p. 818), and (b) the accused was aware that the person he was assisting was involved in drug smuggling (*Ahmed* [1990] Crim LR 648). It is not necessary to establish that the accused intended that the goods be imported into a particular country (*Ahmed*).

INCITEMENT

B20.76 **Misuse of Drugs Act 1971, s. 19**

It is an offence for a person to incite another to commit [an offence under the Act].

The offence of incitement is triable and punishable in the same way as the substantive offence incited (MDA 1971, s. 25(3) and sch. 4). Section 19 applies to all offences under the Act (*Marlow* [1997] 10 CL 119). For the meaning of incitement, see **A6.1** and **A6.5** to **A6.8**.

ENFORCEMENT PROVISIONS

Powers of Entry, Search and Seizure

B20.77 **Misuse of Drugs Act 1971, s. 23**

(1) A constable or other person authorised in that behalf by a general or special order of the Secretary of State (or in Northern Ireland either of the Secretary of State or the Ministry of Home Affairs for Northern Ireland) shall, for the purposes of the execution of this Act, have power to enter the premises of a person carrying on business as a producer or supplier of any controlled drugs and to demand the production of, and to inspect, any books or documents relating to dealings in any such drugs and to inspect any stocks of any such drugs.

(2) If a constable has reasonable grounds to suspect that any person is in possession of a controlled drug in contravention of this Act or of any regulations made thereunder, the constable may—

(a) search that person, and detain him for the purpose of searching him;

(b) search any vehicle or vessel in which the constable suspects that the drug may be found, and for that purpose require the person in control of the vehicle or vessel to stop it;

(c) seize and detain, for the purposes of proceedings under this Act, anything found in the course of the search which appears to the constable to be evidence of an offence under this Act.

In this subsection 'vessel' includes a hovercraft within the meaning of the Hovercraft Act 1968; and nothing in this subsection shall prejudice any power of search or any power to seize or detain property which is exercisable by a constable apart from this subsection.

(3) If a justice of the peace (or in Scotland a justice of the peace, a magistrate or a sheriff) is satisfied by information on oath that there is reasonable ground for suspecting—

(a) that any controlled drugs are, in contravention of this Act or of any regulations made thereunder, in the possession of a person on any premises; or

(b) that a document directly or indirectly relating to, or connected with, a transaction or dealing which was, or an intended transaction or dealing which would if carried out be, an offence under this Act, or in the case of a transaction or dealing carried out or intended to be carried out in a place outside the United Kingdom, an offence against the provisions of a corresponding law in force in that place, is in the possession of a person on any premises,

he may grant a warrant authorising any constable acting for the police area in which the premises are situated at any time or times within one month from the date of the warrant, to enter, if need be by force, the premises named in the warrant, and to search the premises and any persons found therein and, if there is reasonable ground for suspecting that an offence under this Act has been committed in relation to any controlled drugs found on the premises or in the possession of any such persons, or that a document so found is such a document as is mentioned in paragraph (b) above, to seize and detain those drugs or that document, as the case may be.

(3A) The powers conferred by subsection (1) above shall be exercisable also for the purposes of the execution of part II of the Criminal Justice (International Co-operation) Act 1990 and subsection (3) above (excluding paragraph (a)) shall apply also to offences under section 12 or 13 of that Act of 1990, taking references in those provisions to controlled drugs as references to scheduled substances within the meaning of that part.

Note also s. 20 of the Health Act 2006.

Offences of Obstruction, Concealment etc.

The powers of enforcement are supported by offences created by the MDA 1971, s. 23(4). **B20.78**

Misuse of Drugs Act 1971, s. 23

(4) A person commits an offence if he—

(a) intentionally obstructs a person in the exercise of his powers under this section; or

(b) conceals from a person acting in the exercise of his powers under subsection (1) above any such books, documents, stocks or drugs as are mentioned in that subsection; or

(c) without reasonable excuse (proof of which shall lie on him) fails to produce any such books or documents as are so mentioned where their production is demanded by a person in the exercise of his powers under that subsection.

These offences are triable either way (MDA 1971, s. 25 and sch. 4).

As to the time for commencement of proceedings, see **B20.8**. As to sentence, see **B20.105** to **B20.109**.

In *Forde* (1985) 81 Cr App R 19, the Court of Appeal held that a person committed an offence under s. 23(4)(a) only if, on the facts of that case, the accused knew that he was being detained for the purposes of a search under s. 23(2)(a) and if the obstruction was intentional, that is to say the act viewed objectively, through the eyes of a bystander, did obstruct the constable's detention or search, and viewed subjectively, that is to say through the eyes of the accused himself, was intended so to obstruct.

For consideration of the similar phrasing in the offence of the wilful obstruction of a police officer in the execution of his duty contrary to the Police Act 1996, s. 89(2), see **B2.29** to **B2.32**.

Note s. 21 of the Health Act 2006.

OTHER OFFENCES RELATED TO MISUSE OF DRUGS

Contravention of Directions relating to Safe Custody of Controlled Drugs

B20.79 It is an offence, contrary to the MDA 1971, s. 11(2), to contravene any directions given under s. 11(1). The offence is punishable, on summary conviction, with imprisonment for a term not exceeding six months or a fine not exceeding the prescribed sum or both, and, on conviction on indictment, with imprisonment for a term not exceeding two years or a fine or both. Section 11(1) enables the Secretary of State, by notice in writing to be served on the occupier of any premises on which controlled drugs are or are proposed to be kept, to give directions as to the taking of precautions or further precautions for the safe custody of any controlled drugs of a description specified in the notice which are kept on those premises.

Contravention of Direction Prohibiting Practitioner etc. from Possessing, Supplying etc. Controlled Drugs

B20.80 It is an offence, contrary to the MDA 1971, s. 12(6), to contravene a direction given under s. 12(2). The range of sentence for the offence depends upon whether the drug is a Class A, Class B or Class C drug. It should first be noted that the different penalties mean, in accordance with *Courtie* [1984] AC 463, that s. 12(6) creates two offences, since the punishment where the drug is Class A or Class B is the same. For the penalties available on conviction, see sch. 4 to the 1971 Act (set out at **B20.105**).

Directions under s. 12(2) can be made by the Secretary of State with regard to people who fall within s. 12(1), that is, a practitioner or pharmacist who has been convicted of:

(a) an offence under the MDA 1971 or under the Dangerous Drugs Act 1965 or any enactment repealed by that Act; or
(b) an offence under Customs and Excise Act 1952, ss. 45, 56 or 30, the Customs and Excise Management Act 1979, s. 50, 68 or 170, in connection with a prohibition of or restriction on importation or exportation of a controlled drug having effect by virtue of s. 3 of the MDA 1971 or which had effect by virtue of any provision contained in or repealed by the Dangerous Drugs Act 1965;
(c) an offence under the Criminal Justice (International Co-operation) Act 1990, s. 12 or 13.

The directions which the Secretary of State imposes shall:

(a) if that person is a practitioner, be a direction prohibiting him from having in his possession, prescribing, administering, manufacturing, compounding and supplying and from authorising the administration and supply of such controlled drugs as may be specified in the direction;
(b) if that person is a pharmacist, be a direction prohibiting him from having in his possession, manufacturing, compounding and supplying and from supervising and controlling the manufacture, compounding and supply of such controlled drugs as may be specified in the direction.

Such directions may at any time be cancelled or suspended by the Secretary of State by direction under s. 12(3). Any direction must be served on the person in question and be published in the London, Edinburgh and Belfast Gazettes in accordance with s. 12(4). The direction takes effect when a copy is served on the person to whom it applies (s. 12(5)). Section 37(1) of the Act defines 'practitioner' as meaning a doctor, dentist, veterinary practitioner or veterinary surgeon, and 'pharmacist' as having the same meaning as in the Medicines Act 1968.

Contravention of Direction Prohibiting Practitioner etc. from Prescribing etc. Controlled Drugs

It is an offence, contrary to the MDA 1971, s. 13(3), to contravene a direction given under s. 13(1) or (2). The range of sentence for the offence depends upon whether the drug is a Class A, Class B or Class C drug. It should first be noted that the different penalties mean, in accordance with *Courtie* [1984] AC 463, that s. 13(3) creates two offences, since the punishment where the drug is Class A or Class B is the same. For the penalties available on conviction, see sch. 4 to the 1971 Act (set out at **B20.105**). **B20.81**

The Secretary of State's power to give directions under s. 13(1) and (2) are as follows:

(a) Where there has been a contravention of the Misuse of Drugs (Supply to Addicts) Regulations 1997 (SI 1997 No. 1001) (or other regulations concerned with doctors prescribing controlled drugs for addicts made under s. 10(2)(h) or (i)), or contravention of the terms of a licence issued to a doctor in pursuance of those regulations, the Secretary of State may, subject to and in accordance with s. 14, give a direction in respect of the doctor concerning prohibiting him from prescribing, administering and supplying and authorising the administration and supply of such controlled drugs as may be specified in the direction. (Note that s. 12(3) makes clear that contravention of the regulations is not in itself an offence.)

(b) Where the Secretary of State is of the opinion that a practitioner is, or has, after the coming into operation of s. 13(2), been prescribing, administering or supplying or authorising the administration or supply of any controlled drugs in an irresponsible manner, the Secretary of State may, subject to and in accordance with ss. 14 and 15, give a direction in respect of the practitioner concerned prohibiting him from prescribing, administering and supplying and authorising the administration and supply of such controlled drugs as may be specified in the direction.

The supplementary provisions to s. 13 are to be found in the MDA 1971, ss. 14, 15, and 16 and sch. 3.

Failure to Comply with Notice Requiring Information Relating to Prescribing Supply etc. of Drugs

It is an offence, contrary to the MDA 1971, s. 17(3), if a person without reasonable excuse (proof of which shall lie on him) fails to comply with any requirement to which he is subject by virtue of s. 17(1). The offence is punishable, on summary conviction, with a fine not exceeding level 3 on the standard scale. Where the burden of proof lies on D, it is open to challenge in the light of *Lambert* [2002] 2 AC 545 (see **B20.20** and **F3.13**; and consider *Keogh* [2007] 1 WLR 1500). **B20.82**

Giving False Information in Purported Compliance with Notice Requiring Information Relating to Prescribing, Supply etc. of Drugs

It is an offence, contrary to the MDA 1971, s. 17(4), if a person, in purported compliance with a requirement imposed under s. 17, gives any information which he knows to be false in a material particular or recklessly gives any information which is false. The offence is punishable, on summary conviction, with a term of imprisonment not exceeding six months or a fine not exceeding the prescribed sum or both, and, on conviction on indictment, with a term of imprisonment not exceeding two years or a fine or both. **B20.83**

Both this and the offence in **B20.82** rely on the provisions of s. 17(1) and (2):

Misuse of Drugs Act 1971, ss. 17 and 37

17.—(1) If it appears to the Secretary of State that there exists in any area in Great Britain a social problem caused by the extensive misuse of dangerous or otherwise harmful drugs in that area, he may by notice in writing served on any doctor or pharmacist practising in or in the vicinity of that area, or on any person carrying on a retail pharmacy business within the meaning of the Medicines Act 1968 at any premises situated in or in the vicinity of that area, require him to furnish to the Secretary of State, with respect to any such drugs specified in the notice and as regards any period so specified, such particulars as may be so specified relating to the quantities in which and the number and frequency of the occasions on which those drugs—

(a) in the case of a doctor, were prescribed, administered or supplied by him;
(b) in the case of a pharmacist, were supplied by him; or
(c) in the case of a person carrying on a retail pharmacy business, were supplied in the course of that business at any premises so situated which may be specified in the notice.

(2) A notice under this section may require any such particulars to be furnished in such manner and within such time as may be specified in the notice and, if served on a pharmacist or person carrying on a retail pharmacy business, may require him to furnish the names and addresses of doctors on whose prescriptions any dangerous or otherwise harmful drugs to which the notice relates were supplied, but shall not require any person to furnish any particulars relating to the identity of any person for or to whom any such drug has been prescribed, administered or supplied.

37.—(2) References in this Act to misusing a drug are references to misusing it by taking it; . . .

Contravention of Regulations (other than Regulations Relating to Addicts)

B20.84 It is an offence, contrary to the MDA 1971, s. 18(1), for a person to contravene any regulations made under the 1971 Act other than regulations relating to addicts. The offence is punishable, on summary conviction, with a term of imprisonment not exceeding six months or a fine not exceeding the prescribed sum or both, and, on conviction on indictment, with a term of imprisonment not exceeding two years or a fine or both. The significance of this offence, in particular, is that it means any breach of the Misuse of Drugs (Safe Custody) Regulations 1973 (SI 1973 No. 798, as amended by 1999 No. 1403 and SI 2007 No. 2154) is an offence.

Contravention of Terms of Licence or other Authority (other than Licence Issued under Regulations Relating to Addicts)

B20.85 It is an offence, contrary to the MDA 1971, s. 18(2), for a person to contravene a condition or other term of a licence issued under s. 3 of the 1971 Act or of a licence or other authority under regulations made under the 1971 Act, not being a licence issued under regulations relating to addicts. The offence is punishable, on summary conviction, with a term of imprisonment not exceeding six months or a fine not exceeding the prescribed sum or both, and, on conviction on indictment, with a term of imprisonment not exceeding two years or a fine or both.

Giving False Information in Purported Compliance with Obligation to give Information Imposed under Regulations

B20.86 It is an offence, contrary to the MDA 1971, s. 18(3), if a person, in purported compliance with any obligation to give information to which he is subject under or by virtue of regulations made under the 1971 Act, gives any information which he knows to be false in a material particular or recklessly gives any information which is so false. The offence is punishable, on summary conviction, with a term of imprisonment not exceeding six months or a fine not exceeding the prescribed sum or both, and, on conviction on indictment, with a term of imprisonment not exceeding two years or a fine or both. Information has to be supplied under the Misuse of Drugs (Supply to Addicts) Regulations 1997 (SI 1997 No. 1001).

Giving False Information, or Producing Document Containing False Statement etc. for Purpose of Obtaining Issue of Licence

B20.87 It is an offence, contrary to the MDA 1971, s. 18(4), if a person for the purpose of obtaining, whether for himself or another, the issue or renewal of a licence or other authority under the 1971 Act or any regulations made under it:

(a) makes any statement or gives any information which he knows to be false in a material particular or recklessly gives any information which is so false; or
(b) produces or otherwise makes use of any book, record or other document which to his knowledge contains any statement or information which he knows to be false in a material particular.

The offence is punishable, on summary conviction, with a term of imprisonment not exceeding six months or a fine not exceeding the prescribed sum or both, and, on conviction on indictment, with a term of imprisonment not exceeding two years or a fine or both.

SUPPLY OF INTOXICATING SUBSTANCE

Intoxicating Substances (Supply) Act 1985, s. 1 B20.88

(1) It is an offence for a person to supply or offer to supply a substance other than a controlled drug—
  (a) to a person under the age of 18 whom he knows, or has reasonable cause to believe, to be under that age; or
  (b) to a person—
    (i) who is acting on behalf of a person under that age; and
    (ii) whom he knows, or has reasonable cause to believe, to be so acting,

if he knows or has reasonable cause to believe that the substance is, or its fumes are, likely to be inhaled by the person under the age of 18 for the purpose of causing intoxication.

Procedure

The offence is triable summarily only. B20.89

Sentence

The maximum penalty is imprisonment for a term not exceeding six months or a fine not exceeding level 5 or both (Intoxicating Substances (Supply) Act 1985, s. 1(3)). B20.90

Elements and Defence

Since similar concepts apply in the MDA 1971, s. 4(3) (see **B20.28**), it may be that the same meaning of 'supply or offer to supply' appertains in the 1985 Act, but the statute does not make that clear and the point remains open. B20.91

The Intoxicating Substances (Supply) Act 1985, s. 1(4), makes clear that 'controlled drug' has the same meaning as in the MDA 1971 (see **B20.1**).

Intoxicating Substances (Supply) Act 1985, s. 1

(2) In proceedings against any person for an offence under subsection (1) above it is a defence for him to show that at the time he made the supply or offer he was under the age of 18 and was acting otherwise than in the course or furtherance of a business.

As to the incidence of proof, consider *Lambert* [2002] 2 AC 545 (see **F3.13**; and consider *Keogh* [2007] 1 WLR 1500).

MANUFACTURE AND SUPPLY OF SCHEDULED SUBSTANCES

Criminal Justice (International Co-operation) Act 1990, s. 12 B20.92

(1) It is an offence for a person—
  (a) to manufacture a scheduled substance; or
  (b) to supply such a substance to another person,

knowing or suspecting that the substance is to be used in or for the unlawful production of a controlled drug.

Procedure

B20.93 No proceedings may be instituted in England and Wales except by or with the consent of the DPP or the Commissioners of Customs and Excise (Criminal Justice (International Co-operation) Act 1990, s. 21(2)(a)). The offence is triable either way (s. 12(2)). When tried on indictment it is a class 4 offence.

As to the position where the offence is committed on a British ship, see ss. 18 and 24. Section 21 of the MDA 1971 (liability of corporate officers — see **B20.24**) applies to this offence.

Sentence

B20.94 The maximum penalty on conviction on indictment is imprisonment for a term not exceeding 14 years or a fine or both; on summary conviction, the maximum penalty is imprisonment for a term not exceeding six months or a fine not exceeding the statutory maximum or both (Criminal Justice (International Co-operation) Act 1990, s. 12(2)). This is a drug trafficking offence within the meaning of the Proceeds of Crime Act 2002, sch. 2 (see **E21.11**). A minimum custodial sentence of seven years applies for the third Class A drug trafficking offence (see **E6.1**). A confiscation order (see **E21**) or forfeiture order (see **E20.4**) may be imposed for a drug trafficking offence.

Scheduled Substance

B20.95 A scheduled substance is a substance specified in the Criminal Justice (International Co-operation) Act 1990, sch. 2. Schedule 2 may be amended by Her Majesty by Order in Council, except that no substance may be added unless it appears to Her Majesty to be frequently used in or for the unlawful production of a controlled drug, or it has been added to the Annex to the 1988 Vienna Convention against Illicit Traffic in Narcotic Drugs and Psychotic Substances (s. 12(5)).

Criminal Justice (International Co-operation) Act 1990, sch. 2

TABLE I

N-Acetylanthranilic acid	3,4-Methylene-dioxyphenyl-2-propanone
Ephedrine	Norephedrine
Ergometrine	1-Phenyl-2-propanone
Ergotamine	Piperonal
Isosafrole	Pseudoephedrine
Lysergic acid	Safrole

The salts of the substances listed in this table whenever the existence of such salts is possible.

TABLE II

Acetic anhydride	Phenylacetic acid
Acetone	Piperidine
Anthranilic acid	Potassium permanganate
Ethyl ether	Sulphuric acid
Hydrochloric acid	Toluene
Methyl ethyl ketone (also referred to as 2-Butanone or M.E.K.)	

The salts of the substances listed in this table except hydrochloric acid and sulphuric acid whenever the existence of such salts is possible.

Unlawful Production of a Controlled Drug

B20.96 The phrase 'controlled drug' has the same meaning as in the MDA 1971 (Criminal Justice (International Co-operation) Act 1990, s. 12(3)). For that definition, see **B20.1**. 'Unlawful production of a controlled drug' means production of such a drug which is unlawful by virtue of the MDA 1971, s. 4(1)(a) (Criminal Justice (International Co-operation) Act 1990, s. 12(3)). See **B20.40** *et seq.*

A person does not commit this offence if 'he manufactures or, as the case may be, supplies the scheduled substance with the express consent of a constable' (s. 12(1A)).

Supply

Supply is not defined in the Criminal Justice (International Co-operation) Act 1990, but it is presumed that it has the same meaning as in the MDA 1971 (see **B20.28**), as is explicitly the case in the regulations made under the Criminal Justice (International Co-operation) Act 1990, s. 13 (see **B20.98**). **B20.97**

CONTROLLED DRUGS (SUBSTANCES USEFUL FOR MANUFACTURE) REGULATIONS 1991

Making and Preserving Records of Production and Supply of Certain Scheduled Substances

It is an offence for a person to fail to comply with any requirement imposed by regulations made under the Criminal Justice (International Co-operation) Act 1990, s. 13, or, in purported compliance with any such requirement, to furnish information which he knows to be false in a material particular or recklessly to furnish information which is false in a material particular. The offence is triable either way and is punishable, on indictment, with imprisonment for a term not exceeding two years or a fine or both and, on summary conviction, with imprisonment for a term not exceeding six months or a fine not exceeding the statutory maximum or both (s. 13(5)). The Controlled Drugs (Substances Useful for Manufacture) Regulations 1991 (SI 1991 No. 1285) have been made in accordance with s. 13. The regulations have been amended (see the Controlled Drugs (Substances Useful for Manufacture) (Amendment) Regulations 1992 (SI 1992 No. 2914)). Regulation 7 requires a person who produces or supplies a scheduled substance specified in the Criminal Justice (International Co-operation) Act 1990, sch. 2, table I (see **B20.95**) to make a record of each quantity of such scheduled substance produced or supplied by him, and preserve all such records for a period of not less than two years from the end of the calendar year in which the production or supply took place. Regulation 7 provides that 'produce' and 'supply' have the same meaning as in the MDA 1971 (see **B20.43** and **B20.28** respectively). **B20.98**

Enforcement of European Community Obligations

The Controlled Drugs (Substances Useful for Manufacture) Regulations 1991 enforce the obligations imposed on operators and the requirement of notification under Council Regulation (EEC) No. 3677/90 laying down measures to be taken to discourage the diversion of certain substances to the illicit manufacture of narcotic drugs and psychotropic substances (reg. 3). If a person fails to satisfy these obligations, an offence is committed contrary to the Criminal Justice (International Co-operation) Act 1990, s. 13(5) (see **B20.98**). However, on summary conviction, the maximum prison sentence is three and not six months (reg. 6(d)). See also the Controlled Drugs (Substances Useful for Manufacture) (Intra-Community Trade) Regulations 1993 (SI 1993 No. 2166), the Controlled Drugs (Substances Useful for Manufacture) (Intra-Community Trade) (Amendment) Regulations 2001 (SI 2001 No. 3683), and the Controlled Drugs (Substances Useful for Manufacture) (Intra-Community Trade) (Amendment) Regulations 2004 (SI 2004 No. 850). **B20.99**

SHIPS USED FOR ILLICIT TRAFFIC

Criminal Justice (International Co-operation) Act 1990, s. 19 **B20.100**

(2) A person is guilty of an offence if on a ship to which this section applies, wherever it may be, he—
  (a) has a controlled drug in his possession; or
  (b) is in any way knowingly concerned in the carrying or concealing of a controlled drug on the ship,

knowing or having reasonable grounds to suspect that the drug is intended to be imported or has been exported contrary to section 3(1) of the Misuse of Drugs Act 1971 or the law of any state other than the United Kingdom.

Procedure

B20.101 No proceedings shall be instituted except by or with the consent of the DPP or the Commissioners of Customs and Excise (Criminal Justice (International Co-operation) Act 1990, s. 21(2)(a)). Further, no proceedings for the offence which is alleged to have been committed outside the landward limits of the territorial sea of the UK on a ship registered in a state which is a party to the Vienna Convention, may be instituted except in pursuance of the exercise with the authority of the Secretary of State of the powers conferred by sch. 3, and the Territorial Waters Jurisdiction Act 1878, s. 3, does not apply to these proceedings (Criminal Justice (International Co-operation) Act 1990, s. 21(3)).

As sentences for the offence vary according to the class of drug involved, there are three offences created by s. 19(2) (see *Courtie* [1984] AC 463). The offences are all triable either way (s. 19(4)). When tried on indictment they are class 4 offences.

Proceedings for these offences in respect of an offence on a ship may be taken, and the offence may for all incidental purposes by treated as having been committed, in any place in the UK (s. 21(1)).

Section 21 of the MDA 1971 (liability of corporate officers — see **B20.24**) applies to this offence.

Sentence

B20.102 Where a class A drug is involved, the maximum penalty on indictment is imprisonment for life or a fine or both; on summary conviction, the maximum penalty is imprisonment for a term not exceeding six months or a fine not exceeding the statutory maximum or both (Criminal Justice (International Co-operation) Act 1990, s. 15(4)(a)). A minimum custodial sentence of seven years applies for the third Class A drug trafficking offence (see **E6.1**).

Where a Class B drug is involved, the maximum penalty on indictment is imprisonment for a term not exceeding 14 years or a fine or both; on summary conviction, the maximum penalty is imprisonment for a term not exceeding six months or a fine not exceeding the statutory maximum or both (s. 15(4)(b)).

Where a Class C drug is involved, the maximum penalty on indictment is imprisonment for a term not exceeding 14 years or a fine or both; on summary conviction, the maximum penalty is imprisonment for a term not exceeding three months or a fine not exceeding the statutory maximum or both (s. 15(4)(c)).

It is clearly established that where drugs have been intercepted on the high seas and those drugs were destined for a country other than England or Wales, the maximum available sentence for such offences in that other country is not a relevant sentencing consideration (*Maguire* [1997] 1 Cr App R (S) 130; *Wagenaar* [1997] 1 Cr App R (S) 178). The sentencing guidelines laid down by the Court of Appeal should be followed (see **B20.105** ***et seq.***).

These are drug trafficking offences within the meaning of the Proceeds of Crime Act 2002, sch. 2 (see **E21.11**), so a forfeiture order (see **E20.4**) or a confiscation order (see **E21**) may be imposed.

Elements

B20.103 The Criminal Justice (International Co-operation) Act 1990, s. 19(2), applies to a British ship, a ship registered in a state other than the UK which is a party to the Vienna Convention (a Convention state), and a ship not registered in any country or territory (s. 19(1)). Ship includes any vessel used in navigation; British ship means a ship registered in the UK or a colony (s. 24(1)).

'Controlled drug', and the classes of controlled drugs, have the same meaning as in the MDA 1971, see **B20.1** (s. 19(5)). Since the defence in the MDA 1971, s. 28, applies, the meaning of possession in that Act should apply to the present offence. See **B20.11** ***et seq.***

As to the MDA 1971, s. 3(1), see **B17.16**. A certificate purporting to be issued by or on behalf of the government of any state to the effect that the importation or export of a controlled drug is prohibited by the law of that state shall be evidence of the matters stated (s. 19(3)).

It was made clear in *Dean* [1998] 2 Cr App R 171, that it is for the prosecution to prove, to the criminal standard of proof, that the ship in question is one to which s. 19 applies. The Court of Appeal said that it is 'sensible' to decide that issue at the outset of the trial rather than at the end of the prosecution case. On the facts of that particular case, the judge found that the ship was not registered anywhere and thus s. 19 was engaged.

Defence

The defence in the MDA 1971, s. 28, applies (Criminal Justice (International Co-operation) Act 1990, s. 19(5)). See **B20.20** for full details of the defence. **B20.104**

SENTENCING GUIDELINES FOR OFFENCES UNDER THE MISUSE OF DRUGS ACT 1971

Maximum and Minimum Sentences

For sentencing purposes it is necessary to draw a distinction between three different types of drugs: **B20.105**

(a) Class A drugs (especially heroin, morphine, cocaine, LSD, opium and Ecstasy);
(b) Class B drugs (especially amphetamine and codeine); and
(c) Class C drugs (especially cannabis, cannabis resin, benzphetamine and pemoline).

A minimum custodial sentence of seven years must be imposed by the court where an offender aged 18 or over is convicted of a Class A drug trafficking offence committed after 1 October 1997, he has been convicted of two other Class A drug trafficking offences, and there are no particular circumstances relating to any of the offences, or the offender, such that the imposition of a custodial sentence of at least seven years would be unjust in all the circumstances (PCC(S)A 2000, s. 110; see **E6.1**).

Section 25 of the 1971 Act provides for the range of punishment for offences under the Act to be as set out in sch. 4 (see **B20.107**).

Forfeiture and Confiscation

For the court's powers of forfeiture under the MDA 1971, s. 27, see **E20.4**. For powers of confiscation, see **E21**. **B20.106**

Class A Drug Offences

A minimum custodial sentence of seven years applies for the third Class A drug trafficking offence (see **E6.1**). The starting-point for sentencing for Class A offences is the guideline case of *Aramah* (1982) 4 Cr App R (S) 407, modified in certain respects by *Bilinski* (1987) 9 Cr App R (S) 360, *Singh* (1988) 10 Cr App R (S) 402, *Aroyewumi* (1994) 99 Cr App R 347, *Warren* [1996] 1 Cr App R (S) 233, *Hurley* [1998] 1 Cr App R (S) 299, *Mashaollahi* [2001] 1 Cr App R 106 and *Morris* [2001] 1 Cr App R 25. The following guidelines from *Aramah* per **B20.107**

Lord Lane CJ at pp. 408–9 have, therefore, been amended where appropriate to incorporate those modifications:

> Class A Drugs and particularly heroin and morphine: It is common knowledge that these are the most dangerous of all the addictive drugs . . . Consequently anything which the courts of this country can do by way of deterrent sentences on those found guilty of crimes involving these Class A drugs should be done.
>
> I turn to the importation of heroin, morphine and so on: Large scale importation, that is where [the weight of the drugs at 100 per cent purity is of the order of 500 grammes] or more, sentences of [10 years] and upwards are appropriate. There will be cases where [the weight at 100 per cent purity is of the order of 5 kilogrammes] or more, in which case the offence should be visited by sentences of [14 years and upwards]. It will be seldom that an importer of any appreciable amount of the drug will deserve less than four years.
>
> This, however, is one area in which it is particularly important that offenders should be encouraged to give information to the police, and a confession of guilt, coupled with considerable assistance to the police can properly be marked by a substantial reduction in what would otherwise be the proper sentence.
>
> Next, supplying heroin, morphine etc.: It goes without saying that the sentence will largely depend on the degree of involvement, the amount of trafficking and the value of the drug handled. It is seldom that a sentence of less than [five] years will be justified and the nearer the source of supply the defendant is shown to be, the heavier will be the sentence. There may well be cases where sentences similar to those appropriate to large scale importers may be necessary. It is however unhappily all too seldom that those big fish amongst the suppliers get caught.
>
> Possession of heroin, morphine etc. (simple possession): It is at this level that the circumstances of the individual offender become of much greater importance. Indeed the possible variety of considerations is so wide, including often those of a medical nature, that we feel it impossible to lay down any practical guidelines. On the other hand the maximum penalty for simple possession of Class A drugs is seven years' imprisonment and/or a fine, and there will be very many cases where deprivation of liberty is both proper and expedient.

In *Martinez* (1984) 6 Cr App R (S) 364, at p. 365, Lord Lane CJ confirmed that the *Aramah* guidelines on Class A drugs were not confined to heroin and that 'any idea that those who import or deal in cocaine or LSD, as it is known, should be treated more leniently is entirely wrong'. Further, in *Allery* (1993) 14 Cr App R (S) 699, the Court of Appeal rejected an argument that Ecstasy was to be treated as a drug less dangerous than other Class A drugs, such as heroin or cocaine. In *Morris* [2001] 1 Cr App R 25, the Court of Appeal explained that the amount of a Class A drug with which the defendant was involved was a very important factor, but not the sole determinative factor, in sentencing. The amount should generally be based on the weight of the drug involved at 100 per cent purity and not, in general, its street value. In some circumstances, however, reference to street values of the same weight of different drugs might be pertinent simply by way of a cross-check. For example, 1 kg of LSD was worth very much more than 1 kg of heroin. Weight depended on purity. The purity of drugs such as cocaine and heroin, which were not in tablet or dosage form and were often contaminated by other substances, could be appropriately determined only by analysis. Such analysis was essential wherever 500 gm or more of cocaine or heroin were seized and would sometimes be required where smaller amounts were involved. The weight of drugs such as Ecstasy in tablet form or LSD in dosage form could generally be assessed by reference to the number of tablets or doses on an assumed average purity of 100 milligrammes per tablet of Ecstasy and 50 microgrammes per dosage of LSD, unless a different level of purity was shown by expert evidence.

In *Warren* [1996] 1 Cr App R (S) 233, the Court of Appeal said that in cases involving importation of 5,000 or more Ecstasy tablets the appropriate sentence would be in the order of ten years and upwards; for 50,000 tablets or more, it would be 14 years and upwards. These figures were based on the assumption that the tablets were of average, or near average, quality. If analysis showed a substantially different content, then the weight of the constituent

Misuse of Drugs Act, sch. 4

Section 25

SCHEDULE 4 PROTECTION AND PUNISHMENT OF OFFENCES

Section Creating Offence	General Nature of Offence	Mode of Prosecution	Punishment			
			Class A drug involved	Class B drug involved	Class C drug involved	General
Section 4(2)	Production, or being concerned in the production, of a controlled drug	(a) Summary	6 months or the prescribed sum, or both	6 months or the prescribed sum, or both	3 months or £2,500, or both	
		(b) On Indictment	Life or a fine, or both	14 years or a fine, or both	14 years or a fine, or both	
Section 4(3)	Supplying or offering to supply a controlled drug or being concerned in the doing of either activity by another	(a) Summary	6 months or the prescribed sum, or both	6 months or the prescribed sum, or both	3 months or £2,500 or both	
		(b) On indictment	Life or a fine, or both	14 years of a fine, or both	14 years or a fine, or both	
Section 5(2)	Having possession of a controlled drug	(a) Summary	6 months or the prescribed sum, or both	3 months or £2,500 or both	3 months or £1,000 or both	
		(b) On indictment	7 years or a fine, or both	5 years or a fine, or both	2 years or a fine, or both	
Section 5(3)	Having possession of a controlled drug with intent to supply it to another	(a) Summary	6 months or the prescribed sum, or both	6 months or the prescribed sum, or both	3 months or £2,500 or both	
		(b) On indictment	Life or a fine, or both	14 years or a fine, or both	14 years or a fine, or both	
Section 6(2)	Cultivation of cannabis plant	(a) Summary	—	—	—	6 months or the prescribed sum, or both
		(b) On indictment	—	—	—	14 years or a fine, or both
Section 8	Being the occupier, or concerned in the management, of premises and permitting or suffering certain activities to take place there	(a) Summary	6 months or the prescribed sum, or both	6 months or the prescribed sum, or both	3 months or £2,500 or both	
		(b) On indictment	14 years or a fine, or both	14 years or a fine, or both	14 years or a fine, or both	

Section 9	Offences to opium	(a) Summary	—	—	—	6 months or the prescribed sum or both
		(b) On indictment	—	—	—	14 years or a fine, or both
Section 9A	Prohibition of supply etc of articles for administering or preparing controlled drugs	Summary	—	—	—	6 months or level 5 on the standard scale, or both
Section 11(2)	Contravention of direction relating to safe custody of controlled drugs	(a) Summary	—	—	—	6 months or the prescribed sum, or both
		(b) On indictment	—	—	—	2 years or a fine, or both
Section 12(6)	Contravention of direction prohibiting practitioner etc from possessing, supply etc controlled drugs	(a) Summary	6 months or the prescribed sum, or both	6 months or the prescribed sum, or both	3 months or £2,500 or both	
		(b) On indictment	14 years or a fine, or both	14 years or a fine, or both	14 years or a fine, or both	
Section 13(3)	Contravention of direction prohibiting practitioner etc from prescribing, supplying etc controlled drugs	(a) Summary	6 months or the prescribed sum, or both	6 months or the prescribed sum, or both	3 months or £2,500 or both	
		(b) On indictment	14 years or a fine, or both	14 years or a fine, or both	14 years or a fine, or both	
			—	—	—	2 years or a fine, or both
Section 17(3)	Failure to comply with notice requiring information relating to prescribing, supplying etc of drugs	Summary	—	—	—	level 3 on the standard scale
Section 17(4)	Giving false information in purported compliance with notice requiring information relating to prescribing, supply etc of drugs	(a) Summary	—	—	—	6 months or the prescribed sum, or both
		(b) On indictment				2 years or a fine, or both

Section Creating Offence	General Nature of Offence	Mode of Prosecution	Punishment			
			Class A drug involved	Class B drug involved	Class C drug involved	General
Section 18(1)	Contravention of regulations (other than regulations relating to addicts)	(a) Summary	—	—	—	6 months or prescribed sum, or both
Section 18(2)	Contravention of terms of licence or other authority (other than licence issued under regulations relating to addicts)	(a) Summary	—	—	—	6 months or the prescribed sum, or both
		(b) On indictment	—	—	—	2 years or a fine, or both
Section 18(3)	Giving false information in purported compliance with obligation to give information imposed under or by virtue of regulations	(a) Summary	—	—	—	6 months or the prescribed sum, or both
		(b) On indictment	—	—	—	2 years or a fine, or both
Section 18(4)	Giving false information, or producing documents etc containing false statement etc, for purposes of obtaining issue or renewal of a licence or other authority	(a) Summary	—	—	—	6 months or the prescribed sum, or both
		(b) On indictment	—	—	—	2 years or a fine, or both
Section 20	Assisting in or inducing commission outside United Kingdom of an offence punishable under a corresponding law	(a) Summary	—	—	—	6 months or the prescribed sum, or both
		(b) On indictment	—	—	—	14 years or a fine, or both
Section 23(4)	Obstructing exercise of powers of search etc or concealing books, drugs, etc	(a) Summary	—	—	—	6 months or the prescribed sum, or both
		(b) On indictment	—	—	—	2 years or a fine, or both

would be the determinative factor. The Court of Appeal stressed that other matters were also of importance, such as the role of the offender in the offence, his plea, and whether he had provided assistance to the authorities. In *Hurley* [1998] 1 Cr App R (S) 299, the Court of Appeal issued guidance on sentencing levels for importation of LSD. In the case of 25,000 or more quarter-inch squares or dosage units the sentence should in the ordinary case be ten years plus. For 250,000 or more dosage units the sentence should ordinarily be 14 years plus. In each case their lordships were assuming that the dosage unit was of approximately 50 micrograms content pure LSD. Adjustment might be needed when it was shown to vary significantly from that figure. Where the seizure was of tablets or of crystals in a form which enabled a precise weight to be ascertained readily there should be no problem in calculating the number of 50 microgram doses. The Court of Appeal appreciated that cases might arise where, to do justice in individual cases, the sentence level could vary accordingly from the guidelines indicated. In *Mashaollahi* [2001] 1 Cr App R 106, the Court of Appeal issued guidelines on the importation of opium and possession of that drug with intent to supply. The appropriate sentence in a contested case, for possession with intent to supply 40 kilos or more of opium, was 14 years and upwards, and for four kilos or more the sentence was ten years and upwards. There would, however, be an exception where there was evidence that importation of the opium was carried out for conversion into morphine or heroin. Then the appropriate sentence should be based on the equivalent value of those drugs. The sentencing court should proceed on the basis that any given consignment of opium was unadulterated and of 100 per cent purity, although the defence might advance argument in a particular case that the active ingredient was of a lesser percentage.

In *Attuh-Benson* [2005] 2 Cr App R (S) 52, the Court of Appeal stated that it would not be appropriate at present to reconsider the guidelines in *Aramah* with respect to the sentencing of drug couriers, who were often women with dependent children who came from under-developed countries and would suffer considerable hardship from lengthy prison sentences that they would be required to serve in this country. The court did say, however, that there was sufficient flexibility in the *Aramah* guidelines to allow judges to assess the role of the offender, the extent of their culpability, their attitude to the offence and their personal circumstances. In *Robinson* [2004] 2 Cr App R (S) 392, the Court of Appeal observed that in some cases involving importation of drugs where a defence of duress has been run without success, it may still be necessary for the sentencer to hold a *Newton* hearing to determine whether there had been a degree of coercion short of duress.

The *Aramah* guidelines show that most offences relating to Class A drugs are not suitable for summary trial. When cases of simple possession of Class A drugs are dealt with summarily, the Magistrates' Courts Guidelines (2004) indicate the following:

Aggravating Factors For example an amount other than a very small quantity; offence committed on bail; relevant previous convictions and any failures to respond to previous sentences.

Mitigating Factors For example very small quantity.

Guideline: Is it serious enough for a community penalty?

When cases of production and supply of Class A drugs are dealt with summarily, the Guidelines indicate the following:

Aggravating Factors For example commercial production; large amount; deliberate adulteration; venue, e.g. prisons, educational establishments; sophisticated operation; supply to children; offence committed on bail; relevant previous convictions and any failures to respond to previous sentences.

Mitigating Factors For example small amount.

Guideline: Is it so serious that only custody is appropriate? Are magistrates' sentencing powers appropriate?

In all cases, whether of possession or supply, the Guidelines indicate that forfeiture of all drugs and equipment should be considered.

There are numerous Court of Appeal decisions which apply the *Aramah* guidelines in respect of Class A drug offences. The first group is concerned with *importation.* A sentence of 20 years was upheld in *Latif* [1995] 1 Cr App R 270, where 20 kg of heroin had been imported by a 'principal organiser', and 24 years' imprisonment was upheld in *Main* [1997] 2 Cr App R (S) 63, where the offenders were concerned in an attempt to import 1.2 million tablets of Ecstasy in a furniture van. Following interception of the van, a further 111,275 Ecstasy tablets were discovered at their premises. See also *Kaynak* [1998] 2 Cr App R (S) 283. In *Bayley* (1995) 16 Cr App R (S) 605, 15 years' imprisonment was upheld for the importation of 58 kg of Ecstasy. In *Bilinski* (1987) 9 Cr App R (S) 360, the offender pleaded guilty to importing 3.036 kg of heroin. The Court of Appeal said that a sentence of eight years was appropriate, bearing in mind the guilty plea and the assistance the offender gave to the authorities. The case also establishes that an offender's belief that the drugs were in fact Class B and not Class A drugs is relevant to sentence. If this matter is in dispute, a *Newton* hearing may be appropriate to determine it. In *Bilinski*, it seems, a cursory inquiry would have revealed the true nature of the drug and, accordingly, the appropriate reduction was small. Other relevant cases are *Daniel* (1995) 16 Cr App R (S) 892 (offender stopped at Gatwick Airport and found to be in possession of 1.43 kg of heroin at 45 per cent purity; nine years' imprisonment upheld); and *Mouzulukwe* [1996] 2 Cr App R (S) 48 (offender concealed within his body 31 packets containing 231 grammes of powder, including 38 grammes of pure heroin; six years' imprisonment upheld).

As far as *distribution* of Class A drugs is concerned, in *Djahit* [1999] 2 Cr App R (S) 142 the Court of Appeal considered the appropriate sentence for 'a typical low-level retailer of heroin or other Class A drug, with no relevant previous convictions, selling to other addicts in order to be able to buy drugs for his own consumption and to earn enough to live very modestly'. Hooper J stated that such an offender may expect about six years' imprisonment. Selling to the vulnerable or the young would increase the sentence, as would introducing persons to heroin for the first time. A guilty plea will reduce sentence by one quarter to one third and personal circumstances may reduce it further. This sentencing bracket was reviewed in detail by the Court of Appeal in *Twisse* [2001] 2 Cr App R (S) 37, where it was approved as bearing an appropriate relationship to the sentences imposed for importation of Class A drugs. A sentence of six years' imprisonment was reduced to five years in *Weeks* [1999] 2 Cr App R (S) 16, where the offender pleaded guilty to nine counts of supplying heroin. The offender admitted that he was a dealer, claiming that he sold on behalf of someone else but that he was allowed to keep three bags out of every ten that he sold. In *Afonso* [2005] 1 Cr App R (S) 560, however, the Court of Appeal said that there was a group of offenders who supplied Class A drugs for whom sentences in the region of six years following a trial was too high. These were offenders who were out-of-work drug addicts, whose motive was solely to finance the feeding of their own addiction, who held no stock of drugs and were shown to have made a few retail supplies of the drug to which they were addicted to undercover police officers. There would be some adult and young offenders for whom a drug treatment and testing order would be appropriate. Otherwise, an adult offender, for whom this was their first drugs-supply offence, would, following a plea of guilty, receive a term of the order of two to two and half years. For young offenders, the term was likely to be less. In *A-G's Ref (No. 20 of 2002)* [2003] 1 Cr App R (S) 279, the 21-year-old offender pleaded guilty to possession of 786 Ecstasy tablets with intent to supply. The Court of Appeal said that the normal range of sentence in such a case was three to four years' imprisonment, and that the community punishment and rehabilitation order imposed by the judge in this case had been an unduly lenient sentence. Numerous decisions of the Court of Appeal show that supply of drugs to a serving prisoner is a serious aggravating feature of this offence. In *Babbington* [2006] 1 Cr App R (S) 4, where a number of earlier authorities were considered, three years' imprisonment was upheld on the offender who had hidden 520 mg of crack cocaine in her clothing preparatory to passing it to a prisoner on a visit.

As far as sentencing for *possession* of Class A drugs is concerned, the *Aramah* guidelines indicate that sentence may differ widely according to the circumstances, but that 'there will be very many cases where deprivation of liberty is both proper and expedient'. In *Layton* (1988) 10 Cr App R (S) 109, the offender, who had a bad criminal record but no previous drug-related convictions, pleaded guilty to possession of 5.6 grammes of cocaine. A sentence of three months' imprisonment was substituted for the 30 months imposed by the sentencer. Three months' imprisonment was appropriate in *Cox* (1994) 15 Cr App R (S) 216, where the offender was in possession of 16 Ecstasy tablets and 1.5 grammes of crack cocaine. Twelve months was reduced to eight months in *Nawaz* [1999] 1 Cr App R (S) 377, where the offender pleaded guilty to possession of three wraps of crack cocaine for his own use. In *Roberts* [1997] 2 Cr App R (S) 187, a prisoner serving a four-year sentence for possession of heroin with intent to supply was found to be in possession of a small quantity of heroin when searched by prison officers. The Court of Appeal stated that possession of drugs by a prisoner was more serious than possession of drugs outside prison, and upheld a consecutive sentence of 15 months' imprisonment.

Examples of cases of permitting premises to be used for supplying Class A drugs are *Gregory* (1993) 14 Cr App R (S) 403, where a custodial sentence of 15 months' imprisonment, imposed consecutively to terms of imprisonment for other drug offences, was reduced to six months on appeal, and *Bradley* [1997] 1 Cr App R (S) 59, where the offender's premises were used a brothel at which cocaine was supplied. The appropriate sentence for the offence was two years' imprisonment. An exceptional case is *Brock* [2001] 2 Cr App R (S) 249, where the offenders were the project manager and director of a daytime drop-in centre providing shelter for homeless and disadvantaged people. The offenders were convicted of permitting their premises to be used for the supply of heroin. The Court of Appeal quashed sentences of five years and four years, commenting that, in the absence of any evil motive or commercial gain on the part of the offenders (who were of previous good character), sentences of 18 months would have been appropriate.

Class B Drug Offences

B20.108 The Court of Appeal guideline case for these offences is *Aramah* (1982) 4 Cr App R (S) 407, where Lord Lane CJ (at pp. 409–10) distinguished importation, supply and possession of cannabis. The guidelines are set out here as amended by the Court of Appeal in *Ronchetti* [1998] 2 Cr App R (S) 100, on importation of large quantities of cannabis. With effect from 29 January 2004, cannabinol and cannabinol derivatives, cannabis and cannabis resin were reclassified as Class C drugs (see the Misuse of Drugs Act 1971 (Modification) (No. 2) Order 2003 (SI 2003 No. 3201)). The maximum penalties for a range of offences including production, or being concerned in the production, of cannabis under the MDA 1971, s. 4(2), supply or offering to supply under s. 4(3), possession with intent to supply under s. 5(3), and being the occupier of premises and permitting certain activities under s. 8, were, however, all increased with effect from the same date from five years to 14 years by the CJA 2003, s. 284 and sch. 28. It is submitted that the following guidelines are still applicable despite the reclassification.

> Class B Drugs, particularly cannabis: We select this from among the Class B drugs as being the drug most likely to be exercising the minds of the courts.
>
> Importation of cannabis: Importation of very small amounts for personal use can be dealt with as if it were simple possession, with which we will deal later. Otherwise importations of amounts up to about 20 kg of herbal cannabis or cannabis resin, or the equivalent in cannabis oil, will, save in the most exceptional circumstances, attract sentences of between 18 months and three years, with the lowest ranges reserved for pleas of guilty where there has been small profit to the offender. The good character of the courier (as he usually is) is of less importance than the good

> character of the defendant in other cases. The reason for this is, it is well known that the large scale operator looks for couriers of good character and for people of a sort which are likely to exercise the sympathy of the court if they are detected and arrested. Consequently one will frequently find that students and sick and elderly people are used as couriers for two reasons: first of all they are vulnerable to suggestion and vulnerable to the offer of quick profit, and secondly it is felt that the courts may be moved to misplaced sympathy in their case. There are few, if any, occasions when anything other than an immediate custodial sentence is proper in this type of importation.
>
> Medium quantities over 20 kg will attract sentences of three to six years' imprisonment, depending upon the amount involved, and all the other circumstances of the case.
>
> The importation of 100 kg by persons playing more than a subordinate role should attract a sentence of seven to eight years. Ten years was the appropriate starting point following a trial for importation by such persons of 500 kg or more. Larger importations would attract a higher starting point, which should rise according to the roles played, the weight involved and all the other circumstances of the case, up to the statutory maximum of 14 years. A discount from all the figures indicated would, of course, be called for according to the roles played and where there was a plea of guilty.
>
> Supply of cannabis: Here again the supply of massive quantities will justify sentences in the region of 10 years for those playing anything more than a subordinate role. Otherwise the bracket should be between one to four years' imprisonment, depending on the scale of the operation. Supplying a number of small sellers — wholesaling if you like — comes at the top of the bracket. At the lower end will be the retailer of a small amount to a consumer. Where there is no commercial motive (for example, where cannabis is supplied at a party) the offence may well be serious enough to justify a custodial sentence.

In *Wijs* [1998] 2 Cr App R 436, the Court of Appeal issued sentencing guidelines in respect of the unlawful importation of amphetamine and the possession of amphetamine with intent to supply. Lord Bingham CJ referred to the guidelines in *Aramah* and stated that no distinction should be drawn between different drugs included within Class B on the basis that one such drug is more pernicious than another. His lordship noted, however, that weight for weight amphetamine has always been vastly more valuable than cannabis, and that amphetamine was retailed to customers in a highly adulterated form. Goods seized at point of importation may contain a high percentage of the drug, but at a retail level the purity may be 10 per cent to 12 per cent or less. It followed that a trafficker in possession of a given quantity of amphetamine stood to earn very much larger sums than a trafficker in possession of the same weight of cannabis. For amphetamine-related offences, sentencing should not depend on market value but, subject to other considerations, on the quantity of the amphetamine in question calculated on the basis of 100 per cent pure amphetamine base (i.e. the maximum theoretical purity of 73 per cent amphetamine base in amphetamine sulphate, the remaining 27 per cent being the sulphate). On conviction of importing amphetamine following a contested trial, a custodial sentence will almost invariably be called for save in exceptional circumstances or where the quantity of the drug is so small as to be compatible with personal consumption by the importer. The ordinary level of sentence on conviction following a contested trial (subject to all other considerations, and on quantities calculated on the basis of 100 per cent pure amphetamine base) should be:

(a) up to 500 grammes: up to two years' imprisonment;
(b) more than 500 grammes but less than 2.5 kg: two to four years;
(c) more than 2.5 kg but less than 10 kg: four to seven years;
(d) more than 10 kg but less than 15 kg: seven to ten years;
(e) more than 15 kg: upwards of ten years, subject to the statutory maximum of 14 years.

The Court of Appeal in *Morris* [2001] 1 Cr App R 25, observed that, in cases involving more than 500 grammes of amphetamine, purity analysis was essential for sentencing purposes, and analysis might be desirable in cases involving smaller amounts.

When cases of possession of Class B drugs with intent to supply are dealt with summarily the Magistrates' Courts Guidelines (2004) indicate the following for a first-time offender pleading not guilty:

Aggravating Factors For example commercial supply; large amount; venue, e.g. prisons, educational; establishments; supply to children; deliberate adulteration; offence committed on bail; relevant previous convictions and any failures to respond to previous sentences.
Mitigating Factors For example no commercial motive; small amount.

Guideline: Are magistrates' sentencing powers appropriate?

In all cases forfeiture of all drugs and equipment should be considered.

When cases of simple possession of Class B drugs are dealt with summarily, the Magistrates' Courts Guidelines (2004) indicate the following for a first-time offender pleading not guilty:

Aggravating Factors For example large amount; offence committed on bail; relevant previous convictions and any failures to respond to previous sentences.

Mitigating Factors For example small amount.

Guideline: Is discharge or fine appropriate?

The guideline fine is Starting Point B (see E17.5). In all cases forfeiture of all drugs and equipment should be considered.

There are several Court of Appeal decisions following and applying the guidelines in *Aramah*, dealing with the appropriate sentences for offences in connection with Class B drug offences, mainly cannabis. The first group is concerned with *importation*. At the top end of the scale, the offenders in *Royle* [1997] 1 Cr App R (S) 184, received sentences of 13 years and seven years respectively for their roles in the importation by boat of 1,609 kg of cannabis resin, estimated to be worth in excess of £5.5 million. The sentences were upheld, the Court of Appeal noting that only a modest reduction was appropriate for their guilty pleas since the offenders had been caught red-handed by the customs authorities. In *Vickers* [1999] 2 Cr App R (S) 216, the Court of Appeal indicated that, following a trial, the sentence appropriate for importations of the order of 100 kg by persons playing more than a subordinate role, should be seven to eight years. Ten years was appropriate, following a trial, for importations of 500 kg or more. Larger importations would attract higher starting points. In *Frazer* [1998] 1 Cr App R (S) 287, a sentence of six years was upheld in respect of an offender who was found to have 36 kg of cannabis in his suitcase at Gatwick Airport. The sentence, at the top end of the bracket in *Aramah*, was justified since this was the offender's third such conviction. Towards the lower end of the importation scale, in *Watson* (1988) 10 Cr App R (S) 256, the offender and another woman imported 12 kg of cannabis, the offender's suitcase containing 7.4 kg. She was convicted after a trial and sentenced to four years' imprisonment. This was reduced to two years, in line with the *Aramah* guidelines. The offender in *Blyth* [1996] 1 Cr App R (S) 388, arrived in Dover by coach and was found to be in possession of 16 kg of cannabis resin. He admitted having made several previous trips for the purposes of importing cannabis from Spain. A sentence of two years' imprisonment was upheld. In *Astbury* [1997] 2 Cr App R (S) 93, three months' imprisonment was said to be appropriate for importing 1,100 grammes of cannabis, to the value of about £1,500, for personal use. The Court of Appeal in *Elder* (1993) 15 Cr App R (S) 514, found, with some hesitation, that importation by two defendants of 200 grammes of cannabis resin and 700 grammes of herbal cannabis for personal use was an offence which did not cross the custody threshold and could properly be dealt with by way of a community service order.

The second group of cases involves *distribution* of Class B drugs, mainly cannabis. Again, a scale of sentences may be ascertained, following the *Aramah* guidelines. At the top end of the range, the offender in *Netts* [1997] 2 Cr App R (S) 117, was convicted of possessing cannabis with intent to supply. He was stopped while driving his car, which was found to contain 90 kg of cannabis resin in 24 packages. It was accepted that the offender was acting as a courier within the UK. A sentence of seven years' imprisonment was reduced to five years on appeal, the Court of Appeal noting that the very large quantity of cannabis involved took the case above the four year level referred to in *Aramah* but also taking account of the fact that the offender had no previous involvement with drugs and no convictions of any kind. In *Chatfield* (1983) 5 Cr App R (S) 289, the offenders pleaded guilty to possession of 2 kg of cannabis, with intent to supply. Sentences of 30 months were upheld by the Court of Appeal, Watkins LJ commenting that: 'They came somewhere between about half-way towards and the end of the bracket, allowance being made for the fact that they pleaded guilty and for their characters'. Thirty months was said to be 'at the top end of the appropriate scale' but was upheld in *Daley* (1989) 11 Cr App R (S) 242, where the offender, shortly after release from prison for burglary, was seen by a police officer selling cannabis. He sold the officer a small quantity and agreed to supply more; when arrested he was in possession of 450.5 grammes of cannabis resin. He pleaded guilty. In *Hill* (1988) 10 Cr App R (S) 150, the offender had been dealing in cannabis from his home on a regular basis for some time, earning £100 per week from this activity. A 30-month sentence, described by the Court of Appeal as 'near the top end of the bracket for offences of this sort', was reduced to 21 months, since 'although the supply was on a regular basis to a large number of people the amounts involved were comparatively small' and greater recognition should have been given to the offender's guilty plea. Fifteen months' imprisonment was appropriate in *Freeman* [1997] 2 Cr App R (S) 224, where the offender, a man with previous convictions though not related to drugs, pleaded guilty to possession of cannabis resin with intent to supply. The offence was aggravated by the fact that he took the drug into prison to supply a serving prisoner. See also *Doyle* [1998] 1 Cr App R (S) 79.

In cases involving the cultivation of cannabis, the crucial matter is whether the cannabis was for personal use, or for supply. In *Herridge* [2006] 1 Cr App R (S) 252, the Court of Appeal noted that Parliament had now widened the gap between the maximum penalty for supply of cannabis (14 years) and that for simple possession (now two years). The offence of cannabis cultivation involved a wide variation in culpability, but would ordinarily attract a custodial sentence. For cultivation of 52 cannabis plants at home, for personal use, the appropriate sentence, following a guilty plea, was six months' imprisonment. For production of cannabis on a serious commercial scale, imprisonment for four years was upheld in *Booth* [1997] 2 Cr App R (S) 67. It was estimated that the operation would produce between eight and ten kg of cannabis each year. See also *Lyall* (1994) 16 Cr App R (S) 600. In *Blackham* [1997] 2 Cr App R (S) 275, 12 months' imprisonment was appropriate in a case where the offender cultivated 75 cannabis plants at home. The offender was intending to supply the cannabis, though not on a commercial basis, and he had a previous conviction for possession of cannabis with intent to supply.

Where tried summarily, the Magistrates' Courts Guidelines (2004) indicate the following in respect of cultivation of cannabis by a first-time offender pleading not guilty:

> **Aggravating Factors** For example commercial cultivation; large quantity; use of sophisticated system; offence committed on bail; relevant previous convictions and any failures to respond to previous sentences.
>
> **Mitigating Factors** For example for personal use; not responsible for planting; small scale cultivation.
>
> *Guideline*: Is it serious enough for a community penalty?

In all cases forfeiture of all drugs and equipment should be considered.

Few cases are reported on the appropriate sentencing pattern for the offence of permitting premises to be used for smoking cannabis. In *Pusser* (1983) 5 Cr App R (S) 225, however, the offender was the licensee of a public house at which cannabis was smoked, though there was no evidence that he used cannabis himself. After a warning, the police searched the premises and found cannabis in several forms. The Court of Appeal described this as 'a bad case' and upheld the sentence of six months' imprisonment. Twelve months' imprisonment was upheld in *Morrison* [1996] 1 Cr App R (S) 263, where the offender allowed young people aged 14 or 15 to visit his house and smoke cannabis; there was no evidence that the offender supplied cannabis to them.

Class C Drug Offences

B20.109 Class C drugs include cannabis (with effect from 29 January 2004), benzphetamine and pemoline. There is no guideline judgment in respect of these offences, but it is submitted that (save for cases of simple possession) the guidelines in *Aramah* (1982) 4 Cr App R (S) 407 (see **B20.108**) remain valid following the reclassification of cannabis as a Class C drug and the increase in maximum penalties for production, possession with intent to supply etc. of a Class C drug from five years to 14 years. The Magistrates' Courts Guidelines (2004) for possession of Class C drugs with intent to supply, and for simple possession, are the same as those for Class B drugs.

For cases of simple *possession* of small amounts of cannabis for personal use, the guidelines in *Aramah* indicate that a fine will often be an appropriate penalty unless there is repetition involving 'flouting of the law'. Following the reclassification of cannabis as a Class C drug from 29 January 2004, the maximum penalty for simple possession of cannabis was, in effect, reduced from five years to two years.

Section B21 Offences Relating to Dangerous Dogs, Hunting and Animal Welfare

B

Part B Offences

OFFENCES UNDER THE DANGEROUS DOGS ACT 1991

Control and Possession of Dogs Bred for Fighting

The Dangerous Dogs Act 1991, s. 1, controls the possession, disposal and breeding of pit bull terriers. It also applies to the Japanese tosa, dogo Argentino and fila Braziliero. In *Knightsbridge Crown Court, ex parte Dunne* [1994] 1 WLR 296, it was held that s. 1 applies to dogs possessing a substantial number of breed characteristics, even if some other characteristics are missing. Some pit bull/staffordshire crosses may therefore fall within s. 1. As to the burden of proof, s. 5(5) provides: **B21.1**

> If in any proceedings it is alleged by the prosecution that a dog is one to which section 1 . . . applies it shall be presumed that it is such a dog unless the contrary is shown by the accused by such evidence as the court considers sufficient; and the accused shall not be permitted to adduce such evidence unless he has given the prosecution notice of his intention to do so not later than the 14th day before that on which the evidence is to be adduced.

Section 5(5) applies only to criminal proceedings and not where a destruction order is sought without a prosecution (*Walton Street Magistrates' Court, ex parte Crothers* (1996) 160 JP 427). In *Bates v UK* (Commission Application No. 15023/89) the European Human Rights Commission considered the burden imposed by s. 5(5) to be compatible with the presumption of innocence under the ECHR, Article 6(2), but this is difficult to reconcile with *Lambert* [2002] 2 AC 545. It may be necessary for s. 5 to be reinterpreted as imposing only an evidential burden on the defence (see **F3.13**).

Offences

Under s. 1(3) of the Act, it is an offence to possess or have custody of any dog to which s. 1 applies (except under a power of seizure or a destruction order), unless a certificate of exemption has been obtained and its terms complied with (see s. 1(5), SI 1991 Nos. 1744, 2297 and 2636 and the Dangerous Dogs (Amendment) Act 1997, s. 4(1)). Section 1(2) of the 1991 Act creates further offences: **B21.2**

Dangerous Dogs Act 1991, s. 1

(2) No person shall—
- (a) breed, or breed from, a dog to which this section applies;
- (b) sell or exchange such a dog or offer, advertise or expose such a dog for sale or exchange;
- (c) make or offer to make a gift of such a dog or advertise or expose such a dog as a gift;
- (d) allow such a dog of which he is the owner or of which he is for the time being in charge to be in a public place without being muzzled and kept on a lead; or
- (e) abandon such a dog of which he is the owner or, being the owner or for the time being in charge of such a dog, allow it to stray.

Penalties and Defences in relation to Offences under s. 1

Dangerous Dogs Act 1991, s. 1 **B21.3**

(7) Any person who contravenes this section is guilty of an offence and liable on summary conviction to imprisonment for a term not exceeding six months or a fine not exceeding level

5 on the standard scale or both except that a person who publishes an advertisement in contravention of subsection 2(b) or (c)—
(a) shall not on being convicted be liable to imprisonment if he shows that he published the advertisement to the order of someone else and did not himself devise it; and
(b) shall not be convicted if, in addition, he shows that he did not know and had no reasonable cause to suspect that it related to a dog to which this section applies.

Voluntary intoxication is no defence to a charge under s. 1(7) (*DPP v Kellett* [1994] Crim LR 916). Indeed it seems clear from s. 1(7)(b) that the offence is one of strict liability, as are those created by s. 3 (see **B21.5**). As to disqualification and destruction orders, see **B21.6**.

Definitions

B21.4 The term 'advertisement' is defined in the Dangerous Dogs Act 1991, s. 10(2), as including any means of bringing a matter to the attention of the public; 'public place' is defined in s. 10(2) as meaning any street, road or other place to which the public have or are permitted access, whether for payment or otherwise (see *Cummings v DPP* (1999) *The Times*, 26 March 1999), and includes the common parts of a building containing two or more separate dwellings. A pit bull terrier sitting in a car parked in a public place is itself in a public place and must be muzzled in accordance with s. 1(2)(d) (*Bates v DPP* (1993) 157 JP 1004). Muzzling remains necessary even if the dog is ill and would be distressed by muzzling; no defence of necessity applies in such circumstances (*Cichon v DPP* [1994] Crim LR 918). However, a private path or driveway is not a public place merely because visitors or postmen may use it when calling on the owner (*Fellowes v DPP* (1993) 157 JP 936).

Dangerous Dogs Act 1991, ss. 6 and 7

6. Where a dog is owned by a person who is less than sixteen years old any reference to its owner in section 1(2)(d) or (e) or 3 above shall include a reference to the head of the household, if any, of which that person is a member or, in Scotland, to the person who has his actual care and control.

7.—(1) In this Act—
(a) references to a dog being muzzled are to its being securely fitted with a muzzle sufficient to prevent it biting any person; and
(b) references to its being kept on a lead are to its being securely held on a lead by a person who is not less than sixteen years old.

(2) [Power of Secretary of State to prescribe the type of muzzle or lead to be used.]

Failing to Keep Dogs under Proper Control

B21.5 **Dangerous Dogs Act 1991, s. 3**

(1) If a dog is dangerously out of control in a public place—
(a) the owner; and
(b) if different, the person for the time being in charge of the dog,
is guilty of an offence, or, if the dog while so out of control injures any person, an aggravated offence, under this subsection.

(2) In proceedings for an offence under subsection (1) above against a person who is the owner of a dog but was not at the material time in charge of it, it shall be a defence for the accused to prove that the dog was at the material time in the charge of a person whom he reasonably believed to be a fit and proper person to be in charge of it.

(3) If the owner or, if different, the person for the time being in charge of a dog allows it to enter a place which is not a public place but where it is not permitted to be and while it is there—
(a) it injures any person; or
(b) there are grounds for reasonable apprehension that it will do so,
he is guilty of an offence, or, if the dog injures any person, an aggravated offence, under this subsection.

(4) A person guilty of an offence under subsection (1) or (3) above other than an aggravated offence is liable on summary conviction to imprisonment for a term not exceeding six months or a fine not exceeding level 5 on the standard scale or both; and a person guilty of an aggravated offence under either of those subsections is liable—

(a) on summary conviction, to imprisonment for a term not exceeding six months or a fine not exceeding the statutory maximum or both;
(b) on conviction on indictment, to imprisonment for a term not exceeding two years or a fine or both.

As to the meaning of 'public place', see **B21.4**. The question whether someone other than the owner is 'in charge' of the dog is one of fact and degree and should ordinarily be left to the jury (*Rawlings* [1994] Crim LR 433). As to the scope of the defence under s. 3(2), see *Huddart* [1999] Crim LR 568.

Whereas the offences created by s. 3(1) may be committed by both the owner (subject to the s. 3(2) defence) *and* the person in charge of the dog, the s. 3(3) offences can be committed only by an owner *or* person in charge who 'allows' the dog to enter the place in question. This suggests that, if someone else is in charge, the owner cannot ordinarily be liable under s. 3(3), but liability may still arise where, for example, the owner knows that a friend or member of his family regularly exercises the dog in such a place. Failure to take adequate precautions to prevent a dog from escaping and entering such a place may also give rise to liability for 'allowing' entry under s. 3(3). Proof of negligence is not required, as liability is strict (*Greener v DPP* (1996) 160 JP 265).

Under s. 3, the type of dog concerned is irrelevant; it is enough to show that the dog is dangerously out of control. Section 10(3) provides that:

> . . . a dog shall be regarded as dangerously out of control on any occasion on which there are grounds for reasonable apprehension that it will injure any person, whether or not it actually does so, but references to a dog injuring a person or there being grounds for reasonable apprehension that it will do so do not include references to any case in which the dog is being used for a lawful purpose by a constable or a person in the service of the Crown.

It is submitted that references to dogs injuring persons must, in this context, be confined to bites, etc., directly inflicted by dogs and should not include traffic injuries indirectly caused by dogs running loose on a road.

No *mens rea* is specified under s. 3, and the offence would appear to be one of strict liability (see **A4.1** *et seq.*). This legislation was enacted for reasons of public safety, and would become very much harder to enforce if some fault element, such as negligence, had to be proved against the owner of a dog which becomes dangerously out of control. (See *Bezzina* [1994] 1 WLR 1057.) On the other hand, the effect of s. 10(3) is that liability can arise only where the dog behaves in such a way that there are 'reasonable grounds for apprehension that it will injure any person'. This might seem to exclude cases in which a dog suddenly and unexpectedly bites or snaps at some person, assuming it is immediately restrained thereafter, but in *Rafiq v DPP* (1997) 161 JP 412 it was held that, even if a dog bites without warning, it may still be open to a court to infer that there were grounds for reasonable apprehension under s. 10(3) that the dog would renew the attack immediately afterwards.

Even where it seems likely that a dog may injure someone, the words 'dangerously out of control' must be given their natural meaning. If, for example, X teases Y's Doberman in a cruel and stupid way, it may be apparent to any onlooker that X is likely to be bitten unless he desists, but it does not follow that the dog is out of control.

Where the dog is owned by a person under the age of 16, s. 6 (see **B21.4**) applies.

Destruction and Disqualification Orders

As originally drafted, the Dangerous Dogs Act 1991, s. 4(1), demanded the mandatory destruction of the dogs involved wherever offences were committed under s. 1 or aggravated offences committed under s. 3. Trivial incidents, such as the temporary removal of a pit bull's muzzle so that it could drink, could lead to innocent dogs being destroyed, and this rule **B21.6** caused widespread outrage, not least amongst the magistrates and judges who were required to enforce the law (see the attack on the legislation by Rougier J in *Ealing Magistrates' Court, ex parte Fanneran* (1996) 160 JP 409). The severity of the law is now tempered by the Dangerous Dogs (Amendment) Act 1997, which (*inter alia*) adds s. 4(1A) and s. 4A to the original statute.

Dangerous Dogs Act 1991, ss. 4 and 4A

4.—(1) Where a person is convicted of an offence under section 1 or 3(1) or (3) above or of an offence under an order made under section 2 above the court—

(a) may order the destruction of any dog in respect of which the offence was committed and, subject to subsection (1A) below, shall do so in the case of an offence under section 1 or an aggravated offence under section 3(1) or (3) above; and

(b) may order the offender to be disqualified, for such period as the court thinks fit, for having custody of a dog.

(1A) Nothing in subsection (1)(a) above shall require the court to order the destruction of a dog if the court is satisfied—

(a) that the dog would not constitute a danger to public safety; and

(b) where the dog was born before 30th November 1991 and is subject to the prohibition in section 1(3) above, that there is a good reason why the dog has not been exempted from that prohibition.

(2) Where a court makes an order under subsection (1)(a) above for the destruction of a dog owned by a person other than the offender, the owner may appeal to the Crown Court against the order.

(3) A dog shall not be destroyed pursuant to an order under subsection (1)(a) above—

(a) until the end of the period for giving notice of appeal against the conviction, or against the order; and

(b) if notice of appeal is given within that period, until the appeal is determined or withdrawn,

unless the offender and, in a case to which subsection (2) above applies, the owner of the dog give notice to the court that made the order that there is to be no appeal.

(4) Where a court makes an order under subsection (1)(a) above it may—

(a) appoint a person to undertake the destruction of the dog and require any person having custody of it to deliver it up for that purpose; and

(b) order the offender to pay such sum as the court may determine to be the reasonable expenses of destroying the dog and of keeping it pending its destruction.

(5) Any sum ordered to be paid under subsection (4)(b) above shall be treated for the purposes of enforcement as if it were a fine imposed on conviction.

4A.—(1) Where—

(a) a person is convicted of an offence under section 1 above or an aggravated offence under section 3(1) or (3) above;

(b) the court does not order the destruction of the dog under section 4(1)(a) above; and

(c) in the case of an offence under section 1 above, the dog is subject to the prohibition in section 1(3) above,

the court shall order that, unless the dog is exempted from that prohibition within the requisite period, the dog shall be destroyed.

(2) Where an order is made under subsection (1) above in respect of a dog, and the dog is not exempted from the prohibition in section 1(3) above within the requisite period, the court may extend that period.

(3) Subject to subsection (2) above, the requisite period for the purposes of such an order is the period of two months beginning with the date of the order.

(4) Where a person is convicted of an offence under section 3(1) or (3) above, the court may order that, unless the owner of the dog keeps it under proper control, the dog shall be destroyed.

(5) An order under subsection (4) above—

(a) may specify the measures to be taken for keeping the dog under proper control, whether by muzzling, keeping on a lead, excluding it from specified places or otherwise; and

(b) if it appears to the court that the dog is a male and would be less dangerous if neutered, may require it to be neutered.

(6) Subsections (2) to (4) of section 4 above shall apply in relation to an order under subsection (1) or (4) above as they apply in relation to an order under subsection (1)(a) of that section.

As to the making of destruction orders otherwise than on conviction (i.e. where the proceedings are not strictly criminal), see *Walton Street Magistrates' Court, ex parte Crothers* (1996) 160 JP 427 and s. 4B.

Any person who has custody of a dog in contravention of s. 4(1)(b), or who fails to comply with a requirement imposed on him under s. 4(4)(a) commits a summary offence and is liable to a fine not exceeding level 5 on the standard scale (s. 4(8)).

OTHER OFFENCES RELATING TO DANGEROUS DOGS

The Dangerous Dogs Act 1991 does not reduce the powers of courts under the Dogs Act 1871, s. 2. Orders requiring the destruction or proper control of dangerous dogs may still be made under that provision, whether or not any person has been injured, and may require a dog to be muzzled and/or castrated (Dangerous Dogs Act 1991, s. 3(5) and (6)). Under the Dangerous Dogs Act 1989, s. 1(3), it is an offence, punishable on summary conviction by a fine not exceeding level 3 on the standard scale, not to comply with a control or destruction order; and where under that Act an owner has been disqualified from having custody of a dog, contravention of that order is punishable by a fine not exceeding level 5 on the standard scale (Dangerous Dogs Act 1989, s. 1(6)). **B21.7**

Control of Guard Dogs

Guard Dogs Act 1975, s. 1 **B21.8**

(1) A person shall not use or permit the use of a guard dog at any premises unless a person ('the handler') who is capable of controlling the dog is present on the premises and the dog is under the control of the handler at all times while it is being so used except while it is secured so that it is not at liberty to go freely about the premises.

(2) The handler of a guard dog shall keep the dog under his control at all times while it is being used as a guard dog at any premises except—
  (a) while another handler has control over the dog; or
  (b) while the dog is secured so that it is not at liberty to go freely about the premises.

(3) A person shall not use or permit the use of a guard dog at any premises unless a notice containing a warning that a guard dog is present is clearly exhibited at each entrance to the premises.

Under the Guard Dogs Act 1975, s. 5, non-compliance with s. 1 is an offence punishable on summary conviction by a fine not exceeding level 5 on the standard scale.

OFFENCES INVOLVING HUNTING WITH DOGS

The Hunting Act 2004, which came into force on 18 February 2005, imposes a number of prohibitions on the hunting of mammals with dogs, but falls some way short of imposing an outright ban on all such hunting. Challenges to the Act based on alleged incompatibility with the ECHR and EC Treaty have been dismissed by the courts (see *R (Countryside Alliance and others) v A-G and others* [2007] QB 305), as have challenges based on consideration of the Parliament Act 1911 (*R (Jenkins) v A-G* [2006] 1 AC 262). **B21.9**

Hunting Act 2004, s. 1

A person commits an offence if he hunts a wild mammal with a dog, unless his hunting is exempt.

By s. 11(1), the term 'wild mammal' includes, in particular:

(a) a wild mammal which has been bred or tamed for any purpose,
(b) a wild mammal which is in captivity or confinement,

(c) a wild mammal which has escaped or been released from captivity or confinement, and
(d) any mammal which is living wild.

By s. 11(2), any reference in the Act to a person hunting a wild mammal with a dog includes, in particular, any case where:

(a) a person engages or participates in the pursuit of a wild mammal, and
(b) one or more dogs are employed in that pursuit (whether or not by him and whether or not under his control or direction).

Hunting Act 2004, s. 3

(1) A person commits an offence if he knowingly permits land which belongs to him to be entered or used in the course of the commission of an offence under section 1.
(2) A person commits an offence if he knowingly permits a dog which belongs to him to be used in the course of the commission of an offence under section 1.

By s. 11(3), land belongs to a person if he:

(a) owns an interest in it,
(b) manages or controls it, or
(c) occupies it.

And by s. 11(4), a dog belongs to a person if he:

(a) owns it,
(b) is in charge of it, or
(c) has control of it.

As to the taking, killing or injuring of badgers (which may but need not involve the use of dogs), see the Badgers Act 1992.

Procedure, Penalties and Forfeiture

B21.10 Offences under the Hunting Act 2004 (including hare coursing) are triable summarily and the maximum penalty is a fine not exceeding level 5 on the standard scale (s. 6). Section 9 deals with forfeiture of dogs and hunting equipment; but this does not appear to extend to horses.

Hunting Act 2004, s. 9

(1) A court which convicts a person of an offence under part 1 of this Act may order the forfeiture of any dog or hunting article which—
 (a) was used in the commission of the offence, or
 (b) was in the possession of the person convicted at the time of his arrest.
(2) A court which convicts a person of an offence under part 1 of this Act may order the forfeiture of any vehicle which was used in the commission of the offence.
(3) In subsection (1) 'hunting article' means anything designed or adapted for use in connection with—
 (a) hunting a wild mammal, or
 (b) hare coursing.
(4) A forfeiture order—
 (a) may include such provision about the treatment of the dog, vehicle or article forfeited as the court thinks appropriate, and
 (b) subject to provision made under paragraph (a), shall be treated as requiring any person who is in possession of the dog, vehicle or article to surrender it to a constable as soon as is reasonably practicable.
(5) Where a forfeited dog, vehicle or article is retained by or surrendered to a constable, the police force of which the constable is a member shall ensure that such arrangements are made for its destruction or disposal—
 (a) as are specified in the forfeiture order, or
 (b) where no arrangements are specified in the order, as seem to the police force to be appropriate.

(6) The court which makes a forfeiture order may order the return of the forfeited dog, vehicle or article on an application made—
(a) by a person who claims to have an interest in the dog, vehicle or article (other than the person on whose conviction the order was made), and
(b) before the dog, vehicle or article has been destroyed or finally disposed of under subsection (5).
(7) A person commits an offence if he fails to—
(a) comply with a forfeiture order, or
(b) co-operate with a step taken for the purpose of giving effect to a forfeiture order.

Exemptions and Defences

Exemptions from the prohibition in s. 1 are set out in sch. 1 to the Hunting Act 2004. These exemptions are likely to be of central importance in contested cases under s. 1 or s. 3 of the Act. Once the issue is raised, the burden of disproving any claim that hunting was exempt would appear to lie on the prosecution. **B21.11**

Hunting Act 2004, sch. 1

Stalking and flushing out
1.—(1) Stalking a wild mammal, or flushing it out of cover, is exempt hunting if the conditions in this paragraph are satisfied.
(2) The first condition is that the stalking or flushing out is undertaken for the purpose of—
(a) preventing or reducing serious damage which the wild mammal would otherwise cause—
(i) to livestock,
(ii) to game birds or wild birds (within the meaning of section 27 of the Wildlife and Countryside Act 1981),
(iii) to food for livestock,
(iv) to crops (including vegetables and fruit),
(v) to growing timber,
(vi) to fisheries,
(vii) to other property, or
(viii) to the biological diversity of an area (within the meaning of the United Nations Environmental Programme Convention on Biological Diversity of 1992),
(b) obtaining meat to be used for human or animal consumption, or
(c) participation in a field trial.
(3) In subparagraph (2)(c) 'field trial' means a competition (other than a hare coursing event within the meaning of section 5) in which dogs—
(a) flush animals out of cover or retrieve animals that have been shot (or both), and
(b) are assessed as to their likely usefulness in connection with shooting.
(4) The second condition is that the stalking or flushing out takes place on land—
(a) which belongs to the person doing the stalking or flushing out, or
(b) which he has been given permission to use for the purpose by the occupier or, in the case of unoccupied land, by a person to whom it belongs.
(5) The third condition is that the stalking or flushing out does not involve the use of more than two dogs.
(6) The fourth condition is that the stalking or flushing out does not involve the use of a dog below ground otherwise than in accordance with paragraph 2 below.
(7) The fifth condition is that—
(a) reasonable steps are taken for the purpose of ensuring that as soon as possible after being found or flushed out the wild mammal is shot dead by a competent person, and
(b) in particular, each dog used in the stalking or flushing out is kept under sufficiently close control to ensure that it does not prevent or obstruct achievement of the objective in paragraph (a).

Use of dogs below ground to protect birds for shooting
2.—(1) The use of a dog below ground in the course of stalking or flushing out is in accordance with this paragraph if the conditions in this paragraph are satisfied.
(2) The first condition is that the stalking or flushing out is undertaken for the purpose of preventing or reducing serious damage to game birds or wild birds (within the meaning of

section 27 of the Wildlife and Countryside Act 1981) which a person is keeping or preserving for the purpose of their being shot.

(3) The second condition is that the person doing the stalking or flushing out—
  (a) has with him written evidence—
    (i) that the land on which the stalking or flushing out takes place belongs to him, or
    (ii) that he has been given permission to use that land for the purpose by the occupier or, in the case of unoccupied land, by a person to whom it belongs, and
  (b) makes the evidence immediately available for inspection by a constable who asks to see it.

(4) The third condition is that the stalking or flushing out does not involve the use of more than one dog below ground at any one time.

(5) In so far as stalking or flushing out is undertaken with the use of a dog below ground in accordance with this paragraph, paragraph 1 shall have effect as if for the condition in paragraph 1(7) there were substituted the condition that—
  (a) reasonable steps are taken for the purpose of ensuring that as soon as possible after being found the wild mammal is flushed out from below ground,
  (b) reasonable steps are taken for the purpose of ensuring that as soon as possible after being flushed out from below ground the wild mammal is shot dead by a competent person,
  (c) in particular, the dog is brought under sufficiently close control to ensure that it does not prevent or obstruct achievement of the objective in paragraph (b),
  (d) reasonable steps are taken for the purpose of preventing injury to the dog, and
  (e) the manner in which the dog is used complies with any code of practice which is issued or approved for the purpose of this paragraph by the Secretary of State.

Rats

3. The hunting of rats is exempt if it takes place on land—
  (a) which belongs to the hunter, or
  (b) which he has been given permission to use for the purpose by the occupier or, in the case of unoccupied land, by a person to whom it belongs.

Rabbits

4. The hunting of rabbits is exempt if it takes place on land—
  (a) which belongs to the hunter, or
  (b) which he has been given permission to use for the purpose by the occupier or, in the case of unoccupied land, by a person to whom it belongs.

Retrieval of hares

5. The hunting of a hare which has been shot is exempt if it takes place on land—
  (a) which belongs to the hunter, or
  (b) which he has been given permission to use for the purpose of hunting hares by the occupier or, in the case of unoccupied land, by a person to whom it belongs.

Falconry

6. Flushing a wild mammal from cover is exempt hunting if undertaken—
  (a) for the purpose of enabling a bird of prey to hunt the wild mammal, and
  (b) on land which belongs to the hunter or which he has been given permission to use for the purpose by the occupier or, in the case of unoccupied land, by a person to whom it belongs.

Recapture of wild mammal

7.—(1) The hunting of a wild mammal which has escaped or been released from captivity or confinement is exempt if the conditions in this paragraph are satisfied.

(2) The first condition is that the hunting takes place—
  (a) on land which belongs to the hunter,
  (b) on land which he has been given permission to use for the purpose by the occupier or, in the case of unoccupied land, by a person to whom it belongs, or
  (c) with the authority of a constable.

(3) The second condition is that—
  (a) reasonable steps are taken for the purpose of ensuring that as soon as possible after being found the wild mammal is recaptured or shot dead by a competent person, and

(b) in particular, each dog used in the hunt is kept under sufficiently close control to ensure that it does not prevent or obstruct achievement of the objective in paragraph (a).

(4) The third condition is that the wild mammal—

(a) was not released for the purpose of being hunted, and

(b) was not, for that purpose, permitted to escape.

Rescue of wild mammal

8.—(1) The hunting of a wild mammal is exempt if the conditions in this paragraph are satisfied.

(2) The first condition is that the hunter reasonably believes that the wild mammal is or may be injured.

(3) The second condition is that the hunting is undertaken for the purpose of relieving the wild mammal's suffering.

(4) The third condition is that the hunting does not involve the use of more than two dogs.

(5) The fourth condition is that the hunting does not involve the use of a dog below ground.

(6) The fifth condition is that the hunting takes place—

(a) on land which belongs to the hunter,

(b) on land which he has been given permission to use for the purpose by the occupier or, in the case of unoccupied land, by a person to whom it belongs, or

(c) with the authority of a constable.

(7) The sixth condition is that—

(a) reasonable steps are taken for the purpose of ensuring that as soon as possible after the wild mammal is found appropriate action (if any) is taken to relieve its suffering, and

(b) in particular, each dog used in the hunt is kept under sufficiently close control to ensure that it does not prevent or obstruct achievement of the objective in paragraph (a).

(8) The seventh condition is that the wild mammal was not harmed for the purpose of enabling it to be hunted in reliance upon this paragraph.

Research and observation

9.—(1) The hunting of a wild mammal is exempt if the conditions in this paragraph are satisfied.

(2) The first condition is that the hunting is undertaken for the purpose of or in connection with the observation or study of the wild mammal.

(3) The second condition is that the hunting does not involve the use of more than two dogs.

(4) The third condition is that the hunting does not involve the use of a dog below ground.

(5) The fourth condition is that the hunting takes place on land—

(a) which belongs to the hunter, or

(b) which he has been given permission to use for the purpose by the occupier or, in the case of unoccupied land, by a person to whom it belongs.

(6) The fifth condition is that each dog used in the hunt is kept under sufficiently close control to ensure that it does not injure the wild mammal.

In cases where no such exemption can be established, s. 4 of the Act creates a defence of 'reasonable belief' in which a reverse burden of proof appears to be imposed on the accused.

Hunting Act 2004, s. 4

It is a defence for a person charged with an offence under section 1 in respect of hunting to show that he reasonably believed that the hunting was exempt.

Hare Coursing

Hare coursing is proscribed without qualification or exemption by s. 5 of the Hunting Act 2004. **B21.12**

Hunting Act 2004, s. 5

(1) A person commits an offence if he—

(a) participates in a hare coursing event,

(b) attends a hare coursing event,

(c) knowingly facilitates a hare coursing event, or

(d) permits land which belongs to him to be used for the purposes of a hare coursing event.

(2) Each of the following persons commits an offence if a dog participates in a hare coursing event—
  (a) any person who enters the dog for the event,
  (b) any person who permits the dog to be entered, and
  (c) any person who controls or handles the dog in the course of or for the purposes of the event.

(3) A 'hare coursing event' is a competition in which dogs are, by the use of live hares, assessed as to skill in hunting hares.

For penalties and forfeiture provisions, see **B21.10**.

OFFENCES UNDER THE ANIMAL WELFARE ACT 2006

B21.13 The principal provisions of the Animal Welfare Act 2006 came into force in England on 6 April 2007 and in Wales on 28 March 2007. The Act repeals, *inter alia*, the Protection of Animals Act 1911, the Abandonment of Animals Act 1960 and part 1 of the Agriculture (Miscellaneous Provisions) Act 1968, and enables further repeals to be made under secondary legislation. It has no retrospective effect.

The Act does not in its current form apply to any invertebrate creature (see s. 1(1) and (5)), nor to any foetus or embryo (s. 1(2)), but regulations made under the Act may at some future date amend its scope in either respect in accordance with s. 1(3) and (4).

The protection of the Act extends only to 'protected animals'. A protected animal is defined in s. 2 as one of a kind commonly domesticated in the British Isles or one which is under the control of man (whether on a permanent or temporary basis) or not living in a wild state. Feral cats and stray dogs fall within this definition, as do pets, farm animals, animals kept in zoos or wildlife parks, and animals which may recently have escaped from human control, but which are not yet 'living wild'. Wild animals such as foxes or badgers are not ordinarily protected under the Act, but any that have been captured or rescued are protected for as long as they remain in care or captivity. As to the prohibition of certain cruel or potentially cruel methods of taking or killing wild animals, see the Wildlife and Countryside Act 1981, s. 11. Captive wild birds may be protected both under the 2006 Act and under s. 8 of the 1981 Act (*R (RSPCA) v Shinton* (2003) 167 JP 512).

Some offences under the Act can be committed only by a person who is 'responsible for an animal'. An animal for which some person is responsible (such as a pet rat) must necessarily be a protected animal, even if other animals of the same species, living wild, would not be.

By s. 3, a person may be responsible for an animal either on a permanent or temporary basis. Persons running boarding kennels or veterinary practices clearly have temporary responsibility for animals in their care, but responsibility may also extend to a person who agrees to feed, clean and water his neighbour's animals for a few days. A person who owns an animal shall always be regarded as responsible for it, but references to being responsible for an animal include being in charge of it; and by s. 3(4) a person shall be treated as responsible for any animal for which a person under the age of 16 years of whom he has actual care and control is responsible. For an illustration of the kind of case in which this rule may be important, see *R (RSPCA) v C* (2006) 170 JP 463 and **B21.19**.

By ss. 58 and 59, nothing in the Act applies to anything lawfully done under the Animals (Scientific Procedures) Act 1986 or to anything which occurs in the normal course of fishing. As to application to the Crown, see s. 60; as to the liability of directors, managers and officers for offences committed by bodies corporate, see s. 57.

The only offences examined in this work are those created by ss. 4, 7, 8 and 9. Offences to which reference must be made elsewhere include those concerned with the docking of dogs' tails and other prohibited procedures involving protected animals (ss. 5 and 6, together with associated regulations), the unlawful transfer of animals by way of sale or prize to children under the age of 16 (s. 11), and the unlicensed commission of specified activities for which a licence under the Act is required (s. 13).

Prosecutions

The Animal Welfare Act 2006, s. 30, permits prosecutions to be brought by local authorities. No specific provision is made for prosecutions to be brought by the RSPCA, but that society will continue to exercise its common-law powers to bring private prosecutions where it sees fit. **B21.14**

Animal Welfare Act 2006, s. 31

(1) Notwithstanding anything in section 127(1) of the Magistrates' Courts Act 1980, a magistrates' court may try an information relating to an offence under this Act if the information is laid—
   (a) before the end of the period of three years beginning with the date of the commission of the offence, and
   (b) before the end of the period of six months beginning with the date on which evidence which the prosecutor thinks is sufficient to justify the proceedings comes to his knowledge.

(2) For the purposes of subsection (1)(b)—
   (a) a certificate signed by or on behalf of the prosecutor and stating the date on which such evidence came to his knowledge shall be conclusive evidence of that fact, and
   (b) a certificate stating that matter and purporting to be so signed shall be treated as so signed unless the contrary is proved.

Penalties and Orders

Offences under the Animal Welfare Act 2006 are triable only summarily. The maximum penalty in respect of any of the offences considered below (other than an offence under s. 9 or s. 34(9)) is imprisonment for a term not exceeding 51 weeks, or a fine not exceeding £20,000, or both. The maximum penalty for an offence under s. 9 or s. 34(9) is similar, save that the fine may not exceed level 5 on the standard scale (s. 32). **B21.15**

On conviction, a person may be deprived of the animal in question (s. 33), and may be disqualified from owning, keeping or participating in the keeping of animals (s. 34(2)), disqualified from dealing in animals (s. 34(3)) and/or disqualified from transporting or arranging for the transport of animals (s. 34(4)). As to what may amount to 'keeping' an animal, see *R (Arthur) v RSPCA* (2005) 169 JP 676. Disqualification may be ordered in respect of animals generally or in respect of animals of one or more kinds (s. 34(5)) and may be made for such period as the court thinks fit (s. 34(1)). Breach of a disqualification order is an offence under s. 34(9).

Section 34 does not address the problem that arose in *R (RSPCA) v Chester Crown Court* (2006) 170 JP 725, in which the court reluctantly concluded that a disqualification under the Protection of Animals Act 1911, s. 1, could not impose a limit on the number of animals that could be kept. Sedley J suggested in that case that, 'Parliament [may] want to consider whether [that] kind of order . . . should not be authorised by future animal protection legislation', but the new legislation makes no such provision.

As to the seizure of animals in connection with a disqualification order, see ss. 35 and 36. As to the making of orders for the destruction of animals, see ss. 37 and 38. As to the forfeiture of equipment used in connection with offences, see s. 40. As to the cancellation of licences or the disqualification of a person from holding a licence, see s. 42.

Unnecessary Suffering

B21.16 **Animal Welfare Act 2006, s. 4**

(1) A person commits an offence if—
(a) an act of his, or a failure of his to act, causes an animal to suffer,
(b) he knew, or ought reasonably to have known, that the act, or failure to act, would have that effect or be likely to do so,
(c) the animal is a protected animal, and
(d) the suffering is unnecessary.
(2) A person commits an offence if—
(a) he is responsible for an animal,
(b) an act, or failure to act, of another person causes the animal to suffer,
(c) he permitted that to happen or failed to take such steps (whether by way of supervising the other person or otherwise) as were reasonable in all the circumstances to prevent that happening, and
(d) the suffering is unnecessary.
(3) The considerations to which it is relevant to have regard when determining for the purposes of this section whether suffering is unnecessary include—
(a) whether the suffering could reasonably have been avoided or reduced;
(b) whether the conduct which caused the suffering was in compliance with any relevant enactment or any relevant provisions of a licence or code of practice issued under an enactment;
(c) whether the conduct which caused the suffering was for a legitimate purpose, such as—
(i) the purpose of benefiting the animal, or
(ii) the purpose of protecting a person, property or another animal;
(d) whether the suffering was proportionate to the purpose of the conduct concerned;
(e) whether the conduct concerned was in all the circumstances that of a reasonably competent and humane person.
(4) Nothing in this section applies to the destruction of an animal in an appropriate and humane manner.

The offence created by s. 4(1) extends to omissions as well as to positive acts, and to mental suffering as well as physical (see s. 62(1)); but on general principles an omission can be seen as 'causing' suffering only in cases where the person in question was under a duty to prevent it. Thus, if D ignores the suffering of an injured dog he finds lying in the road he will ordinarily commit no offence; but if D was himself responsible for the injury (or care of the dog), he may be under a duty to mitigate the animal's suffering. See generally **A1.10** ***et seq.***

Section 4(3) requires allowance to be made for a number of possible factors when determining whether any suffering was 'unnecessary'. An example suggested in the explanatory notes accompanying the Act involves police horses used for riot control. Such horses may be exposed to a risk of injury from flying stones or even petrol bombs, but the risks involved may well be legitimately incurred in the circumstances.

Administration of Poisons

B21.17 **Animal Welfare Act 2006, s. 7**

(1) A person commits an offence if, without lawful authority or reasonable excuse, he—
(a) administers any poisonous or injurious drug or substance to a protected animal, knowing it to be poisonous or injurious, or
(b) causes any poisonous or injurious drug or substance to be taken by a protected animal, knowing it to be poisonous or injurious.
(2) A person commits an offence if—
(a) he is responsible for an animal,
(b) without lawful authority or reasonable excuse, another person administers a poisonous or injurious drug or substance to the animal or causes the animal to take such a drug or substance, and
(c) he permitted that to happen or, knowing the drug or substance to be poisonous or injurious, he failed to take such steps (whether by way of supervising the other person or otherwise) as were reasonable in all the circumstances to prevent that happening.

(3) In this section, references to a poisonous or injurious drug or substance include a drug or substance which, by virtue of the quantity or manner in which it is administered or taken, has the effect of a poisonous or injurious drug or substance.

This provision, which replaces the offence of wilful poisoning formerly contained in the Protection of Animals Act 1911, s. 1(1)(d), is not intended to cover cases of accidental poisoning. According to the accompanying notes for guidance, the term 'administer' should be understood as indicating a deliberate action.

Animal Fights and Related Activities

Animal Welfare Act 2006, s. 8 **B21.18**

(1) A person commits an offence if he—
  (a) causes an animal fight to take place, or attempts to do so;
  (b) knowingly receives money for admission to an animal fight;
  (c) knowingly publicises a proposed animal fight;
  (d) provides information about an animal fight to another with the intention of enabling or encouraging attendance at the fight;
  (e) makes or accepts a bet on the outcome of an animal fight or on the likelihood of anything occurring or not occurring in the course of an animal fight;
  (f) takes part in an animal fight;
  (g) has in his possession anything designed or adapted for use in connection with an animal fight with the intention of its being so used;
  (h) keeps or trains an animal for use for in connection with an animal fight;
  (i) keeps any premises for use for an animal fight.

(2) A person commits an offence if, without lawful authority or reasonable excuse, he is present at an animal fight.

(3) A person commits an offence if, without lawful authority or reasonable excuse, he—
  (a) knowingly supplies a video recording of an animal fight,
  (b) knowingly publishes a video recording of an animal fight,
  (c) knowingly shows a video recording of an animal fight to another, or
  (d) possesses a video recording of an animal fight, knowing it to be such a recording, with the intention of supplying it.

(4) Subsection (3) does not apply if the video recording is of an animal fight that took place—
  (a) outside Great Britain, or
  (b) before the commencement date.

(5) Subsection (3) does not apply—
  (a) in the case of paragraph (a), to the supply of a video recording for inclusion in a programme service;
  (b) in the case of paragraph (b) or (c), to the publication or showing of a video recording by means of its inclusion in a programme service;
  (c) in the case of paragraph (d), by virtue of intention to supply for inclusion in a programme service.

(6) Provision extending the application of an offence under subsection (3), so far as relating to the provision of information society services, may be made under section 2(2) of the European Communities Act 1972 (powers to implement Community obligations by regulations) notwithstanding the limits imposed by paragraph 1(1)(d) of schedule 2 to that Act on the penalties with which an offence may be punishable on summary conviction.

(7) In this section—
'animal fight' means an occasion on which a protected animal is placed with an animal, or with a human, for the purpose of fighting, wrestling or baiting;
'commencement date' means the date on which subsection (3) comes into force;
'information society services' has the meaning given in Article 2(a) of Directive 2000/31/EC of the European Parliament and of the Council of 8 June 2000 on certain legal aspects of information society services, in particular electronic commerce in the Internal Market (Directive on electronic commerce);
'programme service' has the same meaning as in the Communications Act 2003;
'video recording' means a recording, in any form, from which a moving image may by any means be reproduced and includes data stored on a computer disc or by other electronic means which is capable of conversion into a moving image.

(8) In this section—
 (a) references to supplying or publishing a video recording are to supplying or publishing a video recording in any manner, including, in relation to a video recording in the form of data stored electronically, by means of transmitting such data;
 (b) references to showing a video recording are to showing a moving image reproduced from a video recording by any means.

This provision targets a wide range of activities connected with animal fights. Such fights include fights between humans and protected animals, or between a protected animal and some other animal. A wild animal, such as a badger, which has been captured for the purpose of being baited by dogs, will itself be a protected animal whilst in captivity.

Section 8 does not proscribe the use of an animal (such as a terrier or ferret) for legitimate pest control or the video-recording of an animal being used for such a purpose. Where, however, pest control is combined with sport or betting (e.g., betting on the number of rats killed by a terrier) it would appear to fall within the scope of s. 8.

Note that subss. (3) to (6) have not yet been brought into force.

The Welfare Offence

B21.19 **Animal Welfare Act 2006, s. 9**

(1) A person commits an offence if he does not take such steps as are reasonable in all the circumstances to ensure that the needs of an animal for which he is responsible are met to the extent required by good practice.
(2) For the purposes of this Act, an animal's needs shall be taken to include—
 (a) its need for a suitable environment,
 (b) its need for a suitable diet,
 (c) its need to be able to exhibit normal behaviour patterns,
 (d) any need it has to be housed with, or apart from, other animals, and
 (e) its need to be protected from pain, suffering, injury and disease.
(3) The circumstances to which it is relevant to have regard when applying subsection (1) include, in particular—
 (a) any lawful purpose for which the animal is kept, and
 (b) any lawful activity undertaken in relation to the animal.
(4) Nothing in this section applies to the destruction of an animal in an appropriate and humane manner.

The welfare concept is not wholly new. Regulations made under part 1 of the Agriculture (Miscellaneous Provisions) Act 1968 (repealed by the 2006 Act) imposed detailed welfare obligations on persons responsible for most types of farmed animals. New regulations applicable to farmed animals in England (the Welfare of Farmed Animals (England) Regulations 2007 (SI 2007 No. 2078), in force from 1 October 2007) cover the welfare of all farmed animals (as defined in reg. 3), including those kept on common land, whereas the old Regulations applied only to livestock kept on agricultural land. Animals that are not kept for farming purposes will continue to be exempt from these regulations, but benefit from the general welfare requirement imposed by s. 9 of the 2006 Act.

There is a significant degree of potential overlap between s. 9 and s. 4 (see **B21.16**). Where, for example, an animal that requires human care is abandoned, or deprived of essential veterinary care, an offence will ordinarily be committed under s. 9; if as is likely, this leads to suffering (cold, hunger, distress, etc.) there may be a further offence under s. 4.

What is 'reasonable in all the circumstances' involves an objective test, but it is necessary for a court to consider, not just whether the animal(s) in question received a reasonable standard of care, but whether the accused acted reasonably in the particular circumstances with which he was faced. This principle was established in *R (RSPCA) v C* (2006) 170 JP 463, in which a girl aged 15 was charged under the Protection of Animals Act 1911, s. 1, with causing unnecessary suffering to her cat by 'unreasonably' failing to secure essential veterinary treatment for it. It was held that account must be taken of her youth and of the fact that she had been told by her father (who pleaded guilty) that no such treatment was required. Newman J said (at [15]):

> The issue which the justices had to decide was whether or not this . . . girl had acted reasonably or unreasonably in acceding to the opinion her father had expressed . . . That involved considering whether it was reasonable for her to go along with her father's view of the position, having regard to her age and position in the household, whether it was for her to take any other action, as she could have done, and whether it was reasonable or unreasonable for her to fail to take that other action.

It remains to be seen how strictly the concept of 'good practice' will be interpreted and enforced outside the highly regulated farming context; but arguably any dog or cat owner who fails to keep his animal fully vaccinated against common diseases now risks prosecution under s. 9, because 'good practice' surely requires regular vaccination.

Section 10 of the Act enables inspectors (as defined in s. 51) to issue 'improvement notices' where they are of the opinion that s. 9 requirements are not being met. Such notices must give the responsible person time in which to rectify the problem specified in the notice; but this does not preclude the instigation of proceedings without notice for clear breaches of welfare principles.

Section B22 Offences Relating to the Proceeds of Criminal Conduct

B22.1 Part 7 of the Proceeds of Crime Act 2002 creates a series of 'money laundering' offences (ss. 327–329) which (subject to the transitional arrangements explained below) supplant offences previously contained in the CJA 1988, ss. 93A to 93C and the Drug Trafficking Act 1994, ss. 49 to 51. Sections 330 to 332 of the 2002 Act create offences of failure to disclose cases of suspected money laundering. The non-disclosure offences (which supplant the Drug Trafficking Act 1994, s. 52) are capable of commission only by persons in the 'regulated sector' of the financial services industry as defined in sch. 9 to the Act (as amended by the Proceeds of Crime Act 2002 (Business in the Regulated Sector and Supervisory Authorities) Order 2003 (SI 2003 No. 3074). The current offences differ from s. 52 of the 1994 Act in that they extend to matters concerning the proceeds of all types of criminal conduct, and not just to those concerning the proceeds of drug trafficking. Finally, s. 333 creates an offence of 'tipping off' another person as to the fact that a protected or authorised disclosure (a lawful report of suspected money laundering) has been made, where this tip-off is likely to prejudice any subsequent investigation. This provision supplants s. 93D(2) of the 1998 Act and s. 53(2) of the 1994 Act. As to the origins, scope and purpose of Part 7 generally, see parts 5 to 8 of Brooke LJ's judgment in *Bowman v Fels* [2005] 1 WLR 3083.

In Part 8 of the 2002 Act, s. 342 creates an offence involving conduct that is likely to obstruct or prejudice a money laundering, civil recovery or confiscation investigation. This supplants (but goes well beyond) the offences previously contained in s. 93D(1) of the 1988 Act and s. 53(1) of the 1994 Act.

The current legislation offers the prosecution several advantages over the old, primarily because it avoids the difficulties that could previously arise where, for example, there was clear evidence that D was involved in money laundering but the evidence did not disclose whether this involved the proceeds of drug trafficking or the proceeds of other crimes. D could not then be convicted of either offence. As to the framing of a conspiracy charge in such cases, see *Hussain* [2002] Crim LR 407 and *Rizvi* [2003] EWCA Crim 3575.

Parts 7 and 8 of the Act were brought into force on 24 February 2003 (Proceeds of Crime Act 2002 (Commencement No. 4, Transitional Provisions and Savings) Order 2003 (SI 2003 No. 120)), but subject to article 3 of that Order. This provides that the current provisions do *not* apply where the conduct allegedly constituting an offence under those provisions began before 24 February 2003 and ended on or after that date; and the old money laundering offences continue to have effect in such circumstances. For detailed analysis of the old law, see the 2002 edition of this work and see also *Montila* [2005] 1 All ER 113 and *Saik* [2007] 1 AC 18 (see **A6.21**).

The Money Laundering Regulations

B22.2 The Money Laundering Regulations 2003 (SI 2003 No. 3075) came into force with minor exceptions on 1 March 2004, and impose a wider and more stringent regime than that previously applied by the 1993 Regulations, which they replaced. They will in turn be replaced by the Money Laundering Regulations 2007 (SI 2007 No. 2157) on 15 December 2007, in compliance with the EU 3rd Money Laundering Directive 2005.

Detailed consideration of the regulations falls beyond the scope of this work but the principal implications in terms of criminal liability are as follows: where business relationships are formed, or individual transactions are carried out, in the course of relevant business (as defined in reg. 2), anyone carrying out such a business must maintain certain procedures for identification (reg. 4), record-keeping (reg. 6) and internal reporting (reg. 7). Breaches of those requirements may be punishable under reg. 3, which also contains strict requirements as to the training of employees.

Money Laundering Regulations 2003, reg. 3

(1) Every person must in the course of relevant business carried on by him in the United Kingdom—
   (a) comply with the requirements of regulations 4 (identification procedures), 6 (record-keeping procedures) and 7 (internal reporting procedures);
   (b) establish such other procedures of internal control and communication as may be appropriate for the purposes of forestalling and preventing money laundering; and
   (c) take appropriate measures so that relevant employees are—
      (i) made aware of the provisions of these regulations, part 7 of the Proceeds of Crime Act 2002 (money laundering) and sections 18 and 21A of the Terrorism Act 2000; and
      (ii) given training in how to recognise and deal with transactions which may be related to money laundering.

(2) A person who contravenes this regulation is guilty of an offence and liable—
   (a) on conviction on indictment, to imprisonment for a term not exceeding 2 years, to a fine or to both;
   (b) on summary conviction, to a fine not exceeding the statutory maximum.

(3) In deciding whether a person has committed an offence under this regulation, the court must consider whether he followed any relevant guidance which at the time concerned—
   (a) issued by a supervisory authority or any other appropriate body;
   (b) approved by the Treasury; and
   (c) published in a manner approved by the Treasury as appropriate in their opinion to bring the guidance to the attention of persons likely to be affected by it.

(4) An appropriate body is any body which regulates or is representative of any trade, profession, business or employment carried on by the alleged offender.

(5) In proceedings against any person for an offence under this regulation, it is a defence for that person to show that he took all reasonable steps and exercised all due diligence to avoid committing the offence.

(6) Where a person is convicted of an offence under this regulation, he shall not also be liable to a penalty under regulation 20 (power to impose penalties).

Casinos have sometimes been associated with money laundering activities but, by reg. 8(1), casino operators must obtain satisfactory evidence of a person's identity before allowing him to use the casino's gaming facilities. By reg. 8(2), failure to do so is to be treated as a contravention of reg. 3.

Money Laundering and Criminal Property

B22.3 The term 'money laundering', although widely used in the Proceeds of Crime Act 2002, is potentially misleading. By s. 340(11), 'money laundering' is defined as an act which constitutes an offence under ss. 327, 328 or 329, an inchoate version of such an offence, secondary participation in such an offence or an act which would constitute any of the above if it were done in the UK. The offences under ss. 327 to 329 do not, however, use the terms 'money' or 'laundering' to define their scope. They are concerned instead with 'criminal property', as defined in s. 340(2) to (10).

Proceeds of Crime Act 2002, s. 340

(2) Criminal conduct is conduct which—
(a) constitutes an offence in any part of the United Kingdom, or
(b) would constitute an offence in any part of the United Kingdom if it occurred there.

(3) Property is criminal property if—
(a) it constitutes a person's benefit from criminal conduct or it represents such a benefit (in whole or part and whether directly or indirectly), and
(b) the alleged offender knows or suspects that it constitutes or represents such a benefit.

(4) It is immaterial—
(a) who carried out the conduct;
(b) who benefited from it;
(c) whether the conduct occurred before or after the passing of this Act.

(5) A person benefits from conduct if he obtains property as a result of or in connection with the conduct.

(6) If a person obtains a pecuniary advantage as a result of or in connection with conduct, he is to be taken to obtain as a result of or in connection with the conduct a sum of money equal to the value of the pecuniary advantage.

(7) References to property or a pecuniary advantage obtained in connection with conduct include references to property or a pecuniary advantage obtained in both that connection and some other.

(8) If a person benefits from conduct his benefit is the property obtained as a result of or in connection with the conduct.

(9) Property is all property wherever situated and includes—
(a) money;
(b) all forms of property, real or personal, heritable or moveable;
(c) things in action and other intangible or incorporeal property.

(10) The following rules apply in relation to property—
(a) property is obtained by a person if he obtains an interest in it;
(b) references to an interest, in relation to land in England and Wales or Northern Ireland, are to any legal estate or equitable interest or power;
(c) references to an interest, in relation to land in Scotland, are to any estate, interest, servitude or other heritable right in or over land, including a heritable security;
(d) references to an interest, in relation to property other than land, include references to a right (including a right to possession).

The concept of 'criminal property', which lies at the core of the money laundering offences, is essentially defined in s. 340(2) and (3). See also *Wilkinson v DPP* [2006] EWHC 3012 (Admin). Property that does not fall within the terms of those provisions cannot be criminal property under part 7 of the Act. Subsections (4) to (10) expand upon and illustrate that concept, but are not exhaustive. Section 340(3)(b) purports to be part of this definition of 'criminal property', but for practical purposes it also specifies the key *mens rea* element in money laundering offences.

Criminal property must be proved to represent a person's benefit from *actual* criminal conduct. Unfounded suspicion as to its derivation does not suffice (see *Montila* [2005] 1 WLR 3141 at [41], in which the position under the 2002 Act is specifically addressed). But this criminal quality may in some cases be proved by inference from the way in which the property in question is dealt with, and it is not always necessary to identify the specific underlying offence. If, in other words, money is handled in a manner consistent only with money laundering, it would be open to a court or jury to infer that it must be criminal property because 'no one launders clean money' (see *Director of the Assets Recovery Agency v Olupitan* [2007] EWHC 162 (QB); *El Kurd* [2001] Crim LR 234).

The concept of 'criminal property' may in some circumstances include property derived from activities abroad that are perfectly lawful under local law. As originally drafted, the Act made no concessions to local law, but amendments to the principal money laundering offences came into force on 15 May 2006 (see ss. 327(2A), 328(3) and 329(2A)). These effectively exempt the proceeds of most, but not all, 'locally lawful' activities from the operation of the Act. By virtue of the Proceeds of Crime Act 2002 (Money Laundering: Exceptions to Overseas Conduct Defence) Order 2006 (SI 2006 No. 1070), they do not however exempt the proceeds of conduct which would have constituted an offence punishable by imprisonment for a maximum term in excess of 12 months in any part of the UK if it occurred there, other than the proceeds of conduct that would have amounted to:

(a) an offence under the Gaming Act 1968;
(b) an offence under the Lotteries and Amusements Act 1976, or
(c) an offence under ss. 23 or 25 of the Financial Services and Markets Act 2000.

In *Gabriel* [2006] EWCA Crim 229, the Court of Appeal rejected arguments that profits made from legitimate trading would, if not declared to the Revenue (or, in the case of benefit claimants, to the Department of Work and Pensions) thereby become criminal property. Gage LJ said (at [21] and [22]):

> We recognise that the failure to declare profits for the purposes of income tax may give rise to an offence, but that does not make the legitimate trading in goods an offence of itself. . . .
>
> We can see how benefits obtained on the basis of a false declaration or a failure to disclose a change in circumstances may amount to obtaining a pecuniary advantage, namely the benefits: see section 340(6) . . . But in this case no attempt was made to prove that the appellant or anyone else in her family had made any false declaration or failed to disclose a change of circumstances.

In *Loizou* [2005] 2 Cr App R 618, Clarke LJ said (at [30]), in the context of an alleged offence of transferring criminal property contrary to s. 327(1) of the Act:

> In our view, the natural meaning of s. 327(1) of the 2002 Act is that the property concealed, disguised, converted or transferred, as the case may be, must be criminal property at the time it is concealed, disguised, converted or transferred (as the case may be). Put the other way round, in a case of transfer, if the property is not criminal property at the time of the transfer, the offence is not committed.

If, however, D fraudulently under-declares his profits with the result that he deprives the public revenue of tax, he thereby obtains, in respect of the relevant period, a pecuniary advantage which is derived from cheating the public revenue (see **B16.2**) and this may be a 'benefit' within the meaning of s. 340(3)(a), although this benefit can become criminal property only once a false declaration has been made (*K* [2007] 2 Cr App R 128).

Authorised Disclosure and Appropriate Consent

A person is not guilty of a money laundering offence if he makes an 'authorised disclosure' and acts with the 'appropriate consent'. These terms are defined in the Proceeds of Crime Act 2002, ss. 338 and 335, respectively. **B22.4**

Proceeds of Crime Act 2002, s. 338

(1) For the purposes of this Part a disclosure is authorised if—
(a) it is a disclosure to a constable, a customs officer or a nominated officer by the alleged offender that property is criminal property, and
(b) [repealed]
(c) the first, second or third condition set out below is satisfied.
(2) The first condition is that the disclosure is made before the alleged offender does the prohibited act.
(2A) The second condition is that—
(a) the disclosure is made while the alleged offender is doing the prohibited act,
(b) he began to do the act at a time when, because he did not then know or suspect that the property constituted or represented a person's benefit from criminal conduct, the act was not a prohibited act, and

(c) the disclosure is made on his own initiative and as soon as is practicable after he first knows or suspects that the property constitutes or represents a person's benefit from criminal conduct.

(3) The third condition is that—
(a) the disclosure is made after the alleged offender does the prohibited act,
(b) there is a good reason for his failure to make the disclosure before he did the act, and
(c) the disclosure is made on his own initiative and as soon as it is practicable for him to make it.

(4) An authorised disclosure is not to be taken to breach any restriction on the disclosure of information (however imposed).

(5) A disclosure to a nominated officer is a disclosure which—
(a) is made to a person nominated by the alleged offender's employer to receive authorised disclosures, and
(b) is made in the course of the alleged offender's employment.

(6) References to the prohibited act are to an act mentioned in section 327(1), 328(1) or 329(1) (as the case may be).

References to a constable include a person authorised for these purposes by the Director General of the Serious Organised Crime Agency (SOCA) (s. 340(13)).

Proceeds of Crime Act 2002, s. 335

(1) The appropriate consent is—
(a) the consent of a nominated officer to do a prohibited act if an authorised disclosure is made to the nominated officer;
(b) the consent of a constable to do a prohibited act if an authorised disclosure is made to a constable;
(c) the consent of a customs officer to do a prohibited act if an authorised disclosure is made to a customs officer.

(2) A person must be treated as having the appropriate consent if—
(a) he makes an authorised disclosure to a constable or a customs officer, and
(b) the condition in subsection (3) or the condition in subsection (4) is satisfied.

(3) The condition is that before the end of the notice period he does not receive notice from a constable or customs officer that consent to the doing of the act is refused.

(4) The condition is that—
(a) before the end of the notice period he receives notice from a constable or customs officer that consent to the doing of the act is refused, and
(b) the moratorium period has expired.

(5) The notice period is the period of seven working days starting with the first working day after the person makes the disclosure.

(6) The moratorium period is the period of 31 days starting with the day on which the person receives notice that consent to the doing of the act is refused.

(7) A working day is a day other than a Saturday, a Sunday, Christmas Day, Good Friday or a day which is a bank holiday under the Banking and Financial Dealings Act 1971 in the part of the United Kingdom in which the person is when he makes the disclosure.

(8) References to a prohibited act are to an act mentioned in section 327(1), 328(1) or 329(1) (as the case may be).

(9) A nominated officer is a person nominated to receive disclosures under section 338.

Section 336 details conditions under which a nominated officer may give appropriate consent.

In *Bowman v Fels* [2005] 1 WLR 3083 the Court of Appeal held that, 'the issue or pursuit of ordinary legal proceedings with a view to obtaining the court's adjudication upon the parties' rights and duties is not to be regarded as an arrangement or a prohibited act within ss. 327–9.' It follows that lawyers conducting litigation are not required to make disclosure to the SOCA and obtain SOCA consent merely because of a suspicion that the proceedings might in some way facilitate the acquisition, retention, use or control of criminal property by one or more of the parties.

Where disclosure is required, then as Laddie J explained in *Squirrell Ltd v National Westminster Bank plc* [2006] 1 WLR 637 at [17]: the constable (or SOCA officer) or customs officer may simply give consent (s. 335(1)). Alternatively, consent may be assumed if the party has made an authorised disclosure and has not received, within seven working days, notice that consent is refused. If notice of refusal is indeed given then a further 31 calendar days (the moratorium) must pass before the party can safely deal with the property in question.

Offences of Concealment, etc.

Proceeds of Crime Act 2002, s. 327 **B22.5**

(1) A person commits an offence if he—
 (a) conceals criminal property;
 (b) disguises criminal property;
 (c) converts criminal property;
 (d) transfers criminal property;
 (e) removes criminal property from England and Wales or from Scotland or from Northern Ireland.

(2) But a person does not commit such an offence if—
 (a) he makes an authorised disclosure under section 338 and (if the disclosure is made before he does the act mentioned in subsection (1)) he has the appropriate consent;
 (b) he intended to make such a disclosure but had a reasonable excuse for not doing so;
 (c) the act he does is done in carrying out a function he has relating to the enforcement of any provision of this Act or of any other enactment relating to criminal conduct or benefit from criminal conduct.

(2A) Nor does a person commit an offence under subsection (1) if—
 (a) he knows, or believes on reasonable grounds, that the relevant criminal conduct occurred in a particular country or territory outside the United Kingdom, and
 (b) the relevant criminal conduct—
  (i) was not, at the time it occurred, unlawful under the criminal law then applying in that country or territory, and
  (ii) is not of a description prescribed by an order made by the Secretary of State.

(2B) In subsection (2A) 'the relevant criminal conduct' is the criminal conduct by reference to which the property concerned is criminal property.

(2C) A deposit-taking body that does an act mentioned in paragraph (c) or (d) of subsection (1) does not commit an offence under that subsection if—
 (a) it does the act in operating an account maintained with it, and
 (b) the value of the criminal property concerned is less than the threshold amount determined under section 339A for the act.

(3) Concealing or disguising criminal property includes concealing or disguising its nature, source, location, disposition, movement or ownership or any rights with respect to it.

Indictment

Statement of Offence **B22.6**

Concealing criminal property, contrary to section 327(1)(e) of the Proceeds of Crime Act 2002

Particulars of Offence

D on or about the . . . day of . . . concealed in his home criminal property, namely . . . knowing or suspecting it to represent in whole or in part the proceeds of drug trafficking committed by E.

The explanatory notes to the Act suggest that s. 327 'creates one of three principal money laundering offences', but this may be open to argument. The structure of the section suggests that it creates not one but five separate offences (one in each of s. 327(1)(a) to (1)(e)) and the Act contains no clear indication to the contrary. This contrasts with the Public Order Act 1986, which specifically states in s. 7(2) that ss. 1 to 5 of that Act each create only one offence. An indictment that merely alleges 'money laundering, contrary to s. 327' would thus appear to be duplicitous, although the position is by no means clear and it is possible that the courts will take a different view. The form of indictment above should be acceptable in either case. See generally D11.41 *et seq.*

B22.7 **Procedure and Sentence** Offences under the Proceeds of Crime Act 2002, ss. 327 to 329, are triable either way (s. 334). When tried on indictment they are class 3 offences. The maximum penalty is 14 years' imprisonment and/or a fine following conviction on indictment; six months and/or a fine not exceeding the statutory maximum on summary conviction. Guidance on sentencing for money laundering, albeit in relation to offences replaced by the PCA 2002, may be found in *Basra* [2002] 2 Cr App R (S) 469 and *Gonzalez* [2003] 2 Cr App R (S) 35. In *El-Delbi* [2003] EWCA Crim 1767 the Court of Appeal dealt with a case involving the laundering of the proceeds of drug trafficking. Such offenders can expect to receive severe sentences comparable to those playing a significant role in the supply of drugs. It should be borne in mind, however, that the maximum penalty for money laundering is 14 years while for dealing in Class A drugs it is life imprisonment.

B22.8 **Elements** The Proceeds of Crime Act 2002, s. 327, supplants the Drug Trafficking Act 1994, s. 49, and the CJA 1988, s. 93C. The scope of the offences created is potentially very broad. Dishonesty is not required, nor is knowledge of the provenance of the property. On a literal reading of s. 327, a thief who conceals, disguises or sells property that he has just stolen may thereby commit offences under that section, as may someone who merely suspects that the property he converts or exports represents the benefit of another person's crime (see s. 340(3)(b)). Where property is purchased for 'adequate consideration', s. 329(2) provides a defence to someone who is charged with unlawful acquisition, use or possession under s. 329(1) (see **B22.12**) but this defence cannot apply if he is charged instead with converting, transferring or removing the property under s. 327.

Section 327(2) creates defences to charges under s. 327(1). The accused does not bear any legal or persuasive burden in respect of those defences, but he must presumably bear an evidential burden. The prosecution therefore need not address any such issues unless these are raised by admissible evidence.

Money Laundering Arrangements

B22.9 **Proceeds of Crime Act 2002, s. 328**

(1) A person commits an offence if he enters into or becomes concerned in an arrangement which he knows or suspects facilitates (by whatever means) the acquisition, retention, use or control of criminal property by or on behalf of another person.

(2) But a person does not commit such an offence if—
(a) he makes an authorised disclosure under section 338 and (if the disclosure is made before he does the act mentioned in subsection (1)) he has the appropriate consent;
(b) he intended to make such a disclosure but had a reasonable excuse for not doing so;
(c) the act he does is done in carrying out a function he has relating to the enforcement of any provision of this Act or of any other enactment relating to criminal conduct or benefit from criminal conduct.

(3) Nor does a person commit an offence under subsection (1) if—
(a) he knows, or believes on reasonable grounds, that the relevant criminal conduct occurred in a particular country or territory outside the United Kingdom, and
(b) the relevant criminal conduct—
(i) was not, at the time it occurred, unlawful under the criminal law then applying in that country or territory, and
(ii) is not of a description prescribed by an order made by the Secretary of State.

(4) In subsection (3) 'the relevant criminal conduct' is the criminal conduct by reference to which the property concerned is criminal property.

(5) A deposit-taking body that does an act mentioned in subsection (1) does not commit an offence under that subsection if—
(a) it does the act in operating an account maintained with it, and
(b) the arrangement facilitates the acquisition, retention, use or control of criminal property of a value that is less than the threshold amount determined under section 339A for the act.

Indictment, etc.

B22.10

Statement of Offence

Entering into or becoming concerned in a money laundering arrangement, contrary to section 328(1) of the Proceeds of Crime Act 2002.

Particulars of Offence

D on or about the day of . . . entered into or became concerned in an arrangement, namely the opening by E of an account at . . . . . . under a false name, knowing or suspecting that this arrangement would facilitate the retention, use or control of criminal property by E or by other persons unknown.

In contrast to ss. 327 and 329, s. 328 appears to create a single offence, which may be committed in various ways. It is analogous in this respect to the offence of handling stolen goods (see **B4.127**). As to procedure and sentence, see **B22.7**.

Elements The Proceeds of Crime Act 2002, s. 328, supplants the Drug Trafficking Act 1994, s. 50, and the CJA 1988, s. 93A. It potentially affects not only deliberate or dishonest offenders, but also banks, accountants and legal advisers, etc., who become suspicious as to the legality of the means by which their clients have acquired any of the funds or other property they are asked to deal with or manage. As Laddie J explained in *Squirrell Ltd v National Westminster Bank plc* [2006] 1 WLR 637 at [16]: B22.11

> The purpose of s. 328(1) is not to turn innocent third parties like [banks] into criminals. It is to put them under pressure to provide information to the relevant authorities to enable the latter to obtain information about possible criminal activity and to increase their prospects of being able to freeze the proceeds of crime. To this end, a party caught by s. 328(1) can avoid liability if he brings himself within the statutory defence created by s. 328(2). . . .

The concept of 'suspicion' was considered by the Court of Appeal in *Da Silva* [2007] 1 WLR 303, in the context of an alleged offence under the CJA 1988, s. 93A. Longmore LJ, giving the judgment of the court, said:

> It seems to us that the essential element in the word 'suspect' and its affiliates, in this context, is that the defendant must think that there is a possibility, which is more than fanciful, that the relevant facts exist. A vague feeling of unease would not suffice. But the statute does not require the suspicion to be 'clear' or 'firmly grounded and targeted on specific facts', or based upon 'reasonable grounds'. To require the prosecution to satisfy such criteria as to the strength of the suspicion would, in our view, be putting a gloss on the section.

Arguably, it need not even be proved that such suspicion was well-founded in fact. In *Squirrell*, Laddie J's view was that 'Even if [the client's account] does *not* contain funds which are, in fact, criminal property and no offence has been committed [by the client] s. 328(1) bites if [the bank] has a relevant suspicion'. A similar interpretation seems to have been assumed in *K Ltd v National Westminster Bank plc* [2007] 1 WLR 311. Unfounded suspicions may, if that view is correct, lead to the commission of a s. 328 offence. Such an interpretation nevertheless looks wrong in light of the decision of the House of Lords in *Montila* [2005] 1 WLR 3141 (not referred to in *Squirrell* or *K Ltd*), in which it was held that a conviction for the somewhat similarly worded offence under the CJA 1988, s. 93C(2), required proof that the property in question was *in fact* (and was not merely suspected to be) the proceeds of criminal conduct. The House of Lords thought that this interpretation was strongly supported by the absence of any defence where the property in question was later proved to be 'clean'. Given that the 2002 Act similarly contains no such defence, the same argument would seem to apply. Indeed, the Appellate Committee expressly noted in *Montila* (at [41]) that, in the 2002 legislation, 'there is no room for any ambiguity. The property that is being dealt with in each case must be shown to have been criminal property.' The point did not arise in *Da Silva* where the property in question clearly was criminal property.

In *Bowman v Fels* [2005] 1 WLR 3083, the Court of Appeal rejected arguments that, if a lawyer acting for a client in legal proceedings discovers or suspects anything in the proceedings that may facilitate the acquisition, retention, use or control (usually by his own client or his client's opponent) of criminal property, he must immediately notify the relevant authority (now SOCA) of his belief if he is to avoid being guilty of a s. 328 offence. Brooke LJ said (at [83]):

> [Section 328] is . . . not intended to cover or affect the ordinary conduct of litigation by legal professionals. That includes any step taken by them in litigation from the issue of proceedings and the securing of injunctive relief or a freezing order up to its final disposal by judgment. We do not consider that either the European or the United Kingdom legislator can have envisaged that any of these ordinary activities could fall within the concept of 'becoming concerned in an arrangement which . . . facilitates the acquisition, retention, use or control of criminal property'.

The wording of s. 328(2) does not suggest that the accused bears any legal or persuasive burden in respect of the defences it creates, but he must bear an evidential burden. The prosecution therefore need not address any such issues unless these have been raised by admissible evidence.

Offences of Acquisition, Use or Possession

B22.12 **Proceeds of Crime Act 2002, s. 329**

(1) A person commits an offence if he—
 (a) acquires criminal property;
 (b) uses criminal property;
 (c) has possession of criminal property.

(2) But a person does not commit such an offence if—
 (a) he makes an authorised disclosure under section 338 and (if the disclosure is made before he does the act mentioned in subsection (1)) he has the appropriate consent;
 (b) he intended to make such a disclosure but had a reasonable excuse for not doing so;
 (c) he acquired or used or had possession of the property for adequate consideration;
 (d) the act he does is done in carrying out a function he has relating to the enforcement of any provision of this Act or of any other enactment relating to criminal conduct or benefit from criminal conduct.

(2A) Nor does a person commit an offence under subsection (1) if—
 (a) he knows, or believes on reasonable grounds, that the relevant criminal conduct occurred in a particular country or territory outside the United Kingdom, and
 (b) the relevant criminal conduct—
  (i) was not, at the time it occurred, unlawful under the criminal law then applying in that country or territory, and
  (ii) is not of a description prescribed by an order made by the Secretary of State.

(2B) In subsection (2A) 'the relevant criminal conduct' is the criminal conduct by reference to which the property concerned is criminal property.

(2C) A deposit-taking body that does an act mentioned in subsection (1) does not commit an offence under that subsection if—
 (a) it does the act in operating an account maintained with it, and
 (b) the arrangement facilitates the acquisition, retention, use or control of criminal property of a value that is less than the threshold amount determined under section 339A for the act.

(3) For the purposes of this section—
 (a) a person acquires property for inadequate consideration if the value of the consideration is significantly less than the value of the property;
 (b) a person uses or has possession of property for inadequate consideration if the value of the consideration is significantly less than the value of the use or possession;
 (c) the provision by a person of goods or services which he knows or suspects may help another to carry out criminal conduct is not consideration.

Indictment, etc.

B22.13 *Statement of Offence*

Acquiring criminal property, contrary to section 329(1)(a) of the Proceeds of Crime Act 2002.

Particulars of Offence

D on or about the day of ...... acquired criminal property, namely ...... knowing or suspecting it to represent in whole or in part the proceeds of drug trafficking commited by E.

There may be room for argument as to whether s. 329(1)(a) to (c) each create a distinct offence, or whether they represent three different ways of committing a single offence created by s. 329(1). See the discussion of s. 327 at **B22.6**. The form of indictment shown above should be acceptable in either case. As to procedure and sentence, see **B22.7**.

Elements The Proceeds of Crime Act 2002, s. 329, supplants the Drug Trafficking Act 1994, s. 51 and the CJA 1988, s. 93B. As with s. 327, s. 329 does not distinguish between criminal property that represents the benefit of some other person's crime and that which represents the benefits of a crime which the accused himself has just committed. A thief who uses or retains possession of property that he has just stolen (this being criminal property as defined in s. 340) must therefore be guilty of an offence under s. 29(1)(b) or (c), the maximum penalty for which is twice that for basic theft. It does not follow that such a charge would be appropriate. It might indeed be considered perverse. The structure of the new money laundering offences appears to rely on the assumption that they will be applied sensibly and that prosecutors will not attempt to exploit the more bizarre or extreme possibilities that they create. On the other hand, it is apparent that charges are now being laid under s. 329 in some cases where an accused might previously have faced more charges of theft or handling: see, for example, *Hogan v DPP* (2007) *The Times*, 28 February 2007 and *Wilkinson v DPP* [2006] EWHC 3012 (Admin). **B22.14**

Dishonesty is not required under s. 329, nor need the accused know or believe that the property in question is criminal property. Mere suspicion will suffice (see s. 340(3)(b)).

Defences are provided under s. 329(2) to (2C). The accused bears no legal or persuasive burden in respect of those defences, but he does bear an evidential burden (see *Hogan v DPP*). The prosecution therefore need not address any such issues unless these have been raised by the accused. Where property is purchased for 'adequate consideration', s. 329(2)(c) provides a defence to someone who is charged with unlawful acquisition, use or possession under s. 329(1), but this cannot apply if he is charged instead with an offence under s. 327.

In *Gabriel* [2006] EWCA Crim 229, Gage LJ offered this advice to prosecutors in cases involving s. 329 (at [29]):

> There can be no doubt that the money laundering provisions of the Proceeds of Crime Act 2002 are draconian. The scope of section 329 is wide. It requires proof of no more *mens rea* than suspicion. The danger is that juries will be tempted to think that it is for the defence to prove innocence rather than the prosecution to prove guilt. In *R v Loizou* [2005] EWCA 1579, the prosecution had set out the factors upon which it relied and from which it submitted the jury could draw proper inferences. In our judgment it is a sensible practice for the prosecution, as was done in *Loizou*, either by giving particulars, or at least in opening, to set out the facts upon which it relies and the inferences which it will invite the jury to draw as proof that the property was criminal property. In doing so it may very well be that the prosecution will be able to limit the scope of the criminal conduct alleged.

Money Laundering, Stolen Goods and Wrongful Credits

There are overlaps between the new money laundering offences and several existing offences, including those of assisting offenders, concealing arrestable offences and perverting the course of justice. The most important overlaps, however, appear to be with handling stolen goods (Theft Act 1968, s. 22; see **B4.127** *et seq.*) and dishonestly retaining a wrongful credit (Theft Act 1968, s. 24A, see **B4.145** *et seq.*). **B22.15**

The term, 'stolen goods', as defined in s. 24 of the Theft Act 1968, includes money and other property which directly or indirectly represents (or has previously represented) the proceeds of theft, blackmail, a s. 15 deception offence, or fraud (within the meaning of the Fraud Act 2006) in the hands of the original thief, etc., or in the hands of a dishonest handler of stolen goods. Such property may be criminally 'handled' in a number of ways, but D must be proved to have been dishonest and to have 'known or believed' that the property in question was stolen goods. Mere suspicion is never enough (see **B4.142**). If the goods were allegedly stolen abroad, outside English jurisdiction, it will be necessary to prove the content of the relevant foreign law (see *Ofori* (1994) 99 Cr App R 223). D cannot ordinarily be convicted of handling the proceeds of his own crime, unless he is proved to have done so for the benefit of another. Finally, in cases involving cheques, money transfers or the proceeds of bank accounts, care must be taken to avoid the problems identified (or created) by the House of Lords in *Preddy* [1996] AC 815 (see **B4.148**).

A money laundering offence will often be much easier to establish than any Theft Act offence. By the Proceeds of Crime Act 2002, s. 340(3), the property in question may represent the proceeds of any crime under UK law, and it suffices that D merely suspects this. In *Hickey* [2007] EWCA Crim 542, D pleaded guilty to an offence under s. 327(1)(c) (see **B22.6**) on the basis that he had suspected that a vehicle he delivered to a buyer had been stolen. It is not clear whether a charge of handling could ever have been proved on the facts of that case, but it was accepted that there was no reason to suppose that he had been aware that the theft of the vehicle had been connected to a domestic burglary. See also *Hogan v DPP* (2007) *The Times*, 28 February 2007 and *Wilkinson v DPP* [2006] EWHC 3012 (Admin).

The exact crime from which the property is derived need not be established, nor need anyone have been convicted in respect of it. D may even be guilty of 'money laundering', by using, possessing or retaining the proceeds of his own criminal conduct; but amendments made to the 2002 Act by the SOCPA 2005, s. 102, now ensure that D will not ordinarily be guilty of any of the principal money laundering offences where he knows, or believes on reasonable grounds, that the relevant 'criminal' conduct occurred (or is occurring) in a country or territory outside the UK, and is not (or was not at that time) criminal under the applicable local law. This defence will not apply if the relevant conduct is of a type described by an order made by the Secretary of State.

Where D's bank or building society account contains the proceeds of thefts or frauds, a money laundering charge may similarly be an easier charge to prove than a charge under the Theft Act 1968, s. 24A. Selection of a money laundering charge would again avoid the need for proof of D's dishonesty or of his knowledge as to the provenance of the funds; and D may commit a money laundering offence by retaining or using the proceeds of a crime committed at any time in the past (e.g., a robbery committed by his father 20 years ago) whereas the s. 24A offence can apply only to wrongful credits made on or after 18 December 1996.

Jurisdiction

B22.16 None of the money laundering offences in the Proceeds of Crime Act 2002 are listed as Group A offences for jurisdictional purposes under the CJA 1993, part I (see **A8.7**). This is a surprising omission, given that the offences under ss. 22 and 24A of the Theft Act 1968 are so listed, and that money laundering has been identified as one of the most prevalent transnational offences of recent years; but it must be emphasised that, as long as the money laundering offence takes place in England and Wales, it does not matter if the property concerned is the product of criminal conduct committed elsewhere in the world.

Failure to Disclose Possible Money Laundering

B22.17 Sections 330, 331 and 332 of the Proceeds of Crime Act 2002 create offences of failure to disclose possible money laundering activities (as defined in s. 340(11)). These are not confined (as was the Drug Trafficking Act 1994, s. 52) to cases involving proceeds of drug trafficking. Actual knowledge or suspicion is not required under ss. 330 or 331, nor (apparently) need it be proved that any actual money laundering took place. It suffices in either case that the accused has 'reasonable grounds' for suspicion. Section 330 deals with failures by persons working in the 'regulated sector' (financial services etc.) as defined in sch. 9 to the Act.

Proceeds of Crime Act 2002, s. 330

(1) A person commits an offence if the conditions in subsections (2) to (4) are satisfied.
(2) The first condition is that he—
(a) knows or suspects, or
(b) has reasonable grounds for knowing or suspecting,
that another person is engaged in money laundering.
(3) The second condition is that the information or other matter—
(a) on which his knowledge or suspicion is based, or
(b) which gives reasonable grounds for such knowledge or suspicion,
came to him in the course of a business in the regulated sector.
(3A) The third condition is—
(a) that he can identify the other person mentioned in subsection (2) or the whereabouts of any of the laundered property, or
(b) that he believes, or it is reasonable to expect him to believe, that the information or other matter mentioned in subsection (3) will or may assist in identifying that other person or the whereabouts of any of the laundered property.
(4) The fourth condition is that he does not make the required disclosure to—
(a) a nominated officer, or
(b) a person authorised for the purposes of this Part by the Director General of the Serious Organised Crime Agency,
as soon as is practicable after the information or other matter mentioned in subsection (3) comes to him.
(5) The required disclosure is a disclosure of—
(a) the identity of the other person mentioned in subsection (2), if he knows it,
(b) the whereabouts of the laundered property, so far as he knows it, and
(c) the information or other matter mentioned in subsection (3).
(5A) The laundered property is the property forming the subject-matter of the money laundering that he knows or suspects, or has reasonable grounds for knowing or suspecting, that other person to be engaged in.
(6) But he does not commit an offence under this section if—
(a) he has a reasonable excuse for not making the required disclosure,
(b) he is a professional legal adviser or other relevant professional adviser and—
(i) if he knows either of the things mentioned in subsection (5)(a) and (b), he knows the thing because of information or other matter that came to him in privileged circumstances, or
(ii) the information or other matter mentioned in subsection (3) came to him in privileged circumstances, or
(c) subsection (7) or (7B) applies to him.
(7) This subsection applies to a person if—
(a) he does not know or suspect that another person is engaged in money laundering, and
(b) he has not been provided by his employer with such training as is specified by the Secretary of State by order for the purposes of this section.
(7A) Nor does a person commit an offence under this section if—
(a) he knows, or believes on reasonable grounds, that the money laundering is occurring in a particular country or territory outside the United Kingdom, and
(b) the money laundering—
(i) is not unlawful under the criminal law applying in that country or territory, and
(ii) is not of a description prescribed in an order made by the Secretary of State.
(7B) This subsection applies to a person if—
(a) he is employed by, or is in partnership with, a professional legal adviser or a relevant professional adviser to provide the adviser with assistance or support,
(b) the information or other matter mentioned in subsection (3) comes to the person in connection with the provision of such assistance or support, and
(c) the information or other matter came to the adviser in privileged circumstances.

(8) In deciding whether a person committed an offence under this section the court must consider whether he followed any relevant guidance which was at the time concerned—
(a) issued by a supervisory authority or any other appropriate body,
(b) approved by the Treasury, and
(c) published in a manner it approved as appropriate in its opinion to bring the guidance to the attention of persons likely to be affected by it.

(9) A disclosure to a nominated officer is a disclosure which—
(a) is made to a person nominated by the alleged offender's employer to receive disclosures under this section, and
(b) is made in the course of the alleged offender's employment.

(9A) But a disclosure which satisfies paragraphs (a) and (b) of subsection (9) is not to be taken as a disclosure to a nominated officer if the person making the disclosure—
(a) is a professional legal adviser or other relevant professional adviser,
(b) makes it for the purpose of obtaining advice about making a disclosure under this section, and
(c) does not intend it to be a disclosure under this section.

(10) Information or other matter comes to a professional legal adviser or other relevant professional adviser in privileged circumstances if it is communicated or given to him—
(a) by (or by a representative of) a client of his in connection with the giving by the adviser of legal advice to the client,
(b) by (or by a representative of) a person seeking legal advice from the adviser, or
(c) by a person in connection with legal proceedings or contemplated legal proceedings.

(11) But subsection (10) does not apply to information or other matter which is communicated or given with the intention of furthering a criminal purpose.

(12) Schedule 9 has effect for the purpose of determining what is—
(a) a business in the regulated sector;
(b) a supervisory authority.

(13) An appropriate body is any body which regulates or is representative of any trade, profession, business or employment carried on by the alleged offender.

(14) A relevant professional adviser is an accountant, auditor or tax adviser who is a member of a professional body which is established for accountants, auditors or tax advisers (as the case may be) and which makes provision for—
(a) testing the competence of those seeking admission to membership of such a body as a condition for such admission; and
(b) imposing and maintaining professional and ethical standards for its members, as well as imposing sanctions for non-compliance with those standards.

The guidance referred to in s. 330(8) includes that issued by the Joint Money Laundering Steering Group, in association with the British Bankers' Association. Subscribers to this service may assess their anti-money laundering procedures against current regulatory requirements.

Section 331 creates a broadly similar offence, applicable to nominated officers in the regulated sector, who have themselves received information as to suspected money laundering in consequence of disclosures made to them under s. 330.

Section 332 deals with failures by nominated officers to whom disclosures have been made under s. 337 (protected disclosures) or s. 338 (authorised disclosures).

B22.18 **Penalties and Procedure for Offences under ss. 330 to 332** Offences under the Proceeds of Crime Act 2002, ss. 330 to 332, are triable either way (s. 334). When tried on indictment they are class 3 offences. The maximum penalty is five years' imprisonment and/or a fine following conviction on indictment; six months and/or a fine not exceeding the statutory maximum on summary conviction.

Tipping-off and Prejudicing Investigations

B22.19 The Proceeds of Crime Act 2002, s. 333(1), creates an offence of making a disclosure likely to prejudice a money laundering investigation which is or may in the future be undertaken by law enforcement authorities. It supplants the Drug Trafficking Offences Act 1994, s. 53(2), and the CJA 1988, s. 93D(2).

Proceeds of Crime Act 2002, s. 333

(1) A person commits an offence if—
 (a) he knows or suspects that a disclosure falling within section 337 or 338 has been made, and
 (b) he makes a disclosure which is likely to prejudice any investigation which might be conducted following the disclosure referred to in paragraph (a).

(2) But a person does not commit an offence under subsection (1) if—
 (a) he did not know or suspect that the disclosure was likely to be prejudicial as mentioned in subsection (1);
 (b) the disclosure is made in carrying out a function he has relating to the enforcement of any provision of this Act or of any other enactment relating to criminal conduct or benefit from criminal conduct;
 (c) he is a professional legal adviser and the disclosure falls within subsection (3).

(3) A disclosure falls within this subsection if it is a disclosure—
 (a) to (or to a representative of) a client of the professional legal adviser in connection with the giving by the adviser of legal advice to the client, or
 (b) to any person in connection with legal proceedings or contemplated legal proceedings.

(4) But a disclosure does not fall within subsection (3) if it is made with the intention of furthering a criminal purpose.

The offences previously contained in s. 93D(1) of the 1988 Act and s. 53(1) of the 1994 Act are supplanted by s. 342 of the 2002 Act.

Proceeds of Crime Act 2002, s. 342

(1) This section applies if a person knows or suspects that an appropriate officer . . . is acting (or proposing to act) in connection with a confiscation investigation, a civil recovery investigation or a money laundering investigation which is being or is about to be conducted.

(2) The person commits an offence if—
 (a) he makes a disclosure which is likely to prejudice the investigation, or
 (b) he falsifies, conceals, destroys or otherwise disposes of, or causes or permits the falsification, concealment, destruction or disposal of, documents which are relevant to the investigation.

(3) A person does not commit an offence under subsection (2)(a) if—
 (a) he does not know or suspect that the disclosure is likely to prejudice the investigation,
 (b) the disclosure is made in the exercise of a function under this Act or any other enactment relating to criminal conduct or benefit from criminal conduct or in compliance with a requirement imposed under or by virtue of this Act, or
 (c) he is a professional legal adviser and the disclosure falls within subsection (4).

(4) A disclosure falls within this subsection if it is a disclosure—
 (a) to (or to a representative of) a client of the professional legal adviser in connection with the giving by the adviser of legal advice to the client, or
 (b) to any person in connection with legal proceedings or contemplated legal proceedings.

(5) But a disclosure does not fall within subsection (4) if it is made with the intention of furthering a criminal purpose.

(6) A person does not commit an offence under subsection (2)(b) if—
 (a) he does not know or suspect that the documents are relevant to the investigation, or
 (b) he does not intend to conceal any facts disclosed by the documents from any appropriate officer . . . carrying out the investigation.

It is clear that s. 342(2)(a) and s. 342(2)(b) each create a separate offence. Penalties and procedure for offences under ss. 333 and 342 are the same as for offences under ss. 330 to 332. (See **B22.18**.)

Section B23 Immigration Offences

ILLEGAL ENTRY AND DECEPTION

B23.1 **Immigration Act 1971, ss. 24 and 24A**

24.—(1) A person who is not a British citizen shall be guilty of an offence punishable on summary conviction with a fine of not more than level 5 on the standard scale or with imprisonment for not more than six months, or with both, in any of the following cases—

(a) if contrary to this Act he knowingly enters the United Kingdom in breach of a deportation order or without leave;

(b) if, having only a limited leave to enter or remain in the United Kingdom, he knowingly either—

(i) remains beyond the time limited by the leave; or

(ii) fails to observe a condition of the leave;

(c) if, having lawfully entered the United Kingdom without leave by virtue of section 8(1) above, he remains without leave beyond the time allowed by section 8(1);

(d) if, without reasonable excuse, he fails to comply with any requirement imposed on him under schedule 2 to this Act to report to a medical officer of health, or to attend, or submit to a test or examination, as required by such an officer;

(e) if, without reasonable excuse, he fails to observe any restriction imposed on him under schedule 2 or 3 to this Act as to residence, as to his employment or occupation or as to reporting to the police, to an immigration officer or to the Secretary of State;

(f) if he disembarks in the United Kingdom from a ship or aircraft after being placed on board under schedule 2 or 3 to this Act with a view to his removal from the United Kingdom;

(g) if he embarks in contravention of a restriction imposed by or under an Order in Council under section 3(7) of this Act.

24A.—(1) A person who is not a British citizen is guilty of an offence if, by means which include deception by him:—

(a) he obtains or seeks to obtain leave to enter or remain in the United Kingdom; or

(b) he secures or seeks to secure the avoidance, postponement or revocation of enforcement action against him.

(2) 'Enforcement action', in relation to a person, means—

(a) the giving of directions for his removal from the United Kingdom ('directions') under schedule 2 to this Act or section 10 of the Immigration and Asylum Act 1999;

(b) the making of a deportation order against him under section 5 of this Act; or

(c) his removal from the United Kingdom in consequence of directions or a deportation order.

Procedure

B23.2 An immigration officer may arrest without warrant any person who has committed or attempted to commit any offence under the Immigration Act 1971, ss. 24 (except s. 24(1)(d)) or 24A or whom he has reasonable grounds for suspecting of committing or attempting to commit such an offence (Immigration Act 1971, s. 28A(1) and (2)). The offence of deception can be committed in a control zone in France or Belgium, and powers of arrest are exercisable by police there (Nationality, Immigration and Asylum Act 2002 (Juxtaposed Controls) Order 2003 (SI 2003 No. 2818), arts. 11 to 13).

An offence under the Immigration Act 1971, s. 24, is a purely summary offence (s. 24(1)). An extended time-limit for prosecution applies to offences under s. 24(1)(a) and (c) (ss. 24(3) and 28), but not to the offence of deception under s. 24A. The offence of overstaying under s. 24(1)(b) is committed at any time when the immigrant knows his or her leave has expired but remains in the UK, but can be charged only once for any period of overstay (s. 24(1A)).

The deception offence under s. 24A is triable either way (s. 24A(3)).

Indictment

Statement of Offence

Obtaining leave to enter or remain in the United Kingdom by deception contrary to section 24A(1) and (3) of the Immigration Act 1971 **B23.3**

Particulars of Offence

A on the . . . day of . . ./on a day between the . . . day of . . . and the . . . day of . . . not being a British citizen, obtained/sought to obtain leave to enter or remain in the United Kingdom/the avoidance, postponement or revocation of enforcement against him/her by means of deception namely [*specify deception*]

Sentencing

The maximum sentence for illegal entry and any other offence under the Immigration Act **B23.4** 1971, s. 24, is a fine not exceeding level 5 on the standard scale, six months' imprisonment or both (s. 24(1)). The maximum sentence for the deception offence when tried summarily is the same as that for illegal entry; trial on indictment carries the maximum of two years' imprisonment, a fine or both (s. 24A(3)).

If the defendant is tried or pleads guilty before a magistrates' court in respect of the s. 24A offence, it is likely that he will be committed to the Crown Court for sentence. For all but the most minor offences, an immediate custodial sentence can be expected.

In *Nasir Ali* [2002] 2 Cr App R (S) 32, May LJ in his judgment on appeal against sentence commented on the serious nature of these types of offences because they had the potential to undermine the system of immigration control. He remarked that although a plea of guilty will always attract an appropriate discount, previous good character and personal circumstances of mitigation are of very limited value in cases of this kind which should generally be sentenced on a deterrent basis. In *Nasir Ali* a sentence of 18 months' imprisonment was reduced to 12 months. Similarly, the use of forged documents in support of a fraudulent attempt to gain entry to the UK, where the entry was unconnected with an asylum claim, was held to attract a sentence within the range of 12 to 18 months in *Kolawole* [2005] 2 Cr App R (S) 71. Sentences of 18 months concurrent for seeking leave to enter by deception and possession of a false identity document (under the Identity Cards Act 2006, s. 25) were held excessive in *Compaore* [2006] EWCA Crim 3135, where reliance on *Kolawole* was held to have been a misdirection.

Where the purpose of the entry is to claim asylum, different considerations apply. In *R (K) v Croydon Crown Court* [2005] 2 Cr App R (S) 578, a four-month detention and training order imposed by a youth court on a 17-year-old asylum seeker who used deception on entry was quashed as wrong in principle, and a conditional discharge substituted. The Court emphasised the role and the power of the agent in that case. *Kolawole* was also distinguished in *Mutede* [2006] 2 Cr App R (S) 161, where the offender had a legitimate passport but had obtained counterfeit immigration letters and a counterfeit national insurance card to obtain employment in the UK. In reducing the prison sentence in this case from 14 months to six months, the Court of Appeal commented that there was a difference between using a false passport to gain entry into the country and using false immigration letters to obtain work.

In *Kishientine* [2005] 2 Cr App R (S) 156, the Court of Appeal held that, in passing sentence, a court should not take into consideration the apparent strength of an asylum claim where that claim had not yet been determined by the Secretary of State.

A recommendation for deportation is appropriate in cases which go well beyond the commission of a 'mere' immigration offence, such as entering a bogus marriage in order to remain in the UK (see *Ahemed* [2006] 1 Cr App R (S) 419), or where a fraudulently obtained or forged passport is used to obtain a national insurance number (see *Bennabas* [2005] EWCA Crim 2113).

Elements

B23.5 A person who is a British citizen cannot commit the offences. The offence of illegal entry requires actual entry and will not have been committed if entry has not occurred. The deception offence can be committed by seeking to enter as well as by actually entering, and also embraces action taken to remain in the UK and to prevent or defer removal. It has been used against failed asylum seekers who have sought asylum again under a different identity (*Nagmadeen* [2003] EWCA Crim 2004). The deception must be material (but it does not have to be the sole means of obtaining entry, etc.) and must be by the immigrant personally. The burden of proof for both offences is normally on the prosecution. However, for the illegal entry offence an exception is made in cases brought within six months of the date of entry. In those cases the burden is on the accused to show on the balance of probabilities that he entered the UK legally (Immigration Act 1971, s. 24(4)(b)). It is arguable that this reversal of the legal burden of proof is contrary to the presumption of innocence contained in the ECHR, Article 6(2), particularly since leave to enter may be granted orally (Immigration (Leave to Enter and Remain) Order 2000 (SI 2000 No. 1161), art. 8(3)) and so might be difficult to prove. On the presumption of innocence and Article 6(2), see further **F3.13**.

As to 'deception', see **B5.2**. A conviction for obtaining leave by deception was quashed in *R (Shehi) v Northampton Magistrates' Court* [2007] EWHC 386 (Admin) because s. 24(1) had not been in force when the applicant was convicted.

Defences

B23.6 Section 31 of the Immigration and Asylum Act 1999 sets out defences, based on Article 31 of the Convention Relating to the Status of Refugees ('the Refugee Convention'), to the deception offence. The statutory defence in s. 31 was introduced following the decision of the Divisional Court in *Uxbridge Magistrates' Court, ex parte Adimi* [1999] 4 All ER 520 that the government's obligations under Article 31 of the Refugee Convention required that criminal sanctions were not imposed on refugees who entered the UK illegally provided that they made themselves known to the relevant authorities without delay. Section 31 of the Immigration and Asylum Act 1999 (as amended by the Identity Cards Act 2006) states that it is a defence to the deception offence (and certain other offences, including offences under part I of the Forgery and Counterfeiting Act 1981 and s. 25 of the Identity Cards Act 2006) for a refugee who has come to the UK directly from another country to show that he (a) presented himself to the UK authorities without delay, (b) showed good cause for his illegal entry or presence in the UK, and (c) made a claim for asylum as soon as was reasonably practicable after his arrival in the United Kingdom. The statutory defence applies only to those persons ultimately recognised as refugees, but in *Makuwa* [2006] EWCA Crim 175, the Court of Appeal held that the legal burden fell on the Crown to prove that the accused was not a refugee once she had raised the issue, although the accused had the legal burden of establishing the ingredients of the defence.

The statutory defence under Immigration and Asylum Act 1999, s. 31, does not apply to the offence of illegal entry, and did not apply to the statutory predecessor of s. 24A. A conviction for deception under s. 24A was quashed in *R (Badur) v Birmingham Crown Court and Solihull Magistrates' Court (Director of Public Prosecutions, Secretary of State for the Home Department and Crown Prosecution Service interested parties)* [2006] EWHC 539 (Admin), on the basis that it should have been charged under the statutory predecessor of s. 24A, and the accused would have been able to avail himself of the broader defence which relied directly on the Refugee Convention, Article 31, instead of being limited to the statutory defence under s. 31 of the 1999 Act. In *Asfaw* [2006] EWCA Crim 707, the Court of Appeal expressed concern at the practice of charging the offence of obtaining air services by deception (to which the statutory defence did not apply) as an alternative to offences under the Forgery and Counterfeiting Act 1981 to which the statutory defence applied. The Crown conceded that for compliance with Article 31 there should be no penalty, and the Court substituted an absolute discharge for a nine-month sentence of imprisonment.

FAILURE TO PRODUCE IMMIGRATION DOCUMENTS, ETC

Definition

Asylum and Immigration (Treatment of Claimants, etc.) Act 2004, s. 2 **B23.7**

(1) A person commits an offence if at a leave or asylum interview he does not have with him an immigration document which—
  (a) is in force, and
  (b) satisfactorily establishes his identity and nationality or citizenship.
(2) A person commits an offence if at a leave or asylum interview he does not have with him, in respect of any dependent child with whom he claims to be travelling or living, an immigration document which—
  (a) is in force, and
  (b) satisfactorily establishes the child's identity and nationality or citizenship.
(3) But a person does not commit an offence under subsection (1) or (2) if—
  (a) the interview referred to in that subsection takes place after the person has entered the United Kingdom, and
  (b) within the period of three days beginning with the date of the interview the person provides to an immigration officer or to the Secretary of State a document of the kind referred to in that subsection.
(4) It is a defence for a person charged with an offence under subsection (1)—
  (a) to prove that he is an EEA national,
  (b) to prove that he is a member of the family of an EEA national and that he is exercising a right under the Community Treaties in respect of entry to or residence in the United Kingdom,
  (c) to prove that he has a reasonable excuse for not being in possession of a document of the kind specified in subsection (1),
  (d) to produce a false immigration document and to prove that he used that document as an immigration document for all purposes in connection with his journey to the United Kingdom, or
  (e) to prove that he travelled to the United Kingdom without, at any stage since he set out on the journey, having possession of an immigration document.
(5) It is a defence for a person charged with an offence under subsection (2) in respect of a child—
  (a) to prove that the child is an EEA national,
  (b) to prove that the child is a member of the family of an EEA national and that the child is exercising a right under the Community Treaties in respect of entry to or residence in the United Kingdom,
  (c) to prove that the person has a reasonable excuse for not being in possession of a document of the kind specified in subsection (2),
  (d) to produce a false immigration document and to prove that it was used as an

immigration document for all purposes in connection with the child's journey to the United Kingdom, or

(e) to prove that he travelled to the United Kingdom with the child without, at any stage since he set out on the journey, having possession of an immigration document in respect of the child.

(6) Where the charge for an offence under subsection (1) or (2) relates to an interview which takes place after the defendant has entered the United Kingdom—

(a) subsections (4)(c) and (5)(c) shall not apply, but

(b) it is a defence for the defendant to prove that he has a reasonable excuse for not providing a document in accordance with subsection (3).

(7) For the purposes of subsections (4) to (6)—

(a) the fact that a document was deliberately destroyed or disposed of is not a reasonable excuse for not being in possession of it or for not providing it in accordance with subsection (3), unless it is shown that the destruction or disposal was—

(i) for a reasonable cause, or

(ii) beyond the control of the person charged with the offence, and

(b) in paragraph (a)(i) 'reasonable cause' does not include the purpose of—

(i) delaying the handling or resolution of a claim or application or the taking of a decision,

(ii) increasing the chances of success of a claim or application, or

(iii) complying with instructions or advice given by a person who offers advice about, or facilitates, immigration into the United Kingdom, unless in the circumstances of the case it is unreasonable to expect non-compliance with the instructions or advice.

(8) A person shall be presumed for the purposes of this section not to have a document with him if he fails to produce it to an immigration officer or official of the Secretary of State on request.

Procedure

B23.8 A power of arrest is granted to an immigration officer who reasonably suspects that a person has committed an offence under the Asylum and Immigration (Treatment of Claimants, etc.) Act 2004, s. 2 (s. 2(10)).

The offence is triable either way.

Sentencing

B23.9 The maximum penalty on conviction on indictment is two years' imprisonment, a fine or both. On summary conviction, the maximum is six months, a fine not exceeding the statutory maximum, or both. In normal circumstances, a custodial sentence is inevitable (*Bei Bei Wang* [2005] 2 Cr App R (S) 492, in which a ten-month sentence in a young offenders' institute on an 18-year-old offender was reduced to two months, and a recommendation for deportation quashed). However, in *MJ* (20 July 2007 unreported), the Court of Appeal held that a custodial sentence was generally inappropriate for an unaccompanied minor committing the offence. In *Weng and Wang* [2005] EWCA Crim 2248, sentences of 36 weeks were reduced to three months, and in *Ai (Lu Zhu)* [2006] 1 Cr App R (S) 18, a sentence of nine months imposed on an adult male was reduced to five months. In *Safari and Zanganeh* [2006] 1 Cr App R (S) 1, in reducing a nine-month sentence on an Iranian husband and wife to three months, the Court of Appeal held that it was not open to a trial judge to conclude, without holding a *Newton* hearing, that the offenders gave their documents to an agent to conceal their identities and details of their movements. A recommendation for deportation was upheld as appropriate following conviction for failure to produce immigration documents by an asylum seeker in *Osman (Abdullah)* [2007] EWCA Crim 39.

Elements

B23.10 The Home Office indicated in the Explanatory Notes issued with the Bill that the essence of the offence is that the accused has destroyed a document en route since carriers are required to ensure that their passengers have appropriate documentation prior to embarking on their journey: 'Someone who arrives in the UK, therefore, without a passport may in many cases be assumed to have destroyed it en route.' In addition to defences available to EEA nationals, no offence is committed where a person produces a false immigration document and proves that it was used for all purposes in connection with the journey or where he proves that he was at no stage in possession of an immigration document. Further, a defence is available where a reasonable excuse is provided for not having an immigration document. The Lord Chief Justice held in *Thet v DPP* [2007] 2 All ER 425 that the Asylum and Immigration (Treatment of Claimants, etc.) Act 2004, s. 2(3), (4)(c) and (6) referred to valid documents only. Someone who has been unable to obtain a valid passport in his home country has a reasonable excuse for not producing it, and does not have to prove additionally that he has a reasonable excuse for disposal of a false immigration document used to enter the UK.

The Court of Appeal held in *Embaye* [2005] EWCA Crim 2865 that the imposition of a legal burden of proof on an accused seeking to rely on the statutory defence is not incompatible with the presumption of innocence contained in the ECHR, Article 6(2) (see further **F3.13** ***et seq.***), even if the defence may not fully comply with Article 31 of the Refugee Convention where the defendant is a bona fide asylum claimant. For Article 31, see **B23.5** above.

FAILURE TO COMPLY WITH REQUIREMENT TO PROVIDE INFORMATION REQUIRED TO OBTAIN TRAVEL DOCUMENT

Asylum and Immigration (Treatment of Claimants, etc.) Act 2004, s. 35 **B23.11**

(3) A person commits an offence if he fails without reasonable excuse to comply with a requirement of the Secretary of State under subsection 1.

Under s. 35(1), the Secretary of State may require a person to take specified action if the Secretary of State thinks that the action will or may enable a travel document to be obtained to facilitate the person's deportation or removal.

Procedure

A power of arrest is granted to an immigration officer who reasonably suspects that a person has committed an offence under the Asylum and Immigration (Treatment of Claimants, etc.) Act 2004, s. 35(3) (s. 35(5)). **B23.12**

The offence is triable either way.

Sentencing

The maximum penalty on conviction on indictment is two years' imprisonment, a fine or both. On summary conviction, the maximum is six months, a fine not exceeding the statutory maximum or both (s 35(4)). **B23.13**

Elements

Fear of persecution in the home country was held not to constitute a reasonable excuse for non-compliance with a requirement to attend for interview by officials of that country's Embassy in *Tabnak* [2007] 1 WLR 1317, where the Court of Appeal held that the criminal court should not become a battleground to determine whether deportation was legitimate. It was for the specialist immigration judges and tribunals to assess the merits of an asylum claim. Reasonable excuse should relate to ability, not willingness to comply. Home Office guidance on the Asylum and Immigration (Treatment of Claimants, etc.) Act 2004, s. 35(3) indicates that travel difficulties and health emergencies might constitute reasonable excuses. **B23.14**

ASSISTING UNLAWFUL IMMIGRATION AND RELATED OFFENCES

Definitions

B23.15 **Immigration Act 1971, s. 25**

(1) A person commits an offence if he—

(a) does an act which facilitates the commission of a breach of immigration law by an individual who is not a citizen of the European Union,

(b) knows or has reasonable cause for believing that the act facilitates the commission of a breach of immigration law by the individual, and

(c) knows or has reasonable cause for believing that the individual is not a citizen of the European Union.

Procedure and Jurisdiction

B23.16 An immigration officer may arrest without warrant a person who has committed or is attempting to commit this offence, or whom he has reasonable grounds for suspecting of committing or attempting to commit the offence (Immigration Act 1971, s. 28A(3)).

The offence is triable either way (Immigration Act 1971, s. 25(6)). The offence applies to 'anything done' (to assist unlawful immigration to a Member State) in or out of any part of the United Kingdom (s. 25(4)). The extra-territorial effect applies only to specified categories of British national (s. 25(4) and (5)). The offence applies to assisting unlawful immigration into any Member State of the European Union (s. 25(2)) or Iceland and Norway, who are treated as Member States for this purpose by virtue of art. 2 of the Immigration (Assisting Unlawful Immigration) (Section 25 List of Schengen Acquis States) Order 2004 (SI 2004 No. 2877). This is a measure required to enable the United Kingdom to comply with its obligations under Article 27 of the Schengen Convention to make it a criminal offence to breach the immigration law of the United Kingdom or any Member State.

Indictment

B23.17 *Statement of Offence*

Assisting unlawful immigration to the United Kingdom contrary to section 25 of the Immigration Act 1971.

Particulars of the Offence

A on the . . . day of . . ./on a day between the . . . day of . . . and the . . . day of . . . did an act which facilitated the commission of a breach of immigration law by [*specify name*], who is not a citizen of the European Union, knowing or having reasonable cause to believe that the act facilitated the commission of a breach of immigration law by him, and that he is not a citizen of the European Union.

Sentencing Guidelines

B23.18 The maximum sentence is 14 years' imprisonment, a fine or both on indictment; six months' imprisonment, a fine not exceeding the statutory maximum or both summarily (Immigration Act 1971, s. 25(6)).

This offence is generally regarded as a serious one and would often attract a custodial sentence even where no profit motive or commercial organisation is involved. An important guideline judgment was given by the Court of Appeal in *Le and Stark* [1999] 1 Cr App R (S) 422 in relation to the previous s. 25(1)(a) offence of 'assisting illegal entry' into the United Kingdom. In that case Lord Bingham stated 'The offence is one which calls very often for deterrent sentences and as the statistics make plain, the problem of illegal entry is on the increase'. The Court of Appeal indicated that the appropriate penalty would normally be a custodial sentence and that the offence would be aggravated where (a) it was committed for financial gain,

(b) the illegal entry was facilitated for strangers as opposed to a spouse or a close family member, (c) there had been a high degree of planning, organisation and sophistication, or (d) the offence was committed in relation to a large number of illegal entrants.

In *Akrout (Lofti Ben Salem)* [2003] EWCA Crim 491, the Court of Appeal upheld a sentence of six years' imprisonment for an offence under the previous version of s. 25(1)(a) (when the maximum sentence was ten years). The sentence was said by the Court of Appeal to be severe but not manifestly excessive. In that case a large number of illegal immigrants (24) were involved and the immigrants were strangers to the accused. See also *Saini* [2005] 1 Cr App R (S) 278 (sentence of seven and a half years held not excessive for conspiracy to organise large-scale entry). Sentences totalling ten years for facilitating illegal entry, living on the earnings of prostitution, kidnapping and incitement to rape, for men involved in arranging the illegal entry of women who were then required to work as prostitutes, were increased to a total of 23 years in *A-G's Ref (No. 6 of 2004) (Plakici)* [2005] 1 Cr App R (S) 83. For the offence of trafficking for sexual exploitation, see **B3.210** and **B23.29**.

A person convicted of an offence under the Immigration Act 1971, s. 25 will also be subject to the forfeiture provisions in s. 25C. The provisions under s. 25C confer on the courts the same powers to order the forfeiture of ships, aircrafts and vehicles as previously existed under s. 25A. These powers are extremely wide and, in the current climate of increased illegal immigration, it is to be expected that the courts will make full use of them.

The offence is designated a 'lifestyle offence' under the Proceeds of Crime Act 2002 (see E21.11).

Elements

The offence applies only where the person (or persons) 'assisted' is not a citizen of a Member State of the European Union or a citizen of Iceland or Norway (see **B23.16**), and the term 'citizen of the European Union' is defined so as to include such citizens (s. 25(7)(b)). The offence refers to an act which 'facilitates' a breach of 'immigration law'. 'Immigration law' is defined in s. 25(2) as a law which has effect in a Member State which regulates entitlement to (a) enter the State, (b) transit across the State, or (c) be in the State. The offence thus covers acts facilitating illegal entry or stay in other Member States. The immigration laws of Member States are to be conclusively proved by a certificate from the government concerned (s. 25(3)). It also includes acts assisting non-EU citizens who entered the UK lawfully to remain unlawfully. In *Javaherifard* [2005] EWCA Crim 3231, the Court of Appeal held, following *Singh and Meeuwsen* [1972] 1 WLR 1600, that it is possible to facilitate entry by acts close to but following actual entry (e.g., by making arrangements to get illegal entrants away quickly from the port of disembarkation). But acts done abroad by a person who is not a British national cannot constitute an offence under s. 25 (*Rechack* [2006] EWCA Crim 2975). **B23.19**

There is no longer a separate offence of 'harbouring' an illegal entrant (as there was previously under the Immigration Act 1971, s. 25(2)). This conduct is now included as part of the general offence under the new s. 25.

The wording of s. 25 changed on 10 February 2003 and a count alleging activity both before and after that date charged two separate offences and was impermissible (*Tirnaveanu* [2007] EWCA Crim 1239).

OTHER OFFENCES RELATING TO ASSISTING ENTRY

Helping Asylum-Seeker to Enter the United Kingdom

B23.20 Immigration Act 1971, s. 25A

(1) A person commits an offence if—
(a) he knowingly and for gain facilitates the arrival in the United Kingdom of an individual, and
(b) he knows or has reasonable cause to believe that the individual is an asylum-seeker.

Procedure and Jurisdiction

B23.21 An immigration officer may arrest without warrant a person who has committed or is attempting to commit this offence, or whom he has reasonable grounds for suspecting of committing or attempting to commit the offence (Immigration Act 1971, s. 28A(3)).

The offence is triable either way (Immigration Act 1971, ss. 25A(4) and 25(6)). The offence applies to 'anything done' in or out of any part of the United Kingdom by specified categories of British national (ss. 25A(4) and 25(4) and (5)).

Indictment

B23.22 *Statement of Offence*

Helping an asylum-seeker to enter the United Kingdom contrary to section 25A of the Immigration Act 1971.

Particulars of Offence

A on the . . . day of . . ./on a day between the . . . day of . . . and the . . . day of . . . knowingly and for gain facilitated the arrival in the United Kingdom of [*specify name*], a person whom he knew or had reasonable cause for believing to be an asylum-seeker.

Sentence

B23.23 The maximum sentence is 14 years' imprisonment, a fine or both on indictment; six months' imprisonment, a fine not exceeding the statutory maximum or both summarily (Immigration Act 1971, ss. 25A(4) and 25(6)).

The forfeiture provisions discussed at **B23.18** also apply to this offence (s. 25C(1)). The offence is designated a 'lifestyle offence' for the purposes of the Proceeds of Crime Act 2002 (see **E21.11**).

Elements

B23.24 Section 25A of the Immigration Act 1971 reproduces the offence which was previously set out in Immigration Act 1971, s. 25(1)(b). Since the right to claim asylum is protected by the Universal Declaration on Human Rights, the act of assisting asylum-seekers to arrive in the United Kingdom and claim asylum cannot therefore be unlawful *per se*, and the gravamen of this offence is profiteering. Thus financial gain is an essential element of the offence. The section does not apply to anything done by persons acting on behalf of an organisation which aims to assist asylum-seekers and does not charge for its services (s. 25A(3)). The accused must know or 'have reasonable cause to believe' that the individual he is assisting is an 'asylum-seeker'. 'Asylum-seeker' is defined in s. 25A(2) as someone who 'intends' to claim that to remove him from the United Kingdom would be a breach of the United Kingdom's obligations under (a) the Refugee Convention or (b) the ECHR. This presumably means that a person could be guilty of this offence even though the immigrant did not make a claim under the Refugee Convention or the ECHR, provided it can be established that the immigrant intended to make such a claim.

A conspiracy to 'assist persons claiming asylum in the United Kingdom' is not an offence known to law (*Hadi* [2001] EWCA Crim 2534).

Assisting Entry to the United Kingdom in Breach of Deportation or Exclusion Order

Definitions

Immigration Act 1971, s. 25B **B23.25**

(1) A person commits an offence if he—
  (a) does an act which facilitates a breach of a deportation order in force against an individual who is a citizen of the European Union, and
  (b) knows or has reasonable cause for believing that the act facilitates a breach of the deportation order.

(2) Subsection (3) applies where the Secretary of State personally directs that the exclusion from the United Kingdom of an individual who is a citizen of the European Union is conducive to the public good.

(3) A person commits an offence if he—
  (a) does an act which assists the individual to arrive in, enter or remain in the United Kingdom,
  (b) knows or has reasonable cause for believing that the act assists the individual to arrive in, enter or remain in the United Kingdom, and
  (c) knows or has reasonable cause for believing that the Secretary of State has personally directed that the individual's exclusion from the United Kingdom is conducive to the public good.

Procedure and Jurisdiction

An immigration officer may arrest without warrant a person who has committed or is attempting to commit this offence, or whom he has reasonable grounds for suspecting of committing or attempting to commit the offence (Immigration Act 1971, s. 28A(3)) **B23.26**

The offence is triable either way (Immigration Act 1971, ss. 25A(4) and 25(6)). The offence also applies to 'anything done' in or out of any part of the United Kingdom by specified categories of British national (ss. 25B(4) and 25(4) and (5)).

Sentence

The maximum sentence is 14 years' imprisonment, a fine or both on indictment; six months' imprisonment, a fine not exceeding the statutory maximum or both summarily (Immigration Act 1971, ss. 25B(4) and 25(6)). There are no guideline judgements issued for this offence. **B23.27**

The forfeiture provisions discussed at **B23.18** also apply to this offence (s. 25C(1)). The offence is designated a 'lifestyle offence' for the purposes of the Proceeds of Crime Act 2002 (see E21.11).

Elements

An offence under the Immigration Act 1971 s. 25B, applies only where the person being assisted is a citizen of the European Union. It therefore complements the offence at s. 25, which applies only where the person assisted is not an EU citizen. It is a defence that the accused did not know or have reason to believe that the person being assisted was the subject of a deportation or exclusion order. **B23.28**

TRAFFICKING FOR SEXUAL EXPLOITATION

Trafficking into the UK for Sexual Exploitation

Sexual Offences Act 2003, s. 57(1) **B23.29**

(1) A person commits an offence if he intentionally arranges or facilitates the arrival in the United Kingdom of another person (B) and either—
  (a) he intends to do anything to or in respect of B, after B's arrival but in any part of the world, which if done will involve the commission of a relevant offence, or
  (b) he believes that another person is likely to do something to or in respect of B, after B's

arrival but in any part of the world, which if done will involve the commission of a relevant offence.

Procedure and Jurisdiction

B23.30 The definition of 'relevant offence' for the purposes of this section is set out at the SOA 2003, s. 60(1). The definition includes acts done outside England and Wales and Northern Ireland which, if they had been done in either of those territories, would constitute a 'relevant offence'.

The offence will cover acts committed by any person in the UK (SOA 2003, s. 60(2)(a)). The offence will also cover acts committed outside the UK if committed by a body or person listed in the SOA 2003, s. 60(2)(b), e.g., a body incorporated in the UK or a British citizen.

The offence is triable either way (SOA 2003, s. 57(2)).

Sentencing

B23.31 The maximum sentence is 14 years' imprisonment, a fine or both on indictment; six months' imprisonment, a fine not exceeding the statutory maximum or both summarily (SOA 2003, s. 57(2)). In *Maka* [2005] EWCA Crim 3365, a sentence of 18 years' imprisonment was upheld in respect of five counts of trafficking to and within the UK, relating to the sexual exploitation of a 15-year-old Lithuanian girl. See also *A-G's Ref (No. 6 of 2004) (Plakici)* [2005] 1 Cr App R (S) 83 at **B23.18**..

Forfeiture provisions analogous to those discussed at **B23.18** also apply to this offence (SOA, s. 60A, inserted by the VCRA 2006, s. 54 and sch. 4, in force from 12 February 2007) It is designated a lifestyle offence for the purposes of the Proceeds of Crime Act 2002 (see E21.11).

Elements

B23.32 A person (A) commits the offence of trafficking into the UK for sexual exploitation if he intentionally arranges or facilitates the arrival into the UK of a person (B), where A intends to do anything that would result in the commission of a 'relevant offence' (as defined in SOA 2003, s. 60(1)) involving B. A may also commit the offence if he believes that *another person* (C) is likely to do something to, or in respect of, B that would result in the commission of a relevant offence involving B. It does not appear to matter whether or not C actually carries out the proscribed act so long as A believes that C is likely to do so.

The 'relevant offence' must take place after B's arrival in the UK. However, A may intend the relevant offence to be committed, or believe that it is likely to be committed in any part of the world (SOA 2003, s. 57(1)(a)). This is intended to cover the situation, e.g., where A trafficks B into the UK as an *interim* destination but intends to traffick B on to another country where A intends or believes the relevant offence is likely to be committed.

Third parties (e.g., airline companies) who innocently transport a potential victim to the UK are not covered by the offence. On the other hand the offence is intended to cover any person who is part of the enterprise of trafficking for sexual exploitation provided that person has the necessary intent or belief that a 'relevant offence' is likely to be committed (by himself or any other person).

See also **B3.209** ***et seq.***

Related Offences

B23.33 For the offences of trafficking within the UK for sexual exploitation and trafficking out of the UK for sexual exploitation under the SOA 2003, ss. 58 and 59, see **B3.215** and **B3.220**.

TRAFFICKING PEOPLE FOR EXPLOITATION

Asylum and Immigration (Treatment of Claimants, etc.) Act 2004, s. 4 **B23.34**

(1) A person commits an offence if he arranges or facilitates the arrival in the United Kingdom of an individual (the 'passenger') and—
  (a) he intends to exploit the passenger in the United Kingdom or elsewhere, or
  (b) he believes that another person is likely to exploit the passenger in the United Kingdom or elsewhere.

(2) A person commits an offence if he arranges or facilitates travel within the United Kingdom by an individual (the 'passenger') in respect of whom he believes that an offence under subsection (1) may have been committed and—
  (a) he intends to exploit the passenger in the United Kingdom or elsewhere, or
  (b) he believes that another person is likely to exploit the passenger in the United Kingdom or elsewhere.

(3) A person commits an offence if he arranges or facilitates the departure from the United Kingdom of an individual (the 'passenger') and—
  (a) he intends to exploit the passenger outside the United Kingdom, or
  (b) he believes that another person is likely to exploit the passenger outside the United Kingdom.

(4) For the purposes of this section a person is exploited if (and only if)—
  (a) he is the victim of behaviour that contravenes Article 4 of the Human Rights Convention (slavery and forced labour),
  (b) he is encouraged, required or expected to do anything as a result of which he or another person would commit an offence under the Human Organ Transplants Act 1989 or under section 32 or 33 of the Human Tissue Act 2004,
  (c) he is subjected to force, threats or deception designed to induce him—
    (i) to provide services of any kind,
    (ii) to provide another person with benefits of any kind, or
    (iii) to enable another person to acquire benefits of any kind, or
  (d) he is requested or induced to undertake any activity, having been chosen as the subject of the request or inducement on the grounds that—
    (i) he is mentally or physically ill or disabled, he is young or he has a family relationship with a person, and
    (ii) a person without the illness, disability, youth or family relationship would be likely to refuse the request or resist the inducement.

The 'Human Rights Convention' means the ECHR (s. 5(3)).

Procedure and Jurisdiction

An immigration officer has a power of arrest in respect of this offence (Asylum and Immigration (Treatment of Claimants, etc.) Act 2004, s. 14(2)(p)). **B23.35**

By s. 5(1) and (2), s. 4 applies to anything done in the United Kingdom or outside the United Kingdom by a body incorporated under UK law or by an individual who is a British citizen, a British overseas territories citizen, a British National (Overseas), a British Overseas citizen, a British subject or a British protected person.

Sentencing

The maximum penalty on conviction on indictment is 14 years' imprisonment, a fine or both. On summary conviction, the maximum is 12 months, a fine not exceeding the statutory maximum, or both. The 12 months maximum on summary conviction is stated to be dependent on implementation of the CJA 2003, s. 154 (s. 5(11)). **B23.36**

The forfeiture provisions discussed at **B23.18** also apply to this offence (Asylum and Immigration (Treatment of Claimants, etc.) Act 2004, s. 5(4). The offence is designated a 'lifestyle offence' for the purposes of the Proceeds of Crime Act 2002 (see **E21.11**). The offence is included in the schedule of offences against a child listed in the CJCSA 2000, sch. 4.

Elements

B23.37 A person commits the offence if he arranges for a person to enter or leave the UK to exploit them. The offence is also committed if a person arranges travel within the UK if he believes that the passenger has been brought into the UK to be exploited. Exploitation encompasses slavery or forced labour, organ removal, the use of force or threats to induce the victim to provide services or the abuse of the mentally or physically ill, young persons or relatives.

EMPLOYING PERSONS NOT ENTITLED TO WORK IN THE UK

B23.38 **Asylum and Immigration Act 1996, s. 8**

(1) Subject to subsection (2) below, if any person ('the employer') employs a person subject to immigration control ('the employee') who has attained the age of 16, the employer shall be guilty of an offence if—
   (a) the employee has not been granted leave to enter or remain in the United Kingdom; or
   (b) the employee's leave is not valid and subsisting, or is subject to a condition precluding him from taking up the employment, and (in either case) the employee does not satisfy such conditions as may be specified in an order made by the Secretary of State.

(2) It is a defence for a person charged with an offence under this section to prove that before the employment began any relevant requirement of an order of the Secretary of State under subsection (2A) was complied with.

(2A) An order under this subsection may—
   (a) require the production to an employer of a document of a specified description;
   (b) require the production to an employer of one document of each of a number of specified description;
   (c) require an employer to take specified steps to retain, copy or record the content of a document produced to him in accordance with the order;
   (d) make provisions which apply generally or only in specified circumstances;
   (e) make different provision for different circumstances.

This offence is prospectively repealed by the Immigration, Asylum and Nationality Act 2006 (see B23.45).

Procedure and Jurisdiction

B23.39 The offence is triable either way (Asylum and Immigration Act 1996, s. 8(4)).

Sentencing

B23.40 The maximum penalty on conviction on indictment is a fine, and on summary conviction, a fine of the statutory maximum (Asylum and Immigration Act 1996, s. 8(4)).

Elements

B23.41 It is an offence to employ a person aged 16 or over who is subject to 'immigration control' unless (a) that person has current and valid permission to be in the United Kingdom and (b) that permission does not prevent the person from taking the job in question. It is not an offence if the employee satisfies specified conditions. The conditions, specified in the Immigration (Restrictions on Employment) Order 2004 (SI 2004 No. 755) are that the employee had such leave which has expired and the employee has applied for the leave to be extended or (if an extension has been refused) an appeal may be brought or is pending. The employee must be a person who is permitted to work under the Immigration Rules.

Statutory Defence

B23.42 Employers are given a statutory defence under the Asylum and Immigration Act 1996, s. 8(1) if they have checked and copied certain original documents relating to the employee (s. 8(2)). The Immigration (Restrictions on Employment) Order 2004 (SI 2004 No. 755) sets out in detail the type of documents that employers will be required to check and copy to avail themselves of the statutory defence. The Order applies to all employees employed after 1 May 2004.

The Order contains two separate lists of documents which could go to show a potential employee's entitlement to work in the UK. 'List One' includes such documents as a UK passport describing the holder as a British citizen or as a citizen of the UK and Colonies having a right of abode in the UK and a UK residence permit issued to a national of a European Economic Area Agreement country (the relevant documents are set out in full at part 1 of the schedule to the Order). 'List Two' includes such documents as a work permit issued by Works Permits (UK) and a passport or other travel document endorsed to show that the holder has current leave to enter or remain in the UK and is permitted to take the work permit employment in question (the relevant documents are set out in full at part 2 of the schedule).

The statutory defence does not apply 'in any case where the employer knew that his employment of the employee would constitute an offence under this section' (s. 8(3)).

Establishing the Statutory Defence

An employer will be able to establish the statutory defence by checking and copying one of the *original* 'List One' documents or by checking and copying a combination of two of the *original* 'List Two' documents. The Home Office guidance states that an employer must satisfy himself that the potential employee is the rightful holder of any of the documents relied upon. **B23.43**

Guidance for Employers

The Home Office has issued useful guidance on the effect of the restrictions on employment and on the duties of employers when employing nationals from new European Union Member States after 1 May 2004 and 1 January 2007 (the guidance is available from the Employing Migrant Workers section of the Border and Immigration Agency web site: www.ind.homeoffice.gov.uk). **B23.44**

Penalties under the Immigration, Asylum and Nationality Act 2006 **B23.45**

When the Immigration, Asylum and Nationality Act 2006, ss. 15 to 26 come into force, the Asylum and Immigration Act 1996, ss. 8 and 8A will be repealed and replaced by (i) a regulatory penalty for employers who employ adults who are not entitled to work in the UK under s. 15 of the 2006 Act and (ii) an offence of employing another knowing that he is subject to immigration control and is not entitled to work in the UK under s. 21.

Immigration, Asylum and Nationality Act 2006, s. 21

(1) A person commits an offence if he employs another ('the employee') knowing that the employee is an adult subject to immigration control and that—
- (a) he has not been granted leave to enter or remain in the United Kingdom, or
- (b) his leave to enter or remain in the United Kingdom—
  - (i) is invalid,
  - (ii) has ceased to have effect (whether by means of curtailment, revocation, cancellation, passage of time or otherwise), or
  - (iii) is subject to a condition preventing him from accepting the employment.

Procedure The offence is triable either way (Immigration, Asylum and Nationality Act 2006, s. 21(2)). A body corporate can commit the offence (s. 22). **B23.46**

B23.47 **Sentencing** The maximum penalty on conviction on indictment is two years' imprisonment, a fine or both. On summary conviction, the maximum is six months, a fine not exceeding the statutory maximum, or both.

B23.48 **Elements** The offence is committed only where the employer knows that the employee either has no valid leave to remain or is subject to a condition preventing him from accepting employment. Where the element of knowledge is not made out, there may be scope for the regulatory penalty.

Section C1 Definitions and Basic Principles in Road Traffic Cases

Accident

C1.1 The word 'accident' has been given a number of different meanings depending upon the context in which it is used. In *Chief Constable of West Midlands Police v Billingham* [1979] 1 WLR 747, the Divisional Court expressed a preference for an 'ordinary man' test, stating that the definition of the word by the Court of Appeal in *Morris* [1972] 1 WLR 228 as 'some unintended occurrence which has an adverse physical result' should be understood in relation to the facts of that case. Nonetheless, the court did state (per Bridge LJ) that the word 'accident' was 'capable of applying to an untoward occurrence which has adverse physical results' even if one event in the chain was deliberate. The main doubt was at one time whether an accident could result from one or more intentional or deliberate acts.

In *Chief Constable of Staffordshire v Lees* [1981] RTR 506, the argument that a 'deliberate act' does not constitute an 'accident', at least for the purposes of the Road Traffic Acts, appears to have been finally laid to rest. In that case the defendant deliberately drove his car at a locked gate. The Divisional Court held that an 'accident' could be said to have occurred within the meaning of the RTA 1972, s. 8(2), when arising through a deliberate and intended act, provided that any ordinary person would say that there had been an accident owing to the presence of a motor vehicle on a road. Bingham J stated (at p. 510):

> It would be an insult to common sense if a collision involving a motor car arising from some careless and inadvertent act entitled a constable to exercise his powers under the [Road Traffic] Act but a similar result caused by a deliberate antisocial act did not. Previous cases have made it clear that one should look at the ordinary meaning of the word 'accident'.

See also *Charlton v Fisher* [2001] RTR 479. In *Morris* [1972] 1 WLR 228 Lord Widgery CJ acknowledged the possibility of a *de minimis* argument where the physical consequences were so trivial that an ordinary person would not regard the occurrence as an accident. In *Currie* [2007] EWCA Crim 926, the Court of Appeal held that the term must be given a common-sense meaning and that an accident is not restricted to untoward or unintended consequences having an adverse physical effect, confirming that some physical impact is not an essential element.

Aiding, Abetting, Counselling, Procuring

C1.2 For the meaning of these terms, see generally the Accessories and Abettors Act 1861, s. 8; the MCA 1980, s. 44(1); and A5.1 *et seq.*

By the MCA 1980, s. 44, a person convicted of aiding, abetting, counselling or procuring a summary offence is guilty of the like offence, and if the substantive offence carries endorsement the defendant must have his licence endorsed and may be disqualified.

Where disqualification is mandatory for the principal offence (e.g., driving with excess alcohol in the breath), a person convicted of aiding and abetting etc. is liable to discretionary disqualification by virtue of the RTOA 1988, s. 34(5), and his licence must be endorsed with 10 penalty points (RTOA 1988, s. 28(1)(b)).

Attempts

C1.3 As to attempts generally, see **A6.31** ***et seq.***

By virtue of the Criminal Attempts Act 1981, s. 1(4), it is not possible to attempt the commission of an offence which is purely summary, unless such an offence is created by statute (e.g., the RTA 1988, s. 5(1)(a), attempting to drive a motor vehicle on a road after consuming so much alcohol that the proportion of it in the breath etc. exceeds the prescribed limit). The Criminal Attempts Act 1981, s. 3, enacts similar provisions in relation to statutory attempts as are contained in ss. 1(2), (3) and (4) of the Act.

Automatism and Insanity

C1.4 As to insanity generally, see **A3.13** to **A3.19**. As to automatism generally, see **A3.7**.

Questions of fitness to plead and insanity are triable under the Criminal Procedure (Insanity) Act 1964 (see **D12.2** *et seq.*). In indictable offences, where these issues are raised, the magistrates' court is obliged to commit to the Crown Court in pursuance of that statute.

In the magistrates' court questions relating to automatism usually arise in the form of defences of involuntary behaviour on the part of the driver. (See also mechanical defect at **C1.11**, and duress or necessity at **A3.21** to **A3.29**.)

In *Hill v Baxter* [1958] 1 QB 277, a case on the *mens rea* required under certain sections of the RTA 1930 (now repealed), Lord Goddard CJ, having quoted a famous dictum of Humphreys J in *Kay v Butterworth* (1945) 61 TLR 452, went on to say (at p. 283):

> I agree that there may be cases where the circumstances are such that the accused could not really be said to be driving at all. Suppose he had a stroke or an epileptic fit, both instances of what may properly be called acts of God; he might well be in the driver's seat even with his hands on the wheel, but in such a state of unconsciousness that he could not be said to be driving. A blow from a stone or an attack by a swarm of bees I think introduces some conception akin to *novus actus interveniens.*

In such circumstances, the defendant is not 'driving' but has been rendered incapable of physical control of the vehicle. This is not automatism of the type considered in *Bailey* [1983] 1 WLR 760 and *Hardie* [1985] 1 WLR 64, but nonetheless arises without fault and should not therefore be the subject of any criminal sanction. There must, however, be 'a total destruction of voluntary control'; impaired or reduced control is not enough (per Lord Taylor CJ in *A-G's Ref (No. 2 of 1992)* [1994] QB 91). Sneezing may produce a state of automatism (*Whoolley* (13 November 1997 unreported)). The lack of control must arise from causes which do not bring the defendant within the M'Naghten rules. Thus driving with 'a reduced or imperfect awareness', which is brought on by the repetitive stimuli experienced on a long journey and which reduces a driver's capacity to avoid collisions, cannot, as a matter of law, found a defence of automatism. Similarly, in *Watmore v Jenkins* [1962] 2 QB 572, Winn J pointed out that a finding by the justices that the defendant 'continued to perform the functions of driving, after a fashion' for five miles on a road which was not straight, was inconsistent with a finding of automatism 'extending throughout the whole of the distance . . . to which it related'.

Consequently, in cases involving the use of a motor vehicle, a failure to take precautions appears sufficient to establish criminal liability, where the state of automatism could or should have been reasonably foreseen as a likely result of such a failure. In short, such a failure is tantamount to a self-induced incapacity which will not excuse the defendant from criminal liability in any cases involving a basic or lesser intent.

Causing

A number of offences in the Road Traffic Acts may be committed by causing or permitting the use of, as well as using, a vehicle in a prohibited manner. Each of these gives rise to a separate offence. C1.5

'Causing' demands a positive act on the part of the defendant (*Price v Cromack* [1975] 1 WLR 988). It also requires prior knowledge. In *Milstead v Sexton* [1964] Crim LR 474, the defendant was convicted of causing a car to be used on a road where the car was being towed and he was driving the towing vehicle. In *Ross Hillman Ltd v Bond* [1974] QB 435, the defendant was a limited company which owned a number of vehicles and employed a number of drivers, all of whom had been warned against driving their vehicles whilst overloaded. One of the employees drove his vehicle while it was overloaded. Allowing the defendant's appeal, May J stated (at p. 446):

> Unassisted by any authority I would as a matter of ordinary English construe both the word 'causes' and the word 'permits' in section 40(5)(b) of the Act of 1972 as requiring prior knowledge of the facts constituting the unlawful user . . . if, as I think and as is supported by authority, actual user of a vehicle in contravention of the regulations is an absolute offence, and if, as I also think, a master 'uses' the vehicle which his servant is driving on that master's business, then I think that the mischief against which the regulations are directed, that of having unsafe vehicles on the roads is adequately dealt with. Having regard to the ordinary meaning of 'causes' I do not find it surprising that, whereas on given facts a master charged with using will be convicted, on the same facts a master charged with causing that use will be acquitted.

In *Mounsey v Campbell* [1983] RTR 36, the defendant caused an obstruction by parking his van immediately in front of another motor vehicle so that vehicle was unable to move. The defence had argued that it was only when the defendant refused to move the van that the vehicle became an obstruction, and therefore the proper charge should have been one of 'permitting'. This argument was described as 'nebulous' by the court, who found that the initial act of parking and subsequent refusal to move the vehicle could both constitute 'causing'.

A company which shut its eyes to the failure of its employee to fill in tachograph records could not be said to have 'caused' that failure. Such wilful ignorance may amount to 'permitting' but falls short of the 'positive mandate or . . . other sufficient act required for the offence' (*Redhead Freight Ltd v Shulman* [1989] RTR 1).

Permitting

In *Vehicle Inspectorate v Nuttall* [1999] 1 WLR 629, the House of Lords drew a distinction between positive acts where a person 'allows' or 'authorises' the use of the vehicle by another and omissions which amount to 'failure to take reasonable steps to prevent' such use. When the second, wider meaning applies to the context of the offence charged, it is not an offence of strict liability and, therefore, requires proof of nothing less than wilfulness or recklessness. This may be demonstrated by adducing actual evidence or by raising a rebuttable presumption. For example, in respect of regulatory tachograph requirements, if the employer fails to take reasonable steps to prevent employee drivers from contravening the statutory provisions, it raises a rebuttable presumption that the necessary mental element has been established (per Lord Steyn at p. 637C). The evidence adduced must, however, be capable of supporting such a presumption (*Yorkshire Traction Co. Ltd v Vehicle Inspectorate* [2001] RTR 518). C1.6

For 'permission' involving a positive act, proof of prior knowledge remains necessary (*Ross Hillman Ltd v Bond* [1974] QB 435). This connotes express or implied permission or acquiescence as much as direct participation.

'Knowledge' includes actual and constructive knowledge, such as 'the state of mind of a man who shuts his eyes to the obvious or allows his servant to do something in the circumstances where a contravention is likely, not caring whether a contravention takes place or not' (*James & Son Ltd v Smee* [1955] 1 QB 78, per Parker J at p. 91). Where justices had found that an employer did not know and had no reasonable cause to suspect that one of his vehicles had a defective braking system, it was not open to them to convict of an offence of permitting the vehicle's use, notwithstanding that he would have had no answer to a charge of 'using' the vehicle in a defective condition (*Robinson v DPP* [1991] RTR 315).

Negligence not amounting to recklessness did not justify an inference that a managing director, someone who might be said to be 'the "brains" of the company rather than its hands', was wilfully closing his eyes to the obvious, and therefore that a company was guilty of permitting the use of a vehicle on a road with defective brakes (*Hill & Sons (Botley and Denmead) Ltd v Hampshire Chief Constable* [1972] RTR 29).

That decision closely follows *Magna Plant Ltd v Mitchell* [1966] Crim LR 394, where a plant hire company was charged with unlawfully permitting the use of a vehicle in a dangerous condition. Lord Parker CJ, in giving the judgment of the court, said:

> A company was not criminally liable in the absence of knowledge of the facts constituting the offence for the failure of a servant to whom it had delegated a task. The servant was not in the position of the brains of the company and his knowledge could not be imputed to a director . . .

However, an employer's failure to operate an adequate, or any, system of checking tachograph charts was regarded as sufficiently reckless 'shutting of the eyes' so as to amount to implied knowledge in *Vehicle Inspectorate v Shane Raymond Nuttall t/a Redline Coaches* (1997) 161 JP 701. The test is one of fact and degree. See also *Vehicle Inspectorate v Blakes Chilled Distribution Ltd* [2002] All ER (D) 26 (Feb).

In cases of no insurance, permitting has a stricter interpretation. Where an owner allows the use of a vehicle, believing that use to be insured, such a belief is no defence to a charge of permitting the uninsured use of the vehicle (*Lyons v May* [1948] 2 All ER 1062; *Baugh v Crago* [1975] RTR 453). In exceptional circumstances a conditional permission to use a vehicle only with insurance does not constitute an offence (*Sheldon Deliveries Ltd v Willis* [1972] RTR 217; *Newbury v Davis* [1974] RTR 367), but such a defence must be regarded with extreme caution before it is capable of application (see *DPP v Fisher* [1991] RTR 93, where it was held that the permission must be given direct to the would-be driver).

Using

C1.7 'Using' has a restricted meaning when found in the same section as 'causing' and 'permitting'. In such cases it is only the driver, or his employer, when the driver is driving on his employer's business, who can be said to be 'using' the vehicle (*Mickleborough v BRS (Contracts) Ltd* [1977] RTR 389; *Jones v DPP* [1999] RTR 1; *Interlink Express Parcels Ltd v Night Truckers Ltd* [2000] RTR 324, where the vehicles were owned by another party). 'User' must involve an element of controlling, managing or operating the vehicle by the person concerned (*Hatton v Hall* [1997] RTR 212). For a non-driver of the vehicle, this element could exist as a result of a joint venture to use it for a particular purpose or where the passenger procures the making of the journey (*O'Mahoney v Joliffe* [1999] RTR 245); whether it does is a question of fact and degree.

These propositions extend to cases where the word 'use' is found, either alone, or in conjunction with another word such as 'keeps' (*James & Son Ltd v Smee* [1955] 1 QB 78; *Richardson v Baker* [1976] RTR 56). Use, however, by a person other than a servant, even a business partner, does not constitute use by the owner, albeit that the vehicle is being driven at his request and with his full knowledge (*Crawford v Haughton* [1972] 1 WLR 572; *Garrett v Hooper* [1973] RTR 1). That sort of use may, of course, amount to 'permitting' or even 'causing'. However, *Hallett Silberman v Cheshire County Council* [1993] RTR 32 shows that a vehicle which exceeds its permitted weight may be being used by the owner even if its driver is self-employed and provides the tractor unit. The decision rests heavily on the degree of control exercised by the defendants, who supplied the trailer and chose the route; as such their position was analogous to that of an employer. By contrast, in *DPP v Seawheel Ltd* (1994) 158 JP 444, mere ownership of a part of the assembly on which a load was carried and which was secured to the trailer was insufficient to establish use; the tractor and trailer unit were owned by a person who had contracted to transport the load and there was no finding that the defendants were in possession of any of the relevant parts. It was suggested *obiter*, however, that a wider meaning should be given to 'use' when applied to a trailer rather than when applied to a lorry. However, where 'use' appears in a provision in conjunction with 'drive or cause or permit to be driven', 'use' will be construed more broadly so as to cover the owner of a vehicle used for his purposes or on his behalf and being driven by someone other than an employee (*Richmond upon Thames LBC v Morton* [2000] RTR 79).

Vehicles left unattended on a road can still be regarded as being used, as 'use' has been held to mean 'having the use of' for these purposes (*Eden v Mitchell* [1975] RTR 425). Accordingly, the mere fact of having two defective tyres did not preclude the vehicle's use and the owner's intention in respect of using the vehicle was held to be irrelevant. Similarly, in *Elliott v Grey* [1960] 1 QB 367, despite having an engine that did not work, no battery and no petrol, the vehicle in question was being 'used' without insurance, as it could be moved, albeit not driven. The distinction drawn in *Hewer v Cutler* [1974] RTR 155, that immobile vehicles whose wheels would not rotate were outside the definition of 'use', was found to be unjustified by Mitchell J in *Pumbien v Vines* [1996] RTR 37. In that case the vehicle's tyres were deflated, the handbrake was on, the rear brakes were seized and the gearbox contained no oil because there was a leak in the transmission pipe. It was held that, provided that vehicle was a 'motor vehicle' within the definition of the RTA 1988, s. 185 (see generally C1.12), and was on a road, the owner had the use of it on a road, whether at the material time it could move on its wheels or not. This decision has also apparently removed the requirement of an 'element of controlling, managing or operating the vehicle as a vehicle' (*Nichol v Leach* [1972] RTR 476), in the sense of the vehicle being capable of movement 'as a vehicle'. Consequently, for the purposes of the RTA 1988, ss. 47 and 143, 'use' should be accorded the same meaning and mobility of the vehicle is irrelevant.

Driver and Driving

The definition of 'driver' is set out in the RTA 1988, s. 192. It includes, except in cases of causing death by dangerous driving, a person who is steering, as well as any other person engaged in driving. As respects establishing the identity of the driver of a vehicle concerned in an offence, there is no general presumption that the owner of a vehicle is the driver of it at a particular time, notwithstanding the various statutory provisions which establish owner liability in certain specific circumstances; the question of the driver's identity is one of fact on which the tribunal must be sure (see *Clarke v DPP* (1992) 156 JP 605 and *Powell v DPP* [1992] RTR 270; for directions on car identification, see *Browning* (1991) 94 Cr App R 109). Evidence of ownership is merely one strand in the evidential rope which may go to establish the identity of the driver. C1.8

In *Evans v Walkden* [1956] 1 WLR 1019, occupying the front passenger seat and supervising the driver, thereby being in a position to assume control if necessary, was held not to be equivalent to being in control, with the result that the supervisor was not a 'driver'. *Langman v Valentine* [1952] 2 All ER 803 was distinguished because there the degree of control exercised throughout by the supervisor was considerably greater.

The act of driving is a physical one which can only be performed by a natural person, and the words 'drive' and 'driver' should be construed accordingly. Consequently, the Divisional Court declined to make the respondent, a limited company, vicariously liable for an offence under the RTRA 1984, s. 8(1) (*Richmond London Borough Council v Pinn and Wheeler Ltd* [1989] RTR 354).

In *MacDonagh* [1974] QB 448 (a five-judge Court of Appeal), the essence of driving was said to be the use of 'the driver's controls for the purpose of directing the movement of the vehicle'. The defendant, who was disqualified from driving, had been asked to move his car by a police officer and, on the defendant's version of events, he had pushed it with his two feet on the road and one hand on the steering wheel. The recorder directed the jury that this could properly be described as driving. Lord Widgery CJ, in giving the judgment of the court allowing the appeal, stated (at p. 451):

> There are an infinite number of ways in which a person may control the movement of a motor vehicle, apart from the orthodox one of sitting in the driving seat and using the engine for propulsion. He may be coasting down a hill with the gears in neutral and the engine switched off; he may be steering a vehicle which is being towed by another. As has already been pointed out, he may be sitting in the driving seat while others push, or half sitting in the driving seat but keeping one foot on the road in order to induce the car to move. Finally, as in the present case, he may be standing in the road and himself pushing the car with or without using the steering wheel to direct it. Although the word 'drive' must be given a wide meaning, the courts must be alert to see that the net is not thrown so widely that it includes activities which cannot be said to be driving a motor vehicle in any ordinary use of that word in the English language.

Controlling the movement and direction of a motor cycle by pushing and steering with the ignition and lights on constituted 'driving', as long as the defendant was wearing motor cyclist's clothing and a crash helmet (*McKoen v Ellis* [1987] RTR 26).

In *Selby v DPP* [1994] RTR 157n, Taylor LJ stated (at p. 162) that 'riding' is carried out 'if a person is being carried on a motor cycle as it moves on its wheels, whether propelled by the engine or by his feet or by gravity', which would seem to be equally applicable as the test for 'driving' a motor cycle (*Gunnell v DPP* [1994] RTR 151).

Once the act of driving has commenced, ascertained by applying the *MacDonagh* test, it continues until it terminates, and a person may still be 'driving' although the vehicle is stationary (*Pinner v Everett* [1969] 1 WLR 1266; *Skelton* [1995] Crim LR 635). In *Edkins v Knowles* [1973] QB 748, it was emphasised that the reason for stopping is relevant, as it may be part of the journey, e.g., traffic lights or a junction, or may mark a break in the journey, in which case the length of break and whether the driver leaves the vehicle becomes important. The issue is one of fact and degree, just as it is at the end of a journey, when various activities connected with driving must be completed before the driving is terminated, e.g., switching off the ignition and securing the vehicle. The court must consider the period of time and the circumstances to decide whether the person still in the driving seat was 'driving' (*Planton v DPP* [2002] RTR 107).

C1.9 **Examples of Driving** *MacDonagh* [1974] QB 448 was followed in *McQuaid v Anderton* [1981] 1 WLR 154, in which the appellant, who was disqualified, was steering a towed vehicle which had an operational braking system. The court held that the method of propulsion was irrelevant and dismissed his appeal. See also *Whitfield v DPP* [1998] Crim LR 349.

In *Saycell v Bool* [1948] 2 All ER 83, steering a lorry for 100 yards downhill, without the engine running, was held to be driving.

A person steering a vehicle from the passenger seat, over an appreciable period of time, was driving, as was the person sitting in the driver's seat (*Tyler v Whatmore* [1976] RTR 83), but a momentary seizure of the steering wheel causing the vehicle to leave the road, whilst borderline, could not properly be described as 'driving' (*Jones v Pratt* [1983] RTR 54). In neither case did the court consider the interpretation provisions and any possible definition of 'steersman'. *Jones v Pratt* was followed in *DPP v Hastings* [1993] RTR 205, where there was a similar momentary seizure of the wheel. Although the seizure in *Hastings* was intended to cause danger there was no finding that the driver relinquished control and the seizure was regarded as 'an act of interfering with the driving of the car rather than an act of driving in itself'.

In *Burgoyne v Phillips* [1983] RTR 49, releasing the handbrake and sitting in the car with the steering locked and the engine off whilst the vehicle moved by reason of gravity was held to be driving, although the defendant had left the keys to the car elsewhere. In *Leach v DPP* [1993] RTR 161, however, sitting in the driving seat of a stationary motor vehicle with hands on the steering wheel and the engine off was held not to be, *per se*, driving within the meaning of the RTA 1988, s. 163(1), so as to make it an offence to fail to stop for a constable (cf. *Hoy v McFadyen* 2000 SLT 1060). Where the engine is on but forward propulsion is being prevented because the handbrake remains applied so that the vehicle's wheels merely spin then, applying *MacDonagh*, this amounts to driving (*DPP v Alderton* [2004] RTR 367). However, in *Whelehan v DPP* [1995] RTR 177, quite apart from the defendant's admission to driving to the location where he was found by a constable, the Divisional Court concluded that being discovered in the driving seat of a stationary motor vehicle on a road at 1.20 a.m. with the keys in the ignition switch afforded sufficient evidence from which to infer that the defendant had driven to that location.

Kneeling on the driving seat, releasing the handbrake and attempting to re-apply the handbrake was material upon which justices might find a defendant was driving (*Rowan v Chief Constable of Merseyside* (1985) *The Times*, 10 December 1985).

Duress and Necessity

As to duress generally, see **A3.21** to **A3.29**. As to necessity generally, see **A3.28**. **C1.10**

Mechanical Defect

Where a driver is deprived of control of a motor vehicle as a result of a mechanical defect of **C1.11**
which he has no knowledge, real or constructive, then such a defect is a defence to a charge of careless driving and a charge of contravening the regulations relating to pedestrian crossings.

This defence of mechanical or latent defect stems from *Kay v Butterworth* (1945) 61 TLR 452, *Simpson v Peat* [1952] 2 QB 24, *Hill v Baxter* [1958] 1 QB 227, and the general proposition that in cases not involving fault the law should seek to avoid the imposition of any criminal sanction.

In *Spurge* [1961] 2 QB 205, the appellant had recently purchased a car with a tendency to move to the right when the brakes were applied. His appeal against conviction and sentence for dangerous driving was dismissed on the basis that he was, or should have been, aware of the mechanical defect. The court, stressing that successful reliance on the defence would be rare and that it did not apply where the defect was known, or would have been discovered by the exercise of reasonable prudence, stated (per Salmon J, at p. 212): 'The essence of the defence is that the danger has been created by a sudden total loss of control in no way due to any fault on the part of the driver'. It is for the defence to raise the issue, but the onus of disproving it remains with the prosecution.

In *Burns v Bidder* [1967] 2 QB 227, the defence was recognised as applying to offences under the Pedestrian Crossings Regulations. The defendant's appeal was allowed, as the convicting magistrate, thinking the offence an absolute one and not being satisfied that the brakes had not failed, should have taken the defence of mechanical defect into account in considering whether the prosecution had discharged the onus of proof. In giving the judgment of the court, James J reviewed the authorities, and stated (at pp. 240–41):

> The cases of the driver suddenly stung by a swarm of bees or suffering a sudden epileptic form of disabling attack, or a vehicle being propelled forward by reason of another vehicle hitting it from behind, are illustrations of where no offence may be shown, because control over the vehicle is

> taken completely out of the hands of the driver, and his failure to accord precedence on that account would be no offence.
>
> Likewise in my view a sudden removal of control over the vehicle occasioned by a latent defect of which the driver did not know and could not reasonably be expected to know would render the resulting failure to accord precedence no offence, provided he is in no way at fault himself.

The court again stated that it was for the defence to raise the issue, and it should then be considered with all the other evidence; if a reasonable doubt remained, the prosecution would not have proved the offence. The defence at that time extended to offences of driving in a dangerous manner, and there seems little or no reason why it should not be of general application.

In *Beckford* [1996] 1 Cr App R 96, the Court of Appeal hoped that procedures have been put in place to ensure that vehicles are not scrapped before express permission is given by the police and that such permission will not be forthcoming if serious criminal charges which may involve the possibility of some mechanical defect in the vehicle have been brought.

Motor Vehicle and Mechanically Propelled Vehicle

C1.12 The term 'motor vehicle' is defined in the RTA 1988, s. 185, as a mechanically propelled vehicle intended or adapted for use on roads. A mechanically propelled vehicle does not need to be intended or adapted for such use; whether a vehicle is mechanically propelled remains a question of fact.

A vehicle which has more than one source of power does not cease to be 'mechanically propelled', even though it is propelled by means other than an engine at the relevant time (*Floyd v Bush* [1953] 1 WLR 242). This extends to a vehicle which is being towed, even though that vehicle may be in such a poor condition that it could not be propelled under its own power, and even though it was at the same time a 'trailer', a 'vehicle' drawn by a 'motor vehicle' (*Cobb v Whorton* [1971] RTR 392).

A suitably adapted vehicle, even though originally constructed for use on the roads, may, as a question of fact, cease to be a 'motor vehicle' within the meaning of s. 185, as in *Lawrence v Howlett* [1952] 2 All ER 74, where the auxiliary engine had been removed from a moped making it into a 'pedal cycle'. Normally, however, only when it is clear that a vehicle will not become mobile again can it be said that it ceases to be a 'motor vehicle', and in each case that is a question of fact for the court.

In *Burns v Currell* [1963] 2 QB 433, Lord Parker CJ, adopting a 'reasonable person' test as to the use of the vehicle, stated (at p. 440):

> . . . in the ordinary case . . . there will be little difficulty in saying whether a particular vehicle is a motor vehicle or not. But to define exactly the meaning of the words 'intended or adapted' is by no means easy. I think that the expression 'intended' . . . does not mean 'intended by the user of the vehicle either at the moment of the alleged offence or for the future'.

This case was followed in *Chief Constable of Avon and Somerset Constabulary v F (A Juvenile)* [1987] RTR 378, where justices dismissed seven informations laid against a juvenile on the basis that they could not be sure the vehicle in question came within the definition. The Divisional Court dismissed the prosecution's appeal. Glidewell LJ said (at pp. 382–3):

> I emphasise that that test is what would be the view of the reasonable man as to the general user of this particular vehicle; not what was the particular user to which this particular defendant put it. . . . if a reasonable man were to say 'Yes, this vehicle might well be used on the road', then, applying the test, the vehicle is intended or adapted for such use. If that be the case, it is nothing to the point if the individual defendant says: 'I normally use it for scrambling and I am only pushing it along the road on this occasion because I have no other means of getting it home', or something of that sort.

The test was also applied in *DPP v Saddington* [2001] RTR 227, in relation to a motorised scooter, the 'Go-ped', to conclude that, although the vehicle was incapable of being registered with the Department of Transport and fell foul of the construction and use regulations, it was a 'motor vehicle' for the purposes of the RTA 1988, s. 185(1). This conclusion was reached because a reasonable person would say that one of the scooter's uses would be general use on the roads. See also *DPP v Murray* [2001] EWHC Admin 848.

For a motor vehicle to change its character from that intended by the manufacturer a very substantial or dramatic alteration would be required for it to cease to be a motor vehicle; the addition of something that may make the vehicle unusable on a road might suffice, but the absence of registration plates, reflectors, lights or the speedometer would, it is submitted, be insufficient (see *DPP v Ryan* [1992] RTR 13).

In *Maddox v Storer* [1962] 1 All ER 831, the court stated that it was necessary to look to the context in which the word 'adapted' was used, and when used alone it was held to have the adjectival meaning of 'being fit and apt for the purpose'. If used disjunctively, as an alternative to 'constructed', its meaning was 'being altered so as to make it fit'.

In *Millard v Turvey* [1968] 2 QB 390, a chassis without a cab, doors, roof, windscreen or seats for the accommodation of passengers was held to be a motor vehicle, albeit under construction, but was not a 'motor tractor'. In *Tahsin* [1970] RTR 88, it was held that a moped did not cease to be a 'motor vehicle' merely because its engine would not work. A moped, however, does not become a motor cycle merely because one pedal is missing (*G* (*A Minor*) v *Jarrett* [1981] RTR 186). For a vehicle to change in such a manner requires an alteration in its design or construction.

Owner

See the RTA 1988, s. 192, at **C1.17**. **C1.13**

In relation to a vehicle which is subject to a hiring or hire-purchase agreement, 'owner' includes the person in possession of the vehicle under that agreement. It is submitted that even if the person lawfully in possession of the vehicle under a hiring agreement parts with it to a third party, who may then drive the vehicle without documents, insurance etc., unless the agreement provides for instant termination of the hire, so that property in the vehicle immediately reverts to the person who has legal title to the vehicle, the third party is not guilty of an offence under the Theft Act 1968, s. 12, although both he and the person in possession of the vehicle under the hiring agreement may be guilty of other offences relating to the absence of insurance, etc.

Road or Other Public Place

Road The word 'road' is defined by the RTA 1988, s. 192. It includes any highway and any other road to which the public has access, including bridges over which a road passes. The *Concise Oxford Dictionary* defines 'road' as 'a line of communication between places for use of pedestrians, riders, and vehicles'. Section 34(1)(b) of the 1988 Act includes footpaths and bridleways as being within the definition of a road. **C1.14**

In *Randall v Motor Insurers' Bureau* [1968] 1 WLR 1900, a pedestrian pavement was accepted as forming part of the road, so that a lorry, the greater part of which was on the road, could properly be said to be using the road, even though the plaintiff and that part of the lorry which caused injury to him were at the relevant time on private property. Similarly, in *Price v DPP* [1990] RTR 413, where the defendant drove across a pavement (part of which was maintained at public expense and part of which was privately owned) thereby causing a pedestrian to jump out of the way, it was held that the justices were fully entitled to conclude that the pavement as a whole constituted a road and the defendant was, therefore, properly convicted of driving without reasonable consideration for another road user. In *Clarke v Kato*

[1998] 1 WLR 1647, the House of Lords confirmed that whether a place which is not a highway is a 'road' within the meaning of the RTA 1988, s. 192, is a question of fact to be determined after consideration of its physical character and the function it exists to serve. Lord Clyde gave the following guidance (at p. 1652):

> One obvious feature of a road as commonly understood is that its physical limits are defined or at least definable. It should always be possible to ascertain the sides of a road or to have them ascertained. Its location should be identifiable as a route or way. It will often have a prepared surface and have been manufactured or constructed. But it may simply have developed by the repeated passage of traffic over the same area of land. It may be continuous, like a circular route, or it may come to a termination, as in the case of a cul-de-sac. A road may run on a single line without diversion or it may have branches.
>
> . . . it is also necessary to consider the function of the place in order to see if it qualifies as a road. Essentially a road serves as a means of access. It leads from one place to another and constitutes a route whereby travellers may move conveniently between the places to which and from which it leads. It is thus a defined or at least a definable way intended to enable those who pass over it to reach a destination. Its precise extent will require to be a matter of detailed decision as matter of fact in the particular circumstances. Lines may require to be drawn to determine the point at which the road ends and the destination has been reached. Where there is a door or a gate the problem may be readily resolved. Where there is no physical point which can be readily identified, then by an exercise of reasonable judgment an imaginary line will have to be drawn to mark the point where it should be held that the road has ended. Whether or not a particular area is or is not a road eventually comes to be a matter of fact.

Accordingly, a place that can reasonably be described as a car park does not, save in exceptional circumstances, qualify as a road, and in the event of a carriageway being found to exist within its bounds which does so qualify, the remaining area will retain its integrity as a car park. Trafalgar Square is a road (*Sadiku v DPP* [2000] RTR 155).

In *Holliday v Henry* [1974] RTR 101, a case under the Vehicles (Excise) Act 1971 (now repealed), the respondent kept his car on a road, with a roller skate under each wheel, contending that by this device the car was not 'on' the road. This ingenious defence failed to find favour with the Divisional Court who allowed the prosecutor's appeal, stating that it was perfectly clear that, for the purposes of the 1971 Act, the vehicle was on the road.

In *Hawkins v Phillips* [1980] RTR 197, a filter lane or slip road was held to be part of the main carriageway for the purposes of the RTRA 1967. 'Highway' is defined as a 'public road, main route by land or water'. In *Lang v Hindhaugh* [1986] RTR 271, a footpath which was not designed for motor vehicles or passable by motor cars was held to be a highway. In giving the judgment of the court, Croom-Johnson LJ said (at p. 275):

> Highways are anywhere that the public has a right to pass and repass, either on foot or with animals or in vehicles, as the case may be. If they are only fit for travelling on foot, they are footpaths, but they will still be highways if the public has the right to use them for that purpose. This clearly was a footpath. It also was that kind of a footpath which was a highway.

In *Worth v Brooks* [1959] Crim LR 855, the grass verge by the side of a carriageway was held to form part of the highway which itself constituted a road. In *Dunmill v DPP* (2004) *The Times*, 15 July 2004, a grass area within a camp site, which may have been a public place, was held not to be a road.

The question of whether or not a particular road is one to which the public has access is one of fact and degree (*Waterfield* [1964] 1 QB 164). In *Oxford v Austin* [1981] RTR 416, consideration was given as to whether or not a car park was a road. In giving the judgment of the court, Kilner Brown J said (at p. 418):

> . . . in all these cases there is a well established process which is founded on findings of fact. The first question which has to be asked is whether there is in fact in the ordinary understanding of the word a road, that is to say, whether or not there is a definable way between two points over

which vehicles could pass. The second question is whether or not the public, or a section of the public, has access to that which has the appearance of a definable way.

The primary intention of the place does not appear to be of relevance, as in all cases it remains a question of fact whether or not the area is a road to which the public has access, irrespective of whether it is publicly or privately owned (*Price v DPP* [1990] RTR 413). A road which is not maintainable and manageable at public expense does not preclude it from being 'a road open to the public' as that expression refers to a road to which the public has access (*DPP v Cargo Handling Ltd* [1992] RTR 318).

Other Public Place It is a truism to state that a public place is one to which the public has access. It is not, however, definitive. Whether or not such access is sufficient for a finding that the place is a 'public place' for the purposes of the Road Traffic Acts is a question of fact and degree to be arrived at after consideration of the evidence (see *Planton v DPP* [2002] RTR 107). Justices are entitled to use their 'local knowledge' in arriving at their conclusion on this point, but it is good practice to inform the prosecution and defence so that they can comment (*Bowman v DPP* [1991] RTR 263). **C1.15**

In *Montgomery v Loney* [1959] NILR 171, which concerned a petrol station forecourt, Lord MacDermott drew the distinction between members of the general public and persons who belong to a special class of members of the public and who have 'some reason personal to them for their admittance', such as postmen, meter readers and employees going to work along a factory road.

In *DPP v Vivier* [1991] RTR 205, a case under the RTA 1988, s. 5(1)(a), the Divisional Court gave wide consideration to the meaning of 'public place'. The defendant had been driving a car in a caravan park which covered 80 acres and contained between three and four miles of road. The number of people present in the caravan park, whether admitted as caravanners, campers, or their guests, varied between 800 and 3,500, depending on the time of year. The Divisional Court referred to *Montgomery v Loney* (which in turn had considered *Harrison v Hill* 1932 JC 13, a case concerning access to a farm road adjacent to the public highway) and applied the test adopted there, concluding that:

> the decision whether a place was a place to which the public had access . . . was a matter of fact and degree but whether the material for consideration sufficed to support one view or the other was a matter of law.

Whether a place is a public place or not can be identified by looking at the people who use it and their reasons for doing so. In giving the judgment of the court in *DPP v Vivier*, Simon Brown J separated such persons into two categories, those who seek entry for the purposes of the occupier and those who seek entry for their own purposes (at p. 212):

> How then, in cases where some particular road or place is used by an identifiable category of people, should justices decide whether that category is 'special' or 'restricted' or 'particular' such as to distinguish it from the public at large? What, in short, is the touchstone by which to recognise a special class of people from members of the general public? . . . one asks whether there is about those who obtain permission to enter 'some reason personal to them for their admittance'. If people come to a private house as guests, postmen or meter readers, they come for reasons personal to themselves, to serve the purposes of the occupier.
>
> But what of the rather different type of case such as the present where those seeking entry are doing so for their own, rather than the occupier's purposes and yet are screened in the sense of having to satisfy certain conditions for admission. Does the screening process operate or endow those passing through with some special characteristic whereby they lose their identity as members of the general public and become instead a special class?
>
> Our approach would be as follows. By the same token that one asks in the earlier type of case whether permission is being granted for a reason personal to the user, in these screening cases one must ask: do those admitted pass through the screening process for a reason, or on account of some characteristic, personal to themselves? Or are they in truth merely members of the public

who are being admitted as such and processed simply so as to make them subject to payment and whatever other conditions the landowner chooses to impose.

In *DPP v Coulman* [1993] RTR 230, the respondent's presence in the Freight Immigration Lanes at Dover Eastern Docks after disembarkation, whilst personal to himself, was not material as it was incapable of removing him from being a member of the public and consequently the Lanes constituted a public place for the purposes of the RTA 1988, s. 5. In *Havell v Director of Public Prosecutions* (1994) 158 JP 680, however, use of a car park, which was readily accessible from the road, without restricted access and not marked as being private, as a member of a bona fide club whose membership was not of such a size 'that it was indistinguishable from the public at large in the locality' did not constitute use as a member of the general public; therefore the defendant's appeal against a conviction for being 'in charge' of a motor vehicle on a road or other public place whilst unfit through drink or drugs was allowed. A company car park for the use of staff, customers and other visitors is not a public place unless there is proof of actual use of that car park by members of the public (*Spence* [1999] RTR 353). A car park adjoining a main road and used by members of the public generally is a public place (*May v DPP* [2005] EWHC 1280). (Admin)). In *Filmer v DPP* [2007] RTR 330, Fulford J indicated that 'the critical distinction is between private land to which the public have access at the time in question, on the one hand, and private land which is closed to the public at the material time or is only open to particular people, on the other'.

Vehicle

C1.16 The word 'vehicle' does not appear to have been given any statutory meaning, and may therefore include things as diverse as a bicycle or a poultry shed on wheels (see *Garner v Burr* [1951] 1 KB 31). The *Concise Oxford Dictionary* defines 'vehicle' as a 'carriage or conveyance of any kind used on land'.

Interpretation Provisions of Road Traffic Act 1988

C1.17 **Road Traffic Act 1988, ss. 185, 186, 189, 192**

185.—(1) In this Act—

'heavy locomotive' means a mechanically propelled vehicle which is not constructed itself to carry a load other than any of the excepted articles and the weight of which unladen exceeds 11690 kilograms,

'heavy motor car' means a mechanically propelled vehicle, not being a motor car, which is constructed itself to carry a load or passengers and the weight of which unladen exceeds 2540 kilograms,

'invalid carriage' means a mechanically propelled vehicle the weight of which unladen does not exceed 254 kilograms and which is specially designed and constructed, and not merely adapted, for the use of a person suffering from some physical defect or disability and is used solely by such a person,

'light locomotive' means a mechanically propelled vehicle which is not constructed itself to carry a load other than any of the excepted articles and the weight of which unladen does not exceed 11690 kilograms but does exceed 7370 kilograms,

'motor car' means a mechanically propelled vehicle, not being a motor cycle or an invalid carriage, which is constructed itself to carry a load or passengers and the weight of which unladen—

(a) if it is constructed solely for the carriage of passengers and their effects, is adapted to carry not more than seven passengers exclusive of the driver and is fitted with tyres of such type as may be specified in regulations made by the Secretary of State, does not exceed 3050 kilograms,

(b) if it is constructed or adapted for use for the conveyance of goods or burden of any description, does not exceed 3050 kilograms, or 3500 kilograms if the vehicle carries a container or containers for holding for the purposes of its propulsion any fuel which is wholly gaseous at 17.5 degrees Celsius under a pressure of 1.013 bar or plant and material for producing such fuel,

(c) does not exceed 2540 kilograms in a case not falling within subparagraph (a) or (b) above,

'motor cycle' means a mechanically propelled vehicle, not being an invalid carriage, with less than four wheels and the weight of which unladen does not exceed 410 kilograms,

'motor tractor' means a mechanically propelled vehicle which is not constructed itself to carry a load, other than the excepted articles, and the weight of which unladen does not exceed 7370 kilograms,

'motor vehicle' means, subject to section 20 of the Chronically Sick and Disabled Persons Act 1970 (which makes special provision about invalid carriages, within the meaning of that Act), a mechanically propelled vehicle intended or adapted for use on roads, and

'trailer' means a vehicle drawn by a motor vehicle.

(2) In subsection (1) above 'excepted articles' means any of the following: water, fuel, accumulators and other equipment used for the purpose of propulsion, loose tools and loose equipment.

186.—(1) For the purposes of section 185 of this Act, a side car attached to a motor vehicle, if it complies with such conditions as may be specified in regulations made by the Secretary of State, is to be regarded as forming part of the vehicle to which it is attached and as not being a trailer.

(2) For the purposes of section 185 of this Act, in a case where a motor vehicle is so constructed that a trailer may by partial super-imposition be attached to the vehicle in such a manner as to cause a substantial part of the weight of the trailer to be borne by the vehicle, that vehicle is to be deemed to be a vehicle itself constructed to carry a load.

(3) For the purposes of section 185 of this Act, in the case of a motor vehicle fitted with a crane, dynamo, welding plant or other special appliance or apparatus which is a permanent or essentially permanent fixture, the appliance or apparatus is not to be deemed to constitute a load or goods or burden of any description, but is to be deemed to form part of the vehicle.

(4)–(6) [Regulations.]

189.—(1) For the purposes of the Road Traffic Acts—

(a) a mechanically propelled vehicle being an implement for cutting grass which is controlled by a pedestrian and is not capable of being used or adapted for any other purpose,

(b) any other mechanically propelled vehicle controlled by a pedestrian which may be specified by regulations made by the Secretary of State for the purposes of this section and section 140 of the Road Traffic Regulation Act 1984, and

(c) an electrically assisted pedal cycle of such a class as may be prescribed by regulations so made,

is to be treated as not being a motor vehicle.

(2) In subsection (1) above 'controlled by a pedestrian' means that the vehicle either—

(a) is constructed or adapted for use only under such control, or

(b) is constructed or adapted for use either under such control or under the control of a person carried on it, but is not for the time being in use under, or proceeding under, the control of a person carried on it.

192.—(1) In this Act—

. . .

'bridleway' means a way over which the public have the following, but no other, rights of way: a right of way on foot and a right of way on horseback or leading a horse, with or without a right to drive animals of any description along the way,

'carriage of goods' includes the haulage of goods,

'cycle' means a bicycle, a tricycle, or a cycle having four or more wheels, not being in any case a motor vehicle,

'driver', where a separate person acts as a steersman of a motor vehicle, includes (except for the purposes of section 1 of this Act) that person as well as any other person engaged in the driving of the vehicle, and 'drive' is to be interpreted accordingly,

'footpath', in relation to England and Wales, means a way over which the public have a right of way on foot only,

'goods' includes goods or burden of any description,

'goods vehicle' means a motor vehicle constructed or adapted for use for the carriage of goods, or a trailer so constructed or adapted, 'highway authority', in England and Wales, means—

(a) in relation to a road for which he is the highway authority within the meaning of the Highways Act 1980, the Secretary of State, and

(b) in relation to any other road, the council of the county, metropolitan district or London borough, or the Common Council of the City of London, as the case may be;

'international road haulage permit' means a licence, permit, authorisation or other document issued in pursuance of a Community instrument relating to the carriage of goods by road between member States or an international agreement to which the United Kingdom is a party and which relates to the international carriage of goods by road,

'owner', in relation to a vehicle which is the subject of a hiring agreement or hirepurchase agreement, means the person in possession of the vehicle under that agreement,

'prescribed' means prescribed by regulations made by the Secretary of State,

'road'—

(a) in relation to England and Wales, means any highway and any other road to which the public has access, and includes bridges over which a road passes, and

(b) [Applies only to Scotland.];

'the Road Traffic Acts' means the Road Traffic Offenders Act 1988, the Road Traffic (Consequential Provisions) Act 1988 (so far as it reproduces the effect of provisions repealed by that Act) and this Act,

'statutory', in relation to any prohibition, restriction, requirement or provision, means contained in, or having effect under, any enactment (including any enactment contained in this Act),

'the Traffic Acts' means the Road Traffic Acts and the Road Traffic Regulation Act 1984,

'traffic sign' has the meaning given by section 64(1) of the Road Traffic Regulation Act 1984,

'tramcar' includes any carriage used on any road by virtue of an order under the Light Railways Act 1896, and

'trolley vehicle' means a mechanically propelled vehicle adapted for use on roads without rails under power transmitted to it from some external source (whether or not there is in addition a source of power on board the vehicle).

(1A) In this Act—

(a) any reference to a county shall be construed in relation to Wales as including a reference to a county borough; and

(b) section 17(4) and (5) of the Local Government (Wales) Act 1994 (references to counties and districts to be construed generally in relation to Wales as references to counties and county boroughs) shall not apply.

(2) [Applies only to Scotland.]

(3) References in this Act to a class of vehicles are to be interpreted as references to a class defined or described by reference to any characteristics of the vehicles or to any other circumstances whatsoever and accordingly as authorising the use of 'category' to indicate a class of vehicles, however defined or described.

Section C2 Evidence and Procedure in Road Traffic Cases

Notice of Intended Prosecution

Road Traffic Offenders Act 1988, ss. 1 and 2 **C2.1**

1.—(1) Subject to section 2 of this Act, a person shall not be convicted of an offence to which this section applies unless—

(a) he was warned at the time the offence was committed that the question of prosecuting him for some one or other of the offences to which this section applies would be taken into consideration, or

(b) within 14 days of the commission of the offence a summons (or, in Scotland, a complaint) for the offence was served on him, or

(c) within 14 days of the commission of the offence a notice of the intended prosecution specifying the nature of the alleged offence and the time and place where it is alleged to have been committed, was—

(i) in the case of an offence under section 28 or 29 of the Road Traffic Act 1988 (cycling offences), served on him,

(ii) in the case of any other offence, served on him or on the person, if any, registered as the keeper of the vehicle at the time of the commission of the offence.

(1A) A notice required by this section to be served on any person may be served on that person—

(a) by delivering it to him;

(b) by addressing it to him and leaving it at his last known address;

(c) by sending it by registered post, recorded delivery service or first class post addressed to him at his last known address.

(2) A notice shall be deemed for the purposes of subsection (1)(c) above to have been served on a person if it was sent by registered post or recorded delivery service addressed to him at his last known address, notwithstanding that the notice was returned as undelivered or was for any other reason not received by him.

(3) The requirement of subsection (1) above shall in every case be deemed to have been complied with unless and until the contrary is proved.

(4) Schedule 1 to this Act shows the offences to which this section applies.

2.—(1) The requirement of section 1(1) of this Act does not apply in relation to an offence if, at the time of the offence or immediately after it, an accident occurs owing to the presence on a road of the vehicle in respect of which the offence was committed.

(2) [Exception for fixed penalty notices.]

(3) Failure to comply with the requirement of section 1(1) of this Act is not a bar to the conviction of the accused in a case where the court is satisfied—

(a) that neither the name and address of the accused nor the name and address of the registered keeper, if any, could with reasonable diligence have been ascertained in time for a summons or, as the case may be, a complaint to be served or for a notice to be served or sent in compliance with the requirement, or

(b) that the accused by his own conduct contributed to the failure.

(4) Failure to comply with the requirement of section 1(1) of this Act in relation to an offence is not a bar to the conviction of a person of that offence by virtue of the provisions of—

(a) section 24 of this Act, or
(b) any of the enactments mentioned in section 24(6);

but a person is not to be convicted of an offence by virtue of any of those provisions if section 1 applies to the offence with which he was charged and the requirement of section 1(1) was not satisfied in relation to the offence charged.

The oral warning must have been understood by the defendant. The test was set out in *Gibson v Dalton* [1980] RTR 410, by Donaldson LJ (at pp. 413–14):

> The obligation on the prosecutor is to warn the accused, not merely to address a warning to him or to give a warning. The mischief to which this section is directed is clear. It is that motorists are entitled to have it brought to their attention at a relatively early stage that there is likely to be a prosecution in order that they may recall and, it may be, record the facts as they occurred at the time. . . . But a warning which does not get through to the accused person is of no value at all, and prima facie, therefore, the words might be expected to mean that the warning must get through. . . .
>
> If, viewing the matter objectively, one would expect that the words addressed to the accused person would have been heard and understood by him, then prima facie he was warned within the meaning of the statute. But it is only a prima facie case. It is open to the defendant to prove, if he can, that he did not understand or hear or appreciate the warning and therefore that he was not warned.

The warning must have been given 'at the time' the offence was committed. The latter was held to be a matter of fact and degree, and that the test was what was reasonable (*Okike* [1978] RTR 489). This test was repeated in *Stacey* [1982] RTR 20, where it was added that whether or not the chain of circumstances was unbroken and whether or not all that took place was connected with the incident were relevant factors. In addition, the court held that the issue was to be decided by the judge.

The warning must relate to one or other of the offences to which s. 1 applies (see **C9.1**). It need not specify the particular offence or offences but rather their nature. Alternative verdicts may be entered in accordance with the provisions of the Criminal Law Act 1967, s. 6(3), or the RTOA 1988, s. 24 (see **C2.12**), if the requirements of s. 1(1) have been complied with in relation to the original offence charged.

If the warning was not given at the time, then a summons must be served within 14 days. See the MCA 1980, s. 47, for a saving provision where service by post has not been proved, enabling a second summons to be issued on the same information. In other cases a notice of intended prosecution must be served within 14 days on the driver or registered keeper of the vehicle. Service is deemed under s. 1(2) if sent by registered post or recorded delivery service, as long as it was sent so as to be delivered, in the ordinary course of post, within the 14 days (*Groome v Driscoll* [1969] 3 All ER 1638).

Section 1(3) places the burden of proving failure to comply with the section on the defence on a balance of probabilities.

The requirement in s. 1 does not apply if there has been an accident of which the defendant was aware or to the occurrence of which he has shut his eyes but if the incident was so trivial that the driver was unaware of it a notice of intended prosecution is necessary (*Bentley v Dickinson* [1983] RTR 356, approving *Metropolitan Police v Scarlett* [1978] Crim LR 234, and distinguishing *Harding v Price* [1948] 1 KB 695). For these purposes, 'accident' should be given a commonsense meaning and not be restricted to untoward or unintended consequences having an adverse physical effect (*Currie* [2007] EWCA Crim 926, approving *Bremner v Westwater* 1994 SLT 707). The principle applied in *Bentley v Dickinson*, however, does not extend to cases where the driver's injuries are so severe that he has no recollection of the accident (*DPP v Pidhajeckyj* [1991] RTR 136). There must be a sufficient causal link between the offence and the accident before the warning can be dispensed with (*Myers* [2007] EWCA Crim 599).

Section 2(3) contains a saving where the prosecution have acted with reasonable diligence or the accused has by his own conduct contributed to a failure to comply with s. 1. In the Crown Court, determining this issue is a matter for the judge rather than the jury (*Currie*).

Time-limits

The MCA 1980, s. 127, lays down a general time-limit of six months for the laying of an information for a summary offence, subject to any enactment which expressly permits a longer period. **C2.2**

The RTOA 1988, s. 6, provides for an extended time-limit in relation to certain offences specified in sch. 1 to the Act (see **C9.1**). In those cases proceedings may be commenced within a period of six months from the date on which sufficient evidence came to the prosecutor's knowledge. That date is proved by a signed certificate. No proceedings are to be brought more than three years after the offence.

A traffic examiner employed by the vehicle inspectorate to investigate traffic offences, but not authorised to decide whether to prosecute, is not a prosecutor for the purposes of the 1988 Act (*Swan v Vehicle Inspectorate* [1997] RTR 187).

Duty to Produce Licence to Court

Road Traffic Offenders Act 1988, s. 7 **C2.3**

(1) A person who is prosecuted for an offence involving obligatory or discretionary disqualification and who is the holder of a licence must—
 (a) cause it to be delivered to the proper officer of the court not later than the day before the date appointed for the hearing, or
 (b) post it, at such a time that in the ordinary course of post it would be delivered not later than that day, in a letter duly addressed to the clerk and either registered or sent by the recorded delivery service, or
 (c) have it with him at the hearing,
 and the foregoing obligations imposed on him as respects the licence also apply as respects the counterpart.

'Licence' includes a Community licence (RTOA 1988, s. 91A(1)).

Admissibility of Highway Code

The RTA 1988, s. 38(8), defines 'the Highway Code' as the Code comprising directions for the guidance of persons using roads issued under the RTA 1930, s. 45, and subsequently revised. **C2.4**

Section 38(7) provides that a failure to observe a provision of the Code shall not of itself render a person liable to criminal proceedings, but any such failure may be relied upon by any party to civil or criminal proceedings as tending to establish or negative any liability in question in those proceedings. In appropriate cases, the provisions of the Code can be used as guidance when a judge sums up to the jury, e.g., on what might constitute dangerous driving (*Taylor* [2004] EWCA Crim 213). The subsection does not provide for the admissibility of evidence of due observance of the Code. But a defendant may rely on the failure of any other person to observe a relevant provision of the Code (*Baker v E. Longhurst & Sons Ltd* [1933] 2 KB 461; *Croston v Vaughan* [1938] 1 KB 540).

The Code itself is issued by the Secretary of State under authority of Parliament, pursuant to the RTA 1988, s. 38, and is Crown Copyright. The latest edition was published in 1999. Any copy of it purporting to be printed under the superintendence or authority of Her Majesty's Stationery Office is conclusive evidence of the contents of the Code (Documentary Evidence Act 1882, s. 2).

Evidence by Certificate as to Driver, Owner or User

C2.5 **Road Traffic Offenders Act 1988, s. 11**

(1) In any proceedings in England and Wales for an offence to which this section applies, a certificate in the prescribed form, purporting to be signed by a constable and certifying that a person specified in the certificate stated to the constable—
 (a) that a particular mechanically propelled vehicle was being driven or used by, or belonged to, that person on a particular occasion, or
 (b) that a particular mechanically propelled vehicle on a particular occasion was used by, or belonged to, a firm and that he was, at the time of the statement, a partner in that firm, or
 (c) that a particular mechanically propelled vehicle on a particular occasion was used by, or belonged to, a corporation and that he was, at the time of the statement, a director, officer or employee of that corporation,

shall be admissible as evidence for the purpose of determining by whom the vehicle was being driven or used, or to whom it belonged, as the case may be, on that occasion.

(2) Nothing in subsection (1) above makes a certificate admissible as evidence in proceedings for an offence except in a case where and to the like extent to which oral evidence to the like effect would have been admissible in those proceedings.

(3) Nothing in subsection (1) above makes a certificate admissible as evidence in proceedings for an offence—
 (a) unless a copy of it has, not less than seven days before the hearing or trial, been served in the prescribed manner on the person charged with the offence, or
 (b) if that person, not later than three days before the hearing or trial or within such further time as the court may in special circumstances allow, serves a notice in the prescribed form and manner on the prosecutor requiring attendance at the trial of the person who signed the certificate.

The form of the certificate and rules for service are prescribed by the Evidence by Certificate Rules 1961 (SI 1961 No. 248). The functions of a constable have been extended to traffic wardens by the Functions of Traffic Wardens Order 1970 (SI 1970 No. 1958).

Section 11 provides an exception to the 'hearsay' rule. The offences to which the section applies are set out in sch. 1 to the RTOA 1988 (see **C9.1**).

Proof of Identity of Driver in Summary Proceedings

C2.6 **Road Traffic Offenders Act 1988, s. 12**

(1) Where on the summary trial in England and Wales of an information for an offence to which this subsection applies—
 (a) it is proved to the satisfaction of the court, on oath or in manner prescribed by rules made under section 144 of the Magistrates' Courts Act 1980, that a requirement under section 172(2) of the Road Traffic Act 1988 to give information as to the identity of the driver of a particular vehicle on the particular occasion to which the information relates has been served on the accused by post, and
 (b) a statement in writing is produced to the court purporting to be signed by the accused that the accused was the driver of that vehicle on that occasion,

the court may accept that statement as evidence that the accused was the driver of that vehicle on that occasion.

(2) Schedule 1 to this Act shows the offences to which subsection (1) above applies.

(3) [Enacts a similar provision to subsection (1) above in relation to offences under the RTRA 1984.]

The relevant rule for proving service is the CrimPR, r. 4.11.

In cases where identity becomes an issue and there is no s. 12 statement, the justices will be permitted to assess the sufficiency of the evidence from other sources (*Creed v Scott* [1976] RTR 488), such as relevant information about the registered keeper given to the police when questioned, which, when checked, corresponds to details held on the Police National Computer (*DPP v Bayliff* [2003] EWHC Admin 539). Indeed, where there has been no prior notice that identity is an issue, relying on evidence by way of a dock identification may be permissible (*Karia v DPP* (2002) 166 JP 753).

Although forms returned in accordance with the RTA 1988, s. 172 (see C2.15) which are not signed will not be admissible under s. 12, the contents of the form may amount to a confession admissible in documentary form under the CJA 1988, s. 27 (*Mawdesley v Chief Constable of Cheshire Constabulary* [2004] 1 WLR 1035).

Admissibility of Records of Secretary of State

Road Traffic Offenders Act 1988, s. 13 **C2.7**

(1) This section applies to a statement contained in a document purporting to be—
 (a) a part of the records maintained by the Secretary of State in connection with any functions exercisable by him by virtue of part III of the Road Traffic Act 1988 or a part of any other records maintained by the Secretary of State with respect to vehicles, or
 (b) a copy of a document forming part of those records, or
 (c) a note of any information contained in those records,
 and to be authenticated by a person authorised in that behalf by the Secretary of State.

(2) A statement to which this section applies shall be admissible in any proceedings as evidence (in Scotland, sufficient evidence) of any fact stated in it to the same extent as oral evidence of that fact is admissible in those proceedings.

(3) In the preceding subsections, except in Scotland—
 'copy', in relation to a document, means anything onto which information recorded in the document has been copied, by whatever means and whether directly or indirectly;
 'document' means anything in which information of any description is recorded; and
 'statement' means any representation of fact, however made.

(3A) In any case where—
 (a) a person is convicted by a magistrates' court of a summary offence under the Traffic Acts or the Road Traffic (Driver Licensing and Information Systems) Act 1989,
 (b) a statement to which this section applies is produced to the court in the proceedings,
 (c) the statement specifies an alleged previous conviction of the accused of an offence involving obligatory endorsement or an order made on the conviction, and
 (d) the accused is not present in person before the court when the statement is so produced,
 the court may take account of the previous conviction or order as if the accused had appeared and admitted it.

(3B) Section 104 of the Magistrates' Courts Act 1980 (under which the previous convictions may be adduced in the absence of the accused after giving him seven days' notice of them) does not limit the effect of subsection (3A) above.

(4) In any case where—
 (a) a statement to which this section applies is produced to a magistrates' court in any proceedings for an offence involving obligatory or discretionary disqualification other than a summary offence under any of the enactments mentioned in subsection (3A)(a) above,
 (b) the statement specifies an alleged previous conviction of an accused person of any such offence or any order made on the conviction,
 (c) it is proved to the satisfaction of the court, on oath or in such manner as may be prescribed by rules under section 144 of the Magistrates' Courts Act 1980, that not less than seven days before the statement is so produced a notice was served on the accused, in such form and manner as may be so prescribed, specifying the previous conviction or order and stating that it is proposed to bring it to the notice of the court in the event of or, as the case may be, in view of his conviction, and
 (d) the accused is not present in person before the court when the statement is so produced,
 the court may take account of the previous conviction or order as if the accused had appeared and admitted it.

(5) Nothing in the preceding provisions of this section enables evidence to be given in respect of any matter other than a matter of a description prescribed by regulations made by the Secretary of State.

(6) [Power to make regulations.]

The records to be maintained and which are admissible (see s. 13(5)) are set out in the Vehicle and Driving Licences Records (Evidence) Regulations 1970 (SI 1970 No. 1997). They usually take the form of a computer printout from DVLA at Swansea. For the prescribed manner of proving previous convictions, see the CrimPR, r. 37.5. The form of the document is a computer printout appropriately endorsed.

Records Kept by Operators of Goods Vehicles

C2.8 **Road Traffic Offenders Act 1988, s. 14**

In any proceedings for an offence under section 40A of the Road Traffic Act 1988 or for a contravention of or failure to comply with construction and use requirements (within the meaning of part II of the Road Traffic Act 1988) or regulations under section 74 of that Act, any record purporting to be made and authenticated in accordance with regulations under that section shall be evidence . . . of the matters stated in the record and of its due authentication.

Admissibility of Vehicle Markings as Evidence of Weight or Date

C2.9 **Road Traffic Offenders Act 1988, s. 17**

(1) If in any proceedings for an offence under section 40A, 41A, 41B or 42 of the Road Traffic Act 1988 (using vehicle in dangerous condition or contravention of construction and use regulations)—

(a) any question arises as to a weight of any description specified in the plating certificate for a goods vehicle, and

(b) a weight of that description is marked on the vehicle,

it shall be assumed, unless the contrary is proved, that the weight marked on the vehicle is the weight so specified.

(2) If, in any proceedings for an offence—

(a) under part II of the Road Traffic Act 1988, except sections 47 and 75, or

(b) under section 174(2) or (5) (false statements and deception) of that Act,

any question arises as to the date of manufacture of a vehicle, a date purporting to be such a date and marked on the vehicle in pursuance of regulations under that part of that Act shall be evidence . . . that the vehicle was manufactured on the date so marked.

(3) If in any proceedings for the offence of driving a vehicle on a road, or causing or permitting a vehicle to be so driven, in contravention of a prohibition under section 70(2) of the Road Traffic Act 1988 any question arises whether a weight of any description has been reduced to a limit imposed by construction and use requirements, or so that it has ceased to be excessive, the burden of proof shall lie on the accused.

Admissibility of Evidence from Prescribed Devices

C2.10 **Road Traffic Offenders Act 1988, s. 20**

(1) Evidence (which in Scotland shall be sufficient evidence) of a fact relevant to proceedings for an offence to which this section applies may be given by the production of—

(a) a record produced by a prescribed device, and

(b) (in the same or another document) a certificate as to the circumstances in which the record was produced signed by a constable or by a person authorised by or on behalf of the chief officer of police for the police area in which the offence is alleged to have been committed;

but subject to the following provisions of this section.

(2) [Offences to which section applies.]

(3) [Power to add offences.]

(4) [Requirement of approval of devices.]

(5) [Approval may be subject to conditions concerning the purposes and use of the device.]

(6) In proceedings for an offence to which this section applies, evidence (which in Scotland shall be sufficient evidence)—

(a) of a measurement made by a device, or of the circumstances in which it was made, or

(b) that a device was of a type approved for the purposes of this section, or that any conditions subject to which an approval was given were satisfied,

may be given by the production of a document which is signed as mentioned in subsection (1) above and which, as the case may be, gives particulars of the measurement or of the circumstances in which it was made, or states that the device was of such a type or that, to the best of the knowledge and belief of the person making the statement, all such conditions were satisfied.

(7) For the purposes of this section a document purporting to be a record of the kind mentioned in subsection (1) above, or to be a certificate or other document signed as mentioned in that subsection or in subsection (6) above, shall be deemed to be such a record, or to be so signed, unless the contrary is proved.

(8) Nothing in subsection (1) or (6) above makes a document admissible as evidence in proceedings for an offence unless a copy of it has, not less than seven days before the hearing or trial, been served on the person charged with the offence; and nothing in those subsections makes a document admissible as evidence of anything other than the matters shown on a record produced by a prescribed device if that person, not less than three days before the hearing or trial or within such further time as the court may in special circumstances allow, serves a notice on the prosecutor requiring attendance at the hearing or trial of the person who signed the document.

As to the requirement for corroboration of the opinion evidence of a witness concerning speed in such cases, and the use of measurements as corroboration, see the RTRA 1984, s. 89; *Nicholas v Penny* [1950] 2 KB 466; and *Swain v Gillet* [1974] RTR 446. This section applies to offences under the RTRA 1984, ss. 16, 17(4), 88(7) and 89(1) (speeding offences), offences under that Act in respect of bus lanes or routes for use by buses only, and offences under the RTA 1988, s. 36(1) (failure to comply with automatic traffic light signal).

In the case of any offence to which s. 20 applies, the prosecution will be able to rely on evidence produced by automatic devices of a specified and approved type, without the need for corroboration. The evidence must be accompanied by the appropriate certificate signed by a constable or other authorised person, and, where there is such a certificate, s. 20(7) imposes the burden on the defence of disproving that the document is a record. Where that evidence and certificate are served not less than seven days before the hearing or trial and there is no counter-notice from the defendant in accordance with s. 20(8), they may be tendered in evidence without the necessity of anyone being called to prove them (*DPP v Thornley* (2006) 170 JP 385). Any document served under s. 20(8) must be capable of being used for the purpose intended; if it is only a poor quality copy, that does not constitute 'service' and the document itself is rendered inadmissible under the subsection. However, in any case where s. 20(8) does not apply, the evidence from the prescribed device can be adduced in the conventional way.

A device designed or adapted for measuring by radar the speed of motor vehicles is a prescribed device for the purposes of s. 20 (Road Traffic Offenders (Prescribed Devices) Order 1992 (SI 1992 No. 1209)); a device designed or adapted for recording, by photographic or other image recording means, the position of vehicles in relation to light signals is also a prescribed device (Road Traffic Offenders (Prescribed Devices) (No. 2) Order 1992 (SI 1992 No. 2843)). A camera designed or adapted to record the presence of a vehicle on an area of road which is a bus lane or a route for use by buses only is a prescribed device (Road Traffic Offenders (Additional Offences and Prescribed Devices) Order 1997 (SI 1997 No. 384)); as is a device designed or adapted for recording the measurement of a motor vehicle's speed by capturing two images at predetermined positions on a road, digitally recording each image and the time at which it was captured and calculating the average speed of the vehicle over the distance between those two positions (Road Traffic Offenders (Prescribed Devices) Order 1999 (SI 1999 No. 162)).

In *Roberts v DPP* [1994] RTR 31, the Divisional Court held that the prosecution were required to prove that the Home Secretary had approved the use of the device (in this case a Falcon radar gun) before the measurement of speed could be admitted in evidence. In *DPP v Mura Deva Bharat* (15 November 1999 unreported), the Divisional Court accepted that proof could be through oral evidence from a constable or by inviting the court to take judicial notice of the content of an appropriate practitioners' work. In *Barber v DPP* [2006] EWHC 3137 (Admin), the constable's explanation about why 'Timeout' appeared on stills produced by the device in question was accepted and this did not render the stills inadmissible.

Notification as to Disabilities

C2.11 **Road Traffic Offenders Act 1988, s. 22**

(1) If in any proceedings for an offence committed in respect of a motor vehicle it appears to the court that the accused may be suffering from any relevant disability or prospective disability (within the meaning of part III of the Road Traffic Act 1988) the court must notify the Secretary of State.

(2) A notice sent by a court to the Secretary of State in pursuance of this section must be sent in such manner and to such address and contain such particulars as the Secretary of State may determine.

'Relevant disability' means the disabilities set out in the Motor Vehicles (Driving Licences) Regulations 1999 (SI 1999 No. 2864), part VI. There must be some evidence of such a disability before the court may notify the Secretary of State.

Alternative Verdicts

C2.12 **Road Traffic Offenders Act 1988, s. 24**

(1) Where—

(a) a person charged with an offence under a provision of the Road Traffic Act 1988 specified in the first column of the table below (where the general nature of the offences is also indicated) is found not guilty of that offence, but

(b) the allegations in the indictment or information (or in Scotland complaint) amount to or include an allegation of an offence under one or more of the provisions specified in the corresponding entry in the second column,

he may be convicted of that offence or of one or more of those offences.

Offence charged	Alternative
Section 1 (causing death by dangerous driving)	Section 2 (dangerous driving) Section 3 (careless, and inconsiderate, driving)
Section 2 (dangerous driving)	Section 3 (careless, and inconsiderate, driving)
Section 3A (causing death by careless driving when under influence of drink or drugs)	Section 4(1) (driving when unfit to drive through drink or drugs) Section 5(1)(a) (driving with excess alcohol in breath, blood or urine) Section 7(6) (failing to provide specimen)
Section 4(1) (driving or attempting to drive when unfit to drive through drink or drugs)	Section 4(2) (being in charge of a vehicle when unfit to drive through drink or drugs)
Section 5(1)(a) (driving or attempting to drive with excess alcohol in breath, blood or urine)	Section 5(1)(b) (being in charge of a vehicle with excess alcohol in breath, blood or urine)
Section 28 (dangerous cycling)	Section 29 (careless, and inconsiderate, cycling)

(2) Where the offence with which a person is charged is an offence under section 3A of the Road Traffic Act 1988, subsection (1) above shall not authorise his conviction of any offence of attempting to drive.

(3) Where a person is charged with having committed an offence under section 4(1) or 5(1)(a) of the Road Traffic Act 1988 by driving a vehicle, he may be convicted of having committed an offence under the provision in question by attempting to drive.

(4) Where by virtue of this section a person is convicted before the Crown Court of an offence triable only summarily, the court shall have the same powers and duties as a magistrates' court would have had on convicting him of that offence.

(5) [Applies only to Scotland.]

(6) This section has effect without prejudice to section 6(3) of the Criminal Law Act 1967 (alternative verdicts on trial on indictment) . . . and section 23 of this Act.

When the Road Safety Act 2006, s. 31(4), is brought into force, on a count for an offence under the RTA 1988, s. 3A (causing death by careless driving when under influence of drink or drugs), an alternative verdict of an offence under the RTA 1988, s. 7A(6) (failing to give permission for laboratory test) will, in appropriate cases, be available. Similarly, when s. 20 of the 2006 Act is commenced, in respect of an offence under the RTA 1988, s. 2B (causing death by careless, or inconsiderate, driving), an alternative verdict under the RTA 1988, s. 3 (careless, and inconsiderate, driving), will be available. Finally, when s. 33 of the 2006 Act is commenced, the provisions of the RTA 1988, s. 24 will be enlarged so that, on an unsuccessful manslaughter prosecution in connection with the driving of a mechanically propelled vehicle, an alternative verdict of an offence under the RTA 1988, ss. 1, 2 or 3A, or the OAPA 1865, s. 35 (furious driving) will become available.

Where the offence charged is one under the RTA 1988, s. 4(1) (driving, or attempting to drive, when unfit through drink or drugs) or s. 5(1)(a) (driving, or attempting to drive, with excess alcohol in breath, blood or urine), it is open to the magistrates to convict of the alternative offence of 'being in charge of' or, if the allegation is of driving, to convict of the alternative of attempting to drive (s. 24(3)). However, s. 24(2) states that where the offence charged is that under the RTA 1988, s. 3A, no alternative verdict involving attempting to drive is authorised. If the conviction is in the Crown Court and the offence is one that is triable only summarily, for example, where the conviction is under s. 3 of the 1988 Act (careless driving) as an alternative to a count alleging causing death by dangerous driving under s. 1, the powers of the Crown Court will be the same as those of the magistrates (s. 24(4)).

The six-month time-limit imposed by the MCA 1980, s. 127, does not apply (*Coventry Justices, ex parte Sayers* [1979] RTR 22).

In *Jeavons* [1990] RTR 263, a case of reckless driving, the prosecution alleged that the accused and another were racing, although this was denied in interview. The co-accused pleaded guilty and the appellant did not give evidence. The judge did not leave an alternative verdict of careless driving to the jury. His decision was upheld on the basis that it is for the judge to exclude irrelevant charges and allegations as well as to ensure that the indictment covers offences which the facts might disclose. In the instant case, if the prosecution's case of 'racing' was rejected by the jury there was, in the circumstances, no ground for an allegation of careless driving. However, where there is a live issue as to the quality of a defendant's driving, the alternative verdict of careless driving should be left to the jury (*Cambray* [2007] RTR 128). In *Griffiths* [1998] Crim LR 348, the Court of Appeal held that, in the absence of a verdict of not guilty on the count of dangerous driving, there was no power under s. 24(1) for the jury to return a verdict of guilty of careless driving. For these purposes, a finding of no case to answer is equivalent to a finding of not guilty, thus making available the alternative verdict (*DPP v Smith* [2002] Crim LR 970). Where the defendant has already been acquitted of the 'lesser' charge (by the prosecution offering no evidence or otherwise), the alternative verdict is not available on the trial of the 'greater' charge and that should be made clear to the arbiters of fact (*DPP v Khan* [1997] RTR 82). For a full discussion of alternative verdicts and the relevant procedure, see **D18.41** ***et seq.***

Information as to Date of Birth and Sex

Road Traffic Offenders Act 1988, s. 25 **C2.13**

(1) If on convicting a person of an offence involving obligatory or discretionary disqualification or of such other offence as may be prescribed by regulations under section 105 of the Road Traffic Act 1988 the court does not know his date of birth, the court must order him to give that date to the court in writing.

(2) If a court convicting a person of such an offence in a case where—
 (a) notification has been given to the designated officer for a magistrates' court in pursuance of section 12(4) of the Magistrates' Courts Act 1980 (written pleas of guilty) . . . and

(b) the notification . . . did not include a statement of the person's sex, does not know the person's sex, the court must order the person to give that information to the court in writing.

(3) A person who knowingly fails to comply with an order under subsection (1) or (2) above is guilty of an offence.

(4) Nothing in section 7 of the Powers of Criminal Courts (Sentencing) Act 2000 (where magistrates' court commits a person to the Crown Court to be dealt with, certain powers and duties transferred to that court) applies to any duty imposed upon a magistrates' court by subsection (1) or (2) above.

(5) Where a person has given his date of birth in accordance with this section or section 8 of this Act, the Secretary of State may serve on that person a notice in writing requiring him to provide the Secretary of State—

(a) with such evidence in that person's possession or obtainable by him as the Secretary of State may specify for the purpose of verifying that date, and

(b) if his name differs from his name at the time of his birth, with a statement in writing specifying his name at that time.

(6) A person who knowingly fails to comply with a notice under subsection (5) above is guilty of an offence.

(7) A notice to be served on any person under subsection (5) above may be served on him by delivering it to him or by leaving it at his proper address or by sending it to him by post; and for the purposes of this subsection and section 7 of the Interpretation Act 1978 in its application to this subsection the proper address of any person shall be his latest address as known to the person serving the notice.

Failure to comply with s. 25 is punishable by a fine up to level 3.

Interim Disqualification

C2.14 **Road Traffic Offenders Act 1988, s. 26**

(1) Where a magistrates' court—

(a) commits an offender to the Crown Court under section 6 of the Powers of Criminal Courts (Sentencing) Act 2000 or any enactment mentioned in subsection (4) of that section, or

(b) remits an offender to another magistrates' court under section 10 of that Act, to be dealt with for an offence involving obligatory or discretionary disqualification, it may order him to be disqualified until he has been dealt with in respect of the offence.

(2) Where a court in England and Wales—

(a) defers passing sentence on an offender under section 1 of that Act in respect of an offence involving obligatory or discretionary disqualification, or

(b) adjourns after convicting an offender of such an offence but before dealing with him for the offence,

it may order the offender to be disqualified until he has been dealt with in respect of the offence.

(3) [Applies only to Scotland.]

(4) Subject to subsection (5) below, an order under this section shall cease to have effect at the end of the period of six months beginning with the day on which it is made, if it has not ceased to have effect before that time.

(5) [Applies only to Scotland.]

(6) Where a court orders a person to be disqualified under this section ('the first order'), no court shall make a further order under this section in respect of the same offence or any offence in respect of which an order could have been made under this section at the time the first order was made.

(7) to (9) [Production of licences and consequences of failure to produce.]

(10) to (11) [Duty to send notice of order to Secretary of State and contents of notice.]

(12) Where on any occasion a court deals with an offender—

(a) for an offence in respect of which an order was made under this section, or

(b) for two or more offences in respect of any of which such an order was made, any period of disqualification which is on that occasion imposed under section 34 or 35 of this Act shall be treated as reduced by any period during which he was disqualified by reason only of an order made under this section in respect of any of those offences.

(13) Any reference in this or any other Act (including any Act passed after this Act) to the length of a period of disqualification shall, unless the context otherwise requires, be construed as a reference to its length before any reduction under this section.

(14) [References to counterparts to be disregarded for pre-June 1990 licences.]

Section 26 enables magistrates, when committing an offender to the Crown Court under the PCC(S)A 2000, s. 6 (see **D22.34**), remitting him to another court, deferring sentence or adjourning, to disqualify him from driving until he has been finally dealt with. Any period of disqualification finally imposed by the court, without regard to the period of interim disqualification, is reduced accordingly by the administrative authorities (*Edwards v Wheelan* 1999 SLT 917). Such an order is termed a 'first order' and only one such order may be made under s. 26. The order may only be made for a maximum of six months inclusive of the day on which the order is made. The defendant must produce his licence and, where appropriate, its counterpart, which the court must retain. Failure to do so is an offence unless the licence and its counterpart have been posted in accordance with s. 7 of the Act (see **C2.3**), a new licence and counterpart have been applied for but not received, or the defendant tenders a valid receipt under s. 56 of the Act and immediately produces the licence and counterpart to the court on their return.

Duty to Provide Information

Road Traffic Act 1988, s. 172 **C2.15**

(1) This section applies—
 (a) to any offence under the preceding provisions of this Act except—
  (i) an offence under part V, or
  (ii) an offence under section 13, 16, 51(2), 61(4), 67(9), 68(4), 96 or 120, and to an offence under section 178 of this Act,
 (b) to any offence under sections 25, 26 and 27 of the Road Traffic Offenders Act 1988,
 (c) to any offence against any other enactment relating to the use of vehicles on roads, and
 (d) to manslaughter, or in Scotland culpable homicide, by the driver of a motor vehicle.

(2) Where the driver of a vehicle is alleged to be guilty of an offence to which this section applies—
 (a) the person keeping the vehicle shall give such information as to the identity of the driver as he may be required to give by or on behalf of a chief officer of police, and
 (b) any other person shall if required as stated above give any information which it is in his power to give and may lead to identification of the driver.

(3) Subject to the following provisions, a person who fails to comply with a requirement under subsection (2) above shall be guilty of an offence.

(4) A person shall not be guilty of an offence by virtue of paragraph (a) of subsection (2) above if he shows that he did not know and could not with reasonable diligence have ascertained who the driver of the vehicle was.

(5) Where a body corporate is guilty of an offence under this section and the offence is proved to have been committed with the consent or connivance of, or to be attributable to neglect on the part of, a director, manager, secretary or other similar officer of the body corporate, or a person who was purporting to act in any such capacity, he, as well as the body corporate, is guilty of that offence and liable to be proceeded against and punished accordingly.

(6) Where the alleged offender is a body corporate, . . . or the proceedings are brought against him by virtue of subsection (5) above or subsection (11) below, subsection (4) above shall not apply unless, in addition to the matters there mentioned, the alleged offender shows that no record was kept of the persons who drove the vehicle and that the failure to keep a record was reasonable.

(7) A requirement under subsection (2) may be made by written notice served by post; and where it is so made—
 (a) it shall have effect as a requirement to give the information within the period of 28 days beginning with the day on which the notice is served, and
 (b) the person on whom the notice is served shall not be guilty of an offence under this section if he shows either that he gave the information as soon as reasonably practicable

after the end of that period or that it has not been reasonably practicable for him to give it.

(8) Where the person on whom a notice under subsection (7) above is to be served is a body corporate, the notice is duly served if it is served on the secretary or clerk of that body.

(9) For the purposes of section 7 of the Interpretation Act 1978 as it applies for the purposes of this section the proper address of any person in relation to the service on him of a notice under subsection (7) above is—

(a) in the case of the secretary or clerk of a body corporate, that of the registered or principal office of that body or (if the body corporate is the registered keeper of the vehicle concerned) the registered address, and

(b) in any other case, his last known address at the time of service.

(10) In this section—

'registered address', in relation to the registered keeper of a vehicle, means the address recorded in the record kept under the Vehicle Excise and Registration Act 1994 with respect to that vehicle as being that person's address, and

'registered keeper', in relation to a vehicle, means the person in whose name the vehicle is registered under that Act;

and references to the driver of a vehicle include references to the rider of a cycle.

(11) [Scotland.]

The justices must be satisfied that the document requiring information as to the identity of the driver was sent on behalf of a chief officer of police, but there is no need for that document to be signed, provided the document's authenticity can clearly be established by the prosecution (*Arnold v DPP* [1999] RTR 99).

The obligation to provide information is mandatory. Where a written response is required, giving the information sought orally will not suffice to fulfil the obligation because the scheme of the section is designed to produce a document that can be accepted as evidence against the driver (*DPP v Broomfield* [2003] RTR 108). However, responding in writing, albeit not on the official form, but providing all the information required and signing the letter can suffice to bring the defendant within the defence in s. 172(4) (*Jones v DPP* [2004] RTR 331). Because of the relationship with the RTOA 1988, s. 12, where the form is not signed then, even where it contains the information required, its return will not fulfil the s. 172 requirements (*Mawdesley v Chief Constable of Cheshire Constabulary* [2004] 1 WLR 1035 and *Francis v DPP* (2004) 168 JP 492). If the keeper of the vehicle pleads ignorance as to who was the driver, the onus is on him to show that he did not know, and could not with reasonable diligence have ascertained, the identity of the driver. Where the defendant does not believe he was the driver and knew that only one other person had access to the vehicle, it is a clear inference that that other person was the driver at the time in question and the defendant is obliged to say so (*R (Flegg) v Southampton and New Forest Justices* (2006) 170 JP 373). In those circumstances, the defence in s. 172(4) is unavailable. When the justices reject a defence under s. 172(4), they must exercise care to ensure that they provide readily understandable reasons for doing so (*Weightman v DPP* [2007] EWHC 634 (Admin)). In the case of any person other than the keeper, the onus is on the prosecution to establish that the person had information which may have led to the identification of the driver and which it was in his power to give. For the purpose of submissions on duplicity, s. 172 creates only one offence (*Mohindra v DPP* [2005] RTR 95).

Where the defendant admits to having been the driver concerned in the alleged offence, the statement provided under s. 172 can still be used by the prosecution to prove that fact, because to do so does not violate the right to a fair trial conferred by the ECHR, Article 6 and the privilege against self-incrimination implicit in that general right as s. 172 is not a disproportionate measure (*Brown v Stott* [2003] 1 AC 681, which was applied by the Divisional Court in *DPP v Wilson* [2001] RTR 37 and *Hayes v DPP* [2004] EWHC 227 (Admin). This domestic approach has been endorsed by the European Court of Human Rights in *O'Halloran and Francis v UK* (2007) *The Times,* 13 July 2007, in which it was confirmed that people 'who choose to keep and drive motor cars can be taken to have accepted certain responsibilities and obligation as part of the regulatory regime relating to motor vehicles, and in the legal framework of the United Kingdom, these responsibilities include the obligation, in the event of suspected commission of road traffic offences, to inform the authorities of the identity of the driver on that occasion'. In doing so, the Court focused on the nature and degree of compulsion used to obtain the evidence, the existence of any relevant safeguards in the procedure, and the use to which any material so obtained is put. When balancing these issues the Court concluded that the essence of the right to remain silent and the privilege against self-incrimination had not been destroyed. Where no reply to the requirement is given by the registered keeper, an adverse inference may be drawn that the registered keeper himself was responsible (*Secretary of State for the Environment, Transport and the Regions v Holt* [2000] RTR 309, in relation to a similar requirement under the Vehicle Excise and Registration Act 1994, s. 46).

Contravention of the section constitutes an offence for which the defendant can be disqualified or have his licence endorsed with three penalty points (when the Road Safety Act 2006, s. 29, is brought into force, the number of penalty points will increase to six). It also attracts a fine up to level 3 on the standard scale. An enhanced fixed penalty of £120 is available in respect of this offence.

Section C3 Offences Relating to Driving Triable on Indictment

Manslaughter

C3.1 Manslaughter is considered here only in relation to so-called 'motor' or 'vehicular' manslaughter. As to manslaughter generally, see **B1.32** to **B1.56**.

C3.2 **Indictment** For the form of indictment for manslaughter, see **B1.35**.

C3.3 **Elements** In general see **B1.52** ***et seq.***

The RTA 1988, s. 38, is applicable; see **C2.4**.

Where the prosecution can satisfy the terms of the direction in *Adomako* [1995] 1 AC 171 (see **B1.54**), charging 'motor manslaughter' may still be appropriate, albeit rare, even if the test for dangerous driving in the RTA 1988, s. 2A (see **C3.10** ***et seq.***), is also satisfied.

In 'motor manslaughter', however, the risk of death involved in an offence must be very high (*Pimm* [1994] RTR 391; *Brown (Uriah) v The Queen* [2005] 2 WLR 1558), thereby reflecting the greater degree of turpitude that Parliament must be taken to have intended by restricting the maximum penalty for the statutory offence under s. 1 to 14 years' imprisonment.

C3.4 **Defences** Automatism, mechanical defect, and duress. See **C1.4**, **C1.11** and **A3.21** to **A3.29**. See also *Renouf* [1986] 1 WLR 522 at **C3.35**.

C3.5 **Punishment** See generally, **B1.45**.

Life imprisonment and/or a fine. See *Pimm* [1994] RTR 391.

By the RTOA 1988, s. 34 and sch. 2, part II, disqualification for at least two years and endorsement are obligatory, unless the court finds 'special reasons'. Manslaughter by the use of a motor vehicle carries between 3 and 11 penalty points for the purposes of the RTOA 1988, s. 35. The offence also carries mandatory retesting by way of an extended driving test (see **C7.13**). Forfeiture of a motor vehicle used in connection with the crime may be ordered (see **C7.28** and **E20.1**).

C3.6 **Sentencing** The Court of Appeal has emphasised that real assistance from previous decisions is often unavailable because no two cases are the same (*Brown* [2005] EWCA Crim 2868, where a sentence of ten years' detention in a young offender institution was upheld in respect of a driver who had been trying to kill himself by driving into another vehicle at speed). The sentencing judge must bear in mind that the defendant did not intend to cause serious injury to, or kill, anyone else, which would constitute murder, and that the offence is more serious than causing death by dangerous driving. The risk of death is higher, so the offence will generally merit a proportionately greater sentence than for the statutory offence

(*A-G's Ref (No. 14 of 2001)* [2002] 1 Cr App R (S) 106). Aggravating features include hostility or aggressive action taken towards another and the consumption of alcohol or drugs. Other relevant factors include the number of deaths, whether the gross negligence was prolonged or shortlived and whether it took place in the context of some other offence, e.g., seeking to steal the vehicle (*A-G's Ref (No. 11 of 2006)* [2006] EWCA Crim 3269, which acknowledged that none of the recent cases purport to be guideline cases). In addition to the cases cited in *Brown*, other recent examples of sentencing exercises for motor manslaughter include *Pimm* [1994] RTR 391, *Ripley* [1997] 1 Cr App R (S) 19 and *A-G's Ref (No. 64 of 2001)* [2002] 1 Cr App R (S) 409.

Causing Death by Dangerous Driving

Road Traffic Act 1988, s. 1 **C3.7**

A person who causes the death of another person by driving a mechanically propelled vehicle dangerously on a road or other public place is guilty of an offence.

This offence is triable only on indictment.

Indictment **C3.8**

Statement of Offence

Causing death by dangerous driving, contrary to section 1 of the Road Traffic Act 1988.

Particulars of Offence

D, on the . . . day of . . ., drove a mechanically propelled vehicle dangerously on a road [or public place], namely . . ., and thereby caused the death of V.

Elements The RTA 1988, s. 38, and the RTOA 1988, s. 11, are applicable; see C2.4 and C2.5. For the meaning of 'public place', see C1.15. **C3.9**

For the purposes of the RTA 1988, s. 1, the definition of 'driver' does not include a separate person acting as a steersman. One of the tests for dangerous driving must be satisfied, producing a causal link to the death.

Tests for Dangerous Driving Section 2A sets out to define what constitutes dangerous driving. **C3.10**

Road Traffic Act 1988, s. 2A

(1) For the purposes of sections 1 and 2 above a person is to be regarded as driving dangerously if (and, subject to subsection (2) below, only if)—
  (a) the way he drives falls far below what would be expected of a competent and careful driver, and
  (b) it would be obvious to a competent and careful driver that driving in that way would be dangerous.

(2) A person is also to be regarded as driving dangerously for the purposes of sections 1 and 2 above if it would be obvious to a competent and careful driver that driving the vehicle in its current state would be dangerous.

(3) In subsections (1) and (2) above 'dangerous' refers to danger either of injury to any person or of serious damage to property; and in determining for the purposes of those subsections what would be expected of, or obvious to, a competent and careful driver in a particular case, regard shall be had not only to the circumstances of which he could be expected to be aware but also to any circumstances shown to have been within the knowledge of the accused.

(4) In determining for the purposes of subsection (2) above the state of a vehicle, regard may be had to anything attached to or carried on or in it and to the manner in which it is attached or carried.

Section 2A relies on an objective test. Danger refers to the danger of injury to a person or serious damage to property. *Mens rea* plays no part in the offence. In *Loukes* [1996] 1 Cr App R 444, the Court of Appeal decided that (at p. 450):

> Proof of guilt depends on an objective standard of driving, namely, what would have been obvious to a competent and careful driver. The accused driver's state of mind is relevant only if and to the extent that it attributes additional knowledge to the notional competent and careful driver . . . It should be noted too that the threshold of proof is high. It must be shown that the defect was 'obvious' to a 'competent and careful driver'. It is not enough to show in the case of such a driver that, say, if he had examined the vehicle by going underneath it, he would have seen the defect.

See also *Collins* [1997] RTR 439 and *A-G's Ref (No. 4 of 2000)* [2001] RTR 415.

The standard of driving must fall 'far below' that expected of a 'competent and careful' driver and it must be obvious to a 'competent and careful' driver that the manner of driving is dangerous. The prosecution must demonstrate both elements before s. 2A(1) is satisfied (*Aitken v Lees* 1993 JC 228; see also *Brooks* [2001] EWCA Crim 1944). When directing a jury, the judge must avoid watering down the requirement for the driving to fall 'far below' the standard expected so that it confuses the test with that for careless driving (*Jeshani* [2005] EWCA Crim 146). The introduction of the concept of a careful driver as an objective observer places the question of what constitutes dangerous driving within the province of the tribunal of fact. Speed alone is not sufficient to found a conviction for dangerous driving (*DPP v Milton* [2006] RTR 264). Driving at excessive speeds may constitute the offence depending on the context and all the circumstances (e.g., *Trippick v Orr* 1995 SLT 272 and *McQueen v Buchanan* 1997 SLT 765). In such cases, as it is a matter of fact and degree for the tribunal to determine, it is important to make or elicit specific findings on these issues. When determining what was expected of the competent and careful driver in the situation in which the defendant was driving, the RTA 1988, s. 2A(3) permits favourable circumstances that were known to the accused and are capable of objective proof to be taken into account and is not confined only to circumstances unfavourable to him (*Milton v CPS* [2007] EWHC 532 (Admin), where the magistrates' court had incorrectly ignored the fact that the defendant was a Grade 1 advanced police driver). The provisions of the Highway Code, whilst certainly not conclusive, may still merit careful consideration as guidance as to the standards to be attributed to a careful and competent driver (*Taylor* [2004] EWCA Crim 213).

The Prosecution Team's document 'Driving Offences, incorporating the charging standard' gives the following examples of driving that may support an allegation of dangerous driving: racing or competitive driving; speed, which is highly inappropriate for the prevailing road or traffic conditions; aggressive driving, such as sudden lane changes, cutting into a line of vehicles or driving much too close to the vehicle in front; disregard of traffic lights and other road signs, which, on an objective analysis, would appear to be deliberate, or disregard of warnings from fellow passengers; overtaking that could not have been carried out safely; driving a vehicle with a load that presents a danger to other road users; where the driver is suffering from impaired ability such as having an arm or leg in plaster, or impaired eyesight; driving when too tired to stay awake; driving with actual knowledge of a dangerous defect on a vehicle; using a mobile phone whether as a phone or to compose or read text messages. In addition, by reference to the guidance in *Cooksley* [2003] 3 All ER 40, further factors might be callous behaviour at the time, e.g., throwing a victim off the vehicle or failing to stop, or causing death (and presumably serious injury) in the course of an escape or an attempt to avoid detection. These are indicative only and not conclusive as to the type of behaviour which might constitute dangerous driving.

C3.11 **Dangerous State of Driver** The fact that a driver was adversely affected by alcohol is a circumstance relevant to the issue of dangerous driving, but it is not in itself determinative to prove the offence (*Webster* [2006] 2 Cr App R 103). In *Woodward* [1995] 1 WLR 375, the Court of Appeal distinguished the line of cases which had developed in relation to reckless driving and re-affirmed the earlier principle from *McBride* [1962] 2 QB 167 (a five-judge Court of Appeal), where Ashworth J stated (at p. 172):

> . . . if a driver is adversely affected by drink, this fact is a circumstance relevant to the issue whether he was driving dangerously. Evidence to this effect is of probative value and is admissible in law. In the application of this principle two further points should be noticed. In the first place, the mere fact that the driver has had drink is not of itself relevant: in order to render evidence as to the drink taken by the driver admissible, such evidence must tend to show that the amount of drink taken was such as would adversely affect a driver or, alternatively, that the driver was in fact adversely affected. Secondly, there remains in the court an overriding discretion to exclude such evidence if in the opinion of the court its prejudicial effect outweighs its probative value.

The provisions of the RTOA 1988, s. 15 (see **C5.29**), are applicable only to the alcohol-related offences specified therein. Accordingly, where only a single specimen has been taken from which to assess the level of the defendant's alcohol consumption, such evidence is still admissible on the issue of whether the defendant drove dangerously (*Ash* [1999] RTR 347).

In *Marison* [1997] RTR 457, driving in a dangerously defective state owing to diabetes was considered no different to driving in a dangerously defective state owing to alcohol, constituting circumstances of which the defendant could be expected to be aware and of which he had knowledge, within the meaning of the RTA 1988, s. 2A(3).

Dangerous State of Vehicle The offence may also be committed if the state of a vehicle, including any attachment or load and the way in which it is attached or carried, would make driving it dangerous in the eyes of a 'competent and careful' driver. In relation to the dangerous state of the vehicle being 'obvious', no special definition is required when directing the jury; however it would not be a misdirection to indicate that it can arise from an inspection which is something between a fleeting glance and a long look (*Marsh* [2002] EWCA Crim 137). It could be argued that some loads and vehicles (e.g., certain tractor units and their attachments or a go-kart (*Carstairs v Hamilton* 1997 SCCR 311)) are inherently dangerous. See also *Crossman* (1986) 82 Cr App R 333. However, where the vehicle benefits from specific authorisation from the Secretary of State for use on public roads, there must usually be evidence that the vehicle has been manoeuvred in such a way as to create a danger beyond that otherwise inherent in its use on a road, because 'current state' implies something different from the vehicle's original or manufactured state (*Marchant* [2004] 1 WLR 440). **C3.12**

Where the mere act of taking an inherently dangerous vehicle on the road amounts to dangerous driving, it potentially falls within the RTA 1988, s. 2A(2) and also s. 2A(1)(a) and (b). To that extent s. 2A(2) is superfluous, but it underlines the point that driving a vehicle in a dangerous condition may well constitute an offence under s. 1 or s. 2 (depending on the consequences of the dangerous driving) as well as under the construction and use regulations (see also *Spurge* [1961] 2 QB 205 and *Robert Millar Contractors Ltd* [1970] 2 QB 54). The danger presented by the current state of the vehicle must, however, be capable of being seen or realised at first glance, in the sense of being 'evident to' the competent and careful driver, before it can be regarded as 'obvious'; it should not be discoverable only by taking some additional steps to ascertain the vehicle's defective state (*Strong* [1995] Crim LR 428). Moreover, where the driver is an employee driving the employer's vehicle, it will be important to consider the instructions given to him about checking the vehicle's condition. Unless those instructions appear inadequate, the driver cannot be expected to do more than comply with them (*Roberts* [1997] RTR 462); such compliance satisfies the 'competent and careful driver' test.

Causal Link to Fatality The prosecution need to establish that death resulted from the accused's dangerous driving. It should be noted that danger to the person is not qualified by any adjective and therefore, as long as it is not *de minimis*, any danger to any person, even though slight, if obvious to the 'competent and careful' driver, would suffice. In *Hennigan* [1971] 3 All ER 133, a case of causing death by reckless driving under the RTA 1960, the recklessness consisted mainly of the speed at which the defendant was driving; the driver of **C3.13**

the other car, which contained the two persons who were killed, may well have been substantially to blame for the accident. The court held that there was nothing in the legislation which required the manner of the accused's driving to be a substantial or major cause of the accident, as long as it was 'a cause and something more than *de minimis*'. Similarly, it was said in *Skelton* [1995] Crim LR 635 that no particular degree of contribution to the death, beyond a negligible one, is required. An acceptable direction to the jury is that they do not have to be sure that the defendant's driving 'was the principal, or a substantial, cause of the death, as long as [they] are sure that it was a cause and that there was something more than a slight or a trifling link' (*Kimsey* [1996] Crim LR 35).

C3.14 **Defences** Automatism, mechanical defect, and duress. See **C1.4**, **C1.11** and **A3.21** to **A3.29**. See also *Renouf* [1986] 1 WLR 522 at **C3.35**. No offence is committed under s. 1 where the driving was in a public place other than a road in the course of an authorised motoring event (RTA 1988, s. 13A).

C3.15 **Alternative Verdicts** The RTOA 1988, s. 24, provides alternative verdicts of dangerous driving and careless, and inconsiderate, driving under the RTA 1988, ss. 2 and 3 (see **C2.12**). See also *Fairbanks* [1986] 1 WLR 1202 (discussed at **D18.60**) and *Jeavons* [1990] RTR 263. Section 24 operates without prejudice to the Criminal Law Act 1967, s. 6(3). Accordingly, no separate count for such an offence is required. Indeed, as careless driving has not been specified under the CJA 1988, s. 40, a separate count for that offence would be invalid, thereby rendering ineffective a guilty plea entered in respect of it (*Davis* (19 April 1996 unreported)). By the RTOA 1988, s. 2, a failure to warn a suspect of an intended prosecution or to serve such a warning notice does not act as a bar to conviction of the alternative offences.

C3.16 **Punishment** For offences committed on or after 27 February 2004, the previous maximum of 10 years' imprisonment and/or a fine has been increased to 14 years' imprisonment and/or a fine (CJA 2003, s. 285). Obligatory disqualification for two years and endorsement, unless the court finds 'special reasons' (RTOA 1988, s. 34(4) and sch. 2). The offence carries between 3 and 11 penalty points and mandatory retesting by way of an extended driving test (see **C7.13**). Forfeiture of the motor vehicle used for the purpose of the crime may be ordered (see **C7.28** and **E20.1**).

C3.17 **Sentencing** In *Cooksley* [2003] 3 All ER 40, the Court of Appeal took the opportunity to issue fresh sentencing guidelines, which were of immediate effect, replacing the guidelines in *Boswell* [1984] 1 WLR 1047 and the refinements thereof made over the past decade and discussed in previous editions. It did so with general acceptance of the advice of the Sentencing Advisory Panel published in February 2003. The guidelines are designed to assist sentencers to strike an appropriate balance between the level of culpability of the offender and the magnitude of harm resulting from the offence, with the former being the primary consideration. The court stressed that, because of the need for deterrence and the gravity of the offence, 'no matter what the mitigating circumstances, normally only a custodial sentence will be imposed'.

The court adopted the Panel's list of aggravating and mitigating factors, emphasising that the list should not be regarded as exhaustive (at [15]):

AGGRAVATING FACTORS

. . . *Highly culpable standard of driving at time of offence*

(a) the consumption of drugs (including legal medication known to cause drowsiness) or of alcohol, ranging from a couple of drinks to a 'motorised pub crawl'
(b) greatly excessive speed; racing; competitive driving against another vehicle; 'showing off'
(c) disregard of warnings from fellow passengers
(d) a prolonged, persistent and deliberate course of very bad driving
(e) aggressive driving (such as driving much too close to the vehicle in front, persistent inappropriate attempts to overtake, or cutting in after overtaking)

(f) driving while the driver's attention is avoidably distracted, e.g. by reading or by use of a mobile phone (especially if hand-held)
(g) driving when knowingly suffering from a medical condition which significantly impairs the offender's driving skills
(h) driving when knowingly deprived of adequate sleep or rest
(i) driving a poorly maintained or dangerously loaded vehicle, especially where this has been motivated by commercial concerns

Driving habitually below acceptable standard

(j) other offences committed at the same time, such as driving without ever having held a licence; driving while disqualified; driving without insurance; driving while a learner without supervision; taking a vehicle without consent; driving a stolen vehicle
(k) previous convictions for motoring offences, particularly offences which involve bad driving or the consumption of excessive alcohol before driving

Outcome of offence

(l) more than one person killed as a result of the offence (especially if the offender knowingly put more than one person at risk or the occurrence of multiple deaths was foreseeable)
(m) serious injury to one or more victims, in addition to the death(s)

Irresponsible behaviour at time of offence

(n) behaviour at the time of the offence, such as failing to stop, falsely claiming that one of the victims was responsible for the crash, or trying to throw the victim off the bonnet of the car by swerving in order to escape
(o) causing death in the course of dangerous driving in an attempt to avoid detection or apprehension
(p) offence committed while the offender was on bail.

MITIGATING FACTORS

. . . (a) a good driving record;
(b) the absence of previous convictions;
(c) a timely plea of guilty;
(d) genuine shock or remorse (which may be greater if the victim is either a close relation or a friend);
(e) the offender's age (but only in cases where lack of driving experience has contributed to the commission of the offence), and
(f) the fact that the offender has also been seriously injured as a result of the accident caused by the dangerous driving.

The court expressly approved a number of specific examples of sentencing exercises undertaken by judges and referred to in the Panel's advice. In relation to using mobile phones when driving, the analysis in *Browning* [2002] 1 Cr App R (S) 377, where a sentence of five years' imprisonment was upheld, was regarded as appropriate. Falling asleep at the wheel is clearly an aggravating factor (*A-G's Ref (No. 26 of 1999)* [2000] 1 Cr App R (S) 394), because the prudent driver stops and takes a break before reaching that state of tiredness. Multiple deaths is also an aggravating feature (*France* [2003] 1 Cr App R (S) 108), although it remains necessary to regard the defendant's overall culpability in relation to the driving, rather than the consequences, as the dominant component of the sentencing exercise. However, the defendant's own injuries can be a mitigating factor (*Mallone* [1996] 1 Cr App R (S) 221), but only really where they are very serious and make the defendant's life quite different from what it was before the incident. Care should also be taken when having regard to the views of the family of a victim in accordance with the *Consolidated Criminal Practice Direction*, para. III.28, *Personal statements of victims.*

Bands of Culpability In relation to the appropriate length of sentence, in *Cooksley* [2003] 3 All ER 40 the court identified four bands of culpability, starting with when there are *no aggravating circumstances* (at [21] and [22]). In *Richardson* [2007] 2 All ER 601, following the increase in the maximum term of imprisonment, the court confirmed these bands but adjusted the suggested range of sentence because 'if the level of sentence in cases of the utmost **C3.18**

gravity is significantly increased (as it should be) there should be some corresponding increase in sentences immediately below this level of gravity, continuing down the scale to cases where there are no aggravating features at all' (at [13]). Even at this low level, for an adult offender an immediate custodial sentence will generally be necessary. The starting point has become a custodial sentence of 12 months to two years, although a reduction for a guilty plea should be available. In order to avoid a custodial sentence, there have to be exceptional mitigating features (e.g., *Jenkins* [2001] 2 Cr App R (S) 265).

Cooksley described an offence of *intermediate culpability* as:

> An offence involving a momentary dangerous error of judgment or a short period of bad driving may be aggravated by a habitually unacceptable standard of driving on the part of the offender (factors (j) or (k) listed above), by the death of more than one victim or serious injury to other victims (factors (l) and (m) . . .) or by the offender's irresponsible behaviour at the time of the offence (factors (n) to (p) . . .).

In such a case, the starting point should be two to four and a half years' imprisonment, although, in *Cooksley*, it was suggested that the presence of more than one of the factors listed might justify as much as five years, which post-*Richardson* may now mean higher than five years.

An offence of *higher culpability* was described as when 'the standard of driving is more highly dangerous', as would be indicated, for example, by the presence of one or two of factors (a) to (i) from the list of aggravating factors. Although the 'exact level of sentence would be determined by the dangerousness of the driving and the presence or absence of other aggravating or mitigating factors' (*Cooksley*), the starting point for such an offence is now put at four and a half to seven years' imprisonment.

Finally, for offences of the *most serious culpability*, which 'might be indicated by the presence of three or more of the aggravating factors (a) to (i) ('although an exceptionally bad example of a single aggravating feature could be sufficient to place an offence in this category'), the starting point is now seven years' imprisonment. A sentence of close to, or at, the maximum period of imprisonment 'would be appropriate in a case displaying a large number of these features, or where there were other aggravating factors' (e.g., *Noble* [2003] 1 Cr App R (S) 312).

As regards the appropriate period of disqualification, *Richardson* did not address this aspect and in *Cooksley* the court adopted the advice of the Panel (at [42]):

> . . . matters relevant to fixing the length of the driving disqualification for the offence of causing death by dangerous driving will be much the same as those appearing in the list of aggravating factors for the offence itself. Shorter bans of two years or so will be appropriate where the offender had a good driving record before the offence and where the offence resulted from a momentary error of judgment. Longer bans, between 3 and 5 years, will be appropriate where, having regard to the circumstances of the offence and the offender's record, it is clear that the offender tends to disregard the rules of the road, or to drive carelessly or inappropriately. Bans between 5 and 10 years may be used where the offence itself, and the offender's record, show that he represents a real and continuing danger to other road users. Disqualification for life is a highly exceptional course, but may be appropriate in a case where the danger represented by the offender is an extreme and indefinite one.

These comprehensive guidelines are of general application. They will continue to form the basis of every sentencing exercise and subsequent cases will inevitably be no more than examples of their application.

Causing Death by Careless Driving when under the Influence of Drink or Drugs

C3.19 **Road Traffic Act 1988, s. 3A**

> (1) If a person causes the death of another person by driving a mechanically propelled vehicle on a road or other public place without due care and attention, or without reasonable consideration for other persons using the road or place, and—

(a) he is, at the time when he is driving, unfit to drive through drink or drugs, or
(b) he has consumed so much alcohol that the proportion of it in his breath, blood or urine at that time exceeds the prescribed limit, or
(c) he is, within 18 hours after that time, required to provide a specimen in pursuance of section 7 of this Act, but without reasonable excuse fails to provide it,

he is guilty of an offence.

(2) For the purposes of this section a person shall be taken to be unfit to drive at any time when his ability to drive properly is impaired.

(3) Subsection (1)(b) and (c) above shall not apply in relation to a person driving a mechanically propelled vehicle other than a motor vehicle.

This offence is triable only on indictment.

When the Road Safety Act 2006, s. 31(2) and (3), is brought into force, a new s. 3A(1)(d) will be inserted adding the requirements for an offence under s. 7A(6) (failing without reasonable excuse to give permission for a laboratory test of a specimen taken: see **C5.7**) and making a consequential amendment to s. 3A(3).

Indictment **C3.20**

Statement of Offence

Causing death by careless driving when under the influence of drink or drugs, contrary to s. 3A(1) of the Road Traffic Act 1988.

Particulars of Offence

D, on the . . . day of . . ., caused the death of V by driving a motor [or mechanically propelled] vehicle on a road [or public place], namely . . ., without due care and attention and after having consumed so much alcohol that the proportion of it in his breath [or blood or urine] at the time exceeded the prescribed limit [or when unfit to drive through drink or drugs].

Elements For the meaning of 'careless' and 'without reasonable consideration', see **C6.3** and **C6.4**. When the Road Safety Act 2006, s. 30, is brought into force, the statutory definitions will apply to a s. 3A offence (see **C6.5**). For the meaning of 'public place', see **C1.15**. **C3.21**

The RTA 1988, s. 38, and the RTOA 1988, s. 11, are applicable; see **C2.4** and **C2.5**.

The offence can be committed in six separate ways. The prosecution need to establish either that the accused was driving without due care and attention or without reasonable consideration for other persons using the road, that the death of another person was caused by the manner of his driving and that at the time he came within s. 3A(1)(a) or (b), or that within 18 hours he was required to provide a specimen of breath, blood or urine and failed without reasonable excuse to provide it. The prosecution would therefore have to prove careless driving, the requisite causal link and the related 'drink driving' offence in exactly the same way as if both offences had been charged (see **C6.1** ***et seq.*** and **C5.23** and **C5.37 and C5.7**). The offence does not require any causal connection between the alcohol or drugs and the death (*Shepherd* [1994] 1 WLR 530).

In applying the appropriate test to determine whether a defendant has driven without due care and attention, the jury is entitled to look at all the circumstances of the case, including evidence that the defendant had been affected by alcohol or had taken such an amount of alcohol as would be likely to affect a driver (*Millington* [1996] RTR 80). Thus, the principle stated in *McBride* [1962] 2 QB 167 (see **C3.11**) in relation to causing death by dangerous driving applies equally to the offence in s. 3A(1).

In practice it is submitted that it will be rare to charge this offence in the form of driving without reasonable consideration. It may be that the actions of a driver, for instance, pulling out suddenly and causing another driver to swerve and collide with a person who then dies, could be interpreted as driving without reasonable consideration, but it would also encompass an offence of driving without due care and would normally be charged as such.

Evidence of impairment would normally be provided by a doctor who examines the accused, but evidence may also be provided by non-expert witnesses. It may take the form of a description of the actions of the accused, including the manner of driving, as long as the witness does not express an opinion as to the condition of the accused.

If the offence relates to s. 3A(1)(c), the request to provide a specimen must be made within 18 hours, presumably from the time of driving rather than the time of death.

Section 3A(1)(b) and (c) apply only where the driving is of a 'motor vehicle', but the offence under s. 3A(1)(a) may be committed whilst driving any 'mechanically propelled vehicle'.

C3.22 **Defences** Duress and mechanical defect. See **A3.21** to **A3.29** and **C1.11**. Automatism may be a defence (see **C1.4**), but in practice will be very difficult to establish given the nature of this offence and the possibility of interpreting such a situation as arising from self-induced intoxication. See also **C5.34**.

C3.23 **Alternative Verdicts** The RTOA 1988, s. 24, provides alternative verdicts under the RTA 1988, ss. 3, 4(1), 5(1)(a) and 7(6). When the Road Safety Act 2006, s. 31(4), is commenced, an alternative verdict under the RTA 1988, s. 7A(6) will be added. It would therefore seem that, if someone is accused of an offence based on s. 3A(1)(c), he could theoretically be convicted, for example, of driving whilst unfit even though the indictment contains an allegation that he refused to provide a specimen.

C3.24 **Punishment** For offences committed on or after 27 February 2004, the previous maximum of 10 years' imprisonment and/or a fine has been increased to 14 years' imprisonment and/or a fine (CJA 2003, s. 285). In the absence of 'special reasons', obligatory disqualification for not less than two years and endorsement with between 3 and 11 penalty points. Retesting by way of an extended driving test is mandatory (see **C7.13**). Forfeiture of the motor vehicle used for the purpose of the crime may be ordered (see **C7.28** and **E20.1**).

C3.25 **Sentencing** The sentencing guidelines contained in *Cooksley* [2003] 3 All ER 40, as modified in *Richardson* [2007] 2 All ER 601 (see **C3.17** and **C3.18**) are of equal application to this offence as to causing death by dangerous driving, albeit that the driving may not exhibit the aggravating factors set out in (a) to (i), and the principal or sole aggravating factor may well be the amount of alcohol consumed (*Cooksley* at [34]). In *Richardson* (at [23]), the court noted that 'however excellent the character of the offender, and genuine his remorse, for all effective purposes, a custodial sentence is inevitable'.

Causing Death by Careless, or Inconsiderate, Driving

C3.26 **Road Traffic Act 1988, s. 2B**

> A person who causes the death of another person by driving a mechanically propelled vehicle on a road or other public place without due care and attention, or without reasonable consideration for other persons using the road or place, is guilty of an offence.

This is a new offence that has been prospectively inserted into the RTA 1988 by the Road Safety Act 2006, s. 20. It is a response to concerns about the apparent inadequacy of sentencing powers available to courts where a person's driving has led to fatal consequences but the standard of the driving cannot be shown to amount to dangerous driving and alcohol is not involved (i.e. offences under the RTA 1988, s. 1 or s. 3A), in which case a conviction under the RTA 1988, s. 3 usually follows, for which only a fine can be imposed, coupled, most likely, with disqualification (see **C6.10**). Under s. 2B an offender will be punished not only for the culpability of his poor standard of driving but also for its outcome.

It will have effect only in relation to driving occurring after the coming into force of s. 20 (see s. 61(4) of the 2006 Act). The offence will be triable either way.

Indictment C3.27

Statement of Offence

Causing death by careless [or inconsiderate] driving, contrary to s. 2B of the Road Traffic Act 1988.

Particulars of Offence

D, on the . . . day of . . ., drove a mechanically propelled vehicle on a road [or public place], namely . . ., without due care and attention [or reasonable consideration for other persons using the road [or place]], and thereby caused the death of V.

Elements The offence will require proof of an underlying offence under the RTA 1988, s. 3 (see **C6.1** ***et seq.***), together with a causal link to a fatality (see **C3.13**). C3.28

The RTA 1988, s. 38, and the RTOA 1988, ss. 1, 11 and 12(1), are applicable; see **C2.1**, **C2.4**, **C2.5** and **C2.6**.

Alternative Verdicts The RTOA 1988, s. 24, will provide an alternative verdict under the RTA 1988, s. 3 (see **C2.12**). As for other offences, where the defendant has already been acquitted of the s. 3 charge (by the prosecution offering no evidence), the alternative verdict is no longer available and that should be made clear to the arbiters of fact (*DPP v Khan* [1997] RTR 82). C3.29

Punishment On indictment, five years' imprisonment and/or a fine. On summary trial, 12 months' imprisonment and/or the statutory maximum. Disqualification is obligatory. The offence carries obligatory endorsement with between 3 and 11 penalty points. C3.30

Sentence Given the maximum term available, sentences of imprisonment appear inevitable in circumstances where falling below the standard expected of a competent and careful driver is more likely to lead to disastrous consequences. For example, it is suggested that a court could be more severe with someone driving carelessly through a crowded street rather than out in the country. In *Richardson* [2007] 2 All ER 601 (at [29]), it was suggested that, in order to ensure a fair and balanced sentencing process, it will be important to understand and acknowledge the differences between dangerous and careless driving, because of the comparative ease with which a mistake can lead to the latter offence even amongst experienced drivers who are normally careful. See also **C6.10**. C3.31

Dangerous Driving

Road Traffic Act 1988, s. 2 C3.32

A person who drives a mechanically propelled vehicle dangerously on a road or other public place is guilty of an offence.

This offence is triable either way. In the absence of an election by the defendant, the *Consolidated Criminal Practice Direction*, para. V.51.17 (see **appendix** 7) indicates that such cases should be dealt with summarily unless one or more of the following factors is present, namely (a) alcohol or drugs contributing to the dangerousness, (b) grossly excessive speed, (c) racing, (d) a prolonged course of dangerous driving, (e) other related offences, or (f) significant injury or damage sustained *and* that the court's sentencing powers, taking into account the power to commit for sentence (see **D22.18** ***et seq.***), are insufficient.

Indictment C3.33

Statement of Offence

Dangerous driving, contrary to section 2 of the Road Traffic Act 1988.

Particulars of Offence

D, on the . . . day of . . ., drove a mechanically propelled vehicle dangerously on a road [or public place], namely . . .

Elements For the meaning of 'dangerous' and 'dangerous driving', see **C3.10** ***et seq.*** For the meaning of 'public place', see **C1.15**. C3.34

The RTA 1988, s. 38, and the RTOA 1988, ss. 1, 11 and 12(1), are applicable; see **C2.1**, **C2.4**, **C2.5** and **C2.6**.

Where the evidence permits, charging aggravated vehicle-taking as well as dangerous driving does not result in double jeopardy nor in itself does it amount to an abuse of process (*Harding* [1995] Crim LR 733). However, where the defendant has previously been convicted of another offence arising out of the same incident, e.g., an excess alcohol offence, then pursuing a separate charge of dangerous driving subsequently is wrong; the prosecution must choose its course of action from the outset or no later than before the conclusion of the first set of proceedings (*Phipps* [2005] EWCA Crim 33).

C3.35 **Defences** Automatism, mechanical defect and duress. See **C1.4**, **C1.11** and **A3.21** to **A3.29**. No offence is committed under this section where the driving took place in a public place other than a road in the course of an authorised motoring event (RTA 1988, s. 13A).

In *Renouf* [1986] 1 WLR 522, the appellant pursued a Volvo containing persons who had thrown a barrage of objects which struck the appellant, occasioning actual bodily harm, and damaged the windscreen of his car. The appellant caught up with the Volvo and edged it off the road and on to the grass verge. The only risk caused was that of damage to the Volvo and, in response to a charge of reckless driving, the defence submitted that, in creating that risk, the appellant was using only such force as was reasonable to assist in the lawful arrest of the offenders in accordance with the Criminal Law Act 1967, s. 3(1). The trial judge directed that s. 3(1) of the 1967 Act was incapable of affording a defence to reckless driving. The Court of Appeal, however, held that the jury might, on the unusual evidence in the case, have accepted such a defence, which should therefore have been left to them. If this, albeit unusual, defence could extend to offences of reckless driving, it is submitted that it could also, in appropriate circumstances, be extended to excuse or provide a defence to a charge of dangerous driving, causing death by dangerous driving or manslaughter.

C3.36 **Alternative Verdicts** The RTOA 1988, s. 24, provides an alternative verdict under the RTA 1988, s. 3 (see **C2.12**). Where the defendant has already been acquitted of the s. 3 charge (by the prosecution offering no evidence), the alternative verdict is no longer available and that should be made clear to the arbiters of fact (*DPP v Khan* [1997] RTR 82).

C3.37 **Punishment** On indictment, two years' imprisonment and/or a fine. On summary trial, six months' imprisonment and/or the statutory maximum. Disqualification is obligatory. The offence carries obligatory endorsement with between 3 and 11 penalty points. Retesting by way of an extended driving test is mandatory (see **C7.13**). Forfeiture of the vehicle used may also be ordered (see **C7.28** and **E20.1**).

C3.38 **Sentencing** A plea of guilty will not always attract a discount from the statutory maximum sentence. In *Hastings* [1995] 1 Cr App R (S) 167, the Court of Appeal upheld a sentence of two years' imprisonment, commenting that the appellant had had no realistic option but to plead guilty. The appellant, who had never held a driving licence, drove at 70–90 mph in the early hours of the morning in a densely populated 30 mph area, with the vehicle's lights switched off, caused another moving vehicle to take evasive action, travelled on the wrong side of the road, went through red lights, collided with a moving vehicle and ended up on the pavement. He had also consumed excessive alcohol. *King* [2000] 1 Cr App R (S) 105 offers a different view but *Scarley* [2001] 1 Cr App R (S) 86 adopts the *Hastings* approach.

In *Moore* (1995) 16 Cr App R (S) 536, the Court of Appeal upheld a sentence of nine months' imprisonment, following a guilty plea, referring to the old guidelines in *Boswell* [1984] 1 WLR 1047. The appellant had driven a heavy goods vehicle on a main road in patchy thick fog. On approaching road works, he had been unable to stop in time and collided with a stationary van, injuring the driver and damaging the vehicle. The aggravating features were the speed in those conditions, the nature of vehicle being driven and the appellant's failure to observe the roadside. The period of disqualification, however, was reduced from five years to three. In *Templeton* [1996] 1 Cr App R (S) 380, the defendant drove for nearly four minutes at speeds of up to 70 mph in a built up area, travelling about three miles and crossing seven red lights. Nine months' imprisonment and disqualification for two years was upheld. In *Joseph* [2002] 1 Cr App R (S) 74, dangerous driving resulting in personal injury to a traffic warden attracted a deterrent sentence of ten months' imprisonment and disqualification for two years. See also *Nicholls* [1998] 2 Cr App R (S) 296; *Hicks* [1999] 1 Cr App R (S) 228; *Burman* [2000] 2 Cr App R (S) 3 and *Smith* [2002] 2 Cr App R (S) 103. In *Fitzpatrick* [2003] All ER (D) 120 (Apr), the trial judge was criticised for wrongly taking into account that the driving had resulted in a fatality where this was not the defendant's fault or even part of the prosecution case against him.

In *Kennion* [1997] RTR 421, the Court of Appeal commented that 'where otherwise perfectly respectable people of impeccable character lose control when sitting behind the wheel of a motor car because they imagine in some way that they have been provoked', i.e. road rage, they 'can expect immediate custodial sentences'. Even in such cases, general principles about the appropriate period of disqualification apply (see **C8.6**) and should not be so long as to impair the prospects of rehabilitation (*Chivers* [2005] EWCA Crim 2252, where the disqualification was reduced from five years to 18 months).

Causing Death by Driving: Unlicensed, Disqualified or Uninsured Drivers

Road Traffic Act 1988, s. 3ZB **C3.39**

A person is guilty of an offence under this section if he causes the death of another person by driving a motor vehicle on a road and, at the time when he is driving, the circumstances are such that he is committing an offence under—

(a) section 87(1) of this Act (driving otherwise than in accordance with a licence),
(b) section 103(1)(b) of this Act (driving while disqualified), or
(c) section 143 of this Act (using motor vehicle while uninsured or unsecured against third party risks).

This is a new offence that has been prospectively inserted into the RTA 1988 by the Road Safety Act 2006, s. 21. What it will mean is that, where a fatality results from driving that is not even careless driving (see **C6.1** ***et seq.*** and also the new offence under the RTA 1988, s. 2B: **C3.26**), the fact that the driver should not even have been on the road at the time, whether because he does not hold the requisite driving licence, was disqualified from driving by a court order or did not have the necessary insurance cover to be using the vehicle, that basic offence will be converted into the more serious offence under this provision.

It will have effect only in relation to driving occurring after the coming into force of s. 21 (see s. 61(4) of the 2006 Act). The offence will be triable either way.

Elements The offence will require proof of one of the underlying offences under the RTA 1988 (see **C6.33**, **C3.52** or **C6.36**), together with a causal link to a fatality (see **C3.13**). **C3.40**

The RTOA 1988, ss. 11 and 12(1), are applicable; see **C2.5** and **C2.6**.

Punishment On indictment, two years' imprisonment and/or a fine. On summary trial, 12 months' imprisonment and/or the statutory maximum. Disqualification is obligatory. The offence carries obligatory endorsement with between 3 and 11 penalty points. **C3.41**

Sentence Given the maximum term available, sentences of imprisonment are more likely where the underlying offence is one of the more serious ones. Matters that offer reasonable mitigation for the underlying offence may also provide appropriate mitigation for this aggravated offence. The location at which the fatality is caused may be relevant, e.g., it is suggested that a court could be more severe with someone driving through a crowded street rather than out in the country. **C3.42**

Wanton or Furious Driving

C3.43 **Offences Against the Person Act 1861, s. 35**

Whosoever, having the charge of any carriage or vehicle, shall by wanton or furious driving or racing, or other wilful misconduct, or by wilful neglect, do or cause to be done any bodily harm to any person whatsoever, shall be guilty of an offence . . .

This offence is triable only on indictment.

C3.44 **Indictment**

Statement of Offence

Causing bodily harm, contrary to section 35 of the Offences Against the Person Act 1861.

Particulars of Offence

D, on the . . . day of . . ., having the charge of a taxi cab [or carriage etc.], by wanton [or furious] driving [or racing etc.] caused bodily harm to V.

C3.45 **Elements** The RTA 1988, s. 38, is applicable if the offence is committed on a 'road'. See **C1.14** and **C2.4**.

The offence can be committed whether or not the conduct takes place on a road (*Cooke* [1971] Crim LR 44; *Knight* [2004] EWCA Crim 2998). It also covers any kind of vehicle or carriage, including bicycles (*Parker* (1895) 59 JP 793).

The definition of 'driving' in this context is generally thought to be the older definition, which would include bicycles and even box carts, although such 'vehicles' or 'carriages' would often be propelled manually or by means of pedals and could rarely be said to be 'driven' in the modern sense of that term. 'Wanton' has no technical meaning, and may be construed in the light of its ordinary dictionary definition of irresponsible, capricious, unrestrained or random. In *Knight*, the Court of Appeal accepted as correct the trial judge's direction on the meaning of 'wanton' as effectively recklessness, involving the defendant in 'driving in such a manner as to create an obvious and serious risk of causing physical harm to some other person who might happen to be using the road, or doing substantial damage to property' and 'that in driving in that manner [the defendant] did so without having given any thought to the possibility of there being any such risk, or having recognised that there was some risk involved, had nonetheless gone on to take it'.

C3.46 **Alternative Verdicts** Assault occasioning actual bodily harm, contrary to the OAPA 1861, s. 47. Common assault, contrary to the CJA 1988, s. 39, but only if specifically included as a separate count on the indictment (*Mearns* [1991] QB 82).

C3.47 **Punishment** The offence carries two years' imprisonment and/or a fine. The offence is not endorsable but disqualification may be ordered under the PCC(S)A 2000, s. 147 (see **C8.7**, and for the detail see **E23.10**), if an assault is involved and the accused was driving a motor vehicle. However, when the Road Safety Act 2006, s. 28, is brought into force, if the offence is committed in respect of a mechanically propelled vehicle, endorsement will become obligatory. Further, the offence will carry between 3 and 9 penalty points and disqualification will be discretionary. Forfeiture of the vehicle used for the purposes of the crime may be ordered (see **C7.28** and **E20.1**).

Causing Danger to Road-users

C3.48 **Road Traffic Act 1988, s. 22A**

(1) A person is guilty of an offence if he intentionally and without lawful authority or reasonable cause—

(a) causes anything to be on or over a road, or

(b) interferes with a motor vehicle, trailer or cycle, or

(c) interferes (directly or indirectly) with traffic equipment,

in such circumstances that it would be obvious to a reasonable person that to do so would be dangerous.

(2) In subsection (1) above 'dangerous' refers to danger either of injury to any person while on or near a road, or of serious damage to property on or near a road; and in determining for the purposes of that subsection what would be obvious to a reasonable person in a particular case, regard shall be had not only to the circumstances of which he could be expected to be aware but also to any circumstances shown to have been within the knowledge of the accused.

(3) In subsection (1) above 'traffic equipment' means—
 (a) anything lawfully placed on or near a road by a highway authority;
 (b) a traffic sign lawfully placed on or near a road by a person other than a highway authority;
 (c) any fence, barrier or light lawfully placed on or near a road—
  (i) in pursuance of section 174 of the Highways Act 1980, or section 65 of the New Roads and Street Works Act 1991 (which provide for guarding, lighting and signing in streets where works are undertaken), or
  (ii) by a constable or a person acting under the instructions (whether general or specific) of a chief officer of police.

(4) For the purposes of subsection (3) above anything placed on or near a road shall unless the contrary is proved be deemed to have been lawfully placed there.

(5) In this section 'road' does not include a footpath or bridleway.

This offence is triable either way.

Indictment C3.49

Statement of Offence

Causing danger to road users, contrary to section 22A(1) of the Road Traffic Act 1988.

Particulars of Offence

D, on the . . . day of . . ., intentionally and without lawful authority or reasonable cause interfered with a motor vehicle [or trailer, cycle or traffic equipment], namely . . ., [or caused . . . to be on [or over] a road, namely . . .,] in such circumstances that to do so was dangerous.

Elements The prosecution must establish that the accused intentionally performed the act. As to the burden of proof in relation to a defence of acting with lawful authority or reasonable cause, see **F3.9** ***et seq.*** C3.50

The danger which arises must be of serious damage to property or of injury to any person while on or near a road. The test is an objective one but the danger must exist and must be obvious to a reasonable person. In other words there has to be a serious likelihood that injury or serious damage may be the result of the actions of the accused. In *DPP v D* [2006] RTR 461, where a large road sign had been placed on the carriageway by the defendant and another without authorisation, the Divisional Court held that the proper test is not what would be obvious to a reasonable and prudent driver but rather whether a reasonable bystander, whether a motorist or not and being fully aware that not all drivers do drive carefully and well, would consider the act in question to represent an obvious danger. It is not necessary for injury or damage to result and it seems that any injury, however slight and as long as it could be termed an injury, would qualify. The extent of the potential damage or injury must, of course, have relevance to any sentence.

Punishment On indictment, seven years' imprisonment and/or a fine. On summary trial, six months' imprisonment and/or the statutory maximum fine. The offence is not endorsable. C3.51

Driving while Disqualified

Road Traffic Act 1988, s. 103 C3.52

(1) A person is guilty of an offence if, while disqualified for holding or obtaining a licence, he—
 (a) obtains a licence, or
 (b) drives a motor vehicle on a road.

(2) A licence obtained by a person who is disqualified is of no effect (or, where the disqualification relates only to vehicles of a particular class, is of no effect in relation to vehicles of that class).

(3) [Repealed.]
(4) Subsection (1) above does not apply in relation to disqualification by virtue of section 101 of this Act.
(5) Subsection (1)(b) above does not apply in relation to disqualification by virtue of section 102 of this Act.
(6) In the application of subsection (1) above to a person whose disqualification is limited to the driving of motor vehicles of a particular class by virtue of—
(a) section 102, 117 or 117A of this Act, or
(b) subsection (9) of section 36 of the Road Traffic Offenders Act 1988 (disqualification until test is passed),
the references to disqualification for holding or obtaining a licence and driving motor vehicles are references to disqualification for holding or obtaining a licence to drive and driving motor vehicles of that class.

C3.53 Indictment

Statement of Offence

Driving while disqualified, contrary to section 103(1) of the Road Traffic Act 1988.

Particulars of Offence

D, on the . . . day of . . ., drove a motor vehicle on a road, namely . . ., while disqualified for holding or obtaining a driving licence.

A count charging a person with this offence may be included in an indictment in the circumstances specified in the CJA 1988, s. 40 (see **D11.15**). Sections 6, 11, and 12(1) of the RTOA 1988 apply (see **C2.2**, **C2.5**, and **C2.6**).

C3.54 Elements In the absence of duress, the RTA 1988, s. 103(1)(b), creates an absolute offence. It is usual to produce either the register of the magistrates' court where the defendant was disqualified, or a properly certified extract. These are admissible as evidence of the proceedings of the court by virtue of the CrimPR, r. 6.4. If the conviction was in the Crown Court (or, indeed, the magistrates' court), it may be proved under the PACE 1984, s. 73, by the production of a certificate signed by the clerk of the court. (As to the proof of convictions generally, see **F11.1** *et seq.*) Other authorised methods of proving the conviction are equally admissible, but it is not necessary to prove that the defendant knew of the disqualification (*Taylor v Kenyon* [1952] 2 All ER 726).

In *Derwentside Justices, ex parte Heaviside* [1996] RTR 384, the Divisional Court held that strict proof linking the defendant to the person named in the certificate of conviction is required. In doing so, it identified three methods by which this requirement could be satisfied: an admission under the CJA 1967, s. 10; comparison of fingerprints; or evidence from a person who was present in court when the disqualification was imposed. The fear that this list was exhaustive has been allayed by subsequent decisions of the Divisional Court (*Derwentside Justices, ex parte Swift* [1997] RTR 89; *DPP v Mansfield* [1997] RTR 96; *DPP v Mooney* [1997] RTR 434). Consequently, whilst strict proof is necessary (and failure by the prosecution to adduce any such evidence cannot be cured by information provided by the clerk to the court from computerised court records (*Kingsnorth v DPP* [2003] EWHC 768 (Admin)) the prosecution can rely on any admissible evidence from which it could properly be concluded that the defendant and the individual named in the certificate are one and the same person, and the issue is one for the court to determine on the basis of the evidence placed before it. For example, admissions in an interview with the police provide sufficient evidence (*Moran v CPS* (2000) 164 JP 562). Where the defendant has an unusual name, proof that it is identical to that of a person previously disqualified raises a prima facie case that the defendant is that disqualified person (*Olakunori v DPP* [1998] COD 443), especially if he has also lied about his identity. Even where the personal details of the defendant are not uncommon, a match with those recorded on the certificate of conviction establishes a prima facie case which, in the absence of any contradictory evidence, will be sufficient for the court to convict (*Pattison v DPP* [2006] 2 All ER 317).

If a defendant drives on a 'road', his mistaken belief that it was not a road is incapable of amounting to a defence (*Miller* [1975] 1 WLR 1222).

In *Thames Magistrates' Court, ex parte Levy* (1997) *The Times*, 17 July 1997, it was confirmed that the offence of driving while disqualified can be committed during a period of disqualification which is not suspended pending an appeal (see RTOA 1988, s. 39 and **C7.15**), even where the conviction which led to the disqualification is subsequently quashed. Similarly, the offence can be committed in the period between disqualification following conviction and the swearing of a statutory declaration under the MCA 1980, s. 14, as the earlier proceedings become void from the time of the declaration and not *ab initio* (*Singh v DPP* [1999] RTR 424).

Where a person has been disqualified until he passes a test, under the RTOA 1988, s. 36, a failure to comply with the conditions of a provisional driving licence is an offence under s. 103(1)(b). This would seem to be the case whether or not the defendant has actually obtained such a licence (*Scott v Jelf* [1974] RTR 256). In order to avoid conviction, the defendant bears the burden of showing that he holds a provisional licence and that he was complying with the conditions attached to it at the time of the driving in question (*DPP v Baker* (2004) 168 JP 617). For the purposes of s. 103, such disqualifications persist regardless of whether elements of the original sentence would enable the offence in respect of which disqualification was imposed to be regarded as spent (*Re Hamill* [2001] EWHC Admin 762).

Aiding and abetting the offence of driving while disqualified requires knowledge of the disqualification; this may be actual or constructive, in the sense that the defendant failed to make inquiries which a reasonable man should have made, or deliberately closed his eyes to the possibility of the driver being disqualified (*Pope v Minton* [1954] Crim LR 711; *Bateman v Evans* [1964] Crim LR 601).

The CJA 1988 made the offence summary only, but provides for certain circumstances where it may be included in an indictment and that thereafter it 'shall be tried in the same manner as if it were an indictable offence'. It is submitted that the offence is therefore no longer an 'indictable offence' within the meaning of the Criminal Attempts Act 1981 (see **A6.31**), and the offence of attempting to drive while disqualified has ceased to exist.

Defences Duress or necessity may provide a defence in the proper circumstances. See **C1.10**. **C3.55**

Punishment Six months' imprisonment and/or a fine up to level 5 on the standard scale. Disqualification is discretionary but endorsement is obligatory. The offence carries 6 penalty points. Forfeiture of the vehicle used may also be ordered (see **C7.28** and **E20.1**). In *Morris* (1988) 10 Cr App R (S) 216, where a defendant with five previous convictions for driving while disqualified had elected trial before pleading guilty, the Court of Appeal upheld the imposition of the maximum period of imprisonment of (at that time) one year. There is nothing wrong in principle in imposing a consecutive sentence to that imposed for another offence arising out of the same incident, e.g., aggravated vehicle-taking (*Forbes* [2005] EWCA Crim 2069). Given the nature of the offence, there is often a strong argument against imposing a long period of disqualification (*Mew* (24 January 1997 unreported)). The Magistrates' Courts Guidelines (2004) indicate that a community penalty should be considered. **C3.56**

Other Offences

Other indictable offences that may be related to driving include criminal damage (dealt with at **B8.1** *et seq.*) and taking a motor vehicle without authority (dealt with at **B4.91** *et seq.*) in both the simple and aggravated form. **C3.57**

Section C4 Offences Relating to Documents Triable on Indictment

Forgery, Alteration etc. of Documents etc.

C4.1 **Goods Vehicles (Licensing of Operators) Act 1995, s. 38**

(1) A person is guilty of an offence if, with intent to deceive, he—

(a) forges, alters or uses a document or other thing to which this section applies;
(b) lends to, or allows to be used by, any other person a document or other thing to which this section applies; or
(c) makes or has in his possession any document or other thing so closely resembling a document or other thing to which this section applies as to be calculated to deceive.

(2) This section applies to the following documents and other things, namely—

(a) any operator's licence;
(b) any document, plate, mark or other thing by which, in pursuance of regulations, a vehicle is to be identified as being authorised to be used, or as being used, under an operator's licence;
(c) any document evidencing the authorisation of any person for the purposes of sections 40 and 41;
(d) any certificate of qualification under section 49; and
(e) any certificate or diploma such as is mentioned in paragraph 13(1) of Schedule 3.

C4.2 **Indictment**

Statement of Offence

Forgery [or Use etc.] of a document [or licence etc.] with intent to deceive, contrary to section 38(1) of the Goods Vehicles (Licensing of Operators) Act 1995.

Particulars of Offence

D, on the . . . day of . . ., with intent to deceive, forged [or used etc.] a document [or licence etc.], namely . . .

Statement of Offence

Making [or Possessing] a document [or licence etc.] with intent to deceive, contrary to section 38(1) of the Goods Vehicles (Licensing of Operators) Act 1995.

Particulars of Offence

D, on the . . . day of . . ., with intent to deceive, made [or had in his possession] a document [or thing] so closely resembling an operator's licence [or document etc.] as to be calculated to deceive.

This offence is triable either way.

C4.3 **Elements** The RTOA 1988, s. 6 (see **C2.2**), applies by virtue of the Goods Vehicles (Licensing of Operators) Act 1995, s. 51.

For the meaning of 'intent to deceive' and 'calculated to deceive' see **B5.2 and B6.1**. As to forgery, see s. 38(4) of the 1995 Act and, generally, **B6.1** ***et seq.*** The term 'operator's licence' is defined in s. 2(1) of the 1995 Act and the vehicles authorised to be used under such a licence are set out in s. 5(1). Power to seize documents or articles is contained in s. 41.

Punishment The offence under s. 38 is punishable on summary conviction by a fine up to the statutory maximum, or on indictment by a term of imprisonment not exceeding two years and/or a fine (s. 38(3)). C4.4

Sentencing See *Raven* (1988) 10 Cr App R (S) 354 and C4.9. C4.5

False Records or Entries Relating to Drivers' Hours

Transport Act 1968, s. 99 C4.6

(5) Any person who makes, or causes to be made, any record or entry on a record sheet kept or carried for the purposes of the Community Recording Equipment Regulation or section 97 of this Act or any entry in a book, register or document kept or carried for the purposes of regulations under section 98 thereof or the applicable Community rules which he knows to be false or, with intent to deceive, alters or causes to be altered any such record or entry shall be liable—

(a) on summary conviction, to a fine not exceeding the prescribed sum;

(b) on conviction on indictment, to imprisonment for a term not exceeding two years.

Indictment C4.7

Statement of Offence

Making [or Causing] a false record [or entry] [to be made], contrary to section 99(5) of the Transport Act 1968.

Particulars of Offence

D, on the . . . day of . . ., made [or caused] a record [or entry on a record sheet etc.] kept [or carried] for the purposes of the Community Recording Equipment Regulation [or section 97 of the Transport Act 1968 etc.] [to be made], namely . . ., which he knew to be false.

This offence is triable either way.

Elements For 'intent to deceive', see **B5.2.** C4.8

The 'Community Recording Equipment Regulation' is Council Regulation (EEC) No. 3821/85 of 20 December 1985 on recording equipment in road transport, as it has effect in accordance with other EC Regulations mentioned in reg. 2(1) of the Passenger and Goods Vehicles (Community Recording Equipment Regulation) Regulations 2006 (SI 2006 No. 3276) and as read with the Community Drivers' Hours and Recording Equipment (Exemptions and Supplementary Provisions) Regulations 1986 (SI 1986 No. 1456). The principal Regulation, being directly applicable, requires that drivers of passenger and goods vehicles (see the Transport Act 1968, s. 95(2)) be subject to the 'tachograph' provisions which govern the keeping of records in relation to the hours of work of drivers and their mates whilst on national or international journeys (see, for example, *Skills Motor Coaches Ltd v Vehicle Inspectorate* [2001] All ER (EC) 289). It is given statutory effect by ss. 97, 97A and 97B of the Act, the Passenger and Goods Vehicles (Recording Equipment) Regulations 1979 (SI 1979 No. 1746) and the Community Drivers' Hours and Recording Equipment Regulations 1986 (SI 1986 No. 1457). Regulations made under s. 98 are the Drivers' Hours (Goods Vehicles) (Keeping of Records) Regulations 1987 (SI 1987 No. 1421) which provide for the making of entries in the driver's record book according to the instructions contained therein. These regulations apply where the 'Community rules' do not (i.e. to certain domestic journeys) and impose obligations upon employers, where relevant, as well as drivers. In any proceedings under s. 99(5), it is necessary for the prosecution to establish that the record or book etc. is being 'carried for the purpose' of the relevant regulation or rule, and as certain vehicles are exempt, a thorough examination of the various provisions is essential. In *J. F. Alford Transport Ltd* [1997] 2 Cr App R 326, the Court of Appeal held that knowledge of and passive acquiescence in a principal's offence under s. 99(5) is insufficient to amount to aiding and abetting its commission, but indicated that such knowledge and an ability to control the action of an offender coupled with a deliberate decision to refrain from doing so might suffice.

C4.9 **Sentencing** In *Raven* (1988) 10 Cr App R (S) 354, a sentence of nine months' imprisonment was upheld in a case where the appellant had pleaded guilty to six counts of making a false entry on a driver's record sheet and one of using a document with intent to deceive under the RTA 1960, s. 233 (which s. 38 of the 1995 Act replaced). The appellant was involved in the running of a haulage business, a number of whose vehicles had their tachograph wiring interfered with. He had entered into an agreement with another man to operate using that man's operator's licence and discs. Two drivers said that they were instructed by the appellant, from time to time, to drive with the tachograph switched off. He had been convicted in 1985 and fined for six offences of failing to secure the return of record sheets and one offence of permitting a driver to exceed his permitted hours. In *Potter* [1999] 2 Cr App R (S) 448, the Court of Appeal substituted three months' imprisonment for the nine months imposed and concluded that where the defendant is not in a managerial position and had not therefore corrupted others, a lower sentence may be justified. However, in *Saunders* [2001] 2 Cr App R (S) 301, eight months' imprisonment was upheld in spite of the defendants not occupying managerial positions because of the number of offences and the lengthy period over which they were committed.

The judge who sentenced stressed the importance of safety provisions, the unfairness of competition to 'fair traders', the level of sophistication shown, the public danger which must have arisen, and the fraudulent nature of the appellant's activities. His remarks were quoted and approved by the Court of Appeal.

Forgery, Alteration etc. of Licences, Marks, Trade Plates etc.

C4.10 **Vehicle Excise and Registration Act 1994, ss. 44 and 45**

44.—(1) A person is guilty of an offence if he forges, fraudulently alters, fraudulently uses, fraudulently lends or fraudulently allows to be used by another person anything to which subsection (2) applies.

(2) This subsection applies to—
(a) a vehicle licence,
(b) a trade licence,
(c) a document in the form of a licence which is issued in pursuance of regulations under this Act in respect of a vehicle which is an exempt vehicle under paragraph 19 of schedule 2,
(d) a registration mark,
(e) a registration document, and
(f) a trade plate (including a replacement trade plate).

45.—(1) A person who in connection with—
(a) an application for a vehicle licence or a trade licence,
(b) a claim for a rebate under section 20, or
(c) an application for an allocation of registration marks,

makes a declaration which to his knowledge is either false or in any material respect misleading is guilty of an offence.

(2) A person who makes a declaration which—
(a) is required by regulations under this Act to be made in respect of a vehicle which is an exempt vehicle under paragraph 19 of schedule 2, and
(b) to his knowledge is either false or in any material respect misleading, is guilty of an offence.

(3) A person who—
(a) is required by this Act to furnish particulars relating to, or to the keeper of, a vehicle, and
(b) furnishes particulars which to his knowledge are either false or in any material respect misleading,

is guilty of an offence.

Indictment

Statement of Offence C4.11

Forgery [or Fraudulent use etc.] of a vehicle licence [or trade licence etc.], contrary to section 44(1) of the Vehicle Excise and Registration Act 1994.

Particulars of Offence

D, on the . . . day of . . ., forged [or fraudulently used etc.] a vehicle licence [or trade licence etc.], namely . . .

Statement of Offence

Making a false or misleading declaration, contrary to section 45(1) of the Vehicle Excise and Registration Act 1994.

Particulars of Offence

D, on the . . . day of . . ., in connection with an application for a vehicle licence [or trade licence etc.] knowingly made a declaration, which he knew to be false or in a material respect misleading, namely . . .

Procedure and Evidence The admissibility of records maintained by the Secretary of State is governed by the Vehicle Excise and Registration Act 1994, s. 52. C4.12

Elements Section 53 of the Vehicle Excise and Registration Act 1994 provides that for certain specified matters, relevant to declarations which may be prosecuted under s. 45, the burden of proof shall lie on the defendant. C4.13

For the purposes of s. 44, 'fraudulently' means dishonestly deceiving a police officer or other person responsible for a public duty. There is no requirement to prove an intention to cause any economic loss (*Terry* [1984] AC 374). In *Johnson* [1995] RTR 15, it was held that an offence under the Vehicles (Excise) Act 1971, s. 26 (which s. 44 of the 1994 Act replaced), relating to fraudulent use of a licence could be committed only where there was evidence that the vehicle was being or had been used on a public road while displaying the offending licence.

Forgery does not necessarily connote an intention to defraud but may be taken to include an intention to deceive for the purposes of the Vehicle Excise and Registration Act 1994 (*Clifford v Bloom* [1977] RTR 351; *Clayton* (1980) 72 Cr App R 135).

In *Macrae* (1995) 159 JP 359, the offence of forging a licence was said to involve the defendant making a false licence, with the intent that he or another should use it to induce a third party to accept it as genuine and by reason of so accepting it to do or not to do some act to his own or another's prejudice as a result of such acceptance of the false licence as genuine in connection with the performance of any duty, i.e. akin to the ulterior intent found in the Forgery and Counterfeiting Act 1981, see **B6.32** ***et seq***.

Section 44 applies to any application for a licence in respect of a duty exempt vehicle.

Punishment On indictment, the maximum sentence for an offence under the Vehicle Excise and Registration Act 1994, s. 44 or 45, is two years' imprisonment and/or a fine; on summary conviction, a fine not exceeding the statutory maximum. C4.14

Forgery of Documents etc.: Road Traffic Act 1988, s. 173

Road Traffic Act 1988, s. 173 C4.15

(1) A person who, with intent to deceive—
(a) forges, alters or uses a document or other thing to which this section applies, or
(b) lends to, or allows to be used by, any other person a document or other thing to which this section applies, or
(c) makes or has in his possession any document or other thing so closely resembling a document or other thing to which this section applies as to be calculated to deceive,
is guilty of an offence.

Part C Road Traffic Offences

(2) This section applies to the following documents and other things—
 (a) any licence under any part of this Act or, in the case of a licence to drive, any counterpart of such a licence,
 (aa) any counterpart of a Northern Ireland licence or Community licence,
 (b) any test certificate, goods vehicle test certificate, plating certificate, certificate of conformity or Minister's approval certificate (within the meaning of part II of this Act),
 (c) any certificate required as a condition of any exception prescribed under section 14 of this Act,
 (cc) any seal required by regulations made under section 41 of this Act with respect to speed limiters,
 (d) any plate containing particulars required to be marked on a vehicle by regulations under section 41 of this Act or containing other particulars required to be marked on a goods vehicle by sections 54 to 58 of this Act or regulations under those sections,
 (dd) any document evidencing the appointment of an examiner under section 66A of this Act,
 (e) any records required to be kept by virtue of section 74 of this Act,
 (f) any document which, in pursuance of section 89(3) of this Act, is issued as evidence of the result of a test of competence to drive,
 (ff) any certificate provided for by regulations under section 97(3A) of this Act relating to the completion of a training course for motor cyclists,
 (g) any certificate under section 133A or any badge or certificate prescribed by regulations made by virtue of section 135 of this Act,
 (h) any certificate of insurance or certificate of security under part VI of this Act,
 (j) any document produced as evidence of insurance in pursuance of Regulation 6 of the Motor Vehicles (Compulsory Insurance) (No. 2) Regulations 1973 (SI 1973 No. 2143),
 (k) any document issued under regulations made by the Secretary of State in pursuance of his power under section 165(2)(a) of this Act to prescribe evidence which may be produced in lieu of a certificate of insurance or a certificate of security,
 (l) any international road haulage permit, and
 (m) a certificate of the kind referred to in section 34B(1) of the Road Traffic Offenders Act 1988.

(3) In the application of this section to England and Wales 'forges' means makes a false document or other thing in order that it may be used as genuine.

(4) In this section 'counterpart', 'Community licence' and 'Northern Ireland licence' have the same meanings as in part III of this Act.

When the Road Safety Act 2006, s. 37(8), is brought into force, a new s. 173(2)(n) will be inserted so as to include 'any document produced as evidence of the passing of an appropriate driving test' (as defined in the RTOA 1988, s. 36) within s. 173.

C4.16 **Indictment** The forms provided in **C4.2** may be adapted for use in relation to offences under this section.

C4.17 **Elements** 'Use' extends to use by an employer, see **C1.7**.

Particular words must be read 'against the mischief which that particular section seeks to avoid or prevent'; the production of a driving licence unconnected with any driving on the road is not 'using' it for the purposes of the RTA 1988, s. 173 (*Howe* [1982] RTR 45).

A document which has been completed by someone other than the proper person does not cease to be a document to which the section applies for the purposes of 'using' (*Pilditch* [1981] RTR 303).

A forged document which is not specified within the section, but which closely resembles a document specified within the section, is not 'used' but may fall within paragraph (c) of s. 173(1) (*Holloway v Brown* [1978] RTR 537).

Where an 'intent to deceive' has been established, it is not necessary for the prosecution to prove that the defendant knew the documents were false; if that was the case, the statute would include the word 'knowingly'. Such an intent may be shown by evidence that 'they were irregular documents either by way of irregular acquisition or by the irregular disposing of them' (*Greenberg* [1942] 2 All ER 344, per Birkett J at p. 347). The court in *Greenberg* also stated that it is unnecessary to allege or prove an intent to deceive any particular person. Knowledge that the documents are false may, however, be relevant to the issue of whether the defendant had an 'intent to deceive'.

In *Cleghorn* [1938] 3 All ER 398, a certificate of insurance which had been cancelled was held to be properly described as one resembling a certificate of insurance. Similarly, in *Aworinde* [1996] RTR 66, bogus blank insurance certificates were held to be documents so closely resembling certificates as to be calculated to deceive.

'Calculated to deceive' means 'likely to deceive' (*Davison* [1972] 3 All ER 1121; *Turner v Shearer* [1972] 1 WLR 1387; *Anon.* (1918) 82 JP 447).

Punishment On conviction on indictment, the maximum sentence is two years' imprisonment and/or a fine; on summary conviction, a fine not exceeding the statutory maximum. C4.18

False Statements etc.: Road Traffic Act 1988, s.174

Road Traffic Act 1988, s.174 C4.19

(1) A person who knowingly makes a false statement for the purpose—
- (a) of obtaining the grant of a licence under any part of this Act to himself or any other person, or
- (b) of preventing the grant of any such licence, or
- (c) of procuring the imposition of a condition or limitation in relation to any such licence, or
- (d) of securing the entry or retention of the name of any person in the register of approved instructors maintained under part V of this Act, or
- (dd) of obtaining the grant to any person of a certificate under section 133A of this Act, or
- (e) of obtaining the grant of an international road haulage permit to himself or any other person,

is guilty of an offence.

(2) A person who, in supplying information or producing documents for the purposes either of sections 53 to 60 and 63 of this Act or of regulations made under sections 49 to 51, 61, 62 and 66(3) of this Act—
- (a) makes a statement which he knows to be false in a material particular or recklessly makes a statement which is false in a material particular, or
- (b) produces, provides, sends or otherwise makes use of a document which he knows to be false in a material particular or recklessly produces, provides, sends or otherwise makes use of a document which is false in a material particular,

is guilty of an offence.

(3) A person who—
- (a) knowingly produces false evidence for the purposes of regulations under section 66(1) of this Act, or
- (b) knowingly makes a false statement in a declaration required to be made by the regulations,

is guilty of an offence.

(4) A person who—
- (a) wilfully makes a false entry in any record required to be made or kept by regulations under section 74 of this Act, or
- (b) with intent to deceive, makes use of any such entry which he knows to be false,

is guilty of an offence.

(5) A person who makes a false statement or withholds any material information for the purpose of obtaining the issue—
- (a) of a certificate of insurance or certificate of security under part VI of this Act, or
- (b) of any document issued under regulations made by the Secretary of State in pursuance of his power under section 165(2)(a) of this Act to prescribe evidence which may be produced in lieu of a certificate of insurance or a certificate of security,

is guilty of an offence.

C

Part C Road Traffic Offences

C4.20 **Indictment** The second form set out at **C4.11** may generally be adapted to cover the many different offences created by this section.

C4.21 **Elements** There is no requirement that the making of the false statement results in any gain or advantage accruing to the defendant (*Jones v Meatyard* [1939] 1 All ER 140) or, presumably, to a third person.

The offence in s. 174(5) of making a false statement for the purpose of obtaining the issue of an insurance certificate is an absolute one. However, in *Cummerson* [1968] 2 QB 534, it was indicated that the other offence created by the provision of withholding material information for that purpose may well require proof that the act was done consciously. In *Power v Provincial Insurance plc* [1998] RTR 60, the Court of Appeal decided that a motorist correctly regarded his conviction for driving whilst unfit as being 'spent' by reference to the rehabilitation period applying to the fine imposed and not the period of effectiveness of the endorsement on the driving licence relating to a period of disqualification. This meant that he had been entitled to answer negatively the question whether he had been convicted of an offence for which an order of endorsement had been made, which in turn meant that he had not made a false statement under s.174(5).

C4.22 **Punishment** For offences committed on or after 29 January 2004, on conviction on indictment, the maximum sentence is two years' imprisonment and/or a fine; on summary conviction, six months' imprisonment and/or a fine not exceeding the statutory maximum (CJA 2003, s. 286). For 'older' offences, which are triable summarily only, the maximum sentence is a fine not exceeding level 4 on the standard scale.

Section C5 Drink-Driving Offences

PRELIMINARY TESTING

Road Traffic Act 1988, ss. 6, 6A, 6B, 6C, 6D and 6E **C5.1**

6.—(1) If any of subsections (2) to (5) applies a constable may require a person to co-operate with any one or more preliminary tests administered to the person by that constable or another constable.

(2) This subsection applies if a constable reasonably suspects that the person—
(a) is driving, is attempting to drive or is in charge of a motor vehicle on a road or other public place, and
(b) has alcohol or a drug in his body or is under the influence of a drug.

(3) This subsection applies if a constable reasonably suspects that the person—
(a) has been driving, attempting to drive or in charge of a motor vehicle on a road or other public place while having alcohol or a drug in his body or while unfit to drive because of a drug, and
(b) still has alcohol or a drug in his body or is still under the influence of a drug.

(4) This subsection applies if a constable reasonably suspects that the person—
(a) is or has been driving, attempting to drive or in charge of a motor vehicle on a road or other public place, and
(b) has committed a traffic offence while the vehicle was in motion.

(5) This subsection applies if—
(a) an accident occurs owing to the presence of a motor vehicle on a road or other public place, and
(b) a constable reasonably believes that the person was driving, attempting to drive or in charge of the vehicle at the time of the accident.

(6) A person commits an offence if without reasonable excuse he fails to co-operate with a preliminary test in pursuance of a requirement imposed under this section.

(7) A constable may administer a preliminary test by virtue of any of subsections (2) to (4) only if he is in uniform.

(8) In this section—
(a) a reference to a preliminary test is to any of the tests described in sections 6A to 6C, and
(b) 'traffic offence' means an offence under—
(i) a provision of part II of the Public Passenger Vehicles Act 1981,
(ii) a provision of the Road Traffic Regulation Act 1984,
(iii) a provision of the Road Traffic Offenders Act 1988 other than a provision of part III, or
(iv) a provision of this Act other than a provision of part V.

6A.—(1) A preliminary breath test is a procedure whereby the person to whom the test is administered provides a specimen of breath to be used for the purpose of obtaining, by means of a device of a type approved by the Secretary of State, an indication whether the proportion of alcohol in the person's breath or blood is likely to exceed the prescribed limit.

(2) A preliminary breath test administered in reliance on section 6(2) to (4) may be administered only at or near the place where the requirement to co-operate with the test is imposed.

(3) A preliminary breath test administered in reliance on section 6(5) may be administered—
(a) at or near the place where the requirement to co-operate with the test is imposed, or
(b) if the constable who imposes the requirement thinks it expedient, at a police station specified by him.

6B.—(1) A preliminary impairment test is a procedure whereby the constable administering the test—
(a) observes the person to whom the test is administered in his performance of tasks specified by the constable, and
(b) makes such other observations of the person's physical state as the constable thinks expedient.
(2) The Secretary of State shall issue (and may from time to time revise) a code of practice about—
(a) the kind of task that may be specified for the purpose of a preliminary impairment test,
(b) the kind of observation of physical state that may be made in the course of a preliminary impairment test,
(c) the manner in which a preliminary impairment test should be administered, and
(d) the inferences that may be drawn from observations made in the course of a preliminary impairment test.
(3) In issuing or revising the code of practice the Secretary of State shall aim to ensure that a preliminary impairment test is designed to indicate—
(a) whether a person in unfit to drive, and
(b) if he is, whether or not his unfitness is likely to be due to drink or drugs.
(4) A preliminary impairment test may be administered—
(a) at or near the place where the requirement to co-operate with the test is imposed, or
(b) if the constable who imposes the requirement thinks it expedient, at a police station specified by him.
(5) A constable administering a preliminary impairment test shall have regard to the code of practice under this section.
(6) A constable may administer a preliminary impairment test only if he is approved for that purpose by the chief officer of the police force to which he belongs.
(7) A code of practice under this section may include provision about—
(a) the giving of approval under subsection (6), and
(b) in particular, the kind of training that a constable should have undergone, or the kind of qualification that a constable should possess, before being approved under that subsection.

6C.—(1) A preliminary drug test is a procedure by which a specimen of sweat or saliva is—
(a) obtained, and
(b) used for the purpose of obtaining, by means of a device of a type approved by the Secretary of State, an indication whether the person to whom the test is administered has a drug in his body.
(2) A preliminary drug test may be administered—
(a) at or near the place where the requirement to co-operate with the test is imposed, or
(b) if the constable who imposes the requirement thinks it expedient, at a police station specified by him.

6D.—(1) A constable may arrest a person without warrant if as a result of a preliminary breath test the constable reasonably suspects that the proportion of alcohol in the person's breath or blood exceeds the prescribed limit.
(1A) The fact that specimens of breath have been provided under section 7 of this Act by the person concerned does not prevent subsection (1) above having effect if the constable who imposed on him the requirement to provide the specimens has reasonable cause to believe that the device used to analyse the specimens has not produced a reliable indication of the proportion of alcohol in the breath of the person.
(2) A constable may arrest a person without warrant if—
(a) the person fails to co-operate with a preliminary test in pursuance of a requirement imposed under section 6, and
(b) the constable reasonably suspects that the person has alcohol or a drug in his body or is under the influence of a drug.
(2A) A person arrested under this section may, instead of being taken to a police station, be detained at or near the place where the preliminary test was, or would have been, administered, with a view to imposing on him there a requirement under section 7 of this Act.
(3) A person may not be arrested under this section while at a hospital as a patient.

6E.—(1) A constable may enter any place (using reasonable force if necessary) for the purpose of—

(a) imposing a requirement by virtue of section 6(5) following an accident in a case where the constable reasonably suspects that the accident involved injury of any person, or
(b) arresting a person under section 6D following an accident in a case where the constable reasonably suspects that the accident involved injury of any person.

(2) This section—
(a) does not extend to Scotland, and
(b) is without prejudice to any rule of law or enactment about the right of a constable in Scotland to enter any place.

Constables may now decide to administer preliminary breath, impairment or drug tests as may be appropriate. Accordingly, investigations into 'unfit' offences can properly commence at the earliest opportunity.

Making the Requirement

Circumstances in which Requirement can be Imposed A preliminary test may be required only when one of the situations specified in s. 6(2) to (5) is satisfied. Hospital patients are accorded added protection (see RTA 1988, s. 9, and C5.17). If reliance is placed on 'reasonable belief' following an accident, a higher standard than 'reasonable suspicion' can still be expected (see, e.g., *Johnson v Whitehouse* [1984] RTR 38), although 'belief' does not equate to 'knowledge' (*Bunyard v Hayes* [1985] RTR 348). **C5.2**

The power of the police to stop a vehicle is contained in the RTA 1988, s. 163. There is nothing to prevent random stopping, but the law requires one of the conditions in s. 6(2) to (5) to be complied with before a preliminary test is administered. In *Chief Constable of Gwent v Dash* [1986] RTR 41, police were stopping vehicles at random in order to apprehend drivers who might be suspected of having excess alcohol in their bodies. Macpherson J, giving the judgment of the Divisional Court, said (at p. 46, emphasis added):

> . . . there is no restriction upon the stopping of motorists by a policeman *in the execution of his duty* and the subsequent requirement for a breath test should the policeman then and there genuinely suspect the ingestion of alcohol. It may be said by some to be bad luck that such a situation arises but it is not unlawful provided the officer is in uniform and acts without oppression, or caprice, or some false pretence or proved 'malpractice'.

The court did, however, distinguish cases where a person is arrested in his own house in a situation similar to that in *Morris v Beardmore* [1981] AC 446. See *DPP v Godwin* [1991] RTR 303 and C5.31.

The necessary suspicion may result from information supplied by others and may arise after a motorist has ceased to drive, so long as it relates to the period when he was actually driving (s. 6(3) and (5) and see also *Moss v Jenkins* [1975] RTR 25 and *Blake v Pope* [1986] 1 WLR 1152). Evidence of what the officer has been told is admissible if it goes to his state of mind at the time that he required the specimen of breath. Whilst the absence of a ground under which to administer a preliminary test may invalidate an arrest under s. 6D, it should not invalidate the subsequent procedure unless the court exercises its discretion to exclude evidence under the PACE 1984, s. 78 (see *Griffiths v Willett* [1979] RTR 195) or as a result of human rights violations. In *DPP v Wilson* [1991] RTR 284, it was held that the power to exclude evidence could arise from *Fox* [1986] AC 281 or *Chief Constable of Gwent v Dash*, and co-existed with a wide discretion under s. 78, but there is no duty on the police to warn a driver of a potential offence and failure to do so may not be oppressive.

If the device used to administer a roadside breath test is of a type that could be used to obtain an evidential specimen (see C5.7), the justices must exercise care to ensure that they understand which type of test was being conducted and the consequences flowing therefrom. If the police evidence is that the device was not operating so as to give an accurate evidential reading and that goes unchallenged, or is preferred, the test is a s. 6 preliminary test (*DPP v Karamouzis* [2006] EWHC 2634 (Admin)). Where the test is a preliminary one, the prosecution are not obliged to disclose to the defence the results in figures from that roadside test (*Smith v DPP* [2007] EWHC 100 (Admin)); the test remains indicative only as to whether the constable should arrest the suspect with a view to securing an evidential specimen thereafter.

Where consumption of alcohol is suspected, the constable is likely to continue to require a roadside breath test. Where, however, the suspect appears unfit, the constable may, if he has been given approval by his chief officer in accordance with s. 6B(6), administer an impairment test in accordance with the code of practice issued by the Secretary of State, which is designed to ascertain whether the perceived unfitness to drive is due to drink or drugs. Alternatively, a decision to administer a preliminary drug test by means of an approved device and take a specimen of sweat or saliva might be taken. As s. 6(1) refers to 'any one or more preliminary tests', it is clear that they are not mutually exclusive and the constable could require co-operation with each of the tests in turn, if only to eliminate his suspicions as to both alcohol and drugs.

As regards requiring a preliminary breath test, failing to follow the manufacturer's instructions about allowing a 20-minute gap to elapse after the consumption of alcohol before commencing the test will render the roadside procedure unlawful so that no offence under s. 6(6) will be committed, but that does not of itself affect the lawfulness of the subsequent Intoximeter procedure (*DPP v Kay* [1999] RTR 109).

C5.3 **Other Conditions for Requirement** The constable making a requirement by virtue of any of s. 6(2) to (4) must be 'in uniform', i.e. he should be easily identifiable as a constable. The absence of a helmet (*Wallwork v Giles* [1970] RTR 117) or the wearing of a raincoat (*Taylor v Baldwin* [1976] RTR 265) did not affect the conclusion that the constable was still in uniform. Justices are also able to rely on their knowledge of how the local constabulary operates (*Cooper v Rowlands* [1971] RTR 291, in relation to a motor patrol officer; *Richards v West* [1980] RTR 215, in relation to special constables) and, in the absence of evidence to the contrary, they are entitled to infer or assume from the surrounding circumstances that a constable is in uniform (*Gage v Jones* [1983] RTR 508).

Under s. 6A(2), a preliminary breath test in a situation not involving an accident must be administered at or near the place where the requirement is made but, in relation to a person required to undertake a preliminary breath test as a result of an accident or a preliminary impairment or drug test, it may be administered either at or near the place where the requirement is made (usually the roadside) or at a police station (see, e.g., *Moore* [1994] RTR 360).

The requirement must be made using words of sufficient clarity, although there is no set formula for any particular words to be uttered. In relation to the old s. 6 offence, using 'I wish to give you a breath test' (*Clarke* [1969] 2 QB 91) or 'I intend to give you a breath test' (*O'Boyle* [1973] RTR 445) sufficed. Adapting such wording to cover the impairment or drug test, adding whatever further explanation is appropriate, should be adequate. As long as the words used are reasonably believed by the constable to be capable of, and were, being heard and understood, it is not necessary to prove they were actually both heard and understood (*Nicholls* [1972] 1 WLR 502). There is no need to produce physically a breath test device, provided that an opportunity to comply with the requirement is given (*DPP v Swan* [2004] EWHC 2432 (Admin)).

Failure to Co-operate with a Preliminary Test

C5.4 Section 6(6) creates a single offence of failing, without a reasonable excuse, to co-operate with a preliminary test when required to do so. The RTOA 1988, ss. 11 and 12(1), apply; see **C2.5** and **C2.6**. For the meaning of the terms 'accident', 'driving', 'attempting to drive', 'motor vehicle' and 'road or other public place', see **C1.1**, **C1.8**, **C1.3**, **C1.12**, **C1.14** and **C1.15**. For the meaning of 'in charge', see **C5.25**. The term 'fail' includes a refusal (RTA

1988, s. 11). Whether there is a failure is a question of fact and degree. If a person does not take advantage of the opportunity to take the test provided by the constable, there will in principle be a failure (*Ferguson* [1970] RTR 395).

Reasonable Excuse Once the defence have raised a 'reasonable excuse', it is for the prosecution to negative it (*Rowland v Thorpe* [1970] 3 All ER 195). A claim by the defendant that none of the pre-conditions for making the requirement existed does not constitute a reasonable excuse (*Downey* [1970] RTR 257). In *Chief Constable of Avon and Somerset Constabulary v Singh* [1988] RTR 107, it was held that a failure to provide a roadside breath test merely because the accused claimed that he had not been driving at the time did not constitute a reasonable excuse. His understanding of what was being required of him was held to be irrelevant, because he was putting forward a false story as to the driving of the vehicle. The court did accept that, in certain circumstances, a failure to understand the nature of the obligation might constitute a reasonable excuse, but added that before something could amount to an excuse 'it has to be causative in this sense, that it was the reason why the thing was not done'. This reasoning would seem to be equally valid in relation to the new impairment and drug preliminary tests. A medical condition, such as a chest complaint, may constitute a reasonable excuse for failing to co-operate, or where the person required to provide a specimen is 'physically or mentally unable to provide it or its provision would entail a substantial risk to health' (*Lennard* [1973] 1 WLR 483). See also C5.19 and C5.20. C5.5

Punishment The penalty is a fine up to level 3 on the standard scale. Disqualification is discretionary but, in the absence of 'special reasons', endorsement with 4 penalty points is obligatory. C5.6

EVIDENTIAL SPECIMENS

Road Traffic Act 1988, ss. 7 and 7A C5.7

7.—(1) In the course of an investigation into whether a person has committed an offence under section 3A, 4 or 5 of this Act a constable may, subject to the following provisions of this section and section 9 of this Act, require him—

(a) to provide two specimens of breath for analysis by means of a device of a type approved by the Secretary of State, or

(b) to provide a specimen of blood or urine for a laboratory test.

(2) A requirement under this section to provide specimens of breath can only be made—

(a) at a police station,

(b) at a hospital, or

(c) at or near a place where a relevant breath test has been administered to the person concerned or would have been so administered but for his failure to co-operate with it.

(2A) For the purposes of this section 'a relevant breath test' is a procedure involving the provision by the person concerned of a specimen of breath to be used for the purpose of obtaining an indication whether the proportion of alcohol in his breath or blood is likely to exceed the prescribed limit.

(2B) A requirement under this section to provide specimens of breath may not be made at or near a place mentioned in subsection (2)(c) above unless the constable making it—

(a) is in uniform, or

(b) has imposed a requirement on the person concerned to co-operate with the relevant breath test in circumstances in which section 6(5) of this Act applies.

(2C) Where a constable has imposed a requirement on the person concerned to co-operate with a relevant breath test at any place, he is entitled to remain at or near that place in order to impose on him there a requirement under this section.

(2D) If a requirement under subsection (1)(a) above has been made at a place other than at a police station, such a requirement may subsequently be made at a police station if (but only if)—

(a) a device or a reliable device of the type mentioned in subsection (1)(a) above was not available at that place or it was for any other reason not practicable to use such a device there, or

(b) the constable who made the previous requirement has reasonable cause to believe that the device used there has not produced a reliable indication of the proportion of alcohol in the breath of the person concerned.

(3) A requirement under this section to provide a specimen of blood or urine can only be made at a police station or at a hospital; and it cannot be made at a police station unless—

(a) the constable making the requirement has reasonable cause to believe that for medical reasons a specimen of breath cannot be provided or should not be required, or

(b) specimens of breath have not been provided elsewhere and at the time the requirement is made a device or a reliable device of the type mentioned in subsection (1)(a) above is not available at the police station or it is then for any other reason not practicable to use such a device there,

(bb) a device of the type mentioned in subsection (1)(a) above has been used (at the police station or elsewhere) but the constable who required the specimens of breath has reasonable cause to believe that the device has not produced a reliable indication of the proportion of alcohol in the breath of the person concerned,

(bc) as a result of the administration of a preliminary drug test, the constable making the requirement has reasonable cause to believe that the person required to provide a specimen of blood or urine has a drug in his body, or

(c) the suspected offence is one under section 3A or 4 of this Act and the constable making the requirement has been advised by a medical practitioner that the condition of the person required to provide the specimen might be due to some drug;

but may then be made notwithstanding that the person required to provide the specimen has already provided or been required to provide two specimens of breath.

(4) If the provision of a specimen other than a specimen of breath may be required in pursuance of this section the question whether it is to be a specimen of blood or a specimen of urine and, in the case of a specimen of blood, the question who is to be asked to take it shall be decided (subject to subsection (4A)) by the constable making the requirement.

(4A) Where a constable decides for the purposes of subsection (4) to require the provision of a specimen of blood, there shall be no requirement to provide such a specimen if—

(a) the medical practitioner who is asked to take the specimen is of the opinion that, for medical reasons, it cannot or should not be taken; or

(b) the registered health care professional who is asked to take it is of that opinion and there is no contrary opinion from a medical practitioner;

and, where by virtue of this subsection there can be no requirement to provide a specimen of blood, the constable may require a specimen of urine instead.

(5) A specimen of urine shall be provided within one hour of the requirement for its provision being made and after the provision of a previous specimen of urine.

(6) A person who, without reasonable excuse, fails to provide a specimen when required to do so in pursuance of this section is guilty of an offence.

(7) A constable must, on requiring any person to provide a specimen in pursuance of this section, warn him that a failure to provide it may render him liable to prosecution.

7A.—(1) A constable may make a request to a medical practitioner for him to take a specimen of blood from a person ('the person concerned') irrespective of whether that person consents if—

(a) that person is a person from whom the constable would (in the absence of any incapacity of that person and of any objection under section 9) be entitled under section 7 to require the provision of a specimen of blood for a laboratory test;

(b) it appears to that constable that that person has been involved in an accident that constitutes or is comprised in the matter that is under investigation or the circumstances of that matter;

(c) it appears to that constable that that person is or may be incapable (whether or not he has purported to do so) of giving a valid consent to the taking of a specimen of blood; and

(d) it appears to that constable that that person's incapacity is attributable to medical reasons.

(2) A request under this section—

(a) shall not be made to a medical practitioner who for the time being has any responsibility (apart from the request) for the clinical care of the person concerned; and

(b) shall not be made to a medical practitioner other than a police medical practitioner unless—

(i) it is not reasonably practicable for the request to be made to a police medical practitioner; or
(ii) it is not reasonably practicable for such a medical practitioner (assuming him to be willing to do so) to take the specimen.

(3) It shall be lawful for a medical practitioner to whom a request is made under this section, if he thinks fit—
(a) to take a specimen of blood from the person concerned irrespective of whether that person consents; and
(b) to provide the sample to a constable.

(4) If a specimen is taken in pursuance of a request under this section, the specimen shall not be subjected to a laboratory test unless the person from whom it was taken—
(a) has been informed that it was taken; and
(b) has been required by a constable to give his permission for a laboratory test of the specimen; and
(c) has given his permission.

(5) A constable must, on requiring a person to give his permission for the purposes of this section for a laboratory test of a specimen, warn that person that a failure to give the permission may render him liable to prosecution.

(6) A person who, without reasonable excuse, fails to give his permission for a laboratory test of a specimen of blood taken from him under this section is guilty of an offence.

(7) In this section 'police medical practitioner' means a medical practitioner who is engaged under any agreement to provide medical services for purposes connected with the activities of a police force.

Initial Procedural Requirements

The requirement to provide specimens must arise 'in the course of an investigation', which does not imply any greater formality than is normally involved in the plain and ordinary meaning of the word 'investigation' (*Graham v Albert* [1985] RTR 352). As with a preliminary test (see C5.2), the 'requirement' does not have to be in any formalised language, provided it amounts to a requirement and is made at a permitted location. A requirement made otherwise than by strictly following the guidance contained in a standard form covering the police station testing process is not automatically unlawful (*DPP v Coulter* [2005] EWHC 1533 (Admin)). The requirement can be made at or near the place where a roadside procedure was carried out, at a police station or, when appropriate, at a hospital (see C5.17). Having made the requirement at such a place, the RTA 1988, s. 7, is silent as to the actual taking of the specimen, which implies that it can be done elsewhere (*Pascoe v Nicholson* [1981] 1 WLR 1061; *Russell v Devine* [2003] 1 WLR 1187), when taken by a medical practitioner. Any challenge to the qualifications of the person who took the blood sample must be raised in a timely fashion and not left as a last-minute defence ambush in closing (*Whitfield v DPP* [2006] EWHC 1414 (Admin)). When the requirement is made at a hospital, there is no obligation to explain why a breath specimen cannot be required (*Jones v DPP* [2004] RTR 331). **C5.8**

In *Brown v Gallacher* [2003] RTR 239, the Scottish High Court of Justiciary dismissed an argument that the answers given and specimens provided under this statutory procedure should be disregarded because they infringe the privilege against self-incrimination protected by the ECHR, Article 6.

Where there is some doubt as to who was driving the motor vehicle at the relevant time, a constable may require all the persons suspected of driving to provide a specimen (*Pearson v Metropolitan Police Commissioner* [1988] RTR 276). Indeed, the defendant need not have been driving the motor vehicle on a road or other public place provided the requirement for a specimen is made in the course of an investigation and is made in good faith (*Hawes v DPP* [1993] RTR 116).

At a police station, where there has been a positive result from administering a preliminary drug test, the constable will move directly to requiring a specimen of blood or urine under s. 7(3)(bc), but where consumption of alcohol is suspected, the constable will first consider whether the person should be required to provide two specimens of breath. Unless one of the situations set out in s. 7(3) arises, the constable will proceed to make that requirement, which involves giving the statutory warning necessary under s. 7(7) (see **C5.15**). If the person provides two specimens of breath as required, the lower reading will dictate whether no further action is taken, an offer is made for the person to provide a replacement specimen of blood or urine (see **C5.9**) or a charge under the RTA 1988, s. 5(1), will be pursued (see **C5.23**). If the person fails to provide the specimens as required, the constable may proceed to require an alternative specimen of blood or urine (see **C5.9**) or a charge under the RTA 1988, s. 7(6), may be pursued (see **C5.18**). In order to make himself understood, the constable may repeat any requirement as many times as he feels is appropriate.

Replacement Specimens

C5.9 **Road Traffic Act 1988, s. 8**

(1) Subject to subsection (2) below, of any two specimens of breath provided by any person in pursuance of section 7 of this Act that with the lower proportion of alcohol in the breath shall be used and the other shall be disregarded.

(2) If the specimen with the lower proportion of alcohol contains no more than 50 microgrammes of alcohol in 100 millilitres of breath, the person who provided it may claim that it should be replaced by such specimen as may be required under section 7(4) of this Act and, if he then provides such a specimen, neither specimen of breath shall be used.

(2A) If the person who makes a claim under subsection (2) above was required to provide specimens of breath under section 7 of this Act at or near a place mentioned in subsection (2)(c) of that section, a constable may arrest him without warrant.

(3) The Secretary of State may by regulations substitute another proportion of alcohol in the breath for that specified in subsection (2) above.

If the lower of the two specimens of breath provided is 39 microgrammes in 100 millilitres or less, proceedings under the RTA 1988, s. 5(1), are not usually instituted. For readings of 50 microgrammes or less, the person providing the specimen must be offered the option of supplying another specimen, either of blood or urine, under the RTA 1988, s. 7(4). Failure to offer this statutory option when required is fatal (*Clywd Justices, ex parte Charles* (1990) 154 JP 486). There is however no requirement to give the warning in s. 7(7) when asking a person whether he wishes to give a replacement specimen (*Hayes v DPP* [1994] RTR 163). There is no obligation on the prosecution to prove that the device was operating accurately prior to the defendant being offered a replacement specimen (*Branagan v DPP* [2000] RTR 235; *Wright v DPP* [2005] EWHC 1211 (Admin)) because, if the device were thought to be unreliable, s. 7(3) provides the grounds for requiring blood or urine anyway (see **C5.12**). The driver is not entitled to legal advice before deciding whether to exercise the option (*DPP v Ward* [1999] RTR 11, following *DPP v Billington* [1988] RTR 231: see **C5.20**). When dealing with a juvenile, there is no requirement to delay the investigation so that an appropriate adult can be in attendance before proceeding to allow him to choose whether to provide a replacement specimen (*DPP v Evans* [2003] Crim LR 338). The option must be given fairly and properly so that the person concerned can make an informed choice about exercising it (*Baldwin v DPP* [1996] RTR 238) and the explanation must therefore be sufficiently detailed (*Turner v DPP* [1996] RTR 274n). However, in *Fraser v DPP* [1997] RTR 373, Lord Bingham CJ confirmed that, whilst there were plainly several things for the driver to be told at some stage in the procedure, it did not follow that he had to be told all of them at the very outset; it is the totality of the process that matters. Where a defendant is offered the option of a replacement specimen and refuses but then consents, the prosecution are still entitled to rely on the breath specimen because the statutory procedure ends when the defendant rejects the option (*Smith v DPP* [1989] RTR 159). Where justices found that an unrecorded conversation may have taken place between the police and the defendant, which may have had the effect of dissuading the defendant from exercising the right to provide a replacement specimen, the prosecutor had failed to prove beyond a reasonable doubt that the correct statutory procedure had been followed and an acquittal properly resulted (*Rush v DPP* [1994] RTR 268). Where the defendant consents to providing a replacement blood specimen, then raises issues about how it can or cannot be taken, which are overcome by the investigating officer stating inaccurate information about the consequences of him maintaining that stance, the original consent is not vitiated by the technically improper procedure and the replacement specimen remains admissible, rather than the prosecution having to revert to the original breath analysis (*R (Rainsbury) v DPP* [2007] EWHC 1138 (Admin)).

A failure by the driver to provide a replacement specimen does not render the specimen of breath unavailable for use; a condition precedent to the exclusion of the results of the Intoximeter procedure is the provision of an actual replacement specimen (*DPP v Winstanley* [1993] RTR 222; *Hague v DPP* [1997] RTR 146). In *Winstanley* the defendant wished to provide a replacement specimen and did not object to it being of blood. The doctor was called but did not arrive. After waiting an hour, the investigating officer required two specimens of urine instead. The defendant, through no fault of his own, could not oblige. As no actual specimen had been provided to replace the breath specimens, they remained admissible. Similarly, where a defendant frustrates the efforts of the officer to explain the blood/urine option so that no replacement specimen is supplied, the prosecution are entitled to rely on the breath test results (*DPP v Poole* [1992] RTR 177) and where the defendant's consumption of alcohol results, at least partly, in an inability to comprehend the offer being made, the breath analysis is not rendered inadmissible (*DPP v Berry* (1996) 160 JP 707).

Use of Replaced Specimen Where a replacement specimen is supplied, the effect of the RTA 1988, s. 8(2), is mandatory in precluding the use of the breath specimen, even if the replacement specimen is inadmissible as a result of any irregularity or the prosecution do not, for any reason, rely upon it (*Archbold v Jones* [1986] RTR 178; *Wakely v Hyams* [1987] RTR 49). This principle extends to cases in which the defendant advances 'special reasons' (*Smith v Geraghty* [1986] RTR 222). **C5.10**

In *Yhnell v DPP* [1989] RTR 250, however, evidence of both the breath specimens and the blood specimen supplied as a replacement was admissible to demonstrate to the justices that reliance on the blood sample by the prosecution was correct. The defendant had falsified his part of the blood specimen by injecting into it blood unaffected by alcohol, thereby producing a disproportionately low analysis. The justices were able to have regard to the evidence of the breath readings so as to satisfy themselves that the prosecution analysis of the other part of the blood specimen could be relied upon and that the correct statutory procedure had been followed. In such circumstances, the breath specimens were not being 'used' in the manner prohibited by s. 8(2) so as to found a conviction. Similarly, where a court had regard to the breath specimen (and other matters) to help it determine if the defendant's evidence was capable of belief, the specimen was not being 'used' for the purposes of s. 8(2), which is concerned with the process of proof of the reliability of the sample in order to found a conviction (*Carter v DPP* [2007] RTR 257).

Medical Reason

The question of what constitutes a 'medical reason' by virtue of which a specimen of breath cannot be provided or should not be required for the purposes of the RTA 1988, s. 7(3)(a) (see **C5.7**), is a question for the constable. What is important is the state of knowledge of the constable and his reasonable state of belief, bearing in mind that he is a layman. Unlike under s. 7(4), there is no obligation for the constable to take medical advice before reaching a conclusion (*Steadman v DPP* [2003] RTR 10). As long as he has 'reasonable cause to believe' that a specimen of breath cannot be provided or should not be required for medical reasons, **C5.11** then that is sufficient, whether or not the medical reason advanced appears, 'in the cold light of day', to be an unsatisfactory one for declining to provide a specimen of breath (*Davies v DPP* [1989] RTR 391, per Neill LJ).

Where the defendant does his best to provide a specimen and in the absence of any other reason for not complying, incapacity due to being upset, shaken, intoxicated and distressed can amount to a medical reason (*Webb v DPP* [1992] RTR 299, applying *Davies v DPP*). Intoxication alone may constitute such a medical reason (*Young v DPP* [1992] RTR 328). The taking of tablets is also capable of amounting to a medical reason (*Wade v DPP* [1996] RTR 177). If a medical opinion is given to the constable, it will properly inform the reasonableness of his conclusion on this issue, however wrong that opinion may be (*Andrews v DPP* [1992] RTR 1).

If a medical reason is advanced as to why a specimen of blood, which a constable has decided to be appropriate, cannot or should not be taken, the validity of the reason can be determined under s. 7(4A) only by a medical practitioner (*Townson v DPP* [2006] EWHC 2007 (Admin)).

Reliability of Device

C5.12 Two situations may arise. The constable may already know that the device at the police station is not working properly or may discover its malfunctioning during the procedure (RTA 1988, s. 7(3)(b)) and move directly to consideration of whether to advance the investigation by requiring a blood or urine sample. In this context, the question of reliability is subjective and depends upon the officer's reasonable belief (*Thompson v Thynne* [1986] RTR 293). Alternatively, breath specimens may have been provided as a result of which the investigating officer is presented objectively with reasonable cause to believe in the unreliability of the analysis produced (RTA 1988, s. 7(3)(bb)). This might occur where the difference between the two readings is considerable (e.g., above 20 per cent: *DPP v Smith* [2000] RTR 341; above 15 per cent: *Stewart v DPP* [2003] RTR 529) or where the reading that is produced is wholly inconsistent with the defendant's admitted alcohol consumption and perceived physical state (although this course of action was not taken in the circumstances considered in *DPP v Spurrier* [2000] RTR 60). Where the device is regarded as unreliable, the printout can be adduced in evidence to support the belief of the investigating officer without the need to comply with prior service in accordance with the RTOA, s. 16 (see **C5.26**); in these circumstances, the officer may choose first to invite (but not require) provision of further specimens of breath or proceed directly to considering the requirement for blood or urine (*Jubb v DPP* [2003] RTR 272).

Whether or not a device is reliable depends upon how it functions. If it does not produce the correct date (*Slender v Boothby* [1986] RTR 385n) or if it operates outside its range of tolerance, it may not be regarded as reliable. Even if the malfunctioning is the fault of the operator, the alternative sample provided in accordance with s. 7(4) remains admissible (*Jones v DPP* [1991] RTR 41, where the modem switch on the device was not turned on resulting in no printout being generated).

Challenges to the reliability of a device tend to occur where the defendant claims the reading relied on by the prosecution is falsely high (see **C5.30**) or where the failure to provide the specimens required is attributable to the device rather than the defendant's fault. The principles pointing towards or against reliability can be used by analogy where it is asserted that the investigating officer's decision to proceed to require a blood or urine specimen is flawed.

Choosing Blood or Urine

The choice as to which alternative or replacement specimen to require rests with the investigating officer, unless under the RTA 1988, s. 7(4) and (4A), a medical practitioner or a registered health care professional opines that blood is inappropriate so that urine must be taken. In *DPP v Warren* [1993] AC 319, the House of Lords held that, where an alternative or replacement specimen is required, the driver need not be invited to express a preference for giving blood or urine but, if a specimen of blood is required, he must have the opportunity to raise objection to giving blood on medical grounds (to be determined by a medical practitioner or registered health care professional: see **C5.11**) or for any other reason which might afford a reasonable excuse. The standard wording apparently approved in that case (at p. 327) is as follows: **C5.13**

> I require you to provide an alternative specimen, which will be submitted for laboratory analysis. The specimen may be of blood or urine, but it is for me to decide which. If you provide a specimen you will be offered part of it in a suitable container. If you fail to provide a specimen you may be liable to prosecution. Are there any reasons why a specimen of blood cannot or should not be taken by a doctor?

The officer is entitled to rely on a negative answer specifically given in response (*Jubb v DPP* [2003] RTR 272). In *Baldwin v DPP* [1996] RTR 238, the Divisional Court pointed out that these words were guidelines as to interpretation only rather than having statutory force themselves.

The requirements stated by Lord Bridge in *Warren* were reviewed in *DPP v Jackson* [1999] 1 AC 406. The House of Lords decided that, with three exceptions, those requirements were not to be treated as mandatory but as indicating the matters of which a driver should be aware so that he could know the role of the medical person in the taking of a specimen and in determining any medical objection that he might raise to the giving of such a specimen. The three mandatory exceptions, where particular matters must be mentioned, are:

(a) in a s. 7(3) case, the warning as to the risk of prosecution required by s. 7(7) (see **C5.15**);
(b) in a s. 7(3) case, the statement of the reason under that subsection why breath could not be used; and
(c) in a s. 8(2) case (see **C5.9**), the statement that the specimen of breath which the driver had given containing the lower proportion of alcohol did not exceed 50 microgrammes in 100 millilitres of breath.

As well as complying with those mandatory requirements, investigating officers, in order to seek to ensure that a driver is aware of the role of the medical person, should continue to use the formula set out in *Warren* or words to the same effect. Thus, in addition to telling the driver that a specimen of blood will be taken by an appropriate person unless he considers that there are medical reasons for not taking the blood, the officer should ask the driver if there are any medical reasons why a specimen could not or should not be taken by a medical practitioner or a registered health care professional. The driver should be told of the medical person's role at the outset before he has to make the decision to give blood. Fear of needles may constitute a medical reason in relation to providing blood (*Epping Justices, ex parte Quy* [1998] RTR 158n); thus a failure to investigate further the validity of that claim may preclude the prosecution from relying on any breath specimen already provided but, as it is a question of fact whether any statement by the driver raises a potential medical reason, the justices may be entitled to find that the officer is not obliged to investigate further.

In general, the justices must first decide whether the matters set out in the *Warren* formula were brought to the driver's attention by the investigating officer. If the answer is 'No', the second issue is whether, in relation to the non-mandatory requirements, the officer's failure to give the full formula deprived the driver of the opportunity to express his position or caused him to express it in a way which he would not have done had everything been said. If the answer to the second issue is 'Yes', the driver should be acquitted. But if the answer to the second issue is 'No', the officer's failure to use the full formula should not be a reason for acquittal. Both issues are questions of fact, so that if the justices, having heard the defendant's evidence, are not satisfied beyond a reasonable doubt that he was not prejudiced, they should acquit. However, where any such procedural irregularity is raised where there has been an unequivocal plea of guilty, in the absence of conduct on the part of the prosecutor which is either fraudulent or analogous to fraud, the Divisional Court has doubted its jurisdiction to grant judicial review (*Burton upon Trent Justices, ex parte Woolley* [1995] RTR 139; *Dolgellau Justices, ex parte Cartledge* [1996] RTR 207), thereby significantly reducing the scope for re-opening such convictions.

There is no requirement for a police officer to ask a driver if there is any non-medical reason why a specimen of blood should not be taken (*DPP v Jackson*). However, where such a reason is advanced, the officer should not completely disregard it when deciding how to exercise the discretion between requiring blood or urine, otherwise the decision may be quashed as *Wednesbury* unreasonable (*Joseph v DPP* [2004] RTR 341).

A failure to allow the defendant the right to object to the giving of blood for medical reasons will lead to any subsequent conviction being quashed (*Meade v DPP* [1993] RTR 151; *Edge v DPP* [1993] RTR 146).

C5.14 **Blood and Urine Specimens** The RTA 1988, s. 11(4), and the RTOA 1988, s. 15(4), provide that a blood specimen may be taken only with the consent of the person who provides it and must be taken by a medical practitioner or a registered health care professional in a police station. Otherwise it is to be disregarded.

Under the RTA 1988, s. 7A, a specimen of blood may be taken from a person who is, or may be, incapable of consenting to it being taken for medical reasons without that person actually consenting. Thereafter, before the police can have the sample analysed by a laboratory, the person from whom it was taken must be required by a constable to give permission for that analysis. Failure, without reasonable excuse, to give permission for a laboratory test of the specimen will constitute an offence comparable to the offence under s. 7(6).

An invalid but unproductive request for a specimen of blood does not render evidence of a subsequent correctly-taken specimen of urine inadmissible (*DPP v Garrett* [1995] RTR 302). The investigating officer is entitled to change his mind as to the type of specimen being required until the defendant has complied with the requirement in s. 7(1). However, where the defendant refuses to consent to the taking of blood, in the absence of any medical reason explaining that stance, the officer is not obliged to require a specimen of urine (*DPP v Gibbons* (2001) 165 JP 812).

A specimen of urine provided after the one-hour period referred to in the RTA 1988, s. 7(5), is still admissible to prove an offence under s. 5(1) (*DPP v Baldwin* [2000] RTR 314). The significance of the one-hour limit is that, once it passes, the investigating officer can charge a s. 7(6) offence or rely on the original specimen of breath but, should he so choose to exercise his discretion, he can await provision of the specimen of urine required.

Warning

C5.15 The warning in the RTA 1988, s. 7(7), is mandatory and must be understood by the person required to provide the specimen, although it does not need to be repeated in respect of replacement specimens (see **C5.9**). However, it is mandatory only when a requirement is actually made and is not needed if the constable *invites* a suspect to provide further samples (*Edmond v DPP* [2006] RTR 229). If he does not understand it, the warning is invalid; the subsequent procedure is then ineffectual and a defence becomes available to a charge under s. 7(6) (*Simpson v Spalding* [1987] RTR 221; *Chief Constable of Avon and Somerset Constabulary* *v Singh* [1988] RTR 107). A finding that the defendant understood the request for a specimen being made and the penal warning attached thereto is not affected by the fact that the defendant was being detained under the Mental Health Act 1983, s. 136 (*Francis v DPP* [1997] RTR 113). At a hospital (see **C5.17**), the warning must still be given by a constable and cannot lawfully be given by a doctor (*Beatrice v DPP* [2004] EWHC 2416 (Admin)). However, self-induced intoxication rendering a person incapable of understanding what was being said does not provide such a defence or a reasonable excuse for failing to provide as required (*DPP v Beech* [1992] RTR 239). See also *R (DPP) v Preston* [2003] EWHC 729 (Admin).

A failure to give the warning in s. 7(7) or to comply with any of the appropriate statutory procedures will render evidence of the specimen inadmissible under the RTOA 1988, s. 15(2), even if there is no prejudice to the defendant (*Murray v DPP* [1993] RTR 209). If the defence wish to take issue about the alleged failure to warn, this should occur openly and during the course of the evidence rather than only in closing submissions (*R (Parker) v Crown Court at Bradford* [2007] RTR 369; *Malcolm v DPP* [2007] 1 WLR 1230, where the late timing of the submission provided special circumstances justifying the court, even after retiring to consider its verdict, giving permission for further prosecution evidence to be adduced).

Detention of Persons Affected by Alcohol or a Drug

C5.16 By virtue of the RTA 1988, s. 10, following a requirement for a specimen of breath, blood or urine, a person may be detained at a police station until it appears to a constable that, if he were driving or attempting to drive, he would not be committing an offence under s. 4 or 5 of the Act. If the specimen was provided otherwise than at the police station, the constable may arrest the person and take him to a police station for detention on the same basis, unless the person is at a hospital as a patient and such action would be prejudicial to his proper care and treatment as a patient. If, however, it appears to the constable that there is no likelihood of that person driving or attempting to drive whilst his ability is impaired or he is above the prescribed limit then he may not be detained under s. 10. If a question arises in relation to detention as to whether or not a person's ability to drive is, or might be, impaired through drugs, the constable must consult a medical practitioner and act on his advice.

Protection for Hospital Patients

C5.17 Road Traffic Act 1988, s. 9

(1) While a person is at a hospital as a patient he shall not be required to co-operate with a preliminary test or to provide a specimen under section 7 of this Act unless the medical practitioner in immediate charge of his case has been notified of the proposal to make the requirement; and—
 (a) if the requirement is then made, it shall be for co-operation with a test administered, or for the provision of a specimen, at the hospital, but
 (b) if the medical practitioner objects on the ground specified in subsection (2) below, the requirement shall not be made.

(1A) While a person is at a hospital as a patient, no specimen of blood shall be taken from him under section 7A of this Act and he shall not be required to give his permission for a laboratory test of a specimen taken under that section unless the medical practitioner in immediate charge of his case—
 (a) has been notified of the proposal to take the specimen or to make the requirement; and
 (b) has not objected on the ground specified in subsection (2).

(2) The ground on which the medical practitioner may object is—
 (a) in a case falling within subsection (1), that the requirement or the provision of the specimen or (if one is required) the warning required by section 7(7) of this Act would be prejudicial to the proper care and treatment of the patient; and
 (b) in a case falling within subsection (1A), that the taking of the specimen, the requirement or the warning required by section 7A(5) of this Act would be so prejudicial.

For the RTA 1988, s. 7A, see C5.7.

A person is at a hospital when he is within the hospital's curtilage and he is there for treatment, even as an out-patient. Once the treatment has been completed, the person is no longer a patient within the meaning of s. 9 (*A-G's Ref (No. 1 of 1976*) [1977] 1 WLR 646). The doctor who is directly responsible for the patient is the medical practitioner in immediate charge of his case.

In *Burton upon Trent Justices, ex parte Woolley* [1995] RTR 139, the Divisional Court decided that there is no obligation for the constable to inform a driver who is a patient at a hospital why a specimen of breath cannot be taken but, at some stage during the process at the hospital, the constable has to ask the driver whether there is any reason why a specimen of blood should not be taken. Thereafter, the details of the procedure laid down in *DPP v Warren* [1993] AC 319 and *DPP v Jackson* [1999] 1 AC 406 (see C5.13) should be followed. See also *Jones* v *DPP* [2004] EWHC 3165 (Admin). Where a constable has information supplied by, or presumably about, a person under investigation which relates to a possible medical reason for being unable to provide a specimen, he is required to relay that specific information to the doctor dealing with the patient (*Butler v DPP* [2001] RTR 430). A requirement lawfully made under s. 9 remains valid after the patient's discharge from hospital; it must therefore be complied with unless it is abundantly plain that, following discharge, the investigating officer is setting in train the s. 7 procedure (*Webber v DPP* [1998] RTR 111).

Failure to Provide an Evidential Specimen

C5.18 The RTOA 1988, ss. 11 and 12(1) apply; see C2.5 and C2.6. 'Fail' includes a refusal (RTA 1988, s. 11). Whether there is a refusal is a matter of fact and degree for the justices (*Smyth v DPP* [1996] RTR 59). Where a motorist initially declined to provide the required specimens of breath but indicated a desire to change his mind within some five seconds, the only possible conclusion was that there had not been a refusal. Clear words of denial, such as saying 'No, no, no', even before the investigating officer chooses between a specimen of blood or urine, will probably amount to a refusal (*Burke v DPP* [1999] RTR 387). If the defendant's conduct shows he is not willing to provide the specimen required, or he imposes unacceptable terms for the specimen to be provided, then a failure may well be made out (*DPP v Swan* [2004] EWHC 2432 (Admin), where the court commented that *Mackey* [1977] RTR 146 should not be understood as imposing a threshold of outrageousness in behaviour before it can constitute a failure to provide).

In *DPP v Darwen* [2007] EWHC 337 (Admin), the importance of the conjunctive 'and' in s. 11(3) was stressed, making it clear that the specimen provided must both be sufficient (e.g., in volume) and provided in such a way as to enable the analysis of it to be satisfactorily achieved. If either of these criteria is not satisfied, there will be a failure to provide the required specimen.

In *DPP v Butterworth* [1995] 1 AC 381, the House of Lords confirmed that the RTA 1988, s. 7(6) creates only one offence. Accordingly, a charge stating that 'having been required to provide a specimen of breath/blood/urine for analysis, [the defendant] failed without reasonable excuse to do so' was found not to be duplicitous (*Worsley v DPP* [1995] Crim LR 572, where the prosecution then adduced evidence of failure to provide only one type of specimen), even though the information looks capable of relating to three separate demands for three separate specimens. The essence of the offence is that the police are investigating whether the person committed any of the offences in ss. 3A, 4 and 5 of the 1988 Act and so there is no need to identify in the charge a specific offence to which the mind of the investigating officer was directed.

Although s. 7(6) creates a single offence, two charges can be brought against the same defendant where two separate failures are alleged (*Chichester Justices, ex parte DPP* [1994]

RTR 175). Moreover, the subsequent provision of a different specimen below the prescribed limit as a consequence of a separate request may not cure the initial failure to provide without a reasonable excuse (*Lorimer v Russell* 1996 SLT 501).

In *DPP v Radford* [1995] RTR 86, the Divisional Court recommended that, when prosecuting under the RTA 1988, s. 7(6), the prosecutor should draw the attention of the justices to the relevant authorities set out in the appropriate paragraph of *Stone's Justices' Manual* and to the criteria for consideration set out in *DPP v Curtis* [1993] RTR 72.

Reasonable Excuse It is a defence to a charge under the RTA 1988, s. 7(6), to have had a reasonable excuse for the failure to provide the specimen required. However, where there is a deliberate failure to provide the specimen required, it cannot subsequently be justified by reference to a medical condition which was not alluded to at the time (*DPP v Furby* [2000] RTR 181; *DPP v Lonsdale* [2001] RTR 444; *R (Martiner) v DPP* [2004] EWHC 2484 (Admin)). There must be an attempt to provide which is unsuccessful because of a physical or mental disability before reasonable excuse can be raised as a defence. **C5.19**

Once a defence of reasonable excuse is raised, it is for the prosecution to negative it. What constitutes a 'reasonable excuse' must always remain a matter of fact for the court. But in *Lennard* [1973] 1 WLR 483, Lawton LJ said (at p. 487):

> In our judgment no excuse can be adjudged a reasonable one unless the person from whom the specimen is required is physically or mentally unable to provide it or the provision of the specimen would entail a substantial risk to his health.

Normally, expert medical evidence of the physical or mental incapacity to provide the specimen is required to support the defence and demonstrate the existence of the necessary causative link between the incapacity and the failure to provide (*DPP v Crofton* [1994] RTR 279; *DPP v Brodzky* [1997] RTR 425n; *DPP v Grundy* [2006] EWHC 1157 (Admin)). Where a substantial risk to health is advanced, alternative approaches to the provision of the specimen should be considered before assessing the reasonableness of the excuse (*DPP v Mukandiwa* [2006] RTR 304, where a potentially dangerous trance state triggered by the sight of blood could have been avoided by looking away and did not relate directly to the taking of the blood specimen required).

Post-accident stress cannot, without evidence showing mental or physical disability, constitute a reasonable excuse for failing to provide a specimen (*DPP v Eddowes* [1991] RTR 35). See also *DPP v Ambrose* [1992] RTR 285, *DPP v Falzarano* [2001] RTR 217 and *DPP v Meller* [2002] All ER (D) 33 (Apr). In *De Freitas v DPP* [1993] RTR 98, a phobia of catching AIDS, established by medical evidence, amounted to a reasonable excuse. If a medical reason is claimed as a reason for not providing a specimen of blood, a medical practitioner's opinion that such a reason is not a medical one is conclusive.

Where a medical reason is advanced as a reasonable excuse, the justices should still give proper weight to the other evidence relating to the defendant's failure to provide, e.g., where the defendant, after having satisfactorily provided a roadside test and the first specimen of breath required, put the device's tube to his mouth and no breath was registered (*DPP v Radford* [1995] RTR 86). Only if the justices' decision in this respect is perverse will there be grounds to interfere on appeal.

Even without medical evidence justices are entitled, if they have the test in *Lennard* well in mind, to find that shock combined with inebriation which renders a defendant physically incapable may amount to a reasonable excuse (*DPP v Pearman* [1992] RTR 407; *DPP v Crofton* [1994] RTR 279). Justices should however be wary of using their own knowledge of a medical condition which is not supported by or is beyond the evidence before them (*DPP v Curtis* [1993] RTR 72).

C5.20 **Non-medical Reasons** Omitting to warn the defendant that there is a time-limit for completing the breathalyser process, after which the Intoximeter stops functioning, will not amount to a reasonable excuse (*DPP v Coyle* [1996] RTR 287). Indeed *Cosgrove v DPP* [1997] RTR 153 confirmed that the investigating officer is not obliged to permit the driver the test's full three minutes in which to provide the required specimens. This was re-affirmed in *Watson v DPP* [2006] EWHC 3429 (Admin), where the defendant's insistence on being permitted to go to the lavatory between provision of the first and second breath specimens was not accepted as a reasonable excuse.

Failure to provide a specimen because the defendant was waiting for the arrival of, or telephone advice from, a solicitor did not amount to a reasonable excuse (*DPP v Skinner* [1990] RTR 231 and *DPP v Varley* (1999) 163 JP 443, following *DPP v Billington* [1988] 1 WLR 535). The decision in *Smith v Hand* [1986] RTR 265 was explained as applying only to cases where the defendant has been told positively that he can wait for his solicitor, although *Billington* clearly makes the distinction between imposing a condition and merely making a request in relation to the provision of legal advice. This principle remains unaffected after the HRA 1998 and does not violate the ECHR, Article 6(3) (*Campbell v CPS* (2002) 166 JP 742; *Kennedy v DPP* (2003) 167 JP 267; *Myles v DPP* [2004] 2 All ER 902). See also *Whitley v DPP* (2004) 168 JP 329 and *Causey v DPP* (2005) 169 JP 331. In *Dickinson v DPP* [1989] Crim LR 741, legal advice given to the defendant by a solicitor who accompanied him to the police station to the effect that he should refuse a specimen was held not to constitute a reasonable excuse. Where the defendant makes provision of the specimen required conditional on having sight of a law book, that does not amount to a reasonable excuse (*DPP v Noe* [2000] RTR 351). Neither is insisting upon reading the PACE 1984 codes of practice before providing a specimen of breath a 'reasonable excuse' for failing to provide it (*DPP v Cornell* [1990] RTR 254).

In *DPP v Rous* [1992] RTR 246, it was held that the procedure as to the provision of specimens, whether relating to s. 7(4) or 8(2), does not constitute an interview and therefore there is no discretion under the PACE 1984, s. 78, to exclude evidence relating to the procedure. Indeed para. 11.1A of PACE Code C specifically states that procedures under s. 7 do not constitute interviewing. In *DPP v Whalley* [1991] RTR 161, a finding that the notice given to detained persons misled the accused to think he had a right to consult the codes before further procedures were undertaken was not enough to constitute a reasonable excuse for failing to provide a specimen. It was reiterated that an excuse would not be reasonable unless it followed *Lennard*, or was as a result of failing to understand the obligation to provide a specimen (*Chief Constable of Avon and Somerset Constabulary v Singh* [1988] RTR 107).

C5.21 **Punishment** Where the defendant was driving or attempting to drive, the penalty is six months' imprisonment and/or a fine up to level 5 on the standard scale. Disqualification and endorsement are, in the absence of 'special reasons', obligatory. The offence carries between 3 and 11 penalty points.

In any other case, the penalty is three months' imprisonment and/or a fine up to level 4. Disqualification is discretionary, but endorsement with 10 penalty points, in the absence of 'special reasons', is obligatory.

Forfeiture of the vehicle may be ordered under either situation (see **C7.28** and **E20.1**).

C5.22 **Sentencing** In *Waltham Forest Justices, ex parte Barton* [1990] RTR 49, the Divisional Court indicated that, where a defendant is charged with failing to provide a specimen at the police station, the charge itself should indicate that 'the specimen was required to ascertain the ability of the defendant at the time he was driving or attempting to drive'. The decision in *DPP v Butterworth* [1995] 1 AC 381, however, makes it clear that there is no need to specify in the charge whether the allegation is that the defendant was only 'in charge' or driving or attempting to drive. Lord Slynn stated (at p. 394) that 'the question whether the person was driving or in charge of the motor vehicle is not part of the inquiry into whether there has been a refusal for the purposes of section 7(6). That question only becomes relevant after conviction and goes to the appropriate penalty'. Accordingly, the charge itself does not need to indicate whether the defendant faces a mandatory or discretionary disqualification, although the prosecution might be asked informally on what basis the case is being put.

Where the prosecution case is put on the 'in charge' basis, sentence can be passed only on the basis that the defendant was 'in charge' and not driving (*George v DPP* [1989] RTR 217). Consequently, if there is no evidence adduced that the defendant was driving, the court must sentence only on the 'in charge' basis (*Cawley v DPP* [2001] EWHC Admin 83).

Where the defendant was driving or attempting to drive, the Magistrates' Courts Guidelines (2004) recommend considering disqualification for a minimum period of 18 months for a first offence.

DRIVING, OR BEING IN CHARGE, WITH ALCOHOL CONCENTRATION ABOVE PRESCRIBED LIMIT

Road Traffic Act 1988, s. 5 **C5.23**

(1) If a person—
  (a) drives or attempts to drive a motor vehicle on a road or other public place, or
  (b) is in charge of a motor vehicle on a road or other public place,
  after consuming so much alcohol that the proportion of it in his breath, blood or urine exceeds the prescribed limit he is guilty of an offence.
(2) It is a defence for a person charged with an offence under subsection (1)(b) above to prove that at the time he is alleged to have committed the offence the circumstances were such that there was no likelihood of his driving the vehicle whilst the proportion of alcohol in his breath, blood or urine remained likely to exceed the prescribed limit.
(3) The court may, in determining whether there was such a likelihood as is mentioned in subsection (2) above, disregard any injury to him and any damage to the vehicle.

Elements

The RTOA 1988, ss. 11 and 12(1), apply; see **C2.5** and **C2.6**. For the meaning of the terms 'road or other public place', 'driving' and 'attempting', see **C1.14** and **C1.15**, **C1.8** and **C1.9**, and **C1.3**. The RTA 1988, s. 11, sets out the 'prescribed limit'. If the lower reading in breath is 39 microgrammes in 100 millilitres or less, proceedings are not usually instituted. In *DPP v Johnson* [1995] 1 WLR 728, the Divisional Court held that the meaning of 'consuming' was sufficiently wide to cover ingestion otherwise than by mouth and the important element of the offence was the concentration of alcohol in the driver's body at the relevant time. In *Zafar v DPP* [2005] RTR 220, it confirmed that 'breath' in this context is not confined to deep lung air and should be given its dictionary definition ('air exhaled from any thing'). See also *Woolfe v DPP* [2007] RTR 187. **C5.24**

Section 5 creates nine separate offences of driving, or attempting to drive or being in charge of a vehicle, each with an alcohol concentration above the prescribed limit in relation to breath, blood or urine (*Bolton Justices, ex parte Khan* [1999] Crim LR 912). The charge must state which specimen is to be relied upon by the prosecution. Referring to more than one type of specimen renders the charge bad for duplicity. However, a late amendment to the charge to refer to the correct specimen is likely to be permitted as it should not prejudice the defendant, who knows that driving with excess alcohol in his body is what is being alleged (*Fenwick v Valentine* 1994 SLT 485).

As regards secondary participation in an offence under s. 5, a supervising driver who was aware that the learner driver had drunk so much that the alcohol level in his body must have exceeded the prescribed limit was held to have been properly convicted of aiding and abetting the offence, even though the driver had not been required to provide a specimen

(*Carter v Richardson* [1974] RTR 314, where this was a proper inference to draw from the behaviour of the defendant when the police arrived, because he had lied about who was the driver). Lacing the drinks of a person who then drives may involve procuring an offence under s. 5; the defendant must be proved to have known that the person whose drink was laced was going to drive and that the ordinary result of lacing the drinks would be to raise the driver's alcohol level above the prescribed limit (*A-G's Ref (No. 1 of 1975)* [1975] QB 773). Alternatively, as McCullough J stated in *Blakely v DPP* [1991] RTR 405 (at p. 415):

> It must, at the least, be shown that the accused contemplated that his act would or might bring about or assist the commission of the principal offence: . . . The requirements match those needed to convict principals in the second degree. And they fit well with the liability of the parties to a joint enterprise.

C5.25 **In Charge** It was confirmed in *Drake v DPP* [1994] RTR 411 that a person can be in charge of a motor vehicle when the vehicle is immobile. In *Leach v Evans* [1952] 2 All ER 264, a motorist emerging from a public house considerably under the influence of alcohol told a police officer that he was looking for his van, walked towards it and was then arrested within three yards of it. Lord Goddard CJ posed the question: if the motorist was not in charge of the van who was? This principle was followed in *Haines v Roberts* [1953] 1 WLR 309, where Lord Goddard CJ said (at p. 311):

> It may be that, if a man goes to a public house and leaves his car outside or in the car park and, getting drunk, asks a friend to look after the car for him or to take it home, he has put it in charge of somebody else; but if he has not put it in charge of somebody else he is in charge until he does. His car is out on the road or in the car park—it matters not which— and he is in charge.

In *DPP v Watkins* [1989] QB 821, it was held that a person was in charge of a vehicle if he acted in a manner which showed that he had assumed control or intended to assume control of the vehicle preparatory to driving it. Thereafter the burden of proving the statutory defence in the RTA 1988, s. 7(4), shifts to the defendant. Amongst factors which merited consideration were:

(a) whether and where he was in the vehicle or how far he was from it;
(b) what he was doing at the relevant time;
(c) whether he was in possession of a key that fitted the ignition;
(d) whether there was evidence of an intention to take or assert control of the car by driving or otherwise;
(e) whether any other person was in, at or near the vehicle and, if so, the like particulars in respect of that person.

Where the defendant was the owner of the car in which he was sitting with the ignition keys in his hand, in the absence of any suggestion of another person being in charge, it is an inescapable conclusion that the defendant was in charge (*CPS v Bate* [2004] EWHC 2811 (Admin)).

Evidence as to Specimens

C5.26 **Road Traffic Offenders Act 1988, s. 16**

> (1) Evidence of the proportion of alcohol or a drug in a specimen of breath, blood or urine may, subject to subsections (3) and (4) below and to section 15(5) and (5A) of this Act, be given by the production of a document or documents purporting to be whichever of the following is appropriate, that is to say—
>
> (a) a statement automatically produced by the device by which the proportion of alcohol in a specimen of breath was measured and a certificate signed by a constable (which may but need not be contained in the same document as the statement) that the statement relates to a specimen provided by the accused at the date and time shown in the statement, and

(b) a certificate signed by an authorised analyst as to the proportion of alcohol or any drug found in a specimen of blood or urine identified in the certificate.

(2) Subject to subsections (3) and (4) below, evidence that a specimen of blood was taken from the accused with his consent by a medical practitioner or a registered health care professional may be given by the production of a document purporting to certify that fact and to be signed by a medical practitioner or a registered health care professional.

(3) Subject to subsection (4) below—

(a) a document purporting to be such a statement or such a certificate (or both such a statement and such a certificate) as is mentioned in subsection (1)(a) above is admissible in evidence on behalf of the prosecution in pursuance of this section only if a copy of it either has been handed to the accused when the document was produced or has been served on him not later than seven days before the hearing, and

(b) any other document is so admissible only if a copy of it has been served on the accused not later than seven days before the hearing.

(4) A document purporting to be a certificate (or so much of a document as purports to be a certificate) is not so admissible if the accused, not later than three days before the hearing or within such further time as the court may in special circumstances allow, has served notice on the prosecutor requiring the attendance at the hearing of the person by whom the document purports to be signed.

(5) [Applies only to Scotland.]

(6) A copy of a certificate required by this section to be served on the accused or a notice required by this section to be served on the prosecutor may be served personally or sent by registered post or recorded delivery service.

Printouts In *Garner v DPP* [1990] RTR 208 (following *Castle v Cross* [1984] 1 WLR 1372), the Court of Appeal held that the admissibility of the 'statement automatically produced by the device' (commonly called 'the printout') did not just arise through the RTOA 1988, s. 16(1). The statement is in itself an admissible document and represents real evidence as long as it is properly produced. The purpose and effect of s. 16 is to enable the printout together with an appropriate certificate to be tendered at the hearing and to 'be capable of establishing the facts stated in it without the necessity of anybody being called' (per Stocker LJ at p. 184). In short, s. 16(1)(a) is permissive and provides one method for proving the proportion of alcohol in a breath specimen (*Thom v DPP* [1994] RTR 11; *R (Leong) v DPP* [2006] EWHC 1575 (Admin)). **C5.27**

The printout and the operator's certificate may be separate or contained in the same document. Section 16(4) relates to the operator's, medical practitioner's and analyst's certificates, and not to the printout (*Temple v Botha* [1985] Crim LR 517). On a plea of guilty, there is no need to produce the original printout from the device. If there is a genuine change of plea, reasonable adjournments must be given to the prosecution if there is a problem about production of the printout (*Tower Bridge Magistrates' Court, ex parte DPP* [1989] RTR 118).

A failure to produce the printout in evidence in a case where the officer does not give evidence of the reading, his familiarity with the device, its working or calibration means that the prosecution have failed to establish a case against the defendant (*Hasler v DPP* [1989] RTR 148). Evidence of the breath alcohol reading, in the absence of the printout, is not, in itself, sufficient to found a conviction (*Owen v Chesters* [1985] RTR 191). The prosecution should establish that the device is working correctly by evidence relating to the calibration. An officer giving such evidence has to be trained in the use and manner of performance of the device so as to understand the calibration process and to recognise that, unless the result of the process lies within accepted limits, the device may be unreliable (*Denneny v Harding* [1986] RTR 350). Even where the operator's knowledge of the device has been shown in cross-examination to be less than perfect, provided there is nothing to show the decision was irrational, it is still open to the court to conclude that the operator has been adequately trained so as to be qualified to conduct the procedure and that the device has functioned reliably (*Haggis v DPP* [2004] 3 All ER 382). The operator is entitled to give oral evidence, without production of the printout being a pre-condition, so as to support a conviction, provided that the evidence demonstrates the actual reading on which the charge is founded and demonstrates that the device was working properly and reliably, i.e. by the operator looking at the figures on the device's display (*Thom v DPP*; *Greenaway v DPP* [1994] RTR 17). See also *Sneyd v DPP* [2007] RTR 53. There is also a discretion to permit the prosecution to remedy an oversight to adduce such evidence during their case by calling appropriate evidence later on, especially where the interests of justice outweigh any prejudice to the defendant (*Cook v DPP* [2001] Crim LR 321 and *Leeson v DPP* [2000] RTR 385). The exact procedures of various approved devices differ, so that reliance on the steps in respect of the wrong one, perhaps as a result of references in authorities, will not assist (*Mercer v DPP* (2003) 167 JP 441, which drew the distinction between the Lion Intoxilyser 6000 and the old Lion Intoximeter 3000).

A printout timed according to Greenwich Mean Time is admissible even though British Summer Time was operating at the time the defendant provided the specimen (*Parker v DPP* [1993] RTR 283). Indeed, in *DPP v McKeown* [1997] 1 WLR 295, a printout recording a wholly inaccurate time due to a malfunctioning clock was still held admissible because that malfunction did not affect the way in which the computer processed, stored or retrieved the information used to generate the statement in evidence. This reasoning has been applied to typographical errors on the face of printouts which clearly do not affect the proper functioning of the device (*Reid v DPP* [1999] RTR 357; *DPP v Barber* (1999) 163 JP 457).

C5.28 **Service of Certificate** The certificate under the RTOA 1988, s. 16(2), is termed an HORT/5. Section 16(3) imposes a duty to serve the analyst's certificate, which cannot be waived (*Tobi v Nicholas* [1988] RTR 343). However, where only the lack of a signature on the certificate is an issue, and not service itself, strict proof of service can be waived (*Louis v DPP* [1998] RTR 354). The obligation imposed is treated as being to offer a copy of the printout to the defendant, so that a refusal to accept it in order to argue that it has not been 'handed' as required will not render the contents of the printout inadmissible (*McCormack v DPP* [2002] RTR 355). If the defendant wishes to challenge the lack of service of any of the certificates, this must be done before the contents are put in evidence (*Banks* [1972] 1 WLR 346), although the challenge does not have to be made immediately and may be permitted if made a few minutes later, so that the defendant first has time to consider the implications of the issue (*R (Wooldridge) v DPP* [2003] EWHC 1663 (Admin)), but attempting to do so only in closing is too late (*Jeffreys v DPP* [2006] EWHC 1377 (Admin)).

Section 16(6) provides for service of various notices, and s. 16(4) for the service of a counter-notice. Oral notice will not suffice and, if there is any issue as to whether a document complies with these provisions, the justices will have to determine as a matter of fact whether it constitutes a notice (*R (Stavrinou) v Horseferry Road Justices* [2006] EWHC 566 (Admin); *R (DPP) v Chorley Justices* [2006] EWHC 1795 (Admin)). This procedure provides an alternative method of service to that contained in the CJA 1967, s. 9 (*DPP v Stephens* [2006] EWHC 1860 (Admin), where it was pointed out that the methods specified in s. 16(6) are exhaustively listed).

Admissibility of Specimens

C5.29 **Road Traffic Offenders Act 1988, s. 15**

(1) This section and section 16 of this Act apply in respect of proceedings for an offence under section 3A, 4 or 5 of the Road Traffic Act 1988 (driving offences connected with drink or drugs); and expressions used in this section and section 16 of this Act have the same meaning as in sections 3A to 10 of that Act.

(2) Evidence of the proportion of alcohol or any drug in a specimen of breath, blood or urine provided by or taken from the accused shall, in all cases (including cases where the specimen was not provided or taken in connection with the alleged offence), be taken into account

and, subject to subsection (3) below, it shall be assumed that the proportion of alcohol in the accused's breath, blood or urine at the time of the alleged offence was not less than in the specimen.

(3) That assumption shall not be made if the accused proves—
   (a) that he consumed alcohol before he provided the specimen or had it taken from him and—
      (i) in relation to an offence under section 3A, after the time of the alleged offence, and
      (ii) otherwise, after he had ceased to drive, attempt to drive or be in charge of a vehicle on a road or other public place, and
   (b) that had he not done so the proportion of alcohol in his breath, blood or urine would not have exceeded the prescribed limit and, if it is alleged that he was unfit to drive through drink, would not have been such as to impair his ability to drive properly.

(4) A specimen of blood shall be disregarded unless—
   (a) it was taken from the accused with his consent and either—
      (i) in a police station by a medical practitioner or a registered health care professional; or
      (ii) elsewhere by a medical practitioner; or
   (b) it was taken from the accused by a medical practitioner under section 7A of the Road Traffic Act 1988 and the accused subsequently gave his permission for a laboratory test of the specimen.

(5) Where, at the time a specimen of blood or urine was provided by the accused, he asked to be provided with such a specimen, evidence of the proportion of alcohol or any drug found in the specimen is not admissible on behalf of the prosecution unless—
   (a) the specimen in which the alcohol or drug was found is one of two parts into which the specimen provided by the accused was divided at the time it was provided, and
   (b) the other part was supplied to the accused.

(5A) Where a specimen of blood was taken from the accused under section 7A of the Road Traffic Act 1988, evidence of the proportion of alcohol or any drug found in the specimen is not admissible on behalf of the prosecution unless—
   (a) the specimen in which the alcohol or drug was found is one of two parts into which the specimen taken from the accused was divided at the time it was taken; and
   (b) any request to be supplied with the other part which was made by the accused at the time when he gave his permission for a laboratory test of the specimen was complied with.

Incomplete breath specimens, even if they purport to give a reading, are inadmissible against the defendant (*R (Willicott) v DPP* (2002) 166 JP 385). Under the RTA 1988, s. 7(1)(a), a constable may require provision of two specimens of breath. Accordingly, only the first two specimens actually provided are admissible (*Howard v Hallett* [1984] RTR 353). In this case, the first Intoximeter procedure resulted in only one specimen being provided because of the constable's error, so the full procedure was recommenced resulting in the provision of three specimens in total. The Divisional Court rejected the prosecution's attempt to ignore the first procedure entirely and so rely on the lower of the second and third specimens provided. It ruled that the third specimen was the one to be disregarded as being outside the s. 7 statutory procedure and that the lower of the first two readings was the specimen on which the prosecution was obliged to found its case. On the basis that s. 7(1)(b) enables a constable to require a specimen of blood, only the first specimen of blood or urine taken ought to be admissible.

Where blood has been taken on two occasions and then divided, the resulting analysis is inadmissible (*Dear v DPP* [1988] RTR 148). In *DPP v Elstob* [1992] RTR 45, it was held that the phrase 'divided at the time' in the RTOA 1988, s. 15(5)(a), meant that the taking and division of the specimen had to be closely linked in time and performed as part of the same event, even though it is inevitable that some time will pass between the two acts. It is important to maintain the integrity of what occurs, and therefore it is desirable (albeit not strictly necessary for compliance with the statute) for the defendant to be present. Incorrect labelling by a police doctor of the part specimen handed to the defendant, in pursuance of s. 15(5)(b), is not fatal to the admissibility of evidence relating to the proportion of alcohol or drug found in the specimen, unless it is supplied in such a way as to deter or prevent the defendant from having it analysed (*Butler v DPP* [1990] RTR 377). In order to comply with s. 15(5)(b), the defendant's part does not need to be handed physically to him but can be supplied by being made available, e.g., through provision to a friend in such a way that the defendant must have known what had become of it (*O'Connell v DPP* [2006] EWHC 1419 (Admin)). There is no obligation to give the defendant a choice as to which of the two parts of the sample to take (*R (Lidington) v DPP* [2006] EWHC 1984 (Admin)). As there is no statutory requirement to inform a driver that his breath specimen is above the prescribed limit, failing to do so does not render any replacement specimen provided inadmissible (*DPP v Ormsby* [1997] RTR 394n).

Where the laboratory analysing the sample sub-divides it for the purpose of analysis, it is lawful to use the average result and not necessary to use only the lowest result (*DPP v Welsh* (1997) 161 JP 57). In *Bolton Magistrates' Court, ex parte Scally* [1991] 1 QB 537, where the reliability of the blood analysis was impugned because the sample had been taken using a cleaning swab impregnated with alcohol, the Divisional Court quashed the conviction. Similarly, in *Gregory v DPP* (2002) 166 JP 400, opinion evidence explaining possible discrepancies in the analysis in a borderline case, which resulted from contact with the fluoride preservative in the container into which the blood was transferred after being divided, should not have been disregarded at trial, with the consequence that the conviction was quashed. However, in *Carter v DPP* [2007] RTR 257, following *R (Dhaliwal) v DPP* [2006] EWHC 1149 (Admin), the court concluded that, unless there is something suggesting otherwise, justices are entitled to presume that the procedures laid down for the preparation of analysts' kits have been carried out correctly. Any failure to notify the defendant of the procedure set out in s. 15(5) will harm the prosecution's case irreparably (*Anderton v Lythgoe* [1985] 1 WLR 222); the same consequence is likely in respect of the procedure in s. 15(5A). Where a point is taken on this procedure, it must be taken before evidence of the analysis is adduced (*Hudson v Hornby* [1973] RTR 4).

Where the defendant has exercised the right to provide a replacement specimen under the RTA 1988, s. 8, and then challenges the reliability of the results of the blood analysis, the breath test results, with the benefit of expert evidence linking both, can be admitted to demonstrate compatibility (*Slasor v DPP* [1999] RTR 432). Conversely, the defendant should have the opportunity to adduce evidence of a breath test below the prescribed limit taken shortly after provision of blood analysed as being above the prescribed limit in order to support a challenge to the reliability of that blood analysis (*Parish v DPP* [2000] RTR 143).

C5.30 **Challenging the Specimen Evidence** A general challenge to the admissibility of the printout from the Intoximeter (e.g., relating to the compensatory element where the device detects a substance believed to be acetone, reducing the alcohol reading accordingly) can be made using the PACE 1984, s. 78 (*Ashton v DPP* [1998] RTR 45). However, challenging the reliability of the device so as to render the evidence produced inadmissible is notoriously difficult. The justices should assume the device to have been in good working order until the contrary is proved (*Anderton v Waring* [1986] RTR 74). They can infer from the device being of a type approved by the Secretary of State that it contains the original and approved software (*Skinner v DPP* [2005] RTR 202).

In *Tower Bridge Magistrates' Court, ex parte DPP* [1989] RTR 118, the Divisional Court quashed a witness summons issued by the magistrates' court for a police officer to produce the service record and machine log in respect of the device used, castigating the defence for engaging on a fishing expedition. Disclosure to establish that an approved device has been altered in such a way as to take it out of type approval should be ordered only after production of some material justifying the application not on the basis of mere assertion from the defendant that there had been an unapproved modification (*DPP v Wood* (2006) 170 JP

177). See also *Rothon v DPP* [2006] EWHC 3330 (Admin). Any suggestion that the device was working unreliably must be related to the particular facts of the case before the justices rather than generally (*DPP v Brown* [2002] RTR 395). There should be evidence raising a realistic possibility that the device malfunctioned and a general assertion alleging failure to comply with the manufacturer's recommendations does not amount to such evidence (*Scheiner v DPP* [2006] EWHC 1516 (Admin)). Tests by experts pointing to the unreliability of the device in relation to an aspect of its functions that is wholly irrelevant to the reliability of the evidence adduced in the defendant's case will not deprive the device of its type approval by the Secretary of State (*DPP v Memery* [2003] RTR 249). See also *Grant v DPP* (2003) 167 JP 159.

There is no obligation on the prosecution to disclose to the defence the evidence of the proportion of alcohol found in a roadside breath test where it is not being put in evidence and relied upon in accordance with s. 15(2). Applications under the CPIA 1996, s. 8(2), for such disclosure, with a view to seeing if those readings provided the foundation for a challenge to the evidential specimen on which the prosecutions were based, were rejected in *Murphy v DPP* [2006] EWHC 1753 (Admin) and *Smith v DPP* [2007] EWHC 100 (Admin).

Evidence of the amount of alcohol allegedly taken prior to providing the specimen relied on by the prosecution may be used to challenge the reliability of the evidence relating to the specimen (*Cracknell v Willis* [1988] AC 450). However, this will often depend on the evidence of the defendant alone and, in the absence of the right to provide a sample of blood or urine, he is unlikely to prevail. For example, in *Lafferty v DPP* [1995] Crim LR 429, the defendant adduced evidence as to the amount of alcohol consumed supported by expert evidence indicating that, on such a level of consumption, the Intoximeter reading should not have been as high as it was; if the defendant's evidence to that effect was accepted, it followed that the device was unreliable. The Divisional Court decided that the justices had properly admitted evidence of the results of the roadside breath test, as this went to the veracity of the defendant when attacking the reliability of the device, which attack the prosecution was entitled to rebut by any relevant evidence. See also *Williams v DPP* [2001] EWHC Admin 932. It is not strictly necessary to adduce expert evidence establishing the reading which should have been produced on the basis of what the defendant claims to have consumed (*DPP v Spurrier* [2000] RTR 60) but, except in exceptional circumstances, to do so is always likely to make the defendant's evidence more credible.

In summary, for evidence of a specimen required under the RTA 1988, s. 7(1), to be admissible under the RTOA 1988, s. 15(2), all the procedural requirements of the RTA 1988, ss. 7 and 8, including the mandatory warning under s. 7(7), must be fully complied with, even where no prejudice results from a breach of those requirements (*Murray v DPP* [1993] RTR 209). A blood sample provided voluntarily by the defendant before he is suspected of an excess alcohol offence is also admissible under s. 15(2) (*DPP v Carless* [2005] EWHC 3234 (Admin)).

Excluding Improperly Obtained Specimens

C5.31 Since the decision in *Fox* [1986] AC 281, a lawful arrest is not an essential prerequisite for lawfully requiring a specimen under the RTA 1988, s. 7. Indeed, subject to general principles about the admissibility of evidence illegally or unlawfully obtained (see **F2.8** *et seq.*), it is arguable that no irregularity in the preliminary testing procedure under ss. 6 to 6E can have any effect on the subsequent procedure under s. 7 (*Carmichael v Wilson* 1993 JC 83). See also *DPP v Heywood* [1998] RTR 1 and *Harper v DPP* [2001] EWHC Admin 1071. Similarly, because time is of the essence and the police are not required to delay the breath test procedure in order for the defendant to obtain legal advice (see **C5.19**), the PACE 1984, s. 58 (right of access to solicitor: see **D1.37**) will not usually be breached, enabling s. 78 of that Act to be invoked to justify exclusion of the evidence of the test (*DPP v Rice* [2004] All ER (D) 131 (Mar)).

The decision in *Fox* did, however, recognise a discretion to exclude otherwise admissible evidence obtained by some trick, deception or other impropriety as envisaged in *Sang* [1980] AC 402. In *Matto v Wolverhampton Crown Court* [1987] RTR 337, officers followed the appellant on to private property, continued to administer a breath test to him and thereafter arrested him after their implied licence to remain had been terminated. The Crown Court was of the opinion that, in order to exercise the discretion under the PACE 1984, s. 78, it must find that the police officers were knowingly acting in excess of their powers, and therefore acting in bad faith, and that evidence had been obtained other than voluntarily. In allowing the appeal, Woolf LJ stated that the approach of the Crown Court was wrong (at p. 347):

> . . . it was at least open to the Crown Court, if the matter had been properly left before them, for them to have come to a conclusion that what happened at the house was still affecting the fairness of what happened in the police station and, because it affected the fairness of what happened at the police station, that would in turn give rise to an argument as to the admissibility of the evidence under section 78 of the Police and Criminal Evidence Act 1984.

In *Thomas* [1991] RTR 292, Tudor-Evans J stated (at p. 294):

> . . . in principle and upon authority, it is open to a defendant to argue that the procedures at the police station were so tainted by the previous conduct of the police at the roadside that there was a discretion to exclude the evidence of what happened at the police station.

It is not normally permissible, however, to raise this type of issue before the Divisional Court if it was not raised initially before the justices themselves (*Braham v DPP* [1996] RTR 30).

The Statutory Assumption

C5.32 The assumption in the RTA 1988, s. 15(2) (see **C5.29**), relates to the proportion of alcohol in the defendant's specimen at the time of the offence. The assumption is not rebuttable (*Beauchamp-Thompson v DPP* [1988] RTR 54; *Millard v DPP* [1990] RTR 201) and a court is not competent to receive expert evidence aimed at undermining the assumption (*Griffiths v DPP* (2002) 166 JP 629). The assumption has been found not to be incompatible with the presumption of innocence in the ECHR, Article 6(2) (*Parker v DPP* [2001] RTR 240; *Drummond* [2002] RTR 371).

The assumption provides the 'floor' in relation to the amount of alcohol in the defendant's breath, blood or urine at the relevant time. Accordingly, the prosecution are entitled to produce evidence by way of back-calculation to show that, at the time of driving, attempting to drive or being in charge, the proportion was even higher than the specimen shows and was therefore in excess of the prescribed limit. In *Gumbley v Cunningham* [1988] QB 170, the appellant driver was involved in a fatal accident at 11.15 p.m. Four hours and 20 minutes later, he provided a specimen of blood analysed at 59 milligrammes per 100 millilitres. The prosecution adduced evidence to demonstrate that a person of the height, age, weight and physical condition of the appellant would, at the time of driving, have had alcohol in his body in the range of 120 to 130 milligrammes in blood. In upholding his conviction in the Divisional Court, Mann J said (at p. 181):

> Evidence which is material to the question of what was the proportion of alcohol at the moment of driving must be admissible. The provisions of [the RTOA 1988, s. 15(2) and (3)] do not preclude evidence other than that revealed by a specimen to show a greater level of alcohol although, subject to the 'hip-flask' defence, the specimen will always provide a 'not less' or base figure. If that figure is above the prescribed limit, other evidence is unnecessary to establish the offence.
>
> Our conclusion means that those who drive whilst above the prescribed limits cannot necessarily escape punishment because of the lapse of time. However, our conclusion also means that in cases

> where a sample provided a substantial period of time after driving has ceased shows a level below the prescribed limit justices may find themselves confronted with evidence of a complicated and scientific nature. . . . We think it needs to be said, therefore, that in our view the prosecution should not seek to rely on evidence of back-calculation save where that evidence is easily understood and clearly persuasive of the presence of excess alcohol at the time when a defendant was driving. Moreover, justices must be very careful especially where there is conflicting evidence not to convict unless, upon the scientific and other evidence which they find it safe to rely on, they are sure an excess of alcohol was in the defendant's body when he was actually driving as charged.

Where the analyses of two specimens of blood or urine differ in the amount of alcohol contained in them, it is for the justices to evaluate all the evidence before them. If in any reasonable doubt, they should choose that most favourable to the defendant (*Froggatt v Allcock* [1975] RTR 372n).

Defences

The Statutory 'Hip-flask' Defence Section 15(3) of the RTOA 1988 (see **C5.29**) affords a defence to a charge under the RTA 1988, s. 5, where the defendant claims that the fact that he has alcohol in his body above the prescribed limit is attributable to consumption after the event to an extent that, but for that later consumption of alcohol, evidence from the specimen would not have resulted in an offence being made out. Once the statutory assumption (see **C5.32**) has to be made, the onus shifts to the defendant to raise the 'hip-flask' defence (*Patterson v Charlton* [1986] RTR 18). In *Drummond* [2002] RTR 371, the Court of Appeal decided not to 'read down' s. 15(3) under the HRA 1998, s. 3, so that it imposes only an evidential burden (see e.g., *Lambert* [2002] 2 AC 545 at **F3.13**) and ruled that the persuasive burden imposed does not interfere with the presumption of innocence in the ECHR, Article 6(2), because it is no greater an interference than is necessary. This approach was confirmed as remaining correct post-*Sheldrake* (see **C5.34**) in *DPP v Ellery* [2005] EWHC 2513 (Admin). **C5.33**

The defence also extends to offences under the RTA 1988, ss. 3A and 4 (see **C3.19** and **C5.37**). In the case of an offence under s. 3A, evidence of post-accident consumption of alcohol is admissible even if the defendant drove after the accident because s. 3A looks at the state of intoxication at the time the cause of death arose. In *Dawson v Lunn* [1986] RTR 234, Robert Goff LJ said (at p. 238):

> . . . there are circumstances in which, as a matter of common sense, laymen can reach a perfectly sensible conclusion unaided by scientific evidence. We need only to take the simple case of somebody who satisfies the justices on the evidence that he had drunk only a small amount before driving, and that after ceasing to drive he had drunk a substantial quantity of alcohol. The justices can then conclude as laymen, reliably and confidently . . . that the defendant has satisfied them, on the balance of probabilities, that he has consumed alcohol after ceasing to drive and that had he not done so the proportion of alcohol in his breath, or blood, or urine would not have exceeded the prescribed limit. But there must be cases where the justices cannot sensibly draw that conclusion themselves unaided by expert evidence.

The court then went on to adopt the passage in *Pugsley v Hunter* [1973] 1 WLR 578 (a case on 'special reasons'), where Lord Widgery CJ observed that 'unless the case really is an obvious one . . . the only way in which a defendant can discharge the onus is by calling medical evidence'. The court also discouraged reliance upon extracts from scientific journals. Except perhaps in the clearest of cases, the defendant must therefore call scientific evidence (*DPP v Singh* [1988] RTR 209). Where there is no expert evidence, the justices should avoid drawing their own conclusions about the probable effect of the claimed consumption of alcohol (*Lonergan v DPP* [2003] RTR 188). Where the justices have the benefit of expert evidence, despite apparent discrepancies, they may be entitled to find that the defendant has discharged the onus on him (*DPP v Lowden* [1993] RTR 349).

If expert evidence is to be called, it should be disclosed to the prosecution to avoid unnecessary adjournments (*DPP v O'Connor* [1992] RTR 66).

C5.34 **Other Defences** Section 5(2) of the RTA 1988 provides a defence to an allegation of 'in charge' of the vehicle, based on the likelihood of the defendant driving while still above the prescribed limit. In *Sheldrake v DPP* [2004] 1 AC 264, the House of Lords determined that there was no need to 'read down' this reverse onus of proof as an evidential burden only (as the majority of the Divisional Court had, relying on the presumption of innocence in the ECHR, Article 6(2)) and that this was a provision properly imposing a legal burden on the defendant, which was justified as pursuing a legitimate objective that was neither unreasonable or arbitrary. See **F3.13** for a full discussion of the 'reverse burden'.

In *Drake v DPP* [1994] RTR 411, the Divisional Court held that the presence of a wheel clamp on a motor vehicle could not be disregarded when considering the likelihood of the defendant driving. Medical or other expert evidence will almost inevitably be required to establish the probable alcohol level at the time at which the defendant will next drive (*DPP v Frost* [1989] RTR 11), unless the length of time involved makes that conclusion obvious. As to duress, see **A3.21** to **A3.29**.

Insanity cannot be raised as a defence as there is no *mens rea* element to which it can relate (*DPP v H* [1997] 1 WLR 1406).

Punishment

C5.35 For offences of driving or attempting to drive, the penalty is six months' imprisonment and/or a fine up to level 5 on the standard scale. Disqualification and endorsement are obligatory unless there are 'special reasons', and the offence carries between 3 and 11 penalty points. An order for forfeiture may be made under either offence (see **C7.28** and **E20.1**).

The offence of being 'in charge' is punishable by imprisonment for up to three months and/or a fine up to level 4. Disqualification is discretionary; endorsement with 10 penalty points is obligatory.

Sentencing

C5.36 The Magistrates' Courts Guidelines (2004) indicate that, as a starting point, a custodial sentence might properly be considered for readings of 116 microgrammes in 100 millilitres of breath (equating to 265 milligrammes in 100 millilitres of blood or 355 milligrammes in 100 millilitres of urine). In *Nokes* [1978] RTR 101, it was accepted that there is no rule that a first offence should not attract a custodial sentence if the facts show it to be appropriate. In *Shoult* [1996] RTR 298, Lord Taylor CJ explained that the comment of Sachs J in *Cook* [1996] 1 Cr App R (S) 350, when quashing a sentence of two months' imprisonment and substituting a fine of £500, that it 'can never be appropriate to send a man for this criminality [140 microgrammes in breath], at the lower end of the scale as it is, to prison' had been based on a misunderstanding of the effect of the reading and should not be followed. Instead, the Magistrates' Courts Guidelines were expressly approved as the basic starting point, from which increases or reductions could be made depending on the individual facts of each case.

DRIVING, OR BEING IN CHARGE, WHEN UNDER INFLUENCE OF DRINK OR DRUGS

C5.37 **Road Traffic Act 1988, s. 4**

(1) A person who, when driving or attempting to drive a mechanically propelled vehicle on a road or other public place, is unfit to drive through drink or drugs is guilty of an offence.

(2) Without prejudice to subsection (1) above, a person who, when in charge of a mechanically propelled vehicle which is on a road or other public place, is unfit to drive through drink or drugs is guilty of an offence.

(3) For the purposes of subsection (2) above, a person shall be deemed not to have been in charge of a mechanically propelled vehicle if he proves that at the material time the circumstances were such that there was no likelihood of his driving it so long as he remained unfit to drive through drink or drugs.

(4) The court may, in determining whether there was such a likelihood as is mentioned in subsection (3) above, disregard any injury to him and any damage to the vehicle.

(5) For the purposes of this section, a person shall be taken to be unfit to drive if his ability to drive properly is for the time being impaired.

Elements

The RTOA 1988, ss. 11 and 12(1), apply; see **C2.5** and **C2.6**. The RTA 1988, s. 11 defines 'drugs' as including any intoxicant other than alcohol. For the meaning of the terms 'attempting', 'driving', 'motor vehicle' and 'road or other public place', see **C1.3**, **C1.8** and **C1.9**, **C1.12**, and **C1.14** and **C1.15**. For 'in charge', see **C5.25**. **C5.38**

Section 4 creates three separate offences. The prosecution must establish that the defendant was driving or attempting to drive, or was in charge of a motor vehicle on a road or public place, and that at the time his ability to drive properly was impaired though drink or drugs. The charge may read 'drink or drugs' without either being duplicitous or bad for uncertainty.

Drugs

Medicines are drugs for the purposes of the RTA 1988, s. 4, and include, for instance, insulin and toluene (*Armstrong v Clark* [1957] 2 QB 391; *Bradford v Wilson* (1983) 78 Cr App R 77). In *Watmore v Jenkins* [1962] 2 QB 572, the defendant had been overtaken by a hypoglycaemic episode and coma through a fall in his cortisone level and a consequent increase in his insulin level, brought about by a combination of injected insulin and an improvement in his liver function following recovery from an attack of jaundice. In those unusual circumstances, the Divisional Court upheld an acquittal of driving whilst unfit through drugs as the justices were entitled to 'entertain a reasonable doubt whether the injected insulin was more than a predisposing or historical cause' of the defendant's state. **C5.39**

In *Ealing Magistrates' Court, ex parte Woodman* [1994] RTR 181, the conviction of a diabetic suffering a hypoglycaemic attack was quashed because there was no evidence entitling the stipendiary magistrate to conclude that the presence of insulin in the applicant's blood was the real effective cause of the attack. The Divisional Court decided that it would only be appropriate to rely on s. 4 in such cases where there is evidence of a clear overdose of insulin having been taken by the defendant.

Evidence of Impairment

This may be provided by the opinion evidence of an expert witness, normally a doctor, who has examined the defendant, even if he has refused to be examined, and his testimony should be treated as that of any 'independent expert witness giving evidence to assist the court', whether he be a police surgeon or anyone else (*Lanfear* [1968] 2 QB 77). Opinion evidence of the defendant's state or of the amount he has drunk may be given even by a lay witness, but the opinion of such a lay witness as to whether or not the defendant was fit to drive is not admissible. Nor could a lay witness give evidence as to the amount of alcohol in the defendant's blood. As to opinion evidence by lay witnesses generally, see **F10.2**. **C5.40**

The prosecution are not obliged to adduce opinion evidence of an expert witness in order to establish the defendant's impairment to drive, provided that the totality of the evidence actually adduced suffices to satisfy the justices of this element (*Leetham v DPP* [1999] RTR 29). Such evidence may include the manner of the driving, the defendant's apparent physical state and any admission made relating to the consumption of drugs and, presumably, alcohol. Presumably observations of a defendant's performance in a preliminary impairment test under the RTA 1988, s. 6B, will also be capable of being adduced as relevant evidence on this point.

The prosecution may adduce evidence of the amount of alcohol or a drug in a specimen properly provided by the defendant under the RTA 1988, s. 7. Such evidence is admissible by virtue of the RTOA 1988, ss. 15 and 16 (see **C5.29** and **C5.26**).

Defences

C5.41 The RTA 1988, s. 4(3), provides a defence to an allegation that the defendant was 'in charge' of the vehicle similar to that contained in s. 5(2) (see **C5.34**). The defence imposes a permissible legal burden, rather than just an evidential burden, on the defendant (*Sheldrake v DPP* [2004] 1 AC 264: see **C5.34**).

The defence may also adduce evidence of post-incident consumption to rebut the assumption that he was unfit at the time of the alleged offence (see the RTOA 1988, s. 15(3) and **C5.33**). Evidence of post-incident drug use may provide a defence in comparable circumstances.

Punishment

C5.42 For offences of driving or attempting to drive when unfit, the penalty is a maximum of six months' imprisonment and/or a fine up to level 5 on the standard scale. Endorsement and disqualification for one year are obligatory unless there are 'special reasons'. The offence carries between 3 and 11 penalty points. Forfeiture of the vehicle may be ordered (see **C7.28** and **E20.1**).

The offence of being 'in charge' carries three months' imprisonment and/or a fine up to level 4. Disqualification is discretionary but endorsement with 10 penalty points is obligatory.

INTERPRETATION OF THE ROAD TRAFFIC ACT 1988, ss. 3A TO 10

C5.43 **Road Traffic Act 1988, s. 11**

(1) The following provisions apply for the interpretation of sections 3A to 10 of this Act.

(2) In those sections—

'drug' includes any intoxicant other than alcohol,

'fail' includes refuse,

'hospital' means an institution which provides medical or surgical treatment for in-patients or out-patients,

'the prescribed limit' means, as the case may require—

(a) 35 microgrammes of alcohol in 100 millilitres of breath,

(b) 80 milligrammes of alcohol in 100 millilitres of blood, or

(c) 107 milligrammes of alcohol in 100 millilitres of urine,

or such other proportion as may be prescribed by regulations made by the Secretary of State,

'registered health care professional' means a person (other than a medical practitioner) who is—

(a) a registered nurse; or

(b) a registered member of a health care profession which is designated for the purposes of this paragraph by an order made by the Secretary of State.

(2A) A health care profession is any profession mentioned in section 60(2) of the Health Act 1999 other than the profession of practising medicine and the profession of nursing.

(2B) An order under subsection (2) shall be made by statutory instrument; and any such statutory instrument shall be subject to annulment in pursuance of a resolution of either House of Parliament.

(3) A person does not co-operate with a preliminary test or provide a specimen of breath for analysis unless his co-operation or the specimen—

  (a) is sufficient to enable the test or the analysis to be carried out, and

  (b) is provided in such a way as to enable the objective of the test or analysis to be satisfactorily achieved.

(4) A person provides a specimen of blood if and only if—

  (a) he consents to the taking of such a specimen from him; and

  (b) the specimen is taken from him by a medical practitioner or, if it is taken in a police station, either by a medical practitioner or by a registered health care professional.

Section C6 Summary Traffic Offences

Careless and Inconsiderate Driving

C6.1 **Road Traffic Act 1988, s. 3**

If a person drives a mechanically propelled vehicle on a road or other public place without due care and attention, or without reasonable consideration for other persons using the road or place, he is guilty of an offence.

C6.2 **Elements** The RTOA 1988, ss. 1, 11, and 12(1), apply; see **C2.1**, **C2.5**, and **C2.6**.

For the meaning of the terms 'drive', 'road or other public place' and 'mechanically propelled vehicle', see **C1.8** and **C1.9**, **C1.14** and **C1.15**, and **C1.12**. Section 3 creates two separate offences, commonly called 'careless driving' and 'driving without reasonable consideration'.

The term 'other persons using the road' includes persons who are pedestrians or passengers in vehicles, including that driven by the defendant, as well as other motorists (*Pawley v Wharldall* [1966] 1 QB 373).

C6.3 **Careless Driving** In *Simpson v Peat* [1952] 2 QB 24, Lord Goddard CJ stated that if a driver was 'exercising the degree of care and attention which a reasonable prudent driver would exercise, he ought not to be convicted' of careless driving.

Following the amendment of the RTA 1972 by the Criminal Law Act 1977, Lord Diplock in *Lawrence* [1982] AC 510 considered, albeit *obiter*, the position of offences of careless driving after the offence of dangerous driving (in its former existence) had been abolished (at p. 525):

> Section 3 creates an absolute offence in the sense in which that term is commonly used to denote an offence for which the only *mens rea* needed is simply that the prohibited physical act (*actus reus*) done by the accused was directed by a mind that was conscious of what his body was doing, it being unnecessary to show that his mind was also conscious of the possible consequences of his doing it. So section 3 takes care of the kind of inattention or misjudgment to which the ordinarily careful motorist is occasionally subject without its necessarily involving any moral turpitude, although it causes inconvenience and annoyance to other users of the road.

In *DPP v Cox* (1993) 157 JP 1044, Clarke J explained the underlying principles of the offence, and that in certain circumstances there is effectively a presumption of carelessness, stating (at p. 1047):

> The appellant advances the following propositions of law. First, for justices to convict a defendant of driving without due care and attention contrary to section 3 of the Road Traffic Act 1988, the prosecution must prove beyond reasonable doubt that the defendant was not exercising that degree of care and attention that a reasonable and prudent driver would exercise in the circumstances. Secondly, that standard is an objective one, impersonal and universal, fixed in relation to the safety of other users of the highway. Thirdly, if the facts are such that in the

absence of an explanation put forward by the defendant, or that explanation is objectively inadequate, and the only possible conclusion is that he was careless, he should be convicted. In my judgment, all those propositions of law are correct.

Departure from the standard of driving required by the Highway Code, whilst not in itself an offence, may well establish liability under the RTA 1988, s. 3, but adherence to the Highway Code may, equally, negative such a liability. For the admissibility of the provisions of the Highway Code, see the RTA 1988, s. 38, and C2.4. Each case must be objectively decided on its own facts in the surrounding circumstances. Only if the court considers that the driver has or must have failed to exercise the degree of care and attention which the reasonable, prudent and competent driver would have exercised, should a conviction result. It follows that a particular manner of driving may be careless in one situation but not in another.

On occasions, for example where a driver veers off in the course of overtaking and collides with an oncoming vehicle, the only inference that can be drawn is that the defendant drove carelessly. To draw another inference, such as mechanical defect, without any evidence to support that inference means that the justices have misdirected themselves (*DPP v Tipton* (1992) 156 JP 172). Crossing a road's dividing line is prima facie evidence of carelessness, necessitating an explanation which is acceptable on the facts (*Mundi v Warwickshire Police* [2001] EWHC Admin 447).

In *DPP v Parker* [1989] RTR 413, the respondent had been driving in a line of traffic which came to a halt, and he ran into the back of the car in front which then ran into another car in front. He was not driving fast immediately before the accident and because of the rain, road conditions were wet and slippery. The Divisional Court held that while such driving might in other circumstances be sufficient to constitute an offence, whether it was sufficient in this case had been a question of fact. There was insufficient material to justify a finding that the justices' decision on the facts was perverse, and the appeal accordingly failed.

In *Wilson v MacPhail* 1991 SCCR 170, overtaking a long line of stationary cars at temporary traffic lights and causing obstruction to oncoming traffic after the lights had changed in their favour was held to amount to a failure to exercise the degree of care expected of a reasonable, competent and prudent driver.

The Prosecution Team's document 'Driving Offences, incorporating the charging standard' gives the following examples of driving which may amount to driving without due care and attention: overtaking on the inside; driving inappropriately close to another vehicle; driving through a red light; and emerging from a side road into the path of another vehicle. In addition, the following conduct whilst driving may also amount to driving without due care and attention: using a hand-held mobile phone whilst the vehicle is moving; tuning a car radio; reading a newspaper/map; selecting and lighting a cigarette/cigar/pipe; and talking to or looking at a passenger. These are indicative only and not conclusive as to the type of behaviour which might constitute careless driving.

Although there is no rule of law which requires justices to adjourn any trial involving a fatal road traffic accident until the inquest has been concluded, as a matter of practice it is desirable for them to do so (*Smith v DPP* [2000] RTR 36).

Driving without Reasonable Consideration The essence of this limb of the RTA 1988, s. 3, is that other road users are inconvenienced by the driving of the defendant. Evidence of such inconvenience may be provided either by the direct testimony of another road user, or by inference to be drawn from evidence of the reactions or behaviour of other road users. **C6.4**

The Prosecution Team's document 'Driving Offences, incorporating the charging standard' gives the following examples of conduct appropriate for a charge of driving without reasonable consideration: flashing of lights to *force* other drivers in front to give way; misuse of any lane to avoid queuing or gain some other advantage over other drivers; unnecessarily remaining in an overtaking lane; unnecessarily slow driving or braking without good cause; driving with undipped headlights that dazzle oncoming drivers; driving through a puddle causing pedestrians to be splashed; and driving a bus in such a way as to scare the passengers.

C6.5 **Statutory Definition** When the Road Safety Act 2006, s. 30, is brought into force, both offences under the RTA 1988, s. 3, will benefit from the clarity brought about through codification of the current basic tests. This provision prospectively inserts s. 3ZA into the RTA 1988, which will also apply to s. 2B (the new offence involving fatal consequences: see **C3.26**) and s. 3A (see **C3.19**). This development reflects the inclusion of a test for dangerous driving (s. 2A: see **C3.10**) and, in part, follows its formula. The principles previously used as examples are still likely to constitute the respective offences.

For driving without due care and attention (s. 3ZA(2) and (3)), the single test will be 'if (and only if)' the way the person drives 'falls below what would be expected of a competent and careful driver'. Under this test, not only is it an objective standard, but the court can also consider any particular matters known at the time to the driver because, in determining what would be expected of a careful and competent driver, 'regard shall be had not only to the circumstances of which he could have been expected to be aware but also to any circumstances shown to have been within the knowledge of the accused'.

For driving without reasonable consideration for other persons (s. 3ZA(4)), the offence will be made out *only* if those persons are inconvenienced by the driving in question.

C6.6 **Defences** Mechanical defect, automatism, and necessity (*Backshall* [1998] 1 WLR 1506); see **C1.11, C1.4** and **A3.28**. No offence is committed under s. 3 where the driving took place in a public place other than a road in the course of an authorised motoring event (RTA 1988, s. 13A).

C6.7 **Alternative Verdicts** See the RTOA 1988, s. 24, set out at **C2.12**.

On a trial on indictment for an offence under the RTA 1988, s. 1, 2 or 3A, (and, once the Road Safety Act 2006, s. 20(2), is brought into force, for an offence under the RTA 1988, s. 2B), the jury may find the defendant guilty of an offence under s. 3, (unless he has already been acquitted of it (*DPP v Khan* [1997] RTR 82)), and the Crown Court has the same sentencing powers as a magistrates' court when that occurs. Where the prosecution have not accepted a guilty plea to careless driving and the defendant has been found not guilty of dangerous driving, without an alternative verdict having been entered, the previous guilty plea is a nullity and the court cannot proceed to sentence in respect of it (*McGregor-Read* [1999] Crim LR 860). The requirement for a notice under s. 1(1) of the RTOA 1988 is waived by s. 2(4) of that Act as long as the original requirement for a warning notice, if any, has been complied with.

It is not open to the prosecution to accept a plea of guilty to a charge of careless driving which has been committed for trial under the CJA 1988, s. 41, and offer no evidence on the indictable offence of reckless (now dangerous) driving (*Foote* [1993] RTR 171). Offences committed for trial under s. 41 can be dealt with only following a conviction for an indictable offence arising out of circumstances which are the same as or connected with the summary offence. The question whether the alternative finding of careless driving can be accepted as a guilty plea was left open in *Foote*, and now seems to have been answered in the affirmative in *Davis* (19 April 1996 unreported), which decided that a separate count for careless driving on an indictment containing a fatal driving count was invalid, the inference being that a plea to the latter count is available, despite the wording of s. 24 militating against any alternative finding of guilt other than by the jury.

If a defendant is acquitted, by magistrates, of an offence under s. 2, the court may direct or allow a charge for an offence under s. 3 to be preferred (RTOA 1988, s. 24(3)). This power extends to the Crown Court on an appeal against conviction for dangerous driving (see *Killington v Butcher* [1979] Crim LR 458; Supreme Court Act 1981, s. 79(3)). The requirement for a notice of intended prosecution is waived by the RTOA 1988, s. 2(6), as long as the original requirement for a warning notice, if any, has been complied with.

In *Coventry Justices, ex parte Sayers* [1979] RTR 22, the court held that the six-month time limit did not apply to a charge preferred under s. 24(3).

Powers to Stop, Seize and Remove Vehicles C6.8

Police Reform Act 2002, s. 59

(1) Where a constable in uniform has reasonable grounds for believing that a motor vehicle is being used on any occasion in a manner which—
   (a) contravenes section 3 or 34 of the Road Traffic Act 1988 (careless and inconsiderate driving and prohibition of off-road driving), and
   (b) is causing, or is likely to cause, alarm, distress or annoyance to members of the public,
   he shall have the powers set out in subsection (3).

(2) A constable in uniform shall also have the powers set out in subsection (3) where he has reasonable grounds for believing that a motor vehicle has been used on any occasion in a manner falling within subsection (1).

(3) Those powers are—
   (a) power, if the motor vehicle is moving, to order the person driving it to stop the vehicle;
   (b) power to seize and remove the motor vehicle;
   (c) power, for the purposes of exercising a power falling within paragraph (a) or (b), to enter any premises on which he has reasonable grounds for believing the motor vehicle to be;
   (d) power to use reasonable force, if necessary, in the exercise of any power conferred by any of paragraphs (a) to (c).

(4) A constable shall not seize a motor vehicle in the exercise of the powers conferred on him by this section unless—
   (a) he has warned the person appearing to him to be the person whose use falls within subsection (1) that he will seize it, if that use continues or is repeated; and
   (b) it appears to him that the use has continued or been repeated after the warning.

(5) Subsection (4) does not require a warning to be given by a constable on any occasion on which he would otherwise have the power to seize a motor vehicle under this section if—
   (a) the circumstances make it impracticable for him to give the warning;
   (b) the constable has already on that occasion given a warning under that subsection in respect of any use of that motor vehicle or of another motor vehicle by that person or any other person;
   (c) the constable has reasonable grounds for believing that such a warning has been given on that occasion otherwise than by him; or
   (d) the constable has reasonable grounds for believing that the person whose use of that motor vehicle on that occasion would justify the seizure is a person to whom a warning under that subsection has been given (whether or not by that constable or in respect the same vehicle or the same or a similar use) on a previous occasion in the previous twelve months.

(6) A person who fails to comply with an order under subsection (3)(a) is guilty of an offence and shall be liable, on summary conviction, to a fine not exceeding level 3 on the standard scale.

(7) Subsection (3)(c) does not authorise entry into a private dwelling house.

(8) The powers conferred on a constable by this section shall be exercisable only at a time when regulations under section 60 are in force.

(9) In this section—
   'driving' has the same meaning as in the Road Traffic Act 1988;
   'motor vehicle' means any mechanically propelled vehicle, whether or not it is intended or adapted for use on roads; and
   'private dwelling house' does not include any garage or other structure occupied with the dwelling house, or any land appurtenant to the dwelling house.

The Police (Retention and Disposal of Motor Vehicles) Regulations 2002 (SI 2002 No. 3049) have, as required by s. 59(8), been made under s. 60.

C6.9 **Punishment** The penalty for the offence is a fine up to level 4 on the standard scale. When the Road Safety Act 2006, s. 23, is brought into force, the maximum fine will rise to level 5. Disqualification is discretionary but endorsement, in the absence of 'special reasons', with between three and nine penalty points is obligatory. In appropriate cases, the court may disqualify the defendant until an extended driving test is passed under the RTOA 1988, s. 36 (see *Miller* (1994) 15 Cr App R (S) 505 at **C7.13**).

C6.10 **Sentencing** In *Simpson* (1981) 3 Cr App R (S) 148, a young man of 18 was driving a loaded lorry on a wet road. The lorry had a tendency to pull to the left when the brakes were applied, and on the relevant occasion it did so causing a fatal accident. The court felt the sentence should be in excess of the recommended fine suggested by the Magistrates' Association but, given the otherwise blameless record of the appellant, a disqualification for 12 months should be reduced to three months. In *Farenden* (1984) 6 Cr App R (S) 42, the appellant was indicted for reckless driving, but convicted of careless driving which occurred whilst he was being pursued by the police. He was disqualified for three months. In the magistrates' court he was convicted of driving with excess alcohol in his blood (120 milligrammes). The court reduced the period of disqualification to one month, which it considered sufficient on a first conviction for careless driving. In *Palmer* (1995) 16 Cr App R (S) 85, the appellant, who was driving a fire engine which was responding to an emergency call, pleaded guilty after colliding with a car in a bank of fog and causing injury to two of the car's occupants. The Court of Appeal, noting that disqualification could not be avoided, considered that three months would have been an adequate period.

Sanders (1987) 9 Cr App R (S) 390 was a case where a 44-year-old managing director earning a very considerable salary was fined £750 and disqualified for 12 months. He had driven his car at an excessive speed, lost control on a bridge, and collided with an oncoming car. Russell LJ said (at p. 391):

> Our attention has been drawn by counsel to certain guidelines which are applied in the magistrates' courts, where of course offences of driving without due care and attention have to be dealt with from day to day. Just as on previous occasions this court has taken account of those guidelines, so we do, but we remind ourselves that they are no more than guidelines and that each individual case has to be considered upon its individual merits.

The court, nonetheless, reduced the disqualification from 12 to six months, but felt that the fine (the maximum at that time being £1,000) was entirely appropriate.

In *Soutar* (1994) 15 Cr App R (S) 432, where the appellant had driven at an excessive speed and caused grave injury to a pedestrian in a collision, the fine imposed was halved to £750 and the period of disqualification reduced from two years to 18 months.

Where one or more deaths result from the careless driving, the sentencer is entitled to bear that fact in mind when sentencing, although the defendant's culpability or criminality remains the primary consideration (*Simmonds* [1999] 2 Cr App R 18; *King* [2001] 2 Cr App R (S) 114). This is a departure from the previous line of authority established by *Krawec* [1985] RTR 1 (see Lord Lane CJ at p. 3) and subsequent cases. Henry LJ found 'the concept of a road traffic offence in which the sentencing court is obliged to disregard the fact that a death has been caused as wholly anomalous'. In the years since *Krawec* there has been a general toughening of sentencing policy reflecting public opinion in respect of fatal road traffic incidents which has finally filtered down to offences under the RTA 1988, s. 3. Equally, however, the distinction between careless driving and those other more serious offences is that the latter require a death to have been caused as one of their elements. Two identical pieces of careless driving may currently attract disparate sentences simply because one instance results in death, although this will, when the Road Safety Act 2006, s. 20, is brought into force, result from the considerably increased sentencing powers available for the new offence of causing death by careless, or inconsiderate, driving (see C3.26 *et seq.*).

As to compensation orders, see E18, particularly E18.1.

Motor Racing on Highways

Road Traffic Act 1988, s. 12 C6.11

(1) A person who promotes or takes part in a race or trial of speed between motor vehicles on a public way is guilty of an offence.

Elements The RTOA 1988, ss. 11 and 12(1), apply; see C2.5 and C2.6. C6.12

This offence seems intended to prohibit organised motor racing on a highway, but might equally apply where two or more drivers are engaged in an unofficial race or speed trial. Such conduct may, of course, be an offence under the RTRA 1984, s. 88(7), or the RTA 1988, s. 2 or 3, but its ambit appears to be wider as persons who 'promote' or 'take part' may be convicted, and there is thus no requirement to prove an act of driving but merely of participation.

Punishment The offence carries a fine of up to level 4 on the standard scale. Unless 'special reasons' are established, there is a minimum disqualification from driving for a period of 12 months. Persons who 'promote' or 'take part' must be disqualified even though they are not drivers. The offence is endorsable with between 3 and 11 penalty points. C6.13

Leaving Vehicle in Dangerous Position

Road Traffic Act 1988, s. 22 C6.14

If a person in charge of a vehicle causes or permits the vehicle or a trailer drawn by it to remain at rest on a road in such a position or in such condition or in such circumstances as to involve a danger of injury to other persons using the road, he is guilty of an offence.

Elements For the meaning of the terms 'causing', 'permitting' and 'using', see C1.5, C1.6, and C1.7. The RTOA 1988, ss. 1, 11, and 12(1), apply; see C2.1, C2.5, and C2.6. C6.15

Section 22 applies to any vehicle, not just a motor vehicle. The offence may be established either where the vehicle itself involves a danger of injury (e.g., if it is on fire or parked on a hill without brakes and secured only by stones or bricks placed under the wheels), or where, because of its position on the road, it creates a danger. For example, parking a car or other vehicle on the corner of a busy intersection, obstructing the view of other motorists emerging from a side road, involves a danger of injury, because motorists would be forced to emerge 'blind' and, however cautiously this was done, the likelihood of a collision and consequent injury would remain.

Punishment A fine up to level 3 on the standard scale. If committed in respect of a motor vehicle, disqualification is discretionary and endorsement with 3 penalty points is obligatory. C6.16

Restriction of Carriage of Persons on Motor Cycles

Road Traffic Act 1988, s. 23 C6.17

(1) Not more than one person in addition to the driver may be carried on a motor bicycle.
(2) No person in addition to the driver may be carried on a motor bicycle otherwise than sitting astride the motor cycle and on a proper seat securely fixed to the motor cycle behind the driver's seat.
(3) If a person is carried on a motor cycle in contravention of this section, the driver of the motor cycle is guilty of an offence.

Elements The RTOA 1988, ss. 11 and 12(1), apply; see C2.5 and C2.6. C6.18

Punishment The offence carries a fine up to level 3. Disqualification is discretionary and endorsement with 3 penalty points obligatory. C6.19

Neglect or Refusal to Comply with Traffic Directions Given by Constable

C6.20 **Road Traffic Act 1988, s. 35**

(1) Where a constable or traffic officer is for the time being engaged in the regulation of traffic in a road, a person driving or propelling a vehicle who neglects or refuses—
(a) to stop the vehicle, or
(b) to make it proceed in, or keep to, a particular line of traffic,
when directed to do so by the constable in the execution of his duty or the traffic officer (as the case may be) is guilty of an offence.
(2) Where—
(a) a traffic survey of any description is being carried out on or in the vicinity of a road, and
(b) a constable or traffic officer gives to a person driving or propelling a vehicle a direction—
(i) to stop the vehicle,
(ii) to make it proceed in, or keep to, a particular line of traffic, or
(iii) to proceed to a particular point on or near the road on which the vehicle is being driven or propelled,
being a direction given for the purposes of the survey (but not a direction requiring any person to provide any information for the purposes of a traffic survey),
the person is guilty of an offence if he neglects or refuses to comply with the direction.
(3) The power to give such a direction as is referred to in subsection (2) above for the purposes of a traffic survey shall be so exercised as not to cause any unreasonable delay to a person who indicates that he is unwilling to provide any information for the purposes of the survey.

C6.21 **Elements** The RTOA 1988, ss. 1, 11 and 12(1), apply; see **C2.1**, **C2.5**, and **C2.6**.

This section extends to any vehicle as long as it is being driven or propelled. The reference to a constable includes a traffic warden if he is engaged in accordance with s. 35 in the regulation of traffic in the road.

There are two offences created. For an offence under s. 35(2), the constable must be giving a direction for the purposes of a traffic survey. Under s. 35(1), the constable must be acting in the execution of his duty, which in this case means a duty to protect life and property arising from the dangers created by unregulated traffic (*Hoffman v Thomas* [1974] 1 WLR 374; *Johnson v Phillips* [1976] 1 WLR 65). It is arguable, therefore, that for s. 35 to operate, the constable must have been engaged upon traffic duties and not exercising his powers either under the PACE 1984 or the RTA 1988, s. 163.

C6.22 **Punishment** The offence carries a fine up to level 3. If the offence is committed in respect of a motor vehicle, disqualification is discretionary, but endorsement with 3 penalty points is obligatory.

Failure to Comply with Indication Given by Traffic Sign

C6.23 **Road Traffic Act 1988, s. 36**

(1) Where a traffic sign, being a sign—
(a) of the prescribed size, colour and type, or
(b) of another character authorised by the Secretary of State under the provisions in that behalf of the Road Traffic Regulation Act 1984,
has been lawfully placed on or near a road, a person driving or propelling a vehicle who fails to comply with the indication given by the sign is guilty of an offence.
(2) A traffic sign shall not be treated for the purposes of this section as having been lawfully placed unless either—
(a) the indication given by the sign is an indication of a statutory prohibition, restriction or requirement, or
(b) it is expressly provided by or under any provision of the Traffic Acts that this section shall apply to the sign or to signs of a type of which the sign is one; and, where the indication mentioned in paragraph (a) of this subsection is of the general nature only of the prohibition, restriction or requirement to which the sign relates, a person shall not be convicted of failure to comply with the indication unless he has failed to comply with the prohibition, restriction or requirement to which the sign relates.

Elements The RTOA 1988, ss. 1, 11, 12(1) and 20, apply; see **C2.1**, **C2.5**, **C2.6**, and **C2.10**. **C6.24**

Traffic signs are prescribed by regulations made under the RTRA 1984, s. 64. If a sign indicates a statutory prohibition, restriction or requirement, or if it is expressly provided under any provision of the Traffic Acts that the section applies to the sign, a failure to comply with it is an offence.

The main relevant statutory instrument is the Traffic Signs Regulations and General Directions 2002 (SI 2002 No. 3113). Failure to comply with any traffic sign may constitute an offence but only failure by a person driving a motor vehicle to comply with a sign of a kind specified in reg. 10(2) of the regulations carries endorsement and disqualification. The signs so specified are 'Stop' signs at the junction of minor and major roads; 'double white lines'; 'Drivers of Large or Slow Vehicles Must Phone' signs at automatic half-barrier level crossings or automatic open crossings; and the red signal when shown by light signals prescribed by the regulations.

Emergency traffic signs are included, and all signs are deemed to conform unless the contrary is proved.

Save for possible defences of mechanical defect or automatism (as to which, see **C1.11** and **C1.4**), the section creates an absolute offence.

For contravention of the 'Stop' sign, it is necessary to prove either that the vehicle did not stop before crossing the line or, if the line is unclear, before entering the major road, or that the vehicle when proceeding past the line or entering the major road, if that line is not clearly visible, did so in a manner likely to cause danger to the driver of another vehicle on the major road, or so as to cause that driver to change his speed or course so as to avoid an accident.

For contravention of a red light, it is necessary to prove that the vehicle proceeded beyond the stop line or, if that is not visible or there is no stop line, beyond the mounting of the primary signal.

Regulation 36(1)(b) contains a waiver of the prohibition conveyed by the red light for vehicles being used for fire brigade, ambulance or police purposes, and substitutes instead a requirement that the vehicle will not proceed so as to cause danger to the driver of another vehicle, or to necessitate the driver of any such vehicle to change his speed or course in order to avoid an accident or so as to cause danger to non-vehicular traffic. See also *DPP v Harris* [1995] 1 Cr App R 170.

The prohibition contained by 'double white lines' operates not only to prevent the vehicle crossing those lines, but also to forbid vehicles stopping on any length of road along which the marking has been placed. Regulation 26 does, however, contain certain exemptions for vehicles which have to cross the line for the purposes of obtaining access or to pass a stationary vehicle, to enable passengers to board and alight, and so forth. Stopping within double white lines to pick up a taxi fare is not an offence (*McKenzie v DPP* [1997] RTR 175).

Where there was a failure to place a white arrow before solid double white lines in the centre of the road the lines were not a sign 'lawfully placed' for the purposes of the regulations and directions then in force and failure to comply with the double white lines was, therefore, not an offence contrary to s. 36 of the RTA 1988 (*O'Halloran v DPP* [1990] RTR 62).

Punishment The offence carries a fine up to level 3. If committed in respect of a motor vehicle by a failure to comply with a specified sign (see **C6.24**), disqualification is discretionary, but endorsement with 3 penalty points is obligatory. **C6.25**

Using Vehicle in Dangerous Condition

C6.26 **Road Traffic Act 1988, s. 40A**

A person is guilty of an offence if he uses, or causes or permits another to use, a motor vehicle or trailer on a road when—
(a) the condition of the motor vehicle or trailer, or of its accessories or equipment, or
(b) the purpose for which it is used, or
(c) the number of passengers carried by it, or the manner in which they are carried, or
(d) the weight, position or distribution of its load, or the manner in which it is secured, is such that the use of the motor vehicle or trailer involves a danger of injury to any person.

C6.27 **Elements** The RTOA 1988, ss. 11 and 12(1), apply; see **C2.5** and **C2.6**. For the meaning of the terms 'using', 'causing' and 'permitting' see **C1.7**, **C1.5**, and **C1.6**.

Section 40A puts into statute the more important construction and use requirements and widens the scope of their operation. For example, if the circumstances applying in *Young and C. F. Abraham (Transport) Ltd v CPS* [1992] RTR 194 (see **C6.31**) were to be repeated, s. 40A(d) would apply. Where a passenger is carried in the rear of a van and there are no seats or restraints of any kind there, the speed at which the van is driven will be a material consideration in relation to whether the manner of carriage is such as to involve a danger of injury under s. 40A(c) (*Akelis v Normand* 1997 SLT 136). Section 40A(c) involves considering objectively whether there was a danger inherent in the circumstances in which the vehicle was being driven at the material time (*Gray v DPP* [1999] RTR 339). Accordingly, when assessing that danger, justices can take into account the locality of the offence and the prevailing traffic conditions but must disregard any consequences, such as a serious accident, of the driving involved (*DPP v Potts* [2000] RTR 1).

C6.28 **Punishment** The offence is endorsable with 3 penalty points; disqualification is discretionary. When the Road Safety Act 2006, s. 25(1), is brought into force, in respect of a second offence committed within three years of a previous s. 40A offence, in the absence of 'special reasons', disqualification for six months will be obligatory, although it will remain discretionary only for other offences. Where the offence is committed in respect of a goods vehicle or a vehicle adapted to carry more than eight passengers, a fine of up to level 5 may be imposed; in other cases, a fine up to level 4 may be imposed.

Contravention of Construction and Use Regulations

C6.29 **Road Traffic Act 1988, s. 41A**

A person who—
(a) contravenes or fails to comply with a construction and use requirement as to brakes, steering-gear or tyres, or
(b) uses on a road a motor vehicle or trailer which does not comply with such a requirement, or causes or permits a motor vehicle or trailer to be so used,
is guilty of an offence.

Section 41B makes contravention of a requirement in relation to the weight of a goods vehicle or a passenger vehicle adapted to carry more than eight passengers an offence. It is a defence if the vehicle is proceeding to or from the nearest available weighbridge, which means the nearest one factually, irrespective of the driver's knowledge of its existence (*Vehicle and Operator Services Agency v F & S Gibbs Transport Services Limited* [2007] RTR 193)). In addition a 5 per cent excess may be excluded in certain circumstances. It is not essential for a certificate as to the accuracy of the weighbridge to be produced provided there is other evidence from which its accuracy can be ascertained (*Kelly Communications Ltd v DPP* (2003) 167 JP 73).

When the Road Safety Act 2006, s. 18, is brought into force, a new offence under the RTA 1988, s. 41C, will be created prohibiting vehicles being fitted with, or a person using a vehicle carrying, 'speed assessment equipment detection devices', which are devices 'the purpose, or one of the purposes, of which is to detect, or interfere with the operation of, equipment used to assess the speed of motor vehicles'.

Section 42 makes contravention of the other construction and use requirements an offence and extends this to cover 'using', 'causing' or 'permitting'.

Mobile Telephones, etc. With effect from 27 February 2007 (see SI 2007 No. 237), the Road Safety Act 2006, s. 26, has introduced a new offence under the RTA 1988, s. 41D, dealing specifically with a contravention or failure to comply with a requirement about not driving a motor vehicle in a position which does not give proper control or a full view of the road or traffic ahead or not driving, or supervising the driving, of a motor vehicle while using a hand-held mobile telephone or other hand-held interactive communication device. The offence extends to 'causing' or 'permitting' (see **C1.5** and **C1.6**). The principal reason for carving out such a specific offence was to make endorsement with penalty points obligatory and disqualification discretionary, thereby raising its seriousness closer to the alternative of charging driving without due care and attention. This reflects the dangers associated with needlessly irresponsible use by the driver of, in particular, mobile telephones whilst a vehicle is in motion. **C6.30**

Elements The RTOA 1988, ss. 11 and 12(1), apply to the RTA 1988, ss. 41A, 41B, 41D and 42 (and, in due course, will apply to the RTA 1988, s. 41C); see **C2.5** and **C2.6**. For the meaning of the terms 'using', 'causing' and 'permitting', see **C1.7**, **C1.5**, and **C1.6**. The relevant requirements are those contained in the Road Vehicles (Construction and Use) Regulations 1986 (SI 1986 No. 1078). **C6.31**

In order to show that a vehicle does not fall within any of the definitions contained either in the regulations or the Act, the burden of proof is on the defendant (*Wakeman v Catlow* [1977] RTR 174).

Regulations 13 to 18 and sch. 3 deal with brakes. Even if a trailer is not required to have brakes under reg. 18, any brakes fitted must be maintained in efficient working order (*DPP v Young* [1991] RTR 56). Regulation 27 deals with tyres.

Regulation 100 deals with vehicles which are in a dangerous condition and loads which cause a danger. See the RTA 1988, s. 42(2), for a statutory defence to a summons alleging a failure to comply with a requirement relating to any description of weight applicable to a goods vehicle. In *Young and C. F. Abraham (Transport) Ltd v CPS* [1992] RTR 194, a trailer loaded with an excavator collided with a footbridge because the excavator arms and bucket had not been lowered. The driver and the company were prosecuted for using a trailer for an unsuitable purpose 'as to cause or be likely to cause danger or nuisance to any person . . . on a road'. The Divisional Court decided that the risk came from the incorrect loading rather than the use of the trailer and that, in such circumstances, the offence was not made out.

In respect of an offence under the RTA 1988, s. 41D, reg. 110 imposes a range of restrictions involving driving-related activities that cannot be undertaken whilst the person is using a hand-held mobile telephone or a prescribed hand-held device. Regulation 110(5) contains specific exceptions for calls to the emergency services, where it is a response to a genuine emergency and if it would be unsafe or impracticable to cease the driving-related activity before making the call.

An examination of a vehicle, for the purposes of a prosecution, which involves a permanent alteration to its condition does not render the evidence thereby obtained inadmissible under the PACE 1984, s. 78, merely because the defence are unable to examine the vehicle in its original condition. It would be prudent for the prosecution to inform the defence of their examination and to afford them an opportunity to be present, but justices should hear such evidence and the fact that the defence are denied an opportunity to examine the vehicle goes to weight rather than admissibility (*DPP v British Telecommunications plc* [1991] Crim LR 532).

C6.32 **Punishment** A breach of s. 41A is endorsable with 3 penalty points; disqualification is discretionary. Where an offence is committed in respect of a goods vehicle or a vehicle adapted to carry more than eight passengers, a fine of up to level 5 may be imposed; in other cases, a fine up to level 4.

Breaches of s. 41B or 42 are not endorsable. Section 41B carries a fine up to level 5 and s. 42 carries a fine up to level 4 if committed in respect of a goods vehicle or a vehicle adapted to carry more than eight passengers; in other cases, a fine of up to level 3.

The new s. 41D offence is endorsable with 3 penalty points; disqualification is discretionary. Where an offence is committed in respect of a goods vehicle or a vehicle adapted to carry more than eight passengers, a fine up to level 4 may be imposed; in other cases, a fine up to level 3.

Breach of s. 41C (not yet in force) will be subject to the same penalty as a speeding offence, i.e. it is endorsable with between 3 and 6 penalty points or 3 points when a fixed penalty is imposed. It will carry a fine up to level 4 if committed on a special road (such as a motorway); in other cases, a fine up to level 3.

Driving Otherwise than in Accordance with a Licence

C6.33 **Road Traffic Act 1988, s. 87**

(1) It is an offence for a person to drive on a road a motor vehicle of any class otherwise than in accordance with a licence authorising him to drive a motor vehicle of that class.
(2) It is an offence for a person to cause or permit another person to drive on a road a motor vehicle of any class otherwise than in accordance with a licence authorising that other person to drive a motor vehicle of that class.

This offence encompasses driving without 'L' plates or (an alternative applicable only within Wales) 'D' plates, without supervision, driving under age and driving without a licence.

C6.34 **Elements** The RTOA 1988, ss. 11 and 12(1), apply; see **C2.5** and **C2.6**. For the meaning of 'cause' and 'permit', see **C1.5** and **C1.6**.

Section 88 of the Act creates certain exceptions. The approach to proof is the same as for the offence of no insurance (see **C6.37**).

Foreign drivers are subject to the Motor Vehicles (International Circulation) Order 1975 (SI 1975 No. 1208). If a person resident abroad and temporarily resident in Great Britain holds a Convention driving permit, a foreign driving permit or a British Forces (BFG) driving licence, it shall be lawful for him to drive during a period of 12 months from his last entry into the United Kingdom (unless he is under the minimum age or disqualified by court order). Community licence holders normally resident in Great Britain are no longer obliged to exchange their licences for ones issued under the 1988 Act so as to obtain continuing authorisation to drive (s. 99A of the Act), the only requirement being to deliver their Community licences within the prescribed period to the Secretary of State to enable counterparts to be issued (s. 99B of the Act).

C6.35 **Punishment** The offence carries a fine up to level 3. If the offender's driving would not have been in accordance with a licence that could have been granted, then, in the absence of 'special reasons', disqualification is discretionary and endorsement with between 3 and 6 penalty points is obligatory.

An offence of causing or permitting a person to drive without an appropriate licence contrary to s. 87(2) is punishable only by a fine up to level 3 on the standard scale.

Using etc. Motor Vehicle without Insurance

Road Traffic Act 1988, s. 143 C6.36

(1) Subject to the provisions of this part of this Act—
(a) a person must not use a motor vehicle on a road or other public place unless there is in force in relation to the use of the vehicle by that person such a policy of insurance or such a security in respect of third party risks as complies with the requirements of this part of this Act, and
(b) a person must not cause or permit any other person to use a motor vehicle on a road or other public place unless there is in force in relation to the use of the vehicle by that other person such a policy of insurance or such a security in respect of third party risks as complies with the requirements of this part of this Act.
(2) If a person acts in contravention of subsection (1) above he is guilty of an offence.
(3) A person charged with using a motor vehicle in contravention of this section shall not be convicted if he proves—
(a) that the vehicle did not belong to him and was not in his possession under a contract of hiring or of loan,
(b) that he was using the vehicle in the course of his employment, and
(c) that he neither knew nor had reason to believe that there was not in force in relation to the vehicle such a policy of insurance or security as is mentioned in subsection (1) above.
(4) This part of this Act does not apply to invalid carriages.

Elements The RTOA 1988, ss. 6, 11, and 12(1), apply; see **C2.2**, **C2.5**, and **C2.6**. For the meaning of the terms 'use', 'cause', and 'permit', see **C1.7**, **C1.5**, and **C1.6**. C6.37

The burden of proof rests on the defendant, i.e. he is required to produce evidence of a valid insurance policy (*DPP v Kavaz* [1999] RTR 40), whether or not there has been any requirement to produce this under the proforma HORT/1 or otherwise (*DPP v Hay* [2006] RTR 32).

For the owner of a vehicle to be convicted of using without insurance when it was being driven by someone else, it has to be proved that the defendant owned the vehicle and that the driver at the time was employed by the owner and was, at the material time, acting in the course of his employment (*Jones v DPP* [1999] RTR 1).

The section imposes an absolute liability irrespective of knowledge, even if the charge is for 'causing' or 'permitting' (*Lyons v May* [1948] 2 All ER 1062; *Tapsell v Maslen* [1967] Crim LR 53). However, if the person who allows the use of a vehicle does so on the express condition that the user insures it, he is not 'permitting' the uninsured use of the vehicle within the meaning of s. 143 (*Newbury v Davis* [1974] RTR 367). That case, however, appears to be confined to its own facts. In *DPP v Fisher* [1992] RTR 93, the Divisional Court declined to follow *Newbury* where the driver of the vehicle was not in communication directly with the owner even though the owner only authorised the use of the vehicle by a suitably insured person. Lack of knowledge of unauthorised use of a vehicle does not constitute 'permitting'.

Section 144 of the RTA 1988 contains certain exceptions. The requirements of a policy of insurance are set out in the RTA 1988, s. 145.

By s. 161, 'policy of insurance' includes a covering note. By s. 147(1), a policy of insurance is of no effect under s. 143 until delivered to the party by whom the policy is effected. The burden is on the defendant to prove the facts necessary to establish the statutory defence for employees in s. 143(3).

A policy of insurance obtained by misrepresentation or non-disclosure of material facts is not a 'policy of insurance' for the purposes of the RTA 1930, s. 36(4) (*Guardian Assurance Co. Ltd v Sutherland* [1939] 2 All ER 246, per Branson J). A voidable policy does, however, satisfy the requirements of s. 143 until it is avoided (*Durrant v MacLaren* [1956] 2 Lloyd's Rep 70; *Adams v Dunne* [1978] RTR 281).

Payment of petrol money on a regular 'school run' which went beyond the bounds of mere social kindness may bring the vehicle (if it is adapted to carry more than eight passengers) within the meaning of the term 'public service vehicle' (*DPP v Sikondar* [1993] RTR 90). This may in turn vitiate a policy of insurance so as to bring the driver within the ambit of s. 143.

C6.38 **Punishment** Disqualification is discretionary, but endorsement with between 6 and 8 penalty points is obligatory. A fine up to level 5 may be imposed. An enhanced fixed penalty of £200 has been available in respect of this offence since 1 June 2003 (Fixed Penalty Offences Order 2003 (SI 2003 No. 1253), as amended).

C6.39 **Further Developments** When the Road Safety Act 2006, s. 22, is brought into force, it will introduce a new offence (the RTA 1988, s. 144A) of keeping a vehicle which does not meet the insurance requirements (as defined therein). This is intended as a further clampdown to ensure so far as possible for the protection of other roads users that the use of all relevant vehicles is covered by appropriate minimum levels of insurance. There will be various exceptions to the requirement (under s. 144B) and, in accordance with regulations to be made under s. 159A, information facilitating enforcement may be required from the Motor Insurers' Information Centre. Fixed penalty notices will be available (s. 144C), although the offence will not be endorsable.

Failing to Stop and Failing to Report Accident

C6.40 **Road Traffic Act 1988, s. 170**

(1) This section applies in a case where, owing to the presence of a mechanically propelled vehicle on a road or other public place, an accident occurs by which—
  (a) personal injury is caused to a person other than the driver of that mechanically propelled vehicle, or
  (b) damage is caused—
    (i) to a vehicle other than that mechanically propelled vehicle or a trailer drawn by that mechanically propelled vehicle, or
    (ii) to an animal other than an animal in or on that mechanically propelled vehicle or a trailer drawn by that mechanically propelled vehicle, or
    (iii) to any other property constructed on, fixed to, growing in or otherwise forming part of the land on which the road or place in question is situated or land adjacent to such land.

(2) The driver of the mechanically propelled vehicle must stop and, if required to do so by any person having reasonable grounds for so requiring, give his name and address and also the name and address of the owner and the identification marks of the vehicle.

(3) If for any reason the driver of the mechanically propelled vehicle does not give his name and address under subsection (2) above, he must report the accident.

(4) A person who fails to comply with subsection (2) or (3) above is guilty of an offence.

(5) If, in a case where this section applies by virtue of subsection (1)(a) above, the driver of a motor vehicle does not at the time of the accident produce such a certificate of insurance or security, or other evidence, as is mentioned in section 165(2)(a) of this Act—
  (a) to a constable, or
  (b) to some person who, having reasonable grounds for so doing, has required him to produce it,

the driver must report the accident and produce such a certificate or other evidence. This subsection does not apply to the driver of an invalid carriage.

(6) To comply with a duty under this section to report an accident or to produce such a certificate of insurance or security, or other evidence, as is mentioned in section 165(2)(a) of this Act, the driver—
  (a) must do so at a police station or to a constable, and
  (b) must do so as soon as is reasonably practicable and, in any case, within 24 hours of the occurrence of the accident.

(7) A person who fails to comply with a duty under subsection (5) above is guilty of an offence, but he shall not be convicted by reason only of a failure to produce a certificate or other evidence if, within seven days after the occurrence of the accident, the certificate or other

evidence is produced at a police station that was specified by him at the time when the accident was reported.

(8) In this section 'animal' means horse, cattle, ass, mule, sheep, pig, goat or dog.

Elements For the meaning of the terms 'accident', 'driver' and 'vehicle', see **C1.1**, **C1.8** and **C1.16**. **C6.41**

The RTOA 1988, ss. 11 and 12(1), apply; see **C2.5** and **C2.6**.

Section 170(2) creates one offence which may be committed in a number of different ways. Section 170(3) creates a separate offence, as does s. 170(7) (*DPP v Bennett* [1993] RTR 175). Since 3 April 2000, the offences have applied to use on 'other public places' as well as 'roads'. In *R (Parker) v Crown Court at Bradford* [2007] RTR 369, an attempt to challenge the insertion in s. 170(1) of 'or other public place' by the Motor Vehicles (Compulsory Insurance) Regulations 2000 (SI 2000 No. 726), made under the European Communities Act 1972, was unsuccessful.

The object of s. 170, it is submitted, is to identify the parties involved for the purposes of both civil and criminal proceedings. To that end, it is a question of fact whether providing the name and address of a third party satisfies the requirements of the section (*DPP v McCarthy* [1999] RTR 323); in that case, the driver gave his name and the address of his solicitors, which was found to be sufficient. It is not necessary for the motor vehicle to be directly involved with the accident, but the prosecution must establish causation because of the presence of the defendant's motor vehicle on the road (*Quelch v Phipps* [1955] 2 QB 107). Nor is it necessary for the driver to be physically present in the vehicle at the time of the accident (provided his absence does not terminate the act of 'driving': (see **C1.8** and **C1.9**) (*Cawthorn v DPP* [2000] RTR 45). In *Harding v Price* [1948] 1 KB 695, it was established that where a driver is unaware of an accident, he cannot be aware of a duty to stop or report and is entitled to be acquitted. When it is sought to establish this, the onus of proof rests on the defendant (see also *Hampson v Powell* [1970] 1 All ER 929).

Following such an accident as is mentioned in s. 170(1), the driver is obliged to remain at the scene for a reasonable time so that he can fulfil his obligations under s. 170(2) (*Lee v Knapp* [1967] 2 QB 442; *Ward v Rawson* [1978] RTR 498). The obligation does not extend to searching out persons who might be entitled to the information required under s. 170(2) (*Mutton v Bates* [1984] RTR 256).

Whether or not the vehicle is stopped at the appropriate point is a question of fact; where a driver chose to drive on for 80 yards before stopping and returning to the scene of the accident, the Divisional Court was not prepared to interfere with a decision finding that this constituted a failure to stop as required, because it could not be said to be one which no court, properly directing itself upon the law, could rationally have arrived at (*McDermott v DPP* [1997] RTR 474). Under s. 170(2), a driver is required to stop immediately so that witnesses might make themselves known and any person wishing to request the driver's particulars might do so (*Hallinan v DPP* [1998] Crim LR 754).

Partial compliance with the requirements will not suffice, but if he has stopped and has not been required to provide any or all of the details mentioned in s. 170(2), the driver will fulfil his obligation, subject, however, to a duty to report the accident in the manner prescribed by s. 170(6) if he has not given his name and address. The obligation to report an accident under s. 170(3) therefore exists whenever a driver has not provided his name and address.

In *DPP v Drury* [1989] RTR 165, it was held that a driver who is not aware of an accident but who subsequently becomes aware of it, must report the accident to a police station personally if he becomes aware within 24 hours of the accident occurring. Reporting an accident by telephone is insufficient, and the obligation appears to be one that must, in the absence of physical impossibility, be performed personally (*Wisdom v Macdonald* [1983] RTR 186). The obligations under s. 170 are not negated by police attendance at the scene of the accident and the defendant being conveyed to hospital (*DPP v Hay* [2006] RTR 32).

In an accident involving more than one other person or vehicle, the driver may be required to provide details to a number of people, and failure to provide those details to any one who has reasonable grounds for requiring them is an offence. If, however, the driver has furnished particulars, including his name and address, to at least one person and has satisfied all other requests made, then it is submitted he is not obliged to report the accident in the manner prescribed by s. 170(6), unless personal injury has been caused to someone other than the driver.

Where personal injury is caused to anyone other than the driver of the vehicle, the driver must produce his insurance certificate (or such other documentation as would satisfy s. 165(2)(a) of the Act) at the time of the accident either to a constable or any other person who has reasonable grounds for requesting him to produce it. If he does not produce insurance (or such other documentation as would satisfy s. 165(2)(a) of the Act), either because he was not able to or because he was not so required, he must report the accident in the manner prescribed by s. 170(6).

C6.42 **Punishment** An offence under s. 170(4) is punishable with up to six months' imprisonment and/or a fine up to level 5 on the standard scale. Disqualification is discretionary but endorsement, with between 5 and 10 penalty points, is obligatory. Forfeiture of the vehicle concerned may also be ordered (see **C7.28** and **E20.1**).

Pedestrian Crossing Regulations

C6.43 The RTRA 1984, s. 25, enables the Secretary of State to make regulations in respect of vehicles and pedestrians at and in the vicinity of crossings. The current regulations are the Zebra, Pelican and Puffin Pedestrian Crossings Regulations and General Directions 1997 (SI 1997 No. 2400). Contravention of the regulations is an offence punishable by a fine up to level 3 on the standard scale. Disqualification when a motor vehicle is involved is discretionary, but endorsement with three penalty points is obligatory. The regulations apply to all vehicles.

Failing to Stop at School Crossing

C6.44 **Road Traffic Regulation Act 1984, s. 28**

(1) When between the hours of eight in the morning and half-past five in the afternoon a vehicle is approaching a place in a road where children on their way to or from school, or from one part of a school to another, are crossing or seeking to cross the road, a school crossing patrol wearing a uniform approved by the Secretary of State shall have power, by exhibiting a prescribed sign, to require the person driving or propelling the vehicle to stop it.

(2) When a person has been required under subsection (1) above to stop a vehicle—

(a) he shall cause the vehicle to stop before reaching the place where the children are crossing or seeking to cross and so as not to stop or impede their crossing, and

(b) the vehicle shall not be put in motion again so as to reach the place in question so long as the sign continues to be exhibited.

(3) A person who fails to comply with paragraph (a) of subsection (2) above, or who causes a vehicle to be put in motion in contravention of paragraph (b) of that subsection, shall be guilty of an offence.

C6.45 **Elements** The sign is prescribed by the School Crossing Patrol Sign (England and Wales) Regulations 2006 (SI 2006 No. 2215). The driver of a motor vehicle must stop unless the sign has been removed by the time he arrives at the crossing (*Franklin v Langdown* [1971] 3 All ER 662).

Punishment A fine up to level 3 may be imposed. Discretionary disqualification if the offence is committed by using a motor vehicle, but obligatory endorsement with 3 penalty points. C6.46

Speeding

Road Traffic Regulation Act 1984, s. 89 C6.47

(1) A person who drives a motor vehicle on a road at a speed exceeding a limit imposed by or under any enactment to which this section applies shall be guilty of an offence.

(2) A person prosecuted for such an offence shall not be liable to be convicted solely on the evidence of one witness to the effect that, in the opinion of the witness, the person prosecuted was driving the vehicle at a speed exceeding a specified limit.

(3) The enactments to which this section applies are—
 (a) any enactment contained in this Act except section 17(2);
 (b) section 2 of the Parks Regulation (Amendment) Act 1926; and
 (c) any enactment not contained in this Act, but passed after 1 September 1960, whether before or after the passing of this Act.

(4) If a person who employs other persons to drive motor vehicles on roads publishes or issues any timetable or schedule, or gives any directions, under which any journey, or any stage or part of any journey, is to be completed within some specified time, and it is not practicable in the circumstances of the case for that journey (or that stage or part of it) to be completed in the specified time without the commission of such an offence as is mentioned in subsection (1) above, the publication or issue of the timetable or schedule, or the giving of the directions, may be produced as prima facie evidence that the employer procured or (as the case may be) incited the persons employed by him to drive the vehicle to commit such an offence.

Elements The section applies only to 'motor vehicles', see **C1.12**. The RTOA 1988, ss. 1, 11 and 12(1) apply; see **C2.1**, **C2.5** and **C2.6**. C6.48

Depending on the context and circumstances, driving at grossly excessive speed might constitute dangerous driving (*DPP v Milton* [2006] RTR 264: see **C3.10**).

Section 87 of the 1984 Act exempts motor vehicles being used for fire brigade, ambulance or police purposes, if observance of the speed limit would be likely to hinder the purpose for which they are being used. Where a vehicle is not constructed, adapted or used for the purpose of conveying sick, injured or disabled persons, it may not be an ambulance benefiting from this exemption (*Ashton v CPS* [2005] EWHC 2729 (Admin)). When the Road Safety Act 2006, s. 19, is brought into force, it will substitute a new s. 87, which will enable the coverage to include additional purposes whilst limiting the exemption to drivers who have satisfactorily completed an appropriate course of training.

Incorrectly sited speed restriction signs will not invalidate the speed limit imposed by a relevant enactment (*Wawrzynczyk v Chief Constable of Staffordshire Constabulary* (2000) *The Times*, 16 March 2000), provided no doubt that they sufficiently advise drivers of that speed limit in the location of the alleged offence and do not mislead. At the geographical point where the motorist exceeds the speed limit, the requisite signs must be capable of conveying the reduced limit to the motorist in sufficient time to enable the reduction from a previously lawful speed to within the new limit, which will not be the case if the signs are obscured by overgrown hedgerows (*Coombes v DPP* [2007] RTR 383).

A traffic authority for a road can make an order that a road that is not a restricted road by reason of the positioning of street lighting shall become a restricted road for the purpose of imposing a 30 mph speed limit (see, e.g., *DPP v Evans* [2004] EWHC 2785 (Admin)).

Evidence from an approved device is admissible to prove speeding offences under s. 89 (see RTOA 1988, s. 20 at **C2.10**).

Section 89(2) provides a statutory requirement of corroboration. Opinion evidence as to speed is admissible, but because of the danger of inaccuracy inherent in such evidence, it was felt necessary to require corroboration. See generally, *Nicholas v Penny* [1950] 2 KB 466 and *Swain v Gillet* [1974] RTR 446. The reading of a police car's speedometer is capable of supplying the necessary corroboration, even if there is no evidence of testing, though the weight of such evidence is open to question (see *Swain v Gillet* [1974] RTR 446). It would satisfy the statutory requirement to have the opinion evidence of two or more witnesses, provided that their observations occurred at the same time (*Brighty v Pearson* [1938] 4 All ER 127).

Factual evidence, however, does not require corroboration, and evidence of the speed recorded on the speedometer of a police car, driven at an even distance behind the appellant's car, was held to be sufficient to sustain a conviction (*Nicholas v Penny* [1950] 2 KB 466). The speedometer does not need to be tested, and in the absence of evidence to the contrary can be presumed, as can radar guns, radar speed meters and other mechanical instruments, to be in order at the material time (*Castle v Cross* [1984] 1 WLR 1372; *Burton v Gilbert* [1984] RTR 162). Where the prosecution has been given notice that a serious issue is being raised in relation to evidence based on the radar gun, it is quite simple either for the approval of the device to be established by production of the necessary schedule or for the constable to give evidence that the device used was an approved one; if this line of defence is taken at the last minute, the justices can be invited to take judicial notice on the point or allow the constable to be recalled (*Roberts v DPP* [1994] RTR 31). Where an adjournment is occasioned in these circumstances, the defendant is highly likely to be at risk of having to pay the costs occasioned by it.

The expert evidence of an 'Accident Examiner' which entails the reconstruction of events from various tests, skid marks and damage, is considered to be based on more than mere opinion where he describes the facts on which his opinion is based (*Crossland v DPP* [1988] 3 All ER 712).

It is not open to the prosecution to accept a plea of guilty to a charge of speeding which had been committed for trial under the CJA 1988, s. 41, and offer no evidence on the indictable offence (*Avey* [1994] RTR 419). Offences committed for trial under s. 41 can be dealt with only following a conviction for an indictable offence arising out of circumstances which are the same as or connected with the summary offence. In such circumstances, the proper course for the Crown Court is to remit the s. 41 offence to be dealt with by the justices.

C6.49 **Punishment** A fine up to level 3 may be imposed. Disqualification is discretionary. Endorsement, with 3 penalty points when a fixed penalty is imposed and with between 3 and 6 penalty points in any other case, is obligatory. When the Road Safety Act 2006, s. 17, is brought into force, the range of penalty points applicable will increase to between 2 and 6 points, which will also provide for a more graduated arrangement when a fixed penalty is imposed (see **C7.2**). Special reasons may be capable of being advanced, e.g., when driving too quickly to deal with an emergency situation (see **C8.12**).

Section C7 Sentencing Generally

Production of Licence

Road Traffic Offenders Act 1988, s. 27 C7.1

(1) Where a person who is the holder of a licence is convicted of an offence involving obligatory or discretionary disqualification, and a court proposes to make an order disqualifying him or an order under section 44 of this Act, the court must, unless it has already received them, require the licence and its counterpart to be produced to it.

(2) [Repealed.]

(3) If the holder of the licence has not caused it and its counterpart to be delivered, or posted it and its counterpart, in accordance with section 7 of this Act and does not produce it and its counterpart as required under this section or section 301 of the Criminal Justice Act 2003, section 146 or 147 of the Powers of Criminal Courts (Sentencing) Act 2000, . . . then, unless he satisfies the court that he has applied for a new licence and has not received it—

(a) he is guilty of an offence, and

(b) the licence shall be suspended from the time when its production was required until it and its counterpart are produced to the court and shall, while suspended, be of no effect.

(4) Subsection (3) above does not apply where the holder of the licence—

(a) has caused a current receipt for the licence and its counterpart issued under section 56 of this Act to be delivered to the proper officer of the court not later than the day before the date appointed for the hearing, or

(b) has posted such a receipt, at such time that in the ordinary course of post it would be delivered not later than that day, in a letter duly addressed to the proper officer and either registered or sent by the recorded delivery service, or

(c) surrenders such a receipt to the court at the hearing,

and produces the licence and its counterpart to the court immediately on their return.

'Licence' includes a Community licence and 'new licence' includes a counterpart of a Community licence (RTOA 1988, s. 91A(1) and (2)).

When an offender has been requested to produce his driving licence, a failure to produce it is, unless he has applied for a new licence which he has not received or s.27(4) applies, an offence

C

Part C Road Traffic Offences

punishable by a fine up to level 3 on the standard scale. The licence is also suspended until it is produced, and if the offender drives during that suspension, he is guilty of an offence under the RTA 1988, s. 87(1).

Penalty Points

C7.2 **Road Traffic Offenders Act 1988, s. 28**

(1) Where a person is convicted of an offence involving obligatory endorsement, then, subject to the following provisions of this section, the number of penalty points to be attributed to the offence is—
  (a) the number shown in relation to the offence in the last column of part I or part II of schedule 2 to this Act, or
  (b) where a range of numbers is shown, a number within that range.

(2) Where a person is convicted of an offence committed by aiding, abetting, counselling or procuring, or inciting to the commission of, an offence involving obligatory disqualification, then, subject to the following provisions of this section, the number of penalty points to be attributed to the offence is 10.

(3) Where both a range of numbers and a number followed by the words '(fixed penalty)' is shown in the last column of part I of schedule 2 to this Act in relation to an offence, that number is the number of penalty points to be attributed to the offence for the purposes of sections 57(5) and 77(5) of this Act; and, where only a range of numbers is shown there, the lowest number in the range is the number of penalty points to be attributed to the offence for those purposes.

(4) Where a person is convicted (whether on the same occasion or not) of two or more offences committed on the same occasion and involving obligatory endorsement, the total number of penalty points to be attributed to them is the number or highest number that would be attributed on a conviction of one of them (so that if the convictions are on different occasions the number of penalty points to be attributed to the offences on the later occasion or occasions shall be restricted accordingly).

(5) In a case where (apart from this subsection) subsection (4) above would apply to two or more offences, the court may if it thinks fit determine that that subsection shall not apply to the offences (or, where three or more offences are concerned, to any one or more of them).

(6) Where a court makes such a determination it shall state its reasons in open court and, if it is a magistrates' court . . . shall cause them to be entered in the register . . . of its proceedings.

(7) to (9) [Powers of Secretary of State to alter penalty points and matters consequent.]

When the Road Safety Act 2006, s. 4(2), is brought into force, it will substitute provisions in place of s. 28(3) which introduce graduated fixed penalties. The Secretary of State will be enabled by order to attribute appropriate numbers of penalty points for offences, which may vary depending on the circumstances of the offence (e.g., its nature, its severity, where it has taken place and whether the offender appears to have committed other prescribed offences during a prescribed period).

The effect of s. 28 is to give the court a discretion to impose penalty points in respect of two or more offences committed on the same occasion and thereby aggregate the penalty points imposed in order to disqualify under the 'penalty points' system (s. 28(5)). Reasons must be given in open court and magistrates have to enter them in the register. The power can be used where none of the offences is so serious as to merit disqualification in its own right but the totality of the offending merits disqualification, possibly because of the number of offences or because the offences are of different types.

It should be noted that aiding and abetting etc. an offence involving obligatory disqualification, such as driving with excess alcohol, carries 10 penalty points but does not entail mandatory disqualification. In offences not involving obligatory disqualification, secondary participation entails the same punishment as for the principal.

The expression 'same occasion' was considered in *Johnson v Finbow* [1983] 1 WLR 879, where the appellant was charged with offences of failing to stop after an accident and failing to report the accident to the police. The Divisional Court accepted that there was an argument that the offences were not committed on the same occasion, but Robert Goff LJ, giving the judgment of the court, went on to say (at pp. 882–3):

> . . . looking at the matter more broadly (and, for my part, I think more sensibly), it can be said that the lapse of time, although significant, is not sufficiently great to be able to say, as a matter of common sense, that those offences were committed on different occasions. It is true that they were committed at different moments of time; indeed, they might even have been committed on different days. On the other hand, they certainly arose out of the same accident. And when one sees how closely they are connected with the accident, and how very similar, in fact, the two offences are in their nature, then I think the proper conclusion is that when arising out of the same accident these two offences are committed on the same occasion.

In *Johnston v Over* (1984) 6 Cr App R (S) 420, the defendant had parked two vehicles outside his home. He was charged with two offences of 'using' a vehicle without insurance. The Divisional Court stated that whether or not an offence was 'committed on the same or on different occasions' depended upon the facts of each case, and that in this case, as a matter of common sense, both offences were committed on the same occasion. However, in *McKeever v Walkinshaw* 1996 SLT 1228, the High Court of Justiciary upheld a finding that offences of speeding and crossing a double white line committed at separate points on the same stretch of road during a single course of driving had not occurred on the same occasion. Given the temporal link and the possibility of invoking s. 28(5) to justify imposing separate sets of penalty points, this appears to be an unduly harsh interpretation of s. 28(4).

Offences which are committed on separate occasions have the number or highest number of penalty points awarded separately, and, if committed within three years of each other, those points are added up for the purposes of the RTOA 1988, s. 35.

For further details, see **C8.1** ***et seq.*** and **C9.2**.

Points to be Taken into Account on Conviction

Road Traffic Offenders Act 1988, s. 29 C7.3

(1) Where a person is convicted of an offence involving obligatory endorsement, the penalty points to be taken into account on that occasion are (subject to subsection (2) below)—
 (a) any that are to be attributed to the offence or offences of which he is convicted, disregarding any offence in respect of which an order under section 34 of this Act is made, and
 (b) any that were on a previous occasion ordered to be endorsed on the counterpart of any licence held by him, unless the offender has since that occasion and before the conviction been disqualified under section 35 of this Act.

(2) If any of the offences was committed more than three years before another, the penalty points in respect of that offence shall not be added to those in respect of the other.

The effect of s. 29 is that penalty points remain on the licence; it is not 'wiped clean' by a disqualification under the RTOA 1988, s. 34. If a disqualification is imposed under s. 34, any points attributable to that offence are to be disregarded for the purposes of penalty points to be taken into account on conviction. Thus if a defendant is convicted of two offences committed on the same occasion, one of which carries mandatory disqualification, points on the other offence will be taken into account for the purposes of s. 35. Under the previous legislation, points taken into account were the highest number attributable to one of them. Where there is a disqualification under s. 34, the licence is not endorsed with penalty points.

Even if the offender is disqualified for an offence before the court, the relevant number of penalty points (denoted in sch. 2, part I, col. 7 of the Act) must still be 'taken into account' for the purposes of s. 35.

A previous disqualification under the penalty points system has the effect of wiping the licence clean. Points ordered since the disqualification have to be taken into account even if they are imposed in respect of an offence committed before the disqualification, unless, of course, the offence was committed more than three years before another.

For further details, see **C8.1** *et seq.* and **C9.2**.

For the purposes of this section, the date of conviction means the date on which sentence is imposed (*Brentwood Justices, ex parte Richardson* (1992) 95 Cr App R 187).

C7.4 **Reduced Penalty Points for Attendance on Courses** When the Road Safety Act 2006, s. 34, is brought into force, it will introduce a new range of courses designed, when successfully completed, to remove from the offender's licence three penalty points (or fewer where, for the instant offence, the court endorsed fewer). This is intended to offer an element of re-training for repeat offenders and enable such offenders to benefit from the incentive of reducing the risk of being disqualified on reaching 12 or more penalty points under the RTOA 1988, s. 35 (see **C7.12**).

Sections 30A to 30D will be inserted into the RTOA 1988. The offences to be covered are (i) careless, and inconsiderate, driving; (ii) failing to comply with traffic signs; and (iii) speeding. The opportunity to attend a course will not be available to anyone who has completed a course under s. 30A or 34A (see **C7.10**) in the previous three years or a person who commits the offence during the probationary period for newly qualified drivers (see **C7.8**). These courses will be quite distinct from the Driver Improvement Scheme and Speed Awareness Courses operated by the police without court involvement.

Modification where Fixed Penalty Points also in Question

C7.5 **Road Traffic Offenders Act 1988, s. 30**

(1) Sections 28 and 29 of this Act shall have effect subject to this section in any case where—
  (a) a person is convicted of an offence involving obligatory endorsement, and
  (b) the court is satisfied that the counterpart of his licence has been or is liable to be endorsed under section 57 or 77 of this Act in respect of an offence (referred to in this section as the 'connected offence') committed on the same occasion as the offence of which he is convicted.

(2) The number of penalty points to be attributed to the offence of which he is convicted is—
  (a) the number of penalty points to be attributed to that offence under section 28 of this Act apart from this section, less
  (b) the number of penalty points required to be endorsed on the counterpart of his licence under section 57 or 77 of this Act in respect of the connected offence (except so far as they have already been deducted by virtue of this paragraph).

The offences to which the procedure applies are set out in sch. 3 to the 1988 Act (see **C9.3**). Where the 'fixed penalty' procedure is appropriate, a notice giving reasonable information must either be served on the offender or given to him by a constable in uniform. If the offence is endorsable, the offender must produce his licence to the constable or, within seven days, to an authorised person at a specified police station. If the constable or authorised person is satisfied that the offender is not liable to disqualification under the RTOA 1988, s. 35, the licence is retained and then sent to the 'fixed penalty clerk' so that it can be endorsed.

Every notice must contain a suspended enforcement period during which no proceedings may be brought. That period must be of a minimum duration of 21 days.

If the offender is later convicted of an offence which arose on the 'same occasion' as the offence for which his licence has already been endorsed, the number of penalty points to be imposed in respect of that offence is the highest number of points attributable less the number of points already endorsed under the fixed penalty procedure.

For further details, see **C8.1** *et seq.*, **C9.2** and **C9.3**.

Taking Previously Endorsed Particulars into Consideration

Road Traffic Offenders Act 1988, s. 31 C7.6

(1) Where a person is convicted of an offence involving obligatory or discretionary disqualification and his licence and its counterpart are produced to the court—
   (a) any existing endorsement on his licence is prima facie evidence of the matters endorsed, and
   (b) the court may, in determining what order to make in pursuance of the conviction, take those matters into consideration.

(2) [Applies only to Scotland.]

This is one of a number of ways that previous convictions may be proved. In addition, an extract from the Criminal Records Office may be produced by the prosecution and is admissible if agreed by the defendant. On a number of occasions the only evidence relating to the defendant's driving record will be contained in a computer printout from the DVLA, which may be admitted under the RTOA 1988, s. 13 (see C2.7). In other circumstances previous convictions may be proved under the PACE 1984, ss. 73 to 75 (see generally, **F11.1** ***et seq.***).

Fines and Imprisonment

The RTOA 1988, s. 33, provides that the maximum punishments for offences against the Traffic Acts should be those set out in sch. 2, part I, col. 4. References to years or months are references to terms of imprisonment. Schedule 2 is set out at C9.2. C7.7

Under the provisions inserted into the RTOA 1988, ss. 53 and 84 by the DVCVA 2004, s. 16 (but not yet in force), higher fixed penalties can be imposed where, in the three years prior to committing the offence for which the fixed penalty is offered, the offender had been disqualified or had had penalty points endorsed. Alternatively, when the prospective substitution made by the Road Safety Act 2006, s. 3, is brought into force (see C7.2), an order prescribing fixed penalties may introduce graduated amounts for the offence, depending on circumstances including the nature of the offence, its severity, where it has taken place and, developing the 2004 Act amendment, whether the offender appears to have committed other prescribed offences during a prescribed period. Where it transpires that he is dealing with such an offender to whom such a higher fixed penalty applies, whether before or after the introduction of graduated fixed penalties, the fixed penalty clerk will be empowered to issue a surcharge notice requiring payment of the difference between the normal and enhanced amounts.

Probationary Period for Newly Qualified Drivers

The Road Traffic (New Drivers) Act 1995, s. 1, introduced a probationary period of two years commencing from the day on which a person becomes a qualified driver, during which time a driver who acquires six or more penalty points will have his licence revoked and be required to present himself for retesting before qualifying for a full driving licence. C7.8

A person becomes a 'qualified driver' on the first occasion of passing a United Kingdom driving test or a driving test conducted in any EEA State, the Isle of Man, any of the Channel Islands or Gibraltar (s. 1(2)). Any person who became a qualified driver before the Act entered into force is not affected by its provisions (s. 10(3)). By virtue of s. 7, the period may be terminated early if the person is disqualified until a driving test is passed under the RTOA 1988, s. 36 (see C7.13), or if he has already had to surrender his licence under the terms of the 1995 Act and has since been granted a full driving licence after re-taking and passing a driving test.

During the probationary period, if the driver commits an offence or offences involving obligatory endorsement where the penalty points to be taken into account under the RTOA 1988, s. 29 (see C7.3), are six or more, the sentencing court or fixed penalty clerk must send a notice, together with the driver's licence and its counterpart, to the Secretary of State (s. 2), who must then serve a notice on the driver revoking the licence (s. 3). (Schedule 1 to the 1995 Act makes similar provisions for the surrender and revocation of test certificates and provisional driving licences, where the driver has not yet applied for his full driving licence.) There is no discretion involved although 'special reasons' (see **C8.9**) may, if appropriate, be raised against endorsement to prevent such an eventuality.

Where a licence is revoked the holder has to re-take and pass an 'ordinary' driving test for each class of vehicle affected by the revocation before being able to drive unsupervised and being eligible to apply once again for a full driving licence (s. 4). After passing the retest, the person has the normal two-year period in which to apply for a full driving licence, otherwise the test certificate obtained ceases to have effect. On this occasion, however, no probationary period attaches, otherwise persistent offenders could find themselves in a vicious circle of retesting.

By s. 5, if the driver appeals against the conviction or penalty points that led to his licence being revoked under s. 3 and the Secretary of State receives due notification, his licence will be temporarily restored to him pending determination of the appeal. If the appeal is successful, a new full licence will be granted and, if appropriate, the probationary period will continue to run. If the appeal fails to reduce the relevant penalty points below six, the temporary licence will be treated as revoked. These provisions are supplemented by the New Drivers (Appeals Procedure) Regulations 1997 (SI 1997 No. 1098).

Any penalty points which lead to the revocation of a licence, remain effective for the normal three-year period from the date of commission of the offence (RTOA 1988, s. 29(2); see **C7.3**). Revocation of the driving licence does not 'wipe clean' the person's driving record for the purposes of disqualification for repeated offences under the RTOA 1988, s. 35 (see **C7.12**). A short discretionary disqualification under the RTOA 1988, s. 34(2), would, however, lead to there being no penalty points to be taken into account. As this would result in the retesting requirement and therefore Parliament's clear intention being circumvented, it is suggested that an appropriate approach in a case where the offence might merit a short period of disqualification would be to consider the effect of the 1995 Act first, before turning to the possibility of a discretionary disqualification under the 1988 Act. Conversely, if the sentencer declines to impose a discretionary disqualification, there should be some consideration of the effect on the defendant of awarding six or more penalty points, where the range for the offence permits a lower number (*Edmunds* [2000] 2 Cr App R (S) 62).

Disqualification for Certain Offences

C7.9 **Road Traffic Offenders Act 1988, s. 34**

(1) Where a person is convicted of an offence involving obligatory disqualification, the court must order him to be disqualified for such period not less than 12 months as the court thinks fit unless the court for special reasons thinks fit to order him to be disqualified for a shorter period or not to order him to be disqualified.

(1A) Where a person is convicted of an offence under section 12A of the Theft Act 1968 (aggravated vehicle-taking), the fact that he did not drive the vehicle in question at any particular time or at all shall not be regarded as a special reason for the purposes of subsection (1) above.

(2) Where a person is convicted of an offence involving discretionary disqualification, and either—
  (a) the penalty points to be taken into account on that occasion number fewer than 12, or
  (b) the offence is not one involving obligatory endorsement,
  the court may order him to be disqualified for such period as the court thinks fit.

(3) Where a person convicted of an offence under any of the following provisions of the Road Traffic Act 1988, that is—
  (aa) section 3A (causing death by careless driving when under the influence of drink or drugs),

(a) section 4(1) (driving or attempting to drive while unfit),
(b) section 5(1)(a) (driving or attempting to drive with excess alcohol),
(c) section 7(6) (failing to provide a specimen) where that is an offence involving obligatory disqualification,
(d) section 7A(b) (failing to allow a specimen to be subjected to laboratory test) where that is an offence involving obligatory disqualification; has within the 10 years immediately preceding the commission of the offence been convicted of any such offence, subsection (1) above shall apply in relation to him as if the reference to 12 months were a reference to three years.

(4) Subject to subsection (3) above, subsection (1) above shall apply as if the reference to 12 months were a reference to two years—
(a) in relation to a person convicted of—
(i) manslaughter, . . . or
(ii) an offence under section 1 of the Road Traffic Act 1988 (causing death by dangerous driving), or
(iii) an offence under section 3A of that Act (causing death by careless driving while under the influence of drink or drugs), and
(b) in relation to a person on whom more than one disqualification for a fixed period of 56 days or more has been imposed within the three years immediately preceding the commission of the offence.

(4A) For the purposes of subsection (4)(b) above there shall be disregarded any disqualification imposed under section 26 of this Act or section 147 of the Powers of Criminal Courts (Sentencing) Act 2000 or section 248 of the Criminal Procedure (Scotland) Act 1995 (offences committed by using vehicles) and any disqualification imposed in respect of an offence of stealing a motor vehicle, an offence under section 12 or 25 of the Theft Act 1968, an offence under section 178 of the Road Traffic Act 1988, or an attempt to commit such an offence.

(5) The preceding provisions of this section shall apply in relation to a conviction of an offence committed by aiding, abetting, counselling or procuring, or inciting to the commission of, an offence involving obligatory disqualification as if the offence were an offence involving discretionary disqualification.

(6) This section is subject to section 48 of this Act.

For a more detailed consideration of disqualification, see C8.2 *et seq.*

Where disqualification is mandatory, the minimum period is 12 months, unless the offence is manslaughter or an offence under the RTA 1988, s. 1 or 3A, or the defendant has had more than one disqualification of at least 56 days within the three years preceding the commission of the offence. In those cases the minimum period is two years. If s. 34(3) applies, the minimum period is three years.

In *Learmont v DPP* [1994] RTR 286, the appellant had previously been sentenced to an 18-month disqualification and the four notional penalty points imposed for that offence led to a concurrent disqualification for six months under the penalty points regime then in force. Consequently, the justices had taken the view that two disqualifications of 56 days or more had been imposed within the relevant three-year period when sentencing the appellant for the instant offence of dangerous driving. The Divisional Court held this approach to be wrong as the double disqualification was effectively for a single offence, thereby rendering the increased minimum period for disqualification inapplicable.

Section 48 of the Act deals with exemptions from disqualification and endorsement in construction and use offences (see C7.22).

The penalty points to be taken into account are set out in s. 29 (see C7.3) and include any attributable to the offence or offences for which the defendant is before the court and any points previously endorsed, unless the defendant has been disqualified under s. 35 since their imposition. It is submitted that the effect of s. 29 is that, where an offender has 12 or more points to be taken into account, the court may not disqualify for the substantive offence unless the offence is one which carries discretionary disqualification without obligatory endorsement; in such circumstances, it would seem that Parliament intended the penalty points procedure to take priority.

The effect of s. 34(4A) is that disqualifications under the RTOA 1988, s. 26, the PCC(S)A 2000, s. 147, and any disqualification imposed in respect of an offence of stealing a motor vehicle, or an offence under s. 12 or 25 of the Theft Act 1968, are to be disregarded for the purposes of s. 34(4)(b).

Reduced Disqualification for Attendance on Courses

C7.10 Sections 34A to 34C of the RTOA 1988 set up a procedure for driver retraining for offenders convicted of drink-driving offences and provide an incentive to drivers to attend such courses by reducing the period of disqualification for those who do. After an extended experimental period, the scheme now operates permanently in all areas.

Road Traffic Offenders Act 1988, s. 34A

(1) This section applies where—
   (a) a person is convicted of an offence under section 3A (causing death by careless driving when under influence of drink or drugs), 4 (driving or being in charge when under influence of drink or drugs), 5 (driving or being in charge with excess alcohol) or 7 (failing to provide a specimen) of the Road Traffic Act 1988, and
   (b) the court makes an order under section 34 of this Act disqualifying him for a period of not less than twelve months.

(2) Where this section applies, the court may make an order that the period of disqualification imposed under section 34 shall be reduced if, by a date specified in the order under this section, the offender satisfactorily completes a course approved by the Secretary of State for the purposes of this section and specified in the order.

(3) The reduction made by an order under this section in a period of disqualification imposed under section 34 shall be a period specified in the order of not less than three months and not more than one quarter of the unreduced period (and accordingly where the period imposed under section 34 is 12 months, the reduced period shall be nine months).

(4) The court shall not make an order under this section unless—
   (a) it is satisfied that a place on the course specified in the order will be available for the offender,
   (b) the offender appears to the court to be of or over the age of 17,
   (c) the court has explained the effect of the order to the offender in ordinary language, and has informed him of the amount of the fees for the course and of the requirement that he must pay them before beginning the course, and
   (d) the offender has agreed that the order should be made.

(5) The date specified in an order under this section as the latest date for completion of a course must be at least two months before the last day of the period of disqualification as reduced by the order.

(6) An order under this section shall name the petty sessions area (. . . or, where an order has been made under this section by a stipendiary magistrate, the commission area) in which the offender resides or will reside.

For an order to be made, the period of disqualification must be at least 12 months and the 'reduced period' of disqualification cannot be less than three months or more than a quarter of the entire period of disqualification. The retraining course should be completed at least two months before the expiry of the period of disqualification as reduced by the order. The offender has to be aged at least 17. Before making such an order under s. 34A, the court must be satisfied that a place is available, that the offender agrees to the order and that it is explained to him that he must pay the fees for the course in advance and how much those fees are. This provision has certain disadvantages for the impecunious offender, particularly if that offender has relied on driving for previous employment.

Section 34B deals with certificates in relation to completion of the course. The order reducing the period of disqualification does not come into effect until the certificate has been received by the proper officer of the supervising court. If the certificate is received by the court before the end of the 'reduced period', the order reducing the period of disqualification comes into effect on the day that the certificate is received. The organiser of the retraining course has a power to refuse to give a certificate (s. 34B(4)). If a certificate is not given to the offender in accordance with s. 34B, an application may be made to the supervising court which, if successful, has the effect of a certificate duly received by the court. Section 41A of the RTOA 1988 enables the court to suspend a disqualification pending determination of such an application.

Section 34C deals with the powers of the Secretary of State to give guidance to course organisers and other supplementary matters. See the Road Traffic (Courses for Drink-Drive Offenders) Regulations 1992 (SI 1992 No. 3013) and Courses for Drink-Drive Offenders (Designation of Areas) Order 1997 (SI 1997 No. 2913) for further details.

When the Road Safety Act 2006, s. 35, is brought into force, all these provisions will be substituted and a similar, but extended, Drink Drive Rehabilitation Scheme will be introduced. At the same time, the scheme will no longer be available if the offender has completed an approved course under the RTOA 1988, s. 30A or s. 34A, for a specified offence within the previous three years (see **C7.4**) or for an offender still within the probationary period for newly qualified drivers (see **C7.8**).

Reduced Disqualification under Alcohol Ignition Interlock Programme Order

When the Road Safety Act 2006, s. 15, is brought into force, it will insert into the RTOA 1988, ss. 34D to 34G and 41B, introducing a new means by which an offender convicted of a 'relevant drink offence' may, by agreeing to participate at his own expense in an alcohol ignition interlock programme, obtain a reduced period of disqualification for that offence. This applies only where the offender has committed another relevant drink offence in the 10 years before conviction for the instant offence, the court does not make an order under s. 34A (see **C7.10**) and the period of disqualification to be imposed before considering participation in a programme like this is at least two years. Section 16 of the 2006 Act limits the scheme to an initial experimental period expiring at the end of 2010, although this period may be extended by the Secretary of State. **C7.11**

Whilst the scheme includes elements of education and counselling appropriate for a repeat offender, the core feature is that the offender may drive a motor vehicle only if it is fitted with an alcohol interlock device. Such a vehicle can be driven only after a specimen of breath has been supplied which does not exceed the amount specified (9 microgrammes of alcohol in 100 millilitres or such other proportion as may be prescribed by regulations: s. 34D(10)). Under s. 34D(12), it is an offence (i) for a person to interfere with the device with intent to cause it not to function or not to function properly; and (ii) for a person other than the offender under the order to give, or attempt to give, the specimen of breath required with intent to enable the offender to drive the vehicle.

The reduction secured under this scheme will be at least 12 months but cannot exceed one half of the disqualification (disregarding the period of reduction). Any failure by the offender to comply with the conditions of the programme will result in restoration of the original, unreduced disqualification; under s. 34E, a 'certificate of failing fully to participate' in the programme may be issued. The offender is entitled to apply to the supervising court for a declaration that the certificate has been given otherwise than in accordance with the relevant provisions. If that application is successful, the offender will be able to continue on the programme as if the certificate had never been given.

Disqualification for Repeated Offences

C7.12 **Road Traffic Offenders Act 1988, s. 35**

(1) Where—

(a) a person is convicted of an offence to which this subsection applies, and

(b) the penalty points to be taken into account on that occasion number 12 or more,

the court must order him to be disqualified for not less than the minimum period unless the court is satisfied, having regard to all the circumstances, that there are grounds for mitigating the normal consequences of the conviction and thinks fit to order him to be disqualified for a shorter period or not to order him to be disqualified.

(1A) Subsection (1) above applies to—

(a) an offence involving discretionary disqualification and obligatory endorsement, and

(b) an offence involving obligatory disqualification in respect of which no order is made under section 34 of this Act.

(2) The minimum period referred to in subsection (1) above is—

(a) six months if no previous disqualification imposed on the offender is to be taken into account, and

(b) one year if one, and two years if more than one, such disqualification is to be taken into account;

and a previous disqualification imposed on an offender is to be taken into account if it was for a fixed period of 56 days or more and was imposed within the three years immediately preceding the commission of the latest offence in respect of which penalty points are taken into account under section 29 of this Act.

(3) Where an offender is convicted on the same occasion of more than one offence to which subsection (1) above applies—

(a) not more than one disqualification shall be imposed on him under subsection (1) above,

(b) in determining the period of the disqualification the court must take into account all the offences, and

(c) for the purposes of any appeal any disqualification imposed under subsection (1) above shall be treated as an order made on the conviction of each of the offences.

(4) No account is to be taken under subsection (1) above of any of the following circumstances—

(a) any circumstances that are alleged to make the offence or any of the offences not a serious one,

(b) hardship, other than exceptional hardship, or

(c) any circumstances which, within the three years immediately preceding the conviction, have been taken into account under that subsection in ordering the offender to be disqualified for a shorter period or not ordering him to be disqualified.

(5) References in this section to disqualification do not include a disqualification imposed under section 26 of this Act or section 147 of the Powers of Criminal Courts (Sentencing) Act 2000 . . . or a disqualification imposed in respect of an offence of stealing a motor vehicle, an offence under section 12 or 25 of the Theft Act 1968, an offence under section 178 of the Road Traffic Act 1988, or an attempt to commit such an offence.

(5A) The preceding provisions of this section shall apply in relation to a conviction of an offence committed by aiding, abetting, counselling, procuring, or inciting to the commission of, an offence involving obligatory disqualification as if the offence were an offence involving discretionary disqualification.

(6) [Applies only to Scotland.]

(7) This section is subject to section 48 of this Act.

For further details, see **C8.2** *et seq.*

Disqualification Pending Passing of Driving Test

C7.13 **Road Traffic Offenders Act 1988, s. 36**

(1) Where this subsection applies to a person the court must order him to be disqualified until he passes the appropriate driving test.

(2) Subsection (1) above applies to a person who is disqualified under section 34 of this Act on conviction of—

(a) manslaughter . . . by the driver of a motor vehicle, or

(b) an offence under section 1 (causing death by dangerous driving) or section 2 (dangerous driving) of the Road Traffic Act 1988.

(3) Subsection (1) above also applies—
(a) to a person who is disqualified under section 34 or 35 of this Act in such circumstances or for such period as the Secretary of State may by order prescribe, or
(b) to such other persons convicted of such offences involving obligatory endorsement as may be so prescribed.
(4) Where a person to whom subsection (1) above does not apply is convicted of an offence involving obligatory endorsement, the court may order him to be disqualified until he passes the appropriate driving test (whether or not he has previously passed any test).
(5) In this section—
'appropriate driving test' means—
(a) an extended driving test, where a person is convicted of an offence involving obligatory disqualification or is disqualified under section 35 of this Act,
(b) a test of competence to drive, other than an extended driving test, in any other case,
'extended driving test' means a test of competence to drive prescribed for the purposes of this section, and
'test of competence to drive' means a test prescribed by virtue of section 89(3) of the Road Traffic Act 1988.
(6) In determining whether to make an order under subsection (4) above, the court shall have regard to the safety of road users.
(7) Where a person is disqualified until he passes the extended driving test—
(a) any earlier order under this section shall cease to have effect, and
(b) a court shall not make a further order under this section while he is so disqualified.
(8) Subject to subsection (9) below, a disqualification by virtue of an order under this section shall be deemed to have expired on production to the Secretary of State of evidence, in such form as may be prescribed by regulations under section 105 of the RTA 1988, that the person disqualified has passed the test in question since the order was made.
(9) A disqualification shall be deemed to have expired only in relation to vehicles of such classes as may be prescribed in relation to the test passed by regulations under that section.
(10) Where there is issued to a person a licence on the counterpart of which are endorsed particulars of a disqualification under this section, there shall also be endorsed the particulars of any test of competence to drive that he has passed since the order of disqualification was made.
(11) and (11A) [Extensions to tests taken in Northern Ireland, the Isle of Man, the Channel Islands, an EEA State, Gibraltar, or a designated country or territory or for the purposes of a British Forces licence, if passing such a test would give entitlement to an exchangeable licence.]

The effect of this section is to make disqualification until a test is passed mandatory for those offenders convicted of offences specified in subsection (2). This obligation to disqualify under s. 36 also extends to such persons disqualified under ss. 34 and 35 as may be prescribed and to such other persons convicted of offences involving obligatory endorsement as may be prescribed.

The test to be passed by the offender will be an 'extended driving test' in any case where he has been convicted of an offence involving obligatory disqualification or has been disqualified under s. 35. The matters to be tested are broadly similar to those prescribed for the 'ordinary' driving test, but the minimum length of the extended test is 60 minutes, considerably longer than the normal test of competence to drive (Motor Vehicles (Driving Licences) Regulations 1999 (SI 1999 No. 2864), reg. 41). When the Road Safety Act 2006, s. 37 is brought into force, the definition of 'appropriate driving test' will be modified so that it will enable the Secretary of State to prescribe by regulations the circumstances in which the test to be passed must be an extended one. This is clearly intended to broaden the circumstances in which the more stringent post-disqualification test will be applicable before the driver fully returns to the roads.

The power to order a person to take a driving test where he has been convicted of an offence involving obligatory endorsement which has not been prescribed under s. 36(3)(b) may be exercised only after the court has had regard to the safety of road users in accordance with s. 36(6). The insertion of s. 36(6) seems to indicate that such a regard is paramount in deciding whether to exercise the discretion to disqualify. The fact of its insertion, it is submitted, means that all courts should consider using s. 36 when it is not mandatory to order a retest. Nonetheless, on the previous authorities an order was to be made only on evidence that the ability of the defendant to drive is in some way in question. It should not be used as an additional punishment but only where because of 'age or infirmity or the circumstances of the offence a person may not be a competent driver' (*Buckley* (1988) 10 Cr App R (S) 477).

In *Miller* (1994) 15 Cr App R (S) 505, the Court of Appeal upheld the sentencing judge's order that the appellant be disqualified until passing a driving test on the ground that it was clear his driving was grossly incompetent. The appellant had pleaded guilty to careless driving on an indictment alleging dangerous driving. He had never passed a driving test and had numerous previous convictions, including 10 for driving while disqualified. In *Bannister* [1991] RTR 1, where the appellant was imprisoned for three months and disqualified for two years under s. 36, the court took the view that competence to drive included proper regard for other road users as well as control of the vehicle.

For s. 48, see **C7.22**.

For further details, see **C8.2** ***et seq.***

Effect of Order of Disqualification

C7.14 **Road Traffic Offenders Act 1988, s. 37**

(1) Where the holder of a licence is disqualified by an order of a court, the licence shall be treated as being revoked with effect from the beginning of the period of disqualification.

(1A) Where—

(a) the disqualification is for a fixed period shorter than 56 days in respect of an offence involving obligatory endorsement, or

(b) the order is made under section 26 of this Act, subsection (1) above shall not prevent the licence from again having effect at the end of the period of disqualification.

(2) Where the holder of the licence appeals against the order and the disqualification is suspended under section 39 of this Act, the period of disqualification shall be treated for the purpose of subsection (1) above as beginning on the day on which the disqualification ceases to be suspended.

(3) Notwithstanding anything in part III of the Road Traffic Act 1988, a person disqualified by an order of a court under section 36 of this Act is (unless he is also disqualified otherwise than by virtue of such an order) entitled to obtain and to hold a provisional licence and to drive a motor vehicle in accordance with the conditions subject to which the provisional licence is granted.

For further details, see **C8.2** ***et seq.***

Appeal against and Suspension of Disqualification

C7.15 **Road Traffic Offenders Act 1988, s. 38**

(1) A person disqualified by an order of a magistrates' court under section 34 or 35 of this Act may appeal against the order in the same manner as against a conviction.

Road Traffic Offenders Act 1988, s. 39

(1) Any court in England and Wales (whether a magistrates' court or another) which makes an order disqualifying a person may, if it thinks fit, suspend the disqualification pending an appeal against the order.

Removal of Disqualification

C7.16 **Road Traffic Offenders Act 1988, s. 42**

(1) Subject to the provisions of this section, a person who by an order of a court is disqualified may apply to the court by which the order was made to remove the disqualification.

(2) On any such application the court may, as it thinks proper having regard to—
(a) the character of the person disqualified and his conduct subsequent to the order,
(b) the nature of the offence, and
(c) any other circumstances of the case,
either by order remove the disqualification as from such date as may be specified in the order or refuse the application.

(3) No application shall be made under subsection (1) above for the removal of a disqualification before the expiration of whichever is relevant of the following periods from the date of the order by which the disqualification was imposed, that is—
(a) two years, if the disqualification is for less than four years,
(b) one half of the period of disqualification, if it is for less than 10 years but not less than four years,
(c) five years in any other case;
and in determining the expiration of the period after which under this subsection a person may apply for the removal of a disqualification, any time after the conviction during which the disqualification was suspended or he was not disqualified shall be disregarded.

(4) Where an application under subsection (1) above is refused, a further application under that subsection shall not be entertained if made within three months after the date of the refusal.

(5) If under this section a court orders a disqualification to be removed, the court—
(a) must cause particulars of the order to be endorsed on the counterpart of the licence, if any, previously held by the applicant, and
(b) may in any case order the applicant to pay the whole or any part of the costs of the application.

(5A) Subsection (5)(b) above shall apply only where the disqualification was imposed in respect of an offence involving obligatory endorsement; and in any other case the court must send notice of the order made under this section to the Secretary of State.

(5B) [Manner of sending notice to the Secretary of State.]

(6) The preceding provisions of this section shall not apply where the disqualification was imposed by order under section 36(1) of this Act.

By the RTOA 1988, s. 43, any period of suspension shall be disregarded in determining the expiration of a period of disqualification. Thus, if a defendant is disqualified for three years and during that period the disqualification is suspended for three months, then the expiry of the disqualification is three years and three months after the date of disqualification.

An applicant under s. 42 is eligible to apply for publicly funded representation (*Liverpool Crown Court, ex parte McCann* [1995] RTR 23). The chances of such an application being successful, however, are slim.

The procedure on an application to remove a disqualification is not fixed and is, therefore, a matter for the court. It is usual for the police to respond to the application and they may be represented. One procedure which is often adopted is that the police outline the facts of the offence and give the details of the applicant's record, calling such evidence as they deem appropriate and the court allows. The applicant then gives evidence and may be cross-examined with the permission of the court. Thereafter the applicant or his representative is allowed to address the court. There is no power to award the applicant costs but even if successful he may be ordered to pay the costs of the application. There appears to be nothing to prevent the court from fixing the hearing date at any stage as long as the application is actually heard after the expiry of the 'relevant time'.

Endorsement

Road Traffic Offenders Act 1988, ss. 44 and 45 C7.17

44.—(1) Where a person is convicted of an offence involving obligatory endorsement, the court must order there to be endorsed on the counterpart of any licence held by him particulars of the conviction and also—
(a) if the court orders him to be disqualified, particulars of the disqualification, or
(b) if the court does not order him to be disqualified—

(i) particulars of the offence, including the date when it was committed, and
(ii) the penalty points to be attributed to the offence.

(2) Where the court does not order the person convicted to be disqualified, it need not make an order under subsection (1) above if for special reasons it thinks fit not to do so.

(3) [Applies only to Scotland.]

(4) This section is subject to section 48 of this Act.

45.—(1) An order that any particulars or penalty points are to be endorsed on the counterpart of any licence held by the person convicted shall, whether he is at the time the holder of a licence or not, operate as an order that the counterpart of any licence he may then hold or may subsequently obtain is to be so endorsed until he becomes entitled under subsection (4) below to have a licence issued to him with its counterpart free from the particulars or penalty points.

(2) On the issue of a new licence to a person, any particulars or penalty points ordered to be endorsed on the counterpart of any licence held by him shall be entered on the counterpart of the licence unless he has become entitled under subsection (4) below to have a licence issued to him with its counterpart free from those particulars or penalty points.

(3) [Repealed.]

(4) A person the counterpart of whose licence has been ordered to be endorsed is entitled to have issued to him with effect from the end of the period for which the endorsement remains effective a new licence with a counterpart free from the endorsement if he applies for a new licence in pursuance of section 97(1) of the Road Traffic Act 1988, surrenders any subsisting licence and its counterpart, pays the fee prescribed by regulations under part III of that Act and satisfies the other requirements of section 97(1).

(5) An endorsement ordered on a person's conviction of an offence remains effective (subject to subsections (6) and (7) below)—
(a) if an order is made for the disqualification of the offender, until four years have elapsed since the conviction, and
(b) if no such order is made, until either—
(i) four years have elapsed since the commission of the offence, or
(ii) an order is made for the disqualification of the offender under section 35 of this Act.

(6) Where the offence was one under section 1 or 2 of the Road Traffic Act 1988 (causing death by dangerous driving and dangerous driving), the endorsement remains in any case effective until four years have elapsed since the conviction.

(7) Where the offence was one—
(a) under section 3A, 4(1) or 5(1)(a) of that Act (driving offences connected with drink or drugs), or
(b) under section 7(6) of that Act (failing to provide specimen) involving obligatory disqualification, the endorsement remains effective until 11 years have elapsed since the conviction.

For further details, see **C8.1** ***et seq.*** When the Road Safety Act 2006, s. 14, is brought into force, a reference to an offence under the RTA 1988, s. 7A(6), will be added as s. 45(7)(c). The 2006 Act also includes provision (not yet in force) for the further amendment of the RTOA 1988, s. 44, and the repeal of s. 45 (see **C7.18** and **C7.19**).

The fact that an endorsement to which s. 45(7) applies remains effective beyond the time after which the conviction to which it attaches may be spent under the Rehabilitation of Offenders Act 1974 (see **E26**) does not constitute a violation of the right to private life in the ECHR, Article 8(1) (*R (Pearson) v DVLA* [2003] RTR 292).

New System of Endorsement

C7.18 **Driving Record** Under the Road Safety Act 2006, ss. 8 to 10 (not yet in force), a new approach to endorsement is being introduced. It addresses the concerns held about the inability at present to issue a fixed penalty notice to non-GB licence holders and gives effect to an undertaking given by the government to the EC Commission following a complaint by a Dutch licence holder about the current discrimination.

In order to remove the differences in treatment between those who do and those who do not hold GB driving licences, these provisions introduce the notion of a 'driving record' being established in relation to a person, to be maintained by the Secretary of State and 'designed to be endorsed with particulars relating to offences committed by the person under the Traffic Acts' (RTA 1988, s. 97A, inserted by s. 8 of the 2006 Act). The new provisions will be implemented in two distinct phases; s. 61(8) of the 2006 Act provides for staggered commencement, involving the first phase following the commencement of s. 5 and sch. 1 (giving of fixed penalty notices by vehicle examiners). Initially, in accordance with amendments introduced by the 2006 Act, s. 9 and sch. 2, the driving records will be created and maintained only in respect of unlicensed and foreign drivers. Section 44(3A) will be inserted into the RTOA 1988, making it a requirement to order endorsement on the driving record of an offender who does not hold a driving licence. Notice of that endorsement is then sent to the Secretary of State in accordance with the newly inserted s. 44A.

Endorsement of a driving record will also be available by virtue of amendments made to the RTOA 1988, s. 54 (notices on-the-spot or at a police station). The recipient will be required to deliver the notice to enable an appropriate check to be made as to whether or not he is going to be liable to be disqualified for the offence; if that is not the case, a fixed penalty notice must follow. Similarly, provision is made by the insertion of a new s. 57A into the RTOA 1988, enabling a fixed penalty clerk to deal with a person who does not hold a driving licence in much the same way as someone who does, save that, instead of endorsing the person's counterpart, upon payment of the fixed penalty before the end of the suspended enforcement period, the clerk sends notice to the Secretary of State of the relevant particulars to be endorsed on the person's driving record.

Extension to All Drivers The second phase of the new system will be introduced when the Road Safety Act 2006, s. 10 and sch. 3 (not yet in force), are brought into force. When this stage is reached, driving records will be created for everyone and references to 'the counterpart' will disappear, so that it will no longer have any function. Drivers who hold GB licences will still be required to produce them in order to be given a fixed penalty notice; for all others, they will be dealt with like unlicensed and foreign drivers under the first phase. The benefit will be the centralisation of the offending records in respect of all drivers in a uniform manner. **C7.19**

Combination of Disqualification and Endorsement with Orders for Discharge

The RTOA 1988, s. 46, makes provision as to the combination of orders for disqualification and endorsement with the provisions in the PCC(S)A 2000, s. 14, which have the effect of treating a conviction in respect of which a discharge is imposed as if it were not a conviction at all (see **E14.6**). Section 46(1) provides that the PCC(S)A 2000, s. 14(3), does not operate to prevent the court from endorsing an offender's licence or disqualifying him from driving. Section 46(2) provides that the PCC(S)A 2000, s. 14(1), does not operate to prevent a court from taking into account previous orders of disqualification or endorsement imposed on an occasion when the offender was discharged. **C7.20**

Supplementary Provisions: Decision Not to Disqualify or Endorse or to Shorten Period of Disqualification

Road Traffic Offenders Act 1988, s. 47 **C7.21**

(1) In any case where a court exercises its power under section 34, 35 or 44 of this Act not to order any disqualification or endorsement or to order disqualification for a shorter period than would otherwise be required, it must state the grounds for doing so in open court and, if it is a magistrates' court . . ., must cause them to be entered in the register . . . of its proceedings.

Any court must state, in open court, the grounds on which it has found 'special reasons' or 'mitigating circumstances', but despite the use of the word 'must', the Divisional Court in

Barnes v Gevaux [1981] RTR 236 held that this requirement was discretionary in cases where the power to disqualify is discretionary.

Exemption from Disqualification and Endorsement for Offences against Construction and Use Regulations

C7.22 **Road Traffic Offenders Act 1988, s. 48**

(1) Where a person is convicted of an offence under section 40A of the Road Traffic Act 1988 (using vehicle in dangerous condition etc) the court must not—
(a) order him to be disqualified, or
(b) order any particulars or penalty points to be endorsed on the counterpart of any licence held by him,
if he proves that he did not know, and had no reasonable cause to suspect, that the use of the vehicle involved a danger of injury to any person.

(2) Where a person is convicted of an offence under section 41A of the Road Traffic Act 1988 (breach of requirement as to brakes, steering-gear or tyres) the court must not—
(a) order him to be disqualified, or
(b) order any particulars or penalty points to be endorsed on the counterpart of any licence held by him,
if he proves that he did not know, and had no reasonable cause to suspect, that the facts of the case were such that the offence would be committed.

This provision is, in effect, the equivalent of statutory 'special reasons' in relation to construction and use offences. The onus is on the defendant, on a balance of probabilities, to prove lack of knowledge or reasonable cause for suspicion.

Offender Escaping Consequences of Endorsable Offence by Deception

C7.23 **Road Traffic Offenders Act 1988, s. 49**

(1) This section applies where in dealing with a person convicted of an offence involving obligatory endorsement a court was deceived regarding any circumstances that were or might have been taken into account in deciding whether or for how long to disqualify him.

(2) If—
(a) the deception constituted or was due to an offence committed by that person, and
(b) he is convicted of that offence,
the court by or before which he is convicted shall have the same powers and duties regarding an order for disqualification as had the court which dealt with him for the offence involving obligatory endorsement but must, in dealing with him, take into account any order made on his conviction of the offence involving obligatory endorsement.

Financial Penalty Deposits

C7.24 When the Road Safety Act 2006, s. 11, is brought into force, a new part 3A will be inserted into the RTOA 1988, and sch. 4 to the 2006 Act (prohibition on driving: immobilisation, removal and disposal of vehicles) will also come into force. Part 3A, consisting of ss. 90A to 90F, introduces the new notion of enabling a constable or a vehicle examiner to impose a financial deposit requirement on a person where the specified conditions are satisfied.

The precise extent of the types of person, offences and circumstances when such a requirement can be made will be specified in an order of the Secretary of State. In an appropriate case, where the person believed to have committed such an offence fails to provide 'an address in the United Kingdom at which the constable or vehicle examiner considers it is likely that it would be possible to find the person whenever necessary to do so in connection with the proceedings, fixed penalty notice or conditional offer', a requirement can be made (s. 90A(4)). The requirement is to make payment of 'the appropriate amount' immediately or within 'the relevant period' which varies according to the situation. The amount so paid would be used to pay any uncontested fixed penalty notice. If the person chose to contest the commission of the offence and was unsuccessful, the payment made would be off-set against all, or part, of the fine imposed. If the offender was successful, or the matter did not come to court within the time permitted for a prosecution to be commenced or 12 months, whichever is shorter, the amount would be refunded with interest.

Prohibition on Driving Under the new s. 90D inserted into the RTOA 1988, where a person on whom a financial penalty deposit requirement is imposed does not make an immediate payment of the amount required, the constable or vehicle examiner is entitled, but not obliged, to give notice in writing to the person prohibiting the driving of the vehicle of which the person was in charge at the time of the offence. In doing so, the constable or vehicle examiner may also direct in writing to the person concerned that the vehicle in question must be removed to another specified place. The prohibition on driving will continue until the deposit is paid, a fixed penalty arising from the offence is paid, the person is convicted or acquitted of the offence, the person is told there will be no prosecution for the offence, or the prosecution period expires. **C7.25**

Meaning of 'Offence Involving Obligatory Endorsement'

Road Traffic Offenders Act 1988, s. 96 **C7.26**

For the purposes of this Act, an offence involves obligatory endorsement if it is an offence under a provision of the Traffic Acts specified in column 1 of part I of schedule 2 to this Act or an offence specified in column 1 of part II of that schedule and either—
- (a) the word 'obligatory' (without qualification) appears in column 6 (in the case of part I) or column 3 (in the case of part II) against the offence, or
- (b) that word appears there qualified by conditions relating to the offence which are satisfied.

Meaning of 'Offence Involving Obligatory Disqualification' and 'Offence Involving Discretionary Disqualification'

Road Traffic Offenders Act 1988, s. 97 **C7.27**

(1) For the purposes of this Act, an offence involves obligatory disqualification if it is an offence under a provision of the Traffic Acts specified in column 1 of part I of schedule 2 to this Act or an offence specified in column 1 of part II of that schedule and either—
- (a) the word 'obligatory' (without qualification) appears in column 5 (in the case of part I) or column 2 (in the case of part II) against the offence, or
- (b) that word appears there qualified by conditions or circumstances relating to the offence which are satisfied or obtain.

(2) For the purposes of this Act, an offence involves discretionary disqualification if it is an offence under a provision of the Traffic Acts specified in column 1 of part I of schedule 2 to this Act or an offence specified in column 1 of part II of that schedule and either—
- (a) the word 'discretionary' (without qualification) appears in column 5 (in the case of part I) or column 2 (in the case of part II) against the offence, or
- (b) that word appears there qualified by conditions or circumstances relating to the offence which are satisfied or obtain.

Forfeiture of Motor Vehicle

Section 143 of the PCC(S)A 2000 (see **E20.1** *et seq.*) makes it possible, in some circumstances, for a court to order the forfeiture of a motor vehicle where it has been used in committing or facilitating the commission of an offence. **C7.28**

General Interpretation Provisions

Road Traffic Offenders Act 1988, s. 98 **C7.29**

(1) In this Act—
'disqualified' means disqualified for holding or obtaining a licence and 'disqualification' is to be construed accordingly,
'drive' has the same meaning as in the Road Traffic Act 1988,
'licence' means a licence to drive a motor vehicle granted under part III of that Act,
'provisional licence' means a licence granted by virtue of section 97(2) of that Act,

'the provisions connected with the licensing of drivers' means sections 7, 8, 22, 25 to 29, 31, 32, 34 to 48, 91ZA to 91B, 96 and 97 of this Act,

'road'—

(a) in relation to England and Wales, means any highway and any other road to which the public has access, and includes bridges over which a road passes, and

(b) [Applies only to Scotland.],

'the Road Traffic Acts' means the Road Traffic Act 1988, the Road Traffic (Consequential Provisions) Act 1988 (so far as it reproduces the effect of provisions repealed by that Act) and this Act, and

'the Traffic Acts' means the Road Traffic Acts and the Road Traffic Regulation Act 1984, and 'Community licence', 'counterpart', 'EEA State' and 'Northern Ireland licence' have the same meanings as in part III of the Road Traffic Act 1988.

(2) Sections 185 and 186 of the Road Traffic Act 1988 (meaning of 'motor vehicle' and other expressions relating to vehicles) apply for the purposes of this Act as they apply for the purposes of that Act.

(3) In the schedules to this Act—

'RTRA' is used as an abbreviation for the Road Traffic Regulation Act 1984, and

'RTA' is used as an abbreviation for the Road Traffic Act 1988 or, if followed by '1989', the Road Traffic (Driver Licensing and Information Systems) Act 1989.

(4) Subject to any express exception, references in this Act to any part of this Act include a reference to any schedule to this Act so far as relating to that part.

Section C8 Endorsement, Penalty Points and Disqualification

Endorsement Generally

In all cases involving obligatory or discretionary disqualification, the court, in the absence of 'special reasons' (see **C8.9**) or the operation of the RTOA 1988, s. 48 (see **C7.22**), or the Mental Health Act 1986, s. 37, is obliged to order particulars of the offence to be endorsed on the counterpart of the offender's licence or any licence that might be held by the defendant in the future (or, when the relevant provisions of the Road Safety Act 2006 are brought into force, on the offender's driving record: see **C7.18**). Each offence is denoted by a particular code, and the DVLA is notified. Where the offender is not disqualified, penalty points must also be endorsed (RTOA 1988, s. 44). **C8.1**

The number of points applicable to an offence is set out in the RTOA 1988, sch. 2, part II, col. 5 (see **C9.2**). Certain offences carry a variable number of points (see **C9.2**).

The points to be endorsed should reflect the seriousness of the offence. Therefore, an offence of driving without due care and attention consisting of momentary inattention might be suitably endorsed with three or four penalty points, whereas an offence consisting of prolonged, blatantly bad driving should carry a higher number of points to reflect the greater degree of culpability. In cases involving variable penalty points, the court should allow mitigation before arriving at any decision as to the number of points that might be imposed.

If there are a number of offences committed on the 'same occasion', then, subject to the RTOA 1988, s. 28 (see **C7.2**), the points to be endorsed are those relating to the offence which carries the highest number. Thus, if a defendant is convicted of careless driving and contravention of a street playground order, the highest number of penalty points relates to the careless driving. For the meaning of 'same occasion' see **C7.2**. If the penalty points are the same for both offences, then it is normal practice to endorse the more serious offence with the points. Where penalty points for a fixed penalty have already been endorsed, the maximum number of points available to the court in respect of an offence committed on the same occasion must be reduced accordingly (*Green v O'Donnell* 1997 SCCR 315). If a period of disqualification is obligatory or imposed under the court's discretionary powers, no penalty points in respect of other offences committed on the 'same occasion' are endorsed (*Martin v DPP* [2000] RTR 188 and *Ahmed v McLeod* [2000] RTR 201n, respectively). By virtue of the RTOA 1988, s. 28, the court may, following a determination under s. 28(5), order the endorsement of the counterpart to the licence with penalty points in relation to more than one offence committed on the same occasion. Points would then be aggregated for the purposes of the RTOA 1988, s. 35 (disqualification for repeated offences: see **C7.12**) and the Road Traffic (New Drivers) Act 1995 (surrender of licences: see **C7.8**).

It is not unusual for a defendant to face a number of charges relating to different occasions. In those circumstances the court must establish the total number of points for each occasion, and is then obliged to aggregate those points for the purposes of the penalty points procedure.

If the court disqualifies for any of the substantive offences under the RTOA 1988, s. 34, it does not order endorsement of the counterpart with any penalty points relating to that offence; the counterpart is merely endorsed with particulars of the offence. The points relating to that offence are disregarded for the purposes of s. 35 (see *Martin v DPP* [2000] RTR 188).

The effect of a disqualification under the penalty points procedure is to wipe the licence and its counterpart clean. If the defendant is subsequently convicted of an offence, previously endorsed points are not taken into consideration, but the fact of a penalty points disqualification is relevant to any future points disqualification.

With the exception of offences involving mandatory disqualification, aiders and abettors etc. are punished as principals and the same procedure applies.

As to attempts, see generally **C1.3**. If the offence attempted is summary only, then it must be statutory (e.g., attempting to drive while unfit through drink or drugs), and the penalty is set out in the RTOA 1988, sch. 2, part II, col. 5 (see **C9.2**). If it is triable either way then, by virtue of the Criminal Attempts Act 1981, s. 4(1)(b), the same liability to penalties exists as for the complete offence.

Disqualification under Penalty Points Procedure

C8.2 The penalty points procedure was introduced by the Transport Act 1981 to replace the previous system of 'totting up'. The purpose of the procedure is to punish repeated offences which in themselves are not sufficiently grave to warrant disqualification, but which taken together indicate repeated offences of bad driving or disregard for the law.

When considering the proper sentence for an offence carrying discretionary disqualification, the court should first consider whether that is warranted. In doing so, it will have regard to the defendant's full relevant driving record. If it considers that a mandatory period of disqualification under the RTOA 1988, s. 35, would be the best disposal, the court can exercise its discretion not to disqualify under the RTOA, s. 34 and to impose an appropriate number of penalty points to bring the defendant within s. 35 (*Jones v DPP* [2001] RTR 80). As such, ss. 34 and 35 are complementary rather than mutually exclusive.

Once points have been imposed they are added to any other points imposed in respect of offences committed within three years of the latest offence or offences (points to be taken into consideration). If the total is 12 or more, the court is obliged to disqualify under the RTOA 1988, s. 35. This disqualification is mandatory unless the court finds mitigating circumstances and is in addition to, but not consecutive to, any disqualification which the court may order for the offences before it on that day.

Even if the court disqualifies for a substantive offence, it is obliged to take into account other offences which were committed and to take into account and attribute points in accordance with the RTOA 1988, ss. 28 and 29, with a view to disqualification under s. 35. Points are not endorsed on the counterpart under s. 44 if there is a penalty points disqualification.

C8.3 **Period of Disqualification under Road Traffic Offenders Act 1988, s. 35** The disqualification must be for a minimum period, unless there are grounds for mitigating the normal consequences and the court thinks fit to order a shorter period or no disqualification at all.

If the offender has no previous disqualification of 56 days or more imposed within three years of the commission of the latest offence for which penalty points are to be taken into account, then the period is six months. If there is one such disqualification in the three years, the period is a minimum of one year. If there are two or more such disqualifications imposed within three years of the commission of the latest offence, then the minimum period is two years.

Disqualifications under the RTOA 1988, s. 26, and PCC(S)A 2000, s. 147, are not to be taken into account.

Mitigating Circumstances Mitigating circumstances may be circumstances which relate to the offender and the offence, and may include the offender's record and good works. **C8.4**

The RTOA 1988, s. 35(4), specifically excludes circumstances which are alleged to make the offence not serious, hardship, other than exceptional hardship, and any 'mitigating circumstances' which have been advanced as such during the three years preceding the conviction for the latest offence. For those reasons s. 47 of the 1988 Act requires grounds for mitigating the normal consequences of the conviction to be stated in open court, and entered in the register if the case is heard by a magistrates' court. It is necessary to demonstrate not only that the defendant will lose his employment but also that there are other circumstances associated with that loss which might involve reflected hardship of a serious kind on the defendant's business, family or long-term prospects (*Brennan v McKay* 1997 SLT 603).

It is for the offender to establish that grounds which are advanced are different from any so previously put before the court (*Sandbach Justices, ex parte Pescud* (1983) 5 Cr App R (S) 177). In practice, most of the mitigating circumstances advanced relate to 'exceptional hardship'. In *Owen v Jones* (1987) 9 Cr App R (S) 34, the court expressed the view that in the vast majority of cases justices would need to have evidence to satisfy themselves of the existence of exceptional hardship, but that on occasions they might rely upon their own knowledge. In that case a police officer had acquired a total of 13 points and, if disqualified, would have, by the usual practice of his Chief Constable, been forced to resign, thereby losing his job and his home. This practice was known to the bench, who did not require the defendant to provide evidence, as they found that the facts amounted to exceptional hardship.

'Exceptional hardship' is often advanced in relation to the offender's employment. In those circumstances the court might consider whether or not a licence to drive is necessary for the offender either to go to work or because his occupation is, or entails, driving. Such matters as his hours and pattern of work, together with the distances he must travel in order to reach his work and the availability of public transport, are relevant, as are details of his age and health and any other means of transport available to him. If loss of his licence may mean loss of his job or reduced wages, the court may consider any unusual hardship that may result to the family of the defendant and any unusual hardship that may be occasioned to them if he were to lose his licence. The fact that he is a businessman, with employees dependent upon him and his ability to drive, may be considered, but the court should be careful to inquire as to other means of transport or available methods of effecting his necessary business.

The court must have regard to all the circumstances. This has been held to include, in the case of a young offender with a bad record who was disqualified for two years under the penalty points procedure, the counter-productive nature of long periods of disqualification. In *Thomas* [1983] 1 WLR 1490, Lord Lane CJ said (at p. 1491):

> . . . with persons like the present appellant, who seem to be incapable of leaving motor vehicles alone, to impose a period of disqualification which will extend for a substantial period after their release from prison may well, and in many cases certainly will, invite the offender to commit further offences in relation to motor vehicles. In other words a long period of disqualification may well be counter-productive and so contrary to the public interest. So well established has this sentencing policy become in recent years that it is not necessary to refer to a line of cases.

The disqualification of two years was consequently reduced to one.

Given the breadth of the discretion under s. 35(1), it can be exercised in cases where the unreasonable length of time between the offence resulting in a penalty points disqualification and the imposition of that sentence violates the ECHR, Article 6; in such a case, an appropriate remedy may be the reduction of the usual period of disqualification, or even imposing no disqualification at all (*Miller v DPP* [2005] RTR 44, applying *A-G's Ref (No. 2 of 2001)* [2001] 1 WLR (1869)).

Disqualification Generally

C8.5 Disqualification for an offence may be either obligatory or discretionary (see RTOA 1988, sch. 2, at **C9.2**).

Where a disqualification is discretionary, courts may not consider, except in the more serious cases, that disqualification is appropriate, particularly where it is a first offence. It 'should generally be restricted to cases involving bad driving, persistent motoring offences or the use of vehicles for the purposes of crime' (per Morland J in *Callister* [1993] RTR 70). In that case, theft of a vehicle by sale while it was subject to a credit agreement did not fall into any of those categories. Each case must be taken on its own merits, bearing in mind that certain types of offence will be viewed with greater seriousness. The appropriate test appears to be whether the sentence imposed is 'truly astonishing' (*Tucker v DPP* [1992] 4 All ER 901); if it is not, an appeal is unlikely to succeed. Offences of using a vehicle without insurance and failing to stop after an accident or to report an accident are always viewed seriously and often attract disqualification, even as a first offence. Also viewed seriously is driving while disqualified. In *Pegrum* (1986) 8 Cr App R (S) 27, an appellant, who had numerous previous disqualifications and several convictions for driving while disqualified, was sentenced to the then maximum period of imprisonment of one year. This sentence was upheld by the Court of Appeal.

Where a person is convicted of an offence involving obligatory disqualification, the court must order him to be disqualified for a minimum period of 12 months in the absence of special reasons (see **C8.9**). Where the offence is one of manslaughter by the driver of a motor vehicle or is an offence under s. 1 or 3A of the RTA 1988, the minimum period of disqualification is two years; the minimum period is also two years where the offender has had two or more periods of disqualification of 56 days or more within the period of three years preceding the commission of the offence. A second or subsequent conviction for an offence relating to 'drink driving' (i.e. under s. 3A, 4(1), 5(1)(a), 7(6) or 7A(6)) carries a minimum period of disqualification of three years, if it is committed within 10 years of another such conviction. However, for a s. 7(6) or 7A(6) offence which does not involve driving (in respect of which disqualification is therefore discretionary: see **C5.22**), it would be surprising if the period chosen by the sentencer approached three years by reference to a previous drink-drive offence (*R (Cawley) v Warrington Crown Court* [2001] EWHC Admin 494).

A person convicted of aiding and abetting etc. an offence mentioned in the RTOA 1988, s. 34(3), must be disqualified for three years if he is subsequently convicted of an offence mentioned in s. 34(3) (*Makeham v Donaldson* [1981] RTR 511).

In any case where a magistrates' court is considering imposing a period of disqualification and the person to be disqualified is not present in court, the court must, by virtue of the MCA 1980, s. 11(4), adjourn in order to warn the defendant that they have disqualification in mind. If the defendant fails to attend, they may disqualify in his absence or, more usually, issue a warrant under the MCA 1980, s. 13, to compel his attendance. Before a court imposes disqualification in a case where it is discretionary, either the defendant or his representative should be warned and then given the opportunity to address the court (*Ireland* (1988) 10 Cr App R (S) 474 and *Money* (1988) 10 Cr App R (S) 237).

C8.6 **Length of Disqualification** In general, when considering the length of disqualification courts should attempt to avoid long periods, particularly when the disqualification is imposed at the same time as a sentence of imprisonment as it may have an adverse effect on 'the defendant's prospects of effective rehabilitation upon his release from custody' (per Ognall J in *Russell* [1993] RTR 249n). In addition lengthy disqualifications tend to be counterproductive and often hamper the offender in the job market, sometimes leading to further crime, in particular, driving while disqualified. See *Thomas* (1983) 5 Cr App R (S) 354, *Matthews* (1987) 9 Cr App R (S) 1, *West* (1986) 8 Cr App R (S) 266, *Callum* [1995] RTR 248, *Howson* [2004] EWCA Crim 1850, *Lawson* [2006] 1 Cr App R (S) 323 and *Chivers* [2005] EWCA Crim 2252. Against those considerations the court must also consider its duty to protect the public, and a lengthy period of disqualification to enable the defendant to mature may be justified (*Gibbons* (1987) 9 Cr App R (S) 21).

Where the length of sentence alone is being challenged on appeal (which is preferable to instituting proceedings for judicial review), the appropriate test to apply is whether the sentence is 'truly astonishing' (*Ealing Justices, ex parte Scrafield* [1994] RTR 195). In cases involving additional factors, the 'harsh and oppressive' test might be more appropriate.

Disqualification for life may be imposed (*Tunde-Olarinde* [1967] 1 WLR 911), but such a disqualification is inappropriate and wrong in principle in the absence of either psychiatric evidence or evidence of many previous convictions which indicates that the defendant would indefinitely be a danger to the public if he is allowed to drive (per Morland J in *King* (1992) 13 Cr App R (S) 668). In *King*, although the appellant had used his car as a weapon, he had no previous convictions which related to dangerous or careless driving. The Court of Appeal reduced the period of disqualification from life to five years on the basis that the judge had failed to give weight to the rehabilitative principle set out in *Russell*. Similarly, in *Rivano* (1994) 158 JP 288, the Court of Appeal decided that there were no very exceptional circumstances requiring disqualification for life or leading to the conclusion that, as a man of only 30, the appellant would be a danger to the public indefinitely. See also *Fazal* [1999] 1 Cr App R (S) 152. In *Buckley* (1994) 15 Cr App R (S) 695, however, the fact that the appellant had such an appalling driving record, including six convictions for reckless driving, demonstrated an astonishing readiness to imperil the public and clearly satisfied the second limb in *King*; in those circumstances disqualification for life was justified.

When considering the period for which to disqualify a defendant whose licence has already been revoked because of a relevant disability, it is wrong in principle for the court to disqualify indefinitely (*Harrison* [2004] EWCA Crim 1527). The period of disqualification should reflect the offence and the offender's driving record and concerns about public safety arising from that disability are more appropriately dealt with through DVLA procedures for restoring the licence once the disability is no longer a factor.

Harrington-Griffin [1989] RTR 138 was a case of causing death by reckless driving, where a number of the aggravating features in *Boswell* [1984] 1 WLR 1047 (see C3.17), particularly alcohol, were present. The appellant was sentenced to 30 months' imprisonment and disqualified for seven years after a trial in which the only issue was the location of the point of impact in the collision which caused the fatality. Upholding the sentence, the Court of Appeal said (at p. 141):

> . . . it must be remembered that the discount which attaches to a plea of guilty is not the converse of a penalty for the manner in which a defendant has conducted his defence, but is rather a discount which acknowledges the defendant's contrition. . . .In no class of case is a plea of guilty of more significance than in the present type, for acknowledgement of blame in driving gives some assurance that the driver will remember what has happened and take heed of that lesson.

In arriving at the length of disqualification which is appropriate, the court should not have regard to the application of the RTOA 1988, s. 42, and the power of the court to remove a disqualification, but merely to the length of time that is appropriate for the offence before it. In *Bannister* [1991] RTR 1, the Court of Appeal upheld a disqualification of two years. (See also C7.13.)

Disqualification under Powers of Criminal Courts (Sentencing) Act 2000, ss. 146 and 147 Under the PCC(S)A 2000, s. 147, the Crown Court has power to disqualify where C8.7

a motor vehicle was used for the purpose of committing or facilitating the commission of an offence. In *Fazal* [1999] 1 Cr App R (S) 152, this power was exercised upon conviction for affray. The section also covers offences of assault, including secondary participation, when committed by driving a motor vehicle (s. 147(2)).

Under s. 146, a court has power to disqualify where a person is convicted of any offence in addition to or instead of dealing with the offender in any other way.

For further details of these provisions, see E23.

C8.8 **Disqualification until Test Passed** For the provisions of the RTOA 1988, s. 36, see C7.11. If a defendant is disqualified under the RTOA 1988, s. 36, he must obtain a provisional driving licence before driving and comply with its conditions of use, or else he may run the risk of being convicted under the RTA 1988, s. 103 (*Hunter v Coombs* [1962] 1 WLR 573; *DPP* v *Baker* (2004) 168 JP 617).

Special Reasons

C8.9 A 'special reason' was defined in *Whittal v Kirby* [1947] KB 194 as being special to the facts of the offence and not the offender. In doing so the Divisional Court adopted the definition in *Crossan* [1939] NI 106 (at pp. 112–13):

> A 'special reason' within the exception is one which is special to the facts of the particular case, that is, special to the facts which constitute the offence. It is, in other words, a mitigating or extenuating circumstance, not amounting in law to a defence to the charge, yet directly connected with the commission of the offence, and one which the court ought properly to take into consideration when imposing punishment. A circumstance peculiar to the offender as distinguished from the offence is not a 'special reason' within the exception.

Although *Wickins* (1958) 42 Cr App R 236 broadly confirmed these requirements, in *Jarvis v DPP* (2001) 165 JP 15, in respect of cases where excess alcohol offending is in issue, preference was expressed for the analysis of the position contained in *Jackson and Hart* [1970] 1 QB 647. See also *Kinsella v DPP* [2002] EWHC 545 (Admin). Where a defendant's medical condition is found not to amount to a defence to a charge of failing to provide a specimen, it does not automatically mean that the same medical condition cannot constitute 'special reasons' (*Woolfe v DPP* [2007] RTR 187).

As unreasonable delay in the determination of the charge does not relate to the facts of the offence so such delay cannot constitute a special reason (*Miller v DPP* [2005] RTR 44).

The onus of establishing that there are 'special reasons' lies with the defence on a balance of probabilities. Where there has been a trial resulting in a conviction and the defendant then advances special reasons, justices should readily accede to an application that a defendant be recalled when the earlier evidence has not fully dealt with the relevant facts (see *DPP v Kinnersley* [1993] RTR 105). In most cases (save for obvious ones), the justices might expect to hear expert evidence, particularly where the defence seek to establish that drinks were laced, although where corroboration does not exist or is unavailable for some good reason it is still open to the court to find special reasons where the defendant's evidence is believed (*Watson v Adam* 1996 SLT 459). Notice of the defence's intention to produce evidence of such special reasons should be given to the prosecution so that unnecessary adjournments are avoided. Failure to notify the prosecution could reflect on the *bona fides* of the defendant (*DPP v O'Connor* [1992] RTR 66; see also *Pugsley v Hunter* [1973] 1 WLR 578). The defendant's failure to give an appropriate explanation or account at the time of arrest or commission of the offence does not, as a matter of law, exclude the possibility of a finding that special reasons exist, but it would usually form an important factor for the court in considering all the relevant circumstances of a case (*DPP v Kinnersley*).

'Special reasons' may be advanced on appeal to the Crown Court as part of an appeal against sentence, or, if an appeal against conviction includes an appeal against sentence, where the Crown Court have upheld the conviction. The appeal is by way of rehearing of the evidence relevant to the issue of whether or not there are special reasons and, if so, as to how the discretion is to be exercised. Where special reasons have not been found an appeal by way of case stated is a more convenient procedure than an application for judicial review (see *DPP v O'Connor*).

Exercise of Power Discretionary A finding of 'special reasons' allows the court a discretion as to whether or not it: **C8.10**

(a) disqualifies under the RTOA 1988, s. 34(1); or
(b) endorses under the RTOA 1988, s. 44.

In *St Albans Crown Court, ex parte O'Donovan* [2000] 1 Cr App R (S) 344, the Divisional Court noted that whilst it did not rule out the possibility, following a finding of 'special reasons', of imposing a period of disqualification greater than the mandatory minimum, there would have to be compelling reasons to do so. Here, the defendant was nearly three times above the prescribed limit but had only driven a very short distance and had not posed any appreciable risk of danger to anyone. A disqualification of 12 months was substituted for the original 20 months.

Even though 'special reasons' have been established, there is no obligation to exercise the discretion and the court may still disqualify and endorse as it considers appropriate. In cases involving obligatory disqualification the court may therefore find 'special reasons' and not disqualify but still endorse. In cases where disqualification is discretionary the court may still endorse. In *Agnew v DPP* [1991] RTR 147, a case of careless driving, the Divisional Court found that the conditions were satisfied but refused to exercise their discretion. The applicant was a police officer on a training exercise who had gone through a red light, failing to follow instructions in treating the light in the same way as a 'give way' sign. Morland J, in giving the judgment of the Court, quoted Lord Widgery CJ in *Taylor v Rajan* [1974] QB 424, that 'justices should only exercise the discretion in favour of the driver in clear and compelling circumstances'. He then went on to say (at p. 150):

> There are two competing considerations: the need for realistic police driver training in actual road conditions and the safety of lawful users of the highway, motorists and pedestrians. The second must always be paramount.

Whether or not to exercise the discretion 'is peculiarly a question for [the justices], seeing and hearing the witnesses and making their assessment of the answers which are given to them, to determine whether in the circumstances it is a case in which they, in the exercise of that discretion, feel justified in imposing penalties other than disqualification' (per Beldam J in *Donahue v DPP* [1993] RTR 156). In *DPP v Bristow* [1998] RTR 100, the Divisional Court held that the key question justices should ask themselves when assessing if special reasons exist and whether their discretion should be exercised is what a sober, reasonable and responsible friend of the defendant, who was present at the time but who was a non-driver and thus unable to help, would have advised in the circumstances: drive or not drive. Unless the justices thought it was a real possibility rather than just an off-chance that such a friend would have advised the defendant to drive, they should not find special reasons and exercise their discretion.

Endorsement under s. 44 includes endorsement with penalty points. If the court does exercise the discretion not to endorse with particulars of the conviction, there is no power to endorse penalty points separately. Nor is there any power to endorse either without penalty points or with a lesser number than the amount set out in sch. 2 of the Act.

As shown in the examples that follow, the question of what constitutes 'special reasons' depends upon the facts of any particular case within the overall test as expressed in *Whittal v*

Kirby [1947] KB 194. As long as the justices or Crown Court have properly directed themselves in accordance with that test, the appellate courts will not interfere with their finding. Many of the cases relate to drink-related offences where the defendant may be anxious to avoid a mandatory disqualification. The courts have consistently sought to limit the application of 'special reasons' to cases which are plainly meritorious.

C8.11 **'Laced' Drinks** 'Laced drinks' as a special reason received a comprehensive review in *DPP v O'Connor* [1992] RTR 66. The Divisional Court held that the defence must show:

(a) that the defendant's drink or drinks had been laced;
(b) that the defendant did not know or suspect that his drink had been laced;
(c) that, if the defendant had not taken the laced drink, his level of alcohol would not have exceeded the prescribed limit.

Evidence needs to be examined with some care and expert evidence, which justices should normally expect to receive, is usually highly relevant as it goes to both credibility and whether or not the driver's admitted, voluntary consumption of alcohol would have taken him above the prescribed limit (per Woolf LJ at p. 79). In appropriate cases, public funding should be made available to enable a defendant to adduce expert evidence to support a plea of special reasons in 'laced drinks' cases (*Gravesham Magistrates' Court, ex parte Baker* [1998] RTR 451).

The need for a two-stage process was stressed, and Woolf LJ stated (at p. 81E):

> . . . in cases where there is erratic driving, or there is a substantial amount of alcohol in the defendant's bloodstream, justices will want to consider carefully whether, even if special reasons are established, this is a case where the defendant should have appreciated that he was not in a condition in which he should have driven.

An inability to distinguish between the relative alcoholic strengths of different drinks will not suffice (*Beauchamp-Thompson v DPP* [1988] RTR 54), otherwise it could give rise to a licence to 'lace' one's own drinks. Assuming, without enquiry, that a drink contains no alcohol will not constitute special reasons (*Robinson v DPP* (2004) 168 JP 522, where the court suggested *obiter* that even after enquiry and being told that the drink did not contain alcohol, readings that are very high should still not result in the justices exercising their discretion in favour of the defendant). See also *DPP v Sharma* [2005] RTR 361.

C8.12 **Handling Emergencies** In principle, driving in an emergency is recognised as being capable of amounting to special reasons. When raised, it is the justices' task to decide whether the facts amount to, and were, special reasons and then to decide what effect, if any, this has on the sentence to be imposed (*DPP v Upchurch* [1994] RTR 366; *DPP v Knight* [1994] RTR 374a). In doing so, the court can divide the driving into separate chapters to ascertain whether there was any interruption after which a fresh explanation would be required as to why the defendant had chosen to drive again (*Hamilton v Neizer* 1993 JC 63; *DPP v Goddard* [1998] RTR 463).

In *Aichroth v Cottee* [1954] 1 WLR 1124, Lord Goddard CJ stated (at p. 1127) that the 'mere fact that there is a sudden emergency will not be enough if it is shown that there are other reasonable methods of meeting it'. In *DPP v Cox* [1996] RTR 123, the defendant was a key-holder at a golf club and was contacted in the night when the burglar alarm was activated. Despite the short distance involved and having consumed a considerable amount of alcohol, he drove to the club premises without considering alternative methods of responding to the alarm. The Divisional Court confirmed that the issue of whether an emergency exists must be viewed objectively and held that the justices were justified in concluding that this was an emergency within the guidelines of *Aichroth v Cottee.* Similarly, in *DPP v Tucker* (6 November 1996 unreported), the Divisional Court upheld the justices' view that the defendant, responding to a burglar alarm at a jewellery business he ran, had considered all alternatives to driving himself, none of which were feasible, thereby justifying their finding of special reasons.

A private crisis, such as being blackmailed by a threat of crying rape, can justify a finding of special reasons as long as the justices guard against being taken in by hard luck stories and approach the issue in the proper objective fashion (*DPP v Enston* [1996] RTR 324). Provided justices have considered all the relevant facts, have reached a conclusion on those facts that could not be said to be perverse and have directed themselves properly on the law, the Divisional Court should be very slow to overturn the decision of the justices, even if it does not agree with the conclusions of the justices as to the facts (*Chapman v O'Hagan* [1949] 2 All ER 690). See also *Ashton v CPS* [2005] EWHC 2729 (Admin), which involved a defendant on his way to collect a liveried ambulance to answer a call-out.

In *DPP v Whittle* [1996] RTR 154, however, the Divisional Court overturned a finding of special reasons on grounds of a medical emergency, re-affirming the objective approach required, because the reasonable man would not have regarded the situation as one in which no other course of action was possible. The defendant had taken over the driving from his wife, who had complained of dizziness and blurred vision, but was driving fellow passengers home when stopped by the police. In passing, Simon Brown LJ wondered whether a genuine medical emergency might more properly fall within the complete defence of duress of circumstances (see **A3.29**) rather than being raised only as a special reason. In cases involving the risk of death or serious injury, such a course would certainly be advisable.

Relevance of Distance Driven In *Chatters v Burke* [1986] 1 WLR 1321, following an accident the defendant drove his motor vehicle a very short distance from a field onto the side of the highway, where he stopped, got out, and waited for the arrival of the police. He was charged with driving with excess alcohol in his breath and no insurance. The finding of 'special reasons' was upheld and the court enumerated seven matters which ought to be taken into account in such cases (at p. 1327): **C8.13**

> First of all they should consider how far the vehicle was in fact driven; secondly, in what manner it was driven; thirdly, what was the state of the vehicle; fourthly, whether it was the intention of the driver to drive any further; fifthly, the prevailing conditions with regard to the road and the traffic upon it; sixthly, whether there was any possibility of danger by contact with other road users; and finally, what was the reason for the vehicle being driven at all.

In *DPP v Humphries* [2000] RTR 52, the Divisional Court recognised the importance of this guidance whilst adding that the presence or absence of any factor would not automatically produce a particular conclusion. In this case, an argument in favour of finding 'special reasons' founded on the short distance actually driven was rejected because the intention of the defendant had been to drive much further had he not been apprehended. In contrast, in *DPP v Heritage* (2002) 166 JP 772, where the vehicle had been moved to a parking place and was then involved in a collision, having regard to the very short distance driven and all the surrounding circumstances, the justices were entitled to conclude that special reasons existed on a conviction for no insurance.

In *DPP v Corcoran* [1991] RTR 329, the respondent, having parked in the street because he was late for the theatre, drove some 40 yards to a car park from which a colleague was to collect the car on the following day. The car was travelling without lights, albeit slowly, and there were pedestrians in the vicinity but no other vehicles were visible and no danger was caused to other road users. The lack of danger by contact with other road users and the distance travelled were central to the decision to uphold the justices' finding of special reasons. But other factors, such as the availability of alternative courses of action to that of driving, can lead to the opposite conclusion (*R (DPP) v Oram* [2005] EWHC 964 (Admin)).

In *Daniels v DPP* [1992] RTR 140, the appellant, in the course of attempting to start his motor cycle, travelled 35 yards and was then arrested on suspicion of theft. As the defendant claimed that his refusal to provide the required specimen was attributable to having been distracted by the charge of theft (which was not being pursued), on those particular facts the Divisional Court accepted that this could be found to amount to 'special reasons'.

C8.14 **No Insurance** In cases concerning no insurance, a mistaken, albeit honest, belief that there was insurance has been held to be insufficient to amount to 'special reasons' in the absence of reasonable grounds for the belief (*Knowles v Rennison* [1947] KB 488; *DPP v Robson* [2001] EWHC Admin 496), particularly where responsibility for withdrawal of insurance cover rested on the defendant (*Smith v DPP* [2003] All ER (D) 07 (May)); where a defendant has enquired as to whether he is insured and has been assured that he is, this may amount to reasonable grounds, and special reasons (*Marshall v McLeod* 1998 SCCR 317). The mere fact that a vehicle is parked and unlikely to be driven while uninsured will not amount to 'special reasons' (*Heywood v O'Connor* 1994 SLT 254). In *DPP v Powell* [1993] RTR 266, the defendant's view that he did not require insurance to road test a motorised children's bike, which he regarded as a toy, was held to come within the test set out in *Whittal v Kirby* [1947] KB 194. See also *DPP v Murray* [2001] EWHC Admin 848, which concerned a Go-Ped.

C8.15 **Other Reasons** It can be 'special reasons' where the investigating officer incorrectly informs the defendant that failure to provide the required specimen will not necessarily lead to a period of disqualification (*Bobin v DPP* [1999] RTR 375).

Although fear of AIDS is potentially a defence to a charge of refusing to provide a specimen if it is medically established as a phobia (see *De Freitas v DPP* [1993] RTR 98 at **C5.19**), it was also held, in *DPP v Kinnersley* [1993] RTR 105, to be capable of being a 'special reason' for not disqualifying after a refusal to give a breath specimen.

Section C9 The Schedules to the Road Traffic Offenders Act 1988

Road Traffic Offenders Act 1988, sch. 1

C9.1

SCHEDULE 1

OFFENCES TO WHICH SECTIONS 1, 6, 11 AND 12(1) APPLY

1. (1) Where section 1, 6, 11 and 12(1) of this Act is shown in column 3 of this schedule against a provision of the Road Traffic Act 1988 specified in column 1, the section in question applies to an offence under that provision.
(2) The general nature of the offence is indicated in column 2.

1A. Section 1 also applies to—
(a) an offence under section 16 of the Road Traffic Regulation Act 1984 consisting in the contravention of a restriction on the speed of vehicles imposed under section 14 of that Act,
(b) an offence under subsection (4) of section 17 of that Act consisting in the contravention of a restriction on the speed of vehicles imposed under that section, and
(c) an offence under section 88(7) or 89(1) of that Act (speeding offences).

2. Section 6 also applies—
(a) to an offence under section 67 of this Act,
(b) [Applies only to Scotland.]
(c) [repealed], and
(d) to an offence under paragraph 3(5) of schedule 1 to the Road Traffic (New Drivers) Act 1995.

3. Section 11 also applies to—
(a) any offence to which section 112 of the Road Traffic Regulation Act 1984 (information as to identity of driver or rider) applies except an offence under section 61(5) of that Act,
(b) any offence which is punishable under section 91 of this Act,
(c) any offence against any other enactment relating to the use of vehicles on roads.

4. Section 12(1) also applies to—
(a) any offence which is punishable under section 91 of this Act,
(b) any offence against any other enactment relating to the use of vehicles on roads.

(1) Provision creating offence	(2) General nature of offence	(3) Applicable provisions of this Act
RTA section 1	Causing death by dangerous driving.	Section 11 of this Act.
RTA section 2	Dangerous driving.	Sections 1, 11 and 12(1) of this Act.
RTA section 3	Careless, and inconsiderate, driving.	Sections 1, 11 and 12(1) of this Act.
RTA section 3A	Causing death by careless driving when under influence of drink or drugs.	Section 11 of this Act.
RTA section 4	Driving or attempting to drive, or being in charge of a mechanically propelled vehicle, when unfit to drive through drink or drugs.	Sections 11 and 12(1) of this Act.
RTA section 5	Driving or attempting to drive, or being in charge of a motor vehicle, with excess alcohol in breath, blood or urine.	Sections 11 and 12(1) of this Act.

(1) Provision creating offence	(2) General nature of offence	(3) Applicable provisions of this Act
RTA section 6	Failing to co-operate with a preliminary test.	Sections 11 and 12(1) of this Act.
RTA section 7	Failing to provide specimen for analysis or laboratory test.	Sections 11 and 12(1) of this Act.
RTA section 7A	Failing to allow specimen of blood to be subjected to laboratory test.	Section 11 and 12(1) of this Act.
RTA section 12	Motor racing and speed trials.	Sections 11 and 12(1) of this Act.
RTA section 14	Driving or riding in a motor vehicle in contravention of regulations requiring wearing of seat belts.	Sections 11 and 12(1) of this Act.
RTA section 15	Driving motor vehicle with child not wearing seat belt or with child in a rear-facing child restraint in front seat with an active air bag.	Sections 11 and 12(1) of this Act.
RTA section 19	Prohibition of parking of heavy commercial vehicles on verges and footways.	Sections 11 and 12(1) of this Act.
RTA section 22	Leaving vehicles in dangerous positions.	Sections 1, 11 and 12(1) of this Act.
RTA section 23	Carrying passenger on motor-cycle contrary to section 23.	Sections 11 and 12(1) of this Act.
RTA section 24	Carrying passenger on bicycle contrary to section 24.	Sections 11 and 12(1) of this Act.
RTA section 25	Tampering with motor vehicles.	Section 11 of this Act.
RTA section 26(1)	Holding or getting onto vehicle in order to be carried.	Section 11 of this Act.
RTA section 26(2)	Holding on to vehicle in order to be towed.	Sections 11 and 12(1) of this Act.
RTA section 28	Dangerous cycling.	Sections 1, 11 and 12(1) of this Act.
RTA section 29	Careless, and inconsiderate, cycling.	Sections 1, 11 and 12(1) of this Act.
RTA section 30	Cycling when unfit through drink or drugs.	Sections 11 and 12(1) of this Act.
RTA section 31	Unauthorised or irregular cycle racing, or trials of speed.	Sections 11 and 12(1) of this Act.
RTA section 33	Unauthorised motor vehicle trial on footpaths or bridleways.	Sections 11 and 12(1) of this Act.
RTA section 34	Driving mechanically propelled vehicles elsewhere than on roads.	Sections 11 and 12(1) of this Act.
RTA section 35	Failing to comply with traffic directions.	Sections 1, 11 and 12(1) of this Act.
RTA section 36	Failing to comply with traffic signs.	Sections 1, 11 and 12(1) of this Act.
RTA section 40A	Using vehicle in dangerous condition etc.	Sections 11 and 12(1) of this Act.
RTA section 41A	Breach of requirement as to brakes, steering-gear or tyres.	Sections 11 and 12(1) of this Act.
RTA section 41B	Breach of requirement as to weight: goods and passenger vehicles.	Sections 11 and 12(1) of this Act.
RTA section 41D	Breach of requirements as to control of vehicle, mobile telephones, etc.	Sections 11 and 12(1) of this Act.
RTA section 42	Breach of other construction and use requirements.	Sections 11 and 12(1) of this Act.
RTA section 47	Using, etc., vehicle without required test certificate being in force.	Sections 11 and 12(1) of this Act.

(1) Provision creating offence	(2) General nature of offence	(3) Applicable provisions of this Act
RTA section 53	Using, etc., goods vehicle without required plating certificate or goods vehicle test certificate being in force, or where Secretary of State is required by regulations under section 49 to be notified of an alteration to the vehicle or its equipment but has not been notified.	Sections 11 and 12(1) of this Act.
RTA section 63	Using, etc., vehicle without required certificate being in force showing that it, or a part fitted to it, complies with type approval requirements applicable to it, or using, etc., certain goods vehicles for drawing trailer when plating certificate does not specify maximum laden weight for vehicle and trailer, or using, etc., goods vehicle where Secretary of State has not been but is required to be notified under section 48 of alteration to it or its equipment.	Sections 11 and 12(1) of this Act.
RTA section 71	Driving, etc., vehicle in contravention of prohibition on driving it as being unfit for service or overloaded, or refusing, neglecting or otherwise failing to comply with a direction to remove a vehicle found overloaded.	Sections 11 and 12(1) of this Act.
RTA section 78	Failing to comply with requirement about weighing motor vehicle or obstructing authorised person.	Sections 11 and 12(1) of this Act.
RTA section 87(1)	Driving otherwise than in accordance with a licence.	Sections 11 and 12(1) of this Act.
RTA section 87(2)	Causing or permitting a person to drive otherwise than in accordance with a licence.	Section 11 of this Act.
RTA section 92(10)	Driving after making false declaration as to physical fitness.	Sections 6, 11 and 12(1) of this Act.
RTA section 94(3) and that sub-section as applied by RTA section 99D or 109C	Failure to notify the Secretary of State of onset of, or deterioration in, relevant or prospective disability.	Section 6 of this Act.
RTA section 94(3A) and that subsection as applied by RTA section 99D(b) or 109C(c)	Driving after such a failure.	Sections 6, 11 and 12(1) of this Act.
RTA section 94A	Driving after refusal of licence under section 92(3), revocation under section 93 or service of a notice under section 99C or 109B.	Sections 6, 11 and 12(1) of this Act.
RTA section 99(5)	Driving licence holder failing to surrender licence and counterpart.	Section 6 of this Act.
RTA section 99B(11) and that subsection as applied by RTA section 109A(5)	Driving after failure to comply with a requirement under section 99B(6), (7) or (10) or a requirement under section 99B(6) or (7) as applied by section 109A(5).	Section 6 of this Act.

(1) Provision creating offence	(2) General nature of offence	(3) Applicable provisions of this Act
RTA section 103(1)(a)	Obtaining driving licence while disqualified.	Section 6 of this Act.
RTA section 103(1)(b)	Driving while disqualified.	Sections 6, 11 and 12(1) of this Act.
RTA section 114(1)	Failing to comply with conditions of LGV, PCV licence or LGV Community licence.	Sections 11 and 12(1) of this Act.
RTA section 114(2)	Causing or permitting a person under 21 to drive LGV or PCV in contravention of conditions of that person's licence.	Section 11 of this Act.
RTA section 143	Using motor vehicle, or causing or permitting it to be used, while uninsured or unsecured against third party risks.	Sections 6, 11 and 12(1) of this Act.
RTA section 163	Failing to stop vehicle when required.	Sections 11 and 12(1) of this Act.
RTA section 164(6)	Failing to produce driving licence and counterpart to constable or to state date of birth.	Sections 11 and 12(1) of this Act.
RTA section 165(3)	Failing to give constable certain names and addresses or to produce certificate of insurance or certain test and other like certificates.	Sections 11 and 12(1) of this Act.
RTA section 165(6)	Supervisor of learner driver failing to give constable certain names and addresses	Sections 11 of this Act.
RTA section 168	Refusing to give, or giving false, name and address in case of reckless, careless or inconsiderate driving or cycling.	Sections 11 and 12(1) of this Act.
RTA section 170	Failure by driver to stop, report accident or give information or documents.	Sections 11 and 12(1) of this Act.
RTA section 171	Failure by owner of motor vehicle to give police information for verifying compliance with requirement of compulsory insurance or security.	Sections 11 and 12(1) of this Act.
RTA section 174(1) or (5)	Making false statements in connection with licences under this Act and with registration as an approved driving instructor; or making false statement or withholding material information in order to obtain the issue of insurance certificates, etc.	Section 6 of this Act.
RTA section 175	Issuing false documents.	Section 6 of this Act.

Road Traffic Offenders Act 1988, sch. 2

C9.2

SCHEDULE 2
PROSECUTION AND PUNISHMENT OF OFFENCES
PART I
OFFENCES UNDER THE TRAFFIC ACTS

(1) Provision creating offence	(2) General nature of offence	(3) Mode of prosecution	(4) Punishment	(5) Disqualification	(6) Endorsement	(7) Penalty points
Offences under the Road Traffic Regulation Act 1984						
RTRA section 5	Contravention of traffic regulation order.	Summarily.	Level 3 on the standard scale.			
RTRA section 8	Contravention of order regulating traffic in Greater London.	Summarily.	Level 3 on the standard scale.			
RTRA section 11	Contravention of experimental traffic order.	Summarily.	Level 3 on the standard scale.			
RTRA section 13	Contravention of experimental traffic scheme in Greater London.	Summarily.	Level 3 on the standard scale.			
RTRA section 16(1)	Contravention of temporary prohibition or restriction.	Summarily.	Level 3 on the standard scale.	Discretionary if committed in respect of a speed restriction.	Obligatory if committed in respect of a speed restriction.	3–6 or 3 (fixed penalty).
RTRA section 16C(1)	Contravention of prohibition or restriction relating to relevant event.	Summarily.	Level 3 on the standard scale.			
RTRA section 17(4)	Use of special road contrary to scheme or regulations.	Summarily.	Level 4 on the standard scale.	Discretionary if committed in respect of a motor vehicle otherwise than by unlawfully stopping or allowing the vehicle to remain at rest on a part of a special road on which vehicles are in certain circumstances permitted to remain at rest.	Obligatory if committed as mentioned in the entry in column 5.	3–6 or 3 (fixed penalty) if committed in respect of a speed restriction, 3 in any other case.
RTRA section 18(3)	One-way traffic on trunk road.	Summarily.	Level 3 on the standard scale.			
RTRA section 20(5)	Contravention of prohibition or restriction for roads of certain classes.	Summarily.	Level 3 on the standard scale.			
RTRA section 25(5)	Contravention of pedestrian crossing regulations.	Summarily.	Level 3 on the standard scale.	Discretionary if committed in respect of a motor vehicle.	Obligatory if committed in respect of a motor vehicle.	3
RTRA section 28(3)	Not stopping at school crossing.	Summarily.	Level 3 on the standard scale.	Discretionary if committed in respect of a motor vehicle.	Obligatory if committed in respect of a motor vehicle.	3

(1) Provision creating offence	(2) General nature of offence	(3) Mode of prosecution	(4) Punishment	(5) Disqualification	(6) Endorsement	(7) Penalty points
Offences under the Road Traffic Regulation Act 1984—continued						
RTRA section 29(3)	Contravention of order relating to street playground.	Summarily.	Level 3 on the standard scale.	Discretionary if committed in respect of a motor vehicle.	Obligatory if committed in respect of a motor vehicle.	2
RTRA section 35A(1)	Contravention of order as to use of parking place.	Summarily.	(a) Level 3 on the standard scale in the case of an offence committed by a person in a street parking place reserved for disabled persons' vehicles or in an off-street parking place reserved for such vehicles, where that person would not have been guilty of that offence if the motor vehicle in respect of which it was committed had been a disabled person's vehicle. (b) Level 2 on the standard scale in any other case.			
RTRA section 35A(2)	Misuse of apparatus for collecting charges or of parking device or connected apparatus.	Summarily.	Level 3 on the standard scale.			
RTRA section 35A(5)	Plying for hire in parking place.	Summarily.	Level 2 on the standard scale.			
RTRA section 43(5)	Unauthorised disclosure of information in respect of licensed parking place.	Summarily.	Level 3 on the standard scale.			
RTRA section 43(10)	Failure to comply with term or conditions of licence to operate parking place.	Summarily.	Level 3 on the standard scale.			
RTRA section 43(12)	Operation of public offstreet parking place without licence.	Summarily.	Level 5 on the standard scale.			
RTRA section 47(1)	Contraventions relating to designated parking places.	Summarily.	(a) Level 3 on the standard scale in the case of an offence committed by a person in a street parking place reserved for disabled persons' vehicles where that person would not have been			

(1) Provision creating offence	(2) General nature of offence	(3) Mode of prosecution	(4) Punishment	(5) Disqualification	(6) Endorsement	(7) Penalty points
Offences under the Road Traffic Regulation Act 1984—continued						
RTRA section 47(1)	Contraventions relating to designated parking places.	Summarily.	guilty of the offence if the motor vehicle in respect of which it was committed had been a disabled person's vehicle. (b) Level 2 in any other case.			
RTRA section 47(3)	Tampering with parking meter.	Summarily.	Level 3 on the standard scale.			
RTRA section 52(1)	Misuse of parking device.	Summarily.	Level 2 on the standard scale.			
RTRA section 53(5)	Contravention of certain provisions of designation orders.	Summarily.	Level 3 on the standard scale.			
RTRA section 53(6)	Other contraventions of designation orders.	Summarily.	Level 2 on the standard scale.			
RTRA section 61(5)	Unauthorised use of loading area.	Summarily.	Level 3 on the standard scale.			
RTRA section 88(7)	Contravention of minimum speed limit.	Summarily.	Level 3 on the standard scale.			
RTRA section 89(1)	Exceeding speed limit.	Summarily.	Level 3 on the standard scale.	Discretionary.	Obligatory.	3–6 or 3 (fixed penalty).
RTRA section 104(5)	Interference with notice as to immobilisation device.	Summarily.	Level 2 on the standard scale.			
RTRA section 104(6)	Interference with immobilisation device.	Summarily.	Level 3 on the standard scale.			
RTRA section 105(5)	Misuse of disabled person's badge (immobilisation devices).	Summarily.	Level 3 on the standard scale.			
RTRA section 105(6A)	Misuse of recognised badge (immobilisation devices).	Summarily.	Level 3 on the standard scale.			
RTRA section 108(2) (or that subsection as modified by section 109(2) and (3)).	Non-compliance with notice (excess charge).	Summarily.	Level 3 on the standard scale.			

(1) Provision creating offence	(2) General nature of offence	(3) Mode of prosecution	(4) Punishment	(5) Disqualification	(6) Endorsement	(7) Penalty points
Offences under the Road Traffic Regulation Act 1984—continued						
RTRA section 108(3) (or that sub-section as modified by section 109(2) and (3)).	False response to notice (excess charge).	Summarily.	Level 5 on the standard scale.			
RTRA section 112(4)	Failure to give information as to identity of driver.	Summarily.	Level 3 on the standard scale.			
RTRA section 115(1)	Mishandling or faking parking documents.	(a) Summarily. (b) On indictment.	(a) The statutory maximum. (b) 2 years.			
RTRA section 115(2)	False statement for procuring authorisation.	Summarily.	Level 4 on the standard scale.			
RTRA section 116(1)	Non-delivery of suspect document or article.	Summarily.	Level 3 on the standard scale.			
RTRA section 117	Wrongful use of disabled person's badge.	Summarily.	Level 3 on the standard scale.			
RTRA section 117(1A)	Wrongful use of recognised badge.	Summarily.	Level 3 on the standard scale.			
RTRA section 129(3)	Failure to give evidence at inquiry.	Summarily.	Level 3 on the standard scale.			
Offences under the Road Traffic Act 1988						
RTA section 1	Causing death by dangerous driving	On indictment.	14 years.	Obligatory.	Obligatory.	3–11
RTA section 2	Dangerous Driving.	(a) Summarily. (b) On indictment.	(a) 6 months or the statutory maximum or both. (b) 2 years or a fine or both.	Obligatory.	Obligatory.	3–11
RTA section 3	Careless, and inconsiderate, driving.	Summarily.	Level 4 on the standard scale.	Discretionary.	Obligatory.	3–9
RTA section 3A	Causing death by careless driving when under influence of drink or drugs.	On indictment.	14 years or a fine or both.	Obligatory.	Obligatory.	3–11
RTA section 4(1)	Driving or attempting to drive when unfit to drive through drink or drugs.	Summarily.	6 months or level 5 on the standard scale or both.	Obligatory.	Obligatory.	3–11
RTA section 4(2)	Being in charge of a mechanically propelled vehicle when unfit to drive through drink or drugs	Summarily.	3 months or level 4 on the standard scale or both.	Discretionary.	Obligatory.	10

(1) Provision creating offence	(2) General nature of offence	(3) Mode of prosecution	(4) Punishment	(5) Disqualification	(6) Endorsement	(7) Penalty points
Offences under the Road Traffic Act 1988—continued						
RTA section 5(1)(a)	Driving or attempting to drive with excess alcohol in breath, blood or urine.	Summarily.	6 months or level 5 on the standard scale or both.	Obligatory.	Obligatory.	3–11
RTA section 5(1)(b)	Being in charge of a motor vehicle with excess alcohol in breath, blood or urine.	Summarily.	3 months or level 4 on the standard scale or both.	Discretionary.	Obligatory.	10
RTA section 6	Failing to co-operate with a preliminary test.	Summarily.	Level 3 on the standard scale.	Discretionary.	Obligatory.	4
RTA section 7	Failing to provide specimen for analysis or laboratory test.	Summarily.	(a) Where the specimen was required to ascertain ability to drive or proportion of alcohol at the time offender was driving or attempting to drive, 6 months or level 5 on the standard scale or both. (b) In any other case, 3 months or level 4 on the standard scale or both.	(a) Obligatory in case mentioned in column 4(a). (b) Discretionary in any other case.	Obligatory.	(a) 3–11 in case mentioned in column 4(a). (b) 10 in any other case.
RTA section 7A	Failing to allow specimen to be subjected to laboratory test	Summarily.	(a) Where the test would be for ascertaining ability to drive or proportion of alcohol at the time offender was driving or attempting to drive, 6 months or level 5 on the standard scale or both. (b) In any other case, 3 months or level 4 on the standard scale or both.	(a) Obligatory in the case mentioned in column 4(a). (b) Discretionary in any other case.	Obligatory.	(a) 3–11, in case mentioned in column 4(a). (b) 10 in any other case.
RTA section 12	Motor racing and speed trials on public ways.	Summarily.	Level 4 on the standard scale.	Obligatory.	Obligatory.	3–11
RTA section 13	Other unauthorised or irregular competitions or trials on public ways.	Summarily.	Level 3 on the standard scale.			
RTA section 14	Driving or riding in a motor vehicle in contravention of regulations requiring wearing of seat belts.	Summarily.	Level 2 on the standard scale.			
RTA section 15(2)	Driving motor vehicle with child in front not wearing seat belt.	Summarily.	Level 2 on the standard scale.			

Part C Road Traffic Offences

(1) Provision creating offence	(2) General nature of offence	(3) Mode of prosecution	(4) Punishment	(5) Disqualification	(6) Endorsement	(7) Penalty points
Offences under the Road Traffic Act 1988—continued						
RTA section 15(4)	Driving motor vehicle with child in rear not wearing seat belt or with child in a rear-facing child restraint in front seat with an active air bag.	Summarily.	Level 1 on the standard scale.			
RTA section 15A(3) or (4)	Selling etc. in certain circumstances equipment as conducive to the safety of children in motor vehicles.	Summarily.	Level 3 on the standard scale.			
RTA section 15B	Failure to notify bus passengers of the requirement to wear seat belt.	Summarily.	Level 4 on the standard scale.			
RTA section 16	Driving or riding motor cycles in contravention of regulations requiring wearing of protective headgear.	Summarily.	Level 2 on the standard scale.			
RTA section 17	Selling, etc., helmet not of the prescribed type as helmet for affording protection for motor cyclists.	Summarily.	Level 3 on the standard scale.			
RTA section 18(3)	Contravention of regulations with respect to use of headworn appliances on motor cycles	Summarily.	Level 2 on the standard scale.			
RTA section 18(4)	Selling, etc., appliance not of prescribed type as approved for use on motor cycles.	Summarily.	Level 3 on the standard scale.			
RTA section 19	Prohibition of parking of heavy commercial vehicles on verges, etc.	Summarily.	Level 3 on the standard scale.			
RTA section 21	Driving or parking on cycle track.	Summarily.	Level 3 on the standard scale.			
RTA section 22	Leaving vehicles in dangerous positions.	Summarily.	Level 3 on the standard scale.	Discretionary if committed in respect of a motor vehicle.	Obligatory if committed in respect of a motor vehicle.	3
RTA section 22A	Causing danger to road users.	(a) Summarily. (b) On indictment.	(a) 6 months or the statutory maximum or both. (b) 7 years or a fine or both			
RTA section 23	Carrying passenger on motor-cycle contrary to section 23.	Summarily.	Level 3 on the standard scale.	Discretionary.	Obligatory.	3
RTA section 24	Carrying passenger on bicycle contrary to section 24.	Summarily.	Level 1 on the standard scale.			

(1) Provision creating offence	(2) General nature of offence	(3) Mode of prosecution	(4) Punishment	(5) Disqualification	(6) Endorsement	(7) Penalty points
Offences under the Road Traffic Act 1988—continued						
RTA section 25	Tampering with motor vehicles.	Summarily.	Level 3 on the standard scale.			
RTA section 26	Holding or getting on to vehicle, etc., in order to be towed or carried.	Summarily.	Level 1 on the standard scale.			
RTA section 27	Dogs on designated roads without being held on lead.	Summarily.	Level 1 on the standard scale.			
RTA section 28	Dangerous cycling.	Summarily.	Level 4 on the standard scale.			
RTA section 29	Careless, and inconsiderate, cycling.	Summarily.	Level 3 on the standard scale.			
RTA section 30	Cycling when unfit through drink or drugs	Summarily.	Level 3 on the standard scale.			
RTA section 31	Unauthorised or irregular cycle racing or trials of speed on public ways.	Summarily.	Level 1 on the standard scale.			
RTA section 32	Contravening prohibition on persons under 14 driving electronically assisted pedal cycles.	Summarily.	Level 2 on the standard scale.			
RTA section 33	Unauthorised motor vehicle trial on footpaths or bridleways.	Summarily.	Level 3 on the standard scale.			
RTA section 34	Driving mechanically propelled vehicles elsewhere than on roads.	Summarily.	Level 3 on the standard scale.			
RTA section 35	Failing to comply with traffic directions.	Summarily.	Level 3 on the standard scale.	Discretionary, if committed in respect of a motor vehicle by failure to comply with a direction of a constable, traffic officer or traffic warden.	Obligatory if committed as described in column 5.	3
RTA section 36	Failing to comply with traffic signs.	Summarily.	Level 3 on the standard scale.		Discretionary, if committed in respect of a motor vehicle by failure to comply with an indication given by a sign specified for the purposes of this paragraph in regulations under RTA section 36.	Obligatory if committed as described in column 5.
RTA section 37	Pedestrian failing to stop when directed.	Summarily.	Level 3 on the standard scale.			

C

Part C Road Traffic Offences

(1) Provision creating offence	(2) General nature of offence	(3) Mode of prosecution	(4) Punishment	(5) Disqualification	(6) Endorsement	(7) Penalty points
Offences under the Road Traffic Act 1988—continued						
RTA section 40A	Using vehicle in dangerous condition etc.	Summarily.	(a) Level 5 on the standard scale if committed in respect of a goods vehicle or a vehicle adapted to carry more than eight passengers. (b) Level 4 on the standard scale in any other case.	Discretionary.	Obligatory.	3
RTA section 41A	Breach of requirement as to brakes, steering-gear or tyres.	Summarily.	(a) Level 5 on the standard scale if committed in respect of a goods vehicle or a vehicle adapted to carry more than eight passengers. (b) Level 4 on the standard scale in any other case.	Discretionary.	Obligatory.	3
RTA section 41B	Breach of requirement as to weight: goods and passenger vehicles.	Summarily.	Level 5 on the standard scale.			
RTA section 41D	Breach of requirements as to control of vehicle, mobile telephones etc.	Summarily.	(a) Level 4 on the standard scale if committed in respect of a goods vehicle or a vehicle adapted to carry more than eight passengers. (b) Level 3 on the standard scale in any other case.	Discretionary.	Obligatory.	3
RTA section 42	Breach of other construction and use requirements.	Summarily.	(a) Level 4 on the standard scale if committed in respect of a goods vehicle or a vehicle adapted to carry more than eight passengers. (b) Level 3 on the standard scale in any other case.			
RTA section 47	Using, etc., vehicle without required test certificate being in force.	Summarily.	(a) Level 4 on the standard scale in the case of a vehicle adapted to carry more than eight passengers. (b) Level 3 on the standard scale in any other case.			

(1) Provision creating offence	(2) General nature of offence	(3) Mode of prosecution	(4) Punishment	(5) Disqualification	(6) Endorsement	(7) Penalty points
Offences under the Road Traffic Act 1988—continued						
Regulations under RTA section 49 made by virtue of section 51(2)	Contravention of requirement of regulations (which is declared by regulations to be an offence) that driver of goods vehicle being tested be present throughout tests or drive, etc., vehicle as and when directed.	Summarily.	Level 3 on the standard scale.			
RTA section 53(1)	Using, etc., goods vehicle without required plating certificate being in force.	Summarily.	Level 3 on the standard scale.			
RTA section 53(2)	Using, etc., goods vehicle without required goods vehicle test certificate being in force.	Summarily.	Level 4 on the standard scale.			
RTA section 53(3)	Using, etc., goods vehicle where Secretary of State is required by regulations under section 49 to be notified of an alteration to the vehicle or its equipment but has not been notified.	Summarily.	Level 3 on the standard scale.			
Regulations under RTA section 61 made by virtue of subsection (4)	Contravention of requirement of regulations (which is declared by regulations to be an offence) that driver of goods vehicle being tested after notifiable alteration be present throughout test and drive, etc., vehicle as and when directed.	Summarily.	Level 3 on the standard scale.			
RTA section 63(1)	Using, etc., goods vehicle without required certificate being in force showing that it complies with type approval requirements applicable to it.	Summarily.	Level 4 on the standard scale.			
RTA section 63(2)	Using, etc., certain goods vehicles for drawing trailer when plating certificate does not specify maximum laden weight for vehicle and trailer.	Summarily.	Level 3 on the standard scale.			

(1) Provision creating offence	(2) General nature of offence	(3) Mode of prosecution	(4) Punishment	(5) Disqualification	(6) Endorsement	(7) Penalty points
Offences under the Road Traffic Act 1988—continued						
RTA section 63(3)	Using, etc., goods vehicle where Secretary of State is required to be notified under section 59 of alteration to it or its equipment but has not been notified.	Summarily.	Level 3 on the standard scale.			
RTA section 64	Using goods vehicle with unauthorised weights as well as authorised weights marked on it.	Summarily.	Level 3 on the standard scale.			
RTA section 64A	Failure to hold EC certificate of conformity for unregistered light passenger vehicle or motor cycle.	Summarily.	Level 3 on the standard scale.			
RTA section 65	Supplying vehicle or vehicle part without required certificate being in force showing that it complies with type approval requirements applicable to it.	Summarily.	Level 5 on the standard scale.			
RTA section 65A	Light passenger vehicles and motor cycles not to be sold without EC certificate of conformity.	Summarily.	Level 5 on the standard scale.			
RTA section 67	Obstructing testing of vehicle by examiner on road or failing to comply with requirements of RTA section 67 or Schedule 2.	Summarily.	Level 3 on the standard scale.			
RTA section 68	Obstructing inspection, etc., of vehicle by examiner or failing to comply with requirement to take vehicle for inspection.	Summarily.	Level 3 on the standard scale.			
RTA section 71	Driving, etc., vehicle in contravention of prohibition on driving it as being unfit for service, or refusing, neglecting or otherwise failing to comply with direction to remove a vehicle found overloaded.	Summarily.	Level 5 on the standard scale.			

(1) Provision creating offence	(2) General nature of offence	(3) Mode of prosecution	(4) Punishment	(5) Disqualification	(6) Endorsement	(7) Penalty points
Offences under the Road Traffic Act 1988—continued						
RTA section 74	Contravention of regulations requiring goods vehicle operator to inspect, and keep records of inspection of, goods vehicles.	Summarily.	Level 3 on the standard scale.			
RTA section 75	Selling, etc., unroadworthy vehicle or trailer or altering vehicle or trailer so as to make it unroadworthy.	Summarily.	Level 5 on the standard scale.			
RTA section 76(1)	Fitting of defective or unsuitable vehicle parts.	Summarily.	Level 5 on the standard scale.			
RTA section 76(3)	Supplying defective or unsuitable vehicle parts.	Summarily.	Level 4 on the standard scale.			
RTA section 76(8)	Obstructing examiner testing vehicles to ascertain whether defective or unsuitable part has been fitted, etc.	Summarily.	Level 3 on the standard scale.			
RTA section 77	Obstructing examiner testing condition of used vehicle at sale rooms, etc.	Summarily.	Level 3 on the standard scale.			
RTA section 78	Failing to comply with requirement about weighing motor vehicle or obstructing authorised person.	Summarily.	Level 5 on the standard scale.			
RTA section 81	Selling, etc., pedal cycle in contravention of regulations as to brakes, bells, etc.	Summarily.	Level 3 on the standard scale.			
RTA section 83	Selling, etc., wrongly made tail lamps or reflectors.	Summarily.	Level 5 on the standard scale.			
RTA section 87(1)	Driving otherwise than in accordance with a licence.	Summarily.	Level 3 on the standard scale.	Discretionary in a case where the offender's driving would not have been in accordance with any licence that could have been granted to him.	Obligatory in the case mentioned in column 5.	3–6
RTA section 87(2)	Causing or permitting a person to drive otherwise than in accordance with a licence.	Summarily.	Level 3 on the standard scale.			

Part C Road Traffic Offences

(1) Provision creating offence	(2) General nature of offence	(3) Mode of prosecution	(4) Punishment	(5) Disqualification	(6) Endorsement	(7) Penalty points
Offences under the Road Traffic Act 1988—continued						
RTA section 92(7C)	Failure to deliver licence revoked by virtue of section 92(7A) and counterpart to Secretary of State.	Summarily.	Level 3 on the standard scale.			
RTA section 92(10)	Driving after making false declaration as to physical fitness.	Summarily.	Level 4 on the standard scale.	Discretionary.	Obligatory.	3–6
RTA section 93(3)	Failure to deliver revoked licence and counterpart to Secretary of State.	Summarily.	Level 3 on the standard scale.			
RTA section 94(3) and that subsection as applied by RTA section 99D or 109C	Failure to notify Secretary of State of onset of, or deterioration in, relevant or prospective disability.	Summarily.	Level 3 on the standard scale.			
RTA section 94(3A) and that subsection as applied by RTA section 99D(b) or 109C(c)	Driving after such a failure.	Summarily.	Level 3 on the standard scale.	Discretionary.	Obligatory.	3–6
RTA section 94A	Driving after refusal of licence under section 92(3), revocation under section 93 or service of a notice under section 99C or 109B.	Summarily.	6 months or level 5 on the standard scale or both.	Discretionary.	Obligatory.	3–6
RTA section 96	Driving with uncorrected defective eyesight, or refusing to submit to test of eyesight.	Summarily.	Level 3 on the standard scale.	Discretionary.	Obligatory.	3
RTA section 99(5)	Driving licence holder failing to surrender licence and counterpart.	Summarily.	Level 3 on the standard scale.			
RTA section 99B(11) and that subsection as applied by RTA section 109A(5)	Driving after failure to comply with a requirement under section 99B(6), (7) or (10) or a requirement under section 99B(6) or (7) as applied by section 109A(5).	Summarily.	Level 3 on the standard scale.			

(1) Provision creating offence	(2) General nature of offence	(3) Mode of prosecution	(4) Punishment	(5) Disqualification	(6) Endorsement	(7) Penalty points
Offences under the Road Traffic Act 1988—continued						
RTA section 99C(4)	Failure to deliver Community licence to Secretary of State when required by notice under section 99C.	Summarily.	Level 3 on the standard scale.			
RTA section 103(1)(a)	Obtaining driving licence while disqualified.	Summarily.	Level 3 on the standard scale.			
RTA section 103(1)(b)	Driving while disqualified.	(a) Summarily, in England and Wales. (b) Summarily, in Scotland	(a) 6 months or level 5 on the standard scale or both. (b) 6 months or the statutory maximum or both.	Discretionary.	Obligatory.	6
		(c) On indictment, in Scotland	(c) 12 months or a fine or both.	Discretionary.	Obligatory.	6
RTA section 109B(4)	Failing to deliver Northern Ireland licence to Secretary of State when required by notice under section 109B.	Summarily.	Level 3 on the standard scale.			
RTA section 114	Failing to comply with conditions of LGV, PCV licence or LGV Community licence, or causing or permitting person under 21 to drive LGV or PCV in contravention of such conditions.	Summarily.	Level 3 on the standard scale.			
RTA section 115A(4)	Failure to deliver LGV or PCV Community licence when required by notice under section 115A.	Summarily.	Level 3 on the standard scale.			
RTA section 118	Failing to surrender revoked or suspended LGV or PCV licence and counterpart.	Summarily.	Level 3 on the standard scale.			
Regulations made by virtue of RTA section 120(5)	Contravention of provision of regulations (which is declared by regulations to be an offence) about LGV or PCV drivers; licences or LGV or PCV Community licence.	Summarily.	Level 3 on the standard scale.			
RTA section 123(4)	Giving of paid driving instruction by unregistered and unlicensed person or their employers.	Summarily.	Level 4 on the standard scale.			

(1) Provision creating offence	(2) General nature of offence	(3) Mode of prosecution	(4) Punishment	(5) Disqualification	(6) Endorsement	(7) Penalty points
Offences under the Road Traffic Act 1988—continued						
RTA section 123(6)	Giving of paid instruction without there being exhibited on the motor car a certificate of registration or a licence under RTA part V.	Summarily.	Level 3 on the standard scale.			
RTA section 125A(4)	Failure, on application for registration as disabled driving instructor, to notify Registrar of onset of, or deterioration in, relevant or prospective disability.	Summarily.	Level 3 on the standard scale.			
RTA section 133C(4)	Failure by registered or licensed disabled driving instructor to notify Registrar of onset of, or deterioration in, relevant or prospective disability.	Summarily.	Level 3 on the standard scale.			
RTA section 133D	Giving of paid driving instruction by disabled persons or their employers without emergency control certificate or in unauthorised motor car.	Summarily.	Level 3 on the standard scale.			
RTA section 135	Unregistered instructor using title or displaying badge, etc., prescribed for registered instructor, or employer using such title, etc., in relation to his unregistered instructor or issuing misleading advertisement, etc.	Summarily.	Level 4 on the standard scale.			
RTA section 136	Failure of instructor to surrender to Registrar certificate or licence.	Summarily.	Level 3 on the standard scale.			
RTA section 137	Failing to produce certificate of registration or licence as driving instructor.	Summarily.	Level 3 on the standard scale.			
RTA section 143	Using motor vehicle while uninsured or unsecured against third-party risks.	Summarily.	Level 5 on the standard scale	Discretionary.	Obligatory.	6–8
RTA section 147	Failing to surrender certificate of insurance or security to insurer on cancellation or to make statutory declaration of loss or destruction.	Summarily.	Level 3 on the standard scale.			

(1) Provision creating offence	(2) General nature of offence	(3) Mode of prosecution	(4) Punishment	(5) Disqualification	(6) Endorsement	(7) Penalty points
Offences under the Road Traffic Act 1988—continued						
RTA section 154	Failing to give information, or wilfully making a false statement, as to insurance or security when claim made.	Summarily.	Level 4 on the standard scale.			
RTA section 163	Failing to stop motor vehicle or cycle when required.	Summarily.	Level 3 on the standard scale.			
RTA section 164	Failing to produce driving licence and its counterpart or to state date of birth, or failing to provide the Secretary of State with evidence of date of birth, etc.	Summarily.	Level 3 on the standard scale.			
RTA section 165	Failing to give certain names and addresses or to produce certain documents.	Summarily.	Level 3 on the standard scale.			
RTA section 168	Refusing to give, or giving false, name and address in case of reckless, careless or inconsiderate driving or cycling.	Summarily.	Level 3 on the standard scale.			
RTA section 169	Pedestrian failing to give constable his name and address after failing to stop when directed by constable controlling traffic.	Summarily.	Level 1 on the standard scale.			
RTA section 170(4)	Failing to stop after accident and give particulars or report accident.	Summarily.	6 months or level 5 on the standard scale or both.	Discretionary.	Obligatory.	5–10
RTA section 170(7)	Failure by driver, in case of accident involving injury to another, to produce evidence of insurance or security or to report accident.	Summarily.	Level 3 on the standard scale.			
RTA section 171	Failure by owner of motor vehicle to give police information for verifying compliance with requirement of compulsory insurance or security.	Summarily.	Level 4 on the standard scale.			
RTA section 172	Failure of person keeping vehicle and others to give police information as to identity of driver, etc., in the case of certain offences.	Summarily.	Level 3 on the standard scale.	Discretionary if committed otherwise than by virtue of subsection (5) or (11).	Obligatory if committed otherwise than by virtue of subsection (5) or (11).	3

(1) Provision creating offence	(2) General nature of offence	(3) Mode of prosecution	(4) Punishment	(5) Disqualification	(6) Endorsement	(7) Penalty points
Offences under the Road Traffic Act 1988—continued						
RTA section 173	Forgery, etc., of licences, counterparts of Community licences, certificates of insurance and other documents and things.	(a) Summarily. (b) On indictment.	(a) The statutory maximum. (b) 2 years.			
RTA section 174	Making certain false statements, etc., and withholding certain material information.	(a) Summarily. (b) On indictment.	6 months or the statutory maximum or both. 2 years or a fine or both.			
RTA section 175	Issuing false documents.	Summarily.	Level 4 on the standard scale.			
RTA section 177	Impersonation of, or of person employed by, authorised examiner.	Summarily.	Level 3 on the standard scale.			
RTA section 178	[Scotland.]					
RTA section 180	Failing to attend, give evidence or produce documents to, inquiry held by Secretary of State, etc.	Summarily.	Level 3 on the standard scale.			
RTA section 181	Obstructing inspection of vehicles after accident.	Summarily.	Level 3 on the standard scale.			
RTA schedule 1 paragraph 6	Applying warranty to equipment, protective helmet, appliance or information in defending proceedings under RTA section 15A, 17 or 18(4) where no warranty given, or applying false warranty.	Summarily.	Level 3 on the standard scale.			
Section 25 of this Act.	Failing to give information as to date of birth or sex to court or to provide Secretary of State with evidence of date of birth, etc.	Summarily.	Level 3 on the standard scale.			
Section 26 of this Act.	Failing to produce driving licence and counterpart to court making order for interim disqualification.	Summarily.	Level 3 on the standard scale.			

(1) Provision creating offence	(2) General nature of offence	(3) Mode of prosecution	(4) Punishment	(5) Disqualification	(6) Endorsement	(7) Penalty points
Offences under the Road Traffic Act 1988—continued						
Section 27 of this Act.	Failing to produce licence and counterpart to court for endorsement on conviction of offence involving obligatory endorsement or on committal for sentence, etc., for offence involving obligatory or discretionary disqualification when no interim disqualification ordered.	Summarily.	Level 3 on the standard scale.			
Section 62 of this Act.	Removing fixed penalty notice fixed to vehicle.	Summarily.	Level 2 on the standard scale.			
Section 67 of this Act.	False statement in response to notice to owner.	Summarily.	Level 5 on the standard scale.			

Part II
Other Offences

(1) Offence	(2) Disqualification	(3) Endorsement	(4) Penalty points
Manslaughter or, in Scotland, culpable homicide by the driver of a motor vehicle.	Obligatory.	Obligatory.	3–11
An offence under section 12A of the Theft Act 1968 (aggravated vehicle-taking).	Obligatory.	Obligatory.	3–11
Stealing or attempting to steal a motor vehicle.	Discretionary.		
An offence or attempt to commit an offence in respect of a motor vehicle under section 12 of the Theft Act 1968 (taking conveyance without consent of owner etc. or, knowing it has been so taken, driving it or allowing oneself to be carried in it).	Discretionary.		
An offence under section 25 of the Theft Act 1968 (going equipped for stealing, etc.) committed with reference to the theft or taking of motor vehicles.	Discretionary.		

C

Part C Road Traffic Offences

Road Traffic Offenders Act 1988, sch. 3

C9.3

Schedule 3
Fixed Penalty Offences

(1) Provision creating offence	(2) General nature of offence
Offence under the Highways Act 1835	
Sections 72 of the Highways Act 1835	Cycling/driving on the footway.
Offence under the Greater London Council (General Powers) Act 1974	
Section 15 of the Greater London Council (General Powers) Act 1974.	Parking vehicles on footways, verges, etc.
Offence under the Highways Act 1980	
Section 137 of the Highways Act 1980.	Obstructing a highway, but only where the offence is committed in respect of a vehicle.
Offences under the Road Traffic Regulation Act 1984	
RTRA section 5(1)	Using a vehicle in contravention of a traffic regulation order outside Greater London.
RTRA section 8(1)	Breach of traffic regulation order in Greater London.
RTRA section 11	Breach of experimental traffic order.
RTRA section 13	Breach of experimental traffic scheme regulations in Greater London.
RTRA section 16(1)	Using a vehicle in contravention of temporary prohibition or restriction of traffic in case of execution of works, etc.
RTRA section 17(4)	Wrongful use of special road.
RTRA section 18(3)	Using a vehicle in contravention of provision for oneway traffic on trunk road.
RTRA section 20(5)	Driving a vehicle in contravention of order prohibiting or restricting driving vehicles on certain classes of roads.
RTRA section 25(5)	Breach of pedestrian crossing regulations, except an offence in respect of a moving motor vehicle other than a contravention of regulations 23, 24, 25 and 26 of the Zebra, Pelican and Puffin Pedestrian Crossings Regulations and General Directions 1997.
RTRA section 29(3)	Using a vehicle in contravention of a street playground order.
RTRA section 35A(1)	Breach of an order regulating the use, etc., of a parking place provided by a local authority, but only where the offence is committed in relation to a parking place provided on a road.
RTRA section 47(1)	Breach of a provision of a parking place designation order and other offences committed in relation to a parking place designated by such an order, except any offence of failing to pay an excess charge within the meaning of section 46.

(1) Provision creating offence	(2) General nature of offence
Offences under the Road Traffic Regulation Act 1984—continued	
RTRA section 53(5)	Using vehicle in contravention of any provision of a parking place designation order having effect by virtue of section 53(1)(a) (inclusion of certain traffic regulation provisions).
RTRA section 53(6)	Breach of a provision of a parking place designation order having effect by virtue of section 53(1)(b) (use of any part of a road for parking without charge).
RTRA section 88(7)	Driving a motor vehicle in contravention of an order imposing a minimum speed limit under section 88(1)(b).
RTRA section 89(1)	Speeding offences under RTRA and other Acts.
Offences under the Road Traffic Act 1988	
RTA section 14	Breach of regulations requiring wearing of seat belts.
RTA section 15(2)	Breach of restriction on carrying children in the front of vehicles.
RTA section 15(4)	Breach of restriction on carrying children in the rear of vehicles.
RTA section 16	Breach of regulations relating to protective headgear for motor cycle drivers and passengers.
RTA section 18(3)	Breach of regulations relating to head-worn appliances (eye protectors) for use on motor cycles.
RTA section 19	Parking a heavy commercial vehicle on verge or footway.
RTA section 22	Leaving vehicle in dangerous position.
RTA section 23	Unlawful carrying of passengers on motor cycles.
RTA section 24	Carrying more than one person on a pedal cycle.
RTA section 34	Driving mechanically propelled vehicle elsewhere than on a road.
RTA section 35	Failure to comply with traffic directions.
RTA section 36	Failure to comply with traffic signs.
RTA section 40A	Using vehicle in dangerous condition, etc.
RTA section 41A	Breach of requirement as to brakes, steering-gear or tyres.
RTA section 41B	Breach of requirement as to weight: goods and passenger vehicles.
RTA section 41D	Breach of requirements as to control of vehicle, mobile telephone etc.
RTA section 42	Breach of other construction and use requirements.
RTA section 47	Using, etc., vehicle without required test certificate being in force.
RTA section 87(1)	Driving vehicle otherwise than in accordance with requisite licence.
RTA section 143	Using motor vehicle while uninsured or unsecured against third party risks.
RTA section 163	Failure to stop vehicle on being so required.

(1) Provision creating offence	(2) General nature of offence
Offences under the Road Traffic Regulation Act 1988—continued	
RTA section 172	Failure of person keeping vehicle and others to give the police information as to identity of driver, etc., in the case of certain offences.
Offences under the Vehicle Excise and Registration Act 1994	
Section 33 of the Vehicle Excise and Registration Act 1994.	Using or keeping a vehicle on a public road without vehicle licence, trade licence or nil licence being exhibited in manner prescribed by regulations.
Section 42 of that Act.	Driving or keeping a vehicle without required registration mark.
Section 43 of that Act.	Driving or keeping a vehicle with registration mark obscured, etc.
Section 43C of that Act.	Using an incorrectly registered vehicle.
Section 59 of that Act.	Failure to fix prescribed registration mark to a vehicle in accordance with regulations made under section 23(4)(a) of that Act.

Section D1 Powers of Investigation

POLICE POWERS IN THE INVESTIGATION OF CRIME

Police powers of investigation, including arrest, detention, interrogation, entry and search of premises, personal search and the taking of samples are largely governed by the PACE 1984 and/or the associated PACE Codes of Practice. Most of these powers are dealt with in this section, but see **F2** for the admission (and exclusion) of evidence obtained in breach of the PACE 1984 or the PACE Codes, **F17** for the admission of confession evidence and **F18** for visual and other forms of identification including fingerprints, photographs and samples. **D1.1**

The PACE Codes of Practice are issued by the Secretary of State under the authority of the PACE 1984, ss. 66 and 67. There are eight Codes of Practice, A to H, set out in **appendix** 2. Codes A, B and D to G came into force in their current form on 1 January 2006 (see the Police and Criminal Evidence Act 1984 (Codes of Practice) Order 2005 (SI 2005 No. 3503)), and Code C and H on 25 July 2006 (see the Police and Criminal Evidence Act 1984 (Code of Practice C and Code of Practice H) Order 2006 (SI 2006 No. 1938)). Paragraph 4 of Code A was further revised with effect from 31 August 2006 (see the Police and Criminal Evidence Act 1984 (Codes of Practice) (Revisions to Code A) Order 2006 (SI 2006 No. 2165)). A failure by a police officer or other person required to have regard to provisions of the codes does not, of itself, render him liable to criminal or civil proceedings (PACE 1984, s. 67(10)). However, to the extent that they are relevant, the codes are admissible in evidence in criminal or civil proceedings (PACE 1984, s. 67(11)). See further **F17.5** (in relation to exclusion of confession evidence under the PACE 1984, s. 76) and **F2.30** (in relation to the exclusion of any prosecution evidence under the PACE 1984, s. 78).

The PACE 1984 is principally concerned with regulating police investigation, but it is applied (with modifications) to Customs and Excise officers by the PACE 1984, s. 114(2), and the Police and Criminal Evidence Act 1984 (Application to Customs and Excise) Order 1985 (SI 1985 No. 1800), and to investigations conducted under the Army Act 1955, the Air Force Act 1955 and the Naval Discipline Act 1957 and to persons under arrest under any of those Acts by the PACE 1984, s. 113(1), and the Police and Criminal Evidence Act 1984 (Applications to the Armed Forces) Order 2006 (SI 2006 No. 2015). Note that, when in force, the Armed Forces Act 2006 will replace the disciplinary provisions of the Army Act 1955, the Air Force Act 1955, and the Naval Discipline Act 1957. The Director General of the Serious Organised Crime Agency may designate a member of the Agency staff as having the powers of a police constable, and staff so designated have all the common-law and statutory powers of a constable and the PACE 1984 applies to them and the exercise of their powers, subject to modifications (SOCPA 2005, s. 46(2) and (9), and the Serious Organised Crime and Police Act 2005 (Application and Modification of Certain Enactments to Designated Staff of SOCA) Order 2006 (SI 2006 No. 987)).

Where a person is detained for examination under the TA 2000, s. 53 and sch. 7, their treatment is governed by the TA 2000, sch. 8, part 1. They are not treated as being in police detention for the purpose of the PACE 1984, and the PACE Codes do not apply to them. The detention of persons arrested under the TA 2000, s. 41 (on suspicion of being a terrorist), and associated police powers, is governed by sch. 8 to that Act rather than by the PACE 1984. They are not treated as being arrested for an offence, but whilst they are detained at a police station they are deemed to be in police detention for the purposes of the PACE 1984 (PACE 1984, s. 118(2)). PACE Code H applies to their detention up and until they are charged, released without charge, or transferred to prison (Code H, para. 1.2). If they are charged, Code C will then apply. PACE Code D does apply to persons arrested under the TA 2000, s. 41, except for those provisions relating to photographs, fingerprints, skin impressions, body samples and impressions of people. PACE Code E does not apply, but there is a separate code of practice governing the audio-recording of interviews, issued under the TA 2000, sch. 8, para 3(1). See generally **B10.00** *et seq.*

Persons other than police officers who are charged with the duty of investigating offences or charging offenders are required in the discharge of that duty to have regard to any relevant provision of the codes (PACE 1984, s. 67(9)). A similar duty is placed on persons designated or accredited under the Police Reform Act 2002, ss. 38 or 39 (PACE 1984, s. 67(9A)). Whether a person is charged with such a duty is a question of fact in each case. It has been held to include officers of the Serious Fraud Office (*Director of the Serious Fraud Office, ex parte Saunders* [1988] Crim LR 837 and *Gill* [2004] 1 WLR 469); trading standards officers (*Dudley MBC v Debenhams* (1994) 159 JP 18 and *Tiplady* (1995) 159 JP 548); commercial investigators when interviewing an employee (*Twaites and Brown* (1990) 92 Cr App R 106); store detectives (*Bayliss* (1993) 98 Cr App R 235); and investigators employed by the Federation Against Copyright Theft (*Joy v Federation Against Copyright Theft Ltd.* [1993] Crim LR 588 and *Halawa v Federation Against Copyright Theft* [1995] 1 Cr App R 21). However, it was decided in *Seelig and Spens* [1992] 1 WLR 148, that Department of Trade and Industry inspectors appointed under the Companies Act 1985, ss. 432 and 442, were not persons charged with such a duty, and a similar conclusion was drawn in respect of prison officers in *Martin Taylor* [2000] EWCA Crim 2922.

Although the Police and Criminal Evidence Act 1984 (Application to Customs and Excise) Order 1985 (SI 1985 No. 1800) does not apply ss. 67 and 68 to Customs and Excise officers, it has been held that, by virtue of the PACE 1984, s. 67(9), they must have regard to relevant provisions of the codes when investigating an offence (*Sanusi* [1992] Crim LR 43 and *Okafor* [1994] 3 All ER 741). However, this is not the case where they are interviewing a person under the Value Added Tax Act 1994, s. 60 (*Khan v Revenue and Customs* [2006] EWCA Civ 89), nor under the civil investigation of tax fraud procedure (see HM Revenue and Customs Code of Practice 9 (2005) available at www.hmrc.gov.uk/leaflets/cop9–2005.htm). The PACE codes do not apply where a person is investigated under the Army Act 1955, the Air Force Act 1955 and the Naval Discipline Act 1957 (or the Armed Forces Act 2006, when in force), but dedicated codes have been issued under the PACE 1984, s. 113(2) (Police and Criminal Evidence Act 1984 (Codes of Practice) (Armed Forces) Order 2003 (SI 2003 No. 2315)). For the detention and treatment of a person arrested on a European Arrest Warrant, see **D1.23**.

REASONABLE SUSPICION

D1.2 A number of police powers are premised upon the constable having reasonable grounds for suspicion. For example, stop and search under the PACE 1984, part I, requires a constable to have 'reasonable grounds for suspecting that he will find stolen or prohibited articles' etc. and most, but not all, powers of arrest under s. 24, depend on the officer having reasonable grounds for suspicion. This reflects the ECHR, Article 5(1)(c), which permits a person to be deprived of his liberty 'on reasonable suspicion of having committed an offence or when it is reasonably considered necessary to prevent his committing an offence or fleeing after having done so'. It should be contrasted with the expression 'reasonable grounds for believing', found in the PACE 1984, s. 24(4) (the necessity for arrest), s. 37(2) (detention without charge) and s. 38(1) (bail following charge), which implies a more stringent test. Reasonable suspicion relates to the existence of facts and not to the state of the law. An officer who reasonably but mistakenly proceeds on a particular view of the law, and thus exercises his power of arrest, does not have reasonable suspicion (*Todd v DPP* [1996] Crim LR 344).

Reasonable suspicion is not defined in the PACE 1984. It is explained in relation to stop and search powers in PACE Code A, para. 2.2 of which states that 'there must be an objective basis for that suspicion based on facts, information, and/or intelligence'. It goes on to state that it 'can never be supported on the basis of personal factors alone . . . For example, a person's race, age, appearance, or the fact that the person is known to have a previous conviction, cannot be used alone or in combination with each other as the reason for searching that person'. There is no attempt in Code G to give guidance on reasonable suspicion in relation to arrest.

In relation to arrest it has been held that reasonable suspicion requires both that the constable carrying out the arrest actually suspects (a subjective test) and that a reasonable person in possession of the same facts as the constable would also suspect (an objective test). In addition the arrest must be *Wednesbury* reasonable (*Castorina v Chief Constable of Surrey* (1988) 138 NLJ 180). Whether the constable had reasonable suspicion must be determined according to what he knew and perceived at the time; reasonableness is to be evaluated without reference to hindsight (*Redmond-Bate v DPP* (1999) 163 JP 789). Information required to form a reasonable suspicion is of a lower standard than that required to establish a prima facie case. Prima facie proof must be based on admissible evidence whereas reasonable suspicion may take into account matters which are not admissible in evidence or matters which, while admissible, could not form part of a prima facie case (*Hussien v Chong Fook Kam* [1970] AC 942). Whilst it is not necessary for the constable to have identified the specific offence of which he is suspicious (*Coudrat v Commissioners of Her Majesty's Revenue and Customs* [2005] EWCA Civ 616), he must reasonably suspect the existence of facts amounting to an offence of a kind that he has in mind (*Chapman v DPP* (1988) 89 Cr App R 190).

In forming a reasonable suspicion a constable may rely on hearsay, provided that it is reasonable and that the constable believes it (*Clarke v Chief Constable of North Wales Police* [2000] All ER (D) 477). Thus a constable may arrest a person as a result of radio information, or even an anonymous telephone call, provided that the person arrested corresponds to the description in the message (*King v Gardner* (1979) 71 Cr App R 13; *DPP v Wilson* [1991] RTR 284); he may act on the word of an informant, although such a source should be treated with considerable reserve (*James v Chief Constable of South Wales* [1991] 6 CL 80). The constable may rely on an entry in the police national computer, unless in the light of all the circumstances some further enquiry is called for before suspicion can properly crystallise (*Hough v Chief Constable of Staffordshire Police* [2001] EWCA Civ 39). However, the mere fact that an arresting officer has been instructed by his superior to effect an arrest is not sufficient (*O'Hara v Chief Constable of the Royal Ulster Constabulary* [1997] AC 286; *Olden* [2007] EWCA Crim 726).

Evidence of particular opportunity may give rise to reasonable suspicion. Where police, having taken all reasonable steps to discover the perpetrator of an offence, are left with the fact that one of a number of persons must have been the culprit, this may be sufficient to arrest those persons (*Cummings v Chief Constable of Northumbria Police* [2003] EWCA Civ 1844). The police may be justified in making such arrests even though there is a possibility that another or other persons may have committed the offence. The matter is one of degree (*Al Fayed v Metropolitan Police Commissioner* [2004] EWCA Civ 1579). A constable who has formed reasonable grounds to suspect that an offence has been committed is not obliged to discount all possible defences or seek complete proof before carrying out an arrest (*Ward v Chief Constable of Avon and Somerset Constabulary* (1986) *The Times*, 26 June 1986; *McCarrick v Oxford* [1983] RTR 117).

Use of the power to arrest in order to interview and/or seek further evidence from the suspect, or to arrest as a means of exercising control over a suspect with a view to securing a confession or other information where it is necessary to bring matters to a head speedily, to preserve evidence or to prevent the further commission of crime, is permissible (*Al Fayed v Metropolitan Police Commissioner*). Furthermore, an arrest carried out for an ulterior purpose, e.g., to install a listening device in the arrested person's house for the purpose of investigating another offence, is lawful provided that there are reasonable grounds for suspicion in relation to the offence for which the person was arrested (*Chalkley* [1998] QB 848). However, the police must not mislead the suspect as to the true nature of the investigation, for example, by failing to tell a suspect arrested for burglary that the victim has died (*Kirk* [2000] 1 WLR 567, and see **D1.10**).

THE USE OF FORCE

D1.3 The PACE 1984, s. 117, provides that where any provision of the Act confers a power on a constable and does not provide that the power may be exercised only with the consent of a person other than a police officer, the officer may use reasonable force, if necessary, in the exercise of the power. This would include force used in connection with a stop and search under the PACE 1984, part I, entry and search of premises under s. 17, arrest under s. 24, detention of a person at a police station under the PACE 1984, part IV, search of a person under s. 54, intimate search of a detained person under s. 55, fingerprinting without consent under s. 61 and the taking of a non-intimate sample without consent under s. 63. It would not include the use of force in connection with the conduct of a visual identification procedure governed by PACE Code D, or the taking of an intimate sample under s. 62, since these require consent. A civilian designated under the Police Reform Act 2002, s. 38, may, in exercising powers in respect of which he has been designated, use reasonable force in the same circumstances as a constable (Police Reform Act 2002, s. 38(8)). In addition, the Criminal Law Act 1967, s. 3, empowers any person to use such force as is reasonable in the circumstances in the prevention of crime, or in effecting or assisting in the lawful arrest of an offender or suspected offender or of persons unlawfully at large.

In determining what force is reasonable, the court may take into account all the circumstances including the nature and degree of the force used, the gravity of the offence for which arrest is to be made, the harm that would flow from the use of force against the suspect, and the possibility of effecting the arrest or preventing the harm by other means. The use of excessive force will not, however, render the arrest unlawful (*Simpson v Chief Constable of South Yorkshire Police* (1991) *The Times*, 7 March 1991).

Handcuffs should be used only where they are reasonably necessary to prevent an escape or to prevent a violent breach of the peace by a prisoner (*Lockley* (1864) 4 F & F 155). The same rule applies to the handcuffing of prisoners in court (*Cambridge Justices, ex parte Peacock* (1992) 156 JP 895). It would seem that, where handcuffs are unjustifiably resorted to, their use will constitute a trespass even though the arrest itself is lawful (*Taylor* (1895) 59 JP 393; *Bibby v Chief Constable of Essex* (2000) 164 JP 297). Guidance on the use of handcuffs was issued by the Association of Chief Police Officers in September 2006 and is available at www.acpo.police.uk/asp/policies/Data/guide_use_handcuffs_website_updatedsep06_11x10x06.doc.

POWERS TO STOP AND SEARCH

Police powers to stop and search people and vehicles are conferred by the PACE 1984, and a range of other legislation. See PACE Code A, annex A (see **appendix** 2) for a summary of the main stop and search powers. The PACE 1984, ss. 2 and 3, impose a number of obligations on officers conducting a stop and search irrespective of the legislative authority for it. Code A applies to all powers of stop and search other than those conducted under the Aviation Security Act 1982, s. 27(2), and the PACE 1984, s. 6(1) (see the unnumbered introductory paragraphs to Code A). Community support officers designated under the Police Reform Act 2002, part 4, do not have powers of stop and search under the PACE 1984, but do have such powers under some other legislation (see Code A, annex C for a summary of such powers). **D1.4**

Stop and Search Powers Requiring Reasonable Suspicion

The main stop and search power requiring reasonable suspicion is that under the PACE 1984, part I, although it is also required for stop and search under the TA 2000, s. 43 (but not s. 44). For reasonable suspicion see **D1.2** and PACE Code A, paras. 2.2 to 2.11 (see **appendix** 2). **D1.5**

Police and Criminal Evidence Act 1984, s. 1

(1) A constable may exercise any power conferred by this section—
 (a) in any place to which at the time when he proposes to exercise the power the public or any section of the public has access, on payment or otherwise, as of right or by virtue of express or implied permission; or
 (b) in any other place to which people have ready access at the time when he proposes to exercise the power but which is not a dwelling.

(2) Subject to subsection (3) to (5) below, a constable—
 (a) may search—
  (i) any person or vehicle;
  (ii) anything which is in or on a vehicle,
 for stolen or prohibited articles, any article to which subsection (8A) below applies or any firework to which subsection (8B) below applies; and
 (b) may detain a person or vehicle for the purpose of such a search.

(3) This section does not give a constable power to search a person or vehicle or anything in or on a vehicle unless he has reasonable grounds for suspecting that he will find stolen or prohibited articles or, any article to which subsection (8A) below applies or any firework to which subsection (8B) below applies.

(4) If a person is in a garden or yard occupied with and used for the purposes of a dwelling or on other land so occupied and used, a constable may not search him in the exercise of the power conferred by this section unless the constable has reasonable grounds for believing—
 (a) that he does not reside in the dwelling; and
 (b) that he is not in the place in question with the express or implied permission of a person who resides in the dwelling.

(5) If a vehicle is in a garden or yard occupied with and used for the purposes of a dwelling or on other land so occupied and used, a constable may not search the vehicle or anything in or on it in the exercise of the power conferred by this section unless he has reasonable grounds for believing—
 (a) that the person in charge of the vehicle does not reside in the dwelling; and
 (b) that the vehicle is not in the place in question with the express or implied permission of a person who resides in the dwelling.

(6) If in the course of such a search a constable discovers an article which he has reasonable grounds for suspecting to be a stolen or prohibited article, an article to which subsection (8A) below applies or a firework to which subsection (8B) below applies, he may seize it.

(7) An article is prohibited for the purposes of this part of this Act if it is—
 (a) an offensive weapon; or
 (b) an article—

(i) made or adapted for use in the course of or in connection with an offence to which this sub-paragraph applies; or
(ii) intended by the person having it with him for such use by him or by some other person.

(8) The offences to which subsection (7)(b)(i) above applies are—
(a) burglary;
(b) theft;
(c) offences under section 12 of the Theft Act 1968 (taking motor vehicle or other conveyance without authority);
(d) fraud (contrary to section 1 of the Fraud Act 2006); and
(e) offences under section 1 of the Criminal Damage Act 1971 (destroying or damaging property).

(8A) This subsection applies to any article in relation to which a person has committed, or is committing or is going to commit an offence under section 139 of the Criminal Justice Act 1988.

(8B) This subsection applies to any firework which a person possesses in contravention of a prohibition imposed by fireworks regulations.

(8C) In this section—
(a) 'firework' shall be construed in accordance with the definition of 'fireworks' in section 1(1) of the Fireworks Act 2003; and
(b) 'fireworks regulations' has the same meaning as in that Act.

(9) In this part of this Act 'offensive weapon' means any article—
(a) made or adapted for use for causing injury to persons; or
(b) intended by the person having it with him for such use by him or by some other person.

The power is available only in public places, but this is given a particular meaning by s. 1(1)(a) and (b), (4) and (5).

Stop and Search Powers Not Requiring Reasonable Suspicion

D1.6 Stop and search powers that do not require reasonable suspicion include those under the CJPO 1994, ss. 60 and 60AA, the TA 2000, s. 44, and the CJA 1988, s. 139B. Section 60 of the CJPO 1994 gives the police the power to stop and search in anticipation of violence, but only where an officer of the required rank has given the appropriate authorisation under s. 60(1). Unlike under the PACE power of stop and search, failure of a person to stop when required to under s. 60 is an offence (s. 60(8)).

Criminal Justice and Public Order Act 1994, s. 60

(1) If a police officer of or above the rank of inspector reasonably believes—
(a) that incidents involving serious violence may take place in any locality in his police area, and that it is expedient to give an authorisation under this section to prevent their occurrence, or
(b) that persons are carrying dangerous instruments or offensive weapons in any locality in his police area without good reason,

he may give an authorisation that the powers conferred by this section are to be exercisable at any place within that locality for a specified period not exceeding 24 hours.

. . .

(3) If it appears to an officer of or above the rank of superintendent that it is expedient to do so, having regard to offences which have, or are reasonably suspected to have, been committed in connection with any activity falling within the authorisation, he may direct that the authorisation shall continue in being for a further 24 hours.

(3A) If an inspector gives an authorisation under subsection (1) he must, as soon as it is practicable to do so, cause an officer of or above the rank of superintendent to be informed.

(4) This section confers on any constable in uniform power—
(a) to stop any pedestrian and search him or anything carried by him for offensive weapons or dangerous instruments;
(b) to stop any vehicle and search the vehicle, its driver and any passenger for offensive weapons or dangerous instruments.

(4A) This section also confers on any constable in uniform power—

(a) to require any person to remove any item which the constable reasonably believes that person is wearing wholly or mainly for the purpose of concealing his identity;
(b) to seize any item which the constable reasonably believes any person intends to wear wholly or mainly for that purpose.

(5) A constable may, in the exercise of the powers conferred by subsection (4) above, stop any person or vehicle and make any search he thinks fit whether or not he has any grounds for suspecting that the person or vehicle is carrying weapons or articles of that kind.

(6) If in the course of a search under this section a constable discovers a dangerous instrument or an article which he has reasonable grounds for suspecting to be an offensive weapon, he may seize it.

(7) This section applies (with the necessary modifications) to ships, aircraft and hovercraft as it applies to vehicles.

(8) A person who fails—
(a) to stop, or to stop a vehicle; or
(b) to remove an item worn by him,
when required to do so by a constable in the exercise of his powers under this section shall be liable on summary conviction to imprisonment for a term not exceeding one month or to a fine not exceeding level 3 on the standard scale or both.

(9) Any authorisation under this section shall be in writing signed by the officer giving it and shall specify the grounds on which it is given and the locality in which and the period during which the powers conferred by this section are exercisable and a direction under subsection (3) above shall also be given in writing or, where that is not practicable, recorded in writing as soon as it is practicable to do so.

(9A) The preceding provisions of this section, so far as they relate to an authorisation by a member of the British Transport Police Force (including one who for the time being has the same powers and privileges as a member of a police force for a police area), shall have effect as if the references to a locality in his police area were references to a place specified in section 31(1)(a) to (f) of the Railways and Transport Safety Act 2003.

(10) Where a vehicle is stopped by a constable under this section, the driver shall be entitled to obtain a written statement that the vehicle was stopped under the powers conferred by this section if he applies for such a statement not later than the end of the period of twelve months from the day on which the vehicle was stopped as respects a pedestrian who is stopped and searched under this section.

(10A) A person who is searched by a constable under this section shall be entitled to obtain a written statement that he was searched under the powers conferred by this section if he applies for such a statement not later than the end of the period of twelve months from the day on which he was searched.

(11) In this section—
'dangerous instruments' means instruments which have a blade or are sharply pointed;
'offensive weapon' has the meaning given by section 1(9) of the Police and Criminal Evidence Act 1984 or, in relation to Scotland, section 47(4) of the Criminal Law (Consolidation) (Scotland) Act 1995; and
'vehicle' includes a caravan as defined in section 29(1) of the Caravan Sites and Control of Development Act 1960.

(11A) For the purposes of this section, a person carries a dangerous instrument or an offensive weapon if he has it in his possession.

(12) The powers conferred by this section are in addition to and not in derogation of, any power otherwise conferred.

Under s. 60AA, there is power to require the removal of any item which a constable reasonably believes a person is wearing wholly or mainly for the purpose of concealing his identity, and power to seize an item which a person intends to wear for such a purpose. The power is exercisable where an authorisation under s. 60 is in place, but a separate authorisation may be given under s. 60AA(3) and (4).

Conduct of Stop and Search Powers

The consent of the person concerned is not a sufficient authority for a search. PACE Code A, para. 1.5, provides that a search must not be conducted in the absence of a relevant power. **D1.7**

The various statutory powers contain different provisions regarding the conduct of a stop and search. Most enable both persons and vehicles to be searched, although some are confined to one or the other. Some are exercisable anywhere whereas others can only be carried out in a public place or in specific premises or areas such as schools or ports. Some require the officer to be in uniform, but others do not. For a summary, see Code A, annex A (**appendix 2**).

Code A sets out minimum requirements that must be observed whatever the statutory authority. Reasonable force may be used (PACE 1984, s. 117; Code A, para. 3.2, and see **D1.3**). A person may be detained for the purpose of carrying out a search although the period for which they are detained must be reasonable and be kept to a minimum (PACE 1984, s. 1(2)(b); Code A, para 3.3). It was held in *R (Gillan) v Metropolitan Police Commissioner* [2006] 2 AC 307, that, provided it is properly conducted, a short period of detention (in that case 20 minutes) for the purposes of stop and search does not engage the ECHR, Article. 5. The search must be conducted at or near the place where the person or vehicle was stopped (Code A, para. 3.4), although a place is 'near' if it is within a reasonable travelling distance (Code A, Note for Guidance 6). If a search requires the removal of more than outer clothing this cannot normally be done in public (PACE 1984, s. 2(9)(a); Code A, para. 3.5). Before a search of a person or an attended vehicle is conducted the officer must take reasonable steps to give the person the information set out in the PACE 1984, s. 2, and Code A, paras. 3.8 to 3.11. Recording requirements are set out in the PACE 1984, s. 3, and Code A, sect. 4. There is a similar recording requirement where an officer requests a person in a public place to account for himself, but without a search being conducted (Code A, paras. 4.12 to 4.20).

POWERS OF ARREST: GENERAL PROVISIONS

Powers of Arrest

D1.8 Police powers of arrest without a warrant in relation to criminal offences are principally governed by the PACE 1984, s. 24. Most other statutory powers of arrest were repealed by the SOCPA 2005, s. 111 and sch. 7, although a number of pre-PACE statutory powers are preserved by the PACE 1984, sch. 2, and there are extensive cross-border powers of arrest under the CJPOA 1994 (see **D1.19**). Civilian powers of arrest are governed by the PACE 1984, s. 24A. The other remaining power of arrest without a warrant is the common-law power of arrest for breach of the peace (see **D1.20**). Arrest under a warrant is governed by a number of statutory provisions (see **D1.21**).

Legal Characteristics of Arrest

D1.9 'Arrest' is not defined by the PACE 1984, or other legislation. A person is arrested if, as a result of what is said or done, he is under compulsion and is not free to go as he pleases (*Alderson v Booth* [1969] 2 QB 216; *Inwood* (1973) 57 Cr App R 529). Arrest, it has been said, is an ordinary English word, and whether or not a person has been arrested depends not on the legality of the arrest but on whether he has been deprived of his liberty to go where he pleases (*Lewis v Chief Constable of the South Wales Constabulary* [1991] 1 All ER 206). There is no necessary assumption that an arrest will be followed by a charge (*Holgate-Mohammed v Duke* [1984] AC 437). Although the power to arrest must be exercised for a proper purpose, it was affirmed in *Chalkley* [1998] QB 848 that the fact that an arrest is motivated by a desire to investigate another, more serious, offence does not render it invalid provided there are valid grounds for the arrest. An arrest for an offence will, however, be unlawful, even though made on the basis of reasonable suspicion, where the officer knows at the time of arrest that there is no possibility of a charge being made. Conversely, it is clear that, even though a complainant withdraws his complaint, a constable may still arrest a suspect where he hopes by so doing to obtain a confession (*Plange v Chief Constable of South Humberside Police* (1992) *The Times*, 23 March 1992).

Arrest must be justified by some rule of positive law. In *Rice v Connolly* [1966] 2 QB 414, it was held that a constable may not restrain a person from going about his business unless he acts under powers of stop and search or arrest. On the other hand, taking hold of a person's arm for the purpose of simply drawing his attention to what is being said to him, without an intention to detain or arrest, is neither an arrest nor an actionable trespass to the person unless it goes beyond what is acceptable by the ordinary standards of everyday life (*Mepstead v DPP* (1996) 160 JP 475). Detention of a number of people with a conditional intention to arrest those whom it is lawful and practicable to arrest may be lawful (*Austin and Saxby v Metropolitan Police Commissioner* [2005] EWHC 480).

Reasonable force may be used to effect an arrest (PACE 1984, s. 117; Criminal Law Act 1967, s. 3; and see **D1.3**).

Communication of Fact of and Grounds for Arrest

Where a person is arrested (whether or not for an offence), otherwise than by being informed that he is under arrest, the arrest is unlawful unless he is informed that he is under arrest as soon as is practicable after the arrest (PACE 1984, s. 28(1)). If the arrest is by a constable, this applies even if the fact of arrest is obvious (s. 28(2)).The test for whether the words used were sufficient is whether, having regard to all the circumstances of the case, the person arrested was told, in simple, non-technical language that he could understand, the essential legal and factual grounds for his arrest (*Taylor v Chief Constable of Thames Valley Police* [2004] 1 WLR 3155). According to PACE Code C, Note for Guidance 10B, and Code G, Note for Guidance 3, where a person is arrested for an offence he must be informed of the nature of the suspected offence, and when and where it was allegedly committed. **D1.10**

Further, an arrest is unlawful unless the arrested person is informed of the ground for the arrest at the time of the arrest, or as soon as is practicable after the arrest (s. 28(3)). If the arrest is by a constable, this applies even if the grounds for arrest are obvious (s. 28(4)). The person must also be informed why arrest was believed to be necessary (for the purposes of s. 24(4)), although failure to do so will not render the arrest unlawful (Code G, para. 2.2).

The information need not be given by the arresting officer but may be given by a colleague (*Nicholas v Parsonage* [1987] RTR 199; *Dhesi v Chief Constable of West Midlands Police* (2000) *The Times*, 9 May 2000). Where no reasons are given at the time of arrest because it is impracticable to inform the suspect, acts done at the time of arrest do not become retrospectively invalid because of a later failure to inform him (*DPP v Hawkins* [1988] 1 WLR 1166; *Lewis v Chief Constable of the South Wales Constabulary* [1991] 1 All ER 206). The words used will suffice even though they are apt to describe more than one offence, provided that they aptly describe the offence for which the arrest is made (*Abbassy v Metropolitan Police Commissioner* [1990] 1 WLR 385; *Clarke v Chief Constable of North Wales Police* [2000] All ER (D) 477). An arresting officer may not, however, properly give reasons on which he does not rely; that is, he may not lead a person to think that he is arresting him for one offence when in truth he wishes to arrest him for another (*Christie v Leachinsky* [1947] AC 573; *Abbassy v Metropolitan Police Commissioner*; *Waters v Bigmore* [1981] RTR 356).

In addition to the above information, a person who is arrested, or who is further arrested (e.g., under the PACE 1984, s. 31), must be cautioned at the time of arrest or as soon as is practicable afterwards unless it is impracticable to do so because of his condition or behaviour at the time or he has already been cautioned immediately before arrest (e.g., where he was initially questioned regarding a suspected offence without being arrested) (Code C, para. 10.4, and Code G, para. 3.4). The terms of the caution are set out in Code C, para. 10.4. The alternative caution set out in Code C, annex C, para. 2, does not apply unless the person is already in police detention at the time of arrest. Failure to administer a caution does not render the arrest unlawful, although it may provide grounds for exclusion of evidence under the PACE 1984, ss. 76 or 78.

The nature and circumstances of the offence leading to the arrest, the reason(s) why the arrest was necessary, the giving of the caution, and anything said by the arrested person at the time of his arrest must be recorded by the arresting officer in his pocket book (or other method used for recording information) (Code G, para. 4.1). This record must be made at the time of the arrest unless impracticable, in which case it must be completed as soon as possible thereafter (Code G, para 4.2). If the arrested person is subsequently detained at a police station, the information given by the arresting officer as to the circumstances and reason(s) for the arrest must be recorded in, or attached to, the custody record (Code G, para. 4.3).

Resisting Arrest

D1.11 A person has an unqualified right at common law to resist an unlawful arrest (*Christie v Leachinsky* [1947] AC 573), but he must not use excessive force in doing so (*Wilson* [1955] 1 WLR 493; *Long* (1836) 7 C & P 314). Whilst excessive force in resisting arrest may amount to an offence, the person using excessive force would not be guilty of assaulting a constable in the execution of his duty (*Kenlin v Gardiner* [1967] 2 QB 510).

It would seem that avoiding arrest, or even questioning short of arrest, by running away when approached by police can amount to wilful obstruction of the police in the execution of their duty, contrary to the Police Act 1996, s. 89(2) (*Sekfali v DPP* (2006) 170 JP 393). However, there is some difficulty in reconciling this with the established principle that a person does not commit wilful obstruction or any other offence (except where statute provides otherwise) if he refuses to give police his name and address or to answer police questions (*Rice v Connolly* [1966] 2 QB 414).

Action following Arrest

D1.12 Where a person is arrested at any place other than a police station, or is taken into custody by a constable following an arrest made by a civilian, the constable is normally obliged to take him to a designated police station as soon as is practicable thereafter (PACE 1984, s. 30(1), (1A), (1B) and (2)). In exceptional circumstances the person may be taken to a non-designated station (s. 30(3) to (6)). The constable may delay taking the arrested person to a police station or releasing him on bail under s. 30A if his presence at a place other than a police station is necessary in order to carry out such investigations as it is reasonable to carry out immediately (s. 30(10) and (10A)), but the reasons must be recorded (s. 30(11)). This might include taking the suspect from one place to another to check his alibi (*Dallison v Caffery* [1965] 1 QB 348), search of the arrested person under s. 32(2)(a) (see **D1.65**), or entry and search of premises under s. 32(2)(b) or s. 18(1) and (5) (see **D1.93**). Consistently with the position at common law, a constable who is satisfied that there are no grounds for keeping the arrested person under arrest or releasing them on bail under s. 30A may release him (s. 30(7) and (7A)), but the facts must be recorded (s. 30(8) and (9)).

Notwithstanding the above, an arrested person may, instead of being taken to a police station, be released on bail, to attend at a police station on a future date (s. 30A(1) to (3)). Conditions may be imposed for the purpose of securing surrender, preventing further offences, preventing interference with witnesses or obstruction of the administration of justice, or for the person's own protection (s. 30A(3B)). The person arrested must be given a notice informing him of the offence for which he was arrested, of the grounds of arrest, that he is required to attend a police station and of any conditions imposed, and opportunities for seeking a variation of those conditions. The notice may also specify the police station which he is required to attend and the time when he is required to attend; if it does not do so, it must specify the police station at which a request for variation of a condition may be made. If the notice does not give the requisite information, the arrested person must subsequently be given a further written notice which contains that information. He may be required to attend a different police station from that originally notified (s. 30B(1) to (6)). There is no statutory limit on the period for which bail may be granted under these provisions, but Home Office Circular 61/2003 *Criminal Justice Act 2003: Bail Elsewhere than at a Police Station* suggests a normal maximum of six weeks.

A person released on bail under s. 30A may be re-arrested without warrant if new evidence justifying his arrest has come to light since his release (s. 30C(4)). Any person released under s. 30A who fails to attend at a police station as required and any person whom a constable has reasonable grounds for suspecting has broken any conditions imposed may be arrested without warrant. He must then be taken to a police station (which may be the specified police station or any other police station) as soon as practicable after an arrest. An arrest under these provisions counts as an arrest for an offence (s. 30D(1) to (4)).

ARREST WITHOUT WARRANT

The PACE 1984 s. 24 (police powers of arrest) and s. 24A (civilian powers of arrest), were substituted by the SOCPA 2005, ss. 110 and 111, and s. 110(4) of that Act provides that the substituted sections are to have effect in relation to any offence whenever committed. The changes, which took effect on 1 January 2006, considerably simplified the law on arrest, but also extended them by making powers of arrest available in respect of any offence. On the other hand, both police and civilian powers of arrest are subject to a test of necessity. A new PACE 1984, Code of Practice G, governing statutory powers of arrest by police officers, also came into force on 1 January 2006. Other powers of arrest without warrant, cross-border powers of arrest, and arrest for breach of the peace, are also dealt with under this heading. Powers of arrest are generally discretionary; if the conditions are satisfied the officer may arrest, but is not required to. However, where a person has been arrested for an offence and is at a police station in consequence of that arrest, and it appears to the police that, if released, he would be liable to arrest for some other offence, the person must be arrested for that other offence (PACE 1984, s. 31). **D1.13**

Police Powers of Arrest

Police and Criminal Evidence Act 1984, s. 24 **D1.14**

24.—(1) A constable may arrest without a warrant—
(a) anyone who is about to commit an offence;
(b) anyone who is in the act of committing an offence;
(c) anyone whom he has reasonable grounds for suspecting to be about to commit an offence;
(d) anyone whom he has reasonable grounds for suspecting to be committing an offence.
(2) If a constable has reasonable grounds for suspecting that an offence has been committed, he may arrest without a warrant anyone whom he has reasonable grounds to suspect of being guilty of it.
(3) If an offence has been committed, a constable may arrest without a warrant—
(a) anyone who is guilty of the offence;
(b) anyone whom he has reasonable grounds for suspecting to be guilty of it.
(4) But the power of summary arrest conferred by subsection (1), (2) or (3) is exercisable only if the constable has reasonable grounds for believing that for any of the reasons mentioned in subsection (5) it is necessary to arrest the person in question.
(5) The reasons are—
(a) to enable the name of the person in question to be ascertained (in the case where the constable does not know, and cannot readily ascertain, the person's name, or has reasonable grounds for doubting whether a name given by the person as his name is his real name);
(b) correspondingly as regards the person's address;
(c) to prevent the person in question—
(i) causing physical injury to himself or any other person;
(ii) suffering physical injury;

Part D Procedure

(iii) causing loss of or damage to property;
(iv) committing an offence against public decency (subject to subsection (6)); or
(v) causing an unlawful obstruction of the highway;

(d) to protect a child or other vulnerable person from the person in question;
(e) to allow the prompt and effective investigation of the offence or of the conduct of the person in question;
(f) to prevent any prosecution for the offence from being hindered by the disappearance of the person in question.

(6) Subsection (5)(c)(iv) applies only where members of the public going about their normal business cannot reasonably be expected to avoid the person in question.

D1.15 **Reasonable suspicion** An arrest normally requires the officer to have reasonable grounds for suspicion (see **D1.2**). However, the PACE 1984, s. 24(1)(a) and (b), and (3)(a), permit arrest without reasonable suspicion. Thus, provided that it can be established that the relevant condition is satisfied (e.g., that the person was in the act of committing an offence), the arrest will be lawful even if it cannot be established that the officer had reasonable grounds for suspicion. Note that whereas prior to the amendments to s. 24 by the SOCPA 2005 arrest under this section was limited to 'arrestable' offences, the power of arrest is now available in respect of any offence.

D1.16 **Necessity** In addition to the conditions set out in the PACE 1984, s. 24(1) to (3), the officer must have reasonable grounds for believing that arrest is necessary for any of the reasons set out in s. 24(5) (s. 24(4)). PACE Code G notes that arrest 'represents an obvious and significant interference' with the right to liberty (para. 1.2). A person must not be arrested simply because the power is available. The decision to arrest must be fully justified and the officer must consider whether the necessary objectives can be met by other, less intrusive means. It is essential that the power of arrest is exercised in a 'non-discriminatory and proportionate manner' (Code G, para. 1.3). Code G, para. 2.7, states that whilst the necessity conditions in s. 24(5) are exhaustive, 'the circumstances that may satisfy those criteria remain a matter for the operational discretion of individual officers'. However, the requirement that the officer has reasonable grounds for believing that arrest is necessary implies a similar mixed objective/subjective test to that required for reasonable grounds for suspicion (see **D1.2**). It also denotes a higher threshold than that for reasonable suspicion. The meaning of s. 24(4) was considered in *R (C) v Chief Constable of A* [2006] EWHC 2352 (Admin), but the court declined to make a decision on this point. See **D1.32** for a discussion of the term 'necessary' in relation to the decision to detain under the PACE 1984, s. 37.

Code G, para 2.9, provides some explanation of the various necessity conditions. In relation to s. 24(5)(a) and (b) it states that an address is satisfactory for the purposes of serving a summons if the person will be at the address for a sufficiently long period to facilitate service, or that some other person at the address given will accept service on their behalf. Where the suspect gives their name and/or address, the officer must have reasonable grounds for doubting the name or address given for arrest to be necessary. A constable cannot be said to doubt it simply because in the past other persons suspected of a like offence have not given correct particulars (*G v DPP* [1989] Crim LR 150).

Section 24(5)(c)(i) or (ii) could apply where a constable has grounds for believing that the suspect is likely to commit suicide or is so intoxicated that he is likely to suffer injury. In certain circumstances, loss of or damage to property, for the purposes of s. 24(5)(c)(iii), could include the offender's own property, such as where a violent husband, having assaulted his wife, is believed likely to damage the matrimonial home or objects in it. The condition under s. 24(5)(c)(iv) applies only where members of the public going about their normal business cannot reasonably be expected to avoid the person in question (s. 24(6)). In relation to s. 24(5)(c)(v) it is irrelevant that the police have previously permitted an act of obstruction to take place there (*Arrowsmith v Jenkins* [1963] 2 QB 561).

Section 24(5)(e) permits arrest in order to allow the prompt and effective investigation of the offence or of the conduct of the person in question. It is difficult to see how an arrest could be justified by reference to a need to investigate the conduct of the person unless that involves investigation of the offence of which he is suspected. Code G, para 2.9, gives examples of the circumstances in which this condition may be satisfied, including where there is a need to enter and search property, search the person, or take fingerprints, photographs, etc. Particular attention should be paid to whether this condition is satisfied where the suspect indicates his willingness to co-operate with a police investigation by, e.g., attending voluntarily at a police station, permitting his fingerprints to be taken or allowing a search to be conducted.

In relation to s. 24(5)(f), Code G, para 2.9, states that the condition may be satisfied if there are reasonable grounds for believing that the person will fail to attend court if not arrested, or if the grant of bail under the PACE 1984, s. 30A, would not be enough to deter him from trying to evade prosecution. Given the reasonable belief requirement in s. 24(4), there should be some objective basis for arrest on the basis of this condition. Mere suspicion that the person may not turn up in court should not be sufficient.

Civilian Powers of Arrest

Police and Criminal Evidence Act 1984, s. 24A **D1.17**

24A.—(1) A person other than a constable may arrest without a warrant—
- (a) anyone who is in the act of committing an indictable offence;
- (b) anyone whom he has reasonable grounds for suspecting to be committing an indictable offence.

(2) Where an indictable offence has been committed, a person other than a constable may arrest without a warrant—
- (a) anyone who is guilty of the offence;
- (b) anyone whom he has reasonable grounds for suspecting to be guilty of it.

(3) But the power of summary arrest conferred by subsection (1) or (2) is exercisable only if—
- (a) the person making the arrest has reasonable grounds for believing that for any of the reasons mentioned in subsection (4) it is necessary to arrest the person in question; and
- (b) it appears to the person making the arrest that it is not reasonably practicable for a constable to make it instead.

(4) The reasons are to prevent the person in question—
- (a) causing physical injury to himself or any other person;
- (b) suffering physical injury;
- (c) causing loss of or damage to property; or
- (d) making off before a constable can assume responsibility for him.

(5) This section does not apply in relation to an offence under part 3 or 3A of the Public Order Act 1986.

Section 24A provides for a more restricted scheme of powers of arrest for persons other than constables. These powers apply only to indictable offences (s. 24A(1) and (2)), which includes offences triable either-way as well as indictable-only offences. Unlike a constable, a civilian cannot arrest for an anticipated offence. If a civilian arrests a person under s. 24A(2) for an offence he believes has been committed, the arrest will be unlawful if it cannot be established that an indictable offence was in fact committed (*R v Self* [1992] 3 All ER 476, decided under the former version of s. 24, but the same principles apply). A civilian making an arrest must have reasonable grounds for believing that, for any of the reasons mentioned in s. 24A(4), it is necessary to arrest the person and it must appear to him that it is not practicable for a constable to make the arrest instead (s. 24A(3)). The necessity conditions under s. 24A(4) are more limited than those that apply to constables under s. 24(5).

Other Powers of Arrest

The PACE 1984, s. 26 and sch. 2, preserves certain powers of arrest enacted prior to the PACE 1984. **D1.18**

Police and Criminal Evidence Act 1984, sch. 2

PRESERVED POWERS OF ARREST

1920 c. 55	Section 2 of the Emergency Powers Act 1920.
1952 c. 52	Section 49 of the Prison Act 1952.
1952 c. 67	Section 13 of the Visiting Forces Act 1952.
1955 c. 18	Sections 186 and 190B of the Army Act 1955.
1955 c. 19	Sections 186 and 190B of the Air Force Act 1955.
1957 c. 53	Sections 104 and 105 of the Naval Discipline Act 1957.
1969 c. 54	Section 32 of the Children and Young Persons Act 1969.
1971 c. 77	Section 24(2) of the Immigration Act 1971 and paragraphs 17, 24 and 33 of schedule 2 and paragraph 7 of schedule 3 to that Act.
1976 c. 63	Section 7 of the Bail Act 1976.
1983 c. 2	Rule 36 in schedule 1 to the Representation of the People Act 1983.
1983 c. 20	Sections 18, 35(10), 36(8), 38(7), 136(1) and 138 of the Mental Health Act 1983.
1984 c. 47	Section 5(5) of the Repatriation of Prisoners Act 1984.

A constable has a power to arrest a bailed person whom he has reasonable grounds to believe is not likely to surrender to custody or is likely to break any bail conditions, or reasonable grounds to suspect that he has broken the conditions of his bail (Bail Act 1976, s. 7(3)). A Customs and Excise officer has a similar power to arrest a suspect who he has reasonable grounds for believing is not likely to surrender to custody where the person has been released on bail in respect of possession of controlled drugs, drug trafficking or money laundering (CJA 1988, s. 151). For powers of arrest in respect of a person granted bail at a police station before charge, see **D1.12**.

The general arrest powers in the PACE 1984, s. 25, were repealed by the SOCPA 2005, s. 110(2). Many statutory powers of arrest enacted before and after the PACE 1984 were repealed by the SOCPA 2005, s. 111 and sch. 7, since arrests for any offence are facilitated by the amended s. 24 of the PACE 1984. However, the police continue to enjoy various statutory powers of arrest other than in relation to a criminal offence. For example, they may arrest a person for the purpose of taking fingerprints (PACE 1984, s. 27(3)) or samples (s. 63A(7)). In addition, a constable may arrest without warrant a person whom he reasonably suspects to be a terrorist (see **B10.86** *et seq.*).

Cross-border Powers of Arrest

D1.19 The CJPO 1994, part X (ss. 136 to 140), makes extensive provision for cross-border powers of arrest. Section 136 concerns the cross-border execution of warrants. A warrant issued in one part of the UK in the name of an innocent person (as in the context of personation by the true offender) remains valid until annulled. Where police arrest the person named in the warrant, the arrest will not provoke an action for false arrest or false imprisonment provided that the police acted without malice (*McGrath v Chief Constable of the Royal Ulster Constabulary* [2001] 2 AC 731).

By s. 137, a constable from one part of the UK who has reasonable grounds for suspecting that an offence has been committed or attempted in his jurisdiction may arrest a suspected person in another part of the UK. An arrest can be carried out under this provision where the conditions which would enable the officer to arrest lawfully in his own jurisdiction are satisfied. Following arrest, the arrested person must be taken to a police station in accordance with s. 137(7).

A constable may use reasonable force in effecting an arrest in the other jurisdiction (s. 137(8)(a)). A constable from Scotland arresting or detaining a suspect in England or Wales has the same powers and duties, and the arrested person the same rights, as if the arrest had taken place in Scotland (s. 137(8)(b) and (c) and s. 138(2)). Scottish procedure is modified in certain respects to take account of the exigencies of this scheme.

Search powers are available under these cross-border schemes in respect of arrests under warrant or without warrant. A constable from England and Wales arresting under warrant in Scotland or Northern Ireland, or a constable from Scotland or Northern Ireland arresting under warrant in England or Wales, is given extensive powers under s. 139. The same powers apply to arrests without warrant by a constable from England or Wales making an arrest without warrant in Scotland or Northern Ireland or a constable from Northern Ireland making an arrest in England or Wales (s. 139(1)). Under these powers a constable may search the person if he has reasonable grounds for believing that the person may present a danger to himself or to others (s. 139(2)). The powers are virtually the same as those which apply under the PACE 1984, s. 32, to a search of the person or premises on arrest (see **D1.65** and **D1.95**).

The scheme further provides for reciprocal powers of arrest. Where a police constable in England or Wales would have powers to arrest, a constable from Scotland or Northern Ireland who is in England or Wales has the same powers of arrest (s. 140(1)). Reciprocal powers apply in favour of a constable from England or Wales in Scotland or Northern Ireland (s. 140(3), (4) and (5)). The scheme is premised upon the arresting officer having the same powers and coming under the same obligations as he would were he a local constable operating under local law.

Arrest for Breach of the Peace

Any person, constable or civilian, has a common-law power of arrest where (a) a breach of the peace is committed in his presence, (b) the person effecting the arrest reasonably believes that such a breach will be committed in the immediate future by the person arrested, or (c) a breach of the peace has been committed or the person effecting the arrest reasonably believes that a breach of the peace has occurred and that a further breach is threatened. A breach of the peace occurs whenever harm is actually done or is likely to be done to a person or, in their presence, to their property, or where a person is in fear of being harmed through an assault, affray, riot, unlawful assembly or other disturbance (*Howell* [1982] QB 416). **D1.20**

Reasonable belief is an objective requirement in the sense that the court must determine whether the belief was reasonable having regard to the circumstances as perceived by the person carrying out the arrest at the time (*Redmond-Bate v DPP* (1999) 163 JP 789). Where a reasonable apprehension of an imminent breach of the peace exists, the preventive action taken must be reasonable and proportionate; and there is no power to take action short of an arrest when a breach of the peace is not so imminent as would be necessary to justify arrest (*R (Laporte) v Chief Constable of Gloucestershire* [2007] 2 WLR 46). The power to arrest for an apprehended breach of the peace caused by apparently lawful conduct is exceptional (*Foulkes v Chief Constable of Merseyside Police* [1998] 3 All ER 705; *Bibby v Chief Constable of Essex Police* (2000) 164 JP 297).

Breach of the peace is not an offence under domestic law, although it may be treated as criminal for the purposes of the ECHR (*Steel v UK* (1999) 28 EHRR 603). Consequently, detention of a person arrested for breach of the peace is not governed by the PACE 1984, s. 37. It was held in *Williamson v Chief Constable of West Midlands Police* [2004] 1 WLR 14, that PACE Code C did not apply to a person detained at a police station following arrest for breach of the peace because such a person was not arrested for an offence and therefore was not in police detention. However, Code C, para. 1.10, states that the code (other than the detention review provisions in s. 15) applies to people in custody at police stations 'whether or not they have been arrested'. A person arrested for breach of the peace may be held in custody at a police station, but the officer concerned must have an honest belief, based upon objective and reasonable grounds, that detention is necessary in order to prevent a breach of the peace. If this condition is not satisfied, and no other grounds for detention exist, the person must be released (*Chief Constable of Cleveland Police v McGrogan* [2002] EWCA Civ 86).

ARREST UNDER WARRANT

Warrants Issued by Magistrates' Courts

D1.21 The most important of the statutes which authorise arrest under warrant for a criminal offence is the MCA 1980. Section 1 empowers a justice to issue a warrant on the basis of a written information substantiated on oath that a person has, or is suspected of having, committed an offence. Such a warrant may or may not be endorsed for bail. If endorsed for bail, the warrant will (if relevant) specify the amounts in which any sureties are to be bound. If bail is to be granted with sureties, the police must release the offender if the sureties approved by the officer enter into recognisances in accordance with the endorsement. The person bailed is then obliged to appear before a magistrates' court at the time and place named in the recognisance (s. 117).

The power of a magistrates' court to issue a warrant for the arrest of any person who has attained the age of 18 years is limited by s. 1(4). The offence concerned must be indictable, or punishable with imprisonment, or the person's address must be not sufficiently established for a summons to be served on him. A warrant to arrest any person for non-appearance before a magistrates' court is not to issue unless the offence to which the warrant relates is also punishable with imprisonment or where the court, having convicted the defendant, proposes to impose a disqualification upon him.

Power is given under s. 13 to issue a warrant for the arrest of a suspect who has failed to appear to answer a summons. Power to issue a warrant for arrest in respect of a person who has been granted bail and who fails to surrender to custody or who, having surrendered to custody, then absents himself before the court is ready to deal with the case, is governed by the Bail Act 1976, s. 7.

Warrants Issued by the Crown Court

D1.22 Section 80(2) of the Supreme Court Act 1981 provides that, where an indictment has been signed but the person charged has not been committed for trial, the Crown Court may issue a summons requiring that person to appear before it or may issue a warrant for his arrest. A similar power applies where a person charged with or convicted of an offence has entered into a recognisance to appear at the Crown Court and fails to do so. A warrant for arrest may be endorsed for bail, in which case the officer in charge of the police station to which the accused is taken has the same powers and duties as in the parallel case where the warrant is issued by magistrates (s. 81).

Extradition Cases

D1.23 For powers of arrest in extradition cases, see **D31.3** and **D31.7**.

A person arrested under the provisions may be held in custody at a police station until he is produced before the appropriate court, but is not treated as being in police detention for the purposes of the PACE 1984, s. 118(2). His treatment whilst at a police station is governed by codes of practice issued under the Extradition Act 2003, s. 173 (see the Extradition Act 2003 (Police Powers: Codes of Practice) Order 2003 (SI 2003 No. 3336)).

Irish and Other Warrants

D1.24 Ireland is a category 1 country for the purposes of the Extradition Act 2003, and warrants issued by a judicial authority in Ireland are to be dealt with in accordance with the Extradition Act 2003, part 1 (see **D31.2**). Section 222 provides that an Order in Council may provide for the Act to extend to any of the Channel Islands or the Isle of Man with such modifications as are specified in the Order.

There is provision for the execution of warrants emanating from one part of the UK in another part of the UK. In brief, the scheme provides for the execution of such a warrant either by a constable of the police force of the country of issue or the country of execution. This regime applies to warrants issued in England and Wales, Scotland, or Northern Ireland (CJPO 1994, s. 136). A constable arresting a person under warrant pursuant to these provisions has the same powers of search as apply to a cross-border arrest without warrant (s. 139 and see further D1.19).

Execution of Warrants

The principal provision dealing with the execution of warrants is the MCA 1980, s. 125. This is supplemented by ss. 125A and 125B, which extend powers of execution to civilian enforcement officers and other approved persons and bodies. Section 125 provides that a warrant of arrest issued by a justice of the peace remains in force until it is executed or ceases to have effect in accordance with rules of court, and that it may be executed anywhere in England and Wales by any person to whom it is directed or by any constable acting within his police area. The effect of this, taken together with the Police Act 1996, s. 30, is to enable such a warrant to be executed by a constable anywhere in England and Wales and adjacent UK waters. Furthermore, any constable may execute the warrant in his own police area even though it is addressed to a constable in another police area. Police have a discretion as to when to execute a warrant, but the discretion must be exercised reasonably. The term 'immediately' in such a warrant refers to taking the person before the court and not to when the arrest may be made. In certain circumstances, it may be reasonable for police to investigate a criminal matter before executing a default warrant of which they are aware (*Henderson v Chief Constable of Cleveland Police* [2001] 1 WLR 1103). **D1.25**

A warrant to which s. 125A(1) or s. 125D applies may be executed by any person entitled to execute it even though it is not in his possession at the time (s. 125D(1) and (2)). It must be shown to the person arrested, if he demands it, as soon as practicable (s. 125D(4)). These provisions do not, however, apply to a search warrant or other warrant which must be in the constable's possession at the time (*Purdy* [1975] QB 288).

A constable who arrests a person under warrant must inform the person of the reason for his arrest and that he is acting under warrant (PACE 1984, s. 28).

DETENTION AND TREATMENT OF SUSPECTS

Applicability of PACE and Codes of Practice

General The detention and treatments of suspects is regulated by the PACE 1984, parts IV and V, and PACE Code C. The PACE 1984 distinguishes between persons in police detention and others who may be held in custody at a police station. A person is in police detention if he has been taken to a police station after being arrested for an offence or under the TA 2000, s. 41, or has been arrested at a police station after attending voluntarily or accompanying a constable to it, and he is detained there or detained elsewhere in the charge of a constable (PACE 1984, s. 118(2)). Similarly, a person is in police detention if he is in the custody of a designated civilian detention, investigating or escort officer by virtue of the Police Reform Act 2002, sch. 4, paras. 22, 34(1) or 35(3) (PACE 1984, s. 118(2A)). A person who is at court after being charged is not in police detention (s. 118(2)); neither is a person who attends a police station to answer to live-link bail in accordance with a direction under the CDA 1998, s. 57C (PACE 1984, s. 46ZA(2): in force only in limited areas), unless an exception in s. 46ZA(3) applies). Finally, a person who is arrested and taken to a designated place under the PTA 2005, s. 5, pending the making of a derogating control order is deemed to be in police detention (PTA 2005, s. 5(7)(b)). **D1.26**

Many of the police powers in the PACE 1984 relate only to persons in police detention.

However, certain rights such as the right of intimation (under s. 56) and the right to legal advice (under s. 58), apply to persons arrested and held in custody at a police station or other premises, and apply irrespective of whether the person was arrested for an offence.

Code C applies to persons in custody at a police station whether or not they have been arrested (subject to the exceptions in Code C, para. 1.12), and to persons removed to a police station as a place of safety under the Mental Health Act 1983, ss. 135 and 136. However, sect. 15 of Code C (concerning reviews of detention) applies only to persons in police detention. Whilst a person arrested under the TA 2000, s. 41, and taken to a police station is in police detention, Code H rather than Code C applies unless and until he is charged with an offence (Code H, para. 1.2), and many aspects of detention are governed by the TA 2000, sch. 8. For brief discussion of whether Code C applies to a person detained following arrest for breach of the peace, see **D1.20**.

D1.27 **Persons Remanded to Police Custody** Where a magistrates' court has power to remand a person in custody, it may commit him to detention at a police station (MCA 1980, s. 128(7)). A person so committed is treated as being in police detention for the purposes of the PACE 1984, s. 39 (duty of the custody officer to ensure that detainees are treated in accordance with PACE and the Codes), and his detention is subject to review under the PACE 1984, s. 40 (MCA 1980, s. 128(8)(c) and (d)). The person is not to be kept in police detention unless it is necessary so to detain him for the purpose of inquiring into other offences, and must be taken back before the magistrates' court that committed him as soon as that need ceases (s. 128(8)(a) and (b)). A magistrates' court has a similar power, under the CJA 1988, s. 152(1) and (1A), to commit a person brought before the court in respect of certain drugs offences to the custody of a constable for up to 192 hours, but the legislation is silent on the applicability of the PACE 1984. In any event Code C applies (other than sect. 15) if, as a result, they are held in custody in a police station.

D1.28 **Volunteers** A person who, for the purpose of assisting with an investigation, attends voluntarily at a police station or at any other place where a constable is present, or who accompanies a constable to a police station or such other place without having been arrested, is entitled to leave at will unless he is arrested. This could include victims and witnesses as well as suspects. If the constable decides that the person is to be prevented from leaving at will, he is to inform the suspect at once that he is under arrest and (presumably only if at a police station) bring him before the custody officer (PACE 1984, s. 29; Code C, para. 3.21). If he is not placed under arrest but is cautioned (see **D1.55**), the officer administering the caution must immediately inform him that he is not under arrest, and that he is free to leave if he wishes, and that he may obtain free and independent legal advice if he wishes (Code C, para. 3.21).

Many of the provisions of the PACE 1984 and Code C do not apply to a volunteer even if he is at a police station since he is neither in police detention nor held in custody. However, a volunteer is entitled to legal advice at any time, and to communicate with anyone outside a police station, and must be treated with no less consideration than a person who is in custody (Code C, Note for Guidance 1A).

The Custody Officer

D1.29 Where a person has been arrested, he must normally be taken to a police station (subject to the power to release him under the PACE 1984, ss. 30(7) and 30A (s. 30(1)). He may be taken to any police station, unless it is anticipated that it will be necessary to detain him for more than six hours, in which case he should be taken to a police station designated under s. 35 (s. 30(3) to (6)). One or more custody officers must be appointed for each designated police station (s. 36(1)). A custody officer must be of at least the rank of sergeant (although when the amendment to the PACE 1984, s. 36(1), by the SOCPA 2005, s. 121(1) and (2), is in force a civilian may be appointed to the role) (s. 36(3)). If a custody officer is not readily available, or if a person is taken to a non-designated police station, another officer may perform the role although that officer must normally not be involved in the investigation of an offence for which the person is in detention (s. 36(4) to (7)).

A person who has been arrested for an offence can only be kept in police detention in accordance with the PACE 1984, part IV (s. 34(1)). Such a person may be detained at a police station only on the authority of the custody officer (s. 37(1)), and may not be released except on his authority (s. 34(2) and (3)). Generally, it is the responsibility of the custody officer to ensure that a person in police detention is treated in accordance with the PACE 1984 and the Codes of Practice, although responsibility is temporarily transferred to any officer to whom custody of the person is transferred in accordance with the Codes of Practice (s. 39(1) to (3)).

Custody Records

A custody record must be opened as soon as is practicable in respect of each person who is D1.30 brought to a police station under arrest, or who is arrested at a police station after having attended voluntarily, or who attends a police station in accordance with bail granted under the PACE 1984, s. 30A (Code C, para. 2.1). In the past, custody officers have not opened a custody record if, on an arrested person being produced before them, they have determined that there is sufficient evidence to charge. However, now that charge decisions are frequently made by Crown Prosecutors and this often entails some delay, this policy may be reviewed (see further **D2.5**). A custody record does not have to be opened in respect of a volunteer who is not arrested. The custody officer is responsible for recording in the custody record all matters that are required by the PACE 1984 or the Codes of Practice to be recorded (s. 39(1)(b) and Code C, para. 2.3). If the detained person is transferred to another police station, the custody record or a copy of it must accompany him, and must show the time of and reason for the transfer (Code C, para. 2.3). It is not clear whether a new custody record should be opened where a person is further detained on surrendering to custody following a release on police bail or whether the original custody record should be continued. However, time in police detention before the release on bail will normally count for the purpose of calculating the maximum periods of detention (see **D1.43**).

Both the PACE 1984 and the Codes of Practice provide for the many matters that must be recorded in the custody record. The former requirement to record everything that a person has with him when he is detained is now at the discretion of the custody officer (PACE 1984, s. 54 as amended by CJA 2003, s. 8). If a record is made, it does not have to be in the custody record (s. 54(2A)), although Home Office Circular 60/2003, para. 5.5, states that the detained person should be asked to check any record that is made, and sign it as correct. For details of what must be recorded when a health care professional is called in to examine a detained person, see Code C, paras. 9.15 and 9.16.

A solicitor or appropriate adult must be permitted to see the custody record of a detained person as soon as practicable after his arrival at a police station, and at any time during the period of detention (Code C, para. 2.4). A detained person, his lawyer or his appropriate adult must be permitted, on giving reasonable notice, to inspect the custody record after the person has left police detention (Code C, para. 2.5), and is entitled to receive a copy of the custody record for up to 12 months after release (Code C, para 2.4A).

The Decision to Detain

The Initial Decision Where a person is arrested for an offence, whether without a warrant D1.31 or under a warrant not endorsed for bail, the custody officer at the station where he is detained must determine whether he has sufficient evidence to charge the suspect with the offence for which he is arrested (PACE 1984, s. 37(1)). In making his determination the custody officer is not required to enquire into the lawfulness of the arrest (*DPP v L* [1999] Crim LR 752; *Al Fayed v Metropolitan Police Commissioner* [2004] EWCA Civ 1579). If the custody officer determines that he does not have sufficient evidence to charge, the arrested person is to be dealt with in accordance with the PACE 1984, s. 37(2) (see **D1.32**). If the custody officer determines that he does have sufficient evidence to charge, the arrested person is to be dealt with in accordance with s. 37(7) (see **D2.2**). A person who attends a police station to answer to bail granted under the s. 30A, or returns to a police station to answer to bail otherwise granted by police under the PACE 1984, part IV, or is arrested under s. 30D (having failed to answer to bail granted under s. 30A) or s. 46A (having failed to answer to bail otherwise granted under part IV), is to be treated as arrested for the offence for which he was granted bail (s. 34(7)). A person arrested under the RTA 1988, s. 6(5), or the Transport and Works Act 1992, s. 30(2) (arrest under the breath-test procedure), is also to be treated as having been arrested for an offence (PACE 1984, s. 34(6)). The custody officer must make his determination as soon as is practicable after the arrested person arrives at the station or, if the arrest occurs there, as soon as possible after the arrest (s. 37(10)). He may detain the person at the police station for so long as is necessary to enable him to discharge this function (s. 37(1)).

A custody officer who becomes aware at any time that the grounds for detaining a suspect in police custody have ceased to apply and who is not aware of any other grounds which would justify his continued detention must release him immediately (s. 34(2)), such release normally being without bail (s. 34(5)). He is not, however, to release a suspect who appears to him to have been unlawfully at large when arrested (s. 34(4)). Further, if the offence for which the person was arrested is one in respect of which a sample for the purpose of drug-testing may be taken (see **D1.70**), release may be delayed for up to 24 hours from the relevant time for the purpose of enabling a sample to be taken (s. 37(8A) and (8B)).

D1.32 **Insufficient Evidence to Charge** A custody officer who considers that there are grounds for holding the suspect, but who determines that he does not have sufficient evidence to charge him, must release him with or without bail unless he has reasonable grounds for believing that detention of the suspect without charge is necessary to secure or preserve evidence relating to an offence for which he is under arrest or to obtain evidence by questioning him (PACE 1984, s. 37(2)). If the custody officer does have such a belief, he may authorise the person to be kept in police detention (s. 37(3)), and must make a written record of the grounds for detention as soon as is practicable (s. 37(4); Code C, para. 3.4), normally in the presence of the person (s. 37(5) and (6)).

In determining whether there is sufficient evidence to charge, the custody officer is entitled to rely on the account given by the arresting officer and to assume that the arrest was lawful (see **D1.31**). For the meaning of sufficient evidence to charge, see **D2.3**. The requirement that the officer believes that detention is necessary creates, in principle, a stringent test. That was certainly the view of the then Secretary of State when he explained the provision to Parliament during passage of the original Bill, indicating that it meant more than simply desirable or convenient. It was held in *Al Fayed v Metropolitan Police Commissioner* [2004] EWCA Civ 1579, that whilst the question of reasonable belief that detention is necessary involves an objective element, it is to be determined by reference to whether the custody officer acted reasonably in deciding that detention was necessary. However, it is submitted that if, viewed objectively, detention was not necessary, the officer could not have acted reasonably in so believing.

D1.33 **The Procedural Requirements** Despite the fact that, as noted in **D1.30**, a custody record must be opened in respect of each person who is brought to a police station under arrest, the normal practice has been for a custody record to be opened only if the custody officer determines that the person be detained under the PACE 1984, s. 37(2) and (3). However, given that the charge decision is now normally to be taken by a Crown Prosecutor (see **D2.5**), and that there is normally a delay before a prosecutor makes a charge decision, it is submitted that a custody record should be opened even if the custody officer determines that there is sufficient evidence to charge when the arrested person is first brought before him.

Where the custody officer authorises detention, the procedural requirements are largely governed by PACE Code C. The officer must inform the detained person of his right to legal advice (**D1.37**) and his right to have someone informed of his arrest (**D1.34**), and ask the person whether he wishes to exercise those rights (Code C, paras. 3.1 and 3.5). The officer must also inform the person of his right to consult the Codes of Practice, and give them written notification of his rights (paras. 3.1 and 3.2). The custody officer must conduct a risk assessment and take any necessary action (paras. 3.6 to 3.10).

If the detained person is a juvenile (i.e. under 17 years), the custody officer must ascertain the person responsible for his welfare and inform the person responsible of the arrest and detention (Code C, para. 3.13) and, if the detained person is known to be the subject of a court order under which a person or organisation is responsible for supervising or monitoring him, the custody officer must also inform that person or organisation (para. 3.14). Where the person is a juvenile or mentally disordered or otherwise mentally vulnerable, the officer must inform the appropriate adult and ask that adult to come to the police station (para. 3.15). If the detained person is deaf or there is doubt about his hearing or speaking ability, or doubt about his ability to understand English, and the custody officer cannot establish effective communication, the custody officer must call in an interpreter (para. 3.12). If the person is blind or seriously visually handicapped or is unable to read, the custody officer should ensure that his solicitor, relative, the appropriate adult or some other person likely to take an interest in him is available to help him in checking any documentation. Where Code C requires written consent or signification then the person who is assisting may be asked to sign instead if the detained person so wishes (para. 3.20). In each case, a person who appears to come within the category of persons requiring special treatment must be treated as such.

A detained person who is a foreign national must be informed of his right to communicate with his High Commission, embassy or consulate (Code C, para. 3.3 and sect. 7). If the person is a citizen of a foreign country with which a bilateral consular convention or agreement is in force, the appropriate High Commission, embassy or consulate must be informed, unless the person is a political refugee or is seeking political asylum, in which case this should only be done at his express request (paras. 7.2 and 7.4). These obligations and rights apply in addition to the right to notification of arrest under the PACE 1984, s. 56. There is no provision for delay even where delay in notification of arrest (see **D1.35**) or delay in access to legal advice (see **D1.39**) is authorised.

Notification of Arrest

The Right to Notification A person who has been arrested (whether or not for an offence) and who is being held in custody at a police station or other premises has a right, at his request, to have one friend, or relative or other person who is known to him or who is likely to take an interest in his welfare, told of his arrest and the place where he is being detained. This is to be done as soon as is practicable (PACE 1984, s. 56(1)). His right to have another person notified is exercisable whenever he is transferred from one police station to another (s. 56(8)). The custody officer must inform the suspect of this right (Code C, para. 3.1(i)), and ask him whether he wishes to exercise it (para. 3.5(a)(iii)). **D1.34**

The person chosen by the detainee is to be informed of the detainee's whereabouts at public expense and, if the detainee requests, on each occasion that he is taken to another police station (para. 5.3). If that person cannot be contacted, the detainee may choose up to two alternatives. If they too cannot be contacted, the custody officer or the person in charge of the investigation has discretion to allow further attempts until the information has been conveyed (para. 5.1). If the detainee does not know of anyone to contact for advice, the custody officer should bear in mind local voluntary bodies who may be able to help (Code C, Note for Guidance 5C).

D1.35 **Delaying Notification** Where a person is detained for an indictable offence (i.e. indictable-only or either-way), an officer of the rank of inspector or above may authorise delay in giving notification of a suspect's detention for up to 36 hours from the relevant time (PACE 1984, s. 56(2) and (3)). For the meaning of 'relevant time', see **D1.44**. Authorisation may be given either orally or in writing, but if done orally the authorisation is to be confirmed in writing as soon as practicable (s. 56(4)). The officer may authorise delay only if he has reasonable grounds for believing that any of the conditions in s. 56(5) or (5A) is satisfied. These are the same conditions that apply to a decision to delay access to a lawyer under s. 58 (see **D1.39**). If delay is authorised, the detained person must be told the reason for it, and that reason must be noted on his custody record (s. 56(6)).

D1.36 **Other Similar Rights** A detainee may receive visits at the custody officer's discretion (Code C, para. 5.4), and Code C Note for Guidance 5B indicates that visits should be allowed where possible.

A detainee is entitled to writing materials and to speak on the telephone for a reasonable time to one person, although this may be delayed or denied if the person is detained in respect of an indictable offence and an officer of the rank of inspector or above considers that sending a letter or making a telephone call may result in any of the consequences set out in Code C, annex B, paras. 1 and 2 (Code C, para. 5.6). Any delay or denial of the above rights should be proportionate and should last for no longer than is necessary (para. 5.7A). The detainee must be told that what he says in any communication, other than one to his solicitor, may be read or listened to and may be given in evidence (para. 5.7).

If a friend or relative of a detainee, or a person with an interest in a detainee's welfare, asks where the detainee is then this information must be given provided that the detainee agrees and delay in notification under the PACE 1984, s. 56, has not been authorised (Code C, para. 5.5 and annex B).

Right of Access to Solicitor

D1.37 **The Right to Consult a Solicitor** A person who is arrested (whether or not for an offence) and held in custody at a police station or other premises has a right, at his request, to consult a solicitor privately at any time (PACE 1984, s. 58; Code C, para. 6.1). 'Held in custody' has been given a more restricted meaning than simply 'in custody', and describes the situation where a custody officer has made a decision that the person should be detained (*Kerawalla* [1991] Crim LR 451), although arguably a person has a common-law right to legal advice in those circumstances. The right applies to all persons held in custody including those who are juveniles, or mentally disordered or vulnerable. An appropriate adult has an independent right to legal advice even if the juvenile or vulnerable adult does not want one, although a juvenile cannot be forced to see a solicitor if he does not wish to do so (Code C, paras. 3.19 and 6.5A). While the statutory right does not apply in respect of a prisoner on remand in custody at a magistrates' court, there is a common-law right to consult a solicitor as soon as is reasonably practicable and police cannot refuse access to a prisoner in custody simply because the request falls outside customary hours (*Chief Constable of South Wales, ex parte Merrick* [1994] 1 WLR 663).

A person must be told of his right to free legal advice when: he is brought to a police station under arrest, or when he is arrested having initially attended voluntarily (Code C, para. 3.1); immediately before the beginning or recommencement of any interview at a police station or other authorised place of detention (para. 11.2); before a review of detention is conducted or before a decision is made whether to extend the period of detention (para. 15.4); after charge or being informed that he may be prosecuted, where a police officer wishes to bring to his attention any statement or the content of any interview, or where he is re-interviewed (paras. 16.4 and 16.5); before being asked to provide an intimate sample (Code D, para. 6.3); before an intimate drug search is conducted under the PACE 1984, s. 55(1)(b) (Code C, annex A, para. 2B), or an x-ray or ultrasound scan is taken under s. 55A(1) (Code C, annex K, para. 3); before he is (exceptionally) interviewed after charge (Code C, para. 16.5); and before an identification parade or group or video identification is conducted (Code D, para. 3.17). The person must be told that free independent advice is available from a duty solicitor (Code C, para. 6.1).

If, on being informed or reminded of the right to legal advice, the person declines to speak to a solicitor, the officer must tell him that the right to legal advice includes the right to speak to a solicitor on the telephone, and ask him whether he wishes to do so. If the person still declines legal advice, the officer must ask him why, and record any answer. Once it is clear that the person does not wish to speak to a solicitor at all, the officer must cease to ask him for reasons for his decision (Code C, para. 6.5). No attempt should be made to dissuade a suspect from obtaining legal advice (para. 6.4). Wrongful denial of access to a solicitor may lead to the exclusion of evidence (see **F2.21** and **F17.24**). A suspect cannot be refused access to a solicitor simply because the police fear that the solicitor will advise the suspect not to answer questions (Code C, annex B, para. 4; *Alladice* (1988) 87 Cr App R 380).

The word 'solicitor' is not defined in the PACE 1984, but Code C defines it for the purposes of the Code to include a solicitor holding a practicing certificate, or an accredited or probationary representative included on the register maintained by the Legal Services Commission (Code C, para. 6.12, and see Code D, para. 2.6, Code E, para. 1.5, and Code F, para. 1.5). By Code C, para. 6.12A, an accredited or probationary representative may be denied access to a police station if an officer of the rank of inspector or above considers that to grant access will hinder the investigation. The hindering of the investigation must not arise from the giving of proper legal advice to a detainee. Code C, para. 6.13, reproducing and extending the effect of *Chief Constable of Avon and Somerset, ex parte Robinson* [1989] 1 WLR 793, provides that the officer should take into account whether the credentials of an accredited or probationary representative have been satisfactorily established, whether the person is of suitable character to give advice, and any other matters in any written letter or authorisation provided by the solicitor concerned. A person with a criminal record, save for a minor offence, is unlikely to be suitable. The responsibility for assessing these matters rests with the investigating officer, who may have regard to but is not fettered by general statements of force policy. The primary question is whether allowing a particular individual access to advise the detainee may prejudice the investigation (*R (Thompson) v Chief Constable of the Northumberland Constabulary* [2001] 1 WLR 1342). As the Divisional Court said in *Ex parte Robinson*, where a person is ostensibly capable of giving advice, he cannot be excluded simply because the police believe that he will give poor advice.

There is no similar provision for a solicitor (as opposed to a representative) to be excluded from a police station. However, a solicitor (including a representative) may be required to leave an interview if an officer of the rank of superintendent or above considers that by his misconduct the solicitor has prevented the proper putting of questions to his client (Code C, paras. 6.9 to 6.11). A solicitor is not guilty of misconduct if he seeks to challenge an improper question or the manner in which it is put or if he advises his client not to reply to particular questions or if he wishes to give his client further legal advice. However, Code C, Note for Guidance 6D, suggests that misconduct could include answering questions on the client's behalf or providing written replies for the client to quote.

Section 58(1) of the PACE 1984 grants a right to consult 'privately' with a solicitor. Code C, Note for Guidance 6J, describes this as 'fundamental', and states that facilities to enable private consultation with a solicitor, whether in person or on the telephone, should normally be provided. Covert surveillance of a consultation between a suspect and their solicitor was described in *Grant* [2006] QB 60 as categorically unlawful.

Action When a Request is Made Where a person makes a request to consult a solicitor, he **D1.38**

must be permitted to consult a solicitor as soon as practicable and the custody officer must act without delay to secure that (PACE 1984, s. 58(4), and Code C, para. 6.5). This is subject to the power to delay access to a solicitor under s. 58(8) to (11) (see **D1.39**).

Although s.58 does not expressly give a right to have a solicitor present in a police interview, s. 58(1) does state that the person has a right to consult a solicitor 'at any time', and Code C, para. 6.8, provides that a detainee who has been permitted to consult a solicitor must, on request, be allowed to have him present while he is interviewed unless the exceptions in para. 6.6 apply.

Subject to the power to delay access to a solicitor under s. 58(8) to (11), once a person has asked to consult a solicitor he must not be interviewed or continue to be interviewed until he has been able to have that consultation unless any of the conditions in Code C, para. 6.6 (b) to (d), is satisfied. Note that if an interview is conducted in the absence of legal advice under para. 6.6(b) (but not para. 6.6(c) or (d)), inferences from 'silence' under the CJPOA 1994, ss. 34, 36 or 37, cannot be drawn and the modified caution under Code C, annex C, para. 2, must be given. The statutory drink/driving procedure under the RTA 1988 (or the Transport and Works Act 1992, s.31) is not an interview and is therefore not subject to delay pending legal advice (Code C, para. 11.1A); thus failure to permit access to a solicitor before the procedure is carried out does not afford the suspect with a reasonable excuse for failure to provide a specimen (*DPP v Billington* [1988] 1 WLR 535; and see also *Kennedy v CPS* (2003) 167 JP 267; *Whitley v DPP* (2004) 168 JP 350; and *Myles v DPP* [2004] 2 All ER 902).

D1.39 **Delaying Access to a Solicitor** Delaying access to a solicitor is permitted only where the person is detained in respect of an indictable offence (i.e. indictable-only or either-way), he has not been charged, and delay is authorised by an officer of the rank of superintendent or above (PACE 1984, s. 58(6), and Code C, annex B). The officer may authorise delay only if there are reasonable grounds for believing that exercising the right:

(a) will lead to interference with or harm to evidence connected with an indictable offence or interference with or physical injury to other people (s. 58(8)(a));
(b) will lead to the alerting of other people suspected of having committed such an offence but not yet arrested for it (s. 58(8)(b));
(c) will hinder the recovery of any property obtained as a result of such an offence (s. 58(8)(c)); or
(d) where the person detained for the indictable offence has benefited from his criminal conduct (within the meaning of the Proceeds of Crime Act 2002, part 2), it will hinder the recovery of the value of the property constituting the benefit (s. 58A).

Where these conditions are satisfied, access to a solicitor may be delayed only for as long as the grounds exist, and in any case no longer than 36 hours from the relevant time (s. 58(5); Code C, annex B, para. 6). For the meaning of 'relevant time' see **D1.44**. If the police seek a warrant of further detention (see **D1.46**), the suspect must be allowed access to a solicitor in reasonable time before the hearing even if this is within the 36-hour period (Code C, annex B, para. 7).

These provisions create a stringent test for delaying access to a solicitor and, given that the authorising officer must have 'reasonable grounds' for his 'belief' that access 'will' lead to one or more of the consequences, there should be some objective basis for that belief. In *Samuel* [1988] QB 615, the Court of Appeal held that (a) the police officer must believe that one of the statutory grounds for exclusion applies, and (b) that belief must be reasonable. He must believe that the consequence will very probably happen. It will rarely happen that a police officer will be entitled to believe that a solicitor will knowingly pass on information in breach of the statute, and any grounds put forward would have to be specific to the solicitor concerned. Solicitors are also unlikely to be unwitting dupes, and suspicion that the suspect will try to use the solicitor thus must be specific to him, e.g., where he is known or suspected to be a member of a criminal gang. This is reinforced by Code C, annex B, Note for Guidance B3. In *Alladice* (1988) 87 Cr App R 380, the Court of Appeal seems to have considered the risk of innocent transmission to be greater than that contemplated in *Samuel*, but considered itself to be bound by *Samuel*. In *Davison* [1988] Crim LR 442, the effect of *Samuel* was said to be that if the police seek to deny access to a solicitor they must show more than a substantial risk of their fears being realised. Delaying access to a solicitor under these provisions may infringe the right to fair trial guaranteed by the ECHR, Article 6 (*Murray v UK* (1996) 22 EHRR 29), although it should be noted that inferences under the CJPOA 1994, ss. 34, 36 or 37, are no longer permitted where the person was at an authorised place of detention and he had not been allowed an opportunity to consult a solicitor prior to being questioned (CJPOA 1994, ss. 34(2A), 36(4A) and 37(3A)). See also *Condron v UK* (2001) 31 EHRR 1; *Magee v UK* (2001) 31 EHRR 35; *Averill v UK* (2001) 31 EHRR 36; and *Brennan v UK* (2002) 34 EHRR 18.

If a decision is made to delay access to a particular solicitor the suspect must be allowed to choose another solicitor (Code C, annex B, para. 3). If delay is authorised, the detained person must be told the reason for it, and the reason must be noted on his custody record (annex B, para. 13). Once the grounds for delay cease to exist, the suspect must be asked, as soon as is practicable, whether he wants to exercise the right to a solicitor and the custody record must be noted accordingly (annex B, para. 6).

Juveniles and Mentally Disordered or Vulnerable Persons

For the initial action to be taken in respect of persons who have special needs, see D1.33. In the case of young people, anyone who appears to be under the age of 17 years must be treated as a juvenile for the purposes of the PACE 1984 and the Codes in the absence of clear evidence to the contrary (PACE 1984, s. 37(15); Code C, para. 1.5). With regard to mental disorder or vulnerability, if a police officer has any suspicion, or is told in good faith, that a person of any age may be mentally disordered or otherwise mentally vulnerable, in the absence of clear evidence to dispel that suspicion, the person must be treated as such for the purposes of the Codes of Practice (Code C, para. 1.4). 'Mental disorder' is defined by the Mental Health Act 1983, s. 1(2), as 'mental illness, arrested or incomplete development of mind, psychopathic disorder and any other disorder or disability of the mind'. The term 'mentally vulnerable' applies to any person who, because of their mental state or capacity, may not understand the significance of what is said, of questions or of their replies. Where the custody officer has any doubt about the mental state or capacity of a detainee, the detainee must be treated as mentally vulnerable, and an appropriate adult called (Code C, Note for Guidance 1G). It is imperative that a mentally disordered or otherwise mentally vulnerable person detained under the Mental Health Act 1983, s. 136, be assessed as soon as possible (Code C, para. 3.16). **D1.40**

Appropriate Adult 'Appropriate adult', in the case of a juvenile suspect, is defined as a parent or guardian or, if the juvenile is in care, a representative of the care authority or a voluntary organisation, or a social worker, or (failing these) another responsible adult aged 18 years or older who is not a police officer or police employee (Code C, para. 1.7(a)). An estranged parent whom an arrested juvenile does not wish to attend and to whom the juvenile specifically objects should not act as an appropriate adult (Code C, Note for Guidance 1B; *DPP v Blake* [1989] 1 WLR 432). Similarly, an illiterate parent with a low IQ who cannot appreciate the gravity of the situation in which his child is placed should not act as an appropriate adult (*Morse* [1991] Crim LR 195). Where the juvenile is in care, the relevant social worker or his representative should be prepared to attend as soon as practicable (*DPP v Blake*). **D1.41**

'Appropriate adult' in the case of a person who is mentally disordered or vulnerable is defined as a relative, guardian or other person responsible for care or custody of the person, someone who has experience of dealing with such persons (but who is not a police officer or police employee) or, failing these, some other responsible adult aged 18 years or older who is not a police officer or police employee (Code C, para. 1.7(b)). Code C, Note for Guidance 1D, states that it may be more satisfactory for the appropriate adult to be someone who is experienced or trained in the care of mentally disordered or vulnerable people, although the suspect's wishes should be respected where practicable.

A solicitor attending a police station on a suspect's behalf should not act as an appropriate adult (Code C, Note for Guidance 1F; *Lewis* [1996] Crim LR 260). A person should not be the appropriate adult if he (i) is suspected of involvement in the suspected offence, (ii) is the victim or a witness, (iii) is involved in the investigation, or (iv) has received admissions from the suspect before acting as the appropriate adult (Code C, Note for Guidance 1B). A social worker or a member of a youth offending team should also refrain from acting as an appropriate adult if the suspect has made admissions to them (Code C, Note for Guidance 1C).

D1.42 **Role of the Appropriate Adult** The Codes of Practice do not specify the general role of appropriate adults, although Home Office Guidance for Appropriate Adults states that their role is (i) to ensure that the detained person understands what is happening to him and why; (ii) to support, advise and assist him; (iii) to observe whether the police are acting properly and fairly and to intervene if they are not; (iv) to assist with communication between the detained person and the police; and (v) to ensure that the detained person understands his rights and the appropriate adult's role in protecting those rights. Code C, para. 11.17 describes a similar role for appropriate adults during police interviews. The detainee should be advised of the duties of the appropriate adult and that he can consult with the adult privately at any time (Code C, para. 3.18). If the appropriate adult or the detainee asks for legal advice, the provisions of Code C, s. 6, apply (para. 3.19, and see **D1.37**).

Generally, a juvenile or mentally disordered or vulnerable person must not be interviewed by the police or asked to provide a written statement in the absence of an appropriate adult, unless delay would be likely to lead to interference with or harm to evidence connected with an offence, interference with or physical harm to other people or serious loss of or damage to property, to alerting other suspects not yet arrested, or to hindering the recovery of property obtained in consequence of commission of the offence. If an interview at a police station is necessary for one or more of these reasons, it must be authorised by an officer of the rank of superintendent or above (Code C, paras 11.1, 11.15 and 11.18 to 11.20). Further, the appropriate adult has specific roles in respect of legal advice (para. 3.9) and intimate and strip searches (Code C, annex A, paras 5 and 11(c)). In the case of identification and other evidential procedures that require 'appropriate consent', the PACE 1984, s. 65(1), provides that, in the case of a person who has attained the age of 14 years but is under 17 years, consent is required from the juvenile and their parent or guardian, but that, in the case of a person under 14 years, only the consent of the parent or guardian is required. Note that in a particular case, the appropriate adult may not be a parent or guardian, in which case the adult cannot give consent.

Detention Time-limits

D1.43 The normal maximum period of detention without charge is 24 hours from the relevant time (PACE 1984, s. 41(1)). For the meaning of 'relevant time' see **D1.44**. Subject to the powers to extend detention without charge, if at the expiry of that time the person has not been charged, he must be released, either on bail or without bail (s. 41(7)). The period of detention without charge may be extended in respect of a person under arrest for an indictable offence, for up to a total of 36 hours from the relevant time by an officer of the rank of superintendent or above (see **D1.45**), and for up to a total of 96 hours from the relevant time by a magistrates' court (see **D1.46**). Where a detention time-limit has expired and the person is released without charge, he may not be rearrested without warrant for the offence for which he was previously arrested (subject to the power to arrest for failure to answer to police bail under s. 46A) unless new evidence justifying a further arrest has come to light since the original arrest (ss. 41(9), 42(11) and 43(19)). It is unclear precisely what 'new evidence justifying a further arrest' means, but it is submitted that it means evidence that was not available to the police at the time of the original arrest and detention. If a person is released at the expiry of a detention time-limit, and subsequent analysis of fingerprints or samples taken during their detention implicates him, does this amount to 'new evidence'? Arguably it does, but if that is correct it has the effect of potentially extending the maximum period of detention whenever a person is released pending forensic analysis or further investigation.

For the purpose of calculating maximum periods of detention, time normally runs continuously from the relevant time. However, where a detainee is removed to hospital for medical treatment, time spent at the hospital or travelling to or from hospital does not count, except for any time spent questioning the person for the purpose of obtaining evidence in respect of an offence (s. 41(6)). Note that a person in police detention at a hospital must not be questioned without the agreement of a responsible doctor (Code C, para. 14.2). If a person is questioned in these circumstances, he is entitled to consult a solicitor (see **D1.37**).

The Relevant Time In the usual situation, the relevant time is the time an arrested person arrives at the first police station that he is taken to, or 24 hours after arrest, whichever is the earlier (PACE 1984, s. 41(2)(a)). However, this basic definition is modified in a variety of different circumstances, as follows. **D1.44**

(a) Where a person initially attends a police station as a volunteer (see **D1.28**) and is then arrested at the police station, the relevant time is the time of arrest (s. 41(2)(c)).
(b) Where a person attends a police station to answer to bail granted under the PACE 1984, s. 30A (see **D1.12**), the relevant time is the time he arrives at the police station (s. 41(2)(ca)).
(c) Where the person, having been detained in respect of one offence, is subsequently rearrested for another offence under s. 31, the relevant time is to be calculated by reference to the original offence (s. 41(4)). As a result, a rearrest does not have the effect of extending the maximum period of detention.
(d) Where the person is arrested outside England or Wales, the relevant time is the time that he arrives at the first police station that he is taken to in the police area in England or Wales in which the offence for which he was arrested is being investigated, or 24 hours after he entered England or Wales, whichever is the earlier (s. 41(2)(b)).
(e) Where the person is arrested in police area 1 in connection with an offence for which his arrest is sought in police area 2, the relevant time is the time he arrives at the first police station to which he is taken in police area 2, or 24 hours after he was arrested, whichever is the earlier (s. 41(3)). However, if the person is questioned about the offence in police area 1, the relevant time is calculated in accordance with s. 41(2)(a)). Code C, para. 14.1 states that the person must not be questioned about the offence during transit except in order to clarify any voluntary statement made by him.
(f) Where the person is in police detention (see **D1.26**) in police area 1, his arrest in connection with another offence is sought by police area 2 and he is taken to police area 2 for the purpose of investigating that other offence without being questioned about it in police area 1, the relevant time is the time at which he arrives at the first police station to which he is taken in police area 2, or 24 hours after he leaves the police station in which he was detained in police area 1, whichever is the earlier (s. 41(5)). Again, if the person is questioned about the offence in police area 1, the relevant time is calculated in accordance with s. 41(2)(a)), and the same restrictions on questioning in transit apply as in (e) above.
(g) Where a person is released on police bail under s. 47(3)(b), if he is detained when he

surrenders to bail, the relevant time will be that which applies to the original detention. It makes no difference that the person is arrested under s. 46A for failure to surrender to bail (s. 47(6)). However, if he is arrested other than under s. 46A, e.g., because there is new evidence justifying a further arrest (see **D1.43**), the relevant time will be that relating to the subsequent arrest (s. 47(7)).

Note that the relevant time is not necessarily the same time as that for determining the timing of reviews of detention, which may be some time later (see **D1.48**).

Detention for More than 24 Hours, up to 36 Hours

D1.45 A person can be detained without charge beyond 24 hours only if three conditions are met (PACE 1984, s. 42(1)). These are:

(a) that a police officer of the rank of superintendent or above who is responsible for the police station at which the person is detained has reasonable grounds for believing that such detention is necessary to secure or preserve evidence relating to an offence for which the person is under arrest or to obtain such evidence by questioning him;
(b) that the offence for which he is under arrest is an indictable offence;
(c) that the investigation is being conducted diligently and expeditiously.

As to (a), the requirement for reasonable grounds for belief that detention is necessary is the same as under the PACE 1984, s. 37(2) (see **D1.32**). As to (b), an indictable offence is one that is triable only on indictment or is triable either-way.

If the above conditions are met, the officer may authorise detention for up to 36 hours from the relevant time (see **D1.44**). If he authorises detention for less than 36 hours, he may authorise further detention up to the maximum 36 hours provided that the above conditions still apply (PACE 1984, s. 42(2)). No authorisation under s. 42(1) may be made more than 24 hours after the relevant time. Thus retrospective authorisation is not permitted. Further, by s. 42(4), the decision to authorise detention beyond 24 hours cannot be made before the second review of detention under s. 40 (see **D1.49**). Unlike reviews under s. 40, an extension of detention under these provisions must be dealt with by the officer in person rather than by telephone or video link (Code C, Note for Guidance 15F).

If it is proposed to transfer a person to police detention in another police area, in determining whether to authorise detention without charge beyond 24 hours, the officer must have regard to the distance and the time the journey would take (s. 42(3)). Presumably, if the time involved is likely to take detention beyond the 36 hours permitted, the review officer will have either to refuse the transfer or a warrant of further detention will have to be sought (see **D1.46**).

A person whose extended detention has been ordered under the foregoing procedure must be released from detention either with or without bail at the expiration of 36 hours unless either he has been charged with an offence or a warrant of further detention has been granted by a magistrates' court (s. 42(10)). A person who has been released may not be rearrested for the same offence unless new evidence justifying such a course has come to light (s. 42(11) and see **D1.43**).

Before deciding whether to authorise detention under s. 42(1) or (2), the officer must give the detained person, or his solicitor if he is available at the time that the decision is to be made (and appropriate adult, if relevant (Code C, para. 15.3)), an opportunity to make representations about the decision (s. 42(6)). If the detainee is likely to be asleep at the time the decision is made, it should, if the legal obligations and time constraints permit, be brought forward, but if the detainee is asleep he need not be woken (Code C, Note for Guidance 15C). Representations may be given orally or in writing (s. 42(7)). It has been held that the requirement under s. 42(6) is mandatory, so that a purported authorisation without providing such an opportunity was invalid (*In the matter of an application for a warrant of further detention* [1988] Crim LR 296, although this is a magistrates' court decision). The officer may decline to hear oral representations from the suspect himself if he considers that the detainee's condition or behaviour is such as to render him unfit to do so (s. 42(8)).

If an officer authorises detention beyond 24 hours, and the detainee has not at that time availed himself of the right to have someone informed of his arrest or the right to consult a solicitor, the officer must (a) inform the detainee of his rights, (b) decide whether the detainee should be permitted to exercise them, (c) record his decision in the custody record, and (d) if he decides to refuse to allow the detainee to exercise either of the rights, must also record the grounds for the decision in the detainee's custody record (s. 42(9)).

Detention for More than 36 Hours

Warrant of Further Detention Detention without charge beyond 36 hours from the relevant time (see **D1.44**) is permitted only where a magistrates' court issues a warrant of further detention (PACE 1984, s. 43(1)). A magistrates' court is defined for this purpose as a court consisting of two or more justices sitting otherwise than in open court (PACE 1984, s. 45(1)). **D1.46**

The application must be made on oath by a constable and supported by an information (s. 43(1) and (14)). In order to issue a warrant the court must be satisfied that further detention is justified (s. 43(1)), which must be determined in accordance with the criteria set out in s. 43(4) (which are the same as those applying to the decision to detain beyond 24 hours except that the court must be *satisfied* that detention is necessary for one or more of the specified reasons, as opposed to having to have *reasonable grounds for believing* that detention is necessary; see **D1.2**). The hearing is *inter partes*. The detainee must be given a copy of the information and be brought before the court for the hearing. He is entitled to be legally represented at the hearing. If he is not so represented but wishes to be, the court must adjourn the hearing to enable him to be represented. He may be held in detention during the adjournment. No limit is placed on the time for which an adjournment may be granted (s. 43(1) to (3)).

An application for a warrant of further detention must, as a general rule, be made before the expiry of 36 hours from the relevant time (s. 43(4)(a)). For this purpose, the time of the application is the time that the constable makes the application on oath and gives evidence (*Sedgefield Justices, ex parte Milne* (5 November 1987 unreported). This period may be extended where it is not practicable for the magistrates' court to which the application will be made to sit before the expiry of the period but where it will sit within six hours following the 36-hour period (s. 43(4)(c)). If the application cannot be heard before the expiry of the 36-hour period, the custody officer is to note in the detainee's custody record the fact that he was detained for the extra period and the reason why he was so kept (s. 43(6)). If the application is made outside the 36-hour period and the magistrates' court considers that it would have been reasonable for the police to have made the application before the expiry of the period, it must dismiss the application (s. 43(7), and see *Slough Justices, ex parte Stirling* (1987) 151 JP 603).

If the court is not satisfied that there are reasonable grounds for believing that further detention is justified, it must dismiss the application or adjourn the hearing of it to a time not later than 36 hours from the relevant time (s. 43(8)). The person may be kept in police detention during any period of adjournment (s. 43(9)). If, therefore, the court sits at a time close to the 36-hour limit, it may well not be possible for the police to obtain an adjournment in order to improve their case. Furthermore, where an application for a warrant of further detention has been refused, no further application may be made under s. 43 unless fresh evidence has come to light since the refusal (s. 43(17)). This, of course, assumes that the hearing took place before the expiry of the 36-hour period and that it is possible for the detainee still to be in lawful custody. If the application for a warrant is refused, the police must either charge the detainee or release him, either on bail or without bail (s. 43(15)). However, if the refusal was made before the expiry of the 24-hour limit (**D1.43**) or any extension granted under s. 42 (see **D1.45**), the detainee need not be released before the expiry of that period (provided that the conditions for detention without charge continue to be satisfied) (s. 43(16)).

If the court is satisfied that there are reasonable grounds for believing that further detention is justified, it may issue a warrant of further detention for a maximum period of 36 hours (s. 43(12)). Within that limit, where it is intended to transfer a detainee to another police area, the court must have regard to the distance and time involved in a journey (s. 43(13)). The warrant must state the time at which it is issued and the period for which it is granted (s. 43(10)). At the expiry of a warrant of further detention the detainee must, unless the warrant is extended under the PACE 1984, s. 44, be charged or released, either on bail or without bail. If released on bail, he may not be rearrested without a warrant for the offence for which he was previously arrested unless new evidence justifying a further arrest has come to light since his release (s. 43(19), and see **D1.43**).

D1.47 **Extension of Warrant of Further Detention** A magistrates' court may, on an application on oath and supported by an information, extend a warrant of further detention issued under the PACE 1984, s. 43, provided it is satisfied that there are reasonable grounds for believing that the further detention is justified (s. 44(1)). Such extension may be made for any period which the court thinks fit, having regard to the evidence before it, but it may not be for longer than 36 hours, and the total period for which the person is to be held in detention may not exceed 96 hours from the relevant time (see **D1.44**). There is no formal limit to the number of occasions on which such a further extension may be granted, but the total period of 96 hours cannot be exceeded (s. 44(1) to (4)).

The court must be furnished with the same particulars as are required in the original application, and the detainee has the same rights of representation (s. 44(6)). If the extension is refused, the detainee must either be released (with or without bail) or charged save that, if the application for extension is made before the expiry of the period specified in the warrant itself, he may be held until the expiry of that period (assuming that the conditions for detention without charge continue to apply) (s. 44(7) to (8)).

Reviews of Detention

D1.48 The PACE 1984, s. 40, requires that the detention of persons in police detention (see **D1.26**) be periodically reviewed in order to determine whether continued detention is justified (see also Code C, sect. 15). The review requirement applies both to persons who have not been charged and those who have been charged, but does not apply to a person who is at court after being charged since such a person is not in police detention (PACE 1984, s. 118(2)). The statutory review requirement does not apply to volunteers (see **D1.28**), to persons who have been taken to a police station as a place of safety under the Mental Health Act 1983, nor to persons who have been arrested other than for an offence (e.g., under a fine default warrant or for fingerprints to be taken under the PACE 1984, s. 27). However, the detention of persons who are held in custody but who are not in police detention as defined by the PACE 1984, s. 118(2), should still be reviewed periodically, as a matter of good practice, in order to check the power under which they are held, the conditions of their detention, and that appropriate action is being taken in respect of them (Code C, Note for Guidance 15B). The statutory review requirements do apply to persons who are deemed to be arrested for an offence (see **D1.26**) and to persons who have been remanded to a police station under the MCA 1980, s. 127 (see **D1.27**). They also apply to persons detained at a police station in respect of whom a warrant of further detention has been issued or extended by a magistrates' court (see **D1.46**).

In the case of persons who have been arrested and charged, reviews of detention must be conducted by the custody officer. For persons who have not been charged, they must be conducted by an officer of at least the rank of inspector who has not been directly involved in the investigation (PACE 1984, s. 40(1)). In either case the officer concerned is referred to as a 'review officer' (s. 40(2)).

Timing of Reviews The first review must be conducted no later than six hours after detention was first authorised under the PACE 1984, s. 37 (which may be later than the 'relevant time': see **D1.44**) (PACE 1984, s. 40(3)(a)). The second and subsequent reviews must be carried out no later than nine hours after the previous review (s. 40(3)(b) and (c)). A review may be postponed if it is impracticable to carry it out by the latest time specified (s. 40(4)(a)). The statute gives two examples. The first is where the review officer is satisfied that a review would interrupt questioning then in progress and would prejudice the investigation. The second is where no review officer is readily available at that time (s. 40(4)(b)). However, these are not exhaustive. If a detainee is asleep when a review is conducted, he need not be woken up but, if he is likely to be asleep when a review is due to be conducted, the review officer should consider bringing the review forward (Code C, Note for Guidance 15C). A postponed review must be carried out as soon as is practicable (s. 40(5)), and the review officer is required to record the reasons for any postponement in the custody record (s. 40(7); Code C, para. 15.3). The timing of subsequent reviews is not affected, so that they must be carried out no later than nine hours after the latest time at which the review should have been conducted (s. 40(6)). However, if a review is brought forward, the next review must be conducted no later than nine hours after the time that the review was in fact conducted. **D1.49**

Failure to carry out a timely review of a person's detention in custody before charge renders previously lawful detention unlawful and amounts to the tort of false imprisonment (*Roberts v Chief Constable of the Cheshire Constabulary* [1999] 1 WLR 662).

Criteria for Reviews In the case of a person not yet charged at the time of the review, the review officer must determine whether there is sufficient evidence to charge and, if not, whether detention is necessary for the reasons set out in the PACE 1984, s. 37(2) (s. 40(8) and (8A) and see **D1.32**). If a person is held because he was not in a fit state to be dealt with, the review officer must determine whether or not he is now in a fit state (s. 40(9)). **D1.50**

If a person has already been charged at the time of review, the review officer must consider whether to order his release on bail, applying the same principles as those which the custody officer is obliged to employ under s. 38(1) to (6B) (s. 40(10) and (10A) and see **D2.46**).

If directions relating to a person in police detention given by a higher-ranking officer are at variance with an actual or proposed decision or action of the review officer, the matter must be immediately referred to an officer of the rank of superintendent or above who is in charge of the station (s. 40(11)).

Procedural Requirements Reviews of detention prior to charge (other than those involving consideration of whether detention is to continue beyond 24 hours: see **D1.45**) may be carried out by video-link facilities where regulations have been issued by the Secretary of State under the PACE 1984, s. 45A(1), and the review officer has access to the use of such facilities enabling him to communicate with persons at the police station (s. 45A(1)). In police stations in respect of which such regulations have not been made, or where they have but such facilities are not available, reviews (other than those involving consideration of whether detention is to continue beyond 24 hours) may be conducted by telephone (s. 40A(1)). It is for the officer conducting the review to determine whether to conduct the review in person or by telephone or video-link facilities (where authorised and available), and in making this decision the officer should take into account the factors set out in Code C, para. 15.3C. If a **D1.51**

review is conducted using such facilities, there is provision for representations to be made by telephone or video-link (as appropriate) or by fax (PACE 1984, ss. 40A(3) and (4), and 45A(6) and (7)), and for the review to be entered in the custody record by another officer (ss. 40(A)(3) and 45A(5)). See Code C, paras. 15.9 to 15.11, for further explanation.

Before determining whether to authorise continued detention the review officer must give either the detained person (unless he is asleep), or any solicitor representing him who is available at the time of the review, an opportunity to make representations about the detention (PACE 1984, s. 40(12)). Code C, para. 15.3, however, provides that this opportunity is to be given to the detainee 'and' to his solicitor and, where relevant, to the appropriate adult. The review officer may also, in his discretion, allow other persons having an interest in the person's welfare to make representations to him (para. 15.3A). Before conducting a review, the review officer must ensure that the detained person is reminded of his entitlement to free legal advice (para. 15.4). The detainee or his solicitor may make representations either orally or in writing, but the review officer need not hear oral representations from a detainee whom he considers unfit to make such representations by reason of his condition or behaviour (PACE 1984, s. 40(13) and (14); Code C, para. 15.3B).

A note must be made in the custody record of the fact that the detainee was reminded of his right to legal advice, details of a review conducted by telephone and the outcome of the review (Code C, paras. 15.12, 15.14 and 15.16); if continued detention is authorised, any comment made by the detainee or his solicitor must also be recorded (para. 15.3). Any written representations made must be retained (para. 15.15).

INTERROGATION OF SUSPECTS

D1.52 The interrogation of suspects is governed partly by common law, partly by the PACE 1984, but primarily by PACE Code C. Code C contains rules regulating the treatment of persons who are being questioned, and the questioning itself, principally in sects. 10, 11 and 12. For the application of Code C to the police and to others, see **D1.1**. Recording of interviews is governed by Code E (audio-recording) and Code F (visual recording with sound). Code C, sect. 12, lays down certain rules governing the physical conditions of, and the treatment of detainees in, interviews conducted at police stations. These are not dealt with further here but the full text of the code is set out in **appendix 2**.

Interviews Generally

D1.53 **Definition of Interview** 'Interview' is widely defined by Code C, para. 11.1A, in purposive terms. An interview is the 'questioning of a person regarding their involvement or suspected involvement in a criminal offence or offences which, under para. 10.1, must be carried out under caution'. By para. 10.1, a person whom there are grounds to suspect of an offence 'must be cautioned before any questions about an offence, or further questions if the answers provide the grounds for suspicion, are put to them if either the suspect's answers or their silence, (i.e. failure or refusal to answer or answer satisfactorily) may be given in evidence to a court in a prosecution'. However, it further provides that a caution is not necessary if questions are for other purposes, such as:

(a) solely to establish identify or ownership of a vehicle;
(b) to obtain information in accordance with a statutory requirement, e.g., under the RTA 1988, s. 165 (note that the statutory drink-driving procedure is not an interview: *DPP v D (a Juvenile)* (1992) 94 Cr App R 185);
(c) in furtherance of the proper and effective conduct of a search (although if questioning goes further, e.g., to establish whether drugs found were intended to be supplied to another, a caution will be necessary: *Langiert* [1991] Crim LR 777; *Khan* [1993] Crim LR 54; *Raphaie* [1996] Crim LR 812); or

(d) to seek verification of a written record of comments made by the person outside of an interview.

It follows that questioning of a person in circumstances where a caution does not have to be administered does not amount to an interview for the purposes of Code C. Conversely, questioning of a person about an offence of which there are grounds to suspect him will amount to an interview even if he has not been arrested and no decision to arrest him has been made. The reference to 'an offence' means that a caution must be given if the person is questioned about an offence other than for which he has been arrested if there are grounds to suspect him of it. See further **D1.55** regarding cautioning.

Where an Interview may be Conducted The general rules for the conduct of interviews are contained in Code C, sect. 11. Following a decision to arrest a suspect, he must normally be interviewed only at a police station or other authorised place of detention (Code C, para. 11.1). The reference to 'a decision to arrest' means that if a police officer has decided to arrest a person, he should not delay the arrest in order to question the suspect before doing so. The requirement that an interview be conducted at a police station is subject to exception where delay would be likely to: **D1.54**

(a) lead to interference with or harm to evidence connected with an offence, interference with or physical harm to other persons, or serious loss of, or damage to, property; or
(b) lead to the alerting of other persons suspected of having committed an offence but not yet arrested for it; or
(c) hinder the recovery of property obtained in consequence of the commission of an offence (para. 11.1).

Interviewing in any of these circumstances must cease once the relevant risk has been averted or the necessary questions have been put to avert the risk (Code C, para. 11.1).

Cautions and Special Warnings It follows from Code C, para. 10.1 (see **D1.53**) that a caution must be administered at the commencement of an interview as defined in Code C, para. 11.1A, whether or not it is conducted at a police station. The suspect must also be reminded that he is under caution at the recommencement of an interview after any break, and if there is any doubt, the caution should be given again in full (para. 10.8). The caution must also be given on arrest (para. 10.3, and see **D1.10**). **D1.55**

The normal caution is set out in Code C, para. 10.5, as follows:

> You do not have to say anything. But it may harm your defence if you do not mention when questioned something which you later rely on in Court. Anything you do say may be given in evidence.

Minor deviation from these words is permissible provided that the sense of the caution is preserved (para. 10.7). If it appears that the suspect does not understand the caution, the person giving it should explain it in his own words (Code C, Note for Guidance 10D).

If a suspect is (exceptionally) interviewed after charge (see **D1.63**), of if he is interviewed in circumstances where he has requested a solicitor but has not been permitted to consult with one (see **D1.37** ***et seq.***), the terms of the caution are those set out in Code C, annex C, para. 2 as follows: 'You do not have to say anything, but anything you do say may be given in evidence'. The reason for the different caution is that in such circumstances inferences cannot be drawn under the CJPOA 1994, ss. 34, 36 or 37 (as a result of amendments by the YJCEA 1999, s. 58, following the decision of the European Court of Human Rights in *Murray v UK* (1966) 22 EHRR 29). Although Code C does not require a caution to be given if a statement is taken after charge, it should be given (*Pall* (1992) 156 JP 424).

Whilst Code C, para. 10.1, requires a caution to be given to a person 'whom there are grounds to suspect' of an offence, Note for Guidance 10A explains this phrase by stating that there must be 'some reasonable, objective grounds for the suspicion, based on known facts or information . . .'. This accords with the decision in *James* [1996] Crim LR 650, and this qualification of the expression was not disputed in *Shillibier* [2006] EWCA Crim 793. If correct, however, it means that insofar as the caution has a protective purpose, it does not apply to the questioning of a person in respect of whom there is some suspicion not amounting to a reasonable suspicion, even though what he says may subsequently be used in evidence against him. For examples of interpretation of the cautioning requirement by the courts, see *Senior* [2004] 3 All ER 9, in which it was held that a caution should have been given, and *Perpont* [2004] EWCA Crim 2562, *Ridehalgh v DPP* [2005] RTR 353 and *Sneyd v DPP* (2006) 170 JP 545, in which the decision went the other way. Failure to administer a caution in circumstances where it is required is a significant and substantial breach of Code C, although it will not necessarily result in exclusion of evidence of the interview (*Armas-Rodriguez* [2005] EWCA Crim 1981).

Whenever a person is interviewed he must be informed of the nature of the offence, or further offence, of which he is suspected (Code C, para. 11.1A). In *Kirk* [2000] 1 WLR 567, the suspect was arrested for theft and was not told that his victim had died; believing himself to be facing a charge of theft only, he made admissions. It was held that these should have been excluded.

In addition to the caution, where a suspect is interviewed at a police station or other authorised place of detention following arrest and:

(a) is asked to account for any object, mark or substance, or mark on such objects found on his person, in or on his clothing or footwear, otherwise in his possession, or in the place where he was arrested; or
(b) to account for his presence at the place where he was arrested,

a special warning must be given in the terms set out in Code C, para. 10.11. Inferences cannot be drawn if the warning is not given (CJPOA 1994, ss. 36(4) and 37(3)). The requirement to give a special warning does not apply where the person who has requested a solicitor is interviewed without having been given an opportunity to consult him, since inferences from refusal or failure to account cannot be drawn as a result of CJPOA 1994, ss. 36(4A) and 37(3A) (Code C, para. 10.10).

D1.56 **Information about Legal Advice** The suspect is entitled to legal advice, and this may be delayed only in the specific circumstances specified in the PACE 1984, s. 58 (see **D1.39**). Where the suspect has requested legal advice, he should not normally be interviewed unless he has consulted with a solicitor, although there are exceptions in urgent cases (see **D1.38**). Unless access to a solicitor has been delayed, or one of the exceptions applies, the interviewing officer must remind the suspect of his entitlement to free legal advice immediately prior to the commencement or recommencement of any interview, and that the interview can be delayed for legal advice to be obtained (Code C, para. 11.2). Violations of a suspect's entitlement to legal advice may lead to the exclusion of evidence (see **F2.21** and **F17.24**).

D1.57 **Significant Statement or Silence** At the beginning of an interview carried out at a police station or other authorised place of detention, the interviewing officer must, after cautioning the suspect, put to him any significant statement or silence which occurred in the presence and hearing of a police officer or other police staff (and which has not been put to him in the course of a previous interview) (Code C, para. 11.4). A significant statement is one which appears to be capable of being used in evidence, and in particular a direct admission of guilt. A significant silence is a failure or refusal to answer a question, or answer satisfactorily when under caution which might, allowing for the restrictions on drawing inferences from silence, give rise to an adverse inference under the CJPO 1994 (para. 11.4A).

D1.58 **Conduct of the Interview** No police officer or other interviewer may try to obtain answers to questions or to elicit a statement by the use of oppression, nor shall he indicate, except in answer to a direct question, what action the police will take if the suspect answers or refuses to answer questions or make a statement. If the suspect asks the officer directly what action will be taken in any of those events, the officer may inform the suspect of his proposed action, which could be, e.g., keeping the person in detention if further action is to be taken. The proposed action must, however, be proper and warranted (Code C, para. 11.5). Thus it was improper for the police to tell a church organist accused of theft from choirboys that the police would interview all of the choirboys if he did not confess (*Howden-Simpson* [1991] Crim LR 49). The police should not seek a confession by offering a caution (*R (U) v Metropolitan Police Commissioner* [2003] 1 WLR 897, overturned but not in this respect by *R (R) v Durham Constabulary* [2005] 1 WLR 1184). Home Office Circular 30/2005 *Cautioning of Adult Offenders*, para. 18, states that 'under no circumstances should suspects be pressed, or induced in any way to admit offences in order to receive a Simple Caution as an alternative to being charged'.

Apart from this, the PACE 1984 and Code C provide little, if any, guidance on the proper conduct of interviews. In *Mason* [1988] 1 WLR 139, it was held that a confession should be excluded where the police falsely informed the suspect that incriminating fingerprints had been found, although the fact that his solicitor was also deceived may have been an important factor. In *Maclean* [1993] Crim LR 687, it was noted that not every trick will result in exclusion of evidence, but in *Imran and Hussain* [1997] Crim LR 754, the Court of Appeal stated that there was a positive duty on the police not to actively mislead a suspect. See also **F2.30** and **F17.24** ***et seq.*** on exclusion of evidence.

It is legitimate for police officers to pursue their interrogation of a suspect with a view to eliciting admissions even where the suspect denies involvement in the offence or declines to answer specific questions. Police questioning which is carried on after repeated denials or refusals may become oppressive. In these circumstances, a solicitor present at an interview should not remain passive. In the face of oppressive questioning he should intervene since otherwise police officers may fail to appreciate that their conduct has become oppressive (*Paris* (1993) 97 Cr App R 99). Hectoring and bullying throughout an interview has been held to be oppressive (*Beales* [1991] Crim LR 118), whereas questioning that was rude and discourteous, with raised voices and some bad language, was not (*Emmerson* (1991) 92 Cr App R 284).

When Interviews should Cease The interview of a person who has not been charged **D1.59**
or informed that he may be prosecuted must cease when the officer in charge of the investigation is satisfied that all the questions he considers relevant to obtaining accurate and reliable information about the offence have been put to the suspect, the officer has taken account of other available evidence, and he (or the custody officer in the case of a detained suspect) reasonably believes there is sufficient evidence to provide a realistic prospect of conviction (Code C, para. 11.6). This, of course, is subject to the limits imposed by the PACE 1984 on the maximum periods of detention without charge (see **D1.43**), and the provisions regarding breaks in interviews and rest periods in Code C, sect. 12. The fact that the conditions in para. 11.6 are satisfied does not preclude officers in Revenue cases or acting under the confiscation provisions of the Proceeds of Crime Act 2002 from inviting a suspect to complete a formal question-and-answer record after the interview is completed. (Code C, para. 11.6 refers to the confiscation provisions of the CJA 1988 or the Drug Trafficking Act 1994, but presumably this is an error.)

Code C, para. 11.6, gives the police a large degree of latitude in determining when interviewing should cease since it appears to permit the police to continue questioning beyond the point when they are satisfied that there is sufficient evidence to charge if, e.g., the officer believes that further questions could or should be put to the suspect. However, there is some inconsistency within Code C and thus uncertainty about the effect of para. 11.6. It provides that in the case of a detained suspect (presumably, as opposed to a volunteer) it is for the custody officer and not the investigating officer to determine whether there is sufficient evidence to charge. On the other hand, para. 16.1 states that when the officer in charge of the investigation believes that there is sufficient evidence to provide a realistic prospect of conviction, he must take the suspect to the custody officer without delay. It may be that this is intended to reflect the fact that the custody officer has formal responsibility for making the decision as to whether there is sufficient evidence to charge. However, para. 16.1 implies that when the officer in charge of the investigation is so satisfied he must take the suspect to the custody officer even though the investigating officer still may have further questions to put to the suspect. In any event, by the PACE 1984, s. 37(7), once the custody officer determines that he has before him sufficient evidence to charge the person he must proceed under that subsection, which would normally preclude further interviewing. 'Sufficient evidence to charge' is not defined, but the DPP's *Guidance on Charging* provides that normally the custody officer must apply the threshold test (see further **D2.3**).

Where a person is detained in respect of more than one offence, Code C, para. 16.1, provides that it is permissible to delay informing the custody officer until the conditions are satisfied in respect of each of the offences. This, however, conflicts with the mandatory provisions of s. 37(7).

Recording of Interviews

D1.60 Interviews of suspects must normally be contemporaneously recorded (Code C, para. 11.7). Further, any comment that might be relevant to the suspected offence made by a suspect outside the context of an interview, including unsolicited comments, must be recorded and, where practicable, the suspect must be given the opportunity to verify the record (para. 11.13). Failure to comply with the recording requirements has led to exclusion of evidence of what was allegedly said (see, e.g., *Canale* [1990] 2 All ER 187; *Keenan* [1990] 2 QB 54), but this is not always so (see, e.g., *Waters* [1989] Crim LR 62; *Dures* [1997] 2 Cr App R 247).

Interviews conducted at a police station in respect of any indictable offence must normally be audio-recorded (Code E, para. 3.1). In practice, most interviews are audio-recorded irrespective of the suspected offence. For the provisions governing the audio-recording of interviews generally, see Code E (see **appendix 2**). Visual recording of police interviews is not mandatory in any police force area, but where such facilities are available and a police officer chooses to use them, he must have regard to Code F (see **appendix 2**).

Special Categories of Persons

D1.61 A juvenile or a mentally disordered or vulnerable person (see **D1.40**) must not be interviewed or asked to provide or sign a written statement in the absence of the appropriate adult unless the conditions for conducting an interview away from a police station under Code C, para 11.1, are satisfied (see **D1.54**), or the interview is authorised by an officer of the rank of superintendent or above under Code C, para. 11.18 (Code C, para. 11.15, and annex E). A juvenile should be interviewed at his place of education only in exceptional circumstances and then only if the principal or his nominee agrees. Efforts should be made to notify parents and the appropriate adult. In cases of necessity, and provided that the school was not the victim of the alleged offence, the principal may act as the appropriate adult (Code C, para. 11.16). The appropriate adult is to be reminded of his functions as adviser and observer as well as that of facilitating communication with the person being interviewed (para. 11.17). As to the special rules applying where a child who is to be interviewed is a ward of court, see the *Consolidated Criminal Practice Direction*, para. I.5.1.

A person who appears to be deaf, or where there is doubt about his hearing or speaking ability, must not be interviewed in the absence of an interpreter unless he agrees in writing to being interviewed without one, or the conditions for conducting an interview away from a police station under Code C, para 11.1, are satisfied (see **D1.54**), or such an interview is authorised by an officer of the rank of superintendent or above under Code C, para. 11.18 (Code C, para. 11.15 and annex E). The position is similar for suspects who have difficulty understanding English (Code C, para. 13.2). Where a suspect cannot read and an interview is recorded in writing, the record must be read over to the suspect who must be asked to verify it (Code C, para. 11.11).

Intoxicated Persons

D1.62 Code C, para. 11.18, precludes the questioning of any person who is unable to appreciate the significance of questions and their answers, or to understand what is happening because of the effects of drink, drugs or any illness, ailment or condition, unless the questioning is authorised by an officer of the rank of superintendent or above for a reason set out in the paragraph.

Effect of Charge

D1.63 Generally, a person who has been charged with, or informed that he may be prosecuted for, an offence cannot be interviewed or otherwise asked questions about that offence (Code C, para. 16.5). There are two exceptions to this rule. First, he may be questioned if an officer wishes to bring to the notice of the accused any written statement made by another person or the content of an interview with another person. In such a case, the officer must hand to the accused a true copy of any such statement or interview record, but he must not do or say anything to invite any reply or comment, except to caution him (Code C, para. 16.4). A police officer may read the statement or record to an illiterate person. If the person is a juvenile or is mentally disordered or mentally vulnerable, the copy or interview record must be given or shown to the appropriate adult (para. 16.4A).

The second exception is where an interview is necessary for the purpose of preventing or minimising harm or loss to some other person or to the public, to clear up an ambiguity in a previous answer or statement, or where it is in the interests of justice that the person should have put to him and should have an opportunity to comment on information concerning the offence which has come to light since he was charged or informed that he may be prosecuted (para. 16.5).

In either case, the person must first be cautioned in the terms set out in paras. 16.4(a) or 16.5(a). Inferences under CJPOA 1994 cannot be drawn in such circumstances (see Code C, annex C, para. 1(b)). The person must also be reminded of his right to legal advice.

Serious Fraud and other Serious Crime

D1.64 Different rules apply in relation to investigation of certain serious or complex frauds. While the police are obliged to follow the normal procedure when questioning suspects, including the administration of a caution, the Director of the Serious Fraud Office has power under the CJA 1987, s. 2, to require a person under investigation or any other person whom he has reason to believe has relevant information to produce documents and to provide an explanation of them. This includes the right to re-interview witnesses even following the delivery of a case statement by the defence (*Turner* (1993) *The Times*, 2 July 1993). The Director is not obliged to provide the interviewee with advance information on the subject-matter of the interview but he may do so should he deem it helpful and not likely to prejudice the investigation (*Serious Fraud Office, ex parte Maxwell* (1992) *The Independent*, 7 October 1992). The court has no power to direct liquidators of an insolvent company not to comply with a notice served by the Serious Fraud Office requesting production of transcripts of examinations under the Insolvency Act 1986, s. 236. It is for the judge at the criminal trial to determine whether to admit such a transcript at the criminal trial. A person who without reasonable excuse fails to comply with a requirement under s. 2 commits an offence punishable on summary conviction with up to six months' imprisonment and/or a fine not exceeding level 5. Note however that compulsion to attend for interview or to provide information where the person is at risk of criminal prosecution in respect of those matters is likely to amount to an interference with their rights under the ECHR, Article 6 (*Shannon v UK* (2006) 42 EHRR 31).

It would seem that the fact that a person who is required to answer questions in the course of an enquiry by the Serious Fraud Office is the spouse of a party charged with fraud is not a reasonable excuse for declining to answer questions (*Director of the Serious Fraud Office, ex parte Johnson* [1993] COD 58). This seemingly follows from the consideration that such enquiries are administrative, and must represent something of a triumph of form over function.

For restrictions on the use in evidence of information obtained by virtue of the CJA 1987, s. 2, see s. 2(8) and (8AA), and see further **F9.25** and **F19.1**.

For powers of search under the CJA 1987, s. 2, see the review of the procedure and authorities in *R (Energy Financing Team Ltd) v Bow Street Magistrates' Court* [2006] 1 WLR 1316.

Similar powers to those under CJA 1987, s. 2, are available to the DPP and the Director of Revenue and Customs Prosecutions, or those to whom they delegate them, under the SOCPA 2005, ss. 60 to 70, in respect of the offences listed in s. 61 (SOCPA 2005, s. 60). The list of offences is extensive, and includes the 'lifestyle offences' in the PCA 2002, sch. 2 (see **E21.11**), offences under the TA 2000, ss. 15 to 18 (fund-raising, money laundering, etc.), certain evasion of duty and VAT offences, and certain false accounting and cheating offences.

SEARCH OF THE PERSON

Search on Arrest

D1.65 A constable who arrests a person elsewhere than at a police station may search that person if he has reason to believe that he may present a danger to himself or others (PACE 1984, s. 32(1)), and may seize and retain anything he finds if he has reasonable grounds for believing that the person might use it to cause physical injury to himself or others (s. 32(8)). He may also search the person for anything which that person might use to escape from lawful custody or which might be evidence in relation to an offence, provided that he has reasonable cause to believe that the arrested person has such material on his person (s. 32(2) and (5)). The officer may seize and retain anything, other than an item subject to legal privilege, if he has reasonable grounds for believing that the person may use it to assist with his escape from lawful custody or that it is evidence of an offence or has been obtained in consequence of the commission of an offence (s. 32(9)). 'Reasonable grounds' implies a mixed subjective/objective test (see **D1.2**). Seizure of car keys under s. 32 from a person arrested on suspicion of burglary and who had been placed in a police car was held in *Churchill* [1989] Crim LR 226 to be unlawful since the keys were not evidence of any crime, although they could have been seized under the officer's general duty to preserve property.

Search under s. 32(2) is authorised only to the extent that it is reasonably required for the purpose of discovering any such thing or evidence (s. 32(3)). The reference to 'an' offence means that the power is not limited to search for or seizure of an item which may be evidence relating to the offence for which the person has been arrested. Unlike the power to search premises under s. 32(2)(b), the offence for which the person has been arrested does not have to be an indictable offence. Where the search takes place in public, the constable may only require the arrested person to remove an outer coat, jacket or gloves, but he is authorised to search a person's mouth (s. 32(4)). Hats, including turbans and other forms of head-wear, are not mentioned in s. 32(4) and thus it would seem that a person cannot be required to remove them in public. However, note the power of a constable in uniform, in an area where an authorisation under the CJPOA 1994, s. 60, is in force (see **D1.6**), to require a person to remove any item which the constable reasonably believes is being worn wholly or mainly for the purpose of concealing identity (CJPOA 1994, s. 60AA). Note also that the power to photograph an arrested person without consent under the PACE 1984, s. 64A(1), is supplemented by a power to require the person to remove any item worn on or over the whole or part of the face or head (s. 64A(2)).

Search at the Police Station

With the exception of searches following arrest under the TA 2000, s. 41 (for which see **B10.94**), searches by a constable of persons in detention at a police station, including intimate searches, can take place only under the authority of the PACE 1984 (s. 53(1) and (2)). **D1.66**

The custody officer at a police station is obliged to ascertain everything which a person has with him when he is brought to the station after having been arrested (PACE 1984, s. 54(1); Code C, para. 4.1). In order to do so, the person may be searched if the custody officer considers it necessary in order to ascertain what property the person has, but only to the extent that he considers it necessary for that purpose (s. 54(6); para. 4.1). The custody officer must also ascertain what property the suspect may have acquired for an unlawful or harmful purpose while in custody, and is responsible for the safe-keeping of property taken from the detainee and kept at the police station (Code C, para. 4.1). For recording requirements, see **D1.30**.

The custody officer may seize and retain anything in the possession of the detainee, save for clothes and personal effects. These may be seized only if the custody officer believes that the person from whom they are seized may use them to cause physical injury to himself or another, or to damage property, or to interfere with evidence, or to escape, or if the custody officer has reasonable grounds for believing that they may be evidence relating to an offence (PACE 1984, s. 54(3), (4), (6B) and (6C); Code C, para. 4.2). In respect of most of these criteria, the custody officer need only have a subjective belief that seizure is necessary, but in respect of articles of supposed evidentiary value, his belief must be based on reasonable grounds. Paragraphs 4.2 and 4.3 of Code C expressly state that a detained person may retain clothing and personal effects other than cash and other items of value, at his own risk, unless the custody officer considers that the detainee might use them in the manner noted above or they are needed as evidence.

A person from whom an article is seized is to be told the reason for the seizure unless he is either violent or likely to become so, is incapable of understanding what is said to him, or is in urgent need of medical attention (PACE 1984, s. 54(5); Code C, paras. 1.8 and 4.2).

Under the PACE 1984, s. 54A, searches and examinations may be authorised by an officer of the rank of inspector or above for the purpose of ascertaining whether a detained person has any mark (such as a tattoo) that would tend to identify him as a person involved in the commission of an offence (s. 54A(1)(a)), or so as to facilitate the ascertainment of his identity (s. 54A(1)(b)). By s. 54A(2), authorisation may be given under s. 54A(1)(a) only if appropriate consent (see the PACE 1984, s. 65(1)) has been withheld or it is not practicable to obtain it (for examples, see Code D, Note for Guidance 5D). Authorisation may be given under s. 54A(1)(b) only if the person has refused to identify himself or the officer has reasonable grounds for suspecting that the person is not who he claims to be (s. 54A(3)). An identifying mark found on such a search or examination may be photographed (s. 54A(5)). No intimate search may be carried out under s. 54A (s. 54A(8)), and if the search or examination requires the removal of more than outer clothing it must be treated as a strip search and conducted in accordance with Code C, annex A, para. 11.

Strip Searches

D1.67 A strip search is a search that is not an intimate search, but which involves the removal of more than outer clothing (Code C, annex A, para. 9). It may be conducted only for the purposes of search or examination under the PACE 1984, s. 54A, or where the custody officer thinks it necessary in order to remove an article which the detained person would not be allowed to keep and the officer reasonably considers that the detainee may have concealed such an article (Code C, annex A, para. 10). It is likely that such articles are those referred to in s. 54 (see **D1.66**). It was held in the pre-PACE case of *Lindley v Rutter* [1981] QB 128, that strip searches 'involve an affront to the dignity and privacy of the individual' and that actions such as removal of a brassiere would require considerable justification. The conduct of strip searches is governed by Code C, annex A, para. 11; in particular, they may be carried out only by a constable of the same sex as the person being searched (annex A, para. 11(a)).

Intimate Searches, X-rays and Ultrasound Scans

D1.68 **Intimate Searches** A person who has been arrested and is in police detention (see **D1.26**) may, under certain circumstances, be subjected to an intimate search, i.e. a search consisting of a physical examination of the bodily orifices other than the mouth (PACE 1984, ss. 54 and 65(1)). An intimate search cannot be authorised for the purpose of securing evidence relating to an offence, nor must it be conducted whilst carrying out a search or examination under s. 54A. 'Bodily orifice' is not defined but would include ears, nose, anus and vagina. Physical insertion into a bodily orifice amounts to an intimate search, as does any application of force to an orifice or its immediate surroundings, such as the removal of something within an orifice. Code C, annex A, para. 11(e), also implies that touching an orifice in these circumstances would also amount to an intimate search.

An intimate search can be conducted only if an officer of the rank of inspector or above authorises it. Such officer must have reasonable grounds for believing that the detained person has concealed on him an article which he could use to cause physical injury to himself or others, and which he might so use while he is in police detention or in the custody of a court (s. 55(1)(a)). Authorisation may also be granted if the officer has reasonable grounds for believing that such a person may have concealed on him a Class A drug and is in possession of it with the appropriate criminal intent (i.e. either to supply it to another or to export it with intent to evade a prohibition or restriction: s. 55(17)) (s. 55(1)(b)). In either case the officer must have reasonable grounds for believing that the article in question cannot be found unless the detainee is intimately searched (s. 55(2)). The reasons why an intimate search is considered necessary must be explained to the person before the search takes place (Code C, annex A, para. 2A). Intimate searches are not limited to circumstances where a person has been arrested for an indictable or recordable offence, although searches conducted under s. 55(1)(b) will, by definition, relate to such offences.

Authorisation may be given either orally, subject to confirmation in writing, or in writing (PACE 1984, s. 55(3)). Consent of the person to be searched is not required for a search under s. 55(1)(a), and reasonable force can be used in order to carry it out (PACE 1984, s. 117). Appropriate consent (see s. 65(1) for definition) in writing is required for a search under s. 55(1)(b). In the latter case the person to be searched must be told of the authorisation and the reasons for it (s. 55(3B)). If consent to a search under s. 55(1)(b) (but not a search under s. 55(1)(a)) is refused without good cause, proper inferences may be drawn (s. 55(13A)), but where consent has been refused force may not be used.

The general rule is that an intimate search should be carried out by a suitably qualified person. Searches under s. 55(1)(b) must always be so carried out (s. 55(4) and (5)). Searches under s. 55(1)(a) must normally be carried out by a suitably qualified person, but may be conducted by a constable where an officer of the rank of inspector or above considers that this would not be practicable (s. 55(5) and (6)); such a search may be carried out by a civilian detention officer (Police Reform Act 2002, sch. 4, para. 28). A search under s. 55(1)(a) by anyone other than a suitably qualified person should be considered only as a last resort (Code C, annex A, para. 3A) — an example might be where a suspect is believed to have concealed a poisonous drug in his anus. No intimate search of an arrested juvenile or a mentally vulnerable person may be carried out unless the appropriate adult of the same sex is present or the suspect requests the presence of a particular adult of the opposite sex who is readily available. In the case of a juvenile, the search may take place in the absence of the appropriate adult only if the juvenile approves this in the adult's presence (Code C, annex A, para. 5). A constable may not carry out an intimate search of a person of the opposite sex, but this restriction does not apply to a search carried out by a medically qualified person (Code C, annex A, para. 6). A minimum of two people other than the detainee must be present. The person to be searched, if not legally represented, must be reminded of his entitlement to free legal advice (Code D, para. 6.3).

Intimate searches may be carried out only at a police station, a hospital, surgery or other medical premises, although an intimate search under s. 55(1)(b) may not be carried out at a police station (PACE 1984, s. 55(8) and (9); Code C, annex A, para. 4). 'Medical premises' is not defined but presumably could, e.g., include a factory first-aid post or an industrial health centre. As soon as possible after completion of an intimate search, the parts of the body searched and the reason for the search (and in the case of a search under s. 55(1)(b), the fact of and grounds for the authorisation and the fact that appropriate consent was given) must be recorded in the custody record (s. 55(10) and (11)).

A person from whom anything is seized is to be told the reason why, unless he is incapable of understanding or is violent or likely to become so (s. 55(13)). Articles found in an intimate search may be seized and retained by the police for the same reasons as justify seizure and retention in the case of a non-intimate search (s. 55(12), and see **D1.66**)).

X-rays and Ultrasound Scans By the PACE 1984, s. 55A(1), an x-ray or ultrasound scan may be taken if authorised by an officer of at least the rank of inspector, who has reasonable grounds for believing that a person who has been arrested and is in police detention (see **D1.26**) may have swallowed a Class A drug and was in possession of it with the appropriate criminal intent (see s. 55A(1) and **D1.68**) before his arrest. The officer granting the authorisation must inform the person concerned of the authorisation and of the reasons for it (s. 55A(3)). Neither an X-ray nor an ultrasound scan may be taken without appropriate consent (see s. 65(1) for definition) (s. 55A(2)). The procedures may be carried out by the same categories of person, and at the same places, as for an intimate search under s. 55(1)(b) (s. 55A(4)), and similar recording requirements apply (s. 55A(5)). Adverse inferences may be drawn against a person who refuses consent (s. 55A(9)), but force may not be used. **D1.69**

For the taking of, and identification from, samples, see **F18.30**.

DRUG TESTING FOR CLASS A DRUGS

The power to test for Class A drugs is governed by the PACE 1984 s. 63B, supplemented by s. 63C, and by Code C, sect. 17. The provisions are gradually being introduced in England and Wales, and whilst all of the powers under the provisions are applicable in some police stations, in others they are applicable only where a person has been charged, and in others they are not applicable at all. Further, in some stations they are only applicable in respect of suspects who have attained the age of 18 years, but in others drug-testing following charge (but not before charge) is applicable in respect of suspects who are between the ages of 14 and 17 years. For further information on applicability of the provisions, see Home Office Circular 3/2006. **D1.70**

Where a person is in police detention (see **D1.26**), a sample of urine or a non-intimate sample may be taken from him for the purpose of ascertaining whether he has any specified Class A drug in his body provided that he has been brought before a custody officer (s. 63B(5D)) and the following conditions are satisfied:

(a) either the arrest condition or the charge condition is met;
(b) both the age condition and the request condition are met; and
(c) the notification condition is met in relation to the arrest condition, the charge condition or the age condition (as relevant) (s. 63B(1))a) to (c)).

The Arrest and Charge Conditions

D1.71 The 'arrest condition' is satisfied if the suspect has been arrested for, but not charged with, a trigger offence or any offence where an inspector or above, having reasonable grounds for suspecting that the misuse by that person of any specified Class A drug caused or contributed to the offence, authorises a sample to be taken (PACE 1984, s. 63B(1A)). The 'charge condition' is satisfied if the suspect has been charged with a trigger offence or any offence where an inspector or above, having reasonable grounds for suspecting that the misuse by that person of any specified Class A drug caused or contributed to the offence, authorises a sample to be taken (s. 63B(2)). If a sample is taken on the basis that the arrest condition was satisfied, no further sample can be taken under s. 63B during the same continuous period of detention unless the suspect remains in police detention in respect of another offence in respect of which the arrest condition is satisfied (s. 63B(5B) and (5C); Code C, para. 17.9). A 'specified' Class A drug has the same meaning as in the CJCSA 2000, part III. The term 'trigger offence' is defined in the CJCSA 2000, sch. 6, and the trigger offences are set out in Code C, Note for Guidance 17E (see **appendix** 2).

The Age and Request Conditions

D1.72 Where the arrest condition is met, the 'age condition' is that the person has attained the age of 18; where the charge condition is met, the 'age condition' is that the person has attained the age of 14 (PACE 1984, s. 63B(3)). The 'request condition' is simply that a police officer has requested the suspect to give the sample (s. 63B(4)). Before requesting a sample the suspect must be warned that failure without good cause to provide the sample requested renders him liable to prosecution (s. 63B(5); Code C, Note for Guidance 17A). He must also be told the purpose of taking the sample, that authorisation has been given (where required), and his right to have someone informed of his arrest, to obtain legal advice and to consult the Codes of Practice (Code C, para. 17.6). Where the suspect is a juvenile, the making of the request, the warning that refusal may amount to an offence, and the taking of a sample must be in the presence of an appropriate adult (s. 63B(5A); Code C, para. 17.7).

The Notification Condition

D1.73 The 'notification condition' is that the relevant chief officer has been notified by the Secretary of State that appropriate arrangements have been made for the police area as a whole, or for the particular police station in which the suspect is in police detention (PACE 1984, s. 63B(4A)). As a result, as noted in **D1.70**, the drug-testing powers are not available in all police stations and, where they are, may be available only in respect of suspects who are 18 years or older. In stations where they are available in respect of suspects between the ages of 14 and 17 years, they are available only where the charge condition is satisfied.

The authorisation and grounds for suspicion (where authorisation is required), the warning as to the consequences of refusal, and the time at which the sample is given, must be recorded in the custody record (s. 63C(3) and (4); Code C, para. 17.2).

Failure without good cause to provide a sample is an offence punishable, on summary conviction, with up to three months' imprisonment and/or a fine not exceeding level 4 (ss. 63B(8) and 63C(1)). If the suspect does refuse to provide a sample, the police cannot use force to obtain one (Code C, para. 17.14).

Detention for the Purposes of Drug-testing

D1.74 Where a person has been arrested for a relevant offence (see **D1.71**), he may be detained for up to 24 hours from the relevant time (see **D1.44**) in order for a sample to be taken even though the custody officer would otherwise have decided that the suspect should be released on bail under the PACE 1984, s. 37(2) (bail without charge), s. 37(7)(a) (release without charge and on bail with a view to the CPS making the charge decision), or s. 37(7)(b) (release without charge and on bail but not for that purpose) (s. 37(8A) and (8B); Code C, para. 17.10). Where the arrest condition (but not the charge condition) is satisfied in respect of one offence (offence 1) and the suspect's release would be required before a sample could be taken but for his continued detention in respect of an offence that does not satisfy the arrest condition (offence 2), the suspect may have a sample taken whilst he continues to be detained provided that it is taken within 24 hours of his arrest for offence 1 (s. 63B(5C); Code C, para. 17.10). Thus, if a person is charged with an offence that did satisfy the arrest condition, and a sample could not be taken before he was charged, but he continues to be detained in respect of an offence that does not satisfy the arrest condition, a sample may be taken during that period of further detention, provided that it is taken within 24 hours of the arrest for the first offence. Where a sample may be taken from a person under s. 63B, but he is charged before a sample is taken and the custody officer would otherwise release him on bail under s. 38, the custody officer may authorise his detention for up to six hours from the time of charge in order for a sample to be taken (s. 38(1)(a)(iiia) and (2); Code C, para. 17.10).

Consequences of a Positive Drug-Test

D1.75 Where a suspect aged 18 years or older has tested positive for a specified Class A drug under the PACE 1984, s. 63B, the police may, before the suspect is released, impose a requirement that he attend an initial assessment of his drug misuse and remain for the duration of the assessment. Where the suspect is tested prior to charge, the requirement can be imposed even if the suspect is not subsequently charged with an offence. Failure to attend or to remain at the assessment is an offence carrying imprisonment up to three months and/or a fine not exceeding level 4 (Drugs Act 2005, s. 12(3) and (4); Code C, para. 17.17). When such a requirement is imposed the suspect must be told of the time and place for the assessment and be warned that failure without good cause to attend and to remain renders him liable for prosecution (Code C, para. 17.18). The suspect must also be given a written notice containing this information (Code C, para. 17.19) and the process must be entered in the custody record (Code C, para. 17.20). There are also provisions (in police stations where the chief officer has been notified by the Secretary of State that follow-up assessment arrangements are available) to require a person who is required to attend an initial assessment also to attend a follow-up assessment, and there are similar provisions regarding enforcement (Drugs Act 2005, ss. 10 to 12).

A sample taken under s. 63B may be disclosed only for the purposes set out in s. 63B(7). Although it must be retained until the person has made his first appearance at court (Code C, para. 17.16(b)), it cannot be used for the purpose of prosecuting for an offence, other than those offences mentioned in s. 63B(7). The purposes are:

(a) for the purpose of informing a decision as to bail, whether by the police or by a court (s. 63B(7)(a));
(b) for the purpose of informing a decision about the imposition of a conditional caution (s. 63B(7)(aa));
(c) for the purpose of informing any decision about the supervision of the person in police detention, in custody or on bail (s. 63B(7)(b));

(d) following conviction, for the purpose of informing any decision about sentence, and any decision about supervision or release (s. 63B(7)(c));
(e) for the purpose of a drugs assessment which the suspect is required to attend by the police by virtue of the Drugs Act 2005, s. 9(2) (initial assessment) or s. 10(2) (follow-up assessment) (s. 63B(7)(ca));
(f) for the purposes of a prosecution under the Drugs Act 2005, s. 12(3) (for failure to attend or remain at an initial assessment) or s. 24(3) (for failure to attend or remain at a follow-up assessment) (s. 63B(7)(cb));
(g) for the purpose of ensuring that appropriate advice and treatment is made available to the person concerned (s. 63B(7)(d)).

ENTRY AND SEARCH UNDER WARRANT

D1.76 Powers of entry and search of premises, both under a warrant and without a warrant, are governed by a number of statutes, although the main general power of search under warrant is governed by the PACE 1984, part II. The PACE 1984, ss. 15 (safeguards) and 16 (execution of warrants), apply to warrants issued to a constable under any enactment. For examples of other powers of search under warrant, see PACE Code B, Note for Guidance 2A. Search of premises and seizure is also governed by Code B which applies to search of premises for the purposes and under the powers set out in Code B, para 2.3 (see **appendix 2**). For the powers of designated civilian investigating officers to apply for a warrant under the PACE 1984, s. 8, and the application of other provisions governing search and seizure to such civilians, see the Police Reform Act 2002, sch. 4, part 2. For the powers to search for and seize the proceeds of crime, see **D8** ***et seq.***

All statutory powers of search enacted before the PACE 1984 ceased to have effect in relation to the authorisation of searches for items subject to legal professional privilege, excluded material and special procedure material consisting of documents or other records (PACE 1984, s. 9(2)). The TA 2000 makes separate provision for the search of premises in respect of terrorism (**B10.93**). For powers of search and entry in relation to serious fraud, see the CJA 1987, s. 2; those powers were comprehensively reviewed in *R (Energy Financing Team Ltd) v Bow Street Magistrates' Court* [2006] 1 WLR 1316.

Items Subject to Legal Privilege

D1.77 The term 'items subject to legal privilege' is defined in the PACE 1984, s. 10(1). It includes, of course, lawyer-client communications made in connection with the giving of legal advice to the client, but also includes: (a) communications between either of these or a representative and another person if it was in connection with or in contemplation of and for the purpose of legal proceedings; and (b) items enclosed with or referred to in any of these communications when such items are in the possession of a person entitled to possession of them. If such items are in the possession of a person not so entitled it would appear that the protection afforded by the PACE 1984 is lost. Material in the hands of a solicitor which is not subject to legal privilege is special procedure material (*Norwich Crown Court, ex parte Chethams* [1991] COD 271). However, in accordance with the common-law rule governing privilege (see **F9.36**), if any items are held with the intention of furthering a criminal purpose they are not to be regarded as items subject to legal privilege (s. 10(2): see also *R (Hallinan Blackburn Gittings & Nott (a firm)) v Crown Court at Middlesex Guildhall* [2005] 1 WLR 766).

Excluded Material

D1.78 'Excluded material' means the following material *if it is held in confidence* (PACE 1984, s. 11(1)):

(a) personal records acquired or created in a trade, business, profession or other occupation or for the purpose of any office, paid or unpaid;
(b) human tissue or tissue fluid taken for purposes of diagnosis or medical treatment;
(c) journalistic material consisting of documents or records.

Material of types (a) and (b) is held in confidence if there is an express or implied undertaking to that effect, or a statutory requirement to restrict disclosure or maintain secrecy (s. 11(2)). Material of type (c) will be held in confidence if it is held subject to such an undertaking, restriction or obligation and has been so held since it was first acquired or created for the purpose of journalism (s. 11(3)). It cannot acquire the status of excluded material at a later time just to avoid a search and seizure.

'Personal records' means records concerning an individual (living or dead) who can be identified from them, and relating to that person's physical or mental health, spiritual counselling, or counselling for his personal welfare by a voluntary organisation, or a person with responsibility for so doing, either by virtue of his office or occupation or on authority from a court to supervise that person (e.g., probation officers, members of the clergy) (s. 12). Hospital records of patients' admissions and discharges are excluded material because they relate to the physical or mental health of persons who could be identified from them (*Cardiff Crown Court, ex parte Kellam* (1993) *The Times*, 3 May 1993).

'Journalistic material' means material acquired or created for the purposes of journalism, but only if it is in the possession of a person who acquired it or created it for that purpose. That person will be deemed to have acquired it for that purpose if it was given to him with the intention that it be used for that purpose (s. 13).

Special Procedure Material

D1.79 'Special procedure material' means (PACE 1984, s. 14(1) and (2)):

(a) material, other than items subject to legal privilege and excluded material, acquired or created in a trade, business, profession or occupation, or for the purpose of any office paid or unpaid, where it is held in confidence subject to an express or implied undertaking to that effect or a statutory requirement to restrict disclosure or maintain secrecy; and
(b) 'journalistic material' other than that already falling within the meaning of excluded material.

Material acquired by an employee in the course of his employment, or by a company from an associated company, will be special procedure material only if it was so immediately before it was acquired (s. 14(3)); it cannot later be redesignated as confidential. Material created by an employee in the course of his employment, or by a company on behalf of an associated company, will be special procedure material only if it would have been had the employer or associated company created it (s. 14(4) and (5)).

Warrant Issued by a Justice of the Peace

D1.80 On application by a constable, a justice of the peace may issue a warrant to a constable to enter and search premises if the justice has reasonable grounds for believing: (a) that an indictable offence has been committed; and (b) that there is material on the premises (defined below) which is likely to be of substantial value (whether by itself or together with other material) to the investigation of the offence (PACE 1984, s. 8(1)) and is likely to be admissible in evidence at a trial for the offence (s. 8(4)). Such material must not consist of or include items subject to legal privilege, excluded material or special procedure material (s. 8(1)(d)).

Although warrants under s. 8 relate to premises rather than persons, an 'all premises warrant' may be issued in respect of all premises occupied or controlled by the person named in the application (see below). 'Premises' is defined for all purposes in the PACE 1984 as including any place and, in particular, includes:

(a) any vehicle, vessel, aircraft or hovercraft;
(b) any offshore installation within the meaning of the Mineral Workings (Offshore Installations) Act 1971, s. 1;
(c) any renewable energy installation within the meaning of the Energy Act 2004, part 2, chapter 2;
(d) any tent or movable structure (PACE 1984, s. 23).

D1.81 **All Premises and Specific Premises Warrants** Warrants fall into one of two categories. The first is a 'specific premises warrant' which permits search of one or more sets of premises specified in the application (PACE 1984, s. 8(1A)(a)). The second is an 'all premises warrant' which permits search of any premises occupied or controlled by a person specified in the application, including such sets of premises as are so specified (s. 8(1A)(b)). In addition to the conditions in s. 8(1) (see **D1.80**), before granting an 'all premises warrant' a justice of the peace must be satisfied that, because of the particulars of the indictable offence specified in s. 8(1)(a), there are reasonable grounds for believing that it is necessary to search premises occupied or controlled by the person in question which are not specified in the application in order to find material of substantial value to the investigation and that it is not reasonably practicable to specify in the application all the premises which he controls which might need to be searched (s. 8(1B)). Where an all premises warrant is issued, premises that are not specified in the warrant must not be entered or searched without the prior written authority of an officer of the rank of inspector who is not involved in the investigation (s. 16(3A)).

Either form of warrant may authorise multiple entries and searches of the premises if a justice of the peace is satisfied that it is necessary so to authorise in order to achieve the purpose for which he issues the warrant (s. 8(1C)). A warrant authorising multiple entries may authorise an unlimited number of entries or limit them to a maximum (s. 8(1D)), but any entry or search must be made within three months from the date of issue of the warrant (s. 16(3)). After the first entry and search under such a warrant, subsequent entries or searches may be conducted only with the prior written authority of an officer of the rank of inspector who is not involved in the investigation (s. 16(3B)).

D1.82 **Conditions for Issuing a Warrant** A constable may obtain access to excluded material or special procedure material for the purposes of a criminal investigation by making an application under the PACE 1984, sch. 1 (see **D1.88**). However, a magistrate is not barred from issuing a search warrant under s. 8(1) because there may be special procedure or excluded material on the premises; the issue of a warrant is barred only if the material falls into these categories and is or forms part of the subject-matter of such an application (*Chief Constable of Warwickshire Constabulary, ex parte Fitzpatrick* [1999] 1 WLR 564).

A warrant under s. 8(1) cannot be issued unless at least one of the conditions in s. 8(3) is satisfied:

(a) that it is not practicable to communicate with any person entitled to grant entry to the premises; or
(b) if it is, that it is not practicable to communicate with any person entitled to grant access to the evidence; or
(c) that entry to the premises will not be granted unless a warrant is produced; or
(d) that the purpose of a search may be frustrated or seriously prejudiced unless a constable arriving at the premises can secure immediate entry to them.

It is not a condition precedent to the issue of a magistrates' court warrant that other methods have been tried and failed or would be bound to fail, nor that no other statutory procedure for securing the material exists (*Billericay Justices, ex parte Frank Harris (Coaches) Ltd* [1991] Crim LR 472). Where there are grounds for seeking search warrants, the police are entitled to choose when to apply for them and when, within the time permitted by law, to execute them (*Ex parte Fitzpatrick*).

Powers on Executing a Warrant A constable may seize and retain anything for which a search has been authorised under a warrant issued under the PACE 1984, s. 8 (s. 8(2)). **D1.83**

Unless the statute explicitly so provides, a warrant to enter and search premises does not confer a power to search persons found therein (*Hepburn v Chief Constable of Thames Valley* (2002) *The Times*, 19 December 2002; *DPP v Meaden* [2004] 1 WLR 945). However, it is permissible to take reasonable and necessary steps to detain persons found therein in the course of execution of the warrant (*Connor v Chief Constable of Merseyside* [2006] EWCA Civ 1549).

Access to Excluded or Special Procedure Material

The PACE 1984, s. 9(1), enables access to be obtained to excluded material and special procedure material for the purposes of a criminal investigation if the procedures set out in sch. 1 to the Act are followed. Schedule 1 applies not only to police investigations but also to investigations of indictable offences by the Department of Trade and Industry. A constable may apply for an order or warrant to obtain special procedure material in connection with a DTI investigation (PACE 1984, s. 114A, and Police and Criminal Evidence Act (Department of Trade and Industry Investigations) Order 2002 (SI 2002 No. 2326)). **D1.84**

Access Conditions There are two sets of access conditions in the PACE 1984, sch. 1, one of which must be satisfied. The first set of access conditions (sch. 1, para. 2) requires that: **D1.85**

(a) There are reasonable grounds for believing that an indictable offence has been committed; that there is material which consists of special procedure material or includes special procedure material and does not include excluded material on premises specified in the application or on premises occupied or controlled by a person specified in the application (including all such premises on which there are reasonable grounds for believing that there is such material as it is reasonably practicable so to specify); and that the material is likely to be relevant evidence. Material is not relevant evidence simply because it could be used as the basis for cross-examination (*Norwich Crown Court, ex parte Chethams* [1991] COD 271).
(b) Other methods of obtaining the special procedure material have failed or have not been tried because it appeared they would be bound to fail. Thus if, e.g., a motion under the Bankers' Books Evidence Act 1879 (see **F8.27**) would be possible, it must be shown that such a motion was brought and failed or that the material could not have been secured by such a motion (*Crown Court at Lewes, ex parte Hill* (1991) 93 Cr App R 60). An application cannot however be impugned simply because some further and remote step to uncover evidence might possibly have been taken.
(c) It is in the public interest to produce or allow access to the material, having regard to the benefit to the investigation and the circumstances under which the person holds the material.

The second set of access conditions (sch. 1, para. 3) requires that there are reasonable grounds for believing that there is material which consists of or includes excluded or special procedure material:

(a) on such premises specified in the application; or
(b) on premises occupied or controlled by a person specified in the application (including such premises on which there are reasonable grounds for believing that there is such material as it is reasonably practicable so to specify),

Part D Procedure

in respect of which the issue of a warrant under an enactment other than sch. 1 would have been appropriate and available but for the repeal by s. 9(2) of all the provisions allowing warrants to be issued to search for this type of material.

D1.86 **Procedure** An application must be made to a circuit judge (extended to a High Court judge, recorder, or a district judge (magistrates' court) when the Courts Act 2003, sch. 4, para. 6 is brought into force). Before an order to produce or a search warrant is applied for, careful consideration must be given to what material it is hoped a search might reveal, and the application must also make it clear that the material sought relates to the crime under investigation (*Central Criminal Court, ex parte AJD Holdings* [1992] Crim LR 669). An order to produce special procedure material may be made even though some of the material is not of that description. This avoids making separate but necessarily sequential applications (*Preston Crown Court, ex parte McGrath* [1993] COD 103).

Notice of an application to make an order must be served on the person in possession of the material (sch. 1, para. 8). That person must not conceal, destroy, alter or dispose of the material without leave of a judge or written permission of a constable until the application is dismissed or abandoned, or he has complied with the order (para. 11). Failure to comply with an order is to be treated as a contempt of court (para. 15).

Bodies such as banks in respect of which such applications are made often let them go by default. It is thus particularly important that the judge be given adequate material to enable him to form a reliable judgement. This will include details of the charges, the dates covered by them, whether previous steps to secure the evidence have been tried and failed, and what the nature of the material is.

A suspect has no statutory right to be heard on an application for access, but the judge may in his discretion hear him where this appears likely to be helpful (*Crown Court at Lewes, ex parte Hill* (1991) 93 Cr App R 60).

D1.87 **The Order** If satisfied that one or other of the access conditions is fulfilled, the judge may make an order requiring the person in possession of the material to produce it to a constable for him to take away, or to give a constable access to it, within a specified period, normally seven days (PACE 1984, sch. 1, paras. 1 and 4). Once such an order has been made it cannot be rescinded; the only recourse is judicial review (*Liverpool Crown Court, ex parte Wimpey plc* [1991] Crim LR 635).

The approach which a judge should take towards applications is set out in *Crown Court at Lewes, ex parte Hill* (1991) 93 Cr App R 60 and *R (Bright) v Central Criminal Court* [2001] 1 WLR 662. The Divisional Court in *Ex parte Hill* stated that the Act provides a careful balance between the public interest in the effective investigation and prosecution of crime and the interests of citizens in protecting their personal and property rights. The circuit judge is entrusted with the primary duty of giving effect to that scheme. He must exercise his powers with great care and caution. He must be shown such material as is necessary to enable him to be satisfied before making the order, and he should be told anything which, to the knowledge of the applicant, might weigh against his making such an order (*Leeds Crown Court, ex parte Hill* [1991] COD 197; *Acton Crown Court, ex parte Layton* [1993] Crim LR 458). He should not allow the police to engage in a fishing expedition. Any order which he makes must be specific as to the material sought. In cases involving national security the judge must at least be presented with a properly drafted, careful summary. In particularly sensitive cases he may wish to adapt the procedure which applies to applications for public interest immunity to deal with the matter (*R (Bright) v Central Criminal Court*).

Even if the access conditions are made out, the judge may, in his discretion, refuse to grant the order. Such an exercise of discretion would no doubt be rare. Discretion, however, enables the judge to weigh fundamental principles and, e.g., may in a proper case lead to the conclusion that there would be disproportion between what might be gained to the investigation as against the stifling of public debate (*R (Bright) v Central Criminal Court* per Judge LJ, explaining *Northamptonshire Magistrates' Court, ex parte DPP* (1991) 93 Cr App R 396).

There seems to be doubt whether a judge is inhibited in making an order for production by reason of the fact that the person to whom it is addressed may incriminate himself. In most cases a person against whom an order is made will not be a suspect and the matter may not arise. Where it does, it may be that a simple order to produce does not lead to self-incrimination in any event. In *R (Bright)* there was a lively debate on the issue which, it would seem, cannot be treated as concluded. A production order may be made even though the material sought might incriminate a journalist (*R (Bright) v Central Criminal Court* per Kay and Gibbs JJ).

Where the material consists of information stored in any electronic form, the order is to produce material in a form in which it can be taken away and in which it is visible and legible or from which it can be produced in a visible and legible form. An order to give access is to be understood in the same sense (sch. 1, para. 5).

Where an order to produce requires the presentation or production of e-mails, which require the recipient of the order to modify or interfere with a telecommunications system (an offence under the RIPA 2000), the order 'trumps' the prohibition in the 2000 Act (*R (NTL Group Ltd) v Ipswich Crown Court* [2003] QB 131).

Search Warrant Issued by Judge

A judge may issue a warrant authorising a constable to enter and search premises if one or other of two conditions is satisfied (PACE 1984, sch. 1, para. 12). **D1.88**

The first condition is that he is satisfied that either set of access conditions (see **D1.85**) is fulfilled and that any of the following are also fulfilled (sch. 1, para. 14):

(a) that it is not practicable to communicate with a person entitled to grant entry to the premises;
(b) if it is, that it is not practicable to communicate with a person entitled to grant access to the material;
(c) that there is a statutory restriction on disclosure or obligation of secrecy and disclosure contained in any enactment, and disclosure would be in breach of the statute unless a warrant is issued ; or
(d) that service of notice of an application for an order would seriously prejudice the investigation.

The term 'practicable' bears a wider meaning than feasible or physically possible. The court may consider not only the available means of communication, but also all the circumstances, including the nature of the enquiries and the persons against whom they are directed. For example, the usual procedure where a solicitor's office is to be searched would be by order to produce, but a search warrant may be proper where the firm is under investigation (*Leeds Crown Court, ex parte Switalski* [1991] Crim LR 559; *Maidstone Crown Court, ex parte Waitt* [1988] Crim LR 384; *Central Criminal Court, ex parte Hutchinson* [1996] COD 14).

The second condition is that the second set of access conditions (see **D1.85**) is fulfilled and that there has been a failure to comply with an order under sch. 1, para. 4 (**D1.87**).

The approach which a judge must take towards an application for a search warrant is set out in *Crown Court at Lewes, ex parte Hill* (1991) 93 Cr App R 60 (see **D1.87**).

The judge may not issue an 'all premises warrant' (**D1.81**) unless he is satisfied that there are reasonable grounds for believing that it is necessary to search premises occupied or controlled by the person in question which are not specified in the application, as well as those which are, in order to find the material in question, and that it is not reasonably practicable to specify all the premises that he occupies or controls which might need to be searched (sch. 1, para. 12A).

In searching premises, a constable is entitled to impose reasonable obligations on persons found therein in order to make the search effective. He may, thus, require persons found in the premises to go to or remain in a particular part of the premises while the search is carried out (*DPP v Meaden* [2004] 1 WLR 945, and see **D1.83**).

A constable may seize and retain anything for which such a search has been authorised (sch. 1, para. 13).

Procedural Requirements and Safeguards

D1.89 Courts have consistently held that the issue of a search warrant is a very severe interference with individual liberty. It is a step which should be taken only after mature consideration of the facts and in some, doubtless exceptional instances, the judge should give reasons for his decision (*Southwark Crown Court and HM Customs and Excise, ex parte Sorsky Defries* [1996] Crim LR 195; and see Code B, para. 1.3).

All entries on and searches of premises under a warrant issued *under any enactment* are unlawful unless they comply with ss. 15 and 16 of the PACE 1984. Thus failure by a constable to produce a warrant and provide the occupier with a copy will render the resulting search unlawful and the police will be obliged to return any seized articles (*Chief Constable of Lancashire, ex parte Parker* [1993] QB 577). Assuming the warrant to be valid, the question in respect of any seizure made thereunder is whether the acts performed fell within the acts authorised by the warrant. A trivial excess of power in taking an object not authorised by the warrant will not vitiate the legality of a search (*Inland Revenue Commissioners, ex parte Rossminster* [1980] AC 952; *A-G of Jamaica v Williams* [1998] AC 351; *Chesterfield Justices, ex parte Bramley* [2000] QB 576).

The ideal remains that of a principled search (*Reynolds v Metropolitan Police Commissioner* [1985] QB 881). Thus, where constables are executing a warrant under s. 8 of the PACE 1984, they should ensure both that the material to be seized falls within the terms of the warrant and, because such a warrant is granted to search for material of evidential value, that there are reasonable grounds for believing it to be so and to be likely to be of substantial value in the investigation. While it may not be possible to specify with great precision the nature of the articles to be searched for, the police may not seize items found in the premises to be searched unless they fall within the stated offence or there are reasonable grounds for believing that they are likely to be of value in the investigation or to be evidence of the stated offence.

There is no absolute prohibition on seizing an item which is in fact subject to legal professional privilege provided that the police officer seizing the item did not have reasonable grounds for believing the item to be privileged (*Chesterfield Justices, ex parte Bramley*). If the warrant in question is a magistrates' warrant, the police must, in addition, satisfy themselves as far as possible that the material seized does not fall within the categories of special procedure, excluded, or legally privileged material. It may be that a constable may rely in assessing material for seizure upon information not before the magistrate when a search warrant was issued (*Chief Constable of Warwickshire Constabulary, ex parte Fitzpatrick* [1999] 1 WLR 564). On what may be seized by a constable lawfully in premises, see **D1.97**.

D1.90 **The Application** The PACE 1984, Code B, requires, *inter alia*, that before making an application the officer must take reasonable steps to check the accuracy of his information, that it is recent, and that it has not been provided maliciously or irresponsibly. It also prohibits any application being made on the basis of information provided anonymously unless corroboration has been sought (Code B, para. 3.1). The officer must make reasonable enquiries to ascertain information about the premises to be searched, the likely occupier and the articles concerned (Code B, paras. 3.2 and 3.3). If there is reason to believe that a search might have an adverse effect on community relations, the local police/community liaison officer must be consulted, unless the search is needed urgently in which case he must be consulted as soon as practicable after the search (Code B, para. 3.5). Furthermore, a constable must not, when applying for a warrant, state that the purposes of the search will be frustrated or prejudiced unless immediate access is granted where he does not believe this to be so. In particular no such statement can properly be made where the subject of the search has already demonstrated that he is prepared to co-operate in producing material. Police acting in conjunction with another agency must form their own opinion whether it is necessary to apply for a warrant (*Reading Justices, ex parte South West Meat Ltd* [1992] Crim LR 672).

No application for a search warrant or production order under the PACE 1984, sch. 1, may be made without the prior written authority of an officer of at least the rank of inspector, except in the case of urgency when an application to a justice of the peace may be authorised by the senior officer on duty (Code B, para. 3.4(a)). In the case of an application for a production order under the TA 2000, sch. 5, authorisation must be given by an officer of at least the rank of superintendent (Code B, para 3.4(b)).

A constable who applies for a warrant must state the ground on which he makes the application; the enactment under which the warrant would be issued; and, if the application is for a warrant authorising entry and search on more than one occasion, the ground on which he applies for such a warrant, and whether he seeks a warrant authorising an unlimited number of entries or (if not) the maximum number of entries desired (s. 15(2)(i) to (iii)).

An application for a warrant covering one or more sets of premises specified in the application must specify each set of premises which it is desired to enter and search (s. 15(2A)(a)). Under s. 15(2A)(b), an application for an all premises warrant (see **D1.81**) must specify (i) as many sets of premises which it is desired to enter and search as it is reasonably practicable to specify; (ii) the person who is in occupation or control of those premises and any other premises which it is desired to enter and search; (iii) why it is necessary to search more premises than those specified in sub-para. (i); and (iv) why it is not reasonably practicable to specify all the premises which it is desired to enter and search. A constable who wishes to search only a part of premises divided into separate dwellings and the common parts of those premises must make this clear in the information when applying for the warrant (*South Western Magistrates' Court, ex parte Cofie* [1996] 1 WLR 885). The application must be made *ex parte* and supported by an information in writing (s. 15(3)). The constable must answer on oath any questions put to him by the justice of the peace or the judge at a hearing of an application (s. 15(4)).

If an application is refused, no further application may be made unless supported by additional grounds (Code B, para 3.8).

The Warrant A warrant can authorise entry on only one occasion unless it specifies that it authorises multiple entries (PACE 1984, s. 15(5)). If it authorises multiple entries, it must also specify whether the number of entries authorised is unlimited or limited to a specified maximum (s. 15(5A)). It must specify the name of the person applying for it, the date of issue, the Act under which it is issued, the premises to be searched, and, so far as is practicable, the identity of the articles or persons sought (s. 15(6)). Each set of premises to be searched must be specified or, in the case of an all premises warrant, the person who is in occupation or control of the premises to be searched together with any premises under his occupation or control which can be specified and are to be searched (s. 15(6)(a)(iv)). Two copies must be made of a specific premises warrant which specifies only one set of premises and does not **D1.91**

authorise multiple entries; and as many copies as are reasonably required may be made of any other kind of warrant (s. 15(7)).

D1.92 **Execution of the Warrant** Entry and search under a warrant must be at a reasonable hour unless it appears to the constable executing it that its purpose may otherwise be frustrated (PACE 1984, s. 16(5)). It must carried out within three months from the date of its issue (s. 16(3)). A warrant may be executed by any constable and may authorise persons to accompany him (s. 16(2)). A person so authorised has the same powers as the constable whom he accompanies in respect of the execution of the warrant and the seizure of anything to which it relates (s. 16(2A)). Such a person may, however, exercise those powers only when in the company of and under the supervision of a constable (s. 16(2B)). It permits the police, when executing a warrant to search under the Taxes Management Act 1970, s. 20C, to take with them a lawyer for the purpose of determining whether any of the documents found during the search are subject to legal professional privilege (*Chesterfield Justices, ex parte Bramley* [2000] QB 576; *Middlesex Guildhall Crown Court, ex parte Tamosius & Partners* [2000] 1 WLR 453). Civilians designated as investigating officers under the Police Reform Act 2002 have certain powers to execute warrants (see sch. 4 of that Act).

When acting with another body, it is the police that are responsible for the execution of the warrant. The number of other persons who accompany the police should be limited. The fundamental principle is that the police must not delegate their powers in such a way as to occupy a role ancillary to that of the other agency (*Reading Justices, ex parte South West Meat Ltd* [1992] Crim LR 672).

Where the occupier of premises is present, the constable must identify himself and, if not in uniform, produce his identity (warrant) card, produce the search warrant and supply a copy to the occupier (PACE 1984, s. 16(5)). If the occupier is not present, the constable must do these things for the person who appears to be in charge of the premises (s. 16(6)). If there is no person present who appears to be in charge, a copy of the warrant must be left in a prominent place on the premises (s. 16(7)).

The search may be conducted only to the extent required for the purpose for which it was issued (s. 16(8)). An executed warrant must be endorsed with information about whether the articles or persons sought were found, and whether any other articles were seized. Unless the warrant is a specific premises warrant specifying one set of premises only, the constable must endorse separately in respect of each set of premises entered and searched (s. 16(9)).

A warrant must be returned to the appropriate officer in the magistrates' court or other court that issued it when it has been executed or, in the case of a specific premises warrant which has not been executed, an all premises warrant or any warrant authorising multiple entries, upon the expiry of three months or sooner (s. 16(10) and (10A)). Returned warrants are to be retained by those persons for 12 months (s. 16(11)). This is so that the occupier of the premises to which the warrant related may exercise his right under s. 16(12) to inspect the warrant.

ENTRY AND SEARCH WITHOUT WARRANT

D1.93 A search of premises is always permissible with the consent of a person entitled to grant entry, although consent should be obtained in writing (Code B, sect. 5). Police constables have powers of entry and search under the PACE 1984, ss. 17, 18 and 32, and also under a variety of other statutes (see Code B, Note for Guidance 2B, for examples: see **appendix** 2). The police also have common-law powers in respect of breach of the peace (**D1.20**). Designated civilian investigating officers also have certain powers of entry and search without a warrant (Police Reform Act 2002, s. 38(9) and sch. 4). Code B applies to searches under the PACE

1984, ss. 17, 18 and 32 and to most other searches by police for the purposes of investigation of an alleged offence, whether with or without consent (see Code B, para. 2.3).

Entry for the Purposes of Arrest etc.

The PACE 1984, s. 17(1), empowers a constable to enter and search any premises (for definition, see **D1. 80**): **D1.94**

(a) to execute a warrant of arrest issued in connection with or arising out of criminal proceedings, or a warrant of commitment issued under the MCA 1980, s. 76 (s. 17(1)(a));
(b) to arrest a person for an indictable offence (s. 17(1)(b));
(c) to arrest a person for an offence under the Public Order Act 1936, s. 1 (prohibition of uniforms in connection with political objects) or the Public Order Act 1986, s. 4 (fear or provocation of violence); the RTA 1988, s. 4 (driving etc. when under the influence of drink or drugs) or s. 163 (failure to stop when required to do so by a constable in uniform); the Transport and Works Act 1992, s. 27 (offences involving drink or drugs); for an offence to which the Animals Health Act 1981, s. 61, applies; or an offence under the Animal Welfare Act 2006, ss. 4, 5, 6(1) and (2), 7 and 8(1) and (2) (s. 17(1)(c) and (caa));
(d) provided he is in uniform, to arrest a person for an offence under any enactment contained in the Criminal Law Act 1977, ss. 6 to 8 or 10 (offences relating to entering and remaining on property), or the CJPOA 1994, s. 76 (failure to comply with an interim possession order) (s. 17(1)(c) and (3));
(e) to arrest a child or young person who has been remanded or committed to local authority accommodation under the CYPA 1969, s. 23(1) (s. 17(1)(ca));
(f) to recapture a person who is, or who is deemed to be, unlawfully at large while liable to be detained in a prison, remand centre, young offender institution, or secure training centre, or in pursuance of the PCC(S)A 2000, s. 92 (dealing with children and young persons guilty of grave crimes), or to recapture a person who is unlawfully at large and whom he is pursuing (s 17(1)(cb) and (d));
(g) to save life or limb or prevent serious damage to property (s. 17(1)(e)).

When entering premises to search for a person (except for the purpose of saving life or preventing property damage), the constable must have reasonable grounds for believing that the person he is seeking is on the premises (s. 17(2)(a)). A constable may enter any dwelling in which he has reasonable grounds for believing the suspect may be, and, where the premises consist of two or more dwellings, he may enter any parts of the premises used in common by the occupiers (s. 17(2)(b)).

If a constable has power to arrest a person under an extradition arrest power, he may enter and search any premises for the purposes of exercising the power of arrest if he has reasonable grounds for believing that the person is on the premises (Extradition Act 2003, s. 161(2)). In this case, the relevant Code of Practice is the Extradition Act Code B (see **D1.23**).

Force may be used to enter premises where it is necessary to do so. Where the occupier of the premises is present and can be spoken to, forcible entry will not be justified unless the constable explains by what right and for what purpose he seeks to enter (*Lineham v DPP* [2000] Crim LR 861). That reason must be lawful: a wish to talk to a suspect cannot, e.g., be elided into a wish to arrest a suspect. There is an exception to the duty above where the circumstances are such as to make it impossible, impracticable or unnecessary to give such an explanation to the occupier (*O'Loughlin v Chief Constable of Essex* [1998] 1 WLR 374).

Any search made must be restricted to that which is reasonably required to achieve the object of the search (s. 17(4)).

Other than the power of entry to deal with or prevent a breach of the peace, all common-law powers of a constable to enter premises without a warrant were abolished by the PACE 1984, s. 17(5). A constable does not have the power to enter premises to carry out an investigation as to whether a further breach of the peace would occur (*Friswell v Chief Constable of Essex Police* [2004] EWHC 3009 (QB)). The power of a constable under s. 17(1)(d) to enter and search premises to recapture a person who is unlawfully at large and whom he is pursuing extends to entry to retake a mental patient unlawfully at large provided that such a patient is liable to be retaken and returned to a hospital and provided that the pursuit of such person is almost contemporaneous with the entry to the premises, a term which is somewhat wider than 'hot pursuit'. Where the element of contemporaneity cannot be satisfied, but the situation is one of real emergency, the police could enter the premises under their common-law powers relating to breach of the peace which were specifically preserved by s. 17(6) (*D'Souza v DPP* (1993) 96 Cr App R 278).

Entry and Search on Arrest

D1.95 Where a person is arrested for an indictable offence, a constable may enter and search any premises (for definition, see **D1.80**) where the person was at the time of or immediately before the arrest, for evidence relating to the offence for which he was arrested (PACE 1984, s. 32(2)(b)). Note that unlike the power of personal search under s. 32(2)(a) (**D1.65**), the person must have been arrested for an indictable offence. Where the premises consist of two or more dwellings, the power is confined to the dwelling where the arrest took place, or where the person arrested was immediately before arrest, and to common areas (s. 32(7)). The power extends to the search of vehicles and, in the case of ticket touting (see **B11.145**), extends to the search of any vehicle which the constable has reasonable grounds for believing was being used for any purpose connected with the offence. Unlike the power under the PACE 1984, s. 18, the power under s. 32 applies to premises irrespective of whether the person arrested owns, occupies or controls them. However, it does not extend to the search of premises belonging to the arrested person's friends and associates at which the person was not arrested even though it may be suspected that incriminating items are to be found there (*R (Hewitson) v Chief Constable of Dorset Police* (2004) *The Times*, 6 January 2004).

Entry and search is limited to premises that the person was in at the time of the arrest or 'immediately before' the arrest. In contrast to the power under s. 18, s. 32 is an immediate power and it is not permissible for the police to return to premises to search them several hours after the arrest (*Badham* [1987] Crim LR 202). In *Hewitson* it was indicated that a gap of two hours and ten minutes was too long. Of course, in such circumstances a search may, but will not necessarily, be available under s. 18.

The power of entry and search is available only if the constable has reasonable grounds for believing that there is evidence for which a search is permitted (s. 32(6)). Search is permitted only to the extent that is reasonably required for the purpose of discovering any such thing (s. 32(3)). Whether police entered for that purpose is a question of fact (*Beckford* (1991) 94 Cr App R 43). For an example of a search which would clearly be unlawful today, see *Jeffrey v Black* [1978] QB 490.

Powers of seizure are governed by the PACE 1984, s. 19 (see **D1.97**).

Entry and Search after Arrest

D1.96 Where a person is arrested for an indictable offence, a constable may enter and search any premises (for definition, see **D1.80**) occupied or controlled by that person provided that the constable has reasonable grounds for suspecting that there is on the premises evidence (other than items subject to legal privilege) relating to that offence or to some other indictable offence which is connected with or similar to that offence (PACE 1984, s. 18(1)). It would be possible, provided the conditions are satisfied, for a search to be conducted under both s. 18

and s. 32. For example, where a person is arrested at the house of an acquaintance, that house could be searched under s. 32 and his own house searched under s. 18.

The premises must as a fact, or perhaps as a matter of mixed fact and law, be occupied or controlled by the person under arrest. A senior officer cannot make lawful that which is unlawful simply by granting his authority (*Krohn v DPP* [1997] COD 345). There is no similar provision to PACE 1984, s. 32(7) (see **D1.95**), regarding premises consisting of two or more separate dwellings, although it is submitted that the same principles would apply.

Generally, entry and search under s. 18 is permissible only if it is authorised in writing in advance by an officer of at least the rank of inspector (s. 18(4)). However, a constable can enter and search without such authorisation and before the person is taken to a police station or released on bail under s. 30A (**D1.12**) if the presence of the person at a place other than a police station is necessary for the effective investigation of the offence (s. 18(5) and (5A)). In such a case, the constable must inform an officer of at least the rank of inspector as soon as practicable (s. 18(6)). An officer who authorises or is informed under s. 18(6) of such a search must make a written record of the grounds for the search and the nature of the evidence sought (s. 18(7)). If the person in occupation or control of the premises at the time of the search is in police detention at the time the record is to be made, it must be made a part of his custody record (s. 18(8)).

While the authorisation requirements of s. 18 are mandatory, a failure to comply with them fully (as by not specifying precisely the grounds of the search and the property to be searched for) will not necessarily render the search unlawful. While the section is to be obeyed, the court will, in determining the consequences of any breach, have regard to whether the failure to record prejudiced the person arrested (*Krohn*). As with entry to arrest, it is submitted that a constable must first demand entry (where this is practicable) before resorting to force (see **D1.94**).

The constable may seize and retain anything for which he may search (s. 18(2)). The scope of the search must be restricted to that which is reasonably required for the purpose of discovering such evidence (s. 18(3)).

Where a constable has entered premises in order to arrest under an extradition arrest power (**D1.23**), he may seize and retain anything on the premises that he has reasonable grounds for believing has been obtained in consequence of the commission of an offence, or is evidence in relation to an offence, and that it is necessary to seize it in order to prevent it being concealed, lost, damaged, altered or destroyed (Extradition Act 2003, s. 161(4)). In this case, the relevant code of practice is the Extradition Act Code B (see **D1.23**).

SEIZURE OF, ACCESS TO AND RETENTION OF MATERIALS

Powers of Seizure

Where a constable executes a warrant under the PACE 1984, s. 8 or sch. 1, he has specific powers to seize and retain anything for which the search has been authorised (s. 8(2) and sch. 1, paras. 4 and 13). Similarly, where a search of premises is conducted under s. 18, or a search of the person under s. 32(1) or s. 32(2)(a) (but not of premises under s. 32(2)(b)), a constable has specific powers to seize and retain materials (ss. 18(2), and 32(8) and (9)). In addition to specific powers of seizure and retention, a constable who is lawfully on any premises (see **D1.80** for definition) has power: **D1.97**

(a) to seize anything which is on the premises if he has reasonable grounds to believe that it has been obtained in consequence of the commission of an offence, or that it is evidence in relation to an offence, and that it is necessary to seize it in order to prevent it being concealed, lost, altered or destroyed (PACE 1984, s. 19(2) and (3));

(b) where he has similar reasonable grounds, to require that information which is stored in any electronic form and is accessible from the premises be produced in a form in which it can be taken away and which is in a visible and legible form or in a form (such as a disk) from which a visible and legible version can be produced (s. 19(4)) — this power is in addition to any power otherwise conferred (s. 19(5)), including common-law powers (*Cowan v Condon* [2000] 1 WLR 254).

The power under s. 19(2) and (3) to seize anything 'which is on the premises' includes the premises themselves if they are readily moveable, e.g., a car or caravan (*Cowan v Condon*).

The power to require any information stored in electronic form and which is accessible from the premises to be produced in a form in which it can be taken away etc. is specifically extended to powers of seizure under any enactment contained in an Act passed before or after the PACE 1984, and under the PACE 1984, ss. 8 and 18 and sch. 1, para. 13 (s. 20).

The power under s. 19 is exercisable whether the constable is lawfully on premises by consent or as a result of a statutory or common-law power, and is not limited to indictable offences.

For powers to seize and retain the proceeds of crime, see **D8**.

Seizure of Legally Privileged Material

D1.98 No power to seize conferred under any statute applies to items which the constable has reasonable grounds for believing to be subject to legal privilege (PACE 1984, s. 19(6)). However, this must now be interpreted by reference to the CJPA 2001, s. 50. In *Chesterfield Justices, ex parte Bramley* [2000] QB 576, it was held that the police could not lawfully seize material that included items covered by legal privilege in order to sift and sort them elsewhere. This led to the enactment of the CJPA 2001, s. 50, which enables a person who is lawfully on premises and to whom a power of seizure listed in the CJPA 2001, sch 1, part 1 applies, to seize the whole or part of a suspect item so as to remove it from the premises for the purpose of determining whether it falls within the power. It is a condition of exercise of the power that the determination cannot be reasonably practicably determined on the premises (s. 50(1)). Where the seizable property cannot reasonably practicably be separated from something else in which it is comprised, both the article and that from which it cannot be separated may be seized (s. 50(2)). The factors to be considered in determining reasonable practicability are set out in s. 50(3) and include length of time, numbers of persons needed, damage to property from separation, the apparatus necessary and prejudice to the use of separated property. The powers of seizure referred to in the CJPA 2001, sch. 1, are remarkably comprehensive and include powers of seizure under the PACE 1984, parts II and III. They go beyond the normal range of police activities and include enforcement activities conducted by a wide range of other authorities. Note that Customs officers have the same powers in respect of the provisions concerning legally privileged material as police officers (s. 67).

The CJPA 2001, s. 51, contains similar powers in respect of seizure from the person. The powers to which s. 51 apply are set out in the CJPA 2001, sch. 1, part 2 (s. 51(5)). For guidance on seizure, retention and return of property seized under ss. 50 and 51, see Code B, paras. 7.7 to 7.17 (see **appendix 2**).

Provision is made under s. 52 for giving notice of the exercise of the powers under ss. 50 and 51. Examination and return of anything seized under ss. 50 and 51 is governed by s. 53. Essentially, the examination should be carried out as soon as possible, should be confined to the purpose of verification, and the property should be kept separate from other articles seized.

Specific provision is made in s. 54 for the return of articles seized under ss. 50 or 51 which attract legal privilege. The meaning of 'legal privilege' depends upon the statute in which the phrase is used. The definition in the PACE 1984, s. 10 (see **D1.77**), remains unaltered (see CJPA 2001, s. 65). If at any time after seizure it appears to the person having possession of the seized property that it is an item subject to legal privilege or has such an item comprised in it, that person is under a duty to return the property as soon as reasonably practicable after the seizure. This is subject to exception where the legally privileged item is comprised within property for which the person had power to search and which he is not required to return either under s. 54 or s. 55 (s. 55 concerns excluded and special procedure material). This is itself subject to the proviso that return is not required where separation is not reasonably practicable without prejudicing the use, for lawful purposes, of that part of the article (s. 54(1) and (2)). The power of retention under s. 56 does not authorise retention of anything that must be returned under s. 54 (s. 56(4)).

The CJPA 2001, s. 56, concerns property seized by any constable who is lawfully on premises or by 'relevant persons' (as to which see s. 56(4A) and (5), referring, e.g., to warrants under the Companies Act 1985) accompanying a constable, and to property seized by a constable carrying out a lawful search of any person. Retention of such property is authorised if there are reasonable grounds for believing that it is property obtained in consequence of the commission of an offence and that its retention is necessary to prevent it being concealed, lost, damaged, altered or destroyed (s. 56(2)). The power also extends to property that is believed to be evidence in relation to any offence where its retention is required for the same purposes (s. 56(3)). This is in addition to the powers of retention under the PACE 1984, s. 22 (see **D1.99**).

Powers to obtain hard copies of information stored in electronic form are powers of seizure (s. 60). It follows that the powers of retention etc. apply to such material.

Remedies and safeguards, including applications to the court for return of articles, are contained in s. 59.

Access to and Retention of Seized Property

In respect of seizures under any enactment, on the request of either the occupier of premises **D1.99** on which the property was seized or the person having custody or control of it immediately before seizure, the constable or accompanying person must provide a record of what was seized within a reasonable time of the request (PACE 1984, s. 21(1) and (2)). If requested by the person who had custody or control of the item immediately before it was seized, or by someone acting on his behalf, the officer in charge of the investigation must allow that person access to the item under the supervision of a constable (s. 21(3)). Similarly he must allow access for photographing or copying, or arrange for it to be photographed or copied and supply the photograph or copy to the person requesting it within a reasonable time (s. 21(4), (6) and (7)). A constable may also photograph or copy anything he has power to seize without such a request (s. 21(5)). The requests do not need to be acceded to if there are reasonable grounds to believe that it would prejudice any investigation, or any criminal proceedings resulting therefrom, to do so (s. 21(8)).

The common-law power of the police to preserve *exhibits* is well established (*Lushington, ex parte Otto* [1894] 1 QB 420). Anything seized or taken away by a constable or accompanying person under s. 19 or s. 20 may be retained as long as is necessary in all the circumstances (s. 22(1)). In particular, anything seized for the purposes of a criminal investigation may be retained for use as evidence at a trial, or forensic examination or further investigation, unless a photograph or copy would suffice, and where there are reasonable grounds for believing it has been obtained in consequence of the commission of an offence, anything may be retained in order to establish its lawful owner (s. 22(2) and (4)). In relation to the latter, the police may retain the property only for so long as that purpose continues (*Malone v Metropolitan Police Commissioner* [1980] QB 49; *Gough v Chief Constable of the West Midlands Police* [2004]

EWCA Civ 206; *Settelen v Commissioner of Police for the Metropolis* [2004] EWHC 2171 (Ch).

The police cannot retain items seized because they may be used to cause physical injury, or to damage property, or to interfere with evidence, or to assist in escape from lawful custody, when the person from whom they were seized is no longer in police detention or the custody of the court or has been released on bail (s. 22(3)).

It follows from these provisions that the only permitted use of seized articles is for the purpose of investigating and prosecuting crime, after which they must be returned to their true owner. Documents and information may be communicated to others for the purpose of investigation and prosecution, and may perhaps be disclosed to other public authorities. They may not be made available to private individuals for private purposes (*Marcel v Metropolitan Police Commissioner* [1992] Ch 225).

Section 22(5) declares that the provisions of s. 22 do not affect the power of a court to make an order in respect of property under the Police (Property) Act 1897, s. 1. Anyone claiming property seized by the police should be advised of this procedure where appropriate.

Code B, para. 8.1, requires that records be kept of all searches of premises and specifies the information that must be recorded. At each sub-divisional police station a search register must be kept in which all records of searches must be noted (Code B, para. 9.1).

POLICE BAIL BEFORE CHARGE

Powers to Grant Bail

D1.100 The police have a variety of powers and duties to grant bail to persons arrested for an offence but not charged. For the power to grant bail to an arrested person without taking them to a police station, see **D1.12**. The PACE 1984, s. 34(2), provides that, where a custody officer becomes aware, in relation to a person in police detention (see **D1.26** for definition), that grounds for detention have ceased to apply and the officer is not aware of any other grounds to justify detention, he must order the immediate release from custody of the detained person (unless it appears to the officer that the person was unlawfully at large when arrested: s. 34(4)). Such release must be without bail unless it appears to the custody officer that there is a need for further investigation of any matter in connection with which the person was detained at any time during the period of detention or that in respect of any such matter proceedings may be taken against him (or, if a juvenile, that he may be reprimanded or warned under the CDA 1998, s. 65), in which case the release may be on bail (s. 34(5)).

Where a person arrested either without warrant or under a warrant not endorsed for bail is taken before a custody officer under s. 37(1), and the officer determines that he does not have before him sufficient evidence to charge, the person must be released either without bail or on bail unless the officer has reasonable grounds for believing that detention is necessary for one or more of the specified grounds (s. 37(2), and see **D1.32**). If the officer determines that there is sufficient evidence to charge, the detainee must:

(a) be released without charge and on bail, or kept in police detention, for the purpose of enabling the DPP (in practice a Crown Prosecutor) to make a decision about charge;
(b) released without charge and on bail but not for that purpose;
(c) released without charge and without bail; or
(d) charged (s. 37(7)).

If the officer conducting a review of detention under s. 40 (see **D1.48**) concludes that detention can no longer be justified by reference to the conditions in s. 37, he must release the person with or without bail (s. 40(8)). Where a detained person has not been charged at the expiry of 24 hours after the relevant time, he must be released with or without bail unless further detention is authorised under ss. 42 or 43 (s. 41(7)). A similar provision applies at the expiry of the 36-hour time-limit (s. 42(10)), or where an application for a warrant or extension of a warrant of further detention is refused (unless the 36 hours or the existing warrant has not expired (s. 43(15) and (16) and s. 44(7) and (8)), or where a warrant expires (s. 43(18)). There is no similar provision where an extended warrant expires, but it is submitted that the same principles must apply.

The PACE 1984 imposes no limit on the period for which bail can be granted, and it would seem that a court would only be willing to intervene in exceptional circumstances (*R (C) v Chief Constable of A* [2006] EWHC 2352 (Admin)).

Powers to Impose Conditions

A release on bail under the PACE 1984, part IV (which includes all of the powers to grant bail mentioned in **D1.100** except for bail granted under s. 30A), is deemed to be a release on bail in accordance with the Bail Act 1976, ss. 3, 3A, 5 and 5A, as those sections apply to bail granted by a constable. As a result of amendments to the PACE 1984 by the Police and Justice Act 2006, s. 10 and sch. 6, which came into force on 1 April 2007, the custody officer has power to impose conditions where a person is granted bail under the PACE 1984, s. 37. The officer can impose such conditions as appear necessary for the purpose of securing that the person surrender to custody, does not commit an offence on bail, does not interfere with witnesses or otherwise obstruct the course of justice, and/or for his own protection (or where the person is under 17 years, for his own welfare or in his own interests) (PACE 1984, s. 47(1A), and Bail Act 1976, ss. 3(6) and 3A(5)). Any condition may be imposed other than a condition that the person reside in a bail hostel, make himself available for the purposes of a court report, or attend an interview with a lawyer (Bail Act 1976, s. 3A(2)). It has been held in relation to a court's power to impose bail conditions that in considering whether and what conditions to impose, the court must perceive a real and not merely fanciful risk of the relevant outcome (*Mansfield Justices, ex parte Sharkey* [1985] QB 613), and it is submitted that the same principle must apply to a decision by a police officer. **D1.101**

A person who has been made subject to bail conditions may apply to the same or another custody officer serving at the same station for the conditions to be varied, and in doing so the officer may impose conditions or more onerous conditions (BA 1976, s. 3A(4)). The person may, alternatively or in addition, apply to a magistrates' court for variation, and again the court may impose conditions or more onerous conditions (PACE 1984, s. 47(1D) and (1E)).

Enforcement

A person who has been released on bail under the PACE 1984, part IV, may be rearrested if new evidence justifying a further arrest comes to light after his release (PACE 1984, s. 47(2) and see **D1.43**). Where a person has been released on conditional bail, he may be arrested by a constable having reasonable grounds for suspecting that he has broken any of the conditions (s. 46A(1A)). Further, a person granted bail to return to a police station (whether conditional or not) is under a duty to do so, and may be arrested if he fails to attend the police station at the appointed time (s. 46A(1)). He must then be taken to the police station at which he was required to surrender as soon as practicable (s. 46A(1A)), and he is treated as having been arrested for an offence for the purposes of ss. 30 (duty to take arrested person to a police station) and 31 (arrest for further offence) (s. 46A(2) and (3)). If the person had been released under s. 37(7)(a) and the Crown Prosecutor has not made a charge decision under the PACE 1984, s. 37B, the custody officer may either charge him or release him on bail again (s. 37C(2) and (3)). The duty to attend at the police station on the appointed date is subject to the power of a custody officer to give notice in writing to the person that his attendance is not required (s. 47(4)). **D1.102**

Where a person returns to the police station in accordance with his bail (or fails to surrender and is arrested and taken to the police station), the custody officer may authorise his further detention only if the grounds in s. 37(2) are satisfied (as a result of s. 34(7)). However, this does not apply where the person was released on bail under s. 37(7)(a), in which case he may be kept in police detention to enable a charge decision to be made in accordance with ss. 37B or 37C (s. 37D(4)). Normally, time spent in police detention before the initial release on bail counts for the purpose of calculating the maximum period of detention without charge, whether or not the person surrendered as required, or failed to surrender and was arrested under s. 46A(1) (s. 47(6)). However, this is not the case if he has been arrested under s. 47(2) — in that case the detention clock starts again (s. 47(7)).

INTERCEPTION OF COMMUNICATIONS AND SURVEILLANCE

D1.103 Interception of communications and surveillance is principally regulated by the RIPA 2000, although there are a number of other relevant statutes including the Police Act 1997 and the Intelligence Services Act 1994. A number of RIPA Codes of Practice have been issued by the Secretary of State under the RIPA 2000, s. 71, and they must be taken into account by any court insofar as they are relevant (RIPA 2000, s. 72). Further, a large number of regulations have been issued under the Act. The provisions are complex and only a brief summary is provided here. For more extensive treatment, reference should be made to a specialist text such as V Williams, *Surveillance and Intelligence Law Handbook* (OUP, 2006). A collection of the relevant legislation, regulations, Codes and relevant forms can be found at: http://security.homeoffice.gov.uk/ripa/.

Interception of Communications

D1.104 Chapter 1 of part I of the RIPA 2000 replaced the Interception of Communications Act 1985, and regulates the interception of communications in the course of their transmission by a public postal service or by a public or private telecommunications service. A conversation between two people face-to-face which is overheard by means of a listening device does not constitute a conversation in the course of a transmission (*Allsopp* [2005] EWCA Crim 703). Interception of communications without authorisation under the Act is an offence (s. 1(1) and (2) and see **B9.81**), and may also be a tort (s. 1(3)). Certain interceptions may be lawfully carried out without a warrant (ss. 3 and 4). Note in particular that interception of a communication that is sent by, or intended for, a person who has consented to the interception is lawful provided that it is authorised as directed surveillance (s. 3(2)). Other than interceptions under ss. 3 and 4, interception requires a warrant issued by the Secretary of State (s. 5). The grounds for issuing a warrant are set out in s. 5(2) and (3).

Substantial restrictions apply to the use of intercepted material. In general, no evidence shall be adduced, question asked, assertion or disclosure made, or other thing done in, for the purposes of, or in connection with legal proceedings which would tend to show that an offence under s. 1(1) or (2) was or may have been committed or that an application for an interception warrant had been made (s. 17, and see *A-G's Ref (No. 5 of 2002)* [2005] 1 AC 167)). This is subject to the exceptions under s. 18. The restrictions do not apply to evidence of interceptions conducted outside the jurisdiction (*P* [2001] 2 WLR 463). It is not contrary to s. 17 for evidence to be adduced as to whether an interception was of a public or private telecommunications system (*W* [2003] Crim LR 793).

Surveillance and Covert Human Intelligence Sources

D1.105 Part II of the RIPA 2000 regulates the use of intrusive and directed surveillance, and covert human intelligence sources. Use of these methods without authorisation does not amount to an offence, and there is no similar limitation on evidence to that found in s. 17. They are defined in s. 26, and it is an essential feature of each that the activity be 'covert' (defined in s. 26(9)). Surveillance is intrusive if it is carried out in relation to anything taking place on any residential premises or private vehicle, and involves the presence of an individual on the premises or vehicle or is carried out by means of a surveillance device (s. 26(3)). However, there are certain exceptions to this definition in s. 26(4) to (6). Surveillance is directed if it is undertaken for the purposes of a specific investigation or operation in such a manner as is likely to result in private information being obtained, and is otherwise than by way of an immediate response to events or circumstances the nature of which is that it would not be reasonably practicable for an authorisation to have been sought (s. 26(2)). In this way, surveillance by general CCTV cameras, or by an officer who in the course of a routine patrol decides to follow a suspicious looking person in the street, does not come within the definition, and therefore does not require authorisation under the Act. There is an overlap between the provisions governing the authorisation of intrusive surveillance under the RIPA 2000 and those in the Police Act 1997, part III, and the Intelligence Services Act 1994, s. 5, governing entry on to or interference with property. A covert human intelligence source is defined in the RIPA 2000, s. 26(7) and (8), and could include both an informant and a police officer acting undercover.

Authorisation of intrusive surveillance must be by a senior authorising officer (of the rank of chief constable or equivalent) or by the Secretary of State (s. 32(1)). The grounds for authorisation are set out in s. 32(2) to (4). Authorisation of directed surveillance or the use of a covert human intelligence sources must be by designated persons (of the rank of superintendent or equivalent) (ss. 28(1) and 29(1)). The grounds for authorisation are set out in s. 28(2) and (3), and s. 29(2) and (3) respectively. The person giving authorisation must believe that the operation is necessary (*Brett* [2005] EWCA Crim 983). It was held in *Grant* [2006] QB 60, that surveillance that involved deliberate interference with privileged communications between a person detained at a police station and his solicitor was 'categorically unlawful' notwithstanding the absence of prejudice and that it appeared to have been authorised under the RIPA 2000. However, in the absence of exceptional circumstances, the lawfulness of surveillance would normally be sufficiently demonstrated by the production of the surveillance commissioner's or authorising officer's signed approval and the defence would not normally be entitled to see the authorisation or the material on which it was based (*GS* [2005] EWCA Crim 887).

The RIPA 2000 does not apply to surveillance which is not covert or not conducted by the police (or other regulated agency). Evidence discovered by means of a camera erected by the accused's neighbours and the location of which was known to the accused could be used at the instance of the prosecution and would not be excluded under the PACE 1984, s. 78 (*Rosenberg* [2006] EWCA Crim 6).

INVESTIGATORY POWERS UNDER THE SERIOUS ORGANISED CRIME AND POLICE ACT 2005

Powers of SOCA Staff

The Director General of the SOCA has the power to designate a member of the SOCA staff **D1.106** as a person having the powers of a constable, Revenue and Customs officer, and/or an immigration officer (SOCPA 2005, ss. 43 to 45). Where a person is designated as having powers of a constable, he has all the common-law and statutory powers of a constable (s. 46(2) and (9)), and the PACE 1984 applies to them and the exercise of their powers by virtue of the Serious Organised Crime and Police Act 2005 (Applications and Modification of Certain Enactments to Designated Staff of SOCA) Order 2006 (SI 2006 No. 987), art. 3. For this purpose, the PACE 1984 is subject to the modifications set out in sch. 1 to the Order, the most important of which are:

(a) references to 'police officer' and 'officer' are normally to be treated as references to a 'designated person' under the SOCPA 2005;
(b) where authorisation is required for a search under the PACE 1984, s. 18, reference to an inspector is replaced by reference to a grade 3 officer;
(c) references to 'police station', e.g., in relation to fingerprinting (PACE 1984, s. 27), volunteers (s. 29), and fingerprints and samples (s. 63) are to be treated as references to a 'SOCA office';
(d) 'SOCA office' means a place for the time being occupied by the SOCA.

Powers Relating to Disclosure and Production

D1.107 Part 2 of the SOCPA 2005 confers powers on the DPP and the Director of Revenue and Customs Prosecutions, referred to as 'the Investigating Authority', in relation to the giving of disclosure notices (s. 60(1) and (5)). These may be delegated to a Crown Prosecutor or to a Revenue and Customs Prosecutor (s. 60(2) and (3)).

These powers apply to the offences specified in s. 61(1).

Serious Organised Crime and Police Act 2005, s. 61

(1) This Chapter applies to the following offences—
  (a) any offence listed in schedule 2 to the Proceeds of Crime Act 2002 (lifestyle offences: England and Wales);
  (b) any offence listed in schedule 4 to that Act (lifestyle offences: Scotland);
  (ba) any offence listed in schedule 5 to that Act (lifestyle offences: Northern Ireland);
  (c) any offence under sections 15 to 18 of the Terrorism Act 2000 (offences relating to fund-raising, money laundering etc.);
  (d) any offence under section 170 of the Customs and Excise Management Act 1979 (fraudulent evasion of duty) or section 72 of the Value Added Tax Act 1994 (offences relating to VAT) which is a qualifying offence;
  (e) any offence under section 17 of the Theft Act 1968 (false accounting), or section 17 of the Theft Act (Northern Ireland) 1969 (false accounting) or any offence at common law of cheating in relation to the public revenue, which is a qualifying offence;
  (f) any offence under section 1 of the Criminal Attempts Act 1981, or Article 3 of the Criminal Attempts and Conspiracy (Northern Ireland) Order 1983 or in Scotland at common law, of attempting to commit any offence in paragraph (c) or any offence in paragraph (d) or (e) which is a qualifying offence;
  (g) any offence under section 1 of the Criminal Law Act 1977, or Article 9 of the Criminal Attempts and Conspiracy (Northern Ireland) Order 1983 or in Scotland at common law, of conspiracy to commit any offence in paragraph (c) or any offence in paragraph (d) or (e) which is a qualifying offence;
  (h) in England and Wales—
    (i) any common law offence of bribery;
    (ii) any offence under section 1 of the Public Bodies Corrupt Practices Act 1889 (corruption in office);
    (iii) the first two offences under section 1 of the Prevention of Corruption Act 1906 (bribes obtained by or given to agents).

(2) For the purposes of subsection (1) an offence in paragraph (d) or (e) of that subsection is a qualifying offence if the Investigating Authority certifies that in his opinion—
  (a) in the case of an offence in paragraph (d) or an offence of cheating the public revenue, the offence involved or would have involved a loss, or potential loss, to the public revenue of an amount not less than £5,000;
  (b) in the case of an offence under section 17 of the Theft Act 1968 or section 17 of the Theft Act (Northern Ireland) 1969, the offence involved or would have involved a loss or gain, or potential loss or gain, of an amount not less than £5,000.

The list may be amended by the Secretary of State (s. 61(4)).

Disclosure, Production and Retention The Investigating Authority may issue a disclosure notice where it appears to him: (a) that there are reasonable grounds for suspecting that an offence specified in the SOCPA 2005, s. 61 has been committed; (b) that any person has information, whether documentary or not, which relates to a matter relevant to the investigation of the offence; and (c) that there are reasonable grounds for believing that information which may be provided by that person in compliance with a disclosure notice is likely to be of substantial value (whether or not by itself) to that investigation (s. 62(1)). Note that the information sought need not be directly probative of an offence nor need it be admissible in evidence. **D1.108**

A disclosure notice, which must be in writing and signed or countersigned by the Investigating Authority, may require the person to answer questions, provide information or produce a document, or documents of any particular description, relevant to the offence (s. 62(3) to (5)).

An authorised person may take copies of or extracts from any documents produced and may require the person producing them to provide an explanation for any of them (s. 62(2)). Documents so produced may be retained for so long as the Investigating Authority considers it necessary to retain them (rather than copies) (s. 62(3)). He may retain such documents if he has reasonable grounds for believing that any such documents may have to be produced for the purpose of legal proceedings and that they might otherwise be unavailable for such purposes (s. 62(3)). If a person required to produce documents does not do so, an authorised person may require him to state, to the best of his knowledge and belief, where they are (s. 63(5)).

Privilege Legal professional privilege is fully protected. A person may not be required to answer any privileged question, provide any privileged information, or produce any privileged document (SOCPA 2005, s. 64(1) to (3)), nor may he be required to produce any excluded material (s. 64(5) and PACE 1984, s. 11). Furthermore, a person may not be required to disclose any information or produce any document in respect of which he owes an obligation of confidence by virtue of carrying on any banking business unless the person to whom the obligation is owed consents to disclosure or production, or the requirement is made by or in accordance with a specific authorisation given by the Investigating Authority (s. 64(8) and (9)). It is thus apparent that, while legal professional privilege cannot be overridden by the Investigating Authority, banking secrecy may be so overridden. **D1.109**

Power to Enter, and to Seize Documents

Where a person has been required by a disclosure notice to produce documents but has not done so, or it is not practicable to give a disclosure notice requiring production, or the giving of such a notice might seriously prejudice the investigation into a relevant offence, a justice of the peace may issue a warrant at the instance of the Investigating Authority. Such an application must be made by way of information on oath (SOCPA 2005, s. 66(1) and (2)). The justice must be satisfied that the documents are on the premises specified. **D1.110**

The warrant authorises an appropriate person named in it, accompanied by such other persons as he deems necessary, to enter and search the specified premises using such reasonable force as is necessary, to take possession of documents appearing to be of a description specified in the information or to take any other steps which appear to be necessary for preserving or preventing interference with any such documents. Similar steps may be taken in respect of computer disks which appear to contain the information sought. Copies and extracts of documents may be taken. Any person in the premises may be required to provide an explanation of any such documents or information or to state where any such documents or information may be found and may be required to give the person executing the warrant such assistance as he may reasonably require for the taking of copies or extracts (s. 66(1) and (4)).

It would seem that the obligation to provide an explanation of documents or information must, consistent with the HRA 1998, not require the person directly to incriminate himself.

Provision is made to ensure that premises entered in the absence of the occupier are left secure (s. 66(6)).

As with documents or devices produced under notice, the Investigating Authority may retain the document or device for so long as the Authority considers it necessary to retain it rather than a copy in aid of the investigation (s. 66(7)). Retention of the document or device is also authorised where the Investigating Authority has reasonable grounds for believing that the document or device may have to be produced for the purposes of any legal proceedings and that it might otherwise be unavailable for those purposes (s. 66(8)). Note that that there is no 'reasonable cause to believe' requirement where retention is for the purposes of the investigation but that there is such a requirement where retention is in aid of the possible production of the document or device in legal proceedings.

The power to take possession of or make copies extends only to those items disclosure or production of which can be compelled under this statutory scheme (s. 66(9)).

Failure without reasonable cause to comply with any requirement imposed under ss. r. 62 or 63, is a summary offence punishable with imprisonment not exceeding three months and/or a fine not exceeding level 5 (s. 67(1) and (4)). Knowingly or recklessly making a false or misleading statement in a material particular is an either-way offence punishable on indictment with imprisonment for up to two years and/or an unlimited fine and punishable on summary conviction with six months and/or a fine not exceeding the statutory maximum (s. 67(2) and (5)). Wilful obstruction of any person in the exercise of any of the warrant powers conferred by s. 66 is a summary offence punishable in the same way as an offence under s. 67(1) (s. 67(3) and (4)).

Section D2 The Decision to Prosecute and Diversion

THE DECISION TO PROSECUTE

Significant changes have been made in recent years regarding responsibility for charging suspected offenders. In the past, primary responsibility for charging following a police investigation rested with the police. Once a person was charged with an offence, the prosecution was then taken over by the CPS. The broad thrust of a change in policy was set out in the White Paper *Justice for All* (Cm. 5563, July 2002, ch. 3) which indicated that, in future, primary responsibility for charging was to be transferred to the CPS, with prosecutors also having an enhanced role in advising the police on their investigations and on the gathering of evidence. The purpose was to encourage the police to have more focused investigations, to ensure that appropriate decisions were made regarding charge, and to reduce the number of cases discontinued by the CPS. This policy was given effect by amendments to the PACE 1984, s. 37, by the CJA 2003, part 4 (and further amendment by the Police and Justice Act 2006, s. 11), a revised Code for Crown Prosecutors (see **appendix** 4), and the DPP's *Guidance on Charging* (issued under the PACE 1984, s. 37A, available at http://www.cps.gov.uk/publications/directors_guidance/dpp_guidance.html). Note that in respect of Customs investigations the Director of the Revenue and Customs has issued similar guidance (available at http://www.rcpo.gov.uk/rcpo/guidance/chargingguidance.pdf). In police investigations the custody officer now has responsibility, under the PACE 1984, s. 37, to determine whether there is sufficient evidence to charge, but the charge decision itself is taken by a Crown Prosecutor, although in some circumstances the custody officer retains the power to charge. Crown Prosecutors are now often located in police stations to enable charge decisions to be taken relatively quickly, and where they are not so located, the police may contact a prosecutor under what is known as the CPS Direct scheme. **D2.1**

The Decision to Charge

If the custody officer determines that he has before him sufficient evidence to charge an arrested person with the offence for which he was arrested, the person must be (PACE 1984, s. 37(7)): **D2.2**

(a) released without charge and on bail, or kept in police detention, for the purpose of enabling the DPP (in practice, a Crown Prosecutor) to make a decision under s. 37B (whether there is sufficient evidence to charge and, if so, whether the person should be charged and what the charge should be, or whether he should be given a caution);
(b) released without charge and on bail but not for that purpose;
(c) released without charge and without bail; or
(d) charged.

This is subject to s. 41(7), which provides that at the expiry of a detention time-limit a person who has not been charged must be released either on bail or without, bail (see **D1.43** ***et seq.***). The decision as to how a person is to be dealt with under s. 37(7) is that of the custody officer (s. 37(8)), but in making the decision the custody officer must have regard to the DPP's *Guidance on Charging* (s. 37A(3)). Where the person is dealt with under s. 37(7)(a), an officer involved in the investigation must, as soon as practicable, send to the DPP (in practice a Crown Prosecutor) such information as is specified in the DPP's *Guidance* *on Charging* (s. 37B(1)). The extent of the information to be supplied depends upon a variety of factors such as whether the case is likely to proceed to the Crown Court and the likely plea (see *Guidance on Charging*, para. 7.2).

It would seem to follow from s. 37(7)(b) that, even if the custody officer determines that there is sufficient evidence to charge, the person may be released for the purpose of further investigations. This is supported by Code C, para. 11.6, which provides that the interview or further interview of a person need cease only where the officer in charge of the investigation is satisfied that all relevant questions have been asked, and he has taken into account any other available evidence. Subject to the detention time-limits, there appears to be no limit on the number of times that a person may be bailed under this provision, and no time-limit on the period of bail granted (see **D1.100**). It should be noted that there is some inconsistency between Code C, para. 11.6 and para. 16.1. Whilst the former appears to permit interviewing to continue beyond the point at which the officer in charge of the investigation is satisfied that there is sufficient evidence to provide a realistic prospect of conviction (if he is not satisfied that all relevant questions have been put or he has not had regard to other available evidence), para. 16.1 provides that (unless the person is being investigated in respect of a further offence in respect of which the test has not been satisfied), where the officer in charge of the investigation reasonably believes that there is sufficient evidence to provide a realistic prospect of conviction, he must, without delay, inform the custody officer who will be responsible for considering whether the person should be charged. If the police continue to detain a person without charge beyond the point at which the charge decision should have been made, that detention may be unlawful. Further, it may be argued that inferences should not be drawn from any 'silence' (see **F19.9**) since the CJPOA 1994, s. 34, does not permit inferences from 'silence' after charge.

The PACE 1984, s. 37(7)(c) permits the custody officer to release the person without charge even if he determines that there is sufficient evidence to charge, but it also enables the officer to divert the person from prosecution, such as by means of a caution (**D2.20**).

Where a person is arrested under the provisions of the CJA 2003, which allow a person to be retried after being acquitted of a serious offence which is a qualifying offence under sch. 5, and further prosecution is not precluded by s. 75(3) (see **D12.34** ***et seq.***), the PACE 1984, s. 37, is modified and, in particular, an officer of at least the rank of superintendent (who has not directly been involved in the investigation) must determine whether the evidence available or known to him is sufficient for the case to be referred to a prosecutor to consider whether consent should be sought for an application in respect of that person under the CJA 2003, s. 76 (CJA 2003, s. 87).

D2.3 **Sufficient Evidence to Charge** The phrase 'sufficient evidence to charge' is not defined in the PACE 1984. Code C, paras. 11.6 and 16.1, imply that it means sufficient evidence to provide a realistic prospect of conviction (which is the evidential part of the 'full code test' in the Code for Crown Prosecutors). However, the DPP's *Guidance on Charging*, para. 8.4, provides that, in determining whether there is sufficient evidence to charge, the custody officer must apply the 'threshold test'. The threshold test 'will require an overall assessment of whether in all the circumstances of the case there is at least a reasonable suspicion against the person of having committed an offence (in accordance with Article 5 of the European Convention on Human Rights) and that at that stage it is in the public interest to proceed' (*Guidance on Charging*, para 3.10). This is not dissimilar to the test of reasonable suspicion for an arrest (except for the requirement to apply a public interest test), and clearly provides a lower threshold than that in the 'full code test'. This approach was disapproved by the Divisional Court in *G v Chief Constable of West Yorkshire Police* [2006] EWHC 3485 (Admin), which held that the threshold test is not an appropriate test for determining whether there is sufficient evidence to charge, and that the PACE 1984, s. 37(7), should be interpreted as meaning that the custody officer should normally refer the case to a Crown

Prosecutor without attempting to determine whether there is sufficient evidence to charge. However, the *DPPs' Guidance on Charging* had not yet been changed. In circumstances where the custody officer is permitted under the *Guidance* to take the charge decision without referring the case to a Crown Prosecutor (see D2.5), in determining whether there is sufficient evidence to charge, the custody officer must apply the 'full code test' (D2.6).

Detention for More than One Offence Code C, para. 16.1, provides that where a person is detained in respect of more than one offence it is permissible to delay bringing him before the custody officer with a view to a decision being made under s. 37(7) until the officer in charge of the investigation reasonably believes that there is sufficient evidence to provide a realistic prospect of conviction in respect of all the offences in respect of which the person is being detained. This may be *ultra vires* since s. 37(7) is in mandatory terms and does not cater for such circumstances, but the point does not appear to have been authoritatively determined. **D2.4**

Responsibility for Making the Charge Decision

A Crown Prosecutor, rather than a custody officer, is responsible for making the decision to charge, and for specifying or drafting the charge(s), in all cases except those set out below. **D2.5**

(a) Either-way or summary-only offences where it appears to the custody officer that a guilty plea is likely and that the case is suitable for sentencing in a magistrates' court. However, in the following cases the charge decision must be made by a Crown Prosecutor even if the criteria for charge by a custody officer are otherwise fulfilled:

- offences requiring the consent of the A-G or the DPP;
- either-way offences that are triable only on indictment due to the surrounding circumstances of the commission of the offence or the previous convictions of the person;
- offences under the TA 2000, the A-tCSA 2001, the PTA 2005, or any other offence linked with terrorist activity;
- offences under the Explosive Substances Act 1883;
- offences under any of the Official Secrets Acts;
- offences involving any racial, religious or homophobic aggravation;
- offences classified as domestic violence;
- offences under the SOA 2003 committed by or upon persons under the age of 18 years;
- offences involving persistent young offenders, except those under (b) or (c) below;
- offences arising directly or indirectly out of activities associated with hunting wild mammals with dogs under the Hunting Act 2004;
- wounding or inflicting grievous bodily harm (OAPA 1861, s. 20);
- assault occasioning actual bodily harm (OAPA 1861, s. 47);
- violent disorder (POA 1986, s. 2);
- affray (POA 1986, s. 3);
- deception (TA 1968 and 1978);
- handling stolen goods (TA 1968, s. 22) (*Guidance on Charging*, para. 3.2 and annex A).

(b) Any offence under the Road Traffic Acts or any other offence arising from the presence of a motor vehicle, trailer, or pedal cycle on a road or other public place, other than in the following circumstances, where the charge decision must be made by a Crown Prosecutor:

- the circumstances have resulted in the death of any person;
- there is an allegation of dangerous driving;
- the allegation is one of driving whilst disqualified and there had been no admission in a PACE interview to both the driving and the disqualification;
- the statutory defence to being in charge of a motor vehicle (unfit through drink or drugs or excess alcohol) may be raised under RTA 1988, s. 4(3) or s. 5(2);
- there is an allegation of unlawful taking of a motor vehicle or the aggravated unlawful

taking of a motor vehicle (unless the case is suitable for disposal as an early guilty plea in a magistrates' court (*Guidance on Charging*, para. 3.3(i)).

(c) An offence of absconding (BA 1976), causing harassment, alarm or distress (POA 1986, s. 5), any offence under Town Police Clauses Act 1847, Metropolitan Police Act 1839, Vagrancy Act 1824, Street Offences Act 1959, CJA 1967, s. 91, Licensing Act 1872, s. 12, any offence under any bylaw and any summary offence punishable on conviction with three months' imprisonment or less, except where the DPP publishes other arrangements for the charging and prosecution of these offences (*Guidance on Charging*, para. 3.3(ii)).

(d) In any case where a Crown Prosecutor has responsibility for charging, but it is proposed to withhold bail or to impose bail conditions that may be imposed only by a court, and it is not possible to consult with a Crown Prosecutor before the expiry of the detention time-limit. In these circumstances the custody officer can make the charge decision, but only on the authority of an inspector. The case must then be referred to a Crown Prosecutor as soon as is practicable for authority to proceed with the prosecution (*Guidance on Charging*, para. 3.12).

The Tests for Deciding Whether to Charge

D2.6 In deciding whether to charge, a Crown Prosecutor or custody officer (where they are permitted to charge) must normally apply the 'full code test' set out in the Code for Crown Prosecutors (see **appendix** 4). The full code test has two stages: the evidential stage and the public interest stage.

D2.7 **The Evidential Stage** The evidential stage requires the prosecutor (or custody officer, as the case may be) to be satisfied that there is sufficient evidence to provide a realistic prospect of conviction in respect of each charge. He must consider what the defence case may be and how it is likely to affect the prosecution case. It is an objective test, meaning that a court properly directed in accordance with the law is more likely than not to convict an accused of the alleged offence. See further the Code for Crown Prosecutors, paras. 5.2 to 5.5 at **appendix** 4.

D2.8 **The Public Interest Stage** The public interest stage of the test must be applied only after the prosecutor (or custody officer, as the case may be) has determined that the evidential stage is satisfied. If the prosecutor (or custody officer) has determined that there is sufficient evidence to give a realistic prospect of conviction, a prosecution should normally proceed unless there are public interest factors that outweigh those in favour of prosecution, or it appears more appropriate in all the circumstances of the case to divert the person from prosecution (Code for Crown Prosecutors, para. 5.7). The factors to be taken into account are set out in the Code for Crown Prosecutors, paras. 5.9 to 5.13 (see **appendix** 4).

D2.9 **Selecting the Charges** Charges should be selected which reflect the seriousness and extent of the offending, give the court adequate powers to sentence and impose appropriate post-conviction orders, and enable the case to be presented in a clear and simple way (Code for Crown Prosecutors, para. 7.1). A prosecutor (or custody officer, as the case may be) should not proceed with more charges than are necessary just to encourage an accused to plead guilty to a few nor proceed with a more serious charge just to encourage an accused to plead guilty to a less serious one (Code for Crown Prosecutors, para. 7.2). In making a charge decision, consideration should be given to alternatives to prosecution (see **D2.20**).

D2.10 **Where the Full Code Test does not Apply** Where a custody officer is permitted to make a charge decision (D2.5), if the circumstances are such that bail following charge would not be appropriate (i.e. because one or more of the grounds under the PACE 1984, s. 38 apply), and the evidential material required to apply the full code test is not available, the officer can proceed to charge on the basis of the threshold test (*Guidance on Charging*, para. 3.11: but see D2.3).

Where the charge decision is to be taken by a Crown Prosecutor but the requisite information from the police is not available for the full code test to be applied (see **D2.6**), and it would not be appropriate to release the suspect on bail following charge, the charge decision may be made by reference to the threshold test (but see **D2.3**). In this case, at the time of making the decision the prosecutor must set a date for the full code test to be applied, and on subsequently receiving the relevant information must review the case against the full code test (*Guidance on Charging*, para. 3.9).

The Process of Charging

Where a detained person is charged, he must be cautioned in the terms set out in Code C, para. 16.2, unless the restrictions on drawing inferences apply (see **D1.55**), in which case he must be cautioned in the terms set out in Code C, annex C, para. 2. The person must be given a written notice showing particulars of the offence(s) for which he is charged, including the name of the officer in the case (or warrant number in cases where Code C, para. 2.6A or Code H, para. 2.8 apply), the police station and reference number for the case, and confirmation of the caution. As far as possible, the particulars of the charge must be stated in simple terms, but they must show the precise offence with which the person is charged (Code C, para. 16.3). **D2.11**

Cases Where Consent is Required

Offences Requiring Consent The institution of criminal proceedings for certain offences, or for offences in certain circumstances, requires the consent of either the A-G or the DPP. The most striking example where consent of the A-G is required is under the Law Reform (Year and a Day) Act 1996, where consent is required for commencing proceedings for certain forms of homicide where the victim died more than three years after the event causing death or where the accused has already been convicted in respect of the event which caused the death. Consent need not necessarily be in writing, but may be inferred from the material supplied to the prosecutor (*Jackson* [1997] Crim LR 293). **D2.12**

In general, the A-G's consent is required where issues of public policy, national security or relations with other countries may affect the decision whether to prosecute. An example is the Suppression of Terrorism Act 1978, s. 4(4) (see **A8.15**), by which he must sanction any proceedings in the UK for terrorist offences allegedly committed in a convention country. Other examples are offences of bribery under the Public Bodies Corrupt Practices Act 1889 (s. 4) or Prevention of Corruption Act 1906 (s. 2); offences under the Official Secrets Act 1911 (s. 8); offences of stirring up racial hatred etc. contrary to part III of the POA 1986 (s. 27); contempt of court under the strict liability rule (Contempt of Court Act 1981, s. 7); war crimes (War Crimes Act 1991, s. 1); and offences contrary to the Explosive Substances Act 1883 (s. 7).

Offences for which consent of the DPP is required include: offences of theft or criminal damage where the property in question belongs to the accused's spouse (Theft Act 1968, s. 30(4)); offences of assisting offenders and wasting police time (Criminal Law Act 1967, ss. 4(4) and 5(3)); aiding and abetting suicide (Suicide Act 1961, s. 2(4)); riot (POA 1986, s. 7(1)); and certain terrorism offences under the TA 2000 (TA 2000, s. 117).

CPS guidance *Consents to Prosecute*, appendix 1, contains a useful list of prosecutions requiring consent by the A-G or the DPP (available at www.cps.gov.uk/legal/section1/chapter_i.html).

The Form of Consent The A-G's consent to a prosecution is normally signified in writing, although there would appear to be no bar to its being given orally (per Lord Widgery CJ in *Cain* [1976] QB 496 at p. 502C). The consent need not specify the precise form of charges to which approval is given. Thus, in *Cain*, the Court of Appeal held that the Crown Court had had jurisdiction to try C for possessing explosives under suspicious circumstances contrary to **D2.13**

the Explosive Substances Act 1883, s. 4, even though the A-G's consent did not refer specifically to s. 4, but merely stated in general terms that he consented to the prosecution of C 'for an offence or offences contrary to the provisions of the [1883 Act]'. Although it is theoretically open to an accused to challenge the validity of an apparent consent on the basis that the A-G did not genuinely consider the propriety or otherwise of a prosecution, the initial presumption in the case of a written consent is that it would not have been issued unless the A-G had 'applied himself to his duty, considered the relevant facts, and reached a conclusion upon them' (ibid. at p. 502F).

By the Prosecution of Offences Act 1985, s. 1(7), the consent of the DPP to a prosecution may be given on his behalf by a Crown Prosecutor. However, CPS guidance states that the mere fact that a prosecution is being conducted by the CPS does not imply consent. A prosecutor must specifically consider the case and decide whether proceedings should be instituted or continued. Whilst legislation requiring consent normally states that consent is required in order that proceedings be instituted, proceedings are regarded as instituted for this purpose when an accused appears before a court for the purposes of committal and not earlier (*Whale* [1991] Crim LR 692). CPS guidance states that, in the case of indictable-only offences, consent should be sought and where available served before service of the case or, failing this, prior to the effective plea and directions hearing; in either-way cases, at mode of trial; and in summary offences, at the commencement of trial. In any event, failure to give prior consent does not take away the court's jurisdiction. The court must consider whether there was a 'real possibility that either the prosecution or the defence may suffer prejudice on account of the procedure failure', and if it concludes that there was not such a risk, it may proceed on the charge(s) (*D (Mark Gordon)* [2007] Crim LR 240).

See generally CPS guidance *Consents to Prosecute.*

D2.14 **Supplementary Provisions** Sections 25 and 26 of the Prosecution of Offences Act 1985 contain supplementary provisions relating to consents to prosecution. Section 25 provides that a requirement for consent shall not prevent the arrest of a suspect for the offence in question nor his initial remand (whether in custody or on bail). Section 26 provides that a document duly signed and purporting to be a consent to prosecution shall be admissible as prima facie evidence that consent has in fact been given.

Prosecution of Offences Act 1985, ss. 1(7), 25 and 26

1.—(7) Where any enactment (whenever passed)—
(a) prevents any step from being taken without the consent of the Director or without his consent or the consent of another; . . .
any consent given by . . . a Crown Prosecutor shall be treated, for the purposes of that enactment, as given by . . . the Director.

25.—(1) This section applies to any enactment which prohibits the institution or carrying on of proceedings for any offence except—
(a) with the consent (however expressed) of a Law Officer of the Crown or the Director; or
(b) where the proceedings are instituted or carried on by or on behalf of a Law Officer of the Crown or the Director;
and so applies whether or not there are other exceptions to the prohibition (and in particular whether or not the consent is an alternative to the consent of any other authority or person).
(2) An enactment to which this section applies—
(a) shall not prevent the arrest without warrant, or the issue or execution of a warrant for the arrest, of a person for any offence, or the remand in custody or on bail of a person charged with any offence; and
(b) shall be subject to any enactment concerning the apprehension or detention of children or young persons.

26. Any document purporting to be the consent of a Law Officer of the Crown, the Director or a Crown Prosecutor for, or to—
(a) the institution of any criminal proceedings; or
(b) the institution of criminal proceedings in any particular form;

and to be signed by a Law Officer of the Crown, the Director or, as the case may be, a Crown Prosecutor shall be admissible as prima facie evidence without further proof.

Time-limits

English law starts from the proposition that there is no restriction on the time which may elapse between the commission of an offence and the commencement of a prosecution for it. This applies even if the prosecutor has available to him evidence prima facie establishing the guilt of the accused for a lengthy period before he chooses to initiate proceedings. However, the staleness of the alleged offence is one discretionary factor which the police and the CPS ought to take into account when deciding whether a prosecution is justified (see Code for Crown Prosecutors, para. 5.10, at **appendix** 4). In addition, there are a number of specific statutory provisions prohibiting proceedings once a certain time has elapsed. These include: **D2.15**

(a) MCA 1980, s. 127(1) (see **D20.16**), which provides that a magistrates' court shall not try an information for a summary offence unless it was laid within six months of the offence;
(b) Trade Descriptions Act 1968, s. 19(1) (see **B6.95**), which provides that prosecutions for any indictable offence under the Act must be commenced within three years of the offence or one year from its discovery, whichever is the earlier.

If no time-limit is mentioned for an indictable offence, the general rule applies, and prosecutions may be commenced for it however long ago the relevant events occurred. It should be noted that the restriction in the MCA 1980, s. 127, applies only to trials of *summary* offences. There is no time-limit on the summary trial of either-way offences save in those exceptional cases where a trial on indictment would equally be time-barred (in which event the same limitation applies in the magistrates' court as would apply in the Crown Court: MCA 1980, s. 127(4)). For abuse of process resulting from delay, see **D3.58**.

The commencement of a prosecution is normally regarded as the charging of the accused at the police station or, where proceedings are not taken by way of charge, the laying of an information for the offence. A written information is treated as laid once it is delivered to the clerk's office of a magistrates' court with jurisdiction to issue process for the offence. Consequently, if that is done within any applicable time-limit, proceedings will be held to have been commenced timeously even if the information is not put before a justice or justices' clerk until a later date or, indeed, is never considered by him but is improperly dealt with by an assistant in the clerk's office acting in excess of his powers (see *Manchester Stipendiary Magistrate, ex parte Hill* [1983] 1 AC 328). See generally **D20.16** ***et seq.***

Personal Immunity From Prosecution

The main categories of personal immunity from prosecution are as follows. **D2.16**

(a) Age: children under ten are irrebuttably presumed to be incapable of crime.
(b) Sovereign and diplomatic immunity: the Queen, foreign sovereigns or heads of State, their families and their private servants are all immune from criminal jurisdiction (State Immunity Act 1978, s. 20). In addition, the Diplomatic Privileges Act 1964 gives immunity to diplomatic agents, members of the staff of a diplomatic mission and their families. For further details, see **A8.17**.

Whether the political head of government of a state forming part of a Federal State is entitled to diplomatic immunity is determined by certificate from the Secretary of State which is conclusive of the issue (*R (Alamieyeseigha) v CPS* [2005] EWHC 2704 (Admin), in which *Mellenger v New Brunswick Development Corporation* [1971] 1 WLR 604 was doubted).

Judicial Review of Decision to Prosecute

D2.17 **Decision to Prosecute** Generally, a decision to prosecute is not susceptible to judicial review since it may be challenged within the trial process itself, notably by an application to stay proceedings on the grounds of abuse of process. Arguments relating to abuse of process may and should be raised in the course of the criminal trial itself save in wholly exceptional circumstances (*R (Pepushi) v CPS* (2004) *The Times*, 21 May 2004). It thus appears that in the absence of dishonesty, *mala fides* or some exceptional circumstance, a decision to prosecute cannot be raised by way of judicial review (*DPP, ex parte Kebilene* [2000] 2 AC 326). For abuse of process see **D3.54** ***et seq.***

D2.18 **Decision Not to Prosecute** A decision not to prosecute is susceptible to judicial review because no other remedy is available (*DPP, ex parte Manning* [2001] QB 330), although the cases show that the power to review such a decision will only be exercised sparingly. In general, the DPP is not obliged to give reasons for his decision not to prosecute, and the selection of which charge to bring is for the prosecution. It was not, for example, an abuse of process for the prosecution to charge indecent assault where the time-limit for another, otherwise apt offence, has expired and where the delay in bringing the charge was not attributable to bad faith, fault or administrative delay (*J* [2003] 1 WLR 1590). Where, however, a person has died in custody and an inquest jury has returned a verdict of unlawful killing, implicating an identifiable person against whom there was prima facie evidence, a plausible explanation should be provided. Failure to provide a sufficient explanation may give rise to judicial review (*Manning*); *R (Dennis) v DPP* [2006] EWHC 3211 (Admin)).

A prosecution policy not to prosecute for certain classes of offence or in certain situations is, in principle, susceptible to judicial review (*Metropolitan Police Commissioner, ex parte Blackburn* [1968] 2 QB 118). Conversely, a refusal by the DPP to undertake not to prosecute an offence or a class of offences may not be reviewed. The executive may not suspend or dispense with the execution of the laws without Parliamentary consent. Exercise of the discretion not to prosecute must depend upon a consideration of the public interest in the light of offences already committed (*R (Pretty) v DPP* [2002] 1 AC 800).

When considering whether to issue a summons for a private prosecution after the CPS had discontinued a prosecution in respect of the same facts, magistrates should consider whether the allegation was of an offence known to law and, if so, whether the ingredients of the offence are prima facie present; whether a summons was time barred; whether the court had jurisdiction; whether the informant had the necessary authority to prosecute; and any other relevant facts. However, a private prosecutor is not bound by the full code test in the Code for Crown Prosecutors (*R (Charlson) v Guildford Magistrates' Court* [2006] 1 WLR 3494).

D2.19 **Decision to Caution, Reprimand or Warn** A decision to prosecute rather than caution is susceptible to judicial review, but there is a heavy burden on the applicant which may be insurmountable (*Chief Constable of Kent and CPS, ex parte GL* (1991) 93 Cr App R 416). The courts are reluctant to intervene in a decision unless breach of an authority's clear and settled policy is established (*Metropolitan Police Commissioner, ex parte Thompson* [1977] 1 WLR 1519; *R (Mondelly) v Metropolitan Police Commissioner* (2007) 171 JP 121). Judicial review of a decision to caution was successful in *R (Wyman) v Chief Constable of Hampshire Constabulary* [2006] EWHC 1904 (Admin), where it was held that there was no clear and reliable admission of the alleged offence. This will be particularly significant where a reprimand or warning has been given (see **D2.33**) since, unlike in the case of a caution, consent of the person reprimanded or warned is not required.

A private prosecution commenced after a police decision to caution for the same offence may be stayed as an abuse (*Jones v Whalley* [2007] 1 AC 63). The court indicated that if the complainant had grounds to impugn the decision to caution he could have applied for judicial review to quash the decision and, if successful, could then have commenced a private prosecution. The case of *Jones v Whalley* may be contrasted with *Hayter v L* [1998] 1 WLR 854, where two defendants who had been cautioned were thereafter privately prosecuted, and the prosecution was held by the Divisional Court not to be an abuse of process. The point of distinction between the two cases is that in *Hayter* the forms signed by the defendants indicated, in terms, that such cautions did not preclude the bringing of proceedings by an aggrieved party. In *Jones v Whalley*, the House of Lords declined to rule on the correctness of the decision in *Hayter*. In any event, it should be borne in mind that the DPP has power under the Prosecution of Offences Act 1985 to take over and terminate a private prosecution if it is in the public interest to do so.

ALTERNATIVES TO PROSECUTION

The are two main alternatives to prosecution. The first is the system of cautions (simple cautions and conditional cautions) for adults, along with the system of reprimands and warnings for juveniles. The second is fixed penalty notices. **D2.20**

Cautions

It was noted at D2.2 that even if there is sufficient evidence to charge, the decision whether to initiate a prosecution is discretionary. In deciding whether to prosecute, Crown Prosecutors and custody officers must consider alternatives such as a caution. Cautions, which are available in respect of adults but not those under 18 years (who may be reprimanded or warned: see D2.33), are of two types, the 'simple caution' and the 'conditional caution'. **D2.21**

Simple Cautions

Simple cautions, unlike conditional cautions, are a non-statutory disposal. Their use is governed by Home Office Circular 30/2005. Paragraph 6 of the Circular sets out the aims of the simple caution: **D2.22**

(a) to deal quickly and simply with less serious offences;
(b) to divert offenders, where appropriate, from appearing in the criminal courts; and
(c) to reduce the likelihood of reoffending.

Generally, the decision whether to impose a caution is for the police and not a Crown Prosecutor. However, a Crown Prosecutor has an independent duty to consider whether a caution rather than a charge is appropriate (Code for Crown Prosecutors, para. 8.3; DPP's *Guidance on Charging*, para. 9.5) Paragraph 5 of Home Office Circular 30/2005 suggests that the questions to consider in each case are whether a simple caution is appropriate to the offence and the offender and whether a simple caution is likely to be effective in the circumstances. The decision to issue a simple caution (as distinct from a conditional caution) must be made in accordance with the DPP's *Guidance on Charging* (Circular 30/2005, para. 3; see D2.1). One consequence of this is that indictable-only offences which meet the 'threshold test' (see **D2.3** *et seq.*) must be referred to a Crown Prosecutor.

Criteria for a Simple Caution In determining whether a simple caution is appropriate, the Home Office Circular 30/2005 provides that the following matters must be considered. **D2.23**

(a) Whether there is sufficient evidence of the suspect's guilt to meet the 'threshold test'.
(b) Whether the suspect made a clear and reliable admission of the offence (either verbally or in writing). An admission of the offence which is corroborated by some other evidence will be sufficient to provide a realistic prospect of conviction. This corroboration could be obtained from information in the crime report or obtained during the course of the investigation. A simple caution will not be appropriate where a person has not made a clear and reliable admission of the offence (for example, if intent is denied or there are doubts about their mental health or intellectual capacity, or where a statutory defence is

offered). Where the suspect makes a clear and unequivocal admission, it is acceptable to administer a formal caution (as an alternative to commencing a prosecution) even if the admission was not obtained in an interview complying with the PACE, Code C; however, as a matter of good practice, the police should ensure that a formal interview (complying with Code C) takes place (*Chief Constable of Lancashire Constabulary, ex parte Atkinson* (1998) 192 JP 275). In *R (Wyman) v Chief Constable of Hampshire Constabulary* [2006] EWHC 1904 (Admin), there was not a clear and reliable admission in respect of an offence under the SOA 2003, s. 3, as the comments made by the suspect in interview did not show that he admitted that the complainant did not consent to the touching nor that he did not reasonably believe that the complainant consented. Note that an admission should not be induced by the offer of a caution (*R (R) v Durham Constabulary* [2005] 1 WLR 1184).

(c) Whether it is in the public interest to use a simple caution as the appropriate means of disposal. The same principles are applied as in the case of the decision to prosecute (set out in the Code for Crown Prosecutors: see **appendix** 4) (Circular, para. 7).

If all these requirements are met, the officer must consider whether the seriousness of the offence makes it appropriate for disposal by a simple caution. In determining the seriousness of the offence, the officer has to consider whether there are any aggravating or mitigating factors involved, in accordance with a 'gravity factors matrix' available to the police on the Police National Computer. The Circular gives guidance on interpreting these criteria in relation to offences involving violence against the person, domestic violence, and harassment (Circular, paras. 45 to 50).

D2.24 **Consent of the Suspect** Although consent of the suspect is not identified as one of the criteria for determining whether to impose a caution, paras. 19 and 26 of Home Office Circular 30/2005 clearly indicate that consent is required.

D2.25 **Repeat Cautions** Home Office Circular 30/2005 provides that a person should not normally be cautioned more than once. However, a second or subsequent caution may be appropriate if:

(a) there has been a sufficient lapse of time to suggest that a previous caution has had a significant deterrent effect (the Circular suggests a period of two years or more);
(b) the current offence is trivial or unrelated to the offence for which the previous caution was imposed; or
(c) it is part of a mixed disposal.

The Circular gives as an example of a mixed disposal a case where a person who is arrested for being drunk and disorderly is found in possession of a set of keys which he admits he intended to use in order to steal from cars. A fixed penalty notice could be imposed for the drunk and disorderly offence, and a caution for the 'going equipped' offence (Circular, paras. 17 and 38).

If the suspect has previously received a reprimand or final warning as a juvenile, a caution should not normally be imposed for a subsequent offence unless at least two years has elapsed (Circular, para. 17).

D2.26 **The Decision to Caution** Other than in the case of an indictable-only offence (see D2.22), the decision to impose a caution should normally be referred to a sergeant or above (not necessarily a custody officer) who is not involved in the investigation for approval (Home Office Circular 30/2005, para. 21). The Circular provides that a decision to take no further action should not be made in circumstances where the conditions for imposing a caution are satisfied (para. 23).

D2.27 **Consequences of a Simple Caution** A simple caution should be administered by a suitably trained person to whom authority to administer cautions has been delegated. Unlike a conditional caution, no conditions can be attached, but the offender should be asked to sign a form, which sets out the offender's personal details and details of the offence, accepting the terms of the caution (Home Office Circular 30/2005, para. 26). Although a caution is not a criminal conviction, it will be placed on the person's record and may be cited to a court on a future occasion. Fingerprints and other identification data can be taken and retained, and in the case of a relevant sexual offence the person is placed on the sex offenders register for two years (see **E25.1** *et seq.*). A caution may prevent a further caution being imposed in the future (see **D2.25**).

Conditional Cautions

The 'conditional caution' is a statutory disposal for offenders who have attained the age of 18. The conditional caution is governed by the CJA 2003, part 3, and the Conditional Cautioning Code of Practice (issued under CJA 2003, s. 25: see Criminal Justice Act 2003 (Conditional Cautioning Code of Practice) Order 2004 (SI No. 1683)). Regard should also be had to the DPP's *Guidance on Conditional Cautioning*, issued under the PACE 1984, s. 37A, and available at www.cps.gov.uk/publications/directors_guidance/conditional_cautioning.html. Conditional cautions are not yet available in all police force areas, but should be available throughout England and Wales by March 2008. **D2.28**

A conditional caution is defined as 'a caution which is given in respect of an offence committed by the offender and which has conditions attached to it' (CJA 2003, s. 22(2)). The decision whether to impose a conditional caution is for a Crown Prosecutor, and the police have no power to impose a conditional caution.

Criteria for a Conditional Caution A conditional caution may be imposed on a person aged 18 years or over if each of the five requirements in the CJA 2003, s. 23, are satisfied (CJA 2003, s. 22(1)): **D2.29**

(a) The *authorised person* has evidence that the offender has committed an offence. Although the Conditional Cautioning Code does not say so directly, it would seem that this must be evidence that meets the threshold test (see **D2.3**).
(b) The *relevant prosecutor* decides there is sufficient evidence to charge and that a conditional caution should be given. The prosecutor must apply the full code evidential test and public interest test (see **D2.6** to **D2.8**). In relation to the latter, the prosecutor must be satisfied both that the public interest will be served by a conditional caution and that it would be served by a prosecution if a conditional caution proves impossible to impose, e.g., because the offender does not consent (Conditional Cautioning Code, para. 4.1(i)).
(c) The offender admits the offence. In contrast to the consent requirement for a simple caution, this must be an admission made under caution in interview, and the offender must also admit the offence to the authorised person at the time that the conditional caution is administered (Conditional Cautioning Code, para. 4.1(ii)). The Code provides that, in order to ensure that the offender gives informed consent, he should be advised of his right to legal advice at the point when he is asked to confirm that he committed the offence. It also states that, in order that the offer of a conditional caution should not act as an inducement to confess, the prospect of a conditional caution should not be mentioned to the suspect until he has made a clear and reliable admission (see *R (R) v Durham Constabulary* [2005] 1 WLR 1184).
(d) The *authorised person* explains the effects of the conditional caution to the offender and warns him that failure to comply with any of the conditions renders him liable to being prosecuted for the original offence. The offender must be told that the caution may be cited in future court proceedings, that certain types of potential employer may be informed and, in the case of a relevant sexual offence, that he will be placed on the sex offenders register. The offender must also be told of the consequences of

non-compliance, and that this will usually result in prosecution for the original offence (Conditional Cautioning Code, para. 4.1(iii)).

(e) The offender signs a document which contains details of the offence, an admission that he committed it, his consent to the conditional caution, and the conditions that are attached to the caution. The offender must be told, before he signs the form, that it will be admissible as evidence in court if he is subsequently prosecuted in the event of non-compliance (Conditional Cautioning Code, para. 4.1(iv)).

An *authorised person* is a constable, a designated civilian investigating officer or a person authorised for this purpose by the relevant prosecutor (s. 22(4)). A *relevant prosecutor* means the A-G, Director of the Serious Fraud Office, DPP, Secretary of State, the Director of Revenue and Customs prosecutions, or a person specified in an order made by the Secretary of State (s. 27).

D2.30 **Conditions that may be Imposed** Any condition can be imposed provided it has the purpose of facilitating the rehabilitation of the offender, and/or ensuring that the offender makes reparation for the offence (s. 22(3)). When the Police and Justice Act 2006, s. 17 (amending the CJA 2003, s. 22(3)) is in force, punishing the offender will be added to the possible objectives. In addition, a new s. 22(3A) of the CJA 2003 will permit a condition that the offender pay a financial penalty (limited by a new s. 23A to one quarter of the amount of the maximum fine that could be imposed on summary conviction for the relevant offence, or £250, whichever is the lower) and/or a condition that the offender attend at a specified place at specified times for up to 20 hours.

The Conditional Cautioning Code states that rehabilitation could include taking part in treatment for drug or alcohol dependency, attending an anger management or driving rectification course, or involvement in a restorative justice process (which may lead to reparation). The offender could be required to pay any associated costs. Reparation might include repairing or otherwise making good any damage caused to property, restoring stolen goods, paying 'modest' financial compensation or, in some cases, simply apologising to the victim. Compensation could be to an individual or to an appropriate charity (Conditional Cautioning Code, para. 5.2). A standard condition should be included requiring the offender not to commit further offences until the conditions have been performed. In the event of an offence being committed, the CPS will decide whether to treat this as a breach, with the consequence that the offender is prosecuted for the original offence as well as for the new offence (Conditional Cautioning Code, para. 5.3).

Conditions must be:

(a) proportionate to the offence — they should not be more onerous than the punishment that would be likely to be imposed if the offender was prosecuted;
(b) achievable — they should be realistic, taking into account the offender's circumstances, and offer the reasonable expectation that he could fulfil them within the set time;
(c) appropriate — any conditions should be relevant to the offence and/or the offender (Conditional Cautioning Code, para. 5.1).

In determining the conditions, the prosecutor should take into account whether, in the event of breach, prosecution for the original offence would be possible given that most summary offences have a time-limit of six months within which proceedings must be commenced (Conditional Cautioning Code, para. 6.1). A conditional caution does not have the effect of extending this time-limit.

D2.31 **Repeat Cautions** Simple cautions and conditional cautions do not form a hierarchy in which the former will inevitably be followed by the latter if the person re-offends. A conditional caution could be imposed even though the person has never been made the subject of a simple caution. The Conditional Cautioning Code states that a conditional caution should not be imposed where the person has recently been made the subject of a simple caution unless 'exceptionally' it is believed that a conditional caution might be effective in breaking the pattern of offending. The Code gives no indication of what is meant by 'recent'. However, subject to that qualification, previous cautions (simple or conditional) or convictions for dissimilar offences can be disregarded, as can previous cautions (simple or conditional) or convictions that are more than five years old. However, a previous failure to complete a conditional caution would normally mean that a further conditional caution should not be imposed (Conditional Cautioning Code, para. 3.3).

Consequences of a Conditional Caution Failure without reasonable cause to comply with any of the conditions imposed under a conditional caution renders the person liable to prosecution for the original offence (CJA 2003, s. 24(1)), and the document that the person has signed (see **D2.29**) will be admissible in evidence (s. 24(2)). Although a conditional caution is not a criminal conviction, it will be placed on the person's record and may be cited to a court on a future occasion. Fingerprints and other identification data can be taken and retained and, in the case of a relevant sexual offence, the person is placed on the sex offenders register for two years (see **E25.1** *et seq.*). As indicated in **D2.31**, the imposition of a conditional caution may have consequences for prosecution decisions if the person reoffends. **D2.32**

Under the CJA 2003, s. 24A, which was added by the Police and Justice Act 2006, s. 18 (in force from 29 June 2007), a constable having reasonable grounds for believing that a person who is subject to a conditional caution has failed, without reasonable cause, to comply with any of its conditions, may arrest the person without warrant (s. 24A(1)). Following arrest, the person may be charged with the offence for which the conditional caution was imposed, released without charge to enable a charge decision to be made, or released without charge and without bail (with or without any variation in the conditions attached to the caution) (s. 24A(2)). Where a person is so arrested, various provisions of the PACE 1984 apply with modifications (s. 24B).

Juveniles: Final Warnings and Reprimands

Reprimands and final warnings are a statutory disposal governed by the CDA 1998, ss. 65 and 66, replacing simple cautions for offenders aged 17 and under. Extensive guidance has been issued by the Home Office in *Final Warning Scheme: Guidance for the Police and Youth Offending Teams* (available at www.homeoffice.gov.uk/documents/final-warning-scheme.pdf?view=Binary), supplemented by Home Office Circular 14/2006 *The Final Warning Scheme.* **D2.33**

Criteria for a Warning or Reprimand In order for a reprimand or warning to be given, the following conditions must be satisfied: **D2.34**

(a) a constable must have evidence that the child or young person has committed an offence;
(b) the constable must consider that the evidence is such as to give a realistic prospect of conviction;
(c) the child or young person must admit to the constable that he committed the offence;
(d) the child or young person must not have previously been convicted of an offence; and
(e) the constable must be satisfied that a prosecution would not be in the public interest (CDA 1998, s. 65(1)).

There are two important differences between the final warning scheme and simple and conditional cautions. First, a reprimand or warning cannot be imposed if the person has a previous conviction. Second, there is no requirement that the juvenile (or his parent or guardian) give his consent before a reprimand or warning can be given (*Final Warning Scheme Guidance*, para 4.13). It was held in *R (R) v Durham Constabulary* [2005] 1 WLR 1184, that, since a warning was not the determination of a criminal charge, the absence of a consent requirement was not a breach of the ECHR, Article 6. The determination of a criminal charge has to expose the subject of the charge to the possibility of punishment, whether or not in the event punishment was actually imposed. A process which could culminate only in measures of a preventative, curative, rehabilitative or welfare-promoting kind would not ordinarily be such a determination. Further, the recording of the warning on the police national computer and the sex offenders register was not a public announcement or declaration of guilt, since access to the computer and register is controlled and limited to a small number of authorised persons.

D2.35 **Decision to Reprimand, Warn or Charge** Where the criteria in CDA 1998, s. 65(1), are satisfied, the following factors should be taken into account in determining whether to reprimand, warn or charge:

(a) A child or young person may be reprimanded provided that he has not previously been reprimanded or warned (s. 65(2)). It follows that a child or young person may be reprimanded only once, and that a final warning prevents a future reprimand.
(b) A child or young person may be warned if:
  (i) he has not previously been reprimanded, but the constable considers the offence to be so serious as to require a warning (s. 65(4));
  (ii) he has not previously been warned; or
  (iii) he has previously been warned no more than once, but the current offence was committed more than two years after the date of the previous warning and the constable does not consider the offence to be so serious as to require him to be charged (s. 65(3)). A child or young person cannot be warned more than twice in any circumstances.
(c) A caution administered prior to the CDA 1998, ss. 65 and 66, coming into force is treated as a reprimand, and a second or subsequent caution is treated as a warning (CDA 1998, sch. 9, para. 5).
(d) In addition to the relevance of the child or young person's previous offending history, the key factor in deciding whether he should be reprimanded, warned or charged is the seriousness of the offence, both in terms of the nature of the offence and the surrounding circumstances. In determining seriousness, the police should take into account the ACPO Gravity Factor Matrix (set out in Home Office Circular 14/2006). Under this scheme, a score is determined ranging from 1 to 4, leading to the following recommended action:
  4 Always charge.
  3 Normally warn for a first offence. If the offender does not qualify for a warning, then charge. Only in exceptional circumstances should a reprimand be given. The decision-maker needs to justify a reprimand.
  2 Normally reprimand for a first offence. If the offender does not qualify for a reprimand but qualifies for a warning then give a warning. If the offender does not qualify for a warning then charge.
  1 Always the minimum response applicable to the individual offender, i.e. reprimand, warning or charge.
(e) Where there is more than one offender, each must be considered separately, and different disposals may be justified (*Final Warning Scheme Guidance*, para. 4.29).
(f) Where there is more than one offence, a final warning may be given provided, overall, it is an appropriate and proportionate response (para. 4.30). If the offences arise from one incident, the most serious should be considered and the gravity factors applied to that offence, although the other offences may aggravate or mitigate the gravity factors (para. 4.31).
(g) Where the offence concerned is breach of an ASBO, the police, in consultation with the youth offending team, should make an assessment of both the seriousness of the breach and the young person's offending history. Where breach of the ASBO is effectively a first offence, a warning may be appropriate provided the breach was not a flagrant one. If it

was a flagrant breach, the person should normally be charged 'unless there were some very unusual circumstances' (Home Office Circular 14/2006, para. 5).

(h) Juveniles involved in prostitution should usually be dealt with as victims of abuse and should usually be diverted away from the criminal justice system altogether. However, in exceptional cases where diversion has repeatedly failed, the police may (after consultation with other agencies) initiate criminal proceedings or administer a final warning (*Final Warning Scheme Guidance*, paras. 12.17 and 12.18).

Once a child or young person has been charged, the court will not usually require the police or the CPS to reconsider offering a reprimand or warning (see *R (F) v CPS* (2004) 168 JP 93).

Responsibility for Making the Decision Other than in respect of indictable-only offences, responsibility for making decisions under the statutory scheme is that of the police. In straightforward cases where there are no risk factors, or where the juvenile is in the area only temporarily, a reprimand or warning can be given straightaway (*Final Warning Scheme Guidance*, para. 9.1). However, the police may ask the local youth offending team to carry out an assessment prior to making a decision, especially where consideration is being given to a final warning (para. 3.1). The PACE 1984, s. 34(2) and (5), enables bail to be granted for this purpose. **D2.36**

The Process of giving a Reprimand or Warning Reprimands and warnings can be given only by a police constable (CDA 1998, s. 65) but there is no restriction on the rank of the officer concerned. In the case of an offender under 17 years, the reprimand or warning must be given in the presence of an appropriate adult (s. 65(5)(a)). In the case of a final warning, a youth offending team officer should usually also be present, but is not a replacement for the appropriate adult (*Final Warning Scheme Guidance*, paras. 9.4 and 9.15). There is no statutory obligation for reprimands or warnings of 17-year-olds to be given in the presence of an appropriate adult. **D2.37**

It was originally the case that reprimands and warnings had to be given in a police station. However, that requirement was removed by the CJCSA 2000, s. 56. This gives the police flexibility to arrange for 'restorative conferences' in more suitable locations, such as the offices of the youth offending team responsible for assessing the young offender and providing the intervention programme.

The form of a reprimand or warning is governed by the CDA 1998, s. 65(5)(b) and (6), and is set out in further detail in the *Final Warning Scheme Guidance*, paras. 9.11 and 9.12. Broadly, the officer giving a reprimand or warning must specify the offence(s), explain that it is a serious matter, and explain the consequences. This must be done orally, and be supplemented with a written explanation.

The Consequences of a Reprimand or Warning When a warning (but not a reprimand) is administered, the police must refer the child or young person to a youth offending team (CDA 1998, s. 66(1)). The youth offending team must then make an assessment and, unless it considers it inappropriate to do so, must arrange for the child or young person to participate in an intervention programme (s. 66(2)). Therefore, a warning will usually result in the child or young person participating in some activity determined by the youth offending team. There is no enforcement provision in the CDA 1998 for failure to participate in, or breach of, a rehabilitation programme. **D2.38**

Reprimands and warnings do not count as convictions, but they, or any report on failure to participate in a rehabilitation programme, can be cited in criminal proceedings in the same circumstances as convictions can be cited (s. 66(5)). The juvenile must be told that a record of the reprimand or warning will be kept by the police until the offender is 18 years old or for five years, whichever is the longer (*Final Warning Scheme Guidance*, paras. 9.11 and 9.12). If the offence is one that is covered by the SOA 2003, part II (see **E25.1** *et seq.*), the juvenile will be placed on the sex offenders register for a period of two and a half years. This must be explained to him when he is given the reprimand or warning.

Where a person who has been given a final warning under the CDA 1998, s. 65, is convicted of another offence committed within two years of the warning, the court cannot impose a conditional discharge unless it is of the opinion that there are exceptional circumstances relating to the offence or the offender which justify such a course of action (s. 66(4)). This does not apply if he has been reprimanded rather than warned.

Where a juvenile is informed that he will be reported for a recordable offence, the usual rules regarding the taking of fingerprints apply (see **F18.32**). Where the juvenile is released, on bail or otherwise (for example, for a decision to be taken about a reprimand or warning), and is subsequently reprimanded or warned for a recordable offence, his fingerprints may be taken without consent (PACE 1984, s. 61(6)).

Fixed Penalty Notices

D2.39 **Fixed penalty notices under the CJPA 2001** Fixed penalty notices are a familiar feature of road traffic law. The RTOA 1988, s. 54, provides that where a uniformed police officer has reason to believe that a person is committing, or has on that occasion committed, a fixed penalty offence, the officer may give him a fixed penalty notice in respect of the offence. However, such notices are not confined to road traffic law. The CJPA 2001, ss. 1 and 2, make provision for fixed penalty notices in respect of a range of offences:

- being drunk in a highway, other public place or licensed premises (Licensing Act 1872, s. 12);
- throwing fireworks in a thoroughfare (Explosives Act 1875, s. 80);
- trespassing on a railway (British Transport Commission Act 1949, s. 55);
- throwing stones etc. at trains or other things on railways (British Transport Commission Act 1949, s. 56);
- disorderly behaviour while drunk in a public place (CJA 1967, s. 91);
- wasting police time or giving false report (Criminal Law Act 1967, s. 5(2));
- theft (TA 1968, s. 1);
- destroying or damaging property (Criminal Damage Act 1971, s. 1(1));
- behaviour likely to cause harassment, alarm or distress (POA 1986, s. 5);
- depositing and leaving litter (Environmental Protection Act 1990, s. 87);
- consumption of alcohol in a designated public place (CJPA 2001, s. 12);
- using a public electronic communications network in order to cause annoyance, inconvenience or needless anxiety (Communications Act 2003, s. 127(2));
- contravention of a prohibition or failure to comply with a requirement imposed by or under fireworks regulations or making false statements (Fireworks Act 2003, s. 11);
- sale of alcohol to a person who is drunk (Licensing Act 2003, s. 141);
- sale of alcohol to children (Licensing Act 2003, s. 146(1) and (3));
- purchase of alcohol by or on behalf of children (Licensing Act 2003, s. 149);
- buying or attempting to buy alcohol for consumption on licensed premises by a child (Licensing Act 2003, s. 149(4));
- consumption of alcohol by children or allowing such consumption (Licensing Act 2003, s. 150);
- delivering alcohol to children or allowing such delivery (Licensing Act 2003, s. 151);
- knowingly giving a false alarm of fire (Fire and Rescue Services Act 2004, s. 49).

Penalty notices are defined in the CJPA 2001, s. 2(4), as notices that offer the opportunity, by paying a penalty, 'to discharge any liability to be convicted of the offence to which the notice relates'. Section 2(1) states that, where a police officer has reason to believe that a person aged ten or over has committed a penalty offence, he may give him a penalty notice in respect of the offence. Unless the notice is given in a police station, the constable giving it must be in uniform (s. 2(2)). At a police station, a penalty notice may be given only by an officer who has been authorised by the chief officer of police for that area to give penalty notices (s. 2(3)).

Section 3 sets out the requirements to be met for the notice to be valid. It must:

(a) be in the prescribed form;
(b) state the alleged offence;
(c) give such particulars of the circumstances alleged to constitute the offence as are necessary to provide reasonable information about it;
(d) specify the suspended enforcement period (as to which see s. 5) and explain its effect;
(e) state the amount of the penalty;
(f) state where the penalty may be paid; and
(g) inform the recipient of his right to ask to be tried for the alleged offence and explain how that right may be exercised.

Section 4 sets out the effect of a penalty notice. Where the recipient of the notice asks to be tried for the alleged offence, proceedings may be brought against him. Such a request must be made by the recipient in the manner specified in the penalty notice and before the end of the period of suspended enforcement (defined in s. 5).

If, by the end of the suspended enforcement period, the penalty has not been paid but the recipient has not made a request to be tried, a sum equal to one and a half times the amount of the penalty may be registered under s. 8 of the Act for enforcement against him as a fine.

Under s. 5, proceedings for the offence to which a penalty notice relates may not be brought until the end of the period of 21 days beginning with the date on which the notice was given. If the penalty is paid before the end of this 'suspended enforcement period', no proceedings may be brought for the offence. Section 5 does not apply if the person to whom the penalty notice was given has made a request to be tried.

Fixed penalty notices under the ASBA 2003 The ASBA 2003, s. 43, also makes provision for penalty notices. It applies to the offences listed in s. 44(1), namely: **D2.40**

- affixing posters (Metropolitan Police Act 1839, s. 54, para. 10);
- defacement of streets with slogans etc. (London County Council (General Powers) Act 1954, s. 20(1));
- damaging property (Criminal Damage Act 1971, s. 1(1)) where the damage involves only the painting or writing on, or the soiling, marking or other defacing of, any property by whatever means;
- offences under the Highways Act 1980, s. 131(2) involving only an act of obliteration;
- painting or affixing things on structures on the highway (Highways Act 1980, s. 132(1));
- displaying an advertisement in contravention of regulations (Town and Country Planning Act 1990, s. 224(3)).

Section 43(1) provides that, where an authorised officer of a local authority has reason to believe that a person has committed an offence to which these provisions apply, he may give that person a notice offering him the opportunity of discharging any liability to conviction for that offence by payment of a penalty. However, by virtue of s. 43(2), this does not apply if the authorised officer considers that the commission of the offence, in the case of damage to property, also involves the commission of an offence under the CDA 1998, s. 30 (racially or religiously aggravated criminal damage) or, in the case of any other relevant offence, was motivated (wholly or partly) by hostility towards a person based upon their membership (or presumed membership) of a racial or religious group, or towards members of a racial or religious group based on their membership of that group.

Under s. 43(4), where a person is given a penalty notice in respect of an offence, no proceedings may be instituted for that offence (or any other offence to which the provisions apply arising out of the same circumstances) until 14 days after the date of the notice. The person cannot be convicted of that offence (or any other relevant offence arising out of the same circumstances) if he pays the penalty specified in the notice within 14 days. Section 43(5) stipulates that the penalty notice must 'give such particulars of the circumstances alleged to constitute the offence as are necessary for giving reasonable information of the offence'. Where payment is made by post, it is deemed to have been made at the time at which that letter would be delivered in the ordinary course of post (s. 43(8)).

Section 43B empowers the authorised officer of the local authority to require the person to give his name and address. Failure to give name and address (or giving a false or inaccurate address) is an offence under s. 43B(2), punishable with a fine on level 3 of the standard scale.

D2.41 **Other Fixed Penalty Notice Provisions** There are also a number of statutory provisions for fixed penalty notices in environmental protection legislation. For example, the Environmental Protection Act 1990, s. 88, makes provision for penalty notices for leaving litter. It provides that where an authorised officer of a litter authority finds that a person has committed an offence under s. 87 (leaving litter), or a police officer has reason to believe that a person has committed an offence under that section, he may give that person a notice offering him the opportunity of discharging any liability to conviction for that offence by payment of a fixed penalty. Section 47ZA of that Act makes provision for fixed penalty notices for failure to provide specified receptacles for household or commercial waste, and s. 94A provides for fixed penalty notices relating to ss. 92C (failure to comply with a litter clearing notice served under s. 92A) and 94 (notice to clear litter from a specified area). The Noise Act 1996, s. 8, provides for fixed penalties in respect of offences under ss. 4 (where noise from a dwelling exceeds the permitted level after service of a notice) and 4A (noise from other premises) of that Act. The Refuse Disposal (Amenity) Act 1978, s. 2A, makes provision for fixed penalty notices for the offence of abandoning vehicles contrary to s. 2 of the Act. The Clean Neighbourhoods and Environment Act 2005, s. 59, makes similar provision for dog-fouling; under s. 59(1), where an authorised officer has reason to believe that a person has committed an offence under a dog control order, he may give that person a fixed penalty notice and a fixed penalty notice may also be given under s. 6 for breach of s. 3 or s. 4 of the Act (exposing two or more vehicles for sale on a road or repairing vehicles on a road for profit). Section 73 enables fixed penalty notices to be given where it appears to an authorised officer that a person has committed an offence under s. 71(4) (failure to nominate a key-holder where an audible intruder alarm is installed on premises in an alarm notification area). Section 61 of the Act empowers the authorised officer to require a person to whom he intends to give such a notice to supply his name and address; it is an offence to fail to comply or to give false particulars.

The Environmental Offences (Fixed Penalties) (Miscellaneous Provisions) Regulations 2007 (SI 2007 No. 175) provide that, where the fixed penalty notice for an environmental protection offence is £75, a local authority may choose to specify its own locally applicable amount of between £50 and £80 (reg. 2(1)). If a local authority decides to treat a lesser sum paid within a specified period as full payment of the fixed penalty, that lesser sum must not be less than £50 (reg. 3(1)). In respect of other offences, for which the prescribed amount of the fixed penalty is £100, the local authority may adopt a range of between £75 and £110 (reg. 2(2)); in respect of those offences, the penalty cannot be reduced below £60 for prompt payment (reg. 3(2)).

In respect of other offences, for which the amounts of fixed penalty prescribed in the legislation are, respectively, £100, £200 and £300 (but in each case with no facility for an authority to specify a different locally applicable amount), an authority may nonetheless decide to treat a lesser sum paid within a specified period as full payment of the fixed penalty; the sum cannot be reduced below £60, £120 or £180 respectively (reg. 3(2)).

BAIL FOLLOWING CHARGE

Where a person arrested for an offence otherwise than under a warrant endorsed for bail is charged with an offence the custody officer must, subject to the CJPOA 1994, s. 25 (see **D2.46**), release him from detention either on bail or without bail, unless one or more of the conditions in the PACE 1984, s. 38, is satisfied (PACE 1984, s. 38(1); see **D2.46**). This is subject to the power under the PACE 1984, s. 37(8A) and (8B), to detain the person for the purpose of a Class A drug test (see **D1.74**). If the person is granted bail, the custody officer must appoint for the court appearance a date which is no later than the first sitting of the relevant magistrates' court after the date on which the person is charged, unless notified that the appearance cannot be accommodated until a later date, in which case the officer must appoint that later date (PACE 1984, s. 47(3A)). Alternatively it would seem that when PJA 2006 s. 46, amending the PACE s. 47(3), is in force (beyond the limited areas in which it currently applies), the custody officer may bail a person to attend a police station pursuant to a live-link direction under the CDA 1998, s. 57C. **D2.42**

Power to Impose Conditions

A release on bail under s. 38(1) is deemed to be a release on bail granted in accordance with the BA 1976, ss. 3, 3A, 5 and 5A, as they apply to bail granted by a constable (PACE 1984, s. 47(1)), and the 'normal powers to impose conditions of bail' (as defined in the BA 1976, s. 3(6)) apply (PACE 1984, s. 47(1A)). Conditions can be imposed if it appears necessary for the purpose of securing that the person surrender to custody, does not commit an offence on bail, does not interfere with witnesses or otherwise obstruct the course of justice and/or for his own protection (or where the person is under 17 years, for his own welfare or in his own interests) (PACE 1984, s. 47(1A) and BA 1976, ss. 3(6) and 3A(5)). Any condition may be imposed other than a condition that the person reside in a bail hostel, make himself available for the purposes of a court report, or attend an interview with a lawyer (BA 1976 s. 3A(2)). It has been held in relation to a court's power to impose bail conditions that, in considering whether and what conditions to impose, the court must perceive a real and not merely fanciful risk of the relevant outcome (*Mansfield Justices, ex parte Sharkey* [1985] QB 613), and it is submitted that the same principle must apply to a decision by a police officer. **D2.43**

A person who has been made subject to bail conditions may apply to the same or another custody officer serving at the same station for the conditions to be varied, and in doing so the officer may impose conditions or more onerous conditions (BA 1976, s. 3A(4)). The person may, alternatively or in addition, apply to a magistrates' court for variation, and again the court may impose conditions or more onerous conditions (MCA 1980, s. 43(B)(1) and (2)). Under the Crim PR, r. 19.1(1), an application under s. 43B(1) must be made in writing; contain a statement of the grounds upon which it is made; specify the offence with which the applicant was charged before his release on bail; specify the reasons given by the custody officer for imposing or varying the conditions of bail; and specify the name and address of any surety provided by the applicant before his release on bail to secure his surrender to custody.

Enforcement of Bail

Police bail granted under the PACE 1984, s. 38, is enforceable in the same way as bail granted by a court. Failure to surrender to custody at the appointed time without reasonable cause is an offence under the BA 1976, s. 6, and the person subject to bail may be arrested if he fails to surrender or if a police officer has reasonable grounds for believing that he is not likely to surrender to custody (BA 1976, s. 7). Breach of bail conditions is not an offence but a person released on bail subject to conditions may be arrested if a constable has reasonable grounds for believing that the person is likely to breach any of the conditions, or for suspecting that he has broken any of the conditions. Furthermore, if the person was released subject to a surety, the **D2.44** person on bail may be arrested if the surety notifies the police in writing that the person is unlikely to surrender to custody and that the surety wants to be relieved of the obligations as surety (BA 1976, s. 7(3)). The court at which the suspect is due to appear may extend bail by fixing a later time at which the suspect is to surrender, whether or not bail was granted subject to a surety (MCA 1980, s. 43(1)).

DETENTION FOLLOWING CHARGE

D2.45 As noted in D2.42, where a person arrested for an offence otherwise than under a warrant endorsed for bail is charged with an offence, the custody officer must, subject to the CJPOA 1994, s. 25, release him from detention either on bail or without bail, unless one of more of the conditions in the PACE 1984, s. 38, is satisfied (PACE 1984, s. 38(1)). It was held in *Hutt v Metropolitan Police Commissioner* [2003] EWCA Civ 1911, that where the arrest leading to the detention was unlawful, bail could not be denied under s. 38(1). However, it is submitted that this would not be the case if the nature of the illegality was such that it could be, and was, 'cured' (e.g., where a failure to comply with the requirement under the PACE 1984, s. 28, to inform the arrested person of the grounds for arrest is 'cured' by the arrested person subsequently being given this information).

Where a person charged with an offence is kept in police detention or, in the case of a juvenile, is detained by a local authority in accordance with the PACE 1984, s. 38(6) (see **D2.47**), the police must bring him before a magistrates' court (PACE 1984, s. 46(1)). If he is to be brought before a magistrates' court in the local justice area in which the police station is situated, that must be done as soon as is practicable, and in any event no later than the first sitting after he is charged with the offence (s. 46(2)). This will result in the accused person being brought before the court on the day on which he is charged or on the next day, unless the next day is a Sunday, Christmas Day or Good Friday (s. 46(8)). If no magistrates' court for the area is due to sit in either period, the custody officer must inform the relevant court office that there is a charged and detained person who must be brought before the court (s. 46(3)). Arrangements must then be made for a magistrates' court to sit not later than the day after the day following the date of charge (ss. 46(6)(a) and 46(7)(a)).

Grounds for Withholding Bail

D2.46 The restrictions on bail under the CJPOA 1994, s. 25, mean that where a person is charged with certain specified offences, and they already have a conviction (including a finding of not guilty by reason of insanity, a finding under the Criminal Procedure (Insanity) Act 1964, s. 4A(3) (unfitness to plead) that a person did the act or made the omission charged against him, or conviction for an offence for which the person was absolutely or conditionally discharged) for any of certain specified offences in any part of the UK (or a conviction for culpable homicide), bail may only be granted if the custody officer is satisfied that there are exceptional circumstances which justify the grant of bail. The offences concerned are set out in s. 25(2) (see **D7.8**).

Where the previous conviction was for manslaughter or culpable homicide, the restriction only applies if the person received a custodial sentence (CJPOA 1994, s. 25(3)). No guidance is given in the Act as to the meaning of 'exceptional circumstances' nor as to the relationship between s. 25 and the PACE 1984, s. 38. It would seem that the custody officer would still have to be satisfied that one or more of the s. 38 conditions applies before withholding bail, but in practice, it is highly unlikely that a custody officer would grant bail in the circumstances covered by s. 25. It was held in *R (O) v Crown Court at Harrow* [2003] 1 WLR 2756, that s. 25 does not violate the ECHR, Article 5 (right to liberty and security) provided that it is not construed too narrowly.

The grounds for withholding bail under the PACE 1984, s. 38(1), are as follows.

(a) The suspect's name or address cannot be ascertained, or the custody officer has reasonable grounds for doubting whether the name or address given by the suspect is real (s. 38(1)(a)(i)).
(b) The custody officer has reasonable grounds for believing that the person arrested will fail to appear in court to answer bail (s. 38(1)(a)(ii)).
(c) Where the person was arrested for an imprisonable offence, the custody officer has reasonable grounds for believing that the detention of the person is necessary to prevent him from committing an offence (s. 38(1)(a)(iii)). Note that it refers to a person *arrested* for as opposed to *charged* with an imprisonable offence. It is suggested that the wording follows from the general structure of the section, and that the ground should be relied upon to deny bail only where a person is charged with such an offence.
(d) In a case where a sample may be taken under the PACE 1984, s. 63B (testing for Class A drugs), the custody officer has reasonable grounds for believing that the detention of the person is necessary to enable the sample to be taken (s. 38(1)(a)(iiia)). In this case detention can be for no longer than 24 hours from the relevant time (see **D1.74**).
(e) Where the person was arrested for a non-imprisonable offence, the custody officer has reasonable grounds for believing that detention is necessary to prevent him from causing physical injury to any other person or from causing loss of or damage to property (s. 38(1)(a)(iv)).
(f) The custody officer has reasonable grounds for believing that detention is necessary to prevent the person from interfering with the administration of justice or with the investigation of offences or of a particular offence (s. 38(1)(a)(v)).
(g) The custody officer has reasonable grounds for believing that detention is necessary for the person's own protection (s. 38(1)(a)(vi)).

In considering the above grounds, other than (a) and (g), the custody officer must have regard to the nature and seriousness of the offence, and the probable penalty; the character, antecedents, associations and community ties of the detained person; his record in respect of previous grant of bail; the strength of the evidence; and any other relevant consideration (PACE 1984, s. 38(2A)).

Detention of Juveniles after Charge

The grounds for withholding bail under the PACE 1984, s. 38(1), apply to juveniles in the same way as they apply to adults except that ground (d) applies only if the juvenile has attained the minimum age (see **D1.72**), and that bail may also be withheld if the custody officer has reasonable grounds for believing that the juvenile ought to be detained in his own interests (s. 38(1)(b)). **D2.47**

Where a juvenile is kept in police detention after charge under s. 38(1) (but not where he is detained under some other power), he must be dealt with in accordance with s. 38(6) to (7). Section 38(6) provides that the custody officer must arrange for the juvenile to be transferred to local authority accommodation unless the officer certifies:

(a) that, by reason of such circumstances as are specified in the certificate, it is impracticable for him to do so; or
(b) in the case of an arrested juvenile who has attained the age of 12 years, that no secure accommodation is available and that keeping the juvenile in other local authority accommodation would not be adequate to protect the public from serious harm from him.

With regard to practicability, Code C, Note for Guidance 16D, provides that neither the juvenile's behaviour nor the nature of the offence with which he is charged provides grounds for the custody officer to retain him in police custody rather than to arrange a transfer to local authority accommodation. It also states that lack of secure local authority accommodation does not make it impracticable for the custody officer to transfer the juvenile, noting that the availability of secure accommodation is only a factor in relation to a juvenile aged 12 or over when the local authority accommodation would not be adequate to protect the public from serious harm from the juvenile. Home Office Circular 78/1992 *Criminal Justice Act 1991: Detention, etc, of Juveniles* states that 'impractical' means circumstances where transfer would be physically impossible by reason of, e.g., floods, blizzards, or the impossibility, despite repeated efforts, of contacting the local authority.

Furthermore, Note for Guidance 16D provides that the obligation to transfer a juvenile to local authority accommodation applies as much to a juvenile charged during the daytime as to a juvenile who is to be held overnight, subject to the requirement under s. 46(1) and (2) to bring a person charged and kept in police detention or detained in local authority accommodation under these provisions before a court as soon as is practicable. In *R (M) v Gateshead MBC* [2006] QB 650, the court held that local authorities should have a reasonable system in place to enable them to respond to such requests under s. 38(6), but that they were not under an absolute duty to provide secure accommodation. Where the request was made at 00.20 a.m., with a view to the juvenile being produced in court at 10 a.m. the same day, it was wholly impracticable for the local authority to provide accommodation. If this case is followed, it will in practice significantly reduce the effect of s. 38(6) in seeking to ensure that juveniles are not detained at police stations after charge.

The PACE 1984, s. 38(6)(b), provides that, in the case of juveniles between the ages of 12 and 16, the custody officer can take into account the lack of secure accommodation where keeping the suspect in other local authority accommodation would not be adequate to protect the public from the risk of serious harm from him. It is understood that this subsection was intended to apply only to juveniles of that age who were charged with violent or sexual offences. However, somewhat strangely, s. 38(6A) provides that 'any reference, in relation to an arrested juvenile charged with a violent or sexual offence, to protecting the public from serious harm from him shall be construed as a reference to protecting members of the public from death or serious personal injury, whether physical or psychological, occasioned by further such offences committed by him'. Therefore, the possibility of keeping a juvenile in police custody after charge under s. 38(6) is not confined to those charged with a violent or sexual offence. Furthermore, the justification of 'protecting the public from serious harm' is defined only in respect of those charged with a violent or sexual offence. It is suggested, however, that this definition gives an indication of the gravity of the threat of harm to the public that would be required in order to keep a juvenile charged with any other offence in police custody.

Note that although s. 38(6)(b) refers to the non-availability of secure accommodation, the police cannot insist that the local authority place the juvenile in secure accommodation even if it is available. 'Secure accommodation' has a technical meaning, and a local authority cannot restrict the liberty of a juvenile in its care otherwise than in approved secure accommodation. However, a local authority may decide to hold a juvenile placed with it under s. 38(6) in secure accommodation for up to 72 hours within any 28-day period (Children (Secure Accommodation) Regulations 1991 (SI 1991 No. 1505), reg. 10(1)). The authority may do so only if it appears that non-secure accommodation is inappropriate because:

(a) the juvenile is likely to abscond from other accommodation; or
(b) the juvenile is likely to injure himself or other people if kept in other accommodation (reg. 6).

If a juvenile is kept in police custody under s. 38(6)(a) or (b), the custody officer must certify the reasons, and this certificate must be produced to the court before which the juvenile first appears (s. 38(7)).

Section D3 Courts, Judges and Parties

Introduction

The criminal trial of an adult takes place either in the Crown Court or in a magistrates' court. The criminal trial of a juvenile usually takes place in a special form of magistrates' court, known as the youth court, but sometimes takes place in either the Crown Court or an ordinary magistrates' court. The first part of this section describes the status, structure, judges and main heads of jurisdiction of the Crown Court and ordinary magistrates' courts. Youth courts are described in D23. **D3.1**

The Constitutional Reform Act 2005 contains a number of provisions relevant to criminal justice. Section 3 contains a 'guarantee of continued judicial independence'. It requires the Lord Chancellor, other Ministers of the Crown and everyone with responsibility for matters relating to the judiciary or to the administration of justice to uphold the continued independence of the judiciary. It stipulates that the Lord Chancellor and other Ministers of the Crown must not seek to influence particular judicial decisions through any special access to the judiciary. It requires the Lord Chancellor to have regard to the need to defend that independence, the need for the judiciary to have the support necessary to enable them to exercise their functions, and the need for the public interest in regard to matters relating to the judiciary or to the administration of justice to be properly represented in decisions affecting those matters. Under s. 5, the Lord Chief Justice may lay before Parliament written representations on matters that appear to him to be matters of importance relating to the judiciary, or otherwise to the administration of justice. Under s. 7, the Lord Chief Justice holds the office of President of the Courts of England and Wales and is Head of the Judiciary of England and Wales. As President, he is responsible for representing the views of the judiciary of England and Wales to Parliament, to the Lord Chancellor and to Ministers of the Crown generally, for the maintenance of appropriate arrangements for the welfare, training and guidance of the judiciary of England and Wales (within the resources made available by the Lord Chancellor), and for the maintenance of appropriate arrangements for the deployment of the judiciary of England and Wales and the allocation of work within courts. The President is president of the Court of Appeal, the High Court, the Crown Court, the county courts and the magistrates' courts, and is entitled to sit in any of those courts. Section 8 requires the appointment of a Head of Criminal Justice (the Lord Chief Justice, or someone appointed by the Lord Chief Justice) and empowers the Lord Chief Justice to appoint a Deputy Head of Criminal Justice. Section 61 and sch. 12 establish the Judicial Appointments Commission; ss. 76–84 govern appointment of Lords Justices of Appeal and ss. 85–93 govern the appointment of puisne judges of the High Court. Schedule 1 empowers the Lord Chief Justice to make rules (by statutory instrument); sch. 2 confers on the Lord Chief Justice the power to issue directions.

THE CROWN COURT

Creation and Status

D3.2 The Crown Court was created by the Courts Act 1971, and came into being on 1 January 1972. It replaced the former courts of assize and quarter sessions and a number of other criminal courts. The legislation governing it is largely contained in the Supreme Court Act 1981. Its practice and procedure are prescribed, *inter alia*, by the CrimPR (see **appendix** 1), made by the Criminal Procedure Rules Committee under the Courts Act 2003, s. 69. This Committee (which is chaired by the Lord Chief Justice) has taken over responsibility for the rules of both the Crown Court and the magistrates' courts.

The Crown Court is part of the Supreme Court, and derives its jurisdiction from the provisions of the Supreme Court Act 1981 and any other jurisdiction-conferring enactments (see s. 1(1) of the 1981 Act, which provides that: 'The Supreme Court of England and Wales shall consist of the Court of Appeal, the High Court of Justice and the Crown Court, each having such jurisdiction as is conferred on it by or under this or any other Act'). As is apparent from the use of the singular in s. 1, the Crown Court is a *single* court. It follows that, although the Crown Court sits in many different locations and a case will normally be tried at a location near where the offence allegedly occurred, the trial may take place at any location of the Crown Court. The choice of location will depend on the convenience of the parties, the nature of the offence charged, the desirability of expediting the trial and any directions given by the presiding judge of the relevant circuit as to the locations to which the magistrates' courts in the area of the circuit should normally send cases for trial. (See the *Consolidated Criminal Practice Direction*, para. III.21, *Classification of Crown Court business and allocation to Crown Court centres* reproduced at **appendix** 7.)

In status, the Crown Court occupies a somewhat ambiguous position. Like the High Court, it is part of the Supreme Court and a superior court of record (Supreme Court Act 1981, s. 45(1)), with the same powers in relation to, for example, contempt and enforcement of its orders as are possessed by the High Court (s. 45(4)). Furthermore, when it exercises its jurisdiction in relation to trials on indictment, appeals from its decisions lie only to the Court of Appeal (Criminal Division), just as appeals from the High Court go to the Court of Appeal (Civil Division). On the other hand, decisions of the Crown Court which do not relate to trial on indictment (e.g., a decision taken in respect of an appeal from a magistrates' court) may be challenged in the High Court either by an appeal by way of case stated or by application for judicial review (see ss. 28(2) and 29(3) of the 1981 Act). Thus, for some purposes the Crown Court is treated as on a par with the High Court while for other purposes it is subject to the same supervisory jurisdiction as the High Court exercises in relation to magistrates' courts.

Structure

D3.3 The many different locations in which the Crown Court sits are classified according to (a) geographical position and (b) status. As to (a), every location belongs to one of six 'circuits': (i) Midland and Oxford, (ii) North-Eastern, (iii) Northern, (iv) Wales and Chester, (v) Western, and (vi) South-Eastern. Each circuit is presided over by a High Court judge called the 'presiding judge' who has responsibility for taking certain decisions about the administration and distribution of work on the circuit. If considered desirable, a circuit may have both a senior presiding judge and one or more other presiding judges to assist him. As to (b), locations are either first, second or third tier. At first-tier locations, High Court judges regularly sit; at third-tier locations, High Court judges do not normally sit. Each circuit contains locations of each of the three tiers. The most serious cases will normally be committed to either a first or second-tier location, so that there will be at least the possibility of the trial being conducted by a High Court judge. At each location there is a senior judge (known as the 'resident judge') who is responsible, *inter alia*, for the allocation of business amongst the judges sitting at the location. There may also be 'responsible judges', to whom the resident judge may delegate some of his functions, and 'liaison judges' responsible for liaising between the Crown Court and the local magistrates' courts.

Judges

Supreme Court Act 1981, s. 8 D3.4

(1) The jurisdiction of the Crown Court shall be exercisable by—
   (a) any judge of the High Court; or
   (b) any circuit judge or recorder; or
   (c) subject to and in accordance with the provisions of sections 74 and 75(2), a judge of the High Court, circuit judge or recorder sitting with not more than four justices of the peace, and any such persons when exercising the jurisdiction of the Crown Court shall be judges of the Crown Court.

For ss. 74 and 75(2) (justices sitting in Crown Court), see **D3.9**. Section 8(1) must be read in conjunction with s. 24 (deputy circuit judges) — see **D3.8**.

There are thus three principal categories of Crown Court judge, namely High Court judges, circuit judges and recorders. All proceedings in the Crown Court must be heard and disposed of before a single professional judge of the court except where there is provision for justices to sit with such a judge (s. 73(1)).

High Court Judges About 20 High Court judges may, at any one time, be asked by the Lord Chancellor to sit in the Crown Court. The *Consolidated Criminal Practice Direction*, para. IV. 33, *Allocation of business within the Crown Court* requires that certain categories of case must normally be tried by a High Court judge (see paras. IV.33.1 and IV.33.2 of the *Practice Direction* set out in **appendix** 7). D3.5

Circuit Judges The office of circuit judge was created by the Courts Act 1971 at the same time as the Crown Court. Circuit judges are appointed 'to serve in the Crown Court and county courts and to carry out such other judicial functions as may be conferred on them under this or any other enactment' (Courts Act 1971, s. 16(1)). The minimum qualification for a circuit judge is to be the holder of a ten-year Crown Court or ten-year county court qualification within the meaning of the Courts and Legal Services Act 1990, s. 71, or a recorder, or a person who has held as a full-time appointment for at least three years one of the offices listed in the Courts Act 1971, sch. 2, para. 1A (s. 16(3)). Retirement is normally at the age of 70, though the Lord Chancellor has a discretion to allow the judge to continue in office until his 75th birthday (s. 17(1)). Conversely, the Lord Chancellor (with the agreement of the Lord Chief Justice) may remove a circuit judge from office before retirement age on the ground of 'incapacity or misbehaviour' (s. 17(4)). D3.6

Recorders Recorders are appointed 'to act as part-time judges of the Crown Court and to carry out such other judicial functions as may be conferred on them under this or any other enactment' (Courts Act 1971, s. 21(1) and (2)). The minimum qualification for a recorder is to have a ten-year Crown Court or ten-year county court qualification within the meaning of the Courts and Legal Services Act 1990, s. 71 (s. 21(2)). The appointment must specify the term for which the recorder is appointed and the frequency and duration of the occasions during that term on which he must be available to undertake his duties (s. 21(3)). The original term of appointment must be extended by the Lord Chancellor (with the agreement of the recorder) unless the Lord Chief Justice agrees that the Lord Chancellor should decline to extend the appointment because of the incapacity or misbehaviour of the recorder, s. 21(4A) to (4C)). When not sitting, the recorder may and normally does revert to private practice. Neither the initial term of appointment nor any extension thereof may be such as to D3.7

last beyond the date on which the recorder attains the age of 70 (subject to the power to extend the term of office until the recorder reaches the age of 75) (s. 21(5)). A recorder's appointment may be terminated by the Lord Chancellor on grounds of incapacity, misbehaviour or failure to comply with the terms of his appointment (s. 21(6)). Thus, the major difference between a circuit judge and a recorder is that the former is a full-time and the latter a part-time appointment.

D3.8 **Deputy Circuit Judges** Section 8(1) of the Supreme Court Act 1981 (see **D3.4**) must be read in conjunction with the Courts Act 1971, s. 24, which provides that the Lord Chief Justice may (with the concurrence of the Lord Chancellor) appoint deputy circuit judges or assistant recorders where it is expedient to do so as a temporary measure in order to facilitate the disposal of business in (*inter alia*) the Crown Court. The requirement to be a deputy circuit judge is to have previously held office as a judge of the Court of Appeal or of the High Court or as a circuit judge; an assistant recorder must possess a ten-year Crown Court or a ten-year county court qualification, within the meaning of the Courts and Legal Services Act 1990, s. 71. The retirement age for a deputy circuit judge is 75; the retirement age for an assistant recorder is 70 (subject to the power to extend the term of office until the assistant recorder reaches the age of 75). Although s. 24 still refers to assistant recorders, following the judgment of the High Court of Justiciary in *Starrs v Procurator Fiscal* (2000) 8 BHRC 1 (where it was held that a temporary sheriff was not an 'independent and impartial tribunal'), the Lord Chancellor announced in April 2000 that no useful purpose would be served by maintaining the distinction between assistant recordership and recordership in England and Wales, and so existing assistant recorders were given the status of full recorder.

D3.9 **Justices** For the hearing of appeals from a magistrates' court, the Crown Court *must* normally include not less than two and not more than four justices (the Supreme Court Act 1981, s. 74(1)). The exceptions are that:

(a) If the professional judge is of the opinion that arranging for two justices to sit would cause unreasonable delay, the court may consist of the judge and one justice (CrimPR, r. 63.8(1)).
(b) If one or more of the justices who initially comprised the court subsequently withdraws or is absent for any reason, the proceedings may continue even if the professional judge is left by himself (r. 63.8(2)).

Rule 63.9 prevents a justice from sitting in the Crown Court if he adjudicated in the relevant proceedings in the magistrates' court. Rule 63.7 provides that, where the appeal or committal for sentence is in respect of a juvenile, the justices sitting in the Crown Court must be authorised to sit in the youth court and the court must include both a man and a woman.

By virtue of the Courts Act 2003, s. 66, a Crown Court judge (whether a High Court judge, circuit judge, or recorder) may exercise the powers of a District Judge (Magistrates' Court). So, for example, it would be possible for a Crown Court judge in the Crown Court to deal with a summary offence that is linked with an indictable offence without the case having to go back to a magistrates' court: under s. 66 the judge would be able to deal with the summary offence as if he or she were a magistrate (and doubtless following the procedure that would be adopted in the magistrates' court).

Role of the Justices

D3.10 When the Crown Court comprises a judge sitting with a justice or justices, the decision of the court may be by a majority (Supreme Court Act 1981, s. 73(3)). It follows that the justices may out-vote the professional judge, although if an even-numbered court is equally divided the professional judge has a casting vote (ibid.). The principle that the justices participate equally with the judge in the decisions of the court applies not only to a final decision, such as the sentence to be passed in proceedings on a committal for sentence or the determination of an appeal, but also to interlocutory decisions (e.g., about the admissibility of evidence). Thus, in *Orpin* [1975] QB 283 the Court of Appeal held that a circuit judge and the justices with whom he was sitting acted correctly in retiring to consider together whether a confession which the defence had claimed to be involuntary was admissible or not. In matters of law, however, 'the lay justices must take a ruling from the presiding judge in precisely the same way as the jury is required to take his ruling when the jury considers its verdict' (per Lord Widgery CJ in *Orpin* at p. 287F). The precise facts of *Orpin* would not occur today because justices are not allowed to sit with a professional judge if a case is listed for a plea of not guilty, but the principles on the role of the justices stated in the case do remain valid when the Crown Court is hearing an appeal from a magistrates' court and so includes justices.

The role of the justices was further considered in *Newby* (1984) 6 Cr App R (S) 148, an appeal against sentence passed by a court consisting of a recorder and two justices following N's plea of guilty. Criticising the recorder for announcing sentence immediately after defence counsel's plea in mitigation and without any apparent consultation with the justices (although there had been consultation before coming into court and the passing of notes during counsel's speech), Caulfield J said (at p. 150):

> One would hardly need *Orpin* to recognise that where a recorder or any other judge is sitting with justices, the court consists of the presiding judge and the justices who sit with the judge, and of course on matters of fact the majority decision decides. So obviously there has to be consultation between the presiding judge and the justices who sit with him. [In the present case there had, as a matter of fact, been consultation but there had been no appearance of consultation.] . . .
>
> This court would like to emphasise that where a learned judge is sitting with magistrates, not only should he consult his fellow magistrates by law but he should make sure that the court appreciates that he has consulted. It is not necessary for the court to retire after each particular case. There is nothing wrong in notes being passed between members of the court. But when it comes to the point of sentence having to be given, it is far wiser for the court to show the public that the court is a composite court and that each member has a view which is expressed eventually through the president or chairman of the court.

It is submitted that his lordship's remarks are applicable not only to the passing of sentence but to all decisions (whether interlocutory or final) taken by a court which includes justices.

Modes of Address

Circuit judges, recorders and deputy circuit judges should all be addressed when sitting in court as 'Your Honour', save that any circuit judge sitting at the Central Criminal Court and any senior circuit judge who is the honorary recorder of the city in which he or she sits should be addressed as 'My Lord' or 'My Lady'. **D3.11**

High Court judges sitting in the Crown Court should be addressed as 'My Lord' or 'My Lady' as they would in the High Court.

In cause lists, forms and orders, the following descriptions are appropriate:

Circuit judges	His (or Her) Honour Judge A
Recorders	Mr (or Mrs) Recorder B
Deputy circuit judges	His (or Her) Honour CD, sitting as a deputy circuit judge.

See *Consolidated Criminal Practice Direction*, para. IV.30.

Jurisdiction

By the Supreme Court Act 1981, s. 1(1), the Crown Court has 'such jurisdiction as is conferred on it by or under this or any other Act'. By s. 45(2): **D3.12**

there shall be exercisable by the Crown Court—
(a) all such appellate and other jurisdiction as is conferred on it by or under this or any other Act; and
(b) all such other jurisdiction as was exercisable by it immediately before the commencement of this Act.

Immediately before the commencement of the 1981 Act, the Crown Court exercised the jurisdiction which had been given to it by the Courts Act 1971, which jurisdiction included 'all appellate and other jurisdiction conferred on any court of quarter sessions . . . by or under any Act' (Courts Act 1971, s. 8 and sch. 1, para. 1). The Crown Court has thus inherited the jurisdiction of the older quarter sessions. Furthermore, s. 79(1) of the 1981 Act provides that 'All enactments and rules of law relating to proceedings in connection with indictable offences shall continue to have effect in relation to proceedings in the Crown Court'. It follows that, although the great bulk of the Crown Court's jurisdiction is statute-based, there may still be occasions when — before, during or after a trial on indictment — it is able to exercise a power derived from a rule of common law. An example is the power to release an offender and bind him over to come up for judgment, which is occasionally used in circumstances where the statutory powers to bind a person over to keep the peace or to defer sentence would be inappropriate.

Trial on Indictment

D3.13 The Crown Court has exclusive jurisdiction over trials on indictment (Supreme Court Act 1981, s. 46(1)). The jurisdiction is not geographically restricted: 'The jurisdiction of the Crown Court . . . shall include jurisdiction in proceedings on indictment for offences *wherever committed*, and in particular proceedings on indictment for offences within the jurisdiction of the Admiralty of England' (s. 46(2), emphasis added). This should not, however, be construed to mean that the Crown Court will in general accept jurisdiction over offences committed abroad. The basic rule is that the English criminal courts only inquire into offences allegedly committed in England or Wales or within the jurisdiction of the Admiralty, by which phrase is meant essentially offences committed on British ships on the high seas or on British or foreign ships in British territorial waters (see **A8** both for the general rule and the exceptions to it). Thus, the effect of s. 46(2) is that, assuming the alleged offence is indictable and is an offence in respect of which the English criminal courts accept jurisdiction, the Crown Court will have jurisdiction to try the accused for it.

Appeal

D3.14 A person convicted by a magistrates' court may, if he pleaded not guilty, appeal to the Crown Court against conviction and/or sentence; if he pleaded guilty, he may appeal against sentence (MCA 1980, s. 108, and see **D28.2** *et seq.*).

Committal for Sentence

D3.15 The numerous statutory provisions enabling magistrates' courts to commit an offender to the Crown Court to be sentenced are described fully elsewhere in this work (see **D22.18** *et seq.*).

Summary Offences

D3.16 In certain limited circumstances the Crown Court may have jurisdiction to deal with certain summary offences, pursuant to the CJA 1988, s. 40 and (until its impending repeal is implemented) s. 41. These sections are dealt with in detail in **D10.47** and **D11.15**.

Bail

D3.17 As well as being able to grant bail during the course of a trial on indictment or other proceedings before it, the Crown Court has jurisdiction, *inter alia*, to grant bail to a person: (a) who has been sent to it in custody for trial or sentence; (b) who is appealing to it from a magistrates' court following the imposition of a custodial sentence by the justices; (c) who is appealing from it to the Court of Appeal and has been granted a certificate that the case is fit for appeal; or (d) who has been remanded in custody by a magistrates' court following an argued bail application (see Supreme Court Act 1981, s. 81). Bail is covered in detail in D7.

Contempt etc.

The Supreme Court Act 1981, s. 45(4), provides that 'the Crown Court shall, in relation to the attendance and examination of witnesses, any contempt of court, the enforcement of its orders and all other matters incidental to its jurisdiction, have the like powers, rights, privileges and authority as the High Court'. In particular, the Crown Court is able to deal summarily (i.e. without the empanelling of a jury) with any contempt committed in the face of the court (see generally **B14.69** *et seq.*). The generality of s. 45(4) is subject to the saving that, for purposes of securing the attendance of witnesses, the Crown Court must use the powers given to it by the Criminal Procedure (Attendance of Witnesses) Act 1965, s. 8, and not proceed by way of subpoena. **D3.18**

Judicial Discipline

The Judicial Discipline (Prescribed Procedures) Regulations 2006 (SI 2006 No. 676) set out the procedures to be followed in the investigation and determination of allegations of misconduct by judicial office holders. These procedures govern the exercise of the Lord Chancellor's powers to remove judicial office holders and the Lord Chief Justice's statutory powers formally to advise, warn or reprimand them, or to suspend them from office. Regulation 3 provides for the creation of an Office for Judicial Complaints (the OJC) to support the Lord Chancellor and the Lord Chief Justice in the investigation and determination of allegations of misconduct against judges. Regulation 4 imposes a time-limit of 12 months for the making of a complaint and reg. 5 enables the extension of time-limits. Regulation 9 requires the Lord Chief Justice to make rules for dealing with complaints about justices of the peace, which have to be made to the advisory committee for the local justice area to which the justice is assigned under the Courts Act 2003, s. 10(2). Regulation 14 enables the OJC to dismiss a complaint on any of the grounds set out in reg. 14(1) (including the fact that the complaint does not adequately particularise the matter complained of, or is vexatious, or is without substance, or is untrue, mistaken or misconceived). Under reg. 16, complaints that have not been dismissed by the OJC are referred to the nominated judge, who (under reg. 18) advises the Lord Chief Justice whether the complaint should be dismissed or investigated further or whether disciplinary action should be taken. Where further investigation is required, it is carried out by an investigating judge appointed under reg. 20. The investigating judge advises the Lord Chief Justice and the Lord Chancellor whether the complaint is substantiated and, if so, what disciplinary action should be taken (reg. 22). Regulation 26 sets out the decisions which may be taken after a case has been investigated, including informal action or formal disciplinary action by the Lord Chief Justice or removal from office by the Lord Chancellor. Alternatively, the case may be referred to a review body, established pursuant to reg. 28. The subject of the disciplinary proceedings may also refer the case to a review body (reg. 29(2)). The review body may review any finding of fact and any disciplinary action which has been proposed or taken (reg. 30(1)). **D3.19**

MAGISTRATES' COURTS

Magistrates' courts consist of justices of the peace. The great majority of justices are unpaid lay men or women; a minority are salaried District Judges (Magistrates' Courts), formerly known as stipendiaries, with the minimum qualification of being barristers or solicitors of at least seven years' standing. The bulk of the criminal jurisdiction of magistrates' courts has to be exercised by a court consisting of at least two lay justices sitting in open court. However, **D3.20**

D

Part D Procedure

District Judges almost invariably sit alone. The law on justices and magistrates' courts is contained principally in: (a) the Courts Act 2003 (appointment, removal etc. of justices and organisation of magistrates' courts); (b) the MCA 1980 (jurisdiction and powers of the courts); and (c) the CrimPR (detailed practice and procedure).

The MCA 1980, s. 148(1) provides that: 'the expression "magistrates' court" means any justice or justices of the peace acting under any enactment or by virtue of his or their commission or under the common law'. Thus, whenever a justice or justices sit for the purpose of exercising their jurisdiction as justices they constitute a magistrates' court. Where proceedings fall into a number of distinct stages (as when a magistrates' court, after convicting an offender and imposing a fine, subsequently takes steps to enforce payment of the fine), the court for the later stage need not be constituted by the same justices as constituted the court on the first occasion (s. 148(2)).

Justices of the Peace (Magistrates)

D3.21 The titles 'justice' or 'justice of the peace' and 'magistrate' are interchangeable. Justices are appointed by the Lord Chancellor 'on behalf and in the name of Her Majesty' (Courts Act 2003, s. 10). The Lord Chancellor normally acts on the recommendation of local advisory committees.

Save in the special case of District Judges (Magistrates' Courts) (see **D3.22**), justices are not required to possess any particular qualifications, whether legal or otherwise. There is, however, an obligation on new justices to complete, within a year of appointment, a course of basic instruction in the duties which they will be carrying out. Also a minority of justices are academic lawyers, and there is no objection to the holders or past holders of high judicial office serving as justices. For the special restrictions on the practice of solicitors who are justices, see the Solicitors Act 1974, s. 38. The only significant category of persons actually to be excluded from appointment is undischarged bankrupts.

A justice may be removed from office by the Lord Chancellor with the concurrence of the Lord Chief Justice (Courts Act 2003, s. 11(2)) for incapacity or misbehaviour, persistent failure to meet prescribed standards of competence, or for declining or neglecting to take a proper part in the exercise of his functions as a magistrate. Assuming that does not occur, he retains his status as a justice for life. However, upon his attaining the age of 70 (75 in the case of those who hold or have held high judicial office), a justice's name is put on the 'supplemental list' (see the Courts Act 2003, s. 12), which means that the only functions of a justice which he may perform are insignificant administrative ones, such as authenticating a person's signature. In addition, the Lord Chancellor may direct entry of a name on the supplemental list if either that is expedient because of the justice's age, infirmity or other like cause, or the justice declines or neglects to take a proper part in the work of the bench. A justice may also take the initiative and ask for his name to go on the supplemental list.

Justices, other than District Judges (Magistrates' Courts), are not paid a salary for their work. They are, however, entitled to a travelling and/or subsistence allowance, and to compensation for loss of earnings etc. (Courts Act 2003, s. 15).

District Judges (Magistrates' Courts)

D3.22 Although the great majority of justices are lay, a minority are both paid and legally qualified. The latter (formerly known as stipendiary magistrates) are now properly described as District Judges (Magistrates' Courts). Provisions regarding their appointment, removal, remuneration etc. are contained in the Courts Act 2003, ss. 22 to 26.

Acting on the Lord Chancellor's recommendation, Her Majesty may appoint a barrister or solicitor of not less than seven years' standing to be a District Judge (Magistrates' Courts) or Deputy District Judge and a person so appointed is, by virtue of his office, a justice of the peace for every commission area. One of the District Judges (Magistrates' Courts) is designated the Senior District Judge (Chief Magistrate). District Judges (and Deputy District Judges) sit alone in the magistrates' court.

Under the Courts Act 2003, s. 65, District Judges (Magistrates' Courts) are empowered to exercise some of the powers of a Crown Court judge: sch. 4 sets out a number of interlocutory proceedings and rulings that District Judges will be able to perform before a case is ready to go before a Crown Court judge.

Structure of the Magistrates' Courts System

By contrast with the Crown Court, which is a single court, there are a great number of separate benches of justices who form magistrates' courts as and when required to dispose of the business arising in the areas for which they act. The courts and justices are organised on the basis of local justice areas. **D3.23**

The structure of the system of magistrates' courts changed when the relevant provisions of the Courts Act 2003 came into force on 1 April 2005. Section 7 of the Act creates a single 'commission of the peace' for England and Wales. Under s. 8, England and Wales is divided into areas known as 'local justice areas'; the Local Justice Areas Order 2005 (SI 2005 No. 554), in force from 1 April 2005, specifies the relevant areas. Section 10 makes provision for the appointment of lay justices (that is, justices of the peace who are not District Judges (Magistrates' Courts)). They are appointed for the whole of England and Wales but are assigned to one or more local justice areas by the Lord Chancellor. Under s. 10(3), every lay justice is capable of acting in any local justice area. However, lay justices are deployed to sit in the areas where they live or work, thus continuing the ethos that magistrates' court justice should essentially be local justice.

Jurisdiction

Under the MCA 1980, s. 2(1), a magistrates' court has jurisdiction to try any summary offence and (subject to the mode of trial procedure) any either-way offence (irrespective of where the offence was committed). This re-emphasises the national jurisdiction of the magistracy. If the accused is convicted, the court may sentence him to anything up to the maximum penalty provided for by the statute creating the offence. A court may try offences triable either way allegedly committed by an adult if (a) the offence is not so serious that the court's powers of punishment in the event of conviction would be inadequate, and (b) the accused agrees (ss. 18 to 21). In the event of conviction, the court may impose a penalty of anything up to six months' imprisonment and a fine of £5,000 (s. 32(1)). When implemented, the CJA 2003, s. 282(1), will increase the custodial sentencing powers of a magistrates' court to 12 months for a single offence; a maximum of 65 weeks will apply for two or more offences once the amendment of the MCA 1980, s. 133 by the CJA 2003, s. 155(2) is brought into force. **D3.24**

Where a court has convicted an adult of an offence triable either way it may commit him to the Crown Court for sentence if the court considers its powers of punishment to be inadequate (PCC(S)A 2000, s. 3). When the relevant provisions of the CJA 2003, sch. 3, are in force, the power to commit for sentence under the PCC(S)A 2000, s. 3, will be available only where the accused enters a guilty plea.

A youth court has jurisdiction to try juveniles (persons who have not attained the age of 18) for any offence, whether indictable or summary, other than one of homicide, although in certain circumstances the court may choose instead to send the juvenile to the Crown Court for trial (MCA 1980, s. 24).

A magistrates' court may send someone accused of an indictable offence for trial in the Crown Court irrespective of where the offence was allegedly committed.

A magistrates' court may adjourn proceedings and remand the accused either on bail or in custody (ss. 10(1) and 128). There is also power to bail: (a) an offender whose case has been adjourned for inquiries to be made about him prior to the passing of sentence (s. 10(3)); (b) a person who is being committed to the Crown Court for sentence (PCC(S)A 2000, s. 3); and (c) a person who is appealing to the Crown Court or the High Court against conviction or sentence by the magistrates (MCA 1980, s. 113).

Magistrates' courts are responsible for enforcing the payment of fines, both those fines imposed by a magistrates' court and those imposed by the Crown Court (see Courts Act 2003, s. 97 and schs. 5 and 6, the PCC(S)A 2000, s. 140, and MCA 1980, ss. 75 to 91). Magistrates' courts act as supervising courts for community orders and, if an offender is brought before the court for allegedly failing to comply with the requirements of the order, the court may impose a penalty for the breach of the community order, or (if the community order was imposed by a magistrates' court) re-sentence the offender for the original offence, or (if the original order was made by the Crown Court) commit the offender to the Crown Court to be dealt with (see CJA 2003, sch. 8, part 2). A magistrates' court may deal with a person for misbehaviour etc. in court by imposing imprisonment for up to a month and a fine of £2,500 (Contempt of Court Act 1981, s. 12).

Constitution and Place of Sitting

D3.25 Unless an enactment specifically provides to the contrary, a magistrates' court may not try a charge summarily unless it is composed of at least two justices (MCA 1980, s. 121(1)). This applies whether the offence charged is summary or indictable. Similarly, a court holding a means inquiry under s. 82 of the 1980 Act in respect of a fine defaulter must comprise at least two justices (s. 121(2)). The maximum number of justices who may sit in a criminal case other than in a youth court is three (Justices of the Peace (Size and Chairmanship of Bench) Rules 2005 (SI 2005 No. 553), r. 3). In practice, the court almost always consists of two or three justices. If they include the chairman or one of the deputy chairmen elected by the justices for the local justice area at their annual meeting, then he presides unless he asks one of the others to do so (Courts Act 2003, s. 18). Where neither the chairman nor a deputy chairman is present, precedence will be determined either by any established rule or custom of the bench or, failing that, the order of names on the commission of the peace (see Home Office Circular dated 16 October 1907). The justices composing the court before which any proceedings take place must remain present throughout the proceedings, save that (a) if one or more absent themselves but the court nonetheless is still validly constituted having regard to the nature of the proceedings and the provisions of the MCA 1980, s. 121, then the proceedings may continue before the remaining justices, and (b) where the court has convicted an accused and adjourned before sentencing him, the court which passes sentence need not be composed of the same justices who formed the 'convicting' court (s. 121(6) and (7)). Any decision of the bench may be arrived at by a majority. In the event of an even-numbered court being equally divided, the court must adjourn for re-hearing before a differently constituted bench. The above rules do not apply to District Judges (Magistrates' Courts) who may, and normally do, sit alone unless there is an express provision to the contrary (Courts Act 2003, s. 26). For the special rules governing the constitution of youth courts, see **D23.10** ***et seq.***

Under the MCA 1980, s. 121(4), a magistrates' court must sit in open court if it is conducting a summary trial, imposing imprisonment, or holding an inquiry into the means of an offender under s. 82 of that Act. Moreover, a magistrates' court composed of a single justice may not impose imprisonment for a period exceeding 14 days, and may not order a person to pay more than £1, whether by way of fine, costs, compensation or otherwise (s. 121(5)).

The Courts Act 2003, s. 30(1), empowers the Lord Chancellor to give directions as to the places in England and Wales at which magistrates' courts may sit. Under s. 30(2), the Lord Chancellor may, with the concurrence of the Lord Chief Justice, give directions as to the distribution and transfer of the general business of magistrates' courts between the places so specified. Such directions may (under s. 30(5)) require a defendant to appear at a place in the local justice area in which the offence is alleged to have been committed, or in which the person charged with the offence resides, or in which the witnesses (or the majority of the witnesses) reside; or a place (not necessarily in the same local justice area) where other cases raising similar issues are being dealt with. Section 30(7) empowers the Lord Chancellor to give directions as to the days on which, and times at which, magistrates' courts may sit; subject to these directions, the business of magistrates' courts may be conducted on any day and at any time (s. 30(8)).

Powers of a Single Justice

The Courts Act 2003, s. 49(1), provides that a number of powers of a magistrates' court may be exercised by a single justice of the peace for that area. The list includes extending bail, or imposing or varying conditions of bail; dismissing a charge where no evidence is offered by the prosecution; making an order for the payment of defence costs out of central funds; requesting a pre-sentence report following a plea of guilty and, for that purpose, giving an indication of the seriousness of the offence; requesting a medical report and, for that purpose, remanding the accused in custody or on bail; giving, varying or revoking directions for the conduct of a trial (including directions as to the timetable for the proceedings, the attendance of the parties, the service of documents (including summaries of any legal arguments relied on by the parties), and the manner in which evidence is to be given); and giving, varying or revoking orders for separate or joint trials in the case of two or more accused or two or more charges. **D3.26**

Justices' Clerks

Justices' clerks (and assistant clerks) are appointed by the Lord Chancellor (Courts Act 2003, s. 27(1) and (6)). A justices' clerk must have a five-year magistrates' court qualification (i.e. must have had a right of audience in the magistrates' court for at least five years), or be a barrister or solicitor who has served for not less than five years as an assistant to a justices' clerk, or be a person who has previously been a justices' clerk (s. 27(2)). Section 27(6) also empowers the Lord Chancellor to appoint assistant justices' clerks; a person may be designated if he has a five-year magistrates' court qualification, or has such qualifications as may be prescribed by the Lord Chancellor. Under the Justices' Clerks Rules 2005 (SI 2005 No. 545), r. 2, the acts specified in the schedule to the rules may be done by a justices' clerk or (under r. 3) assistant clerk. The list includes: issuing any summons (including a witness summons); issuing a warrant of arrest (whether or not endorsed for bail) for failure to surrender to the court, where there is no objection on behalf of the accused; dismissing a charge where no evidence is offered by the prosecution; making an order for the payment of defence costs out of central funds; extending bail on the same conditions as those (if any) previously imposed or, with the consent of the prosecutor and the accused, imposing or varying conditions of bail; further adjourning criminal proceedings with the consent of the prosecutor and the accused, provided that the accused either is not remanded or else is remanded on bail on the same terms as previously (or, with the consent of both the prosecutor and the accused, on different terms); further adjourning criminal proceedings, where there has been no objection by the prosecutor and where the accused is remanded on bail in his absence on the same terms as before; where a case is to be tried on indictment, granting a representation order under the AJA 1999, sch. 3, for the purposes of the Crown Court proceedings; asking an accused whether he pleads guilty or not guilty to a charge; fixing or setting aside a date, time and place for the trial of a charge; giving, varying or revoking directions for the conduct of a criminal trial (including directions as to the timetable for proceedings, the attendance of the parties, the service of documents (including summaries of any legal arguments relied on by the parties), and the manner in which evidence is to be given); with the consent of the parties, giving, varying or revoking orders for separate or joint trials in the case of two or more accused or two or more charges; extending, with the consent of the accused, an overall time- **D3.27** limit under the Prosecution of Offences Act 1985, s. 22; requesting a pre-sentence report following a plea of guilty; requesting a medical report and, for that purpose, remanding the accused on bail on the same conditions as those (if any) previously imposed (or, with the consent of the prosecutor and the accused, on other conditions); remitting an offender to another court for sentence; giving consent for another magistrates' court to deal with an offender for breach of a conditional discharge; allowing further time for payment of a sum enforceable by a magistrates' court; varying the number of instalments payable, the amount of any instalment payable and the date on which any instalment becomes payable where a magistrates' court has ordered that a sum adjudged to be paid is to be paid by instalments; requiring an offender to furnish details of his means.

Assistant Clerks

D3.28 The Assistants to Justices' Clerks Regulations 2006 (SI 2006 No. 3405) provide that 'an assistant clerk may be employed as a clerk in court only if he is a barrister or solicitor of the Supreme Court or has passed the necessary examinations for either of those professions, or has been granted an exemption in relation to any examination by the appropriate examining body' (reg. 3). However, under reg. 4, the Lord Chancellor may designate a person to be employed as a clerk in court for a period of up to six months if he is satisfied that the person is a suitable person to be employed as a clerk in court and that no other arrangements can reasonably be made for the hearing of proceedings before the court. Moreover, under reg. 5, the Lord Chancellor may permit a person who is not qualified under reg. 3 to carry out the functions set out in paras. 7, 8, 9(a), 10 to 11 (with the exception of enlarging sureties), 15, 24, 25, 26B and 27 to 36 in the schedule to the Justices' Clerks Rules 2005, to the extent that these functions are performed out of court and provided that that person has been specifically authorised by the justices' clerk for that purpose.

DISQUALIFICATION OF JUSTICES AND JUDGES FROM HEARING PARTICULAR CASES

D3.29 A justice may be disqualified from adjudicating in certain proceedings either by reason of the rule of natural justice that a member of a tribunal must not be biased, or by reason of a specific statutory provision. Where a justice sits when he ought not to have done, the decision of the court is liable to be quashed through the High Court issuing a quashing order upon an application for judicial review. However, the issue of such an order is discretionary, and so, if a party knew of an objection to a justice before the commencement of the proceedings but failed to ask him to withdraw, the order may be refused.

Judicial review is not available to challenge matters relating to trial on indictment (SCA 1981, s. 29(3)), though any issue regarding bias on the part of the trial judge could be raised in any appeal to the Court of Appeal (Criminal Division) to show that the conviction was unsafe.

Actual or Apparent Bias

D3.30 If a justice or judge has a direct interest in the outcome of the case, he will obviously be disqualified from hearing that case. If the justice or judge has an interest other than a direct pecuniary or proprietary one in the outcome of a case, he is disqualified from sitting if there is a real possibility of bias on his part. Although a non-pecuniary interest does not automatically disqualify a justice, it is not essential to show that he was actually biased.

The question in such a case is whether the fair-minded and informed observer, having considered the facts, would conclude that there was a real possibility that the tribunal was biased (*Porter v Magill* [2002] 2 AC 357). In that case, Lord Hope of Craighead notes (at [88]) that there is a close relationship between the concept of independence and that of impartiality. He quotes from the case of *Findlay v UK* (1997) 24 EHRR 221 at pp. 244–5 (para. 73), where the European Court said:

> . . . in order to establish whether a tribunal can be considered as 'independent', regard must be had *inter alia* to the manner of appointment of its members and their term of office, the existence of guarantees against outside pressures and the question whether the body presents an appearance of independence. As to the question of 'impartiality', there are two aspects to this requirement. First, the tribunal must be subjectively free from personal prejudice or bias. Secondly, it must also be impartial from an objective viewpoint, that is, it must offer sufficient guarantees to exclude any legitimate doubt in this respect. The concepts of independence and objective impartiality are closely linked . . .

Lord Hope comments that, in both cases, the concept requires not only that the tribunal must be truly independent and free from actual bias (proof of which is likely to be very difficult), but also that it must not appear, in the objective sense, to lack these essential qualities.

The *Gough* Test The test for apparent bias had been set out by Lord Goff of Chieveley in *Gough* [1993] AC 646 at 670 in these terms: **D3.31**

> I think it unnecessary, in formulating the appropriate test, to require that the court should look at the matter through the eyes of a reasonable man, because the court in cases such as these personifies the reasonable man; and in any event the court has first to ascertain the relevant circumstances from the available evidence, knowledge of which would not necessarily be available to an observer in court at the relevant time . . . I prefer to state the test in terms of real danger rather than real likelihood, to ensure that the court is thinking of possibility rather than probability of bias. Accordingly, having ascertained the relevant circumstances, the court should ask itself whether, having regard to those circumstances, there was a real danger of bias on the part of the relevant member of the tribunal in question, in the sense that he might unfairly regard (or have unfairly regarded) with favour, or disfavour, the case of a party to the issue under consideration by him . . .

In *Porter v Magill*, Lord Hope notes that the 'reasonable likelihood' and 'real danger' tests propounded by Lord Goff in *Gough* had been criticised on the ground that they tend to emphasise the court's view of the facts and to place inadequate emphasis on the public perception of the irregular incident. The Scottish courts (see, for example, *Bradford v McLeod* (1986) SLT 244) had adopted a test which looked at the question whether there was suspicion of bias through the eyes of the reasonable man who was aware of the circumstances. Lord Hope observed that this approach (sometimes described as 'the reasonable apprehension of bias' test) is in line with that adopted in most common-law jurisdictions and by the European Court of Human Rights (which looks at the question whether there was a risk of bias objectively in the light of the circumstances which the court has identified: see *Piersack v Belgium* (1982) 5 EHRR 169 at pp. 179–80 (paras. 30–1); *Pullar v UK* (1996) 22 EHRR 391 at pp. 402–3 (para. 30) and *Hauschildt v Denmark* (1989) 12 EHRR 266 at p. 279 (para. 48)).

The *Gough* Test Revisited In *Bow Street Metropolitan Stipendiary Magistrate, ex parte Pinochet Ugarte (No. 2)* [2000] 1 AC 119 at p. 136, the House of Lords declined to review the *Gough* test. In that case, Lord Hope had expressed the view that the English and Scottish tests were described differently but that their application was likely, in practice, to lead to results that were so similar as to be indistinguishable (p. 142). Moreover, the Court of Appeal, having examined the question whether the 'real danger' test might lead to a different result from that which the informed observer would reach on the same facts, concluded in *Locabail (UK) Ltd v Bayfield Properties Ltd* [2000] QB 451 at p. 477 that, in the overwhelming majority of cases, the application of the two tests would lead to the same outcome. However, in *Re Medicaments and Related Classes of Goods (No. 2)* [2001] 1 WLR 700, the Court of Appeal reconsidered the question of bias. Lord Phillips of Worth Matravers MR, giving the judgment of the court, concluded as follows (at [35]): **D3.32**

> When the Strasbourg jurisprudence is taken into account, we believe that a modest adjustment of the test in *R v Gough* is called for, which makes it plain that it is, in effect, no different from the test applied in most of the Commonwealth and in Scotland. The court must first ascertain all the circumstances which have a bearing on the suggestion that the judge was biased. It must then

D

Part D Procedure

> ask whether those circumstances would lead a fair-minded and informed observer to conclude that there was a real possibility, or a real danger, the two being the same, that the tribunal was biased.

In *Porter v Magill*, Lord Hope (with whom the other Law Lords agreed) approved this 'modest adjustment' of the test in *Gough* subject to one modification. Lord Hope (at [103]) said the test formulated by Lord Phillips:

> expresses in clear and simple language a test which is in harmony with the objective test which the Strasbourg court applies when it is considering whether the circumstances give rise to a reasonable apprehension of bias. It removes any possible conflict with the test which is now applied in most Commonwealth countries and in Scotland. I would however delete from it the reference to 'a real danger'. Those words no longer serve a useful purpose here, and they are not used in the jurisprudence of the Strasbourg court. The question is whether the fair-minded and informed observer, having considered the facts, would conclude that there was a real possibility that the tribunal was biased.

An example of a case where the appearance of bias was alleged is *R (Abdesallam) v Horseferry Road Magistrates' Court* [2006] EWHC 1418 (Admin). The accused's advocate sought to put it to a police officer in cross-examination that he was lying and the chairman of the bench intervened. The advocate objected and, on the advice of their clerk, the justices allowed the advocate to put it to the officer that he was lying. The chairman and the clerk both gave evidence that the advocate had been examining the officer in a hostile tone and that the chairman had intervened to prevent him from doing so. It was held that a fair-minded observer would not have concluded from this exchange that the justices had been biased in favour of the prosecution.

Bench's Knowledge of Accused's Record or Pending Matters

D3.33 There is no blanket rule that the justices must be unaware that there are other charges outstanding against the accused in the same court or that there are offences for which he is awaiting sentence. Where a submission is made that such knowledge disqualifies the justices from acting, they have a discretion to order that the case be tried by a differently constituted bench, but if, having applied the correct test, they conclude that it is proper for them to continue with the case, the Divisional Court will not interfere with their decision (*Weston-super-Mare Justices, ex parte Shaw* [1987] QB 640).

Similar considerations apply where a justice knows from previous dealings with the accused that he is of bad character. The question is whether, having regard to the circumstances of the particular case, there is a real danger of bias on the part of the justice were he to sit. In *Downham Market Magistrates' Court, ex parte Nudd* [1989] RTR 169, Watkins LJ approved earlier authority to the effect that 'mere knowledge of the defendant's previous convictions does not necessarily preclude the court from trying the case. It would only be wrong for the magistrates to proceed where the previous convictions are disclosed to the court in a way which might lead to bias or a suggestion of bias in the minds of the public'. Indeed, in *R (Robinson) v Sutton Coldfield Magistrates' Court* [2006] 4 All ER 1029, the Divisional Court considered the position of the justices where an application is made to adduce bad character evidence pursuant to the CJA 2003, s. 101. Hallett LJ said (at [21]):

> Where an application is made to adduce bad character evidence before a magistrates' court, the justices will, of necessity, hear details of the conviction in order to rule on the application. If the application fails they will put the convictions out of mind when they hear the case. The fact that they know the details of the previous convictions does not disqualify them from discharging their role as fact finders in the trial.

In *Johnson v Leicestershire Constabulary* (1998) *The Times*, 7 October 1998, it was held by the Divisional Court that, where magistrates wrongly become aware that an accused has previous convictions, or has previously been before the court, the test to be applied is whether there is any real danger of bias arising from the magistrates finding out something they should not have discovered. The Court said that it has to be borne in mind that lay justices are capable of putting out of their minds matters which are irrelevant. Similarly, in *R (S) v Camberwell Green Youth Court* [2004] EWHC 1043 (Admin), it was held that a magistrate is not disqualified from hearing the trial of an accused where he has sat in an earlier hearing to issue a bench warrant. The court went on to say that the mere fact that a justice is aware of a previous conviction is not sufficient to disqualify that justice from trying the case of an accused of whose previous conviction the justice is aware. This case involved a district judge (rather than lay justices), but it is submitted that the outcome would have been the same had the court comprised lay justices.

The fact that previous convictions may be admissible in the range of circumstances set out in the CJA 2003, ss. 101 to 106, makes it even less likely that knowledge of previous convictions will be sufficient to disqualify a magistrate from hearing a case. However, specific provision is made for cases where a magistrate becomes aware of a previous conviction through hearing a bail application. The MCA 1980, s. 42, provides that a magistrate may not be a member of the court which tries an accused on a not guilty plea if he has, in the same proceedings, been informed (for the purpose of determining whether bail should be granted) that the accused has one or more previous convictions. This section is repealed by the CJA 2003, sch. 37, part 4, but this repeal has not been brought into effect and so s. 42 remains in force. It is submitted that this must be an oversight. Moreover, it is arguable that a conviction would not necessarily be rendered invalid if a magistrate to whom s. 42 applies was sitting. This argument would be strengthened by the approach taken in *Ashton* [2007] 1 WLR 181, where the key question in the case of procedural failures was held to be whether Parliament intended the proceedings to be invalidated by a procedural irregularity.

Other Interlocutory Rulings

Unless there are special circumstances, the making of an interlocutory ruling on the admissibility of evidence does not deprive justices of the ability to continue the hearing of the trial. Justices should, therefore, not normally disqualify themselves from hearing a trial merely because they have ruled in favour of an *ex parte* application by the prosecution for non-disclosure of material on the ground of public interest immunity (*R (DPP) v Acton Youth Court* [2001] 1 WLR 1828, following *Stipendiary Magistrate for Norfolk, ex parte Taylor* (1997) 161 JP 773 and expressly approved by the House of Lords in *H* [2004] 2 AC 134). **D3.34**

Specific Statutory Provision Disqualifying Justices from Hearing Particular Cases

A justice who is a member of a local authority as defined by the Courts Act 2003, s. 41(6) (e.g., a county council, district council, London borough council, parish or community council or police authority) may not be a member of the Crown Court or of a magistrates' court in any proceedings brought by or against (or by way of appeal from the decision of) the authority or any committee or officer of the authority (Courts Act 2003, s. 41). However, s. 41(5) states that 'no act is invalidated merely because of the disqualification under this section of the person by whom it is done'. **D3.35**

Disqualification of Judges of the Crown Court from Hearing Particular Cases

The rule that nobody may be a judge in his own cause applies to all courts. The position as far as Crown Court judges are concerned was considered in *Mulvihill* [1990] 1 WLR 438. The accused was charged with conspiracy to rob a number of banks and building societies, including the National Westminster Bank. The trial judge owned a number of shares in National Westminster Bank plc. The Court of Appeal, dismissing the appeal against conviction, said that 'a judge in a criminal trial is not, save possibly in some very exceptional circumstances, called upon to declare that he has some remote interest in premises which have become the scene of a crime'. Brooke J said: **D3.36**

> The function of a Crown Court judge conducting a criminal trial on indictment with a jury is very different from that of a lay justice who is one of the primary decision makers in summary proceedings in a magistrates' court; and although [the trial judge] had to make direct decisions on the admissibility of evidence, . . . we do not consider that the hypothetical reasonable bystander would reasonably suspect that it was not possible for him to reach a fair decision because of the existence of his shareholding in one of the institutions whose branch office was robbed.

Rule 63.9 of the CrimPR makes it clear that a justice cannot sit in the Crown Court on the hearing of an appeal in a matter on which he adjudicated. Presumably 'adjudication' is intended to limit the application of the rule to justices who heard the trial itself (or passed sentence following conviction or guilty plea). It is submitted that if a justice was involved in a hearing other than the trial (or sentencing hearing), for example, a bail application or mode of trial hearing, the usual principles governing bias would apply (cf. *Bristol Crown Court, ex parte Cooper* [1989] 1 WLR 878, although it should be borne in mind that this case concerned the licensing jurisdiction of the magistrates, not their criminal jurisdiction).

PARTIES TO CRIMINAL PROCEEDINGS

D3.37 The usual parties to criminal proceedings are the prosecutor and the accused. In *Re Pinochet Ugarte* (2000) *The Times*, 16 February 2000, the Divisional Court stated that there were many bodies representing the interests of victims and other persons who might wish to take part in such proceedings, but there would need to be overwhelming reasons why they should be allowed to intervene in cases other than those which concerned pure points of law, which might well merit different consideration.

Prosecutor

D3.38 The great majority of prosecutions are commenced either by the police and the CPS or by the officers of governmental or quasi-governmental organisations such as local authorities, HM Revenue and Customs, or the Department of Work and Pensions.

So far as 'private' prosecutions are concerned (in other words, those not brought by the police or by another public authority), these have to be brought by the laying of an information (following which the court issues a summons). In *R (Gladstone) v Manchester City Magistrates' Court* [2005] 1 WLR 1987, the Divisional Court held that, unless an information is required by statute to be laid by any particular person, any person may lay it where the offence is not an individual grievance, provided that the prosecution can establish a public interest and benefit as opposed to a purely private interest in criminal proceedings. However, in *Ewing v Davis* [2007] EWHC 1730 (Admin), Mitting J pointed out that, historically, there has never been a requirement that a private prosecutor has to show a public interest where the prosecution is brought under a public general Act. This power has not been fettered by modern statute. Section 6(1) of the Prosecution of Offences Act 1985 neither qualifies nor extends existing rights. His lordship went on to hold that public interest in a private prosecution is established by the nature of the offence as defined in the statute that creates it, not by the circumstances leading up to it. His lordship concluded that *R (Gladstone Plc) v Manchester City Magistrates' Court* should not be taken as an invitation to magistrates to examine the circumstances of alleged offences and their relation to the private prosecutor.

Can an Association Commence a Prosecution?

D3.39 By the CrimPR, r. 7.1(1), 'An information may be laid . . . by the prosecutor . . . in person or by his counsel or solicitor or other person authorised in that behalf'. It might be thought that, by permitting informations to be laid by an agent acting on behalf of the actual prosecutor, r. 4(1) is impliedly recognising that associations may bring prosecutions through the agency of a legal representative or duly authorised member. Such an interpretation of the rule was, however, rejected by the Divisional Court in *Rubin v DPP* [1990] 2 QB 80, in which Watkins LJ expressed the view that a prosecution would not be brought by an inanimate body, whether corporate or unincorporate. This proposition was, however, doubted by Woolf LJ in *Ealing Justices, ex parte Dixon* [1990] 2 QB 91, where his lordship said that 'passages in the judgment of Watkins LJ could be regarded as indicating that a prosecution has to be by an individual rather than a corporate person' but that he (Woolf LJ) had 'reservations as to the reasoning which would lead to this conclusion' (at p. 101D). Even so, his lordship thought it preferable for an individual to lay the information, albeit that he was acting on behalf of a body corporate.

Can Persons Who Are Not Police Officers Commence Prosecutions by Way of Charge?

The procedure for charging a suspect at a police station is described at D2. It is a procedure which, by its very nature, must take place at a police station. Moreover, the PACE 1984, s. 37, places the responsibility for deciding whether or not a person should be charged on the custody officer on duty at the station where the suspect is being detained at the relevant time (see s. 37(7) especially). This, however, has to be read in the light of s. 37B, which provides that where a person is released on bail under s. 37(7)(a), to enable a charging decision to be taken by the CPS, the DPP (in practice, this means a Crown Prosecutor) will decide whether there is sufficient evidence to charge the person with an offence. Moreover, under the Prosecution of Offences Act 1985, s. 3(2), it is the duty of the DPP to take over the conduct of all criminal proceedings instituted on behalf of a police force. Proceedings are instituted on behalf of a police force only where the police force has investigated and arrested the suspect and brought him before the custody officer (*R (Hunt) v Criminal Cases Review Commission* [2001] QB 1108, where the Divisional Court rejected the argument that an Inland Revenue prosecution should have been conducted by the CPS because the suspect had been charged by a custody officer at a police station). Similarly, in *Stafford Justices, ex parte Commissioners of Customs and Excise* [1991] 2 QB 339, where the defendant was arrested by customs officers for alleged drug trafficking offences but was taken to a police station and formally charged by the custody officer, it was held by the Divisional Court that a person such as a customs officer, who has investigated an offence and has arrested a suspect, does not, by taking that suspect to a police station to be charged by a custody officer, thereby surrender prosecution of the proceedings to the DPP. This reasoning was followed in *Croydon Justices, ex parte Holmberg* (1993) 157 JP 277. D3.40

In both cases, the Divisional Court declined to follow *Ealing Justices, ex parte Dixon* [1990] 2 QB 91, where the defendants were charged at a police station with alleged offences under copyright legislation following an investigation by the Federation Against Copyright Theft (FACT) and it was held that a solicitor representing FACT had no right to conduct the prosecution. In light of the later decisions of the Divisional Court, it is submitted that *Dixon* was wrongly decided.

The Director of Public Prosecutions

Insofar as the State plays a direct role in the prosecution system, it does so through the DPP and the law officers of the Crown (the A-G and Solicitor-General). D3.41

The office of DPP is governed by the Prosecution of Offences Act 1985. He is a barrister or solicitor of at least ten years' standing, appointed by the A-G (Prosecution of Offences Act 1985, s. 2). He discharges his functions under the superintendence of the A-G (s. 3(1)). The DPP's duties are listed in s. 3(2) and include the following:

(a) To take over the conduct of all criminal proceedings instituted on behalf of a police force, whether by a member of that force or any other person. An exception is made in the case of 'specified proceedings', that is, those falling within any category specified by the A-G by order made by statutory instrument. The Prosecution of Offences Act 1985 (Specified

Proceedings) Order 1999 (SI 1999 No. 904) exempts from compulsory taking over by the DPP various minor road traffic offences dealt with on a plea of guilty or under the fixed penalty procedure.

(b) To institute and conduct criminal proceedings in any case where it appears to him appropriate to do so either on account of the importance or difficulty of the case or for any other reason.
(c) To take over the conduct of all binding-over proceedings instituted on behalf of a police force.
(d) To have the conduct of extradition proceedings (see **D31**).
(e) To advise police forces, to the extent he considers appropriate, on all matters relating to criminal offences.
(f) To appear for the prosecution when directed by the court to do so on:
  (i) appeals from the High Court to the House of Lords in criminal cases;
  (ii) appeals from the Crown Court to the Court of Appeal (Criminal Division) and from thence to the House of Lords; and
  (iii) appeals to the Crown Court against the exercise by a magistrates' court of its powers under s. 12 of the Contempt of Court Act 1981 to deal with offences of contempt of the court.
(g) To appear, if it seems to him appropriate to do so, to apply for discharge or variation of an ASBO under the CDA 1998, s. 1C.
(h) To discharge such other functions as may from time to time be assigned to him by the A-G.

Where the DPP has the conduct of proceedings in consequence of the duties imposed upon him under s. 3 of the 1985 Act, he may discontinue the proceedings or take any other step in relation to them, including the bringing of an appeal and the making of representations at applications for bail (s. 15(3)).

Further duties imposed on the DPP by the 1985 Act include issuing a code for the guidance of Crown Prosecutors in the performance of various aspects of their duties (s. 10). Another duty resting on the DPP is to give or refuse his consent to a prosecution in those cases where statute provides that the prosecutor may not proceed without it (see **D2.12** for prosecutions requiring the DPP's consent).

The Crown Prosecution Service

D3.42 Section 3(2)(a) of the Prosecution of Offences Act 1985 requires the DPP to 'take over the conduct of all criminal proceedings . . . instituted on behalf of a police force'. To enable him to perform this task, the Act also provided for the creation of the CPS, of which the DPP is the head (s. 1(1)(a)).

The CPS is not instructed by the police — acting on behalf of the DPP it *takes over* prosecutions begun by the police, and therefore exercises an independent judgment in deciding any legal questions which arise.

D3.43 **CPS Involvement in the Charging Process** In light of concerns that the involvement of the CPS was occurring at too late a stage, and that the police were sometimes charging suspects even though there was insufficient evidence for the CPS to allow the case to proceed or were charging suspects with offences which were more serious than the evidence would prove, one of the recommendations of the Auld Review was that the CPS should become involved from the outset. By virtue of the PACE 1984, s. 37B (inserted by CJA 2003, sch. 2, para. 3), if a suspect is released without charge but on police bail, it is then for the CPS to determine whether there is sufficient evidence to charge the suspect with the offence and, if so, whether the suspect should be charged (and, if so, with what offence) or whether he should be given a caution (and, if so, in respect of what offence). The suspect is then to be charged, cautioned, or informed in writing that he is not to be prosecuted. This is subject to general guidance from the DPP (under s. 37A) enabling the police to charge people suspected with particular types of offence without the need to refer the case to the CPS first. Under s. 37B(8) where the CPS decide to charge the suspect, he will be charged either when he returns to the police station to answer his bail etc. or through the new written charge procedure. Under s. 37B(9), a conditional caution (see **D2.28**) can be administered under s. 37B.

Where a suspect is to be charged at the police station by the police, they must first seek advice from the CPS as to whether they have sufficient evidence and what charge(s) are appropriate. This takes place in accordance with the *DPP's Guidance on Charging (Guidance to Police Officers and Crown Prosecutors Issued by the DPP under s 37A of PACE 1984)*, which is available on the CPS web site. It is, of course, still open to a Crown Prosecutor to discontinue the proceedings upon a subsequent review of the case (applying the evidential sufficiency and public interest tests contained in the *Code for Crown Prosecutors*.

The effect of these reforms is that the CPS are involved in deciding what charges (if any) should be preferred in all but the most minor cases (the police may determine the charge for minor road traffic offences and certain other summary offences).

Crown Prosecutors For CPS administrative purposes, the country is divided into areas, with a Chief Crown Prosecutor for each area (Prosecution of Offences Act 1985, s. 1(4)). The DPP may designate any member of the CPS who is a barrister or solicitor to be a Crown Prosecutor (s. 1(3)). Crown Prosecutors have the same rights of audience as practising solicitors, which means essentially that they may appear for the Service in magistrates' courts but, unless they have been granted rights of audience in the higher courts, not in the Crown Court (s. 4 and see **D3.74** for rights of audience in general). Furthermore, without prejudice to any other functions assigned to him as a member of the CPS, a Crown Prosecutor has 'all the powers of the Director as to the institution and conduct of proceedings but shall exercise those powers under the direction of the Director' (s. 1(6)). Where an enactment prevents any step being taken without the DPP's consent or requires any step to be taken by or in relation to him, the consent or step may be taken by or in relation to a Crown Prosecutor (s. 1(7)). Thus, the DPP may delegate to Crown Prosecutors his power to sanction a prosecution in cases where proceedings require his consent. **D3.44**

In *Liverpool Crown Court, ex parte Bray* [1987] Crim LR 51, it was held that the DPP's powers may be exercised by Crown Prosecutors acting within the general authority delegated to them and without express instructions from the DPP. Thus, the DPP's powers to take over the conduct of privately commenced prosecutions and to serve a notice discontinuing a prosecution in its preparatory stages are, in practice, exercised by Crown Prosecutors rather than the DPP himself. The risk of individual Crown Prosecutors coming to widely divergent decisions in similar factual situations is reduced to some extent by s. 10 of the Prosecution of Offences Act 1985, which requires the DPP to issue a code for Crown Prosecutors giving guidance on the general principles to be applied by them in: (a) determining whether proceedings for an offence should be instituted or (if already instituted) discontinued; (b) determining what charges should be preferred; and (c) considering what representations should be made by them to a magistrates' court about the mode of trial suitable for a particular case. The code, which may be altered from time to time, is annexed to the annual report which the DPP is required to make to the A-G, and is reproduced in **appendix** 4.

The Prosecution of Offences Act 1985 also empowers the DPP to appoint persons who are not members of the Service to institute or take over the conduct of such criminal proceedings as he may assign to them (s. 5(1)). The appointed person must have a general qualification (within the meaning of the Courts and Legal Services Act 1990, s. 71). A person appointed under s. 5(1) has, in conducting the proceedings assigned to him, all the powers of a Crown Prosecutor, but has to exercise those powers subject to any instructions given to him by a Crown Prosecutor (s. 5(2)). Section 5 places no fetter on the circumstances in which the DPP may exercise the power to assign cases to non-CPS personnel. In practice, the volume of CPS work in the magistrates' courts is such that some has to be delegated to agents under s. 5. An agent is, however, expected to obtain authority from a CPS lawyer before taking steps in relation to a case such as offering no evidence on a charge or accepting a bind-over (contrast the independence that prosecuting counsel in the Crown Court enjoys: see **D15.4**).

Section 7A of the Prosecution of Offences Act 1985 gives the DPP an additional power of appointment. A member of the Crown Prosecution staff (other than a Crown Prosecutor) can be designated as having the rights of audience of a Crown Prosecutor in relation to bail applications, and the conduct of criminal proceedings in magistrates' courts other than trials. Trials are therefore excluded from the remit of such designated lay staff. The lay staff may also exercise the powers of a Crown Prosecutor except where the offence is triable only on indictment (such offences being excluded by s. 7A(6)).

Prosecutions by Other Persons

D3.45 Section 6(1) of the Prosecution of Offences Act 1985 provides that: 'Nothing in this Part [of the Act] shall preclude any person from instituting any criminal proceedings to which the Director's duty to take over the conduct of proceedings does not apply'. Since the DPP is only required to take over prosecutions begun by the police, it follows that, save in those limited categories of cases where a statute other than the 1985 Act requires a prosecution to have the prior consent of either the DPP or the A-G, there is no restriction on the right of any individual to bring criminal proceedings. This applies whether the individual acts in a purely personal capacity or in the course of his duties for a local authority, government department, business enterprise or other organisation. However, the 1985 Act also gives the DPP a discretion to take over the conduct of proceedings begun by somebody other than himself (s. 6(2)). Since the DPP also has power to discontinue at a preliminary stage proceedings of which he has the conduct, it follows that he can, in effect, bar the continuance of a privately commenced prosecution by taking over its conduct and then serving notice of discontinuance. Alternatively, he can take over a prosecution to ensure its more efficient conduct in the public interest. Where a non-CPS prosecution is withdrawn or not proceeded with within a reasonable time, and there is some ground for suspecting that there is no satisfactory reason for the withdrawal or failure to proceed, the magistrates' court is under a duty to send copies of the documents in the case to the DPP (s. 7(4)); the DPP may then consider whether it is appropriate for him to take over the proceedings.

In *DPP, ex parte Duckenfield* [2000] 1 WLR 55, the Divisional Court considered the basis upon which the DPP ought to take over private prosecutions in order to stop them. It was held that the DPP acted quite properly in not adopting the same test for stopping a prosecution as for starting one. The policy of the DPP was that he would only intervene to stop a private prosecution on evidential grounds where there was clearly no case to answer, and the Divisional Court made it clear that such a policy was in accordance with s. 6(1) of the 1985 Act. It follows that, provided there is evidence to support a private prosecution, the DPP does not have to intervene to stop it, even though he would not have commenced proceedings himself.

In *Bow Street Metropolitan Stipendiary Magistrate, ex parte South Coast Shipping Co.* [1993] QB 645, the Divisional Court held that the fact that the public prosecuting authorities had instituted proceedings for a minor offence arising out of an incident did not preclude a private prosecution for a more serious offence, where there was evidence suggesting culpability. The case arose from the sinking of the Thames pleasure cruiser, the *Marchioness*, by the *Bowbelle*, a disaster in which 51 people died. The master of the *Bowbelle* had been charged under merchant shipping legislation, and was tried twice, the jury failing to reach a verdict on each occasion. A private prosecution for manslaughter was then instituted against the owners of the *Bowbelle* and others. The magistrate's decision to send them for trial was upheld by the Divisional Court.

A private prosecutor may wish to see evidence, including witness statements, that is in the possession of the police or the CPS. However, in *DPP, ex parte Hallas* (1987) 87 Cr App R 340, it was held that s. 6(1) of the 1985 Act does not confer a right to have documents produced in aid of a private prosecution. Nonetheless, once the matter has been sent for trial, the prosecution is deemed to be on behalf of the Crown, and so disclosure may be ordered (*Pawsey* [1989] Crim LR 152).

The Attorney-General

The main functions of the A-G in respect of criminal proceedings are as follows: **D3.46**

(a) He appoints the DPP, who discharges his functions 'under the superintendence of the Attorney-General' (Prosecution of Offences Act 1985, ss. 2 and 3(1)).
(b) Through his office, he may institute and conduct the prosecution of offences of exceptional gravity or complexity, especially those which impinge upon the security of the State and/or this country's relationships with other countries. He may also take over the conduct of a privately commenced prosecution (or direct the DPP to do so). Very occasionally, the A-G appears in court to represent the prosecution.
(c) Certain offences may only be prosecuted by or with the consent of the A-G (see **D2.12**).
(d) From time to time he issues guidelines on aspects of prosecution practice (e.g., in relation to the decision to institute proceedings or the prosecution material which should be made available to the defence).
(e) At any stage after the indictment against an accused has been signed and before the verdict, the A-G may enter a *nolle prosequi*, which terminates the prosecution.

By virtue of the Law Officers Act 1997, s. 1, the functions of the A-G may be discharged by the Solicitor-General.

Nolle Prosequi Either the prosecution or defence may apply informally to the A-G for entry of a *nolle prosequi*. The commonest reason for the power being exercised is that the accused is physically or mentally unfit to be produced in court and his incapacity is likely to be permanent, but there may be other exceptional situations in which a *nolle prosequi* is the best means of halting proceedings which the prosecution agree ought not to be continued. **D3.47**

The power of the A-G to enter a *nolle prosequi* is not shared by the DPP, but it may be viewed as complementing the latter's powers under the Prosecution of Offences Act 1985, s. 23, under which the Director may serve a notice discontinuing proceedings of which he has the conduct if they have not gone beyond the preparatory stages. Once an accused has been sent for trial, a s. 23 notice is impossible, although it would be open to counsel instructed by the Director to offer no evidence when the case comes on for trial.

The Serious Fraud Office

The Serious Fraud Office was set up by the CJA 1987. It is headed by a Director, who is appointed and superintended by the A-G (s. 1(2)). Its functions are to 'investigate any suspected offence which appears to [the Director] on reasonable grounds to involve serious or complex fraud', and to initiate and conduct (or take over and then conduct) any criminal proceedings relating to such fraud (s. 1(3) and (5)). The Director may designate any barrister or solicitor who is a member of the Office to have the same powers as the Director in relation to the institution and conduct of proceedings (s. 1(7) and (8)). The Director of Public Prosecution's duties in relation to the initiation and/or conduct of proceedings where a case appears to be of difficulty or importance do not extend to serious frauds under investigation by the Serious Fraud Office (Prosecution of Offences Act 1985, s. 3(2)). **D3.48**

Serious Organised Crime Agency

D3.49 The SOCPA 2005, s. 1, establishes the Serious Organised Crime Agency (SOCA), to replace both the National Criminal Intelligence Service (NCIS) and the National Crime Squad (NCS). Under s. 2(1), the functions of the SOCA are to (a) prevent and detect serious organised crime, and (b) contribute to the reduction of such crime in other ways and to the mitigation of its consequences. The Serious Fraud Office continues to exist; s. 2(3) provides that if the SOCA becomes aware of conduct which appears to involve serious or complex fraud, it may exercise its functions in relation to that fraud only if the Director of the SFO agrees or if the SFO declines to act in relation to it.

Under s. 5(2)(a), the SOCA may institute criminal proceedings in England and Wales or Northern Ireland. Section 38 governs the prosecution of offences investigated by the SOCA. Under s. 38(1), the Director of Revenue and Customs Prosecutions *may* institute and conduct criminal proceedings in England and Wales that arise out of a criminal investigation by the SOCA relating to a designated offence, and *must* take over the conduct of criminal proceedings instituted by the SOCA in England and Wales in respect of a designated offence. Under s. 38(3), the DPP *may* institute and conduct criminal proceedings in England and Wales that arise out of a criminal investigation by the SOCA relating to a non-designated offence, and *must* (unless the Director of the SFO has the conduct of the proceedings) take over the conduct of criminal proceedings instituted by the SOCA in England and Wales in respect of such an offence. Under s. 38(7)(b), an offence is a 'designated offence' if criminal proceedings instituted by the SOCA in respect of it fall to be referred to the Director of Revenue and Customs Prosecutions by virtue of directions under s. 39(1). Section 39(1) provides that the DPP and the Director of Revenue and Customs Prosecutions, acting jointly, may give directions to the SOCA for enabling the SOCA to determine whether cases arising out of criminal investigations by the SOCA are to be referred to the Director of Revenue and Customs Prosecutions, or to the DPP, in order for him to consider whether to institute proceedings. Under s. 39(7), these directions may make different provision for different cases, circumstances or areas. Section 40 provides that the PACE 1984, ss. 37 to 37B (duties of custody officers etc.) have effect, in relation to a person arrested following a criminal investigation by the SOCA relating to a designated offence, as if references to the DPP were references to the Director of Revenue and Customs Prosecutions.

Under the SOCPA 2005, s. 38(5), the Prosecution of Offences Act 1985, ss. 23 and 23A (power to discontinue proceedings) apply to proceedings conducted by the Director of Revenue and Customs Prosecutions pursuant to s. 38 in the same way that they apply to proceedings conducted by the DPP (see **D3.51**).

Government Departments

D3.50 Several government departments regularly initiate and conduct criminal prosecutions, for example, the Department of Trade and Industry for violations of the Companies Acts and the Department for Work and Pensions for fraudulent benefit claims.

HM Revenue and Customs prosecute offences such as tax evasion, VAT fraud and illegal importation of drugs and other contraband. Under the Commissioners for Revenue and Customs Act 2005, s. 35, the Director of Revenue and Customs Prosecutions may institute and conduct criminal proceedings in England and Wales relating to a criminal investigation by the Revenue and Customs, and must take over the conduct of criminal proceedings instituted in England and Wales by the Revenue and Customs. Section 37 of the Act empowers the Director of Revenue and Customs Prosecutions to designate a member of the Revenue and Customs Prosecutions Office (to be known as a 'Revenue and Customs Prosecutor') to exercise any function of the Director under or by virtue of s. 35. Under s. 37(2), an individual may be designated as a prosecutor only if he has a general qualification within the meaning of the Courts and Legal Services Act 1990, s. 71. Under s. 38, an individual who is not a member of the Revenue and Customs Prosecutions Office, but who has a general qualification within the meaning of the Courts and Legal Services Act 1990, may be appointed by the Director to exercise any function of the Director under s. 35 in relation to specified criminal proceedings, or a specified class or description of criminal proceedings. Moreover, under s. 39, the Director may designate a member of the Revenue and Customs Prosecutions Office who is not legally qualified to conduct summary bail applications (i.e. bail applications in respect of offences that are not triable only on indictment and where the accused has not been sent to the Crown Court for trial) and other ancillary magistrates' court criminal proceedings (i.e. criminal proceedings other than trials in a magistrates' court).

Section 36(3) provides that the Prosecution of Offences Act 1985, ss. 23 and 23A (power to discontinue proceedings) apply to proceedings conducted by the Director of Revenue and Customs Prosecutions in the same way they apply to proceedings conducted by the DPP (see **D3.51**).

DISCONTINUANCE OF AND JUDICIAL RESTRAINT ON CRIMINAL PROSECUTION

Discontinuance of Prosecutions Conducted by the Director of Public Prosecutions

Where the DPP is conducting a prosecution, he may, at any time during the 'preliminary stages' of the proceedings, give notice to the clerk of the court that he does not want the proceedings to continue (Prosecution of Offences Act 1985, s. 23(3)). 'Preliminary stage' does *not* include: (a) any stage of the proceedings after the court has begun to hear evidence for the prosecution at a summary trial of the offence; or (b) any stage of the proceedings after the accused has been sent for trial for the offence. However, the exclusion (by s. 23(2)) of cases that have been sent for trial to the Crown Court is mitigated to a large extent by s. 23A. This specifically provides for a notice of discontinuance to be served where a case has been sent to the Crown Court for trial under the CDA 1998, s. 51. The notice may be served on the Crown Court 'at any time before the indictment is preferred'. This provision will be of even greater importance when the relevant provisions of the CJA 2003, sch. 3, come into force; these extend the scope of the CDA 1998, s. 51, so that it encompasses either-way offences as well as those triable only on indictment. **D3.51**

The effect of the DPP giving notice of discontinuance is that the proceedings are discontinued from the giving of notice. However, they may be revived by the accused himself giving notice that he wishes them to continue (s. 23(3) and (7)). The apparent purpose of allowing the accused to insist on the case continuing is, first, that a full hearing may establish innocence and vindicate him in a way which the mere withdrawal of proceedings could not, and, secondly, if there is an acquittal following trial he may rely on the plea of autrefois acquit if further proceedings are commenced. Conversely, notice of discontinuance does not guarantee that the proceedings will not be revived should additional evidence later be discovered (see s. 23(9), which provides that discontinuance shall not prevent the subsequent institution of fresh proceedings in respect of the same offence).

When giving notice to the court under s. 23(3) the DPP must give his reasons for not wanting the proceedings to continue (s. 23(5)). He must also inform the accused that notice has been given and that he (the accused) has the right to require the proceedings to be continued, but he is not obliged to indicate to the accused his reasons for desiring discontinuance (s. 23(6)). If the accused has been charged at the police station and the DPP wishes to discontinue before there has even been a court appearance, it is merely necessary to serve notice to that effect on the accused himself, and he does not then have the right to require the proceedings to continue (s. 23(4)). Further detailed regulations relating to the giving of notice of discontinuance and 'counter-notices' by the accused are contained in part 8 of the CrimPR. Rule 8.1 states that the period within which the accused may give notice under s. 23(7) that he wants proceedings against him to continue is 35 days from the date when the proceedings were discontinued.

Offering No Evidence

D3.52 Instead of discontinuing proceedings under the Prosecution of Offences Act 1985, s. 23 (see D3.51), the prosecution may simply offer no evidence at the trial. *Cooke v DPP* (1992) 95 Cr App R 233 makes it clear that the statutory power to discontinue a prosecution is additional to the common-law power to offer no evidence.

The court has no power to prevent the offering of no evidence (see Lord Lane CJ in *Canterbury and St Augustine Justices, ex parte Klisiak* [1982] QB 398 at p. 411C–D and *Horseferry Road Magistrates' Court, ex parte O'Regan* (1986) 150 JP 535).

In *Raymond v A-G* [1982] QB 839 the Court of Appeal considered whether it was legitimate for the Director to take over a prosecution with the sole purpose of offering no evidence. It was held that the DPP's decision was not open to attack unless it was so manifestly wrong that it could not have been honestly and reasonably arrived at. Giving the judgment of the court, Sir Sebag Shaw said (at pp. 846H–847D):

> . . . when the Director intervenes in a prosecution which has been privately instituted he may do so not exclusively for the purpose of pursuing it by carrying it on, but also with the object of aborting it; that is to say, he may 'conduct' the proceedings in whatever manner may appear expedient in the public interest. The Director will thus intervene in a private prosecution where the issues in the public interest are so grave that the expertise and the resources of the Director's office should be brought to bear in order to ensure that the proceedings are properly conducted from the point of view of the prosecution.
>
> On the other hand, there may be what appear to the Director substantial reasons in the public interest for not pursuing a prosecution privately commenced. What may emerge from those proceedings might have an adverse effect upon a pending prosecution involving far more serious issues. The Director, in such a case, is called upon to make a value judgment. Unless his decision is manifestly such that it could not be honestly and reasonably arrived at it cannot, in our opinion, be impugned. The safeguard against an unnecessary or gratuitous exercise of this power is that . . . the Director's duties are exercised 'under the superintendence of the Attorney-General' [Prosecution of Offences Act 1985, s. 3(1)]. That officer of the Crown is, in his turn, answerable to Parliament if it should appear that his or the Director's powers under the statute have in any case been abused.

Prosecution of Offences Act 1985, ss. 23 and 23A

23.—(1) Where the Director of Public Prosecutions has the conduct of proceedings for an offence, this section applies in relation to the preliminary stages of those proceedings.

(2) In this section, 'preliminary stage' in relation to proceedings for an offence does not include—

(a) in the case of a summary offence, any stage of the proceedings after the court has begun to hear evidence for the prosecution at the trial;

(b) in the case of an indictable offence, any stage of the proceedings after—

(i) the accused has been committed for trial; or

(ii) the court has begun to hear evidence for the prosecution at a summary trial of the offence;

(c) in the case of any offence, any stage of the proceedings after the accused has been sent for trial under section 51 of the Crime and Disorder Act 1998 (no committal proceedings for indictable-only and related offences).

(3) Where, at any time during the preliminary stages of the proceedings, the Director gives notice under this section to the designated officer for the court that he does not want the proceedings to continue, they shall be discontinued with effect from the giving of that notice but may be revived by notice given by the accused under subsection (7) below.

(4) Where, in the case of a person charged with an offence after being taken into custody without a warrant, the Director gives him notice, at a time when no magistrates' court has been informed of the charge, that the proceedings against him are discontinued, they shall be discontinued with effect from the giving of that notice.
(5) The Director shall, in any notice given under subsection (3) above, give reasons for not wanting the proceedings to continue.
(6) On giving any notice under subsection (3) above the Director shall inform the accused of the notice and of the accused's right to require the proceedings to be continued; but the Director shall not be obliged to give the accused any indication of his reasons for not wanting the proceedings to continue.
(7) Where the Director has given notice under subsection (3) above, the accused shall, if he wants the proceedings to continue, give notice to that effect to the designated officer for the court within the prescribed period; and where notice is so given the proceedings shall continue as if no notice had been given by the Director under subsection (3) above.
(8) Where the designated officer for the court has been so notified by the accused he shall inform the Director.
(9) The discontinuance of any proceedings by virtue of this section shall not prevent the institution of fresh proceedings in respect of the same offence.
[(10) Meaning of 'prescribed'.]

23A.—(1) This section applies where—
(a) the Director of Public Prosecutions, or a public authority (within the meaning of section 17 of this Act), has the conduct of proceedings for an offence; and
(b) the accused has been sent for trial under section 51 of the Crime and Disorder Act 1998 for the offence.
(2) Where, at any time before the indictment is preferred, the Director or authority gives notice under this section to the Crown Court sitting at the place specified in the notice under section 51(7) of the Crime and Disorder Act 1998 that he or it does not want the proceedings to continue, they shall be discontinued with effect from the giving of that notice.
(3) The Director or authority shall, in any notice given under subsection (2) above, give reasons for not wanting the proceedings to continue.
(4) On giving any notice under subsection (2) above the Director or authority shall inform the accused of the notice; but the Director or authority shall not be obliged to give the accused any indication of his reasons for not wanting the proceedings to continue.
(5) The discontinuance of any proceedings by virtue of this section shall not prevent the institution of fresh proceedings in respect of the same offence.

Court Order Restricting the Commencement of a Prosecution

By s. 42 of the Supreme Court Act 1981, the A-G may apply to the High Court for a 'criminal proceedings order'. Such an order prevents the person against whom it is made laying an information or applying for a voluntary bill of indictment unless the High Court gives him leave. Before making the order, the High Court must, after giving the proposed subject the opportunity of making representations, be satisfied that he has 'habitually and persistently and without any reasonable ground . . . instituted vexatious prosecutions (whether against the same person or different persons)'. Where an order has been made, leave to lay an information or apply for a voluntary bill may not be given unless the High Court is satisfied that: (a) the institution of the prosecution would not be an abuse of the criminal process; and (b) the applicant has reasonable grounds for instituting it. There is no appeal against refusal of leave. Thus, instead of being forced to take over the conduct of each prosecution commenced by a vexatious prosecutor and then either offer no evidence or serve a notice of discontinuance, the DPP may request the A-G to obtain a criminal proceedings order, which will prevent further prosecutions by its subject unless he satisfies the High Court that he has good grounds. **D3.53**

ABUSE OF PROCESS: THE POWER TO STAY PROCEEDINGS

D3.54 According to *County of London Quarter Sessions, ex parte Downes* [1954] 1 QB 1, once an indictment has been preferred, the accused must be tried unless:

(a) the indictment is defective (e.g., it contains counts that are improperly joined and so does not comply with the Indictment Rules, r. 9);
(b) a 'plea in bar' applies (such as *autrefois acquit*);
(c) a '*nolle prosequi*' is entered by the A-G to stop the proceedings; or
(d) the indictment discloses no offence that the court has jurisdiction to try (e.g., the offence is based on a statutory provision that was not in force at the date the accused allegedly did the act complained of).

To this list must be added cases where it would amount to an abuse of process to continue with the prosecution. Where proceedings would amount to an abuse of process, the court may order that those proceedings be stayed. The effect of a stay is that the case against the accused is stopped.

In *Beckford* [1996] 1 Cr App R 94, Neill LJ said (at p. 100) that the constitutional principle which underlies the jurisdiction to stay proceedings is that the courts have the power and the duty to protect the law by protecting its own purposes and functions. His lordship quoted the words of Lord Devlin in *Connelly v DPP* [1964] AC 1254, that the courts have 'an inescapable duty to secure fair treatment for those who come or are brought before them'. Neill LJ noted that the jurisdiction to stay proceedings can be exercised in many different circumstances but that two main strands could be detected in the authorities:

(a) cases where the court concludes that the accused cannot receive a fair trial;
(b) cases where the court concludes that it would be unfair for the accused to be tried.

In *Derby Crown Court, ex parte Brooks* (1985) 80 Cr App R 164, Sir Roger Ormrod said (at pp. 168–9) that:

> The power to stop a prosecution arises only when it is an abuse of the process of the court. It may be an abuse of process if either:
> (a) the prosecution have manipulated or misused the process of the court so as to deprive the defendant of a protection provided by the law or to take unfair advantage of a technicality, or;
> (b) on the balance of probability the defendant has been, or will be, prejudiced in the preparation or conduct of his defence by delay on the part of the prosecution which is unjustifiable . . . The ultimate objective of this discretionary power is to ensure that there should be a fair trial according to law, which involves fairness both to the defendant and the prosecution. . . .

The former focuses on the trial process; the latter is applicable where the accused should not be standing trial at all (irrespective of the fairness of the actual trial). Moreover, this is only a partial definition of the scope of abuse of process. In *Horseferry Road Magistrates' Court, ex parte Bennett* [1994] AC 42, Lord Griffiths (at p. 61H) observed that there was no suggestion in the instant case that the appellant could not have a fair trial. However, the court nonetheless had jurisdiction to stay the proceedings. His lordship said:

> If the court is to have the power to interfere with the prosecution in the present circumstances it must be because the judiciary accept a responsibility for the maintenance of the rule of law that embraces a willingness to oversee executive action and to refuse to countenance behaviour that threatens either basic human rights or the rule of law . . . I have no doubt that the judiciary should accept this responsibility in the field of criminal law.

In *DPP v Humphreys* [1977] AC 1, Lord Salmon (at p. 46) commented that a judge does not have 'any power to refuse to allow a prosecution to proceed merely because he considers that, as a matter of policy, it ought not to have been brought. It is only if the prosecution amounts to an abuse of the process of the court and is oppressive and vexatious that the judge has the power to intervene.'

Key Issues

Two key questions run through many of the authorities. (1) To what extent is the accused prejudiced? (2) To what degree are the rule of law and the administration of justice undermined by the behaviour of the investigators or the prosecution? **D3.55**

There is no definitive list of complaints which are capable of amounting to abuse of process but it is possible to derive some categories of abuse from the case law. For example: lengthy delay which causes prejudice to the accused; failure to honour an undertaking given to the accused; failing to secure evidence or destroying evidence; tactical manipulation or misuse of procedures in order to deprive the accused of some protection provided by the law, or taking unfair advantage of a technicality; entrapment; abuse of executive power.

One consequence of the fact that the test for abuse of process is much higher than the judge simply taking the view that the case should not have been brought is that it is not an abuse of process to prosecute someone where the evidence against them is weak. It follows that a judge has no power to prevent the prosecution from presenting their evidence merely on the basis that he considers a conviction unlikely (*A-G's Ref (No. 2 of 2000)* [2001] 1 Cr App R 36).

As well as invoking the right to a fair trial under the ECHR, Article 6, those seeking to establish abuse of process will also rely on the overriding objective set out in the CrimPR, part 1, which requires everyone involved in any way in a criminal case to prepare and conduct the case in accordance with the overriding objective to deal with the case 'justly' (which term includes the requirement to deal with the defence fairly and to deal with the case efficiently and expeditiously: see D4).

Magistrates' Courts

Much of the case law on abuse of process comes from cases tried in the Crown Court. However, abuse of process can also be raised in a magistrates' court. In *Horseferry Road Magistrates' Court, ex parte Bennett* [1994] 1 AC 42, the House of Lords ruled that the jurisdiction exercised by magistrates to protect the court's process from abuse is confined strictly to matters directly affecting the fairness of the trial of the particular accused with whom they were dealing (such as delay or unfair manipulation of court procedures). It does not extend to a wider supervisory jurisdiction to uphold the rule of law. The rationale is that supervision of the use of executive power is a responsibility that is vested in the High Court. Where such an issue arises, the magistrates should adjourn the matter so that an application can be made to the Divisional Court, which is the proper forum for deciding the matter. **D3.56**

In *R (Salubi) v Bow Street Magistrates' Court* [2002] 1 WLR 3073, it was held that the fact that magistrates are required (under the transfer procedure in the CDA 1998, s. 51(1)) to send cases to Crown Court 'forthwith' does not necessarily preclude them from exercising their jurisdiction to stay the proceedings as an abuse of process in an appropriate case. However, it would be appropriate to do so only in rare cases where the defence establish bad faith or serious misconduct. The Divisional Court reiterated that a magistrates' court's power to stay criminal proceedings for abuse of process is strictly confined to matters directly affecting the fairness of a trial before it and that this power should be exercised sparingly. The Court said that where the point is complex or novel it should normally be left for resolution in the Crown Court or the High Court. It should be borne in mind that an abuse of process application may be made immediately after the case arrives at the Crown Court.

In *R (CPS) v City of London Magistrates' Court* [2006] EWHC 1153, the Divisional Court reiterated that, while a magistrates' court has jurisdiction to restrain abuses of its process, that power ought only to be employed in exceptional circumstances. That jurisdiction is, said the Court, usually invoked only where the court concludes either (i) that the accused could not receive a fair trial, or (ii) that it would be unfair for him to be tried.

Where the offence is triable either way, the fact that the defence intend to raise abuse of process as an issue is likely to render the case more suitable for trial on indictment (though it should be borne in mind that it would be possible for the case to be listed before a district judge in the magistrates' court).

Burden and Standard of Proof

D3.57 The normal rule is that he who asserts the abuse of process must prove it; it follows that the defence bear the burden of establishing abuse on the balance of probabilities (*Telford Justices, ex parte Badhan* [1991] 2 QB 78).

It should be noted that in *S (SP)* [2006] 2 Cr App R 341, the Court of Appeal observed that the discretionary decision whether or not to grant a stay by reason of delay is an exercise in judicial assessment dependent on judgement, rather than on any conclusion as to fact based on evidence. It is, therefore, potentially misleading to use the language of burden and standard of proof, which is more apt to an evidence-based fact-finding process. It may well be that this comment should be taken as applying to abuse of process applications generally (i.e. it is not limited to those where delay is an issue), since the balancing of competing interests is at the heart of all abuse claims. It is doubtful, however, that the Court of Appeal intends to signal a new approach to abuse cases: it is likely to remain the case that there is, effectively, a presumption that the trial should go ahead unless there is a compelling reason for stopping the trial from taking place.

Delay

D3.58 There is no general time-limit within which proceedings have to be commenced where the alleged offence is indictable. However, in the case of summary offences, there is a six-month time-limit by virtue of the MCA 1980, s. 127 (see **D20.16**).

Where delay is deliberate, it is likely to be held to amount to an abuse of process. For example, in *Brentford Justices, ex parte Wong* [1981] QB 445, an information against W for careless driving was laid one day within the six-month period permitted by the MCA 1980, s. 127. The prosecutor conceded that he had not then reached a firm decision on whether to take proceedings, but had laid the information simply to keep his options open. Having obtained a summons, he retained it for three months before finally deciding that the prosecution ought to go ahead. W was notified of the decision by letter but a further two months elapsed before the summons was actually served. The magistrates refused an application not to proceed with the trial, since they considered that they were obliged to try an information which had been laid in time. The Divisional Court held that the magistrates had a discretion to decline jurisdiction if there had been an abuse of process, and that what happened in the instant case could properly be regarded as grounds for exercising the discretion in favour of the accused. Donaldson LJ said (at p. 450D–G):

> For my part, I think that it is open to justices to conclude that it is an abuse of the process of the court for a prosecutor to lay an information when he has not reached a decision to prosecute. The process of laying an information is, I think, assumed by Parliament to be the first stage in a continuous process of bringing a prosecution. [Section 127 of the MCA 1980] is designed to ensure that prosecutions shall be brought within a reasonable time. That purpose is wholly frustrated if it is possible for a prosecutor to obtain summonses and then, in his own good time and at his convenience, serve them. Of course there may be delays in service of the summonses due perhaps to the evasiveness of the defendant. There may be delays due to administrative reasons which are excusable, but that is not so in this case.

> Here, as I understand it, there was a deliberate attempt to gain further time in which to reach a decision. It is perhaps hard on the prosecutor to characterise that as an abuse of the process of the court because I am sure there was no intention by the prosecutor to abuse the process of the court. He thought he could legitimately do this. For my part, I do not think that he can. In such a case I think it is open to the justices to say: 'This is an abuse of the process. We, therefore, decline jurisdiction and we dismiss the summonses.' But I think it is a matter which has to be investigated by justices.

The time-limit applicable to summary offences was an important part of Donaldson LJ's reasoning. However, it is submitted that the general thrust of his comments is equally applicable to indictable offences to which that specific time-limit is not applicable.

Inadvertent Delay Where deliberate delay in bringing the case to court cannot be shown, the defence may nonetheless apply for the proceedings to be stayed on the ground of abuse of process if (a) there has been inordinate or unconscionable delay due to the prosecution's inefficiency, and (b) prejudice to the defence from the delay is either proved or to be inferred (per Lloyd LJ in *Gateshead Justices, ex parte Smith* (1985) 149 JP 681). This followed the approach taken by the court in *Grays Justices, ex parte Graham* [1982] QB 1239, where it was held that, although delay alone could be sufficient to justify a stay of proceedings, if sufficiently prolonged, some other impropriety is generally required. The test to be applied is whether the delay in bringing the proceedings is of such magnitude as to render them vexatious and an abuse of the court's process. At p. 1248, May LJ said, 'we do not think that this court should create any form of artificial limitation period for criminal proceedings where it cannot truly be said that the due process of the criminal courts is being used improperly to harass a defendant'. **D3.59**

In *Derby Crown Court, ex parte Brooks* (1985) 80 Cr App R 164, Sir Roger Ormrod propounded a general test for abuse of process but also made specific reference to delay (suggesting a more liberal approach). Two key elements can be derived from this so far as delay is concerned: to amount to abuse of process, the delay must cause prejudice to the accused, and the delay must be unjustified.

In *Bow Street Stipendiary Magistrate, ex parte DPP* (1989) 91 Cr App R 283, the Divisional Court made it clear that, to amount to an abuse of process, delay has to produce genuine prejudice and unfairness. In some cases, however, prejudice would be inferred from substantial delay and the prosecution will have to rebut that inference of prejudice. For example, it is proper to infer prejudice from the mere passage of time where the offence involves an allegation of a single and brief event, which must depend on the recollections of those involved. Similarly, in *Telford Justices, ex parte Badhan* [1991] 2 QB 78, the Court of Appeal said that, whilst it is for the accused to show, on a balance of probabilities, that he is prejudiced in his defence, it is legitimate for the court to infer prejudice where the period of delay is long. The period in question in that case was some 15 or 16 years, and so the court was entitled to infer prejudice and conclude that a fair trial was impossible.

Effect of Delay on Fairness of Trial In *Bell v DPP of Jamaica* [1985] AC 937, the Privy Council laid down guidelines for determining whether delay would deprive the accused of a fair trial. The relevant factors were said to be: **D3.60**

(a) the length of delay;
(b) the prosecution's reasons to justify the delay;
(c) the accused's efforts to assert his rights; and
(d) the prejudice caused to the accused.

In *A-G's Ref (No. 1 of 1990)* [1992] QB 630, the Court of Appeal held that delay would be held to amount to an abuse of process only in exceptional circumstances. This is so even where the delay could not be justified by the prosecution. The Court said that there should be no stay where the delay has been caused by the complexity of the case, or where the actions of the accused have contributed to that delay. In absence of any fault on the part of the prosecution, the accused has to show 'serious prejudice', to the extent that a fair trial is not possible. Whether or not to grant a stay on the basis of delay is a matter for the discretion of the judge. When exercising that discretion, the judge should bear in mind that the trial process itself may enable any prejudice to the accused to be eliminated or reduced (for example, through the power to exclude evidence or by giving directions to the jury on the effect of the delay).

The same approach was adopted by the House of Lords in *A-G's Ref (No. 2 of 2001)* [2004] 2 AC 72. Two questions had been certified by the Court of Appeal: (1) whether criminal proceedings might be stayed on the ground that there had been a breach of the reasonable time requirement imposed by the ECHR, Article 6(1), in circumstances where the accused could not demonstrate that any prejudice had arisen from the delay; and (2) when the relevant time period commences in the determination of whether, for the purposes of Article 6(1), a criminal charge had been heard within a reasonable time. The House of Lords ruled that criminal proceedings may be stayed on the ground that there had been a violation of the reasonable time requirement in the Article 6(1), only if (a) a fair hearing is no longer possible, or (b) there is some other compelling reason why it would be unfair to try the accused (per Lord Bingham at [24]). It was said that it would be anomalous if breach of the reasonable time requirement were to have an effect that is more far-reaching than breach of the accused's other rights in Article 6(1). The House of Lords said that the remedy for such a breach should be effective, just and proportionate. It follows that a stay of the proceedings would never be an appropriate remedy if any lesser remedy would be just and proportionate, adequately vindicating the accused's Convention right. The House of Lords also ruled that, if the breach were established retrospectively (in other words, used as a ground for appeal against conviction), it would not be appropriate to quash any conviction unless the hearing was unfair or it had been unfair to try the accused at all (ibid.).

So far as the second question is concerned, it was held that, for the purposes of the requirement under Article 6(1), a criminal charge must be heard within a reasonable time, the relevant period commences at the earliest time at which a person was officially alerted to the likelihood of criminal proceedings against him (which will normally be when he is charged or served with a summons or written charge).

In *Dyer v Watson* [2004] 1 AC 379, the Privy Council held that the threshold of proving that a trial has not taken place within a reasonable time is a high one, not easily crossed. If the period which has elapsed is one which, on its face, gives ground for real concern, it is necessary to look into the detailed circumstances of the particular case and it must be possible to justify any lapse of time which appears to be excessive. Regard must be had to the complexity of the case, the conduct of the accused (he cannot properly complain of delay of which he is the author) and the manner in which the case has been dealt with by the prosecution and the courts. There is no general obligation on a prosecutor to act with all due expedition and diligence, but a marked lack of expedition, if unjustified, would point towards a breach of the reasonable time requirement.

More recently, the Court of Appeal, in *S (SP)* [2006] 2 Cr App R 341, summarised the position as follows: (a) even where delay is unjustifiable, a permanent stay should be the exception rather than the rule; (b) where there is no fault on the part of the complainant or prosecution, it will be very rare for a stay to be granted; (c) no stay should be granted in the absence of serious prejudice to the accused, so that no fair trial can be held; (d) when assessing possible serious prejudice, the judge should bear in mind his power to regulate the admissibility of evidence, and that the trial process itself should ensure that all the relevant factual issues arising from delay will be placed before the jury for their consideration; (e) if the judge's assessment is that a fair trial is possible, a stay should not be granted (per Rose LJ at [21]).

It is submitted that, where the issue is raised at the stage when the magistrates are contemplating the transfer of the case to the Crown Court, the magistrates should refuse to transfer the case on the basis of delay only in cases where it is patent that a fair trial could not take place; in other cases, the magistrates should send the case to the Crown Court and allow a Crown Court judge to consider whether steps can be taken to enable the accused to have a fair trial (for example, specific directions to the jury about the effect of the delay on the ability of the accused to conduct his defence).

So far as appeals are concerned, *Ali* [2007] EWCA Crim 691 emphasises that the question for the Court of Appeal is not whether the judge was correct to refuse to stay the proceedings, but rather whether the effect of the delay is such as to lead the court to the conclusion that the verdicts were unsafe.

Mitigating the Effects of Delay Where the defence argue that the proceedings amount to an abuse of process, an important consideration, where there has been delay in bringing the prosecution, is whether a direction to the jury about the effect of the delay is a sufficient remedy for the accused. Specimen direction number 37 (issued by the Judicial Studies Board) suggests that the trial judge should point out to the jury that, because they are concerned with events which are said to have taken place a long time ago, they must appreciate that there may be a danger of real prejudice to the accused and this possibility must be borne in mind when considering whether the case against him has been proved. The jury should be directed in terms that they should 'make allowances for the fact that from the defendant's point of view, the longer the time since an alleged incident, the more difficult it may be for him to answer it' and that (even if they believe that the delay is understandable) if they decide that, because of the delay, the accused has been placed at a real disadvantage in putting forward his case, they must take that into account in his favour when deciding if the prosecution has made them sure of his guilt. In *H* [1998] 2 Cr App R 161, the Court of Appeal stated that such a direction was not inevitable, but was required only when some significant difficulty for the defence was raised or became apparent to the judge. In *M* [2000] 1 Cr App R 49, it was said that trial judges should tailor their directions to the circumstances of the particular case and added that, where the evidence was cogent, such a warning might not be necessary and its absence would not necessarily render a conviction unsafe, particularly when counsel's submissions at trial had not highlighted any specific risk of prejudice. **D3.61**

An example of a case where there was held to be a lack of prejudice (and hence no abuse of process) was *Central Criminal Court, ex parte Randle* [1991] 1 WLR 1087. The applicants were charged with offences arising out of the escape from custody of George Blake while he was serving a lengthy prison sentence for spying. They appeared before the Central Criminal Court in 1990, some 23 years after the alleged offences. They applied for the proceedings to be stayed on the grounds of unreasonable delay, but were refused, and they sought judicial review of that decision. The Divisional Court refused their application. They had published a book in 1989, which had provided much of the material upon which the prosecution relied. In the light of its contents, the plea of failing memory could not be advanced, and so there was no prejudice to them. The Divisional Court therefore refused to interfere with the judge's discretion. Similarly, in *Buzalek* [1991] Crim LR 115, the fact that the case turned largely on documentary evidence (and that it was possible for witnesses to refresh their memories from the documents) meant that delay did not cause prejudice to the accused.

Sexual Offences and Delay Cases involving sexual offences, such as child abuse cases, may be regarded as an exceptional category in their own right. It is often the case that such allegations emerge a long time after the alleged abuse took place. The view generally taken by the courts is that the unfairness can be minimised by a direction to the jury to take proper account of the fact that the accused was handicapped in defending the case because of the length of time which has elapsed since the alleged offence was committed. Any residual prejudice is regarded as outweighed by the importance of prosecuting such serious offences. **D3.62**

See, for example, *E* [2004] 2 Cr App R 621, where the Court of Appeal dismissed an appeal against conviction on the basis that the appellant was not put in an impossible position to defend himself; it said that juries should be trusted to make allowances not only for the lapse of time but also for the difficulties faced by an accused who could only deny the offence.

It is important to note that there will be cases where the effect of the delay cannot be assessed until after the evidence has been heard. In *Smolinski* [2004] 2 Cr App R 40, the Court of Appeal said that applications to stay proceedings based on abuse of process where there has been delay should be discouraged. Lord Woolf CJ (at [8] and [9]) pointed out that in cases of alleged sexual offences, it is sometimes very difficult for young children to speak about such matters and therefore it is only many years later that the offences come to light. However, when a long time has elapsed, careful consideration must be given by the prosecution as to whether it is right to bring the prosecution at all. If, having considered the evidence to be called, and the witnesses having been interviewed on behalf of the prosecution, a decision is reached that the case should proceed, then in the normal way it is better not to make an application based on abuse of process. Unless the case is exceptional, the application will be unsuccessful. If an application is to be made to a judge, the best time for doing so is after any evidence has been called and for the judge then, having scrutinised the evidence with particular care, to come to a conclusion whether or not it is safe for the matter to be left to the jury. A similar point about the timing of applications based on abuse of process was made by Hooper LJ in *Burke* [2005] EWCA Crim 29:

> Prior to the start of the case it will often be difficult, if not impossible, to determine whether a defendant can have a fair trial because of the delay coupled with the destruction of documents and the unavailability of witnesses. Issues which might seem very important before the trial may become unimportant or of less importance as a result of developments during the trial, including the evidence of the complainant and of other witnesses including the defendant should he choose to give evidence. Issues which seemed unimportant before the trial may become very important.

Failing to Obtain, Losing or Destroying Evidence

D3.63 In *Medway* [2000] Crim LR 415, the accused was convicted of robbery. It was alleged that he robbed an elderly lady of her handbag. A closed-circuit television camera was operating in the area, but the police, having looked at the film, decided that it contained nothing of value. The tape was destroyed. The judge refused to stay the trial as an abuse of process in the absence of the tape. The Court of Appeal dismissed the appeal. It was said that there was no evidence of malice, and nothing to show that the absence of the tape made the conviction unsafe. An accused could be disadvantaged in a case where evidence had been tampered with, lost or destroyed, but it was only in exceptional circumstances, for example, where such interference was malicious, that a stay was justified.

In *Dobson* [2001] EWCA Crim 1606, the Court of Appeal considered the position where police had failed to obtain CCTV footage relating to the accused's defence of alibi. Their lordships said that, in determining whether there was an abuse of process, it was appropriate to consider:

(a) what was the duty of the police;
(b) whether they had failed in it by not obtaining or retaining the appropriate video footage;
(c) whether there was serious prejudice which rendered a fair trial impossible; and
(d) whether the police failure was a result of bad faith or serious fault.

In the instant case, the police should have looked at the CCTV footage, and had failed in their duty to do so. However, the prejudice was not serious because it was uncertain that the footage would have assisted the defence, the accused was in a position to understand the relevance of the footage and could have requested it and/or sought other evidence to support his alibi. There was no question of malice or intentional omission, as opposed to oversight, on behalf of the police. The judge was therefore right to conclude that a fair trial was possible and the conviction was upheld.

The same approach was taken in what is now to be regarded as the leading authority on such cases, *R (Ebrahim) v Feltham Magistrates' Court* [2001] 2 Cr App R 23. Brooke LJ said (at [74]) that the starting point must be whether there was a duty on the investigator to obtain or retain the material in question. That question will be answered through the provisions of the Code of Practice issued under part II of the CPIA 1996 (see **appendix** 5). If there was no duty to obtain or retain the evidence in question, there can — of course — be no grounds to stay the proceedings for failure to do so. If there was a duty, and that duty has been breached, a stay will be granted only if the accused has been 'seriously prejudiced' by the failure to obtain the evidence, or by its loss or destruction. Brooke LJ said that there has to be either an element of bad faith, or at the very least some serious fault, on the part of the police or the prosecution authorities, for this ground of challenge to succeed. It follows that a stay will, unless there has been bad faith on the part of the prosecution, only be granted where the accused could not have a fair trial. The Court added that the normal forum for challenges to the prosecution case is the trial process itself, which is well equipped to deal with most complaints about how the investigators or prosecution have behaved (for example, through the discretion to exclude evidence under the PACE 1984, s. 78). At [25] Brooke LJ said:

> Two well-known principles are frequently invoked in this context when a court is invited to stay proceedings for abuse of process:
> (i) The ultimate objective of this discretionary power is to ensure that there should be a fair trial according to law, which involves fairness both to the defendant and the prosecution, because the fairness of a trial is not all one sided; it requires that those who are undoubtedly guilty should be convicted as well as that those about whose guilt there is any reasonable doubt should be acquitted.
> (ii) The trial process itself is equipped to deal with the bulk of the complaints on which applications for a stay are founded.

At [27], his lordship went on:

> It must be remembered that it is a commonplace in criminal trials for a defendant to rely on 'holes' in the prosecution case, for example, a failure to take fingerprints or a failure to submit evidential material to forensic examination. If, in such a case, there is sufficient credible evidence, apart from the missing evidence, which, if believed, would justify a safe conviction, then a trial should proceed, leaving the defendant to seek to persuade the jury or justices not to convict because evidence which might otherwise have been available was not before the court through no fault of his. Often the absence of a video film or fingerprints or DNA material is likely to hamper the prosecution as much as the defence.

In *Khalid Ali v Crown Prosecution Service, West Midlands* [2007] EWCA Crim 691, the Court of Appeal emphasised that, in such cases, the mere fact that missing material might have assisted the defence will not necessarily lead to a stay. In considering whether or not to order a stay, the court will have regard to whether there is sufficiently credible evidence, apart from the missing evidence, leaving the defence to exploit the gaps left by the missing evidence. Moses LJ said that the 'rationale for refusing a stay is the existence of credible evidence, itself untainted by what has gone missing'.

Going Back on a Promise

D3.64 In *Croydon Justices, ex parte Dean* [1993] QB 769, the Divisional Court held that, where the police give to a person an undertaking, promise or representation that he will not be charged in exchange for his co-operation, it *may* amount to an abuse of process if he is subsequently prosecuted. In such circumstances, it is not necessary for the accused to show that there was bad faith on the part of the police.

An example of a prosecution change of mind amounting to an abuse of process is *Bloomfield* [1997] 1 Cr App R 135. B was charged with possession of a Class A controlled drug. At a preliminary hearing, prosecuting counsel indicated to the defence that the Crown wished to offer no evidence because it was accepted that B had been the victim of a set-up. Owing to the presence in court of certain people it would have been embarrassing to the police and prosecution if no evidence had been offered that day, so counsel spoke to the judge in his room. An order was then made in open court to adjourn the case and re-list it 'for mention'. The CPS subsequently arranged a conference with new prosecuting counsel and informed the defence that there had been a change of plan and that the Crown intended to continue the prosecution against B. An application at the trial to stay the proceedings as an abuse of process failed. It was held by the Court of Appeal that allowing the prosecution to go ahead amounted to an abuse of process since, whether or not there was prejudice to the accused, it would bring the administration of justice into disrepute if the Crown were permitted to revoke its original decision without any reason being given as to what was wrong with it, particularly as it had been made in the presence of the judge. The Court added that it was irrelevant whether prosecuting counsel had the authority to drop the case, since neither the court nor the accused could be expected to enquire whether prosecuting counsel had authority to conduct a case in court in any particular way and so were entitled to assume, in ordinary circumstances, that counsel did have such authority.

Another example of a prosecution being held an abuse of process is *Jones v Whalley* [2007] 1 AC 63 (see **D2.19**), where a private prosecution was held to be an abuse of process because the accused had previously been cautioned by the police for the offence in question, and the terms of the caution had said, in terms, that he would not have to go before a criminal court in connection with the matter. The House of Lords observed that allowing private prosecutions to proceed, despite an assurance that the offender would not have to go to court, would tend to undermine not only the non-statutory system of cautions, but also the schemes for cautioning young offenders and adult offenders that Parliament had endorsed in the CDA 1998 and the CJA 2003. Their lordships also noted that the abuse complained of was not abuse impairing the fairness of the trial (since evidence of the accused's admission to the offence, and of the caution administered by the police, could be excluded), but went to the fairness of trying the accused at all.

Giving an indication that the case will be dropped does not necessarily mean that it will be an abuse of process for the prosecution to have a change of mind. In *Horseferry Road Magistrates' Court, ex parte DPP* [1999] COD 441, the district judge stayed prosecution where an earlier assurance that no action would be taken had been given to the solicitor acting for the accused. The Divisional Court quashed the stay, holding that the breach of an earlier promise would not, on its own, justify staying the proceedings. There would have to be some particular prejudice or special circumstances to justify a stay. The Court considered *Bloomfield*, and noted that no evidence would have been offered against the accused but for the prosecution request for an adjournment (which they made for their convenience).

Another example is *Mulla* [2004] 1 Cr App R 6. The accused was charged with causing death by dangerous driving. On the morning of the first day of the trial, the prosecution indicated that they would be willing to accept a plea of guilty to careless driving. The judge was dissatisfied with the decision and asked the prosecutor to reconsider. In the afternoon, after having reconsidered the matter, the prosecution indicated that they had decided to proceed with the original charge of causing death by dangerous driving. The Court of Appeal held that this did not amount to an abuse of process. This was not a case in which the accused's hopes were raised, later to be dashed, since he knew from the beginning of the proceedings in court that the judge did not approve of the course which the prosecution were proposing to take. The Court said that factors to be considered include what view is expressed by the judge when the prosecution gives its indication, the period of time over which the prosecution reconsiders the matter before they change their mind, whether or not the accused's hopes have been inappropriately raised, and whether there has been, by reason of the change of course by the prosecution, any prejudice to the defence.

In *Abu Hamza* [2007] 2 WLR 226, the Court of Appeal said that, where a person has been told he will not be prosecuted for an offence, 'it is not likely to constitute an abuse of process to proceed with a prosecution unless (i) there has been an unequivocal representation by those with the conduct of the investigation or prosecution of a case that the defendant will not be prosecuted and (ii) the defendant has acted on that representation to his detriment. Even then, if facts come to light which were not known when the representation was made, these may justify proceeding with the prosecution despite the representation' (per Lord Phillips CJ at [54]). His lordship added (at [51]) that 'it is usually in the public interest that those who are reasonably suspected of criminal conduct should be brought to trial. Only in rare circumstances will it be offensive to justice to give effect to this public interest'.

Immunity from Prosecution

The SOCPA 2005, s. 71, makes provision for immunity from prosecution. It provides that, if a specified prosecutor (i.e. the DPP, the Director of Revenue and Customs Prosecutions, the Director of the Serious Fraud Office or a prosecutor acting on their behalf) thinks that, for the purposes of the investigation or prosecution of any offence, it is appropriate to offer any person immunity from prosecution, he may give the person a written 'immunity notice' (s. 71(1)). A person who has been given such a notice cannot be prosecuted for an offence of a description specified in the notice unless he fails to comply with any of the conditions specified in the notice, in which case the notice ceases to have effect (s. 71(2) and (3)). Given the clear statutory wording, a court would have little option but to regard a prosecution brought in breach of s. 71 as an abuse of process. **D3.65**

Manipulation of Procedure

An example of manipulation of procedure is where a charge alleging a summary offence is replaced with one alleging an indictable offence, or vice versa. Paragraph 7.3 of the Code for Crown Prosecutors (see **appendix** 4) makes it clear that the charge should not be changed simply because of the decision made as to trial venue. In *Canterbury and St Augustine Justices, ex parte Klisiak* [1982] QB 398, it was said that the court should interfere with the prosecution's decision as to what offences to proceed upon only 'in the most obvious circumstances which disclose blatant injustice'. In other words, it has to be clear that the change in the charge is not a bona fide result of a re-assessment of the appropriateness of the original charge. As it was put in *Sheffield Justices, ex parte DPP* [1993] Crim LR 136, it is only appropriate to interfere where the court concludes that the prosecution were acting in bad faith (i.e. deliberately manipulating the system to deprive an accused of his rights). **D3.66**

Another situation where allegations of manipulation can be made is where the accused is charged with a different offence at the time when the custody time-limit for the original offence is about to expire (or has expired), so that a new custody time-limit starts to run. In *R (Wardle) v Leeds Crown Court* [2002] 1 AC 754, a murder charge was replaced with a manslaughter charge when the custody time-limit was about to expire. Their lordships held that the bringing of a new charge would be an abuse of process if the prosecution could not demonstrate, on the facts of the case, that the bringing of the new charge was justified and the magistrates were satisfied that it had been brought solely for the arbitrary and improper purpose of substituting a new custody time-limit.

Abuse of process can also be used in cases which fall just outside the scope of the *autrefois* doctrine but where it would nonetheless be unfair to allow a further prosecution to take place. For example, in *Beedie* [1998] QB 356, the accused was charged with offences under health and safety legislation and, following his conviction, he was charged with manslaughter arising out of the same facts. The Court of Appeal ruled that it was an abuse of process to have sequential trials for offences on an ascending scale of gravity.

Entrapment

D3.67 In *Looseley* [2001] 1 WLR 2060, the House of Lords said that, although entrapment is not a substantive defence in English law, where an accused can show entrapment, the court may stay the proceedings as an abuse of the court's process or it may exclude evidence pursuant to the PACE 1984, s. 78. Of these two remedies, the grant of stay (rather than the exclusion of evidence at the trial) should normally be regarded as the appropriate response, since a prosecution founded on entrapment would be an abuse of the court's process. Police conduct which brings about state-created crime is unacceptable and improper, and to prosecute in such circumstances would be an affront to the public conscience. However, if a person freely took advantage of an opportunity to break the law given to him by a police officer, the police officer is not to be regarded as inciting or instigating the crime. The court should consider whether the police did no more than present the accused with an unexceptional opportunity to commit a crime. The yardstick for the purposes of this test is, in general, whether the police conduct preceding the commission of the offence was no more than might have been expected from others in the circumstances. Whether a police officer can be said to have caused the commission of the offence, rather than merely providing an opportunity for the accused to commit it with a police officer rather than with someone else, will usually be a most important factor, but not necessarily decisive. Ultimately, the overall consideration is always whether the conduct of the police or other law enforcement agency was so seriously improper as to bring the administration of justice into disrepute. In applying this test, the court has regard to all the circumstances of the case, including: (i) the nature of the offence (since the use of proactive techniques is more appropriate in the case of some types of offences (e.g., dealing in unlawful substances, offences with no immediate victim (such as bribery), offences which victims are reluctant to report and conspiracies) — the secrecy and difficulty of detection, and the manner in which the particular criminal activity is carried on, are also relevant considerations; (ii) the reason for the particular police operation and supervision (having reasonable grounds for suspicion is one way good faith may be established, but having grounds for suspicion of a particular individual was not always essential); (iii) the nature and extent of police participation in the crime (the greater the inducement held out by the police, and the more forceful or persistent the police overtures, the more readily might a court conclude that the police overstepped the boundary). Their lordships added that neither the judicial discretion conferred by the PACE 1984, s. 78, nor the court's power to stay proceedings as an abuse of the court, has been modified by the ECHR, Article 6 or the jurisprudence of the European Court of Human Rights. There is no appreciable difference between the requirements of Article 6 (or the Strasbourg jurisprudence on Article 6, such as *Teixeira de Castro v Portugal* (1998) 28 EHRR 101: see **A7.39**) and English law.

Abuse of Executive Power

D3.68 In *Horseferry Road Magistrates' Court, ex parte Bennett* [1994] 1 AC 42, the accused had been brought back forcibly to the UK in disregard of extradition procedures that were available. This was held to amount to an abuse of process even though a fair trial was possible. The point was that the accused should not have been before the court in the first place.

In *Mullen* [2000] QB 520, the security services and police had procured M's unlawful deportation from Zimbabwe. The Court of Appeal ruled that, even if no complaint can be made as to the fairness of the trial itself, unconscionable conduct on the part of the authorities in bringing the accused before the court *may* amount to an abuse of process. Thus, a conviction may be regarded as unsafe on the basis that the trial on which it was founded was an abuse of process. However, it is not invariably an abuse of process: every case should be approached on its own facts, as a court could properly exercise its discretion to allow a conviction to stand where the seriousness of the offence outweighs any abuse of process by the prosecution.

This approach was also adopted by the House of Lords in *Latif* [1996] 1 WLR 104. L was convicted of being knowingly concerned in the importation into the UK of heroin which had been brought into the country by an undercover customs officer. The House of Lords held that whether the proceedings should have been stayed on the ground of abuse was a matter of discretion for the judge, who had to decide whether the matters said to constitute abuse of process amounted to what Lord Steyn described as an 'affront to the public conscience'. His lordship added that this requires the judge to balance the public interest in ensuring that those who are charged with serious crimes should be tried against the competing public interest in not conveying the impression that the court will adopt the approach that the end justifies any means. In the instant case, the judge had been entitled to conclude the proceedings should not be stayed; for similar reasons, the judge had not erred in not exercising his discretion to exclude the core of the prosecution case.

Bringing Justice into Disrepute

Closely related to abuse of executive power are cases where the investigators have behaved in a way that is wholly improper. In *Grant* [2006] QB 60, for example, the police unlawfully intercepted and recorded privileged conversations between the suspect and his legal adviser. No useful evidence was gathered in this way, and so there was nothing to exclude under the PACE 1984, s. 78. The Court of Appeal said that such unlawful acts, amounting as they did to a deliberate violation of a suspect's right to legal professional privilege, were so great an affront to the integrity of the justice system, and therefore the rule of law, that the associated prosecution was thereby rendered abusive and ought not to be countenanced by the court, despite the absence of any actual prejudice to the accused. **D3.69**

Procedure for Making Abuse of Process Applications

Crown Court The procedure to be followed when making an abuse of process application to stay proceedings in the Crown Court is contained the *Consolidated Criminal Practice Direction*, para. IV.36 (see **appendix** 7). In summary, this requires written notice of the application to be given to the prosecutor (and to any co-accused) and to the court at least 14 days before the date fixed for trial. The notice has to specify the nature of the application, and set out the grounds upon which it is made. The advocate appearing for the applicant must serve a skeleton argument on the court and on the other parties at least five working days before the application is due to be heard. The prosecution advocate must serve a responsive skeleton argument at least two working days before the hearing. The skeleton arguments must set out any propositions of law to be advanced, together with any authorities that are relied on. The specific pages in the authorities must be identified. In appropriate cases, the court will order longer lead times when the usual time-limits cannot be complied with (as might be the case if the issues raised are very complex). **D3.70**

The guidance notes to the form which is used for the Plea and Case Management hearing (PCMH) in the Crown Court point out the PCMH itself is the appropriate forum for such applications.

In *Sheffield Stipendiary Magistrate, ex parte Stephens* (1992) 156 JP 555, the Divisional Court warned against the excessive citing of cases in abuse of process applications. Their lordships stressed that each case depends on its own facts. The same point was made in *Newham Justices, ex parte C* [1993] Crim LR 130.

Magistrates' Courts As to the procedure that the magistrates ought to adopt where abuse of process is raised, it is essential that they hear from both the prosecution and the defence. In *Clerkenwell Stipendiary Magistrate, ex parte Bell* (1991) 159 JP 669, the magistrate heard **D3.71**

evidence from a police officer explaining the reason for the delay (of some two and a half years) but he declined to hear evidence from the accused. The Divisional Court held that this was a breach of natural justice and quashed the decision to send the accused to the Crown Court for trial. Similarly, in *Crawley Justices, ex parte DPP* (1991) 155 JP 841, the Divisional Court quashed the decision of the justices to dismiss the case because of delay. The bench had not heard from the prosecution nor enquired fully of the accused as to the facts.

LEGAL REPRESENTATION AND RIGHTS OF AUDIENCE

The Prosecution in the Crown Court

D3.72 At a trial on indictment, the position at common law was that the prosecution had to be legally represented. The only clear modern ruling to that effect was by Judge David QC in *George Maxwell (Developments) Ltd* [1980] 2 All ER 99, where the judge ruled that the case would fail for want of prosecution unless C (a private prosecutor) instructed solicitors and counsel (since, once the indictment was signed, the proceedings continued in the name of the Crown). According to *Southwark Crown Court, ex parte Tawfick* [1995] Crim LR 658, the position has now been altered by the Courts and Legal Services Act 1990, s. 27(2)(c), which provides that a person shall have a right of audience before a court in relation to any proceedings only where he has a right of audience granted by that court in relation to those proceedings. The Divisional Court observed that this gave the Crown Court discretion to allow a private individual to conduct a private prosecution before it. Glidewell LJ added, however, that it was a discretion which would be exercised only occasionally. It is respectfully submitted that this is correct, but that, where there is an appeal against conviction or sentence from a magistrates' court it is arguably anomalous to require the prosecutor to be represented, since he was entitled to conduct the summary proceedings in person.

The Accused in the Crown Court

D3.73 The accused is entitled to decline legal representation and present his case in person. If he is represented during the initial stages of a trial on indictment and then wishes to dispense with counsel's services, application to that effect must be made to the trial judge, who has a discretion to refuse to release counsel. It is, however, rare for the accused's application to be refused. In *Lyons* (1979) 68 Cr App R 104, Waller LJ said (at p. 108) that 'it may well be that in the vast majority of cases a judge, faced with an application to dispense with counsel . . . would allow the application . . . But at the end of the day it is a matter for the discretion of the learned judge'.

The court has the power to prevent an unrepresented accused from cross-examining in an oppressive manner (see *Brown* [1998] 2 Cr App R 364). Moreover, since the YJCEA 1999, ss. 34 to 39, came into effect, unrepresented defendants are prohibited from cross-examining complainants and child witnesses in trials for certain specified offences, and the court has the power to prohibit cross-examination of witnesses by unrepresented defendants in any other case if satisfied that the circumstances of the witness and the case merit it, and that a prohibition would not be contrary to the interests of justice. There are provisions for the appointment of representatives to conduct cross-examination on behalf of unrepresented defendants. The procedural aspects of the restriction on cross-examination by an accused acting in person are set out in the CrimPR, part 31 (which applies both to the Crown Court and to the magistrates' courts).

Rights of Audience in the Crown Court

D3.74 Until comparatively recently, only practising barristers had a right of audience in the Crown Court. The Courts and Legal Services Act 1990 enacted a statutory scheme for the definition and regulation of rights of audience before the courts. It preserves all existing rights of audience (ss. 31 and 32), and sets up a framework for the granting of new rights (s. 27). Machinery has been introduced for advocates who are not barristers to obtain rights of audience formerly held only by barristers. In particular, the right of audience in the Crown Court was extended to solicitors in private practice, subject to compliance with the Higher Courts Qualification Regulations 2000, which are available on the Solicitors Regulation Authority web site and are currently under review.

Magistrates' Courts

In the magistrates' court, neither the prosecutor nor the accused need be legally represented. A private prosecutor (meaning here one who institutes proceedings solely in a personal capacity and not on behalf of a body to which he belongs) will often appear in person, as when the victim of an alleged assault takes out a summons against his assailant and then both argues the case himself and gives the principal evidence for the prosecution. In the case of police prosecutions, the Prosecution of Offences Act 1985, s. 3(2)(a), requires that the DPP, through the CPS, must take over the conduct of the prosecution. **D3.75**

Representation in a magistrates' court may be either by counsel or by solicitor, since both have the right of audience. Furthermore, magistrates have an inherent power to regulate procedure in their courts in the interests of justice, and that would appear to include a limited discretion to allow someone other than counsel, a solicitor or the party himself to present a case.

Arranging for Legal Representation for the Prosecution

It is the responsibility of the CPS to arrange for the prosecution to be legally represented in cases where the DPP has the conduct of the proceedings. Crown Prosecutors may and commonly do represent the CPS at proceedings in magistrates' courts. For trials on indictment (and, in practice, for appeals to the Crown Court and committals for sentence), the CPS are obliged to brief an advocate with the right of audience in the Crown Court unless the case is conducted by a Crown Prosecutor with a right of audience in the higher courts. There is nothing to stop the CPS briefing an advocate for a specific case in a magistrates' court, although the usual practice is to employ counsel or a solicitor as agent to handle the entire CPS list for a court session (under the POA 1985, s. 5). **D3.76**

Major prosecuting authorities other than the CPS (such as HM Revenue and Customs, the Department of Work and Pensions and local authorities) have salaried legal departments to prepare cases. Otherwise, a non-police prosecutor who wishes to be legally represented must instruct solicitors privately, and they will, if necessary, brief counsel. Various enactments also permit certain types of prosecution in the magistrates' courts to be presented by officials who are not practising solicitors and may not even be lawyers (e.g., Local Government Act 1972, s. 223, and Social Security Administration Act 1992, s. 116, which allow authorised persons to prosecute).

Arranging for Legal Representation for the Accused

An accused secures legal representation by instructing solicitors. It is always open to him to apply for public funding to cover the costs. The great majority of defendants in the Crown Court are publicly funded, as are most tried summarily for indictable offences, but only a small minority of those charged with summary offences are granted public funding (see D29.1 *et seq.* for details). Some publicly funded representation is provided through a system of salaried public defenders, but the majority is provided through solicitors in private practice who carry out what is still generally referred to as 'legal aid' work. **D3.77**

OPEN JUSTICE

The General Rule that Proceedings Should be in Open Court

D3.78 It has long been established that criminal trials should take place in open court and be freely reported. On the basis of Lord Diplock's speech in *A-G v Leveller Magazine Ltd* [1979] AC 440 at pp. 449H–450D:

(a) The normal rule is that criminal proceedings (like other litigation) should be conducted publicly.
(b) Nonetheless, courts do have power, by virtue of their general right to control their own procedure, to order that the public be excluded.
(c) The exercise of the power, in common with any other derogation from the principles of open justice, should be strictly confined to cases where the public's presence would genuinely frustrate the administration of justice, and should not be used merely to save parties, witnesses or others from embarrassment or to conceal facts which it might, on more general grounds, be desirable to keep secret.
(d) Insofar as it is correct to speak of a judge or magistrate having a discretion to sit in camera, that discretion may only be exercised in narrowly circumscribed circumstances and consistently with the general spirit of English jurisprudence, which is overwhelmingly in favour of open justice.

A decision to sit in camera is *not* justified merely on the ground that, having regard to the nature of the witness's proposed evidence, he would find it embarrassing to testify publicly (*Malvern Justices, ex parte Evans* [1988] QB 540, in which the Divisional Court held that it was an inappropriate (though not unlawful) exercise of discretion for justices to sit in camera in a case involving special reasons for not disqualifying, for the sole purpose of sparing the defendant the ordeal of giving evidence of 'embarrassing and intimate details' of her personal life). Even when it is claimed that the safety of a witness or party will be endangered by an open hearing, the court should consider carefully whether he can be adequately protected by means less drastic than totally excluding the public. In *Reigate Justices, ex parte Argus Newspapers* (1983) 5 Cr App Rep (S) 181, the Divisional Court emphasised that it is only in exceptional circumstances that a court may depart from the rule that justice has to be administered in public. Hearing a matter in camera is a course of last resort and the justices should have applied their minds to how else they might have dealt with the matter (in the instant case, an order could have been made at the beginning of the proceedings under the Contempt of Court Act 1981, s. 11, protecting the identity of the accused).

It should also be borne in mind that a witness's fears may be overcome by the use of special measures (e.g., under the YJCEA 1999: see **D14.97**), and in other cases it may be more appropriate to deal with a reluctant witness by the threat of contempt proceedings than by depriving the public of access to the courts.

Sitting 'In Camera'

D3.79 **Statutory Provisions** There are a number of statutory provisions which permit or require the exclusion of the public in certain proceedings. The following provide examples.

(a) In proceedings for offences under the Official Secrets Act 1911 or 1920, the court may, on application being made by the prosecution that the publication of any evidence to be given or of any statement to be made in the course of the proceedings would be prejudicial to national safety, order that the public be excluded for some or all of the hearing, though the passing of sentence must take place in public (Official Secrets Act 1920, s. 8(4)).

(b) No child (i.e. person under the age of 14) is permitted to be in court while criminal proceedings are in progress against a person other than himself, save insofar as his presence is required as a witness or 'otherwise for the purposes of justice' (CYPA 1933, s. 36).

(c) Where a juvenile (i.e. person aged under 18) is called as a witness in proceedings in relation to an offence against, or any conduct contrary to, decency or morality, the court may direct that any persons not directly involved in the case be excluded from the court during the taking of the juvenile's evidence, save that bona fide representatives of the press may not be so excluded (s. 37).

(d) The CrimPR, r. 16.11, empowers Crown Court judges to sit in chambers when exercising certain functions, for example hearing bail applications (and appeals under the Bail (Amendment) Act 1993); issuing a summons or warrant; hearing applications relating to procedural matters that are preliminary or incidental to the Crown Court proceedings. Although bail applications in the Crown Court are generally listed to be heard in chambers, any application to sit in public must be approached on the footing that it must be acceded to unless there is a sound reason for excluding the public. When considering such applications, the court must start from the 'fundamental presumption in favour of open justice' (*R (Malik) v Central Criminal Court* [2006] 4 All ER 1141, per Gray J at [40]).

(e) The CrimPR, r. 16.10, makes provision for applications for an order that all or part of a Crown Court trial be held in camera, 'for reasons of national security or for the protection of the identity of a witness or any other person'. The applicant must serve notice of application, seven days before the trial is due to begin, upon the Crown Court and upon his opponent. The appropriate officer of the Crown Court will then ensure that a copy of the notice is prominently displayed within the precincts of the court. The application is then heard, unless the court orders otherwise, in camera, after the accused has been arraigned but before the jury is sworn. The trial is then adjourned for 24 hours or until the appeal is determined or leave to appeal refused.

(f) Special rules govern public access to youth courts (see **D23.11**).

Freedom of the Media to Report Court Proceedings

Section 4 of the Contempt of Court Act 1981 governs liability for the reporting of court proceedings. **D3.80**

Contempt of Court Act 1981, s. 4

(1) Subject to this section a person is not guilty of contempt of court under the strict liability rule in respect of a fair and accurate report of legal proceedings held in public, published contemporaneously and in good faith.

(2) In any such proceedings the court may, where it appears to be necessary for avoiding a substantial risk of prejudice to the administration of justice in those proceedings, or in any other proceedings pending or imminent, order that the publication of any report of the proceedings, or any part of the proceedings, be postponed for such period as the court thinks necessary for that purpose.

(2A) Where in proceedings for any offence which is an administration of justice offence for the purposes of section 54 of the Criminal Procedure and Investigations Act 1996 (acquittal tainted by an administration of justice offence) it appears to the court that there is a possibility that (by virtue of that section) proceedings may be taken against a person for an offence of which he has been acquitted, subsection (2) of this section shall apply as if those proceedings were pending or imminent.

(3) For the purposes of subsection (1) of this section . . . a report of proceedings shall be treated as published contemporaneously—
 (a) in the case of a report of which publication is postponed pursuant to an order under subsection (2) of this section, if published as soon as practicable after that order expires;
 (b) in the case of a report of allocation or sending proceedings of which publication is permitted by virtue only of subsection (6) of section 52A of the Crime and Disorder Act 1998 ('the 1998 Act'), if published as soon as practicable after publication is so permitted;

(c) in the case of a report of an application of which publication is permitted by virtue only of sub-paragraph (5) or (7) of paragraph 3 of schedule 3 to the 1998 Act, if published as soon as practicable after publication is so permitted.

D3.81 **Scope of Order** The *Consolidated Criminal Practice Direction*, para. I.3.3, states that all orders under s. 4(2) must be 'formulated in precise terms having regard to the decision in *R v Horsham Justices, ex parte Farquharson* [1982] QB 762', and must include: (a) the order's precise scope; (b) the time at which it shall cease to have effect; and (c) the specific purpose for which it was made. The order must be put into writing, and the press should be informed. Examples of situations in which the power given to the courts by the Contempt of Court Act 1981, s. 4(2), may be of value are: (a) when an accused is to be tried successively on separate indictments (or several accused are to be tried separately for connected offences) and reports of the evidence given at the trial held first are likely to prejudice jurors for the later trials; and (b) when evidence and/or argument is put before the judge at a trial on indictment in the absence of the jury, the purpose of sending the jury out being to prevent their being prejudiced by, for example, evidence which the judge ultimately rules to be inadmissible.

In *Ex parte The Telegraph plc* [1993] 1 WLR 980, it was held that, in forming a view whether the making of an order under s. 4(2) is necessary for avoiding a substantial risk of prejudice in the administration of justice, the court should have regard to the competing public considerations of ensuring a fair trial and of open justice. The Court of Appeal went on to observe that the two main requirements of s. 4(2) are distinct and so the judge must first identify the risk of substantial prejudice, and then go on to consider whether, in the light of the competing public interests, an order is necessary in order to avoid the risk, whether in his discretion he should make it and, if so, with all or only some of the restrictions sought. It is submitted that the consequence of this is that the court ought not to make an order under s. 4(2) if there is another way of avoiding a substantial risk of prejudice; if an alternative is available, it should be used rather than an order under s. 4(2).

The powers of the court to postpone publication under s. 4(2) are exhaustive, and so the court has no inherent power in addition to the terms of that provision (*Newtownabbey Magistrates' Court, ex parte Belfast Telegraph Newspapers Ltd* (1997) *The Times*, 27 August 1997, where it was held that the court had no power to prohibit the publication of the name and address of the accused, and the nature of the indecent assault charge against him, on the ground that publication might be prejudicial to the accused's own welfare).

In *A-G v Guardian Newspapers Ltd* [1992] 1 WLR 874, one of the issues considered by the Divisional Court was whether the making of an order under s. 4(2), and its terms, could themselves be reported. Mann LJ thought it very doubtful whether such a report could be published. If it could, then that might cause the very mischief which the order was intended to prevent. It might therefore be appropriate in some cases for the judge to make plain whether the making of the order and its terms could be published. Brooke J added that, if the judge needed help in determining whether to make an order, he could adjourn until the press was represented, or he had the help of an *amicus curiae*. In *Clerkenwell Stipendiary Magistrate, ex parte The Telegraph Plc* [1993] QB 462, the Divisional Court made it clear that the court has a discretion to hear representations from the press regarding a s. 4(2) order. Although the power is discretionary, it would generally be right to exercise it by hearing from the press, who are best qualified to represent that public interest in publicity which the court had to take into account in performing the necessary balancing exercise.

D3.82 **Effect of the ECHR** In *Re S (a Child) (Identification: restriction on publication)* [2005] 1 AC 593, the House of Lords reiterated the substance of the decision about the interplay between the ECHR, Articles 8 and 10 in *Campbell v MGN Ltd* [2004] 2 WLR 1232: (a) neither article has precedence over the other; (b) where the values under the two articles are in conflict, an intense focus on the comparative importance of the specific rights being claimed in the individual case is necessary; (c) the justifications for interfering with or restricting each right must be taken into account; (d) the proportionality test must be applied to each. Lord Steyn went on (at [30]),

> A criminal trial is a public event. The principle of open justice puts, as has often been said, the judge and all who participate in the trial under intense scrutiny. The glare of contemporaneous publicity ensures that trials are properly conducted. It is a valuable check on the criminal process. Moreover, the public interest may be as much involved in the circumstances of a remarkable acquittal as in a surprising conviction. Informed public debate is necessary about all such matters. Full contemporaneous reporting of criminal trials in progress promotes public confidence in the administration of justice. It promotes the values of the rule of law.

On this basis, it was held that the press should not be restrained from publishing the identity of the accused in a murder trial in order to protect the privacy of the accused's child, who was not involved in the criminal proceedings.

The same approach was taken in the case of *A Local Authority v W, L, W, T and R* [2006] 1 FLR 1, where the Court considered again the relationship between Articles 8 and 10 of the ECHR. Sir Mark Potter said that each propounds a fundamental right which there is a pressing social need to protect; equally, each qualifies the right it propounds so far as it may be lawful, necessary and proportionate to do so in order to accommodate the other. He went on to say that the exercise to be performed is one of parallel analysis in which the starting point is presumptive parity, in that neither Article 8 nor Article 10 has precedence over or 'trumps' the other. This exercise of parallel analysis requires the court to examine the justification for interfering with each right, and the issue of proportionality is to be considered in respect of each. It is not a mechanical exercise to be decided upon the basis of rival generalities. An intense focus on the comparative importance of the specific rights being claimed in the individual case is necessary before the ultimate balancing test in terms of proportionality is carried out. The interest in open justice is a factor to be accorded great weight in both the parallel analysis and the ultimate balancing test. However, the weight to be accorded to the right freely to report criminal proceedings is not invariably determinative of the outcome; indeed, although it is the ordinary rule that the press, as public watchdog, may report everything that takes place in a criminal court, that rule might nonetheless be displaced in unusual or exceptional circumstances.

Imposition of a Permanent Ban on Reporting Certain Matters

In addition to their power to postpone publication of court reports by virtue of an order under the Contempt of Court Act 1981, s. 4(2), the courts are empowered by a number of statutory provisions to impose a *permanent* ban on the reporting of certain matters. **D3.83**

Contempt of Court Act 1981, s. 11

> In any case where a court (having power to do so) allows a name or other matter to be withheld from the public in proceedings before the court, the court may give such directions prohibiting the publication of that name or matter in connection with the proceedings as appear to the court to be necessary for the purpose for which it was so withheld.

Section 11 complements the common-law power of a court, sitting in public, to receive a small part of the evidence (such as the name and address of a witness) in a form which is not communicated to the public. The terms of the s. 11 show that an order under it may be without limitation of time but may only be made where the court has legitimately exercised its common law power to receive evidence or other information without allowing it to be disclosed to the public (see *Arundel Justices, ex parte Westminster Press Ltd* [1985] 1 WLR 708, *Evesham Justices, ex parte McDonagh* [1988] QB 553). The *Consolidated Criminal Practice Direction*, para. I.3, *Restrictions on reporting proceedings* (see **appendix** 7) applies in part to orders under s. 11 as well as to orders under s. 4(2).

D3.84 **Juveniles** So far as juveniles are concerned, under the CYPA 1933, s. 39, the onus is on the Crown Court or magistrates' court to make an order protecting the juvenile's anonymity. The opposite applies in the youth court, where reporting restrictions to protect the juvenile's identity apply automatically (see CYPA 1933, s. 49, and **D23.12**).

In *Lee* [1993] 1 WLR 103, the Court of Appeal summarised the position in relation to appeals against a decision under s. 39 as follows:

(a) a member of the press who is aggrieved by an order under s. 39 should go back to the Crown Court in the event of a change of circumstances, or should appeal to the Court of Appeal under the CJA 1988, s. 159 (see below);
(b) an accused who is aggrieved by the withholding or discharging of an order under s. 39 should go back to the Crown Court in the event of a change of circumstances or challenge the validity of the order by seeking judicial review;
(c) if an accused indicates that he is intending to apply to the Divisional Court, the Crown Court has power under s. 39 to make a temporary order or grant a stay of the order discharging the direction, pending a decision of the Divisional Court.

Their lordships went on to comment on the approach which the court ought to adopt in considering applications under s. 39. Whereas in *Leicester Crown Court, ex parte S* [1993] 1 WLR 111 the Divisional Court had said that a direction prohibiting publication should only be refused in 'rare and exceptional cases', the Court of Appeal in *Lee* said that, for its part, it would not wish to see the discretion fettered so tightly. This approach was confirmed by the Divisional Court in *Central Criminal Court, ex parte S* (1999) 163 JP 776. Their lordships said that to say that a direction could be discharged only in rare and exceptional circumstances would place an unwarranted gloss upon the broad discretion conferred by statute. The age of the accused is an important factor, but not the only one. The weight to be attributed to the different factors might shift at different stages of proceedings, and particularly after the defendant had been found or pleaded guilty and sentenced. It might then be appropriate to place greater weight on the public interest in knowing the identity of those who had committed crimes, particularly serious ones. The fact that the accused was lodging an appeal might be a material consideration in deciding whether to lift a reporting restriction, but would not always be a weighty factor.

D3.85 **Sexual Offences** The courts also have powers under the Sexual Offences (Amendment) Act 1992. The broad effect of this Act is that the alleged victim in a case of rape or one of the sexual offences listed in s. 2 of the 1992 Act is entitled to anonymity. Once an allegation of one of the offences in question has been made, nothing may be published which is likely to lead members of the public to identify the alleged victim (s. 1(1)). It follows that, in reporting the proceedings at and prior to a trial for rape or one of the offences covered by the 1992 Act, the media are obliged to omit anything likely to disclose the complainant's identity, even if that information was given in open court. Under s. 1(1), the restriction continues for the lifetime of the complainant. The prohibition on publicity may be lifted by order of the court if either: (a) publicity is required by the accused so that witnesses will come forward and the conduct of the defence is likely to be seriously prejudiced if the direction is not given; or (b) the judge at trial is satisfied that imposition of the prohibition imposes a substantial and unreasonable restriction on the reporting of the proceedings and it is in the public interest to relax the restriction (s. 3).

D3.86 **'Reporting Directions'** The CrimPR, part 16, makes provision for the making of 'reporting directions' under the YJCEA 1999, s. 46. The effect of such a direction is that no matter relating to the witness may be included in any publication during the lifetime of the witness, if it is likely to lead members of the public to identify that person as a witness in the proceedings (see **D21.36**).

All the provisions described above relate to the reporting of court proceedings held in public.

The Administration of Justice Act 1960, s. 12 (see **B14.99**), deals with the reporting of proceedings which were held in camera. There is no automatic rule that the reporting of in camera proceedings amounts to contempt — just as when public proceedings were reported, it has to be shown that the reporting involved a substantial risk of prejudice to the administration of justice (per Lord Scarman in *A-G v Leveller Magazine Ltd* [1979] AC 440 at p. 472F–G).

The Principle of Open Justice and Magistrates' Courts

The MCA 1980, s. 121(4), requires a magistrates' court to sit in open court when trying an accused or imposing imprisonment. In *Malvern Justices, ex parte Evans* [1988] QB 540, it was held that (despite the apparently mandatory nature of the wording of s. 121(4)) justices have an inherent power to exclude the public and thus conduct the proceedings in camera, although that power should be exercised only in the exceptional circumstances where it was necessary for the proper administration of justice. Thus, in determining whether to exclude the public, magistrates' courts are in the same position as other courts. **D3.87**

The importance of open justice in the magistrates' court was emphasised in *Faversham and Sittingbourne Justices, ex parte Stickings* (1996) 160 JP 801. The magistrates, during the course of a trial and acting on the advice of their clerk, ruled that certain prosecution evidence was inadmissible. During an adjournment, the prosecutor telephoned the clerk to say that the ruling was wrong in law. The clerk agreed that the ruling was wrong. The defence were not given notice of this until the court reconvened, whereupon the magistrates reversed their earlier ruling and ordered that case be retried by another bench. The Divisional Court said that it was procedurally unfair for a matter to be drawn to the clerk's attention by telephone. The proper method was to do so in writing, sending a copy to all other parties to the case. Furthermore, the general principle was that decisions reached by justices should not be reversed. Accordingly, a retrial should not have been ordered.

Disclosure of the Names of Judges and Magistrates

A further aspect of the principle of open justice is that the names of those administering it shall not be concealed. It has never been suggested that the name of a Crown Court judge should, or could, be kept secret. So far as justices are concerned, there is no statutory rule entitling them to anonymity. Since the principle of open justice requires that nothing should be done to discourage the fair and accurate reporting of proceedings in court, a bona fide inquirer is entitled to know the name of a justice who is sitting or who has sat on a case heard recently. However, a clerk may be justified in refusing (during or after a hearing) to give the name of one of the justices to a person whom the clerk reasonably believes to be seeking that information solely for a mischievous purpose (*Felixstowe Justices, ex parte Leigh* [1987] QB 582, per Watkins LJ). **D3.88**

Appeals against Derogations from Open Justice

Criminal Justice Act 1988, s. 159 **D3.89**

(1) A person aggrieved may appeal to the Court of Appeal, if that court grants leave, against—
  (a) an order under section 4 or 11 of the Contempt of Court Act 1981 made in relation to a trial on indictment;
  (aa) an order made by the Crown Court under section 58(7) or (8) of the Criminal Procedure and Investigations Act 1996 in a case where the court has convicted a person on a trial on indictment;
  (b) any order restricting the access of the public to the whole or any part of a trial on indictment or to any proceedings ancillary to such a trial; and
  (c) any order restricting the publication of any report of the whole or any part of a trial on indictment or any such ancillary proceedings;

and the decision of the Court of Appeal shall be final.

. . .

(5) On the hearing of an appeal under this section the Court of Appeal shall have power—
   (a) to stay any proceedings in any other court until after the appeal is disposed of;
   (b) to confirm, reverse or vary the order complained of; and
   (c) to make such order as to costs as it thinks fit.

The creation of a specific right to appeal against orders of the Crown Court derogating from the principle of open justice was necessary because the ordinary system of appeals to the Court of Appeal (Criminal Division) gives a right of appeal only to the accused following his conviction and/or sentence. It is most unlikely that a decision, for example, to order that media reporting of a trial be postponed would provide a ground of appeal against conviction or sentence, and, even if it did, the Court of Appeal would have no power directly to quash or amend the order — its power would be to quash the conviction or reduce the sentence. Section 159(5), which deals with the Court of Appeal's powers upon disposing of an appeal under the section, contemplates the trial on indictment being stayed while the appeal is determined (see s. 159(5)(a)) as does the CrimPR, r. 16.10(3). The power to stay the trial is necessary because quashing an order derogating from open justice after the relevant proceedings have been completed will often serve no practical purpose, since by that time any harm resulting from the order has already been done.

In *Re A* [2006] 1 WLR 1361, the Court of Appeal confirmed that media representatives and the accused both fall within the description of persons who may be 'aggrieved' within s. 159(1) and went on to consider whether the appeal against an order restricting reporting of proceedings should be determined without a hearing. CrimPR, r. 67.2(6) provides that an application for leave to appeal against an order restricting public access to proceedings 'shall be determined . . . without a hearing'. This is to be contrasted with r. 67.1(6), which provides that an appeal against an order restricting reporting of proceedings 'may be determined without a hearing'. The Court declined to interpret 'shall' in r. 67.2(6) as meaning 'may', saying that the court could not ignore the express requirement that the determination of the appeal is to take place without a hearing. The Court went on to hold that that the absence of a discretion to have a hearing was not incompatible with the ECHR.

D3.90 **Magistrates' Court Cases** Section 159 of the CJA 1988 does not extend to decisions of magistrates' courts or to decisions made by the Crown Court otherwise than in connection with trials on indictment (e.g., on an appeal from magistrates). In respect of such decisions, the remedy of an aggrieved person is to apply to the Divisional Court for judicial review. This has the disadvantage that, even if the remedy sought is granted, it may come too late to be of practical value. Also, an application to quash an order of the lower court or have it declared unlawful is liable to be refused on the basis that, although the order was almost certainly misguided, it was within the court's jurisdiction (see, e.g., *Malvern Justices, ex parte Evans* [1988] QB 540).

Section D4 Criminal Procedure Rules

THE EVOLUTION OF THE RULES

The Criminal Procedure Rules 2005 (CrimPR), which came into effect on 4 April 2005, represent the consolidation, as a concise and simply expressed statement, of the current statutory and common-law procedural rules that apply to criminal cases. The rules applied immediately from their commencement to all cases in the magistrates' court, the Crown Court and the criminal division of the Court of Appeal including those cases already in the system. **D4.1**

The inspiration for the CrimPR came, in large part, from the 'Review of the Criminal Courts of England and Wales' carried out by Auld LJ (the 'Auld report'). At chapter 10, para. 277 it recommended:

> . . . an exercise of both systematic restatement and reform, with the aim of producing a single corpus of rules for a unified criminal court. That instrument should begin with a clear statement of purpose and general rules of application and interpretation, as successfully pioneered in the Civil Justice Rules flowing from Lord Woolf's reforms of the civil law. It should combine the various sources into a concise summary of rules, reducing them so far as possible into a discipline common to all levels of jurisdiction, using the same language and prescribing the same forms. It should make separate provision only in so far as necessary to allow for procedural differences at each level flowing from the court's composition and nature and volume of its work. It should be capable of ready and orderly amendment, by secondary legislation along the lines of that enabling the Lord Chancellor to amend the Civil Procedure Rules, subject to the negative or positive resolution procedure.

In the main, therefore, the CrimPR are a massive exercise in consolidation, bringing together in a structured way the procedural rules pertaining to the criminal courts, replacing particularly the Crown Court Rules (SI 1982 No. 1109), the Magistrates' Court Rules (SI 1981 No. 552) and the Criminal Appeal Rules (SI 1968 No. 1262). Generally, the content of the CrimPR replicates these rules. The process of consolidation has resulted in certain drafting amendments; for example, where rules for the different courts have been unified, with a view to consistency.

The CrimPR are divided into ten main subject divisions, which essentially follow the chronological progress of a criminal case. They are set out in full in **appendix 1**, and individual rules are dealt with in the relevant sections of this work.

Some sections of the CrimPR had not been completed prior to initial commencement in April 2005 (e.g., parts of the section on disclosure and expert witnesses) and the Rules Committee indicated that other sections were likely to be simplified (e.g., those dealing with custody and bail). The Rules have already been significantly amended once as a result, and further regular amendment is to be expected.

A detailed commentary on the rules is to be found in *Blackstone's Guide to the Criminal Procedure Rules 2005* (Oxford University Press).

Two parts of the CrimPR particularly give effect to the intention of the Rules Committee to enhance the efficiency of the criminal justice system. Those parts are:

(a) part 1: the Overriding Objective (see D4.2); and
(b) part 3: Case Management (see D4.6).

THE OVERRIDING OBJECTIVE

D4.2 **Criminal Procedure Rules 2005, r. 1**

1.1—(1) The overriding objective of this new code is that criminal cases be dealt with justly.

(2) Dealing with a criminal case justly includes—

(a) acquitting the innocent and convicting the guilty;
(b) dealing with the prosecution and the defence fairly;
(c) recognising the rights of a defendant, particularly those under Article 6 of the European Convention on Human Rights;
(d) respecting the interests of witnesses, victims and jurors and keeping them informed of the progress of the case;
(e) dealing with the case efficiently and expeditiously;
(f) ensuring that appropriate information is available to the court when bail and sentence are considered; and
(g) dealing with the case in ways that take into account—
(i) the gravity of the offence alleged,
(ii) the complexity of what is in issue,
(iii) the severity of the consequences for the defendant and others affected, and
(iv) the needs of other cases.

1.2—(1) Each participant, in the conduct of each case, must—

(a) prepare and conduct the case in accordance with the overriding objective;
(b) comply with these Rules, practice directions and directions made by the court; and
(c) at once inform the court and all parties of any significant failure (whether or not that participant is responsible for that failure) to take any procedural step required by these Rules, any practice direction or any direction of the court. A failure is significant if it might hinder the court in furthering the overriding objective.

(2) Anyone involved in any way with a criminal case is a participant in its conduct for the purposes of this rule.

1.3 The court must further the overriding objective in particular when—

(a) exercising any power given to it by legislation (including these Rules);
(b) applying any practice direction; or
(c) interpreting any rule or practice direction.

Part 1 of the rules is set out in full in **appendix 1**.

The Balance of Rights and Duties

D4.3 Whilst the overriding objective 'that cases be dealt with justly' (r. 1.1(1)) may appear simply to be an explicit statement of the existing objective of the criminal courts, r. 1.1(2) specifies a number of elements that are included within its ambit. These import recognition that all of those who participate in proceedings have rights to be considered as well as obligations to undertake so as to ensure the efficient expedition of justice.

This approach was elaborated by the Court of Appeal in *Jisl* (2004) *The Times*, 19 April 2004 (at [114]–[118]):

> The starting point is simple. Justice must be done. The defendant is entitled to a fair trial: and, which is sometimes overlooked, the prosecution is equally entitled to a reasonable opportunity to present the evidence against the defendant. It is not however a concomitant of the entitlement to a fair trial that either or both sides are further entitled to take as much time as they like, or for that matter, as long as counsel and solicitors or the defendants themselves think appropriate. Resources are limited. The funding for courts and judges, for prosecuting and the vast majority of defence lawyers is dependent on public money, for which there are many competing demands. Time itself is a resource. Every day unnecessarily used, while the trial meanders sluggishly to its eventual conclusion, represents another day's stressful waiting for the remaining witnesses and

> the jurors in that particular trial, and no less important, continuing and increasing tension and worry for another defendant or defendants, some of whom are remanded in custody, and the witnesses in trials which are waiting their turn to be listed. It follows that the sensible use of time requires judicial management and control. . . .

This has been echoed, more recently, in *R (Robinson) v Sutton Coldfield Magistrates' Court* [2006] EWHC 307 (Admin), where it was made clear that 'the objective of the Criminal Procedure Rules "to deal with all cases efficiently and expeditiously" depends upon adherence to the timetable set out in the rules'.

The Balance of the Criteria

In *Holmes v SGB Services* [2001] EWCA Civ 354, addressing the corresponding provisions of the Civil Procedure Rules, Buxton LJ said that the court had to balance all the criteria identified in r.1.1 without giving any one of them undue weight. However, this should not be interpreted as undermining the traditional status of the presumption of innocence. This was made clear by the Lord Chief Justice when he introduced the CrimPR stating: **D4.4**

> The presumption of innocence and a robust adversarial process are essential features of English legal tradition and of the defendant's right to a fair trial. The overriding objective acknowledges those rights. It must not be read as detracting from a defendant's right to silence or from the confidentiality properly attaching to what passes between a lawyer and his client.

Similarly, the requirement in r. 1.1(2)(b) of 'dealing with the prosecution and the defence fairly' should be read in the context of jurisprudence of the European Court of Human Rights which emphasises the principle of equality of arms (see, e.g., *Kaufman v Belgium* (1986) 50 DR 98 at p. 115). In the same way, there is a notable contrast between the formulae in r. 1.1(2)(c) and (d), which properly reflects the presumption of innocence. Whereas the rights of the defendant (particularly those under the ECHR, Article 6) have to be recognised (r. 1.1(2)(c)), there is a different formula, namely 'respecting the interests', in r. 1.1(2)(d), in relation to other parties in the case. It is therefore clear that proposition (c) takes precedence over proposition (d) where they come into conflict.

Rules 1.1(2)(e) and (f) aim at efficient management of cases. Rule 1(2)(e) is closely related to the new provisions on case management, which are dealt with in **D4.6**. Rule 1.1(2)(f) applies to agencies responsible for records of antecedents, and pre-sentence and medical reports, and underlines their duty to assist the court by ensuring that the relevant information is available at the crucial time when decisions as to bail and sentence are considered.

Rule 1.1(2)(g) imports the civil concept of proportionality into the overall objective, in accordance with the concern for resources identified by the Court of Appeal in *Jisl* (2004) *The Times*, 19 April 2004. It would be unrealistic to expect equivalent resources to be devoted to a case that ought to be tried in the magistrates' court and one that was indictable only. Again, the factors to be taken into account under this element of 'dealing justly' must be fleshed out by the approach of the courts to case management (see **D4.6**).

Duties Imposed on Participants

After the concept of 'dealing justly' has been elaborated in r. 1.1(2), the remaining rules in part 1 deal with the duty of the participants in the case to prepare and conduct the case in accordance with the overriding objective, and to comply with the rules and directions that the court makes. That this applies equally to the legal representatives of the parties was demonstrated in the context of the Civil Procedure Rules by the judgment of Arden LJ in *Geveran Trading v Skjeveslan* [2003] 1 WLR 912 (at [37]): **D4.5**

> It is well established that as an officer of the court an advocate has a duty to the court which overrides his duty to his client — see *Rondell v Worsley*. Accordingly an advocate may not deceive or knowingly mislead the court. The advocate must bring to the attention of the court all relevant decisions and legislative provisions of which he is aware — *Copeland v Smith*. The

> advocate must bring to the attention of the court any procedural irregularity during the course of the trial — *R v Langford.* The advocate must conduct the proceedings economically . . . under the Civil Procedure Rules, it is the express duty of the parties and hence their legal advisers, including advocates, to help the court to further the overriding objective in Rule 1.3. These are merely some examples of the practical application of the advocate's duty to the court.

The obligation on 'participants' does not just relate to their own compliance with the Rules. They are also expected to notify the court and all parties 'at once . . . of any significant failure' of compliance. These so called 'grassing' provisions require one party to report the failures of another. The court itself is fixed with a duty to implement the overriding objective by r. 1.3, through its case management functions.

CASE MANAGEMENT

D4.6 Part 3 of the CrimPR (set out in full at **appendix 1**) applies to the management of all cases in the magistrates' courts and the Crown Court, including the Crown Court acting in its appellate capacity with respect to a magistrates' court (r. 3.1).

The Rationale

D4.7 Rule 3.2(1) lays down that the court must further the overriding objective (see **D4.2**) by 'actively managing the case'. This aim underpinned the recommendations of the Auld report (especially at chapter 10, paras. 229 to 231), and was explicitly the aim of the CrimPR, as is demonstrated by the words of the then Lord Chief Justice when the Consolidated Practice Direction was handed down on 22 March 2005:

> Most importantly, they promote a culture change in criminal case management. They introduce new rules, written in plain English, that give courts explicit powers and responsibilities to manage cases effectively, and to reduce the numbers of ineffective hearings that cause distress to witnesses and inconvenience and expense to everyone.

The need for active case management is a theme that the Court of Appeal has emphasised in a series of recent decisions. For example, in *Jisl* (2004) *The Times*, 19 April 2004, Judge LJ stated (at [116]–[118]):

> Active, hands on, case management, both pre-trial and throughout the trial itself, is now regarded as an essential part of the judge's duty. The profession must understand that this has become and will remain part of the normal trial process, and that cases must be prepared and conducted accordingly.
>
> The issues in this particular trial were identified at a very early stage, indeed during the course of the previous trial itself. In relation to each of the defendants, in a single word, the issue was knowledge. And indeed, the issue in most trials is equally readily identified.
>
> Once the issue has been identified, in a case of any substance at all, (and this particular case was undoubtedly a case of substance and difficulty) the judge should consider whether to direct a timetable to cover pre-trial steps, and eventually the conduct of the trial itself, not rigid, nor immutable, and fully recognising that during the trial at any rate the unexpected must be treated as normal, and making due allowance for it in the interests of justice. To enable the trial judge to manage the case in a way which is fair to every participant, pre-trial, the potential problems, as well as the possible areas for time saving, should be canvassed. In short, a sensible informed discussion about the future management of the case and the most convenient way to present the evidence, whether disputed or not, and where appropriate, with admissions by one or other or both sides, should enable the judge to make a fully informed analysis of the future timetable, and the proper conduct of the trial. The objective is not haste and rush, but greater efficiency and better use of limited resources by closer identification of and focus on critical rather than peripheral issues. When trial judges act in accordance with these principles, the directions they give, and where appropriate, the timetables they prescribe in the exercise of their case management responsibilities, will be supported in this Court. Criticism is more likely to be addressed to those who ignore them.

The Court's Role

Rule 3.2(2) sets out a list of elements of active case management, based upon early identification of the issues and the setting of a procedural timetable. **D4.8**

As far as the conduct of the trial itself is concerned, the duty of the court is set out in r. 3.2(2)(e), which reflects the overriding objective of dealing with each case 'efficiently and expeditiously' (r. 1.1(2)(e)). It states that the court must further the overriding objective by 'ensuring that evidence, whether disputed or not, is presented in the shortest and clearest way'. In addition, r. 3.2(2)(f) charges the court with the duty of 'discouraging delay'.

Judicial action to apply this objective has received the support of the Court of Appeal on a number of occasions. For example:

(a) In *Bryant* [2005] EWCA Crim 2079, the Court of Appeal stated that it will support efforts by the trial judge to move a case forward at a reasonable speed, provided that the accused receives a fair trial.

(b) In *B* [2005] EWCA Crim 805, the case management powers of the judge were exercised to place limits on cross-examination conducted by defence counsel. The Court of Appeal stated that this should not be a routine feature of trial management, but judges were entitled, and indeed obliged, to impose reasonable time-limits where necessary. The entitlement to a fair trial was not inconsistent with proper judicial control over the use of court time.

(c) In *K* [2006] 2 All ER 552, the Court of Appeal made it clear that the case management powers in the CrimPR enabled a judge to deal with issues preliminary to trial by way of written submissions, and to limit the length of those submissions (see **D9.16**).

(d) Similarly, in *Lashley* [2005] EWCA Crim 2016, the Court of Appeal gave guidance on the question of the judge's response to counsel who pressed a judge to reconsider a ruling with which he disagreed. Judge LJ stated:

> Right or wrong, the judge's ruling is or should be the end of an argument, or an application . . . Counsel is not entitled to keep pressing the judge about a ruling with which he disagrees on the basis of his duty to his client. The remedy for an incorrect ruling is provided in this Court. It does not take the form of trying to re-embark on the argument in an endeavour to persuade the judge to a judicial rethink of a ruling that he has already given, at any rate unless and until the circumstances have changed.

For a view on a case management order which required disclosure of details of defence witnesses, and the implications for litigation privilege and legal professional privilege, see *R (Kelly) v Warley Magistrates' Court* [2007] EWHC 1867 (Admin).

Protocols relating to Complex Cases Further guidance as to the way in which case management ought to be conducted is provided in the Protocol for 'Control and Management of Heavy Fraud and Other Complex Criminal Cases'. Whilst the Protocol is primarily directed at the control of complex cases, certain parts of the guidance have equal relevance to shorter and simpler cases. For example, in para. 3(vii) of the Protocol, there is some stress laid upon the need for caution by judges in the use of their case management powers: **D4.9**

> The Criminal Procedure Rules require the court to take a more active part in case management. These are salutary provisions which should bring to an end interminable criminal trials of the kind which the Court of Appeal criticised in *Jisl*. . . . Nevertheless these salutary provisions do not have to be used on every occasion. Where the advocates have done their job properly, by narrowing the issues, pruning the evidence and so forth, it may be quite inappropriate for the judge to 'weigh in' and start cutting out more evidence or more charges of his own volition. It behoves the judge to make a careful assessment of the degree of judicial intervention which is warranted in each case.

The Lord Chief Justice goes on to indicate that this note of caution is supported by the experience gained of the Civil Procedure Rules, which has shown that parties to litigation have been aggrieved on isolated occasions at 'what was perceived to be unnecessary intermeddling by the court'.

There is a similar Protocol relating to the management of terrorism cases, which is available at www.hmcourts-service.gov.uk/cms/files/management_of_terrorism_cases.pdf.

The Role of the Parties

D4.10 Rule 3.2, which lays down the duty of the court, is supplemented by r. 3.3, which fixes the parties with a corresponding duty. To a large extent, the duty on the defence to help identify the 'real issues' is already to be found in the statutory provisions relating to disclosure (see **D9.18**, where detail of the duties in question is to be found). In this regard see *R (DPP) v Chorley Justices* [2006] EWHC 1795 (Admin), where Thomas LJ made clear the importance of co-operation from those defending in narrowing the issues:

> If a defendant refuses to identify what the issues are, one thing is clear: he can derive no advantage from that or seek, as appears to have happened in this case, to attempt an ambush at trial. The days of ambushing and taking last-minute technical points are gone. They are not consistent with the overriding objective of deciding cases justly, acquitting the innocent and convicting the guilty.

Rules 3.5 and 3.8 give the court detailed case management powers and duties, including the power and duty to give directions, which can be varied in accordance with rr. 3.6 and 3.7. Rule 3.9 deals with readiness for trial, while r. 3.10 allows the court to require a party to take various steps to help it manage the trial. Again, the powers involved in this latter set of provisions (e.g., to identify 'any point of law that could affect the conduct of the trial or appeal') in essence reflect the statutory provisions introduced by the CJA 2003 in relation to disclosure (see the CPIA 1996, s. 6A, and **D9.18**).

Case Progression Officers

D4.11 Rule 3.4 requires each of the parties, and the court, to appoint a case progression officer at the commencement of proceedings, and to inform the other participants of how to contact that person. The Case Progression Officer is thereafter responsible for progressing the case. It is their responsibility to ensure that party's compliance with court directions, and to alert other parties to anything which may interfere with the smooth progress of the case. In reality, therefore, it will be the case progression officers who will enforce the 'grassing provisions' described at **D4.5**. The Criminal Case Management Framework describes in detail the obligations imposed on such officers, which makes it clear that it is not a role suitable for court-based professionals, such as barristers or solicitor advocates.

Practical Case Management

D4.12 Part 3 of the CrimPR is supplemented by a case management Practice Direction, which forms part IV.41 of the *Consolidated Criminal Practice Direction* (see **appendix** 7), and the forms to be used for case management purposes, set out in Annex E to the Practice Direction.

The Practice Direction stresses that, at the plea and case management hearing, active case management is necessary in order to reduce the number of ineffective and cracked trials, and the delays that occur within trials. It flags the need for preparation by all concerned. It emphasises the desirability of the presence of the trial advocate at the plea and case management hearing, or at least of an advocate able to make decisions and assist the court to the maximum extent. In order to achieve this objective, listing policy should ensure that list officers as far as possible fix cases to enable the trial advocate to conduct the plea and case management hearing as well as the trial. Plea and case management hearings are addressed at **D14.44**.

Issues of case management that are addressed in more detail later are as follows.

(a) The automatic case management directions made by the magistrates' court at the time that cases are sent or transferred to the Crown Court, including the notice periods for applications for special measures for witnesses and in relation to hearsay, bad character and expert evidence (see **D14.37**).
(b) The provisions relating to issues of disclosure (see **D9**).
(c) The provisions relating to preparatory hearings (see **D14.46**).

Section D5 Preliminary Proceedings in Magistrates' Courts

This section describes the preliminary proceedings in the magistrates' court which precede either the summary trial of an accused or his being sent for trial.

PROCEDURE FOR SECURING PRESENCE OF ACCUSED

Introduction

D5.1 The first appearance of an accused before a magistrates' court is secured by:

(a) his arrest without warrant, followed by his being charged with an offence at a police station, followed by his being bailed to attend the magistrates' court on a specified date to answer the charge; or
(b) as in (a), save that instead of being bailed from the police station, he is held there until he is brought before the court in police custody; or
(c) his arrest without warrant, followed by his being bailed by the police to give CPS time to decide whether to prosecute him and, if so, for what offence(s), such offence(s) being notified to the accused through the written charge and requisition procedure established by the CJA 2003 (the requisition giving details of the date of the first appearance at the magistrates' court); or
(d) in the case of a private prosecution, the laying of an information by the prosecutor before a magistrate (or a magistrates' clerk) resulting in the issue of a summons requiring the accused to attend at court on a specified day to answer the allegation in the information; or
(e) as in (d), save that instead of issuing a summons the magistrate issues a warrant for the accused to be arrested and brought before the court (or, alternatively, a warrant backed for bail by virtue of which the accused is arrested and then released on bail under a duty to attend court on a specified day).

The powers and procedures for arresting an accused without warrant, questioning him in detention at a police station and then charging him are dealt with in **D1**, which also deals with the circumstances in which the police may refuse to bail a person once he has been charged and the period within which they must bring such a person before the magistrates' court. This section considers the other means of securing the presence of the accused before the court (sometimes referred to as 'issue of process').

The Written Charge and Requisition Procedure

D5.2 The CJA 2003, s. 29, creates (in the case of public prosecutions) a new method of commencing criminal proceedings. It has been brought into force in certain areas only (in that it applies only to magistrates' courts sitting in specified locations) by the Criminal Justice Act 2003 (Commencement No.16) Order 2007 (SI 2007 No 1999). Section 29(1) provides that a public prosecutor may institute criminal proceedings against a person by issuing a document (a 'written charge') which charges the person with an offence. Under s. 29(2), where a public prosecutor issues a written charge, a document (called a 'requisition') must be issued at the same time; this requires the accused to appear before a magistrates' court to answer the written charge. The written charge and requisition must be served on the accused and a copy of both must be served on the court named in the requisition (s. 29(3)).

This method of commencing criminal proceedings is available only in the case of public prosecutions. These are defined in s. 29(5) as meaning prosecutions brought by the following (or by someone authorised by that person or body to institute criminal proceedings on their behalf):

(i) a police force;
(ii) the Director of the Serious Fraud Office;
(iii) the DPP (this includes all CPS prosecutions);
(iv) the Director of Revenue and Customs Prosecutions;
(v) the Director General of the Serious Organised Crime Agency;
(vi) the A-G;
(vii) a Secretary of State.

Section 29(5)(h) empowers the Secretary of State to add to the list of people authorised by such a person to institute criminal proceedings by means of a statutory instrument.

Section 29(4) provides that, as a result of the existence of this new procedure, public prosecutors will no longer have the power to commence proceedings by means of the laying of an information for the purpose of obtaining the issue of a summons under the MCA 1980, s. 1 (see below).

The effect of this new procedure is that notification of the requirement to attend court will be communicated to the accused by the prosecutor (not by the magistrates' court, as is the case where a summons is issued). Indeed, in the written charge and requisition procedure, the magistrates' court has no involvement whatsoever in the case until the accused makes his first appearance before the court.

The written charge and requisition procedure does not affect the ability of a public prosecutor to lay an information in order to obtain an arrest warrant. Section 30(4) provides that nothing in s. 29 affects the power of a public prosecutor to lay an information for the purpose of obtaining the issue of a warrant under the MCA 1980, s. 1 (see below). It follows that an information will still have to be laid in order to secure the grant of an arrest warrant.

Under the CJA 2003, s. 30(5), references in any enactment to an 'information' are to be construed as references to a 'written charge', and references to a 'summons' under the MCA 1980, s. 1, are to be construed as references to a 'requisition'.

As the magistrates' court is not involved in the issuing of the written charge and requisition, there will be no possibility of the magistrates preventing a prosecution from being brought in this way. However, it is submitted that the decision to issue a written charge and requisition would be amenable to judicial review and an application for the case to be dismissed as an abuse of process would be available in appropriate cases.

Content of the Written Charge

The CrimPR, r. 7.2(1), provides that a written charge must: **D5.3**

(a) describe the offence with which the accused is charged 'in ordinary language avoiding as far as possible the use of technical terms'; and
(b) give such particulars as may be necessary to provide reasonable information about the nature of the charge.

Under r. 7.2(3), if the offence charged is one created by statute, the description of the offence must contain a reference to the relevant statutory provision. However, under r. 7.2(2), it is not necessary for the written charge either to state all the elements of the offence, or to negative any matter upon which the accused may rely.

Laying an Information and Issuing a Summons

D5.4 **The Information** The written charge and requisition procedure is not available in the case of private prosecutions, which have to be commenced by laying an information (see the CJA 2003, s. 30(4)(b), which provides that nothing in s. 29 affects the power of a person who is not a public prosecutor to lay an information for the purpose of obtaining the issue of a summons (or a warrant) under the MCA 1980, s. 1).

On an information being laid before him, a magistrate may issue either:

(a) a summons requiring the person named in the information to appear before a magistrates' court to answer thereto; or
(b) a warrant to arrest that person and bring him before a magistrates' court (MCA 1980, s. 1(1)).

An information (which is simply an allegation that a person has committed an offence) may be laid orally or in writing (CrimPR, r. 7.1(2)). Indeed, in *Kennet Justices, ex parte Humphrey* [1993] Crim LR 787, the Divisional Court held that an information could be laid by the prosecutor informing the justices' clerk by letter of an intention to charge the defendant at a later date.

In *Manchester Stipendiary Magistrate, ex parte Hill* [1983] 1 AC 328, it was held that a written information is 'laid' when it is received in the office of the clerk to the justices, and so it follows that the laying of the information is the act which determines whether or not the time-limit for bringing a prosecution for a summary offence has been met (see **D20** on time-limits).

In *Rockall v Department for Environment, Food and Rural Affairs* [2007] EWHC 614, the Divisional Court said that the essential concept is that the information should be made available to the justices, or the clerk to the justice, within time. This will be so in relation to postal delivery when it can properly be inferred that it has been received, whether opened or not; and as far as transmissions by fax or other electronic means are concerned, that will be when it can properly be inferred that the information is retrievable, whether retrieved in fact or not.

An oral information is laid by the informant going before a magistrate or clerk to make his allegation. In order to obtain the issue of a warrant for arrest, an information must be in writing (MCA 1980, s. 1(3)).

The information may be laid either by the prosecutor in person, or by counsel or a solicitor on his behalf, or by any other authorised person (r. 7.1(1)). However, an information may not be laid on behalf of an unincorporated association, since the definition of 'person' in the Interpretation Act 1978 as including a 'body of persons corporate or unincorporate' was not intended to apply to the laying of informations (*Rubin v DPP* [1990] 2 QB 80). It follows that an information must be laid by a named, actual person and must disclose the identity of that person. However, the appeal in *Rubin* was dismissed because, although the information was defective in that the informant purported to be 'Thames Valley Police' (such a prosecution would now be commenced by way of written charge and requisition), the appellant could easily have ascertained the identity of the officer who had laid the information.

The decision in *Rubin* may be contrasted with *Norwich Justices, ex parte Texas Homecare* [1991] Crim LR 555. That was a case under the Shops Act 1950, in which the informations were signed by the senior environmental health officer, who had no authority to do so under that Act. The informations were later amended to substitute the signature of the deputy director of administration, who did have the necessary authority, but the amendment took place after the six month deadline for the laying of an information had elapsed. The Divisional Court quashed the convictions, holding that the person laying the informations had no authority to lay them. Since the informations as laid were invalid, they could not found any jurisdiction, and this was not curable by amendment.

The provisions in r. 7.2 on the content of written charges apply equally to every information laid and summons issued.

The Summons The MCA 1980, s. 1(1) (as amended by the Courts Act 2003), provides that: **D5.5**

> (1) On an information being laid before a justice of the peace that a person has, or is suspected of having, committed an offence, the justice may issue—
> (a) a summons directed to that person requiring him to appear before a magistrates' court to answer the information, or
> (b) a warrant to arrest that person and bring him before a magistrates' court.

A justices' clerk (or an assistant clerk who has been specifically authorised by the justices' clerk for that purpose) may issue a summons but not a warrant (see the schedule to the Justices' Clerks Rules 2005 (SI 2005 No. 545), paras. 1 and 2).

The Decisions to Issue a Summons The decision to issue a summons is judicial, not merely administrative (*Gateshead Justices, ex parte Tesco Stores Ltd* [1981] QB 470). Therefore, a justice or clerk must actually apply his mind to the information on the basis of which a summons is sought ('no summons can be issued . . . without a prior judicial consideration by [the justice or clerk] of the information upon which the summons is based': ibid. at p. 478A). The decision whether or not to issue a summons 'is a judicial function which must, therefore, be performed judicially' (per Lord Roskill in *Manchester Stipendiary Magistrate, ex parte Hill* [1983] 1 AC 328). The magistrate or clerk issuing the summons should be satisfied that: **D5.6**

(a) the information alleges an offence known to the law;
(b) it was laid within any time-limit applicable to commencing a prosecution for the offence in question; and
(c) any consent necessary for the bringing of the prosecution has been obtained (per Donaldson LJ in *Ex parte Tesco Stores Ltd*).

There is, however, a residual discretion to refuse to issue a summons. That discretion is not, however, unfettered; the magistrates ought to issue a summons where the information is properly laid unless there are compelling reasons not to do so, for example, if an abuse of the process or impropriety is involved (*R (Mayor and Burgesses of Newham LBC) v Stratford Magistrates' Court* (2004) 168 JP 658). It was held in *Clerk to the Bradford Justices, ex parte Sykes* (1999) 163 JP 224 that the magistrate or clerk is not obliged to make inquiries before issuing a summons. If there is material which persuades him that it would be wrong to issue a summons, he is entitled to act on that information, and should not shut his eyes to it. If he was aware that the individual informant was one who had plagued the court with vexatious informations, for example, he could and probably should act upon that knowledge. The Divisional Court pointed out that, even if a summons is issued, the individual summonsed may apply to the magistrates' court to dismiss it, or stay it on the grounds of abuse of process (see **D3.54** ***et seq.***). It is therefore unnecessary to provide that there should be, at an earlier stage, an obligation to investigate before the summons was issued.

In *R (Charlson) v Guildford Magistrates' Court* [2006] 1 WLR 3494, the court considered the approach to be adopted by magistrates if they are considering whether to issue a summons for a private prosecution where the CPS had already brought and discontinued a prosecution arising out of the same events. Silber J, giving the judgment of the court, said (at [19]) that the magistrates should not require special circumstances before agreeing to the issue of the summons. They should consider: (a) whether the allegation is an offence known to the law and, if so, whether the ingredients of the offence are prima facie present; (b) whether the issue of the summonses is time-barred; (c) whether the court has jurisdiction; (d) whether the informant has the necessary authority to prosecute; and (e) any other relevant facts. He added that, in the different situation where justices are considering whether to accede to an application to issue a summons for a private prosecution where CPS has already brought a prosecution which is still proceeding, the justices should, in the absence of special circumstances, be slow to issue a summons at the behest of a private prosecutor.

It is not the practice for the justice or clerk to consider the evidence before issuing a summons. Neither is it the practice for the person named in the information to attend and oppose the issue of a summons, although the justice or clerk has a discretion to allow him to do so in exceptional circumstances (*West London Stipendiary Magistrate, ex parte Klahn* [1979] 1 WLR 933).

D5.7 **Delay** In providing that a justice may issue a summons 'upon' an information being laid before him, the MCA 1980, s. 1, does not require that the issue of a summons must follow immediately upon the consideration of the information by the justice or clerk (*Fairford Justices, ex parte Brewster* [1976] QB 600). It is open to the prosecutor to lay the information and then suggest that a summons should not be issued immediately (e.g., because the accused is out of the country and service could not be effected for a considerable time). However, if the delay between the laying of the information and issue of the summons is so great as to be unreasonable and to cause prejudice, then the High Court has a discretion to intervene and quash the summons (ibid. at p. 604F–H). Moreover, an information should be laid with the intention of having the consequent summons served as soon as reasonably possible. Therefore, if the prosecutor has not in fact made his mind up whether to proceed at the time of laying his information but is concerned merely that any possible prosecution should not be out of time, then his conduct amounts to an abuse of the process of the court and the magistrates should stay the proceedings if ultimately he does decide to proceed (*Brentford Justices, ex parte Wong* [1981] QB 445).

Service of the Summons or Requisition

D5.8 A summons or requisition must state the name of the justice or public prosecutor responsible for issuing it (CrimPR, r. 7.7(1)). It is acceptable for the necessary signature to be affixed by means of a rubber stamp (see *Brentford Justices, ex parte Catlin* [1975] QB 455 at p. 462E–G for approval of the practice). Rule 7.7(4) permits the use of an electronic signature. The summons or requisition must state (a) the substance of the information or charge, and (b) the time and place at which he is required to appear to answer the charge (r. 7.7(2)). Although r. 7.7(3) permits one summons to be issued in respect of several informations or written charges against a person, it is not uncommon for a separate summons to be issued for each information or charge.

A summons or requisition may be served on an individual by handing it to him (r. 4.3(1)(a)) or by leaving it at, or sending it by first class post to, an address where it is reasonably believed that he will receive it (r. 4.4(1) and (2)(a)).

Service of a summons or requisition on a corporation may be effected by handing it to a person holding a senior position in that corporation (r. 4.3(1)(b)) or by leaving it at, or sending it by first class post to, its principal office in England and Wales or, if there is no readily identifiable principal office, any place in England and Wales where it carries on its activities or business (r. 4.4(1) and (2)(b)).

Issue of Warrant for Arrest

D5.9 The effect of a warrant for arrest is to order and empower the constables of the police force for the area in which it is issued to arrest the person named in the warrant and bring him before a magistrates' court. The MCA 1980, s. 1(1)(b), provides that, whenever a justice before whom an information is laid has power to issue a summons, he may alternatively issue a warrant for the arrest of the person named in the information, provided that:

(a) the information is in writing (s. 1(3)); and
(b) where the person in respect of whom the warrant is to be issued has attained the age of 18, the offence to which the warrant relates is an indictable offence or is punishable with imprisonment or else the person's address is not sufficiently established for a summons, or a written charge and requisition, to be served on him (s. 1(4)).

It is submitted that a magistrate should not issue a warrant if a summons or requisition, as the case may be, would appear to be an effective means of securing the accused's attendance before the court. Moreover, given that a police officer may arrest (without warrant) a person for any offence provided that the officer has reasonable grounds for believing that the arrest is necessary (for example) to allow the prompt and effective investigation of the offence or to prevent any prosecution for the offence from being hindered by the disappearance of the suspect (see PACE 1984, s. 24, and **D1.8**), an application for an arrest warrant will generally be unnecessary, as the suspect can be arrested without one. It follows that the use of a warrant for arrest issued under s. 1 of the 1980 Act is the least common means of commencing proceedings.

Whenever magistrates issue a warrant for arrest they have a discretion to 'back it for bail', i.e. they may direct that, having been arrested, the person arrested shall thereafter be bailed by the police to attend court on a named day (see s. 117 of the 1980 Act). The backing for bail may be unconditional or conditional on the accused providing sureties.

The MCA 1980, s. 1(6), specifically provides that, if the offence alleged is indictable, a warrant for arrest may be issued under s. 1 notwithstanding that a summons (or written charge and requisition) has already been issued on the basis of the information. If the offence is summary and process initially takes the form of a summons or a requisition, it would seem that there is no power to issue a warrant under s. 1, although circumstances may subsequently arise which justify a warrant under other provisions of the Act (e.g., s. 13: issue of a warrant where the accused fails to appear in answer to a summons). Under s. 1(6A), inserted by the CJA 2003, sch. 36, para. 8 (not yet in force), where the offence charged is an indictable offence and a written charge and requisition have previously been issued, a warrant may be issued by a justice upon a copy of the written charge being laid before him by a public prosecutor; this would be appropriate where, for example, the accused has absconded and so the requisition has not been served on him.

Effect of Defect in Process on Jurisdiction of Court

The jurisdiction of a magistrates' court to determine mode of trial for an offence triable either **D5.10**
way, to try such an offence summarily or to send such an offence to the Crown Court to be tried on indictment is dependent, *inter alia,* on the accused appearing or being brought before the court (see MCA 1980, ss. 2(3) to (4) and 18). However, there is no express requirement in those provisions that the accused's presence shall have been obtained by lawful means. Therefore, if he in fact appears before the court (e.g., in answer to a summons or requisition) or is brought before the court following arrest, the magistrates will have jurisdiction to deal with his case even if the process by which his attendance was secured was faulty, provided, of course, that any other preconditions of jurisdiction are satisfied (see *Hughes* (1878–79) LR 4 QBD 614, approved by the House of Lords in *Manchester Stipendiary Magistrate, ex parte Hill* [1983] 1 AC 328).

ADJOURNMENTS AND REMANDS

Power to Adjourn

D5.11 At any stage before the case is sent to the Crown Court for trial or before (or during) a summary trial, a magistrates' court may adjourn the proceedings. Whether to grant an adjournment is always a matter for the court's discretion but it must be exercised judicially. For example, an accused is entitled to a reasonable opportunity to prepare his case (*Thames Magistrates' Court, ex parte Polemis* [1974] 1 WLR 1371). Depending on the nature and complexity of the charge, this will almost certainly necessitate allowing him to take legal advice if he wishes. Similarly, a prosecution application for an adjournment must not be unreasonably refused (*Neath and Port Talbot Justices, ex parte DPP* [2000] 1 WLR 1376). In *S v DPP* (2006) 170 JP 707, it was said that, if it is necessary to adjourn the case to enable justice to be done following a failure by the prosecution properly to disclose matters which ought to be disclosed, then the adjournment must be granted, unless the court is satisfied that no prejudice would be caused to the accused by proceeding.

As regards challenging refusals to adjourn by way of judicial review, a cautionary note was sounded by Clarke J in *R (CPS) v Uxbridge Magistrates* (2007) 171 JP 279, where his lordship said (at [5]) that the Divisional Court should be 'particularly slow' to interfere with a decision to refuse an adjournment, given the discretionary nature of that decision.

D5.12 **Relevant Factors** In *Neath and Port Talbot Justices, ex parte DPP*, Simon Brown LJ identified the factors relevant to the decision whether or not to interfere with the decision of the lower court not to grant an adjournment. Those factors, which are also highly relevant to the original decision whether or not to adjourn, included: '(a) the seriousness of the criminal charges, (b) the nature of the evidence in the case and in particular the extent to which its quality may be affected by the delay, (c) the extent, if any, to which the defendant has brought about or contributed to the justice's error, (d) the extent, if any, to which the defendant has brought about or contributed to the delay in the hearing of the challenge, and (e) how far the complainant would feel justifiably aggrieved by the proceedings being halted and the defendant would feel justifiably aggrieved by their being continued'.

In *Kingston-upon-Thames Justices, ex parte Martin* [1994] Imm AR 172, it was said that the following factors should be taken into account in deciding whether or not to grant an adjournment:

(a) the importance of the proceedings and the likely adverse consequences to the party seeking the adjournment,
(b) the risk of the party being prejudiced in the conduct of the proceedings if the application is refused,
(c) the risk of prejudice or other disadvantage to the other party if the adjournment is granted,
(d) the convenience of the court,
(e) the interests of justice generally in the efficient despatch of court business,
(f) the desirability of not delaying future litigants by adjourning early and thus leaving the court empty,
(g) the extent to which the party applying for the adjournment had been responsible for creating the difficulty which had led to the application.

Ex parte Martin was cited with approval in *R (Costello) v North East Essex Magistrates* (2007) 171 JP 153, where it was held that if, through no fault of the accused, witnesses do not attend who should have attended, or the accused does not attend because he is unfit to attend, the magistrates ought generally to grant an adjournment (Collins J at [11]).

In *CPS v Picton* (2006) 170 JP 567, the Divisional Court once again considered the discretion of the justices to grant an adjournment. Jack J, giving the judgment of the Court, said (at [9]) that the following points emerge from a review of the authorities (including *Essen v DPP* [2005] EWHC 1077 (Admin) and the judgments of Lord Bingham in *Aberdare Justices, ex parte DPP* (1990) 155 JP 324 and *Hereford Magistrates' Court, ex parte Rowlands* [1998] QB 110):

(a) A decision whether to adjourn is a decision within the discretion of the trial court. An appellate court will interfere only if very clear grounds for doing so are shown.
(b) Magistrates should pay great attention to the need for expedition in the prosecution of criminal proceedings; delays are scandalous; they bring the law into disrepute; summary justice should be speedy justice; an application for an adjournment should be rigorously scrutinised.
(c) Where an adjournment is sought by the prosecution, magistrates must consider both the interest of the defendant in getting the matter dealt with, and the interest of the public that criminal charges should be adjudicated upon, and the guilty convicted as well as the innocent acquitted. With a more serious charge the public interest that there be a trial will carry greater weight.
(d) Where an adjournment is sought by the accused, the magistrates must consider whether, if it is not granted, he will be able fully to present his defence and, if he will not be able to do so, the degree to which his ability to do so is compromised.
(e) In considering the competing interests of the parties the magistrates should examine the likely consequences of the proposed adjournment, in particular its likely length, and the need to decide the facts while recollections are fresh.
(f) The reason that the adjournment is required should be examined and, if it arises through the fault of the party asking for the adjournment, that is a factor against granting the adjournment, carrying weight in accordance with the gravity of the fault. If that party was not at fault, that may favour an adjournment. Likewise if the party opposing the adjournment has been at fault, that will favour an adjournment.
(g) The magistrates should take appropriate account of the history of the case, and whether there have been earlier adjournments and at whose request and why.
(h) Lastly, of course the factors to be considered cannot be comprehensively stated but depend upon the particular circumstances of each case, and they will often overlap. The court's duty is to do justice between the parties in the circumstances as they have arisen.

Although not specifically mentioned by Jack J in this summary, it is clear that the Court had the overriding objective in the CrimPR, r. 1, much in mind when formulating this list of considerations.

In *Hereford Magistrates' Court, ex parte Rowlands*, Lord Bingham (at p. 127) said:

> It is not possible or desirable to identify hard and fast rules as to when adjournments should or should not be granted. The guiding principle must be that justices should fully examine the circumstances leading to applications for delay, the reasons for those applications and the consequences both to the prosecution and the defence. Ultimately, they must decide what is fair in the light of all those circumstances. This court will only interfere with the exercise of the justices' discretion whether to grant an adjournment in cases where it is plain that a refusal will cause substantial unfairness to one of the parties. Such unfairness may arise when a defendant is denied a full opportunity to present his case. But neither defendants nor their legal advisers should be permitted to frustrate the objective of a speedy trial without substantial grounds. Applications for adjournments must be subjected to rigorous scrutiny. Any defendant who is guilty of deliberately seeking to postpone a trial without good reason has no cause for complaint if his application for an adjournment is refused . . . In deciding whether to grant an adjournment justices will bear in mind that they have a responsibility for ensuring, so far as possible, that summary justice is speedy justice.

Reasons for granting, or refusing, an adjournment should be given, but they do not have to be elaborate, so long as the basis for the decision is clear (*Essen v DPP*).

Where an application for an adjournment is made on behalf of the defence on the ground that the accused cannot attend court by reason of illness, and there is a medical certificate or

D

Part D Procedure

doctor's letter to support this claim, but the magistrates think that the excuse is spurious, they should nevertheless give the accused the chance to answer their doubts and not simply proceed with the trial (*Bolton Magistrates' Court, ex parte Merna* (1991) 155 JP 612). Similarly, an adjournment should be granted where the absence of the accused is involuntary (as in *R (R) v Thames Youth Court* (2002) 166 JP 613, where the accused failed to attend court because he was in custody, having been arrested in connection with another matter).

D5.13 **Repeated Applications** Where an adjournment has been refused, the court can change its mind only if there is a good reason. In *R (Watson) v Dartford Magistrates' Court* [2005] EWHC 905 (Admin), the prosecution (before the date fixed for trial) sought an adjournment due to the non-availability of two witnesses. The magistrates refused the application. The parties returned to court on the trial date and the prosecution made a further application for an adjournment. This time, the application was successful. The Divisional Court held that the magistrates were wrong to allow the adjournment, since there had not been a change in circumstances since the first request to adjourn the trial. The defendant's case was remitted to the magistrates and the prosecution were to be prohibited from calling the oral evidence of the two witnesses who were previously unavailable.

It follows that, where an adjournment has been refused, a further application should be made only if there has been a material change of circumstances. In *R (F) v Knowsley Youth Court* [2006] EWHC 695 (Admin), for example, the case was listed for trial. Shortly before the trial, the prosecution indicated that they would be applying to vacate the trial date because they had not received the full file from the police. The application for an adjournment was heard by a bench of lay justices on the morning of the day of the trial. The application was refused. In the afternoon, at the beginning of the trial (before a district judge), the prosecution made another application for an adjournment. The district judge, who was made aware that a similar application had been made to a different bench that morning, allowed the application. The defendants sought judicial review of the district judge's decision. The prosecution conceded that the afternoon application was essentially the same application as the morning one, and that there had been no material change in circumstances between the making of the two applications. It was held that the district judge should have refused the application. In the absence of a change of circumstances, he was not entitled to revisit the decision to refuse an adjournment.

D5.14 **Offering No Evidence where Adjournment Refused** If the prosecution seek an adjournment but the magistrates refuse to adjourn and the prosecutor offers no evidence, with the effect that the charge is dismissed, the magistrates cannot subsequently hear the case. In *R (O) v Stratford Youth Court* (2004) 168 JP 469, key prosecution witnesses failed to attend. The justices refused an adjournment; the prosecution thereupon offered no evidence and the justices dismissed the charge. The prosecutor then discovered that the complainant had by then arrived at court and made a request that the court be reconvened. The magistrates agreed to do so; they overturned their refusal to adjourn and rescinded their dismissal of the charge. It was held by the Divisional Court that, where the prosecution have offered no evidence and the court has dismissed the charge, it is not open to the justices to re-open the case. In such a case, the justices are *functus officio*, and any further hearing against the accused in relation to that matter will inevitably give rise to a successful plea of autrefois acquit on his behalf.

D5.15 **Statutory Provisions on Power to Adjourn** The power to adjourn is contained in the MCA 1980, ss. 5, 10(1) and 18(4).

Magistrates' Courts Act 1980, ss. 5, 10 and 18

5.—(1) A magistrates' court may, before beginning to inquire into an offence as examining justices, or at any time during the inquiry, adjourn the hearing, and if it does so shall remand the accused.

(2) The court shall when adjourning fix the time and place at which the hearing is to be resumed; and the time fixed shall be that at which the accused is required to appear or be

brought before the court in pursuance of the remand or would be brought before the court were it not for his agreeing to further remands being in his absence.

[Note: s. 5 will repealed when committal proceedings for either-way offences are abolished.]

10.—(1) A magistrates' court may at any time, whether before or after beginning to try an information, adjourn the trial, and may do so, notwithstanding anything in this Act, when composed of a single justice.

(2) The court may when adjourning either fix the time and place at which the trial is to be resumed, or, unless it remands the accused, leave the time and place to be determined later by the court. . . .

. . .

(4) On adjourning the trial of an information the court may remand the accused and, where the accused has attained the age of 18 years, shall do so if the offence is triable either way and—

(a) on the occasion on which the accused first appeared, or was brought, before the court to answer to the information he was in custody or, having been released on bail, surrendered to the custody of the court; or

(b) the accused has been remanded at any time in the course of proceedings on the information;

and, where the court remands the accused, the time fixed for the resumption of the trial shall be that at which he is required to appear or be brought before the court in pursuance of the remand [or would be brought before the court were it not for his agreeing to further remands being in his absence].

18.—(1) Sections 19 to 23 below shall have effect where a person who has attained the age of 18 years appears or is brought before a magistrates' court on an information charging him with an offence triable either way and—

(a) he indicates under section 17A above that (if the offence were to proceed to trial) he would plead not guilty, or

(b) his representative indicates under section 17B above that (if the offence were to proceed to trial) he would plead not guilty.

. . .

(4) A magistrates' court proceeding under sections 19 to 23 below may adjourn the proceedings at any time, and on doing so on any occasion when the accused is present may remand the accused, and shall remand him if—

(a) on the occasion on which he first appeared, or was brought, before the court to answer to the information he was in custody or, having been released on bail, surrendered to the custody of the court; or

(b) he has been remanded at any time in the course of proceedings on the information;

and where the court remands the accused, the time fixed for the resumption of the proceedings shall be that at which he is required to appear or be brought before the court in pursuance of the remand [or would be brought before the court were it not for his agreeing to further remands being in his absence].

Remanding the Accused on Adjournments References in the MCA 1980, ss. 5, 10 and 18, to 'remanding' an accused mean either remanding him in custody (i.e. committing him to custody to be brought before the court at the end of the period of remand or at such earlier time as the court may require), or remanding him on bail in accordance with the provisions of the Bail Act 1976 (i.e. directing him to appear before the court at the end of the period of the remand or, if bail is made continuous, directing him to appear at every time to which the proceedings may be adjourned) (see MCA 1980, s. 128(1) and (4)). **D5.16**

Section 18 governs adjournments until mode of trial has been determined. Section 10 applies (a) to appearances for summary offences up until conviction, and (b) to appearances for either-way offences from after mode of trial has been determined in favour of summary trial to conviction. Sections 10(4) and 18(4) provide in almost identical terms that, on adjourning proceedings for an offence triable either way, the court must remand the accused unless: (a) he first appeared in answer to a summons or requisition (as opposed to being brought before the court in custody or appearing in answer to police bail); and (b) he has not been remanded at an earlier hearing. The court has a power to remand but may simply adjourn without also remanding. The magistrates may, at their discretion, adjourn without remanding the accused:

(a) at all appearances for summary offences up to conviction; and (b) at appearances for either-way offences up to either a determination for trial on indictment or summary conviction, provided the accused initially appeared in answer to a summons or requisition and has not subsequently been remanded. Where a case is simply adjourned, there is no need to fix the date for the next hearing at the time of adjourning, whereas if there is a remand the adjournment date must be fixed forthwith and is the date to which the accused is remanded. An accused who is not remanded and who then fails to appear on the date to which his case is adjourned commits no offence, but it may be possible either for a warrant to be issued for his arrest or for the proceedings to be conducted in his absence. An accused who has been remanded on bail commits an offence under the Bail Act 1976, s. 6, if he fails without reasonable cause to answer to his bail.

Period of Remand in Custody

D5.17 The maximum period for which a magistrates' court may remand an accused in custody is eight clear days (MCA 1980, s. 128(6)). This is subject to the following exceptions:

(a) following summary conviction, there may be a remand in custody of up to three weeks (four weeks if the remand is not in custody) for inquiries, such as a pre-sentence report, to be made into the most suitable method of dealing with the accused (s. 10(3) of the 1980 Act);
(b) following the court being satisfied that the accused 'did the act or made the omission charged', there may be a remand in custody of up to three weeks (four weeks if on bail) for a medical examination and reports if the court considers that an inquiry should be made into his physical or mental condition before deciding how to deal with him (PCC(S)A 2000, s. 11);
(c) where mode of trial is determined in favour of summary trial but the court is not constituted so as to proceed immediately to trial (e.g., because it consists of a single lay justice), there may be a remand in custody to a date on which the court will be properly constituted (s. 128(6)(c) of the 1980 Act);
(d) where s. 128A of the 1980 Act applies, a second or subsequent remand in custody may be for up to 28 days; and
(e) if the accused is already being detained under a custodial sentence he may be remanded in custody for up to 28 days or his anticipated release date whichever is the shorter (s. 131 of the 1980 Act).

Where the accused is remanded on bail, the remand may exceed eight clear days provided the parties consent (s. 128(6)(a)). In practice, there is virtually never an objection to whatever period of remand on bail appears necessary for the parties to be ready for the next effective stage in dealing with the case.

D5.18 **Further Remands** Where a person is brought before the court after an earlier remand, the court may remand him again (MCA 1980, s. 128(3)). Thus, there may be several remand hearings before the case is sent to the Crown Court or the commencement of summary trial. The only limitation on the number of remands is the general discretion of magistrates to refuse an adjournment if it would be against the interests of justice (e.g., because they consider that the party requesting the adjournment should have been ready to proceed on the present occasion). By s. 130, a court remanding an accused in custody may order that, for subsequent remands, he be brought up before a different magistrates' court nearer to the prison where he is to be confined while on remand. That alternate court then enjoys those powers in relation to remand (and the granting of representation by the Criminal Defence Service) that the original court would otherwise have.

The MCA 1980, s. 128, is without prejudice to the provisions of s. 129 governing further remands where the accused is unable to attend court because of 'illness or accident'. Under

s. 129(1), the magistrates may remand him in his absence to a convenient date, and any restrictions on the period of the remand which would otherwise be imposed by s. 128(6) do not apply. By virtue of s. 129(3), where an accused has been remanded on bail, the court may enlarge his bail in his absence by appointing a later time for him to appear. It will be noted that s. 129(1) applies whether the remand is in custody or on bail, but is restricted to cases where non-attendance on the day originally fixed is due to accident or illness. Section 129(3) applies only to remands on bail but places no restrictions on the reasons for which the court may choose to exercise its powers under the subsection. Thus, bail may be enlarged where it becomes apparent during the remand period that the court will not have time to deal with the case on the day originally fixed, or where the accused fails to attend but some acceptable reason is advanced for his non-appearance (not necessarily sickness or accident). Where bail is enlarged, the court may also enlarge the recognisances of any sureties (i.e. they will be under an obligation to secure the accused's attendance on the new hearing date).

Remands in Custody in the Absence of Accused

To avoid the necessity for an accused to be brought before the court in custody when it is apparent that no effective progress in his case will be possible at the hearing to which he is brought, he may be remanded in custody in his absence under the MCA 1980, s. 128(3A) to (3E). The conditions that must be satisfied for there to be a custodial remand in absence are that: **D5.19**

(a) the accused has consented (at an earlier hearing) to not being present at future remands (s. 128(3A)(a));
(b) he has a legal representative acting for him in the case, although the representative need not be present in court (s. 128(3B));
(c) he has not been remanded in absence on more than two consecutive occasions prior to the present application for remand in absence (s. 128(3A)(b)); and
(d) he has not withdrawn his original consent (s. 128(3A)(d)).

To facilitate the giving of consent to remands in absence, it is provided in s. 128(1A) to (1C) that, where magistrates are proposing to remand in custody an accused who is present in court (s. 128(1A)(b)), they shall, assuming he is legally represented in court (s. 128(1A)(d)), explain to him the possibility of further remands being in his absence and ask him whether he consents to that procedure being adopted. It is a pre-condition of the accused being asked in court for his consent to remands *in absentia* that his legal representative is present in court (s. 128(1B)), whereas (assuming consent has been given) the remands in absence themselves can, and normally do, take place without the attendance of a lawyer, provided the accused still has a solicitor acting for him in the case. The restriction of the number of consecutive remands in absence to a maximum of three means that the accused cannot be remanded for more than approximately a month without being brought before the court. He could, on attending after three remands in his absence, again agree to the next three remands being in his absence. If a case is listed for a formal remand in absence, but it appears to the magistrates that the conditions for such a remand are not in fact satisfied (e.g., because the accused has withdrawn his consent or no longer has solicitors acting for him), they must remand the accused for the shortest period possible that will enable him to be brought before them (s. 128(3C) to (3D)). It should be noted that, although remands in absence are pure formalities, the rule that remands in custody shall not exceed eight clear days must still be complied with in the sense that the accused's case must be listed within each eight-day period so that the magistrates can formally remand him to the next appropriate date.

Remands in absence are limited to cases where the court is adjourning under s. 5, 10(1) or 18(4) of the 1980 Act (i.e. adjournments prior to or during summary trial or sending the case for Crown Court trial). If the adjournment is under s. 10(3) or 30 (adjournments for reports after conviction or after being satisfied that the accused committed the *actus reus* of the offence), the period of a custodial remand may extend to three weeks but there is no power to remand in absence.

Remands in Custody for up to 28 Days

D5.20 By s. 128A of the MCA 1980, a magistrates' court may remand an accused in custody for a period exceeding eight clear days if (s. 128A(2)):

(a) he has previously been remanded in custody for the same offence;
(b) he is now before the court; and
(c) the court (after allowing the parties to make representations) has fixed a date on which it expects that it will be possible for the next stage in the proceedings, other than a hearing relating to a further remand in custody or on bail, to take place.

This final requirement is that the next hearing should be an effective hearing. In the case of either-way offences, the next effective hearing after the accused becomes eligible for an extended remand will be the hearing to determine mode of trial. The maximum period of a remand under s. 128A is 28 days or to the date of the next effective hearing whichever is the shorter (s. 128A(2)(i) and (ii)). Section 128A does not apply on the occasion of a first remand in custody (s. 128A(2)(a)), although the accused may at that stage be invited to consent to the next three remands being in his absence. The making of a remand under s. 128A does not affect the right of the accused to apply for bail during the period of that remand (s. 128A(3)). The preservation of the right to make a bail application even though there has been a 28-day remand in custody entitles the defence to put before the magistrates forthwith any relevant change in circumstances that arises during the period of the remand.

Remand on Bail

D5.21 Under the MCA 1980, s. 128(6)(a), the accused may be remanded for a period greater than eight clear days if he is remanded on bail and both he and the prosecution agree to a longer period of remand.

Statutory Provisions on Duration of Remands

D5.22 **Magistrates' Courts Act 1980, ss. 128, 128A and 129 to 131**

128.—(1) Where a magistrates' court has power to remand any person, then, subject to section 4 of the Bail Act 1976 and to any other enactment modifying that power, the court may—

(a) remand him in custody, that is to say, commit him to custody to be brought before the court, subject to subsection (3A) below, at the end of the period of remand or at such earlier time as the court may require; or
(b) where it is inquiring into or is trying an offence alleged to have been committed by that person or has convicted him of an offence, remand him on bail in accordance with the Bail Act 1976, that is to say, by directing him to appear as provided in subsection (4) below; or
[(c) relates to bail in non-criminal proceedings.]

(1A) Where—

(a) on adjourning a case under section 5, 10(1), 17C or 18(4) above the court proposes to remand or further remand a person in custody; and
(b) he is before the court; and
(c) [repealed]; and
(d) he is legally represented in that court,

it shall be the duty of the court—

(i) to explain the effect of subsections (3A) and (3B) below to him in ordinary language; and
(ii) to inform him in ordinary language that, notwithstanding the procedure for a remand without his being brought before a court, he would be brought before a court for the hearing and determination of at least every fourth application for his remand, and of every application for his remand heard at a time when it appeared to the court that he had no solicitor acting for him in the case.

(1B) For the purposes of subsection (1A) above a person is to be treated as legally represented in a court if, but only if, he has the assistance of counsel or a solicitor to represent him in the proceedings in that court.

(1C) After explaining to an accused as provided by subsection (1A) above the court shall ask him whether he consents to hearing and determination of such applications in his absence.

[(2) If bail is granted subject to the provision of sureties but they are not immediately available, the accused must be remanded in custody until such time as they enter into their recognisances.]

(3) Where a person is brought before the court after remand, the court may further remand him.

(3A) Subject to subsection (3B) below, where a person has been remanded in custody and the remand was not a remand under section 128A below for a period exceeding eight clear days, the court may further remand him (otherwise than in the exercise of the power conferred by that section) on an adjournment under section 5, 10(1), 17C or 18(4) above without his being brought before it if it is satisfied—

(a) that he gave his consent, either in response to a question under subsection (1C) above or otherwise, to the hearing and determination in his absence of any application for his remand on an adjournment of the case under any of those provisions; and

(b) that he has not by virtue of this subsection been remanded without being brought before the court on more than two such applications immediately preceding the application which the court is hearing; and

(c) [repealed]; and

(d) that he has not withdrawn his consent . . .

(3B) The court may not exercise the power conferred by subsection (3A) above if it appears to the court, on an application for a further remand being made to it, that the person to whom the application relates has no solicitor acting for him in the case (whether present in court or not).

(3C) Where—

(a) a person has been remanded in custody on an adjournment of a case under section 4(4), 10(1), 17C or 18(4) above; and

(b) an application is subsequently made for his further remand on such an adjournment; and

(c) he is not brought before the court which hears and determines the application; and

(d) that court is not satisfied as mentioned in subsection (3A) above, the court shall adjourn the case and remand him in custody for the period for which it stands adjourned.

(3D) An adjournment under subsection (3C) above shall be for the shortest period that appears to the court to make it possible for the accused to be brought before it.

[(3E) Procedure to be adopted if it appears to the court at some stage after a remand in absence that the accused ought not have been so remanded.]

(4) Where a person is remanded on bail under subsection (1) above the court may . . . direct him to appear . . .—

(a) before that court at the end of the period of remand; or

(b) at every time and place to which during the course of the proceedings the hearing may be from time to time adjourned;

and, where it remands him on bail conditionally on his providing a surety when it is proceeding with a view to transfer for trial, may direct that the recognisance of the surety be conditioned to secure that the person so bailed appears—

(c) at every time and place to which during the course of the proceedings the hearing may be from time to time adjourned and also before the Crown Court in the event of the person so bailed being committed for trial there.

(5) Where a person is directed to appear or a recognisance is conditioned for a person's appearance in accordance with paragraph (b) or (c) of subsection (4) above, the fixing at any time of the time for him next to appear shall be deemed to be a remand; but nothing in this subsection or subsection (4) above shall deprive the court of power at any subsequent hearing to remand him afresh.

(6) Subject to the provisions of sections 128A and 129 below, a magistrates' court shall not remand a person for a period exceeding eight clear days, except that—

(a) if the court remands him on bail, it may remand him for a longer period if he and the other party consent;

(b) where the court adjourns a trial under section 10(3) or section 11 of the Powers of Criminal Courts (Sentencing) Act 2000, the court may remand him for the period of the adjournment;

(c) where a person is charged with an offence triable either way, then, if it falls to the court to try the case summarily but the court is not at the time so constituted, and sitting in such a place, as will enable it to proceed with the trial, the court may remand him until the next occasion on which it will be practicable for the court to be so constituted, and to sit in such a place, as aforesaid, notwithstanding that the remand is for a period exceeding eight clear days.

[(7) and (8) Concern committing an accused to police detention for a period not exceeding three clear days where there is a need to question him about other offences — see **D1.55**.]

128A.—(1) The Secretary of State may by order made by statutory instrument provide that this section shall have effect—

(a) in an area specified in the order; or

(b) in proceedings of a description so specified,

in relation to any person ('the accused').

(2) A magistrates' court may remand the accused in custody for a period exceeding eight clear days if—

(a) it has previously remanded him in custody for the same offence; and

(b) he is before the court,

but only if, after affording the parties an opportunity to make representations, it has set a date on which it expects that it will be possible for the next stage in the proceedings, other than a hearing relating to a further remand in custody or on bail, to take place, and only—

(i) for a period ending not later than that date; or

(ii) for a period of 28 clear days,

whichever is the less.

(3) Nothing in this section affects the right of the accused to apply for bail during the period of remand.

[(4) Making of statutory instruments under the section.]

129.—(1) If a magistrates' court is satisfied that any person who has been remanded is unable by reason of illness or accident to appear or be brought before the court at the expiration of the period for which he was remanded, the court may, in his absence, remand him for a further time; and section 128(6) above shall not apply.

(2) Notwithstanding anything in section 128(1) above, the power of a court under subsection (1) above to remand a person on bail for a further time—

(a) where he was granted bail in criminal proceedings, includes power to enlarge the recognisance of any surety for him to a later time;

[(b) concerns bail in non-criminal proceedings.]

(3) Where a person remanded on bail is bound to appear before a magistrates' court at any time and the court has no power to remand him under subsection (1) above, the court may in his absence—

(a) where he was granted bail in criminal proceedings, appoint a later time as the time at which he is to appear and enlarge the recognisances of any sureties for him to that time;

[(b) concerns bail in non-criminal proceedings];

and the appointment of the time . . . shall be deemed to be a further remand.

[(4) Concerns enlargement of a surety's recognisance upon committal for trial.]

130.—(1) A magistrates' court adjourning a case under section 5, 10(1), 17C or 18(4) above, and remanding the accused in custody, may, if he has attained the age of 17, order that he be brought up for any subsequent remands before an alternate magistrates' court nearer to the prison where he is to be confined while on remand.

[(2)–(5) and sch. 5 contain detailed provisions governing remands to alternate magistrates' courts.]

131.—(1) When a magistrates' court remands an accused person in custody and he is already detained under a custodial sentence, the period for which he is remanded may be up to 28 clear days.

(2) But the court shall inquire as to the expected date of his release from that detention; and if it appears that it will be before 28 clear days have expired, he shall not be remanded in custody for more than eight clear days or (if longer) a period ending with that date.

PRE-TRIAL HEARINGS BY TELEVISION LINK

The CDA 1998, s. 57, provided for pre-trial hearings involving an accused in custody to be conducted over a live television link between the court and the prison. From 15 January 2007, a new set of provisions, CDA 1998, ss. 57A, 57B, 57D and 57E, is substituted by the Police and Justice Act 2006, s. 45. These provisions enable the courts to direct that an accused in custody may appear at preliminary hearings, and at sentencing hearings, via a 'live link' from prison or from a police station. Under s. 57A(2), the accused is to be treated as present in court when he attends via a live link. D5.23

Under s. 57A(3), a 'live link' is defined so as to require that that the accused be able to see and hear, and to be seen and heard by, the court during the hearing.

Under s. 57B, the court (whether the Crown Court or a magistrates' court) may direct that an accused who is likely to be held in custody during a preliminary hearing is to attend that hearing by way of live link (a 'live link direction'). Under s. 57B(4), if there is a hearing in relation to the making or rescinding of such a direction, the court may require or permit attendance via live link. It follows that the accused does not have to be present in court for a live link direction to be given (and so the court may give such a direction in writing or immediately before the start of a hearing with the accused present via a live link). Under s. 57B(5), the court is required to give the parties the opportunity to make representations before making (or rescinding) a live link direction. If a magistrates' court decides not to give a live link direction where it has power to do so, it must state its reasons in open court and record the reasons in the court register (s. 57B(6)).

Section 57C empowers a magistrates' court (but not the Crown Court) to direct the accused to attend a preliminary hearing via a live link from a police station. By virtue of s. 57C(3) and (4), this provision applies both to an accused who is detained at the police station in connection with the offence in question, and to an accused who has been bailed to return to the police station for a live link appearance in connection with the offence, known as 'live link bail' (PACE, s. 47(3), is amended by the PJA 2006, s. 46, to allow the police to grant bail subject to a duty to appear at a police station for the purpose of a live link hearing). Such a direction may be made only with the consent of the accused (s. 57C(7)). The court may require or permit such consent (or withholding of consent) to be communicated via a live link (s. 57C(9)). Section 57C(10) makes it clear that an accused answering to 'live link bail' is to be treated as having surrendered to the custody of the court as from the time when it makes a live link direction in respect of him.

Under s. 57D, where an accused attends a preliminary hearing over a live link and pleads guilty to the offence (or, if it is an either-way offence, indicates a guilty plea and so is deemed to have pleaded guilty under the 'plea before venue' procedure), and the court proposes to proceed immediately to sentencing, the accused may continue to attend through the link provided that he agrees to do so and the court is satisfied that it is not contrary to the interests of justice for him to do so (s. 57D(2)). Section 57D(3) provides that, where a preliminary hearing over a live link continues as a sentencing hearing, the offender can give oral evidence over the live link only if he has specifically agreed to give evidence in that way and the court is satisfied that it is not contrary to the interests of justice for him to do so.

OPTIONS WHEN THE ACCUSED FAILS TO APPEAR

If an accused who has been bailed to appear at a magistrates' court fails to do so, the court may: D5.24

(a) issue a warrant for his arrest under the Bail Act 1976, s. 7; or

(b) enlarge his bail in accordance with the MCA 1980, s. 129(3); or
(c) proceed in his absence under MCA 1980, s. 11(1) (see below).

If a warrant for arrest is issued the court may, at its discretion, back it for bail (MCA 1980, s. 117). This is a direction that, having been arrested, the person arrested shall thereafter be bailed by the police to attend court on a named day. This is appropriate where, for example, there is some suggestion that the accused has a good reason for non-attendance but there is no evidence to support this suggestion (making it inappropriate simply to enlarge his bail under the MCA 1980, s. 129(3)). The execution of such warrants is sometimes seen as a waste of police resources, and so magistrates' courts have been encouraged to use warning letters instead (see D7.73).

Trial in Absence of the Accused

D5.25 If the accused fails to appear for the trial in the magistrates' court, the case may proceed in his absence provided, where the prosecution commenced by issue of a summons or requisition, that it is proved to the satisfaction of the court that either the summons (or requisition, as the case may be) was served a reasonable time before the hearing or the accused appeared on a previous occasion to answer the charge (MCA 1980, s. 11(1) and (2)). Proof of service of the summons or requisition will entail proving that it came to the accused's knowledge, unless it was sent by post to his last known or usual address, in which case it is deemed to have been served effectively under CrimPR, r. 4.1(4).

Where an adjournment notice has been sent to the accused, it is necessary to satisfy the court that he had 'adequate notice' of the adjournment date (MCA 1980, s. 10(2)). Arguably, this gives the magistrates greater discretion as to what amounts to adequate notice, but courts generally require service of an adjournment notice to be proved in the same way as service of a summons.

It must be borne in mind that, in the case of an offence which is triable either way, the trial cannot proceed in the absence of the accused unless, at an earlier hearing, he consented to summary trial.

Summary trial in the absence of the accused is considered in more detail in **D21.9**.

Bench Warrants

D5.26 Should the court decide to adjourn the trial rather than proceeding in the absence of the accused, it may issue a warrant for his arrest provided: (a) the offence to which the warrant relates is punishable with imprisonment, or the court, having convicted the accused, is proposing to impose a disqualification on him (s. 13(3)), and (b) either it is proved to the satisfaction of the court that the summons (where the proceedings were commenced by summons) was served on the accused a reasonable time before the trial (or adjourned trial, as the case may be), or else the adjournment now being made is a second or subsequent adjournment and the accused was present in court on the occasion of the last adjournment and was informed of the time for the adjourned hearing on that occasion (s. 13(2), (2A) and (2B)). In other words, it has to be proved that the accused knew of the date of the hearing in question and this will be so if either the present hearing is the first hearing, and it is proved that the summons was served on the accused, or the present hearing is a second or subsequent hearing, and the accused was present on the last occasion and the date for the present hearing was fixed at that hearing. Where the accused is under 18, the requirement that the offence is punishable with imprisonment means an offence which, in the case of an adult offender, would be so punishable (s. 13(3A)(a)).

Although warrants under s. 13 are not expressly limited to prosecutions commenced by way of summons, reliance on the section in cases where the accused has been bailed to appear will be unnecessary because non-attendance in answer to bail may always be dealt with by issue of a warrant under the Bail Act 1976, s. 7. If a prosecution for an indictable offence is commenced by way of summons (or by written charge and requisition) and the accused does not appear, a warrant cannot be issued under s. 13 of the 1980 Act unless and until it is determined to try the information summarily, but the prosecutor is entitled to apply for the issue of a warrant for arrest under the MCA 1980, s. 1 (see s. 1(6) which provides that, where the offence charged is indictable, a warrant may be issued under s. 1 notwithstanding that a summons has previously been granted).

Full discussion of the options open to the court where an accused who is on bail fails to attend court may be found in D7.

DELIVERING SIMPLE, SPEEDY, SUMMARY JUSTICE

In 2006, the Government published a paper entitled *Delivering Simple, Speedy, Summary Justice*. It made a number of proposals, which are intended to be rolled out nationally (following local pilot schemes). As well as reorganising the management of magistrates' courts, the proposals seek to streamline case management procedures in order to reduce the overall time between arrest and the conclusion of the case. To this end, the report focuses on four key areas: **D5.27**

(a) making the first hearing effective every time. This requires:
  (i) the prosecution papers to be served on the defence and the court;
  (ii) the court to probe the parties to identify issues to be tried;
  (iii) directions and timescales to be set by the court and a date fixed for trial no later than 6 weeks; and
  (iv) where defendants plead guilty, that they are dealt with there and then.
(b) ensuring that case progression is robustly managed by the judiciary without the need for a court hearing, supported by case progression officers, so that all unnecessary hearings are eliminated and cases proceed on the trial date as ordered;
(c) bringing about a 'change in culture', so that orders are complied with to the right standard at the right time;
(d) ensuring that the judiciary adopts a robust case management approach to adjournments in summary cases so that the expectation is that they will proceed on the day if one of the parties has simply failed to comply with directions or to be adequately prepared.

This report sends a clear signal to magistrates, and to the lawyers who practise in the magistrates' courts, that the case management powers contained in the CrimPR (see **D4.6**) will be applied robustly to ensure that delay is kept to a minimum.

Section D6 Classification of Offences and Determining Mode of Trial

D6.1 Criminal trials in England and Wales are either trials on indictment or summary trials. The former take place in the Crown Court, before a judge and jury; the latter take place in a magistrates' court, before at least two lay justices (or a single district judge). This section deals with (a) the classification of offences according to whether they: (i) must be tried on indictment, or (ii) may be tried either on indictment or summarily, or (iii) must be tried summarily; and (b) the procedure for determining the appropriate mode of trial in those cases where there is a choice.

CLASSIFICATION OF OFFENCES

Definition of the Classes of Offences

D6.2 There are, as regards mode of trial, three classes of offence — namely, (a) those triable only on indictment, (b) those triable only summarily, and (c) those triable either way: see the MCA 1980, ss. 17 to 25. These sections must be read in conjunction with sch. 1 to the Interpretation Act 1978.

Interpretation Act 1978, sch. 1

(a) 'indictable offence' means an offence which, if committed by an adult, is triable on indictment, whether it is exclusively so triable or triable either way;

(b) 'summary offence' means an offence which, if committed by an adult, is triable only summarily;

(c) 'offence triable either way' means an offence, other than an offence triable on indictment only by virtue of [s. 40 or s. 41] of the Criminal Justice Act 1988 which, if committed by an adult, is triable either on indictment or summarily;

and the terms 'indictable', 'summary' and 'triable either way', in their application to offences, are to be construed accordingly.

The Interpretation Act 1978 qualifies the above definitions with the rider that: 'references [in the definitions] to the way or ways in which an offence is triable are to be construed without regard to the effect, if any, of section 22 of the Magistrates' Courts Act 1980 on the mode of trial in a particular case'. The broad effect of s. 22 of the MCA 1980 is that offences under s. 1 of the Criminal Damage Act 1971 involving damage worth less than the relevant sum (currently £5,000) must be dealt with as if they were triable only summarily (see **D6.31**). However, such an offence retains the status of an offence triable either way, even though the magistrates are barred from sending it to the Crown Court for trial (*Considine* (1980) 70 Cr App R 239. In *Fennell* [2000] 1 WLR 2011, the accused was charged with racially aggravated criminal damage (under the CDA 1998, s. 30). The judge allowed the jury to acquit him of that offence but convict him instead (under the Criminal Law Act 1967, s. 6: see **D18.42**) of simple criminal damage. The value involved was less than £5,000. The Court of Appeal held that it was open to the judge to leave an alternative verdict of criminal damage for the jury's consideration even though the value involved was less than £5,000 and, without invoking the

CJA 1988, s. 40, to add that offence of criminal damage to the indictment. Section 22 of the MCA 1980 does not change the classification of the offence, which remains triable either way. In *Alden* (2002) 2 Cr App R (S) 326, where a count of criminal damage was added when the indictment was amended in the Crown Court, the Court of Appeal rejected the argument that *Fennell* was wrongly decided and confirmed that if an offender is to be sentenced by the Crown Court for criminal damage, otherwise than under a particular provision specifically restricting the sentencing powers of the Crown Court (e.g., the CJA 1988, s. 40), then the normal maximum sentence (10 years) is available.

By s. 5 of the Interpretation Act 1978, the definitions set out in sch. 1 are to apply whenever the terms defined are used statutorily unless a contrary intention appears. Consequently, when an Act contains the phrase 'indictable offence' without any further qualification, it must be understood to mean both those offences which, in the case of an adult, *must* be tried on indictment and those which (again in the case of an adult) carry the right to trial on indictment although they can be tried summarily with the agreement of the accused and of the magistrates. In other words, offences triable either way are a subdivision of indictable offences. Summary offences, on the other hand, are entirely distinct from indictable offences and must always be tried summarily, unless s. 40 or s. 41 of the CJA 1988 applies. The reason for the Interpretation Act 1978 definitions referring each time to the possible mode of trial in the case of an adult is that special rules apply to the trial of juveniles, greatly restricting the use of trial on indictment (see s. 24 of the MCA 1980 and D23). However, the fact that a juvenile charged with a certain offence would have to be tried for it summarily in the youth court does not render the offence summary — the question is whether an adult would have to be so tried.

Determining Which Class an Offence Is In

The definitions in the Interpretation Act 1978 do not help to determine whether any particular offence is indictable or summary, or whether, in the former case, it is triable only on indictment or either way. Those questions are answered as follows: **D6.3**

(a) *Statutory offences.* The enactment creating the offence will prescribe the maximum penalty. If the statute provides for a maximum penalty imposable on summary conviction and does not provide for a penalty on conviction on indictment, then the offence is summary. If the statute provides for one penalty on summary conviction and a different (invariably greater) penalty on conviction on indictment, then the offence is triable either way. If the statute provides only for a penalty on conviction on indictment, then the offence is triable only on indictment, unless the offence is listed in the MCA 1980, sch. 1 (see below).
(b) *Common-law offences.* These are all indictable offences. They will be triable only on indictment unless listed in the MCA 1980, sch. 1.

It will be apparent from the above that some statutory offences are triable either way, even though there is no indication in the statute itself that that is so. Similarly, some commonlaw offences are triable either way even though common-law offences are prima facie triable only on indictment. This is because the MCA 1980, s. 17, provides that, without prejudice to any other enactment by virtue of which an offence is triable either way, the offences listed in sch. 1 shall be so triable. As regards determining the mode of trial, it makes no difference whether an offence is listed in sch. 1 or is made triable either way by virtue of the offence-creating statute specifically providing for differing penalties on summary conviction and on conviction on indictment. The significance of the distinction is that, on summary conviction for a sch. 1 offence, the maximum penalty that a magistrates' court may impose is six months' imprisonment and/or a fine not exceeding the 'prescribed sum', presently £5,000, whereas, on summary conviction for an offence made triable either way by the statute creating it, the maximum is basically whatever is prescribed in the statute, save that the maximum prison term imposable may not exceed six months (ss. 31 and 32). The modern tendency when creating new either-way offences is to provide in the statute for the penalties, rather than adding the new offence to the list in sch. 1.

The most important offence-creating statutes covered by sch. 1 are the OAPA 1861, the Perjury Act 1911, the Theft Act 1968 and the Criminal Damage Act 1971. Schedule 1 also deals with the trial of secondary parties and offences of incitement. Attempts are now covered by the Criminal Attempts Act 1981, s. 4(1)(c), the rule being — as it is for allegations of aiding and abetting or inciting — that the offence is triable either way only if the substantive offence is so triable.

Magistrates' Courts Act 1980, s. 17 and sch. 1

17.—(1) The offences listed in Schedule 1 to this Act shall be triable either way.

(2) Subsection (1) above is without prejudice to any other enactment by virtue of which any offence is triable either way.

SCHEDULE 1

OFFENCES TRIABLE EITHER WAY BY VIRTUE OF SECTION 17

1. Offences at common law of public nuisance.
1A. An offence at common law of outraging public decency.
2. Offences under section 8 of the Disorderly Houses Act 1751 (appearing to be keeper of bawdy house etc.).
3. Offences consisting in contravention of section 13 of the Statutory Declarations Act 1835 (administration by a person of an oath etc touching matters in which he has no jurisdiction).
4. Offences under section 36 of the Malicious Damage Act 1861 (obstructing engines or carriages on railways).
5. Offences under the following provisions of the Offences against the Person Act 1861—
   (a) section 16 (threats to kill);
   (b) section 20 (inflicting bodily injury, with or without a weapon);
   (c) section 26 (not providing apprentices or servants with food etc.);
   (d) section 27 (abandoning or exposing a child);
   (e) section 34 (doing or omitting to do anything so as to endanger railway passengers);
   (f) section 36 (assaulting a clergyman at a place of worship etc.);
   (g) section 38 (assault with intent to resist apprehension);
   (h) section 47 (assault occasioning bodily harm);
   (i) section 57 (bigamy);
   (j) section 60 (concealing the birth of a child).
6. Offences under section 20 of the Telegraph Act 1868 (disclosing or intercepting messages).
7. Offences under section 13 of the Debtors Act 1869 (transactions intended to defraud creditors).
8. Offences under section 5 of the Public Stores Act 1875 (obliteration of marks with intent to conceal).
9. Offences under section 12 of the Corn Returns Act 1882 (false returns).
11. Offences under section 3 of the Submarine Telegraph Act 1885 (damaging submarine cables).
12. Offences under section 13 of the Stamp Duties Management Act 1891 (offences in relation to dies and stamps).
13. Offences under section 8(2) of the Cremation Act 1902 (making false representations etc. with a view to procuring the burning of any human remains).
14. All offences under the Perjury Act 1911 except offences under—
   (a) section 1 (perjury in judicial proceedings);
   (b) section 3 (false statements etc. with reference to marriage).
   (c) section 4 (false statements etc. as to births or deaths).
16. Offences under section 17 of the Deeds of Arrangement Act 1914 (trustee making preferential payments).
18. Offences under section 8(2) of the Census Act 1920 (disclosing census information).
19. Offences under section 36 of the Criminal Justice Act 1925 (forgery of passports etc.).
20. Offences under section 11 of the Agricultural Credits Act 1928 (frauds by farmers).

26. The following offences under the Criminal Law Act 1967—
    (a) offences under section 4(1) (assisting offenders); and
    (b) offences under section 5(1) (concealing arrestable offences and giving false information), where the offence to which they relate is triable either way.
28. All indictable offences under the Theft Act 1968 except—
    (a) robbery, aggravated burglary, blackmail and assault with intent to rob;
    (b) burglary comprising the commission of, or an intention to commit, an offence which is triable only on indictment;
    (c) burglary in a dwelling if any person in the dwelling was subjected to violence or the threat of violence.
29. Offences under the following provisions of the Criminal Damage Act 1971—
    section 1(1) (destroying or damaging property);
    section 1(1) and (3) (arson);
    section 2 (threats to destroy or damage property);
    section 3 (possessing anything with intent to destroy or damage property).
32. Committing an indecent assault upon a person whether male or female.
33. Aiding, abetting, counselling or procuring the commission of any offence listed in the preceding paragraphs of this schedule except paragraph 26.
35. Any offence consisting in the incitement to commit an offence triable either way except an offence mentioned in paragraph 33 above.

ADVANCE INFORMATION

If the offence charged is triable either way, the court may not proceed to determine mode of trial unless either the defence have been given advance information about the prosecution case or they have waived their right to it. Although advance information is sometimes both requested and served prior to the accused's first appearance (in which case the court may proceed immediately to determine mode of trial), it is more usual for the provision of the information to necessitate at least one adjournment. Thus, one incidental function of remand hearings is to facilitate the service of advance information. **D6.4**

The right to advance information is contained in part 21 of the CrimPR. The rules are set out in full in **appendix 1**. They apply only when the accused is charged with an offence triable either way (r. 21.1). Since sch. 1 to the Interpretation Act 1978 defines 'offence triable either way' so as to include criminal damage, the rules would seem to apply to any charge of criminal damage, even if it is clear that the value involved is less than the relevant sum and that the matter will therefore have to be dealt with summarily (see **D6.31** *et seq.*) and *Considine* (1980) 70 Cr App R 239 and *Fennell* [2000] 1 WLR 2011).

As soon as possible after the accused has been charged with or summoned for an either-way offence, the prosecutor must give him a written notice, explaining his right to advance information and stating the address at which a request for it may be made (r. 21.2). The request may but need not be in writing. Often it is made orally at court.

If, prior to determination of mode of trial (or, in the case of an accused who is under the age of 18, before he is asked to enter a plea), the accused (or his legal representative) asks for advance information, the prosecutor must serve either copies of the statements of the proposed prosecution witnesses or a summary of the prosecution case (r. 21.3(1)). This is subject to the prosecutor's discretion to withhold disclosure of some or all of his case if he considers that full compliance with r. 21.3(1) might lead to a witness being intimidated or some other interference with the course of justice (r. 21.4).

Where the advance information refers to a document on which the prosecutor proposes to rely, the accused is entitled to see that document (r. 21.3(3)). In an appropriate case, this might include, for example, a video tape which records the accused's participation in the offence. In *Calderdale Magistrates' Court, ex parte Donahue* [2001] Crim LR 141, the accused sought judicial review of a decision by the magistrates refusing to direct the Crown to disclose video tape evidence or accede to a request for an adjournment before proceeding to a plea before venue hearing. Once the defence lawyers saw the video tape, the accused entered a guilty plea. He argued that, as a result of the magistrates' refusal to order disclosure of the tape, he had been unable to make an informed decision on plea and so he had elected for Crown Court trial; it followed that there was a risk that he would not receive the appropriate credit for his guilty plea (given that it was not entered at the plea before venue hearing). The Divisional Court held that the accused was entitled to view the video tape evidence in advance under the Advance Information Rules and that the magistrates had erred in refusing the request for an adjournment. The purpose of part 21 is to enable the accused to make an informed choice as to his plea and mode of trial. It was held that the accused ought to be given the opportunity to withdraw his election for Crown Court trial and be given credit for entering a guilty plea at the earliest opportunity. The footnote to para. 1.6 of the Protocol for the Provision of Advance Information, Prosecution Evidence and Disclosure of Unused Material in the Magistrates' Courts (May 2006) suggests that 'the law is still unclear as to what is to be regarded as a "document" under the rule', and points out that the decision in *Ex parte Donahue* was founded on a concession that the video was a 'document' under the Rules, and so the case cannot be regarded as formally deciding that point. That footnote also refers to *R (DPP) v Croydon Magistrates' Court* [2001] EWHC Admin 552, where reference in a case summary to results of DNA samples was held not to amount to reference to a document and so the prosecution were not obliged to provide further documentary information about the DNA profiling at that stage of the proceedings.

Before proceeding to determination of mode of trial (or, in the case of an accused under the age of 18, before taking a plea), the court must satisfy itself that the accused is aware of his right to advance information (r. 21.5). It is open to the defence to waive their rights (e.g., if the accused has already decided to elect trial on indictment and an adjournment for advance information would be pointless because the prosecution case will in any event be fully disclosed when the case is transferred to the Crown Court).

Should the defence fail to request advance information before mode of trial is determined and the determination is then for summary trial, there is then no obligation under part 21 for the prosecution to make disclosure.

A-G's Guidelines on Disclosure

D6.5 The rules on advance information remain in force but their importance has been superseded, at least to some extent, by the A-G's Guidelines on Disclosure (set out in **appendix** 5). Paragraph 57 provides that, in the case of summary trial:

> The prosecutor should, in addition to complying with the obligations under the CPIA, provide to the defence all evidence upon which the Crown proposes to rely in a summary trial. Such provision should allow the accused or their legal advisers sufficient time properly to consider the evidence before it is called.

The effect of this is to put an accused who is being tried in the magistrates' court in the same position as an accused who is being tried in the Crown Court as regards obtaining copies of the statements of the persons to be called as prosecution witnesses. Standard directions set out in the case progression forms used in magistrates' courts set a time-limit of 28 days from plea for the prosecution to provide the defence with the evidence required by para. 57. However, para. 2.2 of the Protocol says that late provision of such evidence should not automatically result in a trial being adjourned. Rather, the court must take into account the nature of the evidence being provided late and form a view as to how long is required to consider it properly. The Protocol says that, in the majority of cases, 'a competent advocate will be able to deal with the material then and there by the court allowing time before the trial commences, or even during the course of the trial'. However, it is submitted that the robust approach recommended by the Protocol should not be allowed to undermine the requirement in the A-G's Guidelines that the defence should have 'sufficient time properly to consider the evidence before it is called'. See also D9.13.

Right to a Fair Trial

In *Stratford Justices, ex parte Imbert* [1999] 2 Cr App R 276 the Divisional Court considered whether the possibility of an accused being tried summarily without having had sight of the witness statements of the prosecution witnesses was a violation of the right under the ECHR, Article 6(3)(a) 'to be informed promptly . . . and in detail, of the nature and cause of the accusation against him'. The Divisional Court held that it was not, although their lordships recognised that their decision was clearly *obiter* (doubly so when it came to their view that it would still not be a violation after the implementation of the HRA 1998). It is submitted that the absence of advance information might in certain circumstances be a violation of Article 6(3)(b), which lays down the accused's right 'to have adequate time and facilities for his defence', as well as a violation of Article 6(3)(a). In order that the trial should be fair, it is necessary that the defence should be able to consider the prosecution evidence, and prepare upon the basis of knowledge rather than guesswork. Sometimes the nature of that evidence will be predictable, and the defence advocate will be able to respond with the necessary agility of thought. But in other instances, the defence may be ambushed by an unexpected line of evidence. Given the undesirability of adjournments, it is submitted that the requirement of disclosure set out in para. 57 of the A-G's Guidelines should be regarded as necessary in order to accord the accused the rights guaranteed by the Convention. **D6.6**

Failure to Comply

If the prosecution fail to comply with the request for advance information the court must adjourn the proceedings (and, if necessary, may do so more than once) pending compliance by the prosecution with the requirement to provide advance information. An adjournment may be refused only if the court is satisfied that the conduct of the case for the accused will not be substantially prejudiced by non-compliance with the requirement (CrimPR, r. 21.6(1)). According to *Dunmow Justices, ex parte Nash* (1993) 157 JP 1153, this is the only power available to the court where the defence has not had proper disclosure from the prosecution. However, para. 1.7 of the Protocol, when considering the effect of *Ex parte Nash*, makes the point that the court 'should consider relying upon its general case management powers if the interests of justice so require'. It is submitted that, taking account of the overriding objective set out in the CrimPR, part 1, and the case management powers conferred by part 3, the court may now be able to order the provision of advance information despite the absence of a specific power to do so under part 21. **D6.7**

The court cannot dismiss the charge(s) brought by the prosecution because of non-compliance with a request for advance information (*King v Kucharz* (1989) 153 JP 336). In *R (AP, MD and JS)* (2001) 165 JP 684, the Divisional Court held that, even taking into account the ECHR, Article 6, the court does not have jurisdiction to dismiss proceedings for abuse of process simply on the basis of the failure to supply advance information.

Juveniles

The advance information rules apply (with some modifications) in the case of juveniles charged with either-way offences. This is so even though juveniles must be tried summarily unless the MCA 1980, s. 24, provides otherwise and so (unless the case is one to which the provisions of the PCC(S)A 2000, s. 91, apply) there is no mode of trial hearing. **D6.8**

Dealing with Advance Information Expeditiously

Paragraph 1.4 of the Protocol states that, in furtherance of the overriding objective to deal with cases efficiently and expeditiously (CrimPR, r. 1.1(e)), magistrates' courts should expect to deal with both plea and venue on the first hearing of the case. The prosecutor must **D6.9**

D

Part D Procedure

therefore be in a position to comply with any request for advance information either before or at the first hearing. The defence advocates should, save in exceptional circumstances, expect to be ready to go through that material with the accused and advise on venue, plea and any ancillary matters there and then without the need for an adjournment. Paragraph 1.4 adds that, if necessary, cases can be put back in the list to allow the defence sufficient time to consider any material provided. It is submitted, however, that where the material is voluminous or complex, the needs of justice may be best served by an adjournment.

A footnote to para. 1.5 of the Protocol (footnote 7) notes that the CrimPR, part 21 does not specify that a summary of facts and matters supplied in place of the written statements of the prosecution witnesses has to be written or otherwise recorded. It is submitted, however, that the practice should invariably be to comply with the advance information requirements in writing, both so that there is no doubt as to the content of the advance information and to assist the defence advocate when advising the accused.

Paragraph 1.7 of the Protocol indicates that, when faced with applications for adjournments to inspect documents referred to in advance information, the court should consider whether the information already provided is sufficient for the accused to make an informed decision on venue (which is the purpose of the rules on advance information) and, if so, whether any substantial prejudice will arise in refusing that application.

DETERMINATION OF MODE OF TRIAL

Introduction

D6.10 Sections 17A to 21 of the MCA 1980 set out the standard method of determining the mode of trial when an adult is charged with an offence triable either way. Section 22 provides for a special procedure where the charge is one of criminal damage, and s. 23 allows for proceedings under ss. 19 to 22 to be carried out in the absence of the accused provided certain conditions are satisfied. Section 25 relates to changing the decision about mode of trial originally taken.

The Procedure for Determining Mode of Trial

D6.11 The procedure, which is set out in the MCA 1980, s. 17A, applies whenever a person who has attained the age of 18 (i.e. an adult) appears or is brought before a magistrates' court charged with an offence triable either way (MCA 1980, s. 17A(1)). This procedure must be complied with before any evidence is called for purposes of a summary trial or the case is sent for Crown Court trial, and (subject to ss. 17B, 18(3) and 23, considered below) should take place in the presence of the accused (s. 17A(2)). The steps in the standard procedure are as follows:

(a) The charge is written down (if that has not already been done) and read to the accused (s. 17A(3)).
(b) The court explains to the accused that he may indicate whether he would plead guilty or not guilty if the offence proceeded to trial. The court should explain that, if the accused indicates a plea of guilty, the proceedings will be treated as a summary trial at which a guilty plea has been tendered. It must also explain that he may be committed for sentence under the PCC(S)A 2000, s. 3, if it is of the opinion that its powers of punishment are inadequate, or under s. 3A, if it appears to the court that the criteria for the imposition of a sentence under the CJA 2003, s. 225(3) or s. 227(2) (the 'dangerous offender' provisions) apply (s. 17A(4)).
(c) The court asks the accused whether (if the offence went to trial) he would plead guilty or not guilty (s. 17A(5)).
(d) If the accused indicates a guilty plea, the court proceeds as if he had pleaded guilty at summary trial (s. 17A(6)).

(e) If the accused indicates a not guilty plea, the court affords the prosecution and defence the opportunity to make representations about whether the offence is more suitable for summary trial or trial on indictment (s. 19(2)(b)).

(f) The court then considers which mode of trial appears more suitable, having regard to:
  (i) the representations made at stage (e);
  (ii) the nature of the case;
  (iii) whether the circumstances make the offence one of a serious character;
  (iv) whether the punishment which a magistrate's court would have power to inflict for the offence would be adequate; and
  (v) any other circumstances which appear to the court to make the offence more suitable for it to be tried in one way rather than the other (s. 19(1) and (3)).

  When the amendments to s. 19 made by the CJA 2003 come into force, the court will be required, when deciding which mode of trial is more suitable, to consider:
  (i) whether the sentence which a magistrates' court would have power to impose for the offence would be adequate;
  (ii) any representations made by the prosecution or the accused; and
  (iii) any allocation guidelines (or revised allocation guidelines) issued as definitive guidelines under the CJA 2003, s. 170.

  Where the accused is charged with two or more offences which could be tried together, the court has regard to the maximum aggregate sentence which a magistrates' court would have power to impose for all the offences taken together.

(g) If it appears to the court that summary trial is more appropriate, the court (almost invariably through the clerk) explains to the accused:
  (i) that such is the court's view, and he can either consent to be tried summarily or, if he wishes, be tried by a judge and jury in the Crown Court; and
  (ii) if he is tried summarily and convicted, he may be committed for sentence to the Crown Court if the magistrates are of the opinion that greater punishment should be inflicted than they have power to inflict (s. 20(1) and (2)). Note that the power of committal for sentence following summary trial is to be abolished by the CJA 2003 except in cases where the 'dangerous offender' provisions apply (see below).

  The court then asks the accused whether he consents to be tried summarily or wishes to be tried by a jury. Depending on his answer, the court proceeds either to summary trial or to committal proceedings (s. 20(3)).

(h) If it appears to the court that trial on indictment is more appropriate, it tells the accused so and proceeds to committal proceedings (s. 21).

(i) It follows that summary trial is possible only if the magistrates and the accused both agree to summary trial. If the magistrates decline jurisdiction, the case will be sent to the Crown Court; if the magistrates accept jurisdiction but the accused elects trial on indictment, the case will be sent to the Crown Court.

(j) There are equivalent procedures to be followed where the court decides that the accused's disorderly conduct makes it impracticable for proceedings to be conducted in his presence (ss. 17B and 18(3)). Section 17B applies where the accused has attained the age of 18 years, and is represented by a legal representative, and the court considers that, by reason of the accused's disorderly conduct before the court, it is not practicable for proceedings under s. 17A to be conducted in his presence, and it also considers that it should proceed in the absence of the accused. In such a case, the charge is written down (if this has not already been done) and read to the lawyer; the lawyer is then asked whether the accused intends to plead guilty or not guilty; if the lawyer indicates that the accused intends to plead guilty the case is regarded as a summary trial in which the accused has pleaded guilty; if the lawyer indicates that the accused intends to plead not guilty, or if the lawyer declines to indicate the accused's intention regarding the plea, the court proceeds to the mode of trial hearing (s. 17B(2) and (3)); the mode of trial hearing takes place in the absence of the accused (s. 18(3)).

D6.12 **Credit for Guilty Plea** Some guidance on the impact of the 'plea before venue' part of the mode of trial procedure was given by the Court of Appeal in *Rafferty* [1999] 1 Cr App R 235. The court held that (i) where the accused is charged with an either-way offence and indicates a guilty plea at the plea before venue hearing and is then committed for sentence to the Crown Court, he is entitled to a greater discount for his guilty plea than an accused who delays pleading guilty until he appears in the Crown Court (regard should also be had to the Sentencing Guidelines on Guilty Pleas issued by the SGC: see **E1.6** and **appendix 8**); (ii) when a person who is on bail enters a guilty plea at the plea before venue hearing, the usual practice should be to continue his bail, even if it is anticipated that a custodial sentence will be imposed by the Crown Court, unless there is good reason for remanding him in custody.

D6.13 **Legitimate Expectations** Where the court does not pass sentence immediately, the magistrates must be careful not to create an expectation that the accused will ultimately be sentenced in that court if they wish the option of committal for sentence to the Crown Court to remain open. In *Horseferry Road Magistrates' Court ex parte Rugless* (2000) 164 JP 311, the accused indicated a guilty plea at the 'plea before venue' hearing; the court accepted jurisdiction and ordered a pre-sentence report, stating that all sentencing options were to remain open with the exception of committal to the Crown Court for sentence. At the next hearing, the magistrates committed the accused to the Crown Court for sentence (under the PCC(S)A 2000, s. 3). The Divisional Court held that the accused had a legitimate expectation that he would be sentenced in the magistrates' court. The subsequent decision to commit him for sentence was in breach of this legitimate expectation; accordingly it was appropriate to quash the decision to commit for sentence. However, the expectation has to be a legitimate one. In *R (White) v Barking Magistrates' Court* [2004] EWHC 417 (Admin), the accused was charged with production of cannabis contrary to the Misuse of Drugs Act 1971, s. 4(2). The charges related to a large-scale production operation. When he appeared before the justices, they adjourned the matter. At the next hearing they committed him to the Crown Court for sentence. He applied for judicial review of the decision to commit, contending that, at the first hearing, the justices had created a legitimate expectation that they would deal with sentence themselves. It was held that, although an expectation had been created by the justices at the earlier hearing that they would not commit the accused to the Crown Court, that expectation would not be fulfilled, since it would have been an unreasonable decision by the justices. Given the severity of the offending, it would have been unreasonable, and therefore unlawful, for the justices not to have committed the accused for sentencing in the Crown Court.

Statutory Provisions on Mode of Trial

D6.14 **Magistrates' Courts Act 1980, ss. 17A and 17C to 21**

17A.—(1) This section shall have effect where a person who has attained the age of 18 years appears or is brought before a magistrates' court on an information charging him with an offence triable either way.

(2) Everything that the court is required to do under the following provisions of this section must be done with the accused present in court.

(3) The court shall cause the charge to be written down, if this has not already been done, and to be read to the accused.

(4) The court shall then explain to the accused in ordinary language that he may indicate whether (if the offence were to proceed to trial) he would plead guilty or not guilty, and that if he indicates that he would plead guilty—

(a) the court must proceed as mentioned in subsection (6) below; and

(b) he may be committed for sentence to the Crown Court under section 3 of the Powers of Criminal Courts (Sentencing) Act 2000 if the court is of such opinion as is mentioned in subsection (2) of that section.

(5) The court shall then ask the accused whether (if the offence were to proceed to trial) he would plead guilty or not guilty.

(6) If the accused indicates that he would plead guilty the court shall proceed as if—

(a) the proceedings constituted from the beginning the summary trial of the information; and
(b) section 9(1) above was complied with and he pleaded guilty under it.
(7) If the accused indicates that he would plead not guilty section 18(1) below shall apply.
(8) If the accused in fact fails to indicate how he would plead, for the purposes of this section and section 18(1) below he shall be taken to indicate that he would plead not guilty.
(9) Subject to subsection (6) above, the following shall not for any purpose be taken to constitute the taking of a plea—
(a) asking the accused under this section whether (if the offence were to proceed to trial) he would plead guilty or not guilty;
(b) an indication by the accused under this section of how he would plead.

17C. A magistrates' court proceeding under section 17A or 17B above may adjourn the proceedings at any time, and on doing so on any occasion when the accused is present may remand the accused, and shall remand him if—
(a) on the occasion on which he first appeared, or was brought, before the court to answer to the information he was in custody or, having been released on bail, surrendered to the custody of the court; or
(b) he has been remanded at any time in the course of proceedings on the information;
and where the court remands the accused, the time fixed for the resumption of proceedings shall be that at which he is required to appear or be brought before the court in pursuance of the remand or would be required to be brought before the court but for section 128(3A) below.

18.—(1) Sections 19 to 23 below shall have effect where a person who has attained the age of 18 years appears or is brought before a magistrates' court on an information charging him with an offence triable either way and—
(a) he indicates under section 17A above that (if the offence were to proceed to trial) he would plead not guilty, or
(b) his representative indicates under section 17B above that (if the offence were to proceed to trial) he would plead not guilty.
(2) Without prejudice to section 11(1) above [proceeding to summary trial of an information in the absence of the accused if he does not appear], everything that the court is required to do under sections 19 to 22 below must be done before any evidence is called and, subject to subsection (3) below and section 23 below, with the accused present in court.
[(3) Proceeding in the accused's absence if his disorderly conduct makes it impracticable for him to be present: see **D6.19**.]
(4) A magistrates' court proceeding under sections 19 to 23 below may adjourn the proceedings at any time, and on doing so on any occasion when the accused is present may remand the accused, and shall remand him if—
(a) on the occasion on which he first appeared, or was brought, before the court to answer to the information he was in custody or, having been released on bail, surrendered to the custody of the court; or
(b) if he has been remanded at any time in the course of proceedings on the information;
and where the court remands the accused, the time fixed for the resumption of the proceedings shall be that at which he is required to appear or be brought before the court in pursuance of the remand or would be required to be brought before the court but for section 128(3A) below [accused being remanded in custody agreeing to future remands in custody taking place in his absence].
(5) The functions of a magistrates' court under sections 19 to 23 below may be discharged by a single justice, but the foregoing provision shall not be taken to authorise the summary trial of an information by a magistrates' court composed of less than two justices.

19.—(1) The court shall consider whether, having regard to the matters mentioned in subsection (3) below and any representations made by the prosecutor or the accused, the offence appears to the court more suitable for summary trial or for trial on indictment.
(2) Before so considering, the court—
(a) [repealed]
(b) shall afford the prosecutor and then the accused an opportunity to make representations as to which mode of trial would be more suitable.
(3) The matters to which the court is to have regard under subsection (1) above are the nature of the case; whether the circumstances make the offence one of serious character; whether the punishment which a magistrates' court would have power to inflict for it would be adequate;

and any other circumstances which appear to the court to make it more suitable for the offence to be tried in one way rather than the other.

(4) If the prosecution is being carried on by the Attorney-General, the Solicitor- General or the Director of Public Prosecutions and he applies for the offence to be tried on indictment, the preceding provisions of this section and sections 20 and 21 below shall not apply, and the court shall proceed to inquire into the information as examining justices.

(5) The power of the Director of Public Prosecutions under subsection (4) above to apply for an offence to be tried on indictment shall not be exercised except with the consent of the Attorney-General.

20.—(1) If, where the court has considered as required by section 19(1) above, it appears to the court that the offence is more suitable for summary trial, the following provisions of this section shall apply (unless excluded by section 23 below).

(2) The court shall explain to the accused in ordinary language—

(a) that it appears to the court more suitable for him to be tried summarily for the offence, and that he can either consent to be so tried or, if he wishes, be tried by a jury; and

(b) that if he is tried summarily and is convicted by the court, he may be committed for sentence to the Crown Court under section 3 of the Powers of Criminal Courts (Sentencing) Act 2000 if the convicting court is of such opinion as is mentioned in subsection (2) of that section.

(3) After explaining to the accused as provided by subsection (2) above the court shall ask him whether he consents to be tried summarily or wishes to be tried by a jury, and—

(a) if he consents to be tried summarily, shall proceed to the summary trial of the information;

(b) if he does not so consent, shall proceed to inquire into the information as examining justices.

21. If, where the court has considered as required by section 19(1) above, it appears to the court that the offence is more suitable for trial on indictment, the court shall tell the accused that the court has decided that it is more suitable for him to be tried for the offence by a jury, and shall proceed to inquire into the information as examining justices.

Form of Words on Election as to Mode of Trial

D6.15 **Annex to Home Office Circular 45/1997 (excerpt)**

PLEA BEFORE VENUE PROCEDURE: INDICATION OF PLEA

Suggested form of wording for the use of the magistrates' court when inviting the defendant to indicate his plea.

This offence(s) may be tried either by this court or by the Crown Court before a judge and jury. Whether or not this court can deal with your case today will depend upon your answers to the questions which I am going to put to you. Do you understand?

You will shortly be asked to tell the court whether you intend to plead guilty or not guilty to (certain of) the offence(s) with which you are charged. Do you understand?

If you tell us that you intend to plead guilty, you will be convicted of the offence. We may then be able to deal with (part of) your case at this hearing. The prosecutor will tell us about the facts of the case, you (your representative) will have the opportunity to respond (on your behalf), and we shall then go on to consider how to sentence you. Do you understand?

We may be able to sentence you today, or we may need to adjourn the proceedings until a later date for the preparation of a pre-sentence report by the Probation Service. If we believe that you deserve a greater sentence than we have the power to give you in this court, we may decide to send you to the Crown Court, either on bail or in custody, and you will be sentenced by that court which has greater sentencing powers. Do you understand?

[In cases where s. 4 of the PCC(S)A 2000 applies:

If you indicate a guilty plea for this/these offence(s), even if we believe that our own sentencing powers are great enough to deal with you here, we may still send you to the Crown Court to be sentenced there for this/these offence(s) because you have also been charged with a related offence(s) [for which you have already been committed for trial in that court.] [for which you will be committed for trial in that court.] Do you understand?]

If, on the other hand, you tell us that you intend to plead not guilty, or if you do not tell us what you intend to do, we shall go on to consider whether you should be tried by this court or by the

Crown Court on some future date. If we decide that it would be appropriate to deal with your case in this court, we shall ask whether you are content for us to do so or whether you wish your case to be tried in the Crown Court.

Before I ask you how you intend to plead, do you understand everything I have said or is there any part of what I have said which you would like me to repeat or explain?

Changes to Mode of Trial Procedure made by the Criminal Justice Act 2003

The CJA 2003 makes a number of significant changes to the plea before venue and mode of trial procedures, which are yet to come into force. Paragraph 5 of sch. 3 to the CJA 2003 substitutes an amended version of the MCA 1980, s. 19. It requires the prosecution to have the opportunity of informing the magistrates of any previous convictions recorded against the accused and it stipulates that the court must have regard to any allocation guidelines issued under the CJA 2003, s. 170. **D6.16**

Paragraph 6 of sch. 3 substitutes an amended version of the MCA 1980, s. 20. Under the new procedure, the accused is given the opportunity to request an indication from the magistrates of whether, if he were to be tried summarily and were to plead guilty at that stage, the sentence would be custodial or not (s. 20(3)). The magistrates are given a broad discretion whether or not to give such an indication (s. 20(4)). Where an indication is given, the accused will be given the opportunity to reconsider his original indication as to plea (s. 20(5)). If he then decides to plead guilty, the magistrates' court will proceed to sentence, if necessary adjourning for a pre-sentence report; in such a case, a custodial sentence will be available only if such a sentence was indicated by the court (s. 20A(1)). If the accused declines to reconsider his plea indication, or if no sentence indication is given by the magistrates, he will be given the choice of accepting summary trial or electing Crown Court trial. Where an indication of sentence is given and the accused does not choose to plead guilty on the basis of it, the sentence indication is not binding on the magistrates who later try the case summarily, or on the Crown Court if the accused elects trial on indictment (s. 20A(3)).

The CJA 2003, sch. 3, para. 7 will replace the MCA 1980, s. 21, with a new version which provides that, where the magistrates decline jurisdiction (deciding that the case is not suitable for summary trial), they should then send the case to the Crown Court for trial in accordance with the procedure contained in the CDA 1998, s. 51 (which previously applied solely to offences triable only on indictment but which will apply to all indictable offences when sch. 3 comes into force). This amendment will be made necessary by the abolition of committal proceedings for either-way offences.

The CJA 2003, sch. 3, para. 22, amends the PCC(S)A 2000, s. 3. The amended s. 3 will apply only where the accused indicates a guilty plea at the plea before venue hearing. The power to commit for sentence under s. 3 will thus be abolished where the accused is convicted by the magistrates following a summary trial (in other words, where the accused indicates a not guilty plea at the plea before venue hearing, or gives no indication of plea, the magistrates then accept jurisdiction, the accused agrees to summary trial, and is then found guilty). A power to commit for sentence following a guilty plea will necessarily continue to be available, given the fact that an accused may plead guilty to very serious either-way offences at the plea before venue hearing. See **D22.32** for the text of the revised s. 3.

Statutory Provisions on Mode of Trial as Amended by the Criminal Justice Act 2003

Magistrates' Courts Act 1980, ss. 19, 20 and 20A (as substituted and inserted by the CJA 2003, sch. 3, para. 6) (not in force) **D6.17**

19.—(1) The court shall decide whether the offence appears to it more suitable for summary trial or for trial on indictment.

(2) Before making a decision under this section, the court—

(a) shall give the prosecution an opportunity to inform the court of the accused's previous convictions (if any); and

(b) shall give the prosecution and the accused an opportunity to make representations as to whether summary trial or trial on indictment would be more suitable.

(3) In making a decision under this section, the court shall consider—

(a) whether the sentence which a magistrates' court would have power to impose for the offence would be adequate; and

(b) any representations made by the prosecution or the accused under subsection (2)(b) above,

and shall have regard to any allocation guidelines (or revised allocation guidelines) issued as definitive guidelines under section 170 of the Criminal Justice Act 2003.

(4) Where—

(a) the accused is charged with two or more offences; and

(b) it appears to the court that the charges for the offences could be joined in the same indictment or that the offences arise out of the same or connected circumstances,

subsection (3)(a) above shall have effect as if references to the sentence which a magistrates' court would have power to impose for the offence were a reference to the maximum aggregate sentence which a magistrates' court would have power to impose for all of the offences taken together.

(5) In this section any reference to a previous conviction is a reference to—

(a) a previous conviction by a court in the United Kingdom; or

(b) a previous finding of guilt in—

(i) any proceedings under the Army Act 1955, the Air Force Act 1955 or the Naval Discipline Act 1957 (whether before a court-martial or any other court or person authorised under any of those Acts to award a punishment in respect of any offence); or

(ii) any proceedings before a Standing Civilian Court.

(6) If, in respect of the offence, the court receives a notice under section 51B or 51C of the Crime and Disorder Act 1998 (which relate to serious or complex fraud cases and to certain cases involving children respectively), the preceding provisions of this section and sections 20, 20A and 21 below shall not apply, and the court shall proceed in relation to the offence in accordance with section 51(1) of that Act.

20.—(1) If the court decides under section 19 above that the offence appears to it more suitable for summary trial, the following provisions of this section shall apply (unless they are excluded by section 23 below).

(2) The court shall explain to the accused in ordinary language—

(a) that it appears to the court more suitable for him to be tried summarily for the offence;

(b) that he can either consent to be so tried or, if he wishes, be tried on indictment; . . .

(3) The accused may then request an indication ('an indication of sentence') of whether a custodial sentence or non-custodial sentence would be more likely to be imposed if he were to be tried summarily for the offence and to plead guilty.

(4) If the accused requests an indication of sentence, the court may, but need not, give such an indication.

(5) If the accused requests and the court gives an indication of sentence, the court shall ask the accused whether he wishes, on the basis of the indication, to reconsider the indication of plea which was given, or is taken to have been given, under section 17A or 17B above.

(6) If the accused indicates that he wishes to reconsider the indication under section 17A or 17B above, the court shall ask the accused whether (if the offence were to proceed to trial) he would plead guilty or not guilty.

(7) If the accused indicates that he would plead guilty the court shall proceed as if—

(a) the proceedings constituted from that time the summary trial of the information; and

(b) section 9(1) above were complied with and he pleaded guilty under it.

(8) Subsection (9) below applies where—

(a) the court does not give an indication of sentence (whether because the accused does not request one or because the court does not agree to give one);

(b) the accused either—

(i) does not indicate, in accordance with subsection (5) above, that he wishes; or

(ii) indicates, in accordance with subsection (5) above, that he does not wish, to reconsider the indication of plea under section 17A or 17B above; or

(c) the accused does not indicate, in accordance with subsection (6) above, that he would plead guilty.

(9) The court shall ask the accused whether he consents to be tried summarily or wishes to be tried on indictment and—
(a) if he consents to be tried summarily, shall proceed to the summary trial of the information; and
(b) if he does not so consent, shall proceed in relation to the offence in accordance with section 51(1) of the Crime and Disorder Act 1998.

20A.—(1) Where the case is dealt with in accordance with section 20(7) above, no court (whether a magistrates' court or not) may impose a custodial sentence for the offence unless such a sentence was indicated in the indication of sentence referred to in section 20 above.
(2) Subsection (1) above is subject to sections 3A(4), 4(8) and 5(3) of the Powers of Criminal Courts (Sentencing) Act 2000.
(3) Except as provided in subsection (1) above—
(a) an indication of sentence shall not be binding on any court (whether a magistrates' court or not); and
(b) no sentence may be challenged or be the subject of appeal in any court on the ground that it is not consistent with an indication of sentence.

21. If the court decides under section 19 above that the offence appears to it more suitable for trial on indictment, the court shall tell the accused that the court has decided that it is more suitable for him to be tried on indictment, and shall proceed in relation to the offence in accordance with section 51(1) of the Crime and Disorder Act 1998.

Jurisdiction to Conduct Mode of Trial Hearing

The power to conduct a mode-of-trial hearing arises whenever an adult appears or is brought before a magistrates' court charged with an offence triable either way (MCA 1980, s. 18(1)). The proceedings may take place before one magistrate, whether lay or a District Judge (s. 18(5)), but in practice it is almost invariably the case that any lay bench will consist of at least two justices. **D6.18**

The determination of mode of trial need not necessarily take place on the first occasion when an accused charged with an either-way offence appears before magistrates. Section 18(4) allows the court to adjourn at any time before or during proceedings under ss. 19 to 23. If it does so, it must remand the accused (either in custody or on bail) to the date fixed for the resumption of the proceedings, unless he first appeared in answer to a summons and has not subsequently been remanded, in which case the court has a discretion simply to adjourn. Section 17C makes similar provision for the adjournment of the 'plea before venue' hearing. The power of magistrates' courts to adjourn proceedings and the circumstances in which, on adjourning, they are obliged to remand the accused are considered in detail at **D5.11** *et seq*. It is submitted that magistrates are to be regarded as proceeding under the MCA 1980, ss. 17A to 23, from when an accused first appears charged with an either-way offence to when mode of trial is finally determined. Therefore, any adjournment during that period will be by virtue of s. 17C or s. 18(4), rather than s. 5(1) of the 1980 Act (which empowers the court to adjourn before or during committal proceedings).

Where an accused who is a juvenile is charged with an offence triable either way, ss. 17A to 23 of the 1980 Act do not apply (although this will change when the CJA 2003, sch. 3, comes into force, requiring the court to go through a plea before venue procedure in some cases involving defendants under the age of 18). Mode of trial is determined according to entirely different criteria, set out in s. 24 of the Act. The relevant date for determining the age of the accused is 'the date of his appearance before the court on the occasion when the court makes its decision as to the mode of trial' (per Lord Diplock in *Islington North Juvenile Court, ex parte Daley* [1983] 1 AC 347 at p. 364E–F). If he is 18 or over at that date, the fact that he was under 18 when he made his first court appearance in connection with the charge is irrelevant. The procedural problems raised by the accused who celebrates his 18th birthday during the course of the proceedings against him are discussed at **D23.45**.

Presence of the Accused

D6.19 The accused must be present at the plea before venue hearing (MCA 1980, s. 17A(2)) and while the mode of his trial is determined (s. 18(2)), unless any of the exceptions apply.

For the plea before venue hearing the exception is set out in s. 17B. It applies where:

(a) the accused is represented by a legal representative;
(b) the court considers that, by reason of the accused's disorderly conduct before the court, it is not practicable for proceedings under s. 17A to be conducted in his presence; and
(c) the court considers that it should proceed in the absence of the accused.

In such a case the representative is asked to indicate whether the accused intends to plead guilty or not guilty (s. 17B(2)(b)); if the representative indicates a guilty plea, the court proceeds as if the accused had pleaded guilty (s. 17B(2)(c)). Otherwise, the court proceeds to determine mode of trial under s. 18.

Mode of trial can be determined in the absence of the accused under s. 18(3) or s. 23.

(i) Under s. 18(3), the court may determine mode of trial in the absence of the accused if it considers that, by reason of his disorderly conduct before the court, it is not practicable for the proceedings to be conducted in his presence. Where there is a legal representative present in court, he or she speaks on behalf of the accused (s. 18(3)).
(ii) Under s. 23, the court may determine mode of trial in the absence of the accused if he is represented by counsel or a solicitor who signifies to the court that the accused consents to the mode of trial proceedings being conducted in his absence, and the court is satisfied that there is good reason for the proceedings being so conducted (s. 23(1)).

The Act does not define what is meant by the phrase 'good reason' in s. 23(1). Sickness is an obvious example, but it is submitted that 'good reason' extends beyond that. Assuming the court does proceed in the accused's absence and considers that the offence is more suitable for summary trial, his consent to such a trial may be signified by his legal representative, in which event 'the court shall proceed to . . . summary trial' (s. 23(4)(a)). Clearly, this does not require the magistrates to commence the trial forthwith, as they are entitled to adjourn under the general power given them by s. 10(1) of the 1980 Act if an immediate hearing is impracticable or undesirable (e.g., because of the accused's absence). If the court considers that trial on indictment is more appropriate, or if the legal representative does not signify that the accused consents to summary trial, then the court must proceed with a view to sending the case to the Crown Court for trial (s. 23(4)(b) and (5)).

It should also be noted that the court may use a live television link, in a case where the accused is held in custody and facilities are available at the institution where he is held (CDA 1998, s. 57: see D5.23).

D6.20 **Magistrates' Courts Act 1980, ss. 17B, 18(2) and (3) and 23**

17B.—(1) This section shall have effect where—
(a) a person who has attained the age of 18 years appears or is brought before a magistrates' court on an information charging him with an offence triable either way,
(b) the accused is represented by a legal representative,
(c) the court considers that by reason of the accused's disorderly conduct before the court it is not practicable for proceedings under section 17A above to be conducted in his presence, and
(d) the court considers that it should proceed in the absence of the accused.

(2) In such a case—
(a) the court shall cause the charge to be written down, if this has not already been done, and to be read to the representative;
(b) the court shall ask the representative whether (if the offence were to proceed to trial) the accused would plead guilty or not guilty;
(c) if the representative indicates that the accused would plead guilty the court shall proceed

as if the proceedings constituted from the beginning the summary trial of the information, and as if section 9(1) above was complied with and the accused pleaded guilty under it;

(d) if the representative indicates that the accused would plead not guilty section 18(1) below shall apply.

(3) If the representative in fact fails to indicate how the accused would plead, for the purposes of this section and section 18(1) below he shall be taken to indicate that the accused would plead not guilty.

(4) Subject to subsection (2)(c) above, the following shall not for any purpose be taken to constitute the taking of a plea—

(a) asking the representative under this section whether (if the offence were to proceed to trial) the accused would plead guilty or not guilty;

(b) an indication by the representative under this section of how the accused would plead.

18.

. . .

(2) Without prejudice to section 11(1) above [proceeding to summary trial of an information in the absence of the accused if he does not appear], everything that the court is required to do under sections 19 to 22 below must be done before any evidence is called and, subject to subsection (3) below and section 23 below, with the accused present in court.

(3) The court may proceed in the absence of the accused in accordance with such of the provisions of sections 19 to 22 below as are applicable in the circumstances if the court considers that by reason of his disorderly conduct before the court it is not practicable for the proceedings to be conducted in his presence; and the subsections (3) to (5) of section 23 below, so far as applicable, shall have effect in relation to proceedings conducted in the absence of the accused by virtue of this subsection (references in those subsections to the person representing the accused being for this purpose read as references to the person, if any, representing him).

. . .

23.—(1) Where—

(a) the accused is represented by counsel or a solicitor who in his absence signifies to the court the accused's consent to the proceedings for determining how he is to be tried for the offence being conducted in his absence; and

(b) the court is satisfied that there is good reason for proceeding in the absence of the accused,

the following provisions of this section shall apply.

(2) Subject to the following provisions of this section, the court may proceed in the absence of the accused in accordance with such of the provisions of sections 19 to 22 above as are applicable in the circumstances.

(3) If, in a case where subsection (1) of section 22 above applies, it appears to the court as mentioned in subsection (4) of that section, subsections (5) and (6) of that section shall not apply and the court—

(a) if the accused's consent to be tried summarily has been or is signified by the person representing him, shall proceed in accordance with subsection (2) of that section as if that subsection applied; or

(b) if that consent has not been and is not so signified, shall proceed in accordance with subsection (3) of that section as if that subsection applied.

(4) If, where the court has considered as required by section 19(1) above, it appears to the court that the offence is more suitable for summary trial then—

(a) if the accused's consent to be tried summarily has been or is signified by the person representing him, section 20 above shall not apply, and the court shall proceed to the summary trial of the information; or

(b) if that consent has not been and is not so signified, section 20 above shall not apply and the court shall proceed to inquire into the information as examining justices and may adjourn the proceedings without remanding the accused.

(5) If, where the court has considered as required by section 19(1) above, it appears to the court that the offence is more suitable for trial on indictment, section 21 above shall not apply, and the court shall proceed to inquire into the information as examining justices and may adjourn the hearing without remanding the accused.

[26. Powers ancillary to s. 23 to issue a summons or warrant for arrest in respect of the accused if either the court considers that he should be present while the mode of trial is determined or, having proceeded in his absence and adjourned without remanding him prior to committal or transfer proceedings, he does not appear for the resumption of the hearing.]

The Magistrates' Decision

D6.21 Section 19(3) of the MCA 1980 lists the matters to which the magistrates must have regard in considering whether summary trial or trial on indictment is more appropriate. The most important consideration for the magistrates (and for the parties making their representations) is whether or not the sentencing powers of the magistrates would be adequate to deal with the offence(s) in the event of the accused being convicted. Where the accused is charged with more than one offence, the magistrates are required to look at the totality of the allegations, and not at each offence in isolation. Thus the magistrates can, and should, decline jurisdiction if they take the view that their sentencing powers are insufficient to deal with the totality of the offending, even if each offence taken by itself would not merit a harsher sentence than the magistrates could impose for that individual offence. The maximum penalty which magistrates can currently impose on summary conviction for an either-way offence is usually six months' imprisonment and/or a fine of up to £5,000 (an aggregate of one year and/or £5,000 per offence on conviction for two or more such offences). It is plainly wrong for magistrates to agree to summary trial if the offences charged are so serious that the court's powers would be insufficient to deal properly with the accused should he be convicted (see, e.g., *Coe* [1968] 1 WLR 1950). In *Flax Bourton Magistrates' Court, ex parte Commissioners of Customs and Excise* (1996) 160 JP 481, the Divisional Court emphasised that the justices were bound by the statutory obligation set out in s. 19(3) to apply their minds to the question whether or not their powers of punishment would be adequate if they dealt with the case summarily. If they were in doubt as to what the level of sentence should be, they should seek advice from their clerk.

Although the maximum sentence available in the magistrates' court is the most important factor when considering whether or not a case is suitable for summary trial, it is open to the magistrates to consider other factors. In *Horseferry Road Magistrates' Court, ex parte K* [1997] QB 23, for example, the Divisional Court accepted that a possible defence of insanity might make the case more suitable for trial on indictment.

Detailed guidelines on determination of mode of trial are set out in the *Consolidated Criminal Practice Direction*, para. V.51, *Mode of trial* (see **appendix 8**). The guidelines provide that '[in] general, except where otherwise stated, either-way offences should be tried summarily unless the court considers that the particular case has one or more of the features set out in paras. 51.4–51.18 and that its sentencing powers are insufficient'. The guidance is clearly to the effect that there is a presumption that offences triable either way should be tried summarily unless one of the given features is present *and* the magistrates regard their sentencing powers as inadequate. It should be noted that these guidelines are due to be superseded by allocation guidelines issued by the Sentencing Guidelines Council (see below).

D6.22 **Amendments to be made by CJA 2003** The decision of the magistrates to accept jurisdiction will become even more significant when the new version of the PCC(S)A 2000, s. 3, as amended by the CJA 2003, comes into force, with the effect that there will no longer be a power to commit to the Crown Court for sentence if the accused is convicted following a summary trial and, having heard the evidence during the course of the summary trial, the magistrates take the view that their sentencing powers are not in fact adequate. The crucial nature of the initial mode of trial decision is further underlined by the amendments made by the CJA 2003 to the MCA 1980, s. 25. When these amendments come into effect, it will no longer be possible for the magistrates, having accepted jurisdiction at the mode of trial hearing, to start to hear the case by way of summary trial and then to stop the trial and send the accused to the Crown Court for trial on the basis that the evidence they have heard has persuaded them that their sentencing powers are inadequate. Under the amended s. 25, the prosecution may invite the magistrates to reconsider the decision to accept jurisdiction (on the sole ground that the sentencing powers of the magistrates are inadequate) but this application has to be made before the start of the summary trial.

Mode of Trial where there are Co-accused The *Consolidated Practice Direction*, para. V.51.3(e), stipulates that where two or more defendants are jointly charged with an offence, each has an individual right to elect his mode of trial. This follows the approach laid down by the House of Lords in *Brentwood Justices, ex parte Nicholls* [1992] 1 AC 1. In that case, one accused elected Crown Court trial, but the other two wanted to be tried summarily. The magistrates sent all three for Crown Court trial. The House of Lords, however, held that the right of election as to mode of trial given to the accused by the MCA 1980, s. 20(3), is given to each accused individually, and not to all accused collectively. Hence, the election of one defendant is not affected by a different election made by his co-accused. In these circumstances, provided that the court believes summary trial to be appropriate on other grounds, the court should proceed to try summarily the accused who elected summary trial, and should proceed with a view to deciding whether those who elected trial on indictment should be sent to the Crown Court. (See also *Wigan Magistrates' Court, ex parte Layland* (1995) 160 JP 223 and *Ipswich Magistrates' Court, ex parte Callaghan* (1995) 159 JP 748.) In *West Norfolk Justices, ex parte McMullen* (1993) 157 JP 61 and in *Bradford Magistrates' Court, ex parte Grant* (1999) 163 JP 717, the Divisional Court held that the procedure under the MCA 1980 s. 25(2) (the power to vary the mode of trial decision — **D6.36**) may not be used as a device to circumvent the decision in *Ex parte Nicholls* by converting summary proceedings into committal proceedings. **D6.23**

This approach is likely to change when allocation guidelines issued by the Sentencing Guidelines Council (see **D6.28**) become effective.

Previous Convictions In *Colchester Justices, ex parte North East Essex Building Co. Ltd* [1977] 1 WLR 1109, it was held that magistrates should not be told of any previous convictions recorded against the accused at the stage of deciding mode of trial, but should proceed instead on the basis that the defendant is of good character. It is arguable that this no longer represents the law. The current version of the guidelines (to be found in the *Consolidated Practice Direction*) omits the statement contained in the original version of the guidelines to the effect that the accused's antecedents and personal mitigating circumstances were irrelevant for the purpose of deciding mode of trial. It may be argued that this omission was intentional and intended to mark a change in practice. At mode of trial, the magistrates have to consider whether their sentencing powers are adequate, and the existence of previous convictions is highly relevant to that question, particularly previous convictions may be regarded as an 'aggravating factor' under the CJA 2003, s. 143(2); it therefore seems illogical that magistrates should not be aware of previous convictions when deciding mode of trial. Nonetheless, the current practice (see, for example, *Warley Justices, ex parte DPP* [1999] 1 WLR 216) appears to be that magistrates should be kept ignorant of any previous convictions at the mode of trial stage. It may well be that this is partly because, if the magistrates were to become aware of previous convictions when deciding mode of trial, those magistrates would be debarred from trying the accused if summary trial were subsequently to take place. However, when the version of the MCA 1980, s. 19, which is substituted by the CJA 2003, sch. 3, para. 5, comes into effect, the position will be put beyond doubt, since s. 19(2) will specifically provide that the court 'shall give the prosecution an opportunity to inform the court of the accused's previous convictions (if any)'. **D6.24**

The Accused's Decision

It is sometimes asserted that one advantage of summary trial is that there is a limit on the **D6.25** sentence which the magistrates' court can pass (six months' imprisonment for one 'either way' offence, 12 months for two or more). At present, this advantage is largely nullified by the power of the magistrates to commit the defendant to be sentenced in the Crown Court under the PCC(S)A 2000, s. 3. However, when the relevant provisions of the CJA 2003 come into force, magistrates will be empowered to pass a sentence of 12 months' custody for a single either-way offence, but the power to commit for sentence following summary trial of an either-way offence will be abolished.

An advantage of trial on indictment is said to be that submissions on the admissibility of evidence can be made in the absence of the jury, with the obvious benefit that the jury do not find out about any matters that are ruled inadmissible. However under the Courts Act 2003, sch. 3, a bench may give a pre-trial ruling on the admissibility of evidence and that ruling will bind the bench that tries the case (see **D20.32**).

Another supposed advantage of trial on indictment is that the defence are entitled to receive copies of the written statements of the witnesses to be called by the prosecution. However, para. 57 of the Attorney-General's Guidelines on Disclosure (see **appendix 5**) provides that, in the case of summary trial, the prosecutor should provide to the defence all evidence upon which the Crown proposes to rely in a summary trial. Thus, an accused who is to be tried in the magistrates' court should be in the same position as one being tried in the Crown Court as regards obtaining copies of the prosecution witness statements.

D6.26 **Accused Must Understand Mode of Trial Issues** If the magistrates decide that the accused should be given the option of summary trial, it is essential that — at the time he makes his election — he should understand the 'nature and significance of the choice' put to him (*Birmingham Justices, ex parte Hodgson* [1985] QB 1131 per McCullough J at p. 1144E). Since one of the most important factors in the mind of an accused deciding which court he would like to deal with his case is whether or not he believes he has any defence, an election for summary trial made when unrepresented and intending to plead guilty through a misunderstanding of the law is invalid because, even if the accused understands the nature of the choice put to him in the sense of knowing the difference between trial on indictment and summary trial, he does not truly appreciate the *significance* of the choice for him (*Ex parte Hodgson,* see especially p. 1146D–H). Where the accused, at the time of election, intends to plead not guilty but is taken by surprise by the election being put, has not had the opportunity to consult either a lawyer or anybody else able to explain his rights to him and does not properly understand what a Crown Court is, then again his election will be invalid, this time on the ground that he does not understand the *nature* of the choice (*Highbury Corner Metropolitan Stipendiary Magistrate, ex parte Weekes* [1985] QB 1147).

Should an accused claim to have made an invalid election at a time when he was unrepresented, the remedy for the defence is, in the first place, to apply to the magistrates' court to allow him to withdraw his election (see **D6.36** ***et seq.***). If that application is refused, application may be made to the Divisional Court for an order quashing the refusal. It will, however, be necessary to show either that the magistrates took into account irrelevant factors or ignored relevant ones when deciding to hold the accused to his original election, or that their decision was so unreasonable that no bench properly directing itself could have reached it. In *Ex parte Weekes,* the accused's assertion that he had not understood what a Crown Court was when he elected went uncontradicted by the prosecution. In those circumstances, it was plainly unreasonable for the magistrate to have rejected the defence application that the election be withdrawn.

It will be difficult, if not impossible, for the defence to claim that the accused did not appreciate the nature and significance of his choice if he was legally represented at the time. The assumption is that the legal representative will provide whatever advice and explanation are necessary. However, McCullough J in *Ex parte Weekes* held that there is no rule of law that a magistrates' court *must* adjourn before putting an unrepresented accused to his election so as to allow him to apply for legal aid. The accused was 17 years old and charged with assault occasioning actual bodily harm and unlawful wounding. McCullough J said (at pp. 1152F–1153A):

> . . . bearing in mind the applicant's age and the serious nature of the charges, it should have been clear to anyone who had thought about it that the applicant would be granted legal representation and that his election would therefore be a more informed one if he were only asked to elect after he had obtained legal advice. The magistrate had power under section 18(4) of the Magistrates' Courts Act 1980 to adjourn the proceedings at any time prior to putting the accused to his election. However, I am loath to say anything which would appear to lay down as a principle that an unrepresented defendant of any particular age should, in relation to 'serious charges' (whatever they may be), never be put to his election when he first appears before justices, and I find it very difficult to isolate any feature or features here which would make this a special case. It is one thing to say that justices should take account of the fact that a defendant did not understand what was being put to him when this is pointed out to them on an application to re-elect.

On that basis the court quashed the refusal to reconsider the accused's election but not the decision to put him to his election in the first place.

The Prosecution Influence on the Decision

The overall effect of the mode of trial provisions in the MCA 1980 is that summary trial may be vetoed either by the court or by the accused, but not by the prosecution. The most the prosecution can do, generally speaking, is to make representations that trial on indictment would be more appropriate having regard to the gravity of the offence. However, if the prosecution is being carried on by the A-G or Solicitor-General and he applies for the offence to be tried on indictment, that application is binding on the magistrates, who are thereupon obliged to send the case to the Crown Court for trial (s. 19(4)). The same applies if the prosecution is being carried on by the DPP but s. 19(5) contains the important qualification that the DPP must obtain the consent of the A-G before making an application under subs. (4). CPS prosecutions are, as a matter of law, effectively brought by the DPP (as head of the CPS), but the obligation on him to obtain the A-G's consent before applying for trial on indictment under s. 19(4) means that, in practice, the prosecution influence over mode of trial is almost always limited to the making of representations. **D6.27**

Sentencing Guidelines Council: Allocation Guidelines

The MCA 1980, s. 19(3), as amended by the CJA 2003, specifically requires the magistrates to have regard to any allocation guidelines issued by the Sentencing Guidelines Council (SGC) under the CJA 2003, s. 170. In February 2006, the SGC published draft National Allocation Guidelines (<http://www.sentencing-guidelines.gov.uk/docs/allocation_draft_guideline_160206.pdf>). It is anticipated that these will become definitive guidelines, when the connected changes to sentencing procedure in the CJA 2003 are implemented. Key parts of those draft guidelines include the following. **D6.28**

On procedure and principles (para. 3.1), the Guidelines note that the primary test is the adequacy of the sentencing powers of the court; the court will start with a general presumption in favour of trial in a magistrates' court; in deciding whether the powers of the magistrates' court would be adequate, the court is required to have regard to the approach to the assessment of seriousness set out in the SGC Guideline Overarching Principles: Seriousness (see **appendix 8**, part 3).

Paragraph 3.3 notes that the determination of the adequacy of the magistrates' sentencing powers has to be based on the assumption that the prosecution version of the facts is correct. In other words, the issue for the court is the extent of its sentencing powers for the offence(s) charged following conviction based on the prosecution case at its highest. Paragraph 3.3.1

makes the point that, since the allocation decision is required only where the accused has indicated a not guilty plea (or given no indication), the court should allocate either-way cases according to the seriousness of the alleged offence, looking at the case at its worst from the point of view of the accused. In particular, the reduction in sentence for a guilty plea should not influence the court in making an allocation decision. Because previous convictions are relevant to the sentence to be passed, para. 3.3.5 states that, in assessing the seriousness of the current offence(s), the court must consider the existence and relevance of any previous convictions, taking into consideration the nature of the offence(s) to which the conviction(s) relate, the relevance of them to the current offence, and the time that has elapsed since the conviction(s). More significantly, the Guidelines essentially reject reasons that have previously been cited for finding a case unsuitable for summary trial. Paragraph 3.5.1 indicates that 'the procedures in a magistrates' court are generally likely to be adequate for all cases where sentencing is within the powers of that court. Accordingly, it will rarely be appropriate for a magistrates' court to decline summary trial for an offence within its sentencing range for reasons unconnected with the adequacy of sentence'. The Guidelines admit of few exceptions to this. Paragraph 3.5.2 states that there may be 'a few rare and exceptional cases (for example, where unusually complex disclosure issues regarding public interest immunity or sensitivity are to be decided) where it will be especially important to have the separation between judge and jury that is possible in the Crown Court'. The presumption in favour of summary trial, that as many cases as possible should be dealt with in a magistrates' court, is reiterated in para. 3.6.1. However, para. 3.6.1 goes on to state that, since there is no general power to commit for sentence after a determination for summary trial, where any uncertainty remains in relation to the adequacy of the sentencing powers available, it should be resolved in favour of the case being dealt with in the Crown Court.

The Guidelines also reverse the rule that, where there is more than one accused, each case has to be looked at separately. Rather, para. 3.7.1 states that, as a general rule, it is preferable for all issues to be dealt with in a single trial, and para. 3.7.2 says that 'where several defendants are contesting charges that are linked, the presumption is that a single trial will be in the interests of justice for the purpose of considering allocation'.

Paragraph 3.8.1 makes the point that, because the assessment of offence seriousness for the purposes of the allocation decision is based on the prosecution case at its highest, defence representations regarding mode of trial should normally be 'directed to identifying inaccuracies in the factual outline of the case, assessing the adequacy of the court's sentencing powers and determining the relevance of an offender's previous convictions'.

The Guidelines also deal with the new right (under the MCA 1980, s. 20(3) to (8), as amended by the CJA 2003) of the accused to seek an indication from the magistrates of whether they would, or would not, impose a custodial sentence if he were to plead guilty. Paragraph 4.2 states that the key elements of the approach to giving a sentence indication are that the court should assess the type of sentence as realistically as possible in the light of the facts as presented by the prosecution, with the additional element of a guilty plea tendered at this stage in the proceedings, and subject to defence representations as to the accuracy of the factual outline of the case. Wherever possible, the key elements of the basis upon which the indication is given should be recorded in writing. The Guidelines go on to note that the court should proceed with caution where an offender is unrepresented, since raising the possibility of seeking an indication might be seen as putting pressure on the accused to change his plea to guilty. The Guidelines say that the accused should be advised of the availability of independent legal advice and points out that the justices' clerk (or his assistant) present in court has a duty to assist the unrepresented party, and this will include drawing to the attention of an unrepresented defendant that there is an entitlement to request an indication of sentence. The Guidelines also say that the court should not give an indication of sentence where there are alternative charges unless the prosecution has indicated that an agreement as to acceptable pleas has been established following discussions with the defence, and there is an appropriate factual basis upon which an indication could be given (similar principles apply to sentencing indications in the Crown Court: see *Goodyear* [2005] 3 All ER 117). Furthermore, the prosecution must ensure that the court is fully informed of the facts of the case and any relevant background. However, the information presented to the court will not include personal mitigation except insofar as it has influenced the facts of the case presented to the court or it is actively agreed by the prosecution advocate (essentially it would seem that the aim is to avoid a full-blown plea in mitigation when an indication is sought). Finally, the Guidelines say that where a guilty plea is indicated after the court has given an indication of the likely sentence, the appropriate reduction in sentence for the guilty plea should be a maximum of one quarter.

Failure to Comply with the Procedure

In *Kent Justices, ex parte Machin* [1952] 2 QB 355, it was held that, because the jurisdiction of magistrates' courts to try either-way offences derives solely from statute, any failure to comply with the statutory procedure laid down for determining mode of trial renders any summary trial which follows that defective procedure *ultra vires* and therefore a nullity. However, *Ashton* [2007] 1 WLR 181 casts doubt on the authority of *Ex parte Machin*. In *Ashton*, it was held that, in the absence of a clear indication that Parliament intended jurisdiction automatically to be removed following a procedural failure, the decision of the court should be based on an assessment of the interests of justice, with particular focus on whether there was a real possibility that the prosecution or the defence may suffer prejudice. If that risk is present, the court should then decide whether it is just to permit the proceedings to continue. The Court of Appeal reached this conclusion largely through applying the overriding objective in the CrimPR, part 1. This meant, said the court, that a number of authorities, including *Machin*, would have to be reconsidered (see [67]–[69]). **D6.29**

Challenging a Decision to Accept Jurisdiction

It is difficult for the prosecution to mount a challenge against a decision in favour of summary trial, since it is essentially a matter within the magistrates' discretion. Thus, in *McLean, ex parte Metropolitan Police Commissioner* [1975] Crim LR 289, an application to quash a decision to accept jurisdiction failed because the magistrate's decision was not so obviously wrong that no reasonable magistrate could have arrived at it. Nevertheless, in an appropriately clear-cut case, the Divisional Court will grant judicial review. Thus, in *Northampton Magistrates' Court, ex parte the Commissioners of Customs and Excise* [1994] Crim LR 598, the accused was charged with a VAT fraud which, on the prosecution case, had caused a loss of £193,000. The magistrates decided to try him summarily and the prosecution sought judicial review. The Divisional Court said that the correct approach was to ask whether the acceptance of jurisdiction was 'truly astonishing'. Here they must have concluded that it was, as they allowed the application and remitted the matter with a direction to the magistrates to reject jurisdiction. **D6.30**

THE SPECIAL PROCEDURE FOR CRIMINAL DAMAGE CHARGES

Procedure on Criminal Damage Charges

Whenever the accused is charged with a 'scheduled offence', the mode of trial procedure must be preceded by consideration of the value involved in the offence (s. 22(1)). Depending on what that value is, the accused may be deprived of his right to elect trial on indictment, notwithstanding that the offence is otherwise triable either way. **D6.31**

Scheduled offences comprise: (a) offences of damaging or destroying property contrary to s. 1

of the Criminal Damage Act 1971, excluding those committed by fire; and (b) offences of aiding, abetting, counselling or procuring the aforementioned and attempting or inciting them (see MCA 1980, sch. 2). Here, they will be referred to as 'criminal damage offences', although it will be appreciated that a minority of offences under the Criminal Damage Act 1971 are not, in fact, scheduled offences and so are not subject to the special procedure now under consideration.

The minority of criminal damage offences which are *not* scheduled offences comprise:

(a) those committed by damaging or destroying property by fire (these are expressly excluded from scheduled offences by the terms of the MCA 1980, sch. 2); and
(b) those committed with intent to endanger life or being reckless as to the endangering of life contrary to the Criminal Damage Act 1971, s. 1(2): although not expressly dealt with in sch. 2, these cannot be scheduled offences because they are not in the list of offences under the 1971 Act that are triable either way (see MCA 1980, sch. 1, para. 29), and so they are triable only on indictment. It should also be noted that conspiracy to commit criminal damage is not a scheduled offence (*Ward* (1997) 161 JP 297).

D6.32 **Value Involved** If the accused is charged with an offence of criminal damage to which the provisions of the MCA 1980, s. 22, apply, then the court must give the accused the opportunity to indicate his plea (pursuant to s. 17A). It must then consider, having regard to any representations made by the prosecution and defence, whether the value involved in the offence exceeds the relevant sum, currently £5,000 (MCA 1980, s. 22(1)). If the property was allegedly destroyed or damaged beyond repair, the value involved is what it would probably have cost to purchase a replacement in the open market at the time of the offence; if the property was repairable, the value involved is the probable market cost of repairs or the probable market replacement cost, whichever is the less (sch. 2). In *Colchester Magistrates' Court, ex parte Abbott* (2001) 165 JP 386, the Divisional Court made it clear that the value on which the magistrates must focus is the value of the damage to the property itself. They should not concern themselves with any consequential losses which might have been sustained as a result of the damage.

If it appears to the magistrates that the value involved clearly does *not* exceed the relevant sum, they must proceed as if the offence charged were triable only summarily (s. 22(2)). Consequently, the mode of trial provisions of the 1980 Act do not apply and the accused has no right to elect trial on indictment. Nonetheless, the offence is an offence triable either way (see the final paragraph of the note on construction of certain expressions relating to offences in the Interpretation Act 1978, sch. 1, and **D6.2**).

If it appears to the court clear that the value involved exceeds the relevant sum, it is obliged to determine the mode of trial in accordance with the usual mode of trial procedure, just as it would for any other either-way offence (s. 22(3)). Where, for any reason, it is not clear to the court whether the value involved does or does not exceed the relevant sum, it must explain to the accused that he can, if he wishes, consent to summary trial and that, if he does, he will be so tried and his liability to imprisonment or a fine will be limited in accordance with the provisions of s. 33 of the 1980 Act (see below). The accused is then asked if he consents. Depending on his response, the court either proceeds to summary trial or embarks on the ordinary procedure for determining mode of trial, which will presumably result in the accused electing trial on indictment (s. 22(5) and (6)). If the accused is tried summarily for a criminal damage offence as a result *either* of the court deciding that the value involved was clearly less than the relevant sum, *or* of the accused consenting to summary trial in a case where the court was in doubt, then the maximum penalty that may be imposed in the event of conviction is three months' imprisonment or a fine of £2,500, and the offender may not be committed for sentence under the PCC(S)A 2000, s. 3 (s. 33). If the accused is tried summarily in a case where the value involved clearly exceeded the relevant sum but he was nevertheless offered and accepted summary trial, the penalties available are as for any offence listed in sch. 1 to the 1980 Act (i.e. six months' imprisonment and/or a fine of £5,000). Moreover, there may be a committal for sentence under the PCC(S)A 2000, s. 3.

When the CJA 2003, sch. 3, para. 27, comes into force, the maximum sentence of imprisonment under the MCA 1980, s. 33, will be increased to 51 weeks (effectively removing the most significant advantage conferred by s. 33).

When s. 17A of the MCA 1980 was inserted by the CPIA 1996, s. 49, there was no consequential amendment of s. 22. As a result, it is unclear whether a court sentencing an accused who has indicated a plea of guilty to a charge of criminal damage where the value is below £5,000 is limited in its powers to a custodial sentence of three months and/or a fine of £2,500. It would clearly be more logical if the limit did apply. If it were not so, an accused pleading guilty would be at risk of heavier penalties than one found guilty after trial. Moreover, s. 22(1) requires the court to determine the value involved in the offence before proceeding under s. 19; the 'plea before venue' procedure set out in s. 17A necessarily precedes the mode of trial procedure under s. 19.

Procedure for Determining the Value Involved The court is required by the MCA 1980, s. 22(1), to have regard to the 'representations' of the parties when considering the value involved in a criminal damage offence. This does not entail an obligation to hear evidence. In *Canterbury & St Augustine Justices, ex parte Klisiak* [1982] QB 398 at p. 413D–E, Lord Lane CJ said that 'the word "representations" implies something less than evidence. It comprises submissions, coupled with assertions of fact and sometimes production of documents . . . The nearest analogy is, perhaps, the speech in mitigation after a finding or plea of guilty in a criminal trial'. However, the court has a discretion to hear evidence on the question of the value involved if it wishes to do so (ibid.). **D6.33**

In a case where there is real difficulty in arriving at an appropriate basis for calculating the value involved, the prosecution are entitled to say that they will not seek to prove that the accused caused any more damage than can be established with clarity. Acting on that assurance, the court may conclude that the value was clearly less than the relevant sum even though, in the absence of such an assurance and adopting an alternative method of calculation, the question would have remained doubtful and the accused could therefore have elected trial on indictment. An example of this approach may be found in *Salisbury Magistrates' Court, ex parte Mastin* (1986) 84 Cr App R 248, where the prosecution informed the court that, as regards numerous defendants charged with criminal damage to a field by driving their vehicles thereon, they would allege against each individual only that he had caused such damage as was referable to his driving from the gate to the point where his vehicle was eventually parked and would ignore the possibility that he had driven around the field so as to cause damage in excess of the relevant sum. The Divisional Court held that, given the difficulty of establishing precisely what damage each defendant had caused, the prosecution were entitled to limit themselves to proving *vis-à-vis* each individual only that which could be established against him 'with clarity', and, on that basis, the value involved in each offence was clearly under the relevant sum, so the defendants had to be tried summarily).

Two or More Criminal Damage Charges

If the accused is 'charged on the same occasion with two or more scheduled offences and it appears to the court that they constitute or form part of a series of two or more offences of the same or a similar character', then the relevant consideration is the *aggregate* value involved in the offences (MCA 1980, s. 22(11)). In other words, the accused will retain his right to trial on indictment if the value of the offences added together exceeds the relevant sum (£5,000), even if the value of each offence taken individually was under the relevant sum. **D6.34**

The reference in s. 22(11) to a 'series of two or more offences of the same or similar character' connotes that the aggregate value is the relevant value where the offences could be joined together in the same indictment without infringing CrimPR, r. 14.2(3), which governs joinder of counts in an indictment (see **D11.56** ***et seq.***). That rule has been interpreted to mean that, in order for offences to come within its ambit, they must be linked by both a legal and a factual nexus (see *Ludlow v Metropolitan Police Commissioner* [1971] AC 29). When an accused is charged on one occasion with two or more scheduled offences, they will very probably form a series within the meaning of the subsection. Legally, they will be identical (or nearly identical); factually they will amount to a series of offences if linked by closeness in time and geographical location.

Section 22(11) applies where the accused is 'charged on one occasion' with two or more scheduled offences. The phrase could be construed to mean either being charged at the police station or appearing before a magistrates' court to answer charges. It is submitted that the latter interpretation is to be preferred, since there can be no reason of policy why mode of trial should depend on the method of commencing proceedings. A further question arises of whether s. 22(11) is limited to cases where an accused is charged with a series of criminal damage offences on the occasion of his first court appearance or extends also to cases where he originally appears charged with only one offence but further charges are added prior to the determination of mode of trial. Again the latter interpretation seems preferable (otherwise, for example, the prosecution might artificially deprive an accused of the right to trial on indictment by initially bringing him before the court on only one charge even though they already have the evidence to found further charges).

Statutory Provisions on Criminal Damage Mode of Trial

D6.35 **Magistrates' Courts Act 1980, ss. 22 and 33 and sch. 2**

22.—(1)If the offence charged by the information is one of those mentioned in the first column of schedule 2 to this Act (in this section referred to as 'scheduled offences') then the court shall, before proceeding in accordance with section 19 above, consider whether, having regard to any representations made by the prosecutor or the accused, the value involved (as defined in subsection (10) below) appears to exceed the relevant sum. For the purposes of this section the relevant sum is £5,000.

(2) If, where subsection (1) above applies, it appears to the court clear that, for the offence charged, the value involved does not exceed the relevant sum, the court shall proceed as if the offence were triable only summarily, and sections 19 to 21 above shall not apply.

(3) If, where subsection (1) above applies, it appears to the court clear that, for the offence charged, the value involved exceeds that relevant sum, the court shall thereupon proceed in accordance with section 19 above in the ordinary way without further regard to the provisions of this section.

(4) If, where subsection (1) above applies, it appears to the court for any reason not clear whether, for the offence charged, the value involved does or does not exceed the relevant sum, the provisions of subsections (5) and (6) below shall apply.

(5) The court shall cause the charge to be written down, if this has not already been done, and read to the accused, and shall explain to him in ordinary language—

(a) that he can, if he wishes, consent to be tried summarily for the offence and that if he consents to be so tried, he will definitely be tried in that way; and

(b) that if he is tried summarily and is convicted by the court, his liability to imprisonment or a fine will be limited as provided in section 33 below.

(6) After explaining to the accused as provided by subsection (5) above, the court shall ask him whether he consents to be tried summarily and—

(a) if he so consents, shall proceed in accordance with subsection (2) above as if that subsection applied;

(b) if he does not so consent, shall proceed in accordance with subsection (3) above as if that subsection applied.

[(7) Repealed by CJA 1988.]

[(8) No appeal to the Crown Court against conviction for a scheduled offence on the ground that the decision as to the value involved was mistaken.]

[(9) Where a juvenile and an adult are jointly charged with a scheduled offence, the juvenile as well as the adult may make representations as to the value involved.]

[(10) 'The value involved' to be given the meaning set out in sch. 2, and 'material time', when used in sch. 2, means the time of the alleged offence.]

(11) Where—

(a) the accused is charged on the same occasion with two or more scheduled offences and it appears to the court that they constitute or form part of a series of two or more offences of the same or a similar character; or

(b) the offence charged consists in incitement to commit two or more scheduled offences, this section shall have effect as if any reference in it to the value involved were a reference to the aggregate of the values involved.

(12) Subsection (8) of section 12A of the Theft Act 1968 (which determines when a vehicle is recovered) shall apply for the purposes of paragraph 3 of schedule 2 to this Act as it applies for the purposes of that section.

33.—(1)Where in pursuance of subsection (2) of section 22 above a magistrates' court proceeds to the summary trial of an information, then, if the accused is summarily convicted of the offence—

(a) subject to subsection (3) below the court shall not have power to impose on him in respect of that offence imprisonment for more than 3 months or a fine greater than £2,500; and

(b) Section 3 of the Powers of Criminal Courts (Sentencing) Act 2000 [committal for sentence if the magistrates' powers of punishment inadequate] shall not apply as regards that offence.

(2) In subsection (1) above 'fine' includes a pecuniary penalty but does not include a pecuniary forfeiture or pecuniary compensation.

(3) Paragraph (a) of subsection (1) above does not apply to an offence under section 12A of the Theft Act 1968 (aggravated vehicle-taking).

Schedule 2
Offences for which the Value Involved is Relevant to the Mode of Trial

[Column 1 shows the offences subject to the special procedure; column 2 defines the value involved, and column 3 indicates how the value involved is calculated.]

Offence	Value involved	How measured
1. Offences under section 1 of the Criminal Damage Act 1971 (destroying or damaging property), excluding any offence committed by destroying or damaging property by fire.	As regards property alleged to have been destroyed, its value. As regards property alleged to have been damaged, the value of the alleged damage.	What the property would probably have cost to buy in the open market at the material time. (a) If immediately after the material time the damage was capable of repair— (i) what would probably then have been the market price for the repair of the damage, or (ii) what the property alleged to have been damaged would probably have cost to buy in the open market at the material time, whichever is the less; or (b) if immediately after the material time the damage was beyond repair, what the said property would probably have cost to buy in the open market at the material time.
2. The following offences, namely (a) aiding, abetting, counselling or procuring the commission of any offence mentioned in paragraph 1 above; (b) attempting to commit any offence so mentioned; and (c) inciting another to commit any offence so mentioned.	The value indicated in paragraph 1 above for the offence alleged to have been aided, abetted, counselled or procured, or attempted or incited.	As for the corresponding entry in paragraph 1 above.
3. Offences under section 12A of the Theft Act 1968 (aggravated vehicle-taking) where no allegation is made under subsection (1)(b) other than of damage, whether to the vehicle or other property or both.	The total value of the damage alleged to have been caused.	(1) In the case of damage to any property other than the vehicle involved in the offence, as for the corresponding entry in paragraph 1 above, substituting a reference to the time of the accident concerned for any reference to the material time. (2) In the case of damage to the vehicle involved in the offence— (a) if immediately after the vehicle was recovered the damage was capable of repair— (i) what would probably then have been the market price for the repair of the damage, or

Offence	Value involved	How measured
		(ii) what the vehicle would probably have cost to buy in the open market immediately before it was unlawfully taken, whichever is the less; or (b) if immediately after the vehicle was recovered the damage was beyond repair, what the vehicle would probably have cost to buy in the open market immediately before it was unlawfully taken.

VARIATION OF ORIGINAL DECISION AS TO MODE OF TRIAL

Introduction

Variation of the mode of trial decision is governed by the MCA 1980, s. 25. This section will be amended when the relevant provisions of the CJA 2003 come into force. The current version of s. 25 enables the magistrates to switch from summary trial to committal proceedings and *vice versa.* The abolition of committal proceedings by the CJA 2003 means that s. 25 will be radically revised. The new s. 25 is limited to enabling the prosecution to make an application to the magistrates (before the start of the summary trial) to reconsider their acceptance of summary jurisdiction. **D6.36**

Statutory Powers under the Magistrates' Courts Act 1980, s. 25, prior to Amendment by the Criminal Justice Act 2003

Subsections (1) and (2) of the MCA 1980, s. 25, currently govern switching from summary trial to committal for trial; subsections (3) and (4) currently govern switching from committal for trial to summary trial. Section 28 contains an ancillary provision about the use, for purposes of the summary trial, of evidence already considered during the discontinued committal proceedings. **D6.37**

Converting Summary Trial into Committal Proceedings Where a magistrates' court has begun to try an adult summarily for an either-way offence, it may, at any time before the conclusion of the evidence for the prosecution, discontinue the trial and hold committal proceedings instead (MCA 1980, s. 25(1) and (2)). This is subject to the qualification that, if the summary trial is in respect of a scheduled offence of criminal damage and the court is proceeding under s. 22(2) of the 1980 Act because the value involved in the offence clearly did not exceed £5,000, then the court may not alter the mode of trial (see parenthesis in s. 25(2)). **D6.38**

In the context of subsection (2) 'evidence for the prosecution' means evidence adduced in order to establish the guilt of the accused following a not guilty plea (*Dudley Justices, ex parte Gillard* [1986] AC 442). Consequently, if the accused pleads guilty, there is no evidence in the sense intended by s. 25(2), and so no power to switch to committal proceedings. The clear intention of s. 25(2) is to allow the magistrates to withdraw their initial agreement to summary trial if the full facts of the offence, as they emerge during the course of the prosecution evidence following a not guilty plea, make their powers of punishment inadequate. If there is no prosecution case in the sense intended by the subsection because the accused pleads guilty,

D

Part D Procedure

the decision for summary trial is irreversible (although the accused may nonetheless be committed to the Crown Court for sentence under the PCC(S)A 2000, s. 3).

Usually, the magistrates will have to hear at least some prosecution evidence before announcing their decision to change the mode of trial (*Birmingham Stipendiary Magistrate, ex parte Webb* (1992) 95 Cr App R 75), even in a case where the bench has already effectively decided to send the case to the Crown Court for trial, for example, because additional charges have been preferred (see *St Helens Magistrates' Court, ex parte Critchley* (1987) 152 JP 102). The court may be said to have 'begun to try the information summarily', however, after taking a not guilty plea but before hearing evidence (e.g., where it has heard submissions on a preliminary point of law which has a direct and immediate bearing on the process of determining the accused's guilt or innocence: see *Horseferry Road Magistrates' Court, ex parte K* [1997] QB 23, where the submissions related to the availability or otherwise of the defence of insanity in the magistrates' court). However, once the prosecution case is finished, the power to switch to committal proceedings is lost.

D6.39 **Converting Committal Proceedings into Summary Trial** A magistrates' court which has commenced committal proceedings in respect of an either-way offence may switch to summary trial if, having regard to any repesentations made by the prosecution and/or defence and to the nature of the case, it considers that the offence is after all more suitable for summary trial (MCA 1980, s. 25(3)). The switch may take place at any stage during committal proceedings, but is subject to the accused giving his consent (ibid.). Before he is asked for his consent, he must be warned of the possibility of being committed for sentence, unless such a warning has already been given (s. 25(4)(b)). Where the prosecution is being carried on by the A-G or Solicitor-General, exercise of the powers given to the court by s. 25(3) is dependent on the law officer's consent; where it is being carried on by the DPP, the A-G (but not the DPP himself) may direct that the powers shall not be exercised (s. 25(3A)).

Somewhat inconveniently, the power to switch to summary trial contained in s. 25(3) does not arise unless the accused 'appears or is brought before a magistrates' court on an information charging him with an offence triable either way' (see s. 25(1)). Therefore, if the only charge against him is for an offence triable only on indictment (e.g., wounding with intent contrary to s. 18 of the OAPA 1861) but the justices decide that there is a case to answer only for an either-way offence (e.g., unlawful wounding contrary to s. 20 of the 1861 Act), there is no jurisdiction to try the latter offence summarily since the accused did not appear before the bench charged with it as required by s. 25(1) (*Cambridgeshire Justices, ex parte Fraser* [1984] 1 WLR 1391).

The magistrates' court can only change its decision from trial on indictment to summary trial *after* it has begun the committal proceedings. In *Liverpool Justices, ex parte CPS, Liverpool* (1990) 90 Cr App R 261, the Divisional Court held that there is no power to vary the decision for trial on indictment except that contained in the MCA 1980, s. 25. Since committal proceedings had not started, the decision to change to summary trial was a nullity.

Statutory Provision on Variation of Mode of Trial

D6.40 **Magistrates' Courts Act 1980, s. 25 (prior to amendment by the CJA 2003)**

25.—(1) Subsections (2) to (4) below shall have effect where a person who has attained the age of 18 appears or is brought before a magistrates' court on an information charging him with an offence triable either way.

(2) Where the court has (otherwise than in pursuance of section 22(2) above) begun to try the information summarily, the court may, at any time before the conclusion of the evidence for the prosecution, discontinue the summary trial and proceed to inquire into the information as examining justices and, on doing so, shall adjourn the hearing.

(3) Where the court has begun to inquire into the information as examining justices, then, if at any time during the inquiry it appears to the court, having regard to any representations made in the presence of the accused by the prosecutor, or made by the accused, and to the

nature of the case, that the offence is after all more suitable for summary trial, the court may, after doing as provided in subsection (4) below, ask the accused whether he consents to be tried summarily and, if he so consents, may subject to subsection below proceed to try the information summarily.

(3A) Where the prosecution is being carried on by the Attorney-General or the Solicitor-General, the court shall not exercise the power conferred by subsection (3) above without his consent and, where the prosecution is being carried on by the Director of Public Prosecutions, shall not exercise that power if the Attorney-General directs that it should not be exercised.

(4) Before asking the accused under subsection (3) above whether he consents to be tried summarily, the court shall in ordinary language—
 (a) explain to him that it appears to the court more suitable for him to be tried summarily for the offence, but that this can only be done if he consents to be so tried; and
 (b) unless it has already done so, explain to him, as provided in section 20(2)(b) above, about the court's power to commit to the Crown Court for sentence.

[(5) to (7) relate to changing the mode of trial in the case of a juvenile: see **D23.34**.]

(8) If the court adjourns the hearing under subsection (2) or (6) above it may (if it thinks fit) do so without remanding the accused.

Effect of the Criminal Justice Act 2003 on the Variation of Mode of Trial

D6.41 When the CJA 2003, sch. 3, para. 11, comes into force, it will amend the MCA 1980, s. 25. The abolition of committal proceedings for either-way offences necessarily means that it will no longer be possible to switch from committal proceedings to summary trial. The existing power to switch from summary trial to committal proceedings, or vice versa, will therefore be abolished. The former power to switch from summary trial to committal proceedings is replaced with a new power for the prosecution to apply for an either-way case which has been allocated for summary trial to be tried on indictment instead (s. 25(2)). This application must be made before the summary trial begins and must be dealt with by the court before any other application or issue in relation to the summary trial is dealt with (s. 25(2A)). Under s. 25(2B), the court may accede to the application 'only if it is satisfied that the sentence which a magistrates' court would have power to impose for the offence [or offences that constitute or form part of a series of two or more offences of the same or a similar character] would be inadequate'. If the court agrees to the prosecution application, the case is transferred to the Crown Court under the CDA 1998, s. 51. The amended MCA 1980, s. 25, reads as follows:

(1) Subsections (2) to (2D) below shall have effect where a person who has attained the age of 18 appears or is brought before a magistrates' court on an information charging him with an offence triable either way.

(2) Where the court is required under section 20(9) above to proceed to the summary trial of the information, the prosecution may apply to the court for the offence to be tried on indictment instead.

(2A) An application under subsection (2) above—
 (a) must be made before the summary trial begins; and
 (b) must be dealt with by the court before any other application or issue in relation to the summary trial is dealt with.

(2B) The court may grant an application under subsection (2) above but only if it is satisfied that the sentence which a magistrates' court would have power to impose for the offence would be inadequate.

(2C) Where—
 (a) the accused is charged on the same occasion with two or more offences; and
 (b) it appears to the court that they constitute or form part of a series of two or more offences of the same or a similar character,

subsection (2B) above shall have effect as if references to the sentence which a magistrates' court would have power to impose for the offence were a reference to the maximum aggregate sentence which a magistrates' court would have power to impose for all of the offences taken together.

D

Part D Procedure

(2D) Where the court grants an application under subsection (2) above, it shall proceed in relation to the offence in accordance with section 51(1) of the Crime and Disorder Act 1998.

Withdrawal by Accused of Original Election

D6.42 The approach a magistrates' court should adopt when an accused who has already chosen between summary trial and trial on indictment asks to withdraw his original election was fully considered by McCullough J in *Birmingham Justices, ex parte Hodgson* [1985] QB 1131. The following propositions emerge from *Ex parte Hodgson* and the cases mentioned therein:

(a) The magistrates have a discretion to permit the accused to withdraw an election for summary trial, notwithstanding that the MCA 1980, s. 20(3)(a) (s. 20(9)(a) in the version of s. 20 inserted by the CJA 2003), provides that if an accused consents to be tried summarily, the court *shall* proceed to summary trial. The existence of this discretion was affirmed by *Craske, ex parte Metropolitan Police Commissioner* [1957] 2 QB 591. Devlin J said (at pp. 599–600):

> I do not think that [the use of the word 'shall'] means that once the procedure is set in motion, the court has ineluctably to allow the wheels to revolve without any power to stop them if the accused wants to change his mind. . . . I can find nothing . . . which would deprive a magistrate . . . of the ordinary right which they must have in the interests of justice of allowing an accused who has given his consent ill-advisedly to abandoning his right to trial by jury, to be given the opportunity of reconsidering it.

It would seem that the accused can in theory be allowed to re-elect even after his trial on a not guilty plea has begun. However, it is submitted that, once a significant portion of the prosecution evidence has been given, a change of election should be allowed only in very exceptional circumstances, since otherwise the defence would be tempted to ask to re-elect as a tactical ploy whenever the trial seems to be going badly.

(b) In exercising their discretion whether or not to accede to an application to re-elect, magistrates must have regard to the 'broad justice' of the situation (per Lord Widgery CJ in *Southampton Justices, ex parte Briggs* [1972] 1 WLR 277). They are entitled to take into account: (i) that the defendant had his rights as to mode of trial fully explained to him; (ii) that he understood those rights; (iii) that he voluntarily consented to be tried summarily; and (iv) that there were no unusual, difficult or grave features in the case (*Lambeth Metropolitan Stipendiary Magistrate, ex parte Wright* [1974] Crim LR 444, as explained by McCullough J in *Ex parte Hodgson* [1985] QB 1131 at p. 1140A-C). The fact that the accused was unrepresented when he elected summary trial is not sufficient by itself to compel the court to allow a withdrawal of election, even if he is subsequently advised that trial on indictment would be preferable (see, e.g., *Metropolitan Stipendiary Magistrate, ex parte Zardin* (14 May 1971 unreported)). Conversely, although his having had legal advice before electing would obviously be a very powerful argument against an application to re-elect, there is no reason to suppose that it must inevitably be decisive.

(c) Where the material before the magistrates shows that the accused, when he elected summary trial, did not properly understand the nature and significance of the choice put to him, the broad justice of the situation demands that he be allowed to re-elect. Although it is still a matter for the court's discretion, in such a case the discretion may be properly exercised only in favour of the accused (see *Ex parte Hodgson*; *Highbury Corner Metropolitan Stipendiary Magistrates, ex parte Weekes* [1985] QB 1147).

(d) The accused's election as to mode of trial is likely, in practice, to be closely connected to whether he is pleading guilty or not. If, therefore, having elected summary trial, he pleads guilty but is then allowed to change his plea after legal advice, he should be allowed to withdraw his consent to summary trial and be put to his election again (*Bow Street Magistrates' Court, ex parte Welcombe* (1992) 156 JP 609).

(e) At least in cases such as *Ex parte Hodgson* and *Ex parte Weekes*, where it is said that the accused did not understand the nature and significance of his choice, the court's view that the case is more suitable for summary trial is *not* a factor which should tell against an application to withdraw the election (see per McCullough J in *Ex parte Hodgson* [1985] QB 1131 at p. 1145A–B and *Ex parte Weekes* [1985] QB 1147 at p. 1152C–E).

(f) Most of the authorities concern cases where the accused wishes to withdraw his election for summary trial. However, the same general principles apply where he wishes to elect summary trial having originally insisted on trial on indictment. Usually, the court is more willing to accede to such an application because of the saving in time and money which will result. But, if the first election appears to have been nothing more than a tactical ploy (e.g., to obtain a sight of the statements made by the prosecution witnesses), the court is justified in refusing the application to withdraw it (*Warrington Justices, ex parte McDonagh* (5 June 1981, unreported)).

Procedure on Application to Re-elect The Divisional Court has stated that justices should inform themselves of what happened on the occasion of the original election. If they themselves were then sitting, their unaided recollection may be sufficient. If not the clerk should provide the information (e.g., through consulting the court files). If the accused is arguing that he did not understand the consequences of his original election, it is for him to establish that, whether by his own evidence or other means (see *Forest Magistrates' Court, ex parte Spicer* (1989) 153 JP 81). **D6.43**

ADJUSTMENT OF CHARGES TO DICTATE MODE OF TRIAL

It is possible for the prosecution to replace an existing charge with a new charge. In *Cooke v DPP* (1992) 95 Cr App R 233, it was held that the power conferred by s. 23 of the Prosecution of Offences Act 1985 to discontinue proceedings by means of pre-trial or pre-hearing correspondence and without a court appearance, is an additional power to that already possessed by the prosecutor to go before the court and withdraw a charge or offer no evidence on it. **D6.44**

Where the prosecution choose to replace an offence which is triable either way with an offence which is triable only summarily, the accused is thereby deprived of the possibility of trial by jury. In *Canterbury & St Augustine Justices, ex parte Klisiak* [1982] QB 398, it was held that the court can prevent the prosecution from doing this only 'in the most obvious circumstances which disclose blatant injustice' (per Lord Lane CJ at p. 411F). In *Sheffield Justices, ex parte DPP* [1993] Crim LR 136, the Divisional Court said that it would be appropriate to interfere with the prosecutor's decision to replace an either way charge with a summary-only charge only if there was evidence that the prosecutor had done so in order to manipulate the system (in other words, acting in bad faith).

It is also possible for a charge which is triable either way to be replaced with a charge that is triable only on indictment. However, in **Brooks** [1985] Crim LR 385, where the prosecution replaced a charge of unlawful wounding (OAPA 1861, s. 20) with a charge of wounding with intent (s. 18) after the magistrates accepted jurisdiction to try the s. 20 charge despite prosecution representations that the case should be tried on indictment, the Court of Appeal warned that it would be unjust and wrong for the prosecution to do this if the magistrates have already accepted jurisdiction in respect of the either-way offence, since the prosecution would be frustrating the decision reached by the justices.

The principles were summarised by Neill LJ in *Redbridge Justices, ex parte Whitehouse* [1992] 94 Cr App R 332 (at p. 338):

> . . . (3) . . . If the prosecution . . . seek to prefer new charges or to substitute charges or to offer no

> evidence on certain charges the justices should consider the matter on its merits. The fact that the prosecution wish to add or substitute new charges either to ensure that the case is tried summarily or to ensure that it is tried in the Crown Court is not a ground for refusing the issue of a summons or other process provided that on the facts disclosed the justices are satisfied that the course proposed by the prosecution is proper and appropriate in the light of the facts put before them. Thus clearly the justices should not agree to the addition of a charge which is triable only on indictment if the facts are incapable of supporting such a charge and the fresh charge can be seen to be a device designed to deprive the justices of their jurisdiction to try the case themselves. (4) If the justices have already decided to try a matter summarily and the case is then adjourned, any later application by the prosecution to add an additional charge which would have the effect of making summary trial no longer possible should be scrutinised with particular care. The prosecution cannot be allowed improperly to frustrate the earlier decision of the justices. However, I do not understand the decision in *Brooks* . . . as meaning that once the justices have decided on summary trial there are no circumstances in which the prosecutor can properly seek to add a further charge which is triable only on indictment . . . (5) If the justices acting within their jurisdiction exercise their discretion bona fide and bring their minds to bear on the question whether they ought to grant a further summons or not, this Court is very unlikely to interfere except in an exceptional case where the decision satisfies the strict test of being unreasonable in a *Wednesbury* sense.

It must also be borne in mind that the Code for Crown Prosecutors, para. 7.3 (see **appendix** 4), states that 'Crown Prosecutors should not change the charge simply because of the decision made by the court or the defendant about where the case will be heard'.

MODE OF TRIAL FOR SUMMARY OFFENCES

D6.45 It follows from the basic definition of a summary offence as one which is triable *only* summarily that the question of mode of trial for such an offence does not normally arise. However, the provisions of ss. 40 and 41 of the CJA 1988 allow for summary offences to be tried at the Crown Court in two situations. Section 40 provides that where certain summary offences (namely, common assault, driving while disqualified, taking a motor vehicle without the owner's consent, and criminal damage where the value involved is less than £5,000) are disclosed by the evidence on the basis of which an accused has been sent for trial in respect of an indictable offence, and the summary offence is either founded on the same facts as the indictable offence or forms with it a series of offences of the same or similar character, then the prosecution may include a count for the summary offence on the indictment and, if the accused pleads not guilty, the charge will be tried by a jury.

Section 41 provides that where the accused is being sent for trial for an either-way offence and the magistrates take the view that a summary offence punishable with imprisonment or disqualification with which the accused is also charged arose out of circumstances the same as or connected with the circumstances of the either-way offence, then the magistrates may also send the accused for 'trial' in respect of the summary offence. However, that charge will not be put to the accused unless and until he has been convicted of the either-way offence and, if he denies the summary offence, the Crown Court's powers over it cease. Both ss. 40 and 41 thus involve decisions being taken about the mode of trial for a summary offence (see **D10.47** and **D10.15**). Section 41 will be repealed when the relevant provisions of the CJA 2003 come into effect.

Section D7 Bail

Introduction

Bail in criminal proceedings is governed by the Bail Act 1976 (BA 1976) (see s. 1(6) of the Act). 'Bail in criminal proceedings' is defined in s. 1(1) of the Act as: '(a) bail grantable in or in connection with proceedings for an offence to a person who is accused or convicted of the offence, or (b) bail grantable in connection with an offence to a person who is under arrest for the offence or for whose arrest for the offence a warrant (endorsed for bail) is being issued'. This section is chiefly concerned with bail from magistrates' courts and the Crown Court. For bail in appeals to the Court of Appeal, see **D7.4** and **D26.11**. **D7.1**

The BA 1976 is set out at **D7.97**.

COURTS' POWER TO GRANT BAIL

Bail by Magistrates' Court

A magistrates' court, when adjourning a case where the proceedings were commenced by means of a charge (rather than a summons), has to remand the accused. The remand may be in custody or on bail (see MCA 1980, ss. 5(1), 10(1) and 18(4) at **D5.15** for the jurisdiction to adjourn and remand when, respectively, the court is inquiring into an offence as examining justices, trying an information summarily or determining mode of trial for an offence triable either way; and see also s. 128(1) at **D5.16**, which states that, whenever a magistrates' court has power to remand a person, it may either remand him in custody or remand him on bail in accordance with the BA 1976). For the time restrictions on remands in custody and the possibility of remanding an accused in his absence, see **D5.19**. Magistrates also have power to grant bail for the period of any remand for reports etc. after summary conviction (see MCA 1980, s. 10(3), and also PCC(S)A 2000, s. 11, for remands on bail for medical examination). Where a magistrates' court determines to commit an accused to the Crown Court for trial, it may either order that he be kept in custody or release him on bail (MCA 1980, s. 6(8)). Similarly, committals for sentence may be in custody or on bail. Where a magistrates' court has summarily convicted an accused and passed a custodial sentence, it may grant him bail pending the determination of an appeal (MCA 1980, s. 113, which applies both when the accused has given notice of appeal to the Crown Court and when he has asked the magistrates to state a case for the opinion of the Divisional Court). Finally, where the magistrates are sending a defendant to the Crown Court for trial under the CDA 1998, s. 51, which currently relates to indictable-only offences (see **D10**), they may do so in custody or on bail. **D7.2**

Bail by the Crown Court

D7.3 The persons to whom the Crown Court may grant bail are listed in the Supreme Court Act 1981, s. 81(1)(a) to (g). They are as follows:

(a) any person who has been sent in custody for trial in the Crown Court;
(b) any person who has been given a custodial sentence following conviction in the magistrates' court (whether he pleaded guilty or was found guilty) and who is appealing to the Crown Court against conviction and/or sentence;
(c) any person who is in the custody of the Crown Court pending disposal of his case (so whenever the Crown Court adjourns a trial or adjourns between conviction and sentence, it has a discretion to grant the accused bail for the period of the adjournment);
(d) and (e) any person whose case has been decided by the Crown Court but who has applied to the court to state a case for the Divisional Court's opinion or is seeking judicial review of the decision;
(f) any person to whom the Crown Court has granted a certificate that his case is fit for appeal to the Court of Appeal, whether against conviction or against sentence; and
(g) any person who has been remanded in custody by a magistrates' court on adjourning a case under the PCC(S)A 2000, s. 11 or the MCA 1980, s. 5, 10 or 18, provided the magistrates' court has granted a certificate that, before refusing bail, it heard full argument.

All the above powers are subject to the CJPO 1994, s. 25 (see **D7.7**).

In *X* [2004] All ER (D) 400 (Feb), it was held that where a fresh indictment has been preferred in the Crown Court following the quashing of a conviction and the ordering of a re-trial, the Court of Appeal no longer has jurisdiction in relation to bail. It follows that, once a fresh indictment has been preferred, jurisdiction in relation to bail belongs with the Crown Court.

Bail by Court of Appeal

D7.4 The Court of Appeal has jurisdiction to grant bail to a person who has served notice of appeal or notice of application for leave to appeal against his conviction and/or sentence in the Crown Court (Criminal Appeal Act 1968, s. 19). The Court of Appeal also has power to bail a person who is appealing from it to the House of Lords (s. 36).

The above powers are again subject to the CJPO 1994, s. 25 (see **D7.7**).

PRINCIPLES GOVERNING BAIL

Presumption in Favour of Bail

D7.5 Section 4(1) of the BA 1976, in combination with sch. 1, creates a rebuttable presumption in favour of bail. It provides that: 'A person to whom this section applies shall be granted bail except as provided in schedule 1 to this Act'. Subsections (2) to (4) of s. 4 then define the persons to whom subsection (1) applies. They are:

(a) any person who appears before the Crown Court or a magistrates' court in the course of or in connection with proceedings for an offence, or applies to a court for bail in connection with those proceedings (s. 4(2));
(b) any person who has been convicted of an offence and whose case is adjourned for reports before sentencing (s. 4(4)); and
(c) any person brought before the court under the CJA 2003, sch. 8, for alleged breach of a requirement of a community order (s. 4(3)).

Apart from cases where the accused has been convicted and the case has been adjourned for pre-sentence reports, s. 4(1) does *not* apply once a person has been convicted of an offence (as is made clear in the proviso to s. 4(2)). Therefore, an appellant seeking bail pending determination of his appeal has no presumption of bail operating in his favour. Neither does an offender who is committed to the Crown Court for sentence following conviction in a magistrates' court. In both those situations, there is power to grant bail, but its grant or refusal is entirely at the discretion of the court. It should also be noted that s. 4(1) does not apply to bail from the police station, although, once a detainee has been charged, the PACE 1984, s. 38(1), imposes on the custody officer a duty to grant him bail unless its refusal can be justified on grounds similar to those which would justify refusing bail to a person prima facie entitled to bail under s. 4(1). Despite the fact that there is no presumption in favour of bail in the situations mentioned above, it nevertheless remains the case that, if bail is granted, it is 'bail in criminal proceedings' within the definition in the BA 1976, s. 1(1). Therefore, the general provisions of the Act concerning bail in criminal proceedings apply (e.g., if the person bailed fails without reasonable cause to surrender he commits an offence under s. 6).

Bail following Indication of Guilty Plea at 'Plea before Venue' Hearing In *Rafferty* [1991] 1 Cr App R 235, the Court of Appeal dealt with the position where an accused gives an indication, as part of the plea before venue procedure (see **D6.10** ***et seq.***), that he will plead guilty, and is then committed for sentence to the Crown Court. Their lordships stated that, in most such cases, it would not be usual to alter the position as regards bail or custody. When a person who had been on bail pleaded guilty at the plea before venue, the usual practice should be to continue bail, even if it is anticipated that a custodial sentence will be imposed by the Crown Court, unless there are good reasons for remanding the accused in custody. If the accused is in custody, then it would be unusual, if the reasons for remanding him in custody remained unchanged, to alter the position. **D7.6**

No Bail for Homicide or Rape if Previous Conviction

The effect of the CJPO 1994, s. 25, is that the court may not grant bail to an accused who is charged with (or has been convicted of) murder, attempted murder, manslaughter, rape or attempted rape, or certain other offences under the SOA 2003 if he has been convicted of any of these offences (or culpable homicide) in the past unless it is satisfied that there are exceptional circumstances which justify it. In a case where the previous conviction was for manslaughter, the restriction applies only if the accused received a custodial sentence for that offence. 'Conviction' is widely defined to include a finding that the defendant was not guilty by reason of insanity, or was found to have done the act or made the omission charged in a case where he was unfit to plead. **D7.7**

It was suggested by the Law Commission in its paper *Bail and the Human Rights Act 1998* (Law Com No. 269) that the CJPOA 1994, s. 25, is liable to be misunderstood and applied in a way which is incompatible with ECHR, Article 5. The problem with s. 25 is that it appears to create a statutory presumption against the grant of bail in a case to which it applies. If so, it conflicts with the Convention's starting point of the presumption of liberty, and substitutes a presumption of custodial remand. The Commission suggests in its paper that the court should go through the usual process of balancing factors for and against the granting of bail. Because of the provisions of s. 25, however, it should give special weight to those counting against the grant of bail. Thus the court would take all relevant circumstances into account, but might nonetheless deny bail because the case fell within s. 25, where it might not otherwise have done so. Section 25 was considered by the House of Lords in *R (O) v Harrow Crown Court* [2007] 1 AC 247. The House had to consider in particular the effect of s. 25 upon the right to bail of a defendant during the currency of the custody time-limit provided by the Prosecution of Offences Act 1985, s. 22, and upon the expiry of such a custody time-limit (see **D14.6** ***et seq.*** for detailed discussion of custody time-limits). The claimant submitted that, once the court had refused to extend a custody time-limit because of the prosecution's failure to act 'with all due diligence and expedition' within the meaning of s. 22(3)(b) of the 1985 Act, the court could not refuse bail without thereby violating the ECHR, Article 5(3). The House of Lords held that, where an application for bail is made during the currency of the custody time-limit, s. 25 should be read as placing a burden on the defendant to rebut the presumption against bail; if he fails to do so, bail should be denied. Their lordships said that, in the vast majority of cases, the court will be able to reach a clear view one way or the other whether the conditions for withholding bail, specified by the BA 1976, sch. 1, are satisfied. However, the court may occasionally be left unsure as to whether the defendant should be released on bail. This, said their lordships, is the only situation in which the burden of proof assumes any relevance, and in such a case bail would have to be granted. That was described as the 'default position', and s. 25 should be read down to make that plain (per Lord Brown of Eaton-Under-Heywood at [35]). Dealing with the relationship between s. 25 and the custody time-limit provisions, it was held that s. 25 operates to disapply the ordinary requirement under the Prosecution of Offences (Custody Time-limits) Regulations 1987, reg. 6(6), that bail should be granted automatically to anyone whose custody time-limit has expired. Their lordships held that, thus applied, s. 25 is compatible with Article 5(3). They reasoned that the jurisprudence of the Strasbourg court demonstrates that, even where a lack of due diligence is causative of delay, it will not necessarily find a violation of Article 5(3), although in such circumstances the English courts would be likely to refuse an extension of the custody time-limit. Their lordships would not expect there to be many cases where bail is refused notwithstanding the court's refusal to extend the custody time-limit, but there is no necessary inconsistency between the two, and Article 5(3) is not necessarily thereby breached.

D7.8 **Criminal Justice and Public Order Act 1994, s. 25**

(1) A person who in any proceedings has been charged with or convicted of an offence to which this section applies in circumstances to which it applies shall be granted bail in those proceedings only if the court or, as the case may be, the constable considering the grant of bail is satisfied that there are exceptional circumstances which justify it.

(2) This section applies, subject to subsection (3) below, to the following offences, that is to say—
   (a) murder;
   (b) attempted murder;
   (c) manslaughter;
   (d) rape under the law of Scotland or Northern Ireland;
   (e) an offence under section 1 of the Sexual Offences Act 1956 (rape);
   (f) an offence under section 1 of the Sexual Offences Act 2003 (rape);
   (g) an offence under section 2 of that Act (assault by penetration);
   (h) an offence under section 4 of that Act (causing a person to engage in sexual activity without consent), where the activity caused involved penetration within subsection (4)(a) to (d) of that section;
   (i) an offence under section 5 of that Act (rape of a child under 13);
   (j) an offence under section 6 of that Act (assault of a child under 13 by penetration);
   (k) an offence under section 8 of that Act (causing or inciting a child under 13 to engage in sexual activity), where an activity involving penetration within subsection (3)(a) to (d) of that section was caused;
   (l) an offence under section 30 of that Act (sexual activity with a person with a mental disorder impeding choice), where the touching involved penetration within subsection (3)(a) to (d) of that section;
   (m) an offence under section 31 of that Act (causing or inciting a person, with a mental disorder impeding choice, to engage in sexual activity), where an activity involving penetration within subsection (3)(a) to (d) of that section was caused;
   (n) an attempt to commit an offence within any of paragraphs (d) to (m).

(3) This section applies to a person charged with or convicted of any such offence only if he has been previously convicted by or before a court in any part of the United Kingdom of any such offence or of culpable homicide and, in the case of a previous conviction of

manslaughter or of culpable homicide, if he was then sentenced to imprisonment or, if he was then a child or young person, to long-term detention under any of the relevant enactments.

(4) This section applies whether or not an appeal is pending against conviction or sentence.

(5) In this section—

'conviction' includes—

(a) a finding that a person is not guilty by reason of insanity;

(b) a finding under section 4A(3) of the Criminal Procedure (Insanity) Act 1964 (cases of unfitness to plead) that a person did the act or made the omission charged against him; and

(c) a conviction of an offence for which an order is made discharging the offender absolutely or conditionally;

and 'convicted' shall be construed accordingly; and

'the relevant enactments' means—

(a) as respects England and Wales, section 91 of the Powers of Criminal Courts (Sentencing) Act 2000;

(b) as respects Scotland, sections 205(1) to (3) and 208 of the Criminal Procedure (Scotland) Act 1995;

(c) as respects Northern Ireland, section 73(2) of the Children and Young Persons Act (Northern Ireland) 1968.

(6) This section does not apply in relation to proceedings instituted before its commencement.

REFUSING BAIL TO AN ACCUSED CHARGED WITH AN IMPRISONABLE OFFENCE

Part I of sch. 1 to the 1976 Act sets out the circumstances in which an accused may be refused bail if at least one offence with which he is charged (or for which he awaits sentence) is punishable with imprisonment (part II applies when none of the offences are imprisonable). **D7.9**

An unconvicted accused charged with an imprisonable offence need not be granted bail if one or more of the grounds for a remand in custody (listed in the BA 1976, sch. 1, part I, paras. 2 to 7) is applicable. The first — and most commonly relied on — ground subdivides into three. As regards offenders convicted but remanded for reports, there is a further ground on which reliance may also be placed. The statutory grounds for refusing bail are as follows.

Risk of Absconding, Further Offences or Interference with Witnesses **D7.10**

Bail Act 1976, sch. 1, para. 2

(1) The defendant need not be granted bail if the court is satisfied that there are substantial grounds for believing that the defendant, if released on bail (whether subject to conditions or not) would—

(a) fail to surrender to custody, or

(b) commit an offence while on bail, or

(c) interfere with witnesses or otherwise obstruct the course of justice, whether in relation to himself or any other person.

Standard of Proof The opening words of para. 2(1) do *not* require the court to be satisfied that the consequences specified in subparagraphs (a) to (c) actually will occur in the event of bail being granted, or even to be satisfied that they are more likely than not to occur. The court merely has to be satisfied that there are 'substantial grounds for believing' that they would occur. In other words, it is the grounds rather than the putative event itself about which the court must be satisfied. On the other hand, it is not enough for the justices simply to have a subjective perception of a risk of failure to surrender to custody etc. (per Lord Lane CJ in *Mansfield Justices, ex parte Sharkey* [1985] QB 613 at p. 625C–E, where he contrasts the less rigorous requirements which attach when the question is whether an accused who is being granted bail should be granted it subject to conditions with the stricter requirements applying **D7.11**

when the question is whether bail should be refused altogether — in the former situation the court need only perceive a real rather than fanciful risk of absconding etc., whereas in the latter situation the perception must be based on substantial grounds).

Although the question posed by para. 2 is whether substantial grounds exist for believing that a future event will occur and to that extent is a question of fact, it is not a question which can be answered according to the usual rules of evidence. Thus in *Re Moles* [1981] Crim LR 170 it was held that a police officer explaining the objections to bail was entitled to recount what he had been told by a potential witness about the threats the latter had received, with a view to showing that the granting of bail would lead to further interference with witnesses. In *Ex parte Sharkey* Lord Lane referred to *Re Moles* and said (at p. 626A): '. . . there is no requirement for formal evidence to be given [at an application for bail] . . . It was for example sufficient for the facts to be related to the justices at second hand by a police officer.' Current practice when presenting objections to bail in a magistrates' court is not even to have a police officer present, but for the CPS representative to argue that bail is inappropriate on the basis of a police pro forma included in the file.

D7.12 **Application of para. 2** Paragraph 2 of sch. 1 applies some of the later provisions of sch. 1 to para. 2 in order to ensure that para. 2 is interpreted in accordance with those later provisions. Thus para. 2(2) refers to:

(a) para. 2A — where the accused was already on bail in respect of other criminal proceedings on the date of the present offence, he may not be granted bail unless the court is satisfied that there is no significant risk of his committing an offence while on bail — at present, this applies only to offences carrying a life sentence (see **D7.20**);
(b) para. 6 — where the accused was granted bail in the present proceedings but has failed to surrender to custody, he may not be granted bail unless the court is satisfied that there is no significant risk that, if released on bail, he would again fail to surrender to custody — at present, this applies only to offences carrying a life sentence (see **D7.18**);
(c) para. 6B — where a sample lawfully taken from the accused has revealed the presence in his body of a specified Class A drug, the current offence is drug-related and the accused has refused to undergo a relevant assessment or to participate in follow-up to that assessment, the accused may not be granted bail unless the court is satisfied that there is no significant risk of his committing an offence while on bail (see **D7.21**).

D7.13 **Relevant Factors** Certain factors to which the court should have regard when taking a decision under para. 2 are listed in para. 9. These factors are:

(a) the nature and seriousness of the offence and the probable method of dealing with the offender for it;
(b) the character, antecedents, associations and community ties of the accused;
(c) his 'record' for having answered bail in the past; and
(d) the strength of the evidence against him.

Nature and seriousness of offence (para. 9(a)). The relevance of the offence alleged being serious is that the accused will know that, if convicted, he is likely to receive a severe sentence and will therefore be tempted to abscond rather than run the risk of such a sentence. The gravity of the charge is not an automatic reason for refusing bail (although, by virtue of the CJPO 1994, s. 25, an accused must normally be refused bail where the charge is, for example, homicide or rape and he has previously been convicted of such an offence (see **D7.7**)). Indeed, in *Hurnam v State of Mauritius* [2006] 1 WLR 857, the Privy Council said that the seriousness of an offence cannot be treated as a conclusive reason for refusing bail to an unconvicted suspect: the right to personal liberty is an important constitutional right and a suspect should remain at large unless it is necessary to refuse bail in order to serve one of the ends for which detention before trial is permissible.

Character and antecedents (para. 9(b)). This refers primarily to previous convictions. These may make a custodial sentence more likely (especially if the accused, if convicted of the present offence, will be in breach of a suspended sentence of imprisonment). Moreover, a person of previous good character is more likely to be trusted by the courts than one with a record. Previous convictions under the BA 1976, s. 6, for failing to surrender to custody in answer to bail are especially relevant (see subparagraph (c)). It should be borne in mind that, currently, if a magistrate hears about an accused's previous convictions in the course of a bail application, that magistrate is disqualified from trying the accused if a summary trial takes place subsequently (MCA 1980, s. 42). However, this provision will be repealed when the repeals in the CJA 2003, sch. 37, part 4, come into effect.

Associations and community ties (para. 9(b)). The word 'associations' is generally taken to refer to undesirable friends with criminal records. Examining the 'community ties' of the accused involves looking at how easy it would be for the accused to abscond and how much he has to lose by absconding. How long has he lived at his present address? Is he single or married? Does he have dependent children? Is he in employment? How long has he had his present job? Does he have a mortgage or a protected tenancy? An accused of 'no fixed abode' or living in short-term accommodation is not automatically debarred from bail, but the ease with which he could disappear to another address is a factor to be considered.

Bail record (para. 9(c)). Considering the bail record of the accused requires the court to consider whether he has absconded in the past. Absconding in earlier proceedings is regarded as evidence of a risk that he may do so again.

Strength of the prosecution evidence (para. 9(d)). This is relevant to whether an accused would answer bail in the sense that one who knows there is a good chance of being acquitted is less likely to abscond than one who anticipates almost certain conviction. It can be argued that there is no point in the accused absconding if he is likely to be acquitted anyway. Conversely, if the prosecution case is strong, so that conviction is likely, he may abscond rather than 'face the music' (especially if a custodial sentence is likely). It is also relevant that a remand in custody followed by acquittal creates a manifest, if sometimes unavoidable, injustice. In borderline cases, where the arguments against bail are strong but not overwhelming, the court may prefer to run the risk of the accused absconding etc. rather than run the risk of his being acquitted after a long period in custody on remand.

Paragraph 9 concludes with the words 'as well as to any others [i.e. considerations] which appear to be relevant', thus making it clear that the considerations mentioned in para. 9(a) to (d) are *not* exhaustive. Those 'others' might include the fact that the accused has previously committed offences while on bail, or the suggestion that potential prosecution witnesses have already received threats and/or are known to the accused and could easily be contacted by him if he were at liberty. Also, it should be noted that the BA 1976, s. 4(9), stipulates that 'in taking any decisions required by part I or II of schedule 1 to this Act, the considerations to which the court is to have regard include, so far as relevant, any misuse of controlled drugs by the defendant'.

Other Grounds for Withholding Bail

Part 1 of sch. 1 to the BA 1976 sets out a number of other grounds for withholding bail: for the accused's own protection (para. 3); where the accused is already serving a custodial sentence for another offence (para. 4); where the court has insufficient information (para. 5); where the accused has absconded in the present proceedings (para. 6). **D7.14**

Own Protection Under the BA 1976, sch. 1, part I, para. 3, an accused need not be granted bail if the court is satisfied that he should be kept in custody for his own protection. This will cover cases where the offence alleged has caused anger in the area where it was committed and there is a risk of members of the public exacting instant revenge on the person believed to be **D7.15**

D

Part D Procedure

responsible. Where the accused is a juvenile, bail may also be refused if he should be kept in custody 'for his own welfare' (ibid.).

D7.16 **Already in Custody** By the BA 1976, sch. 1, part I, para. 4, an accused need not be granted bail if he is already serving a custodial sentence (whether imposed by a civilian court or by a court-martial). Paragraph 4 applies only if the accused is in custody pursuant to a sentence, not when he is in custody as a result of a remand in other proceedings currently outstanding against him, although in the latter situation bail could almost certainly be refused under para. 2 if the court so wished. In fact, courts often find it more convenient to remand an accused certain to be in custody for the foreseeable future as a result of other matters on technical bail. This avoids the restrictions on the periods for which remands in custody may be ordered and the consequent need to bring the accused back to court for a further remand hearing. A frequently occurring practical problem where an accused is in custody to another court or is a serving prisoner is that the prison authorities are unwilling to bring him to court when required. The onus is on the CPS to obtain a Home Office production order (HOPO) obliging the prison service to arrange for the accused's attendance, but even Home Office production orders by no means always have the desired result. This problem is mitigated to some extent by the availability of live links under the CDA 1998, s. 57B (see **D5.23**).

D7.17 **Insufficient Time** Under the BA 1976, sch. 1, part I, para. 5, the accused need not be granted bail if the court is satisfied that, owing to lack of time since the commencement of the proceedings, it has not been practicable to obtain sufficient information for the purposes of taking the decisions required to be taken by the other paragraphs. In such cases, the court might remand in custody for seven days (or even for a shorter period) to enable the necessary information to be discovered. Examples where para. 5 might apply are if the police are not satisfied that the accused has given them his correct particulars and think he may have previous convictions under another name, or if time is needed to check an address given by the accused, or if inquiries are still in hand which may reveal the offence to be more serious than originally supposed and/or that the accused has committed additional offences. It is submitted that para. 5 should be relied on sparingly, and should not be used to justify dilatoriness on the part of the police or the prosecution in marshalling the objections to bail. A remand in custody under para. 5 does not amount to a decision not to grant bail for the purposes of para. 2 of part IIA. In other words, it does not restrict further applications for bail (see **D7.49**).

D7.18 **Absconded in the Present Proceedings** The BA 1976, sch. 1, part I, para. 6, currently exists in two versions: the original version before the amendments made by the CJA 2003, s. 15(1), and the amended version, which is currently in force only in respect of offences which carry a life sentence (see SI 2006 No. 3217). The original version (which is currently applicable in all cases except those concerning offences that carry a life sentence) reads as follows:

> the defendant need not be granted bail if, having been released on bail in or in connection with the proceedings for the offence . . . , he has been arrested in pursuance of section 7 of this Act

This effectively reverses the presumption in favour of bail, so that there is a burden on the accused to show why bail should be granted despite the fact that he has already absconded in the current proceedings.

The version applicable to offences which carry a life sentence reads as follows:

> (1) If the defendant falls within this paragraph, he may not be granted bail unless the court is satisfied that there is no significant risk that, if released on bail (whether subject to conditions or not), he would fail to surrender to custody.
>
> (2) Subject to sub-paragraph (3) below, the defendant falls within this paragraph if—
> (a) he is aged 18 or over, and
> (b) it appears to the court that, having been released on bail in or in connection with the proceedings for the offence, he failed to surrender to custody.

(3) Where it appears to the court that the defendant had reasonable cause for his failure to surrender to custody, he does not fall within this paragraph unless it also appears to the court that he failed to surrender to custody at the appointed place as soon as reasonably practicable after the appointed time.

Under the revised version of para. 6, the court is required to refuse bail to an adult accused who has failed without reasonable cause to surrender to custody in answer to bail in the same proceedings, unless the court is satisfied that there is no significant risk that he would again fail to surrender if released.

Convicted Offenders: Adjourning for Reports

Under the BA 1976, sch. 1, part I, para. 7, if the case of a convicted offender is adjourned for inquiries or reports, he need not be granted bail if it appears to the court that it would be impracticable to complete the inquiries or make the report without keeping him in custody (e.g., because he would not voluntarily attend for purposes such as seeing a probation officer or being medically examined). Leaving aside the special circumstances posited by para. 7, it has been held that, where a court needs a pre-sentence report before it will be in a position to decide the appropriate sentence, the normal practice should be to grant bail unless there are exceptional reasons for keeping the offender in custody. This is especially so where the court, in order to impose a custodial sentence, has to be satisfied after considering reports that such a sentence is the only appropriate disposition (*McGoldrick v Normand* 1988 SLT 273). Although this was a Scottish case, in which the judgment was delivered by Lord Grieve in the High Court of Justiciary, the statement of principle would seem to be equally applicable to English courts. The reason why bail is normally appropriate is that a remand in custody might appear to be prejudging the question of whether the ultimate sentence should be custodial. **D7.19**

No 'Right to Bail' for Certain Offences Committed on Bail

There are two versions of the BA 1976, sch. 1, part I, para. 2A. The first is the original version, which is currently applicable to all offences except those punishable with a life sentence; the second is the version as amended by the CJA 2003, s. 14(1), which is currently in force only in respect of offences that carry a life sentence (see SI 2006 No. 3217). The original version of para. 2A provides as follows: **D7.20**

> The defendant need not be granted bail if (a) the offence with which he is charged is an indictable offence or an offence triable either way; and (b) it appears to the court that he was on bail in criminal proceedings on the date of the offence.

The version applicable to offences that carry a life sentence is as follows:

> (1) If the defendant falls within this paragraph he may not be granted bail unless the court is satisfied that there is no significant risk of his committing an offence while on bail (whether subject to conditions or not).
> (2) The defendant falls within this paragraph if—
> (a) he is aged 18 or over, and
> (b) it appears to the court that he was on bail in criminal proceedings on the date of the offence.

The original version of para. 2A makes it an exception to the presumption in favour of bail if, at the time of the present offence, the accused was already on bail in respect of earlier alleged offences. The amendment by the CJA 2003 aims to ensure conformity with the HRA 1998. The Law Commission (Law Com No. 269) had recommended that the BA 1976 be amended to make it plain that the fact that the accused was on bail at the time of the alleged offence is not an independent ground for the refusal of bail, as para. 2A (as originally drafted) appeared to suggest; rather it is one of the considerations that the court should take into account when considering withholding bail on the ground that there is a real risk that the accused will commit an offence while on bail. It is, of course, important in this context to remember the presumption of innocence: the accused is *alleged* to have committed an offence while on bail as a result of *allegations* of an earlier offence; at this stage, it cannot be assumed that he is guilty of either offence, since neither offence has been proved.

In *R (Wiggins) v Harrow Crown Court* [2005] EWHC 882 (Admin), Collins J commented (at [24]) that, in the amendments made by the CJA 2003:

> Parliament has added a number of paragraphs which indicate that if there have been particular actions by a defendant it may be in effect presumed that he should not have bail unless the court is satisfied that there is no significant risk that if released on bail he would fail to surrender to custody, or would commit an offence, or whatever the situation in question might be. That, in effect, reverses the usual burden whereby bail must be granted unless the court is satisfied of a particular situation. It then becomes necessary for the court to be persuaded, because of what has happened, that there is no significant risk that he would fail to surrender to custody, or not commit an offence, or whatever.

In fact, the amendments to which Collins J alludes (the new versions of paras. 2A and 6) were not in force at the relevant time. Nonetheless, this does not detract from his view that the effect of the amendments is to reverse the usual presumption in favour of granting bail. The original wording of the provisions in question used the phrase 'need not', which conveys a discretion, whereas the language of the revised version ('may not') is prohibitive and thus reverses the general principle that bail should be refused only if there is good reason to refuse it.

Bail in Cases involving Abuse of Drugs

D7.21 Section 19(4) of the CJA 2003 added paras. 6A to 6C to the BA 1976, sch. 1, part I. These provide that an accused aged 18 or over who has been charged with an imprisonable offence will not be granted bail (unless the court is satisfied that there is no significant risk of his committing an offence while on bail), where the three conditions set out in para. 6B apply, namely:

(1) there is drug test evidence (by way of a lawful test obtained under the PACE 1984, s. 63B, or the CJA 2003, s. 161) that the person has a specified Class A drug in his body;
(2) either he is charged with an offence under the Misuse of Drugs Act 1971, s. 5(2) or (3), and the offence relates to a specified Class A drug, or the court is satisfied that there are substantial grounds for believing that the misuse of a specified Class A drug caused or contributed to the offence with which he is charged or that offence was motivated wholly or partly by his intended misuse of a specified Class A drug; and
(3) the person does not agree to undergo an assessment (carried out by a suitably qualified person) of whether he is dependent upon or has a propensity to misuse any specified Class A drugs, or he has undergone such an assessment but does not agree to participate in any relevant follow-up which has been offered.

If an assessment or follow-up is proposed and agreed to, it will be a condition of bail that it is undertaken (the Bail Act 1976, s. 3(6D)).

Juveniles

D7.22 The CJA 2003, s. 14(2) (in force only in respect of offences that carry a life sentence: see SI 2006 No. 3217) inserts BA 1976, sch. 1, para. 9AA, which applies only where the accused is under the age of 18. Under para. 9AA, if 'it appears to the court that he was on bail in criminal proceedings on the date of the offence', then for the purpose of deciding whether it is satisfied that there are substantial grounds for believing that, if released on bail, he would commit an offence, 'the court shall give particular weight to the fact that the defendant was on bail in criminal proceedings on the date of the offence'. This is similar to the provision applicable to accused aged 18 and over in para. 2A of part 1 of sch. 1 (see **D7.20**). The CJA 2003, s. 15(2) (again, in force only in respect of offences that carry a life sentence), inserts para. 9AB. This provides that, if the accused is under the age of 18 and 'it appears to the court that, having been released on bail in or in connection with the proceedings for the offence, [the accused] failed to surrender to custody', then for the purpose of deciding whether it is satisfied that there are substantial grounds for believing that, if released on bail, he would fail to surrender to custody, 'the court shall give particular weight to (a) where the defendant did not have reasonable cause for his failure to surrender to custody, the fact that he failed to surrender to custody, or (b) where he did have reasonable cause for his failure to surrender to custody, the fact that he failed to surrender to custody at the appointed place as soon as reasonably practicable after the appointed time' (para. 9AB(1) and (3)). Thus, the court is required, in assessing the risk of future absconding in the case of accused under the age of 18, to give particular weight to the fact that he has failed to surrender to custody. Paragraph 9AB(2) makes it clear that, where it appears to the court that the accused had reasonable cause for his failure to surrender to custody, these provisions do not apply unless it also appears to the court that he failed to surrender to custody at the appointed place as soon as reasonably practicable after the appointed time.

REFUSING BAIL TO AN ACCUSED CHARGED WITH A NON-IMPRISONABLE OFFENCE

Part II of sch. 1 to the BA 1976 sets out the reasons justifying refusal of bail to an accused charged solely with non-imprisonable offences. Three of those reasons are identical to reasons for refusing bail to an accused charged with an imprisonable offence, namely, that he should be kept in custody for his own protection (or welfare in the case of a juvenile), that he is serving a custodial sentence, or that he has been arrested in pursuance of s. 7 of the 1976 Act. The grounds of 'risk of absconding etc.,' and 'insufficient time' for refusing bail to someone charged with imprisonable offences do *not* apply where the offences are non-imprisonable. However, para. 5 of part II provides that the accused 'need not be granted bail' if, having been released on bail, he has subsequently been arrested under s. 7 and 'the court is satisfied that there are substantial grounds for believing that the defendant, if released on bail would fail to surrender to custody, commit an offence on bail or interfere with witnesses or otherwise obstruct the course of justice (whether in relation to himself or any other person)'. This version of para. 5 was substituted by the CJA 2003, s. 13(4) (in force from 5 April 2004), to ensure conformity with the HRA 1998 following a recommendation by the Law Commission (Law Com No. 269). **D7.23**

BAIL AND THE EUROPEAN CONVENTION ON HUMAN RIGHTS

Article 5 of the ECHR (see **appendix** 7), which provides that 'everyone has the right to liberty and security of the person', has clear relevance to bail. It lays down that no one shall be deprived of his liberty save in the six sets of circumstances specified in Article 5(1)(a) to (f). The list of exceptions is exhaustive, and has been described in Strasbourg as ensuring that no one is deprived of liberty in an 'arbitrary fashion' (*Engel v Netherlands* (1976) 1 EHRR 647). **D7.24**

The Law Commission (Law Com No. 269, <http://www.lawcom.gov.uk/docs/lc269.pdf>) considered the impact of the HRA 1998 on the law governing decisions taken by the police and the courts to grant or refuse bail in criminal proceedings. The Commission noted that Article 5 of the Convention states that, although reasonable suspicion that the detained person has committed an offence can be sufficient to justify pre-trial detention for a short time, the national authorities must thereafter show additional grounds for detention. They summarised the five additional grounds recognised under the Convention as follows, namely where the purpose of detention is to avoid a real risk that, were the accused to be released:

(1) he would fail to attend trial;
(2) he would interfere with evidence or witnesses, or otherwise obstruct the course of justice;
(3) he would commit an offence while on bail;
(4) he would be at risk of harm against which he would be inadequately protected; or
(5) a disturbance to public order would result.

Strasbourg Case Law

D7.25 Thus, under Article 5, a person charged with an offence must be released pending trial unless there are 'relevant and sufficient' reasons to justify continued detention (*Wemhoff v Germany* (1979) 1 EHRR 55). The case law of the European Court shows that this is interpreted in a way that is very similar to the UK's BA 1976. The grounds accepted by the European Court of Human Rights for withholding bail include:

(1) *the risk that the accused will fail to appear at the trial.* This has been defined as requiring 'a whole set of circumstances which give reason to suppose that the consequences and hazards of flight will seem to him to be a lesser evil than continued imprisonment' (*Stogmuller v Austria* (1979) 1 EHRR 155). The court can take account of 'the character of the person involved, his morals, his home, his occupation, his assets, his family ties, and all kinds of links with the country in which he is being prosecuted' (*Neumeister v Austria* (1979) 1 EHRR 91). The likely sentence is relevant but cannot of itself justify the refusal of bail (*Letellier v France* (1992) 14 EHRR 83);
(2) *the risk that the accused will interfere with the course of justice* (for example, interfering with witnesses, warning other suspects, destroying relevant evidence). There must be an identifiable risk and there must be evidence in support (*Clooth v Belgium* (1992) 14 EHRR 717);
(3) *preventing the commission of further offences.* There must be good reason to believe that the accused will commit offences while on bail (*Toth v Austria* (1992) 14 EHRR 717);
(4) *the preservation of public order.* Bail may be withheld where the nature of the alleged crime and the likely public reaction to it are such that the release of the accused may give rise to public disorder (*Letellier v France*).

Article 5 of the Convention also allows the imposition of conditions on the grant of bail.

'Equality of Arms'

D7.26 It should be noted that the 'equality of arms' principle applies to bail applications (*Woukam Moudefo v France* (1991) 13 EHRR 549). This includes:

(a) the right to disclosure of prosecution evidence for purposes of making a bail application: *Lamy v Belgium* (1989) 11 EHRR 529 (the decision of the Divisional Court, *DPP, ex parte Lee* [1999] 2 Cr App R 304, largely accords with this);
(b) the requirement that the court should give reasons for the refusal of bail (*Tomasi v France* (1993) 15 EHRR 1) and should permit renewed applications for bail at reasonable intervals (*Bezicheri v Italy* (1990) 12 EHRR 210).

The Law Commission concluded that there are no provisions in the BA 1976 which are incompatible with Convention rights. However, the Commission did produce a guide to assist decision-makers to apply the Act in a way that is compatible with the Convention (a copy of the guide can be accessed at <http://www.lawcom.gov.uk/docs/guide.pdf>). The guide emphasises that an accused should be refused bail only where detention is necessary for a purpose which Strasbourg jurisprudence has recognised as legitimate, in the sense that detention may be compatible with the accused's right to release under Article 5(3). Thus, a domestic court exercising its powers in a way which is compatible with the Convention rights should refuse bail only where it can be justified both under the Convention, as interpreted in Strasbourg jurisprudence, and domestic legislation. The guide also points out that detention will be necessary only if the risk relied upon as the ground for withholding bail could not be adequately addressed by the imposition of appropriate bail conditions. Thus, the Commission concluded that conditional bail should be used in preference to detention where a bail condition could adequately address the risk that would otherwise justify detention. Furthermore, the court refusing bail should give reasons for finding that detention is necessary. Those reasons should be closely related to the individual circumstances pertaining to the accused, and be capable of supporting the conclusion of the court.

BAIL AND CUSTODY TIME-LIMITS

Grafted on to the general system of a presumption in favour of bail which is lost if one of the exceptions defined in sch. 1 to the BA 1976 applies, are special rules applying where the prosecution fail to comply with a custody time-limit. Such limits were introduced by the Prosecution of Offences (Custody Time Limits) Regulations 1987 (SI 1987 No. 299), made under the Prosecution of Offences Act 1985, s. 22. Regulation 8 modifies the BA 1976 in that, where a custody time-limit has expired, the words 'except as provided in schedule 1 to this Act' are treated as omitted from s. 4(1) of the Act. The effect is to give the accused an absolute right to bail. Moreover, s. 3 of the 1976 Act (which deals with the conditions which may be imposed when granting bail) is also modified so as to prevent a court, when bailing an accused entitled to bail by reason of the expiry of a custody time-limit, from imposing requirements of a surety or deposit of security or any other condition which has to be complied with *before* release on bail (although it can impose conditions such as residence, curfew or reporting to a police station which have to be complied with *after* release). **D7.27**

Further, reg. 6(6) expressly states that, where the Crown Court is notified that an accused in custody pending his trial on indictment has the benefit of a custody time-limit and that it is about to expire, then it must grant him bail as from the expiry of the time-limit. By reg. 6(1) to (5), the prosecution are obliged to notify the Crown Court at least five days before the limit's expiry of whether they intend to ask the Crown Court to impose conditions on the grant of bail. They must also arrange for the accused to be brought before the court within the two days preceding expiry. This is without prejudice to the prosecution's right to apply for an extension of the time-limit under the Prosecution of Offences Act 1985, s. 22(3). The 1987 Regulations make no express provision as to the procedure to be adopted in a magistrates' court when a custody time-limit is about to expire — the fact that an accused not granted bail has to appear before the magistrates at regular intervals, by reason of the restrictions on the period for which he may be remanded in custody at that stage of the proceedings, perhaps makes it unnecessary to provide expressly for bringing him before the court in anticipation of the expiry of a custody time-limit. For a full discussion of custody time limits, see D14.6 ***et seq.***

CONDITIONS OF BAIL

The BA 1976, s. 3, governs the duties resting on a person granted bail in criminal proceedings and the various requirements which may be attached to a grant of bail. Where the court grants 'unconditional' bail, the accused has simply to surrender to custody (i.e. attend court) at the date and time specified. However, the court may impose a wide range of additional requirements by granting bail subject to specific conditions (known as 'conditional bail'). **D7.28**

Duty to Surrender to Custody

D7.29 A person granted bail in criminal proceedings is under a duty to surrender to custody (BA 1976, s. 3(1)). 'Surrender to custody' is defined in s. 2(2) as surrendering into the custody of the court the accused has been bailed to attend For the problem of what precisely is meant by surrendering to the custody of a court, whether it merely entails reporting to an usher at the court building or extends to being in the dock when the case is called on, see **D7.75**. The date and place at which the accused should surrender is fixed when bail is granted, save that when he is sent to the Crown Court for trial or sentence the obligation is to surrender on the day his case comes up for hearing if it is not possible to notify him of the hearing date at the time the case is sent to the Crown Court. The date originally fixed for surrender to custody may be varied to a later date (see MCA 1980, ss. 43 and 129, for a magistrates' court's powers in this respect). Failure without reasonable cause to surrender to custody is an offence under the BA 1976, s. 6. The introduction of the s. 6 offence coincided with the abolition of the former system whereby the person bailed entered into a recognisance to secure his own attendance and might be ordered to forfeit the amount of the recognisance if he absconded. By s. 3(2) of the 1976 Act an accused granted bail in criminal proceedings may no longer be bailed on his own recognisance (cf. the position where bail is granted otherwise than in criminal proceedings). The accused may, however, be required to provide other people to stand surety for him (see **D7.34**; or he may be required to give security for his surrender to custody (see **D7.38**).

Conditions that May be Imposed by the Court

D7.30 By the BA 1976, s. 3(6), a person bailed may be required by a court to comply with such requirements as appear to the court necessary to secure that he (a) surrenders to custody, (b) does not commit an offence on bail, (c) does not interfere with witnesses or otherwise obstruct the course of justice, (d) makes himself available for the making of inquiries or a report to assist in sentencing, and (e) attends an interview with an authorised advocate or litigator (this will nearly always be a solicitor). The CJA 2003, s. 13(1), adds s. 3(6)(ca), which enables conditions to be imposed for the protection of the accused (or, if he is a child or young person, for his own welfare or in his own interests).

Bail Act 1976, sch. 1, part I

> 8.—(1) . . . where the defendant is granted bail, no conditions shall be imposed under subsections (4) to (7) (except subsection (6)(d) or (e)) of section 3 of this Act unless it appears to the court that it is necessary to do so—
> (a) for the purpose of preventing the occurrence of any of events mentioned in paragraph 2(1) of this part of this schedule, or
> (b) for the defendant's own protection or, if he is a child or young person, for his own welfare or in his own interests.

The events mentioned in para. 2 of part I of sch. 1 are precisely the same as those mentioned in paras. (a) to (c) of s. 3(6): failure to surrender to custody, further offences and interference with witnesses. There is thus an almost complete overlap between s. 3(6) itself and sch. 1, part I, para. 8. This was attributed by Lord Lane CJ in *Mansfield Justices, ex parte Sharkey* [1985] QB 613 to 'indifferent drafting' (at p. 625C). Counsel for the applicants argued that para. 8 impliedly restricted the imposition of requirements to cases where the court was satisfied that there were substantial grounds for believing that one of the adverse consequences would occur unless bail was made conditional. However, this argument was rejected by the Divisional Court. Having quoted s. 3(6) and para. 8, Lord Lane explained their effect in the context of a condition imposed to prevent further offences. His lordship said (at p. 625E):

> In the present circumstances the question the justices should ask themselves is a simple one: 'Is this condition *necessary* for the prevention of the commission of an offence when on bail?' They are not obliged to have substantial grounds. It is enough if they perceive a *real and not a fanciful risk* of the offence being committed. Thus, section 3(6) and paragraph 8 give the court a wide discretion to inquire whether the condition is necessary [emphasis added].

It followed that the justices were *not* obliged to have substantial grounds for believing that a repetition of the accused's conduct would occur. It was enough that they perceived a real risk of that happening. Although given the context of determining the legality of conditions imposed to prevent offences while on bail, the Lord Chief Justice's judgment is obviously applicable, *mutatis mutandis*, to conditions designed to prevent the accused absconding or interfering with witnesses.

A similar approach was adopted in *R (CPS) v Chorley Justices* (2002) 166 JP 764, where the Divisional Court noted that the only pre-requisite for imposing conditions on bail is that, in the circumstances of the particular case, imposition of the condition is necessary to achieve the aims specified in that section (e.g., preventing the accused from absconding, or committing offences while on bail, or interfering with witnesses or otherwise obstructing the course of justice).

The BA 1976 refers to some specific conditions (such as sureties and security) but it does not contain a definitive list of conditions that may be imposed. The court may impose any condition so long as it is necessary to prevent the accused from absconding, committing offences etc.

Commonly imposed conditions include:

(a) a condition of residence, often expressed as a condition that the accused is to live and sleep at a specified address;
(b) a condition that the accused is to notify any changes of address to the police;
(c) a condition of reporting (whether daily, weekly or at other intervals) to a local police station;
(d) a curfew (i.e. the accused must be indoors between certain hours);
(e) a condition that the accused is not to enter a certain area or building or go within a specified distance of a certain address;
(f) a condition that he is not to contact (whether directly or indirectly) the victim of the alleged offence and/or any other probable prosecution witness; and
(g) a condition that he is to surrender his passport to the police.

Conditions (a), (b), (c) and (g) are particularly relevant to reducing the risk of absconding. A special form of residential condition is that the accused is to reside at a bail hostel or probation hostel. When imposing such a condition the court may, and normally will, impose an additional requirement that the accused is to comply with the rules of the hostel (s. 3(6ZA)). In the case of a convicted offender being remanded for reports, a requirement of residence at a hostel may be imposed not simply to reduce the risk of absconding but, additionally or alternatively, to assess his suitability for being dealt with by a means which would involve residence at a probation hostel (see the last words of sch. 1, part I, para. 8). Conditions (d) and (e) are designed to prevent the commission of offences when on bail. A curfew may be appropriate where the offence with which the accused is charged was allegedly committed at night; a geographical restriction is useful if the offence was one of violence committed at a certain address (in effect, the accused is ordered to stay away from the address). Conditions (e) and (f) may be imposed to minimise the risk of interference with witnesses.

In *McDonald v Procurator Fiscal, Elgin* (2003) *The Times*, 17 April 2003 (a case which came before the High Court of Justiciary in Scotland), the accused had been granted bail subject to a condition that he remain in his dwelling at all times except between 10.00 a.m. and noon. It was held that this (rather onerous) requirement did not amount to detention or deprivation of his liberty and did not constitute an infringement of his right to liberty under the ECHR, Article 5.

In *R (CPS) v Chorley Justices*, the question at issue was whether justices are empowered to attach a condition to the grant of bail that the accused present himself at the door of his residence when required to do so by a police officer during the hours of curfew. It was held that there is power under s. 3(6) to impose such 'door-step' conditions, but it is a question of fact in each case whether such a condition is necessary.

D7.31 **Electronic Monitoring** Electronic monitoring ('tagging') is available as a condition of bail in support of a curfew condition. The monitoring enables compliance with the curfew condition to be checked (and the police alerted to any breach). The system does not enable the suspect to be tracked, as it does not provide continuous information on the whereabouts of the accused. Rather, an alert is generated at a monitoring centre if the accused leaves the curfew address during the curfew period set by the court, or attempts to remove or tamper with the tag. Guidance on the use of electronic monitoring is given in Home Office Circular 25/2006. Paragraph 6 of the Circular makes the point that the intention of making tagging available is that it should be used as an alternative to remand in custody. Paragraph 7 notes that there are no statutory minimum or maximum curfew hours for bail cases, and that tagging of adults is not restricted to those who are charged with imprisonable offences (whereas the BA 1976, s. 3AA, restricts the tagging of juveniles to those who are charged with offences which carry imprisonment for adult offenders).

D7.32 **Guidance on Conditions** On 5 May 2006, Thomas LJ, the Senior Presiding Judge for England and Wales, issued a letter of guidance to judges and magistrates on the subject of bail (<http://www.judiciary.gov.uk/docs/judgments_guidance/protocols/bail_trials_absence.pdf>). To enable the court to contact the accused, the guidance notes that, 'where a defendant is reluctant to provide a telephone number and the court considers that conditions are necessary to secure his attendance, the court can consider making as a condition of bail the provision of a telephone number (and notifying the court of any change or of the fact that he/she cannot be contacted on that number)'. The guidance also notes that, if a court decides to use a curfew backed by electronic monitoring, it is 'important to consider including in the conditions of bail a condition that it is the responsibility of the defendant to gain the approval of the court for the designated bail address to be changed'.

D7.33 **Non-imprisonable Offences** In *Bournemouth Magistrates' Court, ex parte Cross* [1989] Crim LR 207, the point at issue was whether conditions could be imposed on bail for non-imprisonable offences. The accused, who was a hunt protester, was charged with a non-imprisonable offence under public order legislation. He was bailed on condition he did not attend another hunt meeting before his next court appearance. He was arrested for alleged breach of this condition and remanded in custody. On application for judicial review, the Divisional Court held that the condition had been validly imposed. The magistrates had been of the view that it was necessary to prevent the commission of further offences, and they were entitled to impose it by the BA 1976, s. 3(6).

Sureties

D7.34 A person granted bail in criminal proceedings may be required, before release on bail, to provide one or more sureties to secure his surrender to custody (BA 1976, s. 3(4)). Section 3(4) does not place any fetter on the discretion to demand a surety (cf. s. 3(6)). However, sch. 1, part I, para. 8 provides that no conditions shall be imposed under any of subsections (4) to (7) of s. 3 unless that appears to the court necessary to prevent the occurrence of any of the events mentioned in sch. 1, part I (i.e. the absconding of the defendant, the commission of offences by him or his interfering with witnesses etc.). However, a surety's only obligation is to ensure the accused's attendance at court — he is not expected to prevent the commission of offences or interference with witnesses. It follows that sureties should be required only in cases where there appears to be a risk of absconding.

It is sometimes argued that where the prosecution object to bail on the basis that the accused is likely to commit further offences, it is possible to require both a surety under the BA 1976 to secure the accused's attendance at court and also a surety to secure his good behaviour under the general powers given to magistrates by the Justices of the Peace Act 1968, s. 1(7) (see **E15** for the power to bind persons over to keep the peace and be of good behaviour). It is submitted, however, that use of s. 1(7) in this way would contravene the BA 1976, s. 3(3)(c), which provides that, 'Except as provided *by this section* . . . no other requirement shall be imposed [on the accused] as a condition of bail' [emphasis added].

Who can be a Surety? The BA 1976, s. 8, contains detailed provisions about the taking of sureties. In considering whether a proposed surety is suitable, regard may be had, *inter alia*, to the factors set out in s. 8(2): (a) the financial resources of the proposed surety: could the surety pay the sum which he is promising to pay?; (b) the character of the proposed surety and whether he has any previous convictions: is the surety a trustworthy person?; and (c) the proximity (whether kinship, place of residence or otherwise) of the proposed surety to the person for whom he is to be surety: is the proposed surety a friend, relative or employer? How far away does he live from the accused? The most important consideration under this heading is the relationship of the proposed surety to the accused: will the surety have the ability to control the accused so as to ensure that he attends court when he should? Put another way, would the fact that the surety stands to lose money if the accused absconds operate on the mind of the accused so as to deter him from absconding? **D7.35**

Taking the Surety The normal consequence for a surety if an accused fails to answer to his bail is that the surety is ordered to forfeit the entire sum in which he stood surety. As the surety is promising to pay money rather than handing over any money at the outset, it is important for the court to be assured that the surety has sufficient funds with which to honour the undertaking to the court. When a surety is taken in court, he is asked how he would pay the sum in which he is to stand surety were the accused to abscond. It is also standard practice for the police to check whether the surety has previous convictions; if he has, and depending on their age and nature, objection may be made to him acting as a surety. If no satisfactory surety is forthcoming at court, but the court is willing to grant bail subject to the provision of a satisfactory surety, the court simply fixes the amount in which the surety is to be bound and the accused remains in custody until the court's requirement can be fulfilled (BA 1976, s. 8(3)). To facilitate early release where the sureties are not at court, they may enter into their recognisances outside court (s. 8(4)). Paragraphs (a) to (d) of s. 8(4), in conjunction with the CrimPR, r. 19.5, list the persons who may accept a surety's recognisance. They are: a justice of the peace; a justices' clerk; a police officer who is either of or above the rank of inspector or is in charge of a police station; the governor of the prison or remand centre where the accused is being held; or, if bail has been granted by the Crown Court, an officer of that court. The court granting bail may, however, specify the person (or class of person) before whom the surety is to be taken or require that the surety be taken in court (see the opening words of s. 8(4)). If a person asked to accept a surety outside court refuses to do so because he is not satisfied about the surety's suitability, the surety may apply either to the court which granted bail or to a magistrates' court for the area where he resides to take his recognisance (s. 8(5)). **D7.36**

In *Birmingham Crown Court, ex parte Rashid Ali* (1999) 163 JP 145, the Divisional Court said (at p. 147, per Kennedy LJ) that 'it is irresponsible (and possibly a matter for consideration by a professional disciplinary body) for a qualified lawyer or legal executive to tender anyone as a surety unless he or she has reasonable grounds for believing that the surety will, if necessary, be able to meet his or her financial undertaking'.

It is quite common to have two or more sureties. If the court will grant bail only subject to a recognisance of a certain amount and that amount is beyond the means of the proposed surety, then one or more additional sureties will have to be found.

For discussion of the consequences for the surety if the accused absconds, see **D7.88**.

Making Sureties Continuous Where an accused is granted bail at a remand hearing and it is **D7.37**

D

Part D Procedure

anticipated that there may be several further appearances in the magistrates' court before his case is finally disposed of or sent to the Crown Court for trial, the court may, instead of simply directing him to appear at the end of the period of the remand, direct that he appear 'at every time and place to which during the course of the proceedings the hearing may be from time to time adjourned' (MCA 1980, s. 128(4)). Similarly, where bail is granted subject to a requirement for sureties, the surety's recognisance may be conditioned to secure that the accused 'appears at every time and place to which during the course of the proceedings the hearing may be from time to time adjourned' and also before the Crown Court in the event of the accused being sent there for trial (ibid.). Making the sureties continuous in this way is a useful device to avoid their having to come to court for each remand hearing. If they have not been made continuous and are not at court, the accused, even if granted bail on precisely the same terms as previously, cannot be released until the undertakings have been renewed (e.g., by going to a local police station). Section 128(4) even empowers magistrates to make the sureties' recognisances extend beyond the date when the case is sent to the Crown Court for trial (i.e. at a remand hearing they undertake to secure the accused's attendance before the Crown Court if he is sent there for trial). Where the accused's bail is conditional both on sureties and other conditions, there is no obligation to inform the sureties should the other conditions be relaxed or varied, but it might be good practice to warn sureties of this possibility at the time they enter into their recognisances (*Wells Street Magistrates' Court, ex parte Albanese* [1982] QB 333).

Deposit of Security

D7.38 Under the BA 1976, s.3(2), a person cannot stand as surety for himself. However, a person granted bail may be required to give security for his surrender to custody, i.e. deposit with the court money or some other valuable item which will be liable to forfeiture in the event of non-attendance in answer to bail (BA 1976, s. 3(5)). As with sureties, security may be required as a condition of bail only if it is considered necessary to prevent absconding. Where security has been given in pursuance of s. 3(5) and the person bailed absconds, the court may, unless there appears to have been reasonable cause for the failure to surrender to custody, order forfeiture of the security (see s. 5(7) to (9)).

In *R (Stevens) v Truro Magistrates' Court* [2002] 1 WLR 144, it was held that it is permissible for a third party to make available an asset to an accused in order to enable him to give it as security for his release on bail and that the court can accept such an asset. However, as it is the accused himself who gives the security, the arrangements the accused might make with those who helped him put up the requisite security are not a matter for the court. There is no obligation for the third party to be notified before the security is forfeited on the accused's non-attendance.

Other Statutory Bail Conditions

D7.39 There are a number of other conditions which may be imposed on the grant of bail pursuant to various provisions of the BA 1976.

D7.40 **Drug Assessments** Section 19(2) of the CJA 2003 added s. 3(6C) to (6E) to the BA 1976. These provide that where:

(a) the conditions set out in para. 6B of part 1 of sch. 1 are satisfied (namely, the accused is aged 18 or over, there is drug test evidence that he has a specified Class A drug in his body, and either the offence is a drugs offence associated with a specified Class A drug or the court is satisfied that there are substantial grounds for believing that the misuse of a specified Class A drug caused or contributed to that offence or provided its motivation), and

(b) the accused has been offered an assessment of whether he is dependent upon or has a propensity to misuse any specified Class A drugs (or such an assessment has been carried out and he has been offered follow-up), and

(c) he has agreed to undergo that assessment or participate in any follow-up,

then the court, if it grants bail, shall impose as a condition of bail that the accused both undergo the relevant assessment and participate in any relevant follow-up proposed to him or, if a relevant assessment has been carried out, that he participate in the relevant follow-up (s. 3(6D)).

Co-operation in the Making of Reports One of the purposes for which the court may impose a requirement under the BA 1976, s. 3(6), is to ensure that the accused will make himself 'available for the purpose of enabling inquiries or a report to be made to assist the court in dealing with him for the offence' (see s. 3(6)(d)). For obvious reasons, such a requirement will not generally be considered until the stage of an adjournment between conviction and sentence. However, there are two situations in which the court is obliged — not merely empowered — to make a requirement under s. 3(6)(d), and both can arise even before conviction. Those situations are: **D7.41**

(a) Where a magistrates' court is dealing with an imprisonable offence, it may adjourn the case under the PCC(S)A 2000, s. 11(1), for a medical examination of the accused provided that the court is satisfied that the accused did the act or made the omission charged, and is of the opinion that an inquiry ought to be made into his physical or mental condition before the method of dealing with him is determined. Although such an adjournment is conditional on the court being satisfied that the accused committed the *actus reus* of the offence, there is no need for a conviction to have been recorded. The purpose of ordering the examination is usually to discover whether the accused's mental condition is such that he might be dealt with by means such as a hospital order (whether with or without a prior conviction for the offence charged) or a community order with a condition for medical treatment. Under s. 11(3), where there is an adjournment under s. 11(1) and the magistrates determine to remand the accused on bail, the court *shall* impose conditions under BA 1976, s. 3(6). Those conditions must include requirements that he: (i) submits to examination by a duly qualified medical practitioner (or, if the inquiry is into his mental condition and the court so directs, by two practitioners); and (ii) for the purpose of the examination, attends at such place or on such practitioner as the court directs and complies with any directions given to him for the purpose.
(b) Where a court grants bail to an accused charged with murder, it must, unless satisfied that satisfactory reports on his mental condition have already been obtained, impose as conditions of bail requirements that he undergo examination by two medical practitioners (including one Home Office approved psychiatrist) and attend such place as directed for the purpose of the examination (BA 1976, s. 3(6A) and (6B)). The importance in such cases of obtaining full medical and, in particular, psychiatric reports on the accused while he is still on remand prior to trial or even committal is that the reports may lay the foundation for a defence of diminished responsibility or, alternatively, assist the prosecution in rebutting such a defence. Subsections (6A) and (6B) ensure that the reports will be forthcoming, even though the granting of bail precludes the necessary examinations being conducted while the accused is detained in prison or remand centre. In *Central Criminal Court, ex parte Porter* [1992] Crim LR 121, the Divisional Court said that if no such condition was imposed, then the decision to grant bail would be a nullity. The court added that disclosure to the Crown of a medical report obtained pursuant to subsection (6A) was within the discretion of the trial judge when he had seen the report (or, exceptionally, the discretion of such other judge as had to conduct any pre-trial review).

Taking Legal Advice The court also has power to require an accused, as a condition of bail, **D7.42**

to attend an interview with a legal adviser before his next appearance in court (BA 1976, s. 3(6)(e)). The aim is to save the time of the court by ensuring that he receives legal advice, in advance of the hearing, to decide on how to respond to the charge. Clearly, if the accused indicates that he does not wish to be legally represented, such a condition should not be imposed. If the condition is attached, then the accused should be told of the consequences of failing to comply. Guidance issued to judges and magistrates has made it clear that, if the accused fails to attend an interview, his solicitor should not be expected to report the breach of the condition (see Home Office Circular 34/1998, para. 11).

D7.43 **Juveniles** Section 3(6ZAA) of the BA 1976, inserted by the CJPA 2001, s. 131(1), provides that, where a juvenile is granted bail, compliance with any bail conditions can be enforced through electronic monitoring. Under s. 3AA such a condition may be imposed provided that:

(a) the juvenile has attained the age of 12;
(b) either:
 (i) he is charged with a violent or sexual offence, or an offence carrying at least 14 years' imprisonment, or
 (ii) he is charged with an imprisonable offence and he has a recent history of repeatedly committing imprisonable offences while remanded on bail or to local authority accommodation; and
(c) electronic monitoring arrangements are available in the area and the necessary provision can be made;
(d) a youth offending team has informed the court of its opinion that the imposition of the requirement is suitable for the juvenile.

Parent Standing Surety for a Juvenile

D7.44 The general rule is that the obligations of a surety extend only to securing the accused's attendance at court. A surety is *not* responsible for preventing any other possible defaults of the accused while on bail (e.g., intimidating witnesses or breaching a condition of bail). However, the BA 1976, s. 3(7), provides that, where the accused is a juvenile and his parent or guardian stands surety for him, the court may require the parent or guardian to secure that the juvenile complies with any condition of bail imposed by virtue of s. 3(6). A requirement under s. 3(7) can be imposed only with the consent of the parent or guardian, and the sum in which he binds himself may not exceed £50.

Applications to Vary the Conditions of Bail

D7.45 Where bail has been granted in criminal proceedings subject to conditions, the accused may apply for the conditions to be varied (BA 1976, s. 3(8)(a)). The application should be made to the court which granted bail (or, in the case of a committal for trial or sentence, the Crown Court). Furthermore, the prosecution may make a similar application either for existing conditions to be varied or, in a case where the court originally granted unconditional bail, for conditions to be imposed (s. 3(8)(b)).

Breach of Bail Conditions

D7.46 Breach of any condition imposed may result in the accused being arrested without warrant under the BA 1976, s. 7(3) and his bail being withdrawn. See D7.76.

PROCEDURE FOR BAIL APPLICATIONS IN MAGISTRATES' COURTS

Application Procedure

The CrimPR do not deal specifically with the procedure to be followed when a person wishes to apply to a magistrates' court for bail in criminal proceedings. Assuming the presumption in favour of bail applies by virtue of the BA 1976, s. 4(1), the onus is on the court to justify any refusal of bail in accordance with sch. 1 to the Act. This applies both when the accused first appears and at all subsequent appearances while he remains within the scope of s. 4(1) (see para. 1 of part IIA of sch. 1). **D7.47**

The question of bail is always a matter for the court. However, when adjourning the case of an unconvicted accused to whom s. 4(1) applies and who is entitled to make an argued bail application under sch. 1, part IIA (see **D7.49**), normal practice is to ask the prosecution if they have any objections to bail. The prosecution representative then summarises the objections (or, as the case may be, states that there are no objections). Usually, there is included in the CPS file a standard form on which the police officer in the case outlines his objections to bail, if any. The prosecution advocate usually has little alternative but to base his remarks on this form, as no officer connected with the case will be present in court. The justices will normally be told of the accused's previous convictions (including any convictions for failure to surrender to custody) when the prosecution give their objections to bail. Following the prosecution objections, the defence representative (or the accused in person if unrepresented) may present the arguments for bail (whether conditional or unconditional). Even where the defence choose not to make a bail application, it is submitted that the prosecution should still be prepared to present at least cursory objections to bail so that the court will be able to base a refusal on one of the reasons contained in sch. 1.

The question of bail is normally dealt with on the basis of submissions from the prosecution and defence. There is no requirement for formal evidence to be given (see *Re Moles* [1981] Crim LR 170 and *Mansfield JJ, ex parte Sharkey* [1985] QB 613 at p. 626, per Lord Lane CJ). Either party may, however, adduce evidence in support of their respective arguments, for example, a police officer to substantiate the objections to bail or proposed sureties to further the application for bail. Such witnesses give their evidence on the *voir dire* form of oath.

The prosecution will not normally reply to the application for bail by the defence. However, the prosecutor does have a right to reply to the defence submissions if this is necessary to correct alleged misstatements of fact in what the defence have said (*Isleworth Crown Court, ex parte Commissioner of Customs and Excise* [1990] Crim LR 859).

Where a case is adjourned for reports following conviction, the prosecution are *not* usually asked if they object to bail. At this stage the question is conventionally regarded as one for the court, subject to representations from the defence. This may reflect the general rule that, in matters of sentencing, the prosecution remain neutral rather than trying to influence the court one way or the other.

Having heard the prosecution objections to bail, and the answer of the defence to those objections, the court announces its decision.

Effect of the Human Rights Act 1998 The form taken by bail hearings may be open to question in the light of the HRA 1998, and the safeguards contained in the ECHR, Article 6. The question is the extent to which the safeguards in Article 6 should apply to the reviews of pre-trial detention that are guaranteed by Article 5. This question was examined (in the context of a hearing involving an accused arrested for breach of a bail condition) in *R (DPP) v Havering Magistrates' Court* [2001] 1 WLR 805. In that case, the need for formal evidence **D7.48**

and procedures was rejected, in favour of a focus upon the quality of the material, with the accused given a right to cross-examine if oral evidence is presented.

Right to Make Repeated Argued Bail Applications

D7.49 Where the accused is remanded in custody, he may make a fully argued application at the next hearing, regardless of whether he is repeating arguments already placed before the previous bench (BA 1976, sch. 1, part IIA, para. 2). Unless he consents to being remanded in his absence, the next hearing will be within eight clear days (MCA 1980, s. 128(6)). (Section 128A of the MCA 1980, which permits remands in custody of up to 28 days, applies only if the accused has already been remanded in custody for the offence on at least one previous occasion.) Therefore, the wait between being refused bail on a first appearance and being able to argue again for bail on a second appearance is relatively short. However, should that second argued application fail, the BA 1976, sch. 1, part IIA, para. 3, is applicable. This provides that, where the accused has been remanded in custody twice and on at least one of those occasions a fully argued bail application was made, the court need not hear arguments as to fact or law which it has heard previously. This is so even though at each hearing the court should nominally consider whether he ought to remain in custody (sch. 1, part IIA, para. 1). Paragraph 3 effectively entitles the magistrates to treat the finding of the previous bench (that there were grounds for refusing bail) as a form of *res iudicata*. They may therefore refuse to hear argument in favour of bail, and need consider the question only to the limited extent of satisfying themselves that the accused has exhausted the argued bail applications to which he is entitled as of right and that there has been no change of circumstances since the last argued application to entitle him to reopen the matter.

The Law Commission Paper *Bail and the Human Rights Act 1998* (Law Com No. 269), contains guidance aiming to ensure that the provisions relating to a change in circumstances are applied in a way that is compatible with the ECHR. This guidance states (at paras. 12.23 and 13.33) that courts should be willing, at regular intervals of 28 days, to consider arguments that the passage of time constitutes, in the particular case before the court, a change in circumstances so as to require full argument. If the court finds that the passage of time does amount to a relevant changed circumstance, or that there are other circumstances which may be relevant to the need to detain the accused that have changed or come to notice since the last fully argued bail hearing, then a full bail application should follow in which all the arguments, old and new, could be put forward and taken into account.

Part IIA of sch. 1 to the BA 1976 was intended to give statutory effect to the decision of the Divisional Court in *Nottingham Justices, ex parte Davies* [1981] QB 38. That decision may therefore be regarded as a useful aid to the interpretation of part IIA. In *Ex parte Davies*, the court was asked to rule on the lawfulness of the policy of the Nottingham Bench that the accused (or his representative) would be allowed to make a full bail application at the first and second hearings; at all subsequent hearings, the bench would refuse to consider matters previously before the court. In other words, from the third remand hearing onwards, they would not entertain an argued bail application unless there had been a change in circumstances since the last such application. Donaldson LJ (with whose judgment Bristow J concurred) upheld the policy. He said (at pp. 43–4, emphasis added):

> . . . I accept that the fact that a bench of the same or a different constitution has decided on a previous occasion or occasions that one or more of the schedule 1 exceptions applies and has accordingly remanded the accused in custody, does not absolve the bench on each subsequent occasion from considering whether the accused is entitled to bail, whether or not an application is made.
>
> However, this does not mean that the justices should ignore their own previous decision or a previous decision of their colleagues. Far from it. On those previous occasions, the court will have been under an obligation to grant bail unless it was satisfied that a schedule 1 exception was made out. If it was so satisfied, it will have recorded the exceptions which in its judgment were

> applicable. This . . . is a finding by the court that schedule 1 circumstances then existed and it is to be treated like every other finding of the court. *It is* res iudicata *or analogous thereto*. It stands as a finding unless and until it is overturned on appeal. . . . It follows that on the next occasion when bail is considered [by the magistrates] the court should treat, as an essential fact, that at the time when the matter of bail was last considered, schedule 1 circumstances did indeed exist. *Strictly speaking, they can and should only investigate whether that situation has changed since then*. . . .
>
> I would inject only one qualification to the general rule that justices can and should only investigate whether the situation has changed since the last remand in custody. The finding on that occasion that schedule 1 circumstances existed will have been based upon matters known to the court at that time. The court considering afresh the question of bail is both entitled and bound to take account not only of a change in circumstances which has occurred since that last occasion, but also of circumstances which, although they then existed, were not brought to the attention of the court. . . . The question is a little wider than 'Has there been a change?' It is 'Are there any new considerations which were not before the court when the accused was last remanded in custody?'

Applying these principles, Donaldson LJ held that the practice of always allowing two (rather than one) argued applications was justified because, although the finding that there were sch. 1 circumstances for refusing bail on the occasion of the first remand in custody was in theory as much a finding of the court as the similar finding on the second occasion and so ought to have precluded the making of the second application, in practice the experience of the justices showed that first bail applications were almost invariably under-prepared, so that there would in fact be new considerations before the second bench which were not before the first.

Interpretation of Part IIA The BA 1976, part IIA, paras. 2 and 3, oblige the court to consider any relevant arguments, whether of fact or of law, which were not before the court when bail was refused. This is so whether the argument arises out of a change in circumstances since the last unsuccessful application, or is an argument that could have been put on the previous occasion but, for whatever reason, was not. Particular points arising from part IIA are: **D7.50**

(a) *Does the accused have to make his argued application on his first and second appearances?* Paragraph 2 does not state, as it might have done, that the accused is entitled to two fully argued bail applications. It merely provides that, *at the first hearing* after he was refused bail, he may support his application with any argument of fact or law, regardless of whether it was previously advanced. Thus, on a literal interpretation of para. 2, if an accused chooses not to make a bail application on the occasion of his first appearance and is accordingly remanded in custody, he may make an argued application at any one of his subsequent appearances, but if that application fails he is debarred from a further argued application unless he can rely on matters which were not earlier placed before the court. It follows that an accused seeking bail who wants two opportunities to do so in the magistrates' court should make applications on both the first and second remand appearances — otherwise a court interpreting part IIA strictly would be justified in saying that he had neglected to avail himself of one opportunity by not making a fully argued application on his first appearance.

(b) *What is the situation where the justices conclude (under para. 5 of part I of sch. 1) that it has not been practicable to obtain sufficient information to decide to grant bail?* In *Calder Justices, ex parte Kennedy* (1992) 156 JP 716, the Divisional Court held that a decision under para. 5 is not a decision not to grant bail. The justices are merely saying that they are not in a position to decide the question of bail. It does not therefore count for the purposes of para. 2 of part IIA of sch. 1.

(c) *What is the position if the accused consents to being remanded in his absence under the MCA 1980, s. 128 (see* **D5.19***)?* In *Dover and East Kent Justices, ex parte Dean* (1991) 156 JP 357, the accused made no bail application on his first appearance and consented to be remanded in his absence for three weeks. He appeared before the justices at the end of that period and wished to make a bail application. The Divisional Court held that the occasions when he was remanded in his absence were not 'hearings' for the purpose of para. 2, and so he had a right to make a bail application when he came before the justices at the end of the period of remand by consent.

(d) *Is the court obliged to consider only the new arguments?* Where the accused has exhausted his automatic entitlement of fully argued applications but claims that a new consideration has arisen which was not placed before the court on the earlier occasions, para. 3 could be construed merely as obliging the court to hear the argument of fact or law not previously advanced, rather than obliging it to reopen the entire question of bail. It is submitted, however, that to consider only the new consideration in isolation from the other arguments for bail would be an artificial exercise, and that the identifying of a new consideration relevant to bail should entitle the accused to make a further full bail application in which both the fresh and the old arguments may be relied on.

(e) *Does the court have a discretion to allow as many argued applications as it wishes?* Paragraph 3 merely states that, at the third and subsequent remand hearings, the court 'need not' hear arguments which it has heard previously. Prima facie the paragraph does not debar the court from entertaining yet another fully argued application, but merely gives it a discretion in the matter. On the other hand, Donaldson LJ in *Nottingham Justices, ex parte Davies* [1981] QB 38 based his approval of the practice of the Nottingham Justices on the principle of *res iudicata.* It is unclear whether para. 3 is meant to override *Ex parte Davies* (in which case magistrates always have a discretion to hear as many fully argued applications for bail as they wish), or is merely giving statutory force to the main thrust of the decision (in which case a scrupulous bench might say that, much as they would like to re-open the question of bail, they are bound by their colleagues' earlier decisions and can do nothing in the absence of fresh arguments or considerations).

(f) *Is the accused always entitled to a fully argued bail application on committal for trial?* In *Reading Crown Court, ex parte Malik* [1981] QB 451, Donaldson LJ said at p. 454, that the moment of committal for trial must be an occasion upon which an accused person is entitled to have his right to bail fully reviewed. This view was based on the proposition that the court will be in a much better position to assess the nature and seriousness of the offence and the strength of the prosecution case. In *Slough Justices, ex parte Duncan* (1982) 75 Cr App R 384, however, the Divisional Court held that, where the accused's legal representative had said that there had been no material change in circumstances except 'the committal proceedings and the changes which flow from those proceedings', the justices were entitled to refuse to hear a bail application. It follows that a committal for trial does not necessarily entitle the accused to re-open the question of bail. Where the committal is without consideration of the evidence, the court will not in fact be made aware of any additional information about the case against the accused. This question will become irrelevant when committal proceedings for either-way offences are replaced with the transfer procedure under the CDA 1998, s. 51, when the relevant provisions of the CJA 2003 come fully into force.

(g) *How should the justices express a decision not to allow an argued application?* Since in theory the court is obliged to consider bail each time an accused who is entitled to the benefit of the BA 1976, s. 4(1), appears before it in custody, it is unwise for the magistrates simply to say that they 'will not allow a fresh application for bail', or words to that effect. The more accurate terminology is: 'As there is no new material before us relevant to bail, bail will be refused'. This avoids giving the impression that they have simply refused to consider the question (per Ormrod LJ in *Ex parte Duncan* at p. 389).

Enlarging Bail

D7.51 The MCA 1980, s. 129, empowers a magistrates' court which has already remanded an accused to make further remands in his absence. This power should be distinguished from the power under s. 128(3A) to remand an accused in custody on up to three consecutive occasions without his being brought before the court if he has consented not to be produced. Section 129(1) applies if the court is satisfied that, on the day to which the accused was remanded, he is unable to attend 'by reason of illness or accident'. It may then remand him again in his absence. The subsection applies regardless of whether the remand is in custody or on bail. Moreover, notwithstanding s. 128(6), a remand in custody under s. 129(1) may exceed eight clear days. Thus, if an accused remanded in custody on an earlier occasion is ill in prison and will not be well enough to attend court for several weeks, the magistrates may extend the period of the remand until such time as he is likely to have recovered.

By contrast with s. 129(1), s. 129(3) applies only if the accused has been remanded on bail. The subsection permits the court to appoint, in his absence, a later time as the time at which he is to appear. The appointment of the new time is deemed to be a further remand (ibid.). This power is useful when unforeseen developments mean that the case will not be able to proceed on the date to which it was originally adjourned. By agreement between the court and the parties, a new date can be fixed without the necessity for the accused appearing. The power is also useful when the accused fails to appear on the date to which he was bailed but an acceptable explanation for his non-appearance is put before the court. Instead of issuing a warrant for his arrest, the magistrates may simply adjourn and enlarge bail in his absence. Whenever bail is enlarged under either s. 129(1) or s. 129(3), the recognisances of the sureties may be correspondingly enlarged to secure the accused's appearance on the new date (s. 129(2) and (3)(a)).

The MCA 1980, s. 129, is supplemented by s. 43(1), which relates to first appearances before a magistrates' court. Section 43(1) provides that, where an accused has been bailed from the police station following charge subject to a duty to surrender at court on a certain date, the court may 'appoint a later time as the time at which he is to appear and may enlarge the recognisances of any sureties'.

STATING AND RECORDING DECISIONS ABOUT BAIL

Section 5 of the BA 1976 imposes a number of requirements about the giving and recording of decisions about bail and the reasons for those decisions. **D7.52**

Duty to Make a Record of the Decision

Where a court grants bail, or withholds bail from someone to whom the BA 1976, s. 4, applies, or appoints a different time or place for a person granted bail to surrender to custody, or varies any conditions of bail or imposes conditions in respect of bail, it must make a record of the decision. The accused is entitled to a copy of the record on request (BA 1976, s. 5(1)). By virtue of the CrimPR, r. 19.11, any record relating to bail that a magistrates' court is required to make must be entered in the court register. As to Crown Court decisions on bail, r. 19.18(8) requires the record to be entered into the court file for the case and to include: (a) the effect of the decision; (b) a statement of any condition imposed in respect of bail or, in a case where the conditions of bail have been varied, a statement of the conditions as varied; and (c) where bail is withheld, a statement of the paragraph of sch. 1 to the BA 1976 on which the decision was based. **D7.53**

Reasons for Decisions relating to Bail

Where a magistrates' court or the Crown Court: (a) withholds bail from an accused prima facie entitled to bail under the BA 1976, s. 4, or (b) imposes conditions on the grant of bail to such a person (or varies conditions already imposed upon him), it must give reasons for withholding bail or, as the case may be, imposing or varying conditions of bail (BA 1976, s. 5(3)). The purpose of the giving of reasons is to enable the accused to consider making an application for bail (or for the variation or removal of conditions of bail) to another court. A **D7.54** note of the reasons must be included in the record of the court's decision (s. 5(4)). Also, the accused must be given a copy of the note (ibid.), unless the decision was taken by the Crown Court and the accused is legally represented, in which case a copy need be provided only if his counsel or solicitor so requests (s. 5(5)). It should be noted that the obligation to give reasons under s. 5(4) arises only if the accused has the benefit of s. 4. If, for example, bail pending appeal is refused to a person summarily convicted and given a custodial sentence, the court is not required by the BA 1976 to explain the refusal, since the case falls outside s. 4.

Reasons for Granting Bail

D7.55 Where a magistrates' court or the Crown Court grants bail to a person to whom the BA 1976, s. 4, applies after hearing representations from the prosecutor in favour of withholding bail, it must give reasons for its decision (s. 5(2A)).

Informing Unrepresented Accused of his Right to Apply to Other Courts

D7.56 Where a magistrates' court withholds bail from an unrepresented accused and sends him for trial to the Crown Court or issues a certificate under s. 5(6A) (see below), he must be informed that he may apply to the Crown Court for bail (BA 1976, s. 5(6)).

Certificates of Full Argument

D7.57 Subsections (6A) to (6C) of s. 5 of the BA 1976 deal with certificates of full argument. Where a magistrates' court adjourns the case under the PCC(S)A 2000, s. 11, or the CDA 1998, s. 52(5), or the MCA 1980, s. 5, 10, 17C, 18 or 24C, and remands the accused in custody after hearing a fully argued bail application, it must, subject to what follows, issue a certificate confirming that full argument was heard (s. 5(6A)). An adjournment during summary trial (under the MCA 1980, s. 10) includes an adjournment for reports after conviction, so the obligation to issue a certificate may arise if the accused is remanded in custody at that stage. Moreover, the obligation to issue a certificate also applies where bail is refused on an adjournment under the PCC(S)A 2000, s. 11, for medical reports.

The obligation arises only if either the court has not previously heard full argument on a bail application made by the accused in the proceedings in question, or it has previously heard such argument but is satisfied that there has been a change in circumstances or that new considerations have been placed before it (s. 5(6A)(b)). In a case where the court heard a second or subsequent fully argued application on the basis of a change in circumstances or new considerations, the certificate must state what the change was (s. 5(6B)). The accused must be given a copy of the certificate (s. 5(6C)). The significance of the issue of a certificate of full argument is that the right to apply to the Crown Court for bail is dependent on it (Supreme Court Act 1981, s. 81(1)(g) and (1J)).

OPTIONS OPEN TO AN ACCUSED REMANDED IN CUSTODY BY MAGISTRATES OR GIVEN BAIL SUBJECT TO CONDITIONS

D7.58 Where the accused is refused bail by the magistrates' court, he may apply for bail to the Crown Court. In certain cases, it may also be possible to seek judicial review of the refusal of bail (see **D7.66**). An appeal can also be made against a decision of the magistrates' court to impose conditions on bail.

Appeal to the Crown Court

D7.59 The restrictions on the right of an accused to make repeated bail applications to the magistrates' court are offset to some extent by the possibility of applying to the Crown Court for bail. The right to apply is contained in the Supreme Court Act 1981, s. 81(1)(g), as qualified by s. 81(1J). Section 81(1)(g) provides that the Crown Court may grant bail to any person who has been remanded in custody by a magistrates' court on adjourning a case under the PCC(S)A 2000, s. 11, or the CDA 1998, s. 52(5), or the MCA 1980, s. 5, 10, 17C, 18 or 24C. Section 81(1J) provides that the Crown Court may grant bail under s. 81(1)(g) only if 'the magistrates' court which remanded [the accused] in custody has certified under section 5(6A) of the Bail Act 1976 that it heard full argument on his application for bail before it refused the application'. As we have seen, the BA 1976, s. 5(6A), imposes a duty on a magistrates' court which refuses bail following full argument to issue a certificate to that effect if either it was the first occasion of such argument or there has been a change in circumstances or new considerations since the previous argued application. Thus, the combined effect of the SCA 1981, s. 81(1)(g) and (1J) and the BA 1976, s. 5(6A), is that, where a fully argued bail application is refused by magistrates, the defence should obtain a certificate of full argument from the court which they may then use to found a further application to the Crown Court. The right to apply to the Crown Court is thus dependent on a fully argued application having been made before the magistrates.

If the Crown Court confirms the refusal of bail, it may be possible for the accused to seek judicial review of that decision (see **D7.66**).

Once the accused has been sent for trial, he may apply to the Crown Court for bail by virtue of s. 81(1)(a) of the 1981 Act, which empowers the Crown Court to grant bail to any person who has been committed or sent in custody to appear before it. At this stage, there is no need to rely on a certificate of full argument.

Appeal against Imposition of Conditions

The CJA 2003, s. 16(1), enables an accused to appeal to the Crown Court against the imposition of certain bail conditions, namely those set out in s. 16(3): **D7.60**

(a) that the person concerned resides away from a particular place or area,
(b) that the person concerned resides at a particular place other than a bail hostel,
(c) for the provision of a surety or sureties or the giving of a security,
(d) that the person concerned remains indoors between certain hours,
(e) imposed under s. 3(6ZAA) of the 1976 Act (requirements with respect to electronic monitoring), or
(f) that the person concerned makes no contact with another person.

The right of appeal under s. 16 can be exercised only if the accused has previously made an application to the magistrates (under the BA 1976, s. 3(8)(a)) for the conditions to be varied (s. 16(4), (5), and (6)). Once the Crown Court has disposed of the appeal, no further appeal can be brought under s. 16 unless an application or further application under the BA 1976, s. 3(8)(a) is made to the magistrates' court after the appeal (see s. 16(8)).

PROCEDURE FOR BAIL APPLICATIONS IN THE CROWN COURT

Notice of Appeal

The procedure for bail applications in the Crown Court is governed by the CrimPR, r. 19.18. **D7.61**
The rule applies only when the application is made otherwise than during the actual hearing of the proceedings (r. 19.18(1)). By r. 19.18(2), written notice of intention to make the application must be given to the prosecutor and, if the prosecution is being carried on by the CPS, to the appropriate Crown Prosecutor; this must be done at least 24 hours before the hearing of the application. The notice must be in the form specified by the *Consolidated Criminal Practice Direction*, annex D, or to like effect (r. 19.18(4)). The applicant is required

to give details of the previous applications for bail (or for variation of conditions of bail), to state the nature and grounds of the present application, to give details of any proposed sureties, to answer any objections to bail that have been raised previously, and to list any previous convictions. The options open to the prosecutor on receiving notice are:

(a) to notify the court and the applicant that he wishes to be represented at the hearing; or
(b) to notify them that he does not oppose the application; or
(c) to send the court a written statement of his reasons for opposing the application, at the same time sending a copy of the statement to the applicant (r. 19.18(3)).

Usually, the CPS will instruct counsel to oppose the application. The accused has no right to be present at the hearing of the application, but may be given leave to attend by the court (r. 19.18(5)). An accused who has been unable to instruct a solicitor to act on his behalf may request the court to assign the Official Solicitor to act for him (r. 19.18(6)). Where that is done, the court may dispense with the requirements of notice etc. and deal with the application in a summary manner (r. 19.18(7)). Since legal aid in criminal proceedings covers bail applications to the Crown Court, it is unlikely that an applicant would be forced to ask for the Official Solicitor's aid.

The Hearing

D7.62 The application is normally heard in chambers (see CrimPR, r. 16.11(2)(a)). Where possible, it should be listed before the judge by whom the case is expected to be tried (see the *Consolidated Criminal Practice Direction*, para. IV.33, *Allocation of business within the Crown Court* at para. IV.33.6). In practice, it is unlikely that any particular judge will have been allocated to the case at such an early stage, and the application will therefore be heard by any circuit judge or recorder sitting at an appropriate location of the Crown Court. The hearing follows the pattern of a bail application in the magistrates' court, with counsel for the prosecution summarising the objections and counsel for the applicant responding.

If bail is granted to an accused who was refused it by magistrates at a remand hearing, the Crown Court may direct him to appear 'at a time and place which the magistrates' court could have directed' (Supreme Court Act 1981, s. 81(1H)). If bail is granted to an accused who was sent for trial in custody, his obligation is simply to appear on the day the case is listed for trial. Any sureties required by the Crown Court may enter into their recognisances before, *inter alia*, an officer of the Crown Court, a police officer who is either in charge of a police station or of the rank of inspector or above, or the governor of the prison or remand centre where the accused is presently detained (CrimPR, r. 19.22(1)).

It is possible for a bail application to be heard in public. According to *R (Malik) v Central Criminal Court* [2006] 4 All ER 1141, when considering such an application, the court must start from the 'fundamental presumption in favour of open justice' (Gray J at [40]). The court therefore has to consider whether it is necessary, in the interests of justice, to depart from the ordinary rule of open justice. The judgment makes it clear that this is not an exercise of discretion (which implies a judicial choice between two or more equally proper courses), but of judgement as to whether a departure from the norm is justified (at [30]). It may, for example, be appropriate for the court to sit in chambers if the delay involved in arranging a public hearing would defeat the purpose of the application (at [31]). It may be in the interests of the accused for the bail application to be heard in private, for example, (i) where the prosecution need to rehearse a damaging case against the accused; (ii) where the prosecution intend to give detailed reasons for fearing that the accused will not surrender if given bail; (iii) where the accused's previous convictions will be referred to; (iv) where it will or may be necessary to reveal personal and confidential information about the accused or about prosecution witnesses or others; and (v) where the court may need to be told about information which has been provided to the prosecuting authorities by the accused or by someone else connected with the case (at [33]). Gray J added that it does not follow that bail applications have to be listed and called on in open court and then adjourned to chambers only if a case is made for doing so. He said that there is nothing objectionable in listing bail applications on the provisional assumption that the interests of justice call for a closed hearing, so long as any application to sit in public is approached on the footing that it must be acceded to unless there is a sound reason for excluding the public. Such an application will ordinarily come from one or both of the parties, but it may also legitimately come from the media or some other third party (at [35]). Another point which emerges from *Malik* is that, where the accused has legal representation, he has no right to be produced from prison for the purposes of a bail application. Gray J pointed out that the increasing use of video links between the court and the prison where the accused is detained effectively removes any disadvantage to the accused by reason of his not being physically present when the application for bail is heard (at [38]). It is submitted that it follows from this that where no video link is available a request for an accused to be produced should be looked on more favourably by the court.

Repeated Bail Applications in the Crown Court

Part IIA of sch. 1 to the BA 1976 applies to bail applications in the Crown Court just as it applies to applications before the magistrates. Therefore, if one application for bail has already been made to the Crown Court, a further argued application may not be presented unless there are fresh arguments or considerations to put before the court (see **D7.43**). **D7.63**

Application for Bail during the Crown Court Proceedings

Paragraph III.25.2 of the *Consolidated Practice Direction* makes the point that, once the trial has begun, the grant of bail during adjournments (such as lunch-time) or overnight, is a matter for the discretion of the trial judge. An important consideration is whether it is possible to segregate the accused from witnesses and jurors. Paragraph III.25.3 states that where the accused was on bail before the trial, he should not be refused overnight bail during the trial unless, in the opinion of the judge, there are positive reasons to justify such refusal. Acceptable reasons are likely to be that (a) a point has been reached where there is a real danger that the accused will abscond, either because the case is going badly for him, or for any other reason, or (b) there is a real danger that he may interfere with witnesses or jurors. Paragraph III.25.4 makes it clear that there is no rule of practice that bail should be revoked when the summing-up has begun, but adds that each case must be decided in the light of its own circumstances and having regard to the judge's assessment of the risks involved. If the accused is convicted, the grant of bail following the verdict depends on the gravity of the offence and the likely sentence (para III.25.5). **D7.64**

BAIL BY THE HIGH COURT

Statutory Bail Jurisdiction of the High Court

The CJA 1967, s. 22(1), formerly gave the High Court jurisdiction to grant bail where it had been refused bail by a magistrates' court, or to vary the conditions of bail granted by a magistrates' court. However, this power was abolished by the CJA 2003, s. 17. There remain, however, a number of instances where the High Court has a statutory jurisdiction to grant bail: **D7.65**

(1) Under the CJA 1967, s. 22(1) (as amended by the CJA 2003, s. 17), where (a) a magistrates' court withholds bail in criminal proceedings or imposes conditions in granting bail in criminal proceedings, and (b) it does so where an application to the court to state a case for the opinion of the High Court is made, the High Court may grant bail or vary the conditions (see **D28.19**). Thus, the High Court can entertain an application for bail (or to vary the conditions) under s. 22 only if the accused is appealing by way of

case stated against conviction (or sentence, although such appeals are rarely appropriate) and the magistrates have withheld bail or granted only conditional bail.

(2) Under the CJA 1948, s. 37, the High Court may also grant bail to a person in three circumstances:
   (a) where he is appealing to the High Court by way of case stated from a decision of the Crown Court (in practice, this will be where an accused appeals from the magistrates' court to the Crown Court and then seeks to appeal to the High Court from the decision of the Crown Court) (see **D28.30**);
   (b) where he is appealing from the Crown Court to the High Court by way of judicial review, seeking an order quashing the decision of the Crown Court (again this will be the case where the accused is challenging a decision of the Crown Court in its appellate capacity) (see **D28.21**); and
   (c) where he has been convicted or sentenced by a magistrates' court and is appealing to the High Court by way of judicial review, seeking an order quashing the decision of the magistrates.

Challenging Refusal of Bail by Way of Judicial Review

D7.66 There is also the possibility of challenging a refusal of bail by way of judicial review. Although Stanley Burnton J in *R (Lipinski) v Wolverhampton Crown Court* [2005] EWHC 1950 (Admin) (at [17]–[20]), expressed doubts about the availability of judicial review to challenge the refusal of bail by a Crown Court judge because of the effect of the Supreme Court Act 1981, s. 29(3) (which excludes judicial review of the Crown Court 'in matters relating to trial on indictment'), the weight of authority clearly establishes that s. 29 is not to be regarded as a bar to judicial review of such decisions. In *R (M) v Isleworth Crown Court* [2005] EWHC 363, it was held that, although the High Court has jurisdiction to judicially review a refusal of bail, that jurisdiction should be exercised sparingly, and the *Wednesbury* principles should be applied robustly. Maurice Kay LJ considered the effect of s. 29(3), and said that 'a decision as to *bail at an early stage of criminal proceedings* [emphasis added] does not relate to trial on indictment as that expression has been interpreted in cases such as *R v Manchester Crown Court, ex parte DPP* (1994) 98 Cr App R 461', in that such a decision does not arise in the issue between the Crown and the accused formulated by the indictment (the test propounded in that case by Lord Browne-Wilkinson). His lordship referred to the case of *Cox* [1997] 1 Cr App R 20, where it had been held that a refusal of bail was not susceptible to judicial review, saying that the rationale of that decision was the availability of an alternative remedy, namely the possibility that then existed of an application to a High Court judge. However, that right has been abolished by the CJA 2003, s. 17. His lordship went on to point out that s. 17(6)(b) of the 2003 Act provides that 'Nothing in this section affects . . . any right of a person to apply for a writ of habeas corpus or any other prerogative remedy'. He said that he had no doubt that 'prerogative remedies' in that context embraced those set out in the Supreme Court Act 1981, s. 29(1), namely mandatory orders, prohibiting orders and quashing orders. That meant, he said, that the Divisional Court now has jurisdiction to review a bail decision by the Crown Court. Having ruled that judicial review was available in such cases, Maurice Kay LJ went on to say (at [11]–[12]):

> Although we have jurisdiction by reason of s. 17(6)(b), I am in no doubt that it is a jurisdiction which we should exercise very sparingly indeed. It would be ironic and retrograde if, having abolished a relatively short and simple remedy on the basis that it amounted to wasteful duplication, Parliament has, by a side wind, created a more protracted and expensive remedy of common application . . . The test must be on *Wednesbury* principles, but robustly applied and with this court always keeping in mind that Parliament has understandably vested the decision in judges in the Crown Court who have everyday experience of, and feel for, bail applications. Of course if bail were to be refused on a basis such as 'I always refuse in this type of case', or some other unjudicial basis, then this court would and should interfere.

This decision was followed in *R (Shergill) v Harrow Crown Court* [2005] EWHC 648, confirming that s. 29(3) of the 1981 Act does not preclude the Divisional Court from considering applications for judicial review of a decision to refuse bail, but that it was only in exceptional cases that the Court would consider it right to review the decision of a Crown Court judge in whom the relevant powers had been vested. The court went on to make two observations. First, a claim for judicial review of the decision of a Crown Court judge to refuse bail should be put before a judge of the Administrative Court or, in the vacation, the vacation judge. The judge may indicate that there is absolutely no chance that the decision would be overturned and reject it out of hand. Otherwise, the matter should then be heard orally as soon as possible, normally within 48 hours (with notice being given to the Crown Court and the prosecution). Secondly, it is essential that reasons given by a Crown Court judge for refusing bail are recorded so that, if any application for judicial review is made, the Administrative Court has a record of the reasons for refusal.

This guidance on procedure was echoed in *R (Allwin) v Snaresbrook Crown Court* [2005] EWHC 742, where it was said that it will not generally be appropriate to grant bail on an interim application on the papers. The Administrative Court judge should direct an oral hearing within a day or two to determine the issue. If, at that hearing, the court is minded to review the Crown Court's decision, permission will be granted, all procedural requirements will be abridged, and the matter will be remitted to the Crown Court to formally grant bail. Such hearings will normally be dealt with by a single judge.

In *R (Galliano) v Crown Court at Manchester* [2005] EWHC 1125 (Admin), the court made it clear that an accused who has been refused bail by a Crown Court judge can succeed on a claim for judicial review only if he persuades the High Court judge that the decision made by the Crown Court judge was one which fell outside the bounds of what could be regarded as reasonable: nothing short of irrationality will entitle the High Court to interfere. Parliament has decided that the right to go to the High Court to seek bail should be abolished, and so the normal court of last resort in questions of bail is the Crown Court. It follows that the High Court will be reluctant to entertain claims for judicial review of a failure to grant bail and will only do so if satisfied that the decision of the Crown Court judge was an irrational one (per Collins J at [11]).

PROSECUTION APPLICATIONS RELATING TO BAIL

Prosecution Right of Appeal against Decision to Grant Bail

The Bail (Amendment) Act 1993 confers upon the prosecution the right to appeal to the Crown Court against a decision by magistrates to grant bail (for text, see D7.98). The right is limited to cases where: D7.67

(a) the accused is charged with or convicted of an offence which is (or would be in the case of an adult) punishable by imprisonment; and
(b) the prosecution is conducted by or on behalf of the DPP (this includes prosecutions conducted by the CPS), or by a person falling within a class prescribed by statutory instrument (the Bail (Amendment) Act 1993 (Prescription of Prosecuting Authorities) Order 1994 (SI 1994 No. 1438) gives the right to the Revenue and Customs Prosecutions Office, the Serious Fraud Office, the Department of Trade and Industry, the Department of Social Security and a universal service provider within the meaning of the Postal Services Act 2000); and
(c) before bail was granted, the prosecution made representations that bail should not granted.

Procedure

The Bail Act 1993 and r. 19.16 of the CrimPR lay down procedural requirements with which D7.68

the prosecution must comply in order to exercise its right. It must give oral notice of appeal at the conclusion of the proceedings in which bail was granted, and before the defendant is released from custody (s. 1(4) of the 1993 Act). In *Isleworth Crown Court, ex parte Clarke* [1998] 1 Cr App R 257, this requirement was held to be satisfied where notice was given to the justices' clerk about five minutes after the court rose and before the accused had been released from custody. The Divisional Court held that a delay of five minutes or so, especially where an accused had not yet been released from custody, did not bring the case into a category in which it could be said that oral notice was not given at the conclusion of the proceedings. This notice must be confirmed in writing and served on the accused within two hours after the conclusion of the proceedings (s. 1(5)); otherwise the appeal is deemed to be disposed of and the accused is released on bail on the terms granted by the magistrates' court (s. 1(7)). Pending appeal, the magistrates must remand the defendant in custody (s. 1(6)). In *R (Jeffrey) v Warwick Crown Court* [2003] Crim LR 190, the prosecutor served the notice of appeal on the accused three minutes late. The Divisional Court held that Parliament did not intend that the time-limit for serving notice of appeal should defeat an appeal if the prosecution had given itself ample time to serve the notice on the accused within the two-hour period, had used due diligence to serve the notice within that period, and the failure to do so was not the fault of the prosecution but was due to circumstances outside its control (per Hooper J at [11]). Furthermore, the court said that the delay of three minutes had not caused the accused any prejudice (since he knew at the conclusion of the proceedings before the magistrates that the prosecution was exercising its right of appeal and he knew that he was being detained in custody as a result of the oral application for him to be remanded in custody until the appeal was disposed of).

The Crown Court must hear the appeal within 48 hours, excluding weekends and public holidays (s. 1(8)). The appeal takes place by way of rehearing, and the judge may then remand the defendant in custody or grant bail with or without conditions (s. 1(9)). In *Middlesex Guildhall Crown Court, ex parte Okoli* [2001] 1 Cr App R 1, the Divisional Court considered how the provision that the appeal must be heard within 48 hours should be interpreted. It was held that an appeal hearing must commence within two working days of the date of the decision of the magistrates' court.

Under the CrimPR, r. 19.17(4), the accused is not entitled to be present at the hearing of the prosecution appeal unless either he is unrepresented or the judge takes the view that the case is of an exceptional nature and that the interests of justice require that the accused be given leave to attend.

Although the MCA 1980, ss. 128, 128A and 129 (see **D5.17** ***et seq.***), do not directly bind the Crown Court, that court has to act consonantly with the rights conferred on an accused by magistrates' courts and, therefore, they were obliged to apply s. 128A(2); where the accused has not yet been sent to the Crown Court for trial, and the judge decides to remand him in custody, the judge must stipulate a date which is in accordance with the powers of the justices under those sections (*Governor of Pentonville Prison, ex parte Bone* (1994) *The Times*, 15 November 1994; *Re Szakal* [2000] 1 Cr App R 248; and *Remice v HMP Belmarsh* [2007] EWCA Crim 936). In *Remice*, the accused was granted conditional bail. The prosecution appealed to the Crown Court. The judge refused bail and remanded the accused in custody but did not set a return date for him to appear again before the magistrates' court. The Divisional Court said that an accused should enjoy no lesser rights in law than he would have done had a prosecutor's appeal not supervened. In the instant case, the Crown Court ought to have deployed the provisions of s. 128A(2) and should have considered whether the accused should have been remanded for more than eight days. If it decided that question in the affirmative, he should have been allowed to make representations.

D7.69 Guidance on the Use of the Power of Prosecution Appeal Guidance issued by the CPS in their Legal Guidance Manual (<http://www.cps.gov.uk/legal/section14/chapter_l.html#55>)

states that the right of appeal against a grant of bail must be used 'judiciously and responsibly'. It should be used only 'in cases of grave concern'. The 'overarching test' is 'whether there is a serious risk of harm to any member of the public or any other significant risk of harm to any member of the public or any other significant public interest ground'. Wherever possible, approval for use of the power has to be sought in advance of the hearing from a Crown Prosecutor of at least four years' standing.

Prosecution Application for Reconsideration of Bail

Under the BA 1976, s. 5B, the prosecution can, in certain circumstances, apply for the grant of bail by a magistrates' court (or by a police officer) to be reconsidered. The power to make such an application is limited to offences that are triable either way or on indictment only (s. 5B(2)). Any application must be based on information which was not available to the court (or police officer) granting bail when the decision was taken (s. 5B(3)). **D7.70**

The accused is not entitled to be present at the hearing of the appeal unless he is unrepresented or 'in any other case of an exceptional nature, a judge of the Crown Court is of the opinion that the interests of justice require him to be present and gives him leave to be so' (CrimPR, r. 19.17(4)). Where the accused has not been able to instruct a solicitor to represent him at the appeal, he may give notice to the Crown Court requesting that the Official Solicitor shall represent him at the appeal, and the court may, if it thinks fit, assign the Official Solicitor to act for him accordingly (r. 19.17(5)).

Rule 19.2 provides that an application under s 5B must be in writing; contain a statement of the grounds on which it is made; specify the offence in respect of which bail was granted; specify the decision to be reconsidered (including any conditions of bail that have been imposed and why they have been imposed); and specify the name and address of any surety provided by the person to whom the application relates to secure his surrender to custody.

When such an application is made by the prosecutor, the court may vary the bail conditions (or impose conditions if the original grant of bail was unconditional), or withhold bail altogether (s. 5B(1)). In deciding what order to make, the court must act in accordance with the presumption in favour of bail contained in s. 4 and sch. 1 (s. 5B(4)). If the decision is to withhold bail and the accused is before the court, he will be remanded in custody. If absent, he must be ordered to surrender to custody and is liable to arrest without warrant (s. 5(5) and (7)). Where the accused is arrested pursuant to s. 5(7), he must be taken before a magistrate within 24 hours (excluding Sundays), and the magistrate must remand him in custody (s. 5(8)).

Section 5B(8A) stipulates that, where the court refuses to withhold bail from the accused after hearing representations from the prosecutor in favour of withholding bail, the court must give reasons for refusing to withhold bail.

FAILURE TO COMPLY WITH BAIL

Where an accused who has been granted bail in criminal proceedings fails to comply with the obligations imposed upon him, two main questions arise. The first is how the court should ensure that he will attend court for the remaining stages of the proceedings; the second is how he (and any sureties) will be dealt with in consequence of his breach of bail. **D7.71**

Powers of the Court when a Bailed Accused Fails to Appear

Whenever a person bailed to attend court fails to surrender to custody in answer to his bail, the court has a number of options. **D7.72**

(1) The court may issue a warrant (often called a 'bench warrant') for his arrest, under the

BA 1976, s. 7(1). This applies whatever court he was bailed to attend and regardless of whether bail was granted by the custody officer at the police station or by the court itself at an earlier hearing. The usual form of warrant simply orders the arrest of the accused and that he be brought to court. However, at the court's discretion, the warrant may be 'backed for bail' (see below), either with or without a requirement for sureties. Where the accused fails to appear, a bench warrant will normally be issued. It should be noted that the schedule to the Justices' Clerks Rules 2005 (SI 2005 No. 545), para. 3, empowers a clerk to issue a warrant of arrest, whether or not endorsed for bail, for failure to surrender to court, where there is no objection on behalf of the accused.

(2) Instead of issuing a warrant, a magistrates' court may adjourn and enlarge the accused's bail under the MCA 1980, s. 129 (see **D7.51**). Similarly, the Crown Court, in appropriate cases, may simply order that the case be stood out of the list and take no further action in respect of the accused (who will remain under an obligation to attend whenever the case is next listed). Such a course of action is appropriate only where the court is satisfied that there is a good reason for the accused's non-attendance (e.g., a doctor's certificate has been sent to the court indicating that he is unfit to attend).

(3) It may be possible to proceed in the absence of the accused (though it should be borne in mind that if the offence is triable either way, a magistrates' court may try the case only with the consent of the accused, and that consent has to be given at a hearing at which the accused is present unless the court is satisfied that there is a good reason for the absence of the accused and he is represented by a lawyer who consents to summary trial on his behalf: see **D6.19**).

D7.73 **Warrants Backed for Bail** Where the court decides to issue an arrest warrant, the warrant may be endorsed with a direction that the person named in it — having been arrested — shall be released on bail (see the MCA 1980, s. 117, and the SCA 1981, s. 81(4), respectively, for the power of magistrates and the Crown Court). This is generally known as 'backing the warrant for bail'. The accused has to be taken to a police station before being bailed only if his bail is subject to one or more sureties. Such warrants are, however, sometimes viewed as consuming a disproportionate amount of police time and effort in return for little or no advantage. Guidance issued by Thomas LJ (the Senior Presiding Judge for England and Wales) in May 2006 (<http://www.judiciary.gov.uk/docs/judgments_guidance/protocols/bail_trials_absence.pdf>) encourages the use of warning letters instead of warrants backed for bail: where the accused does not attend, and the court decides not to proceed in his absence and is considering the issue of a warrant backed for bail (described in the guidance as 'likely to be uncommon cases'), the court should consider whether it is better to send a letter to the accused:

> directing him to attend and warning him of the consequences of non attendance, instead of issuing a warrant backed for bail.

The guidance carries on:

> if the defendant does not attend the rearranged hearing without good reason, the court should then consider proceeding in absence or issuing a warrant not backed for bail. Unless there were unusual circumstances, any other course of action would undermine the process. The letter to the defendant should make it clear that, if the defendant did not attend the rearranged hearing, a court might well proceed in absence or issue a warrant not backed for bail.

D7.74 **Proof of Inability to Attend Court** The guidance issued by Thomas LJ also deals with the question of evidence of inability to attend court through sickness, and makes the point that:

> Proper evidence must be supplied if a defendant claims he is unwell and unable to attend court; the standard 'off-work' or 'unfit to work' sick note will generally not establish that a person is too ill to attend court. There should normally be a letter from a doctor expressly stating that the defendant is too ill to attend court; this should be provided to the court before the date the defendant is due to appear. A letter can be followed up by a phone call from the clerk or legal

adviser to the surgery if the court has doubts about its validity. Unless there is such evidence, the court should consider proceeding in the defendant's absence.

Surrender to Custody

The power to issue a warrant under the BA 1976, s. 7(1), arises only if the accused fails to surrender to custody at the time appointed. In this context, 'surrendering to custody' merely connotes complying with whatever procedure is prescribed by the court for those answering to their bail (*DPP v Richards* [1988] QB 701 per Glidewell LJ at p. 711). Thus, if a court operates a system whereby persons bailed are required to report to an usher and are then allowed to wait in the court precincts until their case is called, a person who so reports has surrendered to custody, even though he is under no physical restraint and is not in the cell area. It follows that, if he subsequently goes away before the court is ready to deal with his case, he has not absconded within the meaning of s. 6, and a warrant may *not* be issued under s. 7(1). However, that situation is covered by s. 7(2), which provides that, where a person who has been released on bail in criminal proceedings absents himself from the court at any time after he has surrendered to custody but before the court is ready to begin or resume the hearing of the proceedings, the court may issue a warrant for his arrest. In *Central Criminal Court, ex parte Guney* [1996] AC 616, the House of Lords held that, where an accused is formally arraigned, the arraignment amounts to a surrender to the custody of the court. The accused's further detention is therefore within the discretion and power of the judge and, unless the judge grants him bail, he will remain in custody pending and during his trial. It also followed that the obligations of any surety are also extinguished at that point. In *Kent Crown Court, ex parte Jodka* (1997) 161 JP 638, the Divisional Court held that bail granted by magistrates ceases when the defendant surrenders to the custody of the Crown Court, whether or not the defendant is arraigned at that hearing.. D7.75

Breach of Bail Conditions

Under s. 7(3) of the BA 1976, where a person has been bailed to attend a court, a police officer may arrest him without warrant prior to the bail date if: D7.76

(a) the officer has reasonable grounds for believing that he is not likely to surrender to custody; or
(b) the officer has reasonable grounds for believing that he either has broken or is likely to break any condition of his bail; or
(c) a surety has given written notice to the police that the person bailed is unlikely to surrender to custody and for that reason the surety wishes to be relieved of his obligations.

Following arrest under s. 7(3), s. 7(4) stipulates that the person arrested must be brought before a magistrate as soon as practicable and, in any event, within 24 hours (excluding Sundays (s. 7(7)), and so a person arrested on a Saturday under s. 7(3) need not be brought before a magistrate until the following Monday). The wording of s. 7(4) makes it clear that the person arrested may be brought before a single justice, who need not be sitting in a courtroom.

In *Governor of Glen Parva Young Offender Institution, ex parte G* [1998] 2 All ER 295, the accused was arrested for breach of bail conditions. He was taken to the cells of a magistrates' court within 24 hours of arrest but was not brought before a magistrate until two hours after the expiry of the 24-hour time-limit. The Divisional Court held that the detention after 24 hours was unlawful as s. 7(4) requires the defendant to be brought before a justice of the peace (not merely brought within the court precincts) within 24 hours of arrest. The importance of dealing with the accused within 24 hours was again emphasised in *R (Culley) v Crown Court sitting at Dorchester* (2007) 171 JP 373, where it was held that the time-limit under s. 7 is a strict one. It follows that the justice is required to complete his investigation and decision-making in relation to this matter within the 24-hour period. If the justice fails to do so, the continued custody of the accused becomes unlawful from the moment the 24-hour period has expired. If the justice purports to remand the accused in custody after that the time, the order is *ultra vires* and unlawful.

D7.77 **Arrest following Grant of Conditional Bail by the Crown Court** In *R (Ellison) v Teeside Magistrates' Court* (2001) 165 JP 355, the Divisional Court held that, where an accused has been sent for trial to the Crown Court, and is subsequently arrested for breach of a bail condition, the jurisdiction to deal with the accused under s. 7 of the BA 1976 must be exercised by the magistrates. Thus, the magistrate must deal with the matter; there is no power to commit the accused to the Crown Court to be dealt with. Lord Woolf CJ (at [9]) said that the appropriate course for the magistrates to take in such a case is to remand the accused to the Crown Court until his trial or further order; if the Crown Court wishes to grant bail, it can then do so, and any order it makes will override the decision of the magistrates.

D7.78 **Approach where the Accused is brought before the Court under s. 7** The question for a magistrate before whom a person is brought in furtherance of the BA 1976, s. 7, is whether that person is likely to fail to surrender to custody, or has broken or is likely to break any condition of his bail. If of the opinion that either of those two matters is established, the magistrate may remand him in custody (s. 7(5)). Alternatively, he may grant him bail subject to different conditions (or even grant him bail on the same conditions as before if he considers that new conditions would not assist but it is nevertheless not a case where a remand in custody would be justified). Where the magistrate is *not* of the opinion that the accused is likely to fail to surrender to custody or has broken, or is likely to break, a condition of his bail, he *must* grant him bail on the same conditions (if any) as were originally imposed.

The guidance to judges and magistrates on the subject of bail from Thomas LJ issued in May 2006 (see **D7.32**) deals with the action to be taken where the accused is arrested for breaching his bail. The guidance says that:

> when the offender is to be re-bailed, the court must always consider whether the conditions need strengthening and give reasons for its decision as to continuing the existing terms or strengthening the terms, such as by adding a tagging condition or requiring a surety or security. If a defendant has failed to surrender to bail, it will usually only be in the unusual case that a defendant will be re-bailed on the same terms.

D7.79 **Human Rights Issues and the Summary Procedure under s. 7** In its Paper *Bail and the Human Rights Act 1998* (Law Com No. 269), the Law Commission expressed the view that the BA 1976, s. 7, is compatible with the ECHR, Article 5 (the right to liberty).

In *R (DPP) v Havering Magistrates' Court* [2001] 1 WLR 805, the Divisional Court considered s. 7 in the context of Articles 5 and 6 (the right to a fair trial) of the Convention. It was held that Article 6 has no direct relevance where justices are exercising their judgement whether or not to remand a person in custody following breach of bail conditions, since s. 7 does not create any criminal offence. However, the court went on to hold that Article 5 is directly relevant. Latham LJ, giving the judgment of the court, summarised the effect of Article 5 and the relevant Strasbourg case law thus (at [35]): 'where a decision is taken to deprive somebody of his liberty, that should only be done after he has been given a fair opportunity to answer the basis upon which such an order is sought'. His lordship went on to hold that the procedure set out in cases such as *Liverpool Justices, ex parte DPP* [1993] QB 233 is entirely compatible with the requirements of Article 5. These proceedings are, by their nature, emergency proceedings to determine whether or not a person, who had not been considered to present risks which would have justified a remand in custody in the first instance, did subsequently present such risks. When exercising the power to detain, the magistrate is not entitled to order detention by reason simply of the finding of a breach, nor is a breach of itself sufficient for the imposition of conditions. The fact of a breach is evidence of a relevant risk arising, but it is no more than one of the factors which the magistrate has to consider in exercising his discretion. The magistrate is required on the material before him to come to an honest and rational opinion, that material not being restricted to admissible evidence in the strict sense. In doing so, he has to bear in mind the consequences for the person arrested, namely the fact that he is at risk of losing his liberty, in the context of the presumption of innocence. The procedural task of the magistrate is to ensure that the person arrested has a full and fair opportunity to comment on, and answer, the material before the court; if that material includes evidence from a witness who gives oral testimony, there must be an opportunity to cross-examine. Likewise, if the person arrested wishes to give oral evidence, he is entitled to do so.

No Power to Adjourn Proceedings under s. 7 In *R (DPP) v Havering Magistrates' Court*, the court confirmed that there is no power for a magistrate to adjourn the hearing once a person has been brought before him under s. 7 of the BA 1976. However, this was held not to result in a breach of Article 5. Parliament has to be taken to have determined that there should be a swift and relatively informal resolution of the issues raised, and so the court has to do its best to come to a fair conclusion on the relevant day; if it cannot do so, it will not be of the opinion that the relevant matters have been made out which could justify detention (per Latham LJ at [44]). In *R (Hussain) v Derby Magistrates' Court* [2002] 1 WLR 2454, the accused was arrested for breach of bail conditions. The magistrates made a preliminary ruling and adjourned the case to the afternoon of the same day. The Divisional Court held that, under s. 7(4) and (5), justices have power to stand an application out of their list after being seized of it and making a preliminary ruling, with the effect that a different bench embark on the hearing afresh and determine it on the same day. What has to be ensured is that the question of continuing detention is placed before a justice or justices within the 24-hour period. The court added that, where such proceedings are heard by a different court following adjournment, the complaint should be put to the accused formally at the start of that hearing. **D7.80**

Nature of a s. 7 Inquiry In *R (Hussain) v Derby Magistrates' Court* [2002] 1 WLR 2454, the court confirmed that investigation into alleged breach of a bail condition is not concerned with the trial of a criminal charge; there is nothing in the language of s. 7(5) which demands that the court should adopt the procedural rigidities appropriate for a more formal hearing such as a summary trial. It follows that there is no need for the court to hear evidence; instead it can base its decision on representations from the prosecution and the defence. **D7.81**

In *R (Vickers) v West London Magistrates' Court* (2003) 167 JP 473, the accused was arrested and brought before the justices for failing to comply with the bail conditions. He sought to raise a defence of reasonable excuse; however, the justices ruled that no such defence exists under the BA 1976, s. 7. The Divisional Court held that s. 7(5) requires a two-stage approach. First, the justices have to determine whether there has been a breach of a bail condition (if there has been no breach of a condition, then the accused is entitled to be granted bail on precisely the same conditions as before); secondly, if there has been a breach, the justices are obliged to consider whether or not the bailed person should be granted bail again. In carrying out the first stage of that process, the justices must act fairly and give the accused a chance to answer the accusations against him. That does not, however, include an inquiry as to whether the arrested person had any reasonable excuse for breaching bail (since s. 7 makes no mention of such a defence and, indeed, s. 7 does not create a criminal offence). The second stage (assuming that the justices are satisfied that there has been a breach) is the point at which the reasons for the breach of bail become relevant, and the justices would be obliged to consider all the evidence, including all the issues relating to any reason for the breach put forward by the accused. The breach of bail will be a factor, but only one factor as to whether or not the bailed person is granted bail again. The court concluded that, if this procedure is followed, there will be no breach of the ECHR, Article 5.

D7.82 **Breach of Bail Conditions as Contempt of Court** Failure to comply with conditions of bail can also amount to contempt of court, but that fact is of limited practical relevance. In *Ashley* [2004] 1 WLR 2057, the accused was convicted of contempt of court, arising out of breaches of bail conditions. He had been released on bail subject to conditions that required him to surrender his passport and not to leave the country. He broke both conditions but returned to face trial on the appointed day. The Divisional Court held that the purpose of placing restrictions on an individual's movement under the BA 1976 is to ensure that he attends the trial. If the conduct breaching bail is known about at the time, that bail could be revoked. Furthermore, there may be cases where breach of a bail condition gives rise to a further offence (e.g., where witnesses are intimidated). However, s. 7 does not itself create any offence. Although the defendant had breached bail conditions by leaving the country, he did return for his trial. It followed that the judge did not have power to deal with him by way of contempt of court.

The Offence of Absconding

D7.83 The BA 1976, s. 6, creates the offence of absconding. Under s. 6(1), if a person released on bail fails without reasonable cause to surrender to custody, he is guilty of an offence. The burden of showing reasonable cause is on the accused (s. 6(3)). Moreover, a person who had reasonable cause for failing to surrender on the appointed day nevertheless commits an offence if he fails to surrender as soon after the appointed time as is reasonably practicable (s. 6(2)). It follows that where an accused has a reasonable excuse for failing to attend court, he must surrender to custody as soon as reasonably practicable after that excuse ceases to apply (and he commits an offence under s. 6 if he does not).

An offence under s. 6(1) or (2) is 'punishable either on summary conviction or as if it were a criminal contempt of court' (s. 6(5)). An offender summarily convicted of a s. 6 offence is liable to imprisonment for up to three months and/or a fine of up to £5,000 (s. 6(7)). An offender dealt with in the Crown Court as if he had been guilty of a criminal contempt is liable to 12 months' imprisonment and/or an unlimited fine (ibid.). Furthermore, a magistrates' court which has convicted the offender of a s. 6 offence may commit him to the Crown Court for sentence if either it considers that the offence merits greater punishment than it has power to inflict, or it is sending the offender for trial to the Crown Court for another offence and it considers that the Crown Court should deal with him for the absconding as well (s. 6(6)). The meaning of 'surrendering to custody' in s. 6(1) and (2) was considered by the Divisional Court in *DPP v Richards* [1988] QB 701 (see **D7.75**).

D7.84 **Procedure for Prosecuting Offences under the Bail Act 1976, s. 6** The BA 1976, s. 6(5), provides that an offence under s. 6(1) or (2) is punishable either on summary conviction or as if it were a criminal contempt of court. The leading authority interpreting this provision is *Schiavo v Anderton* [1987] QB 20, the effect of which is now embodied in *Consolidated Criminal Practice Direction*, part 1, para. I.13, *Failure to surrender* (see **appendix** 7).

In *Schiavo v Anderton*, the accused was arrested some two years after he absconded. It was argued on his behalf that the s. 6(1) offence is summary and that, since no information had been laid within the six-month time-limit prescribed by the MCA 1980, s. 127, the court had no jurisdiction to try the matter. Watkins LJ rejected this contention, holding that s. 6 creates a unique offence which is not a contempt of court but is analogous thereto. It does not fit into the normal classifications of triable only on indictment, triable either way and triable only summarily, but is invariably to be tried by the court disposing of the offence for which the accused was bailed. The offence is also unique in that proceedings for it are not to be initiated by information or charge, but of the court's own motion. Therefore, no time-limit applies. His lordship set out six propositions (at p. 34B–D):

> (1) the magistrates' court and the Crown Court each require separately a power to punish for the offence of absconding. (2) The offence is not subject to the general rule that trial be commenced

> by information. (3) The initiation of the simple procedure for trial by the court's own motion and not by formal charge, as seems to have happened here, is the only proper way to proceed. (4) It is not one of those offences triable on indictment or either way. (5) It is an offence only triable in the court at which proceedings are to be heard in respect of which bail has been granted. (6) It is expected that the trial of the offence will take place immediately following the disposal of the offence in respect of which bail was granted.

In *Lubega* (1999) 163 JP 221, the Court of Appeal held that s. 6(5) did not have the effect of converting an offence under the Act to a contempt of court. It followed that the judge was not entitled to deal with the matter in the same way as a contempt of court.

The procedure to be followed under the BA 1976, s. 6, is now set out in the *Practice Direction*, para. I.13 (see **appendix 8**). The preamble to this section of the *Practice Direction* points out that the failure of an accused to surrender to custody undermines the administration of justice. Accordingly, it is important that the accused appreciates the significance of the obligation to surrender and, where he fails, that courts take appropriate action.

The *Practice Direction* (at para. I.13.9) suggests that there should be a two-stage consideration of whether proceedings should be initiated (i.e. the prosecutor decides whether to invite the court to proceed and the court then decides whether to act on his invitation). In practice, however, many magistrates' courts informally ask the absconder or his legal representative what the reason for his non-appearance was. If the explanation seems prima facie satisfactory, the bench indicates that no further action is necessary; otherwise the clerk is instructed to put the charge.

The *Practice Direction* makes it clear that the absconder should normally be brought before the court at which the proceedings in respect of which bail was granted are to be heard (para. I.13.8). This will usually be the court which granted bail but, where bail was granted by a magistrates' court on sending the accused to the Crown Court for trial or sentence, it will be the Crown Court. A suggestion by Roskill LJ in *Harbax Singh* [1979] QB 319 that the Crown Court might, exceptionally and in its discretion, remit a contested BA 1976 offence to the magistrates for summary trial was rejected by Watkins LJ in *Schiavo v Anderton* [1987] QB 20 (see p. 33D) and it is clear from the *Practice Direction* that trial for the Bail Act offence should take place in the Crown Court if the accused has been sent to that court. The Crown Court judge will sit alone, without a jury (see *Schiavo v Anderton* at p. 34A).

Paragraph I.13.5 of the *Practice Direction* makes it clear that it is no longer appropriate automatically to postpone consideration of the Bail Act offence until the conclusion of the substantive proceedings (as was formerly the practice). Rather, courts should deal with the allegation of absconding as soon as is practicable.

Where a bench, on the occasion of an absconder's first appearance after his absconding, indicates, albeit informally, that no charge need be preferred, that decision is binding on subsequent benches (*France v Dewsbury Magistrates' Court* (1988) 152 JP 301).

A certified copy of the record made under the BA 1976, s. 5(1), of the granting of bail is evidence of the time and place at which the accused should have surrendered. The court file will show whether he did in fact surrender. Thus, although it is in theory for the prosecution to call the evidence of absconding, the basic facts will usually be established from court documents. The prosecution's role is therefore essentially one of testing in cross-examination any reason put forward by the accused to explain his non-appearance.

Failure to Answer Police Bail Failure to answer police bail is dealt with by the police laying an information; the allegation is then tried at the magistrates' court. When this form of commencement of criminal proceedings is abolished (under the CJA 2003), the new written charge and requisition procedure will be used for this purpose. More importantly, the CJA 2003, s. 15(3), disapplies the MCA 1980, s. 127 (which prevents summary proceedings from **D7.85**

being instituted more than six months after the commission of an offence) in respect of offences under the BA 1976, s. 6, and instead provides that such an offence may not be tried unless proceedings are commenced either within six months of the commission of the offence, or within three months of the date when the defendant surrenders to custody, is arrested in connection with the offence for which bail was granted, or appears in court in respect of that offence. This will ensure that a defendant cannot escape prosecution under s. 6 merely by absconding for more than six months.

D7.86 **Reasonable Excuse** The offence under the BA 1976, s. 6, is made out only if the court finds that the accused did not have a 'reasonable cause' for failing to surrender to custody. It follows that it is imperative that the accused be given the opportunity to put forward any explanation he may have for his non-attendance. In *Davis* (1986) 8 Cr App R (S) 64, it was said that the court should give the accused an opportunity to explain himself, and invite submissions from counsel; if the accused was unrepresented he should be given the chance to apply for legal representation or, at the very least, be given the fullest possible opportunity of offering some excuse (if he has any) for absenting himself. In *Boyle* [1993] Crim LR 40, the court made the point that absconding is a serious criminal offence and requires proper proof according to the correct procedure. Therefore, if the accused pleads not guilty to the Bail Act offence, the judge should invite counsel to call evidence or address him on the question of guilt or otherwise. He should then announce his finding, with reasons (see also *How* [1993] Crim LR 201). In *Woods* (1989) 11 Cr App R (S) 551, W was sentenced to 18 months' imprisonment on charges of theft and handling, with three months consecutive for failing to surrender to bail. The Court of Appeal quashed the sentence for the bail offence because the simple procedure laid down in *Davis* had not been followed. In particular, the sentencer had given no indication that he intended to impose a separate consecutive sentence for the bail offence.

In *Hourigan* [2003] EWCA Crim 2306, the accused arrived late at the Crown Court, in breach of his bail. When the case was called on again, the judge proceeded to deal with the question of the breach of bail by treating it as a criminal contempt of court. The Court of Appeal criticised both the judge and counsel, who had overlooked the fact that, for an offence to be committed under s. 6(1), the failure to surrender has to have been without reasonable cause. Therefore, it is incumbent on the court, before deciding whether to impose a penalty, to decide whether the s. 6(1) offence has been made out. The allegation that he has committed an offence under s. 6(1) should be put to the accused (either directly or through counsel). If the accused admits the breach, the court can go on to consider the question of penalty. Where the accused does not admit the breach, the court should make the necessary enquiries (for example, through questioning the accused) and then make a formal announcement of whether the allegation is found to be proven or not, with reasons for that finding. The Court added that, in the ordinary course of things, the s. 6 offence should be dealt with after all the substantive matters have been dealt with, since a pre-sentence report might be of assistance. However, this would seem to be inconsistent with the *Practice Direction*, para. I.13.5, which should be followed in preference to the relevant dictum in *Hourigan*.

Being mistaken about the day on which one should have appeared was held in *Laidlaw v Atkinson* (1986) *The Times*, 2 August 1986 not to amount to a reasonable cause.

D7.87 **Sentencing Guidelines** When sentencing for failure to surrender to bail, under the BA 1976, s. 6, the Magistrates' Courts Guidelines (2004) indicate the following as relevant considerations:

Aggravating Factors For example leaves jurisdiction; long term evasion; results in ineffective trial date; wilful evasion

Mitigating Factors For example appears late on day of hearing; genuine misunderstanding; voluntary surrender.

Guideline: Is discharge or fine appropriate? A curfew order may be particularly suitable. Previous convictions for this offence increase the seriousness — consider custody.

The *Practice Direction* makes reference to the judgment of the Court of Appeal in *White* [2003] 2 Cr App R (S) 133:

> *Sentencing for a Bail Act offence*
> I.13.13 In principle, a custodial sentence for the offence of failing to surrender should be ordered to be served consecutively to any other sentence imposed at the same time for another offence unless there are circumstances that make this inappropriate (see *R v White; R v McKinnon*).

The Court in *White* also held that there is no principle of law that the sentence for failing to surrender to custody should be proportionate to the sentence for the substantive offence of which the accused stands convicted. Indeed, it pointed out that in *Neve* (1986) 8 Cr App R (S) 270, a sentence of six month's imprisonment for failing to surrender to custody was upheld, even though the accused had been acquitted of the substantive offence.

In *Hourigan*, the court made the point that it is inappropriate for a judge in the Crown Court to impose a sentence of less than five days' imprisonment for an offence under s. 6, having regard to the fact that the MCA 1980, s. 132, prohibits magistrates from imposing sentences of less than five days' imprisonment.

Consequences for Sureties when Accused Absconds

If an accused who is granted bail subject to the provision of one or more sureties fails to surrender at the appointed time, the court must forfeit the recognisance(s) (i.e. order the sureties to pay the amounts which they had promised to pay). This is the normal consequence if the accused absconds, although the court has a discretion, in exceptional circumstances, to order that the surety pay less than the full sum or even to order that none of the sum it previously declared forfeited should in fact be forfeited. The power to forfeit recognisances is contained in the MCA 1980, s. 120(1) and (1A), and (in the Crown Court) r. 19.24 of the CrimPR. Section 120(1A)(a) and r. 19.24(1) are in very similar terms, both providing that if the accused fails to appear in court, the Court 'shall declare the recognizance to be forfeited'. The word 'shall' connotes a duty rather than mere power. However, having declared the automatic forfeiture of any recognisance entered into by a surety, the court is required to issue a summons to the surety to appear before it (unless, of course, he is present) to explain why he should not pay the sum (s. 120(1A)(b) and r. 19.24(2)). If the surety fails to answer the summons, the court has the discretion to proceed in his absence provided that it is satisfied that the summons has been correctly served (s. 120(1A) and r. 19.24(3)). The MCA 1980, s. 120(3) provides that the court may, instead of adjudging the surety to pay the whole sum in which he is bound, adjudge him to pay part only of that sum or remit the sum altogether. There is no express provision empowering the Crown Court to remit only part of the recognisance, but that power may be implied from r. 19.24(2), which enables a surety 'to show cause why the Court should not order the recognizance to be estreated'. D7.88

Principles Governing Forfeiture of Surety

The principles governing forfeiture of a surety's recognisance have been set out in a number of cases, including *Southampton Justices, ex parte Green* [1976] QB 11, *Horseferry Road Stipendiary Magistrate, ex parte Pearson* [1976] 1 WLR 511 and *Crown Court at Wood Green, ex parte Howe* [1992] 1 WLR 702. Before making an order, the court should consider both the surety's means and the extent of his responsibility for the accused's non-appearance, including any steps he took to ensure that he would surrender. However, there is a strong presumption that the surety should forfeit the full recognisance. As it was put in *Ex parte Pearson* at p. 514C: D7.89

> . . . the surety has seriously entered into a serious obligation and ought to pay the amount which he or she has promised unless there are circumstances in the case, either relating to . . . means or . . . culpability, which make it fair and just to pay a smaller sum.

The authorities were reviewed extensively by McCullough J in *Uxbridge Justices, ex parte Heward-Mills* [1983] 1 WLR 56. His lordship then summarised their effect thus (at p. 62A–B):

> . . . the more important principles to be derived from the authorities [are] as follows. (1) When a defendant for whose attendance a person has stood surety fails to appear, the full recognisance should be forfeited, unless it appears fair and just that a lesser sum should be forfeited or none at all. (2) The burden of satisfying the court that the full sum should not be forfeited rests on the surety and is a heavy one. It is for him to lay before the court the evidence of want of culpability and of means on which he relies. (3) Where a surety is unrepresented the court should assist him by explaining these principles in ordinary language, and giving him the opportunity to call evidence and advance argument in relation to them.

D7.90 **Want of Means** In both *Southampton Justices, ex parte Green* [1976] QB 11 and *Uxbridge Justices, ex parte Heward-Mills* [1983] 1 WLR 56, the orders for forfeiture were quashed because the magistrates had failed properly to take into account the surety's want of means. Nevertheless, the cases emphasise that the burden is on the surety to show impecuniosity. If he wishes to put forward evidence on the matter, the court is under a duty to consider it, even if he had earlier claimed when being accepted as surety that he was worth the sum which he now states he cannot pay (*Ex parte Heward-Mills*). However, there is no obligation on the court to initiate the inquiry (ibid.). Moreover, it is submitted that, if a proper inquiry was conducted into the surety's means at the time he stood, he should be relieved from his obligations on financial grounds only if something unforeseen has arisen between then and the consideration of forfeiture which prevents him meeting his obligation. Otherwise he benefits from having misled the court which accepted him as surety. The magistrates' error in *Ex parte Heward-Mills* lay in refusing to consider the evidence as to means which the surety wished to advance at the forfeiture hearing, rather than in the conclusion they reached.

In *Leicestershire Stipendiary Magistrate, ex parte Kaur* (2000) 164 JP 127, the appellant had stood surety in the sum of £150,000. To pay that sum she would have had to sell the matrimonial home. Rose LJ, having reviewed the authorities, summarised the guiding principles thus:

> 1. Justices have a wide discretion under section 120 whether to remit in whole or in part;
> 2. In exercising that discretion, they must plainly have regard only to the surety's assets. The assets of other persons are not assets which can properly be called upon to satisfy a surety's liability;
> 3. Want of culpability by a surety in the accused's failure to appear is not in itself a reason for not forfeiting or for remitting a recognisance. But there may be circumstances . . . where the amount forfeited may be reduced because a culpable surety has made very considerable efforts to carry out his or her undertaking;
> 4. Regard may properly be had to a surety's share in the equity of a matrimonial home when a recognizance is being entered into;
> 5. When enforcement of a recognizance is being considered under section 120, the means of the surety at that time is one of the factors to be considered and, at that stage, the impact on both the surety and on others, if the matrimonial home has to be sold to satisfy the recognizance, is a relevant factor when deciding whether to remit a recognizance in whole or in part.

D7.91 **Culpability** According to *Warwick Crown Court, ex parte Smalley* [1987] 1 WLR 237, there is no requirement of proof that any blame attached to the surety for the accused's failure to surrender. The court rejected the suggestion that there had to be some fault on the part of the surety for the recognisance to be forfeited. The authorities on this point were reviewed in *Reading Crown Court, ex parte Bello* [1992] 3 All ER 353. Parker LJ summarised the position as follows:

> The failure of the accused to surrender when required triggers the power to forfeit but the court, before deciding what should be done, must enquire into the question of fault. If it is satisfied that

> the surety was blameless throughout it would then be proper to remit the whole of the amount of the recognisance and in exceptional circumstances this would . . . be the only proper course.

One issue in *Ex parte Bello* was the failure of the court to notify the surety of the date on which the accused had to surrender. Parker LJ said that justice should require that the surety was notified by the court of the date. However, it was impossible to say that ignorance of the date must always be an answer to proceedings for forfeiture: each case will depend on its facts.

In *Maidstone Crown Court, ex parte Lever* [1995] 1 WLR 928, the Court of Appeal signalled a robust approach to the question of culpability. One of two sureties discovered that the accused had not been home for two nights. That surety telephoned the other surety and the police. Attempts by the police to apprehend the accused were unsuccessful. The judge ordered the first surety to forfeit £35,000 (out of a recognisance of £40,000) and the other £16,000 (out of a recognisance of £19,000). The Court of Appeal upheld this decision. Butler-Sloss LJ said (at p. 930) that 'the presence or absence of culpability is a factor but the absence of culpability . . . is not in itself a reason to reduce or set aside the obligations entered into by the surety to pay in the event of a failure to bring the defendant to court'. The reason for the adoption of a fairly strict approach to the forfeiture of recognisances was set out by Butler-Sloss LJ at p. 931, where her ladyship quotes from Lord Widgery CJ in *R v Southampton Justices, ex parte Corker* (1976) 120 SJ 214:

> The real pull of bail, the real effective force that it exerts, is that it may cause the offender to attend his trial rather than subject his nearest and dearest who has gone surety for him to undue pain and discomfort.

Nonetheless, it is clear that there may be circumstances where the amount forfeited might be reduced because the surety has made considerable efforts to carry out his undertakings.

In *Wells Street Magistrates' Court, ex parte Albanese* [1982] QB 333, the court considered the position where the conditions of bail have been varied. Ralph Gibson J, giving the judgment of the court, declined to hold that a court, if it varies the conditions of bail in a case in which there is a surety, is under a duty to give notice of the change to the surety. However, an unnotified variation in bail conditions may be relevant to the question of forfeiture of the recognisance.

Forfeiture of Security

D7.92 Where the accused (or somebody on his behalf) has given security for his surrender to custody in pursuance of a requirement imposed under the BA 1976, s. 3(5), and the court is satisfied that the accused has absconded, then the court may, unless satisfied that he had reasonable cause for his failure, order forfeiture of part or all of the security (s. 5(7) and (8)). Section 5(8A) to (8C) sets out a procedure by which the accused may apply to have an order under s. 5(7) remitted on the grounds that he did in fact have reasonable cause for not surrendering to custody. The principles to be applied in deciding whether or not to order forfeiture of a security are no doubt analogous to those which apply when forfeiture of a surety's recognisance is under consideration.

DETENTION WHEN BAIL IS REFUSED

Detention of Adults

D7.93 Where a court refuses bail to an accused aged 21 or over he is detained in a prison until the next hearing (MCA 1980, ss. 128(1) and 150(1)). As regards an accused aged 17 to 20 inclusive who is remanded in custody, the court — if it has been notified that a remand centre is available for the reception from that court of persons of the accused's class or description —

must commit him to the remand centre (CJA 1948, s. 27(1)). Otherwise it commits him to a prison. When the sentence of detention in a young offender institution is abolished for this age group, committal will be to a prison in any event.

Juveniles Refused Bail

D7.94 As regards a court's decision whether or not to grant bail to a child or young person (defined in the BA 1976, s. 2(2), as someone under the age of 17), the only special rules applying are that (a) bail can be refused if that is necessary for his own welfare, not just if it is necessary for his protection (sch. 1, para. 3), and (b) his parent or guardian may be asked to stand surety for his compliance with such conditions of bail as may have been imposed, as well as standing surety for his appearance at court (s. 3(7)). However, where bail is *refused* in the case of a person aged under 17, the consequences are significantly different.

Under the CYPA 1969, s. 23(1), where a court remands a child or young person in custody, the remand is to local authority accommodation. Under s. 23(4) the court may require the local authority to comply with a security requirement, namely that the accused 'be placed and kept in secure accommodation'. Before a security requirement can be imposed, the conditions set out in ss. 23(5) and 23(5AA) have to be satisfied. Those conditions are that:

(a) the accused has attained the age of 12 and is of a 'prescribed description' (see below); and
(b) the accused has been charged with, or has been convicted of, either (i) a violent or sexual offence, or an offence punishable in the case of an adult with imprisonment for a term of 14 years or more, or (ii) one or more imprisonable offences which amount (or would, if he were to be convicted of the offences with which he is charged, amount) to a 'recent history of repeatedly committing imprisonable offences while remanded on bail or to local authority accommodation'; and
(c) the court is of the opinion, after considering all the options for the remand of the accused, that 'only remanding him to local authority accommodation with a security requirement would be adequate (a) to protect the public from serious harm from him, or (b) to prevent the commission by him of imprisonable offences'.

The 'prescribed description' referred to in s. 23(5) is supplied by the Secure Remands and Committals (Prescribed Description of Children and Young Persons) Order (SI 1999 No. 1265). It applies the provision to girls and boys aged 12, 13 or 14 and to girls aged 15 or 16. However, the CDA 1998, s. 98(1), modifies s. 23 of the 1969 Act to bring boys aged 15 or 16 within the scope of s. 23(5).

The CYPA 1969, s. 23(6), requires the court to state its reasons for deciding that it is appropriate to impose a security requirement. Section 23(5A) provides that a court shall not impose a security requirement in respect of a child or young person who is not legally represented in the court unless he was granted a right to representation funded by the Legal Services Commission but the right was withdrawn, or he applied for such representation but the application was refused because his financial resources were such that he was not eligible, or, having been informed of his right to apply for such representation and having had the opportunity to do so, he refused or failed to apply.

In addition to the powers mentioned above, a youth court can remand a young person aged 15 to 18 years in secure accommodation, by virtue of an application under the CJA 1991, s. 60(3). Section 60(3) provides that where a child or young person has been remanded to local authority accommodation by a youth court (or an adult magistrates' court), any application under the Children Act 1989, s. 25, shall be made to that court. Section 25 provides that a child who is being looked after by a local authority may be placed in accommodation provided for the purpose of restricting liberty ('secure accommodation') only if it appears that either (a) he has a history of absconding and is likely to abscond from any other description of accommodation; and if he absconds, he is likely to suffer significant harm; or (b) if he is kept in any other description of accommodation he is likely to injure himself or other persons. The period of such remand is restricted by the Children (Secure Accommodation) Regulations 1991 (SI 1991 No. 1505), reg. 13, to a period of 28 days at a time. The jurisdiction to make such an order is reserved to the youth court (or adult magistrates' court), and so once the child has been sent to the Crown Court any application under s. 25 would have to be made to the family proceedings court (the detail of which is outside the scope of this work).

Electronic Monitoring The CYPA 1967, s. 23(7), empowers a court remanding a person to local authority accommodation without imposing a security requirement to require that person to comply with any conditions that may be imposed on the grant of bail under the BA 1976, s. 3(6) (s. 23(7)(a)) and 'any conditions imposed for the purpose of securing the electronic monitoring of his compliance' with such conditions (s. 23(7)(b)). Under s. 23AA, the court may impose an 'electronic monitoring condition' only if each of the following requirements is fulfilled: **D7.95**

(a) the accused has attained the age of 12;
(b) the accused has been charged with, or has been convicted of, either (i) a violent or sexual offence, or an offence punishable in the case of an adult with imprisonment for a term of 14 years or more, or (ii) one or more imprisonable offences which amount (or would, if he were to be convicted of the offences with which he is charged, amount) to a 'recent history of repeatedly committing imprisonable offences while remanded on bail or to local authority accommodation' (this is identical to one of the requirements for the imposition of a security requirement);
(c) arrangements for electronic monitoring are available in the relevant area; and
(d) a youth offending team has informed the court that in its opinion the imposition of such a condition will be suitable in the accused's case.

Section 23A enables the arrest of a person who has been remanded to local authority accommodation if the police have reasonable grounds for suspecting that that person has broken any condition imposed under s. 23(7). Under s. 23A(2)(a), a person arrested under s. 23A must be taken before a magistrate within 24 hours of the arrest (excluding Sundays).

Remands to Police Custody

A magistrates' court may, instead of remanding the accused in custody, commit him to detention at a police station for a period not exceeding three clear days (MCA 1980, s. 128(7)). This may be done only if it is necessary for the purposes of inquiries into offences other than the one(s) for which he is appearing before the court (s. 128(8)(a)). He must be brought back before the magistrates' court as soon as that need ceases (s. 128(8)(b)). While detained at the police station, he is entitled to the same protection as regards conditions of detention, and periodic review of the continuing need for detention, as would have been the case had he simply been arrested without warrant on suspicion of having committed an offence (s. 128(8)(c) and (d)). **D7.96**

TEXT OF THE BAIL ACT 1976

Bail Act 1976 **D7.97**

Preliminary

Meaning of 'bail in criminal proceedings'

1.—(1) In this Act 'bail in criminal proceedings' means—
(a) bail grantable in or in connection with proceedings for an offence to a person who is accused or convicted of the offence, or
(b) bail grantable in connection with an offence to a person who is under arrest for the offence or for whose arrest for the offence a warrant (endorsed for bail) is being issued, or

(c) bail grantable in connection with extradition proceedings in respect of an offence.

(2) In this Act 'bail' means bail grantable under the law (including common law) for the time being in force.

(3) Except as provided by section 13(3) of this Act, this section does not apply to bail in or in connection with proceedings outside England and Wales.

. . .

(5) This section applies—

(a) whether the offence was committed in England or Wales or elsewhere, and

(b) whether it is an offence under the law of England and Wales, or of any other country or territory.

(6) Bail in criminal proceedings shall be granted (and in particular shall be granted unconditionally or conditionally), in accordance with this Act.

Other definitions

2.—(1) In this Act, unless the context otherwise requires, 'conviction' includes—

(a) a finding of guilt,

(b) a finding that a person is not guilty by reason of insanity,

(c) a finding under section 11(1) of the Powers of Criminal Courts (Sentencing) Act 2000 (remand for medical examination) that the person in question did the act or made the omission charged, and

(d) a conviction of an offence for which an order is made discharging the offender absolutely or conditionally, and 'convicted' shall be construed accordingly.

(2) In this Act, unless the context otherwise requires—

'bail hostel' means premises for the accommodation of persons remanded on bail,

'child' means a person under the age of fourteen,

'court' includes a judge of a court or a justice of the peace and, in the case of a specified court, includes a judge or (as the case may be) justice having powers to act in connection with proceedings before that court,

'Courts-Martial Appeal rules' means rules made under section 49 of the Courts-Martial (Appeals) Act 1968,

'extradition proceedings' means proceedings under the Extradition Act 2003,

'offence' includes an alleged offence,

'probation hostel' means premises for the accommodation of persons who may be required to reside there by a community order under section 177 of the Criminal Justice Act 2003,

'prosecutor', in relation to extradition proceedings, means the person acting on behalf of the territory to which extradition is sought,

'surrender to custody' means, in relation to a person released on bail, surrendering himself into the custody of the court or of the constable (according to the requirements of the grant of bail) at the time and place for the time being appointed for him to do so,

'vary', in relation to bail, means imposing further conditions after bail is granted, or varying or rescinding conditions,

'young person' means a person who has attained the age of 14 and is under the age of 17.

(3) Where an enactment (whenever passed) which relates to bail in criminal proceedings refers to the person bailed appearing before a court it is to be construed unless the context otherwise requires as referring to his surrendering himself into the custody of the court.

(4) Any reference in this Act to any other enactment is a reference thereto as amended, and includes a reference thereto as extended or applied, by or under any other enactment, including this Act.

Incidents of bail in criminal proceedings

General provisions

3.—(1) A person granted bail in criminal proceedings shall be under a duty to surrender to custody, and that duty is enforceable in accordance with section 6 of this Act.

(2) No recognisance for his surrender to custody shall be taken from him.

(3) Except as provided by this section—

(a) no security for his surrender to custody shall be taken from him,

(b) he shall not be required to provide a surety or sureties for his surrender to custody, and

(c) no other requirement shall be imposed on him as a condition of bail.

(4) He may be required, before release on bail, to provide a surety or sureties to secure his surrender to custody.

(5) He may be required, before release on bail, to give security for his surrender to custody. The security may be given by him or on his behalf.

(6) He may be required to comply, before release on bail or later, with such requirements as appear to the court to be necessary—

(a) to secure that he surrenders to custody,

(b) to secure that he does not commit an offence while on bail,

(c) to secure that he does not interfere with witnesses or otherwise obstruct the course of justice whether in relation to himself or any other person,

(ca) for his own protection or, if he is a child or young person, for his own welfare or in his own interests,

(d) to secure that he makes himself available for the purpose of enabling inquiries or a report to be made to assist the court in dealing with him for the offence,

(e) to secure that before the time appointed for him to surrender to custody, he attends an interview with an authorised advocate or authorised litigator, as defined by section 119(1) of the Courts and Legal Services Act 1990;

and, in any Act, 'the normal powers to impose conditions of bail' means the powers to impose conditions under paragraph (a), (b), (c) or (ca) above.

(6ZAA) Subject to section 3AA below, if he is a child or young person he may be required to comply with requirements imposed for the purpose of securing the electronic monitoring of his compliance with any other requirement imposed on him as a condition of bail.

(6ZA) Where he is required under subsection (6) above to reside in a bail hostel or probation hostel, he may also be required to comply with the rules of the hostel.

(6A) In the case of a person accused of murder the court granting bail shall, unless it considers that satisfactory reports on his mental condition have already been obtained, impose as conditions of bail—

(a) a requirement that the accused shall undergo examination by two medical practitioners for the purpose of enabling such reports to be prepared; and

(b) a requirement that he shall for that purpose attend such an institution or place as the court directs and comply with any other directions which may be given to him for that purpose by either of those practitioners.

(6B) Of the medical practitioners referred to in subsection (6A) above at least one shall be a practitioner approved for the purposes of section 12 of the Mental Health Act 1983.

(6C) Subsection (6D) below applies where—

(a) the court has been notified by the Secretary of State that arrangements for conducting a relevant assessment or, as the case may be, providing relevant follow-up have been made for the local justice area in which it appears to the court that the person referred to in subsection (6D) would reside if granted bail; and

(b) the notice has not been withdrawn.

(6D) In the case of a person ('P')—

(a) in relation to whom paragraphs (a) to (c) of paragraph 6B(1) of part 1 of schedule 1 to this Act apply;

(b) who, after analysis of the sample referred to in paragraph (b) of that paragraph, has been offered a relevant assessment or, if a relevant assessment has been carried out, has had relevant follow-up proposed to him; and

(c) who has agreed to undergo the relevant assessment or, as the case may be, to participate in the relevant follow-up,

the court, if it grants bail, shall impose as a condition of bail that P both undergo the relevant assessment and participate in any relevant follow-up proposed to him or, if a relevant assessment has been carried out, that P participate in the relevant follow-up.

(6E) In subsections (6C) and (6D) above—

(a) 'relevant assessment' means an assessment conducted by a suitably qualified person of whether P is dependent upon or has a propensity to misuse any specified Class A drugs;

(b) 'relevant follow-up' means, in a case where the person who conducted the relevant assessment believes P to have such a dependency or propensity, such further assessment, and such assistance or treatment (or both) in connection with the dependency or propensity, as the person who conducted the relevant assessment (or conducts any later assessment) considers to be appropriate in P's case, and in paragraph (a) above 'Class A drug' and 'misuse' have the same meaning as in the Misuse of Drugs Act 1971, and 'specified' (in relation to a Class A drug) has the same meaning as in part 3 of the Criminal Justice and Court Services Act 2000.

(6F) In subsection (6E)(a) above, 'suitably qualified person' means a person who has such qualifications or experience as are from time to time specified by the Secretary of State for the purposes of this subsection.

(7) If a parent or guardian of a child or young person consents to be surety for the child or young person for the purposes of this subsection, the parent or guardian may be required to secure that the child or young person complies with any requirement imposed on him by virtue of subsection (6), (6ZAA) or (6A) above but—

(a) no requirement shall be imposed on the parent or the guardian of a young person by virtue of this subsection where it appears that the young person will attain the age of 17 before the time to be appointed for him to surrender to custody; and

(b) the parent or guardian shall not be required to secure compliance with any requirement to which his consent does not extend and shall not, in respect of those requirements to which his consent does extend, be bound in a sum greater than £50.

(8) Where a court has granted bail in criminal proceedings that court or, where that court has sent a person on bail to the Crown Court for trial or to be sentenced or otherwise dealt with, that court or the Crown Court may on application—

(a) by or on behalf of the person to whom bail was granted, or

(b) by the prosecutor or a constable,

vary the conditions of bail or impose conditions in respect of bail which has been granted unconditionally.

(8A) Where a notice of transfer is given under a relevant transfer provision, subsection (8) above shall have effect in relation to a person in relation to whose case the notice is given as if he had been committed on bail to the Crown Court for trial.

(8B) Subsection (8) above applies where a court has sent a person on bail to the Crown Court for trial under section 51 of the Crime and Disorder Act 1998 as it applies where a court has committed a person on bail to the Crown Court for trial.

(9) This section is subject to subsection (3) of section 11 of the Powers of Criminal Courts (Sentencing) Act 2000 (conditions of bail on remand for medical examination).

(10) This section is subject, in its application to bail granted by a constable, to section 3A of this Act.

(10) In subsection (8A) above 'relevant transfer provision' means—

(a) section 4 of the Criminal Justice Act 1987, or

(b) section 53 of the Criminal Justice Act 1991.

[Section 3 is prospectively amended by the CJA 2003, s. 41 and sch. 3, part 2. The amendments, which include the repeal of subsections (8A) and (8B) and the second subsection (10), are consequential on the reforms in the 2003 Act on allocation of offences triable either way and the sending of cases to the Crown Court.]

3AA.—(1) A court shall not impose on a child or young person a requirement under section 3(6ZAA) above (an 'electronic monitoring requirement') unless each of the following conditions is satisfied.

(2) The first condition is that the child or young person has attained the age of twelve years.

(3) The second condition is that—

(a) the child or young person is charged with or has been convicted of a violent or sexual offence, or an offence punishable in the case of an adult with imprisonment for a term of fourteen years or more; or

(b) he is charged with or has been convicted of one or more imprisonable offences which, together with any other imprisonable offences of which he has been convicted in any proceedings—

(i) amount, or

(ii) would, if he were convicted of the offences with which he is charged, amount,

to a recent history of repeatedly committing imprisonable offences while remanded on bail or to local authority accommodation.

(4) The third condition is that the court—

(a) has been notified by the Secretary of State that electronic monitoring arrangements are available in each local justice area which is a relevant area; and

(b) is satisfied that the necessary provision can be made under those arrangements.

(5) The fourth condition is that a youth offending team has informed the court that in its

opinion the imposition of such a requirement will be suitable in the case of the child or young person.

(6) Where a court imposes an electronic monitoring requirement, the requirement shall include provision for making a person responsible for the monitoring; and a person who is made so responsible shall be of a description specified in an order made by the Secretary of State.

(7) The Secretary of State may make rules for regulating—

(a) the electronic monitoring of compliance with requirements imposed on a child or young person as a condition of bail; and

(b) without prejudice to the generality of paragraph (a) above, the functions of persons made responsible for securing the electronic monitoring of compliance with such requirements.

(8) Rules under this section may make different provision for different cases.

(9) Any power of the Secretary of State to make an order or rules under this section shall be exercisable by statutory instrument.

(10) A statutory instrument containing rules made under this section shall be subject to annulment in pursuance of a resolution of either House of Parliament.

(11) In this section 'local authority accommodation' has the same meaning as in the Children and Young Persons Act 1969.

(12) For the purposes of this section a local justice area is a relevant area in relation to a proposed electronic monitoring requirement if the court considers that it will not be practicable to secure the electronic monitoring in question unless electronic monitoring arrangements are available in that area.

Conditions of bail in case of police bail

3A.—(1) Section 3 of this Act applies, in relation to bail granted by a custody officer under part IV of the Police and Criminal Evidence Act 1984 in cases where the normal powers to impose conditions of bail are available to him, subject to the following modifications.

(2) Subsection (6) does not authorise the imposition of a requirement to reside in a bail hostel or any requirement under paragraph (d) or (e).

(3) Subsections (6ZAA), (6ZA), (6A) to (6F) shall be omitted.

(4) For subsection (8), substitute the following—

'(8) Where a custody officer has granted bail in criminal proceedings he or another custody officer serving at the same police station may, at the request of the person to whom it was granted, vary the conditions of bail; and in doing so he may impose conditions or more onerous conditions.'

(5) Where a constable grants bail to a person no conditions shall be imposed under subsections (4), (5), (6) or (7) of section 3 of this Act unless it appears to the constable that it is necessary to do so—

(a) for the purpose of preventing that person from failing to surrender to custody, or

(b) for the purpose of preventing that person from committing an offence while on bail, or

(c) for the purpose of preventing that person from interfering with witnesses or otherwise obstructing the course of justice, whether in relation to himself or any other person, or

(d) for that person's own protection or, if he is a child or young person, for his own welfare or in his own interests.

(6) Subsection (5) above also applies on any request to a custody officer under subsection (8) of section 3 of this Act to vary the conditions of bail.

Bail for accused persons and others

General right to bail of accused persons and others

4.—(1) A person to whom this section applies shall be granted bail except as provided in schedule 1 to this Act.

(2) This section applies to a person who is accused of an offence when—

(a) he appears or is brought before a magistrates' court or the Crown Court in the course of or in connection with proceedings for the offence, or

(b) he applies to a court for bail or for a variation of the conditions of bail in connection with the proceedings.

This subsection does not apply as respects proceedings on or after a person's conviction of the offence.

D

Part D Procedure

(2A) This section also applies to a person whose extradition is sought in respect of an offence, when—
(a) he appears or is brought before a court in the course of or in connection with extradition proceedings in respect of the offence, or
(b) he applies to a court for bail or for a variation of the conditions of bail in connection with the proceedings.

(2B) But subsection (2A) above does not apply if the person is alleged to have been convicted of the offence.

(3) This section also applies to a person who, having been convicted of an offence, appears or is brought before a magistrates' court or the Crown Court to be dealt with under—
(a) part 2 of schedule 3 to the Powers of Criminal Courts (Sentencing) Act 2000 (breach of certain youth community orders), or
(b) part 2 of schedule 8 to the Criminal Justice Act 2003 (breach of requirement of community order).

(4) This section also applies to a person who has been convicted of an offence and whose case is adjourned by the court for the purpose of enabling inquiries or a report to be made to assist the court in dealing with him for the offence.

(5) Schedule 1 to this Act also has effect as respects conditions of bail for a person to whom this section applies.

(6) In schedule 1 to this Act 'the defendant' means a person to whom this section applies and any reference to a defendant whose case is adjourned for inquiries or a report is a reference to a person to whom this section applies by virtue of subsection (4) above.

(7) This section is subject to section 41 of the Magistrates' Courts Act 1980 (restriction of bail by magistrates' court in cases of treason).

(8) This section is subject to section 25 of the Criminal Justice and Public Order Act 1994 (exclusion of bail in cases of homicide and rape).

(9) In taking any decisions required by part I or II of schedule 1 to this Act, the considerations to which the court is to have regard include, so far as relevant, any misuse of controlled drugs by the defendant ('controlled drugs' and 'misuse' having the same meanings as in the Misuse of Drugs Act 1971).

[Section 4(3) is prospectively amended by the CJA 2003, sch. 32, para. 22.]

Supplementary

Supplementary provisions about decisions on bail

5.—(1) Subject to subsection (2) below, where—
(a) a court or constable grants bail in criminal proceedings, or
(b) a court withholds bail in criminal proceedings from a person to whom section 4 of this Act applies, or
(c) a court, or officer of a court or constable appoints a different time or place for a person granted bail in criminal proceedings to surrender to custody, or
(d) a court or constable varies any conditions of bail or imposes conditions in respect of bail in criminal proceedings,

that court, officer or constable shall make a record of the decision in the prescribed manner and containing the prescribed particulars and, if requested to do so by the person in relation to whom the decision was taken, shall cause him to be given a copy of the record of the decision as soon as practicable after the record is made.

(2) Where bail in criminal proceedings is granted by endorsing a warrant of arrest for bail the constable who releases on bail the person arrested shall make the record required by subsection (1) above instead of the judge or justice who issued the warrant.

(2A) Where a magistrates' court or the Crown Court grants bail in criminal proceedings to a person to whom section 4 of this Act applies after hearing representations from the prosecutor in favour of withholding bail, then the court shall give reasons for granting bail.

(2B) A court which is by virtue of subsection (2A) above required to give reasons for its decision shall include a note of those reasons in the record of its decision and, if requested to do so by the prosecutor, shall cause the prosecutor to be given a copy of the record of the decision as soon as practicable after the record is made.

(3) Where a magistrates' court or the Crown Court—
(a) withholds bail in criminal proceedings, or
(b) imposes conditions in granting bail in criminal proceedings, or

(c) varies any conditions of bail or imposes conditions in respect of bail in criminal proceedings,

and does so in relation to a person to whom section 4 of this Act applies, then the court shall, with a view to enabling him to consider making an application in the matter to another court, give reasons for withholding bail or for imposing or varying the conditions.

(4) A court which is by virtue of subsection (3) above required to give reasons for its decision shall include a note of those reasons in the record of its decision and shall (except in a case where, by virtue of subsection (5) below, this need not be done) give a copy of that note to the person in relation to whom the decision was taken.

(5) The Crown Court need not give a copy of the note of the reasons for its decision to the person in relation to whom the decision was taken where that person is represented by counsel or a solicitor unless his counsel or solicitor requests the court to do so.

(6) Where a magistrates' court withholds bail in criminal proceedings from a person who is not represented by counsel or a solicitor, the court shall—

(a) if it is sending him for trial to the Crown Court, or if it issues a certificate under subsection (6A) below inform him that he may apply to the High Court or to the Crown Court to be granted bail;

(b) in any other case, inform him that he may apply to the High Court for that purpose.

(6A) Where in criminal proceedings—

(a) a magistrates' court remands a person in custody under section 52(5) of the Crime and Disorder Act 1998, section 11 of the Powers of Criminal Courts (Sentencing) Act 2000 or any of the following provisions of the Magistrates' Courts Act 1980—

(i) section 5 (adjournment of inquiry into offence);

(ii) section 10 (adjournment of trial); or

(iii) section 18 (initial procedure on information against adult for offence triable either way),

after hearing full argument on an application for bail from him; and

(b) either—

(i) it has not previously heard such argument on an application for bail from him in those proceedings; or

(ii) it has previously heard full argument from him on such an application but it is satisfied that there has been a change in his circumstances or that new considerations have been placed before it,

it shall be the duty of the court to issue a certificate in the prescribed form that they heard full argument on his application for bail before they refused the application.

(6B) Where the court issues a certificate under subsection (6A) above in a case to which paragraph (b)(ii) of that subsection applies, it shall state in the certificate the nature of the change of circumstances or the new considerations which caused it to hear a further fully argued bail application.

(6C) Where a court issues a certificate under subsection (6A) above it shall cause the person to whom it refuses bail to be given a copy of the certificate.

(7) Where a person has given security in pursuance of section 3(5) above, and a court is satisfied that he failed to surrender to custody then, unless it appears that he had reasonable cause for his failure, the court may order the forfeiture of the security.

(8) If a court orders the forfeiture of a security under subsection (7) above, the court may declare that the forfeiture extends to such amount less than the full value of the security as it thinks fit to order.

[Subsections (8A) to (9A) detail procedure for taking and forfeiting a security.]

(10) In this section 'prescribed' means, in relation to the decision of a court or an officer of a court, prescribed by Civil Procedure Rules, Courts-Martial Appeal rules or Criminal Procedure Rules, as the case requires or, in relation to a decision of a constable, prescribed by direction of the Secretary of State.

(11) This section is subject, in its application to bail granted by a constable, to section 5A of this Act.

[Section 5 is prospectively amended by the CJA 2003, s. 41, sch. 3, part 2 and sch. 36, part 1.]

Supplementary provisions in cases of police bail

5A.—(1) Section 5 of this Act applies, in relation to bail granted by a custody officer under part IV of the Police and Criminal Evidence Act 1984 in cases where the normal powers to impose conditions of bail are available to him, subject to the following modifications.

(1A) Subsections (2A) and (2B) shall be omitted.
(2) For subsection (3) substitute the following—
'(3) Where a custody officer, in relation to any person,—
(a) imposes conditions in granting bail in criminal proceedings, or
(b) varies any conditions of bail or imposes conditions in respect of bail, in criminal proceedings,
the custody officer shall, with a view to enabling that person to consider requesting him or another custody officer, or making an application to a magistrates' court, to vary the conditions, give reasons for imposing or varying the conditions.'.
(3) For subsection (4) substitute the following—
'(4) A custody officer who is by virtue of subsection (3) above required to give reasons for his decision shall include a note of those reasons in the custody record and shall give a copy of that note to the person in relation to whom the decision was taken.'.
(4) Subsections (5) and (6) shall be omitted.

Reconsideration of decisions granting bail

5B.—(A1) This section applies in any of these cases—
(a) a magistrates' court has granted bail in criminal proceedings in connection with an offence to which this section applies or proceedings for such an offence;
(b) a constable has granted bail in criminal proceedings in connection with proceedings for such an offence;
(c) a magistrates' court or a constable has granted bail in connection with extradition proceedings.
(1) The court or the appropriate court in relation to the constable may, on application by the prosecutor for the decision to be reconsidered,—
(a) vary the conditions of bail,
(b) impose conditions in respect of bail which has been granted unconditionally, or
(c) withhold bail.
(2) The offences to which this section applies are offences triable on indictment and offences triable either way.
(3) No application for the reconsideration of a decision under this section shall be made unless it is based on information which was not available to the court or constable when the decision was taken.
(4) Whether or not the person to whom the application relates appears before it, the magistrates' court shall take the decision in accordance with section 4(1) (and schedule 1) of this Act.
(5) Where the decision of the court on a reconsideration under this section is to withhold bail from the person to whom it was originally granted the court shall—
(a) if that person is before the court, remand him in custody, and
(b) if that person is not before the court, order him to surrender himself forthwith into the custody of the court.
(6) Where a person surrenders himself into the custody of the court in compliance with an order under subsection (5) above, the court shall remand him in custody.
(7) A person who has been ordered to surrender to custody under subsection (5) above may be arrested without warrant by a constable if he fails without reasonable cause to surrender to custody in accordance with the order.
(8) A person arrested in pursuance of subsection (7) above shall be brought as soon as practicable, and in any event within 24 hours after his arrest, before a justice of the peace for the local justice area in which he was arrested and the justice shall remand him in custody. In reckoning for the purposes of this subsection any period of 24 hours, no account shall be taken of Christmas Day, Good Friday or any Sunday.
(8A) Where the court, on a reconsideration under this section, refuses to withhold bail from a relevant person after hearing representations from the prosecutor in favour of withholding bail, then the court shall give reasons for refusing to withhold bail.
(8B) In subsection (8A) above, 'relevant person' means a person to whom section 4(1) (and Schedule 1) of this Act is applicable in accordance with subsection (4) above.
(8C) A court which is by virtue of subsection (8A) above required to give reasons for its decision shall include a note of those reasons in any record of its decision and, if requested to do so by the prosecutor, shall cause the prosecutor to be given a copy of any such record as soon as practicable after the record is made.

(9) Criminal Procedure Rules shall include provision—
(a) requiring notice of an application under this section and of the grounds for it to be given to the person affected, including notice of the powers available to the court under it;
(b) for securing that any representations made by the person affected (whether in writing or orally) are considered by the court before making its decision; and
(c) designating the court which is the appropriate court in relation to the decision of any constable to grant bail.

Offence of absconding by person released on bail

6.—(1) If a person who has been released on bail in criminal proceedings fails without reasonable cause to surrender to custody he shall be guilty of an offence.
(2) If a person who—
(a) has been released on bail in criminal proceedings, and
(b) having reasonable cause therefor, has failed to surrender to custody,
fails to surrender to custody at the appointed place as soon after the appointed time as is reasonably practicable he shall be guilty of an offence.
(3) It shall be for the accused to prove that he had reasonable cause for his failure to surrender to custody.
(4) A failure to give to a person granted bail in criminal proceedings a copy of the record of the decision shall not constitute a reasonable cause for that person's failure to surrender to custody.
(5) An offence under subsection (1) or (2) above shall be punishable either on summary conviction or as if it were a criminal contempt of court.
(6) Where a magistrates' court convicts a person of an offence under subsection (1) or (2) above the court may, if it thinks—
(a) that the circumstances of the offence are such that greater punishment should be inflicted for that offence than the court has power to inflict, or
(b) in a case where it sends that person for trial to the Crown Court for another offence, that it would be appropriate for him to be dealt with for the offence under subsection (1) or (2) above by the court before which he is tried for the other offence, commit him in custody or on bail to the Crown Court for sentence.
(7) A person who is convicted summarily of an offence under subsection (1) or (2) above and is not committed to the Crown Court for sentence shall be liable to imprisonment for a term not exceeding three months or to a fine not exceeding level 5 on the standard scale or to both and a person who is so committed for sentence or is dealt with as for such a contempt shall be liable to imprisonment for a term not exceeding 12 months or to a fine or to both.
(8) In any proceedings for an offence under subsection (1) or (2) above a document purporting to be a copy of the part of the prescribed record which relates to the time and place appointed for the person specified in the record to surrender to custody and to be duly certified to be a true copy of that part of the record shall be evidence of the time and place appointed for that person to surrender to custody.
(9) For the purposes of subsection (8) above—
(a) 'the prescribed record' means the record of the decision of the court, officer or constable made in pursuance of section 5(1) of this Act;
(b) the copy of the prescribed record is duly certified if it is certified by the appropriate officer of the court or, as the case may be, by the constable who took the decision or a constable designated for the purpose by the officer in charge of the police station from which the person to whom the record relates was released;
(c) 'the appropriate officer' of the court is—
(i) in the case of a magistrates' court, the designated officer for the court;
(ii) in the case of the Crown Court, such officer as may be designated for the purpose in accordance with arrangements made by the Lord Chancellor;
(iii) in the case of the High Court, such officer as may be designated for the purpose in accordance with arrangements made by the Lord Chancellor;
(iv) in the case of the Court of Appeal, the registrar of criminal appeals or such other officer as may be authorised by him to act for the purpose;
(v) in the case of the Courts-Martial Appeal Court, the registrar or such other officer as may be authorised by him to act for the purpose.
(10) Section 127 of the Magistrates' Courts Act 1980 shall not apply in relation to an offence under subsection (1) or (2) above.

(11) Where a person has been released on bail in criminal proceedings and that bail was granted by a constable, a magistrates' court shall not try that person for an offence under subsection (1) or (2) above in relation to that bail (the 'relevant offence') unless either or both of subsections (12) and (13) below applies.
(12) This subsection applies if an information is laid for the relevant offence within 6 months from the time of the commission of the relevant offence.
(13) This subsection applies if an information is laid for the relevant offence no later than 3 months from the time of the occurrence of the first of the events mentioned in subsection (14) below to occur after the commission of the relevant offence.
(14) Those events are—
(a) the person surrenders to custody at the appointed place;
(b) the person is arrested, or attends at a police station, in connection with the relevant offence or the offence for which he was granted bail;
(c) the person appears or is brought before a court in connection with the relevant offence or the offence for which he was granted bail.

[Section 6 is prospectively amended by the CJA 2003, s. 41 and sch. 3, part 2.]

Liability to arrest for absconding or breaking conditions of bail

7.—(1) If a person who has been released on bail in criminal proceedings and is under a duty to surrender into the custody of a court fails to surrender to custody at the time appointed for him to do so the court may issue a warrant for his arrest.
(1A) Subsection (1B) applies if—
(a) a person has been released on bail in connection with extradition proceedings,
(b) the person is under a duty to surrender into the custody of a constable, and
(c) the person fails to surrender to custody at the time appointed for him to do so.
(1B) A magistrates' court may issue a warrant for the person's arrest.
(2) If a person who has been released on bail in criminal proceedings absents himself from the court at any time after he has surrendered into the custody of the court and before the court is ready to begin or to resume the hearing of the proceedings, the court may issue a warrant for his arrest; but no warrant shall be issued under this subsection where that person is absent in accordance with leave given to him by or on behalf of the court.
(3) A person who has been released on bail in criminal proceedings and is under a duty to surrender into the custody of a court may be arrested without warrant by a constable—
(a) if the constable has reasonable grounds for believing that that person is not likely to surrender to custody;
(b) if the constable has reasonable grounds for believing that that person is likely to break any of the conditions of his bail or has reasonable grounds for suspecting that that person has broken any of those conditions; or
(c) in a case where that person was released on bail with one or more surety or sureties, if a surety notifies a constable in writing that that person is unlikely to surrender to custody and that for that reason the surety wishes to be relieved of his obligations as a surety.
(4) A person arrested in pursuance of subsection (3) above—
(a) shall, except where he was arrested within 24 hours of the time appointed for him to surrender to custody, be brought as soon as practicable and in any event within 24 hours after his arrest before a justice of the peace; and
(b) in the said excepted case shall be brought before the court at which he was to have surrendered to custody.
(4A) A person who has been released on bail in connection with extradition proceedings and is under a duty to surrender into the custody of a constable may be arrested without warrant by a constable on any of the grounds set out in paragraphs (a) to (c) of subsection (3).
(4B) A person arrested in pursuance of subsection (4A) above shall be brought as soon as practicable and in any event within 24 hours after his arrest before a justice of the peace for the petty sessions area in which he was arrested.
(5) A justice of the peace before whom a person is brought under subsection (4) above may, subject to subsection (6) below, if of the opinion that that person—
(a) is not likely to surrender to custody, or
(b) has broken or is likely to break any condition of his bail,
remand him in custody or commit him to custody, as the case may require, or alternatively, grant him bail subject to the same or to different conditions, but if not of that opinion shall grant him bail subject to the same conditions (if any) as were originally imposed.

(6) Where the person so brought before the justice is a child or young person and the justice does not grant him bail, subsection (5) above shall have effect subject to the provisions of section 23 of the Children and Young Persons Act 1969 (remands to the care of local authorities).

(7) In reckoning for the purposes of this subsection any period of 24 hours, no account shall be taken of Christmas Day, Good Friday or any Sunday.

Bail with sureties

8.—(1) This section applies where a person is granted bail in criminal proceedings on condition that he provides one or more surety or sureties for the purpose of securing that he surrenders to custody.

(2) In considering the suitability for that purpose of a proposed surety, regard may be had (amongst other things) to—
- (a) the surety's financial resources;
- (b) his character and any previous convictions of his; and
- (c) his proximity (whether in point of kinship, place of residence or otherwise) to the person for whom he is to be surety.

(3) Where a court grants a person bail in criminal proceedings on such a condition but is unable to release him because no surety or no suitable surety is available, the court shall fix the amount in which the surety is to be found and subsections (4) and (5) below, or in a case where the proposed surety resides in Scotland subsection (6) below, shall apply for the purpose of enabling the recognisance of the surety to be entered into subsequently.

(4) Where this subsection applies the recognisance of the surety may be entered into before such of the following persons or descriptions of persons as the court may by order specify or, if it makes no such order, before any of the following persons, that is to say—
- (a) where the decision is taken by a magistrates' court, before a justice of the peace, a justices' clerk or a police officer who either is of the rank of inspector or above or is in charge of a police station or, if Criminal Procedure Rules so provide, by a person of such other description as is specified in the rules;
- (b) where the decision is taken by the Crown Court, before any of the persons specified in paragraph (a) above or, if Criminal Procedure Rules so provide, by a person of such other description as is specified in the rules;
- (c) where the decision is taken by the High Court or the Court of Appeal, before any of the persons specified in paragraph (a) above or, if Criminal Procedure Rules so provide, by a person of such other description as is specified in the rules;
- (d) where the decision is taken by the Courts-Martial Appeal Court, before any of the persons specified in paragraph (a) above or, if Courts-Martial Appeal rules so provide, by a person of such other description as is specified in the rules;

and Civil Procedure Rules, Criminal Procedure Rules or Courts-Martial Appeal Rules may also prescribe the manner in which a recognisance which is to be entered into before such a person is to be entered into and the persons by whom and the manner in which the recognisance may be enforced.

(5) Where a surety seeks to enter into his recognisance before any person in accordance with subsection (4) above but that person declines to take his recognisance because he is not satisfied of the surety's suitability, the surety may apply to—
- (a) the court which fixed the amount of the recognisance in which the surety was to be bound, or
- (b) a magistrates' court for the petty sessions area in which he resides, for that court to take his recognisance and that court shall, if satisfied of his suitability, take his recognisance.

(6) Where this subsection applies, the court, if satisfied of the suitability of the proposed surety, may direct that arrangements be made for the recognisance of the surety to be entered into in Scotland before any constable, within the meaning of the Police (Scotland) Act 1967, having charge at any police office or station in like manner as the recognisance would be entered into in England or Wales.

(7) Where, in pursuance of subsection (4) or (6) above, a recognisance is entered into otherwise than before the court that fixed the amount of the recognisance, the same consequences shall follow as if it had been entered into before that court.

Miscellaneous

Offence of agreeing to indemnify sureties in criminal proceedings

9.—(1) If a person agrees with another to indemnify that other against any liability which that other may incur as a surety to secure the surrender to custody of a person accused or convicted of or under arrest for an offence, he and that other person shall be guilty of an offence.

(2) An offence under subsection (1) above is committed whether the agreement is made before or after the person to be indemnified becomes a surety and whether or not he becomes a surety and whether the agreement contemplates compensation in money or in money's worth.

(3) Where a magistrates' court convicts a person of an offence under subsection (1) above the court may, if it thinks—

(a) that the circumstances of the offence are such that greater punishment should be inflicted for that offence than the court has power to inflict, or

(b) in a case where it sends that person for trial to the Crown Court for another offence, that it would be appropriate for him to be dealt with for the offence under subsection (1) above by the court before which he is tried for the other offence,

commit him in custody or on bail to the Crown Court for sentence.

(4) A person guilty of an offence under subsection (1) above shall be liable—

(a) on summary conviction, to imprisonment for a term not exceeding 3 months or to a fine not exceeding the prescribed sum or to both; or

(b) on conviction on indictment or if sentenced by the Crown Court on committal for sentence under subsection (3) above, to imprisonment for a term not exceeding 12 months or to a fine or to both.

(5) No proceedings for an offence under subsection (1) above shall be instituted except by or with the consent of the Director of Public Prosecutions.

[**10.** and **11.** Repealed.]

[**12.** Amendments, repeals and transitional provisions.]

[**13.** Short title, commencement, application and extent.]

Schedule 1

Persons Entitled to Bail: Supplementary Provisions

Part I

Defendants Accused or Convicted of Imprisonable Offences

Defendants to whom part I applies

The following provisions of this part of this schedule apply to the defendant if—

(a) the offence or one of the offences of which he is accused or convicted in the proceedings is punishable with imprisonment, or

(b) his extradition is sought in respect of an offence.

Exceptions to right to bail

2.—(1) The defendant need not be granted bail if the court is satisfied that there are substantial grounds for believing that the defendant, if released on bail (whether subject to conditions or not) would—

(a) fail to surrender to custody, or

(b) commit an offence while on bail, or

(c) interfere with witnesses or otherwise obstruct the course of justice, whether in relation to himself or any other person.

(2) Where the defendant falls within one or more of paragraphs 2A, 6 and 6B of this part of this schedule this paragraph shall not apply unless—

(a) where the defendant falls within paragraph 2A, the court is satisfied as mentioned in sub-paragraph (1) of that paragraph;

(b) where the defendant falls within paragraph 6, the court is satisfied as mentioned in sub-paragraph (1) of that paragraph;

(c) where the defendant falls within paragraph 6B, the court is satisfied as mentioned in paragraph 6A of this part of this schedule or paragraph 6A does not apply by virtue of paragraph 6C of this part of this schedule.

2A. The defendant need not be granted bail if—
(a) the offence is an indictable offence or an offence triable either way; and
(b) it appears to the court that he was on bail in criminal proceedings on the date of the offence.

2A.—(1) If the defendant falls within this paragraph he may not be granted bail unless the court is satisfied that there is no significant risk of his committing an offence while on bail (whether subject to conditions or not).
(2) The defendant falls within this paragraph if—
(a) he is aged 18 or over, and
(b) it appears to the court that he was on bail in criminal proceedings on the date of the offence.

[Note: two versions of para. 2A apply concurrently, depending on circumstances: see SI 2006 No. 3217 and **D7.20**.]

2B. The defendant need not be granted bail in connection with extradition proceedings if—
(a) the conduct constituting the offence would, if carried out by the defendant in England and Wales, constitute an indictable offence or an offence triable either way; and
(b) it appears to the court that the defendant was on bail on the date of the offence.

3. The defendant need not be granted bail if the court is satisfied that the defendant should be kept in custody for his own protection or, if he is a child or young person, for his own welfare.

4. The defendant need not be granted bail if he is in custody in pursuance of the sentence of a court or of any authority acting under any of the Services Acts.

5. The defendant need not be granted bail where the court is satisfied that it has not been practicable to obtain sufficient information for the purpose of taking the decisions required by this part of this schedule for want of time since the institution of the proceedings against him.

6. *The defendant need not be granted bail if, having been released on bail in or in connection with the proceedings for the offence or the extradition proceedings, he has been arrested in pursuance of section 7 of this Act.*

6.—(1) If the defendant falls within this paragraph, he may not be granted bail unless the court is satisfied that there is no significant risk that, if released on bail (whether subject to conditions or not), he would fail to surrender to custody.
(2) Subject to sub-paragraph (3) below, the defendant falls within this paragraph if—
(a) he is aged 18 or over, and
(b) it appears to the court that, having been released on bail in or in connection with the proceedings for the offence, he failed to surrender to custody.
(3) Where it appears to the court that the defendant had reasonable cause for his failure to surrender to custody, he does not fall within this paragraph unless it also appears to the court that he failed to surrender to custody at the appointed place as soon as reasonably practicable after the appointed time.
(4) For the purposes of sub-paragraph (3) above, a failure to give to the defendant a copy of the record of the decision to grant him bail shall not constitute a reasonable cause for his failure to surrender to custody.

[Note: two versions of para. 6 apply concurrently, depending on circumstances: see SI 2006 No. 3217 and **D7.20**.]

Exception applicable to drug users in certain areas

6A. Subject to paragraph 6C below, a defendant who falls within paragraph 6B below may not be granted bail unless the court is satisfied that there is no significant risk of his committing an offence while on bail (whether subject to conditions or not).

6B.—(1) A defendant falls within this paragraph if—
(a) he is aged 18 or over,
(b) a sample taken—
(i) under section 63B of the Police and Criminal Evidence Act 1984 (testing for presence of Class A drugs) in connection with the offence; or
(ii) under section 161 of the Criminal Justice Act 2003 (drug testing after conviction of an offence but before sentence),
has revealed the presence in his body of a specified Class A drug;
(c) either the offence is one under section 5(2) or (3) of the Misuse of Drugs Act 1971 and relates to a specified Class A drug, or the court is satisfied that there are substantial grounds for believing—

(i) that misuse by him of any specified Class A drug caused or contributed to the offence; or
(ii) (even if it did not) that the offence was motivated wholly or partly by his intended misuse of such a drug; and

(d) the condition set out in sub-paragraph (2) below is satisfied or (if the court is considering on a second or subsequent occasion whether or not to grant bail) has been, and continues to be, satisfied.

(2) The condition referred to is that after the taking and analysis of the sample—
(a) a relevant assessment has been offered to the defendant but he does not agree to undergo it; or
(b) he has undergone a relevant assessment, and relevant follow-up has been proposed to him, but he does not agree to participate in it.

(3) In this paragraph and paragraph 6C below—
(a) 'Class A drug' and 'misuse' have the same meaning as in the Misuse of Drugs Act 1971;
(b) 'relevant assessment' and 'relevant follow-up' have the meaning given by section 3(6E) of this Act;
(c) 'specified' (in relation to a Class A drug) has the same meaning as in part 3 of the Criminal Justice and Court Services Act 2000.

6C. Paragraph 6A above does not apply unless—
(a) the court has been notified by the Secretary of State that arrangements for conducting a relevant assessment or, as the case may be, providing relevant follow-up have been made for the local justice area in which it appears to the court that the defendant would reside if granted bail; and
(b) the notice has not been withdrawn.

Exception applicable only to defendant whose case is adjourned for inquiries or a report

7. Where his case is adjourned for inquiries or a report, the defendant need not be granted bail if it appears to the court that it would be impracticable to complete the inquiries or make the report without keeping the defendant in custody.

Restriction of conditions of bail

8.—(1) Subject to subparagraph (3) below, where the defendant is granted bail, no conditions shall be imposed under subsections (4) to (6B) or (7) (except subsection (6)(d) or (e)) of section 3 of this Act unless it appears to the court that it is necessary to do so—
(a) for the purpose of preventing the occurrence of any of the events mentioned in paragraph 2(1) of this part of this schedule, or
(b) for the defendant's own protection or, if he is a child or young person, for his own welfare or in his own interests.

(2) Subparagraph (1) above also applies on any application to the court to vary the conditions of bail or to impose conditions in respect of bail which has been granted unconditionally.

(3) The restriction imposed by subparagraph (1) above shall not apply to the conditions required to be imposed under section 3(6A) of this Act or operate to override the direction in section 11(3) of the Powers of Criminal Courts (Sentencing) Act 2000 to a magistrates' court to impose conditions of bail under section 3(6)(d) of this Act of the description specified in the said section 11(3) in the circumstances so specified.

Decisions under paragraph 2

9. In taking the decisions required by paragraph 2(1), or in deciding whether it is satisfied as mentioned in paragraph 2A(1), 6(1) or 6A of this part of this schedule, the court shall have regard to such of the following considerations as appear to it to be relevant, that is to say—
(a) the nature and seriousness of the offence or default (and the probable method of dealing with the defendant for it),
(b) the character, antecedents, associations and community ties of the defendant,
(c) the defendant's record as respects the fulfilment of his obligations under previous grants of bail in criminal proceedings,
(d) except in the case of a defendant whose case is adjourned for inquiries or a report, the strength of the evidence of his having committed the offence or having defaulted,

as well as to any others which appear to be relevant.

9AA.—(1) This paragraph applies if—
(a) the defendant is under the age of 18, and
(b) it appears to the court that he was on bail in criminal proceedings on the date of the offence.

(2) In deciding for the purposes of paragraph 2(1) of this part of this schedule whether it is satisfied that there are substantial grounds for believing that the defendant, if released on bail (whether subject to conditions or not), would commit an offence while on bail, the court shall give particular weight to the fact that the defendant was on bail in criminal proceedings on the date of the offence.

9AB.—(1) Subject to sub-paragraph (2) below, this paragraph applies if—
(a) the defendant is under the age of 18, and
(b) it appears to the court that, having been released on bail in or in connection with the proceedings for the offence, he failed to surrender to custody.

(2) Where it appears to the court that the defendant had reasonable cause for his failure to surrender to custody, this paragraph does not apply unless it also appears to the court that he failed to surrender to custody at the appointed place as soon as reasonably practicable after the appointed time.

(3) In deciding for the purposes of paragraph 2(1) of this part of this schedule whether it is satisfied that there are substantial grounds for believing that the defendant, if released on bail (whether subject to conditions or not), would fail to surrender to custody, the court shall give particular weight to—
(a) where the defendant did not have reasonable cause for his failure to surrender to custody, the fact that he failed to surrender to custody, or
(b) where he did have reasonable cause for his failure to surrender to custody, the fact that he failed to surrender to custody at the appointed place as soon as reasonably practicable after the appointed time.

(4) For the purposes of this paragraph, a failure to give to the defendant a copy of the record of the decision to grant him bail shall not constitute a reasonable cause for his failure to surrender to custody.

[Note: Paragraphs 9AA and 9AB are in force only in respect of offences which attract a life sentence: see SI 2006 No. 3217 and **D7.20**.]

Cases under section 128A of Magistrates' Courts Act 1980

9B. Where the court is considering exercising the power conferred by section 128A of the Magistrates' Courts Act 1980 (power to remand in custody for more than 8 clear days), it shall have regard to the total length of time which the accused would spend in custody if it were to exercise the power.

Part II

Defendants Accused or Convicted of Non-imprisonable Offences

Defendants to whom part II applies

1. Where the offence or every offence of which the defendant is accused or convicted in the proceedings is one which is not punishable with imprisonment the following provisions of this part of this schedule apply.

Exceptions to right to bail

2. The defendant need not be granted bail if—
(a) it appears to the court that, having been previously granted bail in criminal proceedings, he has failed to surrender to custody in accordance with his obligations under the grant of bail; and
(b) the court believes, in view of that failure, that the defendant, if released on bail (whether subject to conditions or not) would fail to surrender to custody.

3. The defendant need not be granted bail if the court is satisfied that the defendant should be kept in custody for his own protection or, if he is a child or young person, for his own welfare.

4. The defendant need not be granted bail if he is in custody in pursuance of the sentence of a court or of any authority acting under any of the Services Acts.

5. The defendant need not be granted bail if—

(a) having been released on bail in or in connection with the proceedings for the offence, he has been arrested in pursuance of section 7 of this Act; and
(b) the court is satisfied that there are substantial grounds for believing that the defendant, if released on bail (whether subject to conditions or not) would fail to surrender to custody, commit an offence on bail or interfere with witnesses or otherwise obstruct the course of justice (whether in relation to himself or any other person).

PART IIA

DECISIONS WHERE BAIL REFUSED ON PREVIOUS HEARING

1. If the court decides not to grant the defendant bail, it is the court's duty to consider, at each subsequent hearing while the defendant is a person to whom section 4 above applies and remains in custody, whether he ought to be granted bail.
2. At the first hearing after that at which the court decided not to grant the defendant bail he may support an application for bail with any argument as to fact or law that he desires (whether or not he has advanced that argument previously).
3. At subsequent hearings the court need not hear arguments as to fact or law which it has heard previously.

PART III

INTERPRETATION

1. For the purposes of this schedule the question whether an offence is one which is punishable with imprisonment shall be determined without regard to any enactment prohibiting or restricting the imprisonment of young offenders or first offenders.
2. References in this schedule to previous grants of bail in criminal proceedings include references to bail granted before the coming into force of this Act; and so as respects the reference to an offence committed by a person on bail in relation to any period before the coming into force of paragraph 2A of part I of this schedule.
3. References in this schedule to a defendant's being kept in custody or being in custody include (where the defendant is a child or young person) references to his being kept or being in the care of a local authority in pursuance of a warrant of commitment under section 23(1) of the Children and Young Persons Act 1969.
4. In this schedule—

'court', in the expression 'sentence of a court', includes a service court as defined in section 12(1) of the Visiting Forces Act 1952 and 'sentence', in that expression, shall be construed in accordance with that definition;

'default', in relation to the defendant, means the default for which he is to be dealt with under part 2 of schedule 8 to the Criminal Justice Act 2003 (breach of requirement of order)

'the Services Acts' means the Army Act 1955, the Air Force Act 1955 and the Naval Discipline Act 1957.

[Schedule 1, part III, is prospectively amended by the CJA 2003, sch. 36, para. 3.]

TEXT OF THE BAIL (AMENDMENT) ACT 1993

D7.98 **Bail (Amendment) Act 1993, s. 1**

(1) Where a magistrates' court grants bail to a person who is charged with or convicted of an offence punishable by imprisonment, the prosecution may appeal to a judge of the Crown Court against the granting of bail.
(1A) Where a magistrates' court grants bail to a person in connection with extradition proceedings, the prosecution may appeal to the High Court against the granting of bail.
(2) Subsection (1) above applies only where the prosecution is conducted—
  (a) by or on behalf of the Director of Public Prosecutions; or
  (b) by a person who falls within such class or description of person as may be prescribed for the purposes of this section by order made by the Secretary of State.
(3) Such an appeal may be made only if—
  (a) the prosecution made representations that bail should not be granted; and
  (b) the representations were made before it was granted.

(4) In the event of the prosecution wishing to exercise the right of appeal set out in subsection (1) above, oral notice of appeal shall be given to the magistrates' court at the conclusion of the proceedings in which such bail has been granted and before the release from custody of the person concerned.

(5) Written notice of appeal shall thereafter be served on the magistrates' court and the person concerned within two hours of the conclusion of such proceedings.

(6) Upon receipt from the prosecution of oral notice of appeal from its decision to grant bail the magistrates' court shall remand in custody the person concerned, until the appeal is determined or otherwise disposed of.

(7) Where the prosecution fails, within the period of two hours mentioned in subsection (5) above, to serve one or both of the notices required by that subsection, the appeal shall be deemed to have been disposed of.

(8) The hearing of an appeal under subsection (1) above against a decision of the magistrates' court to grant bail shall be commenced within forty-eight hours, excluding weekends and any public holiday (that is to say, Christmas Day, Good Friday or a bank holiday), from the date on which oral notice of appeal is given.

(9) At the hearing of any appeal by the prosecution under this section, such appeal shall be by way of re-hearing, and the judge hearing any such appeal may remand the person concerned in custody or may grant bail subject to such conditions (if any) as he thinks fit.

(10) In relation to a child or young person (within the meaning of the Children and Young Persons Act 1969)—

(a) the reference in subsection (1) above to an offence punishable by imprisonment is to be read as a reference to an offence which would be so punishable in the case of an adult; and

(b) the reference in subsection (5) above to remand in custody is to be read subject to the provisions of section 23 of the Act of 1969 (remands to local authority accommodation).

Section D8 Assets Recovery

D8.1 The PCA 2002 is the embodiment of the 'Assets Recovery Strategy' proposed two years earlier by the Government's Performance and Innovation Unit (see 'Recovering the Proceeds of Crime' (June 2000)). The pursuit and recovery of criminal property is now a principal imperative of crime reduction policy. Statutory responsibility for proactive implementation and direction of the strategy presently lies with the Assets Recovery Agency (ARA) which came into being on 13 January 2003. However, on 11 January 2007, the Home Office laid a Written Ministerial Statement that the ARA is to be merged with the Serious Organised Crime Agency, which will assume overall conduct of the instigation and control of the various forms of recovery proceedings. Subject to the passing of the Serious Crimes Bill, the merger provisions are predicted to come into force in April 2008.

The mechanisms of asset recovery may be broadly divided into six separate categories:

(a) civil recovery of criminal property;
(b) taxation of criminal property;
(c) cash seizure and forfeiture;
(d) powers of investigation;
(e) restraint orders;
(f) post-conviction confiscation (see **E21**).

Civil Procedures: Recovery Orders and Taxation

D8.2 The PCA 2002 makes two forms of civil recovery available to the ARA. (For a more detailed treatment of these procedures, see *Blackstone's Guide to the Proceeds of Crime Act 2002*, 2nd edition.)

First, the Director of the ARA may apply to the High Court for a recovery order (see PCA 2002, part 5). It is proposed to extend the power to apply to the three main prosecutors in England and Wales: the Crown Prosecution Service, the Revenue and Customs Prosecutions Office. If the Director proves to the civil standard the existence of 'recoverable property', defined as 'property obtained through unlawful conduct' or property that represents it, the Court may make an order vesting the property in a trustee for civil recovery. This will be a receiver who has wide powers to realise the property for the benefit of the Director regardless of who then owns it. Where appropriate, an application will be served on, and the proceedings will involve, any person holding associated property; 'associated property' essentially means innocently held property that has a physical or legal connection with the recoverable property.

Secondly, under part 6 of the Act, the Director may take over the tax collection functions of the Inland Revenue in cases where the Director has reasonable grounds to suspect that taxable income, gains or profits are the proceeds of crime.

It should be emphasised that neither of these procedures is conditional upon a successful criminal prosecution. Proceedings are increasingly brought or tax levied whether or not there has been a connected criminal case. Moreover, even an acquittal is no bar to civil recovery proceedings in respect of the very same conduct. Thus, in serious criminal cases, legal advice should include the possibility that, even if acquitted, the defendant's assets (including property that he may have sold or gifted away) could be pursued through the High Court or become the subject of a tax demand. Although civil recovery proceedings are barred in respect of property which has been taken into account for the purposes of a confiscation order under s. 308(9), that will not preclude proceedings for civil recovery where the confiscation order is quashed on appeal (*Director of the Assets Recovery Agency v Singh* [2005] 1 WLR 3747).

THE MAGISTRATES' COURT: CASH SEIZURE AND FORFEITURE

Search and Seizure

Proceeds of Crime Act 2002, s. 289 **D8.3**

(1) If a customs officer or constable who is lawfully on any premises has reasonable grounds for suspecting that there is on the premises cash—
  (a) which is recoverable property or is intended by any person for use in unlawful conduct, and
  (b) the amount of which is not less than the minimum amount,
 he may search for the cash there.

(2) If a customs officer or constable has reasonable grounds for suspecting that a person (the suspect) is carrying cash—
  (a) which is recoverable property or is intended by any person for use in unlawful conduct, and
  (b) the amount of which is not less than the minimum amount,
 he may exercise the following powers.

(3) The officer or constable may, so far as he thinks it necessary or expedient, require the suspect—
  (a) to permit a search of any article he has with him,
  (b) to permit a search of his person.

(4) An officer or constable exercising powers by virtue of subsection (3)(b) may detain the suspect for so long as is necessary for their exercise.

(5) The powers conferred by this section—
  (a) are exercisable only so far as reasonably required for the purpose of finding cash,
  (b) are exercisable by a customs officer only if he has reasonable grounds for suspecting that the unlawful conduct in question relates to an assigned matter (within the meaning of the Customs and Excise Management Act 1979).

(6) Cash means—
  (a) notes and coins in any currency,
  (b) postal orders,
  (c) cheques of any kind, including travellers' cheques,
  (d) bankers' drafts,
  (e) bearer bonds and bearer shares,
 found at any place in the United Kingdom.

(7) Cash also includes any kind of monetary instrument which is found at any place in the United Kingdom, if the instrument is specified by the Secretary of State by an order made after consultation with the Scottish Ministers.

(8) This section does not require a person to submit to an intimate search or strip search (within the meaning of section 164 of the Customs and Excise Management Act 1979).

General Chapter 3 of part 5 of the PCA 2002 provides for powers of search, seizure and forfeiture of cash. 'Cash' includes postal orders, all forms of cheque, bankers' drafts, bearer bonds (and any kind of monetary instrument specified by the Home Secretary) 'found at any place in the United Kingdom' (s. 289(6) and (7)). **D8.4**

Searches A customs officer or constable may search any premises or person for cash 'which is recoverable property or is intended by any person for use in unlawful conduct' (s. 289(1)). 'Recoverable property' is a phrase used throughout the Act and is simply property 'obtained through unlawful conduct' (s. 304(1)). If such property has been disposed of, property that represents 'the original property' is also deemed to be 'recoverable property' (s. 305(1)). Thus, if stolen goods are sold for cash, the cash itself is recoverable property. In broad terms, **D8.5**

unlawful conduct means crime wherever it is committed; more precisely, it is conduct that is unlawful under United Kingdom criminal law or, if it occurs in another country or territory, that is contrary to the criminal law of that country and would be unlawful if it occurred here (s. 241). A person obtains property through unlawful conduct if he obtains it 'by or in return for the conduct' (s. 242(1)). The unlawful conduct need not be his own.

An officer exercising powers under s. 289 must have reasonable grounds for suspecting (a) that such cash is on the premises or is being carried by the person, and (b) that the amount of cash is not less than £1,000 (the Proceeds of Crime Act 2002 (Recovery of Cash in Summary Proceedings: Minimum Amount) Order 2006 (SI 2006 No. 1699) — the amount was reduced from £5,000 with effect from 31 July 2006). Obviously, suspicion that cash is being carried by a person does not of itself justify a search of premises.

Where premises are to be searched, the officer must be on the premises lawfully (i.e. in a public place, on private premises by invitation of the owner or in the exercise of an existing power of entry under the PACE 1984 or the Customs and Excise Management Act 1979). The powers are exercisable 'only so far as reasonably required for the purpose of finding cash'. Involuntary 'intimate' or 'strip searches' within the meaning of the Customs and Excise Management Act 1979, s. 164, are not permitted (s. 289(8)). Searches are governed by a Code of Practice (see the Proceeds of Crime (Cash Searches: Code of Practice) Order 2002 (SI 2002 No. 3115)). Applications to magistrates' court are governed by the Magistrates' Courts (Detention and Forfeiture of Cash) Rules 2002 (SI 2002 No. 2998); applications may be made to any magistrates' court wherever situated.

Searches need prior approval from a magistrate or from a police officer of at least the rank of inspector (or the Customs and Excise equivalent) unless 'in the circumstances it is not practicable to obtain that approval' beforehand (s. 290). If a search is conducted without the authority of a magistrate, and no cash is recovered or any cash is released within 48 hours, a written report must be completed specifying the reasons for the search and why prior approval was not practicable (s. 290(6) and (7)).

D8.6 **Seizure** Constables or customs officers may go on to seize cash if they have reasonable grounds for suspecting that it is recoverable property or is intended by any person for use in unlawful conduct (s. 294(1)). The whole of a cash amount may be seized if it is not reasonably practicable to sever it from a suspected amount (s. 294(2)). Cash seized under the powers of seizure in the PACE 1984 (see **D1.97**) may be re-seized under these provisions. Section 294 imposes no time-limit for doing so. The initial 48-hour limit on detention of the cash (see below) commences only on the re-seizure under s. 294 (*Chief Constable of Merseyside v Hickman* [2006] EWHC (Admin) 451).

Police forces are advised to review cash or account balances in their possession where the money was originally seized as evidence and, at the time of seizure, was more than a £1,000. Police forces need to consider what explanation will be made to the court as to why the cash has not been seized under the PCA 2002 before; for this reason legal advice should always be sought.

Detention of Cash

D8.7 Once seized, cash may be retained for investigation. The initial time-limit for retention is 48 hours, although this may be extended by a magistrate for a further period of three months, and thereafter by further order(s) up to a maximum of two years (s. 295). Weekends, Christmas Day, Good Friday and bank holidays are excluded from the 48-hour calculation (s. 295(1A) and (1B), as inserted by the SOCPA 2005, s. 100). There are two conditions for continued detention of cash: first, that the reasonable suspicion is maintained and, secondly, that either (a) the derivation of the cash is still being investigated, or (b) consideration is being given to bringing 'in the United Kingdom or elsewhere' proceedings against 'any person' for an offence with which the cash is 'connected' or (c) such proceedings have commenced but have not concluded. The cash must be deposited in an interest bearing account.

An order for the return of any part of the cash requires the court to be satisfied that the above conditions no longer apply. A constable or customs officer may release the whole or part of the cash, after notifying the court or justice, which made the order, if satisfied that its retention is no longer justified (s. 297).

Forfeiture

Proceeds of Crime Act 2002, s. 298 **D8.8**

(1) While cash is detained under section 295, an application for the forfeiture of the whole or any part of it may be made—
  (a) to a magistrates' court by the Commissioners of Customs and Excise or a constable,
  (b) (in Scotland) to the sheriff by the Scottish Ministers.

(2) The court or sheriff may order the forfeiture of the cash or any part of it if satisfied that the cash or part—
  (a) is recoverable property, or
  (b) is intended by any person for use in unlawful conduct.

(3) But in the case of recoverable property which belongs to joint tenants, one of whom is an excepted joint owner, the order may not apply to so much of it as the court thinks is attributable to the excepted joint owner's share.

(4) Where an application for the forfeiture of any cash is made under this section, the cash is to be detained (and may not be released under any power conferred by this Chapter) until any proceedings in pursuance of the application (including any proceedings on appeal) are concluded.

The Power A magistrates' court may order the forfeiture of all or part of any cash if satisfied to the civil standard that it is either recoverable property or was intended for use by any person in criminal conduct (s. 298). Plainly, the circumstances will vary greatly from case to case: for example, the cash may be contaminated with traces of drugs that are not explicable in terms of the normal contamination of notes in circulation (see *Pruijsen v Customs and Excise Commissioners* (18 October 1999 unreported)). There may be specific evidence to associate the carrier of cash with illegal activity on a previous occasion. In certain circumstances, even a previous acquittal can be relied upon (see *Customs and Excise Commissioners v Thorpe* (18 November 1996 unreported)). **D8.9**

Third Parties Third parties may lay claim to the cash in the course of detention or forfeiture proceedings 'or at any other time' (s. 301). Thus, the true owner may apply in circumstances where he can show (a) that he was deprived of the cash or of property that it represents by unlawful conduct and (b) that it was not 'recoverable property' immediately before he was deprived of it. **D8.10**

Compensation Where no forfeiture order is made, the person from whom the cash was seized or the person to whom it belongs, may apply for compensation (s. 302). This will normally be no more than the accrued interest. If, however, the court is satisfied that the person has suffered loss as a result of the detention and 'the circumstances are exceptional', it may order reasonable additional compensation. **D8.11**

Any party aggrieved by the making or non-making of a forfeiture order may appeal to the Crown Court (s. 299, as amended by the SOCPA 2005, s. 101). The application must be made within 30 days of the forfeiture order.

Legal Aid Public funding is available to resist an application for forfeiture for respondents and for third parties who claim to be the innocent owners of property (see AJA 1999, sch. 2, para. 3). Such proceedings are treated as civil proceedings and are therefore subject to the required means and merits tests. Representation is 'licensed work'. Solicitors with either civil or criminal franchises may apply. They may 'self-grant' emergency work, otherwise all applications are referred to the Legal Services Commission's Special Investigations Unit. **D8.12**

POWERS OF INVESTIGATION

General

D8.13 Part 8 of the PCA 2002 contains an armoury of judicial orders for the purposes of the investigation and pursuit of criminal property:

(a) production orders;
(b) search and seizure warrants;
(c) disclosure orders;
(d) customer information orders;
(e) account monitoring orders.

The 'Code of Practice Issued Under Section 377 of the PCA 2002' governs the exercise of the five powers. Significantly, the Code emphasises the protections of the ECHR and, in particular, the need 'to satisfy a judge' that the proposed action is proportionate to the investigatory benefit and the public interest. 'This becomes a greater consideration in respect of orders and warrants made against people who are not themselves under investigation' (para. 12).

The Code is admissible in evidence and a court 'may take account of any failure to comply with its provisions 'in determining any question in the proceedings' (s. 377(7)). However, failure to comply with any provision of the Code will not *of itself* render a person liable to criminal or civil proceedings.

All of the orders may be made on *ex parte* application. The conditions for the making of the various orders differ according to the type of investigation involved. There are three types of investigation. The first type of investigation is a 'confiscation investigation', which is an investigation into whether a person has benefited from his criminal conduct or the extent or whereabouts of his benefit from his criminal conduct (s. 341(1)). (See **E21**.) A second type is a 'civil recovery investigation', which is an investigation into whether property 'is recoverable property or associated property, who holds the property or its extent or whereabouts' (s. 341(2)). By s. 341(3), an investigation does not qualify as a civil recovery investigation if proceedings for a recovery order in respect of the property have started, if an interim receiving or administration order applies, or if the property is detained under the cash detention provisions (see **D8.7**). Lastly, a 'money laundering investigation' is an investigation into 'whether a person has committed a money laundering offence' (s. 341(4)). Only a High Court judge may make an order as part of a civil recovery investigation; orders that are part of any other form of investigation may be granted by a judge of the Crown Court (s. 343).

Prejudicing an Investigation

D8.14 A person commits an offence if, knowing or suspecting that an investigation is being, or is about to be conducted, he makes a disclosure that is likely to prejudice it (s. 342(2)(a)) or 'falsifies, conceals, destroys or otherwise disposes of' relevant documents or causes or permits another to do so (s. 342(2)(b)). See **B22.19** for details.

Production Orders

D8.15 **Proceeds of Crime Act 2002, ss. 345 and 346**

345.—(1) A judge may, on an application made to him by an appropriate officer, make a production order if he is satisfied that each of the requirements for the making of the order is fulfilled.

(2) The application for a production order must state that—
(a) a person specified in the application is subject to a confiscation investigation or a money laundering investigation, or
(b) property specified in the application is subject to a civil recovery investigation.

(3) The application must also state that—
(a) the order is sought for the purposes of the investigation;
(b) the order is sought in relation to material, or material of a description, specified in the application;
(c) a person specified in the application appears to be in possession or control of the material.
(4) A production order is an order either—
(a) requiring the person the application for the order specifies as appearing to be in possession or control of material to produce it to an appropriate officer for him to take away, or
(b) requiring that person to give an appropriate officer access to the material,
within the period stated in the order.
(5) The period stated in a production order must be a period of seven days beginning with the day on which the order is made, unless it appears to the judge by whom the order is made that a longer or shorter period would be appropriate in the particular circumstances.

346.—(1) These are the requirements for the making of a production order.
(2) There must be reasonable grounds for suspecting that—
(a) in the case of a confiscation investigation, the person the application for the order specifies as being subject to the investigation has benefited from his criminal conduct;
(b) in the case of a civil recovery investigation, the property the application for the order specifies as being subject to the investigation is recoverable property or associated property;
(c) in the case of a money laundering investigation, the person the application for the order specifies as being subject to the investigation has committed a money laundering offence.
(3) There must be reasonable grounds for believing that the person the application specifies as appearing to be in possession or control of the material so specified is in possession or control of it.
(4) There must be reasonable grounds for believing that the material is likely to be of substantial value (whether or not by itself) to the investigation for the purposes of which the order is sought.
(5) There must be reasonable grounds for believing that it is in the public interest for the material to be produced or for access to it to be given, having regard to—
(a) the benefit likely to accrue to the investigation if the material is obtained;
(b) the circumstances under which the person the application specifies as appearing to be in possession or control of the material holds it.

Requirements A judge may grant a production order if satisfied that each of the necessary requirements is fulfilled (s. 345(1)). The first requirement varies according to the type of investigation: there must be reasonable grounds for 'suspecting' (a) that the subject of a confiscation investigation has benefited from his criminal conduct, (b) that the subject property of a civil recovery investigation is recoverable or associated property, or (c) that the subject of a money laundering investigation has committed a money laundering offence (s. 346(2)). **D8.16**

The remaining three requirements are common to all forms of investigation. There must be reasonable grounds for 'believing' (a) that the person specified in the application is in possession or control of the 'material' (s. 346(3)), (b) that the material 'is likely to be of substantial value (whether or not by itself) to the investigation' (s. 346(4)), and (c) that 'it is in the public interest for the material to be produced or for access to it to be given', having regard to the likely benefit if it is obtained and to the circumstances under which the specified person holds the material (s. 346(5)). Note that the required state of mind is belief and not the lower standard of suspicion necessary for fulfilment of the first requirement.

The application must specify the material and the person believed to be in possession or control of it (s. 345(3)). Only an 'appropriate officer' may apply; the meaning of 'appropriate officer' varies according to the type of investigation (see s. 378).

Terms and Effect of the Order A production order requires the person appearing to be in **D8.17**

possession or control of specified material to produce it to the appropriate officer for removal or for inspection normally within seven days of the order; the period may be lengthened or shortened as 'appropriate in the particular circumstances' (s 345(4) and (5)). Orders may be made in relation to material in the possession or control of a government department (s. 350).

A judge can supplement a production order by making an order requiring entry to premises to allow the appropriate officer to obtain access to the material (s. 347). Specific provisions apply to 'information contained in a computer' (s. 349). The production order has effect to require production of or access to the material in a form in which it is visible and legible. The material may be copied or retained for 'so long as is necessary to retain it' in connection with the relevant investigation and, in particular, until any proceedings are concluded.

An order does not require a person to produce or give access to privileged or excluded material (s. 348). 'Privileged material' is 'any material which the person would be entitled to refuse to produce on grounds of legal professional privilege in proceedings in the High Court' (s. 348(2)). Under s. 379 'excluded material' has the same meaning as in the PACE 1984, s. 11 (see **D1.82**). In broad terms it means material that is held in confidence and that falls into the following categories: (i) personal occupational or business records, (ii) human tissue or tissue fluid taken for medical diagnosis or treatment, (iii) journalistic documents or records.

Production orders and orders to grant entry 'have effect as if they were orders of the court' (s. 351(7)). In other words, breaches of the orders are punishable as contempt of court.

Search and Seizure Warrants

D8.18 Proceeds of Crime Act 2002, ss. 352 and 353

352.—(1) A judge may, on an application made to him by an appropriate officer, issue a search and seizure warrant if he is satisfied that either of the requirements for the issuing of the warrant is fulfilled.

(2) The application for a search and seizure warrant must state that—
- (a) a person specified in the application is subject to a confiscation investigation or a money laundering investigation, or
- (b) property specified in the application is subject to a civil recovery investigation.

(3) The application must also state—
- (a) that the warrant is sought for the purposes of the investigation;
- (b) that the warrant is sought in relation to the premises specified in the application;
- (c) that the warrant is sought in relation to material specified in the application, or that there are reasonable grounds for believing that there is material falling within section 353(6), (7) or (8) on the premises.

(4) A search and seizure warrant is a warrant authorising an appropriate person—
- (a) to enter and search the premises specified in the application for the warrant, and
- (b) to seize and retain any material found there which is likely to be of substantial value (whether or not by itself) to the investigation for the purposes of which the application is made.

(5) An appropriate person is—
- (a) a constable or a customs officer, if the warrant is sought for the purposes of a confiscation investigation or a money laundering investigation;
- (b) a named member of the staff of the Agency, if the warrant is sought for the purposes of a civil recovery investigation.

(6) The requirements for the issue of a search and seizure warrant are—
- (a) that a production order made in relation to material has not been complied with and there are reasonable grounds for believing that the material is on the premises specified in the application for the warrant, or
- (b) that section 353 is satisfied in relation to the warrant.

353.—(1) This section is satisfied in relation to a search and seizure warrant if—
- (a) subsection (2) applies, and
- (b) either the first or the second set of conditions is complied with.

(2) This subsection applies if there are reasonable grounds for suspecting that—

(a) in the case of a confiscation investigation, the person specified in the application for the warrant has benefited from his criminal conduct;
(b) in the case of a civil recovery investigation, the property specified in the application for the warrant is recoverable property or associated property;
(c) in the case of a money laundering investigation, the person specified in the application for the warrant has committed a money laundering offence.

(3) The first set of conditions is that there are reasonable grounds for believing that—
(a) any material on the premises specified in the application for the warrant is likely to be of substantial value (whether or not by itself) to the investigation for the purposes of which the warrant is sought,
(b) it is in the public interest for the material to be obtained, having regard to the benefit likely to accrue to the investigation if the material is obtained, and
(c) it would not be appropriate to make a production order for any one or more of the reasons in subsection (4).

(4) The reasons are—
(a) that it is not practicable to communicate with any person against whom the production order could be made;
(b) that it is not practicable to communicate with any person who would be required to comply with an order to grant entry to the premises;
(c) that the investigation might be seriously prejudiced unless an appropriate person is able to secure immediate access to the material.

(5) The second set of conditions is that—
(a) there are reasonable grounds for believing that there is material on the premises specified in the application for the warrant and that the material falls within subsection (6), (7) or (8),
(b) there are reasonable grounds for believing that it is in the public interest for the material to be obtained, having regard to the benefit likely to accrue to the investigation if the material is obtained, and
(c) any one or more of the requirements in subsection (9) is met.

(6) In the case of a confiscation investigation, material falls within this subsection if it cannot be identified at the time of the application but it—
(a) relates to the person specified in the application, the question whether he has benefited from his criminal conduct or any question as to the extent or whereabouts of his benefit from his criminal conduct, and
(b) is likely to be of substantial value (whether or not by itself) to the investigation for the purposes of which the warrant is sought.

(7) In the case of a civil recovery investigation, material falls within this subsection if it cannot be identified at the time of the application but it—
(a) relates to the property specified in the application, the question whether it is recoverable property or associated property, the question as to who holds any such property, any question as to whether the person who appears to hold any such property holds other property which is recoverable property, or any question as to the extent or whereabouts of any property mentioned in this paragraph, and
(b) is likely to be of substantial value (whether or not by itself) to the investigation for the purposes of which the warrant is sought.

(8) In the case of a money laundering investigation, material falls within this subsection if it cannot be identified at the time of the application but it—
(a) relates to the person specified in the application or the question whether he has committed a money laundering offence, and
(b) is likely to be of substantial value (whether or not by itself) to the investigation for the purposes of which the warrant is sought.

(9) The requirements are—
(a) that it is not practicable to communicate with any person entitled to grant entry to the premises;
(b) that entry to the premises will not be granted unless a warrant is produced;
(c) that the investigation might be seriously prejudiced unless an appropriate person arriving at the premises is able to secure immediate entry to them.

(10) An appropriate person is—
(a) a constable or a customs officer, if the warrant is sought for the purposes of a confiscation investigation or a money laundering investigation;

D

Part D Procedure

(b) a member of the staff of the Agency, if the warrant is sought for the purposes of a civil recovery investigation.

D8.19 **The Powers** A search and seizure warrant authorises an appropriate officer to enter and search specified premises and to seize and retain any material 'which is likely to be of substantial value (whether or not by itself) to the investigation' (s. 352(4)).

Essentially, a warrant is only available (a) where a production order has not been complied with and there are reasonable grounds for believing that the material is on the specified premises (s. 352) or (b)(i) where it is in the public interest to obtain the material and the material is likely to be of substantial value to the investigation but it is not appropriate to make a production order, notwithstanding that the requirements can be made out, because it is not practicable to communicate with the interested parties or because the investigation might be seriously prejudiced unless immediate access is obtained (s. 353(3) and (4)); or (ii) where the material is likely to be of substantial value to the investigation but cannot be identified in advance and it is not practicable to communicate with the interested parties or because the investigation might be seriously prejudiced unless immediate access is obtained (s. 353(5)). A warrant does not confer the right to seize 'privileged' or 'excluded' material (s. 354).

The control of search warrant powers under the PACE 1984 has been extended to embrace searches under a PCA 2002 warrant in confiscation and money laundering investigations (see the PCA 2002, s. 355, and the Proceeds of Crime Act 2002 (Application of Police and Criminal Evidence Act 1984 and Police and Criminal Evidence (Northern Ireland) Order 1989) Order 2003 (SI 2003 No. 174)). The PACE 1984 provisions that apply relate to search warrants (PACE 1984, s. 15), execution of warrants (s. 16), access and copying (s. 21) and retention (s. 22). For details of these provisions, see **D1.90** ***et seq.*** Certain modifications of the provisions are set out in the 2003 Order.

The modifications of the PACE 1984, s. 22, operate to confine the purposes for which seized items may be retained. Section 22 as modified allows retention of items 'as evidence in proceedings relating to the making of a confiscation order' or 'for forensic examination or for investigation in connection with a confiscation investigation or money laundering investigation'. As to the use of documents and materials for purposes other than the purpose of the investigation or resulting criminal proceedings, see *Preston BC v McGrath* (2000) *The Times*, 19 May 2000.

The PCA 2002 itself contains broadly similar but more limited controls on the execution of a warrant granted by a High Court judge in civil recovery investigations (s. 356).

Disclosure Orders

D8.20 **Proceeds of Crime Act 2002, ss. 357 and 358**

357.—(1) A judge may, on an application made to him by the Director, make a disclosure order if he is satisfied that each of the requirements for the making of the order is fulfilled.

(2) No application for a disclosure order may be made in relation to a money laundering investigation.

(3) The application for a disclosure order must state that—

(a) a person specified in the application is subject to a confiscation investigation which is being carried out by the Director and the order is sought for the purposes of the investigation, or

(b) property specified in the application is subject to a civil recovery investigation and the order is sought for the purposes of the investigation.

(4) A disclosure order is an order authorising the Director to give to any person the Director considers has relevant information notice in writing requiring him to do, with respect to any matter relevant to the investigation for the purposes of which the order is sought, any or all of the following—

(a) answer questions, either at a time specified in the notice or at once, at a place so specified;

(b) provide information specified in the notice, by a time and in a manner so specified;
(c) produce documents, or documents of a description, specified in the notice, either at or by a time so specified or at once, and in a manner so specified.

(5) Relevant information is information (whether or not contained in a document) which the Director considers to be relevant to the investigation.

(6) A person is not bound to comply with a requirement imposed by a notice given under a disclosure order unless evidence of authority to give the notice is produced to him.

358.—(1) These are the requirements for the making of a disclosure order.

(2) There must be reasonable grounds for suspecting that—
(a) in the case of a confiscation investigation, the person specified in the application for the order has benefited from his criminal conduct;
(b) in the case of a civil recovery investigation, the property specified in the application for the order is recoverable property or associated property.

(3) There must be reasonable grounds for believing that information which may be provided in compliance with a requirement imposed under the order is likely to be of substantial value (whether or not by itself) to the investigation for the purposes of which the order is sought.

(4) There must be reasonable grounds for believing that it is in the public interest for the information to be provided, having regard to the benefit likely to accrue to the investigation if the information is obtained.

Effect of the Order A disclosure order permits the Director of the ARA to give written notice requiring any person to answer questions at a specified time or place, to provide information in a specified manner or to produce specified documents (s. 357). Notice may be given to anyone 'the Director considers has relevant information'. **D8.21**

The Director may *not* apply for an order in relation to a money laundering investigation. The 'public interest', 'substantial value' and other criteria are similar to those required for the making of production and search and seizure orders.

An order does not confer the right to require persons to answer privileged questions, provide privileged information, produce privileged documents or produce 'excluded material' (s. 361). See **D8.17** for the meaning of these terms. 'A lawyer' may be required to provide the client's name and address.

Generally, a statement made in response to a requirement of a disclosure order may not be used in evidence against the maker in criminal proceedings (s. 360(1)). Its use is permissible, however, in confiscation proceedings, in a prosecution for having failed without reasonable excuse to comply with the disclosure order, or in a prosecution for perjury. More widely, the statement is admissible in any prosecution when the person 'in giving evidence' makes an inconsistent statement (s. 360(2)).

It is an offence to fail to comply with a requirement of a disclosure order without reasonable excuse (s. 359(1)) or if, in purported compliance, he knowingly or recklessly makes a false or misleading statement (s. 359(3)). The latter is triable either way.

Disclosure Notices under the SOCPA 2005 Note that the SOCPA 2005, s. 62 confers powers on the DPP and the Director of Revenue and Customs Prosecutions to issue without a court order their own 'disclosure notices', requiring persons to answer questions, provide information and/or produce documents relevant to specific offences (including all the 'lifestyle offences' listed in the PCA 2002, sch. 2 (see **E21.11**)) . The powers may be delegated to prosecutor level. The conditions are that there are reasonable grounds for suspecting that one of the offences has been committed and that the person has information that 'is likely to be of substantial value' to the investigation. If a notice is not complied with, a justice of the peace may grant a warrant to enter and seize documents. It is an offence not to comply with a notice or to provide false or misleading information. **D8.22**

It is immediately apparent that these provisions are intended to avoid judicial supervision of the extent of the required disclosure. All that will be required for compulsory disclosure in future will be a decision by a Crown Prosecutor.

Customer Information Orders

D8.23 **Proceeds of Crime Act 2002, ss. 363 and 364**

363.—(1) A judge may, on an application made to him by an appropriate officer, make a customer information order if he is satisfied that each of the requirements for the making of the order is fulfilled.

(2) The application for a customer information order must state that—
(a) a person specified in the application is subject to a confiscation investigation or a money laundering investigation, or
(b) property specified in the application is subject to a civil recovery investigation and a person specified in the application appears to hold the property.

(3) The application must also state that—
(a) the order is sought for the purposes of the investigation;
(b) the order is sought against the financial institution or financial institutions specified in the application.

(4) An application for a customer information order may specify—
(a) all financial institutions,
(b) a particular description, or particular descriptions, of financial institutions, or
(c) a particular financial institution or particular financial institutions.

(5) A customer information order is an order that a financial institution covered by the application for the order must, on being required to do so by notice in writing given by an appropriate officer, provide any such customer information as it has relating to the person specified in the application.

(6) A financial institution which is required to provide information under a customer information order must provide the information to an appropriate officer in such manner, and at or by such time, as an appropriate officer requires.

(7) If a financial institution on which a requirement is imposed by a notice given under a customer information order requires the production of evidence of authority to give the notice, it is not bound to comply with the requirement unless evidence of the authority has been produced to it.

364.—(1) 'Customer information', in relation to a person and a financial institution, is information whether the person holds, or has held, an account or accounts at the financial institution (whether solely or jointly with another) and (if so) information as to—
(a) the matters specified in subsection (2) if the person is an individual;
(b) the matters specified in subsection (3) if the person is a company or limited liability partnership or a similar body incorporated or otherwise established outside the United Kingdom.

(2) The matters referred to in subsection (1)(a) are—
(a) the account number or numbers;
(b) the person's full name;
(c) his date of birth;
(d) his most recent address and any previous addresses;
(e) the date or dates on which he began to hold the account or accounts and, if he has ceased to hold the account or any of the accounts, the date or dates on which he did so;
(f) such evidence of his identity as was obtained by the financial institution under or for the purposes of any legislation relating to money laundering;
(g) the full name, date of birth and most recent address, and any previous addresses, of any person who holds, or has held, an account at the financial institution jointly with him;
(h) the account number or numbers of any other account or accounts held at the financial institution to which he is a signatory and details of the person holding the other account or accounts.

(3) The matters referred to in subsection (1)(b) are—
(a) the account number or numbers;
(b) the person's full name;
(c) a description of any business which the person carries on;
(d) the country or territory in which it is incorporated or otherwise established and any number allocated to it under the Companies Act 1985 or the Companies (Northern Ireland) Order 1986 (SI 1986 No. 1032) or corresponding legislation of any country or territory outside the United Kingdom;
(e) any number assigned to it for the purposes of value added tax in the United Kingdom;

(f) its registered office, and any previous registered offices, under the Companies Act 1985 or the Companies (Northern Ireland) Order 1986 (SI 1986 No. 1032) or anything similar under corresponding legislation of any country or territory outside the United Kingdom;
(g) its registered office, and any previous registered offices, under the Limited Liability Partnerships Act 2000 or anything similar under corresponding legislation of any country or territory outside Great Britain;
(h) the date or dates on which it began to hold the account or accounts and, if it has ceased to hold the account or any of the accounts, the date or dates on which it did so;
(i) such evidence of its identity as was obtained by the financial institution under or for the purposes of any legislation relating to money laundering;
(j) the full name, date of birth and most recent address and any previous addresses of any person who is a signatory to the account or any of the accounts.

(4) The Secretary of State may by order provide for information of a description specified in the order—
(a) to be customer information, or
(b) no longer to be customer information.

(5) Money laundering is an act which—
(a) constitutes an offence under section 327, 328 or 329 of this Act or section 18 of the Terrorism Act 2000, or
(aa) constitutes an offence under section 415(1A) of this Act; or
(b) would constitute an offence specified in paragraph (a) or (aa) if done in the United Kingdom.

Effect of the Order A customer information order requires a 'financial institution' on written notice to provide 'customer information' to the 'appropriate officer' (s. 363(5)). 'Customer information' can amount to the most detailed information about financial accounts and account holders (s. 364). Practice and procedure are governed by the CrimPR, r. 62.2. Separate rules apply in civil recovery investigations. The office and rank required of an applicant is determined by the type of investigation (see s. 378). **D8.24**

As with the other types of order, the requirements for the making of an order vary according to the type of investigation. Thus, the nature of the grounds of reasonable suspicion or belief are different in different investigations. 'Public interest' and the 'substantial value (of an order) to the investigation' are constant criteria. In keeping with the provisions relating to disclosure orders, a statement made by a financial institution in response to a customer information order cannot be used against it in criminal proceedings other than in confiscation proceedings, in a prosecution under s. 366 for non-compliance with the order itself or in any prosecution where the financial institution makes an inconsistent statement (s. 367). An application to vary or discharge the order may be made by the original applicant for the order or by 'any person affected by the order' (s. 369).

A financial institution commits an offence if it fails to comply with an order without reasonable excuse (s. 366(1)) or if, in purported compliance, it knowingly or recklessly makes a false or misleading statement (s. 366(3)). The latter is triable either way.

Account Monitoring Orders

Proceeds of Crime Act 2002, ss. 370 and 371 **D8.25**

370.—(1) A judge may, on an application made to him by an appropriate officer, make an account monitoring order if he is satisfied that each of the requirements for the making of the order is fulfilled.

(2) The application for an account monitoring order must state that—
(a) a person specified in the application is subject to a confiscation investigation or a money laundering investigation, or
(b) property specified in the application is subject to a civil recovery investigation and a person specified in the application appears to hold the property.

(3) The application must also state that—

(a) the order is sought for the purposes of the investigation;
(b) the order is sought against the financial institution specified in the application in relation to account information of the description so specified.

(4) Account information is information relating to an account or accounts held at the financial institution specified in the application by the person so specified (whether solely or jointly with another).

(5) The application for an account monitoring order may specify information relating to—
(a) all accounts held by the person specified in the application for the order at the financial institution so specified,
(b) a particular description, or particular descriptions, of accounts so held, or
(c) a particular account, or particular accounts, so held.

(6) An account monitoring order is an order that the financial institution specified in the application for the order must, for the period stated in the order, provide account information of the description specified in the order to an appropriate officer in the manner, and at or by the time or times, stated in the order.

(7) The period stated in an account monitoring order must not exceed the period of 90 days beginning with the day on which the order is made.

371.—(1) These are the requirements for the making of an account monitoring order.

(2) In the case of a confiscation investigation, there must be reasonable grounds for suspecting that the person specified in the application for the order has benefited from his criminal conduct.

(3) In the case of a civil recovery investigation, there must be reasonable grounds for suspecting that—
(a) the property specified in the application for the order is recoverable property or associated property;
(b) the person specified in the application holds all or some of the property.

(4) In the case of a money laundering investigation, there must be reasonable grounds for suspecting that the person specified in the application for the order has committed a money laundering offence.

(5) In the case of any investigation, there must be reasonable grounds for believing that account information which may be provided in compliance with the order is likely to be of substantial value (whether or not by itself) to the investigation for the purposes of which the order is sought.

(6) In the case of any investigation, there must be reasonable grounds for believing that it is in the public interest for the account information to be provided, having regard to the benefit likely to accrue to the investigation if the information is obtained.

D8.26 **Effect, Procedure and Requirements** An account monitoring order requires a financial institution to provide an appropriate officer with specified information 'relating to an account or accounts held' solely or jointly by a specified person ('account information') for the period stated in the order (s. 370). The stated period must not exceed 90 days from the date of the order. An order 'has effect in spite of any restriction on the disclosure of information however imposed' (s. 374). This appears to override any claim of confidentiality or data protection. Procedure is governed by the CrimPR, r. 62.1.

The requirements closely resemble those of the other orders. The general requirements for an order include reasonable belief in the likelihood of the account information being of substantial value to the investigation and that the provision of the information is in the public interest. There are restrictions similar to those relating to other orders on the use in criminal proceedings of a statement by a financial institution in response to an order (s. 372). An application to vary or discharge the order may be made by the original applicant for the order or by 'any person affected by the order' (s. 375).

RESTRAINT ORDERS

D8.27 Proceeds of Crime Act 2002, ss. 40 and 41

40.—(1) The Crown Court may exercise the powers conferred by section 41 if any of the following conditions is satisfied.

(2) The first condition is that—
(a) a criminal investigation has been started in England and Wales with regard to an offence, and
(b) there is reasonable cause to believe that the alleged offender has benefited from his criminal conduct.
(3) The second condition is that—
(a) proceedings for an offence have been started in England and Wales and not concluded, and
(b) there is reasonable cause to believe that the defendant has benefited from his criminal conduct.
(4) The third condition is that—
(a) an application by the prosecutor or the Director has been made under section 19, 20, 27 or 28 and not concluded, or the court believes that such an application is to be made, and
(b) there is reasonable cause to believe that the defendant has benefited from his criminal conduct.
(5) The fourth condition is that—
(a) an application by the prosecutor or the Director has been made under section 21 and not concluded, or the court believes that such an application is to be made, and
(b) there is reasonable cause to believe that the court will decide under that section that the amount found under the new calculation of the defendant's benefit exceeds the relevant amount (as defined in that section).
(6) The fifth condition is that—
(a) an application by the prosecutor or the Director has been made under section 22 and not concluded, or the court believes that such an application is to be made, and
(b) there is reasonable cause to believe that the court will decide under that section that the amount found under the new calculation of the available amount exceeds the relevant amount (as defined in that section).
(7) The second condition is not satisfied if the court believes that—
(a) there has been undue delay in continuing the proceedings, or
(b) the prosecutor does not intend to proceed.
(8) If an application mentioned in the third, fourth or fifth condition has been made the condition is not satisfied if the court believes that—
(a) there has been undue delay in continuing the application, or
(b) the prosecutor or the Director (as the case may be) does not intend to proceed.
(9) If the first condition is satisfied—
(a) references in this Part to the defendant are to the alleged offender;
(b) references in this Part to the prosecutor are to the person the court believes is to have conduct of any proceedings for the offence;
(c) section 77(9) has effect as if proceedings for the offence had been started against the defendant when the investigation was started.

41.—(1) If any condition set out in section 40 is satisfied the Crown Court may make an order (a restraint order) prohibiting any specified person from dealing with any realisable property held by him.
(2) A restraint order may provide that it applies—
(a) to all realisable property held by the specified person whether or not the property is described in the order;
(b) to realisable property transferred to the specified person after the order is made.
(3) A restraint order may be made subject to exceptions, and an exception may in particular—
(a) make provision for reasonable living expenses and reasonable legal expenses;
(b) make provision for the purpose of enabling any person to carry on any trade, business, profession or occupation;
(c) be made subject to conditions.
(4) But an exception to a restraint order must not make provision for any legal expenses which—
(a) relate to an offence which falls within subsection (5), and
(b) are incurred by the defendant or by a recipient of a tainted gift.
(5) These offences fall within this subsection—
(a) the offence mentioned in section 40(2) or (3), if the first or second condition (as the case may be) is satisfied;
(b) the offence (or any of the offences) concerned, if the third, fourth or fifth condition is satisfied.

(6) Subsection (7) applies if—
  (a) a court makes a restraint order, and
  (b) the applicant for the order applies to the court to proceed under subsection (7) (whether as part of the application for the restraint order or at any time afterwards).
(7) The court may make such order as it believes is appropriate for the purpose of ensuring that the restraint order is effective.
(8) A restraint order does not affect property for the time being subject to a charge under any of these provisions—
  (a) section 9 of the Drug Trafficking Offences Act 1986;
  (b) section 78 of the Criminal Justice Act 1988;
  (c) Article 14 of the Criminal Justice (Confiscation) (Northern Ireland) Order 1990 (SI 1990 No. 2588);
  (d) section 27 of the Drug Trafficking Act 1994;
  (e) Article 32 of the Proceeds of Crime (Northern Ireland) Order 1996 (SI 1996 No. 1299).
(9) Dealing with property includes removing it from England and Wales.

D8.28 **Power to make an Order** Under the legislation replaced by the PCA 2002, restraint orders could be granted only by the High Court. Under the PCA 2002, part 2, the jurisdiction is transferred to the Crown Court. A restraint order puts a freeze on the use and disposal of property that is potentially liable for confiscation. A restraint order operates to prohibit 'any specified person from dealing with any realisable property held by him' (s. 41(1)). Realisable property is 'any free property' held by the defendant or by the recipient of a 'tainted gift' (s. 83). The reference to 'tainted gifts' ensures that criminal property can be preserved when it has been 'gifted' away into the hands of another. Property is 'free' unless it is subject to a deprivation or forfeiture order (s. 82: **E21.22**). Property is held by a person who has an 'interest' in it. This is not necessarily confined to the holding of a legal or equitable interest in the property. In the context of a VAT carousel fraud, all the conspirators may have a beneficial 'interest' in the proceeds of the conspiracy which may be the subject of a restraint order (*S* [2005] EWCA Crim 2919).

As an adjunct to a restraint order, the court 'may make such order as it believes is appropriate for the purpose of ensuring that the restraint order is effective' (s. 41(7)). This might cover such things as the surrender of bank books, share certificates and similar items to prevent access to or transfer of property. Frequently, defendants are required to provide statements of their finances. Section 45 empowers a constable or a customs officer to seize any realisable property subject to a restraint order to prevent its removal from England and Wales.

D8.29 **The Exercise of the Power** The underlying purpose of the legislation is to prevent the dissipation of assets in anticipation of an investigation or criminal proceedings. However, as a basic principle, 'if there is no [risk that property will be dissipated] . . . or the risk is merely fanciful, the order ought not to be made since, *ex hypothesi*, it would not be necessary for the achievement of its only proper purpose' (*Re AJ and DJ* (9 December 1992 unreported) per Glidewell LJ). Where dishonesty is alleged, there will usually be reason to fear that assets will be dissipated. Prosecutors should be alive to the possibility that there may be no risk in fact and, where no dissipation has occurred over a long period, they should explain why dissipation is now feared. They have a duty to make full and frank disclosure but, as they act in the public interest, a failure of disclosure should not result in the sanction of discharging the order save where their behaviour was appalling (*Jennings v CPS (Practice Note)* [2006] 1 WLR 182). If the court considers that the prosecution have failed to consider the risk or failed to put relevant material before the court, but that the public interest still requires an order, the court may disallow the prosecution costs (*Jennings v CPS*).

However, the Act has its own 'mission statement' for the exercise of restraint order powers (s. 69). The powers must be exercised:

(a) with a view to securing the availability of the value of the property to satisfy any confiscation order;

(b) in a case where no order has yet been made, with a view to ensuring that the property does not decrease in value;
(c) without taking account of any conflicting obligation of the defendant or a recipient of a tainted gift.

The three objectives are subject to rules that:

(i) a person other than the defendant or a recipient of a tainted gift should be allowed to retain or recover the value of any interest held by him;
(ii) in respect of realisable property held by the recipient of a tainted gift, the powers should be exercised with a view to realising no more than the value for the time being of that gift;
(iii) where no confiscation order has yet been made, and the defendant or a recipient of a tainted gift makes an application, the court should not order the sale of property which cannot be replaced.

Basis for Making an Order

The satisfaction of any one of five 'conditions' in s. 40 provides the basis for a restraint order. The first three conditions are respectively (a) that 'a criminal investigation has been started', (b) that 'proceedings have been started' or (c) that there is an unconcluded application (or an application that the court believes is to be made) for reconsideration of confiscation or an application in respect of an absconded defendant and, in each case, that there is 'reasonable cause to believe that the alleged offender has benefited from his criminal conduct'. The fourth and fifth conditions are that an application to reconsider the amount of benefit or the available amount (see **E21.30**) determined in previous confiscation proceedings is not concluded (or that the court believes such an application is to be made) and there is reasonable cause to believe that the new amount will exceed the original amount. The last four conditions are not satisfied if the court believes that there has been undue delay in continuing the proceedings or that the prosecutor does not intend to proceed. **D8.30**

It appears that, for the purposes of the first two conditions, there need not necessarily be a connection between the current criminal investigation or proceedings and the 'criminal conduct' from which the person is believed to have benefited (see *Re Hill (Restraint Order)* [2005] EWCA Crim 3271). 'Criminal conduct' simply means any conduct that constitutes an offence in England and Wales or that would constitute an offence if it occurred here (s. 76). Accordingly, the conditions for a restraint order simply anticipate the twin components of a confiscation order — a conviction for an offence and a finding that the defendant has benefited from 'his criminal conduct'. In the case of someone found to have a 'criminal lifestyle', this means 'his general criminal conduct' whenever it occurred (see **E21.11** and **E21.12**). It follows that a judge is entitled, in deciding on the terms of the restraint order, to have regard to the likelihood that the defendant, if convicted, would in due course be found to have 'a criminal lifestyle' and that the statutory assumptions of benefit in s. 10 would eventually apply (see **E21.16**). In those circumstances, the judge may make an unlimited restraint order (*Re K and Others* [2005] EWCA Crim 619); where it is so made, a full duty of disclosure is borne by the applicant and the defendant must be given a note of the *ex parte* hearing (*Director of the Assets Recovery Agency v Singh* [2005] 1 WLR 3747).

Procedure

Only 'the prosecutor', the Director of the ARA or an accredited financial investigator may apply (PCA 2002, s. 42(1) and (2)). Procedure is governed by the CrimPR, parts 59 to 61 and part 72 (appeals). An application may be made *ex parte*. **D8.31**

The proceedings are predominantly civil in nature. The standard of proof is the balance of probabilities. Sections 2 to 4 of the Civil Evidence Act 1995, which deal with hearsay evidence, are applied. Indeed, hearsay evidence 'of whatever degree' is expressly admissible (s. 46(1)).

The application must be made in writing and it must be supported by a witness statement, which must contain:

(a) the grounds for the application;
(b) details of the realisable property and of the person holding that property;
(c) the grounds for, and full details of, any application for an ancillary order; and
(d) where the application is made by an accredited financial investigator, a statement that he has been authorised to make the application under s. 68 of the Act.

An application to discharge the order may be made by the original applicant or by 'any person affected by the order' (s. 42(3)). The order must be discharged on the conclusion of the proceedings or, where the order was made for the purposes of an investigation, if proceedings are not started within a reasonable time (s. 42(7)).

The court has a discretion to exempt funds from the order to allow for reasonable living or legal expenses or 'for the purpose of enabling any person to carry on any trade, business, profession or occupation' (s. 41(3)). Paradoxically, the order must not make provision for legal expenses attributable to the investigation or proceedings to which the restraint order relates (see *Re S (Restraint Order: Release of Assets)* [2005] 1 WLR 1338). As a general rule the defendant is entitled to enjoy the standard of life he previously experienced and is entitled to meet continuing expenses as they arise, although this may not extend to keeping up an excessively 'Rolls Royce lifestyle' (*In re Peters* [1988] QB 871; *Re D* (28 October 1992 unreported).

Receivers

D8.32 If necessary, the court may order that property be managed by a management receiver (PCA 2002, s. 48). The court may confer specific powers upon the receiver that include powers to take possession of the property, commence and conduct legal proceedings, enter into contracts, employ agents and to 'take any other steps the court thinks appropriate'. The receiver may realise so much of the property as is necessary to meet his own remuneration and expenses. A court appointed receiver is not an agent of either party but, in effect, an officer of the court (*Re Andrews* [1991] 3 WLR 1236). The order may empower the receiver to (a) search for or inspect anything authorised by the court, (b) make or obtain copies or photographs or records of material (c) remove and take possession of items. In cases of urgency, where it is feared that notice may result in dissipation of the property, the application to appoint a receiver may be made at the same time as an *ex parte* restraint application. The orders made must, however, be in the narrowest terms consistent with the need to act effectively, and ought not to include a general power of sale. In such circumstances, should it become necessary for the receiver to dispose of property, he should return to court on notice for further directions (*Re P* [2000] 1 WLR 473). Where there are third-party interests, the Act itself prevents the court from providing the receiver with power to 'manage or otherwise deal with the property' or to realise any of it for payments to the receiver, without first giving 'persons holding interests in the property a reasonable opportunity to make representations' (s. 49(8)). Moreover, persons who are or who may be affected by the receiver's actions, as well as the receiver, may apply for such directions as the court believes are appropriate (s. 62) or for variation or discharge of the order (s. 63). No distress may be levied against any realisable property, nor may there be forfeiture for breach of a tenancy agreement without leave of the Crown Court (s. 58(2) and (3)). Where other proceedings are pending in respect of the property, the other court has a discretion whether or not to stay those proceedings once it has given an opportunity for the applicant for the restraint order and any receiver to make representations (s. 58(6)).

Self-incrimination

D8.33 Under the High Court jurisdiction, the privilege against self-incrimination was maintained by the inclusion of a prohibition on the use of any statement of assets in a criminal prosecution (*Re O (Disclosure Order: Disclosure of Assets)* [1991] 2 WLR 475). Orders drawn under the new procedures in the Crown Court should contain a clear and specific statement to this effect. This will not prevent the use of such statements in subsequent confiscation proceedings.

Appeal

There is no right to appeal directly against the making of a restraint order. A person affected by the order must first apply to vary or discharge the order. Where such an application is made, both the original applicant or any person affected by the order has a right of appeal therefrom to the Court of Appeal, and thereafter to the House of Lords (PCA 2002, ss. 43 and 44). **D8.34**

Section D9 Disclosure

INTRODUCTION

Types of Disclosure

D9.1 An important issue in criminal procedure is the extent to which the prosecution and the defence must before trial disclose to each other the information pertaining to the case. Concentrating for the moment upon the prosecution, there is a central distinction between:

(a) the disclosure by the prosecution of its case, i.e. the evidence upon which it will rely at trial; and
(b) the disclosure of other material pertaining to the case, which it does not intend to use — 'unused material'.

As far as (a) is concerned, the position differs according to whether trial is taking place summarily or in the Crown Court. The extent to which the prosecution are under a duty to reveal their case is dealt with in **D14.67** ***et seq.*** (so far as trial on indictment is concerned), and in **D20.22** (for the much more limited obligations relating to summary trial); advance disclosure is dealt with in **D6.4** ***et seq.***

This section is concerned with the disclosure by the prosecution of unused material. It also covers the duty of the defence to make disclosure, not of unused material but of the case upon which they will rely at trial. The CJA 2003 made a number of important amendments to the law relating to disclosure. Some of these came into force on 4 April 2005, others are not yet in force.

The Scheme of the Legislation

D9.2 The statutory regime governing the disclosure of unused material by the prosecution and the disclosure of the defence case by the defence is set out in the CPIA 1996, part I (ss. 1 to 21), as amended by the CJA 2003, and supplemented by the Code of Practice issued under the 1996 Act.

The scheme of the legislation is as follows:

(a) there is a statutory duty upon the police officer investigating an offence to record and retain information and material gathered or generated during the investigation (see **D9.7**);
(b) the prosecution should inform the defence of certain categories of that material which they do not intend to use at trial (see **D9.9** to **D9.17**) — as mentioned above, there are separate obligations to inform the defence of material which they do intend to use;
(c) the defence then have a duty to inform the prosecution of the case which they intend to present at trial (**D9.18** to **D9.24**);
(d) the prosecution is under a continuing duty to disclose material which falls within the test for prosecution disclosure (**D9.15**).

The legislation makes provision for applications to be made to the court in certain circumstances where there is a dispute about whether the prosecution should disclose certain material (see **D9.16**); and there are sanctions laid down for defence failure to disclose or disclosure which is late, false or inconsistent (**D9.23**).

The categories of case to which this legislative scheme applies are laid down in s. 1. In summary, it is compulsory in relation to cases sent to the Crown Court to be tried on indictment. It may also apply on a voluntary basis to any summary trial, including those in the youth court (see **D9.21**).

Criminal Procedure and Investigations Act 1996, s. 1

(1) This part applies where—
  (a) a person is charged with a summary offence in respect of which a court proceeds to summary trial and in respect of which he pleads not guilty,
  (b) a person who has attained the age of 18 is charged with an offence which is triable either way, in respect of which a court proceeds to summary trial and in respect of which he pleads not guilty, or
  (c) a person under the age of 18 is charged with an indictable offence in respect of which a court proceeds to summary trial and in respect of which he pleads not guilty.
(2) This part also applies where—
  (a) a person is charged with an indictable offence and he is committed for trial for the offence concerned,
  (b) a person is charged with an indictable offence and proceedings for the trial of the person on the charge concerned are transferred to the Crown Court by virtue of a notice of transfer given under section 4 of the Criminal Justice Act 1987 (serious or complex fraud),
  (c) a person is charged with an indictable offence and proceedings for the trial of the person on the charge concerned are transferred to the Crown Court by virtue of a notice of transfer served on a magistrates' court under section 53 of the Criminal Justice Act 1991 (certain cases involving children),
  (cc) a person is charged with an offence for which he is sent for trial,
  (d) a count charging a person with a summary offence is included in an indictment under the authority of section 40 of the Criminal Justice Act 1988 (common assault etc.),
  (e) a bill of indictment charging a person with an indictable offence is preferred under the authority of section 2(2)(b) of the Administration of Justice (Miscellaneous Provisions) Act 1933 (bill preferred by direction of Court of Appeal, or by direction or with consent of a judge), or
  (f) a bill of indictment charging a person with an indictable offence is referred under section 22B(3)(a) of the Prosecution of Offences Act 1985.
(3) This part applies in relation to alleged offences into which no criminal investigation has begun before the appointed day.
(4) For the purposes of this section a criminal investigation is an investigation which police officers or other persons have a duty to conduct with a view to it being ascertained—
  (a) whether a person should be charged with an offence, or
  (b) whether a person charged with an offence is guilty of it.
(5) The reference in subsection (3) to the appointed day is to such day as is appointed for the purposes of this Part by the Secretary of State by order.
(6) In this Part—
  (a) subsections (3) to (5) of section 3 (in their application for the purposes of section 3, 7 or 9), and
  (b) sections 17 and 18,
  have effect subject to subsections (2) and (3) of section 9 of the Sexual Offences (Protected Material) Act 1997 (by virtue of which those provisions of this Act do not apply in relation to disclosures regulated by that Act).

Section 1(6) was added by the Sexual Offences (Protected Material) Act 1997, s. 9(4), which is not yet in force.

Commencement Dates The disclosure provisions of part I of the CPIA 1996 were brought into effect on 1 April 1997 (the appointed day). They apply to any alleged offence for which a criminal investigation began on or after the appointed day. In order to pinpoint when the **D9.3**

investigation began, it is necessary to look at the definition of criminal investigation contained in s. 1(4). (The scope of the definition in s. 1(4) is potentially broad: see the Code of Practice, para. 2.1, which is set out at **D9.5**). A criminal investigation into an alleged offence can occur before the offence has been committed, for example, in a case of police surveillance in relation to a planned robbery or in relation to a series of offences (*Uxbridge Magistrates' Court, ex parte Patel* (2000) 164 JP 209).

For the law prior to the introduction of the CJA 2003, see the 2005 edition of this book.

Certain of the amendments contained in the CJA 2003 were brought into effect on 4 April 2005. In summary, these were (references are to the sections of the CPIA 1996 as amended):

(a) the change to a single unified objective test for the prosecution duty to disclose (s. 3, inserted by the CJA 2003, s. 32);
(b) a change to the required contents of the defence statement (s. 6A, inserted by the CJA 2003, s. 33(2));
(c) procedural matters relating to the defence statement (s. 6E, inserted by the CJA 2003, s. 36);
(d) the redefined continuing duty of the prosecutor to disclose, replacing secondary prosecution disclosure (s. 7A, inserted by the CJA 2003, s. 37);
(e) certain of the amendments to the sanctions for failure to disclose by the defence (s. 11(1) to (3), (5), (6), (8) to (10) and (12), inserted by the CJA 2003, s. 39).

A further amendment relating to the period when the defence case statement has to be served (s. 5(5C), inserted by the CJA 2003, s.33(1)) was brought into effect on 24 July 2006.

These provisions apply to any alleged offence for which a criminal investigation began on or after 4 April 2005. The reasoning set out above in relation to the commencement of the CPIA 1996 applies equally to these later provisions.

Further amendments contained in the CJA 2003 have yet to be implemented. In summary, they are (references are to the relevant sections of the CPIA 1996):

(a) defence disclosure to co-accused (s. 5(5A), (5B) and (5D), inserted by the CJA 2003, s. 33(1));
(b) updated disclosure by the defence (s. 6B, inserted by the CJA 2003, s. 33(3));
(c) notification of intention to call defence witnesses (s. 6C, inserted by the CJA 2003, s. 34);
(d) notification of names of experts instructed by the defence (s. 6D, inserted by the CJA 2003, s. 35);
(e) further amendments to the sanctions for failure to disclose by the defence (s. 11(4), (7) and (11), inserted by the CJA 2003, s. 39).

In summary therefore:

(1) In relation to offences in respect of which the criminal investigation began prior to 1 April 1997, the common law will apply.
(2) If the investigation commenced on or after 1 April 1997, but before 4 April 2005, the CPIA in its original form will apply.
(3) If the investigation commenced on or after 4 April 2005, the applicable law is the CPIA as amended by part V of the CJA 2003, to the extent that it is in force.

In *Brizzalari* (2004) *The Times*, 3 March 2004, the police investigated B's conduct as a care worker in a residential home in 1991 (years before the commencement of the CPIA 1996), but no prosecution resulted. In 1997 (after the CPIA 1996 came into effect) he was investigated again as part of the 'Operation Juno' investigation. This resulted in his prosecution for a number of offences against the children in his care. At his trial, and again at his appeal, it was argued that his case should be subject to the rules on committal and disclosure in existence prior to 1 April 1997. The Court of Appeal rejected this argument. The case arose from Operation Juno, which was an investigation to which the CPIA 1996 applied. The old law might have applied if the old investigation had been put on hold and then reopened, but that was not the case.

Secondary Sources The legislative scheme is supplemented by a number of secondary sources: **D9.4**

(a) The A-G's Guidelines on Disclosure of Information in Criminal Proceedings, issued in April 2005, which are of considerable importance.
(b) The Court of Appeal's Protocol for the Control and Management of Unused Material in the Crown Court (the 'Crown Court Protocol'). In *K* [2006] 2 All ER 552, the Court of Appeal made it clear that 'the Protocol should be applied by trial judges, and those who act for the prosecution and the defence should ensure that they have familiarised themselves with it'.
(c) The CPS/Police Disclosure Manual, a copy of which can be found online at www.cps.gov.uk/legal/section20/chapter_a.html.
(d) The Protocol for the Provision of Advance Information, Prosecution Evidence and Disclosure of Unused Material in the Magistrates' Courts (the 'Magistrates' Courts Protocol'), a copy of which can be found at www.judiciary.gov.uk/docs/judgments_guidance/protocols/mags_courts_%20disclosure.pdf. The Protocol was issued on 12 May 2006, and is intended to be complementary to the Crown Court Protocol. Although the Magistrates' Courts Protocol is initially intended for use in designated pilot sites, it 'is expected that courts and practitioners in all areas will use and refer to the document for guidance'.
(e) The Protocol for the Control and Management of Heavy Fraud and other Complex Cases, issued in March 2005 (see **appendix** 9).

The full text of the Code of Practice, the A-G's Guidelines and the Crown Court Protocol are to be found at **appendix** 5. Part 25 of the CrimPR (see **appendix** 1) sets out the procedures to be followed for applications to the court concerning unused material.

THE INVESTIGATION STAGE

The responsibilities of investigators are set out in a variety of sources. The primary source is the CPIA Code of Practice (set out in full at **appendix** 5) which has been issued under s. 23 of the CPIA 1996. The code applies to criminal investigations carried out by police officers. By s. 26, those other than police officers charged with the duty of conducting criminal investigations must have regard to the code's provisions. The A-G's Guidelines deal with the duties of investigators and disclosure officers in paras. 23 to 31 (see **appendix** 5). **D9.5**

The CPIA Code of Practice, para. 2.1 defines a criminal investigation as:

> an investigation conducted by police officers with a view to it being ascertained whether a person should be charged with an offence, or whether a person charged with an offence is guilty of it. This will include:

—investigations into crimes that have been committed;
—investigations whose purpose is to ascertain whether a crime has been committed, with a view to the possible institution of criminal proceedings; and
—investigations which begin in the belief that a crime may be committed, for example when the police keep premises or individuals under observation for a period of time, with a view to the possible institution of criminal proceedings.

Criminal Procedure and Investigations Act 1996, ss. 22, 26 and 27

22.—(1) For the purposes of [part II] a criminal investigation is an investigation conducted by police officers with a view to it being ascertained—
(a) whether a person should be charged with an offence, or
(b) whether a person charged with an offence is guilty of it.
(2) In [part II] references to material are to material of all kinds, and in particular include references to—
(a) information and
(b) objects of all descriptions.
(3) In [part II] references to recording information are to putting it in a durable or retrievable form (such as writing or tape).

26.—(1) A person other than a police officer who is charged with the duty of conducting an investigation with a view to it being ascertained—
(a) whether a person should be charged with an offence, or
(b) whether a person charged with an offence is guilty of it,
shall in discharging that duty have regard to any relevant provision of a code which would apply if the investigation were conducted by police officers.
(2) A failure—
(a) by a police officer to comply with any provision of a code for the time being in operation by virtue of an order under section 25, or
(b) by a person to comply with subsection (1),
shall not in itself render him liable to any criminal or civil proceedings.
(3) In all criminal and civil proceedings a code in operation at any time by virtue of an order under section 25 shall be admissible in evidence.
(4) If it appears to a court or tribunal conducting criminal or civil proceedings that—
(a) any provision of a code in operation at any time by virtue of an order under section 25, or
(b) any failure mentioned in subsection (2)(a) or (b),
is relevant to any question arising in the proceedings, the provision or failure shall be taken into account in deciding the question.

27.—(1) Where a code prepared under section 23 and brought into operation under section 25 applies in relation to a suspected or alleged offence, the rules of common law which—
(a) were effective immediately before the appointed day, and
(b) relate to the matter mentioned in subsection (2),
shall not apply in relation to the suspected or alleged offence.
(2) The matter is the revealing of material—
(a) by a police officer or other person charged with the duty of conducting an investigation with a view to it being ascertained whether a person should be charged with an offence or whether a person charged with an offence is guilty of it;
(b) to a person involved in the prosecution of criminal proceedings.
(3) In subsection (1) 'the appointed day' means the day appointed under section 25 with regard to the code as first prepared.

Responsibilities of Investigation Officer and Disclosure Officer

D9.6 Every criminal investigation will involve an investigator and a disclosure officer, though in small cases this might be the same person. An investigator is any police officer involved in the conduct of a criminal investigation; a disclosure officer is the person responsible for examining material retained by the police during the investigation and for revealing material to the prosecutor and, at the request of the prosecutor, the accused (see CPIA Code of Practice, para. 2.1). In recent years there has been increasing emphasis on the need for the investigators and disclosure officers to improve their performance in relation to disclosure. The Crown Court Protocol states that they must perform their tasks thoroughly, scrupulously and fairly (para. 13), and emphasises the importance of appropriate training and the appointment of competent disclosure offices with adequate knowledge of the case. The A-G's Guidelines require investigators and disclosure officers to be objective and to work together with prosecutors on disclosure issues (para. 23). Investigators must err on the side of recording and retaining material if in doubt as to its relevance (para. 24) and must specifically draw to the attention of the prosecutor any material where there is doubt as to whether it is disclosable (para. 30). An individual should not be the disclosure officer if the appointment to or continuation in that role is likely to result in a conflict of interest, e.g., if the disclosure officer is the victim of the alleged offence (para. 25). In larger cases there may be a number of disclosure officers, but in such cases there must always be a lead officer (para. 26). Disclosure officers must inspect, view or listen to all relevant material; generally this will require an examination in detail, but exceptionally alternative approaches are permitted such as the use of software search tools and dip sampling where there are large volumes of material (paras. 26 and 27). Relevant material must be retained but, if it later becomes apparent that it is incapable of impact, retention is no longer required (para. 28). Disclosure officers must seek the advice of prosecutors when in doubt as to their responsibilities (para. 31).

Duty to Record and Retain Material

Investigators must record in a durable or retrievable form any material which may be relevant to the investigation and which is not already recorded. This will include negative information such as the fact that a number of people present at a particular place and time saw nothing unusual (CPIA Code of Practice, para. 4.1). The investigator is responsible for retaining material obtained in a criminal investigation which may be relevant to the investigation (para. 5.1). Material may be 'relevant to an investigation' if it appears to an investigator, or disclosure officer, that it has some bearing on any offence under investigation or any person being investigated, or on the surrounding circumstances of the case. 'Material' includes material gathered in the course of the investigation (e.g., documents seized in the course of searching premises) or generated by the investigation (e.g., interview records) (para. 2.1). The duty to retain material includes, e.g. the following categories: crime reports, including crime report forms, relevant parts of incident report books and police officers' notebooks; final versions of witness statements; draft versions of witness statements where their content differs from the final version; interview records (written or taped); expert reports and schedules; any material casting doubt upon the reliability of a confession; and any material casting doubt on the reliability of a witness (see the list in para. 5.4). However, the duty to retain material does not extend to items purely ancillary to that in the above categories which possess no independent significance, such as duplicate copies of documents. The Disclosure Manual states that reports, advices and other communications between the CPS and police in themselves will usually be of an administrative nature or derivative in that they contain professional opinion based on evidential material or material already subject to revelation. They will usually have no bearing on the case and thus will not be relevant. D9.7

The material must be retained at least until criminal proceedings are concluded. In the event of a conviction, material must be retained until the convicted person is released from custody or discharged from hospital (where the court imposes a custodial sentence or a hospital order) and, in any event, for at least six months from the date of conviction. Where an appeal against conviction is in progress when the release or discharge occurs, or at the end of the six months, the material must be retained until the appeal is determined. A similar rule applies where an application is being considered by the CCRC (paras. 5.8 and 5.9).

Duty to Reveal Material to the Prosecutor

The CPIA Code of Practice, para. 6, requires that where the investigator believes that the person charged with an offence is likely to plead not guilty at a summary trial, or that the offence will be tried in the Crown Court, he must prepare a schedule listing material which has been retained and which does not form part of the case against the accused. This is known as the MG6C. If the investigator has obtained any 'sensitive material', this should be listed in a separate schedule or, in exceptional circumstances, disclosed to the prosecutor separately. Sensitive material is defined as material which the investigator believes would give rise to a D9.8

real risk of serious prejudice to an important public interest if it were to be disclosed. (para. 2.1). Paragraph 6.12 gives a number of examples of such material, which range from material relating to national security to material given in confidence, and includes material relating to informants, undercover police officers, premises used for police surveillance, techniques used in the detection of crime, and material relating to a child witness (e.g., material generated by a local authority social services department). The A-G's Guidelines (see **appendix 5**) emphasise that descriptions by disclosure officers in non-sensitive schedules should be detailed, clear and accurate. Sensitive schedules must contain sufficient information to enable the prosecutor to decide whether the material itself should be viewed, bearing in mind its confidential nature (para. 29).

The investigator should draw the prosecutor's attention to any material which might satisfy the test for prosecution disclosure (see **D9.11**) including certain specified categories detailed in the CPIA Code of Practice, para. 7.3. The disclosure officer must certify that to the best of his knowledge and belief the duties imposed under the code have been complied with.

PROSECUTION DISCLOSURE

Responsibilities of Prosecutor to Review Material

D9.9 Prosecutors must not sit back and leave it to disclosure officers to take responsibility for disclosure issues. The A-G's Guidelines require them to do all that they can to facilitate proper disclosure. This includes probing actions taken by disclosure officers, reviewing schedules and, if necessary, taking action to improve their quality and content, and inspecting, viewing or listening to all material which is believed to satisfy the statutory test for disclosure so as to satisfy themselves that the prosecution can properly be continued (paras. 32 to 35).

Disclosure Post-Charge but Prior to Statutory Obligation

D9.10 The statutory scheme requires service of unused material at particular points (see **D9.14**), but the A-G's Guidelines require investigators and prosecutors to recognise that the interests of justice and fairness in the particular circumstances of any case may require disclosure of material after the commencement of proceedings but before the statutory duty arises (see para. 55). This approach is in line with authority. In *DPP, ex parte Lee* [1999] 1 WLR 1950, the Divisional Court considered whether the prosecution had a duty to disclose unused material in indictable-only offences prior to committal. The court found that there might well be circumstances in which it would be helpful to the defence to know of unused material at an earlier stage. For example:

(a) the previous convictions of the alleged victim when they might be expected to help the defence in a bail application;
(b) material to help an application to stay proceedings as an abuse of process;
(c) material to help the accused's arguments at committal;
(d) material to help the accused prepare for trial, e.g., eye-witnesses whom the prosecution did not intend to use.

Kennedy LJ said that a responsible prosecutor might recognise that fairness required that some of this material might be disclosed. The question was: what immediate disclosure (if any) did justice and fairness require in the circumstances of the case? It is submitted that this approach is consistent with the objective of ensuring that the legitimate rights of the accused are preserved. There has always been an ethical dimension to the duty to disclose, and the decision in *Ex parte Lee* is an indication that it survives the introduction of the CPIA 1996. In line with this approach, the Crown Court Protocol states that CPS lawyers advising the police pre-charge should consider conducting a preliminary review of the unused material so as to give early advice on disclosure issues (para. 17).

The Statutory Test for Disclosure

Section 3 of the CPIA 1996 requires the prosecutor to disclose previously undisclosed material to the accused if it 'might reasonably be considered capable of undermining the case for the prosecution against the accused, or of assisting the case for the accused'. The new test is an objective one (by contrast with the subjective test under the CPIA 1996, which was in force before amendment by the CJA 2003). If there is no such material, the accused must be given a written statement to that effect. Prosecution material includes material which the prosecutor possesses or has been allowed to inspect under the provisions of the CPIA Code of Practice. **D9.11**

In determining whether unused material should be revealed to the defence as part of the disclosure process, the statutory test is whether it might reasonably be considered capable of:

(a) undermining the case for the prosecution against the accused; or
(b) assisting the case for the accused.

Something can be said to be undermined if it becomes more likely to fall (or fail) as a result. The prosecution case will be more likely to fail as a result of evidence which shows a defect, discrepancy or inconsistency in that case. Such evidence ought to be revealed as part of initial disclosure. But it might be undermined as a result of a particular defence, which the accused may or may not run. Clearly it is not possible to say at the stage of initial disclosure with certainty whether the defence will take a particular course. That will become clearer after defence disclosure, although it will actually only be entirely certain once the trial itself takes place. But the mere fact that material in the possession of the prosecution raises a new issue in the case which might reasonably be considered capable of assisting the defence is sufficient, it is submitted, to fulfil the statutory test.

In *H and C* [2004] AC 134, the House of Lords stated that s. 3 does not require disclosure of material which is either neutral in effect or which is adverse to the accused, whether because it strengthens the prosecution or weakens the defence. However, the converse is that: 'Fairness ordinarily requires that any material held by the prosecution which weakens its case or strengthens that of the defendant . . . should be disclosed to the defence. Bitter experience has shown that miscarriages of justice may occur where such material is withheld from disclosure. The golden rule is that full disclosure of such material should be made'.

The Court of Appeal has made plain its view that there has been a wide range of serious misunderstandings as to the ambit of unused material to which the defence is entitled and as to the role to be played by the judge. Having quoted the above statement from *H and C*, the Crown Court Protocol states: 'However, it is also essential that the trial process is not overburdened or diverted by erroneous and inappropriate disclosure. The overarching principle is therefore that unused prosecution material will fall to be disclosed if, and only if, it satisfies the test for disclosure applicable to the proceedings in question [as to which see **D9.3**], subject to any overriding public interest considerations'. For an example of a case where material was rightly withheld because nothing in it served to exculpate the accused, see *Dawson* [2007] EWCA Crim 822.

In *Rowe and Davis v UK* (2000) 30 EHRR 1 (see **D9.28**), the European Court of Human Rights emphasised that the right to a fair trial means that the prosecution authorities should disclose to the defence all material evidence in their possession for and against the accused. Commenting on the case, the House of Lords in *H and C* noted that this had been the domestic law under the A-G's 1981 Guidelines on Disclosure but had ceased to be so in 1996 with the enactment of the CPIA. The A-G's Guidelines had required the disclosure of material which 'has some bearing on the offence(s) charged and the surrounding circumstances of the case'. The House of Lords appear therefore to have been saying in *H and C* that domestic law is now out of line with the Strasbourg jurisprudence, though they did not develop the point. If that is so, the position is that the CPIA must be read and given effect to in a way which is compatible with the ECHR (HRA 1998, s. 3), or the legislation is liable to be declared incompatible by a higher court (s. 4).

Important guidance for prosecutors on the *scope* of the duty of primary disclosure is contained in the A-G's Guidelines (see **appendix** 5). Paragraph 10 of the Guidelines states that, generally, material can reasonably be considered capable of undermining the prosecution case or assisting the defence case if it includes anything that tends to show a fact inconsistent with the elements of the case which must be proved by the prosecution. Paragraphs 12 to 14 describe categories of material which might undermine the case for the prosecution or assist the case for the accused. These categories relate to material which:

(a) casts doubt on the accuracy of any prosecution evidence;
(b) points to another person having involvement in the commission of the offence;
(c) may cast doubt upon the reliability of a confession;
(d) might go to the credibility of a prosecution witness (this will include previous convictions, see *Vasiliou* [2000] Crim LR 845);
(e) might support a defence that is either raised by the defence or apparent from the prosecution papers;
(f) may have a bearing on the admissibility of any prosecution evidence.

In addition, material relating to the accused's mental or physical health, intellectual capacity, or to any ill-treatment which he may have suffered in custody is said to be likely to fall within the test for disclosure.

Material must not be disclosed under the CPIA 1996, s. 3, if a court has concluded that it is not in the public interest that it be disclosed (s. 3(6) and see **D9.26** to **D9.38**). Material must not be disclosed to the extent that its disclosure is prohibited by the Regulation of Investigatory Powers Act 2000, s. 17 (CPIA 1996, s. 3(7)).

Under the Sexual Offences (Protected Material) Act 1997, where material is 'protected', it will not be subject to the usual procedure for prosecution disclosure under the CPIA 1996. The 1997 Act is not in force and there are no plans to bring it into force during the currency of this edition.

Before s. 32 of the CJA 2003 came into force, there was a two-stage procedure for disclosure by the prosecution, involving primary and secondary disclosure.

Criminal Procedure and Investigations Act 1996, s. 3

(1) The prosecutor must—
  (a) disclose to the accused any prosecution material which has not previously been disclosed to the accused and which might reasonably be considered capable of undermining the case for the prosecution against the accused, or of assisting the case for the accused, or
  (b) give to the accused a written statement that there is no material of a description mentioned in paragraph (a).

(2) For the purposes of this section prosecution material is material—
  (a) which is in the prosecutor's possession, and came into his possession in connection with the case for the prosecution against the accused, or
  (b) which, in pursuance of a code operative under part II, he has inspected in connection with the case for the prosecution against the accused.

(3) Where material consists of information which has been recorded in any form the prosecutor discloses it for the purposes of this section—
  (a) by securing that a copy is made of it and that the copy is given to the accused, or
  (b) if in the prosecutor's opinion that is not practicable or not desirable, by allowing the accused to inspect it at a reasonable time and a reasonable place or by taking steps to secure that he is allowed to do so;

and a copy may be in such form as the prosecutor thinks fit and need not be in the same form as that in which the information has already been recorded.

(4) Where material consists of information which has not been recorded the prosecutor discloses it for the purposes of this section by securing that it is recorded in such form as he thinks fit and—
(a) by securing that a copy is made of it and that the copy is given to the accused, or
(b) if in the prosecutor's opinion that is not practicable or not desirable, by allowing the accused to inspect it at a reasonable time and a reasonable place or by taking steps to secure that he is allowed to do so.

(5) Where material does not consist of information the prosecutor discloses it for the purposes of this section by allowing the accused to inspect it at a reasonable time and a reasonable place or by taking steps to secure that he is allowed to do so.

(6) Material must not be disclosed under this section to the extent that the court, on an application by the prosecutor, concludes it is not in the public interest to disclose it and orders accordingly.

(7) Material must not be disclosed under this section to the extent that it is material the disclosure of which is prohibited by section 17 of the Regulation of Investigatory Powers Act 2000.

(8) The prosecutor must act under this section during the period which, by virtue of section 12, is the relevant period for this section.

Service of Schedule

Under the CPIA 1996, s. 4, non-sensitive disclosure schedules must be served on the defence at the same time unused material is served. **D9.12**

Criminal Procedure and Investigations Act 1996, s. 4

4.—(1) This section applies where—
(a) the prosecutor acts under section 3, and
(b) before so doing he was given a document in pursuance of provision included, by virtue of section 24(3), in a code operative under part II.

(2) In such a case the prosecutor must give the document to the accused at the same time as the prosecutor acts under section 3.

Summary Trials — Nature of Prosecution's Obligations

The requirement on the prosecution to serve its own case on the defence arises not from statute but from para. 57 of the A-G's Guidelines. This requires the prosecution to provide the accused with all the evidence on which it intends to rely at trial in sufficient time for the evidence to be considered properly before it is called. The Magistrates' Courts Protocol notes that standard directions require 28 days for service of such material, but it goes on to state that in the majority of cases a competent advocate can deal with late served material on the day by the court allowing time before the trial commences or even during the course of the trial (Magistrates' Courts Protocol, part 2). **D9.13**

As regards disclosure of unused material, by virtue of s. 1(1), the CPIA 1996 partially incorporates summary proceedings into the statutory disclosure scheme (see D9.2). The prosecution's duty of disclosure applies whenever the accused pleads not guilty and the court proceeds to summary trial.

Time-limits for and Method of Disclosure

There are no statutory time-limits for disclosure of unused material. Provision was made in the legislation for a time-limit to be laid down by statutory instrument but no such instrument has ever been made. That being the case, the default position is set out in the CPIA 1996, s. 13(1): disclosure must be made as soon as reasonably practicable after the happening of a particular event, such as the accused being committed for trial. **D9.14**

In Crown Court cases, the Crown Court Protocol requires courts to consider whether it is practicable for the prosecution to comply with its disclosure obligations at the same time as service of papers, in cases sent to the Crown Court under the CDA 1998, s. 51, i.e. 70 days from the date that the matter was sent, or 50 days if the accused is in custody. It recognises that some cases may require an interval. In any event, in all cases, the Protocol emphasises the importance of serving unused material in sufficient time to enable the defence to prepare a defence case statement prior to the plea and case management hearing (see paras. 20 to 28).

In summary trials, disclosure of unused material by the prosecution is usually required by standard directions to be within 28 days following pleas (Magistrates' Courts Protocol, para. 3.1).

Unused material may be disclosed either by giving a copy to the defence or by allowing the defence to inspect the material at a reasonable time and place.

Continuing Duty to Review

D9.15 Under the CPIA 1996, s. 7A, the prosecutor remains under a continuing duty to review questions of disclosure. If, at any time before the accused is acquitted or convicted, the prosecutor forms the opinion that there is material which might undermine the prosecution case, or be reasonably expected to assist the accused's defence, it must be disclosed to the accused as soon as reasonably practicable (provided that the court has not ruled against disclosure in respect of that material). In practice this situation is most likely to arise either on service of the defence case statement or during the trial itself.

After service of the defence case statement, (see **D9.18**), the investigator must look again at the material retained, and draw the prosecutor's attention to any material which might reasonably be considered capable of undermining the prosecution case or of assisting the defence if it were to be disclosed. The disclosure officer must certify compliance with the duties imposed by the CPIA Code of Practice. If the investigator comes into possession of any new material after complying with the duties described above, then he must reveal it to the prosecutor (para. 8). This will then trigger a further requirement for disclosure by the prosecution (A-G's Guidelines, para. 17).

This duty of continuous review will come into play during the trial when, e.g., a prosecution witness gives evidence which is materially inconsistent with a statement made earlier to the police. If the defence are unaware of the statement, prosecuting counsel should disclose it to his opposite number so that he can use it in cross-examination to discredit the testimony of the witness (*Clarke* (1931) 22 Cr App R 58 — although the case was many years before the 1996 Act, it is submitted that the principle still holds).

Where the court has ruled against disclosure on public interest grounds, it must keep under review the question whether it is still in the public interest not to disclose the material affected by its order. The position so far as summary trial is concerned is dealt with in **D9.37**.

Criminal Procedure and Investigations Act 1996, s. 7A

(1) This section applies at all times—
  (a) after the prosecutor has complied with section 3 or purported to comply with it, and
  (b) before the accused is acquitted or convicted or the prosecutor decides not to proceed with the case concerned.

(2) The prosecutor must keep under review the question whether at any given time (and, in particular, following the giving of a defence statement) there is prosecution material which—
  (a) might reasonably be considered capable of undermining the case for the prosecution against the accused or of assisting the case for the accused, and
  (b) has not been disclosed to the accused.

(3) If at any time there is any such material as is mentioned in subsection (2) the prosecutor must disclose it to the accused as soon as is reasonably practicable (or within the period mentioned in subsection (5)(a), where that applies).

(4) In applying subsection (2) by reference to any given time the state of affairs at that time (including the case for the prosecution as it stands at that time) must be taken into account.

(5) Where the accused gives a defence statement under section 5, 6 or 6B—

(a) if as a result of that statement the prosecutor is required by this section to make any disclosure, or further disclosure, he must do so during the period which, by virtue of section 12, is the relevant period for this section;
(b) if the prosecutor considers that he is not so required, he must during that period give to the accused a written statement to that effect.

(6) For the purposes of this section prosecution material is material—
(a) which is in the prosecutor's possession and came into his possession in connection with the case for the prosecution against the accused, or
(b) which, in pursuance of a code operative under part 2, he has inspected in connection with the case for the prosecution against the accused.

(7) Subsections (3) to (5) of section 3 (method by which prosecutor discloses) apply for the purposes of this section as they apply for the purposes of that.

(8) Material must not be disclosed under this section to the extent that the court, on an application by the prosecutor, concludes it is not in the public interest to disclose it and orders accordingly.

(9) Material must not be disclosed under this section to the extent that it is material the disclosure of which is prohibited by section 17 of the Regulation of Investigatory Powers Act 2000.

Defence Applications for Disclosure from the Prosecution

The defence can, under the CPIA 1996, s. 8, apply to the court for an order that the prosecutor should disclose any material which might reasonably be expected to assist the accused's defence. This applies to material held or inspected by the prosecutor (s. 8(3)), but also to any material which the disclosure officer must either supply to the prosecutor or allow the prosecutor to inspect if requested (s. 8(4)). Such an application may be made, however, only after the defence have served a defence statement (s. 8(1)). **D9.16**

In *DPP v Wood* (2006) 170 JP 177, it was held that disclosure of the material sought should have been refused by the magistrates' court as the defence statement served did not raise any issue to which the material was relevant. In the Crown Court Protocol, para. 45 (see **appendix** 5), it is emphasised that defence requests for specific disclosure of unused prosecution material which are not referable to any issue in the case identified by the defence case statement should be rejected.

The procedure for making an application under s. 8 is set out in the CrimPR, r. 25.6. In *K* [2006] 2 All ER 552, the Court of Appeal considered the effect of the case management powers contained in the CrimPR upon the procedure relating to issues of disclosure. Those powers permitted the judge to deal with issues of disclosure exclusively by reference to written submissions, and also to limit their length. A judge was not bound to hear oral submissions, and was entitled to put a time-limit on them. Case management submissions were case specific and no particular method of approach was prescribed. The necessary public element of any hearing was sufficiently achieved if the accused, and any media present for the hearing, were supplied with copies of written submissions if they wished to see them. In *H* [2007] 2 WLR 364, the House of Lords held that an application for defence disclosure under s. 8 can be made at the same time as the court deals with a preparatory hearing but the application cannot be held within the preparatory hearing.

Criminal Procedure and Investigations Act 1996, s. 8

(1) This section applies where the accused has given a defence statement under section 5, 6 or 6B and the prosecutor has complied with section 7A(5) or has purported to comply with it or has failed to comply with it.

(2) If the accused has at any time reasonable cause to believe that there is prosecution material which is required by section 7A to be disclosed to him and has not been, he may apply to the court for an order requiring the prosecutor to disclose it to him.

(3) For the purposes of this section prosecution material is material—
(a) which is in the prosecutor's possession and came into his possession in connection with the case for the prosecution against the accused,

(b) which, in pursuance of a code operative under part II, he has inspected in connection with the case for the prosecution against the accused, or
(c) which falls within subsection (4).

(4) Material falls within this subsection if in pursuance of a code operative under part II the prosecutor must, if he asks for the material, be given a copy of it or be allowed to inspect it in connection with the case for the prosecution against the accused.

(5) Material must not be disclosed under this section to the extent that the court, on an application by the prosecutor, concludes it is not in the public interest to disclose it and orders accordingly.

(6) Material must not be disclosed under this section to the extent that it is material the disclosure of which is prohibited by section 17 of the Regulation of Investigatory Powers Act 2000.

Consequences of Non-disclosure

D9.17 A failure on the part of the prosecution to make proper disclosure might result, in appropriate circumstances, in a defence application to stay proceedings as an abuse of process. For consideration of the factors involved when such an application is made, see **D3.54** ***et seq.***, especially **D3.63**.

A failure on the part of the prosecution to make proper disclosure might result, in appropriate circumstances, in a defence application to stay proceedings as an abuse of process or in a successful appeal. In *Hadley* [2006] EWCA Crim 2544 the prosecution failed to disclose videos relating to surveillance of the appellant's business premises and instead relied on summaries. The conviction was quashed. The court said that a conviction would be regarded as unsafe if the appellant showed that the material which was not disclosed was capable of affecting the jury's mind. The court went on to say that it was likely to be slow to accept that the safety of a conviction was unaffected where a substantial volume of disclosable material had been withheld from the defence. For consideration of the factors involved when an application for a stay is made, see **D3.54** ***et seq.***

DEFENCE DISCLOSURE

The Defence Case Statement

D9.18 By the CPIA 1996, s. 5, once the case is sent to the Crown Court and the prosecution case is served, the accused must give a defence statement to the prosecutor. The defence statement is a written statement setting out the basis on which the case will be defended. In relation to cases where the criminal investigation began on or after 4 April 2005, the areas that the statement must cover are set out in s. 6A of the CPIA 1996, as amended by the CJA 2003, s. 33(2). It must set out: the nature of the accused's defence, including any particular defences upon which he intends to rely; the matters of fact on which he takes issue with the prosecution, with the reasons why; and any points of law which he wishes to take, with any authorities on which he relies. It should be stressed that the duty of disclosure imposed on the defence is of a different kind from what is normally meant when one talks about 'the prosecution duty of disclosure'. The prosecution duty is to disclose unused material, i.e. material which they do not intend to introduce at trial. As far as defence disclosure is concerned, the duty is to reveal the case which will be presented at trial.

The degree of detail which is now required by the CPIA results from a perception among some prosecutors and members of the judiciary that defence lawyers were providing defence statements that were couched in too general terms, so that the intended benefits of their introduction in terms of improved case management were not being realised. In *Bryant* [2005] EWCA Crim 2079, the Court of Appeal had said that a defence statement consisting of a general denial of the counts in the indictment, accompanied by a statement that the accused took issue with any witness giving evidence contrary to his denial, was 'woefully inadequate'. Such a document did not meet the purposes of a defence statement. The Crown Court Protocol, para. 35 (see **appendix** 5), states: 'Judges will expect to see defence case statements that contain a clear and detailed exposition of the issues of fact and law in the case'. The Protocol goes on to say that there must be a complete change of culture. It requires judges to examine the defence statement with care to ensure that it complies with the formalities required by the CPIA (para. 37) and to investigate any failure by the defence to comply with its obligations (see paras. 38 to 41). As to the duty of defence advocates to raise issues of fact and law in the defence statement, see also *Gleeson* [2004] 1 Cr App R 406. In appropriate circumstances the principle that there must be equality of arms will mean that the prosecution must spell out the inferences that it will be asking the trier of fact to draw from the primary facts adduced in its evidence, given that the defence is obliged to set out its reasoning for disputing issues of fact in that evidence. It follows that the scope of the defence statement should be viewed in the context of what might reasonably be required of the defence at a stage when they may not be clear about the way in which the prosecution put their case.

The position as regards disclosure between co-accused is at present governed by common law. In *Cairns* [2003] 1 WLR 796, the judge declined to order disclosure of the defence statements of C's co-accused, ruling that disclosure of such statements was only as between the accused and the Crown. The Court of Appeal held that the Crown should have disclosed the defence statements. Failing that, the judge should have ordered disclosure under s. 8. When s. 33 of the CJA 2003 comes into effect, this matter will be governed by s. 5(5A), (5B) and (5D) of the CPIA 1996. In a multi-accused case, the court will be able to order each of the accused to give copies of his defence statement to his co-accused. The court may act of its own motion, or in response to an application by any party, specifying the period within which the statement must be served.

A further amendment to the defence duty of disclosure is envisaged in the CPIA 1996, s. 6B, which is inserted by the CJA 2003, s. 33(3) but which is not yet in force. It applies where the accused has given a defence statement before the beginning of the relevant period. It requires the defence to provide an 'updated defence statement', or alternatively a statement that it has no changes to make to its initial defence statement.

The question of the authorship of the defence statement (or an updating statement, or a statement that no updating is necessary) is dealt with in s. 6E(1), inserted by the CJA 2003, s. 36. It deems that, where an accused's solicitor purports to give such a statement on behalf of the accused, it is to be treated as given on behalf of the accused unless the contrary is proved. Of course, evidence can be adduced to show that it was not given with the accused's authority, but that may have adverse consequences where legal professional privilege is waived as a result (see **F9.37**).

At trial, the judge may direct that the jury receive a copy of any defence statement (whether initial or updated), edited to exclude any reference to inadmissible evidence. This can be done of the judge's own motion or on application, but only if it would help the jury to understand the case or resolve any issue in it (s. 6E(4) to (6)).

Alibi

If the defence statement discloses an alibi, particulars of alibi must be given. This duty has been expanded as a result of the amendment to the CPIA 1996, s. 6A(2), brought about by the CJA 2003, s. 33(2). The names, addresses and dates of birth (or as much of this information as is known) of any alibi witnesses whom the accused intends to call must be contained within the defence statement. If the accused does not know any of these details, he must give any information in his possession that might assist in identifying or finding any such witness. Changes in relation to alibi witnesses, or the later discovery of the information required by **D9.19** statute, must be dealt with by the procedure for updated disclosure when this is in force. Alibi evidence continues to be defined as 'evidence tending to show that by reason of the presence of the accused at a particular place or in a particular area at a particular time he was not, or was unlikely to have been, at the place where the offence is alleged to have been committed at the time of its alleged commission' (see **D16.15**).

Notification of Details of Defence Witnesses

D9.20 The CJA 2003, s. 34, inserts s. 6C into the CPIA 1996 so as to introduce a duty to notify the court and the prosecutor of any other witnesses. This duty, which is not yet in force, involves notification separately from the defence statement. The accused will be required to give to the court and the prosecutor a notice indicating whether he intends to call any witnesses at trial, other than himself and any alibi witnesses already notified. Again, the defence must provide names, addresses, dates of birth or, if any such details are not known, other identifying information. Notice of intention to call a witness will have to be given within a period to be laid down at the time when this provision comes into effect. Any change in the plans to call witnesses (including a decision not to call a previously notified witness or to call a witness not previously notified) will have to be dealt with by way of an amended notice to the court and the prosecutor. It seems clear from *R (Kelly) v Warley Magistrates' Court* [2007] EWHC 1836 (Admin) that the new provisions, when they come into force, will override legal professional privilege (see **F9.29**). Equally, however, until the new provisions are in force the court cannot compel the defence to disclose the names and addresses of witnesses.

Section 21A of the CPIA 1996 (inserted by the CJA 2003, s. 40) envisages a code of practice for police interviews of witnesses notified by the accused (either to support an alibi or otherwise). It will deal with such matters as the attendance of solicitors on behalf of the accused and the interviewee.

Criminal Procedure and Investigations Act 1996, ss. 5, 6A, 6B and 6E

5.—(1) Subject to subsections (2) to (4), this section applies where—
- (a) [part I] applies by virtue of section 1(2), and
- (b) the prosecutor complies with section 3 or purports to comply with it.

(2) Where [part I] applies by virtue of section 1(2)(b), this section does not apply unless—
- (a) a copy of the notice of transfer, and
- (b) copies of the documents containing the evidence, have been given to the accused under regulations made under section 5(9) of the Criminal Justice Act 1987.

(3) Where [part I] applies by virtue of section 1(2)(c), this section does not apply unless—
- (a) a copy of the notice of transfer, and
- (b) copies of the documents containing the evidence,

have been given to the accused under regulations made under para. 4 of schedule 6 to the Criminal Justice Act 1991.

(3A) Where [part I] applies by virtue of section 1(2)(cc), this section does not apply unless—
- (a) copies of the documents containing the evidence have been served on the accused under regulations made under para. 1 of schedule 3 to the Crime and Disorder Act 1998; and
- (b) a copy of the notice under subsection (7) of section 51 of that Act has been served on him under that subsection.

(4) Where [part I] applies by virtue of section 1(2)(e), this section does not apply unless the prosecutor has served on the accused a copy of the indictment and a copy of the set of documents containing the evidence which is the basis of the charge.

(5) Where this section applies, the accused must give a defence statement to the court and the prosecutor.

(5A) Where there are other accused in the proceedings and the court so orders, the accused must also give a defence statement to each other accused specified by the court.

(5B) The court may make an order under subsection (5A) either of its own motion or on the application of any party.

(5C) A defence statement that has to be given to the court and the prosecutor (under subsection (5)) must be given during the period which, by virtue of section 12, is the relevant period for this section.

(5D) A defence statement that has to be given to a co-accused (under subsection (5A)) must be given within such period as the court may specify.

6A.—(1) For the purposes of this part a defence statement is a written statement—
(a) setting out the nature of the accused's defence, including any particular defences on which he intends to rely,
(b) indicating the matters of fact on which he takes issue with the prosecution,
(c) setting out, in the case of each such matter, why he takes issue with the prosecution, and
(d) indicating any point of law (including any point as to the admissibility of evidence or an abuse of process) which he wishes to take, and any authority on which he intends to rely for that purpose.

(2) A defence statement that discloses an alibi must give particulars of it, including—
(a) the name, address and date of birth of any witness the accused believes is able to give evidence in support of the alibi, or as many of those details as are known to the accused when the statement is given;
(b) any information in the accused's possession which might be of material assistance in identifying or finding any such witness in whose case any of the details mentioned in paragraph (a) are not known to the accused when the statement is given.

(3) For the purposes of this section evidence in support of an alibi is evidence tending to show that by reason of the presence of the accused at a particular place or in a particular area at a particular time he was not, or was unlikely to have been, at the place where the offence is alleged to have been committed at the time of its alleged commission.

(4) The Secretary of State may by regulations make provision as to the details of the matters that, by virtue of subsection (1), are to be included in defence statements.

6B.—(1) Where the accused has, before the beginning of the relevant period for this section, given a defence statement under section 5 or 6, he must during that period give to the court and the prosecutor either—
(a) a defence statement under this section (an 'updated defence statement'), or
(b) a statement of the kind mentioned in subsection (4).

(2) The relevant period for this section is determined under section 12.

(3) An updated defence statement must comply with the requirements imposed by or under section 6A by reference to the state of affairs at the time when the statement is given.

(4) Instead of an updated defence statement, the accused may give a written statement stating that he has no changes to make to the defence statement which was given under section 5 or 6.

(5) Where there are other accused in the proceedings and the court so orders, the accused must also give either an updated defence statement or a statement of the kind mentioned in subsection (4), within such period as may be specified by the court, to each other accused so specified.

(6) The court may make an order under subsection (5) either of its own motion or on the application of any party.

...

6E.—(1) Where an accused's solicitor purports to give on behalf of the accused—
(a) a defence statement under section 5, 6 or 6B, or
(b) a statement of the kind mentioned in section 6B(4),

the statement shall, unless the contrary is proved, be deemed to be given with the authority of the accused.

Defence Disclosure in Cases Tried Summarily

In cases tried summarily there is no obligation on the defence to provide a defence statement. **D9.21** However, once the prosecutor has complied (or purported to comply) with its duty to disclose unused material (see **D9.11**), the accused may give the prosecutor and the court a defence statement (CPIA 1996, s. 6). In the absence of a defence statement, the accused cannot make an application for specific disclosure under s.8, and the court cannot make any orders for disclosure of unused prosecution material (see s.8(1) and **D9.16**).

If the accused provides a defence statement, the requirements in s. 6A as to the contents of the statement apply. The voluntary regime applies to summary trial, whether it is of a summary or an either-way offence or even (in the case of a juvenile) of an indictable-only offence

(s. 1(1)). The Magistrates' Courts Protocol makes the following points in respect of defence statements:

(1) Defence advocates must give consideration at an early stage to whether to serve such a statement.
(2) Defence statements must contain a clear and detailed exposition of the issues of fact and law in the case and courts should examine them with care to ensure that they comply with the formalities required by the CPIA.
(3) Where late service of a defence statement results in potential delay to the proceedings, any application to adjourn for further disclosure or to make an application under s. 8 must be scrutinised carefully by the court.
(4) Any case which raises difficult issues of disclosure should be referred to a district judge, where one is available.

Criminal Procedure and Investigations Act 1996, s. 6

(1) This section applies where—
   (a) [part I] applies by virtue of section 1(1), and
   (b) the prosecutor complies with section 3 or purports to comply with it.
(2) The accused—
   (a) may give a defence statement to the prosecutor, and
   (b) if he does so, must also give such a statement to the court.

. . .

(4) If the accused gives a defence statement under this section he must give it during the period which, by virtue of section 12, is the relevant period for this section.

Defence Disclosure in Cases Tried in the Crown Court — Time-limits

D9.22 By the Criminal Procedure Investigations Act 1996 (Defence Disclosure Time Limits) Regulations 1997 (SI 1997 No. 684), reg. 2, the defence statement must be served within 14 days of the prosecution's compliance (or purported compliance) with the duty of primary disclosure. The defence may apply for an extension, but the application must be made before the deadline expires (reg. 3). The application must not be granted unless the court is satisfied that the accused cannot reasonably give a statement within the deadline. The length of any extension that is granted is entirely at the court's discretion, and it may order further extensions. Time runs from the date of service of a statement by the prosecution under the CPIA 1996, s. 3(1)(h), not from service of the scheduled unused material; however, the right to secondary disclosure is not lost if there is a short delay in serving the defence statement (*DPP v Wood* (2006) 170 JP 177; *Murphy v DPP* [2006] EWHC 1753 (Admin)).

The Crown Court Protocol recognises that there may be some cases where it is not possible to serve a proper defence statement within the 14-day limit and encourages courts to grant well-founded applications for extensions and to put back the plea and case management hearing to enable a sufficient statement to be filed and considered by the prosecution (see para. 33). But, equally, extensions will not be granted as a matter of course. It will not be sufficient for the defence to say that insufficient instructions have been taken for service of the statement within the 14-day time-limit: the court will need to know why, and what arrangements have been made for the taking of such instructions (see para. 28). The Magistrates' Courts Protocol suggests that in cases to be tried summarily it will only be on rare occasions that it will not be possible to serve a statement within the 14-day period.

The amendments introduced by the CJA 2003 to the CPIA 1996 clearly put a burden on defence representatives to embark on detailed preparation at an earlier stage. However, this responsibility cannot be discharged unless the prosecution make timely disclosure of unused material. As it is put in the Crown Court Protocol, para. 25 (see **appendix** 5), 'the defence must have a proper opportunity to read the case papers and to consider the initial or primary disclosure, with a view to timely drafting of a defence case statement (where the matter is to be contested), prior to the PCMH'.

Given the early notification that the defence must now give of its legal arguments, which include those in relation to any alleged abuse of process and admissibility of evidence, there is a strong case for the prosecution to be compelled to give advance notice of its arguments and authorities on such points, if sought. Any failure to do so would seem to offend against the requirement that a fair trial should be based upon the principle of equality of arms.

Criminal Procedure and Investigations Act 1996 (Defence Disclosure Time Limits) Regulations 1997 (SI 1997 No. 684), regs 2 to 5

2. Subject to regulations 3, 4 and 5, the relevant period for sections 5 and 6 of the Act (disclosure by the accused) is a period beginning with the day on which the prosecutor complies, or purports to comply, with section 3 of that Act and ending with the expiration of 14 days from that day.

3.—(1) The period referred to in regulation 2 shall, if the court so orders, be extended by so many days as the court specifies.

(2) The court may only make such an order if an application which complies with para. (3) below is made by the accused before the expiration of the period referred to in regulation 2.

(3) An application under paragraph (2) above shall—

(a) state that the accused believes, on reasonable grounds, that it is not possible for him to give a defence statement under section 5 or, as the case may be, 6 of the Act during the period referred to in regulation 2;

(b) specify the grounds for so believing; and

(c) specify the number of days by which the accused wishes that period to be extended.

(4) The court shall not make an order under paragraph (1) above unless it is satisfied that the accused cannot reasonably give or, as the case may be, could not reasonably have given a defence statement under section 5 or, as the case may be, 6 of the Act during the period referred to in regulation 2.

(5) The number of days by which the period referred to in regulation 2 may be extended shall be entirely at the court's discretion.

4.—(1) Where the court has made an order under regulation 3(1), the period referred to in regulation 2 as extended in accordance with that order shall, if the court so orders, be further extended by so many days as the court specifies.

(2) Paragraphs (2) to (5) of regulation 3 shall, subject to paragraph (4) below, apply for the purposes of an order under paragraph (1) above as they apply for the purposes of an order under regulation 3(1).

(3) There shall be no limit on the number of applications that may be made under regulation 3(2) as applied by paragraph (2) above; and on a second or subsequent such application the court shall have the like powers under paragraph (1) above as on the first such application.

(4) In the application of regulation 3(2) to (5) in accordance with paragraph (2) above, any reference to the period referred to in regulation 2 shall be construed as a reference to that period as extended or, as the case may be, further extended by an order of the court under regulation 3(1) or paragraph (1) or (3) above.

5.—(1) Where the period referred to in regulation 2 or that period as extended or, as the case may be, further extended by an order of the court under regulation 3(1) or 4(1) or (3) would, apart from this regulation, expire on any of the days specified in paragraph (2) below, that period shall be treated as expiring on the next following day which is not one of those days.

(2) The days referred to in paragraph (1) above are Saturday, Sunday, Christmas Day, Good Friday and any day which . . . is a bank holiday in England and Wales.

Sanctions for Failure in Defence Disclosure

Section 11 of the CPIA 1996 lays down sanctions for failure in defence disclosure which apply if the defence: **D9.23**

(a) fail to give the initial defence statement required under s. 5 in respect of Crown Court cases,

(b) in cases tried summarily or in the Crown Court, give the initial defence statement after the 14-day period during which it must be served;

(c) fail to provide an updated statement required under s. 6B(1) or a statement that no updating is necessary under s. 6B(4);

(d) fail to give notice of defence witnesses, as required by s. 6C;
(e) supply the documents in (c) or (d) outside the applicable time-limit;
(f) set out inconsistent defences in the defence statement;
(g) put forward a defence at trial that was not mentioned in the defence statement;
(h) rely on a matter that should have been mentioned in the defence statement to comply with s. 6A, but was not;
(i) give evidence of alibi or call a witness to give evidence in support of alibi without having complied with the provisions relating to notification of alibi witnesses;
(j) call a witness not included or adequately identified in the notice of defence witnesses.

The above list is a summary of s.11 as amended by the CJA 2003, s. 39. As to (c), (d) and (j), the relevant duties have not yet been brought into force.

In the event that any of the above defence deficiencies applies, the court may comment upon the failure in question (s. 11(5)). Other parties (the prosecution and co-accused) may also comment upon any defect in disclosure, but in certain circumstances such comment requires the leave of the court. Those circumstances are where the defect that triggers the sanction is a failure to mention a point of law (including failure to mention a point about admissibility of evidence or abuse of process) or authority to be relied on, failure to give notice of or adequately identify a witness, or failure to give such notice in time (s. 11(6), and (7)).

If any of the above deficiencies applies, the court or jury may also draw such inferences as appear proper in deciding whether the accused is guilty of the offence concerned (s. 11(5)(b)). The accused may not, however, be convicted solely on the basis of such an inference (s. 11(10)). It would seem that the wording of s. 11(5)(b) would preclude the use of an inference from defective disclosure to bolster the prosecution case against a submission of no case to answer, since the phrase 'whether the accused is guilty of the offence concerned' is not apt to describe the decision which the court has to make on such a submission. The context in which such an inference can be drawn is therefore narrower than that applicable to inferences from silence under the CJPO 1994, s. 34 (see **F19.4**), which explicitly allows an inference to be drawn when the court determines whether there is a case to answer, reserving the wording replicated in s. 11(5)(b) of the 1996 Act to apply to the verdict.

Section 6E(2) of the CPIA 1996, inserted by the CJA 2003, s. 36, provides that where it appears to the judge at a pre-trial hearing (see **D14.36** ***et seq***) that the accused has failed to serve a defence statement, or to update it when required to do so, or to serve notice of intention to call defence witnesses, so that there may be comment made or inferences drawn under s. 11(5), he must warn the accused of that possibility. Curiously, this provision is fully in force even though the provisions relating to updated statements and notices to call defence witnesses (ss. 6B and 6C) are not yet in force.

D9.24 **Circumstances in which Comment May Be Made** There is provision about the making of comments and drawing of inferences in three sets of circumstances:

(a) where the defect in question is that the accused put forward a defence different from that set out in his defence statement, the court must have regard to the extent of any difference, and whether there is any justification for it (s. 11(8));
(b) where the defect concerns failure to give notice of, or identify adequately, a defence witness, the court must have regard to whether there is any justification for the failure (s. 11(9)).
(c) where the defect is that the accused issued a notice indicating that no updating is required to the defence statement, the question whether there has been a breach of the requirements for the contents of the defence statement or of the duty to supply particulars of alibi must be determined at the time when the statement under s. 6B(4) was made and as if the original defence statement had been made at that time (s. 11(11), which is not yet in force).

In *Wheeler* (2000) 164 JP 565, the accused was charged with knowingly importing cocaine from Jamaica. He had been arrested at Gatwick when 'swallower' packages of the drug were found in his briefcase. Four further packages were found in the room where he was detained, and a further 17 packages were later excreted from his body. In interview and later in evidence at his trial, he gave an explanation concerning his possession of the drugs which was at odds with the defence statement served by his solicitors prior to the trial. When that statement was put to him in cross-examination, he said that the statement was a mistake. The trial judge gave no specific direction to the jury about the inconsistency between the statement and the accused's evidence. The accused was convicted, and appealed. It was the appellant's case, and was accepted by his solicitors, that the defence statement did not reflect his instructions, and had not been approved by him. The appeal was allowed. In cases where there was a conflict between the defence statement and the accused's evidence at trial, the judge ought to give the jury a specific direction on how to approach that inconsistency. The accused's credibility had been crucial to his case, and the conviction was unsafe in all the circumstances. A retrial was ordered. Their lordships commented that defence statements should be signed by the accused to acknowledge their accuracy and to obviate disputes of the sort which had occurred in the case.

In cases where there is apparent inconsistency between the defence statement and the case run by the defence at trial, the judge needs first to make a decision as to whether the jury should be permitted to draw an inference from the inconsistency, in accordance with the CPIA 1996, s. 11(5)(b). In *Wheeler* it seems that the fault did in fact lie with the solicitors in any event. The Court of Appeal made the point that it would have been wise for the judge to have accepted that, given that the conduct of the defence at trial was in accordance with the version of events that he gave in interview. There will inevitably be a proportion of cases in which defence disclosure is defective, whether due to errors by defence lawyers, a failure by the accused to be organised enough to attend to give instructions, or a lack of focus on the importance of the issues involved. It is right to stress the need for judicial caution before allowing the jury to base a verdict upon foundations which may turn out to be shaky.

When *Wheeler* was decided, there was no presumption that a defence statement was issued with the authority of the accused. The position now is that such a statement is deemed to have been issued with his authority, subject to proof to the contrary (s. 6E(1), inserted by the CJA 2003, s. 36: see **D9.18**). It is submitted that the reasoning of the Court of Appeal is still applicable in the light of the new law. As to the suggestion that defence statements should be signed, this issue arose in *R (Sullivan) v Crown Court at Maidstone* [2002] 1 WLR 2747. In that case the High Court considered a local practice direction by the resident judge that all defence statements were to be signed by the accused before being given to the prosecutor and the court. The practice direction was declared unlawful, on the ground that there was no power to make it.

Where the judge decides to allow the jury to draw an inference, it may trigger the need for a direction in accordance with *Lucas* [1981] QB 720 (see *Bryan* [2004] EWCA Crim 3467 and *Burge* [1996] 1 Cr App R 163 as to the circumstances in which a *Lucas* direction ought to be given). The judge would need to direct the jury to consider whether the defence statement constituted a deliberate lie on a material issue, which was due to the realisation of guilt and the fear of the truth (see **F1.18**).

Criminal Procedure and Investigations Act 1996, s. 11

(1) This section applies in the three cases set out in subsections (2), (3) and (4).
(2) The first case is where section 5 applies and the accused—
  (a) fails to give an initial defence statement,
  (b) gives an initial defence statement but does so after the end of the period which, by virtue of section 12, is the relevant period for section 5,

(c) is required by section 6B to give either an updated defence statement or a statement of the kind mentioned in subsection (4) of that section but fails to do so,
(d) gives an updated defence statement or a statement of the kind mentioned in section 6B(4) but does so after the end of the period which, by virtue of section 12, is the relevant period for section 6B,
(e) sets out inconsistent defences in his defence statement, or
(f) at his trial —
(i) puts forward a defence which was not mentioned in his defence statement or is different from any defence set out in that statement,
(ii) relies on a matter which, in breach of the requirements imposed by or under section 6A, was not mentioned in his defence statement,
(iii) adduces evidence in support of an alibi without having given particulars of the alibi in his defence statement, or
(iv) calls a witness to give evidence in support of an alibi without having complied with section 6A(2)(a) or (b) as regards the witness in his defence statement.

(3) The second case is where section 6 applies, the accused gives an initial defence statement, and the accused —
(a) gives the initial defence statement after the end of the period which, by virtue of section 12, is the relevant period for section 6, or
(b) does any of the things mentioned in paras. (c) to (f) of subsection (2).

(4) The third case is where the accused—
(a) gives a witness notice but does so after the end of the period which, by virtue of section 12, is the relevant period for section 6C, or
(b) at his trial calls a witness (other than himself) not included, or not adequately identified, in a witness notice.

(5) Where this section applies—
(a) the court or any other party may make such comment as appears appropriate;
(b) the court or jury may draw such inferences as appear proper in deciding whether the accused is guilty of the offence concerned.

(6) Where—
(a) this section applies by virtue of subsection (2)(f)(ii) (including that provision as it applies by virtue of subsection (3)(b)), and
(b) the matter which was not mentioned is a point of law (including any point as to the admissibility of evidence or an abuse of process) or an authority,

comment by another party under subsection (5)(a) may be made only with the leave of the court.

(7) Where this section applies by virtue of subsection (4), comment by another party under subsection (5)(a) may be made only with the leave of the court.

(8) Where the accused puts forward a defence which is different from any defence set out in his defence statement, in doing anything under subsection (5) or in deciding whether to do anything under it the court shall have regard —
(a) to the extent of the differences in the defences, and
(b) to whether there is any justification for it.

(9) Where the accused calls a witness whom he has failed to include, or to identify adequately, in a witness notice, in doing anything under subsection (5) or in deciding whether to do anything under it the court shall have regard to whether there is any justification for the failure.

(10) A person shall not be convicted of an offence solely on an inference drawn under subsection (5).

(11) Where the accused has given a statement of the kind mentioned in section 6B(4), then, for the purposes of subsections (2)(f)(ii) and (iv), the question as to whether there has been a breach of the requirements imposed by or under section 6A or a failure to comply with section 6A(2)(a) or (b) shall be determined—
(a) by reference to the state of affairs at the time when that statement was given, and
(b) as if the defence statement was given at the same time as that statement.

(12) In this section—
(a) 'initial defence statement' means a defence statement given under section 5 or 6;
(b) 'updated defence statement' means a defence statement given under section 6B;
(c) a reference simply to an accused's 'defence statement' is a reference—
(i) where he has given only an initial defence statement, to that statement;

(ii) where he has given both an initial and an updated defence statement, to the updated defence statement;

(iii) where he has given both an initial defence statement and a statement of the kind mentioned in section 6B(4), to the initial defence statement;

(d) a reference to evidence in support of an alibi shall be construed in accordance with section 6A(3);

(e) 'witness notice' means a notice given under section 6C.

Section 11 is shown as amended by the CJA 2003, s. 39; s. 11(4), (7) and (9) are not yet in force.

ROLE OF THE COURT

The Court of Appeal has made it plain that it expects the courts to exercise active judicial oversight and management of the handling of disclosure issues. The Crown Court Protocol (which is replicated in key respects by the Magistrates' Courts Protocol) states that there must be a sea-change in the approach of judges and the parties to all aspects of the handling of the material. In the past, applications for disclosure have been based on misunderstandings and misconceptions. The overarching principle to be applied is 'that unused material will fall to be disclosed if, and only if, it satisfies the test for disclosure applicable to the proceedings in question' (Crown Court Protocol, paras. 1 to 5). **D9.25**

The courts are to:

(a) set realistic timetables for prosecution and defence disclosure (paras. 26 to 27);

(b) grant extensions only in response to an appropriately detailed explanation for the request (para. 28);

(c) not allow the prosecution to abdicate their responsibility for reviewing unused material by allowing the defence to inspect everything on the schedule of non-sensitive unused material (para. 30);

(d) examine defence case statements with care to ensure that they comply with the formalities, investigate any failures and, if appropriate, give a warning about the possibility of an adverse inference being drawn (paras. 37 to 41);

(e) cease making blanket orders for disclosure and instead should reject requests which are not referable to an issue identified in the defence case statement and which satisfy the test for disclosure (paras. 42 to 46);

(f) allow adequate time to deal with disclosure issues at the plea and case management hearing (see paras. 47 to 49).

For the equivalent provisions, see the Magistrates' Courts Protocol, part 3.

In *B* [2000] Crim LR 50, the Court of Appeal stressed that the decision as to whether primary disclosure should be made was for the prosecution. The assistance of the judge should be sought only if the questions could properly be decided by him, most obviously where there was an issue relating to public interest immunity. The conviction was quashed as unsafe and a retrial ordered, because the prosecution had asked the judge to read documents and consider whether they should be disclosed to the defence as undermining the prosecution case, thus transferring to him the responsibility for judging the weight and impact of the material. In fact, the defence would have been in a much better position to cross-examine the complainant if they had read the documents in question.

In *Stephenson* [2005] EWCA Crim 1778, the prosecution disclosed material to the defence which suggested that prosecution witnesses were significantly involved in drug-related offences. Prosecution counsel did not, however, place the material before the court, and sought in his closing speech to rely upon the credibility of his witnesses. The Court of Appeal held that the Crown was under a duty, in these circumstances, to place the material before the court. This should have been done as a concession by the Crown.

PUBLIC INTEREST IMMUNITY

D9.26 Circumstances may arise in a case in which material held by the prosecution and tending to undermine the prosecution or assist the defence cannot be disclosed to the defence, fully or even at all, without the risk of prejudice to an important public interest. In such circumstances the courts may be justified in ordering that the material is withheld from disclosure, but they must only allow this to the minimum extent necessary to protect the public interest in question and must never imperil the overall fairness of the trial (*H and C* [2004] AC 134). Applications by the prosecution to the court to withhold material in these circumstances are known as public interest immunity applications. Although the 1996 Act generally disapplies the rules of common law in relation to the prosecution duty of disclosure (s. 21(1)), it preserves 'the rules of common law as to whether disclosure is in the public interest' (s. 21(2)). The provisions of the CPIA 1996 which provide for disclosure to the accused allow relevant material to be withheld on public interest grounds only if the court so decides (ss. 3(6), 7(5), 8(5) and 9(8)).

For the circumstances in which public interest immunity may be claimed, see **F9**. This section deals with the procedure in respect of such claims.

Background

D9.27 The law concerning public interest immunity (previously known as Crown privilege) developed in civil proceedings: see *Duncan v Cammell Laird & Co Ltd* [1942] AC 624; and *Conway v Rimmer* [1968] AC 910. Until the mid-1990s there were few reported cases concerning public interest immunity in criminal proceedings because it was left largely to the judgement of the prosecution as to whether material should be withheld and only exceptionally did courts make a ruling. That position changed with the case of *Ward* [1993] 1 WLR 619. Judith Ward had been convicted of multiple murder and explosives offences. The prosecution had failed to disclose material relevant to her alleged confessions and certain scientific evidence. In upholding her appeal, the Court of Appeal made it clear that the court, rather than the prosecution, had to be the final arbiter as to whether the prosecution was entitled to avoid disclosure on the basis of public interest immunity. It would be wrong to allow the prosecution to withhold material documents without giving notice of that fact to the defence. The court could then, if necessary, be asked to rule on the legitimacy of the prosecution's asserted claim. If the prosecution was not prepared to have the issue of public interest immunity determined by a court, they would inevitably have to abandon the case.

The requirement set out in *Ward* to give notice to the defence of an application in every case seemed likely in some instances to lead to the material in question being compromised. Accordingly, some months after *Ward* was decided, the Court of Appeal laid down guidance as to the procedure to be followed in public interest immunity cases in the case of *Davis* [1993] 1 WLR 613. Lord Taylor CJ stated that:

(a) If the prosecution wish to rely on public interest immunity to justify non-disclosure then, in most cases, they must notify the defence that they are applying for a ruling by the court, and indicate to the defence at least the category of the material which they hold. The defence must then have the opportunity of making representations to the court.

(b) Where, however, the public interest would be injured if disclosure was made of the category of material, the prosecution should still notify the defence of the application, but need not specify the category of material. The defence would be able to address the court on the procedure to be adopted but the application itself would be *ex parte*. If the court on that application found that there should be an *inter partes* application it would so order. If not, it would rule on the *ex parte* application.

(c) In a highly exceptional case where even to reveal that an *ex parte* application was to be made would injure the public interest, the prosecution could apply to the court *ex parte* without notice. Again, if the court on hearing the application considered that notice should have been given to the defence, or even that the normal *inter partes* hearing should have been adopted, it would so order.

Lord Taylor emphasised the importance of the court keeping the situation under review.

Part 25 of the CrimPR in effect reproduces the procedure laid down in *Davis*: see **D9.33**.

Public Interest Immunity and Article 6

The procedural fairness of public interest immunity has been examined in a number of decisions of the European Court of Human Rights. **D9.28**

In *Rowe and Davis v UK* (2000) 30 EHRR 1, the court gave an important ruling concerning the approach to be adopted by the court when public interest immunity issues have to be determined. The following points emerge from the court's unanimous decision.

(a) The right to a fair trial means that the prosecution authorities should disclose to the defence all material evidence in their possession for and against the accused.
(b) That duty of disclosure is not absolute, and 'in any criminal proceedings there may be competing interests, such as national security or the need to protect witnesses at risk of reprisals or keep secret police methods of investigation, which must be weighed against the rights of the accused'.
(c) But only such measures restricting the rights of the defence to disclosure as are strictly necessary are permissible under the ECHR, Article 6(1).
(d) Any difficulties caused to the defence by a limitation on its rights must be sufficiently counterbalanced by the procedure followed by the court.
(e) The task of the European Court is to ascertain whether the decision-making procedure applied in each case complies with the requirements of adversarial proceedings and equality of arms and incorporates adequate safeguards to protect the interest of the accused.

In *Rowe and Davis* it was necessary for the European Court of Human Rights to consider whether procedural failures at first instance could be remedied at a later stage. The judge at first instance had not considered material that had been withheld by the prosecution during the trial. On appeal the Court of Appeal had adopted an *ex parte* procedure to consider the material that had been withheld. The European Court of Human Rights found that this procedure did not remedy the unfairness of the judge at first instance in not considering the material. If he had considered the material he could have monitored the importance of the undisclosed evidence at a stage when it could have affected the course of the trial. Since the Court of Appeal hearing was *ex parte*, the court was reliant upon prosecution counsel and transcripts of the trial for an understanding of the possible relevance of the undisclosed material. The European Court of Human Rights reached the same conclusion in *Atlan v UK* (2002) 34 EHRR 833, a case in which the prosecution had repeatedly denied the existence of undisclosed material and the judge had not been informed of the true position. See also *Dowsett v UK* [2003] Crim LR 890.

The case of *Jasper v UK* (2000) 30 EHRR 441, established that an *ex parte* procedure at first instance would not necessarily breach Article 6(1). The European Court of Human Rights held (by a majority of nine to eight) that there was no breach because, although the application for an order permitting non-disclosure was heard on an *ex parte* basis, the defence were notified that the application had been made, the trial judge gave them as much information regarding the nature of the withheld evidence as possible without revealing what it was, and the defence were permitted to outline their case to the judge. The court reached the same

D

Part D Procedure

conclusion in *Fitt v UK* (2000) 30 EHRR 480, which was decided on the same day on very similar grounds.

In *Botmeh* [2002] 1 WLR 531, it was argued that the *ex parte* procedure could not be followed in the Court of Appeal, but was confined to proceedings at first instance. The argument was rejected. There was nothing in the judgments *Rowe* and *Atlan* to suggest that *ex parte* examination of material by the Court of Appeal was of itself unfair.

In the light of these authorities, it appears that the procedures for handling public interest immunity applications in our domestic courts which are set out in the remaining paragraphs (**D9.29** to **D9.37**) are currently compliant with Article 6 (see also para. 22 of the A-G's Guidelines which state that rigid adherence with the principles set out in *H and C* is necessary to ensure compliance with Article 6).

Approach of the Courts to Public Interest Immunity

D9.29 In the landmark decision of *H and C* [2004] AC 134, the House of Lords provided a template by which courts are to make public interest immunity decisions. Judges are to address a series of questions in sequential order:

(1) The court must first identify whether the material which the prosecution seeks to withhold is material that may weaken the prosecution case or strengthen that of the defence. If the material cannot be so described — because for instance it is neutral or damaging to the accused — then it should not be disclosed. If it can be so described, the golden rule is that disclosure should be made unless public interest immunity considerations prevent it.
(2) Next, in determining whether public interest immunity applies, the court is to apply the test of whether there is a real risk of serious prejudice to an important, and identified, public interest. If the material does not satisfy that test, it does not attract public interest immunity and must be disclosed.
(3) If the material does attract public interest immunity, the court must then consider whether the accused's interests can be protected without disclosure or whether disclosure can be ordered to an extent or in a way which will give adequate protection to the public interest in question and also afford adequate protection to the interests of the defence.
(4) In considering whether limited disclosure is possible, the court must give consideration to ordering the prosecution to make admissions, prepare summaries or extracts of evidence, or provide documents in an edited or anonymised form.
(5) If the court is minded to order limited disclosure of this kind, it must first ask whether it represents the minimum derogation necessary to protect the public interest in question. If not, then it must order more disclosure. If, however, the effect of limited disclosure may be to render the whole trial process unfair to the accused, fuller disclosure should be ordered even if this leads the prosecution to discontinue the proceedings.
(6) The issue of disclosure of the material should be reviewed as the trial unfolds, evidence is adduced and the defence advanced.

If material is capable of being disclosed in redacted or edited form or by way of summaries, it ought not to be necessary to place it before the court for a decision under (4) above. The A-G's Guidelines state that prosecutors should aim to disclose as much of the material as they properly can and should only seek a judicial ruling in truly borderline cases (para. 20). The Crown Court Protocol also encourages redactions, e.g., by removing personal details from a statement (para. 51(c)).

Practice and Procedure of Investigators

D9.30 Material which might in due course be made the subject of a public interest immunity application must be recorded by investigators in a 'sensitive schedule'. As to the contents of the schedule, see **D9.8**. Detailed guidance as to the assessment of sensitivity and the preparation of the schedule is contained in chapter 8 of the Disclosure Manual. Investigators are to specify the reasons why the material is sensitive, the degree of sensitivity attaching to the material, the consequences of revealing it to the defence, the significance of the material to the issues in the trial, the involvement of third parties in bringing the material to the attention of the police, the implications for continuance of the prosecution if disclosure is ordered, and whether it is possible to disclose the material without compromising its sensitivity. In considering the material, prosecutors are to consider the possibility of prejudice to the public interest through direct harm or indirectly through incremental or cumulative harm.

Inclusion of material upon a 'sensitive' schedule is of course in no way conclusive of the question of whether its disclosure is in the public interest. That question is quite clearly one to be answered by the court. The principle in *Ward* [1993] 1 WLR 619 (see **D9.27**), remains intact and is reinforced by the terms of the 1996 Act: the court, rather than the prosecutor (let alone the investigator) is the final arbiter as to whether disclosure can be avoided on the basis of public interest immunity. Further, it is clear that the categories of 'sensitive material' spelt out in the Code of Practice on Disclosure (see **appendix 5**) are wider than the types of material which the courts have been prepared to shield behind public interest immunity. The code gives as an example of sensitive material, 'material given in confidence'; but the fact that material has been given in confidence is not sufficient of itself to ensure that it attracts public interest immunity so as to enable the prosecution to avoid disclosing it (see **F9.1**). Nonetheless public interest immunity applications are likely to founded on material which is contained in the 'sensitive' schedule.

Preparation of Applications

Detailed guidance about the procedure for making a public interest immunity application is contained in chapter 13 of the Disclosure Manual. The guidance emphasises that applications to the court will be rare and should be considered only if the other options of disclosing the material in a way that does not compromise the public interest in issue; or abandoning the case; or disclosing the material because it is in the overall public interest to do so, have been discounted or there is no agreement between the prosecutor, investigators or agencies, or the court's assistance is required to assess whether material should be disclosed. Chapter 13 contains practical details about arranging the application and making the written submission to accompany it. The Crown Court Protocol also deals with the written submission. It discourages formulaic expressions and encourages the use of schedules in complex cases which set out the specific objection in relation to each item and leave a space for the decision (para. 51(d). **D9.31**

The CrimPR, r. 25.2, makes provision for allocation of cases to judges and for service of notices on the accused and interested parties where appropriate (see **appendix 1**).

In *Menga* [1998] Crim LR 58, the Court of Appeal emphasised that prosecution counsel should ensure, as far as he can, that he has sight of all material in respect of which public interest immunity is to be claimed before the trial commences so that the applications can be made at the most convenient time. The CPS, said their lordships, had an obvious obligation to ensure that all such material was in their possession, and the police had a duty to pass the material on.

Procedure in Court

In *Jackson* [2000] Crim LR 377, the Court of Appeal stressed that it is imperative that in all cases the Crown is scrupulously accurate in the information provided in *ex parte* public interest immunity hearings. **D9.32**

The judge must himself examine or view the evidence, so that he can have the facts of what it contained in mind. Only then can he be in a position to balance the competing interests of public interest immunity and fairness to the party claiming disclosure (*K (TD)* (1993) 97 Cr App R 342). In *Law* (1996) *The Times*, 15 August 1996, the Court of Appeal held that, in deciding whether to order the prosecution to disclose information, the judge was not restricted to considering only evidence admissible in a court of law. He was entitled to see additional material, even if it amounted to hearsay evidence.

In *Templar* [2003] EWCA Crim 3186, Latham LJ warned against frequent meetings between the judge and prosecuting counsel in chambers in order to consider public interest immunity issues, where the defendant and his lawyers were absent. In the instant case there were some 36 such meetings. Although there was in fact no impropriety, he warned of the danger that prosecuting counsel and judge might come to use the procedure as a 'mutual support mechanism', with the result that repeated visits to chambers might blur their appreciation of the respective tasks which they faced.

In *G* [2004] EWCA Crim 1368, highly sensitive evidence was disclosed accidentally to the defence counsel and solicitor. The trial judge ordered them not to pass the information in question to anyone else, including their clients. It was held in the course of an interlocutory appeal that this order must be quashed as it would undermine the lawyer-client relationship.

Applications, even if held in private or in secret, must be recorded. The judge should give some short statement of reasons; this is often best done document by document as the hearing proceeds (Crown Court Protocol, para 51(e); CrimPR, r. 25.3).

As to the procedure where the Court of Appeal reviews the conduct by the trial judge of a public interest immunity hearing, see **D26.22** and *McDonald* (2004) *The Times*, 8 November 2004.

Categories of Hearing

D9.33 Rule 25.1 of the CrimPR in effect reproduces the procedure laid down in *Davis* [1993] 1 WLR 613 (see **D9.28**). In Type 1 applications, a notice of application is served on the accused by the prosecutor. Type 2 applications arise where the prosecutor has reason to believe that to reveal to the accused the nature of the material to which the application relates would have the effect of disclosing that which the prosecutor contends should not in the public interest be disclosed. In such cases the prosecutor is not to serve a notice but instead must notify the accused that a Type 2 application has been made. Type 3 applications arise where the prosecutor has reason to believe that to reveal to the accused the fact of an application being made would have the effect of disclosing that which the prosecutor contends should not in the public interest be disclosed. In such cases no notice is required.

The Crown Court Protocol stipulates that in Type 1 and 2 applications proper notice to the defence is necessary to allow them to make focused submissions to the court. The notice should be as specific as possible, though it is accepted that in some cases only the generic nature of the material can properly be identified. The judge should always ask the prosecution to justify the form of notice given or the decision not to give a notice (para. 51(b)). If the judge takes the view that the defence should have had notice of the application, or of the nature of the material, or that the application should be made *inter partes*, then it is plain that he should direct accordingly, as Lord Taylor CJ observed in *Davis* (see **D9.28**).

In *Smith* [1998] 2 Cr App R 1, the Court of Appeal stressed that no *ex parte* application should be made in circumstances where there was nothing to be said which could not be said in the presence of defence counsel.

Use of Special Advocates

In *Rowe and Davis* (2000) 30 EHRR 1 (see **D9.28**), it was argued on behalf of the applicants in Strasbourg that the exclusion of the defence from the *ex parte* procedure conducted by the Court of Appeal should have been counterbalanced by the introduction of a special independent counsel who could argue the relevance of the undisclosed evidence, test the strength of the prosecution claim to public interest immunity, and safeguard against the risk of judicial error or bias. The court found a violation of the ECHR, Article 6 without the need to address this question but the issue arose again in *Edwards v UK* (2003) 15 BHRC 189. In that case, the tribunal of fact was the trial judge, who had to decide whether to exclude evidence because the accused had been entrapped. Material was produced to the trial judge in *ex parte* hearings. The defence was not aware of the material, and was unable to put forward an argument on it. The European Court of Human Rights found that the defence should have been given the opportunity to counter the evidence and show the judge that it was mistaken or unreliable. A procedure which denied the defence that opportunity on an issue which was so fundamental to a fair trial failed to comply 'with the requirements to provide adversarial proceedings and equality of arms' or to incorporate 'adequate safeguards to protect the interests of the accused'. During the course of the judgment, the role of special counsel was again canvassed, and mentioned with some approval by the court. Accordingly, in *H and C* [2004] 2 AC 134, the House of Lords were invited to state that special counsel should be appointed wherever material which the prosecution seeks to withhold is, or may be, relevant to a disputed issue of fact which the judge has to decide in order to rule on an application which will effectively determine the outcome of the proceedings. In particular, it was argued that such an appointment should be made whenever the defence relies on entrapment as a basis for staying the case as an abuse of process or excluding prosecution evidence. The House of Lords declined to hold that special counsel should always be appointed in such circumstances, saying that this would place the trial judge in a straitjacket. Lord Bingham did make it clear, however, that the appointment of special counsel may be a necessary step in appropriate cases to ensure that the contentions of the prosecution are tested and the interests of the accused protected. As to *H and C*, see further **D9.29**. **D9.34**

Interventions of Third Parties

Section 16 of the CPIA 1996 provides for interventions by interested third parties when the court is considering the issue of public interest immunity. **D9.35**

Criminal Procedure and Investigations Act 1996, s. 16

16. Where—

(a) an application is made under section 3(6), 7A(8), 8(5), 14(2) or 15(4),
(b) a person claiming to have an interest in the material applies to be heard by the court, and
(c) he shows that he was involved (whether alone or with others and whether directly or indirectly) in the prosecutor's attention being brought to the material,

the court must not make an order under section 3(6), 7A(8), 8(5), 14(3) or 15(5) (as the case may be) unless the person applying under paragraph (b) has been given an opportunity to be heard.

Categories of Public Interest Material

For examples of circumstances in which the prosecution can successfully claim immunity from disclosure, see **F9.5** *et seq*, especially **F9.9**. **D9.36**

Review of Public Interest Immunity Decisions

Once a court has made a decision to exclude material from consideration on public interest immunity grounds, the approach that is taken with regard to reviewing the decision differs as between cases tried summarily and cases tried on indictment. In summary trials, it is necessary for the accused to apply for the decision to be reviewed, whereas in cases tried on **D9.37** indictment the court is under a duty to keep under review the question whether it is still not in the public interest to disclose the affected material. The difference in approach would appear to stem from the dual role of the magistrates as triers of both fact and law, which was encountered in *South Worcester Justices, ex parte Lilley* [1995] 1 WLR 1595. The problem is that, when the magistrates (in their role as triers of law) conduct a review of documents for which immunity is claimed, it may appear to prejudice them in their role as triers of fact. The problem is compounded when the review is conducted *ex parte*, in the absence of the accused and the defence lawyer. As a result, a new bench may be needed to try the case, after the old bench rules against disclosure. If that new bench were under a duty of continuous review, it would mean that it would be impossible ever to recruit a bench which was proof against the contamination which results from looking at the material. Hence the onus is put on the accused to make the application (see also *Stipendiary Magistrate for Norfolk, ex parte Taylor* (1997) 161 JP 773 and *R (DPP) v Acton Youth Court* [2001] 1 WLR 1828).

Criminal Procedure and Investigations Act 1996, ss. 14 and 15

14.—(1) This section applies where [part I] applies by virtue of section 1(1).

(2) At any time—

(a) after a court makes an order under section 3(6), 7A(8) or 8(5), and

(b) before the accused is acquitted or convicted or the prosecutor decides not to proceed with the case concerned,

the accused may apply to the court for a review of the question whether it is still not in the public interest to disclose material affected by its order.

(3) In such a case the court must review that question, and if it concludes that it is in the public interest to disclose material to any extent—

(a) it shall so order, and

(b) it shall take such steps as are reasonable to inform the prosecutor of its order.

(4) Where the prosecutor is informed of an order made under subsection (3) he must act accordingly having regard to the provisions of [part I] (unless he decides not to proceed with the case concerned).

15.—(1) This section applies where [part I] applies by virtue of section 1(2).

(2) This section applies at all times—

(a) after a court makes an order under section 3(6), 7A(8) or 8(5), and

(b) before the accused is acquitted or convicted or the prosecutor decides not to proceed with the case concerned.

(3) The court must keep under review the question whether at any given time it is still not in the public interest to disclose material affected by its order.

(4) The court must keep the question mentioned in subsection (3) under review without the need for an application; but the accused may apply to the court for a review of that question.

(5) If the court at any time concludes that it is in the public interest to disclose material to any extent—

(a) it shall so order, and

(b) it shall take such steps as are reasonable to inform the prosecutor of its order.

(6) Where the prosecutor is informed of an order made under subsection (5) he must act accordingly having regard to the provisions of [part I] (unless he decides not to proceed with the case concerned).

Intercept Material

D9.38 Section 17 of the RIPA 2000 prevents the fact of interception of a subject's communications and the product of that interception being relied upon or referred to by any party to criminal proceedings. It is given further effect by ss. 3(7), 7(6), 7A(9) and 9(9) of the CPIA 1996. However, s.18 of the RIPA 2000 states that nothing in s. 17 is to prevent disclosure to a prosecutor to enable that person to determine what is required of him by his duty to secure the fairness of the prosecution. This duty may require the prosecutor to make admissions of fact, discontinue part of the case, not rely on certain evidence, or put his case in a different way. It may also require disclosure to the judge so that the judge may sum up the case in a particular way, give appropriate directions to the jury or require admissions of fact from the prosecution. The A-G's Section 18 RIPA Prosecutors Intercept Guidelines (see **appendix** 3) give detailed guidance on the approach to be taken by prosecutors.

DISCLOSURE OF EXPERT EVIDENCE

Disclosure of Findings and Opinions of Experts Intended for Use as Evidence

Part 24 of the CrimPR contains specific rules requiring disclosure of expert evidence, which reflect rules previously contained in the Crown Court (Advance Notice of Expert Evidence) Rules 1987 (SI 1987 No. 716) and the equivalent rules for magistrates' courts. For a detailed discussion, see D14.73 *et seq*. **D9.39**

Responsibilities of Experts and Content of Report

Part 33 of the CrimPR came into effect in November 2006. It contains explicit rules about the responsibilities of expert witnesses to the court, the form in which expert evidence should be introduced, and about the use of the court's case management powers to define what is in dispute between the experts. **D9.40**

Disclosure of Names and Addresses of Experts

There is no obligation on the defence, either at common law or under the CPIA 1996, to reveal material which is not to be used at trial. However, there is a provision in s. 6D, inserted by the CJA 2003, s. 35, which might seem to run counter to this principle. The new provision (which is not yet in force) deals with any expert report commissioned by the accused. If he instructs a person with a view to providing any expert opinion for possible use at trial, he must give the court and the prosecutor the name and address of the expert in question. Potentially, such notification might open the door to the prosecution seeking evidence from the expert in question, as there is no property in a witness (see **F9.32**); however it will not be possible for the expert to provide evidence which involves a breach of privilege, e.g., information provided by the accused in privileged circumstances. No adverse inference may be drawn from failure of the defence to comply with s. 6D or from the fact that an expert has been consulted but not used as a witness. **D9.41**

THIRD-PARTY DISCLOSURE

Sometimes the information which the accused needs for his defence will be in the hands of someone other than the prosecution — a 'third party' as far as the criminal case is concerned. In such cases, there may nonetheless be an obligation on the investigator to obtain the information. Alternatively, the third party may give up the information, voluntarily or under compulsion. **D9.42**

Obligations of Prosecutors

Paragraph 3.5 of the CPIA Code of Practice requires investigators to pursue all reasonable lines of enquiry, whether these point towards or away from the suspect. Where such investigation reveals the existence of material held by a third party which may be relevant to the investigation but such material is not obtained, the third party must be informed of the investigation and invited to retain the material in case a request for disclosure is made. But speculative enquiries of third parties are not required: there must be some reason to believe that they hold relevant material (see para. 3.6). **D9.43**

Voluntary Disclosure Route

There are a number of instances where special procedures have been evolved which will result in voluntary disclosure of material. **D9.44**

(a) *Material held by government departments and other Crown bodies.* The A-G's Guidelines, paras. 47 to 50, establish a procedure by which such material may be disclosed. The prosecution team are not to be regarded as being in constructive possession of such material but they must take reasonable steps to identify such material, including notifying the body of the nature of the prosecution case and of relevant issues. In turn government departments and other Crown bodies have a public law duty to co-operate with a criminal investigation. Statutory prohibitions on disclosure of material usually allow an exception for disclosure for the purposes of criminal proceedings, but questions of legal professional privilege or public interest immunity may nevertheless arise which may affect the willingness of Crown bodies to disclose information in their possession.
(b) *Material held by other agencies.* The A-G's Guidelines, para. 51, provide that the prosecution should take steps to obtain material or information in the possession of a third party (e.g., a local authority, social services department, hospital, doctor or school) if it might reasonably be considered capable of undermining the prosecution case or assisting the defence (i.e. to fulfil the test for primary or secondary disclosure). Paragraph 52 deals with the situation where the police or prosecutors meet with a refusal by the third party to supply such material or information. Such refusal might be made, for instance, if the third party considers that it owes a duty of confidentiality to a person in respect of whom the material relates, or that person's Article 8 right to privacy is engaged, and this overrides its duty to co-operate with the criminal investigation. If, despite the reasons put forward for refusal by the third party, it still appears reasonable to seek its production, and the provisions of the relevant statutes are satisfied, the prosecutor or investigator should apply for a witness summons requiring the third party to produce the material to the court. But there should be consultation with the agency before disclosure is made since there may be public interest reasons justifying withholding disclosure.
(c) *Others.* Third parties which are not public authorities have no public law responsibility to co-operate with an investigation. They may also owe duties of confidentiality arsing out of a professional relationship such as a banking relationship. In such circumstances the third party may feel obliged to insist that he produces material in response to a summons (see **D9.45**).

Compulsory Disclosure Route

D9.45 Investigators have powers, under the PACE 1984, s. 8 and sch. 1, to compel third parties to disclose material for the purposes of a criminal investigation: see **D1.76** to **D1.92**. Where a person is charged and a third party is not prepared to hand over relevant material, the course of action available to the prosecution or the accused is to seek a witness summons. The procedure is laid down by the Criminal Procedure (Attendance of Witnesses) Act 1965, s. 2(1) (for the text, see **D14.90**), as far as Crown Court trial is concerned. In magistrates' courts, it is governed by the MCA 1980, s. 97 (see **D20.24**). The procedure involves issuing a witness summons to compel the third party to attend with the document(s) to give evidence, and/or to produce the document(s) in advance. The person seeking the witness summons must satisfy the court that the third party:

(a) is likely to be able to give or produce material evidence in the case; and
(b) will not voluntarily attend or produce the evidence.

The application should, in the case of Crown Court trial, be made 'as soon as reasonably practicable after the committal' or the equivalent where an alternative to committal has been used. It will usually be heard on notice to the person to whom the summons is directed (the third party), who may appear or be represented at the hearing. The application should be supported by an affidavit, setting out the charges, identifying the evidence or document sought, stating the grounds for believing that the third party is able to give or produce it, and the grounds for believing that it is material. At the hearing, the third party would be able to argue, e.g., that there is no evidence held, or that it is not material, or that it should not be disclosed on grounds of public interest immunity.

In relation to banking material, either the prosecution or the defence may apply to magistrates or to the Crown Court for an order to inspect or take copies. See the Bankers' Books Evidence Act 1879 at **F8.27**.

In *Brushett* [2001] Crim LR 471, the Court of Appeal considered a case where disclosure of reports held by social services departments was sought by the accused in a case of alleged sexual abuse of children. Their lordships characterised the principles governing disclosure by third parties as 'narrower' than those where the prosecution held such material. They indicated that disclosure should nevertheless be granted, e.g., where there had been false accusations by the subject of the report in the past, or where there had been sexual activity with another adult.

In *Alibhai* [2004] EWCA Crim 681, Longmore LJ pointed out various unsatisfactory features of the procedure for disclosure of material held by third parties as follows:

(a) It is not possible to issue a witness summons to a person outside the jurisdiction.
(b) A witness summons to produce a 'document or thing' will not elicit information.
(c) The 'document or thing' must itself be likely to be material evidence, and a witness summons will not be issued for documents which will not themselves constitute evidence in the case but merely give rise to a line of enquiry which might result in evidence being obtained, still less for documents merely capable of use in cross-examination as to credit.
(d) There is no provision for the prosecution or defence, unless they so agree, to examine the documents before they are produced to the court as a result of the witness summons.

The Crown Court Protocol (see **appendix** 5) and the Magistrates' Courts Protocol give guidance as to the approach of the courts to requests for third-party material (see paras. 52 to 62 and part 4 respectively). Both state that fishing expeditions in relation to third-party material (whether by the prosecution or the defence) must be discouraged, and that, in appropriate cases, the court will consider making an order for wasted costs where the application is clearly unmeritorious and ill-conceived.

Section D10 Sending Cases from the Magistrates' Court to the Crown Court

D10.1 All criminal cases begin in the magistrates' court, either through the laying of an information and issue of a summons that requires the accused to attend a magistrates' court (to be replaced, for public prosecutions, by the written charge and requisition procedure) or else the accused is arrested, charged and required to appear at a magistrates' court. If the offence is triable only in the Crown Court, it must be transferred to that court. If it is triable either way, it will be transferred to the Crown Court for trial only if the accused indicates, or is deemed to indicate, a not guilty plea at the plea before venue hearing and the mode of trial hearing that follows results in a decision in favour of Crown Court trial (either because the magistrates decline jurisdiction or because the accused elects Crown Court trial).

The MCA 1980, s. 6, provided two alternative methods for transferring a case from the magistrates' court so that it could be tried in the Crown Court. The first, committal 'without consideration of the evidence' under the MCA 1980, s. 6(2), required a hearing in which the prosecution witness statements were handed to the magistrates; the second, s. 6(1), was a version of committal 'with consideration of the evidence', where the procedure was very similar to an ordinary trial, with witnesses being subject to examination-in-chief, cross-examination and re-examination. A contemporaneous note of the evidence was taken down and, when a witness had finished testifying, the notes were read back to the witness, who was then given an opportunity to make any amendments. The witness then signed the notes (which became a 'deposition'). After the prosecution witnesses had given evidence, the defence had a chance to make a submission that there was no case to answer. If that submission was unsuccessful, the defence had the opportunity to call evidence and make a second submission of no case to answer (though it was, in practice, very rare for the defence to call any evidence at this stage). If a submission of no case to answer was successful, the defendant was 'discharged'.

The CPIA 1996, s. 47, gave effect to a new system of committal proceedings set out in sch. 1 to that Act. Under that system, committal without consideration of the evidence remained in its original version, but committal with consideration of the evidence was amended so that witness statements were read out but witnesses did not attend the hearing.

A further change was made by the enactment of the CDA, s. 51, which effectively abolished committal proceedings in the case of indictable-only offences, replacing them with a system under which the case was transferred (essentially through an administrative exercise) to the Crown Court at a very early stage (often after only one appearance in the magistrates' court).

Finally, sch. 3 to the CJA 2003 abolished committal proceedings for either-way offences, applying the system of transfer in the CDA 1998, s. 51, to either-way offences as well as indictable-only offences. These provisions are not yet in force.

Separate provision is made for the transfer of cases to the Crown Court where the case is a serious fraud case (under the CJA 1987, s. 4) or a case involving one or more child witnesses (under the CJA 1991, s. 53). These provisions are due to be replaced by the CDA 1998, ss. 51B and 51C (inserted by the CJA 2003, sch. 3), respectively. The procedure for sending a juvenile to the Crown Court for trial (where the juvenile is charged alongside an adult or with an offence to which the PCC(S)A 2000, s. 91, applies) is set out in the CDA 1998, s. 51A (again, inserted by the CJA 2003, sch. 3).

Thus, prior to the coming into force of the CJA 2003, sch. 3, the mechanisms for sending a case from the magistrates' court to the Crown Court are:

(a) indictable-only offences: transfer under the CDA 1998, s. 51;
(b) either-way offences: committal proceedings (with or without consideration of the evidence) under the MCA 1980, s. 6;
(c) serious fraud cases: transfer under the CJA 1987, s. 4;
(d) child witness cases: transfer under the CJA 1991, s. 53.

Once the CJA 2003, sch. 3, comes into force, the mechanisms will be:

(a) all indictable offences (adults): transfer under the CDA 1998, s. 51;
(b) juveniles: transfer under the CDA 1998, s. 51A;
(c) serious fraud cases: transfer under the CDA 1998, s. 51B;
(d) child witness cases: transfer under the CDA 1998, s. 51C.

There will remain one other way of securing the Crown Court trial of an accused, namely the voluntary bill of indictment (see **D10.48**).

Need for a Formal Transfer to the Crown Court

The necessity for a formal transfer or sending of the case to the Crown Court for trial arises from the Administration of Justice (Miscellaneous Provisions) Act 1933, s. 2(2). **D10.2**

Administration of Justice Act (Miscellaneous Provisions) Act 1933, s. 2

(2) Subject as hereinafter provided no bill of indictment charging any person with an indictable offence shall be preferred unless either—
  (a) the person charged has sent for trial for the offence; or
  (b) the bill is preferred by the direction of the Court of Criminal Appeal or by the direction or with the consent of a judge of the High Court . . . or
  (c) the bill is preferred under section 22B(3)(a) of the Prosecution of Offences Act 1985:
  Provided that—
  (i) where the person charged has been sent for trial, the bill of indictment against him may include, either in substitution for or in addition to any count charging an offence specified in the notice under section 57D(1) of the Crime and Disorder Act 1998, any counts founded on material which, in pursuance of regulations made under paragraph 1 of Schedule 3 to that Act, was served on the person charged, being counts which may lawfully be joined in the same indictment;
  (ii) a charge of a previous conviction of an offence . . . may, notwithstanding that it was not included in such notice or in any such direction or consent as aforesaid, be included in any bill of indictment

The phrase 'bill of indictment' in s. 2 means simply a draft indictment (which is the term now used in the CrimPR, pt 14), prepared by or on behalf of the prosecution. It is 'preferred', i.e. put before an appropriate officer of the Crown Court for signature. Once signed, it becomes the indictment on which the accused will be tried. If a bill of indictment is preferred without authority, the resulting indictment is liable to be quashed on application to the trial judge, and the accused will be discharged without pleading to the charges against him (see the 1933 Act, s. 2(3)).

Thus, a trial on indictment may not validly take place unless:

(a) the accused has been sent for trial under the CDA 1998 (or, in the case of an either-way offence, the accused has been committed for trial under the MCA 1980, s. 6, until that procedure is replaced by transfer under the CDA 1998, s. 51),

(b) the Court of Appeal has directed the preferment of a bill of indictment (an adjunct of the discretion given to it by the Criminal Appeal Act 1968, s. 7, to quash a conviction on indictment but then to order that the successful appellant be retried); or
(c) the bill is preferred by the direction or with the consent of a High Court judge (a 'voluntary bill of indictment').

The effect of the proviso to s. 2(2) is that, provided the accused was validly sent for trial on a charge of an indictable offence, the indictment against him may include counts for other indictable offences (in respect of which he was not sent for trial) if those offences are disclosed by the evidence on which the transfer to the Crown Court was based.

Court of First Appearance

D10.3 Whether the offence is triable either way or triable only on indictment, the accused will make his first appearance in a magistrates' court. The MCA 1980, s. 2(2) (as amended by the Courts Act 2003, s. 44), provides:

> A magistrates' court has jurisdiction as examining justices over any offence committed by a person who appears or is brought before the court.

When the abolition of committal proceedings for either-way offences takes place, this provision will be further amended (by the CJA 2003, sch. 3, para. 51), to read:

> A magistrates' court has jurisdiction under sections 51 and 51A of the Crime and Disorder Act 1998 in respect of any offence committed by a person who appears or is brought before the court.

Under the CDA 1998, s. 51(13), the functions of a magistrates' court under s. 51 may be discharged by a single justice.

SENDING CASES TO THE CROWN COURT UNDER THE CRIME AND DISORDER ACT 1998, S. 51

D10.4 At the time of writing, the CDA 1998, s. 51, applies only to offences that are triable only on indictment. However, during the lifetime of this edition, the scope of s. 51 may be extended to cover offences that are triable either way. The relevant statutory provisions are set out at **D10.33**.

Section 51(1) provides that, where an adult appears or is brought before a magistrates' court charged with an offence to which these provisions apply, the court shall send him 'forthwith' to the Crown Court for trial for the offence. This is, however, subject to the magistrates' power to adjourn (s. 52(5)), for example, where the situation is developing and it may not be necessary to send the case to the Crown Court, or where the defence needs to muster the necessary information for a bail application.

Section 51(2) says that these provisions apply where the offence is triable only on indictment (unless s. 51B or 51C applies — see **D10.33**), or (when s. 51 is extended to include either-way offences) where the offence is triable either way (provided that the mode of trial stage has resulted in a decision in favour of trial on indictment, in that either the magistrates have declined jurisdiction or the accused has refused the offer of summary trial). Under s. 51(2)(c), the magistrates must also send the accused forthwith to the Crown Court where notice has been given under s. 51B (serious fraud cases) or s. 51C (child witness cases).

Either-way Offences

D10.5 When s. 51 is extended to either-way offences, the CDA 1998, s. 50A(3), will set out the order in which the magistrates must take various steps where the offence is triable either way. It provides that, where an adult is charged with an either-way offence, the procedure involves the following steps:

(a) plea before venue;
(b) in the event of an indication of a not guilty plea, mode of trial procedure;
(c) if the magistrates decline jurisdiction or the accused elects trial on indictment, transfer the case to the Crown Court under s. 51.

Section 51(3) goes on to provide that, where the court sends an adult for trial under s. 51(1), it shall also send him to the Crown Court for trial for any either-way or summary offence with which he is charged and which appears to the court to be related to the offence being sent to the Crown Court under s. 51(1) (provided that, if the offence is a summary offence, it is punishable with imprisonment or disqualification from driving). Under s. 51E(c), an either-way offence is related to an indictable offence if the charge for the either-way offence could be joined in the same indictment as the charge for the indictable offence, and under s. 51E, a summary offence is related to an indictable offence if it arises out of circumstances that are the same as or connected with those giving rise to the indictable offence.

If an adult has already been sent for trial under s. 51(1) and then subsequently appears before a magistrates' court charged with an either-way or summary offence that appears to the court to be related to the offence sent for trial under s. 51(1), the court *may* send him forthwith to the Crown Court for trial for the either-way or summary offence (provided, if the offence is a summary one, that it is punishable with imprisonment or disqualification from driving) (s. 51(4)). Note that this is a discretionary power, not a mandatory duty.

Co-accused

D10.6 Section 51(5) of the CDA 1998 deals with the situation where there are co-accused. It provides that where the court sends an adult for trial (under s. 51(1) or 51(3)), and another adult appears before the court, either on the same or a subsequent occasion, charged jointly with the first adult with an either-way offence, and that offence appears to the court to be related to an offence for which the first adult was sent for trial under s. 51(1) or (3), then the court must (where it is the same occasion) or may (where it is a subsequent occasion), send the other adult forthwith to the Crown Court for trial for the either-way offence. Where the court sends an adult for trial under s. 51(5), it must at the same time send him to the Crown Court for trial for any either-way or summary offence with which he is charged and which appears to the court to be related to the offence for which he is sent for trial (provided that, if it is a summary offence, it is punishable with imprisonment or disqualification from driving).

Section 51(7) covers the situation where an adult and a juvenile are jointly charged. It provides that where the court sends an adult to the Crown Court for trial under s. 51(1), (3) or (5), and a child or young person (i.e. a person under the age of 18) appears before the court (on the same or a subsequent occasion) charged jointly with the adult with an indictable offence for which the adult is sent for trial under s. 51(1), (3) or (5), or charged with an indictable offence that appears to the court to be related to that offence, the court 'shall, if it considers it necessary in the interests of justice to do so, send the juvenile forthwith to the Crown Court for trial for the indictable offence'. Under s. 51(8), where the court sends a juvenile for trial under s. 51(7), it may at the same time send him to the Crown Court for trial for any indictable or summary offence with which he is charged and which appears to the court to be related to the offence for which he is sent for trial (again, if the offence is a summary one, it must be punishable with imprisonment or disqualification from driving).

Subsidiary Matters

D10.7 Where a summary offence is sent to the Crown Court for trial under s. 51, it is to be regarded as having being adjourned by the magistrates *sine die* (s. 51(10)).

Under s. 51(13), the functions of a magistrates' court under s. 51 may be discharged by a single justice.

Section 51A contains equivalent provisions for cases where defendants who are under the age of 18 are to be sent to the Crown Court for trial (see **D10.33**).

Presence of the Accused

D10.8 The CDA 1998, s. 51(1), applies where the accused 'appears or is brought before a magistrates' court'. The term 'appears' covers the situation where the accused attends court in answer to his bail; the term 'brought' applies where the accused was remanded in custody and so has to be produced from the prison to which he has been remanded or where the accused was granted bail but failed to surrender, with the result that a bench warrant for his arrest was issued and so he is now being held in custody.

If the accused does not appear in court for the s. 51 hearing, the court may issue a warrant for his arrest (see MCA 1980, s. 1(6), and Bail Act 1976, s. 7(1), which are respectively applicable where the accused fails to answer to a summons or fails to answer to his bail, whether that bail was granted by the police or by a magistrates' court).

Multiple Charges and Accused

D10.9 A transfer under the CDA 1998, s. 51, may take place in respect of more than one charge and/or more than one accused. Where two or more accused are jointly charged with a single offence, it is clearly appropriate to deal with them together unless there are special reasons for not doing so (e.g., on the date fixed for the proceedings, one of the accused fails to appear, and the court considers that it is in the interests of justice to proceed with the hearing for those who are present, adjourning the hearing in respect of the absent accused until such time as his attendance is secured). Where the accused are charged with separate offences, the question of whether the charges — and hence the accused —may properly be dealt with together is one for the discretion of the court (*Camberwell Green Stipendiary Magistrate, ex parte Christie* [1978] QB 602). The normal practice is to deal with the accused together if, and only if, their alleged offences are so related by time or other factors that, in the event of their being sent for trial, it would be appropriate to draft a single indictment against them all within the principles established by *Assim* [1966] 2 QB 249 (discussed at **D11.67**). In *Ex parte Christie*, a case concerning two accused decided in the context of committal proceedings, the Divisional Court (Lord Widgery CJ) stated (at p. 606E–H):

> [The] principle that joinder is a matter of practice, if established, goes a very long way to solving all the problems which have arisen in this case. I think that it is proper for us to accept the decision in *Assim* as laying down a principle that these are matters of practice, and I think that from there we can inquire into whether there is an established practice of joinder in committal proceedings which will by virtue of the *Assim* doctrine become authoritative properly to be followed by individual courts.
>
> There seems to me to be no answer to the contention that the experience of practice is overwhelming that where two offences, which can properly be tried together on indictment, are the subject of committal proceedings, they can be the subject of concurrent committal proceedings without the necessity of obtaining the consent of the parties concerned. . . .
>
> Since it cannot be challenged that both the defendants in these two informations could be tried together, it seems to me that we can properly adopt the principle that where two offences could be tried together then they could be the subject of concurrent committal proceedings as well.

It is suggested that these comments apply equally to hearings conducted under the CDA 1998, s. 51.

Reporting Restrictions

D10.10 Reporting restrictions in respect of allocation and sending proceedings are governed by the CDA 1998, s. 52A. The only details that may be published or broadcast are those permitted by s. 52A.

The purpose of the restrictions is to prevent potentially prejudicial reporting of the case prior to the conclusion of any trial. Therefore, s. 52A(6) makes it clear that the restrictions do not apply where the accused enters a plea of guilty at the plea before venue hearing or after the conclusion of the accused's trial (or, where there is more than defendant, the trial of the last to be tried).

Nature of Restrictions The matters that may be reported are listed in the CDA 1998, s. 52A(7). They include the identity of the court and the name of the justice(s); the name, age, home address and occupation of the accused; the offence(s) with which the accused is or are charged; the names of counsel and solicitors engaged in the proceedings; arrangements regarding bail; and whether publicly funded representation has been granted. Where notice has been given under s. 51B (serious fraud cases — see **D10.27**), the press may also report 'relevant business information' (defined in s. 52(9) to include the name and address of any business being carried on by the accused). **D10.11**

Contravention of the reporting restrictions is an offence under s. 52B, punishable, on summary conviction, by a fine not exceeding level 5 on the standard scale (currently £5,000). Proceedings may be brought only by or with the consent of the A-G.

Lifting the Restrictions Under the CDA 1998, s. 52A(2), the magistrates can order that the restrictions do not apply to particular proceedings (in other words, they can lift the reporting restrictions). Where there is only one accused and he objects to the lifting of the restrictions, the court may lift the restrictions only if it is satisfied, after hearing representations from the accused, that it is in the interests of justice to do so (s. 52A(3)). Where there are two or more accused and one of them objects to the lifting of the restrictions, the court can lift the restrictions only if it is satisfied, after hearing representations from all the accused, that it is in the interests of justice to do so (s. 52A(4)). **D10.12**

The provisions relating to the lifting of reporting restrictions under s. 52A are slightly different to those contained in the MCA 1980, s. 8, which is replaced by s. 52A. Under s. 8, if there was only one accused, he could insist on the lifting of the restrictions, and if there was more than one defendant and one defendant wanted the restrictions lifted but another did not, the one who wanted the restrictions lifted had to show that it was in the interests of justice for that to happen. However, there was no suggestion that the court could lift the restrictions unless the accused requested an order lifting them. It is submitted that it should be very rare for the court to lift reporting restrictions other than upon an application by the accused, since the restrictions exist for the protection of the accused.

The provisions dealing with cases where there are several accused and one of them wants to have the reporting restrictions lifted are necessary because, even if it were practicable to report only those parts of the proceedings relating to the accused who wants the restrictions lifted and omit everything relating to the others, the court has no power under s. 52A to make an order to that effect. Construing the earlier legislation relating to committal proceedings, the Divisional Court, in *Leeds Justices, ex parte Sykes* [1983] 1 WLR 132, said that 'If the reporting restrictions are to be lifted, then they are to be lifted . . . in their entirety. They cannot be lifted piecemeal' (per Griffiths LJ at p. 136A). The justices therefore cannot pick and choose which of the restrictions are lifted and which remain, but can achieve a similar result by first lifting reporting restrictions through an order under s. 52A and then making a further order under the Contempt of Court Act 1981, s. 4, postponing reporting of some of the evidence until after the trial on indictment (see *Horsham Justices, ex parte Farquharson* [1982] QB 762 and, generally, **D3.78** *et seq.*).

The main question at issue in *Ex parte Sykes* was whether, in the circumstances of that particular case, the magistrates were entitled to hold that it was in the interests of justice to lift reporting restrictions where the lifting of restrictions was opposed by the appellant. The co-accused's argument for an order lifting the restrictions was that, three weeks earlier, a police officer had indicated to his solicitor that the charges against him would be dropped, but the police had gone back on that indication, and the co-accused wished to make a public protest about their behaviour. Griffiths LJ confirmed that, in the event of disagreement between the defendants, the burden was on the accused who wanted reporting to show that it was in the interests of justice for the normal restrictions to be lifted. He went on to say (at pp. 134H–135B):

> Without attempting any comprehensive definition, the interests of justice incorporate as a paramount consideration that the defendants should have a fair trial. When the justices have to balance the request for the committal proceedings to be reported, they must bear in mind that the *prima facie* rule is that committal proceedings should not be reported, and only if a powerful case is made out for their reporting, should they be prepared to make an order when one of the defendants objects, particularly, if the ground of the objection is that very reason that led Parliament to provide that, as a general rule, proceedings should not be reported, namely that there is a risk that if the proceedings are widely reported, the reports may colour the views of the jury which ultimately has to try the case.

On the facts of *Ex parte Sykes*, giving immediate publicity to the co-accused's grievance against the police could be of little or no assistance either to his case or the case of his co-defendants. Therefore, the interests of justice (in the sense of ensuring that the co-accused had a fair trial) would not be advanced by publicity. On the other hand, the appellant believed that 'his trial [would be] prejudiced if there [was] wide publicity of the evidence upon which the prosecution [would] ultimately ask the jury to try the case' (p. 137E). Set against that argument, the co-accused's argument could be 'of no weight', and the justices' order raising reporting restrictions was accordingly quashed. *Obiter*, Griffiths LJ suggested that an application for restrictions to be lifted on the ground that publicity might induce potential witnesses for the defendant making the application to come forward would 'merit really serious consideration by the justices' (*ibid*, p. 137B).

The court must give all the co-accused a chance to make representations. Failure to do so is a serious breach of procedure and is likely to result in the quashing of the order lifting the reporting restrictions (*Wirral District Magistrates' Court, ex parte Meikle* (1990) 154 JP 1035).

D10.13 **Contempt of Court Act 1981** Once the restrictions have been lifted, they cannot be re-imposed (*Bow Street Magistrates, ex parte Kray* [1969] 1 QB 473). However, the same result can be achieved by an order postponing contemporaneous reporting of the proceedings under the Contempt of Court Act 1981, s. 4(2).

In *Sherwood, ex parte The Telegraph Group plc* [2001] 1 WLR 1983, the Court of Appeal issued guidance on applications to postpone media coverage of court proceedings under the Contempt of Court Act 1981, s. 4(2), stating that they should be approached by way of a three-stage test:

(1) The first question is whether reporting would give rise to a not insubstantial risk of prejudice to the administration of justice in the relevant proceedings. If not, that is the end of the matter.
(2) If such a risk is perceived to exist, then the second question arises: would a s. 4(2) order eliminate it? If not, there could clearly be no necessity to impose such a ban and that would be the end of the matter. On the other hand, even if the judge is satisfied that an order would achieve the objective, he would still have to consider whether the risk could satisfactorily be overcome by some less restrictive means. If so, it could not be said to be necessary to take the more drastic approach.
(3) If the judge concludes that there is no other way of eliminating the perceived risk of prejudice, it still does not follow necessarily that an order has to be made. The judge might still have to ask whether the degree of risk contemplated should be regarded as tolerable in the sense of being the lesser of two evils. It is at that stage that value judgements might have to be made as to the priority between competing public interests.

Where there is an appeal, it is the duty of the Court of Appeal not merely to review the decision of the trial judge but to come to its own independent conclusions on the materials placed before it.

Effecting the Transfer: s. 51D

Under s. 51D(1), the magistrates' court specifies, in a notice, the offence(s) for which the accused is being sent for trial and the location of the Crown Court where he is to be tried. A copy of the notice is served on the accused and a copy is sent to the Crown Court (s. 51D(2)). The location of the Crown Court to which the accused is sent for trial is chosen by the magistrates having regard to the convenience of the defence, the prosecution and the witnesses; the desirability of expediting the trial; and any directions given by the Lord Chief Justice under the SCA 1981, s. 75(1). **D10.14**

In *R (Bentham) v Governor of HM Prison Wandsworth* [2006] EWHC 121 (Admin), the accused argued that the notice failed to comply with the requirements of the CDA 1998, s. 51(7) (to be replaced by the CDA 1998, s. 51D when the CJA 2003, sch. 3, comes into force). The Divisional Court (anxious to discourage what was described as a growth industry in unmeritorious complaints based on the drafting of such notices) ruled that the decision of substance is that of magistrates to send the accused to the Crown Court for trial. Only thereafter, and by way of an administrative act, is the notice prepared. No particular form is prescribed, nor is there any provision dealing with the consequences of a defective notice. It follows, said the Court, that defects in the notice do not invalidate (or render ineffective) an otherwise valid (or effective) sending. Gross J added (at [42]) that the notice should, as a matter of good practice, either (a) summarise the offence(s) as carefully as possible, or (b) cross-refer to documents to be sent to the Crown Court, such as the charge sheet or the Memorandum of an Entry entered in the Register of the magistrates' court.

The various documents that the magistrates' court must to send to the Crown Court are listed in the CrimPR, r. 12.1(1) (see **appendix 1**).

In practice, each magistrates' court is informed by the presiding judge of the relevant Crown Court circuit of the location to which it should normally send defendants for trial, and (in the absence of any representations to the contrary by any of the parties) it will automatically send the accused to that location. In other words, the location specified by the presiding judge will be presumed to be the most convenient, and the parties hardly ever seek to persuade the magistrates to send the case elsewhere. Nonetheless, in some cases either the prosecution or the defence may invite the magistrates to transfer the case to a different location of the Crown Court. This may be appropriate if, for example, the offence with which the defendant is charged may have aroused such ill feeling locally that a fair trial at the nearest location of the Crown Court may not be possible. If the magistrates do not accede to a request to transfer the case to a particular location of the Crown Court, or if the location specified by the magistrates subsequently appears unsatisfactory to one of the parties, there are two other ways of moving the trial:

(a) the Supreme Court Act 1981, s. 76(2), empowers an officer of the Crown Court to alter the place of trial;
(b) if the transfer is not effected administratively, either party may make an application to the Crown Court, under s. 76(3) of the 1981 Act for the venue of the trial to be altered. Applications under s. 76(3) formerly had to be heard by a High Court judge sitting in open court; however, the Courts Act 2003, s. 86, amends s. 76 so that it is no longer necessary to apply to a High Court judge. Applications to vary the location of the trial under s. 76 are heard by a Crown Court judge sitting in chambers (pursuant to the CrimPR, r. 16.11(c)). In *Croydon Crown Court, ex parte Britton* (2000) 164 JP 729, it was confirmed that the scope of the SCA 1981, s. 76, extends to altering the place of trial for an offence transferred to the Crown Court under the CDA 1998, s. 51.

Service of Evidence

D10.15 Under the Crime and Disorder Act 1998 (Service of Prosecution Evidence) Regulations 2005 (SI 2005 No. 902), reg. 2, where a person is sent for trial under s. 51, copies of the documents containing the evidence on which the charge(s) are based must, within 70 days from the date of the first hearing in the Crown Court, be served on the accused and on the Crown Court. Under reg. 3, the prosecutor may apply orally or in writing to the Crown Court for an extension (or further extension) of that period. Where the prosecutor wishes to make an oral application under reg. 3 (50 days if the accused is in custody), written notice of the intention to do so must be given to the court and to the accused (reg. 4(1)). Under reg. 5, any written application under reg. 3 must be sent to the court and to the accused. The notice must specify the grounds for the application; the accused may make written representations in response within three days of service of the application on him.

In *Fehily v Governor of Wandsworth Prison* [2003] 1 Cr App R 153, the Divisional Court held that failure by the prosecution to comply with the 42-day time-limit does not render the prosecution a nullity. Furthermore, the Crown Court has jurisdiction to extend time on an application by the prosecution even if the application is made after the expiry of the time-limit.

The bill of indictment must be preferred within 28 days of service of the prosecution case under the CDA 1998, sch. 3, para. 1 (CrimPR, r. 14.2(1)(d)). The indictment may contain any count that is supported by the evidence contained in the papers served by the prosecution, either in addition to or in substitution for the charges upon which the defendant was sent to the Crown Court by the magistrates' court (see the Administration of Justice (Miscellaneous Provisions) Act 1933, s. 2(2)). Any such counts must, however, be capable of being joined in the same indictment without breaching the CrimPR, r. 14.2(3) (and so must be founded on the same facts or form a series of offences of the same or a similar character). See **D10.39**.

Advance Information

D10.16 If an offence is triable either way, the CrimPR, part 21 apply (requiring the prosecution to serve on the defence, if the defence make a request for advance information, either a summary of the prosecution case or copies of the witness statements of the prosecution witnesses — current CPS practice is to supply copies of the statements). If the offence is triable only on indictment, the CrimPR do not apply. However, CPS guidance indicates that in order to ensure that the defendant has equality of arms and is not under an unfair disadvantage, copies of the charges, any disclosable evidence and a copy of any defendant's previous convictions should be served on the defendant or his solicitor prior to the first hearing in the magistrates' court. Prosecutors should also serve any material, if available, which ought to be disclosed in accordance with the common-law rules of disclosure set out in *DPP, ex parte Lee* [1999] 1 WLR 1950 (in particular, anything that might assist the defence in applying for bail). A copy of the same material should be served in good time on the Crown Court for the use of the judge at the preliminary hearing.

Appearance in the Crown Court

D10.17 Under the CDA 1998, s. 52(1), the accused may be sent to the Crown Court in custody or on bail. It should be borne in mind that the presumption in favour of bail (under the Bail Act 1976, s. 4) continues to operate in favour of the accused, and so bail may be withheld only if one or more of the grounds for withholding bail under sch. 1 to the 1976 Act are made out (see **D7.9** *et seq.*).

After the hearing that sends the accused to the Crown Court for trial, the magistrates' court will send a notice to the Crown Court. It used to be the case that the defendant's first appearance in the Crown Court had to take place within eight days if he was in custody, or within 28 days if on bail. However, the rules regarding the listing of the first appearance within set periods of time no longer apply (see the note to the CrimPR, r. 12.2). The preliminary hearing in the Crown Court may be in chambers (r. 16.11(2)(d)). The *Consolidated Criminal Practice Direction*, paras IV.41.3 and V.56.4, state that (unlike the position under the Crown Court Rules, which the CrimPR replace), a preliminary hearing is not required in every case sent for trial under the CDA 1998, s. 51. Rather, a preliminary hearing should be ordered by the magistrates' court (or by the Crown Court) only where such a hearing is considered necessary. If such a hearing is necessary, it should be held approximately 14 days after the accused is sent to the Crown Court. Paragraphs IV.41.5 and V.56.5 provide that, whether or not a magistrates' court orders a preliminary hearing, it should order a plea and case management hearing, to be held approximately 14 weeks after the accused was sent for trial under the CDA 1998, s. 51, if he was remanded in custody (17 weeks if the defendant is on bail). Reference should also be made to para. IV.41.8–12 and to the 'case progression form' in Annex E of the *Consolidated Criminal Practice Direction.* The form sets out a number of standard directions which provide a timetable for the case. For the purpose of the timetable, time starts to run from the date when the prosecution serve the draft indictment, case papers and initial disclosure under the CPIA 1996. Within 14 days of that date:

(i) the defence should notify the prosecution of their witness requirements;
(ii) the prosecution should serve any application for hearsay or defendant's bad character;
(iii) the defence should serve the defence statement (including any alibi details) or notification of a guilty plea, any application for hearsay/bad character, and any notice of an application to dismiss the charges.

Representation by the Criminal Defence Service

Where an indictable offence is transferred to the Crown Court, a representation order allowing representation by the Criminal Defence Service for the Crown Court proceedings may be made either by the magistrates' court or by the Crown Court (see AJA 1999, sch. 3, para. 2, and Criminal Defence Service (General) (No. 2) Regulations 2001, para. 9 (set out at **D29.8**). **D10.18**

Applications for Dismissal

Under the CDA 1998, sch. 3, para. 2(1), the accused may (after the date when he is served with the documents and before the date of the arraignment) apply orally or in writing to the Crown Court for the charge(s) to be dismissed. This application can be made whether or not the indictment has been preferred at the date of the application. Where such an application is made, the judge must dismiss any charge (and quash any count relating to it if an indictment has been preferred) if it appears to him that the evidence against the applicant would not be sufficient for him to be properly convicted (para. 2(2)). **D10.19**

Procedure The accused may make an oral application for dismissal only if he gives written notice of intention to do so (CDA 1998, sch. 3, para. 2(3)). **D10.20**

At the time of writing, under para. 2(4), oral evidence may be given on an application for dismissal only with the leave of the judge; the judge may give leave only if it appears to him, having regard to any matters stated in the application for leave, that the interests of justice require him to do so. If the judge gives leave permitting, or makes an order requiring, a person to give oral evidence but that person does not do so, the judge may disregard any document indicating the evidence that the witness might have given (para. 2(5)). However, when the CJA 2003, sch. 3, para. 20(3)(b) comes into force, the CDA 1998, sch. 3, paras. 2(4) and (5) will be repealed, removing the possibility of oral evidence being adduced at an application for dismissal of a charge transferred under s. 51.

Under the CrimPR, r. 13.2(2), written notice of intention to make an oral application for dismissal must be in the form set out in the *Consolidated Criminal Practice Direction* and must be given not later than 14 days after the day on which the documents were served under the CDA 1998, sch. 3, para. 1. A copy of the notice has to be sent to the prosecution and any co-defendant with whom the applicant is jointly charged. The time for giving notice may be extended, either before or after it expires, by the Crown Court (r. 13.2(3)). An application for an extension of time has to be made in writing to the Crown Court (with copies to the prosecution and any co-defendant with whom the applicant is jointly charged), using the form set out in the *Consolidated Criminal Practice Direction* (r. 13.2(4)).

Written applications for dismissal are governed by the CrimPR, r. 13.3. The application has to be in the form set out in the *Consolidated Criminal Practice Direction* (r. 13.3(1)). Copies of the application and any accompanying documents are sent to the Crown Court, the prosecution, and anyone with whom the applicant is jointly charged. The application has to be made not later than 14 days after the day on which documents required by the CDA 1998, sch. 3, para. 1, were served (r. 13.3(4)). Again, this time may be extended.

Rule 13.4 provides that, not later than seven days from the date of service of notice of intention to apply orally for the dismissal of a charge, the prosecution may apply to the Crown Court under the CDA 1998, sch. 3, para. 2(4) for leave to adduce oral evidence at the hearing of the application, indicating what witnesses it is proposed to call. Under r. 13.4(2), not later than seven days from the date of receiving a copy of a written application for dismissal under r. 13.3, the prosecution may apply to the Crown Court for an oral hearing of the application. This time may be extended by the court (r. 13.4(6)).

Under r. 13.4(5), where the prosecution wish to adduce any written comments or any further evidence in reply to the accused's application for dismissal of the charge(s), they must serve any such comments, copies of the statements or other documents outlining the evidence of any proposed witnesses, and copies of any further documents on the Crown Court and on the accused (and any co-accused) not later than 14 days from the date of receiving the material from the applicant. This time may be extended by the court (r. 13.4(6)).

Where a charge is dismissed under the CDA 1998, sch. 3, para. 2, further proceedings in respect of that charge may be brought only by means of the preferment of a voluntary bill of indictment (para. 2(6)).

D10.21 **Judicial review** The accused cannot challenge the decision of the Crown Court judge not to dismiss a charge under the CDA 1998, sch. 3, para. 2, by way of judicial review. In the context of notices to transfer serious or complex fraud cases to the Crown Court under the CJA 1987, s. 4 (substantially re-enacted in the CDA 1998, s. 51B), it had been held in *Central Criminal Court and Nadir, ex parte Director of the Serious Fraud Office* [1993] 1 WLR 949, that the Divisional Court did have jurisdiction to review the decision under the CJA 1987, s. 6 (which is in similar terms to the CDA 1998, sch. 3, para. 2), but this power should be exercised only in extremely limited circumstances. However, in *R (Snelgrove) v Woolwich Crown Court* [2005] 1 WLR 3223, the accused was charged with an indictable-only offence. He made an application for the charge to be dismissed (under para. 2). The judge refused to dismiss the charge against the accused, who then applied for judicial review. The question at issue was whether the decision under challenge was a matter relating to trial on indictment for the purposes of the Supreme Court Act 1981, s. 29(3), which excludes judicial review in such cases. The Divisional Court held that a decision under sch. 3 not to dismiss the charge is an order in a matter relating to trial on indictment for the purposes of s. 29(3) of the 1981 Act, and so judicial review is not available. Following the sending of a case to the Crown Court, that court is seised of the matter and of all decisions concerning the issue between the accused and the Crown that necessarily relate to the trial on indictment. The availability of judicial review would inject delay and uncertainty into proceedings in the Crown Court, which would be contrary to Parliament's intention. The Court (presided over by Auld LJ) said that

R v Central Criminal Court, ex parte Director of Serious Fraud Office [1993] 1 WLR 949, should no longer be regarded as good law. The decision in *Snelgrove* will be of even greater significance when the s. 51 transfer procedure is extended to include either-way offences. In *R (O) v Central Criminal Court* [2006] EWHC 256 (Admin), the Divisional Court re-affirmed that a judge's decision (i) to refuse to hear oral evidence on an application to dismiss (a possibility that will be removed in any event when the relevant amendment by the CJA 2003 comes into force: see **D10.20**), and (ii) to refuse to dismiss a case under the CDA 1988, sch. 3, para. 2(1), are both matters relating to trial on indictment, and therefore are not susceptible to judicial review (as a result of the Supreme Court Act 1981, s. 29(3)). The Court added that the ECHR, Article 5 has no applicability, since the proceedings concern whether there is a case to go before a jury not any issues of detention or liberty.

Test on Dismissal Applications In *R (Inland Revenue Commissioners) v Crown Court at Kingston* [2001] 4 All ER 721, it was held that the test to be applied by the judge on an application to dismiss under the CJA 1987, s. 6, is whether the evidence would be sufficient for a jury properly to convict. That requires the judge to take into account the whole of the evidence against the accused. On an application under s. 6, it is not appropriate for the judge to view any evidence in isolation from its context and other evidence. The judge is not bound to assume that a jury would make every possible inference capable of being drawn against the accused but has to decide not only whether there is any evidence to go to a jury, but also whether that evidence is sufficient for a jury properly to convict. That exercise requires the judge to assess the weight of the evidence. This is not to say that the judge is entitled to substitute himself for the jury. The question for him is not whether the accused should be convicted on the evidence put forward by the prosecution, but the sufficiency of that evidence. Where the evidence is largely documentary, and the case depends on the inferences or conclusions to be drawn from it, the judge must assess the inferences or conclusions that the prosecution propose to ask the jury to draw from the documents, and decide whether it appears to him that the jury could properly draw those inferences and come to those conclusions. The judge's conclusion as to the weight to be given to any evidence, and his conclusion that the evidence against the accused is or is not sufficient for a jury properly to convict him, can only be impugned if they can be shown to be conclusions that no reasonable judge could have come to, and so the Divisional Court will not interfere if the decision of the judge was within the range of decisions open to a reasonable judge properly directing himself as to the law. Parliament clearly intended the judge to have a wide margin of appreciation in this respect. It is submitted that the same principles would apply to applications to dismiss under the CDA 1998, sch. 3, para. 2. The decision in *R (Snelgrove) v Woolwich Crown Court* [2005] 1 WLR 3223 (see **D10.21**) means that the court in *R (Inland Revenue Commissioners) v Crown Court at Kingston* should not have entertained the application for judicial review of the decision of the Crown Court judge, but the Divisional Court's ruling about the test to be applied in such cases remains valid. **D10.22**

Reporting Restrictions Reporting restrictions in relation to applications for the dismissal of charges are governed by the CDA 1998, sch. 3, para. 3. The restrictions apply automatically but can be lifted under para. 3(2). Under para. 3(8), reporting must be limited to details such as the names, ages, home addresses and occupations of the accused and witnesses; the offence(s) with which the defendant(s) are charged; the names of counsel and solicitors engaged in the proceedings; arrangements as to bail; whether publicly funded representation has been granted. Contravention of these restrictions is a summary offence under para. 3(10), carrying a fine not exceeding level 5 (currently £5,000). Where there is more than one defendant, and one of them objects to the making of an order lifting the restrictions, the judge is required to lift them if, and only if, he is satisfied (after hearing representations from the defendants) that it is in the interests of justice to do so (para. 3(3)). **D10.23**

Power of Crown Court to Deal with Summary Offence

D10.24 The CDA 1998, sch. 3, para. 6, sets out what happens when the accused is sent for trial for a linked summary offence. If the accused is convicted on the indictment, the Crown Court judge has first to consider whether the summary offence is related to the indictable offence(s) for which he was sent for trial. For these purposes, the summary offence is related to the indictable offence if it 'arises out of circumstances which are the same as or connected with those giving rise' to the indictable offence (para. 6(12)). If the judge is so satisfied, the accused is asked to enter a plea. If the accused pleads guilty, the Crown Court will pass sentence (but subject to the limitations on sentence applicable to a magistrates' court). If he pleads not guilty, para. 6(6) provides that the powers of the Crown Court cease in respect of the summary offence (save that the Crown Court may dismiss the charge if the prosecution indicate that they do not wish to proceed with the charge); if the prosecution wish to proceed with the charge, they have to do so in the magistrates' court.

Paragraph 6(8) makes it clear that the provisions of para. 6 do not apply where the summary offence in question is one to which the CJA 1988, s. 40, applies (see **D11.15**) and that offence has been added to the indictment.

The coming into force of the Courts Act 2003, s. 66, affects the power of the Crown Court to deal with summary-only offences in that it confers on Crown Court judges the 'powers of a justice of the peace who is a District Judge (Magistrates' Courts)'. The effect of this provision is that, if the Crown Court is left with a summary offence, the judge may, if the accused pleads not guilty, try the offence as if he were a magistrate instead of remitting the accused to the magistrates' court to be tried for the summary offence. It should be emphasised that this provision simply empowers the Crown Court judge to try the summary offence as if he were a magistrate, and so it is still open to the judge to remit the accused to the magistrates' court to be tried for the summary offence.

If the Court of Appeal quash a conviction for the indictable offence to which a summary offence is related, that Court must also set aside the conviction for the summary offence and may direct that no further proceedings in relation to the offence are to be undertaken (para. 6(9)). If the Court of Appeal does not so direct, it is open to the prosecution to proceed against the accused in the magistrates' court in respect of that summary offence.

Accused No Longer Facing an Offence Sent for Trial

D10.25 The CDA 1998, sch. 3, para. 7 deals with the procedure to be adopted where the accused has been sent for trial for an indictable offence but, as a result of amendment of the indictment or because of a successful application for one or more charges to be dismissed, the accused no longer faces the charge in respect of which he was sent for trial. If he still faces an allegation of an either-way offence, the Crown Court has to go through a mode of trial procedure, which preserves the accused's right to be tried summarily for an either-way offence only where he consents and also preserves the court's discretion to rule that the case is too serious for summary trial. First, he is asked to indicate whether he intends to plead guilty or not guilty (para. 7(5)). If he indicates a guilty plea, the Crown Court proceeds to the sentencing stage for that offence (para. 7(6)). If he indicates a not guilty plea, the court decides whether the case is more suitable for summary trial or for trial on indictment (para. 7(7)). Paragraph 8 enables the court to proceed under para. 7 in the absence of the accused where the accused is legally represented and the court considers that, because of his disorderly conduct before the court, it is not practicable to conduct the proceedings in his presence. In such a case, the representative is asked to give the indication as to plea.

Before deciding whether the case is more suitable for summary trial or for trial on indictment, the court must give the prosecution an opportunity to inform the court of the accused's previous convictions (if any) and must give the prosecution and the accused an opportunity to make representations as to whether summary trial or trial on indictment would be more suitable (para. 9(2)). In reaching the decision, the court has to consider whether the sentence that a magistrates' court would have power to impose for the offence(s) would be adequate and must have regard to any allocation guidelines issued under the CJA 2003, s. 170 (para. 9(3)).

Under para. 10, if the Crown Court considers that an offence is more suitable for summary trial, the accused is given the choice of trial on indictment or summary trial. If the Crown Court considers that the offence is more suitable for trial on indictment, the accused is informed that this is so.

It should be noted that the special procedure for determining mode of trial for criminal damage where the value involved is less than £5,000 (see the MCA 1980, s. 22 at **D6.31**) is also applicable in this context (para. 14).

The plea before venue and mode of trial proceedings can be dealt with in the absence of the accused if the accused is legally represented, the legal representative signifies the accused's consent to the proceedings being conducted in his absence, and the court is satisfied that there is good reason for proceeding in the absence of the accused (para. 15(1)). If the court decides that the case is more suitable for summary trial and the legal representative indicates that the accused wishes to be tried summarily, the court will remit the accused for trial to the magistrates' court; otherwise, the trial will take place in the Crown Court (para. 15(3)).

In *Ashton* [2007] 1 WLR 181, the Court of Appeal held (at [55]) that a Crown Court judge exercising his powers to sit as a district judge under the Courts Act 2003, s. 66, may determine mode of trial and then commit the defendant for sentence and may then (sitting once again as a Crown Court judge) sit as the sentencing court.

Procedural Irregularities In *Haye* [2003] Crim LR 287, the accused was charged with robbery. He was sent for trial at the Crown Court pursuant to the CDA 1998, s. 51. At the plea and directions hearing in the Crown Court, the prosecution dropped the charge of robbery (an indictable-only offence) and replaced it with a charge of theft (triable either way). The accused pleaded not guilty to the theft charge. When the matter came on for trial, the accused was re-arraigned on the theft charge and entered a guilty plea. He subsequently appealed against conviction on the ground that the procedure set out in the CDA 1998, sch. 3, para. 7, had not been followed prior to the arraignment on the theft charge. In particular, he complained that proper consideration was not given to the question of whether he should be tried summarily or whether the Crown Court should continue to deal with the case. He argued that the proceedings that followed the plea of guilty were, therefore, a nullity. The Court of Appeal agreed, holding that any failure to comply with the statutory procedure in relation to the right of an accused to make representations and/or to exercise choice as to mode of trial would have the consequence that, if the matter proceeded to trial, the hearing would be regarded as *ultra vires* and liable to be quashed. In the present case, the accused had been deprived of an opportunity of seeking to persuade the judge that summary trial would be more suitable. It followed that the proceedings in relation to the indictment alleging theft were a nullity. **D10.26**

However, *Haye* was considered by the Court of Appeal in *Ashton* [2007] 1 WLR 181. The Court said that, in the light of the decision of the House of Lords in *Soneji* [2006] 1 AC 340 and the earlier Court of Appeal decision in *Sekhon* [2003] 1 WLR 1655, 'we are confident that if *Haye* was decided now the result would have been the other way' (per Fulford J at [69]). The Court reached this conclusion on the basis that, in the light of those two authorities and of the overriding objective in the CrimPR and in the absence of a clear indication that Parliament intended jurisdiction automatically to be removed following a procedural failure, the decision of the court should be based on an assessment of the interests of justice and, in particular, on whether there is a real possibility that the prosecution or the defence might suffer prejudice. If there is a risk of prejudice, a court should go on to decide whether it is just to permit the proceedings to continue. In other words, procedural failings do not generally render the proceedings invalid, they merely give the court a discretion whether or not to proceed with the case.

The approach laid down by *Ashton* was followed in *Thwaites* [2006] EWCA Crim 3235, where the accused was sent for trial to the Crown Court charged with conspiracy to handle stolen goods. However, he was arraigned and tried on an indictment containing counts of burglary, but no indictable-only offence. During the course of the trial, it was discovered that the judge had failed to conduct the mode of trial procedure required by the CDA 1998, sch. 3, in respect of the either-way charges on the indictment. The trial judge ruled that, had the correct procedure been followed, the case would have been found as suitable only for trial on indictment, and so the accused had suffered no prejudice from the failure to conduct the mode of trial procedure. The Court of Appeal held that earlier authorities such as *Haye* are no longer good law and that there was no unfairness or prejudice to the accused, who had received a fair trial.

Notices in Serious or Complex Fraud Cases: s. 51B

D10.27 A new s. 51B was inserted in the CDA 1998 by the CJA 2003, sch. 3, para. 1. This provision is not yet in force. The CDA 1998, s. 51B, essentially re-enacts the CJA 1987, s. 4 (which remains in force until s. 51B is brought into effect).

Under the CDA 1998, s. 51B(1), an indictable offence may be transferred to the Crown Court by means of a notice given by the prosecution if the prosecution is of the opinion (a subjective test) that the evidence in the case is sufficient for the person charged to be put on trial for the offence and reveals a case of fraud 'of such seriousness or complexity that it is appropriate that the management of the case should without delay be taken over by the Crown Court'. This provision applies only where the prosecution is being brought by a 'designated authority' (or under s. 51B(7), one of its officers). The designated authorities are the DPP, the Serious Fraud Office, the Inland Revenue, the Commissioners of Customs and Excise and a government minister (s. 51B(9)). Thus, although the Serious Fraud Office was set up specifically to coordinate and conduct the investigation and prosecution of serious fraud, the power to give a notice of transfer is not restricted to the Serious Fraud Office, but extends to other bodies, such as the CPS (by virtue of the DPP being head of the CPS and able to delegate his powers to Crown Prosecutors).

In the unlikely event that the magistrates accept jurisdiction at a mode of trial hearing in such a case, any such notice must be given before any summary trial begins (s. 51B(5)). The effect of the notice is that, apart from ancillary matters such as granting bail and publicly funded representation, the functions of the magistrates' court cease in relation to the case (s. 51B(6)). There is no appeal against the decision of the prosecution to give notice under s. 51B (s. 51B(8)). In other words, the prosecution are entitled, simply by virtue of their own notice, to prefer a bill of indictment for the offences concerned.

The notice, which must be given to the magistrates' court at which the person charged appears or before which he is brought (s. 51B(4)), must specify the proposed place of trial; in selecting that place, s. 51B(3) provides that the designated authority must have regard to the same matters as magistrates have to take into account when deciding where to send an accused for trial (see **D10.14**). The indictment must be preferred within 28 days of the giving of notice (subject to the power of the Crown Court to extend that time limit): see the CrimPR, r. 14.2.

In *Wrench* [1996] 1 Cr App R 340 (decided under the 1987 Act), it was held that, if one of the charges is one to which the transfer provisions apply, then the procedure can also be used in respect of any other offences which can validly be joined on the same indictment. It is submitted that the same principle would apply to transfers under s. 51B.

Although the CDA 1998, sch. 3, para. 2(1) refers specifically to s. 51 (and to s. 51A, the equivalent provision for juveniles), it is submitted that the ability to apply to the Crown Court for the charges to be dismissed must apply equally where a notice is given under s. 51B.

Notices in Certain Cases Involving Children: s. 51C

A new s. 51C was inserted in the CDA 1998 by the CJA 2003, sch. 3, para. 18. This provision is not yet in force. The CDA 1998, s. 51C, substantially re-enacts the CJA 1991, s. 53 (which remains in force until s. 51B is brought into effect). **D10.28**

Under the CDA 1998, s. 51C(1), a case may be transferred to the Crown Court by means of a notice given by the DPP (in practice, notice is likely to be given by a Crown Prosecutor) if he is of the opinion (a subjective test) that the evidence in the case is sufficient for the person charged to be put on trial for the offence, that a child will be called as a witness at the trial and that, in order to avoid any prejudice to the welfare of the child, the case should be taken over and proceeded with without delay by the Crown Court. This provision applies only to the offences specified in s. 51C(3), which lists a number of specific sexual or violent offences but also includes any offence that involves an assault on, or injury or a threat of injury to, a person. Under s. 51C(5), the functions of the DPP under s. 51C may be exercised by an officer acting on behalf of the Director; this will include a Crown Prosecutor acting within his general delegated authority delegated to them, even if they have no express instructions from the DPP (*Liverpool Crown Court, ex parte Bray* [1987] Crim LR 51). A decision to give a notice under s. 51C is not subject to appeal or liable to be questioned in any court (s. 51C(6)).

For the purposes of s. 51C, 'child' is defined in s. 51C(7) as a person who is under the age of 17 or any person of whom a video recording (as defined in the YJCEA 1999, s. 63(1)) was made when he was under the age of 17 with a view to its admission as his evidence in chief in the trial.

Under s. 51C(4), the effect of the notice under s. 51C is that, apart from ancillary matters such as granting bail and publicly funded representation, the functions of the magistrates' court cease in relation to the case. The indictment must be preferred within 28 days of the giving of notice (subject to the power of the Crown Court to extend that time limit): see the CrimPR, r. 14.2.

As with notices under s. 51B, it is submitted that the provisions of the CDA 1998, sch. 3, para. 2, should apply to notices given under s. 51C, thus enabling the accused to apply to the Crown Court for the dismissal of the charge(s).

In *Fareham Youth Court and Morey, ex parte CPS* (1999) 161 JP 812, it was held that in the case of a juvenile where the youth court has determined, under the MCA 1980, s. 24(1), that he should be tried summarily, the prosecution cannot reverse that decision by issue of a notice of transfer. In *T and K* [2001] 1 Cr App R 446, the Court of Appeal indicated that, where the defendant is a juvenile, the DPP should not transfer the case to the Crown Court unless satisfied that a magistrates' court would be likely to find that the requirements of the MCA 1980, s. 24, are met (i.e. that it should be possible to sentence the defendant under the PCC(S)A 2000, s. 91 (see **D23.21** ***et seq.***)). It is submitted that there is considerable merit in the approach taken in these two cases, both decided under the 1991 Act, since the interests of both the juvenile defendant and the young witness are best served by a speedy trial. Such a trial should be in the youth court (since that is the court best equipped to deal with juveniles) unless the need to ensure greater powers of punishment provides sufficient reason for Crown Court trial.

Composite Statements and Edited Statements

D10.29 The *Consolidated Criminal Practice Direction*, para. III.24, deals with the procedure to be followed by the prosecution when either a witness has made two or more statements to the police and it is desired to combine them into a single statement potentially admissible at committal, or a witness has included in his statement material on which the prosecution do not after all wish to rely because it is inadmissible, prejudicial or irrelevant. The main points of the direction are listed below.

(a) A composite statement giving the effect of several earlier statements must comply with the statutory requirements and be signed by the witness (para. 24.2).

(b) Any editing of a statement should be done by a Crown Prosecutor (or legal representative of the prosecutor if it is not a CPS case). It should not be done by a police officer (para. 24.1).

(c) There are two acceptable methods of editing a single witness statement, namely, to indicate on the copy statements served on the defence those parts of the original on which the prosecution do not seek to rely, or to prepare and have signed by the witness a fresh statement omitting all mention of the superfluous material (para. 24.3). If the former method is adopted, the original signed statement tendered to the court must be left unmarked, and the deleting of the defence and court copies must be done in such a way (e.g., by bracketing or light striking out) as to permit what is deleted still be to read. It is not permissible to serve a photocopy with the deleted material completely obliterated. The index to the bundle of statements served by the prosecution should contain words to the effect that: 'The prosecution does not propose to adduce evidence of those passages of the attached copy statements that have been struck out and/or bracketed (nor will it seek to do so at the trial unless a notice of further evidence is served)'.

(d) Usually the first course of action described in (c) above will be more appropriate, but the second (i.e. preparing a fresh statement) should be used, for example, when a police officer's original statement refers to interviews with suspects who were not eventually charged and/or to the officer's questioning of the accused about other matters (para. 24.4). The new statement should omit the superfluous material, save that, for the sake of continuity, it might contain a phrase such as, 'After referring to other matters, I then said . . .'.

(e) The direction applies both to statements that the prosecution wish to tender as part of the transfer process under the CDA 1998, s. 51, and to statements which are to be tendered for use at the trial under the CJA 1967, s. 9. Documents exhibited to witness statements (including statements by a suspect under caution and signed contemporaneous notes) should be left in their original state, any editing being left for counsel at the Crown Court (para. 24.6). Similarly, oral answers of the accused recorded in police officers' written statements should not be edited at the preliminary stage save to the extent mentioned in (d) above (i.e. questions about matters not the subject of the present charges to be omitted from a second statement prepared by the officer).

(f) Where two or more statements by a witness are coalesced into a composite statement or when a fresh 'edited' statement is prepared, a copy of the earlier unedited statements should normally be served on the defence (para. 24.7).

Depositions for Use in the Trial

D10.30 The CDA 1998, sch. 3, para. 4, empowers a magistrate to issue a summons requiring a person to attend before a magistrate to have evidence taken in the form of a deposition. Under para. 4(1), before issuing the summons, the magistrate must be satisfied that the person is likely to be able to give material evidence (or to produce a relevant document or other exhibit) on behalf of the prosecution for an offence that has been sent to the Crown Court for trial, and that the witness will not voluntarily make the statement or produce the document or exhibit.

If the prosecutor makes the application on oath and the magistrate is satisfied that the summons would not result in the attendance of the witness, the magistrate may issue an arrest warrant instead of a summons (para. 4(3)). If a summons is issued and the witness fails to attend in answer to the summons, an arrest warrant may be issued (para. 4(5)) and the witness is liable to be committed to custody for up to a month or be fined up to £2,500.

Where evidence has been taken as a deposition under para. 4, para. 5(2) provides that the deposition may be read as evidence at the trial unless (under para. 5(3)) the trial judge orders that this should not be so or a party to the proceedings objects to the use of the deposition.

The deposition is taken before a single magistrate. The accused and his legal representative have no right to attend the taking of the deposition, and if they do attend have no right to cross-examine the witness. Indeed the magistrate does not even have to notify the accused that a deposition is being taken (and would not notify the accused if the prosecution feared that the witness might be the subject of intimidation if the accused knew that a statement was being taken). The prosecutor questions the witness and a note is taken of the answers given by the witness. The witness is then asked to confirm the accuracy of the note. The magistrate must ensure that the questions asked by the prosecutor are relevant to the charge faced by the accused. It is submitted that the absence of the accused and, even more crucially, his legal representative will mean that the prosecutor, the magistrate conducting proceedings and the clerk to the justices in attendance will bear the responsibility for ensuring that evidence is not elicited by means of leading (or otherwise inappropriate) questions.

The Divisional Court considered this power in *R (CPS) v Bolton Magistrates' Court* [2004] 1 WLR 835, holding as follows:

(a) The procedure for taking a deposition from a witness who will not voluntarily make a statement is a proceeding in open court. However, in the circumstances of a particular case, the magistrate might, exceptionally, exclude persons from the taking of the deposition or otherwise modify the procedure where that would assist in the reception of the evidence or is in the interests of justice.

(b) A deposition does not have to be taken at a court-house but can be taken elsewhere. However, that flexibility can properly be exercised only in very unusual circumstances. Any prejudice to the administration of justice caused by members of the public being present can be dealt with by orders under the Contempt of Court Act 1981, s. 4(2), or by the general power to restrict access.

(c) Normally those representing the accused will not be allowed to cross-examine the witness, but there might be cases where the reluctant witness is unlikely to be available at the Crown Court, or could perhaps be spared attendance there if one or two questions were asked; in such a situation it would be open to the justices to permit cross- examination.

(d) Where a witness who has been summoned to give a deposition refuses to answer questions on the ground of privilege against self-incrimination, that claim should be the subject of proper investigation by the justices in respect of each and every question for which it is claimed. Before acceding to a claim to privilege, the court should satisfy itself, from the circumstances of the case and the nature of the evidence that the witness is called to give, that there is a reasonable ground to apprehend real and appreciable danger to the witness with reference to the ordinary operation of the law in the ordinary course of things, and not a danger of an imaginary or insubstantial character.

This procedure is not available to the defence, since its object is to facilitate the gathering of evidence for the prosecution.

Discontinuance of the Prosecution Case

The prosecution may discontinue the case against the accused not only in the magistrates' court, but also, in the case of offences sent up to the Crown Court under the CDA 1998, **D10.31**

s. 51, at any time before the indictment is preferred (Prosecution of Offences Act 1985, s. 23A: see D3.51).

Abuse of Process: the Discretion to Discharge an Accused

D10.32 The fact that a magistrates' court has a duty under the CDA 1998, s. 51(1), to send the case to the Crown Court 'forthwith' does not necessarily preclude the court from exercising its jurisdiction to stay the proceedings as an abuse of process in an appropriate case, though such cases will be very rare (*R (Salubi) v Bow Street Magistrates' Court* [2002] 1 WLR 3073). For discussion of abuse of process, see D3.54 *et seq.*

Statutory Materials

D10.33 **The Crime and Disorder Act 1998, ss. 50A, 51, 51B, 51C, 51D, 51E, 52, 52A and 52B and sch. 3 (as amended by the Criminal Justice Act 2003)**

50A.—(1) Where an adult appears or is brought before a magistrates' court charged with an either-way offence (the 'relevant offence'), the court shall proceed in the manner described in this section.

(2) If notice is given in respect of the relevant offence under section 51B or 51C below, the court shall deal with the offence as provided in section 51 below.

(3) Otherwise—

(a) if the adult (or another adult with whom the adult is charged jointly with the relevant offence) is or has been sent to the Crown Court for trial for an offence under section 51(2)(a) or 51(2)(c) below—

(i) the court shall first consider the relevant offence under subsection (3), (4), (5) or, as the case may be, (6) of section 51 below and, where applicable, deal with it under that subsection;

(ii) if the adult is not sent to the Crown Court for trial for the relevant offence by virtue of sub-paragraph (i) above, the court shall then proceed to deal with the relevant offence in accordance with sections 17A to 23 of the 1980 Act;

(b) in all other cases—

(i) the court shall first consider the relevant offence under sections 17A to 20 (excluding subsections (8) and (9) of section 20) of the 1980 Act;

(ii) if, by virtue of sub-paragraph (i) above, the court would be required to proceed in relation to the offence as mentioned in section 17A(6), 17B(2)(c) or 20(7) of that Act (indication of guilty plea), it shall proceed as so required (and, accordingly, shall not consider the offence under section 51 or 51A below);

(iii) if sub-paragraph (ii) above does not apply—

(a) the court shall consider the relevant offence under sections 51 and 51A below and, where applicable, deal with it under the relevant section;

(b) if the adult is not sent to the Crown Court for trial for the relevant offence by virtue of paragraph (a) of this sub-paragraph, the court shall then proceed to deal with the relevant offence as contemplated by section 20(9) or, as the case may be, section 21 of the 1980 Act.

(4) Subsection (3) above is subject to any requirement to proceed as mentioned in subsections (2) or (6)(a) of section 22 of the 1980 Act (certain offences where value involved is small).

(5) Nothing in this section shall prevent the court from committing the adult to the Crown Court for sentence pursuant to any enactment, if he is convicted of the relevant offence.

51.—(1) Where an adult appears or is brought before a magistrates' court ('the court') charged with an offence and any of the conditions mentioned in subsection (2) below is satisfied, the court shall send him forthwith to the Crown Court for trial for the offence.

(2) Those conditions are—

(a) that the offence is an offence triable only on indictment other than one in respect of which notice has been given under section 51B or 51C below;

(b) that the offence is an either-way offence and the court is required under section 20(9)(b), 21, 23(4)(b) or (5) or 25(2D) of the Magistrates' Courts Act 1980 to proceed in relation to the offence in accordance with subsection (1) above;

(c) that notice is given to the court under section 51B or 51C below in respect of the offence.

(3) Where the court sends an adult for trial under subsection (1) above, it shall at the same time send him to the Crown Court for trial for any either-way or summary offence with which he is charged and which—
 (a) (if it is an either-way offence) appears to the court to be related to the offence mentioned in subsection (1) above; or
 (b) (if it is a summary offence) appears to the court to be related to the offence mentioned in subsection (1) above or to the either-way offence, and which fulfils the requisite condition (as defined in subsection (11) below).

(4) Where an adult who has been sent for trial under subsection (1) above subsequently appears or is brought before a magistrates' court charged with an either-way or summary offence which—
 (a) appears to the court to be related to the offence mentioned in subsection (1) above; and
 (b) (in the case of a summary offence) fulfils the requisite condition,

the court may send him forthwith to the Crown Court for trial for the either-way or summary offence.

(5) Where—
 (a) the court sends an adult ('A') for trial under subsection (1) or (3) above;
 (b) another adult appears or is brought before the court on the same or a subsequent occasion charged jointly with A with an either-way offence; and
 (c) that offence appears to the court to be related to an offence for which A was sent for trial under subsection (1) or (3) above,

the court shall where it is the same occasion, and may where it is a subsequent occasion, send the other adult forthwith to the Crown Court for trial for the either-way offence.

(6) Where the court sends an adult for trial under subsection (5) above, it shall at the same time send him to the Crown Court for trial for any either-way or summary offence with which he is charged and which—
 (a) (if it is an either-way offence) appears to the court to be related to the offence for which he is sent for trial; and
 (b) (if it is a summary offence) appears to the court to be related to the offence for which he is sent for trial or to the either-way offence, and which fulfils the requisite condition.

(7) Where—
 (a) the court sends an adult ('A') for trial under subsection (1), (3) or (5) above; and
 (b) a child or young person appears or is brought before the court on the same or a subsequent occasion charged jointly with A with an indictable offence for which A is sent for trial under subsection (1), (3) or (5) above, or an indictable offence which appears to the court to be related to that offence,

the court shall, if it considers it necessary in the interests of justice to do so, send the child or young person forthwith to the Crown Court for trial for the indictable offence.

(8) Where the court sends a child or young person for trial under subsection (7) above, it may at the same time send him to the Crown Court for trial for any indictable or summary offence with which he is charged and which—
 (a) (if it is an indictable offence) appears to the court to be related to the offence for which he is sent for trial; and
 (b) (if it is a summary offence) appears to the court to be related to the offence for which he is sent for trial or to the indictable offence, and which fulfils the requisite condition.

(9) Subsections (7) and (8) above are subject to sections 24A and 24B of the Magistrates' Courts Act 1980 (which provide for certain cases involving children and young persons to be tried summarily).

(10) The trial of the information charging any summary offence for which a person is sent for trial under this section shall be treated as if the court had adjourned it under section 10 of the 1980 Act and had not fixed the time and place for its resumption.

(11) A summary offence fulfils the requisite condition if it is punishable with imprisonment or involves obligatory or discretionary disqualification from driving.

(12) In the case of an adult charged with an offence—
 (a) if the offence satisfies paragraph (c) of subsection (2) above, the offence shall be dealt with under subsection (1) above and not under any other provision of this section or section 51A below;
 (b) subject to paragraph (a) above, if the offence is one in respect of which the court is required to, or would decide to, send the adult to the Crown Court under—
  (i) subsection (5) above; or

(ii) subsection (6) of section 51A below,

the offence shall be dealt with under that subsection and not under any other provision of this section or section 51A below.

(13) The functions of a magistrates' court under this section, and its related functions under section 51D below, may be discharged by a single justice.

. . .

51B.—(1) A notice may be given by a designated authority under this section in respect of an indictable offence if the authority is of the opinion that the evidence of the offence charged—

(a) is sufficient for the person charged to be put on trial for the offence; and

(b) reveals a case of fraud of such seriousness or complexity that it is appropriate that the management of the case should without delay be taken over by the Crown Court.

(2) That opinion must be certified by the designated authority in the notice.

(3) The notice must also specify the proposed place of trial, and in selecting that place the designated authority must have regard to the same matters as are specified in paragraphs (a) to (c) of section 51D(4) below.

(4) A notice under this section must be given to the magistrates' court at which the person charged appears or before which he is brought.

(5) Such a notice must be given to the magistrates' court before any summary trial begins.

(6) The effect of such a notice is that the functions of the magistrates' court cease in relation to the case, except—

(a) for the purposes of section 51D below;

(b) as provided by paragraph 2 of Schedule 3 to the Access to Justice Act 1999; and

(c) as provided by section 52 below.

(7) The functions of a designated authority under this section may be exercised by an officer of the authority acting on behalf of the authority.

(8) A decision to give a notice under this section shall not be subject to appeal or liable to be questioned in any court (whether a magistrates' court or not).

(9) In this section 'designated authority' means—

(a) the Director of Public Prosecutions;

(b) the Director of the Serious Fraud Office;

(c) the Director of Revenue and Customs Prosecutions;

(d) the Commissioners of Customs and Excise; or

(e) the Secretary of State.

51C.—(1) A notice may be given by the Director of Public Prosecutions under this section in respect of an offence falling within subsection (3) below if he is of the opinion—

(a) that the evidence of the offence would be sufficient for the person charged to be put on trial for the offence;

(b) that a child would be called as a witness at the trial; and

(c) that, for the purpose of avoiding any prejudice to the welfare of the child, the case should be taken over and proceeded with without delay by the Crown Court.

(2) That opinion must be certified by the Director of Public Prosecutions in the notice.

(3) This subsection applies to an offence—

(a) which involves an assault on, or injury or a threat of injury to, a person;

(b) under section 1 of the Children and Young Persons Act 1933 (cruelty to persons under 16);

(c) under the Sexual Offences Act 1956, the Protection of Children Act 1978 or the Sexual Offences Act 2003;

(d) of kidnapping or false imprisonment, or an offence under section 1 or 2 of the Child Abduction Act 1984;

(e) which consists of attempting or conspiring to commit, or of aiding, abetting, counselling, procuring or inciting the commission of, an offence falling within paragraph (a), (b), (c) or (d) above.

(4) Subsections (4), (5) and (6) of section 51B above apply for the purposes of this section as they apply for the purposes of that.

(5) The functions of the Director of Public Prosecutions under this section may be exercised by an officer acting on behalf of the Director.

(6) A decision to give a notice under this section shall not be subject to appeal or liable to be questioned in any court (whether a magistrates' court or not).

(7) In this section 'child' means—

(a) a person who is under the age of 17; or
(b) any person of whom a video recording (as defined in section 63(1) of the Youth Justice and Criminal Evidence Act 1999) was made when he was under the age of 17 with a view to its admission as his evidence in chief in the trial referred to in subsection (1) above.

51D.—(1) The court shall specify in a notice—
(a) the offence or offences for which a person is sent for trial under section 51 or 51A above; and
(b) the place at which he is to be tried (which, if a notice has been given under section 51B above, must be the place specified in that notice).

(2) A copy of the notice shall be served on the accused and given to the Crown Court sitting at that place.

(3) In a case where a person is sent for trial under section 51 or 51A above for more than one offence, the court shall specify in that notice, for each offence—
(a) the subsection under which the person is so sent; and
(b) if applicable, the offence to which that offence appears to the court to be related.

(4) Where the court selects the place of trial for the purposes of subsection (1) above, it shall have regard to—
(a) the convenience of the defence, the prosecution and the witnesses;
(b) the desirability of expediting the trial; and
(c) any direction given by or on behalf of the Lord Chief Justice with the concurrence of the Lord Chancellor under section 75(1) of the Supreme Court Act 1981.

51E. For the purposes of sections 50A to 51D above—
(a) 'adult' means a person aged 18 or over, and references to an adult include a corporation;
(b) 'either-way offence' means an offence triable either way;
(c) an either-way offence is related to an indictable offence if the charge for the either-way offence could be joined in the same indictment as the charge for the indictable offence;
(d) a summary offence is related to an indictable offence if it arises out of circumstances which are the same as or connected with those giving rise to the indictable offence.

52.—(1) Subject to section 4 of the Bail Act 1976, section 41 of the 1980 Act, regulations under section 22 of the 1985 Act and section 25 of the 1994 Act, the court may send a person for trial under section 51 or 51A above—
(a) in custody, that is to say, by committing him to custody there to be safely kept until delivered in due course of law; or
(b) on bail in accordance with the Bail Act 1976, that is to say, by directing him to appear before the Crown Court for trial.

(2) Where—
(a) the person's release on bail under subsection (1)(b) above is conditional on his providing one or more sureties; and
(b) in accordance with subsection (3) of section 8 of the Bail Act 1976, the court fixes the amount in which a surety is to be bound with a view to his entering into his recognisance subsequently in accordance with subsections (4) and (5) or (6) of that section,

the court shall in the meantime make an order such as is mentioned in subsection (1)(a) above.

(3) The court shall treat as an indictable offence for the purposes of section 51 or 51A above an offence which is mentioned in the first column of Schedule 2 to the 1980 Act (offences for which the value involved is relevant to the mode of trial) unless it is clear to the court, having regard to any representations made by the prosecutor or the accused, that the value involved does not exceed the relevant sum.

(4) In subsection (3) above 'the value involved' and 'the relevant sum' have the same meanings as in section 22 of the 1980 Act (certain offences triable either way to be tried summarily if value involved is small).

(5) A magistrates' court may adjourn any proceedings under section 51 or 51A above, and if it does so shall remand the accused.

(6) Schedule 3 to this Act (which makes further provision in relation to persons sent to the Crown Court for trial under section 51 or 51A above) shall have effect.

52A.—(1) Except as provided by this section, it shall not be lawful—
(a) to publish in the United Kingdom a written report of any allocation or sending proceedings in England and Wales; or
(b) to include in a relevant programme for reception in the United Kingdom a report of any such proceedings,

if (in either case) the report contains any matter other than that permitted by this section.

(2) Subject to subsections (3) and (4) below, a magistrates' court may, with reference to any allocation or sending proceedings, order that subsection (1) above shall not apply to reports of those proceedings.

(3) Where there is only one accused and he objects to the making of an order under subsection (2) above, the court shall make the order if, and only if, it is satisfied, after hearing the representations of the accused, that it is in the interests of justice to do so.

(4) Where in the case of two or more accused one of them objects to the making of an order under subsection (2) above, the court shall make the order if, and only if, it is satisfied, after hearing the representations of the accused, that it is in the interests of justice to do so.

(5) An order under subsection (2) above shall not apply to reports of proceedings under subsection (3) or (4) above, but any decision of the court to make or not to make such an order may be contained in reports published or included in a relevant programme before the time authorised by subsection (6) below.

(6) It shall not be unlawful under this section to publish or include in a relevant programme a report of allocation or sending proceedings containing any matter other than that permitted by subsection (7) below—

(a) where, in relation to the accused (or all of them, if there are more than one), the magistrates' court is required to proceed as mentioned in section 20(7) of the 1980 Act, after the court is so required;

(b) where, in relation to the accused (or any of them, if there are more than one), the court proceeds other than as mentioned there, after conclusion of his trial or, as the case may be, the trial of the last to be tried.

(7) The following matters may be contained in a report of allocation or sending proceedings published or included in a relevant programme without an order under subsection (2) above before the time authorised by subsection (6) above—

(a) the identity of the court and the name of the justice or justices;

(b) the name, age, home address and occupation of the accused;

(c) in the case of an accused charged with an offence in respect of which notice has been given to the court under section 51B above, any relevant business information;

(d) the offence or offences, or a summary of them, with which the accused is or are charged;

(e) the names of counsel and solicitors engaged in the proceedings;

(f) where the proceedings are adjourned, the date and place to which they are adjourned;

(g) the arrangements as to bail;

(h) whether a right to representation funded by the Legal Services Commission as part of the Criminal Defence Service was granted to the accused or any of the accused.

(8) The addresses that may be published or included in a relevant programme under subsection (7) above are addresses—

(a) at any relevant time; and

(b) at the time of their publication or inclusion in a relevant programme.

(9) The following is relevant business information for the purposes of subsection (7) above—

(a) any address used by the accused for carrying on a business on his own account;

(b) the name of any business which he was carrying on on his own account at any relevant time;

(c) the name of any firm in which he was a partner at any relevant time or by which he was engaged at any such time;

(d) the address of any such firm;

(e) the name of any company of which he was a director at any relevant time or by which he was otherwise engaged at any such time;

(f) the address of the registered or principal office of any such company;

(g) any working address of the accused in his capacity as a person engaged by any such company;

and here 'engaged' means engaged under a contract of service or a contract for services.

(10) Subsection (1) above shall be in addition to, and not in derogation from, the provisions of any other enactment with respect to the publication of reports of court proceedings.

(11) In this section—

'allocation or sending proceedings' means, in relation to an information charging an indictable offence—

(a) any proceedings in the magistrates' court at which matters are considered under any of the following provisions—
   (i) sections 19 to 23 of the 1980 Act;
   (ii) section 51, 51A or 52 above;

(b) any proceedings in the magistrates' court before the court proceeds to consider any matter mentioned in paragraph (a) above; and

(c) any proceedings in the magistrates' court at which an application under section 25(2) of the 1980 Act is considered;

'publish', in relation to a report, means publish the report, either by itself or as part of a newspaper or periodical, for distribution to the public;

'relevant programme' means a programme included in a programme service (within the meaning of the Broadcasting Act 1990);

'relevant time' means a time when events giving rise to the charges to which the proceedings relate occurred.

52B.—(1) If a report is published or included in a relevant programme in contravention of section 52A above, each of the following persons is guilty of an offence—

(a) in the case of a publication of a written report as part of a newspaper or periodical, any proprietor, editor or publisher of the newspaper or periodical;

(b) in the case of a publication of a written report otherwise than as part of a newspaper or periodical, the person who publishes it;

(c) in the case of the inclusion of a report in a relevant programme, any body corporate which is engaged in providing the service in which the programme is included and any person having functions in relation to the programme corresponding to those of the editor of a newspaper.

(2) A person guilty of an offence under this section is liable on summary conviction to a fine not exceeding level 5 on the standard scale.

(3) Proceedings for an offence under this section shall not, in England and Wales, be instituted otherwise than by or with the consent of the Attorney General.

(4) Proceedings for an offence under this section shall not, in Northern Ireland, be instituted otherwise than by or with the consent of the Attorney General for Northern Ireland.

(5) Subsection (11) of section 52A above applies for the purposes of this section as it applies for the purposes of that section.

. . .

SCHEDULE 3

1. The Attorney General shall by regulations provide that, where a person is sent for trial under section 51 or 51A of this Act on any charge or charges, copies of the documents containing the evidence on which the charge or charges are based shall—

(a) be served on that person; and

(b) be given to the Crown Court sitting at the place specified in the notice under section 51D(1) of this Act

before the expiry of the period prescribed by the regulations; but the judge may at his discretion extend or further extend that period.

(2) The regulations may make provision as to the procedure to be followed on an application for the extension or further extension of a period under sub-paragraph (1) above.

Applications for dismissal

2.—(1) A person who is sent for trial under section 51 or 51A of this Act on any charge or charges may, at any time—

(a) after he is served with copies of the documents containing the evidence on which the charge or charges are based; and

(b) before he is arraigned (and whether or not an indictment has been preferred against him),

apply orally or in writing to the Crown Court sitting at the place specified in the notice under section 51D(1) of this Act for the charge, or any of the charges, in the case to be dismissed.

(2) The judge shall dismiss a charge (and accordingly quash any count relating to it in any indictment preferred against the applicant) which is the subject of any such application if it appears to him that the evidence against the applicant would not be sufficient for him to be properly convicted.

(3) No oral application may be made under sub-paragraph (1) above unless the applicant has given to the Crown Court sitting at the place in question written notice of his intention to make the application.

. . .

(6) If the charge, or any of the charges, against the applicant is dismissed—
(a) no further proceedings may be brought on the dismissed charge or charges except by means of the preferment of a voluntary bill of indictment; and
(b) unless the applicant is in custody otherwise than on the dismissed charge or charges, he shall be discharged.

(7) Criminal Procedure Rules may make provision for the purposes of this paragraph and, without prejudice to the generality of this sub-paragraph, may make provision—
(a) as to the time or stage in the proceedings at which anything required to be done is to be done (unless the court grants leave to do it at some other time or stage);
(b) as to the contents and form of notices or other documents;
(c) as to the manner in which evidence is to be submitted; and
(d) as to persons to be served with notices or other material.

Reporting restrictions

3.—(1) Except as provided by this paragraph, it shall not be lawful—
(a) to publish in the United Kingdom a written report of an application under paragraph 2(1) above; or
(b) to include in a relevant programme for reception in the United Kingdom a report of such an application,
if (in either case) the report contains any matter other than that permitted by this paragraph.

(2) An order that sub-paragraph (1) above shall not apply to reports of an application under paragraph 2(1) above may be made by the judge dealing with the application.

(3) Where in the case of two or more accused one of them objects to the making of an order under sub-paragraph (2) above, the judge shall make the order if, and only if, he is satisfied, after hearing the representations of the accused, that it is in the interests of justice to do so.

(4) An order under sub-paragraph (2) above shall not apply to reports of proceedings under sub-paragraph (3) above, but any decision of the court to make or not to make such an order may be contained in reports published or included in a relevant programme before the time authorised by sub-paragraph (5) below.

(5) It shall not be unlawful under this paragraph to publish or include in a relevant programme a report of an application under paragraph 2(1) above containing any matter other than that permitted by sub-paragraph (8) below where the application is successful.

(6) Where—
(a) two or more persons were jointly charged; and
(b) applications under paragraph 2(1) above are made by more than one of them,
sub-paragraph (5) above shall have effect as if for the words 'the application is' there were substituted the words 'all the applications are'.

(7) It shall not be unlawful under this paragraph to publish or include in a relevant programme a report of an unsuccessful application at the conclusion of the trial of the person charged, or of the last of the persons charged to be tried.

(8) The following matters may be contained in a report published or included in a relevant programme without an order under sub-paragraph (2) above before the time authorised by sub-paragraphs (5) and (6) above, that is to say—
(a) the identity of the court and the name of the judge;
(b) the names, ages, home addresses and occupations of the accused and witnesses;
(bb) where the application made by the accused under paragraph 2(1) above relates to a charge for an offence in respect of which notice has been given to the court under section 51B of this Act, any relevant business information;
(c) the offence or offences, or a summary of them, with which the accused is or are charged;
(d) the names of counsel and solicitors engaged in the proceedings;
(e) where the proceedings are adjourned, the date and place to which they are adjourned;
(f) the arrangements as to bail;
(g) whether a right to representation funded by the Legal Services Commission as part of the Criminal Defence Service was granted to the accused or any of the accused.

(9) The addresses that may be published or included in a relevant programme under sub-paragraph (8) above are addresses—
(a) at any relevant time; and
(b) at the time of their publication or inclusion in a relevant programme.

(9A) The following is relevant business information for the purposes of sub-paragraph (8) above—
(a) any address used by the accused for carrying on a business on his own account;
(b) the name of any business which he was carrying on on his own account at any relevant time;
(c) the name of any firm in which he was a partner at any relevant time or by which he was engaged at any such time;
(d) the address of any such firm;
(e) the name of any company of which he was a director at any relevant time or by which he was otherwise engaged at any such time;
(f) the address of the registered or principal office of any such company;
(g) any working address of the accused in his capacity as a person engaged by any such company;

and here 'engaged' means engaged under a contract of service or a contract for services.

(10) If a report is published or included in a relevant programme in contravention of this paragraph, the following persons, that is to say—
(a) in the case of a publication of a written report as part of a newspaper or periodical, any proprietor, editor or publisher of the newspaper or periodical;
(b) in the case of a publication of a written report otherwise than as part of a newspaper or periodical, the person who publishes it;
(c) in the case of the inclusion of a report in a relevant programme, any body corporate which is engaged in providing the service in which the programme is included and any person having functions in relation to the programme corresponding to those of the editor of a newspaper;

shall be liable on summary conviction to a fine not exceeding level 5 on the standard scale.

(11) Proceedings for an offence under this paragraph shall not, in England and Wales, be instituted otherwise than by or with the consent of the Attorney General.

(11A) Proceedings for an offence under this paragraph shall not, in Northern Ireland, be instituted otherwise than by or with the consent of the Attorney General for Northern Ireland.

(12) Sub-paragraph (1) above shall be in addition to, and not in derogation from, the provisions of any other enactment with respect to the publication of reports of court proceedings.

(13) In this paragraph—
'publish', in relation to a report, means publish the report, either by itself or as part of a newspaper or periodical, for distribution to the public;
'relevant programme' means a programme included in a programme service (within the meaning of the Broadcasting Act 1990);
'relevant time' means a time when events giving rise to the charges to which the proceedings relate occurred.

Power of justice to take depositions etc.

4.—(1) Sub-paragraph (2) below applies where a justice of the peace for any commission area is satisfied that—
(a) any person in England and Wales ('the witness') is likely to be able to make on behalf of the prosecutor a written statement containing material evidence, or produce on behalf of the prosecutor a document or other exhibit likely to be material evidence, for the purposes of proceedings for an offence for which a person has been sent for trial under section 51 or 51A of this Act by a magistrates' court for that area; and
(b) it is in the interests of justice to issue a summons under this paragraph to secure the attendance of the witness to have his evidence taken as a deposition or to produce the document or other exhibit.

(2) In such a case the justice shall issue a summons directed to the witness requiring him to attend before a justice at the time and place appointed in the summons, and to have his evidence taken as a deposition or to produce the document or other exhibit.

(3) If a justice of the peace is satisfied by evidence on oath of the matters mentioned in sub-paragraph (1) above, and also that it is probable that a summons under sub-paragraph (2)

above would not procure the result required by it, the justice may instead of issuing a summons issue a warrant to arrest the witness and to bring him before a justice at the time and place specified in the warrant.

(4) A summons may also be issued under sub-paragraph (2) above if the justice is satisfied that the witness is outside the British Islands, but no warrant may be issued under sub-paragraph (3) above unless the justice is satisfied by evidence on oath that the witness is in England and Wales.

(5) If—
- (a) the witness fails to attend before a justice in answer to a summons under this paragraph;
- (b) the justice is satisfied by evidence on oath that the witness is likely to be able to make a statement or produce a document or other exhibit as mentioned in sub-paragraph (1)(a) above;
- (c) it is proved on oath, or in such other manner as may be prescribed, that he has been duly served with the summons and that a reasonable sum has been paid or tendered to him for costs and expenses; and
- (d) it appears to the justice that there is no just excuse for the failure,

the justice may issue a warrant to arrest the witness and to bring him before a justice at the time and place specified in the warrant.

(6) Where—
- (a) a summons is issued under sub-paragraph (2) above or a warrant is issued under sub-paragraph (3) or (5) above; and
- (b) the summons or warrant is issued with a view to securing that the witness has his evidence taken as a deposition,

the time appointed in the summons or specified in the warrant shall be such as to enable the evidence to be taken as a deposition before the relevant date.

(7) If any person attending or brought before a justice in pursuance of this paragraph refuses without just excuse to have his evidence taken as a deposition, or to produce the document or other exhibit, the justice may do one or both of the following—
- (a) commit him to custody until the expiration of such period not exceeding one month as may be specified in the summons or warrant or until he sooner has his evidence taken as a deposition or produces the document or other exhibit;
- (b) impose on him a fine not exceeding £2,500.

(8) A fine imposed under sub-paragraph (7) above shall be deemed, for the purposes of any enactment, to be a sum adjudged to be paid by a conviction.

(9) If in pursuance of this paragraph a person has his evidence taken as a deposition, the designated officer for the justice concerned shall as soon as is reasonably practicable send a copy of the deposition to the prosecutor and the Crown Court.

(10) If in pursuance of this paragraph a person produces an exhibit which is a document, the designated officer for the justice concerned shall as soon as is reasonably practicable send a copy of the document to the prosecutor and the Crown Court.

(11) If in pursuance of this paragraph a person produces an exhibit which is not a document, the designated officer for the justice concerned shall as soon as is reasonably practicable inform the prosecutor and the Crown Court of that fact and of the nature of the exhibit.

(12) In this paragraph—
'prescribed' means prescribed by Criminal Procedure Rules;
'the relevant date' means the expiry of the period referred to in paragraph 1(1) above.

Use of depositions as evidence

5.—(1) Subject to sub-paragraph (3) below, sub-paragraph (2) below applies where in pursuance of paragraph 4 above a person has his evidence taken as a deposition.

(2) Where this sub-paragraph applies the deposition may without further proof be read as evidence on the trial of the accused, whether for an offence for which he was sent for trial under section 51 or 51A of this Act or for any other offence arising out of the same transaction or set of circumstances.

(3) Sub-paragraph (2) above does not apply if—
- (a) it is proved that the deposition was not signed by the justice by whom it purports to have been signed;
- (b) the court of trial at its discretion orders that sub-paragraph (2) above shall not apply; or
- (c) a party to the proceedings objects to sub-paragraph (2) above applying.

...

Power of Crown Court to deal with summary offence

6.—(1) This paragraph applies where a magistrates' court has sent a person for trial under section 51 or 51A of this Act for offences which include a summary offence.

(2) If the person is convicted on the indictment, the Crown Court shall consider whether the summary offence is related to the indictable offence for which he was sent for trial or, as the case may be, any of the indictable offences for which he was so sent.

(3) If it considers that the summary offence is so related, the court shall state to the person the substance of the offence and ask him whether he pleads guilty or not guilty.

(4) If the person pleads guilty, the Crown Court shall convict him, but may deal with him in respect of the summary offence only in a manner in which a magistrates' court could have dealt with him.

(5) If he does not plead guilty, the powers of the Crown Court shall cease in respect of the summary offence except as provided by sub-paragraph (6) below.

(6) If the prosecution inform the court that they would not desire to submit evidence on the charge relating to the summary offence, the court shall dismiss it.

(7) The Crown Court shall inform the designated officer for the magistrates' court of the outcome of any proceedings under this paragraph.

(8) If the summary offence is one to which section 40 of the Criminal Justice Act 1988 applies, the Crown Court may exercise in relation to the offence the power conferred by that section; but where the person is tried on indictment for such an offence, the functions of the Crown Court under this paragraph in relation to the offence shall cease.

(9) Where the Court of Appeal allows an appeal against conviction of an indictable offence which is related to a summary offence of which the appellant was convicted under this paragraph—

(a) it shall set aside his conviction of the summary offence and give the clerk of the magistrates' court notice that it has done so; and

(b) it may direct that no further proceedings in relation to the offence are to be undertaken;

and the proceedings before the Crown Court in relation to the offence shall thereafter be disregarded for all purposes.

(10) A notice under sub-paragraph (9) above shall include particulars of any direction given under paragraph (b) of that sub-paragraph in relation to the offence.

(11) . . .

(12) An offence is related to another offence for the purposes of this paragraph if it arises out of circumstances which are the same as or connected with those giving rise to the other offence.

Procedure where no indictable-only offence remains

7.—(1) Subject to paragraph 13 below, this paragraph applies where—

(a) a person has been sent for trial under section 51 or 51A of this Act but has not been arraigned; and

(b) the person is charged on an indictment which (following amendment of the indictment, or as a result of an application under paragraph 2 above, or for any other reason) includes no main offence.

(2) Everything that the Crown Court is required to do under the following provisions of this paragraph must be done with the accused present in court.

(3) The court shall cause to be read to the accused each remaining count of the indictment that charges an offence triable either way.

(4) The court shall then explain to the accused in ordinary language that, in relation to each of those offences, he may indicate whether (if it were to proceed to trial) he would plead guilty or not guilty, and that if he indicates that he would plead guilty the court must proceed as mentioned in sub-paragraph (6) below.

(5) The court shall then ask the accused whether (if the offence in question were to proceed to trial) he would plead guilty or not guilty.

(6) If the accused indicates that he would plead guilty the court shall proceed as if he had been arraigned on the count in question and had pleaded guilty.

(7) If the accused indicates that he would plead not guilty, or fails to indicate how he would plead, the court shall decide whether the offence is more suitable for summary trial or for trial on indictment.

(8) Subject to sub-paragraph (6) above, the following shall not for any purpose be taken to constitute the taking of a plea—
(a) asking the accused under this paragraph whether (if the offence were to proceed to trial) he would plead guilty or not guilty;
(b) an indication by the accused under this paragraph of how he would plead.
(9) In this paragraph, a 'main offence' is—
(a) an offence for which the person has been sent to the Crown Court for trial under section 51(1) of this Act; or
(b) an offence—
(i) for which the person has been sent to the Crown Court for trial under subsection (5) of section 51 or subsection (6) of section 51A of this Act ('the applicable subsection'); and
(ii) in respect of which the conditions for sending him to the Crown Court for trial under the applicable subsection (as set out in paragraphs (a) to (c) of section 51(5) or paragraphs (a) and (b) of section 51A(6)) continue to be satisfied.

8.—(1) Subject to paragraph 13 below, this paragraph applies in a case where—
(a) a person has been sent for trial under section 51 or 51A of this Act but has not been arraigned;
(b) he is charged on an indictment which (following amendment of the indictment, or as a result of an application under paragraph 2 above, or for any other reason) includes no main offence (within the meaning of paragraph 7 above);
(c) he is represented by a legal representative;
(d) the Crown Court considers that by reason of his disorderly conduct before the court it is not practicable for proceedings under paragraph 7 above to be conducted in his presence; and
(e) the court considers that it should proceed in his absence.
(2) In such a case—
(a) the court shall cause to be read to the representative each remaining count of the indictment that charges an offence triable either way;
(b) the court shall ask the representative whether (if the offence in question were to proceed to trial) the accused would plead guilty or not guilty;
(c) if the representative indicates that the accused would plead guilty the court shall proceed as if the accused had been arraigned on the count in question and had pleaded guilty;
(d) if the representative indicates that the accused would plead not guilty, or fails to indicate how the accused would plead, the court shall decide whether the offence is more suitable for summary trial or for trial on indictment.
(3) Subject to sub-paragraph (2)(c) above, the following shall not for any purpose be taken to constitute the taking of a plea—
(a) asking the representative under this section whether (if the offence were to proceed to trial) the accused would plead guilty or not guilty;
(b) an indication by the representative under this paragraph of how the accused would plead.

9.—(1) This paragraph applies where the Crown Court is required by paragraph 7(7) or 8(2)(d) above to decide the question whether an offence is more suitable for summary trial or for trial on indictment.
(2) Before deciding the question, the court—
(a) shall give the prosecution an opportunity to inform the court of the accused's previous convictions (if any); and
(b) shall give the prosecution and the accused an opportunity to make representations as to whether summary trial or trial on indictment would be more suitable.
(3) In deciding the question, the court shall consider—
(a) whether the sentence which a magistrates' court would have power to impose for the offence would be adequate; and
(b) any representations made by the prosecution or the accused under sub-paragraph (2)(b) above,

and shall have regard to any allocation guidelines (or revised allocation guidelines) issued as definitive guidelines under section 170 of the Criminal Justice Act 2003.
(4) Where—
(a) the accused is charged on the same occasion with two or more offences; and

(b) it appears to the court that they constitute or form part of a series of two or more offences of the same or a similar character;

sub-paragraph (3)(a) above shall have effect as if references to the sentence which a magistrates' court would have power to impose for the offence were a reference to the maximum aggregate sentence which a magistrates' court would have power to impose for all of the offences taken together.

(5) In this paragraph any reference to a previous conviction is a reference to—

(a) a previous conviction by a court in the United Kingdom, or

(b) a previous finding of guilt in—

(i) any proceedings under the Army Act 1955, the Air Force Act 1955 or the Naval Discipline Act 1957 (whether before a court-martial or any other court or person authorised under any of those Acts to award a punishment in respect of any offence), or

(ii) any proceedings before a Standing Civilian Court.

10.—(1) This paragraph applies (unless excluded by paragraph 15 below) where the Crown Court considers that an offence is more suitable for summary trial.

(2) The court shall explain to the accused in ordinary language—

(a) that it appears to the court more suitable for him to be tried summarily for the offence;

(b) that he can either consent to be so tried or, if he wishes, be tried on indictment; and

(c) in the case of a specified offence (within the meaning of section 224 of the Criminal Justice Act 2003), that if he is tried summarily and is convicted by the court, he may be committed for sentence to the Crown Court under section 3A of the Powers of Criminal Courts (Sentencing) Act 2000 if the committing court is of such opinion as is mentioned in subsection (2) of that section.

(3) After explaining to the accused as provided by sub-paragraph (2) above the court shall ask him whether he wishes to be tried summarily or on indictment, and—

(a) if he indicates that he wishes to be tried summarily, shall remit him for trial to a magistrates' court acting for the place where he was sent to the Crown Court for trial;

(b) if he does not give such an indication, shall retain its functions in relation to the offence and proceed accordingly.

11.—If the Crown Court considers that an offence is more suitable for trial on indictment, the court—

(a) shall tell the accused that it has decided that it is more suitable for him to be tried for the offence on indictment; and

(b) shall retain its functions in relation to the offence and proceed accordingly.

. . .

13.—(1) This paragraph applies, in place of paragraphs 7 to 12 above, in the case of a child or young person who—

(a) has been sent for trial under section 51 or 51A of this Act but has not been arraigned; and

(b) is charged on an indictment which (following amendment of the indictment, or as a result of an application under paragraph 2 above, or for any other reason) includes no main offence.

(2) The Crown Court shall remit the child or young person for trial to a magistrates' court acting for the place where he was sent to the Crown Court for trial.

(3) In this paragraph, a 'main offence' is—

(a) an offence for which the child or young person has been sent to the Crown Court for trial under section 51A(2) of this Act; or

(b) an offence—

(i) for which the child or young person has been sent to the Crown Court for trial under subsection (7) of section 51 of this Act; and

(ii) in respect of which the conditions for sending him to the Crown Court for trial under that subsection (as set out in paragraphs (a) and (b) of that subsection) continue to be satisfied.

Procedure for determining whether offences of criminal damage etc. are summary offences

14.—(1) This paragraph applies where the Crown Court has to determine, for the purposes of this Schedule, whether an offence which is listed in the first column of Schedule 2 to the 1980 Act (offences for which the value involved is relevant to the mode of trial) is a summary offence.

(2) The court shall have regard to any representations made by the prosecutor or the accused.
(3) If it appears clear to the court that the value involved does not exceed the relevant sum, it shall treat the offence as a summary offence.
(4) If it appears clear to the court that the value involved exceeds the relevant sum, it shall treat the offence as an indictable offence.
(5) If it appears to the court for any reason not clear whether the value involved does or does not exceed the relevant sum, the court shall ask the accused whether he wishes the offence to be treated as a summary offence.
(6) Where sub-paragraph (5) above applies—
  (a) if the accused indicates that he wishes the offence to be treated as a summary offence, the court shall so treat it;
  (b) if the accused does not give such an indication, the court shall treat the offence as an indictable offence.
(7) In this paragraph 'the value involved' and 'the relevant sum' have the same meanings as in section 22 of the 1980 Act (certain offences triable either way to be tried summarily if value involved is small).

Power of Crown Court, with consent of legally-represented accused, to proceed in his absence

15.—(1) The Crown Court may proceed in the absence of the accused in accordance with such of the provisions of paragraphs 9 to 14 above as are applicable in the circumstances if—
  (a) the accused is represented by a legal representative who signifies to the court the accused's consent to the proceedings in question being conducted in his absence; and
  (b) the court is satisfied that there is good reason for proceeding in the absence of the accused.
(2) Sub-paragraph (1) above is subject to the following provisions of this paragraph which apply where the court exercises the power conferred by that sub-paragraph.
(3) If, where the court has decided as required by paragraph 7(7) or 8(2)(d) above, it appears to the court that an offence is more suitable for summary trial, paragraph 10 above shall not apply and—
  (a) if the legal representative indicates that the accused wishes to be tried summarily, the court shall remit the accused for trial to a magistrates' court acting for the place where he was sent to the Crown Court for trial;
  (b) if the legal representative does not give such an indication, the court shall retain its functions and proceed accordingly.
(4) If, where the court has decided as required by paragraph 7(7) or 8(2)(d) above, it appears to the court that an offence is more suitable for trial on indictment, paragraph 11 above shall apply with the omission of paragraph (a).
(5) Where paragraph 14 above applies and it appears to the court for any reason not clear whether the value involved does or does not exceed the relevant sum, sub-paragraphs (5) and (6) of that paragraph shall not apply and—
  (a) the court shall ask the legal representative whether the accused wishes the offence to be treated as a summary offence;
  (b) if the legal representative indicates that the accused wishes the offence to be treated as a summary offence, the court shall so treat it;
  (c) if the legal representative does not give such an indication, the court shall treat the offence as an indictable offence.

COMMITTAL PROCEEDINGS FOR EITHER-WAY OFFENCES

D10.34 Until the coming into force of the CJA 2003, sch. 3 (which is not yet in force), either-way offences are transferred from the magistrates' court to the Crown Court by means of committal proceedings pursuant to the MCA 1980, s. 6. Such committal proceedings will be necessary only if the magistrates declined jurisdiction at the mode of trial hearing (usually on the basis that the case is beyond their sentencing powers) or the accused was offered summary trial but decided to elect Crown Court trial.

Committal proceedings under the MCA 1980, s. 6, can take two forms — with consideration of the evidence (comparatively rare) and without consideration of the evidence (much more common). A single lay justice may conduct committal proceedings (MCA 1980, s. 4(1)).

The relevant statutory provisions that are to be superseded on the implementation of the CJA 2003, sch. 3, are set out at **D10.43** *et seq.*

Adjournments

The court may adjourn before or at any time during committal proceedings (MCA 1980, s. 5(1)). If it does so, it must fix the time and place at which the hearing is to be resumed and remand the accused (either on bail or in custody) to appear or be brought before the court on that date (s. 5(2)). It is submitted that s. 5 must be read in conjunction with s. 18(4) (which empowers the court to adjourn proceedings to determine the mode of trial and, in certain circumstances, permits adjournments without an associated remand), so that, if the accused is charged with an either-way offence, the court's power to adjourn is to be found in the latter subsection until the moment when it is determined that the offence shall be tried on indictment. If a decision in favour of trial on indictment is taken in the absence of the accused under the provisions of s. 23 of the 1980 Act and the court decides to adjourn before embarking on the committal proceedings, it may adjourn without remanding the accused (s. 23(4)(b) and (5)). **D10.35**

Presence of the Accused

Evidence tendered at committal proceedings must be tendered in the presence of the accused (MCA 1980, s. 4(3)). This is subject to the qualification that the examining justices may allow evidence to be tendered in his absence if either they consider that, by reason of his disorderly conduct before them, it is not practicable for the evidence to be tendered in his presence, or he cannot be present for health reasons but he is represented by counsel or solicitor and has consented to proceedings *in absentia* (s. 4(4)). Where the necessary conditions are fulfilled, the accused can be committed in his absence, whether the committal is under s. 6(1) or s. 6(2) (*Liverpool City Magistrates' Court, ex parte Quantrell* [1999] 2 Cr App R 24). If the accused does not appear for committal proceedings, the court may issue a warrant for his arrest (see MCA 1980, s. 1(6), and Bail Act 1976, s. 7(1), which are respectively applicable where the accused fails to answer to a summons or fails to answer to his bail). **D10.36**

Where the accused is charged with more than one offence, or there are two or more defendants charged with separate offences, the court can deal with all the offences or defendants if those offences or defendants could properly be joined in the same indictment (see *Camberwell Green Stipendiary Magistrate, ex parte Christie* [1978] QB 602).

Committals Without Consideration of the Evidence

Under the MCA 1980, s. 6(2), committal without consideration of the evidence may take place if: **D10.37**

(a) all the evidence before the court consists of written statements tendered under s. 5A(3) of the 1980 Act;
(b) the accused has a solicitor acting for him in the case, though the solicitor need not necessarily be present in court; and
(c) counsel or solicitor for the accused has not requested the justices to consider a submission that the statements disclose insufficient evidence to put the accused on trial by jury for the offence into which the court is inquiring.

If there are two or more accused, each must have a solicitor acting for him and a request by counsel or solicitor for any of them to make a submission of insufficient evidence will preclude a committal under s. 6(2).

The greater convenience and speed of the procedure make it appropriate for the defence to agree to use it unless there is a specific reason for having the evidence considered. The obvious case for a committal with consideration of the evidence (usually referred to as an 'old style' committal) is when the defence consider that there is a realistic chance of a submission of no case succeeding.

The procedure to be followed for a committal without consideration of the evidence is set out in the CrimPR, r. 10.2. At a committal without consideration of the evidence, the court does not read or have read to it the written evidence tendered under the MCA 1980, s. 5A(2). The documents are simply handed in by the prosecution (together with a copy bundle for transmission to the Crown Court). It may, however, be necessary for the magistrates subsequently to be referred to passages in the statements, e.g., to assist in deciding an application for bail or legal aid. Even though it is not strictly necessary for a solicitor or barrister to be present in court for the accused when a s. 6(2) committal takes place, defence solicitors usually arrange for representation since ancillary questions such as bail, witness orders or legal aid may require legal expertise even if the committal itself is a pure formality. The court's satisfying itself as to the matters mentioned in (b) above usually involves nothing more than the clerk asking the defence advocate whether he agrees to a s. 6(2) committal.

Committals With Consideration of the Evidence

D10.38 The procedure for committals with consideration of the evidence is to be found chiefly in the CrimPR, r. 10.3. These provisions apply where the accused does not have a solicitor acting for him in the case or where the accused's solicitor or barrister has asked the court to consider a submission that there is no case to answer.

The prosecutor is entitled to make an opening speech before tendering the evidence (all of which is written). The evidence may be read through or, with the leave of the court, summarised. The magistrates' court may view any original exhibits and may retain them. No witnesses are called and no evidence can be tendered by the defence. The accused may then make a submission of no case to answer and, if he does so or if the court is minded not to commit for trial, the prosecutor is entitled to respond. The court then reaches its decision as to whether to commit the accused for trial in the Crown Court, on the basis of the test laid down in the MCA 1980, s. 6(1).

Section 5A of the MCA 1980 stipulates that, for evidence to be admissible at committal:

(a) it must be tendered by the prosecutor; and
(b) it must fall within one of the categories of evidence defined in ss. 5B, 5C, 5D and 5E of the Act.

D10.39 **Forms of Evidence** In most cases, the evidence will be in the form of witness statements under s. 5B. Any such statement may be admitted if it is adduced by the prosecutor, has been served on each of the other parties to the committal and complies with the other formalities set out in s. 5B(2) and (3).

Although the usual route for a statement to be admitted in committal proceedings is by s. 5B, there are other possibilities. Section 5C allows for evidence by way of deposition taken in advance of the committal where a prosecution witness is reluctant to provide a written statement. Such a deposition may be taken under the MCA 1980, s. 97A, which enables a magistrate, prior to the sending of a case to the Crown Court, to issue a summons to a potential prosecution witness. The procedure is the same as that laid down in the CDA 1998, sch. 3, para. 4 (see **D10.30**).

A further route of admissibility is provided by s. 5D, which covers statements made by persons now dead, unfit to attend trial, abroad and not reasonably expected to attend or who will be kept away from a trial by fear or threat to their safety, as well as evidence contained in business or trade documents. Documents that 'prove themselves' or are made admissible by other legislation, such as certificates of conviction or DVLA certificates in road traffic proceedings, are made admissible in committal proceedings by s. 5E. Section 5F lays down that any of the documents admissible by virtue of ss. 5B to 5E may be proved by the original or a copy (even if the original is still in existence).

Admissibility Committal proceedings are generally an inappropriate forum in which to raise objections to the admissibility of prosecution evidence. This is because the standard of proof that the prosecution are (at that stage) required to satisfy is a very low one (see **D10.30**), and because, assuming there is a committal for trial, the admissibility of evidence at the trial on indictment is a matter entirely for the Crown Court judge. Furthermore, by virtue of the PACE 1984, ss. 76(9) and 78(3), examining justices are not permitted to consider whether confessions are inadmissible under s. 76 or should be excluded under s. 78 of that Act. **D10.40**

The correct approach appears to be that examining justices should exclude and ignore proposed evidence which no reasonable tribunal could hold to be admissible, but, where the admissibility of evidence is doubtful and especially where its exclusion depends on the exercise of discretion by the court, the evidence should be received by the justices and any challenge to it reserved for the trial (see, e.g., *Highbury Magistrates' Court, ex parte Boyce* (1984) 79 Cr App R 132, where one ground on which the Divisional Court refused judicial review of B's committal for trial was that the examining justices had correctly ruled that they had no discretion to refuse to allow a 'dock identification' of B — the evidence was legally admissible, and the discretion to exclude on the basis that its prejudicial effect exceeded its probative value was to be exercised by the Crown Court, not the justices).

The Decision to Commit The magistrates must commit for trial if they are of the opinion that there is sufficient evidence to put the accused on trial for any indictable offence (whether for the offence for which the prosecution seek committal for trial or some other indictable offence); and they must discharge the accused if they are not of that opinion. In practice, the standard of proof the prosecution are required to satisfy at committal proceedings is very low. It is commonly expressed as establishing a 'prima facie case' or a 'case to answer'. It must also be borne in mind that in committal proceedings under the MCA 1980, s. 6(1), there is no oral testimony: the prosecution simply tender written evidence, and so there is no opportunity for the defence to cross-examine the prosecution witnesses at the committal proceedings. If the written evidence is hopelessly contradictory or makes assertions that are inherently unlikely, this may enable the justices to hold that there is no case to answer. In general, however, it is likely that the magistrates will be concerned only with evidential sufficiency and will leave questions of credibility to the Crown Court, where the jury will have a chance to assess the witnesses at first hand. **D10.41**

Where the accused is charged with several offences, the justices may commit on one or more but not necessarily on all the charges. They are also entitled to commit for an offence that has not been charged by the prosecutor. If examining justices are considering committing for an offence other than that charged by the prosecutor, they should give the defence the opportunity of addressing the court upon that possibility, as well as upon the original charge, before deciding on the submissions as a whole (*Gloucester Magistrates' Court, ex parte Chung* (1989) 153 JP 75).

If there is insufficient evidence to put the accused on trial by jury for any indictable offence, then the examining justices must discharge him. However, discharge at committal proceedings does not amount to an acquittal and so cannot found a plea of *autrefois acquit* to bar proceedings should the accused be prosecuted again on the same charges (*Manchester City Stipendiary Magistrate, ex parte Snelson* [1977] 1 WLR 911). However, the Divisional Court may grant an order of prohibition to prevent successive benches of examining justices repeatedly holding committal proceedings in respect of the same charge if that would be vexatious or an abuse of the process of the court (per Lord Widgery CJ in *Ex parte Snelson* at p. 913G). In fact, the almost invariable practice, where justices refuse to commit after consideration of the evidence and the prosecution are unwilling to accept their decision, is to apply to a High Court judge for a voluntary bill of indictment (see **D10.48**).

D10.42 **Challenging the Decision to Commit** There is very limited scope for the defendant to challenge committal for trial. A decision to commit for trial cannot be appealed to the High Court by way of case stated, since there has not been a 'final determination' (see *Cragg v Lewes District Council* [1986] Crim LR 800); judicial review is available, but only in the case of a really substantial error leading to demonstrable injustice such that the Divisional Court should contemplate granting the remedy (*Neill v North Antrim Magistrates' Court* [1992] 1 WLR 1221). In *Bedwellty Justices, ex parte Williams* [1997] AC 225, the House of Lords held that a committal should be quashed if there was no admissible evidence of the accused's guilt (in that case, the only evidence against the accused consisted of out-of-court statements by co-defendants that were inadmissible against the appellant); their lordships went on to hold that where there was some admissible evidence against the accused, but it was insufficient to amount to a prima facie case against her, the remedy of judicial review is available, but the Divisional Court should be slow to interfere with that decision. Presumably, a decision based on admissible evidence that there is a prima facie case against the accused would only be quashed if no reasonable bench of magistrates could have come to the view that there was sufficient evidence (i.e. the decision to commit the accused for trial was perverse). These cases must be read subject to the statutory prohibition upon consideration by the examining justices of admissibility under the PACE 1984, ss. 76 and 78.

Statutory Materials

[These provisions are due to be superseded by the CJA 2003, sch. 3]

D10.43 **Crime and Disorder Act 1998, s. 51 (prior to amendment by the CJA 2003)**

(1) Where an adult appears or is brought before a magistrates' court ('the court') charged with an offence triable only on indictment ('the indictable-only offence'), the court shall send him forthwith to the Crown Court for trial—
(a) for that offence, and
(b) for any either-way or summary offence with which he is charged which fulfils the requisite conditions (as set out in subsection (11) below).

(2) Where an adult who has been sent for trial under subsection (1) above subsequently appears or is brought before a magistrates' court charged with an either-way or summary offence which fulfils the requisite conditions, the court may send him forthwith to the Crown Court for trial for the either-way or summary offence.

(3) Where—
(a) the court sends an adult for trial under subsection (1) above;
(b) another adult appears or is brought before the court on the same or a subsequent occasion charged jointly with him with an either-way offence; and
(c) that offence appears to the court to be related to the indictable-only offence,
the court shall where it is the same occasion, and may where it is a subsequent occasion, send the other adult forthwith to the Crown Court for trial for the either-way offence.

(4) Where a court sends an adult for trial under subsection (3) above, it shall at the same time send him to the Crown Court for trial for any either-way or summary offence with which he is charged which fulfils the requisite conditions.

(5) Where—
(a) the court sends an adult for trial under subsection (1) or (3) above; and
(b) a child or young person appears or is brought before the court on the same or a subsequent occasion charged jointly with the adult with an indictable offence for which the adult is sent for trial,
the court shall, if it considers it necessary in the interests of justice to do so, send the child or young person forthwith to the Crown Court for trial for the indictable offence.

(6) Where a court sends a child or young person for trial under subsection (5) above, it may at the same time send him to the Crown Court for trial for any either-way or summary offence with which he is charged which fulfils the requisite conditions.

(7) The court shall specify in a notice the offence or offences for which a person is sent for trial

under this section and the place at which he is to be tried; and a copy of the notice shall be served on the accused and given to the Crown Court sitting at that place.

(8) In a case where there is more than one indictable-only offence and the court includes an either-way or a summary offence in the notice under subsection (7) above, the court shall specify in that notice the indictable-only offence to which the either-way offence or, as the case may be, the summary offence appears to the court to be related.

(9) The trial of the information charging any summary offence for which a person is sent for trial under this section shall be treated as if the court had adjourned it under section 10 of the 1980 Act and had not fixed the time and place for its resumption.

(10) In selecting the place of trial for the purpose of subsection (7) above, the court shall have regard to—

(a) the convenience of the defence, the prosecution and the witnesses;

(b) the desirability of expediting the trial; and

(c) any direction given by or on behalf of the Lord Chief Justice with the concurrence of the Lord Chancellor under section 75(1) of the Supreme Court Act 1981.

(11) An offence fulfils the requisite conditions if—

(a) it appears to the court to be related to the indictable-only offence; and

(b) in the case of a summary offence, it is punishable with imprisonment or involves obligatory or discretionary disqualification from driving.

(12) For the purposes of this section—

(a) 'adult' means a person aged 18 or over, and references to an adult include references to a corporation;

(b) 'either-way offence' means an offence which, if committed by an adult, is triable either on indictment or summarily;

(c) an either-way offence is related to an indictable-only offence if the charge for the either-way offence could be joined in the same indictment as the charge for the indictable-only offence;

(d) a summary offence is related to an indictable-only offence if it arises out of circumstances which are the same as or connected with those giving rise to the indictable-only offence.

The Magistrates' Courts Act 1980, ss. 4 to 8 D10.44

[to be repealed by the Criminal Justice Act 2003]

4.—(1) The functions of examining justices may be discharged by a single justice.

(2) Examining justices shall sit in open court except where any enactment contains an express provision to the contrary and except where it appears to them as respects the whole or any part of committal proceedings that the ends of justice would not be served by their sitting in open court.

(3) Subject to subsection (4) below, evidence tendered before examining justices shall be tendered in the presence of the accused.

(4) Examining justices may allow evidence to be tendered before them in the absence of the accused if—

(a) they consider that by reason of his disorderly conduct before them it is not practicable for the evidence to be tendered in his presence, or

(b) he cannot be present for reasons of health but is represented by a legal representative and has consented to the evidence being tendered in his absence.

5.—(1) A magistrates' court may, before beginning to inquire into an offence as examining justices, or at any time during the inquiry, adjourn the hearing, and if it does so shall remand the accused.

(2) The court shall when adjourning fix the time and place at which the hearing is to be resumed; and the time fixed shall be that at which the accused is required to appear or be brought before the court in pursuance of the remand or would be required to be brought before the court but for section 128(3A) below.

5A.—(1) Evidence falling within subsection (2) below, and only that evidence, shall be admissible by a magistrates' court inquiring into an offence as examining justices.

(2) Evidence falls within this subsection if it—

(a) is tendered by or on behalf of the prosecutor, and

(b) falls within subsection (3) below.

(3) The following evidence falls within this subsection—

(a) written statements complying with section 5B below;
(b) the documents or other exhibits (if any) referred to in such statements;
(c) depositions complying with section 5C below;
(d) the documents or other exhibits (if any) referred to in such depositions;
(e) statements complying with section 5D below;
(f) documents falling within section 5E below.

(4) In this section 'document' means anything in which information of any description is recorded.

5B.—(1) For the purposes of section 5A above a written statement complies with this section if—
(a) the conditions falling within subsection (2) below are met, and
(b) such of the conditions falling within subsection (3) below as apply are met.

(2) The conditions falling within this subsection are that—
(a) the statement purports to be signed by the person who made it;
(b) the statement contains a declaration by that person to the effect that it is true to the best of his knowledge and belief and that he made the statement knowing that, if it were tendered in evidence, he would be liable to prosecution if he wilfully stated in it anything which he knew to be false or did not believe to be true;
(c) before the statement is tendered in evidence a copy of the statement is given, by or on behalf of the prosecutor, to each of the other parties to the proceedings.

(3) The conditions falling within this subsection are that—
(a) if the statement is made by a person under 18 years old, it gives his age;
(b) if it is made by a person who cannot read it, it is read to him before he signs it and is accompanied by a declaration by the person who so read the statement to the effect that it was so read;
(c) if it refers to any other document as an exhibit, the copy given to any other party to the proceedings under subsection (2)(c) above is accompanied by a copy of that document or by such information as may be necessary to enable the party to whom it is given to inspect that document or a copy of it.

(3A) In the case of a statement which indicates in pursuance of subsection (3)(a) of this section that the person making it has not attained the age of fourteen, subsection (2)(b) of this section shall have effect as if for the words from 'made' onwards there were substituted the words 'understands the importance of telling the truth in it'.

(4) So much of any statement as is admitted in evidence by virtue of this section shall, unless the court commits the accused for trial by virtue of section 6(2) below or the court otherwise directs, be read aloud at the hearing; and where the court so directs an account shall be given orally of so much of any statement as is not read aloud.

(5) Any document or other object referred to as an exhibit and identified in a statement admitted in evidence by virtue of this section shall be treated as if it had been produced as an exhibit and identified in court by the maker of the statement.

(6) In this section 'document' means anything in which information of any description is recorded.

5C.—(1) For the purposes of section 5A above a deposition complies with this section if—
(a) a copy of it is sent to the prosecutor under section 97A(9) below,
(b) the condition falling within subsection (2) below is met, and
(c) the condition falling within subsection (3) below is met, in a case where it applies.

(2) The condition falling within this subsection is that before the magistrates' court begins to inquire into the offence concerned as examining justices a copy of the deposition is given, by or on behalf of the prosecutor, to each of the other parties to the proceedings.

(3) The condition falling within this subsection is that, if the deposition refers to any other document as an exhibit, the copy given to any other party to the proceedings under subsection (2) above is accompanied by a copy of that document or by such information as may be necessary to enable the party to whom it is given to inspect that document or a copy of it.

(4) So much of any deposition as is admitted in evidence by virtue of this section shall, unless the court commits the accused for trial by virtue of section 6(2) below or the court otherwise directs, be read aloud at the hearing; and where the court so directs an account shall be given orally of so much of any deposition as is not read aloud.

(5) Any document or other object referred to as an exhibit and identified in a deposition

admitted in evidence by virtue of this section shall be treated as if it had been produced as an exhibit and identified in court by the person whose evidence is taken as the deposition.

(6) In this section 'document' means anything in which information of any description is recorded.

5D.—(1) For the purposes of section 5A above a statement complies with this section if the conditions falling within subsections (2) to (4) below are met.

(2) The condition falling within this subsection is that, before the committal proceedings begin, the prosecutor notifies the magistrates' court and each of the other parties to the proceedings that he believes—

(a) that the statement might by virtue of section 23 or 24 of the Criminal Justice Act 1988 (statements in certain documents) be admissible as evidence if the case came to trial, and

(b) that the statement would not be admissible as evidence otherwise than by virtue of section 23 or 24 of that Act if the case came to trial.

(3) The condition falling within this subsection is that—

(a) the prosecutor's belief is based on information available to him at the time he makes the notification,

(b) he has reasonable grounds for his belief, and

(c) he gives the reasons for his belief when he makes the notification.

(4) The condition falling within this subsection is that when the court or a party is notified as mentioned in subsection (2) above a copy of the statement is given, by or on behalf of the prosecutor, to the court or the party concerned.

(5) So much of any statement as is in writing and is admitted in evidence by virtue of this section shall, unless the court commits the accused for trial by virtue of section 6(2) below or the court otherwise directs, be read aloud at the hearing; and where the court so directs an account shall be given orally of so much of any statement as is not read aloud.

[See note below as to the effect of s. 5D.]

5E.—(1) The following documents fall within this section—

(a) any document which by virtue of any enactment is evidence in proceedings before a magistrates' court inquiring into an offence as examining justices;

(b) any document which by virtue of any enactment is admissible, or may be used, or is to be admitted or received, in or as evidence in such proceedings;

(c) any document which by virtue of any enactment may be considered in such proceedings;

(d) any document whose production constitutes proof in such proceedings by virtue of any enactment;

(e) any document by the production of which evidence may be given in such proceedings by virtue of any enactment.

(2) In subsection (1) above—

(a) references to evidence include references to prima facie evidence;

(b) references to any enactment include references to any provision of this Act.

(3) So much of any document as is admitted in evidence by virtue of this section shall, unless the court commits the accused for trial by virtue of section 6(2) below or the court otherwise directs, be read aloud at the hearing; and where the court so directs an account shall be given orally of so much of any document as is not read aloud.

(4) In this section 'document' means anything in which information of any description is recorded.

5F.—(1) Where a statement, deposition or document is admissible in evidence by virtue of section 5B, 5C, 5D or 5E above it may be proved by the production of—

(a) the statement, deposition or document, or

(b) a copy of it or the material part of it.

(2) Subsection (1)(b) above applies whether or not the statement, deposition or document is still in existence.

(3) It is immaterial for the purposes of this section how many removes there are between a copy and the original.

(4) In this section 'copy', in relation to a statement, deposition or document, means anything onto which information recorded in the statement, deposition or document has been copied, by whatever means and whether directly or indirectly.

6.—(1) A magistrates' court inquiring into an offence as examining justices shall on consideration of the evidence—

(a) commit the accused for trial if it is of opinion that there is sufficient evidence to put him on trial by jury for any indictable offence;
(b) discharge him if it is not of that opinion and he is in custody for no other cause than the offence under inquiry;

but the preceding provisions of this subsection have effect subject to the provisions of this and any other Act relating to the summary trial of indictable offences.

(2) If a magistrates' court inquiring into an offence as examining justices is satisfied that all the evidence tendered by or on behalf of the prosecutor falls within section 5A(3) above, it may commit the accused for trial for the offence without consideration of the contents of any statements, depositions or other documents, and without consideration of any exhibits which are not documents, unless—
(a) the accused or one of the accused has no legal representative acting for him in the case, or
(b) a legal representative for the accused or one of the accused, as the case may be, has requested the court to consider a submission that there is insufficient evidence to put that accused on trial by jury for the offence;

and subsection (1) above shall not apply to a committal for trial under this subsection.

(3) Subject to section 4 of the Bail Act 1976 and section 41 below, the court may commit a person for trial—
(a) in custody, that is to say, by committing him to custody there to be safely kept until delivered in due course of law, or
(b) on bail in accordance with the Bail Act 1976, that is to say, by directing him to appear before the Crown Court for trial;

and where his release on bail is conditional on his providing one or more surety or sureties and, in accordance with section 8(3) of the Bail Act 1976, the court fixes the amount in which the surety is to be bound with a view to his entering into his recognizance subsequently in accordance with subsections (4) and (5) or (6) of that section the court shall in the meantime commit the accused to custody in accordance with paragraph (a) of this subsection.

(4) Where the court has committed a person to custody in accordance with paragraph (a) of subsection (3) above, then, if that person is in custody for no other cause, the court may, at any time before his first appearance before the Crown Court, grant him bail in accordance with the Bail Act 1976 subject to a duty to appear before the Crown Court for trial.

(5) Where a magistrates' court acting as examining justices commits any person for trial or determines to discharge him, the designated officer for the court shall, on the day on which the committal proceedings are concluded or the next day, cause to be displayed in a part of the court house to which the public have access a notice—
(a) in either case giving that person's name, address, and age (if known);
(b) in a case where the court so commits him, stating the charge or charges on which he is committed and the court to which he is committed;
(c) in a case where the court determines to discharge him, describing the offence charged and stating that it has so determined;

but this subsection shall have effect subject to section 4 of the Sexual Offences (Amendment) Act 1976 (anonymity of complainant in rape etc. cases).

(6) A notice displayed in pursuance of subsection (5) above shall not contain the name or address of any person under the age of 18 years unless the justices in question have stated that in their opinion he would be mentioned in the notice apart from the preceding provisions of this subsection and should be mentioned in it for the purpose of avoiding injustice to him.

7.—A magistrates' court committing a person for trial shall specify the place at which he is to be tried, and in selecting that place shall have regard to—
(a) the convenience of the defence, the prosecution and the witnesses,
(b) the expediting of the trial, and
(c) any direction given by or on behalf of the Lord Chief Justice with the concurrence of the Lord Chancellor under section 4(5) of the Courts Act 1971.

8.—(1) Except as provided by subsections (2), (3) and (8) below, it shall not be lawful to publish in Great Britain a written report, or to include in a relevant programme for reception in Great Britain a report, of any committal proceedings in England and Wales containing any matter other than that permitted by subsection (4) below.

(2) Subject to subsection (2A) below a magistrates' court shall, on an application for the purpose

made with reference to any committal proceedings by the accused or one of the accused, as the case may be, order that subsection (1) above shall not apply to reports of those proceedings.

(2A) Where in the case of two or more accused one of them objects to the making of an order under subsection (2) above, the court shall make the order if, and only if, it is satisfied, after hearing the representations of the accused, that it is in the interests of justice to do so.

(2B) An order under subsection (2) above shall not apply to reports of proceedings under subsection (2A) above, but any decision of the court to make or not to make such an order may be contained in reports published or included in a relevant programme before the time authorised by subsection (3) below.

(3) It shall not be unlawful under this section to publish or include in a relevant programme a report of committal proceedings containing any matter other than that permitted by subsection (4) below—
 (a) where the magistrates' court determines not to commit the accused, or determines to commit none of the accused, for trial, after it so determines;
 (b) where the court commits the accused or any of the accused for trial, after the conclusion of his trial or, as the case may be, the trial of the last to be tried;

and where at any time during the inquiry the court proceeds to try summarily the case of one or more of the accused under section 25(3) or (7) below, while committing the other accused or one or more of the other accused for trial, it shall not be unlawful under this section to publish or include in a relevant programme as part of a report of the summary trial, after the court determines to proceed as aforesaid, a report of so much of the committal proceedings containing any such matter as takes place before the determination.

(4) The following matters may be contained in a report of committal proceedings published or included in a relevant programme without an order under subsection (2) above before the time authorised by subsection (3) above, that is to say—
 (a) the identity of the court and the names of the examining justices;
 (b) the names, addresses and occupations of the parties and witnesses and the ages of the accused and witnesses;
 (c) the offence or offences, or a summary of them, with which the accused is or are charged;
 (d) the names of the legal representatives engaged in the proceedings;
 (e) any decision of the court to commit the accused or any of the accused for trial, and any decision of the court on the disposal of the case of any accused not committed;
 (f) where the court commits the accused or any of the accused for trial, the charge or charges, or a summary of them, on which he is committed and the court to which he is committed;
 (g) where the committal proceedings are adjourned, the date and place to which they are adjourned;
 (h) any arrangements as to bail on committal or adjournment;
 (i) whether a right to representation funded by the Legal Services Commission as part of the Criminal Defence Service was granted to the accused or any of the accused.

(5) If a report is published or included in a relevant programme in contravention of this section, the following persons, that is to say—
 (a) in the case of a publication of a written report as part of a newspaper or periodical, any proprietor, editor or publisher of the newspaper or periodical;
 (b) in the case of a publication of a written report otherwise than as part of a newspaper or periodical, the person who publishes it;
 (c) in the case of the inclusion of a report in a relevant programme, any body corporate which provides the service in which the programme is included and any person having functions in relation to the programme corresponding to those of an editor of a newspaper,

shall be liable on summary conviction to a fine not exceeding level 5 on the standard scale.

(6) Proceedings for an offence under this section shall not, in England and Wales, be instituted otherwise than by or with the consent of the Attorney-General.

(7) Subsection (1) above shall be in addition to, and not in derogation from, the provisions of any other enactment with respect to the publication of reports and proceedings of magistrates' and other courts.

(8) For the purposes of this section committal proceedings shall, in relation to an information

charging an indictable offence, be deemed to include any proceedings in the magistrates' court before the court proceeds to inquire into the information as examining justices; but where a magistrates' court which has begun to try an information summarily discontinues the summary trial in pursuance of section 25(2) or (6) below and proceeds to inquire into the information as examining justices, that circumstance shall not make it unlawful under this section for a report of any proceedings on the information which was published or included in a relevant programme before the court determined to proceed as aforesaid to have been so published or broadcast.

(9) . . .

(10) In this section—

. . .

'publish', in relation to a report, means publish the report, either by itself or as part of a newspaper or periodical, for distribution to the public.

'relevant programme' means a programme included in a programme service (within the meaning of the Broadcasting Act 1990).

Although the repeal of the MCA 1980, s. 5D, is not yet implemented, it was held in *R (CPS) v City of London Magistrates' Court* [2006] EWHC 1153 (Admin) that evidence which might formerly have been covered by that section was now covered by the hearsay provisions of the CJA 2003. The consequence is that s. 5D has now lost its potency.

D10.45 **Criminal Justice Act 1987, ss. 4 to 6**

4.—(1) If—

(a) a person has been charged with an indictable offence; and

(b) in the opinion of an authority designated by subsection (2) below or of one of such an authority's officers acting on the authority's behalf the evidence of the offence charged—

(i) would be sufficient for the person charged to be committed for trial; and

(ii) reveals a case of fraud of such seriousness or complexity that it is appropriate that the management of the case should without delay be taken over by the Crown Court; and

(c) before the magistrates' court in whose jurisdiction the offence has been charged begins to inquire into the case as examining justices the authority or one of the authority's officers acting on the authority's behalf gives the court a notice (in this Act referred to as a 'notice of transfer') certifying that opinion,

the functions of the magistrates' court shall cease in relation to the case, except as provided by section 5(3), (7A) and (8) below and by paragraph 2 of Schedule 3 to the Access to Justice Act 1999.

(2) The authorities mentioned in subsection (1) above (in this Act referred to as 'designated authorities) are—

(a) the Director of Public Prosecutions;

(b) the Director of the Serious Fraud Office;

(c) the Commissioners of Inland Revenue;

(d) the Commissioners of Customs and Excise; and

(e) the Secretary of State.

(3) A designated authority's decision to give notice of transfer shall not be subject to appeal or liable to be questioned in any court.

(4) This section and sections 5 and 6 below shall not apply in any case in which section 51 of the Crime and Disorder Act 1998 (no committal proceedings for indictable-only offences) applies.

5.—(1) A notice of transfer shall specify the proposed place of trial and in selecting that place the designated authority shall have regard to the considerations to which section 7 of the Magistrates' Courts Act 1980 requires a magistrates' court committing a person for trial to have regard when selecting the place at which he is to be tried.

(2) A notice of transfer shall specify the charge or charges to which it relates and include or be accompanied by such additional matter as regulations under subsection (9) below may require.

(3) If a magistrates' court has remanded a person to whom a notice of transfer relates in custody, it shall have power, subject to section 4 of the Bail Act 1976 and regulations under section 22 of the Prosecution of Offences Act 1985—

(a) to order that he shall be safely kept in custody until delivered in due course of law; or
(b) to release him on bail in accordance with the Bail Act 1976, that is to say, by directing him to appear before the Crown Court for trial;

and where his release on bail is conditional on his providing one or more surety or sureties and, in accordance with section 8(3) of the Bail Act 1976, the court fixes the amount in which the surety is to be bound with a view to his entering into his recognizance subsequently in accordance with subsections (4) and (5) or (6) of that section, the court shall in the meantime make an order such as is mentioned in paragraph (a) of this subsection.

(4) If the conditions specified in subsection (5) below are satisfied, a court may exercise the powers conferred by subsection (3) above in relation to a person charged without his being brought before it in any case in which by virtue of section 128(3A) of the Magistrates' Courts Act 1980 it would have power further to remand him on an adjournment such as is mentioned in that subsection.

(5) The conditions mentioned in subsection (4) above are—
(a) that the person in question has given his written consent to the powers conferred by subsection (3) above being exercised without his being brought before the court; and
(b) that the court is satisfied that, when he gave his consent, he knew that the notice of transfer had been issued.

(6) Where notice of transfer is given after a person to whom it relates has been remanded on bail to appear before a magistrates' court on an appointed day, the requirement that he shall so appear shall cease on the giving of the notice, unless the notice states that it is to continue.

(7) Where the requirement that a person to whom the notice of transfer relates shall appear before a magistrates' court ceases by virtue of subsection (6) above, it shall be his duty to appear before the Crown Court at the place specified by the notice of transfer as the proposed place of trial or at any place substituted for it by a direction under section 76 of the Supreme Court Act 1981.

(7A) If the notice states that the requirement is to continue, when a person to whom the notice relates appears before the magistrates' court, the court shall have—
(a) the powers and duty conferred on a magistrates' court by subsection (3) above, but subject as there provided; and
(b) power to enlarge, in the surety's absence, a recognizance conditioned in accordance with section 128(4)(a) of the Magistrates' Courts Act 1980 so that the surety is bound to secure that the person charged appears also before the Crown Court.

(8) For the purposes of the Criminal Procedure (Attendance of Witnesses) Act 1965—
(a) any magistrates' court for the petty sessions area for which the court from which a case was transferred sits shall be treated as examining magistrates; and
(b) a person indicated in the notice of transfer as a proposed witness shall be treated as a person who has been examined by the court.

(9) The Attorney General—
(a) shall by regulations make provision requiring the giving of a copy of a notice of transfer, together with a statement of the evidence copies of the documents containing the evidence (including oral evidence) on which any charge to which it relates is based—
(i) to any person to whom the notice of transfer relates; and
(ii) to the Crown Court sitting at the place specified by the notice of transfer as the proposed place of trial; and
(b) may by regulations make such further provision in relation to notices of transfer, including provision as to the duties of a designated authority in relation to such notices, as appears to him to be appropriate.

(9A) Regulations under subsection (9)(a) above may provide that there shall be no requirement for copies of documents to accompany the copy of the notice of transfer if they are referred to, in documents sent with the notice of transfer, as having already been supplied.

(10) The power to make regulations conferred by subsection (9) above shall be exercisable by statutory instrument subject to annulment in pursuance of a resolution of either House of Parliament.

(11) Any such regulations may make different provision with respect to different cases or classes of case.

6.—(1) Where notice of transfer has been given, any person to whom the notice relates, at any time before he is arraigned (and whether or not an indictment has been preferred against

D

Part D Procedure

him), may apply orally or in writing to the Crown Court sitting at the place specified by the notice of transfer as the proposed place of trial for the charge, or any of the charges, in the case to be dismissed; and the judge shall dismiss a charge (and accordingly quash a count relating to it in any indictment preferred against the applicant) if it appears to him that the evidence against the applicant would not be sufficient for a jury properly to convict him.

(2) No oral application may be made under subsection (1) above unless the applicant has given the Crown Court sitting at the place specified by the notice of transfer as the proposed place of trial written notice of his intention to make the application.

(3) Oral evidence may be given on such an application only with the leave of the judge or by his order, and the judge shall give leave or make an order only if it appears to him, having regard to any matters stated in the application for leave, that the interests of justice require him to do so.

(4) If the judge gives leave permitting, or makes an order requiring, a person to give oral evidence, but he does not do so, the judge may disregard any document indicating the evidence that he might have given.

(5) Dismissal of the charge, or all the charges, against the applicant shall have the same effect as a refusal by examining magistrates to commit for trial, except that no further proceedings may be brought on a dismissed charge except by means of the preferment of a voluntary bill of indictment.

(6) [Criminal Procedure Rules]

D10.46 **Criminal Justice Act 1991, s. 53 and sch. 6**

53.—(1) If a person has been charged with an offence to which section 32(2) of the 1988 Act applies (sexual offences and offences involving violence or cruelty) and the Director of Public Prosecutions is of the opinion—

(a) that the evidence of the offence would be sufficient for the person charged to be committed for trial;

(b) that a child who is alleged—

(i) to be a person against whom the offence was committed; or

(ii) to have witnessed the commission of the offence,

will be called as a witness at the trial; and

(c) that, for the purpose of avoiding any prejudice to the welfare of the child, the case should be taken over and proceeded with without delay by the Crown Court,

a notice ('notice of transfer') certifying that opinion may be given by or on behalf of the Director to the magistrates' court in whose jurisdiction the offence has been charged.

(2) A notice of transfer shall be given before the magistrates' court begins to inquire into the case as examining justices.

(3) On the giving of a notice of transfer the functions of the magistrates' court shall cease in relation to the case except as provided by paragraphs 2 and 3 of schedule 6 to this Act or by paragraph 2 of schedule 3 to the Access to Justice Act 1999.

(4) The decision to give a notice of transfer shall not be subject to appeal or liable to be questioned in any court.

(5) [Schedule 6]

(6) In this section 'child' means a person who—

(a) in the case of an offence falling within section 32(2)(a) or (b) of the 1988 Act, is under fourteen years of age or, if he was under that age when any such video recording as is mentioned in section 32A(2) of that Act was made in respect of him, is under fifteen years of age; or

(b) in the case of an offence falling within section 32(2)(c) of that Act, is under seventeen years of age or, if he was under that age when any such video recording was made in respect of him, is under eighteen years of age.

(7) Any reference in subsection (6) above to an offence falling within paragraph (a), (b) or (c) of section 32(2) of that Act includes a reference to an offence which consists of attempting or conspiring to commit, or of aiding, abetting, counselling, procuring or inciting the commission of, an offence falling within that paragraph.

(8) This section shall not apply in any case in which section 51 of the Crime and Disorder Act 1998 (no committal proceedings for indictable-only offences) applies.

SCHEDULE 6

1.—(1) A notice of transfer shall specify the proposed place of trial; and in selecting that place the Director of Public Prosecutions shall have regard to the considerations to which a magistrates' court committing a person for trial is required by section 7 of the 1980 Act to have regard when selecting the place at which he is to be tried.

(2) A notice of transfer shall specify the charge or charges to which it relates and include or be accompanied by such additional material as regulations under paragraph 4 below may require.

2.—(1) If a magistrates' court has remanded in custody a person to whom a notice of transfer relates, it shall have power, subject to section 4 of the Bail Act 1976, section 25 of the Criminal Justice and Public Order Act 1994 and regulations under section 22 of the Prosecution of Offences Act 1985—

(a) to order that he shall be safely kept in custody until delivered in due course of law; or

(b) to release him on bail in accordance with the Bail Act 1976, that is to say, by directing him to appear before the Crown Court for trial.

(2) Where—

(a) a person's release on bail under paragraph (b) of sub-paragraph (1) above is conditional on his providing one or more sureties; and

(b) in accordance with subsection (3) of section 8 of the Bail Act 1976, the court fixes the amount in which a surety is to be bound with a view to his entering into his recognisance subsequently in accordance with subsections (4) and (5) or (6) of that section,

the court shall in the meantime make an order such as is mentioned in paragraph (a) of that sub-paragraph.

(3) If the conditions specified in sub-paragraph (4) below are satisfied, a court may exercise the powers conferred by sub-paragraph (1) above in relation to a person charged without his being brought before it in any case in which by virtue of subsection (3A) of section 128 of the 1980 Act it would have the power further to remand him on an adjournment such as is mentioned in that subsection.

(4) The conditions referred to in sub-paragraph (3) above are—

(a) that the person in question has given his written consent to the powers conferred by sub-paragraph (1) above being exercised without his being brought before the court; and

(b) that the court is satisfied that, when he gave his consent, he knew that the notice of transfer had been issued.

(5) Where a notice of transfer is given after a person to whom it relates has been remanded on bail to appear before a magistrates' court on an appointed day, the requirement that he shall so appear shall cease on the giving of the notice unless the notice states that it is to continue.

(6) Where that requirement ceases by virtue of sub-paragraph (5) above, it shall be the duty of the person in question to appear before the Crown Court at the place specified by the notice of transfer as the proposed place of trial or at any place substituted for it by a direction under section 76 of the Supreme Court Act 1981.

(7) If, in a case where the notice states that the requirement mentioned in sub-paragraph (5) above is to continue, a person to whom the notice relates appears before the magistrates' court, the court shall have—

(a) the powers and duties conferred on a magistrates' court by sub-paragraph (1) above but subject as there provided; and

(b) power to enlarge, in the surety's absence, a recognisance conditioned in accordance with section 128(4)(a) of the 1980 Act so that the surety is bound to secure that the person charged appears also before the Crown Court.

3.—For the purposes of the Criminal Procedure (Attendance of Witnesses) Act 1965—

(a) any magistrates' court for the petty sessions area for which the court from which a case was transferred sits shall be treated as examining magistrates; and

(b) a person indicated in the notice of transfer as a proposed witness shall be treated as a person who has been examined by the court.

4. [Regulations]

5.—(1) Where a notice of transfer has been given, any person to whom the notice relates may, at any time before he is arraigned (and whether or not an indictment has been preferred against him), apply orally or in writing to the Crown Court sitting at the place specified by the notice of transfer as the proposed place of trial for the charge, or any of the charges, in the case to be dismissed.

(2) The judge shall dismiss a charge (and accordingly quash a count relating to it in any

indictment preferred against the applicant) which is the subject of any such application if it appears to him that the evidence against the applicant would not be sufficient for a jury properly to convict him.

(3) No oral application may be made under sub-paragraph (1) above unless the applicant has given the Crown Court mentioned in that sub-paragraph written notice of his intention to make the application.

(4) Oral evidence may be given on such an application only with the leave of the judge or by his order; and the judge shall give leave or make an order only if it appears to him, having regard to any matters stated in the application for leave, that the interests of justice require him to do so.

(5) No leave or order under sub-paragraph (4) above shall be given or made in relation to oral evidence from a child (within the meaning of section 53 of this Act) who is alleged—
- (a) to be a person against whom an offence to which the notice of transfer relates was committed; or
- (b) to have witnessed the commission of such an offence.

(6) If the judge gives leave permitting, or makes an order requiring, a person to give oral evidence, but that person does not do so, the judge may disregard any document indicating the evidence that he might have given.

(7) Dismissal of the charge, or all the charges, against the applicant shall have the same effect as a refusal by examining magistrates to commit for trial, except that no further proceedings may be brought on a dismissed charge except by means of the preferment of a voluntary bill of indictment.

(8) [Criminal Procedure Rules].

6.—(1) Except as provided by this paragraph, it shall not be lawful—
- (a) to publish in Great Britain a written report of an application under paragraph 5(1) above; or
- (b) to include in a relevant programme for reception in Great Britain a report of such an application,

if (in either case) the report contains any matter other than that permitted by this paragraph.

(2) An order that sub-paragraph (1) above shall not apply to reports of an application under paragraph 5(1) above may be made by the judge dealing with the application.

(3) Where in the case of two or more accused one of them objects to the making of an order under sub-paragraph (2) above, the judge shall make the order if, and only if, he is satisfied, after hearing the representations of the accused, that it is in the interests of justice to do so.

(4) An order under sub-paragraph (2) above shall not apply to reports of proceedings under sub-paragraph (3) above, but any decision of the court to make or not to make such an order may be contained in reports published or included in a relevant programme before the time authorised by sub-paragraph (5) below.

(5) It shall not be unlawful under this paragraph to publish or include in a relevant programme a report of an application under paragraph 5(1) above containing any matter other than that permitted by sub-paragraph (8) below where the application is successful.

(6) Where—
- (a) two or more persons were jointly charged; and
- (b) applications under paragraph 5(1) above are made by more than one of them,

sub-paragraph (5) above shall have effect as if for the words 'the application is' there were substituted the words 'all the applications are'.

(7) It shall not be unlawful under this paragraph to publish or include in a relevant programme a report of an unsuccessful application at the conclusion of the trial of the person charged, or of the last of the persons charged to be tried.

(8) The following matters may be contained in a report published or included in a relevant programme without an order under sub-paragraph (2) above before the time authorised by sub-paragraphs (5) and (6) sub-paragraphs (5) and (7) above, that is to say—
- (a) the identity of the court and the name of the judge;
- (b) the names, ages, home addresses and occupations of the accused and witnesses;
- (c) the offence or offences, or a summary of them, with which the accused is or are charged;
- (d) the names of counsel and solicitors engaged in the proceedings;
- (e) where the proceedings are adjourned, the date and place to which they are adjourned;
- (f) the arrangements as to bail;
- (g) whether legal aid was granted to the accused or any of the accused.

(9) The addresses that may be published or included in a relevant programme under sub-paragraph (8) above are addresses—
(a) at any relevant time; and
(b) at the time of their publication or inclusion in a relevant programme.

(10) If a report is published or included in a relevant programme in contravention of this paragraph, the following persons, that is to say—
(a) in the case of a publication of a written report as part of a newspaper or periodical, any proprietor, editor or publisher of the newspaper or periodical;
(b) in the case of a publication of a written report otherwise than as part of a newspaper or periodical, the person who publishes it;
(c) in the case of the inclusion of a report in a relevant programme, any body corporate which is engaged in providing the service in which the programme is included and any person having functions in relation to the programme corresponding to those of the editor of a newspaper;

shall be liable on summary conviction to a fine not exceeding level 5 on the standard scale.

(11) Proceedings for an offence under this paragraph shall not, in England and Wales, be instituted otherwise than by or with the consent of the Attorney General.

(12) Sub-paragraph (1) above shall be in addition to, and not in derogation from, the provisions of any other enactment with respect to the publication of reports of court proceedings.

(13) In this paragraph—
'publish', in relation to a report, means publish the report, either by itself or as part of a newspaper or periodical, for distribution to the public;
'relevant programme' means a programme included in a programme service (within the meaning of the Broadcasting Act 1990);
'relevant time' means a time when events giving rise to the charges to which the proceedings relate occurred.

7.—(1) Where a notice of transfer has been given in relation to any case—
(a) the Crown Court before which the case is to be tried; and
(b) any magistrates' court which exercises any functions under paragraph 2 or 3 above or section 20(4) of the Legal Aid Act 1988 in relation to the case,

shall, in exercising any of its powers in relation to the case, have regard to the desirability of avoiding prejudice to the welfare of any relevant child witness that may be occasioned by unnecessary delay in bringing the case to trial.

(2) In this paragraph 'child' has the same meaning as in section 53 of this Act and 'relevant child witness' means a child who will be called as a witness at the trial and who is alleged—
(a) to be a person against whom an offence to which the notice of transfer relates was committed; or
(b) to have witnessed the commission of such an offence.

. . .

COMMITTAL FOR SUMMARY OFFENCES UNDER THE CJA 1988, S. 41

The CJA 1988, s. 41, empowers the magistrates to send a summary offence to the Crown Court for the plea to be taken. This power is available if (s. 41(1)): **D10.47**

(a) the court is sending an accused for trial for one or more either-way offences; and
(b) he is also charged with a summary offence punishable with imprisonment and/or disqualification from driving; and
(c) the summary offence arises out of circumstances which appear to the court to be the same as or connected with the circumstances of the offence or one of those either-way offences.

On exercising the power in s. 41(1), the court must give both the accused and the Crown Court a notice stating which either-way offence is the one that appears to it to be linked with the summary offence (s. 41(2)). A decision to commit under s. 41 is unchallengeable, whether by appeal or by application for judicial review (s. 41(3)), but, before proceeding to deal with the accused for the summary offence, the Crown Court must be satisfied that the conditions for a committal under s. 41 were in fact satisfied.

Following committal under s. 41, the proceedings in the magistrates' court for the summary offence are treated as if they had been adjourned *sine die* (s. 41(1)). The charge for the summary offence is not put to the accused in the Crown Court unless and until he is convicted of one or more of the either-way offences. If he is acquitted of all the either-way offences, the Crown Court has no power to proceed further in the matter, but simply informs the magistrates' court of what has occurred. In *Foote* (1991) 94 Cr App R 82, the accused was committed for trial on a charge of reckless driving (triable either way). At the same time he was committed under the CJA 1988, s. 41, on a charge of careless driving (a summary offence). In effect, the latter was an alternative charge, since both alleged offences related to the same driving. At the Crown Court, he pleaded not guilty to reckless driving. The offence of careless driving was then put to him, and he pleaded guilty. The Crown indicated that the plea was acceptable. The judge directed a verdict of not guilty to be entered on the charge of reckless driving and proceeded to sentence on the careless driving. On appeal, the Court of Appeal quashed the conviction for careless driving, on the basis that, once he had been found not guilty of the either-way offence, the powers of the Crown Court ceased in respect of the summary offence.

Provided that the accused has been validly convicted on a count that has been properly included within the indictment, the Crown Court may deal with an offence sent to it by virtue of s. 41. In *Bird* [1995] Crim LR 745, there were two counts in the indictment, one of possessing an offensive weapon and one of driving whilst disqualified. The latter offence had been included in the indictment by virtue of the CJA 1988, s. 40. In addition, the magistrates sent up to the Crown Court, under s. 41, an offence of having no motor insurance. The accused was acquitted of the offensive weapon count after the prosecution offered no evidence, but was convicted of driving whilst disqualified. The question then arose whether the Crown Court had power to deal with the insurance offence. The Court of Appeal held that the conviction on the driving whilst disqualified count (which had been properly included within the indictment) triggered off the power to deal with the insurance offence under s. 41, and the judge had acted within his jurisdiction in sentencing the accused for the latter offence.

Section 41 has also been amended by the Courts Act 2003, sch. 8, para. 303. Section 41(8), as so amended, provides that where the accused pleads not guilty to the summary offence, 'the Crown Court may try him for the offence', although in the event of a conviction, the Crown Court 'may deal with him only in a manner in which a magistrates' court could have dealt with him'. This amendment is the corollary of the enactment of the Courts Act 2003, s. 66, which empowers Crown Court judges to exercise the powers of magistrates. This means that if an accused is convicted of the either-way offence and then pleads not guilty to the linked summary offence, the Crown Court judge (sitting without a jury) would be able to try the summary offence (following the procedure which would have been adopted had that offence been tried in the magistrates' court). If the judge decides not to try the summary offence, the case can be remitted to the magistrates for them to try it.

Section 41 has also been amended by the DVCVA 2004, sch. 10, so as to insert a new s. 41(4A), which effectively disapplies s. 41 where the accused is convicted of a summary offence to which the provisions of s. 40 of the 1988 Act apply. It provides that the committal of the accused under s. 41 in respect of an offence to which s. 40 applies does not prevent him being found guilty of that offence under the CLA 1967, s. 6(3) (which provides for alternative verdicts in a trial on indictment); if the accused is convicted of the summary offence under s. 6(3), the functions of the Crown Court under s. 41 in relation to that offence cease.

It should also be noted that the CJA 1988, s. 41, will be repealed when the repeal contained in the CJA 2003, sch. 3, para. 60(8) and sch. 37, part 4, comes into effect. This is because the CDA 1998, s. 51(3), as amended by the CJA 2003, sch. 3, will provide that where an accused is sent to the Crown Court for trial in respect of an indictable-only or either-way offence, the justices may also send him for trial in respect of any related offence (provided that, if the related offence is a summary one, it is punishable with imprisonment or disqualification from driving). By virtue of the Courts Act 2003, s. 66, the Crown Court judge would be empowered to try the summary offence if the accused pleads not guilty to it, and to pass sentence if the accused pleads guilty to it or is found guilty of it.

Criminal Justice Act 1988, s. 41

[due to be repealed by the CJA 2003]

(1) Where a magistrates' court commits a person to the Crown Court for trial on indictment for an offence triable either way or a number of such offences, it may also commit him for trial for any summary offence with which he is charged and which—

(a) is punishable with imprisonment or involves obligatory or discretionary disqualification from driving; and

(b) arises out of circumstances which appear to the court to be the same as or connected with those giving rise to the offence, or one of the offences, triable either way,

whether or not evidence relating to that summary offence appears on the depositions or written statements in the case; and the trial of the information charging the summary offence shall then be treated as if the magistrates' court had adjourned it under section 10 of the Magistrates' Courts Act 1980 and had not fixed the time and place for its resumption.

(2) Where a magistrates' court commits a person to the Crown Court for trial on indictment for a number of offences triable either way and exercises the power conferred by subsection (1) above in respect of a summary offence, the magistrates' court shall give the Crown Court and the person who is committed for trial a notice stating which of the offences triable either way appears to the court to arise out of circumstances which are the same as or connected with those giving rise to the summary offence.

(3) A magistrates' court's decision to exercise the power conferred by subsection (1) above shall not be subject to appeal or liable to be questioned in any court.

(4) The committal of a person under this section in respect of an offence to which section 40 above applies shall not preclude the exercise in relation to the offence of the power conferred by that section; but where he is tried on indictment for such an offence, the functions of the Crown Court under this section in relation to the offence shall cease.

(4A) The committal of a person under this section in respect of an offence to which section 40 above applies shall not prevent him being found guilty of that offence under section 6(3) of the Criminal Law Act 1967 (alternative verdicts on trial on indictment); but where he is convicted under that provision of such an offence, the functions of the Crown Court under this section in relation to the offence shall cease.

(5) If he is convicted on the indictment, the Crown Court shall consider whether the conditions specified in subsection (1) above were satisfied.

(6) If it considers that they were satisfied, it shall state to him the substance of the summary offence and ask him whether he pleads guilty or not guilty.

(7) If he pleads guilty, the Crown Court shall convict him, but may deal with him in respect of that offence only in a manner in which a magistrates' court could have dealt with him.

(8) If he does not plead guilty, the Crown Court may try him for the offence, but may deal with him only in a manner in which a magistrates' court could have dealt with him.

(9) . . .

(10) The Crown Court shall inform the designated officer for the magistrates' court of the outcome of any proceedings under this section.

(11) Where the Court of Appeal allows an appeal against conviction of an offence triable either way which arose out of circumstances which were the same as or connected with those giving rise to a summary offence of which the appellant was convicted under this section—

(a) it shall set aside his conviction of the summary offence and give the designated officer for the magistrates' court notice that it has done so; and

(b) it may direct that no further proceedings in relation to the offence are to be undertaken;

and the proceedings before the Crown Court in relation to the offence shall thereafter be disregarded for all purposes.

(12) A notice under subsection (11) above shall include particulars of any direction given under paragraph (b) of that subsection in relation to the offence.

(13) . . .

VOLUNTARY BILLS OF INDICTMENT

D10.48 The Administration of Justice (Miscellaneous Provisions) Act 1933, s. 2(2)(b), provides that a bill of indictment may be preferred 'by the direction or with the consent of a judge of the High Court'.

Procedure for Obtaining a Voluntary Bill

D10.49 The procedure for obtaining a High Court judge's consent to the preferment of a bill of indictment is set out in the Indictments (Procedure) Rules 1971, rr. 6 to 10, and in the *Consolidated Criminal Practice Direction*, para. IV.35 (see **appendix 8**). In summary, the procedure is as follows:

(a) An application must be made in writing, signed by the applicant (i.e. the prosecutor) or his solicitor (Indictments (Procedure) Rules 1971, r. 7).

(b) The application must state:
- (i) whether there has been any previous application for a voluntary bill;
- (ii) whether there have been any committal proceedings or sending for trial;
- (iii) the result of any previous committal proceedings or, in the case of a previous sending for trial, the result of any application to dismiss the charge; and
- (iv) the reason, if there have not been committal proceedings or sending for trial, why it is desired to prefer a voluntary bill instead (rr. 8(b), 9(1) and (3)).

(c) The application must be accompanied by the bill of indictment that it is proposed to prefer (r. 8(1)(a)). This requirement is sufficiently complied with if the application is marked to the effect that the indictment will follow later, and the proposed bill is in fact delivered in time to be placed before the judge when he is making his decision (*Rothfield* (1937) 26 Cr App R 103). The application must also be accompanied by a copy of any existing indictment that has been preferred in consequence of a committal or sending for trial (para. IV.35.2(c)).

(d) Where the accused has already been sent to the Crown Court for trial, the application must also be accompanied by a copy of the documents received in evidence, including any documentary exhibits (r. 9(2) and (3)). A copy of any charges on which the accused has been sent for trial should also accompany the application, and a copy of any charges on which the magistrates refused to send the accused for trial (para. IV.35.2(a) and (b)). If there is any additional evidence the prosecutor intends to rely on which does not appear on the depositions or statements, proofs of that evidence must also be sent. Where there have not been committal proceedings or a sending for trial, the applicant simply sends the proofs of evidence of his proposed witnesses (r. 9(1)(a)). In each case, the application must contain a statement that the evidence contained in the depositions, statements and proofs of evidence will be available at trial and that the case thereby disclosed is (to the best of the applicant's knowledge, information and belief) substantially a true case (ibid). Further, the application must be accompanied by a summary of the evidence or other document, which, in relation to each count in the proposed indictment, identifies the pages in the accompanying statements and exhibits where the essential relevant evidence can be found (para. IV.35.2(d)).

(e) Except where the application is made by or on behalf of the DPP, it must also be accompanied by an affidavit verifying that the statements contained in the application are true to the best of the applicant's knowledge and belief (r. 8(a)). Where a Crown Prosecutor applies for a voluntary bill in exercise of the powers delegated to him by the DPP, the application is made by or on behalf of the DPP and therefore does not have to be supported by an affidavit (see the Prosecution of Offences Act 1985, s. 1(6), and *Ex parte Bray* (1986) *The Times*, 7 October 1986). This is so even if the application was not expressly authorised by the DPP, but merely made by the Crown Prosecutor carrying out his general duties (ibid).

(f) Subject to a contrary direction by the judge, the application is determined without the attendance of the applicant or his witnesses. Should they be required to attend, their attendance is not in open court (r. 10). The judge's decision is signified in writing.

(g) The proposed accused has no right to attend, to be represented before (or even submit written representations to) the judge. In exceptional cases, the judge in his discretion may consider written representations, but it seems likely that he does not even have a discretion to allow the accused to be present in person (*Raymond* [1981] QB 910). Dicta in *Raymond* suggest that, should the accused be allowed to make representations, they must be limited to the question of whether it is appropriate to proceed by way of voluntary bill rather than by another method, and should not extend to the question of whether the statements disclose a prima facie case.

Finality of High Court Judge's Decision

D10.50 Where a High Court judge directs the preferment of a voluntary bill of indictment under the Administration of Justice (Miscellaneous Provisions) Act 1933, s. 2(2)(b), the Court of Appeal will not inquire into the correctness or otherwise of his decision, provided only that he was acting within his jurisdiction (*Rothfield* (1937) 26 Cr App R 103). The issuing of a voluntary bill of indictment is not subject to judicial review (*Manchester Crown Court, ex parte Williams* (1990) 154 JP 589). In *Rothfield*, the accused, having been convicted on an indictment preferred under s. 2(2)(b), argued on appeal that the trial judge should have quashed the indictment and discharged him without trial as the High Court judge had erred in directing preferment of a voluntary bill. Dismissing the appeal, Humphreys J held that a High Court judge's authorisation for the preferring of a bill is binding on a trial judge, and the latter has no jurisdiction to quash the indictment simply on the basis that the former, according to the defence, made a mistake. His lordship continued (at p. 106): '. . . it cannot be made too plain, or stated too definitely, that this court will not inquire into the exercise of the discretion of a judge who is sitting and dealing with an application under the Administration of Justice (Miscellaneous Provisions) Act 1933, so long as it is clear that he had jurisdiction to entertain the application.' Accordingly, the Court of Appeal declined to consider arguments advanced by the appellant that went to whether it had been, in all the circumstances, an appropriate case for a voluntary bill, but their lordships did consider, although ultimately rejected, an argument that the High Court judge had had no power to direct preferment because of an irregularity in the way the prosecutor made his application (failing to accompany the application with a copy of the proposed bill of indictment in breach of what is now the Indictment (Procedure) Rules 1971). Since only High Court judges have jurisdiction to direct preferment of a voluntary bill, a conviction on an indictment purportedly preferred on the direction of a circuit judge will inevitably have to be quashed (see *Thompson* [1975] 1 WLR 1425).

Even though the decision of a High Court judge to issue a voluntary bill of indictment is not subject to judicial review, the decision of a prosecutor to seek a voluntary bill is susceptible to review, but only on very limited grounds (such as alleged malice on the part of the prosecutor: *Inland Revenue Commissioners, ex parte Dhesi* (1995) *Independent*, 14 August 1995).

Circumstances in which it is Appropriate to Apply for a Voluntary Bill

D10.51 Neither the Administration of Justice (Miscellaneous Provisions) Act 1933 nor the Indictments (Procedure) Rules 1971 expressly indicate when it is appropriate to proceed by way of voluntary bill rather than by the normal method of securing a Crown Court trial. The implication of r. 9(1) and (3) is that the normal way to secure authority to prefer a bill of indictment is to bring the accused before a magistrates' court for the case to be sent to the

Crown Court, since the applicant is required to state in his application for a voluntary bill of indictment why the application is being made. Conversely, if the justices have been asked to send the accused to the Crown Court but have declined to do so, the application need not state the reason for its making, presumably because the voluntary bill procedure is accepted as always being appropriate in such cases. This is confirmed by *Horsham Justices, ex parte Reeves* (1980) 75 Cr App R 236 (a case decided before the abolition of committal proceedings), where it was held that the prosecution, having failed after a hearing on the merits to satisfy the examining justices that there was a case to answer, ought to have applied for a voluntary bill rather than initiating a second committal before a different bench of justices. In *Brooks v DPP for Jamaica* [1994] 1 AC 568, however, the Privy Council stressed that the decision to prefer a voluntary bill in these circumstances is one to be exercised with the greatest circumspection, treating the magistrates' decision with the utmost respect.

Decided cases indicate a variety of circumstances in which the prosecution may properly apply for a voluntary bill even before magistrates have been asked to send the accused to the Crown Court for trial. In *Raymond* [1981] QB 910, for example, the reason for the voluntary bill was that the accused, during the early part of committal proceedings, 'gave such unmistakable indications of an intention seriously to disrupt the committal proceedings as to make a mockery of them that counsel for the Crown decided to abandon them' (pp. 913H–914A). Similarly, a voluntary bill was obtained in *Paling* (1978) 67 Cr App R 299, where the committal proceedings for an alleged assault were discontinued after the accused became abusive to the bench and, during a short adjournment, allegedly committed further assaults on officers concerned in the case.

Specific provision is made for the use of the voluntary bill procedure where a charge transferred to the Crown Court (under the CDA 1998, s. 51) has been dismissed (under the CDA 1998, sch. 3, para. 2) and the prosecution wish to seek a trial nonetheless; indeed, in such circumstances, further proceedings may be brought on the dismissed charge(s) by means of the preferment of a voluntary bill of indictment (para. 2(6)).

Section D11 The Indictment

The indictment is the document containing the charges against the accused on which he is arraigned at the commencement of a trial on indictment. In terms of statutory authority, the law on indictments is contained principally in the Indictments Act 1915. Prior to 2 April 2007, this was supplemented by the Indictment Rules 1971 (SI 1971 No. 1253) and the Indictments (Procedure) Rules 1971 (SI 1971 No. 2084). For convenience, these are hereafter referred to collectively as the 1971 Rules. From 2 April 2007, however, the rules relating to indictments have been incorporated by the Criminal Procedure (Amendment) Rules (SI 2007 No. 699) into part 14 of the CrimPR, and those earlier rules have been revoked. See **appendix** 1 for the rules in full. **D11.1**

This new set of rules is supplemented by the fifteenth amendment to the *Consolidated Criminal Practice Direction* (see **appendix** 7), which came into effect on 27 April 2007. Schedule 3 to this amendment contains a new para. IV.34, which relates to the settling of indictments.

The change effected by these amendments is not simply one of form, as was the case when other sets of rules were incorporated unaltered into the CrimPR in April 2005. Significant and potentially far-reaching changes of substance have been made. In this edition, therefore, it is necessary to consider the rules both as they were before April 2007 and as they now are.

The content of this section can be divided into four categories:

(a) rules as to the form of an indictment, which includes rules as to the layout of an indictment, who is responsible for its drafting and the time-limits relevant to its preferment (**D11.2** to **D11.10**);
(b) rules as to the composition of an indictment, in terms of the charges included in an indictment and their wording (**D11.11** to **D11.55**);
(c) rules as to the alteration of an indictment, whether by joinder of charges or offenders, severance or amendment (**D11.56** to **D11.94**);
(d) rules for objecting to an indictment, whether by a motion to quash or as a ground of appeal (**D11.95** to **D11.102**).

REQUIREMENT THAT AN INDICTMENT BE SIGNED

The Rule

Administration of Justice (Miscellaneous Provisions) Act 1933, s. 2 **D11.2**

(1) Subject to the provisions of this section, a bill of indictment charging any person with an indictable offence may be preferred by any person before [the Crown Court], and where a bill of indictment has been so preferred the proper officer of the court shall, if he is satisfied

D

Part D Procedure

> that the requirements of the next following subsection have been complied with, sign the bill, and it shall thereupon become an indictment and be proceeded with accordingly:
>
> Provided that if the judge of the court is satisfied that the said requirements have been complied with, he may, on the application of the prosecutor or of his own motion, direct the proper officer to sign the bill and the bill shall be signed accordingly.

An indictment comes into being only when it is signed by a proper officer of the Crown Court (s. 2(1)). Until it has been so signed, it is a 'bill of indictment' (under the 1971 Rules) or a draft indictment (under the CrimPR, r. 14.1), not an indictment. When the bill of indictment is signed, the date should be added (r. 14.1(3)(a)).

The officer of the Crown Court is required to sign it provided that he is satisfied that the requirements of s. 2(2) of the 1933 Act have been complied with. Section 2(2), reflected in the CrimPR, r. 14.1, provides that no draft indictment may be served unless:

(a) the accused has been sent for trial (pursuant to the CDA 1998, s. 51) or committed for trial;
(b) a notice of transfer has been given to the relevant magistrates' court;
(c) a High Court judge has directed or consented to the preferment of a voluntary bill of indictment; or
(d) the Court of Appeal has ordered a retrial.

Should the officer of the Crown Court wrongly decline to sign a bill of indictment, a judge of the Crown Court may, on the application of the prosecutor or of his own motion, direct him to sign (s. 2(1)).

D11.3 Problems with Compliance with this Rule Simple though the requirement to ensure that the indictment is signed may seem, the courts have had to grapple with the consequences of failure to comply with it. This is because, as the Court of Appeal emphasised in *Morais* [1988] 3 All ER 161, the proper officer's signature is not 'a comparatively meaningless formality' but a 'necessary condition precedent to the existence of a proper indictment'.

The authorities demonstrate that the question is whether or not the failure to sign the indictment in the proper manner is actually no more than a 'meaningless formality'. The following cases provide examples.

(a) In *Jackson* [1997] 2 Cr App R 497, although the judge had directed in open court that the appropriate officer should sign the indictments, she had failed to comply with the judge's direction. Distinguishing *Morais*, their lordships said that in these circumstances, the officer's signature *was* a meaningless formality, and she was deemed to have appended her signature.
(b) In *Laming* (1989) 90 Cr App R 450, where the appropriate officer of the court signed the indictment on the front page rather than at the end, as was required by sch. 1 to the Indictment Rules 1971, the Court of Appeal held that it was nonetheless valid. The important fact was that the appropriate officer of the court had signed the indictment, intending thereby to validate it. The court added, however, that any departure from the normal practice of signing indictments at the end was to be strongly discouraged.

D11.4 Procedural Breaches after *Ashton* In *Ashton* [2007] 1 WLR 181, the Court of Appeal held that the approach to procedural failures in relation to the indictment in cases such as *Morais* [1988] 3 All ER 161, had been superseded by the decision in the House of Lords in *Soneji* [2006] 1 AC 340. Fulford J stated (at [4], [5], [77] and [78]):

> In our judgment it is now wholly clear that whenever a court is confronted by failure to take a required step, properly or at all, before a power is exercised ('a procedural failure'), the court should first ask itself whether the intention of the legislature was that any act done following that procedural failure should be invalid. If the answer to that question is no, then the court should go on to consider the interests of justice generally, and most particularly whether there is a real

possibility that either the prosecution or the defence may suffer prejudice on account of the procedural failure. If there is such a risk, the court must decide whether it is just to allow the proceedings to continue.

On the other hand, if a court acts without jurisdiction—if, for instance, a magistrates' court purports to try a defendant on a charge of homicide—then the proceedings will usually be invalid.

[T]he court should concentrate in future on, first, the intention of Parliament (viz. was it intended that a procedural failure should render the proceedings invalid) and, second, the interests of justice and particularly whether the procedural failure caused any prejudice to any of the parties, such as to make it unjust to proceed further.

Here, the judge and the parties proceeded on the basis that the charges before the court identified the criminality alleged by the prosecution and it was accepted there was no prejudice to the applicant in this particular case when the court dealt with him absent an indictment. We stress that usually a bill of indictment should be preferred and signed and our decision in this case should not be taken as any kind of encouragement to relax that important requirement: an indictment provides a critical safeguard in that it describes the charges an accused faces with clarity and finality. However, applying the test we have described above, there are no indications that Parliament intended that proceedings would be rendered automatically invalid because an indictment had not been preferred or signed, and given no prejudice or consequential injustice have been identified, we see no reason to quash these convictions.

Ashton was followed in *Clarke* [2006] EWCA Crim 1196.

RESPONSIBILITY FOR DRAFTING AN INDICTMENT

Ultimate Responsibility

Ultimate responsibility for the indictment rests with counsel for the prosecution, who must ensure that it is in proper form before arraignment. This principle was affirmed by Watkins LJ, giving the judgment of the Court of Appeal in *Newland* [1988] QB 402, who said (at p. 409): D11.5

Before parting with this case we think the time has come—it may be overdue—when it is necessary to say something about the responsibility for drafting of indictments. It is undertaken by and large by staff of the Crown Courts in this country. The unfortunate fact is, so we are informed and as we from some experience in this court know, that the defective manner in which indictments are drafted is giving cause for concern, having regard to the number of occasions when this occurs.

It is we think necessary for a restatement to be made upon the question of responsibility for the ultimate presentation of an indictment to the court. It was the responsibility of counsel to ensure that the indictment was in proper form before arraignment. A return to that practice—it seems not to be followed generally—may in our view be a salutary thing for everyone concerned, and moreover relieve the staff of the Crown Court of any responsibility it may be felt they have in that respect, and also to have the result of there being fewer appeals to this court based on defective indictments.

Mechanics of Drafting Indictments

The reference in the passage from *Newland* [1988] QB 402 (at D11.5) to Crown Court staff drafting the bulk of indictments reflects the practice at the time Watkins LJ gave his judgment. Perhaps as a result of the dicta in *Newland*, the practice has since changed. Invariably now, the prosecuting authority prepares a schedule of charges for committal drafted in the form of counts suitable for inclusion in an indictment. This schedule, in effect a draft indictment, is sent to the Crown Court with the committal papers, and all the Crown Court officer has to do is to check that there has been no contravention of the Administration of Justice (Miscellaneous Provisions) Act 1933, s. 2(2), and then to sign. D11.6

What has not changed, however, is the ultimate responsibility of counsel, once instructed, to ensure that the indictment is in proper form (*Moss* [1995] Crim LR 828).

TIME-LIMIT FOR PREFERRING A BILL OF INDICTMENT

The Rule

D11.7 A draft indictment should be served on an appropriate officer of the Crown Court within 28 days of the date on which:

(a) the accused is committed (or transferred) for trial;
(b) a notice of transfer is given;
(c) a High Court judge has directed or consented to the preferment of a voluntary bill of indictment; or
(d) copies of documents are served where a person is sent for trial under the CDA 1998, s. 51 (CrimPR, r. 14.1, replacing the previous r. 14.2(1)).

D11.8 **Extension of the Time-limit** Previously (under the pre-2007 version of the Rules), an appropriate court officer had the power to extend the 28-day time-limit for up to a further 28 days (r. 14.3), with any further extension or any review of a refusal by the court officer reserved to a judge of the Crown Court (r. 14.2(2) and (3)). From 1 April 2007, r. 14.1(2) simply permits the Crown Court to extend the time-limit, even after it has expired. Moreover, there are now no specific rules as to the means by which an application for an extension should be made, or what such an application should contain. This is in contrast to the previous requirements (the old r. 14.2(4) and (5)).

D11.9 **Breaches of the Rule** The predecessor to r. 14.2 (r. 5 of the Indictments (Procedure) Rules 1971) was held to be directory, not mandatory. Consequently, breach of the rule is not in itself a good ground of appeal, although it is submitted that inordinate delay of a magnitude sufficient to prejudice the accused in the preparation of his defence might render a conviction unsafe.

The effect of breach has been considered in a number of cases in relation to the form of the rule which simply provided that 'the bill of indictment must be preferred within 28 days of . . . committal or within such longer period as a judge of the Crown Court may allow'.

(a) In *Sheerin* (1976) 64 Cr App R 68, defence counsel moved to quash an indictment preferred 21 days out of time, no application for an extension of time having been made. The trial judge, finding that S had not suffered any prejudice by reason of the delay, gave leave for preferment of a late bill and rejected the motion to quash. On appeal, Lawton LJ held:
    (i) First, that the judge had had jurisdiction to grant the extension of time even though the application was not made until after the 28 days had elapsed (this is now expressly confirmed by r. 14.2).
    (ii) Secondly, as to the status of the rule, his lordship said (at p. 70): 'It is to be noted that the very title of the rules is "Procedure Rules"—that is rules for the guidance of courts in the administration of justice. They are not rules setting boundaries beyond which the courts cannot go.'
    (iii) Thirdly, the judge had properly exercised his discretion in allowing late preferment since preparation of the indictment would have taken longer than the usual period.
(b) In *Soffe* (1982) 75 Cr App R 133, the argument on appeal was that authorisation for an extension of time for preferment had been given by the chief clerk of the Crown Court concerned, not by a judge, and that the 28-day rule (as it then stood) had therefore been breached. Donaldson LJ, giving the Court of Appeal's judgment, said (at p. 136):

> There must be some doubt in this case whether the chief clerk in fact purported to extend the time limited by rule 5 or whether the bill was preferred out of time. So far as this application is concerned, it matters not which occurred. A breach of [the rules] does not constitute a material irregularity in the course of the trial or in any way invalidate the proceedings, and the applicant accordingly has no valid grounds of appeal.

(c) Similarly, when dismissing the appeal in *Farooki* (1983) 77 Cr App R 257, the court relied on the dicta in *Sheerin* and *Soffe*, and could find no valid distinction between the circumstances of the case before them (where an appropriate officer had apparently signed a late-preferred bill without consultation with or authorisation from a judge) and the circumstances of *Sheerin* and *Soffe*.

The approach in these three cases is wholly consistent with the approach of the Court of Appeal to procedural breaches in general in *Ashton* [2007] 1 WLR 181 (see **D11.4**).

The Need for Compliance The lack of effective sanction for breach of the CrimPR, r. 14.2, should not, however, be treated by prosecutors as a licence to take as long as they like to draft the indictment. In *Sheerin*, Lawton LJ gave this warning (at p. 71): **D11.10**

> In coming to the conclusion we have about this matter we would not wish any prosecuting authority to think that they are being given a licence by this court to delay in preparing bills of indictment. As [counsel for the appellant] said in the course of his argument: 'It may well be that in many cases . . . it is from a practical point of view virtually impossible to get the indictment preferred within the period of 28 days, but it is probable that if the prosecution are alive to the existence of [the rule] they could make an application to the court before the expiration of 28 days.' They are encouraged by this court so to do. If there is inordinate delay in preferring a bill of indictment, which clearly has caused, or clearly is likely to cause prejudice to accused persons, then the judge may very well not exercise his discretion and leave the prosecution to take such course as they think fit. Prosecutors should not assume that they will always be granted leave to prefer a voluntary bill of indictment.

Similarly, in *Soffe* (1982) 75 Cr App R 133, Donaldson LJ (at pp. 136–7), 'first and foremost', emphasised 'that it is the duty of all concerned to take all reasonable steps to ensure that bills of indictment are preferred within the 28-day period'.

COUNTS WHICH MAY BE INCLUDED IN AN INDICTMENT

Having identified who is responsible for drafting the indictment, and when that task needs to have been performed, the next question becomes which charges may be included in the indictment. This is a question of which charges may be included in the original draft of the indictment, rather than matters of joinder, severance or amendment to the indictment which may alter its content between the original drafting and the trial (which are dealt with below). The power to amend derives from the Indictment Act 1915, s. 5 (*Wells* (1995) 159 JP 243 and *Osieh* [1996] 1 WLR 1260; and see **D11.86**). **D11.11**

Charges Revealed by the Papers

The Administration of Justice (Miscellaneous Provisions) Act 1933, s. 2(2)(a), allows a bill of indictment charging an offence to be preferred if 'the person charged has been committed for trial for the offence', read in conjunction with proviso (i) to the subsection. The proviso is: 'where the person charged has been committed for trial, the bill of indictment against him may include, either in substitution for or in addition to counts charging the offence for which he was committed, any counts founded on facts or evidence disclosed to the magistrates' court inquiring into that offence as examining justices, being counts which may lawfully be joined in the same indictment'. **D11.12**

This position is reflected by the CrimPR, r. 14.2(5), and para. IV.34(1) of the *Consolidated Criminal Practice Direction*.

It follows that, subject to the rules on when counts and/or defendants are sufficiently closely linked to be properly joined in a single indictment (see **D11.56** and **D11.64**), a draft indictment may include charges for *any* indictable offence disclosed by the evidence from the committal proceedings. Usually the counts in the indictment simply follow the committal charges.

Where the drafter chooses to include a count for an offence in respect of which the examining justices did not commit, he must be careful to ensure that the offence is in fact disclosed by the statements, so as to ensure compliance with the proviso to s. 2(2)(i). He must also ensure, pursuant to para. IV.34(1) of the Practice Direction that as much notice as possible of such charges is provided to the accused.

D11.13 **Application of the Proviso in Section 2(2)(i)** Further points as to the effect of proviso (i) to the Administration of Justice (Miscellaneous Provisions) Act 1933, s. 2(2), are as follows.

(a) The power to depart from the committal charges extends even to including a count for an offence in respect of which the justices were expressly asked to commit but took a considered decision not to do so (*Dawson* [1960] 1 WLR 163). However, the power should be used sparingly in such cases (*Dawson* and *Kempster* [1989] 1 WLR 1125). The potential dangers of reinstating a count after the examining justices have said that there is no case to answer for that offence are graphically illustrated by *Moloney* [1985] AC 905.

(b) The prosecution may not rely on the proviso to s. 2(2) of the 1933 Act to prefer an indictment consisting *entirely* of counts for charges in respect of which there has been no committal for trial, even where the accused has been committed on other charges and the offences charged in the indictment are disclosed by the evidence that was before the justices (*Lombardi* [1989] 1 WLR 73). The reasoning in *Lombardi* was that, in the absence of at least one count on the indictment for a 'committal' offence, the 'non-committal' counts cannot properly be said to be in addition to or in substitution for counts charging the offence in respect of which the accused was committed, as required by the terms of the proviso.

(c) The proviso may not be relied on to add counts to an indictment where that joinder of the committal charges and non-committal charges in one indictment would have contravened the Indictment Rules 1971, r. 9, on the joinder of counts. This was demonstrated in *Lombardi*, in which Lord Lane CJ said (at p. 77):

> Section 2(2) is clearly restrictive. Its primary purpose is to prevent indictments being preferred save after committal or alternative judicial leave. The proviso allows some relaxation, which is itself restricted by the final words 'being counts which may lawfully be joined in the same indictment'.
>
> It would, in our judgement, be contrary to the whole tenor of the section to allow the prosecution to prefer indictments in the way they here suggest without any reference to justices, judge or appellate court . . .
>
> It is true that the words 'bill of indictment' are apt to include more than one bill of indictment. Thus, . . . where the justices have committed on more than one charge, the prosecution are at liberty, in the appropriate case, to prefer a separate indictment in respect of each. However, charges in respect of which there has been no committal, even though based on evidence which was before the justices, can only be the proper subject of indictment where two conditions are satisfied. First, they must be in 'substitution' for or in addition to the counts in respect of which [the] defendant was committed. The contentions advanced by the prosecution involve the necessity . . . of treating this provision as otiose, or, even worse, of allowing the prosecution to prefer two indictments to create a notional 'substitution'.
>
> The second condition which has to be satisfied is that the new counts 'may lawfully be joined in the same indictment'. That must . . . mean the same indictment as that containing the charges on which the appellant was committed. That is clear from the whole context and also from the use of the word 'include'. The prosecution contentions require that those words should mean simply that no indictment must contain counts which cannot lawfully be joined, which scarcely

needs stating. If Parliament had intended the law to be as the prosecution claims it to be, it would have been easy in plain terms to say so.

In short, in the judgment of this court, the words of section 2(2) and its proviso are not apt to entitle the prosecution to prefer the second indictment.

(d) The proviso requires that any offence, other than one on which the accused was committed, must be founded on the committal statements, but it does not require that the evidence which those statements contain must be conclusive (*Biddis* [1993] Crim LR 392). In *Biddis*, it was argued that it was not permissible to add a count of possessing a firearm to the charge of robbery upon which the accused had been committed, because a statement formally proving that it was a firearm within the meaning of the Firearms Act 1968, s. 57(1), was not included in the committal papers. The Court of Appeal held that evidence that the gun had been loaded and fired was sufficient evidence from which the jury could reasonably have inferred that it was an effective weapon.

Limitations to the Application of the Proviso There are two important limitations to objections to indictments on the basis that there has not been compliance with the proviso. **D11.14**

(a) Insofar as an indictment consists of separate counts against several accused who are individually charged (i.e. there is no joint count), the counts against each accused should be treated for purposes of proviso (i) as a separate indictment. Therefore, if two accused, A1 and A2, were separately committed for trial (e.g., because, although their offences are linked, one was not arrested until after the committal of the other) and the prosecution then prefer a single indictment against them both, neither can successfully argue that the counts were preferred without authority simply because the offence alleged against his co-accused happened not to be disclosed by the evidence at the committal proceedings in respect of himself (*Groom* [1977] QB 6). This principle is now embodied in the *Consolidated Criminal Practice Direction*, para. IV.34.2 (see **D11.19** and **appendix** 7).
(b) Section 2(2) and its proviso do not apply to the amendment of an indictment, being concerned with the question of what offences can be included in the bill of indictment when it is *preferred.* The power to amend derives from the Indictments Act 1915, s. 5 (*Wells* (1995) 159 JP 243 and *Osieh* [1996] 1 WLR 1260; and see **D11.86**).

Counts for Summary Offences

In addition to being able to indict the accused for those offences for which he has been committed for trial together with any other indictable offences disclosed by the evidence on which the committal was founded, the drafter of an indictment has a limited power to include counts for certain summary offences. **D11.15**

The power is contained in the CJA 1988, s. 40, and arises when (s. 40(1)):

(a) the accused has been sent for trial for an indictable offence; and
(b) a summary offence to which s. 40 applies is either:
    (i) 'founded on the same facts or evidence as a count charging an indictable offence', or
    (ii) 'is part of a series of offences of the same or similar character as an indictable offence which is also charged'; and
(c) the facts or evidence relating to the summary offence were disclosed 'to a magistrates' court inquiring into the offence as examining justices', or are disclosed by material served on the accused as part of the procedure for sending indictable-only offences to the Crown Court under the CDA 1998, s. 51 and sch. 3 (see **D10**).

Where a count for a summary offence is included in an indictment by virtue of s. 40(1), it is tried exactly as if it were an indictable offence, but, if the accused is convicted, the maximum penalty that may be imposed is that which could have been imposed for the offence by a magistrates' court (s. 40(2)).

Criminal Justice Act 1988, s. 40

(1) A count charging a person with a summary offence to which this section applies may be included in an indictment if the charge—
   (a) is founded on the same facts or evidence as a count charging an indictable offence; or
   (b) is part of a series of offences of the same or similar character as an indictable offence which is also charged,

but only if (in either case) the facts or evidence relating to the offence were disclosed to a magistrates' court inquiring into the offence as examining justices or are disclosed by material which, in pursuance of regulations made under paragraph 1 of schedule 3 to the Crime and Disorder Act 1998 (procedure where person sent for trial under section 51), has been served on the person charged.

(2) Where a count charging an offence to which this section applies is included in an indictment, the offence shall be tried in the same manner as if it were an indictable offence; but the Crown Court may only deal with the offender in respect of it in a manner in which a magistrates' court could have dealt with him.

(3) The offences to which this section applies are—
   (a) common assault;
   (aa) an offence under section 90(1) of the Criminal Justice Act 1991 (assaulting a prisoner custody officer);
   (ab) an offence under section 13(1) of the Criminal Justice and Public Order Act 1994 (assaulting a secure training centre custody officer);
   (b) an offence under section 12(1) of the Theft Act 1968 (taking motor vehicle or other conveyance without authority etc.);
   (c) an offence under section 103(1)(b) of the Road Traffic Act 1988 (driving a motor vehicle while disqualified);
   (d) an offence [of criminal damage etc.] which would otherwise be triable only summarily by virtue of section 22(2) of [MCA 1980]; and
   (e) any summary offence specified under subsection (4) below.

(4) The Secretary of State may by order made by statutory instrument specify for the purposes of this section any summary offence which is punishable with imprisonment or involves obligatory or discretionary disqualification from driving.

D11.16 **The Relevant Summary Offences** The summary offences to which the CJA 1988, s. 40, applies are common assault, assaulting a prisoner custody officer or a secure training centre custody officer, taking a motor vehicle without the owner's consent, driving while disqualified and criminal damage where the value involved is the relevant sum or less (s. 40(3)).

For the purposes of s. 40(3), common assault includes the offence of battery (*Lynsey* [1995] 3 All ER 654).

Although included within the scope of s. 40, criminal damage is not, strictly speaking, a summary offence, even when the value involved is less than the relevant sum. The MCA 1980, s. 22, merely provides that, where it is clear that the value does not exceed the relevant sum of £5,000, the court 'shall proceed *as if* the offence were triable only summarily' (see *Fennell* [2000] 1 WLR 2011 and *Considine* (1980) 70 Cr App R 239). If the committing magistrates have not gone through the s. 22 procedure, the Court of Appeal has held that s. 40 will have no relevance, and the Crown Court is therefore not fettered by s. 40(2) to pass such sentence as could have been passed in a magistrates' court (*Alden* [2002] 2 Cr App R (S) 74).

However, the court came to the opposite view more recently in *Gwynn* [2003] 2 Cr App R (S) 41. The distinction between the two cases lies in the stage at which the criminal damage count was added to the indictment. In *Gwynn* the count had been on the indictment from the outset, and the court had applied its mind to the s. 22 consideration of the value of the criminal damage, whereas in *Alden* the count had been added once the case was in the Crown Court, and s. 22 did not therefore arise.

D11.17 **The Preconditions in s. 40 of the Criminal Justice Act 1988** As to the preconditions for including a count for a summary offence, the CJA 1988, s. 40(1), does *not* require the magistrates actually to have committed the accused for trial for the summary matter, although in practice the prosecution usually ask them so to do. What is essential is that the facts relating to the summary offence shall have been disclosed 'to a magistrates' court inquiring into the offence as examining justices'.

The phrases 'founded on the same facts *or evidence* as a count charging an indictable offence' and 'part of a series of offences of the same or similar character as an indictable offence', are taken almost verbatim from the Indictment Rules 1971, r. 9. The only significant difference between them is that r. 9 does not contain the words 'or evidence', and so to that extent the rule is narrower in ambit.

The Court of Appeal has provided guidance as to interpretation of the phrase:

(a) In *Bird* [1995] Crim LR 745, B was charged on an indictment containing two counts: (1) possession of an offensive weapon (triable either way) which was found in his car when he was stopped and (2) driving while disqualified (summary only), in relation to the fact that he was driving at all. The Court of Appeal, rejecting the argument that charge (2) was improperly joined, held that the two offences were committed at the same time as he drove along and were 'founded on the same facts or evidence'.
(b) In *Smith* [1997] QB 837, the Court of Appeal held that offences of driving a conveyance taken without authority and driving while disqualified were not offences of a similar character to dangerous driving (which was the only indictable offence in the indictment on which the defendant was tried). Since the first two offences were not founded on the same facts as the third offence, they were improperly joined to the indictment, and the convictions in respect of them were quashed (see **D11.57**).

Criminal Justice Act 1988, s. 41 Section 40 of the CJA 1988 should be read in conjunction with s. 41 of the same Act (see **D10.47**), which allows a magistrates' court to commit for *any* summary offence punishable with imprisonment or disqualification which arose out of circumstances the same as or connected with the circumstances of an either-way offence in respect of which they are also committing. Unlike s. 40, s. 41 does not entitle the prosecution to include in the indictment a count for the summary offence. However, if a magistrates' court commit under s. 41 in respect of a summary offence to which s. 40 also applies, the prosecution may in effect elect to proceed under the latter section simply by indicting for the summary offence (s. 41(4)). **D11.18**

DUPLICATION OF INDICTMENTS

Closely linked with the questions of authority to prefer an indictment and counts that may be included in an indictment (see **D11.11**) is the question of whether there may be more than one indictment outstanding against an accused for the same offence. The effect of the somewhat intricate case law is as follows: **D11.19**

(a) Ordinarily, a single committal may be used as authority to prefer several indictments (see, e.g., *Follett* [1989] QB 338 per Lord Lane CJ at p. 344H). Similarly, if several accused are all committed for trial on one occasion, the prosecution may choose to indict them separately if, for example, the offences are not sufficiently linked for a single trial to be in the interests of justice or they wish to use the evidence of one accused against the others.
(b) An accused may have two or more indictments outstanding against him for the same offence (*Poole* [1961] AC 223). Thus, if X has been committed for trial separately for offences A and B, if offences A and B are connected as required by the rules on joinder of counts, the prosecution may serve a joint indictment for both offences. The existence of a

prior indictment for offence A by itself is no bar to the later joint indictment but the prosecution will be required to elect before trial on which of the two they wish to proceed.

(c) Similarly, where two accused are separately committed for trial and it is then wished to have them tried together, the prosecution may prefer a joint indictment regardless of whether separate indictments have already been preferred against the two accused individually (*Groom* [1977] QB 6 and *Consolidated Criminal Practice Direction*, para. IV.34.2, set out in **appendix** 7).

(d) Equally, the prosecution may, where counts in an indictment are improperly joined, ask the judge for leave to prefer two or more fresh indictments out of time and then elect to proceed on those instead of on the original. The consequent duplication of counts between the original and fresh indictments is irrelevant (see *Follett* [1989] QB 338 at p. 345C–D). The prosecution must, however, ensure that the fresh indictments are preferred before the original one is quashed.

D11.20 **The Exception to the Rule** There is one qualification to the rule that a single committal may be used to found several indictments, namely that, if the indictment originally preferred as a result of the committal has been quashed, its effect is exhausted and authority to prefer a replacement indictment must be sought either through fresh proceedings or application to a High Court judge for a voluntary bill of indictment (*Thompson* [1975] 1 WLR 1425). In that case James LJ said (at p. 1429G):

> . . . the Crown is not entitled to prefer indictment after indictment if one indictment, then another and then another fails on a motion to quash. [So] having elected the form of indictment to be put before the trial court on the authority of the committal, if it is found that the election results in the quashing of that indictment the only course open to the Crown is to obtain leave to prefer a new bill and that leave can only be obtained from a High Court judge.

Although the judgment in *Thompson* appears to suggest that it is never permissible to prefer more than one indictment on the basis of one committal, that proposition runs counter to the decision in *Groom* [1977] QB 6, to the *Consolidated Criminal Practice Direction*, para. 34 and to the judgment of Lord Lane CJ in *Follett* [1989] QB 338, where he concluded (at p. 345E) that the narrower *ratio* of *Thompson* (i.e. the one just quoted) was undoubtedly the correct one.

As to voluntary bills of indictment more generally, see **D10.48**.

GENERAL FORM OF AN INDICTMENT

Layout

D11.21 The layout of an indictment should substantially follow the form given in the CrimPR and the Indictments Act 1915. Before 2 April 2007, the layout is given in sch. 1 to the Indictment Rules 1971, thereafter the form is set out in the CrimPR, r. 14.2(1). Hereinafter, the rules are referred to in their amended post-April 2007 form. The basic requirements as to the layout of an indictment are as follows:

(a) Each offence charged should be set out in a separate paragraph or *count* (r. 14.2(1)). If there is more than one count, they should be numbered (r. 14.2(4)).

(b) Each count should be divided into a statement of offence and particulars of offence (r. 14.2(1)(a) and (b)).

(c) The statement of offence describes the offence shortly in ordinary language, and, if the offence is statutory, should specify by section and subsection the provision contravened (Indictments Act 1915, s. 3(1), and r. 14.2(1)(a)).

(d) The particulars of offence should give 'such particulars as may be necessary for giving reasonable information as to the nature of the charge' (Indictments Act 1915, s. 3(1)).

This is supplemented by r. 14.2(1)(b) which states that there should be included 'such particulars of the conduct constituting the commission of the offence as to make clear what the prosecutor alleges against the defendant'.

Under r. 6 of the Indictment Rules 1971 there was a requirement that all the essential elements of the offence should be disclosed (r. 6(b)), save that (a) it was not necessary to allege that the accused fell outside any 'exception, proviso, excuse or qualification' to liability, and (b) failure to disclose an essential element could be disregarded if the accused was not thereby 'prejudiced or embarrassed in his defence' (proviso to r. 6(b) and (c)). This requirement has not been replicated in the CrimPR, part 14. All that is now required is that it is made clear by the statement of offence what legislation underlies the charge, and, by the particulars, what the accused is alleged to have done.

Indictments Act 1915, s. 3

(1) Every indictment shall contain, and shall be sufficient if it contains, a statement of the specific offence or offences with which the accused person is charged, together with such particulars as may be necessary for giving reasonable information as to the nature of the charge.

(2) Notwithstanding any rule of law or practice, an indictment shall, subject to the provisions of this Act, not be open to objection in respect of its form or contents if it is framed in accordance with the rules under this Act.

Degree of Detail Required in the Particulars

In normal circumstances, the particulars of offence are drafted in a short form. Such a course is encouraged as a means to avoid complex, lengthy or unmanageable trials (see *Cohen* (1992) *Independent*, 29 July 1992). **D11.22**

Such brevity does not prejudice the defence since the way the prosecution put their case and the evidence they intend to call will sufficiently emerge from the committal documents. For example, in *Teong Sun Chuah* [1991] Crim LR 463, the appellants were convicted of false accounting and obtaining by deception. One of the grounds of appeal was that no particulars were given of the false representations relied on in support of the counts of deception. The Court of Appeal said that, although it was advantageous for particulars to be given of the false representations in such cases, it was plain in the present case what the particulars were. No injustice was done by failing to spell them out in advance.

There are exceptions to this approach, however. In a complicated conspiracy to defraud, for example, it is established practice to give extended particulars. Similarly, in *Warburton-Pitt* (1991) 92 Cr App R 136, the prosecution's failure to particularise the facts upon which they relied in support of allegations of recklessness formed the basis of a successful appeal. The Court of Appeal said that particulars of the allegations of recklessness were needed because the case was a complicated one; there were a number of possible explanations for the incident.

It appears from a comparison of *Teong Sun Chuah* and *Warburton-Pitt* that the test is: do the particulars provided, whether in the indictment or elsewhere, meet the requirement in r. 14.2(1)(b) that there should be clarity as to the nature of the prosecution case?

This test has recently been reaffirmed by the Court of Appeal in *K* [2005] 1 Cr App R 408. The particulars of offence needed to provide reasonable information as to the nature of the charge and as to the principal matters on which the prosecution relied. In the case of a conspiracy charge, the indictment needed to spell out the agreement alleged, but such further information as is provided to assist the defence does not thereby become an ingredient of the offence that must be proved and on which the jury in due course have to be unanimous.

Moreover, it is open to the defence to ask for additional particulars. One of the purposes of

D

Part D Procedure

doing so is to anchor the prosecution to a particular means by which the charge may be made out (see, e.g., *Landy* [1981] 1 WLR 355 and *Hancock* [1996] 2 Cr App R 554).

Components of the Particulars

D11.23 Rule 5(2) of the Indictment Rules 1971 made provision for the rules to include specimen forms of counts approved by the Lord Chief Justice. No such specimens were provided under the 1971 Rules, and the 2007 redraft removes even reference to them. Such authority as there is on drafting counts for specific offences is therefore derived from decided cases. In addition, the CPS has issued guidance as to how particulars for certain offences should be drafted, and has drafted model forms for such counts (see <http://www.cps.gov.uk/legal/index.html>). A suggested form of count for the major offences will also be found in the section of this work dealing with the offence in question.

The standard components of particulars are:

(a) the names of the defendants charged in the count;
(b) the date of the offence (or the dates of the period within which it occurred if the precise date is not known);
(c) the act constituting the offence (e.g., 'stole' such and such an item of property, or 'inflicted grievous bodily harm' on such and such a person);
(d) the name of the victim of the offence (e.g., the owner of the property stolen or the person wounded or assaulted); and
(e) the state of mind on the part of the accused which the prosecution must establish in order to secure a conviction.

Points of drafting procedure which apply generally, whatever the specific offence alleged, are considered below.

D11.24 **Names** A person named in an indictment (whether as accused, victim or otherwise) should be described by his or her forenames and surname (see 2 Hale 175). Errors in stating names will not, however, affect the validity of the proceedings, provided that the misnamed person is identified with reasonable precision and the parties are not misled. Under r. 8 of the Indictment Rules 1971, it was sufficient where a person's name was not known to describe him as a 'person unknown'. There seems no reason to depart from that practice under the new rules. Trading companies may be described by their corporate name, whether or not they are incorporated.

D11.25 **Date of the Offence** The count should state the date on which the offence occurred insofar as it is known. Normal practice is to give the day of the month, followed by the month, followed by the year (e.g., 'on 1st day of January 2007'). If the precise date is unknown, it is sufficient to allege that the offence occurred 'on or about' a specified date, or 'on a day unknown' before a specified date, or 'on a date other than the date in count one'. Where the formula 'on or about' a date is used, the evidence must show the offence to have been committed 'within some period that has a reasonable approximation to the date mentioned in the indictment' (per Sachs LJ in *Hartley* [1972] 2 QB 1 at p. 7).

An alternative permitted formulation is 'on a day unknown between' two specified dates. If the last-mentioned formula is adopted, the days specified should be those immediately before the earliest and immediately after the latest days on which the offence could have been committed. Thus, if the accused is found in possession of stolen goods on 31 December 2006 and the prosecution case is that the goods were stolen on 1 January 2005, a count for handling would allege that he received the goods 'on a day unknown between 31 December 2004 and 1 January 2007'. See also the section below on duplicity in relation to this formulation.

D11.26 **Materiality of Date** If the evidence at trial as to date differs from that particularised in the count, that is not, as a rule, fatal to a conviction (*Dossi* (1918) 13 Cr App R 158). This position will be different where the allegation as to date is not merely procedural, but may determine the outcome of the case.

For example, in some instances the date on which the act occurred will affect the age of the alleged victim, which may be material. This was the case in *Radcliffe* [1990] Crim LR 524, where, in a case of indecency with a child, the judge in summing up said: 'The dates which are set out in the indictment . . . are immaterial. The prosecution do not have to prove that any particular act happened between those dates. What you have to prove is that it happened.' The Court of Appeal criticised this direction because the jury may have been left with the belief that her age was immaterial and that they could convict even if she was over 14 at the time.

Avoiding Prejudice as to Dates The decision in *Wright v Nicholson* [1970] 1 WLR 142, provides authority for the proposition that where the defence may have been prejudiced in the preparation of their case by a divergence during the evidence from the date specified in the count, the trial may be adjourned to allow them to respond to the altered situation. Alternatively, it might be necessary to discharge the jury and have a second trial on an amended indictment. Failure to allow an adjournment could result in the quashing of any resultant conviction as being unsafe or unsatisfactory. **D11.27**

However, some caution is necessary in applying that decision in the present context because (a) the appeal was not against conviction on indictment but against the dismissal by the Crown Court of an appeal against summary conviction, and (b) the Divisional Court's reasoning was partly based on the faulty premise that the Crown Court had power to amend the information on which the magistrates had convicted the appellant.

Amendment of Dates Since divergence between a count and the evidence as to date is not in itself fatal to conviction, it may be unnecessary for the prosecution to apply for the indictment to be amended on such a divergence becoming apparent (*Dossi* (1918) 13 Cr App R 158; but see *Bonner* [1974] Crim LR 479, where the Court of Appeal apparently overlooked the point). However, as a matter of practice, it may be preferable to eliminate the divergence by an appropriate amendment, thus avoiding confusing the jury. **D11.28**

Continuous Offences

In most instances, the rule against duplicity (i.e. each count may allege only one offence, see D11.41) requires that a count must allege that the offence occurred on *one* day, not on several days. Were it to be otherwise, the only sensible interpretation of such an allegation would be that the accused had committed several distinct offences on different days. Although, the prosecution is permitted to have one count for what are technically distinct criminal acts where those acts formed a single activity or transaction (e.g., pursuant to the CrimPR, r. 14.2(2)), the mention of more than one day (whether conjunctively or disjunctively) in the count is inconsistent with there having been a single activity on the accused's part. **D11.29**

The difference here is between an offence being committed once between a start and end date, and the offence having been committed repeatedly but separately on a number of days.

The exception to the general principle just stated is that where an offence is properly to be regarded as a continuing offence which may take place continuously or intermittently over a period of time, then a count may properly allege that it occurred on more than one day.

Enunciation of the Principle in *Hodgetts v Chiltern District Council* The leading authority on drafting charges for continuous offences is *Hodgetts v Chiltern District Council* [1983] 2 AC 120, in which the House of Lords was concerned with the validity of an information **D11.30**

under the Town and Country Planning Act 1971, s. 89(5). At the time of this case, the provision stated:

> Where, by virtue of an enforcement notice, a use of land is required to be discontinued . . . then if any person uses the land . . . in contravention of the notice, he shall be guilty of an offence and liable on summary conviction to a fine not exceeding £400; . . . and if the use is continued after the conviction, he shall be guilty of a further offence and liable on summary conviction to a fine not exceeding £50 for each day on which the use is so continued.

Interpreting the subsection, Lord Roskill held that it created two offences, an initial one committed immediately there was non-compliance with an enforcement notice requiring the subject of the notice to desist from a certain use of land, and a further offence committed by a person who had already been convicted of the initial offence and who still failed to desist from the prohibited use.

Since the information against H did not allege a prior conviction, it was plainly for an 'initial' offence, not a 'further offence'. The argument for H was that s. 89(5) was separately breached on each day of the period during which an enforcement notice was ignored, and a separate information was required for each day. Rejecting this argument, Lord Roskill said (at p. 128, emphasis added):

> It is not an essential characteristic of a criminal offence that any prohibited act or omission, in order to constitute a single offence, should take place once and for all on a single day. It may take place, whether continuously or intermittently, over a period of time.
>
> . . . as respects non-compliance with a 'desist' notice, it is in my view clear that the initial offence (as well as the further offence) though it too may take place over a period, whether continuously or intermittently (e.g., holding a Sunday market), is a single offence and not a series of separate offences committed each day that the non-compliance prior to the first conviction for non-compliance continues. If it were otherwise it would have the bizarre consequence that upon summary conviction a fine of £400 per diem could be imposed for each such separate offence committed before the offender received his first conviction, whereas for any further offence committed after the offender against a 'desist notice' had been convicted, a daily fine of only £50 could be inflicted. Uniquely a previous conviction would be a positive advantage to the offender. This can hardly have been Parliament's intention.
>
> . . . in the instant case each information . . . charged the offence 'on and since' a specified date . . . I see no objection to [that wording], but it might be preferable if hereafter offences under the first limb of section 89(5) were charged as having been committed between two specified dates, the termini usually being on the one hand the date when compliance with the enforcement notice first became due and on the other hand a date not later than the date when the information was laid, or of course some earlier date if meanwhile the enforcement notice has been complied with. *Indictments frequently charge offences as having been committed between certain dates.* I see no reason in principle why the same practice should not be followed with these informations [emphasis added].

D11.31 **Application of the Principle** Other than in circumstances to which the CrimPR, r. 14.2(2), has application, the following points on drafting counts for continuous offences emerge from the above decision:

(a) Although *Hodgetts v Chiltern District Council* [1983] 2 AC 120 concerned an information for a summary offence, the italicised words above make clear that the same principles apply to counts in an indictment.
(b) Determining whether an offence is properly to be treated as continuous will require detailed analysis of the offence-creating provision. In the absence of specific authority, the drafter of an indictment may have no means of knowing with certainty whether the offence for which he is indicting the accused is continuous or not. In such cases, it may be preferable to avoid potential complications by stating that the offence occurred on one day (not on several), unless the continuation of the misconduct significantly adds to the gravity of the case.

(c) That said, conspiracy is a clear example of a continuous indictable offence. The offence begins when any two or more parties enter into the unlawful agreement and continues until it comes to an end. See, e.g.:
   (i) *Greenfield* [1973] 1 WLR 1151 (and see **D11.42**), where a count for conspiring to cause explosions between 1 January 1968 and July 1971 was held not to be bad for duplicity;
   (ii) *Landy* [1981] 1 WLR 355, where the Court of Appeal, in indicating how the prosecution should have drafted a count for conspiracy to defraud a bank, suggested that the particulars could have begun '[The defendants] *on divers days* between . . . and . . . conspired together and with . . . '.

(d) Theft is clearly not a continuous offence. However, where the evidence is that the accused, on numerous separate occasions over a lengthy period, stole small sums or items of property, but it is not possible to particularise the exact days on which the appropriations occurred, it is possible to have a single count alleging that, on a day within the overall period, the accused stole all the relevant money or property. The cases on this point (known as the general deficiency cases) are considered at **B4.3** (see also the discussion of sample counts at **D11.33**). This problem may also be cured by the CrimPR, r. 14.2(2).

The effect of the CrimPR, r. 14.2(2) In its new form (from 2 April 2007), r. 14.2(2) states: **D11.32**

> More than one incident of the commission of an offence may be included in a count if those incidents taken together amount to a course of conduct having regard to the time, place or purpose of commission

Before this amendment, it had been argued that it was only possible to allege one incident per count, save where a general deficiency count was drafted, or it was asserted that one continuous offence had been committed (see **D11.29**). It was suggested that to allege more than one incident in a count fell foul of the rule against duplicity. The relationship between this amendment and that rule is discussed below (see **D11.44**).

Circumstances in which it is suggested to be appropriate to use r. 14.2(2) to charge a 'multiple offending count' are identified in the most recent version of the *Consolidated Criminal Practice Direction*, at para. IV.34.8:

> Rule 14.2(2) of the Criminal Procedure Rules allows a single count to allege more than one incident of the commission of an offence in certain circumstances. Each incident must be of the same offence. The circumstances in which such a count may be appropriate include, but are not limited to, the following:
> (a) the victim on each occasion was the same, or there was no identifiable individual victim as, for example, in a case of the unlawful importation of controlled drugs or of money laundering;
> (b) the alleged incidents involved a marked degree of repetition in the method employed or in their location, or both;
> (c) the alleged incidents took place over a clearly defined period, typically (but not necessarily) no more than about a year;
> (d) in any event, the defence is such as to apply to every alleged incident without differentiation. Where what is in issue differs between different incidents, a single 'multiple incidents' count will not be appropriate, though it may be appropriate to use two or more such counts according to the circumstances and to the issues raised by the defence.

Counts which allege more than one incident can give rise to certain difficulties. One, which was identified in *Kidd* [1998] 1 WLR 604, is that the accused should be sentenced only for offences on which he has been indicted and of which he has been convicted. This is discussed further at **D19.52**.

Specimen or Sample Counts

D11.33 Where a person is accused of adopting a systematic course of criminal conduct, and where it is not appropriate to allege a continuous offence (see **D11.29**) or a multiple offending count (see **D11.32**), the prosecution sometimes proceeds by way of specimen or sample counts. For example, where dishonesty over a period of time is alleged, a limited number of sample counts are included so as to avoid too lengthy an indictment.

D11.34 **Procedure for Specimen Counts** The practice which the prosecution ought to adopt in these circumstances is as follows:

(a) the defence should be provided with a list of all the similar offences of which it is alleged that those selected in the indictment are samples;
(b) evidence of some or all of these additional offences may in appropriate cases be led as evidence of system;
(c) in other cases, the additional offences need not be referred to until after a verdict of guilty upon the sample offence is returned (*DPP v Anderson* [1978] AC 964).

D11.35 **Potential Problems with Specimen Counts** Potential problems arise with specimen counts in relation to sentencing because the accused should not thereby be denied his right to be tried by a jury for offending for which he may ultimately be sentenced. This is discussed at **D19.56** *et seq.*

In any event, it is crucial that the accused should know the case he has to meet (*Evans* [1995] Crim LR 245). In *Rackham* [1997] 2 Cr App R 222, the Court of Appeal emphasised that the indictment had to be drafted in such a way as to enable the accused to know, with as much particularity as the circumstances would admit, what case he had to meet.

D11.36 **Split Trials** As an alternative to the use of specimen counts, ss. 17 to 21 of the DVCVA 2004 permit a court in certain circumstances to order that the trial of certain counts on an indictment take place before a jury in the normal way and that, if the jury convicts the accused on those counts, the remainder should then be tried before a judge alone. These provisions are set out and discussed at **D13.72**.

The form of such an indictment, and the procedure for their drafting and service is set out at paras. IV.34.4 to 34.7 of the *Consolidated Criminal Practice Direction*. The key points are:

(a) the prosecution must identify when drafting the indictment which counts should be tried by the jury and which should be held in reserve for the judge;
(b) when such an indictment is served, it should be accompanied by an application for a Preparatory Hearing, because it is only at such a hearing that such a mode of trial may be ordered (see **D14.46**).

Place of the Offence

D11.37 Provided the conduct alleged against the accused constitutes an offence regardless of where it occurred, it is unnecessary for the particulars to specify venue. In *Wallwork* (1958) 42 Cr App R 153, the particulars alleged that the offence, in that case of incest, had been committed 'in the county of Sussex or elsewhere'. The Court of Criminal Appeal held that the indictment was not bad for duplicity as the venue need not have been mentioned at all. Lord Goddard CJ said (at pp. 156–7):

> So far as place is concerned, I think [counsel for the prosecution's] point is a perfectly good one, that incest is an offence wherever it is committed, and it matters not whether it is committed in one place or another, provided the prisoner knows the substance of the charge against him. It makes no difference whether the incest in this case was committed in Sussex or Surrey or any other place. It is not intended by this single count to charge him with more than one offence of incest, and the words 'County of Sussex or elsewhere' in the opinion of the court are surplusage.

> It would have been a perfectly good indictment to charge him with the offence if the words 'in the County of Sussex or elsewhere' had been omitted, and there is no pretence for saying that he did not know the nature of the offence with which he was being charged. . . . There are cases . . . in which it is necessary to indicate a particular place in the indictment, and an illustration [is] the offence of larceny on a ship which was at the time of the larceny in a harbour or in a creek or other place of anchorage . . . where it would be necessary to show that the theft took place while the ship was in a harbour or some particular creek, and then it would be necessary to mention the name of the harbour or creek. But . . . it is not necessary to refer to any place in the indictment in an offence of this description.

The example given in the above passage of instances where the place of offence should be particularised may be anachronistic, but current examples of the same requirement are burglary and dangerous driving. Counts for the former should state the building entered as a trespasser, and counts for the latter the roads or other public places where the driving took place. The reason, in both cases, is that, having regard to the definition of the offences, the place where the prohibited conduct occurred is an essential ingredient of the crime.

Allegations as to Money and Property

The Criminal Procedure Act 1851, s. 18, provides that: **D11.38**

> In every indictment in which it shall be necessary to make any averment as to any money or any note of the Bank of England or any other bank, it shall be sufficient to describe such money or bank note simply as money, without specifying any particular coin or bank note; and such allegation, so far as regards the description of the property, shall be sustained by proof of any amount of coin or of any bank note, although the particular nature of the bank note shall not be proved.

Where the offence alleged is one against property, the count must give reasonable particulars of the property concerned. This is normally done by stating what the property was, and who owned it. If that is not known, the count may read 'belonging to a person unknown'. The value of the property need not be stated.

Indicting Secondary Parties

When indicting a secondary party to an offence, namely an aider, abettor, counsellor or procurer, there is no need to indicate, either in the statement of offence or particulars, that such was his role. This convenient rule flows from the Accessories and Abettors Act 1861, s. 8, which provides that: **D11.39**

> Whosoever shall aid, abet, counsel, or procure the commission of any indictable offence, whether the same be an offence at common law or by virtue of any Act passed or to be passed, shall be liable to be tried, *indicted*, and punished as a principal offender [emphasis added].

The usual practice is to take advantage of the 1861 Act and employ the same form of words in indicting a secondary party as would be used against a principal offender.

There is, however, no objection to an express allegation of aiding and abetting, and it may be preferable so to draft if the circumstances are such that the accused could not possibly have been guilty as a principal offender. In such cases, the precedent for a count against a principal offender may be adapted by prefixing the statement of offence with the words 'Aiding and abetting', and by inserting in the particulars 'aided and abetted [name of principal offender] to . . .'.

Where the prosecution are unsure of the precise role played by the accused, it is permissible to allege aiding, abetting, counselling or procuring in the alternative in one count (*Ferguson v Weaving* [1951] 1 KB 814).

The normal practice of indicting secondary parties as if they were principals in the first degree was criticised in *Maxwell* [1978] 1 WLR 1350, where the particulars for an offence of doing an act with intent, contrary to the Explosive Substances Act 1883, s. 3(a), alleged that M had planted a pipe bomb whereas in reality he had merely guided others to the scene where they planted it. The House of Lords dismissed M's appeal against conviction, but Viscount Dilhorne said, *obiter*, at p. 1352G:

> It is desirable that the particulars of the offence should bear some relation to the realities and where, as here, it is clear that the appellant was alleged to have aided and abetted the placing of the bomb and its possession or control, it would . . . have been better if the particulars of offence had made that clear.

Lords Hailsham of St Marylebone, Fraser and Edmund-Davies all commented to like effect; see, e.g., Lord Edmund-Davies at p. 1359G: 'However surprising and unreal such allegations might have sounded to a jury, . . . it has to be said that such wording [of the count] was strictly in accordance with section 8 of the Accessories and Abettors Act 1861'.

Consequences of Errors

D11.40 What if the particulars of offence are incorrect? In *Moses* [1991] Crim LR 617, the Court of Appeal observed that particulars of offence were not like the words of a statute, such that failure of the facts proved to fall precisely within them was fatal. It seems that the test to apply in relation to incorrect particulars is whether the defence were prejudiced by the erroneous description of the offence (see also *Hancock* [1996] 2 Cr App R 554).

THE RULE AGAINST DUPLICITY

The Rule

D11.41 The ordinary rule is that each count in an indictment must allege only one offence. If a count alleges more than one offence, it is said to be bad for duplicity, and should be quashed before arraignment.

D11.42 **Duplicity Revealed by the Wording of the Count** Whether or not a count is bad for duplicity is decided by looking at its wording without reference to the prosecution evidence as disclosed by the committal documents (*Greenfield* [1973] 1 WLR 1151, followed in *Mintern* [2004] EWCA Crim 07).

This is illustrated by *Greenfield* itself, in which the appellants and others were charged in a count which alleged that they had conspired together to cause by explosive substances explosions in the UK. The prosecution relied on evidence of a series of explosions occurring in different parts of England which the jury were invited to conclude had all been the work of the same group.

On appeal, the defence argued that the conspiracy count was bad for duplicity because, as the trial progressed, the evidence was consistent with the existence of more than one conspiracy. The Court of Appeal held that, even if that were so, it did not affect the validity of the count, although it was essential that the jury should be directed to convict only if they found the offence charged proved. Lawton LJ said (at pp. 1155F–1156B):

> [Counsel for the appellants] submitted that count 1 [the conspiracy count] was bad in law because as the trial progressed the evidence was consistent with the existence of more than one conspiracy. In our judgment that did not make the count bad in law. A conspiracy count is bad in law if it *charges* the defendants with having been members of two or more conspiracies. This is elementary law. . . . [Count 1] referred to one conspiracy only . . . judges may be in doubt as to what they should consider before deciding whether a conspiracy count is bad for duplicity. They should look first at the count itself. In most cases it will be unnecessary to look at any other material. If particulars of the count have been requested and given, those too should be

considered. . . . If the prosecution has been requested to give particulars and has refused to do so, the judge may have to look at the depositions to discover the nature of the charge.

Duplicity in a count is a matter of form; it is not a matter relating to the evidence called in support of the count.

Thus, leaving aside the exceptional case of the defence having asked for and been refused additional particulars of a count, the only matters to be considered by a judge determining whether a count is bad for duplicity are the form (i.e. wording) of the count and any additional particulars supplied by the prosecution. The evidence as disclosed on the committal documents is irrelevant.

If the evidence called at trial in fact establishes more than one offence but only one offence is charged in the count, then, subject to any possible amendment of the indictment, the accused will be entitled to an acquittal, not because the count was bad, but because the prosecution have failed to prove him guilty of the precise offence charged in the count, even though they may have proved him guilty of some other offence or offences (see *Griffiths* [1966] 1 QB 589).

Consideration of the Meaning of 'Offence' The proposition that a count must charge only one offence begs the question, what is an offence? The issue came before the House of Lords in *DPP v Merriman* [1973] AC 584. In that case two brothers (FM and JM) were charged in a joint count with wounding with intent. The prosecution case against JM was that, following a dispute in a public house, he stabbed P in the back, after which both he and FM, who had pleaded guilty, joined in stabbing P about seven times. The judge directed the jury that they should ignore any possibility that JM was acting in concert with his brother, and should concentrate solely on whether he had personally stabbed P. **D11.43**

Such a direction was contrary to a line of authority (see especially *Scaramanga* [1963] 2 QB 807) which established that, if one of two defendants charged in a single count was found or pleaded guilty, the other could be convicted only if the jury were satisfied that he had taken part in the *joint* offence. The Court of Appeal had applied *Scaramanga* and quashed JM's conviction. The decision of the House of Lords in *Merriman* was to overrule the *Scaramanga* line of authority.

In reaching their ultimate decision, the House of Lords considered the true import of the rule against duplicity. Lord Morris of Borth-y-Gest said (at p. 593A–E):

It is . . . a general rule that not more than one offence is to be charged in a count in an indictment. . . . The question arises—what is an offence? If A attacks B and, in doing so, stabs B five times with a knife, has A committed one offence or five? If A in the dwelling-house of B steals 10 different chattels, some perhaps from one room and some from others, has he committed one offence or several? In many different situations comparable questions could be asked. In my view, such questions when they arise are best answered by applying common sense and by deciding what is fair in the circumstances. No precise formula can usefully be laid down but I consider that clear and helpful guidance was given by Lord Widgery CJ in . . . *Jemmison v Priddle* [1972] 1 QB 489 at p. 495. I agree . . . that it will often be legitimate to bring a single charge in respect of what might be called one activity even though that activity may involve more than one act. It must, of course, depend upon the circumstances. In the present case, it was not at any time suggested, and in my view could not reasonably have been suggested, that count 1 was open to objection because evidence was to be tendered that the respondent stabbed [P] more than once.

In a similar vein, Lord Diplock said (at p. 607C):

The rule against duplicity, viz. that only one offence should be charged in any count of an indictment . . . has always been applied in a practical, rather than in a strictly analytical, way for the purpose of determining what constituted one offence. Where a number of acts of a similar nature committed by one or more defendants were connected with one another, in the time and place of their commission or by their common purpose, in such a way that they could fairly be regarded as forming part of the same transaction or criminal enterprise, it was the practice, as early as the 18th century, to charge them in a single count of an indictment. Where such a count was laid against more than one defendant, the jury could find each of them guilty of one offence only: but a failure by the prosecution to prove the allegation, formerly expressly stated in the indictment but now only implicit in their joinder in the same count, that the unlawful acts of each were done jointly in aid of one another, did not render the indictment *ex post facto* bad or invalidate the jury's verdict against those found guilty.

D11.44 **The Test Derived from *DPP v Merriman*** In summary, the conclusion in *DPP v Merriman* [1973] AC 584 was that a count is not to be held bad on its face for duplicity merely because its words are logically capable of being construed as alleging more than one criminal act. This applies whether a count is against one accused or several.

The test of whether it is proper to have a single count is: can the separate acts attributed to the accused fairly be said to form a single activity or transaction? (see **D11.51**). It follows from that test that, if the particulars of a count can sensibly be interpreted as alleging a single activity, it will not be bad for duplicity, even if a number of distinct criminal acts are implied.

This interpretation of the rule against duplicity clearly forms the basis for the new rule permitting 'multiple offences' counts to be found in the CrimPR, r. 14.2(2). As the wording of that rule demonstrates, what is permitted is a count alleging a series of offences that amount to a course of conduct, or to use Lord Diplock's words the same 'criminal enterprise'.

Practical Application of the Rule

D11.45 Thus, the rule against duplicity rests ultimately on common sense and pragmatic considerations of what is fair in all the circumstances. That being so, the rule is best understood in terms of past decisions on what is acceptable drafting practice, rather than by applying an artificial concept of what is a single offence. The guidelines below emerge from the cases.

D11.46 **Several Dates** Unless the offence charged is properly to be construed as a continuing offence (see **D11.29**), a count alleging that the accused committed criminal acts on more than one day is bad for duplicity.

For example, in *Thompson* [1914] 2 KB 99, the count charged alleged the commission of incest 'on divers days between the month of January, 1909, and the 4th day of October, 1910'. Although the Court of Criminal Appeal dismissed the appeal because the appellant had had ample notice of the precise dates on which the acts of incest were said to have occurred, it was common ground that the count was 'irregular' because it patently alleged more than one offence.

However, in *DPP v McCabe* [1992] Crim LR 885, a charge alleging that M stole 76 library books from South Glamorgan Library between two specified dates was held not to be bad for duplicity. The Divisional Court held that where there is appropriation of a number of articles, but no evidence as to when the individual appropriations took place, the prosecution is entitled to charge the appropriation of the aggregate number within a specified period.

D11.47 **Several Items of Property** A count for an offence against property may allege that several items were stolen, damaged, obtained by deception, unlawfully possessed or otherwise subjected to the accused's criminal behaviour (per Lord Morris of Borth-y-Gest in the passage from *DPP v Merriman* [1973] AC 584, quoted at **D11.43**, and see *Wilson* (1979) 69 Cr App R 83). Provided there is nothing on the face of the count to indicate to the contrary, it will be presumed that, even if a separate criminal act is being alleged in respect of each item, those acts were so closely related as to form part of a single activity and are therefore properly charged in a single count.

A single count is appropriate if only one act is being alleged, albeit that the act was in respect of several items (e.g., *Thomas* (1800) 2 East PC 934, in which a count for uttering a number of forged receipts in one bundle was upheld). But the special circumstances of a case may make separate counts for each item necessary or desirable even if what is alleged against the accused is a single act or activity. For example, in *Bristol Crown Court, ex parte Willets* (1985) 149 JP 416, where the accused was charged with possession of five obscene videos, the Divisional Court said it would have been better to include five separate counts to allow the jury to consider the obscenity of each video individually (see also *Malhi* [1994] Crim LR 755).

Several Victims Old cases provide examples of a single count naming more than one person as the victim of the offence (see, e.g., *Giddins* (1842) Car & M 634). Modern practice, however, is in general to have a separate count per victim (see, e.g., *Mansfield* [1977] 1 WLR 1102, in which M was charged, *inter alia*, with seven counts of murder, a different victim being named in each count, even though all seven deaths resulted from a single fire allegedly started by M). **D11.48**

Even so, what is appropriate must depend ultimately on the facts of each case. For example:

(a) In *Shillingford* [1968] 1 WLR 566, the Court of Appeal said it was unnecessary to have two separate counts where it was alleged that the appellant had administered a drug to enable both himself and another to have unlawful sexual intercourse with the victim. According to Salmon LJ: '. . . the essence of this offence consists in administering the drug, and . . . accordingly in this particular case there was only one offence under the section. . . . In the view of this court, if there is only one administration there is only one offence, whether the administration was for the purpose of enabling one man or half a dozen men to have intercourse with the woman in question.'
(b) Similarly, in *Jemmison v Priddle* [1972] 1 QB 489, an information for taking and killing two red deer was held not to be bad for duplicity because the deer were shot within seconds of each other. In that case, however, there certainly could not have been any objection to two informations.

Count Alleging Acts or Omissions in the Alternative

A separate question is raised where the statutory provision creating an offence indicates that it may be committed either by one of a number of positive acts or by a failure to act in one of a number of ways. This problem was specifically addressed by the Rules in their pre-April 2007 incarnation. Rule 7 of the Indictment Rules 1971 stated: **D11.49**

> Where an offence created by or under an enactment states the offence to be the doing or the omission to do any one of any different acts in the alternative, or the doing or the omission to do any act in any one of any different capacities, or with any one of any different intentions, or states any part of the offence in the alternative, the acts, omissions, capacities or intentions, or other matters stated in the alternative in the enactment or subordinate instrument may be stated in the alternative in an indictment charging the offence.

Although the new version of the rules relating to indictments does not replicate r. 7, the principle remains that a count containing particulars framed in the alternative is not necessarily bad for duplicity, as is recognised for example by the CrimPR, r. 14.2(2).

However, if an enactment creates several offences and it is desired to charge two or more of those offences in the alternative, the indictment must contain a separate count for each. Furthermore, it is plain that a single section, subsection or paragraph of a statute may be construed as creating more than one offence (see, e.g., *Naismith* [1961] 1 WLR 952 at **D11.50**). What is required, therefore, is a correct assessment of whether a statutory provision is creating one offence that may be committed in a number of alternative ways, or is creating several separate offences. If the former, these statutory alternatives may be particularised as alternatives in one count; if the latter, the rule against duplicity applies and each alternative the prosecution wish to put before the jury must go into a separate count.

D11.50 **Application of the Rule as to Alternative Acts or Omissions** It follows from the discussion at **D11.49** that decisions on whether an enactment creates one or several offences have consistently turned on whether, in defining the conduct prohibited, the enactment refers to a single act (or omission) or to several. If one act is referred to, the enactment will almost certainly be construed as creating one offence, even if the *mens rea* or other elements thereof are defined in the alternative; if more than one, it will be held that the enactment creates a separate offence for each separate act.

For example, in *Naismith* [1961] 1 WLR 952, Ashworth J, in determining whether an allegation under military law that N had 'caused grievous bodily harm to H with intent to do him grievous bodily harm or to maim, disfigure or disable him' was bad for duplicity, said (at p. 954):

> It seems to this court that the proposition with which [counsel for the Crown] started his argument is the right approach. That approach is to keep in mind the distinction between a section creating two or more offences and a section creating one offence but providing that that offence may be committed in more than one way . . . so far as the intents specified in section 18 are concerned, they are variations of method rather than creations of separate offences in themselves. It is probably true to say that the species of assault mentioned in that section, of which there are three, are each in themselves different offences, that is to say, wounding, causing grievous bodily harm and shooting, but that difference does not affect the result of this case in the least because the only act or species of assault alleged was causing grievous bodily harm.

Similarly, it was held in *Thomson v Knights* [1947] KB 336 that a count for being in charge of a motor vehicle when unfit through drink or drugs (contrary to what is now s. 4 of the Road Traffic Act 1988) was valid because the section made criminal one act, namely being in charge of a vehicle, in two situations, namely when under the influence of drink or when under the influence of drugs.

By contrast, in *Mallon v Allon* [1964] 1 QB 385, an information for admitting and allowing to remain in a licensed betting office a person apparently under 18 contrary to s. 5 of the Betting and Gaming Act 1960 (now repealed) was held bad because the enactment referred to two separate acts, first admitting a person on to licensed premises, and secondly allowing him to remain after he had got on to the premises.

Comparison of *Mallon v Allon* with *Thomson v Knights* indicates that the number of offences an enactment is held to create, whether one or several, turns on a fine analysis of the enactment in question, as well as on pragmatic considerations of whether one or several counts would be fairer (for further discussion of this topic see, e.g., **B4.129** and **B4.137**, and *Nicklin* [1977] 1 WLR 403, on the number of counts appropriate when the accused is charged with handling stolen goods).

'Quasi-duplicity'

D11.51 The foregoing discussion of the rule against duplicity has distinguished between a prosecution case to the effect that the accused committed a number of distinct offences, which must always be put in separate counts, and an allegation merely that he committed a number of distinct criminal acts which, since they formed part of one activity or transaction, can properly go into a single count. The distinction was mentioned by both Lord Morris of Borth-y-Gest and Lord Diplock in their opinions in *DPP v Merriman* [1973] AC 584 (quoted at **D11.43**), but the leading authority is the Court of Appeal decision in *Wilson* (1979) 69 Cr App R 83, which incorporates the essential parts of the judgment of Lord Widgery CJ in *Jemmison v Priddle* [1972] 1 QB 489.

D11.52 **The Approach in *Wilson*** In *Wilson* (1979) 69 Cr App R 83, W was charged with two counts alleging thefts from Debenhams and Boots. It was submitted on W's behalf that because the items stolen had come from different departments of the stores in question the counts should have been split so as to have a separate count for the items allegedly stolen from each department. Browne LJ (giving the judgment of the Court of Appeal) distinguished between duplicity in the full sense of the term and what he described as quasi-duplicity or divergence. He said (at p. 85):

> The word duplicity is used in a rather ambiguous sense. . . . First there is a case where it appears on the face of the indictment, or particulars of the indictment, that a count is charging more than one offence. It may sometimes be legitimate to look at the depositions in this context (see *Greenfield* [1973] 1 WLR 1151). That has been referred to in the course of the argument as true duplicity. Secondly, there is a case where, although the indictment is good on its face, it appears at the close of the prosecution case that the evidence establishes that more than one offence was committed on the occasion to which a particular count relates. Perhaps that is best described as divergence or departure, but it often seems to be called duplicity . . . in whatever sense one uses the word duplicity, it is confined to those two situations. But even if a case is not within either the first or the second of those situations, there may be cases where, in the interests of justice, it may be right to make the prosecution split a count or elect on what particular charge they are going to proceed.

In *Wilson* it was argued that the appellant's case fell within the second of the two situations outlined by Browne LJ (i.e. it was a case of divergence or departure rather than true duplicity). Having reviewed the authorities (especially *Jemmison v Priddle* [1972] 1 QB 489), Browne LJ adopted what Lord Widgery CJ had said in *Jemmison v Priddle* as correctly stating the law ((1979) 69 Cr App R 83 at pp. 86–7):

> Lord Widgery CJ said this . . . 'What is the principle which distinguishes between [cases where one count is appropriate and cases where there should be several counts]? . . . one finds that the explanation is given in somewhat inappropriate language, namely, that the test is whether the acts were all one transaction. That is a phrase hallowed by time, but not, in my judgment, of particular assistance in dealing with a particular problem. I find more assistance from somewhat different language used by Lord Parker CJ in *Ware v Fox* [1967] 1 WLR 379.' Then Lord Widgery CJ quotes from what Lord Parker CJ had said at p. 381 . . . and went on: 'I think perhaps that the phraseology of Lord Parker is more helpful to me than the phraseology often found in the text books, and I think that what it means is this, that it is legitimate to charge in a single information one activity even though the activity may involve more than one act. One looks at this case [i.e., *Jemmison v Priddle*] and asks oneself what was the activity with which the appellant was being charged. It was the activity of shooting red deer without a game licence, and although as a nice debating point it might well be contended that each shot was a separate act, indeed that each killing was a separate offence, I find that all these matters, occurring as they must have done within a very few seconds of time and all in the same geographical location are fairly to be described as components of a single activity, and that made it proper for the prosecution in this instance to join them in a single charge.'

Browne LJ concluded that: 'Whether there is one or more offence disclosed is really a question of fact and degree' ((1979) 69 Cr App R 83 at p. 88). On the facts of *Wilson*, the appellant 'entirely failed to satisfy' the court that the counts complained of disclosed more than one offence.

Application of the *Wilson* Principle Thus, the principle emerging from *Wilson* (1979) 69 Cr App R 83 and the earlier cases is simply that more than one criminal act may properly be alleged in one count if the acts formed a single activity. Whether there was one activity or several depends on the facts of each individual case. **D11.53**

This has recently been illustrated in *Iaquaniello* [2005] EWCA Crim 2029. In that case, the accused was charged on an indictment containing a count of doing an act or a series of acts tending and intended to pervert the course of public justice. The Court of Appeal held that it was not duplicitous for a count to state, in this context, 'act or acts'. Where the particulars of offence alleged that the accused did an act or a series of acts tending, and intended, to pervert the course of justice, it was not duplicitous to particularise the acts within one count on the indictment.

The *Wilson* principle is now reflected in the CrimPR, r. 14.2(2), save that the wording there used is that the acts 'amount to a course of conduct' rather than 'one activity'.

Charging Offences Conjunctively in an Effort to Avoid the Rule against Duplicity

D11.54 It has so far been assumed that the rule against duplicity will apply whether separate offences are alleged in one count as alternatives or conjunctively. That assumption is in line with the overwhelming weight of authority. One decision apparently to the contrary, namely *Clow* [1965] 1 QB 598, related to s. 1(1) of the Road Traffic Act 1960, which created three different offences. The particulars of the count alleged two of the three offences under the section in one count. The Court of Criminal Appeal held that, 'it is permissible to charge them [i.e. the separate offences under s. 1(1)] conjunctively as in the present case if the matter relates to one single incident, as of course it does in the present case'.

Clow was distinguished in *Mallon v Allon* [1964] 1 QB 385 (see **D11.50**), where an information under s. 5 of the Betting and Gaming Act 1960 for allowing an under-age person to 'enter *and* remain upon licensed premises' was held to be invalid, despite the use of the conjunctive rather than the disjunctive. Furthermore, the replacement of the offences in s. 1(1) of the Road Traffic Act 1960 with a single offence under s. 1 of the Road Traffic Act 1988 means that, as regards the actual point it decided, *Clow* is no longer significant. The same rule should therefore apply whether a count is framed conjunctively or disjunctively.

Effect of Breach of the Rule against Duplicity

D11.55 Where a count is bad on its face for duplicity, the defence should move to quash it before the accused is arraigned. Although the objection can be taken at a later stage (*Johnson* [1945] KB 419), the Court of Appeal has disapproved of the defence postponing the application to quash for purely tactical reasons (see *Asif* (1982) 82 Cr App R 123). It is open to the prosecution to defeat a motion to quash by asking the judge to allow a suitable amendment of the indictment (see Indictments Act 1915, s. 5(1), for the power to amend indictments at **D11.86**).

The procedure of applying to quash a count will be available only if it is a case of 'true' duplicity, namely that the wording of the count shows that two or more offences are being alleged. Such a motion has to be determined solely by considering the wording of the indictment, without reference to the evidence. In a case of quasi-duplicity or divergence (see *Wilson* (1979) 69 Cr App R 83 and **D11.51**), which becomes apparent only after the evidence has been called, the defence should wait until the close of the prosecution case and then ask the judge to split the count.

Rejection by the trial judge of a motion to quash a count bad on its face for duplicity and/or rejection of an application to split a count open to objection for quasi-duplicity are plainly valid grounds of appeal. In *Donnelly* [1998] Crim LR 131, the Court of Appeal made it clear that cases of true duplicity and quasi-duplicity would be differently treated. In a case where the count was plainly duplicitous in form the appeal must be allowed, even if the point had not been taken at trial (though this does not necessarily follow, see *Thompson* [1914] 2 KB 99). In cases of 'quasi duplicity', a motion to quash the indictment should be moved before the trial judge. If it was not, the appeal would fail unless it was accompanied by an allegation of incompetence by counsel.

JOINDER OF COUNTS IN INDICTMENT

The Rule

D11.56 The circumstances in which the prosecution may lawfully join two or more counts against one accused in a single indictment are prescribed by the CrimPR, r. 14.2(3), which replaces the test formally contained in r. 9 of the Indictment Rules 1971 without any significant alteration to its content. It now states:

> An indictment may contain more than one count if all the offences charged—
> (a) are founded on the same facts; or
> (b) form or are a part of a series of offences of the same or a similar character.

An indictment containing counts which are not linked in either of the ways mentioned in r. 14.2(3) is invalid (although not a nullity), and any convictions returned on such an indictment are liable to be quashed on appeal.

Application of the Rule

Unsurprisingly, cases in which the application of the rule have been considered relate to r. 9 of the Indictment Rules 1971 rather than the CrimPR, r. 14.2(3). There is no reason to anticipate that the slight changes to the wording of the rule would have any bearing on its application, and such cases are therefore still relevant. **D11.57**

In *Newland* [1988] QB 402, N was charged in an indictment containing counts for possessing a Class B drug with intent to supply, and three assaults occasioning actual bodily harm, which offences were entirely unconnected. At trial, when counsel for N submitted that the indictment was invalid, the judge held that he had power under s. 5(3) of the Indictments Act 1915 (see **D11.68**) to sever the indictment. On appeal, the Court of Appeal held as follows.

(a) The power to sever under s. 5(3) applies only to a valid indictment. Watkins LJ, giving the court's judgment, said (at p. 406C–D):

> It was contended by counsel for the prosecution that the [trial judge] rightly derived the power he used from [Indictments Act 1915, s. 5(3)]. But we are in no doubt, in accepting the contrary submission of counsel for the appellant, that that subsection can only apply to a valid indictment. It states what the court may do by way of ordering separate trials of counts in a valid indictment in the interests of a fair trial for a defendant or defendants. The [trial judge] was wrong in his interpretation of that subsection.

(b) The trial judge could have amended the indictment so as to delete either the drugs count or the assault counts. That having been done, the trial could validly have proceeded on what remained (p. 406F). See also *Follett* [1989] QB 338.
(c) Given that no amendment had in fact been made, the unamended indictment was invalid by reason of the contravention of r. 9. Because it was capable of being rendered valid by an appropriate amendment, it was not a nullity (p. 408C–D applying *Bell* (1984) 78 Cr App R 305). But, even though the indictment itself was not a nullity, the fact of its being invalid was sufficient to render null the proceedings flowing from it (p. 408E).
(d) In the circumstances, no valid trial ever commenced and the court's powers under the Criminal Appeal Act 1968, s. 2(1), to quash a conviction and sentence therefore did not come into play. Having concluded that the proceedings against N were null, the court had no option but to exercise its inherent power at common law to quash the convictions (p. 408G–H).

In *Smith* [1997] QB 837, the Court of Appeal disapproved of *Newland* insofar as it related to the effect of misjoinder, as outlined in (c) above. Their lordships held that it was wrong to suggest that all proceedings flowing from an indictment containing a count improperly joined were a nullity (as opposed to the proceedings on the improperly joined count). *Smith* was approved and followed in *Lockley* [1997] Crim LR 455.

First Limb of Rule 14.2(3) of the Criminal Procedure Rules: Charges Founded on the Same Facts

D11.58 The first limb of r. 14.2(3) is clearly satisfied if the offences alleged in counts joined in one indictment arose out of a single incident or an uninterrupted course of conduct (see, e.g., *Mansfield* [1977] 1 WLR 1102, where the indictment against M was held to be properly joined where it contained counts for arson and murder relating to the same fire).

D11.59 **Joinder where One Offence is a Precondition of the Second** Rule 14.2(3) of the CrimPR, like its predecessor, is not restricted to offences that were committed contemporaneously or substantially contemporaneously with each other, as in *Mansfield* [1977] 1 WLR 1102 (see D11.58), but extends to situations where later offences would not have been committed but for the prior commission of an earlier offence.

The leading authority is *Barrell* (1979) 69 Cr App R 250, where the appellants were charged jointly in counts 1 and 2 with affray and assault occasioning actual bodily harm, and W alone was charged in count 3 with attempting to pervert the course of justice. This third count related to an attempt by W to persuade the witness to counts 1 and 2 to 'modify' his evidence. On appeal it was submitted that count 3 did not arise from the same facts as counts 1 and 2. The argument was rejected by the Court of Appeal. Shaw LJ, giving the judgment of the court, said (at pp. 252–3):

> The phrase 'founded on the same facts' does not mean that for charges to be properly joined in the same indictment, the facts in relation to the respective charges must be identical in substance or virtually contemporaneous. The test is whether the charges have a common factual origin. If the charge described by counsel as the subsidiary charge is one that could not have been alleged but for the facts which give rise to what he called the primary charge, then it is true to say for the purposes of rule 9 that those charges are founded, that is to say have their origin, in the same facts and can legitimately be joined in the same indictment.

If W had not been involved in the violence which gave rise to the charges of assault and affray, he would have had no motive for offering the witness a bribe. It followed that all three counts had a common factual origin and were properly joined in one indictment.

D11.60 **Joinder of Mutually Destructive Counts** Difficulty has arisen over whether the principle in *Barrell* (1979) 69 Cr App R 250 can properly be extended to counts that are mutually destructive, that is, the prosecution evidence is such that, if their case on one count is accepted, the accused cannot have committed the offence alleged in the other count and vice versa.

The House of Lords settled the point in *Bellman* [1989] AC 836. The case centred on representations which B had made to obtain money. If they were false, he had obtained the property by deception. If they were true, he had conspired to evade the prohibition on the importation of controlled drugs. The indictment contained counts both for conspiracy and for obtaining by deception.

On appeal, B relied 'upon the more fundamental proposition that under our adversarial procedure of trial in which the burden of establishing the guilt of the accused is placed on the prosecution, it can never be right for mutually contradictory counts to be contained in one indictment. He submitted that to do so would be contrary to the prosecution's duty of proving the case, unfair to the accused and an embarrassment for the jury' (pp. 846H–847A). Lord Griffiths rejected the argument. There was nothing in the Indictments Act 1915 to support it; r. 9 of the Indictment Rules 1971 prima facie contradicted it, and no authority had been cited in which joinder had been refused on the ground that the facts of two counts were mutually destructive (p. 849B–D). On the other hand, it had long been the practice to include in one indictment counts for stealing and handling the same property even though a conviction for theft would necessarily preclude a conviction for handling and vice versa (see *Shelton* (1986) 83 Cr App R 379 for approval of the practice).

Moreover, there will be occasions when justice can be done only by drafting mutually contradictory counts. An example is provided by the facts of *Barnes* (1985) 83 Cr App R 38, where the indictment contained counts for perjury and wounding with intent, the case being that Barnes was either telling the truth at an earlier trial and so was guilty of wounding, or he was telling lies, in which case he was guilty of perjury. The Court of Appeal dismissed the appeal on the ground that, whether or not the joinder of the mutually destructive counts was lawful, there had on the facts been no miscarriage of justice.

In *Bellman*, Lord Griffiths, *obiter*, confirmed the legality of the joinder because the factual origin of both counts was the attack on the victim (see p. 850F–G). Furthermore, the joinder was necessary in the interests of justice since, had Barnes been tried separately for the two offences, he might have 'played the system' by obtaining an acquittal for perjury through testifying that he had indeed wounded the victim and then, at his later trial for wounding, he could have reversed his evidence, secure in the knowledge that he could not be prosecuted again for perjury.

Application of the Decision in *Bellman* Although the decision in *Bellman* [1989] AC 836 puts beyond doubt the propriety of joining mutually destructive counts in one indictment, the prosecution will rarely wish to prefer such an indictment in practice, since it leaves open the risk that a jury will not be able to reach a verdict on either. **D11.61**

As a matter of evidence, it is clear that if, at the end of the prosecution case, it is established that the accused has committed a crime but it is impossible to say which, the judge must direct the jury to acquit. Similarly, if, as in *Bellman* itself, there is evidence on which the jury could properly convict of either count, they must nonetheless be directed in the summing-up that, should they be left in doubt about which of the two offences the accused has committed, they are under a duty to acquit of both, even though they are sure he committed one or other. The various evidential problems that may arise from mutually destructive counts are discussed by Lord Griffiths in *Bellman* at p. 847. See further **D15.60.**

Second Limb of Rule 14.2(3) of the Criminal Procedure Rules: Series of Offences of the Same or a Similar Character

The circumstances in which two or more offences may be said to amount to a series of offences of the same or similar character within the meaning of the second limb of r. 14.2(3) were considered by the House of Lords in *Ludlow v Metropolitan Police Commissioner* [1971] AC 29. The indictment against L contained counts for (a) attempted theft at a public house in Acton on 20 August and (b) robbery at a different public house in Acton on 5 September. The trial judge refused an application that the two charges should be tried separately, and L was convicted on both counts. The case was considered by the House of Lords, where Lord Pearson delivered the leading opinion. The main points emerging from this opinion are as follows. **D11.62**

(a) Two offences are capable of constituting a 'series' for purposes of r. 9 (see p. 38E–G confirming the Court of Appeal decision in *Kray* [1970] 1 QB 125).
(b) In deciding whether offences exhibit the similarity demanded by the rule, the court should take into account both their legal and their factual characteristics (p. 39B). The prosecution submission (that the phrase 'a similar character' means exclusively of a similar legal character) and the defence submission (that the phrase means exclusively of a similar factual character) were each rejected.
(c) To show the existence of a series of offences, the prosecution must be able to point to some nexus between them. This means 'a feature of similarity which in all the circumstances of the case enables the offences to be described as a series' (p. 39D). A

nexus is clearly established if the offences are so connected that the evidence of one would be admissible to prove the commission of the other in accordance with the rules on similar fact evidence, but this is not essential (p. 39D–F, quoting with approval from *Kray* and *Clayton-Wright* [1948] 2 All ER 763).

(d) On the facts of *Ludlow*, the offences were similar in law in that they each had the ingredient of actual or attempted theft. They were also similar in fact because they involved stealing or attempting to steal in neighbouring public houses at a time interval of only 16 days. A sufficient nexus was therefore present to make the offences a series of a similar character within the meaning of r. 9, even though the similarity was not nearly striking enough to bring them within the similar fact evidence rule (p. 39H).

D11.63 **Application of the Principles in *Ludlow*** The following cases are Court of Appeal decisions on whether the degree of similarity between offences justified joinder under r. 9 of the Indictment Rules 1971.

(a) *Mansfield* [1977] 1 WLR 1102, where three counts for arson were held to be properly joined since the offences were committed within a short space of time, and related to premises in the same geographical area, with each of which the accused had some connection.

(b) *Harward* (1981) 73 Cr App R 168, where it was held that an allegation relating to the handling of stolen goods could not be joined to an offence of conspiring to defraud banks by the use of stolen cheques and cheque cards. The only possible nexus between the charges, there being no factual similarity, was the element of dishonesty. However, the dishonesty in the conspiracy count related to H's involvement in fraudulent practices, whereas that in the handling count related to his state of mind when he received the goods. This was therefore insufficient.

(c) *McGlinchey* (1983) 78 Cr App R 282, where two counts for handling stolen goods were held to be properly joined. The only factual similarity between the offences seems to have been their closeness in time. (*McGlinchey* was applied in *Mariou* [1992] Crim LR 511.)

(d) *Marsh* (1985) 83 Cr App R 165, where the indictment included two pairs for criminal damage and reckless driving and a fifth count of assault occasioning actual bodily harm, relating to a wholly separate incident. The joinder was held to be improper because (i) there was no legal similarity between criminal damage and reckless driving on the one hand and assault on the other, and (ii) the common factual element of violence was insufficient by itself to provide a nexus.

(e) *Baird* [1993] Crim LR 778, where the indictment alleged two counts of indecent assault against two boys, the incidents having taken place nine years apart. Although there was no coincidence in time or place, there were similarities in the offences which, their lordships said, 'were truly remarkable'. They concluded that the judge was entitled to hold that the various counts could properly be joined under r. 9, and was justified in refusing to exercise his discretion to sever under the Indictments Act 1915, s. 5(3) (see **D11.68**).

(f) *C* (1993) *The Times*, 4 February 1993, where the accused was charged with rape and attempted rape. Although the counts were separated in time by 11 years, the victim in each case was the accused's daughter. It was held that the counts were properly joined.

(g) *Williams* [1993] Crim LR 533, where it was alleged that W had falsely imprisoned a girl of 13, having indecently assaulted her five days earlier. The Court of Appeal held that these were two separate incidents and the two offences were not of a similar character, despite an evidential nexus.

JOINDER OF ACCUSED

Two or more accused may be joined in one indictment either as a result of being named together in one or more counts on the indictment, or as a result of being named individually in separate counts, albeit that there is no single count against them all. **D11.64**

Joint Counts

All parties to a joint offence may be indicted for it in a single count. In drafting the count: **D11.65**

(a) There is no need to distinguish between principal offenders and secondary parties (Accessories and Abettors Act 1861, s. 8: see **D11.39**).

(b) The count need not expressly allege that the unlawful acts of each accused were done in aid of the others, as that allegation is implicit in the drafting of a single count (see *DPP v Merriman* [1973] AC 584 per Lord Diplock at p. 607C).

Possible Verdicts on Joint Counts Notwithstanding that the accused have been charged in a single count, the jury may convict all or any of them on the basis that they committed the offence charged independently of the others. For example, in *DPP v Merriman*, Lord Diplock said (at p. 607F): **D11.66**

> . . . whenever two or more defendants are charged in the same count of an indictment with any offence which men can help one another to commit it is sufficient to support a conviction against any and each of them to prove *either* that he himself did a physical act which is an essential ingredient of the offence charged *or* that he helped another to do such an act, *and*, that in doing the act or in helping the other defendant to do it, he himself had the necessary criminal intent.

In short, if two accused, A1 and A2, are charged in a joint count the jury may (a) acquit both, or (b) convict both, or (c) acquit one and convict the other.

Should they convict both it will usually be on the basis implicit in the joint count that they helped each other to commit the crime, but the jury may equally convict both where the evidence suggests that they acted independently of each other if they are satisfied that each accused committed the offence.

Similarly, if there is a split verdict, the verdict against the convicted accused is not open to challenge on the ground that the jury must have found that he acted alone without assistance either from his acquitted co-accused or anybody else. The argument that to uphold convictions on a single count in the absence of proof of joint enterprise contravenes the rule against duplicity was rejected in *DPP v Merriman.*

Despite this, the prosecution is well advised only to draft a joint count where the evidence reveals a joint enterprise. If the co-defendants were acting without reference to each other, separate counts are preferable.

Separate Counts

The joining of two or more accused in one indictment notwithstanding the absence of a joint count against them is governed by the decision in *Assim* [1966] 2 QB 249. In that case, the indictment against the two accused, A and C, contained two counts. The first alleged that A had maliciously wounded W, and the second alleged that C, on the same day, had caused actual bodily harm to L. A and C both worked at the premises where the two assaults had allegedly occurred, a nightclub of which both the victims were customers. **D11.67**

On appeal, A argued that it was bad in law to charge two different people in one indictment with two different offences. Offenders could properly be joined in one indictment only as principals said to have jointly committed one offence, or as principals and accessories (see

D

Part D Procedure

p. 251F–G for counsel's argument). A five-judge Court of Appeal extensively reviewed the authorities, and (in a judgment given by Sachs J) reached the following conclusions:

(a) Questions of joinder, whether of offences or offenders, are 'matters of practice on which the court has, unless restrained by statute, inherent power both to formulate its own rules and to vary them in the light of current experience and the needs of justice' (p. 258F). On the assumption that the rule (now the CrimPR, r. 14.2(3)) covers only joinder of offences, the propriety of the joinder of offenders is unaffected either by the Indictments Act 1915 or by any other legislation, whether subordinate or primary, passed since then (p. 258E). Subsequently, Lord Widgery CJ in *Camberwell Green Stipendiary Magistrate, ex parte Christie* [1978] QB 602, said that *Assim* should be accepted as laying down a principle that joinder of offenders is a matter of the practice of the courts.

(b) Since joinder of offenders is merely a matter of practice, errors in the application of the relevant rules, though amounting to an irregularity in the proceedings, will not deprive the trial court of jurisdiction. Consequently, the Court of Appeal is entitled to dismiss an appeal against conviction advanced on this ground if there has been no miscarriage of justice (p. 259D–E), and especially where there has been a failure by the defence to object to the joint trial.

(c) Following an extensive review of the authorities, Sachs J 'came to some general conclusions as to what would nowadays be an appropriate rule of practice on the basis that none of the rules of 1915 deal with the joinder of offenders'. In summary, joinder is appropriate if the offences separately alleged against the accused are, on the evidence, so closely related by time or other factors that the interests of justice are best served by a single trial. His lordship said (at p. 261B–F):

> As a general rule it is, of course, no more proper to have tried by the same jury several offenders on charges of committing individual offences that have nothing to do with each other than it is to try before the same jury offences committed by the same person that have nothing to do with each other. Where, however, the matters which constitute the individual offences of the several offenders are upon the available evidence so related, whether in time or by other factors, that the interests of justice are best served by their being tried together, then they can properly be the subject of counts in one indictment and can, subject always to the discretion of the court, be tried together. Such a rule, of course, includes cases where there is evidence that several offenders acted in concert but is not limited to such cases.
>
> Again, while the court has in mind the classes of case that have been particularly the subject of discussion before it, such as incidents which, irrespective of there appearing a joint charge in the indictment, are contemporaneous (as where there has been something in the nature of an affray), or successive (as in protection racket cases), or linked in a similar manner, as where two persons individually in the course of the same trial commit perjury as regards the same or a closely connected fact, the court does not intend the operation of the rule to be restricted so as to apply only to such cases as have been discussed before it.

(d) It was conceded by the appellant and accepted by the court that, where there is a joint count against two accused, that count may be followed by a separate count or counts against one or more of the accused even in relation to a distinct matter, provided that there is no breach of what is now r. 14.2(3) (p. 257D, quoting *Cox* [1898] 1 QB 179). See also *Barrell* (1979) 69 Cr App R 250 at **D11.59**.

(e) On the facts of *Assim*, the joinder of A and C in one indictment was clearly proper, however narrowly any rule as to joinder of offenders might have been formulated (p. 260G). Having regard to the rule of practice Sachs J had stated, the counts they faced were so closely related by time and other factors that indicting the accused jointly was the correct course.

SEVERANCE

The court has the power to order the separate trial of accused or of offences that are properly joined in one indictment, pursuant to the Indictments Act 1915, s. 5(3). This is supplemented by: D11.68

(a) s. 5(4), which requires the court, following an order for severance under s. 5(3), to make such order for postponement of the trial as appears necessary and expedient; and
(b) s. 5(5), which provides that the procedure on the separate trial of a count following an order under s. 5(3) shall be the same in all respects as if the count had been preferred in a separate indictment.

The power to sever an indictment contained in s. 5(3) was held to apply only to valid indictments in *Newland* [1988] QB 402. However, the decisions of the Court of Appeal in *Smith* [1997] QB 837 and *Lockley* [1997] Crim LR 455 have altered the effect upon the indictment where a count has been improperly joined (see **D11.57**).

Indictments Act 1915, s. 5

(3) Where, before trial, or at any stage of a trial, the court is of opinion that a person accused may be prejudiced or embarrassed in his defence by reason of being charged with more than one offence in the same indictment, or that for any other reason it is desirable to direct that the person should be tried separately for any one or more offences charged in an indictment, the court may order a separate trial of any count or counts of such indictment.

(4) Where, before trial, or at any stage of a trial, the court is of opinion that the postponement of the trial of a person accused is expedient as a consequence of the exercise of any power of the court under this Act to amend an indictment or to order a separate trial of a count, the court shall make such order as to the postponement of the trial as appears necessary.

(5) Where an order of the court is made under this section for the postponement of a trial—
(a) if such an order is made during a trial the court may order that the jury (if there is one) are to be discharged from giving a verdict on the count or counts the trial of which is postponed or on the indictment, as the case may be; and
(b) the procedure on the separate trial of a count shall be the same in all respects as if the count had been found in a separate indictment, and the procedure on the postponed trial shall be the same in all respects (if the jury has been discharged under para (a)) as if the trial had not commenced; and
(c) the court may make such order as to granting the accused person bail and as to the enlargement of recognisances and otherwise as the court thinks fit.

Severance of Counts on an Indictment

The proper exercise of the power was considered by Lord Pearson in *Ludlow v Metropolitan Police Commissioner* [1971] AC 29 (see also **D11.62**). Having held that the joinder of the counts against L for attempted theft and robbery was lawful, his lordship dealt with the appellant's further argument that a single trial of the two offences inevitably prejudiced or embarrassed the accused in his defence since the jury heard evidence on count 1 that was inadmissible on count 2 and vice versa. Therefore, the trial judge should have ordered separate trials in exercise of the discretion given him by s. 5(3). In rejecting this argument Lord Pearson said (at pp. 40–2): D11.69

Before the Indictments Act 1915, it was a tenable theory . . . to say that any joinder of counts relating to distinct alleged offences was necessarily so prejudicial to the accused that such joinder ought not to be permitted. [His lordship then reviewed pre-1915 cases lending support to the theory.]

In my opinion, this theory—that a joinder of counts relating to different transactions is in itself so prejudicial to the accused that such a joinder should never be made—cannot be held to have survived the passing of the Indictments Act 1915. No doubt the juries of that time were much more literate and intelligent than the juries of the late 18th and 19th centuries, and could be relied upon in any ordinary case not to infer that, because the accused is proved to have committed one of the offences charged against him, therefore he must have committed the others as well. I think the experience of judges in modern times is that the verdicts of juries show them to have been careful and conscientious in considering each count separately. Also in most cases it would be oppressive to the accused, as well as expensive and inconvenient for the prosecution, to have two or more trials when one would suffice. *At any rate, . . . the manifest intention of the Act is that charges which either are founded on the same facts or relate to a series of offences of the same or a similar character properly can and normally should be joined in one indictment, and a joint trial of the charges will normally follow, although the judge has a discretionary power to direct separate trials under section 5(3).* If the theory were still correct, it would be the duty of the judge in the proper exercise of his discretion under section 5(3) to direct separate trials in every case where the accused was charged with a series of offences of the same or a similar character, and the manifest intention appearing from section 4 and [r. 9] would be defeated. *The judge has no duty to direct separate trials under section 5(3) unless in his opinion there is some special feature of the case which would make a joint trial of the several counts prejudicial or embarrassing to the accused and separate trials are required in the interests of justice.* In some cases the offences charged may be too numerous and complicated, . . . or too difficult to disentangle, . . . so that a joint trial of all the counts is likely to cause confusion and the defence may be embarrassed or prejudiced. In other cases objection may be taken to the inclusion of a count on the ground that it is of a scandalous nature and likely to arouse in the minds of the jury hostile feelings against the accused. . . . In the present case there was no multiplicity or complexity in the offences charged, and no difficulty for the learned commissioner in dealing separately with the two charges in his summing-up [emphases added].

D11.70 **Application of this Principle** Thus, if counts for separate offences have validly been joined in one indictment, the normal consequence is that they will be tried together. The trial judge should exercise his discretion to order separate trials only if there is a special feature in the case which would make a single trial prejudicial or embarrassing. Although they are not intended to be exhaustive, examples of such special features might include the following.

(a) *The scandalous nature of the evidence as to one of the counts.* For example in *Laycock* [2003] Crim LR 803, the Court of Appeal warned that prosecutors should be careful not to charge counts that would prejudice an accused unless there was a real purpose to be served. In that case, the prosecution was criticised for including in a firearms indictment a count which showed that the accused had been sentenced to a previous sentence of imprisonment with the result that he was prohibited from possession of a firearm.

(b) *The number and/or complexity of the counts.* This may result in difficulties for a jury in disentangling evidence on one count from that on the other count or counts. In this regard, special considerations govern the trial of counts for sexual offences (see D11.71).

The fact that the accused wishes to give evidence in his own defence on one of the counts but not on the others is not, in the normal case, a sufficient reason for severance, even though non-severance will oblige him to choose between not testifying at all and exposing himself to cross-examination about all the charges (*Phillips* (1987) 86 Cr App R 18). See also *Lanford v General Medical Council* [1990] 1 AC 13.

Severance of Multi-count Indictments for Sexual Offences

D11.71 In *DPP v Boardman* [1975] AC 421, the indictment contained counts that B, the headmaster of a boarding-school, had (a) committed buggery on S, a 16-year-old pupil, and (b) had incited H, a 17-year-old pupil, to commit buggery on B. The primary question for the House of Lords was whether the trial judge correctly directed the jury that the evidence of one count was admissible as corroborative evidence in relation to the other. Resolution of this issue involved the answering of two essential questions.

D11.72 **Is the Other Allegation Admissible?** In *DPP v Boardman* [1975] AC 421, Lord Cross of Chelsea stated that questions of the admissibility of similar fact evidence in such cases ought to be decided in the absence of the jury as a preliminary issue. Thus the first question is whether the evidence of one count is admissible supporting evidence of another. Lord Cross said: 'if it is decided that the evidence is inadmissible and the accused is being charged in the same indictment with offences against the other men the charges relating to the different persons ought to be tried separately' (p. 459D).

The reason why this approach was necessary is because '. . . it is asking too much of any jury to tell them to perform mental gymnastics of this sort. If the charges are tried together it is inevitable that the jurors will be influenced, consciously or unconsciously, by the fact that the accused is being charged not with a single offence against one person but with three separate offences against three persons'.

Has there been Contamination? Even where the respective offences bear such a striking similarity to each other that the evidence as to each would be mutually corroborative, the judge should consider whether there is material in the committal statements suggesting that the 'victims' colluded together to tell false stories. Again this should be considered as a preliminary issue. **D11.73**

If there is a real danger that that happened, separate trials should be ordered, but the judge should not use his imagination to invent a conspiracy to make false allegations where there is no evidence in the statements that such a conspiracy existed (see especially *Johannsen* (1977) 65 Cr App R 101, where it was held that the mere fact that four out of the five complainants knew each other gave rise to no more than a speculative possibility that they had collaborated, and there was accordingly no need to direct severance of the counts).

Limitations to the Impact of a Ruling on Severance in Such Cases A decision as to severance does not represent a final decision on the admissibility of each incident alleged in the indictment as similar fact evidence to prove the others. Even where severance is refused, during the course of the ensuing trial it will still be necessary for the court to rule whether the evidence of one victim corroborates that of the other victims. If the court concludes, contrary to the provisional view taken at the application for severance stage, that each victim's evidence is relevant only to the offence against him, then either the jury must be directed accordingly in the summing-up or, more realistically, the jury should be discharged and severance ordered at that stage. **D11.74**

Conversely, if the court initially ordered severance, the prosecution could still ask to be allowed to lead evidence of the other incidents in support of whichever incident the jury is trying. Detailed guidance from Scarman LJ on how trial judges should approach applications for severance and problems of similar fact evidence in multi-count sexual cases will be found in *Scarrott* [1978] 1 QB 1016 at pp. 1027–8.

Application of *Boardman* beyond Indictments for Sexual Offences It might have been thought that the arguments that Lord Cross used in *DPP v Boardman* [1975] AC 421, to justify his dictum that, in cases involving sexual offences, the indictment should be severed if the evidence of one victim could not be used as corroboration of the evidence of the other victims, would apply with equal force whatever the nature of the offence charged. However, the Court of Appeal in subsequent cases has refused to extend the principles stated in *Boardman* and *Scarrott* [1978] 1 QB 1016 beyond multi-count indictments for sexual offences. **D11.75**

Where there is a multi-count indictment for some other type of offence, the principles in *Ludlow v Metropolitan Police Commissioner* [1971] AC 29 apply (see **D11.62**). Accordingly, the judge should order separate trials only if there is a special feature in the case likely to cause the defence prejudice or embarrassment.

(a) In *McGlinchey* (1983) 78 Cr App R 282, the Court of Appeal held that two counts for handling stolen goods on dates approximately six weeks apart were properly joined in one

D

Part D Procedure

indictment even though there was manifestly no striking similarity between the offences. The court approved the judge's exercise of discretion against severance, applying *Ludlow* and distinguishing *Boardman*.

(b) In *Cannan* (1991) 92 Cr App R 16, the Court of Appeal made it clear that, even where an indictment charged a series of sexual offences, the judge had a discretion whether to sever. This was so even though there was no striking similarity between the evidence on the various counts. The indictment in C's case included three sets of offences which were evidentially separate. The Court of Appeal rejected the submission that the judge should have followed 'the general modern practice in sexual cases', and severed the counts in the absence of striking similarity. Lord Lane CJ said (at p. 23):

> It may well be that often the judge in sexual cases will order severance . . . But the fact remains that the Indictments Act 1915 gives the judge a discretion, and . . . that is not a matter with which this Court will interfere, unless it is shown that the judge has failed to exercise his discretion upon the usual and proper principles . . .

D11.76 **Recent Consideration of the *Boardman* Approach** In the case of *DPP v P* [1991] 2 AC 447, the central issue dealt with by the House of Lords was that of similar fact evidence, and particularly whether the evidence of one victim of a sexual offence was admissible to support the allegation of another in the absence of 'striking similarity' between them. However, Lord Mackay (at p. 462) made the following comment about the issue of whether, in the absence of striking similarity, there should have been joinder:

> the evidence referred to is admissible if the similarity is sufficiently strong, or there is other sufficient relationship between the events described in the evidence of the other young children of the family and the abuse charged, that the evidence, if accepted, would so strongly support the truth of that charge that it is fair to admit it notwithstanding its prejudicial effect. It follows that the answer to the second question is no, provided there is a relationship between the offences of a kind which I have just described.

On one interpretation, this could be taken to mean that the rule on joinder in cases of multiple sexual offences is the same as for admissibility, namely that the offences should constitute similar fact evidence in order to be tried together. However, in *Christou* [1997] AC 117, the House of Lords considered the words used by Lord Mackay, and stated that they were *obiter*. The approach to the question of severance in *Cannan* (1991) 92 Cr App R 16 was endorsed.

It follows therefore that the court has a discretion as to severance, with which the appellate courts should interfere only on grounds of *Wednesbury* unreasonableness. In exercising his discretion, the essential task of the trial judge was to achieve a fair resolution of the issues. That required fairness to the accused but also to the prosecution and those involved in it. Among the factors which he might consider were:

(a) how discrete or interrelated were the facts giving rise to the counts;
(b) the impact of ordering two or more trials on the accused and his family, on the victims and their families, and on press publicity; and
(c) importantly, whether directions the judge could give to the jury would suffice to secure a fair trial if the counts were tried together.

(See also *Dixon* (1991) 92 Cr App R 43, *F* [1996] Crim LR 257, *O'Brien* [2000] Crim LR 863 and *Thomas* [2006] EWCA Crim 2442.)

Discretion to Order Separate Trials of Accused

D11.77 The court has a discretion to order separate trials of accused who have properly been joined in one indictment in accordance with the principles stated in *Ludlow v Metropolitan Police Commissioner* [1971] AC 29 (see **D11.62**). The existence of the discretion was acknowledged by Sachs J in *Assim* [1966] 2 QB 249. His lordship said at p. 261B–C):

> Where . . . the matters which constitute the individual offences of the several offenders are upon the available evidence so related . . . that the interests of justice are best served by their being tried together, then they can properly be the subject of counts in one indictment and can, *subject always to the discretion of the court*, be tried together [emphasis added].

Although that was said in the context of an indictment which did not contain a joint count, it has never been doubted that the discretion may be exercised as much in respect of accused charged in a joint count as in respect of those charged in separate counts on one indictment. The discretion may be attributed either to the court's inherent power to control its own proceedings or to the power to sever contained in the Indictments Act 1915, s. 5(3).

Guidance as to the Exercise of the Discretion Because severance of the trial of jointly indicted accused is a matter of discretion, the way in which the discretion is exercised is unlikely to provide a successful ground of appeal (see **D11.99**). Guidance on ordering separate trials does, however, emerge from the decided cases. The following propositions summarise that guidance. **D11.78**

(a) Where the accused are charged in a joint count, the arguments in favour of a joint trial are very strong. These arguments include:
   (i) severance will necessitate much or all of the prosecution evidence being given twice before different juries and increase the risk of inconsistent verdicts;
   (ii) even if the accused are expected to blame each other for the offence (i.e. will run 'cut-throat' defences), the interests of the prosecution and the public in a single trial will generally outweigh the interests of the defence in not having to call each accused before the same jury to give evidence for himself which will incriminate the other (see *Grondkowski* [1946] KB 369, *Moghal* (1977) 65 Cr App R 56, *Edwards* [1998] Crim LR 756 and *Crawford* [1997] 1 WLR 1329).
(b) Where the prosecution case against one accused (A1) includes evidence that is admissible against him but not against his co-accused (A2), there is no obligation to order severance simply because the evidence in question might prejudice the jury against A2. However, the judge should balance the advantages of a single trial against the possible prejudice to A2, and should consider especially how far an appropriate direction to the jury is really likely to ensure that they take into account the evidence only for its proper purpose of proving the case against A1 (see *Lake* (1976) 64 Cr App R 172 and *B* [2004] EWCA Crim 1254).
(c) Where a joint trial of numerous accused would lead to a very long and complicated trial, the judge should consider whether a number of shorter trials, each involving only some of the accused, might make for a fairer and more efficient disposition of the issues. This reason for severance is tied up with the rule against overloading indictments, which is considered at **D11.81**.
(d) There may be some distinction to be drawn between cases where the accused are jointly charged in a single count and those where they allegedly committed separate offences which were nonetheless sufficiently linked to be put in one indictment. In the latter situation, the cases against the accused are unlikely to be as closely intertwined as when a joint offence is alleged, and the public interest argument in favour of a single trial is correspondingly less strong. There should, therefore, be a greater willingness to order separate trials.

Presumption in Favour of Joint Trial The authorities cited above indicate that the decision whether or not to grant severance is one within the discretion of the trial judge, and that the decision should be in favour of joint trial unless the risk of prejudice is unusually great. Thus in *Josephs* (1977) 65 Cr App R 253, where the same issue arose as in *Lake* (1976) 64 Cr App R 172, Lord Widgery CJ said (at p. 255, emphasis added): **D11.79**

> . . . it is a very rare thing for this court to interfere with the trial judge's decision about separate trials. Nothing is more peculiarly left to the trial judge as his concern with that particular point.

> *Of course we have jurisdiction to interfere where something has clearly gone wrong,* but it is very rare, and members of the court today cannot remember a case in which such an interference with the trial judge's decision was made.
>
> . . . the fact that some of [a co-accused's] statements may rub off on the other accused . . . is just one of those things that happens in the course of a multiple criminal trial. The advantages of having co-defendants tried together is so great that the right to order a separate trial will not be granted unless there is good reason for it.

D11.80 **Refusal of Severance as a Ground of Appeal** In general, the Court of Appeal will interfere with the exercise of a discretion only if it can be shown that the trial judge took into account irrelevant considerations, or ignored relevant ones, or arrived at a manifestly unreasonable decision. This was illustrated in *Moghal* (1977) 65 Cr App R 56, where the appeal failed even though the members of the court indicated strongly that, had they been trying the case, they would not have acted as the trial judge had done. The test of whether to intervene is usually stated simply as: did the trial judge's decision cause unacceptable prejudice to the appellant such as might have led to a miscarriage of justice? (*Grondkowski* [1946] KB 369 and *Moghal* (1977) 65 Cr App R 56).

In a suitable case, however, the Court of Appeal has shown that it is willing to exercise its power to intervene where, to use the words of Lord Widgery CJ in *Josephs* (1977) 65 Cr App R 253, 'something has clearly gone wrong'.

(a) In *O'Boyle* (1991) 92 Cr App R 202, O was charged with conspiracy to supply cocaine. His co-defendant R alleged that he had acted under duress from O. At trial, O's confession to US investigators was excluded, but counsel for R sought to cross-examine O on its contents. On appeal, the Court of Appeal held that the trial judge should have ordered severance. The court recognised that the trial judge had a discretion and that, generally, conspirators should be tried together. However, this was an exceptional case, where separate trials would have done little or no harm to the co-defendant or prosecution, while joint trial prejudiced the appellant. See also *Randle* [1995] Crim LR 331.

(b) In *Smith* (1966) 51 Cr App R 22, S and two others were prosecuted in relation to a large-scale theft. The evidence against the co-accused consisted largely of their admissions to the police, in which they also implicated S. The evidence directly admissible against S was scanty. The co-accused were acquitted and S alone convicted. Although the Court of Criminal Appeal accepted that the trial judge had correctly rejected an application for separate trials, the court nevertheless held that the only explanation for S alone being convicted was that the jury must have been prejudiced against him by the material in the co-accused's statements, notwithstanding the judge's direction that those statements were evidence only against the co-accused (see the discussion of *Smith* in *Lake* (1976) 64 Cr App R 172 at p. 177).

What the decisions in *Lake* and *Josephs* demonstrate is a distinction between ordinary prejudice occasioned by a joint trial and what Lord Widgery referred to as 'dangerous prejudice'. The former is almost bound to arise when co-accused run inconsistent defences and does not in general justify severing the indictment. The latter, exemplified by *Smith,* should be dealt with by severance.

Note that the situation may be different where the admissions made by one accused become admissible against another in the circumstances identified in *Hayter* [2005] 1 WLR 605.

Overloading Indictments

D11.81 In drafting indictments and in ruling on applications to sever indictments, both the drafter and the court should have regard not only to what is permitted by the rules on joinder (discussed from **D11.56**) but also to whether one long trial or several shorter ones is more likely to be in the interests of justice.

If a single indictment, containing numerous counts and/or accused, would result in an unduly long or complicated trial and place an unfair burden on the jury, the prosecution should opt for however many shorter indictments are necessary to cover the same ground, notwithstanding that a single indictment would be within the rules. Similarly, if the prosecution have not taken the initiative in this regard, the court should intervene to order separate trials, whether of counts or accused.

In *Wright* [1995] Crim LR 251, it was made clear that the mere length of a trial is not sufficient in itself to characterise convictions as unsafe. (See also *Kellard* [1995] 2 Cr App R 134.) The issue is therefore not that a trial can never be both long and fair, but that no jury ought to be required to try an overloaded indictment.

There are various sources of guidance in this regard, including not only the observations of the Court of Appeal in a number of cases but various recent measures designed to improve the efficiency of the management of cases such as recent amendments to the *Consolidated Criminal Practice Direction* and, in particular, the guidance related to cases of serious fraud (which are discussed in more detail in **D4** and **D14**).

Observations of the Court of Appeal Dicta on overloaded indictments are contained especially in *Novac* (1976) 65 Cr App R 107 and *Thorne* (1977) 66 Cr App R 6. **D11.82**

In *Novac*, there were some 19 counts against four accused (N, R, A-C and A). The major count was against N, R and A-C and alleged a conspiracy to procure males under 21 to commit acts of gross indecency. Further counts alleged specific offences such as living on the earnings of male prostitution, importuning in a public place and buggery or gross indecency with named persons. These had been committed both during the currency of the conspiracy and outside that period. The fourth accused (A) was not alleged to be a member of the conspiracy, but was charged with further indecency offences which had been uncovered during the police investigation.

Bridge LJ, during the course of the judgment of the court, made observations about this complicated indictment (at p. 188):

> We cannot conclude this judgment without pointing out that . . . most of the difficulties which have bedevilled this trial, which have led in the end to the quashing of all convictions except on the conspiracy and related counts, arose directly out of the overloading of the indictment . . . the indictment of 19 counts against four defendants resulted . . . in a trial of quite unnecessary length and complexity. If the specific offence counts against [N, R and A-C] and all the counts against [A] had been tried separately, the main trial of the conspiracy and related counts would have been reasonably manageable and the four separate trials would have been short and straightforward. Quite apart from the question whether the prosecution could find legal justification for joining all these counts in one indictment and resisting severance, the wider and more important question has to be asked whether in such a case the interests of justice were likely to be better served by one very long trial, or by one moderately long and four short separate trials.
>
> We answer unhesitatingly that whatever advantages were expected to accrue from one long trial, . . . they were heavily outweighed by the disadvantages. A trial of such dimensions puts an immense burden on both judge and jury. In the course of a four or five-day summing-up the most careful and conscientious judge may so easily overlook some essential matter. Even if the summing-up is faultless, it is by no means cynical to doubt whether the average juror can be expected to take it all in and apply all the directions given. Some criminal prosecutions involve consideration of matters so plainly inextricable and indivisible that a long and complex trial is an ineluctable necessity. But we are convinced that nothing short of the criterion of absolute necessity can justify the imposition of the burdens of a very long trial on the court.

Much the same sentiments were expressed in *Thorne*, where the trial was even longer. The indictment related essentially to three separate armed robberies. In addition, there were counts for related conspiracies to rob, handling some of the proceeds, and conspiracy to pervert the course of justice by making threats against a potential prosecution witness. In all, there were 10 counts and 14 accused, and the trial lasted nearly seven months. The Court of Appeal (Lawton LJ) commented that the indictment was undoubtedly overloaded, and the trial placed 'a burden on the judge which he should never be asked to bear' (p. 14).

A further aspect of not overloading indictments arises when the conduct of the accused may either be charged in a number of distinct offences or brought under one charge. In those circumstances, the prosecution should have just one count for the obviously appropriate offence, because nothing is gained and much is lost in terms of simplicity of presentation to the jury if the indictment contains counts for all the offences of which the accused might possibly be guilty (see *Staton* [1983] Crim LR 190). This is the situation in which the newly redrafted CrimPR, r. 14.2(2), comes into its own (see **D11.32**).

D11.83 **Putting the Prosecution to its Election** Both *Novac* (1976) 65 Cr App R 107 and *Thorne* (1977) 66 Cr App R 6 were cases in which the complexity of the indictment was in part attributable to the combination of conspiracy and substantive charges. In an effort to meet this particular problem, a practice direction was issued which was again amended in April 2007 and now states:

Consolidated Criminal Practice Direction, para. IV.34

> IV.34.3 Save in the special circumstances described in the following paragraphs of this Practice Direction, it is undesirable that a large number of counts should be contained in one indictment. Where defendants on trial have a variety of offences alleged against them then in the interests of effective case management it is the court's responsibility to exercise its powers in accordance with the overriding objective set out in Part 1 of the Criminal Procedure Rules. The prosecution may be required to identify a selection of counts on which the trial should proceed, leaving a decision to be taken later whether to try any of the remainder. Where an indictment contains substantive counts and one or more related conspiracy counts the court will expect the prosecution to justify the joinder. Failing justification the prosecution should be required to choose whether to proceed on the substantive counts or on the conspiracy counts. In any event, if there is a conviction on any counts that are tried then those that have been postponed can remain on the file marked 'not to be proceeded with without the leave of the court'. In the event that a conviction is later quashed on appeal, the remaining counts can be tried. Where necessary the court has power to order that an indictment be divided and some counts removed to a separate indictment.

The circumstances alluded to in para. IV.34.3 are where there is a split between a trial by jury and a trial by judge alone pursuant to the DVCVA 2004, ss.17 to 21 (see **D11.36**) and where multiple offending counts are used pursuant to the CrimPR, r. 14.2(2), (see **D11.32**).

If a substantive count and a related conspiracy count are joined in the indictment, the prosecution will have to justify their inclusion. If their inclusion is not justified, the prosecution will have to decide on which counts they wish to proceed. It follows that a conspiracy count which adds nothing to the charge of a substantive offence has no place in the indictment (*Jones* (1974) 59 Cr App R 120; see *Watts* (1995) *The Times*, 14 April 1995).

If the prosecution elect to proceed upon the substantive charge, such an election is not necessarily irreversible. In *Findlay* [1992] Crim LR 372, for example, the prosecution, which had elected to proceed on substantive robbery counts, were permitted to reverse that election when the evidence necessary to sustain a conviction on those counts was later ruled inadmissible. The Court of Appeal dismissed the appeal, in view of the fact that there was no demonstrable prejudice to F.

D11.84 **Cases of Serious Fraud** In recent years, the most striking instances of overloaded indictments have emerged in serious fraud cases.

This was illustrated in *Cohen* (1992) *Independent*, 29 July 1992 (the 'Blue Arrow' case), a case in which the indictment was long and complex, and in which the jury did not retire until the 184th day of the trial. The Court of Appeal said that the basic assumption that the jury determined guilt or innocence on evidence which they were able to comprehend and remember had been destroyed in that case. The prosecution had a heavy responsibility not to overload the indictment, but the ultimate responsibility lay with the trial judge, whose powers of severance should have been used at an early stage to overcome the problems of an overloaded indictment.

The prosecution's responsibility to ensure that the indictment was not overloaded was emphasised amongst the conclusions of the HM Crown Prosecution Service Inspectorate report, 'Review of the Investigation and Criminal Proceedings Relating to the Jubilee Line case', June 2006. At paras. 1.30 to 1.32, the Review emphasised that the lack of particularisation in the conspiracy to defraud allegation relied on by the prosecution, and its reliance on broad inferences which necessitated detailed examination of a very considerable number of documents, resulted in a considerable lengthening of the trial without any material effect on the overall level of criminality. The Review underlines the importance of the prosecution ensuring at the outset that their allegations are particularised, focused and aimed at keeping the evidence and length of trial within reasonable bounds.

On the same day as the Jubilee Line case came to an end, 22 March 2005, the then Lord Chief Justice published 'A Protocol for the Control and Management of Heavy Fraud and other Complex Criminal Cases'. The Protocol is examined in more depth elsewhere (e.g., at D14.47) and is set out in full at **appendix 9**; however, in the context of overloaded indictments it has the following to say, under the heading of 'consideration of the length of the trial' (para. 3(vi)):

> (d) One course the judge may consider is pruning the indictment by omitting certain charges and/or by omitting certain defendants. The judge must not usurp the function of the prosecution in this regard, and he must bear in mind that he will, at the outset, know less about the case than the advocates. The aim is to achieve fairness to all parties.
>
> (e) Nevertheless, the judge does have two methods of pruning available for use in appropriate circumstances:
>
> (i) Persuading the prosecution that it is not worthwhile pursuing certain charges and/or certain defendants.
>
> (ii) Severing the indictment. Severance for reasons of case management alone is perfectly proper, although judges should have regard to any representations made by the prosecution that severance would weaken their case. . . . However, before using what may be seen as a blunt instrument, the judge should insist on seeing full defence statements of all affected defendants. Severance may be unfair to the prosecution if, for example, there is a cut-throat defence in prospect. For example, the defence of the principal defendant may be that the defendant relied on the advice of his accountant or solicitor that what was happening was acceptable. The defence of the professional may be that he gave no such advice. Against that background, it might be unfair to the prosecution to order separate trials of the two defendants.

Re-opening an Application for Severance An application to sever the indictment may be made on more than one occasion. Sometimes the second application will be before the same judge but not necessarily so (e.g., where the first application was made at a pre-trial review: see D14.17). **D11.85**

In *Wright* (1989) 90 Cr App R 325, Judge G at the pre-trial review refused to sever a conspiracy count from an indictment which also contained a series of counts relating to substantive offences. Before the trial itself began, defence counsel applied again to sever, this time before Judge C, who rejected the submission on the ground that the matter had been concluded by Judge G. The Court of Appeal held that the question for the second judge was whether there had been a sufficient change to justify re-opening the question. If there had not, he was not obliged to hear the same point argued again.

AMENDING THE INDICTMENT

Statutory Provision

D11.86 The power to amend an indictment, once it has been served, lies in the Indictments Act 1971, s. 5(1).

Indictments Act 1915, s. 5

(1) Where, before trial, or at any stage of a trial, it appears to the court that the indictment is defective, the court shall make such order for the amendment of the indictment as the court thinks necessary to meet the circumstances of the case, unless, having regard to the merits of the case, the required amendments cannot be made without injustice.

Extent of the Power to Amend

D11.87 The power to amend may be exercised both:

(a) in respect of formal defects in the wording of a count, for example when the statement of offence fails to specify the statute contravened or when the particulars do not disclose an essential element of the offence, and
(b) in respect of substantial defects such as divergences between the allegations in the count and the evidence foreshadowed in the committal statements or called at trial.

This was confirmed by the Court of Criminal Appeal in *Pople* [1951] 1 KB 53 at p. 54:

> The argument for the appellants appeared to involve the proposition that an indictment, in order to be defective, must be one which in law did not charge any offence at all and therefore was bad on the face of it. We do not take that view. In our opinion, any alteration in matters of description, and probably in many other respects, may be made in order to meet the evidence in the case so long as the amendment causes no injustice to the accused person.

It followed that the trial judge in *Pople* had been entitled to allow an amendment at the close of the prosecution case to make the property allegedly obtained by deception from a building society a cheque rather than the sum of money. Furthermore, there was no injustice to the accused because the matter in which the indictment was defective was 'the mere description of the thing obtained', while 'in substance, the charge was the same'.

Similarly, in *Radley* (1973) 58 Cr App R 394, Lord Widgery CJ quoted with approval the passage from *Pople* quoted above, and held that an indictment may be defective if it merely fails to allege an offence disclosed by the committal statements. 'Defective', in the context of s. 5(1), is not restricted to defects in form, but 'has got a very much wider meaning' (p. 401). Moreover, this wide meaning is acceptable because the power to amend is subject to the overriding limitation that it must not cause injustice (p. 402).

The power to amend may be exercised in respect of voluntary bills of indictment preferred on the direction of a High Court judge just as it may be exercised in respect of 'ordinary' indictments preferred on the authority of a committal for trial (*Allcock* [1999] 1 Cr App R 227; *Wells* [1995] 2 Cr App R 417 at p. 422; *Walters* (1979) 69 Cr App R 115).

D11.88 **Limitation on Power to Amend** If the indictment is so defective as to be a nullity, it is not capable of amendment and there is a mistrial. An indictment is invalid from the outset in this way where, for example, it alleges an offence unknown to law. Where a count describes a known offence inaccurately, however, it is capable of amendment, subject to the usual considerations of prejudice to the defendant (*McVitie* [1960] 2 QB 483, applied in *Tyler* (1992) 96 Cr App R 332).

D11.89 **Amendment by Insertion of a New Count** As well as enabling amendments to be made to existing counts, s. 5(1) of the Indictments Act 1915 permits the insertion of an entirely new count into an indictment, whether in addition to or in substitution for the original counts (*Johal* [1973] QB 475), where Ashworth J said (at p. 481A), 'there is no rule of law which precludes amendment of an indictment after arraignment, either by addition of a new count or otherwise'.

The words 'after arraignment' appear in the sentence quoted because the main point at issue in that case was whether the amendment was made too late, but obviously the addition of a count before arraignment is even less open to objection than a subsequent addition. Where the addition is made after arraignment, it will be necessary to put the new counts to the accused for him to plead to them.

The amendment to an indictment can be so extensive that the question arises whether it amounts to the substitution of a fresh indictment. This was the issue in *Fyffe* [1992] Crim LR 442, where the Crown amended an 11-count indictment so that it contained 27 counts. It was submitted on appeal that the 27-count indictment was a fresh indictment and therefore the judge should have gone through the procedural steps of staying the 11-count indictment and granting the prosecution leave to prefer the 27-count indictment out of time, whereupon the defendants should have been arraigned once more. The appeal was dismissed since, for all material purposes, the 27 counts reproduced what had appeared in the 11 counts. No new allegations had been added; the amendments were of form rather than substance and it was not necessary to go through the process of re-arraignment.

The Evidential Basis for the New Count A further question arises as to whether it is necessary for the amendment to be founded on facts or evidence disclosed to the examining justices at committal. According to the Court of Appeal in *Osieh* [1996] 1 WLR 1260, it is not necessary. However, it was held in that case that the amendment *had* been founded on evidence disclosed at committal, and this approach ran counter to dicta in *Dixon* (1991) 92 Cr App R 43 and *Hall* [1968] 2 QB 788. In *Hall*, Lord Parker CJ said (at p. 792) that, granted that there was power to amend, the question is really 'whether the amendment asked for and granted was supported by evidence given at the committal proceedings'. **D11.90**

As Professor JC Smith comments in 'Adding Counts to an Indictment' [1996] Crim LR 889, 'Plainly the court thought that an amendment not so supported was invalid'. In any event, the fact that an amendment raises for the first time something not foreshadowed in the committal documents may be a ground for not permitting the amendment, or permitting it only together with an adjournment (per Schiemann LJ in *Osieh*).

Timing of Amendment

The Indictments Act 1915, s. 5(1), makes clear that an indictment may be amended at any stage of a trial, whether before or after arraignment. This was demonstrated in the following cases: **D11.91**

(a) in *Johal* [1973] QB 475, where the insertion of the new counts occurred after arraignment but before the empanelling of the jury;
(b) in *Pople* [1951] 1 KB 53, where the amendment took the form of an alteration in the description of the property obtained by deception and was granted after the close of the prosecution case;
(c) in *Collison* (1980) 71 Cr App R 249, where the amendment was made after the jury had been out considering their verdict for over three hours—on appeal, counsel for C accepted 'that the words in section 5(1) of the Indictments Act 1915 "at any stage of a trial" do permit amendment even after the jury have gone into retirement if the circumstances otherwise justify it and no injustice is caused to the defendant' (p. 253).

The later the amendment, the greater the risk of its causing injustice and therefore the less likely it is to be allowed. However, an indictment may be amended even at the stage of retrial, provided that no injustice is done (*Swaine* [2001] Crim LR 166).

Risk of Injustice

D11.92 The main consideration for a judge deciding whether to allow an amendment is the risk of injustice. If the amendment cannot be made without injustice, it must not be made, as the last clause of s. 5(1) of the Indictments Act 1915 makes clear. The timing of the amendment is a major factor in determining whether there will be injustice. Thus, in *Johal* [1973] QB 475, the Court of Appeal rejected the view in *Harden* [1963] 1 QB 8 that an amendment that substantially substitutes another offence for that originally charged could *never* be made after arraignment, but agreed that such amendments would usually cause injustice. Ashworth J said (at pp. 480G–481C):

> As a statement of principle, to be applied generally, this [i.e., the decision in *Harden*] is . . . too wide. No doubt in many cases in which, after arraignment, an amendment is sought for the purpose of substituting another offence for that originally charged, or for the purpose of adding a further charge, injustice would be caused by granting the amendment. But in some cases (of which the present is an example) no such injustice would be caused and the amendment may properly be allowed . . .
>
> In the judgment of this court there is no rule of law which precludes amendment of an indictment after arraignment, either by addition of a new count or otherwise . . .
>
> On the other hand this court shares the view expressed in some of the earlier cases that amendment of an indictment during the course of a trial is likely to prejudice an accused person. The longer the interval between arraignment and amendment, the more likely it is that injustice will be caused, and in every case in which amendment is sought, it is essential to consider with great care whether the accused person will be prejudiced thereby.

D11.93 **Consideration of the Risk of Injustice Test** On the facts of *Johal* [1973] QB 475, there was no injustice because the amendment was made immediately after arraignment, and 'the situation was to all intents and purposes the same as if application to amend had been made before arraignment'. In *Collison* (1980) 71 Cr App R 249, where the amendment was made after the jury had retired, there was still no injustice because the amendment merely removed a technical impediment to the jury convicting of the lesser offence (see also *Teong Sun Chuah* [1991] Crim LR 463 for an example of amendment at a relatively late stage which was held to be acceptable since it caused no injustice).

On the other hand, in *Gregory* [1972] 1 WLR 991, the Court of Appeal criticised a late amendment to the particulars by the deletion of the allegation as to ownership where that was the central issue in the case and it could not be said that the allegation that the motor belonged to a named person was 'mere surplusage'. In *O'Connor* [1997] Crim LR 516, similarly, there was held to be a risk of injustice where the effect of an amendment made at the close of the prosecution case was to allow the prosecution to shift its ground significantly. The Court of Appeal held that the amendment was unfair, because the Crown's case had changed very significantly, and the appellant had been confronted with a different and more difficult case. It was for the prosecution to decide how to put their case, and they could not rely on the court granting leave to change it as the trial progressed.

Procedure on Amendment

D11.94 In *Moss* [1995] Crim LR 828, it was stated that, where counsel seeks an amendment, he ought to ensure that there is a properly amended form of indictment before the judge, and that any order of the court is clear and is complied with. When amendment is allowed, a note of the order must be endorsed on the indictment (Indictments Act 1915, s. 5(2)).

If necessary, an adjournment may be granted to allow the parties (in particular the defence) to deal with the altered position (s. 5(4)). Where the amendment comes during the course of a trial, there is power to discharge the jury from giving a verdict and order a retrial on the amended indictment (s. 5(5)(a)).

MOTION TO QUASH AN INDICTMENT

Either party may move to quash either the whole indictment or a count thereof. The obvious time for doing so is before the accused is arraigned, although it would seem that the defence may make the application at any stage of the trial. **D11.95**

The effect of a successful application is that the accused may not be tried on the indictment (or particular count thereof to which the motion relates). However, this does not mean that the accused is thereby acquitted. Although the quashing of the indictment exhausts the effect of the committal proceedings on which it was founded (see *Thompson* [1975] 1 WLR 1425), the prosecution may either institute fresh committal proceedings or apply for a voluntary bill of indictment.

Circumstances in which to Bring a Motion A motion to quash may be brought in any of three circumstances. **D11.96**

(a) Where the indictment is bad on its face (e.g., for duplicity or because the particulars of a count do not disclose an offence known to law). Thus, in *Yates* (1872) 12 Cox CC 233, an indictment for criminal libel was quashed because the words attributed to the accused were not prima facie libellous.
(b) Where the indictment (or a count thereof) has been preferred otherwise than in accordance with the provisions of the Administration of Justice (Miscellaneous Provisions) Act 1933, s. 2. Such an indictment must be quashed because it is preferred without authority (see *Lombardi* [1989] 1 WLR 73).
(c) Where the indictment contains a count for an offence in respect of which the accused was not committed for trial and the committal documents do not disclose a case to answer for that offence (*Jones* (1974) 59 Cr App R 120).

It is only in situation (c) that the judge is entitled to consider the prosecution evidence as foreshadowed in the documents (see *Jones* (1974) 59 Cr App R 120). Therefore, where the indictment follows the committal charges and is properly drafted on its face, the defence cannot invite the judge to quash on the basis that committal evidence did not in fact disclose a case to answer and the accused was wrongly committed for trial (*Chairman, County of London Quarter Sessions, ex parte Downes* [1954] 1 QB 1). Where, however, the indictment contains a count on which the accused was not committed the normal rule has to be relaxed in respect of that count, because otherwise the accused would be put on trial for the offence without any prior opportunity of arguing that the evidence is insufficient.

Use of Such Motions by the Defence Motions to quash are of little practical importance for the defence for three main reasons: **D11.97**

(a) the limited grounds on which they may be brought;
(b) the prosecution are often able to prevent a motion succeeding by making a suitable amendment to the indictment (e.g., splitting into two a count that the defence say should be quashed on grounds of duplicity);
(c) a successful motion results in the accused's discharge, not his acquittal.

However, such motions should not be ignored as a defence tool because failure to apply to quash may prejudice the chances of a successful appeal, since it may be argued that, if the defence at trial had felt themselves to be prejudiced by a defect in the indictment rendering it liable to be quashed, they would surely have made the appropriate application. The lack of a motion to quash may show that there was no miscarriage of justice (see, e.g., *Thompson* [1914] 2 KB 99 and *Donnelly* [1998] Crim LR 131).

Use of Such Motions by the Prosecution Although motions to quash are most obviously a remedy available to the defence, the prosecution may wish to quash if they realise that an **D11.98**

indictment they have preferred is invalid. The risk involved in adopting this course is that the committal on which the quashed indictment was founded may not be used as authority to prefer another indictment for the same offence (*Thompson* [1975] 1 WLR 1425 and dicta in *Newland* [1988] QB 402). The better course will usually be to ask the judge to stay (but not quash) the defective indictment and at the same time prefer a fresh indictment correcting the error in the original bill (see *Follett* [1989] QB 338).

DEFECTS IN THE INDICTMENT AS A GROUND OF APPEAL

D11.99 Where a trial proceeds on an unamended but defective indictment, there is an irregularity in the course of the trial which may result in the Court of Appeal finding that the conviction is unsafe (see, e.g., *Ayres* [1984] AC 447).

Decided cases do, however, show a marked reluctance on the part of the Court of Appeal to allow appeals on grounds of errors in the indictment. The precise reasoning varies. Sometimes it is said that the defect concerned a matter which was 'mere surplusage' (see *Dossi* (1918) 13 Cr App R 158). Sometimes a distinction is drawn between an indictment which is a nullity and one which is merely defective (see *McVitie* [1960] 2 QB 483 and *Nelson* (1977) Cr App R 119).

The most helpful approach is that adumbrated by Lord Bridge in *Ayres*. He said (at pp. 460G–461B):

> In a number of cases where an irregularity in the form of the indictment has been discussed in relation to the application of the proviso a distinction, treated as of crucial importance, has been drawn between an indictment which is 'a nullity' and one which is merely 'defective'. For my part, I doubt if this classification provides much assistance in answering the question which the proviso poses. If the statement and particulars of the offence in an indictment disclose no criminal offence whatever or charge some offence which has been abolished, in which case the indictment could fairly be described as a nullity, it is obvious that a conviction under that indictment cannot stand. But if the statement and particulars of offence can be seen fairly to relate to and to be intended to charge a known and subsisting criminal offence but plead it in terms which are inaccurate, incomplete or otherwise imperfect, then the question whether a conviction on that indictment can properly be affirmed under the proviso must depend on whether, in all the circumstances, it can be said with confidence that the particular error in the pleading cannot in any way have prejudiced or embarrassed the defendant.

D11.100 **The Test on Appeal** Normally, therefore, the crucial question is whether the defect has caused prejudice or embarrassment to the defence. This is illustrated by *Ayres* [1984] AC 447 itself. On the facts, the indictment faced by A 'did not charge him accurately with the only offence for which he could properly be convicted' (p. 460C), because it charged a common-law conspiracy when he was in fact guilty of statutory conspiracy. Nonetheless, the House of Lords held that there had been no prejudice, because (at p. 462):

> The particulars of offence in this indictment left no one in doubt that the substance of the crime alleged was a conspiracy to obtain money by deception. The judge in summing up gave all the appropriate directions in relation to that offence . . . the evidence amply proved that offence against the present appellant. The jury in returning a verdict of guilty must have been sure of his guilt of that offence. The judge passed a modest sentence comfortably below the maximum for that offence. The misdescription of the offence in the statement of offence as a common-law conspiracy to defraud had in the circumstances not the slightest practical significance . . . there [cannot] possibly have been any actual miscarriage of justice.

Ayres was referred to in *Graham* [1997] 1 Cr App R 302, where the Court of Appeal made clear that a conviction would not be quashed because of a drafting or clerical error, or a discrepancy, omission or departure from good practice. A conviction would be unsafe only where the particulars did not support a conviction for the offence charged.

Applications of the Test *Ayres* [1984] AC 447 is an extreme and somewhat questionable example of a defect in the indictment not resulting in a successful appeal. Appeals have also failed in the following cases notwithstanding the defects indicated below: **D11.101**

(a) *Thompson* [1914] 2 KB 99, where a count for incest was held to be bad for duplicity because it alleged offences 'on divers days' in a 21-month period;
(b) *McVitie* [1960] 2 QB 483, where the particulars omitted an essential ingredient of the offence charged (a breach of r. 5(1) of the Indictment Rules 1971);
(c) *Nelson* (1977) 65 Cr App R 119, where the statement of offence failed to specify the statute contravened (a breach of r. 6(a)(i) of the 1971 Rules);
(d) *Power* (1977) 66 Cr App R 159, where the statement of offence misdescribed the offence charged (a breach of r. 5(1) of the 1971 Rules).

In each of the above, the reasoning of the court was essentially that the indictment, although defective, was not null as it described an offence known to the law albeit in inaccurate terms, and the accused, on the facts, had not been misled or prejudiced in the conduct of his defence by the error.

COURT'S DISCRETION TO PREVENT ABUSE OF PROCESS

The Crown Court has an inherent power to protect its process from abuse. This includes the capacity to protect against delays in prosecution but other forms of abuse of process have been recognised. For a full discussion of abuse of process, see D3.54. **D11.102**

Section D12 Arraignment and Pleas

D12.1 This chapter address the issues which arise at the stage in proceedings when the accused is normally asked to plead to the indictment. Normal practice is for the accused to enter a plea of not guilty personally when arraigned by the clerk in the absence of any potential jurors There are a number of circumstances in which arraignment should not occur. Those addressed here are circumstances in which the defendant is unfit to plead, or where a claim to autrefois acquit or autrefois convict is raised. Two further bars to arraignment arise where the court has no jurisdiction to proceed (which is addressed at **D13.42** and at **A8.1** to **A8.15**), or where the court orders a stay of proceedings before arraignment because the proceedings represent an abuse of the court's process (which is addressed at **D3.64** ***et seq.***).

Please note that the topic of custody time limits, which was formerly found in this chapter, now appears at **D14.6**.

Where an accused is arraigned, there are then a number of pleas available to him (not guilty, guilty to the offence charged, guilty to a lesser offence etc.) and a variety of possible consequences that can follow from arraignment, including the prosecution offering no evidence or asking for counts to lie on the file. It is at this stage that plea bargains become relevant. There are also, finally, situations where a plea may change.

UNFITNESS TO PLEAD AND OTHER REASONS FOR FAILING TO PLEAD

D12.2 An accused may fail to plead to the indictment when arraigned in three situations:

(a) because he is mentally incapable of doing so, i.e. he is unfit to plead;
(b) in the increasingly rare circumstances in which he is physically incapable, this is sometimes known as 'mute by visitation of God'; or
(c) because he wilfully chooses to stay silent, known as 'mute of malice'.

Unfitness to Plead

D12.3 Whether or not an accused is fit to plead is determined in accordance with tests laid down by common law. The procedure to be followed when an accused might be unfit and the consequences of a finding of unfitness are contained in the Criminal Procedure (Insanity) Act 1964, ss. 4, 4A and 5. Although unfitness to plead in modern times is virtually invariably associated with mental illness or disability, it would be possible for a person who is mentally normal to be found unfit to plead if the circumstances accorded with those enunciated in the relevant test.

D12.4 **The Test of Unfitness to Plead** The leading case of *Pritchard* (1836) 7 C & P 303, concerned a deaf mute who was otherwise of sound mind. Alderson B's direction to the jury empanelled to determine whether P was fit to plead was in terms which Lord Parker CJ was later to say had become 'firmly embodied in our law' (see *Podola* [1960] 1 QB 325 at p. 353). Alderson B said (7 C & P 303 at pp. 304–5):

> There are three points to be inquired into: First, whether the prisoner is mute of malice or not; secondly, whether he can plead to the indictment or not; thirdly, whether he is of sufficient intellect to comprehend the course of proceedings on the trial, so as to make a proper defence — to know that he might challenge [any jurors] to whom he may object — and to comprehend the details of the evidence. . . if you think that there is no certain mode of communicating the details of the trial to the prisoner, so that he can clearly understand them, and be able properly to make his defence to the charge; you ought to find that he is not of sane mind. It is not enough that he may have a general capacity of communicating on ordinary matters.

It will be apparent from the above that there is considerable overlap between the issue of unfitness to plead and the issue of whether an accused is mute of malice or mute by visitation of God. Indeed, the result of Pritchard's case was that he was found unfit to plead, even though his disability (being deaf and speech handicapped) also constitutes the classic example of muteness by visitation of God. Factually, however, *Pritchard* is an atypical case. One would not today expect the issue of unfitness to be raised unless the accused is thought to be suffering from some degree of mental illness or deficiency, even if this may be exacerbated by physical problems.

Nonetheless, Alderson B's direction in *Pritchard* remains the basis of the modern law, and the following points emerge from it:

(a) An accused may be unfit to plead even though he is not insane within the meaning of the M'Naghten rules. The point was expressly decided in *Governor of Stafford Prison, ex parte Emery* [1909] 2 KB 81, a particularly strong decision since the statutory provision then governing unfitness to plead (Lunatics Act 1800, s. 2) actually referred to the jury finding that the person indicted was insane (and see also Lord Parker CJ's judgment in *Podola* [1960] 1 QB 325 at p. 353). It would logically follow that an accused may be unfit even though he is not suffering from any of the forms of mental disorder defined in s. 37(1) of the Mental Health Act 1983 that are a precondition for the making of a hospital order in the case of a convicted offender (see E24.1).

(b) The test of unfitness to plead is whether the accused will be able to comprehend the course of the proceedings so as to make a proper defence (*Pritchard*). Whether he can understand and reply rationally to the indictment is obviously a relevant factor, but the court must also consider whether he would be able to exercise his right to challenge jurors, understand details of the evidence as it is given, instruct his legal advisers and give evidence himself if he so desires.

(c) Assuming the accused can understand the course of the proceedings, he will be fit to plead even though he may act against his own best interests as a consequence of his mental condition (*Robertson* [1968] 1 WLR 1767 — paranoiac who might have made irrational objections to potential jurors, held fit to plead). Similarly, a high degree of abnormality does not *ipso facto* render the accused unfit to plead (*Berry* (1977) 66 Cr App R 156 — finding of unfitness quashed because, although B was in a 'grossly abnormal mental state', the judge failed to direct the jury on the crucial issue of whether those abnormalities made him incapable of following the trial).

(d) Loss of memory through hysterical amnesia does not amount to unfitness to plead if the accused is otherwise normal at the time of trial (*Podola*). Such an accused will be able to comprehend the proceedings and communicate with his legal advisers, although his ability to give instructions as to the prosecution evidence will necessarily be limited.

Burden of Proof Following the evidence, the court must consider whether the accused is capable of understanding the proceedings so that he can: **D12.5**

(a) put forward his defence;
(b) challenge any juror to whom he has cause to object;
(c) give proper instructions to his legal representatives; and
(d) follow the evidence.

If the issue was raised by the defence, the burden of proof is on them to establish on a balance of probabilities that the accused is unfit (*Robertson* [1968] 1 WLR 1767); if raised by the prosecution, they bear the burden of proof beyond reasonable doubt (*Podola* [1960] 1 QB 325).

D12.6 **Procedure for Determining Unfitness to Plead** As indicated above, the issue of whether the accused is fit to plead may be raised by either the prosecution or defence. Whilst it will normally be raised by the latter, the prosecution might wish to assert that the accused is unfit to plead either because of the general principle that prosecuting counsel should act as a 'minister of justice' assisting the court, or because in certain circumstances (e.g., where the offence charged requires proof of a specific or ulterior intent on the part of the accused) it may in practice be difficult to establish guilt if, at the time of trial, the accused is manifestly suffering from mental illness.

D12.7 **Timing of Raising the Issue** Subject to a special procedure contained in the Criminal Procedure (Insanity) Act 1964, s. 4(2) (set out in full at **D12.15**), the issue must be determined as soon as it arises (s. 4(4)). Assuming the possibility of the accused being unfit is known to the parties before trial, it is submitted that the court should be informed of the situation before arraignment so that, if he is unfit, the accused will not be called on to plead.

Section 4(2) of the 1964 Act permits the court to postpone consideration of unfitness until any time up to the opening of the defence case. The court must be of the opinion that, having regard to 'the nature of the supposed disability', postponement is 'expedient' and 'in the interests of the accused'. Such a postponement would be appropriate where there is a reasonable chance that the prosecution evidence may be subject to successful challenge without the need for the defence to be called upon (*Webb* [1969] 2 QB 278; *Burles* [1970] 2 QB 191).

D12.8 **The Issue of Fitness** Until 2005, the issue of fitness to plead was determined by a specially empanelled jury. However, under the DVCVA 2004, s. 22, the decision whether the accused is unfit to plead is taken by a judge alone.

In addition, the Criminal Procedure (Insanity) Act 1964, s. 4(6), lays down that the court may not determine the question of fitness to plead except on the evidence (written or oral) of two or more registered medical practitioners, at least one of whom must have been approved by the Secretary of State as having special experience in the diagnosis or treatment of mental disorder. (See **D19.72** for the power of the court to remand an accused for the preparation of reports on his mental condition under the Mental Health Act 1983, s. 35.) Although such medical evidence is required, the judge is entitled to reject it. He must, however, keep the issue under review (*M* [2006] EWCA Crim 2391).

D12.9 **Trial of the Facts** Section 4A of the Criminal Procedure (Insanity) Act 1964 (which is set out in full at **D12.15**) applies where the court has determined that the accused is unfit to plead. It must then be determined by a jury whether the accused 'did the act or made the omission charged against him as the offence' (s. 4A(2)). If they are satisfied that he did, they must find accordingly (s. 4A(3)). If they are not so satisfied, they must acquit. If the question of fitness to plead was determined on or before arraignment, a jury must be empanelled to try the issue of whether the accused did the act or made the omission. If it was postponed under s. 4(2), the jury by whom the accused was being tried should also determine whether he did the act or made the omission (s. 4A(5)).

The purpose of this 'trial of the facts' is to ensure that the case against an accused who has been found unfit to plead is tested. It aims in this way to avoid the detention of innocent persons in hospital, merely because they are mentally unfit. Although the statute is silent on the standard of proof, it is submitted that the test is 'beyond reasonable doubt', in accordance with general principle.

Relevance of the Mental Element of an Offence at the Trial of the Facts In *Antoine* [2001] 1 AC 340, the House of Lords held that, in this 'trial of the facts', the defence of diminished responsibility could not be raised. In their lordships' view, by using the word 'act' rather than 'offence' in the Criminal Procedure (Insanity) Act 1964, s. 4A(2), Parliament had made it clear that the jury was not to consider the mental ingredients of the offence. The defence could, however, rely on mistake, accident, self-defence or involuntariness. **D12.10**

Similarly in *Grant* [2002] QB 1030, it was held that provocation could not be raised at the s. 4A hearing, since it inevitably required examination of the accused's state of mind, rather than whether he 'did the act charged'.

Only exceptionally, therefore, will it be possible for the intentions of the accused to be considered as part of the enquiry (e.g., see *R (Young) v Central Criminal Court* [2002] 2 Cr App R 178, where the *actus reus* of an offence is that the accused 'concealed' material facts contrary to the Financial Services Act 1986, s. 47(1)).

The ECHR Perspective In *M* [2002] 1 WLR 824, the Court of Appeal considered the above procedures in the light of the ECHR, Article 6. The court held that the criminal charge provisions of Article 6 do not apply to proceedings under ss. 4 and 4A of the 1964 Act, since those proceedings cannot result in a conviction. In any event, they concluded that the procedure under ss. 4 and 4A constituted a fair procedure, providing an opportunity for investigation of the facts on behalf of a disabled person, so far as possible. It fairly balanced the public interest and the interest of the person alleged to have committed the act. In addition, their lordships stated that the defence was able to make an application to stay proceedings for abuse of process when it appeared necessary, and this could be either before arraignment or before any question of disability fell to be determined. **D12.11**

This decision was endorsed by the House of Lords in *H* [2003] 1 WLR 411; any orders made following a finding that the accused did the act in question were said not to be punitive, but to be made only for the purpose of protecting the public.

Consequences of a Finding of Unfitness

Under the Criminal Procedure (Insanity) Act 1964, s. 5 (set out in full at D12.15), if the accused is found unfit to plead, and the jury determines that he did the act or made the omission as charged, the court may make one of the following orders: **D12.12**

(a) an admission order to such hospital as the Secretary of State specifies — such an order may be made the subject of a restriction order without limit of time or for a specified period but, where the offence to which the findings relate is murder, the court must make an admission order without limit of time (see **E24.1**);
(b) a supervision order; or
(c) an order for the accused's absolute discharge.

In *Grant* [2002] QB 1030, the Court of Appeal considered whether the procedure constituted a violation of the ECHR. The accused had been found unfit to plead to a charge of murder, with the result that the trial judge was compelled to make an order for admission to a hospital without limitation of time. The problem identified by their lordships was that the judge could not consider whether such an order was justified on the medical evidence, which was directed to the question of whether the accused was fit to plead. On the facts in *Grant*, the medical evidence supplied had also stated that the accused suffered from mental impairment within the Mental Health Act 1983. The decision left open, however, the possibility of a violation of Article 5 where the medical evidence was more narrowly confined to fitness to plead.

In *Fairley* [2003] EWCA Crim 1625, it was emphasised that the only orders which the judge could make, following a finding that an accused who was unfit to plead had committed the action in question, were confined to those set out in the statute. It followed that a judge had no power in these circumstances to order an accused to be detained in hospital under the Mental Health Act 1983, s. 37(1), nor to add a restriction order under s. 41 of that Act.

D12.13 **Rights of the Victim** Under the DVCVA 2004, s. 38, the victim of a sexual or violent offence has certain rights where an offence is committed by a person who is found not guilty by reason of insanity or who is subject to a finding under the Criminal Procedure (Insanity) Act 1964, ss. 4 and 4A ('the patient'). Where the court makes a hospital order with a restriction order in dealing with the patient for the offence, the probation board for the area must take all reasonable steps to ascertain whether the victim wishes to make representations about any conditions to which the patient should be subject. The victim is also entitled to receive information about any conditions to which the patient is to be subject in the event of his discharge from hospital.

D12.14 **Reversing such an Order** In *R (Hasani) v Crown Court at Blackfriars* [2006] 1 WLR 1992, the accused was found unfit to plead to serious offences against the person. A jury then determined that he had done the acts in question. The judge adjourned the matter to determine the issue of disposal. Before that issue could be determined, evidence was presented to show that the accused was capable of pleading. The judge then directed that the accused be arraigned. On judicial review, the judge's order was quashed, and the case was remitted to the Crown Court. The order to arraign was premature in that a fresh hearing on fitness to plead, in accordance with s. 4, had to be held first. There was nothing in the Criminal Procedure (Insanity) Act 1964 to preclude the holding of a second hearing on the issue of fitness to plead where the evidence justifies that course of action and there has been no final disposition of the case.

D12.15 **Procedure where Accused is Found Fit to Plead** If the accused is found fit to plead before the calling of any prosecution evidence, he will thereafter be arraigned in the usual way and plead to the indictment.

Criminal Procedure (Insanity) Act 1964, ss. 4, 4A and 5

4.—(1) This section applies where on the trial of a person the question arises (at the instance of the defence or otherwise) whether the accused is under a disability, that is to say, under any disability such that apart from this Act it would constitute a bar to his being tried.

(2) If, having regard to the nature of the supposed disability, the court are of opinion that it is expedient to do so and in the interests of the accused, they may postpone consideration of the question of fitness to be tried until any time up to the opening of the case for the defence.

(3) If, before the question of fitness to be tried falls to be determined, the jury return a verdict of acquittal on the count or each of the counts on which the accused is being tried, that question shall not be determined.

(4) Subject to subsections (2) and (3) above, the question of fitness to be tried shall be determined as soon as it arises.

(5) The question of fitness to be tried shall be determined by a court without a jury.

(6) The court shall not make a determination under subsection (5) above except on the written or oral evidence of two or more registered medical practitioners at least one of whom is duly approved.

4A.—(1) This section applies where in accordance with section 4(5) above it is determined by a court that the accused is under a disability.

(2) The trial shall not proceed or further proceed but it shall be determined by a jury—

(a) on the evidence (if any) already given in the trial; and

(b) on such evidence as may be adduced or further adduced by the prosecution, or adduced by a person appointed by the court under this section to put the case for the defence, whether they are satisfied, as respects the count or each of the counts on which the accused was to be or was being tried, that he did the act or made the omission charged against him as the offence.

(3) If as respects that count or any of those counts the jury are satisfied as mentioned in subsection (2) above, they shall make a finding that the accused did the act or made the omission charged against him.

(4) If as respects that count or any of those counts the jury are not so satisfied, they shall return a verdict of acquittal as if on the count in question the trial had proceeded to a conclusion.

(5) Where the question of disability was determined after arraignment of the accused, the determination under subsection (2) is to be made by the jury by whom he was being tried.

5.—(1) This section applies where—

(a) a special verdict is returned that the accused is not guilty by reason of insanity; or

(b) findings have been made that the accused is under a disability and that he did the act or made the omission charged against him.

(2) The court shall make in respect of the accused—

(a) a hospital order (with or without a restriction order);

(b) a supervision order; or

(c) an order for his absolute discharge.

(3) Where—

(a) the offence to which the special verdict or the findings relate is an offence the sentence for which is fixed by law, and

(b) the court have power to make a hospital order,

the court shall make a hospital order with a restriction order (whether or not they would have power to make a restriction order apart from this subsection).

(4) In this section—

'hospital order' has the meaning given in section 37 of the Mental Health Act 1983;

'restriction order' has the meaning given to it by section 41 of that Act;

'supervision order' has the meaning given in part 1 of schedule 1A to this Act.

Sections 4 and 4A are set out as amended by, and s. 5 as substituted by, the DVCVA 2004, ss. 22 and 24, in force from 31 March 2005.

Muteness

If an accused stays silent when arraigned, the issue arises whether he is silent for reasons beyond his control or by deliberate choice. In the former case, he is 'mute by visitation of God' in the latter case, he is said to be 'mute of malice'. **D12.16**

Mute by Visitation of God If the finding of the jury is that the accused is 'mute by visitation of God', the court has the option of adjourning for a short period in order that means of communicating with him may be found (e.g., through bringing an expert in sign language or lip-reading to court, and see also *Harris* (1897) 61 JP 792, where the jury found that a wound in H's throat which prevented him speaking was due to an attempt at suicide and the case was simply adjourned for the wound to heal). **D12.17**

Alternatively, if it seems that the muteness will be permanent and cannot be overcome, the jury should be asked to go on to consider whether the accused is unfit to plead (see **D12.4**; see also *Pritchard* (1836) 7 C & P 303, and *Governor of Stafford Prison, ex parte Emery* [1909] 2 KB 81). Therefore, a finding that the accused is mute by visitation of God is likely to be merely a stage en route to a finding of unfitness to plead, rather than a final determination in itself — indeed, the classic direction of Alderson B in *Pritchard* required the jury to consider in turn whether P was (a) mute of malice, (b) able to plead, and (c) able to comprehend the course of the proceedings.

Mute of Malice Section 6(1)(c) of the Criminal Law Act 1967 provides that: **D12.18**

> Where a person is arraigned on an indictment . . . if he stands mute of malice or will not answer directly to the indictment, the court may order a plea of not guilty to be entered on his behalf, and he shall then be treated as having pleaded not guilty.

D

Part D Procedure

The court may not itself conclude that a silent accused is mute of malice but must empanel a jury to determine the issue (*Schleter* (1866) 10 Cox CC 409), the burden of proof being on the prosecution to establish malice beyond reasonable doubt (*Sharp* [1960] 1 QB 357). The accused has no right of challenge in respect of the jurors so empanelled (*Paling* (1978) 67 Cr App R 299).

If the accused is found mute of malice, there is no objection to the jury that has so found him going on to try the case, subject only to the general rule that a jury empanelled to try one issue may not try a second issue unless the trial of the latter commences within 24 hours of their empanelment to try the first (Juries Act 1974, s. 11).

In modern times, a silent accused will almost certainly be mute of malice. Should there be reasons beyond his control rendering him unable to answer to the indictment, that will have been realised long before arraignment and steps will have been taken to overcome the problem (e.g., by the provision of an interpreter). Alternatively, if he is or may be unfit to plead, either the prosecution or defence will raise that issue with the judge before the indictment is put, thus avoiding the question of muteness arising as a separate issue lest the accused should be found fit to plead and then stay silent when arraigned.

AUTREFOIS ACQUIT AND AUTREFOIS CONVICT

D12.19 The pleas of autrefois acquit and autrefois convict, together with the plea of pardon (see D12.45), are known as pleas in bar, because, if upheld, they bar any further proceedings on the indictment. The basic purpose of the two pleas is to protect the subject against repeated prosecutions for the same offence. Although a large body of case law has developed defining the precise circumstances in which the pleas may be relied on, in reality it will be very rare that a prosecution would occur where the proposed accused has already been acquitted or convicted of the offence that would be charged.

There are a number of important statutory exceptions which will arise under the tainted acquittal provisions of the CPIA 1996, ss. 54 to 57, which are dealt with at **D12.33**, and the retrial provisions of the CJA 2003, ss. 75 to 97, which are dealt with at **D12.34**.

Consideration of the pleas will involve asking: (a) what amounts to an acquittal or a conviction in this context? (b) precisely what is meant by being prosecuted twice for the same offence? and (c) what is the procedure to be followed on the pleas being raised?

Meaning of 'Acquittal' and 'Conviction' in Context of Autrefois Pleas

D12.20 For an autrefois plea to succeed, the earlier conviction or acquittal relied on by the accused must have been by a court of competent jurisdiction and the proceedings must not have been *ultra vires*. This is illustrated in respect of autrefois convict by *Kent Justices, ex parte Machin* [1952] 2 QB 355, in which the Divisional Court quashed by certiorari M's conviction and committal for sentence on the ground that the correct procedure for determining mode of trial had not been complied with and the magistrates therefore acted *ultra vires*. Lord Goddard CJ stated that the prosecution were entitled to recharge the accused as he 'has never been technically in peril and he could be tried again'.

The same applies to *ultra vires* acquittals. For example, where magistrates purport to acquit an accused of an offence triable only on indictment, he cannot rely on the 'acquittal' either to resist committal or to bar a trial on indictment (*West* [1964] 1 QB 15, and see also *Cardiff Magistrates' Court, ex parte Cardiff City Council* (1987) *The Times*, 24 February 1987).

Scope of the Pleas

D12.21 **At Common Law** The leading case is *Connelly v DPP* [1964] AC 1254, the facts of which are illustrative of the general principle. C and three others were jointly charged in two indictments, the first for murder and the second for armed robbery. The prosecution case was that the four accused had all participated in a robbery during the course of which an employee was shot and killed. The preferring of two indictments was necessitated by the then rule of practice that, if there was a count for murder on an indictment, no counts for other offences could be joined with it. The employee named in the second indictment as the victim of the robbery was *not* the murder victim.

The murder indictment was tried first and all the accused were convicted. C successfully appealed against conviction, which meant that he had to be treated as if he had been acquitted of murder, and he could not therefore be reprosecuted either for that offence or for manslaughter. When the prosecution obtained leave from the Court of Criminal Appeal to proceed on the indictment for robbery, C pleaded autrefois acquit.

A jury was empanelled (such an issue would now be determined by the judge — see the CJA 1988, s. 122) to determine the following question: '. . . has this man Connelly proved that he has already been tried and acquitted of the same felony or offence, or of substantially the same offence, or has he already been tried and acquitted on an indictment on which he could have been convicted of the same or substantially the same offence?' The judge directed the jury that the offence of murder could not be regarded as 'substantially or practically the same' as an offence of robbery with aggravation of a sum of money from a different employee. The jury accordingly found that autrefois acquit did not apply. C was convicted of robbery, following a further trial.

The *Connolly* Nine Propositions C appealed against conviction, this time on the ground that his plea of autrefois acquit should have been upheld. The House of Lords dismissed the appeal. The speech of Lord Morris of Borth-y-Gest reviewed at length the old authorities and summarised their effect in nine propositions ([1964] AC 1254 at pp. 1305–6), which may be further summarised as follows: **D12.22**

(a) *A man may not be tried for a crime in respect of which he has previously been acquitted or convicted.* This is the straightforward and obvious application of autrefois, and covers cases where the offence charged in a count is identical in law and on the facts to a crime of which the accused has previously been acquitted or convicted.

(b) *A man cannot be tried for a crime in respect of which he could on some previous indictment have been convicted.* This is the corollary of the power of a jury to return a verdict of not guilty as charged but guilty of a lesser offence. The reasoning is that, where the jury on a certain count could have convicted of a lesser offence but failed to do so, they have impliedly acquitted him both of the offence charged and of the lesser offence. Consequently, their verdict can be relied on to bar a later indictment for either or both offences. Lord Morris traced the principle back to Hale's *Pleas of the Crown* (1778), giving the example of an acquittal for murder barring any later indictment for manslaughter ([1964] AC 1254 at p. 1311) (see *Old Street Magistrates' Court, ex parte Davies* [1995] Crim LR 629, although it is probably confined to its own unusual facts). Logically, the above rule applies whenever an alternative verdict was open to the jury as a matter of law, not whether the judge, as a matter of discretion, drew their attention to the possibility in his summing-up.

(c) *A man cannot be tried for a crime which is in effect the same, or is substantially the same, as a crime of which he has previously been acquitted or convicted (or could have been convicted by way of alternative verdict).* Lord Morris (see pp. 1310–28) undertook a detailed survey of the decided cases (principally from the 19th century) which directly or indirectly indicate when a count is to be regarded as alleging a crime that is substantially (though not exactly) the same as one of which the accused has previously been acquitted or convicted. One clear example of the test being satisfied is provided by an accused being indicted for murder after he has been acquitted of the alleged victim's manslaughter (see *Wrote v Wigges* (1591) 4 Co Rep 45b and *Tancock* (1876) 34 LT 455).

The same will apply whenever proof of an offence of which the accused has already been acquitted is a necessary step towards proving the offence now charged. The strictness of the test is, however, illustrated by *Salvi* (1857) 10 Cox CC 481, where S, after being acquitted on a charge of wounding with intent to murder, was indicted for murder after his victim's death. His plea of autrefois failed because murder could be committed without there being an intention to murder. Therefore, the evidence on the second indictment would not necessarily have to be such as to support a conviction on the first (it could show merely an intention to do the victim grievous bodily harm).

(d) *What has to be considered is whether the crime or offence charged in the later indictment is the same, or is in effect or is substantially the same, as the crime charged in the former indictment and it is immaterial that the facts under examination or the witnesses being called in the later proceedings are the same as those in some earlier proceedings.* The actual decision in *Connelly v DPP* provides the best illustration. The evidence called and facts relied on by the prosecution against C at the trial for robbery were precisely the same as they had called and relied on at the earlier trial for murder. But, despite the coincidence of prosecution facts and evidence at the two trials, the House of Lords were unanimous in holding that autrefois acquit did not avail.

D12.23 **Reconsideration of the Principles in *Beedie*** The above analysis should now be considered in the light of the decision of the Court of Appeal in *Beedie* [1998] QB 356. B was prosecuted first for Health and Safety Act offences and then for manslaughter, both relating to the same death. At his trial for manslaughter, his counsel applied to stay the indictment, relying upon *Connelly*, but the judge refused. He was convicted and he appealed. The Court of Appeal considered the question of whether or not the second offence had to be the same as the first, or whether it was sufficient that it arose from the same facts, and stated the following principles:

(a) The House of Lords in *Connelly* had identified a narrow principle of autrefois. It was applicable only where the *same* offence was alleged in the second indictment. Rose LJ, delivering the judgment of the Court of Appeal in *Beedie*, quoted with approval Lord Devlin in *Connelly* (at p. 1340): 'For the doctrine to apply it must be the same offence both in fact and in law'.

(b) Importantly, however, judicial discretion should be exercised where the second offence arises out of the same or substantially the same set of facts as the first. In addition, there should be no sequential trials for offences on an ascending scale of gravity (relying on the principle in *Elrington* (1861) 1 B & S 688). As it was put in *Forest of Dean Justices, ex parte Farley* [1990] RTR 228 at p. 239, there is an 'almost invariable rule that when a person is tried on a lesser offence he is not to be tried again on the same facts for a more serious offence'.

(c) It was for the prosecution to show that there were special circumstances before the judge should allow the trial to proceed. In *Beedie*, a stay should have been ordered because the manslaughter allegation was based on substantially the same facts as the earlier summary prosecutions, it was a prosecution for an offence of greater gravity, and there were no special circumstances such as to allow the prosecution to proceed; the appeal was allowed (see also *South East Hampshire Magistrates' Court, ex parte CPS* [1998] Crim LR 422) and *Hartnett* [2003] Crim LR 719).

It follows that in such circumstances the plea of autrefois has in reality become a species of abuse of process. This was illustrated more recently, in *Cheong* [2006] EWCA Crim 524, in which it was held that, where an accused has not been acquitted or convicted in a foreign court but the prosecuting authority in that country has acted in some other way in relation to the charge now brought against him, the question for the court is whether the accused could not now receive a fair trial, or it would otherwise be unfair to try him.

Findings that Can Form Basis for Plea of Autrefois Acquit The following findings *do* amount to acquittals and therefore can found a plea of autrefois acquit: **D12.24**

(a) The quashing of a conviction by the Court of Appeal, provided it does not at the same time order a retrial (see Criminal Appeal Act 1968, s. 2(3)).
(b) An acquittal by a foreign court of competent jurisdiction (*Aughet* (1919) 13 Cr App R 101). This was confirmed, *obiter*, by Lord Diplock in *Treacy v DPP* [1971] AC 537, when he said (at p. 562D) that the common-law doctrine of autrefois acquit and convict was 'a doctrine which has always applied whether the previous conviction or acquittal based on the same facts was by an English court or by a foreign court'.

Findings that Cannot Form Basis for Plea of Autrefois Acquit The following findings do *not* amount to acquittals and therefore cannot found a plea of autrefois acquit: **D12.25**

(a) Discharge of the accused at committal proceedings (*Manchester City Stipendiary Magistrate, ex parte Snelson* [1977] 1 WLR 911).
(b) Quashing of an indictment following a motion to quash. This point would not seem to be covered by specific authority but follows inevitably from the nature of the remedy, which is to prevent any proceedings on the indictment in question and, *ex hypothesi*, prevent the returning of a verdict (see *Newland* [1988] QB 402).
(c) The withdrawal of a summons by the prosecution in the magistrates' court prior to the accused having pleaded to it (*Bedford and Sharnbrook Justices, ex parte Ward* [1974] Crim LR 109). In *Grays Justices, ex parte Low* [1990] QB 54, Nolan J reviewed the earlier authorities and concluded (at p. 59A–B):

> . . . it must now be regarded as settled law that . . . the withdrawal of a summons with the consent of the justices will not of itself operate as a bar to the issue of a further summons in respect of the same charge where there has been no adjudication upon the merits of the charge in the original summons, and the defendant has not been put in peril of conviction upon it.

See also *Brookes* [1995] Crim LR 630, where B pleaded not guilty to a charge under the OAPA 1861, s. 20, and the prosecution offered no evidence and laid a charge under s. 18. The Court of Appeal approved the rejection of his plea of autrefois acquit (see also *London Borough of Islington v Michaelides* [2001] Crim LR 843).

(d) The dismissal of an information under s. 15 of the MCA 1980 on account of the non-appearance of the prosecutor (*Bennett and Bond, ex parte Bennet* (1908) 72 JP 362) or where the information is so faulty in form and content that the accused could never have been in jeopardy on it (see *DPP v Porthouse* (1988) 89 Cr App R 21 and *Dabhade* [1993] QB 329).
(e) The dismissal of a charge, pursuant to the CDA 1998, s. 51.
(f) The prosecution serving notice of discontinuance under the Prosecution of Offences Act 1985, s. 23.
(g) The jury being discharged from giving a verdict.
(h) Reliance on evidence of an offence of which the accused has been acquitted as similar fact evidence (*Z* [2000] 2 AC 483).
(i) Where the provisions relating to tainted acquittals in the CPIA 1996, ss. 54 to 57, apply (see **D12.33**).

Findings that Can Form Basis for Plea of Autrefois Convict The following findings *do* amount to convictions and therefore can found a plea of autrefois convict: **D12.26**

(a) A conviction by a foreign court will found autrefois convict, subject to the qualification that if he who now relies on the foreign conviction was found guilty and sentenced in his absence and there is no likelihood of his ever returning to the country concerned to serve his sentence, the plea will fail (*Thomas* [1985] QB 604).
(b) A plea of autrefois convict could only be based upon a complete adjudication against the

accused, including the final disposal of the case by passing sentence or some other order such as an absolute discharge. This was the conclusion of the Privy Council in *Richards v The Queen* [1993] AC 217. The underlying rationale of the plea was to prevent double punishment. But, if a finding of guilt was all that was necessary to support the plea in bar, an accused might escape punishment altogether. The Privy Council thereby concluded that two earlier decisions to the contrary, *Sheridan* [1937] 1 KB 223, and *Grant* [1936] 2 All ER 1156, were wrongly decided.

D12.27 **Findings that Cannot Form Basis for Plea of Autrefois Convict** The following findings do *not* amount to convictions and therefore cannot found a plea of autrefois convict:

(a) The taking of an offence into consideration when passing sentence for other offences of which the offender has been convicted (*Nicholson* [1947] 2 All ER 535).
(b) A finding of guilt in disciplinary proceedings, albeit that the finding is followed by the imposition of a penalty (*Hogan* [1960] 2 QB 513).
(c) A finding of contempt of court in civil proceedings (*Green* [1993] Crim LR 46: but note that the position in relation to non-molestation orders has changed as a result of the DVCVA 2004, s. 1 (see **B14.111**)).

D12.28 **A Note on Issue Estoppel** A further question raised by the appeal in *Connelly v DPP* [1964] AC 1254, was whether the doctrine of issue estoppel applies in criminal cases, i.e. can either the prosecution or the defence prevent the other side reopening a question of fact if that question has already been decided in previous proceedings between the same parties? However, in *DPP v Humphrys* [1977] AC 1, it was held that issue estoppel has no place in criminal proceedings. There is a limited exception in the case of an application for habeas corpus: *Governor of Brixton Prison, ex parte Osman* [1991] 1 WLR 281. For full discussion of issue estoppel, see **F11.12**.

Procedure on Autrefois Pleas

D12.29 The following procedural steps are involved in raising the plea of autrefois, although failure to observe the correct formalities in entering the plea does not prevent reliance on it (*Flatman v Light* [1946] KB 414).

(a) Under the Criminal Procedure Act 1851, s. 28, an accused may raise a plea of autrefois simply by stating that he has already been lawfully acquitted or convicted of the offence now charged. Where, however, he is legally represented, the correct procedure is for the plea to be entered in writing signed by counsel. A suggested form of words is, '[The accused] says that the Queen ought not further to prosecute the indictment against him because he has been lawfully acquitted/convicted of the offence charged therein'.
(b) The obvious time for pleading autrefois is before the indictment is put to the accused, but failure to do so then will not prevent the defence raising the issue at a later stage ('. . . the plea may be raised at any time either as a plea in bar to the second indictment or at any stage in the proceedings': per Lord Hodson in *Connelly v DPP* [1964] AC 1254 at p. 1331).
(c) The prosecution either admit that the plea is good (in which case the accused is discharged) or join issue in writing.
(d) Alternatively, the court may raise the plea of its own motion (*Cooper v New Forest District Council* [1992] Crim LR 877).
(e) Once the plea has been entered and issue joined by the prosecution, the burden of proof is on the accused to make good the plea on a balance of probabilities (*Coughlan* (1976) 63 Cr App R 33).
(f) The parties are not restricted to the formal record of the earlier proceedings (which will establish only the date and place of conviction or acquittal, the wording of the charges and the name of the accused), but may call relevant evidence. In the absence of dispute,

counsel should shorten the proceedings by reading to the court a brief statement of the relevant facts from (a) the previous trial, and (b) the statements in the present case on which they respectively intend to rely in argument (see *Coughlan*).

(g) The issue is determined by the judge without empanelling a jury (CJA 1988, s. 122).

(h) If a plea of autrefois convict or acquit succeeds, it is a bar to any further proceedings on the indictment. If the plea fails, the indictment is put and the accused is entitled to plead not guilty to the general issue notwithstanding his earlier unsuccessful reliance on autrefois (Criminal Law Act 1967, s. 6(1): 'Where a person is arraigned on indictment . . . he shall in all cases be entitled to make a plea of not guilty in addition to any demurrer or special plea').

Statutory Provisions In addition to the procedure to deal with tainted acquittals (D12.33) and a procedure for the retrial of certain serious offences in the light of new evidence (D12.34), the common law on the ambit of autrefois is supplemented by two sets of statutory provisions. **D12.30**

Offences Against the Person Act 1861 Sections. 44 and 45 of the OAPA 1861 provide that, if justices, 'upon the hearing of any case of assault or battery upon the merits, *where the complaint was preferred by or on behalf of the party aggrieved*, shall deem the offence not to be proved, or shall find the assault or battery to have been justified, or so trifling as not to merit any punishment, and shall accordingly dismiss the complaint, they shall forthwith make out a certificate under their hands stating the fact of such dismissal and shall deliver such certificate to the party against whom the complaint was preferred' (s. 44, emphasis added). The obtaining of a s. 44 certificate of dismissal releases the party 'from all further or other proceedings, civil or criminal, *for the same cause*' (s. 45). **D12.31**

The italicised words indicate the main limitations on the scope of ss. 44 and 45. First, a certificate of dismissal may be granted only where the complainant (i.e. prosecutor) in the summary assault proceedings is the victim of the alleged offence. Therefore, if the victim reported the offence to the police and the police commenced proceedings either by charging the accused or laying an information, s. 44 cannot apply since the police, in commencing proceedings, do not act on behalf of the aggrieved. Secondly, a certificate frees the recipient only from further proceedings 'for the same cause'.

Section 18 of the Interpretation Act 1978 Section 18 of the Interpretation Act 1978 states that: **D12.32**

> Where an act or omission constitutes an offence under two or more Acts, or both under an Act and at common law, the offender shall, unless the contrary intention appears, be liable to be prosecuted and punished under either or any of those Acts or at common law, but shall not be liable to be punished more than once for the same offence.

According to Humphreys J in *Thomas* [1950] 1 KB 26, the predecessor of s. 18 of the 1978 Act (s. 33 of the Interpretation Act 1889) 'added nothing and detracted nothing from the common law'. In particular, the prohibition on being punished more than once for the same offence did not protect an accused from being convicted and sentenced on successive occasions for different offences arising out of the same criminal act (conviction for wounding with intent no bar to later indictment for murder).

TAINTED ACQUITTALS

The provisions of the CPIA 1996, ss. 54 to 57, which relate to 'tainted acquittals', constitute a major exception to the availability of autrefois acquit. They enable the prosecution of an accused for a second time for a crime of which he has already been acquitted at trial, provided **D12.33** certain conditions are met. Sections 54 and 55 (set out below) lay down a procedure relating to tainted acquittals where the following conditions are met:

(a) an accused has been acquitted of an offence (s. 54(1)(a)); and
(b) a person has been convicted of an administration of justice offence involving interference with or intimidation of a juror or a witness or potential witness (s. 54(1)(b)); and
(c) the court convicting of the administration of justice offence certifies that there is a real possibility that, but for the interference or intimidation, the acquitted person would not have been acquitted, and that it would not be contrary to the interests of justice to proceed against the acquitted person (s. 54(2) and (5)); and
(d) the High Court grants an order quashing the acquittal after deciding that the four conditions set out in s. 55 are satisfied (s. 55 is set out below).

The provisions of ss. 54 to 57 apply in relation to acquittals in respect of offences alleged to have been committed on or after 15 April 1997. It should be emphasised that it is the *original* offence of which the defendant was acquitted which must be alleged to have been committed on or after that date (s. 54(7)).

The formalities relating to the tainted acquittal procedure are set out in part 40 of the CrimPR. Part 40 makes it clear that the certification referred to in s. 54(2) must take place, at the latest, immediately after sentence (or committal for sentence, or remittal of a juvenile to the youth court to be dealt with for an offence).

Criminal Procedure and Investigations Act 1996, ss. 54 and 55

54.—(1) This section applies where—
(a) a person has been acquitted of an offence, and
(b) a person has been convicted of an administration of justice offence involving interference with or intimidation of a juror or a witness (or potential witness) in any proceedings which led to the acquittal.

(2) Where it appears to the court before which the person was convicted that—
(a) there is a real possibility that, but for the interference or intimidation, the acquitted person would not have been acquitted, and
(b) subsection (5) does not apply,
the court shall certify that it so appears.

(3) Where a court certifies under subsection (2) an application may be made to the High Court for an order quashing the acquittal, and the Court shall make the order if (but shall not do so unless) the four conditions in section 55 are satisfied.

(4) Where an order is made under subsection (3) proceedings may be taken against the acquitted person for the offence of which he was acquitted.

(5) This subsection applies if, because of lapse of time or for any other reason, it would be contrary to the interests of justice to take proceedings against the acquitted person for the offence of which he was acquitted.

(6) For the purposes of this section the following offences are administration of justice offences—
(a) the offence of perverting the course of justice;
(b) the offence under section 51(1) of the Criminal Justice and Public Order Act 1994 (intimidation etc. of witnesses, jurors and others);
(c) an offence of aiding, abetting, counselling, procuring, suborning or inciting another person to commit an offence under section 1 of the Perjury Act 1911.

(7) This section applies in relation to acquittals in respect of offences alleged to be committed on or after the appointed day.

55.—(1) The first condition is that it appears to the High Court likely that, but for the interference or intimidation, the acquitted person would not have been acquitted.

(2) The second condition is that it does not appear to the Court that, because of lapse of time or for any other reason it would be contrary to the interests of justice to take proceedings against the acquitted person for the offence of which he was acquitted.

(3) The third condition is that it appears to the Court that the acquitted person has been given a reasonable opportunity to make written representations to the Court.

(4) The fourth condition is that it appears to the Court that the conviction for the administration of justice offence will stand.
(5) In applying subsection (4) the Court shall—
(a) take into account all the information before it, but
(b) ignore the possibility of new factors coming to light.
(6) Accordingly, the fourth condition has the effect that the Court shall not make an order under section 54(3) if (for instance) it appears to the Court that any time allowed for giving notice of appeal has not expired or that an appeal is pending.

RETRIAL PROVISIONS OF THE CRIMINAL JUSTICE ACT 2003

The CJA 2003 introduced a radical revision to the principles stated above. Sections 75 to 97 of the Act constitute the second major statutory exception to the rule against double jeopardy. In summary, they permit an accused to be retried for a 'qualifying' offence of which he has earlier been acquitted where there is new evidence of his guilt, following an order of the Court of Appeal quashing that acquittal. **D12.34**

Application

As a starting point, the CJA 2003 defines the acquittals to which it has application. **D12.35**

(a) The new provisions apply to offences listed as 'qualifying offences' in the CJA 2003, sch. 5 (set out at **D12.41**). They are all serious offences, which in the main carry a maximum sentence of life imprisonment.
(b) The provisions apply to acquittals after trial on indictment in England and Wales (s. 75(1)) and to acquittals in proceedings outside the UK, except in Scotland, of an offence that would have amounted to or included the commission of a qualifying offence in the UK or elsewhere (s. 75(4)).
(c) The meaning of 'acquittal' in s. 75(1) is extended by s. 75(2) so as to include any qualifying offence of which the accused could have been convicted on the original indictment as an alternative verdict (e.g., manslaughter where the original indictment was for murder). The implied acquittal of the alternative offence (manslaughter in the example) can be quashed by the same procedure as the express acquittal (for murder).
(d) Convictions, special verdicts of not guilty by reason of insanity and findings of unfitness to plead in alternative verdict offences are excluded from the procedure (s. 75(2)(a) to (c)).

By virtue of s. 75(6), the procedure, with its removal of the freedom from double jeopardy, is made fully retrospective. The provisions apply equally to acquittals before and after the passing of the CJA 2003. It is of course possible that the retrospective nature of this provision may be subject to challenge under the ECHR, Article 7 (see **appendix 6**).

Application for a Quashing Order Section 76 of the CJA 2003 allows a prosecutor to apply to the Court of Appeal for an order to quash a person's acquittal for a qualifying offence or a lesser qualifying offence of which he could have been convicted at that time. **D12.36**

The application to the Court of Appeal to quash the acquittal requires the personal written consent of the DPP (s. 76(3)). Before giving his consent, the DPP must be satisfied (s. 76(4)):
(a) that there is evidence that meets the requirements of s. 78 (see **D12.39**);
(b) that it is in the public interest for the application to proceed; and
(c) that any trial would not run counter to our obligations under the Treaty on European Union relating to the principle of *ne bis in idem*.

The principle of '*ne bis in idem*' is equivalent to the prohibition of double jeopardy. The relevant Treaty obligations would appear to be apposite where a retrial is proposed for an offence already dealt with in another country of the EU. In such a case, the DPP would have to certify that such a course of action would not be contrary to the UK's obligations to the EU.

D12.37 **Notice** Notice of the application under the CJA 2003, s. 76(1) or (2), must be given to the Court of Appeal (s. 80(1)). The acquitted person must be served with a copy of the application within two days, and be charged with the offence in question. He is entitled to attend and be represented at the hearing in the Court of Appeal.

Criteria

D12.38 The Court of Appeal must order a retrial if:

(a) 'there is new and compelling evidence in the case' (CJA 2003, s. 78); and
(b) 'it is in the interests of justice for an order to be made' (s. 79).

D12.39 **New Evidence** Under the CJA 2003, s. 78, evidence is 'new' if it was not adduced at the original trial of the acquitted person. This would include evidence that was available at the first trial, but not used. Reliance upon such evidence would raise questions about whether it would be in the interests of justice to order a retrial. Where the failure to use the evidence is because of a lack of diligence or expedition by the prosecutor, that is a factor relevant to the application of the interests of justice test (s. 79(2)(c)). But, as is pointed out in *Blackstone's Guide to the Criminal Justice Act 2003*, p.113, that formula is not apt to cover a tactical decision not to use the evidence in question first time round. The A-G, however, gave to the House of Lords (*Hansard*, HL col. 710 (4 November 2003)), on behalf of the government:

> . . .an undertaking, which I have agreed with the Director of Public Prosecutions, that where evidence was not adduced for tactical reasons, it would not be right to use it as a basis for an application . . . I hope that that will give some comfort. It will be reflected in guidance.

Section 78(5) makes clear that evidence that would have been inadmissible in the original proceedings could form the basis for an application for a retrial as 'new' evidence.

The evidence is 'compelling' if the Court of Appeal considers it to be reliable and substantial and highly probative of the case against the accused. What is compelling will depend on the context of the previous trial. For example, if the identity of the offender was not in issue in the original trial, new evidence as to identification would not fit the evidence criterion so as to justify a retrial.

D12.40 **Interests of Justice** As to the interests of justice test in the CJA 2003, s. 79, the court will consider in particular whether a fair trial is unlikely (e.g., because of adverse publicity about the accused), the length of time since the alleged offence, and whether the police and prosecution have acted with due diligence and expedition with regard to the new evidence. The factors set out in s. 79 are not exhaustive, and the Court of Appeal can consider other relevant issues in determining whether a retrial would be in the interests of justice.

A recent application of this test, in *Dunlop* [2006] EWCA 1354, is illustrative. D had been acquitted, but subsequently not only confessed to the offence but had pleaded guilty to perjury in relation to his evidence at the original trial. The Court of Appeal held that far from it being contrary to the 'interests of justice' to retry him, treating his plea and confession as new evidence (pursuant to s. 78), the public would have been rightly outraged if any other course were taken.

Procedural Issues

D12.41 Reporting restrictions may be imposed by the Court of Appeal in respect of matters surrounding the application for a retrial. The restrictions may last until the end of the retrial or to the point at which it is clear that the acquitted person can no longer be retried (CJA 2003, s. 82). The restrictions may apply to any information in respect of the investigation and to the republication of matters previously published. An application to order or refuse a retrial can be the subject of an appeal to the House of Lords on a point of law (s. 81).

If a retrial is ordered, it must be on an indictment preferred by the direction of the Court of Appeal (s. 84). Arraignment must take place within two months of the date on which the Court of Appeal ordered a retrial, unless it specifies a longer period. The period can be extended only if the Court of Appeal is satisfied that the prosecutor has acted with due expedition since the order was made, and that there is still good and sufficient reason to hold the retrial despite any additional lapse of time.

The procedure in respect of the retrial provisions was considered in *Re D (Acquitted person: Retrial)* [2006] 1 WLR 1998.

Criminal Justice Act 2003, ss. 75 to 80 and 82 to 84 and sch. 5, part 1

75.—(1) This part applies where a person has been acquitted of a qualifying offence in proceedings—
(a) on indictment in England and Wales,
(b) on appeal against a conviction, verdict or finding in proceedings on indictment in England and Wales, or
(c) on appeal from a decision on such an appeal.

(2) A person acquitted of an offence in proceedings mentioned in subsection (1) is treated for the purposes of that subsection as also acquitted of any qualifying offence of which he could have been convicted in the proceedings because of the first-mentioned offence being charged in the indictment, except an offence—
(a) of which he has been convicted,
(b) of which he has been found not guilty by reason of insanity, or
(c) in respect of which, in proceedings where he has been found to be under a disability (as defined by section 4 of the Criminal Procedure (Insanity) Act 1964), a finding has been made that he did the act or made the omission charged against him.

(3) References in subsections (1) and (2) to a qualifying offence do not include references to an offence which, at the time of the acquittal, was the subject of an order under section 77(1) or (3).

(4) This part also applies where a person has been acquitted, in proceedings elsewhere than in the United Kingdom of an offence under the law of the place where the proceedings were held, if the commission of the offence as alleged would have amounted to or included the commission (in the United Kingdom or elsewhere) of a qualifying offence.

(5) Conduct punishable under the law in force elsewhere than in the United Kingdom is an offence under that law for the purposes of subsection (4), however it is described in that law.

(6) This part applies whether the acquittal was before or after the passing of this Act.

(7) References in this part to acquittal are to acquittal in circumstances within subsection (1) or (4).

(8) In this part 'qualifying offence' means an offence listed in part 1 of schedule 5.

76.—(1) A prosecutor may apply to the Court of Appeal for an order—
(a) quashing a person's acquittal in proceedings within section 75(1), and
(b) ordering him to be retried for the qualifying offence.

(2) A prosecutor may apply to the Court of Appeal, in the case of a person acquitted elsewhere than in the United Kingdom, for—
(a) a determination whether the acquittal is a bar to the person being tried in England and Wales for the qualifying offence, and
(b) if it is, an order that the acquittal is not to be a bar.

(3) A prosecutor may make an application under subsection (1) or (2) only with the written consent of the Director of Public Prosecutions.

(4) The Director of Public Prosecutions may give his consent only if satisfied that—
(a) there is evidence as respects which the requirements of section 78 appear to be met,
(b) it is in the public interest for the application to proceed, and
(c) any trial pursuant to an order on the application would not be inconsistent with obligations of the United Kingdom under Article 31 or 34 of the Treaty on European Union relating to the principle of *ne bis in idem*.

D

Part D Procedure

(5) Not more than one application may be made under subsection (1) or (2) in relation to an acquittal.

77.—(1) On an application under section 76(1), the Court of Appeal—

(a) if satisfied that the requirements of sections 78 and 79 are met, must make the order applied for;

(b) otherwise, must dismiss the application.

(2) Subsections (3) and (4) apply to an application under section 76(2).

(3) Where the Court of Appeal determines that the acquittal is a bar to the person being tried for the qualifying offence, the court—

(a) if satisfied that the requirements of sections 78 and 79 are met, must make the order applied for;

(b) otherwise, must make a declaration to the effect that the acquittal is a bar to the person being tried for the offence.

(4) Where the Court of Appeal determines that the acquittal is not a bar to the person being tried for the qualifying offence, it must make a declaration to that effect.

78.—(1) The requirements of this section are met if there is new and compelling evidence against the acquitted person in relation to the qualifying offence.

(2) Evidence is new if it was not adduced in the proceedings in which the person was acquitted (nor, if those were appeal proceedings, in earlier proceedings to which the appeal related).

(3) Evidence is compelling if—

(a) it is reliable,

(b) it is substantial, and

(c) in the context of the outstanding issues, it appears highly probative of the case against the acquitted person.

(4) The outstanding issues are the issues in dispute in the proceedings in which the person was acquitted and, if those were appeal proceedings, any other issues remaining in dispute from earlier proceedings to which the appeal related.

(5) For the purposes of this section, it is irrelevant whether any evidence would have been admissible in earlier proceedings against the acquitted person.

79.—(1) The requirements of this section are met if in all the circumstances it is in the interests of justice for the court to make the order under section 77.

(2) That question is to be determined having regard in particular to—

(a) whether existing circumstances make a fair trial unlikely;

(b) for the purposes of that question and otherwise, the length of time since the qualifying offence was allegedly committed;

(c) whether it is likely that the new evidence would have been adduced in the earlier proceedings against the acquitted person but for a failure by an officer or by a prosecutor to act with due diligence or expedition;

(d) whether, since those proceedings or, if later, since the commencement of this Part, any officer or prosecutor has failed to act with due diligence or expedition.

(3) In subsection (2) references to an officer or prosecutor include references to a person charged with corresponding duties under the law in force elsewhere than in England and Wales.

(4) Where the earlier prosecution was conducted by a person other than a prosecutor, subsection (2)(c) applies in relation to that person as well as in relation to a prosecutor.

80.—(1) A prosecutor who wishes to make an application under section 76(1) or (2) must give notice of the application to the Court of Appeal.

(2) Within two days beginning with the day on which any such notice is given, notice of the application must be served by the prosecutor on the person to whom the application relates, charging him with the offence to which it relates or, if he has been charged with it in accordance with section 87(4), stating that he has been so charged.

(3) Subsection (2) applies whether the person to whom the application relates is in the United Kingdom or elsewhere, but the Court of Appeal may, on application by the prosecutor, extend the time for service under that subsection if it considers it necessary to do so because of that person's absence from the United Kingdom.

(4) The Court of Appeal must consider the application at a hearing.

(5) The person to whom the application relates—

(a) is entitled to be present at the hearing, although he may be in custody, unless he is in custody elsewhere than in England and Wales or Northern Ireland, and

(b) is entitled to be represented at the hearing, whether he is present or not.

(6) For the purposes of the application, the Court of Appeal may, if it thinks it necessary or expedient in the interests of justice—
(a) order the production of any document, exhibit or other thing, the production of which appears to the court to be necessary for the determination of the application, and
(b) order any witness who would be a compellable witness in proceedings pursuant to an order or declaration made on the application to attend for examination and be examined before the court.
(7) The Court of Appeal may at one hearing consider more than one application (whether or not relating to the same person), but only if the offences concerned could be tried on the same indictment.

81. [Consequential amendments: not reproduced]

82.—(1) Where it appears to the Court of Appeal that the inclusion of any matter in a publication would give rise to a substantial risk of prejudice to the administration of justice in a retrial, the court may order that the matter is not to be included in any publication while the order has effect.
(2) In subsection (1) 'retrial' means the trial of an acquitted person for a qualifying offence pursuant to any order made or that may be made under section 77.
(3) The court may make an order under this section only if it appears to it necessary in the interests of justice to do so.
(4) An order under this section may apply to a matter which has been included in a publication published before the order takes effect, but such an order—
(a) applies only to the later inclusion of the matter in a publication (whether directly or by inclusion of the earlier publication), and
(b) does not otherwise affect the earlier publication.
(5) After notice of an application has been given under section 80(1) relating to the acquitted person and the qualifying offence, the court may make an order under this section only—
(a) of its own motion, or
(b) on the application of the Director of Public Prosecutions.
(6) Before such notice has been given, an order under this section—
(a) may be made only on the application of the Director of Public Prosecutions, and
(b) may not be made unless, since the acquittal concerned, an investigation of the commission by the acquitted person of the qualifying offence has been commenced by officers.
(7) The court may at any time, of its own motion or on an application made by the Director of Public Prosecutions or the acquitted person, vary or revoke an order under this section.
(8) Any order made under this section before notice of an application has been given under section 80(1) relating to the acquitted person and the qualifying offence must specify the time when it ceases to have effect.
(9) An order under this section which is made or has effect after such notice has been given ceases to have effect, unless it specifies an earlier time—
(a) when there is no longer any step that could be taken which would lead to the acquitted person being tried pursuant to an order made on the application, or
(b) if he is tried pursuant to such an order, at the conclusion of the trial.
(10) Nothing in this section affects any prohibition or restriction by virtue of any other enactment on the inclusion of any matter in a publication or any power, under an enactment or otherwise, to impose such a prohibition or restriction.
(11) In this section—
'programme service' has the same meaning as in the Broadcasting Act 1990,
'publication' includes any speech, writing, relevant programme or other communication in whatever form, which is addressed to the public at large or any section of the public (and for this purpose every relevant programme is to be taken to be so addressed), but does not include an indictment or other document prepared for use in particular legal proceedings,
'relevant programme' means a programme included in a programme service.

83.—(1) This section applies if—
(a) an order under section 82 is made, whether in England and Wales or Northern Ireland, and
(b) while the order has effect, any matter is included in a publication, in any part of the United Kingdom, in contravention of the order.
(2) Where the publication is a newspaper or periodical, any proprietor, editor or publisher of the newspaper or periodical is guilty of an offence.

(3) Where the publication is a relevant programme—
 (a) any body corporate or Scottish partnership engaged in providing the programme service in which the programme is included, and
 (b) any person having functions in relation to the programme corresponding to those of an editor of a newspaper,
 is guilty of an offence.
(4) In the case of any other publication, any person publishing it is guilty of an offence.
(5) If an offence under this section committed by a body corporate is proved—
 (a) to have been committed with the consent or connivance of, or
 (b) to be attributable to any neglect on the part of,
 an officer, the officer as well as the body corporate is guilty of the offence and liable to be proceeded against and punished accordingly.
(6) In subsection (5), 'officer' means a director, manager, secretary or other similar officer of the body, or a person purporting to act in any such capacity.
(7) If the affairs of a body corporate are managed by its members, 'director' in subsection (6) means a member of that body.
(8) [Applies only to Scotland.]
(9) A person guilty of an offence under this section is liable on summary conviction to a fine not exceeding level 5 on the standard scale.
(10) Proceedings for an offence under this section may not be instituted—
 (a) in England and Wales otherwise than by or with the consent of the Attorney General, or
 (b) [applies only to Northern Ireland].
(11) [Applies only to Northern Ireland.]

84.—(1) Where a person—
 (a) is tried pursuant to an order under section 77(1), or
 (b) is tried on indictment pursuant to an order under section 77(3),
 the trial must be on an indictment preferred by direction of the Court of Appeal.
(2) After the end of 2 months after the date of the order, the person may not be arraigned on an indictment preferred in pursuance of such a direction unless the Court of Appeal gives leave.
(3) The Court of Appeal must not give leave unless satisfied that—
 (a) the prosecutor has acted with due expedition, and
 (b) there is a good and sufficient cause for trial despite the lapse of time since the order under section 77.
(4) Where the person may not be arraigned without leave, he may apply to the Court of Appeal to set aside the order and—
 (a) for any direction required for restoring an earlier judgment and verdict of acquittal of the qualifying offence, or
 (b) in the case of a person acquitted elsewhere than in the United Kingdom, for a declaration to the effect that the acquittal is a bar to his being tried for the qualifying offence.
(5) An indictment under subsection (1) may relate to more than one offence, or more than one person, and may relate to an offence which, or a person who, is not the subject of an order or declaration under section 77.
(6) Evidence given at a trial pursuant to an order under section 77(1) or (3) must be given orally if it was given orally at the original trial, unless—
 (a) all the parties to the trial agree otherwise,
 (b) section 116 applies, or
 (c) the witness is unavailable to give evidence, otherwise than as mentioned in subsection (2) of that section, and section 114(1)(d) applies.
(7) At a trial pursuant to an order under section 77(1), paragraph 5 of schedule 3 to the Crime and Disorder Act 1998 (use of depositions) does not apply to a deposition read as evidence at the original trial.

SCHEDULE 5
QUALIFYING OFFENCES FOR PURPOSES OF PART 10
PART 1
LIST OF OFFENCES FOR ENGLAND AND WALES

Offences Against the Person

Murder

1. Murder.

Attempted murder

2. An offence under section 1 of the Criminal Attempts Act 1981 of attempting to commit murder.

Soliciting murder

3. An offence under section 4 of the Offences against the Person Act 1861.

Manslaughter

4. Manslaughter.

Corporate manslaughter

4A. An offence under section 1 of the Corporate Manslaughter and Corporate Homicide Act 2007.

Kidnapping

5. Kidnapping.

Sexual Offences

Rape

6. An offence under section 1 of the Sexual Offences Act 1956 or section 1 of the Sexual Offences Act 2003.

Attempted rape

7. An offence under section 1 of the Criminal Attempts Act 1981 of attempting to commit an offence under section 1 of the Sexual Offences Act 1956 or section 1 of the Sexual Offences Act 2003.

Intercourse with a girl under thirteen

8. An offence under section 5 of the Sexual Offences Act 1956.

Incest by a man with a girl under thirteen

9. An offence under section 10 of the Sexual Offences Act 1956 alleged to have been committed with a girl under thirteen.

Assault by penetration

10. An offence under section 2 of the Sexual Offences Act 2003 (c. 42).

Causing a person to engage in sexual activity without consent

11. An offence under section 4 of the Sexual Offences Act 2003 where it is alleged that the activity caused involved penetration within subsection (4)(a) to (d) of that section.

Rape of a child under thirteen

12. An offence under section 5 of the Sexual Offences Act 2003.

Attempted rape of a child under thirteen

13. An offence under section 1 of the Criminal Attempts Act 1981 of attempting to commit an offence under section 5 of the Sexual Offences Act 2003.

Assault of a child under thirteen by penetration

14. An offence under section 6 of the Sexual Offences Act 2003.

Causing a child under thirteen to engage in sexual activity

15. An offence under section 8 of the Sexual Offences Act 2003 where it is alleged that an activity involving penetration within subsection (2)(a) to (d) of that section was caused.

Sexual activity with a person with a mental disorder impeding choice

16. An offence under section 30 of the Sexual Offences Act 2003 where it is alleged that the touching involved penetration within subsection (3)(a) to (d) of that section.

Causing a person with a mental disorder impeding choice to engage in sexual activity

17. An offence under section 31 of the Sexual Offences Act 2003 where it is alleged that an activity involving penetration within subsection (3)(a) to (d) of that section was caused.

Drugs Offences

Unlawful importation of Class A drug

18. An offence under section 50(2) of the Customs and Excise Management Act 1979 alleged to have been committed in respect of a Class A drug (as defined by section 2 of the Misuse of Drugs Act 1971).

Unlawful exportation of Class A drug

19. An offence under section 68(2) of the Customs and Excise Management Act 1979 alleged to have been committed in respect of a Class A drug (as defined by section 2 of the Misuse of Drugs Act 1971).

Fraudulent evasion in respect of Class A drug

20. An offence under section 170(1) or (2) of the Customs and Excise Management Act 1979 alleged to have been committed in respect of a Class A drug (as defined by section 2 of the Misuse of Drugs Act 1971).

Producing or being concerned in production of Class A drug

21. An offence under section 4(2) of the Misuse of Drugs Act 1971 alleged to have been committed in relation to a Class A drug (as defined by section 2 of that Act).

Criminal Damage Offences

Arson endangering life

22. An offence under section 1(2) of the Criminal Damage Act 1971 alleged to have been committed by destroying or damaging property by fire.

Causing explosion likely to endanger life or property

23. An offence under section 2 of the Explosive Substances Act 1883.

Intent or conspiracy to cause explosion likely to endanger life or property

24. An offence under section 3(1)(a) of the Explosive Substances Act 1883.

War Crimes and Terrorism

Genocide, crimes against humanity and war crimes

25. An offence under section 51 or 52 of the International Criminal Court Act 2001.

Grave breaches of the Geneva Conventions

26. An offence under section 1 of the Geneva Conventions Act 1957.

Directing terrorist organisation

27. An offence under section 56 of the Terrorism Act 2000.

Hostage-taking

28. An offence under section 1 of the Taking of Hostages Act 1982.

Conspiracy

29. An offence under section 1 of the Criminal Law Act 1977 of conspiracy to commit an offence listed in this Part of this Schedule.

OTHER PLEAS THAT MAY BE TAKEN AT ARRAIGNMENT

D12.42 For convenience, three further objections that may be taken to the arraignment of the accused can briefly be addressed at this point.

Demurrer

D12.43 This is 'an objection to the form or substance of the indictment, apparent on the face of the indictment' (per Cantley J in *Inner London Quarter Sessions, ex parte Metropolitan Police Commissioner* [1970] 2 QB 80 at p. 83G). The guidance given in that case was to the following effect:

(a) the plea must be entered in writing, filed in the Crown Office, and a copy served on the opposite party, preferably prior to the accused being arraigned;
(b) on demurring, the defence are *not* entitled to refer the judge to the contents of the depositions and/or statements tendered at committal proceedings.

The scope of the remedy by demurrer is no wider than the scope of motions to quash. Lord Parker CJ said that he hoped that demurrer would now 'be allowed to die naturally' (ibid. at p. 85G). Similarly, Cantley J said that demurrers had been 'supplanted in practice by the safe and convenient procedures of motion to quash the indictment or motion in arrest of judgment' (a motion that the accused had been convicted of an offence not known to law) (at p. 83C). However, in *Cumberworth* (1989) 89 Cr App R 187, where the defence submitted at the end of the prosecution evidence that the Crown Court lacked jurisdiction in respect of offences allegedly committed on a French ship in Dieppe harbour, the Court of Appeal stated, *obiter*, that it would have been more convenient procedurally to raise the point by way of demurrer at the outset of the trial, thus avoiding the necessity of hearing the evidence if the point were good.

The entry of a demurrer does not affect the accused's right to plead not guilty to the indictment should the demurrer fail (Criminal Law Act 1967, s. 6(1)(a)).

Plea to the Jurisdiction

The purpose of this plea is to assert that the Crown Court has no jurisdiction to try the offence charged (e.g., because it is a summary offence or because it was committed abroad and does not come within the exceptional categories of 'foreign' offences that may be tried in England and Wales). Like a demurrer, the plea should be entered in writing prior to arraignment, although it is always open to the defence to take any jurisdictional point simply under a general not guilty plea (see, e.g., *Treacy v DPP* [1971] AC 537, where that was done). However, in *Cumberworth* (1989) 89 Cr App R 187 (see **D12.43**), the defence were criticised for waiting until the close of the prosecution case to submit that the court had no jurisdiction, since, had the point been good, the court and jury would have heard much evidence on the general issue unnecessarily. **D12.44**

Pardon

This is the third special plea in bar (the other two being autrefois acquit and autrefois convict). It may be relied on where a pardon has been granted by the Crown on the advice of the Home Secretary in exercise of the royal prerogative of mercy. It must be pleaded at the first opportunity (i.e. before arraignment if the pardon has by then been granted). In modern times, the plea has become obsolete. **D12.45**

THE ARRAIGNMENT

Procedure on Arraignment

The arraignment consists of the clerk of the court reading the indictment to the accused and asking him whether he pleads guilty or not guilty to the counts contained therein. If there are several counts, a plea must be taken on each one separately immediately after it is read out (*Boyle* [1954] 2 QB 292); if, however, two counts are in the alternative and the accused pleads guilty to the first count, it is unnecessary to take a plea on the second (ibid.). If there is a joint indictment against several accused, normal practice is to arraign them together. Separate pleas must be taken from each of those named in any joint count. **D12.46**

It is now standard practice to exclude the jurors in waiting from court until after the arraignment has been completed. This avoids the possibility of potential jurors being prejudiced by hearing the accused plead guilty to some but not all the counts on the indictment. After the jury have been sworn, they are told by the clerk the counts to which the accused has pleaded not guilty, no mention being made of any matters to which he has pleaded guilty nor of any co-accused who may have pleaded guilty.

Time for Arraignment

D12.47 The Supreme Court Act 1981, s. 77(1), provides that rules of court are to prescribe the minimum and maximum periods which may elapse between a person's committal for trial and the beginning of the trial (i.e. the arraignment). By s. 77(2), the trial of a person committed for trial (or in respect of whom a notice of transfer has been given) shall not begin within the minimum period prescribed by the rules unless the defence and the prosecution consent, and shall not begin after the maximum period unless a Crown Court judge orders otherwise.

Section 77(3) defines the beginning of the trial as the time when the accused is arraigned. It should be noted, however, that the Crown Court has an unfettered discretion to adjourn proceedings, and there is thus no objection to the accused being arraigned within the eight weeks prescribed by the CrimPR, r. 39.1, and then the case being immediately adjourned to a later date if the parties are still not ready for trial.

D12.48 **Time-limits** Rule 39.1 of the CrimPR (see **appendix 1**) provides that the minimum and maximum periods between committal and arraignment shall be 14 days and eight weeks respectively.

Indictable-only and related offences which are sent for trial direct to the Crown Court by virtue of s. 51 of the CDA 1998 are dealt with in r. 12.2 of the CrimPR, which states that the first Crown Court appearance of the accused should be listed in accordance with any directions given by the magistrates' court. There are no time-limits laid down for the listing of that first appearance.

D12.49 **Failure to Arraign within Time-limit** Leave for late arraignment is left entirely at the Crown Court judge's discretion, and is in practice readily granted. No specific provisions are made as to how or when an application for such leave should be made (cf. the detailed terms of the CrimPR, part 14, which deals with the time within which a bill of indictment must be preferred).

Failure by the prosecution to comply with r. 39.1 is of little or no consequence since the rule has been held to be directory, not mandatory (*Urbanowski* [1976] 1 WLR 455). It follows that a conviction will be upheld even though the arraignment took place more than eight weeks after committal and no leave for late arraignment was sought or obtained until after the expiry of that period (ibid.). Further, by analogy with the cases on failure to obtain leave for preferment of a late bill of indictment (see **D11.9**), a trial will not be invalidated by late arraignment even if no leave was given at any time for the period prescribed by r. 39.1 to be exceeded.

Effect of Lack of Arraignment on the Validity of the Proceedings

D12.50 Failure by the court to have the accused arraigned does not necessarily render invalid subsequent proceedings on the indictment (*Williams* [1978] QB 373). Thus, the defence may waive the accused's right to be arraigned, either expressly or by simply remaining silent while the trial proceeds without arraignment. It was held in *Kepple* [2007] EWCA Crim 1339, where the accused absconded prior to arraignment, that by absenting himself he had waived his right to arraignment.

A dictum of Edmund-Davies LJ in *Ellis* (1973) 57 Cr App R 571 (at p. 575), that the 'only safe and proper course . . . is to say . . . that (apart from a few very special cases) it is an invariable requirement that the initial arraignment must be conducted between the clerk of the court and the accused person himself', should be understood in the context of the facts of that case, namely, the entry of a guilty plea.

On the facts of *Williams*, by contrast, W had always intended to plead not guilty and the trial proceeded in all respects as if he had so pleaded but in fact (through an administrative muddle) the indictment was never put. The pre-trial irregularity did not invalidate the proceedings and W's conviction was upheld despite lack of arraignment.

More recently, the decision of the Court of Appeal in *Ashton* [2007] 1 WLR 181, supports the contention that a failure to follow the correct procedure as to arraignment is not necessarily fatal to proceedings thereafter. Fulford J, giving the judgment of the Court, said (at [4]):

> In our judgement it is now wholly clear that whenever a court is confronted by a failure to take a required step, properly or at all, before a power is exercised ('a procedural failure'), the court should first ask itself whether the intention of the legislature was that any act done following the procedural failure should be invalid. If the answer to that question is no, then the court should go on to consider the interests of justice generally, and most particularly whether there is any real possibility that either the prosecution or the defence may suffer prejudice on account of the procedural failure. If there is such a risk, the court must decide whether it is just to allow the proceedings to continue.

Further, the decision in *Williams* is without prejudice to the principle that a plea of guilty must be entered by the accused personally, the corollary of which is that a conviction on a guilty plea will be valid only if the accused has been properly arraigned (see **D12.64**).

PLEAS THAT MAY BE ENTERED ON ARRAIGNMENT

In the great majority of cases, the plea entered by the accused will be simply one of guilty or not guilty. It is sometimes open to him to plead not guilty as charged but guilty of an alternative (lesser) offence. **D12.51**

The only alternatives to such a plea arise in the circumstances addressed above where it is submitted that it would not be appropriate for the accused to be arraigned at all, namely where the issue arises of whether he has previously been acquitted or convicted of the offence now charged (a plea of autrefois acquit or autrefois convict — see **D12.19**) or where there may be a plea to the jurisdiction (the defence wish to argue that the Crown Court does not have jurisdiction to deal with the case, e.g., because the offence was committed abroad).

PLEA BARGAINING

The issues that arise under this heading are: **D12.52**

(a) the extent to which the judge may properly influence the accused's decision as to plea by indicating the probable sentence, and
(b) the propriety of bargains between the prosecution and defence involving the offering of no evidence in respect of certain charges in return for the accused pleading guilty to others.

Judicial Indications of Sentence

A plea of guilty must be entered voluntarily. If the accused is deprived of a genuine choice as to plea and in consequence purports to plead guilty, the plea is a nullity and the conviction will be quashed on appeal (see **D12.93**). **D12.53**

This was stressed by the Court of Appeal in *Turner* [1970] 2 QB 321. In that case, the reason for holding the appellant's plea to be a nullity was that his counsel, during discussions about whether there should be a change of plea to guilty, went to see the judge, and, on returning to his client, stated that a conviction on a not guilty plea would entail a 'very real possibility' of a prison sentence whereas if T pleaded guilty it would be a 'fine or some other sentence not involving imprisonment'. In the circumstances, the Court of Appeal concluded that the promise of a non-custodial sentence in the event of a guilty plea, coupled with an implied threat of a custodial sentence should the not guilty plea be unsuccessfully maintained, took away T's free choice.

Having decided that the conviction must therefore be quashed, the Court of Appeal made certain observations designed to assist counsel and judges over what was referred to as 'the vexed question of plea bargaining' (at pp. 326E–327D). Those observations have now been superseded by the guidance laid down by the Court of Appeal in *Goodyear* [2005] 1 WLR 2532.

The *Goodyear* Approach

D12.54 The guidelines given in *Goodyear* [2005] 1 WLR 2532, set out the correct approach to judicial indications of sentence. The Court of Appeal identified the proper roles within this process for the court, and those responsible for prosecuting and defending. The guidelines also demonstrate the need to take into account the review of any sentence then passed, either by way of an appeal by the defendant or a reference on behalf of the A-G. In summary, the guidance is as follows.

D12.55 **Responsibilities of the Court** (1) A court should not give an indication of sentence unless one has been sought by the accused.

(2) However, the court remains entitled to exercise the power to indicate that the sentence, or type of sentence, on the accused would be the same whether the case proceeds as a plea of guilty or goes to trial, with a resulting conviction, and is also entitled in an appropriate case to remind the defence advocate that the accused is entitled to seek an advance indication of sentence.

(4) Where an indication is sought, the court may refuse altogether to give an indication, or may postpone doing so, with or without giving reasons.

(5) Where the court has it in mind to defer an indication, the probability is that the judge would explain his reasons, and further indicate the circumstances in which, and when, he would be prepared to respond to a request for a sentence indication.

(6) If the court refuses to give an indication (as opposed to deferring it), it remains open to the defence to make a further request for an indication at a later stage. However, in such circumstances the court should not normally initiate the process, except where appropriate to indicate that the circumstances have changed sufficiently to permit a renewed application for an indication.

(8) Once an indication has been given, it is binding and remains binding on the judge who has given it, and it also binds any other judge who becomes responsible for the case.

(9) If, after a reasonable opportunity to consider his position in the light of the indication, the accused does not plead guilty, the indication will cease to have effect.

(10) Where appropriate, there must be an agreed, written basis of plea, otherwise the judge should refuse to give an indication.

Additional guidance was given in *A-G's Ref (No. 80 of 2005)* [2005] EWCA Crim 3367, when the Court of Appeal stated that:

(a) the principal feature of an appropriate indication of sentence is that an advance indication should be sought by the defence, and not promulgated by the judge;

(b) an indication should not be given that a trial would result in a much longer sentence compared to the one offered if the accused pleads guilty.

Responsibilities of the Defence (1) Subject to the court's power to give an appropriate reminder to the advocate for the accused, the process of seeking a sentence indication should normally be started by the defence. **D12.56**

(2) Whether or not such a reminder has been given, the accused's advocate should not seek an indication without written authority, signed by his client, that he, the client, wishes to seek an indication.

(3) The advocate is personally responsible for ensuring that his client fully appreciates that (a) he should not plead guilty unless he is guilty, (b) any sentence indication given by the court remains subject to the entitlement of the A-G (where it arises) to refer an unduly lenient sentence to the Court of Appeal, (c) any indication given by the court reflects the situation at the time when it is given and if a guilty plea is not tendered in the light of that indication, the indication ceases to have effect, and (d) any indication which may be given relates only to the matters about which an indication is sought.

(4) An indication should not be sought while there is any uncertainty between the prosecution and the defence about an acceptable plea or pleas to the indictment, or the factual basis relating to any plea.

(5) Any agreed basis should be reduced into writing before an indication is sought.

(6) Where there is a dispute about a particular fact which counsel for the accused believes to be effectively immaterial to the sentencing decision, the difference should be recorded for the court to consider.

(7) The court should never be invited to indicate levels of sentence which depend on possible different pleas.

(8) In the unusual event that the accused is unrepresented, he would be entitled to seek a sentence indication of his own initiative, but it would be wrong for either the court or prosecuting counsel to take any initiative in this regard that might too readily be interpreted as or subsequently argued to have been improper pressure.

Responsibilities of the Prosecution (1) As the request for indication comes from the defence, the prosecution is obliged to react, rather than initiate the process. **D12.57**

(2) If there is no final agreement about the plea to the indictment, or the basis of plea, and the defence nevertheless proceeds to seek an indication, which the court appears minded to give, prosecuting counsel should remind the court that an indication of sentence should normally not be given until the basis of the plea has been agreed, or the judge has concluded that he can properly deal with the case without the need for a *Newton* hearing (see **D19.8**).

(3) If an indication is sought, the prosecution should normally enquire whether the court is in possession of or has had access to all the evidence relied on by the prosecution, including any personal impact statement from the victim of the crime, as well as any information of relevant previous convictions recorded against the accused.

(4) If the process has been properly followed, it should not normally be necessary for counsel for the prosecution, before the court gives any indication, to do more than (a) draw the judge's attention to any minimum or mandatory statutory sentencing requirements, and, where applicable or where invited to do so, to any relevant guideline cases or the views of the Sentencing Guidelines Council, and (b) where it applies, to remind the judge that the entitlement of the A-G to refer any eventual sentencing decision as unduly lenient is not affected.

(5) In any event, counsel should not say anything which may create the impression that the sentence indication has the support or approval of the Crown.

Further guidance is given to prosecutors through the A-G's Guidelines on the Acceptance of Pleas (see **appendix 3**) as to their part in any discussion on plea and sentence in chambers.

Such discussions should take place only 'in the most exceptional circumstances'.

(a) Where they do take place, the prosecution advocate should if necessary remind the judge of the desirability of an independent record, and should himself make a full note, recording all decisions and comments. This note should be made available to the prosecuting authority.
(b) Where there is a discussion on plea and sentence and the prosecution advocate does not believe that the circumstances are exceptional, he should remind the judge of the relevant decisions of the Court of Appeal and disassociate himself from any discussion on sentence.
(c) He should not say or do anything which might be taken to agree, expressly or by implication, with a particular sentence.
(d) In cases where s. 35 of the CJA 1988 applies, he should indicate that the A-G may, if he sees fit, seek leave to refer any sentence as unduly lenient (see **D27.3**).

D12.58 **The Indication Process** (1) It is anticipated that any sentence indication would normally be sought at the plea and case management hearing.

(2) In accordance with *A-G's Ref (No. 80 of 2005)* [2005] EWCA Crim 3367, a hearing involving an indication of sentence should normally take place in open court with a full recording of the entire proceedings, and both sides represented, in the presence of the accused (one of the exceptions is where an accused is unaware that he is terminally ill).

(3) The court is most unlikely to be able to give an indication in complicated or difficult cases unless issues between the prosecution and the defence have been addressed and resolved. Therefore, in such cases, no less than seven days' notice of an intention to seek an indication should normally be given in writing to the prosecution and the court.

(4) If an application is made without notice when it should have been given, the court may conclude that any inevitable adjournment should have been avoided and that the discount for the guilty plea should be reduced accordingly.

(5) There should be very little need for the court to be involved in the discussions with the advocates, save to seek better information on any troubling aspect of the case. An opening by the Crown, or a mitigation plea by the defence, is not envisaged.

(6) The fact that notice has been given, and any reference to a request for a sentence indication, or the circumstances in which it was sought, would be inadmissible in any subsequent trial.

(7) Reporting restrictions should normally be imposed, to be lifted if and when the accused pleads or is found guilty.

It is clear from *Goodyear* [2005] 1 WLR 2532, that the Court of Appeal did not envisage a process by which the judge should give some kind of preliminary indication, leading to comments on it by counsel for the Crown, with the judge then reconsidering his indication, and perhaps raising it to a higher level, with counsel for the accused then making further submissions to persuade the judge, after all, to reduce his indication.

D12.59 **Magistrates' Court** It would be impracticable for these new arrangements to be extended to proceedings in magistrates' courts. Accordingly, for the time being, magistrates should confine themselves to the statutory arrangements in the CJA 2003, sch. 3.

References and Appeals Against Sentence If counsel for the prosecution has addressed his responsibilities, the discretion of the A-G to refer a sentence is wholly unaffected by the advance sentence indication process. In such circumstances, the fact that a judge has given an indication of sentence before plea will not bind the Court of Appeal if the A-G appeals on the basis that the sentence is unduly lenient (*A-G's Ref (No. 40 of 1996)* [1997] 1 Cr App R (S) 357: see D27.5). **D12.60**

The accused's entitlement to apply for leave to appeal against sentence if, for example, insufficient allowance has been made for matters of genuine mitigation, is similarly unaffected.

Arrangements between Prosecution and Defence

It is common practice for the prosecution and defence to agree through counsel prior to arraignment that, in the event of the accused pleading guilty to parts of the indictment, the Crown will not seek to prove him guilty as charged. Such an arrangement may take the form of accepting a plea of guilty to a lesser offence, or of offering no evidence on counts to which the accused pleads not guilty, or of asking the judge to allow some counts to remain on the file marked not to be proceeded with. This is addressed in more detail at D12.71 and D12.73. **D12.61**

PLEA OF NOT GUILTY

Entry of Plea of Not Guilty

Normal practice is for the accused to enter a plea of not guilty personally when arraigned by the clerk in the absence of any potential jurors (see D12.1). It is not, however, essential to the validity of a trial that he formally says the words 'not guilty' (see *Williams* [1978] QB 373 at D12.50). If an accused wilfully stays silent when arraigned, or fails to give a direct answer to the charge, or enters a plea which purports to be one of guilty but is in fact ambiguous, the court may and should enter a plea of not guilty on his behalf (see Criminal Law Act 1967, s. 6(1)(c)). **D12.62**

Effect of Plea of Not Guilty

A plea of not guilty puts the prosecution to proof of their entire case. The burden is therefore on them to satisfy the jury beyond reasonable doubt that the accused committed the *actus reus* of the offence (or aided, abetted, counselled or procured its commission), and that in doing so he had the necessary *mens rea*. Should the prosecution fail to adduce sufficient evidence as to *any* element of the offence, the accused is entitled to be acquitted on the judge's direction following a submission of no case to answer made at the close of the prosecution case. **D12.63**

The defence statement should have indicated in advance of trial those parts of the prosecution case which are disputed (see D9.18). Nevertheless defence counsel is still entitled to take advantage of any deficiency in the prosecution evidence (e.g., a witness not coming up to proof) and submit that there is no case to answer, whether or not the element of the offence of which evidence is lacking would otherwise have been contested.

The only method by which the prosecution may be released from their obligation to prove each essential element of the offence is if the defence have made formal admissions under s. 10 of the CJA 1967, or where a fact is presumed (see F3.47 *et seq.*) or judicially noticed (see F1.3 *et seq.*).

D

Part D Procedure

PLEA OF GUILTY

Requirement that Accused Plead Personally

D12.64 A plea of guilty must be entered by the accused personally. If counsel purports to plead guilty on behalf of an accused, the purported plea has no validity and the proceedings constitute a mistrial (*Ellis* (1973) 57 Cr App R 571). On appeal, the Court of Appeal will be obliged either to quash the conviction or to grant a writ of *venire de novo* (i.e. set the conviction aside but order that the accused be retried) (ibid.). In *Ellis,* defence counsel intervened during the arraignment to set out the basis on which the accused would plead guilty, and the judge proceeded to sentence. At no stage did the accused himself say he was guilty, although that was undoubtedly what he would have said had he been allowed to. On appeal, Edmund-Davies LJ reviewed the authorities and then said (at pp. 574–5):

> . . . great mischief would ensue if a legal representative was generally regarded as entitled to plead on an accused's behalf. It would open the door to dispute as to whether, for example, counsel had correctly understood and acted upon the instructions which the accused had given him, and, if a dispute of that kind arose, the consequential embarrassment and difficulty could be difficult in the extreme.
>
> We think that the only safe and proper course accordingly is to say . . . that (apart from a few very special cases) it is an invariable requirement that the initial arraignment must be conducted between the clerk of the court and the accused person himself or herself directly.

Edmund-Davies LJ's dicta do not expressly distinguish between cases where the accused intends to plead guilty and those where he intends to plead not guilty or refuses to plead. As regards the latter, it is possible for a valid trial to take place despite the absence of a personal plea from the accused (see **D12.50**). As regards guilty pleas, however, there can be no derogation whatsoever from the rule that the plea must come from the mouth of the accused. This is confirmed by *Williams* [1978] QB 373, where Shaw LJ, giving the judgment of the Court of Appeal, said (at p. 378G): 'No qualification of or deviation from the rule that a plea of guilty must come from him who acknowledges guilt is . . . permissible. A departure from the rule in a criminal trial would therefore necessarily be a vitiating factor rendering the whole procedure void and ineffectual'.

Effect of Plea of Guilty

D12.65 If the accused pleads guilty, the prosecution are released from their obligation to prove the case. There is no need to empanel a jury, and the accused stands convicted simply by virtue of the word that has come from his own mouth. The only evidence the prosecution then need call in the ordinary case is that of the accused's antecedents and criminal record (see **D19.45** to **D19.51**).

Exceptionally, there may be a dispute between the parties about the material facts of the offence. If the dispute is serious enough to have a significant effect on sentence, the prosecution will either have to call evidence in support of their own version at a so-called '*Newton* hearing' or allow sentence to be passed on the basis of the defence version (for *Newton* hearings, see **D19.8** to **D19.29**). However, even in such cases, the prosecution evidence goes to *how* the offence was committed, not whether it was committed, and the accused remains convicted by his own plea whatever the outcome of the *Newton* hearing.

Adjournments Following Plea of Guilty

D12.66 Once a plea of guilty has been entered, the court may forthwith commence the procedure leading up to the passing of sentence (for which see **D19.1**). It may, on the other hand, take the plea and then adjourn. Whether or not to adjourn is entirely at the discretion of the court. Common reasons for an adjournment are to obtain reports on the accused or to await the outcome of other proceedings outstanding against him with a view to his being sentenced on one occasion for all matters (see *Bennett* (1980) 2 Cr App R (S) 96, for the desirability of linking up outstanding charges).

By virtue of the Supreme Court Act 1981, s. 81(1)(c), on adjourning, the court may either commit the accused to custody or grant him bail. Despite having been convicted, an accused who is remanded for enquiries or report at this stage still has a prima facie right to bail under the Bail Act 1976, s. 4, although in practice bail is usually withdrawn if the accused has pleaded guilty to a serious offence.

MIXED PLEAS

Three scenarios fall to be considered under the head of mixed pleas, namely where an accused pleads guilty to some charges but not others, where an accused pleads guilty and his co-accused do not, and where an accused pleads guilty and gives evidence against those co-accused who have not. D12.67

Mixed Pleas from an Accused

If an accused enters mixed pleas on a multi-count indictment and the prosecution are not prepared to accept those pleas, sentencing for the counts to which he has pleaded guilty should be postponed until after he has been tried on the not guilty counts. This is different from the situation of an accused who pleads guilty to a lesser offence, which is discussed at D12.71. D12.68

Mixed Pleas from Co-accused

Where there are co-accused, one of whom pleads guilty and the other not guilty, normal practice is to adjourn sentencing the former until after the trial of the latter. In the event of a conviction, they can then both be sentenced together. The desirability of co-accused being sentenced on one occasion by the same judge has frequently been stressed. Separate sentencing may lead to unacceptable disparity in the ways they are respectively treated. Also, the judge will hear, during the course of the trial of the accused pleading not guilty, evidence indicating the gravity of the offence charged and the extent of each accused's role in it, which information may ultimately assist him in sentencing the one pleading guilty. D12.69

The above principles were stated by Lord Goddard CJ in *Payne* [1950] 1 All ER 102, when he said:

> [Where several persons are indicted together, and one pleads guilty and the other or others not guilty] the proper course is to postpone sentence on the man who has pleaded guilty until the others have been tried and then to bring up all the prisoners to be dealt with together because by that time the court will be in possession of the facts relating to all of them and will be able to assess properly the degree of guilt of each.

A still stronger statement of the same principle occurs in the judgment of Boreham J in *Weekes* (1980) 74 Cr App R 161, where he said:

> Here are made manifest the difficulties that arise when persons involved with others are sentenced before the full facts have been heard, particularly where a trial is to take place, as it was to take place here. . . . There may be exceptions but generally it is clearly right, it is clearly fairer and it is better for both the public and all the defendants concerned, that all are sentenced at the same time by the same court whenever that is possible.

Practice where Accused Pleads Guilty and Gives Evidence for Prosecution against Co-accused It is now clear that an accused turning Queen's evidence should not be sentenced until after the co-accused's trial. This clarity resulted from 'difficulties' arising in *Weekes* D12.70

(1980) 74 Cr App R 161, to which Boreham J referred in the passage quoted in **D12.69**, namely that W, one of four co-accused charged with armed robbery, was sentenced to seven years' imprisonment while a co-accused (S) was given only 12 months, a term described by the Court of Appeal as 'ludicrously light'. Part of the explanation for the leniency shown to S was that, having intimated an intention to testify for the Crown against his co-accused, he pleaded guilty and was separately sentenced prior to the trial of the others. They were then tried, convicted partly on S's evidence and sentenced by a different judge. At W's appeal, Boreham J criticised the decision to sentence S separately (at p. 166):

> It may be . . . that [S] was sentenced at that early stage by a different court because it had been made known that he was to give evidence on behalf of the Crown against the other three. If that was the reason . . . it is not sufficient reason. . . . it should be left to the judge who may sentence those who have pleaded not guilty to sentence all.

The clear statement in *Weekes* that an accused turning Queen's evidence should not be sentenced until after the co-accused's trial is in direct conflict with the dicta of Lord Goddard CJ in *Payne* [1950] 1 All ER 102, who qualified his general exhortation to sentence co-accused together with this: 'What I have said does not apply in the exceptional case where a man who pleads guilty is going to be called as a witness. In those circumstances it is right that he be sentenced there and then so that there can be no suspicion that his evidence is coloured by the fact that he hopes to get a lighter sentence.'

A reversal of the practice approved in *Payne* was signalled by two unreported cases in 1977, namely *Potter* (15 September 1977 unreported) and *Woods* (25 October 1977 unreported), and that reversal has been confirmed by *Weekes* and *Chan Wai-keung* [1995] 1 WLR 251. In *Coffey* (1976) 74 Cr App R 168, the principle that all should be sentenced at the end of any trial was held to apply when the accused who has pleaded guilty is going to testify for the co-accused, just as it applies when he is to testify for the prosecution. Even so, whether to sentence a co-accused pleading guilty forthwith or adjourn until after the co-accused's trial must, in the last resort, remain a question for the judge (see *Palmer* (1994) 158 JP 138).

A possible issue is whether the accused might attempt to resile from the agreement to give evidence for the prosecution or do so in an unsatisfactory manner. As Lord Denning MR said in *Sheffield Crown Court, ex parte Brownlow* [1980] QB 530, a decision to adjourn is 'a matter in relation to which the trial judge should have the final word'. Moreover, circumstances may arise in which the interests of justice are better served by disposing of the accused pleading guilty before the trial of his co-accused; for example if the latter absconds before his trial, or if the former's offence is self-contained and trivial by comparison with the latter. In all these, and no doubt in other, cases there are, it is submitted, good reasons for departing from the usual practice by sentencing the accused who has pleaded guilty at the first opportunity.

The position is now clarified by the SOCPA 2005, ss. 73 to 75 (see **E1.7**). This demonstrates that the court may take into account the assistance the accused is going to provide to the 'investigator or prosecutor', e.g., by giving evidence or intelligence, when determining his sentence, and should indicate that it has done so unless that would be contrary to the public interest (s. 73). However, if the accused then fails to provide the promised assistance, the prosecution may invite the court to review the sentence and the court may substitute a greater sentence for the sentence originally passed (s. 74, reversing *Stone* [1970] 1 WLR 1112 on that point).

PLEA OF GUILTY TO A LESSER OFFENCE

D12.71 Where the indictment contains a count on which, if the accused were to plead not guilty, the jury could find him not guilty as charged but guilty of an alternative (hereafter referred to as 'lesser') offence, he may enter a plea to the same effect, namely not guilty to the offence charged but guilty only of the lesser offence (Criminal Law Act 1967, s. 6(1)(b)).

If the plea is accepted, he is treated as having been acquitted of the offence actually charged and the court proceeds to sentence him for the lesser offence (Criminal Law Act 1967, s. 6(5)). The circumstances in which a jury have the power to return a verdict of guilty of a lesser offence are defined by legislation, chiefly subsections (2) to (4) of s. 6 of the 1967 Act, which are considered in detail at **D18.41** to **D18.64**.

The considerations relevant to the decision by the prosecution to either accept or reject the plea are considered below.

The extent of the judge's control over the acceptance of a plea to a lesser offence is open to argument. In *Soanes* (1948) 32 Cr App R 136, Lord Goddard CJ said, '. . . it must always be in the discretion of the judge whether he will allow [a plea of guilty to a lesser offence] to be accepted'. However, it is doubtful whether, in an adversarial system of justice, the court can or should insist on one of the parties calling evidence. Neither is there any precedent for the court calling all the witnesses itself. Therefore, if the prosecution absolutely refuse to call evidence to prove the accused guilty as charged, the court would have no real alternative but to accept the situation, subject to any proper question of professional misconduct.

Moreover, in the analogous situation of the accused pleading to some counts on the indictment in exchange for the prosecution offering no evidence on others, the rule seems to be that the prosecution are bound by the judge's views of the bargain if, and only if, they have expressly asked him to approve it in advance (see **D12.78**). If they choose not to seek his prior approval, they may accept the pleas even though the judge indicates in court that they ought to proceed on all counts (see *Coward* (1979) 70 Cr App R 70 and *Broad* (1978) 68 Cr App R 281).

Status of Original Plea in Event of Verdict of Not Guilty

In *Hazeltine* [1967] 2 QB 857, the accused, on being arraigned for wounding with intent contrary to s. 18 of the OAPA 1861, replied, 'Not guilty, but guilty to unlawful wounding'. **D12.72**
The prosecution would not accept the plea, and H was put in charge of a jury who were simply told that he had pleaded not guilty. At his trial, H offered a defence of acting in reasonable self-defence which was inconsistent with his original plea. No evidence was adduced as to that plea, nor was he cross-examined about it. The judge did refer to it in his summing-up but in a manner that almost certainly left the jury confused. When the jury then acquitted H, the judge then sentenced H to nine months' imprisonment. That sentence had to be quashed on appeal as H had not been convicted of any offence. His original plea to unlawful wounding was impliedly withdrawn on the prosecution saying that it was not acceptable, and the jury's verdict implied an acquittal both in respect of the offence charged and in respect of the lesser included offence.

In the course of his speech Salmon LJ explained the purpose and effect of the then equivalent of s. 6(1) of the Criminal Law Act 1967 (s. 39(1) of the Criminal Justice Administration Act 1914). His lordship said (at p. 861A–F):

> Prior to that statutory provision, it was not possible for an accused to plead guilty to unlawful wounding when charged with wounding with intent but it was and always has been possible for a jury, when a man is charged with wounding with intent, to return a verdict of unlawful wounding; so before the Act of 1914 the position was that an accused man might be saying, 'Of course, I am guilty of unlawful wounding but I had no intention of doing grievous bodily harm', the prosecution might be satisfied that a plea of that kind ought to be accepted, and the judge might be so satisfied, yet a great deal of unnecessary time and money had to be wasted by holding a full-dress trial in order to obtain a verdict from a jury which the prosecution, the defence and the judge were satisfied was the only proper verdict in the circumstances.

> This court has no doubt but that section 39(1) of the Act of 1914 was introduced so as to remove this anomaly which resulted in the great waste of time and money to which I have referred. In the view of this court, however, that statutory provision did not get rid of the rule that there can be but one plea to one count should the trial proceed on that count. Accordingly if an accused pleads not guilty to wounding with intent but guilty to unlawful wounding and counsel for the prosecution or the judge takes the view that that plea ought not to be accepted and the trial proceeds, the plea of guilty to unlawful wounding is deemed to be withdrawn and the only plea is the plea of not guilty to wounding with intent. It is then for the jury to consider the evidence and at the end of the case to say either quite simply that the man is not guilty or that he is guilty of wounding with intent or that he is not guilty of wounding with intent but guilty to unlawful wounding.

Although couched in terms of wounding with intent and unlawful wounding, the above passage is obviously applicable whenever a plea of guilty to a lesser offence is rejected.

To avoid a repetition of the manifestly unsatisfactory result in *Hazeltine*, the Court of Appeal suggested that, in cases where the accused offers a defence that is inconsistent with his earlier plea to a lesser offence, the prosecution ought to call evidence of the plea and, if the accused testifies, cross-examine him about it (ibid. at p. 862F–G). There was no need to adopt a policy of always having separate counts for the greater and lesser offences. However, should the prosecution fail to adduce evidence of the plea, it is not open to the judge to repair the omission in his summing-up by informing the jury of what occurred (*Lee* [1985] Crim LR 798). Nor may the judge direct the jury to convict of the lesser offence as opposed to informing them that such a verdict is open to them (ibid., and see *Notman* [1994] Crim LR 518).

PROSECUTION OPTIONS ON PLEA OF NOT GUILTY OR MIXED PLEAS BEING ENTERED

D12.73 Apart from the obvious course of proceeding to a contested trial, there are two options available to the prosecution on the accused pleading not guilty, namely, to offer no evidence or to ask that the indictment remain on the court file. Similar responses are possible where an arraignment results in mixed pleas, with either only some of the accused pleading guilty, or with one accused entering guilty pleas to only some of the charges.

Each of these two options is addressed here. In addition, considerable guidance has been given, notably through guidelines handed down by the A-G and in the report of the Farquharson committee on the role of prosecuting counsel. This guidance is also addressed below.

Offering No Evidence

D12.74 **Criminal Justice Act 1967, s. 17**

> Where a defendant arraigned on an indictment or inquisition pleads not guilty and the prosecutor proposes to offer no evidence against him, the court before which the defendant is arraigned may, if it thinks fit, order that a verdict of not guilty shall be recorded without the defendant being given in charge to a jury, and the verdict shall have the same effect as if the defendant had been tried and acquitted on the verdict of a jury.

The obvious situation for reliance on s. 17 is if the prosecution have reviewed their evidence since committal, or have become aware of additional evidence favourable to the defence, and have concluded that they cannot properly ask a jury to convict. Alternatively, offering no evidence on some counts in an indictment may be part of an agreement with the defence under which the accused pleads guilty to other counts.

Whilst the plain wording of s. 17 gives the court a discretion to decline to order a verdict of not guilty to be entered even though the prosecution intimate that they do not wish to proceed, in the last resort, the prosecution cannot be forced by the court to call evidence.

In *Renshaw* [1989] Crim LR 811, the Court of Appeal stressed the importance of the judge listening to the reasons given by the prosecution for proposing to offer no evidence. The judge should keep in mind that the prosecution will have information which he does not. If he fails to heed what the prosecution say, he will deprive himself of a proper basis for approving or disapproving of their proposed course of action.

Letting Counts Lie on the File

As an alternative to offering no evidence, the prosecution may ask the judge to order that an indictment (or counts thereof) shall lie on the file, marked not to be proceeded with without leave of the court or of the Court of Appeal. Such a course is particularly appropriate where the accused pleads guilty to the bulk of the charges against him (whether contained in one indictment or several) but not guilty to some subsidiary charges. Leaving the latter on the file avoids the necessity of a trial, but also avoids the accused actually being acquitted on the 'not guilty' counts, which might seem inappropriate if the evidence against him is in fact strong. **D12.75**

Contrary to what was previously understood to be the position, there is no objection to an entire indictment remaining on the file, as opposed to merely dealing with some counts of a multi-count indictment in that way (e.g., in *Central Criminal Court, ex parte Raymond* [1986] 1 WLR 710, as a result of R's conviction on one count of a severed 14-count indictment, the trial judge ordered that both the remaining counts of the original indictment and all counts of a completely separate indictment should lie on the file).

The use and practical effect of the order is helpfully summarised by Woolf LJ in *Ex parte Raymond* (at pp. 714H–715B):

> [It is important] to analyse the nature of the order that an indictment should lie on the file. It starts off by having the same effect as an order for an adjournment but an adjournment which it is accepted may never result in a trial. Frequently the order is made to safeguard the position of the prosecution and the defence in case a defendant, who has been convicted, should appeal, it being the intention of the court if there is no appeal or if the appeal is unsuccessful the defendant should never stand trial. That the defendant can still stand trial is indicated by the limits on the discretion of the court (laid down by the House of Lords in *Connelly* v *DPP* [1964] AC 1254) to prevent the Crown proceeding with a prosecution if it wishes to do so. However, in the majority of cases where such an order is made, there will be no trial and there will certainly come a stage when either the prosecution would not seek a trial or if it did seek a trial, the court would regard it as so oppressive to have a trial that leave to proceed would inevitably be refused.

Challenge to an Order to Lie on the File Whether to order that counts lie on the file is a matter totally within the judge's discretion since there is no method by which either party can challenge his decision. There is no appeal to the Court of Appeal as that only arises once there has been a conviction and, if counts remain on the file, there will not be a trial let alone a conviction. See *Mackell* (1981) 74 Cr App R 27, on the Court of Appeal's lack of jurisdiction to reverse an order that counts lie on the file, and Dunn LJ's dictum, quoted with approval in *Central Criminal Court, ex parte Raymond* [1986] 1 WLR 710, that, '. . . there are certain matters upon which the trial judge should have the final say. It seems to us this is one of them'. **D12.76**

Moreover, it was made clear in *Ex parte Raymond* that there cannot be an application to the High Court for judicial review since a decision to leave counts on the file has been held to relate to a trial on indictment and so, by virtue of s. 29(3) of the Supreme Court Act 1981, is not eligible for review. The reasoning of the court was that, although an order to leave counts on the file is effectively an order that a trial shall not take place unless something out of the ordinary subsequently happens to alter the court's mind, it 'starts off by having the same effect as an order for an adjournment' (per Woolf LJ at p. 714H). As to decisions to adjourn, Lord Denning MR's judgment in *Sheffield Crown Court, ex parte Brownlow* [1980]

D

Part D Procedure

QB 530, instanced such decisions as something on which 'the trial judge should have the final word'.

The applicant in *Ex parte Raymond* argued that a Crown Court judge should not order that counts lie on the file unless the defence agree to that course, and, in the absence of such agreement, he ought to require the prosecution to elect between proceeding to trial and offering no evidence. The court ultimately refused to state its view or give any guidance on when orders to lie on the file are appropriate. This reticence was because of its primary decision that it did not in any event have jurisdiction to review the decision of the court below.

D12.77 **Circumstances in which an Order to Lie on the File may be Reversed** The only situation in which the Crown Court or Court of Appeal is likely to give leave for a count or indictment ordered to lie on the file to be tried is if the accused's convictions on the other matters (i.e. the charges on the same or separate indictments to which he pleaded guilty or of which he was found guilty at the same time as the order to lie on the file was made) are quashed on appeal.

Accepting or Rejecting a Plea to a Lesser Offence

D12.78 As was addressed at D12.71, it is possible for an accused to plead guilty to a lesser offence than that charged in the indictment. The prosecution may refuse to accept a plea of guilty to a lesser offence. If so, the plea is deemed to be withdrawn and the case proceeds as if the accused had simply pleaded not guilty (*Hazeltine* [1967] 2 QB 857).

Criteria to be Applied by the Prosecution

D12.79 **Guidelines** The report of the Farquharson committee on the role of prosecuting counsel (May 1986), considered counsel's control over the acceptance of pleas. The committee discussed the authorities, and also made the point that, in the reverse situation of the judge thinking that the evidence on the depositions does not warrant a conviction or that further proceedings would be unfair, he has no power to prevent the prosecution calling their evidence save in the very exceptional case of the proceedings amounting to an abuse of the process of the court.

The principles set out by the Farquharson committee have in any event since been endorsed and developed by the CPS and the General Council of the Bar in a set of Guidelines jointly issued in 2002.

D12.80 **General Rule** In accepting a plea of guilty to a lesser offence or guilty to some counts only on the indictment, prosecuting counsel is in reality making a decision to offer no evidence on a particular charge. Since the committee were of the opinion that counsel was undoubtedly entitled to offer no evidence on the indictment as a whole and could not be forced to call evidence against his will, it followed that he must also be entitled to decide to accept pleas to part only of the indictment.

D12.81 **The Three Qualifications** This general rule is, however, subject to three qualifications:

(a) If prosecuting counsel expressly asks for the court's approval of his proposed acceptance of certain pleas, he must abide by the court's decision (*Broad* (1978) 68 Cr App R 281). There is no obligation on him to seek such approval, but he might feel it right to do so where either it is desirable to reassure the public at large that the course proposed is being properly taken, or he has been unable to reach agreement with his instructing solicitor about what ought to be done.

(b) In a case where the court's approval is not sought beforehand, it is nonetheless usual for counsel to explain in open court his reasons for accepting the plea. It is then open to the judge to express his views. If the judge, on the information available to him, such as the depositions, exhibits, antecedents and perhaps reports on the accused, is 'of the opinion that the course proposed by counsel would lead to serious injustice, he may decline to proceed with the case until counsel has consulted with either the [DPP] or the [Attorney-General] as may be appropriate' (Farquharson, para. k). However, in the final analysis and once the steps just referred to have been taken, the judge has no power to prevent counsel taking the course he thinks fit — 'any attempt by him to do so would give the impression that he was stepping into the arena and pressing the prosecution case'. However, the committee expressed the opinion that 'the occasions when counsel felt it right to resist the judge's views would be rare'.

(c) Should the decision to accept proposed pleas fall to be taken during the course of the trial, prosecuting counsel's position remains as in (b) above until the close of his case. Once, however, he has called his evidence and the judge has either found there is a case to answer or no submission to the contrary has been made, the position is different. At that stage there is, *ex hypothesi*, a case for the accused to answer, and therefore 'it would be an abuse of process for the prosecution to discontinue without leave'. But, even though the judge can rule that the case shall proceed, 'it would not be the duty of counsel to cross-examine the defence witnesses or address the jury if he was of the view that it would not be proper to convict'.

Consideration in *Grafton* The report of the Farquharson committee was referred to with approval in *Grafton* [1993] QB 101. In that case, there was a conflict of evidence between two witnesses called for the Crown. Prosecution counsel consulted those instructing him, and said he would call no further evidence. Apparently, the judge disagreed profoundly with this decision and had an animated argument with prosecuting counsel, who held his ground and took no part in the proceedings thereafter. The judge then himself called a police officer, who was the Crown's remaining witness. G was convicted, and appealed. The appeal was allowed on the basis that the decision whether to continue with the case or not had to be that of the prosecution. By proceeding as he did, the judge was no longer holding the ring between adversaries but took over the prosecution, and the reaction of any neutral bystander could only be that he had become the adversary of the defence. **D12.82**

The Court of Appeal in *Grafton* also approved qualification (c) above. They added, however, that where the prosecution's case is complete, but the judge refuses leave to the Crown to discontinue, it was prosecution counsel's duty to remain in the case. If the prosecution's view later changed (perhaps as a result of hearing the accused testify), he would then be free to cross-examine witnesses or address the jury.

Acceptance of a Plea to a Lesser Offence As to the circumstances in which it is appropriate to accept a plea to a lesser offence, Lord Goddard in *Soanes* (1948) 32 Cr App R 136, declined to lay down a 'hard and fast rule' but expressed the view that, 'where nothing appears on the depositions which can be said to reduce the crime from the more serious offence charged to some lesser offence for which a verdict may be returned, the duty of counsel for the Crown would be to present the offence charged in the indictment'. The possible effect on the prosecution witnesses of testifying at a contested trial (e.g., where the offence charged is of a sexual nature) and/or the reaction of the victim to the charge being reduced may also have a bearing on counsel's ultimate decision (see, e.g., *Coward* (1979) 70 Cr App R 70). **D12.83**

The Attorney-General's Guidelines The A-G's Guidelines on the Acceptance of Pleas (see **appendix 3**) stress that justice should be conducted in public, save in the most exceptional circumstances, and that this includes the acceptance of pleas by the prosecution. Prosecutors are directed to the guidance contained in the Code for Crown Prosecutors, and told that they should be prepared to explain in open court the reasons for accepting pleas to a reduced number of charges or less serious charges. **D12.84**

CHANGE OF PLEA

D12.85 The final topic to be addressed in relation to the arraignment is the procedure to be followed, and criteria to be applied, where an accused seeks to change his plea thereafter. Where he wishes to change his plea from not guilty to guilty (see **D12.86**), this causes little difficulty. Where, however, he seeks to change his plea from guilty to not guilty (see **D12.87**) more difficult considerations arise, not least because such a change represents an assertion that an accused has realised that he did not commit the offence after all. The considerations in this category also include issues as to whether a plea was ambiguous (see **D12.92**) or involuntary (see **D11.93**).

From Not Guilty to Guilty

D12.86 The judge may allow the accused to change his plea from not guilty to guilty at any stage prior to the jury returning their verdict. The procedure is that the defence ask for the indictment to be put again and the accused then pleads guilty. If the change of plea comes after the accused has been put in the charge of a jury, the jury should be directed to return a formal verdict of guilty.

In *Heyes* [1951] 1 KB 29, H pleaded not guilty to charges of stealing and receiving certain property. During the opening of the prosecution case and after advice from counsel who had at that stage been allotted to him, he changed his plea to guilty of receiving. This was done in the jury's presence but they were not asked to return a verdict, and the judge proceeded forthwith to sentence. On appeal, Lord Goddard CJ said:

> Once the jury had heard the appellant say that he wished to withdraw his plea and admit his guilt, the proper proceeding was for the court to ask them to return a verdict. It appears that counsel did suggest to the learned recorder that this was the proper course; but the recorder thought that it did not matter. It does matter because, once a prisoner is in charge of a jury, he can only be either convicted or discharged by the verdict of the jury.
>
> As there was no verdict of the jury here, the trial was a nullity to such an extent that the court could set aside the proceedings and order a retrial or *venire de novo* [but, in the circumstances of this case we] will merely quash the conviction.

In *Poole* [2002] 1 WLR 1528, however, the accused changed her plea to guilty on the second day of the trial. The judge discharged the jury without entering any verdict, and proceedings continued as though the accused had pleaded guilty on arraignment, with an adjournment for reports. The accused then wished to vacate her plea of guilty and, when this was refused, appealed against conviction. The Court of Appeal held that the course taken was permissible and resulted in a valid conviction. In the light of the Court of Appeal decision in *Ashton* [2007] 1 WLR 181 (see **D12.50**), it is difficult now to imagine a court adopting a contrary conclusion.

Although having the indictment put again with a view to a change of plea to guilty is a matter for the judge's discretion, it is difficult to envisage circumstances in which he would be unwilling to allow it to be done. Depending on the stage of the trial at which it comes, the change of plea will provide some mitigation for the accused when sentence is passed. As to the effect of such a change of plea upon the trial of a co-accused, see **D13.57** and the case of *Fedrick* [1990] Crim LR 403 dealt with there.

From Guilty to Not Guilty

D12.87 **Discretion to Allow a Change** The judge has a discretion to allow the accused to withdraw a plea of guilty at any stage before sentence is passed. This was confirmed in *Plummer* [1902] 2 KB 339, where the major question for the court was whether P's conviction on a guilty plea for conspiracy to steal could be sustained in view of his five co-accused (who were the only others named in the conspiracy count) having been acquitted. P was not sentenced until after the acquittal of the others, and, prior to sentence, asked to withdraw his plea. Wright J said (at p. 347):

> Another point is raised in this case, namely, whether the court had power to allow the appellant to withdraw his plea of guilty. There cannot be any doubt that the court had such power at any time before, though not after, judgment [i.e. sentence] and, as we infer that but for the erroneous opinion that there was no such power the withdrawal would have been allowed, this might of itself be a ground for a *venire de novo.*

Similarly, Bruce J held that the first-instance court clearly had a discretion to allow the change of plea; that, if it had exercised its discretion against the appellant, the appellate court might have had no power to interfere; but, in fact, the discretion was never exercised one way or the other and that had deprived the appellant of a chance of an acquittal, with the consequence that the conviction could not stand (at p. 349).

The existence of the discretion was indirectly confirmed by the House of Lords in *S v Recorder of Manchester* [1971] AC 481, when it held that, in the context of change of plea, there is no conviction until sentence has been passed, and therefore magistrates (like the Crown Court) can allow a change to not guilty provided they have not yet passed sentence.

Finally, in *Dodd* (1981) 74 Cr App R 50, the Court of Appeal unhesitatingly accepted the three following propositions from counsel for D, namely that: (a) the court has a discretion to allow a defendant to change a plea of guilty to one of not guilty at any time before sentence; (b) the discretion exists even where the plea of not guilty is unequivocal; and (c) the discretion must be exercised judicially (see p. 57).

Application of the Discretion Whilst confirming the existence of the discretion now under consideration, the case law tends to show that it should be sparingly exercised in favour of the accused. Thus, in *McNally* [1954] 1 WLR 933, where the accused had indicated even in the magistrates' court an intention to plead guilty, could not possibly have misunderstood the nature of a straightforward charge and had unequivocally admitted guilt when the indictment was put to him, the Court of Criminal Appeal approved the trial judge's decision to refuse a change of plea. The same approach was more recently adopted in *Revitt v DPP* [2006] 1 WLR 3172). **D12.88**

Unrepresented Accused Even if the accused was unrepresented when he pleaded but instructs solicitors during an adjournment prior to sentencing and is advised by them that he has a defence, the court is not obliged to accede to a change of plea (*South Tameside Magistrates' Court, ex parte Rowland* [1983] 3 All ER 689). **D12.89**

In *Ex parte Rowland*, in considering such an application for a change of plea, the magistrates, 'rightly, balanced the instructions which the applicant had given to her solicitor after [the original plea] against the prospect that she was changing her story because of the possibility that she might be sentenced to a custodial sentence' (per Glidewell J at p. 692J). Furthermore, the magistrates 'were perfectly entitled to come to the conclusion to which they did come' (i.e. that fear of a custodial sentence was the real motivation for the change of plea), and thus were justified in exercising their discretion against R.

Glidewell J approved the advice given to the magistrates by their clerk that, 'to allow a change of plea was a matter for [the magistrates'] absolute discretion and that once an unequivocal plea had been entered the discretionary power should be exercised judicially, very sparingly and only in clear cases' (at p. 692A). However, the implication is that, had the magistrates thought the plea to have been entered under a misapprehension of law as to the nature of the offence, then their only proper course would have been to allow the application. Although *Ex parte Rowland* was a case concerning change of plea in the magistrates' court, there is no reason why the same principles should not apply in the Crown Court.

In *Revitt v v DPP* [2006] 1 WLR 3172, the accused had been unrepresented, but had been advised by the court legal adviser of the nature and seriousness of the charges and of their right both to legal representations and to advance disclosure before plea. Where the accused proceeded to enter a guilty plea, the Administrative Court found the plea to be both informed and unequivocal.

D12.90 **Represented Accused** If the accused was represented when he entered his plea of guilty, there would seem to be no absolute bar to his applying to withdraw the plea, but it will obviously be very difficult to convince the court that the plea was entered by a genuine mistake. This was demonstrated in *Drew* [1985] 1 WLR 914, where Lord Lane CJ said (at p. 923C): '. . . only rarely would it be appropriate for the trial judge to exercise his undoubted discretion in favour of an accused person wishing to change an unequivocal plea of guilty to one of not guilty. Particularly this is so in cases where, as here, the accused has throughout been advised by experienced counsel'.

Provided the court at first instance recognised that it had a discretion to allow a change of plea and applied the correct principles in determining the application, the Court of Appeal will not interfere with the trial judge's exercise of discretion — see *Dodd* (1981) 74 Cr App R 50 (see **D12.87**), *Cantor* [1991] Crim LR 481, *Anjum* [2004] EWCA Crim 977 and *Towers* [2004] EWCA Crim 1128.

Double Change of Plea

D12.91 Where the accused has changed his plea from not guilty to guilty, the judge still has a discretion to allow him to change back to not guilty (*Drew* [1985] 1 WLR 914). The fact that the jury empanelled to try him as a result of the original not guilty plea formally found him guilty on hearing the change to guilty does not affect the existence of the judge's discretion. In *Drew*, Lord Lane CJ said (at p. 922C):

> There appears to this court no greater difficulty in altering the record following a jury's verdict than doing so upon a change of plea in any other situation. The jury's verdict where, as here, it is entered upon the direction of the judge, is essentially a formality. In our judgment, logic and good sense dictate that the trial judge should have the same power to allow a change of plea even where the verdict of guilty has been returned formally by the jury.

Ambiguous Pleas

D12.92 If an accused purports to enter a plea of guilty but, either at the time he pleads or subsequently in mitigation, qualifies it with words that suggest he may have a defence (e.g., 'Guilty, but it was an accident' or 'Guilty, but I was going to give it back'), then the court must not proceed to sentence on the basis of the plea but should explain the relevant law and seek to ascertain whether he genuinely intends to plead guilty.

If the plea cannot be clarified, the court should order a not guilty plea to be entered on the accused's behalf (Criminal Law Act 1967, s. 6(1)(c): 'if [the accused] stands mute of malice *or will not answer directly to the indictment*, the court may order a plea of not guilty to be entered').

Should the court proceed to sentence on a plea which is imperfect, unfinished or otherwise ambiguous, the accused will have a good ground of appeal. Since the defect in the plea will have rendered the original proceedings a mistrial, the Court of Appeal will have the options either of setting the conviction and sentence aside and ordering a retrial (see, e.g., *Ingleson* [1915] 1 KB 512) or of simply quashing the conviction (see, e.g., *Field* (1943) 29 Cr App R 151). If the former course is chosen (i.e. there is to be a retrial), the court may either then and there direct that a not guilty plea be entered or order that the accused be re-arraigned in the court below (e.g., *Baker* (1912) 7 Cr App R 217).

Involuntary Pleas

A plea of guilty must be entered voluntarily. If, at the time he pleaded, the accused was subject to such pressure that he did not genuinely have a free choice between 'guilty' and 'not guilty', his plea is a nullity (*Turner* [1970] 2 QB 321). On appeal, the Court of Appeal will have the same options as it has when a plea is adjudged ambiguous, namely that it must quash the conviction and sentence but will be able, in its discretion, to issue a writ of *venire de novo* for a retrial as the original proceedings constitute a mistrial. **D12.93**

Pressure to plead may come from a number of sources: the court, defence counsel or other factors. Whatever the source, the effect is the same.

The Court An example of this principle is provided by *Barnes* (1970) 55 Cr App R 100, where the judge, during a submission of no case to answer made in the absence of the jury but in the presence of the accused, said that, having regard to the prosecution evidence, B was plainly guilty and was wasting the court's time by pleading not guilty. Despite this pressure, B did not change his plea. Allowing his appeal against conviction on other grounds, the court indicated that the judge's remarks were 'wholly improper', and, if B had pleaded guilty in consequence of them, the plea would have been null. **D12.94**

Defence Counsel It is the duty of counsel to advise his client on the strength of the evidence and the advantages of a guilty plea as regards sentencing (see, e.g., *Herbert* (1991) 94 Cr App R 233 and *Cain* [1976] QB 496). Such advice may, if necessary, be given in forceful terms (*Peace* [1976] Crim LR 119). **D12.95**

Where an accused is so advised and thereafter pleads guilty reluctantly, his plea is not *ipso facto* to be treated as involuntary (ibid.). It will be involuntary only if the advice was so very forceful as to take away his free choice. Thus, in *Inns* (1974) 60 Cr App R 231, defence counsel, as he was then professionally required to do, relayed to the accused the judge's warning in chambers that, in the event of conviction on a not guilty plea, the accused would definitely be given a sentence of detention whereas if he pleaded guilty a more lenient course might be possible. This rendered the eventual guilty plea a nullity.

However, in the absence of a suggestion that counsel was acting as a conduit to pass on a threat or promise from the judge, it will be extremely difficult for an appellant to satisfy the court that he was deprived by counsel's advice of a voluntary choice when pleading. Thus, in *Hall* [1968] 2 QB 788, H was charged with participation in a major burglary from an art gallery and, alternatively, with handling some of the stolen pictures. The prosecution were willing to accept a plea to the latter. Counsel advised H that, if he pleaded not guilty to both counts, he ran the risk of being convicted of the burglary itself since, although the evidence on that count was not strong, the defence would involve attacks on the prosecution witnesses' characters and the appellant's own bad character would therefore go before the jury. If so convicted, he could expect to receive up to 12 years' imprisonment, whereas if he pleaded guilty to handling the maximum sentence would be five years.

Dismissing H's appeal, Lord Parker CJ said (at pp. 534–7):

> What the court is looking to see is whether a prisoner in these circumstances has a free choice; the election must be his, the responsibility his, to plead guilty or not guilty. At the same time, it is the clear duty of any counsel representing a client to assist the client to make up his mind by putting forward the pros and cons, if need be in strong language, to impress upon the client what the likely results are of certain courses of conduct.

His lordship then paraphrased the advice given by counsel:

> [Defence counsel], in the opinion of this court, was only doing his duty in setting forth the dangers, even, as [he] said, in strong language.

> . . . anybody who has heard the evidence in this case and has understood the workings of the law and our procedure, could not fail to realise that the appellant has no grievance at all . . . and that his counsel performed his duty to the best of his ability. This court has no hesitation in those circumstances in dismissing the appeal.

The position will be different if the advice given by counsel is demonstrably wrong. For example, in *Sorhaindo* [2006] EWCA Crim 1429, the Court of Appeal held that, where an accused had erroneously been advised that his factual case afforded him no defence, he should have been permitted to vacate the guilty plea that he entered in reliance on this advice.

D12.96 **Guidance to Defence Counsel** The Code of Conduct of the Bar, Written Standards for the Conduct of Professional Work, para. 12.3, confirms that defence counsel should explain to the accused the advantages and disadvantages of a guilty plea. It goes on to say that he must make it clear that the client has complete freedom of choice and that the responsibility for the plea is the accused's. It is common practice, endorsed by para. 12.5.1, to tell an accused that he should plead guilty only if he is guilty (see Lord Parker CJ's observation in *Turner* [1970] 2 QB 321 at p. 326F that: 'Counsel of course will emphasise that the accused must not plead guilty unless he has committed the acts constituting the offence charged'). However, it may be felt that, on occasions, realistic advice about the strength of the prosecution case and the sentencing discount for a guilty plea will effectively force an accused into a guilty plea however punctilious defence counsel may be in saying that he should plead guilty only if he is guilty.

Where an accused persists in pleading guilty notwithstanding telling counsel that he is in fact innocent, counsel may continue to act for him but must say nothing in mitigation that is inconsistent with the guilty plea (paras. 12.5.2 and 12.5.3). Counsel may thus be forced to confine his mitigation to the circumstances and background of the offender and any matters minimising the gravity of the offence which are apparent on the face of the prosecution statements; since his only instructions about the offence itself are that the accused is not guilty of it, counsel cannot explain (as he might otherwise do) the immediate temptations etc. that led to its commission.

D12.97 **Other Pressures** Apart from cases where pressure has been brought to bear on the accused to plead guilty, there may be other situations where his mind did not go with his plea and he is therefore entitled to have his conviction set aside. An example is *Swain* [1986] Crim LR 480, in which S changed his plea to guilty half-way through the prosecution case. He gave no coherent explanation to counsel at the time, but it was afterwards discovered that he had been under the influence of the drug LSD. Psychiatric evidence called before the Court of Appeal established that LSD can put the user into a state akin to schizophrenia where he drifts in and out of a delusional world and makes irrational decisions. The court held the change of plea to have been a nullity.

Section D13 Juries

This section deals with the various stages of the process by which a jury is empanelled to try an accused, and the handling of that jury thereafter. The main source of the law on jurors is the Juries Act 1974. Under the heading of the process for empanelment, this section addresses eligibility for jury service, the summoning of jurors, and the selection and empanelling of jurors for a particular case. Under the heading of jury management, this section addresses the conduct of jurors during a trial, and the judge's power to discharge the jury or individual jurors. The rules governing retirement of the jury while they consider their verdict and the verdicts they may return are considered in **D18**. **D13.1**

In addition, this section considers the extent to which errors in the formation of the jury may ground an appeal, and recent legislative measures designed to replace juries with trials by judge alone in certain categories of cases (see **D13.66** ***et seq***).

ELIGIBILITY FOR JURY SERVICE

The basic rule is that all persons aged 18 to 70 who: **D13.2**

(a) are registered either as parliamentary or local government electors; and
(b) have been ordinarily resident in the UK for any period of at least five years since attaining the age of 13,

are eligible for jury service and are therefore under a duty to attend for service if summoned (Juries Act 1974, s. 1).

There are a number of exceptions to this general rule. The first category is of those who are rendered either ineligible or disqualified from serving by the provisions of the Juries Act 1974. The second category is of those who are able to excuse themselves from serving, either as of right under the Act, or at the discretion of the appropriate court officer in accordance with the *Consolidated Criminal Practice Direction*, paras. IV.42.1 to IV.42.3.

Ineligibility and Disqualification

Parts I and II of sch. 1 to the Juries Act 1974, as amended by the CJA 2003, s. 321 and sch. 33, set out those persons who are *ineligible* for jury service and those persons who are *disqualified.* **D13.3**

The ineligible group consists of those defined as mentally disordered (defined in part I of sch.1), meaning those who suffer from mental illness, psychopathic disorder, mental handicap or severe mental handicap and who are consequently either resident in hospital or regularly attending for treatment by a doctor.

The person disqualified (as defined by part II of sch.1), either for life or for ten years, is either disqualified by reason of his previous convictions or by virtue of being on bail in criminal proceedings. If a person serves on a jury knowing that he is disqualified from so doing, he

D

Part D Procedure

commits a summary offence punishable with a fine of up to £5,000 (Juries Act 1974, s. 20(5)).

Juries Act 1974, s. 1 and sch. 1

1.—(1) Subject to the provisions of this Act, every person shall be qualified to serve as a juror in the Crown Court, the High Court and county courts and be liable accordingly to attend for jury service when summoned under this Act if—

(a) he is for the time being registered as a parliamentary or local government elector and is not less than eighteen nor more than seventy years of age;

(b) he has been ordinarily resident in the United Kingdom, the Channel Islands or the Isle of Man for any period of at least five years since attaining the age of thirteen;

(c) he is not a mentally disordered person; and

(d) he is not disqualified for jury service.

(2) In subsection (1) above 'mentally disordered person' means any person listed in part 1 of schedule 1 to this Act.

(3) The persons who are disqualified for jury service are those listed in part 2 of that Schedule.

SCHEDULE 1

MENTALLY DISORDERED PERSONS AND PERSONS DISQUALIFIED FOR JURY SERVICE

PART 1

MENTALLY DISORDERED PERSONS

1. A person who suffers or has suffered from mental illness, psychopathic disorder, mental handicap or severe mental handicap and on account of that condition either—

(a) is resident in a hospital or similar institution; or

(b) regularly attends for treatment by a medical practitioner.

2. A person for the time being under guardianship under section 7 of the Mental Health Act 1983.

3. A person who, under part 7 of that Act, has been determined by a judge to be incapable, by reason of mental disorder, of managing and administering his property and affairs.

4.—(1) In this part of this Schedule—

(a) 'mental handicap' means a state of arrested or incomplete development of mind (not amounting to severe mental handicap) which includes significant impairment of intelligence and social functioning;

(b) 'severe mental handicap' means a state of arrested or incomplete development of mind which includes severe impairment of intelligence and social functioning;

(c) other expressions are to be construed in accordance with the Mental Health Act 1983.

(2) For the purposes of this part a person is to be treated as being under guardianship under section 7 of the Mental Health Act 1983 at any time while he is subject to guardianship pursuant to an order under section 116A(2)(b) of the Army Act 1955, section 116A(2)(b) of the Air Force Act 1955 or section 63A(2)(b) of the Naval Discipline Act 1957 (which are all to be repealed when the Armed Forces Act 2006 comes into force).

PART 2

PERSONS DISQUALIFIED

5. A person who is on bail in criminal proceedings (within the meaning of the Bail Act 1976).

6. A person who has at any time been sentenced in the United Kingdom, the Channel Islands or the Isle of Man—

(a) to imprisonment for life, detention for life or custody for life,

(b) to detention during her Majesty's pleasure or during the pleasure of the Secretary of State,

(c) to imprisonment for public protection or detention for public protection,

(d) to an extended sentence under section 227 or 228 of the Criminal Justice Act 2003 or section 210A of the Criminal Procedure (Scotland) Act 1995, or

(e) to a term of imprisonment of five years or more or a term of detention of five years or more.

7. A person who at any time in the last ten years has—

(a) in the United Kingdom, the Channel Islands or the Isle of Man—
 (i) served any part of a sentence of imprisonment or a sentence of detention, or
 (ii) had passed on him a suspended sentence of imprisonment or had made in respect of him a suspended order for detention,
(b) in England and Wales, had made in respect of him a community order under section 177 of the Criminal Justice Act 2003, a community rehabilitation order, a community punishment order, a community punishment and rehabilitation order, a drug treatment and testing order or a drug abstinence order, or
(c) had made in respect of him any corresponding order under the law of Scotland, Northern Ireland, the Isle of Man or any of the Channel Islands.

8. For the purposes of this Part of this Schedule—
(a) a sentence passed by a court-martial is to be treated as having been passed in the United Kingdom, and
(b) a person is sentenced to a term of detention if, but only if—
 (i) a court passes on him, or makes in respect of him on conviction, any sentence or order which requires him to be detained in custody for any period, and
 (ii) the sentence or order is available only in respect of offenders below a certain age,

and any reference to serving a sentence of detention is to be construed accordingly.

EXCUSAL FROM JURY SERVICE

Excusal as of Right

Certain narrowly defined groups are entitled to be excused from jury service even though they are eligible to serve and have been duly summoned to attend for service under the Juries Act 1974, s. 2. **D13.4**

There are two main categories:

(a) Section 8 of the Juries Act 1974 deals with those excusable by virtue of having served in the recent past.
(b) Section 9(2A) sets out the position with regard to full-time serving members of the armed forces. The Crown Court officer should (within certain limits set out in s. 9A(2A) and (2B)) excuse such members if their commanding officer certifies that their absence would be prejudicial to the efficiency of the service.

If a member of an excusable group is summoned, the onus is on him to apply for excusal and satisfy an appropriate officer of the Crown Court that he does indeed belong to the group in question. Should he not ask to be excused, he (like anybody else who has been summoned) commits an offence by not attending for service. There is also provision for the court itself to excuse the juror without the application first going through an officer (see ss. 8(1) and 9(4)).

In addition, s. 9(3) provides that rules shall enable a juror refused excusal by an officer to appeal to the court against the refusal. Rule 39.2 of the CrimPR requires the juror to give written notice of appeal to the appropriate officer, specifying the matters on which he relies as grounds for excusal. The juror must also be given an opportunity to make representations to the court. The appeal would normally be determined in chambers (see CrimPR, r. 16.11(c)).

Juries Act 1974, ss. 8 and 9

8.—(1) If a person summoned under this Act shows to the satisfaction of the appropriate officer, or of the court (or any of the courts) to which he is summoned—
(a) that he has served on a jury, or duly attended to serve on a jury, in the prescribed period ending with the service of the summons on him, or
(b) that the Crown Court or any other court has excused him from jury service for a period which has not terminated, the officer or court shall excuse him from attending, or further attending, in pursuance of the summons.

(2) In subsection (1) above 'the prescribed period' means two years or such longer period as the Lord Chancellor may prescribe . . .

9.—(1) [Repealed]

(2) If any person summoned under this Act shows to the satisfaction of the appropriate officer that there is good reason why he should be excused from attending in pursuance of the summons, the appropriate officer may, subject to section 9A(1A) of this Act, excuse him from so attending.

(2A) Without prejudice to subsection (2) above, the appropriate officer shall excuse a full-time serving member of Her Majesty's naval, military or air forces from attending in pursuance of a summons if—

(a) that member's commanding officer certifies to the appropriate officer that it would be prejudicial to the efficiency of the service if that member were to be required to be absent from duty, and

(b) subsection (2A) or (2B) of section 9A of this Act applies.

(2B) Subsection (2A) above does not affect the application of subsection (2) above to a full-time serving member of Her Majesty's naval, military or air forces in a case where he is not entitled to be excused under subsection (2A).

(3) Criminal Procedure Rules shall provide a right of appeal to the court (or one of the courts) before which the person is summoned to attend against any refusal of the appropriate officer to excuse him under subsection (2) above or any failure by the appropriate officer to excuse him as required by subsection (2A) above.

(4) Without prejudice to the preceding provisions of this section, the court (or any of the courts) before which a person is summoned to attend under this Act may excuse that person from so attending.

Discretionary Excusal

D13.5 Section 9(2) of the Juries Act 1974 permits a juror discretionary excusal wherever he can show to the satisfaction of the appropriate officer that 'there is good reason why he should be excused from attending'. There is again a right of appeal against the appropriate officer's refusal to excuse. Excusal is dealt with in the *Consolidated Criminal Practice Direction*, paras. IV.42.1 to IV.42.3 (see **appendix** 7).

D13.6 **The Proper Approach to a Discretionary Excusal** Both the proper procedures for determining applications for discretionary excusal, and the extent to which a religious objection to serving on a jury may be a sufficient ground for excusal, were considered by Watkins LJ in the course of his judgment in *Guildford Crown Court, ex parte Siderfin* [1990] 2 QB 683. The case concerned a member of the Plymouth Brethren (a Christian denomination) who took the view that serving on a jury would be contrary to her religious beliefs.

On the broad question of whether and, if so, in what circumstances conscientious and/or religious objection to serving on a jury should entitle a juror to be excused, Watkins LJ stated that the ultimate question for the court is whether the applicant has established a good reason for excusal. A conscientious objection arising out of religious belief is unlikely *on its own* to amount to a good reason, since it will not outweigh the necessity to insist on the observance of the public duty or obligation to perform jury service. 'Adherence to some kind of religious belief cannot be regarded as an unchallengeable right to excusal from jury service' (p. 159F). But, where the applicant's belief would stand in the way of her fulfilling her duty as a juror 'properly, responsibly and honestly', then she should be excused.

As to procedure, Watkins LJ held that the judge at first instance had further erred in refusing an adjournment to enable the juror to be legally represented at the hearing of her appeal. Although there is no right to be represented, the judge hearing the appeal has a discretion to allow it and, in the instant case, there was no reason why an adjournment should not have been allowed for solicitors to be instructed (see p. 158G–H). His lordship also held that any application for excusal from jury service must first be independently considered by an appropriate officer; it is unacceptable for certain types of application to be automatically transferred to a judge.

SUMMONING FOR JURY SERVICE

The procedure for summoning jurors is governed by s. 2 of the Juries Act 1974. Responsibility for summoning jurors for service rests with the Lord Chancellor (s. 2(1)). In making arrangements for the discharge of that duty, the Lord Chancellor is to have regard to the convenience of the persons summoned and the desirability of selecting jurors who live within reasonable daily travelling distance of the Crown Court location they are summoned to attend (s. 2(2)). Subject to that, a person may be required to attend for service anywhere in England and Wales (s. 2(3)). The summons may be served by ordinary post (s. 2(4)). **D13.7**

The Basis for Selection

To enable the Lord Chancellor to perform his duties in relation to the summoning of jurors, he must be provided with as many copies of published electoral registers as he requires (Juries Act 1974, s. 3). The copies must indicate those persons on the register who are either under 18 or over 70 (i.e. ineligible for jury service by reason of age). The choice of those to be summoned is made on a random basis from amongst those who are (a) on the register and (b) of an eligible age. **D13.8**

It follows that a summons may be sent to a person who is ineligible on a ground other than age or who is disqualified by reason of previous convictions. Therefore, s. 2(5) provides that the summons for service shall be accompanied by a notice informing the person summoned of the categories of persons who may not sit on a jury and the possibility of being prosecuted for serving when ineligible or disqualified. The notice must also inform him of his right to apply for excusal from or deferral of jury service.

Panels of those Summoned

As well as summoning jurors, the Lord Chancellor is required to prepare panels (i.e. lists) of those persons who have been summoned (Juries Act 1974, s. 5(1)). The arrangement of and the information contained in the panels is a matter for his discretion (ibid.). At present the only information given is the names and addresses of those summoned and the dates and place of attendance. Parties to a case which will or may be tried by jury are entitled to reasonable facilities for inspecting the panel from which their jurors will be drawn (s. 5(2)). The right must be exercised before the close of the trial (s. 5(3)). **D13.9**

Praying a Tales

In the unlikely event of it appearing to the court that there will be insufficient jurors on the panel to form a complete jury to try an issue, the court may require any persons who are in the vicinity to be summoned without written notice for service (Juries Act 1974, s. 6(1)). This practice is known as '*praying a tales*'. The names of persons so summoned are added to the panel, and the court then proceeds as if they had been on the panel in the first instance (s. 6(2)). It would seem from the wording of s. 6 that the jury must always include at least one person who was on the original panel, since the section refers to 'making up' a full jury by means of additional panellists. Such an interpretation is consistent with the decision in *Solomon* [1958] 1 QB 203 (jury consisting of jurors not on the original panel was held to be no jury at all). **D13.10**

The Obligation Imposed by the Summons

Unless the person summoned has been excused from jury service under the provisions described above, he commits an offence if he either fails to attend on a day covered by the summons, or, having attended, is then either not available when called on to serve or is unfit by reason of drink or drugs (Juries Act 1974, s. 20(1)). The offence is punishable either on **D13.11** summary conviction or as if it were a criminal contempt committed in the face of the court, i.e. the Crown Court judge may and normally would determine whether an offence has been committed rather than causing a summary prosecution to be brought (s. 20(2)). The offence is punishable with a fine of up to £1,000 (ibid.). If the juror can show reasonable cause for his failure to attend etc. he is not liable to any penalty (s. 20(4)).

Juries Act 1974, ss. 2, 5 and 6

2.—(1) Subject to the provisions of this Act, the Lord Chancellor shall be responsible for the summoning of jurors to attend for service in the Crown Court, the High Court and county courts and for determining the occasions on which they are to attend when so summoned, and the number to be summoned.

(2) In making arrangements to discharge his duty under subsection (1) above the Lord Chancellor shall have regard to the convenience of the persons summoned and to their respective places of residence, and in particular to the desirability of selecting jurors within reasonable daily travelling distance of the place where they are to attend.

(3) Subject to subsection (2) above, there shall be no restriction on the places in England and Wales at which a person may be required to attend or serve on a jury under this Act.

[(4) Summons can be served either by post or by hand.]

(5) A written summons sent or delivered to any person under subsection (4) above shall be accompanied by a notice informing him—

(a) of the effect of sections 1 [eligibility for jury service], 9(1) [excusal from jury service], 10 [reference of juror to judge with a view to discharge] and 20(5) [penalties for serving on a jury when disqualified etc.] of this Act; and

(b) that he may make representations to the appropriate officer with a view to obtaining the withdrawal of the summons, if for any reason he is not qualified for jury service, or wishes or is entitled to be excused;

and where a person is summoned under subsection (4) above . . . the appropriate officer may at any time put or cause to be put to him such questions as the officer thinks fit in order to establish whether or not the person is qualified for jury service.

[(6) Proof of service by post may be given by certificate.]

5.—(1) The arrangements to be made by the Lord Chancellor under this Act shall include the preparation of lists (called panels) of persons summoned as jurors, and the information to be included in panels, the court sittings for which they are prepared, their divisions into parts or sets, . . . their enlargement or amendment, and all other matters relating to the contents and form of the panels shall be such as the Lord Chancellor may from time to time direct.

(2) A party to proceedings in which jurors are or may be called on to try an issue, and any person acting on behalf of a party to such proceedings, shall be entitled to reasonable facilities for inspecting the panel from which the jurors are or will be drawn.

(3) The right conferred by subsection (2) above shall not be exercisable after the close of the trial by jury (or after the time when it is no longer possible for there to be a trial by jury).

(4) The court may, if it thinks fit, at any time afford to any person facilities for inspecting the panel, although not given the right by subsection (2) above.

6.—(1) If it appears to the court that a jury to try any issue before the court will be, or probably will be, incomplete, the court may, if the court thinks fit, require any persons who are in, or in the vicinity of, the court, to be summoned (without any written notice) for jury service up to the number needed (after allowing for any who may not be qualified under section 1 of this Act, and for excusals and challenges) to make up a full jury.

(2) The names of the persons so summoned shall be added to the panel and the court shall proceed as if those summoned had been included in the panel in the first instance.

Deferral of Jury Service

D13.12 A power to defer attendance for jury service is contained in the Juries Act 1974, s. 9A, which provides that, if a juror who has been summoned shows to the satisfaction of the appropriate officer that there is good reason why his attendance should be deferred, the officer shall vary the summons accordingly (s. 9A(1)). Obvious reasons for deferral are if the dates in the summons clash with the juror's holiday arrangements or business commitments. Attendance may be deferred only once in respect of one summons (s. 9A(2A)).

An application for deferral may be made direct to the court (s. 9A(4)), and, in any event, there is a right of appeal against the appropriate officer's refusal to defer (s. 9A(3) and CrimPR, r. 39.2).

Reference to the Judge for Discharge of a Summons

Should it appear to the appropriate officer of the court that a person attending for jury service in pursuance of a summons may be unable to act effectively as a juror on account of 'physical disability or insufficient understanding of English', that person may be brought before a judge who 'shall determine whether or not he should act as a juror and, if not, shall discharge the summons' (Juries Act 1974, s. 10). **D13.13**

Furthermore, by s. 2(5), an officer may 'at any time put or cause to be put to [a person summoned for jury service] such questions as the officer thinks fit in order to establish whether or not the person is qualified for jury service'. Knowingly or recklessly to give false answers to such questions is a summary offence punishable with a fine of up to £1,000.

The Procedure The procedure in relation to those who may be unable to act as jurors because of physical disability is governed by the Juries Act 1974, s. 9B. This states that the judge 'shall affirm the summons unless he is of the opinion that the person will not, on account of his disability, be capable of acting effectively as a juror, in which case he shall discharge the summons'. **D13.14**

In *Re Osman* [1996] 1 Cr App R 126, the Recorder of London, Sir Lawrence Verney, held at first instance that a person summoned to be a juror who was profoundly deaf should be discharged from jury service pursuant to s. 9B. The prospective juror could not follow the proceedings in court or the deliberations in the jury room without the assistance of an interpreter in sign language, and it would be an incurable irregularity in the proceedings for the interpreter to retire with the jury when they considered their verdict.

SELECTION OF JURY FOR A PARTICULAR CASE

Once a jury panel has been selected by the process described above, the next stage is to select a jury for a particular case, pursuant to s 11 of the Juries Act 1974. Normally, a jury will be called to try the issue of the accused's guilt or innocence. However, they might alternatively be asked to determine whether an accused whom the court has found to be unfit to plead did the act alleged, or to try the issues mute by visitation of God or of malice (for which see D12.17 and D12.18). **D13.15**

Ballot in Open Court

Juries Act 1974, s. 11 **D13.16**

(1) The jury to try an issue before a court shall be selected by ballot in open court from the panel, or part of the panel, of jurors summoned to attend at the place and time in question.

The 'ballot in open court' is conventionally conducted by the clerk of the court. Part of the jury panel which is sufficient to provide a full jury of 12, allowing for the possibility that some may be successfully challenged, is brought into the back of the court by an usher. These jurors are usually referred to as the 'jury in waiting'. The clerk is given the juror cards for each of the jurors in waiting (i.e. a card on which is printed the juror's name and address). He selects at random 12 of the cards, and reads out the names on them, inviting the jurors in waiting to step into the jury-box should their names be called (see *Salt* [1996] Crim LR 517 and *Tarrant* [1998] Crim LR 342, on the need for selection to be random so far as practicable).

Once 12 jurors are in the box, the clerk informs the accused of his right to challenge jurors. He then reads out the names again, pausing after each name so that the juror may take the juror's oath (or affirm). The form of oath is: 'I swear by almighty God that I will faithfully try the defendant[s] and give [a] true verdict[s] according to the evidence' (see the *Consolidated Criminal Practice Direction*, para. IV.42.4, set out at **appendix** 7, which also states that a solemn affirmation shall be permitted if the juror objects to being sworn. Each juror must take the oath or affirm separately (s. 11(3)).

D13.17 **Anonymity of Jurors** In *Comerford* [1998] 1 WLR 191, the Court of Appeal considered the decision of the trial judge that jurors should be identified, by number not by name, in order to reduce the risk that the jury might be 'nobbled'. Their lordships took the view that, as there was no mandatory requirement that names should be called, such a departure from the normal procedure did not render the trial a nullity, unless it made the proceedings unfair to the appellant. It was made clear, however, that the appellant could have exercised his right to ascertain the names of all the jurors forming the panel if he had so desired and it was said that it is 'highly desirable that in normal circumstances the usual procedure for empanelling a jury should be followed'.

D13.18 **Warnings to the Jury on Empanelment** In the light of the decision of the House of Lords in *Mirza* [2004] 1 AC 1118 (see **D13.46**), the Court of Appeal issued *Practice Direction (Crown Court: Guidance to Jurors)* [2004] 1 WLR 665, which requires that the judge warn the jury that they should alert him to any concerns about the behaviour of fellow jurors at the time, rather than waiting until the conclusion of the case. That Practice Direction is consolidated in the *Consolidated Criminal Practice Direction* at para. IV.42 (see **appendix** 7).

In addition, as was recently restated in *Marshall* [2007] EWCA Crim 35, at the outset of the trial the judge should warn the jury: (a) that they must try the case on the evidence that they hear in court and on nothing else; (b) that they must not discuss the case with others outside court, such as members of their family; and (c) that they should not conduct their own private research, e.g., using the internet.

CHALLENGING JURORS

D13.19 It is fundamental to the jury process that the jurors who try an accused are selected at random. That said, however, it is recognised that there will be circumstances in which the interests of justice require some intervention in that random selection process. The methods of replacing one or more of the prospective jurors called into the box as a result of the clerk's ballot with others from the jury in waiting are:

(a) for either the prosecution or defence to challenge for cause;
(b) for the prosecution to ask a juror to stand by;
(c) for the judge to exercise his discretionary power to remove a juror.

Challenges for Cause

D13.20 A challenge for cause may be made by either the prosecution or defence. It is either a challenge to the whole panel of jurors, known as a challenge 'to the array', or to an individual juror, known as a challenge 'to the polls'.

D13.21 **Challenges to the Array** At common law either party could challenge the whole panel summoned for their case on the ground that the person responsible for the summoning acted improperly or was biased. This right is preserved by the Juries Act 1974, s. 12(6).

Juries Act 1974, s. 12

(6) Without prejudice to subsection (4) above [right to challenge individual jurors], the right of challenge to the array, that is to say the right of challenge on the ground that the person responsible for summoning the jurors in question is biased or has acted improperly, shall continue to be unaffected by the fact that, since the coming into operation of section 31 of

> the Courts Act 1971 (which is replaced by this Act), the responsibility for summoning jurors for service in the Crown Court . . . has lain with the Lord Chancellor.

Nineteenth-century cases indicate that the array was open to challenge when the sheriff responsible for summoning the jury had an apparent interest in the outcome of the trial. More recently, such a challenge is more likely to relate to the racial or religious composition of the jury.

Specific malfeasance in the summoning was also a ground of challenge, as when jurors were summoned at the express request of prosecution or defence, or had been selected on grounds of their religion (see, e.g., *O'Doherty* (1848) 6 St Tr NS 831).

Racial or Religious Composition of the Jury In the absence of evidence of bias or improper conduct by the person responsible for summoning, the jury panel's being imbalanced racially or not reflecting the overall racial or religious composition of the catchment area from which jurors are summoned is *not* sufficient ground for challenge. For example, *Danvers* [1982] Crim LR 680 and *Broderick* [1970] Crim LR 155, which were both approved by the Court of Appeal in *Ford* [1989] QB 868. There is a more detailed analysis of this issue at **D13.35**. The principle of these decisions will apply equally to other apparent imbalances in the jury panel (e.g., as to the proportion of men to women). **D13.22**

The lack of modern authority on challenges to the array indicates that the vesting of responsibility for the summoning of jurors in the Lord Chancellor (i.e. in Crown Court officers) has made even more remote the possibility of challenges to the array being resorted to in practice.

Challenges to the Polls

Juries Act 1974, s. 12 **D13.23**

> (4) The fact that a person summoned to serve on a jury is not qualified to serve shall be a ground of challenge for cause; but subject to that, and to the foregoing provisions of this section, nothing in this Act affects the law relating to challenge of jurors.

Thus, jurors who are too old or too young to be on a jury, or who have not been resident in the UK for a five-year period since attaining the age of 13, or who are not on the electoral roll, or who are disqualified by convictions may all be successfully challenged for cause (see **D13.3**).

In the absence of any challenge from the parties, a juror may in effect challenge himself by stating, if it be the case, that he is not qualified (*Cook* (1696) 13 St Tr 311). The summons sent to each juror is accompanied by a notice which sets out the ineligible and disqualified groups and warns him of his duty to inform the court if he comes within any of them.

Police Officers and Others as Jurors In *Abdroikov* [2005] 1 WLR 3538, the Court of Appeal held that the presence on a jury of a police officer, or a prosecuting solicitor, did not offend against the requirement for a fair trial. When such persons became jurors, they did not do so by reason of their occupation. They could be expected to comply with the terms of their oath and the directions of the judge. A fair-minded observer would not conclude that there was a real possibility that a juror was biased because he was involved in the administration of justice. The position would, however, be different if the juror had special knowledge either of the individuals involved or the facts of the case. **D13.24**

Fear of Bias At common law a qualified juror could be challenged *propter affectum*, i.e. on the ground of some presumed or actual bias which would make him unsuitable to try the case. This ground of challenge is preserved by the last clause of s. 12(4). Most authorities on challenges to the polls *propter affectum* are old, and reflect the very different social and legal conditions of their time. The broad thrust of the decisions is that a juror is challengeable if he has expressed hostility to one side or the other (*O'Coigley* (1798) 26 St Tr 1191), has expressed a wish as to the outcome of the case, is related to a party, or has some other connection with a party (e.g., was his servant or agent). **D13.25**

One modern decision of substantial relevance is *Kray* (1969) 53 Cr App R 412. In that case, the defence wished to object to any jurors who had read newspaper articles published immediately after two of the accused before the court charged with murder had been convicted at an earlier trial for murder. The articles complained of had not only reported the earlier verdict and commented on the evidence, but had also 'set out a number of facts which were not in evidence at the trial and which were discreditable of those to whom they referred'. Lawton J, having criticised the newspapers for publishing these additional facts, then said (at p. 415 emphasis added):

> This does, in my judgment, lead to a prima facie presumption that anybody who may have read that kind of information might find it difficult to reach a verdict in a fair-minded way. It is, however, a matter of human experience . . . first, that the public's recollection is short, and, secondly, that the drama . . . of a trial almost always has the effect of excluding from recollection that which went before. A person summoned for this case would not . . . disqualify himself merely because he had read any of the newspapers containing allegations of the kind I have referred to; but the position would be different if, as a result of reading what he had, *his mind had become so clogged with prejudice that he was unable to try the case impartially.*

Insofar as a general principle may be extracted from the above passage, it seems to be that a juror may be challenged for cause if his mind is so prejudiced that he is unable to try the case impartially, but merely having once been informed of matters discreditable to the accused will not necessarily occasion such prejudice.

Procedure for Challenging for Cause

D13.26 The Juries Act 1974, s. 12(1)(b), provides that 'any challenge for cause shall be tried by the judge before whom [the accused] is to be tried'.

D13.27 **Timing** The challenge must be entered after the juror's name has been drawn by ballot and before he is sworn (s. 12(3)). Conventionally, a challenge is indicated simply by counsel for the challenging party saying the word 'Challenge' as the juror is about to take the oath. Should the challenge not be made until after the juror has begun to take the oath the judge has a discretion to allow it but is not obliged to do so (*Harrington* (1976) 64 Cr App R 1).

It is clear from *Morris* (1991) 93 Cr App R 102, that the right to challenge for cause is limited to the time when the jury is sworn, and cannot be exercised during the course of the trial. M was accused of stealing from a Marks and Spencer store. After the store detective had given evidence, one of the jurors said that she was a personnel assistant with a different branch of the company. The judge refused to discharge the juror saying that the right way to deal with the matter was by a challenge for cause. The Court of Appeal, allowing the appeal, held that by the time the facts about the juror had emerged, it was too late for the defence to challenge for cause.

D13.28 **Process** The burden of proof is on the challenging party, and the judge may order that the hearing be *in camera* or in chambers (CJA 1988, s. 118(2)). If the challenge is of any substance, it will be proper for it to be heard in the absence of the other jurors. The challenged juror should be kept outside the court except insofar as it is necessary to question him. The remaining jurors should leave the court, retiring to the jury room in the charge of the jury bailiff if they have already been sworn. A shorthand note of proceedings should in any event be taken, and the court's decision should be entered on the court record. The judge can hear evidence and question the juror concerned. Counsel may be allowed to ask questions directed to the ground on which the juror is challenged.

After hearing the evidence and any submissions, the judge will decide whether to allow the challenge. If he does so, the juror is discharged and a fresh juror called to replace him. If the challenge is rejected, the judge should tell the juror not to disclose any of the matters dealt with during the challenge to other jurors, and not to allow the fact that the challenge was made to influence him.

Need for Prima Facie Evidence The main difficulty in challenging for cause is that, having indicated a challenge, the challenging party must provide prima facie evidence of his grounds. *After* he has done so, the juror may be asked questions on the *voir dire* to determine whether the challenge is well founded. This is in marked contrast to the practice frequently employed in the USA of parading the jury panel before the challenging party so that he may ask preliminary questions with a view to establishing a prima facie ground of challenge. **D13.29**

The initial requirement of prima facie evidence from the challenger was stated in, e.g., *Dowling* (1848) 7 St Tr NS 382, and was confirmed by Lord Parker CJ in *Chandler (No. 2)* [1964] 2 QB 322, in which his lordship said (at p. 338):

> . . . before any right to cross-examine the juror arose, the defendant would have had to lay a foundation of fact in support of his ground of challenge. It is no good his saying, 'I think this man is antagonistic'. . . . There must be a foundation of fact creating a prima facie case before the juror can be cross-examined.

Similarly, in *Broderick* [1970] Crim LR 155, where defence counsel unsuccessfully sought to cross-examine each member of the panel to determine whether he or she might be biased against B on racial grounds, the Court of Appeal held that it had never been the practice to allow potential jurors to be paraded for cross-examination in a fishing expedition, seeking possible grounds on which a challenge might subsequently be made.

Very occasionally, however, there is a departure from the normal practice. Thus, in *Kray* (1969) 53 Cr App R 412 (see **D13.25**), defence counsel was permitted to examine each juror who came into the box to be sworn on whether he had read certain newspaper articles discreditable to the accused. The only initial evidence of bias adduced was the production of the offending articles. Although Lawton J stated that that evidence was in itself sufficient to raise a prima facie ground of challenge, in reality, the case of *Kray* was simply one in which, because of a wholly exceptional combination of circumstances, the court departed from the usual practice of preventing the preliminary questioning of jurors.

Standing Jurors By

The Right This is a right possessed by the prosecution but not the defence (see *Chandler (No. 2)* [1964] 2 QB 322 at p. 337, where Lord Parker CJ held that the accused, having exhausted the seven peremptory challenges to which he was then entitled, might challenge subsequent jurors for cause but could not require them to stand by, although 'in an exceptional case the judge [could] in his discretion stand by a juror or allow the defendant to do so'). **D13.30**

Standing a juror by differs from challenging him for cause in that counsel need not give a reason for the stand-by. It differs from the peremptory challenges formerly available to the defence in that the juror is not conclusively removed from the jury but will be recalled to the jury-box should the entire jury panel be exhausted without a full jury being obtained, at which stage the prosecution must either accept him or show cause why he should not serve.

In the leading case of *Mason* [1981] QB 881, Lawton LJ, giving the Court of Appeal's judgment, summarised the position thus (at pp. 890H–891A):

> In our judgment, *Mansell* v *The Queen* (1857) 8 E & B 54 established beyond argument that prosecuting counsel have a right to request that a member of the jury panel shall stand by, and that this right can be exercised without there being a provable valid objection, until such time as the panel is exhausted; and when it is, if the Crown still wants to exclude a member of the jury from the panel, a valid objection must be shown.

Lawton LJ added the rider that he expected that prosecuting counsel would act responsibly and would not request a stand-by unnecessarily (p. 891c).

D13.31 **Guidance as to the Use of the Right** Since *Mason* [1981] QB 881 was decided, the defence right of peremptory challenge, which was perceived as a counterbalance to the prosecution right of stand-by, has been abolished. The A-G's guidelines on the exercise by the Crown of its right of stand-by (see **appendix 3**) affirm the general principles that:

(a) members of a jury should be selected at random from the panel subject to any rule of law as to right of challenge by the defence; and
(b) the Juries Act 1974 as amended identifies those classes of persons who *alone* are disqualified from or ineligible for service on a jury, and no other class of person may be so treated (para. 2).

Responsibility for ensuring that an individual does not serve on a jury if he is not competent to discharge his duties properly rests, first, with the appropriate court officer and, ultimately, with the trial judge. In the context of that legislative background, para. 5 of the guidelines defines the two situations in which it is appropriate for prosecuting counsel to use his right of stand-by as follows:

> (a) where a jury check authorised in accordance with the Attorney-General's guidelines on jury checks [see **D13.41** and **appendix 3**] reveals information justifying exercise of the right to stand by in accordance with para. 9 of the guidelines and the Attorney-General personally authorises the exercise of the right to stand by; or
>
> (b) where a person is about to be sworn as a juror who is manifestly unsuitable and the defence agree that, accordingly, the exercise by the prosecution of the right to stand by would be appropriate. An example of the sort of *exceptional* circumstances which might justify stand-by is where it becomes apparent that . . . a juror selected for service to try a complex case is in fact illiterate.

On the assumption that the guidelines are loyally followed, the importance of the right of stand-by has been vastly reduced. Counsel will exercise the right only in (a) the tiny minority of cases which involve national security or terrorism (para. 5(a)), or (b) 'ordinary' cases where a juror is obviously unsuitable *and the defence agree* (para. 5(b)). Thus, the chief function of the right now seems to be to avoid the clumsy mechanics of a challenge for cause where the parties concur that a juror should not serve.

In addition to the example given in para. 5(b) itself, subject to defence consent, jurors could properly be stood by if, e.g., counsel has been informed that they are in fact disqualified by previous convictions, or if they know the accused or any witnesses in the case. The guidelines are presumably not meant to inhibit prosecuting counsel from challenging for cause on grounds of bias if he considers that a juror's previous convictions or other involvement with the police might make him so prejudiced against the Crown as to be unable to try the case fairly. Whether such a challenge would succeed is open to question.

The Court's Power to Exclude Juror

D13.32 Even in the absence of a formal challenge from either party, the trial judge has a residual discretion to exclude from the jury a juror selected by the initial ballot. Existence of the discretion can be traced back to Lord Campbell CJ's judgment in *Mansell v The Queen* (1857) 8 E & B 54, and has since been confirmed by Lord Parker CJ (see *Chandler (No. 2)* [1964] 2 QB 322 at p. 327), by Lawton LJ (see *Mason* [1981] QB 881 at p. 887G–H) and, most recently, by Lord Lane CJ in *Ford* [1989] QB 868.

D13.33 **Reasons for Exclusion** The discretion may and should be exercised where an individual juror is obviously incompetent to act but, for whatever reason, counsel do not challenge or exercise the right of stand-by. It is then the court's duty to prevent the 'scandal and perversion of justice which would arise from compelling or permitting such a juryman to be sworn' (per Lord Campbell CJ in *Mansell v The Queen* (1857) 8 E & B 54, who then gave as specific examples for the judge's intervention cases where the juror was mentally or physically infirm, or insane or drunk, or preoccupied with the dangerous illness of a relative).

Lawton LJ in *Mason* [1981] QB 881, succinctly described modern practice by saying (at p. 887G–H):

> ... trial judges, as an aspect of their duty to see that there is a fair trial, have had a right to intervene to ensure that a competent jury is empanelled. The most common form of judicial intervention is when a judge notices that a member of the panel is infirm or has difficulty in reading or hearing; and nowadays jurors for whom taking part in a long trial would be unusually burdensome are often excluded from the jury by the judge.

Limitations However, judicial intervention should not be extended beyond the kinds of situation mentioned above. The judge must not intervene in a systematic way so as to undermine the random nature of jury selection or influence the overall composition of the jury (per Lord Lane CJ in *Ford* [1989] QB 868). In particular, he has no power to discharge jurors on account of their religion, race or ethnic group in hopes that eventually a more diverse jury will be obtained. Lord Lane said (at p. 872A) that the discretion to exclude a juror 'is to be exercised to prevent individual jurors who are not competent from serving. It has never been held to include a discretion to discharge a competent juror or jurors in an attempt to secure a jury drawn from particular sections of the community, or otherwise to influence the overall composition of the jury.' (See also the discussion of racially balanced juries at D13.35.) **D13.34**

Racial or Religious Balance of Jury

From time to time judicial intervention has been sought to ensure that at least some members of the jury come from the same ethnic group as the accused. Although thus far, examples from the case law have all referred to the racial composition of the jury, there is no basis for them not having equal application to attempts to affect the religious composition of the jury. They include: **D13.35**

(a) *Binns* [1982] Crim LR 522 (trial of West Indian accused of public order offences committed during racial riot in Bristol);
(b) *Bansal* [1985] Crim LR 151 (trial of Asians for offences of violence committed when protesting against a National Front march);
(c) *McCalla* [1986] Crim LR 335 (black accused alleging that his admissions to robbery were extracted from him by racially prejudiced white police officers);
(d) *Danvers* [1982] Crim LR 680 (West Indian accused at Nottingham Crown Court objected to the jury panel because it was entirely white and he was anxious that there should be a substantial representation of black people on the jury; challenge failed, even though the black population in Nottingham apparently represented about 10 per cent of the total);
(e) *Broderick* [1970] Crim LR 155 (black accused simply wished to be tried by an all-black jury).

The precise form of judicial aid sought has varied from case to case. In *Binns*, counsel asked the judge to exercise his right to stand jurors by until a jury representing 'the corporate good sense of the community' had been obtained; in *Bansal* the application was to move the venue of trial to a racially mixed area, while in *Broderick* the defence wished to have the jury panel paraded and asked 'fishing' questions about their possible racial prejudice.

Judicial response to the applications has been equally varied. The judges in *Binns* and *Bansal* were basically sympathetic to the defence request (although in doubt about how far they could go in ordering a certain racial mix on the jury or jury panel). By contrast, Judge Mander

D

Part D Procedure

in *McCalla* ruled that he had no power to order that a jury be racially balanced and, even if he had such power, he would not have chosen to exercise it because a jury should be selected at random subject only to the law on disqualified jurors and challenges for cause. Moreover, to allow interference with jury selection on racial grounds would open the way to further manipulation, e.g., on grounds of political view, sex, or religion, or for some similar reason.

D13.36 **Guidelines for Approaching the Issue** It is the latter view which has found favour with the Court of Appeal. In *Ford* [1989] QB 868, F appealed against his convictions on the ground that the trial judge had refused an application for a racially balanced jury. The main points established by Lord Lane CJ's judgment are as follows:

(a) A challenge to the array of jurors summoned must be on the ground of bias or other irregularity on the part of the summoning officer. Therefore, the fact that the jury panel contains few if any jurors of the same racial group as the accused cannot of itself found a challenge or justify the judge in discharging the panel and ordering the summoning of a new one (see *Danvers* [1982] Crim LR 680 and **D13.22**).
(b) Summoning of jurors is the responsibility of the Lord Chancellor. It is not the judge's function to alter the composition of the jury panel or give directions about the area from which it should be drawn. Woolf J's direction in *Bansal* [1985] Crim LR 151, to the effect that the panel should be drawn from a part of the court's catchment area in which a high proportion of Asians lived, was made without benefit of full argument and was wrong.
(c) Nor should the judge consider a complaint that the jury panel is not truly random because it contains a lower proportion of persons of a certain race or ethnic group than live in the court's catchment area for jurors, unless, of course, the disproportion can be attributed to bias or impropriety on the part of the summoning officer. If the disproportion may be due to maladministration in the procedures for summoning jurors, that must be corrected by *administrative*, not judicial intervention.
(d) The mere fact that a juror is of a particular race or holds a particular religious belief cannot found a challenge for cause by a party on the ground of bias.
(e) The judge may not use his power to stand by or discharge individual jurors selected in the ballot from the jury panel for the purpose of securing a jury of a certain racial mix. To do so would conflict with the principle of random jury selection. In effect, the judge would be altering the composition of the jury panel by his own fiat when no irregularity on the part of the summoning officer had been shown and upholding a challenge when there was no ground in law for it. The judge's intervention should be restricted to the exceptional circumstances indicated in *Mansell v The Queen* (1857) 8 E & B 54 (see **D13.33**). Insofar as the judge in *Binns* [1982] Crim LR 522, had been prepared to stand jurors by until a balanced jury had been obtained, he was in error.
(f) In short, there is not (as had been suggested in *Frazer* [1987] Crim LR 418 and *Bansal*) any principle that a jury should be racially balanced, and it is impermissible for the judge to use his residual discretionary powers over the composition of the jury as a device for obtaining such a balance.

In *Smith* [2003] 1 WLR 2229, the Court of Appeal considered the standing of *Ford* in the light of the HRA 1998 and the ECHR, Article 6. It held that the approach in *Ford* had not been superseded by the HRA 1998. Pill LJ said:

> We do not accept that it was unfair for the appellant to be tried by a randomly selected all white jury or that the fair-minded and informed observer would regard it as unfair. We do not accept that, on the facts of this case, the trial could only be fair if members of the defendant's race were present on the jury. It was not a case where a consideration of the evidence required knowledge of the traditions or social circumstances of a particular racial group.

INVESTIGATION OF THE JURY PANEL

Effective challenging of jurors depends on the amount of information about the jury panel available to the parties. Section 5(2) and (3) of the Juries Act 1974 entitles the parties to inspect the jury panel before or during trial but such inspection will inform them only of the names and addresses of the panel members. It will not of itself yield material capable of founding a challenge for cause. **D13.37**

Proper Enquiries

There would seem to be no objection in theory to a party identifying the panellists summoned to the location of the Crown Court for the time when his case is listed to be heard and then making such inquiries as he sees fit into their employment, background, attitudes etc. on the offchance that grounds for a challenge for cause may emerge. He must, of course, take care not to infringe the general law on privacy or interfere with the jurors in a way which might amount to contempt of court or interference with the course of justice. In practice, the defence do not have the resources to conduct the kind of enquiries mentioned above. **D13.38**

Checks for Previous Convictions

The one inquiry that the prosecution are likely to make is into the criminal records of the panellists. This practice was approved by the Court of Appeal in *Mason* [1981] QB 881. In that case, the police provided prosecution counsel with the results of checks as to whether the panellists summoned had convictions. Counsel stood by certain jurors, some but not all of whom were disqualified by their convictions, without informing defence counsel of the reason. Lawton LJ, giving the judgment of the Court of Appeal, justified the police action as being part of their usual function of preventing crime, it being an offence to serve on a jury when disqualified by convictions (see p. 891D–F). **D13.39**

Further, their lordships could see no reason why the information obtained should not be communicated to prosecuting counsel who could then make such use of it as he considered fit. 'The practice of supplying prosecuting counsel with information about potential jurors' convictions has been followed during the whole of our professional lives. . . . It is not unlawful, and has not until recently been thought to be unsatisfactory' (p. 891G). Prosecuting counsel is under no duty to transmit the information to the defence, although he may do so if he so wishes (p. 891B–D).

Evolution Since *Mason*

The decision in *Mason* that there is no objection to prosecution counsel standing a juror by if he has convictions but they are not such as to disqualify him, has been effectively reversed by the A-G's guidelines on the matter (see below). However, the case remains good authority to justify the practice of 'vetting' jurors by running a preliminary check on their criminal records. **D13.40**

Following the decision in *Mason*, the Association of Chief Police Officers issued recommendations on when the police 'should undertake a check of the names of potential jurors against records of previous convictions'. The recommendations are annexed to the A-G's guidelines on jury checks (see **appendix 3**). They identify three circumstances in which a check may be carried out.

(a) when 'there is reason to believe that attempts are being made to circumvent the statutory provisions excluding disqualified persons from service on a jury, including any case when there is reason to believe that a particular juror may be disqualified';

(b) when it is 'believed that in a previous related abortive trial an attempt was made to interfere with a juror or jurors'; and
(c) when, 'in the opinion of the DPP or the chief constable it is particularly important to ensure that no disqualified person serves on the jury'.

Save when authorised by the A-G's guidelines (see **D13.41**), no further checks on jurors should be carried out. Nor will the police check jurors on behalf of the defence unless requested to do so by the DPP. Should a jury check reveal that a juror, although not disqualified by his criminal record, may be unsuitable to sit as a member of the jury in a particular case, that information will be communicated to prosecuting counsel who will decide what use to make of it (recommendations (2) to (4)).

Jury Vetting

D13.41 In addition to the recommendations of the chief constables, jury vetting by the police or prosecution is controlled by guidelines issued by the A-G (see **appendix 3**). In brief, they affirm that the provisions of the Juries Act 1974 on disqualified and ineligible jurors, combined with majority verdicts (which prevent one perverse juror stopping his colleagues from reaching a verdict) will, in all normal cases, be sufficient to ensure the proper administration of justice without recourse to any investigation of the jury panel going beyond that sanctioned by the Association of Chief Police Officers' recommendations on checking criminal records.

In two classes of case, however, the public interest may demand additional checks (para. 3). Those classes are (a) cases in which national security is involved and part of the evidence is likely to be heard in camera, and (b) terrorist cases (para. 4). In both types of case there is a risk that a juror's political views might be so extreme as to interfere with his fair assessment of the case or lead him to exert improper pressure on his fellow jurors, while in security cases there is the additional risk of the juror either voluntarily or under pressure making improper use of evidence given *in camera* (para. 5).

To ascertain whether a juror might be unsuitable for the above reasons, it may be necessary to investigate the panel by checking the records of Police Special Branches. In security (but not in terrorist) cases the investigation may additionally involve the security services (para. 6). Such checks may be made *only* on the personal authority of the A-G, and are therefore known as 'authorised checks' (para. 7). If a chief officer of police considers that an authorised check is likely to be desirable, he should refer the matter to the DPP, who will make the appropriate application to the A-G (ibid.).

The result of any authorised check will be sent to the DPP, who in turn will decide how much of the information should be passed on to prosecuting counsel (para. 8). In any event, no right of stand-by should be exercised by counsel on the basis of information derived from an authorised check unless he has the personal authority of the A-G and unless the information affords 'strong reason for believing that a particular juror might be a security risk, be susceptible to improper approaches or be influenced in arriving at a verdict for the reasons given [in the guidelines]' (para. 9).

Where a juror is stood by, prosecuting counsel may, in his discretion, disclose to the defence the information on which the stand-by was based, but he is under no duty to do so (para. 10). If an authorised check suggests that a juror might be biased against the accused, the defence should be informed of that in general terms although it may not be possible to give them precise details of the information revealed by the check (para. 11). It will be apparent that authorised checks are a possibility in only a tiny proportion of trials. In the general run of criminal cases, there will either be no check at all on the jury panel or there will be a check only of their criminal records.

COMPOSITION OF THE JURY AS A GROUND OF APPEAL

The Juries Act 1974, s. 18, governs the extent to which the defence may use as a ground of appeal against conviction errors in the way the jury panel was summoned or the particular jury for their case was selected or empanelled. The overall effect is to prevent the verdict being challenged unless the irregularity complained of was raised but not remedied at trial. Moreover, s. 18 prevents lack of qualification or unfitness on the part of an individual juror being a ground of appeal. **D13.42**

Juries Act 1974, s. 18

(1) No judgment after verdict in any trial by jury in any court shall be stayed or reversed by reason—
  (a) that the provisions of this Act about the summoning or empanelling of jurors, or the selection of jurors by ballot, have not been complied with, or
  (b) that a juror was not qualified in accordance with section 1 of this Act, or
  (c) that any juror was misnamed or misdescribed, or
  (d) that any juror was unfit to serve.
(2) Subsection (1)(a) above shall not apply to any irregularity if objection is taken at, or as soon as practicable after, the time it occurs, and the irregularity is not corrected.
(3) Nothing in subsection (1) above shall apply to any objection to a verdict on the ground of personation.

It should be noted that the saving in s. 18(2) applies only to appeals based on contraventions of the Act's provisions as to the summoning or empanelling of jurors or their selection by ballot. If objection to such an irregularity was taken when or as soon as practicable after it occurred and the court did not correct it, it may be relied on as a material irregularity in the course of the trial justifying the quashing of a conviction by virtue of s. 2(1) of the Criminal Appeal Act 1968. Section 18(2) will not assist in a case where the defence did not know of the irregularity in summoning etc. until after conviction, since it will not have been possible to object until a stage at which the Crown Court was *functus officio*.

Unfitness of a Juror

Save in the special case of impersonation of a juror, a juror's having been disqualified from or ineligible for jury service (Juries Act 1974, s. 18(1)(b)) or more generally unfit to serve (s. 18(1)(d)) cannot be a ground of appeal. The statutory provision follows the common law, for example: **D13.43**

(a) *Kelly* [1950] 2 KB 164, in which it was held that the only instances of convictions being quashed on account of a defect in a juror, that defect not having been raised at trial by means of a challenge for cause, were cases in which the juror actually summoned had been impersonated by another;
(b) *Tremearne* (1826) 5 B & C 254, in which the son of the juror called, who was not on the panel and was under age, answered for his father and served. The fact that the defence did not discover the defect in the juror until after conviction (and therefore could not have challenged for cause) is irrelevant to the application of s. 18 (see *Chapman* (1976) 63 Cr App 75 and especially *Pennington* (1985) 81 Cr App R 217).

On a literal reading of s. 18 it is even possible to argue that, where a challenge was made at trial and wrongly rejected, the defence still cannot rely on the error on appeal. However, in such circumstances the proper ground of appeal would in fact be the judge's error of law in ruling against the challenge. Therefore, the appellant would not be caught by s. 18. See also *Tomar* [1997] Crim LR 682.

The broad and somewhat Draconian effect of s. 18 is illustrated by the leading case of *Chapman* (1976) 63 Cr App R 75. After conviction, the defence learnt that one of the jurors who tried the case was deaf and had heard only half the evidence. The defence could not use as their basis of appeal s. 2(1)(c) of the Criminal Appeal Act 1968 (material irregularity in the course of the trial — one of the grounds on which a conviction may normally be quashed) because the express terms of s. 18(1)(d) prevent any unfitness in a juror being used to reverse a verdict, and to argue that a juror was too deaf to hear the evidence with the consequence that there was a material irregularity in the course of the trial is simply to argue that the juror was unfit.

Plainly there had been no wrong decision on a question of law as required by s. 2(1)(b) of the 1968 Act, since the juror (albeit for reasons beyond the defence's control) had never been challenged in the lower court. That left as a possible ground of appeal only the contention that the verdict was unsafe or unsatisfactory (s. 2(1)(a)). On the facts of *Chapman*, their lordships held without difficulty that the verdict was safe. The convictions were unanimous. Therefore, even on the assumption that, had he heard all the evidence, the deaf juror would have been for acquittal, the jury could and no doubt would have convicted by an 11–1 majority.

Moreover, if the juror's incapacity had come to light during the course of the trial, the judge could simply have discharged him from the jury (see **D13.47**), allowing his colleagues to complete the trial and convict. But, even though the argument failed on the facts, the Court of Appeal did indicate, *obiter*, that a juror's unfitness or lack of qualification was in principle a factor capable of rendering a conviction unsafe in conjunction with other circumstances.

Unfitness in General or in Particular

D13.44 It is unclear whether the Juries Act 1974, s. 18(1)(d), prevents a juror's unfitness to serve being used as the ground for reversing a verdict, whether the prohibition is intended to apply only to an argument that the juror was unfit to serve on *any* jury or whether it extends to an argument that, although in general a qualified and competent juror, he was unfit to serve on the jury trying the appellant because of bias arising out of his knowledge of or previous dealings with him.

Whichever is the correct interpretation of s. 18 matters little, since common law, even before the passing of the 1974 Act, had made it virtually impossible to use subsequently discovered bias in a juror as a ground of appeal. For example, in *Box* [1964] 1 QB 430, the foreman of the jury which had convicted the appellants gave evidence before the Court of Appeal that, at the time he served on the jury, he knew the appellants to be ex-burglars and associates of prostitutes. Neither the court nor the parties were aware of the juror's knowledge of the accused when the jury was empanelled; nor did the juror ask to be excused as he plainly should have done.

As to whether the foreman's own evidence justified quashing the conviction, Lord Parker CJ adopted a dictum of Bankes J in *Syme* (1914) 10 Cr App R 284, to the effect that, unless the evidence shows the juror to have been determined *before* trial to come to a certain verdict regardless of the evidence, the court would not interfere. In the instant case, the foreman deposed that, when the trial commenced, he had had no views on the appellant's guilt or innocence but he formed very definite views as the case went along. Such evidence fell far short of that required by Bankes J, and the appeal failed.

Similarly, the foreman's knowledge of the appellant's bad character was not an automatic disqualification from serving on the jury, nor did it mean that he was unable to listen to the evidence and give the accused a fair trial in accordance with his oath. See also *Pennington* (1985) 81 Cr App R 217 and *Bliss* (1986) 84 Cr App R 1.

In practice it will be difficult if not impossible to satisfy the Court of Appeal that a juror was so biased against the accused before the case started that he was determined to convict whatever the evidence might turn out to be.

DISCHARGE OF JURORS OR ENTIRE JURY

The judge has a discretion to discharge up to three jurors from the jury and allow the trial to continue to verdict with the remainder. He also has a discretion to discharge the entire jury from giving a verdict, in which case the accused is not acquitted but may be retried before a fresh jury. Once a jury has been discharged the general rule is that it is *functus officio* and cannot be reconvened to return a verdict, even if it is realised almost immediately after the order for discharge that the order was made in error (see *Russell* (1984) 148 JP 765). **D13.45**

In *Follen* [1994] Crim LR 225, it was stated that there was no fixed rule of law that once the judge had discharged the jury he could not set aside that order, but it would be only in very rare circumstances that this should be done (see *S* [2005] EWCA Crim 1987, for an example of such circumstances). In *Aylott* [1996] 2 Cr App R 169, the Court of Appeal adopted a more flexible approach, and stated that the underlying principle was to ensure that proceedings were fair and to do justice in the particular case (see **D18.75** for more detail).

There are three situations that should be considered in this context. First, where the jury themselves identify a problem; secondly, where there is a problem with a particular juror; and, thirdly, where the problem extends to the jury as a whole. Each of these three situations is addressed here.

In each of these situations the test to be applied is the same, either where there is or may be bias or prejudice against the accused, or misbehaviour that risks injustice to him. This approach is analysed below, together with consideration of how any alleged bias or misconduct can be investigated, and how any ultimate decision as to whether or not to discharge the jury can thereafter be reviewed on appeal.

Jury Monitoring Itself

The House of Lords in *Mirza* [2004] 1 AC 1118, decided in effect that if after verdict a juror raises a concern about a fellow juror's behaviour, the courts will not investigate such behaviour (see **D18.31**). As a result of the views expressed by Lord Hope and Lord Hobhouse, the Court of Appeal issued *Practice Direction (Crown Court: Guidance to Jurors)* [2004] 1 WLR 665, which is consolidated in the *Consolidated Criminal Practice Direction* at para. IV.42 (see appendix 7 and **D13.18**). **D13.46**

As was made clear in *Adams* (2007) 1 Cr App R 449, it is implicit in this approach that the Court of Appeal can hear evidence from jurors to resolve an issue of alleged jury bias when this is raised on appeal, although anyone seeking to interview jurors with a view to investigating such an issue should first obtain the Court of Appeal's leave. It was made clear that this course would only be countenanced in rare and exceptional cases. Equally, a court at first instance would be entitled to question jurors in relation to any alleged impropriety.

Discharge of Individual Jurors

Juries Act 1974, s. 16 **D13.47**

(1) Where in the course of a trial of any person for an offence on indictment any member of the jury dies or is discharged by the court whether as being through illness incapable of continuing to act or for any other reason, but the number of its members is not reduced below nine, the jury shall nevertheless . . . be considered as remaining for all the purposes of that trial properly constituted, and the trial shall proceed and a verdict may be given accordingly.

Section 16(1) is without prejudice to the judge's power to discharge the entire jury if he considers it preferable to do that (for which see **D13.50**), rather than continuing with reduced numbers (s. 16(3)). Discharge of jurors is *not* dependent on the consent of the parties.

In a case where the jury has to consider more than one verdict, the judge retains the power to discharge a juror even after one or more of the verdicts has been given. The reasoning is that the trial (and the accompanying power to discharge) continues in respect of those counts on which the verdict has not been delivered (*Wood* [1997] Crim LR 229).

D13.48 **Judicial Discretion to Discharge a Juror** Section 16(1) does not define the circumstances in which the judge may or should discharge a juror beyond implying that it may be on account of illness making the juror incapable of continuing to act or 'any other reason'. In *Hambery* [1977] QB 924, H's trial exceeded its estimate and was not likely to finish until after the weekend. The judge explained the position to the jury, one of whom indicated that she was due to go on holiday that weekend. After a short discussion with counsel, during which defence counsel raised no express objection, the judge discharged the juror in reliance on s. 16.

On appeal, Lawton LJ held (p. 927D–H) that the extent of the jurisdiction to discharge a juror is a matter of common law, since s. 16 does not confer the power but merely sets out the consequences of exercising it. At common law a jury could be discharged 'in cases of evident necessity' (*Blackstone's Commentaries*, 1857 edn, and see also Erle CJ's judgment in *Winsor v R* (1866) LR 1 QB 390, where he refers (at p. 394) to 'a high degree of need . . . such as . . . might be denoted by the word necessity'). At that time and until 1925, if one juror had to be discharged then so had the whole jury (i.e. there was no power to continue with a reduced jury). Therefore, the present test for jurisdiction to discharge a juror must be the same as the old test for discharging the whole jury, namely, has an evident necessity for it arisen?

Lawton LJ's judgment in *Hambery* does not give specific guidance on what may constitute an evident necessity. However, it would seem to be a fairly elastic concept and is certainly not limited to illness or other cause making it literally impossible for the juror to continue to act. Trial by jury depends on the willing co-operation of the public, and 'If the administration of justice can be carried on without inconveniencing jurors unduly it should be' (see p. 930C–G). Therefore, in the circumstances that had arisen, the judge both had jurisdiction to discharge the juror and could not be criticised for the way he exercised his discretion.

D13.49 **Discharge for Misconduct** Alternatively, there may be misconduct on the juror's part. This is addressed under the heading of misconduct below (see **D13.58**). Misconduct by a juror often necessitates discharge of the whole jury, however, it should be borne in mind that, depending on the precise circumstances, the judge might be able to deal with the problem by discharging only the juror guilty of the misconduct.

Discharge of the Entire Jury

D13.50 The judge has a discretion to discharge the whole jury from giving a verdict. If he does so, the accused is not acquitted but may be retried on the same indictment before a fresh jury (see, e.g., *Winsor v R* (1866) LR 1 QB 390). According to *Blackstone's Commentaries* (1857 edn), a jury should not be discharged unless an 'evident necessity' for it has arisen. In *Winsor v R*, Erle CJ gave some further limited guidance on the subject, which may be summarised as follows:

(a) a jury should not be discharged unless a high degree of need for it arises;
(b) whether to discharge is purely a matter for the judge's discretion; and
(c) if he exercises his discretion wrongly by discharging the jury when he ought not to have done so, the appellate courts are powerless to correct the error (the extent of appellate review of the discharge of a jury, or the refusal to accede to an application for discharge, is addressed below at **D13.63**).

These points must be read subject to the authorities set out at **D13.51** and **D13.58** which identify the proper approach of the court to possible bias or prejudice by a juror or jury and to alleged misconduct on the part of jurors.

The Test for Bias or Prejudice

In *Sander v UK* [2000] Crim LR 767, the European Court of Human Rights emphasised the need for any allegation of bias to be looked at from an objective, as well as a subjective, standpoint. The question, in other words, is not only whether the jury which tried the accused can be shown to be biased, but also whether 'there were sufficient guarantees to exclude any objectively justified or legitimate doubts as to the impartiality of the court'. **D13.51**

S, a British national of Asian origin, had been tried in the Crown Court for conspiracy to defraud. During the trial, the judge received a note from a juror referring to racist remarks and jokes by other jurors. The judge directed the jury to disregard their prejudices and try the case solely on the evidence. The judge subsequently received a letter from the jury refuting the allegation of racial bias, and a letter from another juror apologising for making jokes and denying racial bias. The judge decided not to discharge the jury and S was found guilty. The appeal was dismissed by the Court of Appeal.

The European Court held that the allegations contained in the note were capable of causing objective legitimate doubts about the impartiality of the court, and these doubts were not dispelled by the jury's letter or the judge's directions. Article 6(1) of the ECHR had been violated. (See also *Montgomery v HM Advocate* [2001] 2 WLR 779.)

In *Porter v Magill* [2002] 2 AC 357, the House of Lords considered the question of bias in relation to the courts generally, and approved the test derived from *Re Medicaments and Related Classes of Goods (No. 2)* [2001] 1 WLR 700: would a fair-minded and informed observer conclude that there was a real possibility, or real danger (the two being the same) that the tribunal was biased (see **D3.30**).

This test, which is in accordance with that adopted by the European Court of Human Rights in *Sander*, was applied by the Court of Appeal in *Poole* [2002] 1 WLR 1528, *Brown* [2002] Crim LR 409 and *Mason* [2002] 2 Cr App R 628.

In *Abdroikov* [2005] 1 WLR 3538, it was held that a fair minded and informed observer would not think that there was a real possibility that a juror was biased against a defendant merely because that juror was a serving police officer or was employed by the prosecuting body. The position is, however, different if the juror has a special knowledge either of individuals involved in the case or as to the facts of the case apart from those provided by the evidence, in which case the juror should draw the matter to the attention of the judge (see also **D13.24**).

If an issue arises as to whether a member of the jury has knowledge which makes him unsuitable to sit on that jury, the test in *Porter v Magill* has to be applied in order to determine whether or not the requirements of fairness have been met and, in making that determination, there is no need to distinguish between the position under Article 6 and the position at common law.

Grounds for Discharge

The decided cases deal with four main situations in which the question arises of the discharge of a jury, or in certain circumstances one juror. These are: **D13.52**

(a) when the jury cannot agree on their verdict (as discussed at **D18.82** *et seq.*);
(b) when they may have been inadvertently prejudiced against the accused;
(c) when one or more of their number has misconducted themselves; and
(d) when they acquire or possess personal knowledge of the accused or his bad character.

In addition, there is the related situation in which an application may be made for the discharge of the jury when the misconduct in question is that of the accused himself.

Accidental Prejudice

D13.53 The way in which this most commonly arises is if a witness refers to the accused's bad character during a trial where character has not been put in issue.

D13.54 **The Principle** The leading authority is *Weaver* [1968] 1 QB 353, in which it was held that whether or not to discharge the jury is for the judge's discretion. Although it had been said in *Palmer* (1935) 25 Cr App R 97 that, once a jury was wrongly allowed to hear evidence of a previous conviction, it was very difficult for them to dismiss that evidence from their minds, that case should not now be treated as establishing a general rule that they must inevitably be discharged. How the judge should act will depend on the facts of the particular case, and the court 'will not lightly interfere with' what he does (see Sachs LJ's judgment in *Weaver* [1968] 1 QB 353 at p. 359G).

In *Weaver*, the accused's previous convictions were revealed during incautious cross-examination of the police officer who had interviewed him. Approving the judge's refusal to discharge and dismissing W's appeal against conviction, Sachs LJ said that every decision turned on its own facts and depended especially on 'the nature of what has been admitted into evidence, the circumstances in which it has been admitted and what, in the light of the circumstances of the case as a whole, is the correct course' (p. 360B). The factors which particularly weighed against discharge were (a) that defence counsel had himself been responsible for inviting the answers which he then complained of, and (b) the degree of prejudice had been minimised by the judge's wise summing-up.

Weaver may be contrasted with *Blackford* (1989) 89 Cr App R 239, in which the appellant was convicted of possessing cannabis with intent to supply after a police officer in cross-examination had gratuitously revealed that he had a previous conviction for a similar offence. The Court of Appeal concluded that this had been 'a deliberate attempt by the police to queer the appellant's pitch'. In those circumstances, the trial judge should have discharged the jury and ordered a retrial.

D13.55 **Revelation by a Co-accused** Should an improper indication that one accused may be of bad character come from his co-accused, the Court of Appeal will be particularly loath to interfere with the trial judge's exercise of discretion against discharging the jury. In *Sutton* (1969) 53 Cr App R 504, Fenton Atkinson LJ (giving the Court of Appeal's judgment) said (at pp. 512–3):

> We have considered this matter with some anxiety, but . . . in all the circumstances of this case the judge was justified in exercising his discretion in the manner in which he did, and we would certainly be slow to lay down as a general rule that where one co-defendant says something of this nature about his co-accused, a judge must automatically allow a fresh trial, because it would simply make it too easy if a trial is not going well for one co-accused to say something which would secure his co-accused the advantages, if they are advantages, of a new trial. . . . there was an exercise of discretion by the trial judge, and the court is always slow to interfere with such an exercise of discretion.

D13.56 **Dealing with Prejudicial Revelation** Where the accused is represented by counsel and prejudicial matters are accidentally disclosed, it would seem that counsel must take the initiative and apply at trial for the jury to be discharged. If he fails to do so, any appeal is liable to be dismissed, even if the circumstances were such that, had an application for discharge been made, it would probably have been granted (see *Wattam* [1942] 1 All ER 178).

It is different if the accused is unrepresented. Should circumstances then arise in which an application for discharge might succeed, the judge is under a duty so to inform the accused.

Failure to do so will be a material irregularity in the course of the trial necessitating the quashing of any conviction (*Featherstone* [1942] 2 All ER 672). However, provided the accused is invited to consider applying for discharge, no complaint may be made if the judge, in the proper exercise of his discretion, then decides to rule against the application (ibid.).

Other Forms of Accidental Prejudice Other cases illustrate the same principle, namely that it is proper for a judge to exercise his discretion to discharge the jury when they inadvertently learn something to the accused's potential detriment. For example: **D13.57**

(a) Discovery that the accused faces further charges:
   (i) In *Dubarry* (1976) 64 Cr App R 7, while a jury trying D on one charge were considering their verdict, at least one member of the jury probably saw D being tried on another charge. The Court of Appeal held that the jury should have been discharged.
   (ii) In *Hutton* [1990] Crim LR 875, H was tried on charges of deception and obtaining credit whilst an undischarged bankrupt. Further trials were pending, so an order was made under the Contempt of Court Act 1981, s. 4(2), banning publication of the proceedings. Instead of a notice being pinned to the door, a copy of the order was attached, which published the fact that he faced further trials and which a juror was seen to read. The Court of Appeal held that as the juror who read the order might well have discussed it with his fellow jurors, potential prejudice resulted directly from the irregularity.
   (iii) In *Wilson* (1995) *The Times*, 24 February 1995, the Court of Appeal held that there was a real danger of bias where one of the jurors was the wife of a prison officer at the prison where the accused were held on remand.
(b) Where matters are heard during the trial which, albeit not evidence against the accused, cannot be ignored by the jury:
   (i) In *Fedrick* [1990] Crim LR 403, F's co-accused, S, changed his plea to guilty during the course of the trial. The prosecution had opened the case on the basis that F and S were 'in cahoots'. The judge emphasised to the jury that S's plea of guilty made no difference to F's position both at the time and in his summing-up. The Court of Appeal held that the jury could not properly consider F's case in isolation from S's. They should therefore have been discharged and a fresh trial held.
   (ii) In *Boyes* [1991] Crim LR 717, as the judge concluded his summing-up on charges of rape and indecent assault, the complainant's mother shouted from the public gallery, 'When is it going to come out about the other five girls he has attacked?' The judge told the jury not to pay any attention to the outburst. The Court of Appeal criticised the judge's failure to enquire of the jury whether they had heard the outburst. If they had, one could hardly think of more damaging and prejudicial evidence being taken to the jury room. It was only after such enquiry, with the help of counsel and a very careful contemplation by the judge, that he could decide what to do. He should have considered a fresh trial. His failure to do so was a serious irregularity.
   (iii) In *Maguire* [1997] 1 Cr App R 61, the judge told a defence witness who had refused to answer certain questions that he was to be arrested for contempt of court and would be dealt with at the end of the day. Defence counsel made an application to the judge to discharge the jury on the basis that M had been severely prejudiced. The judge refused, and directed the jury in due course that the arrest of the witness was not to affect their approach to the evidence, had nothing to do with M, and was to be ignored. The Court of Appeal held that the judge should have dealt with the witness in the absence of the jury; the direction given to the jury was not an adequate remedy as it could not have dispelled the inevitable prejudice which had been created.

(iv) In *Brown* [2006] EWCA Crim 827, the Court of Appeal held that an assessment of the consequences of the jury hearing inadmissible material, whether by oversight or deliberate deployment, did not start with the presumption that the jury would be discharged. The same approach was taken in *Lawson* [2005] EWCA Crim 84.

(v) Similarly, in *Tufail* [2006] EWCA Crim 2879, where the judge had inadvertently disclosed matters to the jury during his summing up that had not been adduced during the trial, the Court of Appeal held that the factors to be considered in deciding whether this necessitated the discharge of the jury were (a) the nature of the judge's actions to cure the slip, (b) the strength of the case against the accused, and (c) the degree to which the jury were or may have been influenced by it.

(c) Where publicity or comment on issues relating to the accused's case are reported at a time when they may have an effect on the jury. For example, in *McCann* (1991) 92 Cr App R 239, M and others were tried for conspiracy to murder Mr King, who was then Secretary of State for Northern Ireland, and others. They elected not to give evidence. During the closing stages of the trial, the Home Secretary announced in the House of Commons the government's intention of changing the law on the right to silence. That night, in televised interviews, Mr King himself and Lord Denning expressed in strong terms their view that in terrorist cases a failure to answer questions or give evidence was tantamount to guilt. The Court of Appeal allowed the appeal. Although the court had to give great weight to the trial judge's exercise of discretion, its powers to review were not confined to cases or error of principle or lack of material upon which the judge could properly have arrived at his decision. If necessary, it must examine anew the relevant facts and circumstances, and exercise a discretion by way of review if it considered that the failure to discharge the jury might have resulted in injustice. In this case there was a real risk that the jury had been influenced by the statements and the only way in which justice could be done and be seen to be done was by discharging the jury and ordering a retrial.

(d) Where there has been a material change in circumstances to the detriment of the accused which cannot otherwise be rectified:

(i) In *Ricketts* [1991] Crim LR 915, the trial judge gave leave for the statement of S to be read, on the basis that S's absence was caused by fear. After the jury had retired, S arrived, and the judge saw him in chambers, without informing counsel. Apparently S denied that he had failed to appear because he was frightened. The judge told S that his evidence had been read and was not in dispute and that he was free to go. The judge gave no indication to counsel that S had denied staying away through fear. R was convicted and appealed. The Court of Appeal held that S's evidence had been given prominence on a false basis, i.e. that it was so damning that R or someone on his behalf would seek violent revenge if he testified. In those circumstances, an application to discharge the jury could not properly have been resisted.

(ii) In *Robson* [1992] Crim LR 655, the trial judge decided to direct the jury on a different basis to that on which the parties had presented the evidence. The Court of Appeal found that the fresh issue raised by the judge did not merely introduce a new interpretation of the evidence. It opened up the possibility of conviction on a different factual basis from that put forward by the Crown, and one which had not been fully explored. That resulted in unfairness to the defence, and was a material irregularity. The best course would have been to discharge the jury.

Misconduct by a Juror

D13.58 The judge in his discretion may allow the jury to separate (Juries Act 1974, s. 13). Contrary to the practice of earlier years, it is now standard practice to allow them to separate both for luncheon and overnight adjournments. The discretion of the judge to allow the jury to separate was extended by the CJPO 1994, s. 43. That section allows the judge to permit separation even after the jury have retired to consider their verdict.

It inevitably follows that they will have the opportunity to speak about the case with those who are not of their number. However, they should be warned on the first occasion they separate that that is something they must not do. In *Prime* (1973) 57 Cr App R 632, Lord Widgery CJ said (at p. 637):

> It is important in all criminal cases that the judge should on the first occasion when the jury separate warn them not to talk about the case to anybody who is not one of their number. If he does that and brings that home to them, then it is to be assumed that they will follow the warning and only if it can be shown that they have misbehaved themselves does the opportunity of an application [for discharge] arise.

Most cases coming before the Court of Appeal on discharge of the jury due to misconduct concern allegations that, in defiance of the warning, one or more jurors spoke to prosecution witnesses or members of the public about the case. For example:

(a) In *Davis* [2001] 1 Cr App R 115, the foreman of the jury was found to have visited the scene of the crime during the trial, and the Court of Appeal held that this was a serious material irregularity.

(b) In *Karakaya* [2005] 2 Cr App R 77, the Court of Appeal stated that a juror should not conduct private research for material that might have a bearing on the trial. If such material were obtained or privately used, two fundamental linked rules were violated: the first was of open justice, and the second was that the prosecution and defence were entitled to a fair opportunity to address all material considered by the jury when reaching their verdict.

(c) In *Marshall* [2007] EWCA Crim 35, the Court of Appeal recommended that the judge should warn the jury, at the outset of the trial, that they must try the case on the evidence that they heard in court and on nothing else, which meant that they should not conduct their own private research, e.g., using the Internet.

Juror's Personal Knowledge of a Witness, the Accused or of the Accused's Bad Character

D13.59 A further situation in which the judge will have to consider discharge either of the whole jury or of an individual juror is when it comes to light that a juror knows either the accused or a witness in the case. The problem is particularly acute where the juror may know the accused to be of bad character. The following propositions summarise the Court of Appeal's decisions relating to a juror's possible bias on account of his knowledge of the accused's character, both in cases where the facts were discovered during trial and an application for discharge was accordingly made, and in cases where the defence did not learn of it until after conviction.

(a) A juror who knows the accused or who knows from hearsay of the accused's bad character ought not to sit on the jury, and should ask to be excused from service. Failure to disqualify himself on account of his knowledge of the accused is 'quite improper' (per Lord Parker CJ in *Box* [1964] 1 QB 430 at p. 435, for which see **D13.44**). Depending on the facts of the particular case, previous contact with a witness may not disqualify the juror, but in reality if the juror has any previous acquaintance with the accused, however slight, it is safer for him to be removed.

(b) If the defence are aware at the time the jury is empanelled that a juror is open to objection for the reasons stated in (a) they should obviously challenge for cause or (more simply) ask prosecuting counsel to stand the juror by. Although the Court of Appeal has stated that a juror is not automatically disqualified by knowledge of the accused's previous convictions (see per Lord Parker CJ in *Box*), those statements are in the context of cases where the relevant facts were not known to the defence until after the time for challenging had passed. They do not, it is submitted, cast doubt on the fundamental proposition that a person who knows facts detrimental to the accused should not be on the jury.

D

Part D Procedure

(c) Where a juror's possible knowledge of the accused is not brought to the court's attention until after the trial has commenced, the judge will have to consider discharging the individual juror and/or the entire jury. For example, in *Hood* [1968] 1 WLR 773, defence counsel informed the judge that H's wife, who had just given evidence for the defence, had recognised a jury member as a person who lived in the same road as her mother and would consequently know about her husband's previous convictions. The Court of Appeal confirmed that (a) a juror is not automatically disqualified by knowledge of the accused's previous convictions, and (b) that the Court of Appeal will not enquire into what occurred in the jury room. Moreover, the judge was right not to address questions to the juror himself about the allegations but should have heard evidence from the wife.

(d) If a juror's knowledge of or bias against the accused does not come to the defence's attention until after conviction, an appeal is most unlikely to succeed since the appellant will have to show that the juror had made up his mind before the trial started to convict the accused regardless of the evidence (see *Box* [1964] 1 QB 430).

Misconduct of the Accused

D13.60 In more recent times, the Court of Appeal has made clear that action by the accused, albeit that it may serve to prejudice the jury against him, will not, of itself, form the basis for the discharge of the jury. For example, in *Russell* [2006] EWCA Crim 470, the Court of Appeal considered whether misconduct by the accused during the course of the trial might result in the discharge of the jury. The accused, who was being tried for attempted murder, leapt from the dock and attacked the judge. Once the incident was over, the defence advocate asked the judge to discharge the jury on the basis that they had witnessed the attack and could no longer try the accused impartially. The judge refused to do so. The Court of Appeal dismissed the appeal. The accused's conduct was manipulative and intended to abort the trial. To continue with the trial was neither unfair, nor capable of being seen to be unfair.

Investigation of Misconduct

D13.61 Prior to deciding on the course of action which he will adopt in relation to alleged bias or misconduct, the judge will usually need to question one or more individual jurors, or the entire jury.

In *Blackwell* [1995] 2 Cr App R 625, the Court of Appeal emphasised that the judge has a duty to investigate if there is any realistic suspicion that any juror has been approached or pressurised or otherwise tampered with. Such investigation will probably include questioning of individual jurors or even the jury as a whole. Questioning must be directed to the possibility that the jury's independence has been compromised, rather than to their deliberations on the issues in the case (see also *Oke* [1997] Crim LR 898 and *Appiah* [1998] Crim LR 134, and the standard direction on the need to preserve the privacy of the jury room).

In *Orgles* [1994] 1 WLR 108, the point at issue was whether the recorder at trial had acted correctly in questioning individual jurors, who had complained of dissension in the jury room. The Court of Appeal held that the procedure adopted by the recorder of initially questioning the two jurors separately was wrong and amounted to an irregularity. The circumstances giving rise to an inference that an individual juror or jurors could not fulfil his duties normally arose externally. It was usual in that situation to question the individual juror in open court so that the trial judge might make enquiries without jeopardising the continued participation of the whole jury.

Occasionally, however, the circumstances were internal to the jury, whether through individual characteristics or through interaction with fellow jury members. In the latter circumstances, the problem was not the capacity of one or more individuals to carry out their duties, but the capacity of the jury as a whole. The appropriate course therefore was for the jury as a whole to be asked in open court as to their capacity to continue with the trial. Thereafter, it would then be a matter for the judge's exercise of discretion as to whether he made no order, discharged the whole jury or discharged individual jurors up to three in number. See also *Farooq* [1995] Crim LR 169.

Consultation of the Parties After making such enquiries as are appropriate, it is submitted that the judge should, as a matter of good practice, ask the parties for their views before discharging a juror. However, discharge is not dependent on their consent (see **D13.56**) and it is not absolutely essential even to consult them (see *Richardson* [1979] 1 WLR 1316, where the court received a telephone message from a juror that her husband had died during an overnight adjournment and the judge discharged her without any consultation with counsel, but the conviction was nonetheless upheld). **D13.62**

In *Bryan* [2002] Crim LR 240, members of the jury were overheard discussing the case on a bus, and referring to one elderly juror who had considered the accused guilty throughout the trial. The judge decided not to discharge the jury, but told them that the discussion was scandalous and a possible contempt of court, and directed them to return verdicts based on the evidence, and not on prejudice. The Court of Appeal suggested the following steps should be taken where there was a major crisis of that sort:

(a) the judge should organise a pause for consideration — the jury could be told to cease deliberating and to await the ruling of the court as to when they would be asked to continue their deliberations;
(b) counsel and the judge should then adjourn for half-an-hour or so to allow proper consideration of the steps to take;
(c) the judge should then hear submissions from counsel, and, if necessary, rise to consider what to do.

In the circumstances arising in *Bryan*, it had been wrong to suggest that there was a possibility of contempt proceedings, since the jurors in question might have felt under threat. In the event, however, the jury had not been prevented from considering the case properly, and their verdicts were safe.

Appellate Review of the Exercise of the Discretion to Discharge

In *Winsor v R* (1866) LR 1 QB 390, it was made clear that the decision whether or not to discharge is purely a matter for the judge's discretion; and if he exercises his discretion wrongly by discharging the jury when he ought not to have done so, the appellate courts are powerless to correct the error. **D13.63**

In *Hambley* [1977] QB 924, Lawton LJ reviewed the earlier authorities (especially *Winsor v R*), and concluded that the view that discharge was solely a matter for the trial judge should be understood as referring only to discharge of the entire jury (pp. 928F–929E). A decision to discharge one juror and continue with the remainder is a matter that may be raised on appeal. If the judge acted capriciously, that would be a material irregularity in the course of the trial which could lead to the quashing of any conviction (p. 929F).

However, that the decision to discharge the jury is unlikely to be interfered with on appeal was confirmed in *Gorman* [1987] 1 WLR 545. G, who was convicted at a retrial following the jury at his first trial being discharged, appealed on the ground that a note from the first jury to the judge was to the effect that they were deadlocked, with a split 9–3 in favour of acquittal. The judge simply told counsel that the jury were split and would be incapable of reaching a verdict, without revealing the numbers, and, with counsels' agreement, the jury were discharged. After G's conviction at the retrial, the defence discovered by chance the proportions in which the first jury had been split and argued on appeal that the judge had exercised his discretion to discharge the jury improperly. The Court of Appeal concluded that the law remained as stated in *Winsor v R*, namely that, if the first jury had as a matter of fact been discharged, a court hearing an appeal against the second jury's verdict had no power to review the propriety or otherwise of the discharge.

The position is different should the judge be invited to discharge the jury and refuse to do so. If the accused is then convicted, he may appeal on the basis that continuing with the original jury casts doubt on the safety of his conviction. Such cases have given rise to a considerable amount of authority on when judges ought to discharge juries, although its being a matter for discretion means that the appellate court is unlikely to interfere save in extreme cases.

D13.64 **Risk of Contamination** In *Barraclough* [2000] Crim LR 324, the jury were discharged because they had come to know, as a result of the evidence, of the fact that the accused had previous convictions, in circumstances in which that information should not have been revealed. The judge discharged the jury, who were in their first week of jury service, and a new jury were empanelled on the following day. On appeal it was argued that the retrial should have been delayed until there was an entirely new panel of jurors or that the first jury should have been discharged from further service. The Court of Appeal dismissed the appeal, in view of the fact that the court centre in question was a large one, with a panel of jurors at any one time of over 200, and in the light of the clear warning delivered by the trial judge.

As to the general issue of contamination and retrials, their lordships took the view that in smaller court centres, where there was a greater likelihood of jurors meeting, the court might have to consider discharging the first jury from further attendance or delaying the retrial for, say, a fortnight. In larger court centres, there should be no such problem. Defence counsel should in any event raise any concerns about contamination at the time that the first jury was discharged. If he did not, it would not ordinarily be open to an accused to raise the point on appeal.

ISSUES THAT MAY BE TRIED BY ONE JURY

D13.65 Subject to the exceptions mentioned below, a jury may try only one issue, that is, once it has brought in a verdict on the issue for which it was empanelled, it must be split up with the individual jurors going back into the pool of jurors in waiting with a view to being selected by ballot for further juries.

The exceptional cases in which a jury may be kept together to try a second issue are: (a) where the trial of the second issue begins within 24 hours from the time when the jury was constituted, and (b) where the trial of an issue of unfitness to plead has been postponed until the end of the prosecution evidence and the judge directs that the jury empanelled to try the general issue shall also try unfitness (see Juries Act 1974, s. 11(5)). Even where it is decided that a jury shall try a second issue, the court may order individual members of it to be replaced by others selected by ballot from the jury panel (s. 11(6)).

Juries Act 1974, s. 11

(4) Subject to subsection (5) below, the jury selected by any one ballot shall try only one issue (but any juror shall be liable to be selected on more than one ballot).

(5) Subsection (4) above shall not prevent—

(a) the trial of two or more issues by the same jury if the trial of the second or last issue begins within 24 hours from the time when the jury is constituted, or

. . .

(c) in a criminal case beginning with a special plea, the trial of the accused on the general issue by the jury trying the special plea.

(6) In the cases within subsection (5)(a) [and (b)] above the court may, on the trial of the second or any subsequent issue, instead of proceeding with the same jury in its entirety, order any juror to withdraw, if the court considers that he could be justly challenged or excused, or if the parties to the proceedings consent, and the juror to replace him shall . . . be selected by ballot in open court.

An important corollary of the rule that a jury may try only one issue is that, if an accused is charged in two or more separate indictments, there must be a separate trial for each indictment (see *Crane v DPP* [1921] 2 AC 299), and, subject to s. 11(5)(a), a fresh jury must be empanelled for each trial. A purported trial by one jury of two indictments is a nullity (*Crane*) and that is so even if the parties consented to the course adopted (*Dennis* [1924] 1 KB 867).

JUDGE-ONLY TRIALS ON INDICTMENT

The CJA 2003, ss. 43 to 50, introduced for the first time in England and Wales the concept of trial on indictment without a jury. There are two different sets of circumstances: fraud trials and jury tampering. In addition, the DVCVA 2004, introduces judge-only trials in the case of sample counts. D13.66

Fraud Trials

The prosecution will be able to apply for a trial in the Crown Court to take place without a jury (i.e. in front of a judge sitting alone) in the case of serious or complex fraud (s. 43). D13.67

As the section stands, s. 43 may only be brought into force after an affirmative resolution of each House of Parliament (s. 330(5)(b)). However, the Fraud (Trials without Jury) Bill proposes to repeal that subsection and bring s. 43 into effect.

The application is to be made to a High Court Judge sitting in the Crown Court and would have to be determined at a preparatory hearing. The court must be satisfied that the length and/or complexity of the trial is likely to make it so burdensome that the interests of justice require serious consideration to be given to conducting the trial without a jury.

In considering the matter, the judge must consider whether anything can reasonably be done to make the trial less complex and lengthy. However, in doing so, the judge is not to regard as reasonable any measures which would significantly disadvantage the prosecution. If he is satisfied that the interests of justice require serious consideration of a trial without a jury, then he has a discretion to order that it should proceed without a jury. However, such an order requires the approval of the Lord Chief Justice or a judge nominated by him.

Criminal Justice Act 2003, s. 43 (as amended)

(1) This section applies where—
  (a) one or more defendants are to be tried on indictment for one or more offences, and
  (b) notice has been given under section 51B of the Crime and Disorder Act 1998 (notices in serious or complex fraud cases) in respect of that offence or those offences.

(2) The prosecution may apply to a judge of the High Court exercising the jurisdiction of the Crown Court for the trial to be conducted without a jury.

(3) If an application under subsection (2) is made and the judge is satisfied that the condition in subsection (5) is fulfilled, he may make an order that the trial is to be conducted without a jury; but if he is not so satisfied he must refuse the application.

(4) The judge may not make such an order without the approval of the Lord Chief Justice or a judge nominated by him.

(5) The condition is that the complexity of the trial or the length of the trial (or both) is likely to make the trial so burdensome to the members of a jury hearing the trial that the interests of justice require that serious consideration should be given to the question of whether the trial should be conducted without a jury.

(6) In deciding whether or not he is satisfied that that condition is fulfilled, the judge must have regard to any steps which might reasonably be taken to reduce the complexity or length of the trial.

(7) But a step is not to be regarded as reasonable if it would significantly disadvantage the prosecution.

Jury Tampering

D13.68 Where there is a danger of jury tampering, the prosecution will be able to apply for the trial to be conducted without a jury. Further, where the jury has been discharged in the course of a trial because of jury tampering, the prosecution will be able to apply for it to continue without a jury. 'Jury tampering' is likely to include threatened or actual harm to, or intimidation or bribery of, a jury or any of its members, or their family or friends or property. For the prosecution's application to be granted in respect of a trial which has yet to take place, the court must be satisfied that two conditions are fulfilled:

(a) that there is evidence of a real and present danger that jury tampering would take place (CJA 2003, s. 44(4)); and
(b) that there is so substantial a risk of jury tampering that it is necessary in the interests of justice for the trial to be conducted without a jury, notwithstanding any steps (e.g., police protection) that might reasonably be taken to prevent the risk (s. 44(5)).

D13.69 **The Court's Decision** Where the trial is already under way and the judge is minded to discharge the jury in accordance with his common-law powers because jury tampering appears to have occurred, he must hear representations from the defence and the prosecution as to how he should proceed. If he then decides to discharge the jury, he may order that the trial shall continue without a jury if he is satisfied that this would be fair to the defendant. Alternatively, he may terminate the trial, and has the option of ordering that the retrial is to take place without a jury. Again, he must be satisfied that the danger of jury tampering is such as to make trial without jury necessary in the interests of justice, notwithstanding any steps that could be taken to prevent jury tampering (s. 46(5)).

D13.70 **Right of Appeal** There is a right of appeal to the Court of Appeal by both the defence and the prosecution against any decision made by the court at a preparatory hearing on any application for a trial without a jury (s. 45(5)). There is also a right of appeal against any order to continue a trial in the absence of a jury, or for a retrial to be conducted in the absence of a jury (s. 47).

D13.71 **Application** Where a court orders a trial to be conducted or continued without a jury, the trial will proceed in the usual way, except that functions which a jury would have performed will be performed by the judge alone. If the accused is convicted, the judge will have to give reasons for the conviction (s. 48).

The provisions which relate to judge-only trials where there is a danger of jury tampering came into force on 24 July 2006.

Criminal Justice Act 2003, ss. 44 to 48

44.—(1) This section applies where one or more defendants are to be tried on indictment for one or more offences.
(2) The prosecution may apply to a judge of the Crown Court for the trial to be conducted without a jury.
(3) If an application under subsection (2) is made and the judge is satisfied that both of the following two conditions are fulfilled, he must make an order that the trial is to be conducted without a jury; but if he is not so satisfied he must refuse the application.
(4) The first condition is that there is evidence of a real and present danger that jury tampering would take place.
(5) The second condition is that, notwithstanding any steps (including the provision of police protection) which might reasonably be taken to prevent jury tampering, the likelihood that it would take place would be so substantial as to make it necessary in the interests of justice for the trial to be conducted without a jury.
(6) The following are examples of cases where there may be evidence of a real and present danger that jury tampering would take place—
(a) a case where the trial is a retrial and the jury in the previous trial was discharged because jury tampering had taken place,

(b) a case where jury tampering has taken place in previous criminal proceedings involving the defendant or any of the defendants,
(c) a case where there has been intimidation, or attempted intimidation, of any person who is likely to be a witness in the trial.

45.—(1) This section applies—
(a) to an application under section 43, and
(b) to an application under section 44.
(2) An application to which this section applies must be determined at a preparatory hearing (within the meaning of the 1987 Act or part 3 of the 1996 Act).
(3) The parties to a preparatory hearing at which an application to which this section applies is to be determined must be given an opportunity to make representations with respect to the application.
(4) In section 7(1) of the 1987 Act (which sets out the purposes of preparatory hearings) for paragraphs (a) to (c) there is substituted—
'(a) identifying issues which are likely to be material to the determinations and findings which are likely to be required during the trial,
(b) if there is to be a jury, assisting their comprehension of those issues and expediting the proceedings before them,
(c) determining an application to which section 45 of the Criminal Justice Act 2003 applies,'.
. . .
(10) In this section—
'the 1987 Act' means the Criminal Justice Act 1987,
'the 1996 Act' means the Criminal Procedure and Investigations Act 1996.

46.—(1) This section applies where—
(a) a judge is minded during a trial on indictment to discharge the jury, and
(b) he is so minded because jury tampering appears to have taken place.
(2) Before taking any steps to discharge the jury, the judge must—
(a) inform the parties that he is minded to discharge the jury,
(b) inform the parties of the grounds on which he is so minded, and
(c) allow the parties an opportunity to make representations.
(3) Where the judge, after considering any such representations, discharges the jury, he may make an order that the trial is to continue without a jury if, but only if, he is satisfied—
(a) that jury tampering has taken place, and
(b) that to continue the trial without a jury would be fair to the defendant or defendants;
but this is subject to subsection (4).
(4) If the judge considers that it is necessary in the interests of justice for the trial to be terminated, he must terminate the trial.
(5) Where the judge terminates the trial under subsection (4), he may make an order that any new trial which is to take place must be conducted without a jury if he is satisfied in respect of the new trial that both of the conditions set out in section 44 are likely to be fulfilled.
(6) Subsection (5) is without prejudice to any other power that the judge may have on terminating the trial.
(7) Subject to subsection (5), nothing in this section affects the application of section 43 or 44 in relation to any new trial which takes place following the termination of the trial.

47.—(1) An appeal shall lie to the Court of Appeal from an order under section 46(3) or (5).
(2) Such an appeal may be brought only with the leave of the judge or the Court of Appeal.
(3) An order from which an appeal under this section lies is not to take effect—
(a) before the expiration of the period for bringing an appeal under this section, or
(b) if such an appeal is brought, before the appeal is finally disposed of or abandoned.
(4) On the termination of the hearing of an appeal under this section, the Court of Appeal may confirm or revoke the order.
(5) Subject to rules of court made under section 53(1) of the Supreme Court Act 1981 (power by rules to distribute business of Court of Appeal between its civil and criminal divisions)—
(a) the jurisdiction of the Court of Appeal under this section is to be exercised by the criminal division of that court, and
(b) references in this section to the Court of Appeal are to be construed as references to that division.

48.—(1) The effect of an order under section 43 is that the trial to which the order relates is to be conducted–

(a) without a jury, and
(b) by a judge of the high Court exercising the jurisdiction of the Crown Court

(1A) The effect of an order under section 44 or 46(5) is that the trial to which the order relates is to be conducted without a jury.

(2) The effect of an order under section 46(3) is that the trial to which the order relates is to be continued without a jury.

(3) Where a trial is conducted or continued without a jury, the court is to have all the powers, authorities and jurisdiction which the court would have had if the trial had been conducted or continued with a jury (including power to determine any question and to make any finding which would be required to be determined or made by a jury).

(4) Except where the context otherwise requires, any reference in an enactment to a jury, the verdict of a jury or the finding of a jury is to be read, in relation to a trial conducted or continued without a jury, as a reference to the court, the verdict of the court or the finding of the court.

(5) Where a trial is conducted or continued without a jury and the court convicts a defendant—
(a) the court must give a judgment which states the reasons for the conviction at, or as soon as reasonably practicable after, the time of the conviction, and
(b) the reference in section 18(2) of the Criminal Appeal Act 1968 (notice of appeal or of application for leave to appeal to be given within 28 days from date of conviction etc.) to the date of the conviction is to be read as a reference to the date of the judgment mentioned in paragraph (a).

(6) Nothing in this part affects—
(a) the requirement under section 4 of the Criminal Procedure (Insanity) Act 1964 that a question of fitness to be tried be determined by a jury, or
(b) the requirement under section 4A of that Act that any question, finding or verdict mentioned in that section be determined, made or returned by a jury.

Sections 44, 46 and 47 were brought into force on 24 July 2006, together with s. 45 (insofar as it applies to applications under s. 44) and s. 48 (insofar as it applies to trials ordered under ss. 44 or 46); the provisions are not otherwise in force.

D13.72 **Sample Counts** A further avenue by which the prosecution can seek trial on indictment without a jury is opened up by the DVCVA 2004, s. 17. In essence, it is for the jury to try sample counts, with the remaining counts in the indictment capable of being tried by a judge sitting alone.

The application by the prosecution may be acceded to by the judge if the following conditions are fulfilled:

(a) that the number of counts in the indictment is such that a trial of them all by jury would be impracticable;
(b) that each count to be tried by the jury can be regarded as a sample of counts that could for their part be tried by a judge alone; and
(c) that it is in the interests of justice to grant the order sought.

The judge should have regard to any steps that might be taken to facilitate a jury trial, but not if that might result in the defendant receiving a lesser sentence.

These provisions came into force on 8 January 2007 by virtue of the Domestic Violence, Crime and Victims Act 2004 (Commencement No. 7 and Transitional Provision) Order 2006 (SI 2006 No. 3423). However, they apply only to cases where the accused was committed, transferred under the CJA 1987 or CJA 1991, or served with the case against him pursuant to the CDA 1998, s. 51, *after* 8 January 2007.

Domestic Violence, Crime and Victims Act 2004, ss. 17 and 18

17.—(1) The prosecution may apply to a judge of the Crown Court for a trial on indictment to take place on the basis that the trial of some, but not all, of the counts included in the indictment may be conducted without a jury.

(2) If such an application is made and the judge is satisfied that the following three conditions are fulfilled, he may make an order for the trial to take place on the basis that the trial of

some, but not all, of the counts included in the indictment may be conducted without a jury.

(3) The first condition is that the number of counts included in the indictment is likely to mean that a trial by jury involving all of those counts would be impracticable.

(4) The second condition is that, if an order under subsection (2) were made, each count or group of counts which would accordingly be tried with a jury can be regarded as a sample of counts which could accordingly be tried without a jury.

(5) The third condition is that it is in the interests of justice for an order under subsection (2) to be made.

(6) In deciding whether or not to make an order under subsection (2), the judge must have regard to any steps which might reasonably be taken to facilitate a trial by jury.

(7) But a step is not to be regarded as reasonable if it could lead to the possibility of a defendant in the trial receiving a lesser sentence than would be the case if that step were not taken.

(8) An order under subsection (2) must specify the counts which may be tried without a jury.

(9) For the purposes of this section and sections 18 to 20, a count may not be regarded as a sample of other counts unless the defendant in respect of each count is the same person.

18.—(1) An application under section 17 must be determined at a preparatory hearing.

(2) Section 7(1) of the 1987 Act and section 29(2) of the 1996 Act are to have effect as if the purposes there mentioned included the purpose of determining an application under section 17.

(3) Section 29(1) of the 1996 Act is to have effect as if the grounds on which a judge of the Crown Court may make an order under that provision included the ground that an application under section 17 has been made.

(4) The parties to a preparatory hearing at which an application under section 17 is to be determined must be given an opportunity to make representations with respect to the application.

(5) Section 9(11) of the 1987 Act and section 35(1) of the 1996 Act are to have effect as if they also provided for an appeal to the Court of Appeal to lie from the determination by a judge of an application under section 17.

(6) In this section—

'preparatory hearing' means a preparatory hearing within the meaning of the 1987 Act or part 3 of the 1996 Act;

'the 1987 Act' means the Criminal Justice Act 1987;

'the 1996 Act' means the Criminal Procedure and Investigations Act 1996.

Section D14 Trial on Indictment: General Matters and Pre-trial Procedure

D14.1 Once the accused has pleaded not guilty to the charges he faces (see **D12**), he places himself at the centre of a procedural framework, now governed by the CrimPR and influenced by the strong recent emphasis on effective case management, that is designed to prepare for the ultimate trial. This section addresses those matters of general preliminary application to trials on indictment, the conduct of hearings pre-trial, and the obligations and safeguards imposed by rules at the pre-trial stage.

PLACE OF TRIAL

D14.2 The first issue that arises is the location in which the case is to be tried. Following on from this is the question of transfer of a case between Crown Court centres.

Venue of Trial

D14.3 This is primarily regulated by the Supreme Court Act 1981, s. 75, which empowers the Lord Chief Justice to regulate both the location of the Crown Court to which an accused is initially sent and the nature of the tribunal before which he is ultimately tried (i.e. High Court judge, circuit judge or recorder).

Supreme Court Act 1981, s. 75

(1) The cases or classes of cases in the Crown Court suitable for allocation respectively to a judge of the High Court, circuit judge, recorder or district judge (magistrates' court), and all other matters relating to the distribution of Crown Court business, shall be determined in accordance with directions given by or on behalf of the Lord Chief Justice with the concurrence of the Lord Chancellor.

(2) Subject to section 74(1) [which requires that when hearing an appeal the Crown Court shall normally consist of a professional judge together with at least two justices of the peace], the cases or classes of cases in the Crown Court suitable for allocation to a court comprising justices of the peace (including those by way of trial on indictment which are suitable for allocation to such a court) shall be determined in accordance with directions given by or on behalf of the Lord Chief Justice with the concurrence of the Lord Chancellor.

In addition, the MCA 1980, s. 7 (see **D10.44**) provides that, when specifying the particular location of the Crown Court to which an accused should be sent for trial, a magistrates' court must have regard, *inter alia*, to the directions given by the Lord Chief Justice under s. 75(1) of the Supreme Court Act 1981.

The s. 75 directions currently in force are contained in the *Consolidated Criminal Practice Direction*, paras. III.21 and IV.33 (see **appendix** 7).

Transfer of Cases between Locations of the Crown Court

Section 76(1) of the Supreme Court Act 1981 provides that the Crown Court may give directions altering the place of any trial on indictment, varying either the magistrates' original decision as to venue or any earlier decision of the Crown Court itself (ibid.). Such a change can be brought about in a number of ways: **D14.4**

(a) an officer of the Crown Court may give such directions on behalf of the court (s. 76(2));
(b) either party, if dissatisfied with the place of trial that has been fixed, may apply to the Crown Court for a variation (s. 76(3)), such application to be heard in open court by a High Court judge (s. 76(4)).

The place of trial specified in notices of transfer under s. 4 of the CJA 1987 can be varied in the same way (s. 76(2A)).

Reasons for Transfer The power given to listing officers of the Crown Court to switch a trial from one court centre to another (see Supreme Court Act 1981, s. 76(2)) is used principally to even out the workload between neighbouring courts. Such decisions to switch are made on administrative rather than judicial grounds. **D14.5**

Section 76 is of no assistance as to how the powers it gives are to be exercised. Section 76(1) does contain the qualification that it is 'Without prejudice to the provisions of this Act about the distribution of Crown Court business'. It follows that, on an application by a party under s. 76(3) for variation of the venue specified by the magistrates, the High Court judge determining the application is entitled to consider factors additional to those listed in the MCA 1980, s. 7, which govern the decision of the lower court. Such additional factors may include the possible prejudice to the accused of being tried in the area where the offence was allegedly committed if the nature of the charge has provoked exceptional public hostility.

However, in the light of the Court of Appeal's decision in *Ford* [1989] QB 868 (see **D12.24**), it would be inappropriate to vary the trial venue with a view to obtaining a multiracial jury panel. This was also demonstrated in *Bansal* [1985] Crim LR 151, where Woolf J declined to order that the trial of Asians accused of public order offences arising out of an anti-National Front demonstration be switched from Maidstone to a London Crown Court (although he did give the indication, later criticised in *Ford*, that the jury panel should be drawn from Gravesend rather than from Maidstone itself).

Supreme Court Act 1981, s. 76

(1) Without prejudice to the provisions of this Act about the distribution of Crown Court business, the Crown Court may give directions, or further directions, altering the place of any trial on indictment, whether by varying the decision of the magistrates' court under section 7 of the Magistrates' Courts Act 1980 or by substituting some other place for the place specified in a notice under a relevant transfer provision (notices of transfer from magistrates' court to Crown Court) or by varying a previous decision of the Crown Court.
(2) Directions under subsection (1) may be given on behalf of the Crown Court by an officer of the court.
(2A) Where a preparatory hearing has been ordered under section 7 of the Criminal Justice Act 1987, directions altering the place of trial may be given under subsection (1) at any time before the jury are sworn.
(3) The defendant or the prosecutor, if dissatisfied with the place of trial as fixed by the magistrates' court, as specified in a notice under a relevant transfer provision or as fixed by the Crown Court, may apply to the Crown Court for a direction, or further direction, varying the place of trial; and the court shall take the matter into consideration and may comply with or refuse the application, or give a direction not in compliance with the application, as the court thinks fit.
(4) An application under subsection (3) shall be heard in open court by a judge of the High Court.
(5) In this section 'relevant transfer provision' means—

D

Part D Procedure

(a) section 4 of the Criminal Justice Act 1987, or
(b) section 53 of the Criminal Justice Act 1991.

CUSTODY TIME-LIMITS

D14.6 Section 22 of the Prosecution of Offences Act 1985 was introduced to remedy the manifest inadequacy of the provisions then available to ensure that trials on indictment begin within a reasonable time. The section (set out at **D14.35**) empowers the Secretary of State to make regulations fixing:

(a) the maximum period available to the prosecution to complete any preliminary (pre-trial) stage of proceedings for an offence; and/or
(b) the maximum period for which an accused may be kept in custody while awaiting completion of such a stage.

Definition of Terms

D14.7 Inevitably the main concern of practitioners and the courts is the consequences of a time-limit expiring and applications being made to extend it. Before approaching these issues, however, it is of assistance to define some of the terminology that applies.

D14.8 **Committal** References to 'committal' in this context should be taken to include the giving of a notice of transfer under the CJA 1987, s. 4, or under the CJA 1991, s. 53, and sending for trial under the CDA 1998, s. 51 (subject to specific variations in such cases).

Regulations under the Prosecution of Offences Act 1985, s. 22, have application not only to the time between committal and arraignment, but also to the time between the accused being charged and committal (for offences triable on indictment) or the time between charge and the commencement of summary trial (in other cases). Section 22 is thus relevant to the timing both of committal and summary trial, as well as to the timing of arraignment.

D14.9 **Preliminary Stage of Proceedings** The general effect of s. 22 of the Prosecution of Offences Act 1985 is that the Secretary of State may by regulation impose time-limits in respect of any specified 'preliminary stage' of proceedings for an offence (s. 22(1)). The regulations may relate to any type of offence, whether triable only on indictment, triable either way or summarily. 'Preliminary stage' is defined as *not* including anything after the start of trial.

D14.10 **Start of a Trial on Indictment** As far as trial on indictment is concerned, the 'start of trial' is defined as the point when a jury is sworn, or the court accepts a plea of guilty (Prosecution of Offences Act 1985, s. 22(11A)).

This is significant in cases where a preparatory hearing is held, whether for a long or complex case (in accordance with the CPIA 1996, s. 30: see **D14.55**) or for a serious or complex fraud (in accordance with the CJA 1987, s. 8: see **D14.56**). Under each of those sections, the beginning of the preparatory hearing is deemed to be the beginning of the trial, and therefore custody time-limits will cease to operate from that moment.

In *Re Kanaris* [2003] 1 WLR 443, the House of Lords considered the consequences of the removal of the protection of the custody time-limits regime where a preparatory hearing took place. Lord Hope said:

> . . . a judge who is minded to order a preparatory hearing in a long and complex case should be careful not to deprive an accused who is in custody of the protection of the statutory custody time-limit until it has become necessary for him to do so.

He indicated that the judge could, where appropriate, exercise powers under the CPIA 1996, s. 31(4) to (7) (see **D14.53**), before the preparatory hearing begins to permit effective case management whilst preserving the accused's right to the protection of the statutory custody time-limit.

D14.11 **Start of a Summary Trial** As far as summary trial is concerned, the start of trial is 'when the court begins to hear evidence for the prosecution at trial' or accepts a plea of guilty (Prosecution of Offences Act 1985, s. 22(11B)). There is an exception where the court begins to consider whether to exercise its power, under the Mental Health Act 1983, s. 37(3), to make a hospital order without convicting the accused.

D14.12 **Meaning of Custody** As far as custody time-limits are concerned, 'custody' includes:

(a) local authority accommodation to which a juvenile is committed by virtue of the CYPA 1969, s. 23 (Prosecution of Offences Act 1985, s. 22(11));
(b) the detention of a youth charged with an indictable offence — in *Stratford Youth Court, ex parte S* (1998) 162 JP 552, the Divisional Court held that the 56-day custody time-limit imposed for completion of preliminary stages in indictable offences applied to a young person charged with robbery because, in the case of a young person, it was an offence triable either way;
(c) where an accused remains in custody because he is unable to provide a surety, since he falls within the terms of the MCA 1980, s. 128 (*Re Ofili* [1995] Crim LR 880).

In *Peterborough Crown Court, ex parte L* [2000] Crim LR 470, the Divisional Court held that the whole period during which the accused was remanded in custody for the offence in question should be taken into account when calculating the relevant period for custody time-limits. There was no basis on which part of the period could be disregarded on the basis that the accused was also serving a custodial sentence for an unrelated matter.

Periods Applicable

D14.13 The regulations may prescribe an *overall time-limit* within which the prosecution must complete the stage of the proceedings in question (Prosecution of Offences Act 1985, s. 22(1)(a)). If such an overall time-limit expires, the proceedings in the case are stayed (s. 22(4)). The effects of such a stay are set out in s. 22B. The proceedings for the offence can be reinstituted only if the DPP, a Chief Crown Prosecutor or one of the other senior figures named in s. 22B(2) so directs. Fresh proceedings may be instituted within three months of the original stay of proceedings, or longer with the leave of the court. No overall time-limits currently apply.

Alternatively or additionally, the regulations may prescribe a *custody time-limit*, that being the maximum period for which the accused may be remanded in custody while the stage is being completed (s. 22(1)(b)).

D14.14 **Time-limits** The current regulations relate only to indictable offences and have imposed only custody time-limits. The regulations in question are the Prosecution of Offences (Custody Time-limits) Regulations 1987 (SI 1987 No. 299). The limits are as follows:

(a) *Between first appearance and committal.* By reg. 4(2) and (4), the maximum period for which an accused charged with an indictable offence may be held in the custody of the magistrates' court between his first appearance and committal proceedings is 70 days.
(b) *Between first appearance and summary trial.* If the offence is triable either way and the court determines to try the case summarily, the maximum period in custody between first appearance and the court beginning to hear evidence for the prosecution is again 70 days, unless the decision for summary trial is taken within 56 days, in which case the limit is reduced to 56 days (reg. 4(2) and (3)). In the case of a summary offence, the maximum period is 56 days (reg. 4(4A).
(c) *Between committal and trial on indictment.* By reg. 5(3)(a), the maximum period for

Part D Procedure

which an accused committed for trial to the Crown Court may be held in custody between committal and the start of trial is 112 days.

(d) *Multiple committals.* If a single indictment is preferred containing counts in respect of which the accused was committed for trial on two or more different occasions, the 112-day limit applies separately in relation to each offence (reg. 6(4)). See also **D14.15**.

(e) *Voluntary bill.* Where proceedings are by way of a voluntary bill of indictment (not committal) the 112-day period runs from the date of preferment of the bill (reg. 5(3)(b)).

(f) *Section 51 sending.* Where the accused has been sent for trial under the CDA 1998, s. 51 (provisions relating to indictable-only offences: dealt with in **D9**), the maximum period is 182 days between the date on which he is sent to the Crown Court and the start of the trial. From this maximum must be deducted any period during which the accused was held in custody by the magistrates (reg. 5(6B)).

Separate Time-limits for Each Offence

D14.15 Each offence with which the accused is charged attracts its own time-limit (*Wirral District Magistrates' Court, ex parte Meikle* (1990) 154 JP 1035). In this case, M was charged with five different offences at different dates, being held in custody from the date of the first charge. In view of the fact that the 1987 Regulations repeatedly refer to 'offence' in the singular, the Divisional Court had no difficulty in concluding that each offence attracts its own custody time-limit. (See also *Great Yarmouth Magistrates, ex parte Thomas* [1992] Crim LR 116, *Waltham Forest Magistrates' Court, ex parte Lee* (1993) 157 JP 811, *Leeds Crown Court, ex parte Stubley* [1999] Crim LR 822 and *Wolverhampton Justices and Stafford Crown Court, ex parte Uppal* (1995) 159 JP 86.)

D14.16 **Meaning of Separate Offences** In *R (Wardle) v Leeds Crown Court* [2001] 2 WLR 865, the House of Lords considered the question: what constitutes the charging of an offence, such as to trigger off a fresh custody time-limit? W was originally charged with murder, but the prosecution offered no evidence on that charge and preferred a charge of manslaughter on the day that the original custody time-limit was due to expire. The issue on appeal was whether this new charge gave rise to a new time-limit, given that the original charge of murder could be regarded as including the new charge of manslaughter. Their lordships, by a majority of three to two, dismissed W's appeal, holding as follows.

(a) The word 'offence' in reg. 4 could not be read as including an alternative offence of which the accused could be found guilty under the Criminal Law Act 1967.

(b) The situation would be different if the new charge was simply a restatement of the original charge with different particulars. It had to be a different offence in law to attract a fresh custody time-limit.

(c) The bringing of a fresh charge would be an abuse of process if the prosecution could not demonstrate, on the facts of the case, that it was justified; furthermore the court must be satisfied that the fresh charge had not been brought solely with a view to obtaining the substitution of a fresh custody time-limit.

Effect of Expiry of Custody Time-limit

D14.17 If a custody time-limit expires before completion of the stage of proceedings in question, the accused must be granted bail, in relation at least to the offence to which the limit relates. This is made clear by reg. 6(6), which states that, where the Crown Court is notified that the 112-day time-limit between committal and the start of the trial is about to expire in a certain case, it must bail the accused as from the expiry of the limit, subject to a duty to attend for trial. The regulations do not expressly deal with the procedure for bailing an accused who has the benefit of the 70-day time-limit between charge and committal or summary trial.

D14.18 **The Grant of Bail** The regulations may make provision for the Bail Act 1976 and the MCA 1980 to apply in cases where the accused is bailed as a result of a custody time-limit's expiry with such modifications as the Secretary of State considers necessary (Prosecution of Offences Act 1985, s. 22(2)(d)).

In the case of the Bail Act 1976, its application to accused persons in respect of whom custody time-limits have expired is modified in that:

(a) they are automatically entitled to bail;
(b) on granting bail, the court may not require sureties or the deposit of security; and
(c) following the grant of bail, they may not be arrested without warrant merely on the ground that a police officer believes they are unlikely to surrender to custody (reg. 8).

Other conditions, such as curfew, residence or reporting to a police station, may nevertheless be imposed as in other cases, and the rule that actual or feared breach of such conditions is a ground for arrest without warrant (Bail Act 1976, ss. 3(6) and 7(3)(b)) applies to an accused bailed on expiry of a time-limit just as it applies to an accused granted bail in any other circumstances (see also **D7.27**).

Procedure for Imposing Conditions Regulation 6 requires the prosecution to give notice to the appropriate court and the accused stating whether they intend to ask the court to impose conditions on the bail of an accused in respect of whom a custody time-limit is about to expire. In response to such an indication, the defence must give either: **D14.19**

(a) written notice of a wish to be represented at the hearing of the application;
(b) written notice that the accused does not object to the proposed conditions; or
(c) a written statement of the accused's reasons for objecting.

It is the prosecution's duty to arrange for the accused to be brought before the court within the two days preceding expiry of a custody time-limit (reg. 6(1)(b)).

Where the accused acquires the right to bail as a result of the expiry of a custody time-limit, that right continues until the start of the trial. The decision to the contrary, *Croydon Crown Court, ex parte Lewis* (1994) 158 JP 886, no longer represents the law; it was decided before the CPIA 1996, s. 71, came into effect and at a time when the Prosecution of Offences Act 1985, s. 22, referred to 'arraignment' as the boundary of preliminary proceedings rather than 'start of the trial' (as the new provisions provide).

Limits on the Effect of Expiry Beyond the grant of bail, the expiry of the custody time-limit otherwise has no effect on the proceedings. This was illustrated in *Sheffield Magistrates' Court, ex parte Turner* [1991] 2 QB 472. T had been unlawfully detained, contrary to the Prosecution of Offences Act 1985, s. 22, for a period culminating in his committal for trial. Although the Divisional Court granted a declaration relating to his period of unlawful detention, it was held that this had no effect on the validity of the committal, the fresh custody time-limit, laid down by reg. 5(3), which commenced on that date, or the lawfulness of his detention thereafter. **D14.20**

Consequences of Absconding

Escape from custody during the running of a custody time-limit automatically leads to the regulations imposing the time-limit being disregarded (Prosecution of Offences Act 1985, s. 22(5)). Similarly, if an accused has been released in consequence of the expiry of a custody time-limit and then fails to attend court in answer to his bail, the earlier expiry of the limit is disregarded and the question, once he has been arrested, of whether to bail him again or remand in custody is therefore entirely in the discretion of the court (ibid.). **D14.21**

Procedure for Seeking an Extension of Time-limits

At any time before the expiry of a time-limit, the Crown Court, if the accused has already been committed for trial, or the magistrates' court, in other cases, may extend the limit if satisfied of two matters (Prosecution of Offences Act 1985, s. 22(3)): **D14.22**

(a) that 'the prosecution has acted with all due diligence and expedition' and
(b) that there is 'good and sufficient cause for doing so'.

Instances of 'good and sufficient cause' are given in s. 22(3)(a)(i) and (ii), but they are clearly meant to be no more than examples.

An already extended limit may be further extended (ibid.).

These criteria for the extension of the time-limit are discussed in more detail below.

D14.23 **The Notice Requirement** By reg. 7 of the Prosecution of Offences (Custody Time-Limits) Regulations 1987, an application for extension may be made orally or in writing. Notice of the intention to make the application must be given to the defence and the court not less than five days before an application to the Crown Court and not less than two days before an application to a magistrates' court. Notice may, however, be dispensed with if the court is satisfied that it is not practicable for the prosecution to give it in the time specified (reg. 7(4)).

The effect of a failure by the prosecution to give proper notice was considered in *Governor of Canterbury Prison, ex parte Craig* [1991] 2 QB 195. It was held in that case that the justices still had a discretion under s. 22(3) of the Prosecution of Offences Act 1985 to extend a time-limit 'at any time before . . . expiry'. Hence they could extend the time-limit despite the prosecution's failure to show that it had been impracticable to give the accused two days' notice of an application for extension.

In *R (Haque) v Central Criminal Court* [2004] Crim LR 298, the Divisional Court considered the import of the opening words of s. 22(3): 'The appropriate court may, at any time before the expiry of a time-limit imposed by the regulations, extend, or further extend, that limit'. It was held that they had to be construed as meaning before the expiry of a time-limit imposed by the regulations *as extended, if appropriate* by the court. They did not mean that the application could only be made within the 182 days provided for in reg. 6B following the date on which the accused first appeared in the magistrates' court.

D14.24 **Use of a Chronology** In *Chelmsford Crown Court, ex parte Mills* (2000) 164 JP 1, Lord Bingham CJ said that when a contested application was made for an extension, turning wholly or partly on whether the prosecution had acted with all due expedition, the judge should be given a detailed chronology (preferably agreed), showing the dates of all material events and orders. When the judge ruled on such an application, he should give reasons for his decision, which need not be long or elaborate.

Criteria for Extension

D14.25 The criteria for the extension of a custody time-limit, as set out in the Prosecution of Offences Act 1985, s. 22(3), are that the court must be satisfied (i) that there was good and sufficient cause, and (ii) that the Crown had acted with all due diligence and expedition (the need for 'diligence' was added by the CDA 1998). The authorities since 1985 have provided considerable assistance both in general terms as to the proper approach of the appropriate court to an application, and more specifically as to the proper meaning and ambit of the two criteria.

D14.26 **General Guidance** In *Manchester Crown Court, ex parte McDonald* [1999] 1 WLR 841, Lord Bingham CJ set out the principles underlying the custody time-limit provisions in the Prosecution of Offences Act 1985, s. 23, and gave guidance upon the practicalities of interpreting the tests laid down by the statute. As far as the fundamental principles of the provisions are concerned, he emphasised the presumption of liberty set out in the ECHR, Article 5(3): 'Everyone arrested or detained [for trial] . . . shall be entitled to trial within a reasonable time or to release pending trial'. With that provision in mind, the overriding purposes of the statutory provisions were said to be:

(a) to ensure that the periods for which unconvicted defendants are held in custody are as short as is reasonably and practically possible;
(b) to oblige the prosecution to prepare cases for trial with due diligence and expedition; and
(c) to give the court power to control any extension of the maximum period for which any defendant may be held awaiting trial.

The main points of practical guidance which emerge from *Ex parte McDonald* are:

(1) It is for the prosecution to satisfy the court on the balance of probabilities that the statutory conditions are met.
(2) The necessary standard is that of a competent prosecutor conscious of his duty to bring the case to trial as quickly as is reasonably and fairly possible.
(3) In judging whether this standard was met, the court should consider the nature and complexity of the case, the preparation necessary, the conduct of the defence, and the extent to which the prosecutor was dependent on others outside his control, and other relevant factors.
(4) What amounts to good and sufficient cause is a matter for the court on the facts of the case.
(5) Staff shortages and sickness will be inadequate reasons for extension. The unavailability of a judge or a courtroom may be good and sufficient cause, but such cases should be approached with 'great caution'.
(6) The court should state the reasons for its decision.
(7) Once the court had heard full argument and decided, the Divisional Court would be most reluctant to disturb its decision, and would do so only on the familiar grounds which support an application for judicial review.

Good and Sufficient Cause Factors that have been held not to amount to a good and sufficient cause for the extension of a time-limit include the following. D14.27

(a) *The seriousness of the offence charged.* For example, in *Governor of Winchester Prison, ex parte Roddie* [1991] 1 WLR 303, the Divisional Court held that the seriousness of the offence could not represent a good and sufficient cause, because Parliament had provided the same time-limit for all offences except treason. The more serious the charge, the more important it was for the police to get on with preparing the case.
(b) *Public protection.* For example, in *Central Criminal Court, ex parte Abu-Wardeh* [1997] 1 WLR 1083, the Divisional Court held that the protection of the public was, in itself, an insufficient ground for the extension of a custody time-limit, disagreeing with *Luton Crown Court, ex parte Neaves* (1993) 157 JP 80. In *Birmingham Crown Court, ex parte Bell* [1997] 2 Cr App R 363, the Divisional Court accepted that, although protection of the public might not be enough in itself to constitute good and sufficient cause, where protection of prosecution witnesses was an issue, that might be capable in conjunction with other factors of giving rise to good and sufficient cause.
(c) *Factors that may be relevant to an application for bail.* For example, in *Sheffield Crown Court, ex parte Headley* [2000] Crim LR 374, the Divisional Court stated that it was wrong for a judge in considering an application to extend custody time-limits to take account of matters relevant to the grant of bail under the Bail Act 1976. The custody time-limits regime was a separate and additional safeguard for those in custody, over and above that provided by the Bail Act 1976. Parliament could not have intended that Bail Act considerations could be determinative of a custody time-limit application (see also *R (Eliot) v Reading Crown Court* [2001] Crim LR 811).

Unavailability of a Judge or Courtroom Several cases have turned upon the question of whether the fact that there is no judge or courtroom in which a case may be tried can constitute good and sufficient cause for the grant of an extension. In *Norwich Crown Court, ex parte Cox* (1993) 97 Cr App R 145, the Divisional Court made it plain that, in appropriate D14.28

D

Part D Procedure

circumstances, the lack of a judge and courtroom is capable of constituting the 'good and sufficient cause' which the Act requires. Mann LJ stated that whether the lack of a court and judge should be regarded as being a good and sufficient cause 'must depend upon the facts of that instant case including, in particular, whether a trial date has been specified'. However, in *Maidstone Crown Court, ex parte Schulz* (1993) 157 JP 601, it was held that the grant of an extension of 14 days to enable an earlier trial date to be sought, when the court had been informed that the earliest possible date was in 93 days, was not for good and sufficient cause. More recently, in *R (Miah) v Crown Court at Snaresbrook* [2006] EWHC 2873 (Admin), it was made clear that listing difficulties had to be exceptional to justify an extension; difficulties caused by the pressure of work on a Crown Court in routine cases would not be sufficient.

The court is enjoined, however, to make all reasonable enquiries before permitting an extension on this basis. In particular, it is incumbent on the court to make enquiries as to whether an earlier trial date is possible, either at that court centre or elsewhere (*Preston Crown Court, ex parte Barraclough* [1999] Crim LR 973). This involves the court in satisfying itself that the court staff responsible for fixing the date for trial have fulfilled their duties scrupulously (*Leeds Crown Court, ex parte Wilson* [1999] Crim LR 378).

D14.29 **Convenience of Defence and Witnesses** In *White* v *DPP* [1989] Crim LR 375, the Divisional Court found that the reason for the extension of the time-limit in W's case, namely that the defence had successfully applied for an adjournment to consider the prosecution statements that had only just been served on them, could permit an extension. The reasonable requirement of the defence to consider the papers was capable of being a good and sufficient cause for extension of time, although each case must turn on its own facts. Their lordships did not necessarily agree with the Crown Court judge's approach, namely, that he had to be satisfied beyond reasonable doubt of the existence of good cause before granting an extension (see **D14.32**). The absence or illness of the accused is itself a ground for extension (s. 22(3)(a)(i)).

In *Central Criminal Court, ex parte Bennett* (1999) *The Times*, 25 January 1999, the illness of a prosecution witness, which prevented the trial from taking place, was held to amount to a good and sufficient cause. Likewise, the unexpected non-availability of a prosecution witness may suffice (*Leeds Crown Court, ex parte Redfearn* [1999] COD 437). The fact that a witness is a professional investigator does not make his convenience irrelevant (*Leeds Crown Court, ex parte Wilson* [1999] Crim LR 378).

D14.30 **Due Expedition** In *Norwich Crown Court, ex parte Parker* (1992) 96 Cr App R 68, the Divisional Court said that all concerned with the prosecution were not required to act as though this were their only task at hand; 'all due expedition' meant the expedition appropriate in the circumstances, one of those circumstances being the custody time-limit.

In *Governor of Winchester Prison, ex parte Roddie* [1991] 1 WLR 303, however, it was made clear that due expedition had to be measured against some objective yardstick or it would defeat the Act's objects. Therefore, the fact that the police were understaffed and suffered delays in the receipt of typing and forensic evidence did not mean there was due expedition.

The following factors have relevance to the assessment of this question.

(a) *The stage of the proceedings to which the time-limit relates.* In considering whether the prosecution had acted with all due expedition, the judge ought to consider the matter by reference to the presence or absence of all due expedition at the stage to which the custody time-limit relates (*Birmingham Crown Court, ex parte Bell* [1997] 2 Cr App R 363). For example, in *Central Criminal Court, ex parte Behbehari* [1994] Crim LR 352, the Divisional Court held that, in determining whether the prosecution had acted with 'all due expedition', the court should take into account whether papers were served on the defence in time to allow adequate consideration of the type of committal.

By extension of the same principle, however, the due expedition of the prosecution should be assessed in relation to matters they were obliged to carry out, rather than additional burdens they had assumed (*Southwark Crown Court, ex parte DPP* [1999] Crim LR 394). The decision of the Divisional Court in *R (Hughes) v Woolwich Crown Court* [2006] EWHC 2191 (Admin) underlines the fact that the due expedition of the prosecution in complying with its duties of disclosure will be judged from the time that the obligation in fact arises, rather than necessarily when the formal requirements of the service of a defence statement have been completed.

(b) *Who is responsible for any delay.* The other consideration to which the court should have reference is whether the lack of expedition is actually the fault of the prosecution, or whether it is caused by some third party and beyond the prosecution's control. The most obvious third party in this context is the independent science service. In *Central Criminal Court, ex parte Johnson* [1999] 2 Cr App R 51, the Divisional Court recognised that the prosecution would not have failed to show due expedition where delay had been caused by the independent science service, providing that all reasonable steps had been taken to ensure that the evidence in question was provided in proper time. This includes the obligation to make the laboratory aware of the trial date and time-limit. In *R (Holland) v Leeds Crown Court* [2003] Crim LR 272, failure to inform the laboratory of the time constraints was fatal to a claim to due expedition.

Similarly, delay occasioned by the non-availability of a prosecution witness will translate into a failure by the prosecution to act with due expedition only where it could not be shown that the prosecution had taken reasonable steps in the circumstances to ensure the attendance of the witness. However, the prosecution cannot be expected to 'nursemaid' their witnesses at all times (*Leeds Crown Court, ex parte Redfearn* [1999] COD 437).

The Link between Due Expedition and the Need for an Extension In *Leeds Crown Court, ex parte Bagoutie* (1999) *The Times*, 31 May 1999, Lord Bingham CJ emphasised that the requirement of due expedition was not disciplinary in intention. It aimed to protect the accused from being kept in prison awaiting trial longer than was justifiable. Parliament had intended to insist that prosecutors could not seek extensions where the need for the extension was attributable to their own failure to act with due expedition. Hence, if the court was satisfied that there was good and sufficient cause for the extension, but was not satisfied that the prosecution had acted with all due expedition, it was not obliged to refuse the application if it concluded that the prosecution's failure had neither caused nor contributed to the need for the extension. **D14.31**

In *R (Gibson) v Winchester Crown Court* [2004] 1 WLR 1623, the Divisional Court held that a judge may properly extend custody time-limits even where the prosecution had not acted with all due diligence, if the prosecution's failure is not itself a cause for the required extension.

Applying the Criteria

In *White v DPP* [1989] Crim LR 375, the Divisional Court expressed doubt over the Crown Court judge's approach to the extension of the custody time-limit in W's case, namely that he had to be satisfied beyond reasonable doubt of the existence of good cause before granting an extension. In *Governor of Canterbury Prison, ex parte Craig* [1991] 2 QB 195, Watkins LJ (giving the judgment of the Divisional Court) referred (at p. 132) to the doubt expressed in *White v DPP* and stated: **D14.32**

> In our view, the standard to be applied is that of the balance of probabilities. That is the standard for determining bail applications. It should apply equally, we think, to related interlocutory questions of the sort here in question.

The onus, then, is on the prosecution to satisfy the court as to the criteria for extension.

In *Wildman v DPP* (2001) 165 JP 453, the Divisional Court stated that the prosecution 'have to enable the defendant to test the matters which are relied upon by the Crown'. If the material on which they rely includes oral evidence, the defence must be given an opportunity to cross-examine (*R (DPP) v Havering Magistrates' Court* [2001] 1 WLR 805). However, it is for the prosecution to decide what evidence to call in support of their application, and the defence cannot insist on a witness being called purely to allow him to be criticised (*R (Rippe) v Chelmsford Crown Court* [2002] Crim LR 485).

Crown Court applications for extension of a time-limit may and normally would be determined by a Crown Court judge in chambers (CrimPR, r. 16.11(2)(f)). In *Leeds Crown Court, ex parte Briggs (No. 1)* [1998] 2 Cr App R 413, the Divisional Court stated that the Crown Court judge dealing with an application should give reasons for granting an extension.

Appeals

D14.33 **From the Magistrates' Court to the Crown Court** Following an application to a magistrates' court for extension of a time-limit, the party against whom the magistrates' decision goes may appeal to the Crown Court (Prosecution of Offences Act 1985, s. 22(7) and (8)). An appeal by the prosecution against refusal to extend must be commenced before the actual expiry of the limit, but, provided that is done, the limit is deemed not to have expired until after the determination of the appeal (s. 22(9)).

Rule 20.1 of the CrimPR (see **appendix 1**) sets out the procedure to be followed on such appeals, in particular, the requirement for notice to the court and the other party and the contents of the notice. Appeals against magistrates' decisions on applications to extend are matters that may and normally would be determined by a Crown Court judge in chambers (r. 16.11(2)(g)).

D14.34 **From the Crown Court to the Divisional Court** The mechanism of a challenge to the decision of the Crown Court to grant an extension of time-limits will depend on its basis.

(a) If it is on the basis that there was insufficient evidence to justify that decision, the challenge should be made by way of appeal by case stated to the Divisional Court. In that way, the Crown Court judge will be able to set out clearly the facts found and the material on which the findings were based (*Central Criminal Court, ex parte Behbehari* [1994] Crim LR 352).
(b) In other circumstances, it will be appropriate for a challenge to the decision to be by way of judicial review. In such a case, the requirement for promptness under the Civil Procedure Rules, part 54, will not always be satisfied by commencing proceedings within the three-month period set out therein, but will depend on the circumstances of the case. In *R (Siraju) v Crown Court at Snaresbrook* [2001] EWHC Admin 638, it was stated that a delay which makes it impossible for the matter to be reconsidered by the Crown Court before the original time-limit expires will normally be fatal to a judicial review application.

The exercise of the power to extend a time-limit cannot be used as a ground of appeal should the accused ultimately be convicted (s. 22(10)).

Statutes on Custody Time-limits

D14.35 **Prosecution of Offences Act 1985, ss. 22, 22A and 22B**

22.—(1) The Secretary of State may by regulations make provision, with respect to any specified preliminary stage of proceedings for an offence, as to the maximum period—
(a) to be allowed to the prosecution to complete that stage;
(b) during which the accused may, while awaiting completion of that stage, be—
(i) in the custody of a magistrates' court; or
(ii) in the custody of the Crown Court;
in relation to that offence.

(2) The regulations may, in particular—
(a) be made so as to apply only in relation to proceedings instituted in specified areas or proceedings of, or against persons of, specified classes or descriptions;
(b) make different provision with respect to proceedings instituted in different areas, or different provision with respect to proceedings of, or against persons of, different classes or descriptions;
(c) make such provision with respect to the procedure to be followed in criminal proceedings as the Secretary of State considers appropriate in consequence of any other provision of the regulations;
(d) provide for the Magistrates' Courts Act 1980 and the Bail Act 1976 to apply in relation to cases to which custody or overall time limits apply subject to such modifications as may be specified (being modifications which the Secretary of State considers necessary in consequence of any provision made by the regulations); and
(e) make such transitional provision in relation to proceedings instituted before the commencement of any provision of the regulations as the Secretary of State considers appropriate.

(3) The appropriate court may, at any time before the expiry of a time limit imposed by the regulations, extend, or further extend that limit; but the court shall not do so unless it is satisfied—
(a) that the need for the extension is due to—
(i) the illness or absence of the accused, a necessary witness, a judge or a magistrate;
(ii) a postponement which is occasioned by the ordering by the court of separate trials in the case of two or more accused or two or more offences; or
(iii) some other good and sufficient cause; and
(b) that the prosecution has acted with all due diligence and expedition.

(4) Where, in relation to any proceedings for an offence, an overall time limit has expired before the completion of the stage of the proceedings to which the limit applies, the appropriate court shall stay the proceedings.

(5) Where—
(a) a person escapes from the custody of a magistrates' court or the Crown Court before the expiry of a custody time limit which applies in his case; or
(b) a person who has been released on bail in consequence of the expiry of a custody time limit—
(i) fails to surrender himself into the custody of the court at the appointed time; or
(ii) is arrested by a constable on a ground mentioned in section 7(3)(b) of the Bail Act 1976 (breach, or likely breach, of conditions of bail);

the regulations shall, so far as they provide for any custody time limit in relation to the preliminary stage in question, be disregarded.

(6) Subsection (6A) below applies where—
(a) a person escapes from the custody of a magistrates' court or the Crown Court; or
(b) a person who has been released on bail fails to surrender himself into the custody of the court at the appointed time;

and is accordingly unlawfully at large for any period.

(6A) The following, namely—
(a) the period for which the person is unlawfully at large; and
(b) such additional period (if any) as the appropriate court may direct, having regard to the disruption of the prosecution occasioned by—
(i) the person's escape or failure to surrender; and
(ii) the length of the period mentioned in paragraph (a) above,

shall be disregarded, so far as the offence in question is concerned, for the purposes of the overall time limit which applies in his case in relation to the stage which the proceedings have reached at the time of the escape or, as the case may be, at the appointed time.

(6B) Any period during which proceedings for an offence are adjourned pending the determination of an appeal under part 9 of the Criminal Justice Act 2003 shall be disregarded, so far as the offence is concerned, for the purposes of the overall time limit and the custody time limit which applies to the stage which the proceedings have reached when they are adjourned.

(7) Where a magistrates' court decides to extend, or further extend, a custody or overall time limit, or to give a direction under subsection (6A) above, the accused may appeal against the decision to the Crown Court.

(8) Where a magistrates' court refuses to extend, or further extend, a custody or overall time limit, or to give a direction under subsection (6A) above, the prosecution may appeal against the refusal to the Crown Court.

(9) An appeal under subsection (8) above may not be commenced after the expiry of the limit in question; but where such an appeal is commenced before the expiry of the limit the limit shall be deemed not to have expired before the determination or abandonment of the appeal.

(10) Where a person is convicted of an offence in any proceedings, the exercise, in relation to any preliminary stage of those proceedings, of the power conferred by subsection (3) above shall not be called into question in any appeal against that conviction.

(11) In this section—

'appropriate court' means—

(a) where the accused has been committed for trial, sent for trial under section 51 of the Crime and Disorder Act 1998 or indicted for the offence, the Crown Court; and

(b) in any other case, the magistrates' court specified in the summons or warrant in question or, where the accused has already appeared or been brought before a magistrates' court, a magistrates' court for the same area;

'custody' includes local authority accommodation to which a person is remanded or committed by virtue of section 23 of the Children and Young Persons Act 1969, and references to a person being committed to custody shall be construed accordingly;

'custody of the Crown Court' includes custody to which a person is committed in pursuance of—

(a) section 6 of the Magistrates' Courts Act 1980 (magistrates' court committing accused for trial); or

(b) section 43A of that Act (magistrates' court dealing with a person brought before it following his arrest in pursuance of a warrant issued by the Crown Court); or

(c) section 5(2)(a) of the Criminal Justice Act 1987 (custody after transfer order in fraud case); or

(d) paragraph 2(1)(a) of schedule 6 to the Criminal Justice Act 1991 (custody after transfer order in certain cases involving children).

'custody of a magistrates' court' means custody to which a person is committed in pursuance of section 128 of the Magistrates' Courts Act 1980 (remand);

'custody time limit' means a time limit imposed by regulations made under subsection (1)(b) above or, where any such limit has been extended by a court under subsection (3) above, the limit as so extended;

'preliminary stage', in relation to any proceedings, does not include any stage after the start of the trial (within the meaning given by subsections (11A) and (11B) below);

'overall time limit' means a time limit imposed by regulations made under subsection (1)(a) above or, where any such limit has been extended by a court under subsection (3) above, the limit as so extended; and

'specified' means specified in the regulations.

(11ZA) For the purposes of this section, proceedings for an offence shall be taken to begin when the accused is charged with the offence or, as the case may be, an information is laid charging him with the offence.

(11A) For the purposes of this section, the start of a trial on indictment shall be taken to occur at the time when a jury is sworn to consider the issue of guilt or fitness to plead or, if the court accepts a plea of guilty before the time when a jury is sworn, when that plea is accepted; but this is subject to section 8 of the Criminal Justice Act 1987 and section 30 of the Criminal Procedure and Investigations Act 1996 (preparatory hearings).

(11AA) The references in subsection (11A) above to the time when a jury is sworn include the time when that jury would be sworn but for the making of an order under part 7 of the Criminal Justice Act 2003.

(11B) For the purposes of this section, the start of a summary trial shall be taken to occur—

(a) when the court begins to hear evidence for the prosecution at the trial or to consider whether to exercise its power under section 37(3) of the Mental Health Act 1983 (power to make hospital order without convicting the accused), or

(b) if the court accepts a plea of guilty without proceeding as mentioned above, when that plea is accepted.

(12) For the purposes of the application of any custody time limit in relation to a person who is in

the custody of a magistrates' court or the Crown Court—

(a) all periods during which he is in the custody of a magistrates' court in respect of the same offence shall be aggregated and treated as a single continuous period; and

(b) all periods during which he is in the custody of the Crown Court in respect of the same offence shall be aggregated and treated similarly.

(13) For the purposes of section 29(3) of the Supreme Court Act 1981 (High Court to have power to make prerogative orders in relation to jurisdiction of Crown Court in matters which do not relate to trial on indictment) the jurisdiction conferred on the Crown Court by this section shall be taken to be part of its jurisdiction in matters other than those relating to trial on indictment.

22A.—(1) The Secretary of State may by regulations make provision—

(a) with respect to a person under the age of 18 at the time of his arrest in connection with an offence, as to the maximum period to be allowed for the completion of the stage beginning with his arrest and ending with the date fixed for his first appearance in court in connection with the offence ('the initial stage');

(b) with respect to a person convicted of an offence who was under that age at the time of his arrest for the offence or (where he was not arrested for it) the laying of the information charging him with it, as to the period within which the stage between his conviction and his being sentenced for the offence should be completed.

(2) Subsection (2) of section 22 above applies for the purposes of regulations under subsection (1) above as if—

(a) the reference in paragraph (d) to custody or overall time limits were a reference to time limits imposed by the regulations; and

(b) the reference in paragraph (e) to proceedings instituted before the commencement of any provisions of the regulations were a reference to a stage begun before that commencement.

(3) A magistrates' court may, at any time before the expiry of the time limit imposed by the regulations under subsection (1)(a) above ('the initial stage time limit'), extend, or further extend, that limit; but the court shall not do so unless it is satisfied—

(a) that the need for the extension is due to some good and sufficient cause; and

(b) that the investigation has been conducted, and (where applicable) the prosecution has acted, with all due diligence and expedition.

(4) Where the initial stage time limit (whether as originally imposed or as extended or further extended under subsection (3) above) expires before the person arrested is charged with the offence, he shall not be charged with it unless further evidence relating to it is obtained, and—

(a) if he is then under arrest, he shall be released;

(b) if he is then on bail under part IV of the Police and Criminal Evidence Act 1984, his bail (and any duty or conditions to which it is subject) shall be discharged.

22B.—(1) This section applies where proceedings for an offence ('the original proceedings') are stayed by a court under section 22(4) or 22A(5) of this Act.

(2) If—

(a) in the case of proceedings conducted by the Director, the Director or a Chief Crown Prosecutor so directs;

(b) in the case of proceedings conducted by the Director of the Serious Fraud Office, the Commissioners of Inland Revenue or the Commissioners of Customs and Excise, that Director or those Commissioners so direct; or

(c) in the case of proceedings not conducted as mentioned in paragraph (a) or (b) above, a person designated for the purpose by the Secretary of State so directs,

fresh proceedings for the offence may be instituted within a period of three months (or such longer period as the court may allow) after the date on which the original proceedings were stayed by the court.

(3) Fresh proceedings shall be instituted as follows—

(a) where the original proceedings were stayed by the Crown Court, by preferring a bill of indictment;

(b) where the original proceedings were stayed by a magistrates' court, by laying an information.

(4) Fresh proceedings may be instituted in accordance with subsections (2) and (3)(b) above notwithstanding anything in section 127(1) of the Magistrates' Courts Act 1980

(limitation of time).

(5) Where fresh proceedings are instituted, anything done in relation to the original proceedings shall be treated as done in relation to the fresh proceedings if the court so directs or it was done—

(a) by the prosecutor in compliance or purported compliance with section 3, 4 or 7A of the Criminal Procedure and Investigations Act 1996; or

(b) by the accused in compliance or purported compliance with section 5 or 6 of that Act.

(6) Where a person is convicted of an offence in fresh proceedings under this section, the institution of those proceedings shall not be called into question in any appeal against that conviction.

PRE-TRIAL AND PLEA AND CASE MANAGEMENT HEARINGS

D14.36 As has been emphasised by the Court of Appeal in a series of decisions since the introduction of the CrimPR, a considerably greater emphasis is now placed on case management (see **D3** for a full discussion). At the forefront of this development is the active role played by the court in ensuring that, by the time a case reaches a jury, all necessary preparation has been completed, and completed as efficiently and expeditiously as possible. Nowhere is this approach better demonstrated than in relation to pre-trial hearings, the purpose of which is to reduce delay and focus minds on the key issues that are to occupy the court and jury at trial.

The Impact of Automatic Directions

D14.37 Such pre-trial hearings must now be viewed in the context of the automatic directions that are laid down under part 3 of the CrimPR (see **appendix 1**), and para IV.41 of the *Consolidated Criminal Practice Direction* (see **appendix** 7). The directions are to be made automatically as part of the process of transferring the case to the Crown Court and are set out in the different versions of the case progression form set out in annex E of the Direction — which version is appropriate depends on the methods by which the case is transferred to the Crown Court.

The purpose of the automatic directions, which govern the preparation of the case by the parties, is to ensure that the matters set out have been addressed before the date of the plea and case management hearing at the Crown Court. All of the directions contained in the relevant form 'apply in every case unless the court otherwise orders' [para. V.56.6].

In further guidance provided by the Senior Presiding Judge on 22 April 2005, it was made clear that the magistrates' court must make the directions specified using the prescribed form. The guidance states:

> The standard directions are set out in the magistrates' court case progression forms for cases sent and committed to the Crown Court and *must* be made in every case: this is not discretionary. However, the magistrates' court may decide that additional or alternative directions are required in a particular case.

D14.38 **The Directions** The deadlines for activity by the parties imposed under the directions differ according to the form of committal.

Figure A: Time-line of Standard Directions for Cases Committed to the Crown Court under the Magistrates' Courts Act 1980, s. 6

All Dates calculated from the date of committal

14 DAYS	Defence to provide witness requirements *(CPIA 1996, s. 68 & sch. 2)*	Prosecution to prov.de initial disclosure	Prosecution to serve notice of intention to introduce hearsay evidence *(r. 34.3)*	Defence to give notice of intention to introduce hearsay evidence *(r. 34.4)*	Defence to apply to introduce the bad character of a prosecution witness *(r. 35.2)*	Prosecution to apply to introduce the bad character of the defendant *(r. 35.4)*
21 DAYS						Defence to respond to prosecution's application to introduce the bad character of the defendant *(r. 35.6)*
28 DAYS	Prosecution to prefer indictment *(r. 14.1(1))*	Prosecution to serve any application for special measures *(r. 29.1(4))*	Defence to respond to prosecution's notice of intention to introduce hearsay evidence *(r. 34.5)*	Prosecution to respond to defence's notice of intention to introduce hearsay evidence *(r. 34.5)*	Prosecution to respond to defence's application to introduce the bad character of a prosecution witness *(r. 35.3)*	Defence to serve defence statement *(CPIA 1996 (Defence Disclosure Time Limits) Regs. 1997, reg. 2)*
42 DAYS		Defence to serve any response to the prosecution's application for special measures *(r. 29.1(6))*				

Figure B: Time-line of Standard Directions for Cases Sent to the Crown Court under the Crime and Disorder Act 1998, s. 51

All Dates calculated from the date of sending: dates in bold where defendant is in custody

50/70 DAYS	Prosecution to serve copies of the evidence on which charges are based, initial disclosure and a draft indictment *(CDA 1998, s. 51)]*					
57/77 DAYS (7 DAYS AFTER SERVICE)	Defence to provide witness requirements *(CJA 1967, s. 9(1))*					
64/84 DAYS (14 DAYS AFTER SERVICE)	Defence to give notice of any application to dismiss *(rr. 13.2(2)(c) & 13.3(4)(c))*	Defence to serve defence statement *(CPIA 1996 (Defence Disclosure Time Limits) Regs. 1997, reg. 2)*	Prosecution to serve notice of intention to introduce hearsay evidence *(r. 34.3)*	Defence to give notice of intention to introduce hearsay evidence *(r. 34.4)*	Defence to apply to introduce the bad character of a prosecution witness *(r. 35.2)*	Prosecution to apply to introduce the bad character of the defendant *(r. 35.4)*
71/91 DAYS (21 DAYS AFTER SERVICE)						Defence to respond to prosecution's application to introduce the bad character of the defendant *(r. 35.6)*
78/98 DAYS (28 DAYS AFTER SERVICE)	Prosecution to prefer indictment *(r. 14.1(1))*	Prosecution to serve any application for special measures *(r. 29.1(4))*	Defence to respond to prosecution's notice of intention to introduce hearsay evidence *(r. 34.5)*	Prosecution to respond to defence's notice of intention to introduce hearsay evidence *(r. 34.5)*	Prosecution to respond to defence's application to introduce the bad character of a prosecution witness *(r. 35.3)*	
92/105 DAYS (42 DAYS AFTER SERVICE)		Defence to serve any response to the prosecution's application for special measures *(r. 29.1(6))*				
98/119 DAYS	Plea and Case Management Hearing *(Practice Direction, para. V.56.5)*					

(a) Under the *Consolidated Criminal Practice Direction*, para. V.56.3, at proceedings for committal under the MCA 1980, s. 6, the court is invited to make the series of automatic directions which are summarised in the time-line at Figure A.
(b) Under para. V.56.3, when a case is sent under the CDA 1998, s. 51, the court is invited to make the series of automatic directions which are summarised in the time-line at Figure B. It will be noted that all timings in Figure B are derived from the date on which the prosecution serves its case and completes primary disclosure. With the removal of the need for preliminary hearings, the periods for the service of the case have now become (under the Crime and Disorder Act 1998 (Service of Prosecution Evidence) Regulations 2005 (SI 2005 No. 902): see **D10.14**) 50 days when the accused is in custody (8 days + 42 days) and 70 days when the accused is on bail (28 days + 42 days).

Inconsistent Time-limits The automatic directions for action that is required in response to the service of the case and completion of primary disclosure are culled from a variety of statutory provisions. Because the time-limits imposed by those statutory provisions have, in some cases, been decided in isolation, their combined effect can have unforeseen consequences. For example, the defence are required to provide a defence statement within 14 days of receipt of primary disclosure, because that is the time-limit imposed by the Criminal Procedure and Investigations Act 1996 (Defence Disclosure Time-limits) Regulations 1997 (SI 1997 No. 2680), but the prosecution do not have to prefer the indictment until 28 days after the service of their case, because that is the time-limit in the CrimPR, r. 14.1(1). **D14.39**

Preliminary Hearings

Under the old r. 27(2)(h) of the Crown Court Rules 1982, the Crown Court was obliged to list a defendant's case for a preliminary hearing within eight days of his being sent to the Crown Court in custody, or within 28 days of his being sent on bail. Under CrimPR, r. 12.2, these fixed time-limits no longer apply. **D14.40**

The reason for this can be found in para. IV.41.3 of the *Consolidated Criminal Practice Direction*, which states:

> A preliminary hearing ('PH') is not required in every case sent for trial under section 51 of the Crime and Disorder Act 1998: see rule 12.2 (which altered the Crown Court rule from which it derived). A PH should be ordered only where the court considers such a hearing necessary for some compelling reason.

Circumstances in which there Should be a Preliminary Hearing Paragraph V.56.4 of the *Consolidated Criminal Practice Direction* further makes clear that the decision as to whether or not there should be a preliminary hearing is a decision that may be taken by either the Crown Court or the magistrates. The latter should, if they deem it appropriate for there to be such a hearing, order that it should take place within 14 days. **D14.41**

The Practice Direction itself is silent as to the circumstances in which a preliminary hearing will be appropriate. However, the guidance notes state that a preliminary hearing should be held in the following circumstances:

> (i) there are case management issues which call for such a hearing;
> (ii) the case is likely to last more than 4 weeks;
> (iii) it would be desirable to set an early trial date;
> (iv) the defendant is a child or young person;
> (v) there is likely to be a guilty plea and the defendant could be sentenced at a preliminary hearing; or
> (vi) it seems to the court it is a case suitable for a preparatory hearing in the Crown Court . . .

Pre-trial Hearings

D14.42 The CPIA 1996, ss. 39 to 43, and especially ss. 39 and 40, provide reinforcement in statutory form for the various pre-trial procedures developed in the Crown Court in order to promote the efficient conduct of trials on indictment. They consolidate and bolster the rules for plea and case management hearings (see **D14.44**), which are set out in the *Consolidated Criminal Practice Direction*, para IV.41 (see **appendix** 7) and CrimPR, part 3 (see **D4.6** and, for the text, **appendix** 1).

Criminal Procedure and Investigations Act 1996, ss. 39 and 40

39.—(1) For the purposes of this part a hearing is a pre-trial hearing if it relates to a trial on indictment and it takes place—

(a) after the accused has been sent for trial for the offence and

(b) before the start of the trial.

(2) For the purposes of this part a hearing is also a pre-trial hearing if—

(a) it relates to a trial on indictment to be held in pursuance of a bill of indictment preferred under the authority of section 2(2)(b) of the Administration of Justice (Miscellaneous Provisions) Act 1933 (bill preferred by direction of Court of Appeal or by direction or with consent of a judge), and

(b) it takes place after the bill of indictment has been preferred and before the start of the trial.

(3) For the purposes of this section the start of a trial on indictment occurs at the time when a jury is sworn to consider the issue of guilt or fitness to plead or, if the court accepts a plea of guilty before the time when a jury is sworn, when that plea is accepted; but this is subject to section 8 of the Criminal Justice Act 1987 and section 30 of this Act (preparatory hearings).

(4) The references in subsection (3) to the time when a jury is sworn include the time when that jury would be sworn but for the making of an order under Part 7 of the Criminal Justice Act 2003.

40.—(1) A judge may make at a pre-trial hearing a ruling as to—

(a) any question as to the admissibility of evidence;

(b) any other question of law relating to the case concerned.

(2) A ruling may be made under this section—

(a) on an application by a party to the case, or

(b) of the judge's own motion.

(3) Subject to subsection (4), a ruling made under this section has binding effect from the time it is made until the case against the accused or, if there is more than one, against each of them is disposed of; and the case against an accused is disposed of if—

(a) he is acquitted or convicted, or

(b) the prosecutor decides not to proceed with the case against him.

(4) A judge may discharge or vary (or further vary) a ruling made under this section if it appears to him that it is in the interests of justice to do so; and a judge may act under this subsection—

(a) on an application by a party to the case, or

(b) of the judge's own motion.

(5) No application may be made under subsection (4)(a) unless there has been a material change of circumstances since the ruling was made or, if a previous application has been made, since the application (or last application) was made.

(6) The judge referred to in subsection (4) need not be the judge who made the ruling or, if it has been varied, the judge (or any of the judges) who varied it.

(7) For the purposes of this section the prosecutor is any person acting as prosecutor, whether an individual or a body.

D14.43 **Procedure** As these are pre-trial hearings, they can therefore be conducted by a judge who will not be the eventual trial judge. They differ from preparatory hearings in long or complex cases (see **D14.48**) in this respect. Restrictions on the reporting of pre-trial rulings are contained in the CPIA 1996, ss. 41 and 42. There are no exemptions in respect of the publication of formal details, such as the name, address and occupation of the accused (again, in contrast with the position in relation to preparatory hearings).

In *Diedrick* [1997] 1 Cr App R 361, the appeal concerned the actions of the trial judge in questioning the accused about what he thought was a lie which the accused had told in the questionnaire. The Court of Appeal observed that what was said at the plea and directions hearing was not expected to form part of the material for trial, and it would rarely be appropriate to refer to it. Where the trial judge was considering the use of such material, counsel should be allowed to address the judge first.

Plea and Case Management Hearings

Save in cases where a preparatory hearing is required (discussed at **D14.46**), the major pre-trial hearing will be the plea and case management hearing. The purpose of such hearings is to ensure that all steps necessary for the proper preparation of a case for trial have been taken or are properly timetabled for future attention. These hearings will occur within seven weeks of committal, 14 weeks of sending or notice of transfer where the accused is in custody or 17 weeks of sending or notice of transfer where the accused is on bail. **D14.44**

In the *Consolidated Criminal Practice Direction*, the rationale for such hearings is expressed at para. IV.41.8 as follows:

> Active case management at the PCMH should reduce the number of ineffective and cracked trials and delays during the trial to resolve legal issues. The effectiveness of a PCMH hearing in a contested case depends in large measure upon preparation by all concerned and upon the presence of the trial advocate or advocate who is able to make decisions and give the court the assistance which the trial advocate could be expected to give. Resident Judges in setting the listing policy should ensure that list officers fix cases as far as possible to enable the trial advocate to conduct the PCMH and the trial.

The Form The form to be used at plea and case management hearings is that which appears in annex E of the Practice Direction. In further guidance provided by the Senior Presiding Judge on 22 April 2005, it is made clear that the new plea and case management hearing form is the only form that may be used at such hearings. The purpose of this is to ensure uniformity of forms across the country. The guidance goes on to say that the 'discretionary element in respect of the PCMH form is the manner in which the form is used' and stresses the importance of there being a written record of all orders made at the plea and case management hearing which is made available to all concerned. **D14.45**

The matters of case preparation that are addressed in the form are also addressed at other parts of this book. These include:

(a) orders in relation to witnesses, such as special measures (see **D14.97**) and witness summonses (see **D14.89**);
(b) orders as to disclosure (see **D8** and **D14.67**);
(c) outstanding legal issues, including applications under the bad character and hearsay provisions of the CJA 2003 (see **F12, F14 and F16**).

PREPARATORY HEARINGS

Preparatory hearings are a key pre-trial part of the criminal process in complex cases, the aims of which are very much in keeping with the case management ethos described above, namely the early identification of the issues and the tailoring of the trial process to those issues. Such hearings may be held in long and complex cases (pursuant to the CPIA 1996: see **D14.48**) and in serious fraud cases (pursuant to the CJA 1987: see **D14.56**). **D14.46**

The Fraud Protocol At such hearings, it is important to consider the aspirations behind the Protocol for the control and management of heavy fraud and other complex criminal cases, issued on 22 March 2005 by the then Lord Chief Justice. The document is premised on a **D14.47**

general acceptance that trials of fraud and complex cases take too long, and need to be controlled.

The Protocol seeks to achieve this, in conjunction with the CrimPR, by encouraging continuous case management by judges presiding over trials which may last more than eight weeks. The Protocol, which is set out in **appendix 9**, includes guidance covering the following areas.

(a) There should be initial consideration of the length of trial, requiring the prosecution team to justify the length of trial where it will exceed eight weeks (para. 1(iv)) and to notify the court and others where the case is likely to exceed that length (para. 1(v)). The trial judge is also expected to 'consider what steps should be taken to reduce the length of the trial, whilst still ensuring that the prosecution has the opportunity of placing the full criminality before the court' (para. 3(vi)(b)).
(b) Early appointment of a trial judge is required where the case will last more than four weeks, who will then 'manage the case from cradle to grave' (para. 2). The judge will require a more detailed knowledge of the case than would normally be the case (para. 3(i)(b)).
(c) Case management issues are highlighted, including the matters that should be addressed at directions hearings (para. 3(iii)), with a short preliminary hearing followed by a full case management hearing attended by trial counsel. Prior to that hearing, both prosecution and defence will have identified their cases and at the preliminary hearing there should be 'a real dialogue between the judge and all advocates for the purpose of identifying the focus of the prosecution case, the common ground and the real issues in the case' (para. 3(iv)(b)).
(d) On disclosure, there should be a timetable for structured disclosure which prevents the defence solicitors spending 'a disproportionate amount of time and incur[ring] disproportionate costs trawling through a morass of documents' (para. 4(iii)).

Preparatory Hearings under the Criminal Procedure and Investigations Act 1996, ss. 28 to 38

D14.48 Sections 28 to 38 of the CPIA 1996 contain provisions for preparatory hearings in long or complex cases. They originate from the procedure established for serious fraud cases, which came into force by virtue of the CJA 1987 (see **D14.56**).

D14.49 **Initiating a Preparatory Hearing** The decision to hold a preparatory hearing may be made by a Crown Court judge at any time before a jury is sworn, on the application of any of the parties or by the court of its own motion. The CrimPR, part 15 (see **appendix 1**), lays down deadlines for the defence or prosecution to apply for a preparatory hearing and sets out the procedure for determining any such application. Part 15 also covers the situation where a prosecutor seeks an order for a trial to be conducted with a judge sitting alone, within the terms of the CJA 2003, s. 43 or s. 44 (see **D13.66** ***et seq.***).

D14.50 **The Test for Holding a Hearing** A preparatory hearing can be held, within the scope of the CPIA 1996, only if the case appears to the judge to be complex, serious or likely to lead to a lengthy trial. Where there is no material upon which the judge can properly come to the conclusion that the case will be complex, serious or lengthy, there is no power to hold a preparatory hearing. In such a case, there will be no jurisdiction to entertain an interlocutory appeal (*Ward* [2003] 2 Cr App R 315).

D14.51 **The Status of a Preparatory Hearing** The preparatory hearing is in fact a stage of the trial itself and may be used in order to settle various issues without requiring the jury to attend (s. 30). Since the trial begins with the preparatory hearing, the same judge must preside throughout, save for exceptional circumstances such as death or serious illness (see *Southwark*

Crown Court, ex parte Commissioners for Customs and Excise [1993] 1 WLR 764 and **D14.59**). This contrasts with the position as far as a plea and case management hearing is concerned.

It is possible for a judge to conduct separate preparatory hearings in respect of different accused who are charged in the same indictment (*Re Kanaris* [2003] 1 WLR 443). Each accused is charged jointly and severally, and may thus be dealt with individually if the interests of justice so require.

Matters that may be Addressed during a Preparatory Hearing The purpose of a preparatory hearing is set out in the CPIA 1996, s. 29(2), and may be summarised as: **D14.52**

(a) identifying material issues for the jury;
(b) assisting them to understand those issues;
(c) expediting proceedings before them;
(d) helping the judge to manage the trial; and
(e) considering questions as to the severance or joinder of charges.

Disclosure Among the powers available to the court at a preparatory hearing is the power to order the prosecutor and the defence to make disclosure in advance of the hearing (CPIA 1996, s. 31(4) to (7)), in addition to any disclosure already made as a result of the general duties on the parties (see **D8** and CrimPR, rr. 15.5 and 15.6). In *H* [2007] 2 WLR 364, the House of Lords held that an order or ruling in relation to disclosure under the CPIA, s. 8, did not fall within the purposes for which a preparatory hearing may be held, and therefore could not form the basis for an interlocutory appeal (see also **D14.60**). **D14.53**

Legal Rulings The court may also make rulings as to any question of law relating to the case, including questions as to the admissibility of evidence (CPIA 1996, s. 31(3)), but its powers in this respect may be circumscribed by the principle in *Re Gunawardena* [1990] 1 WLR 703. In that case, it was held that the power to make binding rulings in a preparatory hearing in a serious fraud case was limited by implication to the purposes for which preparatory hearings may be ordered, as set out in s. 29(2) (see **D14.52**). **D14.54**

Applications of this principle include the following.

(a) *Claydon* [2004] 1 WLR 1575, in which the Court of Appeal held that a judge had power to determine, at a preparatory hearing under s. 29, questions of admissibility of evidence under the PACE 1984, s. 78. His rulings on these matters were therefore subject to appeal under the CPIA 1996, s. 35.
(b) *R* (2000) *Independent*, 10 April 2000, in which, similarly, the Court of Appeal held that it had jurisdiction to hear an appeal brought pursuant to s. 35, in respect of evidence sought to be excluded under the PACE 1984, s. 78.
(c) *van Hoogstraaten* [2004] Crim LR 498, where the prosecution appealed against the ruling of the judge which was, in effect, to quash the indictment and, by contrast, the Court of Appeal held that the ruling in question lay outside the scope of the CPIA 1996, s. 29(2), and it therefore had no jurisdiction to entertain an appeal.
(d) *H* [2007] 2 WLR 364, in which it was held that because an order as to disclosure, following an application under the CPIA 1996, s. 8, did not fall within the purposes of a preparatory hearing, it could not form the subject of an appeal. However, there was nothing to prevent a judge dealing with a preparatory hearing from addressing issues of disclosure at the same time and, in effect, in parallel.
(e) In *Shayler* [2001] 1 WLR 2206, the Court of Appeal held that the judge at a preparatory hearing could rule on whether a particular defence (in this case, duress/necessity) was available to an accused as a matter of law.

Note however that in *H* considerable doubts were cast on the correctness of *Re Gunawardena*, *Claydon* and *van Hoogstaaten*.

D14.55 **Reporting Restrictions** Restrictions on reporting preparatory hearings are contained in the CPIA 1996, s. 37, although certain formal details (e.g., the names, ages, home addresses and occupations of the accused and witnesses, and the offence(s) charged) may be published by virtue of s. 37(9). The court has power to lift the restrictions (s. 37(3)).

Criminal Procedure and Investigations Act 1996, ss. 29 to 32 and 34

29.—(1) Where it appears to a judge of the Crown Court that an indictment reveals a case of such complexity, a case of such seriousness or a case whose trial is likely to be of such length, that substantial benefits are likely to accrue from a hearing—
(a) before the time when the jury are sworn, and
(b) for any of the purposes mentioned in subsection (2),
he may order that such a hearing (in this part referred to as a preparatory hearing) shall be held.

(1A) A judge of the Crown Court may also order that a preparatory hearing shall be held if an application to which section 45 of the Criminal Justice Act 2003 applies (application for trial without jury) is made.

(1B) An order that a preparatory hearing shall be held must be made by a judge of the Crown Court in every case which (whether or not it falls within subsection (1) or (1A)) is a case in which at least one of the offences charged by the indictment against at least one of the persons charged is a terrorism offence.

(1C) An order that a preparatory hearing shall be held must also be made by a judge of the Crown Court in every case which (whether or not it falls within subsection (1) or (1A)) is a case in which—
(a) at least one of the offences charged by the indictment against at least one of the persons charged is an offence carrying a maximum of at least 10 years' imprisonment; and
(b) it appears to the judge that evidence on the indictment reveals that conduct in respect of which that offence is charged had a terrorist connection.

(2) The purposes are those of—
(a) identifying issues which are likely to be material to the verdict of the jury;
(b) assisting their comprehension of any such issues;
(c) expediting the proceedings before the jury;
(d) assisting the judge's management of the trial;
(e) considering questions as to the severance or joinder of charges.

[(2) The purposes are those of—
(a) identifying issues which are likely to be material to the determinations and findings which are likely to be required during the trial,
(b) if there is to be a jury, assisting their comprehension of those issues and expediting the proceedings before them,
(c) determining an application to which section 45 of the Criminal Justice Act 2003 applies,]
(d) assisting the judge's management of the trial,
(e) considering questions as to the severance or joinder of charges.]

(3) In a case in which it appears to a judge of the Crown Court that evidence on an indictment reveals a case of fraud of such seriousness or complexity as is mentioned in section 7 of the Criminal Justice Act 1987 (preparatory hearings in cases of serious or complex fraud)—
(a) the judge may make an order for a preparatory hearing under this section only if he is required to do so by subsection (1B) or (1C);
(b) before making an order in pursuance of either of those subsections, he must determine whether to make an order for a preparatory hearing under that section; and
(c) he is not required by either of those subsections to make an order for a preparatory hearing under this section if he determines that an order should be made for a preparatory hearing under that section;
and, in a case in which an order is made for a preparatory hearing under that section, requirements imposed by those subsections apply only if that order ceases to have effect.

(4) An order that a preparatory hearing shall be held may be made—
(a) on the application of the prosecutor,
(b) on the application of the accused or, if there is more than one, any of them, or
(c) of the judge's own motion.

(5) The reference in subsection (1)(a) to the time when the jury are sworn includes the time when the jury would be sworn but for the making of an order under part 7 of the Criminal Justice Act 2003.
(6) In this section 'terrorism offence' means—
(a) an offence under section 11 or 12 of the Terrorism Act 2000 (offences relating to proscribed organisations);
(b) an offence under any of sections 15 to 18 of that Act (offences relating to terrorist property);
(c) an offence under section 38B of that Act (failure to disclose information about acts of terrorism);
(d) an offence under section 54 of that Act (weapons training);
(e) an offence under any of sections 56 to 59 of that Act (directing terrorism, possessing things and collecting information for the purposes of terrorism and inciting terrorism outside the United Kingdom);
(f) an offence in respect of which there is jurisdiction by virtue of section 62 of that Act (extra-territorial jurisdiction in respect of certain offences committed outside the United Kingdom for the purposes of terrorism etc.);
(g) an offence under part 1 of the Terrorism Act 2006 (miscellaneous terrorist related offences);
(h) conspiring or attempting to commit a terrorism offence;
(i) incitement to commit a terrorism offence.
(7) For the purposes of this section an offence carries a maximum of at least 10 years' imprisonment if—
(a) it is punishable, on conviction on indictment, with imprisonment; and
(b) the maximum term of imprisonment that may be imposed on conviction on indictment of that offence is 10 years or more or is imprisonment for life.
(8) For the purposes of this section conduct has a terrorist connection if it is or takes place in the course of an act of terrorism or is for the purposes of terrorism.
(9) In subsection (8) 'terrorism' has the same meaning as in the Terrorism Act 2000 (see section 1 of that Act).

Note: Section 29(5) and the version of s. 29(2) displayed in square brackets are in force only in respect of applications under the CJA 2003, s. 44 (jury tampering).

30. If a judge orders a preparatory hearing—
(a) the trial shall start with that hearing, and
(b) arraignment shall take place at the start of that hearing, unless it has taken place before then.

31.—(1) At the preparatory hearing the judge may exercise any of the powers specified in this section.
(2) The judge may adjourn a preparatory hearing from time to time.
(3) He may make a ruling as to—
(a) any question as to the admissibility of evidence;
(b) any other question of law relating to the case;
(c) any question as to the severance or joinder of charges.
(4) He may order the prosecutor—
(a) to give the court and the accused or, if there is more than one, each of them a written statement (a case statement) of the matters falling within subsection (5);
(b) to prepare the prosecution evidence and any explanatory material in such a form as appears to the judge to be likely to aid comprehension by a jury and to give it in that form to the court and to the accused or, if there is more than one, to each of them;
(c) to give the court and the accused or, if there is more than one, each of them written notice of documents the truth of the contents of which ought in the prosecutor's view to be admitted and of any other matters which in his view ought to be agreed;
(d) to make any amendments of any case statement given in pursuance of an order under paragraph (a) that appear to the judge to be appropriate, having regard to objections made by the accused or, if there is more than one, by any of them.
(5) The matters referred to in subsection (4)(a) are—
(a) the principal facts of the case for the prosecution;
(b) the witnesses who will speak to those facts;
(c) any exhibits relevant to those facts;

(d) any proposition of law on which the prosecutor proposes to rely;
(e) the consequences in relation to any of the counts in the indictment that appear to the prosecutor to flow from the matters falling within paragraphs (a) to (d).

(6) Where a judge has ordered the prosecutor to give a case statement and the prosecutor has complied with the order, the judge may order the accused or, if there is more than one, each of them—
. . .
(b) to give the court and the prosecutor written notice of any objections that he has to the case statement;
. . .

(7) Where a judge has ordered the prosecutor to give notice under subsection (4)(c) and the prosecutor has complied with the order, the judge may order the accused or, if there is more than one, each of them to give the court and the prosecutor a written notice stating—
(a) the extent to which he agrees with the prosecutor as to documents and other matters to which the notice under subsection (4)(c) relates, and
(b) the reason for any disagreement.

(8) A judge making an order under subsection (6) or (7) shall warn the accused or, if there is more than one, each of them of the possible consequence under section 34 of not complying with it.

(9) If it appears to a judge that reasons given in pursuance of subsection (7) are inadequate, he shall so inform the person giving them and may require him to give further or better reasons.

(10) An order under this section may specify the time within which any specified requirement contained in it is to be complied with.

(11) An order or ruling made under this section shall have effect throughout the trial, unless it appears to the judge on application made to him that the interests of justice require him to vary or discharge it.

32.—(1) This section applies where—
(a) a judge orders a preparatory hearing, and
(b) he decides that any order which could be made under section 31(4) to (7) at the hearing should be made before the hearing.

(2) In such a case—
(a) he may make any such order before the hearing (or at the hearing), and
(b) section 31(4) to (11) shall apply accordingly.

34.—(1) Any party may depart from the case he disclosed in pursuance of a requirement imposed under section 31.

(2) Where—
(a) a party departs from the case he disclosed in pursuance of a requirement imposed under section 31, or
(b) a party fails to comply with such a requirement,

the judge or, with the leave of the judge, any other party may make such comment as appears to the judge or the other party (as the case may be) to be appropriate and the jury or, in the case of a trial without a jury, the judge may draw such inference as appears proper.

(3) In doing anything under subsection (2) or in do anything under it the judge shall have regard—
(a) to the extent of the departure or failure, and
(b) to whether there is any justification for it.

(4) Except as provided by this section, in the case of a trial with a jury no part—
(a) of a statement given under section 31(6)(a), or
(b) of any other information relating to the case for the accused or, if there is more than one, the case for any of them, which was given in pursuance of a requirement imposed under section 31,

may be disclosed at a stage in the trial after the jury have been sworn without the consent of the accused concerned.

Preparatory Hearings under the Criminal Justice Act 1987

D14.56 The CJA 1987, enacted as a result of the 1986 report of the Fraud Trials committee (Roskill committee), provides for special 'preparatory hearings' in serious cases of fraud. The relevant provisions are contained in ss. 7 to 11 of the Act, supplemented by the CrimPR, part 15 (see

appendix 1). The provisions are similar to those in the CPIA 1996, ss. 28 to 38 (see **D14.51**), and are therefore described in outline only.

Initiating such a Hearing, and its Purpose By s. 7(1) of the CJA 1987, if it appears to a Crown Court judge that the evidence on an indictment 'reveals a case of fraud of such seriousness or complexity that substantial benefits are likely to accrue from a [preparatory] hearing', then he may order such a hearing. Preparatory hearings are not restricted to cases that have been transferred to the Crown Court by notice under s. 4 of the Act but may be ordered where committal proceedings have been held in the usual way, provided the statements or depositions reveal a fraud case of the requisite gravity. **D14.57**

An order for a preparatory hearing may be made on the application of a party or of the judge's own motion (s. 7(2)). Again, the procedure to be employed in applying for such a hearing is set out in CrimPR, part 15.

The Purpose of a Preparatory Hearing The purposes of the hearing are: (a) to identify the issues which are likely to be material to the verdict of the jury; (b) to assist their comprehension of those issues; (c) to expedite the proceedings before the jury; (d) to assist the judge's management of the trial; (e) the consideration of questions as to the severance or joinder of charges (CJA 1987, s. 7(1)(a) to (e)). **D14.58**

The Status of a Preparatory Hearing The trial is deemed to begin with the preparatory hearing, the accused being arraigned at the start thereof (CJA 1987, s. 8). In *Southwark Crown Court, ex parte Commissioners for Customs and Excise* [1993] 1 WLR 764, the Divisional Court held that a change of judge between preparatory hearing and proceedings in front of the jury could only be accepted in exceptional circumstances, e.g., the death or serious illness of the original judge. **D14.59**

Matters Addressed at Such a Hearing Any question as to the admissibility of evidence and any other question of law relating to the case may be determined at the preparatory hearing (CJA 1987, s. 9(3)). According to *Re Gunawardena* [1990] 1 WLR 703, however, that power is in fact confined to questions related to the purposes of the preparatory hearing, as now outlined in s. 7(1)(a) to (e) (see **D14.58**). **D14.60**

Applications of this principle include the following:

(a) In *G* [2002] Crim LR 59, the trial judge at the preparatory hearing considered the management of the trial of three accused for conspiracy to cheat. He ruled that the indictment related only to one particular 'cell' of the alleged conspiracy, and therefore, only evidence which related to the narrower conspiracy would be admissible. It was held that the purpose of the ruling fell within s. 7(1)(a) since it was 'identifying issues which are likely to be material to the verdict of the jury'. Further, the judge's purpose was pro-active case management to ensure that the jury were not over-burdened.
(b) In *Claydon* [2004] 1 WLR 1575, the Court of Appeal held that the purpose of 'expediting the proceedings before the jury' must include 'questions of evidence such as typically arise under s. 78' of the PACE 1984. Following *Gunawardena*, however, his rulings as to abuse of process would not be subject to appeal because it did not come within the listed purposes of a preparatory hearing, but any resolution of the anomaly 'must be left to a higher court'. That resolution came in *H* [2007] 2 WLR 364, in which the House of Lords concluded that a decision to stay or make other terminatory rulings come within the scope of s. 9. This has the potential to increase the ambit of rulings which may be appealed very dramatically.

Disclosure Either before or at the preparatory hearing, the judge may, under the CJA 1987, s. 9(4), order the prosecution to do any or all of the following: **D14.61**

(a) Supply the court and the accused with a 'case statement' specifying (i) the principal facts

Part D Procedure

of the prosecution case; (ii) the witnesses who will speak to those facts; (iii) any exhibits relevant thereto; (iv) any proposition of law on which the prosecution propose to rely; and (v) the relevance of the aforementioned to any of the counts in the indictment.

(b) Prepare their evidence and other explanatory material in a form that appears to the judge to be likely to aid comprehension by the jury (and to supply it in that form to the court and the accused).

(c) Give the court and the accused notice of matters which, in their view, ought to be agreed (including, where appropriate, the truth of the contents of relevant documents).

(d) Amend the case statement in the light of objections from the defence.

Once an order to the prosecution to supply a case statement has been complied with, the judge may, under s. 9(5), order the defence to do any or all of the following:

(a) Give the court and the prosecution a written statement setting out in general terms the nature of the defence and indicating the principal matters on which they take issue with the prosecution.

(b) Give the court and the prosecution notice of any objection they have to the prosecution case statement.

(c) Inform the court and the prosecution of any point of law (including one of admissibility of evidence) which they wish to take and the authorities on which they will be relying.

(d) Give the court and the prosecution a notice stating the extent to which they are prepared to agree the documents and other matters which the prosecution have asked to have admitted, together with the reason for any refusal to agree.

Once the prosecution has received the defence case statement, it is entitled to make use of it by re-interviewing its own witnesses and asking them questions which arise from that statement. The judge has no power to forbid the prosecution from doing so or to prescribe the way in which they may carry out such re-interviews (*Nadir* [1993] 1 WLR 1322).

D14.62 **Status of Rulings Made at a Preparatory Hearing** Subject to the possibility of being varied on appeal to the Court of Appeal (see **D14.63**), an order or ruling made at the preparatory hearing will have effect at the trial unless it then appears to the judge, on application by a party, that the interests of justice require him to vary or discharge it (CJA 1987, s. 9(10)).

The sanction for a party departing at trial from his case as disclosed at the preparatory hearing and/or failing to comply with an order made at the hearing is that the judge may comment on the departure or failure and the jury may draw such inferences as appear to them proper (s. 10(1)). The judge may also give leave to comment to any of the other parties, but, in deciding whether such leave is appropriate, must have regard to the extent of the departure from the case as earlier disclosed and the justification for it (s. 10(2)). Save as allowed under s. 10(1) and (2), no mention may be made to the jury of any information about the defence case disclosed at the preparatory hearing (s. 10(3)).

APPEALS FROM PREPARATORY HEARINGS

D14.63 There are provisions for appealing from rulings made by the judge at a preparatory hearing to the Court of Appeal and, ultimately, the House of Lords (see the CPIA 1996, ss. 35 and 36, and the CJA 1987, s. 9(11)). Leave to appeal is required from either the judge or the court (ibid.).

Where leave to appeal has been granted, the preparatory hearing may continue, but it cannot be concluded until the appeal has been determined or abandoned (s. 35(2); s. 9(13)). The Court of Appeal may confirm, reverse or vary the decision appealed against (s. 35(3); s. 9(14)).

The Court of Appeal only has jurisdiction to entertain appeals from orders that the Crown Court was entitled to make within a preparatory hearing (see, e.g., *H* [2007] 2 WLR 364).

Part 65 of the CrimPR (**appendix 1**) sets out the rules that govern appeals from both forms of the preparatory hearings.

The Rules

Notice of Appeal Rule 65.1 sets out the requirements imposed on a person making an application for leave to appeal. It requires that an application for leave to the judge of the Crown Court who made the decision to be appealed should be made within two days of the relevant decision. Unless the application for leave is made on the same occasion that the relevant decision is given, the appellant must give written notice of the application (and specify the grounds upon which it is made) to the Crown Court officer and all the parties affected by the decision (r. 65.1(2)). **D14.64**

Under r. 65.1(3) and (4), notice of appeal or an application to the Court of Appeal for leave to appeal must be served on the Registrar, the Crown Court officer and all parties to the preparatory hearing affected by the order or ruling to be appealed. It must be served no later than seven days after the date of the decision to be appealed, or no later than seven days after the determination or withdrawal of any application for leave has been made to the judge of the Crown Court. If written notice of appeal was given to the Crown Court, a copy of it must accompany the notice or application for leave to appeal which is served on the Registrar (r. 65.1(7)). The notice of appeal must (r. 65.1(8) and (9):

(a) specify any question of law to which the appeal relates and must include any facts which are necessary for the consideration of that point of law;
(b) summarise the arguments to be advanced before the Court of Appeal;
(c) list any authorities which are to be cited in argument;
(d) if the judge of the Crown Court has given leave to appeal against his ruling, the notice must refer to that and must set out the grounds on which leave was granted.

The notice should be accompanied by any documents or other things which are necessary for the proper determination of the appeal or application as the case may be (r. 65.1(10)).

Response to a Notice of Appeal If the respondent wishes to oppose the appeal then, within seven days of receipt of the notice, he must serve written notice to that effect in the form set out in the *Consolidated Criminal Practice Direction*. The notice must be served on the Registrar and must state the date on which he received the appellant's notice, summarise his response to the arguments to be advanced by the appellant and set out any authorities he proposes to rely on. Copies must also be served on the Crown Court officer, the appellant and any other parties directly affected by the decision (r. 65.2). **D14.65**

Role of the Court The powers of a single judge of the Court of Appeal are set out in the CrimPR, r. 65.6, and may be exercised as though they were being exercised by the full court. Thus the single judge may give leave to appeal under the appropriate section, extend the time-limit for service of the notice of application and opposition, and give leave for a person in custody to attend a hearing. Any application refused by a single judge can be renewed before the full Court under r. 65.7 by means of service of a written notice. **D14.66**

Criminal Procedure and Investigations Act 1996, ss. 35 and 36

35.—(1) An appeal shall lie to the Court of Appeal from any ruling of a judge under section 31(3), from the refusal by a judge of an application to which section 45 of the Criminal Justice Act 2003 applies or from an order of a judge under section 43 or 44 of that Act which is made on the determination of such an application but only with the leave of the judge or of the Court of Appeal

(2) The judge may continue a preparatory hearing notwithstanding that leave to appeal has been granted under subsection (1), but the preparatory hearing shall not be concluded until after the appeal has been determined or abandoned.

(3) On the termination of the hearing of an appeal, the Court of Appeal may confirm, reverse or vary the decision appealed against.

(4) . . .

36. . . .

(2) The judge may continue a preparatory hearing notwithstanding that leave to appeal has been granted under part II of the Criminal Appeal Act 1968, but the preparatory hearing shall not be concluded until after the appeal has been determined or abandoned.

Section 9(11), (13) and (14) of the CJA 1987, which creates a right of appeal in serious and complex fraud cases, is in identical terms to the CPIA 1996, s. 35.

PRE-TRIAL DISCLOSURE OF INFORMATION: PROSECUTION OBLIGATIONS

D14.67 Regardless of whether the trial is preceded by a preliminary or preparatory hearing, certain obligations rest upon the parties to disclose information about the evidence they intend to call or other material which is in their possession but which they do not intend to use at trial.

Disclosure of Evidence to Be Called

D14.68 The defence at trial on indictment are entitled to know in advance of trial the evidence the prosecution intend to call. Most if not all the evidence will in fact have been disclosed by the statements or depositions. If the prosecution wish to call additional evidence, they are under a duty to serve notice of it.

In *Owens and Owens* [2006] EWCA Crim 2206, the Court of Appeal held that, even where a court had ordered that evidence would only be admissible if served before a certain date, it retained the discretion to vary that order to admit evidence served later.

Disclosure of Information Not Intended to Be Used as Evidence

D14.69 The prosecution's duty to be fair to the defence extends to disclosing information which will not be part of their case and might even contradict their case, and of which the defence might otherwise be unaware. This obligation is now set out in the CPIA 1996, part I (see **D9** for details).

Custody Record etc.

D14.70 By PACE Code C, para. 2.4, the defence are entitled to a copy of the custody record which the custody officer is required to keep in respect of each person detained at a police station (see **appendix** 2). Failure to supply a copy would be a breach of the Code and might lead to the exclusion of evidence through exercise of the court's discretion under the PACE 1984, s. 78 (see **F2.4**). Similarly, if the accused was stopped in the street and searched under the powers given to the police by the PACE 1984, s. 1, the defence are entitled to a copy of the record of search (see s. 2(9)).

PRE-TRIAL DISCLOSURE OF INFORMATION: DEFENCE OBLIGATIONS

D14.71 Historically, there was no general obligation on the defence to disclose the nature of their case, or the evidence they proposed to call before trial. The position altered radically with the implementation of the CPIA 1996, part I (see **D9** for details), which applies to alleged offences for which no criminal investigation began before 1 April 1997 (see **D9.3**).

Defence Statement of Case for a Preparatory Hearing

D14.72 Where a preparatory hearing is held in a case of serious fraud, the defence may be ordered to supply a written statement setting out in general terms the nature of the defence and indicating the principal matters on which they take issue with the prosecution (CJA 1987, s. 9(5)).

This is very similar to the requirements in a defence statement as defined by the CPIA 1996, s. 6A (see **D9.20**).

Expert Evidence

By the PACE 1984, s. 81, rules may require any party to proceedings before the court to disclose to the other parties any expert evidence which he proposes to adduce. Part 24 of the CrimPR contains the rules that now apply under this power. **D14.73**

Application Nominally, the rules apply both to the prosecution and defence but they have little relevance to the prosecution because prosecution expert evidence (like the ordinary prosecution evidence) will normally be disclosed by other means. Also, CrimPR, r. 24.1, makes a saving for expert evidence to be adduced in relation to sentencing (e.g., medical or psychiatric reports). Thus, expert medical evidence to be adduced on the question of guilt or innocence must (like any other expert evidence) be disclosed, but such evidence need not be disclosed if it goes only to sentencing. **D14.74**

Content of the Rules The rules provide that, as soon as practicable after committal, transfer etc., any party intending to rely on expert evidence (whether of fact or opinion) must, unless he has already done so, provide the other parties and the court with a written statement of any finding or opinion which he proposes to adduce by way of such evidence. On request, he must also supply a copy of the record of any 'observation, test, calculation or other procedure' on which the finding or opinion is based or, if it is more practicable, he must allow reasonable opportunity to examine such a record (CrimPR, r. 24.1(1)). **D14.75**

Exceptions Entitlement to the information referred to above may be waived by the other party (r. 24.1(2)). Where there are reasonable grounds for believing that compliance with the rules would lead to intimidation of witnesses or interference with the course of justice, disclosure need not be made but notice must be served on the other parties both that the evidence is being withheld and of the grounds for withholding it (CrimPR, r. 24.2). Otherwise failure to comply with the rules means that the expert evidence will be admissible at trial only with leave of the court (r. 24.3). **D14.76**

PRE-TRIAL DISCLOSURE OF THIRD-PARTY MATERIAL

Another important area of pre-trial disclosure relates to material in the possession of third parties. This will include records held by health and education authorities, or financial institutions. Although applications for such material may commonly be made on behalf of the accused, under para. 51 of the A-G's Guidelines: Disclosure of information for criminal proceedings (set out at **appendix** 5), the prosecution is placed under an obligation to obtain material in the hands of third parties which might be relevant to the prosecution case. **D14.77**

In either event, the mechanism for securing disclosure of third-party material, unless it is volunteered, is through the issuing of a witness summons for the production of documents, pursuant to the Criminal Procedure (Attendance of Witnesses) Act 1965, s. 2A. These provisions are set out at **D14.90**, and this topic is addressed in more detail at **D9.42**.

PRIVATE MEETING BETWEEN JUDGE AND COUNSEL

Before or during the trial, counsel may, with the judge's agreement, see him privately about the case. The basic principles are contained in Lord Parker CJ's observations in *Turner* [1970] 2 QB 321 at p. 324, modified in the light of the decision of the five-judge Court of Appeal in *Goodyear* [2005] 3 All ER 117 (see also **D12.54**). The guidance is as follows. **D14.78**

(a) Freedom of access between counsel and judge is essential. This is because there may be matters calling for communication or discussion which cannot, in the interests of the client, be mentioned in open court.

(b) It is imperative that so far as possible justice be administered in open court. Counsel should therefore ask to see the judge only when it is felt to be really necessary. Equally, the judge should be careful to treat communications made to him out of court as private only when fairness to the accused so requires. In *Llewellyn* (1978) 67 Cr App R 149, the Court of Appeal criticised a trial judge who had asked counsel to come to see him so that they could discuss whether the trial should proceed on a single count for conspiracy or on two conspiracy counts as in the indictment or on charges of substantive offences. The issues should have been aired publicly and a full shorthand note taken which, *inter alia*, might assist the Court of Appeal should the judge's decision later be challenged on appeal.

(c) Any private discussion that does take place should be between the judge and both prosecuting and defence counsel, regardless of who asked for the meeting. If the defence solicitor is in court he should also be allowed to attend if he wishes.

(d) In *Goodyear*, Lord Woolf CJ made it clear (at [67]) that private meetings between judge and counsel should not act as a vehicle for plea bargaining.

D14.79 **Recording the Meeting** Where such a meeting occurs it is essential that a record is made. In *Smith* [1990] 1 WLR 1311, Russell LJ put it this way (at p. 1314B–C):

> Of course, on the authority of the well known case of *Turner* [1970] 2 QB 321, in some circumstances it is permissible for counsel to see the judge in his room to ascertain his reaction to possible sentencing options open to him. But that should never occur, as has been said on almost innumerable occasions in this court, in the absence of a shorthand note-taker or, alternatively, in the absence of some recording device. In this case there was neither a shorthand writer present nor a recording device.

His lordship went on to quote with approval the words of Mustill LJ in *Harper-Taylor* (1988) 138 NLJ 80 at pp. 80–81, which encapsulate the problems posed by 'unnecessary visits to the judge's room':

> Since we regard the discussion in the judge's room as the source of all the subsequent entanglements, some general observations on the practice of meeting the judge in his private room may be appropriate. A first principle of criminal law is that justice is done in public, for all to see and hear. By this standard a meeting in the judge's room is anomalous: the essence, and indeed the purpose, being that neither the defendant nor the jury nor the public are there to hear what is going on. Undeniably, there are circumstances where the public must be excluded. Equally, the jury cannot always be kept in court throughout. The withdrawal of the proceedings into private, without even the defendant being there, is another matter. It is true, as this court stated in *Turner* [1970] 2 QB 321 at p. 326, that there must be freedom of access between counsel and the judge when there are matters calling for communications or discussions of such a nature that counsel cannot in the interests of his client mention them in open court. Criminal trials are so various that a list of situations where an approach to the judge is permissible would only mislead; but it must be clear that communications should never take place unless there is no alternative.
>
> Apart from the question of principle, seeing the judge in private creates risks of more than one kind, as the present case has shown. The need to solve an immediate practical problem may combine with the more relaxed atmosphere of the private room to blur the formal outlines of the trial. Again, if the object of withdrawing the case from open court is to maintain a degree of confidence, as it plainly must be, there is room for misunderstanding about how far the confidence is to extend; and, in particular, there is a risk that counsel and solicitors for the other parties may hear something said to the judge which they would rather not hear, putting them into a state of conflict between their duties to their clients, and their obligation to maintain the confidentiality of the private room.
>
> The absence of the defendant is also a potential source of trouble. He has to learn what the judge has said at second hand, and may afterwards complain (rightly or not) that he was not given an accurate account. Equally, he cannot hear what his counsel has said to the judge, and hence cannot intervene to correct a misstatement or an excess of authority: a factor which may not only be a source of unfairness to the defendant, but which may also deprive the prosecution of the

opportunity to contend that admissions made in open court in the presence of the client and not repudiated by him may be taken to have been made with his authority.

PRESENCE OF THE ACCUSED AT TRIAL

The Principle

As a general principle, an accused should be present throughout his trial. The attendance of the accused at the Crown Court is secured by the magistrates remanding him in custody or on bail when they commit him for trial. If, having been bailed, he fails to attend on the day notified to him as the day of trial, a bench warrant may be issued forthwith for his arrest under the Bail Act 1976, s. 7 (see **D7.72**). **D14.80**

The accused must be present at the commencement of a trial on indictment in order to plead. It is then the almost invariable practice for him to be present throughout his trial. The implication of this rule is that the accused must not only be physically present, but must have the proceedings interpreted to him if that is necessary (*Kunnath v The State* [1993] 1 WLR 1315).

By extension, this also means that the judge ought not to deal with matters which constitute part of the trial proceedings in the absence of counsel for the defence. For example, in *Coolledge* [1996] Crim LR 748, an appeal was allowed because the judge inquired of a witness in chambers and in the absence of defence counsel as to the reason why he had failed to attend court to give evidence. The witness told the judge that he had been threatened by the accused, and the judge then counselled the witness as to how he should give his evidence at trial. The Court of Appeal held that counsel should not have been excluded since the procedure went beyond a mere inquiry, and affected the conduct of the trial itself, which was therefore tainted.

Exceptions to the Principle

Notwithstanding this general rule, the accused's presence may be dispensed with in exceptional circumstances (per Lord Reading CJ in *Lee Kun* [1916] 1 KB 337 at p. 341). The situations in which the court may be justified in proceeding without the accused are as follows. **D14.81**

(a) as a result of the misbehaviour of the accused;
(b) where his absence is voluntary;
(c) when the accused is too ill to attend;
(d) following the death of the accused.

Each of these circumstances and various related matters is considered below.

Misbehaviour by the Accused If the accused behaves in an unruly fashion in the dock, e.g., by shouting out, or if he is apparently trying to intimidate jurors or witnesses by his conduct, and he thereby makes it impracticable for the hearing to continue in his presence, the judge may order that he be removed from court and that the trial proceed without him (*Lee Kun* [1916] 1 KB 337). In practice, the judge would warn the accused before taking the extreme step of barring him from court, and it may be appropriate to allow him to return to the dock at a later stage if he undertakes not to repeat his unruly behaviour. Unruly behaviour may also be deterred by the threat of holding the accused to be guilty of a contempt in the face of the court (see **B14.74**). **D14.82**

Voluntary Absence of the Accused If the accused, having been present for the commencement of his trial, later voluntarily absents himself, either by escaping from custody or by failing to surrender having been bailed by the court for the period of an adjournment, the judge has a discretion to complete the trial in his absence (*Jones (No. 2)* [1972] 1 WLR 887). Should he be convicted, sentence may also be passed in his absence (ibid.). **D14.83**

Whether to proceed in the accused's absence must, however, be a matter for the judge's discretion. The alternative is to discharge the jury from giving a verdict, thus allowing a retrial to take place before a different jury once the accused's presence has been secured. Whether or not the court proceeds in the accused's absence, the judge may and almost certainly will issue a warrant for his arrest under the Bail Act 1976, s. 7 (see **D7.72**).

D14.84 **The Principles to be Considered** In *Hayward* [2001] QB 862, the Court of Appeal considered the principles which the trial judge ought to apply when dealing with an absent defendant, and summarised them as follows.

(a) An accused has, in general, a right to be present at his trial and a right to be legally represented.
(b) Those rights can be waived, separately or together, wholly or in part, by the accused himself:
  (i) they may be wholly waived if, knowing or having the means of knowledge as to when and where his trial is to take place, he deliberately and voluntarily absents himself and/or withdraws instructions from those representing him;
  (ii) they may be waived in part if, being present and represented at the outset, the accused, during the course of the trial, behaves in such a way as to obstruct the proper course of the proceedings and/or withdraws his instructions from those representing him.
(c) The trial judge has a discretion as to whether a trial should take place or continue in the absence of an accused and/or his legal representatives.
(d) That discretion must be exercised with great care and it is only in rare and exceptional cases that it should be exercised in favour of a trial taking place or continuing, particularly if the accused is unrepresented.
(e) In exercising that discretion, fairness to the defence is of prime importance but fairness to the prosecution must also be taken into account. The judge must have regard to all the circumstances of the case including, in particular:
  (i) the nature and circumstances of the accused's behaviour in absenting himself from the trial or disrupting its continuation, and, in particular, whether his behaviour was deliberate, voluntary and such as plainly waived his right to appear;
  (ii) whether an adjournment might result in the accused being caught or attending voluntarily and/or not disrupting the proceedings;
  (iii) the likely length of such an adjournment;
  (iv) whether the accused, though absent, is, or wishes to be, legally represented at the trial or has waived his right to representation;
  (v) the extent to which the absent accused's legal representatives are able to present his defence;
  (vi) the extent of the disadvantage to the accused in not being able to give his account of events, having regard to the nature of the evidence against him;
  (vii) the risk of the jury reaching an improper conclusion about the absence of the accused (but see (f) below);
  (viii) the seriousness of the offence to the accused, victim and public;
  (ix) the general public interest and the particular interest of victims and witnesses that a trial should take place within a reasonable time of the events to which it relates;
  (x) the effect of delay on the memories of witnesses;
  (xi) where there is more than one accused and not all have absconded, the undesirability of separate trials, and the prospects of a fair trial for the defendants who are present.
(f) If the judge decides that a trial should take place or continue in the absence of an unrepresented accused, he must ensure that the trial is as fair as the circumstances permit. He must, in particular, take reasonable steps, both during the giving of evidence and in the summing up, to expose weaknesses in the prosecution case and to make such points on behalf of the accused as the evidence permits. In summing up he must warn the jury that absence is not an admission of guilt and adds nothing to the prosecution case.

The clear emphasis in *Hayward* was on the need for caution before proceeding to try a defendant in his absence. In view of the need to ensure compliance with the ECHR, Article 6, that caution is entirely proper. For the same reason, it is entirely proper that the focus in determining whether to proceed should be upon the accused's right to attend the trial and be represented at it.

The principles outlined by the Court of Appeal in *Hayward* were considered and commended by the House of Lords in *Jones* [2003] 1 AC 1. Lord Bingham endorsed the Court of Appeal's guidelines with two reservations:

(1) the seriousness of the offence should not be considered — the principles would be the same whether the offence was serious or minor;
(2) even if the accused absconded voluntarily, it would generally be desirable that he should be represented.

Absent Defendant's Legal Representatives The position of defence legal representatives when a trial continues in the absence of an accused who has absconded was considered in *Shaw* [1980] 1 WLR 1526. The accused's instructions are not deemed to have been withdrawn and counsel and solicitor are not therefore automatically required to withdraw from the case. Whether counsel should continue to act and to what extent are essentially matters for him having regard to the guidance given in the Code of Conduct of the Bar and the circumstances of the particular case (per Kilner Brown J in *Shaw* at p. 1529G). **D14.85**

The most the judge may do is invite counsel to assist the court in the manner suggested by what are now paras. 15.3.1 and 15.3.2 of the Written Standards for the Conduct of Professional Work in the Code (see also *O'Hare* [2006] EWCA Crim 471).

Where an accused absconds and is convicted in his absence, the limited circumstances in which his legal representatives (assuming they have chosen not to withdraw) may give notice of appeal on his behalf are dealt with in **D25.13**.

Sickness of the Accused If the accused's absence from court is for reasons beyond his control, the trial may *not* continue in his absence unless he consents (see, e.g., the dicta of Williams J in *Abrahams* (1895) 21 VLR 343, adopted by Roskill LJ in *Jones (No. 2)* [1972] 1 WLR 887). The obvious and common example of involuntary absence is sickness. Thus, should the accused become ill during the course of his trial, the judge must either adjourn the case until he recovers or discharge the jury (*Howson* (1981) 74 Cr App R 172). **D14.86**

The above proposition is, however, subject to one possible though limited exception mentioned in *Howson*. The exception is that, if there are several accused and one falls sick, the trial may continue in that accused's absence provided that the evidence and proceedings in his absence relate entirely to the cases against his co-accused and have no possible bearing on his case.

The decision in *Howson* also indicates that it is not enough for an accused to be physically present if he is too unwell to pay proper attention to the proceedings and give instructions to his legal representatives.

Death of the Accused Where the accused dies before the trial is completed, formal evidence of death should be given, and endorsed upon the indictment. This may, e.g., be the evidence of the officer in the case that he has seen and identified the remains of the man named in the indictment. If such evidence is not available, other evidence such as a certified copy of the entry in the register of deaths will suffice. The endorsement of the indictment in such circumstances renders it of no legal effect. **D14.87**

ATTENDANCE OF WITNESSES

Securing the Attendance of Witnesses

D14.88 In most cases, it is the responsibility of the police to secure the attendance of prosecution witnesses, and that of the defence solicitor to ensure that defence witnesses attend. The steps taken will depend on the sensitivity of the witness and whether there is a fixed date for trial, or whether the case is in a warned list in which case an accused, for example, would need to keep in daily contact with his solicitors during the period in which his case might be called on.

D14.89 **Compelling Attendance** Where the prosecution or defence wish to secure the attendance of a witness but are not satisfied that he will attend voluntarily, they can apply for a witness summons. The procedure is set out in the Criminal Procedure (Attendance of Witnesses) Act 1965, ss. 2 to 4, which are set out after **D14.90**. These provisions apply in respect of alleged offences where an investigation did not commence before 1 April 1997. For the position in respect of offences which do not fall within this category, reference should be made to the 1997 edition of this work.

The same provisions are used to secure the production of documents, rather than the attendance of a witness, as evidence. The use of the provisions for this purpose is particularly pertinent to the disclosure of material in the possession of third parties, which is discussed at **D14.77** and **D9.42**.

D14.90 **Punishment for Failure to Attend** A person who 'without just excuse' disobeys a witness order or summons requiring him to attend court is guilty of contempt of the court he fails to attend (Criminal Procedure (Attendance of Witnesses) Act 1965, s. 3(1)). He may be summarily punished as if he had committed a contempt in the court's face (ibid.); it is desirable and appropriate for the judge who issued the warrant to deal in person with the witness (*Yusuf* [2003] 2 Cr App R 488). The maximum penalty is three months' imprisonment (s. 3(2)).

The existence of a 'just excuse' will not be lightly inferred. Witnesses are required to submit even to very substantial inconvenience in their business and private lives. Culpable forgetfulness can certainly never amount to a 'just excuse' (*Lennock* (1993) 97 Cr App R 228). However, the prosecution must prove beyond reasonable doubt that proper notification of the trial date was given (*Abdulaziz* [1989] Crim LR 717).

In *Wang* [2005] EWCA 476, no witness summons had been issued at the time when the defendant was warned that he might be needed at the Crown Court on a particular date. The Court of Appeal quashed his conviction. Nevertheless, the court indicated that, if the defendant had been warned that the prosecution would obtain a witness summons, and had gone to ground to evade it, a conviction under s. 3 of the 1965 Act, or at common law, might have been sustainable.

In *R (H) v Wood Green Crown Court* [2007] 1 WLR 1620, it was made clear that a witness may be remanded for as long as there is a real possibility that he may be required to give evidence, or further evidence, as the case may be.

Criminal Procedure (Attendance of Witnesses) Act 1965, ss. 2 to 4

2.—(1) This section applies where the Crown Court is satisfied that—

(a) a person is likely to be able to give evidence likely to be material evidence, or produce any document or thing likely to be material evidence, for the purpose of any criminal proceedings before the Crown Court, and

(b) it is in the interests of justice to issue a summons under this section to secure the attendance of that person to give evidence or to produce the document or thing.

(2) In such a case the Crown Court shall, subject to the following provisions of this section, issue a summons (a witness summons) directed to the person concerned and requiring him to—

(a) attend before the Crown Court at the time and place stated in the summons, and

(b) give the evidence or produce the document or thing.
(3) A witness summons may only be issued under this section on an application; and the Crown Court may refuse to issue the summons if any requirement relating to the application is not fulfilled.
(4) Where a person has been committed for trial, or sent for trial under section 51 of the Crime and Disorder Act 1998, for any offence to which the proceedings concerned relate, an application must be made as soon as is reasonably practicable after the committal.
(5) Where the proceedings concerned have been transferred to the Crown Court, an application must be made as soon as is reasonably practicable after the transfer.
(6) Where the proceedings concerned relate to an offence in relation to which a bill of indictment has been preferred under the authority of section 2(2)(b) of the Administration of Justice (Miscellaneous Provisions) Act 1933 (bill preferred by direction of Court of Appeal, or by direction or with consent of judge) an application must be made as soon as is reasonably practicable after the bill was preferred.
(7) An application must be made in accordance with Criminal Procedure Rules; and different provision may be made for different cases or descriptions of case.
(8) to (10) [Specify matters which may be covered by the CrimPR.]
2A. A witness summons which is issued under section 2 above and which requires a person to produce a document or thing as mentioned in section 2(2) above may also require him to produce the document or thing—
(a) at a place stated in the summons, and
(b) at a time which is so stated and precedes that stated under section 2(2) above, for inspection by the person applying for the summons.
2B.—(1) If—
(a) a document or thing is produced in pursuance of a requirement imposed by a witness summons under section 2A above,
(b) the person applying for the summons concludes that a requirement imposed by the summons under section 2(2) above is no longer needed, and
(c) he accordingly applies to the Crown Court for a direction that the summons shall be of no further effect,
the court may direct accordingly.
(2) An application under this section must be made in accordance with Criminal Procedure Rules; and different provision may be made for different cases or descriptions of case.
(3) [Specifies matters which may be covered by the CrimPR.]
2C.—(1) If a witness summons issued under section 2 above is directed to a person who—
(a) applies to the Crown Court,
(b) satisfies the court that he was not served with notice of the application to issue the summons and that he was neither present nor represented at the hearing of the application, and
(c) satisfies the court that he cannot give any evidence likely to be material evidence or, as the case may be, produce any document or thing likely to be material evidence,
the court may direct that the summons shall be of no effect.
(2) For the purposes of subsection (1) above it is immaterial—
(a) whether or not Criminal Procedure Rules require the person to be served with notice of the application to issue the summons;
(b) whether or not Criminal Procedure Rules enable the person to be present or represented at the hearing of the application.
(3) In subsection (1)(b) above 'served' means—
(a) served in accordance with Criminal Procedure Rules, in a case where such rules require the person to be served with notice of the application to issue the summons;
(b) served in such way as appears reasonable to the court to which the application is made under this section, in any other case.
(4) The Crown Court may refuse to make a direction under this section if any requirement relating to the application under this section is not fulfilled.
(5) An application under this section must be made in accordance with Criminal Procedure Rules; and different provision may be made for different cases or descriptions of case.
(6) and (7) [Specify matters which may be covered by the CrimPR.]
(8) Where a direction is made under this section that a witness summons shall be of no effect, the person on whose application the summons was issued may be ordered to pay the whole or any part of the costs of the application under this section.

(9) Any costs payable under an order made under subsection (8) above shall be taxed by the proper officer of the court, and payment of those costs shall be enforceable in the same manner as an order for payment of costs made by the High Court in a civil case or as a sum adjudged summarily to be paid as a civil debt.

2D. For the purpose of any criminal proceedings before it, the Crown Court may of its own motion issue a summons (a witness summons) directed to a person and requiring him to—
(a) attend before the court at the time and place stated in the summons, and
(b) give evidence, or produce any document or thing specified in the summons.

2E.—(1) If a witness summons issued under section 2D above is directed to a person who—
(a) applies to the Crown Court, and
(b) satisfies the court that he cannot give any evidence likely to be material evidence or, as the case may be, produce any document or thing likely to be material evidence,
the court may direct that the summons shall be of no effect.
(2) The Crown Court may refuse to make a direction under this section if any requirement relating to the application under this section is not fulfilled.
(3) An application under this section must be made in accordance with Criminal Procedure Rules; and different provision may be made for different cases or descriptions of case.
(4) [Specifies matters which may be covered by the CrimPR.]

3.—(1) Any person who without just excuse disobeys a witness summons requiring him to attend before any court shall be guilty of contempt of that court and may be punished summarily by that court as if his contempt had been committed in the face of the court.
(1A) Any person who without just excuse disobeys a requirement made by any court under section 2A above shall be guilty of contempt of that court and may be punished summarily by that court as if his contempt had been committed in the face of the court.
(2) No person shall by reason of any disobedience mentioned in subsection (1) or (1A) above be liable to imprisonment for a period exceeding three months.

4. [Describes the powers available to ensure compliance with a witness summons, for which see **D9.45**.]

The relevant rules are to be found in the CrimPR, part 18 (see **appendix 1**).

CONTACT WITH WITNESSES, WITNESS COACHING AND FAMILIARISATION

D14.91 An important aspect of the handling of witnesses is consideration of what contact it is appropriate for counsel, and others involved in either the prosecution or defence team, to have with them. This also involves consideration of the prohibition on witnesses being rehearsed by the party that is to call them, which potentially competes with the need to ensure that a witness is able to give his evidence in the best possible way, is not distracted by a lack of familiarity with his surroundings in court, and receives proper support from those responsible for his welfare through what can be a very stressful experience.

Contact between Counsel and Witnesses

D14.92 The relevant provisions of the Code of Conduct may be summarised as follows:

(a) There is no longer a general rule preventing a barrister from having contact with any witness. A barrister may exchange common courtesies with the other side's witnesses, provided he does not discuss the substance of the case with them. More crucially, he may have contact with a witness whom he expects to call and examine in chief, with a view to introducing himself, explaining the court's procedure, and answering any questions about it which the witness might have. The barrister does in fact have a positive responsibility to ensure that a witness facing unfamiliar court procedures is put as much at ease as possible, particularly when that witness is nervous, vulnerable or apparently the victim of criminal conduct (Written Standards, paras. 6.1.2, 6.1.3, 6.1.4 and 6.2.7).

(b) In a contested case in the Crown Court, however, it is generally inappropriate for a barrister to *interview* any potential witness. Interviewing includes discussing the substance of the witness's evidence, or the evidence of other witnesses. Save that, if so instructed, counsel may interview potential witnesses if it is done in accordance with the practice set out in the Code for Pre-Trial Witness Interviews (Written Standards, para. 6.3.2).

(c) Where a barrister has interviewed a potential witness, that fact should be disclosed to all the other parties in the case before the witness is called. The substance of the interview should be recorded, together with the reason for it (para. 6.3.4).

(d) Counsel must not rehearse, practise or coach any witness, in relation either to the evidence itself or to the way in which to give it (para. 705(a)). Particular guidance in this regard was given in the case of *Momodou (Practice Note)* [2005] 1 WLR 3442, where the extent of permissible witness familiarisation was set out (see **D14.95**)

Prosecution Counsel The proper handling of witnesses has become an important part of the role of the prosecutor, not least since the introduction of CPS Standards in this regard. Prosecuting counsel should not confer with any investigator witness unless the latter has a supervisory responsibility in the investigation (e.g., as officer in the case), and should not confer with or receive factual instructions directly from investigators on matters which may be in dispute (Written Standards, para. 6.3.2). **D14.93**

Defence Counsel The interlocking matters of conferences, counsel being attended at court by his professional client, and the seeing of witnesses are dealt with in various provisions of the Code of Conduct of the Bar, which may be summarised as follows: **D14.94**

(a) It is counsel's duty to make himself available for a conference with his client before or on the day of the trial (Written Standards, para. 5.9).

(b) Provided that the interests of justice and of the lay client will not be prejudiced, counsel may agree with his professional client that attendance by the latter's representative may be dispensed with (paras. 706 and 707).

(c) Although, in general, counsel should not interview witnesses or discuss their evidence with them, there may be extraordinary circumstances in which departure from this principle is unavoidable. Paragraph 6.3.3 quotes as an example the circumstances in *Fergus* (1994) 98 Cr App R 313. In that case, Steyn LJ stated (at p. 323) that, since defence solicitors had failed to see the alibi witnesses in order to ask why they had remembered the events of the day in question, counsel should have seen them himself.

(d) Where a barrister has interviewed a potential witness, that fact should be disclosed to all the other parties in the case before the witness is called. The substance of the interview should be recorded, together with the reason for it (para. 6.3.4).

(e) The above rules are all subject to the overriding principle that a barrister must not 'devise facts which will assist in advancing his lay client's case' (para. 5.8). In particular, when defence counsel sees the accused, he must be careful not to suggest a defence that would be more plausible than the one actually being advanced by the lay client.

Witness Familiarisation

In *Momodou (Practice Note)* [2005] 1 WLR 3442, the Court of Appeal made clear that, while familiarisation of witnesses with the court and procedure is legitimate, it must be carefully regulated. Judge LJ stated (at [61] and [62]): **D14.95**

> There is a dramatic distinction between witness training or coaching, and witness familiarisation. Training or coaching for witnesses in criminal proceedings (whether for prosecution or defence) is not permitted. This is the logical consequence of well-known principle that discussions between witnesses should not take place, and that the statements and proofs of one witness should not be disclosed to any other witness. (See [*Richardson* [1971] 2 QB 484, *Arif* (1993) *The Times*, 17 June 1993, *Skinner* (1994) 99 Cr App R 212] and *Shaw* [2002] EWCA Crim 3004.) The witness should give his or her own evidence, so far as practicable uninfluenced by what anyone else has said, whether in formal discussions or informal conversations. The rule reduces, indeed hopefully avoids any possibility, that one witness may tailor his evidence in the light of

what anyone else said, and equally, avoids any unfounded perception that he may have done so. These risks are inherent in witness training. Even if the training takes place one-to-one with someone completely remote from the facts of the case itself, the witness may come, even unconsciously, to appreciate which aspects of his evidence are perhaps not quite consistent with what others are saying, or indeed not quite what is required of him. An honest witness may alter the emphasis of his evidence to accommodate what he thinks may be a different, more accurate, or simply better remembered perception of events. A dishonest witness will very rapidly calculate how his testimony may be 'improved'. These dangers are present in one-to-one witness training. Where however the witness is jointly trained with other witnesses to the same events, the dangers dramatically increase. Recollections change. Memories are contaminated. Witnesses may bring their respective accounts into what they believe to be better alignment with others. They may be encouraged to do so, consciously or unconsciously. They may collude deliberately. They may be inadvertently contaminated. Whether deliberately or inadvertently, the evidence may no longer be their own. Although none of this is inevitable, the risk that training or coaching may adversely affect the accuracy of the evidence of the individual witness is constant. So we repeat, witness training for criminal trials is prohibited.

This principle does not preclude pre-trial arrangements to familiarise witness with the layout of the court, the likely sequence of events when the witness is giving evidence, and a balanced appraisal of the different responsibilities of the various participants. Indeed such arrangements, usually in the form of a pre-trial visit to the court, are generally to be welcomed. Witnesses should not be disadvantaged by ignorance of the process, nor when they come to give evidence, taken by surprise at the way it works. None of this however involves discussions about proposed or intended evidence. Sensible preparation for the experience of giving evidence, which assists the witness to give of his or her best at the forthcoming trial is permissible. Such experience can also be provided by out of court familiarisation techniques. The process may improve the manner in which the witness gives evidence by, for example, reducing the nervous tension arising from inexperience of the process. Nevertheless the evidence remains the witness's own uncontaminated evidence. Equally, the principle does not prohibit training of expert and similar witnesses in, for example, the technique of giving comprehensive evidence of a specialist kind to a jury, both during evidence-in-chief and in cross-examination, and, another example, developing the ability to resist the inevitable pressure of going further in evidence than matters covered by the witnesses' specific expertise. The critical feature of training of this kind is that it should not be arranged in the context of nor related to any forthcoming trial, and it can therefore have no impact whatever on it.

D14.96 **Familiarisation by Outside Agency** The Court of Appeal in *Momodou (Practice Note)* [2005] 1 WLR 3442, went on to give guidance (at [63] to [65]) as to the way in which any familiarisation process ought to be regulated, where it was by an outside agency rather than, as is routine, through the Witness Service. The guidance was as follows:

(a) The CPS should be consulted where prosecution witnesses were involved, and the proposed programme should be put in writing.
(b) Where the defence engaged in such a process, counsel's advice should be sought and the trial judge should be informed.
(c) The familiarisation process should be supervised by a barrister or solicitor, preferably by an organisation accredited for the purpose by the Bar Council and Law Society.
(d) None of those involved should have personal knowledge of the matters in issue, and the material used should not bear any similarity to the issues in the case. Nothing should be done to play on or trigger the witnesses' recollection of events.
(e) Any discussion of the criminal proceedings in question must be stopped and advice given about why it is not permissible.
(f) Careful records should be kept of the programme, those present and those responsible for the process. The records should be handed to the CPS and, in relation to defence witnesses, to the court.
(g) Barristers and solicitors were professionally obliged to see that this guidance was followed.

SPECIAL MEASURES FOR VULNERABLE WITNESSES

D14.97 It had long been recognised at common law that there was a need to make special provision for certain categories of witnesses who, because of their particular vulnerabilities or the nature of their evidence, require special measures to be taken to assist them to give their evidence. Parliament has built on this common-law foundation to develop special measures for particular types of witnesses, especially those who are young, afraid or the victims of sexual assault.

The aim is to ensure that witnesses are able to give their best evidence. This aspiration was summed up by Paul Boateng, then Minister of State for the Home Office, when addressing the House of Commons Standing Committee E on 17 June 1999 in relation to the Youth Justice and Criminal Evidence Bill:

> . . . the Government recognise that in the past the criminal law and the criminal justice system have not always got it right. All too often, witnesses have not been able to give of their best in court, for a variety of reasons. The measure is designed to protect the public interest and thus the interests of justice, striking a proper balance between the interests and rights of the defendant and those of the victim. That demands that the best evidence possible be laid before the jury. Fear, intimidation and the vulnerability of age or incapacity can militate against witnesses giving their best evidence. The proposal will ensure that the best evidence comes before the jury . . .

The YJCEA 1999, part II, chapter I (ss. 16 to 33, set out in full at **D14.119**) contains provision for a series of special measures which the court can direct in respect of certain witnesses. The measures are:

(a) screening the witness from the accused (s. 23);
(b) giving evidence by live link (s. 24);
(c) ordering the removal of wigs and gowns while the witness gives evidence (s. 25);
(d) giving evidence in private, in a sexual case, or where there is a fear that the witness may be intimidated (s. 26);
(e) video recording of evidence-in-chief (s. 27);
(f) video recording of cross-examination and re-examination where the evidence-in-chief of the witness has been video recorded (s. 28);
(g) examination through an intermediary in the case of a young or incapacitated witness (s. 29); and
(h) provision of aids to communication for a young or incapacitated witness (s. 30).

Section 28 is not yet in force. Most of the other measures came into force on 24 July 2002 but s. 29 was brought into force only on 23 February 2004.

The Procedure

D14.98 The measures are available to witnesses who are young or incapable (YJCEA 1999, s. 16) or those the quality of whose evidence 'is likely to be diminished by reason of fear or distress' when giving evidence (s. 17). (See **D14.103** for discussion of qualification for measures.)

In both cases, application has to be made for the appropriate special measure in accordance with s. 19. It requires the court to focus upon whether there are special measures which will improve the quality of the evidence of a witness, as defined in s. 16(5). If there are, the court should determine which of the measures, singly or in combination, would maximise the quality of that evidence.

D14.99 **Application for Measures** Part 29 of the CrimPR now governs the procedure for applying for special measures, which is centred on the completion of a new form, although this is not identified in annex D of the *Consolidated Criminal Practice Direction.*

The stages which apply to applications for special measures in the Crown Court, from the moment that a written application for a special measure is made by completing and submitting the relevant part of the form, are as follows:

(a) Submission of the application on the form — part B for live link, part C for intermediary and part D for use of video recording. There are additional rules for live links (r. 29.6), intermediaries (r. 29.9) and video recordings (r. 29.7). This application has to be made within 28 days of committal, transfer or sending to the Crown Court or service of notice of appeal (r. 29.1(4)(c)).
(b) Any opposition to such an application must be completed in writing, including the reasons for opposition, and served on all parties within 14 days of the receipt of the application (r. 29.1(5) and (6)). The opposition is to state whether issue is taken with the witness's eligibility for the measures, or with the effect of the measure on the quality of the evidence (r. 29.1(8)).
(c) The court shall decide the application without a hearing if no opposition has been received within the prescribed time (r. 29.1(9)).
(d) If opposition has been received, the court shall arrange a hearing and notify the parties of the listing (r. 29.1(10)). All parties thus notified have the right to attend and be heard (r. 29.1(11)).
(e) The court shall notify all parties of its decision and, where it admits a video recording as evidence-in-chief, shall indicate which parts of the video are admitted (r. 29.1(13)).

D14.100 **Varying the Time-limits and Late Applications** The time in which a party can apply for special measures can be extended before or after the period has expired by a written application, served on all parties, and supported by a statement setting out the reasons why extra time is needed (CrimPR, r 29.2). Moreover, r. 29.3 allows a party to make an application for special measures orally once the trial has started, and allows the court to order such measures of its own motion at trial. If an order is refused, the application may be renewed where there has been a material change of circumstances (r. 29.5(2) and (3)).

D14.101 **Varying Special Measures Directions** Once an order has been made for special measures it may be discharged or varied pursuant to the YJCEA 1999, s. 20(2), which allows such a change where there has been a material change of circumstances. Such an application is to be made in writing, as soon as is practicable after the change, setting out the material change in circumstances (CrimPR, r. 29.4). Where the application is to vary or discharge an order permitting the use of a video recording as evidence-in-chief, it should spell out whether it is the whole video or only a specified part of it that is subject to the application (r. 29.7(17)).

Child Witnesses

D14.102 Section 21 of the YJCEA 1999 deals with matters concerning child witnesses and determining the appropriate measures which may be adopted in the case of such a witness. In *R (D) v Camberwell Green Youth Court* [2003] 2 Cr App R 257, it was argued that s. 21(5) (child witnesses in need of special protection) was incompatible with the right to a fair trial under the ECHR, Article 6. The court held that no problem of incompatibility arose. Nothing in the ECHR laid down that vulnerable witnesses must give evidence in the same room as the accused, provided that the accused was able to challenge the witness when the witness gave evidence and provided that the court was able to exclude inadmissible material from the video-recorded interview at the outset.

The court reiterated that the special measures regime in relation to those requiring special protection would only rarely be disapplied and the court should proceed on the presumption that special measures would be used.

The provisions of s. 21 can be extended to apply to certain witnesses who are over the age of 17 if the conditions in s. 22 are met.

Qualification for Special Measures

In order to qualify for special measures, the witness must fall within a category prescribed by the YJCEA 1999. Witnesses may be eligible for the measures on grounds of youth or incapacity (s. 16), or because of the fear or distress they are likely to suffer when giving evidence (s. 17). **D14.103**

In *Brown* [2004] Crim LR 1034, the Court of Appeal made clear that, although s. 17(2) required the court to consider the list of factors in s. 17(2)(a) to (d) in deciding whether a witness was eligible for assistance on the ground that the quality of his evidence would otherwise be diminished by reason of fear or distress, it was entitled to reach that conclusion solely having regard to the nature and circumstances of the offence (the factor specified in s. 17(2)(a)), regardless of the age of the witness or whether he was particularly vulnerable.

Not all eligible witnesses can benefit from all the special measures contained in the YJCEA 1999. Examination through an intermediary and the provision of aids to communication are not available for witnesses eligible only by reason of fear or intimidation.

The Court's Inherent Powers Witnesses who fall outside the assigned categories may in any event be assisted to some extent by the court's inherent powers (e.g., to order the use of screens and the modification of court dress), which are preserved by the YJCEA 1999, s. 19(6)(a) (see, e.g., **D14.106**). **D14.104**

Position of the Accused Prior to 15 January 2006, the accused was specifically and comprehensibly excluded from eligibility under either category (YJCEA 1999, ss. 16(1) and 17(1)). This exclusion may have run counter to the thrust of the decision in *V v UK* (2000) 30 EHRR 121 (see **D23.53**) in respect of juvenile defendants and the spirit of the *Consolidated Criminal Practice Direction*, para. IV.39. The harshness of the exclusion of the accused from eligibility for special measures directions has been mitigated to some extent by two developments. **D14.105**

The first is the suggestion made by the Court of Appeal in *H (Special measures)* (2003) *The Times*, 15 April 2003, that a trial judge, in his discretion, may take the following steps to assist an accused with learning difficulties to give evidence at trial:

(a) ask his legal representatives to provide a detailed defence statement which could be read to the jury if there was concern about the accused's ability to recall events;
(b) if the accused could recall matters only by reference to a past coherent account of events which he had given, the judge might permit him to refer to it;
(c) if the accused could not read, it was open to the judge to conclude that he could be asked leading questions in respect of the account given in the defence statement.

The second relates to the use of live links. Previously, pursuant to the decision of the Divisional Court in *R (S) v Waltham Forest Youth Court* [2004] 2 Cr App R 335, a court could not permit an accused to give evidence by live link, since such permission would not be based upon the common-law discretion to regulate the trial, but on specific statutory measures. However, s. 47 of the Police and Justice Act 2007, which came into effect on 15 January 2007, imports new ss. 33A to 33C into the YJCEA 1999.

Under these sections, a court may permit an accused to give his evidence via a live link (as defined for these purposes by s. 33B) where to do so would permit him to participate more effectively in the proceedings as a witness where the accused is either under the age of 18 and his ability to participate is otherwise compromised by his intellectual ability or lack of social function (s. 33A(4)) or where he is over 18 but suffering from a mental disorder which prevents his effective participation (s. 33A(5)).

Screens

D14.106 Erecting screens to allow the witness to give evidence without being able to see the accused is permitted by s. 23. This provision operates in tandem with the common-law discretion of the court to regulate proceedings to best secure justice by permitting the use of screens which is still of relevance to witnesses to whom the YJCEA 1999, ss. 16 and 17 do not apply. In *X, Y and Z* (1990) 91 Cr App R 36, the Court of Appeal considered the court's power to allow screens for child witnesses. Lord Lane CJ said (at p. 40):

> The learned judge has the duty on this and on all other occasions of endeavouring to see that justice is done. Those are high sounding words. What it really means is, he has got to see that the system operates fairly: fairly not only to the defendants but also to the prosecution and also to the witnesses. Sometimes he has to make decisions as to where the balance of fairness lies. He came to the conclusion that in these circumstances the necessity of trying to ensure that these children would be able to give evidence outweighed any possible prejudice to the defendants by the erection of the screen.

D14.107 **Direction to the Jury where Screens are Used** Where screens are employed, the court should give an appropriate direction to the jury not to draw any inference adverse to the accused from the use of screens (*Ghani* (25 October 1999 unreported)).

D14.108 **Use of Screens for Security Reasons** In *Hugh Jack* (7 April 1998 unreported), Kennedy LJ considered the question of whether screens could be used for witnesses who were not vulnerable, but who ought to be protected in the interests of national security. Kennedy LJ concluded that the interests of justice and national security often merged into one. He then went on to approve the test that had been set out by Evans LJ in *Taylor and Crabb* (22 July 1994 unreported):

> . . . except in 'rare and exceptional circumstances' a defendant is entitled to see and to know the identity of his accusers, including witnesses for the prosecution brought against him, but whether in a particular case an exception should be made is 'pre-eminently a matter for the exercise of discretion by the trial judge'. The court then listed five factors which are or may be relevant to the exercise of that discretion, namely—
>
> (1) there must be real grounds for being fearful of the consequences if the evidence is given and the identity of the witness is revealed;
>
> (2) the evidence must be sufficiently relevant and important to make it unfair to the prosecution to compel them to proceed without it;
>
> (3) the prosecution must satisfy the court that the credit worthiness of the witness has been fully investigated and the result of that enquiry disclosed to the defence so far as is consistent with the anonymity sought. This is a factor which . . . is of no significance in the present case;
>
> (4) the court must be satisfied that no undue prejudice is caused to the defendant;
>
> (5) the court can balance the need for protection, including the extent of the necessary protection, against the unfairness or the appearance of unfairness in the particular case.
>
> That seems to us to be a useful check list in relation to this type of case.

Live Links

D14.109 The use of a live link for the evidence of a witness is permitted by the YJCEA 1999, s. 24. In this context references to live links are references to 'a live television link or other arrangements whereby a witness, whilst absent from the courtroom or other place where the proceedings are being held, is able to see and hear a person there and to be heard and seen' by the judge, legal representatives, and interpreter for the accused (s. 24(8)).

Where the application has been made using part B of the prescribed form, under the CrimPR, r. 29.1(2)(a), opposition to the application must address the question of whether or not the use of the link would maximise the quality of the evidence, unless the witness is a child in need of special protection within the definition in s. 21(1)(b). A witness using a live link is to be accompanied in the room to be used for the link only by persons acceptable to the court (r. 29.6(4)) or by such persons and the intermediary (r. 29.6(5)) as appropriate.

This rule is supplemented by the *Consolidated Criminal Practice Direction* (see **appendix** 7), which states that 'an increased degree of flexibility is now appropriate as to who can act as supporter of a witness giving evidence by live television link' (para. III.29.2). The judge is encouraged to direct who should accompany the witness in advance of the trial. The supporter should be 'completely independent' of, and have no previous knowledge of, the witness and should be trained in accordance with the relevant National Standards. The court usher should additionally be available to assist and to ensure that the judge's directions are complied with (para. III.29.3).

In *R (D) v Camberwell Youth Court* [2005] 1 WLR 393, the House of Lords held that the use of live links was compatible with the accused's right to a fair trial under the ECHR, Article 6. The accused could still hear the evidence, see the witness and had every opportunity to challenge and question them.

Other Permitted Use of Live Links Quite independent of the use of television links pursuant to the YJCEA 1999, s. 24, the CJA 1988, s. 32, provides for the use of live links for witnesses who are overseas. **D14.110**

Criminal Justice Act 1988, s. 32

(1) A person other than the accused may give evidence through a live television link in proceedings to which subsection (1A) applies if (a) the witness is outside the United Kingdom; but the evidence may not be so given without the leave of the court.

(1A) This subsection applies—

(a) to trials on indictment, appeals to the criminal division of the Court of Appeal and hearings of references under section 9 of the Criminal Appeal Act 1995;

(b) to proceedings in youth courts, appeals to the Crown Court arising out of such proceedings and hearings of references under section 11 of the Criminal Appeal Act 1995 so arising.

This section came into force on 5 January 1989 (SI 1988 No. 2073), but only came into operation on 26 November 1990 (SI 1990 No. 2084) when links were permitted in cases of murder, manslaughter, serious frauds and cases initiated by a notice of transfer under the CJA 1987, s. 4. The availability of such links was considerably widened to any trial on indictment starting after 1 September 2004 (SI 2004 No. 1267). Such links are therefore now available at all trials in the Crown Court.

Part 30 of the CrimPR (**appendix 1**) provides the mechanism by which application can now be made to the Crown Court for leave to call a witness via a live television link. It should be remembered that such applications are not limited to the prosecution (r. 30.1(1)). The procedure is as follows:

(a) The application is to be made by completing a form which is to be served within 28 days of the service of the prosecution case following the committal, transfer or sending of the accused to the Crown Court (r. 30.1(4) and (6)).

(b) A party served with an application for a live link has 28 days thereafter to notify the applicant and the court officer whether or not he opposes the application, and if so why, and whether he wishes to be present when the application is heard (r. 30.1(7)).

(c) After that 28-day period has expired, the court will determine the application, either with or without a hearing as appropriate (r. 30.1(8)). Any hearing will take place in chambers (r. 30.1(2)).

Further Extension of the Use of Live Links When the CJA 2003, s. 51, comes into force, a court will be able to authorise witnesses, other than the accused, to give evidence through a 'live link' from another location in the UK, rather than just from overseas. This will usually be via a closed circuit television link, but is defined in such a way as to include any technology with a similar effect, such as video-conferencing facilities or the Internet. **D14.111**

The court may authorise the use of a live link only if:

(a) it is in the interests of the efficient or effective administration of justice for the witness to give evidence in this way (e.g., because he works in a different part of the country and can give his evidence from his place of work via a live link); and
(b) notification has been received that the necessary facilities are available in the area where the criminal proceedings are to take place. (The assumption is that the parties will ensure that there are facilities in the location from which the witness will give evidence.)

Where a direction for a live link has been given, that means that the witness must give all his evidence in that way, so that cross-examination must also be conducted by live link. If it is in the interests of justice to do so, the court can rescind a direction for a live link.

Evidence in Private

D14.112 Under the YJCEA 1999, s. 25, the court may permit a witness to give evidence in private, rather than in front of such members of the public as wish to attend. In *Richards* (1999) 163 JP 246, the Court of Appeal held that there was no conflict between excluding the public from the court and the ECHR, Article 6, because the latter recognised departure from the principle of trial in public where 'publicity would prejudice the interests of justice'.

Video-recorded Evidence-in-chief

D14.113 Section 27 of the YJCEA 1999 permits the evidence-in-chief of a witness to take the form of his video–recorded interview with the police. The conduct of such an interview is governed by the Home Office document *Achieving Best Evidence in Criminal Proceedings: Guidance for Vulnerable or Intimidated Witnesses, including Children,* which sets out good practice for preparing for and conducting such interviews. It is available from the CPS web site. The courts have made clear that failure to comply with such guidance is a factor to be taken into account in deciding whether to permit such a video to be used as evidence at trial (*G v DPP* [1997] 2 Cr App R 78). The test to be applied is that enunciated in *Hanton* [2005] EWCA Crim 2009, namely 'could a reasonable jury properly directed be sure that the witness had given a credible and accurate account on the video tape, notwithstanding any breaches' (approved in *K* [2006] 2 Cr App R 175). See also Ministry of Justice Circular 25/06/2007 on the extended availability of special measures for complainants in cases involving sexual offences.

D14.114 **The Procedure** Where an application is made, using part D of the prescribed form (CrimPR. r. 29.1(2)(c)), the application should be accompanied by a copy of the video itself and must include the details set out in r. 29.7(2) in relation to the defendant, the offence, the witness and the making of the video recording. If the proposal is to show only part of the recorded interview, pursuant to the YJCEA 1999, s. 27(2) and (6), the application must also specify which parts are to be adduced (r. 29.7(3)). The application for the use of a video recording needs to be accompanied by a statement of the circumstances in which the video recording was made, and in particular the matters relating to the time, location, equipment and personnel that are enumerated in r. 29.7(4). The procedural steps to be taken in relation to such an application are similarly contained in r. 29.7 (see **appendix 1**).

The rules in relation to video recorded evidence-in-chief are supplemented by para. IV.40 of the *Consolidated Criminal Practice Direction* (see **appendix** 7), which indicates the following.

(a) The court, when allowing a video recording to be used under s. 27(1), can direct that certain parts of it are to be excluded. The recording must then be edited in accordance with the court's ruling and the edited version is then served on the court officer and on the parties (para. IV.40.2).
(b) Where a video recording is adduced in Crown Court proceedings, it should be produced and proved by the interviewer or another witness who was present at the interview.

Unless that person's statement is agreed, the party relying on the video must ensure that person can attend to give evidence at trial (para. IV.40.3).

(c) If at trial a problem with the editing of the video delays the proceedings, para. IV.40.4 indicates that this is one situation in which the court can consider making an order as to the costs wasted thereby.

Practical Matters Two practical matters that arise in relation to the use of video-recorded evidence-in-chief are: D14.115

(a) where a video recorded interview with a child over the age of 14 is admitted under the YJCEA 1999, s. 27, the oath should be administered before the start of any further questioning, such as cross-examination (*Simmonds* [1996] Crim LR 816);
(b) the court may permit the jury to be provided with a transcript of the video recording whilst it is being played, if that will assist them to follow the evidence in question and it is made clear that it is only being made available for that limited purpose (*Welstead* [1996] 1 Cr App R 59).

Use by the Defence Section 27 of the YJCEA 1999 is not limited to the use of video recordings as evidence-in-chief by the prosecution. Rule 29.7(10) to (16) of the CrimPR regulates the use of this provision by the defence. The concern raised when such special measures were introduced was that the defence would have to disclose the evidence of witnesses they might wish to call in advance, in contradistinction to the position of witnesses to whom the special measure provisions have no application. To overcome this concern, the defence are not obliged to provide the recording to the prosecution until after the prosecution has closed its case (r. 29.7(10)), and the court may determine the application even though the prosecution have not yet seen the video (r. 29.7(11)). Where this occurs, the prosecution may, having seen the video, seek to vary or discharge any order for special measures (r. 29.7(12)). D14.116

Further Extension of the Use of Video Interviews When the CJA 2003, s. 137, comes into effect, the court will be able to permit a video recording of an interview with a witness (other than the accused) to be admitted as the evidence-in-chief of the witness in a wide range of circumstances. The court will be able to authorise such a video recording to replace the witness's evidence-in-chief provided that: D14.117

(a) the person claims to be a witness to the offence, or part of it, or to events closely connected with it; and
(b) the video recording of the statement was made at a time when the events were fresh in the witness's memory; and
(c) the offence is indictable-only, or is an either-way offence prescribed by order of the Home Secretary.

If the recording satisfies (a) to (c), then the court may admit it provided that:

(i) the witness's recollection of events is likely to be significantly better at the time the recording was made than by the time of the trial; and
(ii) it is in the interests of justice to admit it, having regard to whether it is an early and reliable account from the witness, whether the quality is adequate, and the witness's own views about using the recording.

Where a video recording is admitted under these provisions, it is to be treated as the final statement of any matters adequately dealt with in it (s. 138).

Anonymity

The court may take measures, based upon its common-law powers rather than the YJCEA 1999, to ensure that witnesses remain anonymous. In *Davis* [2006] 1 WLR 3130, the Court of Appeal held (at [59]) that: D14.118

In our judgment the discretion to permit evidence to be given by witnesses whose identity may not be known to the defendant is now beyond question. The potential disadvantages to the defendant require the court to examine the application for witness anonymity with scrupulous care, to ensure that it is necessary and that the witness is indeed in genuine and justified fear of serious consequences if his true identity became known to the defendant or the defendant's associates. It is in any event elementary that the court should be alert to potential or actual disadvantages faced by the defendant in consequence of any anonymity ruling, and ensure that necessary and appropriate precautions are taken to ensure that the trial itself will be fair. Provided that appropriate safeguards are applied, and the judge is satisfied that a fair trial can take place, it may proceed. If not, he should not permit anonymity. If he does so, and there is a conviction, it is not to be regarded as unsafe simply because the evidence of anonymous witnesses may have been decisive.

Their lordships recognised the consequences that permitting anonymous witnesses creates for trial advocates. Referring to the two cases which were the subject of the appeal, they said (at [66], [70] and [71]):

Having made orders for anonymity, the trial judges in both cases were content for counsel to be able to see the witness giving evidence, and to observe their demeanour whilst doing so. However, like everyone else in court, counsel were bound by the trial judge's anonymity ruling, and indeed would be in contempt of court if they disobeyed it. Plainly, if the anonymity of the witness were ordered, it would be wholly inappropriate for counsel to provide his client with a physical description of the witness. The effect of doing so would be to dilute, if not altogether extinguish the effect of the order . . .

We cannot provide an answer to every possible combination of circumstances which may arise. Our pragmatic solution to the problems which arise after an order for anonymity is that counsel should identify the issues for his client, and explain the alternatives. The choice is stark, and should be made by the client, on advice. Counsel should inform him that if he, counsel, were able to observe the witness he may be better able to cross-examine him. That is a potential advantage which he would be well able to explain to his client. However, he would also have to explain the pre-condition to such cross-examination, that he could not flout or ignore the order of the court, and could not, at any stage of the trial or afterwards, provide his client with any description of the witness . . .

The alternative is that the defendant may nevertheless instruct his counsel that he should not see the witness if the opportunity to do so is subject to the prohibition on disclosure of his identity, or discussion of his physical description, or . . . the defendant instructs counsel that he should inform him of the appearance of the witness. Alternatively, counsel may believe that the professional relationship with his client would be damaged if he were unable to communicate information which his client wanted from him. In situations like these, the court will order that the anonymous witnesses must be screened from counsel. In this event . . . counsel for the Crown should be in the same position as counsel for the defendant.

Statutes on Special Measures

D14.119 **Youth Justice and Criminal Evidence Act 1999, ss. 16 to 30 and 33A to 33C**

16.—(1) For the purposes of this chapter a witness in criminal proceedings (other than the accused) is eligible for assistance by virtue of this section—

(a) if under the age of 17 at the time of the hearing; or

(b) if the court considers that the quality of evidence given by the witness is likely to be diminished by reason of any circumstances falling within subsection (2).

(2) The circumstances falling within this subsection are—

(a) that the witness—

(i) suffers from mental disorder within the meaning of the Mental Health Act 1983, or

(ii) otherwise has a significant impairment of intelligence and social functioning;

(b) that the witness has a physical disability or is suffering from a physical disorder.

(3) In subsection (1)(a) 'the time of the hearing', in relation to a witness, means the time when it falls to the court to make a determination for the purposes of section 19(2) in relation to the witness.

(4) In determining whether a witness falls within subsection (1)(b) the court must consider any views expressed by the witness.

(5) In this chapter references to the quality of a witness's evidence are to its quality in terms of completeness, coherence and accuracy; and for this purpose 'coherence' refers to a witness's ability in giving evidence to give answers which address the questions put to the witness and can be understood both individually and collectively.

17.—(1) For the purposes of this chapter a witness in criminal proceedings (other than the accused) is eligible for assistance by virtue of this subsection if the court is satisfied that the quality of evidence given by the witness is likely to be diminished by reason of fear or distress on the part of the witness in connection with testifying in the proceedings.

(2) In determining whether a witness falls within subsection (1) the court must take into account, in particular—

(a) the nature and alleged circumstances of the offence to which the proceedings relate;

(b) the age of the witness;

(c) such of the following matters as appear to the court to be relevant, namely—

(i) the social and cultural background and ethnic origins of the witness,

(ii) the domestic and employment circumstances of the witness, and

(iii) any religious beliefs or political opinions of the witness;

(d) any behaviour towards the witness on the part of—

(i) the accused,

(ii) members of the family or associates of the accused, or

(iii) any other person who is likely to be an accused or a witness in the proceedings.

(3) In determining that question the court must in addition consider any views expressed by the witness.

(4) Where the complainant in respect of a sexual offence is a witness in proceedings relating to that offence (or to that offence and any other offences), the witness is eligible for assistance in relation to those proceedings by virtue of this subsection unless the witness has informed the court of the witness's wish not to be so eligible by virtue of this subsection.

18.—(1) For the purposes of this chapter—

(a) the provision which may be made by a special measures direction by virtue of each of sections 23 to 30 is a special measure available in relation to a witness eligible for assistance by virtue of section 16; and

(b) the provision which may be made by such a direction by virtue of each of sections 23 to 28 is a special measure available in relation to a witness eligible for assistance by virtue of section 17;

but this subsection has effect subject to subsection (2).

(2) Where (apart from this subsection) a special measure would, in accordance with subsection (1)(a) or (b), be available in relation to a witness in any proceedings, it shall not be taken by a court to be available in relation to the witness unless—

(a) the court has been notified by the Secretary of State that relevant arrangements may be made available in the area in which it appears to the court that the proceedings will take place, and

(b) the notice has not been withdrawn.

(3) In subsection (2) 'relevant arrangements' means arrangements for implementing the measure in question which cover the witness and the proceedings in question.

(4) The withdrawal of a notice under that subsection relating to a special measure shall not affect the availability of that measure in relation to a witness if a special measures direction providing for that measure to apply to the witness's evidence has been made by the court before the notice is withdrawn.

(5) [Power of Secretary of State to amend so as to alter special measures available.]

19.—(1) This section applies where in any criminal proceedings—

(a) a party to the proceedings makes an application for the court to give a direction under this section in relation to a witness in the proceedings other than the accused, or

(b) the court of its own motion raises the issue whether such a direction should be given.

(2) Where the court determines that the witness is eligible for assistance by virtue of section 16 or 17, the court must then—

(a) determine whether any of the special measures available in relation to the witness (or any combination of them) would, in its opinion, be likely to improve the quality of evidence given by the witness; and

(b) if so—

(i) determine which of those measures (or combination of them) would, in its opinion, be likely to maximise so far as practicable the quality of such evidence; and
(ii) give a direction under this section providing for the measure or measures so determined to apply to evidence given by the witness.

(3) In determining for the purposes of this chapter whether any special measure or measures would or would not be likely to improve, or to maximise so far as practicable, the quality of evidence given by the witness, the court must consider all the circumstances of the case, including in particular—
(a) any views expressed by the witness; and
(b) whether the measure or measures might tend to inhibit such evidence being effectively tested by a party to the proceedings.

(4) A special measures direction must specify particulars of the provision made by the direction in respect of each special measure which is to apply to the witness's evidence.

(5) In this chapter 'special measures direction' means a direction under this section.

(6) Nothing in this chapter is to be regarded as affecting any power of a court to make an order or give leave of any description (in the exercise of its inherent jurisdiction or otherwise)—
(a) in relation to a witness who is not an eligible witness, or
(b) in relation to an eligible witness where (as, for example, in a case where a foreign language interpreter is to be provided) the order is made or the leave is given otherwise than by reason of the fact that the witness is an eligible witness.

20.—(1) Subject to subsection (2) and section 21(8), a special measures direction has binding effect from the time it is made until the proceedings for the purposes of which it is made are either—
(a) determined (by acquittal, conviction or otherwise), or
(b) abandoned,
in relation to the accused or (if there is more than one) in relation to each of the accused.

(2) The court may discharge or vary (or further vary) a special measures direction if it appears to the court to be in the interests of justice to do so, and may do so either—
(a) on an application made by a party to the proceedings, if there has been a material change of circumstances since the relevant time, or
(b) of its own motion.

(3) In subsection (2) 'the relevant time' means—
(a) the time when the direction was given, or
(b) if a previous application has been made under that subsection, the time when the application (or last application) was made.

(4) Nothing in section 24(2) and (3), 27(4) to (7) or 28(4) to (6) is to be regarded as affecting the power of the court to vary or discharge a special measures direction under subsection (2).

(5) The court must state in open court its reasons for—
(a) giving or varying,
(b) refusing an application for, or for the variation or discharge of, or
(c) discharging,
a special measures direction and, if it is a magistrates' court, must cause them to be entered in the register of its proceedings.

(6) [Provision as to rules of court.]

21.—(1) For the purposes of this section—
(a) a witness in criminal proceedings is a 'child witness' if he is an eligible witness by reason of section 16(1)(a) (whether or not he is an eligible witness by reason of any other provision of section 16 or 17);
(b) a child witness is 'in need of special protection' if the offence (or any of the offences) to which the proceedings relate is—
(i) an offence falling within section 35(3)(a) (sexual offences etc.), or
(ii) an offence falling within section 35(3)(b), (c) or (d) (kidnapping, assaults etc.); and
(c) a 'relevant recording', in relation to a child witness, is a video recording of an interview of the witness made with a view to its admission as evidence-in-chief of the witness.

(2) Where the court, in making a determination for the purposes of section 19(2), determines that a witness in criminal proceedings is a child witness, the court must—
(a) first have regard to subsections (3) to (7) below; and
(b) then have regard to section 19(2);

and for the purposes of section 19(2), as it then applies to the witness, any special measures required to be applied in relation to him by virtue of this section shall be treated as if they were measures determined by the court, pursuant to section 19(2)(a) and (b)(i), to be ones that (whether on their own or with any other special measures) would be likely to maximise, so far as practicable, the quality of his evidence.

(3) The primary rule in the case of a child witness is that the court must give a special measures direction in relation to the witness which complies with the following requirements—
(a) it must provide for any relevant recording to be admitted under section 27 (video recorded evidence-in-chief); and
(b) it must provide for any evidence given by the witness in the proceedings which is not given by means of a video recording (whether in chief or otherwise) to be given by means of a live link in accordance with section 24.

(4) The primary rule is subject to the following limitations—
(a) the requirement contained in subsection (3)(a) or (b) has effect subject to the availability (within the meaning of section 18(2)) of the special measure in question in relation to the witness;
(b) the requirement contained in subsection (3)(a) also has effect subject to section 27(2); and
(c) the rule does not apply to the extent that the court is satisfied that compliance with it would not be likely to maximise the quality of the witness's evidence so far as practicable (whether because the application to that evidence of one or more other special measures available in relation to the witness would have that result or for any other reason).

(5) However, subsection (4)(c) does not apply in relation to a child witness in need of special protection.

(6) Where a child witness is in need of special protection by virtue of subsection (1)(b)(i), any special measures direction given by the court which complies with the requirement contained in subsection (3)(a) must in addition provide for the special measure available under section 28 (video recorded cross-examination or re-examination) to apply in relation to—
(a) any cross-examination of the witness otherwise than by the accused in person, and
(b) any subsequent re-examination.

(7) The requirement contained in subsection (6) has effect subject to the following limitations—
(a) it has effect subject to the availability (within the meaning of section 18(2)) of that special measure in relation to the witness; and
(b) it does not apply if the witness has informed the court that he does not want that special measure to apply in relation to him.

(8) Where a special measures direction is given in relation to a child witness who is an eligible witness by reason only of section 16(1)(a), then—
(a) subject to subsection (9) below, and
(b) except where the witness has already begun to give evidence in the proceedings,
the direction shall cease to have effect at the time when the witness attains the age of 17.

(9) Where a special measures direction is given in relation to a child witness who is an eligible witness by reason only of section 16(1)(a) and—
(a) the direction provides—
(i) for any relevant recording to be admitted under section 27 as evidence-in-chief of the witness, or
(ii) for the special measure available under section 28 to apply in relation to the witness, and
(b) if it provides for that special measure to so apply, the witness is still under the age of 17 when the video recording is made for the purposes of section 28,
then, so far as it provides as mentioned in paragraph (a)(i) or (ii) above, the direction shall continue to have effect in accordance with section 20(1) even though the witness subsequently attains that age.

22.—(1) For the purposes of this section—
(a) a witness in criminal proceedings (other than the accused) is a 'qualifying witness' if he—
(i) is not an eligible witness at the time of the hearing (as defined by section 16(3)), but
(ii) was under the age of 17 when a relevant recording was made;
(b) a qualifying witness is 'in need of special protection' if the offence (or any of the offences) to which the proceedings relate is—

D

Part D Procedure

(i) an offence falling within section 35(3)(a) (sexual offences etc.), or
(ii) an offence falling within section 35(3)(b), (c) or (d) (kidnapping, assaults etc.); and
(c) a 'relevant recording', in relation to a witness, is a video recording of an interview of the witness made with a view to its admission as evidence-in-chief of the witness.

(2) Subsections (2) to (7) of section 21 shall apply as follows in relation to a qualifying witness—
(a) subsections (2) to (4), so far as relating to the giving of a direction complying with the requirement contained in subsection (3)(a), shall apply to a qualifying witness in respect of the relevant recording as they apply to a child witness (within the meaning of that section);
(b) subsection (5), so far as relating to the giving of such a direction, shall apply to a qualifying witness in need of special protection as it applies to a child witness in need of special protection (within the meaning of that section); and
(c) subsections (6) and (7) shall apply to a qualifying witness in need of special protection by virtue of subsection (1)(b)(i) above as they apply to such a child witness as is mentioned in subsection (6).

23.—(1) A special measures direction may provide for the witness, while giving testimony or being sworn in court, to be prevented by means of a screen or other arrangement from seeing the accused.
(2) But the screen or other arrangement must not prevent the witness from being able to see, and to be seen by—
(a) the judge or justices (or both) and the jury (if there is one);
(b) legal representatives acting in the proceedings; and
(c) any interpreter or other person appointed (in pursuance of the direction or otherwise) to assist the witness.
(3) Where two or more legal representatives are acting for a party to the proceedings, subsection (2)(b) is to be regarded as satisfied in relation to those representatives if the witness is able at all material times to see and be seen by at least one of them.

24.—(1) A special measures direction may provide for the witness to give evidence by means of a live link.
(2) Where a direction provides for the witness to give evidence by means of a live link, the witness may not give evidence in any other way without the permission of the court.
(3) The court may give permission for the purposes of subsection (2) if it appears to the court to be in the interests of justice to do so, and may do so either—
(a) on an application by a party to the proceedings, if there has been a material change of circumstances since the relevant time, or
(b) of its own motion.
(4) In subsection (3) 'the relevant time' means—
(a) the time when the direction was given, or
(b) if a previous application has been made under that subsection, the time when the application (or last application) was made.

. . .

(8) In this chapter 'live link' means a live television link or other arrangement whereby a witness, while absent from the courtroom or other place where the proceedings are being held, is able to see and hear a person there and to be seen and heard by the persons specified in section 23(2)(a) to (c).

25.—(1) A special measures direction may provide for the exclusion from the court, during the giving of the witness's evidence, of persons of any description specified in the direction.
(2) The persons who may be so excluded do not include—
(a) the accused,
(b) legal representatives acting in the proceedings, or
(c) any interpreter or other person appointed (in pursuance of the direction or otherwise) to assist the witness.
(3) A special measures direction providing for representatives of news gathering or reporting organisations to be so excluded shall be expressed not to apply to one named person who—
(a) is a representative of such an organisation, and
(b) has been nominated for the purpose by one or more such organisations, unless it appears to the court that no such nomination has been made.

(4) A special measures direction may only provide for the exclusion of persons under this section where—
(a) the proceedings relate to a sexual offence; or
(b) it appears to the court that there are reasonable grounds for believing that any person other than the accused has sought, or will seek, to intimidate the witness in connection with testifying in the proceedings.

(5) Any proceedings from which persons are excluded under this section (whether or not those persons include representatives of news gathering or reporting organisations) shall nevertheless be taken to be held in public for the purposes of any privilege or exemption from liability available in respect of fair, accurate and contemporaneous reports of legal proceedings held in public.

26. A special measures direction may provide for the wearing of wigs or gowns to be dispensed with during the giving of the witness's evidence.

27.—(1) A special measures direction may provide for a video recording of an interview of the witness to be admitted as evidence-in-chief of the witness.

(2) A special measures direction may, however, not provide for a video recording, or a part of such a recording, to be admitted under this section if the court is of the opinion, having regard to all the circumstances of the case, that in the interests of justice the recording, or that part of it, should not be so admitted.

(3) In considering for the purposes of subsection (2) whether any part of a recording should not be admitted under this section, the court must consider whether any prejudice to the accused which might result from that part being so admitted is outweighed by the desirability of showing the whole, or substantially the whole, of the recorded interview.

(4) Where a special measures direction provides for a recording to be admitted under this section, the court may nevertheless subsequently direct that it is not to be so admitted if—
(a) it appears to the court that—
(i) the witness will not be available for cross-examination (whether conducted in the ordinary way or in accordance with any such direction), and
(ii) the parties to the proceedings have not agreed that there is no need for the witness to be so available; or
(b) any Criminal Procedure Rules requiring disclosure of the circumstances in which the recording was made have not been complied with to the satisfaction of the court.

(5) Where a recording is admitted under this section—
(a) the witness must be called by the party tendering it in evidence, unless—
(i) a special measures direction provides for the witness's evidence on cross-examination to be given otherwise than by testimony in court, or
(ii) the parties to the proceedings have agreed as mentioned in subsection (4)(a)(ii); and
(b) the witness may not give evidence-in-chief otherwise than by means of the recording—
(i) as to any matter which, in the opinion of the court, has been dealt with adequately in the witness's recorded testimony, or
(ii) without the permission of the court, as to any other matter which, in the opinion of the court, is dealt with in that testimony.

(6) Where in accordance with subsection (2) a special measures direction provides for part only of a recording to be admitted under this section, references in subsections (4) and (5) to the recording or to the witness's recorded testimony are references to the part of the recording or testimony which is to be so admitted.

(7) The court may give permission for the purposes of subsection (5)(b)(ii) if it appears to the court to be in the interests of justice to do so, and may do so either—
(a) on an application by a party to the proceedings, if there has been a material change of circumstances since the relevant time, or
(b) of its own motion.

(8) In subsection (7) 'the relevant time' means—
(a) the time when the direction was given, or
(b) if a previous application has been made under that subsection, the time when the application (or last application) was made.

(9) The court may, in giving permission for the purposes of subsection (5)(b)(ii), direct that the evidence in question is to be given by the witness by means of a live link; and, if the court so directs, subsections (5) to (7) of section 24 shall apply in relation to that evidence as they apply in relation to evidence which is to be given in accordance with a special measures direction.

(10) A magistrates' court inquiring into an offence as examining justices under section 6 of the Magistrates' Courts Act 1980 may consider any video recording in relation to which it is proposed to apply for a special measures direction providing for it to be admitted at the trial in accordance with this section.

(11) Nothing in this section affects the admissibility of any video recording which would be admissible apart from this section.

[28.—(1) Where a special measures direction provides for a video recording to be admitted under section 27 as evidence-in-chief of the witness, the direction may also provide—

(a) for any cross-examination of the witness, and any re-examination, to be recorded by means of a video recording; and

(b) for such a recording to be admitted, so far as it relates to any such cross-examination or re-examination, as evidence of the witness under cross-examination or on re-examination, as the case may be.

(2) Such a recording must be made in the presence of such persons as Criminal Procedure Rules or the direction may provide and in the absence of the accused, but in circumstances in which—

(a) the judge or justices (or both) and legal representatives acting in the proceedings are able to see and hear the examination of the witness and to communicate with the persons in whose presence the recording is being made, and

(b) the accused is able to see and hear any such examination and to communicate with any legal representative acting for him.

(3) Where two or more legal representatives are acting for a party to the proceedings, subsection (2)(a) and (b) are to be regarded as satisfied in relation to those representatives if at all material times they are satisfied in relation to at least one of them.

(4) Where a special measures direction provides for a recording to be admitted under this section, the court may nevertheless subsequently direct that it is not to be so admitted if any requirement of subsection (2) or Criminal Procedure Rules or the direction has not been complied with to the satisfaction of the court.

(5) Where in pursuance of subsection (1) a recording has been made of any examination of the witness, the witness may not be subsequently cross-examined or re-examined in respect of any evidence given by the witness in the proceedings (whether in any recording admissible under section 27 or this section or otherwise than in such a recording) unless the court gives a further special measures direction making such provision as is mentioned in subsection (1)(a) and (b) in relation to any subsequent cross-examination, and re-examination, of the witness.

(6) The court may only give such a further direction if it appears to the court—

(a) that the proposed cross-examination is sought by a party to the proceedings as a result of that party having become aware, since the time when the original recording was made in pursuance of subsection (1), of a matter which that party could not with reasonable diligence have ascertained by then, or

(b) that for any other reason it is in the interests of justice to give the further direction.

(7) Nothing in this section shall be read as applying in relation to any cross-examination of the witness by the accused in person (in a case where the accused is to be able to conduct any such cross-examination).]

Note: Section 28 is not yet in force.

29.—(1) A special measures direction may provide for any examination of the witness (however and wherever conducted) to be conducted through an interpreter or other person approved by the court for the purposes of this section ('an intermediary').

(2) The function of an intermediary is to communicate—

(a) to the witness, questions put to the witness, and

(b) to any person asking such questions, the answers given by the witness in reply to them,

and to explain such questions or answers so far as necessary to enable them to be understood by the witness or person in question.

(3) Any examination of the witness in pursuance of subsection (1) must take place in the presence of such persons as Criminal Procedure Rules or the direction may provide, but in circumstances in which—

(a) the judge or justices (or both) and legal representatives acting in the proceedings are able to see and hear the examination of the witness and to communicate with the intermediary, and

(b) (except in the case of a video recorded examination) the jury (if there is one) are able to see and hear the examination of the witness.

(4) Where two or more legal representatives are acting for a party to the proceedings, subsection (3)(a) is to be regarded as satisfied in relation to those representatives if at all material times it is satisfied in relation to at least one of them.

(5) A person may not act as an intermediary in a particular case except after making a declaration, in such form as may be prescribed by Criminal Procedure Rules, that he will faithfully perform his function as intermediary.

(6) Subsection (1) does not apply to an interview of the witness which is recorded by means of a video recording with a view to its admission as evidence-in-chief of the witness; but a special measures direction may provide for such a recording to be admitted under section 27 if the interview was conducted through an intermediary and—

(a) that person complied with subsection (5) before the interview began, and

(b) the court's approval for the purposes of this section is given before the direction is given.

(7) Section 1 of the Perjury Act 1911 (perjury) shall apply in relation to a person acting as an intermediary as it applies in relation to a person lawfully sworn as an interpreter in a judicial proceeding; and for this purpose, where a person acts as an intermediary in any proceeding which is not a judicial proceeding for the purposes of that section, that proceeding shall be taken to be part of the judicial proceeding in which the witness's evidence is given.

30. A special measures direction may provide for the witness, while giving evidence (whether by testimony in court or otherwise), to be provided with such device as the court considers appropriate with a view to enabling questions or answers to be communicated to or by the witness despite any disability or disorder or other impairment which the witness has or suffers from.

33A.—(1) This section applies to any proceedings (whether in a magistrates' court or before the Crown Court) against a person for an offence.

(2) The court may, on the application of the accused, give a live link direction if it is satisfied—

(a) that the conditions in subsection (4) or, as the case may be, subsection (5) are met in relation to the accused, and

(b) that it is in the interests of justice for the accused to give evidence through a live link.

(3) A live link direction is a direction that any oral evidence to be given before the court by the accused is to be given through a live link.

(4) Where the accused is aged under 18 when the application is made, the conditions are that—

(a) his ability to participate effectively in the proceedings as a witness giving oral evidence in court is compromised by his level of intellectual ability or social functioning, and

(b) use of a live link would enable him to participate more effectively in the proceedings as a witness (whether by improving the quality of his evidence or otherwise).

(5) Where the accused has attained the age of 18 at that time, the conditions are that—

(a) he suffers from a mental disorder (within the meaning of the Mental Health Act 1983) or otherwise has a significant impairment of intelligence and social function,

(b) he is for that reason unable to participate effectively in the proceedings as a witness giving oral evidence in court, and

(c) use of a live link would enable him to participate more effectively in the proceedings as a witness (whether by improving the quality of his evidence or otherwise).

(6) While a live link direction has effect the accused may not give oral evidence before the court in the proceedings otherwise than through a live link.

(7) The court may discharge a live link direction at any time before or during any hearing to which it applies if it appears to the court to be in the interests of justice to do so (but this does not affect the power to give a further live link direction in relation to the accused). The court may exercise this power of its own motion or on an application by a party.

(8) The court must state in open court its reasons for—

(a) giving or discharging a live link direction, or

(b) refusing an application for or for the discharge of a live link direction,

and, if it is a magistrates' court, it must cause those reasons to be entered in the register of its proceedings.

33B.—(1) In section 33A 'live link' means an arrangement by which the accused, while absent from the place where the proceedings are being held, is able—

(a) to see and hear a person there, and

(b) to be seen and heard by the persons mentioned in subsection (2),

and for this purpose any impairment of eyesight or hearing is to be disregarded.

(2) The persons are—
   (a) the judge or justices (or both) and the jury (if there is one),
   (b) where there are two or more accused in the proceedings, each of the other accused,
   (c) legal representatives acting in the proceedings, and
   (d) any interpreter or other person appointed by the court to assist the accused.

33C. Nothing in this Chapter affects—
   (a) any power of a court to make an order, give directions or give leave of any description in relation to any witness (including an accused), or
   (b) the operation of any rule of law relating to evidence in criminal proceedings.

D14.120 **Direction to the Jury about Special Measures** Section 31 deals with the status of evidence where, in accordance with a special measures direction, the witness's evidence is not given by direct oral testimony. Section 32 requires the judge on a trial on indictment to give such warning to the jury as he considers necessary to ensure that the giving of any special measures direction does not prejudice the accused.

In *Brown* [2004] Crim LR 1034, the Court of Appeal made it clear that a judge was not required to repeat a special measures direction in summing up. It was sufficient that he had done so at the time that the evidence in question was given.

Criminal Justice Act 2003, s. 51

(1) A witness (other than the defendant) may, if the court so directs, give evidence through a live link in the following criminal proceedings.
(2) They are—
   (a) a summary trial,
   (b) an appeal to the Crown Court arising out of such a trial,
   (c) a trial on indictment,
   (d) an appeal to the criminal division of the Court of Appeal,
   (e) the hearing of a reference under section 9 or 11 of the Criminal Appeal Act 1995,
   (f) a hearing before a magistrates' court or the Crown Court which is held after the defendant has entered a plea of guilty, and
   (g) a hearing before the Court of Appeal under section 80 of this Act.
(3) A direction may be given under this section—
   (a) on an application by a party to the proceedings, or
   (b) of the court's own motion.
(4) But a direction may not be given under this section unless—
   (a) the court is satisfied that it is in the interests of the efficient or effective administration of justice for the person concerned to give evidence in the proceedings through a live link,
   (b) it has been notified by the Secretary of State that suitable facilities for receiving evidence through a live link are available in the area in which it appears to the court that the proceedings will take place, and
   (c) that notification has not been withdrawn.
(5) The withdrawal of such a notification is not to affect a direction given under this section before that withdrawal.
(6) In deciding whether to give a direction under this section the court must consider all the circumstances of the case.
(7) Those circumstances include in particular—
   (a) the availability of the witness,
   (b) the need for the witness to attend in person,
   (c) the importance of the witness's evidence to the proceedings,
   (d) the views of the witness,
   (e) the suitability of the facilities at the place where the witness would give evidence through a live link,
   (f) whether a direction might tend to inhibit any party to the proceedings from effectively testing the witness's evidence.
(8) The court must state in open court its reasons for refusing an application for a direction under this section and, if it is a magistrates' court, must cause them to be entered in the register of its proceedings.

Section D15 Trial on Indictment: The Prosecution Case

Following a plea of not guilty (see **D12**) and the empanelling of a jury (see **D13**), the trial proper commences with the prosecution case. That falls into two parts, namely (a) counsel's opening speech, and (b) the evidence. **D15.1**

Some evidence that forms the basis for the prosecution case is agreed by the accused, and may therefore be read or summarised in the form of admitted evidence. Other parts of the prosecution case, however, are subjected to challenge on behalf of the accused, either through cross-examination of witnesses called or through objection being taken to the admissibility of evidence. The ultimate challenge to the validity of the prosecution case is that mounted at its conclusion, namely a submission of no case to answer.

Where evidence is excluded which fundamentally undermines the prosecution case, or where the court upholds a submission of no case to answer, the prosecution now has a right of appeal, pursuant to the provisions of the CJA 2003, part IX. Because these provisions operate either during or at the conclusion of the prosecution case, they are addressed at the conclusion of this chapter.

First, however, it is important to consider the obligations that the law, and professional ethics, impose on those who prosecute.

DUTIES AND ROLE OF PROSECUTION COUNSEL

Introduction

The manner in which prosecution counsel should conduct themselves in a criminal trial (in particular a trial on indictment) and the duties resting upon them emerge, to an extent, from dicta in Court of Appeal decisions and, more importantly, from the Code of Conduct of the Bar and from the recommendations of the Farquharson Committee on the role of prosecuting counsel, published in *Counsel*, Trinity 1986. **D15.2**

Ministers of Justice In *Puddick* (1865) 4 F & F 497, Crompton J said (at p. 499) that prosecution counsel 'are to regard themselves as ministers of justice, and not to struggle for a conviction'. See also per Avory J in *Banks* [1916] 2 KB 621 at p. 623. Some of the implications this has on the prosecutor's role are identified in the introductory paragraphs of the Farquharson report: **D15.3**

> There is no doubt that the obligations of prosecution counsel are different from those of counsel instructed for the defence in a criminal case or of counsel instructed in civil matters. His duties are wider both to the court and to the public at large. Furthermore, having regard to his duty to present the case for the prosecution fairly to the jury, he has a greater independence of those instructing him than that enjoyed by other counsel. It is well known to every practitioner that counsel for the prosecution must conduct his case moderately, albeit firmly. He must not strive

> unfairly to obtain a conviction; he must not press his case beyond the limits which the evidence permits; he must not invite the jury to convict on evidence which in his own judgement no longer sustains the charge laid in the indictment. If the evidence of a witness is undermined or severely blemished in the course of cross-examination, prosecution counsel must not present him to the jury as worthy of a credibility he no longer enjoys. . . . Great responsibility is placed upon prosecution counsel and although his description as a 'minister of justice' may sound pompous to modern ears it accurately describes the way in which he should discharge his function.

In *Gonez* [1999] All ER (D) 674, the Court of Appeal endorsed the description of prosecuting counsel as a minister of justice, stating that it was incumbent on him not to be betrayed by personal feelings, not to excite emotions or to inflame the minds of the jury, and not to make comments which could reasonably be construed as racist and bigoted. He was to be clinical and dispassionate.

D15.4 **Relationship of Prosecution Counsel with those Instructing Him** As the Farquharson committee stated in the passage quoted in **D15.3**, prosecution counsel is recognised as enjoying greater independence from those instructing him, whether it be the CPS or other prosecuting agency or private prosecutor, than does defence counsel from his solicitor or lay client. The report considers in detail the limits of this greater independence with special reference to the creation of the CPS.

The committee helpfully summarised their views in the following propositions:

(a) It is the duty of prosecution counsel to read the instructions delivered to him expeditiously and to advise or confer with those instructing him on all aspects of the case well before its commencement.

(b) A solicitor who has briefed counsel to prosecute may withdraw his instructions before the commencement of the trial up to the point when it becomes impracticable to do so, if he disagrees with the advice given by counsel or for any other proper professional reason.

(c) While he remains instructed it is for counsel to take all necessary decisions in the presentation and general conduct of the prosecution.

(d) Where matters of policy fall to be decided after the point indicated in (b) above (including offering no evidence on the indictment or on a particular count, or the acceptance of pleas to lesser counts), it is the duty of counsel to consult those instructing him, as their views at this stage are of crucial importance.

(e) In the rare case where counsel and his instructing solicitor are unable to agree on a matter of policy, it is (subject to (g) below) for prosecution counsel to make the necessary decisions.

(f) Where counsel has taken a decision on a matter of policy with which his instructing solicitor has not agreed, then it would be appropriate for the A-G to require counsel to submit to him a written report of all the circumstances, including his reasons for disagreeing with those who instructed him.

(g) When counsel has had the opportunity to prepare his brief and to confer with those instructing him, but at the last moment before trial unexpectedly advises that the case should not proceed or that pleas to lesser offences should be accepted, and his instructing solicitor does not accept such advice, counsel should apply for an adjournment if instructed so to do.

(h) Subject to the above, it is for prosecution counsel to decide whether to offer no evidence on a particular count or on the indictment as a whole and whether to accept pleas to a lesser count or counts.

Provisions of the Code of Conduct of the Bar Relating to Prosecuting Counsel

D15.5 The CPS and the General Council of the Bar issued Guidelines in 2002 on the application of the Farquharson principles and, where appropriate, these have also been incorporated in the Written Standards for the Conduct of Professional Work in the Code of Conduct of the Bar (the 'Written Standards').

The status of the Code of Conduct of the Bar was explained as follows in *McFadden* (1975) 62 Cr App R 187, by James LJ (at p. 190):

> The Bar Council issues statements from time to time to give guidance to the profession in matters of etiquette and procedure. A barrister who conforms to the Council's rulings knows that he cannot be committing an offence against professional discipline. But such statements, although they have strong persuasive force, do not bind the courts. If therefore a judge requires a barrister to do, or refrain from doing, something in the course of a case, the barrister may protest and may cite any relevant ruling of the Bar Council, but since the judge is the final authority in his own court, if counsel's protest is unavailing, he must either withdraw or comply with the ruling or look for redress in a higher court.

Prosecution Counsel's Duties Paragraph 10 of the Written Standards deals especially with the duties of prosecuting counsel, in the following respects: **D15.6**

(a) Paragraph 10.1 describes the general role and approach of prosecuting counsel in terms similar to those used by Avory J in *Banks* [1916] 2 KB 621, and the Farquharson committee (see **D15.3**). Paragraph 10.6 reflects what is contained in the report of the Farquharson committee.
(b) At the conclusion of the summing-up, it is counsel's duty to draw to the judge's attention any apparent omissions or errors of fact or law (para. 10.7).
(c) Paragraph 10.8 concerns counsel's role at the sentencing stage.

Attendance at Court Paragraph 15.1 of the Written Standards requires counsel to be present throughout the trial (including the summing-up and return of the jury), unless given leave by the court to be absent. If two or more counsel have been instructed, the attendance of one is sufficient. **D15.7**

Documents Coming into Counsel's Possession Paragraphs 7.2, 7.3.1 and 7.3.2 of the Written Standards deal with problems which may arise from counsel coming into possession of documents to which neither he nor his lay or professional clients are entitled. **D15.8**

The provisions of the code are in part the consequence of what occurred in *Tompkins* (1977) 67 Cr App R 181. In that case, a representative of the prosecuting solicitor, having picked up a note from the accused to defence counsel which had apparently been dropped on the floor, handed the note to prosecuting counsel. Prosecution counsel used the note as a previous inconsistent statement of the accused during cross-examination of him. The Court of Appeal upheld the conviction since, although the note was privileged as a communication between client and legal adviser, the doctrine of privilege merely protects a party from the obligation of producing a document and does not determine its admissibility or the use which may be made of it should it come into the hands of the other side. Moreover, even if the note had been inadmissible in itself, that would not have prevented counsel asking questions based upon it without directly revealing its contents to the jury.

The practice adopted in *Tompkins* is not, however, approved by the Code of Conduct, which states that:

(a) a barrister must not try to obtain a document belonging to the other side (or knowledge of its contents) except through the normal and proper channels (para. 7.1);
(b) if he should accidentally come into possession of such a document he should at once return it unread (para. 7.2); and
(c) if he reads a document before realising that he ought not to have done so and would be embarrassed in conducting the case by the knowledge thus inadvertently obtained, he should return his instructions, provided he can do so without prejudice to his lay client (paras. 7.3.1 and 7.3.2).

Speaking to Witnesses The proper handling of witnesses has become an important part of the role of the prosecutor, not least since the introduction of CPS Standards in this regard. It is addressed in more detail at **D14.91**. **D15.9**

D

Part D Procedure

OPENING SPEECH

D15.10 There is little direct authority on what should or should not be said by prosecuting counsel in his opening address to the jury. By convention, it involves an outline of the evidence which the prosecution proposes to call. The following are matters that may affect the style and content of an opening speech.

Emotive Language

D15.11 In making his speeches to the jury, prosecuting counsel must remember his role as a minister of justice who ought not to strive over-zealously for a conviction (see D15.3). He should therefore avoid using emotive language liable to prejudice the jury against the accused. Avory J's oft-quoted description of prosecuting counsel as a minister of justice was given in relation to a trial in which prosecution counsel had made a number of observations 'calculated to prejudice the jury'. The use of emotive language was criticised by his lordship as being 'not in good taste or strictly in accordance with the character which prosecuting counsel should always bear in mind'.

Submissions as to Law

D15.12 The extent to which the prosecutor deals with points of law that may arise during the trial or possible defences which the accused is likely to raise is a matter for his discretion, depending on the circumstances of the particular case. In *Lashley* [2005] EWCA Crim 2016, Judge LJ stated (at [13]):

> The presumption should be that an opening address by counsel for the Crown should not address the law, save in cases of real complication and difficulty where counsel believes and the trial judge agrees that the jury may be assisted by a brief and well-focussed submission.

If counsel deals with a matter of law it is usual to remind the jury that matters of law are ultimately for the judge, and that counsel's remarks should therefore be disregarded insofar as they differ from the judge's directions.

Omission of Evidence Objected to by Defence

D15.13 If defence counsel has intimated that there is an objection to some of the prosecution evidence, no reference should be made to that evidence in opening. If the opening speech cannot be made coherently without reference to the disputed evidence, the judge should be invited to determine whether or not the evidence is admissible as a preliminary issue. See also D15.43.

References to Inadmissible Evidence

D15.14 Should counsel refer in opening to evidence which turns out to be inadmissible or which for any other reason is not called, whether or not this in itself a ground for quashing an accused's conviction depends on the extent to which the accused is prejudiced by it (*Jackson* [1953] 1 WLR 591). A relevant consideration is how the irregularity was dealt with in the summing-up.

In fact, both defence counsel and the judge are likely to point out to the jury that what prosecuting counsel has said is simply not evidence. If the defence, as a result of prosecuting counsel's improper remarks, applied unsuccessfully for the jury to be discharged, the refusal to discharge may be used as a ground of appeal. However, the Court of Appeal is generally reluctant to interfere with a trial judge's exercise of discretion in respect of discharging a jury (see D13.45 *et seq.*).

References to Plea of Guilty by Co-accused

Where the allegation against the accused on trial relates to his actions in concert with another who has pleaded guilty, presentation of the evidence against the accused on trial will involve reference to the actions of that other. Since the jury will inevitably speculate about why this other is not before the court, it is generally desirable to inform them as soon as possible of the reason. This avoids unnecessary mystification of the jury. Therefore, if the defence consent, the jury may be told in opening of the co-accused's plea. **D15.15**

It has been implied that they may be told of it even if the defence do not consent. In *Moore* (1956) 40 Cr App R 50, Lord Goddard CJ said (at pp. 53–4):

> When two people are indicted together for a criminal offence and one pleads guilty and the other does not, it is the commonest thing in the world to tell the jury, as was done in this case, 'You must not pay any attention to the fact that the other man has pleaded guilty'. Even if the plea has not been taken in the presence of the jury, it is very difficult to avoid telling the jury in some way that the other person has pleaded guilty.

The admissibility of convictions of persons other than the accused on trial (including guilty pleas by co-accused) is now governed by the PACE 1984, s. 74(1) (see **F11.5**), and subject to s. 78 of the same Act (exclusion of evidence on grounds of unfairness) (see **F2.14**). Therefore, if it is necessary to address this issue in opening, it should be ventilated at the outset. Unless and until the judge rules the evidence of the co-accused's guilty plea to be admissible, his absence from the dock should be dealt with by a formula such as: 'X, of whom you may hear mention in the course of this case, is not before you and is none of your concern'.

Defence Statements

Under s. 6E(4) of the CPIA 1996, the court has the power to provide a jury with copies of a defence statement served pursuant to that Act. This power is discussed in more detail at **D9**. In the context of the prosecution opening its case, or adducing evidence thereafter as part of its case, it is right to observe that there will be circumstances, such as in relation to proving that notice had been given of a since rejected alibi, where the jury would be entitled to receive a copy of the defence statement to help them, using the wording of s. 6E(5), 'to understand the case or to resolve any issue in the case'. **D15.16**

WITNESSES THE PROSECUTION SHOULD CALL OR TENDER

General Rule: Witnesses on Back of Indictment

Having opened his case, prosecuting counsel calls his witnesses and reads out any written statements admissible under exceptions to the rule against hearsay. As a matter of practice, he should call, or read the statements of, all witnesses whose statements have been served, or, to use the traditional phrase 'witnesses whose names are on the back of the indictment'. **D15.17**

Although counsel has a discretion not to call a witness on the back of the indictment, he must exercise his discretion in a proper manner and not for what Lord Thankerton in *Adel Muhammed El Dabbah v A-G for Palestine* [1944] AC 156, described as 'some oblique motive' (e.g., unfairly so as to surprise or prejudice the defence).

Rationale for the Rule The rationale for the above rule is that, by using a person's evidence at the time of serving its case, the prosecution indicate that he is an intended prosecution witness for the trial. In those circumstances the defence may hesitate to approach the witness or take a further statement from him. Moreover, since it is assumed that the prosecution will ensure that the witness attends at the Crown Court, the defence will take no steps in that regard. Thus, to avoid the defence being taken by surprise and prejudiced by the **D15.18**

loss of evidence of potential value to their case, the prosecution are in general obliged to call him at the trial.

It follows that the rule has no application to witnesses whose statements have never formed part of the prosecution case, but were served upon the defence as unused material. The prosecution is under no duty to call such witnesses to give evidence (*Richardson* (1994) 98 Cr App R 174).

D15.19 **Exceptions to the Rule** The general rule is subject to the following exceptions:

(a) *Witness to be Read.* A witness on the back of the indictment need not be called or even brought to court if the prosecution anticipate being able to read his statement, e.g., by virtue of the CJA 1967, s. 9 (see **D21.24**), or the CJA 2003, ss.116 and 117 (see **F16.3** ***et seq.***).

(b) *Witness not Credible.* Prosecuting counsel has a discretion not to call a witness whose name is on the back of the indictment if the witness no longer appears to counsel to be a credible witness, worthy of belief (*Oliva* [1965] 1 WLR 1028). This exception presupposes that something has occurred between committal and trial to cast doubt on the witness's veracity. In *Oliva*, the prosecution declined to call the victim of an alleged offence who had made a statement to the police naming O as the culprit which he had later retracted. The Court of Criminal Appeal dismissed O's appeal, holding that the prosecution's duty extended only to calling witnesses who appeared capable of belief. As a result of his volte-face, the victim could no longer be regarded as creditworthy and, in the circumstances, prosecuting counsel had a discretion not to call him which he exercised properly.

(c) *Unhelpful but Credible Evidence.* The ruling of Park J in *Nugent* [1977] 1 WLR 789, and the Privy Council cases of *Seneviratne v R* [1936] 3 All ER 36 and *Adel Muhammed El Dabbah v A-G for Palestine* [1944] AC 156, have lent some support to the proposition that the prosecution need not call a witness, even though they regard him as capable of belief, if his anticipated evidence would be likely to confuse the jury about the nature of the prosecution case. However, in *Balmforth* [1992] Crim LR 882, the Court of Appeal held that, once the prosecution had decided that a witness on the back of the indictment was capable of belief, they must call him.

The Reality of the Prosecution's Obligation

D15.20 The problems which arose in *Nugent* [1977] 1 WLR 789, and earlier similar cases over which side should call witnesses were the result of a misguided view that the prosecution at committal proceedings were under a duty to tender the evidence of *all* witnesses who appeared to be (a) credible and (b) capable of giving evidence relevant to the case. If the prosecution are not obliged to use all the evidence favouring their own case at committal (see *Epping and Harlow Justices, ex parte Massaro* [1973] QB 433), there can be no obligation to call evidence or tender statements helpful to the defence (see also **D15.25**).

The prosecution's duty is rather to inform the defence of all unused material, including statements containing evidence which contradicts the prosecution case and/or lays the foundation for a defence (see **D14.69**). Provided that is done, the defence will be able to interview the witnesses and arrange for them to be at the Crown Court to testify as *defence* witnesses if necessary (see also *Russell-Jones* [1995] 3 All ER 239 and *Brown* [1997] 1 Cr App R 112).

D15.21 **Mixed Statements** A grey area still remains where the prosecution have a number of statements broadly agreeing with each other but differing on points of detail, some being more helpful to the defence than others. In such cases, the better practice may be to include all the statements in the committal bundle, and, subject to any later doubts as to credibility, all the statement-makers should then be called by the prosecution at trial (see also *Witts* [1991] Crim

LR 562). Where there is a duty on the prosecution to call or tender a witness, reading the statement of the witness may be an acceptable alternative (*Armstrong* [1995] Crim LR 831).

In *Cairns* [2003] 1 WLR 796, the issue was whether the Crown was entitled to call a witness, rather than whether it was obliged to do so. The Crown called a witness who, they submitted, was worthy of belief in respect of Dl and D2, but not in respect of D3 (their co-accused). The Court of Appeal held that there was no known principle requiring the prosecution to regard the whole of a witness's evidence to be reliable before calling him as a witness. It was not uncommon for part of a witness's evidence to be accepted by a jury and another part rejected. The Crown had acted properly, as had the judge, in admitting the evidence of the witness in question.

Duty to Have the Witnesses at Court

Where the prosecution intend not to call a witness whose name appears on the back of the indictment, they nonetheless have a duty to ensure that he is present at court for the trial so that the defence may call him if they wish (per Lord Parker CJ in *Oliva* [1965] 1 WLR 1028 at p. 1035: 'The prosecution must of course have in court the witnesses whose names are on the back of the indictment, but there is a wide discretion in the prosecution as to whether they should call them'). **D15.22**

The above-stated rule as to attendance of witnesses does not apply if they are absent for reasons beyond the prosecution's control. The considerations relevant to the exercise of the judge's discretion in such cases were summarised by Geoffrey Lane J in giving the judgment of the Court of Appeal in *Cavanagh* [1972] 1 WLR 676. His lordship said (at p. 679B–F):

> The prosecution must take all reasonable steps to secure the attendance of any of their witnesses who are not the subject of a conditional witness order or whom the defence might reasonably expect to be present. The reason for that is obvious and was expressed [by Alderson B] in *Woodhead* (1847) 2 Car & Kir 520. . . .
>
> If, however, it proves impossible, despite such steps, to have the witnesses present, the court may in its discretion permit the trial to proceed provided that no injustice will be done thereby. What considerations will affect the exercise of the court's discretion will vary infinitely from case to case. Would the defence wish to call the witness if the prosecution did not? What are the chances of securing the witness's attendance within a reasonable time? Are the prosecution prepared to proceed in his absence? If so, to what extent would the evidence of the absent witness have been likely to assist the defendant? If the absent witness can be procured, will other witnesses by then have become unavailable? There will be many other matters which may have to be considered.

Does the Judge Have Power to Require the Prosecution to Call a Witness?

The authorities on the prosecution's duty to call witnesses are inconclusive as to whether, in the last resort, the judge may force counsel to call a witness against his will. In *Oliva* [1965] 1 WLR 1028 at p. 1036, Lord Parker CJ stated the position thus: **D15.23**

> If the prosecution appear to be exercising that discretion [not to call a witness] improperly, it is open to the judge of trial to interfere and in his discretion in turn to invite the prosecution to call a particular witness, and if they refuse there is the ultimate sanction in the judge himself calling that witness.

The implication of the dictum is that the judge can 'invite' rather than compel the calling of a witness by prosecution counsel. Counsel has the right to refuse the invitation, but must be aware that, if he does so, the judge could call the witness of his own motion.

A contrary view was taken in *Sterk* [1972] Crim LR 391, where the Court of Appeal held that the trial judge should have *ordered* the prosecution at least to tender a witness on the back of the indictment for cross-examination by the defence.

Tendering a Witness

D15.24 As an alternative to calling a witness and examining him in the normal way, it is open to prosecuting counsel to tender a witness for cross-examination. Counsel merely calls the witness, establishes his name and address, and then invites the defence to ask any questions they wish.

Additional Evidence

D15.25 The prosecution at trial on indictment are not confined to using solely the evidence they relied upon at any committal proceedings. Nor are they obliged to use at committal all the evidence then available to them (*Epping and Harlow Justices, ex parte Massaro* [1973] QB 433; see **D15.20**). If, however, they intend to call evidence at trial additional to the evidence used for committal, whether that be evidence which was not then available or evidence which they simply chose not to adduce, they are required to give the defence notice of their intention.

They must also supply a copy of the statement of the additional witness or, as the case may be, a copy of the further statement made by a witness whose first statement was used at committal, complying with the formal requirements of the CJA 1967, s. 9. If the defence do not object within seven days, it will then be possible to read the statement as evidence at the trial without calling the witness.

D15.26 **Response to the Service of Additional Evidence** In *Wright* (1934) 25 Cr App R 35, the ground of appeal was that the prosecution called a witness to produce two specimens of his writing, and then invited the jury to compare these specimens with the writing on a certain envelope in order to prove that the handwriting was his. Apart from objecting to the lack of evidence from a handwriting expert, the defence contended that they had not been notified of the intention to put the specimens into evidence. Avory J said (at p. 40):

> At most that is a grievance and cannot affect the admissibility of the evidence put before the jury, and, if the appellant or his counsel thought that he was being prejudiced by having had no notice and really desired to call expert evidence to deal with the question of handwriting, he could have applied for an adjournment, but he did not do so.

Thus, the sanction requiring the prosecution to give timely notice of additional evidence is the knowledge that, in the absence of such notice, the trial may have to be adjourned until it has been served and the defence have had time to consider their response to it. Alternatively, if an adjournment is undesirable in the circumstances, the judge could exercise his discretion and exclude the evidence under the PACE 1984, s. 78, on the ground that to admit it would be unfair in view of the lack of notice.

SUPPLYING INCONSISTENT STATEMENTS TO THE DEFENCE

D15.27 As is clear from the discussion above, the prosecution is absolved from calling witnesses whose statements are inconsistent with the broad thrust of its case only if those statements have otherwise been made available to the defence. The prosecution's duty is now set out in the CPIA 1996 (see **D15.29**).

The prosecution duty of disclosure may cover (a) potential witnesses whom they do not intend to call, and (b) statements made by intended prosecution witnesses additional to their main statements included in the committal bundle.

Pre-Criminal Procedure and Investigations Act 1996

D15.28 Whether or not the CPIA 1996 provisions apply, the common law has long identified circumstances in which inconsistent statements should be disclosed. In *Clarke* (1930) 22 Cr App R 58, the issue was whether a police officer was correct in his identification of the accused as the person he had seen in the vicinity of burgled premises. The Court of Appeal were critical of prosecution counsel's refusal to disclose the description which the officer had given to a senior officer of the person he saw. If there had been any serious discrepancy between the description and the officer's testimony, the court 'would have had seriously to consider whether any miscarriage of justice had been caused by this attitude which was unfortunately assumed by the learned counsel for the prosecution'.

Clarke was confirmed in *Liverpool Juvenile Court, ex parte R* [1988] QB 1, where the prosecution failed to inform the defence that a police officer who testified that he had been the victim of a head-butt from the accused had told his sergeant that he 'did not know what had happened but there must have been a clash of heads'. The Divisional Court held that the failure amounted to a breach of the rules of natural justice and quashed the Crown Court's dismissal of the accused's appeal against his summary conviction for assault.

Post Criminal Procedure and Investigations Act 1996

Pursuant to the disclosure regime contained in the CPIA 1996, the prosecution must disclose material which is 'capable of undermining the case for the prosecution against the accused or of assisting the case for the accused' (s. 3(1)(a)). Beyond this, the prosecution have a continuing duty to keep disclosure under review (s. 9). If material becomes 'capable of undermining the case for the prosecution against the accused or of assisting the case for the accused', it must be disclosed 'as soon as reasonably practicable' (s. 9(2)). **D15.29**

Similar considerations apply to material which 'might be reasonably expected to assist the accused's defence as disclosed by the defence statement given under section 5' (s. 9(5)). For further details, see **D9**.

Use of a Witness Summons for a Disclosed Witness

The defence are *not* entitled to a witness summons under s. 2 of the Criminal Procedure (Attendance of Witnesses) Act 1965 ordering its subject to attend court and produce statements in his possession made by anticipated prosecution witnesses, with a view to the contents of the statements being used in cross-examination of the witnesses at the accused's trial (*Cheltenham Justices, ex parte Secretary of State for Trade* [1977] 1 WLR 95). See **D14.90** for the text of s. 2 of the 1965 Act. **D15.30**

EXAMINATION AND CROSS-EXAMINATION OF A WITNESS

Examination-in-Chief

A variety of issues arise in relation to the calling by the prosecution of a witness. The first stage is for the witness to take the oath or affirmation (which is dealt with at **F4.26** *et seq.*). Thereafter, circumstances which may arise, and which are dealt with elsewhere, include: **D15.31**

(a) the use of the special measures provisions contained in the YJCEA 1999, part II, chapter 1 (addressed at **D14.97** *et seq.*);
(b) the use of television live links where the witness is outside the UK, pursuant to the CJA 1988, s. 32 (see **D14.110**), or in the circumstances set out in the CJA 2003, s. 51 (see **D14.120**);
(c) the restriction on the use of leading questions (see **F6.8**);
(d) the rules in relation to memory refreshing, especially pursuant to the CJA 2003, s. 139 (see **F6.9**);
(e) the rules relating to the handling of hostile witnesses, as developed from the Criminal Procedure Act 1865, s. 3 (see **F6.31**).

Use of an Interpreter A decision whether an interpreter should be allowed to assist a **D15.32**

witness to give evidence is a matter for the court to decide. The court is not bound to accept the assertion of a witness that an interpreter is necessary. It can investigate the need itself, and having been told that a witness has some command of English, the court may take the opportunity to assess the limits of the comprehension and fluency of the witness before permitting the use of an interpreter (*Sharma* [2006] EWCA Crim 16).

Cross-examination

D15.33 Cross-examination of witnesses called by the prosecution on behalf of the accused gives rise to a number of issues. Limitations are imposed on the scope of proper cross-examination by a number of sources, which include the following.

(a) The limitations imposed by statute, e.g., the restrictions on cross-examination by an accused in person, contained in the YJCEA 1999, ss. 34 and 35 (discussed at F7.2 *et seq.*), and as to the sexual history of a complainant to whom s. 41 of that Act applies (see F7.17).
(b) It is the duty of the court to restrain lengthy cross-examination on matters not in issue, or which is otherwise unnecessarily prolonging the proceedings (*Kalia* (1974) 60 Cr App R 200).
(c) There are the limitations imposed by the Code of Conduct of the Bar, discussed below.

D15.34 **Limits of Proper Cross-examination** Counsel is required to consider not only whether a proposed question is legally allowable but whether it is ethically justified. He must, therefore, 'not make statements or ask questions which are merely scandalous or intended or calculated only to vilify, insult or annoy either a witness or some other person' (Written Standards, para. 5.10(e)). Moreover, it is for counsel to 'exercise personal judgment upon the substance and purpose of questions asked and statements made', since he is 'personally responsible for the conduct and presentation of his case' (para. 5.10(a)).

Counsel must not suggest that a witness or other person is guilty of crime, fraud or misconduct or attribute to another person the crime or conduct of which his lay client is accused unless such allegations go to a matter in issue (including the credibility of the witness) which is material to his lay client's case, and appear to him to be supported by reasonable grounds (para. 5.10(h)). A witness should never be impugned in a speech by counsel unless counsel has first given him an opportunity in cross-examination to answer the allegation (para. 5.10(g)).

A limitation on defence counsel's unfettered discretion to cross-examine about the issues and impugn the witness's character in the process was suggested by Lord Goddard CJ in *O'Neill* (1950) 34 Cr App R 108, when he criticised defence counsel for his cross-examination, saying that it was 'quite wrong and improper conduct on the part of counsel' to make charges against the police (or any other prosecution witnesses) if he did not intend to call evidence in support of those charges. A distinction had to be drawn between proper and temperate cross-examination as to credit (where one was bound by the witness's answer) and the kind of allegations made by counsel.

READING STATEMENTS AS EVIDENCE AT THE TRIAL ON INDICTMENT

D15.35 The subject-matter of this heading might equally well be regarded as one of the exceptions to the rule against hearsay evidence and therefore allocated to the evidence part of this work. However, it is considered here as it also has crucial implications for the procedural question of which witnesses should attend at trial.

Statements Tendered at Committal

The CPIA 1996, sch. 2, provides for the statements tendered at committal (see **D10.34**) by the prosecution to be read in evidence at the subsequent Crown Court trial. Identical provisions apply to a deposition taken under the MCA 1980, s. 97A, and tendered in evidence at committal. If the defence wishes to prevent the statement or deposition in question being read at trial, it must give written notification to the prosecutor and the Crown Court within 14 days of committal, stating that there is objection to the statement or deposition. **D15.36**

That does not, however, conclude the matter. The objection of the defence can be overruled by the trial judge. According to sch. 2, para. 1(4), 'the court of trial may order that the objection shall have no effect if the court considers it to be in the interests of justice so to order'. This power is potentially most important; if the trial judge overrules the objection, the accused will have no opportunity to cross-examine the witness in question.

In the Parliamentary debate on the subject, it was stated by the government that it was anticipated that the courts, in applying the 'interests of justice' test, would turn for guidance to the CJA 1988, s. 26 (see Baroness Blatch, *Hansard*, HL col. 951 (26 June 1996)). That section referred to the admissibility of certain hearsay statements under the CJA 1988, ss. 23 and 24 (now replaced by the CJA 2003, ss. 116 and 117). Although s. 26 itself has been repealed (see **F16.3**), the test under the CJA 2003 retains many of the features of the 1988 Act.

In considering whether the admission of such a statement under the 2003 Act would be in the interests of justice, the court must have regard to its contents, the risk of unfairness to the accused resulting from the inability to controvert the statement, and any other circumstances which may appear to be relevant. It would appear to have been the intention of Parliament, in the light of the statement of Baroness Blatch quoted above, that the courts should consider the same factors in deciding whether to overrule a defence objection by virtue of the power contained in sch. 2, para. 1(4) of the 1996 Act.

In any event, a trial judge will no doubt be extremely wary about overruling the objections of the defence, and thus denying the accused the right to see those who are giving evidence against him, let alone the right to cross-examine them. Any suspicion that objections were overruled for reasons which were less than compelling would be contrary to well-established principle and, in addition to the normal channels for challenge, would be likely to lead to the prospect of a challenge based upon the ECHR, Article 6(3)(d) (see **A7** and **D29.4**).

Written Statements in Criminal Proceedings other than Committals

The CJA 1967, s. 9, provides for the admissibility of written statements in criminal proceedings other than committal proceedings. Since it is used more frequently in summary trials than in trials on indictment, its terms are set out at **D21.24**. **D15.37**

It is also used in trials on indictment, however; chiefly where the prosecution wish to adduce evidence additional to that which they used at committal proceedings. The party proposing to tender the statement in evidence must serve a copy of it on each of the other parties. If one of those parties, during the period of seven days from the date of service of the copy on him, serves notice on the party wishing to use the statement that he objects to it going into evidence, the statement cannot be read at the trial.

In effect, s. 9 statements are admissible only if all the parties agree. Even if a statement is admissible under s. 9, the court may require that the maker attend to give evidence, e.g., where the defence dispute the contents of the statement but failed to object through an oversight.

Depositions of Children or Young Persons

D15.38 Where a justice has taken a deposition out of court from a juvenile under the provisions of the CYPA 1933, s. 42, the deposition (subject to certain conditions) is admissible in any proceedings in respect of any of the offences mentioned in sch. 1 to the Act (s. 43). Schedule 1 lists numerous specific sexual offences, and also refers to 'any other offence involving bodily injury to a child or young person' (see **F16.50**). The juvenile may but need not have been the victim of the offence.

The conditions of the admissibility of such a deposition are:

(a) that attendance at court would involve serious danger to the juvenile's life or health;
(b) that the deposition is signed by the justice by or before whom it purports to have been taken; and
(c) that, if the deposition is to be admitted against the accused, he was given reasonable notice of the intention to take it and he (or his legal representative) had the opportunity of cross-examining the deponent.

Evidence as to the effect of attending court on the juvenile's health must be provided by a duly qualified medical practitioner.

Address of Witness

D15.39 In its 'Statement of National Standards of Witness Care in the Criminal Justice System' (1996) 161 JP 353, the Criminal Justice Consultative Council's Trial Issues Group proposed that, unless it was necessary for evidential purposes, witnesses should not be required to disclose their addresses in open court. The statement was approved by Lord Bingham CJ in July 1996, but has not been published as a practice direction in any of the law reports. The usual practice followed in the courts is for counsel to ask for the address of the witness at the beginning of evidence-in-chief. If there is a matter of sensitivity, however, the witness does not need to disclose the address in open court, and can write it down for the record. Witnesses are informed by means of a 'Witness Pack' of their right to use this latter method if appropriate.

Formal Admissions

D15.40 As an alternative to the reading of witness statements, facts derived from such witness statements or otherwise may be presented as agreed evidence. These facts, which are admitted by all parties to be true, are presented pursuant to the CJA 1967, s. 10 (see **F1.2**). Where such admissions have been reduced to writing, they should be provided to the jury providing they are relevant to the issues that they are to determine and do not contain inadmissible material (*Pittard* [2006] EWCA Crim 2028).

OBJECTIONS TO PROSECUTION EVIDENCE

Standard Procedure

D15.41 Where the defence intend to object to the admissibility of prosecution evidence disclosed on the committal statements (hereafter referred to as 'disputed evidence'), the standard procedure is as follows.

(a) Defence counsel informs prosecution counsel of the objection before the latter opens his case to the jury. In his opening, prosecution counsel therefore makes no mention of the disputed evidence (as to circumstances where the admissibility issue ought to be resolved before the case starts, see **D15.43**).
(b) At the point at which the admissibility falls to be considered, the jury will withdraw to allow the matter to be resolved by the judge alone (see **D15.42**).

(c) If the admissibility of the disputed evidence raises collateral factual issues as to how it was obtained, it may be necessary to adduce evidence about those facts before the judge in the absence of the jury. This is known as a trial 'on the *voir dire*' because the witnesses testify on a special form of oath (see F4.27). Both prosecution and defence are entitled to call witnesses at this stage. However, their evidence (whether in chief or in cross-examination) should be limited to matters relevant to the admissibility of the disputed evidence. For the application of this rule to the admissibility of confessions, see the PACE 1984, s. 76(2) and *Brophy* [1982] AC 476 (see F17.5 and F17.39).
(d) Whether or not there has been evidence on the *voir dire*, the parties make their representations to the judge about the admissibility of the disputed evidence.
(e) The judge then announces his findings on any factual issues arising on the *voir dire* and rules on whether the disputed evidence should be admitted or not, in the light of the findings of fact, the relevant law on admissibility of evidence and any discretionary power to exclude material which is legally admissible (considerations applicable to this determination are set out at D15.47).
(f) The jury return to court. If the judge ruled against the disputed evidence, the jury will know nothing about it (as to the editing of evidence consequent on such a ruling, see D15.50). If it is ruled admissible, the defence are still entitled to cross-examine on matters they raised on the *voir dire*, although at this stage the cross-examination goes to the weight, if any, that the jury should attach to the disputed evidence, not to its admissibility.

This procedure, and the extent to which it is appropriate to depart from it in certain circumstances, is discussed below.

Presence of Jury in Court during Determination of Question of Admissibility

In *Hendry* (1988) 88 Cr App R 187, where the jury had retired for the *voir dire* contrary to the wishes of the defence, the Court of Appeal refused to follow earlier decisions in *Anderson* (1929) 21 Cr App R 178 and *Ajodha v The State* [1982] AC 204. It was held that the judge had the ultimate discretion as to whether or not the jury retired, as their presence could defeat one of the fundamental objectives of the *voir dire* procedure, namely, to prevent the jury knowing of potentially inadmissible evidence. D15.42

In *Mitchell* [1998] AC 695, the Privy Council stressed that the judge should give no explanation of the outcome of the *voir dire* to the jury, as to do so would risk unfair prejudice to the accused.

Determination of Question of Admissibility as a Preliminary Issue

Where the evidence to which the defence indicate an objection is vital to the prosecution case, so that the prosecution case cannot sensibly be opened without reference to it, the question of admissibility may be determined as a preliminary issue. D15.43

In *Hammond* [1941] 3 All ER 318, the Court of Criminal Appeal, while stating that the appropriate time for determining admissibility of evidence is normally immediately prior to the evidence being called, also indicated that that practice should not be regarded as invariable. Humphreys J (giving the principal judgment) said (at p. 320 emphasis added):

> The ordinary practice in such a case, if there is any objection on the part of the counsel for the defence to the admissibility of a piece of evidence, is that he should inform the prosecution of that fact beforehand, and that that piece of evidence should not be opened to the jury. This court desires to reiterate that what was said by this court in *Cole* (1941) 28 Cr App R 43 is a good practice which should be adhered to, certainly in most cases. *The court cannot lay down as a rule of practice that in no case should the judge decide to hear in advance arguments as to the admissibility of evidence.* There may be cases in which it is convenient, and in which it cannot possibly result in any harm in its being done.

It is unclear whether, if the exceptional course of determining admissibility of evidence as a preliminary issue is adopted, a jury has to be sworn in and then immediately sent out, or whether their empanelment can be delayed until after the preliminary point has been decided. Although for some purposes a trial begins with the arraignment of the accused (see, e.g., the Supreme Court Act 1981, s. 77, which deals with time-limits for commencement of trial), it is arguable that, in general, there is no trial in being until a jury has been sworn and therefore no question connected with the trial (such as whether evidence is admissible) can validly be determined. In deference to this argument, it seems to be the practice to empanel a jury *before* considering objections to evidence (or any other question of law).

Circumstances in which *Voir Dire* Hearing is Necessary

D15.44 Most authorities on the procedure for objecting to evidence concern disputed confessions and the holding of a trial on the *voir dire* to determine their admissibility. However, the procedure is not limited to such circumstances. For example, in *Minors* [1989] 1 WLR 441, Steyn J stated that the trial within a trial procedure ought to be adopted where there is a disputed issue as to the admissibility of a computer printout (for further instances, see **F1.25**).

However, the Court of Appeal in *Flemming* (1987) 86 Cr App R 32, warned against resorting to the procedure unnecessarily. F appealed against his conviction for robbery on the grounds that (a) the identification evidence against him was unsatisfactory and should have been excluded, and (b) the judge was wrong to conclude that he had signed notes of his interview with the police on those pages which contained admissions. The Court of Appeal upheld the rulings of the trial judge but stated that he should have made them without himself hearing evidence on the *voir dire*. The issue of whether the accused had signed the relevant pages of the interview notes was one solely for the jury, the question being whether a confession had been made at all, not whether (assuming it had been made) it had been improperly obtained. As to the identification evidence, the judge could consider the exercise of his discretion to exclude it by reading the depositions and inviting argument from counsel. There was no need to call the witnesses before the judge.

Objecting to Evidence Without a *Voir Dire*

D15.45 The *voir dire* procedure is designed to assist the defence by preventing the jury hearing possibly inadmissible evidence unless and until the judge rules it admissible. It therefore seems logical that the defence should not be forced to adopt the procedure if they consider that the accused's interests will be better served by having the possibly inadmissible evidence and any evidence of how it was obtained adduced before both judge and jury as part of the general case.

The tactical reason sometimes advanced for not wanting a hearing on the *voir dire* is that, if the judge in fact rules the disputed evidence admissible, the prosecution witnesses may have to be asked the same questions before the jury as they were asked before the judge, albeit that the cross-examination before the jury goes to the weight of the evidence, not its admissibility. Having had a 'dry run' before the judge, the witnesses are likely to give a better account of themselves before the jury than they would have done had the questions come as a surprise.

In *Ajodha v The State* [1982] AC 204, the Privy Council affirmed the defence's right to have evidence ruled inadmissible even though they do not seek to exclude it by means of the standard *voir dire* procedure. See **F17.24** to **F17.26** for details.

There are a number of qualifications of this general principle:

(a) If the defence elect not to have a *voir dire*, they are usually entitled to a ruling from the judge on the admissibility of the confession at the close of all the evidence, rather than at the end of the prosecution case (*Jackson* [1985] Crim LR 442). The judge should exclude a confession of his own motion only in a totally exceptional case where the prosecution's own evidence makes it quite clear that the confession was improperly obtained. Otherwise, the judge should not rule or be asked to rule on the confession's admissibility until the close of *all* the evidence, both prosecution and defence. This considerably reduces the attractiveness to the defence of forgoing the normal procedure, since their decision on whether or not to call evidence will have to be taken at a time when they still do not know whether the jury will ultimately be directed to ignore the accused's confession.

(b) In *Cunningham* [1985] Crim LR 374, the Court of Appeal took a liberal attitude to the prosecution being allowed to reopen their case when the defence evidence has raised matters relevant to the admissibility of a confession where there had not been a hearing on the *voir dire*. It that case, it was put to the police officers who had taken a confession statement from C that it was the result of earlier inducements by officers whom the prosecution chose not to call. After C gave evidence repeating what had been put in cross-examination, the trial judge allowed the prosecution to reopen their case so as to call the officers named by C. The Court of Appeal held that it would have been an affront to the course of justice to have done otherwise.

Effect of the Police and Criminal Evidence Act 1984 The above discussion has proceeded on the assumption that the enactment of ss. 76 and 78 of the PACE 1984 (admissibility of confessions and unfairly obtained evidence) has not affected the procedure for excluding confessions. However, Lord Lane CJ stated in *Sat-Bhambra* (1988) 88 Cr App 55 at p. 62, that the wording of those two sections shows that, if it is sought to exclude evidence in reliance on them, the objection must always be made *before* the disputed evidence is adduced. **D15.46**

Lord Lane also drew attention to the PACE 1984, s. 82(3), under which the trial judge's general common-law powers to exclude evidence are preserved. Thus, if the defence do not ask for a *voir dire* but nonetheless evidence is adduced in the course of either the prosecution or defence cases which suggests that a confession was obtained in a manner prohibited by s. 76 or otherwise unfairly, the judge can be invited to exercise his residual common-law powers and either direct the jury to ignore the confession or discharge them from giving a verdict.

Guidance on *Voir Dire* Procedure where Objection to Evidence Taken under Police and Criminal Evidence Act 1984, s. 78

Guidance has been given in *Keenan* [1990] 2 QB 54, on the appropriate procedure for asking the judge to rule under the PACE 1984, s. 78, that evidence obtained in breach of the PACE codes of practice should be excluded because its reception would have such an adverse effect on the fairness of the proceedings that it ought not to be admitted. **D15.47**

The Court of Appeal distinguished between three categories of case:

(a) Cases where a breach of the code is apparent from the custody record or statements of the prosecution witnesses, e.g., where (as in *Keenan* itself) there has been a breach of ss. 11 and 12 of PACE Code C relating to the contemporaneous noting of interviews with a suspect and/or showing him the officer's note. In this situation, it ought only to be necessary for prosecution counsel to make an admission as to the breach, after which there may be legal argument about the consequences for admissibility.

(b) Cases where there may be a prima facie breach which the prosecution seeks to justify, e.g., if access to a solicitor has been refused but the prosecution seek to justify that refusal on grounds such as the risk of interference with evidence if access had been allowed. In such cases, it will clearly be necessary for the prosecution to call evidence on the *voir dire* to explain away the prima facie breach, after which the accused may choose to testify in rebuttal.

D

Part D Procedure

(c) Alleged breaches which can be established only by evidence from the accused himself, e.g., cases of alleged oppression or where the accused claims that he was a person at risk not given the extra protection provided for in PACE Code C. Here, the accused will have to take the initiative by himself giving evidence on the *voir dire* to establish the breach.

Hodgson J (who gave the Court of Appeal's judgment in *Keenan*) thought that cases under (c) would be rare, and that in situations (a) and (b) it would be unlikely that the accused would want to testify in rebuttal. His lordship also said that the trial judge was obliged to give his ruling on whether admission of the evidence would be unfair in ignorance of what the defence's response to the evidence would be if it were admitted. That might seem unsatisfactory, but was simply a consequence of the overall structure of a criminal trial. The judgment helpfully summarises many of the earlier cases dealing with similar issues.

Reviewing a Determination as to Admissibility

D15.48 Prior to the enactment of the PACE 1984, the court was entitled to reconsider a ruling as to the admissibility of evidence where fresh evidence later emerged before the jury which cast doubt on its correctness. This was held in *Watson* [1980] 1 WLR 991, in which Cumming-Bruce LJ adopted the following passage from *Cross on Evidence* (5th edn, Butterworth, 1979) p. 72, as correctly stating the law:

> The judge retains his control over the evidence ultimately to be submitted to the jury throughout the trial. Accordingly, if, having admitted a confession as voluntary on evidence given in the absence of the jury, the judge concludes, in the light of subsequent evidence, that the confession was not voluntary, he may either direct the jury to disregard it, or, where there is no other sufficient evidence against the accused, direct an acquittal or, presumably, direct a new trial.

However, his lordship went on to say that 'the occasions on which a judge should allow counsel to invite him to reconsider a ruling already made are likely to be extremely rare' (p. 995D).

D15.49 **The Effect of the Police and Criminal Evidence Act 1984** The general principle stated in *Watson* (i.e. that a trial judge may in exceptional circumstances be invited to reconsider his decision to admit disputed evidence) was no doubt intended to apply to any disputed evidence, whatever its nature, and not just to possibly inadmissible confessions. However, the position in respect of confession evidence has again been complicated by the wording of the PACE 1984, ss. 76 and 78.

In *Sat-Bhambra* (1988) 88 Cr App R 55, the Court of Appeal held that s. 76 (mandatory exclusion of a confession on grounds of oppression or unreliability) applies only *before* the confession has gone into evidence. There was consequently no statutory obligation on the judge to reconsider his earlier ruling. However, under s. 82(3) of the 1984 Act (preservation of discretionary powers to exclude evidence), the judge could still take whatever steps were necessary to prevent injustice, whether by directing the jury to disregard the evidence they had heard, commenting on its weight in the light of changed evidence, or even discharging them. But he was not, as the appellant contended, *obliged* to discharge them.

The relevant paragraphs from the Court of Appeal's judgment ((1988) 88 Cr App R 55 at p. 62) are set out below:

> In *Watson* [1980] 1 WLR 991, decided before the 1984 Act, it was held that a judge who has second thoughts about the voluntariness of a statement which he has earlier ruled admissible upon the *voir dire* may, where it is appropriate so to do, change his opinion as to its admissibility, and may take such steps as are necessary to put matters right, by, for example, directing the jury to disregard it or discharging the jury.

> The words of section 76 are crucial: 'proposes to give in evidence' and 'shall not allow the confession to be given' are not . . . appropriate to describe something which has happened in the past. They are directed solely to the situation before the statement goes before the jury. Once the judge has ruled that it should do so, section 76 (and section 78, for the same reasons) ceases to have effect. The judge, whatever his change of mind may be, is no longer acting under section 76 as the appellant contends. To that extent the decision in *Watson* does not survive the wording of the 1984 Act.
>
> That does not mean that the judge is powerless to act. He has the power, if only under section 82(3), to take such steps as are necessary, depending on the circumstances, to prevent injustice. He may, if he thinks that the matter is not capable of remedy by a direction, discharge the jury; he may direct the jury to disregard the statement; he may by way of direction point out to the jury matters which affect the weight of the confession and leave the matter in their hands. He is not, as is the submission here, obliged to discharge the jury and to order a new trial.
>
> If a defendant wishes under section 76 to exclude a confession, the time to make his submission to that effect is before the confession is put in evidence and not afterwards.

Editing of Prosecution Evidence

Where the prosecution evidence as foreshadowed in the committal statements contains material which is of such prejudicial effect that the jury clearly ought not to hear it, the practice is for the parties to 'edit' the evidence by agreement before it is called. This practice was recognised by the Court of Appeal in *Weaver* [1968] 1 QB 353. Sachs LJ indicated (at pp. 357G–358A) that the best way for such editing to take place is for the evidence to appear 'unvarnished' in the committal statements. Counsel can then confer at trial to ensure that 'the editing is done in the right way and to the right degree'. If necessary the judge can also play a part in the process. **D15.50**

The *Consolidated Criminal Practice Direction*, para. III.24 (see **appendix** 7), contains detailed instructions on the treatment of committal statements where some of the material contained therein may be inadmissible or unduly prejudicial. It deals partly with the preparation of composite statements to replace several earlier statements made by a witness. It also deals with when it is preferable to prepare a completely fresh statement for a witness to sign, omitting those parts of the first statement which are inadmissible or prejudicial.

Where, however, the prosecution decide that it is unnecessary to have a new statement, the procedure to be adopted is that the *original* of the witness's statement should be tendered to the court unmarked in any way but, on the *copies* served on the defence and provided to the court, the passages on which the prosecution do not propose to rely should either be bracketed or lightly struck out. The striking out should not be done in such a way as to obscure what is being deleted.

Paragraph III.24.3 states that the following note should be attached to the committal bundle: 'The prosecution does not propose to adduce evidence of those passages of the attached copy statements which have been struck out and/or bracketed. (nor will it seek to do so at the trial unless a notice of further evidence is served)'.

As regards (a) documentary exhibits (including statements under caution or interview notes signed by the accused) and (b) police officers' statements referring to oral answers by the accused, the above procedure should *not* be adopted but editing should be left entirely to prosecuting counsel at the Crown Court after discussion with defence counsel and, if appropriate, the trial judge (para. III.24.6).

A difficulty may arise where the jury ask to see the original of an edited document. They may be told that there are technical reasons why this cannot be permitted. Although this is not altogether satisfactory, it may be the only way of dealing with an inherent problem.

SUBMISSION OF NO CASE TO ANSWER

D15.51 After the prosecution have closed their case, the defence may submit that the evidence does not disclose a case to answer in respect of any or all the counts on the indictment. If the submission succeeds on all counts, the judge directs the jury to acquit the accused. If the submission succeeds on only some of the counts, no verdict is taken forthwith on those counts but normal practice is to tell the jury that they will ultimately be directed to acquit the accused of them and they should therefore, for the remainder of the trial, concern themselves only with the counts on which there is a case. If the submission fails on all counts, the jury know nothing about the submission since they are sent out of court while it is made and no mention is made of what occurred in their absence.

The Timing of a Submission in Relation to the Death of a Child

D15.52 A different procedure is to be followed where the accused is charged in the same proceedings with an offence of murder or manslaughter and with an offence under the DVCVA 2004, s. 5 (causing or allowing the death of a child or a vulnerable adult: see **B1.45**), in respect of the same death. The question whether there is a case for him to answer on the charge of murder or manslaughter must not then be considered before the close of all the evidence. If the accused ceases to be charged with the offence under s. 5, then whether there is a case to answer on the murder or manslaughter charge is to be considered before he ceases to be so charged (s. 6). The relevant provisions of the DVCVA 2004 came into force on 21 March 2005.

The Test to Be Applied

D15.53 The leading authority on the test a trial judge should apply in determining whether there is a case to answer is *Galbraith* [1981] 1 WLR 1039. In the course of his judgment in that case, Lord Lane CJ said (at p. 1042B–D):

> How then should the judge approach a submission of 'no case'? (1) If there is no evidence that the crime alleged has been committed by the defendant, there is no difficulty. The judge will of course stop the case. (2) The difficulty arises where there is some evidence but it is of a tenuous character, for example because of inherent weakness or vagueness or because it is inconsistent with other evidence. (a) Where the judge comes to the conclusion that the prosecution evidence, taken at its highest, is such that a jury properly directed could not properly convict upon it, it is his duty, upon a submission being made, to stop the case. (b) Where however the prosecution evidence is such that its strength or weakness depends on the view to be taken of a witness's reliability, or other matters which are generally speaking within the province of the jury and where on one possible view of the facts there *is* evidence upon which a jury could properly come to the conclusion that the defendant is guilty, then the judge should allow the matter to be tried by the jury. . .
>
> There will of course, as always in this branch of the law, be borderline cases. They can safely be left to the discretion of the judge.

D15.54 **The First Limb** As Lord Lane remarked, the first limb of the test set out in *Galbraith* [1981] 1 WLR 1039, does not cause any conceptual problems. The test of there being 'no evidence that the crime alleged has been committed by the defendant' is intended to convey the same meaning as the words of Lord Parker CJ in his *Practice Direction (Submission of No Case)* [1962] 1 WLR 227, when he told magistrates that submissions of no case to answer at summary trial should be upheld, *inter alia*, if 'there has been no evidence to prove an essential element in the alleged offence'.

Such cases may arise, for example, where an essential prosecution witness has failed to come up to proof, or where there is no direct evidence as to an element of the offence and the inferences which the prosecution ask the court to draw from the circumstantial evidence are inferences which, in the judge's view, no reasonable jury could properly draw (see further D21.39).

The Second Limb The second limb of Lord Lane's test in *Galbraith* [1981] 1 WLR 1039, is far less straightforward, and has to be understood in the context of a practice that developed after the passing of the Criminal Appeal Act 1966, s. 4(1)(a) (now Criminal Appeal Act 1968, s. 2(1)), of inviting the judge to hold that there was no case to answer because a conviction on the prosecution evidence would be 'unsafe'. That form of submission reflected the power given to the Court of Appeal by first the 1966 and then the 1968 Act to quash a conviction on the basis that it was, in the court's opinion, 'unsafe or unsatisfactory' (but, since the Criminal Appeal Act 1995, part I, came into force, simply 'unsafe'). **D15.55**

The argument at trial went as follows: since the Court of Appeal can ultimately quash a verdict of guilty if it appears to them unsafe, the jury ought to be prevented from returning such a verdict in the first place. This approach inevitably involved the court considering the *quality* and *reliability* of the evidence, rather than its legal sufficiency, and therefore involved the court carrying out the assessment of evidence and witnesses that would otherwise be the exclusive prerogative of the jury. Lord Lane's judgment makes clear that it is no longer appropriate to argue on a submission of no case that it would be unsafe for the jury to convict, if only because that tempts the judge to impose his own views of the witnesses' veracity (see especially p. 1041B–C).

However, the second limb of the *Galbraith* test does leaves a residual role for the court as assessor of the reliability of the evidence. The court is empowered by the second limb of the *Galbraith* test to consider whether the prosecution's evidence is too inherently weak or vague for any sensible person to rely on it. Thus, if the witness undermines his own testimony by conceding that he is uncertain about vital points, or if what he says is manifestly contrary to reason, the court is entitled to hold that no reasonable jury properly directed could rely on the witness's evidence and therefore (in the absence of any other evidence), there is no case to answer.

Interpretation of the Second Limb in *Shippey* The correct interpretation of the test in *Galbraith* [1981] 1 WLR 1039, was considered by Turner J when ruling on a submission at the trial of *Shippey* [1988] Crim LR 767 for rape. The prosecution relied upon the virtually uncorroborated evidence of the complainant, and the defence conceded that there was some evidence which supported on 'a minimum basis' the allegation that the accused had committed the offence. However, the judge agreed with the defence that parts of the complainant's evidence were totally at variance with other parts supportive of the prosecution case. His lordship found part of her evidence to be 'strikingly and wholly inconsistent with the allegation of rape'. Her evidence as a whole contained 'really significant inherent inconsistencies' and it was 'frankly incredible'. **D15.56**

On a literal view of *Galbraith* and *Barker* (1975) 65 Cr App R 287, the case should therefore have gone to the jury for them to weigh the inconsistencies and implausibilities and decide if she was telling the truth. Turner J took a more robust view. He said that 'taking the prosecution case at its highest' did not mean 'taking out the plums and leaving the duff behind'. It was for the judge to assess the evidence and, if it was 'self-contradictory and out of reason and all common sense', then he could properly conclude that it was 'inherently weak and tenuous' within the meaning of the second limb of Lord Lane's test. Moreover, in forming his judgment, he could take into account both internal inconsistencies in a witness's testimony and inconsistencies between one prosecution witness and another.

The Proper Approach to a Submission of No Case to Answer The following propositions are advanced as representing the position that has now been reached on determining submissions of no case to answer: **D15.57**

(a) If there is no evidence to prove an essential element of the offence, a submission must obviously succeed.
(b) If there is some evidence which, taken at face value, establishes each essential element, the case should normally be left to the jury.
(c) If, however, the evidence is so weak that no reasonable jury properly directed could convict on it, a submission should be upheld. Weakness may arise from the sheer improbability of what the witness is saying, from internal inconsistencies in the evidence or from its being of a type which the accumulated experience of the courts has shown to be of doubtful value (especially in identification evidence cases, which are considered in D15.58).
(d) The question of whether a witness is lying is nearly always one for the jury, but there may be exceptional cases (such as *Shippey* [1988] Crim LR 767) where the inconsistencies are so great that any reasonable tribunal would be forced to the conclusion that the witness is untruthful, and that it would not be proper for the case to proceed on that evidence alone.

Having identified those general principles, it is appropriate to consider various particular types of evidence and categories of cases.

Identification Cases

D15.58 The correct approach to submissions of no case to answer in prosecutions turning upon identification evidence was laid down by the Court of Appeal in *Turnbull* [1977] QB 224 (see F18.2 and F18.26).

As one of several safeguards against erroneous convictions based on witnesses mistakenly identifying the accused, the Court of Appeal stated that, if the quality of the identification evidence on which the prosecution case depends is poor and there is no other evidence to support it, the judge should direct the jury to acquit (pp. 229H–230A). However, supporting evidence capable of justifying leaving a case to the jury, even where the identifying evidence is poor, need not be corroboration in the strict sense (p. 230B–D).

Although *Turnbull* predates *Galbraith* [1981] 1 WLR 1039, there is no suggestion that the principles in it have been affected by the later decision. In fact, the obligation on the trial judge to uphold a submission if the identifying evidence is poor and there is no supporting evidence may be regarded as the clearest example of the application of the second limb of the *Galbraith* test (see *Daley v The Queen* [1994] 1 AC 117).

Confession Cases

D15.59 In *MacKenzie* (1992) 96 Cr App R 98, the Court of Appeal laid down special guidance for trial judges considering a submission of no case to answer in confession cases. Their lordships pointed out that cases depending solely or mainly on confessions, like cases depending upon identification evidence, had given rise to miscarriages of justice. Where certain conditions applied, therefore, the judge should, in the interests of justice, take the initiative and withdraw the case from the jury. The conditions requiring such action by the judge were:

(a) the prosecution case depended wholly upon confessions;
(b) the accused suffered from a significant degree of mental handicap; and
(c) the confessions were unconvincing to a point where a jury properly directed could not properly convict upon them.

Confessions might be unconvincing, e.g., because they lacked the incriminating details to be expected of a guilty and willing confessor, because they were inconsistent with other evidence, or because they were otherwise inherently improbable. See also *Wood* [1994] Crim LR 222.

Mutually Destructive Counts

Where two counts in an indictment are mutually destructive (e.g., alternative counts for theft and handling of the same goods), it may be possible for the defence to submit that, even though the prosecution evidence prima facie shows that the accused must have committed one or other of the offences, no reasonable jury properly directed could be sure which of the two he is guilty of and therefore they must be directed to acquit of both. **D15.60**

The problem arose in *Bellman* [1989] AC 836, a case chiefly important for the House of Lords' decision that mutually destructive counts may be joined in one indictment (see **D11.60**). In the course of reaching that conclusion, the House also considered whether in such cases the judge ought to have upheld a submission of no case in respect of all counts. Lord Griffiths said (at pp. 847G–848G):

> There are, of course, rare situations in which it is clear that the accused has committed a crime but the state of the evidence is such that it is impossible to say which crime he has committed. In such circumstances no prima facie case can be established to support either crime and neither crime can be left to the jury. The classic example arises where a man has given contradictory evidence on oath on two occasions. It is obvious that one statement must be false but in the absence of any evidence to indicate which statement was false it cannot be proved on which occasion the perjury was committed: see *Harris* (1822) 5 B & Ald 926. . . .
>
> An accused is always entitled to have the counts in the indictment considered separately by the judge at the end of the prosecution's evidence and if there is insufficient evidence to provide a prima facie case on any count to have that count withdrawn from the jury.

The situation in *Bellman* was different from that in the perjury example cited by Lord Griffiths. There being prima facie case sufficient in relation to both alternatives, it was a matter for the jury to decide at the end of all the evidence which of the two possible hypotheses based upon the prosecution evidence was the correct one. See also *Tsang Ping-nam v The Queen* [1981] 1 WLR 1462.

Prima Facie Case against Two Accused

Analogous problems to those discussed in **D15.60** arise where there are co-accused and the evidence establishes that one or other committed the offence charged but it is impossible to say which. **D15.61**

In such cases, and assuming there is no evidence of joint enterprise, both are clearly entitled to be acquitted on a submission of no case. Lord Griffiths stated the principle succinctly in his judgment in *Bellman* [1989] AC 836 (at p. 849A): 'It, of course, goes without saying that if the evidence shows that one of two accused must have committed a crime but it is impossible to go further and say which of them committed it, both must be acquitted: see *Lane* (1985) 82 Cr App R 5'. The same point had earlier been made by Lord Goddard CJ in *Abbott* [1955] 2 QB 497 at p. 503.

Whether the evidence really does leave the question of which accused committed the offence in total doubt or whether there is evidence just capable of pointing to one or the other as the person responsible will depend on close analysis of the evidence in the particular case (compare *Gibson* (1984) 80 Cr App R 24, *Lane* (1986) 82 Cr App R 5, *Aston* [1991] Crim LR 701 and *S* [1996] Crim LR 346, all of which involved injuries to young children where it was difficult to determine which of the two parents was responsible).

The position in this regard has been significantly altered by the DVCVA 2004, which delays consideration of a submission of no case to answer in cases where one of two parents may have been responsible for the death of their child until the conclusion of all the evidence (see **D15.52**).

Cases based upon Inferences Drawn from Circumstantial Evidence

D15.62 There has been a degree of debate as to the proper approach to a submission of no case where the prosecution contends that guilt is proved, in whole or in part, by the drawing of certain inferences from circumstantial evidence. In the past, the decision of the Divisional Court in *R (Inland Revenue Commissioners) v Crown Court at Kingston* [2001] EWHC Admin 581, was relied on as support for the contention that a case to answer would only be made out where the prosecution could exclude any alternative inference being drawn from that circumstantial evidence. It is now clear that this is not the case.

Following the test in *Galbraith* [1981] 1 WLR 1039, that, 'where on one possible view of the facts there is evidence upon which a jury could properly come to the conclusion that the defendant is guilty, then the judge should allow the matter to be tried by the jury', the prosecution are not required to show that the jury could not reasonably reach any alternative inference contended for. The question is whether it is properly open to the jury to reach the inferences contended for by the prosecution.

This was the conclusion of Tuckey LJ, giving the judgment of the Court of Appeal in *Bokkum* (7 March 2000 unreported), at [32]:

> Read literally the passage in *Moore* [a reference to the decision of the Court of Appeal in *Moore* (20 August 1992 unreported)] would mean that in any case dependent on circumstantial evidence the judge would be required to withdraw the case from the jury if some inference other than guilt could reasonably be drawn from the facts proved. We do not think that the Court intended to say this and if it did it is contrary to what was said in *Galbraith*. The approach suggested may be appropriate in a case such as *Moore* where the inference of guilt is sought to be drawn from a single fact, but this is much more difficult in a case such as the instant case where the Crown rely on a combination of facts. The judge will, of course, withdraw the case if he considers that it would be unsafe for the jury to conclude that the defendant is guilty on the totality of the circumstantial evidence adduced, but if he concludes that it is open to them to convict then Galbraith requires the judge to leave the decision to them.

This statement of principle was specifically approved by the Court of Appeal in *Edwards* [2004] EWCA Crim 2102 at [84], and the same approach has been adopted more recently in *Jabber* [2006] EWCA Crim 2694 at [21].

Silence in Interview

D15.63 The CJPO 1994, s. 34(2)(c), permits the court, in considering whether the accused has a case to answer, to take into account the fact that he failed to answer questions in interview. However s. 38(3) makes clear that a submission of no case cannot be rejected solely on the basis of such silence (see **F19.6**).

Moreover, as was demonstrated in *Broadhead* [2006] EWCA Crim 1705, care has to be taken to be sure that the accused is relying on facts he failed to mention in interview rather than simply putting the prosecution to proof before inferences can be relied upon at the close of the prosecution case, and therefore before he has given evidence.

Procedure on a Submission of No Case

D15.64 **Jury to be Kept in Ignorance of the Submission** Submissions of no case should be made in the absence of the jury, and should not be referred to in their presence thereafter if they are unsuccessful. This was made clear by the Court of Appeal in *Smith* (1986) 85 Cr App R 197. In that case, the prosecution relied upon identification evidence and a submission of no case to answer based on the sufficiency of that evidence had been made and rejected. In summing up the case, the judge told the jury that, if he had not thought there was sufficient evidence of identification, he would have withdrawn the case from them. Watkins LJ said (at p. 200 emphasis added):

> That is an improper observation for a judge to make to a jury. Submissions [of no case to answer] are made in the absence of the jury. There is very good reason for that as all who take part in trials know. The question as to whether or not there is a sufficiency of evidence is one which is exclusively for the judge following submissions made to him *in the absence of the jury*. His decision *should not be revealed* to the jury lest it wrongly influences them. There is a risk that they might convict because they think the judge's view is a sufficient indication that the evidence is strong enough for that purpose.

In *Crosdale v The Queen* [1995] 1 WLR 864, it was emphasised that a trial judge should ask a jury to withdraw during a submission of no case to answer since it was a matter for him alone whether there was sufficient evidence to go before the jury.

Timing of a Submission Almost invariably, the proper time for making a submission of no case is after the prosecution have called their evidence (*Leadbeater* [1988] Crim LR 463). The only exceptions to this rule are cases where either (a) there is an objection to the jurisdiction of the court (see, e.g., *DPP v Doot* [1973] AC 807, in which the question was whether an offence of conspiracy had been committed inside or outside the jurisdiction), or (b) where there is an agreed statement of facts and the judge is effectively being asked whether what undoubtedly happened amounts to the offence charged. **D15.65**

Procedure following a Successful Submission As already indicated, the procedure upon the judge upholding a submission on all counts of the indictment is for the jury to return to court, whereupon what has occurred is briefly explained to them. One of their number is then asked to stand as foreman and he, on the judge's direction, formally returns a verdict of not guilty. **D15.66**

If the submission has succeeded on some counts but failed on others, the defendant should be regarded during the rest of the trial as no longer being charged on the former (*Plain* [1967] 1 WLR 565). However, in those circumstances no verdict is taken until the end of the trial when the jury both announce their decision on the counts for which there was a case and, on the judge's direction, find the accused not guilty on the remainder of the indictment.

It was made clear in *Carson* (1990) 92 Cr App R 236, and restated in *Livesey* (2007) 1 Cr App R 462, that the court can direct a verdict of not guilty on the only charge indicted but permit the trial to continue in relation to any statutory alternative summary offence.

Initiative for a Submission It is defence counsel's responsibility to make a submission of no case to answer should the circumstances warrant it (*Juett* [1981] Crim LR 113). In general, if experienced counsel fails so to submit in a case where the prosecution evidence is arguably insufficient, it is presumed that he has his own reasons for staying silent, and the trial judge is neither required nor even entitled to intervene. Exceptionally, however, the interests of justice may demand that the judge take the initiative and suggest that there may not be a case to answer. In such exceptional cases and assuming there was not in fact enough evidence to go to the jury at the end of the prosecution case, the Court of Appeal will quash the conviction, notwithstanding that defence counsel did not make a submission (see *Juett*). **D15.67**

Stopping the Case before the End of the Trial

Jury may Acquit at Any Time At common law a jury are entitled to decide at any stage after the prosecution have closed their case that they do not need to hear any further evidence or argument but wish to acquit forthwith. They may not, of course, convict without the trial running its full course. The judge may 'remind' them that this course is open to them. However, he should not go further and issue an invitation to them to acquit (*Kemp* [1995] 1 Cr App R 151, approving the observations of Roskill LJ in *Falconer-Atlee* (1973) 58 Cr App R 348 at p. 357). The judge must make it absolutely clear to the jury that, although they may acquit at this stage, they may not convict. **D15.68**

In *Speechley* [2004] EWCA Crim 3067, counsel for the defence had, when opening the defence at trial, sought to remind the jury of their right to acquit. The judge ruled that he could not do so. The Court of Appeal held that the common-law right of the jury to acquit after the conclusion of the prosecution case was exercisable only where they had been invited to do so by the trial judge. It was the judge's duty to decide when the jury was to be permitted to reach a decision. If a jury was invited by counsel, or sought of its own motion, to return a verdict before the judge asked them to do so, he should direct the jury that it was his duty to ensure that justice was done and that it was not open to them to return a verdict until he had invited them to do so.

D15.69 **Submission at the Close of the Evidence** In *Boakye* (12 March 1992 unreported), Steyn LJ pointed out that, as a matter of principle, the judge was entitled to hold that there was no case to answer even at the end of the defence case:

> [Counsel for the Crown] has made a submission to us that it was not appropriate to make a submission of no case to answer at the end of the defence case. In our judgment a judge is entitled, even at that late stage, if no evidence is available on a count or if there is no evidence of that count upon which a reasonable jury could convict, to rule that there is no case to go before the jury. The contrary proposition would be a startling one. It would contemplate that the judge might be powerless to prevent a real miscarriage of justice in a case where there was a sudden change in the strength of the prosecution case as a result of cogent evidence emerging in the defence case. We rule without any doubt that it was within the power of the judge to make the ruling that was requested of him.

In *Anderson* (1998) *The Independent*, 13 July 1998, the Court of Appeal, similarly, stated that, although it was more usual for defence counsel to make a submission of no case to answer at the close of the prosecution case, a trial judge is not precluded from entertaining and ruling on such a submission at the close of the defence case.

The reasoning of the Court of Appeal in *Brown* [1998] Crim LR 196, reinforces this approach. Their lordships stated that throughout the trial the judge has a duty not to allow a jury to consider evidence on which they could not safely convict. He should not invite them to acquit since, if they convicted, the accused would be left with a sense of grievance. But if, at the conclusion of the evidence, the trial judge is of the opinion that no reasonable jury properly directed could safely convict, he should raise the matter for discussion with counsel even if no submission of no case to answer is made. If, having heard submissions, he is of the same opinion, he should withdraw the case from the jury. See also *Brown* [2002] 1 Cr App R 46.

For the special rule where a defendant is charged with murder or manslaughter, together with an offence under the DVCVA 2004, s. 5, see **D15.52**.

APPEALS BY THE PROSECUTION AGAINST ADVERSE RULINGS

D15.70 Before the introduction of the CJA 2003, the prosecution's ability to challenge a ruling adverse to its position which either terminated a case entirely or excluded evidence in such a way as to fundamentally undermine its ability to continue was extremely limited. It had a right to appeal against rulings made at a preparatory hearing (see **D14.63**) and, after the termination of a prosecution, it was possible for the A-G to refer a point of law to the Court of Appeal, pursuant to the CJA 1977, s. 36, with a view to clarifying the law for the future.

Part 9 of the CJA 2003 (ss. 57 to 74) introduced new provision for appeals by the prosecution against rulings of the Crown Court in relation to trial on indictment. These can be divided into two broad categories:

(a) appeals against terminating rulings (ss. 58 to 61);
(b) appeals against evidentiary rulings which significantly weaken the prosecution case (ss. 62 to 67).

Application

Pursuant to the Criminal Justice Act 2003 (Commencement No. 8 and Transitional and Saving Provisions) Order 2005 (SI 2005 No. 950), a terminating ruling may be the subject of a s. 58 appeal only where proceedings were committed or sent for trial after the date of its commencement (4 April 2005). The provisions relating to s. 62 evidentiary ruling appeals have not yet come into force. D15.71

Terminating Rulings

Section 58 of the CJA 2003 permits the prosecution to challenge rulings of the Crown Court which would otherwise bring proceedings in a particular case to an end, in such a way that, if the ruling in question was found to have been in error, it would be possible for the proceedings to continue. By virtue of s. 58(6), the prosecution may appeal in relation only to certain counts of the indictment. Moreover, s. 58(7) allows the prosecution to appeal other rulings made during the course of the trial in addition to the court's ruling in response to a submission of no case to answer. Such an appeal requires leave either from the trial judge or the Court of Appeal (s. 57(4)). Arguably the wording of s. 58 does not limit the use of such appeals only to terminatory rulings, but it was designed for such rulings. D15.72

The procedural rules which govern such appeals are contained in the CrimPR, part 66 (see **appendix 1**). It involves a series of stages, which are dealt with below.

Consideration of an Appeal

The first step to be taken in relation to such an appeal is for the prosecution, pursuant to the CJA 2003, s. 58(4), either to inform the court that it intends to appeal or to request an adjournment (s. 58(4)(a)(ii)) to consider whether or not to appeal against the ruling of the court. In the latter event the prosecution must, in accordance with the CrimPR, r. 66.2, make the request to the judge of the court immediately following the relevant ruling. D15.73

The court must grant the adjournment unless it is in the interests of justice for the prosecutor to state his intentions immediately; the adjournment will be to the next business day, or longer if the interests of justice so require (s. 58(5) and r. 66.2(3) and (4)).

As soon as reasonably practicable after the prosecutor declares his intention to appeal or asks for an adjournment to consider whether he will appeal, the officer of the Crown Court must serve a transcript of the relevant ruling on the prosecutor, the accused and any interested party (defined in r. 66.1 as a person other than the defendant who is a party to the proceedings, may be affected by the decision under s. 59(1) as to whether to expedite the appeal, and is permitted by the trial judge to make submissions on that issue).

Announcing the Decision to Appeal Following the adjournment (if any) or immediately after the ruling, the prosecutor must inform the judge whether he intends to appeal. If he does, he may apply orally to the judge for leave to appeal (CJA 2003, s. 57(4)). The judge must hear representations from the defence before deciding whether or not to grant leave, but must make the decision on the same day as the oral application for leave is made unless it is in the interests of justice to take longer (CrimPR, r. 66.3). D15.74

Crucially, when appealing against a terminating ruling, the prosecution must undertake to offer no evidence against the accused in the event that the appeal is either abandoned (pursuant to r. 66.10) or refused (s. 58(8)).

Expediting an Appeal Section 59 of the CJA 2003 permits an appeal to be expedited, in the discretion of the trial judge. When the prosecutor signals his intention to appeal, he must also make oral representations as to whether the appeal should be expedited. Before deciding the issue, the judge must hear representations from the defence and any interested party. This D15.75

decision is significant because, if the appeal is not expedited, the court may decide to discharge the jury rather than adjourn the case to allow the appeal to be heard (s. 59(3)).

Any decision by the judge to expedite an appeal may be reversed by him at any time before notice of appeal or application for leave to appeal is served on the Crown Court in accordance with the CrimPR, r. 66.5, or by the Court of Appeal thereafter. The reasons for the reversal of that decision must be provided in writing to the prosecutor, defence and any interested party.

D15.76 **Documentation** Usually a notice of appeal or application for leave to appeal must be served by the prosecutor on the Registrar, the Crown Court officer, the accused and any interested party. If the judge decides to expedite the appeal, that notice must be served before 5 p.m. on the day on which the prosecutor states his intention to appeal. In any other case, the prosecutor has seven days, unless the deadline is extended (CrimPR, r. 66.5). If the appeal or application is resisted, the necessary documentation must be served on the other parties on the next day if the appeal is expedited and otherwise within seven days (r. 66.6). There are special rules for appeals which relate to rulings as to the disclosure of material over which public interest immunity is claimed in r. 66.8.

D15.77 **Conduct by the Court of Appeal** Rule 66.11 of the CrimPR sets out the powers of a single judge in relation to such appeals. The options available to the Court of Appeal in relation to such an appeal are set out in the CJA 2003, s. 61, namely that it may either confirm the ruling at first instance (in which case it orders the acquittal of the accused), reverse it or vary it. If either of the latter options is taken, the orders that the Court of Appeal may then make are those identified in s. 61(4), providing that such an order is in the interests of justice (s. 61(5)).

Evidentiary Rulings

D15.78 Once the relevant provisions come into force, the prosecution may appeal one or more 'qualifying' evidentiary rulings pursuant to the CJA 2003, s. 62. Such rulings are rulings as to the admissibility or exclusion of prosecution material (s. 62(9)), made at any time before the opening of the defence case (s. 62(2)) where the accused is charged with a 'qualifying offence'.

D15.79 **Qualifying Offences** These offences are defined in the CJA 2003, sch. 4, and can be summarised as follows:

(a) offences against the person, including murder, manslaughter, offences under the OAPA 1861, s. 18 and kidnap;
(b) sexual offences, including rape;
(c) drugs offences relating to Class A drugs;
(d) robbery with the use of a firearm or imitation firearm;
(e) arson endangering life and offences contrary to the Explosives Substances Act 1883, ss. 2 and 3;
(f) war crimes and terrorist offences.

D15.80 **Procedure** The CrimPR do not yet provide a procedural framework for such appeals, although it is likely to mirror that in part 66 which relates to s. 58 appeals. The first step, as with terminating ruling appeals, is for the prosecution to inform the court that it seeks to appeal against an identified ruling (CJA 2003, s. 62(5)). Leave to appeal, which may be granted by either the trial judge or the Court of Appeal (s. 57(4)), will be granted only if the ruling, or the rulings taken together, 'significantly weakens the prosecution's case' (s. 63). Again the issue of expedition of appeal is to be determined by the trial judge, and is subject to review (see **D15.73**).

D15.81 **Conduct of the Court of Appeal** The options available to the Court of Appeal in relation to such an appeal are set out in the CJA 2003, s. 61, namely that it may either confirm the ruling at first instance, reverse it or vary it. It may only reverse the ruling if the conditions in s. 67 are satisfied. The orders that it may make are those set out in s. 66(2).

Statutory Extracts on Prosecution Appeals

Criminal Justice Act 2003, ss. 57 to 66

D15.82

57.—(1) In relation to a trial on indictment, the prosecution is to have the rights of appeal for which provision is made by [part 9].

(2) But the prosecution is to have no right of appeal under this part in respect of—
(a) a ruling that a jury be discharged, or
(b) a ruling from which an appeal lies to the Court of Appeal by virtue of any other enactment.

(3) An appeal under this part is to lie to the Court of Appeal.

(4) Such an appeal may be brought only with the leave of the judge or the Court of Appeal.

58.—(1) This section applies where a judge makes a ruling in relation to a trial on indictment at an applicable time and the ruling relates to one or more offences included in the indictment.

(2) The prosecution may appeal in respect of the ruling in accordance with this section.

(3) The ruling is to have no effect whilst the prosecution is able to take any steps under subsection (4).

(4) The prosecution may not appeal in respect of the ruling unless—
(a) following the making of the ruling, it—
(i) informs the court that it intends to appeal, or
(ii) requests an adjournment to consider whether to appeal, and
(b) if such an adjournment is granted, it informs the court following the adjournment that it intends to appeal.

(5) If the prosecution requests an adjournment under subsection (4)(a)(ii), the judge may grant such an adjournment.

(6) Where the ruling relates to two or more offences—
(a) any one or more of those offences may be the subject of the appeal, and
(b) if the prosecution informs the court in accordance with subsection (4) that it intends to appeal, it must at the same time inform the court of the offence or offences which are the subject of the appeal.

(7) Where—
(a) the ruling is a ruling that there is no case to answer, and
(b) the prosecution, at the same time that it informs the court in accordance with subsection (4) that it intends to appeal, nominates one or more other rulings which have been made by a judge in relation to the trial on indictment at an applicable time and which relate to the offence or offences which are the subject of the appeal,

that other ruling, or those other rulings, are also to be treated as the subject of the appeal.

(8) The prosecution may not inform the court in accordance with subsection (4) that it intends to appeal, unless, at or before that time, it informs the court that it agrees that, in respect of the offence or each offence which is the subject of the appeal, the defendant in relation to that offence should be acquitted of that offence if either of the conditions mentioned in subsection (9) is fulfilled.

(9) Those conditions are—
(a) that leave to appeal to the Court of Appeal is not obtained, and
(b) that the appeal is abandoned before it is determined by the Court of Appeal.

(10) If the prosecution informs the court in accordance with subsection (4) that it intends to appeal, the ruling mentioned in subsection (1) is to continue to have no effect in relation to the offence or offences which are the subject of the appeal whilst the appeal is pursued.

(11) If and to the extent that a ruling has no effect in accordance with this section—
(a) any consequences of the ruling are also to have no effect,
(b) the judge may not take any steps in consequence of the ruling, and
(c) if he does so, any such steps are also to have no effect.

(12) Where the prosecution has informed the court of its agreement under subsection (8) and either of the conditions mentioned in subsection (9) is fulfilled, the judge or the Court of Appeal must order that the defendant in relation to the offence or each offence concerned be acquitted of that offence.

(13) In this section 'applicable time', in relation to a trial on indictment, means any time (whether before or after the commencement of the trial) before the time when the judge starts his summing-up to the jury.

(14) The reference in subsection (13) to the time when the judge starts his summing-up to the

jury includes the time when the judge would start his summing-up to the jury but for the making of an order under part 7.

59.—(1) Where the prosecution informs the court in accordance with section 58(4) that it intends to appeal, the judge must decide whether or not the appeal should be expedited.

(2) If the judge decides that the appeal should be expedited, he may order an adjournment.

(3) If the judge decides that the appeal should not be expedited, he may—
(a) order an adjournment, or
(b) discharge the jury (if one has been sworn).

(4) If he decides that the appeal should be expedited, he or the Court of Appeal may subsequently reverse that decision and, if it is reversed, the judge may act as mentioned in subsection (3)(a) or (b).

60.—(1) This section applies where the prosecution informs the court in accordance with section 58(4) that it intends to appeal.

(2) Proceedings may be continued in respect of any offence which is not the subject of the appeal.

61.—(1) On an appeal under section 58, the Court of Appeal may confirm, reverse or vary any ruling to which the appeal relates.

(2) Subsections (3) to (5) apply where the appeal relates to a single ruling.

(3) Where the Court of Appeal confirms the ruling, it must, in respect of the offence or each offence which is the subject of the appeal, order that the defendant in relation to that offence be acquitted of that offence.

(4) Where the Court of Appeal reverses or varies the ruling, it must, in respect of the offence or each offence which is the subject of the appeal, do any of the following—
(a) order that proceedings for that offence may be resumed in the Crown Court,
(b) order that a fresh trial may take place in the Crown Court for that offence,
(c) order that the defendant in relation to that offence be acquitted of that offence.

(5) But the Court of Appeal may not make an order under subsection (4)(a) or (b) in respect of an offence unless it considers it necessary in the interests of justice to do so.

(6) Subsections (7) and (8) apply where the appeal relates to a ruling that there is no case to answer and one or more other rulings.

(7) Where the Court of Appeal confirms the ruling that there is no case to answer, it must, in respect of the offence or each offence which is the subject of the appeal, order that the defendant in relation to that offence be acquitted of that offence.

(8) Where the Court of Appeal reverses or varies the ruling that there is no case to answer, it must in respect of the offence or each offence which is the subject of the appeal, make any of the orders mentioned in subsection (4)(a) to (c) (but subject to subsection (5)).

62.—(1) The prosecution may, in accordance with this section and section 63, appeal in respect of—
(a) a single qualifying evidentiary ruling, or
(b) two or more qualifying evidentiary rulings.

(2) A 'qualifying evidentiary ruling' is an evidentiary ruling of a judge in relation to a trial on indictment which is made at any time (whether before or after the commencement of the trial) before the opening of the case for the defence.

(3) The prosecution may not appeal in respect of a single qualifying evidentiary ruling unless the ruling relates to one or more qualifying offences (whether or not it relates to any other offence).

(4) The prosecution may not appeal in respect of two or more qualifying evidentiary rulings unless each ruling relates to one or more qualifying offences (whether or not it relates to any other offence).

(5) If the prosecution intends to appeal under this section, it must before the opening of the case for the defence inform the court-
(a) of its intention to do so, and
(b) of the ruling or rulings to which the appeal relates.

(6) In respect of the ruling, or each ruling, to which the appeal relates—
(a) the qualifying offence, or at least one of the qualifying offences, to which the ruling relates must be the subject of the appeal, and
(b) any other offence to which the ruling relates may, but need not, be the subject of the appeal.

(7) The prosecution must, at the same time that it informs the court in accordance with

subsection (5), inform the court of the offence or offences which are the subject of the appeal.

(8) For the purposes of this section, the case for the defence opens when, after the conclusion of the prosecution evidence, the earliest of the following events occurs—
  (a) evidence begins to be adduced by or on behalf of a defendant,
  (b) it is indicated to the court that no evidence will be adduced by or on behalf of a defendant,
  (c) a defendant's case is opened, as permitted by section 2 of the Criminal Procedure Act 1865 (c. 18).

(9) In this section—
'evidentiary ruling' means a ruling which relates to the admissibility or exclusion of any prosecution evidence,
'qualifying offence' means an offence described in part 1 of schedule 4.

(10) The Secretary of State may by order amend that part by doing any one or more of the following—
  (a) adding a description of offence,
  (b) removing a description of offence for the time being included,
  (c) modifying a description of offence for the time being included.

(11) Nothing in this section affects the right of the prosecution to appeal in respect of an evidentiary ruling under section 58.

63.—(1) Leave to appeal may not be given in relation to an appeal under section 62 unless the judge or, as the case may be, the Court of Appeal is satisfied that the relevant condition is fulfilled.

(2) In relation to an appeal in respect of a single qualifying evidentiary ruling, the relevant condition is that the ruling significantly weakens the prosecution's case in relation to the offence or offences which are the subject of the appeal.

(3) In relation to an appeal in respect of two or more qualifying evidentiary rulings, the relevant condition is that the rulings taken together significantly weaken the prosecution's case in relation to the offence or offences which are the subject of the appeal.

64.—(1) Where the prosecution informs the court in accordance with section 62(5), the judge must decide whether or not the appeal should be expedited.

(2) If the judge decides that the appeal should be expedited, he may order an adjournment.

(3) If the judge decides that the appeal should not be expedited, he may—
  (a) order an adjournment, or
  (b) discharge the jury (if one has been sworn).

(4) If he decides that the appeal should be expedited, he or the Court of Appeal may subsequently reverse that decision and, if it is reversed, the judge may act as mentioned in subsection (3)(a) or (b).

65.—(1) This section applies where the prosecution informs the court in accordance with section 62(5).

(2) Proceedings may be continued in respect of any offence which is not the subject of the appeal.

66.—(1) On an appeal under section 62, the Court of Appeal may confirm, reverse or vary any ruling to which the appeal relates.

(2) In addition, the Court of Appeal must, in respect of the offence or each offence which is the subject of the appeal, do any of the following—
  (a) order that proceedings for that offence be resumed in the Crown Court,
  (b) order that a fresh trial may take place in the Crown Court for that offence,
  (c) order that the defendant in relation to that offence be acquitted of that offence.

(3) But no order may be made under subsection (2)(c) in respect of an offence unless the prosecution has indicated that it does not intend to continue with the prosecution of that offence.

Section D16 Trial on Indictment: The Defence Case

D16.1 Assuming any submission of no case to answer has been rejected (see **D15.51**), the next stage following the close of the prosecution case is for the defence to call such evidence as they choose. This chapter briefly considers the various potential aspects of a defence case, from opening to the decision to call either the accused himself or any defence witnesses. Of the latter, the only category that calls for special consideration are alibi witnesses. Special considerations also arise where the accused is representing himself (**D16.17**). First, however, it is necessary to assess briefly the professional duties of defence counsel.

DUTIES AND ROLE OF DEFENCE COUNSEL

General Principle

D16.2 Defence counsel is not subject to the constraints of impartiality that apply to prosecuting counsel (addressed at **D15.3**). Subject to the duty resting on any barrister not deliberately to mislead the court, and to the rules of professional conduct generally, he may use all proper means to secure the acquittal or lenient sentencing of his lay client.

In presenting the accused's defence, counsel should not be influenced by his personal opinion of its truth. This cardinal principle was restated by the Professional Conduct Committee of the Bar following the decision of the Court of Appeal in *McFadden* (1975) 62 Cr App R 187, which was to the effect that:

> It is the duty of counsel when defending an accused on a criminal charge to present to the court, fearlessly and without regard to his personal interests, the defence of that accused. It is not his function to determine the truth or falsity of that defence, nor should he permit his personal opinion of that defence to influence his conduct of it. No counsel may refuse to defend because of his opinion of the character of the accused nor of the crime charged. That is a cardinal rule of the Bar, and it would be a grave matter in any free society were it not. Counsel also has a duty to the court and to the public. This duty includes the clear presentation of the issues and the avoidance of waste of time, repetition and prolixity. In the conduct of every case counsel must be mindful of this public responsibility.

More recently, in *Ebanks v The Queen* [2006] 1 WLR 1827, the Privy Council stressed the duty of defence counsel to put his client's case irrespective of whether the accused would ultimately give evidence, that decision being one for the accused alone.

Becoming a Witness

D16.3 Occasionally, the question will arise as to whether it is proper for defence counsel to be called as a witness on behalf of his client. In *Jaquith* [1989] Crim LR 563, the Court of Appeal made certain suggestions for the guidance of the Bar Council and the Law Society as to the circumstances in which this should occur. These include the following:

(a) No advocate should give evidence in a criminal trial if doing so can possibly be avoided.
(b) If an advocate does give evidence, he should thereafter take no further part in the trial. It follows that, unless he has a leader, there must be a retrial.
(c) Counsel should be able to anticipate before the trial whether it will be necessary for him to give evidence. If it will be, he should withdraw as advocate.

(d) If the giving of evidence by an advocate causes real embarrassment or prevents proper cross-examination by other counsel, a retrial should be ordered.

In *Wood* [1996] 1 Cr App R 207, the Court of Appeal said that the rule should be enforced that a member of the Bar giving evidence could no longer act as counsel in the same case. The comment was made in response to a ground of appeal which concerned the tone of voice used by the trial judge and the physical expression of views by sighing, shrugging his shoulders and raising his eyebrows in a way that was said to be hostile to the defence. Their lordships' view was that they could not act on such information unless it was either agreed between counsel or supported by evidence.

Professional Embarrassment

The Court of Appeal has identified other circumstances in which it would be inappropriate for counsel to act. These include the following. **D16.4**

(a) It is generally undesirable for husband and wife, or other partners living together, to appear as advocates against each other in a contested criminal matter (*Batt* [1996] Crim LR 910).
(b) It is undesirable for counsel to prosecute an accused whom he had previously defended. The relevant part of the Code, now para. 603, refers to the risk that a barrister may have confidential information or special knowledge disadvantageous to a former client. In *Dann* [1997] Crim LR 46, it was made clear that it was the *risk* which was material.

Code of Conduct of the Bar

Matters of relevance to defence counsel in the Code can be summarised as follows: **D16.5**

(a) He 'must endeavour to protect his client from conviction except by a competent tribunal and upon legally admissible evidence sufficient to support a conviction for the offence charged' (Written Standards, para. 11.1).
(b) He should satisfy himself, if he is briefed to represent more than one accused, that no conflict of interest is likely to arise (para. 11.2(a)).
(c) He should arrange a conference and if necessary a series of conferences with the accused and the solicitor (para. 11.2(b)).
(d) He should consider whether any enquiries are necessary, and, if so, advise in writing as soon as possible (para. 11.2(c)).
(e) He should consider whether defence witnesses are required (para. 11.2(d)).
(f) He should consider whether a defence case statement is required and, if so, draft it (para. 11.2(e)).
(g) He should consider whether to call expert evidence and notify the prosecution in accordance with the rules (now CrimPR set out at **appendix** 1) if appropriate (para. 11.2(f)).
(h) He should 'ensure that he has sufficient instructions for the purpose of deciding which prosecution witnesses should be cross-examined, and should then ensure that no other witnesses remain fully bound at the request of the defendant' (para. 11.2(g)). This provision does not impede the perfectly proper decision of defence counsel to insist that a witness give evidence to see whether he is 'up to proof', even if there is no intention of cross-examining.
(i) He should consider what admissions can be made, and what admissions and/or exhibits can be requested from the prosecution (para. 11.2(h), (i) and (j)).
(j) He should notify the prosecution in advance if he is instructed to submit in mitigation anything which casts aspersions on the conduct or character of a victim or witness in the case (para. 11.2(k)).
(k) The fact that the accused confesses to counsel that he did commit the offence charged does not bar counsel from appearing or continuing to appear for the defence on a not

guilty plea, nor is counsel released 'from his imperative duty to do all that he honourably can for his client' (para. 12.2). Counsel should bear in mind that, in a criminal trial, the issue is always whether the accused is guilty of the offence charged (never whether he is innocent), and the burden of proof is on the prosecution. However, receiving a confession places very strict limitations on counsel's conduct of the defence since 'he may not assert that which he knows to be a lie' or 'connive at, much less attempt to substantiate, a fraud'. It follows that counsel may properly take objections to the competency of the court, the form of the indictment and the admissibility of any evidence, and may test the prosecution's evidence, but he may not himself call evidence or advance an affirmative defence inconsistent with the confession.

(l) Counsel's duty to advise on pleas and his position if the accused says he is not guilty but for reasons of his own insists on pleading guilty are dealt with (paras. 11.3 and 11.5).

(m) Defence counsel who remains instructed must ensure that the accused is not left unrepresented at any stage of the trial (paras. 15.2.1 to 15.2.4). If two counsel represent the accused, neither may absent himself unless he has good reason and obtains the consent of both his professional and lay client. Where only one counsel is instructed, he may absent himself only if (i) exceptional circumstances have arisen which he could not have been expected to foresee, (ii) he obtains the consent of his professional and lay clients, and (iii) he arranges for a competent deputy to take his place. The client's consent to counsel's absence may be dispensed with in legally aided cases if counsel considers that, by being present, he would involve the fund in unnecessary expenditure (see para. 15.2.3).

(n) The position of counsel should the accused abscond during the trial is considered in paras. 15.3.1 and 15.3.2.

(o) Allegations that may properly be made during a speech in mitigation are dealt with in para. 5.10.

(p) After conviction and sentence, it is counsel's duty to see his client and advise (if necessary in writing) on whether there are grounds of appeal (para. 16.2).

Other Issues

D16.6 Paragraphs 7.2, 7.3.1 and 7.3.2 of the Written Standards deal with the issue of documents coming into counsel's possession (see **D15.8**). The interlocking matters of conferences, counsel being attended at court by his professional client, and the seeing of witnesses are dealt with in various provisions of the Code of Conduct of the Bar, and are summarised at **D14.91**.

DEFENCE OPENING SPEECH

D16.7 If the defence intend to call evidence as to the facts of the case other than or in addition to the evidence of the accused, defence counsel has the right to an opening speech at the beginning of the defence case (*Hill* (1911) 7 Cr App R 1). If, however, the only defence evidence is to come from the accused (or from the accused and character witnesses), then counsel does not have an opening speech. That is the implication of the Criminal Evidence Act 1898, s. 2. In an opening speech, defence counsel may both outline the anticipated defence case and criticise the evidence already given for the prosecution (*Randall* (1973) *The Times*, 11 July 1973). However, the speech should not make assertions of fact that are not to be proved by evidence that is to come.

THE DEFENCE CASE

D16.8 Because the burden of proof is on the prosecution, the defence are never obliged to call evidence, and more particularly to call the accused since he is a competent but not compellable witness (see Criminal Evidence Act 1898, s. 1(1)). Most defence witnesses are governed by the same rules and considerations as prosecution witnesses (discussed at **D15.30**). The only additional limitation is the duty of the court to stop evidence being given where it is irrelevant to the issues in the case (*Brown* [1998] 2 Cr App R 364), or where the court is being used as a political sounding board (*King* (1973) 57 Cr App R 696).

Order of Defence Evidence

The accused should normally be called before any other defence witnesses (PACE 1984, s. 79; Criminal Evidence Act 1898, s. 2). The rationale for this rule is that, whilst witnesses are normally kept out of court until they testify, the accused has the right to be present throughout his trial, and therefore would otherwise have the opportunity to adjust his evidence to accord with that of his witnesses. The court has a discretion to depart from this usual rule (PACE 1984, s. 79), for example to allow a witness whose evidence was not substantially disputed to testify out of the normal order if circumstances made that convenient (see *Morrison* (1911) 6 Cr App R 159 and *Smith* [1968] 1 WLR 636). However, character witnesses must *always* be called after the accused unless there are other witnesses as to the facts (see Criminal Evidence Act 1898, s. 2). **D16.9**

Police and Criminal Evidence Act 1984, s. 79

If at the trial of any person for an offence—
(a) the defence intends to call two or more witnesses to the facts of the case; and
(b) those witnesses include the accused, the accused shall be called before the other witness or witnesses unless the court in its discretion otherwise directs.

Criminal Evidence Act 1898, s. 2

Where the only witness to the facts of the case called by the defence is the person charged, he shall be called as a witness immediately after the close of the evidence for the prosecution.

The Accused as a Witness

The special evidential rules relating to the accused as a witness, for example the application in his case of the rule against self-incrimination and the circumstances in which he may be cross-examined as to character are fully discussed in **part F**. Mentioned below are some further points of a specifically procedural nature concerning evidence from the accused. **D16.10**

Evidence from the Witness Box Subject to a contrary direction from the court, an accused who chooses to testify should give his evidence from the witness-box, not the dock (Criminal Evidence Act 1898, s. 1(4) and see **F4.9**). The obvious situation in which the court might exercise its discretion against allowing the accused physically to enter the witness-box is when there is a perceived risk of violence from him that can be controlled more easily if he remains in the dock while testifying (*Symonds* (1924) 18 Cr App R 100). See also **D14.105** in relation to the use of live links for the accused. **D16.11**

The Decision to Call the Accused The decision whether to testify or not is for the accused himself. This is emphasised in the Code of Conduct of the Bar, Written Standards, para. 12.4: **D16.12**

> A barrister acting for a defendant should advise his client as to whether or not to give evidence in his own defence but the decision must be taken by the client himself.

The Court of Appeal has stated that, when the accused decides not to go into the witness box, it should be the invariable practice of counsel to have that decision recorded and to cause the accused to sign the record giving a clear indication of (i) the fact of his having, of his own accord, decided not to give evidence, and (ii) that he has done that bearing in mind the advice, regardless of what it was, given to him by counsel (*Bevan* (1994) 98 Cr App R 354; *Ebanks v The Queen* [2006] 1 WLR 1827).

Failure to advise the accused properly about the advisability of testifying may, in appropriate circumstances, constitute grounds for the Court of Appeal to decide that a conviction is unsafe and unsatisfactory (*Clinton* [1993] 1 WLR 1181; for further detail, see **D24.19**).

D16.13 **Failure to Give Evidence** Since s. 35 of the CJPO 1994 became law, it is particularly important that the accused should be advised whether to give evidence, since an inference may be drawn from his failure to do so. This section is addressed at **F19.20**, and the procedure which the court should adopt is laid down in the *Consolidated Criminal Practice Direction*, para. IV.44 (see **appendix** 7).

In particular, para. IV.44.3 states that, unless defence counsel has indicated that the accused will give evidence, the court is required to ask:

> Have you advised your client that the stage has now been reached at which he may give evidence and, if he chooses not to do so or, having been sworn, without good cause refuses to answer any question, the jury may draw such inferences as appear proper from his failure to do so?

The approach of the court where the accused is unrepresented is addressed at **D16.17**.

ALIBI EVIDENCE

D16.14 Prior to the commencement of the CPIA 1996, part I, alibi evidence and expert opinion evidence were the only types of evidence of which the defence were required to warn the prosecution in advance. That old regime, pursuant to the CJA 1967, s. 11, applies to offences for which the investigation commenced before 1 April 1997.

For later offences, the duty to give specific notice of alibi has been replaced by the wider duty to provide a defence statement under s. 5 of the 1996 Act (see **D9.18**). The consequences flowing from a defence failure to comply with its duty to notify an alibi now relate not to a potential impediment to the calling of alibi evidence, but to the fact that comment may be made or permitted or inferences drawn in relation to a notice of alibi that is served, or the failure to serve one. (Disclosure of expert evidence is addressed at **D9.39**.)

The Meaning of 'Alibi'

D16.15 The definition of 'alibi' in the CPIA 1996 is provided by s. 6A(3) (see **D9.20**), namely 'evidence tending to show that by reason of the presence of the accused at a particular place or in a particular area at a particular time he was not, or was unlikely to have been, at the place where the offence is alleged to have been committed at the time of its alleged commission'.

It follows that it is only evidence putting the accused at a certain place at the time of the commission of the offence that creates an obligation on the defence to give particulars of alibi if he claims that he was elsewhere (*Lewis* [1969] 2 QB 1).

In *Fields* [1991] Crim LR 38, the Court of Appeal found that a letter from F's solicitor, claiming that F was 25 miles away from the scene of the crime at the time he was allegedly first seen by the witness who later identified him as a participant in the offence, did amount to a notice of alibi. This was because the claim as to where F had been contained in the letter tended to show that F could not have been at the scene of the robbery when it took place.

Similarly, evidence may amount to an alibi even though it comes from the accused only and is to the effect that, at the relevant time, he was by himself at a location other than the scene of the crime (*Jackson* [1973] Crim LR 356).

However, the term 'alibi' presupposes that the offence alleged was committed at a particular place and time, as opposed to being committed in an unspecified geographical area over an unspecified and potentially lengthy period. Therefore, failure by the defence to notify the prosecution that the accused was not where they claimed him to be on one day during the period of three weeks over which the offence allegedly occurred did not mean that an alibi notice was necessary (*Hassan* [1970] 1 QB 423).

In *Johnson* [1995] 2 Cr App R 1, it was held that 'evidence in support of an alibi' must be evidence that the defendant was at some place or in a particular area other than the place where the offence was allegedly committed. J's instructions to his legal representatives were that he had not been present at the club where the offence was committed on the night in question. He was unable to say where he had been, since his arrest took place almost three months later. The Court of Appeal held that the trial judge was wrong to rule that an alibi notice was necessary in those circumstances.

The duty of defence disclosure under the CPIA 1996, s. 5, is addressed at **D9.18**.

Obligation to Consult Accused about Calling Alibi Evidence

Defence counsel is under a duty to consult the accused before deciding not to call alibi evidence. In *Irwin* [1987] 1 WLR 902, the accused's defence was alibi and at his first trial evidence of alibi was called. At the retrial, counsel decided, without consulting the accused, not to call those witnesses. On appeal, it was held that failure to consult the accused about the non-calling of the alibi witnesses was a material irregularity. According to Michael Davies J at p. 906, it is not necessarily vital to consult the client immediately before the alibi witnesses are or, as the case may be, are not called, but it is essential to have discussed the matter thoroughly at some stage. If the client declines to accept counsel's advice that the witnesses should not be called, then counsel should either act on his client's instructions or ask the judge to discharge him from the case (p. 905C–D). If the client accepts counsel's advice, it is preferable to have that confirmed by him in writing (p. 906C). **D16.16**

TREATMENT BY COURT OF UNREPRESENTED ACCUSED

If an accused is not legally represented, the court will, as a matter of practice, seek to give him such assistance in conducting his defence as may seem appropriate. **D16.17**

Alternatively, where the accused dismisses his counsel and/or solicitors during the course of the trial (or they withdraw during trial) and the accused remains entitled to public funding, the judge should grant an adjournment for the accused to be represented (see *Chambers* [1989] Crim LR 367 and *Sansom* [1991] 2 QB 130).

The Accused's Right to Give or Call Evidence

The accused should always be told by the court at the end of the prosecution case of his right to give evidence himself, to call witnesses in his defence (whether or not he himself goes into the witness-box), or to stay silent and call no evidence. Failure to give the accused this information may lead to any conviction being quashed (*Carter* (1960) 44 Cr App R 225). **D16.18**

It is particularly important that an unrepresented accused should be informed of the inferences which may be drawn from a failure to give evidence, pursuant to the CJPOA 1994, s. 35 (see **F19.20**). The court is obliged to address the accused, pursuant to the *Consolidated Criminal Practice Direction*, para. IV.45, in the following terms:

> You have heard the evidence against you. Now is the time for you to make your defence. You may give evidence on oath, and be cross-examined like any other witnes s. If you do not give evidence or, having been sworn, without good cause refuse to answer any question, the jury may draw such inferences as appear proper. That means they may hold it against you. You may also call any witness or witnesses whom you have arranged to attend court. Afterwards you may also, if you wish, address the jury by arguing your case from the dock. But you cannot at that stage give evidence. Do you now intend to give evidence?

Restrictions on the Accused

Since the YJCEA 1999, ss. 34 to 39 (see **F7.12**) came into effect, certain restrictions have applied. Unrepresented defendants are prohibited from cross-examining complainants and **D16.19** child witnesses in trials for certain offences. The courts also have the power to prohibit cross-examination of witnesses by unrepresented defendants if satisfied that the circumstances of the witness and the case merit it, and that a prohibition would not be contrary to the interests of justice. There are provisions for the appointment of representatives to conduct cross-examinations on behalf of unrepresented defendants.

For the position as to cross-examination by an unrepresented accused and related matters, see also *Brown* [1998] 2 Cr App R 364, which is dealt with in detail at F7.12. The procedure on an application for a prohibition on cross-examination of a particular witness is specified by the CrimPR, r. 31.4 (see **appendix 1**).

Section D17 Trial on Indictment: Procedure between Close of Defence Evidence and Retirement of Jury

This chapter addresses the progress of a trial on indictment following the closing of the defence case. This involves consideration of the potential reopening of either the defence or, more usually, the prosecution case thereafter, discussion between the court and counsel of the law relevant to the case, the closing speeches of counsel, and the judge's summing-up. **D17.1**

REOPENING OF PROSECUTION CASE

The general principle is that once prosecuting counsel has stated his case to be closed he may not adduce any further evidence (see Tindal CJ in *Frost* (1839) 4 St Tr NS 85 at col. 386). The exceptions, described below, cannot be listed exhaustively, but as a general rule the court's discretion to admit fresh evidence after the close of the prosecution case must be exercised with great caution (*Munnery* (1991) 94 Cr App R 164). **D17.2**

Matters which Arise *Ex Improviso*

Where a matter arises *ex improviso* in the course of the defence case which no human ingenuity could have foreseen, the judge may allow the prosecution to adduce evidence on the point to rebut that which has been led by the defence (see also **F6.2** *et seq.*). **D17.3**

Evidence Becoming Available to the Prosecution Only after Close of Case

If evidence unexpectedly becomes available to the prosecution between the close of their case and the judge's summing-up, they may exceptionally be given leave to call it even though the issue to which it relates does not arise *ex improviso* (*Doran* (1972) 56 Cr App R 429). For further discussion, see **F6.2**. **D17.4**

Evidence of a Purely Formal Nature Inadvertently Omitted

It has been held that an omission to call evidence of a purely formal nature, the lack of which leaves a technical gap in the prosecution case, may be repaired by allowing them to reopen (*McKenna* (1956) 40 Cr App R 65). However, the circumstances in which this is appropriate are narrowly confined and should not be used as a device for rescuing the prosecution when they have failed to prepare or prove their case properly. **D17.5**

McKenna should be contrasted with *Central Criminal Court, ex parte Garnier* [1988] RTR 42, where G was charged with parking his motorcycle with one or more of its wheels resting on the footway, and the further evidence the court permitted the prosecution to produce related to whether the site of the alleged offence was in fact a footway. The Divisional Court held that the missing evidence was not purely concerned with formalities, and did not arise *ex improviso.* (See further **F6.3**.)

Evidence to Rebut Answers in Cross-examination as to Credit

Although a witness's answers to questions going only to his credit are generally final, there are important exceptions to the rule, notably where the question related to a previous conviction, **D17.6**

D

Part D Procedure

a previous inconsistent statement, possible bias or a reputation for untruthfulness (see F7.27 *et seq.*). It follows that, where the accused or other defence witness is asked in cross-examination a question going to his credit and the question is such that the witness's answer is *not* final because it comes within one of these exceptions, the prosecution must be allowed to reopen their case to adduce evidence to rebut a denial given in cross-examination.

Time for Reopening Prosecution Case

D17.7 As to the latest stage at which the prosecution may be permitted to reopen their case assuming one of the exceptional situations applies, the majority of the decided cases contemplate the additional evidence being called either during or, more probably, at the end of the defence case. However, in *Flynn* (1957) 42 Cr App R 15, the judge gave the prosecution leave to call a witness to rebut an alibi raised *ex improviso* by the defence after counsel's closing speeches but before he began his summing-up.

Use in Cross-examination of Unproved Material

D17.8 The rule that the prosecution must adduce all the material on which they intend to rely as part of their case extends to the use they may make of statements or admissions not earlier proved in evidence in cross-examination.

For example in *Kane* (1977) 65 Cr App R 270, prosecuting counsel was criticised for cross-examining K about 'off the record' answers he had given to police officers, and which had not been adduced in evidence earlier. A distinction has been drawn between cases such as *Kane*, where the cross-examination on fresh material goes to the issues in the case, and cases where the cross-examination goes only to the credit of the defence witness (*Halford* (1978) 67 Cr App R 318). However, it will often be difficult, if not impossible, to determine the borderline between cross-examination as to credit and cross-examination on the issues.

REOPENING OF DEFENCE CASE

D17.9 The judge may in his discretion allow the defence to reopen their case at any stage before the jury retire to consider their verdict. In *Morrison* (1911) 6 Cr App R 159, defence evidence which had only just then come to light was allowed after counsel's closing speeches. In *Sanderson* [1953] 1 WLR 392, the defence were allowed to call a witness even after the end of the summing-up. The Court of Criminal Appeal said that 'it was not a course one would wish to be taken often but, on the particular facts of this case, we think that there is no objection to what was done here. The learned recorder was fully justified in the course he took'. However, once the jury retires to consider its verdict, evidence must never be received, whether it is favourable to the defence or the prosecution (*Owen* [1952] 2 QB 362).

JUDGE CALLING OR RECALLING A WITNESS

D17.10 The judge has a discretion to call a witness whom neither the prosecution nor defence have chosen to call (*Wallwork* (1958) 42 Cr App R 153). The power should be sparingly exercised (*Roberts* (1984) 80 Cr App R 89), and used only where it is necessary in the interests of justice.

Calling a Witness the Prosecution Fail to Call

D17.11 One appropriate situation for the judge taking such a course is where the prosecution have wrongly refused to call a witness whose name is on the back of the indictment (see dicta to that effect in *Oliva* [1965] 1 WLR 1028). If the witness is likely to be adverse to the defence and the prosecution have already closed their case, the judge should not use his power so as to circumvent the restrictions on the prosecution reopening their case (*Cleghorn* [1967] 2 QB 584). If the defence want the judge to call such a witness, he has greater latitude in the exercise of his discretionary powers and any conviction is unlikely to be quashed even if the evidence turns out to be in some respects adverse to the defence (*Tregear* [1967] 2 QB 574).

Consequences of Such Action

The parties require leave to cross-examine a witness called by the judge, but such leave should be given if the witness's evidence has been adverse to the party wishing to put questions (*Cliburn* (1898) 62 JP 232). Moreover, an adjournment may then be necessary to enable a cross-examining party to call his own evidence in rebuttal (*Coleman* (1987) *The Times*, 21 November 1987). **D17.12**

DISCUSSION OF THE RELEVANT LAW

Prior to summing-up, it has become increasingly common for the court to invite counsel, in the absence of the jury, to make representations on how certain aspects of the case should be dealt with. This is especially important where there might otherwise be misunderstanding or doubt as to how points of law and evidence which have arisen during the course of the case should be dealt with (*N* [1998] Crim LR 886; *Wright* [2000] Crim LR 510). **D17.13**

Such a discussion should, ideally, take place before speeches. Only in very exceptional circumstances would it be appropriate for the court to discuss the law with counsel after concluding his summing-up and before the jury's retirement (*Cocks* (1976) 63 Cr App R 79). The course adopted by the judge in *Charles* [1976] 1 WLR 248, of asking counsel to intervene in the course of the summing-up and correct any errors as they arose, was criticised by the Court of Appeal as it detracted from the authority of what the judge was saying.

Assisting the Court

In criminal cases, just as in civil, a barrister is under a duty to bring all relevant authorities to the court's attention even if some are unfavourable to his own argument. Further, he must bring any procedural irregularity to the attention of the court during the hearing and not reserve such matter to be raised on appeal (e.g., where a juror is seen speaking to a witness). **D17.14**

The duties outlined so far apply equally to prosecution and defence counsel (see Written Standards, para. 5.10(c)). In *Smith* [1994] Crim LR 458, one of the grounds of appeal was the fact that contact with a child witness during her evidence was alleged to be irregular. The Court of Appeal said that counsel should have raised the matter at the time with the judge, in the absence of the jury. Failure to do so was reprehensible.

A specific obligation is placed upon prosecuting counsel to assist the court at the conclusion of the judge's summing-up by drawing attention to any apparent errors or omissions of fact or law. No corresponding duty is placed upon defence counsel, but if he ignores a misdirection in the hope of using it as a ground of appeal, he runs a considerable risk. The Court of Appeal may dismiss the appeal on the basis that, if the error had been likely to make a difference to the verdict, counsel should have corrected it at the time (but see *Holden* [1991] Crim LR 478 at D17.23).

CLOSING SPEECHES

Subject to one exception, both the prosecution and defence have the right to a closing speech in which they may sum up their respective cases, criticise the opposition's case and comment **D17.15** upon the evidence. Final speeches are not normally recorded. Where it is apparent that exchanges of importance are likely to take place during final speeches, however, counsel should make this clear to the judge so that the presence of the shorthand writer can be ensured (*Osborne-Odelli* [1998] Crim LR 902). The court should intervene to seek clarification or correction of something said in a speech at its conclusion, or at a convenient break, rather than interrupting counsel in the presence of the jury (*Tuegel* [2000] 2 All ER 872).

Order of Speeches

D17.16 The order of speeches is the result of extensive case law and statutory provisions stretching from the early 19th century to modern times. Those authorities are summarised by Watkins J in the course of his judgment in *Bryant* [1979] QB 108 at pp. 113–18. It is now clear that the prosecution speech is made first.

Restrictions on Prosecution Closing Speeches

D17.17 In *Mondon* (1968) 52 Cr App R 695, the Court of Appeal held that the prosecution lost the right to make a closing speech where the accused was unrepresented and either called no evidence at all or was himself the only witness (apart from character witnesses). Edmund Davies LJ, in giving the judgment of the Court, drew attention to the impact which that speech might have had on the jury's determination of the issues. However, in *Stovell* [2006] EWCA Crim 27, the Court of Appeal concluded (per Rose LJ at [36]):

> . . . in the light of the procedural and evidential changes which have taken place since the decision of this Court in *Mondon*, we are by no means satisfied that in all cases, particularly when a defendant has been represented substantially throughout the trial and there are issues arising during the defence upon which the jury would be assisted by comment from prosecuting counsel, it is necessarily inappropriate for prosecuting counsel to make a second speech.

Even where prosecuting counsel is entitled to make a closing speech, this does not mean that he should as a matter of course exercise the right. In particular, if the accused is legally represented but does not give or call any evidence, the normal practice is for prosecuting counsel *not* to sum up his case. This was confirmed by Watkins J in *Bryant* [1979] QB 108 at p. 117D:

> Prosecuting counsel in the case of a defendant who is himself represented by counsel and gives no evidence and calls none has the right to sum up the prosecution's evidence, or in modern parlance, to make a closing speech at the close of that evidence. It is, however, a right which . . . should only rarely be necessary to use save possibly in long and complex cases and whenever used should bear, as should the majority of speeches by prosecuting and defence counsel, the becoming hallmark of brevity.

In *Hoggard* [1995] Crim LR 747, it was emphasised that the prosecution had the statutory right, by virtue of the Criminal Procedure Act 1865, s. 2, to make a closing speech where the defendant was represented. The length of the speech should, however, be commensurate with the number and complexity of the issues. In a case where the defence relied on self-serving statements made in interviews, or allegations put in cross-examination to witnesses, it would generally be in order for the prosecution to make a closing speech in order to deal with them.

In *Tahir* [1997] Crim LR 837, the Court of Appeal held that prosecuting counsel should not be deprived of the right to make a closing speech in relation to a represented defendant where the co-defendant was unrepresented. In such circumstances, however, the speech must focus on the evidence relating to the represented defendant.

Limitations as to Content

D17.18 Neither counsel in a closing speech should allude to alleged facts or other matters which have not been the subject of evidence (see a resolution of the judges dated 26 November 1881, adopted in *Shimmin* (1882) 15 Cox CC 122). Neither should the jury be invited to add a recommendation of mercy to their verdict should it be one of guilty (*Black* [1963] 1 WLR 1311).

Prosecution Counsel In *Gonez* [1999] All ER (D) 674, the Court of Appeal emphasised that prosecutors must remember their role as a minister of justice in relation to the terms in which they make their speeches (see **D15.3**). In *Ramdhanie* [2005] UKPC 47, the Privy Council upheld an appeal based upon an improper closing speech by the prosecutor. Their lordships concluded that it included passages in which prosecuting counsel strongly implied that there was incriminating material which had not been put before them. The speech also contained emotive and unjustified comments on the defence case, and a number of passages where the prosecutor improperly vouched for the soundness of the prosecution's case. **D17.19**

Prosecuting counsel should not comment to the jury on the potentially serious consequences to police officers of their evidence being disbelieved, even where a police officer has raised the matter in evidence (*Gale* [1994] Crim LR 208).

Equally, prosecution counsel is not entitled to abandon or attack the credit of his own witness (unless he has been given leave to treat him as hostile) and he should not invite inferences contrary to the evidence he has called (*Pacey* (1994) *The Times*, 13 March 1994; *Cairns* [2003] 1 WLR 796).

Pursuant to the PACE 1984, s. 80A, the prosecution should not comment on the failure of the accused's spouse to give evidence. However, prosecution counsel is entitled to comment on the failure of the accused to answer questions in interview and the prohibition on comment on the accused's failure to give evidence was removed by the CJPOA 1994, s. 168(2) and sch. 10, paras. 2 and 11 (see **F19.14**). Similarly, pursuant to the CPIA 1996, s. 11(5), the prosecution may make 'such comment as appears appropriate', providing that the court grants leave, about the failure of the accused to serve a defence statement, or as to divergence between that statement and his evidence (see **D9**).

Defence Counsel In delivering his closing speech defence counsel is not confined to putting forward his client's version of events. He may advance hypotheses which go beyond his client's version of events, always provided that other evidence has been called which supports such hypotheses (*Bateson* (1991) *The Times*, 10 April 1991). **D17.20**

Defence counsel should not refer to the likely consequences of a conviction in terms of punishment since sentencing is no concern of the jury (*A-G for South Australia v Brown* [1960] AC 432).

For the position as to comment by counsel on the defendant's failure to give evidence, see **F19.14**. Defence counsel is obviously entitled to comment upon his own client's not testifying. He is also, in a case where a co-accused runs a defence which conflicts with that of the accused he represents, entitled to comment upon the co-accused's not having entered the witness-box (*Wickham* (1971) 55 Cr App R 199). The judge has no power to prevent or restrict such comment, but may comment upon it himself if he considers it to have been unfair (ibid.).

SUMMING-UP

Preliminary and General Matters

The trial judge's summing-up conventionally falls into two parts, namely, a direction on the law (see **D17.25**) and a summary of the evidence (see **D17.36**). **D17.21**

The Court of Appeal have discouraged courts from commencing a summing-up, or addressing an important aspect of one, at a late hour or just before the weekend (*Rimmer* [1983] Crim LR 250).

Both counsel should take as full a longhand note of the summing-up as is possible. This is especially important where any sentence is likely to be short. A good note may avoid delay caused by waiting for a transcript and thus expedite an appeal (*Campbell*) [1976] Crim LR 508).

D17.22 **Correcting Errors** Where the judge discovers an error in his summing-up, whether as a result of representations by counsel (see **D17.23**) or otherwise, he should expressly acknowledge and refer to the error, tell the jury to disregard it, and then go on to give the correct direction (*Cole* [1993] Crim LR 300). In *Kilbane* [2003] EWCA Crim 607, the judge was alerted in the absence of the jury to a misdirection as to the burden of proof in cases covered by the MDA 1971, s. 28. When the jury returned, the judge gave a correct direction, but described it as an attempt to 'clarify' and 'repeat' what she had previously said. The Court of Appeal quashed the conviction, quoting Salmon LJ in *Moon* [1969] 1 WLR 1705:

> Such a misdirection could be corrected only in the plainest terms. The court must repeat the direction given, acknowledge that it was wrong, tell the jury to put out of their minds all they had heard from the court about the burden of proof . . . and then direct them on the law in clear terms incapable of being misunderstood.

D17.23 **Duties of Counsel in relation to the Summing-up** Prosecuting counsel is under a duty to attend carefully to the summing-up and draw any possible errors (whether of fact or law) to the judge's attention at its close (see *Donoghue* (1987) 86 Cr App R 267 and the Code of Conduct of the Bar, Written Standards, para. 11.7). Moreover, the court is entitled to rely on such assistance (*McVey* [1988] Crim LR 127).

Traditionally, defence counsel has been under no such duty. Beyond the duties described at **D17.14** he may, if he considered it in the best interests of his client, remain silent and take the point on appeal (*Curtin* [1996] Crim LR 831, relying upon *Cocks* (1976) 63 Cr App R 79 and see also *Edwards* (1983) 77 Cr App R 5) (see also **D17.14** in this regard). However, in *Cox* [1995] 2 Cr App R 513, the Court of Appeal held that, where there is evidence on which the jury could find provocation, both prosecution and defence counsel should regard it as their duty to alert the judge to this, before he sums up, invite him to consider whether he agrees that the evidence would justify such a finding and, if so, remind him that he is required by statute to leave the remaining issues to the jury. Similarly, in *Gilbert* [2006] 1 WLR 2108, it was made clear that defence counsel was under a duty to request a good character direction, if the accused was entitled to one, rather than making complaint later if one were not given.

In *Holden* [1991] Crim LR 478, moreover, the Court of Appeal made it clear that the dismissal of the appeal would not be automatic where defence counsel failed to correct an error.

Written Directions

D17.24 Occasionally, in a complex case, the judge may provide the jury with a written list of questions or directions to assist them in their task, setting out the legal issues which must be proved in order to reach their verdict, often described as the 'steps to verdict'. If he does so, he should submit them to counsel well in advance, so that they can comment upon any errors and can base their closing speeches upon the issues raised in the proposed directions. The jury should then be given the written list at the start of the summing-up, so that the judge can take them through the directions one by one, as he deals with each point. See *McKechnie* (1992) 94 Cr App R 51.

The judge is, however, fully entitled to decline to provide the jury with written directions, even where they have been requested (*Lawson* [1998] Crim LR 883). Whilst failure by counsel to comment on such draft directions is not necessarily fatal to an appeal based on any misdirection, such failure is likely to affect the weight accorded to the deficiency (*Gammans* (unreported 13 November 1998)).

Standard Directions

As Lord Hailsham observed in *Lawrence* [1982] AC 510 (at p. 519), a summing-up should be 'custom-built to make the jury understand their task in relation to a particular case'. Which legal directions are necessary will therefore vary and what is set out here is a survey of the standard directions which may be required. **D17.25**

Recently judges have tended to use a standard form for summing up on the law, and this has been encouraged by the Court of Appeal's policy of recommending model or specimen directions, namely standard forms of words by which directions on frequently recurring matters of law may or ought to be given. These specimen directions have been collected in a document issued by the Judicial Studies Board, with the approval of the Lord Chief Justice, to all Crown Court judges. They can be found on the Board's web site: www.jsboard.co.uk.

Whilst the specimen directions are suggested guidelines only and must be adapted to the circumstances of particular cases, their use is intended to 'help to reduce the flow of appeals against conviction' (*Jackson* [1992] Crim LR 214). To this end, where the circumstances or issues in the case required some adaptation of the specimen direction, care should be taken to adapt it appropriately. Specimen directions drafted for one purpose should not be used for a different purpose (for example, it was held in *Taylor* (1994) 98 Cr App R 361 to be wrong to take part of a specimen direction relating to consideration of an accused's bad character for use in relation to the complainant's bad character).

Direction as to the Functions of Judge and Jury At the beginning of the summing-up, the judge ought to remind the jury of their respective roles and hence the different status of the two parts of the summing-up, that part relating to law and that relating to fact (summarising the evidence before them). As regards the law, the judge is the final arbiter (subject to correction in the Court of Appeal) and the jury must therefore accept what he says on the law and apply it to the facts as found by them; as regards the facts, they are the judges (see *Wootton* [1990] Crim LR 201). Therefore, if, in the course of his summing-up, the judge expresses a certain view as to the facts or as to the significance of a piece of evidence but the jury disagree; or he has omitted to mention certain evidence which they consider important; or, conversely, he has stressed something which they consider unimportant — in all such eventualities, it is the *jury's* view which matters. **D17.26**

Burden and Standard of Proof According to *McVey* [1988] Crim LR 127, every summing-up must contain at least a direction to the jury as to the burden and standard of proof, and as to the ingredients of the offence or offences which the jury are called upon to consider. Thus, if the judge fails properly to direct the jury as to the prosecution (a) having the burden of proof and (b) having to discharge that burden beyond reasonable doubt or so that the jury are sure, a conviction is liable to be quashed (see *Donoghue* (1987) 86 Cr App R 267 on the burden of proof and *Edwards* (1983) 77 Cr App R 5 on the standard of proof) (see also F3.38). **D17.27**

In *Bowditch* [1991] Crim LR 831, the Court of Appeal stressed that in cases involving injuries to a small child it was essential that a very clear direction should be given as to the burden of proof. This was to counteract any tendency on the part of the jury, albeit subconsciously, to succumb to their emotions.

Separate Consideration of Counts and Defendants Where there is more than one count on the indictment, the jury should be directed to give separate consideration to each of them (*Lovesey* [1970] 1 QB 352). Similarly, where there is more than one accused on trial, the jury **D17.28**

should be directed to consider the case for and against each separately (*Smith* (1935) 25 Cr App R 119).

Where the allegation against the accused is one of joint enterprise, a direction in accordance with the terms of *Powell and English* [1999] 1 AC 1 will be necessary (see **A5.4** ***et seq.***).

D17.29 **Ingredients of Offence** Appellate decisions reveal a tension between the need for the trial judge to direct the jury as to the ingredients of the offence charged on the one hand, and tailoring such directions to the actual issues in the particular case on the other.

The first of these approaches is exemplified in *McVey* [1988] Crim LR 127, in which the Court of Appeal made clear that it was insufficient for the judge simply to spell out the issue in the case, as the trial judge had in that case. He was required to direct the jury as to the elements of the offence charged. The same approach was adopted in *James* [1997] Crim LR 598, where a conviction for robbery was quashed because the jury had not been directed as to the ingredients of the offence, in particular that the use of force had to be with the intention of stealing.

The second approach was advocated by Diplock LJ in *Mowatt* [1968] 1 QB 421, when he stated that the function of a summing-up was not to give a jury a general dissertation on some aspect of the criminal law, but to isolate the issues for the jury's consideration. Similarly, in *Lawrence* [1982] AC 510, Lord Hailsham of St Marylebone LC remarked (at pp. 519F–520A):

> The purpose of a direction to a jury is not best achieved by a disquisition on jurisprudence or philosophy or a universally applicable circular tour round the area of law affected by the case. The search for universally applicable definitions is often productive of more obscurity than light. . . . A direction to a jury should be custom built to make the jury understand their task in relation to a particular case. Of course it must include references to the burden of proof and the respective roles of jury and judge. But it should also include a succinct but accurate summary of the issues of fact as to which a decision is required, a correct but concise summary of the evidence and arguments on both sides, and a correct statement of the inferences which the jury are entitled to draw from their particular conclusions about the primary facts.

D17.30 **Failure to Answer Questions or Give Evidence** Pursuant to the CJPOA 1994, ss. 34 and 35, the jury are entitled to draw such inferences as they deem appropriate from the failure of the defendant to answer questions in interview (s. 34) or his failure to give evidence (s. 35). Guidance as to the proper form of direction that should be given was provided in *Cowan* [1996] QB 373 and by the Judicial Studies Board Standard direction. No inferences should be drawn from the silence in interview of an accused who does not give or call evidence, and has not advanced a positive case (*Moshaid* [1998] Crim LR 420). Where such inferences should not be drawn, the jury should be specifically directed to that effect (*McGarry* [1999] 1 WLR 1500).

This topic is discussed in more detail at **F19.5** and **F19.14**.

D17.31 **Failure to Call a Witness** One matter which the summing-up ought to avoid dealing with, because of the confusion which it can create in relation to the burden of proof, is the fact that the defence have not called a particular witness or witnesses. In *Wright* [2000] Crim LR 510, the Court of Appeal emphasised the dangers of comment on the failure of the defence to call certain witnesses in the summing-up, since such comments could so easily detract from the realisation that the burden of proof must be upon the prosecution. Such comment has been held to be justified, however, where the prosecution could have had no means of knowing that the witness could have any relevant evidence to give before the defence case (*Gallagher* [1974] 1 WLR 1204) or the witness was one only the defence could have called, such as the accused's solicitor (*Wilmot* (1988) 89 Cr App R 341). See also *Khan* [2001] Crim LR 673.

D17.32 **Other Standard Directions** Other commonly required directions include ones concerning:

(a) the proper approach to circumstantial evidence (see **F1.16** and *Stephens and Clarke* 95/1758/S2);
(b) evidence of lies by the defendant (see **F1.18** for the direction set out in *Lucas* [1981] QB 720, and see also *Burge* [1996] 1 Cr App R 163);
(c) identification evidence (see **F18.19** for the direction set out in *Turnbull* [1977] QB 224), but note that such a direction is not required where the identifying witness retracts his identification (*Davis* [2006] EWCA Crim 2015);
(d) trial in the absence of the accused (see **D14.80**);
(e) the limited admissibility of interviews of co-defendants (see **F17.50** and the decisions in *Rhodes* (1959) 44 Cr App R 23 and *Hayter* [2005] 1 WLR 605) — see also *Knowlden* (1981) 77 Cr App R 94, in relation to the warning that should be given to the jury where one accused gives evidence adverse to another;
(f) pleas of co-accused (see *Dixon* (2001) 164 JP 721: see **D12.69**);
(g) the need for corroboration and care warnings (see **F5.2** for the former and **F5.6**, the CJPOA 1994, s. 32 and *Makanjuola* [1995] 1 WLR 1348, for the latter);
(h) the need for a warning in relation to a witness who may be tainted by improper motives (see *Beck* [1982] 1 WLR 461 and **F5.12**); and
(i) expert evidence (following *Stockwell* (1993) 97 Cr App R 260, the jury should be directed that the jury are not bound to accept expert opinion, see also **F10.14**);
(j) initial remarks to the jury.

Defences

There is an obligation on the trial judge to give the legal directions which apply to the defence advanced on behalf of the accused. Common defences and partial defences to which this applies include: **D17.33**

(a) self-defence (see *Palmer* [1971] AC 814, *Lobell*) [1957] 1 QB 547 and **A3.31**);
(b) alibi (see *Anderson* [1991] Crim LR 361 and **F3.26**) — where an alibi is demonstrated or accepted to be false, a *Lucas*-type direction is appropriate, see *Lesley* [1996] 1 Cr App R 39);
(c) provocation (see *Stewart* [1995] 4 All ER 999 and **B1.22**); and
(d) diminished responsibility (a proper explanation should be given of the terms of the Homicide Act 1957, s. 2: see *Terry* [1961] 2 QB 314 and **A3.12**).

Alternative Defences The jury should not generally be directed on matters which are not issues in the case. Nonetheless, there are occasions when the jury should be directed as to a defence which has not been raised by the evidence or by counsel. The following cases provide examples: **D17.34**

(a) In *Watson* [1992] Crim LR 434, W was charged with buggery, which he denied. The Court of Appeal found that, although the defence of accident had not been raised, there was a duty on the judge to spell out that penetration must have been deliberate (but see *Johnson* [1994] Crim LR 376, where the Court of Appeal concluded to the contrary).
(b) In *Phillips* [1999] All ER (D) 1372, P was charged with unlawful wounding contrary to the OAPA 1861, s. 20. The prosecution case was that P had deliberately attacked the victim with a knife and inflicted wounds upon her by way of retribution. P's case was that the wounding had been accidental. The trial judge summed up on the basis that the defence was accident, mentioning self-defence only to dismiss it. The Court of Appeal held that the judge ought to have left the defence of self-defence to the jury.

The Invisible Burden These cases illustrate what has been described as the 'invisible burden' on the trial judge (S Doran, 'Alternative Defences: the "invisible burden" on the trial judge' [1991] Crim LR 878). This burden arises where a potential defence has not been raised on the accused's behalf, but there is a cogent, rather than speculative, evidential basis for its **D17.35**

consideration (*Bonnick* (1978) 66 Cr App R 266). In such circumstances there is a burden upon the judge to raise such an alternative defence in his summing-up. Circumstances in which this may arise include cases where there is a partial defence to murder, such as provocation (see *Cascoe* [1970] 2 All ER 833 and *Johnson* [1989] 1 WLR 740) and cases where self-defence is lurking in the background (see *Kachikwu* (1965) 52 Cr App R 538).

The Facts

D17.36 In addition to directing the jury on the law, the judge should remind them of and comment upon the evidence. Although in *Attfield* [1961] 1 WLR 1135, it was held that the lack of any summing-up on the facts is not necessarily fatal to a conviction if it is a short and simple case, the Court of Appeal have since made clear that a summary of the evidence is necessary in almost all cases. For example:

(a) In *Brower* [1995] Crim LR 746, it was made clear that in the majority of cases, it was necessary for the judge to sum up on the facts in order to assist the jury and ensure a fair trial. It was incumbent on the judge to define the issues and remind the jury of the evidence they had heard, albeit very recently.
(b) In *Amado-Taylor* [2000] 2 Cr App R 194, it was held to be a procedural irregularity for a judge to sum up without a review of the facts. There were exceptions where this was not required, such as where a case was short and simple. But the closing speeches of counsel were no substitute for a judicial and impartial view of the facts from the trial judge, whose duty it was to focus the attention of the jury upon the issues which he identified.

D17.37 **The Analysis Involved** In simple cases, it will suffice for the judge to sum up the facts by reading out an abbreviated version of his note of the evidence. However, if the trial has been more complex, judges are exhorted to assist the jury by analysing the evidence and relating it to the various issues raised (see *Gregory* [1993] Crim LR 623). Merely reading a note of the evidence in such cases has been criticised, not least because it 'must bore the jury to sleep' (see pp. 339–41 of Lawton LJ's judgment in *Charles* (1976) 68 Cr App R 334).

Similarly, in the passage from Lord Hailsham's speech in *Lawrence* [1982] AC 510 quoted at **D17.29**, reference is made to the desirability of the summing-up including a '*succinct* but accurate summary of the issues of fact as to which a decision is required, a correct but *concise* summary of the evidence and arguments on both sides, and a correct statement of the inferences which the jury are entitled to draw from their particular conclusions about the primary facts' (emphasis added).

D17.38 **Summarising the Defence Case** Crucially, in *Curtin* [1996] Crim LR 831, the Court of Appeal stated that as part of his duty the judge must identify the defence. The way in which he does so will depend on the circumstances of the case, however the following propositions apply:

(a) Where the accused has given evidence, it will be desirable to summarise that evidence.
(b) Where he has given evidence and answered questions in interview, it may be appropriate to draw attention to consistencies and inconsistencies between the two.
(c) When an accused is interviewed at length but does not give evidence, the judge has to decide how, fairly and conveniently, to place the interview before the jury.
(d) When the accused has done neither, it will usually be appropriate to remind the jury of counsel's speech.

On the question whether defence counsel has a duty to draw the judge's attention to a failure to deal adequately with the defence, see **D17.23**.

D17.39 **Judicious Judicial Comment** It is the judge's duty to state matters 'clearly, impartially and logically', and not to indulge in inappropriate sarcasm or extravagant comment (*Berrada* (1989) 91 Cr App R 131). Similarly, in *Marr* (1989) 90 Cr App R 154, the Court of Appeal stressed that observance of the accused's right to have his case presented fairly is never more important than when 'the cards seem to be stacked most heavily against the defendant' (p. 156). Lord Lane CJ added: 'however distasteful the offence, however repulsive the defendant, however laughable his defence, he is nevertheless entitled to have his case fairly presented to the jury both by counsel and by the judge' (p. 156).

However, provided he emphasises that the jury are entitled to ignore his opinions, the judge may comment on the evidence in a way which indicates his own views. Robust comments to the detriment of the defence case are permitted (e.g., *O'Donnell*) (1917) 12 Cr App R 219, in which the judge described the accused's story as a 'remarkable one'), providing the judge is not so critical as effectively to withdraw the issue of guilt or innocence from the jury (*Canny* (1945) 30 Cr App R 143, in which the judge repeatedly told the jury that the defence case was absurd).

Advancing an Alternative Basis for Conviction The question sometimes arises whether the judge is confined, when summarising the case against the accused, to the same basis as that on which the prosecution has put its case. In *Japes* [1994] Crim LR 605, the Court of Appeal said that a judge was not bound by the way in which the Crown opened its case. As the evidence developed, it might become apparent that the offence may have been committed on a somewhat different factual basis. If so, the judge was not debarred from putting that basis before the jury to consider, so long as the accused was not disadvantaged or prejudiced by this course of action (see however *Falconer-Atlee* (1973) 58 Cr App R 348, where the judge was criticised for leaving the case to the jury on a new basis). **D17.40**

Where the judge intends to direct the jury on a new legal basis, it is important that he should give the parties an opportunity to consider and if necessary to argue the point (*Ramzan* [1998] 2 Cr App R 328; see also *Taylor* [1998] Crim LR 582). In appropriate cases, the judge should give the defence the opportunity to call further evidence (*Powell*) [2006] EWCA Crim 685).

Summing-up Amounting to Direction

Application of the principle that the judge should not dictate the jury's verdict through excessively robust comment during his summing-up (see **D17.39**) becomes difficult where the defence case amounts to an admission of guilt. What is clear from the authorities is that the judge must not take the issue of whether the accused is in fact guilty away from the jury. **D17.41**

In *DPP v Stonehouse* [1978] AC 55, one of the issues was whether the admitted facts proved established an attempt to obtain property by deception or merely established acts which were preparatory to such an attempt. Having ruled as a matter of law that the facts proved did constitute an attempt, the judge so directed the jury. The majority of the House of Lords held that, even where any reasonable jury properly directed on the law must upon the facts reach a verdict of guilty, the trial judge should nevertheless leave the issues of fact to them.

That aspect of *Stonehouse* was followed in *Thompson* [1984] 1 WLR 962, a case which turned upon the jurisdiction of the English courts to try an offence of obtaining by deception where the defence argued that the property had been obtained abroad. Having ruled against the defence submissions, the judge in effect directed the jury to convict by telling them that there 'could not be room for any doubt at all' about the elements of the offence being made out, and that he (the judge) had already ruled that the offence was within the jurisdiction of the court. The Court of Appeal held that the judge's direction amounted to an irregularity in the course of the trial.

In *Wang* [2005] 1 WLR 661, the House of Lords considered a number of authorities on the certified question of law: 'In what circumstances, if any, is a judge entitled to direct a jury to return a verdict of guilty?' Their lordships concluded unanimously that there were no such circumstances. There was no distinction to be drawn between cases in which a burden lay on the defence (as it did in the instant case), and those in which the burden lay solely on the Crown. No matter how inescapable a judge might consider a conclusion to be, in the sense that any other conclusion would be perverse, it remained his duty to leave the decision to the jury, and not to dictate what the verdict should be.

The decision in *Wang* was applied in *Caley-Knowles* [2006] 1 WLR 3181, to two cases in which judges had directed the jury to convict. In each case the judge, in doing so, had made clear that he was taking the matter out of the hands of the jury. The Court of Appeal emphasised that it would be a significant misdirection and material irregularity for the decision to be taken away from the jury in that way. However, providing it is clear at all times that the verdict is the sole province of the jury, comment from the judge short of a direction to convict was permissible.

Appointment of a Foreman

D17.42 At the end of the summing-up, the judge should advise the jury to appoint one of their number to be their foreman. The foreman will act as their spokesman and, in due course, announce their verdict.

Unanimity

D17.43 Finally, the judge should invite the jury to retire and to seek to reach a unanimous decision. The *Consolidated Criminal Practice Direction*, para. IV.46.1 (see **D18.34** ***et seq.***), instructs judges that they 'should' direct the jury on unanimous verdicts, and the Specimen Direction from the Judicial Studies Board makes it clear that it is desirable that this should always be done. However, a failure on the part of the judge to give the jury the direction that their verdicts must be unanimous will not necessarily render a conviction unsafe (*Georgiou* (1969) 53 Cr App R 428, see also *Daly* [1999] Crim LR 88).

At the close of his summing-up, it is conventional for the judge to anticipate jury questions about the possibility of a majority verdict by telling them that, at this stage, they should try to reach a unanimous verdict. If the time should come when he can accept a verdict which is not the verdict of them all, he will give them a further direction. The judge should not, however, indicate the precise period which must elapse before a majority verdict becomes a possibility (*Thomas* [1983] Crim LR 745). If he does so, it will not necessarily be improper, e.g., where the effect is to alleviate anxiety or uncertainty which the jury may be feeling (*Guthrie* (1994) *The Times*, 23 February 1994 and *Porter* [1996] Crim LR 126). For the appropriate directions to be given in relation to majority verdicts and verdicts of guilt as to an alternative offence, see **D18**.

D17.44 **Unanimity as to the Basis of a Guilty Verdict** Where the prosecution have put their case on more than one basis, it may be necessary to tell the jury that, in order to convict, they must be unanimous not only as to the accused being guilty but also as to the basis on which he is guilty. For example, in *Brown* (1983) 79 Cr App R 115, the prosecution alleged the obtaining of property by the use of two different deceptions by B. The Court of Appeal held that the jury should have been directed that, if they were not unanimous that B used both deceptions, they should at least all agree as to which one he used.

In *Mitchell* [1994] Crim LR 66, the Court of Appeal stated that the following principles were to be derived from the cases:

(a) Where several matters were set out in a single count, the judge must consider whether to give the jury a direction that they must all be agreed on the particular ingredient which they rely on to find the accused guilty (*Brown*).

(b) Such a direction will be necessary only comparatively rarely. In the great majority of cases (particularly where dishonesty is alleged and where the allegations stand or fall together), it will be unnecessary and may serve only to confuse the jury (*Price* [1991] Crim LR 465 and *More* (1988) 86 Cr App R 234).

(c) In an appropriate case, where there was a realistic danger that the jury might return a verdict of guilty on the basis that some of them found one ingredient proved and others found another ingredient proved, a direction should be given that they must be unanimous as to the proof of the ingredient which demonstrated that offence.

Limitations to this Principle The Court of Appeal have sought to limit the need for a direction that the jury should be unanimous as to the ingredients that should be proved in a number of cases, examples of which are mentioned below: **D17.45**

(a) In *Jones* (1999) *The Times*, 17 February 1999, the Court of Appeal held that the considerations in *Brown* did not have any application to the circumstances where a verdict of manslaughter was returned as an alternative to murder. Provided a jury were agreed that an accused was guilty of manslaughter, in the sense that they were sure that he perpetrated an unlawful act which caused the death of the deceased, there was no need for unanimity as to the basis of that verdict (see **B1.32**).

(b) In *Giannetto* [1997] 1 Cr App R 1, the Court of Appeal stated that there were two cardinal principles involved in the proposition that a jury must find each essential element in an offence proved. First, the jury must be agreed upon the basis on which they found an accused guilty. Second, an accused must know what case he had to meet. Where the Crown alleged that on the evidence the accused must have committed the offence either as principal or as secondary offender, and made it equally clear that they could not say which, the basis on which the jury had to be unanimous was that the accused, having the necessary *mens rea*, by whatever means caused the result which was criminalised by the law (see *Smith* [1997] 1 Cr App R 14, about the application of these principles to an offence of affray).

(c) In *D* [2001] 1 Cr App R 194, D was charged with indecent assaults on his daughter allegedly committed over a three-year period, in some instances in a variety of ways. The Court of Appeal held that where a number of different matters were set out in a single count, the judge should consider whether the jury should be given a direction that they should all be agreed upon the particular ingredient upon which they relied in order to find the accused guilty of the offence charged. Circumstances requiring such a direction would be rare but where there was a realistic danger that the jury might not appreciate that they must all be agreed on the particular ingredient on which they relied to find their guilty verdict, a direction must be given that they should be unanimous as to the proof of that ingredient (see also *Carr* [2000] 2 Cr App R 149, *Boreman* [2000] Crim LR 409 and *Turner* [2000] Crim LR 325).

Section D18 Trial on Indictment: Procedure Relating to Retirement of the Jury and Verdict

D18.1 This chapter addresses the practices and procedures that are engaged with the retirement of the jury to consider its verdict. It also considers the different forms of verdict that can be reached, the directions appropriate to them, and the consequences where the jury conclude that no verdict can be reached.

RETIREMENT OF THE JURY

Basic Rules

D18.2 The principle that governs the keeping of the jury during the period between the close of the judge's summing-up and their returning to court to announce their verdict was succinctly stated by James LJ in *Alexander* [1974] 1 WLR 422 at p. 426H: '. . . once the jury retires to consider their verdict it should not separate, one from another and from the jury bailiffs. They must remain in the charge of the court through the bailiffs throughout.' The purpose of this is to ensure that nobody interferes with the jury while they are considering their verdict.

The Need to Retire

D18.3 In *Rankine* [1997] Crim LR 757, the Court of Appeal considered whether the judge was permitted to ask a jury if they wished to consider their verdict without retiring. Their lordships held that there was nothing in the decided cases to render such an invitation wrong as a matter of course, but stressed the danger that the jury might feel under pressure, and said that such a course would be appropriate only in rare circumstances.

Timing of Retirement

D18.4 If the summing-up concludes late in the day, the jury should not begin to consider their verdict until the following day. For example, in *Birch* (1992) *The Times*, 27 March 1992, the Court of Appeal said that, in a serious case, especially one involving more than one defendant and a number of verdicts, it was undesirable that a jury should be sent out after 3 p.m. unless there were exceptional circumstances. However, see *Buttle* [2006] EWCA Crim 246, where it was held proper for a jury to retire to consider its verdict on a Friday afternoon where there was a reasonable prospect of their reaching a verdict that day.

The decision as to whether the jury should retire late in the afternoon, or wait until the next morning, is one which the judge should take, and he should not leave it up to the jury to decide (*Hawkins* (1994) 98 Cr App R 228). See also *Akano* (1992) *The Times*, 3 April 1992, where retirements continuing until late in the evening were disapproved.

Custody of the Jury Bailiff

D18.5 Immediately before the jury retire, one or more court ushers takes an oath to escort the jurors to some 'private and convenient place' where [he] will not 'suffer anybody to speak to them about the trial this day, nor will he speak to them [himself] without leave of the court, except if it be to ask them if they are agreed upon their verdict'. An usher who has so sworn is thereafter referred to as a 'jury bailiff'.

At all times during their retirement the jury must be in the custody of a jury bailiff in the sense that the bailiff must be near enough to the room where they are to ensure that no non-juror enters the room or otherwise communicates with them.

Communication with the Jury Once the bailiff has escorted the jury to their room, he must not enter it 'unless he is expressly ordered by the court to make a communication to, or enquiry of, the jury, and except in special circumstances and at the express order of the court no other persons should have any communication with the jury' (see para. 4(29)(i) of the Court Manual issued by the Lord Chancellor's office on the creation of the Crown Court). **D18.6**

This wording was adopted by James LJ in his judgment in *Lamb* (1974) 59 Cr App R 196, where the clerk of court had entered the jury room, with the jury bailiff, to tell the jury that they should continue to seek unanimity, they having sent a message via the bailiff asking if they could return a majority verdict. The Court of Appeal held this to have been a material irregularity, there being no special circumstances such as might have justified it. It was further stated that: 'If it be the practice in any Crown Court for directions of this kind between judge and jury to be communicated through the medium of court officers, that practice should cease'.

Similarly, in *Davis (No. 2)* (1960) 44 Cr App R 235, the introduction of a shorthand writer into the jury room and, in *Rose* [1982] 1 WLR 614, the clerk entering the jury room to deliver a message from the judge indicating how much longer the latter was prepared to give them to reach a verdict, were both material irregularities. The correct procedure for answering jury questions has been laid down by the Court of Appeal in, *inter alia*, *Lamb*, and is considered at **D18.18**.

The jury bailiffs are themselves strictly limited in the communication which they can make with the jury. In *Brown* (1989) *The Times*, 25 October 1989, it was stressed that their fundamental duty was to prevent approaches by outsiders and preserve the integrity of the deliberative process. It followed that there was no impropriety, where a juror had indicated to the bailiff that he and his fellow jurors were intimidated by the atmosphere in court, in the bailiff asking him why. The bailiff had then reported the answer to the trial judge, who had addressed the jury as to their duty.

Consequences of a Lapse of Custody If the jury leave the custody of the jury bailiff, it constitutes a material irregularity in the course of the trial which will almost certainly necessitate the quashing of any conviction. **D18.7**

(a) In *Neal* [1949] 2 KB 590, the jury (with the judge's permission) left the court building in order to buy lunch at a restaurant. The conviction was quashed because, even assuming the circumstances justified the judge in allowing the jury to leave the court precincts, it was essential that the bailiff went with them. In his absence, there was no way of knowing who might have spoken to them about the case. It should be noted that the Juries Act 1974, s. 15, now permits the jury to purchase reasonable refreshment at their own expense during the course of their retirement.
(b) In *Ketteridge* [1915] 1 KB 467, where one of the jurors by mistake did not go to the jury room on retirement but left the court and was on his own for some 15 minutes before rejoining his colleagues, there was a breach both of the rule that the jury must not separate (see **D18.8**) and of the rule that the jurors must remain in a bailiff's custody.

Separation of Jury after Retirement By the Juries Act 1974, s. 13, the judge may permit the jury to separate, even after they have retired to consider their verdict. In *Oliver* [1996] 2 Cr App R 514, the Court of Appeal considered the directions which the judge ought to give the **D18.8**

jury when allowing them to separate during consideration of their verdict, and stated that the jury ought to be told:

(a) to decide the case on the evidence and the arguments seen and heard in court, and not on anything seen or heard outside the court;
(b) that the evidence had been completed and it would be wrong for any juror to seek or receive further evidence or information of any sort about the case;
(c) not to talk to anyone about the case save to the other members of the jury and then only when they were deliberating in the jury room;
(d) not to allow anyone to talk to them about the case unless that person was a juror and he or she was in the jury room deliberating about the case; and
(e) on leaving the court, to set the case on one side until they retired to the jury room to continue the process of deliberating about their verdict.

Their lordships added that it was not necessary for the judge to use any precise form of words provided the above points were properly covered. It would be desirable for the direction to be given in full on the first dispersal by the jury, and for a brief reminder to be given at each subsequent dispersal. Further directions might be necessary in particular circumstances.

In *Edwards* [2004] All ER (D) 324 (Nov), the Court of Appeal made it clear that a failure by the judge to direct a jury not to discuss the case with anyone or any outsider did not make a subsequent conviction unsafe. The whole of the circumstances had to be considered, including the absence of any suggestion that any such discussion had taken place, and the strength of the evidence against the defendant.

D18.9 **Keeping the Jury in a Hotel** Rather than allowing the jury to separate and go home at the end of a court day, in appropriate cases arrangements can be made to keep them at a hotel overnight. When this happens, the judge should direct the jury, before they leave court, that their deliberations should not continue at the hotel, but should await their return to court the next day (*Tharakan* [1995] 2 Cr App R 368).

D18.10 **The 'Evident Necessity' Exception** Lord Goddard CJ in *Neal* [1949] 2 KB 590, stated that, by way of exception to the rule that the jury must not separate other than with the permission of the judge, a juror could separate himself from the rest in a case of 'evident necessity'. The examples he gave of 'evident necessity' were if the juror required medical attention or wished to relieve himself. It is submitted that the juror must remain in the custody of a jury bailiff throughout the period that he is absent from the jury room.

D18.11 **Consequences of Improper Separation** The consequences of improper separation of the jury depend upon the extent to which the rule is breached. This is illustrated by a comparison of the Court of Appeal's decisions in *Alexander* [1974] 1 WLR 422, on the one hand, and *Ketteridge* [1915] 1 KB 467 and *Goodson* [1975] 1 WLR 549, on the other.

In *Alexander*, just after the jury had retired, one of them returned by himself to court in order to collect the exhibits. Although the judge had by then risen, defence counsel was still in court, and he told the juror to return to the jury room. Upon the judge being informed what had occurred, the jury were brought back to court; the facts of the incident were confirmed, and they were simply given the exhibits they wanted. James LJ acknowledged that this constituted a procedural irregularity. However, it was so trivial that it did not even amount to a *material* irregularity and there was no possible prejudice to the accused (see also *Farooq* [1995] Crim LR 169).

In *Ketteridge* the separation was for a much more substantial period and the separated juror had been out of the control of the court; the conviction was quashed. Similarly, in *Goodson* [1975] 1 WLR 549, a juror was allowed by the bailiff to leave the jury room and speak to unidentified persons on the telephone. He was prevented from returning to the jury room and discharged. On appeal, it was held that what occurred was a material irregularity which had deprived the appellant of a potential voice in the jury room. The Court of Appeal did not rule on whether the judge had the power to discharge a juror even after the jury have retired (see also *Chandler* [1993] Crim LR 394).

Prohibition of Further Evidence Once Jury Enclosed

It is an absolute rule, subject to no exceptions, that once the jury have retired to consider their verdict no further evidence may be adduced before them. This was the conclusion of the Court of Appeal in *Owen* [1952] 2 QB 362, in which Lord Goddard CJ stated the law thus (at p. 369): **D18.12**

> . . . we think it right to lay down that once the summing-up is concluded, no further evidence ought to be given. The jury can be instructed in reply to any question they may put on any matter on which evidence has been given, but no further evidence should be allowed.

Even where a pertinent request for further evidence is made, the jury 'ought to have been told that the prosecution had laid before them such evidence as they had thought fit and the evidence could not now be reopened' (p. 369).

However, this prohibition only starts once the jury have actually retired. This was made clear in *Sanderson* [1953] 1 WLR 392, where the defence were allowed to call a witness who arrived while the judge was addressing the jury. In a case such as *Sanderson*, however, where evidence is available at the moment the judge finishes his remarks and before the jury have actually retired, there would seem to be no rule of law preventing further evidence, provided it is adduced before the jury retire, and subject to the judge's discretion.

Breach of the Prohibition Although the prohibition on the receipt of fresh evidence after the jury has retired is absolute, its breach will not invariably lead to the discharge of the jury. In *Kaul* [1998] Crim LR 135, the Court of Appeal observed that, although the introduction of fresh evidence after a jury had retired should almost invariably lead to the discharge of that jury, in certain circumstances the defence might properly invite the judge to continue with the trial. Where defence counsel took that risk, it did not necessarily bar the way to an appeal on the basis of the irregularity. **D18.13**

The Extent of the Prohibition The prohibition on evidence after retirement applies to documents as it does to oral evidence. For example: **D18.14**

(a) In *Davis* (1975) 62 Cr App R 194, it was a material irregularity for the jury to be supplied, inadvertently, with a copy of a police statement from a witness which had not been exhibited although it had been used by defence counsel in cross-examination. In *Hulme* (2007) 1 Cr App R 334, it had been an error to allow the jury to retire with a previous inconsistent statement from a hostile witness, even where it had been admitted in evidence pursuant to the CJA 2003, s. 119.

(b) In *Thomas* (3 February 1987 unreported) it was held to have been quite wrong to have provided the jury with a map during their retirement, no map having been exhibited in evidence.

Furthermore, if the jury asks to be supplied with tools or measuring equipment, great care must be taken to ensure that their intention is not to conduct a private experiment germane to the issues in the case. In *Stewart* (1989) 89 Cr App R 273, the Court of Appeal held that the trial judge had erred in permitting the jury, at their request but without asking them why, to have a pair of scales. The case was one in which the weight of a quantity of drugs allegedly concealed in a holdall was highly relevant. The court went on to warn against providing the jury with a ruler or magnifying glass should they request one after retirement. In *Maggs* (1990) 91 Cr App R 243, however, Lord Lane CJ said that the observations in *Stewart* about the supply of a ruler or magnifying glass were too wide. Equipment that was required or designed to enable a jury to carry out unsupervised scientific experiments, such as the scales in *Stewart*, were not permissible, but a magnifying glass or a ruler or a tape-measure were the kind of objects which any person might normally have in his pocket when called to serve on a jury. There could be no objection to his using them in the jury room (see also *Crees* [1996] Crim LR 830).

In *Wallace* [1990] Crim LR 433, the usher supplied the jury in retirement with a dictionary, at their request, but without informing the judge. The jury had not understood what the judge had said about 'grievous' in 'grievous bodily harm'. After seeing the dictionary, they requested further guidance from the judge. The Court of Appeal held that it was an irregularity but not, in the circumstances, a material irregularity such as to lead to the quashing of the convictions.

In *McNamara* [1996] Crim LR 750, the Court of Appeal held that a request from the jury that the accused stand up in the dock and turn around (presumably so that they could perform a dock identification by comparison with video films seen during the trial) should have been treated as a request for further evidence, and was thus impermissible.

D18.15 **Jury's Own Specialist Knowledge or Researches** In *Fricker* (1999) *The Times*, 13 July 1999, the prohibition on new evidence after the jury's retirement was applied to specialist knowledge in the possession of one of the jurors. F was charged with attempting to handle stolen goods, namely certain tyres. After the jury had retired, they sent the judge a note, which stated that one of their number knew from specialist experience that there was very little time for this particular type of tyre to have gone through the normal purchase procedure before being acquired by the accused. The Court of Appeal held that the trial judge had been wrong to rule that the jury had been entitled to take such specialist knowledge into account. It represented entirely new evidence, which neither party had had an opportunity to test. In these circumstances, it would have been appropriate to discharge the jury.

In *Marshall* [2007] EWCA Crim 35, evidence was found in the jury room, at the conclusion of the trial, which showed that at least one of the jurors had carried out research on the Internet into the offences charged and the possible sentences they might attract. The Court of Appeal found this to be an irregularity but not, on the facts, a material one. However, Hughes LJ did observe (at [15]):

> . . . the case underlines the importance of the direction which is conventionally given to jurors at the outset of the trial (and was given to this jury) to the general effect that the golden rule which they must apply is to try the case on the evidence alone which is what they hear in court and nothing else. That can, without drawing attention to any particular risks, conveniently be given in a form which reminds them first of the general rule, secondly of its application in a prohibition on discussion of the case with family, friends or anybody else, and quite often conveniently also with a reminder that private research, whether in the library or on the Internet, should be abjured.

Repetition of Existing Evidence

D18.16 It is, of course, only new evidence which the jury may not have after retirement. The jury may be provided with items that have been exhibited in court. If the jury, after retirement, asks for any exhibits, the matter should be dealt with in open court. Counsel should be given an opportunity to ensure that the exhibits can properly go before the jury (*Ellis* (1991) 95 Cr App R 52; and see also *Devichand* [1991] Crim LR 446).

D18.17 **Application of this Rule to Tape Recordings** In *Emmerson* (1991) 92 Cr App R 284, complaint was made on appeal that the trial judge had refused to provide the jury with the tape of E's interviews, which had been played at trial. The Court of Appeal held that the tape was evidence, becoming an exhibit on production by the officer, regardless of whether it was played during the trial. In *Riaz* (1991) 94 Cr App R 339, it was suggested that, if the jury ask to hear an exhibited tape, the better practice would be for the judge to order the court to reassemble, so that the jury could hear it in open court. The dictum to the contrary in *Emmerson* was disapproved. (For further detail on jury requests for tapes, see **F8.42**.)

Questions from the Jury

The jury are permitted to ask questions of the judge during their retirement. The normal method of so doing is to pass a note to the jury bailiff who takes it to the judge. The procedure to be adopted in answering such questions was set out in *Gorman* [1987] 1 WLR 545. The object of the procedures is: (a) to remove any suspicion of private or secret communication between the court and jury, and (b) to enable the judge to assist the jury properly on any matter of law or fact which appears to be troubling them (per Lord Lane CJ at p. 546C; for the facts, see **D13.24**). **D18.18**

Lord Lane set out three propositions to assist judges who receive a note from a jury who have retired to consider their verdict (at pp. 550H–551B):

> First of all, if the communication raises something unconnected with the trial, for example a request that some message be sent to a relative of one of the jurors, it can simply be dealt with without any reference to counsel and without bringing the jury back to court. [See *Connor* (1985) *The Times*, 26 June 1985 where that very situation seems to have arisen.]
>
> Secondly, in almost every other case a judge should state in open court the nature and content of the communication which he has received from the jury and, if he considers it helpful so to do, seek the assistance of counsel. This assistance will normally be sought before the jury is asked to return to court, and then, when the jury returns, the judge will deal with their communication.
>
> Exceptionally if, as in the present case, the communication from the jury contains information which the jury need not, and indeed should not, have imparted, such as details of voting figures . . . then, so far as possible the communication should be dealt with in the normal way, save that the judge should not disclose the detailed information which the jury ought not to have revealed.

Notes Not Relating to the Trial As to the first proposition, the implication is that, since the jury's note does not concern the trial itself, it need not even be read in open court. Presumably any answer which needs to be given may be conveyed via the jury bailiff. However, to avoid any possible complaint, it is as well to inform defence counsel of what has occurred (see *Connor* (1985) *The Times*, 26 June 1985, and *Brown* [1998] Crim LR 505). **D18.19**

Notes Relating to the Trial Requiring notes connected with the trial to be read in open court, reflects a consistent line of authority going back to *Green* [1950] 1 All ER 38, in which Lord Goddard CJ said: '. . . any communication between a jury and the presiding judge must be read out in court, so that both parties, the prosecution and the defence, may know what the jury are asking and what is the judge's answer' (see also *Furlong* [1950] 1 All ER 636, *Townsend* [1982] 1 All ER 509 and *Rose* [1982] 1 WLR 614). In *Kachikwu* (1968) 52 Cr App R 538 at p. 541, it was further said by Winn LJ that, whenever a jury note is received, immediate steps should be taken to show it to counsel before it is put in the court archives. Whether to ask counsel for assistance about how the note should be answered is within the judge's discretion. **D18.20**

Answering such a Note In *Gorman* [1987] 1 WLR 545 (see **D18.18**), Lord Lane appears to contemplate that, however simple the answer might be, the jury should return to court to be given the answer. Earlier authorities indicate, however, that this is a matter for the judge's discretion, and that there is no objection in principle to an answer being communicated by a note taken in by the jury bailiff, provided he reads out in open court both the jury's note and the answer he is giving. Thus, in *Lamb* (1974) 59 Cr App R 196, James LJ said (at p. 199): **D18.21**

> The practice should be that, on the court being informed by the jury bailiff of the jury's wish to make a request of the court or to communicate something to the court, the request or communication should either be delivered in writing to the court and the contents and any reply

to be delivered through the bailiff, made known in public in court before delivery, or, the jury should be brought back into court to make the request themselves and the judge should answer their request in court.

D18.22 **Answering Only the Question Asked** The jury's usual aim in asking a question of the judge will be to seek assistance on a matter which is troubling them. As *Gascoigne* [1988] Crim LR 317 shows, the judge's response should be within strict limits, particularly as far as any new issue is concerned. In that case the judge, in answering a jury note, proceeded spontaneously to give a direction as to an issue which the prosecution had never raised. The Court of Appeal observed that it would seldom be proper for a trial judge to open up spontaneously with a jury, after they had deliberated for some time, an issue which had not been referred to in the trial or the summing-up.

It might be proper to give a supplementary direction, where a matter canvassed at trial had accidentally been omitted from the summing-up. If this were done, it must be carried out with the utmost caution. It was very much more difficult to envisage any occasion where an entirely new basis for conviction should be volunteered at such a late stage. If, in a very exceptional case, such a direction were to be volunteered, counsel must be given an opportunity to make submissions.

D18.23 **Exceptions to this Requirement** There are two exceptions to the rule that the judge should only answer the question which the jury has asked.

(1) Where the jury's question reveals that they have forgotten or failed to understand a crucial point, it is incumbent on the judge to remind them of it. In *Wickramaratne* [1998] Crim LR 565, it was apparent from the jury's question that they had failed to take the standard direction on the burden of proof on board. The Court of Appeal said that the trial judge should have reminded the jury in forcible terms of that important direction.

(2) Where the jury's question indicates that they are considering an irrelevant matter. The following cases provide examples:
   (a) Where the jury ask the judge if they are allowed to recommend leniency, the Court of Appeal have held that the judge must tell them that they must try the case on the evidence according to their oath and leave questions of penalty to the judge (*Sahota* [1979] Crim LR 678 and *Langham* [1996] Crim LR 430). The reason for this is that the jury might have been influenced by the fact that they could add a rider recommending leniency to come to a verdict which they might not otherwise have done.
   (b) In *Thanki* (1991) 93 Cr App R 12, a note from the jury indicated that they suspected a diary, on which T relied, to be concocted. This had never been suggested by the prosecution. The court held that the accused should have been given an opportunity to meet this line of reasoning (presumably by means other than the production of evidence, in view of the prohibition on new evidence after the jury retires: see D18.12).

D18.24 **Notes Recording Voting Numbers** Lord Lane's third proposition arose directly out of the ground of appeal in *Gorman* [1987] 1 WLR 545. The jury at G's first trial were discharged from giving a verdict after sending a note to the judge indicating that they were 'voting' 9–3 for an acquittal but that the minority were 'adamant and would not change'. The judge simply told counsel that he had received a note that the jury were split, there was no prospect of them reaching a verdict, and, with counsels' agreement, the jury was discharged. The Court of Appeal concluded that there had been no irregularity in not revealing the content of the note, since the proportions in which the jury are split should not be revealed in open court, and the general rule that a jury note should be read out must therefore be qualified. In such circumstances, a judge should do as the judge did in *Gorman*, namely, give the gist of the note (i.e. the jury are split and unlikely to agree even if given more time) but keep secret that which the jury ought not to have communicated.

The Status of a Jury Note A note from any juror is taken to be a note from the jury as a whole, and it was not appropriate to make enquiries as to which juror had written a particular note. This was stressed in *Obellim* [1997] 1 Cr App R 355. In that case a question from the jury caused the judge to suspect that its author might have previous convictions. The judge, without seeking the views of defence counsel, instigated enquiries into the identity of the juror in question, with a view to ascertaining whether he should have been disqualified from jury service. The Court of Appeal said that the only proper check the judge should have made was as to whether the proper enquiries had been made before the juror was called to jury service, and defence counsel should have been informed before even that check. **D18.25**

Consequences of Breach of the *Gorman* Procedure The consequences of failing to observe the procedures described above depend upon the gravity of the breach. It will only represent a material irregularity if it 'goes to the root of the case'. This is illustrated by a comparison of the Court of Appeal's decisions in *Green* [1950] 1 All ER 38 and *Furlong* [1950] 1 All ER 636. **D18.26**

(a) In *Green*, the jury's question and the judge's answer were never read in court at any stage and the judge could not even remember what the question had been about. This was a material irregularity.
(b) In *Furlong* the respective communications were publicly read, albeit after the verdict, and the answer the judge had given was clearly correct. No such irregularity was found.

Investigation of the Jury's Retirement

What occurs in the jury room during the course of the jury's deliberations is absolutely privileged, which is reinforced by the fact that the Contempt of Court Act 1981, s. 8, makes it an offence to disclose, obtain, publish etc. information about what took place in the jury room (see **B14.93**). It follows that alleged irregularities in the way the jury reached their verdict cannot be a ground of appeal. **D18.27**

Enquiries Covered by the Prohibition In *Miah* [1997] 2 Cr App R 12, it was emphasised that the barrier to the Court of Appeal receiving material relating to the jury's deliberations was to be found in the common-law authorities (including *Ellis v Deheer* [1922] 2 KB 113 at p. 121) rather than in the Contempt of Court Act 1981. **D18.28**

A striking example is provided by *Thompson* [1962] 1 All ER 65, where the proposed ground of appeal was that the jury foreman had read to his colleagues a list of T's previous convictions which had somehow come into his possession. The Court of Criminal Appeal simply refused leave for the evidence of the irregularity to be adduced before them, because it would have breached the privacy of the jury room. The case thus demonstrates the absolute nature of the rule that the Court of Appeal will not, metaphorically speaking, enter the jury room (see also *Scholfield* [1993] Crim LR 217).

The decision in *Box* [1964] 1 QB 430, where the complaint also related to a juror's prior knowledge of the accused's character, demonstrates that if the bias can be established without calling evidence of the juror's conduct in the jury room, the appeal is not invalid *ab initio* (see also **D13.44** and **F9.13**).

The prohibition applies to attempts to obtain information about proceedings in the jury room by the defence (*Mickleburgh* [1995] 1 Cr App R 297), the prosecution (*McCluskey* (1994) 98 Cr App R 216), or the court (*Schot* [1997] 2 Cr App R 383). Enquiries may be embarked upon only with the consent of the court, which, as the trial judge is *functus officio* after sentence, means the Court of Appeal (*McCluskey*).

D
Part D Procedure

D18.29 **Enquiries Outside the Prohibition** The prohibition does not extend to events outside the jury room, for example, in the hotel at which a jury is accommodated overnight. For example, in *Young* [1995] QB 324, some of the jurors met in a group and sought the assistance of a ouija board as to the guilt of the accused. The Court of Appeal held that it could enquire into the incident, as it was not in the course of the jury's deliberation.

The Proper Approach to an Investigation

D18.30 The issues surrounding the confidentiality of jury deliberations has been considered in detail by the House of Lords in two recent cases: *Mirza* [2004] 1 AC 1118, and *Smith and Mercieca* [2005] 1 WLR 704.

D18.31 **The Approach in *Mirza*** Their lordships considered two conjoined cases in which letters after the trial indicated irregularities in the jury's deliberations. The Court of Appeal had dismissed both appeals on the basis that evidence as to what had been said by the jurors in private was inadmissible and contravened the Contempt of Court Act 1981, s. 8. Their lordships came to the following conclusions.

(a) The common-law principle prohibiting intrinsic evidence of jury deliberations was in accordance with the ECHR, Article 6. In so doing, they looked at the rationale for the rule of confidentiality, and concluded that it underpinned the independence and impartiality of the jury as a whole.
(b) Consequently, confidentiality reinforced the values in Article 6, and provided essential assistance for the jury to operate as a collective body impartially, and independently of outside influences.
(c) Section 8 of the Contempt of Court Act 1981 did not affect the duty of the trial court and the Court of Appeal to investigate any irregularity in the conduct of the jury within the limits of the common law so as to ensure that the accused received a fair trial.

Their lordships went on to advise that certain measures should be taken to strengthen the jury system. Jurors should be told to inform the court clerk or the judge in writing (either individually or collectively) if anything improper came to their notice. They should be reminded that what was said during their deliberations was confidential to them and could not be repeated or discussed outside the jury room. Their duty of confidentiality continued after the verdict. The *Consolidated Criminal Practice Direction* has been amended as a result (see para. IV.42 at **appendix** 7).

D18.32 **The Approach in *Smith* and *Mercieca*** After the jury had retired and considered its verdict over some period of time, one of its members alleged in some detail that some jurors were disregarding the judge's directions on the law, were indulging in speculation contrary to his instructions and were engaging in a process of horse-trading, whereby some jurors were being pressed to return a guilty verdict on some counts in return for acquittal on others. The judge, with the agreement of counsel, gave the jury a further direction.

On appeal, it was suggested, *inter alia*, that the judge should have carried out an investigation into the alleged irregularities in the jury room. The Court of Appeal (prior to the judgment of the House of Lords in *Mirza* [2004] 1 AC 1118) held that he was precluded from doing so by the Contempt of Court Act 1981, s. 8(1). As a result, the judge was faced with the alternative of discharging the jury or giving a further direction, and could not be criticised for choosing the latter course, particularly since counsel had agreed to it.

On appeal to the House of Lords, it was held that the judge was not obliged as a matter of law in these circumstances to investigate events in the jury room. The common-law prohibition against enquiring into such events certainly extended to matters connected with the subject-matter of the jury's deliberations, and nothing in the opinions in *Mirza* cast doubt upon that basic proposition. Further, their lordships were of the opinion that it would not have been appropriate for the judge to question the jurors about the content of the letter, given that such a course of action would have been likely to make the situation worse. The judge was left with a choice of discharging the jury or giving them a further direction emphasising their duties. He was entitled to adopt the latter course, providing that the direction given was sufficiently comprehensive and emphatic.

Relationship of Jury Room Restrictions to Freedom of Expression

In *A-G v Scotcher* [2005] 1 WLR 1867, the appellant was prosecuted under the Contempt of Court Act 1981, s. 8(1). He had served on a jury which convicted the defendants by a majority. The day after the end of the trial, he wrote to their mother informing her of the discussions which had taken place in the jury room, which he felt would show that the verdict was unsafe. **D18.33**

The Divisional Court held that it was not a defence for a juror to show that he had disclosed the jury's deliberations with the bona fide aim of preventing a miscarriage of justice. He appealed to the House of Lords, which dismissed his appeal holding that he had been in contempt of court in writing to a third party but he would have been entitled to communicate with the Crown Court, the jury bailiff or the clerk of the court, or to have raised the matter directly with the Court of Appeal. Although the appellant's right to freedom of expression under the ECHR, Article 10(1), had been engaged, it was subject to a restriction which was prescribed by law and necessary in a democratic society for preventing the disclosure of information received in confidence. The rule governing the secrecy of jury deliberations was a crucial and legitimate feature of English trial law, with the result that the limitation placed on the juror's freedom of expression was justified.

TYPES OF VERDICT

Before considering the method by which the jury returns its verdict, it is necessary to consider the different types of verdict available to them. As was made clear at **D17.43**, the *Consolidated Criminal Practice Direction*, para. IV.46.1 (see **appendix 7**), instructs judges that they 'should' direct the jury on unanimous verdicts. In circumstances identified below, a jury may return a verdict that represents the view only of the majority (see **D18.35**), or return a verdict in relation to an offence in the alternative to the one charged (see **D18.41**). **D18.34**

MAJORITY VERDICTS

At common law, the verdict of a jury had to be unanimous. This was qualified by what is now the Juries Act 1974, s. 17 (set out at the end of **D18.40**). By s. 17(1) some majority verdicts are permissible, subject to certain conditions being satisfied. The procedure for taking majority verdicts is set out in the *Consolidated Criminal Practice Direction*, para. IV.46 (see **appendix 7**). **D18.35**

Time Requirement

A majority verdict may not be accepted unless the jury have been considering their verdict for such period as the court considers reasonable having regard to the nature and complexity of the case, being in any event a period of not less than two hours (Juries Act 1974, s. 17(4)). Any period during which the jury return to court to ask a question of or receive a communication from the judge should be included when computing the two hours (*Adams* [1969] 1 WLR 106). **D18.36**

Time spent not actually deliberating, for example in making their way to the jury room and electing a foreman, is catered for by the *Consolidated Criminal Practice Direction*, para. IV.46.3 (see **appendix** 7), which states that the jury should be allowed at least two hours and ten minutes for deliberation before the majority direction is given.

D18.37 **Application of the Time Requirement** It is unusual for judges to invite a majority verdict at the earliest moment permitted by the statute and practice direction. However, the time allowed before the majority verdict procedure is set in motion is a matter for the trial judge's discretion, depending largely on the complexity of the case. This is demonstrated by cases such as the following.

In *Wright* (1974) 58 Cr App R 444, following a five-day trial for murder, the judge had the jury back after a bare two hours; told them he could now accept a majority verdict, and asked them to retire for a short time to consider the matter. This was clearly a breach of the practice direction guidance, but that is directory only, not mandatory (see **D18.40**). It was held on appeal that the majority conviction was lawful because (a) there had been no breach of the Juries Act 1974, s. 17, itself, and (b) the judge had not, in the circumstances of the case, unjustifiably rushed the jury into a majority verdict. Although the case had been relatively long and was not easy to decide, the issue was a very simple one, namely whether the jury were satisfied that W's confession to the police had been genuine. In the circumstances, allowing the jury a longer time to reach unanimity would not have helped.

In *Rose* [1982] 1 WLR 614, the Court of Appeal indicated that a period of two hours and 40 minutes was 'a little soon' for the majority verdict direction in a murder trial which had lasted for 15 days.

Minimum Number for Acceptable Majority

D18.38 By the Juries Act 1974, s. 17(1), the minimum majorities permissible are 11–1 or 10–2, or (in the case of a jury from which one or more of the original jurors have been discharged) 10–1 or 9–1. A jury reduced to nine must be unanimous.

Statement of Size of Majority and Minority in Open Court

D18.39 If (and only if) the verdict is guilty, the foreman of the jury must state in open court the number of jurors who respectively agreed to and dissented from the verdict (Juries Act 1974, s. 17(3)).

Since stating the size of a majority for conviction is expressed as a precondition of the court accepting the verdict, failure to comply with s. 17(3) will result in any purported conviction being quashed (*Barry* [1975] 1 WLR 1190 and *Austin* [2003] Crim LR 426). However, it is sufficient for compliance with s. 17(3) if, as happened in *Pigg* [1983] 1 WLR 6, the foreman states the number in the majority leaving the size of the minority to be inferred by the simplest of arithmetic. In *Pigg*, Lord Brandon of Oakbrook (with whose speech all the other Law Lords concurred) stated the position thus (at p. 13G–H, emphasis added):

> . . . compliance with the requirement of section 17(3) of the Act of 1974 is mandatory before a judge can accept a majority verdict of guilty; but the precise form of words used by the clerk of the court when asking questions of the foreman of the jury, and the precise form of words used by the latter in answer to such questions, *as long as they make it clear to an ordinary person how the jury was divided*, do not constitute any essential part of that requirement.

Effect of Failure to Comply

D18.40 The effect of non-compliance with the procedures described above varies depending on whether the non-compliance amounts to a breach of the Juries Act 1974, s. 17, or is merely a breach of the *Consolidated Criminal Practice Direction*, para. IV.46 (see **appendix** 7).

In the former case, since the court's power to accept a majority verdict depends entirely upon the statutory provision, any conviction must be quashed (see *Barry* [1975] 1 WLR 1190 and *Pigg* [1983] 1 WLR 6).

If, on the other hand, there has been failure to comply with the practice direction and nothing more, the conviction may stand since the direction is (as the name implies) directory not mandatory (see *Wright* (1974) 58 Cr App R 444 and *Shields* [1997] Crim LR 758). The Court of Appeal have, however, stressed the importance of following the directions closely (see *Georgiou* (1969) 53 Cr App R 428).

Juries Act 1974, s. 17

(1) Subject to subsections (3) and (4) below, the verdict of a jury in proceedings in the Crown Court . . . need not be unanimous if—
   (a) in a case where there are not less than 11 jurors, 10 of them agree on the verdict; and
   (b) in a case where there are 10 jurors, nine of them agree on the verdict.

. . .

(3) The Crown Court shall not accept a verdict of guilty by virtue of subsection (1) above unless the foreman of the jury has stated in open court the number of jurors who respectively agreed to and dissented from the verdict.

(4) No court shall accept a verdict by virtue of subsection (1) . . . above unless it appears to the court that the jury have had such period of time for deliberation as the court thinks reasonable having regard to the nature and complexity of the case; and the Crown Court shall in any event not accept such a verdict unless it appears to the court that the jury have had at least two hours for deliberation.

VERDICT OF GUILTY OF AN ALTERNATIVE OFFENCE

It is sometimes open to a jury to find the accused not guilty of the offence alleged in a count but guilty of some other alternative offence. This is commonly referred to as a verdict of guilty of a lesser offence. **D18.41**

At common law, a jury could find an accused guilty of a lesser offence if the definition of the greater offence charged necessarily included the definition of the lesser. However, the enactment of a number of statutory provisions has considerably broadened the situations in which alternative verdicts are now permitted. Although the decision of the House of Lords in *Saunders* [1988] AC 148, demonstrates that there is still a residual role for the common law to play, this discussion of alternative verdicts proceeds on the basis that the law is now to be found in statute.

The General Rule

The general provision on the availability of alternative verdicts is contained in the Criminal Law Act 1967, s. 6(3), which provides as follows: **D18.42**

> Where, on a person's trial on indictment for any offence except treason or murder, the jury find him not guilty of the offence specifically charged in the indictment, but the allegations in the indictment amount to or include (expressly or by implication) an allegation of another offence falling within the jurisdiction of the court of trial, the jury may find him guilty of that other offence or of an offence of which he could be found guilty on an indictment specifically charging that other offence.

There are thus two principal situations covered by s. 6(3). One is where the offence charged *expressly* includes an allegation of another indictable offence; the other is where it *impliedly* includes such an allegation.

Express Allegation of Another Offence

To determine whether a count expressly includes an allegation of another offence it is necessary to apply a 'blue-pencil test'. This involves striking from the particulars of the count in the **D18.43** indictment the allegations that the prosecution evidence cannot or may not be able to sustain and, if what remains is a valid count for another offence, that alternative may be left for the jury's consideration (*Lillis* [1972] 2 QB 236).

For example, in *Lillis*, the particulars of a count for burglary contrary to the Theft Act 1968, s. 9(1)(b), alleged that L, on a certain date, entered part of a building, namely the conservatory of a house, and stole therein a lawnmower. However, the complaint of the owners was not that L had taken the mower in the first place but that he had failed to return it when he should have done. Although a submission of no case to answer on the charge of burglary inevitably succeeded, the judge held that there was a case to answer for theft by keeping, and he left that alternative verdict to the jury, who convicted. On appeal, the Court of Appeal applied the 'blue-pencil' test, notionally striking from the count those allegations the prosecution could not prove. What remained were the particulars: 'L stole a lawn-mower'. As this was sufficient to satisfy the Indictment Rules 1971 for a count of theft, the alternative verdict had been open to the jury.

The *Lillis* test was approved by the House of Lords in their decision in *Metropolitan Police Commissioner v Wilson* [1984] AC 242.

Implied Allegation of Another Offence

D18.44 There have been two distinct tests promulgated by the appellate courts for determining when a count impliedly includes an allegation of another offence. The first test was laid down by Sachs LJ in *Springfield* (1969) 53 Cr App R 608 ('the *Springfield* test'), and the second, less restrictive test was laid down by Lord Roskill in *Metropolitan Police Commissioner v Wilson* [1984] AC 242 ('the *Wilson* test').

D18.45 **The *Springfield* Test** Sachs LJ's test in *Springfield* (1969) 53 Cr App R 608, was that a count for offence A impliedly contains an allegation of offence B if, and only if, the commission of offence B is a necessary step towards committing offence A. There were two qualifications to this test:

(a) the court was entitled to look only at the wording of the count and the legal definitions of the offence in the count and the suggested alternative — therefore, if there was any possibility in law that the accused could have committed the 'count' offence without committing the alternative, the latter could not be left to the jury;
(b) it was irrelevant that the prosecution case was that the accused had in fact committed both offences.

D18.46 **Application of the '*Springfield*' Test** Since it has been overtaken by the *Wilson* test, applications of the *Springfield* test are now of limited assistance. However, those cases which would still be decided the same way include the following.

(a) In *Hodgson* [1973] QB 565, it was held that a jury may, on a count of rape, convict of indecent assault. This is because the allegation of rape impliedly includes both an allegation of an assault and an allegation of indecency. This has application only where the victim is under 16 and the accused cannot rely on consent as a defence, otherwise consent would be a complete defence to the charge and no alternative would be needed.
(b) Following the same reasoning, in *McCormack* [1969] 2 QB 442, it was held that, on a count for unlawful sexual intercourse with a girl under 16, the jury may convict of indecent assault.
(c) In *McCready* [1978] 1 WLR 1376, it was held that, on a count for causing grievous bodily harm with intent contrary to the OAPA 1861, s. 18, the jury may not convict either of malicious wounding contrary to s. 20 of the Act or of any form of assault. This is because harm can be caused within the meaning of s. 18 without there having been either an application of force or a wounding. On the other hand, if the count under s. 18

is for wounding, the alternatives mentioned above would be open to the jury since an assault is a necessary step towards a wounding, while an allegation of wounding with intent to do grievous bodily harm expressly includes an allegation of malicious wounding.

The *Wilson* Test The *Springfield* test was disapproved by Lord Roskill in *Metropolitan Police Commissioner v Wilson* [1984] AC 242. The question raised in that case was whether a count for inflicting grievous bodily harm impliedly includes an allegation of assault occasioning actual bodily harm. An allegation that grievous bodily harm occurred obviously and probably expressly includes an allegation that there was actual bodily harm (p. 259C). But do the words 'inflicting harm' impliedly include assault? The crucial passage from Lord Roskill's speech is at pp. 260H–261B: **D18.47**

> The critical question is, therefore, whether it being accepted that a charge of inflicting grievous bodily harm contrary to section 20 [of the Offences against the Person Act 1861] may not necessarily involve an allegation of assault, but may nonetheless do so, and in very many cases will involve such an allegation, the allegations in a section 20 charge 'include either expressly or by implication' allegations of assault occasioning actual bodily harm. If 'inflicting' can, as the cases show, include 'inflicting by assault', then even though such a charge may not necessarily do so, I do not for myself see why on a fair reading of section 6(3) these allegations do not at least impliedly *include* 'inflicting by assault'. That is sufficient for present purposes though I also regard it as also a possible view that those former allegations *expressly* include the other allegations.

Lord Roskill then held that the reasoning in *Springfield* should no longer be followed. Instead the test is that an allegation of the latter offence is impliedly included in the count where commission of the offence alleged in a count may involve commission of another offence, even if it is possible in law for the one offence to be committed without commission of the other.

Applications of the *Wilson* Test Applications of the *Wilson* test include: **D18.48**

(a) In *Metropolitan Police Commissioner v Wilson* [1984] AC 242 itself, the House of Lords restored W's conviction for assault occasioning actual bodily harm on a count alleging inflicting grievous bodily harm contrary to the OAPA 1861, s. 20 (the Court of Appeal, applying the *Springfield* test, had quashed the conviction).
(b) Similarly, in *Jenkins* (which was heard with *Wilson*), a conviction for actual bodily harm was restored on a count alleging burglary contrary to the Theft Act 1968, s. 9(1)(b), in that J, having entered a building as a trespasser, inflicted grievous bodily harm on a person therein.
(c) In *Savage* [1992] 1 AC 699, the House of Lords held that a verdict of assault occasioning actual bodily harm is a permissible alternative verdict on a count alleging unlawful wounding contrary to the OAPA 1861, s. 20.
(d) In *Whiting* (1987) 85 Cr App R 78, the Court of Appeal held that on a count for burglary contrary to the Theft Act 1968, s. 9(1)(b), where the allegation is that the accused, having entered as a trespasser, stole certain property, the jury may convict of entry as a trespasser with intent to steal contrary to s. 9(1)(a).
(e) In *Mandair* [1995] 1 AC 208, the House of Lords held that 'causing' grievous bodily harm contrary to the OAPA 1861, s. 18, was wide enough to include any action that could amount to inflicting grievous bodily harm under s. 20. *Metropolitan Police Commissioner v Wilson* was applied, and *Field* (1993) 97 Cr App R 357 overruled.
(f) In *Morrison* [2003] 1 WLR 1859, the Court of Appeal held that an allegation of attempted murder necessarily involves an allegation of attempt to cause grievous bodily harm, since the act of killing inevitably involves causing serious injury.

Specific Statutory Provisions Relating to Alternative Verdicts

D18.49 The Criminal Law Act 1967, s. 6(3), is supplemented by a number of other provisions prescribing the alternative verdicts which may be returned on counts for certain specific offences.

D18.50 **Murder** Section 6(2) of the Criminal Law Act 1967 provides that:

> On an indictment for murder a person found not guilty of murder may be found guilty—
> (a) of manslaughter, or of causing grievous bodily harm with intent to do so; or
> (b) of any offence of which he may be found guilty under an enactment specifically so providing, or under section 14(2) of this Act; or
> (c) of an attempt to commit murder, or of an attempt to commit any other offence of which he might be found guilty;
>
> but may not be found guilty of any offence not included above.

Paragraph (b) of the subsection preserves the effect of the Infanticide Act 1938, s. 1(2) (upon the trial of a woman for murder of her newly born child the jury may convict of infanticide), and of the Infant Life (Preservation) Act 1929, s. 2(2) (upon a trial for, *inter alia*, murder of a child the jury may convict of child destruction). For s. 4(2) of the Criminal Law Act 1967, see **D18.51**.

D18.51 **Assisting Offenders** By the Criminal Law Act 1967, s. 4(2), if the jury are satisfied that the offence with which the accused is charged (or some other offence of which he might be found guilty on that charge) has been committed by someone, but they find the accused himself not guilty of it, they may, by way of alternative verdict, find him guilty of assisting whoever the offender was contrary to s. 4(1) of the Act.

It has been held that, where it can be foreseen that a charge under s. 4(1) might be a proper way of dealing with the accused's case, the prosecution should not invoke s. 4(2) to put the matter before the jury but should have a separate count for assisting an offender (*Cross* [1971] 3 All ER 641). If, however, the possibility of a conviction under s. 4(1) only arises during the course of the case, then the prosecution are entitled to rely on s. 4(2), although they should still apply to amend the indictment to add an appropriate count before the evidence has been completed so that the defence have a fair opportunity of dealing with the new allegation (*Cross* and see also *Vincent* (1972) 56 Cr App R 281).

D18.52 **Attempts** By the Criminal Law Act 1967, s. 6(4), 'any allegation of an offence shall be taken as including an allegation of attempting to commit that offence'. It follows that, whenever a count charges the accused with a completed indictable offence, he may be convicted of an attempt to commit that offence. Moreover, when s. 6(3) is read in conjunction with s. 6(4), he may be convicted of an attempt to commit any other completed offence of which he could be found guilty on the count.

Conversely, under the second limb of s. 6(4), if the accused is charged merely with an attempt (or with any assault or other act preliminary to an offence, such as assault with intent to rob) but the evidence in fact establishes the completed offence, he may either be convicted as charged, the jury may be discharged with a view to the preferment of an indictment for the completed offence or, following the amendment of s. 6(4) by the CJA 2003, sch. 36, para. 41, the court may 'otherwise act'.

D18.53 **Driving Offences** The Road Traffic Offenders Act 1988, s. 24, makes provision for the alternative verdicts which may be returned where a person is tried for certain offences contrary to the Road Traffic Act 1988 (see **C2.12**).

D18.54 **Offences under the Public Order Act 1986** By the Public Order Act 1986, s. 7, if a jury find the accused not guilty on a count for either violent disorder (contrary to s. 2 of the Act) or affray (contrary to s. 3), they may (without prejudice to the Criminal Law Act 1967,

s. 6(3)) find him guilty of the summary offence of threatening behaviour contrary to s. 4 of the 1986 Act.

In addition, because the offences under ss. 1, 2 and 3 of the 1986 Act (riot, violent disorder and affray) are in descending order of gravity, s. 6(3) of the Criminal Law Act 1967 would have the result that a count under s. 1 will expressly or impliedly include an allegation of offences under the other two sections. Similarly, a count under s. 2 will include an allegation under s. 3.

Taking a Motor Vehicle without the Owner's Consent If, on a count for theft, the jury are not satisfied that the accused committed the offence charged, but it is proved that he committed an offence under the Theft Act 1968, s. 12(1) (taking a motor vehicle without the owner's consent etc.), they may convict him of the latter offence (Theft Act 1968, s. 12(4)). **D18.55**

Common Assault Until the CJA 1988, s. 40, came into force, a person charged under the OAPA 1861, s. 47, with assault occasioning actual bodily harm could be convicted, as an alternative, of common assault. This followed from the Criminal Law Act 1967, s. 6(3), and was the case whether or not there was a specific allegation of common assault as an alternative in the indictment. **D18.56**

By the CJA 1988, s. 40 (see **D11.15**), common assault becomes a summary offence. As a result, in *Mearns* [1991] 1 QB 82, it was held that common assault was not within the jurisdiction of the Crown Court, unless a specific count alleging that offence was added to the indictment. The position is now covered by the DVCVA 2004, s. 11 (see **D18.57**).

Other Offences listed in the CJA 1988, s. 40 In *Mearns* [1991] 1 QB 82, it was suggested that all the offences listed in s. 40 were excluded as alternative offences, unless specific counts were added. The position was altered, however, as a result of the DVCVA 2004, s. 11. This inserted subsections (3A) and (3B) in the Criminal Law Act 1967, which provide that an offence falls within the jurisdiction of the Crown Court if it is an offence to which s. 40 of the CJA 1988 applies, even if a count specifying it is not included in the indictment. **D18.57**

Judge's Discretion in Directing Jury as to Alternative Offences

The judge in summing up is not obliged to direct the jury about the option of finding the accused guilty of an alternative offence, even if that option is available to them as a matter of law. If, however, the possibility that the accused is guilty only of a lesser offence has been obviously raised by the evidence, the judge should, in the interests of justice, leave the alternative to the jury. This is the case even if neither prosecution nor defence counsel wishes the alternative offence to be left to the jury (*Coutts* [2006] 1 WLR 2154). **D18.58**

Considerations Relevant to the Exercise of that Discretion The judge's discretion in relation to alternative verdicts is usually invoked to protect the accused against being prejudiced by the unexpected introduction at a late stage of his trial of a suggestion that he is guilty on a charge that has never been expressly preferred against him and which he has not had a fair opportunity of countering in the course of his defence. Thus in *Metropolitan Police Commissioner v Wilson* [1984] AC 242, Lord Roskill rejected the defence argument that the extension of the availability of alternative verdicts implied in the abandonment of the *Springfield* test (see **D18.45**) might work injustice by referring to the judge's discretion. His lordship said (at p. 261F): **D18.59**

> If it be said that [our conclusion in this case] exposes the defendant to the risk of conviction on a charge which would not have been fully investigated at the trial on the count in the indictment, the answer is that a trial judge must always ensure, before deciding to leave the possibility of conviction of another offence to the jury under section 6(3) [of the Criminal Law Act 1967], that that course will involve no risk of injustice to the defendant and that he has had the opportunity of fully meeting that alternative in the course of his defence.

The proper approach to the exercise of the judge's discretion in this regard is further illustrated in a number of appellate decisions.

D18.60 **Exercise of the Discretion in *Fairbanks*** The exercise of the judge's discretion in relation to alternative verdicts was further considered by the Court of Appeal in *Fairbanks* [1986] 1 WLR 1202, in the context of the defence wanting the alternative to be left. F was indicted for causing death by reckless driving. Defence counsel in his closing speech conceded that F's driving had been careless but the prosecution persuaded the judge to direct the jury to put out of their minds categories of bad driving other than recklessness. The jury, after a four-hour retirement during which a question they asked indicated that they might have wanted to convict of careless driving, found H guilty as charged. On appeal, having reviewed the earlier authorities (*Vaughan* (1908) 1 Cr App R 25, *Naylor* (1910) 5 Cr App R 19 and *Parrott* (1913) 8 Cr App R 186), Mustill LJ said that an alternative offence should be left to the jury 'only if that is in the interests of justice' (p. 1205H).

The application of this test involved a number of possibilities:

(a) Since justice serves the interests of the public as well as those of the accused, there will be cases where, on the evidence, the accused *ought* to be convicted of at least the lesser offence and it would be wrong for the jury to acquit him entirely merely because they cannot be sure that he is guilty as charged (p. 1206D). In such cases the alternative should be left.
(b) Where, on the other hand, the lesser verdict simply did not arise given the way the case had been presented to the court (e.g., the defence was one of alibi), or where it might have arisen had a certain line of questioning been pursued but that had not in fact happened and the possible alternative had therefore ceased to be a live issue, it will be wrong to direct the jury about the alternative.
(c) Similarly, if the possible alternative is very trivial by comparison with the offence charged, introducing it will be an unnecessary and undesirable complication.

Applying those principles to the facts of *Fairbanks*, the judge erred by failing to direct the jury that they could return a verdict of careless driving. The subject-matter of the trial was, broadly speaking, the criminality of F's driving and, although the principal issue had always been whether he was reckless, that had never been the only issue. A verdict of careless driving would not have been fanciful. Neither would a direction on it have confused the jury. In short, not guilty of causing death by reckless driving but guilty of driving without due care and attention was a verdict at which a 'conscientious jury could properly arrive on the evidence', and it should have been available to them notwithstanding that they might use it as a bolt-hole to avoid facing up to the hard decision of whether the accused had been reckless.

D18.61 **Exercise of the Discretion in *Maxwell*** The decision in *Fairbanks* was approved by the House of Lords in *Maxwell* [1990] 1 WLR 401. M, who was charged with robbery, asserted that he was guilty of burglary, but denied that he had intended any violence to the victims. The prosecution declined to apply to amend the indictment to include a count of burglary and directed the jury that they were not entitled to bring in a verdict in relation to burglary. The jury could have been directed that they were entitled to bring in a verdict of guilty to the even lesser charge of theft, but the judge did not deal with that possibility.

On appeal to the House of Lords, it was held that:

(a) the prosecution were entitled, on the evidence, to take the view that the jury should not be distracted by an inappropriate alternative count of burglary;
(b) the judge had been entitled to accept that view;
(c) the judge had been entitled to decline to leave the alternative of theft to the jury since it was relatively trifling, and the essential issue was: did M intend violence to be used?

Lord Ackner, with whose reasons the other Law Lords agreed, stated the test, in cases where the judge has failed to leave an alternative offence to the jury as follows (at p. 408F):

> . . . the court, before interfering with the verdict, must be satisfied that the jury may have convicted out of a reluctance to see the defendant get clean away with what, on any view, was disgraceful conduct. If they are so satisfied then the conviction cannot be safe or satisfactory.

Maxwell has since been followed in *Cambray* [2007] RTR 128.

Exercise of the Discretion in *Coutts* The Court of Appeal and House of Lords judgments in *Coutts* [2005] 1 WLR 1605 and [2006] 1 WLR 2154 clash. **D18.62**

C was charged with murder. His defence was that he and the victim had engaged in an act of consensual sex involving asphyxiation, and that her death was a tragic accident, which resulted from that act. The prosecution took the view that it would be unfair to direct the jury on manslaughter, and the defence agreed with this approach. The trial judge did not direct the jury on manslaughter. C was convicted, and appealed on the basis that the judge should have directed the jury on manslaughter.

The House of Lords allowed the appeal. Lord Bingham, with whom the other Law Lords agreed, stated that, while the murder count against the appellant was clearly a strong one, no appellate court could be sure that a jury to whom the alternative count had been left, would not have convicted of manslaughter. He stated the principle in this way:

> The public interest in the administration of justice is, in my opinion, best served if in any trial on indictment the trial judge leaves to the jury, subject to any appropriate caution or warning, but irrespective of the wishes of trial counsel, any obvious alternative offence which there is evidence to support. I would not extend the rule to summary proceedings since, for all their potential importance to individuals, they do not engage the public interest to the same degree. I would also confine the rule to alternative verdicts obviously raised by the evidence: by that I refer to alternatives which should suggest themselves to the mind of any ordinarily knowledgeable and alert criminal judge, excluding alternatives which ingenious counsel may identify through diligent research after the trial. Application of this rule may in some cases benefit the defendant, protecting him against an excessive conviction. In other cases it may benefit the public, by providing for the conviction of a lawbreaker who deserves punishment. A defendant may, quite reasonably from his point of view, choose to roll the dice. But the interests of society should not depend on such a contingency. . . Nor, with respect, is it an objection that the jury's task would have been more complicated had a manslaughter direction been given. Compared with many directions given to juries, a manslaughter direction in this case would not have been complicated. But even if it would, that cannot be relied on as a reason for not leaving to the jury a verdict which they should on the facts have considered. If juries are to continue to command the respect of the public, they must be trusted to understand the issues raised even by a case of some complexity. For reasons already given, the wishes of counsel cannot override the judge's duty.

Doubt was cast, in the course of the opinions delivered by members of the House of Lords in *Coutts*, on the test for an appellate court to apply, as set out in *Maxwell* [1990] 1 WLR 401 (see **D18.61**). Lord Hutton said that 'that approach is an unsatisfactory one and should no longer be taken'. As Lord Roger put it:

> Since the appeal court cannot inquire into what went on in the jury room, it is very far from clear how they are meant to satisfy themselves in any given case that a jury may have convicted out of a reluctance to see the defendant get clean away.

Consideration of the ECHR The need for the judge to exercise his discretion in such a way as to ensure that the accused is not prejudiced by the unexpected introduction of an alternative offence has been underlined by the European Court of Human Rights in *Pelissier and Sassi v France* (1999) 25 March 1999, App. No. 25444/94. In that case, the defendants, who had been acquitted of the substantive offence of criminal bankruptcy, were convicted on the prosecution's appeal of aiding and abetting the substantive offence. It was not contested that the French court had the power so to do, but it had violated the ECHR, Article 6 by doing so without the possibility having been properly raised in advance of the judgment. **D18.63**

Discussion in Advance with Counsel At the very least, a judge intending to leave an **D18.64**

alternative verdict to the jury should warn counsel beforehand and should give them the opportunity of making representations about the propriety or otherwise of the proposed course (*Hazell* [1985] RTR 369). Counsel should also have an opportunity to address the jury about the alternative verdict, assuming it is to be left (ibid.).

In appropriate cases, giving the defence a fair opportunity to deal with an alternative verdict will involve drawing counsel's attention to the possibility of such a verdict before the close of defence evidence. In *Harris* (1993) *The Times*, 22 March 1993, for example, Steyn LJ in the Court of Appeal stated that it was appropriate to leave an alternative offence to the jury only if the accused had a full opportunity to meet the revised case against him so as to ensure that he was not prejudiced. See also *Griffiths* [2005] EWCA Crim 237.

It is generally assumed that, if the judge does not direct the jury about an alternative verdict or even (as in *Fairbanks* [1986] 1 WLR 1202) expressly tells them to ignore the possibility, they will be guided by him and either find the accused guilty as charged or acquit. However, in *Carter* [1964] 2 QB 1, a conviction for a lesser offence was upheld where prosecuting counsel had told the jury that the verdict was available but the judge made no reference to it in summing up. In order to avoid criticism for flouting the judge's authority, it would seem advisable for counsel first to raise the issue in the absence of the jury after the close of the evidence.

Procedure where the Jury are Unable to Agree that the Accused is Not Guilty as Charged

D18.65 The Criminal Law Act 1967, ss. 4(2) and 6(2) and (3), makes it a precondition of the jury convicting of an alternative offence that they should first find the accused not guilty of the offence specifically charged in the indictment. Where they cannot so agree, the clear wording of the legislation demonstrates that they are not entitled to return a verdict of guilty of the lesser offence. This could lead to the absurd result that the jury would be discharged from giving any verdict whatsoever when they are agreed that the accused is guilty of something.

The solution to this problem reached by the cases is by no means satisfactory. If the possibility of an alternative verdict arises under the Criminal Law Act 1967, s. 6(3) (the general provision), it would seem that, upon being informed that the jury cannot agree as to the greater offence but are agreed on the lesser, the judge may and should amend the indictment by adding a separate count for the lesser offence. A verdict may then be taken on the added count and the jury will be discharged from giving a verdict on the other. Whether the prosecution elect to have a retrial on the original charge is presumably a matter for their discretion.

This approach was approved in *Collison* (1980) 71 Cr App R 249. The offence charged in the original count (on which the jury were split) was wounding with intent and the verdict on which the jury were agreed was guilty of unlawful wounding. Therefore, it was s. 6(3) which would have given them power to return an alternative verdict had they been able to agree that C was not guilty as charged.

In *Saunders* [1988] AC 148, by contrast, it was the effect of s. 6(2) that was in issue. The indictment charged murder only, but it became apparent towards the end of a five-hour retirement that the jury had concluded that S was at least guilty of manslaughter. The judge took a verdict of guilty of manslaughter, although no separate count for manslaughter was added, and discharged the jury from giving a verdict in respect of murder. The House of Lords held that an additional count of manslaughter was unnecessary. Prior to the enactment of the Criminal Law Act 1967, alternative verdicts of manslaughter on a charge of murder had always been allowed by common law. The provisions of the Act did not abrogate the common law but were merely intended to deal with a procedural problem highlighted in *DPP v Nasralla* [1967] 2 AC 238, namely, whether the judge could ask for a verdict as to manslaughter if the jury had initially announced a verdict of not guilty *simpliciter*. Section 6(2) confirmed that he could. However, in situations not covered by s. 6(2), the common law continued to apply.

The Role of the Common Law in the Light of *Saunders* Although the interpretation of s. 6(2) adopted in *Saunders* [1988] AC 148, avoided the necessity of quashing S's conviction for manslaughter and ordering a retrial, it does seem surprising that the common law on alternative verdicts should have survived legislation which was apparently intended to define with some precision when such verdicts are, and when they are not, available. **D18.66**

The further question arises of whether the Criminal Law Act 1967, s. 6(3) (the general provision), was also intended to supplement rather than abrogate the common law. If so, instead of simply asking whether a count expressly or impliedly includes an allegation of another offence, one would also be forced to ask whether, at common law, an alternative verdict would have been available. Such an approach would introduce totally undesirable complications into an area of law which is already far from straightforward.

With respect, the decision in *Saunders* was convenient but ought to be confined to its special facts. If problems similar to those in *Collison* (1970) 71 Cr App R 249, arise in the future it would be safer to deal with them by means of adding a count rather than invoking the court's purported residual powers at common law.

RETURNING THE VERDICT

General Procedure

The jury's verdict is delivered in open court, in the presence of the accused. The invariable practice is for the person the jury have selected to be their foreman to state in response to questions from the clerk of court whether they find the accused guilty or not guilty. **D18.67**

The jury are entitled to return a partial verdict in the sense of finding an accused guilty on one count but not on others, or finding one accused guilty but another not. They are also entitled to find an accused guilty in respect of some only of the allegations set out in the particulars of a count, as when a count for theft specifies several items as the subject-matter of the charge and the jury are satisfied that the accused stole some of them but are left in doubt as to others (see *Furlong* [1950] 1 All ER 636, where the jury sent a note asking the judge if they could return such a verdict and the Court of Criminal Appeal held that the judge's affirmative answer was undoubtedly correct, even though the method by which he had communicated the answer was at fault).

Unanimity of the Verdict Unless a juror indicates dissent at the time, it is conclusively presumed that they all agree with the verdicts announced on their behalf, and the Court of Appeal will not breach the privacy of the jury room by hearing evidence that the necessary unanimity was lacking (*Roads* [1967] 2 QB 108, and see also *Lalchan Nanan v The State* [1986] AC 860, in which, on appeal from the Court of Appeal of Trinidad and Tobago in a capital case, the Privy Council held that the court below had rightly refused to read affidavits from four jurors to the effect that they had not realised the need for unanimity and had wished to acquit the appellant). **D18.68**

If the jury return to court apparently with a verdict prior to their having been given the majority verdict direction, the first question the foreman is asked is whether they have reached a verdict (or verdicts) on which they are all agreed (see *Consolidated Criminal Practice Direction*, para. IV.46.2 at **appendix** 7 and see **D18.71**). If the foreman indicates that they have reached unanimous verdicts, he is then asked in respect of each count on the indictment and each accused charged in a count what the jury's verdict is.

Verdicts of Alternative Counts The general rule that there should be verdicts on each **D18.69**

count is subject to the qualification that, where a jury wishes to convict on one of two counts which are in the alternative, it is preferable to take a verdict only on that count and discharge them from giving a verdict on the other. This is because the Court of Appeal will then, in appropriate circumstances, be able on appeal to substitute for the jury's verdict a verdict of guilty of the alternative count, whereas if the jury are allowed formally to acquit the accused of the alternative their verdict on that must stand, even though the conviction on the other count has to be quashed (see *Seymour* [1954] 1 WLR 678, *Melvin* [1953] 1 QB 481 and *Roma* [1956] Crim LR 46, and also the Criminal Appeal Act 1968, s. 3, for the Court of Appeal's power to substitute for the actual verdict a conviction for another offence of which the jury could lawfully have convicted the appellant on the indictment).

Having regard to the above considerations, the procedure normally adopted where counts are in the alternative is for the clerk to ask the foreman whether the jury find the accused guilty on *either* of the counts. If the answer is yes, the foreman is asked on which count they wish to convict; a verdict is taken on that count, and the judge discharges them from giving a verdict on the other. If the answer is no, not guilty verdicts are taken on each count.

D18.70 **Verdicts on Counts of Descending Gravity** A rather different problem arises where counts are not strict alternatives, but they arise out of the same facts and are of differing degrees of gravity (e.g., counts for wounding with intent to cause grievous bodily harm and malicious wounding contrary to ss. 18 and 20 of the OAPA 1861).

It is usual in such cases for the judge in summing up to tell the jury to consider first the more serious count and only to go on to consider the lesser one if they are not satisfied as to the former. Similarly, when verdicts are taken, the foreman will be asked first for the verdict on the graver count. If it is guilty, the jury will be discharged from giving a verdict on the other; if it is not guilty, a verdict is also taken on the lesser count.

It would not be proper in such cases to allow the jury to convict on both counts because the lesser count really merges into the greater. For example in *Harris* [1969] 1 WLR 745, where H was convicted of both buggery and indecent assault on a boy of 14, the latter offence consisting in playing with the victim's private parts immediately prior to the act of buggery. Edmund-Davies LJ (giving the Court of Appeal's judgment) said:

> There is no suggestion of any indecent assault upon [the victim] except that which formed the preliminary to and was followed very shortly thereafter by the commission of the full act of buggery. It does not seem to this court right or desirable that one and the same incident should be made the subject-matter of distinct charges, so that hereafter it may appear to those not familiar with the circumstances that two entirely separate offences were committed. Were this permitted generally, a single offence could frequently give rise to a multiplicity of charges and great unfairness could ensue. We accordingly allow the application for leave to appeal against the conviction of indecent assault, which really merges into the conviction for the graver charge.

Although his lordship appears to criticise even the formulating of distinct charges based on one incident, the actual mischief was in allowing the jury, once they had convicted of buggery, to go on to convict of the lesser charge also. They should simply have been discharged from giving a verdict in respect of indecent assault.

Where the jury were mistakenly asked for their verdict on the lesser count first, but this error was corrected and the proper procedure then followed, their conviction on the more serious count remained valid (*Fernandez* [1997] 1 Cr App R 123).

Procedure for Taking Majority Verdicts

D18.71 Majority verdicts are discussed at **D18.35**. The procedure for taking majority verdicts is set out in the *Consolidated Criminal Practice Direction*, para. IV.46 (see **appendix** 7). The main features of the procedure are as follows.

(a) If the jury return to court in a period in which it is considered that they should be trying to reach a unanimous verdict (and certainly where they return in less than two hours and ten minutes), the clerk of court asks the foreman if they have reached a verdict on which they are all agreed. If the answer is yes, the verdict is taken; if the answer is no, they are sent back to their room with a direction to continue to try to achieve unanimity.
(b) If the jury return or are sent for after that period has elapsed, the clerk similarly asks the foreman if they have reached a verdict on which they are all agreed. If the answer at this stage is no, the judge directs the jury that he can now accept a majority verdict, and tells them the size of the permissible majorities. However, he must also tell them that, when they again retire, they should make a further attempt to reach a unanimous verdict, and only if that last attempt at unanimity fails should they come back with a majority decision.
(c) Upon the jury returning to court after the majority verdict direction has been given, the clerk asks the foreman whether they have reached a verdict on which the required majority of them are agreed. If the answer is yes, they are asked for the verdict. A verdict of not guilty should be accepted without more ado. If the verdict is guilty, the foreman should be further asked whether it was unanimous or by a majority and, if the latter, how many agreed and how many dissented.

Correcting a Verdict

It occasionally happens that a jury return a verdict and then realise that they have been misunderstood. **D18.72**

Where the Verdict is Incorrect In such cases, the trial judge may allow them to correct their verdict (unless they have been discharged and have dispersed). **D18.73**

This was demonstrated in *Andrews* (1985) 82 Cr App R 148, in which the Court of Appeal held that a jury does have power to alter a verdict from not guilty to guilty provided it acts promptly (see *Parkin* (1824) 1 Mood CC 45 and *Vodden* (1853) Dears CC 229). Whether such an alteration should be allowed is in the discretion of the trial judge, taking into account especially:

(a) the length of time which has elapsed between the original verdict and the moment when the jury express a wish to change;
(b) the apparent reason for the mistake, for example, as in *Andrews* itself, that the jury were mistakenly waiting for a further question from the court clerk; and
(c) the necessity to ensure that justice was done both to the prosecution and to the defence.

In *Andrews*, the accused had been discharged but this was *not* fatal to allowing a change of verdict. However, if the jury had been discharged, and certainly if they had been allowed to disperse, it would then have been too late to rectify the mistake.

Equally, if the jury had heard anything since returning the original verdict that might have affected their earlier thinking, that would preclude any alteration (see *Tantram* [2001] Crim LR 824).

In *Austin* [2003] Crim LR 426, the Court of Appeal stated that, where a verdict was given in the sight and hearing of the entire jury without any dissent by any member of it, there was a presumption that they had all assented to it, albeit that such a presumption could be rebutted.

Correcting an Incomplete Verdict An alteration to the verdict may also be allowed where the original one was not so much incorrect as incomplete (*Carter* [1964] 2 QB 1 — conviction upheld where a jury which had not been directed by the judge about the possibility of finding the accused guilty of a lesser offence (although prosecuting counsel had referred to it) initially found the accused simply not guilty; after the accused had been discharged, the **D18.74**

D

Part D Procedure

foreman explained to the judge that they had wished to convict of the lesser offence and the accused were then recalled for the verdict to be completed and sentence passed).

D18.75 **Otherwise Rectifying the Verdict** Although the general rule is that, once the jury has been discharged, it is *functus officio* (see **D13.45**), there are circumstances in which it can be reconvened in order to rectify its verdict. Examples of such circumstances include the following cases.

(a) In *Aylott* [1996] 2 Cr App R 169, the judge discharged the jury because of a mistaken belief that they were unable to reach a verdict. When he received a further note from the jury which made it clear that they had already reached verdicts, he took the verdicts, as a result of which the appellant was convicted of murder. On appeal it was held that a judge was entitled in certain circumstances to set aside the discharge which he had ordered, for example in that case that the discharge had been based on a fundamental mistake. The underlying principle was to ensure that proceedings were fair and to do justice in the particular case.

(b) In *Maloney* [1996] 2 Cr App R 303, a guilty verdict was taken by the court on Friday afternoon, without asking how many jurors had agreed with the verdict and how many dissented. To rectify this mistake, the jury was reconvened the following Monday and asked about the figures. The Court of Appeal held that the discharge of the jury did not prevent the court carrying out the rectifying procedure. Nor were the lapse of time and the fact that the jury had dispersed fatal, in view of the CJPO 1994, s. 43, which permitted the jury to separate after retirement. There was no suggestion that they had deliberated further after the dispersal, nor that the numbers given as to the size of the majority were incorrect. The position would have been different if the jury had had to deliberate further, or, perhaps, if the verdict was being altered from not guilty to guilty.

Power of Judge to Refuse to Accept Verdict

D18.76 In general, a judge is obliged to accept the jury's verdict however much he may disagree with it (*Robinson* [1975] QB 508, following *Lester* (1938) 27 Cr App R 8). The exceptions to the general rule were succinctly stated by Lord Parker CJ in *Harris* [1964] Crim LR 54. The *Criminal Law Review's* paraphrase of his lordship's judgment reads:

> Where a single verdict is ambiguous, or two verdicts are inconsistent, or the verdict is one which cannot on the indictment or in the circumstances be lawfully returned, the judge is entitled, unless the jury insist, to refuse to accept the first verdict and ask the jury to reconsider the matter and if they change their verdict to record only the second verdict.

Similarly, in *Robinson* [1975] QB 508, James LJ said (at p. 512F):

> . . . once the jury has returned a verdict, then the judge cannot say 'I will not have it', provided, of course, it is a verdict that is not ambiguous and provided it is a verdict that can properly be returned upon the indictment they have been considering.

D18.77 **The Three Categories of Verdicts that a Judge can Refuse** Thus, there are three categories of case in which the first verdict need not be accepted:

(a) *The original verdict is one which the jury cannot lawfully return on the indictment.* An example would be a verdict of guilty of a lesser offence when such a verdict does not, in the circumstances of the case, come within any of the statutory provisions allowing a jury to convict the accused of something other than that with which he is expressly charged in the indictment (see **D18.41**).

(b) *The original verdict is ambiguous.* In such cases the judge should ask whatever questions are necessary to resolve the ambiguity (*Hawkes* (1931) 22 Cr App R 172) and may, if necessary, give a supplementary direction on the law before taking a final verdict (*Sweetland* (1957) 42 Cr App R 62). If the judge proceeds to sentence on a purported verdict of guilty which remains ambiguous, both conviction and sentence will have to be quashed (*Hawkes*).

(c) *Inconsistency in the verdict.* If the individual verdicts on a number of counts or in respect of several accused are inconsistent with each other, having regard to the nature of the evidence that has been adduced, the judge may ask the jury to reconsider their decision. He should only do so, however, if the verdicts are *necessarily* inconsistent. If there is a possible, albeit unlikely, view of the evidence on which the verdicts can be justified, the judge should accept them without further query. An example of this third category is the case of *Burrows* [1970] Crim LR 419. B, P and another were jointly charged with theft of a purse and P alone was charged in the alternative with handling it. The judge declined to accept the jury's initial verdict, acquitting all three of theft but convicting P of handling, because that acquittal implied that they were not satisfied that the goods in question had ever been stolen. Further discussion revealed a misunderstanding by the jury, and when this was corrected the jury found B guilty of theft. On appeal, it was held that the judge should have accepted the original verdicts, because they were not necessarily inconsistent *inter se* since the jury might have been sure that *either* B or the third co-accused had stolen the purse but have been unable to attribute responsibility to one or the other.

If the judge legitimately refuses to accept the jury's first verdict and in consequence they return a proper second verdict, it is the latter which is the operative decision. If the jury, notwithstanding the judge's intervention, persist in returning inconsistent verdicts, the inconsistency may be a good ground of appeal.

Supplementary Questions about the Verdict

It is not in general good practice to ask the jury questions about the basis on which they have returned a verdict of guilty (per Humphreys J in *Larkin* [1943] KB 174). Where the prosecution evidence is such that two or more views of the facts consistent with guilt are tenable, on one of which the accused's culpability is greater than on the other, it is the judge's responsibility to decide what the circumstances of the offence were for the purposes of sentencing (*Solomon* (1984) 6 Cr App R (S) 120 and *Stosiek* (1982) 4 Cr App R (S) 205). Asking the jury to refine their verdict may merely lead to confusion. **D18.78**

Circumstances in which Supplementary Questions may be Asked The one recognised exception to this principle is in cases where the accused is charged with murder and the jury have been left two or more alternative bases on which they might find the accused guilty of manslaughter and not guilty of murder. This is because exactly why the accused was found guilty of manslaughter (whether it was on grounds of provocation or diminished responsibility and, if the latter, whether the abnormality of mind was caused by medication or inherent causes) is of crucial importance to sentence (see *Matheson* [1958] 1 WLR 474, *Frankum* (1983) 5 Cr App R (S) 259 and *Solomon* (1984) 6 Cr App R (S) 120 per Beldam J at p. 126). **D18.79**

There is, however, no absolute requirement to ask supplementary questions even in these circumstances. In *Cawthorne* [1996] Crim LR 526, the Court of Appeal stressed that whether or not the judge asked the jury to indicate the basis of the verdict was a matter for his discretion; following the verdict, he was entitled to sentence on the basis of the facts which he had heard in evidence.

Procedure for Supplementary Questions Because the jury are entitled to decline to answer any supplementary question, beyond delivering its verdict, a judge who intends to ask a jury the basis of a guilty verdict should warn them of his intention before they retire (*Heckstall-Smith* [1989] Crim LR 742). After any such warning, if they convict, they should then be asked the supplementary question immediately after returning the main verdict and before they separate (ibid.). **D18.80**

In complicated cases, it may be a 'sensible precaution' to write the questions down for the jury. In *Frankum* (1983) 5 Cr App R (S) 259, Dunn LJ approved the course adopted by the trial judge in the case who gave the jury a list of questions as follows: 'First, do you think it more probable than not that the accused was suffering from diminished responsibility? If so, you should find him guilty of manslaughter. If you find him guilty of manslaughter, you will be asked (1) is that on the ground of diminished responsibility, and (2) if so, do you think the abnormality (a) arose as a result of inherent causes, (b) was induced by injury from the toxic effects of [a drug F was taking for a peptic ulcer] or (c) was both?'

D18.81 **Factual Basis for Sentence** Subject to the discussion above and **D18.41**, in general, if the judge has summed up the case to the jury on one factual basis, he is entitled to assume that they will acquit or convict on that basis and not on some alternative view of the facts which may theoretically have been open on the evidence but was not a live issue during the trial (*Heckstall-Smith* [1989] Crim LR 742). Where the jury do attempt to indicate, while the judge is passing sentence, that the factual basis on which he is doing so is different from that which they found proved, the judge may refuse to hear what they wish to say (*Ekwuyasi* [1981] Crim LR 574 and see **D18.34**).

JURY UNABLE TO AGREE ON A VERDICT

D18.82 If the jury cannot agree on a verdict, the judge discharges them from giving a verdict. As always when the jury are discharged, the accused is not acquitted but may be retried by a different jury. Whether to ask for a retrial is in the discretion of the prosecution. In the absence of exceptional reasons to the contrary, it is the practice to have a retrial following failure by one jury to agree. If a second jury also fail to agree, the prosecution would not usually seek a third trial but instead offer no evidence.

This convention was examined in *Henworth* [2001] 2 Cr App R 47, and it was stated that it should not be elevated into a proposition of law. In some cases, a further trial might be proper, e.g., if a jury had been tampered with, or some cogent piece of evidence for the Crown had since been discovered. Whether it was an abuse of process for the prosecution to seek a further trial must depend on the facts, including:

(a) the overall period of the delay and the reasons for it;
(b) the results of the previous trials;
(c) the seriousness of the offence; and (possibly)
(d) the extent to which the case against the defendant had changed since previous trials.

Jury Must Not Be Pressurised

D18.83 The jury should be given as much time as they reasonably need to reach a verdict, and must not be pressurised into agreeing against their better judgement. As Cassels J said in *McKenna* [1960] 1 QB 411 at p. 422: 'It is a cardinal principle of our criminal law that in considering their verdict . . . a jury shall deliberate in complete freedom, uninfluenced by any promise, unintimidated by any threat'.

The pressure in *McKenna* itself was extreme, in that the jury were told by the judge that, if they did not reach a verdict within the next ten minutes, they would have to be 'kept all night'. That was at least capable of conveying the impression that they would be kept in their jury room.

Even a much gentler indication of a time-limit may result in unacceptable pressure on the jury. In *Duggan* [1992] Crim LR 513, the jury made it known at 3.52 p.m. that, as some of them had child care commitments, they wished to sit until they had reached a verdict. The judge said that he was prepared to wait until 5 p.m. if it would help. The Court of Appeal held that the judge's intimation of a time-limit was likely to put some of the jury under pressure, in view of their earlier indication of commitments and the fact that it was clear that they would have to spend the night in an hotel if they could not agree.

Proper Discussion of Timing with the Jury Provided the principle in *McKenna* [1960] 1 QB 411 is not breached, there is no objection to the jury being asked if there is any reasonable prospect of their reaching agreement and being told that if there is not the judge will discharge them, while if there is they may have as much time as they want (*Modeste* [1983] Crim LR 746). **D18.84**

Any communication between the judge and jury about the chances of a verdict being reached etc. should take place in open court and should not be conducted by, for example, the clerk going into the jury room with a message (*Rose* [1982] 1 WLR 614). Where the jury request more time to deliberate, the judge may be obliged to allow more time; in any event, he is fully justified in permitting it (*Turner* [1994] Crim LR 287).

Wharton [1990] Crim LR 877 emphasises the importance of the judge enquiring of the jury in open court as to the prospect of a verdict being reached. In that case, the jury retired to consider their verdict at 3 p.m., received the majority direction at 5.34 p.m. and sent a note saying that they had reached a verdict 9–3 at 6.10 p.m. The course then adopted by the judge, with counsel's concurrence, of sending the jury a message asking them to continue their deliberations, was held to represent a material irregularity. Where the jury are unable to reach a verdict, the judge should reassemble them in court and ascertain from the foreman in open court at first hand what prospect there is of reaching a verdict.

When giving a majority direction, the judge should not refer to the possibility of another trial taking place if the jury cannot agree, as to do so might put undue pressure on them to reach agreement (*Boyes* [1991] Crim LR 717).

Saturday Sitting In *Duffin* [2003] EWCA Crim 3064, the Court of Appeal considered the circumstances in which the jury might be asked to consider their verdict on a Saturday. At the trial of the defendant for possession with intent to supply Class A drugs, the jury was sent out at 3.54 p.m. on the Friday of the last day of their scheduled sitting. At 6.07 p.m. the judge told them they were under no pressure to deliver a verdict, and asked them to retire and consider whether they wished to continue their deliberations or return the following day. Majority verdicts of guilty were returned by a majority at 7.31 p.m. The appeal of the accused on the ground that the jury had been placed under improper pressure to deliver the verdicts was allowed. Occasionally a Saturday sitting might be desirable and practicable but, if it was, the proper course was to determine whether the jury had commitments for the following day. Given the lateness of the hour and the fact that the only options had been to stay late or return the following day, the jury had been put under pressure to deliver the verdicts. **D18.85**

Encouraging the Jury to Reach a Verdict

Watson [1988] QB 690 raised the vexed question of whether a judge is entitled to use a form of words encouraging the jury to listen to each other's views and thus, if possible, reach agreement. In particular, the Court of Appeal considered the appropriateness in modern circumstances of a direction approved in *Walhein* (1952) 36 Cr App R 167, which drew attention to the cost and inconvenience caused by a jury not being able to agree. Lord Lane CJ's judgment in *Watson* starts from the proposition that (at p. 700A–B): **D18.86**

> . . . a jury must be free to deliberate without any form of pressure being imposed upon them, whether by way of promise or of threat or otherwise. They must not be made to feel that it is incumbent upon them to express agreement with a view they do not truly hold simply because it might be inconvenient or tiresome or expensive for the prosecution, the defendant, the victim or the public in general if they do not do so.

Experience had shown that the *Walhein* direction potentially put too much pressure on jurors who happened to be in the minority to concur with the majority. There was, however, no reason why a jury should not be directed as follows (at p. 700F–G):

> Each of you has taken an oath to return a true verdict according to the evidence. No one must be false to that oath, but you have a duty not only as individuals but collectively. That is the strength of the jury system. Each of you takes into the jury-box with you your individual experience and wisdom. Your task is to pool that experience and wisdom. You do that by giving your views and listening to the views of the others. There must necessarily be discussion, argument and give and take within the scope of your oath. That is the way in which agreement is reached. If, unhappily, [ten of] you cannot reach agreement you must say so.

It is solely a decision for the trial judge, in the exercise of his discretion, whether or not to give the above direction at all and, if he does decide to give the direction, the time at which he does so.

D18.87 **The Timing of a '*Watson*' Direction** In *Watson* [1988] QB 690, it was held that the direction was probably best given as part of the summing-up or as a last resort should the jury have had the majority verdict direction but still be unable to reach the minimum majority required (pp. 700H–701A). The Court of Appeal have indicated, in any event, that, once a jury has retired, a *Watson* direction should never be given before the majority direction (*Atlan* [2005] Crim LR 63) but, equally, should not be given at the same time as a majority direction (*Buono* (1992) 95 Cr App R 338).

D18.88 **Form of the Direction** If the direction is given, individual variations in its wording may prove dangerous and should if possible be avoided (*Watson* [1988] QB 690). In *Atlan* [2005] Crim LR 63, it was stressed that, if a *Watson* direction is given, it should make it clear that any 'give and take' should be within the scope of the juror's oath. The Court of Appeal suggested that it was just as dangerous to omit words from the *Watson* direction as to add them (see also *Morgan* [1997] Crim LR 593).

Section D19 Trial on Indictment: Sentencing Procedure

This section describes the procedure which applies following, as appropriate, a verdict or a plea of guilty, and which regulates the sentencing of the accused. First there is a need to ascertain the basis of facts, which is of particular importance where the accused has pleaded guilty and the court has therefore not had the opportunity to form a view of the evidence at trial. Secondly there is a need to consider the character of the accused, to obtain such pre-sentence reports as are appropriate about him, and to consider such mitigation as is advanced on his behalf, before either sentencing or adjourning sentence in one of a number of ways. **D19.1**

Sentencing procedure is essentially the same in both the Crown Court and magistrates' courts. It is the former that is under consideration here. For ways in which the summary procedure differs, see **D21**. See also **Part E** as to the sentences that are available, and the procedures and guidelines that apply to them.

ASCERTAINING THE FACTS OF THE OFFENCE

Where the accused pleads guilty, the first stage of the sentencing process is for prosecuting counsel to summarise the facts of the offence. As well as assisting the court, this informs the accused and the public of how the prosecution put their case. **D19.2**

If the accused pleaded not guilty, the facts will have emerged during the course of the evidence and there is normally no need for them to be reiterated. However, in the event of split pleas by co-accused, the sentencing of the accused who pleaded guilty will normally be adjourned until the conclusion of the trial of the accused who pleaded not guilty. If the latter is convicted, the facts will still have to be summarised for the benefit of the one who pleaded guilty.

The Duties of the Prosecutor in Relation to Sentencing

By convention, the prosecution adopt a neutral attitude at the sentencing stage, not seeking to influence the court in favour of a heavy sentence. This is reflected in the Code of Conduct of the Bar, Written Standards, para. 11.8, which should be read in conjunction with the Farquharson committee's report on the general duties of prosecuting counsel (see **D14.7** *et seq.*). Paragraph 11.8(a) states: **D19.3**

> [Prosecuting counsel] should not attempt by advocacy to influence the court with regard to sentence: if, however, a defendant is unrepresented it is proper to inform the court of any mitigating circumstances about which counsel is instructed.

In addition to the general statements of principle just given, the following points may be made about the role of prosecuting counsel at the sentencing stage.

(a) Prosecution counsel can only provide evidence of the impact on its victim of the offence for which the accused is to be sentenced if it accords with the relevant guidelines (see **D19.4**).
(b) Where the possibility arises of the court making an ancillary order in conjunction with the main sentence (e.g., compensation under the PCC(S)A 2000, s. 130, deprivation of property under s. 143 of the same Act, confiscation of the proceeds of crime, or forfeiture of prohibited articles such as drugs or offensive weapons), counsel has a duty to deal with the matter (see Code of Conduct of the Bar, Written Standards, para. 11.8(d)).
(c) Prosecution counsel is under a general duty to assist the court to avoid appealable error. According to the standards applicable to criminal cases, this goes beyond ensuring that the judge does not exceed his maximum powers and extends to reminding him of (i) statutory provisions guiding him in his sentencing task, and (ii) any relevant guidelines laid down by the Court of Appeal. The effect of para. 11.8(b) and (c) is that such assistance should be given either if requested by the court, or on counsel's own initiative if he considers that the judge has erred as a matter of sentencing law (see *Panayioutou* (1989) 11 Cr App R (S) 535 and **D19.6**).

Victim Impact Statements

D19.4 It has become increasingly prevalent in recent years for the court to be provided with an account from the victim of the offence for which the accused is to be sentenced, which can then be taken into account by the court when it passes sentence.

In *Hobstaff* (1993) 14 Cr App R (S) 632, the Court of Appeal stressed that allegations made by prosecuting counsel as to the effect of the offence upon the victim must be backed up by potentially admissible evidence. In that case the Court of Appeal criticised as wholly improper the conduct of prosecution counsel who, without warning to the defence, gave a graphic description of the ill-effects the victims of the offence had suffered as a result of the offences. Evidence of such allegations had to be made in a proper form such as a witness statement, and served in advance on the defence and the court. Defence counsel could then deal with it in such a manner as he thought fit and the judge's judgment would not be influenced by prosecution information alone (see also *A-G's Ref (No. 2 of 1995)* [1996] 1 Cr App R (S) 274).

In *H (Indecent Assault)* (1999) *The Times*, 18 March 1999, the Court of Appeal emphasised that where the prosecution does provide a statement from the victim, the sentencer should approach it with some care. Since it would ill-behove the accused to attempt to investigate such a statement, it would necessarily reflect one side of the case only.

In *Perks* [2001] 1 Cr App R (S) 66, the Court of Appeal laid down guidelines for the courts to take into account in considering 'victim personal statements' for the purpose of sentencing (see **E1.20** for details). The main points of *Perks* are now summarised in the *Consolidated Criminal Practice Direction*, para. III.28, *Personal statements of victims* (see **appendix** 7).

Victim's Advocates

D19.5 In the same regard, a pilot scheme for the introduction of 'victim's advocates' was introduced from April 2006. Trials in the pilot courts (the Central Criminal Court and Crown Courts in Birmingham, Cardiff, Manchester (Crown Square) and Winchester) were permitted to hear from an advocate speaking on behalf of the victim's family in cases where there has been a conviction for murder or manslaughter. The procedure is set out in more detail in the Protocol for Pilot Courts on Victim's Advocates (available at www.judiciary.gov.uk/judgment_guidance).

Counsel's Duty to Assist the Court

Counsel must make himself aware of any legal limitations on the court's sentencing powers and any relevant guidelines as to sentence so as to be in a position to assist the judge if necessary (Code of Conduct of the Bar, Written Standards, para. 11.8(b)). **D19.6**

This statement in the code reflects dicta of the Court of Appeal (e.g., Lawton LJ in *Clarke* (1974) 59 Cr App R 298: '. . . counsel as a matter of professional duty to the court . . . should always before starting a criminal case satisfy themselves as to what the maximum sentence is', and *Kennedy* [1976] Crim LR 508: 'It is the duty of counsel to inform themselves what are the permissible sentences for the offences with which a defendant is charged, so as to be in a position to assist the judge if he makes a mistake').

In *Komsta* (1990) 12 Cr App R (S) 63, it was emphasised that there was a positive obligation on counsel, both for the prosecution and the defence, to ensure that no order is made which the court has no power to make. See also *Brown* [1996] Crim LR 134, *Johnstone* (1996) *The Times*, 18 June 1996, *A-G's Ref. (No. 52 of 2003) (Webb)* [2004] Crim LR 306, and *Reynolds* [2007] EWCA Crim 538.

In *Cain* [2006] EWCA Crim 3233, the Lord Chief Justice observed:

> It is of course the duty of a judge to impose a lawful sentence, but sentencing has become a complex matter and a judge will often not see the papers very long before the hearing and does not have the time for preparation that advocates should enjoy. In these circumstances a judge relies on the advocates to assist him with sentencing. It is unacceptable for advocates not to ascertain and be prepared to assist the judge with the legal restrictions on the sentence that he can impose on their clients.
>
> This duty is not restricted to defence advocates. We emphasise the fact that advocates for the prosecution also owe a duty to assist the judge at the stage of sentencing. It is not satisfactory for a prosecuting advocate, having secured a conviction, to sit back and leave sentencing to the defence. Nor can an advocate, when appearing for the prosecution for the purpose of sentence on a plea of guilty, limit the assistance that he provides to the court to the outlining of the facts and details of the defendant's previous convictions.
>
> The advocate for the prosecution should always be ready to assist the court by drawing attention to any statutory provisions that govern the court's sentencing powers. It is the duty of the prosecuting advocate to ensure that the judge does not, through inadvertence, impose a sentence that is outside his powers. The advocate for the prosecution should also be in a position to offer to draw the judge's attention to any relevant sentencing guidelines or guideline decisions of this court.

The Factual Basis for Sentence

The great majority of summaries of the facts provided by the prosecution raise no procedural problems whatsoever. However, a considerable body of law has developed dealing with the proper approach to that minority of cases in which there is a dispute about the facts of the offence, in the sense that the prosecution version of how the offence was committed differs from that advanced by the defence in mitigation, albeit the accused is clearly guilty on either version. This will arise in particular where the defence advance a written factual basis of plea which is not accepted by the prosecution or the court. The principles to be applied are discussed below. **D19.7**

DISPUTES ABOUT THE FACTS FOLLOWING A PLEA OF GUILTY

Newton Hearings

In *Newton* (1982) 77 Cr App R 13, N pleaded guilty to buggery of his wife, but there was considerable dispute between the prosecution and defence as to whether she had consented **D19.8** both to the buggery and to the other sexual acts alleged. The Court of Appeal indicated three ways in which the judge, in a case where there is such a sharp divergence on the facts of the offence, 'can approach his difficult task of sentencing'. Lord Lane CJ said (at p. 15):

> It is in certain circumstances possible to obtain the answer to the problem from a jury. For example, when it is a question of whether the conviction should be under section 18 or section 20 of the Offences against the Person Act 1861, the jury can determine the issue on a trial under section 18 by deciding whether or not the necessary intent has been proved by the prosecution. . . .
>
> The second method which could be adopted by the judge in these circumstances is himself to hear the evidence on one side and another, and come to his own conclusion, acting so to speak as his own jury on the issue which is the root of the problem.
>
> The third possibility in these circumstances is for him to hear no evidence but to listen to the submissions of counsel and then come to a conclusion. But if he does that, . . . where there is a substantial conflict between the two sides, he must come down on the side of the defendant. In other words where there has been a substantial conflict, the version of the defendant must so far as possible be accepted.

On the facts of *Newton*, the judge had failed to adopt any of the three permissible courses since he had sentenced on the basis that the sexual acts were non-consensual without hearing either evidence or submissions.

The General Approach

D19.9 The basic propositions set out in *Newton* have since been analysed and refined. In particular, in *Underwood* [2005] 1 Cr App R 178, the Court of Appeal gave guidelines on the approach that the sentencer ought to take where an accused pleads guilty on a specific basis that the prosecution may not accept. In summary, and renumbered, they are:

(1) The accused should be sentenced as far as possible on a basis that accurately reflects the facts of the individual case.
(2) If the resolution of the facts in dispute may matter to the sentencing decision, the responsibility for alerting the prosecutor to the areas of dispute rests with the defence (see also **D19.10**).
(3) The prosecution should not be taken by surprise and should if necessary take time to reflect, consult and consider their position and the interests of justice.
(4) Whatever view is formed by the prosecution on any proposed basis of plea is deemed to be conditional on the judge's acceptance of it.
(5) The prosecution may agree the accused's account of the disputed facts. If so, the agreement should be reduced to writing and signed by both advocates (see also **D19.14**).
(6) The agreement should be available to the judge before the prosecution's opening and if possible before he is invited to approve the acceptance of plea, or in any event before the sentencing hearing begins.
(7) If the agreed basis of pleas is not signed by advocates for both sides, or it is not legible, the judge is entitled to ignore it.
(8) If the prosecution rejects the accused's version, the areas of dispute should be identified in a document that focuses the attention of the court on the precise facts which are in dispute.
(9) The most difficult situation arises when the prosecution lacks the evidence positively to dispute the accused's account. In many cases, for example, the matter in issue is outside the knowledge of the prosecution. The prosecution's position may be that they have no evidence to contradict the defence assertions, but that does not mean that the truth of matters outside their own knowledge should be agreed. In those circumstances, particularly if the facts relied upon by the accused arise from his personal knowledge and depend on his own account of the facts, the prosecution should only agree that account if

it is supported by other material. Neither the prosecution nor the judge is bound to agree facts merely because the prosecution cannot gainsay the accused's account.

(10) Whether or not the basis of plea is agreed, the judge is not bound by any such agreement, and is entitled to insist that any evidence relevant to the facts in dispute should be called. The judge is responsible for the sentencing decision and may order a *Newton* hearing to ascertain the truth about disputed facts (see also **D19.15**).

(11) The prosecution and defence should call any relevant evidence. Where the issue arises from facts that are within the exclusive knowledge of the accused, the defence should be willing to call him. If he does not give evidence, the judge may draw such inferences as he thinks fit, subject to any explanation put forward.

(12) An adjournment for these purposes is often unnecessary.

(13) The judge should direct himself on the burden and standard of proof in accordance with ordinary principles.

(14) A *Newton* hearing has the following limitations:

(a) some issues require a verdict from a jury, e.g., intent (see **D18.79**);

(b) a judge cannot make findings of fact and sentence that are inconsistent with the pleas to the counts on the indictment;

(c) where a number of persons are charged with a joint enterprise, the seriousness and context are always relevant;

(d) matters of mitigation are not normally dealt with in a *Newton* hearing, but where there is no evidence to support an accused's account other than his contention, the judge is entitled to invite defence counsel to call his client;

(e) where the impact of the dispute on the eventual sentencing decision is minimal, a *Newton* hearing is unnecessary — the judge will rarely be concerned with minute differences about events on the periphery (see also **D19.18**);

(f) the judge is entitled to decline to hear evidence about disputed facts if the accused's case is absurd or obviously untenable, but he should explain why he has reached that conclusion (see also **D19.20**).

(15) If issues on a *Newton* hearing are resolved in the accused's favour, the credit due to him for a guilty plea should not be reduced.

(16) If the accused is disbelieved or obliges the prosecution to call evidence from a witness causing unnecessary and inappropriate distress, and conveys to the judge that he has no insight into the consequences of his offence and no genuine remorse for it, the judge may reduce the discount for a guilty plea, particularly if it has been tendered at a very late stage.

(17) There might be an exceptional case in which the normal entitlement to credit for a guilty plea is wholly dissipated by the *Newton* hearing, in which case the judge should explain his reasons.

Certain of the more important aspects of these guidelines are analysed below.

Duty of the Accused's Legal Representatives

It is the responsibility of defence solicitors and counsel to notify the prosecution that a plea of guilty will be put forward on the basis that the accused disputes the prosecution version of the facts (*Mohun* (1993) 14 Cr App R (S) 5). **D19.10**

As explained in *Gardener* [1994] Crim LR 301, this notification involves two stages. Where there was a dispute about relevant facts which might affect sentence, defence counsel should make that clear to the prosecution. The court should then be informed, ideally at the outset of the hearing and at the latest during mitigation, not merely that there is a dispute but that the defence wishes to see it resolved in a *Newton* hearing.

The Court of Appeal would not normally consider an argument that the sentencer had failed to order a hearing unless the possibility of such a hearing was raised unequivocally and expressly in the Crown Court (See also *A-G's Refs (Nos. 3 and 4 of 1996)* [1997] 1 Cr App R (S) 29).

Power of Court to Direct a Hearing

D19.11 Ultimately, the decision as to whether or not a *Newton* hearing is required is for the court. The result of this is that such a hearing may arise even where prosecution and defence are agreed on the facts on which the plea is based. This is because the judge is under a duty to hold a *Newton* hearing if an application of the principles stated in **D19.9** leads to that conclusion, even if the defence are against that course.

In *Smith* (1986) 8 Cr App R (S) 169, for example, where the issue was whether an offence of using a firearm with intent to resist arrest had been committed by the deliberate or accidental discharge of the firearm, the judge offered defence counsel a *Newton* hearing to resolve the issue, but counsel declined. The judge then proceeded to sentence on a basis adverse to S. In the Court of Appeal, where the term was reduced, Peter Pain J quoted from Goff LJ in *Williams v Another* (1983) 5 Cr App R (S) 134: '. . . the question whether an issue should be tried does not depend upon the consent of counsel for the appellant or the accused person as the case may be. It is entirely a matter for the decision of the court in any particular case, although the court may of course hear submissions from counsel on the propriety of ordering such an issue to be tried. The question whether counsel for a party agrees or does not agree to the trial of the issue is a matter of no materiality, the decision being entirely within the control of the court' (see also *Myers* [1996] 1 Cr App R (S) 187).

If the judge decides to hold a *Newton* hearing he should avoid giving the impression that he has made up his mind in advance that the defence version is implausible (*Satchell* [1997] 2 Cr App R (S) 258).

D19.12 **Factual Disputes Revealed by the Pre-sentence Report** One way in which the court may be alerted to a factual dispute which may have a bearing on the eventual sentence is where the accused presents to the author of the pre-sentence report a factual account which is at variance with the prosecution case. In such circumstances, the court can initiate a *Newton* hearing. In *Oakley* [1998] 1 Cr App R (S) 100, where there was a conflict over whether the version of the facts presented by the prosecution or that in the pre-sentence report ought to be adopted, the Court of Appeal held that the sentencer should have heard evidence to resolve the conflict, whether or not the prosecution or defence asked for a *Newton* hearing.

However, in *Tolera* [1999] 1 Cr App R 29, the Court of Appeal emphasised that the initiative rested with the defence where it was asking the court to sentence on a basis other than that disclosed by the prosecution case. If the accused wished to rely on the account which he gave to the probation officer and which conflicted with the prosecution case, he should draw the relevant paragraphs to the attention of the court and ask that it be treated as the basis of sentence. The prosecution should be alerted to the fact that such a request would be made. A *Newton* hearing could then follow.

D19.13 **Dispute Arising in Ancillary Proceedings** The court may also be alerted to a material factual dispute during proceedings ancillary to sentencing, such as confiscation. In *McNulty* [1994] Crim LR 385, for example, the judge was engaged in an inquiry as to whether a confiscation order should be made in respect of the proceeds of drug trafficking. This inquiry led the judge to doubt M's basis of plea of non-commercial supply of cannabis resin. The judge therefore embarked on a *Newton* hearing, in which he found that M had been dealing commercially in cannabis. The Court of Appeal held that it was proper to hold a *Newton* hearing in these circumstances, and upheld the sentence and the confiscation order.

In such a situation, it is important to ensure that the *Newton* hearing is governed by the criminal rules of evidence and procedure, regardless of the assumptions and standard of proof which may govern an enquiry under the Proceeds of Crime Act 2002 (see **E21.6**).

Written Basis of Plea

Where an accused pleads guilty on a particular basis (e.g., accepting only a limited version of the allegations made by the prosecution), he should set out the basis of the plea in a written form (*Tolera* [1999] 1 Cr App R 29). The Court of Appeal has indicated that it is reluctant to recognise that a plea was put forward on a particular basis unless there is such a written basis of plea, or the judge has accepted it expressly (*Kesler* [2001] 2 Cr App (S) 542). **D19.14**

Response to an Agreed Basis of Plea In *Beswick* [1996] 1 Cr App R (S) 343, the Court of Appeal dealt with the situation where agreement had been reached between prosecution and defence counsel as to the facts upon which a plea of guilty was to be based, and the judge declined to give effect to that agreement. **D19.15**

Their lordships set out five principles for the guidance of the court in such cases:

(1) Whenever the court has to sentence an offender it should seek to do so on a basis which is true. The prosecution should not, therefore, lend itself to any agreement with the defence which was founded on an unreal and untrue basis.
(2) When that had happened, the judge was entitled to direct a *Newton* hearing in order to determine the true factual basis for sentence.
(3) Such a decision did not create a ground upon which an offender should be allowed to vacate his plea of guilty, provided he does admit his guilt of the offence to which he has pleaded guilty.
(4) The decision that there should be a trial of an issue meant that the judge was entitled to expect the assistance of prosecuting counsel in presenting evidence, and in testing any evidence called by the defence. The agreement which the prosecution has previously entered into with the defence must be viewed as conditional on the approval of the judge. If the judge's approval is not forthcoming, the defence cannot seek to hold the prosecution to the agreement.
(5) Before embarking on the trial of an issue, the judge might consider whether there is any part of the agreement by which the prosecution should be bound. Counsel should also consider which issues are to be tried, and which of the prosecution statements are relevant to them.

Guidance on the issues arising where the basis of a plea is the subject of an agreement between prosecution and defence is to be found in *Underwood* [2005] 1 Cr App R 178 (see **D19.9** and points (1), (4), (5), (6), (7), (8) and (10) in particular).

Longer-than-commensurate Sentence

In *Oudkerk* [1994] Crim LR 700, it was held that, where the imposition of a longer-than-commensurate sentence under the PCC(S)A 2000, s. 80(2)(b) (now repealed), was contemplated, the sentencing court must resolve by a *Newton* hearing any important issue going to the application of that provision. Similar situations may arise in relation to the application of the CJA 2003, ss. 224 to 236 (see **E5.1** ***et seq.***). **D19.16**

Where *Newton* Hearing Unnecessary

Change of Plea Some difficulty arises where the accused changes his plea to guilty after some evidence has been given by prosecution witnesses. In *Mottram* (1981) 3 Cr App R (S) 123, it was held that the judge should then hear evidence from the accused (and, presumably from any witnesses whom he wished to call), before deciding on the version of the facts which would form the basis for sentence. The totality of the evidence received on the point relevant to sentence can then be treated as a *Newton* hearing (see also *Archer* [1994] Crim LR 80). **D19.17**

Insignificant Disputes The principles in *Newton* (1982) 77 Cr App R 13, apply only where the dispute between prosecution and defence is 'substantial' (see the words of Lord Lane's **D19.18**

judgment quoted at **D19.8**). It follows that, where the judge's sentence would be the same whichever version of the facts he were to accept, there is no obligation on him to hear evidence but he can make up his mind one way or the other simply on the basis of counsels' representations.

This was illustrated in *Bent* (1986) 8 Cr App R (S) 19. Where the judge had sentenced on the basis of an actual rather than a threatened assault, it was held that a *Newton* hearing was unnecessary because the gravamen of the charge lay in the offender's having resisted arrest rather than whether a minor assault actually occurred. In cases such as *Bent*, a judge should sentence on the assumption that the defence version is correct, and state that he is doing so (see dicta to that effect by Lincoln J in *Hall* (1984) 6 Cr App R (S) 321 at p. 324).

Further guidance on this topic is to be found in *Underwood* [2005] 1 Cr App R 178 (see **D19.9** and point (14)(e) in particular).

D19.19 **Extraneous Matters** There is no requirement to hold a *Newton* hearing where the matter that is not accepted relates to extraneous mitigation which is outside the prosecution's knowledge (the 'reverse *Newton*' situation). For this see **D19.80** and *Underwood* [2005] 1 Cr App R 178 at **D19.9**, especially point (9).

D19.20 **Defence Version Manifestly Absurd** The guidance in *Newton* (1982) 77 Cr App R 13 requires a sentencer who chooses not to hear evidence about a significant dispute as to the facts of the offence to accept the defence version 'so far as possible'. The implication is that the defence story may be so implausible that a judge ought not to be obliged to waste time by hearing evidence before rejecting it.

Such an interpretation of *Newton* has been confirmed by subsequent decisions, in particular *Hawkins* (1985) 7 Cr App R (S) 351. In that case, H accepted that he had acted as the get-away driver in a joint offence of burglary but he only became aware of the full facts at a very late stage. The judge declined to hear evidence about the facts but sentenced on the prosecution version that H had been a knowing participant throughout. The Court of Appeal dismissed H's appeal because the suggestion that 'he was driving the car around to keep the engine warm or to look for a lavatory for himself, whilst unknown to him his colleagues were burgling a house was an incredible assertion'. The judge did not have to trouble himself with evidence.

The same approach was taken in *Bilinski* (1987) 86 Cr App R 146, and in *Walton* (1987) 9 Cr App R (S) 107 at p. 109 where Kennedy J said, '. . . the words used by this court in *Newton* (1982) 77 Cr App R 13 do not mean that in every case a judge must hear evidence before he rejects a version of the facts put forward in mitigation, but which for good reason he regards as untenable. . . . The judge was fully entitled [in the circumstances of this case] to reject the submission that was put forward [in mitigation] out of hand during the course of argument'.

D19.21 **Evidence of the Accused Incredible** Similar reasoning applies to the case where the accused gives an account on oath at the *Newton* hearing. The fact that the burden of proof is upon the prosecution does not inevitably lead to the conclusion that the accused's testimony must automatically be accepted in the absence of direct evidence to the contrary. If the accused's account on oath is incredible, the judge is entitled to reject it whether or not the prosecution call evidence. Thus, in *Kerr* (1980) 2 Cr App R (S) 54, K, who pleaded guilty to importing cannabis through Heathrow, gave evidence that, until almost the moment of leaving the plane, he had thought the packets in his luggage to be samples of marble, not drugs. It was held that the judge was entitled to reject that explanation even though the prosecution called no evidence, and did not even cross-examine K.

D19.22 **Restrictions on the Court's Right to Reject the Accused's Account** The judge's view that the defence version is manifestly absurd must, however, be in accordance with the facts.

This was illustrated in *Costley* (1989) 11 Cr App R (S) 357. The prosecution alleged that C, who had pleaded guilty to inflicting grievous bodily harm, had used of a piece of wood as a weapon. However, C claimed he had been provoked, and even then had only used his fists. In sentencing (without first hearing evidence), the judge said: 'I find as a fact that the attack was totally unprovoked by anything [V] said or did. . . . I reject your explanation for the use of violence as being wholly incredible'.

The Court of Appeal held that it was not open to the judge to come to these conclusions, and upheld the appeal against sentence. In a case where the sentencer is faced with a substantial conflict on issues such as this, a *Newton* hearing should be held. Where the court feels unable to accept the defence account, it should make that clear, and indicate why (*Tolera* [1999] 1 Cr App R 29).

Procedure

Burden and Standard of Proof In a *Newton* hearing, the burden of proof is on the prosecution to satisfy the judge beyond reasonable doubt that their version of events is the correct one. D19.23

This was demonstrated in *Ahmed* (1984) 80 Cr App R 295, where the issue between prosecution and defence was whether A was a mere courier or the actual seller of a large quantity of diamorphine. The trial judge, after hearing evidence from the offender, decided against his account and sentenced accordingly. On appeal, the defence argument that the judge had misdirected himself as to the standard of proof failed, Parker LJ saying:

> It is apparent . . . that the judge had directed himself and the other members of the court that even if the 'Mr Khan' story might be true, the appellant must be sentenced on the basis that it was true. That direction was in the view of this court entirely proper and follows from *Newton* (1982) 77 Cr App R 13. If it be right that in the absence of evidence the submissions of the defence should be accepted and that the other two possible courses are to have the matter (where circumstances permit) determined by a jury or the judge, then it must in our view follow that the defence version of the facts must be accepted, unless a jury or the judge, as the case may be, is sure that it is wrong.

In *Kerrigan* (1993) 14 Cr App R (S) 179, it was said that it was better for the judge to direct himself openly as to the relevant standard and onus of proof, although the failure to do so was not fatal in every case.

Calling Evidence Once the judge has decreed that there should be a *Newton* hearing, the hearing itself follows normal adversarial lines (per May LJ in *McGrath* (1983) 5 Cr App R (S) 460 at p. 463). The parties are given the opportunity to call such evidence as they wish and to cross-examine the witnesses called by the other side. That said, the position of the parties, and the court, does require consideration. D19.24

Role of the Prosecution Where the basic facts are not in dispute, the prosecution is not obliged to call any evidence, and the judge is then entitled to draw any appropriate inferences, provided that he directs himself properly as to the burden and standard of proof (*Mirza* (1993) 14 Cr App R (S) 64)). D19.25

The prosecution is still required to participate whether or not they have material to dispute the defence account. In *Tolera* [1999] 1 Cr App R 29, the Court of Appeal suggested that, in questioning the offender, the prosecutor should adopt the role of *amicus curiae*, exploring matters which the court wished to be explored. The prosecution should not leave the questioning to the judge.

Role of the Defence On the other hand, the defence cannot be forced to call evidence or otherwise participate, but may simply observe while the prosecution seek to establish their version to the judge's satisfaction. A defendant cannot, however, by declining to give D19.26

evidence, frustrate the exercise which the judge has undertaken so as to enable him subsequently to complain that there has been no *Newton* hearing (*Mirza* (1993) 14 Cr App R (S) 64).

D19.27 **Role of the Court** In order to avoid giving the impression that he has made up his mind in advance, the judge should usually wait until the offender has been examined by his own counsel, and cross-examined by counsel for the prosecution, before questioning him (*Myers* (1996) 1 Cr App R (S) 187).

In assessing the evidence, the judge must, as trier of fact, observe the directions which he would have given the jury for their guidance. This was illustrated in *Gandy* (1989) 11 Cr App R (S) 564. G had pleaded guilty to violent disorder. On the completion of the trial of his co-accused, a *Newton* hearing was held to determine whether G was responsible for throwing a glass which caused serious injury, as the prosecution alleged. The Court of Appeal held that, during that *Newton* hearing, it was important that the judge should have approached the matter and directed himself as if he were a jury. In particular this required the court:

(a) to go through the steps which *Turnbull* [1977] QB 224 required the judge to set out when directing a jury;
(b) to consider the admissibility of identification evidence which breached the PACE 1984 codes of practice; and
(c) to consider the reliability of other aspects of the evidence, e.g., discrepancies between the contemporaneous descriptions of the glass thrower and G's appearance.

Hence it appears that, in the context of a *Newton* hearing: (a) the rules of evidence should be strictly followed, and (b) the judge should direct himself appropriately as the trier of fact.

Consequences of a *Newton* Hearing

D19.28 **Loss of Mitigation for a Guilty Plea** In *Underwood* (2005) 1 Cr App R 178 (see **D19.9**), the Court of Appeal set out guidance as to the extent to which the accused should receive credit for a guilty plea where a *Newton* hearing is necessary (see also *Stevens* (1986) 8 Cr App R (S) 291; *Jauncey* (1986) 8 Cr App R (S) 401; and *Williams* [1991] Crim LR 150). The main points are:

(1) If issues on a *Newton* hearing are resolved in the accused's favour, the credit due to him for a guilty plea should not be reduced.
(2) If the accused is disbelieved or obliges the prosecution to call evidence from a witness causing unnecessary and inappropriate distress, and conveys to the judge that he has no insight into the consequences of his offence and no genuine remorse for it, the judge may reduce the discount for a guilty plea, particularly if it has been tendered at a very late stage.
(3) There might be an exceptional case in which the normal entitlement to credit for a guilty plea is wholly dissipated by the *Newton* hearing, in which case the judge should explain his reasons.

If the judge mentions the prospect of loss of mitigation prior to holding a *Newton* hearing, he should be careful to avoid giving the impression that he has decided against the accused's version in advance (*Satchell* (1997) 2 Cr App R (S) 258).

Appeals in *Newton* Hearing Cases

D19.29 The Court of Appeal does have power to interfere with the decision of the sentencing judge as to the facts of the offence arrived at following a *Newton* hearing (*A-G's Refs (Nos. 3 and 4 of 1996)* (1997) 1 Cr App R (S) 29). However, there are important limitations:

(a) If the judge has properly directed himself as to the burden and standard of proof, the Court of Appeal will exercise its power only in 'exceptional cases' where 'no reasonable jury [properly] directed could have reached the judge's conclusion' (per Parker LJ in *Ahmed* (1984) 80 Cr App R 295).

(b) If the accused himself gave evidence at the *Newton* hearing, the occasions on which interference is justified will be 'rare indeed', bearing in mind the trial judge's advantage in having seen the demeanour etc. of the accused when testifying (ibid.).

In an appropriate case, however, the Court of Appeal will depart from findings of fact made by a judge in a *Newton* hearing (see, e.g., *Gandy* (1989) 11 Cr App R (S) 564, discussed in **D19.27**). In appropriate cases, the Court of Appeal can itself hold a *Newton* hearing (*Guppy* [1994] Crim LR 614).

DISPUTES ABOUT THE FACTS FOLLOWING A VERDICT OF GUILTY

General Principle

Where the accused is convicted following a trial, it is for the sentencer to form his own view as to the facts of the offence established by the evidence, and to sentence accordingly. In general, the jury should not be asked to supplement a verdict of guilty by stating the factual basis on which they reached their decision (see *Stosiek* (1982) 4 Cr App R (S) 205 and *Solomon* (1984) 6 Cr App R (S) 120). **D19.30**

There is a recognised exception to this principle, relating to a verdict of guilty of manslaughter (see **D18.79**). Although *Cranston* (1993) 14 Cr App R (S) 103 appears to give some encouragement to this becoming a wider practice, Dr. Thomas's commentary on that case at [1992] Crim LR 831 correctly identifies the inevitable problems with such a course. A number of propositions emerge from the cases.

Court Not Bound to Accept the Version Most Favourable to the Accused

The court is not obliged to accept the version of events most favourable to the defence consistent with the jury's verdict. For example, in *Solomon* (1984) 6 Cr App R (S) 120, the court was held to be entitled, in a case where the appellant T was found not guilty of attempted murder but guilty of causing grievous bodily harm with intent, to sentence on the basis that T had deliberately caused grievous bodily harm with the shotgun, even though he had not intended to kill, despite the accused's evidence being to a contrary effect (see also *McGlade* (1990) 12 Cr App R (S) 105). **D19.31**

Giving the Accused the Benefit of the Doubt

The court should, however, be 'extremely astute' to give to the offender the benefit of any doubt about the facts of the offence (per Watkins LJ in *Stosiek* (1982) 4 Cr App R (S) 205). In *Stosiek*, S was sentenced for assaulting a plain-clothes police officer occasioning him actual bodily harm on the basis that S realised at the time of the assault that his victim was an officer. The Court of Appeal reduced the sentence because the alternative basis that S had over-reacted to what he took to be a minor assault by an ordinary member of the public was a 'reasonable possibility', and should therefore have been accepted in preference to the unfavourable alternative hypothesis. **D19.32**

In *Efionayi* (1995) 16 Cr App R (S) 380, the defendants were convicted of wilful neglect of a child over a 14-day period. Complaint had been made at trial that it was open to the jury to convict of neglect over the whole period of 14 days, or a part of it. The jury were directed that they could convict if satisfied that any neglect had occurred within the period specified in the count. After they convicted, the judge sentenced on the basis that the neglect covered the whole 14 days. The Court of Appeal allowed the appeal against sentence, stating that the judge should have taken the jury's verdict to relate to the shorter period and sentenced accordingly. The Court of Appeal observed that to prevent this problem, the indictment could easily have been amended to secure the jury's finding on the point.

The Basis Must be Consistent with the Verdict

D19.33 The court must not adopt a view of the facts which is adverse to the offender and inconsistent with the jury's verdict, even if that verdict is difficult to understand. Thus, in *Hazelwood* (1984) 6 Cr App R (S) 52, H was acquitted of assault with intent to resist arrest but convicted of common assault in the alternative. His sentence was reduced because a sentence as severe as that passed was explicable only on the basis that the judge really thought H to be guilty as charged. Although the jury's verdict was difficult to understand except as an illogical compromise, 'the court has . . . to have respect for the jury's verdict and must avoid concluding or indeed suspecting that the appellant was in fact resisting arrest' (per Stephen Brown LJ).

This is really an aspect of the broader principle (see **D19.41**) that an offender must be sentenced only for those offences of which he has been found guilty or which he has admitted to the court whether by way of a guilty plea or by asking for them to be taken into consideration, or by otherwise agreeing that the indictment does not represent the full extent of his criminal conduct.

Impact of any Expressed Jury Opinion

D19.34 If the jury indicate on their own initiative a view of the facts which is relevant to sentence, the judge is not bound by that view when he decides upon sentence. In *Mills* [2004] 1 Cr App R (S) 332, the offender, on being convicted of being knowingly concerned in fraudulently evading the prohibition on the importation of cocaine and other drugs, was sentenced on the basis that he knew he was importing drugs with a high value. The jury submitted a note, stating that their verdict of guilty was based on a view that the offender genuinely believed that the goods he was importing were not drugs but were prohibited. The sentencing judge concluded that he was not bound by the note, and refused to vary the sentence. The Court of Appeal agreed that he was not bound by the jury's finding, and dismissed the appeal.

Newton Hearing following a Trial

D19.35 The court can hold a *Newton* hearing after the jury has returned a verdict of guilty (*Finch* (1993) 14 Cr App R (S) 226). This would be appropriate where an issue material to sentence was not properly canvassed during the trial because it was not relevant to guilt. In *Finch* itself, it was held that a *Newton* hearing should have been held to determine whether or not F had been entrapped, because it could, if true, amount to substantial mitigation, whilst not in law constituting a defence.

Ascertaining Facts by Verdict of Jury

D19.36 In *Newton* (1982) 77 Cr App R 13, the third alternative method of identifying the factual basis for sentence to which Lord Lane referred was to obtain the answer from a jury (see **D19.8**). The method for achieving this is to include a count on the indictment which will indicate how, in the jury's view, the primary offence to which the accused pleads guilty was committed.

For example, in *Gandy* (1989) 11 Cr App R (S) 564 (see **D19.27** for the facts), where the issue was whether G, charged with violent disorder, had caused a particular injury, the Court of Appeal felt 'some regret that the Crown had not seen fit in the circumstances of this case to include a specific count against [the appellant] for either wounding with intent under section 18 of the Offences against the Person Act 1861 or alternatively under section 20 of that Act for unlawful wounding' (see also *Efionayi* (1995) 16 Cr App R (S) 380 and **D19.32**).

In *Dowdall* (1992) 13 Cr App R (S) 441, however, the Court of Appeal held that the jury should be used to decide the issue only where the difference in the versions of the facts alleged by the prosecution and the defence reflects different offences. In that case, D was charged with stealing a pension book from a bag. He maintained that he had found the book, rather than removing it from the bag. The prosecution therefore amended the indictment to reflect these two possibilities: finding and taking. On appeal, the Court of Appeal held that the count should not have been split in two as the alternative averments added in each case were immaterial to guilt. The right course where sentence turned on which version was right was for the judge either to adopt D's version, or to try the issue himself.

ASCERTAINING THE FACTS OF THE OFFENCE WHERE ONE ACCUSED PLEADS GUILTY AND THE OTHER NOT GUILTY

The rule that, if there has been a not guilty plea followed by a verdict of guilty, it is for the judge to decide for sentencing purposes how the offence was committed on the basis of the evidence he has heard during the course of the trial, and the rule that, if the accused pleads guilty, the judge must accept the defence version of the facts unless he is satisfied at a *Newton* hearing that the prosecution version is correct, come into conflict with each other when one accused pleads guilty and the co-accused not guilty. **D19.37**

The Court of Appeal has wavered in its approach to the problem. In *Taggart* (1979) 1 Cr App R (S) 144 and *Depledge* (1979) 1 Cr App R (S) 183, it was held that, when sentencing the accused who pleaded guilty, the judge could take into account the evidence he had heard at the co-accused's trial. However, in *Michaels* (1981) 3 Cr App R (S) 188, the judge was criticised for taking a view of the facts adverse to the appellants without having all the witnesses who had testified at the trial of their co-accused recalled for cross-examination.

The Court of Appeal have since been afforded the opportunity of resolving the conflict between the earlier authorities on two occasions, namely in *Smith* (1988) 87 Cr App R 393 and *Mahoney* (1993) 14 Cr App R (S) 291.

The Approach in *Smith*

In *Smith* (1988) 87 Cr App R 393, *Taggart* and *Depledge* were preferred to *Michaels*. S pleaded guilty to conspiracy to obtain property by deception. At their trial, certain of his co-accused offered the defence that they acted under duress stemming from S. When the time came to sentence, the judge indicated that he had taken a preliminary view that S was the ringleader in the enterprise, albeit that the jury had rejected the co-accused's claim that they had been subjected to duress by him. None of the evidence called at the trial was recalled but S was offered the opportunity to testify in his own defence that he was not the ringleader. **D19.38**

The Court of Appeal upheld the sentence and said that the judge had handled the procedural problem 'impeccably'. His primary task when sentencing was to decide what had been the facts of the conspiracy and, in doing that, he *was* entitled to take into account evidence he had heard at the trial of the co-accused and even witness statements. There was no need to have the witnesses recalled for cross-examination by the accused pleading guilty. To hold otherwise might have led to a situation where the judge felt constrained to sentence one conspirator on a view of the facts which he had rejected when sentencing a co-conspirator. It was, however, necessary for S himself to be offered the opportunity of giving evidence about the extent of his involvement. The judge had done that more than once, and the appeal was accordingly dismissed.

Difficulties with *Smith* The decision in *Smith* (1988) 87 Cr App R 393, while understandable as a pragmatic solution to a difficult problem, may lead to a sense of unfairness being felt by an offender who is sentenced on a view of the facts which he disputes and which his **D19.39**

counsel has not been able to test. In *Smith*, counsel was present in court during the trial of the co-accused, holding a noting brief. Thus, the defence at least knew what had been said against S. However, counsel had no standing to cross-examine the witnesses who impugned his client, and S himself never heard the evidence on the basis of which he was sentenced.

A further anomaly appears when one compares the approach outlined in *Smith* with that adopted in a case such as *Gandy* (1989) 11 Cr App R (S) 564 (see **D19.27**). In *Gandy*, a *Newton* hearing was held in relation to G, who had pleaded guilty, at the end of the trial of others. In that *Newton* hearing the judge was required to follow the rules which would govern the use of evidence in a jury trial. Clearly, there is no equivalent protection for the accused where the *Smith* procedure is concerned. The resultant distinction exacerbates the sense of unfairness already referred to (see also *Winter* [1997] Crim LR 66).

The Approach in *Mahoney*

D19.40 In *Mahoney* (1993) 14 Cr App R (S) 291, the Court of Appeal favoured the approach suggested in *Michaels*, although neither that case nor *Taggart* nor *Depledge* was referred to. Twenty-one prisoners were indicted in relation to a prison riot. There were two trials, and M pleaded guilty to the lesser offence of violent disorder and was sentenced at the end of the second trial. The Court of Appeal reduced M's sentence, stating (Leonard J at p. 293):

> A further submission is made that in this case what happened was that the learned judge heard the evidence in the first trial and in the second trial which led to acquittal, and that in large part he passed sentence upon the appellant on the basis of that material. The problem about that was that the appellant was neither present at, nor represented at, either of those two trials. It was, in our view, wrong therefore, for the learned judge to pay regard to what he had heard in those trials when he was passing sentence upon the appellant.
>
> It is quite clear that the judge formed the view that the prosecution had been somewhat supine in accepting the pleas to violent disorder at the threshold of the second trial. That seems to be the point of his observation about his sentencing on the basis of the facts rather than the title of the offence. If there were matters which were in dispute, the learned judge should either have adopted the course which he indicated at the earlier stage and have sentenced on the basis of what the appellant through his counsel was accepting to be the appropriate facts of the case, or alternatively, if there was a need to resolve the dispute, it should have been resolved by means of a *Newton* hearing.

DUTY TO MAKE SENTENCE CONFORM TO FACTS CONSISTENT WITH VERDICT

D19.41 The above heading may seem a statement of the obvious. It is, however, a cardinal principle of sentencing, confirmed by *Ralf* (1989) 11 Cr App R (S) 121. It has a number of implications for determining the facts of the offence, which are addressed below.

Respecting the Verdict

D19.42 First, as explained immediately above, the sentencer must respect the jury's verdict when determining the facts of the offence and not pass a sentence appropriate to a more serious charge of which the offender has been acquitted (*Gillespie* [1998] 2 Cr App R (S) 61). Similarly, if the prosecution accept a plea to a lesser offence or to one of several counts, the judge must be careful to sentence for that only and not for the more serious matters left on the file (*Booker* (1982) 4 Cr App R (S) 53). The Court of Appeal emphasised this in *Stubbs* (1988) 89 Cr App R 53, saying 'the court must abide loyally by the plea which had been tendered'.

Not Inflating the Offending

Secondly, the judge must not sentence on the basis that the offender has committed other similar offences on other occasions, even if the circumstances of the offence charged or admissions made by the offender when being questioned by the police strongly indicate that it was not a 'one-off' occurrence (*Reeves* (1983) 5 Cr App R (S) 292 and *Ayensu* (1982) 4 Cr App R (S) 248). This is subject to the major exception that the defence may concede that the counts in the indictment are merely samples of a continuing course of conduct or ask for other offences to be taken into consideration (see **D19.52**). **D19.43**

Similarly, the judge must not, under the pretence of determining the facts of the offence at a *Newton* hearing, in effect find the accused guilty of an offence more serious than that with which he is charged (*Courtie* [1984] AC 463; *Druce* (1993) 14 Cr App R (S) 691).

Secondary Offending

Difficult problems also arise where the prosecution version of the facts of the offence on the indictment (the primary offence) implies that the accused is guilty of an additional offence (the secondary offence) with which he is not charged. There are some cases which seem to suggest that, provided the secondary offence is of no greater gravity than the primary offence, the judge may (subject to the need for a *Newton* hearing) sentence on the basis that the latter did indeed involve commission of the former as alleged by the prosecution. **D19.44**

This is illustrated in the cases of *Ribas* (1976) 63 Cr App R 147 and *Rubinstein* (1982) 4 Cr App R (S) 202, which concerned, respectively, counts for importing controlled drugs and conspiracy to cultivate controlled drugs. The question arose whether the sentencers were right to reject the defence mitigation that the drugs were intended only for personal consumption, given that there was no count on either indictment for possession with intent to supply or conspiracy to supply. The Court of Appeal in both cases upheld the judges' approach.

These cases may be contrasted with *Lawrence* (1981) 3 Cr App R (S) 49, where L pleaded guilty to cultivating cannabis and the Court of Appeal held that the sentencer had to 'banish from his mind' the possibility that L was growing the cannabis in order to sell it. *Lawrence* was considered and applied in *O'Prey* [1999] 2 Cr App R (S) 83, where the Court of Appeal stressed that it was not permissible for the sentencer to sentence for criminality not reflected in the indictment (for the solution of adding a count to the indictment to reflect the secondary offence, see **D19.36**).

However, in other circumstances the Court of Appeal has positively exhorted sentencers to take into account other offences in this way. For example in *Boswell* [1984] 1 WLR 1047, in the course of giving guidelines on sentencing for causing death by reckless driving, Lord Lane CJ said that an aggravating feature conclusive towards a custodial sentence was if the offender's driving had involved other offences such as driving while disqualified or under the influence of drink.

EVIDENCE OF CHARACTER AND ANTECEDENTS

Requirement for Evidence of Character and Antecedents

After the prosecution summary of the facts, or immediately after the jury's verdict of guilty if it was a not guilty plea, it is the responsibility of the prosecution to adduce evidence about the offender's character and antecedents. The evidence is based upon a copy of written antecedents prepared in advance by the police according to a basic pattern prescribed in the *Consolidated Criminal Practice Direction*, para. III.27 (see **appendix 7**). **D19.45**

Procedure for Giving Antecedents

D19.46 Evidence of the offender's antecedents can either be presented through the calling of a police officer to give evidence on oath, or presented by prosecuting counsel, provided that the defence has agreed that the antecedents are not in dispute. Where the evidence is given by an officer, he takes the *voir dire* oath (see **F4.27**) and, in effect, reads from the antecedents and previous convictions forms. The normal rules of evidence are relaxed in that counsel may ask leading questions. Moreover, the antecedents will not necessarily have been prepared by the officer giving the evidence or contain matters within his personal knowledge. In fact, most of the information will have come from the offender himself, either on the occasion of his present arrest or in the course of his previous dealings with the police. Once the officer has completed his evidence in chief, he may be asked further questions by counsel for the defence.

Contents of Antecedents

D19.47 The prosecution are not necessarily restricted to the basic and essentially uncontroversial form of antecedents specifically sanctioned by the *Consolidated Criminal Practice Direction*, para. III.27. Further guidance has been provided as to what may or may not be included in the presentation of antecedents.

(a) It must not contain allegations of a generalised nature which are prejudicial to the offender and, by their very nature, incapable of proof (*Van Pelz* [1943] KB 157).

(b) In exceptional cases, it may be proper to adduce additional information about the offender's involvement in gangland crime and organised prostitution (*Wilkins* (1977) 66 Cr App R 49) or his position in a chain of criminals supplying drugs (*Robinson* (1969) 53 Cr App R 314). As to whether it is proper to adduce evidence of the offender's criminal associates, in *Bibby* [1972] Crim LR 513 the Court of Appeal ruled that it was unfair but Lord Goddard CJ in *Crabtree* [1952] 2 All ER 974 could see nothing wrong with such evidence provided that the officer could give it from first-hand knowledge.

(c) Such allegations are likely to be challenged by the defence, and, in the event of challenge, it is essential that the prosecution prove what they allege in accordance with the ordinary rules of criminal evidence.

(d) 'Evidence' from the antecedents officer based on hearsay is inadmissible, even if it takes the form of recounting information supplied to him by colleagues (*Wilkins*). This reflects a principle first stated in *Campbell* (1911) 6 Cr App R 131 that, whenever antecedents evidence is challenged by the defence, the onus is on the prosecution to prove their case by strict evidence. If they fail to do so, the judge should ignore the challenged allegation and state that he is ignoring it (ibid., and also *Sargeant* (1974) 60 Cr App R 74).

If the prosecution anticipate that the antecedents will be disputed by the defence, it is good practice to give the defence notice of the proposed evidence (see dicta in both *Robinson* and *Wilkins*).

Proof of the Offender's Convictions

D19.48 Like any other disputed part of the antecedents, if the offender disputes a previous conviction alleged against him at the antecedents stage, it must either be proved in accordance with the strict rules of evidence or ignored. For the methods of proving a previous conviction, see **F11**. If the offender has a long record, it is rare for it to be given in full. The judge will indicate which of the convictions he considers it necessary to read.

Spent Convictions

D19.49 The Rehabilitation of Offenders Act 1974, as applied to criminal proceedings by the *Consolidated Criminal Practice Direction*, para. I.6 (see **appendix** 7), restricts the circumstances in which it is proper to refer to 'spent convictions'.

The scheme of the 1974 Act is that, where an offender is sentenced to 30 months' imprisonment or less for an offence, his conviction becomes spent upon the expiry of the 'rehabilitation period'. That period runs from the date of conviction and varies in length depending upon the sentence imposed (e.g., ten years for a prison sentence exceeding six months but not exceeding 30 months; six months for an absolute discharge). Commission of a further offence during the rehabilitation period for an earlier one usually means that neither conviction becomes spent until the rehabilitation date for the later one. Thus, recidivist offenders rarely enjoy the advantages of their convictions becoming spent. For further details of periods of rehabilitation, see **E26.3**; for evidential considerations, see **F12.51**.

The Proper Approach to Spent Convictions The main function of the Rehabilitation of Offenders Act 1974 is to protect a person with spent convictions from having to reveal his record in civil proceedings or when applying for a job. Indeed, s. 7(2) provides that the protection against questions relating to spent convictions afforded by s. 4(1) of the Act does *not* apply to evidence given in criminal proceedings. However, the *Consolidated Criminal Practice Direction*, para I.6, gives guidance on how the criminal courts should deal with spent convictions (see **appendix** 7). The main points emerge from the following quotations from the direction: **D19.50**

(a) '. . . it is recommended that both court and advocates should give effect to the general intention of Parliament [in passing the 1974 Act] by never referring to a spent conviction when such reference can reasonably be avoided' (para. I.6.4).
(b) 'After a verdict of guilty the court must be provided with a statement of the defendant's record for the purposes of sentence. The record supplied should contain all previous convictions, but those which are spent should, so far as practicable, be marked as such' (para. I.6.5).
(c) 'No one should refer in open court to a spent conviction without the authority of the judge, which authority should not be given unless the interests of justice so require' (para. I.6.6).
(d) 'When passing sentence the judge should make no reference to a spent conviction unless it is necessary to do so for the purpose of explaining the sentence to be passed' (para. I.6.7).

Breach of Court Orders

If the offender's present conviction apparently puts him in breach of an existing court order such as a suspended sentence (for which see **E8.7**) or a conditional discharge (for which see **E14.5**), it will be necessary to put that breach to him. If he denies the breach, the matter must be proved by strict evidence. Upon the breach being admitted or proved, prosecuting counsel should, if possible, be able to give the court details of the offence in respect of which the order breached was made. **D19.51**

SENTENCING THE OFFENDER FOR MATTERS OF WHICH HE HAS NOT BEEN CONVICTED

It is a basic principle of sentencing that the offender should be sentenced only for those crimes of which he has been convicted and not for anything else which the court may consider him to have done (see **D19.43**). **D19.52**

There are three identifiable exceptions to this principle where a sentencer may properly be influenced by other offences not officially before the court. These are as follows:

(a) taking into account a less serious secondary offence which has not been charged but the commission of which is implicit in, and represents an aggravating feature of, the more serious primary offence (see *Rubinstein* (1982) 4 Cr App R (S) 202 at **D19.44**).

(b) if the offender expressly asks for the other offences to be taken into consideration (see D19.53), and

(c) if the prosecution case is that the offences on the indictment are merely samples of a continuing course of conduct and the defence accept that to be so (see **D19.56**).

Taking Other Offences into Consideration

D19.53 This is a common practice with no set rules governing its operation. It is based upon convention rather than statute or common law. It requires the co-operation of the police, the court and, most importantly, the offender himself. It operates to the benefit of both the police and the offender. The police are enabled to clear up numerous offences which might otherwise remain unsolved. The offender is able to 'wipe the slate completely clean' at a minimal cost in terms of increased sentence.

D19.54 **Normal Practice** The normal procedure involves the following stages.

(a) The police, having arrested a suspect for a certain offence and obtained admissions from him, will then invite him to tell them about other crimes they think he may have committed.

(b) Depending on the suspect's response, a list is then drawn up of the other offences.

(c) The suspect is charged with a limited number of offences, is prosecuted in the normal way, and pleads guilty.

(d) At some time before his court appearance, the offender is served with the list of the other offences and asked to sign it if he agrees that he committed them. He may, of course, accept some but not all of the offences.

(e) Copies of the list (the 't.i.c.s') are then given to the defence and included in prosecuting counsel's brief.

(f) At a convenient moment during the counsel's summary of the facts of the offence to which the offender has pleaded guilty, the court is told that he wishes to have other offences taken into consideration. The court is given the original of the list, signed by the accused.

(g) The offender then confirms with the court that he does admit the offences and wants them taken into consideration.

(h) The court then decides whether to comply with the offender's request. Assuming it does, prosecuting counsel gives brief details of the offences, and the sentencing process thereafter continues in the normal way. When passing sentence, the judge should state that he has taken so many other offences into consideration.

Although the t.i.c. procedure is geared for offenders expected to plead guilty, there is no objection to adapting it for an accused pleading not guilty. Thus, in anticipation of a guilty verdict, the police might prepare a t.i.c. list and then use an adjournment between conviction and sentence to invite the accused to sign the list.

D19.55 **Assessment of the Procedure** A number of matters arise in relation to the t.i.c. procedure.

(a) Since the offender is never charged with or convicted of the t.i.c.s, the court's powers of sentence are limited to the maximum for the offences on the indictment of which the offender has been convicted, whether by way of guilty plea or jury verdict (hereafter referred to as 'the conviction offences'). This is not a significant restriction since it is rare that a court would wish to impose a sentence nearing the maximum penalties. The exception to this limitation is that the court may order the offender to pay compensation for a matter taken into consideration, and to that extent may sentence directly for the offence — see PCC(S)A 2000, s. 130(1)(a).

(b) An offence should not be taken into consideration if it carries endorsement of the licence and discretionary or obligatory disqualification if the conviction offences are non-endorsable (*Collins* [1947] KB 560 and *Simons* (1953) 37 Cr App R 120). Otherwise, the offender would escape even endorsement whereas, had the t.i.c. offence been prosecuted in the normal way, the court would have been obliged to endorse in the absence of special reasons and might have chosen also to disqualify.

(c) Offences should not be taken into consideration unless the offender clearly requests the sentencer to do so and admits commission of the offences (*Griffiths* (1932) 23 Cr App R 153). In *Walsh* (8 March 1973 unreported), Scarman J stressed the importance of the offender understanding what is being done, admitting the offences and genuinely wanting them taken into consideration.

(d) It is not necessary to read the list out in full. It is sufficient if the judge confirms with the offender that he has signed the list containing a specified number of offences which he agrees that he committed, and confirms that he now wants them borne in mind when sentence is passed for the offences on the indictment. The request to take offences into consideration should come from the offender himself, not counsel (*Mortimer* (10 March 1970 unreported)).

(e) The judge always has a discretion whether or not to comply with a request to take an offence into consideration. He should not take into consideration an offence which the offender is willing to admit if the public interest requires that the offence be dealt with by indictment (*McLean* (1910) 6 Cr App R 26). Further, it would be bad practice to take offences into consideration which are either more serious than or of a completely different type from the conviction offences.

(f) The fact that an offence has been taken into consideration does not entitle the offender to rely on autrefois convict should he subsequently be prosecuted for it (*Nicholson* [1947] 2 All ER 535). However, in the absence of quite exceptional circumstances, the prosecution would not consider instituting proceedings for a matter that they know to have been taken into consideration by a court on a previous occasion.

(g) In passing sentence, the judge may increase the penalty somewhat because of the t.i.c.s. However, the amount of the increase will almost certainly be considerably less than what would have been the sentence had the offences been separately prosecuted.

Sample Offences

As an alternative to following strictly the procedure for taking other offences into consideration, the prosecution may invite the judge to treat the offences on the indictment of which the accused has been convicted, or to which he has pleaded guilty, as samples of a continuing course of conduct. (See **D11.33** for detail on the implications of sample counts when considering the indictment.) **D19.56**

This is an attractive course where the offender appears to have committed a large number of similar offences over a protracted period. Although there is no reason, in such a case, why a list of t.i.c.s should not be prepared as described in **D19.53**, the list can become inordinately long (see, e.g., *Sequeira* (1982) 4 Cr App R (S) 65, where, in respect of an offender who had claimed social security benefit for four years when ineligible, the t.i.c. procedure resulted in a list of 150 offences).

Sentencing for Sample Offences Following a Guilty Plea It is generally accepted, that where the accused pleads guilty and the defence agree with the prosecution that the offences on the indictment are merely samples, the court may sentence on that basis even though the offender does not formally ask for other offences to be taken into consideration. **D19.57**

Such an approach was approved in *Huchison* [1972] 1 WLR 398 per Phillimore LJ at p. 400C:

> Of course, there are cases where the prosecution puts forward a count as a sample count, and in those cases it is well understood that if that course is taken and the defence are notified, a judge is entitled to deal with the whole matter on the basis that the offence in fact was repeated more than once, or that there were other similar incidents.

If, however, the defence dispute the other occasions on which similar offences were allegedly committed, the judge should sentence the offender only for those occasions which he does admit, whether by way of guilty plea or by asking for a limited number of other occasions to be taken into consideration.

This, again, was demonstrated in *Huchison*. H pleaded guilty to one count of incest with his daughter, and there was dispute as to how often intercourse had occurred. The Court of Appeal criticised the sentencing procedure adopted. Upon it becoming obvious that the defence denied the suggestion that the offence on the indictment was a sample one, the judge's options were either to sentence H strictly for the one act of intercourse he had admitted, or to adjourn so that counts for the other occasions could be added to the indictment.

Huchison has been followed in *McKenzie* (1984) 6 Cr App R (S) 99 (sentence reduced for seven cheque card offences involving loss to the victims of £640 because the judge had apparently sentenced on the basis denied by the defence that the counts on the indictment were samples of continuing conduct in which £11,000 had been obtained), and *Ralf* (1989) 11 Cr App R (S) 121 (sentence for assault on a child reduced because the judge referred to the appellant having caused various injuries to the child over and above those she actually admitted).

D19.58 **Sentencing for Sample Offences Following a Trial** Where the accused pleads not guilty to the offences on the indictment but is found guilty, more recent authorities support the proposition that the accused should only be sentenced for offences which he has admitted to the court, whether by plea, by asking the court to take them into consideration, or in some other clear fashion (*Perkins* (1994) 15 Cr App R (S) 402).

Hence, the fact that the charges upon which the accused was found guilty were described by the prosecution as 'specimens' does not entitle the judge to sentence him as if he had been found guilty of other offences not included in the indictment. This is the view adopted in *Burfoot* (1990) 12 Cr App R (S) 252. The accused ought not to be deprived of his right to jury trial merely because offences are omitted from the indictment.

In *Clark* [1996] 2 Cr App R (S) 351, the Court of Appeal followed the reasoning in *Burfoot* and in *McKenzie* (1984) 6 Cr App R 99. Their lordships said that the weight of authority supported the proposition that, where an offender was convicted on a single count, the sentencer must not sentence him on the basis that he was guilty of further offences of a similar nature unless the offender admitted that this was so. Such authority as had been cited to the contrary (*Mills* (1979) 68 Cr App R 154 and *Singh* (1981) 3 Cr App R (S) 90) was rejected. The court suggested that prosecutors should charge sufficient offences fairly to reflect the criminality of the offending.

A different conclusion was reached by the Court of Appeal in *Bradshaw* [1997] 2 Cr App R (S) 128. However, in *Canavan* [1998] 1 Cr App R 79, the Court of Appeal considered the conflict of authority and said that *Clark* was to be preferred to *Bradshaw*. Lord Bingham CJ stated in *Canavan* that the court could not base its decision as to sentence on the commission of offences not forming part of the offence for which the offender was to be sentenced. It is respectfully submitted that the decision in *Canavan* upholding that in *Clark* has resolved the question both authoritatively and in accordance with principle.

An alternative to the above procedure is now set out in the DVCVA 2004, s. 17. This allows the prosecution to apply for trial by jury on sample counts, with the judge trying the remaining counts alone (see **D13.72** for details).

REPORTS ON THE ACCUSED

After the prosecution summary of the facts and antecedents evidence, the court considers any reports that have been prepared on the offender. These may include pre-sentence reports, medical and psychiatric reports and assessments for suitability for a community sentence. In many cases, it will have been necessary to delay sentencing to allow such reports to be prepared (see **D19.101**). **D19.59**

Judicial Promise of Non-custodial Sentence on Adjournment for Reports

Where the court adjourns for reports in circumstances which justifiably lead the offender to expect that, if the report turns out to be favourable, the sentence will be non-custodial, the court is bound by the implied promise it has given. Consequently, if the report is indeed favourable, a custodial sentence should not be passed, and will be quashed on appeal, however deserved it would otherwise have been. **D19.60**

The principle was first stated in *Gillam* (1980) 2 Cr App R (S) 267. G, a serving prisoner, appeared to be sentenced for offences for which it was likely that he would receive a further prison term. However, the judge adjourned so that G's suitability for community service could be assessed, and ordered that, upon the expiry of his present sentence, G should be released on bail. The Court of Appeal's judgment observed that the main purpose of the adjournment was 'to ascertain whether community service was available for such a person as [G] and whether he was a fit subject to perform that service'. In the event, although G was assessed suitable for community service he received a sentence of imprisonment.

The Court of Appeal allowed the appeal for the following reasons (per Watkins LJ at p. 269, emphasis added):

> . . . an important principle of sentencing is involved in this case. All the signs, when the appellant first appeared before the deputy circuit judge, . . . pointed to the imposition of an immediate prison sentence. For reasons best known to himself he decided against that course but to request the production of a report with a view to considering whether or not this man should perform community service. There was, therefore, created in the appellant's mind an expectation, not unnaturally, of performing that service if the probation officer and others who were called upon to assist in the production of the report were disposed to recommend such a course to the court. It was recommended. *When a judge in these circumstances purposely postpones sentence so that an alternative to prison can be examined and that alternative is found to be a satisfactory one in all respects the court ought to adopt the alternative.* A feeling of injustice is otherwise aroused.

Application of the *Gillam* principle The decision in *Gillam* has been followed in a number of cases since in which reports prepared on offenders during adjournments were favourable, and the custodial sentences ultimately imposed had to be quashed. These included: **D19.61**

(a) *Ward* (1982) 4 Cr App R (S) 103 (three-week adjournment so that W could stay at a probation hostel with a view to the making of a probation order with a condition of residence at the hostel);
(b) *McMurray* (1987) 9 Cr App R (S) 101 (four-week adjournment so that McM could attend a day assessment centre);
(c) *Wilkinson* (1988) 9 Cr App R (S) 468, the facts of which were similar to *Ward*, where the sentencing judge conceded that the judge who adjourned for social enquiry reports had, by so doing, more or less promised a non-custodial disposition, but said that the offence was so serious that he (the sentencing judge) was not prepared to incur public wrath by such a lenient course — the Court of Appeal held that, in the circumstances, he had no option but to honour the first judge's implied promise, whatever the public reaction.

Adjournment for Reports Not Binding the Judge However, there is no rule that adjourning for reports *inevitably* carries the implication that the sentence will be non-custodial if the **D19.62**

report so recommends. The application of the *Gillam* principle depends upon 'there having been something in the nature of a promise, express or implied, that if a particular proposal is recommended, it will be adopted' (per Croom-Johnson J in *Moss* (1983) 5 Cr App R (S) 209).

Thus, if the judge makes it clear when adjourning that he is *not* committing himself to a non-custodial disposition even if the report is generally favourable and recommends such a course, the offender can have no complaints about the recommendation being rejected. That was held in *Horton* (1985) 7 Cr App R (S) 299, where the judge, on adjourning for reports, said that he thought that an immediate custodial sentence would be the likely conclusion. One reason for the judge adjourning in *Horton* was the fact that the offender was under 21, and there was then a statutory requirement for a report in respect of such offenders.

The combination of such a statutory requirement and the principle in *Gillam's* case creates a difficulty for the judge. He may well feel it necessary to obtain a report to comply with the statutory provisions. Silence about his ultimate intentions may be construed as an implied promise to pass a non-custodial sentence but equally he ought not to give the impression that a custodial sentence is inevitable. It may be thought that the judge in *Horton* steered a judicious middle course, indicating that custody was probable but leaving open the possibility that something truly exceptional in the reports might persuade him to change his mind. See also *Norton* (1989) 11 Cr App R (S) 143.

In *Renan* (1994) 15 Cr App R (S) 722, the Court of Appeal said that the silence of the judge when adjourning for a pre-sentence report should never be taken as an indication that a non-custodial sentence would be passed, even when the accused was granted bail. It was the duty of counsel in these circumstances to warn the defendant that the grant of bail did not mean that custody would be avoided.

D19.63 **Committal for Sentence** The *Gillam* principle applies not only when the Crown Court is passing sentence following a conviction on indictment, but also when it is dealing with a committal for sentence or appeal from a magistrates' court. In both cases, if the ordering of reports by the court below created a reasonable expectation of a non-custodial sentence, the Crown Court is bound by the lower court's implied promise (see *Rennes* (1985) 7 Cr App R (S) 343 and *Gutteridge v DPP* (1987) 9 Cr App R (S) 279).

D19.64 **Effect of an Adjournment for Enquiries** It need not be an adjournment for reports which creates the expectation of a non-custodial sentence. In *McMillan* (1988) 10 Cr App R (S) 205, counsel addressed the Crown Court judge on the basis that sentence might be deferred in view of the fact that employment was available to M. The judge adjourned for an hour to allow confirmation that the employment was still open to be obtained. The Court of Appeal held that M's hopes had been raised by the judge's actions, resulting in a sense of grievance when a custodial sentence was nevertheless imposed. See also *Jackson* [1996] Crim LR 355.

D19.65 **Effect of Judicial Indications as to Sentence** Another situation in which the accused might have a legitimate expectation of a non-custodial sentence is where the judge has indicated that he will impose such a sentence. *Turner* [1970] 2 QB 321 (see **D12.53**) establishes that any judicial indication of sentence must be given on the basis that it is irrespective of plea. If an indication is given on the basis that it applies only if the accused pleads guilty, the judge will be bound by the indication if the accused pleads not guilty and is convicted (see *Bird* (1978) 67 Cr App R 203 and *Atkinson* [1978] 1 WLR 425).

An example of the application of this principle is *Keily* [1990] Crim LR 204. The judge at a pre-trial review in chambers had indicated that if K pleaded guilty he would not receive a sentence of immediate imprisonment. K was told this, but pleaded not guilty, and was convicted following trial before a different judge. The second judge was told of the first judge's indication but sentenced K to immediate imprisonment. The Court of Appeal found:

(a) the indication given by the first judge bound the second judge (see *Wilkinson* (1988) 9 Cr App R (S) 468 at **D19.61**); and
(b) an indication given on the basis of a guilty plea binds the sentencer on conviction after a not guilty plea (*Turner*; *Bird*; *Atkinson*).

The fact that a judge gave an indication of sentence before plea will not bind the Court of Appeal if the A-G appeals against the sentence as unduly lenient (*A-G's Ref (No. 40 of 1996)* [1997] 1 Cr App R (S) 357: see **D27.5**).

Pre-sentence Report

Meaning The term 'Pre-Sentence Report' is defined by the CJA 2003, s. 158(1), as a report which: **D19.66**

> (a) with a view to assisting the court in determining the most suitable method of dealing with an offender, is made or submitted by an appropriate officer [defined in subsection (2)]; and
> (b) contains information as to such matters, presented in such manner, as may be prescribed by rules made by the Secretary of State.

Preparation of the Report Pre-sentence reports on adults are compiled by probation officers. In the cases of children under 13, reports are prepared by local authority social workers. In the cases of those aged 13 to 16 inclusive, responsibility is shared between the probation service and social services, precise arrangements varying from area to area (see CYPA 1969, ss. 9 and 34(3)). **D19.67**

Circumstances in which a Report Must be Obtained The CJA 2003 places an obligation on the court to obtain a pre-sentence report in two circumstances. **D19.68**

(a) Under s. 156(3)(a), the court 'shall obtain and consider a pre-sentence report' in determining whether a custodial sentence should be imposed. This is not obligatory, however, where the court is of the opinion that it is unnecessary and the accused is over 18. In the case of a juvenile, a pre-sentence report is obligatory unless 'the offence or any other offence associated with it is triable only on indictment'. Even then, the court need not order a new pre-sentence report, but may have regard to an existing one (see **E1.16**).
(b) Under s. 156(3)(b), the court is required to obtain and consider a pre-sentence report before forming an opinion as to the suitability of an offender for various types of community sentence (for further details, see **E10.1**).

Circumstances in which a Report May Be Prepared It is the duty of the probation service or, as the case may be, social services to prepare a report if one is requested by the court. Alternatively, the service may take the initiative and prepare a report without being asked to do so if: **D19.69**

(a) it is anticipated that the accused will plead guilty and he is either aged 30 or less; or
(b) the conviction will put him in breach of a suspended sentence or other court order;
(c) he has recently been in contact with the probation service, or medical reports are also being prepared;
(d) if the accused is female and pleading guilty, there will usually be a pre-trial report even if she does not fall within any of the aforementioned categories.

The probation service will be reluctant to prepare a report if the accused indicates a not guilty plea, both because it will be wasted effort in the event of an acquittal and also because one of the main purposes of a report is to assess the offender's attitude to his offence and that cannot be done if he denies having committed it. Where the court desires a report and one has not already been prepared, it will be necessary to adjourn. It may be made a condition of bail that the accused co-operates in the preparation of the report (Bail Act 1976, s. 3(6): see **D7.41**).

Procedure on Receiving Pre-sentence Report A copy of the pre-sentence report must be **D19.70**

given either to the offender or to his legal representative and to the prosecutor. In the case of an unrepresented offender aged under 18, the report need not be given to him personally but must be given to his parent or guardian if present. Where the offender is aged under 18 and disclosure to him or any parent or guardian would be likely to create a risk of significant harm to the offender, the copy provided need not be a complete copy of the report (CJA 2003, s. 159(2) and (3)).

A copy of the report may be withheld from the prosecutor if the prosecutor is not of a prescribed description and the court considers it inappropriate for him to be given it (s. 159(4)). The prescribed description of a prosecutor for these purposes is contained in the Pre-Sentence (Prescription of Prosecutors) Order 1998 (SI 1998 No. 191).

The probation officer who prepared the report is not usually present in court when the report is submitted, but the defence may require his attendance if they wish in order to challenge what has been written. The report is not read out in full in open court, but counsel may refer to passages of it in mitigation if he so desires.

D19.71 **New Disclosures in a Pre-Sentence Report** In *Cunnah* [1996] 1 Cr App R (S) 393, the Court of Appeal stressed that when fresh and highly relevant material appeared in a pre-sentence report it must be discussed with counsel. This is particularly important, as was the case in *Cunnah,* where pleas had been entered on a limited basis.

Medical and Psychiatric Reports

D19.72 It is a precondition of the making of a hospital order under the Mental Health Act 1983, s. 37(1) (or an interim hospital order under s. 38), that the court be satisfied on the written or oral evidence of two medical practitioners that the offender is suffering from mental disorder within the meaning of the Act such as to warrant the making of an order (see E24.1). Equally, a report from at least one medical practitioner is required before a custodial sentence is passed on a mentally disordered offender (CJA 2003, s. 157: see E24.1).

Where a medical report is to be tendered in evidence under the provisions of the Mental Health Act 1983, a copy must be given to defence solicitors (Mental Health Act 1983, s. 54(3)(a)). If the accused is unrepresented, the gist of the report should be disclosed to him although he is not entitled to a copy; in the case of a juvenile, the substance of the report must be disclosed to any parent or guardian present in court (s. 54(3)(b)). The medical practitioner who made the report may be required to attend for cross-examination (s. 54(3)(c)).

D19.73 **Power to Remand to Obtain a Report** A magistrates' court has various powers in relation to obtaining such a report.

(a) When remanding an accused in custody the court may, in appropriate cases, request the prison medical service to prepare a report.
(b) If a magistrates' court is satisfied that the accused 'did the act or made the omission charged', it has the power to remand him for up to three weeks in custody or four weeks on bail for a medical examination to be made and report prepared (PCC(S)A 2000, s. 11(1) and (2)). A remand under s. 11(1) and (2) may be ordered notwithstanding that the accused is unconvicted. If the accused is granted bail, it *must* be made a condition of his bail that he co-operate in the preparation of the reports (s. 11(3)).

No specific provisions govern the obtaining of medical reports by the Crown Court. If none have been prepared as a result of proceedings in the court below, the court may exercise its inherent power to adjourn so as to give the opportunity for a report to be made.

D19.74 **Remand to Hospital** The courts have been given the power, under the Mental Health Act 1983, s. 35, to remand an accused or convicted person to hospital, for the preparation of reports on his mental condition (see below). This may arise either on the court's own motion or at the initiative of defence solicitors. There are special requirements for medical evidence in the case of mentally disordered offenders.

Mental Health Act 1983, s. 35

(1) Subject to the provisions of this section, the Crown Court or a magistrates' court may remand an accused person to a hospital specified by the court for a report on his mental condition.

(2) For the purposes of this section an accused person is—

(a) in relation to the Crown Court, any person who is awaiting trial before the court for an offence punishable with imprisonment or who has been arraigned before the court for such an offence and has not yet been sentenced or otherwise dealt with for the offence on which he has been arraigned;

(b) in relation to a magistrates' court, any person who has been convicted by the court of an offence punishable on summary conviction with imprisonment and any person charged with such an offence if the court is satisfied that he did the act or made the omission charged or he has consented to the exercise by the court of the powers conferred by this section.

(3) Subject to subsection (4) below, the powers conferred by this section may be exercised if—

(a) the court is satisfied, on the written or oral evidence of a registered medical practitioner that there is reason to suspect that the accused person is suffering from mental illness, psychopathic disorder, severe mental impairment or mental impairment; and

(b) the court is of the opinion that it would be impracticable for a report on his mental condition to be made if he were remanded on bail;

but those powers shall not be exercised by the Crown Court in respect of a person who has been convicted before the court if the sentence for the offence of which he has been convicted is fixed by law.

(4) The court shall not remand an accused person to a hospital under this section unless satisfied, on the written or oral evidence of the registered medical practitioner who would be responsible for making the report or of some other person representing the managers of the hospital, that arrangements have been made for his admission to that hospital and for his admission to it within the period of seven days beginning with the date of the remand; and if the court is so satisfied it may, pending his admission, give directions for his conveyance to and detention in a place of safety.

Other Reports

Before passing a community sentence, the court must normally be satisfied, on the basis of a report from a probation officer (or social worker of a local authority social services department) that the offender is a suitable person to perform work under a community order (CJA 2003, s. 148 and s. 156: see **E10.1**). An assessment for suitability for a community penalty is usually ordered in conjunction with a pre-sentence report. **D19.75**

Various other types of report may also be before the court. In particular, in the cases of juveniles, detailed reports by social workers may be prepared during the period of a remand in care prior to sentence. There may also be a report from the juvenile's school, dealing with his attendance, behaviour, performance etc. When it comes into force, the CJA 2003, s. 161, will permit the drug testing of offenders before any community penalty is imposed upon them.

MITIGATION OF SENTENCE

The final stage in the sentencing process before the sentence is pronounced is the presentation of defence mitigation. According to Comyn J in *Gross v O'Toole* (1982) 4 Cr App R (S) 283, this is 'purported to be the province of the most junior of counsel' but 'is in fact amongst the most difficult tasks any barrister can ever face'. The plea in mitigation usually consists solely of a speech by defence counsel. In his discretion, counsel may additionally call witnesses to speak to the offender's generally good character or to explain why, in their view, he acted as he did on the occasion in question. **D19.76**

Legal Representation at the Sentencing Stage

D19.77 An unrepresented offender may, of course, put forward mitigation on his own behalf. However, if the court is considering a custodial disposition it is generally desirable that the mitigation should be professionally presented. This is especially so if the offender is either young or has not previously been given a custodial sentence.

D19.78 **Statutory Requirement for Representation** Section 83 of the PCC(S)A 2000, which applies to both the Crown Court and magistrates' courts, provides that (a) adult offenders who have not previously been sentenced to imprisonment and (b) offenders aged under 21 whether or not they have previously lost their liberty shall not be sentenced to imprisonment or, as the case may be, one of the custodial sentences available for the offenders aged under 21 unless they are legally represented. The exception to that requirement is where the accused was granted representation funded as part of the Criminal Defence Service but it was withdrawn because of his conduct, or where it was withdrawn or refused because he was not financially eligible or where (having been informed of the right to apply for such representation and having the opportunity to do so) he has refused or failed to do so (s. 83(3)).

Section 83 extends to the passing of suspended sentences of imprisonment, but a suspended sentence which has not taken effect is ignored for purposes of deciding if an offender has previously had a prison sentence (s. 83(5)). Section 83(4) lays down that a person is to be treated as legally represented if he had legal assistance after conviction and before sentence.

D19.79 **Consequences of Breach** Failure to comply has been held to have differing consequences depending upon the court in error. If the failure occurred in the magistrates' court, the Crown Court, on appeal, must pass a sentence which the lower court could *lawfully* have passed, and therefore it must replace the custodial sentence with a non-custodial one (*Birmingham Justices, ex parte Wyatt* [1976] 1 WLR 260). If, however, the Crown Court was the sentencing court and the appeal is to the Court of Appeal, the latter may uphold the sentence below if they consider that it was the right one in all the circumstances (*McGinlay* (1975) 62 Cr App R 156; *Hollywood* (1990) 154 JP 705; *Wilson* [1995] Crim LR 510).

Powers of Criminal Courts (Sentencing) Act 2000, s. 83

(1) A magistrates' court on summary conviction, or the Crown Court on committal for sentence or on conviction on indictment, shall not pass a sentence of imprisonment on a person who—
- (a) is not legally represented in that court, and
- (b) has not been previously sentenced to that punishment by a court in any part of the United Kingdom,

unless he is a person to whom subsection (3) below applies.

(2) A magistrates' court on summary conviction, or the Crown Court on committal for sentence or on conviction on indictment, shall not—
- (a) pass a sentence of detention under section 90 or 91 below,
- (b) pass a sentence of custody for life under section 93 or 94 below,
- (c) pass a sentence of detention in a young offender institution, or
- (d) make a detention and training order,

on or in respect of a person who is not legally represented in that court unless he is a person to whom subsection (3) below applies.

(3) This subsection applies to a person if either—
- (a) he was granted a right to representation funded by the Legal Services Commission as part of the Criminal Defence Service but the right was withdrawn because of his conduct or because it appeared that his financial resources were such that he was not eligible to be granted such a right;
- (aa) he applied for such representation and the application was refused because it appeared that his financial resources were such that he was not eligible to be granted a right to it; or
- (b) having been informed of his right to apply for such representation and having had the opportunity to do so, he refused or failed to apply.

(4) For the purposes of this section a person is to be treated as legally represented in a court if, but only if, he has the assistance of counsel or a solicitor to represent him in the proceedings in that court at some time after he is found guilty and before he is sentenced.

(5) For the purposes of subsection (1)(b) above a previous sentence of imprisonment which has been suspended and which has not taken effect under section 119 below . . . shall be disregarded.

(6) In this section 'sentence of imprisonment' does not include a committal for contempt of court or any kindred offence.

Requirement to Prove Mitigation

Although normally a plea in mitigation consists solely of a speech by counsel, exceptionally, counsel may also decide to call evidence in order to establish the facts he is advancing in mitigation. Whether to call evidence and, if so, whether to call it before, in the middle or at the end of his speech is a matter for counsel (per Comyn J in *Gross v O'Toole* (1982) 4 Cr App R (S) 283). Having made his choice, he 'cannot easily go back on it' (ibid.). **D19.80**

The requirement to prove mitigation should not be confused with the resolution of a factual dispute as to the circumstances of offence in a *Newton* hearing (see **D19.8** ***et seq.***). The cases appear to draw a distinction between 'true *Newton*' situations, where the dispute is about the immediate circumstances of the offence, and what have been described by Dr. Thomas in his case commentaries in the *Criminal Law Review* as 'reverse *Newton*' situations. In the latter, the dispute is about extraneous matters about which the prosecution witnesses are unlikely to have any knowledge. Since these matters would not have formed part of the prosecution case, or be within the prosecution's knowledge, and may well be within the peculiar knowledge of the accused, the rule is that the onus of satisfying the judge rests on the defence.

Applicable Principles The general principles as to proving mitigation were stated by the Divisional Court in *Gross v O'Toole* (1982) 4 Cr App R (S) 283. G's mitigation, in relation to offering his services as a taxi driver, was that he had offered his services gratuitously. This mitigation was rejected by the court. The Divisional Court rejected the argument that the court ought not to have rejected a substantial part of the mitigation without giving an opportunity for affirmative evidence to be called. The decision whether to call evidence or rely solely on his own submissions was one for the defence advocate. Ormrod LJ said: **D19.81**

> The main point of the mitigation is a rather interesting one. It involves the question as to what should magistrates do when they do not accept statements made by defending advocates in mitigation which are essentially statements of fact. Are they entitled to look at such propositions as mitigation in general terms? Are they entitled to relate what has been said to them to the other facts of the case, and perhaps, find themselves in difficulty in accepting the statement made by the advocate, as often happens, of course, in mitigation? I think, for my part, that if an advocate is going to put forward in mitigation something which is, on the face of it, quite inconsistent with the other information that the magistrates have so far as sentence is concerned, e.g. the list of previous convictions, it really is for the defending advocate to indicate that he wishes to make good the submission . . . he takes the chance himself if he does not offer to call evidence. . . .
>
> I do not think [the magistrates] were obliged to tell the defending advocate that they did not accept his mitigation, because I do not think anyone in court, least of all the defending advocate, could have supposed for a moment that they would accept his mitigation.

Comyn J, in a supplementary judgment, slightly qualified Ormrod LJ's remarks by stating that if, on a significant point on which there is room for some doubt, the magistrates do in fact doubt what the advocate is saying, they ought to tell him before he concludes his mitigation so he can try to remedy it. However, both their lordships clearly accepted the basic premise that it is for the defence to establish its own mitigation to the court's satisfaction, and whether they do that by a speech or evidence or both is essentially a matter for them, not the court.

D19.82 **Court's Discretion to Reject Such Evidence** It follows from the principles stated in *Gross v O'Toole* (1982) 4 Cr App R (S) 283, that the court may reject matters advanced in mitigation even if the offender or other defence witnesses testify in support of those facts and no contradictory evidence is adduced by the prosecution (see *Kerr* (1980) 2 Cr App R (S) 54).

This has been demonstrated in a number of cases.

(a) In *Ogunti* (1987) 9 Cr App R (S) 325, following O's guilty plea to possessing heroin with intent to supply, the court was held to be entitled to disbelieve counsel's mitigation to the effect that O had acted under duress. The Court of Appeal held that it was a 'reverse *Newton*' situation and the onus of proving the facts rested on the defence. The judge was entitled to draw reasonable inferences from the statements of the witnesses (e.g., as to the value of the drugs and the skilful way they were hidden in O's car), and therefore reject the defence account of the nature of O's involvement.

(b) In *Guppy* [1994] Crim LR 614, the Court of Appeal held that, where the offender raised extraneous matters of mitigation, a burden of proof rested upon him to the civil standard. Their lordships did state, however, that in the general run of cases the sentencer would readily accept the accuracy of defence counsel's statements.

(c) In *Broderick* (1993) 15 Cr App R (S) 476, it was held that the mitigation alleging duress went to matters outside the prosecution's knowledge so that *Newton* principles did not apply.

However, in *Tolera* [1999] 1 Cr App R 29, the Court of Appeal held that there was an onus on the prosecution to rebut the appellant's explanation that he had been under a degree of compulsion, falling short of duress, to carry the heroin which was the subject of the charge.

Content of Mitigation

D19.83 Guidance on matters of mitigation within the knowledge of the defence is provided by *Underwood* [2005] 1 Cr App R 178 (see **D19.9** and points (9), (11) and (14)(d) in particular). Guidance has similarly been provided in relation to other aspects of mitigation.

D19.84 **Mitigation Following Conviction** Where counsel delivers a plea in mitigation after a trial and a verdict of guilty, it is generally unrealistic for him to reiterate in strong terms his client's innocence and at the same time ask for leniency. It should not therefore be taken as an admission of guilt on his client's behalf, so as to undermine a subsequent appeal, if he accepts the jury's verdict and mitigates on that basis (*Wu Chun-piu v The Queen* [1996] 1 WLR 1113).

D19.85 **Citing of Authority** The Court of Appeal has encouraged the practice of counsel citing its previous decisions when mitigating at first instance (see *Ozair Ahmed* (1993) 15 Cr App R (S) 286, and *Johnson* [1994] Crim LR 537 and the commentary thereon). Reference should also be made, where appropriate, to Sentencing Council Guidelines.

D19.86 **Judicial Indications as to Sentence** Where the judge is contemplating imposing a sentence which defence counsel might not be anticipating, he is under a duty in fairness to the offender to give notice of what is in his mind so that defence counsel can then make submissions on that issue.

(a) In *Scott* (1989) 11 Cr App R (S) 249, the judge disqualified S for life without giving his counsel the opportunity to make submissions on that aspect of the sentence; the Court of Appeal reduced the disqualification.

(b) In *Woods* (1989) 11 Cr App R (S) 551, the Court of Appeal said that if the judge intended to impose a separate custodial sentence for an offence under the Bail Act 1976 he should invite submissions from counsel. (See also *O'Brien* (1995) 16 Cr App R (S) 556.)

Derogatory Assertions in Mitigation

D19.87 There are two restrictions placed on the content of mitigation where that involved derogatory assertions, which in turn impose obligations on prosecution counsel. These are the contained in the Bar Code of Conduct and the CPIA 1996.

D19.88 **Code of Conduct** Defence counsel 'must not make statements or ask questions which are merely scandalous or intended or calculated only to vilify, insult or annoy' any person (Code of Conduct of the Bar, para. 708(g)). Further he must, if possible, avoid the naming in open court of a third party whose character would be impugned thereby (para. 708(h)).

The Code of Conduct of the Bar, Written Standards, para. 11.8(e), gives guidance to prosecution counsel on what to do if the defence assert facts in the course of mitigation which the prosecution believe to be untrue. Counsel's duty is first to draw the attention of defence counsel to the assertion in question. If the defence persist, the prosecution should invite the court to hold a *Newton* hearing on the issue (see **D19.8**).

D19.89 **Criminal Procedure and Investigations Act 1996** The CPIA 1996, ss. 58 to 61, allow the judge to impose reporting restrictions on false or irrelevant assertions made during a speech in mitigation. There is power to make a full order where there are substantial grounds for believing that the assertion is derogatory to a person's character, and either false or irrelevant to the proceedings. Whilst considering the matter, the court is empowered to make an interim order, provided that there is a real possibility that a full order will be made. The powers do not apply if the assertion has been made earlier in proceedings, e.g., at trial. Full orders may be revoked at any time by the court, and if not revoked will cease to have effect after one year. It is an offence to publish or broadcast in breach of a full or interim order, rendering the offender liable to a fine on summary conviction not exceeding level 5 on the standard scale.

Criminal Procedure and Investigations Act 1996, s. 58

(1) This section applies where a person has been convicted of an offence and a speech in mitigation is made by him or on his behalf before—
- (a) a court determining what sentence should be passed on him in respect of the offence, or
- (b) a magistrates' court determining whether he should be committed to the Crown Court for sentence.

(2) This section also applies where a sentence has been passed on a person in respect of an offence and a submission relating to the sentence is made by him or on his behalf before—
- (a) a court hearing an appeal against or reviewing the sentence, or
- (b) a court determining whether to grant leave to appeal against the sentence.

(3) Where it appears to the court that there is a real possibility that an order under subsection (8) will be made in relation to the assertion, the court may make an order under subsection (7) in relation to the assertion.

(4) Where there are substantial grounds for believing—
- (a) that an assertion forming part of the speech or submission is derogatory to a person's character (for instance, because it suggests that his conduct is or has been criminal, immoral or improper), and
- (b) that the assertion is false or that the facts asserted are irrelevant to the sentence,

the court may make an order under subsection (8) in relation to the assertion.

(5) An order under subsection (7) or (8) must not be made in relation to an assertion if it appears to the court that the assertion was previously made—
- (a) at the trial at which the person was convicted of the offence, or
- (b) during any other proceedings relating to the offence.

(6) Section 59 has effect where a court makes an order under subsection (7) or (8).

(7) An order under this subsection—
- (a) may be made at any time before the court has made a determination with regard to sentencing;
- (b) may be revoked at any time by the court;
- (c) subject to paragraph (b), shall cease to have effect when the court makes a determination with regard to sentencing.

D

Part D Procedure

(8) An order under this subsection—
  (a) may be made after the court has made a determination with regard to sentencing, but only if it is made as soon as is reasonably practicable after the making of the determination;
  (b) may be revoked at any time by the court;
  (c) subject to paragraph (b), shall cease to have effect at the end of the period of 12 months beginning with the day on which it is made;
  (d) may be made whether or not an order has been made under subsection (7) with regard to the case concerned.

(9) For the purposes of subsections (7) and (8) the court makes a determination with regard to sentencing—
  (a) when it determines what sentence should be passed (where this section applies by virtue of subsection (1)(a));
  (b) when it determines whether the person should be committed to the Crown Court for sentence (where this section applies by virtue of subsection (1)(b));
  (c) when it determines what the sentence should be (where this section applies by virtue of subsection (2)(a));
  (d) when it determines whether to grant leave to appeal (where this section applies by virtue of subsection (2)(b)).

PRONOUNCEMENT OF SENTENCE

D19.90 After the defence mitigation, the judge pronounces sentence. Normally he does so immediately upon the close of defence counsel's address, but there is no objection to his adjourning briefly to consider his decision.

Giving Reasons

D19.91 Section 174 of the CJA 2003 creates an obligation on the judge to give reasons for, and explain the effects of, the sentence passed, save where the sentence is fixed by law or is otherwise mandatory (s. 174(3)). The information that the sentencer is required to give the offender is set out in s. 174(1) and para. I.7 of the *Consolidated Criminal Practice Direction* (see **appendix** 7). In summary:

(a) The court must explain in non-technical terms its reasons for deciding on the sentence passed, the structure of the sentence, what it requires the offender to do, what will happen if it is not done, and any power which exists to vary or review the sentence (s. 174(1)).

(b) In addition, if the court is departing from any definitive guidelines issued by the Sentencing Guidelines Council, it must say why (s. 174(2)(a)).

(c) If a custodial sentence is being passed, the court must explain why the offence is sufficiently serious to warrant such a sentence (s. 174(2)(b)).

(d) Any reduction for a guilty plea must be mentioned in the reasons, together with any aggravating or mitigating factors which the court regarded as being of particular importance (s. 174(2)(d) to (e)).

Criminal Justice Act 2003, s. 174

(1) Subject to subsections (3) and (4), any court passing sentence on an offender—
  (a) must state in open court, in ordinary language and in general terms, its reasons for deciding on the sentence passed, and
  (b) must explain to the offender in ordinary language—
    (i) the effect of the sentence,
    (ii) where the offender is required to comply with any order of the court forming part of the sentence, the effects of non-compliance with the order,
    (iii) any power of the court, on the application of the offender or any other person, to vary or review any order of the court forming part of the sentence, and
    (iv) where the sentence consists of or includes a fine, the effects of failure to pay the fine.

(2) In complying with subsection (1)(a), the court must—
(a) where guidelines indicate that a sentence of a particular kind, or within a particular range, would normally be appropriate for the offence and the sentence is of a different kind, or is outside that range, state the court's reasons for deciding on a sentence of a different kind or outside that range,
(b) where the sentence is a custodial sentence and the duty in subsection (2) of section 152 is not excluded by subsection (1)(a) or (b) or (3) of that section, state that it is of the opinion referred to in section 152(2) and why it is of that opinion,
(c) where the sentence is a community sentence and the case does not fall within section 151(2), state that it is of the opinion that section 148(1) applies and why it is of that opinion,
(d) where as a result of taking into account any matter referred to in section 144(1), the court imposes a punishment on the offender which is less severe than the punishment it would otherwise have imposed, state that fact, and
(e) in any case, mention any aggravating or mitigating factors which the court has regarded as being of particular importance.

(3) Subsection (1)(a) does not apply—
(a) to an offence the sentence for which is fixed by law (provision relating to sentencing for such an offence being made by section 270), or
(b) to an offence the sentence for which falls to be imposed under section 51A(2) of the Firearms Act 1968, under subsection (2) of section 110 or 111 of the Sentencing Act or under section 29(4) or (6) of the Violent Crime Reduction Act 2006 (required custodial sentences).

The *Consolidated Criminal Practice Direction*, para. I.7 (see **E1.15**) requires that whenever a custodial sentence is imposed, the court should explain the practical effect of the sentence. The Practice Direction (set out at **appendix** 7) includes a series of short statements which can be adapted by the sentencer, but prescribes no form of words, and makes it clear that what is to be given is merely an explanation; the sentence will be that which is pronounced by the court.

Statutory obligations to give reasons are also imposed by the following:

(a) PCC(S)A 2000, s. 130(3) — a court with power to make a compensation order in an offender's case must explain its reasons for not doing so.
(b) RTOA 1988, s. 47(1) — where the court does not order disqualification or endorsement on account of special reasons or hardship.

Court of Appeal Guidance Even before the introduction of the CJA 2003, s. 174, the Court of Appeal had encouraged sentencers to give reasons, and had indicated that that should certainly be done if the sentence might seem unduly severe in the absence of explanation (*Newton* (1979) 1 Cr App R (S) 252). **D19.92**

It has been held that failure by the sentencing court to give reasons when required to do so does not invalidate the sentence (*McQueen* (1989) 11 Cr App R (S) 305), although the failure may no doubt be taken into account by the appellate court should the offender appeal. Where the sentencer does give reasons and what he says indicates an error of principle in the way he approached his task, the Court of Appeal sometimes reduces the sentence even though the penalty was not in itself excessive. Similarly, a failure by the judge to state expressly that he is taking into account any guilty plea does not oblige the Court of Appeal to interfere with what is otherwise an appropriate sentence (*Wharton* (2001) *The Times*, 27 March 2001).

VARIATION OF SENTENCE

By the PCC(S)A 2000, s. 155(1), a sentence imposed or other order made by the Crown Court when dealing with an offender may be varied or rescinded within 28 days of being passed or made. The judge who makes the variation must be the judge who originally passed **D19.93** sentence; if, however, he was accompanied by justices on the first occasion, they need not be present for the variation (s. 155(4) and see *Morrison* [2005] EWCA Crim 2705).

The 28-day limitation on exercising the power to vary is qualified in the case of accused who are jointly tried inasmuch as the period is 28 days from the conclusion of the joint trial or 56 days from the date of the sentence or order to be varied, whichever is the shorter (s. 155(2)). Conclusion of the trial, in this context, means the latest of any of the dates on which one of the accused was sentenced or acquitted (s. 155(3)).

Extent of the Power to Vary

D19.94 The power in the PCC(S)A 2000, s. 155, may be used to replace one form of sentence with a quite different form. This was illustrated in:

(a) *Sodhi* (1978) 66 Cr App R 260, where the Crown Court, upon learning that S had been diagnosed by psychiatrists as suffering from paranoid psychosis and was dangerous, substituted for a six-month prison sentence a hospital order plus restriction order without time-limit; and
(b) *Iqbal* (1985) 7 Cr App R (S) 35, in which an unlawful sentence of 30 months' youth custody passed on a juvenile was replaced by an equivalent term of detention under what is now the PCC(S)A 2000, s. 91(3).

The Court of Appeal upheld both variations, saying in *Sodhi* that the word 'varied' in s. 155(1) has a wide meaning and the court's power is therefore not restricted to changing the length of a sentence. The section may also be used to add an extra order to the sentence already passed (*Reilly* [1982] QB 1208).

Increasing the Sentence by Variation

D19.95 The obvious use of the power in the PCC(S)A 2000, s. 155, is to correct minor errors made by the court when passing sentence. It is also clear that the power may be used to benefit the offender by reducing his sentence if, on reflection, the judge considers that he was originally too harsh. Recent decisions also show that the power may be used to increase a sentence substantially in appropriate circumstances.

(a) In *Newsome* [1970] 2 QB 711, the sentencer had overlooked legislation then in force which obliged the court to suspend any sentence of imprisonment it passed on the appellants unless the term thereof exceeded six months. The Court of Appeal held that he had jurisdiction to increase the sentence to address this problem because he had always intended to pass a short, immediate custodial sentence, and the increase he ordered was virtually the minimum necessary to achieve his original object.
(b) In *Grice* (1977) 66 Cr App R 167, a more restrictive view was taken of the court's power to vary sentence. The sentencer had varied a suspended sentence to make the term one of immediate imprisonment where G had during the 28-day period for variation breached an undertaking given to the court pre-sentence. The Court of Appeal restored the original sentence, holding that only in exceptional circumstances (such as in *Newsome*) should s. 155 be used to make a substantial increase in penalty.
(c) In *Reilly* [1982] QB 1208, the sentencer initially declined to make a criminal bankruptcy order when he passed sentence. He was then persuaded to make the order, and varied the sentence accordingly. Kerr LJ, giving the Court of Appeal's judgment, held that *Grice* had to be considered in the light of *Sodhi* (1978) 66 Cr App R 260 and dicta of the House of Lords in *Menocal* [1980] AC 598, in which Lord Edmund-Davies said that, contrary to *Grice*, the statutory power to vary is not 'restricted to mere slips of the tongue or slips of the memory'. It was therefore clear 'almost beyond argument' that the judge in *Reilly* had jurisdiction to change his mind and add the criminal bankruptcy order.
(d) In *Hart* (1983) 5 Cr App R (S) 25, the sentencer became aware the he had been induced

to pass a sentence of six months' imprisonment suspended for 18 months by a false story which H had invented to gain a lenient sentence. Unfortunately, the sentencer did not vary the sentence within the prescribed period. However, Lord Lane CJ said: '. . . the learned judge was absolutely correct . . . to take this opportunity to review the sentence, had he done it within the stipulated time. Where someone makes it known after the event that he, as this appellant put it, has "conned the court", in other words told lies to the court and has thereby escaped his just punishment, is one of the plain cases for which [section 155(1)] is designed'.

The Correct Approach to Upward Variation General guidance was given in *McLean* (1988) 10 Cr App R (S) 18, where the sentencer had passed a sentence of three years' imprisonment on the strength of M's promise that he had turned over a new leaf, but had varied his sentence to four years' imprisonment when he then promptly escaped from custody. The Court of Appeal held that the judge did have the power to increase the sentence. **D19.96**

In the course of argument, McCullough J put to counsel that the proper approach of the court was to ask: (i) Did M's conduct create an exceptional situation? (ii) If it did, was the judge reasonably entitled to take the view that the exceptional situation undermined the whole basis upon which he passed sentence? If the answer to both questions was yes, then the judge could properly exercise the wide discretion given by the statute to increase the sentence. In delivering the court's judgment, Woolf LJ confirmed that this was the correct approach (at p. 22).

The upshot of the above cases seems to be that the Crown Court may increase sentence by a variation under s. 155(1), even to the extent of substituting an immediate custodial sentence for a suspended one, where additional argument put before the court (as in *Reilly* [1982] QB 1208) or information that the original sentence was passed on an incorrect factual basis (as in *Hart* (1983) 5 Cr App R (S) 25 and *McLean*) justifies such variation. It is clear from *McLean* that the principle advanced in *Grice* (1977) 66 Cr App R 167 remains good law: namely, that variations to the detriment of the offender are justified only in exceptional circumstances.

More recently, in *Reynolds* [2007] EWCA Crim 538, the Court of Appeal held that the power to vary could be used within the 28-day period to increase sentence when the impact of chapter 5 of the CJA 2003 (in that the offence was a 'specified' offence, or that a 'specified' offence was a 'serious' offence) had not originally been appreciated. If a sentence is rescinded in such circumstances, the court may then adjourn sentence, e.g., to allow a report to be prepared to address the question of dangerousness, even if that results in sentencing finally occurring after the 28-day period.

Procedure for Variation of Sentence

Presence of the Offender In both *May* (1981) 3 Cr App R (S) 165 and *Cleere* (1983) 5 Cr App R (S) 465, it was held that the offender has a right to be present when his sentence is varied, and variations made in the absence of the respective appellants and without their having the benefit of legal representation were quashed. **D19.97**

This was slightly qualified in *Shacklady* (1987) 9 Cr App R (S) 258, where Rose J, quoting a sentence from Watkins LJ's judgment in *Cleere*, stated the principle to be that 'the defendant or his counsel must have an opportunity to address the court' (p. 261). Accordingly, a variation made in the absence of the offender but with counsel in attendance on his behalf was upheld.

In *McLean* (1988) 10 Cr App R (S) 18 (see **D19.96**), M's sentence was increased from three to four years after his escape from custody and hence in his absence (voluntary on his part, unavoidable from the court's point of view). The judge heard representations from M's counsel on the occasion when he varied sentence. With the obvious exception of such circumstances, it is submitted that a genuine increase by variation should not be made unless both the offender and counsel are present.

D19.98 **Hearing in Open Court** In *Dowling* (1988) 88 Cr App R 88, it was stressed that any variation of sentence should take place in open court. In that case, the judge purported to vary the sentence, as a result of a query from his clerk, without returning to court, or discussing the matter with counsel. The Court of Appeal emphasised that where the 'judge is minded to vary a sentence he has passed or even to clarify a doubt or ambiguity as to the effect of it, he should do so in open court'. Only in this manner would all those concerned hear the final decision from the judge directly, and in such a way that a shorthand note would be available. The court may rescind a sentence on one occasion, and then resentence at a later date, provided that the whole process is completed within the 28-day period (*Dunham* [1996] 1 Cr App R (S) 438).

Variations Outside the 28-day Period

D19.99 A sentence may not be varied outside the period specified in the PCC(S)A 2000, s. 155(1) (*Menocal* [1980] AC 598, where the House of Lords quashed an order depriving the offender of £4,000 found in her possession when arrested because the order was not added to the original sentence until after the expiry of the time for variation). *Menocal* was followed in *Hart* (1983) 5 Cr App R (S) 25. The 28-day limit cannot be extended by rescinding the original sentence within the time-limit, and then not sentencing until after the time-limit has expired (*Stillwell* (1991) 94 Cr App R 65).

D19.100 **Correcting Rather than Varying** A distinction is drawn, however, between varying the sentence by changing its length, adding an order to it or replacing it with a different type of disposition and merely correcting a technical defect in the sentence as originally announced. For example, in *Saville* [1981] QB 12, the Court of Appeal upheld the correction of the terms of a criminal bankruptcy order because the Crown Court has an inherent jurisdiction, apart from the statutory jurisdiction, to remedy mistakes in its record and the correction or variation was of such a minor nature that it was appropriate to exercise the inherent jurisdiction.

DEFERRING SENTENCE

Purpose of Deferring Sentence

D19.101 Under the PCC(S)A 2000, ss. 1 to 1D (set out at **D19.107**), the purpose for which sentence may be deferred is to enable the court, when it does deal with the offender, to have regard to:

(a) his conduct after conviction (including, where appropriate, the making by him of reparation for his offence), or
(b) any change in his circumstances (s. 1(1)).

The court must fix the date to which sentence is deferred, the maximum period allowed being six months (s. 1(4)). Subject to an exception mentioned below, sentence may be deferred only once (ibid.).

Deferment requires the offender's consent and the court must be satisfied that exercise of the power would be in the interests of justice (s. 1(3)). The court dealing with the offender after the period of deferment may deal with him in any way the deferring court could have done (s. 1D(2)(a)). By s. 1D(2)(b), that includes, where sentence was deferred by a magistrates' court, committing the offender for sentence under s. 3. Where a magistrates' court defers sentence and then commits under s. 3, the Crown Court may also defer sentence, that being the exception to the rule that sentence may be deferred only once (s. 1D(3)).

Where there is a requirement to make a referral order on a young offender (see **E12.3**), the court may not defer passing sentence on him.

Requirements that May be Imposed The most important requirement imposed on an offender when his sentence is deferred is to return on the specified day. Upon deferring sentence, the court does not bail the offender but, if he should fail to appear on the deferment date, a warrant may be issued for his arrest (PCC(S)A 2000, s. 1(7)). D19.102

The requirements imposed by the court when deferring sentence may include reparative and other activity to be undertaken during the period of deferment. When the court comes to impose sentence at the end of the period of deferment, it is able to have regard to the conduct of the offender and any change in his circumstances. In this context, 'conduct' includes reference to how well the offender has complied with any requirements imposed by the court.

The court may appoint a supervisor to monitor the offender's compliance with the requirements imposed, who may be a probation officer. Those requirements may include one as to residence (s. 1A). 1f the court is satisfied that the offender has failed to comply with one or more requirements, it may deal with him before the end of the period of deferment (s. 1B). He may in any event be dealt with before the end of the period of deferment if he commits another offence (s. 1C).

Challenge to a Deferred Sentence A deferred sentence may, in appropriate circumstances, be referred by the A-G to the Court of Appeal for review, where he considers that it constitutes an unduly lenient sentence (*A-G's Ref (No. 27 of 1992)* [1993] Crim LR 630: see D27.6). D19.103

Appropriate Circumstances for Deferring

In *George* [1984] 1 WLR 1082, Lord Lane CJ gave some indication of when it may be appropriate to defer sentence. He referred especially to cases where the improvement in the offender's conduct or steps which the court wants him to take are not sufficiently specific to be made the subject of a requirement in a probation order, but nonetheless the court wishes to see what progress he makes before sentencing (p. 1085G–H). However, deferment should not be used either as an easy option when the sentencer's intentions could in fact be achieved by other means (*George*, at p. 1086A) or where it imposes such a restriction on the offender's freedom of action that another order was more appropriate (*Skelton* [1983] Crim LR 686). D19.104

Recommended Procedure when Deferring Sentence

Lord Lane CJ in his judgment in *George* [1984] 1 WLR 1082, gave guidance on the procedure which should be adopted when deferring sentence. The chief points to be noted are: D19.105

(a) When deferring sentence the court must make it clear to the offender the particular purposes under the PCC(S)A 2000, s. 1(1), that it has in mind, and the conduct that is expected of him during deferment. The court should also make it clear that it is deferring sentence as opposed to merely adjourning (*Fairhead* [1975] 2 All ER 737).
(b) A careful note should be made by the court of what the offender is told. Ideally, the offender himself should also be given a written note of the conduct expected of him.
(c) The court eventually passing sentence should:
    (i) ascertain the purpose of the deferment and any requirement as to conduct then imposed;
    (ii) determine whether the offender has substantially conformed (or attempted to conform) with the proper expectations of the deferring court.
(d) In order to decide whether the offender has lived up to expectations, the sentencing court will almost certainly require an up-to-date social enquiry report. To avoid unnecessary delay, it may be appropriate to order the report when sentence is deferred. If the offender has conformed with the sentencing court's expectations, he may expect a non-custodial sentence; if he has not, the sentencing court should state with precision in what respects he has failed. Failure to do so may lead to any custodial sentence being quashed because

of the appearance given that the sentencing court merely disagrees with the original decision to defer as opposed to being genuinely disappointed in the offender's conduct (*Glossop* (1981) 3 Cr App R (S) 347).

The above procedure is recommended in part because the judge who passes sentence need not necessarily be the judge who deferred sentence, and it is therefore necessary to ensure as far as possible that the former knows how the latter was thinking. However, whenever possible, both the judge who deferred sentence and counsel who then represented the offender should make themselves available for the eventual sentencing (see *Gurney* [1974] Crim LR 472 and *Ryan* [1976] Crim LR 508).

(e) Every effort should be made to sentence the offender on the date to which sentence was deferred (per Lord Lane CJ in *Anderson* (1983) 78 Cr App R 251). In exceptional circumstances, however, the court may adjourn to a later date, even if that is more than six months after the original deferment (see *Ingle* [1974] 3 All ER 811). In *Anderson* the Court of Appeal held that the Crown Court had not been deprived of its jurisdiction to sentence by reason of the delay, but the sentence eventually passed should reflect how stale the offence had become.

Custodial Sentence after Deferment

D19.106 As indicated by Lord Lane CJ in *George* [1984] 1 WLR 1082, the tacit understanding between the court and the offender when sentence is deferred is that, if he substantially conforms (or, at least, tries to conform) with the deferring court's proper expectations, the sentencing court will pass a non-custodial sentence. It follows that, although conviction for further offences during a deferment period will almost certainly lead to a custodial sentence (see, e.g., *Hope* (1980) 2 Cr App R (S) 6), merely staying out of trouble does not guarantee the opposite. For example, in *Smith* (1976) 64 Cr App R 116, where sentence was deferred to see if S could (a) work regularly and (b) reduce his alcohol consumption, the Court of Appeal upheld an eventual custodial sentence because he had done neither of those things, even though he had avoided further offending.

There are qualifications to this approach.

(a) Where the offender falls short of the deferring court's expectations in only a minor way, this should not be used as a justification for a custodial sentence (*Smith* (1979) 1 Cr App R (S) 339).

(b) Offences which were allegedly committed during the period of deferment but which are unresolved by the time the period expires should not influence the sentencer in any way unless and until the offender has been convicted of the later alleged offences (*Aquilina* [1990] Crim LR 134).

Sentencing before the End of the Deferment Period

D19.107 Once sentence has been deferred, the court may not proceed to sentence until the deferment period has expired, unless either it revokes the order for deferment within 28 days by virtue of the PCC(S)A 2000, s. 155(1) (see **D19.93**), or s. 1C applies (see *McQuaide* (1974) 60 Cr App R 239).

The effect of the latter provisions is that, if an offender is convicted of an offence (the subsequent offence) during a deferment period, the court passing sentence on him for the subsequent offence may also sentence for the deferment offence (s. 1C(3)). This does not apply if sentence was deferred by the Crown Court and the sentencing court for the subsequent offence is a magistrates' court (proviso (a) to s. 1C(3)).

In the converse case of the Crown Court sentencing for the subsequent offence, sentence having been deferred by a magistrates' court, the Crown Court's powers in respect of the deferment offence are limited to those of a magistrates' court (proviso (b)). Apart from the possibility of the court that sentences an offender for a subsequent offence also sentencing him for the deferment offence, conviction for a subsequent offence during a deferment period always entitles the *deferring* court to sentence forthwith for the deferment offence, even though the deferment period has not expired (s. 1C(1)).

Powers of Criminal Courts (Sentencing) Act 2000, ss. 1 to 1D

1.—(1) The Crown Court or a magistrates' court may defer passing sentence on an offender for the purpose of enabling the court, or any other court to which it falls to deal with him, to have regard in dealing with him to—

(a) his conduct after conviction (including, where appropriate, the making by him of reparation for his offence); or

(b) any change in his circumstances;

but this is subject to subsections (3) and (4) below.

(2) Without prejudice to the generality of subsection (1) above, the matters to which the court to which it falls to deal with the offender may have regard by virtue of paragraph (a) of that subsection include the extent to which the offender has complied with any requirements imposed under subsection (3)(b) below.

(3) The power conferred by subsection (1) above shall be exercisable only if—

(a) the offender consents;

(b) the offender undertakes to comply with any requirements as to his conduct during the period of the deferment that the court considers it appropriate to impose; and

(c) the court is satisfied, having regard to the nature of the offence and the character and circumstances of the offender, that it would be in the interests of justice to exercise the power.

(4) Any deferment under this section shall be until such date as may be specified by the court, not being more than six months after the date on which the deferment is announced by the court; and, subject to section 1D(3) below, where the passing of sentence has been deferred under this section it shall not be further so deferred.

(5) Where a court has under this section deferred passing sentence on an offender, it shall forthwith give a copy of the order deferring the passing of sentence and setting out any requirements imposed under subsection (3)(b) above—

(a) to the offender,

(b) where an officer of a local probation board has been appointed to act as a supervisor in relation to him, to that board, and

(c) where a person has been appointed under section 1A(2)(b) below to act as a supervisor in relation to him, to that person.

(6) Notwithstanding any enactment, a court which under this section defers passing sentence on an offender shall not on the same occasion remand him.

(7) Where—

(a) a court which under this section has deferred passing sentence on an offender proposes to deal with him on the date originally specified by the court, or

(b) the offender does not appear on the day so specified,

the court may issue a summons requiring him to appear before the court at a time and place specified in the summons, or may issue a warrant to arrest him and bring him before the court at a time and place specified in the warrant.

(8) Nothing in this section or sections 1A to 1D below shall affect—

(a) the power of the Crown Court to bind over an offender to come up for judgment when called upon; or

(b) the power of any court to defer passing sentence for any purpose for which it may lawfully do so apart from this section.

1A.—(1) Without prejudice to the generality of paragraph (b) of section 1(3) above, the requirements that may be imposed by virtue of that paragraph include requirements as to the residence of the offender during the whole or any part of the period of deferment.

(2) Where an offender has undertaken to comply with any requirements imposed under section 1(3)(b) above the court may appoint—

(a) an officer of a local probation board, or

(b) any other person whom the court thinks appropriate,

to act as a supervisor in relation to him.

(3) A person shall not be appointed under subsection (2)(b) above without his consent.

(4) It shall be the duty of a supervisor appointed under subsection (2) above—
  (a) to monitor the offender's compliance with the requirements; and
  (b) to provide the court to which it falls to deal with the offender in respect of the offence in question with such information as the court may require relating to the offender's compliance with the requirements.

1B.—(1) A court which under section 1 above has deferred passing sentence on an offender may deal with him before the end of the period of deferment if—
  (a) he appears or is brought before the court under subsection (3) below; and
  (b) the court is satisfied that he has failed to comply with one or more requirements imposed under section 1(3)(b) above in connection with the deferment.

(2) Subsection (3) below applies where—
  (a) a court has under section 1 above deferred passing sentence on an offender;
  (b) the offender undertook to comply with one or more requirements imposed under section 1(3)(b) above in connection with the deferment; and
  (c) a person appointed under section 1A(2) above to act as a supervisor in relation to the offender has reported to the court that the offender has failed to comply with one or more of those requirements.

(3) Where this subsection applies, the court may issue—
  (a) a summons requiring the offender to appear before the court at a time and place specified in the summons; or
  (b) a warrant to arrest him and bring him before the court at a time and place specified in the warrant.

1C.—(1) A court which under section 1 above has deferred passing sentence on an offender may deal with him before the end of the period of deferment if during that period he is convicted in Great Britain of any offence.

(2) Subsection (3) below applies where a court has under section 1 above deferred passing sentence on an offender in respect of one or more offences and during the period of deferment the offender is convicted in England and Wales of any offence ('the later offence').

(3) Where this subsection applies, then (without prejudice to subsection (1) above and whether or not the offender is sentenced for the later offence during the period of deferment), the court which passes sentence on him for the later offence may also, if this has not already been done, deal with him for the offence or offences for which passing of sentence has been deferred, except that—
  (a) the power conferred by this subsection shall not be exercised by a magistrates' court if the court which deferred passing sentence was the Crown Court; and
  (b) the Crown Court, in exercising that power in a case in which the court which deferred passing sentence was a magistrates' court, shall not pass any sentence which could not have been passed by a magistrates' court in exercising that power.

(4) Where a court which under section 1 above has deferred passing sentence on an offender proposes to deal with him by virtue of subsection (1) above before the end of the period of deferment, the court may issue—
  (a) a summons requiring him to appear before the court at a time and place specified in the summons; or
  (b) a warrant to arrest him and bring him before the court at a time and place specified in the warrant.

1D.—(1) In deferring the passing of sentence under section 1 above a magistrates' court shall be regarded as exercising the power of adjourning the trial conferred by section 10(1) of the Magistrates' Courts Act 1980, and accordingly sections 11(1) and 13(1) to (3A) and (5) of that Act (non-appearance of the accused) apply (without prejudice to section 1(7) above) if the offender does not appear on the date specified under section 1(4) above.

(2) Where the passing of sentence on an offender has been deferred by a court ('the original court') under section 1 above, the power of that court under that section to deal with the offender at the end of the period of deferment and any power of that court under section 1B(1) or 1C(1) above, or of any court under section 1C(3) above, to deal with the offender—
  (a) is power to deal with him, in respect of the offence for which passing of sentence has been deferred, in any way in which the original court could have dealt with him if it had not deferred passing sentence; and
  (b) without prejudice to the generality of paragraph (a) above, in the case of a magistrates'

court, includes the power conferred by section 3 below to commit him to the Crown Court for sentence.

(3) Where—
  (a) the passing of sentence on an offender in respect of one or more offences has been deferred under section 1 above, and
  (b) a magistrates' court deals with him in respect of the offence or any of the offences by committing him to the Crown Court under section 3 below,

the power of the Crown Court to deal with him includes the same power to defer passing sentence on him as if he had just been convicted of the offence or offences on indictment before the court.

(4) Subsection (5) below applies where—
  (a) the passing of sentence on an offender in respect of one or more offences has been deferred under section 1 above;
  (b) it falls to a magistrates' court to determine a relevant matter; and
  (c) a justice of the peace is satisfied—
    (i) that a person appointed under section 1A(2)(b) above to act as a supervisor in relation to the offender is likely to be able to give evidence that may assist the court in determining that matter; and
    (ii) that that person will not voluntarily attend as a witness.

(5) The justice may issue a summons directed to that person requiring him to attend before the court at the time and place appointed in the summons to give evidence.

(6) For the purposes of subsection (4) above a court determines a relevant matter if it—
  (a) deals with the offender in respect of the offence, or any of the offences, for which the passing of sentence has been deferred; or
  (b) determines, for the purposes of section 1B(1)(b) above, whether the offender has failed to comply with any requirements imposed under section 1(3)(b) above.

ADJOURNMENTS

Apart from its power under the PCC(S)A 2000, s. 1, to defer passing sentence for up to six months, the Crown Court has inherent jurisdiction at common law to adjourn before sentencing an offender. In other words, it need not sentence on the occasion on which an offender pleads guilty or is found guilty. **D19.108**

Although there are no express limitations on the grounds for adjourning or the length of the adjournment, by analogy with the decision in *Arthur v Stringer* (1986) 84 Cr App R 361, it would be improper to adjourn solely because the offender is slightly too young for the form of sentence the court considers desirable in his case and adjourning will allow him to attain the minimum age necessary. In that case the Divisional Court stated that the discretion vested in the court to adjourn has to be exercised judicially. It cannot be said to have been exercised judicially if the only reason for exercising it was to ensure that the offender had reached the age of 21 by the time he was sentenced, thus enabling the court to pass a sentence of imprisonment.

During the period of the adjournment, the offender may be remanded in custody or granted bail at the court's discretion (see the Supreme Court Act 1981, s. 81(1)(c), for the power to grant bail).

Maximum Length

As to the maximum period for an adjournment, analogous guidance is provided by the MCA 1980, s. 10(3), which restricts an adjournment after conviction to a maximum of three weeks at a time if the offender is remanded in custody, four weeks if he is granted bail. Although the subsection does not directly apply to the Crown Court when dealing with an offender convicted on indictment, it is an indication of the kind of periods Parliament considers appropriate for post-conviction adjournments, at least where the ultimate sentence is likely to be relatively short. **D19.109**

Where the Crown Court is dealing with an offender who has appealed against his conviction and/or sentence in the magistrates' court, the higher court is directly bound by the provisions of s. 10(3) since the appeal takes the form of a rehearing, and the Crown Court's powers are therefore no greater than those of the magistrates (see *Arthur v Stringer* (1986) 84 Cr App R 361).

Binding Over

D19.110 A final power possessed by the Crown Court, analogous to adjourning, is to bind the offender over to come up for judgment if called upon to do so. Although in form a postponement of sentence, this is used more as a means of avoiding sentencing an offender if, exceptionally, the court does not want to impose a penalty but the ordinary alternatives to a penalty (such as a conditional discharge or a probation order) are inappropriate to meet the court's concerns in the particular circumstances of the case. The understanding is that, if the offender does not reoffend and complies with any conditions the court imposes when binding him over, he will not in fact be required to return before the court.

Section D20 Summary Trial: General and Preliminary Matters

The subject-matter of this section is the procedure for summary trial, concentrating on those respects in which it differs from that for trial on indictment. It should be read in conjunction with D5 and D6 which deal with the proceedings in a magistrates' court prior to the commencement of trial (or the sending of the case to the Crown Court), including the commencement of criminal proceedings. **D20.1**

THE INFORMATION OR WRITTEN CHARGE

Contents of the Information or Written Charge

Criminal proceedings may be commenced in a number of different ways: **D20.2**

(a) The accused may be arrested and, after the police have sought advice from the CPS, charged by the police (the details of the offence(s) will appear on a charge sheet).

(b) The accused may be arrested and then be granted police bail while the CPS decide whether there is sufficient evidence to justify a charge. When the CJA 2003, s. 29, comes into force, the CPS (or other public prosecuting bodies) will commence proceedings by prosecutor issuing a document (a 'written charge'), charging the person with an offence, and a 'requisition', requiring the person to appear before a magistrates' court to answer the written charge.

(c) An information may be laid at a magistrates' court and the court then issues a summons (or an arrest warrant) requiring the accused to attend before it. By virtue of the CJA 2003, s. 29, laying an information (followed by issue of a summons by the court) will be available only in the case of private prosecutions however it has been brought into force in certain areas only (in that it applies only to magistrates' courts sitting in specified locations: see the Criminal Justice Act 2003 (Commencement No.16) Order 2007 (SI 2007 No 1999)).

Much of the relevant legislation (such as the MCA 1980) refers to trial of the 'information' by a magistrates' court. The CJA 2003, s. 30(5), provides that references to an information are to be construed as references to a written charge, and references to a summons are to be construed as referring to a requisition. By convention, if an accused is charged at a police station, the charge sheet is regarded as an information.

Content Rule 7.2(1) of the CrimPR states that: **D20.3**

> (1) Every written charge issued by a public prosecutor and every information, summons or warrant laid in or issued by a magistrates' court shall be sufficient if it—
>
> (a) describes the offence with which the accused is charged, or of which he is convicted, in ordinary language avoiding as far as possible the use of technical terms; and

D

Part D Procedure

(b) gives such particulars as may be necessary to provide reasonable information about the nature of the charge.

Rule 7.2(3) further provides that, if the offence is statutory, the 'section of the Act, or, as the case may be, the rule, order, regulation, bylaw or other instrument creating the offence' must be referred to. By r. 7.2(2), it is not necessary to state all the elements of the offence or negative any matter on which the accused may rely. The latter provision is a procedural corollary of the evidential rule that it is for the accused to prove that he comes within a statutory exception etc., not for the prosecution to show that he falls outside it (see MCA 1980, s. 101).

Beyond the general statement in r. 7.2 that informations (and written charges) should avoid the use of technical terms and give reasonable information about the nature of the charge, there is little guidance on how they should be drafted. However, reference to a particular statutory provision may cure an apparent defect by making plain what might otherwise be ambiguous (*Karpinski v City of Westminster* [1993] Crim LR 606, followed in *DPP v Short* (2002) 166 JP 474).

D20.4 **Insufficient particulars** If the information (or written charge) as originally drafted gives insufficient particulars, application for further particulars may be made at any time after the charge has been preferred (*Aylesbury Justices, ex parte Wisbey* [1965] 1 WLR 339).

In *Nash v Birmingham Crown Court* (2005) 169 JP 157, it was held that if the information (or written charge) fails to give sufficient information to the accused as to the nature of the charge he faces, that does not of itself render the proceedings a nullity or any resulting conviction unsafe, provided that the requisite information is given to the accused in good time for him to be able fairly to meet the case against him. The accused is entitled to that information and its provision is capable of curing the defect in the information or written charge. In such a case it may well be appropriate for the prosecution to apply to amend the information or charge (under the MCA 1980, s. 123), with the defence being granted an adjournment if they may have been misled by the original error (see **D20.9**).

Rule against Duplicity

D20.5 An information or written charge may allege only one offence. This follows from the CrimPR, r. 7.3(1), which provides that 'a magistrates' court shall not proceed to the trial of an information or written charge that charges more than one offence'. However, r. 7.3(1) does not mean that an accused who appears before a magistrates' court may face only one offence at a time, as r. 7.3(2) goes on to provide that: 'Nothing in this rule shall prohibit two or more informations or written charges being set out in one document'.

In *Carrington Carr v Leicestershire County Council* (1994) 158 JP 570, it was said that there are five situations where informations (or written charges) may be duplicitous:

(a) where two or more discrete offences are charged conjunctively in one information (for example, where a single information alleges both dangerous driving and careless driving);
(b) where two offences are charged disjunctively or in the alternative in one information (for example, where a single information alleges dangerous driving or careless driving);
(c) where an offence was capable of being committed in more ways than one (for example, driving under the influence of drink or drugs) and both ways are referred to in one information;
(d) where a single offence was charged in respect of an activity but the activity involved more than one act, and
(e) where a single activity was charged but a number of particulars are relied on by the prosecution to prove the offence (for example, a single act of obtaining by deception where the deception involved several misrepresentations).

In the latter two situations, a single information or written charge may well be appropriate. However, if the accused wishes to admit some, but not all, of the allegations (or wishes to raise different defences to different allegations), separate informations or charges will be necessary.

In *Asda Stores Ltd v Wandsworth London Borough Council* [2007] EWHC 433 (Admin), the defendant company was charged with two offences under a single paragraph of food hygiene regulations (one for failure to control pests and one for failure to minimise the risk of contamination). The company argued that there should have been a single charge. The Divisional Court held that the paragraph in question created more than one offence and so the company had been charged correctly.

Thus, each case turns on the construction of the statute creating the particular offence.

See also **D11.41** to **D11.55** for discussion of the rule against duplicity in the context of indictments.

Whether One or More than One Act is Being Alleged (a) *Jemmison v Priddle* [1972] 1 QB 489: an information alleging that the unlawful killing of two red deer was held not to be bad for duplicity because, although the killing of each of the deer was a potential offence (in the absence of a game licence), the killings had occurred in the same geographical location within a very short time of each other. Thus, what was being alleged was a single activity of shooting deer, not two separate offences. **D20.6**

(b) *Horrix v Malam* [1984] RTR 112: a conviction on a single information alleging careless driving was upheld where the prosecution case was that the accused had driven badly on three different roads, the driving complained of being divided into two distinct incidents, witnessed by different police officers and with a 10-minute gap between them.

(c) *Cullen v Jardine* [1985] Crim LR 668: an information for felling 90 trees without a licence was held not to be bad for duplicity. Even though the felling had taken place over a three-day period and there might have been separate defences advanced in respect of different trees, it was still possible to regard the felling as one activity. The fact that a number of distinct issues might arise in the course of the trial did not of itself necessitate separate informations. The magistrates were perfectly capable on the information as drafted of determining how many trees the accused had illegally felled and adjusting the penalty accordingly. Whether an information is bad for duplicity is a matter of fact and degree in each case.

(d) *Anderton v Cooper* (1980) 72 Cr App R 232: the information concerned alleged management of a brothel between specified dates. This was held not to amount to duplicity, as the offences in question could take place over a period of time and so the information was alleging a single continuing offence.

(e) *Bristol Crown Court, ex parte Willets* (1985) 149 JP 416: a single information alleging possession of obscene video tapes was held not to be bad for duplicity since all the tapes had been found on the accused's premises as a result of a single search and the information was alleging a single activity (but cf. *Ward* [1988] Crim LR 57 where an information for possessing by way of trade 15 videotaped films in breach of copyright, was held duplicitous).

(f) *Heaton v Costello* (1984) 148 JP 688: an information for stealing a bottle of cider, a pair of trousers and a cardigan from a supermarket was held not to be bad for duplicity since all the items were stolen on one visit to the supermarket. The case goes a little beyond the leading authority of *Wilson* (1979) 69 Cr App R 83, since the theft of the cider was effected by switching price labels and the theft of the clothing by walking through the checkouts without paying. Thus, one theft had been completed within the store, while the other remained incomplete until the accused had passed the checkout. Nevertheless, the Divisional Court held that there was but a single activity.

(g) *Barton v DPP* (2001) 165 JP 779: an information alleging theft of a total of £1,338.23 was held not to be bad for duplicity. The prosecution case was that on 94 separate occasions, the accused had taken small amounts of cash from the till. The accused gave no specific explanation for the individual takings and put forward the same defence for all. Further, to lay 94 separate informations would clearly be oppressive. See also *Smith* [2005] Crim LR 575.

(h) *Ministry of Agriculture, Fisheries and Food v Nunn Corn (1987) Ltd* [1990] Crim LR 268: it was held that an information will be duplicitous if it alleges more than one victim of the offence. It is submitted that this should not be seen as an invariable rule. In most cases the fact that there are separate victims will indeed mean that there were separate offences (e.g., theft of an item belonging to A and theft of an item belonging to B will necessarily be separate offences). However, there may be circumstances where a single offence can be committed against more than one victim (for example, where the accused is charged with stealing property that is owned jointly by A and B or where a single unlawful act on the part of the accused causes loss to more than one victim, as where a single act of fraud causes property in which several people have an interest to lose value).

Whether a Statutory Provision Creates One or More than One Offence

D20.7 An important issue that may arise when the question of duplicity is under consideration is whether the statutory provision in question creates a single offence or more than one offence. This is a matter of statutory interpretation, but case law may serve as a guide to the approach taken by the courts.

(a) *Mallon v Allon* [1964] 1 QB 385: an information for admitting and allowing a person under 18 to remain in a licensed betting office was held to be duplicitous because the relevant provision prohibited two separate acts, namely (i) admitting an under-age person on to licensed premises and (ii) allowing him to remain after he had entered the premises. The information was therefore charging two separate offences even though they arose out of one continuing incident.

(b) *Surrey Justices, ex parte Witherick* [1932] 1 KB 450: an information for driving without due care and attention or without reasonable consideration (contrary to what is now the Road Traffic Act 1988, s. 3) was held to be duplicitous because the section creates two separate offences, one of driving without due care and the other of driving without reasonable consideration. Accordingly, they must be alleged in separate informations, not as alternatives in a single information.

(c) *Ware v Fox* [1967] 1 WLR 379: a conviction on an information alleging that the defendant had permitted the premises he occupied to be used for the purposes of smoking cannabis or dealing in cannabis was quashed because the relevant statutory provision created separate offences of (i) allowing premises to be used for smoking cannabis and (ii) allowing them to be used for dealing in it.

(d) *Thomson v Knights* [1947] KB 336: an information alleging driving when unfit through drink or drugs (contrary to what is now the RTA 1988, s. 4: see **C5.30**) was upheld since the section creates a single offence of driving when in a self-induced state of incapacity, not two separate offences of driving while unfit through drink, and driving while unfit through drugs.

(e) *Amos v DPP* [1988] RTR 198: an information alleging that a bus driver was guilty of 'failing to behave in a civil and orderly manner and to take all reasonable precautions to ensure the safety of passengers alighting from the vehicle', contrary to regulations governing the conduct of drivers, was held to be defective. The structure of the regulation in question, with its division of different types of misconduct into separate paragraphs, showed that it was creating a number of separate offences (one per paragraph), not a single compendious offence of misconduct.

(f) *Mohindra v DPP* [2005] RTR 95: this case concerned the RTA 1988, s. 172(3) (see **C2.15** for details) in which the court rejected the argument that the subsection creates two separate offences, one based on the obligation created by s. 172(2)(a) and the other based on

s. 172(2)(b). It follows that an information that simply refers to s. 172(3) is not bad for duplicity. In holding that s. 172(3) creates only one offence, the Divisional Court observed that whether the failure to comply with the requirement is a breach of an obligation under s. 172(2)(a) or (2)(b) is not an issue unless and until the addressee asserts that he was not the keeper or, as a keeper, he seeks to rely on the defence in s. 172(4).

Action where an Information or Written Charge is Duplicitous If an information, in breach of the CrimPR, r. 7.3(1), alleges more than one offence, the court is required, under r. 7.3(3), 'to call upon the prosecutor to elect on which offence he desires the court to proceed, whereupon the offence or offences on which the prosecutor does not wish to proceed shall be struck out of the information or written charge; and the court shall then proceed to try that information or written charge afresh'. **D20.8**

If a prosecutor who is called upon to make an election under r. 7.3(3) fails to do so, the court shall dismiss the information or written charge (r. 7.3(4)). Under r. 7.3(5), where one or more offences have been struck out under r. 7.3(3), if 'the accused requests an adjournment and it appears to the court that he has been unfairly prejudiced, it shall adjourn the trial'.

Thus, if a single information or written charge alleges more than one offence, the court must call upon the prosecution to decide with which offence to proceed. The other offence will then be struck out. If the prosecution fail to choose between the offences, the court must strike out the entire information or written charge.

AMENDMENT OF INFORMATION OR WRITTEN CHARGE

Before or during the course of a summary trial it may become apparent that the information or written charge is defective, either in the sense that it does not comply with the CrimPR, part 7 (see above) or in the sense that there is a discrepancy between the particulars alleged in it and the prosecution evidence adduced at trial. The MCA 1980, s. 123, greatly limits the extent to which any such defect may be used as a ground for objecting to the proceedings, but at the same time requires the court to grant an adjournment if a variation between the information (or written charge) and the evidence adduced may have misled the defence. **D20.9**

Magistrates' Courts Act 1980, s. 123

(1) No objection shall be allowed to any information or complaint, or to any summons or warrant to procure the presence of the defendant, for any defect in it in substance or in form, or for any variance between it and the evidence adduced on behalf of the prosecutor or complainant at the hearing of the information or complaint.

(2) If it appears to a magistrates' court that any variance between a summons or warrant and the evidence adduced on behalf of the prosecutor or complainant is such that the defendant has been misled by the variance, the court shall, on the application of the defendant, adjourn the hearing.

If read literally, the wording of s. 123 requires the magistrates to ignore any defect in an information (or written charge), however gross it might be, save to the extent of granting the defence an adjournment in the circumstances set out in s. 123(2). The appellate courts have not, however, allowed the section to have such a sweeping effect. Lord Widgery CJ in *Garfield v Maddocks* [1974] QB 7 summarised the modern approach thus:

> Those extremely wide words, which on their face seem to legalise almost any discrepancy between the evidence and the information, have in fact always been given a more restricted meaning, and in modern times the section is construed in this way, that if the variance between the evidence and the information is slight and does no injustice to the defence, the information may be allowed to stand notwithstanding the variance which occurred. On the other hand, if the variance is so substantial that it is unjust to the defendant to allow it to be adopted without a proper amendment of the information, then the practice is for the court to require the prosecution to amend in order to bring their information into line. Once they do that, of course,

there is provision in [s. 123(2)] whereby an adjournment can be ordered in the interests of the defence if the amendment requires him to seek an adjournment.

In *New Southgate Metals Ltd v London Borough of Islington* [1996] Crim LR 334, the Divisional Court held that there are three types of error which can occur in an information (or written charge):

(a) an error so fundamental that it cannot be rescued by any appropriate and reasonable amendment: this will cause the prosecution to fail without more;
(b) a defect that is substantial enough to require amendment: the magistrates have power to allow amendment (subject to granting an adjournment if the defence are placed at any disadvantage by the amendment) — if such an error is not corrected, any conviction obtained upon the defective information is at risk of being quashed by the Divisional Court;
(c) an error that is so trivial that no amendment is required: the conviction may be upheld even on the unamended information.

Minor Defects which Do Not Require Amendment

D20.10 In *Sandwell Justices, ex parte West Midlands Passenger Transport Executive* [1979] RTR 17, the Divisional Court held that a variation between the information (which alleged that the company had put a vehicle on the road with a defective rear nearside tyre) and the evidence (which was that it was a defective rear offside tyre) was so trivial that, even in the absence of the amendment which was in fact made, the conviction would have been upheld. It was clear that the company was always aware of which tyre was the subject of the complaint, and had in fact brought it to court for inspection at the hearing.

Defects which Require Amendment but which are Not Incurable

D20.11 In such cases, if an amendment is sought and allowed, the court must go on to consider whether the defence have been misled by the original error and, if they have, it should grant an adjournment. Failure by the prosecution to ask for the amendment, or failure by the court to grant an adjournment, may lead to any conviction being quashed by the Divisional Court. Examples of this category of defect include:

(a) *Meek v Powell* [1952] 1 KB 164: the information set out the offence under a repealed section of an Act which had later been re-enacted in identical terms; it was held that the justices could have allowed the information to be amended (granting an adjournment if sought), or they could have dismissed it, allowing the prosecution to commence fresh proceedings under the correct Act, but it was not open to them to convict on the un-amended information.

(b) *New Southgate Metals Ltd v London Borough of Islington* [1996] Crim LR 334: the information referred to the wrong statute. No point was taken before the justices, but on appeal to the Crown Court a submission of no case to answer was based on the argument that the summons disclosed no offence known to law. The Divisional Court dismissed the appeal, holding that the full particulars of the offence were accurately set out in the information and the prosecution were not put on notice in the court below. The same approach was adopted in *Harlow Magistrates Court, ex parte O'Farrell* [2000] Crim LR 589 (where the information contained a reference to the wrong statutory instrument).

(c) *Newcastle-upon-Tyne Justices, ex parte John Bryce (Contractors) Ltd* [1976] 1 WLR 517: the justices permitted the amendment of an information which originally alleged *permitting* the use of an overladen lorry so as to allege actual use of it. It was held that, even though the amendment was more than six months from the date of the alleged offence (cf. the MCA 1980, s. 127) and even though it substituted a different offence for that originally charged (on a true construction of the legislation 'use' and 'permitting use' were two separate offences), nonetheless the amendment was permissible under what is now the MCA 1980, s. 123. The defence were not misled or taken by surprise, *inter alia,* because the nature of the prosecution case had always been apparent from the statement of facts on the summons.

(d) *Scunthorpe Justices, ex parte McPhee* (1998) 162 JP 635. The accused had been charged with robbery, but the CPS subsequently agreed to accept pleas of guilty to theft and common assault. The justices granted an application to amend the information to allege theft, but, on the clerk's objection, refused to allow an amendment to charge common assault. The objection was based on the ground that the six-month time-limit (see the MCA 1980, s. 127) for the summary offence of common assault had elapsed. The Divisional Court held that an information could be amended after expiry of the six-month period to allege a different offence or offences provided that (i) such offence(s) alleged the 'same wrongdoing' as the original offence, and (ii) the amendment could be made in the interests of justice. The phrase 'same wrongdoing' meant that the new offence should arise out of the same, or substantially the same, facts as gave rise to the original offence. In considering whether it is in the interests of justice for the amendment to be made, the court should pay particular regard to the interests of the accused. If the amendment would result in the accused facing a 'significantly more serious charge', it is likely to be against the interests of justice to allow such an amendment; similarly, the need for an adjournment would militate against the court granting leave for the amendment of the information. Both conditions were met in the instant case, and the information could have been amended accordingly.

(e) *Thames Magistrates' Court, ex parte Stevens* (2000) 164 JP 233: the accused was charged with assault occasioning actual bodily harm (OAPA 1861, s. 47). The prosecution subsequently indicated that they wished to withdraw the s. 47 charge and lay a charge alleging the summary offence of common assault (CJA 1988, s. 39) instead. However, it was more than six months since the commission of the offence. The Divisional Court held that the magistrate had correctly concluded that what was being sought by the prosecution was an amendment of the original charge rather than a substitution or withdrawal of that charge. The MCA 1980, s. 127, therefore did not apply to prevent the court from dealing with the charge of common assault. The magistrate, in considering whether the amendment was in the interests of justice, had taken proper account of the fact that: (i) the offences had arisen out of the same facts; (ii) the applicant had not been misled or prejudiced by the amendment; (iii) she was not deprived by the amendment of any substantive defence that she had; (iv) the evidence to be adduced by the prosecution was not different after the amendment; and (v) the effect of the amendment was in fact to reduce the gravity of the original charge.

(f) *Wyllie v CPS* [1988] Crim LR 753: an information for an offence under what is now the RTA 1988, s. 7, alleged failure to provide a specimen of urine for analysis. The justices correctly allowed it to be amended so as to allege failure to provide a specimen of blood, because, on the facts of the particular case, the evidence would have been the same whichever limb of the section the case was prosecuted under, and the defence had not been misled.

(g) *Wright v Nicholson* [1970] 1 WLR 142: the information alleged gross indecency with a child on 17 August 1967; however, the child's evidence as to time was vague and the incident he described could have occurred on some other day in August and the accused had credible alibi evidence for the date given in the information. The Divisional Court quashed the conviction because the variation between the information and the prosecution evidence adduced was so substantial as to give rise to a risk of 'grave injustice' to the accused. The Divisional Court indicated that, had the information been amended and the defence granted an adjournment to consider the altered basis of the prosecution case, the conviction could have been upheld. Insofar as *Wright v Nicholson* suggests that the Crown Court on appeal may amend an information, it has been overruled by *Garfield v Maddocks* [1974] QB 7, but the case remains authority for the proposition stated here. (See also *Norwich Crown Court, ex parte Russell* [1993] Crim LR 518, where the information alleged that the offence of criminal damage had been committed on 19 February 1991 whereas it was the prosecution's case that the offence was committed on 18 February; the discrepancy was not noticed until after conviction and the Divisional Court said that the justices had clearly ignored the confusion as to dates and there was no reason why the conviction could not stand, even though the information had not been amended.)

(h) In *DPP v Short* (2002) 166 JP 474, the information alleged that the defendant 'used' a vehicle with excess alcohol (rather than 'drove') under the RTA 1988, s. 5. At the end of the evidence, the prosecution invited the justices to exercise their power under the MCA 1980, s. 123, to amend the information to substitute 'drove' for 'used', thus bringing the information within the wording of the RTA 1988, s. 5. The magistrates refused to allow the information to be amended. The Divisional Court said that, taking account of the express reference to s. 5 of the 1988 Act, it could not be said that the information disclosed an offence not known to law. The court went on to say that the MCA 1980, s. 123, confers a wide discretion on justices to amend an information, and that discretion should ordinarily be exercised in favour of amendment unless so amending would result in injustice to an accused. In the present case, no injustice would have been caused to the accused by the proposed amendment, since he was fully aware of the case against him. It followed that the justices had erred in refusing the prosecution amendment.

(i) In *R (James) v DPP* (2004) 168 JP 596, the accused was charged with supplying a Class B drug. At the close of her case, it was submitted on her behalf that the evidence, although demonstrating an attempt to supply the drug, did not demonstrate an actual supply. The prosecution, relying on s. 123, applied to amend the information to allege an offence of attempting to supply a Class B drug (contrary to the Criminal Attempts Act 1981). Issues arose as to whether the justices were right to allow the amendment after the close of the defence case and whether they were right not to hold fresh mode of trial proceedings after allowing the amendment. The Divisional Court held that there is no fetter on the justices relying on the very wide wording of s. 123 to substitute a different offence, even where that offence arises under a different Act of Parliament, provided that no injustice is caused to the accused in so doing. There is, said the court, no reason why magistrates' courts should apply different principles to the Crown Court, which has the power to make such amendments. In the present case, the court decided that the accused had suffered no prejudice and went on to hold that, where there is no such injustice to the accused, there is no requirement on the magistrates to undertake the mode of trial procedure upon the amendment of an information, even where one offence is substituted for another.

(j) In *Shaw v DPP* (2007) 171 JP 254, the justices allowed an information to be amended to allege a different offence. The new offence carried imprisonment, whereas the original one did not. The Divisional Court held that the substitution of a new offence with a significantly heavier penalty, especially one where the accused faces the possibility of a custodial sentence, should have led the justices to reach the conclusion that it was not in the interests of justice to allow such an amendment.

Fundamental Defects that Cannot be Rescued by Amendment

D20.12 In *Atterton v Browne* [1945] KB 122, Humphreys J said: 'There have been . . . many decisions [under the predecessor of s. 123] which show that the section does not operate to prevent an objection being effective where the error alleged is fundamental, such as, for instance, where one offence is charged in the information and a different offence is found in the conviction recorded by the justices, even though the two matters may seem to be very much the same thing'. Similarly, it has been held that an information laid against the wrong person (e.g., the company secretary when it should have been the company itself) is so flawed that amendment cannot assist (*City of Oxford Tramway Co. v Sankey* (1890) 54 JP 564 and compare *Allan v Wiseman* [1975] RTR 217 with *Marco (Croydon) Ltd v Metropolitan Police* [1984] RTR 24 on the possibly fine distinction between an information which charges the wrong person and one which merely inaccurately describes the correct person). The only remedy for the prosecution in the case of an irremediable defect is to start the proceedings afresh (which, in the case of a summary offence, is possible only if less than six months have elapsed since the commission of the offence). There must then be an adjournment so that a fresh summons or requisition can be served on the new defendant (*Greater Manchester Justices, ex parte Aldi GmbH & Co KG* (1995) 159 JP 717).

An example of the operation of these principles may be found in *R (J Sainsbury plc) v Plymouth Magistrates' Court* (2006) 170 JP 690. An information had been laid under the Food Safety Act 1990 naming the defendant company as 'J Sainsbury plc (trading as Sainsburys Supermarket Ltd)'. J Sainsbury plc asserted that it was not the proper defendant, since the relevant store was operated by J Sainsbury Supermarkets Ltd. The prosecution applied under the MCA 1980, s. 123, to substitute J Sainsbury Supermarkets Ltd as defendant. The district judge acknowledged that the two companies were two separate legal entities, but allowed the amendment notwithstanding that the time-limit for bringing a prosecution had since expired. The Divisional Court held that the proper defendant had not been before the court and so the effect of the decision of the district judge was impermissibly to prefer a charge against it out of time.

JURISDICTION TO TRY CASES SUMMARILY

Basis of Jurisdiction

The jurisdiction of a magistrates' court to try cases summarily is set out in the MCA 1980, s. 2. See also **D3.23** and **D3.24**. Under s. 2: **D20.13**

(a) A magistrates' court has jurisdiction to try any summary offence (s. 2(1)).
(b) A magistrates' court has jurisdiction to try an either-way offence provided only that the procedure for determining mode of trial contained in the MCA 1980, ss. 18 to 22, has resulted in a decision for summary trial (s. 2(4)).

The venue of the offence is therefore irrelevant to jurisdiction, save in the sense that the English courts as a whole do not claim jurisdiction over offences committed abroad.

The jurisdiction to try offences conferred by s. 2 is without prejudice to any jurisdiction to try that magistrates' courts may be granted by other enactments. The other jurisdiction-conferring enactments relate chiefly to offences committed outside the UK. They include the Merchant Shipping Act 1995, s. 281 (jurisdiction over offences committed on British ships on the high seas); s. 282 of the same Act (jurisdiction over offences committed abroad if the accused was a member of the crew of a British merchant ship at the time or within the preceding three months); the Territorial Waters Jurisdiction Act 1878, s. 2 (jurisdiction over offences committed on foreign or British ships which are lying off the coast within British territorial waters), and the Civil Aviation Act 1982, s. 92 (jurisdiction over offences on British-controlled aircraft while they are in flight, whether or not within UK airspace).

Magistrates' Courts Act 1980, s. 2

(1) A magistrates' court has jurisdiction to try any summary offence.
(2) A magistrates' court has jurisdiction as examining justices over any offence committed by a person who appears or is brought before the court.
(3) Subject to—
   (a) sections 18 to 22, and
   (b) any other enactment (wherever contained) relating to the mode of trial of offences triable either way,

a magistrates' court has jurisdiction to try summarily any offence which is triable either way.

When the CJA 2003, sch. 3, para. 51, is brought fully into force, the words 'as examining justices over' in s. 2(2) will be replaced by 'under sections 51 and 51A of the Crime and Disorder Act 1998 in respect of'. That amendment is already partly in force (to the extent that the court is dealing with indictable-only offences or dangerous young offenders).

Determining the Place of the Trial

D20.14 The Courts Act 2003, s. 30(3), empowers the Lord Chancellor (with the concurrence of the Lord Chief Justice) to give directions as to the distribution and transfer of magistrates' courts business. Where a person is charged with an offence, the prosecution decide which court that person should appear before and this decision will have to take account of any such directions (s. 30(4)).

According to the *Directions Regarding Where Magistrates' Courts Can Sit and Criminal and Civil Jurisdiction and Procedure in Magistrates' Courts in England and Wales* (<http://www.hmcourts-service.gov.uk/cms/files/Section_30_Direction_9_March_05.doc>), the 'guiding principle' governing which magistrates' court should hear a case is that it should be heard either at a magistrates' court for the local justice area in which (i) the offence is alleged to have been committed, or (ii) the person charged with the offence resides (para. 5). However, this guiding principle may be departed from for good reason. Examples of what might be good reasons in individual cases are set out in para. 6:

(a) the consolidation of similar complaints/offences against the same defendant or co-accused;
(b) the place in which the witnesses, or the majority of the witnesses, reside;
(c) the place where other cases raising similar issues are being dealt with;
(d) the need to prevent an appearance of bias on the part of the tribunal.

Paragraph 7 gives examples of what might be good reasons based on management issues unconnected with the individual case, such as:

(a) the consolidation of cases to be conducted by the same prosecutor;
(b) the efficient management of all court accommodation;
(c) the need to ensure an efficient distribution of cases between local justice areas;
(d) the place where other cases raising similar issues are being dealt with;
(e) the need to deal with cases of a specialist nature.

Transfer of Cases between Magistrates' Courts

D20.15 It sometimes proves necessary, or desirable, to transfer cases from one magistrates' court to another. The MCA 1980, s. 27A, contains a general power to effect such a transfer at any stage in the proceedings. This power may be exercised by the court of its own motion, or on the application of one of the parties to the case. Where the court is minded to transfer a case, it should invite representations from all parties before doing so. There is to be no appeal from a decision on transfer.

Magistrates' Courts Act 1980, s. 27A

(1) Where a person appears or is brought before a magistrates' court—
 (a) to be tried by the court for an offence, or
 (b) for the court to inquire into the offence as examining justices,
 the court may transfer the matter to another magistrates' court.
(2) The court may transfer the matter before or after beginning the trial or inquiry.
(3) But if the court transfers the matter after it has begun to hear the evidence and the parties, the court to which the matter is transferred must begin hearing the evidence and the parties again.
(4) The power of the court under this section to transfer any matter must be exercised in accordance with any directions given under section 30(3) of the Courts Act 2003.

In addition to the general power conferred by s. 27A, there are specific statutory provisions relevant to sentencing hearings and remand hearings:

(a) By virtue of the PCC(S)A 2000, s. 10(1), where a magistrates' court has convicted an offender of an offence (the 'instant offence') and is then informed that he also stands convicted in another magistrates' court of some other offence for which he is yet to be sentenced, it may remit him to that other court to be dealt with for the instant offence. This power applies only if (i) the offender is aged 18 or over; (ii) the other court agrees to the remittal, and (iii) the instant offence is either imprisonable or punishable with disqualification from driving (s. 10(1) and (2)). The provisions of the MCA 1980, s. 128 (power to remand in custody or on bail and maximum period for remands in custody) apply upon a remittal to another court just as they would apply if the court were adjourning with a view to the offender being brought back before itself (PCC(S)A 2000, s. 10(3)(a)). In consequence of the remittal, the other court may deal with the case as if all the proceedings before the convicting court had in fact taken place before itself (s. 10(3)(b)). This includes the power to remit the offender to a third magistrates' court (s. 10(4)) or even to remit him back to the original convicting court (s. 10(5)). It will be noted that s. 10 can be of assistance only if the person to be remitted has already been convicted (though not sentenced or committed for sentence) in *both* the courts concerned.

(b) To avoid inconveniently long journeys from remand prison to court, a magistrates' court remanding an accused in custody under the MCA 1980, ss. 5 (remands prior to committal proceedings), 10(1) (remands prior to summary trial of an information), 17C (remands before 'plea before venue' hearing), 18(4) (remands prior to determining mode of trial for an offence triable either way) or 24C (adjournments prior to 'plea before venue' hearings in the case of juveniles — not yet in force), may order that he be brought up for any subsequent remands before an alternate magistrates' court nearer to the prison where is to be confined while on remand (s. 130(1)). While the order under s. 130(1) is in force, the alternate court exercises all the powers relating to a further remand (whether in custody or on bail) and the granting of legal aid which would otherwise fall to be exercised by the original court (s. 130(3)). The order ceases to have force when either the alternate court — upon making a further remand in custody — orders that the defendant be brought before the original court at the end of the remand, or it grants the accused bail (s. 130(4)). The alternate court would no doubt remand the defendant to be brought back before the original court on the occasion of the last remand before it is anticipated that a substantive step will be taken in the proceedings (e.g., it will ensure that the defendant appears in the original court for the commencement of a summary trial or the determination of mode of trial).

TIME WITHIN WHICH SUMMARY TRIAL SHOULD TAKE PLACE

General Rule

A magistrates' court may not try an accused for a *summary* offence unless the information was laid within six months of the time when the offence was allegedly committed (MCA 1980, s. 127(1). Section 127(2)(a) makes it clear that s. 127(1) does not apply to indictable offences (which term includes either-way offences). Where a statute creates a *continuing* summary offence, a prosecution can be brought at any time until six months have elapsed from the date when the offence ceased to be committed (*British Telecommunications plc v Nottinghamshire CC* [1999] Crim LR 217). D20.16

Section 127 does not make it clear when time starts to run in the case of proceedings brought by the new written charge and requisition procedure (established by the CJA 2003, s. 29). The possibilities are either the date of the issue of the written charge and requisition, or the date when they are received by the accused (or deemed to be received under the CrimPR, r. 4.10). It is submitted that the relevant date ought to be the date when the written charge and requisition are issued. This would be consistent with the position in the case of proceedings brought by the laying of an information and issue of a summons, where time starts to run when the information is laid (not when the summons is received by the accused).

In *Atkinson v DPP* [2005] 1 WLR 96, it was held that, where there is uncertainty as to whether an information has been laid in time, the question should be determined according to the criminal standard of proof and the magistrates should decline to hear the matter unless satisfied so that they are sure that the information was laid in time (see also *Lloyd v Young* [1963] Crim LR 703).

As regards either-way offences, there is no time-limit within which proceedings must be started (see *Kemp v Liebherr (Great Britain) Ltd* [1987] 1 WLR 607) unless it is one of the exceptional offences for which there is statutory limitation on the time for taking proceedings on indictment, in which case that limitation applies equally to summary proceedings (s. 127(2) and (4)).

Even where a statute creates an offence triable either way and then appears to impose a time-limit in respect of summary proceedings (but not proceedings on indictment), the limitation is overridden by the MCA 1980, s. 127(2). In *Kemp v Liebherr (Great Britain) Ltd*, a prosecution under the Health and Safety at Work etc. Act 1974 was commenced more than six months after evidence justifying a prosecution had become available to the prosecutor. By s. 34(3) of the Act, summary proceedings for contravening the Act apparently had to be commenced within six months of obtaining the evidence. The Divisional Court held that the proceedings were nonetheless within time since, on a true construction of the Act, the offence charged was triable either way and therefore s. 34(3) was effectively negated by the MCA 1980, s. 127(2). It should be noted, however, that this case involved a statute that pre-dated the MCA 1980. It is submitted that the same result might not occur in the case of a statute that was enacted after the MCA 1980, since Parliament could be taken as overriding s. 127(2) in the later Act if it chose to place a time-limit on the commencement of summary proceedings, but not proceedings on indictment.

Service of Summons or Requisition

D20.17 There is no specific time-limit within which the summons (or requisition) must be served once the information has been laid (or the written charge issued). However, excessive delay in serving the summons could amount to an abuse of process giving the court the power to dismiss the case (see **D20.19**).

Start of Time-limit

D20.18 The time-limit begins to run from the commission of the offence, rather than the date alleged in the information. Hence where there is an application to amend the date in the information to a later date, so that it falls within the six-month time-limit, the fact that six months had elapsed from the date alleged in the information is not in itself a valid objection to the amendment (*Blackburn Justices, ex parte Holmes* (2000) 164 JP 163).

For the position where the information is amended after the expiry of the time-limit so as to charge a different offence, see *Scunthorpe Justices, ex parte McPhee* (1998) 162 JP 635 at **D20.11**.

Magistrates' Courts Act 1980, s. 127

(1) Except as otherwise expressly provided by any enactment and subject to subsection (2) below, a magistrates' court shall not try an information . . . unless the information was laid . . . within six months from the time when the offence was committed. . . .

(2) Nothing in—

(a) subsection (1) above; or

(b) subject to subsection (4) below, any other enactment (however framed or worded) which, as regards any offence to which it applies, would but for this section impose a time-limit on the power of a magistrates' court to try an information summarily or impose a limitation on the time for taking summary proceedings,

shall apply in relation to any indictable offence.

(3) Without prejudice to the generality of paragraph (b) of subsection (2) above, that paragraph includes enactments which impose a time-limit that applies only in certain circumstances (for example, where the proceedings are not instituted by or with the consent of the Director of Public Prosecutions or some other specified authority).

(4) Where, as regards any indictable offence, there is imposed by any enactment (however framed or worded, and whether falling within subsection (2)(b) above or not) a limitation on the time for taking proceedings on indictment for that offence no summary proceedings for that offence shall be taken after the latest time for taking proceedings on indictment.

DISCRETION NOT TO PROCEED ON ACCOUNT OF DELAY

Effect of Delay

Even where proceedings were commenced within time, a magistrates' court has a discretion to refuse to try an information and acquit the accused without trial if there has been delay amounting to an abuse of the process of the court (see *Brentford Justices, ex parte Wong* [1981] QB 445). Delay as a possible abuse of process is dealt with fully at D3.58 *et seq.* **D20.19**

Where the delay is deliberate, it is likely to amount to an abuse of process, as in *Brentford Justices, ex parte Wong*, where the prosecutor deliberately delayed in effecting service of the summons in order to gain more time in which to decide whether or not to continue the case against the accused.

Where deliberate delay in bringing the case to court cannot be shown, the defence may nonetheless apply for the magistrates to exercise their discretion not to proceed if (i) there has been inordinate or unconscionable delay due to the prosecution's inefficiency, and (ii) prejudice to the defence from the delay is either proved or to be inferred (per Lloyd LJ in *Gateshead Justices, ex parte Smith* (1985) 149 JP 681, summarising the effect of earlier decisions). It is clear that where there is an element of deliberate delay on the part of the prosecution, the courts are more willing to stay the prosecution than if there has been mere inefficiency. Conversely, if the delay was in part attributable to the accused's own conduct, an application to stay is unlikely to succeed (*Canterbury and St Augustine Justices, ex parte Turner* (1983) 147 JP 193).

Delay in Service of Summons or Requisition Several of the decisions relating to delay in the context of summary trial have been in the context of delays in serving the summons. For example, in *Watford Justices, ex parte Outrim* [1983] RTR 26, the summons was served almost two years after issue. It was held that when service of the summons is delayed so long as to produce substantial prejudice to an accused or to be unconscionable, the justices have a discretion to decline to proceed to hear the summons. Where the accused has not tried to evade service or in any way contributed to the failure to serve him, there is a clear inference that something had gone wrong with the process serving procedures, and in such circumstances the justices are entitled and, in appropriate cases, bound to refuse to proceed with the summons. Such delay is unlikely to arise in the case of public prosecutions commenced by way of written charge and requisition, as the two documents should be issued together. **D20.20**

Application to Summary Offences and Either-way Offences The discretion to halt the proceedings applies both to proposed trials of summary offences and to summary trials of offences triable either way. However, it is submitted that the discretion to stay the proceedings is more likely to be exercised in the former class of case since Parliament, by enacting the MCA 1980, s. 127, has indicated that proceedings for summary offences should take place within a reasonably short period, and delays between information and service of the summons indirectly thwart Parliament's intention. **D20.21**

DISCLOSURE BY THE PROSECUTION

Advance Warning of the Prosecution Case

D20.22 Where the offence is triable either way, the defence may learn the nature of the prosecution case by requesting advance information (see the CrimPR, part 21). The rules are considered and set out in full at **D6.4** *et seq.* The main purpose of the information is to assist the defence in determining the mode of trial. Accordingly, the time at which it should be requested and provided is *before* the magistrates consider whether the case is more suitable for summary trial or for trial on indictment (see r. 21.3(1)). Advance information may take the form of copies of the proposed prosecution witnesses' statements or of a summary of the prosecution case (r. 21.3(1)(a) and (b)). The former is of much greater assistance to the defence than the latter in the conduct of a summary trial, and it is submitted that the prosecution should provide copies of the witness statements rather than a mere summary. This is especially the case bearing in mind para. 57 of the A-G's Guidelines on Disclosure (see **appendix 6**), which states that the prosecution should 'provide to the defence all evidence upon which the Crown proposes to rely in a summary trial. Such provision should allow the accused and their legal advisers sufficient time properly to consider the evidence before it is called'.

Where the offence charged is a summary one, the CrimPR, part 21, does not apply. However, para. 57 of the A-G's Guidelines does apply (since it refers to summary trials generally, not just to summary trial of either-way offences), and so prosecutors should provide the defence with copies of the statements of their witnesses even if the offence is triable only summarily.

Disclosure of Unused Prosecution Material

D20.23 The position relating to disclosure in summary trial under the CPIA 1996 is dealt with at **D9.21**. The main difference between disclosure under the CPIA in the magistrates' court, as against the Crown Court, is that in the magistrates' court the provision of a 'defence statement' is voluntary, not mandatory (see CPIA 1996, s. 6). If the defence choose to serve a defence statement, it must fulfil the requirements that are applicable to defence statements, and adverse inferences can be drawn (under s. 11) if it does not comply with those requirements or if, for example, the accused serves the defence statement late or puts forward a different case at trial. The only advantage of serving a defence statement in the magistrates' court is that it triggers a check by the prosecution to see if they have any hitherto undisclosed material which might assist the accused's defence as set out in the defence statement. If the defence statement would not add anything to what the accused said when interviewed by the police (and so the prosecution are already aware of the nature of the defence case), it is submitted that there is little to be gained from serving a defence statement where the case is to be heard by a magistrates' court.

SECURING THE ATTENDANCE OF WITNESSES: WITNESS SUMMONSES

D20.24 The attendance of witnesses for purposes of criminal proceedings in magistrates' courts may be secured by the issue of a summons or warrant under the powers given in the MCA 1980, s. 97, which applies equally to proposed prosecution and proposed defence witnesses.

Section 97 provides, essentially, that, where a magistrate is satisfied that:

(a) any person within the jurisdiction is likely to be able to give material evidence, or produce any document or thing likely to be material evidence, for purposes of a summary trial to be held in a magistrates' court, and

(b) it is in the interests of justice to issue a summons under this subsection to secure the attendance of that person to give evidence or produce the document or thing,

then the magistrate may issue a summons requiring the person to attend before the court on the date specified in the summons (s. 97(1)).

A similar power is given to justices' clerks by para. 2 of the schedule to the Justices' Clerks Rules 2005 (SI 2005 No. 545). If a magistrate (but not a clerk) is further satisfied by evidence on oath that it is probable that a summons issued under s. 97(1) would not procure the witness's attendance, then he may issue a warrant (s. 97(2)).

Should a person summoned under s. 97(1) fail to attend as required, the court may issue a warrant (s. 97(3)). It must, however, be satisfied that:

(a) the witness is indeed likely to be able to give material evidence or produce a material document or thing;
(b) that he has been duly served with the summons and been paid or tendered a reasonable sum for costs and expenses; and
(c) that there is no just excuse for the failure to attend.

Requirement (a) must be established by evidence on oath; requirement (b) may be established either by evidence on oath or in such other manner as is prescribed. By virtue of the CrimPR, part 4, a witness summons may be served in one of the following ways:

(i) by handing it to individual (r. 4.3(1)(a));
(ii) by leaving it at, or sending it by first class post to, an address where it is reasonable to believe that the individual will receive it (r. 4.4(1) and r. 4.4(2)(a)).

Material Admissible Evidence

The power to issue a witness summons is conditional upon the magistrate being satisfied that the witness will be able to give or produce material evidence. In *Peterborough Magistrates' Court, ex parte Willis* (1987) 151 JP 785, it was held that a witness summons should not be issued to enable someone to find out whether the witness can give any material evidence, as there has to be material before the court on which it may be satisfied that the witness will be able to give material evidence. The Divisional Court added that, when it reviews a s. 97 order, it will consider only the material before the magistrates who issued the summons. **D20.25**

Similarly, where the summons is to produce a document or thing, the applicant must be able to show that the item to be produced would be admissible evidence and not, for example, material subject to legal professional privilege (*Derby Magistrates' Court, ex parte B* [1996] AC 487). In the context of prosecutions for drink-driving offences, summonses requiring the police to produce the logbook and service records for the Intoximeter machine on which the accused was tested have been quashed on the basis that the requests amount to a 'fishing expedition' which it was hoped might lead to some information being disclosed which would be of assistance to the defence (see *Coventry Magistrates' Court, ex parte Perks* [1985] RTR 74 and *Tower Bridge Magistrates' Court, ex parte DPP* [1989] RTR 118). Similarly, in *R (Cunliffe) v Hastings Magistrates' Court* [2006] EWHC 2081 (Admin), the court quashed witness summonses to produce documents relating to the functioning and design of the breath-testing instrument, since the request had amounted to a 'fishing expedition' and because the documents were not admissible *per se* because they would need an expert witness to interpret them (the court only has power to order the production of admissible evidence).

In *Reading Justices, ex parte Berkshire County Council* [1996] 1 Cr App R 239, Simon Brown LJ summarised the key principles governing such applications as follows (at p. 246–7):

(i) to be material evidence documents must be not only relevant to the issues arising in the criminal proceedings, but also documents admissible as such in evidence;

(ii) documents which are desired merely for the purpose of possible cross-examination are not admissible in evidence and, thus, are not material for the purposes of s. 97;
(iii) whoever seeks production of documents must satisfy the justices with some material that the documents are 'likely to be material' in the sense indicated, likelihood for this purpose involving a real possibility, although not necessarily a probability;
(iv) it is not sufficient that the applicant merely wants to find out whether or not the third party has such material documents. This procedure must not be used as a disguised attempt to obtain discovery.

Procedure

D20.26 The CrimPR, r. 28.2, provides that the court may issue (or withdraw) a witness summons, warrant or order with or without a hearing, and that any hearing under part 28 must be in private unless the court otherwise directs. Under r. 28.3(1), a party seeking a witness summons (or warrant) must apply as soon as practicable after becoming aware of the grounds for doing so. It should also be noted that, under the MCA 1980, s. 97(2B), an application for a witness summons may be refused if the magistrate or clerk is not satisfied that an application for the summons has been made as soon as reasonably practicable after the accused pleaded not guilty. Rule 28.3(2) requires the applicant to explain:

(i) what evidence the proposed witness can give or produce;
(ii) why it is likely to be material evidence; and
(iii) why it would be in the interests of justice to issue a summons or warrant.

The application may be made orally (unless r. 28.5 applies — see below) except where the court directs otherwise (r. 28.3(3)). Where the application is in writing, it has to be in the prescribed form (r. 28(4)).

Rule 28.5 applies where the application is for a witness summons requiring the proposed witness to produce in evidence a document or thing, or to give evidence about information apparently held in confidence, that relates to another person. Under r. 28.5(4), the court must not issue a witness summons in such a case unless everyone served with the application has had at least 14 days in which to make representations, and the court is satisfied that it has been able to take adequate account of the duties and rights, including rights of confidentiality, of the proposed witness and of any person to whom the proposed evidence relates.

Under r. 28.6, a person served with an application for a witness summons requiring production of a document or thing may object to its production on the ground that either it is not likely to be material evidence, or the duties or rights (including rights of confidentiality) of the proposed witness or of any person to whom the document or thing relates outweigh the reasons for issuing a summons. Under r. 28.6(2), the court may require the proposed witness to make the document or thing available for the objection to be assessed.

Rule 28.7 makes provision for the withdrawal of a witness summons or warrant. The party who applied for it may seek its withdrawal on the ground that it no longer is needed; the witness (or any person to whom the evidence relates) may seek its withdrawal on the grounds that he was not aware of the application for it, and either he cannot give or produce evidence likely to be material evidence, or his duties or rights (including rights of confidentiality) outweigh the reasons for the issue of the summons, warrant or order.

Failure to Testify

D20.27 If a proposed witness attending or brought before a magistrates' court refuses without just excuse to be sworn or give evidence (or to produce a document or thing), he may be imprisoned for up to a month and/or fined up to £2,500 (MCA 1980, s. 97(4)). This applies whether the witness attended court entirely voluntarily or in answer to a summons or was brought there following execution of a warrant.

Statutory Provision on Witness Summonses and Warrants

Magistrates' Courts Act 1980, s. 97 D20.28

(1) Where a justice of the peace is satisfied that—
  (a) any person in England or Wales is likely to be able to give material evidence, or produce any document or thing likely to be material evidence, at the summary trial of an information or hearing of a complaint by a magistrates' court, and
  (b) it is in the interests of justice to issue a summons under this subsection to secure the attendance of that person to give evidence or produce the document or thing,

  the justice shall issue a summons directed to that person requiring him to attend before the court at the time and place appointed in the summons to give evidence or to produce the document or thing.

(2) If a justice of the peace is satisfied by evidence on oath of the matters mentioned in subsection (1) above, and also that it is probable that a summons under that subsection would not procure the attendance of the person in question, the justice may instead of issuing a summons issue a warrant to arrest that person and bring him before such a court as aforesaid at a time and place specified in the warrant ...

(2A) A summons may also be issued under subsection (1) above if the justice is satisfied that the person in question is outside the British Islands but no warrant shall be issued under subsection (2) above unless the justice is satisfied by evidence on oath that the person in question is in England or Wales.

(2B) A justice may refuse to issue a summons under subsection (1) above in relation to the summary trial of an information if he is not satisfied that an application for the summons was made by a party to the case as soon as reasonably practicable after the accused pleaded not guilty.

(2C) In relation to the summary trial of an information, subsection (2) above shall have effect as if the reference to the matters mentioned in subsection (1) above included a reference to the matter mentioned in subsection (2B) above.

(3) On the failure of any person to attend before a magistrates' court in answer to a summons under this section, if—
  (a) the court is satisfied by evidence on oath that he is likely to be able to give material evidence or produce any document or thing likely to be material evidence in the proceedings; and
  (b) it is proved on oath, or in such other manner as may be prescribed, that he has been duly served with the summons, and that a reasonable sum has been paid or tendered to him for costs and expenses; and
  (c) it appears to the court that there is no just excuse for the failure, the court may issue a warrant to arrest him and bring him before the court at a time and place specified in the warrant.

(4) If any person attending or brought before a magistrates' court refuses without just excuse to be sworn or give evidence, or to produce any document or thing, the court or justice, as the case may be, may commit him to custody until the expiration of such period not exceeding one month as may be specified in the warrant or until he sooner gives evidence or produces the document or thing or impose on him a fine not exceeding £2,500 or both.

(5) A fine imposed under subsection (4) above shall be deemed, for the purposes of any enactment, to be a sum adjudged to be paid by a conviction.

AUTREFOIS IN THE CONTEXT OF SUMMARY TRIAL

There is no special procedure for pleading autrefois acquit or autrefois convict at summary trial. However, it is well established that a previous acquittal or conviction for the same matter is as much a bar to summary proceedings as it is to proceedings on indictment (per Lord Morris in *Connelly v DPP* [1964] AC 1254). The issue may be raised simply on a not guilty plea. D20.29

The question most frequently raised by autrefois arising out of summary proceedings is whether there has been a genuine acquittal or, as the case may be, conviction by magistrates acting properly within their jurisdiction. If there has not, the accused is said never to have

D

Part D Procedure

been in jeopardy and therefore unable to rely on autrefois. Thus, as explained in **D20.35**, the withdrawal of a charge before a plea is entered does *not* found autrefois, whereas the dismissal of the charge following a not guilty plea and the offering of no evidence normally does (see **D20.36**). However, a distinction is drawn between cases where, for whatever reason, no evidence is offered and those where the proceedings in the magistrates' courts are so flawed that the accused was never in danger of a valid conviction. In the latter type of case, a purported acquittal (or conviction) does not prevent the magistrates re-trying the accused for the same offence: see *Dabhade* [1993] QB 329, where it was confirmed that fresh proceedings may be brought if (but only if) the accused was never in jeopardy of a valid conviction. Thus, where magistrates purport to acquit the accused without giving the prosecution the opportunity to call evidence, the purported acquittal is liable to be quashed and the autrefois doctrine will not prevent fresh proceedings for the same offence being instituted (*Dorking Justices, ex parte Harrington* [1984] AC 743). For example, in *Holmes v Campbell* (1998) 162 JP 655, a magistrates' court dismissed the information against the accused when the prosecutor failed to appear at the hearing. The prosecutor subsequently brought fresh proceedings (making the same allegations) but the magistrates' court declined to try the case on the ground that it would be an abuse of process. The Divisional Court held that by virtue of the MCA 1980, s. 15, the accused could not have been convicted at a hearing where the prosecutor was absent, and so had not been in jeopardy of conviction at that hearing. It followed that the doctrine of autrefois acquit did not prevent the hearing of the fresh charge.

Where the prosecution have preferred two charges in the alternative arising out of the same facts and the court puts them to their election as to the one on which they wish to proceed, the immediate dismissal of the information on which they are not proceeding does not enable the accused to rely on autrefois in respect of the other (*Broadbent v High* [1985] RTR 359).

UNFITNESS TO PLEAD IN THE CONTEXT OF SUMMARY TRIAL

D20.30 There is no specific procedure by which a person's fitness to plead may be determined in the magistrates' court. If the accused is thought to be suffering from a mental disability such as to render him unable to comprehend the course of the proceedings or make a proper defence to the charge (i.e. he would be found unfit to plead if he were facing trial on indictment), the defence have the following options:

(a) Assuming the offence is triable either way, they may elect trial on indictment and have the question of fitness determined by a jury in the Crown Court. Indeed, it would be open to the justices to decline jurisdiction on the basis that the Crown Court is the more appropriate forum for a case where fitness to plead is an issue.

(b) Assuming there is to be a summary trial, they may allow the accused to plead not guilty (or indicate a not guilty plea if he is incapable even of doing that) and put the prosecution to proof of their case. If the definition of the offence involves the prosecution in proving *mens rea* and especially if it involves a specific intent, the accused's mental condition may make it difficult for the prosecution to discharge their burden. It seems that the common-law defence of insanity is available to an accused in a summary trial where *mens rea* is in issue (*Horseferry Road Magistrates' Court, ex parte K* [1997] QB 23).

(c) They may invite the court to make a hospital order under the Mental Health Act 1983, s. 37(3), without convicting the accused.

The Mental Health Act 1983, s. 37(3), enables magistrates to achieve a result very similar to that which follows upon an accused being found unfit to plead to an indictment. It must be read in conjunction with the PCC(S)A 2000, s. 11(1).

In *R (Singh) v Stratford Magistrates' Court* [2007] EWHC 1582 (Admin), the Divisional Court confirmed that the defence of insanity can be relied upon in magistrates' courts (following *Horseferry Road Magistrates' Court, ex parte K* [1997]). The court went on to consider the effect of the Mental Health Act 1983, s 37(3), holding that it provides the magistrates with the power, in an appropriate case, to abstain from either convicting or acquitting the accused, but instead to make a hospital or guardianship order. Hughes LJ went on (at [39]–[41]) to hold that a magistrates' court has the power, in an appropriate case, to try the issue of insanity and pronounce its conclusion upon it, without convicting or acquitting the accused, provided that the conditions for making a hospital or guardianship order under s. 37(3) are met. However, if satisfied that there is no purpose in resolving the issue of insanity, and if a s. 37(3) order is going to be made, the court can deal with the case without trying that issue. If it is clear that no s. 37(3) order is going to be possible on the medical evidence whatever happens then, in the absence of some other compelling factor, the case must proceed to trial. Before embarking on a case in which s. 37(3) may be applied, magistrates should make it clear that it is a possibility and should invite submissions from the parties upon the course to be adopted. In particular, careful consideration must be given to any reason advanced why the issue of insanity should be tried. Such an application should be resolved having regard to the interests of justice, which include, but are not limited to, justice to the accused.

The same principles are to be followed in respect of a young person facing trial in the youth court (*R (P) v Barking Youth Court* (2002) 2 Cr App R 294). It should also be noted that the MCA 1980, s. 142, can be used to reopen decisions under the Mental Health Act 1983, s. 37, where that is appropriate (*R (Bartram) v Southend Magistrates' Court* [2004] EWHC 2691 (Admin)). For detailed guidance on the approach to be taken, see *CPS v P* (2007) 171 JP 349 (see **D23.4**).

Powers of Criminal Courts (Sentencing) Act 2000, s. 11

(1) If, on the trial by a magistrates' court of an offence punishable on summary conviction with imprisonment the court—
 (a) is satisfied that the accused did the act or made the omission charged, but
 (b) is of the opinion that an inquiry ought to be made into his physical or mental condition before the method of dealing with him is determined,

the court shall adjourn the case to enable a medical examination and report to be made, and shall remand him.

(2) An adjournment under subsection (1) above shall not be for more than three weeks at a time where the court remands the accused in custody, nor for more than four weeks at a time where it remands him on bail.

(3) Where on an adjournment under subsection (1) above the accused is remanded on bail, the court shall impose conditions under paragraph (d) of section 3(6) of the Bail Act 1976 and the requirements imposed as conditions under that paragraph shall be or shall include requirements that the accused—
 (a) undergo medical examination by a registered medical practitioner or, where the inquiry is into his mental condition and the court so directs, two such practitioners; and
 (b) for that purpose attend such an institution or place, or on such practitioner, as the court directs and, where the inquiry is into his mental condition, comply with any other directions which may be given to him for that purpose by any person specified by the court or by a person of any class so specified.

Mental Health Act 1983, s. 37(3)

Where a person is charged before a magistrates' court with any act or omission as an offence and the court would have power, on convicting him of that offence, to make a [hospital] order under subsection (1) above in his case as being a person suffering from mental illness or severe mental impairment, then, if the court is satisfied that the accused did the act or made the omission charged, the court may, if it thinks fit, make such an order without convicting him.

It will be noted that the power to order medical reports under the PCC(S)A 2000, s. 11(1), and the power to make a hospital order under the Mental Health Act 1983, s. 37(3), both depend merely upon the court being satisfied that the accused committed the *actus reus* of the offence with which he is charged. Therefore, in a case where the accused is apparently suffering from mental illness or impairment, the court may cause a not guilty plea to be entered on his behalf and hear the prosecution evidence. Assuming that evidence establishes the *actus reus*, the court may then adjourn for reports. If, on the basis of those reports, the medical criteria for the making of a hospital order are satisfied, the court may make such an order *without convicting the accused*. For details about the pre-conditions for a hospital order and, in particular, the need for reports from two medical practitioners (including a Home Office approved psychiatrist) confirming that the accused is suffering from mental illness or severe mental impairment as defined by the Mental Health Act 1983, see **E24.1**.

Where the information is for an either-way offence an added difficulty arises, namely that the magistrates' court will not have jurisdiction to hear evidence establishing the *actus reus* of the offence unless the accused consents to summary trial. *Ex hypothesi*, he is unlikely to be in a fit state to give his consent. In *Lincoln (Kesteven) Justices, ex parte O'Connor* [1983] 1 WLR 335, the accused was charged with assault occasioning actual bodily harm. His mental state was such that he was incapable of consenting to summary trial. The Divisional Court held that a trial is *not* a necessary precondition of the court being satisfied for the purposes of s. 37(3) that the accused committed the *actus reus* of the offence. In an exceptional case such as the instant one, where the accused was legally represented and everybody agreed that he had assaulted the victim, the justices could conclude without evidence that the offence had occurred. Therefore, they had jurisdiction to make a hospital order. It is, however, clear that the magistrates have no jurisdiction under s. 37(3) to make a hospital order in respect of a person charged with an offence triable only on indictment (*Chippenham Magistrates' Court, ex parte Thompson* (1996) 160 JP 207).

PRE-TRIAL HEARINGS

Early Hearings and Early Administrative Hearings

D20.31 There is a system of pre-trial hearings in the magistrates' courts: where a guilty plea is anticipated, an 'Early First Hearing' is scheduled; where a not guilty plea is expected, there will be an 'Early Administrative Hearing'.

The statutory basis for such hearings is found in the CDA 1998, s. 50, which provides that where the accused has been charged with an offence at a police station, the magistrates' court before whom he appears or is brought for the first time in relation to the charge may, unless the accused falls to be dealt with under s. 51 below, consist of a single justice. At a hearing conducted by a single justice under s. 50, the accused is asked whether he wishes to apply for legal aid (if necessary, the hearing may be adjourned for this purpose under s. 50(4A)). On adjourning the hearing, the magistrate may remand the accused in custody or on bail. Under s. 50(4), an early administrative hearing may be conducted by a justices' clerk (or an assistant clerk who has been specifically authorised by the justices' clerk for that purpose), but the clerk is not empowered to remand the accused in custody or, without the consent of the prosecutor and the accused, to remand the accused on bail on conditions other than those (if any) previously imposed.

It will be noted that s. 50 applies only where the accused was charged at the police station, and so does not apply where the accused is granted police bail and is then charged by the CPS using the written charge and requisition procedure. However, there is nothing to prevent magistrates' courts operating a system of early administrative hearings in all cases where a not guilty plea is expected. In due course, provision will be made for pre-trial hearings in magistrates' courts by the CrimPR, part 9.

Pre-trial Hearings and Pre-trial Rulings

The Courts Act 2003, s. 45 and sch. 3, makes specific provision for binding rulings to be made at pre-trial hearings in criminal cases that are to be heard in the magistrates' courts. Schedule 3 inserts new sections into the MCA 1980 (in force from April 2005). The MCA 1980, s. 8A, applies to cases that are to be tried summarily where the accused has entered a not guilty plea (s. 8A(1)). For these purposes, a pre-trial hearing is a hearing that takes place before the court begins to hear evidence from the prosecution at the trial (or, in those cases where fitness to plead is an issue, before the court considers whether to exercise its power under the Mental Health Act 1983, s. 37(3), to make a hospital order without convicting the accused (s. 8A(2)). At a pre-trial hearing, the magistrates may decide any question as to the admissibility of evidence and any other question of law relating to the case (s. 8A(4)). Such rulings may be made only if it appears to the court that it is in the interests of justice to make the ruling (s. 8A(3)(c)). If the accused is unrepresented, he must be given the chance to apply for publicly funded representation (s. 8A(5)). Pre-trial rulings may be made on the application of the defence or prosecution, or of the court's own motion (s. 8A(6)). **D20.32**

Under s. 8B(1), a pre-trial ruling is binding until the case against the accused (or, where there is more than one, against each of them) is disposed of. However, under s. 8B(3), the court may (on application by a party or of its own motion) discharge or vary a pre-trial ruling provided it appears to the court that it is in the interests of justice to do so, and the court has given the parties an opportunity to be heard. A party can apply for the ruling to be discharged or varied only if there has been a material change of circumstances since the ruling was made or, if there has been a previous application under s. 8B, since that application was made (s. 8B(5)).

Under the MCA 1980, s. 25, where the magistrates have accepted jurisdiction in the case of an either-way offence, the prosecution may ask the magistrates (before the start of the summary trial) to reconsider that decision (on the ground that the magistrates' sentencing powers are inadequate to deal with the offence if the accused is convicted); under the MCA 1980, s. 8B(6)(a), any pre-trial ruling in respect of such an offence is discharged when the case is sent to the Crown Court for trial (so, unsurprisingly, the Crown Court would not be bound by that ruling).

Statutory Provisions on Pre-trial Hearings and Rulings

Magistrates' Courts Act 1980, ss. 8A and 8B **D20.33**

8A.—(1) For the purposes of this section a hearing is a pre-trial hearing if—
(a) it relates to an information—
(i) which is to be tried summarily, and
(ii) to which the accused has pleaded not guilty, and
(b) it takes place before the start of the trial.

(2) For the purposes of subsection (1)(b), the start of a summary trial occurs when the court begins—
(a) to hear evidence from the prosecution at the trial, or
(b) to consider whether to exercise its power under section 37(3) of the Mental Health Act 1983 (power to make hospital order without convicting the accused).

(3) At a pre-trial hearing, a magistrates' court may make a ruling as to any matter mentioned in subsection (4) if—
(a) the condition in subsection (5) is met,
(b) the court has given the parties an opportunity to be heard, and
(c) it appears to the court that it is in the interests of justice to make the ruling.

(4) The matters are—
(a) any question as to the admissibility of evidence;
(b) any other question of law relating to the case.

(5) The condition is that, if the accused is not legally represented, the court must—
(a) ask whether he wishes to be granted a right to representation funded by the Legal Services Commission as part of the Criminal Defence Service, and

(b) if he does, decide whether or not to grant him that right.

(6) A ruling may be made under this section—

(a) on an application by a party to the case, or

(b) of the court's own motion.

(7) For the purposes of this section and section 8B, references to the prosecutor are to any person acting as prosecutor, whether an individual or body.

8B.—(1) Subject to subsections (3) and (6), a ruling under section 8A has binding effect from the time it is made until the case against the accused or, if there is more than one, against each of them, is disposed of.

(2) The case against an accused is disposed of if—

(a) he is acquitted or convicted,

(b) the prosecutor decides not to proceed with the case against him, or

(c) the information is dismissed.

(3) A magistrates' court may discharge or vary (or further vary) a ruling under section 8A if—

(a) the condition in section 8A(5) is met,

(b) the court has given the parties an opportunity to be heard, and

(c) it appears to the court that it is in the interests of justice to do so.

(4) The court may act under subsection (3)—

(a) on an application by a party to the case, or

(b) of its own motion.

(5) No application may be made under subsection (4)(a) unless there has been a material change of circumstances since the ruling was made or, if a previous application has been made, since the application (or last application) was made.

(6) A ruling under section 8A is discharged in relation to an accused if—

(a) the magistrates' court commits or sends him to the Crown Court for trial for the offence charged in the information, or

(b) a count charging him with the offence is included in an indictment by virtue of section 40 of the Criminal Justice Act 1988.

Reporting Restrictions applicable to Pre-trial Hearings

D20.34 Section 8C of the MCA 1980 imposes restrictions on reporting of pre-trial hearings in order to avoid prejudicing the right to a fair trial (particularly important if the case is ultimately tried in the Crown Court). The publishing of anything other than the basic factual information permitted by s. 8C(7) is prohibited — unless the court orders that reporting restrictions should not apply — until such time as the case against the defendant is disposed of. Section 8C(7) permits the publication of the identity of the court and the names of the justices; the names, ages, home addresses and occupations of the accused and witnesses; the offence(s) with which the accused is charged; the names of counsel and solicitors in the proceedings; where the proceedings are adjourned, the date and place to which they are adjourned; any arrangements as to bail; whether a right to representation by the Criminal Defence Service was granted to the accused.

The power to lift the reporting restrictions is conferred by s. 8C(3). Where the court is minded to order that the reporting restrictions do not apply and there is only one accused, and he objects to the making of an order removing the restrictions, the court may make the order if (and only if) satisfied after hearing his representations that it is in the interests of justice to do so (subsection (4)(a)); where there are two or more accused and one or more of them objects to the lifting of the restrictions, the court may make the order if (and only if) satisfied after hearing the representations of each of the accused that it is in the interests of justice to do so (s. 8C(5)(b)). Breach of these reporting restrictions is a summary offence punishable under s. 8D with a level 5 fine (currently £5,000). Under s. 8D(6), proceedings for this offence may not be instituted otherwise than by or with the consent of the A-G.

The implementation of this power to make binding pre-trial rulings will bring the powers of magistrates at pre-trial hearings into line with those of the judges in the Crown Court (where the CPIA 1996, s. 40, empowers a judge to give binding pre-trial rulings on matters of law and admissibility of evidence).

CASE MANAGEMENT

Part V.56 of the *Consolidated Practice Direction* governs case management in magistrates' courts (supplementing the rules set out in the CrimPR, part 3). Paragraph V.56.1 makes it clear that once the time-limits set out in the CrimPR and other legislation have expired, the parties will be expected to be fully prepared. D20.35

Paragraph V.56.2 requires use of the case progression form set out in Annex E of the *Practice Direction* and makes the point that the form, together with the accompanying guidance notes, constitutes a case progression timetable for the effective preparation of a case. Moreover, the case progression forms to be used in magistrates' courts contain directions, all of which apply in every case unless the court orders otherwise (para. V.56.6).

The case progression form for the magistrates' court draws attention to a number of questions:

(i) Has the accused been advised that the case may proceed in his absence?
(ii) Has the accused been advised about credit for pleading guilty?
(iii) What are the 'trial issues' (e.g., identification — with details)?
(iv) What applications are to be made (e.g., special measures, bad character, hearsay)?
(v) What is the likely number of witnesses (both prosecution and defence) and, in the case of the former, will their statement be read under the CJA 1967, s. 9)?
(vi) What is the estimated length of trial?

The court will fix the trial date at (or shortly after) the hearing at which the accused pleads not guilty.

Standard Directions

A number of standard directions are applicable to a summary trial unless the court orders otherwise. Time for compliance with the directions starts to run from the date of the hearing at which the trial date is fixed (unless the court orders otherwise). The standard directions are as follows: D20.36

Special measures. The prosecution must serve any application for 'special measures' directions within 14 days, and the defence have 14 days thereafter in which to serve any response.

Prosecution case and disclosure. The prosecution (if they have not done so already) must serve copies of the witness statements, along with any documentary exhibits, tapes of interview, and vidco or CCTV tapes within 28 days. The prosecution must also comply with its initial duty of disclosure under the CPIA 1996 within 28 days.

Hearsay evidence. The prosecution must serve any notice of intention to introduce hearsay evidence at the same time as it complies with its initial duty of disclosure, and the defence must serve any notice opposing the prosecution's notice within 14 days of receipt thereof.

The defence must serve any notice of intention to introduce hearsay evidence within 14 days of the date on which the prosecution complied with its initial duty of disclosure, and the prosecution must serve any notice opposing the defence notice within 14 days of receipt thereof.

Bad character evidence. The defence must serve any application to introduce the bad character of a prosecution witness within 14 days of the date on which the prosecution complied with its initial duty of disclosure. The prosecution must serve any notice opposing the defence application within 14 days of receipt thereof.

The prosecution must serve any notice to introduce the accused's bad character at the same time as it complies with its initial duty of disclosure, and the defence must serve any application to exclude evidence of the accused's bad character within seven days of receipt of the prosecution application.

Defence statement. If a defence statement is to be given, the defence must serve it within 14 days of the prosecution complying with its initial duty of disclosure.

Witness statements. If the defence wish a prosecution witness to give evidence in person at the trial (rather than allowing their statement to be read to the court under the CJA 1967, s. 9), the defence must notify the prosecution within seven days of receiving the prosecution case (i.e. the witness statements etc.).

The defence must serve any statements of defence witnesses who the defence propose not to give evidence in person at the trial within 14 days of receiving the prosecution case, and a party who wishes such a witness to give evidence in person at the trial must notify the prosecution within seven days of service of the statement.

Further disclosure. The prosecution must complete any further disclosure at least 14 days before the trial.

Written admissions. The parties must file any written admissions made under the CJA 1967, s. 10, within 56 days.

Expert evidence. A party seeking to rely on expert evidence must serve the expert's report within 28 days.

A party served with expert evidence must indicate whether the expert is required to attend at the trial, and either serve their own expert evidence in response, or indicate that they are not intending to rely on expert evidence, within 28 days of receipt of the other party's expert evidence.

A meeting of experts to agree non-contentious matters and identify issues (if appropriate and if the parties agree) should take place within 28 days of service of both parties' expert evidence, and the parties must notify the court within 14 days of an experts' meeting whether the length of the trial is affected by the outcome of the meeting.

Points of law. If any point of law is to be taken by a party and a skeleton argument would be helpful, it must be served, together with the relevant authorities, at least 21 days prior to the trial. The other party must serve a skeleton argument in reply, together with the relevant authorities, at least seven days prior to the trial.

Trial readiness. The parties must certify readiness for trial, by filing a certificate of readiness, at least seven days prior to the trial.

The guidance notes to these directions point out the directions allow the parties eight weeks in which to prepare for trial (or 14 weeks where there is to be expert evidence). If the court fixes a trial date less than eight weeks after the date of the not guilty plea then directions relevant to the case will need to be modified.

The notes also make the point that not all the standard directions will be needed in every case where the defendant is pleading not guilty. If the accused intends to plead guilty but there is a dispute over the facts of the offence, and a *Newton* hearing is to be held, any reference to the trial in the standard directions should be read as a reference to the *Newton* hearing (with the timetable beginning on the date of the guilty plea).

The standard directions are described in the guidance notes as 'default directions', which will apply where the accused pleads not guilty unless the justices, a District Judge (Magistrates' Court), a justices' clerk or an assistant to a justices' clerk, as the case may be, direct otherwise.

TRIAL OF INFORMATIONS AND WRITTEN CHARGES

Discretion Not to Try an Information

Save in cases where there has been inordinate delay amounting to an abuse of the process of the court (see **D20.19**), magistrates are almost always obliged to hear the prosecution evidence. In *Birmingham Justices, ex parte Lamb* [1983] 1 WLR 339, the Divisional Court held that the justices erred in refusing to try informations for reasons such as the relative triviality of the charge, the apparent frailty of the prosecution evidence insofar as it had been disclosed, and the long period that would elapse before the court would have time to hear the case on the basis of a not guilty plea. McNeill J said (at p. 344D): **D20.37**

> At the end of the day, the law does not permit cases, on grounds of supposed injustice, to be dismissed out of hand without hearing any evidence. The justices can reflect their sense of injustice at the end of the prosecution case if they are not satisfied that the offence has been made out. They can reflect it at the end of the whole of the evidence by acquitting the defendant or, if they feel obliged to convict, they can reflect it by imposing such a penalty as reflects their view of the case.
>
> In the magistrates' court, there is no power which enables the justices to dismiss a summons simply on the basis that it would be . . . 'unjust to let it continue' [or] 'that the continuation of the proceedings was prejudicial to the defendant'.

It is submitted that this statement may be too wide insofar as it suggests that magistrates may *never* dismiss an information without a hearing. They may do so where there has been unconscionable delay (see **D20.19**). Furthermore, even in cases where there has not been delay, it would seem that the court may very exceptionally stay a prosecution on the grounds that there has been some other irregularity amounting to an abuse of process (*Grays Justices, ex parte Low* [1990] 1 QB 54). In *ex parte Low*, the Divisional Court held that even though the withdrawal of an earlier summons in exchange for the accused agreeing to be bound over did not enable the defence to rely on autrefois acquit when fresh proceedings were brought for the same offence, the magistrates should have declined to proceed on the second summons because (a) the circumstances of the withdrawal of the first summons had not been brought to the attention of the magistrates issuing the second summons, and (b) that withdrawal, coupled with the bind-over, had involved the concurrence not just of the CPS but of the first court (which had to decide whether the conditions for a bind-over were met) and the accused himself (who voluntarily took upon himself the risk of having his recognisance estreated if he offended during the relevant period).

Apparent bad faith on the part of the prosecutor has also been held sufficient to justify dismissal without hearing (see *Sherwood v Ross* [1989] Crim LR 576, where a private prosecution was brought apparently as a bargaining counter in negotiations over a civil claim).

In *Watford Justices, ex parte DPP* [1990] RTR 374, a magistrate's court refused to hear evidence and dismissed two charges of burglary. The decision was taken on the basis that the accused had spent time in custody, and the charges were rather trivial. The Divisional Court granted a declaration to the Crown (who decided to proceed no further) that the magistrates had acted contrary to the MCA 1980, s. 9(2), which required them to hear evidence before convicting an accused or dismissing the information. Thus, if the prosecution wish to adduce evidence, the magistrates must hear that evidence unless the information can be dismissed on the basis that the prosecution have been guilty of abuse of process. (See also *DPP v Gane* [1991] Crim LR 711 and *Milton Keynes Justices, ex parte DPP* [1991] Crim LR 712.)

Discretion to Try Informations Separately

Where an accused faces several charges or there are several accused charged with separate offences, the decision whether the charges or accused should be tried together or separately is **D20.38** one for the magistrates (*Chief Constable of Norfolk v Clayton* [1983] 2 AC 473). In *Clayton*, Lord Roskill set out the practice which should be adopted in such cases. His lordship said (at pp. 491G–492E):

> . . . I see no compelling reason why your lordships should not say that the practice in magistrates' courts in these matters should henceforth be analogous to the practice prescribed in *Assim* [1966] 2 QB 249 in relation to trials on indictment. Where a defendant is charged on several informations and the facts are connected, for example motoring offences or several charges of shoplifting, I can see no reason why those informations should not, if the justices think fit, be heard together. Similarly, if two or more defendants are charged on separate informations but the facts are connected, I can see no reason why they should not, if the justices think fit, be heard together. In the present cases there were separate informations against the husband and the wife and a joint information against them both. I can see no rational objection to all those informations being heard and determined together. Of course, when this question arises, justices will be well advised to inquire both of the prosecution and of the defence whether either side has any objection to all the informations being heard together. If consent is forthcoming on both sides, there is no problem. If such consent is not forthcoming, the justices should then consider the rival submissions and . . . rule as they think right in the overall interests of justice . . . Absence of consent, either express where the defendant is present or represented and objects or necessarily brought about by his absence or the absence of representation, should no longer in practice be regarded as a complete and automatic bar to hearing more than one information at the same time or informations against more than one defendant charged on separate informations at the same time when in the justices' view the facts are sufficiently closely connected to justify this course and there is no risk of injustice to defendants by its adoption. Accordingly, the justices should always ask themselves whether it would be fair and just to the defendant or defendants to allow a joint trial. Only if the answer is clearly in the affirmative should they order joint trial in the absence of consent by or on behalf of the defendant.

The above passage implies that where all parties (including the prosecution) are in favour of a joint trial, the court should automatically agree to that course. In the case of both prosecution and defence being *against* a joint trial, the ultimate decision is still with the magistrates, but they should be slow to exercise their discretion against the parties' wishes (*Highbury Corner Magistrates' Court, ex parte McGinley* (1986) 150 JP 257).

Trial of Successive Informations by Same Bench

D20.39 If an accused who is charged with two or more offences applies successfully for the offences to be tried separately, the question then arises whether the bench that decided in favour of separate trials may properly hear any or all of the cases. This is part of the broader question of whether knowledge that the accused faces more than one charge in their court should disqualify magistrates on the ground of possible bias (see also **D3.33**). The following propositions emerge from the cases:

(a) The test to be applied if magistrates know that the accused has other matters outstanding against him in their court (whether they are matters for which he is yet to be tried or matters in respect of which he has been convicted but awaits sentence) is now that laid down by the House of Lords in *Gough* [1993] AC 646 as being generally 'applicable in all cases of apparent bias, whether concerned with justices or members of other inferior tribunals, or with jurors, or with arbitrators', namely, is there a real danger of bias on the part of the member(s) of the tribunal in question? (see Lord Goff of Chieveley at p. 904).

(b) Procedurally, there is no objection to the court sheet or sheets put before the magistrates in respect of an accused listing not only the information which they are about to try on a not guilty plea, but also other charges against him which are in the court list for the day (per Mann LJ in *Weston-super-Mare Justices, ex parte Shaw* [1987] QB 640 at pp. 646–8 and Watkins LJ at pp. 648–9). A declaration to the contrary in *Liverpool City Justices, ex parte Topping* [1983] 1 WLR 119 by Ackner LJ was granted upon a misunderstanding of the distinction between the court register (which is completed by the clerk after the relevant adjudication by the magistrates) and the court sheets or court list which are given to the magistrates simply for their information (see per Watkins LJ in *Ex parte Shaw*).

(c) Where a bench orders separate trials, it would seem that it may proceed forthwith to trial of one of those charges, notwithstanding that it inevitably knows of the others, provided that there is no real danger of bias. Whether, having tried one case, the same bench can then properly try the others, either on the same day or after an adjournment, is again a matter for their discretion (*Sandwich Justices, ex parte Berry* (1982) 74 Cr App R 132).

Alternative Charges

In *R (CPS) v Blaydon Youth Court* (2004) 168 JP 638, the accused faced two charges. One alleged a public order offence in the racially aggravated form; the other alleged the same offence in the non-aggravated form. The prosecution intended the second charge to be an alternative to the first and sought a joint trial of the two charges. The justices, surprisingly, declined to try the two charges together. The Divisional Court confirmed that, in accordance with *Clayton*, a magistrates' court can conduct a joint trial of two charges when the prosecution have brought those charges in the alternative. It was argued that this could mean that two convictions are recorded against the accused. The court answered this by saying that, if the magistrates convict the accused of the more serious offence, they can adjourn the less serious offence *sine die* (under the MCA 1980, s. 10) or else grant an absolute discharge in respect of the less serious offence, although the court emphasised that it would be 'unwise' to do the latter until the time for an appeal against the more serious conviction has expired. It is submitted that the best course of action in such a case is to adjourn the less serious matter under the MCA 1980, s. 10. D20.40

Informations against Two or More Defendants Jointly

A single charge may be brought against two or more defendants who allegedly committed an offence jointly. The principles governing such cases are analogous to those governing trial of joint counts on indictment. In other words, the justices may convict either or both, whether on the basis that they did indeed commit the offence jointly or on the basis that they acted independently of each other. The acquittal of one does not prevent the conviction of the other (see, for example, *Barsted v Jones* (1964) 124 JP 400). As at trial on indictment, there is a discretion to order separate trials where two or more defendants are jointly charged in an information. However, it is submitted that a joint trial will generally be preferable. D20.41

Section D21 Summary Trial: The Course of the Trial

PLEAS WHICH MAY BE TENDERED TO THE INFORMATION/WRITTEN CHARGE

Pleas That May Be Tendered

D21.1 The first stage in a summary trial is for the court (through the clerk) to read the charge to the accused and ask him if he pleads guilty or not guilty (MCA 1980, s. 9(1)). If he pleads guilty, the court may convict him without hearing evidence (s. 9(3)).

The requirement to record a conviction following a guilty plea is without prejudice to the power (indeed duty) of the court to hold a *Newton* hearing (*Newton* (1982) 77 Cr App R 13) if there is a substantial variation between the prosecution and defence versions of the facts of the offence. In *Warley Magistrates' Court, ex parte DPP* [1999] 1 WLR 216, the Divisional Court said that where there is a significant difference between the prosecution and defence versions of the facts of the offence:

(a) if the magistrates think that their sentencing powers will be adequate however the dispute is resolved, they should follow the *Newton* procedure and either accept the defence version or hear evidence and then make findings of fact;
(b) if they think that their sentencing powers will not be adequate however the dispute is resolved, they should simply commit for sentence, leaving the Crown Court to follow the *Newton* procedure;
(c) if the decision whether or not to commit for sentence turns or may turn on which version is found to be correct, the magistrates should follow the *Newton* procedure.

In the absence of a guilty plea, the court is under a duty to hear evidence and either convict the accused or dismiss the charge (s. 9(2)).

Magistrates' Courts Act 1980, s. 9

(1) On the summary trial of an information, the court shall, if the accused appears, state to him the substance of the information and ask him whether he pleads guilty or not guilty.
(2) The court, after hearing the evidence and the parties, shall convict the accused or dismiss the information.
(3) If the accused pleads guilty, the court may convict him without hearing evidence.

Alternative Offences

D21.2 The only pleas which may be entered to an information are those of guilty or not guilty. A magistrates' court has no power to return a verdict of not guilty as charged but guilty of a lesser offence (see *Lawrence v Same* [1968] 2 QB 93), and it follows that a plea to like effect is not an option available to the accused even if the prosecution would be willing to accept it. However, in a case where a plea to something other than the offence charged would be acceptable to the parties, the procedural difficulty may be overcome by charging the accused with the lesser offence (assuming any relevant time-limit has not expired). The accused may then plead guilty to the new charge in exchange for the prosecution offering no evidence on the original one.

There are, however, certain statutory exceptions to the rule that a magistrates' court cannot convict an accused of an offence with which he is not charged but which forms part and parcel of the offence with which he is charged: for example, the Road Traffic Offenders Act 1998, s. 24, allows an accused charged with dangerous driving (RTA 1988, s. 2) to be convicted instead of careless driving (RTA 1988, s. 3) and an accused charged with driving while unfit through drink or drugs (RTA 1988, s. 4) or driving with excess alcohol (RTA 1988, s. 5) to be convicted of being 'in charge' of a vehicle while unfit or with excess alcohol as the case may be (see **C2.12**).

Plea of Guilty

The same basic principles govern the entry of a guilty plea at summary trial as govern the entry of such a plea at trial on indictment (see **D12.64** ***et seq.***). It is essential that the plea be *unequivocal.* If, when the charge is put, the accused does not answer directly or qualifies what purports to be a guilty plea with words suggesting that he is really putting forward a defence, then the court must try to resolve the ambiguity. If the plea remains ambiguous, the court must reject it and hear evidence before convicting or acquitting. The concept of an equivocal plea has been extended to pleas which, although unambiguous when made, are thrown into doubt by something which occurs between plea and sentence (e.g., the presentation of mitigation which is inconsistent with guilt, as in *Durham Quarter Sessions, ex parte Virgo* [1952] 2 QB 1). It has also been extended to pleas entered under duress (*Huntingdon Crown Court, ex parte Jordan* [1981] QB 857). One reason why justices must be careful to ensure that a purported plea of guilty is unequivocal is that if they convict and sentence on an equivocal plea the accused may appeal to the Crown Court against conviction, notwithstanding the general rule that a person who pleads guilty in the magistrates' court may appeal only against sentence. If the Crown Court finds the plea to have been equivocal, it remits the case to the lower court with a direction to hear the evidence on a not guilty plea (see *Plymouth Justices, ex parte Hart* [1986] QB 950). **D21.3**

There is little direct authority on the manner in which a guilty plea should be entered before a magistrates' court. If the accused attends court, the plea must come from him personally and may not be entered by his counsel or solicitor on his behalf (*Wakefield Justices, ex parte Butterworth* [1970] 1 All ER 1181). This accords with the judgment in *Williams* [1978] QB 373 where it was stated (at p. 378G) that: 'No qualification of or deviation from the rule that a plea of guilty must come from him who acknowledges guilt is . . . permissible. A departure from the rule in a criminal trial would therefore necessarily be a vitiating factor rendering the whole procedure void and ineffectual.' While that was said in the context of an appeal against conviction on indictment, the Court of Appeal appears to have been laying down a general principle of application to *all* criminal proceedings. However, a special difficulty arises in magistrates' courts when the accused does not appear in person but is deemed to be present because he is legally represented (see MCA 1980, s. 122). It is submitted that, in the light of *Williams,* it is doubtful whether a legal representative can enter a binding guilty plea in the absence of the accused.

Where the accused is a corporation, however, a duly appointed 'representative' of the corporation may, *inter alia,* consent to summary trial (where the offence is triable either way) and enter a plea of guilty or not guilty to the information (MCA 1980, sch. 3, para. 2(b) and (c)).

Plea of Not Guilty

A not guilty plea to an information will normally be entered by the accused personally. If, however, he is absent and the court decides to proceed without him, or he remains silent **D21.4**

D

Part D Procedure

when asked to plead, or enters an ambiguous plea, then the court simply hears the evidence in accordance with the requirement of the MCA 1980, s. 9(2), as if there had been a not guilty plea.

The options open to the prosecution (other than proceeding to summary trial) where an accused does not plead guilty are as follows.

D21.5 **Withdrawal of Summons** The prosecution may, with the leave of the court, withdraw the summons (*Redbridge Justices, ex parte Sainty* [1981] RTR 13). If the prosecution are not in a position to prove guilt on the day appointed for the hearing, or for any other reason do not wish to proceed forthwith to trial, they may prefer to withdraw the summons (rather than offering no evidence or asking for an adjournment), since such withdrawal avoids there being a verdict of not guilty. Consequently, a fresh summons may later be obtained in respect of the same offence, and the accused will not be able to rely upon autrefois acquit to prevent the trial on that summons proceeding.

That withdrawal of a summons is not equivalent to an acquittal was confirmed in *Grays Justices, ex parte Low* [1990] 1 QB 54. Nolan J said (at p. 59A–B):

> I think it must now be regarded as settled law that . . . the withdrawal of a summons with the consent of the justices will not of itself operate as a bar to the issue of a further summons in respect of the same charge where there has been no adjudication upon the merits of the charge in the original summons, and the defendant has not been put in peril of conviction upon it.

It is submitted that the same principles will apply to prosecutions commenced by way of charge at the police station and to prosecutions brought under the written charge and requisition procedure: the prosecution can avert a not guilty verdict by withdrawing the charge and then re-prosecute.

D21.6 **Offering No Evidence** Once the accused has entered a plea of not guilty, the option of asking for the summons to be withdrawn ceases to be open to the prosecution. Therefore, if they are not ready to proceed on the date that has been fixed for trial, the only course available to them is to ask for an adjournment. If the adjournment is refused, they must either call whatever evidence they do have at court or, if that evidence would plainly be insufficient for a conviction, offer no evidence.

Other situations where it may be appropriate for the prosecution to offer no evidence are where the accused has pleaded guilty to one offence and the prosecution do not wish to proceed with another (related) charge, or where new evidence exonerating the accused has come to light, or where the CPS have reviewed the evidence and have decided that there is insufficient prospect of securing a conviction to merit continuing the proceedings.

Where the charge is dismissed following the prosecution deciding to offer no evidence, this counts as an acquittal for the purpose of the doctrine of autrefois acquit. In *R (A) v South Staffordshire Youth Court* (2007) 171 JP 36, the accused was charged with assault occasioning actual bodily harm. He pleaded not guilty. The prosecution subsequently preferred the more serious charge of inflicting grievous bodily harm and offered no evidence in respect of the lesser charge, which was formally dismissed by the court. During the trial of the grievous bodily harm charge, the prosecutor concluded that he would not be able to establish that charge and offered the accused the opportunity to plead guilty to the original lesser charge. The question at issue was whether the court had jurisdiction to re-open the case on the charge of occasioning actual bodily harm. It was held that, in a case where a not guilty verdict is entered in the Crown Court under the CJA 1967, s. 17 (which provides that where the prosecutor offers no evidence, the court may order that a verdict of not guilty be recorded without the need for a verdict from a jury), an accused is entitled to rely on the defence of autrefois acquit if charged again with that offence. This principle applies equally where a magistrates' court dismisses a charge pursuant to the MCA 1980, s. 27 (which provides that where on the summary trial of an either-way offence the court dismisses the information, the dismissal shall have the same effect as an acquittal on indictment), since s. 27 is, for all practical purposes, the same as s. 17. The court was therefore *functus officio* and the decision to proceed on the lesser charge was wrong.

Change of Plea

A magistrates' court may allow an accused to change his plea from guilty to not guilty at any stage before sentence is passed (*S (an infant) v Recorder of Manchester* [1971] AC 481). D21.7

Whether to accede to an application for a change of plea is in the court's discretion and there is no automatic rule that an accused who was unrepresented when he entered his plea is entitled to change it upon obtaining legal representation during the period of an adjournment before sentence (*South Tameside Magistrates' Court, ex parte Rowland* [1983] 3 All ER 689). The question for the bench is whether the original plea was unequivocal and entered with a proper understanding of what the charge entailed. If it was, then the magistrates are entitled to refuse any application to change.

In *Revitt v DPP* [2006] 1 WLR 3172, the Divisional Court applied the guidance given in *S v Recorder of Manchester*, holding that if, after an unequivocal plea of guilty has been made, it becomes apparent that the accused did not appreciate the elements of the offence to which he was pleading guilty, then it is likely to be appropriate to permit him to withdraw his plea. Similarly, if the facts relied upon by the prosecution do not add up to the offence charged, justice will normally demand that the accused be permitted to withdraw his plea. Lord Phillips CJ (at [19]) added that the onus lies on a party seeking to vacate a guilty plea to demonstrate that justice requires that this should be permitted.

Once the court has passed sentence, it is *functus officio* and the conviction recorded upon the guilty plea can be set aside only by appealing to the Crown Court on the basis that the plea was equivocal. On the other hand, if the court does consent to a change of plea from guilty to not guilty, it must (in the case of an either-way offence) go on to allow the accused to consider afresh whether to consent to summary trial and he should be put to his election again (*Bow Street Magistrates' Court, ex parte Welcombe* (1992) 156 JP 609; see also D6.42).

A magistrates' court has an unfettered discretion to allow a change of plea from not guilty to guilty at any time before a verdict is returned.

FAILURE OF PARTIES TO APPEAR

Failure of an Accused to Appear

These paragraphs should be read in conjunction with D5, which deals with adjournments and with the options available to a magistrates' court upon non-appearance in answer to a summons or requisition, and D7, which deals with bail. D21.8

Trial in the Absence of the Accused: Powers and Procedure A summary trial may take place in the absence of the accused (MCA 1980, s. 11(1)). However, where proceedings were commenced by summons or by written charge and requisition, then (unless the accused has appeared on a previous occasion in answer to the summons) it must be proved to the satisfaction of the court that it was served on him a reasonable time before the hearing (s. 11(2)). Proof of service of a summons or requisition is governed by the Crim PR, part 4. A summons or requisition may be served: D21.9

(a) on an individual, by handing it to him (r. 4.3(1)(a)) or by leaving it at, or sending it by first-class post to, an address where it is reasonably believed that he will receive it (r. 4.4(1) and (2)(a));

(b) on a corporation, by handing it to a person holding a senior position in that corporation (r. 4.3(1)(b)) or by leaving it at, or sending it by first class post to, its principal office in England and Wales, or if there is no readily identifiable principal office, any place in England and Wales where it carries on its activities or business (r. 4.4(1) and (2)(b)).

If the accused does not appear and the conditions for proceeding in his absence described above are satisfied, a not guilty plea is entered on his behalf. The burden is then on the prosecution to prove their case to the normal criminal standard, whether by calling oral evidence or by reading statements served on the accused under the CJA 1967, s. 9 (such statements are admissible in the absence of objection from the defence — positive consent is not required: see s. 9(2)(d)). Should the prosecution evidence turn out to be insufficient, the court is obliged to acquit the accused, notwithstanding his absence. Assuming, however, that the case is proved, the court may either proceed immediately to sentence or, in certain circumstances, it may adjourn to give the accused notice that he should attend for sentencing (see MCA 1980, s. 10(3) and (4)). The MCA 1980, s. 11(3), prevents the court from passing a custodial sentence upon an offender who is absent and s. 11(4) prevents the court from imposing any disqualification on an offender who is absent unless he has been warned by means of a notice that the court is contemplating that course of action. Under s. 13(5) the court also has the option of issuing a warrant for the offender's arrest if it is undesirable, by reason of the gravity of the offence, to continue in his absence.

The power to try an information in the absence of the accused applies to either-way offences just as it applies to summary offences. However, if the proceedings are for an either-way offence, it will normally be necessary for the accused to have attended in person for the determination of mode of trial (see **D6.19**). Assuming he has done so and consented to summary trial, the actual trial may then take place in his absence.

D21.10 **Determining whether to Proceed to Trial in Accused's Absence** The discretion to proceed in the absence of the accused has to be exercised with some caution. In *Dewsbury Magistrates' Court, ex parte K* (1994) *The Times*, 16 March 1994, the Divisional Court quashed the conviction in his absence of a juvenile aged 16, for burglary of a dwelling-house. Their lordships held that the convenience of the court in processing the case could not possibly outweigh the facts that he was 16, on a very serious charge entailing the risk of a custodial sentence if convicted, had no record of non-attendance and had not been put on bail (he had been remanded into the care of the local authority).

In *Bolton Magistrates' Court, ex parte Merna* (1991) 155 JP 612, the Divisional Court considered the position where the accused is absent, and seeks an adjournment on medical grounds. It was held that if the court suspects the grounds to be spurious or inadequate, it should ordinarily express its doubts, giving the defendant an opportunity to seek to resolve them. The court may call for better evidence, require further inquiries to be made or adopt any further fair expedient. A claim of illness with apparently responsible professional support should not be rejected without the court satisfying itself that it is proper to reject it and that no unfairness would result. McCullough J, at p. 616C–G, said:

> Plainly applications to adjourn will be necessitated when there are genuine reasons for an accused being unable to attend court. Equally plainly there will be occasions when unmeritorious applications are made on behalf of defendants who are in fact fit to attend court but have chosen not to do so. The circumstances in which such applications are made will vary widely and, for my part, I would find it impossibly difficult to try to lay down, other than in the most general terms, the principles upon which justices should act. I will say no more than this. The discretion should be exercised judicially. It should be exercised with proper regard to the principle that a defendant is entitled to a fair trial; this must include a fair opportunity to be present to hear the evidence given against him and, should he want to do so, to give evidence in his own defence and call witnesses . . . Inevitably, there will be occasions when the justices are not satisfied with the

> [medical certificate] and may want to hear more. They may want somebody to get in touch with the doctor; they may even want to hear the doctor give evidence before them. I am not attempting to lay down any principles. In many cases it may be that the sensible course is to adjourn for long enough for a telephone call to be made to the doctor by a court official or perhaps a police officer and that this will provide confirmation that the accused is indeed unfit to attend. If the justices should, after such an adjournment, still not be satisfied it may be the only reasonable thing to do will be to adjourn again to enable some further approach to be made. It will always be necessary to bear in mind that it is a serious step to proceed with a man's trial for an allegation of a criminal offence in his absence.

However, the fact that a medical certificate has been received from the accused is not conclusive. In *Ealing Magistrates' Court, ex parte Burgess* (2001) 165 JP 82, the Divisional Court said that justices have a discretion to reject an accused's medical certificate, refuse an adjournment and proceed to hear the case in his absence. That discretion has to be exercised with proper regard to the principle that a defendant has a right to a fair trial and a fair opportunity to be present. However, the principle only extended to a fair opportunity to be present and not an unlimited one.

In *R (R (a Juvenile)) v Thames Youth Court* (2002) 166 JP 613, the accused was a juvenile. On the day his trial was listed for hearing before the youth court, he was arrested in connection with an unrelated offence and so was unable to attend the youth court. The district judge decided to try the case in his absence. The Divisional Court said that in cases where an accused has plainly not absented himself from his trial voluntarily, but fully expected to be present, the threshold of prejudice and fairness that the accused has to demonstrate for the purposes of establishing that a guilty verdict might be unsafe is a comparatively low one, particularly where he is a juvenile and where there is material about which his counsel would have wished to have taken instructions. It is an important consideration that a juvenile might not have the same level of understanding as an adult. Even though the case concerned a juvenile, it is submitted that it would be wrong in principle for an accused to be tried in his absence in any case where the court is aware that the absence is unavoidable and out of the accused's control. Some support for this view may be derived from the decision in *Jones* [2003] 1 AC 1 (see **D14.84**), where the House of Lords held (in the context of trial on indictment) that a judge has a discretion to commence a trial in the absence of the accused, but this discretion should be exercised with great caution; if the absence is attributable to involuntary illness or incapacity it would be very rarely, if ever, right to do so, at any rate unless the accused was represented and asked that the trial should begin (per Lord Bingham at [13]).

Adjournments It is rare for the prosecution to have their witnesses at court for the return date specified on the summons or requisition. It follows that, unless the accused appears and pleads guilty, or has sent a plea of guilty by post, the case will have to be adjourned for proof. The MCA 1980, s. 10(1), gives magistrates a general discretionary power to adjourn before trial. However, s. 10(2) provides that the trial shall not be resumed on the date to which it was adjourned unless the court is satisfied that the parties have had adequate notice. Assuming the accused was not present when the case was adjourned, it will be necessary to send an adjournment notice to him. If the adjournment notice is not served, the prosecution will not be able to proceed to prove their case in his absence, even though there has been proof of service of the summons itself. Service is governed by the Crim PR, part 4. As well as the methods for serving a summons or requisition (see above), where the accused is legally represented, the notice may be served by handing it to that representative (r. 4.3(1)(c)) or leaving it at, or sending it by first-class post to, the office of the representative (r. 4.4(2)(c)). **D21.11**

Warrant for Arrest Where the accused fails to appear, there is power to grant an arrest warrant under the MCA 1980, s. 13. Section 13(1) provides that where the court, instead of proceeding in the absence of the accused, adjourns or further adjourns the trial, the court may **D21.12**

issue a warrant for his arrest. For this power to apply, it has to be proved to the satisfaction of the court that the summons (or requisition) was served on the accused within what appears to the court to be a reasonable time before the trial or adjourned trial, unless the present adjournment is a second or subsequent adjournment of the trial, the accused was present when the trial was adjourned, and date for the present hearing was fixed when the case was adjourned.

If the accused appears to be evading service of the summons or requisition, and the offence is an indictable one, it is open to the prosecution to start proceedings again by seeking an arrest warrant. The MCA 1980, s. 1(6), provides that, 'Where the offence charged is an indictable offence, a warrant under this section may be issued at any time notwithstanding that a summons has, or a written charge and requisition have, previously been issued'.

If the accused is currently on bail and fails to attend court, a warrant for his arrest may, in any event, be issued under the Bail Act 1976, s. 7(1).

Declaration that the Accused Did Not Know of the Proceedings

D21.13 The provisions as to service of a summons or requisition, and the possibility of trial in absence, make it possible for an accused to be tried and sentenced when, in fact, he knew nothing of the proceedings (e.g., if the summons was left for him with someone else at his address who failed to pass it on). The MCA 1980, s. 14, therefore provides a procedure by which a conviction in absence may be set aside. The accused must make a statutory declaration that he did not know of the summons (or requisition) or of the proceedings until a date after the court had begun to try the case. The declaration must specify the date on which he first had knowledge of the proceedings, and must be served on the court within 21 days thereof. The effect of a timeous statutory declaration is to make void the summons (or requisition) and all subsequent proceedings, although the information (or written charge) itself is unaffected. Consequently, the prosecution may serve a fresh summons (or requisition) for the same offence, even if it is a summary offence and more than six months have elapsed since the date of commission. Under s. 14(3), the court may allow a statutory declaration to take effect even though it is served out of time if, in the circumstances, it appears to the court that it was not reasonable for the accused to serve the declaration within the 21 days permitted. The accused may appear before the court in person to make a statutory declaration, or he may send the declaration to the clerk's office by registered letter or recorded delivery (s. 14(2)).

Magistrates' Courts Act 1980, s. 14

(1) Where a summons has been issued under section 1 above and a magistrates' court has begun to try the information to which the summons relates, then, if—

(a) the accused, at any time during or after the trial, makes a statutory declaration that he did not know of the summons or the proceedings until a date specified in the declaration, being a date after the court has begun to try the information; and

(b) within 21 days of that date the declaration is served on the designated officer for the court,

without prejudice to the validity of the information, the summons and all subsequent proceedings shall be void.

(2) For the purposes of subsection (1) above a statutory declaration shall be deemed to be duly served on the designated officer if it is delivered to him, or left at his office, or is sent in a registered letter or by the recorded delivery service addressed to him at his office.

(3) If on the application of the accused it appears to a magistrates' court (which for this purpose may be composed of a single justice) that it was not reasonable to expect the accused to serve such a statutory declaration as is mentioned in subsection (1) above within the period allowed by that subsection, the court may accept service of such a declaration by the accused after that period has expired; and a statutory declaration accepted under this subsection shall be deemed to have been served as required by that subsection.

(4) Where any proceedings have become void by virtue of subsection (1) above, the information shall not be tried again by any of the same justices.

Plea of Guilty by Post

To avoid the inconvenience of putting the prosecution to proof in cases where the accused does not wish to contest the charge but is unwilling to attend court to plead guilty, the MCA 1980, s. 12, sets out a procedure allowing the accused to plead guilty by post. **D21.14**

Procedure The procedure applies to proceedings by way of summons (or written charge and requisition) in an adult magistrates' court for summary offences (s. 12(1)). Section 12 also applies to a summons (or requisition) issued in respect of such an offence requiring a person aged 16 or 17 to appear before a youth court (s. 12(2)). Whether to give the accused the option of pleading by post is at the discretion of the prosecutor. The main steps in the procedure are: **D21.15**

(a) With the summons (or requisition), the prosecutor serves (i) a notice summarising the effect of s. 12, (ii) a concise statement of the facts of the offence or a copy of the written statements under the CJA 1967, s. 9, and (iii) a notice setting out any information relating to the accused which will, or may, be placed before the court by or on behalf of the prosecutor (s. 12(3)). If the witness statements are served, they are admissible as evidence unless the accused objects. If the accused fails to plead guilty by post or to attend court to plead not guilty, and so fails to object to the use of the witness statements as evidence, the court can proceed to try him in his absence, the prosecution case being based upon the witness statements already served on him.

(b) The prosecutor notifies the court that the above documents have been served (s. 12(1)(b)).

(c) Assuming he wishes to take advantage of the procedure, the accused (or his solicitor) must notify the court in writing that he desires to plead guilty without attending court (s. 12(4)). A form is normally enclosed with the summons for the purpose. On the form (or in an accompanying letter), the accused may state any mitigating circumstances that he wants brought to the court's attention. Provided the notification is received before the actual hearing, it does not matter that it arrives after the return date specified in the summons or requisition (*Norham and Islandshire Justices, ex parte Sunter Bros Ltd* [1961] 1 WLR 364). If there are several charges, it is essential that the accused makes it clear that he is pleading guilty to each of them (*Burnham, Bucks, Justices, ex parte Ansorge* [1959] 1 WLR 1041). If the offence is endorsable, he must also send his driving licence, plus a statement of his date of birth and sex (RTOA 1988, s. 8).

(d) If the court is satisfied that all the above has been done, it may proceed to hear and dispose of the case as if the accused had appeared and pleaded guilty (s. 12(5)). The prosecutor may, but need not, be present (ibid.). The notification of a guilty plea, the statement of facts served by the prosecution or (unless the court otherwise directs) the written statement or statements under the CJA 1967, s. 9, and any statement submitted in mitigation must be read out by the clerk in open court (s. 12(7) to (7B)). Failure to do so will render the proceedings a nullity. In *Epping and Ongar Justices, ex parte Breach* [1987] RTR 233, for example, the Divisional Court quashed a company's conviction and sentence for using an overloaded goods vehicle because, although the company had entered a plea of guilty by post, its statement in mitigation had not been read out. The result occurred in *Oldham Justices, ex parte Morrissey* [1959] 1 WLR 58, where the statement in mitigation had merely been handed to the magistrates for them to read. Moreover, such errors cannot be remedied by the bench reconsidering its decision within 28 days under the provisions of the MCA 1980, s. 142(2), since that subsection only applies where the accused has been *found* guilty, not where he has given notice of intention to plead guilty (ibid.). All the prosecution can do is re-start the prosecution process by serving a fresh summons or requisition (see *Ex parte Breach*). It is also a strict rule that the only statement about the facts of the offence allowed to be given by or on behalf of the prosecution is that which they served on the accused with the summons (s. 12(8)). Thus, when he pleads guilty by post, the accused knows exactly how the case against him will be put.

(e) The court is not obliged to hear and dispose of the case on a plea of guilty by post simply because the parties have chosen to adopt the procedure. The magistrates may, in their discretion, decide that the case is not appropriate for such disposal. If so, they must adjourn so that (at the resumed hearing) the case may be dealt with as if the plea had never been notified (s. 12(9)). The adjournment notice sent to the accused must state the reason for the adjournment (s. 12(10)). Alternatively, the magistrates may accept the plea, hear the statement of facts and mitigation, and then decide that the accused ought to be given an opportunity to attend before sentence is pronounced. If so, they adjourn after convicting. Again the notice of adjournment must specify the reason for it (s. 12(10) and see *Mason* [1965] 2 All ER 308, where a disqualification from driving imposed in the absence of the accused after he had been convicted on a plea of guilty by post at an earlier hearing was quashed because the adjournment notice failed to state that the reason why the magistrates adjourned on the first occasion was because they were considering disqualification). Indeed it should be borne in mind that a sentence of imprisonment, or disqualification from driving, cannot be imposed in the absence of the accused. If the court is minded to impose such a sentence, the accused will be summoned to attend on a later occasion (see the MCA 1980, s. 11(3) and (4)).

(f) At any time before the hearing, the accused may withdraw his plea of guilty by post simply by giving written notice to that effect to the clerk (s. 12(6)). The magistrates have jurisdiction at the hearing itself to allow a change of plea, enabling an accused who earlier pleaded guilty by post to contest the matter (*Bristol Justices, ex parte Sawyers* [1988] Crim LR 754).

D21.16 Where Accused Attends Court after Plea of Guilty by Post The MCA 1980, s. 12A, makes provision for the application of s. 12 where the accused appears in court. If the accused has indicated that he wishes to plead guilty by post but nevertheless appears before the court, the court may (if the accused consents) proceed as if the accused were absent. Similarly, if the accused has not indicated that he wishes to plead guilty by post but, when he attends court, indicates that he wishes to plead guilty, the court may (if he consents) proceed as if he were absent and he had indicated an intention to plead guilty by post. Where the court proceeds as if the accused were absent, the prosecution summary of the facts of the case must not go beyond the statement served on the accused when he was given the option of pleading guilty by post. However, if the accused is in fact present in court, he must be given the opportunity to make an oral submission with a view to mitigation of sentence.

D21.17 DVLA Printout The 'pleading guilty by post' system is used most commonly for driving offences, and so the RTOA 1988 also makes provision for a printout from the DVLA to be admissible as evidence of previous convictions for traffic offences without the need to give the defendant advance notice of intention to refer to these previous convictions (see C2.7).

Statutory Material

D21.18 **Magistrates' Courts Act 1980, s. 12**

(1) This section shall apply where—

(a) a summons has been issued requiring a person to appear before a magistrates' court, other than a youth court, to answer to an information for a summary offence, not being—

(i) [repealed]

(ii) an offence specified in an order made by the Secretary of State by statutory instrument; and

(b) the designated officer for the court is notified by or on behalf of the prosecutor that the documents mentioned in subsection (3) below have been served upon the accused with the summons.

(2) The reference in subsection (1)(a) above to the issue of a summons requiring a person to appear before a magistrates' court other than a youth court includes a reference to the issue of a summons requiring a person who has attained the age of 16 at the time when it is issued to appear before a youth court.

(3) The documents referred to in subsection (1)(b) above are—

(a) a notice containing such statement of the effect of this section as may be prescribed;

(b) either of the following, namely—

(i) a concise statement of such facts relating to the charge as will be placed before the court by the prosecutor if the accused pleads guilty without appearing before the court, or

(ii) a copy of such written statement or statements complying with subsections (2)(a) and (b) and (3) of section 9 of the Criminal Justice Act 1967 (proof by written statement) as will be so placed in those circumstances; and

(c) if any information relating to the accused will or may, in those circumstances, be placed before the court by or on behalf of the prosecutor, a notice containing or describing that information.

(4) Where the designated officer for the court receives a notification in writing purporting to be given by the accused or by a legal representative acting on his behalf that the accused desires to plead guilty without appearing before the court—

(a) the designated officer for the court shall inform the prosecutor of the receipt of the notification; and

(b) the following provisions of this section shall apply.

(5) If at the time and place appointed for the trial or adjourned trial of the information—

(a) the accused does not appear; and

(b) it is proved to the satisfaction of the court, on oath or in such manner as may be prescribed, that the documents mentioned in subsection (3) above have been served upon the accused with the summons,

the court may, subject to section 11(3) and (4) above and subsections (6) to (8) below, proceed to hear and dispose of the case in the absence of the accused, whether or not the prosecutor is also absent, in like manner as if both parties had appeared and the accused had pleaded guilty.

(6) If at any time before the hearing the designated officer for the court receives an indication in writing purporting to be given by or on behalf of the accused that he wishes to withdraw the notification—

(a) the designated officer for the court shall inform the prosecutor of the withdrawal; and

(b) the court shall deal with the information as if the notification had not been given.

(7) Before accepting the plea of guilty and convicting the accused under subsection (5) above, the court shall cause the following to be read out before the court by the clerk of the court, namely—

(a) in a case where a statement of facts as mentioned in subsection (3)(b)(i) above was served on the accused with the summons, that statement;

(aa) in a case where a statement or statements as mentioned in subsection (3)(b)(ii) above was served on the accused with the summons and the court does not otherwise direct, that statement or those statement;

(b) any information contained in a notice so served, and any information described in such a notice and produced by or on behalf of the prosecutor;

(c) the notification under subsection (4) above; and

(d) any submission received with the notification which the accused wishes to be brought to the attention of the court with a view to mitigation of sentence.

(7A) Where the court gives a direction under subsection (7)(aa) above the court shall cause an account to be given orally before the court by the clerk of the court of so much of any statement as is not read aloud.

(7B) Whether or not a direction under paragraph (aa) of subsection (7) above is given in relation to any statement served as mentioned in that paragraph the court need not cause to be read out the declaration required by section 9(2)(b) of the Criminal Justice Act 1967.

(8) If the court proceeds under subsection (5) above to hear and dispose of the case in the absence of the accused, the court shall not permit—
(a) any other statement with respect to any facts relating to the offence charged; or
(b) any other information relating to the accused,
to be made or placed before the court by or on behalf of the prosecutor except on a resumption of the trial after an adjournment under section 10(3) above.
(9) If the court decides not to proceed under subsection (5) above to hear and dispose of the case in the absence of the accused, it shall adjourn or further adjourn the trial for the purpose of dealing with the information as if the notification under subsection (4) above had not been given.
(10) In relation to an adjournment on the occasion of the accused's conviction in his absence under subsection (5) above or to an adjournment required by subsection (9) above, the notice required by section 10(2) above shall include notice of the reason for the adjournment.
(11) No notice shall be required by section 10(2) above in relation to an adjournment—
(a) which is for not more than 4 weeks; and
(b) the purpose of which is to enable the court to proceed under subsection (5) above at a later time.

Failure of Prosecutor to Appear

D21.19 If the prosecutor does not appear for the trial or adjourned trial (but the accused is present), the court may at its discretion either (a) dismiss the information, or (b) adjourn the trial, or (c) proceed in the prosecutor's absence (MCA 1980, s. 15(1)). The third option is available only if the court has received evidence on a previous occasion (i.e. the case was adjourned part-heard after prosecution evidence sufficient to raise a case to answer had been adduced — if that has not been done, the court obviously cannot proceed in the prosecutor's absence because there will be no one with standing to call the evidence). Should the court decide to adjourn, it may not remand the accused in custody unless (a) he has been brought from custody or (b) he cannot be remanded on bail because of his failure to find sureties (s. 15(2)).

The discretion under s. 15(1) to dismiss the information has not been conferred for punitive purposes. The justices must not, therefore, exercise their power to dismiss where they know that a prosecutor is on the way to court, and that the case is otherwise ready to be presented (*Hendon Justices, ex parte DPP* [1994] QB 167); nor should the power be invoked where the prosecutor is present but unable to proceed because of the absence of the prosecution file (*DPP v Shuttleworth* (2002) 166 JP 417).

Where a magistrates' court dismisses a charge under s. 15 without consideration of the merits of the case because of the non-attendance of the prosecutor, there is no rule of law which prevents the court dealing with an identical charge subsequently preferred against the same accused; the question to be decided is whether the new charge amounts to an abuse of process, and so the court must consider what prejudice would be caused by the preferment of that new charge (*Holmes v Campbell* (1998) 162 JP 655).

Failure of Both Parties to Appear

D21.20 Should neither the prosecutor nor the accused appear for the trial (or adjourned trial) of an information, the court may either dismiss the information or — if evidence has been received on a previous occasion — proceed in their absence (MCA 1980, s. 16).

Appearance by Legal Representative

D21.21 The parties to proceedings in magistrates' courts may be represented by legal representatives (MCA 1980, s. 122(1)). Alternatively, they may conduct their case in person. It is not the practice to grant persons other than the parties or the legal representative a right of audience, unless statute expressly allows for alternative representation in a particular category of case.

(In certain circumstances, the CPS may be represented by a member of staff, designated by the DPP, who is not a barrister or solicitor). However, where a party wishes to have the assistance of a friend, the friend may sit by the party, advise during the course of the hearing, suggest questions or points for argument etc., although he will not be permitted actually to ask questions of witnesses himself or address the court (see *McKenzie v McKenzie* [1971] P 33).

The nature of the assistance permitted was examined by the Court of Appeal in *Leicester City Justices, ex parte Barrow* [1991] 2 QB 260. Watkins LJ, giving the judgment of the court, emphasised that what was at issue was a party's right to reasonable assistance. The court confirmed that a party was entitled to have someone attend as a friend, to take notes, to quietly make suggestions, and to give advice. A litigant has the right to present his own case and, in doing so, to arm himself with such assistance as he thought necessary, subject to the right of the court to intervene; he did not have to seek the leave of the court to exercise that right. Nevertheless, the court should be informed of the fact that a party would have his adviser with him; and, if the assistance was unreasonable in manner or degree, was provided for an improper purpose or was in any way inimical to the administration of justice, the court could restrict him in the use of that assistance.

Where a party does not attend court but is represented by a legal representative, he is deemed not to be absent (s. 122(2)). The prosecution is customarily conducted by a Crown Prosecutor, or counsel or a solicitor acting on behalf of the CPS. If the accused chooses not to attend but to be legally represented, his representative may cross-examine the prosecution witnesses, make submissions and speeches, and even call witnesses other than the accused, exactly as if his client were present. Furthermore, the effect of s. 122(2) is that the presence of the legal representative precludes the issue of a warrant for the accused's arrest under s. 13 (warrants for arrest where the court adjourns instead of proceeding in the absence of the accused). However, s. 122(3) limits the effect of the deeming provision to the extent that a represented party is *not* deemed to be present if his presence was required to 'satisfy any provision of any enactment or any condition of a recognisance expressly requiring his presence'. Consequently, an accused who fails to surrender to custody in answer to his bail may have a warrant issued for his arrest whether or not he is legally represented in court (see the Bail Act 1976, s. 3(1), which provides that a person granted bail in criminal proceedings shall be under a duty to surrender to custody, and s. 7(1) which empowers the court to issue a bench warrant if he does not do so). Similarly, the terms of the MCA 1980, s. 23, make it clear that proceedings to determine mode of trial require the actual presence of the accused save in the exceptional circumstances defined in the section.

Magistrates' Courts Act 1980, s. 122

(1) A party to any proceedings before a magistrates' court may be represented by a legal representative.

(2) Subject to subsection (3) below, an absent party so represented shall be deemed not to be absent.

(3) Appearance of a party by a legal representative shall not satisfy any provision of any enactment or any condition of a recognisance expressly requiring his presence.

THE PROSECUTION CASE

Opening Speech

The prosecution representative has the right to make an opening speech (CrimPR, r. 37.1(1)): 'On the summary trial of an information, where the accused does not plead guilty, the prosecutor shall call the evidence for the prosecution, and before doing so may address the court'). The opening is usually kept short and, in straightforward cases, may be dispensed with completely. D21.22

In *L and B v DPP* [1998] 2 Cr App R 69, the case had been adjourned for a month after the main prosecution witnesses had given evidence. At the resumed hearing, the justices invited the prosecutor to deliver a second speech in order to remind them of evidence which they were having difficulty remembering. On appeal to the Divisional Court, the appellants contended that the prosecution should not have been allowed to address the justices again. The Divisional Court dismissed the appeal. There was nothing unfair in the prosecutor being asked to remind the court of evidence which had been given, subject to the safeguard that the defence should invariably be asked to address the court in reply, to correct any errors or draw attention to any differences of recollection.

Witnesses whom the Prosecution Must Call

D21.23 Where a prosecution witness attends court to give evidence in a summary trial, the prosecutor is obliged to call him to give evidence if the defence so requests, or at least tender him for cross-examination (*Wellingborough Magistrates' Court, ex parte Francois* (1994) 158 JP 813). If the prosecutor serves a bundle of witness statements on the defence prior to summary trial, the prosecution must call as witnesses all the people whose statements have been served (unless any of the exceptions which relate to Crown Court trials are applicable). If the prosecutor refuses to do so, it is open to the justices to call such a person as a witness, which is preferable to leaving it to the defence to call that person as a witness (see *Haringey Justices, ex parte DPP* [1996] QB 351).

WRITTEN EVIDENCE AT SUMMARY TRIAL: CJA 1967, s. 9

D21.24 A party wishing to tender a written statement as evidence at a summary trial rather than calling the maker of the statement may make use of the provisions of the CJA 1967, s. 9. The main points about s. 9 of the CJA 1967 are that:

(a) The statement must be signed by the maker, and must contain a declaration that it is true to the best of his knowledge and belief, and that he made it knowing that if it were tendered in evidence he might be prosecuted for wilfully stating in it anything he knew to be false or did not believe to be true (s. 9(2)(a) and (b)).

(b) A copy of the statement (together with a copy of any documentary exhibit referred to therein) must be served on each of the other parties (s. 9(2)(c)). If, within seven days of service, any of them serves a counter-notice objecting to the statement being put in evidence, it may not be used (s. 9(2)(d)). It follows that a party wishing to avail himself of s. 9 should serve the copy statement at least seven days before the proposed hearing date. The onus is then on his opponent to object to the statement within the week. However, the strict requirements of service of the copy statement may be waived by the opposing party (proviso to s. 9(2)). Conversely, even where the copy statement was served more than a week before the hearing and no objection to its being read was indicated, the court may, of its own volition or on the application of a party, require the maker of the statement to attend and give oral evidence (s. 9(4)(b)). In practice, where a s. 9 statement has been served on the defence but, by inadvertence, no notice objecting it was given within the statutory time, the court is likely to adjourn for the witness to be called rather than insisting upon the strict letter of s. 9(2). This is particularly so where the accused is unrepresented.

(c) The CrimPR, r. 27.1, requires that written statements to be tendered in evidence under s. 9 must be in the form set out in the *Consolidated Practice Direction* (<http://www.dca.gov.uk/criminal/procrules_fin/contents/formssection/formspage.htm>). There is also a prescribed form to accompany the statements, indicating the intention of the prosecutor to tender those statements in evidence in the absence of objection from the defence.

(d) Where a statement is admitted in evidence under s. 9, it is either read in full to the court or, at the court's discretion, parts of it may be summarised (s. 9(6)). The CrimPR, r. 27.1(6), provides that where a written statement is tendered in accordance with s. 9, the name of the maker of the statement must be read aloud unless the court otherwise directs. Rule 27.1(7) requires that where, under s. 9(6), any part of the evidence is read out aloud (or summarised), the evidence shall be read (or summarised) by or on behalf of the party who has tendered the evidence. The statement is *not* to be taken conclusively to be true, but is merely 'admissible as evidence to the like extent as oral evidence to the like effect by [the maker]' would be admissible (s. 9(1)). It follows that if the defence fail to serve a notice objecting to the admissibility of the statement, they are not precluded at trial from adducing evidence inconsistent with it (*Lister v Quaife* [1983] 1 WLR 48). The position is then analogous to that which arises when a prosecution witness is called in person but significant differences between his evidence and the anticipated defence evidence are not put to him in cross-examination as they ought to be. Although the court may then treat the defence case on the disputed areas with some scepticism, they are not entitled to reject it out of hand and — if left in doubt by the combined effect of the defence evidence and the formally unchallenged prosecution evidence — would be obliged to give the benefit of the doubt to the defence. However, the defence should not use the reasoning in *Lister v Quaife* as a tactical device so as to avoid the necessity of putting the defence case to a prosecution witness in person (per May LJ at p. 55B). If there are differences between the defence case and the contents of a proposed s. 9 statement, then a notice should be served objecting to the statement. In the event of failure to give such notice and defence witnesses then contradicting the statement, the prosecution should ask for an adjournment so that the maker of the statement can be called. The court ought not only to agree to the adjournment but should also consider ordering that the costs thrown away be paid by the defence whatever the eventual outcome of the case (ibid. pp. 54H–55A). In any event, the prosecution should hesitate before making use of the s. 9 procedure in respect of evidence crucial to their case (per Stephen Brown J who said at p. 55E: 'Section 9 of the CJA 1967 is a very valuable provision designed to save expense and trouble in very many instances, but where the evidence which is in written statements, served under the provisions of the notice, is central to the issues in the case, prosecutors should give very careful consideration as to whether or not they should call the actual witness so that the proper impact of that evidence can be made upon the court').

(e) The *Consolidated Practice Direction*, para III.24.5 (see **appendix** 7), notes that where statements are to be tendered under s. 9 in the course of summary proceedings, and the statement contains evidence which is inadmissible or prejudicial, that evidence cannot be excised by means of striking out or bracketing (a method that would otherwise be permissible) and so there will be a need to prepare fresh statements excluding any inadmissible or prejudicial material.

Criminal Justice Act 1967, s. 9

(1) In any criminal proceedings, a written statement by any person shall, if such of the conditions mentioned in the next following subsection as are applicable are satisfied, be admissible as evidence to the like extent as oral evidence to the like effect by that person.

(2) The said conditions are—

(a) the statement purports to be signed by the person who made it;

(b) the statement contains a declaration by that person to the effect that it is true to the best of his knowledge and belief and that he made the statement knowing that, if it were tendered in evidence, he would be liable to prosecution if he wilfully stated in it anything which he knew to be false or did not believe to be true;

(c) before the hearing at which the statement is tendered in evidence, a copy of the statement is served, by or on behalf of the party proposing to tender it, on each of the other parties to the proceedings; and

(d) none of the other parties or their solicitors, within seven days from the service of the copy of the statement, serves a notice on the party so proposing objecting to the statement being tendered in evidence under this section:

Provided that the conditions mentioned in paragraphs (c) and (d) of this subsection shall not apply if the parties agree before or during the hearing that the statement shall be so tendered.

(3) The following provisions shall also have effect in relation to any written statement tendered in evidence under this section, that is to say—

(a) if the statement is made by a person under the age of 18, it shall give his age;

(b) if it is made by a person who cannot read it, it shall be read to him before he signs it and shall be accompanied by a declaration by the person who so read the statement to the effect that it was so read; and

(c) if it refers to any other document as an exhibit, the copy served on any other party to the proceedings under paragraph (c) of the last foregoing subsection shall be accompanied by a copy of that document or by such information as may be necessary in order to enable the person on whom it is served to inspect that document or a copy thereof.

(3A) In the case of a statement which indicates in pursuance of subsection (3)(a) of this section that the person making it has not attained the age of fourteen, subsection (2)(b) of this section shall have effect as if for the words from 'made' onwards there were substituted the words 'understands the importance of telling the truth in it'.

(4) Notwithstanding that a written statement made by any person may be admissible as evidence by virtue of this section—

(a) the party by whom or on whose behalf a copy of the statement was served may call that person to give evidence; and

(b) the court may, of its own motion or on the application of any party to the proceedings, require that person to attend before the court and give evidence.

[(5) Applications before trial under subsection (4)(b) above to courts other than a magistrates' court.]

(6) So much of any statement as is admitted in evidence by virtue of this section shall, unless the court otherwise directs, be read aloud at the hearing and where the court so directs an account shall be given orally of so much of any statement as is not read aloud.

(7) Any document or object referred to as an exhibit and identified in a written statement tendered in evidence under this section shall be treated as if it had been produced as an exhibit and identified in court by the maker of the statement.

(8) A document required by this section to be served on any person may be served—

(a) by delivering it to him or to his solicitor; or

(b) by addressing it to him and leaving it at his usual or last known place of abode or place of business or by addressing it to his solicitor and leaving it at his office; or

(c) by sending it in a registered letter or by the recorded delivery service or by first class post addressed to him at his usual or last known place of abode or place of business or addressed to his solicitor at his office; or

(d) in the case of a body corporate, by delivering it to the secretary or clerk of the body at its registered or principal office or sending it in a registered letter or by the recorded delivery service or by first class post addressed to the secretary or clerk of that body at that office; and in paragraph (d) of this subsection references to the secretary, in relation to a limited liability partnership, are to any designated member of the limited liability partnership.

OBJECTIONS TO PROSECUTION EVIDENCE

D21.25 The procedure to be followed where the defence object, during the course of a summary trial, to proposed prosecution evidence (or have some other preliminary point of law to argue before the magistrates) is a matter of considerable difficulty. The difficulty arises from the magistrates being the judges of both fact and law. Especially if the issue is one of admissibility of evidence, there is a danger that the magistrates will learn the nature of the evidence in the course of the presentation of arguments about its admissibility. Should they then rule it inadmissible, they may nonetheless have difficulty in ignoring it when reaching a verdict. Furthermore, where the objection to the evidence is based upon the manner in which it was obtained, there is the further difficulty that, if a *voir dire* (or 'trial within a trial') procedure were to be adopted by the magistrates and they admitted the primary evidence, they might have to hear the secondary evidence they had heard on the *voir dire* all over again in the course of the ordinary defence case, because it would still be relevant to the weight of the primary evidence even though the question of admissibility had been settled.

The stage of the trial at which the magistrates rule upon a question of admissibility of evidence (or other incidental issue) is a matter for their discretion (see Lord Lane CJ's judgment in *F v Chief Constable of Kent* [1982] Crim LR 682, followed in *Epping and Ongar Justices, ex parte Manby* [1986] Crim LR 555 and *A v DPP* (2000) 164 JP 317).

Notwithstanding this general proposition, delaying the determination of a question of admissibility of a confession until after the conclusion of the prosecution evidence may be unfair to the defence, in that the accused will not be able to give evidence about alleged irregularities in the obtaining of the confession unless he testifies in his own defence, which will expose him to cross-examination about the general issues. Moreover, in taking the decision whether to call evidence at all, the defence advocate ought to know whether evidence as crucial as a confession is to be part of the case against his client. These special considerations were recognised by Lord Lane in the following passage from his judgment in *F v Chief Constable of Kent* (quoted in *A v DPP*), where the admissibility of a confession was at issue:

> It is impossible to lay down any general rule as to when magistrates should announce their decision on this type of point, and indeed when the point itself should be taken. Every case will be different. Some sort of preliminary point, for instance with regard to the admissibility of a document or something like that, can plainly, with the assistance of the clerk, be decided straight away. Other points, such as the one with which we are dealing here, may require a decision at a later stage of the case, possibly after further argument. It may be that in some cases the defendant will be entitled to know what the decision of the justices with regard to the admissibility of a confession is at the close of the prosecution case in order to enable him to know what proper course he should take with regard to giving evidence and calling evidence and so on.

It is submitted that, where the confession is the main evidence against the accused, so that without it there might not be a case to answer, the interests of justice dictate that admissibility should be determined as a preliminary issue (see the comments of Goff LJ in *ADC v Chief Constable of Greater Manchester* (Divisional Court, unreported, 14 March 1983), quoted in *Halawa v Federation against Copyright Theft* [1995] 1 Cr App R 21 at p. 27).

PACE 1984, s. 78

It should be borne in mind that, where the defence argue that a confession should be excluded under the PACE 1984, s. 76, the court is obliged to hear evidence about the obtaining of the confession (as the prosecution have to prove that the confession was not obtained in the manner forbidden by s. 76); however, where the admissibility of prosecution evidence falls to be considered under the general exclusionary discretion in s. 78, the court has a discretion to hear evidence on the issue of admissibility but is not obliged to do so (and so may rule on the matter following submissions on behalf of the parties). In the latter type of case, it is still a matter for the justices' discretion when they determine admissibility: *Vel v Chief Constable of North Wales* (1987) 151 JP 510 and *Halawa v Federation Against Copyright Theft* [1995] 1 Cr App R 21. In *Vel*, it was held that, in relation to s. 78, magistrates may deal with an application to exclude evidence when it arises but in other cases may leave the decision until the end of the hearing. The court declined to lay down any general rule, other than that the object should always be to secure a trial which is fair and just to both sides. In *Halawa*, the Divisional Court said that, in most cases, it is generally better for the magistrates to hear all the prosecution evidence (including the disputed evidence) before considering an application to exclude evidence under s. 78. This does of course leave the justices with the very difficult (some might say impossible) task of putting from their minds prejudicial evidence that they have heard but then decide is inadmissible. **D21.26**

PACE 1984, s. 76

D21.27 Where an objection to evidence is based upon the PACE 1984, s. 76, the terms of the section require that the court shall not admit the confession unless satisfied that it was not obtained by oppression or by words or conduct likely to render it unreliable. It follows that magistrates (just like the Crown Court) are obliged to determine such an issue as soon as it is raised and, if necessary, hear evidence on the obtaining of the confession (*Liverpool Juvenile Court, ex parte R* [1988] QB 1). At the conclusion of his judgment in *Ex parte R*, Russell LJ summarised its effect as follows:

> 1. The effect of section 76(2) of the Police and Criminal Evidence Act 1984 is that in summary proceedings justices must now hold a trial within a trial if it is represented to them by the defence that a confession was or may have been obtained by either of the improper processes appearing in subparagraphs (a) or (b) of section 76(2).
>
> 2. In such a trial within a trial the defendant may give evidence confined to the question of admissibility and the justices will not be concerned with the truth or otherwise of the confession.
>
> 3. In consequence of paragraphs 1 and 2 above, the defendant is entitled to a ruling upon admissibility of a confession before, or at, the end of the prosecution case.
>
> 4. There remains a discretion open to the defendant as to the stage at which an attack is to be made upon an alleged confession. A trial within a trial will only take place before the close of the prosecution case if it is represented to the court that the confession was, or may have been, obtained by one or other of the processes set out in subparagraphs (a) or (b) of section 76(2). If no such representation is made the defendant is at liberty to raise admissibility or weight of the confession at any subsequent stage of the trial. For the avoidance of doubt, I consider that 'representation' is not the same as, nor does it include, cross-examination. Thus the court is not required to embark upon, nor is the defence bound to proceed upon, a *voir dire* merely because of a suggestion in cross-examination that the alleged confession was obtained improperly.
>
> 5. It should never be necessary to call the prosecution evidence relating to the obtaining of a confession twice.

In his fourth proposition, Russell LJ would seem to be encouraging defence advocates to delay formally objecting to a confession until their own case, at which stage the magistrates may still exclude the confession if the accused's evidence raises a reasonable possibility that there was a breach of s. 76(2). This suggestion would seem to be at odds with the case law on challenging confessions at trials on indictment (see **D15.46** and especially *Sat-Bhambra* (1988) 88 Cr App R 55, where it was held that, once a confession had been adduced by the prosecution, it is too late for the defence to represent that it was obtained by oppression or in circumstances likely to render it unreliable).

'Dock Identifications'

D21.28 One particular element of some prosecution cases is the use of the so-called 'dock identification' (see **F6.25** and **F18.16**). Where the identity of the accused as the person who committed the offence is in issue, the court will rarely allow a witness who has not previously identified the accused at an identification parade or video identification procedure to be asked 'do you see the person who committed the offence in court today?' (*North Yorkshire Trading Standards Dept v Williams* (1995) 159 JP 383). The reason for not allowing this to be done is that the accused is at a great disadvantage — the eyes of the witness are bound to go to the person sitting in the dock. However, in *Barnes v DPP* [1997] 2 Cr App R 505, the defendant was charged with failing to provide a breath specimen. There had been no identification procedure and the only evidence that the defendant was the person who refused to provide a specimen was a 'dock identification' by a police officer. The Divisional Court held that the justices had a discretion to allow a defendant to be identified in court even if there had not been a previous identification parade. In *Karia v DPP* (2002) 166 JP 753, the defendant appealed against conviction for a number of motoring offences on the ground that the magistrates should not have allowed the police officer who had stopped the vehicle to make a 'dock identification' of him, and that an identification parade should have been held. He argued that the decision in *Barnes v DPP* permitting dock identifications in such cases was incompatible with the HRA 1998. It was held that the aim of a dock identification in such a case is usually to avoid an unmeritorious dismissal of a prosecution case resulting from a failure to make a purely formal identification of the defendant. In *Karia* the defendant had not notified the prosecution that identity was in issue, and so the dock identification was not unfair because there was no basis on which the police could have considered that it would be useful to hold an identification procedure. As far as the human rights point was concerned, the court said that a requirement that the issues should be made known to the court before or during the proceedings cannot infringe the ECHR, Article 6; moreover, a requirement that a defendant should indicate before or at his trial what are the issues in the trial does not infringe his right to silence. On this basis, it would appear that dock identifications are to be ruled out only where the defendant has already indicated that identity is in issue in the case. In *Holland v HM Advocate* [2005] HRLR 25, the Privy Council held that there is no basis, except perhaps in an extreme case, for regarding dock identifications as inadmissible *per se*.

'SPECIAL MEASURES' DIRECTIONS

The court has power to make arrangements both under its inherent jurisdiction and under the YJCEA 1999. The latter powers are the most commonly used. **D21.29**

An application can be made under the YJCEA 1999, s. 19, for special measures:

(a) screening the witness from the accused (s. 23);
(b) giving evidence by live link (s. 24), although this provision will become less relevant as the CJA 2003, s. 51 (when in force), will enable a court to authorise witnesses, other than the accused, to give evidence through a live link in criminal proceedings;
(c) giving evidence in private, in a sexual case, or where there is a fear that the witness may be intimidated (s. 25);
(d) video recording of evidence-in-chief (s. 27) — again, this provision will be made less relevant once the CJA 2003, s. 137, extends the circumstances in which evidence-in-chief can take the form of a video-recorded statement;
(e) video recording of cross-examination and re-examination where the evidence-in-chief of the witness has been video recorded (s. 28);
(f) examination through an intermediary in the case of a young or incapacitated witness (s. 29);
(g) provision of aids to communication for a young or incapacitated witness (s. 30).

These measures are also applicable in the Crown Court, and are dealt with fully at **D14.97**. The procedure for making (and opposing) applications for special measures directions is set out in the CrimPR, part 29 (see **appendix 1**).

In *R (S) v Waltham Forest Youth Court* [2004] 2 Cr App R 335, the accused (who was aged 13) wanted to testify in her own defence but said that she was too scared to do so because of the physical presence in court of her co-accused. The question arose whether the court could make a 'special measures' direction in respect of the accused. The Divisional Court held that there is no power to make a direction under the Act in relation to the evidence of the accused. It was Parliament's clear intention to exclude defendants from those provisions. It should, however, be borne in mind that one special measure (namely, testifying via a 'live link') is available for the accused under the YJCEA 1999, s. 33A (inserted by the PJA 2006, s. 47, with effect from January 2007 (see **D21.32**)).

Procedure for Seeking Special Measures Directions

D21.30 Applications under the rules have to be made in the prescribed form (specified by the *Consolidated Criminal Practice Direction*, Annex D). In the magistrates' court, the application must be received within 14 days of the accused indicating his intention to plead not guilty to any charge brought against him and in relation to which a special measures direction may be sought; in the youth court, the application must be received within 28 days of the date on which the accused first appears before the court in connection with the offence (r. 29.1(4)). An application may be made to extend this time-limit (under r. 29.2) or the application may be made at the hearing itself (r. 29.3), though in both cases the delay in making the application must be explained.

The other parties to the proceedings may serve notice of opposition to the application. Where a party wishes to oppose the application, he must, within 14 days of the date on which the application was served on him, notify the applicant and the court in writing of his opposition and give reasons for it (r. 29.1(6)). There will then be a hearing to determine the application. Rule 29.4, makes provision for applications to vary or discharge a special measures direction (see also the YJCEA 1999, s. 20(2)); such applications must be based on a material change of circumstances since the direction was made. Also, where an application for a special measures direction has been refused by the court, the application may be renewed if there is a material change of circumstances since the court refused the application (r. 29.5).

D21.31 **Live Television Links** Rule 29.6 deals with applications for special measures directions for witnesses to give evidence by means of a live television link. A party who seeks to oppose an application for a child witness to give evidence by means of a live link must state why, in his view, the giving of a special measures direction would not be likely to maximise the quality of the witness's evidence (unless the application relates to a child witness in need of special protection within the meaning of the YJCEA 1999, s. 21(1)(b), in which case this provision does not apply). Where a special measures direction is made enabling a witness to give evidence by means of a live link, the witness must be accompanied at the live link only by persons acceptable to the court (and the intermediary where one is used) (r. 29.6(5)).

In *R (D) v Camberwell Green Youth Court* [2005] 1 WLR 393, the House of Lords held that the use of live television links is compatible with the accused's right to a fair trial under the ECHR, Article 6. Their lordships noted that the accused can see and hear all the evidence produced at the trial and has every opportunity to challenge and question the witnesses against him at the trial itself, and that the Convention does not guarantee a right to a face-to-face confrontation.

In *R (S) v Waltham Forest Youth Court* [2004] 2 Cr App R 335, the Divisional Court held that there is no power to make a special measures direction under the 1999 Act in relation to the evidence of the accused. Nor, said the Court, is there any common law power to permit an accused to give evidence by live link.

Part 8 of the CJA 2003, when brought into force, will extend the circumstances where live links can be used. A 'live link' (defined in s. 56(2)) will usually mean a closed circuit television link, but could apply to any technology with the same effect, such as video-conferencing facilities or the internet. Section 51(2)(a) makes it clear that these provisions apply to summary trial (as well as trial on indictment) and, under s. 51(2)(f), to a hearing before a magistrates' court which is held after the defendant has entered a plea of guilty (i.e. a *Newton* hearing). Under s. 51(3), a direction may be given on an application by a party to the proceedings or of the court's own motion. However, s. 51(4) provides that a direction may not be given unless the court is satisfied that it is 'in the interests of the efficient or effective administration of justice for the person concerned to give evidence in the proceedings through a live link'. Under s. 51(6), the court must consider all the circumstances of the case, and in particular (s. 51(7)):

(a) the availability of the witness;
(b) the need for the witness to attend in person;
(c) the importance of the witness's evidence to the proceedings;
(d) the views of the witness;
(e) the suitability of the facilities at the place where the witness would give evidence through a live link;
(f) whether a direction might tend to inhibit any party to the proceedings from effectively testing the witness's evidence.

Under s. 51(8), the court must state in open court its reasons for refusing an application for a direction where one is sought.

Under s. 52(2), where the court has given a direction under s. 51 for a person to give evidence through a live link in particular proceedings, the person concerned may not give evidence in those proceedings after the direction is given otherwise than through a live link unless the court rescinds the direction, which it can do under s. 52(3) (on the application of a party or of its own motion), if it appears to the court to be in the interests of justice to do so.

Accused Testifying via Live Link

The Police and Justice Act 2006, s. 47, inserts new sections – ss. 33A to 33C – into the YJCEA 1999. Section 33A allows the court (whether the Crown Court or a magistrates' court), on application by the accused, to direct that any evidence given by him should be given via a 'live link'. Section 33B defines 'live link' very broadly: it encompasses any technology that enables the accused to see and hear a person in the courtroom, and to be seen and heard by the persons listed in s. 33B(2), namely the judge or justices (or both) and the jury (if there is one), any co-accused, the legal representatives acting in the proceedings and any interpreter or other person appointed by the court to assist the accused. D21.32

Before giving a live link direction, the court must be satisfied that it would be in the interests of justice to do so, and:

(a) if the accused is under the age of 18, that his ability to participate effectively as a witness giving oral evidence is compromised by his 'level of intellectual ability or social functioning', and that use of a live link would enable him to participate more effectively as a witness, whether by improving the quality of his evidence or otherwise (s. 33A(4)); or
(b) if the accused is aged 18 or over, that he is unable to participate effectively in the proceedings effectively as a witness giving oral evidence because he has a mental disorder (within the meaning of the Mental Health Act 1983) or a 'significant impairment of intelligence and social function', and that use of a live link would enable him to participate more effectively as a witness, whether by improving the quality of his evidence or otherwise (s. 33A(5)).

The Explanatory Notes that accompany the 2006 Act make it clear that the presumption in the case of adult defendants is that they should give evidence in court. The criteria set out in s. 33A(5) are intended to ensure that the use of live links is reserved for exceptional cases where the accused has a condition that prevents effective participation as a witness and so may prevent a fair trial from taking place. In the case of a juvenile accused, however, the test is less strict (in that there is no reference to a mental disorder or impairment); it is sufficient that the accused's ability to participate is compromised. The Notes make the point that this 'lower threshold recognises that it may be more common for juveniles to experience difficulties during the trial through limited intelligence and social development, than it would be for adults' but goes on the emphasise that s. 33A(4) 'is aimed at juvenile defendants with a low level of intelligence or a particular problem in dealing with social situations, and is not intended to operate merely because an accused is a juvenile and is nervous, for example'.

Section 33A(6) provides that, where a live link direction has been given, the accused must give all his evidence in that way. It follows that any cross-examination of the accused also has to take place via a live link. However, the court may, in the exercise of its discretion, discharge a live link direction if it appears to the court to be in the interests of justice to do so (s. 33A(7)). This may be appropriate where, for example, the accused finds that giving evidence over a live link is more difficult than expected and believes that giving evidence in open court would allow him to give better quality evidence.

D21.33 **Video-recorded Testimony** Rule 29.7 of the CrimPR deals with video recording of testimony from witnesses. Where an application is made for a special measures direction enabling a video recording of an interview of a witness to be admitted as evidence-in-chief of the witness, the application must be accompanied by the video recording which it is proposed to tender in evidence and must include the information specified by r. 29.7(2), which includes a statement of the circumstances in which the recording was made. This statement must comply with the requirements of r. 29.7(4), which sets out a series of detailed questions about the making of the recording.

Where a party opposes the use of the video recording, he must lodge a notice giving reasons why it would not be in the interests of justice for the recording (or part of it) to be admitted (r. 29.7(7)(a) and (8)).

Rule 29.7(10) stipulates that any video recording which the defendant proposes to tender in evidence need not be sent to the prosecution until the close of the prosecution case at the trial.

Section 137(1) of the CJA 2003, when brought into force, will extend the cases where evidence can be given by means of a video recording. It empowers the court to allow a video recording of an interview with a witness (other than the accused), or a part of such a recording, to be admitted as the evidence-in-chief of the witness (i.e. to replace live evidence-in-chief of that witness) provided that the person is called as a witness in proceedings for an offence which is triable only on indictment, or for an either-way offence prescribed in regulations made under the section, and:

> (b) the person claims to have witnessed (whether visually or in any other way)—
>   (i) events alleged by the prosecution to include conduct constituting the offence or part of the offence, or
>   (ii) events closely connected with such events,
> (c) he has previously given an account of the events in question (whether in response to questions asked or otherwise),
> (d) the account was given at a time when those events were fresh in the person's memory (or would have been, assuming the truth of the claim mentioned in paragraph (b)),
> (e) a video recording was made of the account,
> (f) the court has made a direction that the recording should be admitted as evidence in chief of the witness, and the direction has not been rescinded, and
> (g) the recording is played in the proceedings in accordance with the direction.

Section 137(3) provides that a direction under s. 137(1)(f) may not be made in relation to a recorded account given by the accused, and may be made only if it appears to the court that (a) the witness's recollection of the events in question is likely to have been significantly better when he gave the recorded account than it will be when he gives oral evidence in the proceedings, and (b) it is in the interests of justice for the recording to be admitted, having regard in particular to the matters set out in s. 137(4), namely:

(a) the interval between the time of the events in question and the time when the recorded account was made;
(b) any other factors that might affect the reliability of what the witness said in that account;
(c) the quality of the recording;
(d) any views of the witness as to whether his evidence-in-chief should be given orally or by means of the recording.

It does not matter if the statements in the recorded account were not made on oath (s. 137(5)). Section 138(1) stipulates that where a video recording has been admitted into evidence under s. 137, the witness cannot give evidence-in-chief in any other way.

Intermediaries The YJCEA 1999, s. 29, allows, as part of the special measures provision, for the use of intermediaries to facilitate communication with witnesses with special communication difficulties. Section 29 specifies that: **D21.34**

> the function of an intermediary is to communicate:
> (a) to the witness, questions put to the witness, and
> (b) to any person asking such questions, the answers given by the witness in reply to them,
> and to explain such questions and answers so far as necessary to enable them to be understood by the witness or person in question.

Such intermediaries have to be professionally experienced in their own specialist area of communication, and are subject to a Code of Practice and a Code of Ethics.

Use of Expert Evidence Under the CrimPR, r. 29.8, a party who proposes to adduce expert evidence (whether of fact or opinion) in connection with an application or renewal application for, or for varying or discharging, a special measures direction must furnish the other party or parties to the proceedings with a statement in writing of any finding or opinion which he proposes to adduce by way of such evidence and (if the other party so requests) provide a reasonable opportunity to examine the record of any observation, test, calculation or other procedure on which the finding or opinion is based. **D21.35**

'Reporting Directions' Part 16 of the CrimPR makes provision for the making of 'reporting directions' under the YJCEA 1999, s. 46. The effect is that no matter relating to the witness may be included in any publication during the lifetime of the witness, if that matter is likely to lead members of the public to identify that person as a witness in the proceedings. The application may be made in writing or orally (r. 16.1). Under r. 16.2, any party may oppose the application for a 'reporting direction' and must state whether they dispute that the witness is eligible for protection under s. 46 or that the granting of protection would be likely to improve the quality of the evidence given by the witness or the level of co-operation given by the witness to any party to the proceedings in connection with that party's preparation of its case. Under r. 16.7(4), the court may hear and take into account representations made to it by any person who in the court's view has a legitimate interest in the application before it. **D21.36**

Inherent Powers As well as the specific powers conferred by the YJCEA 1999, the court has inherent powers to safeguard the interests of witnesses, for example by ensuring their anonymity. **D21.37**

In a case concerning those inherent powers, *Davis* [2006] 1 WLR 3130 (see **D14.47**), the Court of Appeal noted that, in *Krasniki v Czech Republic* (Application No. 51277/99), the European Court of Human Rights had accepted that the Convention rights of witnesses include, where necessary, the preservation of their anonymity and that the concealment of the identity of witnesses is not inconsistent with the right to a fair trial, provided that the need for anonymity is clearly established. The ultimate requirement is that the trial should be fair. A conviction is not to be regarded as unsafe simply because the evidence of anonymous witnesses might have been decisive.

Position of Justices Following Application Justices who have ruled on an application for special measures are not disqualified from hearing the case against the accused. In *KL and LK v DPP* (2002) 166 JP 369, the prosecution made an application for the use of screens in relation to a prosecution witness, on the grounds that she would feel intimidated having to give evidence in the accused's presence and had been intimidated. The question to be decided was whether the justices should withdraw from the case after hearing the application. Richards J said (at [13]) that: **D21.38**

> there can be no objection in principle to justices continuing to hear a case after listening to and ruling on an application for the witness to be screened from a defendant. The fact that evidence or submissions adverse to the defendant are advanced in support of such an application does not necessarily prevent fair-minded consideration of the case after the application has been determined, whether it has been allowed or refused.

It is submitted that the same approach would be taken with regard to any other applications for special measures (whether under the YJCEA 1999 or under the court's inherent powers).

SUBMISSION OF NO CASE TO ANSWER

D21.39 At the close of the prosecution evidence the defence may submit that there is no case to answer (see **D15.51** for the position in trial on indictment). The test to be applied when a submission is made was laid formerly down by Lord Parker CJ in *Practice Direction (Submission of No Case)* [1962] 1 WLR 227. This provided that a submission of no case to answer in a summary trial should be upheld if either (a) there was no evidence to prove an essential element in the alleged offence, or (b) the evidence adduced by the prosecution had been so discredited as a result of cross-examination, or was so manifestly unreliable, that no reasonable tribunal could safely convict upon it. This practice direction was revoked by the *Consolidated Criminal Practice Direction* but nothing was put in its place. This leaves justices without clear guidance on the test to be applied when considering a submission of no case.

It is submitted that justices should continue to take the view that, if a submission of no case to answer is made, the decision should depend not on whether they would at that stage convict or acquit but on whether the evidence is such that a reasonable tribunal might convict. If a reasonable tribunal might convict on the evidence so far laid before it, there is a case to answer. The submission should succeed if a conviction would be perverse, in the sense that no reasonable bench could convict.

There is no obligation on justices to give reasons for rejecting a submission of no case to answer (*Moran v DPP* (2002) 166 JP 467).

Credibility of Prosecution Witnesses

D21.40 An important issue is the extent to which justices may have regard to the credibility of prosecution witnesses when considering a submission of no case to answer. In the Crown Court, the test to be applied by the judge when ruling on a submission of no case is set out in *Galbraith* [1981] 1 WLR 1039: is the prosecution evidence so tenuous that, even taken at its highest, a jury properly directed could not properly convict on it? The requirement that the Crown Court judge should 'take the prosecution evidence at its highest' is intended to leave questions of credibility to the jury. In *Barking and Dagenham Justices, ex parte DPP* (1995) 159 JP 373, the Divisional Court said that questions of credibility should, except in the clearest of cases, not normally be taken into account by justices considering a submission of no case. Nonetheless, it is submitted that some justices may well take the pragmatic view that it would be inappropriate for them to go through the motions of hearing defence evidence if they have already formed the view that the prosecution evidence is so unconvincing that they will not be able to convict on it in any event. However, the general principle remains that, so long as the necessary minimum amount of prosecution evidence has been adduced so as to raise a case on which a reasonable tribunal *could* convict, the justices should allow the trial to run its course rather than acquitting on a submission.

Prosecution Right of Reply

D21.41 When the justices are provisionally minded to uphold the submission of no case to answer, they should first call on the prosecution to address them (*Barking and Dagenham Justices, ex parte DPP*), so that the prosecutor has an opportunity to address the court to show why the case should not be dismissed. This means that the prosecution have the right to reply to the defence submission that there is no case to answer unless, having heard the defence submission, the magistrates decide to rule against the defence and indicate this fact to the prosecutor.

Re-opening the Case following a Submission

D21.42 In some cases, the deficiency in the prosecution case which is highlighted by the defence submission of no case to answer may be cured by allowing the prosecution to re-open their case, rather than upholding the submission of no case to answer and acquitting the accused. In *Hughes v DPP* (2003) 167 JP 589, it was said that when, on a submission of no case to answer, a point is raised which has no bearing on the merits of the prosecution, and the defect in the prosecution case is one of omission (and probably oversight), the advocate acting for the prosecution should request leave to re-call the relevant witness to supplement the prosecution evidence. The Divisional Court added that, in such a case, the magistrates should normally exercise their discretion to permit the prosecution to re-open their case so that such evidence can be given, particularly where the fact in question is likely to be uncontroversial. Indeed, if necessary, the magistrates should consider inviting the prosecution to re-call the relevant witness. It is submitted that it may well be appropriate for the justices to allow the prosecution to re-open their case, and thus adduce evidence that was inadvertently omitted, even if the missing evidence does have a more direct bearing on the merits of the prosecution case. If the defect in the prosecution case is one that could be cured simply and speedily by allowing them to re-open their case and re-call a witness, it may well be that the interests of justice require that the prosecution be given the chance to remedy the defect. It is difficult to see how the defendant would be prejudiced by this decision. However, if the re-opening of the prosecution case would require an adjournment, and thus cause delay in the disposal of the case, the balance of the interests of justice might require that the submission be upheld and the defendant acquitted.

From the perspective of professional conduct and ethics, it is also noteworthy that in his judgment in *Hughes*, Stanley Burnton J went on to say (echoing comments made by Auld LJ in *Gleeson* [2004] 1 Cr App R 406) that 'Ambushes of the kind attempted in this case are to be discouraged and discountenanced. Criminal proceedings are not a game: their object is to achieve a fair determination of the innocence or guilt of the defendant'. A similar point was made in *R (DPP) v Chorley Justices and Andrew Forrest* [2006] EWHC 1795 (Admin), where Thomas LJ gave a warning (at [26]) that the defence must raise issues as early as possible in the case:

> If a defendant refuses to identify what the issues are, one thing is clear: he can derive no advantage from that or seek, as appears to have happened in this case, to attempt an ambush at trial. The days of ambushing and taking last-minute technical points are gone. They are not consistent with the overriding objective of deciding cases justly, acquitting the innocent and convicting the guilty.

In *Tuck v Vehicle Inspectorate* [2004] EWHC 728 (Admin), a Divisional Court, consisting of Kennedy LJ and McKay J considered another case in which magistrates had permitted the prosecution to repair omissions in their evidence after they had closed their case, following a submission of no case to answer. McKay J, in a judgment with which Kennedy LJ agreed, summarised the principles applicable as follows (at [15]):

(1) The discretion to allow the case to be re-opened is not limited to matters arising *ex improviso* or mere technicalities, but is a more general discretion.
(2) The exercise of this discretion should not be interfered with by a higher court unless its exercise was wrong in principle or perverse.
(3) The general rule remains that the prosecution must finish its case once and for all and the test to be applied is narrower than consideration of whether the additional evidence

would be of value to the tribunal. The discretion will only be exercised on the rarest of occasions.

(4) The discretion must be exercised carefully having regard to the need to be fair to the defence, and giving consideration to the question of whether any prejudice will be caused.

(5) The courts have in the past differed as to whether the mere loss of a tactical advantage can constitute such prejudice.

(6) Criminal procedure while adversarial is not a game, and the overall interests of justice include giving effect to the requirement that a prosecution should not fail through inefficiency, carelessness or oversight.

(7) Of particular significance is the consideration of whether there is any risk of prejudice to the accused.

In *Steward v DPP* [2003] 1 WLR 592, the justices acceded to a submission of no case to answer. The prosecutor then pointed out that the reasons given by the magistrates contained an error of fact. The justices reviewed their decision, and concluded that there was a case to answer. The accused, who was subsequently convicted, appealed by way of case stated on the basis that the justices had been acting *functus officio* by proceeding to hear the case after reaching a finding of no case to answer. The Divisional Court held that the justices were entitled to re-open a case, despite having acceded to a submission of no case to answer, where an error in the reasons has been identified by the prosecution and the accused agrees that there was an error. In those circumstances, the process of adjudication has not been completed and the justices are not *functus officio*. The case was said to be distinguishable from *Essex Justices, ex parte Final* [1963] 2 QB 816 (where it was held that justices should not re-open a case once they have reached their decision), as that case had been re-opened in order to hear further submissions on the evidence, whereas in the present case the error was identified immediately, and the justices admitted it and rectified it; also, the earlier case was decided at a time when it was less common for justices to give reasons for accepting a submission of no case to answer (and so errors in their reasoning were less likely to be immediately apparent).

DEFENCE CASE AND SPEECHES

D21.43 If a submission of no case to answer is not made, or is unsuccessful, the defence then have the opportunity to present evidence to the court. If the defendant is going to call other witnesses as well as giving evidence himself, the defendant should give evidence first unless the court otherwise directs (see PACE 1984, s. 79).

If the defendant decides not to give evidence, he runs the risk that the magistrates will be entitled to draw adverse inferences from his silence under the CJPOA 1994, s. 35 (see **F19.20**). The magistrates should warn the defendant of the possible consequences of not testifying (see s. 35(2)). In *Radford v Kent County Council* (1998) 162 JP 697, the magistrates failed to warn the defendant that adverse inferences could be drawn if he failed to testify. However, in their stated case, the justices said that 'we drew no inferences whatsoever from the failure of the appellant to give evidence, but simply were aware that the evidence for the prosecution was not rebutted by evidence from or on behalf of the appellant'. The Divisional Court held that, although the warning of the consequences of not testifying is very important, the failure to give the warning in the particular case did not render the appellant's conviction unsafe.

It should be noted that the restrictions on an accused cross-examining witnesses in cases involving alleged sexual offences (see the YJCEA 1999, ss. 34 to 36) apply equally in magistrates' courts. The procedural aspects are contained in the CrimPR, part 31.

Speeches

D21.44 The CrimPR, r. 37.1, sets out the order of evidence and speeches in a summary trial (see **appendix 1** for the text). At the close of the defence case, the defence advocate may make a closing speech, provided that he or she did not make an opening speech. This is because, under r. 37.1(4), the defence are entitled to make only one speech, and so they may make either an opening speech or a closing speech; most defence advocates would choose to make a closing speech, since that is the last chance to address the magistrates before they consider their verdict and it is useful to be able to draw together the threads of the defence case and highlight reasonable doubt in the prosecution case. Under r. 37.1, the prosecutor (although entitled to make an opening speech) has no right to make a closing speech. However, r. 37.1(5) says that either party may, with the leave of the court, make a second speech. Thus, if the prosecutor wishes to make a closing speech or the defence wish to make a closing speech as well as an opening speech, an application must be made to the magistrates for permission to do so. Where one party is allowed to make a second speech, r. 37.1(5) stipulates that the other party must also be allowed to make a second speech. Where the case is a complex one, the justices may well allow both parties to make two speeches. Rule 37.1(6) states that where both parties address the court twice, the closing speech for the accused takes place after the closing speech for the prosecution. Thus, the defence always have the last word.

Evidence in Rebuttal

D21.45 Rule 37.1(3) provides that after any evidence called by the defence, 'the prosecutor may call evidence to rebut that evidence'. Rebuttal evidence may be appropriate if something has arisen *ex improviso* (i.e. something that could not reasonably have been foreseen) during the course of the defence case (see **F6.2**), or where the evidence which the prosecution seek to adduce is intended to remedy a technical deficiency in their case. In those circumstances, the justices may allow the prosecution case to be reopened (*Price v Humphries* [1958] 2 QB 353; *Hammond v Wilkinson* (2001) 165 JP 786). However, the power to allow the prosecution to re-open their case can go beyond such technical difficulties. For example, in *James v South Glamorgan County Council* (1994) 99 Cr App R 321, the main prosecution witness had not arrived but the trial proceeded nonetheless; after the prosecution case had been closed and while the defendant was giving evidence, the witness arrived. It was accepted by the magistrates that the witness had a good reason for being late and the prosecution were allowed to call him as a witness. It was held by the Divisional Court that, since the evidence had not been available at the proper time and there was no unfairness to the defendant (not least because there was no suggestion that the accused's case would have been differently conducted had the evidence of the witness been given timeously), the decision of the magistrates was correct.

Similarly, in *Khatibi v DPP* (2004) 168 JP 361, the court said that the discretion to admit evidence after the close of the prosecution case is not confined to the well established exceptions of rebuttal and mere formality. The discretion must, however, be exercised with great caution. The magistrates should bear in mind the strictly adversarial nature of the English criminal process, whereby the cases for the prosecution and the defence are presented consecutively in their entirety. The normal order of events should not be departed from substantially unless justice really demands such a course of action. In deciding whether to exercise their discretion to permit the calling of evidence after the close of the prosecution case, the magistrates must look carefully at the interests of justice overall, and in particular the risk of any prejudice to the defendant.

In *Khatibi*, the court also pointed out that it has generally been accepted that an application to call further evidence cannot succeed after the bench has retired to consider its verdict. It is only in the rarest of cases that further evidence may be adduced once the justices have retired to consider their verdict. In *Webb v Leadbetter* [1966] 1 WLR 245, one of two prosecution witnesses failed to arrive. The one available witness was called. The prosecution case closed.

The accused gave evidence and his case closed. The justices had retired to consider their decision when they were informed that the second prosecution witness, whose car had broken down, had arrived. They returned to court and allowed the prosecution to call him. His evidence corroborated that of the first prosecution witness. The accused was convicted. The Divisional Court held that, although justices have a discretion to allow further evidence to be called in particular circumstances, the manner of the exercise of that discretion depends on the stage of the case. In the absence of 'special circumstances' (per Lord Parker CJ) or even 'very special circumstances' (per Winn LJ), they should not allow evidence to be called after they have retired. In the instant case, such circumstances were absent and so the further evidence had been wrongly admitted. This decision was followed in *R (Traves) v DPP* (2005) 169 JP 421, where the accused was charged with driving whilst disqualified. At the trial, the prosecution failed to produce the memorandum of conviction which was necessary in order to prove that the accused was driving whilst disqualified. The defence made a submission of no case to answer. The justices retired to consider their decision but, before they returned to court to announce their decision, they were informed that the prosecution now had the evidence that had been lacking. The prosecution sought, and were granted, leave to re-open their case. The prosecution produced evidence of the disqualification and the defendant was convicted. The Divisional Court held that the moment of retiring to consider the decision is a critical point, after which only very special circumstances could allow further evidence to be called. In the instant case, there existed no such very special circumstances and so the conviction was quashed.

However, in *Malcolm v DPP* [2007] 1 WLR 1230, the Divisional Court took a broader of view of what would amount to 'special circumstances', enabling the case to be re-opened even after the justices had retired to consider their verdict. The accused had been charged with driving with excess alcohol. In her final speech, defence counsel submitted that there had been no warning, as required by the RTA 1988, s. 7(7), that a failure to provide a specimen might render the accused liable to prosecution and that, accordingly, there was no admissible evidence of the analysis of alcohol in her breath. The magistrates retired to consider the submissions. They returned to court and gave their conclusions that the case would have to be dismissed because of the lack of admissible evidence of the proportion of alcohol in the appellant's breath. Before they formally dismissed the case, however, counsel for the prosecution requested leave to recall the officer in charge of the breath test procedure. The Divisional Court reiterated the test established by *Webb v Leadbetter*, that special circumstances are required before they can receive further evidence after they have retired to consider their verdict. However, Stanley Burnton J, with whom Maurice Kay LJ agreed, said (at [31]):

> [Counsel for the appellant's] submissions, which emphasised the obligation of the prosecution to prove its case in its entirety before closing its case, and certainly before the end of the final speech for the defence, had an anachronistic, and obsolete, ring. Criminal trials are no longer to be treated as a game, in which each move is final and any omission by the prosecution leads to its failure. It is the duty of the defence to make its defence and the issues it raises clear to the prosecution and to the court at an early stage . . . Even in a relatively straightforward trial such as the present, in the magistrates' court (where there is not yet any requirement of a defence statement or a pre-trial review), it is the duty of the defence to make the real issues clear at the latest before the prosecution closes its case. In *Pydar Justices, ex parte Foster* [1995] 160 JP 87 at 90B Curtis J. commented on the submission that a defending advocate was entitled to 'keep his powder dry'. He said:
>
> Without any doubt whatsoever, it is the duty of a defending advocate properly to lay the ground for a submission, either by cross examination or, if appropriate, by calling evidence.
>
> That was not done in this case.

The court concluded that there were, therefore, special circumstances entitling the magistrates to allow the case to be re-opened. Moreover, Stanley Burnton J added that, 'I respectfully disagree with the decision of Bean J in *Traves*. In my judgment it was wrongly decided'.

His lordship appears to be saying that Bean J should have decided that the facts in that case did, in fact, disclose 'special circumstances'.

The position in magistrates' courts may be contrasted in this regard with the absolute rule applicable in the Crown Court that, once a jury has retired to consider its verdict, no further evidence may be adduced before them (*Owen* [1952] QB 362).

SEEING THE MAGISTRATES IN CHAMBERS

The bench has an inherent discretion to hear representations in chambers during the course of a trial (*Nottingham Magistrates' Court, ex parte Furnell* (1996) 160 JP 201). However, the discretion has to be exercised with even greater caution than applies to the analogous procedure of seeing the judge in a trial on indictment (for details of which, see **D14.78**). In any event, all parties should be made aware of what is happening and be represented in chambers (except where there is an issue of public interest immunity to be heard on an *ex parte* basis) and a contemporaneous note should be taken, normally by the clerk. **D21.46**

DECISION ON THE ISSUE OF GUILT

Manner of Arriving at and Announcing Decision

In the event of disagreement, a lay bench reaches its decisions (including a decision to acquit or convict) by a majority. Where the bench is even-numbered, the chairman does *not* have a casting vote. Therefore, in the event of the justices being equally divided, it will be necessary for the case to be adjourned for rehearing before a differently constituted court (*Redbridge Justices, ex parte Ram* [1992] QB 384). Watkins LJ said that this is not a matter of discretion; the decision to adjourn for this purpose arises from a duty so to do. **D21.47**

Assuming there is the possibility of a majority, justices trying an information are under a duty to reach a decision, and a mandatory order will lie against them if they do not. In both *Bridgend Justices, ex parte Randall* [1975] Crim LR 287 and *Bromley Justices, ex parte Haymills (Contractors) Ltd* [1984] Crim LR 235, benches of three magistrates pronounced themselves unable to decide on the charge against the accused and remitted the case for re-hearing by another bench. In each case, the Divisional Court ordered the original justices to reach a decision, saying that if two of them were unhappy about convicting then the prosecution had failed to prove its case and the finding would have to be one of not guilty.

The decision is announced in open court by the chairman. He does not state whether it is unanimous or by a majority.

The justices have to give reasons for their decision to convict the accused. However, it is sufficient for them to indicate the basis of their decision, without stating their reasons in the form of a judgment or giving reasons in any elaborate form (see *McKerry v Teesdale & Wear Valley Justices* (2000) 164 JP 355, per Lord Bingham, at [23]). If a party wishes to obtain more detailed reasons, a request can be made to the magistrates to state a case.

In *R (McGowan) v Brent Justices* (2002) 166 JP 29, the Divisional Court confirmed that *McKerry v Teesdale & Wear Valley Justices* is still good law following the coming into force of the HRA 1998. Tuckey LJ (at [18]), said that 'the essence of the exercise in a criminal case such as this is to inform the defendant why he has been found guilty. That can usually be done in a few simple sentences'.

Use of Personal Knowledge **D21.48**

In reaching their decision on a question of fact, it is open to magistrates to use their personal local knowledge. However, they should inform the prosecution and the defence that they are doing so, so that those representing the parties have the opportunity of commenting upon the knowledge which the magistrates claim to have (*Bowman v DPP* [1991] RTR 263; *Norbrook Laboratories (GB) Ltd v Health & Safety Executive* [1998] EHLR 207). In *Gibbons v DPP* (2001) 165 JP 812, the appellants were charged with assault. They said they had been acting in self-defence. An eye-witness gave evidence that she was 25 yards from the fight and that the appellants were responsible. After the closing speeches had been made, the district judge had cause to visit the place where the alleged offence had occurred. While there, he checked the site of the assault, the distance the witness was located from the attack and whether her view would have been obstructed. The Divisional Court held that the matters checked were all critical issues at the trial. At the very least, the district judge should have informed the parties of his intention of taking a view, so that they could have had the opportunity to make submissions as to where the witness had actually been located. It followed that there had been a defect in the trial process; the convictions were quashed and a retrial ordered.

Guilty of a Lesser Offence

D21.49 The justices are restricted to reaching a decision of guilty or not guilty on the charge actually before them. They have no power to find an accused not guilty as charged but guilty of a lesser offence (*Lawrence v Same* [1968] 2 QB 93). This applies even when a jury, on an equivalently worded count for an either-way offence, would be entitled under the Criminal Law Act 1967, s. 6(3), to return an alternative verdict. Thus, in *Lawrence v Same* a purported summary conviction for common assault on a charge of unlawful wounding was quashed. It would have been otherwise had there been two separate charges, and the court had decided to convict only on the lesser offence.

There are, however, certain exceptions to the above rule. By virtue of the RTOA 1988, s. 24, magistrates may, whenever trying certain driving offences, find the accused not guilty of the offence charged, but guilty of another statutorily specified driving offence (e.g., convicting the accused of careless driving instead of dangerous driving, even though the only charge before the court is one of dangerous driving: see **C2.12**). The Theft Act 1968, s. 12A(5), constitutes a further statutory exception to the general rule: where an accused is charged with an aggravated offence of taking a vehicle without the owner's consent contrary to s. 12A, he may be found guilty of the lesser offence of unauthorised taking of a vehicle contrary to s. 12. The authority for this course of action, which is contained in s. 12A(5) and is not confined to trial on indictment, overrides the general principle (*R (H) v Liverpool City Youth Court* [2001] Crim LR 487).

Where an information charges an attempt but the evidence establishes the full offence, the justices may nonetheless convict of the attempt (*Webley v Buxton* [1977] QB 481).

If the accused is charged with alternative offences at the outset and pleads not guilty to both, the magistrates may convict him of the more serious of the two offences and adjourn the other charge (under the MCA 1980, s. 10) *sine die* (i.e. on the understanding that the accused will hear no more about that charge) or else convict him of the lesser offence as well but impose only a nominal penalty in respect of it (*DPP v Gane* (1991) 155 JP 846 and *R (CPS) v Blaydon Youth Court* (2004) 168 JP 638).

Setting Aside a Conviction for Rehearing before Differently Constituted Bench

D21.50 Magistrates' Courts Act 1980, s. 142

(2) Where a person is convicted by a magistrates' court and it subsequently appears to the court that it would be in the interests of justice that the case should be heard again by different justices, the court may so direct.

(2A) The power conferred on a magistrates' court by subsection (2) above shall not be exercisable in relation to a conviction if—

(a) the Crown Court has determined an appeal against—

(i) the conviction; or

(ii) any sentence or order imposed or made by the magistrates' court when dealing with the offender in respect of the conviction; or

(b) the High Court has determined a case stated for the opinion of that court on any question arising in any proceeding leading to or resulting from the conviction.

The MCA 1980, s. 142(2), thus enables an accused who was convicted in the magistrates' court (whether he pleaded guilty or was found guilty) to ask the magistrates to set the conviction aside. This application can be considered by the same magistrates who convicted the accused or by a different bench. If the conviction is set aside, the case is re-heard by different magistrates from those who convicted. An application under s. 142(2) may be appropriate if, for example, the magistrates made an error of law or there was some defect in the procedure which led to the conviction.

In *Dewsbury Magistrates, ex parte K* (1994) *The Times*, 16 March 1994, the accused (who was aware that the case was due to be heard) was convicted in his absence, but his failure to attend court was not intentional. He sought a re-hearing but the justices refused. This refusal was quashed by the Divisional Court, which said that any inconvenience to the court or to the prosecution should not outweigh the right of the accused to have an opportunity of defending himself. However, in *Gwent Magistrates' Court, ex parte Carey* (1996) 160 JP 613, the Divisional Court held that magistrates have a broad discretion in deciding whether or not to re-open a case under s. 142. They are entitled to have regard to the fact that the accused failed to attend the original hearing through his own fault and that witnesses would be inconvenienced if a retrial were to be ordered. Henry LJ also said that the magistrates were entitled to take account of the apparent strength of the prosecution case, although little weight should be given to it, since an apparently strong case can collapse during the course of a trial. His lordship also pointed out that the magistrates, by refusing to re-open the case, were not 'finally shutting out the defendant from the judgment seat' because he still had his unfettered right of appeal to the Crown Court under the MCA 1980, s. 108.

There is no time-limit for making an application under s. 142. However, where an accused applies under s. 142(2) for the trial to be re-heard, delay in making the application is a relevant consideration for the magistrates in deciding whether or not to grant that application (*Ealing Magistrates' Court, ex parte Sahota* (1998) 162 JP 73).

THE ROLE OF THE JUSTICES' CLERK/LEGAL ADVISER

Introduction

The qualifications and appointment of justices' clerks are described at D3.27. There is a distinction between clerks in the strict sense of the word and the legal advisers who form part of the court staff. The function of a clerk in court is the same whether he be a legal adviser or the actual clerk to the justices, although a legal adviser may and ought to seek assistance from *the* clerk if a point of difficulty arises on which the adviser does not feel qualified to advise the magistrates. **D21.51**

A justices' clerk must perform his legal functions independently. He is not subject to the directions of the Lord Chancellor or any other person when performing such legal functions, e.g., giving advice to the justices (see the Courts Act 2003, s. 29). An assistant clerk is similarly independent save that he is subject to the directions of the justices' clerk (s. 29(2)).

The functions of the clerk are set out in the Courts Act 2003, s. 28, and in the *Consolidated Criminal Practice Direction (Criminal Proceedings: Consolidation)*, para. V.55 (see **appendix** 7). Section 28 provides:

(4) The functions of a justices' clerk include giving advice to any or all of the justices of the peace to whom he is clerk about matters of law (including procedure and practice) on questions

arising in connection with the discharge of their functions, including questions arising when the clerk is not personally attending on them.

(5) The powers of a justices' clerk include, at any time when he thinks he should do so, bringing to the attention of any or all of the justices of the peace to whom he is clerk any point of law (including procedure and practice) that is or may be involved in any question so arising.

Paragraph V.55.3 of the Practice Direction provides a list of matters on which the clerk or legal adviser may legitimately advise the magistrates:

(a) questions of law (including human rights issues);
(b) questions of mixed law and fact;
(c) matters of practice and procedure;
(d) the range of penalties available;
(e) any relevant decisions of the superior courts or other guidelines;
(f) other issues relevant to the matter before the court; and
(g) the appropriate decision-making structure to be applied in any given case.

Duties of Clerk with Regard to Questions of Law

D21.52 The role of the clerk (or authorised legal adviser) is to *advise* on law, practice and procedure. Since the magistrates are the ultimate arbiters of both law and fact there is no obligation on them to adopt the clerk's advice on law, but it is accepted practice that they do in fact do so. Thus, in *Jones v Nicks* [1977] RTR 72, Lord Widgery CJ strongly criticised magistrates for rejecting the clerk's advice that mitigation advanced by a motorist in respect of an offence of speeding could not amount to special reasons for not endorsing his licence. His lordship said: 'Justices really must accept legal advice from their clerk in circumstances like this; if they do not, all that happens is that a great deal of time and money is wasted in bringing the matter up here to be put right.' If the clerk forms the view that the justices are wrong, however, he has no power to ignore their order and treat it as a nullity (*Liverpool Magistrates' Court, ex parte Abiaka* (1999) 163 JP 497). In those circumstances, he should put the matter before the same bench, or a different bench if the original bench is unavailable, so that they can consider his fresh legal advice and alter the original order, or arrange for reconsideration by a superior court.

When a point of law arises during the course of proceedings, any advice given by the clerk to the magistrates should be given publicly in open court.

In *Chichester Justices, ex parte DPP* [1994] RTR 175, it was held (*obiter*) that, if the clerk who advises the justices is not the clerk who was present in court when the parties made their submissions on the point of law at issue, it is essential that the clerk should hear informal submissions on the relevant law from the parties before advising the justices.

Advice on law will certainly include advice on the elements of the offence charged and on questions of admissibility of evidence. So far as sentencing is concerned, the clerk should be careful not to go beyond advising on the range of penalties available and any relevant guidelines (whether from case law or from the Sentencing Guidelines Council); he should certainly not advocate a certain type of disposal, as this would be to interfere with a decision which is for the bench alone.

Clerk to Play No Part in Decisions on Questions of Fact

D21.53 Paragraph V.55.4 of the *Consolidated Criminal Practice Direction* makes it clear the clerk or legal adviser must play no part in making findings of fact. Contravention of the rule may lead to judicial review of the court's decision (see, for example, *Stafford Justices, ex parte Ross* [1962] 1 WLR 456, where the conviction was quashed because, while the accused was giving evidence in his own defence, the clerk handed the bench a note which, in effect, argued that the evidence ought not to be believed).

Retirement of Clerk with Bench

The clerk should not leave the court-room with the justices when they retire to consider their verdict. If the magistrates require assistance from the clerk, he should join them only when asked to do so and should return to the court-room once the advice has been given, so as to avoid giving the impression that he is participating improperly in the decision-making process (*Eccles Justices, ex parte Farrelly* (1993) 157 JP 77). Where the justices request their adviser to join them in the retiring room, this request should be made in the presence of the parties in court. The *Practice Direction*, para. V.55.7, stipulates that any legal advice given to the justices in their retiring room should be regarded as provisional, and the adviser should then repeat the substance of the advice in open court and give the parties an opportunity to make representations on the correctness of that provisional advice; the legal adviser should state in open court whether the provisional advice is confirmed or if he has varied it (and, if so, how). The same point was made in *Clark v Kelly* [2004] 1 AC 681 (a case which concerned the role of the clerk to the justices in the district court (the Scottish equivalent of the magistrates' court), where the Privy Council said that the role of the clerk is compatible with the defendant's right to a fair trial under the ECHR, Article 6. **D21.54**

It is submitted that this procedure may legitimately not be followed if the substance of the clerk's advice is simply repeating advice he has already given in open court, and on which the parties have already had the chance to make submissions. However, if the clerk advises the justices after they have retired to consider their decision and the clerk cites authority which was not cited in open court, he should inform the advocates in the case and give them the opportunity to make further submissions to the magistrates (*W v W* (1993) *The Times*, 4 June 1993).

In *R (Murchison) v Southend Magistrates' Court* (2006) 170 JP 230, the justices had retired to consider their verdict. They reached their decision and then invited the court legal adviser to assist in the compilation of reasons. After the legal adviser had done so, she informed the justices of the accused's antecedents. The justices then returned to court and gave their verdict. The accused was convicted. Immediately afterwards, the justices announced that they had seen the antecedents and were minded to adjourn sentence for a pre-sentence report. Judicial review of the conviction was sought on the ground that the justices had been made aware of the accused's antecedents before they had announced their decision in open court. The Divisional Court dismissed the appeal because the magistrates had not known of the accused's previous convictions until after they had concluded their deliberations and had reached a reasoned decision. However, it was said that, as a matter of procedure, 'no advice should be offered by a legal adviser, provisional or otherwise, on sentence until the magistrates have returned to court, announced their decision on conviction, heard about the accused's antecedents and listened to counsel's submissions' (per Hallett LJ at [20]). The court added that 'legal advisers should only attend upon the bench . . . when called upon to do so; and then only to assist with matters arising at that stage' and that (given the possibility that in the instant case the legal adviser went into the retiring room with a copy of the appellant's previous convictions in her hand) legal advisers should ensure that any such documentation is left elsewhere when they retire to give the justices legal advice (ibid. [21]).

Noting the Evidence

It is implicit in the duties of the clerk that he should take a note of evidence (see para. V.55.4 of the *Consolidated Criminal Practice Direction*, which states that he 'may assist the bench by reminding them of the evidence, using any notes of the proceedings for this purpose'). As to the desirability of supplying the defence with a copy of the clerk's note if they are appealing against conviction to the Crown Court, see *Clerk to Highbury Corner Justices, ex parte Hussein* [1986] 1 WLR 1266. **D21.55**

Role of Clerk where Accused is Unrepresented

D21.56 The legal adviser is under a duty to assist unrepresented parties to present their case, but must do so without appearing to become an advocate for the party concerned (*Consolidated Criminal Practice Direction,* para. V.55.9). In *Simms v Moore* [1970] 2 QB 327, Lord Parker CJ gave guidance which is summarised below.

(1) In general neither the court nor the justices' clerk should take an active part in the proceedings except to clear up ambiguities in the evidence.
(2) So far as examining witnesses is concerned, this should never be done if the party concerned is legally represented or where a party, even though unrepresented, is competent to and desires to examine the witnesses himself.
(3) Where an unrepresented party is not competent, through a lack of knowledge of court procedure or rules of evidence or otherwise, to examine the witnesses properly, the court can at its discretion permit the clerk to do so.
(4) When this is permitted, there is no reason why the clerk should not do so by reference to a proof of evidence or statement handed in to him, provided always that an opportunity is given to the other side to see it or to have a copy.
(5) Where notes of evidence have to be or are taken, care should be taken not to use the proof or statement as the basis of the notes. The best course is for it to be arranged that someone else, possibly a member of the court itself, should take the note.
(6) Generally, the discretion in the court should be so exercised that examination of witnesses by the clerk should be permitted only when there are reasonable grounds for thinking that thereby the interests of justice would be best promoted, care being taken to see that nothing is done which conflicts with the rules of natural justice or the principle that justice must manifestly be seen to be done.

Thus, it is common practice for clerks to explain to an unrepresented accused the purpose of cross-examination and, if the accused himself still seems incapable of doing it properly, to frame suitable questions on his behalf. Moreover, under the CrimPR, r. 37.2 (see **appendix 1**), the court must explain to an unrepresented accused the substance of the charge in simple language. The same rule states that if the accused, instead of asking questions in cross-examination, makes assertions, then the court should put any necessary questions to the witness on his behalf and may for this purpose question the accused in order to bring out or clear up any point arising out of such assertions. Both of these functions are in practice usually discharged by the clerk. At the close of the prosecution case, the clerk will inform the accused of his right to give and call evidence if he so wishes.

Section D22 Sentencing in the Magistrates' Court

The procedures to be followed between a plea or verdict of guilty and the court pronouncing sentence are described in section **D18** with special reference to sentencing in the Crown Court. Sentencing procedure in the magistrates' courts follows the same basic pattern. The following paragraphs, which should be read in conjunction with section **D19** and with **Part E** (which deals with sentencing generally), cover topics of relevance only to magistrates' courts. **D22.1**

ADJOURNMENTS PRIOR TO SENTENCE

Magistrates' Courts Act 1980, s. 10(3)

> A magistrates' court may, for the purpose of enabling inquiries to be made or of determining the most suitable method of dealing with the case, exercise its power to adjourn after convicting the accused and before sentencing him or otherwise dealing with him; but, if it does so, the adjournment shall not be for more than four weeks at a time unless the court remands the accused in custody and, where it so remands him, the adjournment shall not be for more than three weeks at a time. **D22.2**

It is apparent from the latter half of s. 10(3) that, although the maximum period for adjournment after conviction is four weeks on bail or three weeks in custody, the court is not obliged to sentence at the end of the first such adjournment but may adjourn again (e.g. if the pre-sentence report it needs is not ready at the end of the first period). Where an offender is granted bail for a post-conviction adjournment, the court may impose a condition that he make himself available for the purpose of enabling inquiries or a report to be made to assist the court in dealing with him for the offence (Bail Act 1976, s. 3(6)(d)).

There is some overlap between the MCA 1980, s. 10(3), and the PCC(S)A 2000, s. 11, which empowers magistrates to adjourn for medical reports once they are satisfied that the accused committed the *actus reus* of the offence. If magistrates have convicted, they must *ex hypothesi* be satisfied as to the *actus reus*, and may therefore adjourn under s. 11. However, the chief value of s. 11 is not so much at the post-conviction stage (as the magistrates may adjourn for medical reports under the general powers of the MCA 1980, s. 10(3)) but before conviction when the obtaining of suitable reports and recommendations may enable the court to make a hospital order without finding the accused guilty. Where the court adjourns under the PCC(S)A 2000, s. 11 and bails the accused it *must* make it a condition of bail that he undergo a medical examination by either one or two duly qualified medical practitioners (s. 11(3)). See **D19.35** for the court's power to remand an accused to hospital for the preparation of full medical reports.

SENTENCING IN ABSENCE

The power in the MCA 1980, s. 11(1), to proceed in the accused's absence extends to passing sentence without him there, once the court has found the case proved. However, this is qualified by s. 11(3) and (4): **D22.3**

(3) A magistrates' court shall not in a person's absence sentence him to imprisonment or detention in a young offender institution or make a detention and training order or an order under paragraph 8(2)(a) or (b) of schedule 12 to the Criminal Justice Act 2003 that a suspended sentence shall take effect.

(4) A magistrates' court shall not in a person's absence impose any disqualification on him, except on resumption of the hearing after an adjournment under section 10(3) above; and where a trial is adjourned in pursuance of this subsection the notice required by section 10(2) above shall include notice of the reason for the adjournment.

In short, magistrates may not pass a custodial sentence or a disqualification on an absent accused save that (in the case of disqualification only) they may do so provided they have adjourned after conviction and given him notice of the reason for the adjournment.

Where an accused is represented by counsel or solicitor, the deeming provision in the MCA 1980, s. 122 (see **D21.21**), presumably has the effect of allowing the normally prohibited sentences to be passed even though the offender is not physically present, but in practice the court would almost certainly adjourn rather than take such extreme steps *in absentia.* A sentence passed in contravention of s. 11(3) or (4) will be a nullity and liable to be quashed (see, for example, *Llandrindod Wells Justices, ex parte Gibson* [1968] 1 WLR 598, where a disqualification from driving was quashed because the accused, having pleaded guilty by post, was disqualified from driving forthwith, no adjournment being granted). Although the prohibition in s. 11(4) will, in the majority of cases, be relevant to proposed disqualification from driving, it extends to any form of disqualification that a magistrates' court may order.

In the case of an absent offender being sentenced for a summary offence, the court may take account of any previous convictions that he may have, provided notice of intention to cite the convictions was served on him at least seven days prior to the hearing (MCA 1980, s. 104). The section does not apply to sentencing for either-way offences or to sentencing in a youth court.

As regards sentencing for endorsable offences, an accused who does not intend to attend court is under a duty to send in his licence before the hearing date, and the court may then take account of any endorsements on the licence when sentencing. If the licence is not duly delivered, the court may adjourn for production of it. Alternatively, if the prosecution have obtained from the DVLA a printout of the details recorded there in respect of the accused, the court may proceed to sentence on the basis of the printout.

Warrants

D22.4 Depending on the penalty they have in mind, magistrates may consider it undesirable to proceed to sentence in the offender's absence. If so, they will adjourn. They may also be able to issue a warrant for the offender's arrest. The power to issue a warrant upon adjourning is contained in the MCA 1980, s. 13(1). The same basic conditions apply to issuing a warrant at the post-conviction stage as apply before conviction (i.e. where the proceedings were commenced by way of summons or written charge and requisition, it must be proved that the summons was served on the accused a reasonable time before the trial or adjourned trial, and the offence must be imprisonable). However, following conviction, the powers of the court are widened in that it may issue a warrant even though the offence is non-imprisonable, provided it is proposing to impose a disqualification on the offender (s. 13(3)(b)). On the other hand, an additional restriction is imposed, namely that it must think it 'undesirable, by reason of the gravity of the offence, to continue the trial in the absence of the accused' (s. 13(5)). This restriction applies whether the accused was convicted following a trial or upon a guilty plea and also applies immediately evidence has been adduced for purposes of a not guilty trial (whether or not the court has found the accused guilty by the time of adjournment). In cases where the accused has entered a plea of guilty by post, there is no power to issue a warrant if either the magistrates decide to adjourn rather than accept the plea, or, having convicted, they adjourn before sentence (e.g., because they are considering disqualification) (s. 13(4)). However, if the court has adjourned once without issuing a warrant in the circumstances predicated by s. 13(4) and the accused fails to appear for the adjourned hearing, then (subject to proof that the adjournment notice was duly served) a warrant may be issued.

Attendance at Sentencing Hearings via Live Link

D22.5 The PJA 2006, s. 45, replaces the existing CDA 1998, s. 57, with a series of new provisions (ss. 57A to 57E). These provisions enable the courts to direct that an accused in custody may appear at sentencing hearings via a 'live link' from the place at which he is being held. Section 57D deals with preliminary hearings which turn into sentencing hearings because the accused is convicted (see **D5.23**). Section 57E deals with other sentencing hearings. Section 57E(2) provides that, where it is likely that an offender who has been convicted by a court of an offence will be held in custody during the sentencing hearing, the court may direct that the offender attend via a live link. Under s. 57E(4), such a direction may be given by the court of its own motion or following an application from either party, and may include subsequent sentencing hearings in relation to that offence. A direction may be given only if the offender consents to it and the court is satisfied that it is not contrary to the interests of justice to give the direction (s. 57E(5)). The court may, if it is in the interests of justice to do so, rescind the live link direction, either of its own motion or on the application of either party (s. 57E(6)). Under s. 57E(7), the offender can give oral evidence via the live link under s. 57E only if he has specifically agreed to do so and the court is satisfied that it is not contrary to the interests of justice for him to give his evidence in that way. If the court refuses an application for, or rescinds, a live link direction under s. 57E, it must state its reasons in open court and, in the case of a magistrates' courts, must record the reasons in the court register (s. 57E(8)).

RESTRICTIONS ON MAGISTRATES' COURTS' POWERS OF SENTENCE

Offences Triable Either Way

D22.6 The maximum sentence that magistrates may currently impose upon an offender summarily convicted of an offence triable either way listed in sch. 1 to the Act is six months' imprisonment and/or a fine of up to £5,000. Where an offence is made triable either way by the statute creating it, the maximum sentence on summary conviction is six months or the term prescribed by the statute whichever is the less, and/or a fine of up to £5,000 or the amount prescribed by the statute, whichever is the greater (PCC(S)A 2000, s. 78, and MCA 1980, s. 32(2)).

The six-month ceiling on magistrates' powers of imprisonment contained in s. 78(1) may be expressly excluded. Thus, if an offence-creating enactment simply provides that the maximum term on summary conviction for an offence triable either way shall be nine months' imprisonment, the effect of s. 78(1) is to reduce the maximum to six months, but, if it provides that 'notwithstanding anything in section 78(1) of the PCC(S)A 2000, the maximum term shall be nine months', then s. 78(1) is overridden and the maximum is indeed nine months.

The CJA 2003, s. 154 (not yet in force), empowers a magistrates' court to impose up to 12 months' imprisonment for a single offence and s. 282 increases the maximum penalty on summary conviction for an either-way offence from six months to 12 months.

As to the maximum fine for an offence triable either way always being £5,000, this does not apply if the offence-creating enactment is a 'relevant enactment' (i.e. one passed after 1977), and so the maximum fine in such cases is whatever the statute prescribes, whether more or less than £5,000. Nor does the £5,000 maximum apply to fines for continuing offences where the court may impose a penalty for each day on which the offence is continued after a specified date, or to certain specified either-way offences under the Misuse of Drugs Act 1971 (see the MCA 1980, s. 32(4) and (5), qualifying the effect of s. 32(2)).

By virtue of the MCA 1980, s. 34(3), if the statute creating the offence empowers the court to impose a custodial sentence on the offender but makes no mention of a fine, then (unless this provision is expressly excluded), the court may, instead of imposing a custodial sentence, impose a fine of up to £5,000 if the offence is triable either way, or £1,000 (level 3) if the offence is a summary one.

Summary Offences

D22.7 The maximum sentence of imprisonment (if any) for a summary offence is six months or that prescribed by the statute creating the offence, whichever is the less (PCC(S)A 2000, s. 78(1)). Again this is subject to the six-month ceiling in s. 78(1) being expressly overridden by any other enactment. The maximum fine for a summary offence is whatever the offence-creating provision specifies. Nearly always, the enactment will fix the fine by reference to a level on the standard scale of fines rather than by reference to a specific sum of money (see E17.5 for the standard scale of fines). The offence-creating provision will indicate whether a fine may be imposed in addition to any sentence of imprisonment or only as an alternative thereto.

The CJA 2003, sch. 26 (not yet in force), increases the penalty for a number of summary offences to 51 weeks.

Aggregate Prison Terms

D22.8 Magistrates may make a sentence of imprisonment run concurrently with or consecutively to the term of any such sentence that the offender is already serving (MCA 1980, s. 133(1)). Similarly, magistrates sentencing an offender for several offences and imposing imprisonment for two or more of them may make the terms concurrent or consecutive (ibid.). This is subject to the maximum *aggregate* term that a magistrates' court may impose on one occasion for several offences, which is six months, unless it is sentencing for two or more either-way offences, in which case it is 12 months (proviso to s. 133(1) and s. 133(2)). Where magistrates have power to deal with an offender for breach of a suspended sentence, they may (if they choose to activate part or all of the suspended term) make it run consecutively to any term of imprisonment they impose for the offences that put the offender in breach (see PCC(S)A 2000, s. 119(3)). In such a case, the aggregate of the suspended term and the terms for the present offences may exceed the aggregate normally permitted by s. 133(1) and (2) (see *Chamberlain* (1992) 13 Cr App R (S) 525). An order under the PCC(S)A 2000, s. 116 (that an offender should return to custody to serve his original sentence), is to be treated in the same way, i.e. it does not count towards the aggregate permitted by s. 133 of the MCA 1980 (*Worthing Justices, ex parte Varley* [1998] 1 WLR 819).

The CJA 2003, s. 155(2) (not yet in force), amends the MCA 1980, s. 133(1), to empower a magistrates' court to impose a maximum aggregate term of 65 weeks.

Aggregate Fines

D22.9 When magistrates are dealing with an offender for several offences (whether summary or triable either way), they may fine him up to the statutory maximum for each offence. In other words, there is no special restriction on the aggregate fine that may be imposed.

Criminal Damage Cases

D22.10 Where magistrates deal with a charge of criminal damage under the special procedure in the

MCA 1980, s. 22, as if it were a summary offence (see **D6.31**) and the accused is convicted, their powers of sentencing are restricted to three months' imprisonment or to a fine at level 4 (currently £2,500, see **E17.5**). If, on the other hand, they conclude that the value involved in the offence exceeded the relevant sum (£5,000) and therefore adopt the usual procedure for determining mode of trial, the maximum sentence, should there be a decision for summary trial and conviction, is that which may be imposed for any other either-way offence listed in sch. 1 to the MCA 1980 (i.e. six months' imprisonment and/or a fine of £5,000). When the CJA 2003, sch. 32, para. 27, comes into force, the maximum sentence of imprisonment for criminal damage where the value does not exceed the relevant sum will be increased to 51 weeks.

Compensation Orders

The maximum amount of compensation that a magistrates' court may order in respect of any one offence (whether summary or triable either way) is £5,000 (PCC(S)A 2000, s. 131(1)). Where an offender is convicted of several offences there is no special aggregate restriction on the compensation (i.e. he may be ordered to pay £5,000 for each offence). Where he is convicted of one or more offences and also asks for other offences to be taken into consideration, compensation may be ordered for the offences taken into consideration in a sum not exceeding the difference (if any) between the maximum compensation that could be ordered for the conviction offences and the sum actually awarded for those offences (s. 131(2)). **D22.11**

Custody for Young Offenders

A magistrates' powers may impose a sentence of detention in a young offender institution on an offender aged 18 to 20. The court's powers are limited to the same extent as are their powers to imprison. This flows from the PCC(S)A 2000, s. 97(1), which provides that (subject to certain additional restrictions which apply in the case of juvenile offenders), 'the maximum term of detention in a young offender institution that a court may impose for an offence is the same as the maximum term of imprisonment that it may impose for that offence'. **D22.13**

A youth court may impose a detention and training order, for which the maximum duration is 24 months (12 months' custody and 12 months' supervision in the community). See **E9.10**.

Other Sentencing Powers

Magistrates are also entitled to suspend a prison sentence, although the term suspended must not exceed that which they could have imposed as a sentence of immediate imprisonment. **D22.13**

As to the various non-custodial sentencing options, these are all at the disposal of magistrates' courts to the same extent and in the same circumstances as they are at the disposal of the Crown Court.

Provisions of the Magistrates' Courts Act 1980 and the Powers of Criminal Courts (Sentencing) Act 2000 relating to Magistrates' Sentencing Powers

Magistrates' Courts Act 1980, ss. 32, 33 and 133 **D22.14**

32.—(1) On summary conviction of any of the offences triable either way listed in schedule 1 to this Act a person shall be liable to imprisonment for a term not exceeding six months or to a fine not exceeding the prescribed sum or both, except that—

(a) a magistrates' court shall not have power to impose imprisonment for an offence so listed if the Crown Court would not have that power in the case of an adult convicted of it on indictment;

(b) on summary conviction of an offence consisting in the incitement to commit an offence triable either way a person shall not be liable to any greater penalty than he would be liable to on summary conviction of the last-mentioned offence.

(2) For any offence triable either way which is not listed in schedule 1 to this Act, being an offence under a relevant enactment, the maximum fine which may be imposed on summary conviction shall by virtue of this subsection be the prescribed sum unless the offence is one for which by virtue of an enactment other than this subsection a larger fine may be imposed on summary conviction.

(3) Where, by virtue of any relevant enactment, a person summarily convicted of an offence triable either way would, apart from this section, be liable to a maximum fine of one amount in the case of a first conviction and of a different amount in the case of a second or subsequent conviction, subsection (2) above shall apply irrespective of whether the conviction is a first, second or subsequent one.

(4) Subsection (2) above shall not affect so much of any enactment as (in whatever words) makes a person liable on summary conviction to a fine not exceeding a specified amount for each day on which a continuing offence is continued after conviction or the occurrence of any other specified event.

(5) Subsection (2) above shall not apply on summary conviction of any of the following offences:—

(a) offences under section 5(2) of the Misuse of Drugs Act 1971 (having possession of a controlled drug) where the controlled drug in relation to which the offence was committed was a Class B or Class C drug;

(b) offences under the following provisions of that Act, where the controlled drug in relation to which the offence was committed was a Class C drug, namely—

(i) section 4(2) (production, or being concerned in the production, of a controlled drug);

(ii) section 4(3) (supplying or offering a controlled drug or being concerned in the doing of either activity by another);

(iii) section 5(3) (having possession of a controlled drug with intent to supply it to another);

(iv) section 8 (being the occupier, or concerned in the management, of premises and permitting or suffering certain activities to take place there);

(v) section 12(6) (contravention of direction prohibiting practitioner etc. from possessing, supplying etc. controlled drugs); or

(vi) section 13(3) (contravention of direction prohibiting practitioner etc. from prescribing, supplying etc. controlled drugs).

[(6) Any power by subordinate instrument to restrict the amount of fine which may be imposed on summary conviction for an offence triable either way shall not be affected by subsection (2) above.]

(9) In this section—

'fine' includes a pecuniary penalty but does not include a pecuniary forfeiture or pecuniary compensation;

'the prescribed sum' means £5,000 or such sum as is for the time being substituted in this definition by an order in force under section 143(3) below;

'relevant enactment' means an enactment contained in the Criminal Law Act 1977 or in any Act passed before, or in the same session as, that Act.

33.—(1) Where in pursuance of subsection (2) of section 22 above a magistrates' court proceeds to the summary trial of an information, then, if the accused is summarily convicted of the offence—

(a) subject to subsection (3) below the court shall not have power to impose on him in respect of that offence imprisonment for more than three months or a fine on level 4 on the standard scale; and

(b) section 3 of the Powers of Criminal Courts (Sentencing) Act 2000 (committal to Crown Court for sentence) shall not apply as regards that offence.

(2) In subsection (1) above 'fine' includes a pecuniary penalty but does not include a pecuniary forfeiture or pecuniary compensation.

(3) Paragraph (a) of subsection (1) does not apply to an offence under section 12A of the Theft Act 1968 (aggravated vehicle-taking).

133.—(1) Subject to section 265 of the Criminal Justice Act 2003, a magistrates' court imposing imprisonment or a sentence of detention in a young offender institution on any person may order that the term of imprisonment or detention in a young offender institution shall commence on the expiration of any other term of imprisonment or detention in a young offender institution imposed by that or any other court; but where a magistrates' court imposes two or more terms of imprisonment or detention in a young offender institution to run consecutively the aggregate of such terms shall not, subject to the provisions of this section, exceed six months.

(2) If two or more of the terms imposed by the court are imposed in respect of an offence triable either way which was tried summarily otherwise than in pursuance of section 22(2) above [criminal damage triable only summarily if the value involved was less than £5,000], the aggregate of the terms so imposed and any other terms imposed by the court may exceed six months but shall not, subject to the following provisions of this section, exceed 12 months.

(2A) In relation to the imposition of terms of detention in a young offender institution subsection (2) above shall have effect as if the reference to an offence triable either way were a reference to such an offence or an offence triable only on indictment.

(3) The limitations imposed by the preceding subsections shall not operate to reduce the aggregate of the terms that the court may impose in respect of any offences below the term which the court has power to impose in respect of any one of those offences.

(4) Where a person has been sentenced by a magistrates' court to imprisonment and a fine for the same offence, a period of imprisonment imposed for non-payment of the fine, or for want of sufficient distress to satisfy the fine, shall not be subject to the limitations imposed by the preceding subsections.

(5) For the purposes of this section a term of imprisonment shall be deemed to be imposed in respect of an offence if it is imposed as a sentence or in default of payment of a fine adjudged to be paid by the conviction or for want of sufficient distress to satisfy such a sum.

Powers of Criminal Courts (Sentencing) Act 2000, ss. 78 and 131

78.—(1) A magistrates' court shall not have power to impose imprisonment, or detention in a young offender institution, for more than six months in respect of any one offence.

(2) Unless expressly excluded, subsection (1) above shall apply even if the offence in question is one for which a person would otherwise be liable on summary conviction to imprisonment or detention in a young offender institution for more than six months.

(3) Subsection (1) above is without prejudice to section 133 of the Magistrates' Courts Act 1980 (consecutive terms of imprisonment).

(4) Any power of a magistrates' court to impose a term of imprisonment for non-payment of a fine, or for want of sufficient distress to satisfy a fine, shall not be limited by virtue of subsection (1) above.

(5) In subsection (4) above 'fine' includes a pecuniary penalty but does not include a pecuniary forfeiture or pecuniary compensation.

(6) In this section 'impose imprisonment' means pass a sentence of imprisonment or fix a term of imprisonment for failure to pay any sum of money, or for want of sufficient distress to satisfy any sum of money, or for failure to do or abstain from doing anything required to be done or left undone.

(7) Section 132 of the Magistrates' Courts Act 1980 contains provision about the minimum term of imprisonment which may be imposed by a magistrates' court.

131.—(1) The compensation to be paid under a compensation order made by a magistrates' court in respect of any offence of which the court has convicted the offender shall not exceed £5,000.

(2) The compensation or total compensation to be paid under a compensation order or compensation orders made by a magistrates' court in respect of any offence or offences taken into consideration in determining sentence shall not exceed the difference (if any) between—

(a) the amount or total amount which under subsection (1) above is the maximum for the offence or offences of which the offender has been convicted; and

(b) the amount or total amounts (if any) which are in fact ordered to be paid in respect of that offence or those offences.

PRESENTING THE FACTS, CHARACTER AND ANTECEDENTS

D22.15 The procedure before sentence is passed is basically the same as in the Crown Court — the prosecution representative summarises the facts if there has been a guilty plea, the pre-sentence report (if any) is read, and mitigation is presented. In road traffic cases, it is not the practice to provide antecedents or even a list of convictions, although the bench will know of current endorsements from the offender's licence or (failing that) a printout from the DVLA.

ADJUDICATION ON AND PRONOUNCEMENT OF SENTENCE

D22.16 As with any adjudication of a magistrates' court, the decision as to sentence may be by a majority of those sitting. In the event of an equal division, the court could adjourn under the MCA 1980, s. 10 (adjournments after conviction and before sentence), and reconsider the matter at the resumed hearing.

The court which passes sentence need not be composed of the justices who convicted the offender (or who sat at an earlier post-conviction hearing when the case was adjourned) but, where the court which is to pass sentence consists of, or includes, justices who were not sitting when the offender was convicted, the court must 'make such inquiry into the facts and circumstances of the case as will enable the justices who were not sitting when the offender was convicted to be fully acquainted with those facts and circumstances' (MCA 1980, s. 121(7)). This will invariably be done through a summary of the relevant facts presented by the prosecutor (prior to any plea in mitigation by the defence).

When announcing the sentence, magistrates are obliged to give their reasons in circumstances similar to those in which the Crown Court is obliged to give reasons (see **D19.56**). In particular, the CJA 2003, s. 174(1), imposes a duty to give reasons for, and explain the effect of, any sentence (see **E1.16**). In the case of a custodial sentence or a community sentence, the court must explain why it regards the offence as being sufficiently serious to warrant such a sentence (s. 174(2)(b) and (c)). The court must also mention any aggravating or mitigating factors which it regarded as being of particular importance (s. 174(2)(e)). Where the Sentencing Guidelines Council has issued definitive guidelines relevant to the sentence, and the court departs from those guidelines, it must give reasons for doing so (s. 174(2)(a)). A magistrates' court is also required to record the reason for passing a custodial sentence in the warrant of commitment and in the court register (s. 174(5)).

VARIATION OF SENTENCE UNDER THE MCA 1980, s. 142

D22.17 The MCA 1980, s. 142(1), allows a magistrates' court to vary or rescind its decision as to sentence if it is in the interests of justice to do so. The power is similar to that in respect of setting aside a conviction (see **D21.50**).

The magistrates can re-open the case under s. 142 regardless of whether the accused pleaded guilty or was found guilty. However, s. 142 cannot operate where the accused was acquitted (see *Coles v East Penwith Justices* (1998) 162 JP 687, where the Divisional Court held that there was no power under s. 142(1) to revoke a defendant's costs order where the prosecution had withdrawn the charges).

For the general principles to be applied when considering whether to vary a sentence by increasing it, see **D19.93**, where the question is considered in relation to the Crown Court.

Section 142 can only be used to increase sentence in exceptional circumstances. In *Holme v*

Liverpool City Justices (2005) 169 JP 306, the accused pleaded guilty to dangerous driving, a pedestrian having sustained serious injuries. A community sentence was imposed. The magistrates agreed to a request from CPS to re-open the case under s. 142, on the basis that the original counsel for the prosecution had not addressed the extent of the pedestrian's injuries and that the difference between the sentence imposed and the custodial sentence that would probably have been imposed had the court known all the facts offended the principles of justice. On appeal to the Divisional Court, Collins J (at [30] said:

> the power under s. 142 is to be used in a relatively limited situation, namely one which is akin to mistake or, as the court says, the slip rule. But there is no reason, on the face of it, to limit it further. It seems to me that if a court has been misled into imposing a particular sentence, and it is discovered that it has been so misled, then the sentence may properly be said to have been imposed because of a mistake; the mistake being the failure of the court to appreciate a relevant fact. That may well give power to the court to exercise the jurisdiction conferred by s. 142, but it does not indicate that that power should necessarily be used.

At [42]–[43], his lordship said that it is:

> possible to envisage circumstances where the failure of the court to be aware of such material factors could properly mean that there could be resort to s. 142 [but] it would only be in very rare circumstances that it would be appropriate to resort to s. 142 to consider an increase in sentence, particularly if that increase . . . brought the possibility of custody as opposed to another form of disposal.

The facts of the instant case, said the Court, did not come anywhere near justifying such a use of s. 142.

The power should not be used to punish an offender who has misbehaved in the dock after pronouncement of sentence by increasing what was first announced (*Powell* (1985) 7 Cr App R (S) 247, a case which in fact concerned misbehaviour by an offender at the Crown Court).

Magistrates' Courts Act 1980, s. 142

(1) A magistrates' court may vary or rescind a sentence or other order imposed or made by it when dealing with an offender if it appears to the court to be in the interests of justice to do so; and it is hereby declared that this power extends to replacing a sentence or order which for any reason appears to be invalid by another which the court has power to impose or make.

(1A) The power conferred on a magistrates' court by subsection (1) above shall not be exercisable in relation to any sentence or order imposed or made by it when dealing with an offender if—

(a) the Crown Court has determined an appeal against—
  (i) that sentence or order;
  (ii) the conviction in respect of which that sentence or order was imposed or made; or
  (iii) any other sentence or order imposed or made by the magistrates' court when dealing with the offender in respect of that conviction (including a sentence or order replaced by that sentence or order); or

(b) the High Court has determined a case stated for the opinion of that court on any question arising in any proceeding leading to or resulting from the imposition or making of the sentence or order.

[(2), (2A) and (3) Relate to setting aside a conviction: D21.50.]

(5) Where a sentence or order is varied under subsection (1) above, the sentence or other order, as so varied, shall take effect from the beginning of the day on which it was originally imposed or made, unless the court otherwise directs.

COMMITTAL FOR SENTENCE

Powers to Commit for Sentence

D22.18 As an alternative to passing sentence themselves, magistrates may in some circumstances commit the offender to the Crown Court to be sentenced. The major powers to commit for sentence are as follows:

(a) PCC(S)A 2000, s. 3: general power to commit an adult offender who is summarily convicted of an either-way offence.
(b) PCC(S)A 2000, s. 3A: power to commit adult offenders summarily convicted of an offence triable either way in a case where the 'dangerous offender' provisions of the CJA 2003 are applicable. This provision is not yet in force.
(c) PCC(S)A 2000, s. 4: power to commit an adult offenders convicted of an either-way offence as a result of a guilty plea indicated before the mode of trial procedure has been embarked upon.
(d) CJA 2003, sch. 12, para. 8(6) and para. 11(2): power to commit an offender who is in breach of a requirement under a Crown Court suspended sentence and power to commit an offender convicted of an offence committed during the operational period of a Crown Court suspended sentence, respectively.
(e) PCC(S)A 2000, s. 13(5): power to commit an offender convicted of an offence committed during the period of Crown Court conditional discharge.
(f) CJA 2003, sch. 8, para. 9(6): power to commit an offender who is in breach of a Crown Court community order or conditional discharge to be dealt with for the breach.
(g) PCC(S)A 2000, s. 6: supplementary power to commit offenders who are being committed under the PCC(S)A 2000, ss. 3 to 4A, or 13(5) or the CJA 2003, sch. 12, para. 11(2), to be sentenced also for other matters that would otherwise fall to be dealt with by the magistrates.

Where the defence wish to quash a committal for sentence on the basis that it was in excess of jurisdiction, the remedy is by way of judicial review (see **D28.28**).

Committal under the Powers of Criminal Courts (Sentencing) Act 2000, s. 3

D22.19 **Powers of Criminal Courts (Sentencing) Act 2000, s. 3**
(prior to amendment by the CJA 2003)

(1) Subject to subsection (4) below, this section applies where on the summary trial of an offence triable either way a person aged 18 or over is convicted of the offence.
(2) If the court is of the opinion—
  (a) that the offence or the combination of the offence and one or more offences associated with it was so serious that greater punishment should be inflicted for the offence than the court has power to impose, or
  (b) in the case of a violent or sexual offence, that a custodial sentence for a term longer than the court has power to impose is necessary to protect the public from serious harm from him,

  the court may commit the offender in custody or on bail to the Crown Court for sentence in accordance with section 5(1) below.
(3) Where the court commits a person under subsection (2) above, section 6 below (which enables a magistrates' court, where it commits a person under this section in respect of an offence, also to commit him to the Crown Court to be dealt with in respect of certain other offences) shall apply accordingly.
(4) This section does not apply in relation to an offence as regards which this section is excluded by section 33 of the Magistrates' Courts Act 1980 (certain offences where value involved is small).
(5) The preceding provisions of this section shall apply in relation to a corporation as if—
  (a) the corporation were an individual aged 18 or over; and

(b) in subsection (2) above, paragraph (b) and the words 'in custody or on bail' were omitted.

For the changes to the powers under s. 3 when the relevant provisions of the CJA 2003 are implemented, see **D22.32**.

Limitations on the Power to Commit under s. 3 (prior to amendment by the CJA 2003)

Nature of the Offence The offender must have been convicted of an either-way offence (not a summary offence). Furthermore, the MCA 1980, s. 33, provides that the power to commit for sentence contained in the PCC(S)A 2000, s. 3 does not apply when an offender is convicted of an offence of criminal damage which the magistrates dealt with as if it were a summary offence because the value involved was less than £5,000 (see **D6.31** for the special procedure for criminal damage charges). **D22.20**

Reason for Powers of Punishment Being Insufficient In order to commit to the Crown Court for sentence, the magistrates must be of the opinion: **D22.21**

(a) that the offence (in combination, where appropriate, with associated offences) is so serious that the proper punishment exceeds their powers; or
(b) that, in the case of a violent or sexual offence, a custodial sentence longer than it can impose is necessary to protect the public from serious harm from the offender.

The circumstances which usually give rise to a committal based upon s. 3(2)(a) are:

(i) the accused is revealed as having a record of previous convictions (the CJA 2003, s. 143, indicates that each previous conviction may be treated as an aggravating factor); or
(ii) the accused asks for further offences to be taken into consideration ('TICs' may result in an increase in the sentence eventually passed).

So far as committals in other circumstances are concerned, the Divisional Court has considered on several occasions whether the magistrates have an unfettered discretion to commit for sentence under s. 3, or are bound (in the absence of new material) by their original acceptance of jurisdiction. In *Manchester Magistrates' Court, ex parte Kaymanesh* (1994) 15 Cr App R (S) 838, Balcombe LJ stated that, if nothing further came to light after the decision to try the case summarily had been made, the magistrates should not normally commit for sentence to the Crown Court. However, the court took a different view in *Sheffield Crown Court, ex parte DPP* (1994) 15 Cr App R (S) 768 and *Dover Justices, ex parte Pamment* (1994) 15 Cr App R (S) 778. In both of these cases, the Divisional Court held that the power of the magistrates to commit under what is now s. 3 is unfettered. The court held that there was nothing unreasonable or illogical about permitting a court to form one view at the stage of deciding on summary trial, and a different view at the stage of deciding to commit for sentence. In *North Sefton Magistrates' Court, ex parte Marsh* (1995) 16 Cr App R (S) 401, the Divisional Court came down firmly in favour of a broad interpretation of s. 3, and stated that *Ex parte Kaymanesh* was wrongly decided. The magistrates had 'an open textured decision' on whether to commit under s. 3, which was apparently separate from their decision on mode of trial. However, the Divisional Court in both *Ex parte Marsh* and *Ex parte Pamment* did stress that magistrates should think carefully when deciding to accept jurisdiction because normally an offender should be able to conclude that, once jurisdiction had been accepted, he would not on the same facts be committed for sentence. In *Southampton Magistrates' Court, ex parte Sansome* [1999] 1 Cr App R (S) 112, the Divisional Court confirmed that the correct approach was that taken in *Marsh* and *Pamment.*

Thus, it is submitted that, as a matter of good practice, magistrates should not normally commit an offender for sentence under s. 3 unless new information has come to light since the mode of trial decision was taken. However, if magistrates do commit for sentence on the basis of information which was already known to the court when the decision to try the case

Part D Procedure

was reached, judicial review will not be granted since the magistrates have not acted beyond their powers. It should also be borne in mind that the question of whether a s. 3 committal can only be triggered by new information, or whether the magistrates can, in effect, simply change their minds about the adequacy of their sentencing powers, is now relevant only in those cases where the accused indicates an intention to plead not guilty (or gives no indication as to plea) at the 'plea before venue' hearing and is subsequently convicted by the magistrates. Where the accused indicates an intention to plead guilty, he will do so in the magistrates' court, and so will be convicted by the magistrates, however serious the offence is and before the magistrates are given any information about the seriousness of the offence.

When the relevant provisions of the CJA 2003 come into force (see below), magistrates will no longer be able to commit an offender for sentence under s. 3 when he has been found guilty of an either-way offence following summary trial: that power will be available only where the accused pleads guilty to the either-way offence.

In *Wirral Magistrates' Court, ex parte Jermyn* [2001] 1 Cr App R (S) 137, it was held that a decision to commit for sentence is not the sort of decision for which reasons have to be given, as any person so committed has the opportunity to make full representations to the sentencing court in due course as to the appropriate penalty (per Penry-Davey J at [39]).

D22.22 **Legitimate Expectation** The discretion of the magistrates to commit for sentence is subject to the general principle of 'legitimate expectation'. If the offender has been led to believe, whether expressly or by implication, that he will be sentenced by the magistrates, then he should not subsequently be committed for sentence, whether by the same or a differently constituted bench. In *Nottingham Magistrates' Court, ex parte Davidson* [2000] 1 Cr App R (S) 167, Lord Bingham CJ summarised the 'legitimate expectation' principle as follows:

> if a court at a preliminary stage of the sentencing process gives to a defendant any indication as to the sentence which will or will not be thereafter passed upon him, in terms sufficiently unqualified to found a legitimate expectation in the mind of the defendant that any court which later passes sentence upon him will act in accordance with the indication given, and if on a later occasion a court, without reasons which justify departure from the earlier indication, and whether or not it is aware of that indication, passes a sentence inconsistent with, and more severe than, the sentence indicated, the court will ordinarily feel obliged, however reluctantly, to adjust the sentence passed so as to bring it into line with that indicated.

It followed that where the offender had received an indication when the case was adjourned for a pre-sentence report that there would be no committal for sentence, he could not subsequently be committed for sentence. The same approach was adopted by Otton LJ in *Norwich Magistrates' Court, ex parte Elliott* [2000] 1 Cr App R (S) 152). Similarly, in *Wirral Magistrates' Court, ex parte Jermyn,* it was clear that the offender was warned of the court's power to commit, but the warning gave the impression that the court was satisfied on the material that it had that the matter should remain in the magistrates' court and that would change only if new material emerged; no such material did emerge and so the offender had a legitimate expectation that he would be sentenced in the magistrates' court.

The burden is on the offender to show that there was a 'clear and unequivocal representation' that sentence would be determined by the magistrates (*Sheffield Magistrates' Court, ex parte Ojo* (2000) 164 JP 659).

Magistrates sometimes use the phrase that they are keeping 'all options open' when adjourning for a pre-sentence report, in an effort to avoid arousing the expectations of the accused. In *Norwich Magistrates' Court, ex parte Elliott,* Otton LJ said (at p. 159) that:

> care should be taken that nothing is said or done which might indicate to the accused that committal has been ruled out. If the court wishes to retain the discretion to commit to the Crown Court it should say so. For the court properly to retain the discretion to commit for sentence in such circumstances, it is necessary for it to make absolutely clear to the accused that

> the decision whether or not to commit for sentence has not been taken, and would only be taken at the adjourned hearing . . . [However,] the mere fact of adjourning for pre-sentence reports, without more, cannot amount to a promise by the court that the subsequent justices will not commit the defendant to the Crown Court for sentence.

In *Feltham Justices, ex parte Rees* [2001] 2 Cr App R (S) 1, the justices invited the accused's solicitor to mitigate before them and then adjourned for the preparation of a pre-sentence report; at the time of the adjournment they stated that they were leaving 'all options open' but did not say that committal to the Crown Court was one of those options. This was held to have given rise to a legitimate expectation that the justices themselves would pass sentence (and that the phrase 'all options open' meant that a custodial sentence was a possibility). Rose LJ said that, 'if justices have in mind that one of the options which is open to them is to commit for sentence, they should specifically say so'. Elias J, in a short concurring judgement, said:

> If the legitimate expectation is not to be created in those circumstances, it is incumbent on the justices to make it absolutely clear to the accused that the decision whether or not to commit for sentence has not been taken, and that he might yet be sent for sentence before the Crown Court. The simple issue in this case is whether the words 'all options open' did make it absolutely clear that the defendant might be sent to the Crown Court for sentence. In my judgment, they did not . . .

If the Crown Court does pass sentence on an offender who has been committed for sentence despite the magistrates having adjourned for reports in circumstances giving rise to a legitimate expectation that the sentence would be non-custodial if the reports should be favourable, the Crown Court on committal for sentence is as much precluded from imposing a custodial sentence as the magistrates would have been (*Rennes* (1985) 7 Cr App R (S) 343, applying the general principle in *Gillam* (1980) 2 Cr App R (S) 267).

Inadequacy of Maximum Fine

The PCC(S)A 2000, s. 3, is usually invoked because the offence merits a longer custodial sentence than the magistrates can impose. However, it also allows the magistrates to commit for sentence because of the limitations on the amount of the fine which they can impose. In *North Essex Justices, ex parte Lloyd* [2001] 2 Cr App R (S) 15, the magistrates committed for sentence on the basis that, even though imprisonment was not appropriate, a larger fine should be imposed than the £5,000 to which they were restricted. The Divisional Court held that there was no reason why they should not commit on this basis. It would have been sensible, however, for them to spell out the reason for their decision to commit. Although the Crown Court judge would not be bound by their statement, it would be extremely valuable for him to know the basis on which the committal had been made. Nevertheless, they were entitled to act as they did, and the application for judicial review of their decision was refused. D22.23

Guilty Plea at Plea before Venue and Committal for Sentence

Guidance on several issues that may arise in this context was given by the Divisional Court in *Warley Magistrates' Court, ex parte DPP* [1999] 1 WLR 216. The court held as follows: D22.24

(a) The magistrates must have regard to the discount to be granted on a plea of guilty when deciding whether the punishment which they would have power to inflict would be adequate.
(b) Where the gravity of the offence is such that, even when allowance has been made for the indicated plea, it will be obvious that whatever may be the mitigation the punishment should be greater than the magistrates' court has power to impose, then the court should be prepared to commit the offender to the Crown Court for sentence without seeking any pre-sentence report or hearing in full any mitigation which he may wish to advance. However, if that course is to be adopted, the offender should be told what the court has

in mind, and he or his legal representative should be allowed to make brief submissions in opposition to that course. If the court is persuaded by the submission to change its mind, it should invite the prosecutor to make any submission he may wish to make in reply.

(c) In other cases (i.e. where, after allowance has been made for the plea of guilty, it appears that the court sentencing powers are or may be adequate), the hearing should proceed as usual. If a court, initially minded to commit at an early stage of the proceedings, is persuaded not to adopt that course at that stage, it can keep the option open by saying that the option of committal remains available, and then arranging for the preparation of a pre-sentence report. If, at the end of the hearing, whether or not to commit for sentence remains a live issue, the court should seek assistance from the prosecution and from the offender or his representative in relation to that issue.

(d) If the accused indicates a plea of guilty but there is a dispute as to the facts which must be resolved before sentence can be passed, necessitating a *Newton* hearing (see **D19.5**):
   (i) if the magistrates consider that, whatever the outcome of the *Newton* hearing, they will have adequate powers of sentencing, they should proceed to hold a *Newton* hearing;
   (ii) if the magistrates consider that, whatever the outcome, the offender will have to be committed for sentence, it is clearly preferable to leave the Crown Court to conduct the *Newton* hearing;
   (iii) if the decision as to whether or not to commit for sentence turns, or may turn, on the outcome of the *Newton* hearing, the magistrates' court should proceed to conduct the *Newton* hearing.

(e) If a magistrates' court does conduct a *Newton* hearing and then commits to the Crown Court, it should record its findings for the benefit of the Crown Court, but it is open to the offender to seek to challenge those findings in the Crown Court (which may conduct a fresh *Newton* hearing).

Bail

D22.25 In *Rafferty* [1999] 1 Cr App R 235, the Court of Appeal dealt with the question of whether a committal should be on bail or in custody where the accused indicates a plea of guilty in the plea before venue procedure. Thomas J said:

> in most cases where a plea of guilty is made at the plea before venue, it will not be usual to alter the position as regards bail or custody. In the usual case, when a person who has been on bail pleads guilty at the plea before venue, the usual practice should be to continue bail, even if it is anticipated that a custodial sentence will be imposed by the Crown Court, unless there are good reasons for remanding the defendant in custody. If the defendant is in custody, then after entering a plea of guilty at the plea before venue, it would be unusual, if the reasons for remanding him in custody remained unchanged, to alter the position.

It should be borne in mind, however, that there is no statutory presumption in favour of bail, since the BA 1976, s. 4, does not apply where an offender is being committed for sentence. *Rafferty* removed the principle, which dated back to *Coe* [1968] 1 WLR 1950, that an offender committed for sentence should normally be committed in custody, since he faces a relatively long custodial sentence.

Challenging the Decision to Commit or to Refuse to Commit

D22.26 If an offender is aggrieved at a decision to commit him for sentence to the Crown Court, there is little that can be done about it. The Crown Court usually has no power to remit the case back to the magistrates' court. If the order is plainly bad (for example, s. 3 is invoked by the magistrates in respect of an offence which is triable only summarily), the Crown Court could remit the case to the magistrates' court but the proper course of action is usually for the offender to apply to the Divisional Court for judicial review (*Sheffield Crown Court, ex parte DPP* (1994) 15 Cr App R (S) 768). Such a challenge would succeed only if the committal were perverse in the *Wednesbury* sense that no reasonable bench of magistrates could have decided to commit the defendant for sentence (for example, where the committal defeated a legitimate expectation that there would be no committal for sentence — see above).

However, two points should be noted. First, it is by no means inevitable that the Crown Court will in fact impose a sentence which is more severe than the sentence which the magistrates' court could have imposed. Secondly, there is the option of appealing to the Court of Appeal against the sentence imposed by the Crown Court (under the Criminal Appeal Act 1968, s. 10) if that sentence is in fact excessive.

If the prosecution are unhappy with a decision *not* to commit for sentence, judicial review may be available. However, in *R (DPP) v Devizes Magistrates' Court* [2006] EWHC 1072 (Admin), Maurice Kay LJ said (at [24]) that the Divisional Court will interfere with such decisions only where they are properly categorised as 'truly astonishing'.

Committal for Sentence under the Powers of Criminal Courts (Sentencing) Act 2000, s. 4

The PCC(S)A 2000, s. 4(1) and (2), provides that, where the accused has indicated that he will plead guilty to an either-way offence (and so is deemed to have pleaded guilty to it) and he is also sent for trial for one or more related offences, the magistrates may commit him to the Crown Court for sentence in respect of the either-way offence to which he has pleaded guilty. For the purposes of these provisions, one offence is related to another if the charges for them could be joined (under the CrimPR, r. 14.2(3): see **D11.56**) in the same indictment if both were to be tried in the Crown Court (s. 4(7)). So the two charges must be founded on the same facts or must be, or be part of, a series of offences of the same or a similar character. **D22.27**

Section 4(4) provides that, where the justices have committed an offender for sentence pursuant to s. 4(2), the Crown Court can exceed the sentencing powers of the magistrates' court in respect of the either-way offence only if:

(a) the magistrates stated that they considered their sentencing powers were inadequate to deal with the offender for that offence (and so they also had power to commit him for sentence under s. 3); or else
(b) he is also convicted by the Crown Court of one or more of the related offences.

If the magistrates take the view that their sentencing powers are adequate to deal with the offence in respect of which the offender has indicated a guilty plea, then only s. 4 allows the justices to commit him to the Crown Court for sentence for that offence. On the other hand, if the magistrates take the view that their sentencing powers are not adequate to deal with that offence, they have two options: they can either commit him for sentence for that offence under s. 3, or they can commit him for sentence under s. 4 but indicate that they took the view that their sentencing powers were inadequate and so could have invoked s. 3. Obviously, the best practice will be to use s. 3 where the magistrates' sentencing powers are not adequate and to use s. 4 where their powers are adequate.

When committing an offender for sentence, the court should state whether it is doing so under s. 3 or s. 4. If the magistrates use s. 4 but do not consider that their sentencing powers are adequate to deal with the offence, they should state (under s. 4(4)) that they also had the power to commit the defendant for sentence under s. 3, so as to avoid inadvertently fettering the powers of the Crown Court when dealing with the offence.

Powers of Criminal Courts (Sentencing) Act 2000, s. 4

(1) This section applies where—
  (a) a person aged 18 or over appears or is brought before a magistrates' court ('the court') on an information charging him with an offence triable either way ('the offence');

D

Part D Procedure

(b) he or his representative indicates that he would plead guilty if the offence were to proceed to trial; and
(c) proceeding as if section 9(1) of the Magistrates' Courts Act 1980 were complied with and he pleaded guilty under it, the court convicts him of the offence.

(2) If the court has committed the offender to the Crown Court for trial for one or more related offences, that is to say, one or more offences which, in its opinion, are related to the offence, it may commit him in custody or on bail to the Crown Court to be dealt with in respect of the offence in accordance with section 5(1) below.

(3) If the power conferred by subsection (2) above is not exercisable but the court is still to inquire, as examining justices, into one or more related offences—
(a) it shall adjourn the proceedings relating to the offence until after the conclusion of its inquiries; and
(b) if it commits the offender to the Crown Court for trial for one or more related offences, it may then exercise that power.

(4) Where the court—
(a) under subsection (2) above commits the offender to the Crown Court to be dealt with in respect of the offence; and
(b) does not state that, in its opinion, it also has power so to commit him under section 3(2) above,

section 5(1) below shall not apply unless he is convicted before the Crown Court of one or more of the related offences.

(5) Where section 5(1) below does not apply, the Crown Court may deal with the offender in respect of the offence in any way in which the magistrates' court could deal with him if it had just convicted him of the offence.

(6) Where the court commits a person under subsection (2) above, section 6 below (which enables a magistrates' court, where it commits a person under this section in respect of an offence, also to commit him to the Crown Court to be dealt with in respect of certain other offences) shall apply accordingly.

(7) For the purposes of this section one offence is related to another if, were they both to be prosecuted on indictment, the charges for them could be joined in the same indictment.

Procedure and Powers of the Crown Court following a committal under the PCC(S)A 2000, s. 3 or s. 4

D22.28 **Procedural Issues** Committal under the PCC(S)A 2000, s. 3, will be to the most convenient location of the Crown Court, having regard to any relevant local direction on the matter. The Crown Court, when hearing a s. 3 committal, comprises a circuit judge or recorder (the presence of lay justices is required only for appeals from magistrates' courts (Supreme Court Act 1981, s. 74).

Before proceeding to hear the case, the Crown Court should confirm that the person before it has indeed been committed for sentence by the magistrates' court. This is usually done by asking the offender if he admits that fact. In the absence of such admission, the prosecution must prove the committal by formal evidence. The evidence might come from a certified copy of the magistrates' court register or from someone present in the magistrates' court at the time of the committal. Once the committal has been admitted or proved, the procedure before sentence is passed is exactly the same as when there is a guilty plea, with a prosecution summary of the facts and a plea in mitigation on behalf of the offender.

Where the offender indicates that he is appealing against his conviction in the lower court, the sentencing proceedings should be adjourned until the conclusion of the appeal (*Faithful* [1950] 2 All ER 1251). If, however, the court inadvertently disposes of the committal for sentence in ignorance of the fact that the offender is appealing against conviction, the appeal should be heard nonetheless and, if it succeeds, the sentence passed on the committal will simply fall with the conviction (*Croydon Crown Court, ex parte Bernard* [1981] 1 WLR 116).

Where the offender asked the lower court to take other offences into consideration, he is not bound to take the same course in the Crown Court (i.e. the normal procedure for taking offences into consideration should be followed in the Crown Court and, in the absence of a request to consider the other matters, they must be ignored (*Davies* (1980) 2 Cr App R (S) 364).

Powers of Crown Court The PCC(S)A 2000, s. 5, provides that, following a committal for sentence under s. 3 or s. 4, the Crown Court may deal with the offender as if he had just been convicted on indictment. Therefore, the combined effect of these provisions is to provide a mechanism by which a summarily convicted offender, who merits more than the maximum sentence the magistrates could impose, may be dealt with for his offence with appropriate severity. D22.29

Powers of Criminal Courts (Sentencing) Act 2000, s. 5

(1) Where an offender is committed by a magistrates' court for sentence under section 3 or 4 above, the Crown Court shall inquire into the circumstances of the case and may deal with the offender in any way in which it could deal with him if he had just been convicted of the offence on indictment before the court.

***Newton* hearings** If a *Newton* hearing took place at the magistrates' court, the Crown Court should adopt the outcome. In *Warley Justices, ex parte DPP* [1999] 1 WLR 216, Kennedy LJ said that it may be that the offender will seek to challenge the magistrates' findings in the Crown Court, but 'I would not expect him to be allowed to do so unless he could point to some significant development, such as the discovery of important further evidence, having occurred since the magistrates' court reached its conclusion'. A similar point was made in *Gillan v DPP* (2007) 171 JP 330, where the court considered the question: 'Where magistrates have determined the factual basis for sentencing at a *Newton* hearing, and then commit the defendant for sentence in the Crown Court, does the duty of the Crown Court to enquire into the circumstances of the case include a power to hear evidence in a second *Newton* hearing to determine afresh the factual basis on which the defendant shall be sentenced?'. Forbes J, giving the judgment of the Divisional Court said (at [28]–[29]): D22.30

> I am completely satisfied that the Crown Court does have jurisdiction to hold a further *Newton* hearing if it is in the interests of fairness and justice to do so . . . However, the fact that the Crown Court has jurisdiction or a power to hold a further *Newton* hearing does not mean, ipso facto, that it should accede to an application to do so in any case where it is apparent that the magistrates have already conducted such a hearing and made clear findings of fact as part of their perfectly proper decision-making with regard to committing the defendant to the Crown Court for sentence. Essentially, the matter is a question for the discretion of the judge, in the proper exercise of which he or she must be fully mindful of his or her obligation to carry out a proper inquiry into the circumstances of the case . . . I would not expect the judge in the Crown Court to exercise his discretion in favour of allowing a defendant to re-open the magistrates' findings of fact unless the defendant was able to point to some significant development or matter, such as (but not confined to) the discovery of important further evidence having occurred since the Magistrates' Court reached its conclusion on the facts. In saying that, I would not wish it to be thought that I was laying down any absolute or strict formula as to how the judge should exercise his or her discretion in any particular case. Everything will depend upon the facts and circumstances of the particular case; each case must be considered individually.

If the divergence between prosecution and defence versions becomes apparent for the first time at the Crown Court (or no *Newton* hearing was held at the magistrates' court), the Crown Court should, of course, hold a *Newton* hearing to determine the issue (see *Munroe v DPP* (1988) 152 JP 657).

Age of Offender In *Robson* [2007] 1 All ER 506, the Court of Appeal considered the position where the offender has attained an age of relevance to sentencing powers during the period between the magistrates' court and Crown Court proceedings. In that case, a 17-year-old offender was convicted of sexual assault and was committed to the Crown Court for sentence under the PCC(S)A 2000, s. 3C (part of the 'dangerous offender' provisions established by the CJA 2003). When he appeared for sentencing, he had attained the age of 18. D22.31

The Court of Appeal considered whether the age of an offender committed to the Crown Court for sentence is to be treated, for the purpose of sentence, differently from the age of an offender convicted after trial. The latter has to be sentenced on the basis of his age at the date of his conviction, whether he is convicted following a guilty plea or a guilty verdict (*Danga* (1992) 94 Cr App R 252 and *Robinson* (1993) 96 Cr App R 418). The court held that, at least for the purposes of the sentencing regime created for dangerous offenders by the CJA 2003, ss. 224 to 236 (see E5), the matter should be decided on the basis of the wording of the relevant statutory provisions. For dangerous offenders, these refer to age at the date of conviction (not sentence), and so the relevant date for sentence purposes is the date of the conviction, not the date of the Crown Court appearance following committal for sentence. Given that the PCC(S)A 2000, s. 89(1), provides that a sentence of imprisonment may not be passed on a person 'if he is aged under 21 when *convicted* of the offence', it would seem that the use of the word 'convicted' requires the court to pass a sentence appropriate to the age at the date of conviction, not the date of sentence (and so an offender who attains the age of 21 between conviction in the magistrates' court and appearance in the Crown Court for sentence should be sentenced as if he were under 21, and therefore is not eligible for a sentence of imprisonment).

Committal for Sentence following Implementation of Criminal Justice Act 2003

D22.32 The power to commit for sentence where the accused has been convicted in the magistrates' court following a not guilty plea will be abolished when the relevant provisions of the CJA 2003 come into force. There will, however, still be a power to commit for sentence where the accused indicates a guilty plea at the plea before venue hearing and the court considers that the offence is so serious that the Crown Court ought to be able to deal with him as if he had just been convicted on indictment. The CJA 2003, sch. 3, para. 22, substitutes an amended version of the PCC(S)A 2003, s. 3.

Powers of Criminal Courts (Sentencing) Act 2000, s. 3 (as substituted by the CJA 2003: not yet in force)

(1) Subject to subsection (4) below, this section applies where—
   (a) a person aged 18 or over appears or is brought before a magistrates' court ('the court') on an information charging him with an offence triable either way ('the offence');
   (b) he or his representative indicates under section 17A or (as the case may be) 17B of the Magistrates' Courts Act 1980 (initial procedure: accused to indicate intention as to plea), but not section 20(7) of that Act, that he would plead guilty if the offence were to proceed to trial; and
   (c) proceeding as if section 9(1) of that Act were complied with and he pleaded guilty under it, the court convicts him of the offence.

(2) If the court is of the opinion that—
   (a) the offence; or
   (b) the combination of the offence and one or more offences associated with it, was so serious that the Crown Court should, in the court's opinion, have the power to deal with the offender in any way it could deal with him if he had been convicted on indictment, the court may commit him in custody or on bail to the Crown Court for sentence in accordance with section 5(1) below.

(3) Where the court commits a person under subsection (2) above, section 6 below (which enables a magistrates' court, where it commits a person under this section in respect of an offence, also to commit him to the Crown Court to be dealt with in respect of certain other offences) shall apply accordingly.

(4) This section does not apply in relation to an offence as regards which this section is excluded by section 17D of the Magistrates' Courts Act 1980 (certain offences where value involved is small).

(5) The preceding provisions of this section shall apply in relation to a corporation as if—
   (a) the corporation were an individual aged 18 or over; and
   (b) in subsection (2) above the words 'in custody or on bail' were omitted.

Under the substituted section, if the accused indicates a not guilty plea (or gives no indication) at the plea before venue hearing, the court accepts jurisdiction and the accused consents to summary trial, but information emerges during the summary trial which makes the offence appear more serious than it did when the magistrates accepted jurisdiction, it will no longer be open to magistrates to commit the accused for sentence if they convict him. It should also be noted that the power to terminate a summary trial and hold committal proceedings instead, so that the trial will start again in the Crown Court (under MCA 1980, s. 25(2)), is to be curtailed when the amendments to the MCA 1980, s. 25, contained in the CJA 2003, sch. 3, para. 11, come into effect. The power under s. 25(2) will be altered so that, where the magistrates have accepted jurisdiction and the accused has consented to summary trial, the prosecution may apply for the case to be transferred to the Crown Court for trial (on the ground that the sentencing powers of the magistrates' court are inadequate) but such application may only be made before the summary trial begins.

Dangerous Offenders

The CJA 2003, sch. 3, para. 23, also enacts a new power of committal in the PCC(S)A 2000, s. 3A (not yet in force). This enables a magistrates' court which convicts an adult defendant to commit him to the Crown Court for sentence when the criteria for an extended sentence or a sentence for public protection appear to be met under the 'dangerous offender' provisions of the CJA 2003 (see E5). **D22.33**

Powers of Criminal Courts (Sentencing) Act 2000, s. 3A

(1) This section applies where on the summary trial of a specified offence triable either way a person aged 18 or over is convicted of the offence.
(2) If, in relation to the offence, it appears to the court that the criteria for the imposition of a sentence under section 225(3) or 227(2) of the Criminal Justice Act 2003 would be met, the court must commit the offender in custody or on bail to the Crown Court for sentence in accordance with section 5(1) below.
(3) Where the court commits a person under subsection (2) above, section 6 below (which enables a magistrates' court, where it commits a person under this section in respect of an offence, also to commit him to the Crown Court to be dealt with in respect of certain other offences) shall apply accordingly.
(4) In reaching any decision under or taking any step contemplated by this section—
  (a) the court shall not be bound by any indication of sentence given in respect of the offence under section 20 of the Magistrates' Courts Act 1980 (procedure where summary trial appears more suitable); and
  (b) nothing the court does under this section may be challenged or be the subject of any appeal in any court on the ground that it is not consistent with an indication of sentence.
(5) Nothing in this section shall prevent the court from committing a specified offence to the Crown Court for sentence under section 3 above if the provisions of that section are satisfied.
(6) In this section, references to a specified offence are to a specified offence within the meaning of section 224 of the Criminal Justice Act 2003.

Committal under the Powers of Criminal Courts (Sentencing) Act 2000, s. 6

The PCC(S)A 2000 gives a power to commit for sentence which may be used to supplement a committal under any of the following provisions: **D22.34**

(a) PCC(S)A 2000, ss. 3 to 4A (committal for sentence for either-way offences);
(b) PCC(S)A 2000, s. 13(5) (conditionally discharged person convicted of further offence);
(c) CJA 2003, sch. 12, para. 11(2) (committal to Crown Court where offender convicted during operational period of suspended sentence).

These committal powers are referred to below as 'primary powers'.

By the PCC(S)A 2000, s. 6(2), when a magistrates' court exercises a primary committal power in respect of an indictable offence, it may also commit the offender to the Crown Court to be dealt with in respect of any other offence of which he stands convicted (whether summary or indictable) that the magistrates' court has jurisdiction to deal with; s. 6(2) expressly states that, provided the committing court would be able to deal with the matter if it were not to commit, the power to commit arises even if the conviction was by a different court. Thus, to take the example of a magistrates' court which has decided to commit an offender under s. 3, for one either-way offence, a committal under s. 6 may, *inter alia*, relate to:

(a) another, less serious, either-way offence of which the magistrates have convicted the offender on the same occasion;
(b) a summary offence of which they have convicted the offender on the same occasion.

The reason a committal under s. 3 for the secondary offence would be inappropriate in situation (a) is that, because the offence is not sufficiently serious, the magistrates' powers of sentencing for it are adequate. In situation (b), a committal under s. 3 would be inappropriate simply because the section does not extend to summary offences.

The other use of s. 6 is where a summary conviction puts the offender in breach of a suspended sentence passed by the Crown Court and the magistrates consider that, although the breach should be committed to the Crown Court under the CJA 2003, sch. 12, para 11(2)(a), the offence giving rise to the breach is not in itself serious enough to warrant committal under s. 3. The court should then commit the offender under para. 11(2)(a), for possible activation of the suspended sentence, and under s. 6, for sentence for the present offence.

Where the offence in respect of which the *primary* power of committal arises is a summary offence, the magistrates' powers under s. 6 are slightly more limited in that they may commit only in respect of (a) any other offence carrying imprisonment or disqualification from driving of which their court has convicted the offender, or (b) breach of a suspended sentence passed on the offender by their or another magistrates' court (s. 6(3)). In fact, the primary power of committal will, in practice, nearly always relate to an indictable offence, and so s. 6(3) is of little practical significance.

Following a committal under s. 6, the Crown Court may, after inquiring into the circumstances of the case, deal with the offender in any way the magistrates' court might have done had it not committed (s. 7). The Crown Court's powers on a committal under s. 6 are thus identical to the powers of the lower court (cf. the position where there is a committal under s. 3). This limitation on the Crown Court's powers reveals the basic purpose of a committal under s. 6, namely to enable one court to deal with an offender for all matters outstanding against him rather than have the sentencing function split between the Crown Court and the magistrates. The purpose of s. 6 is *not* to expose the offender to risk of greater punishment than the lower court could inflict.

Section D23 Trial of Juveniles

INTRODUCTION

The Aims of the Youth Justice System

The CDA 1998, s. 37(1), provides that 'It shall be the principal aim of the youth justice system to prevent offending by children and young persons'. Section 37(2) goes on to require that 'In addition to any other duty to which they are subject, it shall be the duty of all persons and bodies carrying out functions in relation to the youth justice system to have regard to that aim'. However, the CYPA 1933, s. 44(1), provides that: D23.1

> Every court in dealing with a child or young person who is brought before it, either as an offender or otherwise, shall have regard to the welfare of the child or young person and shall in a proper case take steps for removing him from undesirable surroundings, and for securing that proper provision is made for his education and training.

Terminology: 'Juvenile', 'Adult', 'Child' and 'Young Person'

(a) *Juvenile*. The term is not expressly defined by the relevant legislation. It is, however, convenient shorthand for a person who has not attained the age of 18. There are some examples of the word being used in this way. For example, the MCA 1980, s. 29(1)(a), refers to 'a person under the age of 18 ("the juvenile")'. 'Juvenile' is, therefore, used in this sense throughout. D23.2

(b) *Adult*. In the context of criminal procedure and mode of trial, the definition of 'adult' is simply a function of the definition of juvenile — i.e. an adult is any person aged 18 or over. In the context of sentencing, however, 'adult' is sometimes used to mean those aged 21 or over, since it is at that age that an offender currently becomes liable to imprisonment rather than detention in a young offender institution.

(c) *Child*. By the CYPA 1933, s. 107(1), 'child' (when used in that Act) means a person under the age of 14 years, unless the context otherwise requires. The CYPA 1969, s. 70(1), contains a similar provision in respect of the majority of the provisions of that Act, while the CYPA 1963, s. 65(3), provides that the 1963 Act shall be construed 'as one with' the 1933 Act. It should be noted, however, that in some contexts 'child' is given an extended meaning (e.g., for purposes of children in care where it connotes any person under 18).

(d) *Young person*. The definition sections referred to in (c) above also define 'young person' as a 'person who has attained the age of 14 years and is under the age of 18 years'. Thus, juveniles divide into children (aged under 14) and young persons (aged 14 to 17 inclusive).

Youth Offending Teams

Pursuant to the CDA 1998, s. 39, each local authority has to establish a youth offending team (YOT). The YOT has to comprise: D23.3

(a) a probation officer;
(b) a person with experience of social work in relation to children, nominated by the director of children's services appointed by the local authority;
(c) a social worker;
(d) a police officer;
(e) a person nominated by a Primary Care Trust or a health authority any part of whose area lies within the local authority's area; and
(f) a person with experience in education nominated by the director of children's services.

Other people may be co-opted on to the YOT (for example, housing officers and people with experience of dealing with drugs and alcohol misuse). The functions of the YOT are to co-ordinate the provision of youth justice services for all those in the authority's area who need them, and to carry out such functions as are assigned to it in the local authority's 'youth justice plan'. The plan (made under the CDA 1998, s. 40) sets out how youth justice services in the area are to be provided and funded, and the functions of the YOTs in that area. The YOT is able to ascertain the needs of each young offender, identifying the specific problems that make that young person offend and measuring the risk that the young person poses to others. This enables the YOT to identify suitable programmes to address the needs of the young person in order to prevent further offending.

Prosecuting Young Defendants

D23.4 Detailed guidance (entitled *The CPS: Youth Offenders*) on prosecuting young defendants from the perspective of the CPS is to be found on their website (<http://www.cps.gov.uk/legal/section4/chapter_b.html>). That guidance makes reference to *Chief Constable of Kent, ex parte L* (1991) 93 Cr App R 416, where it was held that the discretion of the CPS to continue or to discontinue criminal proceedings against a juvenile is reviewable by the Divisional Court, but only where it can be demonstrated that the decision was made regardless of or clearly contrary to a settled policy of the DPP evolved in the public interest (see generally **D2.19**). This means that Crown Prosecutors have to be careful to follow the guidance contained in the Code for Crown Prosecutors and in the published guidance on 'youth offenders'.

There is an irrebuttable presumption that a person who is under the age of 10 cannot be guilty of a criminal offence. There used to be a rebuttable presumption that a child aged between 10 and 14 was incapable of committing an offence. This presumption, often called *doli incapax*, was that children under 14 did not know the difference between right and wrong (and therefore were incapable of committing a crime) unless the prosecution were able to prove that they did have this understanding. Hence, a child aged under 14 could be convicted of a criminal offence only if the presumption of *doli incapax* was first rebutted. To rebut the presumption, the prosecution had to adduce evidence to prove that the child knew that what he or she was doing was seriously wrong, rather than simply naughty. The presumption was, however, abolished by the CDA 1998, s. 34.

In *CPS v P* (2007) 171 JP 349, Smith LJ considered whether the *doli incapax* doctrine exists despite the abolition of the presumption by the CDA 1998, s. 34. Her ladyship said (at [46]):

> It appears to me that the effect of section 34 is to abolish the presumption that a child is *doli incapax* but not the defence itself . . . [I]t seems to me that the defence must be capable of existing without being attached to the presumption. The two are distinct concepts. The defence is 'I did not know that this act was seriously wrong'. The practical problems arose because this was presumed to apply in every case of a child of 10 but under 14 and extraneous evidence had to be called to rebut the presumption. If the presumption is removed, . . . there remains a perfectly workable defence.

Her ladyship made it clear that her observations on this point were *obiter* (a point reinforced by Gross J in a short judgment concurring in the result) but she went on to consider the evidential issues that arise if there remains a defence of *doli incapax*. She said (at [47]):

> If the defence remains available, . . . there would have to be an evidential burden on the defence to raise the issue . . . [A]s a matter of general principle the burden should remain on the Crown to prove that the child had the requisite understanding. Moreover, the standard of proof should be the usual criminal standard.

In *CPS v P* the court went on to consider the issues that arise where a youth court has to consider the question of the juvenile's capacity to stand trial and related it to the question of fitness to plead and (if it remains a defence) *doli incapax*. At [48] her ladyship said:

> Usually, a defendant will only be found unfit to plead when s/he has either mental illness or substantial impairment of intellectual capacity. A child might be *doli incapax* without any such impairment but simply on account of immaturity or the unusual nature of his upbringing . . .
> [I]t appears to me that there is a large measure of overlap between the issues of 'sufficient understanding of right from wrong', 'fitness to plead', 'ability to participate effectively in a trial' and 'the fairness of the trial' . . . A child who, due to immaturity or lack of understanding, does not know that what is alleged against him is seriously wrong may well also, for the same reasons, be unable to participate effectively in a trial.

Her ladyship then considered the procedure to be adopted in such cases and, in particular, whether there should ever be a stay before evidence is heard. Her ladyship said, at [51]:

> [N]otwithstanding the fact that the youth court is a creature of statute (like any other magistrates' court) it has an inherent jurisdiction to stay proceedings as an abuse of process at any stage. The jurisdiction is limited to matters directly affecting the fairness of the trial of the particular defendant concerned and does not extend to the wider supervisory jurisdiction for upholding the rule of law, which is vested in the High Court . . . However . . . it will be in only exceptional cases that it should be exercised, on the ground of one or more of the capacity issues, before any evidence is heard.

Her ladyship then addressed the weight to be accorded to medical evidence in such cases (at [52] and [53]):

> Medical evidence . . . will rarely provide the whole answer to the question of whether the child ought to be tried for a criminal offence. This is an issue which the court has to decide, not the doctors, although of course the medical evidence may be of great importance. But, the medical evidence must almost always be set in the context of other evidence relating to the child, which may well bear upon the issues of his understanding, mental capacity and ability to participate effectively in a trial . . . The court must be willing, in an appropriate case, to disagree with and reject the medical opinion. It is the court's opinion of the child's level of understanding which must determine whether a criminal trial proceeds.
> . . . [I]n most cases, the medical evidence should be considered as part of the evidence in the case and not as the sole evidence on a freestanding application . . .

Smith LJ also emphasised (at [54]–[57]) the need to keep the issue of capacity under review and, as part of that review process, to consider whether the case was one where the court should simply make a finding of fact whether the juvenile committed the *actus reus* of the offence (thus enabling a disposal under the Mental Health Act 1983 rather than convicting the accused):

> [T]he court has a duty to keep under continuing review the question of whether the criminal trial ought to continue. If at any stage the court concludes that the child is unable to participate effectively in the trial, it may decide to call a halt. However, the court may consider that it is in the interests of the child that the trial should continue . . .
> If the court decides that it should call a halt to the criminal trial on the ground that the child cannot take an effective part in the proceedings, it should then consider whether to switch to a consideration of whether the child has done the acts alleged . . .
> The decision as to whether or not to switch to fact-finding is one for the discretion of the court . . . I consider that proceedings should be stayed as an abuse of process before fact-finding only if

no useful purpose at all could be served by finding the facts.
If the court decides to find the facts and finds that the defendant did the acts alleged, it would then consider whether to seek further medical evidence with a view to making an order under the Mental Health Act 1983. If the court finds that the defendant did not do the acts alleged, the proceedings would be brought to an end by a finding of not guilty.

Court of First Appearance

D23.5 The juvenile's first court appearance in respect of an offence will be in the youth court unless the case is one of the exceptional ones where the first appearance is in the adult magistrates' court. Those exceptional cases are where:

(a) the juvenile is jointly charged with an adult; or
(b) the juvenile is charged with aiding and abetting an adult to commit an offence (or vice versa); or
(c) the juvenile is charged with an offence which arises out of circumstances which are the same as (or connected with) those which resulted in the charge faced by an adult accused.

Bail

D23.6 So far as bail is concerned, the Bail Act 1976 (with the presumption in favour of bail) applies to juveniles. The criteria for granting bail are virtually the same as for adults. There are three important differences. First, a juvenile can be refused bail where this is necessary for his own 'welfare' (not just if necessary for his own 'protection', as is the case with adults). Secondly, a parent or guardian may be asked to act as a surety not only for the juvenile's attendance at court (the function of the surety in the case of adult defendants) but also for compliance with any other conditions of bail which the court may impose (BA 1976, s. 3(7)). The third, and most significant, difference between adults and juveniles is in what happens to a juvenile under the age of 17 if bail is withheld, whether before or after conviction. Where juveniles are refused bail, they are remanded to local authority accommodation unless the criteria laid down in the CYPA 1969, s. 23(5), are satisfied, in which case the court may require the local authority to place and keep the juvenile in 'secure accommodation' (run by the local authority). For details, see D7.94.

Mode of Trial

D23.7 The normal rules governing mode of trial are modified to a large extent in the case of juveniles. The great majority of juveniles are tried and sentenced in *youth courts*. By virtue of the CYPA 1933, s. 45, youth courts are magistrates' courts. It follows that trial in the youth court is merely a form of summary trial (even though there are special rules relating to the constitution and proceedings of youth courts). However, the youth court has jurisdiction to try offences which, in the case of an adult, are triable only on indictment (with the exception of homicide and certain firearms offences). Whereas an adult may never be tried summarily for an offence triable only on indictment and always has the right to elect trial on indictment for an offence triable either way, a juvenile may be (and normally is) tried summarily for indictable offences, whatever his wishes as to mode of trial may be. In other words, he has no right to election of a Crown Court trial. If a juvenile is sent to the Crown Court for trial, it is because the *magistrates* have decided that they should not accept jurisdiction — the most the juvenile may do is to make representations for or against staying in the youth court.

In summary, a juvenile either may or must be tried in an adult court if he is charged:

(a) with homicide, or
(b) with an offence to which the PCC(S)A 2000, s. 91, applies (mostly offences carrying at least 14 years' imprisonment in the case of an adult), or
(c) with a firearms offence to which the mandatory minimum sentence provisions of the Firearms Act 1968, s. 51A, applies, or

(d) with an offence which falls within the ambit of the 'dangerous offender' provisions of the CJA 2003 (these offences are listed in sch. 15 to that Act), or
(e) alongside an adult defendant.

The procedure for determining where the juvenile will be tried in those cases where mode of trial is an issue is discussed in D23.17 *et seq.*

TRIAL OF JUVENILES IN THE YOUTH COURT

As we have seen, the youth court has jurisdiction to try offences which would be triable only on indictment in the case of an adult. Most juveniles are therefore tried in the youth court. **D23.8**

Constitution and Operation of the Youth Court

The CYPA 1933, s. 45 (as amended by the Courts Act 2003, s. 50) sets out the framework under which lay magistrates and district judges are authorised to hear youth court cases. Under s. 45(2), a justice of the peace is not qualified to sit as a member of a youth court unless he has an authorisation to do so under s. 45(3). Under s. 45(3) the authorisation is given by the Lord Chief Justice, with concurrence of the Lord Chancellor. These personal authorisations are valid throughout England and Wales. A magistrate can be given authorisation for particular proceedings (set out in the authorisation) or for all youth court proceedings (s. 45(3)). To quote from the Explanatory Notes that accompany the Courts Act 2003, 'because of the often sensitive nature of youth cases, and the specific knowledge and understanding that is required, these rules [will] help to ensure that only trained and suitable magistrates (or District Judges (Magistrates' Courts)) sit on youth courts'. **D23.9**

The CYPA 1933, s. 45, has to be read alongside the Youth Courts (Constitution of Committees and Right to Preside) Rules 2007 (SI 2007 No. 1611), which came into force on 13 July 2007 (and replaced the Youth Courts (Constitution) Rules 1954). Under r. 3 of the 2007 Rules, there has to be a committee, known as a 'youth panel' for each local justice area. The panel consists of the youth justices (i.e. the justices authorised to sit as members of a youth panel is to advise the Bench Training and Development Committee (or, for Inner London, the Inner London Youth Training and Development Committee) in relation to the number of justices required to sit and preside in youth courts in its local justice area and to liaise with other bodies to share information and represent the views of youth justices.

Composition of the Youth Court The composition of the youth court is governed by the Youth Courts (Constitution of Committees and Right to Preside) Rules 2007, r. 10(1). This requires a youth court to consist of either (a) a district judge (magistrates' courts) sitting alone, or (b) not more than three justices, including a man and a woman. **D23.10**

Under r. 10(2) and (3), if no male justice or (as the case may be) no female justice is available due to circumstances that were unforeseen when the justices to sit were chosen, or if the only male (or female) justice present cannot properly sit as a member of the court, then the court may be constituted without a male (or female) justice if the other members of the youth court think it inexpedient in the interests of justice for there to be an adjournment.

In *Birmingham Justices, ex parte F* (2000) 164 JP 523, the juvenile was tried by a youth court which consisted of two male magistrates. No point as to the absence of a female magistrate was taken by prosecution, defence or the clerk. The juvenile was found guilty, and sought judicial review on the ground that there should have been at least three magistrates, including a man and a woman, in accordance with the requirement for a mixed bench. The Divisional Court granted judicial review, and ordered a retrial, holding that what is now r. 10(1) is mandatory unless the justices decide in their discretion to proceed under what is now r. 10(2) and (3). Such discretion has to be exercised publicly and with submissions from the parties. In the present case, it had not been exercised in that way.

Under r. 11(1), a youth court (unless it consists of a district judge sitting alone) must be chaired by a district judge (if he is sitting as a member of the court)) or by a youth justice who is on the list of approved youth court chairmen. Rule 11(2) provides that a youth justice may preside before he has been included on a list of approved youth court chairmen only if he is under the supervision of a youth justice who is on a list of approved chairmen and has completed the necessary training course. Rule 12 deals with the exceptional situation where no youth justice entitled to preside at the hearing is present. Rule 12(1) states that the youth justices present may appoint one of their number to preside provided that they are satisfied as to the suitability of the justice they propose as chair and (unless the absence of a qualified chairman arises because of illness, circumstances unforeseen when the youth justices to sit were chosen or some other emergency) the justice in question has completed, or is undergoing, a chairman training course.

D23.11 **Exclusion of Public** The public are excluded from the court-room of a youth court. The CYPA 1933, s. 47(2), stipulates that the only persons permitted to be present in the youth court are:

(a) members and officers of the court;
(b) parties to the case before the court, their solicitors and counsel, and witnesses and other persons directly concerned in that case;
(c) bona fide representatives of news gathering or reporting organisations; and
(d) such other persons as the court may specially authorise to be present.

Thus, the only persons entitled to be present in the youth court apart from the accused, the parents and the justices and their clerk are:

(a) the lawyers representing the juvenile or the prosecution in the case — lawyers cannot enter the court-room if a case they are appearing in is not yet being dealt with;
(b) court officials (for example, the usher);
(c) reporters (but note the reporting restrictions set out below);
(d) probation officers and social workers;
(e) witnesses giving evidence (who are allowed to remain in court once they have given evidence);
(f) anyone else directly concerned in the case;
(g) anyone whom the magistrates specifically allow to be present.

Under the VCRA 2006, s. 11(7), where the youth court is dealing with proceedings for an offence under s. 11(1) (breach of a drinking banning order), one person authorised to be present by a relevant authority may be in the courtroom.

The position in the youth court should be contrasted with those cases where a juvenile is appearing as an accused, or as a witness, in the adult magistrates' court or the Crown Court – in those courts, the public has the right to be present unless the court takes the exceptional step of sitting 'in camera'.

Press Reports

D23.12 Restrictions on what can be reported are contained in the CYPA 1933, s. 49 (which is prospectively amended by the YJCEA 1999, sch. 2, para 3). Under s. 49(1), no report of proceedings in a youth court may be published or broadcast which reveals the name, address or other identifying detail of any juvenile concerned in the proceedings, whether he be concerned as a party or merely as a witness. The overarching test is whether the particulars in question are likely to lead to the juvenile being identified as someone concerned in the proceedings. The court may, however, lift the ban on publicity to the extent it considers necessary either to avoid injustice to the juvenile himself (s. 49(5)(a)) or, as respects a juvenile who is unlawfully at large, where it is necessary to do so for the purpose of apprehending him and bringing him before a court or returning him to custody (s. 49(5)(b)). Section 49(5)(b) applies only to a juvenile who is charged with or convicted of a violent or sexual offence or an offence punishable in the case of an adult with imprisonment for 14 years or more. Moreover, the power conferred by s. 49(5)(b) may be exercised only upon the application of the DPP (this includes Crown Prosecutors), and notice of the application must be given to the juvenile's legal representative (s. 49(7)). The power to lift the reporting restrictions may be exercised by a single justice (s. 49(8)).

The automatic restrictions on publishing or broadcasting identifying details of a juvenile involved in youth court proceedings apply only while that person is a juvenile. In *T v DPP; North East Press Ltd* (2004) 168 JP 194, the accused was convicted and sentenced in the youth court. During the course of those proceedings he attained the age of 18. The justices ruled that the CYPA 1933, s. 49, no longer applied, since the accused was no longer aged under 18. It was held by the Divisional Court that an accused in proceedings before the youth court ceases to benefit from the reporting restrictions contained in s. 49 as soon as he attains the age of 18, because the specific purpose of s. 49 is to protect children and young persons from adverse publicity. Such restrictions are an exception to the general right to report proceedings, and so should be interpreted narrowly. The fact that a person had been a young person at the commencement of proceedings could not justify such a person continuing to benefit from s. 49 once he has ceased to be a young person.

In addition, the court may also lift the ban on publicity where a juvenile has been convicted of an offence, if it is satisfied that it is in the public interest to do so (s. 49(4A)). Before doing so, it must afford an opportunity to the parties to make representations (s. 49(4B)).

In *McKerry v Teesdale and Wear Valley Justices* (2000) 164 JP 355, the Divisional Court recognised that there was a tension between the young person's right to privacy and the 'hallowed principle that justice is administered in public, open to full and fair reporting of the proceedings in court'. Lord Bingham CJ stressed that the power to dispense with anonymity, as permitted in certain circumstances by s. 49(4A), had to be exercised with very great care, caution and circumspection. His lordship said that it would be wholly wrong for any court to dispense with a young person's prima facie right to anonymity as an additional punishment, and that it was also very difficult to see any place for 'naming and shaming'. The court must be satisfied that the statutory criterion, that it was in the public interest to dispense with the reporting restrictions, is satisfied. His lordship observed that this will very rarely be the case, and justices making an order under s. 49(4A) must be clear *why* it is in the public interest to dispense with the restrictions. In weighing up the public interest, it is entirely proper for the justices to ask a reporter who was present in court if he wished to say anything. His lordship said that inviting the observations of the press could be a valuable process in these circumstances, and the justices had not been in error in doing so in the instant case.

It should be borne in mind that the rule on publicity in the youth court is the reverse of that which applies in the adult magistrates' court and the Crown Court, where the media are permitted to identify a juvenile concerned in proceedings unless an order to the contrary is made under s. 39 of the 1933 Act. In the youth court, on the other hand, the juvenile must not be identified unless the court gives permission.

Attendance of Parent or Guardian The CYPA 1933, s. 34A(1), provides that if the juvenile is aged under 16 the court *must* (and if the juvenile is aged 16 or 17, the court *may*) require a parent or guardian to 'attend at the court during all the stages of the proceedings, unless and to the extent that the court is satisfied that it would be unreasonable to require such attendance, having regard to the circumstances of the case'. 'Guardian' is defined as any person who, **D23.13**

in the opinion of the court, has for the time being 'the care of the child or young person' (CYPA 1933, s. 107). 'Parent' is not defined in the 1933 Act, but, by the Adoption Act 1976, s. 39, includes the adopter of an adopted child. In cases where the local authority has parental responsibility, their representative, rather than, or in certain cases as well as, the parent must (or may) be required to attend (CYPA 1933, s. 34A(2)). If the juvenile is not legally represented, the parent or guardian may assist in the conduct of the defence, for example, in cross-examination of prosecution witnesses (see CrimPR, r. 38.2). If the juvenile is not legally represented and no parent or guardian is present, r. 38.5(3) effectively enables the clerk to ask questions on the juvenile's behalf.

D23.14 **Advance Information** The CrimPR, r. 21.3(1) stipulates that, where the offence is triable either way in the case of an adult, and the accused has not attained the age of 18 when he appears or is brought before a magistrates' court (which term must be taken to include a youth court), he is entitled to receive, before he is asked whether he pleads guilty or not guilty, either copies of the prosecution witness statements or a summary of the prosecution case (see also **D6.4**). The provisions on disclosure in the CPIA 1996 are applicable to cases involving juveniles (see **D9**). Similarly, the A-G's Guidelines on Disclosure (see **appendix** 5) apply equally to youth court cases; this includes para. 57, which stipulates that the prosecutor should provide to the defence all evidence upon which the Crown proposes to rely in a summary trial, allowing the accused and his legal advisers sufficient time properly to consider the evidence before it is called.

Course of the Trial in a Youth Court

D23.15 The course of a trial in the youth court is essentially the same as the course of a trial in an adult magistrates' court. The CrimPR, part 38 (see **appendix 1** for the full text), governs the procedure. Under r. 38.3, the court is required to explain to the juvenile the substance of the charge in simple language suitable to his age and understanding, but that obligation does not extend to giving a detailed elaboration of the elements of the offence (*Blandford Justices, ex parte G* [1967] 1 QB 82). Having explained the charge, the court asks the juvenile if he pleads guilty or not guilty (r. 38.4). If, after the prosecution evidence, there is a case to answer, an unrepresented juvenile must be told of his right to give evidence and to address the court (r. 38.6). As a matter of terminology, the words 'conviction' and 'sentence' are not to be used in connection with juveniles tried summarily (CYPA 1933, s. 59). They are replaced by, respectively, the terms 'finding of guilt' and 'order made upon a finding of guilt'. This applies both to proceedings in the youth court and to proceedings against juveniles in the adult magistrates' court. It does not, however, apply to proceedings on indictment.

The procedure in the youth court is intended to be less formal than in the adult magistrates' court. So, for example, the accused sits on a chair, not in a dock, and usually has a parent or guardian sitting nearby; the accused and any juvenile witnesses are addressed by their first names; the oath taken by witnesses is to 'promise' (not 'swear') to tell the truth (CYPA 1963, s. 28(1)).

Statutes and Rules Relating to Procedure in Youth Court

D23.16 **Children and Young Persons Act 1933, ss. 34A, 45, 47, 49 and 59**

34A.—(1) Where a child or young person is charged with an offence or is for any other reason brought before a court, the court—

(a) may in any case; and

(b) shall in the case of a child or a young person who is under the age of sixteen years,

require a person who is a parent or guardian of his to attend at the court during all the stages of the proceedings, unless and to the extent that the court is satisfied that it would be unreasonable to require such attendance, having regard to the circumstances of the case.

(2) In relation to a child or young person for whom a local authority have parental responsibility and who—

(a) is in their care; or

(b) is provided with accommodation by them in the exercise of any functions (in particular those under the Children Act 1989) which are social services functions within the meaning of the Local Authority Social Services Act 1970,

the reference in subsection (1) above to a person who is a parent or guardian of his shall be construed as a reference to that authority or, where he is allowed to live with such a person, as including such a reference.

In this subsection 'local authority' and 'parental responsibility' have the same meanings as in the Children Act 1989.

45.—(1) Magistrates' courts—

(a) constituted in accordance with this section or section 66 of the Courts Act 2003 (judges having powers of District Judges (Magistrates' Courts)), and

(b) sitting for the purpose of—

(i) hearing any charge against a child or young person, or

(ii) exercising any other jurisdiction conferred on youth courts by or under this or any other Act,

are to be known as youth courts.

(2) A justice of the peace is not qualified to sit as a member of a youth court for the purpose of dealing with any proceedings unless he has an authorisation extending to the proceedings.

(3) He has an authorisation extending to the proceedings only if he has been authorised by the Lord Chief Justice with the concurrence of the Lord Chancellor or a person acting on his behalf to sit as a member of a youth court to deal with—

(a) proceedings of that description, or

(b) all proceedings dealt with by youth courts.

(4) The Lord Chief Justice with the concurrence of the Lord Chancellor may by rules make provision about—

(a) the grant and revocation of authorisations,

(b) the appointment of chairmen of youth courts, and

(c) the composition of youth courts.

. . .

47.—(1) Youth courts shall sit as often as may be necessary for the purposes of exercising any jurisdiction conferred on them by or under this or any other Act.

(2) No person shall be present at any sitting of a youth court except—

(a) members and officers of the court;

(b) parties to the case before the court, their solicitors and counsel, and witnesses and other persons directly concerned in that case;

(c) bona fide representatives of newspapers or news agencies;

(d) such other persons as the court may specially authorise to be present.

49.—(1) The following prohibitions apply (subject to subsection (5) below) in relation to any proceedings to which this section applies, that is to say—

(a) no report shall be published which reveals the name, address or school of any child or young person concerned in the proceedings or includes any particulars likely to lead to the identification of any child or young person concerned in the proceedings; and

(b) no picture shall be published or included in a programme service as being or including a picture of any child or young person concerned in the proceedings.

(2) The proceedings to which this section applies are—

(a) proceedings in a youth court;

(b) proceedings on appeal from a youth court (including proceedings by way of case stated);

(c) proceedings under schedule 7 to the Powers of Criminal Courts (Sentencing) Act 2000 (proceedings for varying or revoking supervision orders); and

(d) proceedings on appeal from a magistrates' court arising out of proceedings under schedule 7 to that Act (including proceedings by way of case stated).

(3) The reports to which this section applies are reports in a newspaper and reports included in a programme service; and similarly as respects pictures.

(4) For the purposes of this section a child or young person is 'concerned' in any proceedings whether as being the person against or in respect of whom the proceedings are taken or as being a witness in the proceedings.

(4A) If a court is satisfied that it is in the public interest to do so, it may, in relation to a child or young person who has been convicted of an offence, by order dispense to any specified extent

D

Part D Procedure

with the requirements of this section in relation to any proceedings before it to which this section applies by virtue of subsection (2)(a) or (b) above, being proceedings relating to—
(a) the prosecution or conviction of the offender for the offence;
(b) the manner in which he, or his parent or guardian, should be dealt with in respect of the offence;
(c) the enforcement, amendment, variation, revocation or discharge of any order made in respect of the offence;
(d) where an attendance centre order is made in respect of the offence, the enforcement of any rules made under section 221(1)(d) or (e) of the Criminal Justice Act 2003; or
(e) where a detention and training order is made, the enforcement of any requirements imposed under section 103(6)(b) of the Powers of Criminal Courts (Sentencing) Act 2000.

(4B) A court shall not exercise its power under subsection (4A) above without—
(a) affording the parties to the proceedings an opportunity to make representations; and
(b) taking into account any representations which are duly made.

(5) Subject to subsection (7) below, a court may, in relation to proceedings before it to which this section applies, by order dispense to any specified extent with the requirements of this section in relation to a child or young person who is concerned in the proceedings if it is satisfied—
(a) that it is appropriate to do so for the purpose of avoiding injustice to the child or young person; or
(b) that, as respects a child or young person to whom this paragraph applies who is unlawfully at large, it is necessary to dispense with those requirements for the purpose of apprehending him and bringing him before a court or returning him to the place in which he was in custody.

(6) Paragraph (b) of subsection (5) above applies to any child or young person who is charged with or has been convicted of—
(a) a violent offence,
(b) a sexual offence, or
(c) an offence punishable in the case of a person aged 21 or over with imprisonment for fourteen years or more.

(7) The court shall not exercise its power under subsection (5)(b) above—
(a) except in pursuance of an application by or on behalf of the Director of Public Prosecutions; and
(b) unless notice of the application has been given by the Director of Public Prosecutions to any legal representative of the child or young person.

(8) The court's power under subsection (5) above may be exercised by a single justice.

(9) If a report or picture is published or included in a programme service in contravention of subsection (1) above, the following persons, that is to say—
(a) in the case of publication of a written report or a picture as part of a newspaper, any proprietor, editor or publisher of the newspaper;
(b) in the case of the inclusion of a report or picture in a programme service, any body corporate which provides the service and any person having functions in relation to the programme corresponding to those of an editor of a newspaper,

shall be liable on summary conviction to a fine not exceeding level 5 on the standard scale.

(10) In any proceedings under schedule 7 to the Powers of Criminal Courts (Sentencing) Act 2000 (proceedings for varying or revoking supervision orders) before a magistrates' court other than a youth court or on appeal from such a court it shall be the duty of the magistrates' court or the appellate court to announce in the course of the proceedings that this section applies to the proceedings; and if the court fails to do so this section shall not apply to the proceedings.

(11) In this section—

'legal representative' means an authorised advocate or authorised litigator, as defined by section 119(1) of the Courts and Legal Services Act 1990;

'programme' and 'programme service' have the same meaning as in the Broadcasting Act 1990;

'sexual offence' means an offence listed in part 2 of Schedule 15 to the Criminal Justice Act 2003;

'specified' means specified in an order under this section;

'violent offence' means an offence listed in part 1 of Schedule 15 to the Criminal Justice Act 2003;

and a person who, having been granted bail, is liable to arrest (whether with or without a warrant) shall be treated as unlawfully at large.

59. The words 'conviction' and 'sentence' shall cease to be used in relation to children and young persons dealt with summarily and any reference in any enactment . . . to a person convicted, a conviction or a sentence shall, in the case of a child or young person, be construed as including a reference to a person found guilty of an offence, a finding of guilt or an order made upon such finding, as the case may be.

Substantial amendments to s. 49 are made by the YJCEA 1999, sch. 2; these amendments are not yet in force.

DETERMINING MODE OF TRIAL OF JUVENILES

Most trials involving juvenile defendants take place in the youth court. However, there are cases where a juvenile may, or must, be tried in an adult court (either an adult magistrates' court or the Crown Court). The law on mode of trial for juveniles is to be found (somewhat confusingly) in a combination of statutory sources, including the CYPA 1933, s. 46, the CYPA 1963, s. 18, and the MCA 1980, ss. 24 and 29. The key points may be summarised thus. **D23.17**

There are five circumstances in which the trial of a juvenile may take place in the Crown Court:

(a) where the juvenile is accused of homicide (i.e. murder or manslaughter); or
(b) where the juvenile is charged with a firearms offence where the Firearms Act 1968, s. 51A, applies; or
(c) where the juvenile is accused of an offence to which the PCC(S)A 2000, s. 91, applies (i.e. an offence carrying at least 14 years' imprisonment in the case of an adult or one specified in s. 91 itself); or
(d) where the juvenile is charged with a 'specified' offence as defined by the CJA 2003, s. 224 (and so falls within the ambit of the 'dangerous offender' provisions of that Act); or
(e) where the juvenile is charged alongside an adult.

There is only one situation where the trial of a juvenile may take place in an adult magistrates' court, namely where the juvenile is charged alongside an adult.

Trial on Indictment The limited circumstances in which it is possible for a juvenile to be tried on indictment are set out in the MCA 1980, s. 24. The Criminal Justice Act 2003 (Commencement No. 2 and Saving Provisions) Order 2004 (SI 2004 No. 81) brought into force, on 22 January 2004, the CJA 2003, s. 42. This amended the MCA 1980, s. 24, in a manner said by the headnote to s. 42 to be transitional in nature (pending the full implementation of the relevant provisions of the CJA 2003). Section 24, in presently amended form, provides as follows: **D23.18**

Magistrates' Courts Act 1980, s. 24

(1) Where a person under the age of 18 years appears or is brought before a magistrates' court on an information charging him with an indictable offence other than one falling within subsection (1B) below, he shall be tried summarily unless—
   (a) the offence is such as is mentioned in subsection (1) or (2) of section 91 of the Powers of Criminal Courts (Sentencing) Act 2000 (under which young persons convicted on indictment of certain grave crimes may be sentenced to be detained for long periods) and the court considers that if he is found guilty of the offence it ought to be possible to sentence him in pursuance of subsection (3) of that section; or
   (b) he is charged jointly with a person who has attained the age of 18 years and the court considers it necessary in the interests of justice to commit them both for trial;

and accordingly in a case falling within paragraph (a) or (b) of this subsection the court shall commit the accused for trial if either it is of opinion that there is sufficient evidence to put him on trial or it has power under section 6(2) above so to commit him without consideration of the evidence.

[When the other amendments made by the CJA 2003 come into effect, s. 24(1) will read as follows:

(1) Where a person under the age of 18 years appears or is brought before a magistrates' court on an information charging him with an indictable offence he shall, subject to sections 51 and 51A of the Crime and Disorder Act 1998 and to sections 24A and 24B below, be tried summarily.]

(1A) Where a magistrates' court—

(a) commits a person under the age of 18 for trial for an offence falling within subsection (1B) below; or

(b) in a case falling within subsection (1)(a) above, commits such a person for trial for an offence,

the court may also commit him for trial for any other indictable offence with which he is charged at the same time if the charges for both offences could be joined in the same indictment.

[Subs. (1A) will be repealed when the amendments made by the CJA 2003 come into effect.]

(1B) An offence falls within this subsection if—

(a) it is an offence of homicide; or

(b) each of the requirements of section 51A(1) of the Firearms Act 1968 would be satisfied with respect to—

(i) the offence; and

(ii) the person charged with it,

if he were convicted of the offence; or

(c) section 29(3) of the Violent Crime Reduction Act 2006 (minimum sentences in certain cases of using someone to mind a weapon) would apply if he were convicted of the offence.

(2) Where, in a case falling within subsection (1)(b) above, a magistrates' court commits a person under the age of 18 for trial for an offence with which he is charged jointly with a person who has attained that age, the court may also commit him for trial for any other indictable offence with which he is charged at the same time (whether jointly with the person who has attained that age or not) if the charges for both offences could be joined in the same indictment.

[(3) and (4) concern maximum powers of punishment when a juvenile is tried summarily for an indictable offence.]

It will be apparent from s. 24(1) that there are three categories of case in which either a juvenile must be tried on indictment or the magistrates have a discretion whether to deal with him themselves or send him to the Crown Court. The categories are as follows.

D23.19 **Homicide Cases** The MCA 1980, s. 24(1A) and (1B), require juveniles to be sent for trial in the Crown Court in homicide cases. The term 'homicide' is not defined but obviously includes murder and manslaughter; however, it does not include causing death by dangerous driving, as that offence falls within the ambit of the PCC(S)A 2000, s. 91 (see **D23.21**). Under the DVCVA 2004, s. 6(5), an offence under s. 5 of that Act (causing or allowing the death of a child or vulnerable adult) is an offence of homicide for the purposes of the MCA 1980, s. 24. Where a juvenile is charged with homicide, there is no determination of mode of trial, since the case has to be sent to the Crown Court. Until they are abolished, that sending is achieved through committal proceedings. When the relevant provisions of the CJA 2003 come into force, the case will be sent to the Crown Court under the CDA 1998, s. 51A(3)(a).

D23.20 **Firearms Offences** Under the MCA 1980, s. 24(1) and (1B), a juvenile must be sent to the Crown Court for trial on any charge where, if convicted, he would be subject to the mandatory minimum sentence under the Firearms Act 1968, s. 51 (see **E6.6**), or where he is charged with an offence to which the VCRA 2006, s. 29(3), would apply if he were convicted. In such circumstances, he has to be sent to the Crown Court (through committal proceedings until the CDA 1998, s 51A(3)(a), becomes applicable), and so there is no determination of mode of trial.

Cases Falling within the PCC(S)A 2000, s. 91 ('grave crimes')

The MCA 1980, s. 24(1)(a), must be read in conjunction with the PCC(S)A 2000, s. 91, which provides for the punishment of juveniles convicted on indictment of certain serious offences, sometimes referred to as 'grave' crimes. Section 91, which empowers the Crown Court to order that a juvenile be detained for a period not exceeding the maximum sentence of imprisonment which may be imposed on an adult offender for the offence in question, applies only in the following cases: **D23.21**

(a) where a juvenile who has attained the age of 10 is convicted of an offence which carries at least 14 years' imprisonment in the case of an adult offender;
(b) where a juvenile who has attained the age of 10 is convicted of an offence under the Sexual Offences Act 2003, ss. 3, 13, 25 or 26;

This provision is necessary because of the relatively limited ambit of the normal custodial sentence for young offenders, namely the detention and training order: this order is limited to a total of 24 months (12 months custody followed by 12 months supervision); where the offender has not attained the age of 15, a detention and training order can be made only if he is a 'persistent offender'; the detention and training order is not available where the offender is under 12. In other words, s. 91 achieves two key objectives: (a) it enables the Crown Court to pass a longer term of detention than would otherwise be possible (given the 24-month limit on the duration of the detention and training order); and (b) it enables the Crown Court to impose a term of detention where otherwise no detention would be possible (in the case of an offender under the age of 12, or an offender under the age of 15 who is not a persistent offender).

Scope of s. 91 The power to sentence under s. 91 is currently conditional upon there having been a conviction on indictment. If the allegations against a young person are of such a nature that — in the event of his being convicted — there ought to be the option of sentencing him to a long term of detention under s. 91, MCA 1980, s. 24(1)(a), enables the magistrates in the youth court to decline jurisdiction and to send the case to the Crown Court for trial. At the moment, the transfer to the Crown Court is achieved through committal proceedings, but these will be replaced when the CDA 1998, s 51A(3)(b), comes into force. **D23.22**

In *AM* [1998] 1 WLR 63, the Court of Appeal confirmed that, where a juvenile is charged with more than one offence, and the PCC(S)A 2000, s. 91, applies to one or some, but not all, of those offences, the court may, when considering the seriousness of the offence(s) to which s. 91 applies, consider the seriousness of the combination of all offences, since they are 'associated offences' within the meaning of the PCC(S)A 2000, s. 161(1).

Section 24(1A) of the MCA 1980 (inserted by the CDA 1998, s. 47(6), to confirm the effect of *Stephenson* [1999] 1 Cr App R 1) provides that, where a magistrates' court sends a juvenile to the Crown Court in a case to which the PCC(S)A 2000, s. 91, applies, the court may also send him for trial for any other indictable offence with which he is charged at the same time, even if the other indictable offence is not within the ambit of s. 91, provided that the charges for both offences can properly be joined in the same indictment. This will be the case where the offences are founded on the same facts or form (part of) a series of offences of the same (or a similar) character. In the event of conviction, the Crown Court may order long-term detention only in respect of those offences to which s. 91 applies.

Where a juvenile appears before a youth court charged with a number of offences and is sent to the Crown Court in respect of some (but not all) of them, the youth court is not required to adjourn proceedings in respect of the other offences (MCA 1980, s. 10(3A)).

Deciding Mode of Trial where s. 91 Applies

D23.23 Where the appropriateness of summary trial is canvassed in a case falling within the ambit of the PCC(S)A 2000, s. 91, the court should hear representations from both the prosecution and defence, but *evidence* about the gravity of the offence (as opposed to representations) is not appropriate at this stage (see the observations of the Divisional Court in *South Hackney Juvenile Court, ex parte RB and CB* (1983) 77 Cr App R 294).

It must be emphasised that the juvenile has no right to elect Crown Court trial. Where he is tried is a matter for the magistrates, who will take account of the representations made by the prosecution and defence in coming to their decision.

When a youth court is deciding whether or not to send a juvenile to be tried in the Crown Court in a case where s. 91 applies, the court is entitled to know about any previous findings of guilt recorded against the juvenile (*R (Tullet) v Medway Magistrates' Court* (2003) 167 JP 541).

In *R (W) v Brent Youth Court* (2006) 170 JP 198, the Divisional Court observed that if the youth court is to make a satisfactory decision it must have all the necessary information before it. The facts of the case as alleged, which must be assumed to be true unless manifestly not, should be put accurately before the court. It is the duty of both advocates to ensure that the summary of the facts is scrupulously fair and balanced. The court should also be told of any undisputed mitigation that will be available to the accused including (where applicable) an indication of an intention to plead guilty. The accused's previous record must, said the court, be accurately described.

There have been several recent Divisional Court cases offering guidance to youth court justices on how to decide whether a case to which s. 91 applies should be sent to the Crown Court or tried in the youth court.

In *R (D) v Manchester City Youth Court* [2002] 1 Cr App R (S) 573, Gage J said that the effect of s. 24 is that a magistrates' court should not decline jurisdiction unless the offence and the circumstances surrounding it and the offender are such as to make it 'more than a vague or theoretical possibility that a sentence of detention for a long period may be passed'.

This necessarily means that the justices must take into account the sentencing practice of the Crown Court (and the Court of Appeal) in relation to s. 91. As Stanley Burnton J observed in *R (D) v Sheffield Youth Court* (2003) 167 JP 159, 'in deciding whether it considers that it ought to be possible to sentence a defendant pursuant to s. 91, the youth court must consider the sentencing powers of the Crown Court and the guidance that has been given as to their exercise. If, on the basis of that guidance, there is no real possibility of such a sentence, [sending the juvenile to the Crown Court] is inappropriate'. His lordship added that, in making its decision, the youth court should take into account any undisputed facts put forward as mitigation (such as the good character of the accused). However, contentious mitigation should be ignored: if the case is sent to the Crown Court and the accused convicted, mitigation will be a matter for that court.

In *R (W) v Thetford Youth Court* [2003] 1 Cr App R (S) 323, Gage J said that, where an offence is likely to attract a sentence of less than two years' custody, the appropriate sentence will be a detention and training order. In the case of an offender under 15 who is not a persistent offender, or a child under 12, the most likely sentence will be a non-custodial sentence. It follows that, in most cases, the appropriate place of trial will be the youth court. However, his lordship went on to say that there may be cases where, despite the fact that the offender is under 15 and no detention and training order can be made, the only appropriate sentence is a custodial sentence pursuant to s. 91, possibly for a period of less than two years. However, such cases would rarely call for a sentence pursuant to s. 91, particularly if the court is dealing with an offender under the age of 12. He emphasised that the mere fact that a youth court, unable to make a short detention and training order, considers that the option to pass a short custodial sentence should be available, does not mean that it should decline jurisdiction:

> It seems to me that in such circumstances the fact that a detention and training order is not available indicates that Parliament intended that generally a non-custodial sentence should be passed . . . [C]ases involving offenders under 15 for whom a detention and training order is not available will only rarely attract a period of detention, under s. 91; the more rarely if the offender is under 12.

In *R (C) v Balham Youth Court* [2004] 1 Cr App R (S) 143, Scott Baker LJ (at [33]) adopted a similar view:

> the fact than an offender . . . does not qualify for a detention and training order because he is only 14 and not a persistent offender is not an exceptional circumstance to justify passing a sentence of less than two years under section 91 of the 2000 Act.

He went on to say that the relevant question in that case was whether it was such a serious case that detention above two years would or might realistically be required.

In *R (M and W) v West London Youth Court* [2004] EWHC (Admin) 1144, Leveson J (at [17]) expressed the test in slightly different terms:

> Whether there is a real prospect that a custodial sentence of, or in excess of, 2 years might be required, or is there any unusual feature of this case which might justify a sentence of less than two years, pursuant to section 91(3), for which purpose the absence of a power to impose a detention and training order because the offender is under the age of 15 is not an unusual feature?

In *R (H) v Southampton Youth Court* [2005] 2 Cr App R (S) 171, it was emphasised that offenders under 18, and in particular those under 15, should be tried in the youth court, with Crown Court jurisdiction being reserved for the most serious crimes. It would only be in exceptional cases that an offender aged between 12 and 14 should be sent for trial to the Crown Court. Leveson J summarised the relevant principles as follows (paras. [33]–[35]):

> The general policy of the legislature is that those who are under 18 years of age, and in particular children of under 15 years of age, should, wherever possible, be tried in the youth court. It is that court which is best designed to meet their specific needs. A trial in the Crown Court with the inevitably greater formality and greatly increased number of people involved (including a jury and the public) should be reserved for the most serious cases.
>
> It is a further policy of the legislature that, generally speaking, first-time offenders aged 12 to 14 and all offenders under 12 should not be detained in custody and decisions as to jurisdiction should have regard to the fact that the exceptional power to detain for grave offences should not be used to water down the general principle. Those under 15 will rarely attract a period of detention and, even more rarely, those who are under 12.
>
> In each case the court should ask itself whether there is a real prospect, having regard to his or her age, that this defendant whose case they are considering might require a sentence of, or in excess of, two years or, alternatively, whether although the sentence might be less than two years, there is some unusual feature of the case which justifies declining jurisdiction, bearing in mind that the absence of a power to impose a detention and training order because the defendant is under 15 is not an unusual feature.

If the accused before the youth court is charged with an offence to which s. 91 applies, the only question for the youth court is whether it considers that, if he is found guilty of the offence, it ought to be possible to sentence him pursuant to s. 91. Once it so considers, the youth court has no discretion in the matter. Questions of the suitability of the Crown Court for the trial of the offender are irrelevant to the decision to be made by the youth court. In *Devizes Youth Court, ex parte A* (2000) 164 JP 330, the Divisional Court specifically ruled out the argument that the Crown Court is not a suitable place to deal with a case against a youth, holding that the relevant provisions of international conventions (such as the United Nations' Standard Minimum Rules for the Administration of Juvenile Justice, the United Nations' Convention on the Rights of the Child and the ECHR) affect the way in which the trial is conducted, not the decision as to whether the case is dealt with in the Crown Court or the youth court: if the justices form the judgment that, if the accused is found guilty of the offence, it ought to be possible to sentence him to detention under s. 91, they are bound to send the juvenile to the Crown Court for trial (see the judgment of Brooke LJ at p. 334).

This view seemed to be doubted in *R (W) v Southampton Youth Court* (2003) 1 Cr App R (S) 455, Lord Woolf (sitting with Kay LJ) said (at [16] and [18]):

> While the need to impose the appropriate sentence is important, so is the need to ensure that wherever possible the trial should take place in the appropriate setting. That is more satisfactorily achieved in a youth court than in a Crown Court . . . [J]ustices should start off with a strong presumption against sending young offenders to the Crown Court unless they are satisfied that that is clearly required, notwithstanding the fact that the forum for trial will not be so appropriate as the youth court.

However, in *R (D) v Sheffield Youth Court*, Stanley Burnton J said that he did not think that Lord Woolf intended to suggest that a youth court which considers that it ought to be possible to sentence the accused pursuant to s. 91 nonetheless has a discretion whether or not to commit him to the Crown Court (at [38]):

> If he did, his observation was inconsistent with the decision in *Devizes*, where the point was the basis of its decision, and I should follow *Devizes*. In any event, in my judgment, *Devizes* was correctly decided. Section 24(1) unambiguously requires the youth court to commit to the Crown Court if the conditions for the exercise of the power to commit are satisfied: the words are 'the Court shall commit the accused for trial'. Parliament has decided that the Crown Court is the suitable venue for the trial of persons under the age of 18 if the conditions expressly laid down by section 24(1) are satisfied.

D23.24 **Summary of Approach to be taken in s. 91 Cases** The relevant law was restated in *R (CPS) v Redbridge Youth Court* (2005) 169 JP 393, where the court summarised the legal framework. Although it is not necessary, in order to invoke the PCC(S)A 2000, s. 91, that the crime be one of exceptional gravity, the power to make an order for detention is a long-stop reserved for very serious offences. When considering the MCA 1980, s. 24, the youth court should start with a strong presumption against sending a young defendant to the Crown Court unless it is satisfied that it is clearly required (since the general policy of the legislature is that those under 18 years of age and, in particular, children under 15 years of age, should, wherever possible, be tried in the youth court). It follows that a trial in the Crown Court should be reserved for the most serious cases. A magistrates' court should not decline jurisdiction unless the offence and the circumstances surrounding it and the offender are such as to make it more than a vague or theoretical possibility that a sentence of detention for a long period might be passed under s. 91. Section 91 is primarily applicable to cases of such gravity that the court is or might be considering a sentence of at least two years, and there has to be a real possibility or a real prospect of such a sentence.

Challenging the Decision to Send a Juvenile to the Crown Court

D23.25 The appropriate means of challenging a decision to send a juvenile to the Crown Court is by way of judicial review. In *AH* (2003) 167 JP 30, the accused (who was 14 years old) was charged with robbery. The youth court declined jurisdiction on the ground of insufficient sentencing powers and sent him for trial in the Crown Court under the MCA 1980, s.

24(1)(a). At the start of the trial in the Crown Court, an application to stay the proceedings as an abuse of process was made on the ground that the case should not have been sent for trial. It was held that the appropriate forum for challenging the decision to commit for trial is the Divisional Court (by way of an application for judicial review) rather than by making an abuse of process application in the Crown Court.

It used to be thought that the Divisional Court would apply the well-known *Wednesbury* 'perversity' test to any challenge to a decision to send for trial. However, it is clear from *R (W) v Thetford Youth Court* [2003] 1 Cr App R (S) 323, *R (W) v Southampton Youth Court* [2003] 1 Cr App R (S) 455 and *R (D) v Sheffield Youth Court* (2003) 167 JP 159 that the test is less restrictive than that. As Stanley Burnton J put it in the latter case (at [41]):

> The test to be applied by the High Court on judicial review of a decision of a youth court under section 24(1) is: in the judgment of the High Court, was the decision of the youth court wrong? . . . It is not sufficient for the High Court to consider that it would have made a different decision under section 24(1) to that of the youth court. Only if the High Court is satisfied that the original decision was wrong may it interfere.

Where a youth court intends to send a juvenile to the Crown Court for trial with a view to the imposition of a sentence of detention under the PCC(S)A 2000, s. 91, in the event of conviction, the court should give reasons for its decision (*R (C) v Balham Youth Court* [2004] 1 Cr App R (S) 143).

It should be noted that, even if a juvenile is tried and convicted in the Crown Court, the Crown Court is not obliged to pass a sentence of detention under s. 91. The Crown Court retains the power to deal with the offender in any way that the youth court could have done. It would, however, generally be undesirable for the Crown Court to remit the case to the youth court for sentence under s. 8 of the 2000 Act (see **D23.66**), since the youth court will already have expressed the view that the case is too serious for its powers (see *Allen* (1999) 163 JP 841).

Challenging a Refusal to Send Juvenile to the Crown Court

If the justices refuse to send the juvenile to the Crown Court in a case where a sentence under **D23.26** s. 91 of the 2000 Act would be available, the procedure to be used to challenge that decision should be an application for judicial review (and not the seeking of a voluntary bill of indictment). In *R (DPP) v Camberwell Youth Court* [2005] 1 WLR 810, the Divisional Court said that, in order that the matter can be dealt with within the sort of time-scale that would be involved in seeking a voluntary bill of indictment, an expedited hearing of the application for judicial review should be sought (by completing Form N463). It follows that if, without adequate explanation, an application for a voluntary bill is made, the court will probably refuse consent on the basis that no good reason has been shown to depart from the normal procedure, and the interests of justice do not require it.

Dangerous Offenders The CDA 1998, s. 51(3)(d) (in force from April 2005), stipulates **D23.27** that where the offence is a 'specified offence' (within the meaning of the CJA 2003, s. 224) and it appears to the court that if a juvenile is found guilty of the offence the criteria for the imposition of a sentence under s. 226(3) or s. 228(2) of that Act would be met, the court shall send him forthwith to the Crown Court for trial for that offence. This is a 'sending' under s. 51A, and so there are no committal proceedings.

Offences that come within the definition of 'specified' offences for these purposes are listed in sch. 15 of the 2003 Act. The 'public protection' provisions of the CJA 2003 (ss. 226 and 228 in the case of juveniles) come into play where the court takes the view 'that there is a significant risk to members of the public of serious harm occasioned by the commission by the offender of further specified offences'. If the Crown Court were to come to that view and the specified offence is a 'serious' one (i.e. punishable with a life sentence or a determinate sentence of at least 10 years), the court would have to impose a life sentence if the seriousness of the offence so merits (if the offence carries custody for life) or an indeterminate sentence of detention for public protection (if the offence does not carry custody for life and an extended sentence under s. 228 would not be adequate to protect the public). Where the offence is a 'specified offence' but not a 'serious' one (i.e. it carries less than 10 years' imprisonment), the Crown Court is required to impose an extended sentence so that the juvenile is under licence, following his release from custody, for an extended period for the purpose of protecting members of the public from serious harm occasioned by the commission by him of further specified offences. These sentences are considered in more detail in **E5**.

It follows that where a juvenile is charged with a 'specified' offence, the youth court has to consider whether the Crown Court would take the view 'that there is a significant risk to members of the public of serious harm occasioned by the commission by the offender of further specified offences' and would go on to impose a sentence under s. 226 or s. 228, as the case may be. In *Lang* [2006] 1 WLR 2509, Rose LJ at [17(iv)] pointed out that 'if the foreseen specified offence is not serious, there will be comparatively few cases in which a risk of serious harm will properly be regarded as significant'.

It should be noted that, if the youth court tries a 'specified' offence, it retains the power to commit the juvenile to the Crown Court for sentence if the justices decide at that stage that the criteria for the imposition of a sentence for public protection or an extended sentence (as the case may be) appear to be satisfied (see the PCC(S)A 2000, s. 3C, discussed at **D23.40**).

In *R (DPP) v East Surrey Youth Court (Ghanbari, interested party)* [2006] 1 WLR 2543, the Divisional Court considered the guidance on the dangerous offender provisions of the CJA 2003, ss. 224 to 229, given by the Court of Appeal in *Lang*, and went on to highlight the need, in relation to those under 18, to be 'particularly rigorous before concluding that there is a significant risk of serious harm by the commission of further offences': such a conclusion is unlikely to be appropriate in the absence of a pre-sentence report following assessment by a young offender team. In most cases where a non-serious specified offence is charged, an assessment of dangerousness will not be appropriate until after conviction, when, if the dangerousness criteria are met, the accused can be committed to the Crown Court for sentence (per Rose LJ at [17]). The advice given by Laws LJ in *R (B) v Barking Youth Court* [2006] EWHC 2121 (Admin), that 'those advising young offenders should make shift to obtain material by which the magistrates may be informed of the degree of their client's dangerousness on the first occasion of his appearance before the court' (para. 11) would seem to conflict with *Lang* on this point. It is submitted that the view of the Court of Appeal in *Lang* is to be preferred.

The CPS guidance on 'youth offenders' suggests that there will be few cases in which it will be appropriate to exercise the power conferred by the CDA 1998, s. 51(3)(d), and that such power should be exercised only where there is there is sufficient information (which will usually include a risk assessment in a recent pre-sentence report, about the nature and circumstances of the offender, the offence and any pattern of behaviour of which the offence forms part, to enable the court to assess the offender as dangerous), and it is in the interests of justice for the youth to be tried on indictment. The guidance goes on to say that 'prosecutors should usually recommend summary trial on the basis that the youth court is the appropriate tribunal for youth trials' and that trial on indictment is unnecessary as the youth can be committed for sentence under the PCC(S)A 2000, s. 3C, if, having heard all the facts about the offence and the offender, the court decides that a sentence under the dangerousness provisions may be necessary. On this basis, sending a juvenile to the Crown Court for trial is described as an 'exceptional' course of action.

The provisions on committal for sentence are considered in more detail below (at **D23.38** *et seq.*).

Where Juvenile is Charged with an Adult

The MCA 1980, s. 24(1)(b), provides that a juvenile may be sent to the Crown Court to be tried jointly with an adult if: **D23.28**

(a) the juvenile is jointly charged with the adult (in practice, this will include cases where one is alleged to have aided and abetted the other, since both will usually be charged as principal offenders); and
(b) the adult is going to be tried in the Crown Court (either because the offence is triable only on indictment in the case of an adult, or else the mode of trial hearing resulted in a decision in favour of trial on indictment rather than summary trial); and
(c) the justices decide that it is 'necessary in the interests of justice' that the juvenile and the adult should both be sent to the Crown Court for trial.

Where one offender is charged with taking a conveyance without the owner's consent and another is charged with allowing himself to be carried in a conveyance which has been taken without the owner's consent, although these are in reality separate offences, they are to be regarded as jointly charged for the purposes of the MCA 1980, s. 24(1)(b): *Peterborough Justices, ex parte Allgood* (1995) 159 JP 627.

Determining Mode of Trial The juvenile has no right to elect Crown Court trial, as it is up to the magistrates to decide where he will be tried. The court will invite representations from the prosecution and defence on the issue of whether or not it is 'necessary in the interests of justice' to send the juvenile to the Crown Court. **D23.29**

In coming to their decision on this question, the justices have to balance what may well be conflicting interests. On one hand, it is desirable that there should be a joint trial (to avoid prosecution witnesses having to give their evidence twice, to avoid the risk of inconsistent verdicts, and to avoid the risk of disparity in the sentences which are passed in the event of conviction). On the other hand, a juvenile may well find appearing in the Crown Court an unduly traumatic experience. It is submitted that the younger the juvenile and the less serious the charge, the more reluctant the justices should be to send the juvenile to the Crown Court. Also relevant are the likely plea of the juvenile and the degree of his involvement in the offence: if the juvenile is likely to plead guilty and it is accepted by the prosecution that he played only a minor role in the offence, it is likely to be more appropriate to deal with him separately.

In *R (DPP) v East Surrey Youth Court (Ghanbari, interested party)* [2006] 1 WLR 2543, the Divisional Court said that, when deciding whether or not to send a juvenile for trial in the Crown Court, justices should bear in mind the policy of the legislature is that those who are under 18 should, wherever possible, be tried in a youth court, which is designed for their specific needs. When an accused under the age of 18 is jointly charged with an adult, an exercise of judgement is called for by the youth court when assessing the competing presumptions in favour of (i) joint trial of those jointly charged, and (ii) the trial of young defendants in the youth court. Factors relevant to that judgement will include the age and maturity of the young defendant, the comparative culpability in relation to the offence and the previous convictions of the two and whether the trial can be severed without either injustice or undue inconvenience to witnesses (per Rose LJ at [17]).

The Draft Guidelines on allocation issued by the Sentencing Guidelines Council in February 2006 make the point that, where one or more of the defendants is a juvenile, any presumption in favour of sending the juvenile to the Crown Court to be tried jointly with an adult who is being sent there must be balanced with the general presumption that young defendants should be dealt with in a youth court. The Draft Guidelines give examples of factors that should be considered when deciding whether to separate the youth and adult defendants:

(a) the young age of the offender, particularly where the age gap between the adult and youth offender is substantial;
(b) the immaturity and intellect of the youth;
(c) the relative culpability of the youth compared with the adult and whether or not the role played by the youth was minor;
(d) lack of previous convictions on the part of the youth compared with the adult offender;
(e) whether the trial of the adult and youth can be severed without inconvenience to witnesses or injustice to the case as a whole.

Similar points are made in the CPS guidance on 'youth offenders', where the relevant factors are said to include:

(a) the respective ages of the adult and youth;
(b) the respective roles of the youth and adult in the commission of the offence;
(c) the likely plea;
(d) whether there are existing charges against the youth before the youth court;
(e) the need to deal with the youth as expeditiously as possible consistent with the interests of justice; and
(f) the likely sentence upon conviction.

In *R (W) v Brent Youth Court* (2006) 170 JP 198, Smith LJ considered how to approach the case where there are several defendants (at [9]):

> Where several defendants are charged together I would stress the need . . . for the court to consider the position of each defendant separately. Where all the defendants are under the age of 18 there is no power to commit a young person to the Crown Court in the interests of justice, as there is where one defendant is over the age of 18 and must be committed to the Crown Court. If all are under 18, the court must make an appropriate decision for each defendant, even if this results in one defendant being tried in the youth court and others in the Crown Court.

Normally, s. 24(1)(b) will be relevant where a juvenile and an adult appear together in an adult magistrates' court. However, in *Coventry City Magistrates, ex parte M* [1992] Crim LR 810, it was held that the power to send a juvenile for trial in the Crown Court under s. 24(1)(b) is not confined to an adult magistrates' court in which the adult and the juvenile appear together. A youth court can also exercise this power in a case where a juvenile before it is to be jointly indicted with an adult who has already been sent for trial by an adult magistrates' court.

D23.30 **Procedure where Juvenile is Not Sent with Adult to the Crown Court for Trial** If the justices decide that it is not necessary in the interests of justice to send the juvenile to the Crown Court, even though the adult co-accused is to be tried by the Crown Court, the charge will be put to the juvenile in the adult magistrates' court and a plea taken from him. If the juvenile pleads guilty, the magistrates will consider whether their sentencing powers in respect of the juvenile are adequate. Those powers are to make any one or more of the following orders:

(a) absolute discharge;
(b) conditional discharge;
(c) a fine (up to £1,000 for a juvenile who has attained the age of 14; up to £250 for one who has not: PCC(S)A 2000, s. 135);
(d) requiring the juvenile's parents to enter into a recognisance to keep proper control of him.

If these powers, which are contained in the PCC(S)A 2000, s. 8(8), are not sufficient, the justices will remit the juvenile to the youth court to be sentenced (under PCC(S)A 2000, s. 8(6)).

If the juvenile pleads not guilty, the adult magistrates' court may try him (under MCA 1980, s. 29(2)); however, in the absence of a good reason to the contrary (for example, the prosecution wishing to offer no evidence), it is submitted that he should normally be remitted to the youth court for trial.

Procedure where Adult Co-accused is Tried Summarily Where the juvenile is jointly charged with an adult who is to be tried summarily (i.e. the offence is a summary one or an either-way offence where the adult defendant and the justices both agree to summary trial), the procedure is as follows. If the adult pleads not guilty, the court will ask the juvenile to enter a plea. If the juvenile pleads not guilty, the adult court *must* try him (CYPA 1933, s. 46(1)(a)). If he pleads or is found guilty, the magistrates will remit him to the youth court for sentence if the sentences which the adult court can impose (see **D23.30**) are inappropriate. If the adult pleads guilty and the juvenile pleads not guilty, the adult magistrates' court *may* try him under the MCA 1980, s. 29(2), or remit him to the youth court for trial. Although the magistrates could theoretically try the juvenile (even though the adult has pleaded guilty, so that there will be no trial of the adult), it is much more likely that they will remit him to the youth court for trial. There is little justification for trying a juvenile on his own in the adult magistrates' court. If the juvenile pleads guilty (or the adult court does try him and he is found guilty), the adult court will remit him to the youth court if none of the sentences which the adult court can impose are appropriate. **D23.31**

Where the juvenile is charged with aiding and abetting the adult or the adult is charged with aiding and abetting the juvenile, the adult magistrates' court has a discretion to try them both if they both plead not guilty (CYPA 1933, s. 46(1)(b); CYPA 1963, s. 18(a)). If the adult and juvenile are charged with offences which arise out of the same circumstances and both plead not guilty, the adult magistrates' court may either try the juvenile or remit him to the youth court for trial (CYPA 1963, s. 18(b)). If the adult pleads guilty and the juvenile not guilty, the magistrates are likely to remit the juvenile to the youth court for trial; if the adult magistrates' court tries the juvenile and convicts him, he will be remitted to the youth court for sentence if the magistrates' sentencing powers (see above) are inappropriate.

Where the PCC(S)A 2000, s. 91, Applies There will be cases where a juvenile and an adult are charged with an offence to which the PCC(S)A 2000, s. 91, applies, and so both s. 24(1)(a) and s. 24(1)(b) of the MCA 1980 will be relevant. If the adult is sent to the Crown Court for trial, the question of whether a sentence under s. 91 would be appropriate in the event of the juvenile being convicted of the offence will be highly relevant to the decision whether to send the juvenile to the Crown Court for trial. As both defendants will be appearing in the adult magistrates' court, it will be that court which takes the decision on where the juvenile is to be tried. The adult court has no power to remit the juvenile to the youth court for that court to decide mode of trial (*Tottenham Youth Court, ex parte Fawzy* [1999] 1 WLR 1350). **D23.32**

Severance The *Consolidated Practice Direction*, para. III.30.4, says that if a juvenile is indicted jointly with an adult, the court should consider (at the plea and case management hearing) whether the juvenile should be tried on his own. The court should so order 'unless of the opinion that a joint trial would be in accordance with part 1 of the Criminal Procedure Rules (the overriding objective) and in the interests of justice'. **D23.33**

If the offence with which the adult and juvenile are charged is one which falls within the ambit of the PCC(S)A 2000, s. 91, or the 'dangerous offender' provisions of the CJA 2003, but the court orders that the adult and the juvenile be tried separately, the juvenile would still be tried in the Crown Court (with its procedures modified as appropriate). However, if the offence does not fall within the scope of these provisions, it seems anomalous that the juvenile should still be tried in the Crown Court even though he is being tried separately from the adult. It may be that this is inevitable, as there seems to be no specific statutory power enabling the Crown Court to remit the juvenile to the youth court for trial in such a case.

Varying the Decision on Mode of Trial

D23.34 The court is given power by the MCA 1980, s. 25(5) to (7), to switch during the course of a hearing from committal proceedings to summary trial or vice versa. Subsections (5) to (7) parallel the earlier part of s. 25 which deals with the same situation in the case of adult accused.

In *R (K) v Leeds Youth Court* (2001) 165 JP 694, the Divisional Court held that where the youth court decides to try the case, it is entitled to change its decision if the original decision is no longer appropriate. Circumstances justifying such a decision include a change in circumstances, and instances where new material is adduced. There will also be cases where, as the evidence unfolds, the manner in which it is presented would justify such a decision. However, the summary trial must be in progress, and the prosecution must have commenced its evidence, before a decision to change the mode of trial is made (see *Liverpool Justices, ex parte CPS* (1990) 90 Cr App R 261). It follows from this that it is not possible for the mode of trial to be changed where there has been an unequivocal plea of guilty (see *Herefordshire Youth Court, ex parte J* (1998) *The Times*, 4 May 1998, and also *Dudley Justices, ex parte Gillard* [1986] AC 442 for a decision to that effect in respect of an adult accused).

In *R (H) v Balham Youth Court* [2003] EWHC 3267 (Admin), the Divisional Court confirmed that a youth court has the power under s. 25(7) to reopen its decision as to mode of trial once it has embarked upon committal proceedings, and to switch from committal proceedings to summary trial.

The power to vary the decision as to mode of trial will change significantly when the relevant provisions of the CJA 2003 come into force (see D23.36).

Challenging the Decision to Try a Case Summarily

D23.35 Where the decision of the justices to try the case summarily is alleged to be unreasonable, the appropriate remedy is to seek judicial review (*Inner London Youth Court, ex parte DPP* (1996) 161 JP 178).

Procedures Introduced by the Criminal Justice Act 2003

D23.36 The CDA 1998, s. 51A (to which the MCA 1980, s. 24(1) in its amended form will refer) was brought into force, save in relation to subs. (3)(a) to (c), from 4 April 2005 (see para. 29 of sch. 1 to the Criminal Justice Act 2003 (Commencement No. 8 and Transitional and Saving Provisions) Order 2005 (SI 2005 No. 950).

When fully in force, the CDA 1998, s. 51A(2) and (3) (added by the CJA 2003, sch. 3, para. 18), will enable the court to send the juvenile forthwith to the Crown Court for trial where the juvenile is charged with:

(a) homicide, or
(b) a firearms offence where there is a mandatory minimum sentence (Firearms Act 1968, s. 51A), or
(c) an offence to which the provisions of the PCC(S)A 2000, s. 91, apply and the court considers that it ought to be possible to sentence the juvenile to detention under that section in the event of his being convicted of the offence, or
(d) the offence is a 'specified' offence (under the CJA 2003, s. 224) and it appears to the court that, if he is found guilty of the offence, the criteria for the imposition of a sentence

under the CJA 2003, s. 226 (detention for life or detention for public protection for serious offences), or s. 228 (extended sentence for certain violent or sexual offences) would be met.

For these purposes, the term 'homicide' includes an offence under the DVCVA 2004, s. 5 (causing or allowing the death of a child or vulnerable adult) (see s. 6(5) of that Act). The procedure also applies where notice has been given to the court under the CDA 1998, s. 51B (serious or complex fraud cases) or s. 51C (certain cases involving child witnesses). The CDA 1998, s. 51A(4), enables linked offences to be transferred to the Crown Court at the same time (if the linked offence is a summary one, it can only be sent to the Crown Court if it is punishable with imprisonment or disqualification from driving). The functions of the court under s. 51A can be exercised by a single justice (s. 51A(11)).

Where the juvenile is charged jointly with an adult who has been sent for trial for the same or a related offence, the court shall, if it considers it necessary in the interests of justice to do so, send the juvenile forthwith to the Crown Court for trial for the indictable offence (and any related offences, though if a related offence is a summary offence this provision will apply only if it is punishable with imprisonment or involves obligatory or discretionary disqualification from driving) (CDA 1998, s. 51(7) and (8)).

Matters are made rather complicated by the fact that only parts of the CDA 1998, s.51A, are in force. However, the position may be summarised thus: at the time of writing, only offences which fall under the 'dangerous offender' provisions of the CJA 2003 are sent to the Crown Court under s. 51A; homicide, offences to which the Firearms Act 1968, s. 51A, applies, and offences falling under the PCC(S)A 2000, s. 91, are sent to the Crown Court by means of committal proceedings. When s. 51A is brought fully into force, all such offences will be sent to the Crown Court under s. 51A.

Crime and Disorder Act 1998, s. 51A

(1) This section is subject to sections 24A and 24B of the Magistrates' Courts Act 1980 (which provide for certain offences involving children or young persons to be tried summarily).

(2) Where a child or young person appears or is brought before a magistrates' court ('the court') charged with an offence and any of the conditions mentioned in subsection (3) below is satisfied, the court shall send him forthwith to the Crown Court for trial for the offence.

(3) Those conditions are—

(a) that the offence falls within subsection (12) below;

(b) that the offence is such as is mentioned in subsection (1) of section 91 of the Powers of Criminal Courts (Sentencing) Act 2000 (other than one mentioned in paragraph (d) below in relation to which it appears to the court as mentioned there) and the court considers that if he is found guilty of the offence it ought to be possible to sentence him in pursuance of subsection (3) of that section;

(c) that notice is given to the court under section 51B or 51C below in respect of the offence;

(d) that the offence is a specified offence (within the meaning of section 224 of the Criminal Justice Act 2003) and it appears to the court that if he is found guilty of the offence the criteria for the imposition of a sentence under section 226(3) or 228(2) of that Act would be met.

(4) Where the court sends a child or young person for trial under subsection (2) above, it may at the same time send him to the Crown Court for trial for any indictable or summary offence with which he is charged and which—

(a) (if it is an indictable offence) appears to the court to be related to the offence mentioned in subsection (2) above; or

(b) (if it is a summary offence) appears to the court to be related to the offence mentioned in subsection (2) above or to the indictable offence, and which fulfils the requisite condition (as defined in subsection (9) below).

(5) Where a child or young person who has been sent for trial under subsection (2) above subsequently appears or is brought before a magistrates' court charged with an indictable or summary offence which—

(a) appears to the court to be related to the offence mentioned in subsection (2) above; and
(b) (in the case of a summary offence) fulfils the requisite condition,

the court may send him forthwith to the Crown Court for trial for the indictable or summary offence.

(6) Where—

(a) the court sends a child or young person ('C') for trial under subsection (2) or (4) above; and
(b) an adult appears or is brought before the court on the same or a subsequent occasion charged jointly with C with an either-way offence for which C is sent for trial under subsection (2) or (4) above, or an either-way offence which appears to the court to be related to that offence,

the court shall where it is the same occasion, and may where it is a subsequent occasion, send the adult forthwith to the Crown Court for trial for the either-way offence.

(7) Where the court sends an adult for trial under subsection (6) above, it shall at the same time send him to the Crown Court for trial for any either-way or summary offence with which he is charged and which—

(a) (if it is an either-way offence) appears to the court to be related to the offence for which he was sent for trial; and
(b) (if it is a summary offence) appears to the court to be related to the offence for which he was sent for trial or to the either-way offence, and which fulfils the requisite condition.

(8) The trial of the information charging any summary offence for which a person is sent for trial under this section shall be treated as if the court had adjourned it under section 10 of the 1980 Act and had not fixed the time and place for its resumption.

(9) A summary offence fulfils the requisite condition if it is punishable with imprisonment or involves obligatory or discretionary disqualification from driving.

(10) In the case of a child or young person charged with an offence—

(a) if the offence satisfies any of the conditions in subsection (3) above, the offence shall be dealt with under subsection (2) above and not under any other provision of this section or section 51 above;
(b) subject to paragraph (a) above, if the offence is one in respect of which the requirements of subsection (7) of section 51 above for sending the child or young person to the Crown Court are satisfied, the offence shall be dealt with under that subsection and not under any other provision of this section or section 51 above.

(11) The functions of a magistrates' court under this section, and its related functions under section 51D below, may be discharged by a single justice.

(12) An offence falls within this subsection if—

(a) it is an offence of homicide; or
(b) each of the requirements of section 51A(1) of the Firearms Act 1968 would be satisfied with respect to—
(i) the offence; and
(ii) the person charged with it,
if he were convicted of the offence; or
(c) section 29(3) of the Violent Crime Reduction Act 2006 (minimum sentences in certain cases of using someone to mind a weapon) would apply if he were convicted of the offence.

'Plea before Venue' Procedure for Juveniles

D23.37 The CJA 2003, sch. 3, para. 10, inserts new ss. 24A to 24D into the MCA 1980. The effect of these new sections (which are not yet in force) is to apply a procedure similar to that contained in ss. 17A to 17C of that Act (the 'plea before venue' hearing) to cases involving an accused who is under the age of 18.

The plea before venue procedure set out in s. 24A applies where there is a possibility of the juvenile being tried in the Crown Court, either because he is charged jointly with an adult and the magistrates consider that it is necessary in the interests of justice to send the juvenile to the Crown Court for trial alongside the adult (under the CDA 1998, s. 51(7)), or because the juvenile is charged with an offence to which the PCC(S)A 2000, s. 91, applies and the court considers that, if he is found guilty of the offence, it ought to be possible to sentence him to long-term detention under s. 91 (see the MCA 1980, s. 24A(1)). In those cases, the juvenile is invited to indicate whether he intends to plead guilty or not guilty (s. 24A(6)). If he indicates that he intends to enter a guilty plea, he is deemed to have pleaded guilty at that point (s. 24A(7)). The magistrates then proceed to the sentencing stage; if the offence is one to which the PCC(S)A 2000, s. 91, applies, the magistrates may commit the juvenile to the Crown Court for sentence under the PCC(S)A 2000, s. 3B. If the juvenile indicates a not guilty plea (or gives no indication as to intended plea), the magistrates proceed to determine mode of trial in the usual way (s. 24A(8) and (9)). Thus, if the case is one to which s. 91 of the 2000 Act applies, the magistrates go on to consider whether it ought to be possible to impose a sentence of detention under that section if the juvenile is convicted; if the case is one where the juvenile is charged alongside an adult who is to be tried in the Crown Court, the magistrates consider whether it is necessary in the interests of justice for the juvenile to be sent to the Crown Court for trial as well.

Section 24B enables the plea before venue procedure to be determined in the absence of the juvenile if he is legally represented, and the court considers that, because of the juvenile's disorderly conduct before the court, it is not practicable for proceedings to be conducted in his presence, and the court considers that it should proceed in his absence. In such cases, the legal representative is invited to enter a plea on behalf of the juvenile (and an indication by the representative of an intended guilty plea is deemed to be a plea of guilty under s. 24B(2)(c)).

Proceedings under s. 24A or 24B can be adjourned. Where the accused is present, the adjournment may take the form of a remand, either in custody or on bail (s. 24C). The functions of the magistrates' court under ss. 24A to 24C may be exercised by a single justice (s. 24D(1)).

Magistrates' Courts Act 1980, ss. 24A to 24D

24A.—(1) This section applies where—
  (a) a person under the age of 18 years appears or is brought before a magistrates' court on an information charging him with an offence other than one falling within section 51A(12) of the Crime and Disorder Act 1998 ('the 1998 Act'); and
  (b) but for the application of the following provisions of this section, the court would be required at that stage, by virtue of section 51(7) or (8) or 51A(3)(b), (4) or (5) of the 1998 Act to determine, in relation to the offence, whether to send the person to the Crown Court for trial (or to determine any matter, the effect of which would be to determine whether he is sent to the Crown Court for trial).

(2) Where this section applies, the court shall, before proceeding to make any such determination as is referred to in subsection (1)(b) above (the 'relevant determination'), follow the procedure set out in this section.

(3) Everything that the court is required to do under the following provisions of this section must be done with the accused person in court.

(4) The court shall cause the charge to be written down, if this has not already been done, and to be read to the accused.

(5) The court shall then explain to the accused in ordinary language that he may indicate whether (if the offence were to proceed to trial) he would plead guilty or not guilty, and that if he indicates that he would plead guilty—
  (a) the court must proceed as mentioned in subsection (7) below; and
  (b) (in cases where the offence is one mentioned in section 91(1) of the Powers of Criminal Courts (Sentencing) Act 2000) he may be sent to the Crown Court for sentencing under section 3B or (if applicable) 3C of that Act if the court is of such opinion as is mentioned in subsection (2) of the applicable section.

(6) The court shall then ask the accused whether (if the offence were to proceed to trial) he would plead guilty or not guilty.

(7) If the accused indicates that he would plead guilty, the court shall proceed as if—
  (a) the proceedings constituted from the beginning the summary trial of the information; and
  (b) section 9(1) above was complied with and he pleaded guilty under it,

and, accordingly, the court shall not (and shall not be required to) proceed to make the relevant determination or to proceed further under section 51 or (as the case may be) section 51A of the 1998 Act in relation to the offence.

(8) If the accused indicates that he would plead not guilty, the court shall proceed to make the relevant determination and this section shall cease to apply.

(9) If the accused in fact fails to indicate how he would plead, for the purposes of this section he shall be taken to indicate that he would plead not guilty.

(10) Subject to subsection (7) above, the following shall not for any purpose be taken to constitute the taking of a plea—

(a) asking the accused under this section whether (if the offence were to proceed to trial) he would plead guilty or not guilty;

(b) an indication by the accused under this section of how he would plead.

24B.—(1) This section shall have effect where—

(a) a person under the age of 18 years appears or is brought before a magistrates' court on an information charging him with an offence other than one falling within section 51A(12) of the Crime and Disorder Act 1998;

(b) but for the application of the following provisions of this section, the court would be required at that stage to make one of the determinations referred to in paragraph (b) of section 24A(1) above ('the relevant determination');

(c) the accused is represented by a legal representative;

(d) the court considers that by reason of the accused's disorderly conduct before the court it is not practicable for proceedings under section 24A above to be conducted in his presence; and

(e) the court considers that it should proceed in the absence of the accused.

(2) In such a case—

(a) the court shall cause the charge to be written down, if this has not already been done, and to be read to the representative;

(b) the court shall ask the representative whether (if the offence were to proceed to trial) the accused would plead guilty or not guilty;

(c) if the representative indicates that the accused would plead guilty the court shall proceed as if the proceedings constituted from the beginning the summary trial of the information, and as if section 9(1) above was complied with and the accused pleaded guilty under it;

(d) if the representative indicates that the accused would plead not guilty the court shall proceed to make the relevant determination and this section shall cease to apply.

(3) If the representative in fact fails to indicate how the accused would plead, for the purposes of this section he shall be taken to indicate that the accused would plead not guilty.

(4) Subject to subsection (2)(c) above, the following shall not for any purpose be taken to constitute the taking of a plea—

(a) asking the representative under this section whether (if the offence were to proceed to trial) the accused would plead guilty or not guilty;

(b) an indication by the representative under this section of how the accused would plead.

24C.—(1) A magistrates' court proceeding under section 24A or 24B above may adjourn the proceedings at any time, and on doing so on any occasion when the accused is present may remand the accused.

(2) Where the court remands the accused, the time fixed for the resumption of proceedings shall be that at which he is required to appear or be brought before the court in pursuance of the remand or would be required to be brought before the court but for section 128(3A) below.

24D.—(1) The functions of a magistrates' court under sections 24A to 24C above may be discharged by a single justice.

(2) Subsection (1) above shall not be taken as authorising—

(a) the summary trial of an information (other than a summary trial by virtue of section 24A(7) or 24B(2)(c) above); or

(b) the imposition of a sentence,

by a magistrates' court composed of fewer than two justices.

It should also be noted that the CJA 2003, sch. 3, para. 11(4), repeals the MCA 1980, s. 25(3) to (8) (the power to switch between summary trial and committal proceedings) to reflect the abolition of committal proceedings.

Committal for Sentence and the PCC(S)A 2000, s. 91

At the time of writing, the power to pass a sentence of detention under the PCC(S)A 2000, s. 91, can be exercised by the Crown Court only where the juvenile was convicted on indictment (i.e. where the juvenile either pleaded guilty in the Crown Court or was convicted in that court). However, under the MCA 1980, s. 24A or 24B, where the juvenile is charged with an offence to which the PCC(S)A 2000, s. 91, applies or is charged alongside an adult who is to be tried in the Crown Court, and the juvenile indicates a guilty plea, he will be deemed to have pleaded guilty before the justices. If the offence is one to which the provisions of s. 91 apply, the magistrates will then be empowered by the PCC(S)A 2000, s. 3B (added by CJA 2003, sch. 3, para. 23), to commit the juvenile to the Crown Court for sentence. This power to commit for sentence is available where the court is of the opinion that the offence (or the combination of the offence and one or more offences associated with it) is such that the Crown Court should, in the court's opinion, have power to deal with the offender under s. 91. In such a case, the court may commit the juvenile (in custody or on bail) to the Crown Court for sentence. Section 3B(3) provides that, where a juvenile is committed for sentence under s. 3B(2), s. 6 of the 2000 Act (which enables a magistrates' court to commit the offender to the Crown Court to be dealt with in respect of certain other offences) is applicable. It should be noted that s. 3B does not apply where the young defendant indicates an intention to plead not guilty (or gives no indication) and is convicted after summary trial; in such cases, the youth court must pass sentence itself. **D23.38**

Powers of Criminal Courts (Sentencing) Act 2000, s. 3B

(1) This section applies where—
   (a) a person aged under 18 appears or is brought before a magistrates' court ('the court') on an information charging him with an offence mentioned in subsection (1) of section 91 below ('the offence');
   (b) he or his representative indicates under section 24A or (as the case may be) 24B of the Magistrates' Courts Act 1980 (child or young person to indicate intention as to plea in certain cases) that he would plead guilty if the offence were to proceed to trial; and
   (c) proceeding as if section 9(1) of that Act were complied with and he pleaded guilty under it, the court convicts him of the offence.

(2) If the court is of the opinion that—
   (a) the offence; or
   (b) the combination of the offence and one or more offences associated with it, was such that the Crown Court should, in the court's opinion, have power to deal with the offender as if the provisions of section 91(3) below applied, the court may commit him in custody or on bail to the Crown Court for sentence in accordance with section 5A(1) below.

(3) Where the court commits a person under subsection (2) above, section 6 below (which enables a magistrates' court, where it commits a person under this section in respect of an offence, also to commit him to the Crown Court to be dealt with in respect of certain other offences) shall apply accordingly.

Committal for Sentence: Associated Offences Sent for Trial The CJA 2003, sch. 3, para. 25, inserts a new s. 4A into the PCC(S)A 2000. This section applies where a juvenile is charged with an offence to which s. 91 of the 2000 Act applies and, at the plea before venue hearing, the juvenile indicates an intention to plead guilty to that offence. Under s. 4A(2), if the court has sent the offender to the Crown Court for trial for one or more offences that are related to the s. 91 offence, it may commit him (in custody or on bail) to the Crown Court to be dealt with in respect of the s. 91 offence. Under s. 4A(4), if the magistrates commit the s. 91 offence to the Crown Court for sentence but do not state that, in their opinion, the case is one where it ought to be possible to impose detention under s. 91, the Crown Court cannot impose detention under s. 91 for that offence (and so is limited to the sentences that could be imposed by the youth court). This provision thus mirrors the PCC(S)A 2000, s. 4, which is applicable to adult offenders. **D23.39**

D23.40 **Committal for Sentence: Dangerous Offenders** The PCC(S)A 2000, s. 3C (added by CJA 2003, sch. 3, para. 23, and brought into force on 4 April 2005) enables committal for sentence of dangerous young offenders. Where a juvenile is convicted of an offence specified in the CJA 2003, s. 224, and it appears to the court that the criteria for the imposition of a sentence under s. 226(3) or s. 228(2) (dangerous offenders), would be met, the court must commit the offender (in custody or on bail) to the Crown Court for sentence. The offender can also be committed (under PCC(S)A 2000, s. 6) to be sentenced for other offences that the magistrates would otherwise be dealing with.

The CJA 2003, sch. 3, para. 27, inserts a new s. 5A into the PCC(S)A 2000 (in force, but only in relation to cases committed for sentence under s. 3C, from 4 April 2005). This provides that, where an offender is committed for sentence under s. 3B, 3C or 4A, the Crown Court may deal with the offender in any way in which it could deal with him if he had just been convicted of the offence on indictment. In *Robson* [2007] 1 All ER 506, the Court of Appeal ruled that the Crown Court is required to pass sentence on the basis of the age of the offender at the date of conviction (not the age of appearance before the Crown Court).

Powers of Criminal Courts (Sentencing) Act 2000, ss. 3C, 4A and 5A

3C.—(1) This section applies where on the summary trial of a specified offence a person aged under 18 is convicted of the offence.

(2) If, in relation to the offence, it appears to the court that the criteria for the imposition of a sentence under section 226(3) or 228(2) of the Criminal Justice Act 2003 would be met, the court must commit the offender in custody or on bail to the Crown Court for sentence in accordance with section 5A(1) below.

(3) Where the court commits a person under subsection (2) above, section 6 below (which enables a magistrates' court, where it commits a person under this section in respect of an offence, also to commit him to the Crown Court to be dealt with in respect of certain other offences) shall apply accordingly.

(4) Nothing in this section shall prevent the court from committing a specified offence to the Crown Court for sentence under section 3B above if the provisions of that section are satisfied.

(5) In this section, references to a specified offence are to a specified offence within the meaning of section 224 of the Criminal Justice Act 2003.

4A.—(1) This section applies where—

(a) a person aged under 18 appears or brought before a magistrates' court ('the court') on an information charging him with an offence mentioned in subsection (1) of section 91 below ('the offence');

(b) he or his representative indicates under section 24A or (as the case may be) 24B of the Magistrates' Courts Act 1980 (child or young person to indicate intention as to plea in certain cases) that he would plead guilty if the offence were to proceed to trial; and

(c) proceeding as if section 9(1) of that Act were complied with and he pleaded guilty under it, the court convicts him of the offence.

(2) If the court has sent the offender to the Crown Court for trial for one or more related offences, that is to say one or more offences which, in its opinion, are related to the offence, it may commit him in custody or on bail to the Crown Court to be dealt with in respect of the offence in accordance with section 5A(1) below.

(3) If the power conferred by subsection (2) above is not exercisable but the court is still to determine to, or to determine whether to, send the offender to the Crown Court for trial under section 51 or 51A of the Crime and Disorder Act 1998 for one or more related offences—

(a) it shall adjourn the proceedings relating to the offence until after it has made those determinations; and

(b) if it sends the offender to the Crown Court for trial for one or more related offences, it may then exercise that power.

(4) Where the court—

(a) under subsection (2) above commits the offender to the Crown Court to be dealt with in respect of the offence; and

(b) does not state that, in its opinion, it also has power so to commit him under section 38(2) or, as the case may be, section 3C(2) above,

section 5A(1) below shall not apply unless he is convicted before the Crown Court of one or more of the related offences.

(5) Where section 5A(1) below does not apply, the Crown Court may deal with the offender in respect of the offence in any way in which the magistrates' court could deal with him if it had just convicted him of the offence.

(6) Where the court commits a person under subsection (2) above, section 6 below (which enables a magistrates' court, where it commits a person under this section in respect of an offence, also to commit him to the Crown Court to be dealt with in respect of certain other offences) shall apply accordingly.

(7) Section 4(7) above applies for the purposes of this section as it applies for the purposes of that section.

5A.—(1) Where an offender is committed by a magistrates' court for sentence under section 3B, 3C or 4A above, the Crown Court shall inquire into the circumstances of the case and may deal with the offender in any way in which it could deal with him if he had just been convicted of the offence on indictment before the court.

(2) In relation to committals under section 4A above, subsection (1) above has effect subject to section 4A(4) and (5) above.

Relationship between the PCC(S)A 2000 and Dangerous Offender Provisions

D23.41 The coming into force of s. 3C of the 2000 Act necessitates consideration of the relationship between s. 91 of that Act and the CJA 2003, ss. 226 and 228. If the offence is a 'specified offence' (as defined by the CJA 2003, s. 224(1) — i.e. an offence specified in sch. 15), the youth court must send the juvenile to the Crown Court (under the CDA 1998, s. 51A(3)(d)) if the justices are of the opinion that the Crown Court will take the view that there is a significant risk to members of the public of serious harm occasioned by the commission by the offender of further specified offences. (If the Crown Court takes that view, it must impose an 'extension period' for which the offender is subject to a licence following the end of the custodial term.) If the offence is a 'serious offence' (as defined by s. 224(2) — i.e. an offence specified in sch. 15 and punishable with at least 10 years' imprisonment), the youth court must similarly send the juvenile to the Crown Court for trial (under the CDA 1998, s. 51 A(3)(d)) if the justices are of the opinion that the Crown Court would take the view that there is a significant risk to members of the public of serious harm occasioned by the commission by the offender of further specified offences. (If the Crown Court takes that view, it has to pass a sentence of detention for life.) Thus there are, essentially, three categories of offence:

(a) offences which fall within s. 91 but which are not 'specified offences' under s. 224: the court follows the plea before venue procedure (under the MCA 1980, s. 24A), once it is brought into force, and may commit the juvenile to the Crown Court, under the PCC(S)A 2000, s. 3B, if he indicates a guilty plea.

(b) offences which are 'specified offences' but which do not fall within s. 91: the justices must decide whether it appears to them that the criteria for the imposition of a sentence under the CJA 2003, s. 226 or s. 228, are satisfied. If the justices take the view that the criteria are satisfied, they must send the juvenile to the Crown Court for trial. If the justices take the view that the criteria are not satisfied, they will try the case summarily. If they try the case and convict the juvenile, and decide at that stage that the criteria are, in fact, satisfied (they will, of course, have much more information by that stage), they must commit the juvenile to the Crown Court for sentence under s. 3C(2).

(c) offences that are both 'specified' offences and fall within s. 91: the justices will go through the plea before venue procedure. If the juvenile indicates a guilty plea, he may be committed for sentence either under s. 3B (when in force), on the basis that the justices are of the opinion that the Crown Court should have power to impose detention under s. 91 (a test that depends on the seriousness of the offence), or under s. 3C, on the basis that it appears to the court that the criteria for the imposition of a sentence under s. 226 or s.

228 would be met (a test that depends largely on there being a significant risk of future serious harm). If the juvenile indicates an intention to plead not guilty (or gives no indication), the justices have to decide whether to try the case summarily or to send the juvenile for trial in the Crown Court. If the justices take the view that the Crown Court ought to be able to pass a sentence under s. 91 or that the defendant is likely to satisfy the criteria for a sentence under s. 226 or s. 228, they must send the juvenile for trial in the Crown Court. If the justices decide to try the case themselves and they find the juvenile guilty, they will be able to commit him to the Crown Court for sentence under s. 3C (if they decide, at that stage, that the criteria for a sentence under s. 226 or s. 228 are met) but not under s. 3B (which applies only to guilty pleas). If the juvenile is committed for sentence under s. 3C, the Crown Court has power (under s. 5A) to impose a sentence under s. 91 if it decides that the criteria for a sentence under s. 226 or s. 228 are not in fact met.

MODE OF TRIAL AND PROCEDURE FOR PERSONS CLOSE TO 18TH BIRTHDAY

D23.42 This section deals with the various provisions relevant to persons whose age at the time of proceedings against them places them on the borderline between being a juvenile or an adult (i.e. close to their 18th birthday). Some of the decided cases deal with the situation where the determining event was the accused's 17th birthday, and so it needs to be borne in mind that the coming into force of the CJA 1991, s. 68, made the 18th birthday the watershed at which a juvenile becomes an adult.

Determining Age

D23.43 By the CYPA 1933, s. 99(1), where a person apparently under 18 is brought before a court, the court is to make 'due inquiry' as to his age and must take into account such evidence on the matter as may be forthcoming at the hearing of the case. However, any order or judgment of the court is not to be invalidated by subsequent proof that the person's age was incorrectly stated, and he is deemed for purposes of the 1933 Act to be whatever age he is presumed or declared to be by the court (ibid.). The court is entitled to accept what he (or his parent, if present) says on the matter, although in cases of doubt it may ask for further inquiries to be undertaken. The MCA 1980, s. 150(4), makes similar provision in respect of age-dependent powers granted to magistrates by that Act. For the purposes of the PCC(S)A 2000, a person's age 'shall be deemed to be that which it appears to the court . . . after considering any available evidence' (s. 164(1)).

Children and Young Persons Act 1933, s. 99

(1) Where a person, whether charged with an offence or not, is brought before any court otherwise than for the purposes of giving evidence, and it appears to the court that he is a child or young person, the court shall make due inquiry as to the age of that person, and for that purpose shall take such evidence as may be forthcoming at the hearing of the case, but an order or judgment of the court shall not be invalidated by any subsequent proof that the age of that person has not been correctly stated to the court, and the age presumed or declared by the court to be the age of the person so brought before it shall, for the purposes of this Act, be deemed to be the true age of that person, and, where it appears to the court that the person so brought before it has attained the age of 18 years, that person shall for the purposes of this Act be deemed not to be a child or young person.

[(2) to (4) deal with proof of age of the victim of an offence where the charge alleges that he was a child or young person.]

Magistrates' Courts Act 1980, s. 150

(4) Where the age of any person at any time is material for the purposes of any provision of this Act regulating the powers of a magistrates' court, his age at the material time shall be deemed

to be or to have been that which appears to the court after considering any available evidence to be or to have been his age at that time.

Discovery of True Age during Proceedings

The statutory presumption that an accused who is apparently around the age of 17 or 18 is whatever age he is declared to be by the court prevents judgments or orders of the court (in particular, findings of guilt and sentences) being disturbed should it be discovered after the court is *functus officio* that it was misled as to age. The presumption cannot assist where it emerges during the course of the proceedings that the court's initial view about age was erroneous. However, proviso (c) of the CYPA 1933, s. 46(1), gives an adult magistrates' court which has embarked upon the trial of an accused in the belief that he was an adult a discretion to complete the hearing even if it should appear to the court during the course of the proceedings that he is in fact a juvenile. Conversely, s. 48(1) of the 1933 Act provides that 'A youth court sitting for the purpose of hearing a charge against a person who is believed to be a child or young person may, if it thinks fit to do so, proceed with the hearing and determination of the charge notwithstanding that it is discovered that the person in question is not a child or young person'. **D23.44**

Mode of Trial where the Accused Attains the Age of 18 during Proceedings

Relevant Date In *Islington North Juvenile Court, ex parte Daley* [1983] 1 AC 347, the House of Lords had to consider at what stage of the proceedings an accused charged with an either-way offence must attain the relevant age (then 17, now 18) in order to entitle him to elect to be tried by a jury. Lord Diplock, with whom the other Law Lords agreed, held that 'the only appropriate date at which to determine whether an accused person has attained an age which entitles him to elect to be tried by jury for offences which . . . are triable either way is the date of his appearance before the court on the occasion when the court makes its decision as to the mode of trial'. In *Ex parte Daley*, the accused was 16 when he made his first appearance in the juvenile court (when the case was simply adjourned). By the time he next appeared, he had attained the age of 17 and so had ceased to be a juvenile according to the law at the time. The effect of the decision of the House of Lords was that he was entitled to elect trial by jury, because he became an adult before mode of trial was determined. Thus, in *Nottingham Justices, ex parte Taylor* [1992] QB 557, the accused was aged 16 when he pleaded not guilty to charges of robbery. He attained the age of 17 (and hence, according to the law at the time, became an adult) before the court was ready to try the case. The Divisional Court held that the material date was that at which the mode of trial was determined, when he was still aged 16, and so he had to be tried summarily in the youth court. Similarly, in *Uxbridge Youth Court, ex parte H* (1998) 162 JP 327, the accused was 17 (and so a juvenile) when arrested and charged but, by the time he made his first appearance at the youth court, he had turned 18. The Divisional Court held that the youth court did not have jurisdiction to deal with the accused, since he had attained the age of 18 (and so was an adult) by the time of his first court appearance. **D23.45**

The reference by Lord Diplock in *Ex parte Daley* to the moment when the youth court 'makes its decision as to the mode of trial' is unhelpful to the extent that the only situations in which the court has to choose between summary trial and trial on indictment are when either the juvenile is jointly charged with an adult who is being sent or when the juvenile is charged with an offence which falls within the ambit of the PCC(S)A 2000, s. 91, or the 'dangerous offender' provisions of the CJA 2003. In all other cases, there is no choice, since the juvenile *must* be tried summarily whether the magistrates like it or not (save when homicide is alleged or in the case of the other exceptions (see **D23.19**), in which case he must be tried on indictment). Thus, in the great majority of cases, there is no separate occasion on which mode of trial for a juvenile is determined — he is simply asked to plead guilty or not guilty, and such decision as there is as to mode of trial is implicit in the clerk being allowed to put the charge to him. Therefore, it is submitted that Lord Diplock must be taken as having meant that the right of a person who attains the relevant age during the currency of proceedings against him to be tried on indictment for an indictable offence depends either upon his age when mode of trial is determined, or — if there is no express determination of mode of trial — upon his age when the court is ready for the charge to be put. If he is under that age on the occasion of entering a plea, he had no right to elect trial on indictment, even if the matter is forthwith adjourned for trial at a later date and he attains the age before any evidence is heard.

The corollary of *Ex parte Daley* is that, where the offence charged is triable only on indictment in the case of an adult, an erstwhile juvenile must go to the Crown Court for trial if he is 18 before a plea is taken. In *Vale of Glamorgan Juvenile Justices, ex parte Beattie* (1985) 82 Cr App R 1, the youth court was held to have no power or discretion to proceed summarily on a charge of robbery because, even though the accused was 16 when he first appeared before the court, because he had had his 17th birthday before the court was ready to take a plea (and, according to the law at the time, then became an adult). The Divisional Court held that the material date for determining the mode of trial was the date when the charge was put to him and the proceedings were ready to be commenced.

It must also follow that, in cases where the sequence of events is as in *Ex parte Beattie* but the offence is triable either way, the 'juvenile', if he wants to be dealt with summarily, can only make representations to that effect, the court being entitled to refuse jurisdiction if it considers that the charge is too serious for summary disposal. Moreover, any summary trial would take place in the adult magistrates' court, not the youth court.

Additional Charges after Accused Attains the Age of 18

D23.46 Where an accused against whom proceedings have properly been commenced in the youth court attains the age of 18 and is then charged with an additional matter, the latter charge may not in any circumstances be heard in the youth court (*Chelsea Justices, ex parte DPP* [1963] 1 WLR 1138). That applies regardless of whether the youth court is able to retain jurisdiction over the original charge. Accordingly, in *Chelsea Justices, ex parte DPP*, the Divisional Court issued an order prohibiting the youth court from hearing a charge of attempted murder first preferred when the accused was 17 (and hence, at that time, an adult), even though it arose out of the same facts as a charge of wounding with intent preferred when he was 16.

Deliberate Delay until Accused Becomes 18

D23.47 The position where the prosecution deliberately delays the issue of process, so that the accused is no longer a juvenile when he appears in court, was considered in *Rotherham Justices, ex parte Brough* [1991] Crim LR 522. The prosecution wanted the juvenile to be tried for an offence under s. 18 of the OAPA 1861, which would be triable only on indictment in the case of an adult. In order to avoid any possibility that the youth court might try him, his first court appearance was fixed for a date after his 17th birthday, which at that time was when he became an adult. The Divisional Court held that the accused had not been prejudiced since the delay was under a week, and the justices would probably have sent the case to the Crown Court under the MCA 1980, s. 24(1)(a), anyway. It is submitted that this sort of manipulation of procedure could easily be held to amount to an abuse of process, particularly if there were any evidence of bad faith on the part of the prosecution or if the accused could point to particular prejudice from the delay in instituting proceedings.

TRIAL OF JUVENILES ON INDICTMENT

The procedure for trying a juvenile on indictment is identical to that for trying an adult, subject to necessary modifications, which are discussed below. D23.48

Reporting Restrictions

Under the CYPA 1933, s. 39(1), a court may direct that no newspaper report of proceedings before it shall reveal the name, address, or school, or any particulars calculated to lead to the identification of any juvenile concerned in the proceedings. A direction may also be given that no picture of the juvenile shall be published. Section 39 applies to sound and television broadcasts just as it applies to reports in newspapers (CYPA 1963, s. 57(4)). D23.49

Section 39 applies to any court — Crown Court, adult magistrates' court or civil courts. It is otiose in respect of youth courts, since publicity for such proceedings is governed by s. 49 (see **D23.12**). Under s. 39, the onus is on the court to make an order restricting publicity. If no order is made, the media are at liberty to report the names etc. of juveniles just as they are at liberty to report the names of adults. The protection of the section may be extended not just to a juvenile accused but to any juvenile involved in the proceedings (e.g., as a witness).

Publication of matter in contravention of a direction given under s. 39(1) is a summary offence punishable with a fine of up to £5,000 (s. 39(2)). Where an order under s. 39 is breached, the proper course is for the judge to report the matter so that proceedings for the summary offence created by s. 39 may be taken, not to treat it as a contempt of court (*Tyne Tees Television Ltd* (1997) *The Times*, 20 October 1997).

In *Central Criminal Court, ex parte S* (1999) 163 JP 776, the Divisional Court held that there has to be a good reason for making an order under s. 39 preventing identification of a juvenile who appears before an adult court. The court said that in deciding whether or not to make such an order, the weight which the court should attach to the various factors relevant to the decision might be different at differing stages of the proceedings. For example, after the juvenile has been convicted, it might be appropriate to place greater weight on the interest of the public in knowing the identity of those who have committed serious crimes.

The court has the power to lift the restrictions imposed under s. 39. In *Central Criminal Court, ex parte S*, the Divisional Court declined to follow *Leicester Crown Court, ex parte S* (1992) 94 Cr App R 153 and held that it is not the case that a s. 39 order should be discharged only in rare and exceptional circumstances.

Children and Young Persons Act 1933, s. 39

(1) In relation to any proceedings in any court the court may direct that—
  (a) no newspaper report of the proceedings shall reveal the name, address, or school, or include any particulars calculated to lead to the identification, of any child or young person concerned in the proceedings, either as being the person by or against or in respect of whom the proceedings are taken, or as being a witness therein;
  (b) no picture shall be published in any newspaper as being or including a picture of any child or young person so concerned in the proceedings as aforesaid; except insofar (if at all) as may be permitted by the direction of the court.

(2) Any person who publishes any matter in contravention of any such direction shall on summary conviction be liable in respect of each offence to a fine not exceeding level 5 on the standard scale.

Drafting Orders under the CYPA 1933, s. 39 Orders under s. 39 must be drafted with some care. In *Briffet & Bradshaw v DPP* (2002) 166 JP 841, it was held that a person would be guilty of an offence under s. 39 only if the terms of the order imposing reporting restrictions are clear and unambiguous: the order must leave no doubt in the mind of a reasonable reader as to precisely what it is that is prohibited. The court added that the making of an D23.50

order under s. 39 is justified only if the ECHR, Article 10, is complied with, in the sense that the restriction of free expression is required to meet a pressing social need.

In *R (Gazette Media) v Teeside Crown Court* [2005] EWCA Crim 1983 the Court of Appeal declined an invitation to modify the approach taken in *Southwark Crown Court, ex parte Godwin* [1992] QB 190, where it was held that a court has no power, when making an order under s. 39, to order in terms that the name of a defendant is not to be published in any report of the proceedings, since an order under s. 39 has to be restricted to the terms of the section, either using the words of the section or words to the like effect and no more. Glidewell LJ said that if the inevitable effect of making an order is that it is apparent that some details, including names of defendants, may not be published because publication would breach the order then that is the practical application of the order but it is not a part of the terms of the order itself.

D23.51 **Replacement of s. 39** The YJCEA 1999, s. 45 (not yet in force) repeals s. 39 of the 1933 Act and provides that, in proceedings formerly covered by s. 39 (i.e. proceedings other than in the youth court), the court may direct that no matter relating to the accused or a witness shall, while he is under the age of 18, be included in any publication if it is likely to lead members of the public to identify him as a person concerned in the proceedings (s. 45(3)). The court may make an 'excepting direction', which dispenses, to the extent specified in the direction, with the restrictions imposed by a direction under s. 45(3) if it is satisfied that it is necessary in the interests of justice to do so (s. 45(4)) or if satisfied that the effect of the restrictions is to impose a substantial and unreasonable restriction on the reporting of the proceedings, and that it is in the public interest to remove or relax that restriction (s. 45(5)). The mere fact that the proceedings have been determined or abandoned is not sufficient in itself (ibid.). In deciding whether to impose reporting restrictions or to make an excepting direction, the court must have regard to the welfare of the juvenile in question (s. 45(6)). The restrictions apply to any identifying details, but include (in particular) the juvenile's name and address, the identity of any school or other educational establishment attended by him, the identity of any place of work, and any still or moving picture of him (s. 45(8)).

Attendance of Parent or Guardian

D23.52 The CYPA 1933, s. 34A (power of court to order that the juvenile's parent or guardian attend), applies to proceedings in the Crown Court and adult magistrates' court in the same way as it applies in proceedings in the youth court (see **D23.13**).

Procedure at Trial

D23.53 In *V v UK* (2000) 30 EHRR 121, the European Court of Human Rights scrutinised the procedure adopted for the trial of juveniles in the Crown Court. T and V (both aged 10) abducted Jamie Bulger, aged two, from a shopping precinct, took him on a two-mile journey, battered him to death and left him on a railway line to be run over. The trial took place over three weeks in November 1993, in public, at the Crown Court in Preston. It was preceded and accompanied by massive publicity. Throughout the proceedings, the arrival of the accused was greeted by a hostile crowd. On occasion, attempts were made to attack the vehicles bringing the accused to court. In the court-room, the press benches and public gallery were full. At the opening of the trial, the judge made an order under the CYPA 1933, s. 39, that there should be no publication of the names, addresses or other identifying details of the accused, or publication of their photographs. Nevertheless, the trial took place in the full glare of national and international publicity. At the end of the trial, the accused were found guilty, and the judge modified the reporting restriction order to allow publication of the names of T and V, but no other details.

In due course, T and V appealed to the European Court of Human Rights, on the grounds *inter alia* that their trial in the Crown Court amounted to inhuman and degrading treatment within the meaning of the ECHR, Article 3, and that they had been denied a fair trial under Article 6(1).

The court held (by twelve votes to five) that the trial did not amount to inhuman and degrading treatment contrary to Article 3. It did, however, violate the right to a fair trial under Article 6(1) (this decision was reached by sixteen votes to one). The Court stated that it is essential that a young child charged with a serious offence attracting high levels of media interest should be tried in such a way as to reduce as far as possible any feelings of intimidation. It considered that the formality and ritual of the Crown Court must at times have seemed incomprehensible and intimidating for a child aged 11. It noted that less serious crimes in England and Wales were dealt with in the youth courts, from which the general public is excluded and in which there are automatic reporting restrictions. It laid emphasis upon the blaze of publicity surrounding the trial, and the judge's comments on the effect which this must have had on witnesses. The implication was that this must have been even more traumatic for the accused. There was evidence that certain of the modifications to the courtroom, in particular the raised dock which was designed to enable the accused to see what was going on, had the adverse effect of increasing their sense of discomfort during the trial, since they felt exposed to the scrutiny of the press and public. Further, there was evidence that the post-traumatic stress disorder suffered by the accused, combined with the lack of any therapeutic work since the offence, had limited their ability to instruct lawyers or testify in their own defence. The Court found that they were unable to follow the trial or take decisions in their own best interests. They were therefore unable to participate effectively in the criminal proceedings against them and were, in consequence, denied a fair hearing in breach of Article 6(1). However, it should be emphasised that the Court did not find that trial of juveniles in the Crown Court is necessarily unfair, only that appropriate adaptations to the procedure have to be made to accommodate the needs of the young defendant. To ensure that future Crown Court trials of juveniles are not open to the same criticisms, the *Consolidated Practice Direction* contains detailed guidance on the adaptations that should be made to the trial process (see **D23.57**).

Fairness of Crown Court *per se*

D23.54 In *SC v UK* (2005) 40 EHRR 226, the applicant, who was aged 11 years at the time, challenged the fairness of his Crown Court trial. The European Court held that there had been a breach of the applicant's right to a fair trial. The court said that the right of an accused to effective participation in his criminal trial generally includes not only the right to be present, but also the right to hear and follow the proceedings. In the case of a child, it is essential that he be dealt with in a manner which takes full account of his age, level of maturity and intellectual and emotional capacities, and that steps are taken to promote his ability to understand and participate in the proceedings, including conducting the hearing in such a way as to reduce as far as possible his feelings of intimidation and inhibition. In the present case, two experts had assessed the juvenile as having a very low intellectual level for his age. The court said that it could not conclude that the juvenile was capable of participating effectively in his trial. The court considered that, when the decision is taken to deal with a child who risks not being able to participate effectively because of his young age and limited intellectual capacity, by way of criminal proceedings rather than some other form of disposal directed primarily at determining the child's best interests and those of the community, it is essential that he be tried in a specialist tribunal which is able to give full consideration to and make proper allowance for the handicaps under which he labours, and adapt its procedure accordingly. The trial in this case took place before the Practice Direction came into effect but it is unlikely that the measures in that Practice Direction would have brought about a different result. However, the effect of decision of the European Court would seem to be confined to children whose intellectual level is unusually low.

SC v United Kingdom was considered in *R (P) v West London Youth Court* [2006] 1 WLR

1219, in which the main issue was whether the intellectual capacity of the accused (who was aged 15 but had a mental age of 8) was such that he could not effectively participate in the proceedings. It was held that neither youth nor limited intellectual capacity necessarily leads to a breach of Article 6. What is crucial is whether the tribunal hearing the case (in the instant case, a youth court) is able to adapt its procedures so that the defendant can effectively participate in the proceedings. Scott Baker LJ ruled (at [7]) that the district judge had correctly directed himself that the minimum requirements for a fair trial for the accused were:

(i) he had to understand what he is said to have done wrong;
(ii) the court had to be satisfied that the [juvenile] when he had done wrong by act or omission had the means of knowing that was wrong;
(iii) he had to understand what, if any, defences were available to him;
(iv) he had to have a reasonable opportunity to make relevant representations if he wished;
(v) he had to have the opportunity to consider what representations he wished to make once he had understood the issues involved.

He had therefore to be able to give proper instructions and to participate by way of providing answers to questions and suggesting questions to his lawyers in the circumstances of the trial as they arose.

TRIAL OF JUVENILES IN ADULT MAGISTRATES' COURTS

D23.55 The exceptional circumstances in which a juvenile who is to be tried summarily is tried in an adult magistrates' court rather than a youth court are set out in the CYPA 1933, s. 46, and the CYPA 1963, s. 18. Their effect is as follows:

(a) Where an adult and juvenile are charged jointly with an offence, and both plead not guilty to that offence, the trial must take place in the adult magistrates' court (first proviso to the CYPA 1933, s. 46(1)). If, however, (i) the adult pleads guilty, or (ii) the adult is sent to the Crown Court for trial but the magistrates decide that it is not in the interests of justice for the juvenile to be sent to the Crown Court as well, and the juvenile pleads not guilty, then the juvenile may be remitted to the youth court for trial (by virtue of the MCA 1980, s. 29(2)). Whether to remit the juvenile in these circumstances is a matter for the adult court's discretion, but it is submitted that it would normally be appropriate to remit the juvenile for trial in the youth court.

(b) Where an adult is charged with aiding, abetting, causing, procuring, allowing or permitting a juvenile to commit an offence, and at the same time the juvenile himself is charged with the offence as principal offender, the adult magistrates' court may, in its discretion, hear the charge against the juvenile (second proviso to the CYPA 1933, s. 46(1)). The same applies in the reverse situation (where a juvenile is charged with aiding, abetting etc. an adult: CYPA 1963, s. 18). The normal practice, however, is simply to join aiders and abettors with the principal offender in a single charge, in which event the first proviso to the CYPA 1933, s. 46(1), applies. Thus, the situation envisaged by the second proviso will rarely arise.

(c) Where a juvenile is charged separately from but at the same time as an adult, and the charge against the one arises out of circumstances which are the same as or linked with the charge against the other, then the adult court may try the charge against the juvenile (CYPA 1963, s. 18). It is not entirely clear whether, when referring to a juvenile and adult being charged at the same time, the second proviso to the CYPA 1933, s. 46(2), and the CYPA 1963, s. 18, are referring to the moment when proceedings are commenced or to the time when the accused appear before the court. The latter construction of the sections would appear more sensible.

(d) Where it becomes apparent during the course of proceedings before an adult magistrates' court that an accused who had been thought to be over 18 is in fact a juvenile, the adult court may, if it thinks fit, complete the hearing (third proviso to the CYPA 1933, s. 46(1)).

Similarly, the CYPA 1933, s. 46(1A), provides that, where a plea of guilty by post is received from a person who is in fact a juvenile but the court has no reason to be aware of his true age, then he shall be deemed to be an adult.

It will be noted that in situation (a) the adult magistrates' court is obliged to try both the juvenile and adult together unless the MCA 1980, s. 29, comes into play, whereas in situations (b) to (d), whether to try the juvenile or remit him to the youth court is in the court's discretion. It should also be noted that the fact that a juvenile will ultimately have to be tried before the youth court does not prevent him being brought before an adult court for purposes of a bail application and remand (CYPA 1933, s. 46(2)).

Summary Trial Procedure for Juveniles Tried in an Adult Magistrates' Court

The procedure in an adult magistrates' court when a juvenile is being tried is the same as the procedure for trial of an adult, subject to the application of the CYPA 1933, ss. 34A and 39 (attendance of parent or guardian and order restricting divulgence of juvenile's name etc. in the media). Reference should also be made to the CrimPR, part 38 (see **D23.15 and appendix 1**) which apply equally to trial in a youth court and trial of a juvenile in the adult court. **D23.56**

Where a juvenile is tried in an adult magistrates' court, the automatic reporting restrictions contained in the CYPA 1933, s. 49, do not apply. However, the court has a discretion to impose reporting restrictions under the CYPA 1933, s. 39, to prevent identifying details of the juvenile being published or broadcast (see **D23.49**).

Under the CYPA 1933, s. 34A(1), a parent or guardian must (if the juvenile is under 16), or may (if the juvenile is 16 or 17) be ordered to attend each hearing in the case unless it is unreasonable so to require (see **D23.13**).

Children and Young Persons Act 1933, s. 46

(1) Subject as hereinafter provided, no charge against a child or young person, and no application whereof the hearing is by rules made under this section assigned to youth courts, shall be heard by a magistrates' court which is not a youth court: Provided that—
  (a) a charge made jointly against a child or young person and a person who has attained the age of 18 years shall be heard by a magistrates' court other than a youth court, and
  (b) where a child or young person is charged with an offence, the charge may be heard by a magistrates' court which is not a youth court if a person who has attained the age of 18 years is charged at the same time with aiding, abetting, causing, procuring, allowing or permitting that offence; and
  (c) where in the course of any proceedings before any magistrates' court other than a youth court it appears that the person to whom the proceedings relate is a child or young person, nothing in this subsection shall be construed as preventing the court, if it thinks fit so to do, from proceeding with the hearing and determination of those proceedings.

(1A) If a notification that the accused desires to plead guilty without appearing before the court is received by the designated officer for a court in pursuance of section 12 of the Magistrates' Courts Act 1980 and the court has no reason to believe that the accused is a child or young person, then, if he is a child or young person he shall be deemed to have attained the age of 18 for the purposes of subsection (1) of this section in its application to the proceedings in question.

(2) No direction, whether contained in this or any other Act, that a charge shall be brought before a youth court shall be construed as restricting the powers of any justice or justices to entertain an application for bail or for a remand, and to hear such evidence as may be necessary for that purpose.

Children and Young Persons Act 1963, s. 18

Notwithstanding section 46(1) of [the CYPA 1933] . . . a magistrates' court which is not a youth court may hear an information against a child or young person if he is charged—
  (a) with aiding, abetting, causing, procuring, allowing or permitting an offence with which a person who has attained the age of 18 is charged at the same time; or
  (b) with an offence arising out of circumstances which are the same as or connected with those

giving rise to an offence with which a person who has attained the age of 18 is charged at the same time.

Magistrates' Courts Act 1980, s. 29

(1) Where—

(a) a person under the age of 18 ('the juvenile') appears or is brought before a magistrates' court other than a youth court on an information jointly charging him and one or more other persons with an offence; and

(b) that other person, or any of those other persons, has attained that age,

subsection (2) below shall have effect notwithstanding proviso (a) in section 46(1) of the Children and Young Persons Act 1933 (which would otherwise require the charge against the juvenile to be heard by a magistrates' court other than a youth court).

In the following provisions of this section 'the older accused' means such one or more of the accused as have attained the age of 18.

(2) If—

(a) the court proceeds to the summary trial of the information in the case of both or all of the accused, and the older accused or each of the older accused pleads guilty; or

(b) the court—

(i) in the case of the older accused or each of the older accused, proceeds to inquire into the information as examining justices and either commits him for trial or discharges him; and

(ii) in the case of the juvenile, proceeds to the summary trial of the information,

then, if in either situation the juvenile pleads not guilty, the court may before any evidence is called in his case remit him for trial to a youth court acting for the same place as the remitting court or for the place where he habitually resides.

(3) A person remitted to a youth court under subsection (2) above shall be brought before and tried by a youth court accordingly.

(4) Where a person is so remitted to a youth court—

(a) he shall have no right of appeal against the order of remission; and

(b) the remitting court may give such directions as appear to be necessary with respect to his custody or for his release on bail until he can be brought before the youth court.

(5) The preceding provisions of this section shall apply in relation to a corporation as if it were an individual who has attained the age of 18.

ADAPTATIONS TO NORMAL TRIAL PROCESS FOR VULNERABLE DEFENDANTS

D23.57 The *Consolidated Practice Direction*, para. III.30 (see **appendix** 7), makes detailed provision for the trial of 'vulnerable defendants', which term necessarily includes juveniles. It applies (unlike the original version of these provisions) to proceedings in the Crown Court and in the adult magistrates' court. The stated purpose of the direction is to extend to proceedings in relation to vulnerable defendants in the adult courts procedures analogous to those used in the youth court.

Paragraph III.30.2 says that the adaptations needed will vary according to the age, maturity and development (intellectual, social and emotional) of the accused. However, in all cases involving vulnerable defendants, the overriding principle is that 'all possible steps should be taken to assist a vulnerable defendant to understand and participate in those proceedings. The ordinary trial process should, so far as necessary, be adapted to meet those ends' (para. III.30.3).

Paragraph III.30.4 stipulates that if a young defendant is to be tried jointly with an adult, the court should consider at the plea and case management hearing, or at a case management hearing in a magistrates' court, whether the young defendant should be tried on his own. The court should so order unless of the opinion that a joint trial would be in accordance with the overriding objective and in the interests of justice. If the juvenile is tried jointly with the adult, the court should consider whether any of the modifications to the trial process are required. Possible modifications include:

(a) arranging for the juvenile to visit, out of court hours and before the trial, the court-room in which that hearing is to take place, so that he can familiarise himself with it;
(b) making appropriate reporting restrictions;
(c) ensuring, so far as possible, that all the participants are on the same or almost the same level.;
(d) allowing the juvenile to sit with members of his family and a social worker, and in a place which permits easy, informal communication with his legal representatives;
(e) ensuring that each step of the trial is explained in language that the juvenile can understand;
(f) conducting the trial to a timetable which takes full account of a vulnerable defendant's ability to concentrate, including frequent and regular breaks;
(g) ensuring that the trial is conducted in simple, clear language that the defendant can understand and that cross-examination is conducted by questions that are short and clear;
(h) in the Crown Court, not wearing robes and wigs;
(i) if necessary, restricting attendance by members of the public in the court-room to a small number (e.g., those with an immediate and direct interest in the outcome of the case) and restricting the number of reporters attending in the courtroom to such number as is judged practicable and desirable.

Live Links for Accused

The YJCEA 1999, s. 33A (inserted by the Police and Justice Act 2006, s. 47), enables the court, on application by the accused, to direct that any evidence given by him should be given via live video link. Before giving such a direction, the court must be satisfied that it would be in the interests of justice to do so and, where the accused is under the age of 18, that his ability to participate effectively as a witness is compromised by his level of intelligence or social functioning, and that his ability to participate effectively would be improved by giving evidence via a live link (s. 33A(4)). See **D21.32** for fuller discussion of s. 33A. **D23.58**

The Explanatory Notes that accompany the 2006 Act note that this provision 'is aimed at juvenile defendants with a low level of intelligence or a particular problem in dealing with social situations, and is not intended to operate merely because an accused is a juvenile and is nervous, for example'. Thus, it is not intended that this power should be invoked routinely. This provision applies to all criminal courts, including the youth court, but it is submitted that orders are most likely to be appropriate under s. 33A when the juvenile is being tried in the Crown Court or in an adult magistrates' court.

SENTENCING POWERS AND PROCEDURE IN THE YOUTH COURT

Sentencing Powers Generally

All the sentences and other orders provided for by statute for use in respect of juvenile offenders are at the disposal of the youth court following conviction of a juvenile, with the exception of detention under the PCC(S)A 2000, which is available only to the Crown Court. The general nature and limitations on the use of these sentences are discussed in **Part** E of this work. In brief, the principal sentences are as follows: **D23.59**

(a) detention and training orders (see **E9.10** for details);
(b) fines (see E17) — in the case of juveniles, fines are limited by virtue of the MCA 1980, s. 24(3) and (4), to a maximum of £1,000 in the case of offenders who are aged 14 to 17,

and a maximum of £250 where the offender is aged 10 to 13 (or the maximum specified for the offence, if less);

(c) adult community orders where the offender is aged 16 or 17; youth community orders for offenders aged 10 to 17 (see **E11**);
(d) referral orders and reparation orders (see **E12** and **E13** for details); and
(e) absolute and conditional discharges (see **E14** for details).

The youth court is also empowered to make certain orders against the parents of a juvenile whom it has convicted, namely binding the parents over or making a parenting order (see **E16** for details).

Procedure before Sentence in the Youth Court

D23.60 Part 44 of the CrimPR (see **appendix 1**) makes supplementary provisions about the procedure to be followed before a juvenile is sentenced by the youth court (or an adult magistrates' court). The juvenile, and his parent or guardian, if present, must be given an opportunity to make a statement as to sentence (r. 44.1(2)(a)), and the court is also obliged to consider any available information about the juvenile's general conduct, home environment, school record and medical history (r. 44.1(2)(b)). If the necessary information is not immediately available, the court must consider the desirability of adjourning for inquiries to be made (r. 44.1(2)(c)). Reports from probation officers, local authorities, local education authorities, schools or doctors may be considered without being read aloud (r. 44.1(2)(d)). If the reports are read out, r. 44.1(2)(e) provides that, if the court considers it necessary in the interests of the juvenile, it may require him or his parent or guardian, if present, to withdraw from the court. However, under r. 44.1(3), the court is required to arrange for copies of any written report before the court to be made available to the juvenile's legal representative, to a parent or guardian if present at the hearing, and to the juvenile (unless the court decides that it would be impracticable to disclose the report to the juvenile, having regard to his age and understanding or that it would be undesirable to do so having regard to potential serious harm which might thereby be suffered by him). If the juvenile is not legally represented and a particular report is not made available to him and has been considered by the court without being read aloud, or the juvenile or the parent/guardian has been required to withdraw from the court, then the juvenile must be told 'the substance of any part of the information given to the court bearing on his character or conduct which the court considers to be material to the manner in which the case should be dealt with unless it appears to it impracticable so to do having regard to his age and understanding' (r. 44.1(4)(a)), and the parent/guardian (if present) must be told 'the substance of any part of such information which the court considers to be material as aforesaid and which has reference to his character or conduct or to the character, conduct, home surroundings or health of the relevant minors, and if such a person, having been told the substance of any part of such information, desires to produce further evidence with reference thereto, the court, if it thinks the further evidence would be material, shall adjourn the proceedings for the production thereof and shall, if necessary in the case of a report, require the attendance at the adjourned hearing of the person who made the report' (r. 44.1(4)(b)). Before finally disposing of the case, the court must inform the juvenile and his parent or guardian (if present) of the way it proposes to deal with him, and give them an opportunity to make final representations (r. 44.2(1)). On making its order, the court must explain its nature and effect (r. 44.2(2)).

The court will also receive information about any previous finding of guilt recorded against the juvenile, and details of any reprimands or warnings previously administered by the police.

Preparation of Reports

D23.61 The responsibility for preparing reports on juveniles rests primarily on the local authority in whose area the juvenile resides (CYPA 1969, s. 9), although in the cases of juveniles who have attained the age of 13, the justices or probation and after-care committee for a particular area may direct that the task be undertaken by probation officers (see s. 34(3) of the 1969 Act and SI 1970 No. 1882).

Children and Young Persons Act 1969, s. 9

(1) Where a local authority or a local education authority bring proceedings for an offence alleged to have been committed by a [juvenile] or are notified that any such proceedings are being brought, it shall be the duty of the authority, unless they are of opinion that it is unnecessary to do so, to make such investigations and provide the court before which the proceedings are heard with such information relating to the home surroundings, school record, health and character of the person in respect of whom the proceedings are brought as appear to the authority likely to assist the court.

(2) If the court mentioned in subsection (1) of this section requests the authority aforesaid to make investigations and provide information or to make further investigations and provide further information relating to the matters aforesaid, it shall be the duty of the authority to comply with the request.

Children and Young Persons Act 1969, s. 34

(3) In the case of a person who has attained such age as the Secretary of State may by order specify, an authority shall, without prejudice to subsection (2) of section 9 of this Act, not be required by virtue of subsection (1) of that section to make investigations or provide information which it does not already possess with respect to his home surroundings if, by direction of the justices or local probation board acting for any relevant area, arrangements are in force for information with respect to his home surroundings to be furnished to the court in question by an officer of a local probation board.

Sending to another Youth Court

Instead of itself sentencing a juvenile who pleads or is found guilty before it, a youth court may remit him to the youth court for the area where he habitually resides, which court may then deal with him as if it had just convicted him (PCC(S)A 2000, s. 8(3)). The receiving court also has all the powers of jurisdiction that it would have had in the first place. It can, for example, accept a change of plea during the course of proceedings (*Stratford Youth Court, ex parte Conde* [1997] 1 WLR 113). **D23.62**

Sentencing Powers where Accused Attains the Age of 18 after Finding of Guilt

Children and Young Persons Act 1963, s. 29 **D23.63**

Where proceedings in respect of a young person are begun for an offence and he attains the age of 18 before the conclusion of the proceedings, the court may deal with the case and make any order which it could have made if he had not attained that age.

Prima facie, s. 29 could be interpreted as permitting the youth court to retain jurisdiction to try an indictable offence even where the 'juvenile' attains the age of 18 before mode of trial is determined, provided the proceedings were commenced when he was still 17. In the light of *Islington North Juvenile Court, ex parte Daley* [1983] 1 AC 347 (see **D23.45**), such a broad interpretation is clearly untenable. In *St Albans Juvenile Court, ex parte Goodman* [1981] QB 964, Skinner J accepted the submissions of both counsel that s. 29 applies only to questions of disposal and not to questions of trial. This dictum was referred to with approval by Stephen Brown LJ in *Lewes Juvenile Court, ex parte T* (1984) 149 JP 186.

Section 29 is, however, plainly relevant to sentencing. Thus, where an accused pleads or is found guilty when still a juvenile but attains the age of 18 during an adjournment before sentence, the court may deal with him as if he remained under that age. In *Aldis v DPP* [2002] 2 Cr App R (S) 400, the accused attained the age of 18 before conviction and sentence, and two questions were posed: (a) whether the youth court could impose a detention and training order on a youth who had attained the age of 18 prior to conviction and sentence, and (b) whether the CYPA 1963, s. 29, applied in such situations. It was held that the justices were entitled, pursuant to s. 29, to sentence an offender to a detention and training order even though he had attained the age of 18 prior to the sentencing hearing, provided he was under 18 at the date when the court decided whether they were obliged to try him summarily. In his commentary on this decision, Dr David Thomas (at [2002] Crim LR 434) concludes: '[a]gainst the background of the changes in sentencing powers since 1963, and the language of the current legislation, the reasoning of the court is unconvincing. If Parliament had meant to qualify [the PCC(S)A 2000,] ss. 96 and 100 [detention in a young offenders' institution and detention and training orders, respectively] in the way suggested, it could have done so by express provision, . . . rather than rely on a provision enacted almost 40 years ago in a totally different context'. Nonetheless, the Divisional Court did make the point, not unreasonably, that because the relevant age for determining the type of sentence is the date of conviction, not the date when sentence is passed (see *Danga* [1992] QB 476), the effect of the CYPA 1963, s. 29, is not as anomalous as it may at first seem.

In *Bowker* [2007] EWCA Crim 1608, the Court of Appeal again considered the approach to be taken where an offender who has attained the age of 18 is convicted of an offence committed whilst under the age of 18. The Court emphasised that the principle that his culpability should be judged by reference to his age at the time of the offence is only a starting point. The sentence that would have been imposed at the time of the commission of the offence is a 'powerful' factor, not the sole or determining factor. The sentencer also has to take account of the matters set out in the CJA 2003, s. 142, including deterrence.

Remittal to Adult Magistrates' Court

D23.64 The PCC(S)A 2000, s. 9, gives the youth court a discretionary power to remit a juvenile to an adult magistrates' court once he reaches the age of 18. The adult magistrates' court may then 'deal with the case in any way in which it would have power to deal with it if all proceedings relating to the offence which took place before the youth court had taken place before [the adult court]' (s. 9(2)(b)). There is no right of appeal against the order of remission (s. 9(4)).

In *R (Denny) v Acton Youth Court* [2004] 1 WLR 3051, a 17-year-old was charged with attempted robbery. He entered a plea of not guilty at the youth court. By the time the matter came on for trial and he was found guilty, he was 18. The justices in the youth court adjourned sentence and remitted him to the adult magistrates' court pursuant to s. 9. The Divisional Court held that the order remitting the case to the adult court was unlawful: youth courts should never remit an offender to a magistrates' court for sentence in relation to an offence which, in the case of an adult, is triable only on indictment. The court went on to say that, provided the adult court has not reached the stage of considering sentence, it is possible for the youth court to rescind a remittal to an adult magistrates' court under the MCA 1980, s. 142(1), since a remittal under s. 9 is an 'order made when dealing with an offender'.

It should be noted that the *type* of sentence is generally fixed by the offender's age at the date of conviction (*Danga* [1992] QB 476). This was confirmed in *Robson* [2007] 1 All ER 506, where the accused was aged 17 when he was convicted of sexual assault. The youth court committed him to the Crown Court for sentence under the PCC(S)A 2000, s. 3C. When he appeared for sentencing, he had attained the age of 18. The Court of Appeal held that, as a matter of statutory construction, the age of the offender for the purpose of determining which of the statutory regimes under the CJA 2003, ss. 224 to 236 (dangerous offenders: see E5), applies to him is the offender's age at the date of conviction. The court reached this conclusion on the basis that the relevant provisions refer to cases where 'a person aged 18 or over is *convicted*' and where 'a person aged under 18 is *convicted*'. The use of the word 'convicted', rather than 'sentenced', was held to be determinative of the question of which date is relevant. Where appropriate, however, the court should have regard to the offender's age at the date when the offence was committed when considering the severity of the penalty to impose.

In *Jones* [2004] 1 Cr App R (S) 18, the offender was aged 17 at the time of the offence; however, by the time he was convicted and sentenced, he had attained the age of 18. He was sentenced to 15 months' detention in a young offender's institution. It was held (following *Ghafoor* [2003] 1 Cr App R (S) 84) that, where an offender crossed a relevant age threshold between the date of the commission of the offence and the date of conviction, the starting point for sentence was the sentence which the offender would have been likely to receive if he had been sentenced on the date of the commission of the offence. It is then appropriate to consider other factors, and if there are good reasons to depart from that starting point then that can be done. It follows that the type of sentence is determined by the offender's age at the date of conviction, but the severity of the sentence imposed should take proper account of the offender's age when the offence was committed.

Powers of Criminal Courts (Sentencing) Act 2000, s. 9

(1) Where a person who appears or is brought before a youth court charged with an offence subsequently attains the age of 18, the youth court may, at any time after conviction and before sentence, remit him for sentence to a magistrates' court (other than a youth court).

SENTENCING PROCEDURE AND POWERS IN THE CROWN COURT

Sentencing Powers Generally

The Crown Court has the same powers as the youth court when sentencing a young offender (see **D23.59**) save that: **D23.65**

(a) the Crown Court may impose a sentence of detention under the PCC(S)A 2000, s. 91;
(b) the MCA 1980, s. 24(3) and (4), do not apply to the Crown Court, and so there is no limitation on the maximum amount of a fine that the Crown Court may impose; and
(c) in order to make a referral order (under the PCC(S)A 2000, s. 16) the Crown Court judge would have to act as a district judge under the Courts Act 2003, s. 66, since only magistrates' courts and youth courts are empowered to make such an order).

Remission to the Youth Court

Save in cases of homicide, where a juvenile has been convicted on indictment, the Crown Court 'shall unless satisfied that it would be undesirable to do so', remit the case to a youth court acting for the place where the offender was sent for trial' (PCC(S)A 2000, s. 8(2)). The youth court may then deal with the offender as if he had been tried and found guilty by itself (s. 8(3)). There is no appeal against the order of remission, although the sentence eventually passed by the youth court may be appealed to the Crown Court (or the Divisional Court, if wrong in law) in the usual way (s. 8(5)). When making the order for remission, the Crown Court gives such directions as appear necessary in relation to the granting or withholding of bail (s. 8(4)). **D23.66**

The obligation imposed on the Crown Court by s. 8(2) to remit a juvenile convicted before it to the youth court for sentence 'unless satisfied that it would be undesirable to do so' might seem to be a major fetter on the power of the Crown Court to deal with juveniles. However, s. 8(2) has been interpreted so as to give the Crown Court an almost unfettered discretion to retain the sentencing function for itself if it so wishes, and, in practice, the great majority of juveniles convicted in the Crown Court are also sentenced there. Guidance on the application of s. 8 was given by Lord Lane CJ in *Lewis* (1984) 79 Cr App R 94. His lordship indicated that reasons for *not* remitting include:

(a) that, in a case where the juvenile pleaded not guilty and was convicted, the Crown Court judge who presided at the trial will be better informed about the facts of the offence and general nature of the case than the youth court could hope to be;

(b) that, in a case where an adult and juvenile have been jointly tried on indictment and both convicted, sentencing the juvenile in the Crown Court will avoid the risk of unjustifiable disparity in sentencing that would arise if he were to be remitted to the youth court;

(c) that remitting would cause delay, unnecessary duplication of proceedings and extra expense.

Lord Lane did suggest that it may become desirable to remit the case where a report has to be obtained and the Crown Court judge will be unable to sit when the report becomes available, but added that this situation should be avoided wherever possible. It is submitted that, in virtually any case, the Crown Court will be able to justify a decision not to remit on the basis of one or other of the reasons put forward by Lord Lane.

Cases where the PCC(S)A 2000, s. 91, Applies

D23.67 Where the juvenile was sent to the Crown Court because he was charged with an offence to which the PCC(S)A 2000, s. 91, applies, the Crown Court is not obliged to pass a sentence of detention under s. 91. The Crown Court retains the power to deal with the offender in any way that the youth court could have done. It will generally be undesirable for the Crown Court to remit the case to the youth court for sentence under the PCC(S)A 2000, s. 8(2), since the youth court will already have expressed the view that the case is too serious for its powers (see *Allen* (1999) 163 JP 841).

Powers of Criminal Courts (Sentencing) Act 2000, s. 8

(1) Subsection (2) below applies where a child or young person (that is to say, any person aged under 18) is convicted by or before any court of an offence other than homicide.

(2) The court may and, if it is not a youth court, shall unless satisfied that it would be undesirable to do so, remit the case—

(a) if the offender was sent to the Crown Court for trial under section 51 or 51A of the Crime and Disorder Act 1998, to a youth court acting for the place where he was committed for trial or sent to the Crown Court for trial;

(b) in any other case, to a youth court acting either for the same place as the remitting court or for the place where the offender habitually resides;

but in relation to a magistrates' court other than a youth court this subsection has effect subject to subsection (6) below.

(3) Where a case is remitted under subsection (2) above, the offender shall be brought before a youth court accordingly, and that court may deal with him in any way in which it might have dealt with him if he had been tried and convicted by that court.

(4) A court by which an order remitting a case to a youth court is made under subsection (2) above—

(a) may, subject to section 25 of the Criminal Justice and Public Order Act 1994 (restrictions on granting bail), give such directions as appear to be necessary with respect to the custody of the offender or for his release on bail until he can be brought before the youth court; and

(b) shall cause to be transmitted to the designated officer for the youth court a certificate setting out the nature of the offence and stating—

(i) that the offender has been convicted of the offence; and

(ii) that the case has been remitted for the purpose of being dealt with under the preceding provisions of this section.

(5) Where a case is remitted under subsection (2) above, the offender shall have no right of appeal against the order of remission, but shall have the same right of appeal against any order of the court to which the case is remitted as if he had been convicted by that court.

SENTENCING PROCEDURE AND POWERS IN THE ADULT MAGISTRATES' COURT

The powers of the adult magistrates' court to deal with a juvenile offender are restricted by the PCC(S)A 2000, s. 8(6) to (8). Under s. 8(6), the magistrates must remit the juvenile to the youth court to be sentenced unless the case is one where the court is required by the PCC(S)A 2000, s. 16(2), to refer the offender to a youth offender panel (in which event the court may, but need not, remit the case to the youth court) or where the magistrates' court's very limited sentencing powers are appropriate. Those powers are: **D23.68**

(a) absolute or conditional discharge;
(b) a fine (the maximum fine that an adult magistrates' court may impose on a juvenile is restricted in the same way as the maximum fine that may be imposed by a youth court (see **D23.59**);
(c) binding over the juvenile's parents;
(d) ancillary orders (such as disqualification from driving, endorsement of the driving licence and orders ancillary to the sentence proper such as orders to pay compensation or costs).

Powers of Criminal Courts (Sentencing) Act 2000, s. 8

(6) Without prejudice to the power to remit any case to a youth court which is conferred on a magistrates' court other than a youth court by subsections (1) and (2) above, where such a magistrates' court convicts a child or young person of an offence it must exercise that power unless the case falls within subsection (7) or (8) below.

(7) The case falls within this subsection if the court would, were it not so to remit the case, be required by section 16(2) below to refer the offender to a youth offender panel (in which event the court may, but need not, so remit the case).

(8) The case falls within this subsection if it does not fall within subsection (7) above but the court is of the opinion that the case is one which can properly be dealt with by means of—
(a) an order discharging the offender absolutely or conditionally, or
(b) an order for the payment of a fine, or
(c) an order (under section 150 below) requiring the offender's parent or guardian to enter into a recognizance to take proper care of him and exercise proper control over him,
with or without any order that the court has powers to make when absolutely or conditionally discharging an offender.

Where the juvenile is remitted to the youth court, the remission must be either to the youth court acting for the same place as the remitting court or to the court for the place where the juvenile habitually resides (see s. 8(2)). The remitting court may grant the juvenile bail (s. 8(4)).

Section D24 Anti-social Behaviour Orders

Introduction

D24.1 The Crime and Disorder Act 1998, s. 1, provides for anti-social behaviour orders (usually referred to as ASBOs). An ASBO is an order that 'prohibits the defendant from doing anything described in the order' (CDA 1998, s. 1(4)). Under the CDA 1998, s. 1(6), the prohibitions that may be imposed under an ASBO are those necessary for 'protecting persons (whether relevant persons or persons elsewhere in England and Wales) from further anti-social acts by the defendant'. Detailed guidance on ASBOs may be found in a Home Office document entitled *A Guide to Anti-social Behaviour Orders*, available at <http://www.harassment-law.co.uk/pdf/asbogide.pdf>.

APPLICATIONS FOR ASBOS IN CIVIL PROCEEDINGS

Nature of the Offending Behaviour

D24.2 The CDA 1998, s. 1(1), provides that a 'relevant authority' (see below) may apply for an ASBO if it appears to the authority that two conditions are fulfilled in respect of any person aged 10 or over:

(a) the person has acted 'in an anti-social manner, that is to say, in a manner that caused or was likely to cause harassment, alarm or distress to one or more persons not of the same household as himself' (s. 1(1)(a)); and

(b) 'such an order is necessary to protect relevant persons from further anti-social acts by him' (s. 1(1)(b)).

In *R (Gosport Borough Council) v Fareham Magistrates' Court* [2007)] 1 WLR 634, the Divisional Court held that, in order to show that behaviour 'caused' harassment, alarm or distress within the meaning of s. 1(1)(a), it would probably be necessary for a court to hear evidence from one of the harassed, alarmed or distressed victims. In contrast, the alternative formulation in s. 1(1)(a), 'or was likely to cause', enables police witnesses to demonstrate that there were potential victims present, who it was likely were caused harassment, alarm or distress.

Standard of Proof

D24.3 In *R (McCann) v Crown Court at Manchester* [2003] 1 AC 787, the House of Lords held that applications for ASBOs under the CDA 1998, s. 1, are civil (not criminal) in nature (but see **D24.12**). This is because the defendant is not being convicted of a criminal offence. Indeed, the behaviour which prompts the application for an ASBO need not amount to a criminal offence. Nonetheless, their lordships went on to hold that, although in principle the standard of proof ordinarily applicable in civil proceedings (namely the balance of probabilities) should apply to applications for ASBOs, there are good reasons for applying the higher, criminal, standard when allegations are being made, which, if proved, would have serious consequences for the defendant. It follows that, when applying s. 1(1)(a), the magistrates must be sure that the defendant acted in the manner specified in that provision. In other words, the proceedings are civil in nature but the court must apply the criminal standard of proof.

Under the CDA 1998, s. 1(5), the court has to 'disregard any act of the defendant which he shows was reasonable in the circumstances'. The burden is on the defendant to show this on the balance of probabilities.

'Relevant Authority'

An application for an ASBO may be made only by a 'relevant authority'. This term is defined by s. 1(1A), as including local authorities, the police (including the British Transport Police), social landlords (registered under the Housing Act 1996, s. 1), and housing action trusts (established under the Housing Act 1988, s. 62). The CDA 1998, s. 1A(2), enables the Secretary of State to add to the list of 'relevant authorities' that may apply for anti-social behaviour orders. The Crime and Disorder Act 1998 (Relevant Authorities and Relevant Persons) Order 2006 (SI 2006 No. 2137) adds the Environment Agency and Transport for London to the list of bodies that are 'relevant authorities'. **D24.4**

'Relevant Persons'

The court has to be satisfied that 'relevant persons' are in need of protection by an ASBO. This term is defined by the CDA 1998, s. 1(1B). Essentially, relevant persons are people who are local to the person in respect of whom the order is being sought. Where the applicant is a social landlord or a housing action trust, it means people who are residing in, or who are otherwise on or likely to be on, premises provided or managed by that authority, and people who are, or who are likely to be, in the vicinity of such premises (s. 1(1B)(d)). Where the British Transport Police apply for an ASBO, 'relevant persons' means 'persons who are within or likely to be within a place specified in s. 31(1)(a) to (f) of the Railways and Transport Safety Act 2003 (that is, on the track, on the network, in a station, in a light maintenance depot, on other land used for purposes of or in relation to a railway, on other land in which a person who provides railway services has a freehold or leasehold interest, and throughout Great Britain for a purpose connected to a railway or to anything occurring on or in relation to a railway); or persons who are within or likely to be within such a place'. Where the applicant is the Environment Agency, relevant persons are those on or in the vicinity (or likely to be on or in the vicinity) of land in respect of which the Agency has a statutory function. In the case of Transport for London (TfL), it connotes persons who are on or in the vicinity (or likely to be on or in the vicinity) of land or vehicles used in connection with TfL services. **D24.5**

Application Procedure

The application for an ASBO has to be made to the magistrates' court that serves the area concerned (CDA 1998, s. 1(3)). **D24.6**

In *R (Chief Constable of West Mercia Constabulary) v Boorman* (2005) 169 JP 669, it was held that evidence of events that took place more than six months before an application for an ASBO (i.e. outside the time-limit under the MCA 1980, s. 127, for commencing a prosecution in the case of summary offences) is admissible both for the purposes of proving that a person acted in an anti-social manner during the relevant period and to show that such an order is necessary.

Practice Direction (Magistrates' Courts: Composition) [2006] 1 WLR 636 stipulates that, where there is an application to a magistrates' court for an ASBO (or for an ASBO to be varied or discharged) and the person against whom the order is sought is under 18, the justices constituting the court should normally be qualified to sit in the youth court. However, applications for interim orders under s. 1D (see **D24.10**), including those made without notice, may be listed before justices who are not so qualified. If it is not practicable to constitute a bench in accordance with the direction, in particular where to do so would result in a delayed hearing, para. 3 provides that 'this direction does not apply'.

Where an ASBO is being sought by a local authority, failure by the local authority to consult the person against whom they are seeking the ASBO during the decision-making process is not a breach of that person's rights under Article 6 or 8 of the ECHR, since he can resist the application in court (*Wareham v Purbeck District Council* (2005) 169 JP 217).

In *R (M) v Sheffield Magistrates' Court* [2005] 1 FLR 81, the Divisional Court gave detailed guidance on cases where a local authority applies for an ASBO against a child in its care, to ensure that the interests of the child are protected properly.

It should be noted that the same power to make an ASBO is available to a county court under s. 1B of the Act (see the guidance given by the Court of Appeal in *Moat Housing Group-South Ltd v Harris* [2005] EWCA Civ 287).

Duration

D24.7 An ASBO has effect for the period specified in the order (which must be at least two years) or until further order of the court (CDA 1998, s. 1(7)). Under s. 1(9), except with the consent of both parties, an ASBO cannot be discharged before the end of the period of two years beginning with the date of service of the order. In *R (Lonergan) v Crown Court at Lewes* [2005] 1 WLR 2570, Kay LJ said that, just because the ASBO must run for a minimum of two years, it does not follow that each and every prohibition within a particular order must endure for the life of the order. For example, a curfew for two years in the life of a teenager is a very considerable restriction of freedom. Kay LJ said that in many cases it is likely that either the period of curfew could properly be set at less than the full life of the order or that, in the light of behavioural progress, an application to vary the curfew under s. 1(8) (see below) might well succeed.

Variation or Discharge of an ASBO

D24.8 Subject to the proviso that the order cannot be discharged before two years have elapsed unless both parties consent, s. 1(8) of the CDA 1998 enables the applicant or the defendant to apply to the magistrates' court for the order to be varied or discharged.

Under the Magistrates' Courts (Anti-Social Behaviour Orders) Rules 2002 (SI 2000 No. 2784), r. 6(2), an application to vary or discharge an ASBO must be made in writing to the magistrates' court which made the order, or, in the case of an application under s. 1C, to any magistrates' court in the same area, specifying the reason why the court should vary or discharge the order. If the court considers that there are no grounds upon which it might conclude that the order should be varied or discharged, it may determine the application without a hearing (r. 6(3)). Otherwise, a hearing of the application takes place under r. 6(4).

The period of an ASBO made under s. 1(1) can be extended on an application to vary its terms under s. 1(8) (*Leeds City Council v RG* [2007] EWHC 1612 (Admin)). However, an application to impose more stringent obligations on a defendant can succeed only if the applying authority can put before the justices material which justifies the extension as necessary in order to achieve the statutory objective (and the usual burden and standard of proof apply to the determination of that question). In the case of an application to vary the length of the ASBO, the applying authority has to persuade the court that it is appropriate to do so rather than make an application for a new ASBO. Moreover, there must be a clear rationale for asking for an extension of an ASBO for less than two years, namely that the authority does not consider that it is necessary to have a further period as long as the minimum period of two years.

Appeals

The CDA 1998, s. 4, provides for an appeal to the Crown Court against the making of an ASBO by a magistrates' court. Under s. 4(2), the Crown Court may make 'such orders as may be necessary to give effect to its determination of the appeal'. D24.9

It is also possible to seek judicial review of the making of an ASBO. However, in *R (W) v Acton Youth Court* (2006) 170 JP 31, the Divisional Court held that, in a claim for judicial review, it is not enough for the claimant to demonstrate that there were some errors in procedure, or that the terms of the order can be criticised (since the remedy for such complaints where the order is made by a magistrates' court is by way of appeal to the Crown Court); to succeed in having the order quashed by judicial review the claimant must demonstrate that the process before the magistrates was so flawed that the making of the order amounted to an excess of jurisdiction (per Pitchers J at [26]).

Interim ASBOs

The CDA 1998, s. 1D(2), enables an interim ASBO to be made if the court considers that it is just to do so pending the determination of the main application. The effect of the order is to prohibit the defendant from doing anything described in the order (s. 1D(3)). Under s. 1D(4), an interim order has to be for a fixed period; it may be varied, renewed or discharged; and, if it has not previously ceased to have effect, must cease to have effect on the determination of the main application. D24.10

The Magistrates' Court (Anti-Social Behaviour Orders) Rules 2002 (SI 2002 No. 2784), r. 5(1), provides that an application for an interim ASBO may, with leave of the justices' clerk, be made without notice being given to the defendant. The justices' clerk may grant such leave only if satisfied that it is 'necessary for the application to be made without notice being given to the defendant' (r. 5(2)). In *R (Manchester City Council) v Manchester Justices* (2005) *The Times*, 8 March 2005, the Divisional Court held that, in deciding whether he is satisfied that it is necessary for the application to be made without notice being given to the defendant, the clerk should have regard, *inter alia*, to:

(a) the likely response of the defendant on receiving notice of such an application;
(b) whether such a response was liable to prejudice the complaint having regard to the complainant's vulnerability;
(c) the gravity of the conduct complained of within the scale tackled by ASBOs in general as opposed to the locality of the magistrates' court;
(d) the urgency of the matter;
(e) the nature of the prohibitions sought;
(f) the right of the defendant to know about the proceedings; and
(g) the counterbalancing protections in the defendant's favour, namely (i) the ineffectiveness of the order until served, (ii) the limited period of time for which the order would be effective, and (iii) the defendant's right to apply to vary or discharge the order.

The Court made the point that the test in r. 5(2) is substantially less stringent than the test applied by the justices following the granting of leave.

Where an interim order is granted, the interim order and the application, together with a summons giving a date for the defendant to attend court, must be served on the defendant in person as soon as practicable after the making of the interim order (r. 5(3)).

Under r. 5(4), an interim order made without notice does not take effect until it has been served on the defendant. If it is not served on the defendant within seven days of being made, it ceases to have effect (r. 5(5)). An interim order also ceases to have effect if the application for an ASBO is withdrawn (r. 6(6)).

Under r. 5(7), where the court refuses to make an interim order without notice being given to the defendant it may direct that the application be made on notice.

Rule 5(8) stipulates that, if an interim order is made without notice, and the defendant subsequently applies to the court for the order to be discharged or varied, his application cannot be dismissed without his being given the opportunity to make oral representations to the court.

Given the fact that the defendant can seek a review of the interim ASBO, the power to make an interim order without notice is not inconsistent with the ECHR, Article 6 (see *R (M) v Secretary of State for Constitutional Affairs* [2004] 1 WLR 2298).

The SOCPA, s. 139 (in force from 1 July 2005), extends the ambit of s. 1D to enable interim orders to be made additionally where a request is made by the prosecution for an order under s. 1C (see **D24.11**) or the court is minded to make an order under s. 1C of its own motion. There is thus a power to grant an interim ASBO following conviction, pending a full hearing.

ASBOS FOLLOWING CONVICTION IN CRIMINAL PROCEEDINGS

D24.11 An ASBO may be imposed following a conviction.

Crime and Disorder Act 1998, s. 1C(2)

(2) If the court considers—
  (a) that the offender has acted, at any time since the commencement, in an anti-social manner, that is to say in a manner that caused or was likely to cause harassment, alarm or distress to one or more persons not of the same household as himself, and
  (b) that an order under this section is necessary to protect persons in any place in England and Wales from further anti-social acts by him,

it may make an order which prohibits the offender from doing anything described in the order.

Section 1C(3) stipulates that the court may make such an order either if the prosecutor asks it to do so, or of its own volition.

Section 1C(4) provides that an ASBO can be made only in addition to a sentence imposed in respect of the offence of which the offender has been convicted, or in addition to an order for a conditional discharge.

Section 1C(9A) allows a local authority, where a person subject to an ASBO resides in its area, to prosecute for breach of the ASBO.

The SOCPA 2005, s. 139, amends s. 1C to empower the court to adjourn any proceedings in relation to an order under s. 1C, even after sentencing the offender. If the offender does not appear for any adjourned proceedings, the court may further adjourn the proceedings or (if satisfied that he has had adequate notice of the time and place of the adjourned proceedings) issue a warrant for his arrest.

The SOCPA 2005, s. 140, makes fresh provision for the variation and discharge of ASBOs made under s. 1C through the insertion of a new section, s. 1CA. This provides that the offender, the DPP, or a relevant authority (see **D24.4**), may apply for the order to be varied or discharged. An order under s. 1C cannot be discharged within two years of the date when the order was made unless (if the offender is the applicant) the DPP consents or (if the application is made by the DPP or by a relevant authority) the offender consents. A relevant authority may apply for variation or discharge of the order only (in the case of variation) if the protection of relevant persons from anti-social acts by the person subject to the order would be more appropriately effected by a variation of the order, or (in the case of discharge) if it is no longer necessary to protect relevant persons from anti-social acts by him by means of such an order.

Nature of ASBOs under s. 1C and Evidential Issues

In *C v Sunderland Youth Court* [2004] 1 Cr App R (S) 443, the Divisional Court declined to decide whether proceedings under the CDA 1998, s. 1C, are civil or criminal in nature, holding that, in any event, the court must act fairly and have regard to all relevant considerations. However, in *R (W) v Acton Youth Court* (2006) 170 JP 31, the Court decided that proceedings under s. 1C are civil, not criminal, in nature. It follows that hearsay is admissible (and so the machinery of the Civil Evidence Act 1995, and the Magistrates' Courts (Hearsay Evidence in Civil Proceedings) Rules 1999, is applicable), but the court must consider the weight of the evidence. As Pitchers J put it at [24], the court 'must distinguish between hearsay which, on examination, they find to be cogent and what is more properly to be regarded as unreliable tittle tattle'. In *W and F* [2007] 1 WLR 339, the civil nature of the proceedings was endorsed, as was the admissibility of hearsay. But Aikens J indicated (at [40]) that a court must be satisfied to a criminal standard that the defendant has acted in the anti-social manner alleged. **D24.12**

In *M v DPP* [2007] EWHC 1032 (Admin), the Divisional Court observed that it is wrong to regard the requirements of the Magistrates' Courts (Hearsay Evidence in Civil Proceedings) Rules 1999 as mere formalities. However, where the substance of the evidence has been provided to the defendant's solicitors in sufficient time before the hearing, and there is no prejudice to the defendant, it is open to the justices to hold that it is not in the interests of justice for there to be an adjournment for the serving of a formal notice.

Section 1C(3A) provides that, for the purpose of deciding whether to make an ASBO, the court may consider evidence led by the prosecution and the defence. It is immaterial whether such evidence would have been admissible in the proceedings in which the offender was convicted (s. 1C(3B)).

Use of ASBOs

General guidance in respect of the terms of any ASBO was provided by the Court of Appeal in *P (Shane Tony)* [2004] 2 Cr App R (S) 343. Giving the judgment of the Court, which was presided over by Lord Woolf CJ, Henriques J said (at [34]): **D24.13**

> (1) The test for making an order is one of necessity to protect the public from further anti-social acts by the offender.
> (2) The terms of the order must be precise and capable of being understood by offender.
> (3) The findings of fact giving rise to the making of the order must be recorded.
> (4) The order must be explained to the offender.
> (5) The exact terms of the order must be pronounced in open court and the written order must accurately reflect the order as pronounced.

In *Boness* (2005) 169 JP 621, the Court of Appeal gave detailed guidance on the use of ASBOs:

(1) An ASBO must be precise and capable of being understood by the offender. It follows that the court should ask itself before making an order: 'Are the terms of this order clear so that the offender will know precisely what it is that he is prohibited from doing?' ([20]).

(2) Following a finding that the offender has acted in an anti-social manner (whether or not the act constituted a criminal offence), the test for making an order that prohibits the offender from doing something is one of necessity. Each separate order prohibiting a person from doing a specified thing has to be necessary to protect persons from further anti-social acts by him. Accordingly, any order has to be tailor-made for the individual offender ([29]).

D

Part D Procedure

(3) Given the requirement that the order has to be necessary to protect persons from further anti-social acts by the offender, the purpose of an ASBO is not to punish. It follows that the use of an ASBO to punish an offender is unlawful.

(4) A court should not impose an ASBO as an alternative to prison or other sanction; rather, the court should decide the appropriate sentence and then move on to consider whether an ASBO should be made after sentence has been passed.

(5) It also follows from the requirement that the order has to be necessary to protect persons from further anti-social acts by the offender that the court should not impose an order which prohibits an offender from committing a specified criminal offence, if the sentence which can be passed following conviction for the offence should be a sufficient deterrent. An ASBO should not be used merely to increase the sentence of imprisonment which an offender is liable to receive.

(6) As well as considering whether an order is necessary to protect persons from further anti-social acts by him, the court must ensure that the terms of the order are proportionate, in the sense that they must be commensurate with the risk to be guarded against.

Further guidance on the making of ASBOs under the CDA 1998, s. 1C, was handed down by the Court of Appeal in *W and F* [2007] 1 WLR 339. Aikens J, giving the judgment of the Court, set out (at [40]) a number of rules which are summarised below:

(1) The test of 'necessity' set out in s. 1C(2)(b) requires the exercise of judgement or evaluation; it does not require proof beyond reasonable doubt that the order is 'necessary'.

(2) The findings of fact giving rise to the making of the order must be recorded by the court.

(3) The terms of the order made must be precise and capable of being understood by the offender.

(4) The conditions in the order must be enforceable in the sense that the conditions should allow a breach to be readily identified and capable of being proved. Therefore the conditions should not impose generic prohibitions, but should identify and prohibit the particular type of anti-social behaviour that gives rise to the necessity of an ASBO.

(5) There is power under s. 1C(5) of the CDA 1998 to suspend the starting point of an ASBO until an offender has been released from a custodial sentence. However, where custodial sentences in excess of a few months are passed and the offender is liable to be released on licence and is thus subject to recall, the circumstances in which there would be a demonstrable necessity to make a suspended ASBO, to take effect on release, will be limited. But there might be cases where geographical restraints could supplement licence conditions.

(6) Because the test for making an ASBO and prohibiting an offender from doing something is one of necessity, each separate order prohibiting a person from doing a specified thing must be necessary to protect persons from anti-social behaviour by the offender. Therefore, each order must be specifically fashioned to deal with the offender concerned. The court has to ask: 'is this order necessary to protect persons in any place in England and Wales from further anti-social acts by him?'.

(7) Not all conditions set out in an ASBO have to run for the full term of the ASBO itself. The test must always be what is necessary to deal with the particular anti-social behaviour of the offender and what is proportionate in the circumstances.

(8) The order is there to protect others from anti-social behaviour by the offender. Therefore the court should not impose an order which prohibits an offender from committing specified criminal offences if the sentence which could be passed following conviction (or a guilty plea) for the offence should be a sufficient deterrent.

(9) It is unlawful to make an ASBO as if it were a further sentence or punishment. An ASBO must therefore not be used merely to increase the sentence of imprisonment that the offender is to receive.

In *McGrath* [2005] 2 Cr App R (S) 525, the court said that there is no requirement that the acts prohibited by an ASBO should, by themselves, give rise to harassment, alarm or distress. However, the terms of an ASBO must be clear and commensurate with the risk they seek to guard against, hence not disproportionate. Whether the terms of an ASBO are disproportionate depends on the facts of each case. The court added that it is not appropriate to take account of the fact that it is a matter for the discretion of prosecution whether or not charges are to be preferred for breaching an ASBO: 'a party at risk of a prison sentence should not be left to the discretion of the prosecution as to whether to prefer charges' (per Gross J at [15]).

Breach of the ASBO

The CDA 1998, s. 1(10), provides that if, without reasonable excuse, a person does anything that he is prohibited from doing by an ASBO, he commits an offence. The maximum penalty is six months' imprisonment and/or a fine up to £5,000 following summary conviction, or up to five years' imprisonment and/or an unlimited fine following conviction in the Crown Court. Section 1(11) stipulates that the court cannot grant a conditional discharge when it convicts a defendant under s. 1(10). **D24.14**

The gravity of the breach of an ASBO depends on all the circumstances of the case, including the nature of the conduct giving rise to the breach, and the flagrancy of the breach. For example, the court might take a more serious view of a breach occurring shortly after the imposition of the ASBO, or repetition of the same breach (*Parker v DPP* [2005] EWHC 1485).

In *Tripp* [2005] EWCA Crim 2253, Leveson J added (at [19]) that, where breaches of ASBOs do not involve harassment, alarm or distress, community penalties, rather than custody, should be considered in order to help the offender learn to live within the terms of the ASBO to which he is subject. In those cases when there is no available community penalty, custodial sentences which are necessary to maintain the authority of the court should be kept as short as possible.

In *Stevens* [2006] 2 Cr App R (S) 453, the Court of Appeal had to consider whether it was wrong in principle for a sentence of imprisonment to be imposed in respect of breach of an ASBO, where the conduct amounting to that breach constituted an offence for which the statutory maximum sentence was a fine. The Court held that any sentence for breach of an ASBO has to be proportionate, or 'commensurate'. It follows that, where conduct constituting breach of the ASBO is also a distinct criminal offence, the maximum sentence for that offence is a factor to be borne in mind when considering proportionality. However, the Court of Appeal said that it could not be right for the court's power to be limited to maximum sentence for the criminal offence, since breach of an ASBO is an offence in its own right. Accordingly, it is not wrong in principle for the court to impose a custodial sentence for breach of an ASBO even if the maximum sentence for the 'offence' was a fine (or to pass a prison sentence greater than the maximum for that offence). The Court added that its decision should not be taken to suggest that ASBOs should be imposed as a device to circumvent a maximum penalty for an offence which might be believed to be too modest. That, said the Court, was a distinct issue which relates to the circumstances in which it was proper to make an ASBO in the first place, not to the consequences which follow breach of an order properly made.

Prohibition of Conduct Amounting to an Offence

The question of whether an ASBO may include a term prohibiting the defendant from committing a specific criminal offence (see (8) at **D24.13**) has vexed the Court of Appeal. In **D24.15**

Kirby [2006] 1 Cr App R (S) 151, the offender pleaded guilty to driving offences. The judge imposed an ASBO because it effectively increased the penalty that the court could impose for further similar offences to five years. The Court of Appeal held that the power to make an ASBO should not normally be exercised where the underlying objective is to give the court higher sentencing powers in the event of future similar offending. The court added that the making of an ASBO should not be a normal part of a sentencing process, particularly in cases which do not in themselves specifically involve intimidation, harassment and distress. Rather, it is an exceptional course to be taken in particular circumstances. *Kirby* was approved in *Williams* [2006] 1 Cr App R (S) 305.

In *Morrison* [2006] 1 Cr App R (S) 488, the Court of Appeal held that an ASBO, though it may prohibit conduct which is also a distinct offence, must be justified by reference to the statutory requirements of the CDA 1998, s. 1C(2)(a) and (b). Caution should be exercised in the making of an ASBO if the behaviour in question would, in any event, be a criminal offence; an ASBO should not be made simply for the purpose of increasing the available sentence beyond the maximum which would otherwise be laid down by statute for the conduct which is prohibited. If a breach of an ASBO consists of no more than the commission of an offence for which a maximum penalty is prescribed by statute, it is wrong in principle to pass a sentence for that breach calculated by reference to the five-year maximum for breach of an ASBO. Rather the tariff is determined by the statutory maximum for the offence in question; there may, however, be exceptional cases in which it can properly be said that the vice of the breach of an ASBO, although it amounts to an offence, goes beyond that offence, for example, repeated offences of criminal damage directed against a particular and perhaps vulnerable victim or group of victims (per Hughes J at [19]).

In *Lamb* [2005] EWCA Crim 2487, however, the Court of Appeal said the view expressed in *Morrison* appears to ignore the impact of anti-social behaviour on the wider public which was the purpose of the legislation in the first place and means that anti-social behaviour short of a criminal offence could be more heavily punished than anti-social behaviour that coincidentally was also a criminal offence (per Leveson J at [16]). The court said that the contrary approach in *Tripp* [2005] EWCA Crim 2253 and *Braxton* [2005] 1 Cr App R (S) 167 is to be preferred.

It is submitted that the following principles can be derived from this body of case law:

(i) it is permissible to include in an ASBO a clause which prohibits the offender from committing a specific criminal offence (or which prohibits the offender from engaging in conduct which also amounts to a specific criminal offence);
(ii) however, this should not be done solely in order to increase the penalty which can be imposed on the offender if he commits that offence;
(iii) if the offender breaches that term of the ASBO, the court dealing with the breach should have regard to the maximum penalty applicable for the specific criminal offence but may, if it is just and proportionate to do so, impose a sentence for the breach of the ASBO which exceeds the maximum sentence for the specific criminal offence (subject of course to the maximum sentence available for breach of an ASBO).

Drafting of ASBOs

D24.16 What if the terms of an ASBO are drafted too widely? In *R (W) v DPP* (2005) 169 JP 435, the defendant had been made subject to an ASBO which contained a number of specific clauses and one which prohibited him from committing any criminal offence. He committed an offence of theft during the currency of the order. It was held that the clause of the order restricting the defendant from committing any criminal offence was plainly too wide. It is, said the court, well established that a person subject to a restraining order is entitled to know what he can and cannot do (see *B v Chief Constable of Avon and Somerset Constabulary* [2001]

1 WLR 340). The court went on to hold that the clause in question was plainly invalid and, therefore, unenforceable. In *M v DPP* [2007] EWHC 1032 (Admin), the Divisional Court reiterated that, where a clause is too broad, it cannot stand.

The question of the raising of arguments as to the validity in the context of proceedings for breach (rather than on appeal from the making of the order) was revisited in *DPP v T* [2007] 1 WLR 209. The Divisional Court held that the normal rule in relation to an order of the court is that it must be treated as valid and be obeyed unless and until it is set aside. Even if the order should not have been made in the first place, a person may be liable for any breach of it committed before it is set aside. The person against whom an ASBO is made has a full opportunity to challenge that order on appeal or to apply to vary it; accordingly, insofar as any question does arise as to the validity of such an order, there is no obvious reason why the person against whom the order was made should be allowed to raise that issue as a defence in subsequent breach proceedings rather than by way of appeal against the original order, or possibly an application for judicial review (per Richards LJ at [27] and [34]). Therefore, there are strong arguments in favour of the view that, whichever court makes the order, the order must be treated as valid and must be obeyed unless and until it is set aside or varied on appeal or on an application to vary: during the intervening period it cannot be treated as a nullity and of no legal effect. His lordship went on (at [35]):

> . . . although it is alleged that the relevant provision of the ASBO is unduly wide and uncertain and unnecessary for the purpose of protecting against further anti-social acts, we very much doubt whether that could be said to go to the validity of the order. The magistrates' court plainly had jurisdiction under the Crime and Disorder Act 1998 to make an ASBO. It seems to us that if the court was in error in including a provision in these terms . . . that did not have the consequence of taking the order outside the court's jurisdiction; and if the order was within the court's jurisdiction, it would remain valid even if there were errors in it that were open to correction on appeal. With great respect to the Divisional Court in *R (W)*, we do not accept that because an order is 'plainly too wide' it is also 'plainly invalid'.

Where the court is concerned that one or more of the terms of the ASBO is drafted too widely, Richards LJ indicated (at [37]) that the court may:

> consider whether the relevant provision lacked sufficient clarity to warrant a finding that the respondent's conduct amounted to a breach of the order; whether the lack of clarity provided a reasonable excuse for non-compliance with the order; and whether, if a breach was established, it was appropriate in the circumstances to impose any penalty for the breach.

It is submitted that the careful wording of the judgment of Richards LJ does not entirely rule out the possibility of arguing, in the course of proceedings for alleged breach of an ASBO, that the ASBO is invalid. The Court does, however, appear to be suggesting that complaints about the wording of a particular clause — for example, that it is drafted too widely — are likely to be insufficient to render the clause invalid. It is very clear from this judgment that the Divisional Court wishes to discourage arguments on the validity of the ASBO, or particular clauses thereof, being put forward in proceedings for the breach of that ASBO (rather than on an appeal from the making of the order). It is significant that his lordship suggests that a person subject to an ASBO may have a defence (of reasonable excuse for non-compliance) if a particular clause is not drafted with sufficient precision.

REPORTING RESTRICTIONS

Where the offender is under the age of 18, the CDA 1998, s. 1C(9B) and (9C), removes, in the case of ASBOs made under s. 1C (i.e. following conviction), the automatic reporting restrictions (which would normally apply, pursuant to the CYPA 1933, s. 49 (see **D23.12**), to prevent reporting of the identity of the juvenile), although the court retains a discretion (under s. 39 of the 1933 Act) to apply reporting restrictions. The SOCPA 2005, s. 141, **D24.17** makes the same provision in respect of proceedings for breaches under s. 1(10) of the Act. Under ss. 1(10D) and (10E) of the 1998 Act (inserted by the 2005 Act), the CYPA 1933, s. 49, does not apply to such proceedings, but s. 39 of the 1933 Act does apply (see **D23.49**). (Note that s. 39 is to be replaced by the YJCEA 1999, s. 45, when that section is brought into force.)

Publicity in the context of interim ASBOs was considered by the Divisional Court in *R (K) v Knowsley MBC* (2004) 168 JP 461. The defendant applied for reporting restrictions to be imposed pursuant to s. 39 of the 1933 Act following the making of an interim ASBO. The justices took the view that the public had a legitimate interest in being made aware of the interim ASBO and that, despite concerns for the defendant's welfare and privacy, those interests were outweighed by the interests of the public, and so it was not appropriate to make an order under s. 39. The Divisional Court held that the justices had erred in that they had failed to consider, or to attach any importance to, the interim nature of the proceedings. Although they had quite properly attached weight to the interest of the public in allowing the terms of the interim ASBO to be known, the fact that the order was an interim one and the fact that the authority's allegations were unproven (and might or might not be proven at a full hearing) were matters of importance to be borne in mind on an application for a s. 39 order at the interim stage. The Court made it clear that this does not mean that a s. 39 order should be the norm on an application for an interim ASBO against a minor.

In *R (Stanley, Marshall and Kelly) v Metropolitan Police Commissioner* (2004) 168 JP 623, the Divisional Court gave further guidance on publicity in connection with the making of ASBOs. When questions of publicity arise in such cases, the police and local authorities should recognise that those subject to the orders might have their rights under the ECHR, art. 8(1), infringed; they should consider whether the publicity that is envisaged is necessary and proportionate to the authorities' legitimate aims. Whether publicity is intended to inform, to reassure, to assist in enforcing the existing orders by policing, to inhibit the behaviour of those against whom the orders have been made or to deter others, it is unlikely to be effective unless it includes photographs, names and at least partial addresses. Those responsible for publicity must leave no room for mis-identification. As to the remainder of the content of any publicity, that has to depend upon the facts of the case. If residents have been exposed to criminal behaviour for years and orders have been obtained by reference to that behaviour and in order to bring it to an end, there is no reason why publicity material should not say so. It must not assert that those against whom orders have been made have been convicted of any crime (since ASBO proceedings are civil, not criminal).

See also the guidance on publicity issued in October 2005 by the Home Office and available at <http://www.respect.gov.uk/uploadedFiles/Members_site/Documents_and_images/Enforcement_tools_and_powers/ASBOs_PublicisingGuidance_0032.doc>. This guidance makes the point that, 'each individual case should be judged on its merits as to whether or not to publicise the details of an individual subject to an ASBO' and that the decision-making process should aim to consider and record several key factors:

(a) the need for publicity;
(b) a consideration of the human rights of the public;
(c) a consideration of the human rights of those against whom ASBOs are made;
(d) what the publicity should look like and whether it is proportionate to the aims of the publicity.

The guidance goes on to note that 'publicity must be necessary to achieve the identified aim — this will involve a necessity test. The identified aim for publicising could be (1) to notify the public that ASBOs have been obtained in order to reassure the public that action has been taken; (2) to notify the public of specific ASBOs so that they can help in their enforcement; or (3) to act as a deterrent to others involved in anti-social behaviour. In some cases two or all three aims will be relevant'. In any event, 'the decision-maker should recognise and acknowledge that for publicity to achieve its aim it might interfere with the individual's human rights and potentially those of his or her family. Publicity should be proportionate to this interference'. The document then gives detailed guidance about the type of information that may be included in publicity.

SPECIAL MEASURES IN ASBO CASES

The SOCPA 2005, s. 143, makes provision for 'special measures' for witnesses in proceedings for ASBOs. It inserts s. 1I into the 1998 Act. This provision applies to magistrates' court proceedings for a civil ASBO, magistrates' court or Crown Court proceedings for an ASBO under s. 1C (i.e. after conviction) or to an application in the magistrates' court for an interim ASBO under s. 1D. It applies to such proceedings the special measures provisions contained in the YJCEA 1999 (with the omission of those that are applicable only in the context of criminal proceedings). For discussion of special measures, see **D14.97** and **D21.29**. **D24.18**

INDIVIDUAL SUPPORT ORDERS

Individual support orders (made under the CDA 1998, ss. 1AA and 1AB, inserted by the CJA 2003, s. 322) are aimed at preventing further anti-social behaviour where an ASBO has already been made against a person under the age of 18. Section 1AA(1) stipulates that the court must consider making an individual support order after it has made an ASBO against a child or young person (that is, a person aged 10 to 17). Under s. 1AA(2), the court must make an individual support order if three conditions are fulfilled. Those conditions (set out in s. 1AA(3)) are: **D24.19**

(a) that an individual support order 'would be desirable in the interests of preventing any repetition of the kind of behaviour which led to the making of the anti-social behaviour order';
(b) that the defendant is not already subject to an individual support order; and
(c) that arrangements for implementing individual support orders are available in the area in which the defendant resides or will reside.

The effect of an individual support order is set out in s. 1AA(2): it requires the defendant to comply, for a period not exceeding six months, with such requirements as are specified in the order, and to comply with any directions given by the responsible officer (who supervises the defendant under the order) with a view to the implementation of those requirements.

The requirements specified under s. 1AA(2) must be ones 'that the court considers desirable in the interests of preventing any repetition of the kind of behaviour which led to the making of the anti-social behaviour order' (s. 1AA(5)). Under s. 1AA(6), the defendant may be required to participate in activities, present himself to a person or persons and comply with any arrangements for his education. The offender cannot be required to attend a place (or different places) on more than two days per week (s. 1AA(7)). Section 1AA(8) obliges the court, when imposing requirements, to avoid (as far as practicable) any conflict with the defendant's religious beliefs and any interference with the times, if any, at which he normally works or attends school or any other educational establishment. Under s. 1AA(9), the court is required to obtain and consider information from a social worker of a local authority social services department or a member of a youth offending team in order to determine whether the individual support conditions are fulfilled and, if so, what requirements should be included in the order.

Section 1AB(1) requires the court to explain to the defendant, in ordinary language and in open court, the effect of the order, the consequences of failure to comply with its requirements, and the court's power to review the order. Under s. 1AB(3), failure without reasonable excuse to comply with any of the requirements included in the individual support order is a summary offence, punishable with a fine of up to £1,000 (where the offender is aged 14 to 17), or £250 (where the offender is aged 10 to 13). Section 1AB(4) stipulates that a referral order cannot be made in respect of a conviction under s. 1AB(1).

Under s. 1AB(5), an individual support order ceases to have effect (if it has not already expired) when the anti-social behaviour order to which it is linked ceases to have effect. Section 1AB(6) allows the defendant or the responsible officer to apply to the court for the order to be varied or discharged; s. 1AB(7) allows a court to vary or discharge an individual support order if it is varying the ASBO to which it is linked.

The CDA 1998, s. 4(2), enables an appeal to the Crown Court against the making of an individual support order by a magistrates' court.

PARENTING ORDERS

D24.20 The CDA 1998, s. 9(1B) provides that, where a court makes an ASBO against a person under the age of 16, it must also make a parenting order (see **E16.1**) against the parents of that child if it is satisfied that the parenting order would be desirable in the interests of preventing any repetition of the kind of behaviour that led to making of the ASBO.

INTERVENTION ORDERS

D24.21 Intervention orders, which may be sought be a relevant authority (see **D24.4**) may be attached to an ASBO by virtue of the CDA 1998, s. 1G (inserted by the Drugs Act 2005, s. 20, and in force from 1 October 2006), in order to tackle anti-social behaviour resulting from drug abuse. Measures specified by the order are aimed at the prevention of further drug-related anti-social behaviour. Intervention orders are available only where the court is making an ASBO in respect of a defendant who has attained the age of 18, a report from an appropriately qualified person shows that the individual's anti-social behaviour is linked to misuse of drugs, and the court is satisfied that a number of conditions are satisfied, namely:

(a) an intervention order is desirable in the interests of preventing a repetition of the behaviour which led to the behaviour order being made (the 'trigger behaviour');
(b) appropriate activities relating to the trigger behaviour or its cause are available for the defendant;
(c) the defendant is not currently subject to another intervention order or to any other treatment relating to the trigger behaviour or its cause (whether on a voluntary basis or by virtue of a requirement imposed by a court);
(d) arrangements for implementing intervention orders are available in the area in which the defendant resides.

The intervention order requires the defendant to comply, for a period not exceeding six months, with such requirements as are specified in the order, and with any directions given by a person authorised to do so under the order. The defendant may be required to participate in the activities specified in those requirements or directions at the time(s) specified or to present himself to a specified person at specified times. Failure without reasonable excuse to comply with the intervention order is an offence under s. 1H(3) punishable with a fine on level 4 (currently £2,500).

By virtue of s. 1H(4), the intervention order ceases to have effect (if it has not already done so) when the ASBO as a result of which it was made ceases to have effect.

Section 1H(5) enables the applicant or the relevant authority to apply to the court for the intervention order to be varied or discharged.

RELEVANT STATUTES

Crime and Disorder Act 1998, ss. 1, 1A, 1AA, 1AB, 1C, 1CA, 1D, 1E, 1G, 1I and 4

1.—(1) An application for an order under this section may be made by a relevant authority if it appears to the authority that the following conditions are fulfilled with respect to any person aged 10 or over, namely— D24.22

(a) that the person has acted, since the commencement date, in an anti-social manner, that is to say, in a manner that caused or was likely to cause harassment, alarm or distress to one or more persons not of the same household as himself; and

(b) that such an order is necessary to protect relevant persons from further anti-social acts by him.

. . .

(1A) In this section and sections 1B, 1CA, 1E and 1F 'relevant authority' means—

(a) the council for a local government area;

(aa) in relation to England, a county council;

(b) the chief officer of police of any police force maintained for a police area;

(c) the chief constable of the British Transport Police Force; . . .

(d) any person registered under section 1 of the Housing Act 1996 as a social landlord who provides or manages any houses or hostel in a local government area; or

(e) a housing action trust established by order in pursuance of section 62 of the Housing Act 1988.

(1B) In this section 'relevant persons' means—

(a) in relation to a relevant authority falling within paragraph (a) of subsection (1A), persons within the local government area of that council;

(aa) in relation to a relevant authority falling within paragraph (aa) of subsection (1A), persons within the county of the county council;

(b) in relation to a relevant authority falling within paragraph (b) of that subsection, persons within the police area;

(c) in relation to a relevant authority falling within paragraph (c) of that subsection—

(i) persons who are within or likely to be within a place specified in section 31(1)(a) to (f) of the Railways and Transport Safety Act 2003 in a local government area; or

(ii) persons who are within or likely to be within such a place;

(d) in relation to a relevant authority falling within paragraph (d) or (e) of that subsection—

(i) persons who are residing in or who are otherwise on or likely to be on premises provided or managed by that authority; or

(ii) persons who are in the vicinity of or likely to be in the vicinity of such premises.

(2) . . .

(3) Such an application shall be made by complaint to a magistrates' court.

(4) If, on such an application, it is proved that the conditions mentioned in subsection (1) above are fulfilled, the magistrates' court may make an order under this section (an 'anti-social behaviour order') which prohibits the defendant from doing anything described in the order.

(5) For the purpose of determining whether the condition mentioned in subsection (1)(a) above is fulfilled, the court shall disregard any act of the defendant which he shows was reasonable in the circumstances.

(5A) *Nothing in this section affects the operation of section 127 of the Magistrates' Courts Act 1980 (limitation of time in respect of informations laid or complaints made in magistrates' court).*

(6) The prohibitions that may be imposed by an anti-social behaviour order are those necessary for the purpose of protecting persons (whether relevant persons or persons elsewhere in England and Wales) from further anti-social acts by the defendant.

(7) An anti-social behaviour order shall have effect for a period (not less than two years) specified in the order or until further order.

(8) Subject to subsection (9) below, the applicant or the defendant may apply by complaint to the court which made an anti-social behaviour order for it to be varied or discharged by a further order.

(9) Except with the consent of both parties, no anti-social behaviour order shall be discharged before the end of the period of two years beginning with the date of service of the order.

(10) If without reasonable excuse a person does anything which he is prohibited from doing by an anti-social behaviour order, he is guilty of an offence and liable—

(a) on summary conviction, to imprisonment for a term not exceeding six months or to a fine not exceeding the statutory maximum, or to both; or
(b) on conviction on indictment, to imprisonment for a term not exceeding five years or to a fine, or to both.

(10A) The following may bring proceedings for an offence under subsection (10)—
(a) a council which is a relevant authority;
(b) the council for the local government area in which a person in respect of whom an anti-social behaviour order has been made resides or appears to reside.

(10B) If proceedings for an offence under subsection (10) are brought in a youth court section 47(2) of the Children and Young Persons Act 1933 has effect as if the persons entitled to be present at a sitting for the purposes of those proceedings include one person authorised to be present by a relevant authority.

(10C) In proceedings for an offence under subsection (10), a copy of the original anti-social behaviour order, certified as such by the proper officer of the court which made it, is admissible as evidence of its having been made and of its contents to the same extent that oral evidence of those things is admissible in those proceedings.

(10D) In relation to proceedings brought against a child or a young person for an offence under subsection (10)—
(a) section 49 of the Children and Young Persons Act 1933 (restrictions on reports of proceedings in which children and young persons are concerned) does not apply in respect of the child or young person against whom the proceedings are brought;
(b) section 45 of the Youth Justice and Criminal Evidence Act 1999 (power to restrict reporting of criminal proceedings involving persons under 18) does so apply.

(10E) If, in relation to any such proceedings, the court does exercise its power to give a direction under section 45 of the Youth Justice and Criminal Evidence Act 1999, it shall give its reasons for doing so.

(11) Where a person is convicted of an offence under subsection (10) above, it shall not be open to the court by or before which he is so convicted to make an order under subsection (1)(b) (conditional discharge) of section 12 of the Powers of Criminal Courts (Sentencing) Act 2000 in respect of the offence.

(12) In this section—
'British Transport Police Force' means the force of constables appointed under section 53 of the British Transport Commission Act 1949;
'the commencement date' means the date of the commencement of this section;
'child' and 'young person' shall have the same meaning as in the Children and Young Persons Act 1933;
'local government area' means—
(a) in relation to England, a district or London borough, the City of London, the Isle of Wight and the Isles of Scilly;
(b) in relation to Wales, a county or county borough,

. . .

[Section 1(5A) is inserted by the VCRA 2006, s. 59(1), which is not yet in force.]

1A.—(1) The Secretary of State may by order provide that the chief officer of a body of constables maintained otherwise than by a police authority is, in such cases and circumstances as may be prescribed by the order, to be a relevant authority for the purposes of section 1 above.

(2) The Secretary of State may by order—
(a) provide that a person or body of any other description specified in the order is, in such cases and circumstances as may be prescribed by the order, to be a relevant authority for the purposes of such of sections 1 above and 1B, 1CA and 1E below as are specified in the order; and
(b) prescribe the description of persons who are to be 'relevant persons' in relation to that person or body.

1AA.—(1) Where a court makes an anti-social behaviour order in respect of a defendant who is a child or young person when that order is made, it must consider whether the individual support conditions are fulfilled.

(2) If it is satisfied that those conditions are fulfilled, the court must make an order under this section ('an individual support order') which—
(a) requires the defendant to comply, for a period not exceeding six months, with such requirements as are specified in the order; and

(b) requires the defendant to comply with any directions given by the responsible officer with a view to the implementation of the requirements under paragraph (a) above.

(3) The individual support conditions are—

(a) that an individual support order would be desirable in the interests of preventing any repetition of the kind of behaviour which led to the making of the anti-social behaviour order;

(b) that the defendant is not already subject to an individual support order; and

(c) that the court has been notified by the Secretary of State that arrangements for implementing individual support orders are available in the area in which it appears to it that the defendant resides or will reside and the notice has not been withdrawn.

(4) If the court is not satisfied that the individual support conditions are fulfilled, it shall state in open court that it is not so satisfied and why it is not.

(5) The requirements that may be specified under subsection (2)(a) above are those that the court considers desirable in the interests of preventing any repetition of the kind of behaviour which led to the making of the anti-social behaviour order.

(6) Requirements included in an individual support order, or directions given under such an order by a responsible officer, may require the defendant to do all or any of the following things—

(a) to participate in activities specified in the requirements or directions at a time or times so specified;

(b) to present himself to a person or persons so specified at a place or places and at a time or times so specified;

(c) to comply with any arrangements for his education so specified.

(7) But requirements included in, or directions given under, such an order may not require the defendant to attend (whether at the same place or at different places) on more than two days in any week; and 'week' here means a period of seven days beginning with a Sunday.

(8) Requirements included in, and directions given under, an individual support order shall, as far as practicable, be such as to avoid—

(a) any conflict with the defendant's religious beliefs; and

(b) any interference with the times, if any, at which he normally works or attends school or any other educational establishment.

(9) Before making an individual support order, the court shall obtain from a social worker of a local authority or a member of a youth offending team any information which it considers necessary in order—

(a) to determine whether the individual support conditions are fulfilled, or

(b) to determine what requirements should be imposed by an individual support order if made,

and shall consider that information.

(10) In this section and section 1AB below 'responsible officer', in relation to an individual support order, means one of the following who is specified in the order, namely—

(a) a social worker of a local authority;

(b) a person nominated by a person appointed as chief education officer under section 532 of the Education Act 1996;

(c) a member of a youth offending team.

1AB.—(1) Before making an individual support order, the court shall explain to the defendant in ordinary language—

(a) the effect of the order and of the requirements proposed to be included in it;

(b) the consequences which may follow (under subsection (3) below) if he fails to comply with any of those requirements; and

(c) that the court has power (under subsection (6) below) to review the order on the application either of the defendant or of the responsible officer.

(2) The power of the Secretary of State under section 174(4) of the Criminal Justice Act 2003 includes power by order to—

(a) prescribe cases in which subsection (1) above does not apply; and

(b) prescribe cases in which the explanation referred to in that subsection may be made in the absence of the defendant, or may be provided in written form.

(3) If the person in respect of whom an individual support order is made fails without reasonable excuse to comply with any requirement included in the order, he is guilty of an offence and liable on summary conviction to a fine not exceeding—

(a) if he is aged 14 or over at the date of his conviction, £1,000;
(b) if he is aged under 14 then, £250.

(4) No referral order under section 16(2) or (3) of the Powers of Criminal Courts (Sentencing) Act 2000 (referral of young offenders to youth offender panels) may be made in respect of an offence under subsection (3) above.

(5) If the anti-social behaviour order as a result of which an individual support order was made ceases to have effect, the individual support order (if it has not previously ceased to have effect) ceases to have effect when the anti-social behaviour order does.

(6) On an application made by complaint by—
(a) the person subject to an individual support order, or
(b) the responsible officer,
the court which made the individual support order may vary or discharge it by a further order.

(7) If the anti-social behaviour order as a result of which an individual support order was made is varied, the court varying the anti-social behaviour order may by a further order vary or discharge the individual support order.

1C.—(1) This section applies where a person (the 'offender') is convicted of a relevant offence.

(2) If the court considers—
(a) that the offender has acted, at any time since the commencement date, in an anti-social manner, that is to say in a manner that caused or was likely to cause harassment, alarm or distress to one or more persons not of the same household as himself, and
(b) that an order under this section is necessary to protect persons in any place in England and Wales from further anti-social acts by him,
it may make an order which prohibits the offender from doing anything described in the order.

(3) The court may make an order under this section—
(a) if the prosecutor asks it to do so, or
(b) if the court thinks it is appropriate to do so.

(3A) For the purpose of deciding whether to make an order under this section the court may consider evidence led by the prosecution and the defence.

(3B) It is immaterial whether evidence led in pursuance of subsection (3A) would have been admissible in the proceedings in which the offender was convicted.

(4) An order under this section shall not be made except—
(a) in addition to a sentence imposed in respect of the relevant offence; or
(b) in addition to an order discharging him conditionally.

(4A) The court may adjourn any proceedings in relation to an order under this section even after sentencing the offender.

(4B) If the offender does not appear for any adjourned proceedings, the court may further adjourn the proceedings or may issue a warrant for his arrest.

(4C) But the court may not issue a warrant for the offender's arrest unless it is satisfied that he has had adequate notice of the time and place of the adjourned proceedings.

(5) An order under this section takes effect on the day on which it is made, but the court may provide in any such order that such requirements of the order as it may specify shall, during any period when the offender is detained in legal custody, be suspended until his release from that custody.

(9) Subsections (7), (10), (10C), (10D), (10E) and (11) of section 1 apply for the purposes of the making and effect of orders made by virtue of this section as they apply for the purposes of the making and effect of anti-social behaviour orders.

(9A) The council for the local government area in which a person in respect of whom an anti-social behaviour order has been made resides or appears to reside may bring proceedings under section 1(10) (as applied by subsection (9) above) for breach of an order under subsection (2) above.

(9B) Subsection (9C) applies in relation to proceedings in which an order under subsection (2) is made against a child or young person who is convicted of an offence.

(9C) In so far as the proceedings relate to the making of the order—
(a) section 49 of the Children and Young Persons Act 1933 (restrictions on reports of proceedings in which children and young persons are concerned) does not apply in respect of the child or young person against whom the order is made;
(b) section 39 of that Act (power to prohibit publication of certain matter) does so apply.

(10) In this section—
'child' and 'young person' have the same meaning as in the Children and Young Persons Act 1933;
'the commencement date' has the same meaning as in section 1 above;
'the court' in relation to an offender means—
(a) the court by or before which he is convicted of the relevant offence; or
(b) if he is committed to the Crown Court to be dealt with for that offence, the Crown Court; and
'relevant offence' means an offence committed after the coming into force of section 64 of the Police Reform Act 2002.

1CA.—(1) An offender subject to an order under section 1C may apply to the court which made it for it to be varied or discharged.
(2) If he does so, he must also send written notice of his application to the Director of Public Prosecutions.
(3) The Director of Public Prosecutions may apply to the court which made an order under section 1C for it to be varied or discharged.
(4) A relevant authority may also apply to the court which made an order under section 1C for it to be varied or discharged if it appears to it that—
(a) in the case of variation, the protection of relevant persons from anti-social acts by the person subject to the order would be more appropriately effected by a variation of the order;
(b) in the case of discharge, that it is no longer necessary to protect relevant persons from anti-social acts by him by means of such an order.
(5) If the Director of Public Prosecutions or a relevant authority applies for the variation or discharge of an order under section 1C, he or it must also send written notice of the application to the person subject to the order.
(6) In the case of an order under section 1C made by a magistrates' court, the references in subsections (1), (3) and (4) to the court by which the order was made include a reference to any magistrates' court acting in the same local justice area as that court.
(7) No order under section 1C shall be discharged on an application under this section before the end of the period of two years beginning with the day on which the order takes effect, unless—
(a) in the case of an application under subsection (1), the Director of Public Prosecutions consents, or
(b) in the case of an application under subsection (3) or (4), the offender consents.

1D.—(1) This section applies where—
(a) an application is made for an anti-social behaviour order;
(b) an application is made for an order under section 1B;
(c) a request is made by the prosecution for an order under section 1C; or
(d) the court is minded to make an order under section 1C of its own motion.
(2) If, before determining the application or request, or before deciding whether to make an order under section 1C of its own motion, the court considers that it is just to make an order under this section pending the determination of that application or request or before making that decision, it may make such an order.
(3) An order under this section is an order which prohibits the defendant from doing anything described in the order.
(4) An order under this section—
(a) shall be for a fixed period;
(b) may be varied, renewed or discharged;
(c) shall, if it has not previously ceased to have effect, cease to have effect on the determination of the application or request mentioned in subsection (1), or on the court's making a decision as to whether or not to make an order under section 1C of its own motion.
(5) In relation to cases to which this section applies by virtue of paragraph (a) or (b) of subsection (1), subsections (6), (8) and (10) to (12) of section 1 apply for the purposes of the making and effect of orders under this section as they apply for the purposes of the making and effect of anti-social behaviour orders.
(6) In relation to cases to which this section applies by virtue of paragraph (c) or (d) of subsection (1)—
(a) subsections (6) and (10) to (12) of section 1 apply for the purposes of the making and

effect of orders under this section as they apply for the purposes of the making and effect of anti-social behaviour orders;

and

(b) section 1CA applies for the purposes of the variation or discharge of an order under this section as it applies for the purposes of the variation or discharge of an order under section 1C.

1E.—(1) This section applies to—

(a) applications for an anti-social behaviour order; and

(b) applications for an order under section 1B.

(2) Before making an application to which this section applies, the council for a local government area shall consult the chief officer of police of the police force maintained for the police area within which that local government area lies.

(3) Before making an application to which this section applies, a chief officer of police shall consult the council for the local government area in which the person in relation to whom the application is to be made resides or appears to reside.

(4) Before making an application to which this section applies, a relevant authority other than a council for a local government area or a chief officer of police shall consult—

(a) the council for the local government area in which the person in relation to whom the application is to be made resides or appears to reside; and

(b) the chief officer of police of the police force maintained for the police area within which that local government area lies.

(5) Subsection (4)(a) does not apply if the relevant authority is a county council for a county in which there are no districts.

1G.—(1) This section applies if, in relation to a person who has attained the age of 18, a relevant authority—

(a) makes an application for an anti-social behaviour order or an order under section 1B above (the behaviour order),

(b) has obtained from an appropriately qualified person a report relating to the effect on the person's behaviour of the misuse of controlled drugs or of such other factors as the Secretary of State by order prescribes, and

(c) has engaged in consultation with such persons as the Secretary of State by order prescribes for the purpose of ascertaining that, if the report recommends that an order under this section is made, appropriate activities will be available.

(2) The relevant authority may make an application to the court which is considering the application for the behaviour order for an order under this section (an intervention order).

(3) If the court—

(a) makes the behaviour order, and

(b) is satisfied that the relevant conditions are met,

it may also make an intervention order.

(4) The relevant conditions are—

(a) that an intervention order is desirable in the interests of preventing a repetition of the behaviour which led to the behaviour order being made (trigger behaviour);

(b) that appropriate activities relating to the trigger behaviour or its cause are available for the defendant;

(c) that the defendant is not (at the time the intervention order is made) subject to another intervention order or to any other treatment relating to the trigger behaviour or its cause (whether on a voluntary basis or by virtue of a requirement imposed in pursuance of any enactment);

(d) that the court has been notified by the Secretary of State that arrangements for implementing intervention orders are available in the area in which it appears that the defendant resides or will reside and the notice has not been withdrawn.

(5) An intervention order is an order which—

(a) requires the defendant to comply, for a period not exceeding six months, with such requirements as are specified in the order, and

(b) requires the defendant to comply with any directions given by a person authorised to do so under the order with a view to the implementation of the requirements under paragraph (a) above.

(6) An intervention order or directions given under the order may require the defendant—

(a) to participate in the activities specified in the requirement or directions at a time or times so specified;

(b) to present himself to a person or persons so specified at a time or times so specified.

(7) Requirements included in, or directions given under, an intervention order must, as far as practicable, be such as to avoid—

(a) any conflict with the defendant's religious beliefs, and

(b) any interference with the times (if any) at which he normally works or attends an educational establishment.

(8) If the defendant fails to comply with a requirement included in or a direction given under an intervention order, the person responsible for the provision or supervision of appropriate activities under the order must inform the relevant authority of that fact.

(9) The person responsible for the provision or supervision of appropriate activities is a person of such description as is prescribed by order made by the Secretary of State.

(10) In this section—

'appropriate activities' means such activities, or activities of such a description, as are prescribed by order made by the Secretary of State for the purposes of this section;

'appropriately qualified person' means a person who has such qualifications or experience as the Secretary of State by order prescribes;

'controlled drug' has the same meaning as in the Misuse of Drugs Act 1971;

'relevant authority' means a relevant authority for the purposes of section 1 above.

(11) An order under this section made by the Secretary of State may make different provision for different purposes.

(12) This section and section 1H below apply to a person in respect of whom a behaviour order has been made subject to the following modifications—

(a) in subsection (1) above paragraph (a) must be ignored;

(b) in subsection (2) above, for 'is considering the application for' substitute 'made';

(c) in subsection (3) above paragraph (a), the word 'and' following it and the word 'also' must be ignored.

1H.—(1) Before making an intervention order the court must explain to the defendant in ordinary language—

(a) the effect of the order and of the requirements proposed to be included in it,

(b) the consequences which may follow (under subsection (3) below) if he fails to comply with any of those requirements, and

(c) that the court has power (under subsection (5) below) to review the order on the application either of the defendant or of the relevant authority.

(2) The power of the Secretary of State under section 174(4) of the Criminal Justice Act 2003 includes power by order to—

(a) prescribe cases in which subsection (1) does not apply, and

(b) prescribe cases in which the explanation referred to in that subsection may be made in the absence of the defendant, or may be provided in written form.

(3) If a person in respect of whom an intervention order is made fails without reasonable excuse to comply with any requirement included in the order he is guilty of an offence and liable on summary conviction to a fine not exceeding level 4 on the standard scale.

(4) If the behaviour order as a result of which an intervention order is made ceases to have effect, the intervention order (if it has not previously ceased to have effect) ceases to have effect when the behaviour order does.

(5) On an application made by—

(a) a person subject to an intervention order, or

(b) the relevant authority,

the court which made the intervention order may vary or discharge it by a further order.

(6) An application under subsection (5) made to a magistrates' court must be made by complaint.

(7) If the behaviour order as a result of which an intervention order was made is varied, the court varying the behaviour order may by a further order vary or discharge the intervention order.

(8) Expressions used in this section and in section 1G have the same meaning in this section as in that section.

1I.—(1) This section applies to the following proceedings—

(a) any proceedings in a magistrates' court on an application for an anti-social behaviour order,

(b) any proceedings in a magistrates' court or the Crown Court so far as relating to the issue whether to make an order under section 1C, and

(c) any proceedings in a magistrates' court so far as relating to the issue whether to make an order under section 1D.

(2) Chapter 1 of part 2 of the Youth Justice and Criminal Evidence Act 1999 (special measures directions in the case of vulnerable and intimidated witnesses) shall apply in relation to any such proceedings as it applies in relation to criminal proceedings, but with—

(a) the omission of the provisions of that Act mentioned in subsection (3) (which make provision appropriate only in the context of criminal proceedings), and

(b) any other necessary modifications.

(3) The provisions are—

(a) section 17(4),

(b) section 21(1)(b) and (5) to (7),

(c) section 22(1)(b) and (2)(b) and (c),

(d) section 27(10), and

(e) section 32.

(4) Any rules of court made under or for the purposes of chapter 1 of part 2 of that Act shall apply in relation to proceedings to which this section applies—

(a) to such extent as may be provided by rules of court, and

(b) subject to such modifications as may be so provided.

(5) Section 47 of that Act (restrictions on reporting special measures directions etc.) applies, with any necessary modifications, in relation to—

(a) a direction under section 19 of the Act as applied by this section, or

(b) a direction discharging or varying such a direction,

and sections 49 and 51 of that Act (offences) apply accordingly.

4.—(1) An appeal shall lie to the Crown Court against the making by a magistrates' court of an anti-social behaviour order, an individual support order, an order under section 1D above, . . .

(2) On such an appeal the Crown Court—

(a) may make such orders as may be necessary to give effect to its determination of the appeal; and

(b) may also make such incidental or consequential orders as appear to it to be just.

(3) Any order of the Crown Court made on an appeal under this section (other than one directing that an application be re-heard by a magistrates' court) shall, for the purposes of section 1(8), 1AB(6), be treated as if it were an order of the magistrates' court from which the appeal was brought and not an order of the Crown Court.

Section D25 Appeal to the Court of Appeal (Criminal Division) following Trial on Indictment

BASES OF JURISDICTION OF THE COURT OF APPEAL (CRIMINAL DIVISION)

Statutory Bases

The vast majority of appeals against conviction and sentence are disposed of by the Court of Appeal (Criminal Division) under its statutory jurisdiction. Section 15(2) of the Supreme Court Act 1981 enables the exercise of the statutory powers conferred under the following legislative provisions: **D25.1**

Criminal Appeal Act 1968, ss. 1 and 2	Jurisdiction to determine appeals against conviction on indictment.
Criminal Appeal Act 1968, ss. 9 and 11	Jurisdiction to determine appeals against sentence passed following conviction on indictment.
Criminal Appeal Act 1968, ss. 10 and 11	Jurisdiction to determine appeals against sentence passed on a committal for sentence.
Criminal Justice Act 1982, s. 36	Jurisdiction to give an opinion on a point of law referred to the court by the A-G following an acquittal on indictment.
Criminal Justice Act 1987, s. 9(11) to (14)	Jurisdiction to determine appeals against rulings made at preparatory hearings in serious fraud cases.
Criminal Justice Act 1988, ss. 35 and 36	Jurisdiction to increase sentence on a reference by the A-G following an unduly lenient sentence for an offence triable only on indictment.
Criminal Appeal Act 1995, s. 13	Jurisdiction to determine appeals on a reference by the CCRC.

Venire de Novo

In addition to its statutory jurisdiction, the Court of Appeal retains the power to deal with appeals by way of a writ of *venire de novo*. The power has its origins in the jurisdiction of the Court for Crown Cases Reserved, a forerunner of the modern Court of Appeal (Criminal Division). In essence, the power is exercised when there has been such a fundamental irregularity in procedure that no valid trial has taken place. In *Rose* [1982] AC 822, the House of Lords referred with approval to an article by Sir Robin Cooke (published at (1955) 71 **D25.2**

LQR 100) in which he identified categories of procedural irregularity which had been found sufficient to ensure that the trial was in effect a nullity and hence justify the issue of a writ of *venire de novo.* The categories identified were as follows:

(a) where there was error as to the true plea of the defendant or some doubt about the nature of his plea, whether guilty or not guilty;
(b) where there was misjoinder of defendants (*Crane v DPP* [1921] 2 AC 299);
(c) where there was failure to take the verdict of the jury on a change of plea from not guilty to guilty (*Hancock* (1931) 23 Cr App R 16);
(d) where there was some irregularity in the committal proceedings (*Gee* [1936] 2 KB 442);
(e) where there was personation of a juror (*Wakefield* [1918] 1 KB 216);
(f) where there was denial of the right to challenge a juror (*Williams* (1925) 19 Cr App R 67); and
(g) where the judge was unqualified to act as such.

When *Rose* was before the Court of Appeal, Lord Lane CJ added an eighth category of case in which retrials had historically been ordered, namely when the verdict of the jury was so ambiguous or ill-expressed that no judgment could properly be given on it. His reasoning was approved in the House of Lords.

The effect of the procedure is that the Court of Appeal orders a retrial and the prosecution prefers a fresh indictment against the accused.

ALLOCATION OF BUSINESS

Matters Dealt with by the Full Court

D25.3 A court consisting of an uneven number of judges no fewer than three is required to determine (a) an appeal against conviction, (b) an appeal against a verdict of not guilty by reason of insanity, (c) an appeal against a finding of unfitness to plead, (d) an application for leave to appeal to the Court of Appeal which has not previously been refused by the single judge, or (e) an application for leave to appeal to the House of Lords.

Ordinarily, a court sitting to deal with any of the above hearings will comprise just three judges. But, exceptionally, five or even seven judges will sit when the matter to be decided is very important and would benefit from the authority of a five-judge court (see, e.g., *Goodyear* [2005] 3 All ER 117, or there have been conflicting decisions of the Court of Appeal on the same point: *Newsome* [1970] 2 QB 711).

Matters Dealt with by a Two-judge Court

D25.4 By virtue of s. 55(4) of the Supreme Court Act 1981, a court comprised of two judges may deal with any matter other than those mentioned at **D25.3**. Thus a two-judge court may (a) determine an appeal against sentence, (b) refuse leave to appeal to the Court of Appeal, provided the application for leave has already been refused by a single judge, (c) grant leave to appeal to the Court of Appeal, (d) deal with all interlocutory applications, and (e) direct that the CCRC investigate a particular issue and report to the court.

Matters Dealt With By a Single Judge

D25.5 Sections 31 and 44 of the Criminal Appeal Act 1968 set out the matters which may be dealt with by a single judge. Rule 68.6 of the CrimPR sets out the procedure governing the renewal before the full court of any application refused by the single judge (see **D26.8**).

DECIDING OUTCOME OF APPEAL AND GIVING JUDGMENT

The Court of Appeal may determine an appeal by majority decision. If a two-judge court is equally divided then, under the Supreme Court Act 1981, s. 55(5), the case must be reargued before a reconstituted court comprised of an uneven number of judges. A case is finally determined once the decision of the court has been announced in open court, even if no reasons have yet been given, as it is then properly binding on the judges (*Coates* [2004] 1 WLR 3043). Consequently in *Steele* [2007] 1 WLR 222, it was held that when the court circulated the transcript of its judgment in advance of handing it down, the appeal was determined even though, when the judgment was handed down, not all members of the original constitution were present. The handing down of the judgment was merely its formal promulgation. **D25.6**

APPEAL AGAINST CONVICTION

Statutory Basis of Appeal against Conviction

Criminal Appeal Act 1968, s. 1 **D25.7**

(1) Subject to subsection (3) below a person convicted of an offence on indictment may appeal to the Court of Appeal against his conviction.
(2) An appeal under this section lies only—
  (a) with the leave of the Court of Appeal; or
  (b) if the judge of the court of trial grants a certificate that the case is fit for appeal.

Unless the trial judge certifies that a case is fit for appeal, leave to appeal to the Court of Appeal is required (see D25.8). A certificate from the trial judge can be granted of the judge's own motion or on application on behalf of the convicted person (see *Consolidated Criminal Practice Direction*, para. IV.50.3). Such a certificate should be granted only when there is a cogent ground of appeal with substantial prospects of success (see *Consolidated Criminal Practice Direction*, para. IV.50.4). In *Inskip* [2005] EWCA Crim 3372, it was said that a certificate should be granted only in exceptional circumstances.

Appeal against Conviction with Leave

Unless the trial judge has granted a certificate that the case is fit for appeal, any would-be appellant needs leave to appeal. Written grounds of appeal must be submitted within 28 days of the conviction. The initial decision either to grant or refuse leave is usually taken on the papers by the single judge (see the Criminal Appeal Act 1968, s. 31(2)(a)), but sometimes the decision as to leave may be made by a two-judge or full court at the discretion of the Registrar of Criminal Appeals ('the Registrar'). The need for expedition is the usual reason for such a leave hearing. **D25.8**

If leave is refused by the single judge, the applicant is entitled to renew his application before a two-judge or full court under s. 31(3).

Appeal against Conviction following a Plea of Guilty

The fact that a plea of guilty has been entered does not preclude an appeal against the resultant conviction. If the conviction is found to be unsafe despite the plea of guilty (see D25.14), it will be quashed. However, the fact that an appellant was fit to plead, had received expert advice, had been aware of what he was doing and had intended to plead guilty would be highly relevant to the consideration of the safety of the conviction (*Lee* [1984] 1 WLR 578). The most common basis upon which an unequivocal plea of guilty is challenged is where there has been an incorrect ruling on a point of law by the trial judge which allows the appellant no escape from a guilty verdict. But if an appellant has simply been influenced to **D25.9** enter a plea of guilty because of a decision to admit evidence which meant that his prospects of acquittal were hopeless, the conviction would not normally be held to be unsafe (*Chalkley* [1998] QB 848). That aspect of the judgment in *Chalkley* was approved in *Togher* [2001] 3 All ER 463, and has found relatively recent reflection in *Hanson* [2005] 1 WLR 3169, where Rose V-P observed that it was highly unlikely that an appeal would be entertained when a defendant pleaded guilty following a decision to admit evidence of bad character.

The Court of Appeal may also quash a conviction arising from a guilty plea following the admission of fresh evidence on appeal under the Criminal Appeal Act 1968, s. 23 (see *Swain* [1986] Crim LR 480).

A conviction may also be held to be unsafe when the guilty plea which led to it flowed from inappropriate legal advice. In *W (AG)* [1999] Crim LR 87, the Court of Appeal quashed the appellant's convictions when he had pleaded guilty to two counts of an indictment following advice that if he did not do so then the evidence in relation to those counts would be very damaging to his defence on the remaining counts. He was advised that, if he pleaded guilty, no evidence would be given about the allegations in those counts. The appellant did not admit his guilt of the counts but pleaded guilty to them and the prosecution successfully applied to admit the evidence of those guilty pleas.

Single Right of Appeal

D25.10 If an appeal is unsuccessful (either because leave is refused or leave is granted and the appeal is dismissed), there is usually no opportunity for a further appeal even if the point to be argued is new or fresh evidence has arisen (*Pinfold* [1988] QB 462).

Two minor caveats to that rule were acknowledged in *Pinfold*:

(a) where the appeal has been abandoned, the Court of Appeal may in exceptional circumstances treat the abandonment as a nullity (see *Medway* [1976] QB 779); and
(b) if the dismissal of the first appeal involved some procedural irregularity which led to injustice for the appellant, the court may treat the dismissal as a nullity.

Unless either of those caveats apply, an unsuccessful appellant's only remedy is to ask the CCRC to refer his case back to the Court of Appeal (see **D27.1**).

Right of Appeal Vests only in the Convicted Person

D25.11 Section 1(1) of the Criminal Appeal Act 1968 confers a right of appeal only on a person convicted on indictment. However s. 44A provides that the Court of Appeal may allow an approved person to begin or continue an appeal on behalf of a deceased appellant (see, e.g., *Whelan* [1997] Crim LR 659).

Directions Concerning Loss of Time and Frivolous and Vexatious Appeals

D25.12 Section 29 of the Criminal Appeal Act 1968 enables the Court of Appeal to direct that all or part of the time an applicant for leave to appeal has spent in custody since the commencement of the appeal proceedings shall not count in relation to the sentence he is required to serve. Paragraph II.16.1 of the *Consolidated Criminal Practice Direction* amplifies the provisions of s. 29 (see **appendix** 7). In *Kuimba* [2005] EWCA Crim 955, the Court of Appeal suggested that the power under s. 29 should be invoked more frequently given the large number of unmeritorious appeals which produced a heavy burden on the court's resources. In *Hart* [2007] 1 Cr App R 412, the Court of Appeal re-emphasised and, more significantly, followed that advice. The court directed that, for two of the four named applicants, days in custody whilst awaiting disposition of their appeal should not count towards sentence. In both cases, counsel for the applicant had advised negatively on appeal and the applicant had renewed the application for leave to the full court despite the single judge concluding that the grounds of appeal were without merit.

By virtue of s. 20 of the 1968 Act, the Court of Appeal may summarily dismiss an appeal or application for leave to appeal without either of the parties being called on to attend if it considers the appeal to be frivolous or vexatious. A ground of appeal is 'frivolous or vexatious' if it is so unmeritorious that there is no realistic prospect of it succeeding after full argument (*Taylor* [1979] Crim LR 649).

Appellant who Absconds

The Court of Appeal may consider and determine the appeal of a person who has absconded. In *Charles* [2001] 2 Cr App R 233, the court expressed the view that it might be contrary to the ECHR, Article 6, if the appeal of a person was shut out solely because he had absconded. **D25.13**

DETERMINATION OF APPEALS AGAINST CONVICTION

Statutory Basis of Determination of Appeal

Criminal Appeal Act 1968, s. 2 **D25.14**

(1) Subject to the provisions of this Act, the Court of Appeal—
  (a) shall allow an appeal against conviction if they think that the conviction is unsafe; and
  (b) shall dismiss such an appeal in any other case.

The Safety Test

By virtue of s.2 of the Criminal Appeal Act 1968 (as amended by s. 2(1) of the Criminal Appeal Act 1995), the principal question for the Court of Appeal in the determination of an appeal against conviction is now whether or not the conviction is unsafe. **D25.15**

Prior to the amendment by the 1995 Act, s. 2 provided that the Court of Appeal should allow an appeal if it was of the view that the conviction was unsafe or unsatisfactory, or that the judgment of the court of trial should be set aside because of an error of law, or that there had been a material irregularity in the course of the trial. Even if the point in issue concerning a point of law or material irregularity was decided in favour of the appellant, the Court of Appeal could exercise the proviso and dismiss the appeal if they were satisfied that no miscarriage of justice had occurred. Despite the change in wording, the authorities which developed in relation to the application of the earlier version of s. 2 are relevant to the operation of the provision as now amended and the consideration of the ultimate question of the safety of the conviction.

The classic analysis of the Court of Appeal's powers under the old s. 2 was set out in *Cooper* [1969] 1 QB 267, where Lord Widgery said (at p. 271C–G):

> [This is] a case in which every issue was before the jury and in which the jury was properly instructed, and, accordingly, a case in which this court will be very reluctant indeed to intervene. It has been said over and over again throughout the years that this court must recognise the advantage which a jury has in seeing and hearing the witnesses, and if all the material was before the jury and the summing-up was impeccable, this court should not lightly interfere. Indeed, until the passing of the Criminal Appeal Act 1966 [which somewhat widened the court's powers to quash a conviction] it was almost unheard of for this court to interfere in such a case.
>
> However, now our powers are somewhat different, and we are indeed charged to allow an appeal against conviction if we think that the verdict of the jury should be set aside on the ground that under all the circumstances of the case it is unsafe or unsatisfactory. That means that in cases of this kind the court must in the end ask itself a subjective question, whether we are content to let the matter stand as it is, or whether there is not some lurking doubt in our minds which makes us wonder whether an injustice has been done. This is a reaction which may not be based strictly on the evidence as such; it is a reaction which can be produced by the general feel of the case as the court experiences it.

Despite the comments by the Court of Appeal in *F* [1998] Crim LR 307 to the effect that there was no need to add to the simple words of the new section and the concept of lurking doubt was inappropriate, *Cooper* is still regularly used as guidance for the approach to be taken in relation to the issue of whether or not a conviction is safe, and the Court of Appeal have continued to refer to the test (see, e.g., *Litchfield* [1998] Crim LR 507). As Professor Sir John Smith points out in his commentary on *F*, the repealed words 'or unsatisfactory' played no part in the decision in *Cooper*, and that case has not been overruled.

In addition, in *Mullen* [2000] QB 520, an appeal was based upon the circumstances in which the appellant was brought to trial. The English authorities had colluded with their Zimbabwean counterparts to ensure M's deportation from Zimbabwe to England in a manner which amounted to an abuse of process. The Court of Appeal held that abuse of process could still amount to a ground for the quashing of a conviction under the new wording of s. 2. Any safe conviction must of necessity be lawful and, if a trial should never have taken place, the conviction could not be safe.

In *Smith* [1999] 2 Cr App R 238, the Court of Appeal dealt with an appeal which was based on a contention that the trial judge had been wrong to reject a submission of no case to answer. After the judge had rejected the submission, the accused gave evidence and admitted his guilt. Under the authorities developed prior to the amendment of s. 2, the Court of Appeal could have quashed the conviction if it thought that the rejection of the submission of no case was erroneous. The court in *Smith* was faced with the question of whether the change in the wording had changed that position. The court held that it had not and, even though the appellant had admitted his guilt, the conviction was quashed.

The test applied by the Court of Appeal is different to that applied by the trial judge on a submission of no case to answer (see *Arobieke* [1988] Crim LR 314).

So far as 'fresh evidence' cases are concerned, the classic statement relating to the old s. 2 is to be found in *Stafford v DPP* [1974] AC 878 where Lord Kilbrandon approved *Cooper* and summarised the test to be applied by each member of the appellate court as: 'Have I a reasonable doubt, or perhaps even a lurking doubt, that this conviction may be unsafe or unsatisfactory?' Their lordships rejected the central submission by the appellants that the consideration by the court should be of the likely effect that the fresh evidence would have had on the minds of the jury; the test was no different in a fresh evidence case than in any other appeal against conviction.

In *Pendleton* [2002] 1 WLR 72, the House of Lords approved *Stafford*. The court must ask itself whether the conviction is unsafe, and it is not incumbent on it to ask what effect it would have had on the jury. Lord Bingham said (at [19]):

> I am not persuaded that the House laid down any incorrect principle in Stafford, so long as the Court of Appeal bears very clearly in mind that the question for its consideration is whether the conviction is safe and not whether the accused is guilty. . .The Court of Appeal can make its assessment of the fresh evidence it has heard, but save in a clear case it is at a disadvantage in seeking to relate that evidence to the rest of the evidence which the jury heard. For these reasons it will usually be wise for the Court of Appeal, in a case of any difficulty, to test their own provisional view by asking whether the evidence, if given at the trial, might reasonably have affected the decision of the trial jury to convict. If it might, the conviction must be thought to be unsafe.

In *Dial* [2005] 1 WLR 1660, the Privy Council reaffirmed the decision in *Pendleton*. But in language which is not in keeping with the exhortation of Lord Bingham as to what the Court of Appeal should bear in mind, Lord Brown said (at [31] and [42]):

> If the Court concludes that the fresh evidence raises no reasonable doubt as to the guilt of the accused it will dismiss the appeal. The primary question is for the Court itself and is not what effect the fresh evidence would have on the mind of the jury.

> Wherever fresh evidence establishes that a material prosecution witness has told a lie, the question arising for the Appeal Court's determination is whether that realistically places the appellant's guilt in reasonable doubt.

Dial has since been cited with approval in *Harris* [2006] 1 Cr App R 55, a decision of the Court of Appeal which concerned fresh expert evidence in a number of shaken baby syndrome cases.

APPROACH OF COURT OF APPEAL TO COMMONLY OCCURRING ERRORS IN THE COURSE OF A TRIAL

Exhaustive consideration of the many errors and irregularities which can found a successful appeal against conviction is not possible within this section and regard should be had to other parts of this work dealing with matters of procedure and substantive law. Nevertheless, it is possible to identify commonly occurring errors which are dealt with below. **D25.16**

Wrongful Admission or Exclusion of Evidence

The wrongful exclusion of admissible evidence or wrongful inclusion of inadmissible evidence will lead to the quashing of a conviction if the error means that the conviction is unsafe. That remains true even if the appellant's advocate failed to object to the admission of the evidence when it was adduced. But the fact that the advocate did not object to the evidence will be a factor in determining whether its admission was sufficiently prejudicial to render the conviction unsafe (*Stirland v DPP* [1944] AC 315; *Mustafa* (1977) 65 Cr App R 26). **D25.17**

If the evidence of a witness is wrongfully admitted or excluded because of an error as to that witness's competence or compellability, the same principle applies as that relating to the admissibility of a specific piece of evidence.

Erroneous Exercise of Discretion

The Court of Appeal have often said that they will not interfere to quash a conviction on the basis of an erroneous exercise of discretion save in very limited circumstances (*Grondkowski* [1946] KB 369; *Selvey v DPP* [1970] AC 304; *Moghal* (1977) 65 Cr App R 56). The prospects of an appeal succeeding in relation to a matter in the trial judge's discretion are much improved if there has been a failure to exercise the discretion or a failure to take relevant factors into account, or the judge has taken irrelevant factors into account in the exercise of his discretion (*Sullivan* [1971] 1 QB 253; *Quinn* [1996] Crim LR 516). Occasionally, the Court of Appeal have suggested a wider approach to their function of reviewing the exercise of the trial judge's discretion. In *McCann* (1991) 92 Cr App R 239, the Court of Appeal said that the review was not limited to cases in which a trial judge had erred in principle or where there was no material on which the decision he reached could properly have been arrived at. If necessary, the court could examine afresh the relevant facts and circumstances in order to exercise a discretion by way of review where the judge's ruling may have resulted in injustice to the appellants. **D25.18**

Conduct of Lawyers

Errors on the part of advocates may lead to a conviction being found to be unsafe. If the decision of the advocate is taken in good faith, having weighed the competing considerations and having consulted his client where appropriate, the court is much less likely to interfere than where the decision is taken in defiance of instructions and without reference to the client (*Clinton* [1993] 1 WLR 1181). **D25.19**

A number of formulations of the test for determining when an advocate's conduct is sufficient to lead to the quashing of a conviction have found favour at different times. That the advocate's conduct must be flagrantly incompetent was said to be necessary in *Ensor* [1989] 1 WLR 497, whilst in *Richards* [2000] All ER (D) 900, the court held that the test to be applied in relation to the conduct of the lawyer was that contained in *Associated Provincial Picture Houses Ltd. v Wednesbury Corporation* [1948] 1 KB 223, i.e. the *Wednesbury* unreasonableness test.

The Court of Appeal have recognised the difficulties associated with such tests and in *Clinton* stressed that the real test to be applied was not the extent or quality of the advocate's incompetence but whether the conduct affected the safety of the conviction in accordance with s. 2(1) of the Criminal Appeal Act 1968. In *Scollan* [1999] Crim LR 566, the Court of Appeal approved that approach and said that the position had been unaffected by the amendment of s. 2(1) by the Criminal Appeal Act 1995 (see **D25.15**). Similarly in *Nangle* [2001] Crim LR 506, the Court of Appeal emphasised that a test requiring flagrant incompetence might not be appropriate in the light of the ECHR, Article 6. What mattered was whether the appellant had had a fair trial; if the conduct of his lawyers was such that that requirement had not been met, the court might have to intervene. In *Boodram v State of Trinidad and Tobago* [2002] 1 Cr App R 103, the Privy Council observed that, if the conduct of an appellant's lawyers was such that he had been denied due process, the conclusion would be that he had not had a fair trial and the conviction should be quashed without the need for an investigation of the impact of the lawyers' failings on the outcome of the trial.

Guidance as to the procedure to be followed by an advocate when dealing with an appeal involving criticism of counsel was issued by the Bar Council and approved by Lord Taylor CJ in December 1995. The guidance was quoted with approval by Judge LJ in *Doherty* [1997] 2 Cr App R 218, and the importance of advocates following that guidance was emphasised in *Nasser* (1998) *The Times*, 19 February 1998.

Rejection of Submission of No Case to Answer

D25.20 The wrongful rejection of a submission of no case to answer at the close of the prosecution case will lead to the conclusion that a conviction is unsafe (*Abbott* [1955] 2 QB 497). That can be so even when the appellant has given evidence and admitted his guilt in cross-examination (*Smith* [1999] 2 Cr App R 238). The failure of an experienced advocate to make a submission of no case will not preclude the quashing of a conviction on the basis that there was in fact no case to answer, but the Court of Appeal will presume that the advocate had reason to not make the submission and will look at the whole of the evidence in making its decision. The court will not ordinarily interfere if a submission would have succeeded but was not made, and evidence of guilt emerged later in the trial (*Juett* [1981] Crim LR 113).

Defects in the Indictment

D25.21 There are a number of different challenges to the safety of a conviction which can be made by reference to defects in the indictment.

Where the indictment charges an offence not known to law, the conviction will be quashed (*DPP v Bhagwan* [1972] AC 60). That will be the case even if the defendant pleads guilty or no point is taken at trial (*Whitehouse* (1977) 65 Cr App R 33).

Where the indictment is preferred and signed without jurisdiction, the proceedings will be a nullity (*Thompson* (1975) 61 Cr App R 108, but see *Ashton* [2007] 1 WLR 181 and **D11.4**).

Where an indictment is duplicitous, a conviction may be quashed if the duplicity results in the conviction being unsafe (*Cain* [1983] Crim LR 802; *Levantiz* [1999] 1 Cr App R 465). That is so whether objection was taken at trial or not (*Molloy* [1921] 2 KB 364).

When counts are improperly joined or included in an indictment contrary to r. 14.2 of the CrimPR, s. 2(2) of the Administration of Justice (Miscellaneous Provisions) Act 1933, or

s. 40 of the CJA 1988, the conviction may be quashed. If the joinder of counts falls foul of s. 2(2) of the 1933 Act, the conviction will be quashed subject to the caveat that application must be made at trial to quash the indictment. In *Morry* [1946] KB 153, the appellant had been unrepresented at trial but the trial judge raised the point and that was held to be sufficient. In *Nisbet* [1972] 1 QB 37, the Court of Appeal expressed the *obiter* view that it had inherent jurisdiction to quash added or substituted counts if they might result in injustice even though they were founded on the committal papers and no objection was taken at trial. If counts are improperly joined contrary to r. 14.2 or s. 40, the conviction in relation to the wrongly joined count will be quashed (*Smith* [1997] 1 Cr App R 390).

Inconsistent Verdicts

The Court of Appeal will quash a conviction based on apparently inconsistent verdicts only if those verdicts are such that no reasonable jury applying its mind to the evidence could have reached the conclusions that it did (*Durante* [1972] 1 WLR 1612, adopting the judgment of Devlin J in *Stone* (unreported 13 December 1954)). For examples of the importance of the scrutiny of the facts of a case in the application of this rule, see *Drury* (1971) 56 Cr App R 104; *Kirby* (1972) 56 Cr App R 758; *Grizzle* [1991] Crim LR 553; *McKechnie* (1991) 94 Cr App R 51; *Harrison* [1994] Crim LR 859; *Aldred* [1995] Crim LR 160; *Malashev* [1997] Crim LR 587; *G* [1998] Crim LR 483; *Hayward* [2000] Crim LR 189 and *B & Q plc* [2005] EWCA Crim. 2297; *Burke* [2006] EWCA Crim 3122. **D25.22**

Conduct of the Trial Judge

Excessive judicial intervention during the course of the evidence of the accused has sometimes led to the quashing of a conviction. In *Hulusi* (1974) 58 Cr App R 378, Lawton LJ summed up the principle underlying such appeals (at p. 385): **D25.23**

> It is a fundamental principle of an English trial that, if an accused gives evidence, he must be allowed to do so without being badgered and interrupted. Judges should remember that most people go into the witness-box, whether they be witnesses for the Crown or the defence, in a state of nervousness. They are anxious to do their best. They expect to receive a courteous hearing, and when they find, almost as soon as they get into the witness-box and are starting to tell their story, that the judge of all people is intervening in a hostile way, then, human nature being what it is, they are liable to become confused and not to do as well as they would have done had they not been badgered and interrupted.

Conduct other than interruption which prevents justice being done to the defence case can also give rise to a successful ground of appeal against conviction (*Barnes* (1970) 55 Cr App R 100). In *Alves* [1997] 1 Cr App R 78, the Court of Appeal held that dismissive remarks about the prospects of acquittal, albeit in the absence of the jury, when the accused was in the course of giving evidence, would have the same inhibiting effect on an accused as interruption, and quashed the conviction. In *Lashley* [2005] EWCA Crim 2015, the attacks upon defence counsel made by the judge amounted to inappropriate personal animosity involving criticism of her ability and integrity. The court said that such conduct would undermine the accused's confidence in the administration of justice and would likely do so for a reasonable observer — the conviction was quashed.

APPROACH OF COURT OF APPEAL TO COMMONLY OCCURRING ERRORS IN SUMMING-UP

Plainly, errors in the summing-up may found a successful appeal against conviction if the error leads to the conclusion that the conviction is unsafe. **D25.24**

Misdirection on Law

D25.25 A misdirection as to law will lead to the quashing of a conviction only if that misdirection causes the conviction to be unsafe. Thus, in *Edwards* (1983) 77 Cr App R 5 and *Donoghue* (1987) 86 Cr App R 267, the Court of Appeal dismissed the appeals despite the trial judge having failed to direct the jury as to the standard and burden of proof respectively. In each case the court observed that the evidence against the defendant was very strong and justified the exercise of the proviso which then applied under s. 2(1) of the Criminal Appeal Act 1968. By contrast, in *James* [1997] Crim LR 598, the Court of Appeal quashed the conviction for robbery where the trial judge had failed to direct the jury that it was necessary for the force used to be for the purpose of stealing. That direction was crucial to distinguish between robbery and theft.

Wrongful Withdrawal of Issues from the Jury

D25.26 In *Sheaf* (1925) 19 Cr App R 46, Avory J said 'When we once arrive at the conclusion that a vital question of fact has not been left to the jury, the only ground on which we can affirm a conviction is that there has been no miscarriage of justice, on the ground that if the question had been left to the jury, they must necessarily have come to the conclusion that the appellant was guilty'. Thus, if a trial judge fails to direct a jury as to an issue of fact going to an element of the offence, the conviction may be quashed if it is, as a result, unsafe.

Where the evidence on a particular issue is agreed, it can be appropriate for a trial judge to direct a jury that the jury could draw an adverse inference against the accused on that issue. But if the judge removes all issues of fact and law from the jury so that the jury are effectively directed to convict the defendant, the conviction is highly likely to be quashed (*Stonehouse* [1978] AC 55). That is not inevitably so if a not guilty verdict from a properly directed jury would have been perverse (*Thompson* [1984] 1 WLR 962).

Misdirection on Facts

D25.27 A misstatement or omission of a fact in the course of the summing-up may lead to the quashing of a conviction if the fact was of such importance that, if it had been correctly stated, the jury may not have reached the same verdict. In *Bateson* [1969] 3 All ER 1372, the Court of Appeal quashed the conviction where the trial judge told the jury that the accused had first mentioned his defence when the trial had commenced. The court took the view that it was at least 'on the cards' that the jury would have acquitted if the facts had been correctly stated to them. Conversely in *Wright* [1974] 58 Cr App R 444, the Court of Appeal dismissed an appeal when the misdirection as to facts was not sufficiently central. Scarman LJ said (at p. 452):

> At the end of the day, when the appellant's case is not that the judge erred in law but that the judge erred in his handling of the facts, the question must be, first of all, was there error, and secondly, if there was, was it significant error which might have misled the jury? If this court has a lurking doubt it is its duty to quash the conviction as unsafe, but this court . . . has reached the clear conclusion that this verdict was safe and satisfactory.

Improper Comment on Facts or Defence Case

D25.28 A trial judge is entitled to comment on the facts and express an opinion as to those facts, so it is rare that an appeal will be successful when it is based on such judicial comments. It is only when a trial judge exhibits blatant unfairness and pro-prosecution bias that the conviction will be imperilled. In *Canny* (1945) 30 Cr App R 143, the conviction was quashed when the judge repeatedly described the defence case as absurd. Similarly, in *Berrada* (1989) 91 Cr App R 131, the conviction was quashed when the judge described allegations put by the defence to a prosecution witness as 'really monstrous' and 'wicked'.

Comment on Failure of Accused to Testify

A direction by a trial judge on the failure of an accused to testify is an important one and an error as to that direction may give rise to an arguable ground of appeal. Detailed consideration of the appropriate direction to the jury can be found at F19.19. **D25.29**

Comment on the Accused's Character

Detailed consideration of the elements of directions as to character may be found at F12. An inappropriate direction may lead to the quashing of a conviction. **D25.30**

EFFECT OF SUCCESSFUL APPEAL AGAINST CONVICTION

Criminal Appeal Act 1968, ss. 2 and 7 **D25.31**

2.—(2) In the case of an appeal against conviction the court shall, if they allow the appeal, quash the conviction.

(3) An order of the Court of Appeal quashing a conviction shall, except when under section 7 below the appellant is ordered to be retried, operate as a direction to the court of trial to enter, instead of the record of conviction, a judgment and verdict of acquittal.

7.— (1) Where the Court of Appeal allow an appeal against conviction and it appears to the court that the interests of justice so require, they may order the appellant to be retried.

(2) A person shall not under this section be ordered to be retried for any offence other than –
- (a) the offence of which he was convicted at the original trial and in respect of which his appeal is allowed as mentioned in subsection (1) above;
- (b) an offence of which he could have been convicted at the original trial on an indictment for the first mentioned offence; or
- (c) an offence charged in an alternative count of the indictment in respect of which no verdict was given in consequence of his being convicted of the first-mentioned offence.

Decision to Order a Retrial

Under s. 2(2) of the Criminal Appeal Act 1968, the Court of Appeal may quash a conviction and order that the court of trial enter a verdict of not guilty against the accused. Alternatively, the court may order a retrial of the successful appellant under s. 7. There are currently no reliable statistics on the percentage of successful appeals which result in a retrial. **D25.32**

The factors which the court will take into account when deciding whether or not to order a retrial will include the length of time which has elapsed between the appellant's original conviction and the successful appeal and the extent to which any fresh evidence received by the court undermines the strength of the case against the appellant (see *Saunders* (1974) 58 Cr App R 248; *Flower* [1966] 1 QB 146; *McIlkenny* (1991) 93 Cr App R 287).

Occasionally, a retrial will not be ordered because of considerable publicity surrounding the alleged offences which is adverse to the defendant (*Taylor* (1994) 98 Cr App R 361). But, it is submitted, an application that the appellant should not be retried because of prejudicial publicity is highly unlikely to succeed. The Court of Appeal will allow such an application only if it is satisfied on the balance of probabilities that, as a result of the publicity, one or all of the verdicts returned by a jury would be unsafe The court may take account of the time between the publicity and the retrial and can seek to minimise its effect by a change of trial venue and suitable questions to the jury (*Stone* [2001] Crim LR 465).

Section 8 includes a number of procedural requirements to be followed when a retrial is ordered. The most important of those requirements are as follows:

(a) a new indictment must be preferred by the Court of Appeal;
(b) arraignment must be within two months of the quashing of the conviction unless the Court of Appeal allows longer;

(c) at any time after the two months has elapsed, the appellant may apply for the order for retrial to be set aside and for a verdict of not guilty to be entered;
(d) upon receipt of such an application, the Court of Appeal may quash the order for retrial or may allow late arraignment — the court will allow late arraignment only if the prosecution has acted with due expedition and there is good and sufficient cause that the retrial take place despite the delay following the order for a retrial.

In *Horne* [1992] Crim LR 304, the prosecution papers were lost and, as a result, the accused was not arraigned within the two-month time-limit. The prosecution was held not to have acted with due expedition despite an early trial date being set down. In *Jones* [2003] 1 Cr App R 313, an adjourned date for the arraignment was set down outside the two-month period without the prosecution noticing the difficulties that listing would produce. The Court of Appeal held that the prosecution had acted with due expedition but if the applicable test had been of due diligence (as in relation to custody time-limits), the position would have been different. Defence lawyers were also criticised for failing to draw the difficulties to the attention of the prosecution in order that they could comply with the order of the court.

Partially Successful Appeal: Substituting Verdict

D25.33 **Criminal Appeal Act 1968, s. 3**

(1) This section applies on an appeal against conviction, where the appellant has been convicted of an offence and the jury could on the indictment have found him guilty of some other offence, and on the finding of the jury it appears to the Court of Appeal that the jury must have been satisfied of facts which proved him guilty of the other offence.
(2) The Court may, instead of allowing or dismissing the appeal, substitute for the verdict found by the jury a verdict of guilty of the other offence, and pass such sentence in substitution for the sentence passed at the trial as may be authorised by law for the other offence, not being a sentence of greater severity.

Section 3 of the Criminal Appeal Act 1968 allows the Court of Appeal to substitute a verdict of guilty for an offence other than that of which the appellant was convicted if it appears to the court that:

(a) the jury could on the indictment have found the appellant guilty of the substituted offence, the allegation of which was expressly or impliedly included in the allegation in the particular count in the indictment, and
(b) the jury must have been satisfied of facts which proved the appellant guilty of the substituted offence (*Graham* [1997] 1 Cr App R 302).

Section 3 of the 1968 Act applies to two broad categories of cases. The first is where the appellant was tried and convicted on a single count but the evidence was such that the jury could have convicted of the substituted offence. In *Spratt* [1980] 1 WLR 554, following the appellant's conviction for murder, the Court of Appeal received fresh evidence going to the issue of whether he was suffering from diminished responsibility when the alleged offence was committed. As it was not in dispute that an unlawful killing had been perpetrated, the court was able to substitute a conviction for manslaughter.

The second category of case is where there are counts charged in the alternative and the jury have convicted on a count which is not supported by the evidence. The court may substitute the alternative count provided the jury have not already entered a not guilty count in relation to that count (*Seymour* [1954] 1 WLR 678; but see also *Smythe* (1980) 72 Cr App R 8 for a minor variation of the rule).

Sentence when Appeal Allowed on Part Only of an Indictment

D25.34 If an appellant has been convicted in the Crown Court of a number of offences and the Court of Appeal quashes some of the convictions but not others, the court is entitled to resentence the offender on the counts on which he remains convicted. The power, which arises under the

Criminal Appeal Act 1968, s. 4, is limited to the extent that the court may not pass a sentence of greater totality or severity than that which was originally passed by the Crown Court. The Court of Appeal may resentence even on those counts for which the Crown Court imposed no separate penalty (*O'Grady* (1941) 28 Cr App R 33; *Dolan* (1975) 62 Cr App R 36).

RIGHT OF APPEAL AGAINST SENTENCE

Statutory Basis of Appeal against Sentence

The right to appeal against sentence is statutory and derives from the Criminal Appeal Act 1968. Section 9 governs appeals against sentence following conviction on indictment. Appeals from sentences imposed in the Crown Court following summary conviction are covered by s. 10. The definition of sentence for the purposes of the sections is to be found in s. 50. **D25.35**

Whether the appeal lies under s. 9 or s. 10, the appellant must, by virtue of s. 11, either have leave to appeal from the Court of Appeal or the sentencing judge must certify that the case is fit for appeal against sentence. Paragraph IV.50 of the *Consolidated Criminal Practice Direction* deals with bail pending appeal and directs that a sentencing judge should not certify an appeal against sentence 'merely in the light of mitigation to which, in his opinion, he has given due weight'. The Court of Appeal have also reminded sentencing judges of the terms of the Practice Direction in stating that a certificate should not be granted in the absence of a 'particular and cogent ground of appeal' (*Dawson* (1984) *The Times*, 28 June 1984). The reality in practice is that certificates of appeal against sentence are rarely applied for and are even less seldom granted.

Unless the sentencing judge certifies that the case is fit for appeal, an applicant needs leave from the Court of Appeal to appeal against his sentence (s. 11; see **D25.38**).

Sentence Following Conviction on Indictment

Criminal Appeal Act 1968, ss. 9 and 50 **D25.36**

9.—(1) A person who has been convicted of an offence on indictment may appeal to the Court of Appeal against any sentence (not being a sentence fixed by law) passed on him for the offence, whether passed on his conviction or in subsequent proceedings.

(1A) In subsection (1) of this section, the reference to a sentence fixed by law does not include a reference to an order made under subsection (2) or (4) of section 269 of the Criminal Justice Act 2003 in relation to a life sentence (as defined in section 277 of that Act) that is fixed by law.

(2) A person who on conviction on indictment has also been convicted of a summary offence under section 41 of the Criminal Justice Act 1988 (power of Crown Court to deal with summary offence where person committed for either-way offence) or paragraph 6 of schedule 3 to the Crime and Disorder Act 1998 (power of Crown Court to deal with summary offence where person sent for trial for indictable-only offence) may appeal to the Court of Appeal against any sentence passed on him for the summary offence (whether on his conviction or in subsequent proceedings) under subsection (7) of that section or sub-paragraph (4) of that paragraph.

50.—(1) In this Act, 'sentence', in relation to an offence, includes any order made by a court when dealing with an offender including, in particular—

(a) a hospital order under part III of the Mental Health Act 1983, with or without a restriction order;
(b) an interim hospital order under that part;
(bb) a hospital direction and a limitation direction under that part;
(c) a recommendation for deportation;
(ca) a confiscation order under part 2 of the Proceeds of Crime Act 2002;
(cb) an order which varies a confiscation order made under part 2 of the Proceeds of Crime Act 2002 if the varying order is made under section 21, 22 or 29 of that Act (but not otherwise);

(cc) a direction under section 20(3) or 21(3) of the Crime (Sentences) Act 1997 (extended supervision for sexual or violent offenders);
(d) a confiscation order under the Drug Trafficking Act 1994 other than one made by the High Court;
(e) a confiscation order under part VI of the Criminal Justice Act 1988;
(f) an order varying a confiscation order of a kind which is included by virtue of paragraph (d) or (e) above;
(g) an order made by the Crown Court varying a confiscation order which was made by the High Court by virtue of section 19 of the Act of 1994;
(h) a declaration of relevance under the Football Spectators Act 1989; and
(i) an order under section 129(2) of the Licensing Act 2003 (forfeiture or suspension of personal licence).

(1A) Section 14 of the Powers of Criminal Courts (Sentencing) Act 2000 (under which a conviction of an offence for which an order for conditional or absolute discharge is made is deemed not to be a conviction except for certain purposes) shall not prevent an appeal under this Act, whether against conviction or otherwise.

(2) Any power of the Criminal Division of the Court of Appeal to pass a sentence includes a power to make a recommendation for deportation in cases where the court from which the appeal lies had power to make such a recommendation.

(3) An order under section 17 of the Access to Justice Act 1999 is not a sentence for the purposes of this Act.

A person convicted on indictment may appeal to the Court of Appeal against *any* sentence passed on him for the offence, unless it is one fixed by law (i.e. the life sentence for murder) (s. 9(1)). If an offender is convicted on indictment and pleads guilty to an additional offence which was committed or transferred to the Crown Court by the magistrates under the CJA 1988, s. 41 (see **D6.45**), his right of appeal extends to his sentence for that matter also (s. 9(2)). The appeal is available if the sentence is passed at the time of the conviction or later. Thus, the right of appeal exists if an offender is resentenced for an offence following subsequent offending. Equally, if an offender is convicted of drug trafficking offences and is subsequently made the subject of a confiscation order, the offender may appeal against the confiscation order (*Neal* [1999] Crim LR 509).

Section 50(1) states that 'sentence' includes any order made by a court when dealing with an offender'. The definition therefore covers not only the penalty but also many orders made ancillary to that sentence. Thus an order to pay costs (*Hayden* [1975] 1 WLR 852) or compensation (see the numerous cases such as *Vivian* [1979] 1 WLR 291) may be the subject of appeal to the Court of Appeal. Other ancillary orders which have been held to be part of the sentence for the purposes of an appeal are restitution orders under the Theft Act 1968, s. 28 (*Parker* [1970] 1 WLR 1003); orders binding an offender over to come up for judgment if required to do so (*Williams* [1982] 1 WLR 1398); and orders revoking a parole licence (*Welch* [1982] 1 WLR 976). Section 50(1) also specifically provides that hospital orders under part III of the Mental Health Act 1983 (whether with or without a restriction order) and recommendations for deportation are part of the sentence.

Although by virtue of s. 9(1) it is not possible to appeal against the mandatory life sentence for murder, it is possible to appeal against the minimum term set by the court or against a whole life term (s. 9(1A), inserted by the CJA 2003, s. 271). Moreover, the period specified in respect of a discretionary life sentence under s. 82A of the PCC(S)A 2000 is susceptible to appeal. An appeal can be instituted against either the failure of a sentencer to specify a period (*Hollies* (1995) 16 Cr App R (S) 463), or against the actual period which the sentencer fixes (*D* (1995) 16 Cr App R (S) 564). (For details of s. 82A, see **E5.15**.)

Sentence Following Summary Conviction and Crown Court Disposal

Criminal Appeal Act 1968, s. 10 **D25.37**

(1) This section has effect for providing rights of appeal against sentence when a person is dealt with by the Crown Court (otherwise than on appeal from a magistrates' court) for an offence of which he was not convicted on indictment.

(2) The proceedings from which an appeal against sentence lies under this section are those where an offender convicted of an offence by a magistrates' court—
   (a) is committed by the court to be dealt with for his offence at the Crown Court; or
   (b) having been made the subject of an order for conditional discharge or a youth community order within the meaning of the Powers of Criminal Courts (Sentencing) Act 2000 or a community order within the meaning of the Criminal Justice Act 2003 or given a suspended sentence, appears or is brought before the Crown Court to be further dealt with for his offence.

(3) An offender dealt with for an offence at the Crown Court in a proceeding to which subsection (2) of this section applies may appeal to the Court of Appeal against any sentence passed on him for the offence by the Crown Court.

The right of appeal against a sentence imposed by the Crown Court for which the offender was summarily convicted is governed by s. 10. The appeal arises when (a) an offender is committed for sentence (e.g., under the PCC(S)A 2000, s. 3 or s. 6), or (b) having been made the subject of an order for conditional discharge or a community order or given a suspended sentence of imprisonment, he breaches the order or suspended sentence by a subsequent conviction and falls to be dealt with by the Crown Court for the breach (s. 10(2)(a) and (b)). Although such cases are dealt with relatively infrequently, there are two main situations in which such matters come before the Crown Court, namely:

(a) the offender is summarily convicted of an offence which puts him in breach of an order mentioned in s. 10(2)(b) that was made by a magistrates' court and the convicting magistrates' court decides to commit him for sentence in respect of the subsequent offence and also decides to commit him to be dealt with for the breach;
(b) the offender is summarily convicted of an offence which puts him in breach of a relevant order previously made against him by the Crown Court when dealing with him following committal for sentence for a summary conviction. In such a case, the magistrates' court may either commit the offender to be dealt with for the breach or may decline to commit him but, in the latter case, the Crown Court may secure the attendance of the offender before it by the appropriate process.

The previous limitation of the right of appeal to a sentence imposing a term of imprisonment of six months or more has been removed by the CJA 2003, s. 319. Thus any offender committed to the Crown Court for sentence may institute an appeal against the sentence imposed upon him.

Powers of the Court of Appeal when Determining an Appeal against Sentence

Criminal Appeal Act 1968, s. 11 **D25.38**

(1) Subject to subsection (1A) below, an appeal against sentence, whether under section 9 or section 10 of this Act, lies only with the leave of the Court of Appeal.

(1A) If the judge who passed the sentence grants a certificate that the case is fit for appeal under section 9 or 10 of this Act, an appeal lies under this section without the leave of the Court of Appeal.

(2) Where the Crown Court, in dealing with an offender either on his conviction on indictment or in a proceeding to which section 10(2) of this Act applies, has passed on him two or more sentences in the same proceeding, being sentences against which an appeal lies under section 9(1) or section 10, an appeal or application for leave to appeal against any one of those sentences shall be treated as an appeal or application in respect of both or all of them.

(2A) Where following conviction on indictment a person has been convicted under section 41 of the Criminal Justice Act 1988 of a summary offence an appeal or application for leave to appeal against any sentence for the offence triable either way shall be treated also as an appeal or application in respect of any sentence for the summary offence and an appeal or application for leave to appeal against any sentence for the summary offence shall be treated also as an appeal or application in respect of the offence triable either way.

(2B) If the appellant or applicant was convicted on indictment of two or more offences triable either way, the references to the offence triable either way in subsection (2A) above are to be construed, in relation to any summary offence of which he was convicted under section 41 of the Criminal Justice Act 1988 following the conviction on indictment, as references to the offence triable either way specified in the notice relating to that summary offence which was given under subsection (2) of that section.

(3) On an appeal against sentence the Court of Appeal, if they consider that the appellant should be sentenced differently for an offence for which he was dealt with by the court below may—

(a) quash any sentence or order which is the subject of the appeal; and

(b) in place of it pass such sentence or make such order as they think appropriate for the case and as the court below had power to pass or make when dealing with him for the offence;

but the court shall so exercise their powers under this subsection that, taking the case as a whole, the appellant is not more severely dealt with on appeal than he was dealt with by the court below.

(4) [repealed]

[(5) and (6) Concern respectively the position where the Court of Appeal quashes an interim hospital order but does not replace it with its own sentence, and the position where the court replaces the sentence of the court below with an interim hospital order.]

(7) For the purposes of this section, any two or more sentences are to be treated as passed in the same proceeding if—

(a) they are passed on the same day; or

(b) they are passed on different days but the court in passing any one of them states that it is treating that one together with the other or others as substantially one sentence.

Upon appeal against sentence, the Court of Appeal may quash the sentence and substitute any other sentence or order that it deems appropriate, provided that the substituted sentence could lawfully have been passed by the Crown Court and provided also that the appellant is not dealt with more severely when the case is viewed as a whole. The Court of Appeal may not impose a mandatory sentence where a Crown Court has failed to impose or if it would mean treating the appellant more severely (*Reynolds* [2007] EWCA Crim 538).

As the Court of Appeal must look at the position as a whole when deciding whether the substituted sentence would constitute treating the appellant more severely, it follows that, if the offender was sentenced for two or more matters, the Court of Appeal may increase the sentence for one of them and adjust the others accordingly. As just one example of a not infrequent practice, in *McKenna* (1985) 7 Cr App R (S) 348, a youth was convicted on indictment of rape and sentenced to two years' detention. He was further sentenced to a year's detention to run consecutively for an offence of robbery in respect of which he had been committed to the Crown Court for sentence. The latter sentence was unlawful and so the Court of Appeal had no option but to quash it. But it replaced the two-year sentence for rape with one of three years and imposed no separate penalty for the robbery. Overall, the substituted sentence was therefore not more severe than that imposed at the Crown Court.

Infrequently, the relative severity of a substituted sentence to the original sentence is not immediately obvious. Examples of such situations include:

(a) 'Taking the case as a whole' means taking together the totality of the matters in respect of which the appellant was being dealt with in the court below on the day he was sentenced' (per Glidewell J in *Sandwell* (1984) 80 Cr App R 78 at p. 81). In *Sandwell*, S pleaded guilty on the same day to two offences charged in separate indictments, and was sentenced for each to, *inter alia*, 12 months' disqualification to run consecutively. There is no power to impose consecutive disqualifications and so those disqualifications fell to be quashed, but the Court of Appeal varied the sentence to two years' disqualification for each offence to run concurrently.

(b) A sentence of life imprisonment may not be substituted for a sentence of imprisonment for a fixed term of years (*Whittaker* [1967] Crim LR 431).

(c) An immediate custodial term may not be imposed in place of a suspended sentence *Peppard* (1990) 12 Cr App R (S) 88 (following *McCabe* (1988) 10 Cr App R (S) 134).

(d) A hospital order coupled with a restriction order for an indefinite period has been held to be no more severe than a sentence of three years' imprisonment (*Bennett* [1968] 1 WLR 988, cited with approval in *Crozier* (1990) 12 Cr App R (S) 206). Furthermore, a hospital order without restriction has been substituted for a sentence of Borstal training (*Marsden* [1968] 1 WLR 785). It would appear that the rationale underlying those decisions is that, in contrast to a custodial term, a hospital order is intended to be a remedial treatment and not a punishment.

(e) A fine in combination with a custodial term may properly be substituted for a reduced custodial term (*Walton* (29 August 1989 unreported)). W had been sentenced by the court below to four months' imprisonment. He served 11 days in custody and was then released on bail. At the appeal, such term of imprisonment as would allow immediate release was substituted, with the addition of a fine of £1,000.

(f) A period of disqualification from driving may be imposed or increased where a sentence of imprisonment is reduced (*Ardani* (1983) 77 Cr App R 302). Conversely, in *McLaren* (1983) 5 Cr App R (S) 332, the appellant's fine was increased but his period of disqualification was reduced.

Commonly Occurring Grounds of Appeal against Sentence

From the existing case law, it is possible to identify a number of heads of appeal against sentence which have emerged. What follows is a summary of the more conspicuous of those heads of appeal. **D25.39**

Sentence Wrong in Law The Court of Appeal will intervene when the sentence imposed on an appellant could not legally be passed. A simple example is *Corcoran* (1986) 8 Cr App R(S) 118, in which a youth convicted summarily was sentenced to three years detention, ostensibly in accordance with s. 53(3) of the CYPA 1933. That sentence was imposed in the Crown Court following committal for sentence. As s. 53(3) detention can only be imposed following conviction on indictment, the Court of Appeal was forced to substitute the maximum available sentence in the youth court of 12 months' youth custody, despite observing that a sentence of three years was richly deserved. **D25.40**

Sentence Wrong in Principle or Manifestly Excessive The Court of Appeal will interfere with the sentence imposed by the Crown Court if it is of the view that it was outside the broad range of appropriate penalties. The fact that a sentence is merely severe will not be sufficient to move the Court as has been stated in a number of cases. In *Nuttall* (1908) 1 Cr App R 180, Channell J said, 'This court will . . . be reluctant to interfere with sentences which do not seem to it to be wrong in principle, though they may appear heavy to individual judges'. Likewise, in *Gumbs* (1926) 19 Cr App R 74, Lord Hewart CJ stated: **D25.41**

> . . . this court never interferes with the discretion of the court below merely on the ground that this court might have passed a somewhat different sentence; for this court to revise a sentence there must be some error in principle.

If the Crown Court imposes a sentence which is not of the appropriate form (because for example an offender was not eligible for the custodial sentence imposed upon him), the more appropriate description is that the sentence is 'wrong in principle'. Equally, an inappropriate combination of sentences can be most appropriately described as 'wrong in principle' (see *Socratous* (1984) 6 Cr App R (S) 33, in which the imposition of a short custodial term combined with a probation order was held to be wrong in principle).

That a sentence passed is 'manifestly excessive' is the basis that is most commonly used in the modern appeal process. An appeal will succeed only if the sentence was excessive in the sense of being outside the appropriate range for the offence and offender in question, as opposed to being merely more than the Court of Appeal itself would have passed. For example in *Withers* [1983] Crim LR 339, the principal submission was that a sentence of nine months' imprisonment for stealing £1,000 from employers was too long by three months. The court held that a sentence of six months would not have been wrong, but to reduce the sentence by such a small amount would have been 'tinkering' with the Crown Court judge's decision and the appeal was consequently dismissed. Although the sentence was 'excessive' in one sense, it was not so excessive as to be outside the appropriate range. Equally, where a sentence was not manifestly excessive at the time that it was passed, the Court of Appeal will not interfere with the level of that sentence just because the 'tariff' for that offence is reduced after the sentence is passed or legislation alters the level of sentence to be imposed (*Graham* [1999] 2 Cr App R (S) 312).

By virtue of the CJA 2003, s. 172, a sentencing judge ought to have regard to a relevant guideline when sentencing (see **E1.2**). If a judge clearly departs from a relevant definitive guideline, that is likely to give rise to an arguable ground of appeal, especially if he does not give reasons for that departure. Whilst a court does not have to follow a guideline, it ought to have regard to it. If it does not follow the guideline, it must give reasons as to why it does not (*Bowering* [2006] 2 Cr App R(S) 80).

D25.42 **Judge's Remarks when Sentencing** If the judge's sentencing remarks tend to reveal that he has taken irrelevant factors into account in deciding the appropriate sentence to impose on the appellant, the Court of Appeal may allow the appeal and substitute a different sentence. But if the Court of Appeal takes the view that the sentence was appropriate despite the flaws in the decision-making by the judge, it may nonetheless uphold the sentence. Examples of circumstances in which the judge's sentencing remarks might lead to a reduction in sentence include where the judge implies that he has increased the sentence because the offender elected trial on indictment, pleaded not guilty, or made attacks on the character of prosecution witnesses (see *Skone* (1966) 51 Cr App R 165; *Scott* (1983) 5 Cr App R (S) 90; *Doab* [1983] Crim LR 569).

D25.43 **Procedural Errors** The failure of a sentencing judge to follow the correct procedure can lead to a variation in the sentence by the Court of Appeal. But that is by no means necessarily the case. The failure of a sentencing judge to secure a pre-sentence report before passing sentence in circumstances where one was required will not necessarily lead to a reduction in sentence, but the Court of Appeal will secure such a report before dealing with the appeal. Similarly, where information about an offender's antecedents has been inappropriately given to the court of sentence, the Court of Appeal may either reduce the sentence or maintain it as the correct sentence in all the circumstances (*Wilkins* (1977) 66 Cr App R (S) 49; *Van Pelz* [1943] KB 157). The failure of the judge to hold a *Newton* hearing when asked to do so is more likely to result in a reduction in sentence, as the sentencing judge may well have proceeded on a basis adverse to the defendant (see *Costley* (1989) 11 Cr App R (S) 357 and **D19.22**).

D25.44 **Sense of Grievance** The Court of Appeal will intervene when the appellant has a justifiable sense of grievance at the sentence imposed upon him following events preceding sentence. In practice, this principle applies most often when a sentencing judge orders pre-sentence reports and indicates that, if the reports are satisfactory, a non-custodial sentence will be passed, but then proceeds to send the offender into custody despite positive reports (*Gillam* (1980) 2 Cr App R (S) 267; *Ward* (1982) 4 Cr App R (S) 103). Moreover, if an indication of a non-custodial sentence is given privately to an advocate and a guilty plea follows, any subsequent sentencing judge will be bound by the indication of the first judge (*Moss* (1983) 5 Cr App R (S) 209). But if a judge indicates that the fact of his ordering reports should not be taken as any indication that he would eventually pass a non-custodial sentence, or indicates that he is 'making no promises', then obviously the court will not be moved to vary the sentence imposed if a custodial sentence follows, as the appellant's hopes could not be said to have been legitimately raised (*Horton* (1985) 7 Cr App R (S) 299).

Disparity of Sentence There has been some inconsistency in the approach taken by the Court of Appeal to the question of the circumstances in which a difference in sentence between co-accused can form a ground of appeal against sentence. In *Stroud* (1977) 65 Cr App R 150, Scarman LJ stated that disparity can never in itself be a sufficient ground of appeal. Instead, the question for the Court of Appeal is simply whether the sentence received by the appellant was wrong in principle or manifestly excessive. If it was not, the appeal should be dismissed, even though a co-offender was, in the Court of Appeal's view, treated with undue leniency. To reduce the heavier sentence would simply result in two, rather than one, over-lenient penalties. Decisions in the same vein include *Brown* [1975] Crim LR 177, *Hair* [1978] Crim LR 698 and *Weekes* (1980) 74 Cr App R 161. D25.45

By contrast, in *Fawcett* (1983) 5 Cr App R (S) 158, the Court of Appeal held that where an offender had received a sentence which in and of itself was not objectionable but, for no apparent good reason, was more severe than that of his co-accused, the court could intervene if the disparity was serious. Lawton LJ said that the question to be asked is:

> would right-thinking members of the public, with full knowledge of all the relevant facts and circumstances, learning of this sentence consider that something had gone wrong with the administration of justice?

(See also *Wood* (1983) 5 Cr App R (S) 381 and *Sigston* [2004] EWCA Crim 1595.)

In more recent cases the Court of Appeal have followed the approach in *Fawcett* (but see *Tate* (2006) 150 SJ 1192, for a recent example of a case following the line of reasoning in *Stroud*).

The fact that offenders who are sentenced at roughly the same time as an appellant in the same Crown Court have received more lenient sentences for comparable offences can never be relied on as a ground of appeal. The court will not allow such comparisons to be made (*Large* (1981) 3 Cr App R (S) 80).

Failure to Distinguish between Offenders The failure of the court of sentence to distinguish between offenders when one has powerful mitigation and the other does not can give rise to a successful ground of appeal against sentence. In *Ekwubiri* (unreported 15 February 1999), a large number of drug dealers trapped by undercover officers had been on bail for a considerable period of time when they were eventually sentenced. The Court of Appeal held that, given E's exceptional mitigation, it would have been appropriate for the judge to distinguish between him and other co-accused whom the judge was sentencing for similar offending and reduced his sentence accordingly (see also *Fraser* (1982) 4 Cr App R (S) 254). D25.46

APPEAL AGAINST VERDICT OF NOT GUILTY BY REASON OF INSANITY

Criminal Appeal Act 1968, ss. 12 and 13 D25.47

12. A person in whose case there is returned a verdict of not guilty by reason of insanity may appeal to the Court of Appeal against the verdict—
    (a) with the leave of the Court of Appeal; or
    (b) if the judge of the court of trial grants a certificate that the case is fit for appeal.

13.—(1) Subject to the provisions of this section, the Court of Appeal—
    (a) shall allow an appeal under section 12 of this Act if they think that the verdict is unsafe; and
    (b) shall dismiss such an appeal in any other case.
(2) [Repealed.]
(3) Where apart from this subsection—

D

Part D Procedure

(a) an appeal under section 12 of this Act would fall to be allowed; and
(b) none of the grounds for allowing it relates to the question of the insanity of the accused,
the Court of Appeal may dismiss the appeal if they are of opinion that, but for the insanity of the accused, the proper verdict would have been that he was guilty of an offence other than the offence charged.

(4) Where an appeal under section 12 of this Act is allowed, the following provisions apply—
(a) if the ground, or one of the grounds, for allowing the appeal is that the finding of the jury as to the insanity of the accused ought not to stand and the Court of Appeal are of opinion that the proper verdict would have been that he was guilty of an offence (whether the offence charged or any other offence of which the jury could have found him guilty), the court—
(i) shall substitute for the verdict of not guilty by reason of insanity a verdict of guilty of that offence; and
(ii) shall, subject to subsection (5) below, have the like powers of punishing or otherwise dealing with the appellant, and other powers, as the court of trial would have had if the jury had come to the substituted verdict; and
(b) in any other case, the Court of Appeal shall substitute for the verdict of the jury a verdict of acquittal.

As with appeals against other findings in the Crown Court, leave is required to appeal a finding of not guilty by reason of insanity unless the trial judge certifies that the case is fit for appeal. Equally, just as s. 2 of the 1968 Act stipulates that the Court of Appeal will allow an appeal against conviction only if the verdict is unsafe, the court takes the same approach under s. 12 to any appeal against a finding of not guilty by reason of insanity.

If the basis for allowing the appeal is that the appellant is not insane, the court will substitute a finding of guilt of the appropriate offence and sentence accordingly. If the court reaches the view that the appeal should be allowed on grounds which are not related to the insanity of the appellant, but which grounds undermine the safety of the conviction (such as fresh evidence showing that the appellant did not commit the offence), a verdict of not guilty will be recorded. In such circumstances, under s. 14A, the court can order the detention of the appellant so that he may be assessed in accordance with sch. 1 to the Criminal Procedure (Insanity and Unfitness to Plead) Act 1991. The Court of Appeal may do so if it considers that the appellant is suffering from a mental disorder which warrants his detention in hospital for assessment and that he ought to be so detained in the interests of his own health and safety or with a view to the protection of other persons. If the court reaches the view that a verdict of not guilty would not have been appropriate, but findings that the appellant did the act or omission charged and was under a disability were appropriate, it may make any of the orders which could have been made by the court of sentence (s. 14).

APPEAL AGAINST FINDING OF UNFITNESS TO PLEAD

D25.48 **Criminal Appeal Act 1968 s. 15**

(1) Where there has been a determination under section 4 of the Criminal Procedure (Insanity) Act 1964 of the question of a person's fitness to be tried, and there have been findings that he is under a disability and that he did the act or made the omission charged against him, the person may appeal to the Court of Appeal against either or both of those findings.
(2) An appeal under this section lies only—
(a) with the leave of the Court of Appeal; or
(b) if the judge of the court of trial grants a certificate that the case is fit for appeal.

Section 15 enables the Court of Appeal to quash a finding of unfitness to plead. If the finding was made after arraignment and the court is of the view that the appellant should have been acquitted, the court may order the acquittal of the appellant. In other cases, following the finding that the appellant is fit to plead, the court will ensure that the appellant is brought to trial.

APPEAL AGAINST CONVICTION: SUBSTITUTION OF FINDING OF INSANITY OR UNFITNESS TO PLEAD

Under s. 6 of the Criminal Appeal Act 1968, the Court of Appeal may quash a conviction on the basis that the offender should have been found not guilty by reason of insanity or unfit to plead. In such circumstances, the court may then make any appropriate order which would have been available to the court of sentence. **D25.49**

JUDICIAL REVIEW OF ORDERS RESTRICTING OPEN JUSTICE

Section 159 of the CJA 1988 allows for appeals to the Court of Appeal (Criminal Division) against orders made by the Crown Court restricting reporting in relation to a trial on indictment (under either s. 4 or s. 11 of the Contempt of Court Act 1981) or public access to the trial. **D25.50**

It appears that the Court of Appeal have no power to grant an order which would act to restrict reporting or access when the Crown Court has refused to make such an order (*Lee* [1993] 1 WLR 103).

Section D26 Procedure on Appeal to the Court of Appeal (Criminal Division)

THE RULES AND THE GUIDE

D26.1 The procedure for appealing to the Court of Appeal (Criminal Division) is governed by relevant sections of the Criminal Appeal Act 1968 combined with parts 67, 68 and 74 of the CrimPR (see **appendix 1**). Appeals under the Proceeds of Crime Act 2002 are dealt with under the Proceeds of Crime Act 2002 (Appeals under Part 2) Order 2003 (SI 2003 No. 82). Appeals under the CJA 2003, sch. 22 (see **E4.4**) are dealt with under the Criminal Justice Act 2003 (Mandatory Life Sentences: Appeals in Transitional Cases) Order (SI 2005 No. 2798).

A booklet produced by the Registrar of Criminal Appeals, *A Guide to Proceedings in the Court of Appeal Criminal Division* ('the Guide'), gives an overview of the procedure and provides a good deal of useful, practical advice.

This section deals with the procedure for appealing both against conviction and against sentence.

NOTICE OF APPEAL AND NOTICE OF APPLICATION FOR LEAVE TO APPEAL

D26.2 **Criminal Appeal Act 1968, s. 18**

(1) A person who wishes to appeal under this part of this Act to the Court of Appeal, or to obtain the leave of that court to appeal, shall give notice of appeal or, as the case may be, notice of application for leave to appeal, in such manner as may be directed by rules of court.
(2) Notice of appeal, or of application for leave to appeal, shall be given within 28 days of the conviction, verdict or finding appealed against, or in the case of appeal against sentence, from the date on which sentence was passed or, in the case of an order made or treated as made on conviction, from the date of the making of the order.
(3) The time for giving notice under this section may be extended, either before or after it expires, by the Court of Appeal.

Notice of appeal (if the trial judge has granted a certificate that the case is fit for appeal) or notice of application for leave to appeal (required in all other cases) must be lodged in the manner prescribed by the rules of the court in accordance with s. 18(1). Under s. 18(2), the notice must be lodged within 28 days of either conviction or sentence, depending on which is being appealed. By virtue of s. 18A, the same rule applies in respect of cases of contempt of court. If a conviction is the subject of appeal, then time runs from the date of conviction and not sentence (if the sentence hearing takes place at a later date) (*Long* (1997) 161 JP 769). Rule 68.3(1) of the CrimPR (see **appendix** 1) requires an applicant to serve the relevant notice on an officer of the Crown Court. That service will be on an officer of the Crown

Court which convicted and sentenced the applicant. The notice must be in the form specified in the *Consolidated Criminal Practice Direction* (until relatively recently it was commonly referred to as 'Form NG'). The notice should be accompanied by the grounds of appeal. By virtue of r. 68.3(1) and (2) both the notice and grounds are required to be set out in the form specified in the Practice Direction.

The form submitting the notice and grounds of appeal should be signed by the appellant or applicant unless he has indicated a firm intent to appeal. In that case his solicitor may sign for him.

The Crown Court forwards the notice and grounds of appeal to the office of the Registrar of Criminal Appeals.

A strict timetable for the preparation of advice and grounds of appeal is suggested in the Guide. It recommends that all briefs to counsel to represent a person who has the benefit of a representation order should contain instructions to give advice in the event of a conviction. It is now common for solicitors to include such instructions in the brief to counsel and they are usually phrased so as to include the timetable envisaged by the Guide. In the event of a conviction, if he is able to do so, counsel should immediately orally indicate his final view as to the prospects of a successful appeal against conviction or sentence. If he cannot do so at that time, counsel should indicate his provisional view as to the prospects of any appeal succeeding or indicate that he needs time to consider the position. If counsel has not reached a settled view by the time he sees his client after the conviction and/or sentence, he should send a written advice as to his final view to his instructing solicitor within 14 days. If appropriate, he should also append signed grounds of appeal. His instructing solicitor should then ensure that the advice and/or grounds reach the lay client within a further seven days. If the advice on appeal is positive, the lay client will then decide whether or not he wishes to proceed with the appeal against conviction and/or sentence. If he does so wish, the relevant notice and grounds should be lodged as described in **D26.2**.

The *Consolidated Criminal Practice Direction*, para. II.2.5, specifies target times within which appeals should be heard. The target times run from when the case is received by the listing officer; for an appeal against sentence the target time is 28 days, whilst for an appeal against conviction it is 63 days rising to 80 days if evidence is to be called.

Paragraph II.2.2 stipulates that the listing of matters before the Court of Appeal takes precedence over all lower courts and, wherever possible, the Crown Court should have regard to that when arranging to release an advocate to attend the Court of Appeal.

GROUNDS OF APPEAL

Drafting and Contents of Grounds of Appeal

At para. 2.2 of the Guide it is stated that grounds of appeal should be sufficiently detailed to enable the Registrar and the Court of Appeal to identify clearly the matters relied on. Paragraph 2.3 requires that any authorities on which the potential appellant wishes to rely should be cited. Any misdirections or omissions in the summing-up should be clearly identified (*Fielding* (1938) 26 Cr App R 211), and it is the duty of counsel to ensure that grounds are properly particularised (*Nicco* [1972] Crim LR 420). In *Singh* [1973] Crim LR 36, the Court of Appeal urged caution in quoting sentences from the summing-up out of context in the grounds of appeal when, if the sentence was read in context, it would not be seen as objectionable. **D26.3**

Advice with Grounds

D26.4 Paragraph 1.6 of the Guide suggests that it may be helpful for an advocate to include his advice on appeal with the grounds of appeal. There is no obligation on the advocate to do this and an adverse advice should never be included. The practice is very common and allows an opportunity for the advocate to rehearse his argument before the single judge in a way that would be much more difficult if attempted within the grounds. In such circumstances, it is advisable that the advocate include within the appended grounds a request that the grounds be read in conjunction with the advice.

Perfection and Variation

D26.5 The grounds of appeal first lodged may be varied or amplified within such time as the Court of Appeal will allow (CrimPR, r. 63.6). If counsel wishes to perfect grounds, he should normally indicate that wish in a note to the Registrar accompanying the original grounds. Failure to do so may result in the original grounds being placed before the single judge without being perfected (para. 4.1 of the Guide). When grounds of appeal are lodged, the advocate will usually identify any transcripts which are necessary for him to perfect the grounds of appeal. If the Registrar agrees, the transcripts are secured and sent to the advocate. When the Registrar's office sends the transcripts to the advocate, an accompanying letter usually sets out the date by which the grounds should be perfected. If an advocate is not able to comply with the deadline set by the Court of Appeal, he should contact the relevant lawyer or caseworker in the Registrar's office in order to ask for an extension of time within which to perfect the grounds. Paragraph 4.4 of the Guide suggests that the perfected grounds should comprise a fresh document which includes references to the appropriate part of the transcript by page number and letter and also includes appropriately cited authorities. If, having read the transcript, the advocate forms the view that the appeal is no longer arguable, he should inform his solicitors of that in an appropriate advice (para. 4.5) He should also inform the Registrar but should not send him a copy of the advice. If the advocate advises abandonment and the applicant for leave continues with the appeal, he is at risk of a direction that time served does not count (see D25.12).

Duty of Counsel with Regards to Grounds of Appeal

D26.6 Paragraph 2.4 of the Guide states that 'Counsel should not settle or sign grounds unless they are reasonable, have some real prospect of success and are such that he is prepared to argue before the court'. If counsel is unable to be sure that he is settling reasonable grounds of appeal until after having had sight of the transcript, he should settle the grounds nonetheless and include a note to the Registrar setting out his position. It is not unknown for counsel to be criticised for grounds of appeal which the Court of Appeal considers improper. In *Morson* (1976) 62 Cr App R 236, grounds of appeal drafted by counsel suggested that the summing-up was unfair and amounted to a direction to convict. Scarman LJ said that the description of the summing-up was a travesty and that the court deplored the fact that that ground of appeal was put forward.

Appellant Drafting Notice and Grounds of Appeal

D26.7 An appeal may be conducted in person, without the benefit of legal representation. The necessary forms are available to prospective appellants in custody as well as those who are at liberty. However, the unrepresented applicant who has had the benefit of negative advice as to the prospects of success of his appeal runs an increasing risk of a direction that any time he has served in custody between the commencement of appeal proceedings and their conclusion not count towards time served (see D25.12).

LEAVE TO APPEAL

Procedure for Obtaining Leave to Appeal

D26.8 Ordinarily, once the grounds have been perfected, the case is referred to a single judge for the consideration of whether leave to appeal should be granted. Alternatively, the case may be referred to a full court to determine the issues of leave and the prosecution will be asked to attend. If the full court grants leave, the court may then forthwith proceed to a substantive hearing of the appeal. Such a course is usually taken when there is a need for expedition in the proceedings. An example of where such expedition might be necessary is when the trial of an accused is due to start in the very near future but he has an outstanding appeal in relation to a previous conviction. If the Crown is seeking to adduce evidence of the conviction subject to appeal before the jury at the new trial, it will be necessary to resolve the appeal before starting the trial.

The far more usual procedure is for the single judge to consider the issue of leave on the papers. The single judge should notify the applicant of his decision as soon as possible (CrimPR, r. 68.29). If the application for leave is refused, the applicant has 14 days to notify his intention to renew the application before the court (r. 68.6(1)). The time for notification may be extended either before or after that 14-day period has expired (r. 68.6(1)), but the applicant must have good reason for not being able to comply with the deadline. That reason cannot be to do with the merits of the case. If the applicant has received misleading advice as to the need to notify his renewal from the prison in which he is held, that is capable of being sufficient (*Doherty* [1971] 1 WLR 1454).

If the single judge grants leave on a particular ground without deciding the issue of leave in respect of the other grounds, the appellant is free to argue the other grounds at the substantive hearing of the appeal. But if the single judge grants leave on one ground but refuses leave on others, the appellant must renew his application for leave in relation to those other grounds, having previously informed the respondents and the Registrar's office of his intention, before he is allowed to argue them at the substantive hearing (*Cox* [1999] 2 Cr App R 6).

A renewed application for leave to appeal is heard by the court. The court will be comprised of at least two judges and usually three. The applicant has no right to attend, so if he is in custody he will not be present. Even though legal aid is not available for representation at such hearings, it is common for counsel to provide their services free of charge and the applications are fully argued. It is even very common for counsel to submit written skeleton arguments for renewed applications for leave to appeal. Where counsel does not appear, renewed applications for leave to appeal are often placed in a 'non-counsel list'. Such hearings then simply involve the calling on of the case followed by one of the court giving judgment in the case.

Extension of Time for Leave to Appeal

D26.9 Although the time period for lodging the notice of application for leave to appeal is 28 days, that period may be extended either before or after its expiry (Criminal Appeal Act 1968, s. 18(3)). The period may be extended either by the Registrar's office or the single judge; its extension is a matter of discretion. An appellant is usually required to show good reason for the extension of time to be granted (*Ramsden* [1972] Crim LR 547; *Burley* (1994) *The Times* 9 November 1994). In exceptional circumstances, the Court of Appeal will allow an extension even where the period of delay is inordinate and unexplained because, if the appeal has merit, the refusal might lead to a reference to the CCRC, with all the attendant delay and cost associated (see *King* [2000] Crim LR 835). There is no incompatibility with the ECHR in imposing time-limits on appeal proceedings provided that they are not too short or too rigorously enforced (*Ballinger* [2005] 2 Cr App R 433). If the appellant has commenced an appeal against sentence and subsequently seeks to commence an appeal against conviction, the court will usually allow an extension of time so as to avoid any difficulties associated with resolving an appeal against sentence before the conviction appeal is resolved (*Mitchell* [1977] 1 WLR 753).

TRANSCRIPTS

D26.10 When counsel lodges grounds of appeal, he will ordinarily indicate to the Registrar the transcripts which he needs to perfect the grounds of appeal that he has settled. Those transcripts may include, for example, the evidence of particular witnesses and rulings on issues of law. The Registrar will usually provide those transcripts; if there is any disagreement as to the need for them, the matter should be referred to the single judge for resolution (para. 3.1 of the Guide). Given the cost associated with the provision of a transcript, counsel should request one only if it is essential for the conduct of the appeal (*Flemming* (1987) 86 Cr App R 32). In *Lifely* (1990) *The Times*, 16 July 1990, the Court of Appeal said that transcripts of submissions made by counsel to the trial judge were costly and time-consuming to prepare and were usually unnecessary.

BAIL PENDING APPEAL

Bail by the Court of Appeal

D26.11 Criminal Appeal Act 1968, s. 19

(1) The Court of Appeal may, subject to section 25 of the Criminal Justice and Public Order Act 1994, if they think fit,—
   (a) grant an appellant bail pending the determination of his appeal; or
   (b) revoke bail granted to an appellant by the Crown Court under paragraph (f) of section 81(1) of the Supreme Court Act 1981 or paragraph (a) above; or
   (c) vary the conditions of bail granted to an appellant in the exercise of the power conferred by either of those paragraphs.

(2) The powers conferred by subsection (1) above may be exercised—
   (a) on the application of an appellant; or
   (b) if it appears to the registrar of criminal appeals of the Court of Appeal . . . that any of them ought to be exercised, on a reference to the court by him.

The Court of Appeal may grant bail to an appellant under s. 19. The applicant or appellant may apply for bail or the Registrar may refer the case to the court for consideration of whether bail should be granted. An applicant for bail must complete a form B (see para. 16.1 of the Guide), and the issue of bail may be dealt with by the single judge at the same time that he considers whether or not leave to appeal should be granted. If the question needs to be considered urgently (e.g., because the appellant has been given a short custodial sentence by the Crown Court and will have served most or all of it by the time the papers would be ready for a judge to consider leave to appeal), a separate application for bail may be made. In such circumstances, the Registrar is asked to list the application before a single judge at the earliest opportunity. Unless the court or a single judge directs to the contrary, the prosecution must be given at least 24 hours' written notice of the intention to make the application (CrimPR, r. 68.7(3)). An urgent application should normally be made first to the Crown Court judge under the Supreme Court Act 1981, s. 81 (see **D26.12**), and the Court of Appeal may decline to treat the application as urgent if that was not done (*Consolidated Criminal Practice Direction*, para. V.50.6).

Under the CrimPR, r. 67.8(2), an application for bail to the single judge may be made orally. Whilst funding is not available for such applications, counsel often appear on behalf of applicants at such hearings.

In *Watton* (1978) 68 Cr App R 293, the Court of Appeal said that the question that the court should ask itself is whether there are exceptional circumstances which drive the court to the conclusion that justice can only be done with the granting of bail. The strength of the grounds of appeal will be a relevant factor in the decision as to whether to grant bail. Equally, the likely length of time before the appeal is heard will be relevant depending on how long the appellant has to serve. If an appellant is granted bail but his appeal is unsuccessful, he will be returned to custody.

Rules 68.8 and 68.9 of the CrimPR contain detailed provisions as to the forfeiture of sureties should the appellant abscond. Under ss. 19(1) (b) and (c) the court may vary or revoke bail previously granted by the Court of Appeal or the Crown Court.

The Registrar may vary bail in certain circumstances (see **D26.25**).

In *Ofori* (1994) 99 Cr App R 219, it was held that there is a power to grant bail even where the applicant is subject to a recommendation for deportation but, if the court was considering granting bail, it might think it wise to inform the Secretary of State to give him the opportunity to make representations.

Bail Granted by the Crown Court

D26.12

Supreme Court Act 1981 s. 81

(1) The Crown Court may, subject to section 25 of the Criminal Justice and Public Order Act 1994, grant bail to any person—
  - (a) [bail following committal, transfer or sending to the Crown Court: see **D6**];
  - (b) who is in custody pursuant to a sentence imposed by a magistrates' court, and who has appealed to the Crown Court against his conviction or sentence; or
  - (c) who is in the custody of the Crown Court pending the disposal of his case by that court; or
  - (d) who, after the decision of his case by the Crown Court, has applied to that court for the statement of a case for the High Court on that decision; or
  - (e) who has applied to the High Court for a quashing order to remove proceedings in the Crown Court in his case into the High Court, or has applied to the High Court for leave to make such an application; or
  - (f) to whom the Crown Court has granted a certificate under section 1(2) or 11(1A) of the Criminal Appeal Act 1968 or under subsection(1B) below; or
  - (g) who has been remanded in custody by a magistrates' court on adjourning a case under section 11 of the Powers of Criminal Courts (Sentencing) Act 2000 (remand for medical examination) or—
    - (i) section 5 (adjournment of inquiry into offence);
    - (ii) section 10(adjournment of trial);
    - (iii) section 18 (initial procedure on information against adult for offence triable either way);

  and the time during which a person is released on bail under any provision of this subsection shall not count as part of any term of imprisonment or detention under his sentence.

(1A) The power conferred by subsection (1)(f) does not extend to a case to which section 12 or 15 of the Criminal Appeal Act 1968 (appeal against verdict of not guilty by reason of insanity or against findings that the accused is under a disability and that he did the act or made the omission charged against him) applies.

(1B) A certificate under this subsection is a certificate that a case is fit for appeal on a ground which involves a question of law alone.

(1C) The power conferred by subsection (1)(f) is to be exercised—
  - (a) where the appeal is under section 1 or 9 of the Criminal Appeal Act 1968, by the judge who tried the case; and
  - (b) where it is under section 10 of that Act, by the judge who passed the sentence.

(1D) The power may only be exercised within twenty-eight days from the date of the conviction appealed against, or in the case of appeal against sentence, from the date on which sentence was passed or, in the case of an order made or treated as made on conviction, from the date of the making of the order.

(1E) The power may not be exercised if the appellant has made an application to the Court of Appeal for bail in respect of the offence or offences to which the appeal relates.

(1F) It shall be a condition of bail granted in the exercise of the power that, unless a notice of appeal has previously been lodged in accordance with subsection (1) of section 18 of the Criminal Appeal Act 1968—

(a) such a notice shall be so lodged within the period specified in subsection (2) of that section; and

(b) not later than 14 days from the end of that period, the appellant shall lodge with the Crown Court a certificate from the registrar of criminal appeals that a notice of appeal was given within that period.

(1G) If the Crown Court grants bail to a person in the exercise of the power, it may direct him to appear—

(a) if a notice of appeal is lodged within the period specified in section 18(2) of the Criminal Appeal Act 1968 at such time and place as the Court of Appeal may require; and

(b) if no such notice is lodged within that period, at such time and place as the Crown Court may require.

(1H) Where the Crown Court grants a person bail under subsection (1)(g) it may direct him to appear at a time and place which the magistrates' court could have directed and the recognizance of any surety shall be conditioned accordingly.

(1J) The Crown Court may only grant bail to a person under subsection(1)(g) if the magistrates' court which remanded him in custody has certified under section 5(6A) of the Bail Act 1976 that it heard full argument on his application for bail before it refused the application.

(2) Provision may be made by rules of court as respects the powers of the Crown Court relating to bail, including any provision—

(a) except in the case of bail in criminal proceedings (within the meaning of the Bail Act 1976), allowing the court instead of requiring a person to enter into a recognizance, to consent to his giving other security;

(b) allowing the court to direct that a recognizance shall be entered into or other security given before a magistrates' court or a justice of the peace, or, if the rules so provide, a person of such other description as is specified in the rules;

(c) prescribing the manner in which a recognizance is to be entered into or other security given, and the persons by whom and the manner in which the recognizance or security may be enforced;

(d) authorising the recommittal, in such cases and by such courts or justices as may be prescribed by the rules, of persons released from custody in pursuance of the powers;

(e) making provision corresponding to sections 118 and 119 of the Magistrates' Courts Act 1980 (varying or dispensing with requirements as to sureties, and postponement of taking recognizances).

(3) Any reference in any enactment to a recognizance shall include, unless the context otherwise requires, a reference to any other description of security given instead of a recognizance, whether in pursuance of subsection (2)(a) or otherwise.

(4) The Crown Court, on issuing a warrant for the arrest of any person, may endorse the warrant for bail, and in any such case—

(a) the person arrested under the warrant shall, unless the Crown Court otherwise directs, be taken to a police station; and

(b) the officer in charge of the station shall release him from custody if he, and any sureties required by the endorsement and approved by the officer, enter into recognizances of such amount as may be fixed by the endorsement:

Provided that in the case of bail in criminal proceedings (within the meaning of the Bail Act 1976) the person arrested shall not be required to enter into a recognizance.

(5) A person in custody in pursuance of a warrant issued by the Crown Court with a view to his appearance before that court shall be brought forthwith before either the Crown Court or a magistrates' court.

(6) A magistrates' court shall have jurisdiction, and a justice of the peace may act, under or in pursuance of rules under subsection (2) whether or not the offence was committed, or the arrest was made, within the court's area, or the area for which he was appointed.

Section 81(1) of the Supreme Court Act 1981 provides that the Crown Court may grant bail to any person to whom it has granted a certificate under ss. 1(2) or 11(1A) of the Criminal Appeal Act 1968.

Section 81 also provides for the means by which the Crown Court may exercise the power. The Court of Appeal may revoke or vary bail granted by the Crown Court (Criminal Appeal Act 1968, s. 19(1)(b) and (c)).

The *Consolidated Criminal Practice Direction*, para. IV.50 (see **appendix** 7), gives guidance both on the granting of certificates that a case is fit for appeal and on the consequent granting of bail. Paragraph IV.50.3 states that the judge 'may well think it right' to hear the application for a certificate in chambers with a shorthand writer present, and also to invite defence counsel to submit in advance of the hearing a draft of the grounds of appeal which he will ask the judge to certify. A copy of the draft grounds of appeal should also preferably be sent to the prosecution as they will thus be better able to assist the judge at the hearing. The first question for the judge is whether there exists a particular and cogent ground of appeal and hence whether a certificate should be granted (para. IV.50.4). The length of the period which might elapse before the hearing of any appeal is not relevant to the granting of a certificate but, if the judge does decide to grant a certificate, it is one factor in the decision whether also to grant bail. However, a judge who intends to take such a factor into account 'may find it advisable' to obtain from the listing officer of the Court of Appeal an accurate and up-to-date assessment of the likely waiting time (para. IV.50.5). If the defence are of the view that the issue of bail is an urgent matter, an application to the trial judge should be made in the first instance. If the defence fail to apply to the Crown Court judge for bail pending appeal, the Court of Appeal may decline to treat as urgent any application to itself for bail (para. IV.50.6) (see also **D26.11**). In *Harries* [2007] EWCA Crim 820, the Court of Appeal cautioned that a Crown Court judge should grant a certificate of appeal only where there was an unresolved issue of law or where there were clear reasons for considering that an appeal would be allowed. In the instant case, the judge expressly declined to give any view as to the substance of the grounds of appeal when granting a certificate; if he had sought the assistance of the prosecution as to the grounds advanced, he might have realised that the appeal was extremely unlikely to succeed.

Suspension of Other Sentences Pending Appeal

D26.13 The Court of Appeal may suspend the disqualification of a driver pending appeal (RTOA 1988, s. 40(2)). By virtue of s. 30(1) and (2) of the Criminal Appeal Act 1968, an order for the restitution of property to a person made by the Crown Court under the PCC(S)A 2000, s. 148, shall, unless the Court of Appeal directs to the contrary in a case in which, in its opinion, title to the property is not in dispute, be suspended until there is no further possibility of an appeal which might result in the order being varied or set aside. In determining whether there is any possibility of an appeal, the power of a court to give leave to appeal out of time is to be disregarded. Thus, a restitution order will take effect 28 days from sentence if no notice of application for leave to appeal is given but, if notice is given, it will be suspended until determination of the appeal unless the Court of Appeal gives a direction to the contrary because title to the property does not appear to be disputed. The Court of Appeal may annul or vary the order for restitution even though the conviction is not quashed (s. 30(2)). Under the PCC(S)A 2000, s. 132(1), compensation orders are treated for the purposes of the Criminal Appeal Act 1968, s. 30, in the same way as restitution orders. The enforcement of any fine the appellant was ordered to pay is suspended upon notice of appeal or application for leave to appeal being given.

PRESENCE OF THE APPELLANT AT THE APPEAL

D26.14 **Criminal Appeal Act 1968, s. 22**

(1) Except as provided by this section, an appellant shall be entitled to be present, if he wishes it, on the hearing of his appeal, although he may be in custody.

(2) A person in custody shall not be entitled to be present—

(a) where his appeal is on some ground involving a question of law alone; or

(b) on an application by him for leave to appeal; or

(c) on any proceedings preliminary or incidental to an appeal; or

(d) where he is in custody in consequence of a verdict of not guilty by reason of insanity or of a finding of disability,

unless the Court of Appeal give him leave to be present.

(3) The power of the Court of Appeal to pass sentence on a person may be exercised although he is for any reason not present.

(4) The Court of Appeal may give a live link direction in relation to a hearing at which the appellant is expected to be in custody but is entitled to be present (by virtue of subsection (1) or leave given under subsection (2)) at any time before the beginning of that hearing.

(5) For this purpose—

(a) a 'live link direction' is a direction that the appellant (if he is being held in custody at the time of the hearing) is to attend the hearing through a live link from the place at which he is held; and

(b) 'live link' means an arrangement by which the appellant is able to see and hear, and to be seen and heard by, the Court of Appeal (and for this purpose any impairment of eyesight or hearing is to be disregarded).

(6) The Court of Appeal—

(a) must not give a live link direction unless the parties to the appeal have had the opportunity to make representations about the giving of such a direction; and

(b) may rescind a live link direction at any time before or during any hearing to which it applies (whether of its own motion or on the application of a party).

An appellant who is not in custody has the right to be present at his appeal. Appellants in custody are entitled to be present at the hearing of their appeal if it is based on fact or a mixed question of law and fact. In theory, there is no right to be present if the question to be resolved at the appeal against conviction is one of pure law, but it is very rare that an appellant is not present at his appeal against conviction. If the appellant wishes to be present at the hearing of the appeal, he should normally indicate his wishes on form 1A. The single judge is normally responsible for granting leave for the appellant to be present. An appellant may be present for the purposes of this section via live link (s. 22(4) to (6), inserted by the Police and Justice Act 2006, s. 48).

If an appellant is not in custody or bailed to appear at the hearing, he is not required to be present at the hearing. If he is not present, but has been given notice of the hearing, the court may proceed in his absence. If an appellant absconds before the hearing of his appeal, the court may adjourn the appeal, find against the appellant in his absence or, exceptionally, agree to hear the appeal on its merits (*Flower* [1966] 1 QB 146; *Carter* (1994) 98 Cr App R 106).

HEARING OF AN APPEAL

Practice in Usual Case

D26.15 Rule 68.23(2) of the CrimPR requires the Registrar to give as much notice as reasonably possible of the date on which the court will hear any appeal or application. The notice must be served on (a) the appellant himself, (b) any person having custody of him, and (c) any other interested party. Plainly, 'any other interested party' will include the prosecution. The duty to give notice of hearing dates does not apply to applications before a single judge (r. 68.23(3)). Representation for the hearing is normally granted either by the Registrar or by the single judge at the same time as he gives leave to appeal. In most cases, a representation order will be granted only if the single judge grants leave. The representation order is usually limited to an advocate, but if necessary it will be extended to provide for the services of a solicitor. The Registrar will forward the necessary papers to counsel and will try to agree a date for the hearing with counsel's clerk (para. 10.1 of the Guide). It is usual for various dates to be offered to counsel's clerk. The respondent is not usually represented at an appeal against sentence, and that remains the practice despite the observations by Lord Lane CJ in *Dempster* (1987) 85 Cr App R 176, to the effect that the increasing complexity of sentencing law and procedure made it desirable for the prosecution to be in attendance more frequently than before. At an appeal against conviction, the respondent is invariably represented.

The Registrar's staff prepare a summary of the case for the benefit of the single judge and, if necessary, the judges who hear the substantive appeal. Case summaries are now disclosed to all advocates in the case unless there is a specific direction to the contrary (*Consolidated Criminal Practice Direction*, para. II.18, *Criminal Appeal Office summaries*).

Paragraph II.17 of the *Consolidated Criminal Practice Direction* stipulates the time-limits for the service of the skeleton arguments on appeal against conviction. The appellant's advocate must serve a skeleton argument on the Registrar and the respondent within 14 days of the granting of leave. The respondent should then serve a skeleton in response within 14 days thereafter.

Under para. 10.7 of the Guide, the advocate for the appellant should assume that the court is familiar with the facts of the case and the grounds as settled. Counsel for the appellant makes his submissions first, followed by counsel for the respondent.

Receipt of Evidence by the Court of Appeal

Criminal Appeal Act 1968, s. 23 **D26.16**

(1) For purposes of an appeal under this part of this Act [appeals against conviction and/or sentence and references to the Court of Appeal by the Home Secretary] the Court of Appeal may, if they think it necessary or expedient in the interests of justice—
  (a) order the production of any document, exhibit or other thing connected with the proceedings, the production of which appears to them necessary for the determination of the case;
  (b) order any witness who would have been a compellable witness in the proceedings from which the appeal lies to attend for examination and be examined before the court, whether or not he was called in those proceedings; and
  (c) receive any evidence which was not adduced in the proceedings from which the appeal lies.

(2) The Court of Appeal shall, in considering whether to receive any evidence, have regard in particular to—
  (a) whether the evidence appears to the Court to be capable of belief;
  (b) whether it appears to the Court that the evidence may afford any ground for allowing the appeal;
  (c) whether the evidence would have been admissible in the proceedings from which the appeal lies on an issue which is the subject of the appeal; and
  (d) whether there is a reasonable explanation for the failure to adduce the evidence in those proceedings.

(3) Subsection (1)(c) above [power to receive evidence of any witness if tendered] applies to any evidence of a witness (including the appellant) who is competent but not compellable, and applies also to the appellant's husband or wife where the appellant makes an application for that purpose and the evidence appeal lies except on such an application.

At any appeal against conviction, the Court of Appeal may admit evidence which is relevant to that appeal by virtue of s. 23. In appropriate cases, that evidence may be introduced in the interests of justice at the request of the respondents and is not limited to rebuttal of fresh evidence adduced by the appellant (*Hanratty* [2002] EWCA Crim 1141). However, it will not be admitted where its purpose is to advance a basis for conviction not argued previously and not put before the jury (*Fitzgerald* [2006] EWCA Crim 1565). The admission of evidence under s. 23 is a matter of discretion for the court. The court will admit evidence if it is necessary or expedient in the interests of justice.(s. 23(1)). The factors listed in s. 23(2) are not preconditions for the admission of evidence, but are merely factors which the court will take into account in deciding whether evidence should be received.

D26.17 **Capable of Belief** The Court of Appeal will often make a judgment as to whether the evidence is capable of belief before actually hearing it. Thus the Court gives an indication as to whether or not the evidence appears to be capable of belief. Matters which will be important in that consideration will include the contents of any statement produced and the compatibility of those contents with the evidence at trial, along with any explanation as to how the evidence came to light. In *Sale* [2000] 2 Cr App R 431, Rose LJ said that fresh evidence falls into three categories. First, evidence which is plainly capable of belief; there is no difficulty with such evidence and the court will ordinarily receive it. Second, evidence which is plainly incapable of belief; such evidence again presents no difficulty and the court will usually not receive such evidence. The third type of evidence is that which is possibly capable of belief; it may be necessary for the court to hear the witness *de bene esse* in order to determine whether the evidence is capable of belief, and that course is frequently followed.

D26.18 **Capable of Founding a Ground of Appeal** Even if fresh evidence potentially fulfils all the other criteria in the Criminal Appeal Act 1968, s. 23, it is necessary that it is capable of founding an arguable ground of appeal before it can be admitted. For example, an appellant may produce evidence of a statement by the complainant which was inconsistent with his evidence at trial. Unless the inconsistency of the statement is of sufficient magnitude to be capable of disturbing the safety of the conviction, it will not be admissible.

D26.19 **Admissible in the Proceedings from which the Appeal Lies** Plainly, evidence which would not have been admissible at the trial proceedings cannot form the basis of a successful appeal against conviction. The importance of that point has been most keenly felt in appeals involving misconduct by police officers which only comes to light after conviction (*Twitchell* [2000] 1 Cr App R 373).

D26.20 **Reasonable Explanation for the Failure to Adduce the Evidence** In *Stafford and Luvaglio (No. 1)* (1969) 53 Cr App R 1, Edmund-Davies LJ said 'public mischief would ensue and legal process could become indefinitely prolonged were it the case that evidence produced at any time will generally be admitted by this court when verdicts are being reviewed'. That warning against the potential dangers of admitting fresh evidence is indicative of a general reluctance on the part of the court to admit evidence without a reasonable explanation for the failure to adduce the evidence at trial.

An appellant will not have a reasonable explanation for failing to adduce evidence at trial if he has taken a decision not to call particular evidence following advice from his lawyers (*Hampton* (2004) *The Times*, 13 October 2004). Similarly, it will not assist an appellant that alibi witnesses have not been called because his lawyers had been unable to trace them, if the appellant could have made his lawyers aware of information which would have enabled them to trace the witnesses in good time (*Beresford* (1971) 56 Cr App R 143). If witnesses could genuinely not be found in time for trial, that may amount to a reasonable explanation. But before the Court of Appeal will admit the evidence, it is likely to be necessary for each person involved in the process of finding and taking a proof of evidence from the witnesses to serve a statement of truth about their role in that process (*Gogana* (1999) *The Times*, 12 July 1999; *James* [2000] Crim LR 571).

Procedure for Calling Evidence

D26.21 Rule 68.15 of the CrimPR requires that an appellant who wishes the Court of Appeal to exercise its power to receive evidence should give notice to that effect. The prescribed form for such notice (form 6) should be used. An oral application may be made to the court. If the appellant additionally wishes the witness to be ordered to attend court for examination, he should give notice of that also. An order for a witness to attend may be made only if the witness would have been a compellable witness before the Crown Court (see Criminal Appeal Act 1968, s. 23(1)(b)). It may be made by a single judge (s. 31(2); see **D26.24**). The decision to receive the evidence is for a court and not a single judge or the Registrar. Indeed, even an order under s. 23(4) that the witness be examined by an officer of the court etc. prior to determination of the appeal is one that only a court can make.

By virtue of s. 23(4), if the court thinks it necessary or expedient in the interests of justice, the court may order that the examination of any compellable witness be conducted before any judge, officer of the court or other person appointed by the court for the purpose. The single judge has no such power (see **D26.24**). The examination of such a witness must be conducted by the taking of a deposition in public unless the court otherwise directs (r. 68.16(2)). The deposition may then be admitted as evidence before the Court of Appeal, so avoiding the need for oral evidence (s. 23(4)). By virtue of s. 23(1)(c) and (3), whilst the power to order a witness to attend and to order that his evidence be taken in deposition form before an examiner is exercisable only in respect of compellable witnesses, the discretion to receive evidence tendered by the appellant applies not only to compellable witnesses but also to those who are merely competent. Paragraph 14.4 of the Guide suggests that, where a witness is not formally examined prior to determination of the appeal in the manner described above (either because he was not compellable or because the court simply did not choose to make an order for examination), the appellant should serve on the Registrar either an affidavit sworn by the witness or a s. 9 statement. Sometimes, the court can rely on the written statement or affidavit of the witness without hearing oral evidence.

Whilst the rules do not specify the precise way in which a witness's evidence should be given, the usual route is the same as that adopted in first instance proceedings. The witness is examined in chief by the party tendering his evidence, cross-examined by the opposite party and then, if need be, re-examined and questioned directly by the court. The procedure followed by the Court of Appeal will more often than not be a matter for the court, and so the court itself may commence the questioning of the witness and allow the parties to ask any additional questions they see fit. Where the appellant is allowed to call evidence, the prosecution may be allowed to call their own evidence in rebuttal. See *Lee* [1984] 1 WLR 578, for a case where the court contemplated hearing virtually the whole of the prosecution and defence cases in order to determine an appeal against conviction where the appellant had pleaded guilty at the Crown Court. The Court of Appeal noted that there were exceptional circumstances and stipulated that it was not to provide a precedent for the hearing of such extensive evidence.

REVIEW OF PUBLIC INTEREST IMMUNITY

In *McDonald* (2004) *The Times*, 8 November 2004, the Court of Appeal set out the principles that applied to a review of a trial judge's conduct of a public interest immunity hearing. **D26.22**

(a) The approach was to be the same whether the hearing had been on notice or not. The principles regarding the appointment of special counsel or the need for a judge to recuse himself are the same in both cases.
(b) The Court of Appeal would have to review all the material with the prosecution present. A prosecution summary by itself is not sufficient. However, such a summary is usually desirable, especially where the material is voluminous.
(c) The review of the material should be carried out by a court of the same constitution as hears the substantive appeal.

(d) The review is to take place sufficiently in advance of the substantive hearing to permit special counsel to be appointed and prepared if the need arises.
(e) In the majority of cases where the material can be read in an hour or two and where there are no listing difficulties, the review should take place in the first week of that constitution of the court sitting, with the substantive hearing following in the third week.
(f) Where the public interest immunity material is unusually voluminous, special listing arrangements have to be made over a longer time-scale

ABANDONING AN APPEAL

D26.23 Rule 68.22 of the CrimPR governs the abandonment of an appeal. The appellant must serve the necessary form (IA4) on the Registrar's office and the form must be signed by or on behalf of the applicant or appellant (r. 68.22(1) and (2)). The proceedings are then deemed to have been dismissed or refused (r. 68.22(4)). Abandonment of the appeal does not preclude the making of a loss of time order or the award of costs against the appellant. Once an appeal has commenced, the appellant may still abandon the appeal but needs the leave of the court (*De Courcy* [1964] 1 WLR 1245).

If an appellant abandons his appeal, he may reinstate it with the leave of the court. The court will allow such a reinstatement if it is of the view that the abandonment was a nullity because, for example, of fraud, mistake or erroneous advice. The important question will be whether the appellant's mind goes with the abandonment. If he cannot show that it did not, the abandonment will not be held to be a nullity. In *Grant* [2005] EWCA Crim 2018, correspondence between G and his lawyers culminated in his lawyers advising that if they did not hear from him within seven days they would abandon the appeal. Because of a delay in the post, caused by G being transferred between prisons, he had no opportunity to communicate a change of mind about his appeal. The Court of Appeal held that by virtue of G's original letter his mind had gone with the notice and the abandonment was therefore not a nullity.

APPLICATIONS TO A SINGLE JUDGE

D26.24 **Criminal Appeal Act 1968, ss. 31 and 44**

31.—(1) There may be exercised by a single judge in the same manner as by the Court of Appeal and subject to the same provisions—
(a) the powers of the Court of Appeal under this part of this Act specified in subsection (2) below;
(aa) the power to give leave under section 14(4B) of the Criminal Appeal Act 1995;
(b) the power to give directions under section 4(4) of the Sexual Offences (Amendment) Act 1976; and
(c) the powers to make orders for the payment of costs under sections 16 to 18 of the Prosecution of Offences Act 1985 in proceedings under this part of this Act.

(2) The powers mentioned in subsection (1)(a) above are the following—
(a) to give leave to appeal;
(b) to extend the time within which notice of appeal or of application for leave to appeal may be given;
(c) to allow an appellant to be present at any proceedings;
(ca) to give a live link direction under section 22(4);
(d) to order a witness to attend for examination;
(e) to exercise the powers conferred by section 19 of this Act [bail pending determination of appeal];
(f) to make orders under section 8(2) of this Act and discharge or vary such orders [orders relating to procedure on a retrial];
[(g) repealed];
(h) to give directions under section 29(1) of this Act [directions for loss of time].

(2A) The power of the Court of Appeal to suspend a person's disqualification under section

40(2) of the Road Traffic Offenders Act 1988 may be exercised by a single judge in the same manner as it may be exercised by the court.

(2B) The power of the Court of Appeal to grant leave to appeal under section 159 of the Criminal Justice Act 1988 [appeals against orders restricting publicity] may be exercised by a single judge in the same manner as it may be exercised by the court.

(3) If the single judge refuses an application on the part of an appellant to exercise in his favour any of the powers above specified, the appellant shall be entitled to have the application determined by the Court of Appeal.

44.—(1) There may be exercised by a single judge—

(a) the powers of the Court of Appeal under this part of this Act—

(i) to extend the time for making an application for leave to appeal;

(ii) to make an order for or in relation to bail; and

(iii) to give leave for a person to be present at the hearing of any proceedings preliminary or incidental to an appeal; and

(b) their powers to make orders for the payment of costs under sections 16 and 17 of the Prosecution of Offences Act 1985 in proceedings under this Part of this Act,

but where the judge refuses an application to exercise any of the said powers the applicant shall be entitled to have the application determined by the Court of Appeal.

(2) The power of the Court of Appeal to suspend a person's disqualification under section 40(3) of the Road Traffic Offenders Act 1988 may be exercised by a single judge, but where the judge refuses an application to exercise that power the applicant shall be entitled to have the application determined by the Court of Appeal.

The single judge may be either a judge of the High Court or a Lord Justice of Appeal (s. 44)). The functions of the single judge are ordinarily carried out by a High Court judge. By virtue of ss. 31 and 44, a single judge may exercise a number of powers in the same manner as the Court of Appeal. It should be noted that the single judge may order a witness to attend for examination, but it is a matter for the court as to whether the evidence will be received (*Ahmed* (1996) Crim LR 339). Rule 68.5(5) of the CrimPR governs the procedure relating to the exercise of the powers available to the single judge.

APPLICATIONS TO THE REGISTRAR

Criminal Appeal Act 1968, s. 31A **D26.25**

(1) The powers of the Court of Appeal under this part of this Act which are specified in subsection (2) below may be exercised by the registrar.

(2) The powers mentioned in subsection (1) above are the following—

(a) to extend the time within which notice of appeal or of application for leave to appeal may be given;

(b) to order a witness to attend for examination;

(c) to vary the conditions of bail granted to an appellant by the Court of Appeal or the Crown Court;

(d) to make orders under section 23(1)(a).

(3) No variation of the conditions of bail granted to an appellant may be made by the registrar unless he is satisfied that the respondent does not object to the variation; but, subject to that, the powers specified in that subsection are to be exercised by the registrar in the same manner as by the Court of Appeal and subject to the same provisions.

(4) If the registrar refuses an application on the part of an appellant to exercise in his favour any of the powers specified in subsection (2) above, the appellant shall be entitled to have the application determined by a single judge.

(5) In this section 'respondent' includes a person who will be a respondent if leave to appeal is granted.

The powers exercisable by the Registrar in connection with appeals are set out in s. 31A of the Criminal Appeal Act 1968. Rule 68.5 of the CrimPR governs the procedure applicable to the exercise of the powers available to the Registrar.

Section D27 Reference to the Court of Appeal (Criminal Division) Following Trial on Indictment

REFERENCE BY THE CRIMINAL CASES REVIEW COMMISSION

D27.1 The 'CCRC' was created by the Criminal Appeal Act 1995. Under s. 9, the CCRC may at any time refer a conviction on indictment or any sentence imposed in relation to that conviction (unless it is a sentence fixed by law) to the Court of Appeal. Under s. 11, the CCRC may refer any summary conviction or associated sentence to the Crown Court. For the CCRC to refer a case, there must be a real possibility that the Court of Appeal or Crown Court will quash the original conviction or sentence. The reference will ordinarily only be made in respect of an argument or information not available in the court of first instance or on appeal (s. 13). However, in exceptional circumstances, the CCRC may refer a case without any such development in the proceedings (s. 14).

Sections 17 to 21 set out the investigative powers of the CCRC. Under s. 17, the CCRC may require any public body to produce any document or information. In *R (Director of Revenue and Customs Prosecutions) v Criminal Cases Review Commission* (2007)1 Cr App R 395 the Divisional Court held that, when deciding whether to refer a case, the CCRC is not required to have a regard to, let alone follow, a practice of the Court of Appeal Criminal Division operating at a stage with which the CCRC is not concerned. Thus, whilst it may be the usual practice of the Court of Appeal Criminal Division to refuse applications for extension of time to appeal when the appeal is based on a change in the law, the CCRC is not required to adopt the same practice. By contrast, the CCRC is required to have regard to the way in which the Court of Appeal Criminal Division approaches the 'unsafe' test when deciding whether to refer a case.

That guidance to the CCRC on the relevance of the practice of the Court of Appeal in relation to extensions of time in change of law cases was forcefully overturned in *Cottrell* [2007] EWCA Crim 2016. The President said that it is not open to the CCRC lawfully to apply a policy based on the decision in *R (DRCP) v CCRC.* The practice of the court must be addressed and evaluated in every case. Just as the court will not normally allow an application for an extension of time for leave to appeal in a change of law case, a conviction should not normally be referred on the basis of a change of law. In the final analysis, however, it is for the CCRC to exercise its own independent and fact specific judgment whether to refer a case, provided it gives proper weight to the law and practice of the court.

In *R (Dorsett) v Criminal Cases Review Commission* [2007] All ER (D) 63 (Jun), the Divisional Court held that the CCRC is not required to refer a case to the Court of Appeal Criminal Division simply because the Strasbourg court has ruled that there has been a breach of the ECHR. The Court of Appeal does not automatically quash convictions in such cases and so the CCRC should apply the test set out in the Criminal Appeal Act 1995, s. 13(1)(a), and refer a case only if there is a real possibility that the conviction would not be upheld.

By the CJA 2003, s. 315, leave from the Court of Appeal is required if an appellant is to argue any grounds additional to those upon which the CCRC has referred his case to the Court of Appeal.

In *Siddall* [2006] EWCA Crim 1353, the Court of Appeal suggested a timetable for the progress of an appeal referred by the CCRC. For complex cases, the timetable is likely to be viewed as onerous by lawyers regularly involved in the conduct of such appeals. It suggests:

(1) Within six weeks of the date of referral, the appellant's solicitors must cause all relevant papers to be bundled into files and paginated; counsel must lodge a skeleton argument referring to the documents as paginated and apply to the Criminal Appeal Office for a date (giving estimated length of hearing) and any other directions considered necessary.
(2) Within four weeks thereafter, the Crown must propose the inclusion of any further documentation which it requires;
(3) Within two further weeks, the Crown must lodge its skeleton with any suggested change to the estimate it deems to be necessary.
(4) Any response skeleton must be lodged within two further weeks thereafter.
(5) Consideration must be given to whether a core bundle should be provided for the hearing.

The court observed that a reference by the CCRC should be treated with the respect it deserved. Any failure to follow the suggested timetable could result in the case being stood out from the list and risk a wasted costs order being made.

REFERENCES BY THE ATTORNEY-GENERAL

Reference on a Point of Law Following Acquittal

Criminal Justice Act 1972, s. 36 **D27.2**

(1) Where a person tried on indictment has been acquitted (whether in respect of the whole or part of the indictment) the Attorney-General may, if he desires the opinion of the Court of Appeal on a point of law which has arisen in the case, refer that point to the court, and the court shall, in accordance with this section, consider the point and give their opinion on it.
(2) For the purpose of their consideration of a point referred to them under this section the Court of Appeal shall hear argument—
   (a) by, or by counsel on behalf of, the Attorney-General; and
   (b) if the acquitted person desires to present any argument to the court, by counsel on his behalf or, with the leave of the court, by the acquitted person himself.
(3) Where the Court of Appeal have given their opinion on a point referred to them under this section, the court may, of their own motion or in pursuance of an application in that behalf, refer the point to the House of Lords if it appears to the court that the point ought to be considered by that House.
(4) If a point is referred to the House of Lords under subsection (3) of this section, the House shall consider the point and give their opinion on it accordingly; and section 35(1) of the Criminal Appeal Act 1968 (composition of House for appeals) shall apply also in relation to any proceedings of the House under this section
(5) Where, on a point being referred to the Court of Appeal under this section or further referred to the House of Lords, the acquitted person appears by counsel for the purpose of presenting any argument to the court or the House, he shall be entitled to his costs, that is to say to the payment out of central funds of such sums as are reasonably sufficient to compensate him for expenses properly incurred by him for the purpose of being represented on the reference or further reference; and any amount recoverable under this subsection shall be ascertained, as soon as practicable, by the registrar of criminal appeals or, as the case may be, such officer as may be prescribed by order of the House of Lords.

Section 36 provides for the reference of a point of law to the Court of Appeal by the A-G. The use of the power is confined to circumstances following the acquittal of an accused where the A-G requires the opinion of the Court of Appeal on a point of law. There is no provision for the referral of points of law which do not arise from proceedings resulting in an acquittal. In *A-G's Reference (No. 1 of 1975)* [1975] QB 773, Lord Widgery stated that the procedure should not be used simply for very heavy questions of law but should be used for short but important points requiring a quick ruling.

Whatever the opinion of the Court of Appeal, the acquittal is unaffected. Nevertheless, the acquitted defendant is entitled to be represented at the hearing (s. 36(5)). The process of referral of a point of law by the A-G is governed by the CrimPR, part 69 (see **appendix 1**).

Section 36 provides for the further referral of the point of law to the House of Lords following the judgment of the Court of Appeal. The point may be referred to the House of Lords upon application by the parties or on the Court of Appeal's own motion.

Reference for Review of Sentence

D27.3 **Criminal Justice Act 1988, part IV (ss. 35 and 36)**

PART IV REVIEWS OF SENTENCING

35.—(1) A case to which this part of this Act applies may be referred to the Court of Appeal under section 36 below.

(2) Subject to rules of court, the jurisdiction of the Court of Appeal under section 36 below shall be exercised by the criminal division of the Court, and references to the Court of Appeal in this part of this Act shall be construed as references to that division.

(3) This part of this Act applies to any case—

(a) of a description specified in an order under this section; or

(b) in which sentence is passed on a person—

(i) for an offence triable only on indictment; or

(ii) for an offence of a description specified in an order under this section.

(4) The Secretary of State may by order made by statutory instrument provide that this part of this Act shall apply to any case of a description specified in the order or to any case in which sentence is passed on a person for an offence triable either way of a description specified in the order.

(5) A statutory instrument containing an order under this section shall be subject to annulment in pursuance of a resolution of either House of Parliament.

(6) In this part of this Act 'sentence' has the same meaning as in the Criminal Appeal Act 1968, except that it does not include an interim hospital order under part III of the Mental Health Act 1983, and 'sentencing' shall be construed accordingly.

36.—(1) If it appears to the Attorney-General—

(a) that the sentencing of a person in a proceeding in the Crown Court has been unduly lenient; and

(b) that the case is one to which this part of this Act applies,

he may, with the leave of the Court of Appeal, refer the case to them for them to review the sentencing of that person; and on such a reference the Court of Appeal may—

(i) quash any sentence passed on him in the proceeding; and

(ii) in place of it pass such sentence as they think appropriate for the case and as the court below had power to pass when dealing with him.

(2) Without prejudice to the generality of subsection (1) above, the condition specified in paragraph (a) of that subsection may be satisfied if it appears to the Attorney-General that the judge—

(a) erred in law as to his powers of sentencing; or

(b) failed to pass a sentence required by—

(i) section 51A of the Firearms Act 1968;

(ii) section 110(2) or 111(2) of the Powers of Criminal Courts (Sentencing) Act 2000; or

(iii) any of the sections 225 to 228 of the Criminal Justice Act 2003.

(3) For the purposes of this part of this Act any two or more sentences are to be treated as passed in the same proceeding if they would be so treated for the purposes of section 11 of the Criminal Appeal Act 1968.

(3A) Where a reference under this section relates to an order under subsection (2) of section 269 of the Criminal Justice Act 2003 (determination of minimum term in relation to mandatory life sentence), the Court of Appeal shall not, in deciding what order under that section is appropriate for the case, make any allowance for the fact that the person to whom it relates is being sentenced for a second time.

(4) No judge shall sit as a member of the Court of Appeal on the hearing of, or shall determine any application in proceedings incidental or preliminary to, a reference under this section of a sentence passed by himself.

(5) Where the Court of Appeal have concluded their review of a case referred to them under this section the Attorney-General or the person to whose sentencing the reference relates may refer a point of law involved in any sentence passed on that person in the proceeding to the House of Lords for their opinion, and the House shall consider the point and give their opinion on it accordingly, and either remit the case to the Court of Appeal to be dealt with or deal with it themselves; and section 35(1) of the Criminal Appeal Act 1968 (composition of House for appeals) shall apply also in relation to any proceedings of the House under this section.

(6) A reference under subsection (5) above shall be made only with the leave of the Court of Appeal or the House of Lords; and leave shall not be granted unless it is certified by the Court of Appeal that the point of law is of general public importance and it appears to the Court of Appeal or the House of Lords (as the case may be) that the point is one which ought to be considered by that House.

(7) For the purpose of dealing with a case under this section the House of Lords may exercise any powers of the Court of Appeal.

The scope of the power to refer now extends beyond indictable-only offences to include a number of offences, and combinations of offences, set out in the Criminal Justice Act 1988 (Reviews of Sentencing) Order 2006 (SI 2006 No. 1116), sch. 1 (see **D27.6**). An offence is deemed to be triable only on indictment for the purposes of s. 35 if it is so for an adult and it is irrelevant that a youth can be tried summarily on such an allegation (*W* (1993) *The Times*, 16 March 1993). It is for the A-G personally to consider whether leave should be sought for a reference to the Court of Appeal on the basis that the sentence was unduly lenient and if appropriate to apply for leave. The procedure to be followed is set out in the CJA 1988, sch. 3, supplemented by the CrimPR, part 70 (see **appendix 1**). If leave is granted, the reference proceeds according to the facts before the sentencing judge, and the Court of Appeal will not alter the sentence on the grounds of new material that was not before the sentencing judge, but will decide whether the sentence was unduly lenient on the basis of what was before the sentencing judge (*A-G's Ref (No. 19 of 2005)* [2006] EWCA Crim 785).

Double Jeopardy When the Court of Appeal increases a sentence under the reference procedure, its practice has often been to allow some discount on the sentence it would consider appropriate because of what is usually termed the 'double jeopardy' of an offender having to wait before knowing if his sentence is to be increased. In *A-G's Refs (Nos. 14 and 15 of 2006)* [2007] 1 All ER 718, the Court of Appeal gave some guidance as to the relevance and applicability of such double jeopardy. The effect of the principle on the actions of the court will vary significantly according to the circumstances. Where an offender has a substantial part of a long determinate sentence remaining to be served or is serving a discretionary life sentence, the principle has limited effect, if any, because the anxiety occasioned by the process will consequently be less keenly felt. Where, however, an offender had completely served a custodial sentence, was close to release, had a custodial sentence substituted for a non-custodial sentence or was very young, the discount for double jeopardy should be near the upper end of the range, at about 30 per cent. **D27.4**

Additional Matters Taken into Account on Reference The following additional points apply to references under the CJA 1988, s. 35. **D27.5**

(a) If an indication of sentence is given to an offender by the sentencing judge, the Court of Appeal will take that into account but is not necessarily bound by it. In *A-G's Refs (Nos. 86 and 87 of 1999)* [2001] 1 Cr App R (S) 505, an indication was given by the judge before trial that a non-custodial sentence would be imposed whether the accused pleaded guilty or proceeded to a contested trial. The indication was repeated after a finding of guilty. That indication plainly could have had no effect on any decision made by the offender as to plea and so would be no bar to the increase of sentence under the reference procedure (cf. *A-G's Ref (No. 44 of 2000)* [2001] Cr App R 416, relevance of prosecution representations to the accused).

(b) By virtue of s. 35(6), a 'sentence' for the purposes of the reference procedure has the same meaning as in the Criminal Appeal Act 1968, s. 50 (see **D25.36**) (except that it does not include an interim hospital order under part III of the Mental Health Act 1983) and thus is any order made by a court when dealing with an offender.

(c) The Court of Appeal will act in relation to a sentence only if it is unduly lenient and not simply lenient. The test to be applied is whether the sentence was outside the range which the judge, applying his mind to all relevant factors, could reasonably consider appropriate (*A-G's Ref (No. 4 of 1989)* [1990] 1 WLR 41).

(d) The Court of Appeal's decision following the reference may be the subject of appeal to the House of Lords by the A-G or the offender. That appeal must be by leave of either the Court of Appeal or the House of Lords and must concern a point of law of public importance.

Reviewable Sentences and Procedure: Statutory Provisions

D27.6 **Criminal Justice Act 1988 (Reviews of Sentencing) Order 2006 (SI 2006 No. 1116), sch. 1**

1. Any case tried on indictment—
   (a) following a notice of transfer given under section 4 of the Criminal Justice Act 1987 (notices of transfer and designated authorities) by an authority designated for that purpose under subsection (2) of that section; or
   (b) in which one or more of the counts in respect of which sentence is passed relates to a charge which was dismissed under section 6(1) of the Criminal Justice Act 1987 (applications for dismissal) and on which further proceedings were brought by means of preferment of a voluntary bill of indictment.
2. Any case in which sentence is passed on a person for one of the following offences:
   (a) an offence under section 16 of the Offences against the Person Act 1861 (threats to kill);
   (b) an offence under section 5(1) of the Criminal Law Amendment Act 1885 (defilement of a girl between 14 and 17);
   (c) an offence under section 1 of the Children and Young Persons Act 1933 (cruelty to persons under 16) or section 20 of the Children and Young Persons Act (Northern Ireland) 1968 (cruelty to persons under 16);
   (d) an offence under section 6 of the Sexual Offences Act 1956 (unlawful sexual intercourse with a girl under 16), section 14 or 15 of that Act (indecent assault on a woman or on a man), section 52 of the Offences against the Person Act 1861 (indecent assault upon a female), or Article 21 of the Criminal Justice (Northern Ireland) Order 2003 (indecent assault on a male);
   (e) an offence under section 1 of the Indecency with Children Act 1960 or section 22 of the Children and Young Persons Act (Northern Ireland) 1968 (indecent conduct with a child);
   (f) an offence under section 4(2) or (3) (production or supply of a controlled drug), section 5(3) (possession of a controlled drug with intent to supply) or section 6(2) (cultivation of cannabis plant) of the Misuse of Drugs Act 1971;
   (g) an offence under section 54 of the Criminal Law Act 1977 or Article 9 of the Criminal Justice (Northern Ireland) Order 1980 (inciting a girl under 16 to have incestuous sexual intercourse);
   (h) an offence under section 50(2) or (3), section 68(2) or section 170(1) or (2) of the Customs and Excise Management Act 1979, insofar as those offences are in connection with a prohibition or restriction on importation or exportation of either:
      (i) a controlled drug within the meaning of section 2 of the Misuse of Drugs Act 1971, such prohibition or restriction having effect by virtue of section 3 of that Act; or
      (ii) an article prohibited by virtue of section 42 of the Customs Consolidation Act 1876 but only insofar as it relates to or depicts a person under the age of 16;
   (i) offences under sections 29 to 32 of the Crime and Disorder Act 1998 (racially or religiously aggravated assaults; racially or religiously aggravated criminal damage; racially or religiously aggravated public order offences; racially or religiously aggravated harassment etc).
3. To the extent that part IV of the Criminal Justice Act 1988 does not apply by virtue of section 35(3)(b)(i), any case in which sentence is passed on a person for an offence under one of the following sections of the Sexual Offences Act 2003:

(a) section 3 (sexual assault);
(b) section 4 (causing a person to engage in sexual activity without consent);
(c) section 7 (sexual assault of a child under 13);
(d) section 8 (causing or inciting a child under 13 to engage in sexual activity);
(e) section 9 (sexual activity with a child);
(f) section 10 (causing or inciting a child to engage in sexual activity);
(g) section 11 (engaging in sexual activity in the presence of a child);
(h) section 12 (causing a child to watch a sexual act);
(i) section 14 (arranging or facilitating commission of a child sex offence);
(j) section 15 (meeting a child following sexual grooming etc);
(k) section 25 (sexual activity with a child family member);
(l) section 47 (paying for sexual services of a child);
(m) section 48 (causing or inciting child prostitution or pornography);
(n) section 49 (controlling a child prostitute or a child involved in pornography);
(o) section 50 (arranging or facilitating child prostitution or pornography);
(p) section 52 (causing or inciting prostitution for gain);
(q) section 57 (trafficking into the UK for sexual exploitation);
(r) section 58 (trafficking within the UK for sexual exploitation);
(s) section 59 (trafficking out of the UK for sexual exploitation);
(t) section 61 (administering a substance with intent).

4. Any case in which sentence is passed on a person for attempting to commit or inciting the commission of an offence set out in paragraph 2(a) to (h) or paragraph 3.

Criminal Justice Act 1988, sch. 3

Reviews of Sentencing — Supplementary

1. Notice of an application for leave to refer a case to the Court of Appeal under section 36 above shall be given within 28 days from the day on which the sentence, or the last of the sentences, in the case was passed.
2. If the registrar of criminal appeals is given notice of a reference or application to the Court of Appeal under section 36 above, he shall—
   (a) take all necessary steps for obtaining a hearing of the reference of application; and
   (b) obtain and lay before the court in proper form all documents, exhibits and other things which appear necessary for the proper determination of the reference or application.
3. Rules of court may enable a person to whose sentencing such a reference or application relates to obtain from the registrar any documents or things, including copies or reproductions of documents, required for the reference or application and may authorise the registrar to make charges for them in accordance with scales and rates fixed from time to time by the Treasury.
4. An application to the Court of Appeal for leave to refer a case to the House of Lords under section 36(5) above shall be made within the period of 14 days beginning with the date on which the Court of Appeal conclude their review of the case; and an application to the House of Lords for leave shall be made within the period of 14 days beginning with the date on which the Court of Appeal conclude their review or refuse leave to refer the case to the House of Lords.
5. The time during which a person whose case has been referred for review under section 36 above is in custody pending its review and pending any reference to the House of Lords under subsection (5) of that section shall be reckoned as part of the term of any sentence to which he is for the time being subject.
6. Except as provided by paragraphs 7 and 8 below, a person whose sentencing is the subject of a reference to the Court of Appeal under section 36 above shall be entitled to be present, if he wishes it, on the hearing of the reference, although he may be in custody.
7. A person in custody shall not be entitled to be present—
   (a) on an application by the Attorney-General for leave to refer a case; or
   (b) on any proceedings preliminary or incidental to a reference,
   unless the Court of Appeal give him leave to be present.
8. The power of the Court of Appeal to pass sentence on a person may be exercised although he is not present.
9. A person whose sentencing is the subject of a reference to the House of Lords under section 36(5) above and who is detained pending the hearing of that reference shall not be entitled to be present on the hearing of the reference or of any proceeding preliminary or incidental

thereto except where an order of the House authorises him to be present, or where the House or the Court of Appeal, as the case may be, give him leave to be present.

10. The term of any sentence passed by the Court of Appeal or House of Lords under section 36 above shall, unless they otherwise direct, begin to run from the time when it would have begun to run if passed in the proceeding in relation to which the reference was made.

11. Where on a reference to the Court of Appeal under section 36 above or a reference to the House of Lords under subsection (5) of that section the person whose sentencing is the subject of the reference appears by counsel for the purpose of presenting any argument to the court or the House, he shall be entitled to his costs, that is to say to the payment out of central funds of such funds as are reasonably sufficient to compensate him for expenses properly incurred by him for the purpose of being represented on the reference; and any amount recoverable under this paragraph shall be ascertained, as soon as practicable, by the registrar of criminal appeals or, as the case may be, such officer as may be prescribed by order of the House of Lords.

Section D28 Challenging Decisions of Magistrates' Courts and of the Crown Court in its Appellate Capacity

ROUTES OF CHALLENGE OF DECISIONS OF MAGISTRATES' COURTS

A person aggrieved by a decision of the magistrates' court has three means of challenge to that decision available to him. They are as follows: **D28.1**

(a) appeal to the Crown Court;
(b) appeal to the High Court by way of case stated;
(c) application to the High Court for judicial review.

Any person convicted by a magistrates' court may appeal against either the conviction and/or sentence. If the offender pleaded guilty in the magistrates' court, then he may also appeal against conviction and sentence to the Crown Court. An appeal to the High Court by way of case stated or an application for judicial review is available to either party in the magistrates' court if they are aggrieved at the outcome of proceedings. An appeal by way of case stated or application for judicial review is heard by a Divisional Court of the Queen's Bench Division of the High Court.

APPEAL TO THE CROWN COURT

Magistrates' Courts Act 1980, s. 108 **D28.2**

(1) A person convicted by a magistrates' court may appeal to the Crown Court—
  (a) if he pleaded guilty, against his sentence;
  (b) if he did not, against the conviction or sentence.

(1A) Section 14 of the Powers of Criminal Courts (Sentencing) Act 2000 (under which a conviction of an offence for which a conditional or absolute discharge is made is deemed not to be a conviction except for certain purposes) shall not prevent an appeal under this section, whether against conviction or otherwise.

(2) A person sentenced by a magistrates' court for an offence in respect of which an order for conditional discharge has been previously made may appeal to the Crown Court against the sentence.

(3) In this section 'sentence' includes any order made on conviction by a magistrates' court, not being—
  [(a) repealed by Criminal Justice Act 1982, sch. 16]
  (b) an order for the payment of costs;
  (c) an order under section 2 of the Protection of Animals Act 1911 (which enables a court to order the destruction of an animal); or
  (d) an order made in pursuance of any enactment under which the court has no discretion as to the making of the order or its terms;

D

Part D Procedure

and also includes a declaration of relevance, within the meaning of section 23 of the Football Spectators Act 1989.

(4) Subsection (3)(d) above does not prevent an appeal against a surcharge imposed under section 161A of the Criminal Justice Act 2003.

Appeals against Conviction and Sentence

D28.3 Appeals to the Crown Court are governed by the MCA 1980, s. 108, and the CrimPR, part 3. Appeals from the youth court are governed by the same provisions (as a youth court is part of the magistrates' court), but an important procedural difference between an appeal from a youth court and one from an adult magistrates' court lies in the composition of the court. An appeal from the youth court must be heard by a judge or recorder of the Crown Court sitting with two lay justices (one man and one woman) who are authorised to sit in the youth court (r. 68.3). Exceptionally, a judge may allow an appeal to commence with only one lay justice authorised to sit in the youth court if unreasonable delay would be occasioned whilst a second authorised lay justice attended.

The broad definition of 'sentence' contained within s. 108(3) mirrors that in the equivalent provision for the Court of Appeal Criminal Division in s. 50 of the Criminal Appeal Act 1968.

Appeal against Conviction Following Plea of Guilty

D28.4 Generally, if a plea of guilty is entered in the magistrates' court, no appeal against the resulting conviction is available to the Crown Court. There are exceptions to that rule as follows:

(a) *When a plea is equivocal when made.* A plea is equivocal when made if a defendant enters a plea of guilty but, by additional comment following the plea, suggests that he is not guilty and has a defence. For example, if on a charge of assault a defendant pleads guilty but adds that he was only defending himself, then the plea is equivocal. The usual practice would then be for the clerk of the court to explain any necessary matters of law to the defendant and retake the plea. If the defendant then unambiguously pleads guilty the court may proceed to sentence, but if the plea remains equivocal, the court enters a not guilty plea. If the court does not follow that procedure and the Crown Court is satisfied on appeal that the plea was equivocal, the case will be remitted back to the magistrates' court for a fresh plea to be entered. The magistrates' court is required to co-operate with any investigation by the Crown Court into whether or not the plea is equivocal. Such co-operation extends to the provision of affidavits explaining the circumstances in which the guilty plea came to be entered (*Rochdale Justices, ex parte Allwork* [1981] 3 All ER 434). If, having conducted a proper enquiry into whether or not the initial plea was equivocal, the Crown Court remits the proceedings with a direction that a trial take place, the magistrates' court must comply with that direction (*Plymouth Justices, ex parte Hart* [1986] QB 950).

(b) *When a plea is subsequently shown to be equivocal.* The usual circumstances in which an unambiguous plea of guilty subsequently becomes equivocal are when material emerges in mitigation which undermines the unambiguous nature of the plea. On appeal on such a basis, the Crown Court should remit the case for trial (*Durham Quarter Sessions, ex parte Virgo* [1952] 2 QB 1; *Blandford Justices, ex parte G* [1967] 1 QB 82).

(c) *When a plea is entered under duress.* Plainly, any plea entered under duress is not a true plea and the Crown Court may remit a case back to the magistrates' court for trial if a plea of guilty has been entered under duress. In *Huntingdon Justices, ex parte Jordan* [1981] QB 857, J had pleaded guilty to shoplifting under duress from her husband. Her defence to the shoplifting allegations would similarly have been one of duress. The Divisional Court held that the Crown Court had jurisdiction to remit the case for trial in such circumstances if they were made out.

(d) *When autrefois convict or acquit arises.* The Crown Court in its appellate capacity may examine a plea in bar of *autrefois convict* or *acquit* even where the defendant has pleaded guilty in an entirely unambiguous way in the magistrates' court (*Cooper v New Forest District Council* [1992] Crim LR 877).

(e) *When a reference is made by the CCRC.* Under s. 11 of the Criminal Appeal Act 1995, the CCRC may refer any conviction in the magistrates' court to the Crown Court irrespective of whether the conviction arose from a plea of guilty or following a trial. Thus all of the bases of challenge to a conviction following a guilty plea in the Crown Court are available through the CCRC.

Appeal against Binding Over

Under s. 1(1) of the Magistrates' Courts (Appeals from Binding Over Orders) Act 1956, any defendant who feels aggrieved at being bound over by the magistrates may appeal that binding over order to the Crown Court. The appeal is by way of rehearing, and so if the facts which led to the binding over are not accepted by the appellant, they must be proved to the satisfaction of the court (*Shaw v Hamilton* [1982] 1 WLR 1308). **D28.5**

Procedure on Appeal to the Crown Court

Rule 63.2(1) and (3) of the CrimPR requires notice of appeal to be given in writing to the clerk of the relevant magistrates' court and to the prosecutor within 21 days of sentence being passed or the defendant being otherwise dealt with by the magistrates, e.g., by committal for sentence. The appellant has 21 days from the date of sentence or committal even if that is after the date of conviction and he is appealing only against conviction. That is to be contrasted with the position in respect of an appeal against conviction from the Crown Court to the Court of Appeal Criminal Division (see **D26.2**). The notice should state whether the appeal is against conviction or sentence or both, but no particular form is prescribed. Rule 63.2(4) requires that the notice state the grounds of appeal. If a notice is served within time, no leave to appeal is required. By virtue of r. 63.2(5), the Crown Court may give leave to appeal out of time but, under r. 63.2(6), an application for an extension of time must be made in writing, and must specify the grounds of the application. The grounds of the application should include the proposed grounds of appeal as well as any reasons for applying out of time. In exercising its discretion, the court will take into account the merits of the case and any reasons for the delay. The court has discretion in exceptional circumstances to grant an oral hearing in order that representations for leave to apply out of time may be made. There is no general duty on a judge to give reasons for refusing leave to appeal out of time (see *Croydon Crown Court, ex parte Smith* (1983) 77 Cr App R 277). **D28.6**

Bail pending appeal is dealt with at **D28.13**.

An appeal is heard by a circuit judge or recorder who must normally sit with two lay magistrates who were not involved with the original proceedings (Supreme Court Act 1981, s. 74). Prior to the hearing, the defence may request a copy of the clerk's notes of evidence of the summary trial (see also **D19.53**).

Hearing Any request the appellant might make for a copy should be 'viewed sympathetically' (per Lord Lane CJ in *Clerk to Highbury Corner Justices, ex parte Hussein* [1986] 1 WLR 1266). Under s. 79(3), the appeal proceeds by way of complete rehearing. Thus, at an appeal against conviction, counsel for the respondent (i.e. the prosecution) makes an opening speech and calls evidence, after which counsel for the appellant may make a submission of no case to answer. If that fails, defence evidence is called, counsel makes a closing speech, and the court announces its decision. The parties may call evidence which has only become available to them since the trial, or evidence they decided not to use in the magistrates' court. The information on which the appellant was convicted may not be amended by the Crown Court **D28.7**

D

Part D Procedure

(*Garfield v Maddocks* [1974] QB 7). In *Swansea Crown Court, ex parte Stacey* [1990] RTR 183, it was held that the judge erred in allowing a prosecution application to amend the information in respect of the date of the alleged offences. Equally, the Crown Court cannot strike out an amendment made by the magistrates (*Fairgrieve v Newman* (1985) 82 Cr App R 60).

An appeal against sentence is, in essence, a fresh sentencing hearing. The prosecution opens the facts and antecedents of the appellant, and defence counsel then mitigates. The court then decides the sentence to be imposed. When dealing with an appeal against sentence, the Crown Court should not ask itself whether the sentence was within the discretion of the magistrates (as would be the appropriate question in judicial review proceedings) but should consider whether, in the light of all the matters which the Crown Court had heard, the sentence passed by the magistrates was the correct one. If what the court thinks is the appropriate sentence differs significantly from the sentence imposed by the magistrates, the appeal should be allowed and the sentence of the Crown Court substituted for that of the magistrates (*Swindon Crown Court, ex parte Murray* (1998) 162 JP 36). The Crown Court is not entitled to increase the sentence on appeal from the magistrates' court on the basis that the magistrates ought to have committed the offender to the Crown Court for sentence in the first place (*R (Lees-Sandey) v Chichester Crown Court* (2004) *The Times*, 15 October 2004).

If a defendant pleads guilty in the magistrates' court but disputes the version of events put forward by the prosecution, and the magistrates decide to accept the defendant's version of events without hearing evidence, the Crown Court hearing an appeal against sentence is not bound by that action. As the appeal is a rehearing, the court may determine the appeal and hence pass a different sentence on a different factual basis to that which formed the basis of the sentence imposed by the magistrates' court. However, if the Crown Court intends to decide the appeal on a different factual basis, the court should inform the appellant of that intention in clear terms and allow him the opportunity of a *Newton* hearing (*Bussey v DPP* [1999] 1 Cr App R (S) 125).

D28.8 **Reasons for Decision** Reasons for the decision of the Crown Court should be given by the judge presiding over the hearing. The reasons should include a statement of the main contentious issues in the case and how the court had resolved them. A refusal to give reasons might amount to a denial of natural justice (*Harrow Crown Court, ex parte Dave* [1994] 1 WLR 98). The duty to provide reasons exists whether the court allows or dismisses the appeal against conviction (*Inner London Crown Court, ex parte London Borough of Lambeth Council* [2000] Crim LR 303). If reasons are not given the decision of the Crown Court will usually be vitiated, but that is not an unqualified rule. If, for example, the reasons are obvious, the failure to set them out will not necessarily be fatal (*Kingston Crown Court, ex parte Bell* (2000) 164 JP 633). In *Snaresbrook Crown Court, ex parte Input Management Ltd* (1999) 163 JP 533, the Divisional Court defined the obligation to give reasons, holding that the reasons given by the Crown Court should enable the defendant: (i) to see the nature of the criminality found to exist by the court; and (ii) to consider properly whether there are grounds for a further appeal to the Divisional Court by way of case stated.

Powers of the Crown Court on Appeal

D28.9 The powers of the Crown Court when disposing of an appeal are set out in the Supreme Court Act 1981, s. 48. The decision of the Crown Court may be a majority decision. This means that the lay justices can out-vote the judge. The lay justices must, however, accept any decisions on questions of law made by the judge.

The Supreme Court Act 1981, s. 48(2), provides that, following an appeal from the magistrates' court, the Crown Court:

(a) may confirm, reverse or vary any part of the decision appealed against, including a determination not to impose a separate penalty in respect of an offence; or
(b) may remit the matter with its opinion thereon to the authority whose decision is appealed against; or
(c) may make such other order in the matter as the court thinks just, and by such order exercise any power which the said authority might have exercised.

Section 48(4) and (5) further provide that:

> . . . if the appeal is against a conviction or a sentence, the preceding provisions of this section shall be construed as including power to award any punishment, whether more or less severe than that awarded by the magistrates' court whose decision is appealed against, if that is a punishment which that magistrates' court might have awarded.
> (5) This section applies whether or not the appeal is against the whole of the decision.

Thus, s. 48 allows the Crown Court to:

(a) quash the conviction;
(b) remit the case to the magistrates' court (for example, in the case of an equivocal plea);
(c) vary the sentence imposed by the magistrates (this includes the power to increase the sentence, but not beyond the maximum sentence which the magistrates' court could have passed: s. 48(4)).

Under s. 11(5) of the Criminal Appeal Act 1995, if a reference to the Crown Court is made by the CCRC, the Crown Court has no power to increase the sentence.

If a defendant's hopes of a non-custodial sentence are legitimately raised as a result of an indication given by magistrates that favourable pre-sentence reports would be likely to result in a non-custodial sentence, the Crown Court should not impose or uphold a custodial sentence. Whilst the appeal proceedings constitute a complete rehearing, the expectation created in the appellant should be respected (*Isleworth Crown Court, ex parte Irvin* [1992] RTR 281).

In *Portsmouth Crown Court, ex parte Ballard* (1989) 154 JP 109, it was held that the Crown Court had no power to impose a sentence consecutive to one imposed *after* the date of imposition of the sentence being appealed.

An unsuccessful appellant may be required to pay the prosecution's costs (Prosecution of Offences Act 1985, s. 18(1)(b) (see **D30.17**) and CrimPR, r. 78.1(2)). A successful appellant may be awarded his costs (s. 16(3)) as may a private prosecutor (s. 17(1) and (2)), but there is no provision for a public prosecutor to be awarded costs from the public purse.

Abandonment of Appeal

Magistrates' Courts Act 1980, s. 109 D28.10

> (1) Where notice to abandon an appeal has been duly given by the appellant—
> (a) the court against whose decision the appeal was brought may issue process for enforcing that decision, subject to anything already suffered or done under it by the appellant; and
> (b) the said court may, on the application of the other party to the appeal, order the appellant to pay to that party such costs as appear to the court to be just and reasonable in respect of expenses properly incurred by that party in connection with the appeal before notice of the abandonment was given to that party.
> (2) In this section 'appeal' means an appeal from a magistrates' court to the Crown Court, and the reference to a notice to abandon an appeal is a reference to a notice shown to the satisfaction of the magistrates' court to have been given in accordance with rules of court.

Rule 63.5 of the CrimPR sets out the procedure for abandonment of an appeal under the MCA 1980, s. 109. The appellant may abandon his appeal by giving notice in writing to that effect to the magistrates' court, to the appropriate officer of the Crown Court and to the prosecution and to any other party to the appeal (CrimPR, r. 63.5(2)). The notice should be given at least three days before the hearing of the appeal. Where notice to abandon an appeal has been duly given by the appellant, the court against whose decision the appeal was brought may issue process for enforcing that decision, subject to anything already suffered or done under it by the appellant (MCA 1980, s. 109(1)(a)). If notice to abandon an appeal is duly given, the Crown Court is thereby deprived of its power to order the appellant to pay costs, but the magistrates may make an order in respect of expenses properly incurred by the prosecutor before he received the notice (s. 109(1)(b) and r. 78.1(3)).

An appeal cannot be abandoned simply by an appellant failing to attend or failing to instruct an advocate. But, even if no notice in writing is given in accordance with the CrimPR, r. 63.5, the Crown Court may still allow an appeal to be abandoned (r. 63.5(1)).

Upon the abandonment of an appeal, the Crown Court has no power to increase sentence (*Gloucester Crown Court, ex parte Betteridge* (1997) 161 JP 721; CrimPR r. 63.5). Once an appeal has been abandoned, the Crown Court has no power to reinstate the appeal unless the abandonment was a nullity (*Knightsbridge Crown Court, ex parte Commissioners of Customs and Excise* [1986] Crim LR 324) If an appellant does not proceed with an appeal, but equally does not formally abandon it, the Crown Court may award costs against him (r. 78.1(4)).

Proceeding in the Absence of the Parties

D28.11 If an appellant fails to attend at the appeal hearing when required but is represented by an advocate, the Crown Court should hear the appeal. It is not open to the Crown Court to treat the non-attendance as an effective abandonment of the appeal (*R (Hayes) v Chelmsford Crown Court* (2003) 167 JP 65).

Where neither party appears or is represented, the proper course is to dismiss the appeal (*Croydon Crown Court, ex parte Clair* [1986] 1 WLR 746).

Enforcement of Orders of Crown Court on Appeal

D28.12 **Magistrates' Courts Act 1980, s. 110**

After the determination by the Crown Court of an appeal from a magistrates' court the decision appealed against as confirmed or varied by the Crown Court, or any decision of the Crown Court substituted for the decision appealed against, may, without prejudice to the powers of the Crown Court to enforce the decision, be enforced—

(a) by the issue by the court by which the decision appealed against was given of any process that it could have issued if it had decided the case as the Crown Court decided it;

(b) so far as the nature of any process already issued to enforce the decision appealed against permits, by that process;

and the decision of the Crown Court shall have effect as if it had been made by the magistrates' court against whose decision the appeal is brought.

Bail Pending Appeal

D28.13 Under the MCA 1980, s. 113, bail may be granted pending appeal to the Crown Court in respect of either conviction or sentence. The Bail Act 1976 does not apply so there is no right to bail. Under the Supreme Court Act 1981, s. 81(1), an appellant refused bail by the magistrates may apply to the Crown Court for bail. Since the implementation of the CJA 2003, s. 17, it is no longer possible to apply to the High Court for bail pending appeal if the Crown Court refuses bail.

APPEAL TO DIVISIONAL COURT BY WAY OF CASE STATED

Principles of Appeal by Way of Case Stated

D28.14 **Magistrates' Courts Act 1980, ss. 111 to 114**

111.—(1) Any person who was a party to any proceeding before a magistrates' court or is aggrieved by the conviction, order, determination or other proceeding of the court may question the proceeding on the ground that it is wrong in law or is in excess of jurisdiction by applying to the justices composing the court to state a case for the opinion of the High Court on the question of law or jurisdiction involved; but a person shall not make an application under this section in respect of a decision against which he has a right of appeal to the High Court or which by virtue of any enactment passed after 31st December 1879 is final.

(2) An application under subsection (1) above shall be made within 21 days after the day on which the decision of the magistrates' court was given.

(3) For the purpose of subsection (2) above, the day on which the decision of the magistrates' court is given shall, where the court has adjourned the trial of an information after conviction, be the day on which the court sentences or otherwise deals with the offender.

(4) On the making of an application under this section in respect of a decision any right of the applicant to appeal against the decision to the Crown Court shall cease.

(5) If the justices are of opinion that an application under this section is frivolous, they may refuse to state a case, and, if the applicant so requires, shall give him a certificate stating that the application has been refused; but the justices shall not refuse to state a case if the application is made by or under the direction of the Attorney-General.

(6) Where justices refuse to state a case, the High Court may, on the application of the person who applied for the case to be stated, make an order of mandamus requiring the justices to state a case.

112. Any conviction, order, determination or other proceeding of a magistrates' court varied by the High Court on an appeal by case stated, and any judgment or order of the High Court on such an appeal, may be enforced as if it were a decision of the magistrates' court from which the appeal was brought.

113.—(1) Where a person has given notice of appeal to the Crown Court against the decision of a magistrates' court or has applied to a magistrates' court to state a case for the opinion of the High Court, then, if he is in custody, the magistrates' court may, subject to section 25 of the Criminal Justice and Public Order Act 1994, grant him bail.

(2) If a person is granted bail under subsection (1) above, the time and place at which he is to appear (except in the event of the determination in respect of which the case is stated being reversed by the High Court) shall be—

(a) if he has given notice of appeal, the Crown Court at the time appointed for the hearing of the appeal;

(b) if he has applied for the statement of a case, the magistrates' court at such time within 10 days after the judgment of the High Court has been given as may be specified by the magistrates' court;

and any recognisance that may be taken from him or from any surety for him shall be conditioned accordingly.

(3) Subsection (1) above shall not apply where the accused has been committed to the Crown Court for sentence under section 37 above or section 3 of the Powers of Criminal Courts (Sentencing) Act 2000.

(4) Section 37(6) of the Criminal Justice Act 1948 (which relates to the currency of a sentence while a person is released on bail by the High Court) shall apply to a person released on bail by a magistrates' court under this section pending the hearing of a case stated as it applies to a person released on bail by the High Court under section 22 of the Criminal Justice Act 1967.

114. Justices to whom application has been made to state a case for the opinion of the High Court on any proceeding of a magistrates' court shall not be required to state the case until the applicant has entered into a recognisance, with or without sureties, before the magistrates' court, conditioned to prosecute the appeal without delay and to submit to the judgment of the High Court and pay such costs as that court may award; and (except in any criminal matter) a justices' clerk shall not be required to deliver the case to the applicant until the applicant has paid him the fees payable for the case and for the recognisances to the designated officer for the court.

Appeal from the magistrates' court by way of case stated is provided for in the MCA 1980, s. 111(1), and the procedure is governed by ss. 111 to 114 of that Act, part 64 of the CrimPR, and the Civil Procedure Rules, part 52. The appeal is to a Divisional Court of the Queen's Bench Division of the High Court. The essence of the procedure is an appeal on a point of law which is identified in a document known as the 'case'. The case is initially drafted by the justices' clerk in conjunction with the bench whose decision is being appealed.

Features of the 'case stated' process which emerge from s. 111 include:

(a) The remedy is available to both the prosecution and defence.
(b) The remedy operates only in relation to an error of law or a decision taken in excess of jurisdiction. A decision as to a question of fact will ordinarily not give rise to an appeal by way of case stated but may do so if the finding of fact is alleged to be such that no reasonable bench could have properly reached that factual conclusion on the evidence (*Bracegirdle v Oxley* [1947] KB 349; *Braintree District Council v Thompson* [2005] EWCA Civ 178). In *Oladimeji v DPP* [2006] EWHC Admin 1199, the court stated that any defendant who believes that the justices should not have arrived at a finding for which there was evidence because, for example, it was against the weight of the evidence, has his remedy in an appeal to the Crown Court and not to the High Court. Under s. 111(4), any appellant who employs the case stated procedure forfeits his right to appeal to the Crown Court.
(c) The remedy is available only after the final determination of proceedings in the magistrates' court. Thus the procedure is not available in relation to decisions made in respect of committal proceedings (*Dewing v Cummings* [1971] RTR 295). Similarly, if trial proceedings are adjourned the procedure cannot be employed during the period of adjournment (*Streames v Copping* [1985] QB 920).
(d) The remedy is available in respect of errors made in relation to sentence as well as conviction. Such appeals have often been successfully established by the prosecution where the court has wrongly held that there were 'special reasons' for not disqualifying a driver (see, e.g., *Haime v Walklett* [1983] RTR 512). On a defendant's part, he may use the case stated procedure if the bench has passed a sentence which is so far beyond the usual level of sentence for such an offence that it is 'harsh and oppressive' (*Tucker v DPP* [1992] 4 All ER 901).

Procedure on Appeal by way of Case Stated

D28.15 By virtue of the MCA 1980, s. 111(2) and (3), an application to state a case must be made within 21 days of the 'day on which the court sentences or otherwise deals with the offender'. The procedure to be followed upon application by way of case stated is contained in the CrimPR, part 64. Rule 64.1 governs the initial application to the bench for it to state a case. Under r. 64.1(1), the application must be in writing and should stipulate the question(s) of law on which the opinion of the High Court is sought. If it is asserted that the magistrates' court reached a conclusion of fact for which there was no evidential basis, the fact in question must be identified (r. 64.1(2)). Rule 64.1(3) requires that the initial application be sent to the relevant magistrates' court. The bench may refuse to state a case on the basis that it is frivolous. Frivolous, in this context, has been defined as 'futile, misconceived, hopeless or academic' and it should be rare that the magistrates' court reach such a conclusion (*Mildenhall Magistrates' Court, ex parte Forest Heath District Council* (1997) 161 JP 401). If the magistrates' court does refuse to state a case because it is of the opinion that the application is frivolous, it must issue the applicant with a statement to that effect (MCA 1980, s. 115) and should also provide a short statement of its reasons.

The applicant may challenge the decision to refuse to state a case by way of judicial review. Upon the applicant doing so, the Divisional Court may quash the decision to refuse to state a case and decide to proceed to a substantive hearing of the case stated application, using the affidavit evidence provided by the parties as the 'case stated'. Such procedure has the advantage that the Divisional Court does not have to wait for the case to be returned to the magistrates' court for a case to be stated before quashing a conviction (*Reigate Justices, ex parte Counsell* (1983) 148 JP 193; *Ealing Justices, ex parte Woodman* [1994] Crim LR 372). In

Blackfriars Crown Court, ex parte Sunworld Ltd [2000] 1 WLR 2102, the Divisional Court said that if the court below has given a reasoned judgment which contains all the necessary findings of fact and identifies the points of law in question in its refusal to state a case, the single judge should grant permission for judicial review if it considers the point to be arguable. In that way, the need for a case to be stated is obviated.

Under s. 114 of the MCA 1980, if a magistrates' court does state a case, it may require an applicant to enter into a recognisance that he will prosecute the appeal without delay and pay any costs ultimately awarded against him by the High Court.

Drafting of Case Stated It is the justices' clerk who is responsible for drafting the case following consultation with the bench and taking any representations from the parties into account. The required contents of a statement of case are governed by the CrimPR, r. 64.6 (see **appendix 1**). It must contain the facts found by the court and any questions of law or jurisdiction upon which the opinion of the court is sought. No statement of evidence is necessary unless one of the questions on which the opinion of the High Court is sought is whether there was evidence before the magistrates' court which would justify a particular finding of fact by that court. If there is such a question, then the particular finding of fact which it is claimed could not be supported by the evidence must be specified in the case. **D28.16**

Service and Representations The draft case must be sent to the parties within 21 days of receipt of the application (r. 64.2(1)). Within 21 days thereof, the parties must make written, signed representations on the draft case and they must be sent to the magistrates' court officer. Rule 64.3 dictates that within 21 days of the last day for the making of representations, the justices may make any amendments to the draft case that they see fit, having taken into account any representations made by the parties. Any two or more of the justices whose decision is questioned may state a case and it must be signed. It may be signed by them or, if they so direct, may be signed on their behalf by a justices' clerk. The case must then be sent forthwith to the applicant or his legal representative (r. 64.3(3)). A failure to comply with the time-limits set out for the various participants is not necessarily fatal to an application. In particular, rr. 64.2(1) and 64.4 make specific provision for steps to be taken if the time-limits are not satisfied. Within ten days of receiving the case, under para. 18.4 of the *Civil Procedure Rules Part 52 Practice Direction*, the applicant or his legal representative must lodge it at the Administrative Court Office. Paragraph 18.6 of that Practice Direction requires the applicant to serve the appellant's notice and accompanying documents on the respondents within four days of their being lodged at the Divisional Court. The time for lodging the case may be extended by the Divisional Court, but without such an extension the claim may be struck out if the applicant fails to lodge within ten days. **D28.17**

Whilst the time-limits applying after an application for the magistrates to state a case has been made may be extended, the initial 21-day time-limit within which an application must be made cannot be varied as it is prescribed by statute. If the application arrives late when sent by post, the 21-day time-limit is met if the application would have arrived on time in the normal course of events (*P and M Supplies (Essex) Ltd v Hackney London Borough Council* (1990) 154 JP 814).

Amendment of Case Plainly, where there is a difference between an earlier draft of the case and the final version, the Divisional Court will act on the final version (*Thomas* [1990] Crim LR 269). On an appeal by way of case stated, the court is confined to the facts set out in the case. Thus if any party wishes to add any evidential matter to the case, he should seek to have the case amended either by agreement with the other party and the lower court or by application to the Divisional Court under the Supreme Court Act 1981, s. 28A(2) (*Skipaway Ltd v Environment Agency* [2006] EWHC 983 (Admin)). **D28.18**

Bail Pending Appeal

D28.19 An appellant by way of case stated who has been sentenced to a term of immediate custody may be granted bail pending appeal by the magistrates' court under the MCA 1980, s. 113. If granted bail, he must surrender to the magistrates' court no later than ten days after the final determination of the appeal. The exact date on which he must surrender will be fixed by the magistrates' court after the appeal. If refused bail, he may apply to a judge in chambers in the High Court under s. 37(1)(b) of the CJA 1948. The procedure for an application for bail to the High Court in such circumstances is set out in the Rules of the Supreme Court, ord. 79, r. 9.

Determination by Divisional Court of an Appeal by Way of Case Stated

D28.20 The Divisional Court which hears an application by way of case stated will be comprised of at least two judges, and often three. If a two-judge court cannot agree, the appeal is unsuccessful (see the *obiter* remarks of Scrutton LJ in *Flannagan v Shaw* [1920] 3 KB 96 at p. 107). No evidence is called at the hearing as all evidence which needs to be referred to will be contained in the stated case (see **D27.14**). Instead the appeal is conducted by way of submissions from the parties. If the facts contained within the case give rise to a point of law which was not argued before the magistrates but would have provided the defendant with a defence, the court may consider the point provided no further evidence is necessary (*Whitehead v Haines* [1965] 1 QB 200).

Under s. 28A(3) of the Supreme Court Act 1981, the court may 'reverse, affirm or amend' the decision of the magistrates' court, or remit the case with its opinion, or make any other order (including an order as to costs) as it sees fit. Thus the Divisional Court may quash an acquittal with a direction that the magistrates' court convicts and sentences. Alternatively, the court may simply substitute a conviction for the previous acquittal and proceed to sentence. Similarly, if the appeal concerns sentence only, the court may substitute the appropriate sentence.

An appellant may abandon an appeal by way of case stated without leave (*Collet v Bromsgrove District Council* (1996) 160 JP 593).

The Divisional Court is entitled to order a retrial before the same bench or a different bench where a fair trial is still possible (*Griffith v Jenkins* [1992] 2 AC 76).

APPLICATION FOR JUDICIAL REVIEW

Prerogative Orders Generally

D28.21 The High Court polices the decision-making of inferior public bodies by way of judicial review. Consequently, decisions of the magistrates' court and some of those of the Crown Court (those which are not concerned with matters relating to trial on indictment) are susceptible to review. The High Court does so by means of prerogative orders, foremost of which are quashing orders, mandatory orders and prohibiting orders.

The application for judicial review is dealt with by a Divisional Court of the Queen's Bench Division of the High Court.

The granting of prerogative orders is discretionary and the Divisional Court will sometimes withhold relief despite it being open to the court to grant it where fairness and the due administration of justice demand it. Undue delay on behalf of the applicant for judicial review may sometimes result in the withholding of relief. In *Neath and Port Talbot Justices, ex parte DPP* [2000] 1 WLR 1376, the Divisional Court identified the principal factors to be taken into account in considering whether delay should lead to a refusal of relief. They are:

(a) the seriousness of the offence;
(b) the nature of the evidence in the case (and in particular the extent to which the quality of the evidence would be affected by delay);
(c) the extent of any contribution by the defendant to the error of the magistrates' court;
(d) the extent of any contribution by the defendant to any delay in the review process;
(e) the extent to which the complainant would be justifiably aggrieved by the abandonment of the proceedings;
(f) the extent to which the defendant would be justifiably aggrieved by the continuation of the proceedings.

Rule 54.5(1) of the Civil Procedure Rules provides that a claim form must be filed promptly and, in any event, not later than three months after the grounds to make the claim first arose. But a judicial review claim will not necessarily be regarded as being in time merely because it is made within a three-month period. Instead, the claim form must be lodged promptly, and applications for judicial review have been rejected as being out of time where delay has occurred within the three-month period (see, e.g., *Independent Television Commission, ex parte TV NI Ltd* (1991) *The Times*, 30 December 1991).

The Divisional Court has also refused relief when the defendant had an appeal to the Crown Court available to him (see *Peterborough Justices, ex parte Dowler* [1996] 2 Cr App R 561). But in *Hereford Magistrates' Court, ex parte Rowlands* [1998] QB 110, Lord Bingham CJ emphasised the importance of the supervisory jurisdiction of the High Court in ensuring continued high standards in magistrates' courts, and concluded that the existence of a right to appeal to the Crown Court, particularly if unexercised, should not ordinarily preclude permission for judicial review, nor substantive relief in a proper case.

The principal grounds upon which judicial review may be sought are:

(a) error of law on the face of the record — i.e. an error disclosed by the court records;
(b) excess of jurisdiction;
(c) breach of natural justice.

The concept of breach of natural justice has frequently been litigated and has been widely drawn. It has been held to include:

(i) failing to give the accused adequate time to prepare a defence (*Thames Magistrates' Court, ex parte Polemis* [1974] 1 WLR 1371);
(ii) failing to grant an adjournment to allow for the attendance of a witness (*Bracknell Justices, ex parte Hughes* [1990] Crim LR 266);
(iii) the prosecution failing to call or disclose the statement of a witness who might assist the defence (*Leyland Justices, ex parte Hawthorn* [1979] QB 283);
(iv) the prosecution failing to disclose the previous convictions of prosecution witnesses (*Knightsbridge Crown Court, ex parte Goonatilleke* [1986] QB 1);
(v) making an order as to costs against a defendant without enquiring as to his means (*Newham Justices, ex parte Samuels* [1991] COD 412).

The proceedings in the magistrates' court must ordinarily be concluded before any application for judicial review. Interlocutory decisions by the magistrates' court are not generally amenable to review (*Greater Manchester Justices, ex parte Aldi GmbH & Co KG* [1995] RTR 207), but it is possible to review a decision as whether proceedings should commence (*R (Hoar-Stevens) v Richmond-upon-Thames Magistrates* [2004] Crim LR 474; *Rochford Justices, ex parte Buck* (1979) 68 Cr App R 114).

Whilst it is possible to challenge a sentence by way of judicial review, it is not usually appropriate and the defendant should seek his remedy through appeal to the Crown Court unless there are clear and substantial grounds for proceeding by way of review (*Allen v West Yorkshire Probation Service* (2001) 165 JP 313; *Tucker v DPP* [1992] 4 All ER 901). Both of

D

Part D Procedure

these cases were appeals by way of case stated but the court made it clear that judicial review was also inappropriate.

Quashing Orders

D28.22 Quashing orders are used to nullify decisions and orders made by the magistrates' court, such as decisions to commit for trial, committals for sentence and convictions. Its use in respect of acquittals is more limited than in the case stated procedure because of the double jeopardy principle. Even if the prosecution are prejudiced to the extent that, had the defence had been similarly prejudiced it would have required the quashing of the conviction, review will still not be available. That principle was reaffirmed by the House of Lords in *Dorking Justices, ex parte Harrington* [1984] AC 743, but an important exception to the rule was established. In simple terms, the rule will not apply where the magistrates acquit where they have no jurisdiction to do so. If that occurs, the acquittal is a nullity and a quashing order may be made. Such a situation may come about when the magistrates acquit in respect of an indictable-only offence (*West* [1964] 1 QB 15) or a defendant is acquitted of an either-way offence when the correct mode of trial procedures have not been followed (*Cardiff Magistrates' Court, ex parte Cardiff City Council* (1987) *The Times*, 24 February 1987), or the magistrates' court, in the absence of good reason, acquits without listening to any of the prosecution witnesses available at court (*Hendon Justices, ex parte DPP* [1994] QB 167).

D28.23 **Excess of Jurisdiction** When a magistrates' court acts in excess of jurisdiction, the Divisional Court may issue a quashing order. In *Kent Justices, ex parte Machin* [1952] 2 QB 355, a conviction was quashed when magistrates failed to explain to a defendant the possibility that he could be committed for sentence before he consented to summary trial.

Judicial review is rarely the most appropriate means of challenge to a sentence imposed by the magistrates but it can in very limited circumstances be used to challenge a sentence passed in excess of jurisdiction. In *St. Albans Crown Court, ex parte Cinnamond* [1981] QB 480, the Divisional Court extended the concept of excess of jurisdiction to include a sentence that was so harsh that no reasonable tribunal, properly understanding its powers, could have passed it. Not surprisingly, the courts have repeatedly sought to confine the applicability of *Ex parte Cinnamond* to very limited circumstances. In *Croydon Crown Court, ex parte Miller* (1986) 85 Cr App R 152, it was said that the sentence would have to appear in all the circumstances to be, by any acceptable standard, truly astonishing. Whilst in *Truro Crown Court, ex parte Adair* [1997] COD 296, Lord Bingham CJ questioned whether the sentence needed to be truly astonishing but asserted that it needed to fall clearly outside the broad area of the lower court's sentencing discretion.

D28.24 **Breach of Rules of Natural Justice** A number of decisions of magistrates' courts have been quashed where a magistrate or clerk has an interest of either a pecuniary or non-pecuniary nature such as to give rise to a reasonable suspicion of bias. In addition, procedural irregularities have often led to the quashing of decisions on the grounds of breach of natural justice (see D27.21).

D28.25 **Error of Law** An error of law made by a magistrates' court is amenable to review. As an example, in *Southampton Justices, ex parte Green* [1976] QB 11, the Court of Appeal quashed an order made by the magistrates that G should forfeit the surety provided as the decision-making process was wrong in law. So far as the exercise of discretion on questions of law is concerned, the court will apply the test in *Associated Provincial Picture Houses Ltd v Wednesbury Corporation* [1948] 1 KB 223 (*Re Proulx* [2001] 1 All ER 57).

Mandatory Orders

D28.26 A mandatory order is issued to compel a magistrates' court to comply with its obligations and usually flows from an order quashing the original decision. One may be issued where the magistrates' court has wrongly refused jurisdiction (*Rochford Justices, ex parte Buck* (1978) 68 Cr App R 114; *Wells Street Stipendiary Magistrate, ex parte Seillon* [1978] 1 WLR 1002). In matters of discretion, if the magistrates' court overlooked the fact that it had a discretionary power, or applied the wrong principles in deciding whether or not to exercise it, the Divisional Court will issue a mandatory order requiring the court to consider or reconsider the matter, applying the correct principles as stated by the High Court (*Highgate Justices, ex parte Lewis* [1977] Crim LR 611). The court will not be required to exercise the power in a particular way unless it is clear that that would be the only conclusion to which a reasonable tribunal directing itself properly could come.

Prohibiting Orders

A prohibiting order prevents a magistrates' court from taking a particular course of action which would be in excess of its jurisdiction (*Hatfield Justices, ex parte Castle* [1981] 1 WLR 217). **D28.27**

Procedure on Application for Judicial Review

The procedure to be followed on an application for judicial review is governed by the Supreme Court Act 1981, s. 31, along with part 54 of the Civil Procedure Rules and the Part 54 Practice Direction. The Judicial Review Pre-Action Protocol usually requires that a claimant for judicial review write to the proposed defendant explaining the basis of the challenge. Such a letter gives the decision-maker an opportunity to reverse the decision before proceedings are started. But a decision by a court will normally be a final decision and so the court will not be able to reverse that decision as it will often be *functus officio*. The Protocol recognises that in such circumstances a letter before claim is not necessary. If an interim decision of a court is to be challenged, the court will not be *functus officio* and the court should be put on notice that an application for judicial review will be made. The claimant should then apply for an adjournment in order to bring the judicial review proceedings (*Streames v Copping* [1985] QB 920). If the application for an adjournment is refused, the Administrative Court may stay the magistrates' court proceedings as interim relief under para. 6.4 of the Pre-Action Protocol. **D28.28**

Any claimant for judicial review requires permission to pursue the claim. The issue of permission is usually resolved on the papers by the single judge. If permission is granted, the matter proceeds to a substantive hearing.

(a) The first stage of the process is to submit a claim form. As well as the matters that normally have to appear in a claim form (see the Civil Procedure Rules, r. 8.2), r. 54.6 provides that the claimant has to identify interested parties and must state the remedy sought. The claim form has to be accompanied by the documents required by the Practice Direction which supplements part 54. Paragraph 5.6 of the Practice Direction provides that the claim form must include or be accompanied by a detailed statement of the claimant's grounds for bringing the claim for judicial review, a statement of the facts relied upon, and a time estimate for the hearing. The statement of facts and the grounds to be relied on are usually drafted by counsel if the claimant is legally represented. The claim form must also be accompanied by any written evidence in support of the claim (or in support of any application to extend time), a copy of any order that the claimant seeks to have quashed, an approved copy of the lower court's reasons for reaching the decision under challenge, copies of any documents on which the claimant proposes to rely, copies of any relevant statutory material, and a list of essential documents for reading in advance by the court (with page references to the passages relied on) (para. 5.7). The prosecution must always be named as an interested party where the claim is for judicial review of a decision of a magistrates' court or the Crown Court (para. 5.2). Not more than 21 days after the service of the claim form the defendant must file an acknowledgement of service. The acknowledgement of service must be served on the claimant, and on any other person named in the claim form, not later than seven days after it is filed. If the person serving it intends to contest the claim, the acknowledgement of service must set out a summary of the grounds for contesting the claim, known as 'summary grounds of resistance', and must state the name and address of anyone whom the person filing it considers to be an interested party.

(b) The court will generally consider the question of permission without a hearing (para. 8.4 of the Practice Direction) Where there is a hearing, neither the defendant nor any other interested party need attend the hearing unless the court directs otherwise (para. 8.5). The court will not usually make an order for costs where the defendant or any interested party does attend a hearing (para. 8.6). The single judge will grant permission if the claimant's application for judicial review discloses an arguable case. Rule 54.12 provides that, if the court (without a hearing) refuses permission to proceed or gives permission that is subject to conditions or on certain grounds only, the court will serve its reasons for making the order along with the order itself. Under r. 54.12, 'the claimant may not appeal but may request the decision to be reconsidered at a hearing' (and must file a request for such a hearing within seven days of the service of the court's reasons for the decision). The renewed application will be before a Divisional Court in a criminal cause or matter. Neither the defendant, nor anyone else served with the claim form, may apply to set aside an order giving the claimant permission to proceed (r. 54.13).

(c) Once permission has been granted, the defendant (and anyone else served with the claim form who wishes to contest the claim or support it on additional grounds) must serve detailed grounds for contesting the claim (or supporting it on additional grounds), and any written evidence, within 35 days after the service of the order granting permission.

(d) The court may decide the claim for judicial review without a hearing where all the parties agree (r. 54.18). In all other circumstances, the claimant must file and serve a skeleton argument not less than 21 working days before the date of the hearing of the judicial review claim (para. 15.1 of the Practice Direction). Under para. 15.2 of the Practice Direction, the defendant (and any other party wishing to make representations at the hearing) must file and serve a skeleton argument not less than 14 working days before the date of the hearing. The skeleton arguments must contain a list of issues, a list of the legal points to be taken (together with any relevant authorities), a chronology of events, a list of essential reading by the court in advance of the hearing and a list of persons referred to.

(e) The claimant must have the court's permission if he is to rely on grounds other than those for which the court gave permission to proceed (r. 54.15). The claimant must give notice no later than seven clear days before the hearing to any person served with the claim form if he intends to rely on additional grounds at the hearing of the claim for judicial review.

(f) The usual procedure followed at the hearing is one of legal argument supported by affidavits or witness statements. However, it is possible for oral evidence to be called if necessary.

Bail Pending Judicial Review

D28.29 In contrast to the position in respect of appeals by way of case stated, the magistrates' court has no power to grant bail pending an application for judicial review. Bail may be secured through an application to a judge in chambers under s. 37(1)(d) of the CJA 1948.

ROUTES TO CHALLENGE DECISIONS OF THE CROWN COURT ACTING IN ITS APPELLATE CAPACITY

Appeal by Way of Case Stated

D28.30 Supreme Court Act 1981, s. 28

(1) Subject to subsection (2), any order, judgment or other decision of the Crown Court may be questioned by any party to the proceedings, on the ground that it is wrong in law or is in excess of jurisdiction, by applying to the Crown Court to have a case stated by that court for the opinion of the High Court.

(2) Subsection (1) shall not apply to—

(a) a judgment or other decision of the Crown Court relating to trial on indictment; or

(b) any decision of that court under the Local Government (Miscellaneous Provisions) Act 1982 which, by any provision of any of those Acts, is to be final.

(3) Subject to the provisions of this Act and to rules of court, the High Court shall, in accordance with section 19(2), have jurisdiction to hear and determine—

(a) any application, or any appeal (whether by way of case stated or otherwise), which it has power to hear and determine under or by virtue of this or any other Act; and

(b) all such other appeals as it had jurisdiction to hear and determine immediately before the commencement of this Act.

(4) In subsection (2)(a) the reference to a decision of the Crown Court relating to trial on indictment does not include a decision relating to an order under section 17 of the Access to Justice Act 1999.

In common with applications by way of case stated from the magistrates' court, an application to appeal by way of case stated from the Crown Court may be made in respect of an error of law or where it is alleged that the Crown Court acted in excess of jurisdiction. There can be no challenge on the basis that a decision is against the weight of the evidence. Similarly, as with appeals by way of case stated from the magistrates' court, the proceedings in the Crown Court must have been finally decided before the case stated procedure may be employed (*Loade v DPP* [1990] 1 QB 1052). By virtue of s. 28 of the Supreme Court Act 1981, no appeal by way of case stated is possible in respect of matters relating to trial on indictment (see D28.31 for further explanation). The means of challenge is plainly available in respect of any decision of the Crown Court relating to an appeal against conviction or sentence from the magistrates' court.

The procedure to be followed in respect of an appeal by way of case stated from the Crown Court is set out in the CrimPR, r. 64.7. An application to the Crown Court to state a case should be made to the appropriate officer of the court within 21 days of the decision challenged being made (CrimPR, r. 64.7(1)). Rule 64.7(14) allows any time-limit (including the initial 21-day period) under r. 64.7 to be extended by the Crown Court. That stands in contrast to the position in relation to appeals by way of case stated from the magistrates' court. Extensions of time may be granted by a judge sitting without lay justices but should only be granted for cogent reasons (*DPP v Coleman* [1998] 1 WLR 1708). Where the prosecution seek to extend the time in which to apply for a case to be stated following the acquittal of a defendant:

(a) the defendant should be notified of the application;

(b) the terms on which the extension was being sought should be disclosed to him, and he should be told of his right to make representations;

(c) the court should then consider the representations of both parties, and the defendant should be given the opportunity to deal with all the representations made by the prosecution;

(d) normally the court would consider the application on paper without the necessity for an oral hearing.

The judge had not considered representations from the defendant in *Coleman* and thus the procedure was flawed and the defendant's acquittal stood.

In contrast to the position in the magistrates' court, the party seeking to state a case from the Crown Court draws an initial draft case which is put before the judge who presided at the relevant proceedings (r. 64.7(8)). The respondent may also submit a draft case to the judge (r. 64.7(9)(c)). Having read the draft(s), the judge states and signs a case (r. 64.7(12)). The case is then sent to the appellant and he must lodge it in the Crown Office. By virtue of ord. 56, r. 1 of the Rules of the Supreme Court, he must also lodge copies of the judgments or orders made both in the Crown Court and the magistrates' court. The appeal is normally heard within six months of the Crown Court decision. The Divisional Court's powers of disposal in relation to the appeal are identical to those it possesses on an appeal from the magistrates.

Under s. 81(1)(d) of the Supreme Court Act 1981, bail pending appeal by way of case stated from the Crown Court may be granted by a judge in chambers.

Application for Judicial Review

D28.31 By virtue of s. 29(3) of the Supreme Court Act 1981, it is possible to challenge a decision of the Crown Court by way of judicial review provided that that decision does not concern a matter relating to trial on indictment. In *Re Smalley* [1985] AC 622, the House of Lords held that the phrase 'relating to trial on indictment' covered all decisions relating to the conduct of the trial. It has thus been held that the decision to stay any part of an indictment as an abuse of process is a matter relating to trial on indictment (*Ashton* [1994] AC 9), as is an order that counts should lie on the file in the usual way (*Central Criminal Court, ex parte Raymond* [1986] 1 WLR 710), a decision as to the order in which indictments are tried (*Southwark Crown Court, ex parte Ward* [1996] Crim LR 123) and decisions as to disclosure (*Chester Crown Court, ex parte Cheshire County Council* [1996] Crim LR 336). It has also been held that the decision to hold a trial on the issue of fitness to plead is a matter relating to trial on indictment (*Bradford Crown Court, ex parte Bottomley* [1994] Crim LR 753) as is the imposition of a mandatory life sentence (*R (Lichniak) v Secretary of State for the Home Department* [2002] QB 296).

Matters which do not relate to trial on indictment include forfeiture of a surety (*Re Smalley*), forfeiture of property used in the course of an offence belonging to a third party (*Maidstone Crown Court, ex parte Gill* [1986] 1 WLR 1405), binding over of an acquitted accused (*Inner London Crown Court, ex parte Benjamin* (1986) 85 Cr App R 265) and restrictions on the publication of the identity of a convicted youth (*Leicester Crown Court, ex parte S (A Minor)* [1993] 1 WLR 111).

Under s. 81(1)(e) of the 1981 Act, bail may be granted pending judicial review of a decision of the Crown Court.

If a defendant convicted in the magistrates' court appeals to the Crown Court, any further appeal to the High Court on a point of law should be by way of case stated and not judicial review (*Gloucester Crown Court, ex parte Chester* [1998] COD 365).

NO POWER OF JUDICIAL REVIEW OVER DECISIONS OF THE HIGH COURT

D28.32 There is no power available to the High Court to judicially review the decisions of the High Court. In that vein, the decision of a judge of the High Court to issue a voluntary bill of indictment is not amenable to judicial review (*Manchester Crown Court, ex parte Williams* (1990) 154 JP 589).

THE CHOICE BETWEEN JUDICIAL REVIEW AND CASE STATED

Both judicial review and the case stated procedure set aside the decision of the court below, and a choice must be made as to which route to pursue. In *R (P) v Liverpool City Magistrates* (2006) 170 JP 453, Collins J stated: **D28.33**

(a) the normal route for an appeal against a decision of justices where it is alleged there has been an error of law is by way of case stated;
(b) it would be wrong to seek judicial review where case stated was appropriate, merely in order to avoid the more stringent time-limit;
(c) however, judicial review is more appropriate where there is an issue of fact to be raised and decided which the justices did not decide themselves;
(d) judicial review may also be appropriate where it is alleged that there has been unfairness or bias in the conduct of the case by the justices but, where it is alleged that there has been a misdirection or an error of law, case stated is the appropriate remedy.

In *North Essex Justices, ex parte Lloyd* [2001] 2 Cr App R (S) 86, the Divisional Court said that judicial review should be pursued where the inferior court has acted in excess of jurisdiction.

Judicial review is the only remedy available where the defence wish to challenge a committal for trial or sentence, as the case stated procedure is not available where there has not been a final determination of the case.

In *Essen v DPP* [2005] EWHC 1077 (Admin), Sedley LJ said that the authorities restricting appeal by way of case stated to those where there has been a final determination 'could usefully be revisited'. This was borne partly out of a concern that an appellant might be left without a remedy. If the interlocutory decision had been made more than 21 days before the final determination of the case, the case stated procedure would not be available. In addition, on one view, the court lacks jurisdiction to undertake judicial review of interlocutory decisions of justices (a view based on *Rochford Justices, ex parte Buck* (1979) 68 Cr App R 114). But it is submitted that the rule is not without exception. In *R (Watson) v Dartford Magistrates' Court* [2005] EWHC 905 (Admin), it was held that the normal rule is that the High Court should not interfere with interlocutory rulings made by justices; but if the prosecution would say at the end of the trial that it was too late for the defendant to complain, there is no fetter on the High Court intervening.

APPEAL FROM THE DIVISIONAL COURT

Any appeal from the High Court in a criminal cause or matter, either in relation to an appeal by way of case stated or a judicial review, is direct to the House of Lords (see D29.2). **D28.34**

Section D29 Appeal to the House of Lords, the European Court of Justice and the European Convention on Human Rights

APPEAL TO THE HOUSE OF LORDS

From the Court of Appeal (Criminal Division)

D29.1 **Criminal Appeal Act 1968, ss. 33 and 34**

33.—(1) An appeal lies to the House of Lords, at the instance of the defendant or the prosecutor, from any decision of the Court of Appeal on an appeal to that court under part I of this Act or part 9 of the Criminal Justice Act 2003 or section 9 (preparatory hearings) of the Criminal Justice Act 1987 or section 35 of the Criminal Procedure and Investigations Act 1996 or section 47 of the Criminal Justice Act 2003.

(1A) In subsection (1) above the reference to the prosecutor includes a reference to the director of the Assets Recovery Agency in a case where (and to the extent that) he is a party to the appeal to the Court of Appeal.

(1B) An appeal lies to the House of Lords, at the instance of the acquitted person or the prosecutor, from any decision of the Court of Appeal on an application under section 76(1) or (2) of the Criminal Justice Act 2003 (retrial for serious offences).

(2) The appeal lies only with the leave of the Court of Appeal or the House of Lords; and leave shall not be granted unless it is certified by the Court of Appeal that a point of law of general public importance is involved in the decision and it appears to the Court of Appeal or the House of Lords (as the case may be) that the point is one which ought to be considered by that House.

(3) Except as provided by this part of this Act and section 13 of the Administration of Justice Act 1960 (appeal in cases of contempt of court), no appeal shall lie from any decision of the criminal division of the Court of Appeal.

(4) In relation to an appeal under subsection (1B), references in this Part to a defendant are references to the acquitted person.

34.—(1) An application to the Court of Appeal for leave to appeal to the House of Lords shall be made within the period of 28 days beginning with the relevant date; and an application to the House of Lords for leave shall be made within the period of 28 days beginning with the date on which the application for leave is refused by the Court of Appeal.

(1A) In subsection (1), 'the relevant date' means—

(a) the date of the Court of Appeal's decision, or

(b) if later, the date on which the Court gives reasons for its decision.

(2) The House of Lords or the Court of Appeal may, upon application made at any time by the defendant or, in the case of an appeal under section 33(1B), by the prosecutor, extend the time within which an application may be made by him to that House or the court under subsection (1) above.

(3) An appeal to the House of Lords shall be treated as pending until any application for leave to appeal is disposed of and, if leave to appeal is granted, until the appeal is disposed of; and for purposes of this part of this Act an application for leave to appeal shall be treated as disposed of at the expiration of the time within which it may be made, if it is not made within that time.

Either the prosecution or defence may appeal a decision of the Court of Appeal to the House of Lords, but only if the Court of Appeal or the House of Lords itself considers that the appeal involves a point of law of general public importance which should be considered by the House of Lords. In addition, the Court of Appeal must certify that the appeal involves a question concerning a point of law of general public importance. An application to the Court of Appeal for leave to appeal to the House of Lords must be made by the party seeking to appeal within 28 days of the judgment to be appealed (or the reasons for the decision, if given later). Where the Court of Appeal is of the view that the prospective appeal raises no point of law of public importance, it may decide so on the papers (*Daines* [1961] 1 WLR 52). A refusal to allow oral submissions will not amount to a violation of a person's rights under the ECHR, Article 6 (*Steele* [2007] 1 WLR 222).

A refusal by the Court of Appeal to certify a question cannot be appealed. If the Court of Appeal certifies a question but leave to appeal to the House of Lords is refused, then the party may apply for leave to the House of Lords within 28 days of the refusal by the Court of Appeal.

The procedure to be followed in the preparation of appeals for the House of Lords can be found in *House of Lords: Practice Directions and Standing Orders Applicable to Criminal Appeals* (December 2006). The document, known as the 'Red Book' is available on request from the Judicial Office of the House of Lords (020 7219 3111/3) or from the House of Lords website at www.parliament.uk/judicial_work/judicial_work2.cfm.

If the Court of Appeal decides an appeal on one ground but leaves others undecided and the House of Lords hears the appeal of that decision, the House of Lords may either rule on those grounds as if it were the Court of Appeal or may remit them back to the Court of Appeal for its decision. In *Mandair* [1995] 1 AC 208, the House of Lords stated that the undecided grounds of appeal should be identified and written submissions should be made as to whether and how the House of Lords should dispose of them.

Part 3 of the Constitutional Reform Act 2005 provides for the establishment of the Supreme Court of the United Kingdom. The Supreme Court will consist of 12 judges and the jurisdiction of the House of Lords will be transferred to it on a day to be appointed.

From a Divisional Court of the Queen's Bench Division

Section 1(1)(a) of the Administration of Justice Act 1980 provides that any appeal from a Divisional Court of the Queen's Bench Division in a criminal cause or matter is direct to the House of Lords, leapfrogging the Court of Appeal. In a similar leave process to that operating in the Court of Appeal (see **D29.1**), the Divisional Court must certify that the appeal involves a point of law of general public importance and leave to appeal must be granted by either the Divisional Court or the House of Lords. **D29.2**

THE EUROPEAN COURT OF JUSTICE

Treaty of Rome, Article 234 (formerly Article 177) **D29.3**

The Court of Justice shall have jurisdiction to give preliminary ruling concerning:

(a) the interpretation of this Treaty;
(b) the validity and interpretation of acts of the institutions of the Community and of the ECB;
(c) the interpretation of the statutes of bodies established by an act of the Council, where those statutes so provide.

Where such a question is raised before any court or tribunal of a member State, that court or tribunal may, if it considers that a decision on the question is necessary to enable it to give judgment, request the Court of Justice to give a ruling thereon.

Where any such question is raised in a case pending before a court or tribunal of a member State, against whose decisions there is no judicial remedy under national law, that court or tribunal shall bring the matter before the Court of Justice.

Provision for references of points of interpretation to the European Court of Justice is made in Article 234 of the Treaty of Rome.

If a reference is made, the domestic proceedings are suspended pending the ruling of the European Court of Justice. When the ruling is given, the domestic court applies it and continues to the conclusion of the proceedings.

Article 234 dictates that any court against whose decisions there is no remedy shall bring the matter before the Court of Justice. For practical purposes, in English criminal law, that means that the House of Lords must refer a relevant point. Any other court or tribunal has discretion as to whether such a reference should be made, but what authority exists discourages magistrates' courts and the Crown Court from referring a point.

Thus in *Plymouth Justices, ex parte Rogers* [1982] QB 863, it was held that a magistrates' court has the power to make such a reference and the Divisional Court will not interfere with the exercise of the justices' discretion to make such a reference unless they act unreasonably in doing so, or misdirect themselves. Nevertheless the Divisional Court advised that justices should exercise considerable caution before making such a reference. If a magistrates' court erred in the interpretation of community law, that could always be corrected by the higher courts. When making a reference, the form of the question to be answered is very important and the higher courts will normally be in a better position to assess the appropriateness of the question and assist in formulating it appropriately.

So far as the Crown Court is concerned, the House of Lords stated in *Henn* [1981] AC 850 (per Lord Diplock at p. 904):

> . . . in a criminal trial upon indictment it can seldom be a proper exercise of the presiding judge's discretion to seek a preliminary ruling before the facts of the alleged offence have been ascertained, with the result that the proceedings will be held up for nine months or more in order that at the end of the trial he may give to the jury an accurate instruction as to the relevant law, if the evidence turns out in the event to be as was anticipated at the time the reference was made — which may not always be the case. It is generally better, as the judge himself put it, that the question be decided by him in the first instance and reviewed thereafter if necessary through the hierarchy of the national courts.

The procedure to be adopted in an application for a reference by the Crown Court is set out in the CrimPR, part 75 (see **appendix 1**).

THE EUROPEAN CONVENTION ON HUMAN RIGHTS

D29.4 An individual has the power to petition the European Court of Human Rights if he feels that his human rights under the ECHR have been violated (see A7).

In order that a complaint be admissible before the European Court, the applicant must have exhausted all domestic remedies. The applicant is not required, however, to have pursued points which have no chance of success. Thus in *V v UK* (2000) 30 EHRR 121, the court was concerned with the case of two boys convicted of the murder of James Bulger. The court ruled that Article 6 requires a specially adapted procedure for the trial of juveniles in the Crown Court which promotes the welfare of the young defendant, respects his right to privacy and enables him to understand and take part fully in the proceedings. The court rejected an argument by the UK government that the complaint was inadmissible because the boys had not exhausted all domestic remedies as they had failed to argue in the domestic courts that their inability to understand and participate fully in the proceedings meant that they were in effect unfit to plead. The court observed that the government could not point to one example where such an application had been successful.

In addition, the petition must raise an issue which is not substantially the same as one upon which the commission or court has already ruled and, equally, the petition cannot have been submitted to another 'procedure of international investigation or settlement'.

Under Article 35, the petition must be brought within six months of the date when the final decision is taken. That date was defined in *Greenock Ltd v UK* (1985) 42 DJR 33, as the date of a final decision taken in the exhaustion of an effective and sufficient domestic remedy, or from the date of the act or decision complained of where that act or decision finally determines the applicant's position in the domestic jurisdiction. Time usually ceases to run when the petitioner sends the first letter to the court giving an indication of the issue and indicating an intention to lodge an application (*Kelly v UK* (1985) 42 DR 205) but the court may look at all the circumstances to determine the relevant date. If the violation of the applicant's rights is a continuing one, time will not start to run until the violation ceases (*Temple v UK* (1985) 8 EHRR 319).

The court sits in committees of three judges, chambers of seven judges and, exceptionally, in Grand Chambers of 17 judges. The parties are required to file written evidence within certain time-limits and, if the court considers it necessary, an oral hearing at which the applicant is represented takes place. The decision of the court may be by way of majority. The court can compel any state which is in breach of the ECHR to make 'just satisfaction', and if it finds that the state's laws are incompatible with the Convention, can impose a duty on the state to rectify the position.

Section D30 Public Funding and Costs

D30.1 This section deals with the financing of criminal proceedings through orders for public funding and costs.

PUBLIC FUNDING IN CRIMINAL PROCEEDINGS

D30.2 The primary sources of the law on public funding in criminal matters are the AJA 1999 and Criminal Defence Service Act 2006. The Acts are supplemented by various statutory instruments, reproduced throughout this chapter as appropriate. Grant of legal aid in most criminal cases is authorised by Her Majesty's Courts Service, operating under a service level agreement on behalf of the Legal Services Commission.

Grant of Right to Representation

D30.3 The Legal Services Commission funds individuals who are granted the right to representation in accordance with sch. 3 to the AJA 1999 (AJA 1999, s. 14(1)). Paragraph 1 of sch. 3 lays down that a right to representation may be granted to an individual in relation to any kind of criminal proceedings mentioned in s. 12(2), and to enable him to resist an appeal to the Crown Court otherwise than in an official capacity. The Criminal Defence Service Act 2006 removed the general right of a court to grant legal aid in criminal proceedings and passed the power to court officials, save where regulations provide otherwise (AJA 1999, sch. 3, para. 2(1A)). Where the right is granted, it includes representation for any related bail or other preliminary or incidental proceedings (para. 2(2)). Under the AJA 1999, s. 12(2), the term 'criminal proceedings' is defined as including, for example:

(i) proceedings before any court for dealing with an individual accused of an offence;
(ii) proceedings before any court for dealing with an individual convicted of an offence (including proceedings in respect of a sentence or order);
(iii) extradition proceedings;
(iv) proceedings for binding an individual over to keep the peace or to be of good behaviour under the MCA 1980, s. 115, and for dealing with an individual who fails to comply with an order under that section;
(v) proceedings for contempt committed, or alleged to have been committed, by an individual in the face of a court.

Section 12(2)(g) enables other proceedings to be brought within the ambit of representation orders by deeming those proceedings to be criminal proceedings.

Under the Criminal Defence Service (General) (No. 2) Regulations 2001 (SI 2001 No. 1437), reg. 3, such proceedings include, for example:

(a) civil proceedings in a magistrates' court arising from failure to pay a sum due or to obey an order of that court where such failure carries the risk of imprisonment;
(b) proceedings under the CDA 1998, ss. 1, 1D and 4, relating to anti-social behaviour orders;
(c) proceedings under the CDA 1998, s. 8(1)(b), relating to parenting orders made where an anti-social behaviour order or a sex offender order is made in respect of a child;

(d) proceedings under the CDA 1998, s. 8(1)(c), relating to parenting orders made on the conviction of a child;
(e) proceedings under ss. 14B, 14D, 14G, 14H, 21B and 21D of the Football Spectators Act 1989;
(f) proceedings under s. 137 of the Financial Services and Markets Act 2000 to appeal against a decision of the Financial Services and Markets Tribunal;
(g) proceedings under ss. 20, 22, 26 and 28 of the ASBA 2003 relating to parenting orders in cases of exclusion from school and parenting orders in respect of criminal conduct and anti-social behaviour;
(h) proceedings relating to orders under part 2 of the SOA 2003.

The decision whether or not to grant a representation order is to be determined by a two-stage test, incorporating an assessment on means (for magistrates' court proceedings) and 'according to the interests of justice' (AJA 1999, sch. 3, para. 5(1)). Representation orders for Crown Court proceedings are not subject to any means test.

Financial eligibility for a grant of representation is determined under the Criminal Defence Service (Financial Eligibility) Regulations 2006 (SI 2006 No. 2492). Applicants who fall into one or more of the following categories will automatically pass the means test assessment:

(i) under the age of 18 and in full-time education;
(ii) aged 16 or 17 with no income and living with a parent or guardian;
(iii) under the age of 16;
(iv) directly or indirectly in receipt of income support, income based jobseeker's allowance or guarantee state pension credit.

The specific factors which must be taken into account when determining whether a grant of representation is in the interests of justice are:

(a) whether, in the event of conviction, the accused is likely to lose his liberty or livelihood, or suffer serious damage to his reputation;
(b) whether the proceedings may involve consideration of a substantial (i.e. complex) question of law;
(c) whether the accused may be unable to understand the proceedings or to state his own case;
(d) whether the proceedings may involve the tracing and interviewing of witnesses, or expert cross-examination of witnesses;
(e) whether it is in the interests of someone other than the accused that he should be represented.

In assessing whether the accused is likely to lose his liberty, regard must be had to the facts alleged by the prosecution, rather than the maximum penalty that could theoretically be imposed (*Highgate Justices, ex parte Lewis* [1977] Crim LR 611). So it is not enough that the offence carries a custodial sentence: the court must consider whether a custodial sentence might be imposed in the particular case. In *Liverpool City Magistrates, ex parte McGhee* [1993] Crim LR 609, the Divisional Court rejected the contention that what is now called an unpaid work requirement could be regarded as a sentence which deprives the accused of liberty. However, Rose LJ did add that the list of criteria in what is now sch. 3, para. 5 is not exhaustive, and so the possibility of a community punishment order may be a factor in deciding whether or not to make a representation order.

In *R (Punatar) v Horseferry Road Magistrates' Court* [2002] EWHC 1196 (Admin), an application for representation submitted at the end of court proceedings was refused because the prosecution substituted a charge for a non-imprisonable offence in place of an imprisonable one. The Divisional Court held that representation should have been granted due to the fact that when the solicitor decided to attend court the offence that was charged at that time merited representation. It was wrong to apply hindsight.

The factor which includes expert cross-examination of witnesses (para. (d) above) means expert cross-examination of witnesses, not cross-examination of expert witnesses (*Liverpool City Magistrates, ex parte McGhee*).

In *Scunthorpe Justices, ex parte* S (1998) *The Times*, 5 March 1998, the Divisional Court considered that refusal of legal aid to an accused aged 16 who sought to challenge whether a police officer had acted in the execution of his duty was irrational. The expertise needed to cross-examine police witnesses, and to find, select and proof defence witnesses was beyond an accused aged 16.

In *R (Matara) v Brent Magistrates' Court* (2005) 169 JP 576, the accused was charged with failure to provide a specimen of breath. He made an application for legal aid. It was argued that he would be unable to understand the court proceedings because his understanding of English was inadequate; the court's response was that an interpreter would be provided. On appeal, it was held that at least one of the 'interests of justice' criteria in the AJA 1999, sch. 3, para. 5 was met, making the refusal of legal aid unreasonable to a degree which entitled the Divisional Court to intervene. The availability of an interpreter did not meet the point that it was the claimant's case that he was unable to understand what was being said at the time of his arrest, a point which lay at the heart of his defence. It went to his ability to state his own case and the overall fairness of the trial. The decision to refuse legal aid was therefore quashed and the case remitted to a differently constituted bench for reconsideration.

In *Oates* [2002] 1 WLR 2833, the applicant sought permission to appeal to the Court of Appeal against her conviction; the application was refused by the single judge and she wished to renew the application orally. She sought legal aid for representations to be made on her behalf. It was held that legal assistance by way of a representation order will not, save in exceptional circumstances, be granted on a renewed application for permission to appeal against conviction following refusal by the single judge. It was held that this is not contrary to the right of an accused to defend himself through legal assistance of his own choosing under the ECHR, Article 6(3)(c).

Applying for a Representation Order

D30.4 Under the Criminal Defence Service (General) (No. 2) Regulations 2001, reg. 4:

> The Commission shall fund such advice and assistance, including advocacy assistance, as it considers appropriate in relation to any individual who:
> (a) is the subject of an investigation which may lead to criminal proceedings;
> (b) is the subject of criminal proceedings;
> (c) requires advice and assistance regarding his appeal or potential appeal against the outcome of any criminal proceedings or an application to vary a sentence;
> (d) requires advice and assistance regarding his sentence;
> (e) requires advice and assistance regarding his application or potential application to the Criminal Cases Review Commission;
> (f) requires advice and assistance regarding his treatment or discipline in prison (other than in respect of actual or contemplated proceedings regarding personal injury, death or damage to property);
> (g) is the subject of proceedings before the Parole Board;
> (h) requires advice and assistance regarding representations to the Home Office in relation to a mandatory life sentence or other parole review;
> (i) is a witness in criminal proceedings and requires advice regarding self-incrimination; or
> (j) is a volunteer [a person attending a police station voluntarily, 'helping the police with their enquiries'] or
> (k) is detained under schedule 7 to the Terrorism Act 2000.

Regulation 4A deals with advice given prior to the grant of a representation order. It provides that:

Advice given prior to the grant of a representation order in the Crown Court shall be deemed to have been given under that order where:
(a) the interests of justice required that the advice was provided as a matter of urgency;
(b) there was no undue delay in making the application for a representation order; and
(c) the advice was given by the representative who was subsequently assigned under the representation order.

Regulation 5 sets out the representation that may be granted irrespective of the means of the accused:

(1) The following advice and assistance may be granted without reference to the financial resources of the individual:
(a) all advice and assistance provided to an individual who is arrested and held in custody at a police station or other premises;
(b) all advocacy assistance before a magistrates' court or the Crown Court;
(c) all advice and assistance provided by a court duty solicitor in accordance with his contract with the Commission;
(d) all advice and assistance provided to a volunteer during his period of voluntary attendance;
(e) all advice and assistance provided to an individual being interviewed in connection with a serious service offence; and
(f) all advice and assistance provided in respect of an individual who is the subject of an identification procedure carried out by means of video recordings in connection with that procedure, notwithstanding the individual's non-attendance at a police station at the time the procedure is carried out.
(2) For the purposes of paragraph (1), a serious service offence is an offence under the Army Act 1955, the Air Force Act 1955 or the Naval Discipline Act 1957 which cannot be dealt with summarily.
(3) Advocacy assistance may be granted to an individual regarding his treatment or discipline in prison (other than in respect of actual or contemplated proceedings regarding personal injury, death or damage to property), or where he is the subject of proceedings before the Parole Board, if his weekly disposable income does not exceed [a figure specified in regulations, varied annually, currently £201] and his disposable capital does not exceed £3,000 [for applicants with dependants this figure is adjusted upwards].
(4) Except where paragraph (1) applies, the Commission, or a person acting on behalf of the Commission where such function has been delegated in accordance with section 3(4) of the Act, shall determine the financial eligibility of the individual . . .
(5) Except where paragraph (1) . . . applies, an individual is eligible for advice and assistance if his weekly disposable income does not exceed [a figure specified in regulations, varied annually, currently £95] and his disposable capital does not exceed £1,000 [for applicants with dependants this figure is adjusted upwards].
(6) The Commission shall assess the disposable income and disposable capital of the individual and, where appropriate, of any person whose financial resources may be treated as those of the individual, in accordance with schedule 1 to these Regulations.
(7) Where the Commission is satisfied that any person whose disposable income is to be assessed under paragraph (6) is directly or indirectly in receipt of any qualifying benefit, it shall take that person's disposable income as not exceeding the [eligibility limit].
(8) The following are qualifying benefits for the purposes of paragraph (7):
(a) income support;
(b) income-based jobseeker's allowance;
(c) working tax credit claimed together with child tax credit where the gross annual income is not more than [a figure specified in regulations, varied annually, currently £14,213]
(d) working tax credit with a disability element or severe disability element (or both) where the gross annual income is not more than [a figure specified in regulations, varied annually, currently £14,213]; and
(e) guarantee credit under section 1(3)(a) of the State Pension Credit Act 2002.
(9) Where the Commission is satisfied that any person whose disposable capital is to be assessed under paragraph (3) is directly or indirectly in receipt of income support, income-based

jobseeker's allowance or guarantee state pension credit, it shall take that person's disposable capital as not exceeding the [eligibility limit].

Regulation 6 requires the application for a representation order to be made on a standard form and stipulates that public funding is effective from the date of the receipt of a properly completed application form:

(1) The date of any representation order is the date on which the application for the grant of such an order is received in accordance with these regulations.
(2) Any application for the grant of a representation order in respect of proceedings in the Crown Court or the Court of Appeal which are mentioned in section 12(2)(a) to (f) of the Act and in regulation 3(2)(h) shall be made in accordance with regulations 9 and 10.

The power to make a representation order, for criminal proceedings other than in a magistrates' court, is contained in reg. 7:

The court, a judge of the court, the head of the Civil Appeals Office, or the registrar of criminal appeals may grant a representation order at any stage of criminal proceedings (other than criminal proceedings in a magistrates' court) in the circumstances set out in these regulations whether or not an application has been made for such an order.

Regulations 9 and 10 go on to set out the procedure governing an application for a representation order. In respect of proceedings in the magistrates' court, application must be made in writing to the justices' clerk. For proceedings in the Crown Court, the application may be made orally or in writing to the Crown Court or in writing to the court manager. Applications in respect of Crown Court proceedings may also be made to the appropriate officer at the magistrates' court, in the manner specified in reg. 9(1)(c) to (g). Where a retrial is ordered as a result of an appeal, application is to the court ordering the retrial.

In all the above cases, where an application is refused, the applicant must be provided with written reasons for the refusal and details of the appeal process.

In *K* (2005) *The Times*, 15 February 2005, the Court of Appeal emphasised that when a court grants a representation order for an appeal, the representation order only covers work on, and attendance or appearance at, the hearing in respect of the grounds upon which the court has granted leave to appeal. It does not cover any work, preparation or time in court that is done or spent in respect of any renewed application in respect of a ground on which leave to appeal has been refused. If, on a renewed application made at the same time as an appeal, leave is granted, the practice of the court is exactly the same as applies when a renewed application is made separately.

Criminal Defence Service (General) (No. 2) Regulations 2001 (SI 2001 No. 1437), regs. 9 and 10

9.—(1) Other than where regulation 6(3) applies, an application for a representation order in respect of proceedings in the Crown Court may be made, where an application for such an order in respect of the proceedings in a magistrates' court has not been made or has been refused:
(a) orally or in writing to the Crown Court;
(b) in writing to the appropriate officer of that court;
(c) in writing to a magistrates' court at the conclusion of any proceedings in that magistrates' court;
(d) in writing to a magistrates' court inquiring into the offence as examining justices or sending for trial under section 51 of the Crime and Disorder Act 1998;
(e) where a magistrates' court has been given a notice of transfer under section 4 of the Criminal Justice Act 1987 (serious fraud cases), in writing to the appropriate officer of that magistrates' court;
(f) in the case of an appeal to the Crown Court from a magistrates' court, in writing to the appropriate officer of that magistrates' court;
(g) where the applicant was committed for trial in the Crown Court under section 6(2) of the Magistrates' Courts Act 1980, in writing to the appropriate officer of the magistrates' court ordering the committal; and

(h) in the case of a retrial ordered under section 7 of the Criminal Appeal Act 1968, orally or in writing to the court ordering the retrial.

(2) An application for a representation order in respect of representations to the High Court against a voluntary bill of indictment may be made:

(a) in writing to the appropriate officer of the Crown Court; or

(b) orally to the judge considering the voluntary bill

and where any such order is granted it shall also apply to any proceedings to which the applicant is indicted.

(3) Where an application is made to the court, it may refer it to the appropriate officer for determination.

(4) Where an application is refused, the appropriate officer shall provide to the applicant:

(a) written reasons for the refusal; and

(b) details of the appeal process.

10.—(1) An application for a representation order in respect of proceedings in the Court of Appeal or the House of Lords may be made:

(a) orally to the Court of Appeal, or a judge of the court; or

(b) in writing to the Court of Appeal, a judge of the court, or the appropriate officer of the court.

(2) Where an application is made to the court, it may refer it to a judge or the appropriate officer for determination.

(3) Where an application is made to a judge, he may refer it to the appropriate officer for determination.

(4) The appropriate officer may:

(a) grant the application; or

(b) refer it to the court or a judge of the court.

(5) A representation order shall not be granted until notice of leave to appeal has been given in respect of the proceedings which are the subject of the application.

(6) Where a representation order is granted in respect of proceedings in the Court of Appeal, a judge or the appropriate officer may specify the stage of the proceedings at which the representation order shall take effect.

(7) The House of Lords may not grant a representation order in respect of any proceedings.

Nature of Representation

The AJA 1999, s. 15(1), provides: **D30.5**

> An individual who has been granted a right to representation in accordance with schedule 3 may select any representative or representatives willing to act for him; and, where he does so, the Commission is to comply with the duty imposed by section 14(1) by funding representation by the selected representative or representatives.

The form taken by the representation is dealt with in the Criminal Defence Service (General) (No. 2) Regulations 2001, regs. 11 to 17 and 19 to 24. These regulations deal with the circumstances in which orders for representation by an advocate or advocates (including Queen's Counsel) may be granted. They also lay down the procedure for a change of representative, for withdrawal of representation, and for the authorisation and restriction of expenditure incurred.

In *A-G's Ref (No. 82a of 2000)* [2002] 2 Cr App R 342, the Court of Appeal held that the principle of equality of arms does not require that, where the Crown instructs leading counsel and the defence is being funded at public expense, the accused is entitled to be represented by leading counsel as well.

Regulation 11 deals with representation in magistrates' courts and some Crown Court proceedings; reg. 12 with advocates in magistrates' courts; reg. 13 makes similar provision for the Crown Court, Court of Appeal and House of Lords. Regulation 14 provides for the appointment of Queen's Counsel or more than one advocate; reg. 15 enables representation to be by way of an advocate alone in certain cases and reg. 16 enables one representative to be replaced by another. Regulation 16A requires that co-accused should have the same representative unless there is a conflict of interest. Regulation 17 deals with withdrawal of representation. Regulation 19 covers the authorisation of certain types of expenditure and regs. 20 to 24 deal with miscellaneous matters.

Under the Criminal Defence Service (Representation Orders and Consequential Amendments) Regulations 2006 (SI 2006 No. 2493), reg. 4, a representation order extends to the Crown Court, if the proceedings continue there and to any proceedings incidental to the proceedings (but does not extend to an appeal).

Criminal Defence Service (General) (No. 2) Regulations 2001, regs. 11 to 17 and 19 to 24

11.—(1) The right conferred by section 15(1) of the Act, as regards representation in respect of any proceedings to which this regulation applies, shall be exercisable only in relation to those representatives who are:

(a) employed by the Commission to provide such representation; or
(b) authorised to provide such representation under a crime franchise contract with the Commission which commences on or after 2nd April 2001 and specifies the rate of remuneration for such representation.

(2) This regulation applies to:

(a) any criminal proceedings in a magistrates' court;
(b) any proceedings in the Crown Court mentioned in regulation 3(2);
(c) any appeal by way of case stated from a magistrates' court; and
(d) any proceedings which are preliminary or incidental to proceedings mentioned in sub-paragraphs (a) to (c).

(3) This regulation does not apply to proceedings referred to in section 12(2)(f) of the Act (proceedings for contempt in the face of a court).

12.—(1) A representation order for the purposes of proceedings before a magistrates' court may only include representation by an advocate in the case of:

(a) any indictable offence, including an offence which is triable either way; or
(b) proceedings under section 9 of, or paragraph 6 of schedule 1 to, the Extradition Act 1989,

where the court is of the opinion that, because of circumstances which make the proceedings unusually grave or difficult, representation by both a solicitor and an advocate would be desirable.

(2) A representation order for the purposes of proceedings before a magistrates' court may not include representation by an advocate other than as provided in paragraph (1).

13.—(1) Subject to paragraph (2) and regulation 11, the right conferred by section 15(1) of the Act, as regards representation in respect of any proceedings in the Crown Court (other than proceedings mentioned in regulation 3(2)), Court of Appeal or House of Lords, shall be exercisable only in relation to those representatives who are:

(a) employed by the Commission to provide such representation; or
(b) authorised to provide such representation under a crime franchise contract with the Commission or
(c) in respect of an appeal from the Financial Services and Markets Tribunal, the representatives of the assisted person before the Court of Appeal.

(2) Where the Commission has determined that representation in a very high cost serious fraud case shall be provided by members of the Serious Fraud Panel, such right shall be limited to representatives who are for the time being members of that Panel.

(3) For the purposes of this regulation:

(a) a very high cost serious fraud case is a very high cost case with regard to which the offence with which the defendant is charged is primarily or substantially founded on allegations of fraud or other serious financial impropriety, or involves complex financial transactions; and
(b) the Serious Fraud Panel is a panel of solicitors appointed under arrangements made by the Commission to deal with such cases.

(4) This regulation does not apply to any proceedings referred to in section 12(2)(f) of the Act [contempt in the face of the court].

14.—(1) A representation order may provide for the services of a Queen's Counsel or of more than one advocate in respect of the whole or any specified part of any proceedings only in the cases specified and in the manner provided for by the following paragraphs of this regulation; and in this regulation 'junior counsel' means any advocate other than a Queen's Counsel.

(2) Subject to paragraphs (3) to (9), a representation order may provide for the services of a Queen's Counsel or of more than one advocate in any of the following terms:
  (a) a Queen's Counsel alone;
  (b) where two advocates are required:
    (i) a Queen's Counsel with a junior counsel;
    (ii) a Queen's Counsel with a noting junior counsel;
    (iii) two junior counsel; or
    (iv) a junior counsel with a noting junior counsel;
  (c) where three advocates are required:
    (i) in any of the terms provided for in sub-paragraph (b) plus an extra junior counsel; or
    (ii) in any of the terms provided for in sub-paragraph (b) plus an extra noting junior counsel.

(3) A representation order relating to proceedings in the Crown Court may be made in the terms of paragraph (2)(a) if and only if:
  (a) in the opinion of the court the case for the assisted person involves substantial novel or complex issues of law or fact which could not be adequately presented except by a Queen's Counsel; and
  (b) either:
    (i) a Queen's Counsel or senior Treasury counsel has been instructed on behalf of the prosecution; or
    (ii) the case for the assisted person is exceptional compared with the generality of cases involving similar offences.

(4) A representation order relating to proceedings in the Crown Court may be made in the terms of paragraph (2)(b)(iii) or (iv) if and only if:
  (a) in the opinion of the court the case for the assisted person involves substantial novel or complex issues of law or fact which could not be adequately presented by a single advocate; and
  (b) either:
    (i) two or more advocates have been instructed on behalf of the prosecution;
    (ii) the case for the assisted person is exceptional compared with the generality of cases involving similar offences;
    (iii) the number of prosecution witnesses exceeds 80; or
    (iv) the number of pages of prosecution evidence exceeds 1,000

  and for this purpose the number of pages of prosecution evidence shall include all witness statements, documentary and pictorial exhibits and records of interview with the assisted person and with other defendants forming part of the committal documents or included in any notice of additional evidence.

(5) A representation order relating to proceedings in the Crown Court may be made in the terms of paragraph (2)(b)(i) or (ii) if and only if:
  (a) in the opinion of the court the case for the assisted person involves substantial novel or complex issues of law or fact which could not be adequately presented except by a Queen's Counsel assisted by junior counsel; and
  (b) either:
    (i) the case for the assisted person is exceptional compared with the generality of cases involving similar offences; or
    (ii) a Queen's Counsel or senior Treasury counsel has been instructed on behalf of the prosecution and one of the conditions in paragraph (4)(b)(i), (iii) or (iv) is satisfied.

(6) A representation order may be made in the terms of paragraph (2)(c) if and only if:
  (a) the proceedings arise from a prosecution brought by the Serious Fraud Office;
  (b) the court making the order considers that three advocates are required; and
  (c) in the case of proceedings in the Crown Court, the conditions in paragraph (4) or (5) are satisfied.

(7) The fact that a Queen's Counsel has been or is proposed to be assigned under this regulation shall not by itself be a reason for making an order in any of the terms provided for by paragraph (2)(b) or (c).

(8) Where a Queen's Counsel has been or is proposed to be assigned under this regulation, no order in any of the terms provided for by paragraph (2)(b) or (c) shall be made where the case relates to an appeal to the Court of Appeal or to the House of Lords and it appears to the court at the time of making the order that representation can properly be undertaken by a Queen's Counsel alone.

(9) No order shall be made or amended so as to provide for representation:

(a) in the terms of paragraph (2)(b) unless the court making the order is of the opinion that the assisted person could not be adequately represented under an order in the terms of paragraph (2)(a);

(b) in the terms of paragraph (2)(b)(i) unless the court making the order is of the opinion that the assisted person could not be adequately represented under an order in the terms of paragraph (2)(b)(ii),(iii) or (iv);

(c) in the terms of paragraph (2)(b)(ii) unless the court making the order is of the opinion that the assisted person could not be adequately represented under an order in the terms of paragraph (2)(b)(iii) or (iv);

(d) in the terms of paragraph (2)(b)(iii) unless the court making the order is of the opinion that the assisted person could not be adequately represented under an order in the terms of paragraph (2)(b)(iv);

(e) in any of the terms provided for by paragraph (2)(c)(i) unless the court making the order is of the opinion that the assisted person could not be adequately represented under the corresponding order under paragraph (2)(c)(ii).

(10) Every application for a representation order in any of the terms provided for by paragraph (2), or for an amendment under paragraph (15), shall be in writing specifying:

(a) the terms of the order sought and the grounds of the application; and

(b) which of the conditions in paragraphs (3), (4), (5), (6) and (9) is relied upon in support of the order sought, and on what grounds it is contended that each such condition is fulfilled.

(11) A court may, before making a representation order in the terms provided for by paragraph (2) or amending the order under paragraph (15), require written advice from any advocate already assigned to the applicant on the question of what representation is needed in the proceedings.

(12) A court making a decision whether to make an order under paragraph (2) or to amend an order under paragraph (15) shall make annotations to the written application under paragraph (10), stating whether each of the conditions relied upon in support of the order made or sought is fulfilled.

(13) Subject to paragraph (14), a decision to make or amend a representation order so as to provide for the services of a Queen's Counsel or of more than one advocate may only be made:

(a) in the course of a trial or of a preliminary hearing, pre-trial review or pleas and directions hearing, by the judge presiding at that trial or hearing;

(b) where the proceedings are in the Crown Court, by a High Court judge, the resident judge of the Crown Court or (in the absence of the resident judge) a judge nominated for that purpose by the presiding judge of the circuit; or

(c) where the proceedings are in the Court of Appeal, by the registrar, a High Court judge or a judge of the Court of Appeal.

(14) A magistrates' court which may grant a representation order as respects any proceedings in the Crown Court by virtue of these Regulations may make:

(a) a representation order providing for the services of a Queen's Counsel without a junior counsel where the proceedings are a trial for murder and the order is made upon committal, transfer or sending for trial; or

(b) a representation order providing for the services of a Queen's Counsel with one junior counsel where the prosecution is brought by the Serious Fraud Office and the order is made upon receiving a notice of transfer under section 4 of the Criminal Justice Act 1987

but shall have no other power to make an order under this regulation.

(15) In proceedings to which paragraph (3), (4), (5) or (6) applies, a representation order may be amended:

(a) in any terms provided for by paragraph (2) in accordance with the provisions of this regulation; or

(b) to provide for representation by one junior counsel only.

(16) In every case in which a representation order is made under this regulation for the provision of funded services in terms provided for by paragraph (2)(b) or (c), it shall be the duty of:

(a) each representative:

(i) to keep under review the need for more than one advocate to be present in court or otherwise providing services; and

(ii) to consider whether the representation order should be amended as provided for in paragraph (15);

(b) Queen's Counsel, where the services of a Queen's Counsel are provided, to keep under review the question whether he could act alone.

(17) It shall be the duty of each representative, if of the opinion that the representation order should be amended as provided for in paragraph (15), to notify that opinion in writing:

(a) to the other representatives for the assisted person; and

(b) to the court

and the court shall, after considering the opinion and any representations made by any other representatives for the assisted person, determine whether and in what manner the representation order should be amended.

15. The court may grant a representation order for representation by an advocate alone:

(a) in any proceedings referred to in section 12(2)(f) of the Act [contempt in the face of the court];

(b) in respect of an appeal to the Court of Appeal or the Courts-Martial Appeal Court; or

(c) in cases of urgency where it appears to the court that there is no time to instruct a solicitor:

(i) in respect of an appeal to the Crown Court; or

(ii) in proceedings in which a person is committed to or appears before the Crown Court for trial or sentence, or appears or is brought before that court to be dealt with.

16.—(1) Where a representation order has been granted an application may be made to the court before which the proceedings are heard to select a representative in place of a representative previously selected, and any such application shall state the grounds on which it is made.

(2) The court may:

(a) grant the application where:

(i) the representative considers himself to be under a duty to withdraw from the case in accordance with his professional rules of conduct and, in such a case, the representative shall provide details of the nature of such duty;

(ii) there is a breakdown in the relationship between the assisted person and the representative such that effective representation can no longer be provided and, in such a case, the representative shall provide details of the nature of such breakdown;

(iii) through circumstances beyond his control, the representative is no longer able to represent the assisted person; or

(iv) some other substantial compelling reason exists; or

(b) refuse the application.

16A. Where an individual who is granted a right to representation is one of two or more co-defendants whose cases are to be heard together, that individual must select the same representative as a co-defendant unless there is, or is likely to be, a conflict of interest.

17.—(1) Where any charge or proceedings against the assisted person are varied, the court before which the proceedings are heard or, in respect of any proceedings mentioned in regulation 3(2)(a) to (g), the Commission, must—

(a) consider whether the interests of justice continue to require that he be represented in respect of the varied charge or proceedings; and

(b) withdraw the representation order if the interests of justice do not so require.

(1A) The court before which the proceedings are heard or, in respect of any proceedings mentioned in regulation 3(2)(a) to (g), the Commission, must consider whether to withdraw the representation order in any of the following circumstances—

(a) where the assisted person declines to accept the order in the terms which are offered;

(b) otherwise at the request of the assisted person; or

(c) where the representative named in the representation order declines to continue to represent the assisted person.;

(2) Where representation is withdrawn, the appropriate officer or the Commission, as appropriate, shall provide written notification to the assisted person and to the solicitor (or, where there was no solicitor assigned, to the advocate), who shall inform any assigned advocate (or, where notification is given to the advocate, any other assigned advocate).

(3) On any subsequent application by the assisted person for a representation order in respect of the same proceedings,

(a) he must declare the withdrawal of the previous representation order and the reason for it; and

(b) where the representation order was withdrawn in the circumstances set out in paragraph (1) or paragraph (1A)(a) or (b) and a representation order is subsequently granted, the court or the Commission, as appropriate, must select the same representative, unless it considers that there are good reasons why it should select a different representative.

19.—(1) Where it appears to the solicitor necessary for the proper conduct of proceedings in the Crown Court for costs to be incurred under the representation order by taking any of the following steps:

(a) obtaining a written report or opinion of one or more experts;

(b) employing a person to provide a written report or opinion (otherwise than as an expert);

(c) obtaining any transcripts or recordings; or

(d) performing an act which is either unusual in its nature or involves unusually large expenditure

he may apply to the Costs Committee for prior authority to do so.

(2) The Commission may authorise a person acting on behalf of the Costs Committee to grant prior authority in respect of any application made under paragraph (1).

(3) Where the Costs Committee or a person acting on its behalf authorises the taking of any step specified in paragraph (1), it shall also authorise the maximum to be paid in respect of that step.

20. A representative assigned to an assisted person in any proceedings in the Crown Court may apply to the court for prior authority for the incurring of travelling and accommodation expenses in order to attend at the trial or other main hearing in those proceedings.

21.—(1) No question as to the propriety of any step, or as to the amount of the payment within the maximum authorised, with regard to which prior authority has been given under regulation 19 or 20 or under any contract, shall be raised on any determination of costs unless the representative knew or should reasonably have known that the purpose for which it was given had become unnecessary.

(2) Payment may be allowed on a determination of costs in respect of any step with regard to which prior authority may be given, notwithstanding that no such authority was given or that the maximum authorised was exceeded.

22. Where a representation order has been made, the assisted person's solicitor or advocate, whether acting under a representation order or otherwise, shall not receive or be a party to the making of any payment for work done in connection with the proceedings in respect of which the representation order was made except such payments as may be made:

(a) by the Lord Chancellor or the Commission; or

(b) in respect of any expenses or fees incurred in:

(i) preparing, obtaining or considering any report, opinion or further evidence, whether provided by an expert witness or otherwise; or

(ii) obtaining any transcripts or recordings

where an application for an authority to incur such fees or expenses has been refused by the Costs Committee.

23.—(1) This regulation applies to very high cost cases where funded services are provided.

(2) Any solicitor who has conduct of a case which is a very high cost case shall notify the Commission in writing accordingly as soon as is practicable.

(3) Where a solicitor fails to comply with the provisions of this regulation without good reason, and as a result there is a loss to public funds, the court or Costs Committee, as appropriate, may refuse payment of his costs up to the extent of such loss.

(4) No payment under paragraph (3) shall be refused unless the solicitor has been given a reasonable opportunity to show why it should not be refused.

24. Notwithstanding the relationship between or rights of a representative and client or any privilege arising out of such relationship, where the representative for an applicant or assisted person knows or suspects that that person:
(a) has intentionally failed to comply with any provision of regulations made under the Act concerning the information to be furnished by him; or
(b) in furnishing such information has knowingly made a false statement or false representation
the representative shall immediately report the circumstances to the Commission.

Appeals against Refusal of Representation

Where an applicant for the grant of a representation order is refused, he may appeal by way of a renewed application to the body which refused the application. The procedure is set out in the Criminal Defence Service (Representation Orders: Appeals etc.) Regulations 2006 (SI 2006 No. 2494). **D30.6**

Regulation 4 deals with the magistrates' court, reg. 6 the Crown Court, and reg. 7 with the Court of Appeal. Regulation 8 deals with refusals of representation by the Legal Services Commission and reg. 9 provides for appeals against withdrawals of representation orders. No appeal lies against a refusal of representation in the magistrates' court on the grounds that the individual is not financially eligible (reg. 5).

Criminal Defence Service (Representation Orders: Appeals etc.) Regulations 2006, regs. 4 to 9

4.—(1) In this regulation 'court' means the magistrates' court in which the proceedings in respect of which the individual is seeking a representation order are being or are to be heard and includes a single justice.
(2) An individual may appeal to the court against a decision to refuse to grant a representation order made on the grounds that the interests of justice do not require such an order to be granted.
(3) The court must either—
(a) uphold the decision; or
(b) decide that it would be in the interests of justice for a representation order to be granted.
(4) Where the court makes a decision under paragraph (3)(b), the individual may apply to the representation authority for a representation order; and—
(a) if the individual states in writing, verified by a statement of truth, that his financial resources have not changed since the date of his original application so as to make him financially ineligible for a representation order, the representation authority must grant the order; or
(b) if his financial resources may have so changed, the representation authority—
(i) must determine whether the individual is financially eligible to be granted a representation order in accordance with the Criminal Defence Service (Financial Eligibility) Regulations 2006; and
(ii) if he is so eligible, must grant the order.
5. An appeal does not lie against a decision to refuse to grant a representation order in respect of proceedings in a magistrates' court made on the grounds that the individual is not financially eligible to be granted such an order.
6.—(1) An individual whose application for the grant of a representation order in respect of proceedings in the Crown Court has been refused on the grounds that the interests of justice do not require such an order to be granted may make a renewed application to the appropriate officer who, or court which, refused the application.
(2) Where a renewed application is made to the appropriate officer, he may—
(a) grant the order; or
(b) refer the application—
(i) in the Crown Court, to a judge of the Crown Court; or
(ii) in a magistrates' court, to the court or a District Judge (Magistrates' Court),
who may grant the order or refuse the application.
7.—(1) An individual whose application for the grant of a representation order in respect of proceedings in the Court of Appeal has been refused by the court or the appropriate officer on the grounds that the interests of justice do not require such an order to be

granted may make a renewed application to the court or the appropriate officer (as the case may be).

(2) Where a renewed application is made to the appropriate officer, he may—

(a) grant the order; or

(b) refer the application to a judge of the Court of Appeal, who may grant the order or refuse the application.

8. An individual whose application for the grant of a representation order in respect of proceedings, other than proceedings in a magistrates' court, has been refused by the Commission on the grounds that the interests of justice do not require such an order to be granted may make a renewed application to the Commission, which may grant the order or refuse the application.

9.—(1) An individual whose representation order has been withdrawn may apply on one occasion to the person who, or body which, withdrew the order to set aside the withdrawal.

(2) Any application must be made on such form as is from time to time specified—

(a) by the Commission, in the case of withdrawal by the Commission or by the representation authority in proceedings in a magistrates' court; and

(b) by the Lord Chancellor, in the case of withdrawal by the appropriate officer or the court in proceedings in the Crown Court or the Court of Appeal.

(3) Where an application is made to the appropriate officer, he may—

(a) set aside the withdrawal; or

(b) refer the application—

(i) in a magistrates' court, to the court or a District Judge (Magistrates' Court);

(ii) in the Crown Court, to a judge of the Crown Court; or

(iii) in the Court of Appeal, to a judge of the Court of Appeal,

who may set aside the withdrawal or refuse the application.

Funding of Judicial Review and Appeal by Way of Case Stated

D30.7 Work undertaken in relation to judicial review of criminal proceedings is not treated as being incidental to those proceedings. Solicitors working under either a general criminal or civil contract can obtain funding for legal help, investigative help and legal representation from the community legal service.

Appeals by way of case stated are covered within the definition of criminal proceedings (AJA 1999, s. 12(2)(b)). Verbal or written advice following conviction and, if appropriate, an application for representation to the High Court is treated as incidental to the proceedings and should be claimed as part of representation in those proceedings. If there is no representation order in force, advice and assistance can be given in the appeals and review class of work under the terms of the general criminal contract. Following the lodging of a stated case, an application for representation should be made to the High Court.

Funding of Certain Proceeds of Crime Act Proceedings

D30.8 The POCA 2002 contains a range of measures designed to deprive criminals of the proceeds from criminal conduct. Cases involving earlier legislation continue to have effect in appropriate cases. Funding is provided under the Community Legal Service (CLS) or Criminal Defence Service, but firms operating solely under a criminal defence service contract are authorised to carry out associated civil work in relation to POCA proceedings.

Type of proceedings	Funding position	Notes
Criminal Justice Act 1988 and Drug Trafficking Act 1994. Proceedings for confiscation, restraint and receivership arising from criminal proceedings (in the Crown Court or the civil courts).	Considered ancillary to the proceedings from which they arise, so covered by any current representation order.	This covers work for the defendant only. CLS funding may be available for third parties if the application is in the civil courts and the firm has a civil contract. Work for third parties in the criminal courts can only be covered by exceptional funding.
Enforcement proceedings in the magistrates' court for confiscation orders.	Fresh criminal proceedings: apply for representation to the court hearing the matter.	
Applications for certificates of inadequacy (in the High Court).	Fresh criminal proceedings: apply for representation to the court hearing the matter. The court may make a recovery of defence costs order at the end of the proceedings.	
Proceeds of Crime Act 2002. Proceedings under part 2 of the Act for confiscation, restraint and receivership arising from criminal proceedings (in the Crown Court) after the defendant has been charged.	Considered ancillary to the proceedings from which they arise, so covered by any current representation order (extended to Crown Court if necessary). If the original substantive proceedings have ended or there is no representation order in place, then you should apply to the Crown Court for a fresh representation order.	This covers work for the defendant only.
Proceeds of Crime Act 2002. Proceedings under part 2 of the Act for confiscation, restraint and receivership arising from criminal proceedings (in the Crown Court) before the defendant has been charged, or where the client is not the defendant; proceedings under part 5 of the Act ('civil confiscation proceedings') for confiscation, restraint and receivership (in the Crown Court), whether the work is for the defendant or someone else; cash forfeiture proceedings under part 5 of the Act (in the magistrates' court).	Insofar as the work relates to a criminal investigation in which the client is involved, the CDS Advice and Assistance scheme should be used until the defendant is charged. In other circumstances CLS funding may be available.	All civil proceedings under the 2002 Act are classed as Associated CLS Work under the General Criminal Contract.

D

Part D Procedure

Recovery of Costs

D30.9 The AJA 1999, s. 17, provides that:

(1) An individual for whom services are funded by the Commission as part of the Criminal Defence Service shall not be required to make any payment in respect of the services except where subsection (2) applies or regulations under section 17A or otherwise provide.
(2) Where representation for an individual in respect of criminal proceedings in any court other than a magistrates' court is funded by the Commission as part of the Criminal Defence Service, the court may, subject to regulations under subsection (3), make an order requiring him to pay some or all of the cost of any representation so funded for him (in proceedings in that or any other court), except insofar as he has already been ordered under regulations under section 17A to pay that cost.

Section 17A provides for contribution orders in respect to the costs of legal representation, but no regulations have been made under that section. However, a court other than a magistrates' court must make an order that an individual repay some or all of the cost of any such representation. Such an order is known as a Recovery of Defence Costs Order ('RDCO'). The procedure relating to the RDCO is set out in the Criminal Defence Service (Recovery of Defence Costs Orders) Regulations 2001 (SI 2001 No. 856).

Regulation 3 enables a court *other than a magistrates' court*, to make an RDCO (the power to make an RDCO became a duty to make such an order where the defendant is convicted following amendment of the 2001 Regulations by the Criminal Defence Service (Recovery of Defence Costs) Order 2004 (SI 2004 No. 1195)):

(1) Where an individual receives representation in respect of criminal proceedings which is funded by the Commission or the Lord Chancellor as part of the Criminal Defence Service, the court before which the proceedings are heard, other than a magistrates' court, shall make an order requiring him to pay some or all of the cost of any representation so funded for him in the circumstances set out in these Regulations.
(2) An order of the type mentioned in paragraph (1) shall be known as a Recovery of Defence Costs Order (an 'RDCO').

It follows from the exclusion of magistrates' courts from reg. 3 that a person convicted by a magistrates' court cannot be required to contribute to the costs incurred on their behalf by the Criminal Defence Service.

Under reg. 4:

(1) The judge hearing the case shall make an RDCO against a funded defendant except as provided in paragraph (2).
(2) An RDCO shall not be made against a funded defendant who:
  (a) has appeared in the magistrates' court only;
  (b) is committed for sentence to the Crown Court;
  (c) is appealing against sentence to the Crown Court; or
  (d) has been acquitted, other than in exceptional circumstances.

The judge may not make an RDCO against a defendant who has appeared in the magistrates' court but who is committed for sentence to the Crown Court or who appeals against sentence to the Crown Court. Nor may a judge make an RDCO against a defendant who has been acquitted, other than in exceptional circumstances (which phrase is not further defined). It is implicit in reg. 4 that RDCOs will most commonly be made where a publicly-funded defendant is convicted on indictment, or unsuccessfully appeals from the magistrates' court to the Crown Court (reg. 4(2)(c) excludes only appeals against sentence), or unsuccessfully appeals against conviction and/or sentence to the Court of Appeal. Paragraph XI.1.6 of the *Practice Direction (Costs: Criminal Proceedings)* [2004] 2 All ER 1070, says that where a person of modest means properly brings an appeal against conviction, it should be borne in mind that it will not usually be desirable or appropriate for the court to make an RDCO for a significant amount if to do so would inhibit an appellant from bringing an appeal. This would appear to conflict with the mandatory obligation to make an RDCO but the spirit of this paragraph may perhaps be reflected in the amount of the RDCO.

The amount of the RDCO is governed by reg. 5:

(1) An RDCO may be made up to a maximum amount of the full cost of the representation incurred in any court under the representation order.
(2) An RDCO may provide for payment to be made forthwith, or in specified instalments.

Regulation 6 requires that, except in the circumstances mentioned in reg. 4(2)(a), (b) or (c), such information and evidence as is required by the court with regard to the financial resources of a funded defendant must be provided. Regulation 7(1) empowers the appropriate officer to refer the financial resources of a funded defendant to the Commission for a report. In compiling such a report, the Commission may investigate the financial resources of the defendant and may subsequently require him to provide further information or evidence, and details of any change in his financial circumstances (reg. 7(2)).

Regulation 8 contains anti-avoidance provisions:

(1) Without prejudice to regulation 9(1)(a), where it appears to the judge, the appropriate officer or the Commission that:
  (a) the funded defendant has directly or indirectly transferred any resources to another person;
  (b) another person is or has been maintaining him in any proceedings; or
  (c) any of the resources of another person are or have been made available to him

  the judge, the appropriate officer or the Commission (as the case may be) may assess or estimate the value of the resources of that other person and may treat all or any of such resources as those of the funded defendant.
(2) In this regulation, 'person' includes a company, partnership, body of trustees and any body of persons whether corporate or not corporate.

Regulation 9 lays down rules for calculating the financial resources of the defendant:

(1) Except as provided in paragraph (2), for the purpose of calculating the financial resources of the funded defendant:
  (a) the amount or value of every source of income and every resource of a capital nature available to him may be taken into account; and
  (b) the financial resources of the funded defendant's partner shall be treated as the financial resources of the funded defendant.
(2) Other than in exceptional circumstances, the following assets of the funded defendant shall not be taken into account:
  (a) the first £3,000 of capital available to him;
  (b) the first £100,000 of equity in his principal residence; and
  (c) his income, where the court or the Commission are satisfied that his gross annual income does not exceed £25,250.
(3) In this regulation, 'funded defendant's partner' means a person with whom the funded defendant lives as a couple, and includes a person with whom the funded defendant is not currently living but from whom he is not living separate and apart.

Regulation 10 states that 'where he is requested to do so by the judge, the solicitor for the funded defendant shall provide an estimate of the total costs which are likely to be incurred under the representation order'. Regulation 11 requires that, 'at the conclusion of the relevant proceedings, the judge shall: '(a) subject to regulation 4(2), make an RDCO; and (b) where an RDCO may be made under regulation 4(2)(d), consider whether it is reasonable in all the circumstances of the case to make such an order' (see also part XI of the *Practice Direction*). Regulation 12 goes on:

Where the judge considers that it is, or may be, reasonable to make an RDCO, he may:
  (a) make the order; or

(b) if further information is required in order to decide whether to make the order:
  (i) adjourn the making of the order; and
  (ii) order that any further information which is required should be provided.

The sanction for failure to supply information that is sought is set out in reg. 13:

> Where information is required under regulation 6, 7(2) or 12(b)(ii) and such information fails to be provided, an RDCO shall be made for the full cost of the representation incurred under the representation order.

Regulation 14 provides that the solicitor for the funded defendant must inform the Commission if it subsequently transpires that the costs incurred under the representation order were lower than the amount ordered to be paid under an RDCO. If the defendant has already paid the amount ordered to be paid under the RDCO, the balance must be repaid to him (para. 14(2)).

Regulations 15 to 17 cover enforcement of RDCOs.

Criminal Defence Service (Recovery of Defence Costs Orders) Regulations 2001, regs. 15 to 17

15. The judge may make an order prohibiting an individual who is required to furnish information or evidence from dealing with property where:
(a) information has failed to be provided in accordance with these Regulations;
(b) he considers that there is a real risk that relevant property will be disposed of; or
(c) at the conclusion of the case, the assessment of the costs incurred under the representation order or of the financial resources of the funded defendant has not yet been completed.

16. Any payment required to be made under an RDCO shall be made to the Commission in accordance with the order.

17. The Commission may enforce an RDCO in any manner which would be applicable to a civil debt between parties and may add any costs incurred in connection with the enforcement to the amount to be paid under the RDCO.

Detailed guidance on RDCOs may be found in part XI of *Practice Direction (Costs: Criminal Proceedings)* [2004] 2 All ER 1070.

COSTS

Power to Award Costs

D30.10 The power of the courts to award costs in criminal proceedings is contained in ss. 16 to 21 of the Prosecution of Offences Act 1985, supplemented by the Costs in Criminal Cases (General) Regulations 1986 (SI 1986 No. 1335). The Prosecution of Offences Act 1985, s. 16, deals with costs out of central funds in favour of an acquitted accused, known as 'defendant's costs orders'; s. 17 deals with prosecution costs out of central funds; s. 18 with orders that a convicted accused pay prosecution costs; s. 19 with orders that a party guilty of improper acts or omissions in the course of the proceedings pay any costs thrown away by his opponent in consequence; and s. 19A with awards of costs against legal representatives. Section 20 authorises the Lord Chancellor to make supplemental regulations, and s. 21 contains definitions. A detailed commentary of the costs in criminal cases is contained in *Practice Direction (Costs: Criminal Proceedings)* [2004] 2 All ER 1070.

Defendants' Costs Orders

D30.11 **Jurisdiction to Make a Defendant's Costs Order** In any of the situations listed below the appropriate court may make a defendant's costs order in favour of a successful accused or, as the case may be, appellant. The effect of a defendant's costs order is that the defence costs are paid out of central funds. The principal cases in which power to make such an order arises are as follows:

Section of Prosecution of Offences Act 1985	*Nature and result of proceedings*	*Court with power to make order*
16(1)	An information is not proceeded with, or the magistrates decide not to commit for trial, or the accused is acquitted after a summary trial.	The magistrates' court which refuses to commit or, as the case may be, acquits the accused. The fact that the court would not have tried the case because the information was laid out of time does not prevent the court from making a defendant's costs order (*Patel v Blakey* [1988] RTR 65). There is no power to award costs in relation to pre-charge work, for example in relation to providing advice and assistance at a police station.
16(2)	An accused is not tried for an offence for which he has been committed for trial (or in respect of which notice of transfer has been given), or he is tried on indictment and acquitted on any count in the indictment.	The Crown Court
16(3)	An accused convicted in the magistrates' court appeals against conviction and it is set aside by the Crown Court, or he appeals against sentence and is awarded a less severe punishment by the Crown Court.	The Crown Court
16(4)	Where the Court of Appeal allows an appeal against conviction or substitutes a verdict of guilty of another offence or, on an appeal against sentence, exercises its powers under the Criminal Appeal Act 1968, s. 11(3) (where the court considers that the appellant should be sentenced differently for an offence for which he was dealt with by the court below).	Court of Appeal
16(4A)	On an appeal under the CJA 1987, s. 9(11) (appeals against orders or rulings at preparatory hearings).	Court of Appeal

The references to committal proceedings will cease to be relevant when committal proceedings for either-way offences are abolished (when the relevant provisions of the CJA 2003 come into force) save for the exceptional cases where the magistrates refuse to send a case for trial to the Crown Court on the basis that it would be an abuse of process.

In *Liverpool Magistrates' Court, ex parte Abiaka* (1999) 163 JP 497, the Divisional Court held that s. 16(1) gave power to any constitution of the magistrates' court to make a defendant's costs order, and was not confined to the same constitution of justices who had dismissed the case.

D30.12 **Proper Approach to Making of a Defendant's Costs Order** The Prosecution of Offences Act 1985, s. 16, merely empowers courts to make defendants' costs orders but gives no guidance on when and how the power should be exercised. Such guidance is, however, provided by the *Practice Direction (Costs: Criminal Proceedings)* [2004] 2 All ER 1070.

The Practice Direction applies whenever a magistrates' court, the Crown Court, Divisional Court or the Court of Appeal considers an award of costs in criminal proceedings. Paragraph II.1.1 makes it clear that magistrates' courts may make defendant's costs orders, whether inquiring into an indictable offence as examining justices (or with a view to sending the proceedings to the Crown Court for trial), or dealing summarily with an offence. In deciding whether to make an order, magistrates' courts should take into account the same factors as the Crown Court (see below).

Paragraphs II.1.1 (magistrates' courts) and II.2.1 (Crown Court) of the Practice Direction stipulate that, where s. 16 of the Act applies, an order should normally be made 'unless there are positive reasons for not doing so'. An example for not making an order is that 'the defendant's own conduct has brought suspicion on himself and has misled the prosecution into thinking that the case against him was stronger than it was'; in such a case, 'the defendant can be left to pay his own costs'. Paragraph II.1.2 (in the section on magistrates' courts) makes it clear that the decision whether to make an order under s. 16 'is a matter in the discretion of the court in the light of the circumstances of each particular case', effectively reducing the scope for challenging a refusal to make an order under s. 16. Paragraph II.2.1 (in the section on the Crown Court) says that the court, if it declines to make a costs order, should explain that the reason for not making an order does not involve any suggestion that the defendant is guilty of any criminal conduct but that the order is being refused because of a particular positive reason, which should be specifically identified. Paragraph II.4.3 of the Practice Direction provides that where the Court of Appeal has jurisdiction to make an order under s. 16, it will have in mind the principles applied by the Crown Court in relation to acquitted defendants.

When considering whether the defendant brought the prosecution on himself, the court is entitled to rely on a statement of facts from the prosecution. Thus, the court does not have to hear oral evidence on this matter (*Mooney v Cardiff Justices* (2000) 164 JP 220).

The limited nature of the circumstances in which a defendant's costs order may be refused is illustrated by *Sainsbury's Supermarkets Ltd v HM Courts Service (South West Region, Devon and Cornwall Area)* (2006) 170 JP 690. An information had been laid under the Food Safety Act 1990 naming the defendant as 'J Sainsbury plc (trading as Sainsburys Supermarket Ltd)'. J Sainsbury plc asserted that it was not the proper defendant, since the relevant store was operated by J Sainsbury Supermarkets Ltd. The prosecution applied under the MCA 1980, s. 123, to substitute J Sainsbury Supermarkets Ltd as defendant. The district judge incorrectly allowed the amendment (see **D20.21**) and also refused to make a defendant's costs order in favour of J Sainsbury plc. The Divisional Court quashed this refusal, since J Sainsbury plc had not lulled the prosecution into a sense of false security, nor had it been responsible for any delay in bringing the proceedings; as it was not the party responsible for the relevant sale, that company had a complete defence and so was entitled to a defendant's costs order.

In *R (Stoddard) v Oxford Magistrates' Court* (2005) 169 JP 683, the defendants were charged with selling alcohol to an under-age purchaser. After considerable delay, the prosecution indicated that they were willing to conclude the proceedings by way of a formal caution, and the defendants accepted that offer. The charges were subsequently dismissed, with the prosecution offering no evidence. The defendants applied for a defendant's costs order under s. 16, but the application was refused. The Divisional Court held that a caution is not to be equated with a conviction. Although by accepting a formal caution a defendant is acknowledging that he has committed the alleged offence, and the existence of the caution can be drawn to the attention of a court on a subsequent occasion, it can be distinguished from a conviction since a defendant does not receive a criminal record, there is no penalty, and no risk of publicity. It follows that, where a prosecution is withdrawn following the acceptance by the accused of a caution, the defendant stands acquitted for the purposes of the making of a defendant's costs order under s. 16.

The ECHR can also be relevant to the way in which costs applications are dealt with. In *Hussain v UK* (2006) 43 EHRR 437, counsel for the Crown informed the court that a key witness did not want to give evidence and that the prosecution did not feel that she ought to be compelled to give evidence; accordingly, they offered no evidence. The applicant was duly acquitted. He made an application for a defendant's costs order under s. 16. The trial judge stated that there was compelling evidence against the defendant on the court papers and that he was not going to exercise his discretion to make an order for costs in his favour. The European Court of Human Rights noted that the presumption of innocence enshrined in the ECHR, Article 6(2), is one of the elements of a fair criminal trial required by Article 6 and will be violated if a statement of a public official concerning a person charged with a criminal offence reflects an opinion that he is guilty unless he has been proved so according to law. The court observed that, although the ECHR does not guarantee a defendant who had been acquitted the right to reimbursement of his costs, there was no question of any conduct by the applicant which could have brought him within the sort of cases in which a costs order might be refused, and no suggestion that he was in any way responsible for the non-attendance of the witness. The only natural interpretation which could be put on the trial judge's words was that he was refusing the order because he was of the view that, although the applicant had been acquitted, he was in fact guilty of the offence. That was incompatible with the presumption of innocence, and it followed that there had been a violation of Article 6(2).

In *R (Harry A Coff Ltd) v Environment Agency* [2003] EWHC 1305 (Admin), a district judge declined to make a defendant's costs order under s. 16 on the ground that the amount sought was unreasonable on its face and the court should not allow costs that reflect extravagance. The Divisional Court held that the district judge was wrong to refuse to make a defendant's costs order on this basis. What had been asked for was an order for costs to be assessed. It would therefore be for the person subsequently assessing the costs to determine whether the costs claimed were excessive.

Costs should not be denied merely because the prosecution acted properly in bringing the case. See, e.g., *Birmingham Juvenile Court, ex parte H* (1992) 156 JP 445, where the defence solicitor admitted that the prosecution was not malicious, but the Divisional Court held that this was no reason for the justices to refuse to make a defendant's costs order.

Paragraph II.2.2 of the Practice Direction deals with the problem of an accused being acquitted on some but not all counts. The Prosecution of Offences Act 1985, s. 16(2)(b), expressly allows a defendant's costs order to be made in such cases. Paragraph II.2.2 provides that where the accused is convicted of one or more counts in the indictment but acquitted on others, the court may order that only part of the costs incurred be paid (see also s. 16(7) of the Act). Thus, the making of a costs order in such a case is left completely to the discretion of the court. The court 'should make whatever order seems just having regard to the relative importance of the two charges and the conduct of the parties generally'. The same approach applies in the magistrates' court (see para. II.1.1). No doubt the court's decision will in practice depend on whether the accused was acquitted on the major part of the indictment or only on subsidiary counts. Whether a plea to the matters of which he was ultimately convicted was offered to the prosecution but rejected will also be of importance.

Paragraph II.2.3 of the Practice Direction points out that the Crown Court may make a defendants' costs order in favour of a successful appellant. In *R (Barrington) v Preston Crown Court* [2001] EWHC Admin 599, the accused was convicted in the magistrates' court of failing to provide a breath specimen. She appealed to the Crown Court. At the Crown Court, the prosecution offered no evidence after a crucial witness failed to attend. The conviction was quashed. However, the judge refused an application for a defendant's costs order. On appeal, it was held that, having regard to the fact that the case collapsed not because of anything the accused had said or done, or any misleading behaviour on her part, but simply because a prosecution witness had failed to attend court, an application for a defendant's costs order should have been successful. Similarly, in *R (Cunningham) v Exeter Crown Court* [2003] 2 Cr App R (S) 374, the Divisional Court reiterated that, where the Crown Court allows an appeal from the magistrates' court, the successful defendant should be awarded his costs under s. 16 unless there are positive reasons for not doing so. Where the court takes the view that there are such reasons for not awarding costs, it should set out its reasons for coming to that view (albeit briefly, but in sufficient detail that the defendant can see the basis for the decision).

D30.13 **Costs Payable under a Defendant's Costs Order: the General Rule** Unless the court orders otherwise, the effect of a defendant's costs order is that the accused or appellant is paid out of central funds such amount as the court considers reasonably sufficient to compensate him for any expenses properly incurred by him in the proceedings (Prosecution of Offences Act 1985, s. 16(6) and *Practice Direction (Costs: Criminal Proceedings)* [2004] 2 All ER 1070, para. I.3.1g). 'Proceedings' include any there may have been in a court below that making the costs order (see the definition of 'proceedings' in s. 21(1)). Thus, where the Crown Court on trial on indictment or appeal from the magistrates makes a defendant's costs order, the order will (in the absence of express provision to the contrary) cover the costs of the committal proceedings or summary trial. Similarly, an order by the Court of Appeal following a successful appeal from the Crown Court will extend to the costs of the trial on indictment. Paragraph I.3.1 of the Practice Direction says that where the court is sitting in an appellate capacity, the order 'will include the costs incurred in the proceedings in the lower courts unless for good reason the court directs that such costs are not included in the order'.

The term 'costs' covers only expenses properly incurred in the proceedings; it cannot include expenses that do not relate directly to the proceedings themselves, such as loss of earnings (see para. I.1.3 of the Practice Direction). The paragraph goes on to note that where the party in whose favour the costs order is made is funded by the Criminal Defence Service, he will only recover his 'personal costs' (see the Prosecution of Offences Act 1985, s. 21(4A)(a)).

If the accused agrees, the amount payable under s. 16(6) may be fixed forthwith and specified in the order (s. 16(9)(a)). Otherwise it is determined in accordance with regulations made by the Lord Chancellor (s. 16(9)(b)). The relevant provisions are part III (regs. 4 to 13) of the Costs in Criminal Cases (General) Regulations 1986 (SI 1986 No. 1335). These provide in essence that the 'appropriate authority' (or officers appointed to act on his behalf) shall consider the claim for costs submitted by or on behalf of the accused, and shall allow reasonable costs in respect of work that appears to have been actually and reasonably done and disbursements that have been actually and reasonably incurred (reg. 7). The 'appropriate authority' is (a) the Registrar in the case of Court of Appeal proceedings; (b) the Master of the Crown Office in the case of Divisional Court proceedings; (c) an officer appointed by the Lord Chancellor in the case of Crown Court proceedings, and (d) the justices' clerk in the case of magistrates' court proceedings (reg. 5). An applicant (i.e. any person in whose favour an order for costs out of central funds has been made) who is dissatisfied with the appropriate authority's decision as to the costs payable may first apply for redetermination by the authority. If the result of that is unsatisfactory, there is an appeal to a costs judge, and a further appeal from him to the High Court if a point of principle of general importance is involved (regs. 9 to 12). The procedure on appeal to the High Court against the decision of a costs judge is governed by the Civil Procedure Rules, part 52. The above provisions for redetermination and appeal do not apply where the costs determined are in respect of magistrates' courts proceedings (see reg. 9), although presumably the decision of the justices' clerk may be challenged by judicial review in accordance with the usual principles governing such applications.

Paragraph I.4.1 of the Practice Direction says that unless the court has specified the sum to be paid, the amount payable is to be determined by the appropriate officer of the court. However, the court may disallow any costs not properly incurred or direct the determining officer to consider whether particular costs were properly incurred. Paragraph V.1.1 provides that costs not properly incurred include costs in respect of 'work unreasonably done' (e.g., where unjustified expense has been incurred) or where costs have been wasted because of 'failure to conduct the proceedings with reasonable competence and expedition'. Where the court is minded to make such an order, it should give the relevant party a chance to make representations on the matter (para. V.1.2).

R (McCormick) v Liverpool City Magistrates' Court [2001] 2 All ER 705 concerned costs incurred before legal aid was granted. The accused did not have the means to pay those costs. It was held that costs are incurred by an accused for the purpose of s. 16(6) if he is contractually obliged to pay for them; there is no requirement to prove that he had in fact paid, or was likely to pay, those costs.

Orders for Less than the Full Costs Incurred By the Prosecution of Offences Act 1985, s. 16(7), where the court making a defendant's costs order is of the opinion that there are circumstances making it inappropriate for the accused to recover the full amount of the costs that would otherwise be assessed payable under s. 16(6), it shall assess what amount would be just and reasonable and specify it in the order. One obvious situation for fixing the costs at less than the full amount is where an accused is acquitted on some but not all the counts on the indictment. **D30.14**

In *Dudley Magistrates' Court, ex parte Power City Stores Ltd* (1990) 154 JP 654, where the defendant wanted to recover the cost of employing leading counsel, the Divisional Court held that, in calculating the amount of costs to be paid under s. 16, the officer doing the assessment has to carry out a two-stage test. First, he has to consider whether the expenses claimed were properly incurred by the defendant. If so, the second step is to ask what amount would be reasonably sufficient to compensate the defendant for those costs. The test is whether the defendant acted reasonably in instructing the counsel he did. There are cases in which junior counsel or a solicitor could conduct the case, but in which it is reasonable to instruct leading counsel. In *R (Hale) v Southport Justices* (2002) *The Times*, 29 January 2002, it was held that the question was whether the accused had acted reasonably in the circumstances by instructing a solicitor at a particular hourly rate, not whether he could have instructed a more junior solicitor. In that case, the justices' clerk had applied the statutory criterion of reasonable sufficiency in s. 16(6) to the wrong issue, namely the quality of representation, rather than the costs incurred.

It should be noted that a court acting under s. 16(7) is obliged to specify the sum that shall be paid rather than allowing a percentage of the total costs as assessed by the appropriate authority (see the terms of the subsection).

Order in Favour of a Publicly Funded Accused By the Prosecution of Offences Act 1985, s. 21(4A)(a), the costs of a publicly funded accused shall *not* — for purposes of a defendant's **D30.15**

costs order — be taken to include any expenses incurred on his behalf by the Legal Services Commission. It follows that a defendant's costs order will generally be pointless in the case of such an accused since all the costs properly incurred on his behalf will have been defrayed out of legal aid, and there will be nothing left on which the order can bite. A costs order will, however, be appropriate if, for example, the accused was not aided until a late stage of the proceedings and paid for the costs of his early representation privately, or if there were unusual expenditures incurred on his behalf and an application under the Criminal Defence Service (General) (No. 2) Regulations 2001, reg. 19 or 20, failed to obtain authorisation for the expenditure from the Legal Services Commission. Similarly, he can, as a result of a defendant's costs order, become entitled to an allowance for travelling and subsistence under reg. 23, as if he had been a witness. The upshot of s. 21(4A)(a) is that, save in a minority of exceptional cases, defendants' costs orders are relevant only to accused who have paid for their defences privately.

Prosecution Costs

D30.16 **Power to Make Order for Prosecution Costs** Subject to what follows, the Prosecution of Offences Act 1985, s. 17(1), provides that the court may award a prosecutor such amount out of central funds as it considers reasonably necessary to compensate him for any expenses properly incurred by him in the proceedings. This applies whether or not the accused is convicted, but applies only to proceedings in respect of an indictable offence (whether tried summarily or on indictment) and proceedings before a Divisional Court in respect of a summary offence (s. 17(1)(a) and (b)). An important restriction on the ambit of s. 17(1) is that no order may be made in favour of a public authority (s. 17(2)), which term is defined by s. 17(3) as comprising a police force, the CPS, local authorities and any other authority appointed by the Crown or financed by money voted by Parliament. Thus, s. 17(1) is of potential value only in that tiny proportion of prosecutions brought by private individuals or organisations. Where the subsection does potentially apply, an order *should* be made unless there is good reason for not doing so — e.g., the proceedings have been instituted or continued without good cause (see para. III.1.1 of the *Practice Direction (Costs: Criminal Proceedings)* [2004] 2 All ER 1070). Even so, an express application must be made, rather than assuming that the court will automatically order costs of its own motion (ibid.). Regulations 4 to 13 of the Costs in Criminal Cases (General) Regulations 1986 apply to assessment of prosecutors' costs out of central funds just as they apply to costs under defendants' costs orders. Under earlier regulations, it was held that a private prosecutor could not claim for the time he had spent in preparation and presentation of the prosecution, although he was entitled to recover travelling and secretarial expenses (*Stockport Magistrates' Court, ex parte Cooper* (1984) 149 JP 261).

D30.17 **Order that the Accused Pay Prosecution Costs** Subsections (1) and (2) of the Prosecution of Offences Act 1985, s. 18, authorise the making of orders that a convicted accused or unsuccessful appellant shall pay costs as indicated in the table below. The first column describes the event giving rise to the liability to a costs order; the second states the court with power to make the order, and the third states the person in whose favour the order is to be made.

Relevant event	*Court*	*Beneficiary of order*
Summary conviction (whether for a summary offence or for one triable either way).	The convicting magistrates' court.	The prosecutor.
Conviction on indictment.	The Crown Court.	The prosecutor.
Dismissal of an appeal to the Crown Court against conviction or sentence by the magistrates.	The Crown Court.	The prosecutor.

Relevant event	*Court*	*Beneficiary of order*
Dismissal of an appeal to the Court of Appeal against conviction or sentence (including application for leave to appeal); dismissal of an application for leave to appeal from the Court of Appeal to the House of Lords; dismissal of an appeal or application for leave to appeal under the CJA 1987, s. 9(11), or an appeal or application for leave to appeal under the CPIA 1996, s. 35(1) (latter was added by CJA 2003, s. 312(3)).	The Court of Appeal.	Such person as may be named in the order (not necessarily the prosecutor).

In addition, reg. 14 of the Costs in Criminal Cases (General) Regulations 1986 provides, *inter alia*, that the Prosecution of Offences Act 1985, s. 18, is to apply to proceedings in the Crown Court on committals for sentence (including committals to be dealt with for breach of a suspended sentence, probation order or conditional discharge) just as it applies to trials on indictment. In short, the Crown Court when dealing with the committed offender may order him to pay costs.

In *Hamilton-Johnson v RSPCA* [2002] 2 Cr App R (S) 390, the issue was whether the Crown Court had jurisdiction to order a defendant who appealed unsuccessfully from the magistrates' court to the Crown Court to pay to the prosecutor sums by way of costs which the magistrates had refused to award to the prosecutor. The Court of Appeal, Civil Division, concluded that the Crown Court had the requisite jurisdiction to make such an order, but should hesitate before doing so as the magistrates would be far better placed than the Crown Court to decide the issue.

Amount of Order for Prosecution Costs When a court makes an order under the Prosecution of Offences Act 1985, s. 18, for the payment of prosecution costs, it orders the payment of an amount that it considers 'just and reasonable'. That sum must be specified in the order (s. 18(3)). The court may not delegate (e.g., to a justices' clerk or Crown Court officer) the duty of determining what the accused should pay (*Bunston v Rawlings* [1982] 1 WLR 473). See also para. I.4.3 of the *Practice Direction (Costs: Criminal Proceedings)* [2004] 2 All ER 1070. Therefore, the prosecution should if possible be able to inform the court of the costs that have been incurred at each stage of the relevant proceedings, thus enabling the court to make an appropriate order (ibid.). Where the prosecution are unable to provide a figure forthwith, the court should adjourn for enquiries to be made by an appropriate officer (ibid.). D30.18

When seeking an order for costs against a defendant, the prosecution must give notice to the defendant of its intention to apply for such an order (*Emmett* (1999) *The Times*, 15 October 1999).

In *Associated Octel Ltd* [1997] 1 Cr App R (S) 435, the Court of Appeal held that the costs of the prosecution for the purposes of s. 18(1) might include the costs of the prosecuting authority in carrying out investigations. In *Octel*, the offence was both investigated and prosecuted by the Health and Safety Executive. It is submitted that the position would be different where different bodies investigated and prosecuted (e.g., the police and the CPS respectively). It would not seem to be 'just and reasonable' for the court to order the defendant to pay the prosecution in respect of costs for which it was not liable. As to the procedure to be adopted in cases where the prosecution seeks an order requiring the defendant to pay costs, the Court of Appeal observed that:

(a) the prosecution should serve on the defence, at the earliest time, full details of its costs, so as to give the defence a proper opportunity to consider them and make representations on them, if appropriate;

(b) if the defendant, once served with a schedule of the prosecution's costs, wished to dispute the whole or any part of the schedule, he should give proper notice to the prosecution of the objections which it was proposed to make and should at least make it clear to the court what the objections were — in some exceptional cases, a full hearing would need to be held for the objections to be resolved, as there was no provision for the taxation of the prosecution's costs in a criminal case.

In *Bow Street Stipendiary Magistrate, ex parte Multimedia Screen Ltd* (1998) *The Times*, 28 January 1998, the defendant sought judicial review of a costs order requiring him to pay £15,000 although he had made only a tiny profit from the offence of which he was convicted. The Divisional Court held that the prosecution had had to do a lot of research and so the order was appropriate. In most cases, precise assessment of prosecution costs will be irrelevant, since the principles discussed below as to the exercise of the court's discretion in the making of orders will result in the amount the accused is required to pay being well below the actual costs, however restrictively interpreted.

Section 18(1) is subject to two specific qualifications. First, where a person is, on summary conviction, fined £5 or less, no order for costs may be made 'unless in the particular circumstances of the case [the court] considers it right to do so'. Secondly, where a juvenile is convicted before a magistrates' court, the amount of any costs he is ordered to pay shall not exceed the amount of any fine imposed on him (s. 18(5)). It is submitted that, where a juvenile is dealt with by means other than a fine, the costs that may be awarded against him are entirely discretionary and not subject to any statutory upper limit.

D30.19 **Proper Approach to Orders that the Accused Pay Prosecution Costs** Paragraph VI.1.4 of the *Practice Direction (Costs: Criminal Proceedings)* [2004] 2 All ER 1070 states that an order should be made under the Prosecution of Offences Act 1985, s. 18, where the court is satisfied that the offender or appellant has the means and ability to pay. This is the fundamental principle governing costs against the accused and merely confirms pre-existing case law; see, e.g., *Mountain* (1978) 68 Cr App R 41, where the Court of Appeal varied orders that M and K pay the entire prosecution costs as assessed (probably £1,000) to orders that they pay £150 and £250 respectively, Lawton LJ saying that when imposing financial penalties, including costs, the court must have regard to the means of a convicted person. Similarly, in *Nottingham Justices, ex parte Fohmann* (1986) 84 Cr App R 316, the Divisional Court quashed an order by magistrates that F pay a fine of £400 (for offences of obtaining by deception by turning back the odometers on cars he was selling at auction) and prosecution costs of £600, since he was on supplementary benefit and — even if able to maintain the rate of £10 per week ordered by the court — would have taken two years to pay the combined fine and costs. Glidewell LJ indicated that the amount of costs ordered should not exceed that which the offender can reasonably pay within a year. The case also illustrates that the propriety or otherwise of the decision on costs must be viewed in the light of the overall financial orders made by the court, in particular, any fines or compensation the offender is required to pay. Although *Ex parte Fohmann* remains important for its statement of principle, the suggested time-limit of a year for payment of costs may no longer be appropriate in view of the Court of Appeal having held that fines and compensation may now be fixed at amounts requiring payment by instalments over a two or even three-year period (see **E17.12** and **E18.5**). In deciding whether the offender has sufficient means to pay an order for costs, mortgage debts should be taken into account (*Ghadami* [1998] 1 Cr App R (S) 42).

In *Northallerton Magistrates' Court, ex parte Dove* (1999) 163 JP 657, the Divisional Court gave the following series of guidelines on the imposition of costs.

(1) The order to pay costs should never exceed the sum which the offender is able to pay, and which it is reasonable to expect him to pay, having regard to his means and any other financial order imposed on him.

(2) Nor should it exceed the sum which the prosecutor has actually and reasonably incurred.
(3) The purpose of such an order is to compensate the prosecutor and not to punish the offender, e.g., for exercising his constitutional right to defend himself.
(4) Any costs ordered should not in the ordinary way be grossly disproportionate to any fine imposed. Where the fine and the costs exceeded the sum which the offender could reasonably be ordered to pay, the costs should be reduced, rather than the fine.
(5) An offender facing a fine or an order as to costs should disclose to the magistrates the data relevant to his financial position, so that they can assess what he can reasonably afford to pay. Failure to make such disclosure could lead the court to draw reasonable inferences as to his means.
(6) The court should give the offender a fair opportunity to adduce any relevant financial information and make submissions prior to the determination of any financial order.

In addition to these factors, the following matters may influence the court's decisions on costs against him:

(a) *Plea.* A plea of guilty certainly does not preclude the making of an order for costs. However, combined with other factors such as the offender's limited means, it may persuade the court not to make an order or to make one for considerably less than the actual costs (see O'Connor LJ's judgment in *Maher* [1983] QB 784 at p. 789D–H). The weight to be attached to the plea in this context will depend, *inter alia*, on the stage at which it was entered and the gravity of the case. Thus, in *Maher*, the Court of Appeal (distinguishing the earlier case of *Matthews* (1979) 1 Cr App R (S) 346) ordered that the three appellants should pay a total of £180,000 costs, even though they had all eventually pleaded guilty and one of them had done so at the earliest possible opportunity. The costs orders were justified, *inter alia*, because the offences were exceptionally serious — murder and a major conspiracy to import heroin.

(b) *Remainder of the sentence.* Where the offender is given an immediate custodial sentence it is unusual to impose an order for costs, if only because he will for the time being have no income out of which to make the required payments. But, again, it is ultimately a matter for the court's discretion. Thus, if there is good reason to suppose that he has substantial capital assets (in particular if they are the proceeds of crime), an order may properly be made (see *Maher* [1983] QB 784 for an example). Where the sentence is non-custodial, one line of authority suggests that any order for costs should not be out of proportion to the penalty proper. This principle was clearly stated by Phillimore LJ in *Whalley* (1972) 56 Cr App R 304:

> This court takes the view that whenever a court is imposing a financial penalty, or making an order in regard to costs, it must have regard to the means of the individual. . . .

The Court of Appeal has considered on a number of occasions the question whether the court should make an order for the payment of prosecution costs which is larger than the fine imposed for the offence itself. For example, in *Whalley*, an order to pay the whole costs of prosecuting a drink-driving offence, for which W had been disqualified and fined £20, was reduced to an order to pay costs not exceeding £50. Similarly, in *Firmston* (1984) 6 Cr App R (S) 189, costs of £400 ordered following F's conviction on indictment for theft from a shop were reduced to £100 because he had been given an absolute discharge for the offence itself. These cases were cited in *Boyle* [1995] Crim LR 514, in which the Court of Appeal nonetheless decided to follow instead the case of *Bushell* (1980) 2 Cr App R (S) 77. Their lordships upheld an order to pay £1,000 prosecution costs where the offender had been fined £250 after electing trial on indictment when the case could conveniently have been tried summarily; in such a case, which was otherwise appropriate for an order for him to pay prosecution costs, the offender could properly be ordered to pay costs on the Crown Court scale.

D

Part D Procedure

(c) *Conduct of the defence.* At least in theory, an offender who is found guilty on indictment of an either-way offence should not be punished in costs for having exercised his constitutional right to trial by jury (*Hayden* [1975] 1 WLR 852). However, any order made will inevitably reflect the fact that he has chosen the more expensive method of trial (ibid., and see also *Bushell* (1980) 2 Cr App R (S) 77 where orders to pay £250 costs against each of two accused were upheld because, even though the offence was merely one of obtaining services worth £21 and the fines imposed were only £100, they had elected Crown Court trial in a matter eminently suitable for summary disposition and thus greatly increased the costs incurred by the prosecution). The exercise of the court's discretion may also be affected by the accused having chosen to plead not guilty when the prosecution case against him was manifestly strong and he must have known all along that he was guilty (see dicta in *Singh* (1982) 4 Cr App R (S) 38 where an order of £400 costs against S following his conviction on indictment for a minor assault occasioning actual bodily harm was upheld partly because he had 'extravagantly' elected trial on indictment when there was 'really no need in the circumstances' for him to do so). The relevance of the reasonableness of the defence (albeit disbelieved) to costs was also referred to, *obiter*, by Lawton LJ in *Mountain* (1978) 68 Cr App R 41 (at pp. 43–44 emphasis added):

> In many cases at the trial the accused says, as he is entitled to say and frequently is justified in saying, that there has been some mistake on the part of the prosecution witnesses; that they have confused themselves in thinking that they saw something which they did not see, that their memories have failed them or that the accused has some explanation for what at first sight seems to be criminal conduct. *In that class of case it may be unfair to make an order that the accused should pay the costs of the prosecution.* But there are other kinds of cases which come before the Crown Court where the defence is that everybody except the accused is telling lies and that the prosecution's case is virtually a concocted one. . . .
>
> It is in that kind of case that courts are entitled to make an order that the accused should pay the costs of the prosecution.

(d) *Conduct of the prosecution.* Where a minor case is in the Crown Court through the prosecution's choice, they cannot expect to recover their full costs from the accused. In *Hall* (1988) 10 Cr App R (S) 456, H was willing to plead guilty to careless driving. The case went to the Crown Court because the prosecution insisted on a charge of reckless (now 'dangerous') driving. In the Crown Court, H pleaded guilty to careless driving, and the Crown offered no evidence on the reckless driving charge. H was conditionally discharged and ordered to pay £372 prosecution costs. On appeal, the order was reduced to £25 (the amount appropriate to a guilty plea in the magistrates' court at the time). See also *Clark* (1993) 14 Cr App R (S) 360.

(e) *Apportionment between co-defendants.* Where there is more than one accused, each should be liable only for that portion of the prosecution's costs which is attributable to him. In *Ronson* [1991] Crim LR 794, the appellant and two co-defendants were each ordered to pay a third of the prosecution costs (£440,000 each). The fourth defendant was unable to pay. On appeal, the Court of Appeal held that the right approach was to see what would be a reasonable estimate of the cost of trying each defendant alone. That could not be done here. It was not right that the three defendants who could pay should bear the burden of the fourth. Hence the costs of each defendant were reduced from a third to a quarter. Thus, the court should divide the total amount payable between the number of defendants (not just those who are able to pay) so that each defendant pays only his own share of the costs and does not subsidise a defendant who cannot pay. However, in *Harrison* (1993) 14 Cr App R (S) 419, the Court of Appeal upheld an order made against only one of a number of defendants: he was the principal offender (the other defendants having played relatively minor roles in the offences) and he had the means to pay the amount ordered. In *Durose* [2004] EWCA Crim 2188, it was argued by counsel that the court had power to make an order for costs which imposed joint and several liability. The court did not hear full argument on the point but said that their 'instinctive reaction' was that that is not an appropriate kind of order to make in a criminal case. The point was left open for decision in a later case.

Paragraph VI.1.5 of the Practice Direction notes that the amount of an order made under s. 18 of the 1985 Act must be specified in the order by the court. Paragraph VI.1.6 points out that the Administrative Court is not covered by s. 18 but adds that the court has 'complete discretion over all costs between the parties in relation to proceedings before it'. Paragraph VI.1.7 notes that (under the Prosecution of Offences Act 1985, s. 21(4A)(b)) an order under s. 18 includes costs funded by the Legal Services Commission.

Appeals on Costs

D30.20 Neither party has a right of appeal to the Crown Court in respect of a costs order made by a magistrates' court: the prosecution have no right of appeal to the Crown Court, and the MCA 1980, s. 108(3)(b), precludes a defence appeal to the Crown Court against a costs order. However, it was held in *Hamilton-Johnson v RSPCA* [2002] 2 Cr App R (S) 390, that the Crown Court does have jurisdiction to make an order as to costs incurred before the conclusion of the magistrates' court proceedings (either under the Prosecution of Offences Act 1985, s. 18(1), or the Supreme Court Act 1981, s. 48(2)). Usually, following an unsuccessful appeal against conviction, the Crown Court should hesitate to modify the magistrates' costs order. If the prosecutor wishes to seek an increase in the costs the defendant has to pay, he should give written notice to this effect to the defendant, so that the defendant is aware of the possible consequences of pursuing an appeal against conviction.

Orders to Pay Costs Thrown Away

D30.21 The Prosecution of Offences Act 1985, s. 19(1) and (2), empowered the Lord Chancellor to make regulations by virtue of which a party to criminal proceedings may be ordered to pay costs thrown away as a result of his 'unnecessary or improper act or omission'. Regulation 3 of the Costs in Criminal Cases (General) Regulations 1986 provides that, before making such an order, the court shall hear the parties concerned, and shall take into account any other order as to costs which has been made in the proceedings (reg. 3(2)). Conversely, when the time comes to make a general order as to costs, the court shall take into account any order that has already been made under reg. 3 (reg. 3(4)). The amount to be paid by the 'guilty' party must be specified in the order (reg. 3(3)). In the case of a juvenile who has been convicted of an offence, any sum he is ordered to pay by a magistrates' court under reg. 3 shall not exceed the amount of any fine imposed on him (reg. 3(5)). If, during the period of an adjournment, the prosecution serves a notice of discontinuance, the court retains jurisdiction to determine applications for costs (*DPP v Denning* [1991] 2 QB 532). For an order as to costs to be made under reg. 3, there must be a causal relationship between the unnecessary or improper act, and the incurring of the costs to be paid under the order (*Wood Green Crown Court, ex parte DPP* [1993] 1 WLR 723). In *Leicester Crown Court, ex parte Commissioners of Customs and Excise* (2001) *The Times*, 23 February 2001, it was said that, under reg. 3, the judge has to consider first whether there has been an unnecessary or improper act or omission by, or on behalf of, the prosecution. Secondly, he has to determine whether the costs that were incurred by the accused were as a result of that unnecessary or improper act or omission. Thirdly, he has to decide whether he will, as a matter of discretion, order all or part of the costs to be paid by the party in default. It is implicit in the last stage that, before an order can be made, the judge is required to identify the costs incurred as a result of the unnecessary or improper act or omission. Having performed those exercises, the judge has to specify the amount to be paid.

Regulation 3 is the only provision under which the prosecution may be ordered to pay costs to the accused personally. According to para. VII.1.1 of the *Practice Direction (Costs: Criminal Proceedings)* [2004] 2 All ER 1070, an order is appropriate only where the improper act or omission which has caused costs to be thrown away is that of the accused or prosecutor personally, not where it is that of the legal representatives. For orders that legal representatives pay costs, see D29.24.

In *Leicester Crown Court, ex parte Commissioners of Customs and Excise*, the prosecution had refused to disclose some documents and there was an application to stay the trial as an abuse of process. The prosecution offered no evidence and the judge ordered verdicts of not guilty to be recorded. The judge ordered the prosecution to pay the defence costs incurred. The question to be decided was whether the costs order was a matter relating to trial on indictment and so excluded from judicial review by the Supreme Court Act 1981, s. 29. The Divisional Court held that, under reg. 3 of the Costs in Criminal Cases Regulations 1986, the judge has to consider first whether there had been an unnecessary or improper act or omission by, or on behalf, of the prosecution. Secondly, he has to determine whether the costs that were incurred by the defendants were as a result of that unnecessary or improper act or omission. Thirdly, he has to decide whether he would, as a matter of discretion, order all or part of the costs to be paid by the party in default. It is implicit in the last stage that, before an order can be made, the judge is required to identify the costs incurred as a result of the unnecessary or improper act or omission. Having performed those exercises, the judge has to specify the amount to be paid. In the present case, the judge had not complied with reg. 3. However, that was not a decision made without jurisdiction, since the judge was entitled to make a costs order once he was seised of the issue of whether the relevant documents had been disclosed. In those circumstances, the High Court had no jurisdiction to reconsider the judge's decision on an application for judicial review.

Witness Expenses

D30.22 Section 19(3) of the Prosecution of Offences Act 1985 empowers the Lord Chancellor to make regulations authorising the payment out of central funds of (a) witness expenses, (b) the cost of obtaining medical reports, and (c) the fees of an interpreter. Part V of the Costs in Criminal Cases (General) Regulations 1986 (regs. 15 to 25) deals with such payments. By reg. 16(1), the expenses properly incurred by the witness or, as the case may be, maker of a medical report or interpreter are to be allowed out of central funds unless the court directs otherwise. This applies whatever the outcome of the proceedings and regardless of whether the witness etc. is required by the prosecution or defence. A non-expert witness (other than police or prison officers) is entitled to travelling expenses, a subsistence allowance and a loss allowance (e.g., for loss of earnings) (see reg. 18). Payment of professional witnesses, experts, suppliers of medical reports and interpreters is dealt with in regs. 19 and 20. If a defendant's costs order is made in favour of the accused, he may also be allowed a subsistence allowance and travelling expenses, but he is not entitled to compensation for loss of earnings (reg. 23). See also paras. IV.1 and IV.2 of the *Practice Direction (Costs: Criminal Proceedings)* [2004] 2 All ER 1070.

Claw-back by the Lord Chancellor

D30.23 Section 20(2) of the Prosecution of Offences Act 1985 empowers the Lord Chancellor to make regulations enabling sums paid by the Legal Services Commission or out of central funds to be recovered from a person who is the beneficiary of an *inter partes* costs order. The Costs in Criminal Cases (General) Regulations 1986, regs 26 and 27, have been made in pursuance of s. 20(2). The effect of the subsection and regulations is that the Lord Chancellor may claw back for the Legal Services Commission or for central funds money received by:

(a) a defendant who is funded by the Commission where the prosecution are ordered to pay costs under reg. 3 (costs thrown away by a party's default), or
(b) a defendant who is granted costs out of central funds where the prosecution are ordered to pay costs under reg. 3, or
(c) a private prosecutor who is granted costs out of central funds and also obtains an order that the accused pay prosecution costs.

Orders for Costs against Legal Representatives

An order to pay costs may be made against a legal representative (as distinct from a party) by virtue of the inherent jurisdiction of the Crown Court (in the case of a solicitor) or under the Prosecution of Offences Act 1985, s. 19A (in respect of a solicitor or a barrister). **D30.24**

The Crown Court, as part of the Supreme Court, has inherent jurisdiction to order that a solicitor pay personally any costs thrown away by his or his staff's improper act or omission (see para. IX.1.1 of the *Practice Direction (Costs: Criminal Proceedings)* [2004] 2 All ER 1070). Such an order may not be made unless reasonable notice is given to the solicitor and he has a reasonable opportunity of being heard in reply (para. IX.1.2). This power should be used only in exceptional circumstances and not where a statutory power would be available (see para. IX.1.3). In *Holden and Co. v CPS* [1990] 2 QB 261, it was held that mistake, error of judgment or mere negligence were not sufficient to trigger off such an order. The court's jurisdiction arose only where there was a serious dereliction of the solicitor's duty to the court. The primary object of such an order was to reimburse a litigant for costs incurred because of the solicitor's default, but there were also punitive and deterrent elements in the order.

The power to order legal representatives to pay costs has been extended by the Prosecution of Offences Act 1985, s. 19A. This statutory power is in addition to the inherent jurisdiction discussed in the preceding paragraph. A magistrates' court, the Crown Court or the Court of Appeal may disallow costs or order the legal representative concerned to meet the whole or part of any wasted costs. Paragraph VIII.1.1 of the Practice Direction makes it clear that an order under s. 19A can be made against any person exercising a right of audience or a right to conduct litigation. It therefore covers both solicitors and barristers. Wasted costs are costs which are incurred as a result of any improper, unreasonable or negligent act or omission by the representative or his employee, or which the court considers it unreasonable to expect a party to pay in the light of such act or omission occurring after the costs were incurred (s. 19A(3)). The test is therefore extended to cover negligence, in addition to improper or unreasonable acts or omissions. The procedure for the exercise of the power is laid down in regs 3A to 3D of the Costs in Criminal Cases (General) Regulations 1986. These require the court to specify the amount of the wasted costs order, and allow the representative and any party to the proceedings to make representations. The hearing should normally be in chambers, with a shorthand writer present. The court should give reasons for its order, which it may announce in public. Paragraph VIII.1.2 of the Practice Direction says that judges in criminal cases have more direct responsibility for costs than their civil counterparts and so should keep the question of costs in the forefront of their mind at every stage of the case. They ought to be prepared to take the initiative themselves without any prompting from the parties. Paragraph VIII.1.4 provides that judges contemplating making a wasted costs order should bear in mind the guidance given by the Court of Appeal in *Re a Barrister (Wasted Costs Order) (No. 1 of 1991)* [1993] QB 293, and para. VIII.1.5 goes on to refer to the additional guidance given by the Court of Appeal in *Re P (a Barrister) (Wasted Costs Order)* [2002] 1 Cr App R 207.

In *Re a Barrister (Wasted Costs Order) (No. 1 of 1991)*, the Court of Appeal considered an order made against defence counsel in the Crown Court. The trial judge purported to 'disallow such part of the brief fee which would otherwise have been payable on the partial trial as exceeds what would be the proper enhanced refresher for the retrial'. His order was based upon his finding that the barrister was guilty of an 'unreasonable act or omission'. On appeal by the barrister, the Court of Appeal held that the order was *ultra vires* and fatally flawed, since it did not specify the amount of the wasted costs. In any event, the barrister was not, their lordships held, guilty of any unreasonable act or omission such as could found a wasted costs order. They went on to lay down the following guidelines as to the practice to be adopted in deciding upon a wasted costs order:

1 There is a clear need for any judge or court intending to exercise the wasted costs jurisdiction to formulate carefully and concisely the complaint and grounds upon which such an order might be sought. Those measures were draconian, and, as in contempt proceedings, the grounds had to be clear and particular.

2 Where necessary a transcript of the relevant part of the proceedings under discussion should be available. And, in accordance with the rules, a transcript of any wasted costs hearing had to be made.

3 A defendant involved in a case where such proceedings were contemplated should be present if, after discussion with counsel, it was thought that his interests might be affected. And he should certainly be present and represented if the matter might affect the course of his trial. Regulation 3B(2) [of the Costs in Criminal Cases Regulations 1986: see D29.26] furthermore required that before a wasted costs order was made 'the court shall allow the legal or other representative and any party to the proceedings to make representations'. There might be cases where it might be appropriate for counsel for the Crown to be present.

4 A three-stage test or approach is recommended when a wasted costs order was contemplated:

(i) Had there been an improper, unreasonable or negligent act or omission?

(ii) As a result, had any costs been incurred by a party?

(iii) If the answers to (i) and (ii) were yes; should the court exercise its discretion to disallow or order the representative to meet the whole or any part of the relevant costs, and if so what specific sum was involved?

5 It was inappropriate to propose any deal or settlement, such as was suggested in the present case, that the representative might forgo fees. The judge should formally state his complaint, in chambers, and invite the representative to make his own comments. After any other party had been heard the judge should give his formal ruling. Discursive conversations such as took place in the present case might be unfair and should certainly not take place.

6 As was indicated above the judge had to specify the sum to be disallowed or ordered. Alternatively, the relevant available procedure should be substituted, should it be impossible to fix the sum [see A Guide to the Award of Costs in Criminal Proceedings (RCJ (1991) HMSO), para. 6.7].

Further guidance was given in *Re P (a Barrister) (Wasted Costs Order)*, where the Court of Appeal reiterated that the crucial questions in determining whether to make a wasted costs order were those set out in 4(i) to (iii) above, and stated that the standard of proof to be applied was on the balance of probability. Generally, it would be appropriate for any application in respect of costs to be heard by the trial judge. It was, however, open for the trial judge to decline to consider such an application if, for example, he was personally embarrassed by the appearance of bias. It was only in the most exceptional circumstances that it would be appropriate to pass the matter to another judge, and the fact that, in the proper exercise of judicial functions, a judge had expressed views in relation to the conduct of a lawyer against whom an order was sought did not of itself normally constitute bias or the appearance of bias so as to necessitate a transfer.

In *Ridehalgh v Horsefield* [1994] Ch 205, the Court of Appeal gave guidance on the discretion to make a wasted costs order in favour of one party to litigation against the legal representative of the other. Sir Thomas Bingham MR made it clear that the judgment was applicable to criminal as well as civil courts, and made the following points.

(a) 'Improper' covered, but was not confined to, conduct which would ordinarily justify serious professional penalty. It was not limited to significant breach of the relevant code of professional conduct. It included conduct which was improper according to the consensus of professional, including judicial, opinion, whether it violated the letter of a professional code or not.

(b) 'Unreasonable' described conduct which was vexatious, i.e. designed to harass the other side rather than advance the resolution of the dispute. Conduct could not be described as unreasonable simply because it led to an unsuccessful result, or because other more cautious legal representatives would have acted differently. The acid test was whether the conduct permitted of a reasonable explanation. If it did, the course adopted might be regarded as optimistic and reflecting on a practitioner's judgment, but it was not unreasonable.

(c) 'Negligent' should be understood in an untechnical way to denote failure to act with the competence reasonably expected of ordinary members of the profession. It was not a term of art and did not necessarily involve an actionable breach of the legal representative's duty to his own client.

(d) A legal representative was not acting improperly, unreasonably or negligently simply because he acted for a party who pursued a claim or defence which was plainly doomed to fail.

(e) However, a legal representative could not lend his assistance to proceedings which were an abuse of process, and was not entitled to use litigious procedures for purposes for which they were not intended, e.g., by issuing proceedings for reasons unconnected with success in the action, pursuing a case which was known to be dishonest or knowingly conniving at incomplete disclosure of documents.

(f) Any judge considering making a wasted costs order must make full allowance for the fact that an advocate in court often had to make decisions quickly and under pressure.

(g) Legal professional privilege might be relevant. If so, the privilege was the client's which he alone could waive. Judges should make full allowance for the inability of respondent lawyers to tell the whole story. Where there was room for doubt, the respondent lawyers were entitled to the benefit of it. It was only when, with all allowance made, a lawyer's conduct of proceedings was quite plainly unjustifiable, that it could be appropriate to make the order.

(h) When a solicitor sought the advice of counsel, he did not abdicate his own professional responsibility. He had to apply his mind to the advice received. But the more specialised the advice, the more reasonable it was likely to be for him to accept it.

(i) A threat to apply for a wasted costs order should not be used as a means of intimidation. However, if one side considered that the conduct of the other was improper, unreasonable or negligent and likely to cause a waste of costs, it was not objectionable to alert the other side to that view.

(j) In the ordinary way, such applications were best left until after the end of the trial.

(k) As to procedure, the respondent lawyer should be told very clearly what he was said to have done wrong. No formal process of discovery would be appropriate. Elaborate pleadings should in general be avoided. The court could not imagine circumstances in which the applicant could interrogate the respondent lawyer or vice versa. The legal representative must have opportunity to show cause why an order should not be made, but this did not mean that the burden was on the legal representative to exculpate himself.

Paragraph VIII.1.7 of the Practice Direction says that the court may postpone the making of a wasted costs order to the end of the case if it appears more appropriate to do so, e.g., where there may be conflict between the legal representatives as to the apportionment of blame, or the legal representative concerned is unable to make full representations because of a possible conflict with his duty to the client.

In *Re a Barrister (Wasted Costs Order) (No. 4 of 1992)* (1994) *The Times*, 15 March 1994, the Court of Appeal held that a barrister who practised at home without a clerk must not rely wholly on instructing solicitors to notify him of the dates and times of his cases. He was responsible for keeping abreast of listing details and should have adopted a system which enabled him to do so.

In *Rodney (Wasted Costs Order)* (9 December 1996 unreported), counsel failed to appear before the Court of Appeal due to an error by a junior clerk. A wasted costs order was made although counsel was in no way personally to blame. He was liable for the actions of a clerk in chambers in the same way as a solicitor was vicariously liable on a wasted costs order for the actions of a clerk in his firm.

In *Re A Barrister (Wasted Costs Order No. 4 of 1993)* (1995) *The Times*, 21 April 1995, the Court of Appeal held that a judge should not impose such a Draconian penalty as a wasted costs order without taking into account the daily demands of practice and the difficulties associated with time estimates.

In *Re a Firm of Solicitors (Wasted Costs Order)* [1999] All ER (D) 728, Q, who was on trial in the Crown Court, was unhappy with his barrister and wished to dispense with her services. Defence counsel suggested that this should be put in writing, and when the court had risen, the experienced solicitor's clerk took a statement from Q to that effect. Whilst the clerk was reading the statement back to Q, the usher brought the jury past them. It was later contended that some of them must have heard what was said, and the jury had to be discharged. The judge made a wasted costs order, which was upheld by the Court of Appeal. The question was whether taking those instructions at a place where he knew the jury was likely to appear and then being oblivious to their appearance constituted negligence on the part of the clerk. In the circumstances, he had been negligent.

In *Re Boodhoo (A Solicitor)* (2007) 1 Cr App R 422, the Court of Appeal held that it was not unreasonable for a solicitor to withdraw from proceedings in circumstances where a client had warned in advance that he would not attend the trial, and no instructions in relation to continuing to act in the client's absence had been obtained.

The reference to 'criminal proceedings' in the Prosecution of Offences Act 1985, s. 19A(1), is wide enough to include proceedings relating to the issue of a witness summons. A local authority attending to answer an application for disclosure of social services files relating to the complainant in a criminal case is a party to criminal proceedings, and can be the beneficiary of a wasted costs order (*Re A Solicitor (Wasted Costs Order)* [1996] 1 FLR 40).

Paragraph VIII.1.8 of the Practice Direction stipulates that a wasted costs order should normally be made regardless of the fact that the client of the legal representative concerned is funded by the Criminal Defence Service. However where the court is minded to disallow substantial costs out of the Criminal Defence Service fund, it may, instead of making a wasted costs order, make observations to the determining authority that work may have been unreasonably done (see para. X.1.1).

Paragraph VIII.2.1 notes that the Administrative Court is governed by a different regime, namely making a wasted costs order under the Supreme Court Act 1981, s. 51(6), and has to comply with the Civil Procedure Rules, r. 48.7 (which contains similar provisions as to giving the legal representative a reasonable opportunity to attend a hearing to give reasons why the court should not make such an order). This paragraph also notes that the Administrative Court can invoke the Civil Procedure Rules, r. 44.14, which enables the court to make an order against a party or his legal representative where it appears to the court that the conduct of a party or his legal representative before or during the proceedings which gave rise to the summary or detailed assessment proceedings was unreasonable or improper.

Awards of Costs against Third Parties

D30.25 The Courts Act 2003, s. 93, added a new s. 19B to the Prosecution of Offences Act 1985, which enables costs to be awarded against third parties where there has been serious misconduct by a third party. See also para. VII.3 of the *Practice Direction (Costs: Criminal Proceedings)* [2004] 2 All ER 1070.

The Costs in Criminal Cases (General) (Amendment) Regulations 2004 (SI 2004 No. 2408) inserted a new part IIB into the Costs in Criminal Cases (General) Regulations 1986 with effect from 18 October 2004 (and applicable only to misconduct that occurred on or after that date). The power to make a third-party costs order is available to magistrates' courts, the Crown Court and the Court of Appeal.

Regulation 3F(1) provides that if (a) there has been serious misconduct (whether or not constituting a contempt of court) by a third party; and (b) the court considers it appropriate, having regard to that misconduct, to make a third-party costs order against him, the court may order the third party to pay all or part of the costs incurred or wasted by any party as a result of that misconduct. Under reg. 3F(2), the court may make a third-party costs order at any time during or after the proceedings, either on the application of any party or of its own initiative. This is qualified by reg. 3F(3), which stipulates that the court may make a third-party costs order during the proceedings only if it decides that there are good reasons to do so, rather than making the order after the proceedings; the parties to the proceedings, and the third party, must be allowed to make representations on the issue of the timing of the order.

Regulation 3F(4) requires the court, before making a third-party costs order, to allow the third party, and any party to the proceedings, to make representations; the court is also empowered to hear evidence.

Under reg. 3G, where a party applies to the court for a third-party costs order or the court decides that it might make a third-party costs order of its own initiative, the third party must receive written notice of the application; this written notice must include details of the alleged misconduct of the third party. If the third party or any other party does not attend the hearing, the court may proceed in his absence if satisfied that he have been duly served with notice of the hearing; if an order is made, it can be set aside if it is later shown that the third party did not receive notice (reg. 3G(8)).

Regulation 3H makes provision for appeals against third-party costs orders. In the case of an order made by a magistrates' court, the appeal lies to the Crown Court; in the case of an order made at first instance by the Crown Court, the appeal lies to the Court of Appeal. The appeal has to be instituted (with written notice to the court that made the order, stating the grounds of appeal) within 21 days of the order being made. This time-limit may be extended where there is good reason (reg. 3H(4)). Under reg. 3H(6), the appeal court may affirm, vary or revoke the order, as it thinks fit.

STATUTES AND REGULATIONS RELATING TO COSTS

Prosecution of Offences Act 1985, ss. 16 to 21 D30.26

PART II COSTS IN CRIMINAL CASES

Award of costs out of central funds

Defence costs

16.—(1) Where—

(a) an information laid before a justice of the peace for any area, charging any person with an offence, is not proceeded with;

(b) a magistrates' court inquiring into an indictable offence as examining justices determines not to commit the accused for trial;

(c) a magistrates' court dealing summarily with an offence dismisses the information;

that court or, in a case falling within paragraph (a) above, a magistrates' court for that area, may make an order in favour of the accused for a payment to be made out of central funds in respect of his costs (a 'defendant's costs order').

(2) Where—

(a) any person is not tried for an offence for which he has been indicted or sent for trial; or

(aa) a notice of transfer is given under a relevant transfer provision but a person in relation to whose case it is given is not tried on a charge to which it relates; or

(b) any person is tried on indictment and acquitted on any count in the indictment;

the Crown Court may make a defendant's costs order in favour of the accused.

(3) Where a person convicted of an offence by a magistrates' court appeals to the Crown Court under section 108 of the Magistrates' Courts Act 1980 (right of appeal against conviction or sentence) and, in consequence of the decision on appeal—

(a) his conviction is set aside; or

(b) a less severe punishment is awarded;

the Crown Court may make a defendant's costs order in favour of the accused.

(4) Where the Court of Appeal—

(a) allows an appeal under part I of the Criminal Appeal Act 1968 against—

(i) conviction;

(ii) a verdict of not guilty by reason of insanity; or

(iii) a finding under of the Criminal Procedure (Insanity) Act 1964 that the appellant is under disability that he did the act or made the omission charged against him; or

(aa) directs under section 8(1B) of the Criminal Appeal Act 1968 the entry of a judgment and verdict of acquittal;

(b) on an appeal under that part against conviction—

(i) substitutes a verdict of guilty of another offence;

(ii) in a case where a special verdict has been found, orders a different conclusion on the effect of that verdict to be recorded; or

(iii) is of the opinion that the case falls within paragraph (a) or (b) of section 6(1) of that Act (cases where the court substitutes a finding of insanity or unfitness to plead);

(c) on an appeal under that part against sentence, exercises its powers under section 11(3) of that Act (powers where the court considers that the appellant should be sentenced differently for an offence for which he was dealt with by the court below);

the court may make a defendant's costs order in favour of the accused; or

(d) allows, to any extent, an appeal under section 16A of that Act (appeal against order made in cases of insanity or unfitness to plead).

(4A) The court may also make a defendant's costs order in favour of the accused on an appeal under section 9(11) of the Criminal Justice Act 1987 (appeals against orders or rulings at preparatory hearings) or section 35(1) of the Criminal Procedure and Investigations Act 1996] (appeals against orders or rulings at preparatory hearings) or under part 9 of the Criminal Justice Act 2003.

(5) Where—

(a) any proceedings in a criminal cause or matter are determined before a Divisional Court of the Queen's Bench Division;

(b) the House of Lords determines an appeal, or application for leave to appeal, from such a Divisional Court in a criminal cause or matter;

(c) the Court of Appeal determines an application for leave to appeal to the House of Lords under part II of the Criminal Appeal Act 1968; or

(d) the House of Lords determines an appeal, or application for leave to appeal, under part II of that Act;

the court may make a defendant's costs order in favour of the accused.

(6) A defendant's costs order shall, subject to the following provisions of this section, be for the payment out of central funds, to the person in whose favour the order is made, of such amount as the court considers reasonably sufficient to compensate him for any expenses properly incurred by him in the proceedings.

(7) Where a court makes a defendant's costs order but is of the opinion that there are circumstances which make it inappropriate that the person in whose favour the order is made should recover the full amount mentioned in subsection (6) above, the court shall—

(a) assess what amount would, in its opinion, be just and reasonable; and

(b) specify that amount in the order.

[(8) Repealed.]

(9) Subject to subsection (7) above, the amount to be paid out of central funds in pursuance of a defendant's costs order shall—

(a) be specified in the order, in any case where the court considers it appropriate for the amount to be so specified and the person in whose favour the order is made agrees the amount; and

(b) in any other case, be determined in accordance with regulations made by the Lord Chancellor for the purposes of this section.

(10) Subsection (6) above shall have effect, in relation to any case falling within subsection (1)(a) or (2)(a) above, as if for the words 'in the proceedings' there were substituted the words 'in or about the defence'.

(11) Where a person ordered to be retried is acquitted at his retrial, the costs which may be ordered to be paid out of central funds under this section shall include—

(a) any costs which, at the original trial, could have been ordered to be so paid under this section if he had been acquitted; and

(b) if no order was made under this section in respect of his expenses on appeal, any sums for the payment of which such an order could have been made.

(12) In subsection 2(aa) 'relevant transfer provision' means—

(a) section 4 of the Criminal Justice Act 1987, or

(b) section 53 of the Criminal Justice Act 1991.

Prosecution costs

17.—(1) Subject to subsection (2) below, the court may—

(a) in any proceedings in respect of an indictable offence; and

(b) in any proceedings before a Divisional Court of the Queen's Bench Division or the House of Lords in respect of a summary offence;

order the payment out of central funds of such amount as the court considers reasonably sufficient to compensate the prosecutor for any expenses properly incurred by him in the proceedings.

(2) No order under this section may be made in favour of—

(a) a public authority; or

(b) a person acting—

(i) on behalf of a public authority; or

(ii) in his capacity as an official appointed by such an authority.

(3) Where a court makes an order under this section but is of the opinion that there are circumstances which make it inappropriate that the prosecution should recover the full amount mentioned in subsection (1) above, the court shall—

(a) assess what amount would, in its opinion, be just and reasonable; and

(b) specify that amount in the order.

(4) Subject to subsection (3) above, the amount to be paid out of central funds in pursuance of an order under this section shall—

(a) be specified in the order, in any case where the court considers it appropriate for the amount to be so specified and the prosecutor agrees the amount; and

(b) in any other case, be determined in accordance with regulations made by the Lord Chancellor for the purposes of this section.

(5) Where the conduct of proceedings to which subsection (1) above applies is taken over by the Crown Prosecution Service, that subsection shall have effect as if it referred to the prosecutor who had the conduct of the proceedings before the intervention of the Service and to expenses incurred by him up to the time of intervention.

(6) In this section 'public authority' means—

(a) a police force within the meaning of section 3 of this Act;

(b) the Crown Prosecution Service or any other government department;

(c) a local authority or other authority or body constituted for purposes of—

(i) the public service or of local government; or

(ii) carrying on under national ownership any industry or undertaking or part of an industry or undertaking; or

(d) any other authority or body whose members are appointed by Her Majesty or by any Minister of the Crown or government department or whose revenue consist wholly or mainly of money provided by Parliament.

Award of costs against accused

18.—(1) Where—

(a) any person is convicted of an offence before a magistrates' court;

(b) the Crown Court dismisses an appeal against such a conviction or against the sentence imposed on that conviction; or

(c) any person is convicted of an offence before the Crown Court;

the court may make such order as to the costs to be paid by the accused to the prosecutor as it considers just and reasonable.

(2) Where the Court of Appeal dismisses—
   (a) an appeal or application for leave to appeal under part I of the Criminal Appeal Act 1968; or
   (b) an application by the accused for leave to appeal to the House of Lords under part II of that Act; or
   (c) an appeal or application for leave to appeal under section 9(11) of the Criminal Justice Act 1987;

   it may make such order as to the costs to be paid by the accused, to such person as may be named in the order, as it considers just and reasonable.

(2A) Where the Court of Appeal reverses or varies a ruling on an appeal under Part 9 of the Criminal Justice Act 2003, it may make such order as to the costs to be paid by the accused, to such person as may be named in the order, as it considers just and reasonable.

(3) The amount to be paid by the accused in pursuance of an order under this section shall be specified in the order.

(4) Where any person is convicted of an offence before a magistrates' court and—
   (a) under the conviction the court orders payment of any sum as a fine, penalty, forfeiture or compensation; and
   (b) the sum so ordered to be paid does not exceed £5;

   the court shall not order the accused to pay any costs under this section unless in the particular circumstances of the case it considers it right to do so.

(5) Where any person under the age of 18 is convicted of an offence before a magistrates' court, the amount of any costs ordered to be paid by the accused under this section shall not exceed the amount of any fine imposed on him.

(6) Costs ordered to be paid under subsection (2) or (2A) above may include the reasonable cost of any transcript of a record of proceedings made in accordance with rules of court made for the purposes of section 32 of the Act of 1968.

Other awards

Provision for orders as to costs in other circumstances

19.—(1) The Lord Chancellor may by regulations make provision empowering magistrates' courts, the Crown Court and the Court of Appeal, in any case where the court is satisfied that one party to criminal proceedings has incurred costs as a result of an unnecessary or improper act or omission by, or on behalf of, another party to the proceedings, to make an order as to the payment of those costs.

(2) Regulations made under subsection (1) above may, in particular—
   (a) allow the making of such an order at any time during the proceedings;
   (b) make provision as to the account to be taken, in making such an order, of any other order as to costs which has been made in respect of the proceedings or any grant of representation funded by the Legal Services Commission as part of the Criminal Defence Service; of representation for the purposes of the proceedings which has been made under the Legal Aid Act 1988;
   (c) make provision as to the account to be taken of any such order in the making of any other order as to costs in respect of the proceedings; and
   (d) contain provisions similar to those in section 18(4) and (5) of this Act.

(3) The Lord Chancellor may by regulations make provision for the payment out of central funds, in such circumstances and in relation to such criminal proceedings as may be specified, of such sums as appear to the court to be reasonably necessary—
   (a) to compensate any witness in the proceedings, and any other person who in the opinion of the court necessarily attends for the purpose of proceedings otherwise than to give evidence, for the expense, trouble or loss of time properly incurred in or incidental to his attendance;
   (b) to cover the proper expenses of an interpreter who is required because of the accused's lack of English;
   (c) to compensate a duly qualified medical practitioner who—
      (i) makes a report otherwise than in writing for the purpose of section 11 of the Powers of Criminal Courts (Sentencing) Act 2000 (remand for medical examination); or

(ii) makes a written report to a court in pursuance of a request to which section 32(2) of the Criminal Justice Act 1967 (report by medical practitioner on medical condition of offender) applies;

for the expenses properly incurred in or incidental to his reporting to the court;

(d) to cover the proper fee or costs of a person appointed by the Crown Court under section 4A of the Criminal Procedure (Insanity) Act 1964 to put the case for the defence;

(e) to cover the proper fee or costs of a legal representative appointed under section 38(4) of the Youth Justice and Criminal Evidence Act 1999 (defence representation for purposes of cross-examination) and any expenses properly incurred in providing such a person with evidence or other material in connection with his appointment.

(3A) In subsection (3)(a) above 'attendance' means attendance at the court or elsewhere.

(4) The Court of Appeal may order the payment out of central funds of such sums as appear to it to be reasonably sufficient to compensate an appellant who is not in custody and who appears before it on, or in connection with, his appeal under part I of the Criminal Appeal Act 1968.

(5) The Lord Chancellor may by regulations provide that any provision made by or under this part which would not otherwise apply in relation to any category of proceedings in which an offender is before a magistrates' court or the Crown Court shall apply in relation to proceedings of that category, subject to any specified modifications.

19A.—(1) In any criminal proceedings—

(a) the Court of Appeal;

(b) the Crown Court; or

(c) a magistrates' court,

may disallow, or (as the case may be) order the legal or other representative concerned to meet, the whole of any wasted costs or such part of them as may be determined in accordance with regulations.

(2) Regulations shall provide that a legal or other representative against whom action is taken by a magistrates' court under subsection (1) may appeal to the Crown Court and that a legal or other representative against whom action is taken by the Crown Court under subsection (1) may appeal to the Court of Appeal.

(3) In this section—

'legal or other representative', in relation to any proceedings, means a person who is exercising a right of audience, or a right to conduct litigation, on behalf of any party to the proceedings;

'regulations' means regulations made by the Lord Chancellor; and

'wasted costs' means any costs incurred by a party—

(a) as a result of any improper, unreasonable or negligent act or omission on the part of any representative or any employee of a representative; or

(b) which, in the light of any such act or omission occurring after they were incurred, the court considers it is unreasonable to expect that party to pay.

19B.—(1) The Lord Chancellor may by regulations make provision empowering magistrates' courts, the Crown Court and the Court of Appeal to make a third party costs order if the condition in subsection (3) is satisfied.

(2) A 'third party costs order' is an order as to the payment of costs incurred by a party to criminal proceedings by a person who is not a party to those proceedings ('the third party').

(3) The condition is that—

(a) there has been serious misconduct (whether or not constituting a contempt of court) by the third party, and

(b) the court considers it appropriate, having regard to that misconduct, to make a third party costs order against him.

(4) Regulations made under this section may, in particular—

(a) specify types of misconduct in respect of which a third party costs order may not be made;

(b) allow the making of a third party costs order at any time;

(c) make provision for any other order as to costs which has been made in respect of the proceedings to be varied on, or taken account of in, the making of a third party costs order;

(d) make provision for account to be taken of any third party costs order in the making of any other order as to costs in respect of the proceedings.

(5) Regulations made under this section in relation to magistrates' courts must provide that the third party may appeal to the Crown Court against a third party costs order made by a magistrates' court.

(6) Regulations made under this section in relation to the Crown Court must provide that the third party may appeal to the Court of Appeal against a third party costs order made by the Crown Court.

[**20.** The Lord Chancellor may make regulations for carrying this part of the Act into effect.]

Interpretation, etc.

21.—(1) In this Part—

'accused' and 'appellant', in a case where section 44A of the Criminal Appeal Act 1968 (death of convicted person) applies, include the person approved under that section;

'defendant's costs order' has the meaning given in section 16 of this Act;

'legally assisted person', in relation to any proceedings, means a person to whom a right to representation funded by the Legal Services Commission as part of the Criminal Defence Service has been granted for the purposes of the proceedings;

'proceedings' includes—

(a) proceedings in any court below; and

(b) in relation to the determination of an appeal by any court, any application made to that court for leave to bring the appeal; and

'witness' means any person properly attending to give evidence, whether or not he gives evidence or is called at the instance of one of the parties or of the court, but does not include a person attending as a witness to character only unless the court has certified that the interests of justice required his attendance.

(2) Except as provided by or under this part no costs shall be allowed on the hearing or determination of, or of any proceedings preliminary or incidental to, an appeal to the Court of Appeal under part I of the Criminal Appeal Act 1968.

(3) Subject to rules of court made under section 53(1) of the Supreme Court Act 1981 (power by rules to distribute business of Court of Appeal between its civil and criminal divisions), the jurisdiction of the Court of Appeal under this part, or under regulations made under this part, shall be exercised by the Criminal Division of that court; and references in this part to the Court of Appeal shall be construed as references to that division.

(4) For the purposes of sections 16 and 17 of this Act, the costs of any party to proceedings shall be taken to include the expense of compensating any witness for the expenses, trouble or loss of time properly incurred in or incidental to his attendance.

(4A) Where one party to any proceedings is a legally assisted person then—

(a) for the purposes of sections 16 and 17 of this Act, his costs shall be taken not to include the cost of representation funded for him by the Legal Services Commission as part of the Criminal Defence Service; and

(b) for the purposes of sections 18 to 19B of this Act, his costs shall be taken to include the cost of representation funded for him by the Legal Services Commission as part of the Criminal Defence Service.

(5) Where, in any proceedings in a criminal cause or matter or in either of the cases mentioned in subsection (6) below, an interpreter is required because of the accused's lack of English, the expenses properly incurred on his employment shall not be treated as costs of any party to the proceedings.

(6) The cases are—

(a) where an information charging the accused with an offence is laid before a justice of the peace for any area but not proceeded with and the expenses are incurred on the employment of the interpreter for the proceedings on the information; and

(b) where the accused is sent for trial but not tried and the expenses are incurred on the employment of the interpreter for the proceedings in the Crown Court.

Costs in Criminal Cases (General) Regulations 1986 (SI 1986 No. 1335)

Part I Preliminary

1 and 2 Concern citation, commencement and revocations.

Part II Costs Unnecessarily or Improperly Incurred

Unnecessary or improper acts and omissions

3.—(1) Subject to the provisions of this regulation, where at any time during criminal proceedings—

(a) a magistrates' court,
(b) the Crown Court, or
(c) the Court of Appeal

is satisfied that costs have been incurred in respect of the proceedings by one of the parties as a result of an unnecessary or improper act or omission by, or on behalf of, another party to the proceedings, the court may, after hearing the parties, order that all or part of the costs so incurred by that party shall be paid to him by the other party.

(2) Before making an order under paragraph (1), the court shall take into account any other order as to costs (including any legal aid order) which has been made in respect of the proceedings.

(3) An order made under paragraph (1) shall specify the amount of costs to be paid in pursuance of the order.

(4) Where an order under paragraph (1) has been made, the court may take that order into account when making any other order as to costs in respect of the proceedings.

(5) No order under paragraph (1) shall be made by a magistrates' court which requires a person under the age of 17 who has been convicted of an offence to pay an amount by way of costs which exceeds the amount of any fine imposed on him.

Part IIA Wasted Costs Orders

Application and definitions

3A.— This part of these regulations applies to action taken by a court under section 19A of the Act and in this part of these regulations:—

'wasted costs order' means any action taken by a court under section 19A of the Act; and

'interested party' means the party benefiting from the wasted costs order and, where he was receiving services funded for him as part of the Criminal Defence Service, or an order for the payment of costs out of central funds was made in his favour, shall include the authority responsible for determining costs payable in respect of work done under the representation order or out of central funds as the case may be.

General

3B.—(1) A wasted costs order may provide for the whole or any part of the wasted costs to be disallowed or ordered to be paid and the court shall specify the amount of such costs.

(2) Before making a wasted costs order the court shall allow the legal or other representative and any party to the proceedings to make representations.

(3) When making a wasted costs order the court may take into account any other order as to costs in respect of the proceedings and may take the wasted costs order into account when making any other such order.

(4) Where a wasted costs order has been made the court shall notify any interested party of the order and the amount disallowed or ordered to be paid.

Appeals

3C.—(1) A legal or other representative against whom the wasted costs order is made may appeal—

(a) in the case of an order made by a magistrates' court, to the Crown Court, and
(b) in the case of an order made at first instance by the Crown Court, to the Court of Appeal.

(2) Subject to paragraph (4), an appeal shall be instituted within 21 days of the wasted costs order being made by the appellant's giving notice in writing to the court which made the order, stating the grounds of appeal.

(3) The appellant shall serve a copy of the notice of appeal and grounds, including any application for an extension of time in which to appeal, on any interested party.

(4) The time limit within which an appeal may be instituted may, for good reason, be extended before or after it expires—

(a) in the case of an appeal to the Crown Court, by a judge of that court;
(b) in the case of an appeal to the Court of Appeal, by a judge of the High Court or Court of Appeal or by the Registrar of Criminal Appeals,

and in each case the court to which the appeal is made shall give notice of the extension to the appellant, the court which made the wasted costs order and any interested party.

(5) The court shall give notice of the hearing date to the appellant, the court which made the wasted costs order and any interested party and shall allow the interested party to make representations which may be made orally or in writing.

(6) The court may affirm, vary or revoke the order as it thinks fit and shall notify its decision to the appellant, any interested party and the court which made the order.

Recovery of sums due under a wasted costs order

3D.—Where the person required to make a payment in respect of sums due under a wasted costs order fails to do so, the payment may be recovered summarily as a sum adjudged to be paid as a civil debt by order of a magistrates' court by the party benefiting from the order, save that where he was receiving services funded for him as part of the Criminal Defence Service or an order for the payment of costs out of central funds was made in his favour, the power to recover shall be exercisable by the Lord Chancellor.

PART IIB THIRD PARTY COST ORDERS

Application and definitions

3E.—(1) This Part of these Regulations applies where there are, or have been criminal proceedings in a magistrates' court, the Crown Court or the Court of Appeal.

(2) In this Part of these Regulations—

'court' means the court in which the criminal proceedings are taking, or took, place;

'interested party' means the party benefiting from the third party costs order and, where he was receiving services funded for him as part of the Criminal Defence Service, shall include the authority responsible for determining costs payable in respect of work done under the representation order or out of central funds as the case may be;

'party' means a party to the criminal proceedings;

'third party' means a person who is not a party;

'third party costs order' means an order as to the payment, by a third party, of costs incurred by a party in accordance with regulation 3F.

General

3F.—(1) If—

(a) there has been serious misconduct (whether or not constituting a contempt of court) by a third party; and

(b) the court considers it appropriate, having regard to that misconduct, to make a third party costs order against him

the court may order the third party to pay all or part of the costs incurred or wasted by any party as a result of the misconduct.

(2) The court may make a third party costs order—

(a) subject to paragraph (3), at any time during or after the criminal proceedings; and

(b) on the application of any party or of its own initiative (but not otherwise).

(3) The court shall make a third party costs order during the proceedings only if it decides that there are good reasons to do so, rather than making the order after the proceedings, and it shall notify the parties and the third party of those reasons and allow any of them to make representations.

(4) Before making a third party costs order the court shall allow the third party and any party to make representations and may hear evidence.

(5) When making a third party costs order the court may vary or take into account any other order as to costs in respect of the criminal proceedings and may take the third party costs order into account when making any other order as to costs in respect of the criminal proceedings.

(6) A third party costs order shall specify the amount of costs to be paid in pursuance of the order.

(7) When a third party costs order has been made the court shall notify the third party and any interested party of the order and the amount ordered to be paid.

Procedure for third party costs orders

3G.—(1) This regulation applies where a party ('the applicant') applies to the court for a third party costs order or the court decides that it might make a third party costs order of its own initiative.

(2) In this regulation—

'appropriate officer' means—

(a) in relation to a magistrates' court, a designated officer (as defined in section 37(1) of the Courts Act 2003);

(b) in relation to the Crown Court, an officer appointed by the Lord Chancellor; and

(c) in relation to the Court of Appeal, the Registrar of Criminal Appeals;

'serve' means serve in accordance with rules of court.

(3) An application for a third party costs order shall be in writing and shall contain—

(a) the name and address of the applicant;

(b) the names and addresses of the other parties;

(c) the name and address of the third party against whom the order is sought;

(d) the date of the end of the criminal proceedings;

(e) a summary of the facts upon which the applicant intends to rely in making the application, including details of the alleged misconduct of the third party.

(4) The application shall be sent to the appropriate officer and, upon receiving it, the appropriate officer shall serve copies of it on the third party and to the other parties.

(5) Where the court decides that it might make a third party costs order of its own initiative the appropriate officer shall serve notice in writing accordingly on the third party and the parties.

(6) At the same time as serving notice under paragraph (5) the appropriate officer shall serve a summary of the reasons why the court might make a third party costs order, including details of the alleged misconduct of the third party.

(7) When the appropriate officer serves copies of an application under paragraph (4) or serves notice under paragraph (5) he shall at the same time serve notice on the parties and the third party of the time and place fixed for the hearing.

(8) At the time notified the court may proceed in the absence of the third party and of any party if it is satisfied that they have been duly served with the notice given under paragraph (7) and the copy of the application or (as the case may be) the notices given under paragraphs (5) and (6), but the court may set aside any third party costs order if it is later shown that the third party did not receive them.

Appeals

3H.—(1) A third party against whom a third party costs order is made may appeal—

(a) in the case of an order made by a magistrates' court, to the Crown Court; and

(b) in the case of an order made at first instance by the Crown Court, to the Court of Appeal.

(2) Subject to paragraph (4), an appeal shall be instituted within 21 days of the third party costs order being made by the appellant giving notice in writing to the court which made the order, stating the grounds of appeal.

(3) The appellant shall serve a copy of the notice of appeal and grounds, including any application for extension of time in which to appeal, on any interested party.

(4) The time limit within which an appeal may be instituted may, for good reason, be extended beforc or after it expires—

(a) in the case of an appeal to the Crown Court, by a judge of that court;

(b) in the case of an appeal to the Court of Appeal, by a judge of the High Court or Court of Appeal, or by the Registrar of Criminal Appeals,

and in each case the court to which the appeal is made ('the appeal court') shall give notice of the extension to the appellant, the court which made the third party costs order and any interested party.

(5) The appeal court shall give notice of the hearing date to the appellant, the court which made the third party costs order and any interested party and shall allow the interested party to make representations which may be made orally or in writing.

(6) The appeal court may affirm, vary or revoke the order as it thinks fit and shall notify its decision to the appellant, any interested party and the court which made the order.

Recovery of sums due under a third party costs order

3I. Where the person required to make a payment in respect of sums due under a third party costs order fails to do so, the payment may be recovered summarily as a sum adjudged to be paid as a civil debt by order of a magistrates' court by the party benefiting from the order, save that where he was receiving services funded for him as part of the Criminal Defence Service or an order for the payment of costs out of central funds was made in his favour, the power to recover shall be exercisable by the Lord Chancellor.

PART III COSTS OUT OF CENTRAL FUNDS

[4 to 13 Prescribe the procedure to be followed by a person in whose favour an order for costs out of central funds has been made; define the 'appropriate authority' to whom the claim for costs should be submitted; prescribe the manner in which the appropriate authority should determine and authorise payment of costs, and provide for redetermination of the costs or an appeal to the taxing master and ultimately the High Court where the applicant for costs is dissatisfied with the appropriate authority's decision.]

PART IIIA FEES OF COURT APPOINTEES

[**13A** to **13C** Provide for modifications of the regulations to allow for payment of court appointees, acting under the Criminal Procedure (Insanity) Act 1964, s. 4A, or the YJCEA 1999, s. 38.]

PART IV MISCELLANEOUS APPLICATIONS OF THE ACT

Application of sections 16, 17 and 18 of the Act

14.—(1) Sections 17 and 18 of the Act [orders for private prosecutors' costs out of central funds and orders that accused pay prosecution costs] shall apply to proceedings in the Crown Court in respect of a person committed by a magistrates' court to that Court—

(a) with a view to his being sentenced for an indictable offence in accordance with [the PCC(S)A 2000, ss. 3 and 4]; or

(b) with a view to his being sentenced by the Crown Court under section 6(6) or 9(3) of the Bail Act 1976 [committal where magistrates consider that an offence of absconding is too serious to be punished adequately by them etc.]; or

(c) with a view to the making of a hospital order with an order restricting his discharge under part III of the Mental Health Act 1983,

as they apply where a person is convicted in proceedings before the Crown Court.

[(2) Section 18 of the Act to apply to certain committals and appeals under the Vagrancy Act 1824 — incorrigible rogues etc.]

[(3) Section 18 to apply to proceedings in either a magistrates' court or the Crown Court when the proceedings concern (a) breach of conditional discharge, community service order or probation order; (b) breach of a suspended sentence or a suspended sentence supervision order; or (c) breach of an attendance centre order.]

PART V ALLOWANCES TO WITNESSES

Definitions

15. In this part of these regulations—

'expenses' include compensation to a witness for his trouble or loss of time and out of pocket expenses;

'proceedings in a criminal cause or matter' includes any case in which—

(a) an information charging the accused with an offence is laid before a justice of the peace for any area but not proceeded with; or

(b) the accused is committed for trial but not tried;

'professional witness' means a witness practising as a member of the legal or medical profession or as a dentist, veterinary surgeon or accountant who attends to give professional evidence as to matters of fact;

'private prosecutor' means any person in whose favour an order for the payment of costs out of central funds could be made under section 17 of the Act;

'the relevant amount' has the meaning assigned to it by regulation 17;

'witness' means any person properly attending to give evidence, whether or not he gives evidence or is called at the instance of one of the parties or of the court, but does not include—

(a) a person attending as a witness to character only unless the court has certified that the interests of justice required his attendance;

(b) a member of a police force attending court in his capacity as such;

(c) a full-time officer of an institution to which the Prison Act 1952 applies attending court in his capacity as such; or

(d) a prisoner in respect of any occasion on which he is conveyed to court in custody.

General

16.—(1) Where, in any proceedings in a criminal cause or matter in a magistrates' court, the Crown Court, a Divisional Court of the Queen's Bench Division, the Court of Appeal or the House of Lords—

(a) a witness attends at the instance of the accused, a private prosecutor or the court; or
(b) an interpreter is required because of the accused's lack of English; or
(c) a medical practitioner makes a report otherwise than in writing,

the expenses properly incurred by that witness, interpreter or medical practitioner shall be allowed out of central funds in accordance with this part of these regulations, unless the court directs that the expenses are not to be allowed out of central funds.

(2) Subject to paragraph (3), any entitlement to an allowance under this part of these regulations shall be the same whether the witness, interpreter or medical practitioner attends on the same day in one case or more than one case.

(3) Paragraph (2) shall not apply to allowances under regulation 25.

Determination of rates or scales of allowances payable out of central funds

17.—(1) The Lord Chancellor shall, with the consent of the Treasury, determine the rates or scales of allowances payable out of central funds to witnesses, interpreters or medical practitioners and a reference in this part of these regulations to an allowance not exceeding the relevant amount means an amount calculated in accordance with the rates or scales so determined.

[**18.**—(1) Witnesses other than professional or expert witnesses may be allowed (a) a loss allowance not exceeding the relevant amount in respect of (i) expenditure to which he would not otherwise have been subject or (ii) any loss of earnings or of State benefit, and (b) a subsistence allowance not exceeding the relevant amount (para. (1)). This also applies to persons who necessarily attend for the purposes of the proceedings but not to give evidence (para. (2)). It does not apply to police officers, prison officers or prisoners conveyed to court in custody (para. (3)).]

Professional witnesses

[**19.** A professional witness may be allowed a professional witness allowance not exceeding the relevant amount.]

Expert witnesses etc.

20.—(1) The court may make an allowance in respect of an expert witness for attending to give expert evidence and for work in connection with its preparation of such an amount as it may consider reasonable having regard to the nature and difficulty of the case and the work necessarily involved.

(2) Paragraph (1) shall apply, with the necessary modifications, to—

(a) an interpreter, or
(b) a medical practitioner who makes a report otherwise than in writing for the purpose of [the PCC(S)A 2000, s. 11],

as it applies to an expert witness.

[**21** and **22** Deal respectively with night allowances for professional and expert witnesses, and allowances for seamen detained on shore.]

Prosecutors and defendants

23. A person in whose favour an order is made under section 16, 17 or 19(4) of the Act may be allowed the same subsistence allowance and travelling expenses as if he attended as a witness other than a professional or expert witness.

[**24.** Detailed provisions as to the travelling expenses a witness may be allowed.]

[**25.** Concerns payment for medical reports requested by the court under the PCC(S) A 2000, s. 11, or with a view to making a hospital order or a probation order with a condition of treatment.]

Part VI Recovery of Sums Paid out of the Legal Aid Fund or Central Funds

Directions by the Lord Chancellor

26.—(1) The Lord Chancellor shall recover in accordance with directions given by him any sums paid as part of the Criminal Defence Service or central funds where a costs order has been made against a person in favour of—

(a) a person receiving services funded for him as part of the Criminal Defence Service, or

(b) a person in whose favour an order for the payment of costs out of central funds has been made.

(2) [Nature of directions.]

(3) In this regulation and regulation 27 'costs order' shall include a wasted costs order as defined by regulation 3A, or a third party costs order as defined by regulation 3E, of these Regulations.

Section D31 Extradition

Extradition is the process by which, at the request of another jurisdiction, a person accused or convicted of an offence is sent by the UK to that jurisdiction, or where a person is sent to the UK from another jurisdiction, at the request of the UK, to stand trial or serve a custodial sentence. Extradition is governed by the Extradition Act 2003 (in force from 1 January 2004), which has been amended by the Extradition Act 2003 (Multiple Offences) Order 2003 (SI 2003 No. 3150) and the Police and Justice Act 2006, sch. 13 (in force from 15 January 2007, except paras. 4, 5 and 6). The Act applies to all requests for extradition received by the relevant authority in the UK on or after 1 January 2004. Any request for extradition received before that date is governed by the previous extradition regime, namely the Extradition Act 1989 or the Backing of Warrants (Republic of Ireland) Act 1965. The Extradition Act 2003 reformed the law of extradition and was intended to provide a more effective framework to extradition. This section provides a general introduction to the framework of extradition and procedure. **D31.1**

Under the Extradition Act 2003, a foreign territory is designated as a part 1 or part 2 territory by order made by the Secretary of State under powers conferred on him by ss. 1 and 69. References in the Act to a category 1 territory are to the territories designated for the purposes of part 1 and references to a category 2 territory are to the territories designated for the purposes of part 2. Parts 1 and 2 govern requests for extradition made by a foreign jurisdiction. Part 3 governs requests made by the UK.

PART 1 OF THE ACT

Part 1 of the Extradition Act 2003 (ss. 1 to 68) adopts the framework decision of the Council of the European Union made on 13 June 2002 on the European arrest warrant and the surrender procedures between Member States (2002/584/JHA). It applies to any territory which has been designated as a part 1 territory under s. 1 and is signatory to the framework decision. The framework decision introduced the European arrest warrant and was intended to abolish formal extradition procedures between Member States. The format and content of the European arrest warrant is set out in the annex to the framework decision. Part 1 makes no reference to the European arrest warrant. Instead, what is required is a part 1 warrant. **D31.2**

A Part 1 Warrant

Under s. 2(1), a part 1 warrant must be received by the authority designated for the purposes of part 1 by order made by the Secretary of State. The Serious Organised Crime Agency replaced the National Criminal Intelligence Service as the designated authority on 1 April 2006. The designated authority may issue a certificate certifying that the authority which issued the part 1 warrant has the function of issuing arrest warrants in the category 1 territory (s. 2(7) and (8)). **D31.3**

A part 1 warrant is an arrest warrant issued by a judicial authority of a category 1 territory which contains the information required by s. 2. A warrant which does not satisfy the requirements of s. 2 is not a part 1 warrant within the meaning of s. 2 (see, for example, *The Office of the King's Prosecutor, Brussels v Armas* [2006] 2 AC 1 per Lord Hope at [42]). Whether a warrant satisfies s. 2 may be the subject of legal argument. One of the recurring difficulties faced has been removed by the recent amendments to the 2003 Act introduced by the Police and Justice Act 2006, sch. 13. The difficulty was that, where extradition was sought of a person who had been convicted of an offence in a category 1 territory, s. 2 of the 2003 Act required the part 1 warrant to contain a statement that the person in respect of whom the warrant was issued is alleged to be unlawfully at large after conviction of an offence specified in the warrant. This requirement was removed and replaced with the simpler requirement that the part 1 warrant contains the statement that the person has been convicted of an offence. The amended provision is in keeping with the framework decision which does not contain any requirement for the Member State to declare that the person sought is unlawfully at large. The House of Lords in *Moutez Almallah Dabas v Spain* [2007] UKHL 6 (see, for example, Lord Bingham at [4]) emphasised that part 1 of the 2003 Act must be read in the context of the Council framework decision which was conceived and adopted as a ground-breaking measure intended to simplify and expedite procedures for the surrender, between Member States, of those accused of crimes committed in other Member States or required to be sentenced or serve sentences for such crimes following convictions in other Member States. He added (at [5]) that no Member State may seek to frustrate or impede the achievement of the purpose of the Decision.

A person may be arrested after a part 1 warrant has been certified (arrest under part 1 warrant) or where a part 1 warrant has been or will be issued (provisional arrest). Once arrested, the person must be brought before the appropriate judge (defined in s. 67) as soon as practicable (where arrested under a certified part 1 warrant) or within 48 hours (where provisionally arrested). He must be given a copy of the warrant as soon as practicable after arrest (ss. 3, 4, 5 and 6) and may apply to the judge to be discharged if he has not been brought before the appropriate judge in compliance with the Act or has not been provided with a copy of the warrant.

The Initial Hearing

D31.4 Once before the appropriate judge, there must be an initial hearing (ss. 7 and 8). At the hearing the judge must decide whether, on a balance of probabilities, the person brought before him is the person in respect of whom the warrant was issued. The judge has the power to adjourn the proceedings (s. 7(6), (9) and (10)). If not satisfied, the judge must order the person's discharge; otherwise he must proceed under s. 8.

Section 8 requires the judge to fix a date on which the extradition hearing is to begin, to inform the person of the contents of the part 1 warrant and to give the person the required information about consent. Consent involves the irrevocable waiver of the protections provided by part 1 (and part 2) of the Act (e.g., speciality which does not permit the requesting territory to try the person whose return has been sought for offences not specified in the request unless certain conditions are satisfied). Section 8 also requires the judge to remand the person in custody or on bail although he may later grant bail to a person he has remanded in custody.

The dated fixed for the extradition hearing must not be later than 21 days starting with the date of arrest (whether under a part 1 warrant or provisional arrest) (s. 8(4)). Before the date fixed for the extradition hearing, an application may be made to the judge for a later date. Section 8(5) has been interpreted as prohibiting an application for the extradition hearing to be adjourned *on the day* of the hearing itself. If no application is made for the extradition hearing to take place on a later date and the extradition hearing does not begin on or before that date, the person arrested may apply to be discharged and the judge must discharge him unless reasonable cause is shown for the delay. The judge must order his discharge on the first occasion after the date fixed for the hearing when the person appears or is brought before the judge unless reasonable cause is shown for the delay even if there is no application made on his behalf.

The Extradition Hearing

At the extradition hearing the judge has the same powers (as nearly as may be) as a magistrates' court would have if the proceedings were the summary trial of an information against the person (s. 9(1)). Once started, the extradition hearing may be adjourned. Part 1 sets out a number of questions to be decided by the judge at the hearing and in a sequential order. However, in practice, the judge may wish to hear submissions on all issues and to provide a single judgment dealing with all matters at the end of the hearing. After each decision, the judge must either discharge the person or proceed under the next relevant provision. The first question is whether the offence specified in the part 1 warrant is an extradition offence (see D31.9). If the judge is satisfied that the offence is an extradition offence, he must proceed under s. 11 and decide whether there are any bars to extradition. These are set out in s. 11 and exhaustively defined in ss. 12 to 19A. The case law decided under the Extradition Act 1989 remains relevant to proceedings under the 2003 Act and in particular to the bars to extradition. The bars to extradition are: D31.5

(a) the rule against double jeopardy;
(b) extraneous considerations;
(c) the passage of time;
(d) the person's age;
(e) hostage-taking considerations;
(f) speciality;
(g) the person's earlier extradition to the United Kingdom from another territory;
(h) the person's earlier extradition to the United Kingdom from a non-category 1 territory.
(i) the person's earlier transfer to the United Kingdom by the International Criminal Court.

If the judge is satisfied that there are no bars to extradition and the person has not been convicted of the extradition offence, the judge must proceed under s. 21. Where a person has been convicted of the extradition offence, the judge must proceed under s. 20.

Extradition Act 2003, s. 20

(1) If the judge is required to proceed under this section (by virtue of section 11) he must decide whether the person was convicted in his presence.
(2) If the judge decides the question in subsection (1) in the affirmative he must proceed under section 21.
(3) If the judge decides that question in the negative he must decide whether the person deliberately absented himself from his trial.
(4) If the judge decides the question in subsection (3) in the affirmative he must proceed under section 21.
(5) If the judge decides that question in the negative he must decide whether the person would be entitled to a retrial or (on appeal) to a review amounting to a retrial.
(6) If the judge decides the question in subsection (5) in the affirmative he must proceed under section 21.
(7) If the judge decides that question in the negative he must order the person's discharge.
(8) The judge must not decide the question in subsection (5) in the affirmative unless, in any proceedings that it is alleged would constitute a retrial or a review amounting to a retrial, the person would have these rights—
 (a) the right to defend himself in person or through legal assistance of his own choosing or, if he had not sufficient means to pay for legal assistance, to be given it free when the interests of justice so required;
 (b) the right to examine or have examined witnesses against him and to obtain the attendance and examination of witnesses on his behalf under the same conditions as witnesses against him.

Finally, the judge must decide under s. 21 whether the person's extradition would be compatible with his rights under the ECHR within the meaning of the HRA 1998. If it is compatible, the judge must order the person's extradition to the category 1 territory (s. 21(3)). Once such an order is made and no notice of appeal is given before the end of the permitted period (seven days starting with the day on which the order is made: s. 26(4)), the person must be extradited to the category 1 territory before the end of the required period (s. 35(3)). The required period is (a) 10 days starting with the first day after the period permitted under s. 26 for giving notice of appeal against the judge's order, or (b) if the judge and the authority which issued the part 1 warrant agree a later date, 10 days starting with the later date (s. 35(4)). A person may apply to be discharged if he is not extradited before the end of the required period.

PART 2 OF THE ACT

D31.6 Part 2 of the Extradition Act 2003 (ss. 69 to 141) applies to the territories designated for the purposes of part 2. Part 2 was intended to reduce the complexity of proceedings and to simplify the rules governing authentication of foreign documents. (The authentication of documents is dealt with in s. 202.) Territories designated as part 2 territories are divided into two groups: the territories which must provide a prima facie case and those which are not required to do so. Article 3 of the Extradition Act 2003 (Designation of Part 2 Territories) Order 2003 (SI 2003 No. 3334) designates certain category 2 territories for the purposes of ss. 71(4), 73(5), 84(7) and 86(7), i.e. as territories which do not have to make a prima facie case.

The procedure under part 2 requires the involvement of the Secretary of State, who may issue a certificate under s. 70 (certifying that the request has been made in the approved way) if he receives a valid request for the extradition to a category 2 territory of a person who is in the UK (s. 70(1)). Section 2 provides for the limited circumstances in which the Secretary of State may refuse to issue a certificate. A request is valid if:

(a) it contains a statement that:
  - (i) the person sought is accused in the category 2 territory of the commission of an offence specified in the request and the request is made with a view to his arrest and extradition to the category 2 territory for the purpose of being prosecuted for the offence, or
  - (ii) the person has been convicted of an offence specified in the request by a court in the category 2 territory and the request is made with a view to his arrest and extradition to the category 2 territory for the purpose of being sentenced for the offence or of serving a sentence of imprisonment or another form of detention imposed in respect of the offence (s. 70(3), (4) and (4A)); and

(b) it is made in the approved way.

A request is made in the approved way, in most instances, if it is made by an authority of the territory which the Secretary of State believes has the function of making requests for extradition in that territory, or by a person recognised by the Secretary of State as a diplomatic or consular representative of the territory (s. 70(5), (6) and (7)). Once the Secretary of State has issued a certificate (in which he must identify the Order by which the territory is designated as a category 2 territory) he must send the request and the certificate to the appropriate judge (s. 70(9)). The 'appropriate judge' is a District Judge (magistrates' courts) designated for the purposes of parts 1 and 2 by the Lord Chancellor.

Arrest under Part 2

D31.7 As in part 1, a person may be the subject of a provisional arrest or an arrest after the Secretary of State has complied with s. 70(9). If provisionally arrested and brought before the judge, the judge must discharge the person if the documents referred to in s. 70(9) are not received by him within the required period, which is either 45 days starting with the day on which the person was arrested or a longer period designated by the Secretary of State. Longer periods are specified in relation to particular territories in the Extradition Act 2003 (Designation of Part 2 Territories) Order 2003 (SI 2003 No. 3334), art. 4.

The Extradition Hearing

D31.8 Under part 2, the extradition hearing must begin no later than the end of the permitted period, which is either two months starting with the date on which the person first appears before the judge or, where the person has been provisionally arrested, two months starting with the date on which the judge received the documents referred to in s. 70(9). There is no initial hearing. At the extradition hearing, the judge is required to decide a series of questions.

At the initial stages of the extradition hearing the judge is required to decide whether the documents sent to him by the Secretary of State consist of or include certain documents and information. He is also required to decide, on a balance of probabilities, the question of identity, whether the offence specified in the request is an extradition offence and whether copies of the documents have been served on the person (s. 78). Once satisfied of these matters, the judge must proceed under s. 79 and decide whether there are any bars to extradition. The bars to extradition are (a) the rule against double jeopardy, (b) extraneous considerations, (c) the passage of time, and (d) hostage-taking considerations. These are exhaustively defined in ss. 80 to 83.

If the judge decides there are no bars to extradition, the person has not been convicted of the offence and the territory has been designated for the purposes of s. 84(7), the judge must proceed under s. 87. If the category 2 territory has not been designated for the purpose of s. 84(7), s. 84 requires the judge to decide whether there is evidence which would be sufficient to make a case requiring an answer by the person if the proceedings were the summary trial of an information against him (a prima facie case). If so satisfied, the judge must proceed under s. 87.

If the judge is satisfied that there are no bars to extradition and the person has been convicted of the extradition offence, the judge must answer a series of questions under s. 85 before proceeding further. Section 85 is identical to s. 20 save that, if the judge decides that a person is entitled to a retrial or (on appeal) a review amounting to a retrial, he must under s. 86 (unless the territory has been designated for these purposes) decide whether the evidence discloses a prima facie case. Once ss. 85 and 86 are satisfied, the judge must proceed under s. 87.

Section 87 requires the judge to decide whether extradition would be compatible with the person's rights under the ECHR. If so satisfied, the judge must send the case to the Secretary of State for his decision as to whether the person is to be extradited. The judge must remand the person in custody or on bail pending the decision of the Secretary of State. The judge does not order extradition. The order under part 2 is to be made by the Secretary of State whose functions are set out in ss. 93 to 102. The Secretary of State's order for extradition or discharge must be made within two months starting with the day on which the judge sends the case to the Secretary of State for his decision (ss. 99 and 102).

EXTRADITION OFFENCE

D31.9 The term 'extradition offence' is defined in the Extradition Act 2003, ss. 64 and 65 (part 1) and ss. 137 and 138 (part 2). There are several categories of extradition offence and it is possible for conduct to fall into more than one category. The key concept in determining whether the offence specified constitutes an extradition offence is 'conduct'. The judge is not concerned with the criminal law in the requesting territory or the legal ingredients of the offence specified in the request. The question whether conduct constitutes an extradition offence, in general terms, involves a consideration of where the conduct occurred, whether the conduct would constitute an offence in the relevant part of the UK punishable with a minimum term of 12 months' imprisonment or another form of detention and the penalty which may be imposed in the requesting territory. There are a number of exceptions to this general rule. For example, under part 1, for the first time, extradition may be granted where the conduct specified in the warrant would not constitute an offence in the relevant part of the UK provided no part of the conduct occurred in the UK and the conduct falls within the European framework list. Schedule 2 to the Act sets out the European framework list of conduct which may be amended by the Secretary of State to ensure that it corresponds to the list of conduct set out in Article 2.2 of the European framework decision. (See *The Office of the King's Prosecutor, Brussels v Armas* [2006] 2 AC 1 and *Bermingham* [2006] EWHC 200 (Admin).) Sections 64 and 65 and ss. 137 and 138 set out in detail the definition of an extradition offence and it is necessary to refer to the provisions in any particular case.

PHYSICAL OR MENTAL CONDITION

D31.10 Under part 1 (s. 25) and part 2 (s. 91) of the Extradition Act 2003, the judge may be addressed in relation to the physical or mental condition of the person sought. The judge may discharge the person or adjourn the extradition hearing if it appears to the judge that the person's physical or mental condition is such that it would be unjust or oppressive to extradite him. (See *R (Warren) v Secretary of State for the Home Department* [2003] EWHC 1177 and *Re Davies* (unreported 30 July 1997, HC).)

APPEAL

D31.11 Sections 26 to 34 govern appeals under part 1 and ss. 103 to 116 govern appeals under part 2. An appeal to the High Court on a question of law or fact may be brought under part 1 and part 2 by the requesting territory or the person whose extradition is sought. Leave is not required. Under part 1, notice of appeal must be given within seven days, starting with the day on which the order for extradition is made. Under part 2, notice of appeal must be given within 14 days, starting with the day on which the order for the person's discharge is made or the day on which the Secretary of State informs the person of his decision. (An appeal cannot be heard until after the Secretary of State has made his decision.) In part 2, the parties may also appeal against the Secretary of State's order to discharge or order extradition. An appeal lies to the House of Lords, with leave, from a decision of the High Court on an appeal under part 1 or part 2.

DOMESTIC PROCEEDINGS

D31.12 Under both parts 1 and 2 of the Extradition Act 2003, the existence of domestic proceedings against the person sought affects whether the extradition proceedings may continue without interruption. Where, at any time in the extradition proceedings, a person is charged with an offence in the UK, the judge *must* adjourn the proceedings until the charge is disposed of, withdrawn, proceedings are discontinued or an order is made for the charge to lie on the file (ss. 22 and 88). Where the person is serving a sentence in the UK, the judge *may* adjourn the hearing until the sentence has been served (ss. 23 and 89).

Section E1 Sentencing: General Provisions

Purposes of Sentencing

The CJA 2003, s. 142, sets out a list of the purposes of sentencing. It came into effect on 4 April 2005 and applies in respect of offences committed on or after that date. **E1.1**

Criminal Justice Act 2003, s. 142

(1) Any court dealing with an offender in respect of his offence must have regard to the following purposes of sentencing—
   (a) the punishment of offenders,
   (b) the reduction of crime (including its reduction by deterrence),
   (c) the reform and rehabilitation of offenders,
   (d) the protection of the public, and
   (e) the making of reparation by offenders to persons affected by their offences.

Section 142(2) limits the scope of this by stating that s. 142(1) does not apply in relation to an offender who is aged under 18 at the time of conviction (in respect of whom the CDA 1998, s. 37, states that the principal purpose of the youth justice system 'is to prevent offending by children and young persons'), and where there is also a statutory duty under the CYPA 1933, s. 44, to 'have regard to the welfare of the child or young person'. Nor does s. 142(1) apply where the offence is fixed by law (murder), where the sentence falls to be imposed under the PCC(S)A 2000, s. 110(2) or 111(2) (required custodial sentences: see **E6.1** and **E6.3**), the FA 1968, s. 51A(2) (minimum sentence for certain firearms offences: see **E6.6**), or the VCRA 2006, s. 29 (minimum sentence in certain cases of using someone to mind a weapon: see **E6.9**) or any of ss. 225 to 228 of the CJA 2003 (dangerous offenders: see **E5**), or in relation to the making of a hospital order (with or without restriction), an interim hospital order, a hospital direction or a limitation direction (as to which, see **E24**). Section 142(3) states that 'sentence' includes any order made by a court when dealing with an offender in respect of his offence, and so would clearly extend to ancillary orders as well as custodial, community, and financial penalties.

The SGC Guideline, *Overarching Principles: Seriousness* (Dec 2004), states that 'The Act does not indicate that any one purpose should be more important than any other and in practice they may all be relevant to a greater or lesser degree in any individual case — the sentencer has the task of determining the manner in which they apply' (para. 1.2).

Sentencing Guidelines

Existing arrangements for the promulgation of sentencing guidelines, by the Sentencing **E1.2**

Part E Sentencing

Guidelines Council (chaired by the Lord Chief Justice) on advice from the Sentencing Advisory Panel, are set out in the CJA 2003, ss. 167 to 173. Such guidelines may relate to the sentencing of offenders (which may be general in nature or limited to a particular category of offence or offender) or be allocation guidelines relating to decisions by a magistrates' court as to whether an offence is more suitable for summary trial or trial on indictment (CJA 2003, s. 170(1)).

Criminal Justice Act 2003, s. 172

(1) Every court must—
(a) in sentencing an offender, have regard to any guidelines which are relevant to the offender's case, and
(b) in exercising any other function relating to the sentencing of offenders, have regard to any guidelines which are relevant to the exercise of the function.

(2) In subsection (1) 'guidelines' means sentencing guidelines issued by the Council under section 170(9) as definitive guidelines, as revised by subsequent guidelines so issued.

The SGC has to date issued eight definitive guidelines on (i) reduction of sentence for a guilty plea (revised July 2007), (ii) seriousness and (iii) new sentences: CJA 2003 (all December 2004), (iv) manslaughter by reason of provocation (November 2005), (v) robbery (July 2006), (vi) domestic violence and (vii) breach of a protective order (both December 2006) and (viii) Sexual Offences Act 2003 (April 2007). Under the statutory provisions that existed before the CJA 2003, the Court of Appeal had issued sentencing guidelines on the court's own initiative since the 1980s and, since 1999, subject to the advice of the Sentencing Advisory Panel. Such guidelines have always been regarded as authoritative, but not strictly binding, in that a sentencer may, having given reason, depart from them (see *Johnson* (1994) 15 Cr App R (S) 827). According to the Court of Appeal in *Oosthuizen* [2006] 1 Cr App R (S) 385, s. 172(1)(a) requires the court to 'have regard' to any guidelines which are relevant, and it was not open to judges to disregard the guidelines. On the other hand it did not follow that in every case a guideline would be followed. For comment along similar lines, see *Last* [2005] 2 Cr App R (S) 381, *Peters* [2005] 2 Cr App R (S) 627 and *Bowering* [2006] 2 Cr App R (S) 80.

Appellate judges have stressed that it is the duty of counsel to bring any guideline authority to the attention of the sentencer, in case they might otherwise be overlooked. An example is *Panayioutou* (1989) 11 Cr App R (S) 535, where it was said that 'if this Court has laid down guidelines, then the time has come when judges are entitled to have those guideline cases drawn to their attention.' Both prosecution and defence advocates should be prepared to assist the judge by drawing relevant statutory provisions to his attention (*Cain* [2006] EWCA 3233). In *Lyon* (2005) *The Times*, 19 May 2005, Rose LJ said that, on an appeal against sentence, earlier decisions of the Court of Appeal which were neither guideline cases, nor cases expressed to be of general application in sentencing, were unlikely to be a reliable guide to sentencing brackets for particular offences since the facts and circumstances of cases varied infinitely. Particular caution was needed if relying on references by the A-G, unless they clearly expressed statements of general application. In *Doidge* (2005) *The Times*, 10 March 2005, the Court of Appeal stated that it would not in general be appropriate for advice tendered by the Sentencing Advisory Panel to the Sentencing Guidelines Council to be cited to the Court of Appeal or the single judge, since that advice might not be adopted by the SGC. It was only the final guidelines of the SGC to which courts had to have regard.

Determining the Seriousness of an Offence

E1.3 **Criminal Justice Act 2003, s. 143**

(1) In considering the seriousness of any offence, the court must consider the offender's culpability in committing the offence and any harm which the offence caused, was intended to cause or might foreseeably have caused.

Section 143 came into effect on 4 April 2005, and applies to offences committed on or after that date. The SGC Guideline, *Overarching Principles: Seriousness* (Dec 2004), states that 'The sentencer must start by considering the *seriousness* of the offence, the assessment of which will determine which of the sentencing thresholds has been crossed, indicate whether a custodial, community or other sentence is the most appropriate, be a key factor in determining the length of a custodial sentence, the onerousness of the requirements to be incorporated in a community sentence and the amount of any fine imposed' (para. 1.3).

The guidelines go on to consider various levels of culpability and varieties of harm, before indicating that 'harm must always be judged in the light of culpability' and that 'if much *more* harm, or much *less* harm has been caused by the offence than the offender intended or foresaw, the culpability of the offender, depending on the circumstances, may be regarded as carrying greater or lesser weight as appropriate'. For the full text of the SGC guidelines, see **appendix 8**.

Relevance of Previous Convictions to Offence Seriousness

Criminal Justice Act 2003, s. 143(2) E1.4

(2) In considering the seriousness of an offence ('the current offence') committed by an offender who has one or more previous convictions, the court must treat each previous conviction as an aggravating factor if (in the case of that conviction) the court considers that it can reasonably be so treated having regard, in particular, to—
(a) the nature of the offence to which the conviction relates and its relevance to the current offence, and
(b) the time that has elapsed since the conviction.

Section 143 came into effect on 4 April 2005, and applies to offences committed on or after that date. The SGC Guidelines do not deal with s. 143(2), and it is unclear to what extent it changes the earlier sentencing principles. The PCC(S)A 2000, s. 151(1), which remains relevant to offences committed before 4 April 2005, stated that 'in considering the seriousness of any offence, the court may take into account any previous convictions of the offender or any failure of his to respond to previous sentences'. Section 151(1) clearly conferred a discretion to take account of previous convictions, but the Court of Appeal authorities indicated that it was wrong to impose a sentence disproportionate to the seriousness of the offence purely on the basis of a bad record (*Galloway* (1979) 1 Cr App R (S) 311; *Queen* (1981) 3 Cr App R (S) 245; *Bailey* (1988) 10 Cr App R (S) 231). In any case, a clean record, or a record of few convictions, will often be regarded as a significant mitigating factor and may be taken into account under the CJA 2003, s. 166(1) (see **E1.13**).

The CJA 2003, s. 143(4), makes it clear that 'previous conviction' in this context means a previous conviction by a court in the UK or a previous finding of guilt in service disciplinary proceedings but, by s. 143(5), this does not prevent the court from treating a previous conviction by a court outside the UK as an aggravating factor in any case where the court considers it appropriate to do so.

For the provision of information on antecedents in the Crown Court and magistrates' courts, see the *Consolidated Criminal Practice Direction*, III.27.1 to III.27.11 at **appendix 7**.

Offending on Bail

The CJA 2003, s. 143(3), states: 'In considering the seriousness of any offence committed while the offender was on bail, the court must treat the fact that it was committed in those circumstances as an aggravating factor'. This is particularly so where the offence committed on bail is of the same type as the offence for which bail was granted (see *Jeffrey* [2004] 1 Cr App R (S) 179). E1.5

Section 143 came into effect on 4 April 2005, and applies to offences committed on or after that date, but s. 143(3) replaces the PCC(S)A 2000, s. 151(2), which is identically worded in all material respects and which applies to offences committed before that date.

While s. 143(2) is expressed in mandatory terms, it has to be set against the established sentencing principle that consecutive sentences are appropriate where one offence is committed while the offender is on bail in respect of another (see E2.11). Operation of these rules together might result in a disproportionately severe sentence.

Reduction in Sentence for Guilty Plea

E1.6 **Criminal Justice Act 2003, s. 144**

(1) In determining what sentence to pass on an offender who has pleaded guilty to an offence in proceedings before that or another court, a court must take into account—
  (a) the stage in the proceedings for the offence at which the offender indicated his intention to plead guilty, and
  (b) the circumstances in which this indication was given

(2) In the case of an offence the sentence for which falls to be imposed under subsection (2) of section 110 or 111 of the [PCC(S)A 2000], nothing in that subsection prevents the court, after taking into account any matter referred to in subsection (1) of this section, from imposing any sentence which is not less than 80 per cent of that specified in that subsection.

Section 144 came into effect on 4 April 2005, and applies to offences committed on or after that date, but s. 144 replaces the PCC(S)A 2000, s. 152(1) and (3), which is identically worded in all material respects and which applies to offences committed before that date.

The SGC Revised Guideline, *Reduction in Sentence for a Guilty Plea* (July 2007), explains that a reduction in sentence in such circumstances 'is appropriate because a guilty plea avoids the need for a trial (thus enabling other cases to be disposed of more expeditiously), shortens the gap between charge and sentence, saves considerable cost, and, in the case of an early plea, saves victims and witnesses from the concern about having to give evidence' (para. 2.2). Reduction for plea is a separate matter from remorse and other aspects of mitigation, and is separate from any reduction which may be appropriate to reflect assistance to the prosecuting or enforcement authorities (para. 2.3).

The SGC Revised Guideline makes it clear that the principle of a reduction applies in the Crown Court, a magistrates' court, and, whenever practicable, in a youth court (para. 1.1). It should be applied to any of the punitive elements of a sentence, but not to the rehabilitative elements, and to any ancillary order including a disqualification from driving (para. 2.5). The effect of the plea may, in an appropriate case, be to change a community sentence to a fine or discharge, or to change a custodial sentence to a community one, in which case the change in form of the sentence incorporates the reduction for plea (para. 2.6).

In *A-G's Refs (Nos. 14 and 15 of 2006)* [2006] 2 Cr App R (S) 215 the Court of Appeal invited the SGC to review, as a matter of urgency, whether it was appropriate to award a one-third reduction in sentence for a timely guilty plea (i) if the case against the offender had been overwhelming and (ii) where the appropriate sentence was very long (so that the discount might appear too generous). The SGC Revised Guideline retains the structure of the original guideline and confirms that the level of reduction should be a proportion of the total sentence imposed, with the proportion calculated by reference to the circumstances in which the guilty plea was indicated, in particular the stage in the proceedings. The greatest reduction (recommended one-third) will be given where the plea was indicated at the 'first reasonable opportunity', reducing to a recommended one-quarter (where a trial date has been set) to a recommended one-tenth (for a guilty plea entered at the 'door of the court' or after the trial has begun (para. 4.2). In each case there is a presumption that the recommended reduction will be given unless there are good reasons for a lower amount. However, where the prosecution case is overwhelming, it may not be appropriate to give the full reduction that would otherwise be given (para. 5.3). Where a court is satisfied that a lower reduction should be given for this reason, a recommended reduction of 20 per cent is likely to be appropriate where the guilty plea was indicated at the first reasonable opportunity (para. 5.4). A court departing from a guideline must state the reasons for doing so (para. 5.5).

The Revised Guideline says that, if an offender is being sentenced as a dangerous offender, any specified minimum custodial term should be reduced in the normal way to reflect the guilty plea (para. 5.1). A sentencer cannot remedy a perceived defect in the law, such as where a maximum penalty appears to be too low, by refusal of the appropriate discount (para. 5.6). If after pleading guilty there is a *Newton* hearing and the offender's version of the facts is rejected, some or all of the recommended reduction for plea may be lost (para. 4.3(v) and *Williams* (1990) 12 Cr App R (S) 415). For the application of a guilty plea to setting the minimum term in murder cases see the Revised Guideline, Part F and **E4.1**, and for application of the guilty plea to setting the specified period under the PCC(S)A 2000, s. 82A, see the Revised Guideline, Part G and **E5.4**. For further details, and examples, see the full text of the Revised Guideline set out in Part 1 of **appendix 8** of this work.

The CJA 2003, s. 174(2)(d), states that where, as a result of taking into account any matter referred to in s. 144(1), the court imposes a punishment on the offender which is less severe than it otherwise would have imposed, it must state that fact. Section 174(2)(d) came into effect on 4 April 2005, and applies to offences committed on or after that date. It replaces the PCC(S)A 2000, s. 152(2), which is identically worded in all material respects and which applies to offences committed before that date.

In *Fearon* [1996] 2 Cr App R (S) 406 the Court of Appeal stressed that the sentencing judge should always make it clear that a reduction for the guilty plea had been made. The SGC Revised Guideline provides additional guidance, that 'when pronouncing sentence the court should usually state what the sentence would have been if there had been no reduction as a result of the guilty plea' (para. 3.1).

Section 144(2) refers to the minimum required custodial sentences that fall to be imposed under the PCC(S)A 2000, s. 110(2) or 111(2) (see further **E6.1** and **E6.2**). In those two circumstances the reduction for guilty plea can be no more than 20 per cent of the sentence. Section 144(2) makes no reference to minimum sentences for certain firearm offences under the FA 1968, s. 51A. The Court of Appeal decided in *Jordan* [2005] 2 Cr App R (S) 266 that s. 51A did not permit a reduction to reflect a guilty plea (see further **E6.8**).

Reduction in Sentence for Assistance by Offender

E1.7 The SOCPA 2005, s. 73, makes provision for reduction in an offender's sentence to reflect assistance given or offered to the authorities by that offender. Any reduction on this ground has been regarded as separate from and additional to the appropriate discount for pleading guilty (*Wood* [1997] 1 Cr App R (S) 347) and it is submitted that this continues to apply following the SGC Guideline. The relevant provisions came into effect on 1 April 2006.

Serious Organised Crime and Police Act 2005, s. 73

(1) This section applies if a defendant—
- (a) following a plea of guilty is either convicted of an offence in proceedings in the Crown Court or is committed to the Crown Court for sentence, and
- (b) has, pursuant to a written agreement made with a specified prosecutor, assisted or offered to assist the investigator or prosecutor in relation to that or any other offence.

(2) In determining what sentence to pass on the defendant the court may take into account the extent and nature of the assistance given or offered.

(3) If the court passes a sentence which is less than it would have passed but for the assistance given or offered, it must state in open court—
- (a) that it has passed a lesser sentence than it would otherwise have passed, and
- (b) what the greater sentence would have been.

(4) Subsection (3) does not apply if the court thinks that it would not be in the public interest to disclose that the sentence has been discounted; but in such a case the court must give written notice of the matters specified in paragraphs (a) and (b) of subsection (3) to both the prosecutor and the defendant.

(5) Nothing in any enactment which—
(a) requires that a minimum sentence is passed in respect of any offence or an offence of any description or by reference to the circumstances of any offender (whether or not the enactment also permits the court to pass a lesser sentence in particular circumstances), or
(b) in the case of a sentence which is fixed by law, requires the court to take into account certain matters for the purposes of making an order which determines or has the effect of determining the minimum period of imprisonment which the offender must serve (whether or not the enactment also permits the court to fix a lesser period in particular circumstances),
affects the power of a court to act under subsection (2).
(6) If, in determining what sentence to pass on the defendant, the court takes into account the extent and nature of the assistance given or offered as mentioned in subsection (2), that does not prevent the court from also taking account of any other matter which it is entitled by virtue of any other enactment to take account of for the purposes of determining—
(a) the sentence, or
(b) in the case of a sentence which is fixed by law, any minimum period of imprisonment which an offender must serve.

The reference to 'minimum sentence' in s. 73(5)(a) presumably would cover sentences imposed under the PCC(S)A 2000, s. 110 (see **E6.1**) or s. 111 (see **E6.3**) or under the FA 1968, s. 51A (see **E6.6**). Section 73(5)(b) deals with murder cases.

Section 73(7) provides that where a court thinks that it would not be in the public interest to state in open court that a discount has been given, CJA 2003, s. 174 (which requires the court to explain its reasons) does not apply to the extent that the explanation would reveal that a discount has been given for that reason. Further, CJA 2003, s. 270, which requires the court to give reasons for its selection of the minimum term in a case of murder, is qualified to the same extent.

Section 74 provides for a subsequent review of a sentence passed (a) on an offender who received a discounted sentence under s. 73 on the basis of a promise to assist which he did not fulfil, or (b) on an offender who received a discounted sentence at the time, but has since given or offered to give further assistance, or (c) on an offender who did not receive a discounted sentence within s. 73(2) but has subsequently given or offered to give assistance.

E1.8 **Extent of Discount** These provisions are silent as to the appropriate extent of any reduction to reflect actual or promised assistance by the offender. There are a number of long-standing Court of Appeal authorities which appear still to be relevant despite the introduction of the statutory scheme. The decision in *Sinfield* (1981) 3 Cr App R (S) 258 establishes that, where an offender has given significant assistance to the police or prosecuting authorities, especially where it leads to the apprehension of other offenders or the prevention of other offences, he may expect a discount, possibly a substantial one, from his sentence. The extent of the discount varies in accordance with a number of circumstances, and there is no set scale of discount. The level of discount will depend on the quality, quantity, accuracy and timeliness of the information given, the offender's willingness to testify if required, and the extent to which his co-operation with the authorities has put himself or his family at serious risk of reprisal. The discount should be set at a level appropriate to show to offenders that it was worthwhile to provide such assistance (*Sivan* (1988) 10 Cr App R (S) 282). While it was said in *Wood* (1987) 9 Cr App R (S) 238 that, in a case where a discount had been given for assistance, that fact should be made clear in open court, there are many cases where such a course would put the informant at greater danger. The statutory scheme in s. 73(4) preserves the possibility of dealing with a difficult and sensitive matter other than in open court. In *A and B* [1999] 1 Cr App R (S) 52, the Court of Appeal reviewed earlier authorities and re-stated the applicable general principles. It was there noted that the Court of Appeal might on occasion increase the level of discount which had been granted by the trial judge, on the basis of later information which showed that the material provided by the offender had turned out to be of greater value to the authorities than initially had been thought. Section 74 provides for any such adjustment to be carried out by bringing the matter back before the sentencer, rather than by way of an appeal against sentence.

Increase in Sentences for Racial or Religious Aggravation

The CJA 2003, s. 145, states that where a court is considering the seriousness of an offence other than one under the CDA 1988, ss. 29 to 32, if the offence was racially or religiously aggravated, the court must treat that fact as an aggravating factor on sentence and must state in open court that the offence was so aggravated. **E1.9**

Section 145 came into effect on 4 April 2005, and applies to offences committed on or after that date. The section replaces the PCC(S)A 2000, s. 153, which is identically worded in all material respects. The Anti-Terrorism, Crime and Security Act 2001, s. 39, extended 'racial aggravation' to 'racial or religious aggravation' with effect from 14 December 2001. For the definition of 'racial or religious aggravation', see **B11.160**. In *Morrison* [2001] 1 Cr App R (S) 12, the Court of Appeal said that the appropriate additional punishment to reflect racial aggravation would depend on all the circumstances, but in that case approved the enhancement by two years of a nominal sentence of four and a half years for burglary committed in circumstances of racial aggravation.

Section 145 is of general application in sentencing, except that it does *not* apply where the court is imposing sentence for one of the racially or religiously aggravated offences under the CDA 1998, ss. 29 to 32 (certain aggravated assaults, aggravated criminal damage, certain aggravated public order offences, or aggravated harassment: see **B11.160**). The racially or religiously aggravated forms of these offences carry higher maximum penalties. The cases of *Saunders* [2000] 1 Cr App R (S) 548 and *Kelly* [2001] 2 Cr App R (S) 341 provide sentencing guidelines for cases involving racial aggravation. They are both cases of racially aggravated actual bodily harm and are considered at **B2.26**. Nor does s. 145 apply where the offender has been convicted of the basic offence where a racially or religiously aggravated version exists. In *McGillivray* [2005] 2 Cr App R (S) 366, the offender pleaded guilty to assault occasioning actual bodily harm. The racially aggravated version of that offence had originally been charged as well, but no evidence was adduced on that count and a verdict of not guilty was entered. The judge passed a sentence of three years' imprisonment on the basis that the assault had been racially aggravated. The Court of Appeal said that it had not been open to the judge to sentence on that basis, since the offender had not been convicted of the racially aggravated form of the offence. The sentence was reduced to two years, a sentence appropriate for the basic offence.

Increase in Sentences for Aggravation Related to Disability or Sexual Orientation

The CJA 2003, s. 146, applies where the court is considering the seriousness of an offence committed in any of the following circumstances: **E1.10**

(a) that, at the time of committing the offence, or immediately before or after doing so, the offender demonstrated towards the victim of the offence hostility based on—
  (i) the sexual orientation (or presumed sexual orientation) of the victim, or
  (ii) a disability (or presumed disability) of the victim

or

(b) that the offence is motivated (wholly or partly)—
  (i) by hostility towards persons who are of a particular sexual orientation, or
  (ii) by hostility towards persons who have a disability or a particular disability.

The court must treat the fact that the offence was committed in any of those circumstances as an aggravating factor, and must state in open court that the offence was committed in such circumstances (s. 146(1) to (3)).

E

Part E Sentencing

It is immaterial whether or not the offender's hostility is based, to any extent, on any other factor (s. 146(4)). 'Disability' means 'any physical or mental impairment' (s. 146(5)).

Section 145 came into effect on 4 April 2005 and applies to offences committed on or after that date.

General Aggravating Factors

E1.11 **Criminal Justice Act 2003, s. 156**

(1) In forming any such opinion as is mentioned in section 148(1), (2)(b) or (3)(b), section 152(2) or section 153(2), a court must take into account all such information as is available to it about the circumstances of the offence or (as the case may be) of the offence and the offence or offences associated with it, including any aggravating or mitigating factors.
(2) In forming any such opinion as is mentioned in section 148(2)(a) or (3)(a), the court may take into account any information about the offender which is before it.

The SGC Guideline, *Overarching Principles: Seriousness* (Dec 2004), sets out a list of aggravating factors relevant to sentencing. Some of these reflect higher culpability on the part of the defendant, others reflect a more than usually serious degree of harm. The Guideline is set out at **appendix 8** to this work. It is submitted that aggravating factors affecting the seriousness of the offence should always be taken into account when deciding, *inter alia*, whether an offence is 'serious enough' to warrant a community sentence (CJA 2003, s. 148(1)) or 'so serious that neither a fine alone nor a community sentence can be justified' (CJA 2003, s. 152(2)).

General Mitigating Factors

E1.12 See the CJA 2003, s. 156(2), set out at **E1.11**.

The SGC Guideline, *Overarching Principles: Seriousness* (Dec 2004), sets out a list of mitigating factors relevant to sentencing. Some of these reflect significantly lower culpability on the part of the defendant, others that the harm caused by the offence is less than usually serious. The Guideline is set out at **appendix 8** to this work.

Personal Mitigation

E1.13 The CJA 2003, s. 166(1), makes provision for a sentencer to take account of any matters that 'in the opinion of the court, are relevant in mitigation of sentence'. Whether to take account of personal mitigation is a matter within the discretion of the court (see Scarman LJ in *Inwood* (1974) 60 Cr App R 70) and, in particular, the serious nature of the offence may mean that little weight can be given to what would otherwise be regarded as significant personal mitigation.

The CJA 2003, s. 166(2), states that even though the offence, or the combination of the offence and one or more offences associated with it, was so serious that a community sentence could not normally be justified for the offence, the court may, after taking matters of personal mitigation into account, pass a community sentence. This subsection had no equivalent in the PCC(S)A 2000, but the principle contained within it has been clear at least since the early case law on the CJA 1991, especially *Cox* [1993] 1 WLR 188. In that case Lord Taylor CJ stated that although 'on all the known facts of the case, we have reached the conclusion that only a custodial sentence could be justified for this offence', a community sentence was the proper sentence having regard to personal mitigation, in particular the offender's youth and clean record. Section 166(2) confirms that the *Cox* principle survives the 2003 Act. In *Seed* [2007] EWCA Crim 254, the Court of Appeal stressed that a clean record could be important personal mitigation and might make a custodial sentence inappropriate notwithstanding that the custodial threshold had been crossed.

Regard to be had to Totality of Offending Conduct

E1.14 The CJA 2003, s. 166(3), states that nothing prevents a court

(a) from mitigating any penalty included in an offender's sentence by taking into account any other penalty included in that sentence, and
(b) in the case of an offender who is convicted of one or more other offences, from mitigating his sentence by applying any rule of law as to the totality of sentences.

This provision re-enacts PCC(S)A 2000, s. 158(2)(b). Section 166(3) came into effect on 4 April 2005, and applies to offences committed on or after that date.

Sentencers must have regard to the total length of sentence passed, particularly where consecutive sentences have been imposed, to ensure that the sentence properly reflects the overall seriousness of the behaviour (*Jones* [1996] 1 Cr App R (S) 153). Overall sentences have been reduced on appeal for this reason in a range of situations, including: where a suspended sentence is activated consecutively to an immediate sentence (*Bocskei* (1970) 54 Cr App R 519); where the offender has committed several offences of moderate gravity (*Holderness* (1974) CSP A5–3B01); where a new custodial sentence is ordered to run consecutively to a custodial sentence which the offender is already serving (*Stevens* [1997] 2 Cr App R (S) 180); and where the offender receives a long sentence together with a short one (consecutive sentences of 11 years and six months adjusted on appeal to run concurrently (*Smith* (1981) 3 Cr App R (S) 201).

Prevalence

The SGC Guideline, *Overarching Principles: Seriousness* (Dec 2004), states (at paras. 1.38 and 1.39) that the seriousness of an individual case should be judged on its own dimensions of harm and culpability rather than as part of a collective social harm. It is legitimate for the overall approach to sentencing levels for particular offences to be guided by their cumulative effect. However, it would be wrong to further penalise individual offenders by increasing sentence length for committing an individual offence of that type. **E1.15**

There may be exceptional circumstances that arise that may lead a court to decide that local prevalence should influence sentencing levels. The pivotal issue in such cases will be the harm being caused to the community. It is essential that sentencers both have supporting evidence from an external source (for example the local Criminal Justice Board) to justify claims that a particular crime is prevalent in their area and are satisfied that there is a compelling need to treat the offence more seriously than elsewhere. This principle was endorsed by the Court of Appeal in *Oosthuizen* [2006] 1 Cr App R (S) 385.

Duty to Give Reasons for, and Explain Effect of, Sentence

Criminal Justice Act 2003, s. 174 **E1.16**

(1) Subject to subsections (3) and (4), any court passing sentence on an offender—
 (a) must state in open court, in ordinary language and in general terms, its reasons for deciding on the sentence passed, and
 (b) must explain to the offender in ordinary language—
  (i) the effect of the sentence,
  (ii) where the offender is required to comply with any order of the court forming part of the sentence, the effects of non-compliance with the order,
  (iii) any power of the court, on the application of the offender or any other person, to vary or review any order of the court forming part of the sentence, and
  (iv) where the sentence consists of or includes a fine, the effects of failure to pay the fine.
(2) In complying with subsection (1)(a), the court must—
 (a) where guidelines indicate that a sentence of a particular kind, or within a particular range, would normally be appropriate for the offence and the sentence is of a different kind, or is outside that range, state the court's reasons for deciding on a sentence of a different kind or outside that range,
 (b) where the sentence is a custodial sentence and the duty in subsection (2) of section 152 is not excluded by subsection (1)(a) or (b) or (3) of that section, state that it is of the opinion referred to in section 152(2) and why it is of that opinion,

(c) where the sentence is a community sentence and the case does not fall within section 151(2), state that it is of the opinion that section 148(1) applies and why it is of that opinion,

(d) where as a result of taking into account any matter referred to in section 144(1), the court imposes a punishment on the offender which is less severe than the punishment it would otherwise have imposed, state that fact, and

(e) in any case, mention any aggravating or mitigating factors which the court has regarded as being of particular importance.

(3) Subsection (1)(a) does not apply—

(a) to an offence the sentence for which is fixed by law (provision relating to sentencing for such an offence being made by section 270), or

(b) to an offence the sentence for which falls to be imposed under section 51A(2) of the Firearms Act 1968 (c. 27) or under subsection (2) of section 110 or 111 of the Sentencing Act (required custodial sentences).

(4) The Secretary of State may by order—

(a) prescribe cases in which subsection (1)(a) or (b) does not apply, and

(b) prescribe cases in which the statement referred to in subsection (1)(a) or the explanation referred to in subsection (1)(b) may be made in the absence of the offender, or may be provided in written form.

(5) Where a magistrates' court passes a custodial sentence, it must cause any reason stated by virtue of subsection (2)(b) to be specified in the warrant of commitment and entered on the register.

(6) In this section—

'guidelines' has the same meaning as in section 172;

'the register' has the meaning given by section 163 of the Sentencing Act.

Section 174 imposes a general duty on courts to give reasons for, and to explain the effect of, the sentence which is being passed on an offender. It brings together in one place various obligations to give reasons that, prior to the 2003 Act, were scattered in various other statutes. It also creates some new requirements, such as explaining the relevance of any sentencing guidelines applicable to the offender's case and, if the court has departed from them, to explain why. See further E1.2.

The list of requirements is not exhaustive. It must be set alongside the obligations on a sentencer who passes a custodial sentence on an offender, to explain the practical effect of the early release provisions on the duration of that sentence arising from the *Consolidated Criminal Practice Direction*, para. I.7, *Explanations for the imposition of custodial sentences* (see **appendix** 7). This indicates that the statutory provisions governing the early release of offenders are not widely understood by the general public, and states that it is desirable when a custodial sentence is passed that its practical effect should be fully understood by the defendant, any victim, and any member of the public who is present in court or reads a full report of the proceedings. Such explanation of the practical effect of the sentence is to be provided by the sentencer in addition to the need to comply with pre-existing statutory requirements. Sentencers should give the explanation in terms of their own choosing, while taking care to ensure that the explanation is clear and accurate. No form of words is prescribed, although annex C to the Practice Direction contains short statements which may, adapted as necessary, be of value as models.

Some provisions, which require a court to explain why it has *not* taken a particular course of action in sentencing the offender, have not been brought within s. 174. Examples are the duty imposed by the PCC(S)A 2000, s. 130(3), to give reasons on passing sentence if the court does not make a compensation order, the duty imposed under the CJCSA 2000, s. 28, to give reasons when sentencing an offender aged over 18 for an offence against a child for not disqualifying that offender from working with children in the future, the duty imposed under the Football Spectators Act 1989 where the offender is convicted of a relevant offence for the court to give reasons why it is not making a football banning order, and the duty imposed under the CDA 1998, s. 9, to impose a parenting order on the parent of a young offender aged under 16 unless the court is not satisfied that such an order would be desirable in the interests of preventing offending by the young offender (in which case the sentencer must give reasons in open court that this criterion is not satisfied, and why not).

Failure to Comply No consequence of any failure to comply with these requirements is specified in s. 174. In the past the Court of Appeal has taken the view that a failure to comply with procedural requirements cannot invalidate the sentence nor can it, as such, provide a sufficient basis for an appeal against sentence. In commenting upon provisions in the CJA 1991, which required sentencers to explain in ordinary language the justification for imposing a custodial sentence on an offender, Lord Taylor CJ said in *Baverstock* (1993) 14 Cr App R (S) 471 (at p. 475) that the statutory provisions were 'not to be treated as a verbal tightrope for judges to walk' and that even if judges made a mistake and failed to explain something they should have explained, the Court of Appeal would not interfere with the resultant sentence 'unless it is wrong in principle or excessive'. **E1.17**

Pre-sentence Reports

Criminal Justice Act 2003, ss. 156 and 158 **E1.18**

156.—(1) [See **E1.11**.]

(2) [See **E1.11**.]

(3) Subject to subsection (4), a court must obtain and consider a pre-sentence report before—

(a) in the case of a custodial sentence, forming any such opinion as is mentioned in section 152(2), section 153(2), section 225(1)(b), section 226(1)(b), section 227(1)(b) or section 228(1)(b)(i), or

(b) in the case of a community sentence, forming any such opinion as is mentioned in section 148(1), (2)(b) or (3)(b) or any opinion as to the suitability for the offender of the particular requirement or requirements to be imposed by the community order.

(4) Subsection (3) does not apply if, in the circumstances of the case, the court is of the opinion that it is unnecessary to obtain a pre-sentence report.

(5) In a case where the offender is aged under 18, the court must not form the opinion mentioned in subsection (4) unless—

(a) there exists a previous pre-sentence report obtained in respect of the offender, and

(b) the court has had regard to the information contained in that report, or, if there is more than one such report, the most recent report.

(6) No custodial sentence or community sentence is invalidated by the failure of a court to obtain and consider a pre-sentence report before forming an opinion referred to in subsection (3), but any court on an appeal against such a sentence—

(a) must, subject to subsection (7), obtain a pre-sentence report if none was obtained by the court below, and

(b) must consider any such report obtained by it or by that court.

(7) Subsection (6)(a) does not apply if the court is of the opinion—

(a) that the court below was justified in forming an opinion that it was unnecessary to obtain a pre-sentence report, or

(b) that, although the court below was not justified in forming that opinion, in the circumstances of the case at the time it is before the court, it is unnecessary to obtain a pre-sentence report.

(8) In a case where the offender is aged under 18, the court must not form the opinion mentioned in subsection (7) unless—

(a) there exists a previous pre-sentence report obtained in respect of the offender, and

(b) the court has had regard to the information contained in that report, or, if there is more than one such report, the most recent report.

158.—(1) In this Part 'pre-sentence report' means a report which—

(a) with a view to assisting the court in determining the most suitable method of dealing with an offender, is made or submitted by an appropriate officer, and

(b) contains information as to such matters, presented in such manner, as may be prescribed by rules made by the Secretary of State.

(2) In subsection (1) 'an appropriate officer' means—

(a) where the offender is aged 18 or over, an officer of a local probation board, and

(b) where the offender is aged under 18, an officer of a local probation board, a social worker of a local authority social services department or a member of a youth offending team.

These sections came into effect on 4 April 2005 and apply to offences committed on or after that date.

The normal requirement (as stated in s. 156(3)) is that the court should obtain a pre-sentence report before making a decision to impose a custodial or community sentence. The court has discretion to dispense with that requirement whenever it appears to the court to be 'unnecessary' to obtain one (s. 156(4)). This discretion is, however, subsequently narrowed (in s. 156(5)) in respect of offenders who are under the age of 18. Section 156(6) provides that no sentence shall be invalidated by failure of the court to comply with these requirements, but, on appeal against a custodial or community sentence passed without the court having obtained and considered a pre-sentence report, the appellate court must obtain and consider one unless, in accordance with s. 156(7), the appellate court is of opinion that the court below was justified in not calling for a report or that the court below was not so justified but, in the circumstances of the case at the time when it is before the appellate court, it is unnecessary to obtain a pre-sentence report. The appellate court cannot, however, take this line in respect of an offender who is under the age of 18. In such a case the appellate court must order a pre-sentence report, or at least have sight of the most recent previous pre-sentence report prepared on the offender (s. 156(8)).

In *Armsaramah* [2001] 1 Cr App R (S) 467, the Court of Appeal approved the decision of the sentencer to impose a custodial sentence of five years on an adult offender convicted of kidnapping and robbery, without the benefit of a pre-sentence report. The Court of Appeal noted that the defence had not called for a report, the offender had been convicted after a trial, and the judge had made every possible assumption in favour of the defendant in light of the information available. An earlier decision in *Gillette* (1999) *The Times*, 3 December 1999, to the effect that whenever a sentencer was considering passing a first custodial sentence (apart perhaps from a very short one) on an offender, a pre-sentence report should always be ordered, was distinguished not least because in that case counsel had requested adjournment for a report to be prepared but the judge had declined to do so.

The CJA 2003, s. 159, deals with disclosure of pre-sentence reports to the defence (to the offender or his counsel or solicitor, and if the offender is under 18 to any parent or guardian present in court) and to the prosecution, and substantially re-enacts PCC(S)A 2000, s. 156. Section 159 specifically states, however, that the disclosure provision does not apply to pre-sentence reports given orally. This section came into effect on 4 April 2005 and applies to offences committed on or after that date.

Other Reports

E1.19 The CJA 2003, s. 160, applies where a report (other than a pre-sentence report) is made by an officer of a local probation board or a member of the youth offending team with a view to assisting the court (except a youth court) in deciding how best to deal with an offender. The section provides for disclosure of the contents of the report to the defence (but not to the prosecution), and substantially re-enacts PCC(S)A 2000, s. 157. This section came into effect on 4 April 2005 and applies to offences committed on or after that date.

Victim Personal Statements

E1.20 The *Consolidated Criminal Practice Direction*, para.III.28, *Personal statements of victims* (see **appendix** 7) and the decision of the Court of Appeal in *Perks* [2001] 1 Cr App R (S) 66 together provide guidance on the relevance of victim personal statements placed before the sentencer on the impact which the offence had on the victim or, in a case where the victim had died, the impact on their surviving close family. The guidance is as follows:

(a) A sentencer must not make assumptions, unsupported by evidence, about the effects of an offence on the victim (see further *Hobstaff* (1993) 14 Cr App R (S) 605, where it was said that if there was no admissible evidence of the effects of the offence on the victim it should be disregarded, and *O'S* (1993) 14 Cr App R (S) 632);
(b) If an offence has had a particularly damaging or distressing effect upon the victim, this should be made known to and be taken into account by the court when passing sentence (said to be an 'elementary principle of sentencing' in *Nunn* [1996] 2 Cr App R (S) 136; see also *Doe* (1995) 16 Cr App R (S) 718);
(c) Evidence of the effects of an offence on the victim must be in proper form, and a witness statement, an expert report or otherwise, duly served upon the defendant or his representatives prior to sentence;
(d) Evidence of the victim alone should be approached with care, the more so if it related to matters which the defence could not realistically be expected to investigate; and
(e) The opinions of the victim and the victim's close relatives on the appropriate level of sentence should not be taken into account (see also *Nunn* and *Hird* [1998] 2 Cr App R (S) 241). The court must pass what it judged to be the appropriate sentence having regard to the circumstances of the offence and of the offender. It could not accede to a plea for vengeance by the relatives, and had to be very cautious about paying attention to pleas for mercy. This was, however, subject to two exceptions:
    (i) where the sentence passed on the offender was aggravating the victim's distress, the sentence might be moderated to some degree 'as an act of mercy' (examples are *Nunn* and *Roche* [1999] 2 Cr App R (S) 105); and
    (ii) where the victim's forgiveness or unwillingness to press charges provided evidence that his physical or mental suffering must be very much less than would normally be the case (examples are *Hutchinson* (1994) 15 Cr App R (S) 134 and *Mills* [1998] 2 Cr App R (S) 229).

In *Ismail* [2005] 2 Cr App R (S) 542, where the 18-year-old offender pleaded guilty to rape and sexual assault of a 16-year-old girl, the Court of Appeal said that it was essential for the sentencer to have, and to take into account, a victim personal statement in a case of that kind.

Mentally Disordered Offenders

The CJA 2003, s. 157(1), states that in any case where an offender is or appears to be mentally disordered, the court must obtain and consider a medical report before passing a custodial sentence other than one fixed by law. This is subject to s. 157(2), which states that the court need not order such a report if, in the circumstances of the case, it is of the opinion that it is unnecessary to do so. Section 157(6) defines 'medical report'. A medical report is distinct from a pre-sentence report, and s. 157(7) clearly states that the ordering of a medical report does not displace the need to order a pre-sentence report under s. 156. **E1.21**

Criminal Justice Act 2003, s. 166

(1) Nothing in—
    (a) section 148 (imposing community sentences),
    (b) section 152, 153 or 157 (imposing custodial sentences),
    (c) section 156 (pre-sentence reports and other requirements),
    (d) section 164 (fixing of fines),
    prevents a court from mitigating an offender's sentence by taking into account any such matters as, in the opinion of the court, are relevant in mitigation of sentence.

Section 166(5) further provides that nothing in the sections mentioned in s. 166(1)(a) to (d) is to be taken as requiring a court to pass a custodial sentence, or any particular custodial sentence, on a mentally disordered offender, or as restricting any power (under the Mental Health Act 1983 or otherwise), which enables a court to deal with such an offender in the manner it considers to be the most appropriate in all the circumstances. 'Mentally disordered', in relation to a person, means suffering from a mental disorder within the meaning of the Mental Health Act 1983 (s. 166(6)).

These sections came into effect on 4 April 2005 and apply to offences committed on or after that date.

Section E2 Custodial Sentences: General Provisions

Available Custodial Sentences

By the PCC(S)A 2000, s. 76(1), the term 'custodial sentence' means (a) a sentence of imprisonment, (b) a sentence of detention under the PCC(S)A 2000, s. 90 or 91, (c) a sentence of custody for life under the PCC(S)A 2000, s. 93 or 94, a sentence of detention in a young offender institution, or (d) a detention and training order. The term 'sentence of imprisonment' does not include a committal for contempt of court or any kindred offence (s. 76(2)). **E2.1**

Offenders aged under 21 at the date of conviction cannot be sentenced to imprisonment (PCC(S)A 2000, s. 89(1)). Those under 21 cannot be committed to prison for any reason, such as non-payment of a fine, but if a person under 21 is remanded in custody for trial or sentence, or sent in custody for trial under the CDA 1998, s. 51, he may be committed to prison for the period before his case is disposed of (PCC(S)A 2000, s. 89(2)).

When the CJCSA 2000, s. 61, is brought into force, the sentences of detention in a young offender institution and custody for life will be abolished. Offenders who would have received such sentences will thereafter be sentenced to imprisonment, which will become the standard custodial sentence for offenders aged 18 to 20 inclusive as well as for offenders aged 21 and over. No date for implementation of s. 61 has yet been set.

Maximum Custodial Sentences

Maximum prison terms for indictable offences and offences triable either way are almost always laid down by statutes creating those offences. Maximum terms are indicated in respect of each of the offences dealt with in **part B**. Where a person is convicted on indictment and is liable to be sentenced to imprisonment, but the sentence is not limited to a specified term or life by any enactment, the maximum prison sentence available is two years (PCC(S)A 2000, s. 77). This provision does not apply to common-law offences, such as incitement, for which the penalty which may be imposed by the Crown Court is not subject to any limitation except that it must not be disproportionate to the actual offence committed (*Higgins* [1952] 1 KB 7). For sentencing by magistrates' courts, and by the Crown Court when exercising the powers of a magistrates' court, see **E2.3**. **E2.2**

There are special rules in respect of statutory conspiracies and attempts, as to which see **A6.13** and **A6.33** respectively.

The effect of statutory changes to maximum sentences is as follows. Unless there is clear provision to the contrary, where a defendant falls to be sentenced for an offence committed before an increase in the relevant maximum sentence, he should be sentenced on the basis of the old maximum (*Penwith Justices, ex parte Hay* (1979) 1 Cr App R (S) 265; *North* [2001]

1 Cr App R (S) 109). Article 7 of the ECHR states that no heavier penalty shall be imposed than the one applicable at the time the offence was committed (see *Welch v UK* (1995) 20 EHRR 247; *Ibbotson v UK* [1999] Crim LR 153). When the offence is charged as having been committed on a day unknown between specified dates and the maximum sentence was increased between those dates, the lower maximum applies (*Street* [1997] 2 Cr App R (S) 309; *Cairns* [1998] 1 Cr App R (S) 434). If the maximum penalty is reduced between the time of commission of the offence and the date of conviction then, in the absence of guidance from the relevant provision or commencement order, it seems that the sentencing court should infer the intention of Parliament in a common sense way (see *A-G's Ref (No. 48 of 1994)* (1995) 16 Cr App R (S) 980 and *Shaw* [1996] 2 Cr App R (S) 278).

In *Carroll* (1995) 16 Cr App R (S) 488, the judge, on imposing the maximum sentence of two years' detention in a young offender institution on an offender who had pleaded guilty to aggravated vehicle-taking, commented that the maximum sentence provided by statute was too low. The Court of Appeal, reducing the sentence to 18 months, said that sentencers must abide loyally by the maximum sentence provided, that the maximum sentence should be reserved for the most serious examples of that offence and that an appropriate discount (such as for a guilty plea) should be made from the sentence which was commensurate with the seriousness of the offence. See **E1.6**

In considering whether a particular offence is one of the worst examples of its kind, sentencers should have regard to the range of cases which is actually encountered in practice, 'and ask themselves whether the particular case they are dealing with comes within the broad band of that type' but 'should not use their imaginations to conjure up unlikely worst possible kinds of case' (per Lawton LJ in *Ambler* (1975) CSP A1–4C01, followed and applied in *Butt* [2006] 2 Cr App R (S) 364). A 'worst case' of dangerous driving was identified in *Hastings* [1996] 1 Cr App R (S) 167; the Court of Appeal upheld the maximum two-year term. The statutory maximum should not normally be imposed where there is significant mitigation. An example is *Pinto* [2006] 2 Cr App R (S) 579, where the maximum sentence of ten years imposed for an offence of cruelty to a child was reduced to eight years on appeal.

In general the maximum sentence should not be imposed where the accused has pleaded guilty. In *Greene* (1993) 14 Cr App R (S) 682, the maximum sentence of five years' imprisonment for violent disorder was reduced to three years on the ground that the offender had pleaded guilty; in *Barnes* (1983) 5 Cr App R (S) 368 a maximum sentence imposed for attempted rape (which was then seven years) was reduced on the grounds of the guilty plea and saving the victim from the ordeal of giving testimony. See **E1.6**

Limits on Imposition of Imprisonment: Magistrates' Courts

E2.3 General limits on the power of magistrates' courts to impose imprisonment are specified by the PCC(S)A 2000, s. 78 and the MCA 1980, s. 32. The minimum prison sentence which may be imposed is one of five days (MCA 1980, s. 132) and the maximum is six months in respect of any one offence (PCC(S)A 2000, s. 78(1)) unless a shorter maximum term is provided by statute. The six-month limit does not, however, apply to imprisonment for non-payment of a fine (see **E17.7**). The maximum aggregate term which magistrates can impose is six months, unless two of the terms are imposed for offences triable either way, in which case the maximum aggregate term is 12 months (MCA 1980, s. 133). These provisions also apply to the sentence of detention in a young offender institution but not to the detention and training order. For more detailed treatment of the sentencing powers of a magistrates' court, see **D22**. Magistrates' courts are, of course, subject to the criteria for determining both the imposition and length of a custodial sentence (see **E2.5** and **E2.7**). When the CJA 2003, s. 154(1) is brought into force, the maximum prison sentence which may be imposed by a magistrates' court will be increased from six months to 12 months. By ss. 154(3) and 155, the maximum aggregate term which may be imposed by a magistrates' court will be increased from six months to 65 weeks. No date has been set for this change. The increased powers will also apply to the sentence of detention in a young offender institution, for so long as that sentence continues to exist. When the CJCSA 2000, s. 61, is brought into force, the sentence of detention in a young offender institution will be abolished and offenders who would have received such sentences will thereafter be eligible to be sentenced to imprisonment. No date for the implementation of s. 61 has yet been set, but by the CJA 2003, s. 333(1) and sch. 38, para. 1, if relevant sentencing provisions of the 2003 Act are brought into force before the sentence of detention in a young offender institution is abolished, the sentencing provisions may be modified accordingly. This means that s. 154(1) should be read as if it contained the words 'or detention in a young offender institution' after 'imprisonment' until such time as the former sentence is abolished.

A magistrates' court having power to imprison a person may instead order him to be detained within the precincts of the court-house or at any police station until such hour, not later than 8 p.m. on the day on which the order is made, as the court directs (MCA 1980, s. 135(1)). Such order shall not operate to deprive the person of a reasonable opportunity of returning home on the same day (s. 135(2)).

Restriction on Imposing Custodial Sentences on Persons Not Legally Represented

The PCC(S)A 2000, s. 83(1), states that a magistrates' court on summary conviction, or the Crown Court on committal for sentence or on conviction on indictment shall not pass a sentence of imprisonment on a person who (a) is not legally represented in that court, and (b) has not been previously sentenced to that punishment by a court in any part of the UK unless he is a person to whom s. 83(3) applies. For the purposes of s. 83(1)(b), a previous sentence of imprisonment, which has been suspended and which has not taken effect, shall be disregarded. This is a reference to the 'old-style' suspended sentence and not to suspended sentences under the CJA 2003. Section 83(3) applies to a person if either (a) he was granted a right to representation funded by the Legal Services Commission as part of the Criminal Defence Service but the right was withdrawn because of his conduct, or (b) having been informed of his right to apply for such representation and having had the opportunity to do so, he refused or failed to apply (s. 83(3)). **E2.4**

Section 83(2) extends the effect of these provisions to custodial sentences other than imprisonment: (a) detention under the PCC(S)A 2000, s. 91, (b) custody for life, (c) detention in a young offender institution and (d) the detention and training order.

For the purposes of s. 83, a person is to be treated as legally represented if, but only if, he has the assistance of counsel or a solicitor to represent him in the proceedings in that court at some time after he is found guilty and before he is sentenced (s. 83(4)).

A custodial sentence passed contrary to the provisions of s. 83 is unlawful, but may be substituted by a lawful sentence on appeal (see *Howden* [2007] 1 Cr App R (S) 164, *Hollywood* (1990) 12 Cr App R (S) 325, *Wilson* (1995) 16 Cr App R (S) 997).

General Restrictions on Imposing Discretionary Custodial Sentences

Criminal Justice Act 2003, s. 152 **E2.5**

(1) This section applies where a person is convicted of an offence punishable with a custodial sentence other than one—
  (a) fixed by law, or
  (b) falling to be imposed under section 51A(2) of the Firearms Act 1968, under [section] 110(2) or 111(2) of the Sentencing Act or under any of sections 225 to 228 of this Act.

(2) The court must not pass a custodial sentence unless it is of the opinion that the offence, or

the combination of the offence and one or more offences associated with it, was so serious that neither a fine alone nor a community sentence can be justified for the offence.

(3) Nothing in subsection (2) prevents the court from passing a custodial sentence on the offender if—
  (a) he fails to express his willingness to comply with a requirement which is proposed by the court to be included in a community order and which requires an expression of such willingness, or
  (b) he fails to comply with an order under section 161(2) (pre-sentence drug testing).

Section 152 came into effect on 4 April 2005 and applies in respect of offences committed on or after that date. It is closely similar to the PCC(S)A 2000, s. 79(1), (2)(a) and (3). The whole of s. 79 was repealed by the CJA 2003 with effect from 4 April 2005. It may be noted that the previous wording, that 'only such a sentence can be justified by the offence' is replaced by 'neither a fine alone nor a community sentence can be justified for the offence'. It is doubtful whether this change in wording makes any practical difference, as both formulae require the sentencer to turn to a custodial sentence only when all other sentencing options have been considered and rejected. Custody remains as a last resort. As Lord Woolf CJ observed in *Kefford* [2002] 2 Cr App R (S) 495, 'the message is imprisonment only when necessary and for no longer than necessary'. The message was reinforced in *Seed* [2007] EWCA Crim 254, when Lord Phillips CJ noted that at times of prison overcrowding the custodial regime would be more punitive and the opportunities for rehabilitative intervention in prison would be restricted.

The SGC Guideline, *Overarching Principles: Seriousness* (Dec 2004), states that the clear intention of this 'threshold test' is to reserve prison as a punishment for the most serious offences, but that it is impossible to determine definitively which features of a particular offence make it serious enough to merit a custodial sentence (para. 1.32).

Section 152(3) deals with the exceptional situation where a court may pass a custodial sentence on an offender who has failed to express his willingness to comply with a requirement proposed to be included in a community order and where the requirement requires an expression of such willingness. Requirements which require the offender's expression of willingness to comply are a mental health treatment requirement (s. 207(3)(c)), a drug rehabilitation requirement (s. 209(2)(d)), and an alcohol treatment requirement (s. 212(3)). Pre-sentence drug testing is considered at **E10.2**.

E2.6 **Two or More Offences** Where the offender stands convicted of two or more offences the court, in deciding whether custody is justified under s. 152(2) must consider the seriousness of the sum of the offences, provided that these are 'associated' with one another. Section 161(1) of the 2000 Act specifies when one offence is to be regarded as associated with another.

Powers of Criminal Courts (Sentencing) Act 2000, s. 161

(1) For the purposes of this Act, an offence is associated with another if—
  (a) the offender is convicted of it in the proceedings in which he is convicted of the other offence, or (although convicted of it in earlier proceedings) is sentenced for it at the same time as he is sentenced for that offence; or
  (b) the offender admits the commission of it in the proceedings in which he is sentenced for the other offence and requests the court to take it into consideration in sentencing him for that offence.

In *Baverstock* [1993] 1 WLR 202 the offender was dealt with for two offences; the second having been committed while the offender was on bail in respect of the first. The offender was sentenced for the two offences on the same occasion; hence, they were 'associated' for the purposes of s. 161(1). It is clear from the case of *Godfrey* (1993) 14 Cr App R (S) 804 that, where a sentencer is sentencing for a new offence and at the same time revokes a community sentence which had earlier been passed on the offender and re-sentences for that offence, or where the sentencer passes a sentence for an offence in respect of which a conditional discharge had earlier been granted, the new offence and the earlier offence are associated offences. In *Godfrey* itself, however, the judge imposed 'no separate penalty' for a breach of conditional discharge. This meant that the earlier offence was not being sentenced on the same occasion as the new offence, and thus the two offences could not be regarded as associated. In *Crawford* (1993) 98 Cr App R 297, it was held that, where the offender had been committed to the Crown Court in respect of an offence of theft which placed him in breach of a suspended sentence imposed for an earlier offence of theft, the two offences were not associated offences. *Crawford* was followed and applied in *Cawley* (1994) 15 Cr App R (S) 25. Where an offender has been convicted in respect of a number of charges which are represented as 'sample counts', offences which are not included in the indictment or formally taken into consideration are not associated offences (*Canavan* [1998] 1 Cr App R (S) 79; *Tovey* [2005] 2 Cr App R (S) 606). See further **D19.53**.

Length of Discretionary Custodial Sentences: General Provision

Criminal Justice Act 2003, s. 153 **E2.7**

(1) This section applies where a court passes a custodial sentence other than one fixed by law or falling to be imposed under section 225 or 226.
(2) Subject to section 51A(2) of the Firearms Act 1968, sections 110(2) and 11(2) of the Sentencing Act and sections 227(2) and 228(2) of this Act, the custodial sentence must be for the shortest term (not exceeding the permitted maximum) that in the opinion of the court is commensurate with the seriousness of the offence, or the combination of the offence and one or more offences associated with it.

Section 153 came into effect on 4 April 2005 and applies to offences committed on or after that date. It is closely similar to the PCC(S)A 2000, s. 80(1) and (2)(a). The whole of s. 80 was repealed by the CJA 2003 with effect from 4 April 2005. It may be noted that the previous wording, 'for such term' is replaced by 'for the shortest term'. The wording in s. 153(2) is a clearer reflection of the well-established principle that, when it is necessary to impose a custodial sentence, that sentence should be as short as possible to achieve the goals of that sentence.

Section 153(2) states that the court may have regard to 'the combination of the offence and one or more offences associated with it' when determining the length of a custodial sentence. Section 161(1)of the PCC(S)A of 2000 (see **E2.6**) defines when one offence may be regarded for these purposes as 'associated with' another.

Where the offender is being sentenced for several offences, this approach could lead to a total sentence which is disproportionate to the overall seriousness of the offending behaviour. The CJA 2003, s. 166(3)(b), in an attempt to avoid this, declares that nothing shall prevent a court 'in a case of an offender who is convicted of one or more other offences, from mitigating his sentence by applying any rule of law as to the totality of sentences'. This provision gives statutory recognition to the totality principle, which has been developed by the Court of Appeal. For discussion of that principle, see **E1.14**.

Where a court is dealing with an offender for several offences, one (or more) of which is (or are) so serious that only custody can be justified but the remainder of which are not so serious, the court is not precluded from passing custodial sentences for the lesser offences. However, those sentences should normally be ordered to run concurrently with the sentences for the more serious offences and should not increase the length of the overall term (*Oliver* [1993] 1 WLR 177).

In *Bibi* [1980] 1 WLR 1193 Lord Lane CJ said (at p. 1195):

> . . . sentencing courts must be particularly careful to examine each case to ensure, if an immediate custodial sentence is necessary, that the sentence is as short as possible, consistent only with the duty to protect the interests of the public and to punish and deter the criminal.

The Court of Appeal in *Ollerenshaw* [1999] 1 Cr App R (S) 65 stated that the approach in *Bibi* was no less valid in the light of current prison overcrowding. Rose LJ said that, when a court is considering imposing a custodial sentence of about 12 months or less, it should ask itself (especially where this will be the offender's first prison sentence) whether a shorter period might be equally effective. Six months may be just as effective as nine, or two months may be just as effective as four. In *Kefford* [2002] 2 Cr App R (S) 495, Lord Woolf CJ said that the overcrowding of the prison system was a matter of grave concern and that all courts should heed the message, which was 'imprisonment only when necessary and for no longer than necessary'. See also *Mills* [2002] 2 Cr App R (S) 229, with respect to the female prison population and *Seed* [2007] EWCA Crim 254.

Crediting of Periods of Remand in Custody

E2.8 **Criminal Justice Act 2003, s. 240**

(1) This section applies where—
  (a) a court sentences an offender to imprisonment for a term in respect of an offence committed after the commencement of this section, and
  (b) the offender has been remanded in custody (within the meaning given by section 242) in connection with the offence or a related offence, that is to say, any other offence the charge for which was founded on the same facts or evidence.

(2) It is immaterial for that purpose whether the offender—
  (a) has also been remanded in custody in connection with other offences; or
  (b) has also been detained in connection with other matters.

(3) Subject to subsection (4), the court must direct that the number of days for which the offender was remanded in custody in connection with the offence or a related offence is to count as time served by him as part of the sentence.

(4) Subsection (3) does not apply if and to the extent that—
  (a) rules made by the Secretary of State so provide in the case of—
    (i) a remand in custody which is wholly or partly concurrent with a sentence of imprisonment, or
    (ii) sentences of imprisonment for consecutive terms or for terms which are wholly or partly concurrent, or
  (b) it is in the opinion of the court just in all the circumstances not to give a direction under that subsection.

(5) Where the court gives a direction under subsection (3), it shall state in open court—
  (a) the number of days for which the offender was remanded in custody, and
  (b) the number of days in relation to which the direction is given.

(6) Where the court does not give a direction under subsection (3), or gives such a direction in relation to a number of days less than that for which the offender was remanded in custody, it shall state in open court—
  (a) that its decision is in accordance with rules made under paragraph (a) of subsection (4), or
  (b) that it is of the opinion mentioned in paragraph (b) of that subsection and what the circumstances are.

(7) For the purposes of this section a suspended sentence—
  (a) is to be treated as a sentence of imprisonment when it takes effect under paragraph 8(2)(a) or (b) of Schedule 12, and
  (b) is to be treated as being imposed by the order under which it takes effect.

(8) For the purposes of the reference in subsection (3) to the term of imprisonment to which a person has been sentenced (that is to say, the reference to his 'sentence'), consecutive terms and terms which are wholly or partly concurrent are to be treated as a single term if—
  (a) the sentences were passed on the same occasion, or
  (b) where they were passed on different occasions, the person has not been released under this Chapter at any time during the period beginning with the first and ending with the last of those occasions.

(9) Where an offence is found to have been committed over a period of two or more days, or at some time during a period of two or more days, it shall be taken for the purposes of subsection (1) to have been committed on the last of those days.

(10) This section applies to a determinate sentence of detention under section 91 of the Sentencing Act or section 228 of this Act as it applies to an equivalent sentence of imprisonment.

Section 240 replaces the CJA 1967, s. 67, by which the length of a sentence of imprisonment, detention in a young offender institution or determinate period of detention imposed under the PCC(S)A 2000, s. 91, was automatically treated as reduced by any period during which the offender was in custody. Section 240 now requires the sentencer imposing any of these custodial sentences normally to direct in open court that the number of days so spent by the offender shall count as part of the custodial sentence (s. 240(3)), unless the sentencer decides in accordance with s. 240(4) that no credit, or reduced credit, should be given. If no credit, or reduced credit, is given, then the sentencer must explain the reasons (s. 240(6)).

Section 240(1) refers to 'imprisonment', which includes the extended sentence of imprisonment under the CJA 2003, s. 227. The section also applies to sentences of detention in a young offender institution and (by s. 240(10)) to determinate sentences of detention under the PCC(S)A 2000, s. 91, and to the extended sentence provisions for offenders aged under 18, under the CJA 2003, s. 228. In respect of other sentences where the law requires the setting of a specified period under the PCC(S)A 2000, s. 82A (discretionary life sentence, custody for life, detention for life, imprisonment for public protection under the CJA 2003, s. 225 or detention for public protection under the CJA 2003, s. 226), s. 82A(3)(b) of that Act requires the court when fixing the specified minimum period to take into account any direction which it would have given under s. 240 (see **E5.13**). In fixing the minimum term applicable in a case of murder, the court is also required to take into account the effect of any direction which it would have given under the CJA 2003, s. 240 (see **E4.1**).

Section 240 does not apply to any committal in default of payment of any sum of money, other than one adjudged to be paid on a conviction (s. 242(1)), nor does it apply to the detention and training order, in respect of which there are separate provisions for crediting periods of remand in custody (see **E9.15**).

The Court of Appeal provided guidance on the operation of s. 240 in *Barber* [2006] 2 Cr App R (S) 539. The court stressed the importance of the sentencer giving a clear direction in open court that all of the days which the offender has spent on remand (other than those excluded by virtue of the Remand in Custody (Effect of Concurrent and Consecutive Sentences of Imprisonment) Rules 2005) should count as part of the sentence unless the court considers that it would be just in all the circumstances not to give such a direction with respect to all, or some, of those days. If the court decides that it would be just not to give such a direction, the judge should consider alerting counsel in advance in order to hear representations on the point and, in any event, should give reasons for the decision. Clearly it is important that all parties are agreed on the number of days which have been served. If there is uncertainty over that matter, the Court of Appeal in *Norman* [2007] 1 Cr App R (S) 509 suggested that it may be necessary to adjourn sentence, or to adjourn determination of the issue under s. 240, until such time as accurate information is available. A later adjustment to a sentence already imposed should be made within the 28-day slip rule under the PCC(S)A 2000, s. 155 (see **D19.93**). According to the Court of Appeal in *Gordon* [2007] 2 All ER 768 there was no reason why a judge could not make it clear that the offender should receive credit for the full period of time spent in custody on remand (or any particular part of that period), that on the current information that amounted to X days, but if that information proved to be wrong the court would order an amendment of the record for the correct period to be entered.

The CJA 2003, s. 241, provides for time spent by the offender on remand to be treated as time served under the sentence for the purpose of calculating whether a prisoner has served a certain proportion of the sentence and whether he is therefore eligible for early release.

Section 242(2), explains that 'remanded in custody' means 'remanded in or committed to custody by order of a court', or 'remanded or committed to local authority accommodation' under the CYPA 1969, s. 23 (but see the decision of the House of Lords in *Secretary of State for the Home Department, ex parte A* [2000] 2 AC 276, which held that under the previous legislative regime, this applied only if the remand was to 'secure accommodation'), or 'remanded, admitted or removed to hospital' under the Mental Health Act 1983. It does not include time spent in police detention. Section 242(2) appears to provide a closed list of what can amount to 'remanded in custody'. In *Watson* [2000] 2 Cr App R (S) 301, the Court of Appeal said that it was right to take into account a period of 11 months that the offender had spent on remand in a bail hostel under restrictive conditions, although the court clearly stated that a period in a bail hostel was not to be equated with a period on remand in custody.

E2.9 **Extradited Prisoners** The CJA 2003, s. 243, relates to extradited prisoners, and replaces the CJA 1991, s. 47. Section 243 provides that days kept in custody awaiting extradition are to be treated as though they were days remanded in custody. This brings extradited offenders within the scope of s. 240, and earlier decisions in respect of such offenders may still be regarded as relevant. In *Stone* (1988) 10 Cr App R (S) 322, the Court of Appeal upheld the judge's decision to take only part of the period into account, in view of the appellant's challenge to extradition proceedings (see also *De Simone* [2000] 2 Cr App R (S) 332 and *Andre* [2002] 1 Cr App R (S) 98).

E2.10 **Effect of Time on Remand on Community Sentence** Section 240 does not deal with the situation where an offender has been remanded in custody for a period of time before being sentenced to a community sentence. This is dealt with in the CJA 2003, s. 149, which states that the court may have regard to any such period in determining the restrictions on liberty to be imposed by a community order or by a youth community order. See further Sentencing Guideline, *New Sentences: CJA 2003* (Dec 04), paras. 1.1.37 to 1.140, set out in **appendix 8, Part 2.**

Concurrent and Consecutive Custodial Sentences

E2.11 Where an offender is convicted on more than one count, the court should impose separate sentences on each count. Prison sentences may run concurrently or consecutively, or there may be a mixture of concurrent and consecutive sentences. The court should make it clear which sentence relates to which count and whether the sentences are concurrent or consecutive. If it fails to do so, it is presumed that the sentences are concurrent. Where a court passes a prison sentence on a person who is already serving one or more sentences of imprisonment, it must make clear whether the fresh sentence is to be served concurrently with or consecutively to the existing sentence or sentences. It is unlawful to pass a sentence partly concurrent with and partly consecutive to another sentence (*Salmon* [2003] 1 Cr App R (S) 414). There is no power to antedate the commencement of a sentence (PCC(S)A 2000, s. 154; *Whitfield* [2002] 2 Cr App R (S) 186), so the new sentence takes effect from the date on which it is imposed, unless the sentencer specifies a later date. A court imposing a prison sentence must not direct that the new sentence shall commence on the expiration of any other prison sentence from which the offender has been released under the CJA 1991, part II (PCC(S)A 2000, s. 84).

Terms of imprisonment may be ordered to run consecutively even where that results in a total term greater than the maximum which could have been imposed for any of the offences (e.g., *Prime* (1983) 5 Cr App R (S) 127).

A fixed-term prison sentence may not run consecutively to a life sentence (*Foy* [1962] 1 WLR 609) nor vice versa (*Jones v DPP* [1962] AC 635, at p. 647). For relevant principles applicable to sentences for public protection, see **E5.11**.

Generally, where offences arise out of the same incident, sentences should be concurrent. Concurrent sentences should be imposed where multiple deaths arise from a single act of dangerous driving (*Noble* [2003] 1 Cr App R (S) 312) or where convictions for dangerous driving and for inflicting grievous bodily harm relate to the same incident (*Bain* [2005] 2 Cr App R (S) 319). In *Cosco* [2005] 2 Cr App R (S) 405, where the offender committed three offences of indecent exposure during the course of one afternoon, the Court of Appeal said that the three offences were part of a single course of conduct and concurrent sentences were appropriate. Occasionally, however, consecutive sentences are upheld for offences committed on the same occasion. An example is *Hardy* [2006] 2 Cr App R (S) 47, where the Court of Appeal upheld consecutive sentences totalling two years' imprisonment for dangerous driving, driving while disqualified and failing to provide a specimen. Steel J said that, while the offence of dangerous driving carried the main custodial sentence, it would be bizarre to add no further custodial term for the other matters. There was well established authority, deriving from *Wheatley* (1983) 5 Cr App R (S) 417, that consecutive sentences should usually be imposed in cases such as these.

Consecutive sentences should normally be imposed where an offender has used violence to resist arrest for another offence (*Wellington* (1988) 10 Cr App R (S) 384) or has used violence to make good his escape (*Bunch* (1971) CSP A5–2C01). In the case of robbery involving the use of a real or imitation firearm, earlier decisions such as *French* (1982) 4 Cr App R (S) 57, *McGrath* (1986) 8 Cr App R (S) 372 and *Greaves* [2004] 2 Cr App R (S) 41 state that consecutive sentences are generally appropriate. In *A-G's Refs (Nos 21 and 22 of 2003)* [2004] 2 Cr App R (S) 63, however, the Court of Appeal said that, in many cases of robbery, the possession or use of the firearm was intrinsic to the seriousness of the robbery itself, and concurrent sentences would not be inappropriate so long as the sentence as a whole reflected the overall criminality in the case. The Court of Appeal also said that, if the offender is in possession of a firearm at the time of committing another offence, such as criminal damage or dealing in drugs, it will often be appropriate to impose consecutive sentences for the firearms offence and the other offence. Consecutive sentences should normally be imposed where the offender commits an offence on bail which was granted in respect of the other offence (*Whittaker* [1998] 1 Cr App R (S) 172), although it is not clear how the principle squares with the CJA 2003, s. 143(3): see **E1.5**). A custodial sentence imposed for a failure to surrender to bail should normally be ordered to be served consecutively (*White* [2003] 2 Cr App R (S) 133 and **D7.83**). A custodial sentence imposed for escape from lawful custody should run consecutively to the sentence being served at the time of the escape (*Clarke* (1994) 15 Cr App R (S) 825) as should a custodial sentence for offences committed within prison by a serving prisoner (*Ali* [1998] 2 Cr App R (S) 123). Where an offender has attempted to interfere with the course of justice in relation to an offence committed by him, sentence for the interference offence should normally be consecutive to the sentence for the other offence (*A-G's Ref (No. 1 of 1990)* (1990) 12 Cr App R (S) 245).

Consecutive sentences are always subject to the totality principle: see **E1.14**.

Relevance to Sentence of Early Release Provisions

E2.12 The *Practice Statement (Crime: Sentencing)* [1992] 1 WLR 948 established that, when passing a custodial sentence in the Crown Court, it is necessary for the sentencer to have regard to the actual period which was likely to be served by the offender, having regard to current arrangements for the early release of prisoners. In *Cunningham* [1993] 1 WLR 183, however, Lord Taylor CJ warned that the Court of Appeal would be unmoved 'by nice mathematical comparisons' on the effective length of custodial sentences. A sentencer may wish to adjust sentence length to avoid an unusual, adverse effect upon an offender's release date (see *Waite* (1992) 13 Cr App R (S) 26, *Cozens* [1996] 2 Cr App R (S) 321 and *Harrison* [1998] 2 Cr App R (S) 174). The decision in *Cozens* does not require a sentencer to pass an unduly lenient sentence to avoid that result (*Parker* [2000] 2 Cr App R (S) 295). Nothing in *Practice Statement (Crime: Sentencing)* should be taken to detract from the principle that a sentencer should not increase sentence length merely to bring an offender within a different early release category (*Kenway* (1985) 7 Cr App R (S) 457).

In *Al-Buhairi* [2004] 1 Cr App R (S) 496, and in *Alkazraji* [2004] 2 Cr App R (S) 295, the Court of Appeal held that it was not proper for a judge to adjust sentence to take account of the fact that the offender may be released early on the home detention curfew scheme. Such release was a matter within the discretion of the individual prison governor. There was always a degree of uncertainty and it was undesirable for judges to become involved in that possibility when they dealt with offenders.

Relevance to Sentence of Allocation to Particular Custodial Regime

E2.13 The sentencer should not recommend that an offender serve a custodial sentence at a specified prison, such as Grendon Underwood, since it may not always be possible for this to be arranged (*Hook* (1980) 2 Cr App R (S) 353; *Lancaster* (1995) 16 Cr App R (S) 184). The fact that a prisoner will be required to serve his sentence under rule 43 (in isolation for his own protection) is not normally a relevant consideration when passing sentence (*Kay* (1980) 2 Cr App R (S) 284; *Parker* [1996] 2 Cr App R (S) 275). An exceptional case is *Holmes* (1979) 1 Cr App R (S) 233.

Section E3 Discretionary Custodial Sentences

Prison Sentences of 12 Months or More

The SGC Guideline, *New Sentences: CJA 2003* (Dec 2004), set out in **Part 2 of appendix 8**, **E3.1**
explains that, following the implementation of the relevant early release provisions of the CJA 2003, where a prison sentence or sentence of detention in a young offender institution of 12 months or more is imposed on an offender who is not a 'dangerous offender' (as to which, see E5), the offender will be entitled to be released from custody after serving half the sentence, but the whole of the second half will be subject to licence requirements. These requirements will be set by the Secretary of State shortly before release (para. 2.1.3).

As well as restricting liberty to a greater extent, the new requirements will last until the very end of the sentence, rather than to the three-quarter point as at present, potentially making a custodial sentence significantly more demanding than under the previous legislation. Breach of these requirements at any stage is likely to result in the offender being returned to custody and this risk continues, therefore, for longer under the new framework than under the previous legislation (para. 2.16).

The Council's conclusion is that the sentencer should seek to achieve the best match between a sentence under the new framework and its equivalent under the old framework so as to maintain the same level of punishment. As a guide the Council suggests the sentence length should be reduced by in the region of 15 per cent (para. 2.19).

The reference in these provisions to sentences of imprisonment must be taken also to include sentences of detention in a young offender institution (the Criminal Justice Act 2003 (Sentencing) (Transitory Provisions) Order 2005 (SI 2005 No. 643)). When the CJCSA 2000, s. 61, is brought into force, the sentence of detention in a young offender institution will be abolished. Offenders who would have received such a sentence will thereafter be sentenced to imprisonment, which will become the standard custodial sentence for offenders aged 18 to 20 inclusive as well as for offenders aged 21 and over. No date for implementation of s. 61 has yet been set.

By the CJA 2003, s. 238, where the court imposes a determinate sentence of imprisonment of 12 months or more on an offender for any offence (but not a sentence of detention under PCC(S)A 2000, s. 91), the part of the sentence to be served after release from custody will be subject to prescribed standard conditions, and may be made subject to further conditions similar to the requirements applicable to the community sentence. The conditions to be imposed on licence will be determined shortly before release of the offender by the Secretary of State (on advice from the probation service), but the court, at the time of passing sentence, will be able to make recommendation as to the content of those conditions (s. 238(1)), and the Secretary of State must have regard to any such recommendation (s. 238(2)). The conditions that the Secretary of State may attach to a licence are to be prescribed by order (s. 250), and the sentencer will wish to bear these in mind when making a recommendation at the point of sentence. A recommendation made by the sentencer as to licence conditions is not to be treated as part of the sentence (s. 238(3)), and so cannot be the subject of an appeal against sentence.

The SGC Guideline, *New Sentences: CJA 2003* states that a court may sensibly suggest interventions that could be useful when passing sentence, but should only make specific recommendations about the requirements to be imposed on licence when announcing short sentences and where it is reasonable to anticipate their relevance at the point of release. The governor and the probation service should have due regard to any recommendations made by the sentencing court but its decision should be contingent upon any changed circumstances during the custodial period (para. 2.1.14).

Prison Sentences of Less than 12 Months (Custody Plus)

E3.2 The CJA 2003, ss. 181 and 182, contain provisions that, when brought into force, will restrict the powers of the courts to impose sentences of imprisonment under 12 months in length. Any power of a court to impose a sentence of less than 12 months may be exercised only in accordance with these provisions. No date has been set for these provisions to be brought into force.

Criminal Justice Act 2003, s. 181

(1) Any power of a court to impose a sentence of imprisonment for a term of less than 12 months on an offender may be exercised only in accordance with the following provisions of this section unless the court makes an intermittent custody order (as defined by section 183).

(2) The term of the sentence—
- (a) must be expressed in weeks,
- (b) must be at least 28 weeks,
- (c) must not be more than 51 weeks in respect of any one offence, and
- (d) must not exceed the maximum term permitted for the offence.

(3) The court, when passing sentence, must—
- (a) specify a period (in this chapter referred to as 'the custodial period') at the end of which the offender is to be released on a licence, and
- (b) by order require the licence to be granted subject to conditions requiring the offender's compliance during the remainder of the term (in this chapter referred to as 'the licence period') or any part of it with one or more requirements falling within section 182(1) and specified in the order.

(4) In this part 'custody plus order' means an order under subsection (3)(b).

(5) The custodial period—
- (a) must be at least 2 weeks, and
- (b) in respect of any one offence, must not be more than 13 weeks.

(6) In determining the term of the sentence and the length of the custodial period, the court must ensure that the licence period is at least 26 weeks in length.

(7) Where a court imposes two or more terms of imprisonment in accordance with this section to be served consecutively—
- (a) the aggregate length of the terms of imprisonment must not be more than 65 weeks, and
- (b) the aggregate length of the custodial periods must not be more than 26 weeks.

(8) A custody plus order which specifies two or more requirements may, in relation to any requirement, refer to compliance within such part of the licence period as is specified in the order.

(9) Subsection (3)(b) does not apply where the sentence is a suspended sentence.

The term of the sentence must be expressed in weeks, must be at least 28 weeks, must not be more than 51 weeks in respect of any one offence, and must not exceed the maximum term permitted for the offence (s. 181(2)). The court must specify a custodial period (of at least two weeks but, in respect of any one offence, of not more than 13 weeks) at the end of which the offender is to be released on licence. In any case the licence period must be at least 26 weeks. This is to be known as a 'custody plus' order. If two or more terms are to be served consecutively, the aggregate length of the terms must not be more than 65 weeks and the aggregate length of the custodial periods must not be more than 26 weeks.

Criminal Justice Act 2003, s. 182

(1) The requirements falling within this subsection are—

(a) an unpaid work requirement (as defined by section 199),
(b) an activity requirement (as defined by section 201),
(c) a programme requirement (as defined by section 202),
(d) a prohibited activity requirement (as defined by section 203),
(e) a curfew requirement (as defined by section 204),
(f) an exclusion requirement (as defined by section 205),
(g) a supervision requirement (as defined by section 213), and
(h) in a case where the offender is aged under 25, an attendance centre requirement (as defined by section 214).

(2) The power under section 181(3)(b) to determine the conditions of the licence has effect subject to section 218 and to the following provisions of chapter 4 relating to particular requirements—
(a) section 199(3) (unpaid work requirement),
(b) section 201(3) and (4) (activity requirement),
(c) section 202(4) and (5) (programme requirement), and
(d) section 203(2) (prohibited activity requirement).

(3) Where the court makes a custody plus order requiring a licence to contain a curfew requirement or an exclusion requirement, the court must also require the licence to contain an electronic monitoring requirement (as defined by section 215) unless—
(a) the court is prevented from doing so by section 215(2) or 218(4), or
(b) in the particular circumstances of the case, it considers it inappropriate to do so.

(4) Where the court makes a custody plus order requiring a licence to contain an unpaid work requirement, an activity requirement, a programme requirement, a prohibited activity requirement, a supervision requirement or an attendance centre requirement, the court may also require the licence to contain an electronic monitoring requirement unless the court is prevented from doing so by section 215(2) or 218(4).

(5) Before making a custody plus order requiring a licence to contain two or more different requirements falling within subsection (1), the court must consider whether, in the circumstances of the case, the requirements are compatible with each other.

The custody plus order may require the licence to be granted subject to conditions requiring the offender's compliance during the remainder of the term. Licence conditions may be selected from a list set out in s. 182.

These eight requirements are drawn from the list of 12 specified requirements which a sentencer may insert into a community order. The operational details of these eight requirements are considered at **E10.6** to **E10.11**, **E10.16** and (where the offender is under the age of 25) **E10.17**.

Whenever the court makes a custody plus order which requires a licence to contain two or more different requirements, it must consider whether, in the circumstances of the case, the requirements are compatible with each other (s. 182(5)). Power to insert such requirements into the licence is made subject to the court ensuring, so far as possible, that the condition or conditions avoid conflict with the offender's religious beliefs, and the requirements of any other relevant order to which he may be subject, and avoid interference with the offender's work, schooling or other educational commitments (s. 217). The court must also be satisfied that local facilities exist, and that local arrangements are in place, for the carrying out of relevant requirements (s. 218). A custody plus order must specify the petty sessions area in which the offender will reside during the licence period (s. 216(2)(a)).

The court cannot make an unpaid work requirement unless satisfied that the offender is a suitable person to perform such work (s. 199(3)). The court cannot impose an activity requirement unless it has consulted an officer of a local probation board or a member of a youth offending team (as appropriate), is satisfied that it is feasible to secure compliance with the requirement (s. 201(3)) and has secured the agreement of any person other than the offender and the responsible officer whose co-operation is required (s. 201(4)). The court cannot insert a programme requirement unless the relevant accredited programme has been recommended to the court by an officer of a local probation board or a member of a youth offending team (as appropriate) as being suitable for the offender, the court is satisfied that the programme will be available (s. 202(4)) and the court has secured the agreement of any person other than the offender and the responsible officer whose co-operation is required. The court cannot insert a prohibited activity requirement unless it has consulted an officer of a local probation board or a member of a youth offending team (as appropriate) (s. 203(2)).

If the custody plus order contains a curfew requirement or an exclusion requirement, the court must also require the licence to contain an electronic monitoring requirement, as defined by s. 215, unless it is unable to do so because there is some person, other than the offender, whose co-operation is required but who does not consent (s. 215(2)), or because electronic monitoring arrangements are not available in the local area (s. 218(4)) or because in the particular circumstances of the case the court considers it inappropriate to do so.

If the custody plus order contains an unpaid work requirement, an activity requirement, a programme requirement, a prohibited activity requirement, a supervision requirement or an attendance centre requirement, the court may also require the licence to contain an electronic monitoring requirement, unless it is unable to do so because there is some person, other than the offender, whose co-operation is required but who does not consent (s. 215(2)), or because electronic monitoring arrangements are not available in the local area (s. 218(4)).

Section E4 Mandatory Life Sentences

An offender aged 21 and over who is convicted of murder (but not related offences such as attempted murder or conspiracy to murder) must be sentenced to imprisonment for life (Murder (Abolition of Death Penalty) Act 1965, s. 1(1)). For an offender aged under 21 on the date of conviction, the equivalent sentence is custody for life (see PCC(S)A 2000, s. 93 and **E4.6**). If, however, the offender who is convicted of murder was aged under 18 when the offence was committed, the sentence is one of detention at Her Majesty's pleasure (see PCC(S)A 2000, s. 90 and **E4.7**). The setting of the specified period in relation to other forms of life sentence, such as the discretionary life sentence, is governed by the PCC(S)A 2000, s. 82A (see **E5.13**). When the CJCSA 2000, s. 61, is brought into force, the sentence of custody for life will be abolished, and offenders in this age group who are convicted of murder will then be sentenced to life imprisonment instead. No date has been set for this change.

Murder: Life Imprisonment

Following the decision of the House of Lords in *R (Anderson)* v *Secretary of State for the Home Department* [2003] 1 AC 837, the Home Secretary now plays no role in the setting of the minimum term to be served by an offender sentenced to life imprisonment for murder. It was decided in that case that former powers enjoyed by the Home Secretary under the C(S)A 1997, s. 29, to amend the minimum term recommended by the judiciary, infringed the right of an offender under the ECHR, Article 6, to have his sentence imposed by an independent and impartial tribunal and, accordingly, a declaration of incompatibility under the HRA 1998 with respect to that section was made. Section 29 was repealed by the CJA 2003, sch. 37, part 8. When passing a sentence of life imprisonment for murder the court was formerly empowered under the Murder (Abolition of Death Penalty) Act 1965, s. 1(2), to 'declare the period which it recommends to the Secretary of State as the minimum period which should elapse' before the offender is released on licence. The power under s. 1(2) was also repealed by the CJA 2003, sch. 37, part 8. **E4.1**

The CJA 2003, ss. 269 to 277 and schs. 21 and 22, provide a statutory scheme for the setting of minimum terms in murder cases, together with transitory provisions. These provisions came into effect on 18 December 2003. They apply to all cases in which a court passes, on or after the commencement date, a mandatory life sentence for murder. This applies to sentences of life imprisonment for murder, detention at Her Majesty's pleasure under the PCC(S)A 2000, s. 90 and, until that sentence is abolished, custody for life imposed for murder committed by an 18, 19 or 20-year-old offender under the PCC(S)A 2000, s. 93. By the CJA 2003, s. 269(2), the court must normally make an order that the early release provisions of the C(S)A 1997, s. 28(5) to (8) are to apply to the offender as soon as he has served the part of his sentence which is specified in the order. That part is to be such as the court considers appropriate, taking into account (a) the seriousness of the offence, or the combination of the offence and any one or more offences associated with it, and (b) the effect of any direction which it would have given under the CJA 2003, s. 240 (crediting periods of remand in custody) if it had sentenced him to a term of imprisonment (s. 269(3)). If the offender is aged 21 or over when he committed the offence, the court may, however, because of the seriousness of the offence, order that the early release provisions are not to apply to the offender (s. 269(4)). An order under s. 269(4) would have the effect of imposing a 'whole life' minimum term. A judge fixing the minimum term to be served as part of the mandatory life sentence for murder is concerned with the seriousness of the offence and not the dangerousness of the offender. The element of public protection is provided by the indeterminate nature of the life sentence itself and becomes the responsibility of the Parole Board once the minimum term has been served (*Leigers* [2005] 2 Cr App R (S) 654; *Jones* [2006] 2 Cr App R (S) 121). In considering the seriousness of an offence under s. 269(3) or (4), the court must have regard to (a) the 'general principles' set out in sch. 21 and (b) any guidelines relating to offences in general which are relevant to the case and are not incompatible with the provisions of sch. 21 (s. 269(5)). Any court making an order under s. 269(2) or (4) must state in open court, in ordinary language, its reasons; in stating its reasons it must, in particular, state which of the starting points in sch. 21 it has chosen and its reasons for doing so and state its reasons for any departure from that starting point (s. 270).

E4.2 Schedule 21 Principles Schedule 21 sets out a detailed scheme of 'general principles' for determination of the minimum term in relation to mandatory life sentences. It should be noted that, for the purposes of sch. 21, 'child' means a person under 18 years of age, 'minimum term' means the part of the sentence to be specified by the sentencer under s. 269(2), and 'whole life order' means an order under s. 269(4). Section 28 of the CDA 1998 (meaning of 'racially or religiously aggravated') applies for the purposes of sch. 21 as it does for ss. 29 to 32 of the 1998 Act (see **B11.160**), and for the purposes of sch. 21 an offence is aggravated by sexual orientation if it is committed in circumstances falling within the CJA 2003, s. 146(2)(a)(i) or (b)(i) (see **E1.10**).

Criminal Justice Act 2003, sch. 21, paras. 4 to 11

Starting points

4.—(1) If—

(a) the court considers that the seriousness of the offence (or the combination of the offence and one or more offences associated with it) is exceptionally high, and

(b) the offender was aged 21 or over when he committed the offence,

the appropriate starting point is a whole life order.

(2) Cases that would normally fall within sub-paragraph (1)(a) include—

(a) the murder of two or more persons, where each murder involves any of the following—

(i) a substantial degree of premeditation or planning,

(ii) the abduction of the victim, or

(iii) sexual or sadistic conduct,

(b) the murder of a child if involving the abduction of the child or sexual or sadistic motivation,

(c) a murder done for the purpose of advancing a political, religious or ideological cause, or

(d) a murder by an offender previously convicted of murder.

5.—(1) If—

(a) the case does not fall within paragraph 4(1) but the court considers that the seriousness of the offence (or the combination of the offence and one or more offences associated with it) is particularly high, and

(b) the offender was aged 18 or over when he committed the offence,

the appropriate starting point, in determining the minimum term, is 30 years.

(2) Cases that (if not falling within paragraph 4(1)) would normally fall within sub-paragraph (1)(a) include—

(a) the murder of a police officer or prison officer in the course of his duty,

(b) a murder involving the use of a firearm or explosive,

(c) a murder done for gain (such as a murder done in the course or furtherance of robbery or burglary, done for payment or done in the expectation of gain as a result of the death),

(d) a murder intended to obstruct or interfere with the course of justice,

(e) a murder involving sexual or sadistic conduct,

(f) the murder of two or more persons,

(g) a murder that is racially or religiously aggravated or aggravated by sexual orientation, or

(h) a murder falling within paragraph 4(2) committed by an offender who was aged under 21 when he committed the offence.

6. If the offender was aged 18 or over when he committed the offence and the case does not fall within paragraph 4(1) or 5(1), the appropriate starting point, in determining the minimum term, is 15 years.

7. If the offender was aged under 18 when he committed the offence, the appropriate starting point, in determining the minimum term, is 12 years.

Aggravating and mitigating factors

8. Having chosen a starting point, the court should take into account any aggravating or mitigating factors, to the extent that it has not allowed for them in its choice of starting point.

9. Detailed consideration of aggravating or mitigating factors may result in a minimum term of any length (whatever the starting point), or in the making of a whole life order.

10. Aggravating factors (additional to those mentioned in paragraph 4(2) and 5(2)) that may be relevant to the offence of murder include—
(a) a significant degree of planning or premeditation,
(b) the fact that the victim was particularly vulnerable because of age or disability,
(c) mental or physical suffering inflicted on the victim before death,
(d) the abuse of a position of trust,
(e) the use of duress or threats against another person to facilitate the commission of the offence,
(f) the fact that the victim was providing a public service or performing a public duty; and
(g) concealment, destruction or dismemberment of the body.

11. Mitigating factors that may be relevant to the offence of murder include—
(a) an intention to cause serious bodily harm rather than to kill,
(b) lack of premeditation,
(c) the fact that the offender suffered from any mental disorder or mental disability which (although not falling within section 2(1) of the Homicide Act 1957) lowered his degree of culpability,
(d) the fact that the offender was provoked (for example, by prolonged stress) in a way not amounting to a defence of provocation,
(e) the fact that the offender acted to any extent in self-defence,
(f) a belief by the offender that the murder was an act of mercy, and
(g) the age of the offender.

Paragraph 12 states that nothing in sch. 21 restricts the application of the CJA 2003, s. 143(2) (circumstances in which each previous conviction of the offender is to be treated as an aggravating factor: see **E1.4**), s. 143(3) (commission of an offence while on bail to be treated as an aggravating factor: see **E1.5**) or s. 144 (reduction in sentences for guilty pleas: see **E1.6**). Detailed guidance as to the procedure for passing a mandatory life sentence under s. 269 and sch. 21 were issued by the Lord Chief Justice on 18 May 2004 and can be found in the *Consolidated Criminal Practice Direction*, para. IV.49 (see **appendix** 7). The SGC Guideline, *Reduction in Sentence for a Guilty Plea* (see **E1.6**), is applicable when setting the minimum term to be served in a mandatory life sentence. For the text of the guidelines, see **appendix 8**. In *Last* [2005] 2 Cr App R (S) 381, the Court of Appeal gave guidance on the application of that Guideline in murder cases. Lord Woolf CJ said that except in the 'unlikely circumstances' that an offender would be prejudiced by the application of the Guideline, it was sensible for it to be adopted. In *Jones* [2005] EWCA Crim 3115, the Court said that while the reduction for guilty plea could have no direct effect on a whole life minimum term, the offender's guilty plea was one among many factors to bear in mind when considering whether a whole life minimum term was appropriate. If it was not a borderline case, a whole life minimum term would be appropriate despite a guilty plea. In *Peters* [2005] 2 Cr App R (S) 627, the Court said that, when considering whether the offender had pleaded guilty at the first reasonable opportunity, there may be some cases where that opportunity would not arise until the accused had obtained advice from leading counsel.

Appeal Since the sentence for murder is a mandatory sentence, there is no appeal against it. **E4.3**

By the Criminal Appeal Act 1968, s. 9(1A) (as inserted by CJA 2003, s. 271), however, an offender may appeal against an order specifying a minimum term made under the CJA 2003, s. 269(2), or against an order under s. 269(4) that the early release provisions are not to apply. The A-G may refer an order specifying a minimum term under s. 269(2) to the Court of Appeal under the CJA 1988, s. 36(3A) (as inserted by CJA 2003, s. 272). In such a case, subsection (3A) states that the Court of Appeal 'shall not, in deciding what order under that section is appropriate for the case, make any allowance for the fact that the person to whom it relates is being sentenced for a second time'. This is a reference to the normal recognition on an A-G's reference for review of a sentence on the basis that it was unduly lenient, that some reduction from the increased sentence is appropriate to reflect the fact that the offender has had to face the prospect of being sentenced twice over (see **D27.4**). Subsection (3A) creates an exception to that principle.

E4.4 **Commencement and Transitional Provisions** It will be noted that, for the purposes of commencement of these provisions, the relevant date of 18 December 2003, is the date of *sentence*, and not the date of commission of the offence. This opens up a *prima facie* challenge to these provisions under the ECHR, Article 7, if it could be shown that a particular offender who committed a murder before the commencement date, has received a minimum term imposed under the CJA 2003, sch. 21, which is longer than the minimum term which he would have received at the time the murder was committed. Schedule 22, paras. 9 and 10 refer to those cases where sentence is passed on or after the commencement date, in respect of a murder committed before that date. They state that, when dealing with such a case, the court fixing the minimum term must not fix a minimum term which, in the opinion of the court, is greater than that which the Home Secretary would have been likely to have imposed prior to December 2002, and must not make a 'whole life' minimum term in any case where, in the opinion of the court, the Home Secretary would not have imposed a 'whole life tariff' before December 2002. In *Sullivan* [2005] 1 Cr App R 23, the Court of Appeal said that the main difference in practice would be in the minority of cases where the new higher starting points applied. Amendments to para. 49 of the *Practice Direction* were issued in consequence (see **appendix** 7).

Schedule 22 also makes provision for transitional cases, where either (a) existing mandatory life sentence prisoners have already been notified of their minimum term by the Home Secretary or (b) existing mandatory life sentence prisoners have not been so notified. In the first case, on an application of the prisoner to a single judge of the High Court, the judge must review the minimum term which has been notified to the prisoner by the Home Secretary and, if appropriate, amend it, but not increase it. In the second case the Home Secretary must refer such prisoners to a single judge of the High Court for the setting of the minimum term by that judge. The minimum term so set must not be greater than that which the Home Secretary would have been likely to have imposed prior to December 2002. Reasons need to be given by the High Court in each case. There is a right of appeal by the offender to the Court of Appeal against a minimum term set by the judge under either of these procedures, and the A-G may refer any minimum term to the Court of Appeal which he regards as being unduly lenient.

E4.5 **Court of Appeal Guidance** Guidance on the operation of these provisions for the setting of minimum terms in murder cases can be found in a series of Court of Appeal decisions, the most prominent of which are *Last* [2005] 2 Cr App R (S) 381, *Peters* [2005] 2 Cr App R (S) 627, and *Jones* [2006] 2 Cr App R (S) 121. See also *A-G's Ref (No. 106 of 2004)* [2004] EWCA Crim 2751, *Warsame* [2005] 1 Cr App R (S) 699, and *Reid* [2005] 2 Cr App R (S) 60. Taken together, these cases show that while judges must pay close attention to the scheme of sch. 21, to identify the correct starting point and relevant aggravating and mitigating factors, there is considerable flexibility within the scheme, which requires the exercise of judicial discretion. In *Jones*, the Court of Appeal pointed out the huge gap which exists between the specified starting points, which could only provide 'a very broad framework' for the sentencing exercise. Care must be taken not to 'double count' an aggravating factor which was already catered for in a specified starting point. The list of aggravating and mitigating features is not exhaustive. In *Richardson* [2006] 1 Cr App R (S) 240, it was held that the judge was entitled to regard the offender's possession of a knife at the time of the murder as an aggravating feature of the offence although it was not mentioned in sch. 21. The relative weight to be accorded to each, or to any particular combination of those features, will vary greatly, depending on the circumstances of the case, and sch. 21, para. 9 indicates that 'detailed consideration' of aggravating and mitigating factors may result in a final minimum term of any length. In *Peters*, it was noted that, although sch. 21, para. 11(a) treats as a mitigating factor an intention to cause grievous bodily harm rather than to kill, there would be circumstances where the absence of that intention would provide little or no mitigation. The same was true of para. 11(e), where the offender had acted to some extent in self-defence.

Murder: Offenders under 21

For an offender convicted of murder who is aged under 21 at the date of conviction, the mandatory sentence is custody for life under the PCC(S)A 2000, s. 93, unless the offender was under 18 when the offence was committed, in which case the mandatory sentence is detention at Her Majesty's pleasure. When the CJCSA 2000, s. 61, is brought into force, the sentence of custody for life will be abolished, and offenders in this age group who are convicted of murder will be sentenced to the mandatory sentence of life imprisonment instead. No date has been set for this change. **E4.6**

Guidance on the setting of a minimum term for the sentence of custody for life is now set out in the CJA 2003, ss. 269 to 277 and schs. 21 and 22. These provisions came into effect on 18 December 2003, and were considered at **E4.1**. It should be noted that an offender aged 18, 19 or 20 cannot attract a 'whole life' starting point but may, in a case where the seriousness of the offence is 'particularly high' attract a starting point of 30 years. Otherwise, the starting point is 15 years.

Murder: Detention at Her Majesty's Pleasure

The PCC(S)A 2000, s. 90, prescribes a mandatory sentence of detention at Her Majesty's pleasure for murder committed by an offender who was under 18 at the time of the offence. It is confined to murder cases *(Abbott* [1964] 1 QB 489). A person so sentenced will be detained in such place and under such conditions as the Secretary of State may direct or may arrange (s. 92). **E4.7**

Guidance on the setting of a minimum term for the sentence of detention at Her Majesty's pleasure is now set out in the CJA 2003, ss. 269 to 277 and schs. 21 and 22 (see **E4.1**). See *M* [2006] 1 Cr App R (S) 293.

It should be noted that an offender who was aged under 18 when he committed the offence cannot attract a 'whole life' starting point or a starting point of 30 or 15 years. The starting point is always 12 years.

Section E5 Custodial Sentences for Dangerous Offenders under the Criminal Justice Act 2003

APPLICATION OF THE SCHEME

Overview of Provisions

E5.1 Sections 224 to 236 of and sch. 15 to the CJA 2003 provide measures for sentencing 'dangerous offenders'. They came into effect on 4 April 2005 and apply in respect of offences committed on or after that date.

(1) They replace measures in the PCC(S)A 2000, for the imposition of 'longer than commensurate' determinate custodial sentences, which could be imposed on an offender convicted of a violent offence or a sexual offence, and from whom it is necessary to protect the public from serious harm.
(2) They replace Crown Court powers to make an order extending the period of supervision on licence appropriate for an offender convicted of a violent offence or a sexual offence (extended sentence provisions under s. 85 of the 2000 Act. Section 86 (see **E5.17**) remains in force and is not affected.
(3) They replace the 'automatic' life sentence for the second 'serious offence', under the PCC(S)A 2000, s. 109.

It should be noted, however, that in any case where the sentence for the offence would otherwise fall within the provisions for the sentencing of dangerous offenders, nothing shall prevent the sentencing court from imposing a hospital or guardianship order under the Mental Health Act 1983 instead (CJA 2003, sch. 32, para. 38: see **E24**). In *Johnson* [2007] 1 WLR 608, a case which provides a valuable overview of the provisions, the Court of Appeal stressed that the sentences under ss. 225 to 228 of the CJA 2003 were concerned with future risk and public protection, rather than with punishment for past offences.

The scheme applies to an offender aged 18 or over who has been convicted of a specified 'sexual offence' or 'violent offence', where the court is of the opinion that 'there is a significant risk to members of the public of serious harm occasioned by the commission by him of further specified offences'. Under the scheme, dangerous offenders who have been convicted of such an offence (all of which are listed in sch. 15, and for which the maximum penalty is between two and 10 years) will be given an 'extended sentence' under s. 227. The extended sentence is a determinate sentence, served in custody at least to the half-way point. Release during the whole of the second half of the sentence is subject to the positive recommendation of the Parole Board. Additionally, extended supervision periods of up to five years for violent offenders, and up to eight years for sexual offenders *must* be added to the sentence.

If an offender is aged 18 or over and has been convicted of an offence listed in sch. 15 whose maximum penalty is ten years or more, and the court is of the opinion that 'there is a significant risk to members of the public of serious harm occasioned by the commission by him of further specified offences, he will receive *either* a discretionary life sentence *or* a sentence of imprisonment or detention in a young offender institution for public protection under s. 225. If the offender has been assessed as dangerous, and has been convicted of an offence listed in sch. 15 which carries a maximum sentence of life imprisonment, the court must consider the seriousness of the offence when deciding which of the two possible sentences to impose. For either sentence the court *must* specify a minimum term under the PCC(S)A 2000, s. 82A (see **E5.16**), which the offender is required to serve in custody. After this point the offender will remain in custody until the Parole Board is satisfied that the risk which he represents has diminished, such that he can be released and be supervised in the community.

Offenders aged under 18 are made subject to similar though not identical provisions under ss. 226 and 228. In *Robson* [2007] 1 All ER 507, a case involving committal for sentence from the youth court to the Crown Court, the Court of Appeal confirmed that eligibility for any of the public protection sentences in the Act turns upon the date of conviction, rather than the date of the offence or the date of sentence. This decision is consistent with authorities on other forms of custodial sentences for young offenders: see *Danga* [1992] QB 476 and **E9.2**.

Offence Classification

Section 224 of the CJA 2003 defines 'specified offence', 'serious offence', and 'serious harm' for the purposes of these provisions. 'Specified offences' are those sexual offences or violent offences which are listed in sch. 15 (s. 224(1)). All of the 'sexual offences' or 'violent offences' in sch. 15 carry a maximum penalty of two years' imprisonment or more. A 'serious offence' is defined as a specified sexual or violent offence which carries a maximum penalty of 10 years' imprisonment or detention in a young offender institution or more, including life imprisonment or custody for life (s. 224(2)). 'Serious harm' means death or serious personal injury, whether physical or psychological (s. 224(3)). **E5.2**

Violent Offences The specified violent offences are manslaughter; kidnapping, false imprisonment and offences under the following enactments: OAPA 1861, ss. 4, 16, 18, 20 to 23, 27 to 32, 35, 37, 38, and 47; Explosive Substances Act 1883, ss. 2 and 3; Infant Life (Preservation) Act 1929, s. 1; CYPA 1933, s. 1; Infanticide Act 1938, s. 1; FA 1968, ss. 16, 16A, 17(1), 17(2) and 18; Theft Act 1968, ss. 8 and 9 (where the burglary is committed with intent to inflict grievous bodily harm, or to do unlawful damage), 10 and 12A (involving an accident which caused the death of any person); Criminal Damage Act 1971, ss. 1 (arson) and 1(2); Taking of Hostages Act 1982, s. 1; Aviation Security Act 1982, ss. 1 to 4; Mental Health Act 1983, s. 127; Prohibition of Female Circumcision Act 1985, s. 12; POA 1986, ss. 1 to 3; CJA 1988, s. 134; RTA 1988, ss. 1 and 3A; Aviation and Maritime Security Act 1990, ss. 1 and 9 to 13; offences under the Channel Tunnel (Security) Order 1994; Protection from Harassment Act 1997, s. 4; CDA 1998, ss. 29, 31(1)(a) and 31(1)(b); International Criminal Court Act 2001, ss. 51 and 52; Female Genital Mutilation Act 2003, ss. 1 to 3. The DVCVA 2004, s. 58(1), adds an offence under s. 5 of that Act to this list. Paragraph 64 of sch. 15 also makes it clear that aiding, abetting, counselling, procuring, inciting, conspiring or attempting to commit any of the specified violent offences is also covered. Attempt to commit murder and conspiracy to commit murder are also listed. **E5.3**

Sexual Offences The specified sexual offences are: the SOA 1956, ss. 1 to 7, 9 to 11, 14 to 17, 19 to 29, 32 and 33; the MHA 1983, s. 128; the Indecency with Children Act 1960, s. 1; the SOA 1967, ss. 4 and 5; the Theft Act 1968, s. 9 (burglary with intent to commit rape); the CLA 1977, s. 54; the Protection of Children Act 1978, s. 1; the Customs and Excise Management Act 1979, s. 170 (indecent or obscene articles); the CJA 1988, s. 160; SOA 2003, ss. 1 to 19, 25, 26, 30 to 41, 47 to 50, 52, 53, 57 to 59, 61 to 67, 69 and 70. Paragraph 153 of sch. 15 also makes it clear that aiding, abetting, counselling, procuring, inciting, conspiring or attempting to commit any of the specified sexual offences is also covered. **E5.4**

IMPRISONMENT OR DETENTION FOR PUBLIC PROTECTION

Life Sentence or Imprisonment for Public Protection

E5.5 Section 225(1) of the CJA 2003 applies where:

'(a) a person aged 18 or over is convicted of a serious offence [i.e. which carries life imprisonment or custody for life or a maximum penalty of ten years' imprisonment or detention in a young offender institution or more] committed after the commencement of this section, and

(b) the court is of the opinion that there is a significant risk to members of the public of serious harm occasioned by the commission by him of further specified offences'.

If the offence with which the person has been convicted carries life imprisonment as its maximum penalty and 'the court considers that the seriousness of the offence, or of the offence and one or more offences associated with it, is such as to justify the imposition of a sentence of imprisonment for life', the court *must* impose a life sentence (s. 225(2)). If the offence does not carry life imprisonment as its maximum penalty, or if it does but the court considers that the seriousness of the offence does not justify a life sentence, it *must* impose a sentence of public protection (s. 225(3)).

Guidance on the choice between a life sentence or a sentence of imprisonment for public protection may be found in *Lang* [2006] 1 WLR 2509 (see **E5.6**), as applied in *Samuel B* [2006] 2 Cr App R (S) 472. In *Lang* Rose LJ stated that in these provisions Parliament must be taken to have adopted the Court of Appeal's long-standing criteria for the imposition of a discretionary life sentence (see **E5.13**), and was not seeking to introduce a new and more restrictive criterion for the imposition of discretionary life sentences in the future. In *Samuel B* the Court of Appeal quashed a discretionary life sentence imposed for an offence of rape of a 14-year-old girl and substituted a sentence of imprisonment for public protection, on the basis that in the past the current offence would not have justified a life sentence.

Detention for Life or Detention for Public Protection

E5.6 Section 226(1) of the CJA 2003 applies where:

'(a) a person aged under 18 is convicted of a serious offence [i.e. one which carries detention for life or has a maximum penalty of ten years' detention under the PCC(S)A 2000, s. 91, or more] committed after the commencement of this section, and

(b) the court is of the opinion that there is a significant risk to members of the public of serious harm occasioned by the commission by him of further specified offences'.

If the offence with which the person under 18 has been convicted carries detention for life under the PCC(S)A 2000, s. 91, as its maximum penalty and 'the court considers that the seriousness of the offence, or of the offence and one or more offences associated with it, is such as to justify the imposition of a sentence of detention for life', the court *must* impose a sentence of detention for life (s. 226(2)). If the case does not come within s. 226(2), the court must choose between a sentence of detention for public protection and an extended sentence. If the court considers that an extended sentence under s. 228 would not be adequate for public protection, the court must impose a sentence of detention for public protection (s. 226(3)).

In *Lang* [2006] 1 WLR 2509, the Court of Appeal said that when sentencing young offenders it was important to bear in mind that they may change and develop in a shorter time than an adult. This, together with their level of maturity, may be highly relevant when assessing future conduct and whether that may give rise to a significant risk of serious harm. For an offender aged under 18 the statutory scheme allows greater discretion over choice of sentence. The court may impose an extended sentence even where a 'serious offence' has been committed. Where the offender is very young, an indeterminate sentence may be inappropriate even where a serious offence has been committed and there is a significant risk of serious harm from further offence. This issue arose in *D* [2006] 1 Cr App R 616, where the 13-year-old offender pleaded guilty to robbery. She carried out a sustained violent attack on another girl in a public park and stole various items from her. The offender asked for other offences including a burglary and an offence of assaulting a police officer to be taken into consideration. The robbery was a specified violent offence for the purposes of the CJA 2003. Reports before the judge indicated that the offender presented a considerable risk to others and that the risk of further offending was very high. The judge concluded that there was a significant risk of serious harm for the purposes of s. 226(1)(b) and s. 228(1)(b) (see below). The judge did not consider that detention for life was required, but that an extended sentence would not be sufficient for the purposes of the case. The offender was sentenced to detention for public protection for 12 months for the robbery, with no separate penalty for the other offences. The Court of Appeal, having regard to a psychology report which had not been available to the judge, quashed the sentence of detention for public protection and substituted an extended sentence, with a custodial period of 12 months and an extension period of three years.

EXTENDED SENTENCE

Extended Sentence: Persons 18 or Over

Section 227 of the CJA 2003 applies where: E5.7

'(a) a person aged 18 or over is convicted of a specified offence other than a serious offence [i.e. one which carries a maximum penalty of between two years and ten years' imprisonment or detention in a young offender institution], committed after the commencement of this section, and

(b) the court is of the opinion that there is a significant risk to members of the public of serious harm occasioned by the commission by him of further specified offences'.

In these circumstances the court *must* impose an extended sentence of imprisonment or detention in a young offender institution, which is a sentence of imprisonment etc. (not exceeding the maximum for the offence) the term of which is equal to the aggregate of (a) the appropriate custodial term (not exceeding the maximum for the offence) and (b) a further period (the extension period) on licence, of such length as the court considers necessary to protect members of the public from serious harm occasioned by the commission by the offender of further specified offences (s. 227(2)).

The custodial term of the extended sentence is the commensurate sentence appropriate to the offence or (if that commensurate sentence would be less than 12 months) a term of 12 months (s. 227(3) and see *Smith* [2007] 1 Cr App R (S) 607). The extension period must not exceed five years in the case of a specified violent offence and must not exceed eight years in the case of a specified sexual offence (s. 227(4)). During the second half of the appropriate custodial term the offender may be released on the recommendation of the Parole Board (s. 247). The Court of Appeal in *S* [2006] 2 Cr App R (S) 224 reached the 'tentative conclusion' that the extension period in an extended sentence began to run at the end of the custodial period set by the court, whether or not part of that custodial period was served on licence. The extension period followed the custodial period; it did not follow the custodial period as reduced by release on licence.

Extended Sentence: Persons Under 18

Section 228 of the CJA 2003 applies the extended sentence provisions to young offenders aged under 18, who are convicted of a specified violent or sexual offence. Section 228 applies where: E5.8

'(a) a person aged under 18 is convicted of a specified offence committed after the commencement of this section, and
(b) the court considers—
(i) that there is a significant risk to members of the public of serious harm occasioned by the commission by him of further specified offences, and
(ii) where the specified offence is a serious offence that the case is not one in which the court is required by section 226(2) to impose a sentence of detention for life or by section 226(3) to impose a sentence of detention for public protection'.

In these circumstances the court *must* impose an extended sentence of detention under the PCC(S)A 2000, s. 91, which is a sentence of detention the term of which is equal to the aggregate of (a) the appropriate custodial term (not exceeding the maximum for the offence) and (b) a further period (the extension period) on licence, of such length as the court considers necessary to protect members of the public from serious harm occasioned by the commission by the young offender of further specified offences (s. 228(2)).

The custodial term of the extended sentence is such term as the court considers appropriate which must be at least 12 months (s. 228(3)). The extension period must not exceed five years in the case of a specified violent offence and must not exceed eight years in the case of a specified sexual offence (s. 228(4)). During the second half of the appropriate custodial term the young offender may be released on the recommendation of the Parole Board (s. 247). A person sentenced to be detained under s. 228 is liable to be detained in such place as may be determined by the Secretary of State (s. 235). See *S* [2006] 2 Cr App R (S) 224 at E5.7 for the Court of Appeal's 'tentative conclusion' that the extension period in an extended sentence began to run at the end of the custodial period set by the court.

ASSESSMENT OF DANGEROUSNESS

E5.9 Section 229 of the CJA 2003 is an important section which deals with the necessary evidence base for the assessment of dangerousness required for the court to establish whether, under any of the ss. 225 to 228, the offender poses a 'significant risk to members of the public of serious harm occasioned by the commission by him of further specified offences'.

In the leading case of *Lang* [2006] 1 WLR 2509, Rose LJ said that the requirement that a risk be 'significant' means more than a possibility — it must be 'noteworthy, of considerable amount or importance'. A wide variety of information will need to be considered before such an assessment is made by the court. The court will rely upon the pre-sentence report (prepared in accordance with the *Guide for Sentences of Public Protection* issued by the National Probation Service in June 2005) and the details of the offender's previous convictions, where relevant. A psychiatric report would be appropriate in some cases, but should be clearly directed to the issue of dangerousness. In *Pluck* [2007] 1 Cr App R (S) 43 the Court of Appeal commented that reports before the courts were not binding on the sentencer but, if the judge was minded to depart from the conclusion set out in a report, counsel should be warned in advance. It would only rarely be appropriate for a judge to permit cross-examination of the author of a pre-sentence report on the assessment of risk (*S* [2006] 2 Cr App R (S) 224). Wherever possible the prosecution should be in a position to describe to the court the facts of any previous specified offences on the record. If there is doubt over the accuracy of the facts or circumstances of previous convictions of the offender, it may be necessary, according to *Samuels* (1995) 16 Cr App R (S) 856, to investigate the context of an earlier offence to see if the offender really does constitute a risk, but adjournment in such circumstances was not obligatory. It may be possible to proceed on the basis of the information before the court, and in some cases the court might infer the seriousness of past offences from the sentences which had been imposed for them. It is clear that in the assessment of dangerousness it is not just previous *specified* offences which are relevant. The court may have regard to offences on the record which are not specified offences, especially where they indicate an escalating pattern of seriousness. Indeed, it is not a pre-requisite to a finding of dangerousness that the offender has any previous convictions. A first offender might qualify. Nor is it necessary that serious harm (or indeed any harm) has been caused by the offender in the course of past offences, since that may have been simply a matter of good fortune — a public protection sentence may properly be imposed where there is a significant risk of serious harm from such offences in the future (see further *Johnson* [2007] 1 WLR 608).

In *Lang*, Rose LJ said that since the CJA 2003 defines 'serious harm' as 'death or serious personal injury, whether physical or psychological', and that was a phrase familiar to courts from earlier legislation, earlier guidance might be helpful. See, in particular, *Creasey* (1994) 15 Cr App R (S) 671 and *A-G's Ref (No. 47 of 1998)* [1999] 1 Cr App R (S) 464. His lordship said that the fact that the further offence that is foreseen is a 'serious offence' does not automatically mean that commission of such an offence would result in 'serious harm', and if the offence foreseen is not a 'serious offence', it will be rare that there is a 'significant risk of serious harm'. The Court of Appeal confirmed that risk to 'members of the public' was a general term, and should not be construed so as to exclude any particular group, such as prison officers or staff in mental hospitals. It seems safe to assume that such a risk could properly be made out where the risk is specific to a small group of individuals, or just to one potential victim (applying the pre-Act authorities of *Hashi* (1995) 16 Cr App R (S) 121 and *S* (1994) 15 Cr App R (S) 765.

If, at the time the specified offence was committed, the offender had not been previously convicted of any specified offence, or was aged under 18, the court in deciding whether the offender poses the relevant 'significant risk':

(a) *must* take into account all such information as is available to it about the nature and circumstances of the offence,
(b) *may* take into account any information which is before it about any pattern of behaviour of which the offence forms part, and
(c) *may* take into account any information about the offender which is before it (s. 229(2)).

It seems that in such a case the court will be relying upon the facts of the offence (especially where these have emerged in some detail during the course of a contested trial), the contents of a pre-sentence report, and the contents of any other relevant report, such as a psychiatric report. Other material may be taken into account, as in *Hillman* [2006] 2 Cr App R (S) 565 where the judge properly had regard to a synopsis of material prepared by the prosecution containing details of earlier alleged misconduct by the offender which had resulted in the making of an ASBO against him. The Court of Appeal said that although the incidents referred to in the synopsis had not been tested in adversarial judicial proceedings, they could be regarded as 'hard information' and could be relied upon.

Statutory Presumption of Dangerousness If, at the time the specified offence was committed, the offender was aged 18 or over and had been previously convicted of one or more specified offence, the court *must assume that* the offender poses a 'significant risk' *unless*, after taking into account: **E5.10**

(a) all such information as is available to it about the nature and circumstances of each of the offences,
(b) where appropriate, any information which is before it about any pattern of behaviour of which any of the offences forms part, and
(c) any information about the offender which is before it,

the court considers that it would be *unreasonable to conclude* that there is such a risk (CJA 2003, s. 229(3)).

According to the decision in *Lang* [2006] 1 WLR 2509, an exercise of judgement on the part of the sentencer is always required here, and although the court must start from the presumption that such an offender poses a significant risk, there is discretion, and the judge is expected to reach a reasonable conclusion in the light of the available information. It was the express intention of Parliament to protect the public from serious harm. It follows that it was not the intention to require the imposition of indeterminate sentences for relatively minor offences. The presumption does not, of course, in any event apply to offenders aged under 18 nor to adults with no previous convictions. *Lang* was applied in *Isa* [2006] 2 Cr App R (S) 192, where the offender pleaded guilty to an offence of sexual assault, contrary to the SOA 2003, s. 3. He approached a 13-year-old girl, who was walking along the street in the company of her mother. He put one hand on the victim's breast and held her arm with his other hand. Her mother intervened and the offender was arrested. The victim was shocked by what had happened. The offender had four previous convictions for indecent assault on girls and women and had received various custodial sentences. Sexual assault is a serious specified sexual offence under the Act and, since the earlier indecent assaults were specified offences, by the CJA 2003, s. 229(3) the court had to assume that there was a significant risk of serious harm. The judge, having taken into account the offender's record and relevant reports, imposed a sentence of imprisonment for public protection with a minimum period of six months. The Court of Appeal quashed that sentence and substituted a sentence of 12 months' imprisonment, saying that repetitive violent or sexual offending at a relatively low level without serious harm did not, of itself, give rise to a significant risk of serious harm in the future.

E5.11 **Multiple Offences and Concurrent Terms** In *O'Brien* [2007] 1 WLR 833, where the Court of Appeal held that, although a sentence of imprisonment for public protection could, as a matter of law, be ordered to run consecutively to another such sentence, it was undesirable in practice to do so. If the sentencer intends that the minimum period to be served under a sentence of imprisonment for public protection should run consecutively to an existing sentence (or consecutively to a period imposed under the PCC(S)A 2000, s. 116), the notional determinate term for the sentence of imprisonment for public protection should be lengthened by including the balance of the existing sentence (or s. 116 period). The notional determinate term should then be divided by two to fix the minimum period. In *Brown* [2007] 1 Cr App R (S) 468, the Court of Appeal said that the passing of consecutive extended sentences, or the passing of an extended sentence followed by a consecutive determinate sentence, was undesirable and should be avoided. Where otherwise appropriate, however, an extended sentence could be made to run consecutively to a determinate sentence.

If an offender falls to be sentenced for one or more 'serious specified offences' (i.e. punishable with a maximum penalty of ten years or more) and, at the same time, for one or more 'specified offences' (i.e. punishable with a maximum penalty of between two years and ten years), the court should impose separate sentences on each count (*Edwards* [2007] 1 Cr App R (S) 646; *Meade* [2007] 1 Cr App R (S) 762). If the court is of the opinion that the offender is dangerous, on application of the test set out in s. 225(1)(b), it will be appropriate to impose one or more sentences of imprisonment for public protection for the serious specified offences and one or more extended sentences for the specified offences. Following the principles set out in *O'Brien* and in *Brown*, such sentences will normally be concurrent rather than consecutive. The gravity of the offence or offences which are not 'serious specified offences' and which are dealt with by way of one or more extended sentence, should be taken into account when determining the length of the minimum term specified by the court under the PCC(S)A 2000, s. 82A, for the sentence(s) of imprisonment for public protection.

Giving of Reasons

E5.12 In *Lang* [2006] 1 WLR 2509, the Court of Appeal said that the sentencer should be careful to give reasons for all conclusions, particularly for the finding of whether or not there is a significant risk. Reasons should include reference to the information which has been taken into account. If the sentencer is minded to come to a different conclusion from the report(s) presented, it would be wise to alert counsel so that representations can be made on the issue.

DISCRETIONARY LIFE SENTENCES

A discretionary life sentence may be passed only in respect of an offence for which life imprisonment is provided as the maximum penalty. The statutory criteria in the CJA 2003 for determining whether the imposition of a custodial sentence is justified and, if so, for fixing its length (set out at E2.5 and E2.7) apply to discretionary life sentences. **E5.13**

An offender serving a life sentence may be sentenced to a further life sentence where the criteria for imposition of that sentence are made out (*A-G's Ref (No. 32 of 1996)* [1997] 1 Cr App R (S) 261). A discretionary life sentence and a fixed-term sentence may run concurrently, but the fixed-term sentence should not be made disproportionate to the offence for which it is passed in order to delay the offender's release on licence from the life sentence (*Middleton* (1981) 3 Cr App R (S) 273). Determinate sentences may be ordered to run consecutively to each other and concurrently with a life sentence (*Nugent* (1984) 6 Cr App R (S) 93). A life sentence and a fixed term sentence may not, however, run consecutively.

The following sentencing principles have been developed by the Court of Appeal to distinguish the use of the discretionary life sentence from the use of fixed-term custodial sentences. According to Lawton LJ in *Pither* (1979) 1 Cr App R (S) 209, '. . . life sentences for offences other than homicide should not be imposed unless there are exceptional circumstances in the case'. These principles remain relevant when the sentencer is exercising a choice between imposing a sentence of life imprisonment or a sentence of imprisonment for public protection under s. 225.

Where the court is considering imposing a life sentence, defence counsel should be informed so that the matter may be addressed by argument (*McDougall* (1983) 5 Cr App R (S) 78; *Morgan* (1987) 9 Cr App R (S) 201). In *Virgo* (1988) 10 Cr App R (S) 427, the judge heard submissions from both counsel.

Gravity of the Immediate Offence

In *A-G's Ref (No. 32 of 1996)* [1997] 1 Cr App R (S) 261 Lord Bingham CJ stated that unless the offender was convicted of a very serious offence there could be no question of imposing a life sentence. In *Chapman* [2000] 1 Cr App R (S) 377, the Court of Appeal observed that in a number of earlier decisions on discretionary life sentences less emphasis had been given to the seriousness of the instant offence than might have been expected. Lord Bingham CJ said in *Chapman* that there was an interrelationship between the gravity of the offence, the likelihood of further offending, and the gravity of further offending should it occur. The more likely it was that an offender would reoffend, and the more grave such re-offending was likely to be, the less emphasis the court might lay on the gravity of the original offence. There was, however, no ground for doubting the indispensability of the offence seriousness condition laid down in *Hodgson* (1967) 52 Cr App R 113 and confirmed in *A-G's Ref (No. 32 of 1996)*. In *Simmonds* [2001] 2 Cr App R (S) 328 and in *Barker* [2003] 1 Cr App R (S) 212, the Court of Appeal quashed discretionary life sentences on the ground, *inter alia*, that the offences of 'simple arson' and attempted robbery, respectively, were not sufficiently grave in themselves to justify life sentences. **E5.14**

On the other hand, the commission of a very grave offence does not of itself require the imposition of a life sentence (*Owen* (1980) 2 Cr App R (S) 45; *Terence Patrick J* (1993) 14 Cr App R (S) 500), nor does persistence in offending (*Pither* (1979) 1 Cr App R (S) 209; *Wilkinson* (1983) 5 Cr App R (S) 105).

Serious Danger for Indeterminate Period

E5.15 In *A-G's Ref (No. 32 of 1996)* [1997] 1 Cr App R (S) 261, it was said that before a discretionary life sentence could be justified there must be good grounds for believing that the offender would constitute a serious danger to the public for a period of time which could not reliably be estimated at the time of the sentence. Since a discretionary life sentence cannot be passed unless the offence of conviction is a violent offence or a sexual offence (see **E5.13**), the sentencer will have in mind the risk of particularly serious violent or sexual offences being committed by the offender in the future. The basis for such an assessment will often be the mental condition of the offender, but it is not necessary to show that the offender is suffering from a specific form of mental disorder (*Powell* [2002] 1 Cr App R (S) 199). In *A-G's Ref (No. 32 of 1996)* the offender was convicted of causing grievous bodily harm with intent and, the offence was committed the day after the offender had been released on home leave from a life sentence for murder. A sentence of seven years' imprisonment was increased to a further life sentence by the Court of Appeal. Lord Bingham CJ observed that, while the offender's mental state was often highly relevant in life sentence cases, the crucial point was that the offender would represent a serious danger to the public for an indeterminate period. See also *Trowbridge* [2002] 2 Cr App R (S) 154 and *Szczerba* [2002] 2 Cr App R (S) 387. Medical evidence on the offender's mental state should normally be available to the court (*Roche* (1995) 16 Cr App R (S) 849), but such evidence is not essential and a discretionary life sentence may be imposed even where the medical evidence is inconclusive (*Cobb* [2002] 1 Cr App R (S) 67). In some cases the court has inferred that the offender represents a serious continuing danger from the circumstances of the offence and the offender's criminal record. An example is *Chandler* (1993) 14 Cr App R (S) 586. In *A-G's Ref (No. 76 of 1995)* [1997] 1 Cr App R (S) 81, a case of false imprisonment and repeated rape by an offender with a previous conviction for rape, a longer-than-commensurate sentence of nine years' imprisonment was increased to a life sentence by the Court of Appeal, without having received any medical evidence. The danger represented by the offender will usually be to members of the public generally, but a threat to a particular person may be sufficient (*Allen* (1987) 9 Cr App R (S) 169).

PERIOD SPECIFIED UNDER THE POWERS OF CRIMINAL COURTS (SENTENCING) ACT 2000, s. 82A

Section 82A applies where a court imposes:

(a) a discretionary sentence of life imprisonment (see **E5.13**);
(b) a sentence of imprisonment or detention in a young offender institution for public protection under the CJA 2003, s. 225 (see **E5.5**);
(c) a sentence of detention for public protection under the CJA 2003, s. 226 (see **E5.6**);
(d) a sentence of custody for life under the PCC(S)A 2000, s. 94, where that sentence is *not* imposed as the mandatory sentence for murder (see **E9.6**); and
(e) a sentence of detention for life on a person under the age of 18 pursuant to PCC(S)A 2000, s. 91 (see **E9.9**).

E5.16 **Powers of Criminal Courts (Sentencing) Act 2000, s. 82A**

(1) This section applies if a court passes a life sentence in circumstances where the sentence is not fixed by law.
(2) The court shall, unless it makes an order under subsection (4) below, order that the provisions of section 28(5) to (8) of the Crime (Sentences) Act 1997 (referred to in this section as the 'early release provisions') shall apply to the offender as soon as he has served the part of his sentence which is specified in the order.
(3) The part of his sentence shall be such as the court considers appropriate taking into account—

(a) the seriousness of the offence, or of the combination of the offence and one or more offences associated with it;
(b) the effect of any direction which it would have given under section 240 of the Criminal Justice Act 2003 (crediting periods of remand in custody) if it had sentenced him to a term of imprisonment; and
(c) the early release provisions as compared with section 244(1) of the Criminal Justice Act 2003.

(4) If the offender was aged 21 or over when he committed the offence and the court is of the opinion that, because of the seriousness of the offence or of the combination of the offence and one or more offences associated with it, no order should be made under subsection (2) above, the court shall order that the early release provisions shall not apply to the offender.

(4A) No order under subsection (4) above may be made where the life sentence is—
(a) a sentence of imprisonment for public protection under section 225 of the Criminal Justice Act 2003, or
(b) a sentence of detention for public protection under section 226 of that Act.

The imposition of a life or indeterminate sentence is designed to protect the public from the offender, whereas the period specified under s. 82A is meant to reflect the degree of punishment, retribution and deterrence appropriate for the offence, aside from the question of public protection (*Wheaton* [2005] 1 Cr App R (S) 425). The specified period should not be lengthened with a view to protecting the public (*Adams* [2000] 2 Cr App R (S) 274). The effect of specifying part of the sentence under s. 82A is that the life or indeterminate sentence prisoner will not become eligible to be considered for early release until the expiry of that period. If the court is of the view that, because of the seriousness of the offence or offences no order should be made under s. 82A(2), it should make an order under s. 82A(4), to the effect that the early release provisions shall not apply to the offender, subject to s. 82A(4A).

Some of the cases referred to below relate to earlier versions of these provisions but, it is submitted, still represent the law.

The *Consolidated Criminal Practice Direction*, para. IV.47, *Imposition of discretionary life sentences* (see **appendix** 7) indicates that the sentencer should specify the relevant period, save in the very exceptional case where he considers that the offence is so serious that detention for life is justified by that alone, irrespective of the risk to the public. In that case, he should state this in open court when passing sentence. A decision not to specify might be the subject of an appeal (*Hollies* (1995) 16 Cr App R (S) 463). When specifying the relevant period, the judge should have regard to the specific terms of the section, and should indicate the reasons for the decision. Before specifying the relevant period, the sentencer should permit counsel for the defence to address the court on the appropriate length of the relevant part. An order under s. 82A may be the subject of an appeal (*McBean* [2002] 1 Cr App R (S) 430) or might constitute an unduly lenient sentence (*A-G's Ref (No. 82 of 2000)* [2001] 2 Cr App R (S) 289).

Section 82A(3)(a). In *A-G's Ref (No. 3 of 2004)* [2005] 1 Cr App R (S) 230, the Court of Appeal emphasised that, when having regard to the seriousness of the offence (or the combination of the offence and other offences associated with it), the section permitted the sentencer to look at the totality of the associated offences, rather than just the offence for which the life sentence was being passed, and to consider whether the sentences for the associated offences would have been consecutive to the main sentence if a life sentence had not been given. The court followed *Lundberg* (1955) 16 Cr App R (S) 948 and *Haan* [1996] 1 Cr App R (S) 267. In a case where the offender falls to be sentenced on the same occasion for more than one serious specified offence, or for one or more serious specified offence and one or more specified offence, such sentences should take effect concurrently rather than consecutively but the seriousness of the totality of the offences should be reflected in the length of the period selected by the judge under s. 82A (see *Edwards* [2007] 1 Cr App R (S) 646 and *Meade* [2007] 1 Cr App R (S) 762).

Section 82A(3)(b). This subsection refers to the CJA 2003, s. 240 (effect of time spent in custody on remand: see **E2.8**). According to the Court of Appeal in *Marklew* [1999] 1 WLR 485, the sentencer should normally give full credit for the period spent by the defendant on remand. Accurate information should be made available to the court by the prosecution or prison authorities as to the number of days spent in custody before the life sentence is imposed, and the Court of Appeal in *McStay* [2003] 1 Cr App R (S) 176 said that this figure should not be rounded up or down. *Marklew* also indicates, however, that there may be some circumstances in which the giving of full credit to the offender would not be appropriate.

Section 82A(3)(c). A sentencer exercising power under s. 82A is required to take into account the fact that under the CJA 2003, s. 244, a prisoner who has received a determinate sentence is entitled to be released after serving one half of his sentence. In *Marklew* the Court of Appeal issued guidance on the setting of the period to be specified under s. 82A; Thomas J stated that henceforth sentencers should make clear what the determinate sentence would have been and should then normally fix the specified period at *one-half* of the notional term. In fixing the notional determinate sentence, allowance should be made for a guilty plea (*Meek* (1995) 16 Cr App R (S) 1003). The principle of setting the specified period at *one-half* of the notional determinate sentence has been followed and applied in subsequent cases, including *McBean* [2002] 1 Cr App R (S) 430 and *Szczerba* [2002] 2 Cr App R (S) 387. The rationale, according to Pill LJ in *West* [2001] 1 Cr App R (S) 103, is that a life sentence prisoner should be in no worse a position on an application for early release than a determinate sentence prisoner. Nonetheless, it seems that there may be exceptional cases where it is appropriate to fix a longer specified term, especially for an adult offender, of up to two-thirds of the notional determinate sentence (*Marklew*).

SEXUAL OFFENCE COMMITTED BEFORE 30 SEPTEMBER 1998: EXTENDED LICENCE PERIOD

E5.17 **Powers of Criminal Courts (Sentencing) Act 2000, s. 86**

(1) Where, in the case of a long-term or short-term prisoner—
  (a) the whole or any part of his sentence was imposed for a sexual offence committed before 30th September 1998, and
  (b) the court by which he was sentenced for that offence, having had regard to the matters mentioned in section 32(6)(a) and (b) of the Criminal Justice Act 1991, ordered that this section should apply,

  sections 33(3) and 37(1) of that Act shall each have effect as if for the reference to three-quarters of his sentence there were substituted a reference to the whole of that sentence.

(2) Expressions used in this section shall be construed as if they were contained in part II of the Criminal Justice Act 1991.

(3) The reference in subsection (1) above to section 33(3) of the Criminal Justice Act 1991 is to section 33(3) as it has effect without the amendment made by section 104(1) of the Crime and Disorder Act 1998 (which substituted the words 'on licence' for the word 'unconditionally' and does not apply in relation to a prisoner whose sentence or any part of whose sentence was imposed for an offence committed before 30th September 1998).

Section 86 of the 2000 Act preserves the effect of what was formerly CJA 1991, s. 44, but is applicable only where the relevant offence was committed before 30 September 1998. The CJA 1991, s. 44, came into effect on 1 October 1992. The Court of Appeal in *R v R* [2003] 1 WLR 490 held, somewhat surprisingly, that an order under s. 86 in respect of sexual offences committed ten or more years before that date did not infringe the ECHR, Article 7, because an order under s. 86 was preventive rather than punitive in character. The Court concluded that its own previous decision in *JT* [2003] EWCA Crim 1011 was incorrect on this point. It also follows that an order under s. 86 was unnecessarily set aside in *MG* [2002] 2 Cr App R (S) 1.

Section 86 applies in respect of an offender who committed an offence before the relevant date the whole or part of whose sentence is imposed for a 'sexual offence' (as defined in s. 161 of the 2000 Act). Note that s. 86 applies to sexual, but not violent, offences. Under s. 86, if the sentencing court so specifies, the offender, after release on licence, is required to serve out the full term of his sentence under supervision in the community rather than, as would otherwise be the case, receiving unconditional release after completing three-quarters of his term. In deciding whether to make an order under s. 86, the court is required to have regard to the need to protect the public from serious harm, and the desirability of preventing the commission by the offender of further offences and of securing his rehabilitation. For examples of the use of this section (in its earlier form as CJA 1991, s. 44), see *Apelt* (1994) 15 Cr App R (S) 420 and *Kennan* [1996] 1 Cr App R (S) 1. In *A-G's Ref (No. 7 of 1996)* [1997] 1 Cr App R (S) 39, Lord Bingham CJ in the Court of Appeal commended the use of this sentencing power.

Section E6 Prescribed Custodial Sentences

MINIMUM CUSTODIAL SENTENCES FOR CLASS A DRUG OFFENCES

E6.1 Section 110 of the PCC(S)A 2000 provides that where:

(a) a person is convicted of a Class A drug trafficking offence committed after 30 September 1997,
(b) at the time when that offence was committed he was aged 18 or over and had been convicted in any part of the United Kingdom of two other Class A drug trafficking offences, and
(c) one of those offences was committed after he had been convicted of the other,

the Crown Court shall impose a custodial sentence for a term of at least seven years, unless the court is of the opinion that there are particular circumstances which relate to any of the offences or to the offender which would make it unjust to do so in all the circumstances (s. 110(2) and (3)).

For the purposes of s. 110, 'Class A drug trafficking offence' means a drug trafficking offence committed in respect of a Class A drug (see **B20.1**); s. 110(5) defines 'drug trafficking offence' by reference to the Proceeds of Crime Act 2002, sch. 2 (see **E21.11**) (s. 110(5)); and 'custodial sentence' means imprisonment or detention in a young offender institution (s. 110(6)). Nothing in s. 110 prevents a hospital order being imposed on an offender in an appropriate case (Mental Health Act 1983, s. 37(1A)). In *Harvey* [2000] 1 Cr App R (S) 368, the Court of Appeal upheld a sentence of seven years' imprisonment on an offender imposed under this power. Lord Bingham CJ said that the object of the provision plainly was to require courts to impose a sentence of at least seven years in cases where otherwise they would not, or might not, have done so. His lordship declined to indicate what might amount to circumstances 'which would make it unjust' to impose the prescribed sentence, but for subsequent examples see *Pearce* [2005] 1 Cr App R (S) 364, *Turner* [2006] 1 Cr App R (S) 565 and *McDonough* [2006] 1 Cr App R (S) 647.

In a case where either of the earlier Class A drug trafficking offences was dealt with by way of an absolute or conditional discharge (admittedly rather unlikely) or, before 1 October 1992, by way of a probation order, and the offender was not subsequently sentenced for the offence, the conviction for that offence is a conviction for limited purposes only (see the PCC(S)A 2000, s. 14 and **E14.6**) and would not count as a qualifying conviction for the purposes of s. 110.

Guilty Plea

E6.2 Where the offender has pleaded guilty, the sentencing court is required to take into account the stage at which he indicated his intention to plead guilty and the circumstances in which this indication was given (CJA 2003, s. 144). Section 144(2) states that in the case of an offence coming within s. 110 the maximum reduction for a guilty plea shall be 20 per cent of the determinate sentence of at least seven years which would otherwise have been imposed. A discount of 20 per cent on seven years produces a sentence slightly less than five years and eight months. It is desirable for the judge to explain how the final sentence has been arrived at

(*Brown* [2000] 2 Cr App R (S) 435). It is not appropriate to reduce the sentence further by reference to the SGC, *New Sentences: CJA 2003* (Dec 2004), para. 2.1.7, since the guidelines did not apply to prescribed custodial sentences such as s. 110 (*AG's Ref (No. 6 of 2006) (Farish)* [2007] 1 Cr App R (S) 58).

MINIMUM CUSTODIAL SENTENCES FOR DOMESTIC BURGLARY

Section 111 of the PCC(S)A 2000 provides that where: **E6.3**

(a) a person is convicted of a domestic burglary committed after 30 November 1999;
(b) at the time when the domestic burglary was committed he was aged 18 or over and had been convicted in England and Wales of two other domestic burglaries; and
(c) one of those other burglaries was committed after he had been convicted of the other, and both of them were committed after 30 November 1999,

the Crown Court shall impose a custodial term of at least three years except where the court is of the opinion that there are particular circumstances which relate to any of the offences or the offender which would make it unjust to do so in all the circumstances.

In *McInerney* [2003] 1 Cr App R 627, the guideline case on sentencing for domestic burglary (see **B4.58**), Lord Woolf CJ said at [16]:

> It may be helpful to give examples of the type of situation where a three year sentence may be unjust. The sentence could be unjust if two of the offences were committed many years earlier than the third offence, or if the offender has made real efforts to reform or conquer his drug addiction, but some personal tragedy triggers the third offence, or if the first two offences were committed when the offender was not yet 16. As we read s. 111 it gives the sentencer a fairly substantial degree of discretion as to the categories of situations where the presumption can be rebutted.

In *Gibson* [2004] 2 Cr App R (S) 451, the Court of Appeal held that, where the judge had adjourned sentence to obtain an assessment of the offender's suitability for a community penalty in circumstances where that gave rise to an expectation on the offender's part that, if the report was positive, he would receive such a sentence, it was unjust then to impose the prescribed sentence under s. 111.

For the purposes of s. 111 'domestic burglary' means a burglary committed in respect of a building or part of a building which is a dwelling (s. 111(5)). The maximum penalty on indictment for such an offence is 14 years' imprisonment (see further **B4.58**). An attempt to commit a domestic burglary is not a qualifying offence (*Maguire* [2003] 2 Cr App R (S) 40, in which the Court of Appeal agreed with the view expressed in a previous edition of this work). 'Custodial sentence' means imprisonment or detention in a young offender institution (s. 110(6)). Nothing in s. 111 prevents a hospital order being imposed on an offender in an appropriate case (Mental Health Act 1983, s. 37(1A)).

Sequence of Offences

The key considerations in the PCC(S)A 2000, s. 111, are the dates on which the qualifying offences were committed and the dates on which the defendant was convicted. The sequence must be (i) commission, then conviction, (ii) commission, then conviction, (iii) commission, then conviction. The section would not bite in a case where the offender commits a third domestic burglary before being convicted of the second (*Hoare* [2004] 2 Cr App R (S) 261). 'Convicted' must be distinguished from 'sentenced'. So, commission of a third domestic burglary at a time when the offender is on bail awaiting sentence for a second domestic burglary does trigger the operation of the section (*Webster* [2004] 2 Cr App R (S) 126). **E6.4**

Section 111 can operate in an uneven way, so that one offender will infringe the provision after having been convicted of just three domestic burglaries, while another might have been convicted of (or had taken into consideration) many more such offences without yet having infringed it.

A finding of guilt in a youth court is equivalent to a conviction and counts for these purposes (*Frost* [2001] 2 Cr App R (S) 124). It is unclear whether an earlier spent conviction for domestic burglary counts as a qualifying conviction. It is submitted that such a conviction does count, but that the fact that the conviction was spent may be a particular circumstance relating to that offence making the imposition of the prescribed sentence unjust in all the circumstances.

Guilty Plea

E6.5 Where the offender has pleaded guilty, the sentencing court is required to take into account the stage at which he indicated his intention to plead guilty and the circumstances in which this indication was given (CJA 2003, s. 144: see **E1.6**). Section 144(2) states that in the case of an offence coming within s. 111, the maximum reduction for a guilty plea shall be 20 per cent of the determinate sentence of at least three years which would otherwise have been imposed. A discount of 20 per cent on three years produces a sentence of just less than two years and five months. It would seem, by analogy with *Brown* [2002] 2 Cr App R (S) 435, that where discount has been given for plea the sentencer should explain how the final sentence has been arrived at.

MINIMUM CUSTODIAL SENTENCES FOR FIREARMS OFFENCES

E6.6 Section 51A of the FA 1968 (as inserted by CJA 2003, s. 287) provides for minimum custodial sentences for certain firearms offences. Section 51A applies to offences committed on or after 22 January 2004. For details of the offences listed in s. 51A, see **B12.50**.

Firearms Act 1968, s. 51A

(1) This section applies where—
  (a) an individual is convicted of
    (i) an offence under s. 5(1)(a), (ab), (aba), (ac), (ad), (ae), (af) or (c) of this Act, or
    (ii) an offence under s. 5(1A)(a) of this Act, and
  (b) the offence was committed after the commencement of this section and at a time when he was aged 16 or over.

(2) The court shall impose an appropriate custodial sentence (or order for detention) for a term of at least the required minimum term (with or without a fine) unless the court is of the opinion that there are exceptional circumstances relating to the offence or to the offender which justify its not doing so.

(3) Where an offence is found to have been committed over a period of two or more days, or at some time during a period of two or more days, it shall be taken for the purposes of this section to have been committed on the last of those days.

In *A-G's Ref (No. 114 of 2004)* [2005] 2 Cr App R (S) 24, the Court of Appeal made it clear that s. 51A applies only where one of the specific offences listed there is proved or admitted. Although the offender in the case considered by the Court might properly have been charged with an offence under the FA 1968, s. 5, no such count had been included on the indictment and so the minimum sentence could not apply.

The minimum sentences specified in the section are five years' imprisonment in the case of an offender aged 18 or over when convicted, and three years' detention under the PCC(S)A 2000, s. 91 (long-term detention), for any offender aged at least 16 but under 18 at the time he committed the offence (s. 51A(4)). It will be noted that the specified minimum sentences refer to 'imprisonment' in the case of an offender aged 18 or over. This wording anticipates the abolition of the sentence of detention in a young offender institution, by the CJCSA 2000, s. 61. In the important decision of *Campbell* [2006] 2 Cr App R (S) 627 the Court of Appeal held that until s. 61 is brought into force, or the wording of the FA 1968, s. 51A is appropriately amended, the minimum custodial sentence provisions do not apply to offenders aged 18, 19 or 20. Parliament has now rectified this anomaly by way of the Firearms (Sentencing) (Transitory Provisions) Order 2007, which amends s. 51A(4) so as to make it clear that for an offender aged 18, 19 or 20 the appropriate custodial sentence is one of detention in a young offender institution rather than one of imprisonment. The amendment applies to offences committed on or after 28 May 2007. For offences committed on or after 22 January 2004 but before 28 May 2007, the decision in *Campbell* will apply. The specified minimum sentence on an offender aged under 18 is the sentence of long-term detention under the PCC(S)A 2000, s. 91. In general, detention under s. 91 can be imposed on a young offender only where the maximum penalty for the offence is at least 14 years' imprisonment in the case of an adult. The relevant firearms offences all carry a maximum penalty of 10 years' imprisonment. Section 91 is therefore amended by the CJA 2003, s. 289, to bring the relevant firearms offences within its scope. Section 289 came into force on 22 January 2004, together with consequential amendments in sch. 32, paras. 48 to 50. Nothing in s. 51A prevents a hospital order being imposed on an offender in an appropriate case (Mental Health Act 1983, s. 37(1A)). See *McEneaney* [2005] 2 Cr App R (S) 531.

The Exceptional Circumstances Proviso

The 'exceptional circumstances' proviso in the FA 1968, s. 51A(2), brings the minimum sentence provision on firearms offences broadly into line with the provisions for a minimum custodial sentence for the third Class A drug trafficking offence under the PCC(S)A 2000, s. 110 (see **E6.1**) and for the third domestic burglary under the PCC(S)A 2000, s. 111 (see **E6.3**). Those provisions are differently worded, however, in that they permit the sentencer to avoid the prescribed sentence if there are 'particular circumstances . . . which would make it unjust' to impose the minimum sentence. It is important to note, however, that the minimum sentence for the firearms offences listed in the FA 1968, s. 51A, applies to *all* such offences, whereas ss. 110 and 111 apply only to repeat offenders. **E6.7**

The Court of Appeal has given some indication of the factors which might amount to 'exceptional circumstances' in respect of this provision, building on the early declaration in *Jordan* [2005] 2 Cr App R (S) 266 that such cases would be 'rare'. General guidance was given in *Rehman* [2006] 1 Cr App R (S) 404. The Court of Appeal said that, in determining whether the case involved 'exceptional circumstances', it was necessary to look at the case as a whole. Sometimes there would be a single isolated factor that would amount to an exceptional circumstance, but in other cases it would be the collective impact of all the relevant circumstances. The Court said that, so far as it could identify a rationale for this sentencing provision, it was to do with deterrence, rather than public protection (which had been the case for the PCC(S)A 2000, s. 109), so that it could not be treated in the same way. Lord Woolf CJ said that s. 51A was capable of causing considerable injustice, especially bearing in mind that possession of a prohibited firearm was an absolute offence. Reading s. 51A in the light of the HRA 1998, s. 3, his lordship said that the circumstances would be 'exceptional' if it would mean that to impose the minimum sentence would result in an arbitrary and disproportionate sentence. Unless a judge was clearly wrong in *not* identifying exceptional circumstances when they were present, the Court of Appeal would not readily interfere with the trial judge's decision. It may be that the formulation of the test in *Rehman* permits greater discretion for the trial judge than exists in relation to the minimum custodial sentences at **E6.1** and **E6.3**.

In *Rehman* itself, the Court of Appeal held that the judge had erred in not finding exceptional circumstances in the case, where the offender's background (in particular his previous good character), his early plea of guilty, his ignorance of the unlawfulness of the weapon (he had purchased it as a collector's model), and the fact that there was just one weapon, taken together amounted to exceptional circumstances. The sentence was reduced from five years to one year, allowing the offender's immediate release. In *Blackall* [2006] 1 Cr App R (S) 131, the exceptional circumstances were matters personal to the offender. He was paraplegic, with many consequential physical disabilities, such that the imposition of any sentence of imprisonment on him would be much more severe than would usually be the case. The fact that the offender was keeping the prohibited weapon for his own protection could not amount to an exceptional circumstance, since that was a common feature of such cases and the minimum sentence was designed to deter people from keeping such firearms, whatever their reason might be. In *McEneaney* [2005] 2 Cr App R (S) 531, the offender suffered from schizophrenia following a head injury incurred in his youth. The illness was controlled by medication and a hospital order was not recommended. The Court of Appeal said that the offender's psychiatric history did not amount to exceptional circumstances. In *Evans* [2006] 1 Cr App R (S) 346, the offender's obsessive compulsive symptoms, which had apparently led him to hoard guns, did not amount to exceptional circumstances. It was relevant in this case that the offender was a civilian reception officer at a police station, who had abused his position to steal ammunition which had been handed in. Exceptional circumstances were found in *Mehmet* [2006] 1 Cr App R (S) 397, where the offender, a man of good character, had acquired the gun from a friend some years before possession became unlawful in 2004. By then the offender was ill with depression and he did not become aware of the change in the law. He had no ammunition for the gun. The Court of Appeal said that, taken together, these factors amounted to exceptional circumstances, and the sentence of imprisonment was reduced from five years to 30 months. Finally, exceptional circumstances were found in *Harrison* [2006] 2 Cr App R (S) 353, where the offender was apprehended while on the way to dispose of the weapon, which belonged to another person, by throwing it into a lake.

Guilty Plea

E6.8 In contrast to the PCC(S)A 2000, ss. 110(2) and 111(2), there is no provision in the FA 1968, s. 51A, limiting the extent to which the offender's guilty plea can affect the sentence imposed. The Court of Appeal in *Jordan* [2005] 2 Cr App R (S) 266 held that, in respect of s. 51A, Parliament must have intended to exclude the normal principles of reduction of sentence to reflect a guilty plea. No discount was available for plea. The rigour of s. 51A was mitigated by the possibility of exceptional circumstances being found. Such cases would be rare, but if the judge had properly identified exceptional circumstances the sentence would then be at large.

MINIMUM CUSTODIAL SENTENCES FOR USING SOMEONE TO MIND A WEAPON

E6.9 The VCRA 2006, s. 28 (in force from 6 April 2007) creates an offence where the offender uses another person to look after, hide or transport a dangerous weapon for him under arrangements or in circumstances that facilitate, or are intended to facilitate, the weapon's being available to the offender for an unlawful purpose (see **B12.150**)

Violent Crime Reduction Act 1996, s. 29

(1) This section applies where a person ('the offender') is guilty of an offence under section 28.

(2) Where the dangerous weapon in respect of which the offence is committed is a weapon to which section 141 or 141A of the Criminal Justice Act 1988 (specified offensive weapons, knives and bladed weapons) applies, the offender shall be liable, on conviction on indictment for a term not exceeding 4 years or to a fine, or to both.

(3) Where—

(a) at the time of the offence, the offender was aged 16 or over, and

(b) the dangerous weapon in respect of which the offence was committed was a firearm mentioned in section 5(1)(a) to (af) or (c) or section 5(1A)(a) of the 1968 Act (firearms possession of which attracts a minimum sentence),

the offender shall be liable, on conviction on indictment, to imprisonment for a term not exceeding 10 years or to a fine, or to both.

(4) On a conviction in England and Wales, where—
(a) subsection 3 applies, and
(b) the offender is aged 18 or over at the time of conviction, the court must impose (with or without a fine) a term of imprisonment of not less than 5 years, unless it is of the opinion that there are exceptional circumstances relating to the offence or to the offender which justify its not doing so.

(5) In relation to times before the commencement of paragraph 80 of schedule 7 to the Criminal Justice and Court Services Act 2000, the reference in subsection (4) to a sentence of imprisonment, in relation to an offender aged under 21 at the time of conviction, is to be read as a reference to a sentence of detention in a young offender institution.

(6) On a conviction in England and Wales, where—
(a) subsection (3) applies, and
(b) the offender is aged 18 at the time of conviction, the court must impose (with or without a fine) a term of detention under section 91 of the Powers of Criminal Courts Sentencing Act 2000 of not less than 3 years, unless it is of the opinion that there are exceptional circumstances relating to the offender or to the offence which justify its not doing so.

(7)–(9) [Scotland]

(10) In any case not mentioned in subsection (2) or (3), the offender shall be liable, on conviction on indictment, to imprisonment for a term not exceeding 5 years or to a fine, or to both.

Statutory Aggravating Factor

Where a court is considering the seriousness of an offence under the VCRA 2006, s. 28, the fact that the offender was aged 18 or over and used a person to look after etc. the weapon who was under 18, the court must treat that fact as increasing the seriousness of the offence (s. 29(11)). The judge should state in open court that the offence was so aggravated (s. 29(12)). **E6.10**

Section E7 Intermittent Custody

E7.1 Provisions on intermittent custody were brought into force on 26 January 2004. Intermittent custody was made available only to certain trial courts on a pilot basis, from that date. On 3 November 2006 the Home Office announced its intention not to implement the intermittent custody order nationally.

Section E8 Suspended Sentences under the Criminal Justice Act 2003

Power to impose a suspended sentence under the CJA 2003 came into effect on 4 April 2005 in respect of offences committed on or after that date. The power to impose a suspended sentence of imprisonment under the PCC(S)A 2000, s. 118, was repealed and replaced. The power to impose a suspended sentence under the CJA 2003 applies to sentences of imprisonment and, until the CJCSA 2000, s. 61, is brought into force, to sentences of detention in a young offender institution. The pre-2003 Act suspended sentence was available only in respect of offenders aged 21 and over; the new scheme applies to offenders aged 18 and over sentenced to detention in a young offender institution, subject to what is said below. See further the Criminal Justice Act 2003 (Sentencing) (Transitory Provisions) Order 2005 (SI 2005 No. 643). The suspended sentence is available to the Crown Court where that court imposes a determinate custodial sentence of 12 months or less or where a magistrates' court imposes a determinate custodial sentence of 6 months or less. Sentences of less than 14 days cannot be suspended. Detention and training order sentences cannot be suspended. **E8.1**

Power to Impose Suspended Sentences

Criminal Justice Act 2003, s. 189 **E8.2**

(1) A court which passes a sentence of imprisonment or, in the case of a person aged at least 18 but under 21, detention in a young offender institution for a term of at least 14 days but not more than 12 months, or in the case of a magistrates' court, at least 14 days but not more than 6 months may—

(a) order the offender to comply during a period specified for the purposes of this paragraph in the order (in this chapter referred to as 'the supervision period') with one or more requirements falling within section 190(1) and specified in the order, and

(b) order that the sentence of imprisonment or detention in a young offender institution is not to take effect unless either—

(i) during the supervision period the offender fails to comply with a requirement imposed under paragraph (a), or

(ii) during a period specified in the order for the purposes of this sub-paragraph (in this chapter referred to as the 'operational period') the offender commits in the United Kingdom another offence (whether or not punishable with imprisonment),

and (in either case) a court having power to do so subsequently orders under paragraph 8 of schedule 12 that the original sentence is to take effect.

This section is printed as modified by SI 2005 No. 643. Section 181(2) states that the term of the suspended sentence 'must be expressed in weeks'.

The period in the suspended sentence during which the offender is to undertake specified requirements is called the 'supervision period' of the suspended sentence, and the entire length of the order is called the 'operational period' of the suspended sentence. The supervision period must not end later than the operational period (s. 189(3)), but each of the two periods must last for not less than six months and not more than two years (s. 189(4)). It should be noted that a suspended sentence must specify at least one requirement (*Lees-Wolfenden* [2007] 1 Cr App R (S) 730). The sentence of imprisonment or detention in a young offender institution imposed by the court will not take effect unless the offender fails to comply with the requirements imposed by the court, or he commits another offence (whether punishable with imprisonment or not) during the operational period of the suspended sentence.

Section 189(6) states that a suspended sentence is to be treated as a sentence of imprisonment or detention in a young offender institution. A suspended sentence cannot be ordered unless all the statutory provisions as to the imposition of a sentence of immediate imprisonment have been observed. Before a suspended sentence can be passed, the court must take account of the relevant provisions of the CJA 2003, ss. 152 and 153, which must be complied with before any custodial sentence is passed (see **E2.5** and **E2.8**). The power to impose a suspended sentence in a magistrates' court is limited in the same way in which magistrates' powers to impose prison sentences are limited (see **E2.3**).

The SGC Guideline, *New Sentences: CJA 2003* (Dec 2004), provides that while there are many similarities between the suspended sentence and the community order, the crucial difference is that the suspended sentence is a prison sentence (or a sentence of detention in a young offender institution) and is only appropriate for an offence that crosses the custody threshold, and for which custody is the only option (para. 2.2.10). As far as the length of the sentence is concerned, before making the decision to suspend, the court must first have decided that a prison sentence (or sentence of detention in a young offender institution) is justified and should also have decided the length of that sentence, which should be the shortest term commensurate with the seriousness of the offence if it were to be imposed immediately. The decision to suspend the sentence should not lead to a longer term being imposed than if the sentence were to take effect immediately (para. 2.2.12).

Suspended Sentence: Consecutive Terms

E8.3 Section 189(2) of the CJA 2003 as modified by SI 2005 No. 643 states that where two or more sentences imposed on the same occasion are to be served consecutively, the power to suspend sentence is not exercisable in relation to any of the sentences unless the aggregate of the terms does not exceed 12 months, or in the case of a magistrates' court, six months.

Suspended Sentence: Combining with Other Sentences or Orders

E8.4 It is submitted that an immediate prison sentence and a suspended sentence should not be imposed on the same occasion (by analogy with *Sapiano* (1968) 52 Cr App R 674), nor should a suspended sentence be imposed on an offender currently serving a term of imprisonment (by analogy with *Butters* (1971) 55 Cr App R 515). A court which passes a suspended sentence on an offender must not on the same occasion impose a community sentence in respect of that offence or any other offence for which he is dealt with by the court (CJA 2003, s. 189(5)). It is submitted that a suspended sentence cannot be combined with a discharge when sentencing for a single offence (see **E14.4**) but a discharge could be given for one offence when a suspended sentence was passed in respect of another offence sentenced on the same occasion. A fine may be combined with a suspended sentence, but it is improper to combine them when a fine standing alone would have been the proper sentence. A fine may be added to a suspended sentence, but a suspended sentence should not be added to a fine. There is no restriction on imposing ancillary provisions such as compensation orders, restitution orders, or deprivation orders, at the same time as a suspended sentence.

Suspended Sentence: Imposition of Requirements

E8.5 Section 190 of the CJA 2003 lists the requirements with which the court may order the offender to comply during the supervision period of the suspended sentence. These are:

(a) an unpaid work requirement (as defined by s. 199),
(b) an activity requirement (s. 201),
(c) a programme requirement (s. 202),
(d) a prohibited activity requirement (s. 203),
(e) a curfew requirement (s. 204),
(f) an exclusion requirement (s. 205),
(g) a residence requirement (s. 206),
(h) a mental health requirement (s. 207),
(i) a drug rehabilitation requirement (s. 209),
(j) an alcohol treatment requirement (s. 212),
(k) a supervision requirement (s. 213), and
(l) in a case where the offender is aged under 25, an attendance centre requirement (s. 214).

For details of these requirements, see **E10.6** to **E10.17**.

The SGC Guideline, *New Sentences: CJA 2003* (Dec 2004), provides that the court will set the requirements to be complied with during the supervision period. Whilst the offence for which a suspended sentence is imposed is generally likely to be more serious than one for which a community sentence is imposed, the imposition of the custodial sentence is a clear punishment and deterrent. In order to ensure that the overall terms of the sentence are commensurate with the seriousness of the offence, it is likely that the requirements to be undertaken during the supervision period would be less onerous than if a community sentence had been imposed. These requirements will need to ensure that they properly address those factors that are most likely to reduce the risk of re-offending.

Whenever the court passes a suspended sentence which contains two or more different requirements, it must consider whether, in the circumstances of the case, the requirements are compatible with each other (s. 190(5)). Power to insert such conditions into the licence is made subject to the court ensuring, so far as possible, that the condition or conditions avoid any conflict with the offender's religious beliefs, or with the requirements of any other relevant order to which he may be subject, and avoid interference with the times, if any, at which he normally works or attends school or any other educational establishment (s. 217). The court must also be satisfied that local facilities exist, and that local arrangements are in place, for the carrying out of relevant requirements (s. 218). A suspended sentence must specify the petty sessions area in which the offender will reside (s. 216(1)).

Restrictions on Imposition of Requirements The court cannot make an unpaid work requirement unless satisfied that the offender is a suitable person to perform such work (CJA 2003, s. 199(3)). Thehe court cannot impose an activity requirement unless it has consulted an officer of a local probation board or a member of a youth offending team (as appropriate), is satisfied that it is feasible to secure compliance with the requirement (s. 201(3)) and has secured the agreement of any person other than the offender and the responsible officer whose co-operation is required (s. 201(4)). The court cannot insert a programme requirement unless the relevant accredited programme has been recommended to the court by an officer of a local probation board or a member of a youth offending team (as appropriate) as being suitable for the offender, the court is satisfied that the programme will be available (s. 202(4)) and the court has secured the agreement of any person other than the offender and the responsible officer whose co-operation is required. The court cannot insert a prohibited activity requirement unless it has consulted an officer of a local probation board or a member of a youth offending team (as appropriate) (s. 203(2)). The court cannot insert a mental health requirement unless the court is satisfied on the evidence of a registered medical practitioner that the mental condition of the offender is such as requires and is susceptible to treatment and does not warrant the making of a hospital or guardianship order, that arrangements have been made for the treatment to be carried out, and that the offender has consented to the inclusion **E8.6**

of the mental health requirement into the suspended sentence (s. 207(3)). The court may not insert a drug rehabilitation requirement unless it is satisfied that the offender is dependent on, or has a propensity to misuse, a controlled drug and that his dependency or propensity is such as requires and may be susceptible to treatment, that arrangements can be made for the treatment to be carried out, that the requirement has been recommended by the responsible officer, and that the offender has expressed his willingness to comply with the requirement (s. 209(2)). The court may not impose an alcohol treatment requirement unless it is satisfied that the offender is dependent on alcohol, that his dependency is such as requires and may be susceptible to treatment, that arrangements can be made for the treatment to be carried out, and that the offender has expressed his willingness to comply with the requirement (s. 212(2)).

If the suspended sentence contains a curfew requirement or an exclusion requirement, the court *must* also require the licence to contain an electronic monitoring requirement, as defined by s. 215 of the Act, *unless* the court is unable to do so because there is some person, other than the offender, whose co-operation is required but who does not consent (s. 215(2)), or because electronic monitoring arrangements are not available in the local area (s. 218(4)), or because, in the particular circumstances of the case, the court considers it inappropriate to do so.

If the suspended sentence contains an unpaid work requirement, an activity requirement, a programme requirement, a prohibited activity requirement, a residence requirement, a mental health treatment requirement, a drug rehabilitation requirement, an alcohol treatment requirement, a supervision requirement or an attendance centre requirement, the court *may* also require the licence to contain an electronic monitoring requirement, unless the court is unable to do so because there is some person, other than the offender, whose co-operation is required but who does not consent (s. 215(2)), or because electronic monitoring arrangements are not available in the local area (s. 218(4)).

Suspended Sentence: Power to Provide for Review

E8.7 Section 191(1) of the CJA 2003 confers a discretion on the court to provide that a suspended sentence is made subject to periodic review, at review hearings, at specified intervals of time. The court may order the offender to attend those hearings, and it may order the responsible officer, before each review, to provide to the court a report on the offender's progress under the suspended sentence. If the offender is subject to a suspended sentence which contains a drug rehabilitation requirement, such requirement will already be subject to court review hearings under the CJA 2003, s. 210, so s. 191(2) provides that in those circumstances the suspended sentence cannot be subject to review under s. 191(1). A review hearing is conducted by the court responsible for the order, and s. 191(3) to (5) specifies which court is responsible for review of the suspended sentence in particular situations.

Section 192 describes what is to happen at the review hearings. Section 192(1) permits the court to amend any community requirement of the suspended sentence order, after consideration of the report from the supervising officer. This is limited by s. 192(2) which explains that the court cannot amend the order by adding a requirement of a different kind unless the offender consents to that new requirement, but it can impose a requirement of the same kind. The offender's consent is always required before the court amends a drug rehabilitation requirement, an alcohol treatment requirement, or a mental health treatment requirement (s. 192(2)(b)). The court may also extend the supervision period, but not so that it infringes the normal rules on suspended sentences in s. 189(3) or (4), by lasting for longer than two years from the date of the original order or ending later than the operational period.

Under s. 192(4), if on the basis of the report from the responsible officer the court is of the opinion that the offender is making satisfactory progress, it can dispense with the next pending review hearing, or may amend the order so that subsequent reviews can be held by considering the papers rather than by a full hearing. The court may order the offender to attend a review hearing if progress is no longer satisfactory, or it may adjust the intervals of time between review hearings (s. 192(5) and (7)).

Suspended Sentence: Breach, Commission of Further Offence, and Amendment

Section 193 refers to the CJA 2003, sch. 12, which contains provisions relating to the breach, revocation and amendment of the community requirements of suspended sentence orders, and to the effect of the offender being convicted of a further offence. **E8.8**

Paragraphs 4 and 5 of sch. 12 are the key provisions here. By para. 4, if the responsible officer is of the opinion that the offender has failed without reasonable excuse to comply with any of the community requirements of the suspended sentence, the officer must give a *warning* describing the circumstances of the failure, stating that the failure is unacceptable, and informing the offender that if within the next 12 months he again fails to comply with any requirement of the order, he will be brought back before the court. By para. 5, if there has been a warning, and within 12 months there is a further failure without reasonable excuse to comply, the responsible officer must cause an information to be laid before a magistrate, or before the Crown Court, in respect of that second failure. Paragraphs 6 and 7 deal in detail with the arrangements for issue of a summons or warrant by the magistrate or by the Crown Court.

Powers Available to Deal with Breach Paragraph 8 of sch. 12 to the CJA 2003 describes the powers of the court when dealing with a breach of a community requirement in a suspended sentence, or on conviction of a further offence. If it is proved to the satisfaction of the court before which the offender is brought that he has failed without reasonable cause to comply with any of the community requirements, or has been convicted of an offence committed during the operational period of the suspended sentence, the court must deal with him in one of the following ways set out in para. 8(2): **E8.9**

(a) order that the suspended sentence takes effect with the original term and custodial period unaltered, or
(b) order that the suspended sentence takes effect with the substitution of a *lesser term* (which, however, cannot be less than 28 weeks) and/or the substitution of a *lesser custodial period* (which, however, cannot be less than two weeks), or
(c) amend the order by imposing more onerous community requirements or extending the supervision period (but not so that it exceeds two years in total or ends later than the operational period) or extending the operational period (but not so that it exceeds two years in total).

By para. 8(3), the court must make an order under para. 8(2)(a) or (b) unless it is of the opinion that it would be unjust to do so in view of all the circumstances. These circumstances include (by para. 8(4)), the extent to which the offender has complied with the community requirements of the suspended sentence order, and (where the offender has breached the suspended sentence by committing a further offence) the facts of that subsequent offence. If the court is of the opinion that it would be unjust to order that the suspended sentence should take effect in full, it should state its reasons.

The pre-existing principles derived from case-law on breach of community sentences (where the offender has failed to comply with community requirements) and breach of suspended sentence (where the offender has committed a further offence) will continue to be of some value, at least in the short term, in applying these provisions.

The SGC Guideline, *New Sentences: CJA 2003* (Dec 2004), provides that where proceedings are brought for breach the court has several options, including extending the operational period. However, the presumption (which also applies where breach is by commission of a further offence) is that the suspended prison sentence will be activated (whether with its original custodial term or a lesser term) unless the court takes the view that this would, in all the circumstances, be unjust. In reaching that decision, the court may take into account both the extent to which the offender has complied with the requirements and the facts of the new offence (para. 2.2.15). Where a court considers that the sentence needs to be activated, it may activate it in full or with a reduced term. Again, the extent to which the requirements have been complied with will be very relevant to this decision (para. 2.2.17). If a court amends the order rather than activating the suspended prison sentence, it must either make the requirements more onerous, or extend the supervision or operational periods (provided that these remain within the limits defined by the CJA 2003). In such cases, the court must state its reasons for not activating the suspended sentence, which could include the extent to which the offender has complied with the requirements or the facts of the subsequent offence (para. 2.2.18). If an offender near the end of an operational period (having complied with the requirements imposed) commits another offence, it may be more appropriate to amend the order rather than activate it (para. 2.2.19). If a new offence committed is of a less serious nature than the offence for which the suspended sentence was passed, it may justify activating the sentence with a reduced term or amending the terms of the order (para. 2.2.20). It is expected that any activated suspended sentence will be consecutive to the sentence imposed for the new offence (para. 2.2.21). If the new offence is non-imprisonable, the sentencer should consider whether it is appropriate to activate the suspended sentence at all (para. 2.2.22).

Under the CJA 2003, sch 12, para. 9, if the court makes an order under para. 8(2)(a) or (b) that the suspended sentence is to take effect, the court *must* also make a custody plus order (assuming that those provisions have already been brought into effect) and *may* order that the sentence takes effect immediately or on the expiry of another term of imprisonment imposed on the offender.

E8.10 **Amendment of Requirements** Paragraphs 13 to 18 of sch. 12 to the CJA 2003 deal with various forms of amendment to community requirements in a suspended sentence order which may be made by an appropriate court on application by the offender or the responsible officer, or as to change of residence and other matters.

Section E9 Custodial Sentences: Detention and Custody of Offenders under 21

For the restriction on imposing imprisonment on persons aged under 21, see E2.1. The custodial sentences which are available for offenders under the age of 21 are detention in a young offender institution (determinate custodial sentence for those aged 18 to 20 inclusive: see E9.3), custody for life (indeterminate custodial sentence for those aged 18 to 20 inclusive; see E9.6), detention under the PCC(S)A 2000, s. 91 (see E9.8) and the detention and training order (determinate custodial sentence for those aged under 18: see E9.10). **E9.1**

The PCC(S)A 2000, s. 83(2), prohibits the passing of any of these custodial sentences on an offender aged under 21 who is not legally represented. This prohibition does not apply, however, if the offender has been granted a right to legal representation but the right has been withdrawn because of his conduct or, having been informed of his right to apply for legal representation and having had the opportunity to do so, he has refused or failed to comply (s. 83(3)). A person is to be treated as 'legally represented' for these purposes if, but only if, he has the assistance of counsel or a solicitor to represent him in that court at some time after he is found guilty and before he is sentenced (s. 83(4)).

When the CJCSA 2000, s. 61, is brought into force, the sentences of detention in a young offender institution and custody for life will be abolished. Offenders who would have received such sentences will thereafter be sentenced to imprisonment, which will become the standard custodial sentence for offenders aged 18 to 20 inclusive as well as for offenders aged 21 and over. No date has been set for this change.

Determining the Age of the Offender

Criminal Justice Act 1982, s. 1 **E9.2**

(6) For the purposes of any provision of this Act which requires the determination of the age of a person by the court or the Secretary of State his age shall be deemed to be that which it appears to the court or the Secretary of State (as the case may be) to be after considering any available evidence.

When a court imposes a sentence on an assumption of the offender's age made under s. 1(6), the sentence is not rendered unlawful when it is discovered subsequently that the assumption was incorrect (*Brown* (1989) 11 Cr App R (S) 263). If there is a dispute about the offender's age, the best course may be to adjourn until the matter can be resolved (*Steed* (1990) 12 Cr App R (S) 230).

In *Danga* [1992] QB 476, where the offender was aged 20 when convicted but aged 21 when sentenced, it was held that the relevant age of the offender for the purposes of s. 96(1) was the age at the date of conviction. In *Ghafoor* [2003] 1 Cr App R (S) 428, the offender, who was 17 when the offence was committed but 18 when convicted, pleaded guilty to riot. It was noted that the maximum penalty for the offence was 10 years' detention in a young offender institution but, had the offender been convicted when still 17, the maximum penalty would have been a detention and training order of 24 months, less an appropriate discount for guilty plea. The Court of Appeal stated that, when fixing the appropriate term of detention in a young offender institution, the starting point for sentence should be that term which the offender would have been likely to receive if he had been sentenced at the date of the commission of the offence. The sentence of four and a half years' detention in a young offender institution was reduced to 18 months. *Ghafoor* was followed and applied in *Jones* [2004] 1 Cr App R (S) 126 and *Britton* [2007] 1 Cr App R (S) 745.

In *Robinson* [1993] 1 WLR 168 it was held, following *Danga* [1992] QB 476, that in determining whether an offender was eligible for a sentence under s. 91 the relevant age was the age of the offender at the time of conviction, rather than his age at the time of sentence.

Detention in a Young Offender Institution

E9.3 **Power to Order Detention**

Powers of Criminal Courts (Sentencing) Act 2000, s. 96

(1) Subject to sections 90, 93 and 94 above, where—
 (a) a person aged at least 18 but under 21 is convicted of an offence which is punishable with imprisonment in the case of a person aged 21 or over, and
 (b) the court is of the opinion that either or both of paragraphs (a) and (b) of section 79(2) above apply or the case falls within section 79(3),
the sentence that the court is to pass is a sentence of detention in a young offender institution.

It should be noted that the procedural provisions which must be complied with before a custodial sentence may lawfully be imposed upon an adult offender must also be complied with in respect of an offender aged under 21 (see **E2.5** and **E2.7**).

A sentence of detention in a young offender institution may be suspended, in accordance with the provisions of the CJA 2003, s. 189. To be eligible for suspension the sentence of detention in a young offender institution must be for at least 14 days and not more than 12 months in the Crown Court and for at least 14 days but not more than 6 months in the magistrates' court. See **E8.1**.

Time spent in custody on remand may be deducted from a sentence of detention in a young offender institution (CJA 2003, s. 240). See **E2.8**.

E9.4 **Minimum and Maximum Terms** The PCC(S)A 2000, s. 97, provides for minimum and maximum terms for this sentence.

Powers of Criminal Courts (Sentencing) Act 2000, s. 97

(1) The maximum term of detention in a young offender institution that a court may impose for an offence is the same as the maximum term of imprisonment that it may impose for that offence.
(2) Subject to subsection (3) below, a court shall not pass a sentence for an offender's detention in a young offender institution for less than 21 days.
(3) A court may pass a sentence of detention in a young offender institution for less than 21 days for an offence under section 65(6) of the Criminal Justice Act 1991 (breach of requirement imposed on young offender on his release from detention).

In *Dover Youth Court, ex parte K (A Minor)* [1999] 1 WLR 27, the Divisional Court held that, on a proper construction of the word 'sentence', s. 97(2) should be taken to refer to the sentence imposed for a particular offence, rather than to the total sentence produced by aggregating more than one custodial term.

Concurrent and Consecutive Sentences of Detention E9.5

Powers of Criminal Courts (Sentencing) Act 2000, s. 97

(4) Where—
- (a) an offender is convicted of more than one offence for which he is liable to a sentence of detention in a young offender institution, or
- (b) an offender who is serving a sentence of detention in a young offender institution is convicted of one or more further offences for which he is liable to such a sentence,

the court shall have the same power to pass consecutive sentences of detention in a young offender institution as if they were sentences of imprisonment.

(5) Subject to section 84 above (restriction on consecutive sentences for released prisoners) where an offender who—
- (a) is serving a sentence of detention in a young offender institution, and
- (b) is aged 21 or over,

is convicted of one or more further offences for which he is liable to imprisonment, the court shall have the power to pass one or more sentences of imprisonment to run consecutively upon the sentence of detention in a young offender institution.

For concurrent and consecutive custodial sentences, see **E2.11**.

The sentence of detention in a young offender institution is subject to the statutory criteria for determining whether a custodial sentence should be imposed (see **E2.5**) and for determining custodial sentence length (see **E2.7**).

Although the statutory criteria are equally applicable to sentences of detention in a young offender institution as they are to imprisonment, the authorities suggest that it is often appropriate to pass a shorter custodial sentence on an offender who has not yet attained the age of 21 than the term which would be imposed on an adult who has committed the same offence, although this may be outweighed by other factors in the case. Comment to this effect can be found in *A-G's Ref (No. 42 of 1996)* [1997] 1 Cr App R (S) 388 and in *Howells* [1999] 1 WLR 307.

The length of a sentence of detention in a young offender institution is normally reduced following a plea of guilty. The general principle and relevant statutory provision are set out at **E1.6**.

In *George* (1993) 14 Cr App R (S) 12, where the young offender pleaded guilty to a 'disgraceful' offence of criminal damage committed in a church at night, the Court of Appeal said that a guilty plea should normally attract a discount, and reduced the maximum available term of 12 months (as it then was) to 10 months. In *Sharkey* (1995) 16 Cr App R (S) 257, the Court of Appeal said that it was 'wrong in principle' to impose the maximum term of detention in a young offender institution on an offender who had pleaded guilty, and the same view was taken in *Carroll* (1995) 16 Cr App R (S) 488. These last two cases involved serious incidents of aggravated vehicle-taking.

Custody for Life

Powers of Criminal Courts (Sentencing) Act 2000, s. 94 E9.6

94.—(1) Where a person aged at least 18 but under 21 is convicted of an offence—
- (a) for which the sentence is not fixed by law, but
- (b) for which a person aged 21 or over would be liable to imprisonment for life, the court shall, if it considers that a sentence for life would be appropriate, sentence him to custody for life.

The criteria for the imposition for the sentence of custody for life, where it is imposed as a discretionary sentence, are those contained in the CJA 2003, ss. 152 and 153. The PCC(S)A 2000, s. 82A, provides that a sentencer imposing a sentence of custody for life as a discretionary life sentence under s. 94, may specify that part of the sentence which must expire before the offender becomes eligible for consideration for early release. The sentencer should start by deciding what determinate sentence would have been appropriate if custody for life had not been imposed, and then specify a period which will normally be one half of that notional sentence as the part to be specified under s. 82A (*Marklew* [1999] 1 WLR 485). Credit should be given for relevant mitigating factors, such as the youth of the offender and for any period spent on remand in custody or in local authority secure accommodation.

The sentence of custody for life has, in the past, been distinguished from the imposition of a determinate sentence of detention in a young offender institution by the requirement that custody for life should be imposed only in exceptional circumstances and only where the offender displays a degree of mental instability. This is very similar to the requirement for the imposition of a life sentence of imprisonment on an adult. The Court of Appeal has stressed that custody for life is reserved for exceptional cases where there is a marked degree of mental instability, and should not be passed on the assumption that it is a more merciful disposal than a fixed-term sentence (*Hall* (1986) 8 Cr App R (S) 458 and *Lynas* (1992) 13 Cr App R (S) 363, following *Pither* (1979) 1 Cr App R (S) 209).

Cases where the Court has quashed sentences of custody for life imposed at trial are: *Hall* (1986) 8 Cr App R (S) 458 (sentence inappropriate after a guilty plea to arson, since 'no real evidence that the offender was suffering from any mental illness or abnormality, although he was immature and a young criminal who had committed many offences'; sentence varied to seven years); and *Powell* (1989) 11 Cr App R (S) 113 (sentence inappropriate after a guilty plea to wounding with intent, taking a conveyance and violent disorder, since the offender had shown a degree of remorse and because there was 'an insufficient degree of mental instability, or dangerousness, to call for the exceptional course which the judge felt obliged to take'; sentence varied to eight years). On the other hand, a sentence of custody for life was upheld in *Silson* (1987) 9 Cr App R (S) 282, where the accused, who pleaded guilty to two counts of arson, one with intent to endanger life, involving damage of £20,000, was described as not suffering from any psychiatric illness, but as being of dull/normal intelligence, immature and inadequate, and whose behaviour was attributed in part to alcohol and solvent abuse. Such a sentence was similarly upheld in *Busby* (1992) 13 Cr App R (S) 291, where the offender, aged 18, pleaded guilty to buggery of a girl aged three. He was not suffering from any mental illness but was described as 'flat and detached' and showed no remorse. He had committed two earlier assaults on young children and, in the light of that, it was held that the primary responsibility of the court was to protect the public.

Detention under PCC(S)A 2000, s. 91

E9.7 **Powers of Criminal Courts (Sentencing) Act 2000, s. 91**

(1) Subsection (3) below applies where a person aged under 18 is convicted on indictment of—
- (a) an offence punishable in the case of a person aged 21 or over with imprisonment for 14 years or more, not being an offence the sentence for which is fixed by law; or
- (b) an offence under section 3 of the Sexual Offences Act 2003 (in this section, 'the 2003 Act' (sexual assault); or
- (c) an offence under section 13 of the 2003 Act (child sex offences committed by children or young persons); or
- (d) an offence under section 25 of the 2003 Act (sexual activity with a child family member); or
- (e) an offence under section 26 of the 2003 Act (inciting a child family member to engage in sexual activity).

(1A) Subsection (3) below also applies where—
- (a) a person aged under 18 is convicted on indictment of an offence—
  - (i) under subsection (1)(a), (ab), (aba), (ac), (ad), (ae), (af) or (c) of section 5 of the Firearms Act 1968 (prohibited weapons), or
  - (ii) under subsection (1A)(a) of that section,
- (b) the offence was committed after the commencement of section 51A of that Act and at a time when he was aged 16 or over, and

(c) the court is of the opinion mentioned in section 51A(2) of that Act (exceptional circumstances which justify its not imposing required custodial sentence).

(2) Repealed

(3) If the court is of the opinion that neither a community sentence nor a detention and training order is suitable, the court may sentence the offender to be detained for such period, not exceeding the maximum term of imprisonment with which the offence is punishable in the case of a person aged 21 or over, as may be specified in the sentence.

(4) Subsection (3) above is subject to (in particular) sections 152 and 153 of the Criminal Justice Act 2003.

(5) Where subsection (2) of section 51A of the Firearms Act 1968 requires the imposition of a sentence of detention under this section for a term of at least the required minimum term (within the meaning of that section), the court shall sentence the offender to be detained for such period, of at least that term but not exceeding the maximum term of imprisonment with which the offence is punishable in the case of a person aged 18 or over, as may be specified in the sentence.

When the relevant provisions of the VCRA 2006 are brought into force, s. 91 will be amended. In particular, s. 49 and sch. 1, para. 7(2) of the 2006 Act will insert new subsections (1B) and (1C) as follows:

(1B) Subsection (3) below also applies where—
(a) a person aged under 18 is convicted on indictment of an offence under the Firearms Act 1968 that is listed in section 51A(1A)(b), (e) or (f) of that Act and was committed in respect of a firearm or ammunition specified in section 5(1)(a), (ab), (ac), (ad), (af) or (c) or section 5(1A)(a) of that Act;
(b) the offence was committed after the commencement of section 30 of the Violent Crime Reduction Act 2006 and for the purposes of section 51A(3) of the Firearms Act 1968 at a time when he was aged 16 or over; and
(c) the court is of the opinion mentioned in section 51A(2) of the Firearms Act 1968.

(1C) Subsection (3) below also applies where—
(a) a person aged under 18 is convicted of an offence under section 28 of the Violent Crime Reduction Act 2006 (using someone to mind a weapon);
(b) section 29(3) of that Act applies (minimum sentences in certain cases); and
(c) the court is of the opinion mentioned in section 29(6) of that Act (exceptional circumstances which justify not imposing the minimum sentence).

Section 91 is also prospectively amended by the 2006 Act, s. 49, sch. 1, para. 7(1) and (3)

It should be noted that s. 91 is not available in respect of burglary of commercial premises, where the maximum penalty is ten years' imprisonment (*Brown* (1995) 16 Cr App R (S) 932). In *Ganley* [2001] 1 Cr App R (S) 60 the Court of Appeal noted that the power to impose detention under s. 91 was unaffected by the introduction of detention and training orders. If detention for two years or less is called for, it will generally be appropriate to make a detention and training order rather than an order under s. 91. It should be noted, however, that the detention and training order may be imposed on an offender aged under 15 only where he is a 'persistent offender'. There is no such restriction in relation to detention under s. 91. In *S J-R and DG* [2001] 1 Cr App R (S) 377 two boys aged 14 were convicted of robbery. Neither qualified as a persistent offender, but the Court of Appeal endorsed sentences of 15 months and 30 months' detention under s. 91.

Powers under s. 91 are limited to conviction in the Crown Court; a youth court may not exercise them. In a case where the offence merits a greater penalty than is permitted by the scheme of maximum penalties for the detention and training order (see **E9.10**), the proper course is for the magistrates to commit to the Crown Court for trial to allow for the possibility of an order under s. 91 being made. In *AM* [1998] 1 WLR 363, the Court of Appeal again reminded magistrates of the need to commit for trial any case which might merit detention under s. 91. In *R (D) v Manchester City Youth Court* [2002] 1 Cr App R (S) 573, however, the Divisional Court quashed a committal for a trial of a boy aged 13 charged with indecent assault. The boy was not a 'persistent offender', and so a detention and training order could not be imposed. Gage J said that committal with a view to sentence under s. 91 should normally be ordered only where a custodial sentence in excess of two years was envisaged by the youth court. That approach was endorsed by the Divisional Court in *R(W) v Southampton Youth Court* [2003] 1 Cr App R (S) 455, where Lord Woolf CJ said that the general policy of the legislation was that young offenders should, wherever possible, be tried by a youth court. If an offender did not qualify for a detention and training order because he was under 15 and not a persistent offender, the most likely outcome was a non-custodial penalty. Only exceptionally, if the appropriate sentence would be 24 months or thereabouts, would committal to Crown Court with a view to sentence under s. 91 be appropriate. See also *R(C) v Balham Youth Court* [2004] 1 Cr App R (S) 143.

Time spent in custody (or local authority secure accommodation) on remand may be deducted from a sentence imposed under s. 91 (CJA 2003, s. 240, set out at **E2.8**). The PCC(S)A 2000, s. 83 (restriction on imposing sentence where offender not legally represented), applies (see **E2.4**). A detention and training order cannot be ordered to run consecutively to an order of detention under s. 91 (*Hayward* [2001] 2 Cr App R (S) 149), nor *vice versa* (*Lang* [2001] 2 Cr App R (S) 175).

Detention under PCC(S)A 2000, s. 91: Sentencing Principles

E9.8 Where a young offender has been convicted of more than one offence, and power to sentence the offender under s. 91 is available in respect of one of the offences but not the other(s), *Fairhurst* [1986] 1 WLR 1374 established that it was wrong to pass a sentence under s. 91 for an offence which did not warrant such a sentence to compensate for the inability to pass such a sentence for an offence which did justify a longer term of detention but which did not carry power to sentence under s. 91. In *Walsh* [1997] 2 Cr App R (S) 210 there were five offenders, all girls aged 14 or 15. They pleaded guilty to false imprisonment and unlawful wounding, committed while carrying out a sustained violent attack on another girl aged 14. Sentences of detention under s. 91 were imposed, for terms varying between three and a half years and three years eleven months. It was argued on appeal that the sentences were wrong since the real gravamen of the offending lay in respect of the unlawful wounding, an offence for which s. 91 is not available. The Court of Appeal, however, held that the two offences were associated with each other and s. 91 was available for the offence of false imprisonment. Sentence lengths were, however, reduced in this case for other reasons. The approach taken in *Walsh* was endorsed in *AM* [1998] 1 WLR 363.

General guidance on the use of the PCC(S)A 2000, s. 91, was provided by Lord Lane CJ in *Fairhurst*, in which his lordship commented that it was not necessary, in order to invoke the provisions of s. 91, that the crime committed should be one of exceptional gravity, such as attempted murder, manslaughter, wounding with intent, armed robbery or the like but, on the other hand, that it was not good sentencing practice to pass a sentence of detention under s. 91 simply because the maximum available sentence of youth custody (now a detention and training order) appeared to be on the low side for the particular offence committed. These comments were endorsed by Lord Bingham CJ in *AM*.

The Court of Appeal held in *Wainfur* [1997] 1 Cr App R (S) 43 that, for offenders under 18, for whom the maximum custodial sentence was 24 months, the court should be satisfied before imposing a sentence under s. 91 that a sentence 'substantially greater' than 24 months was appropriate. In *AM*, however, the Court of Appeal signalled a change of approach, stating that the effect of the earlier law had been to 'create a sentencing no-man's land' between that maximum sentence and the shortest term which might appropriately be imposed under s. 91. Accordingly, Lord Bingham CJ in *AM* stated that while a Crown Court sentencer should not exceed the 24-month limit without much careful thought, if it was concluded that a longer (even if not much longer) sentence was called for, then the court should impose whatever it considered the appropriate period of detention under s. 91 to be.

In *Bennett* (1995) 16 Cr App R (S) 438, five years' detention was upheld on a boy aged 15, for damaging property being reckless whether life was endangered and for aggravated vehicle-taking. He took a van from a garage and drove it at high speed, starting a police chase during which the van was driven at police vehicles, causing damage to the value of £3,500. The offender had committed over 100 previous offences, and the sentence was justified on punitive and deterrent grounds and having regard to the prevalence of such offending in the area in question. In *Jephson* [2001] 1 Cr App R (S) 18, a 17-year-old young woman pleaded guilty to taking part in an attempted robbery at a bank in which an imitation firearm had been produced. The offender was of previous good character and from a stable home. She was not the instigator of the offence and had expressed remorse. The Court of Appeal reduced a term of five years' detention to one of four years. In *P* [2006] 1 Cr App R (S) 659 a sentence of three years' detention under s. 91 was upheld on a 12-year-old boy who pleaded guilty to kidnapping a boy aged eight and subjecting him to violence and abuse. The offender was assessed as being of very low intelligence and as having special educational needs. After giving 'anxious consideration' to the case, the Court of Appeal concluded that although the sentence was long for an offender of this age, it was justified and not excessive.

Detention for Life under PCC(S)A 2000, s. 91

If the offence carries imprisonment for life as the maximum penalty in respect of an adult, **E9.9**
then detention for life may be ordered under s. 91.

The PCC(S)A 2000, s. 82A, provides that a sentencer imposing a sentence of detention for life may specify what part of the sentence must expire before the offender becomes eligible for consideration for early release. The sentencer should start by deciding what determinate sentence would have been appropriate if detention for life had not been imposed, and then specify a period which will normally be one half of that notional sentence as the part to be specified under s. 82A (*Marklew* [1999] 1 WLR 485). Credit should be given for relevant mitigating factors, and for any period spent on remand in custody or in local authority secure accommodation.

In *Carr* [1996] 1 Cr App R (S) 191, the offender was a 15-year-old girl who pleaded guilty to causing grievous bodily harm with intent, having stabbed another schoolgirl in the back with a knife. She asked for two other offences, in which she had tried to strangle other schoolgirls, to be taken into consideration. Reports revealed other instances of disturbed and aggressive behaviour and indicated that the defendant was 'exceptionally dangerous'. An indeterminate sentence under s. 91 was imposed. In *JM* [2003] 1 Cr App R (S) 245, a sentence of detention for life was upheld in the case of a boy of 14 convicted of causing grievous bodily harm with intent, who had a history of violent and disturbed behaviour. He had struck a man on the back of the head with a wooden stake, fracturing his skull and causing long-lasting injuries. It was accepted that the offender was likely to remain a serious danger to the community for the foreseeable future, and no confident prediction of improvement could be made. Taking a notional determinate sentence of seven years, a period of three and a half years was specified under the PCC(S)A 2000, s. 82A. This was reduced by the Court of Appeal by four months, to take account of time spent in custody on remand.

Detention and Training Orders

Sections 100 to 107 of the PCC(S)A 2000 provide for the detention and training order. **E9.10**
Powers to impose this sentence came into force on 1 April 2000, and apply to offenders convicted on or after that date. The detention and training order is available to youth courts and to the Crown Court, in respect of offenders aged under 18 who have been convicted of an offence punishable with imprisonment in the case of an adult. Where an offender is aged 17 at the date of conviction but is aged 18 when sentenced, the sentence takes effect as a detention

and training order rather than a sentence of detention in a young offender institution (*Danga* (1992) 13 Cr App R (S) 408; *Hahn* [2003] 2 Cr App R (S) 636).

Powers of Criminal Courts (Sentencing) Act 2000, s. 100

(1) Subject to sections 90 and 91 above, sections 226 and 228 of the Criminal Justice Act 2003, and subsection (2) below, where—
 (a) a child or young person (that is to say, any person aged under 18) is convicted of an offence which is punishable with imprisonment in the case of a person aged 21 or over, and
 (b) the court is of the opinion that subsection (2) of section 152 of the Criminal Justice Act 2003 applies or the case falls within subsection (3) of that section, the sentence that the courts is to pass is a detention and training order.

(2) A court shall not make a detention and training order—
 (a) in the case of an offender under the age of 15 at the time of the conviction, unless it is of the opinion that he is a persistent offender;
 (b) in the case of an offender under the age of 12 at that time, unless—
  (i) it is of the opinion that only a custodial sentence would be adequate to protect the public from further offending by him; and
  (ii) the offence was committed on or after such date as the Secretary of State may by order appoint.

(3) A detention and training order is an order that the offender in respect of whom it is made shall be subject, for the term specified in the order, to a period of detention and training followed by a period of supervision.

For s. 90 (detention at Her Majesty's pleasure), see **E4.7**; for s. 91 (long-term detention), see **E9.9**. No day has yet been appointed for the purposes of s. 100(2)(b).

Power to pass a detention and training order on a young offender aged under 15 at the time of conviction is limited to cases in which the offender qualifies as a 'persistent' offender. In *S (A)* [2001] 1 Cr App R (S) 62, the Court of Appeal found a 14-year-old offender who had no previous convictions to be a 'persistent offender' for the purposes of s. 100(2)(a). S pleaded guilty to three counts of robbery, two of possession of an offensive weapon (a kitchen knife) and one count of false imprisonment. The offences were committed in the company of two other youths, and the victims were boys of 14 and 12 years of age. The seriousness of the offences (which were violent and intimidating) and the fact that they were committed over two days qualified the offender as 'persistent', despite the absence of a criminal record. The appropriate sentence was said to be a detention and training order of 24 months. A similar approach was adopted by the Court of Appeal in *C* [2001] 1 Cr App R (S) 415, where a 14-year-old who had committed a burglary and an offence of allowing himself to be carried on a vehicle taken without consent, committed two further burglaries and an offence of aggravated vehicle-taking while on bail for the earlier offences. Astill J said that this criminal behaviour demonstrated a sufficient degree of persistence to satisfy the terms of the section. A detention and training order for 12 months was upheld. In *A. D.* [2001] 1 Cr App R (S) 202, it was held that formal cautions on the record are relevant in determining persistence. Formal cautions for juveniles have been replaced by reprimands and warnings under the CDA 1998, but it is clear that these are to be regarded as relevant in the same way. Section 100(4) of the PCC(S)A 2000 states that, where the court makes a detention and training order on an offender aged under 15, it must state in open court that it is of the opinion mentioned in s. 100(2)(a) and, where applicable, (b)(i). This is in addition to the normal obligations on the sentencer under s. 79(4), to give reasons for imposing a custodial sentence.

Duration of Order and Consecutive Orders

E9.11 **Powers of Criminal Courts (Sentencing) Act 2000, s. 101**

(1) Subject to subsections (2) and (2A) below, the term of a detention and training order made in respect of an offence (whether by a magistrates' court or otherwise) shall be 4, 6, 8, 10, 12, 18 or 24 months.

(2) The term of a detention and training order may not exceed the maximum term of imprisonment that the Crown Court could (in the case of an offender aged 21 or over) impose for the offence.

(2A) Where—

(a) the offence is a summary offence,

(b) the maximum term of imprisonment that a court could (in the case of an offender aged 18 or over) impose for the offence is 51 weeks,

the term of a detention and training order may not exceed six months.

(3) Subject to subsections (4) and (6) below, a court making a detention and training order may order that its term shall commence on the expiry of the term of any other detention and training order made by that or any other court.

(4) A court shall not make in respect of an offender a detention and training order the effect of which would be that he would be subject to detention and training orders for a term which exceeds 24 months.

(5) Where the term of the detention and training orders to which an offender would otherwise be subject exceeds 24 months, the excess shall be treated as remitted.

(6) A court making a detention and training order shall not order that its term shall commence on the expiry of the term of a detention and training order under which the period of supervision has already begun (under section 103(1) below).

(7) Where a detention and training order ('the new order') is made in respect of an offender who is subject to a detention and training order under which the period of supervision has begun ('the old order'), the old order shall be disregarded in determining—

(a) for the purposes of subsection (4) above whether the effect of the new order would be that the offender would be subject to detention and training orders for a term which exceeds 24 months; and

(b) for the purposes of subsection (5) above whether the term of the detention and training orders to which the offender would (apart from that subsection) be subject exceeds 24 months.

Subsection (2A) and the reference to it in subsection (1) are inserted by the CJA 2003, s. 298. That section is not in force.

By s. 101(1), the term of a detention and training order must be for one of the specified periods set out in that subsection, the minimum period being four months and the maximum period 24 months. It follows that in a case where the court would otherwise have imposed a detention and training order for four months but there is a guilty plea or other significant mitigation (or the offender has spent a period on time on remand in custody: see **E9.15**) then the court cannot impose a detention and training order at all. It was noted by the Divisional Court in *Inner London Crown Court, ex parte N and S* [2001] 1 Cr App R (S) 343, that one effect of the introduction of detention and training orders had been to raise the custody threshold for young offenders. In *Ganley* [2001] 1 Cr App R (S) 60, the Court of Appeal said that terms of less than four months could not be aggregated so as to reach the four-month minimum. Individual terms of less than four months would not comply with s. 101(1). Section 101(1) is expressed as being 'subject to' s. 101(2), which explains that when imposing such a sentence the court may not exceed the maximum term of imprisonment which the Crown Court could have imposed on an adult for that offence. It follows from this that, if the maximum sentence for an offence is three months' imprisonment, a detention and training order cannot be imposed at all. An example is the offence of interfering with a motor vehicle (see **B4.108**). Where a court is sentencing for a summary-only offence, the longest detention and training order it may impose is normally six months, because that is the maximum term which the Crown Court could impose for that offence (see CJA 1988, s. 40(2) at **D11.15**, and s. 41(7)). An exception is the offence of absconding, under the Bail Act 1976, s. 6, where the maximum penalty in the Crown Court is 12 months. Otherwise, the maximum sentence of 24 months is available to the youth court as well as to the Crown Court, since the restrictions on the imposition of imprisonment and detention in a young offender institution by magistrates' courts (see **E2.3**) are not applicable to the detention and training order. In accordance with general principles, the maximum sentence of 24 months should not be imposed where the offender has pleaded guilty or there is other significant mitigation (*Kelly* [2002] 1 Cr App R (S) 40; *Dalby* [2006] 1 Cr App R (S) 216). If, however, the offence for which the offender is being sentenced is one which would have attracted a sentence of long-term detention under PCC(S)A 2000, s. 91, for a term in excess of 24 months, it is possible that (making due allowance for mitigation) the proper sentence would be a detention and training order for 24 months. This approach was taken in *Fieldhouse* [2001] 1 Cr App R (S) 361, where there was a guilty plea and a significant period in custody. See also *S (A)* [2001] 1 Cr App R (S) 62 (see **E9.10**), where the maximum sentence may be explicable on the same basis. Restricting the sentencing courts to the specific terms identified in s. 101(1) has given rise to practical difficulty. If the appropriate duration of a detention and training order would otherwise be, say, 18 months, but the offender enters a timely guilty plea and/or there is other significant mitigation, the court must reduce the term, at least to 12 months, to take such matters into account. There is no stopping point between 18 and 12 months (see *Pitt* [2002] 1 Cr App R (S) 195).

E9.12 **Consecutive Orders** As far as consecutive detention and training orders are concerned, it is clear that the terms of each order must comply with the PCC(S)A 2000, s. 101(1) and (2), but the Court of Appeal has held in *Norris* [2001] 1 Cr App R (S) 401 that it is not necessary for the total term to add up to one of the periods listed. When imposing consecutive detention and training orders for two summary-only offences, the youth court may exceed a total term of six months, although that is the maximum aggregate term of imprisonment which the Crown Court can impose, by virtue of the MCA 1980, s. 133 (*C v DPP* [2002] 1 Cr App R (S) 189).

A detention and training order cannot run consecutively to an order under s. 91 (*Hayward* [2001] 2 Cr App R (S) 149) nor vice versa (*Lang* [2001] 2 Cr App R (S) 175).

E9.13 **Imposition of Excessive Term** If a term, or aggregate term, longer than 24 months is imposed by the court, the excess is automatically remitted (PCC(S)A 2000, s. 101(5)). The period of 24 months was formerly the maximum aggregate term of detention in a young offender institution which might be imposed on an offender aged 15, 16 or 17, in which context there was a similar rule relating to automatic remission of sentence length over 24 months. That rule frequently caused difficulty for sentencers and in *AM* [1998] 1 WLR 363 the Court of Appeal reminded sentencers once again of the need to make it clear whether the sentence being imposed on the offender was one of detention in a young offender institution (now a detention and training order) or one of long-term detention under the PCC(S)A 2000, s. 91. See further *GF* [2000] Crim LR 608 and commentary.

E9.14 **Early Release** Ordinarily, the period of detention and training shall be one-half of the full term of the order, although the Secretary of State retains a discretion to release a person under such an order at a somewhat earlier date (PCC(S)A 2000, s. 102). The second half of the order is the period of supervision, although again the Secretary of State retains power to provide by order that the period of supervision shall be curtailed (s. 103). Supervision will be carried out by an officer of a local probation board, a social worker of a local authority social services department, or a member of a youth offending team.

Requirement to Take Into Account Period Spent on Remand

E9.15 **Powers of Criminal Courts (Sentencing) Act 2000, s. 101**

(8) In determining the term of a detention and training order for an offence, the court shall take account of any period for which the offender has been remanded in custody in connection with the offence, or any other offence the charge for which was founded on the same facts or evidence.

(9) Where a court proposes to make detention and training orders in respect of an offender for two or more offences—
  (a) subsection (8) above shall not apply; but
  (b) in determining the total term of the detention and training orders it proposes to make in respect of the offender, the court shall take account of the total period (if any) for

which he has been remanded in custody in connection with any of those offences, or any other offence the charge for which was founded on the same facts or evidence.

(10) Once a period of remand has, under subsection (8) or (9) above, been taken account of in relation to a detention and training order made in respect of an offender for any offence or offences, it shall not subsequently be taken account of (under either of those subsections) in relation to such an order made in respect of the offender for any other offence or offences.

It is important to note that, with respect to the detention and training order, the court *must* take into account any period for which the offender has been remanded in custody. The CJA 2003, s. 240, which applies to detention in a young offender institution and detention under the PCC(S)A 2000, s. 91, does not apply to the detention and training order. Where a young offender has spent time on remand prior to the imposition of a detention and training order, in order to achieve the same effect which the operation of s. 240 would have, it will be necessary for the sentencer to double the number of days spent on remand before deducting that total from the length of the order imposed (see further *Eagles* [2007] 1 Cr App R (S) 612). The requirement on the court to make such reduction has caused difficulty in relation to the specified duration of a detention and training order, which must be for one of the seven periods set out in the PCC(S)A 2000, s. 101(1). In *Inner London Crown Court, ex parte I* (2000) *The Times*, 12 May 2000, the Divisional Court stated that the duty imposed by s. 101(8) was to 'take account' of the time spent on remand in custody, but this did not require the sentencer to make a 'one-for-one discount'. This general approach was confirmed by the Court of Appeal in *B* [2001] 1 Cr App R (S) 89 and by the Divisional Court in *Inner London Crown Court, ex parte N and S* [2001] 1 Cr App R (S) 343. In the latter case, where the young offender had spent three days in custody on remand, the Court said that it was impossible to fine tune a detention and training order by reference to a few days. This, with respect, is clearly right since the detention and training order imposed (after making appropriate adjustment) must be for one of the specified periods set out in s. 101(1).

Breach of Order

Section 104 of the PCC(S)A 2000 provides powers in relation to breach of supervision requirements in a detention and training order. If it is proved to the satisfaction of a youth court acting for the relevant local justice area that the offender has failed to comply with supervision requirements specified in the order, the court may order the offender to be detained in secure accommodation for three months or the remainder of the term of the order (whichever is the shorter), or it may impose on the offender a fine not exceeding level 3. An offender may appeal against such an order to the Crown Court. **E9.16**

Section 105 relates to the commission of a further imprisonable offence by the offender during the currency of a detention and training order. The court, whether or not it passes any other sentence on the offender, may order him to be detained in secure accommodation from the date of the new order for the whole or part of the period between the date of commission of the new offence and the date at which the full term of the original order would have come to an end. Such an order may be made even where the offender is convicted of the new offence after the full term of the original order has come to an end, as long as the offence was committed within the supervision part of the order. The reinstated part of the sentence may be served before any sentence imposed for the new offence, or it may be served concurrently with that sentence, but the reinstated period shall be disregarded in determining the appropriate length of the new sentence.

Section 106 deals with the effect of imposing a detention and training order on a person already subject to a term of detention in a young offender institution, and *vice versa*. Section 106A deals with the effect of imposing a sentence of detention under the PCC(S)A 2000, s. 91, or a sentence of detention under the CJA 2003, s. 228, on an offender already subject to a detention and training order.

Section E10 Community Order under the Criminal Justice Act 2003

E10.1 If the offender is aged 18 or over at the date of the offence, *and the offence was committed on or after 4 April 2005*, the appropriate sentence is a community order under the CJA 2003.

If the offender is aged 18 or over at the date of the offence, *and the offence was committed before 4 April 2005*, the available community sentences are a community rehabilitation order, a community punishment order, a community punishment and rehabilitation order, a drug treatment and testing order, a curfew order, an exclusion order, and (if the offender is aged under 21 or in some cases under 25) an attendance centre order. These orders continue to be available for offenders aged 16 and 17 *for offences committed on or after 4 April 2005 but before 4 April 2009*. The first four of these orders are considered at **E11.11** (community rehabilitation order), **E11.26** (community punishment order), **E11.34** (community punishment and rehabilitation order) and **E11.37** (drug treatment and testing order). The other three are considered at **E11.45** (curfew order), **E11.47** (exclusion order) and **E11.49** (attendance centre order).

POWER TO MAKE COMMUNITY ORDER UNDER THE CJA 2003

Criteria for the Imposition of Community Order

E10.2 By the CJA 2003, s. 147, a 'community sentence' means a sentence that consists of or includes a 'community order' (as defined by s. 177) or 'one or more youth community orders'. By s. 177, a 'community order' is an order imposed on an offender aged 18 or over in respect of an offence committed on or after 4 April 2005. The order will contain one or more requirements imposed by the court. These requirements are considered in detail at **E10.5**. All the requirements closely reflect community orders which existed prior to implementation of the relevant provisions of the CJA 2003, although there are changes of detail. A number of general provisions apply to the imposition of all community sentences. These are dealt with now, before turning to the details of the individual requirements.

Criminal Justice Act 2003, s. 148

(1) A court must not pass a community sentence on an offender unless it is of the opinion that the offence, or the combination of the offence and one or more offences associated with it, was serious enough to warrant such a sentence.

(2) Where a court passes a community sentence which consists of or includes a community order—

(a) the particular requirement or requirements forming part of the community order must be such as, in the opinion of the court, is, or taken together are, the most suitable for the offender, and

(b) the restrictions on liberty imposed by the order must be such as in the opinion of the court are commensurate with the seriousness of the offence, or the combination of the offence and one or more offences associated with it.

Section 149 deals with the situation where an offender was remanded in custody in connection with that offence before being convicted of, or pleading guilty to, it. The section states that the sentencing court 'may have regard' to any such period of remand when determining the restrictions on liberty to be imposed by a community order or youth community order. This clearly confers a discretion to take account of such period, rather than requiring the court to do so. 'Remanded in custody' is given a wide meaning here, to include remands to local authority accommodation where the offender was kept in local authority secure accommodation or in a secure training centre, or was removed to a hospital: see further the CJA 2003, s. 242(2) and **E2.8**.

Section 150 provides, for the avoidance of doubt, that the power to make a community order or youth community order is not available where the sentence for the offence is fixed by law (murder), or where it falls to be imposed under the FA 1968, s. 51A, the PCC(S)A 2000, s. 110(2) or 111(2) or (when the relevant provisions are brought into force) the VCRA 2006, s. 29(4) or (6) (see **E6**), or where it falls to be imposed under the CJA 2003, ss. 225 to 228 (dangerous offenders: see **E5**).

Section 151 will, when the section is brought into force, allow the sentencer to impose a community order on certain offenders aged 16 or over, instead of imposing a fine, if the offender is a 'persistent offender previously fined'. This status requires that the offender has, on three or more previous occasions since attaining the age of 16, been convicted and had passed on him a sentence consisting only of a fine. It is not relevant for these purposes whether he has, on other occasions, been given a custodial sentence or a community order. If, despite the general effect of the CJA 2003, s. 143(2) (aggravation of sentence to reflect previous convictions: see **E1.4**) the sentencing court would not (apart from s. 151) have regarded the latest offence as being serious enough to justify a community sentence, the court may still pass a community sentence if, having regard to all the circumstances including the previous convictions, it is in the interests of justice to make such an order. This section bears some similarity to the PCC(S)A 2000, s. 59 (see **E17.14**), which is prospectively repealed by the CJA 2003. Section 59 is restricted to imposing a curfew order, or a community punishment order, on a 'petty persistent offender' for whom a fine would normally have been the appropriate sentence for the latest offence, but against whom there were outstanding fines which had not been paid. It will be seen that s. 151 will be more general in its effect, allowing the court to move from a fine to a community sentence in light of all the circumstances of the case, including the offender's record.

Reports Section 156 of the CJA 2003 deals with pre-sentence reports and other requirements, with respect to community sentences. It substantially re-enacts the PCC(S)A 2000, s. 36 (community sentences: pre-sentence reports) and is set out at **E1.18**. Whenever a court is considering whether to impose a community sentence, and what restrictions to put on the offender's liberty as part of that sentence, the court must take into account all the information available to it, including information about the offence and about the offender. Before imposing a community sentence, the sentencing court must normally obtain a pre-sentence report but, reflecting the earlier provisions, the court need not obtain such a report if it considers it 'unnecessary' to do so. Given the information and specialist advice contained in pre-sentence reports, it would surely be rare for a court to impose a community sentence without first considering such a report. **E10.3**

Section 159 deals with disclosure of pre-sentence reports to the defence and the prosecution (see **E1.18**).

Section 160 applies where a report (other than a pre-sentence report) is made by an officer of a local probation board with a view to assisting any court in deciding how best to deal with an offender. This section provides for disclosure of the contents of that report to the defence (but not the prosecution).

Drug Testing Section 161 of the CJA 2003 provides for pre-sentence drug testing, but is not in force. In any case where the court is considering imposing a community sentence, it **E10.4**

may make an order that the offender undergo pre-sentence drug testing, to ascertain whether the offender has any specified Class A drug in his body. Failure without reasonable excuse to comply with the testing as required by the court is punishable by a fine of an amount not exceeding level 4 (currently £2,500). It should be noted that power to order pre-sentence drug testing is only exercisable in areas where the court has been notified by the Secretary of State that the power is available by that court and the notice has not been withdrawn. When s. 161 is brought into force, it will replace the PCC(S)A 2000, s. 36A, which is applicable only in respect of offenders aged 18 or over where the court is considering passing a community sentence.

Community Orders Requirements

E10.5 Section 177 lists the requirements with which the court may order an offender aged 18 or over to comply during the course of a community sentence. They are:

(a) an unpaid work requirement (as defined in s. 199),
(b) an activity requirement (s. 201),
(c) a programme requirement (s. 202),
(d) a prohibited activity requirement (s. 203),
(e) a curfew requirement (s. 204),
(f) an exclusion requirement (s. 205),
(g) a residence requirement (s. 206),
(h) a mental health treatment requirement (s. 207),
(i) a drug rehabilitation requirement (s. 209),
(j) an alcohol treatment requirement (s. 212),
(k) a supervision requirement (s. 213), and
(l) in a case where the offender is aged under 25, an attendance centre requirement (s. 214).

A number of general provisions apply, which are dealt with now, before turning to the details of the individual requirements.

Any community order must specify the petty sessions area in which the offender resides or will reside (s. 216(1)). The court must ensure, so far as practicable, that any requirement imposed in a community sentence is such as to avoid (a) any conflict with the offender's religious beliefs, or with the requirements of any other relevant order to which the offender may be subject, and (b) any interference with the times, if any, at which the offender normally works, attends school or any other educational establishment (s. 217(1)). The court which makes the relevant order must forthwith provide copies of the order to the offender and to the appropriate responsible officer (s. 219(1)), and to certain other persons affected by the order (s. 219(2) and sch. 14). There is also a general duty on the offender made subject to a community order to keep in touch with the responsible officer in accordance with such instructions as he may from time to time be given by that officer, and the offender must notify the officer of any change of address (s. 220). A community sentence must specify a date, not more than three years after the date of the order, by which all the requirements in it must have been complied with, but if there are two or more different requirements in the order the court may specify different dates (s. 177(5)). See, however, s. 200(2) in relation to an unpaid work requirement at **E10.6**. Before making a community sentence which contains two or more requirements, the court must consider whether, in the circumstances of the case, the requirements are compatible with each other (s. 177(6)).

The SGC Guideline, *New Sentences: CJA 2003* (Dec 2004), provides that, in many cases, a pre-sentence report will be pivotal in helping a sentencer decide whether to impose a custodial sentence or whether to impose a community sentence and, if so, whether particular requirements, or combinations of requirements, are suitable for an individual offender. The court must always ensure (especially where there are multiple requirements) that the restriction on liberty placed on the offender is proportionate to the seriousness of the offence committed.

The court must also consider the likely effect of one requirement on another, and that they do not place conflicting demands upon the offender (para. 1.1.15).

Having reached the provisional view that a community sentence is the most appropriate disposal, the sentencer should request a pre-sentence report, indicating which of the three sentencing ranges is relevant and the purpose(s) of sentencing that the package of requirements is designed to fulfil (para. 1.1.16). Paragraph 1.1.23 provides:

> There should be three sentencing ranges (low, medium and high) within the community sentence band, based upon offence seriousness. It is not intended that an offender necessarily progresses from one range to the next on each sentencing occasion. The decision as to the appropriate range each time is based upon the seriousness of the new offence(s). The decision on the nature and severity of the requirements to be included in a community sentence should be guided by:
> (i) the assessment of offence seriousness (low, medium or high);
> (ii) the purpose(s) of sentencing the court wishes to achieve;
> (iii) the risk of re-offending;
> (iv) the ability of the offender to comply, and
> (v) the availability of requirements in the local area.
> The resulting restriction on liberty must be a proportionate response to the offence that was committed.

For the full text of the guidelines, which contain examples of requirements suitable to each of the three sentencing ranges, see **appendix 8, Part 2**.

Unpaid Work Requirement

The number of hours of unpaid work which may be ordered by the court under the CJA 2003, s. 199, must be not less than 40 and not more than 300 (s. 199(2)). Before inserting an unpaid work requirement into a community order, the court must, if it thinks necessary, hear from an appropriate officer that the offender is a suitable person to perform work under the requirement (s. 199(3)) and that local arrangements exist for the requirement to be carried out (s. 218(1)). The appropriate officer is an officer of the local probation board. **E10.6**

If the court makes community orders on the offender in respect of two or more offences of which the offender has been convicted on the same occasion and includes unpaid work requirements in each of them, the court may direct that the hours of work may run concurrently or consecutively, but the total number of hours must not exceed 300 (s. 199(5)). The work required should normally be completed within 12 months (s. 200(2)). The Secretary of State may by order amend the maximum number of hours of unpaid work which may be specified under an unpaid work requirement (s. 223(1)(a)).

Activity Requirement

Section 201(1) of the CJA 2003 defines an activity requirement as a requirement that the offender must either present himself to a specified person, at a specified place such as a community rehabilitation centre, for a certain number of days, and/or take part in specified activities for a certain number of days. The aggregate number of days must not exceed 60 (s. 201(5)). An activity requirement may include such tasks as receiving help with employment, or group work on social problems. Reparative activities, involving contact between offenders and persons affected by their offences, are also within the compass of this requirement (s. 201(2)). Before inserting an activity requirement into a community sentence, the court must consult an appropriate officer, be satisfied that it is feasible to secure compliance with the requirement (s. 201(3)), and be satisfied that local arrangements exist for persons to participate in such activities (s. 218(2)). The appropriate officer is an officer of the local probation board. If the activity requirement would involve the co-operation of a person other than the offender and the responsible officer, the consent of that other person must be obtained before the requirement can be inserted into the order (s. 201(4)). **E10.7**

Programme Requirement

E10.8 Section 202(1) of the CJA 2003 defines a programme requirement as a requirement that the offender must participate in an accredited programme at a specified place on a certain number of days. Such programmes include those which address offending behaviour and cover such topics as anger management, sex offending, substance misuse and so on. The court may not insert a programme requirement into a community sentence unless the relevant accredited programme has been recommended to the court as being suitable for the offender by an officer of the local probation board, and the court is satisfied that the programme is or will be available at the place specified in the community order (s. 202(4)). If the activity requirement would involve the co-operation of a person other than the offender and the responsible officer, the consent of that other person must be obtained before the requirement can be inserted into the order (s. 202(5)).

Prohibited Activity Requirement

E10.9 Section 203(1) of the CJA 2003 defines a prohibited activity requirement. The court can require an offender to refrain from taking part in certain activities, on a certain day or days (such as attending football matches), or over a period of time. The requirement may include forbidding him to contact a certain person, and may be that the offender does not possess, use or carry a firearm (s. 203(3)). Before inserting a prohibited activity requirement into a community sentence, the court must consult an officer of the local probation board.

Curfew Requirement

E10.10 By the CJA 2003, s. 104, a curfew requirement is a requirement that the offender remain at a place specified by the court for certain periods of time. These periods of time must not be less than two hours and not more than 12 hours in any given day (s. 204(2)). An order might require the offender to be indoors at home between 7 p.m. and 7 a.m. A curfew requirement within a community order must not last for more than six months from the day on which it is made (s. 204(3)). The Secretary of State may by order amend the number of hours or the periods of time which can be specified in a curfew requirement (s. 223(1)(b) and (3)(a)). Before inserting a curfew requirement into a community order, the court must obtain and consider information about the place proposed to be specified in the order, including information as to the attitude of persons likely to be affected by the enforced presence there of the offender (s. 204(6)). Where the court makes a community sentence which includes a curfew requirement, it must normally also impose an electronic monitoring requirement unless the court considers it inappropriate to do so (s. 177(3)).

Exclusion Requirement

E10.11 Under the CJA 2003, s. 205, an exclusion requirement is a requirement which prohibits an offender from entering a specified place, or places, or area (such as a specified town centre), during a period specified in the order. The order can exclude the offender from different places for different periods of time. It may also be used as a means of keeping the offender away from a specified person, in which case the person for whose protection the order is made should be given a copy of the requirement made by the court (s. 219 and sch. 14). An exclusion requirement cannot last longer than two years. The Secretary of State may by order amend the periods of time which can be specified in an exclusion requirement (s. 223(3)(b)). Where the court makes a community order which includes an exclusion requirement, it must normally also impose an electronic monitoring requirement unless the court considers it inappropriate to do so (s. 177(3)).

Residence Requirement

E10.12 A residence requirement is a requirement that the offender resides at a place specified in the order for a specified period of time (CJA 2003, s. 206(2)). Before making such a requirement, the court must consider the home surroundings of the offender (s. 206(3)). A court may not specify residence at a hostel or other institution except on the recommendation of an officer of a local probation board (s. 206(4)).

Mental Health Treatment Requirement

The mental health treatment requirement in the CJA 2003, s. 207, is based on requirements as to treatment that could formerly be inserted into a community rehabilitation order. The court may direct an offender to undergo mental health treatment, by or under the direction of a doctor or chartered psychologist. The treatment may take the form of treatment as a resident patient in a hospital or care home, treatment as a non-resident patient, or treatment under the direction of a doctor or chartered psychologist as may be specified (s. 207(2)). Before the court can insert a mental health treatment requirement, it must be satisfied, on the evidence of a doctor approved for the purposes of the Mental Health Act 1983, s. 12, that the mental condition of the offender is such as requires and may be susceptible to treatment and is not such as to warrant the making of a hospital order or a guardianship order. The court must also be satisfied that arrangements have been made or can be made for the treatment to be specified in the order, and that the offender has expressed his willingness to comply with such an order (s. 207(3)). The supervising officer will supervise the offender only to the extent necessary for revoking or amending the order (s. 207(4)). **E10.13**

Section 208 deals with provision for the doctor or chartered psychologist subsequently to change the place at which the offender is to receive treatment to a place where treatment can be better or more conveniently given. The doctor or registered psychologist must notify the responsible officer in advance, and the offender must consent to any such change.

Drug Rehabilitation Requirement

By the CJA 2003, s. 209, the court may insert into a community sentence a drug rehabilitation requirement, which includes drug treatment and testing. It requires that, during a period specified in the order (the treatment and testing period), the offender must submit to treatment by or under the direction of a specified person having the necessary qualifications or experience and must provide samples, at such times and in such circumstances as are requested, to determine whether he has any drug in his body during that period (s. 209(1)). **E10.14**

Before imposing a drug rehabilitation requirement, the court must be satisfied that the offender is dependent on, or has a propensity to misuse, any controlled drug (as defined by MDA 1971, s. 2) and that his dependency or propensity is such as requires and may be susceptible to treatment (s. 209(2)(a)). The court must also be satisfied that arrangements have been made or can be made for the proposed treatment (s. 209(2)(b)), and that the insertion of a drug rehabilitation requirement has been recommended to the court as being suitable for the offender by an officer of the local probation board (s. 209(2)(c)). The offender must express his willingness to comply with the requirement (s. 209(2)(d)). The treatment and testing period must be for at least six months (s. 209(3)), and may take the form of treatment as a resident in a specified institution or place, or treatment as a non-resident (s. 209(4)). The Secretary of State may by order amend the periods of time which can be specified in a drug rehabilitation requirement (s. 223(3)(c)).

Section 210 states that the court may provide for the drug rehabilitation requirement to be reviewed periodically at intervals of not less than one month, provide for these reviews to be held by the court responsible for the order (a review hearing) and require the offender to attend each review hearing. The responsible officer will provide a written report, which will include the results of the offender's drug tests, on the offender's progress under the requirement in advance of each review hearing (s. 210(1)). Section 211 sets out what is to happen at each review of a drug rehabilitation requirement. The court, after considering the report from the responsible officer, may amend the requirement, but cannot do so unless the offender consents. It cannot reduce the term of the treatment and testing period below six months (s. 211(2)). If the offender does not consent to the proposed amendment to the requirement, the court may revoke the order and re-sentence the offender as if he had just been convicted (s. 211(3)). If it does so, the court must take into account the extent to which the offender has complied with the requirements of the order. If the court wishes it may impose a custodial sentence on the offender, provided the offence was punishable with imprisonment (s. 211(4)). If the offender's progress is satisfactory, the court can state that in future reviews can be on paper and without a hearing (s. 211(6)). If the offender's progress then becomes unsatisfactory and he is not present, the court can require him to attend in future (s. 211(7)). The court may also amend the order to provide for future review hearings (s. 211(8)).

Alcohol Treatment Requirement

E10.15 By the CJA 2003, s. 212, the court may insert into a community order an alcohol treatment requirement. It requires that, during a period specified in the order, the offender must submit to treatment by or under the direction of a specified person having the necessary qualifications or experience with a view to the reduction or elimination of the offender's dependency on alcohol.

Before imposing an alcohol treatment requirement, the court must be satisfied that the offender is dependent on alcohol and that his dependency is such as requires and may be susceptible to treatment (s. 212(2)). The court must also be satisfied that arrangements have been made or can be made for the proposed treatment. The offender must express his willingness to comply with the requirement (s. 212(3)). The alcohol treatment requirement must be in effect for at least six months (s. 212(4)), and may take the form of treatment as a resident in a specified institution or place, or treatment as a non-resident or treatment by or under the direction of such person having the necessary qualification or experience (s. 212(5)). The Secretary of State may by order amend the periods of time which can be specified in an alcohol treatment requirement (s. 223(3)(d)).

Supervision Requirement

E10.16 A supervision requirement is a requirement that, during the relevant period, the offender must attend appointments with the responsible officer or another person determined by the responsible officer at such time and place as may be determined by the officer (CJA 2003, s. 213(1)), with a view to promoting the offender's rehabilitation (s. 213(2)). The 'relevant period' in this context means the full duration of the community sentence.

Attendance Centre Requirement

E10.17 Section 214 of the CJA 2003 provides for an attendance centre requirement to be inserted into a community order. An attendance centre requirement is available only in respect of offenders aged under 25 years (see s. 177 and the cross-heading before s. 214).

Under an attendance centre requirement in a community sentence, the offender must attend at an attendance centre specified in the relevant order for a specified number of hours which must be not less than 12 nor more than 36 (s. 214(2)). The offender must not be required to attend more than once on any single day or for more than three hours on any occasion (s. 214(6)). The court cannot make an attendance centre requirement unless satisfied that there is an attendance centre available locally (s. 218(3)) and that the attendance centre order specified is reasonably accessible to the offender (s. 214(3)). The responsible officer will notify the offender of the date and time required for the first attendance, and subsequent hours are fixed by the officer in charge of the attendance centre (s. 214(5) and (6)). Sections 221 and 222 set out the powers of the Secretary of State to continue to provide attendance centres and to regulate a number of aspects of their provision.

Electronic Monitoring Requirement

Section 215 of the CJA 2003 provides that the court passing a community sentence can order the electronic monitoring of the offender's compliance with any of the other requirements in the sentence. Where the court makes a community order which includes a curfew requirement or an exclusion requirement, it *must* also impose an electronic monitoring requirement, unless the court considers it inappropriate to do so (s. 177(3)), and it *may* do so in respect of any other requirement (s. 177(4)). The periods of electronic monitoring can be specified by the court in the order, or set by the responsible officer (s. 215(1)). If the court is proposing to include such a requirement but there is a person other than the offender without whose co-operation it will not be practicable to secure the monitoring, the requirement cannot be included without that person's consent (s. 215(2)). The court must ensure that electronic monitoring arrangements are available in the local area and that the necessary provision can be made under those arrangements (s. 218(4)). **E10.18**

ENFORCEMENT OF COMMUNITY ORDERS

Section 179 of the CJA 2003 introduces sch. 8 to that Act, which contains provisions dealing with breach, revocation and amendment of community orders, and the effect of the offender being convicted of a further offence. **E10.19**

Breach of Community Order

Paragraphs 5 and 6 of sch. 8 to the CJA 2003 are the key provisions here. By para. 5, if the responsible officer is of the opinion that the offender has failed without reasonable excuse to comply with any of the requirements of a community order, the officer must give a *warning* describing the circumstances of the failure, stating that the failure is unacceptable, and informing the offender that if within the next 12 months he again fails to comply with any requirement of the order, he will be brought back before the court. By para. 6, if there has been a warning, and within 12 months there is a further failure without reasonable excuse to comply, the responsible officer must cause an information to be laid before a magistrates' court, or before the Crown Court in respect of that second failure. Paragraphs 7 and 8 deal in detail with the arrangements for issue of summons or warrant by the justice of the peace or by the Crown Court. **E10.20**

Paragraph 9 describes the powers of a magistrates' court when dealing with a breach of a community order. If it is proved to the satisfaction of the court before which the offender is brought that he has failed without reasonable excuse to comply with any of the requirements of the community order, the court must deal with him in one of the following ways (set out in para. 9(1)):

(a) by amending the terms of the community order so as to impose more onerous requirements (subject to para. 9(3)), or
(b) where the community order was made by a magistrates' court, revoke the order and deal with him for the offence in any way in which the court could deal with him if he had just been convicted, or
(c) where the community order was made by a magistrates' court in respect of an offence which was not punishable with imprisonment, and the offender is aged 18 or over, and he has wilfully and persistently failed to comply with the requirements of the order, revoke the order and impose a sentence of imprisonment for a term not exceeding 51 weeks.

When dealing with the offender under para. 9(1), the magistrates' court must take into account the extent to which the offender has complied with the requirements of the com-

E

Part E Sentencing

munity order (para. 9(2)). If the community order was made by the Crown Court, the magistrates' court may instead commit the offender in custody or release him on bail to appear before the Crown Court (para. 9(6)).

Paragraph 10 describes the powers of the Crown Court when dealing with a breach of a community order. If it is proved to the satisfaction of the court before which the offender is brought that he has failed without reasonable excuse to comply with any of the requirements of the community order, the court must deal with him in one of the following ways (set out in para. 10(1)):

(a) by amending the terms of the community order so as to impose more onerous requirements (subject to para. 10(3)), or
(b) by revoking the order and dealing with him for the offence in any way in which he could have been dealt with for that offence by the court which made the order, or
(c) where the offence in respect of which the order was made which was not punishable with imprisonment, and he has wilfully and persistently failed to comply with the requirements of the order, revoke the order and impose a sentence of imprisonment or detention in a young offender institution for a term not exceeding 51 weeks.

When dealing with the offender under para. 10(1), the Crown Court must take into account the extent to which the offender has complied with the requirements of the community order (para. 10(2)).

Revocation of Community Order

E10.21 Paragraphs 13 to 15 of sch. 8 to the CJA 2003 deal with revocation of a community order where, on application by the offender or the responsible officer, having regard to changed circumstances since the order was made, it is in the interests of justice to revoke the order or to deal with the offender for the offence in some other way. These circumstances would include the offender making good progress under the order or responding satisfactorily to the requirements in the order.

Paragraphs 21 to 23 deal with the powers of a magistrates' court and the Crown Court in circumstances where an offender subject to a community order has been convicted of a further offence. If a magistrates' court is dealing with the subsequent offence, and the community order was made by a magistrates' court, the magistrates' court may revoke the community order, or revoke it and deal with the offender for that original offence in any way in which he could have been dealt with by the court for that offence (para. 21(2)). When dealing with the offender under para. 21(2), the magistrates' court must take into account the extent to which the offender has complied with the requirements of the community order (para. 21(3)). If the community order was made by the Crown Court, the magistrates' court may instead commit the offender in custody or release him on bail to appear before the Crown Court (para. 22(1)). If the Crown Court is dealing with the subsequent offence, it may revoke the community order, or revoke it and deal with the offender for that original offence in any way in which he could have been dealt with for the offence by the court which made the order (para. 23(2)). When dealing with the offender under para. 23(2), the Crown Court must take into account the extent to which the offender has complied with the requirements of the community order (para. 23(3)).

Amendment of Community Order

E10.22 Paragraphs 16 to 20 of sch. 8 to the CJA 2003 deal with various forms of amendment to requirements in a community order which may be made by an appropriate court, on application by the offender or the responsible officer, as to change of residence, change of circumstances of the offender, and other matters.

Withdrawal or Reduction of Benefit

Section 62 of the Child Support, Pensions and Social Security Act 2000 makes provision for the Secretary of State to withdraw or reduce social security benefit where a person has failed to comply with a designated community sentence imposed under the CJA 2003. The sanction period is set at four weeks. See the Child Support, Pensions and Social Security Act 2000 (Commencement No. 10) Order 2001 (SI 2001 No. 2619) restricting the operation of this power to offenders so sentenced and who fall to be supervised in Derbyshire, Hertfordshire, Teesside or the West Midlands probation areas. E10.23

Section E11 Community Sentences: Offenders Aged under 18

E11.1 If the offender is aged 16 or 17 at the date of the offence, irrespective of the date on which the offence was committed, the available community sentences are a community rehabilitation order, a community punishment order, a community punishment and rehabilitation order, a drug treatment and testing order, a curfew order, an exclusion order, an attendance centre order, a supervision order, and an action plan order. The first four of these orders are considered at **E11.11**, **E11.26**, **E11.34** and **E11.37**. The other five are considered at **E11.45**, **E11.47**, **E11.49**, **E11.54** and **E11.64**. The provisions applicable to offenders aged 16 or 17 at the date of the offence are now expected to continue until 4 April 2009 (Criminal Justice Act 2003 (Commencement No. 8 and Transitional and Saving Provisions) (Amendment) Order 2007 (SI 2007 No. 391)).

If the offender is aged under 16 at the date of the offence, irrespective of the date on which the offence was committed, the appropriate sentence is a youth community order under the CJA 2003. Youth community orders are considered are **E11.45**, **E11.47**, **E11.49**, **E11.54** and **E11.64**.

PROVISIONS COMMON TO COMMUNITY SENTENCES UNDER PCC(S)A 2000

Statutory Criteria for the Imposition of a Community Order

E11.2 By the PCC(S)A 2000, s. 33(1), a 'community order' means any of the following: a community punishment order, a community rehabilitation order, a community punishment and rehabilitation order, a curfew order, a supervision order, an attendance centre order, a drug treatment and testing order, a drug abstinence order, an action plan order and an exclusion order. Section 35(1) restricts the imposition of community orders.

Powers of Criminal Courts (Sentencing) Act 2000, s. 35

(1) A court shall not pass a community sentence on an offender unless it is of the opinion that the offence, or the combination of the offence and one or more offences associated with it, was serious enough to warrant such a sentence.

The requirement in s. 35(1) that the court must consider 'the offence, or the combination of the offence and one or more offences associated with it' mirrors s. 79(2)(a), which relates to justifying the imposition of a custodial sentence. A definition of the phrase 'associated with' is provided by s. 161(1) and is considered at **E2.5**. An offence which is taken into consideration may count as an offence to be weighed in accordance with s. 161(1). In contrast with the justification for imposing custody, however, where the offence, or the combination of one or more offences, must be 'so serious that only such a sentence can be justified', a community sentence can be justified whenever the offence, or the combination of one or more offences, 'is serious enough to warrant such a sentence'. In *T* [1999] 2 Cr App R (S) 304 Maurice Kay J said that the phrase 'serious enough' should not be given too exacting an interpretation, since it was often one of the purposes of a community sentence to help the offender. There is no provision in s. 35 equivalent to s. 79(2)(b) (violent or sexual offences). The offender's previous convictions and response to previous sentences are relevant when determining the seriousness of an offence; so is the fact that the offence was committed when the offender was on bail, and the fact that the offence was racially or religiously aggravated. Section 35 should also be read subject to the provision relating to persistent petty offenders (see **E17.14**).

Powers of Criminal Courts (Sentencing) Act 2000, s. 35

(3) Subject to subsection (2) above and to section 69(5) below (which limits the community orders that may be combined with an action plan order), where a court passes a community sentence—

(a) the particular order or orders comprising or forming part of the sentence shall be such as in the opinion of the court is, or taken together are, the most suitable for the offender; and

(b) the restrictions on liberty imposed by the order or orders shall be such as in the opinion of the court are commensurate with the seriousness of the offence, or the combination of the offence and one or more offences associated with it.

Where an offender is being sentenced for several offences, the court's power to consider the whole pattern of the offending could lead it to pass a total sentence which is disproportionate to the overall seriousness of the offending behaviour. Section 158(2)(b) of the PCC(S)A 2000, in an attempt to avoid this, makes reference to the totality principle (see **E1.14**) by stating that the sentencer may mitigate the sentence by 'applying any rule of law as to the totality of sentences'. A difficulty with s. 35(3) is that the twin objectives of 'suitability' and 'seriousness' sometimes conflict, and the statute gives no indication of which objective should then prevail.

Matters to be Taken into Account In forming its opinion that a community sentence is justified under the PCCS(A) 2000, s. 35(1), and in determining the appropriate restrictions on liberty imposed by the community order or orders comprising the community sentence, s. 36(1) requires the court to 'take into account all such information about the circumstances of the offence or (as the case may be) of the offence or offences associated with it (including any aggravating or mitigating factors) as is available to it' and, by s. 36(2), in forming an opinion about the suitability of the community order or orders for the offender, the court 'may take into account any information about the offender which is before it'. Further, by s. 158(1) nothing shall prevent a court from 'mitigating an offender's sentence by taking into account any such matters as, in the opinion of the court, are relevant in mitigation of sentence', and, by s. 158(2)(a) and without prejudice to the generality of s. 158(1), the court may mitigate any penalty included in an offender's sentence by taking into account any other penalty included in that sentence. By s. 151(1), the court may take into account any previous convictions of the offender or any failure of his to respond to previous sentences. **E11.3**

Section 36(4) requires that, subject to s. 36(5), the court 'shall obtain and consider a pre-sentence report' before forming an opinion as to the suitability for the offender of one or more of the following orders:

(a) a community rehabilitation order which includes additional requirements authorised by sch. 2 to the PCC(S)A 2000;
(b) a community punishment order;
(c) a community punishment and rehabilitation order;

(d) a drug treatment and testing order; or
(e) a supervision order which includes requirements authorised by sch. 6 to the Act.

For the definition of a pre-sentence report, see s. 162 and **E1.18**. It follows from s. 36(4) that a pre-sentence report is not required by law whenever the court is considering imposing a community rehabilitation order which does not include additional requirements, a supervision order which does not include the specified requirements mentioned above, a curfew order, an attendance centre order, a drug abstinence order, an exclusion order or an action plan order. No doubt in many cases, however, it would constitute good sentencing practice to obtain a report. Section 36(4) is subject to s. 36(5), which states that the court may dispense with a report in any case where the offender is aged 18 or over and the court considers it to be unnecessary to obtain one. For offenders who are under the age of 18 years, s. 36(6) provides that, in a case where the offence or any other offence associated with it is triable only on indictment, the court may dispense with a pre-sentence report if it considers a report to be unnecessary, but that if none of the offences before the court is triable only on indictment, the court must not dispense with obtaining a pre-sentence report 'unless there exists a previous pre-sentence report obtained in respect of the offender and the court has had regard to the information contained in that report or, if there is more than one such report, the most recent report'.

Section 36(7) states that no relevant community sentence shall be invalidated by failure of the court to obtain and consider a pre-sentence report but, on appeal against a relevant community sentence passed without the court having obtained a pre-sentence report, the appellate court must obtain and consider one, unless the court is of the opinion that the court below was justified in not calling for a report or that the court below was not so justified but, in the circumstances of the case at the time it is before the appellate court, it is unnecessary to obtain one.

ENFORCEMENT OF CERTAIN COMMUNITY ORDERS UNDER PCC(S)A 2000

E11.4 The PCC(S)A 2000 contains provisions for breach, revocation and amendment of various community orders. Schedule 3 applies to community punishment orders, community rehabilitation orders, community punishment and rehabilitation orders, curfew orders, drug treatment and testing orders, and exclusion orders; all of these are designated 'community orders' in s. 33(1). Although supervision orders, attendance centre orders and action plan orders are also community orders within the meaning of the 2000 Act, sch. 3 does not apply to them. For enforcement provisions in relation to them, see **E11.62**, **E11.53** and **E11.66** respectively. Nor does sch. 3 apply to discharges, which are not community orders within s. 33(1); for breach of conditional discharge, see **E14.5**. Where an offender is convicted of a further offence while a relevant order is in force, the appropriate procedure is revocation (see **E11.6**) and not breach (sch. 3, para. 6(1)).

Breach of Community Order

E11.5 Schedule 3, para. 3, states that, if at any time while a relevant order is in force in respect of an offender, it appears on information to a justice of the peace acting for the petty sessions area concerned that the offender has failed to comply with any of the requirements of the order, the justice may either issue a summons requiring the offender to appear or, if the information is in writing and on oath, issue a warrant for his arrest. Paragraph 4 deals with the relevant powers of the magistrates' court, para. 5 deals with the powers of the Crown Court. It should be noted that a magistrates' court dealing with breach of an order imposed by that court has no power to commit the offender to the Crown Court for sentence for the original offence (*Chute* [2003] 2 Cr App R (S) 445).

Powers of Criminal Courts (Sentencing) Act 2000, sch. 3, paras. 4 and 5

4.—(1) If it is proved to the satisfaction of a magistrates' court before which an offender appears or is brought under paragraph 3 above that he has failed without reasonable excuse to comply with any of the requirements of the relevant order, the court may deal with him in respect of the failure in any one of the following ways—

(a) it may impose on him a fine not exceeding £1,000;

(b) where the offender is aged 16 or over it may, subject to paragraph 7 below, make a community punishment order in respect of him;

(c) where—

(i) the relevant order is a curfew order and the offender is aged under 16, or

(ii) the relevant order is a community rehabilitation order or community punishment and rehabilitation order and the offender is aged under 21,

it may, subject to paragraph 8 below, make an attendance centre order in respect of him; or

(d) where the relevant order was made by a magistrates' court, it may deal with him, for the offence in respect of which the order was made, in any way in which it could deal with him if he had just been convicted by the court of the offence.

(2) In dealing with an offender under sub-paragraph (1)(d) above, a magistrates' court—

(a) shall take into account the extent to which the offender has complied with the requirements of the relevant order; and

(b) in the case of an offender who has wilfully and persistently failed to comply with those requirements, may impose a custodial sentence (where the relevant order was made in respect of an offence punishable with such a sentence) notwithstanding anything in section 79(2) of this Act.

(3) Where a magistrates' court deals with an offender under sub-paragraph (1)(d) above, it shall revoke the relevant order if it is still in force.

(4) Where a relevant order was made by the Crown Court and a magistrates' court has power to deal with the offender under sub-paragraph (1)(a), (b) or (c) above, it may instead commit him to custody or release him on bail until he can be brought or appear before the Crown Court.

(5) A magistrates' court which deals with an offender's case under sub-paragraph (4) above shall send to the Crown Court—

(a) a certificate signed by a justice of the peace certifying that the offender has failed to comply with the requirements of the relevant order in the respect specified in the certificate; and

(b) such other particulars of the case as may be desirable;

and a certificate purporting to be so signed shall be admissible as evidence of the failure before the Crown Court.

(6) A person sentenced under sub-paragraph (1)(d) above for an offence may appeal to the Crown Court against the sentence.

5.—(1) Where under paragraph 3 or by virtue of paragraph 4(4) above an offender is brought or appears before the Crown Court and it is proved to the satisfaction of that court that he has failed without reasonable excuse to comply with any of the requirements of the relevant order, the Crown Court may deal with him in respect of the failure in any one of the following ways—

[(a) to (c) identical to sch. 3, para. 4(1)(a) to (c) above]; or

(d) it may deal with him, for the offence in respect of which the order was made, in any way in which it could deal with him if he had just been convicted before the Crown Court of the offence.

(2) In dealing with an offender under sub-paragraph (1)(d) above, the Crown Court—

[(a) and (b) identical to sch. 3, para. 4(1)(a) and (b) above].

(3) Where the Crown Court deals with an offender under sub-paragraph (1)(d) above, it shall revoke the relevant order if it is still in force.

(4) In proceedings before the Crown Court under this paragraph any question whether the offender has failed to comply with the requirements of the relevant order shall be determined by the court and not by the verdict of a jury.

Any breach should either be admitted by the offender or be formally proved (*Devine* [1956] 1 WLR 236) and the prosecution should be in a position to put before the court the facts of the original offence, at least in outline, as well as the facts of the breach (*Clarke* [1997] 2 Cr

Part E Sentencing

App R (S) 163). Where the court employs the option provided by para. 4(1)(b) or 5(1)(b) in respect of an offender who is in breach of a community punishment order or a community punishment and rehabilitation order, the number of hours which the offender may be required to work under the secondary order (imposed in consequence of the breach) must not exceed 60, and the total number of hours of community punishment in the original order and the secondary order must not exceed 240 (where the original order was a community punishment order) or 100 (where the original order was a community punishment and rehabilitation order) (para. 7(3)). For PCC(S)A 2000, s. 60, see **E11.49** (attendance centre orders). The exercise of any of the options in para. 4(1)(a) to (c) or para. 5(1)(a) to (c) is without prejudice to the continuation of the original order. There would appear, in principle, to be no limit to the number of occasions upon which the court might exercise these options in respect of subsequent breaches of the same order by an offender but, if the offender can be said to have 'wilfully and persistently failed to comply' with the order, para. 4(2)(b) or 5(2)(b) may be invoked. The effect of a court exercising its powers under para. 4(1)(d) or 5(1)(d) is that the original order will cease to have effect. There is perhaps an expectation that, once the court turns to para. 4(1)(d) or 5(1)(d), the offender is facing a custodial sentence, but this is not inevitable, particularly where, having regard to para. 4(2)(a) or 5(2)(a), the offender has completed a substantial portion of the original order. Paragraphs 4(2)(b) and 5(2)(b) deal with the case of an offender who has 'wilfully and persistently failed to comply' with the terms of the community order, and empower the court to substitute a custodial sentence instead, notwithstanding the general restrictions on the imposition of custodial sentences contained in s. 79(2). Custody is not inevitable in such a case; the paragraphs state that the court 'may' impose such a sentence. In *Platts* [1998] 2 Cr App R (S) 34 the offender failed to comply with a condition of his community rehabilitation order, and subsequently he could not be found. By the time he was arrested and the matter came before the Crown Court dealing with the breach, the term of the community rehabilitation order had expired. It was argued that the court had no power to revoke an order which had expired, by analogy with *Cousin* (1994) 15 Cr App R (S) 516. The Court of Appeal held, however, that the cases were distinguishable. Where the offender was before the court for breach of the order, rather than for commission of a further offence, it was open to the court where appropriate to revoke the community order and re-sentence for the original offence. Otherwise, the offender could escape the consequences of breach simply by keeping out of the way until the order had expired.

E11.6 **Imposition of Custodial Sentences** Where a custodial sentence is imposed consequent upon breach of a community sentence, the court must, of course, have regard to the normal limitations upon the imposition of custodial sentences, such as the restriction on the maximum custodial sentence which may be imposed by a magistrates' court. If the court imposes a custodial sentence in place of a community order, it seems that it should also normally observe the statutory restrictions with respect to the imposition and length of custodial sentence. This means that custody should be imposed consequent upon breach only where the original offence was so serious that only custody could be justified for it. It was explained by the Court of Appeal in *Oliver* [1993] 1 WLR 177 that the mere fact that the offender has been dealt with by way of a community sentence need not be inconsistent with a finding that the offence was so serious that only custody could be justified for it, since the court which passed the original sentence may have taken account of matters of personal mitigation which may be less persuasive now, in light of breach of the order. If, however, the court is relying upon the PCC(S)A 2000, sch. 3, para. 4(2)(b) or 5(2)(b), that the offender has 'wilfully and persistently failed to comply' with the requirements of the community order, it is clear that the court is not required to justify the imposition of custody in accordance with s. 79(2).

In *Robinson* (1986) 8 Cr App R (S) 327, the Court of Appeal held that a court should not deal with an offender for breach of a community punishment order by way of a suspended sentence, where the effect of that would be to place the offender at risk of custody long after the original offence had been committed.

It is clear that where custody is imposed consequent upon breach of a community order, allowance should be made for any period spent by the offender in custody on remand before the community order was passed, since such time will not count as part of that sentence for the purposes of the CJA 1967, s. 67, though the extent of any allowance is a matter for judicial discretion (*Henderson* [1997] 2 Cr App R (S) 266; *Armstrong* [2002] 2 Cr App R (S) 396). The extent of the allowance given should be indicated when custody is imposed (*Henderson*).

Powers of Crown Court and a Magistrates' Court Where the original community order was made by the Crown Court, a magistrates' court has power to deal with the offender under para. 4(1)(a), (b) or (c) but may not revoke the order. It may, instead of dealing with him, commit the offender to the Crown Court to be dealt with there. The Crown Court has no jurisdiction to deal with the breach of a community order unless the matter has first come to the magistrates' court and the offender is then sent to the Crown Court under para. 4(3). The Crown Court's powers are identical to those of the magistrates' court, except that, under the equivalent power to para. 4(1)(d) (which for the Crown Court is para. 5(1)(d)), it is empowered to deal with the offender in any manner in which it could deal with him if he had just been convicted of that offence before the Crown Court. The words 'before the Crown Court' make it clear that where the Crown Court is dealing with an offender on breach the Crown Court is not restricted to the sentencing powers of the magistrates' courts. E11.7

Investigation of Allegations of Breach Where an offender who suffered from arthritis was sentenced to 100 hours' community punishment, but did not commence the work as required and subsequently produced a medical certificate, the Court of Appeal indicated that the best way of dealing with such a case was to proceed by way of breach under the PCC(S)A 2000, sch. 3, paras. 3 and 4, and for the court to determine whether there was 'reasonable excuse' for the failure to comply with the terms of the order or whether the offender had simply tried to 'con' the court (*Booth* [1998] 1 Cr App R (S) 132, following *Jackson* (1984) 6 Cr App R (S) 202 where the offender had claimed that work commitments rendered her unable to comply with the terms of the order). Breach procedure was more appropriate here than making application for revocation of the order, to ensure that the allegations of breach were properly explored and proved. See also *Hammon* [1998] 2 Cr App R (S) 202. E11.8

Revocation of Community Order

The relevant provisions are paras. 10 to 15 of sch. 3 to the PCC(S)A 2000. Paragraph 10 allows for the revocation of a community order, on application to a magistrates' court acting for the petty sessions area concerned, by the offender or by the responsible officer, on a number of grounds to do with the offender's change of circumstances since the order was imposed. The court may, on such application, revoke the order or (taking account of the extent to which the offender has complied with the order) make an order that the offender should be dealt with in some other manner for the offence in respect of which the order was made (para. 10(3)(a)); if the original order was made by the Crown Court, the court may commit the offender to the Crown Court (para. 10(3)(b)). A common situation in which para. 10 is employed is an application to bring a community rehabilitation order to an end early, in light of the offender's good progress under para. 10(4). E11.9

Powers of Criminal Courts (Sentencing) Act 2000, sch. 3, para. 11

(1) This paragraph applies where—
  (a) a relevant order made by the Crown Court is in force in respect of an offender and the offender or the responsible officer applies to the Crown Court for the order to be revoked or for the offender to be dealt with in some other way for the offence in respect of which the order was made; or

(b) an offender in respect of whom a relevant order is in force is convicted of an offence before the Crown Court or, having been committed by a magistrates' court to the Crown Court for sentence, is brought or appears before the Crown Court.

(2) If it appears to the Crown Court to be in the interests of justice to do so, having regard to circumstances which have arisen since the order was made, the Crown Court may—

(a) revoke the order; or

(b) both—

(i) revoke the order; and

(ii) deal with the offender, for the offence in respect of which the order was made, in any way in which the court which made the order could deal with him if he had just been convicted of that offence by or before the court which made the order.

The circumstances in which a community rehabilitation order, community punishment and rehabilitation order or drug treatment and testing order may be revoked under para. 11(2)(a) include the offender's making good progress or his responding satisfactorily to supervision or treatment (para. 11(3)). The Crown Court may revoke a community order and sentence the offender for the offence in respect of which the order was made even though there is no application for termination of the order, and no failure by the offender to comply with it (*Williams* (1979) 1 Cr App R (S) 78), but when dealing with an offender under para. 11(2)(b) the Crown Court must take into account the extent to which the offender has complied with the requirements of the order (para. 11(4)). When exercising its powers under para. 11(2)(b) to revoke a community order passed by a magistrates' court and deal with the offender for the original offence, the Crown Court is limited to the powers of the magistrates' court. In *Ogden* [1996] 2 Cr App R (S) 386 the Court of Appeal held that the Crown Court was so limited and the wording of para. 11(2)(b) now makes the matter clear beyond doubt. It should be noted that it is not necessary for the application of these powers that the new offence must be committed during the period of the community order but, where an offender subject to a community order is convicted by the Crown Court of an offence committed before it was passed, it will seldom be appropriate, if the community order is revoked, to pass a further sentence for the offence in respect of which the community order was made. This is because the offender has not broken the terms of the order by committing a further offence whilst it was current (*Cawley* (1994) 15 Cr App R (S) 209, followed in *Saphier* [1997] 1 Cr App R (S) 235 and *Reid* [1998] 2 Cr App R (S) 40, but see *Kenny* [1996] 1 Cr App R (S) 397 and *Day* [1997] 2 Cr App R (S) 328). Further, the decisions in *Bennett* (1994) 15 Cr App R (S) 213 and *Cousin* (1994) 15 Cr App R (S) 516 establish that, where the offender has committed an offence during the currency of a community order but is convicted by the Crown Court of that offence after the term of the community order to which he was subject has come to an end, the Crown Court has no power to revoke that order and no power to deal with the offender for the original offence.

Where an offender is convicted of a further offence by a magistrates' court while he is subject to a community order imposed by the Crown Court, the Crown Court ordinarily has power to revoke the community order only if there has been an application under para. 10(3)(b) or on a committal for sentence under s. 3 (*Adams* (1994) 15 Cr App R (S) 417).

It is clear that where custody is imposed consequent upon revocation of a community order, allowance should be made for any period spent by the offender in custody on remand before the community order was passed, since such time will not count as part of that sentence for the purposes of the CJA 1967, s. 67, though the extent of any allowance is a matter for judicial discretion (*McDonald* (1988) 10 Cr App R (S) 458; *Gyorgy* (1989) 11 Cr App R (S) 1).

Case law indicates that where a community order is revoked and the offender is sentenced for a further offence a separate sentence should normally be passed for the original offence (*Fry* [1955] 1 WLR 28; *Rowsell* (1988) 10 Cr App R (S) 411). It was held in *Anderson* (1982) 4 Cr App R (S) 252 that, where a custodial sentence is imposed for the new offence and a consecutive custodial sentence is imposed for the original offence, this is subject to the totality principle (see E1.14). In *Anderson*, the Court of Appeal varied two consecutive sentences of six months' imprisonment, imposed for the offences for which the community order had been made, so as to make them run concurrently with the substantial sentence of imprisonment which had been imposed in respect of the new offences. *Anderson* was followed in *Cook* (1985) 7 Cr App R (S) 249.

Powers of Criminal Courts (Sentencing) Act 2000, sch. 3, para. 13

(1) This paragraph applies where—
   (a) an offender in respect of whom a relevant order is in force is convicted of an offence by a magistrates' court unconnected with the order;
   (b) the court imposes a custodial sentence on the offender; and
   (c) it appears to the court, on the application of the offender or the responsible officer, that it would be in the interests of justice to exercise its powers under this paragraph, having regard to circumstances which have arisen since the order was made.

(2) In sub-paragraph (1) above 'a magistrates' court unconnected with the order' means—
   (a) in the case of a drug treatment and testing order, a magistrates' court which is not responsible for the order;
   (b) in the case of any other relevant order, a magistrates' court not acting for the petty sessions area concerned.

Where, by virtue of para. 13(3)(b), an offender is before the Crown Court that court may revoke the order (para. 14). In such a case the Crown Court may revoke the order but has no power to deal with the original offence by imposing a fresh sentence for it.

Amendment of Community Order

Schedule 3 to the PCC(S)A 2000 (paras. 18 to 25) deals with various powers of amendment of community orders. Paragraph 18 allows for amendments to be made to a community order other than a drug treatment and testing order to take account of a change in the offender's place of residence from one petty sessions area to another; para. 19 deals with amendment of the requirements or duration of a community rehabilitation order, community punishment and rehabilitation order or a curfew order; para. 20 relates to community rehabilitation orders or community punishment and rehabilitation orders which contain a requirement of mental treatment or treatment for alcohol or drug dependence and provides for variation or cancellation of that requirement; para. 21 regulates the amendment of drug treatment and testing orders; para. 22 allows for the extension of the period of a community punishment order or community punishment and rehabilitation order beyond 12 months for reasons such as the offender's changed work commitments or ill health. **E11.10**

COMMUNITY REHABILITATION ORDERS

A community rehabilitation order may be imposed on an offender aged 18 or over convicted of an offence committed before 4 April 2005, or on an offender aged 16 or 17 convicted of an offence committed before or after that date. The PCC(S)A 2000, ss. 41 and 42, are prospectively repealed by the CJA 2003 but the repeal is not expected to take effect before April 2009. **E11.11**

Power to Make Community Rehabilitation Orders

A community rehabilitation order is a 'community order' within the meaning of the PCC(S)A 2000, s. 33(1), so that the imposition of a community rehabilitation order requires justification in terms of the seriousness of the offence, or the offence and one or more offences associated with it. **E11.12**

Powers of Criminal Courts (Sentencing) Act 2000, s. 41

(1) Where a person aged 16 or over is convicted of an offence and the court by or before which he is convicted is of the opinion that his supervision is desirable in the interests of—
(a) securing his rehabilitation, or
(b) protecting the public from harm from him or preventing the commission by him of further offences,
the court may (subject to sections 34 to 36 above) make an order requiring him to be under supervision for a period specified in the order of not less than six months nor more than three years.

(2) An order under subsection (1) above is in this Act referred to as a 'community rehabilitation order'.

(3) A community rehabilitation order shall specify the petty sessions area in which the offender resides or will reside.

(4) If the offender is aged 18 or over at the time when the community rehabilitation order is made, he shall, subject to paragraph 18 of schedule 3 to this Act (offender's change of area), be required to be under the supervision of an officer of a local probation board appointed for or assigned to the petty sessions area specified in the order.

(5) If the offender is aged under 18 at that time, he shall, subject to paragraph 18 of schedule 3, be required to be under the supervision of—
(a) an officer of a local probation board appointed for or assigned to the petty sessions area specified in the order; or
(b) a member of a youth offending team established by a local authority specified in the order;
and if an order specifies a local authority for the purposes of paragraph (b) above, the authority specified must be the local authority within whose area it appears to the court that the offender resides or will reside.

(6) In this Act, 'responsible officer', in relation to an offender who is subject to a community rehabilitation order, means the officer of a local probation board or member of a youth offending team responsible for his supervision.

The minimum qualifying age for a community rehabilitation order is 16, the same as for community punishment orders. There is an overlap between community rehabilitation orders and supervision orders, in that offenders aged 16 and 17 will qualify for either sentence (for supervision orders, see **E11.54**).

Powers of Criminal Courts (Sentencing) Act 2000, s. 41

(7) Before making a community rehabilitation order, the court shall explain to the offender in ordinary language—
(a) the effect of the order (including any additional requirements proposed to be included in the order in accordance with section 42 below);
(b) the consequences which may follow (under part II of schedule 3 to this Act) if he fails to comply with any of the requirements of the order; and
(c) that the court has power (under parts III and IV of that schedule) to review the order on the application of either the offender or of the responsible officer.

(8) On making a community rehabilitation order, the court may, if it thinks it expedient for the purpose of the offender's reformation, allow any person who consents to do so to give security for the good behaviour of the offender.

(9) The court by which a community rehabilitation order is made shall forthwith give copies of the order to—
(a) if the offender is aged 18 or over, an officer of a local probation board assigned to the court, or
(b) if the offender is aged under 18, an officer of a local probation board or member of a youth offending team so assigned,
and he shall give a copy to the offender, to the responsible officer and to the person in charge of any institution in which the offender is required by the order to reside.

(10) The court by which such an order is made shall also, except where it itself acts for the petty sessions area specified in the order, send to the justices' chief executive for that area—
(a) a copy of the order; and
(b) such documents and information relating to the case as it considers likely to be of

assistance to a court acting for that area in the exercise of its functions in relation to the order.

(11) An offender in respect of whom a community rehabilitation order is made shall keep in touch with the responsible officer in accordance with such instructions as he may from time to time be given by that officer, and shall notify him of any change of address.

For the PCC(S)A 2000, s. 42, see **E11.13**; for sch. 3 (breach of community orders), see **E11.5**. It should be noted that, where a requirement as to treatment for drug or alcohol dependency or a requirement as to treatment for a mental condition is to be included in a community rehabilitation order, the offender must express his willingness to comply with that requirement. Section 79(3) of the 2000 Act states that a court may pass a custodial sentence on an offender 'if he fails to express his willingness to comply with a requirement which is proposed by the court to be included in a community rehabilitation order . . . and which requires an expression of such willingness'. Although s. 41(7) requires 'the court' to explain the effect of the order to the offender in ordinary language, see, by analogy, *Wehner* [1977] 1 WLR 1142, where it was held that explanation of the effect of a conditional discharge might be left to the offender's lawyer. On a failure to give a copy of the order to the offender, see, by analogy, *Walsh v Barlow* [1985] 1 WLR 90, considered at **E11.29**. It was held in *Palmer* (1992) 13 Cr App R (S) 595 that a court dealing with a person for contempt of court has no power to make a community rehabilitation order.

Additional Requirements in Community Rehabilitation Orders

Powers of Criminal Courts (Sentencing) Act 2000, s. 42 **E11.13**

(1) Subject to subsection (3) below, a community rehabilitation order may in addition require the offender to comply during the whole or any part of the probation period with such requirements as the court, having regard to the circumstances of the case, considers desirable in the interests of—
  (a) securing the rehabilitation of the offender; or
  (b) protecting the public from harm from him or preventing the commission by him of further offences.

(2) Without prejudice to the generality of subsection (1) above, the additional requirements which may be included in a community rehabilitation order shall include the requirements which are authorised by schedule 2 to this Act.

(2A) For the purposes of this Part of this Act, a drug abstinence requirement is a requirement for the offender—
  (a) to abstain from misusing specified Class A drugs; and
  (b) to provide, when instructed to do so by the responsible officer, any sample mentioned in the instruction for the purpose of ascertaining whether he has any specified Class A drug in his body.

(2B) The first set of conditions is—
  (a) that the offender was aged 18 or over on the date of his conviction for the offence;
  (b) that, in the opinion of the court, the offender is dependent on or has a propensity to misuse specified Class A drugs; and
  (c) that the offence is a trigger offence.

(2C) The second set of conditions is—
  (a) that the offender was aged 18 or over on the date of his conviction for the offence; and
  (b) that, in the opinion of the court—
    (i) the offender is dependent on or has a propensity to misuse specified Class A drugs; and
    (ii) the misuse by the offender of any specified Class A drug caused or contributed to the offence.

(2D) The order may not include a drug abstinence requirement if—
  (a) the community rehabilitation order includes any requirement in respect of drugs under paragraph 6 of Schedule 2 to this Act; or
  (b) the community sentence includes a drug treatment and testing order or a drug abstinence order.

(2E) The function of giving instructions for the purposes of subsection (2A)(b) above shall be

E

Part E Sentencing

exercised in accordance with guidance given from time to time by the Secretary of State; and the Secretary of State may make rules for regulating the provision of samples in pursuance of such instructions.

(2F) The court shall not include a drug abstinence requirement in the order unless the court has been notified by the Secretary of State that arrangements for implementing such requirements are available in the area proposed to be specified under section 41(3) above and the notice has not been withdrawn.

(3) Without prejudice to the power of the court under section 130 below to make a compensation order, the payment of sums by way of damages for injury or compensation for loss shall not be included among the additional requirements of a community rehabilitation order.

For the PCC(S)A 2000, sch. 2, see below. In *Rogers v Cullen* [1982] 1 WLR 729, Lord Bridge indicated that no requirement should be included in a community rehabilitation order which would 'introduce a custodial or other element', and that any discretion conferred on the probation officer to regulate the probationer's activities should be 'confined within well defined limits'. By the Firearms Act 1968, s. 52(1), the court may include a requirement in a community rehabilitation order that the offender shall not possess, use, or carry a firearm.

Additional Requirements Authorised by the PCC(S)A 2000, sch. 2

E11.14 For the normal requirement to obtain a pre-sentence report before imposing a community rehabilitation order containing any of the additional requirements authorised by sch. 2, see **E11.1**.

E11.15 **Requirements as to Residence** By sch. 2, para. 1, the order may include a requirement as to the residence of the offender, but before inserting such a requirement the court must consider the home surroundings of the offender. If the order is to require the offender to reside in an approved hostel or any other institution, the period of residence must be specified in the order.

E11.16 **Requirements as to Activities, etc.**

Powers of Criminal Courts (Sentencing) Act 2000, sch. 2, para. 2

(1) Subject to the provisions of this paragraph, a community rehabilitation order may require the offender—
   (a) to present himself to a person or persons specified in the order at a place or places so specified;
   (b) to participate or refrain from participating in activities specified in the order—
      (i) on a day or days so specified; or
      (ii) during the probation period or such portion of it as may be so specified.

Before making a requirement under para. 2(1), the court must consult an officer of the local probation board or, if the offender is aged under 18, either such officer or a member of a youth offending team, and must be satisfied that it is feasible to secure compliance with it (para. 2(2)). A place specified in the order must have been approved by the relevant probation committee as providing facilities suitable for persons subject to community rehabilitation orders (para. 2(5)). By para. 2(3), no requirement which is mentioned in para. 2(1)(a) or which involves participation in activities may be included in an order if it involves the co-operation of a person other than the offender and the offender's responsible officer, unless that other person consents to its inclusion.

A requirement mentioned in para. 2(1)(a) or involving participation in activities must require the offender to present himself at a place or participate in activities for not more than a total of 60 days and, while there or so participating, comply with instructions given by, or under the authority of, the person in charge of the place or activities (para. 2(4) and (6)). These arrangements must be such as to avoid, so far as practicable, any conflict with the offender's religious beliefs, with the requirements of any other community order to which he may be subject, or interference with the times, if any, at which the offender normally works or attends a school or any other educational establishment (para. 2(7)). A requirement which involves the offender from refraining from specified activities (such as attending football matches, where the offence arose out of football-related violence) may be imposed in respect of a day or days specified in the order, or during such portion of the order as may be specified (para. 2(1)(b)).

Requirements as to Attendance at Community Rehabilitation Centre E11.17

Powers of Criminal Courts (Sentencing) Act 2000, sch. 2, para. 3

(1) Subject to the provisions of this paragraph, a community rehabilitation order may require the offender during the probation period to attend at a community rehabilitation centre specified in the order.
(2) A court shall not include in a community rehabilitation order such a requirement as is mentioned in sub-paragraph (1) above unless it has consulted—
(a) in the case of an offender aged 18 or over, an officer of a local probation board; or
(b) in the case of an offender aged under 18, either an officer of a local probation board or a member of a youth offending team.
(3) A court shall not include such a requirement in a community rehabilitation order unless it is satisfied—
(a) that arrangements can be made for the offender's attendance at a centre; and
(b) that the person in charge of the centre consents to the inclusion of the requirement.

A 'community rehabilitation centre' is defined in para. 3(8) as premises '(a) at which non-residential facilities are provided for use in connection with the rehabilitation of offenders; and (b) which are for the time being approved by the Secretary of State as providing facilities suitable for persons subject to community rehabilitation orders.'

A requirement imposed under para. 3(1) shall involve attendance at the centre for not more than 60 days during the course of the order, during which time the offender must comply with all the instructions of the staff at the centre (para. 3(4)). The instructions for attendance must, so far as is practicable, avoid any conflict with the offender's religious beliefs, with the requirements of any other community order to which he may be subject, and avoid any interference with the times, if any, when the offender normally works or attends school or any other educational establishment (para. 3(5)).

Extension of Requirements for Sexual Offenders Paragraph 4 of sch. 2 provides that where an offender has been convicted of a sexual offence (as defined in PCC(S)A 2000, s. 161(2)), the normal 60-day limit in relation to being present at a place or required activities (under para. 2(4) and (6)) and in relation to attendance at a community rehabilitation centre (under para. 3(4)) does not apply. The duration may, in the case of an offender convicted of a sexual offence, be for 'such greater number of days as may be specified in the direction'. E11.18

Requirements as to Treatment for Mental Condition etc. Requirements relating to treatment for a mental condition are provided in sch. 2, para. 5. E11.19

Requirements as to Treatment for Drug or Alcohol Dependency Schedule 2, para. 6(1) provides for the insertion of a requirement of treatment for drug or alcohol dependency where: E11.20

a court proposing to make a community rehabilitation order is satisfied—
(a) that the offender is dependent on drugs or alcohol;
(b) that his dependency caused or contributed to the offence in respect of which the order is proposed to be made; and
(c) that his dependency is such as requires and may be susceptible to treatment.

In these provisions 'dependency' is widely construed and includes cases where the offender has 'a propensity towards the misuse of drugs or alcohol' (para. 6(9)). Treatment for the dependency must be carried out at a place specified in the order or be carried out by or under the direction of a person meeting the description so specified (para. 6(4)). Treatment may continue for the whole period of the community rehabilitation order or for such specific part of it as is required by the court (para. 6(3)). Before such a requirement can be imposed, the court must be satisfied that arrangements have been or can be made for the treatment to be carried out and that the offender has expressed his willingness to comply with the requirement (para. 6(5)). While the offender is under treatment as a resident in pursuance of such a requirement, the responsible officer's normal supervision duties are relevant only insofar as is necessary for the purpose of revocation or amendment of the order (para. 6(6)).

It would seem from the words 'caused or contributed to the offence' in para. 6(1) that the court is not confined in the use of these powers to cases where the offender has been convicted of an offence which is directly related to drugs or alcohol or committed under the influence of drugs or alcohol. The powers could, for example, be used where an offender had committed theft to obtain money to purchase alcohol or drugs. If the court has been notified that arrangements are in place in the area proposed to be specified in the community rehabilitation order for implementing drug treatment and testing orders (see **E11.38**), para. 6(1) shall be construed as being limited only to offenders dependent on alcohol (para. 6(2)).

E11.21 **Curfew Requirements** Schedule 2 para. 7 provides that a community rehabilitation order may include a requirement that the offender remain, for periods specified in the requirement, at a place so specified. The terms of the requirement are very similar to those of a curfew order, and a curfew requirement cannot be included in the order if the order forms part of a community sentence which contains a curfew order. See **E11.44**.

E11.22 **Exclusion Requirements** When the CJCSA 2000, s. 51, is brought into force, a new para. 8 will be inserted into the PCC(S)A 2000, sch. 2, providing that a community rehabilitation order may include a requirement prohibiting the offender from entering a place for a specified period (not exceeding two years). The terms of the requirement are very similar to those of an exclusion order, and an exclusion requirement cannot be included in the order if the order forms part of a community sentence which contains an exclusion order. See **E11.47**.

MAKING OF COMMUNITY REHABILITATION ORDERS: SENTENCING PRINCIPLES

General Guidance

E11.23 The PCC(S)A 2000, s. 41(1) provides that the purposes of a community rehabilitation order are to be either securing the rehabilitation of the offender or protecting the public from harm from him or preventing the commission by him of further offences. Additionally, since a community rehabilitation order is a 'community order' within the meaning of s. 33(1), its imposition in any case must be justified by the sentencer in terms of the seriousness of the offence, or the seriousness of the offence and one or more offences associated with it.

Mixing Community Rehabilitation Orders with Other Sentences or Orders

E11.24 It is impermissible to combine a community rehabilitation order with an immediate custodial sentence, whether in respect of the same offence or for different offences sentenced on the same occasion (*Carr-Thompson* [2000] 2 Cr App R (S) 335). Exceptionally, a community rehabilitation order might be imposed on an offender nearing the end of a custodial sentence imposed on a different occasion (*Fontenau v DPP* [2001] 1 Cr App R (S) 48). A community rehabilitation order may not be combined with a community punishment order when sentencing for a single offence (s. 35(2)), except where imposed in a specified mix to form a community punishment and rehabilitation order. Nor can a community rehabilitation order and a community punishment order be imposed for separate offences sentenced on the same occasion (*Gilding v DPP* (1998) *The Times*, 20 May 1998). A community rehabilitation order cannot be combined with a hospital order (Mental Health Act 1983, s. 37(8)). A community rehabilitation order may, however, be combined with a fine, whether imposed in respect of the same or different offences. A community rehabilitation order may not be combined with a discharge when sentencing for a single offence, since a discharge is imposed only where 'it is inexpedient to inflict punishment' (PCC(S)A 2000, s. 12(1)), but these two measures may, of course, be used for different offences sentenced on the same occasion. When combining measures, regard should be had to s. 158(2)(a), which states that nothing 'shall prevent a court from mitigating any penalty included in an offender's sentence by taking into account any other penalty included in that sentence'.

A community rehabilitation order can be combined with an order of disqualification from driving (Road Traffic Offenders Act 1988, s. 46(1)). Compensation may not be ordered as a requirement of a community rehabilitation order (PCC(S)A 2000, s. 42(3)), but a court may make an order for compensation or for costs, or for restitution of property (s. 148(2)) at the same time as making a community rehabilitation order. The court may combine with a community rehabilitation order an order for deportation (Immigration Act 1971, s. 6(3), though see **E22.5**), or an exclusion order in respect of licensed premises (Licensed Premises (Exclusion of Certain Persons) Act 1980, s. 1(2) (see **E23.1**)). A community rehabilitation order may be combined with a deprivation order under the PCC(S)A 2000, s. 143.

Breach, Revocation and Amendment of Community Rehabilitation Orders

The relevant enforcement provisions are described at **E11.4** *et seq.* **E11.25**

COMMUNITY PUNISHMENT ORDERS

A community punishment order may be imposed on an offender aged 18 or over convicted of an offence committed before 4 April 2005, or on an offender aged 16 or 17 convicted of an offence committed before or after that date. The PCC(S)A 2000, ss. 46 and 51, are prospectively repealed by the CJA 2003 but the repeal is not expected to take effect before April 2009. **E11.26**

Powers of Criminal Courts (Sentencing) Act 2000, s. 46

(1) Where a person aged 16 or over is convicted of an offence punishable with imprisonment, the court by or before which he is convicted may (subject to sections 34 to 36 above) make an order requiring him to perform unpaid work in accordance with section 47 below.

(2) An order under subsection (1) above is in this Act referred to as a 'community punishment order'.

(3) The number of hours which a person may be required to work under a community punishment order shall be specified in the order and shall be in the aggregate—
   (a) not less than 40; and
   (b) not more than 240.

(4) A court shall not make a community punishment order in respect of an offender unless, after hearing (if the court thinks it necessary) an appropriate officer, the court is satisfied that the offender is a suitable person to perform work under such an order.

(5) In subsection (4) above 'an appropriate officer' means—
   (a) in the case of an offender aged 18 or over, an officer of a local probation board or social worker of a local authority social services department; and
   (b) in the case of an offender aged under 18, an officer of a local probation board, a social worker of a local authority social services department or a member of a youth offending team.

(6) A court shall not make a community punishment order in respect of an offender unless it is satisfied that provision for him to perform work under such an order can be made under the arrangements for persons to perform work under such orders which exist in the petty sessions area in which he resides or will reside.

Unless the period during which the community punishment order is to be performed is extended, by virtue of sch. 3, para. 22, the work must be completed during the period of 12 months beginning with the date of the order but, unless revoked, the order remains in force until the offender has completed the number of hours specified in it (s. 47(3)).

E11.27 **Reports** For the normal requirement to obtain a pre-sentence report, see **E11.2**.

Where a court adjourns for the purpose of obtaining a report to assess the offender's suitability for a community punishment order, and if the report shows the offender to be suitable, the court should normally make such an order to avoid feelings of injustice which would otherwise be aroused in the offender (referred to as 'an important principle of sentencing' in *Gillam* (1980) 2 Cr App R (S) 267; followed in *Millwood* (1982) 4 Cr App R (S) 281). For further discussion of this issue, see **D19.59**.

Two or More Orders

E11.28 **Powers of Criminal Courts (Sentencing) Act 2000, s. 46**

(8) Where a court makes community punishment orders in respect of two or more offences of which the offender has been convicted by or before the court, the court may direct that the hours of work specified in any of those orders shall be concurrent with or additional to those specified in any other of those orders, but so that the total number of hours which are not concurrent shall not exceed the maximum specified in subsection (3)(b) above.

Section 46(8) has direct application to the situation where a court is imposing two community punishment orders on the same occasion. In such a case, the total number of hours ordered must not exceed 240. In *Evans* [1977] 1 WLR 27, the offender was convicted in a magistrates' court and a sentence of 60 hours' community punishment was ordered. Three days later he appeared before the Crown Court in respect of a burglary and was given a further 60 hours for that offence, consecutive to the first. The Court of Appeal referred to s. 46(8) and said that nothing in that subsection prevented consecutive community punishment orders, whether they were imposed on the same or different occasions, provided that 'there should not be orders totalling more than 240 hours in existence at the same time in respect of the same offender'. According to *Anderson* (1989) 11 Cr App R (S) 147, when consecutive community punishment orders are made, the limitation to 240 hours refers to the total number of hours ordered, rather than to the total which remain to be served. In *Siha* (1992) 13 Cr App R (S) 588, the Court of Appeal said that while s. 46(8) did not actually prevent the imposition of consecutive community punishment orders on different occasions which together totalled more than 240 hours, sentencers should remember that Parliament had prescribed 240 hours as the maximum to be imposed on a single occasion. Where an offender is made subject to consecutive community punishment orders, those orders should be regarded 'for all practical purposes' as a single order (*Meredith* (1994) 15 Cr App R (S) 528).

Procedural Requirements

E11.29 **Powers of Criminal Courts (Sentencing) Act 2000, s. 46**

(9) A community punishment order—
- (a) shall specify the petty sessions area in which the offender resides or will reside; and
- (b) where the offender is aged under 18 at the time the order is made, may also specify a local authority for the purposes of section 47(5)(b) below (cases where functions are to be discharged by member of a youth offending team);

and if the order specifies a local authority for those purposes, the authority specified must be the local authority within whose area it appears to the court that the offender resides or will reside.

(10) Before making a community punishment order, the court shall explain to the offender in ordinary language—
- (a) the purpose and effect of the order (and in particular the requirements of the order as specified in section 47(1) to (3) below);
- (b) the consequences which may follow (under part II of schedule 3 to this Act) if he fails to comply with any of those requirements; and

(c) that the court has power (under parts III and IV of that schedule) to review the order on the application either of the offender or of the responsible officer.

(11) The court by which a community punishment order is made shall forthwith give copies of the order to—

(a) if the offender is aged 18 or over, an officer of a local probation board assigned to the court, or

(b) if the offender is aged under 18, an officer of a local probation board or member of a youth offending team so assigned,

and he shall give a copy to the offender and to the responsible officer.

(12) The court by which such an order is made shall also, except where it itself acts for the petty sessions area specified in the order, send to the justices' chief executive for that area—

(a) a copy of the order; and

(b) such documents and information relating to the case as it considers likely to be of assistance to a court acting for that area in the exercise of its functions in relation to the order.

In *Walsh v Barlow* [1985] 1 WLR 90, it was argued by the offender, without success, that a community punishment order which had been made in respect of him by a magistrates' court was ineffective, as no copy had been delivered to him by the relevant officer. Stephen Brown LJ held (at pp. 100–1) that such delivery was 'not a prerequisite to the coming into force of the order; the order comes into force as soon as the court has pronounced the sentence . . . '.

Obligations under the Order

Powers of Criminal Courts (Sentencing) Act 2000, s. 47 **E11.30**

(1) An offender in respect of whom a community punishment order is in force shall—

(a) keep in touch with the responsible officer in accordance with such instructions as he may from time to time be given by that officer and notify him of any change of address; and

(b) perform for the number of hours specified in the order such work at such times as he may be instructed by the responsible officer.

For the meaning of 'the responsible officer', see s. 47(4). The instructions given by the responsible officer under s. 47(1) 'shall, so far as practicable, be such as to avoid (a) any conflict with the offender's religious beliefs, or with the requirements of any other community order to which he may be subject; and (b) any interference with the times, if any, at which he normally works or attends a school or any other educational establishment' (s. 47(2)).

Provision is made in s. 47(3A) to (3C) for the inclusion of drug abstinence requirements into community punishment orders. In a case where (a) the offender is aged 18 or over on the date of his conviction for the offence; (b) in the opinion of the court the offender is dependent on, or has a prospensity to misuse, specified Class A drugs; and (c) the offence is a 'trigger offence', then the community punishment order must contain a drug abstinence requirement, unless the community punishment order forms part of a community sentence which includes a drug treatment and testing order or a drug abstinence order. In a case where conditions (a) and (b) are made out, but the offence is not a 'trigger offence', the court may insert a drug abstinence requirement where it is of the opinion that misuse by the offender of any Class A drug caused or contributed to the offence, but again subject to there being none of the other drug-related requirements or orders in place.

COMMUNITY PUNISHMENT ORDERS: SENTENCING PRINCIPLES

Range of Hours in Relation to Sentence Offender Would Otherwise Have Received

The sentencing principles described in this paragraph must be read in the light of the criteria for the imposition of community sentences in general (see E11.2). An example of the **E11.31** application of these criteria by the Court of Appeal is *Small* (1993) 14 Cr App R (S) 405. The 20-year-old offender, who was employed as operations manager by a company supplying pizzas, pleaded guilty to three counts of theft. On three occasions he failed to pay into the bank money received in the shop, totalling £1,080. The sentencer considered that the offences were so serious that only a custodial sentence could be justified, and imposed a term of three months' detention in a young offender institution. The Court of Appeal, having regard to the offender's age, good record and information in the pre-sentence report that the offender had been insufficiently mature to cope with the volume of work and degree of responsibility imposed upon him, quashed the custodial sentence but held that the offences were serious enough to warrant a community sentence. The pre-sentence report suggested that the offender did not need supervision, but that a sentence commensurate with the seriousness of the offence would be a 'mid-length term of community service'. The Court of Appeal substituted a community punishment order for 50 hours, though this sentence made some unspecified allowance for the fact that the offender had already spent one month in custody.

In *Davies* (1984) 6 Cr App R (S) 224, the Court of Appeal imposed a community punishment order of 60 hours on an offender who was peripherally involved in an attack on another youth, and who pleaded guilty to stealing the victim's jacket, where 'it was wrong in principle to have imposed an immediate custodial sentence'. Sixty hours' community punishment was held to be appropriate in *Hamilton* (1988) 10 Cr App R (S) 383, where the offender stole property worth £180 and was also approved in *Zaman* (1992) 12 Cr App R (S) 657, where a 19-year-old stole a radio from a car. In a case of offenders who were involved in the spraying of paint on carriages at a London Underground depot (*Ferreira* (1988) 10 Cr App R (S) 343), the Court of Appeal replaced custodial sentences with community punishment orders of 120 hours, Farquharson J commenting that community punishment was 'designed' for such a case: 'They have done this wanton damage and therefore it behoves them to do some service to the public to put it right.'

Appropriateness with Respect to Serious Offences

E11.32 The sentencing principles described in this paragraph must now be read in the light of the criteria for the imposition of community sentences in general (see **E11.2**).

A community punishment order may, on occasion, be appropriate in a case involving violence (*McDiarmid* (1980) 2 Cr App R (S) 130, where the offender, aged 18 and of previous good character, in the course of a disturbance in a public house, threw a beer glass at a man, causing a cut lip). However, in a case involving more serious violence (*Heyfron* (1980) 2 Cr App R (S) 230), it was held that community punishment was 'wholly wrong'. In that case the accused attacked a man who had apparently made sexual advances to his common-law wife, causing severe facial injuries.

Community punishment orders may be imposed in cases of burglary, even, on occasion, of dwelling houses. In *Coleman* (1981) 3 Cr App R (S) 178, the Court of Appeal, while agreeing with the trial judge that those who commit burglary in dwellings must expect custodial sentences, varied the sentence to a community punishment order in the light of the offender's 'fairly minor' previous convictions. In *Seymour* (1983) 5 Cr App R (S) 85, the offender was aged 28 and had been sentenced on several previous occasions for burglary, including four custodial sentences. The Court of Appeal varied an 18-month custodial sentence to a community punishment order, commenting that 'there are other ways of protecting society than merely taking a young criminal out of circulation for what must be a limited period. If one can achieve at any rate some change of heart by some alternative sentence, one may be doing as well for society.' In *Brown* (1981) 3 Cr App R (S) 294, community punishment was 'tailor-made' for a 19-year-old with no previous convictions, who, in breach of trust, had, together with a co-defendant, committed burglary of his employer's premises, with loss of goods to the value of £2,850. The Court emphasised the offender's clean record (though a 'light' criminal record would, apparently, have produced the same result), his stable home background with wife and young child, good work record, genuine remorse, and only slight chance of re-offending.

Mixing Community Punishment Orders with Other Sentences or Orders

A community punishment order and a community rehabilitation order may not be combined together *per se* when sentencing for the same offence (PCC(S)A 2000, s. 35(2)) but in a certain mix they form a community punishment and rehabilitation order (see **E11.35**). Nor can a community punishment order and a community rehabilitation order be imposed for separate offences sentenced on the same occasion (*Gilding v DPP* (1998) *The Times*, 20 May 1998). It is possible to combine a community punishment order with a curfew order (see **E11.45**). A community punishment order may be combined with an order for costs, a disqualification of any kind imposed upon the offender, a compensation order or a deprivation order made under s. 143. **E11.33**

A community punishment order should not be imposed on the same occasion as an immediate sentence of imprisonment (nor, it is submitted, any other custodial sentence), even though the sentences relate to different counts (*Starie* (1979) 69 Cr App R 239). It was held in *Ray* (1984) 6 Cr App R (S) 26 that a community punishment order and a suspended sentence of imprisonment could not be imposed on the same occasion. Exceptionally, a community punishment order might be imposed on an offender nearing the end of a custodial sentence imposed on a different occasion (*Fontenau v DPP* [2001] 1 Cr App R (S) 48). A community punishment order cannot be combined with a discharge when sentencing for a single offence, since a discharge is imposed only where 'it is inexpedient to inflict punishment' (s. 12(1)), but these two measures may, of course, be used for different offences sentenced on the same occasion.

When combining measures on sentence, regard should be had to s. 158(2)(a), which states that nothing 'shall prevent a court from mitigating any penalty included in an offender's sentence by taking into account any other penalty included in that sentence'.

COMMUNITY PUNISHMENT AND REHABILITATION ORDERS

A community punishment and rehabilitation order may be imposed on an offender aged 18 or over convicted of an offence committed before 4 April 2005, or on an offender aged 16 or 17 convicted of an offence committed before or after that date. The PCC(S)A 2000, s. 51, is prospectively repealed by the CJA 2003, but the repeal is not expected to be brought into force before April 2009. **E11.34**

Power to Make Community Punishment and Rehabilitation Orders

Powers of Criminal Courts (Sentencing) Act 2000, s. 51 **E11.35**

(1) Where a person aged 16 or over is convicted of an offence punishable with imprisonment and the court by or before which he is convicted is of the opinion mentioned in subsection (3) below, the court may (subject to sections 34 to 36 above) make an order requiring him both—
   (a) to be under supervision for a period specified in the order, being not less than twelve months nor more than three years; and
   (b) to perform unpaid work for a number of hours so specified, being in the aggregate not less than 40 nor more than 100.

(2) An order under subsection (1) above is in this Act referred to as a 'community punishment and rehabilitation order'.

(3) The opinion referred to in subsection (1) above is that the making of a community punishment and rehabilitation order is desirable in the interests of—

(a) securing the rehabilitation of the offender; or
(b) protecting the public from harm from him or preventing the commission by him of further offences.

(4) Subject to subsection (1) above, sections 41, 42, 46 and 47 above and schedule 2 to this Act shall apply in relation to community punishment and rehabilitation orders—
(a) in so far as those orders impose such a requirement as is mentioned in paragraph (a) of subsection (1) above, as if they were community rehabilitation orders; and
(b) in so far as they impose such a requirement as is mentioned in paragraph (b) of that subsection, as if they were community punishment orders.

A community punishment and rehabilitation order is a 'community order', and its imposition requires justification by the court in terms of the seriousness of the offence, or the seriousness of the offence and one or more offences associated with it. These requirements are set out at **E11.2**. Before making a community punishment and rehabilitation order, the court must comply with all the relevant procedural requirements for imposing a community punishment order and a community rehabilitation order. For the normal requirement to obtain a pre-sentence report, see **E11.2**.

One effect of s. 51(4) is that the court may insert any of the additional requirements into the community rehabilitation part of the order which are provided for in sch. 2 (see **E11.14 *et seq.***), though this must be subject to the proviso that their inclusion is not logically incompatible with the performance of the community punishment part of the order.

Section 35(2) states that 'a community sentence shall not consist of or include both a community rehabilitation order and a community punishment order'. These elements can be mixed together only in the form of a community punishment and rehabilitation order. Nor can a community rehabilitation order and a community punishment order be imposed for separate offences sentenced on the same occasion. See further **E11.24**.

Breach, Revocation and Amendment of Community Punishment and Rehabilitation Orders

E11.36 The relevant enforcement provisions are described at **E11.3 *et seq.***

DRUG TREATMENT AND TESTING ORDERS

E11.37 A drug treatment and testing order may be imposed on an offender aged 18 or over convicted of an offence committed before 4 April 2005, or on an offender aged 16 or 17 convicted of an offence committed before or after that date. The PCC(S)A 2000, ss. 52 to 55, will be repealed but the repeal is not expected to take effect before April 2009.

Power to Make Drug Treatment and Testing Order

E11.38 A drug treatment and testing order is a 'community order' within the meaning of the PCC(S)A 2000, s. 33(1), so that the imposition of a drug treatment and testing order requires justification in terms of the seriousness of the offence, or the offence and one or more offences associated with it. The relevant statutory criteria are set out at **E11.2**. The statutory provisions do not refer to the type of drugs, but according to the Court of Appeal in *A-G's Ref (No. 64 of 2003)* [2004] 2 Cr App R (S) 106, such orders will usually be made in relation to Class A drugs, predominantly heroin and crack cocaine.

Powers of Criminal Courts (Sentencing) Act 2000, s. 52

(1) Where a person aged 16 or over is convicted of an offence, the court by or before which he is convicted may (subject to sections 34 to 36 above) make an order which—
(a) has effect for a period specified in the order of not less than six months nor more than three years ('the treatment and testing period'); and
(b) includes the requirements and provisions mentioned in sections 53 and 54 below;

but this section does not apply in relation to an offence committed before 30th September 1998.

(2) An order under subsection (1) above is in this Act referred to as a 'drug treatment and testing order'.

(3) A court shall not make a drug treatment and testing order in respect of an offender unless it is satisfied—
  (a) that he is dependent on or has a propensity to misuse drugs; and
  (b) that his dependency or propensity is such as requires and may be susceptible to treatment.

(4) For the purpose of ascertaining for the purposes of subsection (3) above whether the offender has any drug in his body, the court may by order require him to provide samples of such description as it may specify; but the court shall not make such an order unless the offender expresses his willingness to comply with its requirements.

(5) A court shall not make a drug treatment and testing order unless it has been notified by the Secretary of State that arrangements for implementing such orders are available in the area proposed to be specified in the order under section 54(1) below and the notice has not been withdrawn.

(6) Before making a drug treatment and testing order, the court shall explain to the offender in ordinary language—
  (a) the effect of the order and of the requirements proposed to be included in it;
  (b) the consequences which may follow (under part II of schedule 3 to this Act) if he fails to comply with any of those requirements;
  (c) that the order will be periodically reviewed at intervals as provided for in the order (by virtue of section 54(6) below); and
  (d) that the order may be reviewed (under parts III and IV of schedule 3) on the application either of the offender or of the responsible officer;

and 'responsible officer' here has the meaning given by section 54(3) below.

(7) A court shall not make a drug treatment and testing order unless the offender expresses his willingness to comply with its requirements.

Section 52(4) (pre-sentence drug testing) applies to offenders aged 16 or 17. For offenders aged 18 or over, see PCC(S)A 2000, s. 36A. The requirement in s. 52(7) is one of the occasions on which the court must secure the offender's willingness to comply with the order before it can be imposed. Section 79(3) states that 'nothing [in s. 79(2)] shall prevent the court from passing a custodial sentence on the offender if he fails to express his willingness to comply . . .'.

Treatment Requirement

Powers of Criminal Courts (Sentencing) Act 2000, ss. 53 and 54 **E11.39**

53.—(1) A drug treatment and testing order shall include a requirement ('the treatment requirement') that the offender shall submit, during the whole of the treatment and testing period, to treatment by or under the direction of a specified person having the necessary qualifications or experience ('the treatment provider') with a view to the reduction or elimination of the offender's dependency on or propensity to misuse drugs.

(2) The required treatment for any particular period shall be—
  (a) treatment as a resident in such institution or place as may be specified in the order; or
  (b) treatment as a non-resident in or at such institution or place, and at such intervals, as may be so specified;

but the nature of the treatment shall not be specified in the order except as mentioned in paragraph (a) or (b) above.

(3) A court shall not make a drug treatment and testing order unless it is satisfied that arrangements have been or can be made for the treatment intended to be specified in the order (including arrangements for the reception of the offender where he is to be required to submit to treatment as a resident).

(4) A drug treatment and testing order shall include a requirement ('the testing requirement') that, for the purpose of ascertaining whether he has any drug in his body during the treatment and testing period, the offender shall during that period, at such times or in such circumstances as may (subject to the provisions of the order) be determined by the treatment provider, provide samples of such description as may be so determined.

(5) The testing requirement shall specify for each month the minimum number of occasions on which samples are to be provided.

54.—(1) A drug treatment and testing order shall include a provision specifying the petty sessions area in which it appears to the court making the order that the offender resides or will reside.

(2) A drug treatment and testing order shall provide that, for the treatment and testing period, the offender shall be under the supervision of an officer of a local probation board appointed for or assigned to the petty sessions area specified in the order.

(3) In this Act 'responsible officer', in relation to an offender who is subject to a drug treatment and testing order, means the officer of a local probation board responsible for his supervision.

(4) A drug treatment and testing order shall—
(a) require the offender to keep in touch with the responsible officer in accordance with such instructions as he may from time to time be given by that officer, and to notify him of any change of address; and
(b) provide that the results of the tests carried out on the samples provided by the offender in pursuance of the testing requirement shall be communicated to the responsible officer.

(5) Supervision by the responsible officer shall be carried out to such extent only as may be necessary for the purpose of enabling him—
(a) to report on the offender's progress to the court responsible for the order;
(b) to report to that court any failure by the offender to comply with the requirements of the order; and
(c) to determine whether the circumstances are such that he should apply to that court for the revocation or amendment of the order.

(6) A drug treatment and testing order shall—
(a) provide for the order to be reviewed periodically at intervals of not less than one month;
(b) provide for each review of the order to be made, subject to section 55(6) below, at a hearing held for the purpose by the court responsible for the order (a 'review hearing');
(c) require the offender to attend each review hearing;
(d) provide for the responsible officer to make to the court responsible for the order, before each review, a report in writing on the offender's progress under the order; and
(e) provide for each such report to include the test results communicated to the responsible officer under subsection (4)(b) above and the views of the treatment provider as to the treatment and testing of the offender.

(7) In this section references to the court responsible for a drug treatment and testing order are references to—
(a) where a court is specified in the order in accordance with subsection (8) below, that court;
(b) in any other case, the court by which the order is made.

(8) Where the area specified in a drug treatment and testing order made by a magistrates' court is not the area for which the court acts, the court may, if it thinks fit, include in the order provision specifying for the purposes of subsection (7) above a magistrates' court which acts for the area specified in the order.

(9) Where a drug treatment and testing order has been made on an appeal brought from the Crown Court or from the criminal division of the Court of Appeal, for the purposes of subsection (7) (b) above it shall be deemed to have been made by the Crown Court.

E11.40 **Procedural Requirements** Before making a drug treatment and testing order the court must explain to the offender in ordinary language the effect of the order and the requirements proposed to be included in it, the consequences which may follow if he fails to comply with any of those requirements, that the order may be reviewed on application either of the offender or of the responsible officer and that the order will be reviewed periodically by the court making the order (s. 52(6)). According to the Divisional Court in *R (Inner London Probation Service v Tower Bridge Magistrates' Court* [2002] 1 Cr App R (S) 179, it is important, particularly where the offender is unrepresented, that the prosecutor should check that all necessary steps required to be taken by the sentencer in accordance with ss. 52 to 54 have been complied with. Although these strictly do not require the agreement of the probation service, a court should be slow to make an order in the face of a reasoned probation service assessment that the offender was unsuitable for it. The court shall forthwith give copies of the order to an officer of the local probation board, and he shall give copies to the offender, to the treatment provider, and to the responsible officer (s. 57(1)). It is unlikely that non-compliance with the provision of the copies of the order would render the drug treatment and testing order invalid, by analogy with *Walsh v Barlow* [1985] 1 WLR 90 (see **E11.29**).

Court of Appeal Guidance In *A-G's Ref (No. 64 of 2003)* [2004] 2 Cr App R (S) 106 the Court of Appeal gave important guidance on the appropriate use of drug treatment and testing orders. The Court stated that (a) judges should be alert to pass sentences which had a realistic prospect of reducing drug addiction whenever it was possible sensibly to do so; (b) many offences were committed by an offender under the influence of drugs, but the fact that the defendant was so acting was not itself a reason for making a DTTO; (c) a necessary prerequisite of the making of a DTTO was clear evidence that the defendant was determined to free himself from drugs; (d) a DTTO was likely to have a better prospect of success earlier rather than later in a criminal career, but there would be exceptional cases; (e) it would be very rare for a DTTO to be appropriate for an offence involving serious violence or threat of violence with a lethal weapon; (f) the type of offence for which a DTTO would generally be appropriate would be an acquisitive offence carried out to obtain money for drugs; (g) a DTTO might be appropriate even when a substantial number of offences had been committed; (h) a DTTO was unlikely to be appropriate for a substantial number of serious offences which either involved violence or had a particularly damaging effect on the victim(s), and there must be a degree of proportionality between offence and sentence so that excessive weight was not given to the prospect of rehabilitation; (i) material about the offender which became available between sentencing and appeal might be of particular significance as to the propriety of a DTTO, so that an up-to-date assessment of the offender might be ordered at that stage. **E11.41**

This guidance consolidates, and expands upon, earlier guidance in *Robinson* [2002] 2 Cr App R (S) 434 and *Kelly* [2003] 1 Cr App R (S) 472. See also *Woods* [2006] 1 Cr App R (S) 477.

Review Hearings

Section 55 provides that periodic reviews of the offender's progress under the terms of the drug treatment and testing order shall be carried out, by the court which made the order, at intervals of not less than one month. These reviews, at least initially, will require the offender's attendance at each 'review hearing' in court, at which the offender's test results, the responsible officer's written report on his progress under the order, and the views of the person providing the treatment will all be considered by the court (s. 54(6)). At a review hearing the court, after considering the report of the responsible officer, may amend any requirement or provision of the order (s. 55(1)), except that the court may not amend the treatment or testing requirement in the order unless the offender expresses his willingness to comply with the amendment, and the court may not reduce the treatment and testing period below the minimum, or increase it above the maximum, specified in s. 52(1). If the offender fails to express his willingness to comply with the treatment or testing requirement as proposed to be amended, the court may revoke the order and deal with him for the offence in respect of which the order was made in any manner in which it could deal with him if he had just been convicted by the court of the offence (s. 55(3)). In so dealing with the offender the court must take into account the extent to which the offender has complied with the order's requirements, and may impose a custodial sentence notwithstanding s. 79(2) (s. 55(4)). Further, if the drug treatment and testing order was made by a magistrates' court on an offender under the age of 18 for an offence triable only on indictment in the case of an adult, the court's power to re-sentence for the original offence is limited to the imposition of a fine not exceeding £5,000 or to deal with him in any way in which it could deal with him if it had just convicted him of an offence punishable with imprisonment for a term not exceeding six months (s. 55(5)). If, at a review hearing it appears that the offender's progress under the **E11.42** order is satisfactory, subsequent reviews may be carried out by the court without a full review hearing (in the case of the Crown Court, by a judge; in the case of a magistrates' court, by a justice of the peace acting for the relevant commission area) but, if progress subsequently becomes unsatisfactory, a further review hearing in court must be convened (s. 55(7) to (9)).

Breach, Revocation and Amendment of Drug Treatment and Testing Order

E11.43 Schedule 3 to the PCC(S)A 2000 makes provision for breach, revocation and amendment of certain community orders, and sch. 3 applies to drug treatment and testing orders. See **E11.3**.

The Court of Appeal in *A-G's Ref (No. 64 of 2003)* [2004] 2 Cr App R (S) 106 observed that the relevant National Standards provided that breach action might be taken after one unacceptable failure, and must be taken after a second unacceptable failure to comply with the requirements of the order. A failed drug test was not a breach by itself, but regular failures often indicated unsatisfactory progress. For detailed guidance on the options available to the Crown Court when sentencing an offender subject to a drug treatment and testing order who commits further offences, see *Robinson* [2002] 2 Cr App R (S) 434.

YOUTH COMMUNITY ORDERS: GENERAL PROVISIONS

E11.44 The CJA 2003, s. 147(1), states that 'community sentence' means 'a sentence that consists of or includes . . . (b) one or more youth community orders', and that 'youth community order' means:

(a) a curfew order as defined by the PCC(S)A, 2000, s. 163;
(b) an exclusion order under the PCC(S)A 2000, s. 40A(1) (which defines it as an order under s. 37(1) of that Act);
(c) an attendance centre order as defined by the PCC(S)A 2000, s. 163;
(d) a supervision order under the PCC(S)A 2000, s. 63(1); or
(e) an action plan order under the PCC(S)A 2000, s. 69(1).

Criminal Justice Act 2003, s. 148

(3) Where a court passes a community sentence which consists of or includes one or more youth community orders—
(a) the particular order or orders forming part of the sentence must be such as, in the opinion of the court, is, or taken together are, the most suitable for the offender, and
(b) the restrictions on liberty imposed by the order or orders must be such as in the opinion of the court are commensurate with the seriousness of the offence, or the combination of the offence and one or more offences associated with it.

In determining the restrictions on liberty to be imposed by a youth community order, the court may have regard to any period for which the offender has been remanded in custody (s. 149). The power to make a youth community order is not available for an offence for which the sentence is fixed by law (murder) or falls to be imposed under the CJA 2003, ss. 226 or 228 (dangerous offenders) (s. 150).

For the requirement to order a pre-sentence report before passing a youth community order, see CJA 2003, s. 156, at **E1.18**.

By the CJA 2003, s. 36B(1), a youth community order may include requirements for securing the electronic monitoring of the offender's compliance with any other requirements imposed by the order. This is subject to s. 36B(2), which states that such a requirement shall not be included unless the court has been notified that electronic monitoring arrangements are available in the local area and the court is satisfied that the necessary provisions can be made.

CURFEW ORDERS

A curfew order may be imposed on an offender aged 18 or over only if the offence was committed before 4 April 2005, but the order may be imposed on an offender aged under 18 irrespective of the date on which the offence was committed. Curfew orders will no longer be available for offenders aged 16 or 17 once the new provisions in the CJA 2003 are fully in force, but that change is not expected to take place before April 2009. E11.45

Powers of Criminal Courts (Sentencing) Act 2000, s. 37

(1) Where a person aged [under 16] is convicted of an offence, the court by or before which he is convicted may (subject to sections 148, 150 and 156 of the Criminal Justice Act 2003) make an order requiring him to remain, for periods specified in the order, at a place so specified.

(2) An order under subsection (1) above is in this Act referred to as a 'curfew order'.

(3) A curfew order may specify different places or different periods for different days, but shall not specify—
  (a) periods which fall outside the period of six months beginning with the day on which it is made; or
  (b) periods which amount to less than two hours or more than twelve hours in any one day.

(4) [Repealed]

(5) The requirements in a curfew order shall, as far as practicable, be such as to avoid—
  (a) any conflict with the offender's religious beliefs or with the requirements of any other youth community order to which he may be subject; and
  (b) any interference with the times, if any, at which he normally works or attends school or any other educational establishment.

(6) A curfew order shall include provision for making a person responsible for monitoring the offender's whereabouts during the curfew periods specified in the order; and a person who is made so responsible shall be of a description specified in an order made by the Secretary of State.

(7) A court shall not make a curfew order unless the court has been notified by the Secretary of State that arrangements for monitoring the offender's whereabouts are available in the area in which the place proposed to be specified in the order is situated and the notice has not been withdrawn.

(8) Before making a curfew order, the court shall obtain and consider information about the place proposed to be specified in the order (including information as to the attitude of persons likely to be affected by the enforced presence there of the offender).

(9) Before making a curfew order in respect of an offender who on conviction is under 16, the court shall obtain and consider information about his family circumstances and the likely effect of such an order on those circumstances.

(10) [Repealed]

(11) The court by which a curfew order is made shall give a copy of the order to the offender and to the responsible officer.

(12) In this Act, 'responsible officer', in relation to an offender subject to a curfew order, means the person who is responsible for monitoring the offender's whereabouts during the curfew periods specified in the order.

Enforcement of Curfew Orders

Schedule 3 to the PCC(S)A 2000 makes provision for breach, revocation and amendment to youth community orders, and sch. 3 applies to curfew orders. See s. 40B of that Act. E11.46

EXCLUSION ORDERS

An exclusion order may be imposed on an offender aged 18 or over only if the offence was committed before 4 April 2005, but the order may be imposed on an offender aged under 18 irrespective of the date on which the offence was committed. In any case the court must have E11.47

been notified that arrangements are available in the local area. Exclusion orders will no longer be available for offenders aged 16 or 17 once the new provisions in the CJA 2003 are fully in force, but that change is not expected to take place before April 2009.

An exclusion order is a youth community order within the meaning of the CJA 2003, s. 147. A number of general provisions relate to youth community orders, and these are set out at **E11.44**.

Powers of Criminal Courts (Sentencing) Act 2000, s. 40A

(1) Where a person aged [under 16] is convicted of an offence, the court by or before which he is convicted may (subject to sections 148, 150 and 156 of the Criminal Justice Act 2003) make an order prohibiting him from entering a place specified in the order for a period so specified of not more than three months.

(2) An order under subsection (1) above is in this Act referred to as an 'exclusion order'.

(3) An exclusion order—

(a) may provide for the prohibition to operate only during the periods specified in the order;

(b) may specify different places for different periods or days.

(4) [Repealed]

(5) The requirements in an exclusion order shall, as far as practicable, be such as to avoid—

(a) any conflict with the offender's religious beliefs or with the requirements of any other youth community order to which he may be subject; and

(b) any interference with the times, if any, at which he normally works or attends school or any other educational establishment.

(6) An exclusion order shall include provision for making a person responsible for monitoring the offender's whereabouts during the periods when the prohibition operates; and a person who is made so responsible shall be of a description specified in an order made by the Secretary of State.

An exclusion order shall specify the local justice area in which the offender resides or will reside (s. 40A(7)). The court must not make an exclusion order unless the court has been notified that arrangements for monitoring the offender are available in the relevant area (s. 40A(8)). The court must, before making an exclusion order, obtain and consider information about the young offender's family circumstances and the likely effect of such an order on those circumstances (s. 40A(9)). The court must give a copy of the order to the offender and the responsible officer, and give to any affected person any information relating to the order that the court considers appropriate (s. 40A(11)). An 'affected person' is either a person whose consent is required to the inclusion of a requirement under s. 36B (electronic monitoring of the exclusion order) or a person for whom the exclusion is designed (wholly or partly) to protect from being approached by the young offender (s. 40A(13)).

Breach, Revocation and Amendment of Exclusion Order

E11.48 The PCC(S)A 2000, sch. 3, makes provision for breach, revocation and amendment of youth community orders (see s. 40B of that Act) and sch. 3 applies to exclusion orders.

ATTENDANCE CENTRE ORDERS

E11.49 An attendance centre order may be imposed on an offender aged 18, 19 or 20 only if the offence is punishable with imprisonment and was committed before 4 April 2005, but the order may be imposed on an offender aged under 18 irrespective of the date on which the offence was committed. Attendance centre orders will no longer be available for offenders aged 16 or 17 once the new provisions in the CJA 2003 are fully in force, but that change is not expected to take place before April 2009.

An attendance centre order may also be made in respect of an offender aged under 25 who would be liable to be committed to custody for default or in contempt.

Powers of Criminal Courts (Sentencing) Act 2000, s. 60

(1) Where—

(a) (subject to sections 148, 150 and 156 of the Criminal Justice Act 2003) a person aged [under 16] is convicted by or before a court of an offence punishable with imprisonment, or

(b) a court has power or would have power, but for section 89 below (restrictions on imprisonment of young offenders and defaulters), to commit a person aged under 16 to prison in default of payment of any sum of money or for failing to do or abstain from doing anything required to be done or left undone,

the court may, if it has been notified by the Secretary of State that an attendance centre is available for the reception of persons of his description, order him to attend at such a centre, to be specified in the order, for such number of hours as may be so specified.

(2) An order under subsection (1) above is in this Act referred to as an 'attendance centre order'.

The words 'has power or' in s. 60(1)(b) were added by the CJCSA 2000, sch. 7, para. 173, which is not yet in force.

Attendance centre orders may be made by a youth court or the Crown Court. Section 89 prohibits a court from passing a sentence of imprisonment on a person under 21.

An attendance centre order can be made by a court only if:

(a) it has been so notified by the Secretary of State in accordance with s. 60(1); and
(b) the court is satisfied that the centre to be specified in the order is reasonably accessible to the offender, having regard to his age, the means of access available to him and any other circumstances (s. 60(6)).

Hours of Attendance Section 60(3) and (4) of the PCC(S)A 2000 contain provisions relating to the aggregate number of hours of attendance. First, the aggregate number of hours which form the duration of the order must be specified in the order and must be not less than 12, except where the offender is aged under 14 and in the opinion of the court 12 hours would be excessive, having regard to his age or other circumstances (s. 60(3)). Secondly, the aggregate number of hours must not exceed 12, except where the court is of opinion, having regard to all the circumstances, that 12 hours would be inadequate, in which case it must not exceed 24 hours (s. 60(4)). **E11.50**

A court may, however, pass a further attendance centre order upon an offender before an earlier one imposed on him has ceased to have effect, without regard to the number of hours specified in the earlier order or to the fact that it is still in effect (s. 60(5)). The order must specify the time at which the offender is first to attend (s. 60(8)), but subsequent times shall be fixed by the officer in charge of the centre (s. 60(9)). In any event, an offender shall not be required to attend a centre on more than one occasion on any day, or for more than three hours on any one occasion (s. 60(10)). The times at which an offender is required to attend at an attendance centre shall, as far as practicable, avoid any conflict with the offender's religious beliefs or with the requirements of any other youth community order to which he may be subject and interference with the times at which he works, attends school or any other educational establishment (s. 60(7)).

Order in Default of Payment Where the attendance centre order is passed in default of payment of any sum of money, payment of the whole sum discharges the order, and payment of a proportion of the sum reduces the number of hours to be served under the order by the same proportion, rounded down to the nearest complete hour (PCC(S)A 2000, s. 60(12)). **E11.51**

Revocation and Amendment of Attendance Centre Orders

An attendance centre order may be revoked on application to a court by the offender or the officer in charge of the centre. Such court shall be either a magistrates' court acting for the petty sessions area in which the attendance centre is situated or the court which made the **E11.52** order (PCC(S)A 2000, sch. 5, para. 4(2)(b)). The Crown Court may reserve to itself the power to revoke the order (para. 4(2)(a)).

Paragraph 4(3) provides that, where a magistrates' court revokes an attendance centre order made by a magistrates' court, or the Crown Court revokes such an order made by the Crown Court, the court has power to deal with the original offence in any manner in which the offender could have been dealt with for that offence by the court which made the order, if the order had not been made.

An application for variation may be made by the offender or the officer in charge of the centre, to a magistrates' court acting for the petty sessions area in which the centre is situated (para. 5(1)). The court may vary the starting day or hour of the order, or may substitute another attendance centre (para. 5(2)).

Breach of Attendance Centre Orders

E11.53 Where it appears on information to a justice acting for the petty sessions area in which the attendance centre is situated, or if the order was made by a magistrates' court, the petty sessions area for which that court was acting (PCC(S)A 2000, sch. 5, para. 1(1)), that the offender has failed without reasonable excuse to attend or has committed a breach of the rules for the regulation and management of attendance centres made by the Secretary of State by statutory instrument, which cannot be adequately dealt with under those rules, and it is proved to the satisfaction of the court that he has so failed or has so committed a breach of the rules, the court may, without revoking the order, impose a fine not exceeding £1,000, or, if the order was made by a magistrates' court, the magistrates' court before which the offender is brought has power to revoke the order and deal with the offender for the original offence, in any manner in which he could have been dealt with for that offence by the court which made the order if that order had not been made (sch. 5, para. 2(1)). If the order was made by the Crown Court, the magistrates' court may commit him in custody or release him on bail until he can appear before the Crown Court. The magistrates' court should provide a certificate signed by a justice of the peace giving particulars of the case (para. 2(7)), though this is not conclusive of the failure to attend or breach of the rules, which must be specifically proved before the Crown Court. The Crown Court has powers to revoke the order and deal with the offender for the original offence which are parallel to those of the magistrates' court.

If the court, when dealing with a breach, acts to revoke the order and deal with the offender in respect of which the order was made, it must take into account the extent to which the offender has complied with the requirements of the attendance centre order (para. 2(5)(a)). Further, where the offender has 'wilfully and persistently failed to comply' with the requirements of the order, the court may then deal with the offender by way of a custodial sentence (para. 2(5)(b)). For the situation where an attendance centre order is made on appeal, see para. 6.

SUPERVISION ORDERS

Power to Make Supervision Orders

E11.54 By virtue of the PCC(S)A 2000, s. 63, a supervision order may be made by a youth court or by the Crown Court, where a person aged under 18 is found guilty of an offence.

Powers of Criminal Courts (Sentencing) Act 2000, s. 63

(1) Where a child or young person (that is to say, a person aged under 18) is convicted of an offence, the court by or before which he is convicted may (subject to sections 148, 150 and 156 of the Criminal Justice Act 2003) make an order placing him under the supervision of—
 (a) a local authority designated by the order;

(b) an officer of a local probation board; or
(c) a member of a youth offending team.
(2) An order under subsection (1) above is in this Act referred to as a 'supervision order'.
(3) In this Act 'supervisor', in relation to a supervision order, means the person under whose supervision the offender is placed or to be placed by the order.
(4) Schedule 6 to this Act (which specifies requirements that may be included in supervision orders) shall have effect.
(5) A court shall not make a supervision order unless it is satisfied that the offender resides or will reside in the area of a local authority; and a court shall be entitled to be satisfied that the offender will so reside if he is to be required so to reside by a provision to be included in the order in pursuance of paragraph 1 of schedule 6 to this Act.
(6) A supervision order—
(a) shall name the area of the local authority and the local justice area in which it appears to the court making the order (or to the court amending under schedule 7 to this Act any provision included in the order in pursuance of this paragraph) that the offender resides or will reside; and
(b) may contain such prescribed provisions as the court making the order (or amending it under that schedule) considers appropriate for facilitating the performance by the supervisor of his functions under section 64(4) below, including any prescribed functions for requiring visits to be made by the offender to the supervisor;

and in paragraph (b) above 'prescribed' means prescribed by Criminal Procedure Rules.

A supervision order will last for three years from the date on which it was made, or for such shorter period as may be specified in the order (s. 63(7)). In every case, the duty of the supervisor is to 'advise, assist and befriend the offender (s. 64(4)). Section 64 provides further details as to the selection and duty of the supervisor, and s. 67 is a definition section. A supervision order does not require the consent of the offender, but the court may not insert a requirement of treatment for a mental condition (see **E24.3**) without the offender's consent where the offender has attained the age of 14.

The PCC(S)A 2000, s. 64A, provides that nothing prevents a court which makes a supervision order on an offender from also making a curfew order.

Requirements in Supervision Orders

The basic supervision order may be supplemented where appropriate with various requirements. **E11.55**

Powers of Criminal Courts (Sentencing) Act 2000, sch. 6, para. 1

(1) A supervision order may require the offender to reside with an individual named in the order who agrees to the requirement, but a requirement imposed by a supervision order in pursuance of this paragraph shall be subject to any such requirement of the order as is authorised by paragraph 2, 3, 6, 6A or 7 below.

The exceptions relate to cases where a supervised person may from time to time be obliged to reside elsewhere by virtue of a requirement made under one of the other paragraphs of sch. 6.

Powers of Criminal Courts (Sentencing) Act 2000, sch. 6, para. 2

(1) Subject to sub-paragraph (2) below, a supervision order may require the offender to comply with any directions given from time to time by the supervisor and requiring him to do all or any of the following things—
(a) to live at a place or places specified in the directions for a period or periods so specified;
(b) to present himself to a person or persons specified in the directions at a place or places and on a day or days so specified;
(c) to participate in activities specified in the directions on a day or days so specified.

The number of days in respect of which the supervisor may give directions is fixed by the court up to a maximum of 180 (para. 2(5)). It shall be for the supervisor to decide whether and to what extent he exercises power to give directions conferred on him by virtue of para.

2(1) and the form of any directions (para. 2(4)). A requirement imposed in pursuance of para. 2(1) shall be subject to any requirement authorised by para. 6 (treatment for offender's mental condition) (para. 2(3)). Intermediate treatment ordered under para. 2 leaves the implementation to the discretion of the supervisor.

E11.56 **Court Imposed Requirements** Requirements as to activities may be included by virtue of sch. 6, para. 3, rather than under para. 2. Under para. 3, the court may itself require the offender to do anything which the supervisor may have required him to do under para. 2, and nominate the place where the offender is to live or attend, and the activities he is to participate in.

Powers of Criminal Courts (Sentencing) Act 2000, sch. 6, para. 3

(1) This paragraph applies to a supervision order unless the order requires the offender to comply with directions given by the supervisor under paragraph 2(1) above.
(2) Subject to the following provisions of this paragraph and paragraph 4 below, a supervision order to which this paragraph applies may require the offender—
  (a) to live at a place or places specified in the order for a period or periods so specified;
  (b) to present himself to a person or persons specified in the order at a place or places and on a day or days so specified;
  (c) to participate in activities specified in the order on a day or days so specified;
  (d) to make reparation specified in the order to a person or persons specified or to the community at large;
  (e) [repealed]
  (f) to refrain from participating in activities specified in the order—
    (i) on a specified day or days during the period for which the supervision order is in force; or
    (ii) during the whole of that period or a specified portion of it;
  and in this paragraph 'make reparation' means make reparation for the offence otherwise than by payment of compensation.

The maximum number of days in respect of which such requirements may be made under para. 3(2)(a) to (e) is 180. Before making any order under para. 3(2), the court must be satisfied, after consultation with the supervisor as to the offender's circumstances and the feasibility of securing compliance with the requirements, that compliance is feasible; that the requirements are necessary for securing the good conduct of the offender or for preventing a repetition by him of the same offence or the commission of other offences; and that, if the offender is under the age of 16, it has obtained and considered information about his family circumstances and the likely effect of the requirements on those circumstances (para. 3(4)). The court must not by para. 3(2) include any requirement that would require the cooperation of a person other than the supervisor and the offender, without that other person's consent; or include any requirement to make reparation to any person unless that person is identified as a victim of the offence or a person otherwise affected by it, and consents to the inclusion of the requirement. Nor may the court include by para. 3(2) any requirement that the person resides with a specified individual or a requirement as to treatment for the offender's mental condition (para. 3(5)).

Local Authority Residence Requirement

E11.57 **Powers of Criminal Courts (Sentencing) Act 2000, sch. 6, para. 5**

(1) Where the conditions mentioned in sub-paragraph (2) below are satisfied, a supervision order may impose a requirement ('a local authority residence requirement') that the offender shall live for a specified period in local authority accommodation (as defined by section 163 of this Act).
(2) The conditions are that—
  (a) a supervision order has previously been made in respect of the offender;
  (b) that order imposed—
    (i) a requirement under paragraph 1, 2, 3 or 7 of this schedule; or
    (ii) a local authority residence requirement;

(c) the offender fails to comply with that requirement, or is convicted of an offence committed while that order was in force; and
(d) the court is satisfied that—
(i) the failure to comply with the requirement, or the behaviour which constituted the offence, was due to a significant extent to the circumstances in which the offender was living; and
(ii) the imposition of a local authority residence requirement will assist in his rehabilitation;

except that sub-paragraph (i) of paragraph (d) above does not apply where the condition in paragraph (b)(ii) above is satisfied.

A local authority residence requirement must designate the local authority in whose area the offender resides, and the court must first consult the designated authority. The requirement may last for a maximum of six months. It may stipulate that the offender shall *not* live with a named person. A local authority residence requirement cannot be imposed by a court on an offender who is not represented at the relevant time in that court unless the offender was granted a right to representation but the right was withdrawn because of his conduct, or he has been informed of his right to apply for representation and has had the opportunity to do so, but has refused or failed to apply. A supervision order which includes a local authority residence requirement may also include any of the requirements mentioned in paras. 2, 3, 6 and 7 (para. 5(3) to (9)).

Foster Parent Residence Requirement

Powers of Criminal Courts (Sentencing) Act 2000, sch. 6, para. 5A **E11.58**

(1) Where the conditions mentioned in sub-paragraph (2) below are satisfied, a supervision order may impose a requirement ('a foster parent residence requirement') that the offender shall live for a specified period with a local authority foster parent.
(2) The conditions are that—
(a) the offence is punishable with imprisonment in the case of an offender aged 18 or over;
(b) the offence, or the combination of the offence and one or more offences associated with it, was so serious that a custodial sentence would normally be appropriate (or, where the offender is aged 10 or 11, would normally be appropriate if the offender were aged 12 or over); and
(c) the court is satisfied that—
(i) the behaviour which constituted the offence was due to a significant extent to the circumstances in which the offender was living, and
(ii) the imposition of a foster parent residence requirement will assist in his rehabilitation.

The normal maximum period which may be specified is 12 months (para. 5A(5)). A supervision order imposing such a requirement may also impose any of the requirements mentioned in paras 2, 3, 6 and 7 of sch. 6.

Treatment of Mental Condition

Powers of Criminal Courts (Sentencing) Act 2000, sch. 6, para. 6 **E11.59**

(1) This paragraph applies where a court which proposes to make a supervision order is satisfied, on the evidence of a registered medical practitioner approved for the purposes of section 12 of the Mental Health Act 1983, that the mental health of the offender—
(a) is such as requires and may be susceptible to treatment; but
(b) is not such as to warrant the making of a hospital order or guardianship order within the meaning of that Act.
(2) Where this paragraph applies, the court may include in the supervision order a requirement that the offender shall, for a period specified in the order, submit to treatment of one of the following descriptions so specified, that is to say—
(a) treatment as a resident patient in an independent hospital or care home within the meaning of the Care Standards Act 2000, or a hospital within the meaning of the Mental Health Act 1983, but not a hospital at which high security psychiatric services within the meaning of that Act are provided;
(b) treatment as a non-resident patient at an institution or place specified in the order;

(c) treatment by or under the direction of a registered medical practitioner specified in the order;
(d) treatment by or under the direction of a chartered psychologist specified in the order.

A requirement of treatment for a mental condition cannot be included unless the court is satisfied that arrangements have been made or can be made for the treatment in question, and in the case of treatment as a resident patient, for the reception of that patient (para. 6(3)). If the offender is aged 14 or over, such a requirement cannot be included by the court unless the offender consents to its inclusion. In no case must such a requirement continue in force after the supervised person has attained the age of 18 (para. 6(3)).

Drug Treatment

E11.60 **Powers of Criminal Courts (Sentencing) Act 2000, sch. 6, para. 6A**

(1) This paragraph applies where a court proposing to make a supervision order is satisfied—
(a) that the offender is dependent on, or has a propensity to misuse, drugs, and
(b) that his dependency or propensity is such as requires and may be susceptible to treatment.
(2) Where this paragraph applies, the court may include in the supervision order a requirement that the offender shall, for a period specified in the order ('the treatment period') submit to treatment by or under the direction of a specified person having the necessary qualifications and experience ('the treatment provider') with a view to the reduction or elimination of the offender's dependency on or propensity to misuse drugs.
(3) The required treatment shall be—
(a) treatment in such institution or place as may be specified in the order, or
(b) treatment as a non-resident at such institution or place, and at such intervals, as may be so specified;
but the nature of the treatment shall not be specified in the order except as mentioned in paragraph (a) or (b) above.

A requirement under para. 6A cannot be included in a supervision order unless the court is satisfied that arrangements have been made or can be made for the treatment intended to be specified in the order and that the requirement has been recommended to the court as suitable for the offender by an officer of the local probation board or by a member of a youth offending team and (in the case of an offender aged 14 or over) unless he consents to its inclusion (para. 6(4)). A supervision order with such a treatment requirement may also include a requirement (a testing requirement) that the offender provide samples of such description as may be determined (para. 6(5)), but a testing requirement cannot be included unless the offender is aged 14 or over and consents to its requirement and the court has been notified that arrangements for implementing such requirements are in force in the relevant area (para. 6(6)).

Education Requirement

E11.61 **Powers of Criminal Courts (Sentencing) Act 2000, sch. 6, para. 7**

(1) This paragraph applies to a supervision order unless the order requires the offender to comply with directions given by the supervisor under paragraph 2(1) above.
(2) Subject to the following provisions of this paragraph, a supervision order to which this paragraph applies may require the offender, if he is of compulsory school age, to comply, for as long as he is of that age and the order remains in force, with such arrangements for his education as may from time to time be made by his parent, being arrangements for the time being approved by the local education authority.

The court must not include such an education requirement under para. 7 unless it has consulted the relevant local education authority and it is satisfied of the authority's view that educational arrangements appropriate for the offender can be made (para. 7(3)).

Expressions used in para. 7 and in the Education Act 1996 have the same meaning as in that Act (para. 7(4)). The court may not make a requirement under para. 7 unless it has consulted the supervisor about the offender's circumstances, and thereby considers the requirement necessary for securing the good conduct of the offender or for preventing a repetition by him of the same offence or the commission of other offences (para. 7(5)).

Breach of Supervision Order

By the PCC(S)A 2000, sch. 7, para. 2, where it is proved to the satisfaction of a relevant court, on the application of the supervisor, that the offender has failed to comply with any of the requirements of the order included pursuant to paras. 1, 2, 3, 5, 5A, 6A, or 7 of sch. 6 or s. 63(6)(b) of the 2000 Act, then, whether or not it also revokes or amends the supervision order, the court may order payment of a fine not exceeding £1,000, or, subject to sch. 7, para. 3, may make a curfew order under s. 37 (unless the offender is subject to a curfew order) or, subject to para. 4, may make an attendance centre order. The term 'relevant court' means, in the case of an offender under the age of 18, a youth court and, in the case of an offender who has attained that age, an adult magistrates' court (para. 1). If the supervision order was made by a relevant court, it may revoke the order and deal with the offender for the offence in respect of which the order was made in any manner in which he could have been dealt with for that offence by the court which made the order if the order had not been made. If the supervision order was made by the Crown Court, the relevant court may commit him in custody or release him on bail until he can be brought or appear before the Crown Court. Where the original order was made by the Crown Court, the relevant court should send to the Crown Court a certificate giving details of the offender's failure to comply with the requirement in question and such other particulars as may be desirable. Where the offender is committed to the Crown Court and it is proved to the satisfaction of the Crown Court that the offender has failed to comply with the requirement, the Crown Court may deal with him for the offence in respect of which the order was made in any manner in which it could have dealt with him for that offence if it had not made the order. Where the Crown Court so deals with an offender, it must also discharge the supervision order if it is still in force (para. 2(5)). E11.62

The court dealing with the breach must take account of the extent to which the offender has complied with the requirements of the supervision order (para. 2(7)).

Revocation and Amendment of Supervision Order

During the currency of a supervision order a relevant court may, if appropriate, on the application of the supervisor or the offender, make an order revoking the supervision order (PCC(S)A 2000, sch. 7, para. 5(1)). The relevant court may also vary the supervision order by cancelling any requirement included in it under sch. 6 or s. 63(6)(b) or by inserting any provision which could have been included in the order. There are also limitations upon the court's powers to vary a requirement under para. 6 relating to medical treatment. E11.63

ACTION PLAN ORDERS

An action plan order is available only in respect of offenders aged under 18 at the time of commission of the offence. E11.64

Powers of Criminal Courts (Sentencing) Act 2000, ss. 69 and 70

69.—(1) Where a child or young person (that is to say, any person aged under 18) is convicted of an offence and the court by or before which he is convicted is of the opinion mentioned in subsection (3) below, the court may (subject to sections 148, 150 and 156 of the Criminal Justice Act 2003) make an order which—

(a) requires the offender, for a period of three months beginning with the date of the order, to comply with an action plan, that is to say, a series of requirements with respect to his actions and whereabouts during that period;

(b) places the offender for that period under the supervision of the responsible officer; and

(c) requires the offender to comply with any directions given by the responsible officer with a view to the implementation of that plan;

and the requirements included in the order, and any directions given by the responsible officer, may include requirements authorised by section 70 below.

(2) An order under subsection (1) above is in this Act referred to as an 'action plan order'.

(3) The opinion referred to in subsection (1) above is that the making of an action plan order is desirable in the interests of—

(a) securing the rehabilitation of the offender; or

(b) preventing the commission by him of further offences.

(4) In this Act 'responsible officer', in relation to an offender subject to an action plan order, means one of the following who is specified in the order, namely—

(a) an officer of a local probation board;

(b) a social worker of a local authority social services department;

(c) a member of a youth offending team.

(5) The court shall not make an action plan order in respect of the offender if—

(a) he is already the subject of such an order; or

(b) the court proposes to pass on him a custodial sentence or to make in respect of him a community order under section 177 of the Criminal Justice Act 2003, an attendance centre order, a supervision order or a referral order.

(6) Before making an action plan order, the court shall obtain and consider—

(a) a written report by an officer of a local probation board, a social worker of a local authority social services department or a member of a youth offending team indicating—

(i) the requirements proposed by that person to be included in the order;

(ii) the benefits to the offender that the proposed requirements are designed to achieve; and

(iii) the attitude of a parent or guardian of the offender to the proposed requirements; and

(b) where the offender is aged under 16, information about the offender's family circumstances and the likely effect of the order on those circumstances.

(7) The court shall not make an action plan order unless it has been notified by the Secretary of State that arrangements for implementing such orders are available in the area proposed to be named in the order under subsection (8) below and the notice has not been withdrawn.

(8) An action plan order shall name the local justice area in which it appears to the court making the order (or to the court amending under schedule 8 to this Act any provision included in the order in pursuance of this subsection) that the offender resides or will reside.

(9) Where an action plan order specifies an officer of a local probation board under subsection (4) above, the officer specified must be an officer appointed for or assigned to the local justice area named in the order.

(10) Where an action plan order specifies under that subsection—

(a) a social worker of a local authority social services department, or

(b) a member of a youth offending team,

the social worker or member specified must be a social worker of, or a member of a youth offending team established by, the local authority within whose area it appears to the court that the offender resides or will reside.

(11) [Repealed]

70.—(1) Requirements included in an action plan order, or directions given by a responsible officer, may require the offender to do all or any of the following things, namely—

(a) to participate in activities specified in the requirements or directions at a time or times so specified;

(b) to present himself to a person or persons specified in the requirements or directions at a place or places and at a time or times so specified;

(c) subject to subsection (2) below, to attend at an attendance centre specified in the requirements or directions for a number of hours so specified;

(d) to stay away from a place or places specified in the requirements or directions;

(e) to comply with any arrangements for his education specified in the requirements or directions;

(f) to make reparation specified in the requirements or directions to a person or persons so specified or to the community at large; and

(g) to attend any hearing fixed by the court under section 71 below.

(2) Subsection (1)(c) above applies only where the offence committed by the offender is an offence punishable with imprisonment.

(3) In subsection (1) (f) above 'make reparation', in relation to an offender, means make reparation for the offence otherwise than by the payment of compensation.

(4) A person shall not be specified in requirements or directions under subsection (1)(f) above unless—

(a) he is identified by the court or (as the case may be) the responsible officer as a victim of the offence or a person otherwise affected by it; and

(b) he consents to the reparation being made.

(4A) Subsection (4B) below applies where a court proposing to make an action plan order is satisfied—

(a) that the offender is dependent on, or has a propensity to misuse, drugs, and

(b) that his dependency or propensity is such as requires and is susceptible to treatment.

(4B) Where this subsection applies, requirements included in an action plan order may require the offender for a period specified in the order ('the treatment period') to submit to treatment by or under the direction of a specified person having the necessary qualifications and experience ('the treatment provider') with a view to the reduction or elimination of the offender's dependency on or propensity to misuse drugs.

(4C) to (4H) [These subsections are omitted here but are in virtually identical terms to the PCC(S)A 2000, sch. 6, para. 6A(3) to (8) (supervision orders: requirements as to drug treatment and testing) see **E11.60**].

(5) Requirements included in an action plan order and directions given by a responsible officer shall, as far as practicable, be such as to avoid—

(a) any conflict with the offender's religious beliefs or with the requirements of any other youth community order or any community order to which he may be subject; and

(b) any interference with the times, if any, at which he normally works or attends school or any other educational establishment.

Subsections (4A) to (4H) of s. 70 came into force on 1 December 2004 and apply to offences committed on or after that date. They apply in certain areas only (SI 2004 No. 3033), namely Bradford, Calderdale, Keighley, Manchester and Newham and part of Teesside.

The requirement of attendance at an attendance centre in s. 70(1)(c) is restricted by s. 70(2) to cases in which the offender has committed an offence punishable with imprisonment in the case of an adult. For attendance centre orders, see **E11.49**. The requirement to make reparation in s. 70(1)(f) may be compared with the equivalent provision in relation to reparation orders: see **E13**. The wording of s. 70(4) indicates that the court may require reparation to be made to a person who is the victim of the offence or someone 'otherwise affected' by it. Thus the court might require reparation to be made by the offender to the victim of an assault committed by him, and/or to be made to a bystander who suffered shock as a result of witnessing the assault.

The court may pass an action plan order without first obtaining a pre-sentence report, but s. 69(6) requires that before making such an order the court must obtain and consider a written report by a probation officer, a social worker or a member of a youth offending team.

Immediately after making the order the court may fix a further hearing for a date not more than 21 days ahead and direct the officer to make at that hearing a report as to the effectiveness of the order and the extent to which it has been implemented (s. 71(1)). At such a hearing, the court, after considering the officer's report may, on the application of the officer or the offender, vary the order by cancelling any provision included in it or by inserting in it any provision which that court could originally have included (s. 71(2)).

Mixing Action Plan Orders with Other Sentences or Orders

Section 69(5) of the PCC(S)A 2000 makes it clear that an action plan order cannot be imposed where the court also passes on the offender a custodial sentence or one of a range of **E11.65** other community orders. Section 69(5) does not mention curfew orders, so presumably an action plan order could be combined with a curfew order. Although s. 69(5) does not mention reparation orders, the relevant provision on reparation orders (s. 73(4)) states that reparation orders and action plan orders cannot be combined. There is nothing to prevent an action plan order being combined with a fine, or with ancillary orders such as a compensation order or a deprivation order under s. 143.

Breach and Revocation of Action Plan Orders and Reparation Orders

E11.66 Arrangements for discharge or variation, and for dealing with the offender's failure to comply with the terms of an action plan order (or reparation order) are set out in the PCC(S)A 2000, sch. 8. Where an action plan order or reparation order is in force and it is proved to the satisfaction of the appropriate youth court, on the application of the responsible officer, that the offender has failed to comply with any requirement in the order, the court shall proceed as follows.

Powers of Criminal Courts (Sentencing) Act 2000, sch. 8, para. 2

(1) This paragraph applies if while an action plan order or reparation order is in force in respect of an offender it is proved to the satisfaction of the appropriate court, on the application of the responsible officer, that the offender has failed to comply with any requirement included in the order.

(2) Where this paragraph applies, the court—

(a) whether or not it also makes an order under paragraph 5(1) below (revocation or amendment of order)—

(i) may order the offender to pay a fine of an amount not exceeding £1,000; or

(ii) subject to paragraph 3 below, may make a curfew order in respect of him; or

(iii) subject to paragraph 4 below, may make an attendance centre order in respect of him; or

(b) if the action plan order or reparation order was made by a magistrates' court, may revoke the order and deal with the offender, for the offence in respect of which the order was made, in any way in which he could have been dealt with for that offence by the court which made the order if the order had not been made; or

(c) if the action plan order or reparation order was made by the Crown Court, may commit him in custody or release him on bail until he can be brought or appear before the Crown Court.

Where the youth court proceeds under para. 2(2)(c), it must send to the Crown Court a certificate detailing the offender's failure to comply, together with such other particulars as may be desirable. Where the offender appears before the Crown Court, and it is proved to the satisfaction of the court that he has failed to comply with the relevant order, that court may deal with him for the offence in respect of which the order was made, in any manner in which it could have dealt with him for the offence if it had not made the order. Where the Crown Court so deals with the offender, it must revoke the action plan order or reparation order, if it is still in force. Whether the offender is dealt with by the youth court or the Crown Court, the court when dealing with the failure to comply must take into account the extent to which the offender has complied with the terms of the order (para. 3(3) to (7)).

Paragraphs 5 and 7 deal with further procedural and supplemental matters, including the requirement that the offender shall normally be present before the court which is dealing with his failure to comply with the order.

Section E12 Referral Order

Under part III of the PCC(S)A 2000, a youth court or, exceptionally, an adult magistrates' court, dealing with an offender under the age of 18 for whom this is his first conviction, is in certain circumstances required to sentence the young offender by ordering him to be referred to a youth offender panel. In other circumstances the court has a discretion to deal with the young offender in that way. The youth offender panel is composed of people with an interest or expertise in dealing with young people. The panel agrees a 'contract' with the offender and his family which is aimed at tackling the offending behaviour and its causes. The contract sets out certain requirements, which may include the young offender being required to apologise to, and carry out some form of reparation for, the victim of the offence, or to carry out community work, or to take part in family counselling or drug rehabilitation. These requirements are specified by the youth offender panel rather than the sentencing court, and are not dealt with further here.

Requirement to Refer, and Power to Refer, Young Offender to a Youth Offender Panel

The circumstances which must exist before the court is *required* to make a referral order are set out in PCC(S)A 2000, ss. 16 and 17(1). In respect of s. 16, they are as follows: **E12.1**

(a) that the youth court (or other magistrates' court) is dealing with an offender under the age of 18 where neither the offence nor any associated offence is one for which the sentence is fixed by law;
(b) the court is not proposing to pass a custodial sentence or make a hospital order in respect of the offence or any associated offence;
(c) the court is not proposing to grant an absolute discharge in respect of the offence;
(d) the compulsory referral conditions set out in s. 17 are satisfied; and
(e) the court has been notified by the Secretary of State that arrangements for the implementation of referral orders are available in the area in which the young offender resides or will reside.

The compulsory referral conditions referred to are set out in s. 17(1). They are satisfied in relation to an offence if the offence is punishable with imprisonment and the offender:

(a) pleaded guilty to the offence and to any associated offence;
(b) has never been convicted by or before a court in the United Kingdom of any offence other than the offence and any associated offence; and
(c) has never been bound over in criminal proceedings in England and Wales or Northern Ireland to keep the peace or to be of good behaviour.

Non-imprisonable offences were removed from the scope of compulsory referral by the Reference Orders (Amendment of Referral Conditions) Regulations 2003 (SI 2003 No. 1605), which came into force on 18 August 2003.

The circumstances which must exist before a court has *power* to make a referral order, but is not under a requirement to do so, are set out in ss. 16 and 17(2). The applicable parts of s. 16 (referred to above) are (a) to (c) and (e). The terms of s. 17(2) are satisfied in relation to an offence if:

(a) the offender is being dealt with by the court for the offence and one or more associated offences, whether or not any of them is an offence punishable with imprisonment;
(b) although he pleaded guilty to at least one of the offences mentioned in paragraph (a), he also pleaded not guilty to at least one of them;
(c) he has never been convicted by or before a court in the United Kingdom of any offence other than the offences mentioned in paragraph (a); and
(d) he has never been bound over in criminal proceedings in England and Wales or Northern Ireland to keep the peace or to be of good behaviour.

In relation to s. 17(1)(b) and (2)(c), s. 17(5) makes it clear that an offence in respect of which the offender has previously been conditionally discharged does count as a conviction for these purposes, notwithstanding the PCC(S)A 2000, s. 14 (see **E14.6**). It appears that the wording of s. 17(2)(b) is satisfied even if the young offender is acquitted of the offence or offences to which he pleaded not guilty.

Making of Referral Orders

E12.2 The referral order must specify the relevant youth offending team responsible for implementing the order, require the offender to attend each of the appropriate meetings of the panel, and specify the period (the 'compliance period') during which the youth offender contract is to have effect. The minimum compliance period is three months and the maximum period is one year (s. 18(1)). It is submitted that the length of the compliance period should reflect the seriousness of the offending behaviour and the age of the offender. When making the order, the court must explain to the young offender in ordinary language the effect of the order and the consequences which may follow if there is a failure to agree the terms of the contract or if the young offender breaches the terms of the contract (s. 18(3)). Where the court is dealing with the young offender for associated offences and is passing more than one referral order, the court may order that the specified periods of the orders shall run concurrently or consecutively to one another, but the total period shall not exceed 12 months (s. 18(4) to (7)).

In the case of a young offender who is under the age of 16 when the order is made, the court must, and in any other case may, make an order requiring the parent or guardian of the young offender (or a representative of a local authority where that local authority has parental responsibility and the young offender is in the authority's care or is provided by them with accommodation under any statutory provision) to attend the relevant meetings of the youth offender panel (s. 20(1) and (2)). This does not apply if the court is satisfied that in the circumstances of the case it would be unreasonable to require such attendance (s. 20(3)).

Mixing Referral Orders with Other Sentences or Orders

E12.3 There are very strict limitations on the mixing of a referral order with other sentences or orders. A referral order cannot be made where the court imposes a custodial sentence or hospital order on the offender for the offence or for any associated offence, or where it grants an absolute discharge for the offence (PCC(S)A 2000, s. 16(1)(c)). Where the court makes a referral order for an offence, it must not at the same time deal with the offender for that offence in any of the 'prohibited ways', which are to impose any community sentence, fine, reparation order or conditional discharge (s. 19(4)). Where the court makes a referral order for an offence, it is required to deal with any associated offence either by making a referral order or by passing an absolute discharge, and it must not deal with any associated offence in any of the 'prohibited ways' (s. 19(3)). Whether in respect of the offence for which the referral order is made or for any associated offence, the court must not make an order binding over the young offender to keep the peace (see **E15.1**) or binding over the parent or guardian of the young offender under s. 150 (see **E16.5**). Finally, where there is a requirement rather than a power to make a referral order, the court may not defer passing sentence on the young offender (see **D19.101**), although other specified powers of adjournment, remand, remission for sentence and committal for sentence are unaffected (s. 19(7)). Notwithstanding all these restrictions, it would still be permissible for the court, at the same time as making a referral order, in an appropriate case to make a compensation order under s. 130, a restitution order under s. 148 (see **E19**) or a deprivation order under s. 143 (see **E20**). By the CJA 2003, s. 324 and sch. 34, a court sentencing a young offender by referral order may at the same time make a parenting order under the CDA 1998, s. 8 (see **E16.1**). This combination was formerly not permissible.

Breach, Revocation and Amendment of Referral Orders

Provisions for dealing with a young offender who is referred back to court in breach of a referral order, or is convicted while subject to a referral order, are set out in the PCC(S)A 2000, sch. 1. In the case of a young offender who is under the age of 18 when he appears in court having been referred back, the appropriate court is the youth court acting for the relevant petty sessions area and, if he is 18 or over at that time, it is a magistrates' court acting for that area (para. 1). **E12.4**

If it is proved to the satisfaction of the court that the youth offender panel was entitled to make the finding of breach of the referral order which resulted in the young offender being referred back to court, or that any discretion of the panel in that respect was exercised reasonably, the court may (provided that the young offender is present before it) revoke the referral order and may deal with the young offender in any other manner in which he could have been dealt with for that offence by the court which made the order (para. 5(5)(a)). The court must have regard to the circumstances of his referral back to court and, where a contract has taken effect, the extent of his compliance with it (para. 5(5)(b)). The court may, on the other hand, decide not to revoke the referral order, either because the court does not endorse the decision of the panel to refer the order back to the court or for any other reason (para. 7).

Where an offender who is subject to a referral order is convicted of an offence, the court dealing with the offence may, if that offence was committed before the referral order was made, sentence the offender for the new offence by extending the compliance period of the referral order (para. 11). The court may adopt a similar course even where the offence was committed after the referral order was made, but only if the court is satisfied that 'exceptional circumstances' exist, and states in open court why it is so satisfied (para. 12). In neither of these situations, however, can the compliance period be extended so as to exceed 12 months. Apart from cases falling within para. 11 or 12, the court will deal with the commission of a further offence under para. 14, which states that, unless the court sentencing for the new offence deals with the case by way of absolute discharge, the effect of dealing with the offender for the further offence is to revoke the referral order. The court may, if it is in the interests of justice, deal with the offender for the original offence in any other manner in which the offender could have been dealt with for that offence by the court which made the referral order (para. 14(3)). The court must have regard, where a contract has taken effect, to the extent to which the young offender has complied with its terms (para. 14(4)).

The court which made the referral order may vary the youth offending team specified in the order because of the young offender's change of residence (s. 21(5)).

Section E13 Reparation Orders

Under ss. 73 and 74 of the PCC(S)A 2000, the Crown Court and youth courts have power to impose a reparation order on an offender aged under 18 who is convicted of any offence except murder.

Power to Make a Reparation Order

E13.1 A reparation order is *not* a 'community sentence' within the meaning of the CJA 2003, s. 147.

Powers of Criminal Courts (Sentencing) Act 2000, ss. 73 and 74

73.—(1) Where a child or young person (that is to say, any person aged under 18) is convicted of an offence other than one for which the sentence is fixed by law, the court by or before which he is convicted may make an order requiring him to make reparation specified in the order—

(a) to a person or persons so specified; or

(b) to the community at large;

and any person so specified must be a person identified by the court as a victim of the offence or a person otherwise affected by it.

(2) An order under subsection (1) above is in this Act referred to as a 'reparation order'.

(3) In this section and section 74 below 'make reparation', in relation to an offender, means make reparation for the offence otherwise than by the payment of compensation; and the requirements that may be specified in a reparation order are subject to section 74(1) to (3).

(4) The court shall not make a reparation order in respect of the offender if it proposes—

(a) to pass on him a custodial sentence; or

(b) to make in respect of him a community order under section 177 of the Criminal Justice Act 2003, a supervision order which includes requirements authorised by schedule 6 to this Act, an action plan order or a referral order.

(5) Before making a reparation order, a court shall obtain and consider a written report by an officer of a local probation board, a social worker of a local authority social services department or a member of a youth offending team indicating—

(a) the type of work that is suitable for the offender; and

(b) the attitude of the victim or victims to the requirements proposed to be included in the order.

(6) The court shall not make a reparation order unless it has been notified by the Secretary of State that arrangements for implementing such orders are available in the area proposed to be named in the order under section 74(4) below and the notice has not been withdrawn.

(7) [Repealed]

(8) The court shall give reasons if it does not make a reparation order in a case where it has power to do so.

74.—(1) A reparation order shall not require the offender—

(a) to work for more than 24 hours in aggregate; or

(b) to make reparation to any person without the consent of that person.

(2) Subject to subsection (1) above, requirements specified in a reparation order shall be such as in the opinion of the court are commensurate with the seriousness of the offence, or the combination of the offence and one or more offences associated with it.

(3) Requirements so specified shall, as far as practicable, be such as to avoid—

(a) any conflict with the offender's religious beliefs or with the requirements of any community order or any youth community order to which he may be subject; and

(b) any interference with the times, if any, at which he normally works or attends school or any other educational establishment.

(4) A reparation order shall name the local justice area in which it appears to the court making the order (or to the court amending under schedule 8 to this Act any provision included in the order in pursuance of this subsection) that the offender resides or will reside.
(5) In this Act 'responsible officer', in relation to an offender subject to a reparation order, means one of the following who is specified in the order, namely—
(a) an officer of a local probation board;
(b) a social worker of a local authority social services department;
(c) a member of a youth offending team.
(6) Where a reparation order specifies an officer of a local probation board under subsection (5) above, the officer specified must be an officer appointed for or assigned to the local justice area named in the order.
(7) Where a reparation order specifies under that subsection—
(a) a social worker of a local authority social services department, or
(b) a member of a youth offending team,
the social worker or member specified must be a social worker of, or a member of a youth offending team established by, the local authority within whose area it appears to the court that the offender resides or will reside.
(8) Any reparation required by a reparation order—
(a) shall be made under the supervision of the responsible officer; and
(b) shall be made within a period of three months from the date of the making of the order.

The wording of s. 73(2) indicates that the court may require reparation to be made to a person who is the victim of the offence, or to someone 'otherwise affected' by it. In a case of assault, this might include not just the victim of the assault but, instead or in addition, a bystander who suffered shock as a result of witnessing the assault. Since the reparation order is not a community order, it may be used where the offender has committed an offence which is not serious enough to justify the use of a community sentence although there seems to be no reason why, in an appropriate case, the reparation order could not be used as an alternative to one of the less onerous community orders. Section 74(2) makes it clear that the number of hours of work required of the young offender and, presumably, the nature of that work, must be such as in the opinion of the court are commensurate with the seriousness of the offence committed. A reparation order may be imposed without the court first obtaining a pre-sentence report but, by s. 73(5), before making a reparation order the court must obtain and consider a report from a probation officer, a social worker or a member of a youth offending team indicating the type of work which is suitable for the young offender, and the attitude of the victim, or victims, to the requirements to be included in the order. Before making a reparation order, the court must explain to the offender in ordinary language the effect of the order and of the requirements proposed to be included in it, the consequences which may follow if he fails to comply with any of those requirements, and that the order may be reviewed by the court on the application either of the offender or of the responsible officer (s. 73(7)). Section 73(8) requires the court to give reasons why it has not made a reparation order in a case where it had power to do so. A similar provision exists in relation to compensation orders (see s. 130(3) at **E18.1**).

Mixing Reparation Orders with Other Sentences or Orders

Section 73(4) of the PCC(S)A 2000 makes it clear that a reparation order cannot be imposed where the court also passes on the offender a custodial sentence, or a community order. There is nothing to prevent a reparation order being combined with ancillary orders such as a compensation order or a deprivation order under s. 143. **E13.2**

Breach and Revocation of Reparation Orders

Arrangements for dealing with the offender's failure to comply with the terms of a reparation order are set out in the PCC(S)A 2000, sch. 8. The relevant provisions were considered at E11.66. **E13.3**

Section E14 Absolute and Conditional Discharges

Power to Grant Absolute and Conditional Discharges

E14.1 Powers of Criminal Courts (Sentencing) Act 2000, s. 12

(1) Where a court by or before which a person is convicted of an offence (not being an offence the sentence for which is fixed by law or falls to be imposed under section 110(2) or 111(2) below, section 51A(2) of the Firearms Act 1968 or section 225, 226, 227 or 228 of the Criminal Justice Act 2003 or section 29(4) or (6) of the Violent Crime Reduction Act 2006 is of the opinion, having regard to the circumstances including the nature of the offence and the character of the offender, that it is inexpedient to inflict punishment, the court may make an order either—

(a) discharging him absolutely; or

(b) if the court thinks fit, discharging him subject to the condition that he commits no offence during such period, not exceeding three years from the date of the order, as may be specified in the order.

(2) Subsection 1(b) above has effect subject to section 66(4) of the Crime and Disorder Act 1998 (effect of reprimands and warnings).

(3) An order discharging a person subject to such a condition as is mentioned in subsection (1)(b) above is in this Act referred to as 'an order for conditional discharge'; and the period specified in any such order is in this Act referred to as 'the period of conditional discharge'.

(4) [Repealed]

(5) If (by virtue of section 13 below) a person conditionally discharged under this section is sentenced for the offence in respect of which the order for conditional discharge was made, that order shall cease to have effect.

A discharge is *not* a community sentence within the meaning of the CJA 2003, s. 147.

In *Wehner* [1977] 1 WLR 1143, it was held that while it was 'sound practice' for the court to explain the effect of a conditional discharge to the offender personally, the delegation of the task of explanation to the offender's lawyer is not prohibited, provided that the court is satisfied that the explanation has been made and understood before it makes the order. By s. 12(6), any court may, on making an order for conditional discharge, allow any person who consents to do so to give security for the good behaviour of the offender. Where a conditional discharge has been imposed on appeal, it shall be deemed, if made on appeal from a magistrates' court to have been imposed by that court and, if made on appeal from the Crown Court or the Court of Appeal, to have been made by the Crown Court (s. 15(2)).

SENTENCING PRINCIPLES

Use of Absolute Discharge

E14.2 The power to grant an absolute discharge is available to all criminal courts whatever the age of the offender and, apart from the exceptional cases in which the PCC(S)A 2000, s. 12(1), applies whatever the offence committed. Its imposition may reflect the triviality of the offence, the circumstances in which it came to be prosecuted, or special factors relating to the offender. Cases in which the Court of Appeal has advocated the use of the absolute discharge include *Smedleys Ltd v Breed* [1974] AC 839 and *King* [1977] Crim LR 627.

Use of Conditional Discharge

E14.3 The power to grant a conditional discharge is available to all criminal courts whatever the age of the offender. The conditional discharge cannot be used in murder cases or where the FA 1968, s. 51A(2), or the PCC(S)A 2000, s. 110 or 111, applies, nor where the offender has been convicted of doing something which he is prohibited from doing by an anti-social behaviour order without reasonable excuse (CDA 1998, s. 1(11)), nor where the offender has been convicted of without reasonable excuse doing anything which he is prohibited from doing by a sex offender order (CDA 1998, s. 2(9)), nor, except where there are 'exceptional circumstances' relating to the offence or the offender which justify its doing so, where the offender is convicted of an offence within two years of receiving a warning from a police officer (CDA 1998, ss. 65 and 66(4)).

When a discharge is conditional, the sole condition is that the offender should commit no further offence during the period of the conditional discharge. No other condition or requirement may be inserted. The period of the conditional discharge is fixed by the court but must not exceed three years. Cases in which the Court of Appeal has advocated the use of the conditional discharge include *Whitehead* (1979) 1 Cr App R (S) 187 and *Watts* (1984) 6 Cr App R (S) 61.

Combining Discharge with Other Sentences or Orders

A discharge cannot be combined with a punitive measure for the same offence (*Savage* (1983) 5 Cr App R (S) 216) except where permitted by statute. Thus a discharge cannot be combined with a custodial sentence, a community order or a fine (*Sanck* (1990) 12 Cr App R (S) 155). If, however, an offender is given a discharge for one of a number of offences, the court is free to exercise its normal powers of sentence with respect to his other offences (*Bainbridge* (1979) 1 Cr App R (S) 36). There are restrictions on the use of the discharge where the court is proposing to make a referral order (see **E12.3**). Section 12(7) of the PCC(S)A 2000, states that: **E14.4**

> (7) Nothing in this section shall be construed as preventing a court, on discharging an offender absolutely or conditionally in respect of any offence, from making an order for costs against the offender or imposing any disqualification on him or from making in respect of the offence an order under section 130, 143 or 148 below (compensation orders, deprivation orders and restitution orders).

For s. 130 (compensation orders), see **E18.12**; for s. 143 (deprivation orders) see **E20.3**; and for s. 148 (restitution orders), see **E19.2**. The wording of s. 12(7) permits the combination of a discharge with 'any disqualification'. Thus, for example, a discharge may be combined with an order for disqualification from driving, whether imposed under the RTOA 1988 (see also s. 46 of that Act), or the PCC(S)A 2000, s. 146 (see **E23.9**) or 147 (see **E23.10**). A discharge may be combined with an order to disqualify a person from acting as a company director (reversing the decision in *Young* (1990) 12 Cr App R (S) 262) or with a recommendation for deportation (*Akan* [1973] 1 QB 491).

Breach of Conditional Discharge

A conditional discharge can be breached only by the conviction of the offender of a further offence committed during the period of the discharge (PCC(S)A 2000, s. 13(1)). A court dealing with the breach (the Crown Court if it made the conditional discharge, or the magistrates' court if it made it) may sentence the offender for the original offence in any manner in which it could have dealt with him if he had just been convicted before the court for that offence (s. 13(6)), but the Crown Court dealing with a person conditionally discharged by a magistrates' court is limited to the lower court's powers (s. 13(7)). One magistrates' court may deal with breach of a conditional discharge imposed by a different magistrates' court, but only with the consent of the original magistrates' court (s. 13(8)). Where an offender aged under 18 has been conditionally discharged by a magistrates' court in respect of an offence triable only on indictment in the case of an adult, and the offender has **E14.5** now attained the age of 18, the powers exercisable by the court under s. 13(6), (7) or (8) are to impose a fine not exceeding £5,000 for the original offence, or to deal with the offender in any way in which a magistrates' court could deal with him if it had just convicted him of an offence punishable with imprisonment for a term not exceeding six months (s. 13(9)). Sentencing for the original offence always terminates the conditional discharge itself, but any order for compensation or costs made at the time of the discharge remains valid (*Evans* [1963] 1 QB 979).

Limited Effect of Conviction on the Grant of Absolute or Conditional Discharge

E14.6 **Powers of Criminal Courts (Sentencing) Act 2000, s. 14**

(1) Subject to subsection (2) below, a conviction of an offence for which an order is made under section 12 above discharging the offender absolutely or conditionally shall be deemed not to be a conviction for any purpose other than the purposes of the proceedings in which the order is made and of any subsequent proceedings which may be taken against the offender under section 13 above.

(2) Where the offender was aged 18 or over at the time of his conviction of the offence in question and is subsequently sentenced (under section 13 above) for that offence, subsection (1) above shall cease to apply to the conviction.

(3) Without prejudice to subsections (1) and (2) above, the conviction of an offender who is discharged absolutely or conditionally under section 12 above shall in any event be disregarded for the purposes of any enactment or instrument which—
  (a) imposes any disqualification or disability upon convicted persons; or
  (b) authorises or requires the imposition of any such disqualification or disability.

(4) Subsections (1) to (3) above shall not affect—
  (a) any right of any offender discharged absolutely or conditionally under section 12 above to rely on his conviction in bar of any subsequent proceedings for the same offence; or
  (b) the restoration of any property in consequence of the conviction of any such offender; or
  (c) . . .

An offender who has been discharged by the Crown Court or a magistrates' court may appeal against his conviction, sentence or other ancillary order made in conjunction with the discharge (s. 14(6). A conviction in respect of which a discharge is granted does not count for the purpose of putting a suspended sentence imposed under the PCC(S)A 2000 into effect nor, it is submitted, does it count as a previous conviction for the purposes of s. 110 or 111 of the 2000 Act. The phrase 'subsequently sentenced' in s. 14(2) refers to the situation where the offender originally granted a discharge is in breach of that order so that he becomes liable to be sentenced for the original offence. Where the court dealing with the breach chooses not to deal with the original offence, therefore, the conviction in respect of it counts for limited purposes only.

Section E15 Binding Over

This section deals with the court's power to bind over a person to keep the peace and the Crown Court's power to bind a person over to come up for judgment. The power to bind over a parent or guardian of an offender aged under 16 is dealt with at **E16.5**.

BINDING OVER TO KEEP THE PEACE

Power to Bind Over to Keep the Peace

Powers of a magistrates' court to bind over a person to keep the peace arise either on complaint (under the MCA 1980, s. 115) or of the court's own motion under common-law powers and pursuant to various statutes, most importantly the Justices of the Peace Act 1361. While an order under s. 115 can be made only after a full hearing of the complaint, where the court binds over of its own motion it may do so at any time before the conclusion of criminal proceedings, on withdrawal of the case by the prosecution, on a decision by the prosecution to offer no evidence, on an adjournment, or upon acquittal of the defendant, where a justice considers that the person's conduct is such that there might be a breach of peace in the future, whether committed by him or by others. These powers, which are exercisable 'not by reason of any offence having been committed, but as a measure of preventive justice' (*Veater v Glennon* [1981] 1 WLR 567), may be used in a wide variety of situations, including as a sentencing option against a convicted offender. A person bound over to keep the peace may be made subject to a condition that he shall not possess, use, or carry a firearm (Firearms Act 1968, s. 52(1)). Formerly, there was power to bind over a person 'to be of good behaviour' in cases where that person's behaviour did not amount to a breach of the peace but was found to be *contra bonos mores* (described by the Divisional Court in *Hughes v Holley* (1988) 86 Cr App R 130 as conduct which was ' . . . wrong rather than right in the judgment of the majority of contemporary citizens'). In *Hashman and Harrup v UK* (2000) 30 EHRR 241, however, the European Court of Human Rights said that the nature of requirements imposed on a person bound over to be of good behaviour was insufficiently precise to qualify as a 'restriction . . . prescribed by law' under the ECHR, Article 10(2), so that binding over the applicants to be of good behaviour had been a breach of their rights under that Article. **E15.1**

The power to bind over is frequently used as a method of disposal in cases involving minor assaults or minor incidents of public disorder, where the prosecution are prepared not to proceed, provided that the defendant agrees to be bound over. The person bound over is required to enter into a recognizance in an amount which will be forfeited if he fails to keep the peace for a specified period.

Justices of the Peace Act 1968, s. 1

> (7) It is hereby declared that any court of record having a criminal jurisdiction has, as ancillary to that jurisdiction, the power to bind over to be of good behaviour, a person who or whose case is before the court, by requiring him to enter into his own recognisances or to find sureties or both, and committing him to prison if he does not comply.

The Crown Court is a court of record (Supreme Court Act 1981, s. 45), so that both magistrates' courts and the Crown Court have powers to bind over offenders and others who are before the court. The Court of Appeal (Criminal Division) also possesses these powers (*Sharp* [1957] 1 QB 552). Those who may be bound over include an acquitted defendant

(*Inner London Crown Court, ex parte Benjamin* (1986) 85 Cr App R 267), a defendant before the court in respect of whom the prosecution has been unable to proceed (*Lincoln Crown Court, ex parte Jude* [1998] 1 WLR 24), a witness before the court (*Sheldon v Bromfield Justices* [1964] 2 QB 573), and a complainant (*Wilkins* [1907] 2 KB 380). On the other hand, the victim of an assault who is not a party to the proceedings and has not been called to give evidence against the assailant, who has pleaded guilty, cannot be bound over (*Swindon Crown Court, ex parte Pawitter Singh* [1984] 1 WLR 449), nor can a person who is the subject of an unconditional witness order, but who is in the event not required to give evidence (*Kingston-upon-Thames Crown Court, ex parte Guarino* [1986] Crim LR 325).

Bind Over: Procedural Requirements

E15.2 Where a court contemplates exercising its power against a person who has not been charged with an offence, it should ensure that the person concerned understands what the court has in mind and give him the opportunity to make representations (*Hendon Justices, ex parte Gorchein* [1973] 1 WLR 1502). It is also good practice to allow an acquitted defendant, upon whom the court proposes to make a bind over, an opportunity to address the court on the matter (*Woking Justices, ex parte Gossage* [1973] QB 448). In *Middlesex Crown Court, ex parte Khan* (1997) 161 JP 240, the Divisional Court stated that before binding over an acquitted defendant the judge should be satisfied beyond reasonable doubt that the defendant posed a potential threat to other persons and was a man of violence. A mere belief that the acquitted person might pose such a threat was not enough. In the case of a disturbance in the face of the court, natural justice does not require that the person concerned be given a warning or a chance to make representations before being bound over (*North London Metropolitan Magistrate, ex parte Haywood* [1973] 1 WLR 965). Where the court proposes to bind over a person who has been convicted, in anything other than a trivial sum, his means and other personal circumstances should be investigated and representations allowed in respect of them (*Central Criminal Court, ex parte Boulding* [1984] QB 813). It was held in *Lincoln Crown Court, ex parte Jude* [1998] 1 WLR 24 that a sum of £500 was not so trivial an amount as to dispense with the requirement of a means inquiry. The court should fix the period of the recognisance and the sum of money to be forfeited upon breach at the time when it orders the bind over. There is no upper limit to the amount, save that it must be reasonable. A person may, therefore, be bound over in a sum which exceeds the maximum fine which could be exacted for the relevant offence (*Sandbach Justices, ex parte Williams* [1935] 2 KB 192).

The period for which the order may run is entirely within the discretion of the court. Although an order to bind over may name a person or persons for whose special protection it is made (e.g., *Wilson v Skeock* (1949) 65 TLR 418), there is no power to insert specific conditions in an order binding a person over to keep the peace or to be of good behaviour (*Randall* (1986) 8 Cr App R (S) 433). Under the Magistrates' Courts (Appeals from Binding Over Orders) Act 1956, there is a right of appeal to the Crown Court against an order by a magistrates' court to enter into recognisances to keep the peace. See, further, *Preston Crown Court, ex parte Pamplin* [1981] Crim LR 338. Where the bind over is made by the Crown Court on sentence, an appeal lies to the Court of Appeal by virtue of Criminal Appeal Act 1968, s. 50(1).

Requirement for Additional Penalty

E15.3 It is unclear whether a convicted offender may be bound over to keep the peace without the passing of some other sentence. The wording of the Justices of the Peace Act 1968, s. 1(7) (see **E15.1**), indicates that the bind over is 'ancillary' to the court's criminal jurisdiction, and this may mean that a court should determine the penalty for the offence before the ancillary power of binding over to keep the peace is considered. There is evidence, however, that bind overs are sometimes imposed on sentence without any additional penalty.

Refusal or Failure to Enter into Recognisance

The sanction available to a magistrates' court in the case of a failure or a refusal to enter into a recognisance is imprisonment. This may be for a maximum period of six months or until the person complies with the order, if sooner (MCA 1980, s. 115(3)). Imprisonment cannot be imposed on a person who is under the age of 21 (PCC(S)A 2000, s. 89). Such a person may properly consent to be bound over even though his refusal to consent could not lead to imprisonment (*Conlan v Oxford* (1983) 5 Cr App R (S) 237). A person aged between 18 and 20 inclusive who refuses to consent to be bound over by a magistrates' court may be detained under the PCC(S)A 2000, s. 108 (see *Howley v Oxford* (1985) 81 Cr App R 246 and **E17.2**). There is no power in these circumstances to order the detention of a person who is under the age of 18, but a magistrates' court may order such a person to attend at an attendance centre (see s. 60(1)(b) and **E11.49**). It seems that the Crown Court may deal with a refusal to be bound over as a contempt of court. **E15.4**

Failure to Comply with Conditions of Order

If a person who has been bound over by the Crown Court is adjudged to have failed to comply with the conditions of the order, the court may forfeit the whole or part of the recognisance in its discretion, allow time for payment, direct payment by instalments or reduce or discharge the recognisance (PCC(S)A 2000, s. 139(1)), but it is not empowered to impose a prison term (*Finch* (1962) 47 Cr App R 58, *Gilbert* (1974) CSP D10–3A01). The Crown Court, when forfeiting a recognisance, must fix a term of imprisonment or detention, to be served in default (PCC(S)A 2000, s. 139(2)). See further **E17.2** and **E17.3**. **E15.5**

In a magistrates' court, a recognisance can be declared to be forfeit only by way of an order on complaint (MCA 1980, s. 120), by virtue of whichever power the bind over was originally imposed. Such proceedings are civil in character, and require only the civil standard of proof (*Marlow Justices, ex parte O'Sullivan* [1984] QB 381), but the person concerned should be told the nature of the breach alleged and be given opportunity to present evidence, call witnesses or give an explanation (*McGregor* [1945] 2 All ER 180). There is no right of appeal against an adjudication of forfeiture (*Durham Justices, ex parte Laurent* [1945] KB 33).

BINDING OVER TO COME UP FOR JUDGMENT

Powers to Bind Over to Come Up for Judgment

The common-law power (see *Spratling* [1911] 1 KB 77) to bind over to come up for judgment, which can be exercised only by the Crown Court, may be exercised in respect of any offence except one where the penalty is fixed by law. The effect of such an order is that the offender is bound over on recognisance on specified conditions. If he breaks one or more of the conditions, he will be brought back before the court for sentence but, if he does not break any of the conditions during the specified period, he will either not be sentenced for the offence, or will receive a nominal penalty. **E15.6**

A bind over to come up for judgment is in lieu of sentence, and it is therefore wrong to impose it in addition to a sentence for the offence (*Ayu* [1958] 1 WLR 1264). An offender must consent to the making of the order, though consent would not be vitiated by a realistic expectation of a custodial sentence in the alternative (*Williams* [1982] 1 WLR 1398). Where the judge proposes to call an offender to come up for judgment, notice shall be given to him (*David* (1939) 27 Cr App R 50).

If the offender is in breach of the order, he may forfeit the recognisance as well as being sentenced for the original offence. Where a person is brought back before the court on the ground that a recognisance entered into by him has been broken, the facts against him must be proved beyond reasonable doubt (*McGarry* (1945) 30 Cr App R 187). The order is a 'sentence' made on conviction on indictment (*Abrahams* (1952) 36 Cr App R 147) and an appeal lies to the Court of Appeal (Criminal Appeal Act 1968, s. 50(1); *Williams* [1982] 1 WLR 1398).

Section E16 Orders Against Parents

PARENTING ORDERS

Under ss. 8 to 10 of the CDA 1998, the Crown Court and youth courts have power to impose a parenting order on a parent or guardian of a child or young person where, *inter alia*, that child or young person has been convicted of any offence (s. 8(1)(c)). The court must be notified by the Secretary of State that local arrangements for implementation have been made. Section 8(1)(a), (b) and (d) allow for the imposing of parenting orders in consequence of the making of a child safety order in the case of a child, an anti-social behaviour order or sex offender order in the case of a child or young person, or where a parent is convicted of an offence involving failure to comply with a school attendance order or failure to secure the regular attendance at school of a registered pupil. These provisions are not considered further here. **E16.1**

Power to Make Parenting Order

Crime and Disorder Act 1998, s. 8 **E16.2**

(4) A parenting order is an order which requires the parent—
  (a) to comply, for a period not exceeding twelve months, with such requirements as are specified in the order; and
  (b) subject to subsection (5) below, to attend, for a concurrent period not exceeding three months, such counselling or guidance sessions as may be specified in directions given by the responsible officer.

(5) A parenting order may, but need not, include such a requirement as is mentioned in subsection (4)(b) above in any case where a parenting order under this section or any other enactment has been made in respect of the parent on a previous occasion.

(6) The relevant condition is that the parenting order would be desirable in the interests of preventing—
  . . .
  (b) in a case falling within paragraph (c) of that subsection, the commission of any further offence by the child or young person;
  . . .

(7) The requirements that may be specified under subsection (4)(a) above are those which the court considers desirable in the interests of preventing any such repetition or, as the case may be, the commission of any such further offence.

(7A) A counselling or guidance programme which a parent is required to attend by virtue of subsection (4)(b) above may be or include a residential course but only if the court is satisfied—
  (a) that the attendance of the parent at a residential course is likely to be more effective than his attendance at a non-residential course in preventing any such repetition or, as the case may be, the commission of any such further offence, and
  (b) that any interference with family life which is likely to result from the attendance of the parent at a residential course is proportionate in all the circumstances.

(8) In this section and section 9 below 'responsible officer', in relation to a parenting order, means one of the following who is specified in the order, namely—
  (a) a probation officer;
  (b) a social worker of a local authority social services department; and
  (c) a member of a youth offending team.

Requirements specified in s. 8(4)(a) might commonly include that the parent ensure that the child is accompanied to and from school each day, and is indoors by a certain hour in the evening. It is clear from s. 8(4)(b) and (5) that the court has no discretion to dispense with the requirement of attendance at counselling sessions, unless the parent has been the subject of a parenting order on a previous occasion. While s. 8 creates a power to pass a parenting order where the young offender is aged under 18, s. 9 goes further and places a duty on the court to make a parenting order where the young offender is aged under 16. If, however, the court is not satisfied that the 'relevant condition' is fulfilled (i.e. that the making of a parenting order would be desirable in the interests of preventing the commission of any further offence by the child or young person under 16) then the court must state in open court that it is not so satisfied, and why it is not (s. 9(1)). A similar duty, and similar exception, applies where the offender has been made subject to an anti-social behaviour order (s. 9(1B)).

By the CJA 2003, s. 324 and sch. 34, a youth court has power to make a parenting order at the same time as sentencing the young offender by referral order (see E12). This combination was formerly not permitted. If the offender is aged under 16, such that the youth court would normally be under a duty to impose a parenting order unless not satisfied that the 'relevant condition' is fulfilled, such a duty does *not* extend to cases where the youth court is considering whether to make a parenting order at the same time as sentencing the young offender by referral order.

Before making a parenting order the court need not obtain a presentence report, but, by s. 9(2), before making a parenting order in a case where the young offender is aged under 16, the court must obtain and consider information about the young offender's family circumstances and the likely effect of the order on those circumstances. By s. 9(2A), if the court proposes to make a parenting order at the same time as sentencing the young offender by referral order, the court must obtain and consider a report by an appropriate officer indicating the requirements proposed to be included in the parenting order and indicating their desirability in preventing the commission of further offences by the young offender. Section 9(3) requires that before making a parenting order the court must explain to the parent in ordinary language the effect of the order and of the requirements proposed to be included in it, the consequences which may follow if he fails to comply with any of those requirements, and that the court has power to review the order on the application either of the parent or of the responsible officer. Requirements specified in, and directions given under, a parenting order shall, as far as practicable, be such as to avoid any conflict with the parent's religious beliefs and any interference with the times, if any, at which he normally works or attends an educational establishment (s. 9(4)). In *R (M) v Inner London Crown Court* (2003) *The Times*, 27 February 2003, the Divisional Court held that the making of parenting orders did not contravene the ECHR, Article 8, guaranteeing respect for private and family life.

Variation and Appeal

E16.3 If, while the parenting order is in force, application is made to the court either by the responsible officer or by the parent, the court may, where appropriate, make an order discharging the parenting order or varying it by cancelling any provision included within it or by inserting in it any provision which could have been included in the order if the court had then the power to make it and were exercising that power (s. 9(5)). If an application is made for the discharge of a parenting order and that application is dismissed, no fresh application for discharge can be made without the consent of the court which made the order (s. 9(6)).

A person in respect of whom a parenting order has been made by virtue of s. 8(1)(c) (commission of offence by offender aged under 18) has the same right of appeal against that order as if the offence that led to the making of the order were an offence committed by him and the order were a sentence passed on him for the offence (s. 10(4)).

Breach of Parenting Order

If while a parenting order is in force the parent without reasonable excuse fails to comply with any requirement included in the order or specified in directions given by the responsible officer, he shall be liable on summary conviction to a fine not exceeding level 3 on the standard scale (s. 9(7)). It would appear that in the absence of such failure to comply by the parent, commission of a further offence by the child does not constitute a breach of the parenting order. E16.4

BINDING OVER OF PARENT OR GUARDIAN OF OFFENDER AGED UNDER 16

The PCC(S)A 2000, s. 150(1), places an obligation upon magistrates' courts and the Crown Court to bind over the parent or guardian of an offender who is under the age of 16, whenever the court is satisfied that to do so would be desirable in the interests of preventing the commission by the young offender of further offences. If the court is not satisfied of that on the particular facts of the case, it should state in open court that it is not, and give reasons for that view. Such an order cannot be made where the young offender has been sentenced by way of referral order (see E12). E16.5

By s. 150(2), the court is empowered to order the parent or guardian to enter into a recognisance (in a sum not exceeding £1,000: s. 150(3)) to take proper care of the offender and exercise proper control over him. Entry into the recognisance requires the consent of the parent or guardian, but if consent is refused and the court considers that refusal unreasonable, the parent or guardian may be punished by a fine not exceeding £1,000. A court which has passed a community sentence on the relevant minor may include in the recognisance a provision that the minor's parent or guardian ensure that the minor complies with the requirements of that sentence. The maximum duration of the recognisance is until the offender reaches the age of 18, or for a period of three years, whichever is the shorter period (s. 150(4)).

In fixing the level of the recognisance, the court shall take into account, among other things, the means of the parent or guardian, whether doing so has the effect of increasing or reducing the level of the recognisance (s. 150(7)).

As far as forfeiture of the recognisance is concerned, s. 150(5) states that the MCA 1980, s. 120, shall apply in relation to a recognisance under s. 150 as it does to a recognisance to keep the peace (see E15.5). The court may order forfeiture of the whole, or part, of the recognisance, together with costs. A right of appeal against an order under s. 150 made by a magistrates' court is created by s. 150(8) and where the order is made by the Crown Court, a similar right applies under s. 150(9).

FINE, COMPENSATION OR COSTS TO BE PAID BY PARENT OR GUARDIAN

The parent or guardian of a juvenile may be ordered by the court to pay the fine, costs or order for compensation imposed upon a juvenile by virtue of the PCC(S)A 2000, s. 137. E16.6

Powers of Criminal Courts (Sentencing) Act 2000, s. 137

(1) Where—

(a) a child or young person (that is to say, any person aged under 18) is convicted of any offence for the commission of which a fine or costs may be imposed or a compensation order may be made, and

(b) the court is of opinion that the case would best be met by the imposition of a fine or

> costs or the making of such an order, whether with or without any other punishment, the court shall order that the fine, compensation or costs awarded be paid by the parent or guardian of the child or young person instead of by the child or young person himself, unless the court is satisfied—
> (i) that the parent or guardian cannot be found; or
> (ii) that it would be unreasonable to make an order for payment, having regard to the circumstances of the case.

Section 137(2) further provides that where a person under 18 would otherwise be required to pay a fine in respect of breach of a community order or reparation order or for breach of supervision requirements under a detention and training order, the court shall order the fine to be paid by the parent or guardian, subject to the same qualifications as appear in s. 137(1). The court may make a financial circumstances order with respect to the parent or guardian (s. 136(1)). As a consequence of the CJA 2003, s. 161A (surcharges: see **E18.14**), which was brought into force on 7 April 2007, the PCC(S)A 2000, s. 137, has been amended to provide that the surcharge be paid by the parent or guardian unless he cannot be found or it is unreasonable to require him to pay; the amendment has effect only in relation to offences committed after that date.

Section 137(3) states that in the case of a young person who has attained the age of 16 years, subsections (1) and (2) shall have effect as if, instead of imposing a duty, they conferred a power to make such an order. While an order under s. 137 may be made against a parent or guardian who has failed to attend court after having been required to do so, apart from such case no order should be made without giving the parent or guardian an opportunity of being heard (s. 137(4)). An appeal against an order made by a magistrates' court under s. 137 lies to the Crown Court (s. 137(6)) and an appeal against an order made by the Crown Court under s. 137 lies to the Court of Appeal (s. 137(7)).

The court should not make an order under s. 137 against a parent or guardian without first considering the means of that parent or guardian (*Lenihan v West Yorkshire Metropolitan Police* (1981) 3 Cr App R (S) 42). It may be 'unreasonable' for the court to make an order under s. 137 in a case where the parent or guardian has done all that he or she reasonably could to prevent the offending (*Sheffield Crown Court, ex parte Clarkson* (1986) 8 Cr App R (S) 454; *TA v DPP* [1997] 1 Cr App R (S) 1; *J-B* [2004] 2 Cr App R (S) 211). Assessment of the means of the parent or guardian, or assessment of the extent to which the parent or guardian has been neglectful of the offender, should be made on the basis of properly admissible evidence and not simply assumed from the pre-sentence report prepared upon the offender.

Section 137(8) provides that where a local authority has parental responsibility for a child or young person, and the child or young person is in the care of a local authority, or is being provided with accommodation by them in the exercise of their functions, references in s. 137 to 'parent or guardian' should be construed as references to that local authority. In *D v DPP* (1995) 16 Cr App R (S) 1040, the Divisional Court held that a court should not make an order against the local authority in a case where the authority had done all that it reasonably and properly could to protect the public from the young offender and to keep the young offender from criminal ways. Where the local authority so contends, it should be ready to provide evidence to the court of the steps which it has taken. In *Bedfordshire County Council v DPP* [1996] 1 Cr App R (S) 322, the Divisional Court further held that before an order for payment by a local authority could be made a causative link should normally be established between any fault proved on the part of the council and the offences committed. If no such causative fault was shown to the satisfaction of the court, it would be unreasonable to order compensation. 'Local authority' and 'parental responsibility' have the same meaning as in the Children Act 1989.

Section E17 Fines

IN THE CROWN COURT

Powers of Crown Court to Impose Fines

Criminal Justice Act 2003, s. 163 **E17.1**

Where a person is convicted on indictment of any offence, other than an offence for which the sentence is fixed by law or falls to be imposed under section 110(2) or 111(2) of the Sentencing Act or under any of sections 225 to 228 of this Act, the court, if not precluded from sentencing the offender by its exercise of some other power, may impose a fine instead of or in addition to dealing with him in any other way in which the court has power to deal with him, subject however to any enactment requiring the offender to be dealt with in a particular way.

Section 163 deals with the general power of the Crown Court to impose a fine on an offender convicted on indictment. In general the Crown Court can impose a fine on an offender either instead of, or in addition to, dealing with him in any other way. There are some sentences which cannot be combined with a fine. A fine cannot be combined with a hospital order (see Mental Health Act 1983, s. 37(8)), nor with a discharge when sentencing for a single offence (*McClelland* [1951] 1 All ER 557). There are also the exceptional cases, referred to in s. 163, where a fine is not available as a penalty.

There is no statutory limit to the amount of fine which may be imposed by the Crown Court (see also Criminal Law Act 1977, s. 32(1)), and this includes a case where an offender is committed for sentence under the PCC(S)A 2000, s. 3, following conviction in a magistrates' court of an offence triable either way. If, however, the magistrates' court commits a person to the Crown Court under s. 6 (see **D22.34**), the Crown Court must observe all the limitations on sentencing powers which would have applied in the magistrates' court with regard, for example, to the limitations on magistrates' powers to imprison and financial limitations on fines (see **E17.4**) or compensation orders. These limitations apply even where the offence is triable either way and the magistrates' court might have committed to the Crown Court under s. 3.

Powers of Criminal Courts (Sentencing) Act 2000, s. 139

(1) Subject to the provisions of this section, if the Crown Court imposes a fine on any person or forfeits his recognizance, the court may make an order—
  (a) allowing time for the payment of the amount of the fine or the amount due under the recognizance;
  (b) directing payment of that amount by instalments of such amounts and on such dates respectively as may be specified in the order;
  (c) in the case of a recognizance, discharging the recognizance or reducing the amount due under it.

(2) Subject to the provisions of this section, if the Crown Court imposes a fine on any person or forfeits his recognizance, the court shall make an order fixing a term of imprisonment or of detention under section 108 above (detention of persons aged 18 to 20 for default) which he is to undergo if any sum which he is liable to pay is not duly paid or recovered.

Power and Duty of Court to Fix Term in Default

Although a term of imprisonment or detention to be served in default must be fixed in every case where the Crown Court imposes a fine or forfeits a recognisance (unless the offender is **E17.2** under 18 years of age), it seems that a failure to fix such a term does not invalidate the fine itself (*Hamilton* (1980) 2 Cr App R (S) 1). For the PCC(S)A 2000, s. 108, see below, and for the table of maximum periods of imprisonment or detention in a young offender institution which may be fixed in default, see **E17.3**. The term which is fixed should relate to the whole sum, rather than to any instalment (*Power* (1986) 8 Cr App R (S) 8). Where fines are imposed in respect of more than one offence, the terms to be served in default may be ordered to run concurrently or consecutively (*Savundranayagan* [1968] 1 WLR 1761), and the court may order that the term(s) to be served in default may run concurrently or consecutively to any term of imprisonment or detention in a young offender institution to which the offender is sentenced at that time by the court or which he is currently serving (s. 139(5)). A term of imprisonment in default may be imposed consecutively to a maximum prison sentence imposed for the same offence (*Carver* [1955] 1 WLR 181). Consecutive custodial terms are, however, subject to the totality principle (*Savundranayagan* [1968] 1 WLR 1761). See, further, *Benmore* (1983) 5 Cr App R (S) 468.

Where the Crown Court imposes a fine on committal for sentence from a magistrates' court, in circumstances where the powers of the Crown Court are limited to those of the magistrates' court, the Crown Court must specify the term to be served in default (s. 139(7)).

Powers of Criminal Courts (Sentencing) Act 2000, s. 139

(3) No person shall on the occasion when a fine is imposed on him or his recognizance is forfeited by the Crown Court be committed to prison or detained in pursuance of an order under subsection (2) above unless—
  (a) in the case of an offence punishable with imprisonment, he appears to the court to have sufficient means to pay the sum forthwith;
  (b) it appears to the court that he is unlikely to remain long enough at a place of abode in the United Kingdom to enable payment of the sum to be enforced by other methods; or
  (c) on the occasion when the order is made the court sentences him to immediate imprisonment, custody for life or detention in a young offender institution for that or another offence, or so sentences him for an offence in addition to forfeiting his recognizance, or he is already serving a sentence of custody for life or a term—
    (i) of imprisonment
    (ii) of detention in a young offender institution; or
    (iii) of detention under section 108 above.

Powers of Criminal Courts (Sentencing) Act 2000, s. 108

(1) In any case where, but for section 89(1) above, a court would have power—
  (a) to commit a person aged at least 18 but under 21 to prison for default in payment of a fine or any other sum of money, or
  (b) to make an order fixing a term of imprisonment in the event of such a default by such a person, or
  (c) to commit such a person to prison for contempt of court or any kindred offence,

  the court shall have power, subject to subsection (3) below, to commit him to be detained under this section or, as the case may be, to make an order fixing a term of detention under this section in the event of default, for a term not exceeding the term of imprisonment.

(2) For the purposes of subsection (1) above, the power of a court to order a person to be imprisoned under section 23 of the Attachment of Earnings Act 1971 shall be taken to be a power to commit him to prison.

(3) No court shall commit a person to be detained under this section unless it is of the opinion that no other method of dealing with him is appropriate; and in forming any such opinion, the court—
  (a) shall take into account all such information about the circumstances of the default or contempt (including any aggravating or mitigating factors) as is available to it; and
  (b) may take into account any information about that person which is before it.

(4) Where a magistrates' court commits a person to be detained under this section, it shall—
  (a) state in open court the reason for its opinion that no other method of dealing with him is appropriate; and
  (b) cause that reason to be specified in the warrant of commitment and to be entered in the register.

There is no power to fix a term of detention under s. 108 in relation to an offender aged under 18 (*Basid* [1996] 1 Cr App R (S) 421, *Byas* (1995) 16 Cr App R (S) 869). It should be noted that, although s. 108(3) states that no court shall commit an offender to be detained unless 'no other method of dealing with him is appropriate', the statutory criteria in ss. 79 to 81 (relating to the imposition and length of custodial sentences), and the normal requirement to obtain a pre-sentence report, do not apply to a term of detention in default or for contempt. This is because a sentence of detention under s. 108, is not a 'custodial sentence' for the purposes of the PCC(S)A 2000. The obligation in s. 83 (restriction on imposing custodial sentence on persons under 21 not legally represented), also does not apply in the present context.

When the CJCSA 2000, s. 75, is brought into force, the power under the PCC(S)A 2000, s. 108, will be abolished. A term of imprisonment in default will then be set for offenders aged 18 to 20 inclusive, as for offenders aged 21 and over.

Table of Maximum Periods in Default

The periods set out in the following table are the maximum periods of imprisonment or detention to be served in default, applicable to the corresponding fine values (PCC(S)A 2000, s. 139(4)): **E17.3**

Not exceeding £200	7 days
Over £200, not exceeding £500	14 days
Over £500, not exceeding £1,000	28 days
Over £1,000, not exceeding £2,500	45 days
Over £2,500, not exceeding £5,000	3 months
Over £5,000, not exceeding £10,000	6 months
Over £10,000, not exceeding £20,000	12 months
Over £20,000, not exceeding £50,000	18 months
Over £50,000, not exceeding £100,000	2 years
Over £100,000, not exceeding £250,000	3 years
Over £250,000, not exceeding £1 million	5 years
Over £1 million	10 years

These are maximum periods, and the Crown Court has discretion to fix a shorter term within the appropriate bracket. Where more than one fine is imposed, consecutive terms may be fixed. Where, exceptionally, a magistrates' court is empowered to fix a term in default of payment of a fine, the same periods apply, except that a default term in excess of 12 months cannot be exceeded (MCA 1980, sch. 4).

IN THE MAGISTRATES' COURT

Powers of Magistrates' Court to Impose Fines

Where an offender has been summarily convicted of an offence triable either way which is **E17.4**
listed in MCA 1980, sch. 1, the magistrates may fine him an amount not exceeding the 'prescribed sum' (MCA 1980, s. 32(1)). By s. 32(9) of that Act, 'the prescribed sum' means £5,000. Where, however, the offender has been summarily convicted of an offence triable either way, and the statute creating the offence prescribes a particular maximum penalty upon summary conviction, the magistrates may fine him an amount not exceeding the maximum penalty indicated in the statute creating the offence or the prescribed sum, whichever is the greater (s. 32(2)), and subject to the exception of certain drug offences listed in s. 32(5). Where the maximum penalty indicated in the statute creating the offence is expressed to be 'the statutory maximum', that maximum shall be the prescribed sum, i.e. £5,000. In the case of an offender under 18 years of age, a lower maximum fine applies (see E17.6)

The maximum fine which may be imposed for a summary offence is nearly always prescribed in the statute which creates the offence. If the statute refers only to punishment by means of imprisonment, power to impose a fine at level 3 is nonetheless included (MCA 1980, s. 34(3)).

Standard Scale of Maximum Fines for Summary Offences and Guideline Fines in Magistrates' Courts

E17.5 The 'standard scale' of maximum fines for summary offences is contained in the CJA 1982, s. 37(2). This scale applies to summary offences only; for offences triable either way dealt with summarily, see **E17.4**. For offenders under 18, a special maximum fine applies (see **E17.6**).

Level on the scale	*Amount of fine*
1	£200
2	£500
3	£1,000
4	£2,500
5	£5,000

The Magistrates' Courts Sentencing Guidelines (2004) provide guideline fines for magistrates' courts, based on the weekly take home pay or weekly benefit payment of the offender. Other relevant outgoings should be considered by the court before the final determination of the fine is made. There are three levels of guideline fine, A, B and C, which indicate offence seriousness and are set out in relation to particular offences where appropriate in **parts B** and C of this work. Fine level A is one half of net weekly income, fine level B equates to net weekly income, and fine level C is one and a half times net weekly income. The Guidelines also state that the fine should be reduced where discount is given for a timely guilty plea (see **E1.6**), and adjusted upwards or downwards to reflect the presence of substantial aggravating or mitigating factors.

Fining Juveniles

E17.6 Under the PCC(S)A 2000, s. 135, where a person under 18 years of age is found guilty by a magistrates' court of an offence in respect of which the court would normally be empowered to impose a fine exceeding £1,000, the amount of the fine imposed shall not exceed £1,000. Section 135 also provides that, if the offender is under the age of 14 and the court could otherwise have imposed a fine exceeding £250, the amount of the fine imposed shall not exceed £250.

There is no limit upon the fine which may be imposed by a Crown Court upon a juvenile convicted on indictment.

See **E16.6** for the court's power to order that a fine be paid by a parent or guardian.

Enforcement of Fines

E17.7 Enforcement of all fines is carried out by magistrates' courts, whether the fine was imposed in a magistrates' court or in the Crown Court. The procedure for enforcement of fines is contained in the MCA 1980, ss. 75 to 91. By virtue of the definition of 'fine' in s. 150 of the 1980 Act, the same procedures also apply to the enforcement of compensation orders, the recovery of recognisances which the court has ordered to be forfeited and any other 'sum adjudged to be paid by a conviction or order of a magistrates' court', subject to certain exceptions which are indicated where appropriate below. The magistrates' court which is responsible for enforcement is that court which imposed the fine or, if the fine was imposed by the Crown Court, the court specified in the fine order or, if none was specified, the court which committed the offender for trial or sentence to the Crown Court. If the offender is now residing in a different local justice area, a transfer of fine order may be made (MCA 1980, s. 89). When ordering a fine, the Crown Court must fix a term to be served in default (see E17.2) but a magistrates' court should not normally do so (ss. 82(3) and 77(2)).

When a fine is imposed it becomes due for payment immediately. The magistrates' court may, however, instead of requiring immediate payment, allow time for payment or order payment by instalments (s. 75(1)). Subsequently, further time may be given (s. 75(2)). If the court orders payment by instalments, default in any one instalment is taken to be a default in payment of all instalments then unpaid (s. 75(3)). Where the court allows time for payment, it may fix a day on which the offender must appear in person before the court (unless he is serving a custodial sentence) if any part of the sum remains unpaid, to enable an inquiry into his means to be conducted (s. 86). Before the court can impose imprisonment or order detention it must inquire into the means of the defaulter in his presence (s. 82(3)). The Courts Act 2003, sch. 5 (as amended), requires a court, where appropriate, to make an attachment of earnings order or a deduction from benefit order in respect of a fine, compensation order, or any other sum imposed on conviction. The provisions apply whether the offender is required to pay immediately or is given time to pay, and no distinction is drawn between existing defaulters and other offenders. The consent of the offender is not required. The final version of these provisions came into force on 3 July 2006 (Collection of Fines (Final Scheme) Order 2006 (SI 2006 No. 1737)).

Enforcement Pursuant to Means Inquiry

If the offender fails to pay the whole or any part of the sum within the time allowed by the court, the magistrates' court may issue a summons or warrant requiring the offender to appear or issue a warrant to arrest him and bring him before the court to conduct a means inquiry to investigate the offender's ability to pay (MCA 1980, s. 83). The court may require that the offender produce evidence of his income and outgoings. If the court orders the offender to produce a statement of means and the offender fails to do so, such failure is an offence punishable by a fine up to level 3 (s. 84(2)). If the offender knowingly or recklessly furnishes a statement which is false in a material particular, or knowingly fails to disclose any material fact, this is an offence punishable with imprisonment not exceeding four months, a fine not exceeding level 3, or both (s. 84(3)). **E17.8**

In the light of information received by the court at the means inquiry, the magistrates may grant further time to the offender for payment of the fine, or arrange payment by instalments, or reduce the amount of each instalment (s. 75). The court may remit the whole or any part of the fine having regard to any change in the offender's circumstances since his conviction (s. 85(1)). The court may also remit or reduce the fine where the fine was imposed in the absence of adequate information about the offender's means, either because he was convicted in his absence or failed to comply with an order to furnish information concerning his means. If the Crown Court imposed the fine, the magistrates may remit the fine in whole or in part only if they first obtain the consent of the Crown Court. It should be noted that the power to remit is restricted to fines and there is no equivalent power in respect of compensation orders (s. 85(4)).

The court may order the offender's *immediate imprisonment*, (or, in the case of an offender aged 18 or over but under 21, detention under the PCC(S)A 2000, s. 108), for the term originally specified as being the time to be served in default or, if no such time was specified, a term specified by the court having regard to the table in the MCA 1980, sch. 4. This table corresponds to the first seven entries listed in the PCC(S)A 2000, s. 139(4), which is set out at E17.3. An immediate committal to custody can be ordered only where, since the conviction, the court has inquired into the offender's means in his presence on at least one occasion and where:

(a) in the case of an offence punishable with imprisonment the offender appears to the court to have sufficient means to pay the sum outstanding forthwith, or
(b) the court is satisfied that the default is due to the offender's wilful refusal or culpable

neglect and has considered or tried all other methods of enforcing payment of the sum but it appears to the court that they are inappropriate or unsuccessful (MCA 1980, s. 82(4)).

Further restrictions on the use of immediate committal to prison are set out in s. 82(5) to (5F). The court must have 'considered or tried' all other methods of enforcement: these words must be complied with and allow no room for the exercise of discretion (*Norwich Magistrates' Court, ex parte Tigger (formerly Lilly)* (1987) 151 JP 689). The warrant of commitment should state the grounds on which the court was satisfied that it was undesirable or impracticable to use the other methods of enforcement (*Oldham Justices, ex parte Cawley* [1997] QB 1). For an offender aged over 18 but under 21, the PCC(S)A 2000, s. 108(4), further requires the justices to specify in the warrant their reasons for concluding that detention is the only appropriate method of dealing with the defaulter (see E17.2). 'Wilful refusal', which means a deliberate defiance of the court order, or 'culpable neglect', which means a reckless disregard of the court order, must be established by proof beyond reasonable doubt (*South Tyneside Justices, ex parte Martin* (1995) *The Independent*, 20 September 1995).

FINES: SENTENCING PRINCIPLES

E17.9 The CJA 2003, s. 162, provides that, where an individual has been convicted of an offence, the court may, before sentencing him, make a 'financial circumstances order' with respect to him. Both magistrates' courts and the Crown Court may make such an order. Where a magistrates' court has been notified in accordance with the MCA 1980, s. 12(4), that an individual wishes to plead guilty without appearing before the court, the court also has power to make a financial circumstances order (s. 162(2)). A 'financial circumstances order' is an order requiring the relevant individual 'to give to the court, within such period as may be specified in the order, such a statement of his financial circumstances as the court may require' (s. 162(3)). An individual who, without reasonable excuse, fails to comply with a financial circumstances order is liable on summary conviction to a fine not exceeding level 3 (s. 162(4)), and if such individual makes, in pursuance of a financial circumstances order, a statement which he knows to be false in a material particular, is reckless as to its falsity or knowingly fails to disclose any material fact he is liable on summary conviction to a fine not exceeding level 4 (s. 162(5)).

Under the CJA 2003, s. 164, the following statutory principles are applicable to the fixing of fines, both in the Crown Court and in magistrates' courts.

Criminal Justice Act 2003, s. 164

(1) Before fixing the amount of any fine to be imposed on an offender who is an individual, a court must inquire into his financial circumstances.

(2) The amount of any fine fixed by a court must be such as, in the opinion of the court, reflects the seriousness of the offence.

(3) In fixing the amount of any fine to be imposed on an offender (whether an individual or other person), a court must take into account the circumstances of the case including, among other things, the financial circumstances of the offender so far as they are known, or appear, to the court.

(4) Subsection (3) above applies whether taking into account the financial circumstances of the offender has the effect of increasing or reducing the amount of the fine.

(4A) In applying subsection (3), a court must not reduce the amount of a fine on account of any surcharge it orders the offender to pay under section 161A, except to the extent that he has insufficient means to pay both.

(5) Where—

(a) an offender has been convicted in his absence in pursuance of section 11 or 12 of the Magistrates' Courts Act 1980 (non-appearance of accused), or

(b) an offender—

(i) has failed to furnish a statement of his financial circumstances in response to a request which is an official request for the purposes of section 20A of the Criminal Justice Act 1991 (offence of making false statement as to financial circumstances).
(ii) has failed to comply with an order under section 162(1) above, or
(iii) has otherwise failed to cooperate with the court in its inquiry into his financial circumstances,

and the court considers that it has insufficient information to make a proper determination of the financial circumstances of the offender, it may make such determination as it thinks fit.

For the MCA 1980, ss. 11 and 12, see **D21.9** and **D21.14** respectively. Section 164 is an important section concerned with fixing the amount of a fine. The court must inquire into the financial circumstances of an offender before fixing the amount of a fine. When determining the amount of the fine, the court must take into account the financial circumstances of the offender, the seriousness of the offence, and the circumstances of the case.

Proportionality to Gravity of Offence

The first principle in relation to the use of the fine, whether in the Crown Court or in magistrates' courts, is that the selection of the fine as a sentence, and the determination of the appropriate level of any fine, should reflect the seriousness of the offence. A fine is an inappropriate penalty where the seriousness of the offence requires an immediate custodial sentence. An example is *A-G's Ref (No. 41 of 1994)* (1995) 16 Cr App R (S) 792, where fines totalling £350 had been imposed on the offender who had pleaded guilty to wounding with intent to cause grievous bodily harm. He had struck the victim on the head with a beer bottle, causing a wound which required stitches, and subsequently threatened him with a knife. The Court of Appeal held that the sentence was 'absurd', and unduly lenient and substituted a custodial term of 30 months. On the other hand, there are cases which are not so serious as to justify a fine. In *Jamieson* (1975) 60 Cr App R 318 the offender, who had a clean record and substantial personal mitigation, was convicted of theft of a half bottle of whisky from a supermarket and fined £300. The Court of Appeal varied the sentence to a conditional discharge. **E17.10**

It is clear from the PCC(S)A 2000, s. 164(2), that the level of the fine imposed should reflect the seriousness of the offence. The imposition of the maximum available fine should be reserved for the most serious instances of the offence which are reasonably likely to occur. The existence of significant mitigation, such as the offender's guilty plea, should normally preclude the imposition of the maximum fine. In *Universal Salvage v Boothby* (1983) 5 Cr App R (S) 428 a company was fined for breach of regulations requiring it to have in its lorry proper equipment to record the journeys made. It was accepted that, in reliance on a letter from the relevant government department, the company had reasonably believed that the regulations were not applicable to them. Liability for the offence was strict, but the Divisional Court held that the circumstances provided considerable mitigation and that the imposition of the maximum fine on the company by the magistrates' court constituted an error of law. In all cases involving fines it is the 'first duty' of the sentencer to 'measure that fine against the gravity of the offence' (per Kenneth Jones LJ in *Messana* (1981) 3 Cr App R (S) 88), having regard to all relevant matters in aggravation and mitigation.

The court should not calculate the level of the fine on the basis of the compensation which would have been received if the victim had made application to the Criminal Injuries Compensation Board (*Roberts* (1980) 2 Cr App R (S) 121).

In *Warden* [1996] 2 Cr App (S) 269, the Court of Appeal observed that, where an offender had spent time on remand in custody but had subsequently received a fine as the appropriate sentence for the offence, some credit should normally be given for the time spent in custody. The amount of the credit was a matter for the discretion of the sentencer.

Helpful guidance on the proper use of fines, when imposed for several different offences, was provided by the Court of Appeal in *Yorkshire Water Services* [2002] 2 Cr App R (S) 37, where the defendant company pleaded guilty to 17 counts of supplying water unfit for human consumption. The counts related to four separate incidents in which contaminated water was supplied, and a large number of households were affected. In reducing the total fine imposed from £119,000 to £80,000, Rougier J stated that the relevant considerations in setting the fine in a case of this sort were (1) the degree of culpability involved in the commission of the offence, (2) the damage done, considering both its spacial and temporal ambit together with the physical and economic ill effects, (3) the offender's previous record, including failure to heed warnings, (4) the need to strike a balance between a fitting punishment and avoiding counter-productive effects on the offending organisation, (5) the offender's plea, attitude, and performance after the event. In determining the appropriate fine, the court should determine the penalty for any one incident rather than 'tot up' the various manifestations of that incident. In *Chelmsford Crown Court, ex parte Birchall* (1989) 11 Cr App R (S) 510, the Divisional Court said that the application of a 'rigid formula' to the calculation of a fine was incorrect, even for a single offence, and it was wrong to apply it to each of 10 offences and add the figures up: the courts had to consider all the circumstances and apply the principles of sentencing which were well known. The main importance of this decision is its clear endorsement of the application to fines of the totality principle (see, in relation to custodial sentences, **E1.14**). When fining in respect of a number of offences, the sentencer must review the total sentence and ensure that it remains proportionate to the totality of the offending, as well as being within the offender's capacity to pay. The PCC(S)A 2000, s. 158(2)(b), reinforces this sentencing principle by stating that the court may mitigate the overall sentence 'by applying any rule of law as to the totality of sentences'.

Further guidance on the appropriate level of fines for particular offences may be obtained from the Magistrates' Courts Sentencing Guidelines (2004). Their guideline fines are explained in **E17.5** and set out in **parts B** and **C** of this work in relation to each of the offences dealt with.

Taking into Account Means of Offender

E17.11 It is well established that while a fine is meant to be a punishment and it is perfectly proper for the offender to have to endure a degree of hardship in paying the fine, since 'one of the objects of the fine is to remind the offender that what he has done is wrong' (per Lord Lane CJ in *Olliver* (1989) 11 Cr App R (S) 10), the imposition of a fine which is quite beyond the means of the offender is wrong in principle.

Where the offender lacks the means to pay the level of fine which is proportionate to the seriousness of the offence, it is contrary to principle to impose a custodial sentence instead. According to Roskill LJ in *Reeves* (1972) 56 Cr App R 366, where the offender had pleaded guilty to obtaining £600 by deception and had received a prison sentence of nine months, the comments made by the sentencer 'must plainly have indicated to the appellant . . . that he was being sent to prison not because the offence itself merited a sentence of immediate imprisonment but because he had not the financial wherewithal to pay a substantial fine. That . . . is, of course, completely wrong'.

Where the offender is well-off and paying the fine proportionate to the offence would cause him little inconvenience, it is contrary to principle to impose a custodial sentence instead (*Gillies* [1965] Crim LR 64). It is, however, right to raise the level of the fine in such a case, so as to increase its impact on the offender, although the Court of Appeal in *Jerome* [2001] 1 Cr App R (S) 316 said that there must remain some proportionality between the offence and the fine. In that case a fine of £10,000 imposed on a relatively affluent offender for handling stolen goods worth £2,739 was said to be manifestly excessive, and was reduced to £6,000. It should be noted that PCC(S)A 2000, s. 128(4), makes it clear that the level of a fine should be adjusted upwards or downwards to take account of the offender's ability to pay. The Magistrates' Courts Sentencing Guidelines (2004) state that 'the aim should be for the fine to have equal impact on rich or poor'. Section 128(4) does not, of course, affect the principle that an offender who is well-off should not be dealt with by financial penalty where the offence itself merits custody and an offender who is less well-off would have gone to prison (*Markwick* (1953) 37 Cr App R 125). The principle that a rich offender must not be permitted to 'buy his way out of prison' is a fundamental one, and it applies equally where the offender has family or friends who are able to meet a substantial fine (*Curtis* (1984) 6 Cr App R (S) 250).

The requirement that the court should adjust the level of the fine in accordance with the offender's means entails that the court should not assume that someone other than the offender will be paying the fine. In *Charambous* (1984) 6 Cr App R (S) 389, where a fine was imposed on a married woman who had limited income of her own, the Court of Appeal stressed that the fine must reflect the offender's means and was not a fine on the family.

If a defendant company wishes to make a submission as to its ability to pay a fine, it should supply copies of its accounts and other financial information to the court. Where such information has been withheld, the court is entitled to assume that the company is able to pay any fine it is minded to impose (*F. Howe and Sons (Engineers) Ltd* [1999] 2 All ER 249).

Instalments should Require Payment within a Reasonable Time

It seems that, apart from exceptional circumstances, where a fine is ordered to be paid by instalments, it should be capable of being paid off by the offender within 12 months (*Knight* (1980) 2 Cr App R (S) 82, *Nunn* (1983) 5 Cr App R (S) 203). In *Olliver* (1989) 11 Cr App R (S) 10, however, it was held by the Court of Appeal that the maximum time is not limited to 12 months. Lord Lane CJ said (at p. 15): E17.12

> . . . there is nothing wrong in principle in the period of payment being longer, indeed much longer than one year, providing it is not an undue burden and so too severe a punishment having regard to the nature of the offence and the nature of the offender. Certainly it seems to us that a two-year period will seldom be too long, and in an appropriate case three years will be unassailable, again of course depending on the nature of the offender and the nature of the offence.

The Magistrates' Courts Sentencing Guidelines (2004) state that 'The fine is payable in full on the day and the offender should always be asked for immediate payment. If periodic payments are allowed, the fine should normally be payable within a maximum of 12 months. It should be remembered, however, that for those on very low incomes it is often unrealistic to expect them to maintain weekly payments for as long as a year.'

There is an exception in relation to corporate defendants, where the fine may be payable over a substantially longer period than for an individual (*Rollco Screw and Rivet Co.* [1999] 2 Cr App R (S) 436).

Combining Fines with Other Sentences or Orders

For restrictions imposed by statute on combining a fine with certain custodial sentences see the CJA 2003, s. 163, at E17.1. Apart from those cases, there is no statutory general restriction on combining fines with imprisonment or other custodial sentences, whether in respect of the same offence or different offences sentenced on the same occasion, though this will not often be a desirable combination, since incarceration may well deprive the offender of the means to pay the fine. In any event, a fine and a custodial sentence will be an inappropriate combination where the offender lacks the means to pay the fine, and hence will serve the term fixed in default of payment (*Maund* (1980) 2 Cr App R (S) 289), or where the offender will be saddled with a significant financial burden on his release from prison. E17.13

A fine may be combined with an immediate custodial sentence, exceptionally where the custodial term imposed is considered to be inadequate and additional punishment is required (*Garner* [1986] 1 WLR 73, per Hodgson J) but also where the fine is being used as a means of removing an offender's profit from his offending. In *Garner* the Court of Appeal approved the imposition of a fine of £150,000 in addition to the maximum prison term available for the offence of conspiracy to contravene the Finance Act 1972, s. 38(1), relating to payment of VAT. In the 'removal of profit' cases the existence of a 'substantial financial benefit' by the offender must be established (*Forsythe* (1980) 2 Cr App R (S) 15), and the offence which gave rise to the profit must be proved or admitted before a fine may be used in this way (*Ayensu* (1982) 4 Cr App R (S) 248). In *Garner* Hodgson J described the fine in these cases as 'a rough and ready method of confiscating the profits of crime'. A more sophisticated approach to the removal of substantial proceeds of offending, which was not available to the courts at the time of these decisions, is to make a confiscation order (see **E21**).

It is possible, whether sentencing for a single offence or for different offences sentenced on the same occasion, to combine a fine with a community sentence of any kind, or a reparation order. A fine cannot, however, be combined with a discharge when sentencing for a single offence (*McClelland* [1951] 1 All ER 557), although it may be combined with a discharge when sentencing for different offences sentenced on the same occasion. A fine cannot be combined with a hospital order (Mental Health Act 1983, s. 37(8)).

A fine and a compensation order may be combined. The PCC(S)A 2000, s. 130(12), provides that, where the offender has insufficient means to pay both an appropriate fine and appropriate compensation, the court shall give preference to compensation. In a particular case this will mean that the level of the fine is reduced to enable the full compensation order to stand, or that no fine is ordered and the compensation order stands alone. Fines may be combined with other financial orders, such as an order to pay the costs of the prosecution, though the court must consider the total effect of the orders it is making, and should ensure that the whole sum the offender has to pay is not beyond his means. There is some authority to the effect that a small fine should not be combined with a large order for costs (*Whalley* (1972) 56 Cr App R 304). A fine may also be combined with a restitution order under the PCC(S)A 2000, s. 148(1), with a deprivation order under s. 143, and with a disqualification order, where the vehicle was used for the purposes of crime, under s. 147.

Persistent Petty Offenders

E17.14 By the PCC(S)A 2000, s. 59(1), where a person aged 16 or over is convicted of an offence by a magistrates' court or the Crown Court, the court is satisfied that each of the conditions mentioned in s. 59(2) is fulfilled and, if it were not so satisfied, the court would have imposed a fine in respect of the offence, the court may, instead of fining the offender (and notwithstanding the general restrictions on the imposition of community sentences contained in s. 35), make a community punishment order or a curfew order. The conditions in s. 59(2) are that:

(a) one or more fines imposed on the offender in respect of one or more previous offences have not been paid; and
(b) if a fine were imposed in an amount which was commensurate with the seriousness of the offence, the offender would not have sufficient means to pay it.

Clearly the purpose of this provision is to allow the court to impose a community punishment order or a curfew order in a case where the seriousness of the offence itself would not justify the use of a community sentence, but where the existence of outstanding fines in the offender's case seems to make the use of the fine unrealistic.

When the relevant provisions are brought into force, s. 59 will be repealed and replaced by the CJA 2003, s. 151 (see **E10.1**).

Surcharge

As from 1 April 2007, the DVCVA 2004, s. 14, inserts new ss. 161A and 161B into the CJA 2003. Sections 161A and 161B apply only in relation to offences committed on or after that date. E17.15

Criminal Justice Act 2003, ss. 161A and 161B

161A.—(1) A court when dealing with a person for one or more offences must also (subject to subsections (2) and (3)) order him to pay a surcharge.

(2) Subsection (1) does not apply in such cases as may be prescribed by an order made by the Secretary of State.

(3) Where a court dealing with an offender considers—

(a) that it would be appropriate to make a compensation order, but

(a) that it would be appropriate to make a compensation order, but

(b) that he has insufficient means to pay both the surcharge and appropriate compensation,

the court must reduce the surcharge accordingly (if necessary to nil).

(4) For the purposes of this section a court does not 'deal with' a person if it—

(a) discharges him absolutely, or

(b) makes an order under the Mental Health Act 1983 in respect of him.

161B.—(1) The surcharge payable under section 161A is such amount as the Secretary of State may specify by order.

(2) An order under this section may provide for the amount to depend on—

(a) the offence or offences committed,

(b) how the offender is otherwise dealt with (including, where the offender is fined, the amount of the fine),

(c) the age of the offender.

This is not to be read as limiting section 330(3) (power to make different provisions for different purposes etc.).

The Secretary of State has made an order (the Criminal Justice Act 2003 (Surcharge) (No. 2) Order 2007 (SI 2007 No. 1079)) as specified in s. 161B(1). An earlier Order was made, but was revoked prior to the commencement date of April 1. The (No. 2) Order states that a court dealing with an offender by way of a fine, whether standing alone or in combination with any other order, must order the offender to pay the surcharge, which is set at £15. No other disposal triggers the surcharge requirement. The number of offences being dealt with on the sentencing occasion is irrelevant. The sum of £15 is a fixed amount and is not affected by the size of the fine or fines imposed, except that, if the offender has insufficient means to pay both the surcharge and the fine, the fine should be reduced to enable the surcharge to be paid (CJA 2003, s. 164(4A)). If the offender has insufficient means to pay both the surcharge and the compensation order, the court should reduce the surcharge to enable the compensation order to be paid.

Section E18 Compensation Orders

POWER TO MAKE COMPENSATION ORDERS

E18.1 The power of the court to make compensation orders is governed by the PCC(S)A 2000, ss. 130 to 134.

Powers of Criminal Courts (Sentencing) Act 2000, s. 130

(1) A court by or before which a person is convicted of an offence, instead of or in addition to dealing with him in any other way, may, on application or otherwise, make an order (in this Act referred to as a 'compensation order') requiring him—
   (a) to pay compensation for any personal injury, loss or damage resulting from that offence or any other offence which is taken into consideration by the court in determining sentence; or
   (b) to make payments for funeral expenses or bereavement in respect of a death resulting from any such offence, other than a death due to an accident arising out of the presence of a motor vehicle on a road;

   but this is subject to the following provisions of this section and to section 131 below.

(2) Where the person is convicted of an offence the sentence for which is fixed by law or falls to be imposed under section 110(2) or 111(2) above, section 51A(2) of the Firearms Act 1968 or section 225, 226, 227 or 228 of the Criminal Justice Act 2003 or section 29(4) or (6) of the Violent Crime Reduction Act 2006, subsection (1) above shall have effect as if the words 'instead of or' were omitted.

(3) A court shall give reasons, on passing sentence, if it does not make a compensation order in a case where this section empowers it to do so.

(4) Compensation under subsection (1) above shall be of such amount as the court considers appropriate, having regard to any evidence and to any representations that are made by or on behalf of the accused or the prosecutor.

The victim does not have to apply to the court before a compensation order can be made. In *Holt v DPP* [1996] 2 Cr App R (S) 314, the Divisional Court held that a compensation order could be made in respect of a victim of theft who had died before sentence was passed. There is no limit to the amount of compensation which the Crown Court may order, though it must have regard to the offender's means (see **E18.9**). In the magistrates' court, s. 131 provides that the maximum sum which may be ordered by way of compensation for any offence is £5,000. Section 131 also places a limit on the total sum which may be ordered by way of compensation in a magistrates' court where the offender asks for offences to be taken into consideration. The total amount ordered must not exceed the maximum which could be ordered for the offences in respect of which the offender has been formally convicted. In *Crutchley* (1994) 15 Cr App R (S) 627, followed in *Hose* (1995) 16 Cr App R (S) 682, the Court of Appeal held that it is not open to a court to make a compensation order in respect of an offence admitted by the offender (as a sample count) but never charged or taken into consideration.

The court should make clear which amounts of compensation relate to which offences: the fixing of a 'global figure' is inappropriate (*Oddy* [1974] 1 WLR 1212), unless the offences were committed against the same victim (*Warton* [1976] Crim LR 520). Where there are competing claimants for available funds, the total compensation available should normally be apportioned on a pro rata basis (*Miller* [1976] Crim LR 694), though in *Amey* [1983] 1 WLR 345 the court selected some claimants for compensation and excluded others. Where there are co-defendants, it is preferable to make separate orders against each of them (*Grundy* [1974] 1 WLR 139).

Nature of Payment

Liability for, and Evidence of, Injury, Loss or Damage 'Any personal injury, loss or damage': it is not a prerequisite of making a compensation order that the offender would be civilly liable for the loss (*Chappell* (1984) 80 Cr App R 31), though this will generally be the case. The court may compensate distress and anxiety (*Bond v Chief Constable of Kent* [1983] 1 WLR 40, *Godfrey* (1994) 15 Cr App R (S) 536). 'Loss' may include a sum by way of interest (*Schofield* [1978] 1 WLR 979). An award may be made whenever it can fairly be said that a particular loss results from the offence (*Rowlston v Kenny* (1982) 4 Cr App R (S) 85), without having regard to technical issues of causation (*Thomson Holidays Ltd* [1974] QB 592). Thus in *Taylor* (1993) 14 Cr App R (S) 276 it was held to be appropriate to require the offender to pay £50 compensation to a man who had been kicked in the course of an affray in which the offender and four others had accosted another group of men and a fight had developed. It could not be established that Taylor had kicked the victim, but it was said to be 'artificial and unjust to look narrowly at the physical acts of each defendant'. A case which fell on the other side of the line was *Derby* (1990) 12 Cr App R (S) 502, where the offender had threatened the victim with a knife and his co-accused had seriously injured the victim by attacking him with a piece of wood. It was held that a compensation order for £4,000 made against the offender was improper, since the offender had clearly not been responsible for inflicting the injuries. This approach was followed in *Denness* [1996] 1 Cr App R (S) 159. See also *Deary* (1994) 14 Cr App R (S) 648. **E18.2**

Where there has been no damage or loss (e.g., where a stolen article is recovered and returned undamaged and is of no less value to the owner), no compensation order can be made (*Hier* (1976) 62 Cr App R 233, *Tyce* (1994) 15 Cr App R (S) 415), since the issue in compensation is the loss to the victim rather than the benefit to the offender. Conversely, where there has been damage or loss to the victim, a compensation order is not precluded by the fact that the offender has made no profit from the offence. The amount of the victim's loss should either be agreed by the offender or established by evidence. The case of *Vivian* [1979] 1 WLR 291 is clear authority for this point. In *Horsham Justices, ex parte Richards* [1985] 1 WLR 986, Neill LJ said (at p. 993): '. . . in my judgment the court has no jurisdiction to make a compensation order without receiving any evidence where there are real issues raised as to whether the claimants have suffered any, and if so what, loss'. The court should, however, hesitate to embark on a complex inquiry into the scale of loss, since compensation orders are designed to be used only in clear, straightforward cases (see **E18.11**).

In the case of an offence under the Theft Act 1968 or the Fraud Act 2006, where the property in question is recovered, any damage to the property occurring while it was out of the owner's possession is treated as having resulted from the offence, however and by whomsoever it was caused (PCC(S)A 2000, s. 130(5); see *Quigley v Stokes* [1977] 1 WLR 434).

Motor Accidents A compensation order may only be made in respect of injury, loss or damage (other than loss suffered by a person's dependants in consequence of his death) which was due to an accident arising out of the presence of a motor vehicle on a road, if: **E18.3**

(a) it is damage which falls within s. 130(5); or
(b) it is in respect of injury, loss or damage for which the offender is uninsured in relation to the use of the vehicle, and compensation is not payable under any arrangements to which the Secretary of State is a party (i.e. the Motor Insurers' Bureau Agreement) (s. 130(6)).

In the case of property damage, the Agreement does not cover the first £300 of the damage, and a compensation order up to that amount may be made in an appropriate case (*DPP v Scott* (1995) 16 Cr App R (S) 292). See further *Austin* [1996] 2 Cr App R (S) 191. If a compensation order is made in respect of such an accident, the compensation can include a sum representing the whole or part of any loss of or reduction in preferential rates of insurance attributable to the accident ('no claims' bonus) (s. 130(7)). A vehicle which is exempted from insurance (see Road Traffic Act 1988, s. 144) is not uninsured for these purposes (s. 130(8)).

E18.4 **Compensation for Loss Arising from Death** A compensation order in respect of funeral expenses may be made for the benefit of anyone who incurred the expenses (s. 130(9)). A compensation order in respect of bereavement may only be made for the benefit of a person who could claim damages for bereavement under the Fatal Accidents Act 1976, s. 1A (i.e. the spouse of the deceased or, in the case of a deceased minor, his parents, or mother if the minor is illegitimate), and the amount of that compensation shall not exceed the sum specified in the Fatal Accidents Act 1976, s. 1A(3) (currently £10,000) (s. 130(10)).

Offender's Means and Parental Liability

E18.5 In determining whether to make a compensation order, and in determining the amount to be paid, it is the duty of the court to have regard to the offender's means so far as they appear or are known to the court (s. 130(11), and see further, **E18.9**). The court may allow the offender time to pay the sum due under the compensation order, or direct payment of the sum by instalments of such amounts and on such dates as the court may specify (PCC(S)A 2000, s. 141 and MCA 1980, s. 75(1)).

Where a child or young person is convicted of an offence and the court makes an order for compensation, it should, under PCC(S)A 2000, s. 137, normally order the parent or guardian of the child or young person to pay the compensation order (see **E16.6**).

Payment, Discharge and Review

E18.6 The victim of the offence shall not receive the compensation until there is no further possibility of an appeal on which the order could be varied or set aside (s. 132(1)). By s. 133, at any time before the offender has paid into court the whole of the money under the order, the magistrates' court having power to enforce the order may, on the application of the offender, discharge the order or reduce it, on the ground that:

(a) the injury, loss or damage in respect of which the order was made has been held in civil proceedings to be less than it was taken to be for the purposes of the order;
(b) that property, the loss of which was the subject of the order, has now been recovered;
(c) that the means of the offender are insufficient to satisfy both the compensation order and a confiscation order made against him in the same proceedings under the CJA 1988, part IV or the Proceeds of Crime Act 2002, part 2; or
(d) that the offender's means have suffered a substantial reduction, which was unexpected at the time of making the order.

Before the magistrates can act to discharge or reduce the order under (c) or (d), they must have the consent of the Crown Court if the Crown Court made the order.

Enforcement of Compensation Orders

E18.7 Enforcement of compensation orders is the function of the magistrates' courts. The maximum terms of imprisonment which a magistrates' court may impose in default of payment of compensation orders are specified in the MCA 1980, sch. 4. These are the same periods which apply in the case of fines, and which are set out in the table at **E17.3**, except that the magistrates have no power to specify a term in default in excess of 12 months. These are maximum terms, and the magistrates have discretion to fix a lower term. The Crown Court is not empowered to make an order fixing the term to be served in default of payment of a compensation order (in contrast to its duty to do so in respect of fines: *Komsta* (1990)

12 Cr App R (S) 63, and see **E17.2**). The maximum terms indicated in sch. 4 will thus normally also apply in default of compensation orders imposed by the Crown Court. Exceptionally, however, if the Crown Court makes a compensation order for an amount in excess of £20,000 and considers that a maximum default term of 12 months is inadequate, it may fix a longer period, not exceeding the term specified for the equivalent amount in the PCC(S)A 2000, s. 139(4). As with fines, part payment of the compensation order will result in a proportionate reduction in the term to be served in default. A court may make an order for sums payable in respect of a compensation order made by a magistrates' court or the Crown Court to be deducted from the offender's income support payments in accordance with the Fines (Deduction from Income Support) Regulations 1992 (SI 1992 No. 2182).

COMPENSATION ORDERS: SENTENCING PRINCIPLES

Compensation Order Not Alternative to Sentence

In *Inwood* (1974) 60 Cr App R 70, Scarman LJ said (at p. 73): 'Compensation orders were not introduced into our law to enable the convicted to buy themselves out of the penalties for crime. Compensation orders were introduced into our law as a convenient and rapid means of avoiding the expense of resort to civil litigation when the criminal clearly has means which would enable the compensation to be paid.' It follows from this important principle that the imposition of a compensation order should not affect the punishment imposed for the offence and, in particular, should not 'permit the offender to buy his way out of a custodial sentence'. **E18.8**

This principle is, however, subject to the PCC(S)A 2000, s. 130(12), which gives priority to the imposition of a compensation order over a fine. This, to some extent, permits the offender to 'buy his way out of the penalties for crime', by reducing the fine in order for compensation to be paid, but s. 130(12) does not affect sentences other than fines. Some watering down of the principle in *Inwood* (1974) 60 Cr App R 70 may be detected in other decisions of the Court of Appeal such as *Huish* (1985) 7 Cr App R (S) 272, but its importance was re-emphasised by Lord Taylor CJ in *A-G's Ref (No. 5 of 1993)* (1994) 15 Cr App R (S) 201.

Taking into Account Means of Offender

It is the responsibility of the offender to inform the court of his resources, and not for the sentencer to initiate inquiries into the matter (*Bolden* (1987) 9 Cr App R (S) 83). It is not the duty of the prosecutor to establish the offender's means (*Johnstone* (1982) 4 Cr App R (S) 141), but where the offender's lawyer advances mitigation on the basis that the offender will pay substantial compensation, the lawyer is under an obligation to ensure that the necessary means exist (*Coughlin* (1984) 6 Cr App R (S) 102, *Huish* (1985) 7 Cr App R (S) 272, *Bond* (1986) 8 Cr App R (S) 11). If the offender misleads the court into believing that he has the means to pay compensation, a subsequent appeal by the offender against the compensation order will not succeed (*Hayes* (1992) 13 Cr App R (S) 454; *Dando* [1996] 1 Cr App R (S) 155). He must pay the compensation, or serve the appropriate term in default of payment. **E18.9**

It is generally wrong to make a compensation order which will require the sale of the offender's home (*Harrison* (1980) 2 Cr App R (S) 313), but it is not unreasonable to expect the offender to sell other items to pay the compensation (*Workman* (1979) 1 Cr App R (S) 335). In such a case the court must ascertain the value of the asset (*Chambers* (1981) 3 Cr App R (S) 318). An order should not be made on the basis of the sale of an asset where it is not certain that the offender will be able to dispose of that asset (*Hackett* (1988) 10 Cr App R (S) 388: family home, in joint names).

Co-defendants may be required to pay different sums by way of compensation if their capacity to pay is different. See *Beddow* (1987) 9 Cr App R (S) 235, where the offender was one of two defendants who pleaded guilty to being carried in a vehicle taken without consent by a third defendant, who had fallen asleep at the wheel, causing the van to crash. The offender was conditionally charged and ordered to pay £300 in compensation. The other two defendants received a suspended sentence and a conditional discharge respectively, but neither was required to pay compensation. The Court of Appeal approved the sentences on the basis that the offender was the only one of the defendants who was in work and could afford to pay. See also *Stapleton* [1977] Crim LR 366. A compensation order should not be imposed on the assumption that persons other than the offender will pay, or contribute to, the order (*Hunt* [1983] Crim LR 270).

Compensation Should be Payable within Reasonable Time

E18.10 In *Webb* (1979) 1 Cr App R (S) 16, Cantley J observed (at p. 18) that: 'It is no use making a compensation order (particularly one with a sentence of imprisonment in default of compliance) if there is no realistic possibility of the compensation order being complied with'. This may be because the offender has very limited means (as in *Webb*) or because the offender is serving a custodial sentence with no immediate prospect of work (e.g., *Grafton* (1979) 1 Cr App R (S) 305). A compensation order should not be made which involves payments by instalment over an unreasonable length of time. In *Bradburn* (1973) 57 Cr App R 948, Lord Widgery CJ said that, in general, compensation orders 'should be sharp in their effect rather than protracted' and that an order which would take four years to complete was 'unreasonably long'. In *Olliver* (1989) 11 Cr App R (S) 10, the Court of Appeal indicated that a fine (or compensation order) might properly be repaid over a period of up to three years. Lord Lane CJ said (at p. 15) that: 'Certainly it seems to us that a two-year period will seldom be too long, and in an appropriate case three years will be unassailable'. See also *Yehou* [1997] 2 Cr App R (S) 48.

Compensation Order Should be Made Only in Clear Case

E18.11 In *Donovan* (1981) 3 Cr App R (S) 192, the offender pleaded guilty to taking a conveyance, having hired a car for two days and failed to return it. The car had suffered no damage. The offender was fined £250, with £100 costs and £1,388 compensation, on the basis of the hire company's loss of use. Eveleigh LJ said that: 'A compensation order is designed for the simple, straightforward case where the amount of the compensation can be readily and easily ascertained'. Since the amount of damages in a civil case of loss of use 'is notoriously open to argument', the compensation order was quashed, and the hire company left to pursue its civil remedy if it wished to do so. In *Hyde v Emery* (1984) 6 Cr App R (S) 206 the offender pleaded guilty to three charges of obtaining unemployment benefit by false representation. There was a dispute over whether the sum claimed in compensation by the DHSS should be reduced by the amount of supplementary benefit which he could legitimately have claimed. Watkins LJ said in the Divisional Court that the magistrates should have declined to deal with the matter. See also *Briscoe* (1994) 15 Cr App R (S) 699 and *White* [1996] 2 Cr App R (S) 58. A slightly different line was taken in *James* [2003] 2 Cr App R (S) 574. The offender pleaded guilty to 20 counts of false accounting. The total sum involved was in dispute, but there was an agreed minimum loss of £8,000 to the victim. The Court of Appeal said that it was proper for a compensation order in that sum to be ordered, bearing in mind that the only realistic chance for the victim to receive any compensation from the offender was through the criminal court.

Combining Compensation Orders with Other Sentences or Orders

E18.12 Compensation orders may be imposed on an offender 'instead of or in addition to dealing with him in any other way' (PCC(S)A 2000, s. 130(1): see **E18.1**). It is expressly provided that a compensation order may be combined with a discharge (s. 12(7)).

While a compensation order may be combined with a sentence of immediate custody where the offender is clearly able to pay or has good prospects of employment on his release from custody (*Love* [1999] 1 Cr App R (S) 484), it is often inappropriate to impose a compensation order as well as a custodial sentence. It may well be undesirable for a compensation order to be hanging over the offender's head after release, and the order may be 'counterproductive, and force him back into crime to find the money' (*Inwood* (1974) 60 Cr App R 70). See also *Morgan* (1982) 4 Cr App R (S) 358, *Clark* (1992) 13 Cr App R (S) 124 and *Jorge* [1999] 2 Cr App R (S) 1. While it is not wrong to combine a compensation order with a suspended sentence, and, indeed, that combination is positively encouraged by s. 118(5), regard should be had to the fact that if the offender is in breach of the suspended sentence, its activation may bring to an end any prospect of the payment of compensation (*McGee* [1978] Crim LR 370). It is contrary to principle to suspend a custodial sentence merely because of the offender's ability to pay compensation.

Where it would be appropriate both to impose a fine and to make a compensation order, but the offender has insufficient means to pay both, the court shall give preference to compensation, though it may impose a fine as well (s. 130(12)). This means that the fine should be reduced or, if necessary, dispensed with altogether, to enable the compensation to be paid. A compensation order may, thus, stand alone on sentence.

Guidelines for Compensation

E18.13 The guidelines set out below are provided in the Magistrates' Courts Sentencing Guidelines (2004):

Type of Injury		*Suggested Award*
Graze	Depending on size	Up to £75
Bruise	Depending on size	Up to £100
Black eye		£125
Cut (no permanent scarring)	Depending on size and whether stitched	£100–£500
Sprain	Depending on loss of mobility	£100–£1,000
Loss of a non-front tooth	Depending on cosmetic effect	£500–£1,000
Loss of front tooth		£1,500
Eye	Blurred or double vision	£1,000
Facial scar	However small (resulting in permanent disfigurement)	£1,500
Nasal	Undisplaced fracture of the nasal bone	£1,000
Nasal	Displaced fracture of bone requiring manipulation	£1,500
Nasal	Not causing fracture but displaced septum requiring sub-mucous resection	£2,000
Wrist	Simple fracture with recovery within month	£3,000
Wrist	Displaced fracture (limb in plaster; recovery 6 months)	£3,500
Finger	Fractured little finger, recovery within month	£1,000
Leg or arm	Closed fracture of tibia, fibula, ulna or radius with recovery within month	£3,500
Laparotomy	Stomach scar 6–8 inches long (resulting from operation)	£3,500

The Guidelines state that these are 'general guidance on appropriate starting points for general damages'. It is for the criminal courts to decide what use should be made of the information in this table, but a sentencer certainly cannot be criticised for having had recourse to it (*Broughton* (1986) 8 Cr App R (S) 379).

Surcharge

E18.14 As from 1 April 2007, the DVCVA 2004, s. 14, inserts new ss. 161A and 161B into the CJA 2003. Sections 161A and 161B apply only in relation to offences committed on or after that date. See E17.15.

Section E19 Restitution Orders

Power to Make Restitution Orders

A restitution order is designed to restore to a person entitled to them goods which have been stolen or otherwise unlawfully removed from him, or to restore to him a sum of money representing the proceeds of the goods, out of money found in the offender's possession on apprehension. Either the Crown Court or a magistrates' court may make such an order. **E19.1**

Powers of Criminal Courts (Sentencing) Act 2000, s. 148

(1) This section applies where goods have been stolen, and either—
 (a) a person is convicted of any offence with reference to the theft (whether or not the stealing is the gist of his offence); or
 (b) a person is convicted of any other offence, but such an offence as is mentioned in paragraph (a) above is taken into consideration in determining his sentence.

(2) Where this section applies, the court by or before which the offender is convicted may on the conviction (whether or not the passing of sentence is in other respects deferred) exercise any of the following powers—
 (a) the court may order anyone having possession or control of the stolen goods to restore them to any person entitled to recover them from him; or
 (b) on the application of a person entitled to recover from the person convicted any other goods directly or indirectly representing the stolen goods (as being the proceeds of any disposal or realisation of the whole or part of them or of goods so representing them), the court may order those other goods to be delivered or transferred to the applicant; or
 (c) the court may order that a sum not exceeding the value of the stolen goods shall be paid, out of any money of the person convicted which was taken out of his possession on his apprehension, to any person who, if those goods were in the possession of the person convicted, would be entitled to recover them from him;

and in this subsection 'the stolen goods' means the goods referred to in subsection (1) above.

For the purposes of this section, 'stealing' is very widely construed, to include not just theft and offences where theft is a constituent element, such as robbery and burglary, but also where the goods were obtained by blackmail or fraud (or deception where the act in question was prior to the commencement of the Fraud Act 2006), or were stolen goods handled following any of these offences (Theft Act 1968, s. 24(4)). A restitution order should not be made unless the evidence on which it is based is clear and has been given before sentence is imposed (PCC(S)A 2000, s. 148(5); *Church* (1970) 55 Cr App R 65). A restitution order should not be made where the question of title to goods is unclear. According to Woolf J:

> . . . the criminal courts are not the appropriate forum in which to satisfactorily ventilate complex issues as to the ownership of such money or goods. In cases of doubt it is better to leave the victim to pursue his civil remedies or, alternatively, to apply to the magistrates' court under the Police (Property) Act 1897. On the other hand, in appropriate cases where the evidence is clear, it is important that the court should make proper use of the power to order restitution since this can frequently avoid unnecessary expense and delay in the victim receiving the return of his property. (*Calcutt* (1985) 7 Cr App R (S) 385, at p. 390)

For obvious reasons, there is no requirement under these provisions that account should be taken of the offender's means: contrast compensation orders at **E18.9**.

If an order is made under s. 148(2)(a), it will be inappropriate to order restitution under s. 148(2)(b) or (c) in addition, since the person will thereby recover more than the value of the goods (*Parsons* (1976) CSP J3–2F01). Under s. 148(2)(a), the person in 'possession or control' need not be the offender, but may be an innocent purchaser. Where a person has, in good faith, bought the goods from the convicted person, or has, in good faith, lent money to the convicted person on the security of the goods, the court may order payment of compensation to that person out of money taken from the offender under s. 148(2)(c) (s. 148(4)). Such an order may be made with or without that person's application (s. 149(2)).

Under s. 148(2)(b), an application must be made by the person claiming, and may not relate to goods held by a third party. Where the offender is no longer in possession of the goods, orders may be made under both s. 148(2)(b) and (c), with reference to the same goods, providing that the person does not thereby recover more than the value of the goods (s. 148(3)).

An order may be made under s. 148(2)(c) with or without an application being made (s. 149(2)). Again, where the offender is no longer in possession of the goods, orders may be made under both s. 148(2)(b) and (c), with reference to the same goods, providing that the person does not thereby recover more than the value of the goods (s. 148(3)).

Money seized from the offender after he has been arrested may be the subject of an order (*Ferguson* [1970] 1 WLR 1246, where £2,000, taken from the offender's safe deposit box 11 days after his arrest, was held to have been in his possession at the time of his apprehension). But it seems that money seized prior to his arrest may not (*Hinde* (1977) 64 Cr App R 213, a case decided in relation to forfeiture orders but applicable by analogy here). There is no need to show that the money is the proceeds of the relevant offence; all that is necessary is that it be shown that the money belongs to the offender (*Lewis* [1975] Crim LR 353). It was also established in *Lewis* that under s. 148(2)(c), a restitution order may be made against an offender for a greater sum than he received from the offence, provided that it is not for a sum greater than the total loss occasioned by the offence (in contrast to *Grundy* [1974] 1 WLR 139, which established that joint and several liability should not apply in relation to a compensation order).

An offender may appeal against a restitution order as against any other sentence. Such an order is, however, where made on conviction on indictment, subject to an automatic suspension for 28 days from the date of conviction (unless the trial court directs to the contrary on the ground that 'the title to the property is not in dispute': Criminal Appeal Act 1968, s. 30(1)) or, further, until the determination of any appeal, and, where made by a magistrates' court, it is subject to an automatic suspension for 21 days from the date of conviction (unless the court directs to the contrary as above: s. 149(4)) or, further, until the determination of any appeal (s. 149(4)).

Combining Restitution Orders with Other Sentences or Orders

E19.2 A restitution order may be made in combination with any other sentence passed by the court.

Section E20 Deprivation Orders

POWERS TO MAKE DEPRIVATION ORDERS UNDER THE PCC(S)A 2000, s. 143

The main power of the courts to order the forfeiture of property connected with the commission of an offence is created by the PCC(S)A 2000, s. 143(1). Other powers of forfeiture under specific statutes are considered at E20.4. The power under s. 143 may be exercised by the Crown Court or a magistrates' court, in respect of any offence. E20.1

Powers of Criminal Courts (Sentencing) Act 2000, s. 143

(1) Where a person is convicted of an offence and the court by or before which he is convicted is satisfied that any property which has been lawfully seized from him, or which was in his possession or under his control at the time when he was apprehended for the offence or when a summons in respect of it was issued—
   (a) has been used for the purpose of committing, or facilitating the commission of, any offence, or
   (b) was intended by him to be used for that purpose,

the court may (subject to subsection (5) below) make an order under this section in respect of that property.

(2) Where a person is convicted of an offence and the offence, or an offence which the court has taken into consideration in determining his sentence, consists of unlawful possession of property which—
   (a) has been lawfully seized from him, or
   (b) was in his possession or under his control at the time when he was apprehended for the offence of which he has been convicted or when a summons in respect of that offence was issued,

the court may (subject to subsection (5) below) make an order under this section in respect of that property.

(3) An order under this section shall operate to deprive the offender of his rights, if any, in the property to which it relates, and the property shall (if not already in their possession) be taken into the possession of the police.

(4) Any power conferred on a court by subsection (1) or (2) above may be exercised—
   (a) whether or not the court also deals with the offender in any other way in respect of the offence of which he has been convicted; and
   (b) without regard to any restrictions on forfeiture in any enactment contained in an Act passed before 29th July 1988.

(5) In considering whether to make an order under this section in respect of any property, a court shall have regard—
   (a) to the value of the property; and
   (b) to the likely financial and other effects on the offender of the making of the order (taken together with any other order that the court contemplates making).

(6) Where a person commits an offence to which this subsection applies by—
   (a) driving, attempting to drive, or being in charge of a vehicle, or
   (b) failing to comply with a requirement made under section 7 or 7A of the Road Traffic Act 1988 (failure to provide specimen for analysis or laboratory test or to give permission for such a test) in the course of an investigation into whether the offender had committed an offence while driving, attempting to drive or being in charge of a vehicle, or
   (c) failing, as the driver of a vehicle, to comply with subsection (2) or (3) of section 170 of the Road Traffic Act 1988 (duty to stop and give information or report accident),

the vehicle shall be regarded for the purposes of subsection (1) above (and section 144(1)(b) below) as used for the purpose of committing the offence (and for the purpose of committing any offence of aiding, abetting, counselling or procuring the commission of the offence).

(7) Subsection (6) above applies to—
  (a) an offence under the Road Traffic Act 1988 which is punishable with imprisonment;
  (b) an offence of manslaughter; and
  (c) an offence under section 35 of the Offences Against the Person Act 1861 (wanton and furious driving).

(8) Facilitating the commission of an offence shall be taken for the purposes of subsection (1) above to include the taking of any steps after it has been committed for the purpose of disposing of any property to which it relates or of avoiding apprehension or detection.

The effect of an order under s. 143 is to deprive the offender of his rights, if any, in the property (s. 143(3)), but it does not affect the rights of any other person, who may apply for recovery of the property (see below). The power does not extend to real property, such as the offender's home (*Khan* (1982) 4 Cr App R (S) 298). Nor should an order be made where the property is subject to joint ownership (*Troth* (1980) 71 Cr App R 1, where it was said that deprivation orders should be confined to 'simple, uncomplicated cases'). The power does not extend to property which was associated with an offence committed by some person other than the offender: s. 143(1)(a)(i) should be read as if the words 'by him' rather than 'by anyone' appeared after the word 'offence' (*Slater* [1986] 1 WLR 1340, *Neville* (1987) 9 Cr App R (S) 222). The phrase 'facilitating the commission of, any offence' in s. 143 includes the taking of any steps after it has been committed for the purpose of disposing of any property to which it relates or of avoiding apprehension or detection (s. 143(8)). Section 143(6) and (7) make it clear that an offender's vehicle *shall* be regarded as having been used for the purpose of any offence specified therein. Sections 143(6) and (7), however, in no way limit the courts' power to order forfeiture of an offender's car in respect of other offences under the general provision in s. 143(1). See also the important sentencing principle as to totality at **E20.2**. Where the making of a deprivation order is being considered by the court, *Pemberton* (1982) 4 Cr App R (S) 328 requires that evidence be laid before the judge on the issue and that 'full and proper investigation' must be made into the prosecution's application. See also *Ball* [2003] 2 Cr App R (S) 92.

The property shall be taken into the possession of the police, if not in their possession already, and the Police (Property) Act 1897 shall apply to such property. However, no application can be made by a claimant after six months from the date of the deprivation order. And no such order can be made unless the claimant satisfies the court either that he had not consented to the offender having possession of the property or, where the order was made under s. 143(1)(a), that he did not know, and had no reason to suspect, that the property was likely to be used for the purpose mentioned in that subsection (s. 144(1)). The police have power under the 1897 Act to dispose of property where its ownership has not been ascertained and no court order has been made in respect of it. In relation to s. 143, the police have similar powers where no application has been made within six months or no such application has succeeded (s. 144(2)).

Powers of Criminal Courts (Sentencing) Act 2000, s. 145

(1) Where a court makes an order under section 143 above in a case where—
  (a) the offender has been convicted of an offence which has resulted in a person suffering personal injury, loss or damage, or
  (b) any such offence is taken into consideration by the court in determining sentence,

  the court may also make an order that any proceeds which arise from the disposal of the property and which do not exceed a sum specified by the court shall be paid to that person.

(2) The court may only make an order under this section if it is satisfied that but for the inadequacy of the offender's means it would have made a compensation order under which the offender would have been required to pay compensation of an amount not less than the specified amount.

No order can be made under this provision before the expiry of the six-month period mentioned above, or where a successful application has been made under the Police (Property) Act 1897 in respect of the property (s. 145(3)).

DEPRIVATION ORDERS: SENTENCING PRINCIPLES

Deprivation Order Affects Totality of Sentence

See the PCC(S)A 2000, s. 143(5), at **E20.1**. In *Buddo* (1982) 4 Cr App R (S) 268, the offender pleaded guilty to burglary and assault. In addition to a total prison sentence of two years, the offender was deprived of his rights in a motor caravan in which he had driven to commit the burglary. The Court of Appeal was of the view that such an order could properly be made on the facts but that sentencers were 'not required to make such an order in every case in which a vehicle is used in the commission of a crime'. In this case, according to Park J, the deprivation order was 'overdoing the punishment', and the order was quashed. See also *Scully* (1985) 7 Cr App R (S) 119 and *Priestley* [1996] 2 Cr App R (S) 144. **E20.2**

Where the order would have a disproportionately severe impact upon the offender, it is also inappropriate. In *Tavernor* [1976] RTR 242, an order depriving the offender of his rights in a car, imposed in addition to a suspended prison sentence and a fine, was quashed in view of the offender's physical disability. See also *Highbury Corner Metropolitan Stipendiary Magistrate, ex parte Di Matteo* [1991] 1 WLR 1374.

In a case where several offenders are equally implicated and receive comparable sentences, it is wrong to impose in addition a deprivation order upon one of them (*Ottey* (1984) 6 Cr App R (S) 163; but see *Burgess* [2001] 2 Cr App R (S) 5, where it was said that the principle can be taken so far but no further). This may be contrasted with the principle applicable to compensation orders, the object of which is to compensate the victim, rather than to punish the offender (see **E18.8**).

Combining Deprivation Orders with Other Sentences or Orders

A deprivation order may be combined with a compensation order, and provision is made under the PCC(S)A 2000, s. 145, to allow the sale of property connected with the offence in order to finance compensation for the victim where the means of the offender would otherwise have been inadequate to meet a compensation order. A deprivation order may be combined with a discharge or a community rehabilitation order (s. 12(7)). **E20.3**

OTHER STATUTORY POWERS TO MAKE FORFEITURE ORDERS

Many other statutes contain their own forfeiture provisions relating to offences committed under those statutes, or to property regulated under those statutes. **E20.4**

Misuse of Drugs Act 1971, s. 27

(1) Subject to subsection (2) below, the court by or before which a person is convicted of an offence under this Act or an offence falling within subsection (3) below or an offence to which section 1 of the Proceeds of Crime (Scotland) Act 1995 relates may order anything shown to the satisfaction of the court to relate to the offence, to be forfeited and either destroyed or dealt with in such other manner as the court may order.

(2) The court shall not order anything to be forfeited under this section, where a person claiming to be the owner of or otherwise interested in it applies to be heard by the court, unless an opportunity has been given to him to show cause why the order should not be made.

(3) An offence falls within this subsection if it is an offence which is specified in—

(a) paragraph 1 of schedule 2 to the Proceeds of Crime Act 2002 (drug trafficking offences), or
(b) so far as it relates to that paragraph, paragraph 10 of that schedule.

Any personal property which relates to the offence may be forfeited, including money (*Beard* [1974] 1 WLR 1549), but s. 27 does not extend to intangibles, or to property situated outside the jurisdiction of the English courts (*Cuthbertson* [1981] AC 470). Nor, apparently, does s. 27 permit the forfeiture of real property such as a house (*Pearce* [1996] 2 Cr App R (S) 316). The property must be shown to relate to the offence of which the offender has been convicted; its relation to intended offences is insufficient (*Morgan* [1977] Crim LR 488, *Ribeyre* (1982) 4 Cr App R (S) 165, *Llewellyn* (1985) 7 Cr App R (S) 225 and *Cox* (1986) 8 Cr App R (S) 384). Thus, where the offender was convicted of possession of cocaine, which was hidden in his car, a forfeiture order under s. 27 could not be made in respect of £1,489 also found in his possession and accepted to be the proceeds of drug dealing, since this was the proceeds of drugs other than those to which the conviction related (*Boothe* (1987) 9 Cr App R (S) 8). In *Boothe* an order made under the predecessor to the PCC(S)A 2000, s. 143 (see **E20.1**), for forfeiture of a car was upheld. It is clear that an order in relation to the car might have been made under s. 27 of the 1971 Act (*Bowers* (1994) 15 Cr App R (S) 315). If the offender disputes that property is related to the offence of which he has been convicted, he must be permitted to call evidence (*Churcher* (1986) 8 Cr App R (S) 94). Under s. 27(2), it seems that the court may order forfeiture notwithstanding such an application: contrast the position under the PCC(S)A 2000, s. 143 at **E20.1**.

It may be assumed that the sentencing principles listed in relation to the PCC(S)A 2000, s. 143, also apply here. There is, however, under s. 27, no power to sell property to generate compensation.

Firearms Act 1968, s. 52

(1) Where a person—
(a) is convicted of an offence under this Act (other than an offence under section 22(3) or an offence relating specifically to air weapons) or is convicted of a crime for which he is sentenced to imprisonment, or detention in a young offender institution or a young offender's institution in Scotland or is subject to a secure training order; or
(b) has been ordered to enter into a recognisance to keep the peace or to be of good behaviour, a condition of which is that he shall not possess, use or carry a firearm; or
(c) is subject to a community order containing a requirement that he shall not possess, use or carry a firearm;

the court by or before which he is convicted, or by which the order is made, may make such order as to the forfeiture or disposal of any firearm or ammunition found in his possession as the court thinks fit and may cancel any firearm certificate or shot gun certificate held by him.

The wording of s. 52(1) is broad, and does not require the offence to relate in any way to the firearm, or the offender to be in possession of the firearm at any particular time. Firearms forfeited under s. 52 may be disposed of by the court in accordance with s. 52(4) of and sch. 6 to the 1968 Act.

Prevention of Crime Act 1953, s. 1

(2) Where any person is convicted of an offence under subsection (1) of this section the court may make an order for the forfeiture or disposal of any weapon in respect of which the offence was committed.

The offence relates to having in any public place any offensive weapon without lawful authority or reasonable excuse.

Section E21 Confiscation Orders

GENERAL

Part 2 of the Proceeds of Crime Act (the PCA 2002) provides a single model for the making of confiscation orders following conviction in criminal cases (other than for certain terrorist offences which have separate legislation). The basic framework is a merger and extension of the two similar but separate schemes contained in the Drug Trafficking Act 1994 for drug offences and in the CJA 1988, as heavily amended by the PCA 1995, for other offences (see the 2002 edition of this work). Many of the earlier cases remain useful guides to the application of the 2002 Act. The Act came into force on 24 March 2003 but does not apply if *any* of the index offences of which the defendant has been convicted took place before that date (PCA 2002 (Transitional Provisions, Savings and Amendment) Order (SI 2003 No. 333)). The Assets Recovery Agency (ARA) may initiate and conduct confiscation proceedings. See **D8** for all other asset recovery measures. (Note that on 11 January 2007, the Home Office laid a Written Ministerial Statement that the ARA is to be merged with the Serious Organised Crime Agency which will assume overall conduct of the instigation and control of the various forms of recovery proceedings. Subject to the passing of the Serious Crime Bill, the merger provisions are predicted to come into force in April 2008.) **E21.1**

The PCA 2002 changed the previous law in five important ways:

(a) the Crown Court is now the 'one-stop shop' for confiscation and ancillary orders;
(b) the Act creates a single, unified system for confiscation following a criminal conviction;
(c) an enquiry is mandatory in all cases if the prosecution applies for a hearing;
(d) the Act introduces the notion of a 'criminal lifestyle', which triggers an unlimited review of the proceeds of the defendant's 'general criminal conduct';
(e) it gives the prosecution a right of appeal.

The Human Rights Act 1998

Article 6 Viewed overall, the process of confiscation amounts to thc 'determination of a criminal charge' and 'a defendant enjoys full benefit of all the rights conferred by Article 6(1) [of the ECHR] in all aspects of confiscation proceedings' including the guarantee of a hearing within a reasonable time. Article 6(1) is engaged, for example, in late enforcement proceedings to commit a defaulting defendant to prison (*Lloyd v Bow St Magistrates' Court* [2004] 1 Cr App R 132; *Crowther v UK* (2005) *The Times*, 11 February 2005) and in a late prosecution application for reconsideration of the available amount (*Re Saggar* [2005] 1 WLR 2693). **E21.2**

Paradoxically, however, it has been firmly held that, in principle, confiscation proceedings are part of the sentencing process and the defendant is not then 'charged with a criminal offence' within the meaning of Article 6(2). Once he is convicted, Article 6(2) has no application in relation to allegations made about the defendant's character and conduct as part of the sentencing process, unless such accusations are of such a nature and degree as to amount to the bringing of a new 'charge' within the autonomous Convention meaning (*Benjafield* [2003] 1 AC 1099; *McIntosh v Lord Advocate* [2003] 1 AC 1078; *Phillips v UK* (2001) Appln. 41087/98 [2001] Crim LR 817: see also **A7.86**). Accordingly, the use of the mandatory assumptions of fact and reverse burdens of proof in the determination of benefit (see **E21.16**) do not engage, let alone breach, the specific protections of Article 6(2), including the presumption of innocence. In *Geering v Netherlands* (Appln. No. 30810/03, 3 March 2007) the European Court did encounter a situation in which a defendant in confiscation proceedings may be treated as 'charged with a criminal offence' and entitled to the presumption of innocence. The defendant had been acquitted on appeal of most of the charges which he had faced. Following this, a confiscation order was nevertheless made by another court which found, on the balance of probabilities, that there were 'sufficient indications' that he had committed the offences of which he had been acquitted and that it was 'implausible' that he had not benefited from the proceeds which it then estimated. It appears that the distinguishing features of the European Court's decision are (a) that the defendant was 'charged with a criminal offence' in the sense that the confiscation hearing was a redetermination of his guilt of the offences of which he had been acquitted; and (b) that there was no evidence, other than 'conjecture', that he actually had benefited.

Similar provisions in earlier legislation have been held to achieve a proportionate balance between the interests of the defendant and those of the public (see *Benjafield*). Nor does the application of the legislation as intended amount to an arbitrary interference with the right to peaceful enjoyment of possessions within the meaning of Protocol 1, Article 1 (*Ellingham* [2005] 2 Cr App R (S) 192).

E21.3 **Article 7** Article 7 of the ECHR prohibits retrospective penalties (see **A7.87**). However, there is no breach where the determination of benefit or of the available amount includes property acquired by the defendant before the legislation came into force, provided that the offence giving rise to the confiscation proceedings was committed after that date (*Welch v UK* (1995) 20 EHRR 247; *Taylor v UK* (1998) Appln. 31209/96).

E21.4 **Article 8** Hardship and the exercise of discretion are not considerations in the determination of the amount of the confiscation order. 'The court is merely concerned with the arithmetic exercise of computing what is, in effect, a statutory debt' (*Ahmed* [2005] 1 WLR 122). Thus, Article 8 (the right to respect for private and family life, home and correspondence) is not engaged when the value of the matrimonial home is accounted as part of the 'available amount' (see **E21.22**). 'The extent of the relevance' of a spouse's interest in the matrimonial home is 'within the appreciation' of the Contracting State (*Danison v UK* (1998) Appln. 45042/98). However, consideration of the rights of third parties under Article 8 and consequent issues of proportionality may become relevant at the enforcement stage (see **E21.29**) if, for example, the prosecutor attempts to realise the value of the family home in order to meet an unpaid confiscation order (*Ahmed*).

The Process: A Summary

E21.5 **Proceeds of Crime Act 2002, s. 6**

(1) The Crown Court must proceed under this section if the following two conditions are satisfied.

(2) The first condition is that a defendant falls within any of the following paragraphs—

(a) he is convicted of an offence or offences in proceedings before the Crown Court;

(b) he is committed to the Crown Court for sentence in respect of an offence or offences under section 3, 4 or 6 of the Sentencing Act;

(c) he is committed to the Crown Court in respect of an offence or offences under section 70 below (committal with a view to a confiscation order being considered).

(3) The second condition is that—

(a) the prosecutor or the Director asks the court to proceed under this section, or

(b) the court believes it is appropriate for it to do so.

(4) The court must proceed as follows—

(a) it must decide whether the defendant has a criminal lifestyle;

(b) if it decides that he has a criminal lifestyle it must decide whether he has benefited from his general criminal conduct;

(c) if it decides that he does not have a criminal lifestyle it must decide whether he has benefited from his particular criminal conduct.

(5) If the court decides under subsection (4)(b) or (c) that the defendant has benefited from the conduct referred to it must—
(a) decide the recoverable amount, and
(b) make an order (a confiscation order) requiring him to pay that amount.

(6) But the court must treat the duty in subsection (5) as a power if it believes that any victim of the conduct has at any time started or intends to start proceedings against the defendant in respect of loss, injury or damage sustained in connection with the conduct.

(7) The court must decide any question arising under subsection (4) or (5) on a balance of probabilities.

(8) The first condition is not satisfied if the defendant absconds (but section 27 may apply).

(9) References in this Part to the offence (or offences) concerned are to the offence (or offences) mentioned in subsection (2).

A confiscation order does not itself confiscate any property but, instead, requires the offender to pay over a sum of money: 'the recoverable amount' (see **E21.18** to **E21.20**). This will be either (a) the full amount of what the court has found to be his 'benefit' from his 'criminal conduct' or (b) the value of all his assets at the time of the order, if he can prove that amount to be less: 'the available amount' (see **E21.22**)

Under s. 6(2) an order may be made in the Crown Court against anyone (a) convicted of an offence in the Crown Court; (b) committed to the Crown Court for sentence; or (c) committed to the Crown Court for specific consideration of a confiscation order. The process is inexorable and must proceed to its conclusion when either (a) the prosecutor asks the Crown Court to proceed, or (b) the court itself considers that it is appropriate to do so (s. 6(3)).

The PCA 2002 abolished the power of magistrates to make confiscation orders. However, this is likely to be revived for amounts not exceeding £10,000 if and when the Home Secretary makes an order to that effect under the SOCPA 2005, s. 97. At present, magistrates must commit a convicted defendant to the Crown Court 'with a view to a confiscation order being considered' if the prosecution so requests (PCA 2002, s. 70).

Procedure is now governed by the CrimPR, parts 56 to 62 and 72 (see **appendix 1**).

Normally, the confiscation order must be made before sentence. However, the court may postpone the confiscation hearing for up to two years from the date of conviction and proceed instead to sentence the defendant or to order compensation (although not other monetary penalties). In 'exceptional circumstances' longer postponements are possible.

A strict order of events must be followed after conviction or committal as above:

(a) The process starts when the prosecution asks for an enquiry or when 'the court believes it is appropriate' to hold one.

(b) The court must then decide whether the defendant has a 'criminal lifestyle'. This depends solely upon the nature of the offence or offences of which he has been convicted in the current or earlier proceedings.

(c) The judge must then determine whether the defendant has benefited from 'criminal conduct'. There are two alternatives:
(i) if the defendant has been found to have a criminal lifestyle, the court must determine whether he has benefited from 'his *general* criminal conduct'.
(ii) if, on the other hand, the defendant does not have a criminal lifestyle, the court must determine whether he has benefited from 'his *particular* criminal conduct' (i.e. from the particular offence(s) of which he has been convicted or has had taken into consideration).

(d) Next, the judge must determine the gross market value of the defendant's proceeds of crime or benefit — 'the recoverable amount'. In calculating benefit from 'general criminal conduct', the judge must apply the relevant assumptions as to income and expenditure in the previous six years and as to property 'held' by the defendant on conviction (unless the defendant can show an assumption to be incorrect or that 'there would be a serious risk of injustice if an assumption were made').

(e) Lastly, the judge must make a confiscation order in that sum *unless* the defendant can prove that the value of all his existing assets, known as 'the available amount' (including artificial or 'tainted' gifts to others), is less than the value of the benefit. If so, the 'available amount' becomes the 'recoverable amount' and, therefore, is the amount of the confiscation order.

Information, Evidence and Proof

E21.6 **Proceeds of Crime Act 2002, ss. 16 to 18**

16.—(1) If the court is proceeding under section 6 in a case where section 6(3)(a) applies, the prosecutor or the Director (as the case may be) must give the court a statement of information within the period the court orders.

(2) If the court is proceeding under section 6 in a case where section 6(3)(b) applies and it orders the prosecutor to give it a statement of information, the prosecutor must give it such a statement within the period the court orders.

(3) If the prosecutor or the Director (as the case may be) believes the defendant has a criminal lifestyle the statement of information is a statement of matters the prosecutor or the Director believes are relevant in connection with deciding these issues—

(a) whether the defendant has a criminal lifestyle;

(b) whether he has benefited from his general criminal conduct;

(c) his benefit from the conduct.

(4) A statement under subsection (3) must include information the prosecutor or Director believes is relevant—

(a) in connection with the making by the court of a required assumption under section 10;

(b) for the purpose of enabling the court to decide if the circumstances are such that it must not make such an assumption.

(5) If the prosecutor or the Director (as the case may be) does not believe the defendant has a criminal lifestyle the statement of information is a statement of matters the prosecutor or the Director believes are relevant in connection with deciding these issues—

(a) whether the defendant has benefited from his particular criminal conduct;

(b) his benefit from the conduct.

(6) If the prosecutor or the Director gives the court a statement of information—

(a) he may at any time give the court a further statement of information;

(b) he must give the court a further statement of information if it orders him to do so, and he must give it within the period the court orders.

(7) If the court makes an order under this section it may at any time vary it by making another one.

17.—(1) If the prosecutor or the Director gives the court a statement of information and a copy is served on the defendant, the court may order the defendant—

(a) to indicate (within the period it orders) the extent to which he accepts each allegation in the statement, and

(b) so far as he does not accept such an allegation, to give particulars of any matters he proposes to rely on.

(2) If the defendant accepts to any extent an allegation in a statement of information the court may treat his acceptance as conclusive of the matters to which it relates for the purpose of deciding the issues referred to in section 16(3) or (5) (as the case may be).

(3) If the defendant fails in any respect to comply with an order under subsection (1) he may be treated for the purposes of subsection (2) as accepting every allegation in the statement of information apart from—

(a) any allegation in respect of which he has complied with the requirement;

(b) any allegation that he has benefited from his general or particular criminal conduct.

(4) For the purposes of this section an allegation may be accepted or particulars may be given in a manner ordered by the court.

(5) If the court makes an order under this section it may at any time vary it by making another one.

(6) No acceptance under this section that the defendant has benefited from conduct is admissible in evidence in proceedings for an offence.

18.—(1) This section applies if—
(a) the court is proceeding under section 6 in a case where section 6(3)(a) applies, or
(b) it is proceeding under section 6 in a case where section 6(3)(b) applies or it is considering whether to proceed.

(2) For the purpose of obtaining information to help it in carrying out its functions the court may at any time order the defendant to give it information specified in the order.

(3) An order under this section may require all or a specified part of the information to be given in a specified manner and before a specified date.

(4) If the defendant fails without reasonable excuse to comply with an order under this section the court may draw such inference as it believes is appropriate.

(5) Subsection (4) does not affect any power of the court to deal with the defendant in respect of a failure to comply with an order under this section.

(6) If the prosecutor or the Director (as the case may be) accepts to any extent an allegation made by the defendant—
(a) in giving information required by an order under this section, or
(b) in any other statement given to the court in relation to any matter relevant to deciding the available amount under section 9,
the court may treat the acceptance as conclusive of the matters to which it relates.

(7) For the purposes of this section an allegation may be accepted in a manner ordered by the court.

(8) If the court makes an order under this section it may at any time vary it by making another one.

(9) No information given under this section which amounts to an admission by the defendant that he has benefited from criminal conduct is admissible in evidence in proceedings for an offence.

Exchange of Information The procedure has its own form of pleadings now governed by the CrimPR, r. 58(1) (see **appendix** 1). First, the prosecution must serve a 'Statement of Information' outlining the matters that it believes are relevant to the various stages of the PCA enquiry (PCA 2002, s. 16). **E21.7**

In return, the defendant may be ordered to 'indicate . . . in a manner ordered by the court' the extent to which he accepts the allegations in the statement and, if he does not accept any allegation, 'to give particulars of any matters he proposes to rely on' (s. 17). If the offender fails 'in any respect' to comply with such an order, he can be treated as having accepted 'every allegation' in the statement apart from (a) those to which he has responded and (b) the basic allegation that he has benefited from criminal conduct (see *Crutchley* (1994) 15 Cr App R (S) 627).

In addition, the court has a free-standing power at any time to order the defendant to provide written information 'to help it in carrying out its functions' (s. 18). Failure to comply without reasonable excuse entitles the court to draw adverse inferences. The judge cannot order a third party such as a solicitor to provide information (*R (Dechert Solicitors) v Southwark Crown Court* [2001] EWHC Admin 477).

Evidence and Proof The standard of proof throughout the PCA 2002 is that of 'the balance of probabilities' (s. 6(7)). In strict terms the prosecution carry the burden of proving both the fact that the defendant has benefited from criminal conduct and the amount of his benefit. However, in lifestyle cases, once the prosecution establish any income, expenditure or interest in property, the burden is considerably lightened by the mandatory assumptions of benefit. Moreover, it has been held that 'the ordinary rules of criminal evidence (do) not apply' to confiscation hearings (*Silcock* [2004] 2 Cr App R (S) 323). **E21.8**

Where the hearing has been preceded by a contested trial, the judge is entitled to form his own view from the evidence (*Threapleton* [2002] Crim LR 229; *Boyer* (1981) 3 Cr App R (S) 35; *Solomon* (1984) 6 Cr App R (S) 120; *McGlade* (1990) 12 Cr App R (S) 105). The defendant must be allowed to give evidence at this stage (*Jenkins* (1990) 12 Cr App R (S) 582). The judge may take account of discrepancies between a defendant's evidence in the trial and his evidence in the confiscation hearing (*O'Connell* [2005] EWCA Crim 1520).

E21.9 **The Effect of the Basis of a Guilty Plea** The agreed basis of a guilty plea, while obviously relevant to sentence, will not necessarily limit the ambit of the confiscation inquiry. The prosecution should consider whether any sentencing concession might conflict with the assumptions of benefit which must ordinarily be applied in subsequent confiscation proceedings (see **E21.16**). 'What is plainly unacceptable is for the concession to be made for part of the sentencing process, without qualification, but for reliance to be placed, tacitly, on the assumptions when it comes to the confiscation hearing' (*Lunnon* [2005] 1 Cr App R (S) 111). In *Lunnon*, it had been accepted by the Crown that the defendant had no prior involvement in drug trafficking. In those circumstances, to apply a mandatory assumption that the defendant had previously benefited from drug trafficking would amount to 'injustice' and allow the court to disapply the assumption. The determining feature is the extent of the concession made by the prosecution rather than the fact that the defendant's plea has been entered on a limited basis. In *Lazarus* [2005] 1 Cr App R (S) 552, the prosecution accepted a guilty plea to a drugs offence on the basis of limited involvement in the offence. The Court of Appeal nevertheless upheld a confiscation order that 'assumed' that monies passing through a bank account in previous years were the proceeds of drug trafficking. It held that the basis of the plea was not inconsistent with prior drug trafficking; the prosecution had never been invited to agree, as they had in *Lunnon*, that there had been no previous trafficking and the defendant had known shortly after the acceptance of his plea that the prosecution were seeking to rely on the statutory assumptions and had the opportunity to rebut them. See also *Green* [2007] EWCA Crim 1248. In *Bakewell* [2006] 2 Cr App R (S) 277, the prosecution accepted a written basis of plea limiting the amount of the defendant's payment for participation in a fraudulent evasion of duty. Significantly, they were not prepared to accept the defendant's assertion that this was the extent of his benefit. Without that concession, the payment was merely to be regarded as his 'reward'; correctly applying s. 76(5), his benefit, in contrast to his reward, was the whole value of the pecuniary advantage obtained in the evasion of duty. Moreover, *Bakewell* was a case involving the evasion of duty payable to H.M. Customs and Excise; in a later but similar decision, *Rowbotham* [2006] 2 Cr App R (S) 642, the Court of Appeal implied that, notwithstanding a basis for plea, 'Customs and Excise' cases are *sui generis* because of the liability for the whole duty evaded borne by 'any . . . person acting on behalf of the importer of the excise goods' (Excise Goods (Holding, Movement, Warehousing and REDS) Regulations 1992 (SI 1992 No. 3135), reg. 5).

In most cases the prosecution are advised to say no more than that they do not dispute a defence assertion for the purposes of sentence but that they cannot say what information may arise in the course of the confiscation inquiry (*Lazarus*).

E21.10 **Special Counsel** Frequently, the judge will have seen and reviewed material which has not been disclosed for reasons of public interest immunity. The material may be highly adverse to a defendant in subsequent confiscation proceedings and, in particular, damaging to his credibility — for example, information that he has been a highly successful criminal for many years. In such a situation, the appointment of special counsel should be considered (*May* [2005] 1 WLR 2902).

MAKING OF CONFISCATION ORDER

Stage One — Determining Criminal Lifestyle

E21.11 **Proceeds of Crime Act 2002, s. 75**

(1) A defendant has a criminal lifestyle if (and only if) the following condition is satisfied.

(2) The condition is that the offence (or any of the offences) concerned satisfies any of these tests—
  (a) it is specified in Schedule 2;
  (b) it constitutes conduct forming part of a course of criminal activity;
  (c) it is an offence committed over a period of at least six months and the defendant has benefited from the conduct which constitutes the offence.

(3) Conduct forms part of a course of criminal activity if the defendant has benefited from the conduct and—
  (a) in the proceedings in which he was convicted he was convicted of three or more other offences, each of three or more of them constituting conduct from which he has benefited, or
  (b) in the period of six years ending with the day when those proceedings were started (or, if there is more than one such day, the earliest day) he was convicted on at least two separate occasions of an offence constituting conduct from which he has benefited.

(4) But an offence does not satisfy the test in subsection (2)(b) or (c) unless the defendant obtains relevant benefit of not less than £5000.

(5) Relevant benefit for the purposes of subsection (2)(b) is—
  (a) benefit from conduct which constitutes the offence;
  (b) benefit from any other conduct which forms part of the course of criminal activity and which constitutes an offence of which the defendant has been convicted;
  (c) benefit from conduct which constitutes an offence which has been or will be taken into consideration by the court in sentencing the defendant for an offence mentioned in paragraph (a) or (b).

(6) Relevant benefit for the purposes of subsection (2)(c) is—
  (a) benefit from conduct which constitutes the offence;
  (b) benefit from conduct which constitutes an offence which has been or will be taken into consideration by the court in sentencing the defendant for the offence mentioned in paragraph (a).
  (c) benefit from conduct which constitutes an offence which has been or will be taken into consideration by the court in sentencing the defendant for an offence mentioned in paragraph (a) or (b).

The court must first decide whether the defendant has a 'criminal lifestyle' (s. 6(4)(a)). This is a purely formulaic exercise in which the defendant qualifies if one of the offences of which he has been convicted falls within the statutory catalogue in s. 75. There are three sub-divisions:

(a) Offences specified in sch. 2 (including their inchoate forms). The specified offences fall under the following broad headings: (i) drug trafficking; (ii) money laundering; (iii) directing terrorism; (iv) people trafficking; (v) arms trafficking; (vi) counterfeiting; (vii) intellectual property; (viii) prostitution and child sex; (ix) blackmail. An offence under the Gangmasters (Licensing) Act 2004, s. 12, is also specified.

(b) An offence that 'constitutes conduct forming part of a course of criminal activity'. To qualify, a defendant must have been convicted of:
  (i) three or more other offences in the current proceedings, each of which was committed on or after 24 March 2003 and which constitutes conduct from which he has benefited (i.e. at least four offences in all), or
  (ii) such an offence on at least two separate occasions in the six years before the current proceedings were started.

  A conviction for these purposes includes an offence taken into consideration. The total benefit from the offences or offences taken into consideration must be at least £5,000.

(c) An offence committed over a period of at least six months resulting in benefit of not less than £5,000.

Stage Two — Determination of Benefit from Criminal Conduct

Proceeds of Crime Act 2002, s. 76 **E21.12**

(1) Criminal conduct is conduct which—
  (a) constitutes an offence in England and Wales, or
  (b) would constitute such an offence if it occurred in England and Wales.

(2) General criminal conduct of the defendant is all his criminal conduct, and it is immaterial—
  (a) whether conduct occurred before or after the passing of this Act;
  (b) whether property constituting a benefit from conduct was obtained before or after the passing of this Act.

(3) Particular criminal conduct of the defendant is all his criminal conduct which falls within the following paragraphs—
  (a) conduct which constitutes the offence or offences concerned;
  (b) conduct which constitutes offences of which he was convicted in the same proceedings as those in which he was convicted of the offence or offences concerned;
  (c) conduct which constitutes offences which the court will be taking into consideration in deciding his sentence for the offence or offences concerned.

(4) A person benefits from conduct if he obtains property as a result of or in connection with the conduct.

(5) If a person obtains a pecuniary advantage as a result of or in connection with conduct, he is to be taken to obtain as a result of or in connection with the conduct a sum of money equal to the value of the pecuniary advantage.

(6) References to property or a pecuniary advantage obtained in connection with conduct include references to property or a pecuniary advantage obtained both in that connection and some other.

(7) If a person benefits from conduct his benefit is the value of the property obtained.

Criminal conduct is conduct that either constitutes an offence in England and Wales or which would constitute an offence if it occurred here (s. 76(1)).

If the defendant does not have a criminal lifestyle, the court must nevertheless determine the benefit of 'his *particular* criminal conduct' (s. 6(4)(a)). The enquiry is restricted to the offences that are proved or admitted in the current proceedings, including offences taken into consideration (s. 76(3)). The assumptions do not apply.

If, on the other hand, he does have a criminal lifestyle, the court must determine his benefit from 'his general criminal conduct' (s. 6(4)(b)). General criminal conduct is all of the defendant's criminal conduct regardless of when it occurred (s. 76(2)). In determining benefit from general criminal conduct in the previous six years, the court must apply the required assumptions (see **E21.16**).

A person benefits from criminal conduct 'if he obtains property as a result of or in connection with the conduct' (s. 76(4)). Property is all property wherever situated and includes (a) money, (b) all forms of real or personal property, (c) things in action and other intangible or incorporeal property. The benefit to the 'defendant is the value of the property obtained' (s. 76(7)). Property is 'obtained' by a person 'if he obtains an interest in it' (s. 84(2)(b)). An interest in land includes 'any legal estate or equitable interest or power' (s. 84(2)(f)); an interest in property other than land includes a right including a right to possession (s. 84(2)(h)). Where the defendant has obtained a pecuniary advantage, the benefit is an amount equal to the value of the advantage (s. 76(5)).

Obviously, obtaining state benefits on the basis of a false declaration or failure to declare a change in circumstances will amount to obtaining a pecuniary advantage, i.e. the amount of the state benefits. However, legitimate trading profit which has not been declared to the Inland Revenue or Department of Works and Pensions does not *per se* amount to criminal property (*Gabriel* [2006] EWCA Crim 229). Even so, 'these words do not mean more than that profits from legitimate trading can never without more give rise to criminal property' (*IK* [2007] EWCA Crim 491). Where the defendant has been proved to have cheated the Revenue, legitimate but undeclared cash profits may amount to criminal property in that they represent 'in part' the tax of which the Revenue has been cheated.

E21.13 **Temporary Benefit** It is not necessary for the property to pass to the defendant. A temporary obtaining is sufficient (see *Patel* [2000] 2 Cr App R (S) 10; *Simpson* [1998] 2 Cr App R (S) 111; *Alagobola* [2004] 2 Cr App R (S) 248; *Wilkes* [2003] Cr App R (S) 625). A pecuniary advantage can be obtained by deferment of a debt or by temporary evasion of payable duty. In *Smith* [2002] 1 WLR 54 the defendant fraudulently imported cigarettes by sea, sailing past Customs houses at Immingham and Hull without paying the excise duty. The boat was intercepted before the cigarettes could be offloaded and sold. The House of Lords upheld a confiscation order in the amount of the duty temporarily evaded. See also *Dimsey* [2000] 2 All ER 142 and *Edwards* [2004] EWCA Crim 2923.

However, no pecuniary advantage is obtained by a temporary and unrealised increase in the value of shares. In *Rigby* [2006] 1 WLR 3067 company shares had been inflated by misleading statements; following corrective statements the value of the shares then fell dramatically before they could be sold. The court distinguished *Smith*: 'In *Smith*, the benefit or pecuniary advantage — the evaded duty — was the very thing obtained by the offence. Here, the temporary increased value of the shares was not obtained at all . . . absent a sale of the shares. The increase in value was . . . purely notional and soon disappeared'.

Joint Enterprise and Individual Benefit In strict theory the prosecution must prove that the defendant has, in fact, obtained property or a pecuniary advantage himself and not simply that it has been obtained by others, for example, co-conspirators. Accordingly, no benefit is obtained if the defendant withdraws from a conspiracy to rob before any robbery occurs and he has not been 'instrumental in obtaining the cash in any realistic way' (*Byatt* [2006] 2 Cr App R (S) 779). However, 'robust inferences' may be drawn if defendants are 'unhelpful as to which of them obtained what benefit' (*Houareau* [2006] 1 Cr App R (S) 509; *Olubitan* [2004] 2 Cr App R (S) 70; *Davy* [2003] EWCA Crim 781; *Gokal* (11 March 1999 unreported, CA); *Martens* (20 April 1999 unreported, Langley J)). **E21.14**

An order cannot be made jointly and severally against defendants. As a general rule, the court should attempt to apportion the amount of the proceeds and make separate orders against each individual according to the degree of involvement. In the absence of any explanation from the defendant and of evidence to the contrary, it may be taken that the proceeds were equally shared (*Porter* (1990) 12 Cr App R (S) 377; *Gibbons* [2003] 2 Cr App R (S) 169). However, where the benefit consists of property that is *jointly* controlled by defendants, for example, monies in the bank accounts of companies used and jointly controlled by defendants, as in VAT frauds involving multiple companies, each defendant obtains the whole of the amount obtained by the companies in which he has a controlling interest (*May* [2005] 1 WLR 2902). If an offender has sufficient control to realise property jointly held with an absent defendant, the whole of the property is treated as his benefit (*Chrastny (No. 2)* [1991] 1 WLR 1385).

Where one defendant receives the benefit and then shares it with other members of the enterprise, for example, by passing it through a bank account of which he is the sole signatory, that defendant is treated as having obtained the whole amount of the benefit. The amount of his benefit is not reduced by the share that he passes to the other members. Simultaneously and additionally, the benefit of each of the others is the amount that they, in turn, obtain from him. As Newman J stated in *Sharma* [2006] 2 Cr App R (S) 416 (at [19] and [25]):

> Where the proceeds of crime are concerned, there is no room for the application of trust principles and the application of the normal legal consequences which flow from the receipt of money for others. Nor in this area of the law would the purpose of the statute, namely to deprive criminals of the benefits of their criminal enterprise, be assisted by the introduction of collateral inquiries on an issue as to whether, when the benefit or part of the benefit is paid on to another criminal or other person participating in the crime, the original recipient is to be regarded as having never held the benefit for himself and to have obtained no fresh or continuing benefit from making the disposal to another.
>
> . . . The amount of money which might be recovered pursuant to a confiscation order is irrelevant. In every case, at the time a confiscation order is made, there can be no certainty that the amount to be paid will be paid and thus, where more than one confiscation order is made in respect of a victim's loss, the question of double recovery may not arise.

However, it appears that, in drugs cases at least, where payment is obtained by one defendant on behalf of several defendants jointly, others who have joint control may be liable for the whole of the common pool: 'It does not matter that proceeds of sale may have been received by one conspirator who retains his share before passing on the remainder; what matters is the capacity in which he received them' (*Green* [2007] EWCA Crim 1248). Whether proceeds of sale were initially received on the individual's own personal behalf or on behalf of the conspirators as a whole is a question of fact for the judge to decide on the evidence before him. Where there is evidence that another defendant was the ringleader and controller of the conspiracy, the judge is entitled to infer that the others were acting in accordance with his instructions, receiving proceeds of sale on behalf of the conspirators as a whole before retaining for themselves such amounts as had been agreed.

Lastly, there may be exceptions to the basic rule where joint and several liability is separately imposed by other legislation. For example, where the offender has been convicted of obtaining by deception or of conspiracy to obtain by deception, his benefit may be the whole of the property obtained as, under the Theft Act 1968, s. 15(2), '"obtains" includes obtaining for another or enabling another to obtain or to retain' (*Rees* 19 July 1990 unreported, Auld J). Also, in *Rowbotham* [2006] 2 Cr App R (S) 642, the Court of Appeal implied that the rule in 'Customs and Excise cases' that 'any . . . person acting on behalf of the importer of the excise goods' is liable for the whole duty is overriding (see the Excise Goods (Holding, Movement, Warehousing and REDS) Regulations 1992 , reg. 5).

E21.15 **Connection with Criminal Conduct** The obtaining of the property need not be exclusively connected with or result from the criminal conduct as long as it has some 'connection' with it (ss. 76(4) and (6)) (see *Osei* (1998) 10 Cr App R (S) 289 (an airline ticket and money given to a drugs courier for showing to an immigration officer in order to obtain entry); *Finch* (1993) 14 Cr App R (S) 226 (money obtained by 'ripping-off' a drug dealer; *Randle and Pottle* [1991] COD 369 (profits from the sale of a book about the prison escape of the spy, George Blake, in which the defendants had participated).

E21.16 **The role of the assumptions** Where the court determines that the defendant has a criminal lifestyle, all the assumptions in the PCA 2002, s. 10, are mandatory.

Proceeds of Crime Act 2002, s. 10

(1) If the court decides under section 6 that the defendant has a criminal lifestyle it must make the following four assumptions for the purpose of—
   (a) deciding whether he has benefited from his general criminal conduct, and
   (b) deciding his benefit from the conduct.
(2) The first assumption is that any property transferred to the defendant at any time after the relevant day was obtained by him—
   (a) as a result of his general criminal conduct, and
   (b) at the earliest time he appears to have held it.
(3) The second assumption is that any property held by the defendant at any time after the date of conviction was obtained by him—
   (a) as a result of his general criminal conduct, and
   (b) at the earliest time he appears to have held it.
(4) The third assumption is that any expenditure incurred by the defendant at any time after the relevant day was met from property obtained by him as a result of his general criminal conduct.
(5) The fourth assumption is that, for the purpose of valuing any property obtained (or assumed to have been obtained) by the defendant, he obtained it free of any other interests in it.
(6) But the court must not make a required assumption in relation to particular property or expenditure if—
   (a) the assumption is shown to be incorrect, or
   (b) there would be a serious risk of injustice if the assumption were made.
(7) If the court does not make one or more of the required assumptions it must state its reasons.

The first assumption is that any property transferred to the defendant within the six-year period that preceded the start of the proceedings was obtained by him (a) as a result of his general criminal conduct, and (b) at the earliest time he appears to have held it (s. 10(2)). Proceedings start when a summons or warrant is issued or when a defendant is charged following arrest without warrant or when a voluntary bill of indictment is preferred (s. 85). Property is transferred if 'an interest' in it is transferred or granted by another (s. 84(2)(c)).

The second assumption is that any property held by the defendant at any time after the date of conviction was obtained as a result of his general criminal conduct at the earliest time he appears to have held it (s. 10(3)). It is irrelevant when he acquired the property (*Chrastny (No. 2)* [1991] 1 WLR 1385).

The third assumption is that any expenditure incurred by the defendant at any time after the start of the six-year period was met from property obtained by him as a result of his general criminal conduct (s. 10(4)). In other words, once some expenditure is proved, the court must assume it was funded from property obtained as a result of earlier criminal conduct. The benefit is the amount of *that* property but there must be some evidential basis for calculation of the amount of *that* property (*Williams (Errol)* [2001] 2 Cr App R (S) 44). The fact of expenditure, classically in drugs cases, may be inferred from the circumstances (*Dellaway* [2001] 1 Cr App R (S) 77). Arguably the legitimate boundaries of inference have been stretched on occasions. In *Barnham* [2006] 1 Cr App R (S) 83, the defendant was convicted of two conspiracies to import drugs but no importation had actually occurred. The judge was entitled to infer, 'provided he keeps well in mind that the risk of serious injustice must be avoided' that the defendant had in fact available to him quantities of drugs intended for importation and that those drugs had been paid for out of earlier trafficking. Moreover, where the judge concluded that the defendant was the lead organiser, he was entitled to discount the possibility that other conspirators had contributed to the cost of the drugs. In *Odesanya* [2005] All ER (D) 221, the defendant had been convicted of a drugs importation. In the confiscation proceedings he could be linked to an earlier importation of drugs, although there was no evidence proving the amount or value of the earlier drugs. The Court of Appeal nevertheless upheld an inference that the amount and value of the first importation were identical with those of the second, noting that there was no evidence from the defendant on the point.

The limits of the exercise were illustrated in *Williams* [2001] 2 Cr App R (S) 44. The judge properly calculated drugs expenditure of £0.5 million. However, treating this sum as profit from a notional earlier transaction, he then purported to work out the gross amount of *that* transaction. Deciding arbitrarily that the expenditure represented a 25 per cent profit on the earlier transaction, he multiplied the expenditure by four, making nearly £2 million, to which he then added to the net benefit, making a total of nearly £2.5 million. The Court of Appeal quashed the order, observing:

> The mistake of the judge in the present case was to take the figure produced by the application of the proper approach, (£1/2 million), and then to subject it to a series of further hypotheses for which there was no evidential basis, namely:
>
> (i) that it was the product of a particular form of drug trafficking i.e. wholesale supply,
>
> (ii) that it represented net profits of such activity and
>
> (iii) that a hypothetical quantity and value of drugs must have been required to be purchased during the preceding 6 years to enable such a profit to be calculated.
>
> The judge was wrong to employ the 'expenditure' assumption . . . for this purpose and his device of calculating a figure for the working capital required to produce a profit equal to the proceeds figure . . . was incorrect. There was simply no evidence as to the defendant's possession of such drugs, or that they were funded from previous dealing . . . the problem seems to us to have stemmed from the fact that the sentencing judge . . . sought to redefine (the proceeds) and treat them as 'profits', and to base his further calculations on that redefinition. That approach does not

seem to us to be one permitted by the Act. It is also one likely to lead to arbitrary and unjust results.

A finding or concession that a minder or courier had no beneficial interest in property such as drugs or that it is the defendant's first such offence, should prevent any inference that he paid for the property (*J* [2001] 1 Cr App R (S) 273; *Butler* (1993) 14 Cr App R (S) 537; *Johannes* [2002] Crim LR 14).

The fourth assumption is that the defendant is or was the only person with an interest in any property which he is proven or assumed to have obtained (s. 10(5)). (For the later deduction of third-party interests from the available amount, see **E21.22**.)

E21.17 **Defeating the Assumptions** An assumption may not be made if the defendant proves on the balance of probabilities that it is 'incorrect', for example, by evidence of legitimate income (s. 10(6)(a)). See, for example, *Hesketh* [2006] EWCA Crim 2596.

The only other circumstance in which an assumption can be avoided is when 'there would be a serious risk of injustice if the assumption were made' (s. 10(6)(b)). 'It is putting it too high' to require the defendant to prove injustice on the balance of probabilities; 'the judge must avoid any real risk of injustice'. The court 'should step back and determine whether there is or might be a risk of serious or real injustice and, if there is or might be, then such an order should not be made' (*Benjafield* [2003] 1 AC 1099).

In *Jones* [2007] 1 WLR 7 the Court of Appeal expressly approved the following statement from an earlier edition of this work: the risk of injustice must arise from the operation of the assumptions in the calculation of benefit and not from eventual hardship in the making of a confiscation order (see also *Dore* [1997] 2 Cr App R (S) 152; *Ahmed* [2005] 1 WLR 122). What is contemplated is some unjust contradiction in the process of assumption and an agreed factual basis for sentence (see **E21.9** and *Lunnon* [2005] 1 Cr App R (S) 111, *Lazarus* [2005] Crim LR 64 and *Bakewell* [2006] 2 Cr App R (S) 277) or in the process of assumption itself — for example in the double counting of income and expenditure. Thus, in cases of multiple drug transactions, the judge should not automatically aggregate the proceeds from the sales and the cost of purchase (as expenditure assumed to have been met each time from a preceding sale): 'The proceeds of sale and the money used to buy the new stock is the same money and that it would be wrong to treat the defendant as having received two separate sums of money when in fact he has received only one' (*Green* [2007] EWCA Crim 1248).

There is no double penalty when drugs are both forfeited under the Misuse of Drugs Act 1971, s. 27 (see **E20.4**) and their value counted as expenditure (*Dore*).

If the court is satisfied of a serious risk of injustice 'in an appropriate case', it may temper the full force of the assumptions by making a percentage discount to guard against 'a remote possibility that a small part of the property . . . had a legitimate source' (*Deprince* [2004] 2 Cr App R (S) 463).

Stage Three — Determination of the Recoverable Amount

E21.18 **Proceeds of Crime Act 2002, ss. 7 and 80**

7.—(1) The recoverable amount for the purposes of section 6 is an amount equal to the defendant's benefit from the conduct concerned.

(2) But if the defendant shows that the available amount is less than that benefit the recoverable amount is—
- (a) the available amount, or
- (b) a nominal amount, if the available amount is nil.

(3) But if section 6(6) applies the recoverable amount is such amount as—
- (a) the court believes is just, but
- (b) does not exceed the amount found under subsection (1) or (2) (as the case may be).

(4) In calculating the defendant's benefit from the conduct concerned for the purposes of subsection (1), any property in respect of which—

(a) a recovery order is in force under section 266, or
(b) a forfeiture order is in force under section 298(2),
must be ignored.

(5) If the court decides the available amount, it must include in the confiscation order a statement of its findings as to the matters relevant for deciding that amount.

80.—(1) This section applies for the purpose of deciding the value of property obtained by a person as a result of or in connection with his criminal conduct; and the material time is the time the court makes its decision.

(2) The value of the property at the material time is the greater of the following—
(a) the value of the property (at the time the person obtained it) adjusted to take account of later changes in the value of money;
(b) the value (at the material time) of the property found under subsection (3).

(3) The property found under this subsection is as follows—
(a) if the person holds the property obtained, the property found under this subsection is that property;
(b) if he holds no part of the property obtained, the property found under this subsection is any property which directly or indirectly represents it in his hands;
(c) if he holds part of the property obtained, the property found under this subsection is that part and any property which directly or indirectly represents the other part in his hands.

(4) The references in subsection (2)(a) and (b) to the value are to the value found in accordance with section 79.

The Amount of Benefit The first rule is that 'the recoverable amount . . . is an amount equal to the defendant's benefit from the conduct concerned' (PCA 2002, s. 7(1)). The amount of the defendant's benefit is literally 'the value of the property obtained' (s. 76(7)). It follows that benefit does not merely mean the profit element (see *Smith* (1989) 11 Cr App R (S) 290; *Simons* (1994) 15 Cr App R (S) 126; *Banks* [1997] 2 Cr App R (S) 110; *Simpson* [1998] 2 Cr App R (S) 111; *Currey* (1995) 16 Cr App R (S) 42); *Carter* [2006] EWCA Crim 416). As a general rule, the recoverable amount should not be reduced to reflect, for example, the notional outlay of expenses in the acquisition of controlled drugs (*Versluis* [2005] 2 Cr App R (S) 144). There may be specific circumstances in which this may be possible (*Ilsemann* (1990) 12 Cr App R (S) 398; *Cukovic* [1996] 1 Cr App R (S) 131). **E21.19**

No discount can be given to reflect income which the defendant would have derived from the loser had there been no misconduct — for example, where a defendant had falsely claimed income support, no account was to be taken of working families tax credit to which he would have been entitled but for his misrepresentations (*Richards* [2005] 2 Cr App R (S) 583). Nor is there any discretion to reduce the amount of benefit by taking into account voluntary repayments made to a loser. In these circumstances, it is obviously possible that the determined benefit, when added to the repayment, could exceed the actual loss. It is important to recognise that it is in the general interests of justice to encourage such agreements without the need for confiscation proceedings. An abuse of process could arise where the prosecution were unjustly and without proper cause seeking to go behind such an agreement, reached with full and proper disclosure (*Mahmood* [2006] 1 Cr App R (S) 570).

There appears to be a conflict of authority under the earlier legislation as to whether a defendant is liable for the full value of property obtained where he has contributed some legitimate funds towards its acquisition — 'the full value approach' (see *In Re K* (6 July 1990, unreported, CA); *Layode* (12 March 1993, unreported, CA); *Rees* (19 July 1990, unreported, Auld LJ); cf. *Walls (Andrew)* [2003] 1 WLR 731; *Moulden* [2005] 1 Cr App R(S) 691).

Valuation of Benefit Secondly, 'the basic rule' of valuation throughout the PCA 2002 is that the value of any property is its market value at the material time (s. 79(2)). The material time for valuing benefit 'is the time the court makes its decision' (s. 80(1)). Its value at that time is the *greater* of the following: **E21.20**

(a) its (market) value at the time it was obtained by the defendant (adjusted for subsequent inflation); or

(b) if he still holds the property, its current market value or, if he no longer holds the property, the market value of any property that 'directly or indirectly represents' it, or a combination of both if he has converted only part of the property which he originally obtained (s. 80(2)).

Thus, if the market value of the property has declined since the defendant obtained it, then his benefit is its original market value adjusted upwards for inflation (*Foxley* (1995) 16 Cr App R (S) 879). For the determination of value in relation to property which has increased in value, and for the treatment of mortgage monies which contributed to the acquisition of such property and the effect of such monies on the defendant's benefit, see *Moulden* [2005] 1 Cr App R (S) 691.

The fraudulent purchase and subsequent sale of vehicles is a single process leading to a single benefit for these purposes. There are not two separate benefits consisting of the value of the vehicle when the defendant dishonestly obtained it and, additionally, the proceeds of sale of the same vehicle. The judge should first look at the value of the vehicle when the defendant obtained it and then go on to see whether there were any proceeds of sale in his hands that exceeded (or were less than) the value of the vehicle when he obtained it. The benefit is the greater of the two values. 'It is not in our view realistic to treat the purchase and sale of the same vehicle as separate criminal enterprises': (*Scragg* [2006] EWCA Crim 2916).

Market value may vary according to whether goods have been obtained wholesale, for example by theft from containers in transit, or from a retail outlet (see *Ascroft* [2003] EWCA Crim 2365). The value as benefit of controlled drugs in the past or present possession of the defendant is nil. Controlled drugs have no 'market value' as they cannot be sold or realised lawfully (*Dore* [1997] 2 Cr App R (S) 152; *Ajibade* [2006] 2 Cr App R (S) 168); nor does a worthless cheque (*Johnson* (1990) 91 Cr App R 332). The price which the defendant paid for controlled drugs in his possession is, however, relevant as evidence of expenditure incurred by the defendant for the purposes of applying the third assumption.

E21.21 **Effect of Recovery or Forfeiture Order or Claim by Victim** The court must ignore any property over which there is a recovery or forfeiture order in force (s. 7(4)) and, in the case of general criminal conduct, the court must deduct any previous confiscation orders (s. 8(3)). A court need not calculate the recoverable amount and make an order 'if it believes that any victim of the conduct has at any time started or intends to start proceedings against the defendant in respect of loss, injury or damage sustained in connection with the conduct' (s. 6(6)). If it does decide to do so, the benefit is 'such amount as the court believes just'.

Stage Four — Determination of the Available Amount

E21.22 **Proceeds of Crime Act 2002, s. 9**

(1) For the purposes of deciding the recoverable amount, the available amount is the aggregate of—
   (a) the total of the values (at the time the confiscation order is made) of all the free property then held by the defendant minus the total amount payable in pursuance of obligations which then have priority, and
   (b) the total of the values (at that time) of all tainted gifts.
(2) An obligation has priority if it is an obligation of the defendant—
   (a) to pay an amount due in respect of a fine or other order of a court which was imposed or made on conviction of an offence and at any time before the time the confiscation order is made, or
   (b) to pay a sum which would be included among the preferential debts if the defendant's bankruptcy had commenced on the date of the confiscation order or his winding up had been ordered on that date.
(3) 'Preferential debts' has the meaning given by section 386 of the Insolvency Act 1986.

A court cannot confiscate more than a defendant is worth — 'the available amount'. The assessments, first of the amount of benefit, and then of the available amount, are entirely separate exercises. The calculation of the available amount is simply a computation of the defendant's realisable assets, including tainted gifts, regardless of their origins, illegitimate or not. If the offender proves on the balance of probabilities that he is worth less than the amount of his benefit then the 'available amount' becomes the 'recoverable amount' and, therefore, the amount of the order (s. 7(2)(a); see *Ilsemann* (1990) 12 Cr App R (S) 398 and *Comiskey* (1991) 93 Cr App R 227).

The 'available amount' is the aggregate of:

(a) the total value at the time of the order of 'all the free property then held by the defendant' (minus the total amount of any priority obligations), *and*
(b) the total value of all 'tainted gifts' (s. 9(1)).

Property is 'held' by a person 'if he holds an interest in it' (s. 84). Property, therefore, includes a beneficial interest under a will (*Walbrook* (1993) 15 Cr App R (S) 783) but not a possible lump sum pension payment which would, if paid, go to a trustee in bankruptcy (*Cornfield* [2007] 1 Cr App R (S) 771). A defendant's 'interest' is not necessarily confined to the holding of a legal or equitable interest in the property. In the context of a VAT carousel fraud, all the conspirators have been held to have a beneficial interest in the proceeds of the conspiracy; the prosecution do not have to show that there is any enforceable right to the money as between the fraudsters (*S* [2005] EWCA Crim 2919). Where a defendant controls a company and the company controls property which represents the benefit, the corporate veil may be lifted and company assets treated as those of the defendant (*Omar* [2005] 1 Cr App R (S) 446). Property is free unless there is already a forfeiture or deprivation order in force (s. 82). The value is the market value. Costs of sale may be deducted (*Cramer* (1992) 13 Cr App R (S) 390). Where the judge is satisfied that there are hidden assets, it is for the defendant to prove that their value is less than the benefit figure (*Siddique* [2005] EWCA Crim 1812; *Barnham* [2006] 1 Cr App R (S) 83; *Valentine* [2006] EWCA Crim 2717).

Where a defendant's benefit comprises the gross amount which he has obtained from the sale of drugs, it is permissible, where the defendant so proves, to reach a lower available amount by reducing the benefit figure to reflect the cost to him of purchasing those drugs (*Singh* [2005] EWCA Crim 1448).

The process of calculation is as follows:

(a) identify the free property in which the defendant has an interest at the time of the order;
(b) calculate the total current market value of his beneficial interests in that property;
(c) deduct the amount of his priority obligations (i.e. fines, etc., and preferential debts);
(d) lastly, add the total value of any 'tainted gifts'.

In Customs and Excise cases, seizure of the instruments of crime, such as motor vehicles, results in their immediate forfeiture under the Customs and Excise Management Act 1979 so that they no longer form part of the available amount (*Thacker* (1995) 16 Cr App R (S) 461).

Tainted Gifts The total value of 'all tainted gifts' must be added to the available amount **E21.23**
(s. 9(1)(b)). Any difficulty that the defendant may have in retrieving the actual gift is immaterial (*Tighe* [1996] 1 Cr App R (S) 314). A defendant makes a gift if he transfers property to another for 'significantly less' consideration than its value at the time he obtained it (s. 78(1)). The process of then identifying whether a gift is 'tainted' varies according to whether or not the defendant has been found to have a criminal lifestyle. Where a defendant has a criminal lifestyle or where 'no court has made a decision', a gift is tainted if it was made since the start of the six-year period preceding the commencement of the proceedings (s. 77(2) and (9)). Alternatively, a gift is tainted, regardless of when it was made, if it is proved to consist of property obtained by the defendant 'as a result of or in connection with his general criminal conduct' or of property in his hands which represented such property 'in whole or part . . . directly or indirectly' (s. 77(3)). If the defendant does not have a criminal

lifestyle, any gift is tainted if made 'after the date on which the offence concerned was committed' (s. 77(5)). Note that the slightly different language of the CJA 1988, s. 74(10) ('if made by the defendant at any time after the commission of the offence') was given a wide construction in *Stannard* [2005] EWCA Crim 217, where the defendant was convicted of the offence of cheating the public revenue particularised as submitting false company tax claims. The claims were submitted after the relevant gifts were made. The court was 'not confined to the particulars' and held instead that 'the substance of the cheat' was the earlier creation of false documents and the transfer of company funds. Under the PCA 2002, a continuing offence is deemed to be committed 'on the first occasion when it is committed' (s. 77(6)).

The value of the tainted gift is the value of 'the property given' so that in a transaction for consideration, the property given is the proportion of the whole that represents the gift element (s. 78(2)). The value of the property given is its market value. The market value is the greater of the following: (a) its value at the time it was given (adjusted for subsequent inflation); or (b) its value at the time of the confiscation order. If the recipient of the gift has retained none or only part of the property, its value is that of 'any property which directly or indirectly represents it in his hands' or a combination of the value of what he has retained and such property (s. 81).

The court should first determine whether the defendant himself has any beneficial interest. If so, it should then go on to consider whether the other party's share is genuinely beneficial or whether it is a tainted gift (*Buckman* [1997] 1 Cr App R (S) 325). The genuineness of an encumbrance, such as a mortgage, is a question of fact to be determined on the evidence (*Harvey* [1999] 1 Cr App R (S) 354). The balance of a negative equity cannot be set off against the available amount (*Ghadami* [1998] 1 Cr App R (S) 42).

E21.24 **Family Home** Frequently, the defendant's share in the value of the family home will be included in the available amount. At this stage the fact that the home may need to be sold to meet the order, and innocent family members suffer hardship as a result, is irrelevant to 'the arithmetic exercise' of calculating the defendant's worth (*Ahmed* [2005] 1 WLR 122). The provisions are compatible with the ECHR (*Danison v UK* (1998) Appln. 45042/98: see E21.4). Nevertheless, the position may be very different at the enforcement stage. If the order is not met and the prosecutor applies for permission to realise the property, the court is obliged to receive representations from third parties. The Article 8 rights of those affected by the loss of the family home are engaged and the court must now consider whether loss of the home is proportionate (*Ahmed*). Secondly, where there are concurrent matrimonial proceedings, it may be possible to order the transfer of the innocent partner's share as ancillary relief in those proceedings thus taking that share out of the calculation of the available amount (see *Customs and Excise Commissioners v MCA* (2002) *The Times*, 25 July 2002; *CPS v Grimes; Grimes v Grimes* [2003] FLR 510; *Hedges* [2004] EWCA Crim 2133; *X v X* [2005] 2 FLR 487). However, since the abolition by the PCA 2002 of the High Court jurisdiction over restraint and enforcement, there is no longer any dual procedure under which confiscation and matrimonial ancillary relief can be combined. The proper course is for the matrimonial aspects to be dealt with first (*Webber v CPS* [2006] EWHC 2893 (Fam)). It was stated in *CPS v Richards* [2006] EWCA Civ 848 that 'as a matter of justice and public policy', where the family assets are themselves tainted, they should not be distributed to satisfy ancillary relief claims; when conducting its discretionary balance exercise, 'the only decisive factor' for the court is whether the assets are tainted as having been derived from crime.

Confiscation Orders and Sentence

E21.25 **Proceeds of Crime Act 2002, ss. 13 to 15**

13.—(1) If the court makes a confiscation order it must proceed as mentioned in subsections (2) and (4) in respect of the offence or offences concerned.

(2) The court must take account of the confiscation order before—

(a) it imposes a fine on the defendant, or
(b) it makes an order falling within subsection (3).
(3) These orders fall within this subsection—
(a) an order involving payment by the defendant, other than an order under section 130 of the Sentencing Act (compensation orders);
(b) an order under section 27 of the Misuse of Drugs Act 1971 (forfeiture orders);
(c) an order under section 143 of the Sentencing Act (deprivation orders);
(d) an order under section 23 of the Terrorism Act 2000 (forfeiture orders).
(4) Subject to subsection (2), the court must leave the confiscation order out of account in deciding the appropriate sentence for the defendant.
(5) Subsection (6) applies if—
(a) the Crown Court makes both a confiscation order and an order for the payment of compensation under section 130 of the Sentencing Act against the same person in the same proceedings, and
(b) the court believes he will not have sufficient means to satisfy both the orders in full.
(6) In such a case the court must direct that so much of the compensation as it specifies is to be paid out of any sums recovered under the confiscation order; and the amount it specifies must be the amount it believes will not be recoverable because of the insufficiency of the person's means.

14.—(1) The court may—
(a) proceed under section 6 before it sentences the defendant for the offence (or any of the offences) concerned, or
(b) postpone proceedings under section 6 for a specified period.
(2) A period of postponement may be extended.
(3) A period of postponement (including one as extended) must not end after the permitted period ends.
(4) But subsection (3) does not apply if there are exceptional circumstances.
(5) The permitted period is the period of two years starting with the date of conviction.
(6) But if—
(a) the defendant appeals against his conviction for the offence (or any of the offences) concerned, and
(b) the period of three months (starting with the day when the appeal is determined or otherwise disposed of) ends after the period found under subsection (5),
the permitted period is that period of three months.
(7) A postponement or extension may be made—
(a) on application by the defendant;
(b) on application by the prosecutor or the Director (as the case may be);
(c) by the court of its own motion.
(8) If—
(a) proceedings are postponed for a period, and
(b) an application to extend the period is made before it ends,
the application may be granted even after the period ends.
(9) The date of conviction is—
(a) the date on which the defendant was convicted of the offence concerned, or
(b) if there are two or more offences and the convictions were on different dates, the date of the latest.
(10) References to appealing include references to applying under section 111 of the Magistrates' Courts Act 1980 (statement of case).
(11) A confiscation order must not be quashed only on the ground that there was a defect or omission in the procedure connected with the application for or the granting of a postponement.
(12) But subsection (11) does not apply if before it made the confiscation order the court—
(a) imposed a fine on the defendant;
(b) made an order falling within section 13(3);
(c) made an order under section 130 of the Sentencing Act (compensation orders).

15.—(1) If the court postpones proceedings under section 6 it may proceed to sentence the defendant for the offence (or any of the offences) concerned.
(2) In sentencing the defendant for the offence (or any of the offences) concerned in the postponement period the court must not—
(a) impose a fine on him,

(b) make an order falling within section 13(3), or
(c) make an order for the payment of compensation under section 130 of the Sentencing Act.

(3) If the court sentences the defendant for the offence (or any of the offences) concerned in the postponement period, after that period ends it may vary the sentence by—
(a) imposing a fine on him,
(b) making an order falling within section 13(3), or
(c) making an order for the payment of compensation under section 130 of the Sentencing Act.

(4) But the court may proceed under subsection (3) only within the period of 28 days which starts with the last day of the postponement period.

(5) For the purposes of—
(a) section 18(2) of the Criminal Appeal Act 1968 (time limit for notice of appeal or of application for leave to appeal), and
(b) paragraph 1 of Schedule 3 to the Criminal Justice Act 1988 (time limit for notice of application for leave to refer a case under section 36 of that Act),
the sentence must be regarded as imposed or made on the day on which it is varied under subsection (3).

(6) If the court proceeds to sentence the defendant under subsection (1), section 6 has effect as if the defendant's particular criminal conduct included conduct which constitutes offences which the court has taken into consideration in deciding his sentence for the offence or offences concerned.

(7) The postponement period is the period for which proceedings under section 6 are postponed.

The judge may make a confiscation order before sentence or postpone the determination and proceed to sentence (PCA 2002, s. 14(1)). When sentence follows the confiscation proceedings, circumstantial differences are sometimes exposed. The most basic principle of sentencing must still prevail — that a person cannot be sentenced for offences of which he has not been convicted (or had taken into consideration), unless he accepts that the offences are specimen examples of a wider course of conduct (see *Bragazon* (1998) 10 Cr App R (S) 258; *Ayensu* (1982) 4 Cr App R (S) 248). The judge 'should be careful not to take into account factual matters of which he has not been satisfied beyond reasonable doubt. Above all, he should not allow the unusual and . . . very adverse assumptions to lead him to make findings adverse to the defendant in the realm of sentencing which he would not have made applying the ordinary burden of proof' (*Saunders* (1990) 12 Cr App R (S) 344). It is, therefore, wrong to deny credit for having no previous convictions where the application of the assumptions has resulted in a finding of previous involvement in drug trafficking (*Callan* (1994) 15 Cr App R (S) 574). Even so, the sentencer may 'pay some regard to the evidence placed before him . . . in the same way as he might pay regard to general evidence placed before him' to find, for example, that this was not the first occasion on which the defendant had offended (*Harper* (1989) 11 Cr App R (S) 240; *Thompson* [1997] 1 Cr App R (S) 289). Where the outcome of a confiscation enquiry does result in a conflict with other features of the case, the judge is entitled to hold a *Newton* hearing to resolve the conflict (*McNulty* (1994) 15 Cr App R (S) 606).

Relationship with Other Orders

E21.26 The interaction between confiscation orders and other sentencing powers is regulated by the PCA 2002, s. 13. The effect of the confiscation order on the sentence varies according to the type of sentencing order. A distinction is made between the principal financial orders (but not including compensation) and other orders. The court cannot make certain financial orders (fines, deprivation orders or forfeiture orders under the Misuse of Drugs Act 1971 or the Terrorism Act 2000) without taking account of the confiscation order and reducing the defendant's available means accordingly (s. 13(2) and (3)). Generally, however, the judge must 'leave the confiscation order out of account in deciding the appropriate sentence' (s. 13(4)) for example, in deciding whether to impose a custodial sentence (see *Rogers* [2002]

1 Cr App R (S) 337; *Andrews* [1997] 1 Cr App R (S) 279). A fine is not appropriate when a court has sentenced a defendant to imprisonment and made a confiscation order (*Hedley* (1989) 11 Cr App R (S) 298).

The PCA 2002 has particular rules to ensure the primacy of compensation for victims and losers over confiscation. The court must still go through the process of making the confiscation order, then fixing the amount of compensation without regard to the existence of the confiscation order. If 'the court (then) believes . . . [the defendant] will not have sufficient means to satisfy both the orders in full', it must order the shortfall in compensation to be paid out of the confiscated sum (s. 13(5) and (6); see also *Mitchell* [2001] 2 Cr App R (S) 141; *Williams* [2001] 1 Cr App R 500). On the other hand, if the defendant does have the means, he can be ordered to pay the money twice over both as confiscation and compensation (see *Brazil* (12 January 1995, unreported, CA); *Williams* and *Mitchell*).

An order for costs ought not to be made where the judge has assessed the available amount to be less than the benefit figure. The implication of such an assessment is that no further funds are available (*Ahmed* [1997] 2 Cr App R (S) 8; *Szrajber* [1994] 15 Cr App R (S) 821; *Hopes* (1989) 11 Cr App R (S) 38).

Postponement

Either the prosecution or defence may apply for a postponement or the court may order a postponement of its own motion (PCA 2002, s. 14(7)). The court has an unfettered discretion to postpone the determination for specified periods up to a maximum of two years from the date of conviction (or longer in exceptional circumstances) (s. 14(4) and (5)). If a determination is postponed, the judge may sentence in the meantime so long as he does not impose a fine or make a compensation, forfeiture or deprivation order (s. 15(2)); these orders may be imposed after a postponed determination but only in the 28 days immediately following. Even so, a postponed confiscation order is not invalidated by the making of such orders beforehand (*Donohoe* [2006] EWCA Crim 2200). Costs should not be awarded before making the confiscation order (*Threapleton* [2002] Crim LR 229; *Smart* [2003] 2 Cr App R (S) 384). **E21.27**

Numerous problems arose under earlier legislation when judges misapplied the postponement provisions. It is now unlikely that a procedurally incorrect order would sustain a subsequent appeal as orders are not to be quashed only on the ground that 'the procedure connected with the application for or the granting of a postponement' was defective (s. 14(11)).

'Mere temporising, delay or inaction (does) not amount to a postponement of a determination . . . a judicial decision (is) needed' (*Steele* [2001] 2 Cr App R (S) 178). However, while not departing from this principle, a trend towards increasing latitude in its application is evident from the authorities — to the point where in *Knights* [2006] 1 AC 368 the House of Lords held that flaws in the postponement procedure will not invalidate a subsequent confiscation order if the judge has acted in good faith. A decision to postpone need not be expressed in any particular form of words. The fact that the judge has so decided may be inferred from the circumstances; for example, where he has made plain his intention to sentence first and it was understood by all concerned that confiscation would be dealt with at a later date (*Tahir* [2006] EWCA Crim 792). It is preferable for a precise date to be set, but not fatal to the subsequent order if it is not. (See *Ruddick* [2003] 2 Cr App R (S) 52; *Haisman* [2004] 1 Cr App R (S) 383; *Sekhon* [2003] 1 WLR 1655.) The court may restore the proceedings to the list and make a confiscation order 'provided that the judge acts in good faith and in the purported exercise of his statutory power' (*Knights*).

The two-year period may be exceeded in 'exceptional circumstances' (s. 14(4)). The phrase 'must take its colour from the setting in which it appears' and should not be strictly construed

(*Soneji* [2006] 1 AC 340). The failure to refer expressly to 'exceptional circumstances' will not invalidate a postponement if it can be inferred that the court made an appraisal of the circumstances and had the appropriate test in mind, and if the order can be justified (*Chuni* [2002] 2 Cr App R (S) 82; *Gadsby* [2001] Crim LR 828). It is only if the timetable initially set makes it likely that the two-year period will be exceeded that the court must on the first occasion address itself to 'exceptional circumstances' (*Knights*). Listing difficulties are capable of amounting to exceptional circumstances (see *Soneji*; *Young* [2003] EWCA Crim 3481; *Groombridge* [2004] 1 Cr App R (S) 84). The wording of similar provisions in the CJA 1988, s. 72(A)(3), has been held to exclude any parallel common-law power of adjournment (*Soneji*). Although the language of the PCA 2002, s. 14, is different, the interpretation may be similar.

The court may also postpone the determination while the defendant appeals against conviction. If the appeal takes more than two years, postponement for up to three months after the appeal is permitted (s. 14(6)). The court may grant a postponement without a hearing — presumably only where the parties agree (CrimPR, r. 58.2).

Form of Order and Payment of Amount

E21.28 The court must fix the recoverable amount. An order confiscating the equity of a particular property 'valued at not less than £26,000' is defective (*Jubb* [2002] 2 Cr App R (S) 8).

The ordinary principle is that the order must be satisfied immediately (s. 11(1)). However, if the defendant shows that he needs time to pay, he can be allowed a specified period of up to six months to meet the order. If he applies before the end of that period, it can be extended in exceptional circumstances to a maximum of 12 months from the date of the order. There is no inherent jurisdiction to extend time to pay further (*Revenue and Customs Prosecution Service v Kearney* [2007] EWHC (Admin) 640).

ENFORCEMENT, RECONSIDERATION AND APPEALS

Enforcement

E21.29 In most cases, the order is effectively treated as a fine to be collected and enforced by a specified magistrates' court or, if none is specified, by the committing magistrates' court (s. 35(2)). However, the Director of the Assets Recovery Agency must be appointed as 'the enforcement authority' in any case in which the Director applied for the determination or has applied to be the enforcement authority (s. 34). If the amount of the order is not paid in time, interest accrues on the unpaid amount for the period for which it remains unpaid (s. 12).

The mechanism for imposing terms of imprisonment or detention for default is almost identical to that used in the enforcement of fines and many of the provisions of the PCC(S)A 2000 are expressly incorporated in the PCA 2002. Thus, the Crown Court must fix a default term in accordance with the scale set out in the PCC(S)A, s. 139(4) (see **E17.3**). Failure to do so, however, will not invalidate the order (*Ellis* [1996] 2 Cr App R (S) 403). The scale ranges from seven days for an amount not exceeding £200 up to ten years for anything over £1 million. These are maximum terms and it follows that the Crown Court may fix lesser terms within the bands (*Szrajber* (1994) 15 Cr App R (S) 821).

The Crown Court may itself go on to commit the defendant to serve the default period immediately but only where: (a) he appears to have the means to pay forthwith; (b) he is unlikely to remain in the jurisdiction long enough for payment to be enforced by another method; or (c) he is serving or is sentenced to imprisonment or detention. The default period is served consecutively but 'serving that term does not prevent the confiscation order from continuing to have effect so far as any other method of enforcement is concerned' (s. 38(5)). Default imprisonment is remitted if payment is made. If the non-imprisoned defendant does default, the magistrates must summons and then commit him to serve the default period. They may not allow further time or payment by instalments or hold a further means enquiry (s. 35(3)). See also *CPS v Greenacre* [2007] EWHC 1193 (Admin). Where the Director is the enforcement authority he may apply to the Crown Court *ex parte* for a summons directing the defendant to re-appear before the Crown Court; the court may then commit the defendant (s. 37).

Proceedings to enforce an order by commitment to prison are part of the determination of a criminal charge within the meaning of the ECHR, Article 6(1), and must be determined 'within a reasonable time' (*Lloyd v Bow Street Magistrates' Court* [2004] 1 Cr App R 132; *Crowther v UK* (2005) *The Times*, 11 February 2005).

If the order is not satisfied, the prosecution may ask the Crown Court to appoint an enforcement receiver (s. 50). The court may then confer powers on the receiver to: (a) take possession of realisable property; (b) manage 'or otherwise deal with' the property; (c) realise the property 'in such manner as the court may specify'; (d) bring, continue or defend legal proceedings (s. 51(2)). If the Director is the enforcement authority, the court 'must make an order for the appointment of a receiver', who may be a member of the ARA staff (s. 52(3) and (6)). Where the prosecutor or Director believes that realisable property is situated outside the United Kingdom, a Request for Assistance may be sent to the Home Secretary who may, in turn, forward the request to the relevant government (s. 74). A Request for Assistance asks the receiving country to apply the various co-operation treaties and, in particular, to prohibit anyone from dealing in the property and to ensure that the proceeds 'are applied in accordance with the law of the receiving country'. If property is realised abroad, the amount which the defendant has been ordered to pay under the order is reduced accordingly.

Reconsideration

Confiscation orders may be varied within 28 days under the general 'slip-rule', particularly where further information comes to light (PCC(S)A 2000, s. 155; see *Miller* (1990) 12 Cr App R (S) 519). However, the PCA 2002 itself anticipates that the full extent of the defendant's assets may not emerge for some considerable time or, alternatively, that his assets actually amount to less than originally thought. Accordingly, the court retains powers to vary findings (a) as to the existence or amount of benefit for up to six years from conviction or (b) indefinitely as to the available amount. Procedure is governed by the CrimPR, rr. 58.3 and 58.4. **E21.30**

The prosecution or the Director have six years from the date of conviction in which to ask the court to consider evidence of benefit which was 'not available' to them at the time of conviction or when the court decided not to proceed with a determination (ss. 19 to 21). The court may fix the recoverable amount as such amount that 'the court believes is just'. It may not apply the s. 10 assumptions to property obtained or expenditure made after that date. Secondly, the prosecutor or Director (or a receiver) may apply at any point for reconsideration of the available amount (s. 22). Section 22 even catches property that has accrued to the defendant after the date of the confiscation order and regardless of whether the prosecution can prove that it is the result of crime (*Tivnan* [1999] 1 Cr App R (S) 92; *Bates* [2007] 1 Cr App R (S) 9). Note that the ECHR entitlement to 'a hearing within a reasonable time' applies to reconsideration of the available amount notwithstanding that Parliament has stipulated no statutory time limit. The issue of delay must be determined by reference to the entirety of the proceedings and not on the basis that the reconsideration proceedings are distinct and separate (*Re Saggar* [2005] 1 WLR 2693).

The defendant (or an appointed receiver) may apply to the Crown Court for the amount of the order to be reduced if the available amount is inadequate for payment in full (s. 23). An application does not provide an opportunity to try and make good deficiencies in the case presented at the time of the confiscation order (*Gokal v Serious Fraud Office* [2001] EWCA Civ 368; see also *C* (18 November 1997 unreported, CA); *W* (29 January 1998 unreported, CA); *Re McKinsley* [2006] 1 WLR 3420; *Rooney* [2007] EWCA Crim 236).

Appeals

E21.31 A confiscation order or variation (apart from variations based upon inadequacy of the available amount) constitutes a sentence for the purposes of appeal (Criminal Appeal Act 1968, s. 50(1): see **D25.36**). Accordingly, the defendant may appeal against the making or the amount of an order with the leave of the Court of Appeal. The court may confirm, quash or vary the order. An order remains subject to appeal 'until there is no possibility of an appeal on which the order could be varied or quashed' (s. 87(2)). It follows that the right of appeal exists while there remains a possibility of variation or reconsideration. New rules bring the procedural aspects broadly in line with the Criminal Appeal Act 1968 and the rules that formerly applied under the 1968 Act (see the CrimPR, parts 71 to 73). The prosecutor or Director have a general right of appeal under the PCA 2002 itself 'in respect of' the making of an order and against a decision not to make an order. This requires leave. The prosecutor or Director cannot appeal against refusals to reconsider whether to proceed, to reconsider the amount of benefit or to hold an enquiry for an absconder (s. 31). The parties may appeal further to the House of Lords (s. 33).

MISCELLANEOUS

Absconding Defendants

E21.32 It seems that, once a *convicted* defendant absconds, the prosecution cannot proceed in the normal way (PCA 2002, s. 6(8)). They may, instead, apply to proceed under s. 27 but the court has a discretion rather than a duty to do so and the price is a more limited form of enquiry. The court may proceed if it 'believes it is appropriate for it do so' (s. 27(3)) and the prosecution has taken reasonable steps to contact the defendant. The court then proceeds as if the defendant were present but the required assumptions and the provisions requiring defence disclosure must be ignored (s. 27(5)). 'Any person the court believes is likely to be affected by an order' is entitled to appear and to make representations; if the defendant re-appears following the making of an order, he can then do little other than to apply for a variation on the basis that the available amount is inadequate (s. 23). If the prosecution applied to proceed under s. 27 in the defendant's absence but 'no court has proceeded' under that section, the prosecution may make a second attempt within six years if it has fresh evidence.

There is a similar discretion to proceed where an unconvicted defendant absconds before the proceedings for the index offence(s) have been concluded (s. 28). Once two years have elapsed from the day that 'the court believes he absconded', a similarly modified form of enquiry can take place. If he then re-appears before the proceedings for the offence(s) are concluded, the court may discharge the order if it finds either that there has been 'undue delay' in continuing the prosecution or that the prosecutor does not intend to continue with the prosecution (s. 30(4)). However, if on his re-appearance, the defendant is 'tried and acquitted', the order must be discharged (s. 30(2)).

Compensation

E21.33 There are detailed provisions under which the court may order 'such compensation it believes is just' where there has been a 'serious default' by the prosecuting authorities (PCA 2002, s. 72). In order to qualify for compensation three conditions must be met: (a) a criminal investigation has been started but has not resulted in conviction (or the conviction is quashed on appeal); (b) there has been a serious default without which the investigation would not have continued; and (c) a person who held realisable property suffered loss in consequence of an order under the PCA 2002, part 2. Procedures are governed by the CrimPR, r. 58.10 (see **appendix 1**).

POWER TO RECOMMEND FOR DEPORTATION

Section E22 Recommendation for Deportation

POWER TO RECOMMEND FOR DEPORTATION

E22.1 The Secretary of State is empowered under the Immigration Act 1971 to order the deportation from the United Kingdom of persons who are not British citizens. A court may, on sentencing an offender, make a recommendation that the offender be deported, by virtue of that Act and the British Nationality Act 1981. The final decision on deportation is taken by the Home Secretary, who is able to take account of a wider range of considerations than is the court, such as the political situation in the country to which the offender will go (*Nazari* [1980] 1 WLR 1366). The fact that the offender has overstayed a limited permission to be in the UK is a matter for the Home Secretary, and is not a ground, in itself, for the court to make a recommendation for deportation (*Aziz* [2004] EWCA Crim 1700). The fact that the offender has refugee status is not a ground, in itself, for not making an order (*Villa* (1992) 14 Cr App R (S) 34).

By the Immigration Act 1971, s. 3(6), a recommendation may be made in respect of any person who is not a British citizen, who is aged 17 or over, and who is convicted of an offence punishable with imprisonment as an adult. A 'British citizen' is a person who has a right of abode in the United Kingdom (see, for the definition, the British Nationality Act 1981, part I), but, in addition, a Commonwealth citizen or a citizen of the Irish Republic shall not be recommended for deportation if that person was resident in the UK when the 1971 Act came into force, and has been ordinarily resident in the UK for at least the five years immediately prior to the date of conviction (s. 7(1)) (for the definition of 'Commonwealth citizen' see the British Nationality Act 1981, s. 37 and sch. 3; the Immigration Act 1971 came into force on 1 January 1973). Periods of six months or more spent in prison or detention do not count towards the five-year period (s. 7(3)). Whether continuity of residence has been broken by periods spent abroad is a matter for the sentencer to decide (*Hussain* (1972) 56 Cr App R 165), but temporary absence on holiday is not relevant (*Edgehill* [1963] 1 QB 593).

Whenever an offender's citizenship is questioned for these purposes, s. 3(8) places the onus on the offender to prove citizenship or entitlement to any exemption under the Act (see further, s. 8 for exemptions in relation to crews of ships and aircraft, military personnel and persons subject to diplomatic immunity). Section 6(2), however, provides that a court shall not make a recommendation for deportation unless the offender has been given at least seven days' written notice. This may require adjournment after conviction. If the court is considering making a recommendation for deportation, the defence should be given an opportunity to address the court on that matter (*Antypas* (1973) 57 Cr App R 207).

In the past it has been possible to make a recommendation for deportation against a person protected by the EEC Treaty, Article 48, only if the conditions specified in Articles 3 and 9 of Directive 64/221 were satisfied. These were considered in *Bouchereau* [1978] QB 732, and the principles which emerged have been followed in subsequent cases, particularly *Secretary of State, ex parte Santillo* (1980) 2 Cr App R (S) 274, *Krauss* (1982) 4 Cr App R (S) 113, *Compassi* (1987) 9 Cr App R (S) 270, *Escauriaza* (1987) 87 Cr App R 344 and *Spura* (1988) 10 Cr App R (S) 376. The principles applicable here appear to be the same as those which apply in respect of any other non-British subject who does not come within one of the exceptions in the Immigration Act 1971. In *Escauriaza* (1987) 87 Cr App R 344, it was accepted by the Court of Appeal that EEC law 'simply mirrors the law and practice of this country'. These principles are stated in E22.2. Directive 64/221 has been repealed and replaced by Directive 2004/38, which came into effect on 30 April 2006. The new Directive confers enhanced rights on EU citizens and their families to reside within the territory of Member States, and Articles 27 to 33 of the new Directive regulate and limit the powers of Member States to expel an EU citizen or family members on grounds of public policy or security. The Court of Appeal in *Carmona* [2006] 1 WLR 2264 questioned whether Article 28 of the new Directive would apply to a recommendation for deportation, since the recommendation was not an 'expulsion decision' within the meaning of the Article. However, it would not be appropriate for a court to recommend deportation in circumstances where it was clear that the Directive would preclude deportation itself.

Before making a recommendation for deportation the sentencing court should always give careful consideration to the circumstances of the case, and full reasons for the decision to recommend deportation should always be given, in fairness to the offender and also to provide assistance to the Secretary of State who would have to make the final decision (*Nazari* [1980] 1 WLR 1366; *Rodney* [1996] 2 Cr App R (S) 230). The Court of Appeal in *Bozat* [1997] 1 Cr App R (S) 270, while endorsing these requirements, said that a failure to give reasons did not necessarily mean that a recommendation should be quashed; the Court of Appeal could provide its own reasons if it considered deportation to be appropriate.

The Crown Court's common-law power to bind over an offender to come up for judgment has on occasion been used as a means of requiring an offender to leave the country indefinitely (see E15). Such power is not restricted by the Immigration Act 1971.

RECOMMENDATION FOR DEPORTATION: SENTENCING PRINCIPLES

Whether the Accused's Continued Presence in UK to Detriment of Community

In *Nazari* [1980] 1 WLR 1366, Lawton LJ said (at p. 1373): E22.2

> This country has no use for criminals of other nationalities, particularly if they have committed serious crimes or have long criminal records. That is self-evident. The more serious the crime and the longer the record the more obvious it is that there should be an order recommending deportation. On the other hand, a minor offence would not merit an order.

The Court of Appeal in *Benabbas* [2006] 1 Cr App R (S) 550 reviewed a large number of authorities on the power to recommend deportation, and affirmed the continuing importance of the principles set out in *Nazari*. It was said that the required 'detriment to the community' had to be judged by reference to the public interest and the requirements of public policy. In *Benabbas* the offender had used a stolen French passport to support an application for a national insurance number; the issue of detriment was bound up with the protection of public order afforded by confidence in the system of passports. The appeal against the recommendation for deportation was dismissed. In *Ahemed* [2006] 1 Cr App R (S) 419, the Court of Appeal upheld a recommendation for deportation where the offender had entered the UK by deception on the basis of a sham marriage. It was said that entering into a bogus marriage and then trying to use it to deceive the authorities was sufficient to justify a finding that the offender's continued presence in the UK would be to the detriment of the community. See also *Carmona* [2006] 1 WLR 2264 at E22.4.

While the seriousness of the offence committed is always a relevant consideration, there are circumstances where, despite the commission of a serious offence, the offender's continued presence in the UK would not be to the detriment of the community. In *Maftonian* [2006] 1 Cr App R (S) 76, a recommendation for deportation was quashed in a case where the offender, formerly a man of good character, had admitted wounding with intent to cause grievous bodily harm by stabbing the victim a number of times. The Court of Appeal found that the offence was completely out of character and arose from particular circumstances which were very unlikely to recur.

A recommendation for deportation should not be made purely on the basis of an offender's criminal record (*Secretary of State, ex parte Santillo* (1980) 2 Cr App R (S) 274), a principle described by Donaldson LJ as 'not only the law in accordance with Article 3 of the Council Directive [but] also only common sense and fairness'. A recommendation may be made, however, if the court considers that the offender's previous record, in the light of the current offence, renders it likely that he will offend again.

Harshness of Foreign Regime Not to Be Considered

E22.3 In *Nazari* [1980] 1 WLR 1366, Lawton LJ said (at p. 1373): '. . . the courts are not concerned with the political systems which operate in other countries. . . . The court has no knowledge of those matters over and above that which is common knowledge; and that may be wrong. . . . It is for the Home Secretary to decide in each case whether an offender's return to his country of origin would have consequences which would make his compulsory return unduly harsh.' This principle was applied in *Antypas* (1972) 57 Cr App R 211 and *Bali* [2001] 2 Cr App R (S) 464, though a different line was taken in *Thoseby* (1979) 1 Cr App R (S) 280. The principle in *Nazari* was reaffirmed in *Ukoh* [2005] 2 Cr App R (S) 231, where the Court of Appeal said that the apparent policy of the Nigerian government, by which Nigerian nationals convicted abroad of importation of drugs would be liable to be sentenced to a further five years' imprisonment in Nigeria on their return, was not a matter which a sentencing court could properly consider. It was a matter for the Home Secretary, when deciding whether to act upon any recommendation.

Likely Impact on Third Parties

E22.4 The Court of Appeal in *Nazari* [1980] 1 WLR 1366 said that it had no wish to break up families or impose hardship on innocent people by making a recommendation for deportation. In *Benabbas* [2006] 1 Cr App R (S) 550, the Court of Appeal, following *Nazari*, said that in most cases the decision whether to make a recommendation for deportation was a matter of balancing the offender's wrongdoing against his mitigation, which included the interests of his family. The balance might on occasions be difficult to find, but the test and the elements were plain and, subject to the interests of the family, personal to the defendant. Section 6 of the HRA 1998 provides that it is unlawful for a court to act in a way which is incompatible with a right under the ECHR, and formerly it had been thought that the decision over whether to recommend deportation must engage with Convention rights, including the right to family life under Article 8 (see *Boultif v Switzerland* (2001) 33 EHRR 50 and *Mokrani v France* (2005) 40 EHRR 5). In the important case of *Carmona* [2006] 1 WLR 2264, however, the Court of Appeal preferred the view that, since the sentencing court was involved only in making a recommendation, and the final decision on deportation rested with the Home Secretary, the issue of engagement with Article 8, as well as the offender's rights under Articles 2 and 3, were for the Home Secretary and not the court. See further *Samaroo and Sezek v Secretary of State for the Home Department* [2001] EWCA Civ 1139. According to Stanley Burnton J [at 22]:

> In our judgment . . . there is now no need for a sentencing court to consider the Convention rights of an offender whose offence justifies a recommendation for deportation. It is moreover undesirable that the sentencing court should undertake an assessment for which it is not qualified or equipped, and which will in any event be undertaken by the Home Secretary and the Tribunal. His Convention rights will be considered if the Home Secretary makes a deportation order against which the offender appeals to the Tribunal. In the case of non-EU citizens, sentencing courts should consider only whether the offence committed by the offender, in the light of the

information before the court, justifies the conclusion that his continued presence in the contrary is contrary to the public interest. Different considerations will arise in relation to EU citizens.

Combining Recommendation with Other Sentences or Orders

A recommendation for deportation is ancillary to sentence. The sentence should be selected first, and should not be mitigated on the ground that the offender is also to be recommended for deportation (*Edgehill* [1963] 1 QB 593). There is no statutory restriction upon combining a recommendation for deportation with any other sentence or order. It may be combined with a sentence of life imprisonment (Immigration Act 1971, s. 6(4)). A recommendation for deportation is most commonly combined with a fine or a custodial sentence. The imposition of a non-custodial penalty would frequently run contrary to the sentencing principle that the continued presence of the accused in the UK would be to the detriment of the community (E22.2). In *Akan* [1973] QB 491, however, the Court of Appeal upheld a recommendation for deportation in conjunction with a conditional discharge. Although a conviction followed by a conditional discharge is treated as a conviction for limited purposes only (see **E14.6**), the Immigration Act 1971, s. 6(3), provides that, for the purposes of a recommendation for deportation, a person who has been found to have committed an offence 'shall . . . be regarded as a person convicted of the offence'. **E22.5**

Section E23 Exclusions and Disqualifications

Licensed Premises

E23.1 When the VCRA 2006, s. 65 and sch. 5, are brought into force, the Licensed Premises (Exclusion of Certain Persons) Act 1980 will be repealed. No date has yet been set for this change.

Licensed Premises (Exclusion of Certain Persons) Act 1980, s. 1

(1) Where a court by or before which a person is convicted of an offence committed on licensed premises is satisfied that in committing that offence he resorted to violence or offered or threatened to resort to violence, the court may, subject to subsection (2) below, make an order (in this Act referred to as an 'exclusion order') prohibiting him from entering those premises or any other specified premises, without the express consent of the licensee of the premises or his servant or agent.

(2) An exclusion order may be made either—

(a) in addition to any sentence which is imposed in respect of the offence of which the person is convicted; or

(b) where the offence was committed in England or Wales, notwithstanding the provisions of sections 12 and 14 of the Powers of Criminal Courts (Sentencing) Act 2000 (cases in which absolute and conditional discharges may be made, and their effect), in addition to an order discharging him absolutely or conditionally; but not otherwise.

(3) An exclusion order shall have effect for such period, not less than three months or more than two years, as is specified in the order, unless it is terminated under section 2(2) below.

Such order may be made by the court either of its own motion, on the application of the victim or prosecutor or on the application of an interested third party made by way of representation to the prosecutor (*Penn* [1996] 2 Cr App R (S) 214).

The expression 'licensed premises' means premises in respect of which there is in force a justices' on-licence. In *Grady* (1990) 12 Cr App R (S) 152, the offender pleaded guilty to assault occasioning actual bodily harm, after having been involved in an altercation in a public house, during which she pushed or punched the landlady, causing bruising to her back. The Court of Appeal quashed an order excluding the offender from entering licensed premises within the county of Norfolk for 12 months. It was said that exclusion orders were designed for those who might be described as making a nuisance of themselves in public houses, to the annoyance of other customers and possible danger to the licensee; it was inappropriate to make such an order in the case of a woman of mature years with a clean record. In *Arrowsmith* [2003] 2 Cr App R (S) 301, the offender had head-butted a man in a public house, breaking his nose. The sentencer, in addition to passing a sentence of 12 months' imprisonment for the offence, made an exclusion order relating to 165 specified licensed premises within the Borough of Crewe and Nantwich, where the offender resided.

The Court of Appeal upheld the order on the particular facts of the case, but said that courts should not regard the decision as an invitation to draft overly wide exclusion orders.

Section 2 of the Act states that anyone who enters premises in breach of an exclusion order shall be guilty of an offence punishable on summary conviction with a fine not exceeding £200, or to imprisonment for one month or both. At the time of such conviction, the court shall consider whether the exclusion order should continue in force, and may terminate it, or vary it by deleting the name of any specified premises, if it thinks fit. There is no power to extend the order. By s. 4, a copy of any exclusion order, or order terminating or varying an exclusion order, shall be sent by the court to the licensee of the premises concerned.

Drinking Banning Orders

When the relevant provisions are brought into force, the VCRA 2006, chapter 1, will repeal the 1980 Act and provide power for a court to make a 'drinking banning order' on conviction in criminal proceedings where the court is satisfied that the offender has engaged in criminal or disorderly conduct while under the influence of alcohol and that such an order is necessary to protect other persons from further conduct by him of that kind while he is under the influence of alcohol. Such an order may impose any prohibition which is necessary for that purpose (s. 1(2)) and must be for not less than two months nor more than two years (s. 2(1)). Breach of a drinking banning order is a summary offence punishable with a fine not exceeding level 4 on the standard scale. **E23.2**

Football Banning Orders

Powers contained in the Football Spectators Act 1989 to exclude offenders who have been convicted of 'a relevant offence' from attendance at football matches, were amended by the Football (Disorder) Act 2000, which came into effect on 28 August 2000 and applies to relevant offences committed after that date. The 2000 Act inserted new ss. 14 to 14J for ss. 14 to 17 of the 1989 Act. Accordingly there is now no s. 15, 16 or 17 of that Act. Section 14B has been amended by the Football (Disorder) (Amendment) Act 2002. The 2000 Act also repealed ss. 30 to 34 and s. 36 of the POA 1986 which hitherto had applied in this context; s. 35 of that Act remains in place. The 2000 Act has the effect of removing the distinction, found in earlier versions of these provisions, between 'domestic' and 'international' football banning orders. When the VCRA 2006, ss. 52(1) and 65 and sch. 5, are brought into force, the Football (Disorder) Act 2000 will be repealed; sch. 3 to the VCRA 2006 contains amendments of the 1989 Act. **E23.3**

In *Gough v Chief Constable of Derbyshire* [2002] QB 459, the Divisional Court held that football banning orders were a lawful and proportionate restriction on a national citizen's freedom of movement under European Community law. The Court also held that such an order imposed after conviction was not a 'penalty' and accordingly there could be no infringement of the ECHR, Article 7 when, after conviction for a public order offence, the criminal court had imposed a ban for six years (twice the maximum ban available when the offence was committed).

Relevant Offences The 'relevant offences' are listed in sch. 1 to the 1989 Act, as substituted by the 2000 Act. A wide range of offences involving violence, possession of an offensive weapon, drunkenness, public disorder, damage to property and road traffic offences are 'relevant offences' if they were committed at or in connection with a football match, or when travelling to or from a football match (whether or not the match was actually attended by the offender). The offence under the POA 1986, s. 5, is included in sch. 1, but the offence under s. 4 of that Act is not. In *O'Keefe* [2004] 1 Cr App R (S) 402, the Court of Appeal held that any offence under s. 4 was a 'relevant offence' provided it had been committed in the relevant circumstances of connection with a football match. Specified offences under the 1989 Act, **E23.4**

offences under the Sporting Events (Control of Alcohol etc.) Act 1985, any offence under the Football (Offences) Act 1991 and the ticket tout offence under the CJPO 1994, s. 166, are also included. The offences listed extend to any attempt, conspiracy or incitement to commit such an offence, and to aiding, abetting, counselling or procuring the commission of such an offence. The racially aggravated offences in the CDA 1998, ss. 29 to 32, are not, however, listed.

E23.5 **Declaration of Relevance** In respect respect of a number of the offences listed in the Football Spectators Act 1989, sch. 1, before making a banning order the court is required to make a 'declaration that the offence related to a particular football match or matches' (a 'declaration of relevance'), which ordinarily requires that the prosecutor shall have given notice to the accused, at least five days before the first day of the trial, that it was proposed to show that the offence charged did relate to a particular football match or matches. Exceptionally, however, the court may make such a declaration in a case where the required notice has not been given, but only if the accused consents to waive the giving of full notice or the court is satisfied that the interests of justice do not require further notice to be given (s. 23).

E23.6 **Regulated Football Match** The provisions as amended now relate to any 'regulated football match', which means 'an association football match (whether in England and Wales or elsewhere) which is a prescribed match or a match of a prescribed description' (Football Spectators Act 1989, s. 14(2)). See also the Football Spectators (Prescription) Order 2004 (SI 2004 No. 2409).

E23.7 **Miscellaneous Matters** A 'banning order' means an order made by the court which (in relation to regulated football matches in England and Wales), prohibits the person under the order from entering any premises for the purpose of attending such a match, and (in relation to regulated football matches outside England and Wales), requires that person to report at a police station (s. 14(4)). A magistrates' court or the Crown Court has power to make a banning order. Such an order can only be made in addition to a sentence imposed in respect of the relevant offence, or in addition to a conditional discharge for that offence (s. 14A(4)). A banning order may be made in combination with a conditional discharge notwithstanding the PCC(S)A 2000, s. 14 (s. 14A(5) and see **E14.6**). A banning order cannot be made where the offender has received an absolute discharge for the offence.

By the Football Spectators Act 1989, s. 14A, where the offender is convicted of a relevant offence, if the court is satisfied that there are reasonable grounds to believe that making a banning order would help to prevent violence or disorder at or in connection with any regulated football matches, it is required to make a banning order in respect of the offender (s. 14A(2)). For discussion of what might amount to 'reasonable grounds', see *Smith* [2004] 1 Cr App R (S) 341. It is clear that a banning order may on the facts be justified on the basis of a single offence, without further evidence of repetition or propensity (*Hughes* [2006] 1 Cr App R (S) 632). For the purposes of deciding whether to make an order, the court may consider evidence led by the prosecution and the defence (s. 14(3A)) and it is immaterial whether that evidence would have been admissible in the proceedings (s. 14A(3B)). If it is not so satisfied, it must state that fact in open court and give its reasons (s. 14A(3)). On making a banning order, the court must explain the effect of that order to the offender in ordinary language (s. 14E(1)). The order requires the person to report initially at a specified police station within five days of the order being made (s. 14E(2)) and, unless there are exceptional circumstances, the order also requires that the offender (in connection with regulated football matches taking place outside the United Kingdom) shall surrender his passport (s. 14E(3)). If it appears to the court that there are exceptional circumstances, it must state in open court what they are (s. 14E(4)). There is power whereby the court may impose additional requirements on the person subject to the order in relation to any regulated football matches (s. 14G(1)). In particular, the court may make an order under the POA 1986, s. 35, requiring the offender to attend at a police station within seven days of the making of the order to have his photograph taken (s. 35(1)). This particular requirement, however, can be made by the court only where it has been requested by the prosecutor (s. 35(3)). A banning order takes effect on the day when the order is made (Football Spectators Act s. 14F(1)). If the order is made in addition to a sentence of immediate imprisonment (that term in this context 'includes any form of detention'), the maximum duration of the order is ten years and the minimum is six years (s. 14F(3)). Where any other sentence has been imposed for the offence, the maximum duration of the order is five years and the minimum is three years (s. 14F(4)).

If a banning order has been in force for at least two-thirds of the period of the order, the person subject to it may apply to the court by which it was made to terminate it early (s. 14H).

A person subject to a banning order who fails to comply with any requirement imposed by the order is guilty of an offence punishable on summary conviction with imprisonment for a term not exceeding six months, or a fine not exceeding level 5, or both (s. 14J).

Disqualification of Company Director

By the Company Directors Disqualification Act 1986, ss. 1 and 2, a court may make a disqualification order against an offender, wherever he is convicted of an indictable offence, whether tried on indictment or summarily, in connection with the promotion, formation, management or liquidation of a company (widely construed in *Georgiou* (1988) 87 Cr App R 207 and *Goodman* (1993) 14 Cr App R (S) 147, approving *Corbin* (1984) 6 Cr App R (S) 17), or in connection with the receivership or management of a company's property. This has the effect that the offender must not, without the leave of the court, be a director of a company, a liquidator or administrator of a company, a receiver or manager of a company's property, or in any way, directly or indirectly, be concerned or take part in the promotion, formation or management of a company, for a specified period beginning with the date of the order. Such a disqualification has general effect; a court has no power to limit the order to a particular type of company (*Ward* (2001) *The Times*, 10 August 2001). The purpose of the order is to protect the public from those who, for reasons of dishonesty, or naivety or incompetence, abuse their role and status as director (*per* Potter LJ in *Edwards* [1998] 2 Cr App R (S) 213). **E23.8**

The maximum period of disqualification which may be imposed by a magistrates' court is five years, and the maximum for the Crown Court is 15 years. There is no minimum period. In *Millard* (1994) 15 Cr App R (S) 445, the Court of Appeal identified an 'upper bracket' or disqualification for more than 10 years, which should be reserved for particularly serious cases (including those where the director has been disqualified previously), and a 'middle bracket' of six to ten years. The decision in *Edwards* appears to recognise a third bracket, of between two and five years, reflecting the distinctions drawn in the civil case of *Re Sevenoaks Stationery (Retail)* [1991] Ch 164, but this may overlook the fact that in a criminal case there is no equivalent to the two-year minimum disqualification period which applies in a civil case.

Disqualification for 15 years was appropriate in *Vanderwell* [1998] 2 Cr App R (S) 439 for a 'thoroughly dishonest fraudster' who pleaded guilty to managing a company while an undischarged bankrupt, obtaining property by deception and failing to keep proper accounts, and who had served an earlier prison sentence for fraud and received an earlier disqualification. See also *Atterbury* [1996] 2 Cr App R (S) 151, when disqualification for 12 years was imposed on the offender who had acted as a company director in contravention of an earlier disqualification order. Seven years' disqualification was upheld in *Bott-Walters* [2005] 2 Cr App R (S) 438, where the offender, the managing director of a company, had obtained £200,000 from another company by deception. Disqualification for five years was appropriate in *Theivendran* (1992) 13 Cr App R (S) 601 (managing a company whilst an undischarged bankrupt and obtaining excessive credit contrary to the Insolvency Act 1986) and in *Ashby* [1998] 2 Cr App R (S) 37. In *Victory* [1999] 2 Cr App R (S) 102, two years' disqualification was reduced to 12 months in the case of a director who was 'careless to the point of incompetence' in keeping accounting records.

A contravention of a disqualification order is, in itself, a criminal offence punishable with up to two years' imprisonment (s. 13). Where a disqualification order is made against a person who is already subject to one, the periods specified shall run concurrently (see *Johnson* [1996] 2 Cr App R (S) 228).

Disqualification from Driving on Commission of an Offence

E23.9 By s. 146 of the PCC(S)A 2000, a court by or before which a person is convicted of an offence may, instead of or in addition to dealing with him in any other way, order him to be disqualified, for such period as it thinks fit, from holding or obtaining a driving licence (s. 146(1)). The power is made available to the Crown Court and magistrates' courts and applies in relation to any offence. Section 146 came into effect on 1 January 1998, but power to disqualify under that section was extended to all courts only from 1 January 2004 (see HOC 59/2003).

On a literal reading of s. 146, the section renders redundant all the provisions on disqualification from driving which are contained in the RTOA 1988 (see **C7** and **C8**), as well as the power to disqualify from driving contained in the PCC(S)A 2000, s. 147 (see **E23.10**). According to s. 146, conviction for an offence may, without more, attract a period of disqualification from driving for such period as the court thinks fit. It may be, however, that the courts will interpret s. 146 so as to confer an additional power to disqualify offenders who have not committed a driving-related offence (so that the disqualification provisions in the 1988 Act are inapplicable) and who have not otherwise used a vehicle in the commission, or in facilitating the commission, of the offence (so that disqualification under s. 147, is not available). So construed, s. 146 empowers the court to disqualify from driving an offender whose offence is completely unrelated to motor vehicles. In *Cliff* [2005] 2 Cr App R (S) 118, the offender was convicted of affray following a serious disturbance at student accommodation. The offender discharged a ball-bearing gun and tried to kick down the door to a room in which students were hiding. He was sentenced to 15 months' imprisonment together with a disqualification under s. 146 for two years. The Court of Appeal upheld the disqualification, saying that it was not necessary for the offence of conviction to be related in any way to the use of a motor vehicle. The Court added, however, that an order under s. 146 could not be made arbitrarily, and there must be sufficient reason for it. In this case, the offender had admitted that, before the incident of affray he had driven his car while affected by drink or drugs or both. In *Bye* [2006] 1 Cr App R (S) 157, disqualification for 12 months under s. 146 in conjunction with a prison sentence of eight months was upheld by the Court of Appeal in a case where the offender got out of his car and attacked another motorist; in *Waring* [2006] 1 Cr App R (S) 56, disqualification for 18 months in conjunction with a prison sentence of four months for escape from lawful custody was upheld. In the latter case the offender had been stopped by the police, provided a positive breath test but, in the process of being taken to the police station, had jumped from the police car and escaped. He thereby avoided a second breath test and any possibility of being prosecuted for driving with excess alcohol. There is no power under s. 146 to order an offender to take an extended driving test on the expiry of the disqualification under the RTOA 1988, s. 36.

It is unclear whether an order made under s. 146 affects the totality of the sentence (by analogy with the power to order forfeiture of the offender's property under s. 143: see **E20.2**) or whether it should be regarded as an ancillary order (by analogy with compensation orders: see **E18.8**) imposition of which should not affect the punishment imposed for the offence. It is suggested that where disqualification is imposed under s. 146 it is imposed as an additional form of punishment, and so the former view is the preferable one.

Disqualification from Driving where Motor Vehicle Used for Committing or Facilitating Commission of an Offence

Section 147 of the PCC(S)A 2000 provides that the Crown Court may disqualify an offender from holding or obtaining a licence to drive a motor vehicle in cases where a motor vehicle has been used for the purpose of committing, or facilitating the commission of, the offence. This power is available: **E23.10**

(a) where a person is convicted before the Crown Court of an offence punishable on indictment with imprisonment for a term of two years or more, or where the offender has been convicted by a magistrates' court of such an offence and he is committed under s. 3 of the 2000 Act to the Crown Court for sentence (s. 147(1)), or
(b) where he is convicted before any court of common assault or any other offence involving assault (including an offence of aiding, abetting, counselling or procuring, or inciting the commission of an offence)(s. 147(2)),

and the Crown Court is satisfied that the motor vehicle was used (whether by the person convicted or by anyone else) for the purpose of committing, or facilitating the commission of the offence in question (s. 147(3)). Section 147(6) provides that facilitating the commission of an offence includes the taking of any steps after it has been committed for the purpose of disposing of any property to which it relates or of avoiding apprehension or detection.

In a case falling within s. 147, the Crown Court may order the person convicted to be disqualified, for such period as the court thinks fit, from holding or obtaining a licence (s. 147(3) and (4)), but there is no power under s. 147 to order the defendant to take an extended driving test on the expiry of the disqualification under the Road Traffic Offenders Act 1988, s. 36.

It should be noted that there is no requirement under s. 147 that the person convicted was the driver of the vehicle (*Matthews* [1975] RTR 32; *Skitt* [2005] 2 Cr App R (S) 122), nor that the vehicle was directly involved in the commission of the offence, although use of the vehicle must at least have facilitated its commission (see *Patel* (1994) 16 Cr App R (S) 756). If there is no causal link at all, an order under s. 147 cannot be made (see *Parrington* (1985) 7 Cr App R (S) 18, although disqualification might now be ordered instead under s. 146 (see E23.9)).

Before disqualifying the offender, the court must warn counsel of the possibility of disqualification under s. 147, and counsel should be given an opportunity to address the court on that matter. Failure to warn may result in the disqualification being quashed on appeal (*Powell* (1984) 6 Cr App R (S) 354). A court imposing a disqualification under s. 147 should take account of its likely effects on the offender's employment prospects (*Davegun* (1985) 7 Cr App R (S) 110; *Liddey* [1999] 2 Cr App R (S) 122).

Disqualification from Working with Children

The CJCSA 2000, ss. 26 to 34, provide a power for, and in certain cases a duty on, the Crown Court to impose a disqualification order on a person who has committed an offence against a child and who has received a qualifying sentence. The effect of the order is to disqualify that person from working with children in the future. When the relevant provisions of the Safeguarding Vulnerable Groups Act 2006 are brought into force, these provisions will be repealed. No date has yet been set for this change. **E23.11**

In *Field* [2003] 1 WLR 882, the Court of Appeal held that an order disqualifying the offender from working with children was not a 'penalty', and accordingly there was no infringement of the ECHR, Article 7, when the disqualification was imposed on the basis of sexual offences committed by the offender before the relevant provisions were brought into force. In *G*

[2006] 1 Cr App R (S) 173, the order survived challenge under the ECHR, Articles 3 and 8 (as well as renewed argument under Article 7).

For the purposes of these provisions, a person commits an offence against a child if he commits any offence specified in the CJCSA 2000, sch. 4, para. 1, or commits against a child any offence mentioned in sch. 4, para. 2, or he falls within sch. 4, para. 3 (s. 26). 'Child' means a person under the age of 18 (s. 42). The offence under the Child Abduction Act 1984, s. 2, is not included in the schedule (see *Prime* [2005] 1 Cr App R (S) 203).

Where the person who has committed the qualifying offence is aged 18 or over and the Crown Court imposed a 'qualifying sentence' in respect of that offence, the court shall order that the offender is to be disqualified from working with children *unless* the court is satisfied, having regard to all the circumstances, that it is unlikely that the offender will commit any further offence against a child. The burden of proof is on the offender and the standard of proof is the civil standard (*MG* [2002] 2 Cr App R (S) 1; *Clayton* [2004] 1 Cr App R (S) 201). If the court so finds, it must state its reasons (s. 28). If the person who has committed the qualifying offence is aged under 18 and a qualifying sentence is imposed in respect of that offence, the Crown Court may order that the offender is to be disqualified from working with children *if* the court is satisfied, having regard to all the circumstances, that it is likely that the offender will commit a further offence against a child. If the court makes a disqualification order on an offender under 18, it must state its reasons for doing so (s. 29).

The qualifying sentences are imprisonment for 12 months or more, detention in a young offender institution for 12 months or more, detention at Her Majesty's pleasure, detention under the PCC(S)A 2000, s. 91, for 12 months or more, a sentence of detention under the CJA 2003, s. 226 or 228, a detention and training order for 12 months or more, a hospital order or a guardianship order (s. 30). An (old-style) extended sentence is a qualifying sentence if its total length (rather than the length of the custodial term) is for 12 months or more (*Wiles* [2004] 2 Cr App R (S) 467).

By the CJA 2003, s. 299 and sch. 30, ss. 29A and 29B are inserted into the CJCSA 2000. Section 29A adds a further category of case in which the Crown Court *may* order disqualification. This is where the offender, *irrespective of age*, is convicted of an offence against a child and where *no* qualifying sentence is imposed in respect of the conviction. The court may order disqualification in such a case *if* the court is satisfied, having regard to all the circumstances, that it is likely that the offender will commit a further offence against a child. If the court makes an order for disqualification against an offender under s. 29A it must state its reasons for doing so.

Section 29B provides that, if the Crown Court has, in respect of an offender aged 18 or over, not made a disqualification order under s. 28 and has not given reasons for not doing so or, in respect of an offender aged under 18, it has not made a disqualification order under s. 29 and it appears to the prosecutor that it has failed to consider whether it should have done so, then in either case the prosecutor may apply to the court for a disqualification order to be made. It should be noted that s. 29B applies to cases falling within s. 28 or s. 29 of the Act, but does not apply to cases falling within s. 29A.

Sexual Offences Prevention Orders

E23.12 The SOA 2003, ss. 104 to 113, create powers for the courts to impose a sexual offences prevention order. The relevant provisions came into force on 1 May 2004 and from that date replace powers to impose a restraining order under previous legislation. It seems clear from the wording of the relevant provisions that the sexual offences prevention order is available in respect of relevant sexual offences committed before the commencement date as well as those committed on or after that date.

A court may make a sexual offences prevention order under the SOA 2003, s. 104, where the court deals with an offender in respect of an offence listed in sch. 3 (see **E25.2**) or sch. 5 to the SOA 2003 (both schedules are amended by SI 2007 No. 296 to cover a wider range of offences), or where the offender is found not guilty of such an offence by reason of insanity, or where there is a finding that he is under a disability and has done the act charged against him in respect of such an offence, and where the court is satisfied that it is necessary to make such an order, for the purpose of 'protecting the public or any particular members of the public from serious sexual harm from the defendant' (s. 104(1) to (3)). This phrase means 'protecting the public in the United Kingdom or any particular members of that public from serious physical or psychological harm, caused by the defendant committing one or more offences listed in sch. 3' (s. 106(3)). Acts, behaviour, convictions and findings include those occurring before the commencement date (s. 106(4)). An order may also be made following a conviction on an application by a chief officer of police in respect of a qualifying offender (s. 104(1) and (4) to (6)). A court may make a sexual offences prevention order even though a sentence of imprisonment for public protection has not been passed (*Rampley* [2007] 1 Cr App R (S) 543).

A sexual offences prevention order prohibits the offender from doing anything described in the order and has effect for a fixed period (not less than five years) specified in the order or until further order (s. 107(1)). The only prohibitions that may be included in the order are those necessary for the purpose of protecting the public or any particular members of the public from serious sexual harm from the defendant (s. 107(2)). Where (a) the order is made in respect of an offender who was a relevant offender immediately before the making of the order, and (b) the offender would otherwise cease to be subject to the notification requirements (see **E25**) while the order has effect, the offender remains subject to the notification requirements (s. 107(3)). Where an order is made in respect of an offender who was not a relevant offender immediately before the making of the order (a) the order causes the offender to become subject to the notification requirements from the making of the order until the order (as renewed from time to time) ceases to have effect (s. 107(4)).

Provisions relating to the variation, renewal and discharge of sexual offences prevention orders are set out in s. 108, and provisions relating to appeals against sexual offences prevention orders are set out in s. 110.

If an offender who is subject to a sexual offences prevention order, without reasonable excuse does anything which he is prohibited from doing by that order, he commits an offence which is punishable on summary conviction to imprisonment for a term not exceeding six months or a fine not exceeding the statutory maximum or both, or on conviction on indictment to imprisonment for a term not exceeding five years. Where a person is convicted of such an offence, it is not open to the court to make a conditional discharge in respect of the offence (s. 113).

In *Yates* [2004] 1 Cr App R (S) 269, the Court of Appeal stressed the importance of a sentencer distinguishing between a restraining order under the SOA 1997 and a disqualification from working with children (see **E23.11**). A restraining order under the Sex Offenders Act 1997, s. 5A (now a prevention order under the SOA 2003, s. 104), was primarily designed for those who presented a serious ongoing risk of danger to the public in general, or any particular member of the public, from serious harm. An order under the section could impose a significant restriction on the liberty of the offender and should be construed as authorising no more severe interference with that liberty than was proportionate to the risk. In *Halloran* [2004] 2 Cr App R (S) 155, another case under the Sex Offenders Act 1997, s. 5A, the offender received a sentence of eight months' imprisonment after pleading guilty to 13 counts of making indecent photographs of children by downloading from the Internet. The sentencer in addition imposed a restraining order prohibiting the offender from ever owning or having access to a computer except at his place of work. The Court of Appeal quashed the restraining order, stating that the 'restrictive test', requiring the judge to be satisfied that the order was 'necessary' to protect the public from serious harm, had not been passed in this case. 'serious harm' was not defined in the 1997 Act, but the Court bore in mind the meaning of 'serious harm' in the PCC(S)A 2000, s. 161(4) (now repealed). If the prosecution invited the judge to make such an order they should be in a position to put before him material to show that the statutory requirements had been met. In *D* [2006] 2 Cr App R (S) 204 the Court of Appeal held that it had been appropriate in the particular case, where the offender had committed sexual offences against his daughter when she was aged between 10 and 13, to impose an order prohibiting the offender from contacting his young son. The son had not been the victim of offending but had suffered psychological harm and was at risk of further such harm if the offender committed more offences.

Restraining Orders under the Protection from Harassment Act 1997

E23.13 A court which is sentencing or otherwise dealing with a person convicted of an offence under the Protection from Harassment Act 1977, s. 2 or s. 4 (see **B11.78** and **B11.87**) may, as well as dealing with the offender in any other way, make a restraining order under s. 5 of the 1997 Act. For the purpose of protecting the victim of the offence (or any other person mentioned in the order) from further conduct which amounts to harassment, or will cause a fear of violence, the order may prohibit the offender from doing anything described in the order. The order must be drafted in clear and precise terms so that there is no doubt as to its conditions, and may make reference to specific roads or addresses from which the offender is prohibited, if necessary by the inclusion of a map (*Debnath* [2006] 2 Cr App R (S) 169). In considering the terms and extent of the restraining order, the court should have regard to proportionality with the seriousness of the offence. The order has effect for a specified period or until further order. The prosecutor, the defendant or any other person mentioned in the order may apply to the court which made the order for it to be varied or discharged by a further order. The Court of Appeal may decline to interfere with the terms of a restraining order if the appropriate remedy was an application to the court to vary or discharge the order (*Debnath*).

If without reasonable excuse the offender does anything which he is prohibited from doing under the order, he is guilty of an offence punishable, on conviction on indictment, with imprisonment for a term not exceeding five years, or a fine, or both; or on summary conviction to imprisonment for a term not exceeding six months, or a fine not exceeding the statutory maximum, or both.

In *Liddle* [2000] 1 Cr App R (S) 131 the Court of Appeal considered the approach to sentence for breach of a restraining order imposed by a court under s. 5, following conviction under s. 2 or s. 4. Curtis J observed that relevant sentencing factors would be the relative seriousness and persistence of the offender's conduct, whether there was a history of disobedience to court orders, and the actual impact of the harassment on the victim. The attitude of the offender was also relevant, such as whether he had pleaded guilty, expressed remorse, and was willing to receive appropriate treatment or help. See also *Lumley* [2001] 2 Cr App R (S) 110, *Pace* [2005] 1 Cr App R (S) 370 and *Bennett* [2005] 2 Cr App R (S) 362. These decisions should now be read in the light of the SGC Definitive Guideline on *Breach of a Protective Order* (effective from 18 December 2006). The guidelines suggest:

(i) a custodial sentence of more than 12 months where breach (whether one or more) involved significant physical violence and significant physical or psychological harm to the victim;

(ii) a range of 26 to 39 weeks' custody where there was more than one breach involving some violence and/or significant physical or psychological harm to the victim or a single breach involving some violence and/or significant physical or psychological harm to the victim;

(iii) a range of 13 to 26 weeks' custody where there was a single breach involving some violence and/or significant physical or psychological harm to the victim;
(iv) a medium range community order where there was more than one breach involving no or minimal contact or some direct contact; and
(v) a low range community order where there was a single breach involving no or minimal direct contact.

For the full text of the guideline, see **appendix 8, Part 6.**

Travel Restriction Orders: Drug Trafficking Offenders

By the CJPA 2001, ss. 33 to 37, any criminal court (but, in practice, the Crown Court) is given power to impose a travel restriction order on an offender who is convicted of a drug trafficking offence committed after that date, and who has been sentenced by that court to a term of imprisonment for four years or more (s. 33(1)). The effect of the order is to restrict the offender's freedom to leave the UK for a period specified by the court, and it may require delivery up of his passport. The minimum duration of a travel restriction order is two years, starting from the date of the offender's release from custody. There is no maximum period prescribed in the legislation. The court must always consider whether such an order should be made and must give reasons where it does not consider such an order to be appropriate (s. 33(2)). **E23.14**

'Drug trafficking offence' is defined by s. 34. It may be noted that this is a different definition from that provided by the Proceeds of Crime Act 2002, sch. 2. Section 35 provides for revocation and suspension of travel restriction orders. Section 36 creates various offences in relation to contravention of these orders.

Guidance on the imposition of travel restriction orders was given by the Court of Appeal in *Mee* [2004] 2 Cr App R (S) 434. The order was designed to prevent or reduce the risk of offending after the offender's release from prison. It was not confined to cases involving importation, but those were the cases in which it was most likely to be appropriate. The restriction on a person's freedom to travel was a significant restriction and should not be taken away for a number of years unless there were grounds for doing so. The length of the order should be that which was required to protect the public in the light of the assessment of risk of reoffending, taking into account the offender's age, previous convictions, family contacts and employment considerations. *Mee* was followed and applied in *Fuller* [2006] 1 Cr App R (S) 52, where a travel restriction order, imposed on a woman aged 25 who had pleaded guilty to importation of cocaine was quashed on the basis that there was no significant risk of re-offending and that the order would prevent contact between the offender's child and his grandparents in Jamaica for a period of seven years. See also *Onung* [2007] 2 Cr App R (S) 9.

Financial Reporting Orders

With effect from 1 April 2006, by the SOCPA 2005, s. 76(1) and (2), a court sentencing an offender for an offence listed in s. 76(3) may also make a financial reporting order in respect of that offender, provided that it is satisfied that the risk of the person's committing another offence of the kind mentioned in s. 76(3) is sufficiently high to justify the making of the order. The relevant offences are offences under the TA 1968, ss. 15, 15A, 16 and 20(2), under the TA 1978, ss. 1 and 2, and, with effect from 15 January 2007, offences under the Fraud Act 2006, ss. 1 and 11, together with any offence specified in the PCA 2002, sch. 2 ('lifestyle offences': see **E21.11**). Further, with effect from 4 May 2007, the following offences have been added: conspiracy to defraud; offences of false accounting under the TA 1968, s. 17; offences under the Public Bodies Corrupt Practices Act 1889, s. 1, the Prevention of Corruption Act 1906, s. 1, the CJA 1988, s. 93A, 93B or 93C, the Drug Trafficking Act 1994, s. 49, **E23.15**

50 or 51, or the Terrorism Act 2000, s. 15, 16, 17 or 18; attempt, conspiracy or incitement, or aiding, abetting, counselling or procuring any of the relevant offences.

The purpose of the financial reporting order is to require the person on whom the order is imposed to make a report to a person specified in the order as to such particulars of his financial affairs as may be specified in the order (s. 79(3)). The report may relate to a specified period of time beginning with the date on which the order comes into force and to subsequent specified periods of time, each beginning immediately after the end of the previous one (s. 79(2)). Each report must be made within a number of days after the end of the period in question, as specified in the order (s. 79(5)).

A financial reporting order comes into force when it is made and has effect for the period specified in the order, beginning with the date in which it is made. If made by a magistrates' court, the period must not exceed five years (s. 76(6)). If made by the Crown Court, the period must not exceed 20 years, where the person has been sentenced to imprisonment for life, or 15 years, in any other case (s. 76(7)).

A person who without reasonable excuse includes false or misleading information in a report, or who otherwise fails to comply with any requirement of s. 79, is guilty of an offence and liable on summary conviction to imprisonment for a term not exceeding 51 weeks, or to a fine not exceeding level 5 on the standard scale, or to both (s. 79(10)).

Section 80 provides for the variation and revocation of financial reporting orders by the court which made the order, and s. 81 provides for verification and disclosure of such orders.

Orders under the Crime and Disorder Act 1998, s. 1C (Anti-social Behaviour)

E23.16 The CDA 1998, s. 1C, applies where an offender is convicted of an offence and the court considers that the offender has acted, at any time since the commencement date of s. 1C, in an anti-social manner, i.e. a manner that caused or was likely to cause harassment, alarm or distress to one or more persons not of the same household as himself. These orders are discussed at D23.

Section E24 Mentally Disordered Offenders

HOSPITAL ORDERS

E24.1 An admission to a hospital by means of a hospital order has the same effect for most purposes as a compulsory civil commitment under part II of the Mental Health Act 1983. The order lapses after six months, but may be renewed for a further six months and then at yearly intervals thereafter, where the responsible medical officer considers further detention necessary for the protection of the public or in the interests of the patient's health or safety (Mental Health Act 1983, s. 20 and sch. 1). There is no limit to the number of renewals which might subsequently be made, but the patient may be discharged from hospital by way of various powers exercised by the responsible medical officer, the hospital managers, or a mental health review tribunal.

Mental Health Act 1983, s. 37

(1) Where a person is convicted before the Crown Court of an offence punishable with imprisonment other than an offence the sentence for which is fixed by law, or is convicted by a magistrates' court of an offence punishable on summary conviction with imprisonment, and the conditions mentioned in subsection (2) below are satisfied, the court may by order authorise his admission to and detention in such hospital as may be specified in the order or, as the case may be, place him under the guardianship of a local social services authority or of such other person approved by a local social services authority as may be so specified.

(1A) In the case of an offence the sentence for which would otherwise fall to be imposed—

(a) under section 51A of the Firearms Act 1968,

(b) under section 110(2) or 111(2) of the Powers of Criminal Courts (Sentencing) Act 2000, or

(c) under any of sections 225 to 228 of the Criminal Justice Act 2003,

(d) under section 29(4) or (6) of the Violent Crime Reduction Act 2006 (minimum sentences in certain cases of using someone to mind a weapon)

nothing in those provisions shall prevent a court from making an order under subsection (1) above for the admission of the offender to a hospital.

(1B) References in subsection (1A) above to a sentence falling to be imposed under any of the provisions mentioned in that subsection are to be read in accordance with section 305(4) of the Criminal Justice Act 2003.

(2) The conditions referred to in subsection (1) above are that —

(a) the court is satisfied, on the written or oral evidence of two registered medical practitioners, that the offender is suffering from mental illness, psychopathic disorder, severe mental impairment or mental impairment and that either—

(i) the mental disorder from which the offender is suffering is of a nature or degree which makes it appropriate for him to be detained in a hospital for medical treatment and, in the case of psychopathic disorder or mental impairment, that such treatment is likely to alleviate or prevent a deterioration of his condition; or

(ii) in the case of an offender who has attained the age of 16 years, the mental disorder is of a nature or degree which warrants his reception into guardianship under this Act; and

(b) the court is of the opinion, having regard to all the circumstances including the nature of the offence and the character and antecedents of the offender, and to the other available methods of dealing with him, that the most suitable method of disposing of the case is by means of an order under this section.

At least one of the two medical practitioners referred to in s. 37(2) must be approved, for the purposes of s. 12, by the Secretary of State, as having special experience in the diagnosis or treatment of mental disorder (s. 54(1)). Three of the four forms of mental disorder specified in s. 37(2)(a) are defined in s. 1 of the 1983 Act. This section also describes other conditions which do not amount to mental disorder within the Act. Whenever a hospital order (or guardianship order) is made, the court must specify from which of these forms of mental disorder the offender is found by the court to be suffering (s. 37(7)), and an order cannot be made unless the offender is described by each of the medical practitioners as suffering from the same form of mental disorder (s. 37(7)). A hospital order may be appropriate, even though no causal link is established between the offender's mental disorder and the offence in respect of which the order is made (*McBride* (1972) CSP F2- 2A01). In *Blackwood* (1974) 59 Cr App R 170, the Court of Appeal said that a court should not normally make a hospital order if the offender was not legally represented. Only a youth court may make a hospital order or guardianship order on a juvenile (PCC(S)A 2000, s. 8(6)).

Section 37(3) of the Mental Health Act 1983 deals with the power of a magistrates' court to make a hospital order, where the court is satisfied that the person did the act or made the omission charged, without proceeding to conviction. This power is to be very sparingly used (see *Lincoln (Kesteven) Justices, ex parte O'Connor* [1983] 1 WLR 335).

A hospital order or guardianship order cannot be made unless the court is satisfied, on the written or oral evidence of the registered medical practitioner who would be in charge of the offender's treatment, or of some other person representing the managers of the hospital, that arrangements have been made for the offender's admission to that hospital within 28 days of the date of the order (s. 37(4)). The health authorities are under no legal obligation to accept offenders from the courts (see, for example, the comments of Field J in *Barker* [2003] 1 Cr App R (S) 212). They are, however, under a legal obligation to supply information to the courts about the availability of beds in their regions for the admission of persons under hospital orders (s. 39(1)). In an emergency or other special situation arising within that 28 days, the Secretary of State may give directions for the admission of the offender to a hospital different from that specified in the order (s. 37(5)).

The decision whether to make a hospital order under s. 37 or impose a sentence of imprisonment is within the discretion of the court (*Khelifi* [2006] 2 Cr App R (S) 650). The fact that the conditions in s. 37(2) are all made out does not compel the making of a hospital order, or give rise to a presumption that one will be made. The welfare of the offender is always an important consideration, but must be assessed in light of the seriousness of the offence.

By s. 37(8), when a hospital order or a guardianship order is made, the court shall not pass a sentence of imprisonment, make an order for detention, impose a fine, make a community order or a supervision order in respect of the offence, or require a parent of a juvenile so dealt with to enter into a recognisance (see **E16.5**). A hospital order cannot be combined with a referral order (see **E12**). The court may, however, 'make any other order which the court has power to make apart from this section': this would include ancillary orders such as a compensation order.

E24.2 **Interim Hospital Orders** Section 38 provides for the making of an 'interim hospital order' for the purposes of establishing whether a convicted person is suitable to be the subject of a hospital order. The qualifying conditions are virtually the same as for the making of a hospital order under s. 37, but the interim order is available to the court 'before making a hospital order or dealing with him in some other way'. One difference in the powers is that an interim order can be made only where one of the registered medical practitioners who gives evidence is employed at the hospital where the person is to be detained. An interim hospital order is not a final disposal of the case; such an order may last for up to 12 weeks, renewable for further periods of not more than 28 days at a time, though in no case may it last for more than a total of 12 months. No minimum period is specified. Power to make an interim hospital order under s. 38 may also be exercised for the purposes of determining whether a person should be made subject to a hospital direction or a limitation direction under s. 45A (s. 45A(8): see E24.6). At the end of the interim period the court must make a final disposal of the case, and the interim order comes to an end. In a case where a court renews an interim hospital order, or where it finally disposes of the case by making a hospital order under s. 37, the offender need not appear before the court, provided that he is legally represented and his representative has had an opportunity of being heard (s. 38(2) and (6)).

GUARDIANSHIP ORDERS

By the Mental Health Act 1983, s. 40(2), a guardianship order shall confer on the authority or person named in the order as guardian, the same powers as a guardianship application made and accepted under part II of the 1983 Act. These powers, in outline, are to determine place of residence, require attendance for treatment, occupation, education or training, and to require access to the patient in any place of residence for a doctor, social worker or other specified person (Mental Health Act 1983, s. 8). E24.3

The relevant statutory provisions are the same as those which relate to the courts' powers to make hospital orders (see E24.1), except that there is no requirement in respect of the making of a guardianship order that the mental disorder must be treatable, and see the requirement in s. 37(2)(a)(ii), set out at E24.1. In addition, by s. 37(6), a guardianship order cannot be made unless the relevant authority or person is willing to receive the offender into guardianship. Section 39A empowers a court which is minded to make a guardianship order to request the local social services authority to inform the court whether it would be willing to comply with the order and, if so, to give information about how it would exercise its powers under s. 40(2). A guardianship order lasts for six months, but may be renewed for a further six months and thereafter annually (s. 20).

RESTRICTION ORDERS

Power to Make Restriction Orders

Mental Health Act 1983, s. 41 E24.4

(1) Where a hospital order is made in respect of an offender by the Crown Court, and it appears to the court, having regard to the nature of the offence, the antecedents of the offender and the risk of his committing further offences if set at large, that it is necessary for the protection of the public from serious harm so to do, the court may, subject to the provisions of this section, further order that the offender shall be subject to the special restrictions set out in this section, either without limit of time or during such period as may be specified in the order; and an order under this section shall be known as 'a restriction order'.

(2) A restriction order shall not be made in the case of any person unless at least one of the registered medical practitioners whose evidence is taken into account by the court under section 37(2)(a) above has given evidence orally before the court.

For hospital orders, see E24.1. The special restrictions applicable to a patient under a restriction order are set out in s. 41(3). In particular, powers under the 1983 Act to transfer or discharge the patient are exercisable only with the consent of the Secretary of State. Only the Crown Court may make a restriction order, though magistrates may commit an offender to the Crown Court, provided the offender is aged 14 or over, with a view to such a disposal (s. 43 and see *Avbunudje* [1999] 2 Cr App R (S) 189). If the magistrates' court commits the offender to the Crown Court, but the Crown Court decides not to make a restriction order, the Crown Court's powers of sentence are limited to those which the magistrates could have imposed, unless there is also in effect a general committal for sentence.

A restriction order cannot be made unless there is evidence that it is necessary to protect the public from serious harm (*Courtney* (1987) 9 Cr App R (S) 404; *Kearney* [2003] 2 Cr App R (S) 85). A court is not bound to accept medical evidence for or against restricting discharge when a hospital order is made (*Royse* (1981) 3 Cr App R (S) 58, *Birch* (1989) 11 Cr App R (S) 202). There is no requirement for a causal connection between the disorder and the offence (*Hatt* [1962] Crim LR 647, approved in *Birch*).

Unlike a hospital order under s. 37, a restriction order does not lapse in the ordinary way unless renewed, but continues for as long as the restriction order is in place. If the restriction order is for a fixed period, at the end of that period the restrictions no longer apply but the hospital order continues in effect (s. 41(5)). Neither the responsible medical officer nor the hospital managers may discharge the patient without the Secretary of State's consent. The Secretary of State or a mental health review tribunal may release a patient who is subject to a restriction order at any time, either absolutely or conditionally (s. 42(1) and (2)). If the patient is discharged conditionally, the restriction order remains in force and the patient may be recalled to hospital.

Sentencing Principles

E24.5 In *Birch* (1989) 11 Cr App R (S) 202, the Court of Appeal gave important guidance upon the selection of sentence for mentally disordered offenders generally, and in particular the appropriate use of restriction orders under the Mental Health Act 1983, s. 41. Earlier cases on the use of restriction orders should be read subject to this decision. The following general points emerge:

(a) In a case involving a degree of mental disorder, the sentencer should consider whether a period of compulsory detention is apposite.
(b) If such an order is inappropriate, the sentencer must consider whether the conditions contained in s. 37, for the making of a hospital order (see **E24.1**), are satisfied. If in doubt, he may wish to make an interim hospital order, giving the court and the doctors further time to decide. If the conditions in s. 37 are satisfied, he will consider whether to make a hospital order or impose a custodial sentence.
(c) The sentencer should then consider whether the conditions of s. 41 are satisfied.

Mustill LJ held in *Birch* that the choice between a hospital order and a restriction order depends on a prognosis which the judge must make (rather than the medical experts). A sentencer should not add a restriction order to a hospital order simply to mark the gravity of the offence, nor as a means of punishment. The words 'from serious harm' in the Mental Health Act 1983, s. 41, mean that the court is required to assess, not the seriousness of the risk that the offender will reoffend, but the risk that if he does so the public will suffer serious harm. His lordship said (at p. 213):

> The harm in question need not, in our view, be limited to personal injury. Nor need it relate to the public in general, for it would in our judgment suffice if a category of persons, or even a single person, were adjudged to be at risk: although the category of person so protected would no doubt exclude the offender himself. Nevertheless the potential harm must be serious, and a high possibility of a recurrence of minor offences will no longer be sufficient.

His lordship also held that it would be a mistake to equate the seriousness of the offence with the likelihood of a restriction order being made. It is only one factor, but the court would have to be very sure of its ground to pass a restriction order where the commission of a serious offence was coupled with a very low risk of reoffending. On the other hand, a relatively minor offence committed by a person who is shown by the medical evidence to be mentally disordered and dangerous may justify the passing of a restriction order. It is not necessary to wait until someone has been seriously injured before a hospital order with restrictions can be made (see *Nwohia* [1996] 1 Cr App R (S) 170).

If the sentencer decides on a restriction order, he must then choose an unlimited order, or one for a fixed term. It is regarded as imprudent in any but the most exceptional circumstances to impose a restriction for a fixed rather than an unlimited period (*Gardiner* [1967] 1 WLR 464, *Birch* and *Nwohia*).

If the criteria within the Mental Health Act 1983, s. 41, are established, the sentencer may, but is not obliged to, make a restriction order. The decision is that of the judge, and a restriction order may be made even though not recommended by the medical evidence (*Royce* (1981) 3 Cr App R (S) 58). The alternative sentences are life imprisonment, imprisonment for public protection (if the offence was committed on or after 4 April 2005), or a fixed-term sentence. The cases make it clear that an indeterminate sentence is to be preferred to a fixed-term sentence where the offender is subject to a degree of mental instability which makes it probable that he will continue to offend unless detained for an indefinite period (*Pither* (1979) 1 Cr App R (S) 209). Where the conditions for a restriction order under the Mental Health Act 1983 are made out, a bed in an appropriate hospital is available, and the medical evidence is that the mental disorder is treatable and that successful treatment will greatly diminish the risk posed by the offender, a restriction order should normally be imposed in preference to a life sentence (*Mbatha* (1985) 7 Cr App R (S) 373; *Hutchinson* [1997] 2 Cr App R (S) 60; *Mitchell* [1997] 1 Cr App R (S) 90). In the decision of the House of Lords in *Drew* [2004] 2 Cr App R (S) 65, however, it was noted that offenders subject to hospital orders (with or without restriction) are entitled to release when their medical condition has been successfully treated, while release from a life sentence is a matter for the Parole Board, which can take into account all relevant matters of risk rather than just mental health. A life sentence thereby provided a greater degree of control over the offender. See further *IA* [2006] 1 Cr App R (S) 521.

Mustill LJ in *Birch* also gave guidance (at p. 215) on the choice between a restriction order and a custodial sentence, suggesting that this choice may arise in two distinct situations:

(a) 'If the offender is dangerous and no suitable secure hospital accommodation is available: here the judge will be driven to impose a prison sentence.' A number of earlier cases indicate that where a determinate custodial sentence is imposed rather than a hospital order, it must be proportionate to the offence committed (*Clarke* (1975) 61 Cr App R 320, *Hook* (1980) 2 Cr App R (S) 353 and *Fisher* (1981) 3 Cr App R (S) 112). In other cases, however, the Court of Appeal has upheld a disproportionate term of custody, on the grounds of the protection of the public, on an offender for whom no place was available in a hospital (*Scanlon* (1979) 1 Cr App R (S) 60, *Gouws* (1981) 3 Cr App R (S) 325).

(b) 'Where the sentencer considers that notwithstanding the offender's mental disorder there was an element of culpability in the offence which merits punishment. This may happen where there is no connection between the mental disorder and the offence, or where the defendant's responsibility for the offence is "diminished" but not wholly extinguished.' Although *Mbatha* (1985) 7 Cr App R (S) 373 indicates that in such a case a hospital order is to be preferred, there is no rule to that effect and in *Nafei* [2005] 2 Cr App R (S) 127 the Court of Appeal upheld a sentence of imprisonment on an offender who was suffering from schizophrenia and for whom a hospital order was recommended, but where there was no causal connection between the mental condition and the offence.

HOSPITAL AND LIMITATION DIRECTIONS

Sections 45A and 45B of the Mental Health Act 1983 are designed to apply where the court **E24.6** has heard evidence that the offender is suffering from a psychopathic disorder and the making of a hospital order is appropriate, but the court wishes to ensure that the offender (if found not to be capable of responding to treatment for his condition or upon completion of his period of treatment) will thence be transferred to prison for the remainder of the sentence rather than being released from hospital.

Section 45A applies where a person is convicted before the Crown Court of an offence the sentence for which is not fixed by law and the court considers making a hospital order before deciding to impose a sentence of imprisonment (s. 45A(1)). By s. 45A(2), the court must be satisfied on the written or oral evidence of two registered medical practitioners (at least one of whom must give oral evidence: s. 45A(4)):

(a) that the offender is suffering from psychopathic disorder;
(b) that the mental disorder from which the offender is suffering is of a nature or degree which makes it appropriate for him to be detained in a hospital for medical treatment; and
(c) that such treatment is likely to alleviate or prevent a deterioration of his condition.

In these circumstances the court may make a 'hospital direction', which is a direction that, instead of being detained in prison, the offender be detained in a specified hospital. The court may also make a 'limitation direction', which is a direction that the offender also be made subject to the restrictions set out in s. 41 of the 1983 Act (see **E24.4**). The court must also be satisfied on the written or oral evidence of the registered medical practitioner who would be in charge of the offender's treatment, or of some other person representing the managers of the hospital, that arrangements have been made for the offender's admission to that hospital and for his admission within the period of 28 days from the making of the order. The court may, pending admission within that period, give directions for the offender's detention in a place of safety (s. 45A(5)). A hospital direction and a limitation direction given in respect of an offender have effect not only as regards the sentence of imprisonment imposed but also as regards any other sentence of imprisonment imposed on the same or a previous occasion (s. 45A(9)).

By s. 45A(10), the Secretary of State may by order provide that directions made under s. 45A may apply to offenders suffering from other forms of mental disorder apart from psychopathic disorder. No such order has been made. The House of Lords in *Drew* [2004] 1 Cr App R (S) 65 and the Court of Appeal in *IA* [2006] 1 Cr App R (S) 521 have both expressed the hope that the Secretary of State might extend the power to make a limitation direction at the same time as imposing a custodial sentence to offenders suffering from mental illness or impairment not involving psychopathic disorder. In *Staines* [2006] 2 Cr App R (S) 376, after a helpful review of the authorities, the Court of Appeal upheld a sentence of life imprisonment together with a hospital and limitation direction under s. 45A in a case of manslaughter by diminished responsibility.

Section 45B provides that with respect to any person a hospital direction shall have effect as a transfer direction and a limitation direction shall have effect as a restriction direction. While a person is subject to a hospital direction and a limitation direction the responsible medical officer must supply to the Secretary of State a report on the offender at least every 12 months.

Section E25 Notification Requirements under the Sexual Offences Act 2003

The Sex Offenders Act 1997 required certain categories of sex offenders to notify the police of their name and home address and subsequent changes. With effect from 1 May 2004, the Sex Offenders Act 1997 was repealed and replaced by the SOA 2003. A person is subject to the notification requirements of the 2003 Act if he is convicted of an offence listed in sch. 3 to that Act, or is found not guilty of such an offence by reason of insanity, or is found to be under a disability and to have done the act charged against him in respect of such an offence, or is cautioned in respect of such an offence (SOA 2003, s. 80). A person subject to the notification requirements is referred to in the Act as a 'relevant offender'. The notification requirements are set out in s. 83. They are that the offender must, within the period of three days of the conviction, finding or caution, notify to the police the offender's date of birth, national insurance number, name (and any aliases), home address and any other address at which he regularly stays. Subsequent changes to these details must also be notified to the police (s. 84). Persons who were formerly subject to registration under the Sex Offenders Act 1997 are now made subject to the notification requirements under the SOA 2003 (s. 81). The retrospective element in the notification requirements under the Sex Offenders Act 1997 was held by the European Commission on Human Rights not to breach the ECHR, Article 7(1), since registration under that Act was not a 'penalty' within the meaning of Article 7 (see *Ibbotson v UK* [1999] Crim LR 153). Although the requirements of the 1997 Act did not extend to offenders conditionally discharged (according to the House of Lords in *Longworth* [2006] 1 WLR 313) the requirements of the 2003 Act do apply to such offenders from 1 May 2004 (see **E25.3**). **E25.1**

The requirements of the 1997 Act (and, it is submitted, the 2003 Act) are not an additional form of punishment, and so should not be taken into account when determining the sentence to be passed. See *A-G's Ref (No. 50 of 1997)* [1998] 2 Cr App R (S) 155. The provisions of the Act are automatic in their effect and, in principle, do not require the sentencer dealing with a case involving one of the listed offences to make reference to them, although the SOA 2003, s. 92 provides that, where a sentencer states in open court that an offender has been convicted of a listed offence and certifies those facts, the certificate shall be sufficient evidence of those facts. In respect of the equivalent provision under the 1997 Act, s. 5, Rose LJ stated in *A-G's Ref (No. 50 of 1997)* that there was 'an expectation that a judge passing sentence will make use of section 5, in order to make a statement . . . in an appropriate case'. It may well be, however, that the duty imposed on the sentencer by the CJA 2003, s. 174 (see **E1.16**), to explain the effect of sentence, now requires an explanation in open court of the nature and effect of the notification requirements of the 2003 Act.

Listed Offences

Offences listed in sch. 3 to the SOA 2003 are offences under: **E25.2**

SOA 1956, s. 1 (rape);
SOA 1956, s. 5 (intercourse with a girl under 13);
SOA 1956, s. 6 (intercourse with a girl under 16) if the offender was 20 or over;
SOA 1956, s. 10 (incest by a man) if the victim or other party was under 18;

SOA 1956, s. 12 (buggery) if the offender was 20 or over and the victim or other party was under 18;
SOA 1956, s. 13 (indecency between men) if the offender was 20 or over and the victim or other party was under 18;
SOA 1956, s. 14 (indecent assault on a woman) if the victim was under 18 or the offender was sentenced to at least 30 months' imprisonment or was admitted to hospital and subject to a restriction order;
SOA 1956, s. 15 (indecent assault on a man) if the victim was under 18 or the offender was sentenced to at least 30 months' imprisonment or was admitted to hospital subject to a restriction order;
SOA 1956, s. 16 (assault with intent to commit buggery) if the victim or other party was under 18;
SOA 1956, s. 28 (causing or encouraging the prostitution of, intercourse with, or indecent assault on, a girl under 16);
Indecency with Children Act 1960, s. 1 (indecent conduct towards young child);
Criminal Law Act 1977, s. 54 (inciting girl under 16 to have incestuous sexual intercourse);
Protection of Children Act 1978, s. 1 (indecent photographs of children) if the photographs showed persons under 16 and subject to age of offender and sentence imposed;
Customs and Excise Management Act 1979, s. 170 (penalty for fraudulent evasion of duty) in relation to indecent or obscene articles, if the prohibited goods included indecent photographs of persons under 16 and the offender was 18 or over or received a sentence of at least 12 months' imprisonment
CJA 1988, s. 160 (possession of indecent photograph of child) if the indecent photograph showed persons under 16 and the offender was 18 or over or received a sentence of at least 12 months' imprisonment;
SO(A)A 2000 (abuse of position of trust) if the offender was 20 or over;
SOA 2003, s. 1 or s. 2 (rape, assault by penetration);
SOA 2003, s. 3 (sexual assault) subject to age of offender and sentence imposed;
SOA 2003, s. 4, 5 or 6 (causing sexual activity without consent, rape of child under 13, assault of child under 13 by penetration);
SOA 2003, s. 7 (sexual assault of child under 13) where the offender was aged 18 or over or was sentenced to at least 12 months' imprisonment;
SOA 2003, ss. 8 to 12 (causing or inciting a child under 13 to engage in sexual activity; child sex offences committed by adults);
SOA 2003, s. 13 (child sex offences committed by children or young persons), if the offender was sentenced to at least 12 months' imprisonment;
SOA 2003, s. 14 (arranging or facilitating the commission of a child sex offence), where the offender was aged 18 or over or was sentenced to at least 12 months' imprisonment;
SOA 2003, s. 15 (meeting a child following sexual grooming);
SOA 2003, ss. 16 to 19 (abuse of a position of trust), if the offender is imprisoned, detained in a hospital or receives a community sentence of at least 12 months;
SOA 2003, s. 25 or s. 26 (familial child sex offences) where the offender was aged 18 or over or was sentenced to at least 12 months' imprisonment;
SOA 2003, ss. 30 to 37 (offences against persons with a mental disorder impeding choice);
SOA 2003, ss. 38 to 41 (care workers for persons with mental disorder) subject to age of offender and sentence imposed;
SOA 2003, s. 47 (paying for sexual services of a child) where the victim was under 16 and where the offender was aged 18 or over or was sentenced to at least 12 months' imprisonment;
SOA 2003, s. 48 (causing or inciting child prostitution or pornography) where the offender was aged 18 or over or was sentenced to at least 12 months' imprisonment;
SOA 2003, s. 49 (controlling a child prostitute or child involved in pornography) where the offender was aged 18 or over or was sentenced to at least 12 months' imprisonment;

SOA 2003, s. 50 (arranging or facilitating child prostitution or pornography) where the offender was aged 18 or over or was sentenced to at least 12 months' imprisonment;
SOA 2003, s. 61 (administering a substance with intent);
SOA 2003, s. 62 or s. 63 (committing an offence, or trespassing, with intent to commit a sexual offence) subject to age of offender and sentence passed and subject to age of intended victim;
SOA 2003, s. 64 or s. 65 (sex with an adult relative) subject to age of offender and sentence imposed;
SOA 2003, s. 66 (exposure), subject to age of offender, age of victim and sentence imposed;
SOA 2003, s. 67 (voyeurism), subject to age of offender and sentence imposed;
SOA 2003, s. 69 or s. 70 (intercourse with animal or sexual penetration of corpse), subject to age of offender and sentence imposed.
An attempt, conspiracy or incitement to commit the relevant offences is also covered (sch. 3, para. 94).

Notification Period

The length of the notification period depends on the sentence which was imposed, and is set out in a Table in s. 82(1): E25.3

Description of relevant offender	*Notification period*
A person sentenced to imprisonment for life, or a term of 30 months or more, or admitted to a hospital subject to a restriction order	indefinite period
A person sentenced to imprisonment for a term of more than six months but less than 30 months	10 years
A person sentenced to imprisonment for a term of six months or less or admitted to hospital without being subject to a restriction order	7 years
A person cautioned	2 years
A person conditionally discharged	The period of the conditional discharge
A person of any other description	5 years

This table applies to sentences of detention in a young offender institution, detention and training order, long-term detention under the PCC(S)A 2000, s. 91 and a sentence of custody for life, as they do to imprisonment (s. 131). It should be noted that, if the person is under 18 on the relevant date, this table has effect as if for the periods of 10 years, seven years, five years and two years there were substituted a reference to one half of those periods (s. 82(1)). There are special provisions for determining the notification period where consecutive or partly concurrent custodial terms have been imposed (s. 82(2)). Where an offender is sentenced to an extended sentence under the PCC(S)A 2000, s. 85, the extension period should be included when the notification period is determined. This appears to be the effect of *Wiles* [2004] Crim LR 596, in which the Court of Appeal held that its decision in *S (Graham)* [2001] 1 Cr App R 111 was made *per incuriam.*

Unreasonable Failure to Comply

Unreasonable failure to comply with notification requirements or the deliberate provision of false information is an offence punishable on summary conviction with imprisonment for a term not exceeding six months, or a fine not exceeding the statutory maximum, or both; on conviction on indictment, the maximum penalty is five years' imprisonment (SOA 2003, s. 91). See *B* [2005] 2 Cr App R (S) 403 and *Bowman* [2006] 2 Cr App R (S) 268. E25.4

Section E26 Rehabilitation of Offenders

General Principle

E26.1 Under the Rehabilitation of Offenders Act 1974, after the passage of time convictions may become 'spent' and a convicted person may consider himself 'rehabilitated'. When a conviction is spent the offender is treated for a range of purposes as if he had never been convicted of the offence concerned. While s. 7(2) of the Act excludes from its scope the operation of criminal proceedings, the *Consolidated Criminal Practice Direction*, para. I.6, *Spent convictions* nonetheless requires that spent convictions which appear on an offender's record should be marked as such, and that nobody should refer in open court to such spent convictions without the authority of the judge, which should only be given where the interests of justice so require. When passing sentence, the sentencer should make no reference to spent convictions unless it is necessary to do so to explain the sentence being passed. Similar arrangements apply to magistrates' courts, following Home Office Circular No. 98 of 1975.

The Act's protection applies to all convictions, except those which result in an excluded sentence (see **E26.2**). 'Conviction' is given a broad meaning in the Act, but would not extend to cover the imposition of a bind over to keep the peace which has been imposed at any time except at sentence. It is unclear whether the Act applies to a recommendation for deportation. Offences in respect of which orders for absolute or conditional discharge are made do not count as convictions for a variety of purposes, but s. 1(4) of the Act provides that these are convictions which may be the subject of rehabilitation.

Sentences Falling outside the Scope of Rehabilitation

E26.2 Certain sentences fall outside the scope of the Rehabilitation of Offenders Act 1974, and an offender who has received such a sentence can never become rehabilitated with respect to that conviction. Those sentences are:

(a) life imprisonment;
(b) imprisonment, detention in a young offender institution or youth custody for a term exceeding 30 months;
(c) detention during Her Majesty's pleasure;
(d) detention under the PCC(S)A 2000, s. 91, for life or for a term exceeding 30 months;
(e) custody for life.
(f) imprisonment for public protection under the CJA 2003, s. 225, detention for public protection under the CJA 2003, s. 226, or an extended sentence under the CJA 2003, ss. 227 or 228.

Rehabilitation Periods

E26.3 Rehabilitation periods in respect of sentences not specified in the Rehabilitation of Offenders Act 1974, s. 5(1) (see **E26.2**) are set out in Tables A and B of s. 5(2). The relevant period runs from the date of conviction, even where sentence is deferred. Some of the rehabilitation periods are reduced where the offender was under 18 years of age at the date of conviction. The table below summarises the principal provisions of Tables A and B.

Sentence	*Rehabilitation period*
A sentence of imprisonment, detention in a young offender institution, or youth custody, for more than six months but not more than 30 months	Ten years for an adult, five years for a juvenile
A sentence of imprisonment, detention in a young offender institution, or youth custody, of six months or less	Seven years for an adult, three and a half years for a juvenile
Detention and training order where person aged at least 15 at date of conviction	Five years if the order exceeded six months, three and a half years if six months or less
Detention and training order where person aged under 15 at date of conviction	One year after the order expires
A fine	Five years for an adult, two and a half years for a juvenile
A community punishment order or community punishment and rehabilitation order	Five years for an adult, two and a half years for a juvenile
Community rehabilitation order (offenders so sentenced before 3 February 1995), bind over to keep the peace or to be of good behaviour, conditional discharge	The date the order or bind over ceases or one year, whichever is the longer
Community rehabilitation order (offenders so sentenced on or after 3 February 1995) or a community order under the CJA 2003, s. 177	Five years for an adult, two and a half years for a juvenile
Supervision order	The date the order ceases or one year, whichever is the longer
Attendance centre order	One year after the order expires
Referral order	When the contract ceases to have effect
Secure training order	One year after the order expires
Hospital order	Five years from the date of conviction or two years after the order expires, whichever is the longer
Disqualification and other orders imposing disability, prohibition or other penalty	The date the order ceases to have effect
Absolute discharge	Six months

For the purposes of the Act, a suspended sentence of imprisonment counts as a sentence of immediate imprisonment of the same length. Two consecutive custodial sentences are aggregated for the purposes of the Act (s. 5(9)(b)). Where an offender receives more than one sentence or order in respect of a single offence, the relevant rehabilitation period is the longest of those applicable (s. 6(2)). A driving licence endorsement is not a 'disability, prohibition or other penalty' within the terms of the Act (*Power v Provincial Insurance* [1998] RTR 60).

Effect of Further Conviction

E26.4 A person who has been convicted can only become rehabilitated under the Rehabilitation of Offenders Act 1974 if he is not reconvicted within the relevant rehabilitation period (s. 6(4)). If he is reconvicted of anything other than a summary offence (s. 6(6)), the rehabilitation period for the first offence continues to run until the expiry of the period for the second offence. If an excluded sentence (see **E26.2**) is passed for the second offence, then this excludes both convictions permanently from the possibility of rehabilitation.

Section F1 General Principles of Evidence in Criminal Cases

FACTS IN ISSUE

The facts in issue comprise: (a) the facts which the prosecution bear the burden of proving or disproving (in order to establish the guilt of the accused) and (b) the facts which, in exceptional cases, the accused bears the burden of proving (in order to succeed in his defence). '[W]henever there is a plea of not guilty, everything is in issue and the prosecution have to prove the whole of their case, including the identity of the accused, the nature of the act and the existence of any necessary knowledge or intent' (*Sims* [1946] KB 531, per Lord Goddard CJ at p. 539). Thus the nature of the facts in issue in any given case is determinable by reference to the legal ingredients of the offence charged and any defence raised. Any fact which is formally admitted under the CJA 1967, s. 10, ceases to be in issue — it must be taken to have been proved and is not open to contradictory proof. Under s. 10(1) of the Act, a formal admission may be made of 'any fact of which oral evidence may be given in any criminal proceedings', words which make it clear that the section cannot be used to admit what would otherwise fall to be excluded because, say, it is inadmissible opinion or hearsay (*Coulson* [1997] Crim LR 886). **F1.1**

FORMAL ADMISSIONS

Criminal Justice Act 1967, s. 10 **F1.2**

(1) Subject to the provisions of this section, any fact of which oral evidence may be given in any criminal proceedings may be admitted for the purpose of those proceedings by or on behalf of the prosecutor or defendant, and the admission by any party of any such fact under this section shall as against that party be conclusive evidence in those proceedings of the fact admitted.

(2) An admission under this section—

(a) may be made before or at the proceedings;

(b) if made otherwise than in court, shall be in writing;

(c) if made in writing by an individual, shall purport to be signed by the person making it and, if so made by a body corporate, shall purport to be signed by a director or manager, or the secretary or clerk, or some other similar officer of the body corporate;

(d) if made on behalf of a defendant who is an individual, shall be made by his counsel or solicitor;

(e) if made at any stage before the trial by a defendant who is an individual, must be approved by his counsel or solicitor (whether at the time it was made or subsequently) before or at the proceedings in question.

(3) An admission under this section for the purpose of proceedings relating to any matter shall be treated as an admission for the purpose of any subsequent criminal proceedings relating to that matter (including any appeal or retrial).

(4) An admission under this section may with the leave of the court be withdrawn in the proceedings for the purpose of which it is made or any subsequent criminal proceedings relating to the same matter.

Ordinarily, written admissions should be put before the jury, provided at least that they are relevant to an issue before the jury and do not contain any material which should not go before the jury (*Pittard* [2006] EWCA Crim 2028). In court, a formal admission may be made by counsel or a solicitor *orally* (see s. 10(2)(b) and (d), and *Lewis* [1989] Crim LR 61). However, where an admission is made in this way by or on behalf of the prosecutor or accused for the purposes of summary trial, the court shall cause the admission to be written down and signed by or on behalf of the party making the admission (CrimPR, r. 37.4). Whatever the manner of making a formal admission under s. 10 of the 1967 Act, it should be such that what has been admitted should appear clearly on the shorthand note (*Lennard* [1973] 1 WLR 483). It is also important that the jury are clear as to what has been formally admitted. Thus in *Lewis* (1971) 55 Cr App R 386, in which counsel for the accused formally admitted every fact alleged in the prosecution's opening speech and the prosecution called no evidence, relying solely on admissions, leave to appeal against conviction was refused. The Court added, however, that such a procedure should be adopted only rarely and with caution, because jurors, when considering the opening speech, might find it difficult to distinguish between law, mixed fact and law, and comment.

Formal admissions made with the benefit of advice are an important and cogent part of the evidence in a trial. If it is sought to resile from them, leave to withdraw them is unlikely to be given under s. 10(4) without cogent evidence from the accused and those advising him that the admissions were made by reason of mistake or misunderstanding (*Kolton* [2000] Crim LR 761).

As to the application of CJA 1967, s. 10 to proceedings before courts-martial, see Criminal Justice Act 1967 (Application to Courts-Martial) (Evidence) Regulations 1997 (SI 1997 No. 173), reg. 2.

JUDICIAL NOTICE

F1.3 Generally speaking, the doctrine of judicial notice allows the tribunal of fact to treat a fact as established, notwithstanding that no evidence has been adduced to establish it. The doctrine, however, takes three distinct forms. The first two, judicial notice without inquiry and judicial notice after inquiry, were defined and distinguished by Lord Sumner in *Commonwealth Shipping Representative v Peninsular and Oriental Branch Service* [1923] AC 191, at p. 212: 'Judicial notice refers to facts, which a judge can be called upon to receive and to act upon, either from his general knowledge of them, or from inquiries to be made by himself for his own information from sources to which it is proper for him to refer'. The phrase 'judicial notice' is also used, in a third sense, to refer to the use which may be made by jurors or magistrates of their personal knowledge of facts in issue or relevant to the facts in issue. This has been referred to as jury or magistrate notice. These three forms of judicial notice require separate analysis.

Judicial Notice without Inquiry at Common Law

F1.4 If a fact is sufficiently notorious or of such common knowledge that it requires no proof, the judge, without recourse to any extraneous sources of information, may take judicial notice of it and direct the jury to treat it as established, notwithstanding that it has not been established by evidence. Examples include: the fact that a fortnight is too short a period for human gestation (*Luffe* (1807) 8 East 193); the fact that the streets of London are full of traffic (*Dennis v A.J. White & Co.* [1916] 2 KB 1, at p. 6); and the fact that reconstructed trials with a striking degree of realism are among the popular forms of modern television entertainment (*Yap Chuan Ching* (1976) 63 Cr App R 7). Judicial notice may also be taken of the fact that cocaine hydrochloride is a form of cocaine (*A-G for the Cayman Islands v Roberts* [2002] 1 WLR 1842) and that goldfinches are British wild birds (*Hughes v DPP* (2003) 167 JP 589). In criminal cases, foreign law, being a question of fact generally calling for the evidence of an appropriately qualified expert, cannot be the subject of judicial notice (*Ofori* (1994) 99 Cr App R 223). There is one exception: the common law of Northern Ireland (*Re Nesbitt* (1844) 14 LJ MC 30 at p. 33).

Judicial Notice without Inquiry Pursuant to Statute

Judicial notice of a fact may be required by statute. The most important examples are the Evidence Act 1845, s. 2 and the Interpretation Act 1978, s. 3. Section 2 of the 1845 Act requires judicial notice to be taken of the fact that a judicial or official document purporting to have been signed by a judge of the Supreme Court was signed by that judge. See also the County Courts Act 1984, s. 134(2) (summonses and other documents issuing out of a county court and sealed or stamped with the seal of the court). **F1.5**

Evidence Act 1845, s. 2

> All courts, judges, justices, masters in Chancery, masters of courts, commissioners judicially acting, and other judicial officers, shall henceforth take judicial notice of the signature of any of the equity or common law judges of the superior courts at Westminster, provided such signature be attached or appended to any decree, order, certificate, or other judicial or official document.

Section 3 of the Interpretation Act 1978, as supplemented by s. 22(1) and sch. 2, para. 2, requires judicial notice to be taken of statutes of the UK (whether general, local and personal, or private) passed after 1850.

Interpretation Act 1978, s. 3

> Every Act is a public Act to be judicially noticed as such, unless the contrary is expressly provided by the Act.

Thus in the absence of express provision to the contrary, evidence is not required to prove either the contents of an Act passed after 1850 or that such an act has been duly passed by both Houses of Parliament. At common law, the courts are bound to take judicial notice of Public Acts passed before 1850. Private Acts passed before 1850 require to be proved by the production of a Queen's Printer's or Stationery Office copy (see Evidence Act 1845, s. 3 and the Documentary Evidence Act 1882, s. 2).

Statutory instruments may be proved by Queen's Printer's or Stationery Office copies (see *Ashley* (1967) 52 Cr App R 42 and the Documentary Evidence Act 1868, s. 2, at **F8.10**). There is no equivalent to the Interpretation Act 1978, s. 3, for judicial notice to be taken of statutory instruments, although some instruments have acquired such notoriety that judicial notice may be taken of them (*Jones* (1968) 54 Cr App R 63).

Judicial Notice after Inquiry

In a number of cases, judges have taken judicial notice of a fact only after referring to extraneous sources of information, such as certificates from ministers or officials, learned treatises, works of reference and expert witnesses. Such a judicial inquiry is distinct from proof by evidence in the normal way: the rules of evidence are inapplicable; the result of the inquiry is not open to evidence in rebuttal; and the result, except in the case of facts lacking constancy (e.g., the status of a foreign government), constitutes a legal precedent. The justification for judicial notice after inquiry is that some facts, although not sufficiently notorious to be the subject of judicial notice without inquiry, are readily demonstrable by reference to sources of virtually indisputable authority, or arise so frequently that proof in the normal way is undesirable because of the cost and the need for uniformity of decision. Judicial notice after inquiry has been taken of the following three kinds of fact: **F1.6**

(a) Facts of a political nature, such as relations between the government of the UK and a foreign state, the status of foreign sovereigns or governments, the membership of diplomatic suites, and the extent of territorial sovereignty. The source of information is usually a minister, whose certificate will be treated as an indisputably accurate source for reasons of public policy, namely the desirability of avoiding conflict between the courts and the executive. In *Bottrill, ex parte Kuechenmeister* [1947] KB 41, the Court of Appeal, treating as conclusive the certificate of the Foreign Secretary that Germany still existed as a State and German nationality as a nationality, and that His Majesty was still in a state of war with Germany, held that the applicant for a writ of *habeas corpus* was still an enemy alien. See also *Duff Development Co. Ltd v Government of Kelantan* [1924] AC 797; *Engelke v Musmann* [1928] AC 433; and *Carl Zeiss Stiftung v Rayner and Keeler Ltd (No. 2)* [1967] 1 AC 853.

(b) Facts which are readily demonstrable after reference to appropriate authoritative works of reference or learned treatises. Illustrations would be the day of the week on which a certain date fell, after reference to an almanac or diary; the longitude and latitude of a certain place, after reference to an atlas or other geographical work; and the date and location of a well-known historical event, after reference to an appropriate authoritative history. See *Read v Bishop of Lincoln* [1892] AC 644.

(c) Customs and professional practices, after consultation with suitably qualified experts. See *Brandao v Barnett* (1846) 12 Cl & F 787 (the custom of bankers' lien); *Re Rosher* (1884) 26 ChD 801 (conveyancers' practices); *Davey v Harrow Corporation* [1958] 1 QB 60 (ordnance surveyors' practices); and *Heather v P-E Consulting Group Ltd* [1973] 1 Ch 189 (accountants' practices).

PERSONAL KNOWLEDGE OF COURT OR JURY

Judges

F1.7 It has been held that a judge may use personal knowledge of matters within the common knowledge of people in the locality, a principle which derives from cases decided under the Workmen's Compensation Acts, under which county court judges sat as arbitrators and took into account, in assessing compensation, personal knowledge of the labour market, conditions of work, and wages (see, e.g., *Keane v Mount Vernon Colliery Co. Ltd* [1933] AC 309 and *Reynolds v Llanelly Associated Tinplate Co. Ltd* [1948] 1 All ER 140). In *Mullen v Hackney London Borough Council* [1997] 1 WLR 1103 it was held that a county court judge, in deciding which penalty to impose on the council for its failure to carry out an undertaking to the court to repair housing, was entitled to take judicial notice of his own knowledge of the council's conduct in relation to previous undertakings. The decision, it is submitted, is difficult to justify. As to judicial notice, the facts were clearly not notorious or of common knowledge, and were not of the kind of which judicial notice has been held to have been properly taken after enquiry. As to personal knowledge, the Court of Appeal has treated the principle established in the cases decided under the Workmen's Compensation Acts as if it were a principle of general application in any county court case: see Christopher Allen, *The International Journal of Evidence and Proof*, 1998 Vol 2, No. 1, 37.

Magistrates

F1.8 In *Wetherall v Harrison* [1976] QB 773 the issue was whether the accused had a reasonable excuse for failure to give a blood sample. The accused said that he had had a sort of fit, which the prosecution alleged had been simulated. One of the justices, a practising registered medical practitioner, gave his professional view on the matter to the other justices, who also drew on their own experience of wartime inoculations and the fear that they could create in certain cases. Dismissing the appeal, the Divisional Court held that justices, unlike judges, lack the ability to exclude certain factors from their consideration. In particular, if a magistrate is a specialist, whether doctor, engineer or accountant, it is not possible for him to approach the decision in the case as though he did not have that training, and it would be a very bad thing if he had to. One of the advantages of justices is that they bring a lot of varied experience into the court-room, and use it. Although it would be quite wrong for a justice to give evidence to himself or the other justices in contradiction of that which had been heard in court, he can employ his basic knowledge, for the benefit of himself and the other justices, in considering, weighing up and assessing the evidence given before the court.

'It has always been recognised that justices may and should — after all, they are local justices — take into consideration matters which they know of their own knowledge, and particularly matters in regard to the locality' (*Ingram v Percival* [1969] 1 QB 548 per Lord Parker CJ at p. 555). The appellant had been convicted of unlawfully using a net secured by anchors for taking salmon or trout in tidal waters. It was held that the justices were fully entitled to make use of their own knowledge that the place where the net was fixed was in tidal waters. See also *Paul v DPP* (1989) 90 Cr App R 173 concerning a charge of soliciting a woman for the purposes of prostitution from a motor vehicle in a street in such manner or in such circumstances as to be likely to cause nuisance to other persons in the neighbourhood, contrary to the Sexual Offences Act 1985, s. 1(1). It was held that the justices, who had no evidence before them that anyone had actually been caused nuisance, were entitled to take into account two matters within their local knowledge: first, that the area in question was often frequented by prostitutes and that there was a constant procession of cars driving around the area at night; and secondly, that it was a heavily populated residential area. In *Field, ex parte White* (1895) 64 LJ MC 158, the issue being whether cocoa necessarily contains foreign ingredients, no evidence was adduced. The justices, relying on their own knowledge of the subject, found for the accused. Although Wills J observed that perhaps in future evidence should be heard on such a matter, the Divisional Court refused to disturb the justices' finding. Local knowledge of the prevalence of a particular kind of offence may be taken into account, but should be applied with care (see generally Stockdale and Devlin, *Sentencing*, 1987, paras. 1.69 and 1.70). However, it is submitted that magistrates should exercise extreme caution in using personal knowledge, particularly where the facts are not matters of local notoriety.

Jurors

The doctrine of judicial notice also applies to jurors in relation to matters coming within the sphere of their everyday knowledge and experience (*Rosser* (1836) 7 C & P 648, approved in *Jones* [1970] 1 WLR 16). In *Jones* it was argued that it had not been proved that the accused had been given an opportunity to provide a specimen of breath for a breath test, because there had been no evidence to show that the device used, the Alcotest R80, was 'of a type approved by the Secretary of State' for the purposes of the Road Safety Act, 1967, s. 7. Rejecting this argument, Edmund-Davies LJ said, at p. 20: '. . . the number of decided cases in which it has been proved that the Alcotest R80 device is of an approved type has by now become so large and so widely reported that, in our judgment, a court (including the jury) is entitled to take judicial notice of that fact, and its formal proof is accordingly no longer necessary'. **F1.9**

However, although jurors may use their *general* knowledge, they may not use their *personal* knowledge to supplement or contradict the evidence given in the case. The older authorities suggest that a juror with particular knowledge of a matter should be sworn as a witness and give evidence in the normal way (see *Rosser* (1836) 7 C & P 648; *Manley v Shaw* (1840) Car & M 361; *Antrim Justices* [1895] 2 IR 603). A preferable solution, it is submitted, is the course adopted in *Blick* (1966) 50 Cr App R 280. In that case a juror passed a note to the judge to the effect that his own local knowledge contradicted the alibi evidence given by the accused. In consequence the judge allowed the prosecution to call evidence, relating to the matters contained in the note, to rebut the alibi. This decision was upheld by the Court of Criminal Appeal.

RELEVANCE

F1.10 The cardinal rule of the law of evidence is that, subject to the exclusionary rules, all evidence which is sufficiently relevant to the facts in issue is admissible, and all evidence which is irrelevant or insufficiently relevant to the facts in issue should be excluded. As to the former, however, evidence which is relevant may nonetheless be excluded if it is such that no reasonable jury, properly directed as to its defects, could place any weight on it (*Robinson* [2006] 1 Cr App R 221, a case concerning voice recognition evidence). As to the latter, inasmuch as an offence of strict liability involves no proof of *mens rea*, evidence of motive, intention or knowledge is inadmissible, being irrelevant to what the Crown has to prove and merely prejudicial to the accused (*Sandhu* [1997] Crim LR 288; and see also *Byrne* [2002] 2 Cr App R 311). The classic formulation of relevance is to be found in Article 1 of Stephen's *Digest of the Law of Evidence* (12th ed.), according to which the word signifies that 'any two facts to which it is applied are so related to each other that according to the common course of events one either taken by itself or in connection with other facts proves or renders probable the past, present or future existence or non-existence of the other'. *Nethercott* [2002] Cr App R 117 provides an example of a fact which was relevant to the past existence of another fact. N's defence was that he had acted under duress as a result of threats by his co-accused G. Evidence of the fact that G had subsequently attacked N with a knife was relevant to the defence because it made it more likely that N, at the time of the offence, had genuinely feared for his safety.

On the question of relevance, Lord Simon of Glaisdale has said:

> Evidence is relevant if it is logically probative or disprobative of some matter which requires proof. I do not pause to analyse what is involved in 'logical probativeness', except to note that the term does not of itself express the element of experience which is so significant of its operation in law, and possibly elsewhere. It is sufficient to say, even at the risk of etymological tautology, that relevant (i.e., logically probative or disprobative) evidence is evidence which makes the matter which requires proof more or less probable. (*DPP v Kilbourne* [1973] AC 729, at p. 756.)

The question of relevance is typically a matter of degree to be determined, for the most part, by common sense and experience (*Randall* [2004] 1 WLR 56, *per* Lord Steyn at [20]).

For some of the more frequently recurring examples of relevant evidence, see **F1.16** to **F1.21**.

Strict Application of the Test

F1.11 There is a long-standing practice on the part of the prosecution to make admissions in relation to facts that may point to a third party having committed the crime with which the accused is charged, such admissions being relevant and admissible material to weigh in the scales in deciding whether it might have been the third party and not the accused who committed the offence (*Greenwood* [2005] 1 Cr App R 99). Such admissions were made in *Blastland* [1986] AC 41, but the test of 'logical probativeness' was strictly applied to exclude additional evidence relating to the state of mind of the third party. The appellant, B, was convicted of the buggery and murder of F, a boy. At the trial, B admitted that he had met F and engaged in homosexual activity with him (including attempted buggery), but said that shortly afterwards he saw another man nearby and, fearing that he had been observed committing a serious offence, panicked and ran away. B's description of the other man corresponded closely to one M. B said that M must have committed both offences charged. There were formal admissions by the prosecution showing M to have been known to engage in the past in homosexual activities with adults but not with children. There were also both formal admissions and evidence relating to M's movements on the evening of F's murder. The defence sought leave to call a number of witnesses to give evidence that before F's body had been found, M had made statements to them that a boy had been murdered. The trial judge ruled that this evidence was inadmissible. Before the House of Lords, the appellant submitted that the statements made by M were admissible as original evidence to show M's state of mind, i.e. his knowledge of the murder before the body had been found. Lord Bridge, giving the judgment of the House, held that such evidence would only have been admissible if M's state of mind had been either directly in issue itself or of direct and immediate relevance to an issue arising at the trial. The evidence had been properly rejected because the issue at the trial was whether B had committed the crimes, and what was relevant to that was not the fact of M's knowledge but how he had come by it; since he might have come by that knowledge in a number of different ways, there was no rational basis on which the jury could be invited to draw an inference as to the source of that knowledge. To do so would have been mere speculation. The evidence of what M said, therefore, could not be put before the jury to support the conclusion that he, rather than B, may have been the criminal. See also *Kearley* [1992] 2 AC 228 at **F15.12**, *Williams* [1998] Crim LR 494 and *Akram* [1995] Crim LR 50. However, in *Gadsby* [2006] EWCA Crim 3206, it was held, *obiter*, that evidence may be relevant if it is capable of increasing or diminishing the probability of facts indicating that some other person committed the crime (e.g. evidence that a person with the opportunity of committing the crime had a propensity to do so).

The strict approach taken in *Blastland* was also adopted in *T (AB)* [2007] 1 Cr App R 43. The complainant alleged that she had been sexually abused by the appellant, who was her uncle, and by her grandfather and her step-grandfather, but it was not alleged that they were acting in concert. The grandfather admitted the allegations against him but died before the matter reached court. The step-grandfather pleaded guilty to counts of indecently assaulting the complainant. It was held that evidence of the grandfather's admission and of the step-grandfather's guilty plea should not have been admitted, because it was not relevant, in itself, to the issue whether the appellant abused the complainant; and that while it was 'tempting' to say that it was relevant to the issue of her credibility, that would amount to a form of 'oath helping' which has never been permissible as a ground for admitting evidence.

Relevance of Demeanour of Victim

In *Keast* [1998] Crim LR 748 (applied in *Venn* [2003] EWCA Crim 236) it was held that unless there is some concrete basis for regarding long-term demeanour and state of mind of a victim of sexual abuse as confirming or disproving the occurrence of such abuse, it cannot assist a jury bringing their common-sense to bear on who is telling the truth. However, demeanour witnessed close in time to the event in question may have probative value, by analogy with the principle of *res gestae* (*Townsend* [2003] EWCA Crim 3173). On a charge of causing death by dangerous driving, evidence that the accused used cocaine shortly before the accident is relevant, even in the absence of evidence as to the amount of cocaine used (*Pleydell* [2006] 1 Cr App R 212; contrast, in the case of alcohol consumed, *Woodward* [1995] 2 Cr App R 388). **F1.12**

Relevance in Drug Cases

Concerning the offence of possession of drugs with intent to supply, evidence which is arguably relevant to the question of intent may fall to be excluded because of its prejudicial effect in indicating dealing in drugs in the past or generally. This principle and the following cases will need to be read subject to the provisions in the CJA 2003, ss. 98 to 113, relating to the accused's bad character (see **F12**). Under the principle, it has been held that evidence of the possession of weights and scales on which there are traces of the drug in question will be admitted (*Batt* [1994] Crim LR 592), but not evidence of past deposits in and withdrawals from savings accounts, because that can only found an inference of past drug dealing (*Gordon* [1995] 2 Cr App R 61). In *Batt* it was also held that evidence of the discovery of £150 in an ornamental kettle in B's house was inadmissible because it had nothing to do with intent to supply in future the drugs found, but had a highly prejudicial effect as evidence of propensity **F1.13** to supply or of past or future supplying generally. *Batt*, however, has not laid down a general principle that evidence of possession of money is never admissible (*Nicholas* [1995] Crim LR 942; *Okusanya* [1995] Crim LR 941). On one view the decision in *Batt* turned on the fact that the trial judge had failed to direct the jury as to how they could properly use the evidence of the money found (*Morris* [1995] 2 Cr App R 69). Alternatively *Batt* should be seen as a case strictly confined to its own facts, bearing in mind that £150 was too small, and its hiding place too unremarkable, to be the hallmark of present drug dealing (*Okusanya*). In *Wright* [1994] Crim LR 55, it was held that drug traders needed to keep by them large sums of cash and therefore evidence of the discovery of £16,000 was capable of giving rise to an inference of dealing and tended to prove that the drugs found were for supply. In *Gordon* [1995] 2 Cr App R 61, it was held that evidence of the discovery of £4,200 was admissible subject to an appropriate direction. Similarly in *Smith* [1995] Crim LR 940, it was held that evidence that in recent months £9,000 had been deposited in S's account, £2,100 of which could not be explained by legitimate transactions, was admissible, subject to an appropriate direction. The jury should be directed (i) that evidence of the discovery of money is relevant only if they reject any innocent explanation for it advanced by the accused, (ii) that if there is any possibility of the money having been in the accused's possession for reasons other than drug dealing, then the evidence is not probative, but (iii) that if they conclude that it indicates not merely past dealing but an on-going dealing in drugs, they may take into account the finding of it, together with the drugs, in considering the issue of intent to supply (*Grant* [1996] 1 Cr App R 73; cf. *Antill* [2002] EWCA Crim 214). The same principles apply where the prosecution relies on a list of names or drugs paraphernalia (*Lovelock* [1997] Crim LR 821 and *Haye* [2002] EWCA Crim 2476). Such a direction, however, will not always need to be given in terms (*Malik* [2000] 2 Cr App R 8). The jury should also be directed not to treat it as evidence of propensity, i.e. not to pursue the line of reasoning that because of the past dealing the accused is likely to be guilty (*Simms* [1995] Crim LR 304 and *Lucas* [1995] Crim LR 400). In *Guney* [1998] 2 Cr App R 242 the Court of Appeal declined to follow earlier authorities to the effect that, where possession of the drugs is in issue, evidence of possession of money or drugs paraphernalia can never be relevant to that issue (see *Halpin* [1996] Crim LR 112 and *Richards* [1997] Crim LR 499). It was held that, although evidence of possession of a large sum of cash or enjoyment of a wealthy lifestyle does not, on its own, prove possession, there are numerous sets of circumstances in which it may be relevant to that issue, not least to the issue of knowledge as an ingredient of possession. The real issue in the case was whether G was knowingly in possession of nearly five kilos of heroin or whether it had been 'planted', the defence having conceded that, if possession were to be proved, then it would be open to the jury to infer intent to supply. It was held that, in all the circumstances, evidence of the finding of nearly £25,000 in cash in the wardrobe of G's bedroom and in close proximity to the drugs was relevant to the issue of possession. *Guney* was applied in *Griffiths* [1998] Crim LR 567. See also *Edwards* [1998] Crim LR 207 and *Scott* [1996] Crim LR 652.

In cases of illegal importation of controlled drugs in which the accused denies any knowledge of how the drugs came to be in his possession, evidence of finding drugs in his home is relevant and admissible because the jury are entitled to consider such a coincidence, which may go to rebut the defence raised (*Willis* (unreported 29 January 1979) and *Peters* [1995] 2 Cr App R 77). The principle is not confined to couriers, but extends to those who claim to have been unknowingly involved in the importation of drugs, such as those meeting couriers at airports (*Groves* [1998] Crim LR 200). Evidence admissible to rebut such a defence includes evidence of the possession of drugs or drugs paraphernalia, and evidence suggesting a pattern of the accused having been involved in previous importations: see, as to the latter, *Ilomuanya* [2005] EWCA Crim 58, where the evidence relied on was held to be irrelevant because it neither established nor tended to suggest any such pattern.

Relevance as a Matter of Degree

Relevance is a question of degree. For example, evidence of facts which supply a motive for an accused to have committed a particular crime is generally admissible to show that it is more likely that he committed that crime (see *Ball* [1911] AC 47, per Lord Atkinson at p. 68 and *Phillips* [2003] Crim LR 629; but see also, in the case of offences of strict liability, *Sandhu* [1997] Crim LR 288). However, evidence of motive will be excluded if it is so remote from the offence charged that it can be said to be without any probative value at all (see *Berry* (1986) 83 Cr App R 7). Similarly, on a charge of manslaughter against a doctor, although expert evidence of his skill as shown by his treatment of the case under investigation is admissible, expert evidence as to his skilful treatment of patients on other occasions is inadmissible (*Whitehead* (1848) 3 Car & Kir 202). Evidence of marginal relevance may be excluded on the grounds that it would lead to a multiplicity of subsidiary issues, involving the court in a protracted investigation and distracting it from the main issue (see *A-G v Hitchcock* (1847) 1 Exch 91 per Rolfe B at p. 105 and *Patel* [1951] 2 All ER 29, per Byrne J at p. 30). On occasions, the effect of evidence which is technically admissible is so slight that it is wiser not to adduce it, especially if there is any danger of a contravention of the PACE 1984, s. 78 (see **F2.6**), i.e. where its admission would have such an adverse effect on the fairness of the proceedings that the court ought not to admit it (*Robertson* [1987] QB 920, per Lord Lane CJ at p. 928; and see also *Williams* [1990] Crim LR 409). **F1.14**

Evidence of Earlier Trial

Where two trials arise out of the same transaction, evidence of the outcome of the first is generally inadmissible at the second, because the verdict in the first, whether reached on the same or different evidence, is usually irrelevant; some exceptional feature is needed before it will be considered relevant (*Hui Chi-ming v The Queen* [1992] 1 AC 34). The principle applies *a fortiori* if the first trial arose out of a different transaction (*Terry* [2005] 2 Cr App R 118 at [34]). On one view, the rationale of the principle is that the evidence amounts to nothing more than evidence of the opinion of the first jury (*Hui-chi Ming v The Queen*), but by itself that would be a reason for never admitting evidence of a previous verdict. The true rationale, in the case of an earlier acquittal, is that in most cases it is impossible to be certain why a jury acquitted (*Deboussi* [2007] EWCA Crim 684), although the principle appears also to apply in the case of an acquittal following a ruling by a trial judge that there was insufficient evidence to go to the jury (see *Hudson* [1994] Crim LR 920 and cf. *Colman* [2004] EWCA Crim 3252). The cases indicate that the 'exceptional feature' arises where there is a clear inference from the verdict that the jury rejected a witness's evidence because they did not believe him and his credibility is directly in issue in the second trial, as when it is alleged that an officer has fabricated an admission, the officer having given evidence of an admission in an earlier trial resulting in an acquittal by virtue of which his evidence can be shown to have been disbelieved (*Edwards* [1991] 2 All ER 226). See also *Hay* (1983) 77 Cr App R 70, *Cooke* (1986) 84 Cr App R 286 and *Deboussi*). As to the relevance (and admissibility) of previous convictions or acquittals as evidence of the facts on which they were based, see **F11.5** ***et seq.*** **F1.15**

CIRCUMSTANTIAL EVIDENCE

Circumstantial evidence is to be contrasted with direct evidence. Direct evidence is evidence of *facts in issue*. In the case of testimonial evidence, it is evidence about facts in issue of which the witness claims to have personal knowledge, for example, 'I saw the accused strike the victim'. Circumstantial evidence is evidence of *relevant facts*, i.e. facts from which the existence or non-existence of facts in issue may be inferred. It does not necessarily follow that the weight to be attached to circumstantial evidence will be less than that to be attached to direct evidence. For example, the tribunal of fact is likely to attach more weight to a variety of **F1.16** individual items of circumstantial evidence, all of which lead to the same conclusion, than to direct evidence to the contrary coming from witnesses lacking in credibility.

Circumstantial evidence 'works by cumulatively, in geometrical progression, eliminating other possibilities' (*DPP v Kilbourne* [1973] AC 729 per Lord Simon at p. 758). Pollock CB, likening circumstantial evidence to a rope comprised of several cords, said:

> One strand of the cord might be insufficient to sustain the weight, but three stranded together may be quite of sufficient strength.
>
> Thus it may be in circumstantial evidence — there may be a combination of circumstances, no one of which would raise a reasonable conviction, or more than a mere suspicion; but the whole, taken together, may create a strong conclusion of guilt, that is, with as much certainty as human affairs can require or admit of. (*Exall* (1866) 4 F & F 922, at p. 929)

However, although circumstantial evidence may sometimes be conclusive, it must always be narrowly examined, if only because it may be fabricated to cast suspicion on another. For this reason, it has been said that: 'It is also necessary before drawing the inference of the accused's guilt from circumstantial evidence to be sure that there are no other co-existing circumstances which would weaken or destroy the inference' (*Teper v The Queen* [1952] AC 480, per Lord Normand at p. 489). Nonetheless, there is no requirement, in cases in which the prosecution's case is based on circumstantial evidence, that the judge direct the jury to acquit unless they are sure that the facts proved are not only consistent with guilt but also inconsistent with any other reasonable conclusion (*McGreevy v DPP* [1973] 1 WLR 276).

Certain varieties of circumstantial evidence have arisen so frequently in practice as to attract the label 'presumption of fact'. For the presumption of continuance of life, see **F3.48**; for the presumption of intention, see **F3.49**; and for the presumption of guilty knowledge in cases of handling, theft etc., see **F3.50**. Other frequently recurring examples of circumstantial evidence include evidence of plans and acts preparatory to the commission of an offence (to show intention to commit the offence); evidence of opportunity or lack of opportunity, i.e. alibi evidence (to show presence or absence at the time and place of the crime committed); and evidence of identity, including evidence of physical idiosyncrasy, manner of vocal or written expression, fingerprints and DNA genetic fingerprint tests. Circumstantial evidence of identity can also take the form of evidence that a tracker dog tracked the accused from the scene of the crime (see *Haas* (1962) 35 DLR (2d) 172 (British Columbia) and, for the conditions of admissibility of such evidence, *Pieterson* [1995] 1 WLR 293 and *Sykes* [1997] Crim LR 752). Other typical examples of circumstantial evidence are dealt with below.

Motive

F1.17

> Surely in an ordinary prosecution for murder you can prove previous acts or words of the accused to show that he entertained feelings of enmity towards the deceased, and this is evidence not merely of the malicious mind with which he killed the deceased, but of the fact that he killed him. . . . it is more probable that men are killed by those who have some motive for killing them than by those who have not. (*Ball* [1911] AC 47 per Lord Atkinson (during argument) at p. 68, affirmed in *Williams* (1986) 84 Cr App R 299.)

This classic statement remains good law and any doubt that may have been cast upon it in *Berry* (1986) 83 Cr App R 7 should be disregarded (*Phillips* [2003] 2 Cr App R 528 at [26]). Evidence of motive may be admissible notwithstanding that the motive is irrational and *Berry*, insofar as it suggests otherwise, has been disapproved (*Phillips* at [30]). Evidence of motive may also be admissible notwithstanding that it reveals the accused's criminal disposition. In *Williams* W was charged with making a threat to kill E, intending that she would fear that the threat would be carried out. Evidence was admitted of previous acts of violence by W against E, including an assault in respect of which he had been convicted and sentenced to a term of imprisonment which had come to an end six weeks before the time of the present offence. The prosecution case was that: (a) the threat had been made because of resentment arising from the imprisonment; and (b) the previous acts of violence tended to show that W intended his threat to be taken seriously. In the same way, evidence that the accused lacked a motive to commit the crime charged may be admissible to show the comparative improbability of his having committed it (see *Grant* (1865) 4 F & F 322). He may also adduce evidence that someone else had such a motive, as in *Greenwood* [2005] 1 Cr App R 99 where, in the case of an undisputed murder, it was held that the accused was entitled to adduce evidence to show that the victim's ex-boyfriend was near the murder scene and appeared to have a motive. It does not follow from the foregoing, however, that evidence of motive (or its absence) is necessarily relevant to the facts in issue on a particular charge (see for example *Graham-Kerr* (1989) 88 Cr App R 302 (the indecency of a photograph), applied in *Rowley* (1991) 94 Cr App R 95 (an act outraging public decency), and compare *Court* [1989] AC 28).

Lies

Lies told by the accused, on their own, do not make a positive case of any crime (*Strudwick* (1994) 99 Cr App R 326 at p. 331). However, they may indicate a consciousness of guilt and in appropriate circumstances may therefore be relied upon by the prosecution as evidence supportive of guilt, as in *Goodway* [1993] 4 All ER 894 where the accused's lies to the police as to his whereabouts at the time of the offence were used in support of the identification evidence adduced by the prosecution. In that case it was held that, whenever a lie told by an accused is relied on by the Crown or may be used by the jury to support evidence of guilt, as opposed merely to reflecting on his credibility (and not only when it is relied on as corroboration or as support for identification evidence), a threefold *Lucas* ([1981] QB 720) direction should generally be given to the jury: **F1.18**

(a) The lie must be deliberate and must relate to a material issue.
(b) They must be satisfied that there was no innocent motive for the lie, reminding them that people sometimes lie, for example, in an attempt to bolster up a just cause, or out of shame or a wish to conceal disgraceful behaviour.
(c) The lie must be established by evidence other than that of the witness who is to be corroborated.

See also *Taylor* [1994] Crim LR 680. In *Taylor* [1998] Crim LR 822, a trial for murder in which the only issue was provocation, T admitted that he had lied in saying that he had never had any contact with the victim. The jury were directed that if they were sure that the lies were told to conceal T's guilt in relation to the death, then they might use them as evidence of that guilt. The Court of Appeal held that the jury should also have been told that the lies could support the prosecution case of murder only if they were sure that they were told to conceal the fact that T had murdered the victim, rather than merely to conceal his connection with the death, i.e. to avoid responsibility for deliberate murder rather than a provoked killing.

In *Goodway* it was also held that a direction need not be given where it is otiose as indicated in *Dehar* [1969] NZLR 763, i.e. where the rejection of the explanation given by the accused almost necessarily leaves the jury with no choice but to convict as a matter of logic. For an example, see *Barsoum* [1994] Crim LR 194 and cf. *Wood* [1995] Crim LR 154. See also *Gordon* [1995] Crim LR 306. Nor, it seems, does a judge need to give a *Lucas* direction where the accused has offered an explanation for his lies and the judge has dealt with that explanation fairly in his summing-up (*Saunders* [1996] 1 Cr App R 463 at pp. 518–19).

The Four *Burge* Situations In *Burge* [1996] 1 Cr App R 163, the Court of Appeal held that a *Lucas* direction is usually required in four situations, which may overlap (Kennedy LJ at p. 173): **F1.19**

1. Where the defence relies on an alibi.

2. Where the judge considers it desirable or necessary to suggest that the jury should look for support or corroboration of one piece of evidence from other evidence in the case, and amongst that other evidence draws attention to lies told, or allegedly told, by the defendant.
3. Where the prosecution seek to show that something said, either in or out of the court, in relation to a separate and distinct issue was a lie, and to rely on that lie as evidence of guilt in relation to the charge which is sought to be proved.
4. Where although the prosecution have not adopted the approach to which we have just referred, the judge reasonably envisages that there is a real danger that the jury may do so.

The Court of Appeal held that the direction (if given) should, so far as possible, be tailored to the circumstances of the case, but that it will normally suffice to make two points: first that the lie must be admitted or proved beyond reasonable doubt, and second that the mere fact that the accused lied is not in itself evidence of guilt since defendants may lie for innocent reasons, so only if the jury is sure that the accused did not lie for an innocent reason can a lie support the prosecution case. The Court also stressed that the need for the direction arises only in cases where the prosecution say, or the judge envisages that the jury may say, that the lie is evidence against the accused, in effect using it as an implied admission of guilt. The direction is not needed in run-of-the-mill cases where the defence case is contradicted by the evidence of prosecution witnesses in such a way as to make it necessary for the prosecution to say that, insofar as the two sides are in conflict, the accused's account is untrue. Equally, a *Goodway* direction is not required simply because the jury may reject the evidence of an accused about a central issue in the case, because that situation is covered by the general direction on the burden and standard of proof (*Hill* [1996] Crim LR 419).

As to the first situation identified in *Burge*, in *Lesley* [1996] 1 Cr App R 39 it was held that where evidence is adduced in support of an alibi, the Judicial Studies Board specimen direction (which ends with the words 'An alibi is sometimes invented to bolster a genuine defence') should routinely be given. It was also held, however, that whether failure to do so renders a conviction unsafe depends on the facts of each case and the strength of the evidence. The accused had served an alibi notice but did not call the person named in it and gave no evidence himself. The prosecution inferentially invited the jury to conclude that the alibi was false and therefore evidence of guilt. Taking account of the fact that the chief prosecution witness was not altogether satisfactory, it was held that failure to give the direction rendered the verdict unsafe (cf. *Drake* [1996] Crim LR 109, in which the proviso was applied). See also *Peacock* [1998] Crim LR 681, in which P, when first interviewed, said that he had spent the evening of the robbery with his girlfriend, but at trial gave evidence that he had spent the evening with his former girlfriend and that what he had said initially was not a lie but a mistake. *Lesley* was distinguished in *Harron* [1996] 2 Cr App R 457, where it was held that the judge had not erred in failing to direct the jury that an alibi is sometimes falsified to bolster a genuine defence because the central issue in the case was whether the prosecution witnesses were lying or whether H was. Lies had not played a part in the way the Crown had put their case nor constituted a matter which the jury might have taken into account separate from their determination of the main issue, which turned upon the truthfulness of the witnesses. If they accepted the evidence for the Crown it necessarily involved a conclusion that the evidence of the accused was untrue, and that he was lying. See also *Gultutan* [2006] EWCA Crim 207 and *House* [1994] Crim LR 682.

As to the third situation identified in *Burge*, in *Genus* [1996] Crim LR 502, where the accused claimed to have been acting under duress and the prosecution case was that the accused had told lies to the police and in evidence on collateral issues (i.e. on issues not directly relevant to the question of duress) and that the jury should, by reason of those lies, disbelieve their account of acting under duress, it was held that the case cried out for a *Lucas* direction. In *Robinson* [1996] Crim LR 417, where the judge in his summing-up gave considerable prominence to the issue whether R had lied about when his defence was first made known to the police, it was held that the case fell clearly within the fourth situation identified in *Burge*.

As to the fourth situation identified in *Burge*, the Court of Appeal is unlikely to be persuaded that there was a real danger of the jury treating a particular lie as evidence of guilt if defence counsel at the trial did not alert the judge to that danger and ask him to consider whether a direction should be given to meet it (per Kennedy LJ in *Burge* [1996] 1 Cr App R 163 at p. 174). The failure of defence counsel to raise the matter at the trial may also be taken into account in cases in which both the third and the fourth situations identified in *Burge* arise, and may lead the Court of Appeal to conclude that the matter was not a large or important feature of the case and that the absence of the usual direction did not make the conviction unsafe (*McGuinness* [1999] Crim LR 318).

Situations Where a *Lucas* Direction is Unnecessary A *Lucas* direction is required only where lies are directly related in some way to the offence charged, for example a lie which amounts to a false alibi (*Smith* [1995] Crim LR 305), but not a lie concerning some matter which is relevant only to the credibility of the accused (*Landon*) [1995] Crim LR 338). However, even if a lie is relied on merely to attack credibility, a *Lucas* direction is appropriate in exceptional circumstances, for example where the lie figures largely in the case and there is a risk that the jury may think that the accused must be guilty because he lied (*Tucker* [1994] Crim LR 683). **F1.20**

In *Middleton* [2001] Crim LR 251, it was said *per curiam* that if the question arises at trial whether a *Lucas* direction is required, it will generally be more useful to consider the application to the facts of the case of the principles derived from the many cases on the point, rather than to trawl through the cases themselves. The court stressed that the point of a *Lucas* direction is to warn against the 'forbidden reasoning' that lies necessarily demonstrate guilt. Where there is no risk of such forbidden reasoning on the part of the jury, a direction is unnecessary. According to the court, a direction is also generally unnecessary in relation to lies told by an accused in evidence, because the position is covered by the general directions on the burden and standard of proof. In cases where a direction could be given about a lie told in evidence, a judge may not be obliged to give a direction, especially if it would do more harm than good (*Nyanteh* [2005] EWCA Crim 686).

A *Lucas* direction is not likely to be required in the many cases of handling stolen goods in which the accused denies knowledge or belief that the goods were stolen, including those in which the accused gives different and inconsistent versions as to how he came by the goods, and the Crown's case is that he is not telling the truth (*Barnett* [2002] 2 Cr App R 168).

Continuance of Events over Period of Time

Evidence of the speed at which someone was driving at a particular point in time may be admitted to prove the speed at which he was driving a short time earlier or, as the case may be, later (see, respectively, *Dalloz* (1908) 1 Cr App R 258 and *Beresford v St Albans Justices* (1905) 22 TLR 1). **F1.21**

MULTIPLE ADMISSIBILITY

Evidence which is admissible in law for one purpose cannot be excluded because it is inadmissible for some other purpose (although if it is tendered by the prosecution it may be excluded as a matter of discretion). '[I]t often happens, both in civil and criminal cases, that evidence is tendered on several alternative grounds, and yet it is never objected that if on any ground it is admissible, that ground must not prevail, because on some other ground it would be inadmissible and prejudicial' (*Bond* [1906] 2 KB 389, per Jelf J at pp. 411–12). The principle has attracted the somewhat misleading label of 'multiple admissibility' (J. H. Wigmore, *Evidence in Trials at Common Law*, vol. 1 (revised by Peter Tillers) (Boston Mass: Little, Brown & Co. **F1.22**

1983), sect. 13). A typical example would be a case in which evidence of the previous convictions of the accused is admitted for the purpose of impugning his credibility, notwithstanding that it is inadmissible for the purpose of showing that it is more likely that he is guilty of the offence charged (*Jenkins* (1945) 31 Cr App R 1; *Cook* [1959] 2 QB 340). Similarly, a confession which implicates both its maker and a co-accused may be admitted in evidence against its maker, notwithstanding that it is inadmissible evidence against the co-accused.

Where the principle applies, it has been said that 'it is usual for the judge (not always very successfully) to caution the jury against being biased by treating the evidence in the objectionable sense' (*Bond* [1906] 2 KB 389 per Jelf J at p. 412). Nowadays such a warning is often mandatory: see e.g., *Gunewardene* [1951] KB 600 (a confession admissible for use only against its maker and not against any co-accused); *Flicker* [1995] Crim LR 493 (statements in which a confession is inextricably linked with material relating to the accused's propensity to offend); and *Norman* [2006] EWCA Crim 1662 (evidence of the discovery of drugs on a previous occasion inadmissible on the issue of intention to supply drugs subsequently found in the same place). Where evidence of the bad character of an accused, D1, is relevant to an issue between the Crown and a co-accused, D2, as when D2 adduces evidence of D1's bad character in support of D2's defence of having acted under duress, although the judge may direct the jury to ignore the evidence when considering the case against D1, such a direction need not be given if, in the circumstances of the case, it would needlessly perplex the jury and require them to indulge in mental gymnastics for very little, if any, benefit to D1 (see *Randall* [2004] 1 WLR 56 at [35] and *Robinson* [2006] 1 Cr App R 480). In the case of a confession tendered by the prosecution and implicating both its maker and his co-accused, one solution is to edit the confession by omitting references to the co-accused or by replacing their names with letters of the alphabet or expressions such as 'another person' (see *Rogers* [1971] Crim LR 413; *Silcott* [1987] Crim LR 765; and generally **F17.58**). Alternatively, but only in exceptional circumstances, the judge may find it necessary to order separate trials for the accused (see *Lake* (1976) 64 Cr App R 172).

CONDITIONAL ADMISSIBILITY

F1.23 The relevance of a particular item of evidence may become apparent only if considered together with other evidence. However, because evidence is given in order and by one witness at a time, it often happens that the other evidence can only be adduced at a later stage. Prima facie, therefore, the first item of evidence is irrelevant, and for that reason inadmissible. In these circumstances, upon an undertaking by counsel to demonstrate the relevance of the first item by introducing the further evidence, the court may allow the first item of evidence to be admitted conditionally or *de bene esse.* If, notwithstanding the introduction of the further evidence, the first item remains irrelevant, the judge will direct the jury to disregard it. For example, in the case of a conspiracy, if the judge is satisfied that a statement was made by one conspirator that is reasonably open to the interpretation that it was made in furtherance of the common design, it is admissible in evidence against another party to the conspiracy, provided that the judge is also satisfied that there is sufficient further evidence beyond the statement itself to show that the other party was a party to the conspiracy. Admitting evidence of such a statement may be conditional upon the adduction of the further evidence. If it transpires that there is insufficient further evidence, or no such evidence, the statement should be disregarded (see generally **F16.40** ***et seq.***). See also the cases on accusations made in the presence of the accused, the relevance of which depends on evidence of the accused's reaction to them (see Lords Atkinson and Reading in *Christie* [1914] AC 545 at pp. 554 and 565 respectively and **F17.66**). In an extreme case, where great prejudice may be caused to an accused, a warning by the judge may be insufficient, and it may be necessary for the judge to discharge the jury.

THE BEST EVIDENCE RULE

As an Inclusionary Rule

The best evidence rule is moribund. In *Omychund v Barker* (1745) 1 Atk 21, in which depositions of Hindu witnesses were admitted in evidence, notwithstanding that they did not accept the authority of the Gospel, Lord Hardwicke said (at p. 49): 'The judges and sages of the law have laid it down that there is but one general rule of evidence, the best that the nature of the case will admit'. This case suggests an inclusionary rule permitting the admission of the best evidence available in the circumstances of the case. Subsequent authorities, however, show that the rule has rarely been used in this way. Under the modern law of evidence, there exists no general rule, of an inclusionary nature, to the effect indicated in *Omychund v Barker*. **F1.24**

As an Exclusionary Rule

The best evidence rule, which was used in the 18th and early 19th centuries as an exclusionary principle, i.e. to prevent the admission of certain evidence where better was available, is now all but defunct. In *Francis* (1874) LR 2 CCR 128, in which the accused was indicted for false pretences, in that he falsely represented a ring to be a diamond ring, evidence was admitted of his attempts on other occasions to obtain money on a cluster ring in order to prove guilty knowledge. Rejecting an argument that because the cluster ring itself was not produced in court, evidence of witnesses who saw it and swore to its being false had been improperly admitted, Lord Coleridge CJ said: 'No doubt if there was not admissible evidence that this ring was false it ought not to have been left to the jury; but though the non-production of the article may afford ground for observation more or less weighty, according to circumstances, it only goes to the weight, not to the admissibility, of the evidence'. **F1.25**

However, very occasionally reliance is placed upon the rule. In *Quinn* [1962] 2 QB 245, on a charge of keeping a disorderly house, arising out of the performance of allegedly indecent striptease acts, one of the accused sought to put in evidence a film made three months after the events complained of and purporting to depict the acts performed, together with evidence that the acts depicted in the film were identical to the acts performed. It was held that the evidence had been properly rejected. Ashworth J said (at p. 257): '. . . it was admitted that some of the movements in the film (for instance, that of a snake used in one scene) could not be said with any certainty to be the same movements as were made at the material time. In our judgment, this objection goes not only to weight, as was argued, but to admissibility: it is not the best evidence.' Compare *Thomas* [1986] Crim LR 682, a case of reckless driving in which a video recording of the route taken by the accused was ruled admissible to remove the need for maps and photographs and to convey a more accurate picture of the roads in question. The reasoning in *Quinn* [1962] 2 QB 245 is difficult to reconcile with the clear statement of Lord Denning MR in *Garton v Hunter* [1969] 2 QB 37. Referring to the best evidence rule, his lordship said (at p. 44):

> That old rule has gone by the board long ago. The only remaining instance of it that I know is that if an original document is available in your hands, you must produce it. You cannot give secondary evidence by producing a copy. Nowadays we do not confine ourselves to the best evidence. We admit all relevant evidence. The goodness or badness of it goes only to weight, and not to admissibility.

See also Ackner LJ in *Kajala v Noble* (1982) 75 Cr App R 149 at p. 152 and *Governor of Pentonville Prison, ex parte Osman* [1990] 1 WLR 277 at p. 308; and cf. *Springsteen v Masquerade Music Ltd* [2001] EWCA Civ 563, discussed at **F8.2**. As to proof of the contents of documents, see **F8**.

QUESTIONS OF LAW AND FACT

In a Trial on Indictment: General Principles

F1.26 As a general rule, questions of law (including practice) are for the judge, and questions of fact for the jury. In trials on indictment without a jury, the judge decides all questions of both law and fact and, if the accused is convicted, must give a judgment which states the reasons for the conviction (CJA 2003, s. 48(3) and (5)). Lay magistrates, when sitting with a judge in the Crown Court, are also judges of the court (see the Supreme Court Act 1981, ss. 8 and 73); they should participate in all questions to be determined by the court, including the factual aspect of any question relating to the admissibility of evidence, but must accept the ruling of the judge on any question of law (*Orpin* [1975] QB 283). In jury trials, questions of law for the judge include those relating to:

(a) challenges to jurors — see **D13.19** ***et seq***;
(b) the discharge of a juror or the whole jury — see **D13.45** ***et seq***;
(c) the competence of persons to give sworn or unsworn evidence;
(d) the admissibility of evidence;
(e) the withdrawal of an issue from the jury;
(f) submissions of no case to answer — see **D15.51** ***et seq***;
(g) the numerous issues on which the jury should be directed in the summing up, such as the substantive law governing the charge, the burden and standard of proof, the use which the jury is entitled to make of the evidence adduced, the operation of any presumptions, the nature of, and any requirement for, corroboration, etc. — see further **D17.21** ***et seq*** and **F5**; and
(h) matters ancillary to the trial itself, such as questions of bail, costs and leave to appeal.

Questions of fact for the jury include:
(a) whether the accused stands mute of malice or by visitation of God;
(b) the credibility of the witnesses called and the weight of the evidence adduced; and
(c) whether, applying the burden and standard of proof applicable to the case, they are satisfied as to the existence or non-existence of the facts in issue.

In jury trials, questions of fact which fall to be determined by the *judge* are the existence or non-existence of preliminary facts, i.e. facts which must be proved as a condition precedent to the admissibility of certain types of evidence; the sufficiency of evidence (in deciding whether an issue should be withdrawn from the jury); and the evaluation of evidence adduced by the parties (for the purpose of commenting on its weight in his summing up to the jury). There are also a number of special cases, dealt with below, in which questions of fact fall to be determined, either wholly or in part, by the judge.

F1.27 **Construction of Words** As a general rule, the construction of ordinary words in a statute is a question for the tribunal of fact (see *Manning* (1871) LR 1 CCR 338, at p. 430 — 'a building' under the Malicious Damage Act 1861, s. 6; *Cozens v Brutus* [1973] AC 854 — 'insulting behaviour' under the Public Order Act 1936, s. 5; *Chambers v DPP* [1995] Crim LR 896 — 'disorderly behaviour' under the Public Order Act 1986, s. 5; *Feely* [1973] QB 530 — 'dishonestly' under the Theft Act 1968, s. 1(1); *Harris* (1968) 84 Cr App R 75 — 'knowledge or belief' under the Theft Act 1968, s. 22(1); *Jones* [1987] 1 WLR 692 — 'armed' under the Customs and Excise Management Act 1979, s. 86; *Garwood* [1987] 1 WLR 319 — 'menaces' under the Theft Act 1968, s. 21(1); *Howard* [1993] Crim LR 213 — an 'explosive substance' under the OAPA 1861, s. 29; and *Kirk* [2006] EWCA Crim LR 725 — 'indecent or obscene' under the Postal Services Act 2000, s. 85(4)). Thus, although a judge is perfectly at liberty to direct a jury that it is not open to them to give to a word a particular meaning (being a meaning so unreasonable that if it were adopted and the accused convicted, the

Court of Appeal would treat the verdict as perverse), normally he should not direct the jury as to the meaning of an ordinary word. The exception to this rule is where the word has been used in a context which indicates that it is being used in an unusual sense or has acquired a special meaning as a result of the authorities, as happened in relation to the word 'fraudulently' under the Larceny Act 1916, s. 1(1) — see Lawton LJ in *Feely* [1973] QB 530. In *Brutus v Cozens* [1973] AC 854, Lord Reid said (at p. 861 C–E):

> The meaning of an ordinary word of the English language is not a question of law. The proper construction of a statute is a question of law. If the context shows that a word is used in an unusual sense the court will determine in other words what that unusual sense is. But here there is in my opinion no question of the word 'insulting' being used in any unusual sense. . . . It is for the tribunal which decides the case to consider, not as law but as fact, whether in the whole circumstances the words of the statute do or do not as a matter of ordinary usage of the English language cover or apply to the facts which have been proved. If it is alleged that the tribunal has reached a wrong decision then there can be a question of law but only of a limited character. The question would normally be whether their decision was unreasonable in the sense that no tribunal acquainted with the ordinary use of language could reasonably reach that decision.

When a statutory provision is dealing with a technical subject and can only be understood with the assistance of an expert, then the words used must be given their ordinary and natural meaning to a person qualified to understand them, and evidence as to that meaning may be received from an appropriate expert (*Couzens* [1992] Crim LR 822).

As to the construction of *documents*, this is generally a matter of fact for determination by the jury, with the exception of binding agreements between parties and all forms of parliamentary and local government legislation, which are for the judge to construe as a matter of law. The City Code on Take-overs and Mergers sufficiently resembles legislation as to require construction of its provisions by a judge (*Spens* [1991] 1 WLR 624). In a case of obtaining by deception, arising out of an allegedly false written representation, in which the central question is not as to the legal effect of the document but whether the representation was made and, if so, whether it was false, then both aspects of that question are for the jury (*Adams* [1993] Crim LR 525; and see also *Morris* [1994] Crim LR 596).

Foreign Law Questions relating to the law of any jurisdiction other than that of England and Wales are questions of fact to be determined, on the evidence adduced, by the judge alone. **F1.28**

Administration of Justice Act 1920, s. 15

> Where for the purpose of disposing of any action or other matter which is being tried by a judge with a jury in any court in England or Wales, it is necessary to ascertain the law of any other country which is applicable to the facts of the case, any question as to the effect of the evidence given with respect to that law shall, instead of being submitted to the jury, be decided by the judge alone.

Section 15 of the 1920 Act applies to criminal proceedings (*Hammer* [1923] 2 KB 786). As to the proof of foreign law, see **F8.14** and **F10.16**.

Autrefois Acquit or Convict Where an accused pleads autrefois acquit or convict, it shall be for the judge, without the presence of a jury, to decide the issue (CJA 1988, s. 122). See also **D12.19** *et seq.* **F1.29**

Perjury The question whether a statement on which perjury is assigned was 'material' in the judicial proceeding in which it was made is a question of law to be determined by the court of trial (Perjury Act 1911, s. 11(6)). **F1.30**

Defamation On every trial of an indictment or information for the making or publishing of any libel, it is for the jury to give a verdict of guilty or not guilty upon the whole matter put in issue (see the Libel Act 1792 (Fox's Act), s. 1). However, it is for the judge to determine **F1.31**

whether the writing in question is capable of bearing the defamatory meaning ascribed to it by the prosecutor (*Capital and Counties Bank Ltd v George Henty and Sons* (1882) 7 App Cas 741). If it can be said that 12 jurors could reasonably come to the conclusion that the writing was defamatory, the question whether the writing does in fact constitute a criminal libel should be left to the jury (*Turner v Metro-Goldwyn-Mayer Pictures Ltd* [1950] 1 All ER 449; *Lewis v Daily Telegraph Ltd* [1964] AC 334).

In Summary Trials

F1.32 In the case of proceedings presided over by lay justices, the justices decide all questions of both law and fact, but on questions of law, including the law of evidence, should seek and accept the advice of the clerk. As to the proper role of the justices' clerk in a summary trial, see the *Consolidated Criminal Practice Direction*, para. V.55, *Clerk retiring with justices* which is set out in **appendix** 7 and discussed in detail at **D21.51** *et seq.* In theory, District Judges (Magistrates' Courts) are in the same position as lay justices. In practice, however, the District Judge will be the more experienced lawyer, so that the occasions for asking for advice will be quite rare.

HEARINGS ON THE *VOIR DIRE*

General Principles

F1.33 The hearing on the *voir dire*, or trial within a trial, is the procedure whereby the court determines disputed preliminary facts, i.e. facts which must be established as a condition precedent to the admission of certain items of evidence. The procedure is set out at **D15.20** to **D15.41** (trial on indictment) and **D21.25** (summary trial).

Concerning what evidence is admissible for the purpose of proving or disproving disputed preliminary facts, there is some authority to suggest that the judge is bound by the exclusionary rules of evidence which apply in relation to the admissibility of evidence at the trial proper. Thus, at common law, it has been held that it is wrong for a judge to determine the admissibility of a confession on the basis of the depositions (*Chadwick* (1934) 24 Cr App R 138). Most of the decisions concern specific statutory provisions governing the admissibility of evidence. In *O'Loughlin* [1988] 3 All ER 431, a decision on the conditions of admissibility imposed by the CJA 1925, s. 13(3) (now repealed), Kenneth Jones J ruled that in a criminal statute, unless other methods of proof are specified (for example, 'by information or belief'), 'proof' means proof by admissible evidence. Preliminary facts under the CJA 1988, s. 23 (now repealed) called for proof by admissible evidence (see *Neill v North Antrim Magistrates' Court* [1992] 1 WLR 1221, *obiter* but applied in *Belmarsh Magistrates' Court, ex parte Gilligan* [1998] 1 Cr App R 14 and *Wood* [1998] Crim LR 213, at **F16.8**; and *Case* [1991] Crim LR 192 and *Mattey* [1995] 2 Cr App R 409, at **F16.7**). However, it was also held that a written statement could be admitted under the CJA 1988, s. 23(3)(b), on the basis of the *unsworn* evidence of its maker that he was not giving oral evidence through fear (*Greer* [1998] Crim LR 572; *Jennings* [1995] Crim LR 810). As regards the preliminary facts set out in s. 24(1)(i) and (ii) of the CJA 1988 (now repealed), it was held that, although evidence was often desirable, it was not always essential, because in appropriate circumstances the judge could infer the facts from the document sought to be admitted under s. 24 and the method or route by which it had been produced before the court (*Foxley* [1995] 2 Cr App R 523 and *Ilyas* [1996] Crim LR 810).

In trials on indictment, the various matters which may fall to be determined in a hearing on the *voir dire* include the following:

(a) the competence of a witness (see **F4.2** and **F4.21**);

(b) the admissibility of a confession (see **F17.39** to **F17.47**) or some other variety of admissible hearsay, such as a dying declaration or a *res gestae* statement (see, for example, *Jenkins* (1869) LR 1 CCR 187);

(c) the admissibility of a tape recording (see *Robson* [1972] 1 WLR 651 and **F8.41**);
(d) the admissibility of a statement contained in a document produced by a computer (see **F8.37**); and
(e) the admissibility of a plea of guilty against an accused who subsequently changes his plea to not guilty (see *Rimmer* [1972] 1 WLR 268 at **F17.2** and cf. *Hetherington* [1972] Crim LR 703).

Cases in which a Hearing on *Voir Dire* Usually Not Required

A hearing on the *voir dire* is not normally required to determine the admissibility of evidence relating to an identification parade. In *Walshe* (1980) 74 Cr App R 85 Boreham J said (at p. 87): **F1.34**

> . . . those representing the applicant drew some close analogy between the admissibility of evidence of an identification parade and the admissibility of a voluntary statement. But those are very different matters. As soon as a statement is challenged the law places on the Crown the burden of showing that it is admissible by proving that it was voluntarily made. [See now the PACE 1984, s. 76(2).] That is a separate and different matter. Here there was no burden on the Crown to prove the admissibility of the evidence relating to the identification parade and what flowed from it. It was clearly admissible evidence and should have been admitted. Its quality is, of course, another matter, to be considered by the jury.

In *Beveridge* (1987) 85 Cr App R 255, it was argued on appeal that in the light of the PACE 1984, s. 78, *Walshe* could no longer stand. It was held, dismissing the appeal, that where a question arises under s. 78 as to the admissibility of identification parade evidence, although there may be rare occasions when it will be desirable to hold a trial within a trial, in general the judge should decide on the basis of the depositions, statements and submissions of counsel.

In *Flemming* (1987) 86 Cr App R 32, a decision under the law prior to the 1984 Act, the appellant argued that identification evidence was inadmissible on the grounds, *inter alia*, that the identification at the police station was carried out in circumstances which contravened Home Office Circular No. 109 of 1978. It was submitted that the result was that the probative value of the evidence was minimal compared to its prejudicial effect, so that it would be unfair for the evidence to be admitted. The Court of Appeal held that it was quite unnecessary to hold a trial within a trial for this purpose. Woolf LJ (referring to one of the guidelines laid down by Lord Widgery LCJ in *Turnbull* [1977] QB 224, at p. 229, namely that when, in the opinion of the judge, the quality of the identifying evidence is poor, the judge should withdraw the case from the jury unless there is other evidence which goes to support its correctness) said, at pp. 36–7:

> In the normal way the trial judge will make his assessment whether he needs to take the action referred to by the Lord Chief Justice either at the end of the case for the prosecution or after all the evidence in the case has been called. There may be exceptional cases where the position is so clear on the depositions that he can give a ruling at an earlier stage. However, the trial judge should not decide the matter by holding a preliminary trial, as in this case, before the evidence for the prosecution has been placed before the jury.
>
> It is, of course, true that the trial judge has a residual discretion to exclude evidence which is strictly admissible if he comes to the conclusion that its probative value is outweighed by its prejudicial effect, so that its admission would be unfair to the defendant. However, this residual discretion cannot justify the holding of trials within a trial as occurred here. Issues of this sort can be satisfactorily dealt with by the judge perusing the depositions, together with any facts that are common ground between the prosecution and the defence.

See also *Martin* [1994] Crim LR 218.

Application to Summary Trial

F1.35 There can be no question of a trial within a trial in proceedings before magistrates, because the function of the *voir dire* is to allow the tribunal of law to decide a point of law in the absence of the tribunal of fact, and magistrates are judges of both fact and law. Thus, if the admissibility of a confession is in dispute, and the magistrates decide that matter as a separate issue by hearing evidence as to the preliminary facts and ruling in favour of admissibility, it is unnecessary to repeat the evidence about the confession in the trial proper. See generally, **D21.25**.

It is impossible to lay down any general rule as to when the question of admissibility should be determined by magistrates, or as to when their decision on it should be announced, every case being different (*F v Chief Constable of Kent* [1982] Crim LR 682). These principles, insofar as they relate to confessions, are subject to the statutory constraint of the PACE 1984, s. 76(2), and the decision in *Liverpool Juvenile Court, ex parte R* [1988] QB 1. However, subject to this and other similar statutory constraints, there is still no general rule as to when admissibility should be determined and the decision on it announced. In *Epping and Ongar Justices, ex parte Manby* [1986] Crim LR 555 the applicant, convicted as the proprietor of a firm on whose behalf an overweight vehicle had been driven, contested the admissibility of a certificate of a police officer to the effect that the applicant had admitted responsibility for the vehicle (see **C2.5**), and sought leave to have the question resolved as a preliminary issue. It was held that the justices had not erred in refusing the application and admitting the evidence as providing a prima facie case for the applicant to deal with later, if he saw fit.

If, during the course of a summary trial, the defence challenge the admissibility of a confession under the PACE 1984, s. 76(2) (see **F17.6**), the magistrates are bound by the terms of that subsection to hold a trial within a trial. In *Liverpool Juvenile Court, ex parte R* [1988] QB 1, Russell LJ held as follows:

(a) During the course of a summary trial, if the defence, before the close of the prosecution case, make a representation to the court that a confession made by the defendant was or may have been obtained by either of the improper methods set out in s. 76(2), the magistrates must hold a trial within a trial and make a ruling on the admissibility of the confession during or at the end of the prosecution case. (If the defence make an alternative submission based on the PACE 1984, s. 78, this should be examined at the same trial within a trial at the same time: *Halawa v Federation Against Copyright Theft* [1995] 1 Cr App R 21.)
(b) In such a trial within a trial, the defendant may give evidence confined to the question of admissibility.
(c) At this stage, the magistrates will not be concerned with whether or not the confession is true.
(d) If the defence do not make a representation before the close of the prosecution case, the defendant may raise the question of the admissibility or weight of the confession at any subsequent stage at the trial.
(e) At this later stage, however, although the court retains an inherent jurisdiction to exclude the confession, as well as the power to exclude by virtue of the PACE 1984, s. 78 (see **F2.29**), it is not required to embark on a trial within a trial.

Nothing in the court's judgment was intended to lay down guidance as to the trial of indictable offences in the Crown Court.

Where the defence make a submission that the magistrates should exercise their discretion to exclude evidence under s. 78 of the 1984 Act, they are not entitled to have that issue settled as a preliminary issue in a trial within a trial (*Vel v Chief Constable of North Wales* (1987) 151 JP 510). In *Halawa v Federation Against Copyright Theft* [1995] 1 Cr App R 21, it was held that the duty of a magistrate, on an application under s. 78, is either to deal with the issue when it arises or to leave the decision until the end of the hearing, the objective being to secure a trial that is fair and just to both parties. Thus in some cases the accused will be given the opportunity to exclude the evidence before giving evidence on the main issues, because if denied that opportunity his right to remain silent on the main issues will be impaired, but in most cases it is better for the whole of the prosecution case, including the disputed evidence, to be heard first, because under s. 78 regard should be had to 'all the circumstances' and fairness to the prosecution requires that the whole of its case, in this regard, be before the court. In deciding, the court may take account of the extent of the issues to be raised by the evidence of the accused in the trial within a trial. A trial within a trial may be appropriate if the issues are limited, but not if it is likely to be protracted and to raise issues which will need to be re-examined in the trial itself.

Section F2 The Discretion to Exclude Evidence; Evidence Unlawfully, Improperly or Unfairly Obtained

THE DISCRETION TO EXCLUDE AT COMMON LAW

General Principles

F2.1 Although there is no authority to suggest that a criminal court has any power to *admit* as a matter of discretion evidence which is inadmissible under an exclusionary rule of law, it is well established that a judge, as part of his inherent power and overriding duty in every case to ensure that the accused receives a fair trial, always has a discretion to *exclude* otherwise admissible prosecution evidence if, in his opinion, its prejudicial effect on the minds of the jury outweighs its true probative value. The classic description of the discretion is that of Lord du Parcq, delivering the reasons of the Board in *Noor Mohamed v The King* [1949] AC 182. Referring to cases in which the prosecution seek to admit similar-fact evidence, his lordship said (at p. 192):

> . . . in all such cases the judge ought to consider whether the evidence which it is proposed to adduce is sufficiently substantial, having regard to the purpose to which it is professedly directed, to make it desirable in the interest of justice that it should be admitted. If, so far as that purpose is concerned, it can in the circumstances of the case have only trifling weight, the judge will be right to exclude it. To say this is not to confuse weight with admissibility. The distinction is plain, but cases must occur in which it would be unjust to admit evidence of a character gravely prejudicial to the accused even though there may be some tenuous ground for holding it technically admissible.

The first clear statements as to the existence of this exclusionary discretion are to be found in the speeches of Lord Moulton and Lord Reading CJ in *Christie* [1914] AC 545, at pp. 559 and 564 respectively. Thereafter, the discretion developed on a case-by-case basis in relation to particular and different types of otherwise admissible evidence. In relation to similar fact evidence, for example, see *Harris v DPP* [1952] AC 694, at p. 707 (in which Viscount Simon cited and applied the passage from *Noor Mohamed v The King* set out above) and *DPP v Boardman* [1975] AC 421, at pp. 438, 441, 453, and 463. In relation to evidence otherwise admissible under the Theft Act 1968, s. 27(3), see *List* [1966] 1 WLR 9; *Herron* [1967] 1 QB 107; *Perry* [1984] Crim LR 680; and generally **F12.48 to F12.50**. The discretion may be invoked by a trial judge to exclude statements tendered in committal proceedings (*Blithing* (1983) 77 Cr App R 86), but the judge's power to exclude the sworn deposition of a deceased witness should be exercised with great restraint: see *Scott v The Queen* [1989] AC 1242 per Lord Griffiths at pp. 1258–9 and *Neshet* [1990] Crim LR 578. Concerning exercise of the discretion in relation to identification evidence, see **F18**. See also *Eatough* [1989] Crim LR 289.

In *Sang* [1980] AC 402, the House of Lords was firmly of the opinion that, notwithstanding its case-by-case development, under the modern law the discretion is a general one. The cases, therefore, are not to be treated as a closed list of the situations in which the discretion may be exercised (see Viscount Dilhorne and Lord Salmon, at pp. 438 and 445 respectively). The cases are nothing more than examples of a single discretion founded on the duty of the judge to ensure that every accused person has a fair trial (per Lords Scarman and Fraser, at pp. 452 and 447 respectively). Lord Salmon said (at p. 445):

> I recognise that there may have been no categories of cases, other than those to which I have referred, in which technically admissible evidence proffered by the Crown has been rejected by the court on the ground that it would make the trial unfair. I cannot, however, accept that a judge's undoubted duty to ensure that the accused has a fair trial is confined to such cases. In my opinion the category of such cases is not and never can be closed except by statute.

Discretion to Exclude only Prosecution Evidence The discretion may only be exercised to exclude evidence on which the prosecution, as opposed to any co-accused, proposes to rely. In *Lobban v The Queen* [1995] 1 WLR 877 (at p. 887), the Privy Council cited with approval the following description of this principle in Keane, *The Modern Law of Evidence* (3rd edn, 1994) at p. 36: F2.2

> There is no discretion to exclude, at the request of one co-accused, evidence tendered by another. Thus although . . . there is a discretion to exclude similar fact evidence tendered by the prosecution, such evidence, when tendered by an accused to show the misconduct on another occasion of a co-accused is, if relevant to the defence of the accused, admissible whether or not it prejudices the co-accused (see per Devlin J in *Miller* [1952] 2 All ER 667 (Winchester Assizes), approved in *Neale* (1977) 65 Cr App R 304). Similarly, there is no discretion to prevent an accused from cross-examining a co-accused about his previous convictions and bad character when, as a matter of law, he becomes entitled to do so under s. 1(f)(iii) [now s. 1(3)(iii)] Criminal Evidence Act 1898, i.e. where the co-accused has 'given evidence against' the accused, because, it is said, the accused in seeking to defend himself should not be fettered in any way (see *Murdoch v Taylor* [1965] AC 574 (HL)).

In *Lobban v The Queen* itself, it was held that there is no discretion to exclude the exculpatory part of a 'mixed' statement (see **F6.22**) on which one co-accused wishes to rely on the grounds that it implicates another. R made a statement containing admissions as well as an exculpatory explanation, an integral part of which implicated L, his co-accused. The prosecution tendered the statement against R; it was no evidence against L. Counsel for L submitted that the trial judge should have exercised his discretion to edit the statement to exclude the parts implicating L. The Privy Council held that no such discretion existed. The discretionary power applies only to evidence on which the prosecution proposes to rely. Although the prosecution had *tendered* the statement, they could not rely on it as evidence against L and the disputed material supported R's defence. There was therefore no discretionary power to exclude the disputed material. See also, however, per Evans LJ in *Thompson* [1995] 2 Cr App R 589 at pp. 596–7: where evidence is inadmissible against and prejudicial to an accused, but relevant to and therefore admissible for a co-accused, the only safeguard is the cumbersome device of separate trials, and it might be preferable to allow a discretion to exclude where the prejudice to the accused is substantial and the evidence of only limited benefit to the co-accused.

Admissions, Confessions and Evidence obtained Improperly or Unfairly The discretion founded on the duty of the judge to ensure that every accused has a fair trial is not limited to excluding evidence which is likely to have prejudicial value out of proportion to its probative value, but extends to other evidence which might operate unfairly against the accused, namely admissions, confessions and other evidence obtained from the accused after the commission of the offence by improper or unfair means (see *Sang* [1980] AC 402 per Lords Diplock, Fraser and Scarman, at pp. 436, 450 and 456 respectively). The discretion, in its extended form, merits discrete analysis: as to admissions and confessions, see **F2.10**; as to evidence obtained from the accused by improper or unfair means, see generally **F2.8** to **F2.20**. F2.3

Exercise of Discretion as Basis of Appeal

Exercise of the discretion is a subjective matter, and each case has to be decided in the context of its own particular facts (see *Sang* [1980] AC 402, per Lords Fraser and Scarman, at pp. 450 F2.4

and 456 respectively). In *Selvey v DPP* [1970] AC 304 Lord Guest went so far as to say (at p. 352): 'If it is suggested that the exercise of this discretion may be whimsical and depend on the individual idiosyncrasies of the judge, this is inevitable where it is a question of discretion'. It follows from this that the Court of Appeal will not lightly interfere with judicial exercise of the discretion. In the context of cross-examination under the Criminal Evidence Act 1898, s.1(3)(ii) (now repealed) it was held that the Court of Appeal will not interfere unless:

(a) the judge has failed even to consider exercise of the discretion, in which case the appeal court may exercise its own discretion (see *Cook* [1959] 2 QB 340); or
(b) he has erred in principle, or there is no material on which he could properly have arrived at his decision (*Cook* per Devlin J, at p. 348, approved by Viscount Dilhorne in *Selvey v DPP* at p. 342 and applied in *Burke* (1985) 82 Cr App R 156).

Application to Summary Trial

F2.5 In *Sang* [1980] AC 402, Lord Scarman made the following *obiter* observations relating to summary trials (at p. 456):

> The development of the discretion has, of necessity, been largely associated with jury trial. In the result, legal discussion of it is apt to proceed in terms of the distinctive functions of judge and jury. No harm arises from such traditional habits of thought, provided always it be borne in mind that the principles of the criminal law and its administration are the same, whether trial be (as in more than 90 per cent of the cases it is) in the magistrates' court or on indictment before judge and jury. The magistrates are bound, as is the judge in a jury trial, to ensure that the accused has a fair trial according to law; and have the same discretion as he has in the interests of a fair trial to exclude legally admissible evidence. No doubt, it will be rarely exercised. And certainly magistrates would be wise not to rule until the evidence is tendered and objection is taken. . . . They must wait and see what is tendered; and only then, if objection be taken, rule. When asked to rule, they should bear in mind that it is their duty to have regard to legally admissible evidence, unless in their judgment the use of the evidence would make the trial unfair.

THE DISCRETION TO EXCLUDE: STATUTORY PROVISIONS

Police and Criminal Evidence Act 1984, s. 78

F2.6 The common-law discretion founded on the duty of the judge or magistrates to ensure that every accused person has a fair trial has now been buttressed by statute. The PACE 1984, s. 78(1), provides that in any criminal proceedings 'the court may refuse to allow evidence on which the prosecution propose to rely to be given if it appears to the court that, having regard to all the circumstances, including the circumstances in which the evidence was obtained, the admission of the evidence would have such an adverse effect on the fairness of the proceedings that the court ought not to admit it'. Section 78 applies to 'evidence on which the prosecution *proposes* to rely' and therefore applications to exclude evidence under the section should be made before the evidence is adduced (and, if reference is to be made to it in the prosecution opening speech, before that speech): see, in the case of a confession, *Sat-Bhambra* (1988) 88 Cr App R 55, considered at **F17.42**, and, in the case of identification evidence, *Lashley* [2005] EWCA Crim 2016.

Section 78(1) is generally regarded as conferring a discretionary power, but strictly speaking it does not involve an exercise of discretion because if a court decides that admission of the evidence in question would have such an adverse effect on the fairness of the proceedings that it ought not to admit it, it cannot logically exercise a discretion to admit it (per Auld LJ in *Chalkley* [1998] QB 848 at p. 874). Either way, the Court of Appeal has been loath to interfere with the decisions of trial judges under s. 78. It has been said that the Court of Appeal will intervene only if the judge has not exercised his discretion under s. 78 at all or has done so but in a *Wednesbury* unreasonable manner (*Associated Provincial Picture Houses Ltd v*

Wednesbury Corporation [1948] 1 KB 223) and that where the Court of Appeal does intervene, it will exercise its own discretion (see *O'Leary* (1988) 87 Cr App R 387 per May LJ at p. 391, *Quinn* [1995] 1 Cr App R 480 at p. 498, *Christou* [1992] QB 979, *Khan* [1997] Crim LR 508, and *Dures* [1997] 2 Cr App R 247). However, it is submitted that the true test for the Court of Appeal should be whether the admission of the evidence in question renders the conviction unsafe, since that is now the only ground on which it may allow an appeal against conviction (see the Criminal Appeal Act 1968, s. 2(1) at **D25.25** to **D25.32**, and generally Adrian Clarke 'Safety or Supervision' [1999] Crim LR 108).

The subsection may be used to attempt to exclude *any* evidence on which the prosecution propose to rely (see, e.g., *O'Loughlin* [1988] 3 All ER 431 (depositions and documentary records); *Mason* [1988] 1 WLR 139 (confessions); *Beveridge* (1987) 85 Cr App R 255 (identification parades); *Deenik* [1992] Crim LR 578 (voice identifications); and *McGrath v Field* [1987] RTR 349 (intoximeter readings)). Thus in the case of (a) any admissible evidence which is likely to have a prejudicial effect out of proportion to its probative value, and (b) admissions, confessions and other evidence obtained from the accused after the commission of the offence by improper or unfair means, and which might operate unfairly against the accused (see *Sang* [1980] AC 402), the court may now exclude *either* under its powers at common law *or* pursuant to s. 78. In *Matto v Wolverhampton Crown Court* [1987] RTR 337 Woolf LJ said (at p. 346): 'Whatever is the right interpretation of s. 78, I am quite satisfied that it certainly does not reduce the discretion of the court to exclude unfair evidence which existed at common law. Indeed, in my view in any case where the evidence could properly be excluded at common law, it can certainly be excluded under s. 78.' An example is *O'Connor* (1986) 85 Cr App R 298. A and B were jointly charged with having conspired to commit an offence. A pleaded guilty and B not guilty. At the trial of B the prosecution sought to admit the conviction of A under the PACE 1984, s. 74. The prejudicial effect of this evidence clearly outweighed its probative value, because A's admission of the offence charged might have led the jury to infer that B must have conspired with A, and therefore the common-law discretion to exclude could have been invoked. Instead, the Court of Appeal held that the evidence should have been excluded under s. 78. See also *Kempster* [1989] 1 WLR 1125 and *Mattison* [1990] Crim LR 117, which are considered at **F11.8**.

The primary importance of s. 78, however, is not the degree of overlap with the common law, but the fact that it extends the common-law powers by reason of its potential for the exclusion of evidence obtained by improper or unfair means. Concerning evidence improperly or unfairly obtained, the common-law powers are restricted to admissions, confessions and other evidence obtained from the accused after the commission of the offence (*Sang* [1980] AC 402). In *Sang*, their lordships, despite their apparent unanimity, were neither clear nor in agreement as to the precise meaning of the phrase 'evidence obtained from the accused after the commission of the offence'. Section 78, however, is capable of application to *any* evidence obtained by improper or unfair means and on which the prosecution seek to rely. The application of s. 78 to such evidence is considered separately at **F2.21**.

Other Statutory Provisions

Unlike the PACE 1984, s. 78(1), which is of general application, other statutory provisions empower the court, in the exercise of its discretion, to exclude specific types of otherwise admissible evidence. Thus the CJA 2003, s. 101(3), confers a discretion to exclude otherwise admissible evidence of the bad character of the accused, having regard to the particular factors set out in s. 101(4) (see **F12.11**) and the CJA 2003, s. 126, confers a discretion to exclude otherwise admissible hearsay statements (see **F16.56**). **F2.7**

ADMISSIBILITY OF EVIDENCE OBTAINED UNLAWFULLY, IMPROPERLY OR UNFAIRLY

General Rule of Admissibility

F2.8 Subject to the exceptions considered in **F2.9** to **F2.12**, evidence obtained unlawfully, improperly or unfairly is admissible as a matter of *law.* (Concerning the existence and extent of the *discretion* to exclude evidence thus obtained, see **F2.13** ***et seq.***) In *Kuruma, Son of Kaniu v The Queen* [1955] AC 197, Lord Goddard CJ, on behalf of the Board, said (at p. 203):

> . . . the test to be applied in considering whether evidence is admissible is whether it is relevant to the matters in issue. If it is, it is admissible and the court is not concerned with how the evidence was obtained. While this proposition may not have been stated in so many words in any English case there are decisions which support it, and in their lordships' opinion it is plainly right in principle.

Referring to this pronouncement in *Jeffrey v Black* [1978] QB 490, Lord Widgery CJ said (at p. 497): 'I have not the least doubt that we must firmly accept the proposition that an irregularity in obtaining evidence does not render the evidence inadmissible.' Evidence is admissible, therefore, if it has been obtained by any of the following means:

(a) Theft (see *Leatham* (1861) 8 Cox CC 498 per Crompton J at p. 501).
(b) Unlawful search of persons (see *Jones v Owen* (1870) 34 JP 759 and *Kuruma, Son of Kaniu v The Queen* [1955] AC 197).
(c) Unlawful search of premises (see *Jeffrey v Black* [1978] QB 490).
(d) The use of *agents provocateurs* (*Sang* [1980] AC 402).
(e) Eavesdropping (see *Stewart* [1970] 1 WLR 907, *Keeton* (1970) 54 Cr App R 267, *Maqsud Ali* [1966] 1 QB 688 and *Senat* (1968) 52 Cr App R 282).
(f) Invasion of privacy (see *Khan* [1997] AC 558, in which evidence of an incriminating conversation was obtained by means of a secret electronic surveillance device).

Procedures for Obtaining Evidence Prescribed by Statute

F2.9 Although in general the court is not concerned with how evidence is obtained, where it is a necessary step towards procuring a conviction for an offence that the evidence be obtained in accordance with a procedure prescribed by statute, evidence obtained other than in accordance with that procedure will not be admissible. See *Scott v Baker* [1969] 1 QB 659 (the procedure for providing a specimen in relation to an offence of drinkdriving), approved in *Spicer v Holt* [1977] AC 987; and contrast *Trump* (1979) 70 Cr App R 300 (see **F2.17**), *Adams* [1980] QB 575 and *Tunbridge Wells Borough Council v Quietlynn Ltd* [1985] Crim LR 594.

Confessions

F2.10 If it is represented to the court that a confession made by an accused person was or may have been obtained by the means set out in the PACE 1984, s. 76(2), the court shall not allow the confession to be given in evidence against him, except to the extent that the prosecution prove to the court beyond reasonable doubt that the confession was not so obtained. Concerning the admissibility of both confessions and facts discovered in consequence of inadmissible confessions, see generally **F17**.

Evidence Obtained by Torture

F2.11 If it is represented to the court that a confession made by an accused was or may have been obtained by oppression, which is defined to include torture, the court shall not allow the confession to be given in evidence against him except insofar as the prosecution proves to the court beyond reasonable doubt that the confession (notwithstanding that it may be true) was not so obtained (see **F17.5** and **F17.6**). At common law, however, there is a broader general principle, established in *A v Secretary of State for the Home Department (No. 2)* [2006] 2 AC 221, that evidence obtained by torture is inadmissible. In that case, seven members of the House of Lords unanimously held that the Special Immigration Appeals Commission (SIAC), a superior court of record, on hearing an appeal under the Anti-terrorism, Crime and Security Act 2001, s. 25 (since repealed) by a person detained under the Act, may not rely on evidence procured by torture inflicted by officials of a foreign state, with or without the complicity of the British authorities. According to Lord Bingham, as a matter of constitutional principle, evidence obtained by torturing another human being may not lawfully be admitted against a party to proceedings in a British court, irrespective of where, or by whom, or on whose authority the torture was inflicted. His lordship said (at [52]): 'The principles of the common law, standing alone . . . compel the exclusion of third party torture evidence as unreliable, unfair, offensive to ordinary standards of humanity and decency and incompatible with the principles which should animate a tribunal seeking to administer justice. But the principles of the common law do not stand alone. Effect must be given to the European Convention, which itself takes account of the all but universal consensus embodied in the Torture Convention'. The House of Lords did not clearly define torture for these purposes, but Lord Hoffmann (at [97]) expressed a preference for the definition adopted by Parliament in the CJA 1988, s. 134, namely the infliction of severe pain or suffering on someone by a public official in the performance or purported performance of his official duties. The House of Lords also held that a conventional approach to the burden of proof was inappropriate in the context of such a hearing before the SIAC (in which, for example, the appellant may not see the statement or know what it says and may not know the name or identity of its author) and, by a majority, that the SIAC should refuse to admit the evidence if it concludes, on a balance of probabilities, that it was obtained by torture. However, it is submitted that in a criminal trial, if the defence can establish a prima facie case that evidence on which the prosecution seeks to rely was obtained by torture, the burden will be on the prosecution to prove beyond reasonable doubt that it was not so obtained.

Privileged Documents

If a document protected by legal professional privilege (or secondary evidence of it) has been obtained by the opponent of the party entitled to assert the privilege, then the document (or secondary evidence of it) will be admissible in evidence. This principle applies whether the document was obtained by the inadvertence of the party entitled to assert the privilege or by the wrongful act of his opponent (see *Calcraft v Guest* [1898] 1 QB 759; *Tompkins* (1977) 67 Cr App R 181). In civil proceedings, the party in whom the privilege is vested may apply for an injunction to restrain his opponent from making any use of the confidential information obtained in the document (*Lord Ashburton v Pape* [1913] 2 Ch 469). However, the principle of *Lord Ashburton v Pape* cannot be used to prevent the prosecution from tendering relevant evidence in a public prosecution (see *Butler v Board of Trade* [1971] Ch 680, a decision which is consistent with the general rule that criminal courts are not concerned with the method by which the evidence they consider has been obtained). **F2.12**

In *ITC Film Distributors Ltd v Video Exchange Ltd* [1982] Ch 431, one party to civil proceedings obtained by a trick in court privileged documents belonging to the other party. By that stage in the case there were difficulties in the way of granting injunctive relief under the principle established in *Lord Ashburton v Pape* [1913] 2 Ch 469. Warner J held that the public interest that litigants should be able to bring their documents into court without fear that they might be filched by their opponents required an exception to the rule in *Calcraft v Guest* [1898] 1 QB 759; and he observed that to obtain documents in such circumstances is probably a contempt of court which the court should not countenance by admitting the documents in evidence. It is submitted that if the same facts were to arise in a public prosecution rather than civil proceedings, then, notwithstanding the principles established in

Calcraft v Guest and *Butler v Board of Trade* [1971] Ch 680, the result, on the reasoning employed by Warner J, would be the same.

DISCRETIONARY EXCLUSION OF EVIDENCE OBTAINED UNLAWFULLY, IMPROPERLY OR UNFAIRLY

Cases before *Sang*

F2.13 Prior to *Sang* [1980] AC 402, the cases revealed an unbroken chain of dicta to the effect that in criminal proceedings the court has a general discretion to exclude otherwise admissible prosecution evidence which has been obtained by improper or unfair means, e.g.:

(a) Evidence obtained 'by a trick' (*Kuruma, Son of Kaniu v The Queen* [1955] AC 197, per Lord Goddard CJ at p. 204.

(b) Evidence obtained 'oppressively, by false representations, by a trick, by threats, by bribes' (*Callis v Gunn* [1964] 1 QB 495, per Lord Parker CJ at pp. 501–2).

(c) Evidence obtained 'by conduct of which the Crown ought not to take advantage' (*King v The Queen* [1969] 1 AC 304, per Lord Hodson at p. 319).

(d) In the context of an illegal search, exceptional cases in which 'not only have the police officers entered without authority, but they have been guilty of trickery or they have misled someone, or they have been oppressive or they have been unfair, or in other respects they have behaved in a manner which is morally reprehensible' (*Jeffrey v Black* [1978] QB 490, per Lord Widgery CJ at p. 498).

Despite these various dicta as to the existence of a discretion to exclude evidence which has been obtained oppressively, improperly or unfairly, there were very few cases in which such a discretion was in fact exercised. It was exercised in *Ameer* [1977] Crim LR 104 to exclude evidence which had been obtained as a result of the activities of an *agent provocateur*, and a similar course was taken in *Foulder* [1973] Crim LR 45 and in *Burnett* [1973] Crim LR 748; but all three cases were overruled in *Sang* [1980] AC 402. The only other case in which the discretion was exercised was *Payne* [1963] 1 WLR 637. P was charged with drunken driving. He had been induced to submit himself to examination by a doctor to see if he was suffering from any illness or disability, on the understanding that the doctor would not examine him for the purpose of seeing whether he was fit to drive; but at the trial the doctor gave evidence of P's unfitness to drive based on his symptoms and behaviour in the course of that examination. The conviction was quashed on the ground that the judge should have exercised his discretion to exclude the doctor's evidence. In *Sang* [1980] AC 402, however, *Payne* was regarded as analogous to cases in which an accused is unfairly induced to confess to an offence, and the judgment of the Court of Criminal Appeal was therefore seen to be based on the maxim *nemo tenetur se ipsum prodere* (no man is to be compelled to incriminate himself). In *McDonald* [1991] Crim LR 122, a decision under the PACE 1984, s. 78, it was held that it was not unfair to adduce evidence of a damaging admission, made by the accused in the course of a psychiatric examination, on a non-medical issue. See also *Gayle* [1994] Crim LR 679 and, in the case of confessions made to probation officers, *Elleray* [2003] 2 Cr App R 165.

Sang

F2.14 In *Sang* [1980] AC 402, the point of law on which the appeal actually turned was whether a judge has a discretion to exclude the prosecution evidence if satisfied that the offence charged was instigated by an *agent provocateur* and, but for this, would not have been committed by the accused. The House of Lords held that, whatever the ambit of the judicial discretion to exclude admissible evidence, it does not extend to excluding evidence of a crime on the grounds that it was instigated by an *agent provocateur*, because if it did so extend it would amount to a procedural device whereby the trial judge could avoid the substantive law, under which it is clearly established that there is no defence of entrapment (see *McEvilly* (1973) 60 Cr App R 150 and *Mealey* (1974) 60 Cr App R 59). The point of law of general importance certified by the Court of Appeal, however, went beyond the issue of *agents provocateurs* and raised a much wider question, namely: 'Does a trial judge have a discretion to refuse to allow evidence, being evidence other than evidence of an admission, to be given in any circumstances in which such evidence is relevant and of more than minimal probative value?' Although it was not strictly necessary for their lordships to answer the certified question in its full breadth, they proceeded to do so, and the primary importance of *Sang* is the *obiter* answer given. Treating the certified question as if it were not confined to trial by jury but concerned the existence of the discretion in any criminal trial, whether in the Crown Court or in a magistrates' court, their lordships, by way of answer, agreed on the following form of words suggested by Viscount Dilhorne (at p. 437):

> (1) A trial judge in a criminal trial has always a discretion to refuse to admit evidence if in his opinion its prejudicial effect outweighs its probative value. (2) Save with regard to admissions and confessions and generally with regard to evidence obtained from the accused after commission of the offence, he has no discretion to refuse to admit relevant admissible evidence on the ground that it was obtained by improper or unfair means. The court is not concerned with how it was obtained. It is no ground for the exercise of discretion to exclude that the evidence was obtained as the result of the activities of an *agent provocateur*.

The first of the above propositions is considered at **F2.1** to **F2.5**. As to the second proposition, despite the apparent unanimity, their lordships expressed various differing views, especially as to the meaning to be ascribed to the words 'and generally with regard to evidence obtained from the accused after commission of the offence', as the following extracts from the speeches illustrate:

(a) Lord Diplock (at p. 436) treated the phrase as referring to 'evidence tantamount to a self-incriminatory admission which was obtained from the defendant, after the offence had been committed, by means which would justify a judge in excluding an actual confession which had the like self-incriminating effect', and cited, by way of illustration, *Barker* [1941] 2 KB 381 (in which fraudulently prepared documents produced to a tax inspector were held to stand on precisely the same footing as an oral or written confession brought into existence as the result of a promise, inducement or threat) and *Payne* [1963] 1 WLR 637 (see **F2.13**). Lord Diplock said (at p. 436):

> The underlying rationale of this branch of the criminal law . . . is . . . now to be found in the maxim *nemo debet prodere se ipsum*. . . . That is why there is no discretion to exclude evidence discovered as the result of an illegal search but there is discretion to exclude evidence which the accused has been induced to produce voluntarily if the method of inducement was unfair.

(b) Viscount Dilhorne was largely in agreement with Lord Diplock. Thus, although he found it unnecessary to decide whether *Payne* [1963] 1 WLR 637 was correctly decided, he sought to explain the statement of Lord Goddard CJ in *Kuruma, Son of Kaniu v The Queen* [1955] AC 197 at p. 203 (that a judge might exercise his discretion to exclude a document obtained by a trick: see **F2.13**) on the basis that the Lord Chief Justice was perhaps thinking of admissions, confessions and the decision in *Barker* [1941] 2 KB 381. Viscount Dilhorne was also of the opinion that the observations made by Lord Parker CJ in *Callis v Gunn* [1964] 1 QB 495 at p. 501 and by Lord Widgery CJ in *Jeffrey v Black* [1978] QB 490 at p. 498 (see **F2.8**) were not correct.

(c) Lord Salmon, taking a less restrictive view as to the meaning of the phrase, said (at p. 444) 'In my opinion, the decision as to whether evidence may be excluded depends entirely on the particular facts of each case and the circumstances surrounding it — which are infinitely variable'. The category of cases in which evidence may be rejected on the grounds that it would make a trial unfair was not closed and could never be closed except by statute (at p. 445).

(d) Lord Fraser of Tullybelton, who agreed with Lord Diplock that the decision in *Payne* [1963] 1 WLR 637 was based, at least in part, on the maxim *nemo tenetur se ipsum accusare*, concluded, in apparent reliance on the *obiter dicta* in *Kuruma, Callis v Gunn* and *Jeffrey v Black*, that the phrase under discussion applied 'only to evidence and documents obtained from an accused person or from premises occupied by him' and would 'leave judges with a discretion to be exercised in accordance with their individual views of what is unfair or oppressive or morally reprehensible' (at p. 450).

(e) Lord Scarman treated the phrase as referring exclusively to the obtaining of evidence from the accused. His lordship said (at pp. 456–7):

> If an accused is misled or tricked into providing evidence (whether it be an admission or the provision of fingerprints or medical evidence or some other evidence), the rule against selfincrimination, — *nemo tenetur se ipsum prodere* — is likely to be infringed. Each case must, of course, depend on its circumstances. All I would say is that the principle of fairness, though concerned exclusively with the use of evidence at trial, is not susceptible to categorisation or classification and is wide enough in some circumstances to embrace the way in which, after the crime, evidence has been obtained from the accused.

Cases after *Sang*

F2.15 Much of the case law subsequent to *Sang* [1980] AC 402 has neither clarified nor refined the principles laid down in that case; see, for example, *Winter v Barlow* [1980] RTR 209; *Doyle v Leroux* [1981] RTR 438; *Clarke* (1984) 80 Cr App R 344; and *Morris v Beardmore* [1981] AC 446, in which Lord Roskill said (at p. 469) that in *Sang* the House had carefully defined the limits of judicial discretion to exclude evidence otherwise clearly admissible, setting at rest many doubts which had previously existed as to its existence and scope, and that it would be a retrograde step to enlarge upon its now narrow limits or to engraft an exception, merely in order to meet the situation under discussion in that case. However, other authorities, such as *Khan* [1997] AC 558, *Trump* (1979) 70 Cr App R 300, *Adams* [1980] QB 575 and *Apicella* (1985) 82 Cr App R 295, are illustrative of what evidence is and is not capable of being treated as 'evidence tantamount to a self-incriminatory admission'; and *Fox* [1986] AC 281 has put a major gloss on the principles established in *Sang* [1980] AC 402, to the effect that where evidence has been unlawfully obtained from the accused after the commission of the offence, the discretion will not be exercised if those who obtained the evidence did so on the basis of a bona fide mistake as to their powers. In this regard, see also *Trump* (1979) 70 Cr App R 300. These cases are considered below.

F2.16 *Khan* In *Khan* [1997] AC 558, the House of Lords, relying upon the dictum of Lord Diplock in *Sang* set out at **F2.14**, held that evidence of an incriminating conversation obtained by means of a secret electronic surveillance device was not subject to the discretion recognised in *Sang* to exist in the case of admissions and confessions, because the accused had not been 'induced' to make the admissions recorded.

F2.17 *Trump* In *Trump* (1979) 70 Cr App R 300, the appellant was convicted of driving while unfit through drink. He was given a breathalyser test which proved positive. The officer administering the test then arrested him unlawfully. The appellant was taken to the police station and given a statutory warning that he might be prosecuted if he failed to provide a specimen. Under the relevant procedures, no such warning was required. As a result of the warning, the accused consented to the provision of a specimen of blood which was found to contain a proportion of alcohol above the prescribed limit. He appealed on the ground that the specimen of blood had been unlawfully obtained and that the result of its analysis should have been excluded. It was conceded by the appellant that after the breath test had proved positive, the officer had a statutory power of arrest (but not under the statutory provision which the officer purported to use) and that had he exercised that power the result of the analysis of blood would have been admissible as evidence. The Court of Appeal held that:

(a) the giving of blood by the accused was very close to his making an admission that he had consumed an excessive amount of alcohol, and therefore was subject to the discretion recognised in *Sang* [1980] AC 402 to exist in cases analogous to improperly obtained admissions; but
(b) the judge would have erred if he had excluded the evidence because, although the blood was given as the result of a threat, the officer was acting in good faith and the evidence could not have undermined the fairness of the trial.

Apicella In *Apicella* (1985) 82 Cr App R 295 the appellant was convicted on three counts of rape. Each of the victims had contracted an unusual strain of gonorrhoea. The appellant, whilst held on remand, was suspected by the prison doctor to be suffering from gonorrhoea. The doctor, for solely therapeutic reasons, called in a consultant physician who, on the assumption that the appellant was consenting, took a sample of body fluid in order to make a diagnosis. In fact, the appellant submitted because he had been told by a prison officer that, being a prisoner, he had to submit. The sample showed that the appellant was suffering from the same strain of gonorrhoea as the victims, and the prosecution called evidence to that effect. On appeal, although no reference to *Trump* (1979) 70 Cr App R 300 appears to have been made, the Court of Appeal rejected a submission that the body fluid taken without consent was the physical equivalent of an oral confession. Lawton LJ, giving the judgment of the court, held that the pertinent question was whether the intended use of the evidence was likely to make the trial unfair; that the appellant was not tricked into submitting to the examination in the way which led the court in *Payne* [1963] 1 WLR 637 (see **F2.13**) to exclude evidence; and that the prosecution's use of the evidence was not unfair. **F2.18**

Adams In *Adams* [1980] QB 575 the accused was charged with offences under the Obscene Publications Act 1959, s. 2. On 6 April 1977, the police, acting under a search warrant issued under s. 3(1) of the 1959 Act, entered and searched the accused's bookshop and seized certain articles. On 12 April 1977, officers purporting to act under the same warrant, entered and searched the shop and seized further articles. The Court of Appeal held that since a warrant issued under s. 3(1) authorised only one entry, search and seizure of premises, and was spent once that had been carried out, the entry, search and seizure on 12 April was unlawful. On the question whether the judge should have exercised his discretion to exclude the articles seized on 12 April, it was held that there was no material suggesting that the error of the police as to the continuing validity of the warrant after the search on 6 April was oppressive in the sense that the adjective was used in *Sang* [1980] AC 402. This assumes, contrary to the view of Lord Diplock in *Sang* (see **F2.14**), that evidence discovered as a result of an illegal search *is* subject to the discretion recognised in that case and, in appropriate circumstances, may be excluded. **F2.19**

Fox In *Fox* [1986] AC 281 the appellant was convicted under the Road Traffic Act 1972, s. 6(1), on the basis of the proportion of alcohol in a breath specimen which he had been required to provide at a police station following his wrongful arrest. Officers had entered the appellant's house without his consent and without statutory authority, and required him to provide a specimen of breath. He refused. He was then arrested and taken to the police station where he was required to provide the specimen of breath which was the crucial item of evidence which led to his conviction. The requirement to provide a specimen in the appellant's house was not valid and the appellant had committed no offence by failing to comply with it. Consequently, his arrest for failure to provide a specimen was unlawful. On appeal, it was submitted that the evidence of the specimen obtained at the police station, although relevant and admissible, ought to have been excluded by the justices in the exercise of their discretion. This submission was rejected by both the Divisional Court and the House of Lords. Lord Fraser of Tullybelton, whose reasoning was expressly adopted by Lords Elwyn-Jones, Edmund-Davies, Bridge of Harwich and Brightman, said (at p. 293): 'Of course, if the appellant had been lured to the police station by some trick or deception, or if the police **F2.20** officers had behaved oppressively towards the appellant, the justices' jurisdiction to exclude otherwise admissible evidence recognised in *Sang* might have come into play. But there is nothing of that sort suggested here. The police officers did no more than make a bona fide mistake as to their powers.' This passage was cited and applied by McNeill J in *Gull v Scarborough* [1987] RTR 261. See also *DPP v Wilson* [1991] RTR 284, a decision under the PACE 1984, s. 78.

Police and Criminal Evidence Act 1984, s. 78

F2.21 (1) In any proceedings the court may refuse to allow evidence on which the prosecution proposes to rely to be given if it appears to the court that, having regard to all the circumstances, including the circumstances in which the evidence was obtained, the admission of the evidence would have such an adverse effect on the fairness of the proceedings that the court ought not to admit it.

(2) Nothing in this section shall prejudice any rule of law requiring a court to exclude evidence.

(3) This section shall not apply in the case of proceedings before a magistrates' court inquiring into an offence as examining justices.

The importance of s. 78(1) is reflected in the large volume of reported cases in which it has arisen for consideration since it came into force. It is important to stress at the outset, however, the salutary warning given by Auld J in *Jelen* (1989) 90 Cr App R 456 at pp. 464–5:

> . . . the decision of a judge whether or not to exclude evidence under section 78 of the 1984 Act is made as a result of the exercise by him of a discretion based upon the particular circumstances of the case and upon his assessment of the adverse effect, if any, it would have on the fairness of the proceedings. The circumstances of each case are almost always different, and judges may well take different views in the proper exercise of their discretion even when the circumstances are similar. This is not an apt field for hard case law and wellfounded distinctions between cases.

The following paragraphs make a number of general observations. The cases concerning confessions and identification evidence are also considered separately and in more detail at **F17** and **F18** respectively.

F2.22 **Procedure** As to procedure, the issue of unfairness may be raised by counsel for any accused against whom the evidence may be used (by the prosecution). Section 78(1) applies not to evidence which the prosecution have adduced, but to evidence on which the prosecution *propose* to rely. In *Harwood* [1989] Crim LR 285, in which a submission that evidence should be excluded under s. 78 was made *after* the evidence had been given, the Court of Appeal doubted whether s. 78 could in any circumstances entitle the judge to withdraw the evidence or to direct the jury to acquit when the judge had not been invited to refuse to allow the evidence to be given. However, where a judge has excluded evidence on which the prosecution propose to rely but, at some later stage in the trial, in his opinion the balance of fairness shifts, he then has a discretion to reconsider his ruling and admit the evidence (*Allen* [1992] Crim LR 297).

It seems reasonable to suppose that if the court is prepared to entertain a submission that a particular item would have such an adverse effect on the fairness of the proceedings that the court ought not to admit it, argument should take place in the absence of the jury and, in cases in which evidence needs to be called as to the circumstances in which the evidence was obtained (because they are in dispute), there should be a hearing on the *voir dire*. In *Manji* [1990] Crim LR 512 the accused denied that he had made certain damaging admissions in a conversation with police officers and alleged that he had not been cautioned. On a defence application under s. 78 to exclude this evidence as having been obtained in breach of the Codes of Practice under the PACE 1984, the trial judge refused to hold a trial within a trial on the issue of whether the accused had been cautioned. It was held that the judge had erred. However, where a question arises under s. 78(1) as to the admissibility of identification parade evidence, it has been held that, although there may be rare occasions when it will be desirable to hold a trial within a trial, in general the judge should decide on the basis of the depositions, statements and submissions of counsel (*Beveridge* (1987) 85 Cr App R 255). See **F1.34**.

In *Anderson* [1993] Crim LR 447 it was acknowledged, *per curiam*, that it is not entirely clear under s. 78(1) where the burden of proof lies. It is submitted that, if there is no dispute as to the circumstances in which the evidence was obtained, there will be no issue of fact and no question of burden of proof will arise; if there is such a dispute, evidence is called for and, in accordance with the general rule, the burden should be on the prosecution to disprove beyond reasonable doubt the circumstances on which the accused relies. However, in *R (Saifi) v Governor of Brixton Prison* [2001] 1 WLR 1134, which concerned the application of s. 78 in extradition proceedings, it was held that the absence from s. 78 of any suggestion that facts are to be proved to any particular standard is deliberate; that a magistrate may simply evaluate the evidence tendered both by the government and the accused as to the circumstances in which the evidence was obtained and may decide, on that evidence, the question of adverse effect on the fairness of the proceedings; and therefore that there is no need for a magistrate to make a specific finding in relation to every issue raised.

As to the procedure in summary trials, see **F1.35**.

The Test for Exclusion Section 78(1) of the PACE 1984 directs the court, in deciding whether to exercise the statutory discretion, to have regard to all the circumstances, including those in which the evidence was obtained. In some cases, of course, the submission to exclude under the subsection will *not* be based on the circumstances in which the evidence was obtained; see, for example, the cases in which an application has been made under s. 78(1) to exclude evidence of the conviction of a person otherwise admissible under s. 74 of the 1984 Act, which are considered at **F11.5**. **F2.23**

In other cases, however, counsel will be fully justified in basing a submission to exclude on the circumstances in which the evidence was obtained, because it is implicit in the subsection that there can be circumstances in which the evidence was obtained which makes it have such an adverse effect on the fairness of the proceedings that the court ought not to admit it (see *Matto v Wolverhampton Crown Court* [1987] RTR 337 per Woolf LJ). Thus, the court may have regard to any unlawful, improper or unfair conduct by means of which the evidence was obtained, including, in particular, conduct in breach of the ECHR or the provisions of the 1984 Act (or the codes of practice issued under the Act) relating to such matters as search, seizure, arrest, detention, treatment, questioning and identification. Even where the evidence in question was obtained by someone who is not 'charged with the duty of investigating offences' for the purposes of s. 67(9) of the 1984 Act, the principles underlying Code C may be of assistance in considering the discretion to exclude under s. 78(1) (*Smith* [1994] 1 WLR 1396). Regard may also be had to the Cleveland Guidelines on best practice when children are interviewed in connection with sexual abuse and 'Achieving Best Evidence in Criminal Proceedings: Guidance for Vulnerable or Intimidated Witnesses, Including Children' (the 'Memorandum'): see *Dunphy* (1993) 98 Cr App R 393, a decision on an earlier version of the Memorandum, the Memorandum of Good Practice on Video- Recorded Interviews with Child Witnesses. However, breach of the European Convention on Human Rights, the 1984 Act or the PACE codes etc. will not necessarily result in exclusion: every case has to be determined on its own particular facts (see *Parris* (1988) 89 Cr App R 65, per Lord Lane CJ at p. 72, *Khan* [1995] QB 27 and *Keenan* [1990] 2 QB 54 per Hodgson J at p. 69). Equally, the fact that evidence has been obtained by 'oppressive' conduct will not automatically result in exclusion, because oppressive conduct, depending on its degree and actual or possible effect, may or may not affect the fairness of admitting particular evidence (*Chalkley* [1998] QB 848 at p. 874).

'The Fairness of the Proceedings' In cases in which the court takes the view that there was serious or reprehensible conduct, and this results in exclusion, the decision should not be **F2.24**

taken in order to discipline the police (*Mason* [1988] 1 WLR 139 per Watkins LJ and *Delaney* (1988) 88 Cr App R 338 per Lord Lane CJ at p. 341). The critical test under s. 78 is whether any impropriety affects the fairness of the proceedings: the court cannot exclude evidence under the section simply as a mark of its disapproval of the way in which it was obtained (per Auld LJ in *Chalkley*).

Thus if a sample of hair is obtained by an assault and not in accordance with ss. 63 and 65 of the 1984 Act and is then used to prepare a DNA profile which implicates the accused, the evidence will be admitted on the basis that the means used to obtain it have done nothing to cast doubt on its reliability and strength (see *Cooke* [1995] 1 Cr App R 318 and cf. *Nathaniel* [1995] 2 Cr App R 565). The same reasoning may also justify the admission in evidence of the fruits of an improper search (see *Stewart* [1995] Crim LR 500, where the entry involved a number of breaches of Code B; and see also *McCarthy* [1996] Crim LR 818). The evidence should be excluded, however, where there is a real risk that the improper means used to obtain it have affected its reliability, and therefore the fairness of the trial, for example a case involving a complete flouting of Code B in which the accused claims that the property allegedly found must have been planted. (But see *Wright* [1994] Crim LR 55 at **F2.30**.) Equally, where officers are justified in delaying taking a suspect to a police station in order that a search may be conducted with his assistance, but abuse that opportunity to circumvent Code C by asking a series of questions, beyond those necessary to the search, on matters which properly ought to be asked under the rules of the Code applying at a police station, the answers may be excluded on the grounds of unfairness (*Khan* [1993] Crim LR 54, applied in *Raphaie* [1996] Crim LR 812).

In *Quinn* [1990] Crim LR 581 Lord Lane CJ said:

> The function of the judge is therefore *to protect the fairness of the proceedings*, and normally proceedings are fair if a jury hears *all* relevant evidence which either side wishes to place before it, but proceedings may become unfair if, for example, one side is allowed to adduce relevant evidence which, for one reason or another, the other side cannot properly challenge or meet, or where there has been an abuse of process, e.g. because evidence has been obtained in deliberate breach of procedures laid down in an official code of practice.

In *Quinn*, identification evidence had come into existence abroad as a result of arrangements made by a foreign police force. A police officer went to a criminal court in Dublin, where the accused was on trial in respect of other offences committed in the Republic of Ireland, and identified the accused. It was held that, in the circumstances of the case, the judge had to have regard to such factors as (a) the possible cross-examination handicap to the defence; (b) the possibility of mistake being increased because of the way in which the identification was arranged and the fact that both the judge himself and the defence could warn the jury of the disadvantages of the procedure adopted and the consequent danger of relying upon the evidence; (c) the fact that the accused was deprived of the opportunity to stand on an identification parade or to consult a solicitor or to record what happened when the identification was carried out; (d) that the accused was not told of the identification at the time; and (e) the fact that the identification evidence did not stand alone but could be tested by other evidence. The Court of Appeal could find nothing to indicate that the trial judge had misdirected himself, had regard to irrelevant matters or failed to have regard to relevant matters. In *Konscol* [1993] Crim LR 950, the trial judge admitted evidence of an interview with K, containing lies, conducted by a Belgian customs officer. There was no dispute that K had said what was recorded, and the interview was conducted fairly according to Belgian law, but K was neither cautioned nor advised that he could have a lawyer present. The Court of Appeal dismissed the appeal and declined to lay down guidelines as to when a court should admit a statement made overseas according to rules which did not coincide with the provisions of the PACE 1984. See also *McNab* [2002] Crim LR 129.

In *Mason* [1988] 1 WLR 139 the accused was convicted of arson. After arrest, the accused and his solicitor were told by police officers that a fingerprint of the accused had been identified on glass from a bottle found at the scene of the crime. This was a deliberate falsehood designed to elicit a confession. The solicitor advised the accused to explain any involvement on his part in the incident, whereupon the accused confessed. There was no other prosecution evidence. Quashing the conviction, the Court of Appeal held that had the judge, in the exercise of the statutory discretion, taken into account the deceit practised on the solicitor, which he had failed to do, he would have been driven to exclude the confession. See also *Samuel* [1988] QB 615. *Mason* was distinguished in *DPP v Marshall* [1988] 3 All ER 683. On a charge of selling intoxicating liquor without a licence, evidence was adduced that officers, wearing plain clothes, and without announcing their office, had purchased liquor from the premises in question. It was held that this evidence could not have any effect on the fairness of the trial and therefore was not to be excluded under the PACE 1984, s. 78.

Scope of s. 78(1) As regards the scope of the PACE 1984, s. 78(1), in *Mason* [1988] 1 WLR 139 Watkins LJ said that it 'does no more than to restate the power which judges had at common law before the 1984 Act was passed'. It is submitted that this view is erroneous in principle and inconsistent with the authorities to date. **F2.25**

(a) Concerning the provisions of part VIII of the PACE 1984, s. 82(3) expressly preserves the discretion to exclude which the court possessed at common law prior to the coming into force of the Act, and therefore Parliament, in enacting s. 78, must be taken to have extended the pre-existing discretion.
(b) Section 78(1), insofar as it may be used to exclude evidence obtained by improper or unfair means, is not confined, as is the common-law power described in *Sang* [1980] AC 402 (at p. 437), to 'admissions, confessions and generally with regard to evidence obtained from the accused after the commission of the offence', but extends to any evidence on which the prosecution propose to rely.
(c) Nor, in relation to evidence obtained improperly or unfairly, is s. 78(1) necessarily confined, in the way that the common-law power apparently is, to cases in which those who obtained the evidence acted *mala fide* (*Fox* [1986] AC 281, see **F2.20**). See further **F2.29**.

Section 78(1) *may* be used to exclude evidence obtained illegally, improperly or unfairly. Insofar as it may be used in this way to exclude admissions, confessions and evidence obtained from the accused after the commission of the offence, it overlaps with the common-law discretion as defined in *Sang*. The subsection, however, has the potential for the exclusion of *any* evidence on which the prosecution propose to rely, whether obtained from the accused, his premises, or from any other source. Thus, in *Gaynor* [1988] Crim LR 242, evidence that a witness had picked out the accused at a group identification was excluded under s. 78 on the basis of a breach of PACE Code D.

Prosecutions Founded on Entrapment The leading authority on the application of the PACE 1984, s. 78(1), to a prosecution founded on entrapment is the decision of the House of Lords in *Loosely* [2001] 1 WLR 2060, from which the following propositions derive. **F2.26**

(a) Although in English law entrapment is not a substantive defence, where an accused can show entrapment, the court may stay the proceedings as an abuse of the court's process or it may exclude evidence pursuant to s. 78.
(b) Of these two remedies, the grant of stay, rather than the exclusion of evidence at the trial, should, as a matter of principle, normally be regarded as the appropriate response. A prosecution founded on entrapment would be an abuse of the court's process. Police conduct which brings about state-created crime is unacceptable and improper. To prosecute in such circumstances would be an affront to the public conscience.

(c) A decision on whether to stay criminal proceedings is distinct from a decision on the forensic fairness of admitting evidence (see *Chalkley* [1998] 2 Cr App R 79 at p. 105). Thus if the court is not satisfied that a stay should be granted and the trial proceeds, the question under s. 78 is not whether the proceedings should have been brought but whether the fairness of the proceedings will be adversely affected by, e.g., admitting the evidence of the agent provocateur or evidence which is available as a result of his activities (see *Shannon* [2001] 1 WLR 51 at p. 68). However, if an application to exclude evidence under s. 78 is in substance a belated application for a stay, it should be treated as such and decided according to the principles appropriate to the grant of a stay.

(d) In deciding whether conduct amounts to state-created crime, the existence or absence of a predisposition on the part of the accused to commit the crime is not the criterion by which the acceptability of police conduct is to be decided, because predisposition does not make acceptable what would otherwise be unacceptable conduct on the part of the police or other law enforcement agencies. (But cf. *Moon* [2004] EWCA Crim 2872, where absence of disposition on the part of M to deal with or supply heroin was regarded as a critical factor.) A useful guide is to consider whether the police did no more than present the defendant with an unexceptional opportunity to commit a crime. The yardstick for the purposes of this test is, in general, whether the police conduct preceding the commission of the offence was no more than might have been expected from others in the circumstances. McHugh J had this approach in mind in *Ridgeway v The Queen* (1995) 184 CLR 19 at p. 92, when he said:

> The State can justify the use of entrapment techniques to induce the commission of an offence only when the inducement is consistent with the ordinary temptations and stratagems that are likely to be encountered in the course of criminal activity. That may mean that some degree of deception, importunity and even threats on the part of the authorities may be acceptable. But once the State goes beyond the ordinary, it is likely to increase the incidence of crime by artificial means.

Of its nature, the technique of providing an opportunity to commit a crime is intrusive. The greater the degree of intrusiveness, the closer will the courts scrutinise the reason for using it. On this, proportionality has a role to play. Whether a police officer can be said to have caused the commission of the offence, rather than merely providing an opportunity for the accused to commit it with a police officer rather than in secrecy with someone else, will usually be a most important factor, but not necessarily decisive.

(e) Ultimately, the overall consideration is always whether the conduct of the police or other law enforcement agency was so seriously improper as to bring the administration of justice into disrepute. In applying this test, the court has regard to all the circumstances of the case. The following circumstances are of particular relevance. (i) The nature of the offence. The use of proactive techniques is more appropriate in the case of some offences, e.g., dealing in unlawful substances, offences with no immediate victim (such as bribery), offences which victims are reluctant to report and conspiracies. The secrecy and difficulty of detection, and the manner in which the particular criminal activity is carried on, are relevant considerations. (ii) The reason for the particular police operation and supervision. The police must act in good faith. Having reasonable grounds for suspicion is one way good faith may be established. It is not normally considered a legitimate use of police power to provide people not suspected of being engaged in any criminal activity with the opportunity to commit crimes. The principle is that the police should prevent and detect crime, not create it. Closely linked with the question whether the police were creating or detecting crime is the supervision of their activities. To allow police officers or controlled informers to undertake entrapment activities unsupervised carries great danger, not merely that they will try to improve their performances in court, but of oppression, extortion and corruption. The need for reasonable suspicion and proper supervision are both stressed in the Undercover Operations Code of Practice issued jointly by all UK police authorities and HM Customs and Excise in response to the HRA 1998. However, the requirement of reasonable suspicion does not necessarily mean that there must have been suspicion of the accused. The police may, in the course of a bona fide investigation into suspected criminality, provide an opportunity for the commission of an offence which is taken by someone to whom no suspicion previously attached (see, e.g., *Williams v DPP* [1993] 3 All ER 365). Sometimes random testing may be the only practicable way of policing a particular trading activity. (iii) The nature and extent of police participation in the crime. The greater the inducement held out by the police, and the more forceful or persistent the police overtures, the more readily may a court conclude that the police overstepped the boundary. In assessing the weight to be attached to the police inducement, regard is to be had to the defendant's circumstances, including his vulnerability. For the police to behave as would an ordinary customer of a trade, whether lawful or unlawful, being carried on by the accused will not normally be regarded as objectionable. (iv) The accused's criminal record. This is unlikely to be relevant unless it can be linked to other factors grounding reasonable suspicion that the accused is currently engaged in criminal activity.

(f) Neither the judicial discretion conferred by s. 78, nor the court's power to stay proceedings as an abuse of the court, has been modified by the ECHR, Article 6 and the jurisprudence of the European Court of Human Rights. There is no appreciable difference between the requirements of Article 6, or the Strasbourg jurisprudence on Article 6, and the English law as it has developed in recent years. There is nothing in either the general principle applied by the European court in *Teixeira de Castro v Portugal* (1998) 28 EHRR 101 or in the cluster of factors to which it attached importance which suggests any difference from the current English approach to entrapment.

Undercover Operations In *Smurthwaite* [1994] 1 All ER 898 it was held that the relevant factors, in deciding whether to exclude under the PACE 1984, s. 78 evidence obtained as a result of police undercover operations, *include* whether the undercover officer was acting as an *agent provocateur* in the sense that he was enticing the accused to commit an offence he would not otherwise have committed; the nature of any entrapment; whether the evidence consists of admissions to a completed offence or relates to the actual commission of an offence; how active the officer's role was in obtaining the evidence; whether there is an unassailable record of what occurred or whether it is strongly corroborated; and whether the officer abused his role to ask questions which ought properly to have been asked as a police officer and in accordance with the codes (see *Christou* [1992] QB 979 and *Bryce* [1992] 4 All ER 567, **F2.28**). It was held that if in all the circumstances the evidence would have the adverse effect described in s. 78(1) then the judge will exclude it. The factors recited in *Smurthwaite* also apply in the case of evidence obtained by undercover journalists acting not on police instructions, but on their own initiative (*Shannon* [2001] 1 WLR 51 and *Shannon v UK* [2005] Crim LR 133). Section 78(1) cannot be circumvented by the police using, as *agents provocateurs*, informants who will not be called as witnesses. Thus if an informant, acting on police instructions, entraps an accused into committing an offence and the accused is then approached by an undercover police officer in whose presence the offence is committed, a submission may be made under s. 78(1) to exclude the officer's evidence notwithstanding that his behaviour throughout cannot be criticised having regard to the relevant factors in *Smurthwaite* (see *Smith* [1995] Crim LR 658; cf. *Mann* [1995] Crim LR 647). However, entrapment, whether direct or indirect, is not in itself sufficient to require exclusion under s. 78. The facts and circumstances amounting to entrapment may be taken into account (and in an appropriate case may prove decisive), but the principal focus must be the procedural fairness of the proceedings, the nature and reliability of the prosecution evidence and the fullness and fairness of the opportunity available to the accused to deal with it (per Potter LJ in *Shannon* [2001] 1 WLR 51 at [38]; and see also *Governor of Pentonville Prison, ex parte Chinoy* [1992] 1 All ER 317). **F2.27**

In *Smurthwaite*, the two appellants, S and G had been tried for soliciting to murder. In each case the person solicited was an undercover police officer posing as a contract killer, and the prosecution case depended upon secret tape recordings of meetings held between the undercover officer and the accused. In S's case, the Court of Appeal was not persuaded that the officer was an *agent provocateur*. There was an element of entrapment and a trick, but (a) the tapes recorded not admissions about some previous offence but the actual offence being committed, (b) the tapes showed that S made the running and that the officer had taken a minimal role in the planning and had used no persuasion towards S, (c) the tapes were an accurate and unchallenged record and (d) the officer had not abused his role to ask questions which ought properly to have been asked as a police officer. In these circumstances, the judge's decision not to exclude the evidence was upheld. The outcome was the same in G's case: the facts were very similar and, although the first meeting between G and the officer was not recorded and there was a stark conflict of evidence as to what was said at that meeting, the existence of a total record was only one factor, and both the contents of the subsequent taped conversations and statements made by G in her formal police interviews supported the officer's account of the first meeting. In *Latif* [1996] 1 WLR 104, the accused was convicted of being knowingly concerned in the importation of drugs which had been brought into the country by an undercover customs officer. Although the accused had been lured into England by the deceit of an informer and both he and the undercover officer had possibly committed the offence of possessing heroin in Pakistan, the House of Lords upheld the trial judge's refusal to exclude the informer's evidence under s. 78. See also *Pattemore* [1994] Crim LR 836 and *Morley* [1994] Crim LR 919.

In *Williams v DPP* plain-clothes officers, as part of an investigation into thefts from vehicles in Essex, which was not directed at any specific individual, parked an insecure and unattended van, which appeared to contain a valuable load of cigarettes, in a busy street. Concealed officers later observed the accused removing cartons from the van. It was held that magistrates were entitled, in exercising their discretion under s. 78, to admit the police evidence. The officers were not acting as *agents provocateurs* and, following *DPP v Marshall* [1988] 3 All ER 683 (see **F2.24**) and the reasoning in *Christou* [1992] QB 979 (see **F2.28**), the trick was not applied to the accused: they voluntarily applied themselves to the trick. The argument that *Christou* could be distinguished, because in that case the police were seeking to obtain evidence of offences which had already been committed, was rejected. See also *London Borough of Ealing v Woolworths plc* [1995] Crim LR 58, where a boy aged 11, acting on the instructions of trading standards officers, had purchased an 18-category video film. In *Nottingham City Council v Amin* [2000] 1 WLR 1071, a taxi driver who was not licensed to ply for hire in a certain district, was flagged down there by plain-clothes officers who were then taken to their destination. A stipendiary magistrate used s. 78 to exclude the officers' evidence, having regard to the HRA 1998 and decisions of the European Court of Human Rights. On appeal, the respondent relied on *Teixeira de Castro v Portugal* (1998) 28 EHRR 101. In that case two undercover agents had instigated an offence and, since there was nothing to suggest that without their intervention it would have been committed, it was held that the intervention and use made of it at the trial amounted to a violation of the right to a fair trial under Article 6. Lord Bingham CJ distinguished the case on the basis that 'the facts . . . simply cannot lend themselves to the construction that this respondent was in any way prevailed upon or overborne or persuaded or pressured or instigated or incited to commit the offence'. Lord Bingham said (at pp. 1076–77):

> On the one hand it has been recognised as deeply offensive to ordinary notions of fairness if a defendant were to be convicted and punished for committing a crime which he only committed because he had been incited, instigated, persuaded, pressurised or wheedled into committing it by a law enforcement officer. On the other hand, it has been recognised that law enforcement agencies have a general duty to the public to enforce the law and it has been regarded as unobjectionable if a law enforcement officer gives a defendant an opportunity to break the law, of

> which the defendant freely takes advantage, in circumstances where it appears that the defendant would have behaved in the same way if the opportunity had been made by anyone else.

In *Loosely*, Lord Hoffmann made two important comments on this passage. First (at [54] and [55]), it was observed in relation to the final sentence that Lord Bingham obviously did not mean only that the accused would have responded in the same way to someone who was not a policeman, because the accused in such cases *ex hypothesi* has no knowledge that he is dealing with a policeman, and therefore such a condition would invariably be satisfied:

> What he meant was that the policemen behaved like ordinary members of the public in flagging the taxi down. They did not wave £50 notes or pretend to be in distress. The test of whether the law enforcement officer behaved like an ordinary member of the public works well and is likely to be decisive in many cases of regulatory offences committed with ordinary members of the public, such as selling liquor in unlicensed quantities (*DPP v Marshall* [1988] 3 All ER 683) . . . But ordinary members of the public do not become involved in large scale drug dealing, conspiracy to rob . . . or hiring assassins (. . . *Smurthwaite* [1994] 1 All ER 898). The appropriate standards of behaviour are in such cases more problematic. And even in the case of offences committed with ordinary members of the public, other factors may require a purely causal test to be modified.

Secondly (at [70]), Lord Hoffmann observed that when Lord Bingham said that the accused should not be 'incited, instigated, persuaded, pressurised or wheedled' into committing the offence he was not intending each of those verbs to be given a disjunctive and technical meaning, but was intending to evoke a more general concept of conduct which causes the accused to commit the offence as opposed to giving him the opportunity to do so. 'No doubt a test purchaser who asks someone to sell him a drug is counselling and procuring, perhaps inciting the commission of an offence. Furthermore, he has no statutory defence to a prosecution. But the fact that his actions are technically unlawful is not regarded in English law as a ground for treating them as an abuse of power: see *R v Latif* [1996] 1 WLR 104. . . .'

Undercover Operations after Commission of the Offence As to evidence obtained by undercover operations *after* commission of the offence, although the PACE 1984, s. 78(1) does apply, each case must be decided on its own facts. In *Jelen* (1989) 90 Cr App R 456, D, J and K were charged with conspiracy to commit false accounting. D pleaded guilty and after he was sentenced gave evidence for the prosecution in the case against J and K. D had been the first to be arrested. He made admissions and implicated J. That was the first that the police had heard of J's involvement and their view was that they would have had to caution J if they had sought to question him then but that they had insufficient evidence upon which they could have arrested and charged him. They accordingly asked D if he would obtain some corroboration of what he had told them by arranging to have a recorded conversation with J without J knowing that it was being recorded. D then held such a conversation with J in the course of which D lied to J, telling him that he had not said anything to the police. During the conversation, J made remarks from which his guilt could have been inferred. The trial judge admitted the evidence and the Court of Appeal held that although there was an element of entrapment, it could see no reason to disagree with the judge's conclusion. Cf. *H* [1987] Crim LR 47, which the court distinguished. **F2.28**

In *Bailey* [1993] 3 All ER 513, two co-accused exercised their right to silence when interviewed by the police. They were charged, remanded in police custody and placed together in a bugged cell by officers who, in order to lull them into a false sense of security, pretended that they had been forced to put them in the same cell by an uncooperative custody officer. It was held that evidence of incriminating conversations between them, obtained by this police subterfuge, was admissible. Although the police were not entitled to question the accused further, they did not have to protect them from any opportunity to hold incriminating conversations, if they chose to do so, and there was nothing in the 1984 Act or Code of Practice C to prohibit them from bugging a cell, even after an accused had been charged and had exercised his right to silence. The judge was therefore entitled to admit the evidence. See also *Shaukat Ali* (1991) *The Times*, 19 February 1991, *Roberts* [1997] 1 Cr App R 217 and *Mason* [2002] 2 Cr App R 628.

In *Khan* [1997] AC 558 the police made a recording of an incriminating conversation relating to the importation of heroin, by means of a secret electronic surveillance device. The House of Lords held that the fact that evidence has been obtained in apparent or probable breach of the right to privacy set out in the ECHR, Article 8, or for that matter the law of a foreign country, is relevant to exercise of the s. 78 power, but the significance of such conduct is its effect, if any, upon the fairness of the proceedings. It therefore upheld the decision of the trial judge that the circumstances in which the evidence had been obtained, even if they constituted a breach of Article 8, did not require exclusion. In *Khan v United Kingdom* (2001) 31 EHRR 1016, the European Court of Human Rights held that, although the recording was obtained in breach of Article 8, its use at the trial did not violate the right to a fair hearing under Article 6. The court, repeating what it had said in previous judgments such as *Schenk v Switzerland*, held that the central question was whether the proceedings as a whole were fair. Noting that the accused had had the opportunity to challenge the admissibility of the evidence under s. 78, as well as its authenticity, the court found that the use of the evidence did not conflict with the requirements of fairness guaranteed by Article 6(1). Similar conclusions have also been reached by the European Court of Human Rights in respect of evidence obtained in breach of Article 8 by the unlawful installation of a listening device in the applicant's home (*Chalkley v United Kingdom* [2003] Crim LR 51) and by the unlawful use of covert listening devices at a police station (*PG and JH v United Kingdom* [2002] Crim LR 308). See also *Mason* [2002] 2 Cr App R 628. In *Perry v United Kingdom* [2003] ECHR 375 there are *dicta* (at [40]) to suggest that where personal data is recorded in breach of Article 8, its use at trial in a public court-room may also constitute a breach of Article 8. However, in *Button* [2005] EWCA Crim 516, where video evidence had been obtained in breach of Article 8, the proposition that the court was bound to exclude such evidence because otherwise it would act unlawfully was rejected on the basis that the court played no part in the covert surveillance, which had already occurred, and breach of Article 8 was subsumed by the Article 6 duty to ensure a fair trial. As to covert filming, see also *Loveridge* [2001] 2 Cr App R 591 in which the accused was covertly and unlawfully filmed at court; *Marriner* [2002] EWCA Crim 2855, in which undercover journalists had made secret videos (as well as tape-recordings) of the accused; and *Rosenberg* [2006] EWCA Crim 6, where both R and the police were aware of surveillance carried out by the complainant but neither initiated nor encouraged by the police.

In *P* [2002] 1 AC 46, the House of Lords rejected an argument that the admissibility of telephone intercepts made overseas, in accordance with both the laws of the country in question and the ECHR, would infringe Article 6. It was held that (1) the criterion of fairness under Article 6 is the same as that to be applied by a judge under s. 78; (2) the fair use of intercept evidence at a trial is not a breach of Article 6 even if the evidence was unlawfully obtained; (3) it is a cogent factor in favour of the admission of such evidence that one of the parties to the conversation is to be a witness and give evidence of what was said during it; and (4) there is no principle of exclusion of intercept evidence in English law independent of the Interception of Communications Act 1985 (see now the RIPA 2000). In *Sargent* [2003] 1 AC 347, a decision under the 1985 Act, it was held that there is no rule prohibiting the use of inadmissible intercepts at police interviews and that, subject to s. 78, such use will not render the interview evidence inadmissible.

Khan v United Kingdom was distinguished in *Allan v United Kingdom* (2002) 36 EHRR 143, in which it was held that the use of statements obtained in a way which effectively undermines a suspect's right to make a meaningful choice whether to speak to the authorities or remain silent infringed procedural rights inherent in the ECHR, Article 6. A was convicted of murder. He had been interviewed by officers on several occasions, but acting on legal advice had consistently refused to answer questions. H, an experienced informer, who had undergone coaching by police officers, was fitted with recording devices and placed in A's cell for the specific purpose of questioning him to obtain information about the murder. At the trial H gave evidence that A had admitted his presence at the scene of the murder. However, this conversation, which proved to be decisive evidence at trial, was not recorded on tape. The court acknowledged that whether the right to silence is undermined to such an extent as to invoke Article 6 depends on the circumstances of the case, but was satisfied that evidence of the conversations with H had been obtained without sufficient regard to fair trial guarantees. The admissions allegedly made formed decisive evidence against him. They were not spontaneous but induced by persistent questioning of H who, at the instigation of the police, in effect interrogated A, but without any of the safeguards of a formal interview, including the issuing of a caution and the attendance of a solicitor. When the case returned to the Court of Appeal (*Allan* [2004] EWCA Crim 2236), the conviction was quashed. It was held that H was a 'police stooge', an agent of the State carrying out the equivalent of interrogation after A had exercised a right of silence. The use of H to obtain admissions impinged on A's common-law right of silence and privilege against self-incrimination. The admission of H's evidence was in effect to allow the subversion of the provisions of PACE Code C serving to give procedural effect to the right to silence.

In *Christou*, the police set up a shop staffed by two undercover officers who purported to be willing to buy stolen jewellery. Transactions in the shop were recorded (on tape and video) in order to recover stolen property and obtain evidence against thieves and receivers. The accused, charged in consequence of the operation, sought to exclude evidence on the grounds that it had been obtained, without administering a caution in accordance with para. 10.1 of the Code of Practice C, by a trick designed to deprive them of their privilege against self-incrimination. The Court of Appeal, distinguishing *Payne* [1963] 1 WLR 637 (see **F2.13**) and *Mason* [1988] 1 WLR 139 (see **F2.24**), held that the accused had voluntarily applied themselves to the trick and this had resulted in no unfairness. It was further held that although the officers had grounds to suspect the accused of having committed an offence, para. 10.1 of Code of Practice C was not intended to apply to the facts in question. It was designed to protect suspects who are vulnerable to abuse or pressure from officers, or who may believe themselves to be so. Where a suspect, even if not in detention, is being questioned by an officer acting as such, for the purpose of obtaining evidence, the parties are not on equal terms; the officer is perceived to be in a position of authority and the suspect may be intimidated or undermined. The accused, however, were not questioned by officers acting as such, conversation was on equal terms and there was no question of pressure or intimidation. *Christou* was applied in *Maclean* [1993] Crim LR 687, a very similar case in which a person suspected of the illegal importation of drugs 'applied himself to the trick', which was the opportunity of holding a conversation with a car salvage operator, who was in reality a customs officer. In *Cadette* [1995] Crim LR 229 a suspected drug courier, at the request of customs officers, telephoned C, pretended that she had not been arrested and tried to persuade C to come to the airport. Evidence of their conversation was admitted. It was held that although there comes a point when officers may move from following up available lines of inquiry in order to obtain evidence to a stage where they seek in effect to deprive a suspect of the protection afforded by the 1984 Act and Codes, the officers had not crossed the line. See also *Mason* [2002] 2 Cr App R 628.

In *Christou*, Lord Taylor CJ further held that it *would* be wrong for the police to adopt an undercover pose or disguise to enable them to ask questions about an offence uninhibited by Code of Practice C and with the effect of circumventing it, and a judge could then exclude under s. 78. In that case, however, questions asked by the officers about the origin of the goods formed a part of their undercover pose as receivers — such information would prevent them from reselling the goods in the area from which they were stolen. See also *Lin* [1995] Crim LR 817, where an undercover officer was introduced to the accused not for the purpose of obtaining evidence about a past offence involving a stolen Inland Revenue cheque, but to discover the future plans of the accused in relation to an on-going conspiracy to handle stolen cheques. It was held that a conversation about the Inland Revenue cheque was a necessary part of establishing the officer's credentials as a 'criminal'. The position was different in *Bryce* [1992] 4 All ER 567, where an undercover officer, in conversations with the accused about a car, asked how recently it had been stolen. The accused replied 'two to three days' and added 'we are having two a week away. Would you be interested in any others?'. The Court of Appeal, quashing the conviction for handling, held that the evidence of these conversations should have been excluded. The questions were not necessary to the maintenance of the undercover pose. They went directly to the issue of guilty knowledge, they were disputed, there was no caution and there were no contemporary records.

F2.29 **Bad Faith** The common-law discretion to exclude evidence obtained unlawfully will not be exercised if those who obtained the evidence made a *bona fide* mistake as to their powers; but it may be exercised if such persons resorted to trickery, deception or oppression (*Fox* [1986] AC 281). Some of the authorities on the PACE 1984, s. 78, draw the same distinction, laying great stress on whether the police acted *mala fide*, *knowingly* exceeding their powers. In *Matto v Wolverhampton Crown Court* [1987] RTR 337, the accused was convicted of driving with excess alcohol. Police officers, when requesting a specimen of breath on the accused's property, realised that they were acting illegally. The specimen proved positive. The accused was then arrested and, at the police station, provided another positive specimen. The appeal was allowed on the grounds that, the officers having acted *mala fide* and oppressively, the Crown Court, had it directed itself properly, could have exercised its discretion under s. 78 to exclude the evidence. See also *Mason* [1988] 1 WLR 139, in which a *deliberate* deceit was practised on both the accused and his solicitor and *Canale* [1990] 2 All ER 187, in which it was held that had the trial judge directed his mind to breaches of the interview rules under Code of Practice C which were 'flagrant', 'deliberate' and 'cynical', he would and should have concluded that the interviews should be excluded under s. 78.

Other authorities, however, adopting an approach designed to protect the suspect from being denied his civil rights, make it clear that the statutory discretion may be exercised even in the absence of *deliberate* or *wilful* misconduct. Thus, in *DPP v McGladrigan* [1991] RTR 297, the Divisional Court held that the argument on *mala fides* originated from *Fox*, a case decided before the PACE 1984 came into force, and that s. 78(1) of the 1984 Act gave the courts a new and considerably wider discretion. The court relied upon *Samuel* [1988] QB 615 to reject the argument that *mala fides* had to be established before the statutory discretion could be exercised. The court also pointed out that, insofar as *Matto v Wolverhampton Crown Court* suggested that in breathalyser cases *Fox* still applied, it should be noted that the case was not only a successful appeal by the accused, but also preceded *Samuel*. See also *Brine* [1992] Crim LR 123.

In *Foster* [1987] Crim LR 821 a confession was made after caution during an 'exchange' initiated by arresting officers at the police station. Evidence of the confession, based on a note compiled in the absence of the accused, was excluded under s. 78 on the grounds of breach of Code of Practice C: a contemporaneous record should have been made of the 'exchange', which was 'an interview'; a record should have been made of the reason why no contemporaneous record had been made; and the accused should have been given the opportunity to read and sign the written record of the interview. It was ruled that it was irrelevant whether the breaches were wilful or merely ignorant; in the absence of a contemporaneous record at the trial, the accused was deprived of the opportunity to demonstrate that his denial of the offence was not an afterthought but a denial which he made at the time of his arrest.

In *Alladice* (1988) 87 Cr App R 380, a case in which the accused had been improperly denied the right of access to a solicitor pursuant to the PACE 1984, s. 58, Lord Lane CJ, giving the reserved judgment of the Court of Appeal, held that if the police had acted in bad faith, the court would have little difficulty in ruling any confession inadmissible under s. 78; but that if the police, albeit in good faith, had nevertheless fallen foul of s. 58, it was still necessary for the court to decide whether admission of the evidence would adversely affect the fairness of the proceedings to such an extent that the confession ought to be excluded. (On the facts, however, it was held that had the trial judge considered s. 78, he would not have been obliged to exclude the evidence because the accused was well able to cope with the interviews, understood the cautions that he had been given — at times exercising his right to silence — and was aware of his rights. Thus if the solicitor had been present, his advice would have added nothing to the knowledge of his rights which the accused already had.) See also *Dunford* (1990) 91 Cr App R 150; *Parris* (1988) 89 Cr App R 68; *Walsh* (1989) 91 Cr App R 161; and *Anderson* [1993] Crim LR 447. In *Walsh*, Saville J, referring to breaches of s. 58 or the provisions of the Codes of Practice, said (at p. 163):

> . . . although bad faith may make substantial or significant that which might not otherwise be so, the contrary does not follow. Breaches which are themselves significant and substantial are not rendered otherwise by the good faith of the officers concerned.

Significant and Substantial Breaches In *Quinn* [1990] Crim LR 581, *Walsh* (1989) 91 Cr App R 161 and *Keenan* [1990] 2 QB 54 were referred to with approval as authority for the general proposition that a significant and substantial breach of a PACE Code may well result in the exclusion of evidence obtained in consequence, even in the absence of bad faith. Whether a breach is 'significant and substantial' for these purposes is clearly a question of fact and degree. In *Sparks* [1991] Crim LR 128 (in which the proviso to s. 2(1) of the Criminal Appeal Act 1968 was applied), breaches of Code C (failure to caution and failure to keep a proper interview record) were held to be substantial. See also *Okafor* [1994] 3 All ER 741 (failure to caution, to remind of the right to legal advice and to make a contemporaneous record of interview); and *Joseph* [1993] Crim LR 206 (failure to make contemporaneous record of interview), but cf. *Watson v DPP* (2004) 168 JP 116. In *Pall* (1992) 156 JP 424, it was held that the absence of a caution was bound to be significant in most circumstances. See also, concerning breaches of Code D, *Samms* [1991] Crim LR 197 (identification by confrontation: failure to show that it was impracticable to hold a parade or a group identification) and *Marcus* [2005] Crim LR 384 (failure in a video identification procedure to use images of persons bearing a sufficient resemblance to the accused). Contrast *Rajakuruna* [1991] Crim LR 458, where a breach of Code C (failure to inform a person not under arrest that he is not obliged to remain with the officer) was held to be not significant or substantial. In appropriate circumstances, breach of the right to legal advice in the PACE 1984, s. 58, and in the ECHR, Article 6(3)(c), may result in the exclusion of evidence (see generally **F17.20**). However, in the case of drink-driving offences the public interest requires that the obtaining of breath specimens should not be delayed to any significant extent in order to enable a suspect to take legal advice (*Kennedy v DPP* (2002) 166 JP 742 and *Campbell v DPP CPS* (2003) 167 JP 267); and it is a question of fact and degree in any given case whether the custody officer acted without delay to secure the provision of legal advice and whether the person held in custody was permitted to consult a solicitor as soon as was practicable (*Kirkup v DPP* (2004) 168 JP 255; *Whitley v DPP* (2004) 168 JP 350. Similarly, in the case of juveniles, there is no reason to delay the obtaining of specimens in order for an appropriate adult to be present (*R (DPP) v B* (2003) 167 JP 144). **F2.30**

It is important to stress that the test for exclusion is not the seriousness of the breach *per se*, but the extent of any unfairness caused thereby (see **F2.23**). In *Ryan* [1992] Crim LR 187, it was argued that the judge's conclusion that there had been a major breach of the identification code (Code of Practice D) should have sufficed to exclude the evidence. Rejecting this argument, the Court of Appeal pointed out that there had been occasions when there had been quite serious breaches but, it being established that this had not caused unjust prejudice to the accused, the judge had quite properly allowed the evidence in. In *Hoyte* [1994] Crim LR 215 a confession was admitted, despite a failure to caution, on the basis that the police had acted in good faith and, in the circumstances, there could have been no unfairness under

s. 78. The outcome was the same in *Senior* [2004] 3 All ER 9, where customs officers had asked a series of preliminary 'routine' questions without first cautioning the accused. See also, applying *Senior, Rehman* [2006] EWCA Crim 1900. Similarly in *Gill* [2004] 1 WLR 49 evidence obtained in a 'Hansard' interview was admitted, despite a failure to caution, on the basis that the interviewers had not acted in bad faith and the interviewees knew that criminal proceedings were in prospect and must have known that they were not obliged to answer questions. See also *Law-Thompson* [1997] Crim LR 674 (confessions made by a mentally disordered accused in the absence of an appropriate adult).

In *Wright* [1994] Crim LR 55, evidence of a search was admitted notwithstanding that a record of the search had not been made in W's custody record (contrary to s. 18(8) of the 1984 Act) and that there were said to have been breaches of PACE Code B (no communication had been made with W, he was not present at the search and no proper list had been made of the property). Noting that there had been no deliberate breach of Code B, it was held that the judge had taken into account the breach of s. 18(8) and the other matters could not have placed W at any disadvantage. See also *Khan* [1997] Crim LR 508 and *Sanghera* [2001] 1 Cr App R 299.

Section F3 Burden and Standard of Proof and Presumptions

BURDEN OF PROOF

Legal and Evidential Burdens

There are two principal kinds of burden, the legal burden and the evidential burden. The legal burden is a burden of proof, i.e. a burden imposed on a party to prove a fact or facts in issue. In some cases the legal burden in relation to some of the facts in issue will be on one party, and the legal burden in relation to another (or others) will be on the other party. For example, if insanity is raised by way of defence, the legal burden on that issue is on the defence, whereas the legal burden on the other facts in issue is on the prosecution (*M'Naghten's Case* (1843) 10 Cl & F 200; *Smith* (1910) 6 Cr App R 19). Any statutory provision imposing a legal burden on the accused may be open to challenge on the basis of incompatibility with Article 6(2) of the ECHR (see **F3.13**). Questions of construction are questions of law in respect of which no burden lies on either party (*Scott v Martin* [1987] 1 WLR 841). **F3.1**

The Legal Burden The legal burden is sometimes referred to as the persuasive burden or the risk of non-persuasion, phrases which indicate that a party bearing the legal burden on a fact in issue will lose on that issue if the burden is not discharged to the required standard of proof. The standard of proof required to discharge the legal burden varies according to whether the burden is borne by the prosecution or defence. If the legal burden is borne by the prosecution, the standard required is proof beyond reasonable doubt (*Woolmington v DPP* [1935] AC 462 — see further **F3.38**). If the legal burden is borne by the accused, the standard required is proof on a balance of probabilities (*Carr-Briant* [1943] KB 607); the accused never bears the heavier burden of proof beyond reasonable doubt — see further **F3.40**). The question whether a party has discharged a legal burden borne by him is decided by the tribunal of fact, whether jury or magistrates, at the end of the trial after all the evidence has been presented. **F3.2**

The Evidential Burden The evidential burden is not a burden of proof but the burden of adducing evidence or 'the duty of passing the judge', in other words the burden imposed on a party to adduce sufficient evidence on a fact or facts in issue to satisfy the judge that such issue or issues should be left before the tribunal of fact. In some cases, the evidential burden on some of the facts in issue will be on one party and the evidential burden on another (or others) will be on the other party. Very often a party bearing the legal burden on an issue also bears the evidential burden on that issue. However, in the case of many defences (including, for example, provocation and self-defence), the evidential burden in relation to the defence is on the accused and the legal burden in relation to the defence is on the prosecution. Thus, if the evidential burden is not discharged and there is insufficient evidence for that defence to be put before the jury, the issue will be withdrawn from the jury and nothing more will be heard of it; but if the evidential burden is discharged or, whether discharged or not, there is in any event sufficient evidence for that defence to be put before the jury, the legal burden of **F3.3**

negativing or disproving that defence will be on the prosecution (see, e.g., *Lobell* [1957] 1 QB 547, and generally **F3.28** to **F3.36**). Although normally a judge will not leave a particular defence to the jury until the conclusion of the evidence, in rare cases in which the precise nature of the evidence to be called is clear it may be appropriate for the judge to indicate at an earlier stage what his ruling is likely to be (*Pommell* [1995] 2 Cr App R 607 at p. 612). If, during a trial, a judge indicates that he will leave a particular defence to the jury, but later changes his view, he should inform the defence, because they may then wish to give more evidence on the matter and defence counsel may wish to seek to persuade the judge not to withdraw the issue (*Wright* [1992] Crim LR 596).

F3.4 **Discharge of Burdens Borne by the Prosecution** If the evidential burden on a particular issue is borne by the prosecution, it is discharged by the adduction of sufficient evidence to justify as a possibility a finding by the tribunal of fact that the legal burden on the same issue has been discharged, in other words 'such evidence as, if believed and if left uncontradicted and unexplained, could be accepted by the jury as proof' (*Jayasena v The Queen* [1970] AC 618, per Lord Devlin at p. 624). If the prosecution bear both the evidential and legal burden on a particular issue and discharge the evidential burden, it does not necessarily follow that they will succeed on that issue — the issue in question will go before the jury for them to determine whether or not the legal burden has been discharged. However, if the prosecution bear both the legal and evidential burden on an issue and fail to discharge the evidential burden, they will necessarily fail on that issue, since the judge will withdraw that issue from the jury. Questions relating to the sufficiency of the evidence adduced by the prosecution may be raised by the judge of his own motion, but usually arise on a defence submission of no case to answer after the prosecution have closed their case. As to submissions of no case to answer more generally, see **D15.51** ***et seq.***

F3.5 **Discharge of Burdens Borne by the Defence** If the accused bears both the evidential and the legal burden on a particular issue, for example insanity, the evidential burden is discharged by the adduction of such evidence as might satisfy the jury on the probability of that which the accused is called upon to establish (*Carr-Briant* [1943] KB 607, per Humphreys J at p. 612). If the accused bears the evidential but not the legal burden on a particular issue, for example self-defence, the evidential burden is discharged by the adduction of such evidence as 'might leave a jury in reasonable doubt' (*Bratty v A-G for Northern Ireland* [1963] AC 386, per Lord Morris at p. 419). In no case is the accused called upon to prove a fact beyond reasonable doubt: the standard of proof is proof on the balance of probabilities (*Carr-Briant*).

Incidence of Legal Burden: General Rule

F3.6 The general rule is that the prosecution bear the legal burden of proving all the elements in the offence necessary to establish guilt (*Woolmington v DPP* [1935] AC 462). See also *Mancini v DPP* [1942] AC 1, per Lord Simon at p. 11. In *Woolmington*, W was charged with the murder of his wife, who had left him to return to her mother. He visited her with a sawn-off shotgun concealed under his coat, and when they met she was killed by a shot from the gun. W said that while attempting to induce his wife to return to him by threatening to kill himself, the gun went off accidentally. Swift J directed the jury that, once it was proved that W shot his wife, W bore the burden of disproving malice aforethought. The House of Lords held this to be a misdirection. Viscount Sankey LC said, at pp. 481–2:

> But while the prosecution must prove the guilt of the prisoner, there is no such burden laid on the prisoner to prove his innocence and it is sufficient for him to raise a doubt as to his guilt; he is not bound to satisfy the jury of his innocence. . . .
>
> Throughout the web of the English criminal law one golden thread is always to be seen, that it is the duty of the prosecution to prove the prisoner's guilt subject to what I have already said as to the defence of insanity and subject also to any statutory exception. . . . No matter what the charge or where the trial, the principle that the prosecution must prove the guilt of the prisoner is part of the common law of England and no attempt to whittle it down can be entertained. . . . It

> is not the law of England to say, as was said in the summing-up in the present case: 'if the Crown satisfy you that this woman died at the prisoner's hands then he has to show that there are circumstances to be found in the evidence which has been given from the witness-box in this case which alleviate the crime so that it is only manslaughter or which excuse the homicide altogether by showing it was a pure accident'.

The prosecution bear the burden of proving all the elements in the offence, even if this involves proving negative averments. Thus, in a case of rape the prosecution bear the burden of proving that the complainant did not consent (*Horn* (1912) 7 Cr App R 200). Similarly, the prosecution bear the burden of proving absence of consent on a charge of assault (*Donovan* [1934] 2 KB 498). On a charge of obtaining property by deception, the prosecution bear the burden of proving the falsity of the statement, even if that involves proving a negative (*Mandry* [1973] 1 WLR 1232, in which the statement, made by street traders selling scent for £1, was 'You can go down the road and buy it for two guineas in the big stores'). *Mandry* also illustrates that there is a limit to what can reasonably be required of the prosecution when seeking to prove a negative. A constable gave evidence that he had visited four shops in the area and that the scent was not sold at any of them. In cross-examination, he admitted that he had not visited a well-known department store. The judge directed the jury that the police could not be expected to visit every shop in London in order to prove that the scent was not being sold for two guineas in any shop; and that if the accused knew of any shop where it could be bought at that price, they were perfectly entitled to adduce such evidence. The Court of Appeal held that no criticism could be made of this direction. In many cases, however, because of the difficulties of proving a negative proposition, statute may, exceptionally, require the accused to bear the burden of proving certain facts (see **F3.8** to **F3.12** and **F3.9**).

There are only three categories of exception to the general rule as laid down in *Woolmington v DPP* [1935] AC 462:

(a) insanity;
(b) express statutory exceptions; and
(c) implied statutory exceptions.

Statutory exceptions are sometimes referred to as reverse onus provisions.

Exception in Case of Defence of Insanity If the accused raises the defence of insanity, he will bear the burden of proving it (on a balance of probabilities) (*M'Naghten's Case* (1843) 10 Cl & F 200; *Smith* (1910) 6 Cr App R 19; *Sodeman v The King* [1936] 2 All ER 1138). Under the Criminal Procedure (Insanity) Act 1964, s. 6, if the accused is charged with murder and raises one of two issues, either insanity or diminished responsibility, the court shall allow the prosecution to adduce evidence tending to prove the other of those issues. The burden on the prosecution will be to prove the other of those issues beyond reasonable doubt (*Grant* [1960] Crim LR 424, per Paul J). **F3.7**

Criminal Procedure (Insanity) Act 1964, s. 6

> Where on a trial for murder the accused contends—
> (a) that at the time of the alleged offence he was insane so as not to be responsible according to law for his actions; or
> (b) that at that time he was suffering from such abnormality of mind as is specified in subsection (1) of section 2 of the Homicide Act 1957 (diminished responsibility), the court shall allow the prosecution to adduce or elicit evidence tending to prove the other of those contentions, and may give directions as to the stage of the proceedings at which the prosecution may adduce such evidence.

If an accused is alleged to be under a disability rendering him unfit to plead and stand trial on indictment, the issue may be raised by either the prosecution or defence (see the Criminal Procedure (Insanity) Act 1964, s. 4, and generally **D12.2** *et seq*). If the prosecution contend that the accused is under such a disability and this is disputed by the defence, the burden of proof is on the prosecution to satisfy the jury beyond reasonable doubt (*Robertson* [1968] 1 WLR 1767). If the defence contend that the accused is under such a disability, the burden is on the defence to satisfy the jury on a balance of probabilities (*Podola* [1960] 1 QB 325).

F3.8 **Express Statutory Exceptions** Statute may expressly cast on the accused the burden of proving a particular issue or issues. The legal burden in relation to all other issues in such cases will remain on the prosecution, in accordance with the general rule as laid down in *Woolmington v DPP* [1935] AC 462. An example is the Homicide Act 1957, s. 2.

Homicide Act 1957, s. 2

(2) On a charge of murder, it shall be for the defence to prove that the person charged is by virtue of this section [persons suffering from diminished responsibility] not liable to be convicted of murder.

Where the defence of diminished responsibility is raised, the onus is on the defence to prove it on a balance of probabilities (*Dunbar* [1958] 1 QB 1; *Grant* [1960] Crim LR 424). According to the Court of Appeal in *Lambert, Ali and Jordan* [2001] 2 WLR 211, s. 2(2) does not contravene the ECHR, Article 6(2).

Section 2(2) leaves it to the defence to decide whether the issue of diminished responsibility should be raised; if, therefore, the judge detects evidence of diminished responsibility but the defence do not raise the issue, the judge is not bound to direct the jury to consider the matter, but, at most, should in the absence of the jury draw the matter to the attention of the defence so that they may decide whether they wish the issue to be considered by the jury (*Campbell* (1986) 84 Cr App R 255, per Lord Lane CJ, *obiter*).

Prior to the coming into force of the HRA 1998, it could be said with confidence that statutory provisions which put on the accused an obligation to 'prove' a particular matter, had thereby cast a legal burden on the defence. However provisions of this kind and the decisions pertaining to them must now be read subject to the decision of the House of Lords in *Lambert* [2002] 2 AC 545 (discussed at **F3.13**) that in appropriate circumstances the words 'to prove' may be read down under the HRA 1998, s. 3 so as to impose on an accused no more than an evidential burden.

Prevention of Corruption Act 1916, s. 2 (see **B15.10**). Where corruption is presumed under s. 2, the onus is on the accused to prove on a balance of probabilities that a payment was not corrupt (*Carr-Briant* [1943] KB 607). The presumption in s. 2 does not apply to a conspiracy, contrary to the Criminal Law Act 1977, s. 1(1), to make corrupt payments contrary to the Prevention of Corruption Act 1906, s. 1 (*A-G, ex parte Rockall* [2000] 1 WLR 882).

Prevention of Crime Act 1953, s. 1 (see **B12.118**). In the case of an offensive weapon *per se*, the prosecution are not required to prove that the accused had it with him with the intention of using it to cause injury to the person; if possession in a public place is proved, the onus is on the accused to prove on a balance of probabilities lawful authority or reasonable excuse for the possession (*Davis v Alexander* (1970) 54 Cr App R 398). In the case of an article not made or adapted for use for causing injury to the person, the onus is on the prosecution to prove that the accused carried it with the intention of using it to injure; and if the jury are satisfied as to this, and the issue of lawful authority or reasonable excuse has been raised, the onus is on the accused to prove on a balance of probabilities such authority or excuse (*Petrie* [1961] 1 WLR 358; *Brown* (1971) 55 Cr App R 478).

For other examples, see the CJA 1925, s. 47 (see **A3.30**), and the Homicide Act 1957, s. 4(2) ('Where it is shown that a person charged with the murder of another killed the other or was a party to his . . . being killed, it shall be for the defence to prove that the person charged was acting in pursuance of a suicide pact between him and the other').

Implied Statutory Exceptions A statute can place the legal burden of proof on the accused not only expressly but also by implication, i.e. on its true construction. In summary trials, the matter is governed by the MCA 1980, s. 101. Concerning trials on indictment, the leading authorities are *Edwards* [1975] QB 27 and *Hunt* [1987] AC 352; in the latter it was made clear that when, in *Woolmington v DPP* [1935] AC 462, Viscount Sankey LC referred to 'any statutory exception' (see **F3.6**), he was referring to statutory exceptions in which Parliament had placed the burden of proof on the accused *either* expressly *or* by implication (per Lords Griffiths and Ackner). **F3.9**

Magistrates' Courts Act 1980, s. 101

> Where the defendant to an information or complaint relies for his defence on any exception, exemption, proviso, excuse or qualification, whether or not it accompanies the description of the offence or matter of complaint in the enactment creating the offence or on which the complaint is founded, the burden of proving the exception, exemption, proviso, excuse or qualification shall be on him; and this notwithstanding that the information or complaint contains an allegation negativing the exception, exemption, proviso, excuse or qualification.

The cases, in the ensuing commentary, in which statutory provisions have been so construed as to place a legal burden on the accused, must now be read subject to the HRA 1998 and the decisions discussed at **F3.13** *et seq.* Any implied statutory exception must now be open to challenge on the basis of incompatibility with the ECHR, Article 6(2). As to summary trials, it is submitted that 'the burden of proving' to which the MCA 1980, s. 101, refers always means the legal burden and therefore any implied statutory exception is capable of derogating from Article 6(2). It follows that for each such exception the question of compatibility will need to be considered by reference to the three-stage test set out in *Lambert* [2002] 2 AC 545, discussed at **F3.14** (cf. *per* Clarke LJ in *R (Grundy & Co Excavations Ltd) v Halton Division Magistrates' Court* (2003) 167 JP 387 at [60] and [61]).

Concerning the construction of s. 101, the following matters of general importance should also be noted:

(a) On its wording, s. 101 applies to summary trials. However, it is now established that where a statute, on its true construction, places the legal burden of proof on an accused, the burden is on the accused whether the case be tried summarily or on indictment; s. 101 reflects and applies to summary trials the common-law rule relating to the incidence of the burden of proof evolved by judges on trials on indictment (*Hunt* [1987] AC 352).
(b) The section applies where the words of exception etc. amount to a defence.
(c) In *Nimmo v Alexander Cowan & Sons Ltd* [1968] AC 107, Lord Pearson gave the following *obiter* guidance (at p. 135) as to the construction of the Scottish equivalent of s. 101. An exemption, exception or proviso is easily recognisable from the wording of the enactment — an exception would naturally begin with the word 'except' and a proviso with the words 'Provided always that'. The addition of the words 'excuse' and 'qualification' showed an intention to widen the provision. There is no usual formula for an 'excuse'. A 'qualification', if understood in a grammatical sense, might cover any adjective, adverb or adjectival or adverbial phrase. More probably it means some qualification, such as a licence, for doing what would otherwise be unlawful. There is no usual formula for 'qualification' in that sense. The court should look at the substance and effect of the enactment in question, as well as its form, in order to ascertain whether it contains an 'excuse or qualification'.

In a case of driving without a licence, it is for the accused driver to prove that he has a current driving licence (*John v Humphreys* [1955] 1 WLR 325). Similarly, in cases of driving without insurance, it is for the accused driver to prove that he is insured (*Williams v Russell* (1933) 149 LT 190; *Philcox v Carberry* [1960] Crim LR 563). In *Gatland v Metropolitan Police Commissioner* [1968] 2 QB 279, the accused had left a skip on the road with which a car had collided. They were charged with an offence under the Highways Act 1959, s. 140(1), which provided that 'if a person, without lawful authority or excuse, deposits anything whatsoever on a highway in consequence whereof a user of the highway is injured or endangered, that person shall be guilty of an offence'. The Divisional Court held that it was for the prosecution to prove that a thing had been deposited on the highway and that in consequence a user of the highway had been injured or endangered; but that it was for the accused to prove lawful authority or excuse. Contrast, *Westminster City Council v Croyalgrange* [1986] 1 WLR 674. See also, construing Environmental Protection Act 1990, s. 33(1)(a), *Environment Agency v M E Foley Contractors Ltd* [2002] 1 WLR 1754.

F3.10 *Nimmo v Alexander Cowan & Sons Ltd* *Nimmo v Alexander Cowan & Sons Ltd* [1968] AC 107 was a Scottish civil action brought by a workman under the Factories Act 1961, s. 29(1). Section 29(1) provides that every place at which any person has at any time to work 'shall, so far as is reasonably practicable, be made and kept safe for any person working there'. The question before the House of Lords was whether the burden of proving that it was not reasonably practicable to make the working place safe lay on the defendant or the plaintiff. The same question could have arisen in a criminal action: s. 155(1) of the 1961 Act makes a breach of s. 29(1) a summary offence. Both Lord Pearson (at p. 134) and Lord Reid (at p. 115) observed that the incidence of the burden of proof would be the same whether the proceedings were civil or criminal. The House divided on the construction of the section. The majority, Lords Guest, Upjohn and Pearson, held that it was for the plaintiff (or prosecution) to prove that the working place was not safe, and for the defendant (or accused) to excuse himself by proving that it was not reasonably practicable to make it safe. The minority, Lords Reid and Wilberforce, held that it was for the plaintiff (or prosecution) to prove that it was reasonably practicable to make the working place safe. Their lordships were in agreement, however, that if the linguistic construction of a statute does not clearly indicate on whom the burden should lie, the court should look to other considerations to determine the intention of Parliament, such as the mischief at which the Act was aimed and the ease or difficulty that the respective parties would encounter in discharging the burden.

F3.11 *Edwards* The MCA 1980, s. 101, sets out in statutory form the common-law rule which applies to trials on indictment. This was established in *Edwards* (1975) QB 27. Prior to *Edwards* there was a rule of statutory interpretation that 'if a negative averment be made by one party which is peculiarly within the knowledge of the other, the party within whose knowledge it lies, and who asserts the affirmative, is to prove it and not he who asserts the negative' (*Turner* (1816) 5 M & S 206, per Bayley J at p. 211). This approach was followed in *Oliver* [1944] KB 68 and *Ewens* [1967] 1 QB 322.

In *Edwards* [1975] QB 27, the accused was convicted on indictment of selling intoxicating liquor without a licence, contrary to the Licensing Act 1964, s. 160(1)(a). He appealed on the ground that the prosecution had failed to adduce any evidence to show that he was not the holder of a licence. It was submitted that at common law the burden of proving an exception, exemption and the like is borne by the accused only if the facts constituting such exception or exemption are peculiarly within the accused's own knowledge which, in the instant case, they were not, because the police had access to the public register of local licences. The Court of Appeal, dismissing the appeal, held that it was for the accused to prove that he was the holder of a licence. Referring to the common-law exception to the fundamental rule that the prosecution must prove every element of the offence charged, Lawton LJ said, at p. 40:

> It is limited to offences arising under enactments which prohibit the doing of an act save in specified circumstances or by persons of specified classes or with specified qualifications or with the licence or permission of specified authorities. Whenever the prosecution seeks to rely on this exception, the court must construe the enactment under which the charge is laid. If the true construction is that the enactment prohibits the doing of acts, subject to provisos, exemptions and the like, then the prosecution can rely upon the exception.

In our judgment its application does not depend upon either the fact, or the presumption, that the defendant has peculiar knowledge enabling him to prove the positive of any negative averment.

Hunt In *Hunt* [1987] AC 352, the House of Lords held that: F3.12

(a) *Edwards* was decided correctly, subject to one qualification. The formula given by Lawton LJ was 'a helpful approach' and 'an excellent guide to construction' but was not intended to be, and is not, exclusive in its effect — on rare occasions a statute will be construed as imposing the legal burden on the accused although outside the ambit of the formula (see the speech of Lord Griffiths, with which Lords Keith and Mackay agreed, at p. 365 and that of Lord Ackner at p. 379).
(b) In the final analysis each case must turn on the construction of the particular legislation to determine whether the defence is an exception within the meaning of the MCA 1980, s. 101, which reflects the rule for trials on indictment (per Lord Griffiths at p. 375).
(c) In construing an enactment in order to ascertain where the burden of proof lies, the court is not restricted to the form or wording of the statutory provision but is entitled to have regard to matters of policy. The court must look at the substance and effect of the enactment and practical considerations affecting the burden of proof, particularly the ease or difficulty that the respective parties would encounter in discharging the burden (per Lord Griffiths at p. 375 and per Lord Ackner at pp. 380 and 382). However, Parliament can never lightly be taken to have intended to impose an onerous duty on an accused to prove his innocence in a criminal case, and a court should be very slow to draw any such inference from the language of a statute (per Lord Griffiths at p. 374).

In *Hunt* [1987] AC 352, the appellant was found to be in possession of a powder containing morphine mixed with two other substances which were not controlled drugs. He was convicted of the unlawful possession of morphine, contrary to the Misuse of Drugs Act 1971, s. 5(2). Under the Misuse of Drugs Regulations 1973, sch. 1, para. 3, any preparation of morphine containing not more that 0.2 per cent of morphine compounded with other ingredients was excepted from the prohibition on possession contained in s. 5 of the 1971 Act. The question, on appeal, was whether it was for the prosecution to prove that the accused did not come within the exception contained in para. 3, or for the accused to prove that he did come within it. Quashing the conviction, the House of Lords held that:

(a) The case did not come within the formula, laid down by Lawton LJ in *Edwards* [1975] QB 27, as to when the legal burden is on the accused.
(b) On the true construction of the provisions, it was for the prosecution to prove not only that the powder contained morphine, but also that it was not morphine in the form permitted by para. 3. This would not place an undue burden on the prosecution. In the normal case the substance in question would be analysed for the police, and there would be no difficulty in producing evidence to show that it did not fall within sch. 1 to the 1973 Regulations. However, if the burden were to be placed on the accused, he would be faced with very real difficulties in discharging it, because the suspected substance is usually seized by the police and there is no statutory provision entitling the accused to a portion of it. Often there is very little of the substance, and it may have been destroyed in the process of analysis on behalf of the prosecution.
(c) Since the question of construction was obviously one of real difficulty, regard should be had to the fact that offences involving the misuse of hard drugs are among the most serious in the criminal calendar, and in these circumstances any ambiguity should be resolved in favour of the accused by placing the burden of proving the nature of the substance involved on the prosecution.

See also, in similar vein, *Makuwa* [2006] 1 WLR 2755: where the language of a statute does not make it clear whether the defence has to be established by the accused or negatived by the prosecution, the court should consider the mischief at which the statute was aimed and practical considerations affecting the burden of proof, in particular the ease or difficulty that the respective parties would encounter in discharging the burden.

The ruling in *Hunt* that regard may be had to the ease or otherwise that the respective parties will encounter if required to discharge the legal burden, gives an added validity, it is submitted, to a number of cases decided prior to *Edwards* [1975] QB 27 and difficult to reconcile with it. See, for example, *Curgerwen* (1865) LR 1 CCR 1 and *Putland* [1946] 1 All ER 85.

Incidence of the Legal Burden: the Human Rights Act 1998

F3.13 Any reverse onus provision is open to challenge on the basis of incompatibility with the ECHR, Article 6(2), which provides that 'everyone charged with a criminal offence shall be presumed innocent until proved guilty according to the law'. However, a reverse onus provision will not inevitably give rise to a finding of incompatibility (per Lord Hope in *Lambert* [2002] 2 AC 545 at [87]). It is now well settled that, in deciding the issue, the court should focus on the particular circumstances of the case and strike a reasonable balance between the general interest of the community and the protection of the fundamental rights of the individual. The relevant principles to be found in the jurisprudence of the European Court were summarised by Lord Bingham in *Sheldrake v DPP* [2005] 1 AC 264 at [21].

> The overriding concern is that a trial should be fair, and the presumption of innocence is a fundamental right directed to that end. The Convention does not outlaw presumptions of fact or law but requires that these should be kept within reasonable limits and should not be arbitrary. It is open to states to define the constituent elements of a criminal offence, excluding the requirement of *mens rea*. But the substance and effect of any presumption adverse to a defendant must be examined, and must be reasonable. Relevant to any judgment on reasonableness or proportionality will be the opportunity given to the defendant to rebut the presumption, maintenance of the rights of the defence, flexibility in application of the presumption, retention by the court of a power to assess the evidence, the importance of what is at stake and the difficulty which a prosecutor may face in the absence of a presumption. Security concerns do not absolve member states from their duty to observe basic standards of fairness. The justifiability of any infringement of the presumption of innocence cannot be resolved by any rule of thumb, but on examination of all the facts and circumstances of the particular provision as applied in the particular case.

The obvious drawback to a test so reliant on notions of fairness, reasonableness and proportionality is that views may reasonably differ so that in many cases it will be as possible to reach a rational conclusion of compatibility as incompatibility. A good example, in this respect, is furnished by *Keogh* [2007] 1 WLR 1500, where the Court of Appeal, reversing the decision of Aikens J, held that the Official Secrets Act 1989, ss. 2(3) and 3(4), could be 'read down' so as to impose only an evidential burden on the accused, on the basis that a reverse burden was not a necessary element in the operation of ss. 2 and 3, it being 'practicable' to require the prosecution to prove that the accused knew or had reasonable cause to believe that the information that he disclosed related to such matters as 'defence', and that its disclosure would be damaging.

The leading domestic authorities are *Johnstone* [2003] 1 WLR 1736 and *Sheldrake v DPP*, but it is useful to consider first the decision in *Lambert* and the subsequent cases in which it has been followed or distinguished.

F3.14 ***Lambert*: Misuse of Drugs Act 1971, s. 28** In *Lambert* [2002] 2 AC 545, the accused was charged with possession of cocaine with intent to supply contrary to the Misuse of Drugs Act 1971, s. 5(3). In his defence, he relied on s. 28 of the 1971 Act (see **B20.20**), asserting that he did not believe or suspect or have reason to suspect that the bag which he had carried contained cocaine. The trial judge directed the jury that under s. 28 the legal burden was on the accused. The Court of Appeal dismissed the appeal against conviction. One of the principal issues before the House of Lords was whether s. 28 as applied by the trial judge contravened Article 6(2) or could be interpreted, under the HRA 1998, s. 3(1), as placing on the accused an evidential burden only, i.e. in a way which would be compatible with Article 6. The House of Lords held (Lord Steyn dissenting) that, since the trial had taken place before the coming into force of the 1998 Act, the accused was not entitled to rely in an appeal after the Act had come into force on an alleged breach of his rights under the ECHR by the trial judge. On the question of compatibility with Article 6, the House was of the view (Lord Hutton dissenting) that s. 28 is not compatible with Article 6(2) but, under s. 3 of the 1998 Act, may be read as imposing only an evidential burden on the accused. The words 'to prove' in s. 28(2) (and 'if he proves' in s. 28(3)) can be taken to mean 'to give sufficient evidence' (see per Lord Steyn at [42] and Lord Hope at [94]).

In his judgment, Lord Steyn approached the question of compatibility in three stages by asking first whether s. 5(3) of the 1971 Act, read with s. 28, interfered with Article 6(2) and, if so, secondly whether there was an objective justification for such interference and thirdly whether it was proportionate, i.e. no greater than was necessary. As to the first question, it was held that s. 28 was an ingredient of the offence under s. 5(3) in that knowledge of the existence and control of the contents of the container is the gravamen of the offence, taking into account that s. 28 deals directly with the situation where the accused is denying moral blameworthiness and the fact that the maximum prescribed penalty is life imprisonment, and therefore s. 28 derogates from the presumption of innocence. Lord Steyn also reached this conclusion on broader grounds. He held that the answer should not turn on the distinction between constituent elements of the crime and defensive issues, which will sometimes be unprincipled and arbitrary. Lord Steyn said (at [35]; cf. Lord Hutton at [185]):

> After all, it is sometimes simply a matter of which drafting technique is adopted: a true constituent element can be removed from the definition of the crime and cast as a defensive issue whereas any definition of an offence can be reformulated so as to include all possible defences within it. It is necessary to concentrate not on technicalities and niceties of language but rather on matters of substance.

Lord Steyn (at [35]) adopted the reasoning of Dickson CJC, giving the judgment of the Canadian Supreme Court in *Whyte* (1988) 51 DLR 4th 481: 'If an accused is required to prove some fact on the balance of probabilities to avoid conviction, the provision violates the presumption of innocence because it permits a conviction in spite of a reasonable doubt in the mind of the tribunal of fact as to the guilt of the accused'. As to the second question, Lord Steyn was satisfied that there was an objective justification for interference with the burden of proof in the 1971 Act. Sophisticated drug smugglers, dealers and couriers typically secrete drugs in some container, enabling the person in possession to say that he was unaware of the contents. Such defences are commonplace and pose real difficulties for the police and prosecuting authorities. Turning to the third question, the principle of proportionality required the House to consider whether it was necessary to impose a legal rather than an evidential burden on the accused. Lord Steyn noted that to put a legal burden on the accused had a far-reaching consequence, that a guilty verdict may be returned in respect of an offence punishable by life imprisonment even though the jury may consider that it is reasonably possible that the accused had been duped. The burden of showing that *only* a reverse legal burden can overcome the difficulties of the prosecution in drugs cases was a heavy one. A 'new realism' had significantly reduced the problems faced by the prosecution in drugs cases. First, the relevant facts usually being peculiarly within the knowledge of the possessor of the container, such possession presumptively suggests, in the absence of exculpatory evidence, knowledge of the contents. Secondly, the judge can now comment on an accused's failure to mention facts when questioned or charged under the CJPOA 1994, s. 34 (see **F19.4**). Thirdly, in cases where a 'mixed statement' is received in evidence, the judge may direct that excuses do not have the same weight as the incriminating part of the statement (see **F17.63**). For these reasons, s. 28 did not satisfy the criterion of proportionality but was a disproportionate reaction to the perceived difficulties facing the prosecution in drugs cases. However, under s. 3 of the HRA 1998, the words 'to prove' in s. 28(2) (and 'if he proves' in s. 28(3)) could be read as placing only an evidential burden on the accused.

F3.15 ***L v DPP*: CJA 1988, s. 139(4)** *Lambert* [2002] 2 AC 545 was distinguished in *L v DPP* [2003] QB 137, a case of being in possession of a lock-knife contrary to the CJA 1988, s. 139 (see **B12.131**), in relation to s. 139(4), whereby it is a defence for an accused 'to prove that he had good reason or lawful authority for having the article with him in a public place'. Striking 'a fair balance', it was held that s. 139(4) does not conflict with the ECHR, Article 6. Six reasons were given. (1) Under s. 139 it is for the prosecution to prove that the accused knowingly had the article in his possession. (2) There is a strong public interest in bladed articles not being carried in public without good reason. (3) The accused is proving something within his own knowledge. (4) Notwithstanding the adversarial nature of English proceedings, an accused, whether he gives evidence or not, is entitled, under Article 6, to expect the court to scrutinise the evidence with a view to deciding if a good reason exists. (5) In the great majority of cases the tribunal of fact makes a judgment as to whether there was a good reason without the decision depending on whether it has to be proved that there is a good reason. (6) Limited weight should be given, in striking the balance, to the much more restricted power of sentence for an offence under s. 139 than for an offence under the MDA 1971, s. 28. See also *Mathews* [2004] QB 690, applying *L v DPP* in relation to both s. 139(4) and (5) of the 1988 Act.

F3.16 ***Drummond*: RTOA 1988, s. 15** *Lambert* [2002] 2 AC 545 was also distinguished in *Drummond* [2002] 2 Cr App R 352, in relation to the 'hip flask' defence in RTOA 1988, s. 15, whereby it is for the accused to prove that he consumed alcohol before providing a specimen and after the offence (see **C5.33**). The court noted that the offence of driving while over the limit does not require the court to ascertain the accused's intent; that conviction follows a scientific test which is intended to be as exact as possible; that if an accused drinks after the event, it is he who defeats the aim of the legislature by making the test potentially unreliable; and that the relevant scientific evidence to set against the specimen result is within the knowledge or means of access of the accused. For these reasons it was held that the legislative interference with the presumption of innocence in s. 15 was not only justified, but was no greater than was necessary.

F3.17 ***DPP v Barker*: RTOA 1988, s. 37(3)** In *DPP v Barker* (2004) 168 JP 617, B was charged with driving while disqualified and relied on the RTOA 1988, s. 37(3), whereby a person disqualified from driving is entitled to hold a provisional licence and to drive a vehicle in accordance with its conditions. It was held that the MCA 1980, s. 101 applied (see **F3.9**) and therefore the burden was on B to show that he had a provisional licence and was driving in accordance with its conditions. The burden was held to be wholly proportionate; as to being the holder of a provisional licence, the burden could easily be discharged by producing the licence; and as to the conditions of the licence, in some cases, in the absence of any information from the accused as to the identity of a passenger, it would be impossible for the prosecution to establish his identity and that he was the holder of a licence and therefore qualified to be supervising the driver.

F3.18 ***Johnstone*: Trade Marks Act 1994, s. 92(5)** *Johnstone* [2003] 1 WLR 1736 concerned the Trade Marks Act 1994, s. 92(5), whereby it is a defence for a person charged with an offence under s. 92 (unauthorised use of a trade mark) to show that he believed on reasonable grounds that use of a sign was not an infringement of the trade mark. The House of Lords, approving the decision of the Court of Appeal in *S* [2003] 1 Cr App R 602 was of the unanimous *obiter* view that s. 92(5) should be interpreted as imposing on the accused the legal burden and that this interpretation was compatible with Article 6(2). According to Lord Nicholls (at [50] and [51]):

> A sound starting point is to remember that if an accused is required to prove a fact on the balance of probability . . . this permits a conviction in spite of the fact-finding tribunal having a reasonable doubt as to the guilt of the accused . . . This consequence of a reverse burden of proof should colour one's approach when evaluating the reasons why it is said that, in the absence of a persuasive burden on the accused, the public interest will be prejudiced to an extent which justifies placing a persuasive burden on the accused. The more serious the punishment which may flow from conviction, the more compelling must be the reasons. The extent and nature of the factual matters required to be proved by the accused, and their importance relative to the matters required to be proved by the prosecution, have to be taken into account. So also does the extent to which the burden on the accused relates to facts which, if they exist, are readily provable by him as matters within his own knowledge or to which he has ready access.
>
> In evaluating these factors the court's role is one of review. Parliament, not the court, is charged with the primary responsibility for deciding, as a matter of policy, what should be the constituent elements of a criminal offence . . . The court will reach a different conclusion from the legislature only when it is apparent the legislature has attached insufficient importance to the fundamental right of an individual to be presumed innocent until proved guilty.

In relation to s. 92, it was held that two particular factors constituted compelling reasons why s. 92(5) put a legal burden on the accused. First, those who trade in brand products are aware of the need to be on guard against counterfeit goods. They are aware of the need to deal with reputable suppliers and to keep records and of the risks they take if they do not. Second, that whereas the s. 92(5) defence relates to facts within the accused's own knowledge and his sources of supply are known to him, by and large it is to be expected that those who supply traders with counterfeit products, if traceable at all by outside investigators, are unlikely to be cooperative. So, in practice, if the prosecution must prove that a trader acted dishonestly, there would be fewer investigations and prosecutions. Among the other factors considered was an important policy consideration: to protect consumers and honest manufacturers and traders. Counterfeiting is a serious contemporary problem with adverse economic effects on genuine trade and on consumers, in terms of quality of goods, and, sometimes, on health or safety.

***A-G's Ref (No. 1 of 2004)*: Insolvency Act 1986** In *A-G's Ref (No. 1 of 2004)* [2004] 1 WLR 2111, a five-judge Court of Appeal was convened to hear five appeals. The first two appeals concerned the same statutory provisions in the Insolvency Act 1986, namely s. 353(1), whereby a bankrupt is guilty of an offence if he does not inform the official receiver of a disposal of property comprised in his estate (see **B7.43**), s. 357(1), whereby a bankrupt is guilty of an offence if he makes, or in the five years before the start of the bankruptcy made, any gift or transfer of, or any charge on, his property (see **B7.47**) and s. 352, under which a person is not guilty of an offence under either s. 353(1) or s. 357(1), among others, if he had no intent to defraud or to conceal the state of his affairs (see **B7.42**). It was held that (1) s. 352, if interpreted as imposing a legal burden on the accused for the purposes of s. 353(1), does not breach Article 6 and (2) s. 352, if interpreted as imposing a legal burden on the accused for the purposes of s. 357(1), does breach Article 6 but can be read down so as to impose only an evidential burden. The reason given for the conclusion in (1) was that the proper working of insolvency law depends on the inclusion in the assets of an insolvent company, and in the estate of a bankrupt, of all the assets that should be comprised in them; that concealment or disposal of such assets to the disadvantage of the creditors can be done alone and in private; and that whether there has been fraud will often be known only to the individuals in question. These considerations normally justify the imposition on an accused who is proved to have deliberately acted in a manner that gives rise to an inference that he sought to defraud his creditors, of the burden of proving that he did not intend to do so. It was further held that the decision in *Carass* [2002] 1 WLR 1714 cannot stand with *Johnstone* [2003] 1 WLR 1736 and must be treated as impliedly overruled. In *Carass* it was held that s. 206(4) of the 1986 Act, whereby, in relation to various offences of fraud in anticipation of winding up, it is a defence for an accused to prove that he had no intent to defraud F3.19

(see **B7.30**), must be regarded as imposing only an evidential burden. The reason given for the conclusion in (2) above was the very wide ambit of s. 357. For example, it applies to disposals made long before the commencement of bankruptcy, and possibly at a time when there was no indication of insolvency, and the prosecution does not have to prove that the bankrupt was aware of the possibility of his insolvency. In these circumstances, to require the bankrupt to prove that he had no intent to defraud is not justified and infringes Article 6.

F3.20 *A-G's Ref (No. 1 of 2004)*: **Protection from Eviction Act 1977** The third appeal in *A-G's Ref (No. 1 of 2004)* [2004] 1 WLR 2111 concerned the Protection from Eviction Act 1977, s. 1(2), whereby if a person unlawfully deprives the residential occupier of any premises of his occupation or the premises, he shall be guilty of an offence 'unless he proves that he believed, and had reasonable cause to believe, that the residential occupier had ceased to reside in the premises' (see **B13.1**). It was held that this reverse burden was justified for three reasons. First, the essence of the offence is unlawfully depriving the occupier of his occupation of the premises, and the defence is only available if the accused can bring himself within a narrow class of exception. Second, the circumstances relied upon by the accused are peculiarly within his own knowledge. Third, the imposition of a criminal penalty is designed to regulate conduct in the public interest and there is a strong public interest in deterring landlords from ejecting tenants unlawfully.

F3.21 *A-G's Ref (No. 1 of 2004)*: **Homicide Act 1957, s. 4(2)** The fourth appeal in *A-G's Ref (No. 1 of 2004)* [2004] 1 WLR 2111 concerned the Homicide Act 1957, s. 4(2), which provides that 'Where it is shown that a person charged with the murder of another killed the other it shall be for the defence to prove that the person charged was acting in pursuance of a suicide pact between him and the other'. It was held that the legal burden is on the accused. The defence only arises once the prosecution has proved all the elements of murder and therefore the burden to justify the reverse burden of showing that it is proportional is more readily discharged. The penalty for murder is of the harshest kind, but in the Homicide Act 1957 Parliament singled out the defences of diminished responsibility and suicide pacts as requiring proof by an accused. Parliament no doubt had in mind the fact that in many cases the only evidence of a suicide pact would emanate from the survivor. The facts to establish the defence lie within the accused's knowledge and the reverse burden provides protection for society from murder disguised as a suicide pact killing.

F3.22 *A-G's Ref (No. 1 of 2004)*: **CJPOA 1994, s. 51(7)** The fifth appeal in *A-G's Ref (No. 1 of 2004)* [2004] 1 WLR 2111 concerned the CJPO 1994, s. 51(7), whereby if it is proved that the accused did an act which intimidated or was intended to intimidate another person ('the victim'), and that he did so knowing or believing that the victim was assisting in the investigation of an offence or was a witness or potential witness or a juror or potential juror in proceedings for an offence, he shall be presumed, 'unless the contrary is proved', to have done the act with the intention of thereby causing the investigation or the course of justice to be obstructed, perverted or interfered with (see **B14.41**). It was held that although the reverse burden involved an ingredient of the offence, not a special defence, the imposition of a legal burden on the accused was both justified and proportional. Witness and jury intimidation is a very serious threat to the administration of criminal justice which has substantially increased and continues to do so and it is understandable that Parliament should wish to take strong measures to stamp it out. Once all the matters that give rise to the presumption are proved, it is entirely reasonable that the burden of proving lack of intention should rest with the accused. In balancing the potential detriment to the accused and the mischief Parliament is seeking to eradicate, the balance comes down firmly in favour of the prosecution.

F3.23 *Sheldrake v DPP*: **General** In *A-G's Ref (No. 1 of 2004)*, [2004] 1 WLR 2111 Lord Woolf CJ, giving the judgment of the court, saw the need to simplify the task of lower courts when faced with reverse onus provisions by providing them with guidance on the relevant principles to be applied. The court noted the large number of authorities on the subject and the conflicting messages some of them gave. In particular the court noted the significant difference in emphasis between the approaches of Lord Steyn in *Lambert* [2002] 2 AC 545 and Lord Nicholls in *Johnstone* [2003] 1 WLR 1736, and that 'few provisions will be left as imposing a legal burden on Lord Steyn's approach' (at [38]). It was suggested that until clarification by a further decision of the House of Lords, the lower courts, if in doubt as to what should be the outcome of a challenge to a reverse burden, should follow the approach of Lord Nicholls rather than that of Lord Steyn. Lord Woolf also set out 'General Guidance' in the form of ten general principles. However, in *Sheldrake v DPP* [2005] 1 AC 264, the House of Lords held that both *Lambert* and *Johnstone*, unless or until revised or supplemented, should be regarded as the primary domestic authorities on reverse burdens; that nothing said in *Johnstone* suggested an intention to depart from or modify *Lambert*, which should not be treated as superseded or implicitly overruled; and that the differences in emphasis were explicable by the difference in the subject matter of the two cases. The House also expressly declined to endorse Lord Woolf's 'General Guidance', save to the extent that it was in accordance with the opinions of the House in *Lambert* and *Johnstone*. Lord Bingham said that the task of the court is never to decide whether a reverse burden should be imposed on an accused, but always to assess whether a burden enacted by Parliament unjustifiably infringes the presumption of innocence, and questioned Lord Woolf's assumption that Parliament would not make an exception without good reason. Such an assumption, it was held, may lead the court to give too much weight to the enactment under review and too little weight to the presumption of innocence and the obligation imposed on the court by s. 3.

***Sheldrake v DPP*: RTA 1988, s. 5(2)** In *Sheldrake v DPP* [2005] 1 AC 264, the House heard two conjoined appeals. The first concerned the RTA 1988, s. 5(2) (see C5.23), whereby it is a defence for a person charged with an offence of being in charge of a motor vehicle on a road or other public place after consuming excess alcohol to prove that, at the time of the alleged offence, the circumstances were such that there was no likelihood of his driving the vehicle whilst the proportion of alcohol in his breath, blood or urine remained likely to exceed the prescribed limit. It was held that even on the assumption that s. 5(2) infringes the presumption of innocence, it was directed to the legitimate object of preventing death, injury and damage caused by unfit drivers and met the tests of acceptability identified in the Strasbourg jurisprudence. It was not objectionable to criminalise conduct in these circumstances without requiring the prosecutor to prove criminal intent. The accused has a full opportunity to show that there was no likelihood of his driving, a matter so closely conditioned by his own knowledge at the time as to make it much more appropriate for him to prove the absence of a likelihood of his driving on the balance of probabilities than for the prosecutor to prove such a likelihood beyond reasonable doubt. The imposition of a legal burden did not go beyond what was necessary. Counsel had submitted that all burdens on the defence should be evidential only. It was held that such a fundamental change was not mandated by Strasbourg authority and remained a matter for Parliament and not the House of Lords. **F3.24**

***Sheldrake v DPP*: Terrorism Act 2000, s. 11(2)** The second appeal in *Sheldrake v DPP* [2005] 1 AC 264 concerned the Terrorism Act 2000, s. 11(1) and (2). **F3.25**

Terrorism Act 2000, s. 11

(1) A person commits an offence if he belongs or professes to belong to a proscribed organisation.

(2) It is a defence for a person charged with an offence under subsection (1) to prove—
 (a) that the organisation was not proscribed on the last (or only) occasion on which he became a member or began to profess to be a member, and
 (b) that he has not taken part in the activities of the organisation at any time while it was proscribed.

The House was of the unanimous opinion that the ingredients of the offence are set out fully in s. 11(1) and that s. 11(2) adds no further ingredient. The House also held, by majority,

F

Part F Evidence

that s. 11(2) is incompatible with art. 6 and should be read and given effect as imposing on the accused an evidential burden only. Six reasons were given for the conclusion of incompatibility.

(1) The extraordinary breadth of s. 11(1) and the uncertain scope of the word 'profess' are such that some of those liable to be convicted and punished under s. 11(1) may be guilty of no conduct that can reasonably be regarded as blameworthy or such as should properly attract criminal sanctions. As to the breadth of the subsection, it covers, for example, a person who joined an organisation when it was not a terrorist organisation or not a proscribed organisation, or when, if it was, he did not know that it was. There would be a clear breach of the presumption of innocence and a real risk of unfair conviction if such a person could exonerate himself only by establishing the defence provided and it was the clear duty of the courts to protect an accused against such a risk.
(2) As to s. 11(2)(b), it may be all but impossible for an accused to show that he has not taken part in the activities of the organisation. Terrorist organisations do not generate minutes or records on which he can rely and although he can assert his non-participation, his evidence may well be discounted as unreliable.
(3) If s. 11(2) imposes a legal burden and the accused fails to prove the matters specified, there is no room for the exercise of discretion — the court must convict him.
(4) The penalty for the offence, imprisonment for up to 10 years, is severe.
(5) Security considerations carry weight, but they do not absolve member states from their duty to ensure that basic standards of fairness are observed.
(6) Little significance can be attached to the requirement in s. 117 that the DPP gives his consent to a prosecution because art. 6 is concerned with the procedure relating to the trial of a criminal case and not the decision to prosecute.

As to the reading down of s. 11(2), there could be no doubt that Parliament intended it to impose a legal burden on the accused, because s. 118 of the Act lists a number of sections that are to be understood as imposing an evidential burden only and s. 11(2) is not among those listed. However, the majority held that s. 11(2) should be treated as if s. 118 applied to it, on the basis that, although that was not the intention of Parliament when enacting the 2000 Act, it was the intention of Parliament when enacting the HRA 1998, s. 3.

F3.26 *Makuwa*: **Immigration and Asylum Act 1999, s. 31(1)** *Makuwa* [2006] 1 WLR 2755 concerned the Immigration and Asylum Act 1999, s. 31(1), whereby it is a defence to various offences, including using a false instrument contrary to the Forgery and Counterfeiting Act 1981, s. 3, for a refugee to show that, having come to the UK directly from another country where his life was threatened, he (a) presented himself to the UK authorities without delay, (b) showed good cause for his illegal entry or presence, and (c) made a claim for asylum as soon as was reasonably practicable after his arrival in the UK. The accused was charged with using a false instrument — a false passport — contrary to s. 3 of the 1981 Act and relied upon s. 31(1) of the 1999 Act. The Court of Appeal held that the accused bore the legal burden in relation to all the matters in s. 31(1) except the issue of refugee status and that the infringement of ECHR, Article 6(2) was justifiable as a proportionate way of achieving the legitimate objective of maintaining proper immigration controls by restricting the use of forged passports, one of the principal means by which they were likely to be overcome.

F3.27 **Regulatory Offences** According to Lord Clyde in *Lambert* [2002] 2 AC 545 the imposition of a legal burden on the accused may be acceptable in the case of statutory offences which are concerned to regulate the conduct of some particular activity in the public interest. Lord Clyde said at [154]: 'The requirement to have a licence in order to carry on certain kinds of activity is an obvious example. The promotion of health and safety and the avoidance of pollution are among the purposes to be served by such controls. These kinds of cases may properly be seen as not truly criminal. Many may be relatively trivial and only involve a monetary penalty. Many may carry with them no real social disgrace of infamy'. This line of reasoning has been relied upon in subsequent cases, including *S* (see above) in which the Court of Appeal (at [48]) regarded the Trade Marks Act 1994, s. 92, as being in the nature of a regulatory offence with a degree of moral obloquy rather less than the 'truly criminal' cases. *Davies v Health and Safety Executive* (2002) *The Times*, 27 December 2002 concerned the Health and Safety at Work Act 1974, ss. 3(1) and 33(1), which together make it an offence for an employer to fail to discharge the duty to conduct his undertaking in such a way as to ensure, so far as is reasonably practicable, that persons not in his employment who may be affected thereby are not exposed to risks to their health and safety, and s. 40 of the Act whereby, for these purposes, 'it shall be for the accused to prove . . . that it was not reasonably practicable to do more than was in fact done to satisfy the duty'. It was held that since s. 40 related to an ingredient of the offence under ss. 3 and 33, it did make some inroad into the presumption of innocence, but that the imposition of a legal burden on the accused was justified, necessary and proportionate. Important reasons given for reaching this conclusion included the fact that the Act was regulatory, its purpose to secure the health, safety and welfare of employees and others, that the offences in question involved no risk of imprisonment and that the moral obloquy was less than that of truly criminal offences. See also *R (Grundy & Co Excavations Ltd) v Halton Division Magistrates' Court* (2003) 167 JP 387, in relation to the exceptions from the necessity for a licence for the felling of trees in the Forestry Act 1967, s. 9 and the relevant regulations. In that case it was held that the offence of tree felling was a classic regulatory offence, designed to protect the nation's trees, which involved only a monetary penalty and carried no real social disgrace, infamy, or moral stigma or obloquy.

Incidence of the Evidential Burden: General Rule

Generally speaking, a party bearing the legal burden on a particular issue will also bear the evidential burden on that issue. Thus, as a general rule, the prosecution bear both the legal and evidential burden in relation to all the elements in the offence necessary to establish guilt; and where the defence bear the legal burden of proving insanity or, by virtue of an express or implied statutory exception, some other issue, they will also bear the evidential burden in that regard (although, concerning insanity, in rare and exceptional cases the judge may of his own motion raise the issue and leave it to the jury: *Thomas* [1995] Crim LR 314). In relation to numerous common-law and statutory defences, however, the evidential burden is on the defence, and, if it is discharged so that the defence in question is put before the jury, the legal burden is then on the prosecution to disprove such defence. Although it is said in these cases that the evidential burden is on the defence, that burden will be discharged *whenever* there is sufficient evidence in relation to the defence to leave it to the jury; the evidence may be adduced by the defence (or elicited by them in cross-examination), *or* it may be given by a prosecution witness (or a co-accused) giving his evidence in chief *or* it may be given in any other way (*Bullard v The Queen* [1957] AC 635). Where such a defence arises upon the evidence called by any party, then whether or not it has been mentioned by the defence, the judge must leave it to the jury (*Palmer v The Queen* [1971] AC 814 at p. 823). See also *Bonnick* (1978) 66 Cr App R 266, *Hopper* [1915] 2 KB 431 at p. 435 and *DPP (Jamaica) v Bailey* [1995] 1 Cr App R 257; and cf. *Groark* [1999] Crim LR 669, considered at **F3.33**. If there is no evidence to support the defence upon which an accused seeks to rely, the judge is entitled to withdraw the case from the jury (see *Hill* (1988) 89 Cr App R 74 and *Pommell* [1995] 2 Cr App R 607). However it has been said that even if there is no evidence in support of a defence and it is not raised by defence counsel (perhaps for tactical reasons), if there is a reasonable possibility on one interpretation of the evidence adduced that the accused may have that defence, the judge should put it to the jury (*Watson* [1992] Crim LR 434). The defences to which the foregoing principles relate are as follows. **F3.28**

Provocation A judge is under no duty to put before the jury strained and implausible inferences for the purpose of creating a defence of provocation for which, in truth, there is no **F3.29**

basis (*Walch* [1993] Crim LR 714; see also *Wellington* [1993] Crim LR 616). The judge is required to leave the defence to the jury only if there is some evidence, from whatever source, suggestive of the reasonable possibility that the accused might have lost his self-control due to provoking words or conduct, because without some evidence of the specific nature of the provocation, the jury cannot decide either the subjective or the objective condition under the Homicide Act 1957, s. 3. If there is no such evidence, but merely the speculative possibility of an act of provocation, the issue does not arise, and suggestions in cross-examination cannot by themselves raise the issue (*Acott* [1997] 1 WLR 306; see also *Kromer* [2002] EWCA Crim 1278 and *Miao* (2003) *The Times*, 26 November 2003; and cf. *Stewart* [1995] 4 All ER 999). If there is sufficient evidence of provocation, whether called by the Crown or the defence, the issue should be put before the jury and the prosecution bear the burden of disproving it beyond reasonable doubt (*Mancini v DPP* [1942] AC 1; *Cascoe* [1970] 2 All ER 833; *McPherson* (1957) 41 Cr App R 213). In *Hopper* [1915] 2 KB 431, it was held that provocation should have been left to the jury in a murder trial at which the defence had been accident. See also *Rossiter* [1994] 2 All ER 752 in which the issue of provocation was not raised by the defence, the accused maintaining that she was defending herself. It was held that whenever there is material, on a charge of murder, which is capable of amounting to provocation, however tenuous it may be, the judge should leave that issue to the jury. This principle applies even if the defence do not rely on provocation but rely instead on accident (*Dhillon* [1997] 2 Cr App R 104) or maintain that the accused was not at the scene of the crime or that he was there but that the crime was committed by someone else (*Cambridge* [1994] 1 WLR 971, also explaining that the word 'tenuous', as used in *Rossiter*, described the provocative acts and words, not the evidence of their existence). The principle also applies even if the defence have conveyed to the judge that in their opinion the issue should *not* be left to the jury (*Burgess* [1995] Crim LR 425). However, it is most unsatisfactory that where the defence do not rely on provocation at the trial, the judge's failure to direct the jury on it can found an appeal against conviction. For this reason, in *Cox* [1995] 2 Cr App R 513 it was held that if it appears to *either* counsel that there is evidence on which the jury could find provocation, they should regard it as their duty to point it out to the judge before he sums up. There are compelling grounds, it is submitted, for extending this duty so that it applies in relation to other defences, and not just provocation. Where there is sufficient evidence of provocation, but the trial judge fails to leave the issue before the jury, so that they are deprived of the opportunity, in accordance with the Homicide Act 1957, s. 3, to consider whether any provocation was enough to make a reasonable man do as the accused did, the Court of Appeal may nonetheless conclude that the conviction is safe. The proper approach is to take the evidence in support of the possible defence at the highest it can reasonably be put and to ask whether at least ten members of the jury, not being perverse, inevitably and surely would have concluded that the provocative conduct was not enough to make a reasonable man do as the accused did, taking into account everything done or said according to the effect which it would have had on a reasonable man (*Van Dongen* [2005] 2 Cr App R 632).

F3.30 **Self-defence** In *Lobell* [1957] 1 QB 547 the appellant was convicted of wounding with intent to cause grievous bodily harm. There was some evidence to support his defence of self-defence. The trial judge directed the jury that it was for the defence to establish that plea to their satisfaction. The conviction was quashed on the grounds that this was a misdirection. Although the prosecution are not obliged to give evidence in chief to rebut a suggestion of self-defence before the issue is raised, once there is sufficient evidence to leave the issue before the jury, it is for the prosecution to disprove it beyond reasonable doubt. In *Wheeler* [1967] 3 All ER 829, Winn LJ said (at p. 830) that wherever there has been a killing or the infliction of violence not proving fatal, in circumstances in which the accused puts forward a justification such as self-defence, it is quite essential that the jury should understand that the issue is not properly to be regarded as a defence; and where the judge does slip into the error of referring to such justification as a defence, it is particularly important that he should use language which suffices to make it clear to the jury that it is not a defence in respect of which any onus rests upon the accused, but a matter which the prosecution must disprove as an essential part of their case before a verdict of guilty is justified. See also *Abraham* [1973] 1 WLR 1270, at p. 1273. There may be evidence of self-defence even if the defence of the accused is one of alibi. In *Bonnick* (1978) 66 Cr App R 266, a case of stabbing in which the defence was one of alibi, it was held, rejecting the contention that the evidence of the Crown witnesses had raised the issue of self-defence, that the question whether there was sufficient evidence to leave an issue before the jury was a question for the trial judge to answer by applying common sense to the evidence; but when there was sufficient evidence to raise a prima facie case, the issue should be left to the jury. In *Dickens* [2005] EWCA Crim 2017, it was held that since, in the particular circumstances of the case, it was extremely difficult to disentangle the defences of self-defence and accident and unwise to approach the facts as if they fell within mutually exclusive compartments, both defences should have been left to the jury.

Duress The Crown are not called upon to anticipate a defence of duress and destroy it in advance, but if the accused places before the court such material as makes duress a live issue, fit and proper to be left to the jury, it is for the Crown to destroy that defence in such a manner as to leave in the jury's mind no reasonable doubt that the accused cannot be absolved on the grounds of the alleged compulsion (*Gill* [1963] 1 WLR 841, per Edmund Davies J at p. 846). See also *Bone* [1968] 1 WLR 983, per Lord Parker CJ at p. 985. As to duress of circumstances, see also *Pommell* [1995] 2 Cr App R 607. **F3.31**

Non-insane Automatism Although the onus is on the defence to prove insanity on a balance of probabilities, where there is evidence on which a jury could find automatism not due to a disease of the mind, the onus is on the prosecution to disprove such automatism beyond reasonable doubt: the *obiter* view of the majority in *Bratty v A-G for Northern Ireland* [1963] AC 386. See also *Stripp* (1978) 69 Cr App R 318 and *Pullen* [1991] Crim LR 457. Where the defence of automatism is raised by an accused, two questions fall to be decided by the judge before the defence can be left to the jury: (1) whether a proper evidential foundation for the defence has been laid and (2) whether the evidence shows the case to be one of insane automatism, i.e. a case which falls within the M'Naghten Rules, or one of non-insane automatism. If the judge rules that the case is one of insanity, the jury then has to decide, on the basis of the judge's direction, whether the accused is guilty or not guilty by reason of insanity (*Burgess* [1991] 1 QB 92). Where the issues of both insanity and non-insane automatism arise in the same case, the judge should distinguish between them in his summing-up and explain that, whereas it is for the defence to prove insanity, it is not for them to prove automatism; it is for the prosecution to negative it once the defence lay a foundation for it (*Burns* (1973) 58 Cr App R 364, per Stephenson LJ at p. 374). **F3.32**

Drunkenness Insofar as drunkenness may constitute a defence, once there is evidence before the court to support it, the onus of disproof rests on the prosecution (*Kennedy v HM Advocate* 1944 JC 171; *Foote* [1964] Crim LR 405). However, in *Groark* [1999] Crim LR 669 it was held that if, in a case of wounding with intent, there is evidence of drunkenness which might give rise to the issue whether the accused did form the specific intent, but the defence is that the accused knew what was happening but acted in self-defence, defence counsel is not obliged to seek a direction on self-induced intoxication in relation to intent; the judge may ask him if he has any objection to such a direction and, if he does object, then the direction need not be given. **F3.33**

Alibi Although there is no general rule of law that in every case where alibi is raised the judge must specifically direct the jury, quite apart from the general direction on burden and standard of proof, that it is for the prosecution to negative the alibi, it is the clear duty of the judge to give such a direction if there is a danger of the jury thinking that an alibi, because it is called a defence, raises some burden on the defence to establish it (*Wood (No. 2)* (1967) 52 Cr App R 74 per Lord Parker CJ). It is a common and good *practice* to give such a specific and **F3.34**

additional direction in any event (*Preece* (1992) 96 Cr App R 264); and ideally it should be given (*Anderson* [1991] Crim LR 361; *Johnson* [1995] Crim LR 242). In *Mussell* [1995] Crim LR 887, it was held that a special direction is necessary if the nature of the alibi is that the accused was at a specific place elsewhere, raising the question why he did not call witnesses in support, but is unnecessary if the evidence amounts to little more than a denial that he committed the crime.

F3.35 **Mistaken Belief in Consent** Where a case involves a charge of rape under the SOA 1956 (i.e. brought before 1 May 2004), if there is evidence before the court that the accused mistakenly believed that the complainant had consented, the onus of disproof lies on the prosecution (*Thomas* (1983) 77 Cr App R 63; *Gardiner* [1994] Crim LR 455). For the position on consent under the SOA 2003, see **B3.10** ***et seq.***

F3.36 **Statutory Defences** The principles set out above also apply in relation to a variety of statutory defences. Thus where an accused puts forward an explanation for his conduct based on the Criminal Law Act 1967, s. 3 (see **A3.31**), the jury should be clearly directed that it is for the Crown to destroy the validity of such an explanation and that it is not for the accused to establish it (see *Cameron* [1973] Crim LR 520 and *Khan* [1995] Crim LR 78). For further examples, see the SOA 2003, s.75 (see **B3.11**), the Terrorism Act 2000, s. 118(2) (see **B10.4**) and the Regulation of Investigatory Powers Act 2000, s. 53(3).

STANDARD OF PROOF

General Rule

F3.37 The standard of proof means the degree to which proof must be established by a party bearing a burden of proof. The standard required of the prosecution before the tribunal of fact can find the accused guilty is proof beyond reasonable doubt. Where the legal burden on a particular issue is borne by the accused, the standard required of the defence before the tribunal of fact can find in favour of the accused on that issue is proof on a balance of probabilities. These subjects call for discrete analysis.

Usual Direction Where Legal Burden on Prosecution

F3.38 It is the duty of the judge in the summing-up to make it clear to the jury what standard of proof the prosecution are required to meet. However, it is not a matter of some precise formula or particular form of words being used (*Allan* [1969] 1 WLR 33, per Fenton Atkinson LJ at p. 36).

> It is not the particular formula that matters: it is the effect of the summing-up. If the jury are made to understand that they have to be satisfied and must not return a verdict against a defendant unless they feel sure, and that the onus is all the time on the prosecution and not on the defence, then whether the judge uses one form of language or another is neither here nor there. (*Kritz* [1950] 1 KB 82, per Lord Goddard CJ at p. 89, *obiter*, but cited with approval in *Walters v The Queen* [1969] 2 AC 26.)

However, though the law requires no particular formula, judges are wise, as a general rule, to adopt one; the time-honoured formula is that the jury must be satisfied beyond reasonable doubt (*Ferguson v The Queen* [1979] 1 WLR 94 per Lord Scarman). This phrase has been approved by the House of Lords (*Woolmington v DPP* [1935] AC 462; *Mancini v DPP* [1942] AC 1).

Another well-established formulation of the standard is to direct the jury that in order to find the accused guilty they must be 'sure' or 'satisfied so that they feel sure' (*Kritz* [1950] 1 KB 82, per Lord Goddard CJ at pp. 89–90, approved in *Walters v The Queen* [1969] 2 AC 26; and *Summers* [1952] 1 All ER 1059 at p. 1060). Directions using the words 'reasonably sure', 'pretty sure', 'pretty certain' and 'sure, which is less than being certain' have all been disapproved (see *Head* (1961) 45 Cr App R 225, *Woods* [1961] Crim LR 324, *Law* [1961] Crim LR 52 and *Stephens* (2002) *The Times*, 27 June 2002 respectively). It is inadequate merely to direct the jury that they must be 'satisfied' without any indication of the degree of satisfaction required (*Hepworth* [1955] 2 QB 600; and *Allan* [1969] 1 WLR 33, per Fenton Atkinson LJ). It is proper to direct that 'You, the jury, must be completely satisfied' or 'You must feel sure of the prisoner's guilt' (*Hepworth* [1955] 2 QB 600, per Lord Goddard CJ at p. 603). It is generally sufficient and safe to combine the two classic formulations of the standard and direct that 'You must be satisfied beyond reasonable doubt so that you feel sure of the defendant's guilt' (*Ferguson v The Queen* [1979] 1 WLR 94, per Lord Scarman at p. 99).

In *McGreevy v DPP* [1973] 1 WLR 276, it was argued on the basis of *Hodge* (1838) 2 Lew CC 227, that if the case against the accused depends wholly or substantially on circumstantial evidence, the judge should direct the jury that not only must they be satisfied that the circumstances are consistent with the accused having committed the offence, but also they must be satisfied that the circumstances are inconsistent with any other rational conclusion than that the accused is the guilty person. The House of Lords held that there is no rule of law requiring such a direction. It suffices, in such a case, to give the usual direction that they, the jury, must be satisfied of the guilt of the accused beyond reasonable doubt.

Cases Requiring Explanation of Usual Direction

Judges have used a variety of expressions with a view to explaining to the jury the meaning of **F3.39**
'reasonable doubt', some of which have suggested too low a standard of proof and resulted in a conviction being quashed. For example, in *Gray* (1973) 58 Cr App R 177 the trial judge defined a reasonable doubt as 'a doubt based upon good reason and not a fanciful doubt' and as 'the sort of doubt which might affect you in the conduct of your everyday affairs'. The Court of Appeal, quashing the conviction, held that if the judge had referred to the sort of doubt which may affect the mind of a person in the conduct of important affairs, there could have been no criticism, but the reference to everyday affairs might have suggested too low a standard. See also *Stafford* (1968) 53 Cr App R 1, in which Edmund-Davies LJ said (at p. 2): 'We do not . . . agree with the trial judge when, directing the jury upon the standard of proof he told them to "Remember that a reasonable doubt is one for which you could give reasons if you were asked", and we dislike such a description or definition.' It was against a background of cases of this kind that in *Ching* (1976) 63 Cr App R 7 Lawton LJ, delivering the judgment of the Court, said (at p. 11): 'We point out and emphasise that if judges stopped trying to define that which is almost impossible to define there would be fewer appeals. We hope that there will not be any more for some considerable time.' Earlier, his lordship said (at p. 10):

> . . . in most cases . . . judges would be well advised not to attempt any gloss upon what is meant by 'sure' or what is meant by 'reasonable doubt'. In the last two decades there have been numerous cases before this court, some of which have been successful, some of which have not, which have come here because judges have thought it helpful to a jury to comment on what the standard of proof is. Experience in this court has shown that such comments usually create difficulties. They are more likely to confuse than help. But the exceptional case does sometimes arise.

Ching itself illustrates the kind of exceptional case in which a judge should explain to a jury what is meant by reasonable doubt. In that case the judge, in his summing-up, had directed the jury on the standard of proof by using the two classic formulations, 'sure' and 'beyond reasonable doubt', and had explained that these were two ways of saying the same thing. After retirement the jury returned to court, and the judge understood the foreman to ask for a further direction on the standard of proof. The judge said:

> A reasonable doubt . . . is a doubt to which you can give a reason as opposed to a mere fanciful sort of speculation such as 'Well, nothing in this world is certain, nothing in this world can be

proved' . . . It is sometimes said the sort of matter which might influence you if you were to consider some business matter. A matter, for example, of a mortgage concerning your house, or something of that nature.

The Court of Appeal held that:

(a) in the light of the foreman's request, the case was an exceptional one, calling for a further direction; and
(b) although it disliked that part of the additional direction in which the judge had defined a reasonable doubt as one to which you can give a reason, taking the effect of both the summing-up and the additional direction together, the judge was right in what he did.

In exceptional cases in which the jury do ask for an explanation of 'reasonable doubt', a suitable form of words is provided by *Walters v The Queen* [1969] 2 AC 26. There, the Privy Council, while of the opinion that it is a matter of discretion for the judge to choose the most appropriate set of words to enable the particular jury in question to understand the standard of proof, upheld the following direction of the trial judge: 'A reasonable doubt is that quality and kind of doubt which, when you are dealing with matters of importance in your own affairs, you allow to influence you one way or the other.' The decision was affirmed in *Gray* (1973) 58 Cr App R 177.

It is not helpful for a judge to direct a jury to distinguish between being sure and being certain, and if necessary the judge should say that his direction to be sure is the limit of the help he can give (*Stephens* (2002) *The Times*, 27 June 2002).

Direction Where Legal Burden on Defence

F3.40 In the exceptional cases in which the legal burden of proving an issue is borne by the defence (see F3.7 *et seq.*), it is discharged by proof on a balance of probabilities. See, in the case of insanity, *Sodeman v The King* [1936] 2 All ER 1138; in the case of the Prevention of Crime Act 1953, s. 1, an express statutory exception, *Brown* (1971) 55 Cr App R 478; in the case of the Homicide Act 1957, s. 2(2), another express statutory exception, *Dunbar* [1958] 1 QB 1; and in the case of implied statutory exceptions under the MCA 1980, s. 101, *Islington London Borough Council v Panico* [1973] 1 WLR 1166. In *Carr-Briant* [1943] KB 607, the accused, who was convicted of an offence under the Prevention of Corruption Acts 1906 and 1916, bore the legal burden of proving that money given or lent to an employee of a Government Department was not paid or given corruptly. The trial judge directed the jury that the burden on the accused was as heavy as that normally resting on the prosecution. Humphreys J, quashing the conviction, said (at p. 612) that 'the jury should be directed that . . . the burden of proof required is less than that required at the hands of the prosecution in proving the case beyond a reasonable doubt, and that the burden may be discharged by evidence satisfying the jury of the probability of that which the accused is called upon to establish'.

The classic definition of proof on a 'balance of probabilities' is that of Denning J in *Miller v Minister of Pensions* [1947] 2 All ER 372, at p. 374: 'If the evidence is such that the tribunal can say: "We think it more probable than not", the burden is discharged, but, if the probabilities are equal, it is not.'

BURDEN OF PROOF ON FACTS AFFECTING ADMISSIBILITY OF EVIDENCE

F3.41 When the admissibility of a particular item of evidence is in dispute, the burden of proving preliminary facts, that is those facts which must be proved as a condition precedent to the admission of the disputed evidence, lies on the party seeking to admit that evidence. Thus, at common law the prosecution bore the burden of proving the facts constituting the condition precedent to the admissibility of confessions, a rule which has now been put on a statutory basis (see *Thompson* [1893] 2 QB 12 and the PACE 1984, s. 76(2)). Likewise, it has been held that the onus of establishing the preliminary facts in relation to a dying declaration is on the party who seeks to admit such a declaration (*Jenkins* (1869) LR 1 CCR 187). The burden of proving the competence of a witness is on the party seeking to call that witness. In *Yacoob* (1981) 72 Cr App R 313 the defence objected to the prosecution calling a woman whom they alleged to be incompetent because she had gone through a ceremony of marriage with the accused. The prosecution alleged that the marriage was bigamous. The trial judge ruled that it was for the defence to prove the validity of the marriage. The Court of Appeal held that this was wrong: it was for the prosecution to prove the woman's competence beyond reasonable doubt. As to the requirement to satisfy the judge of the originality and genuineness of a tape recording, see *Robson* [1972] 1 WLR 651, *Stevenson* [1971] 1 WLR 1, *Rampling* [1987] Crim LR 823, and the Code of Practice for Tape Recording of Police Interviews (Code E).

STANDARD OF PROOF ON FACTS AFFECTING ADMISSIBILITY OF EVIDENCE

When the burden of proving the admissibility of a particular item of evidence is borne by the prosecution, the standard to be met is proof beyond reasonable doubt. See, in the case of confessions at common law, *Sartori* [1961] Crim LR 397, *Cave* [1963] Crim LR 371 and *DPP v Ping Lin* [1976] AC 574, at p. 580 (a rule now put on a statutory basis by the PACE 1984, s. 76(2)); in the case of dying declarations, *Jenkins* (1869) LR 1 CCR 187; in the case of the competence of a witness, *Yacoob* (1931) 72 Cr App R 313; and on the issue of the genuineness of samples of writing which it is sought to admit under the Criminal Procedure Act 1865, s. 8, for the purposes of comparison with a disputed writing, *Ewing* [1983] QB 1039. In *Ewing*, the Court of Appeal held that since s. 8 of the 1865 Act did not itself deal with the standard of proof required to satisfy the judge as to the genuineness of the sample writing, the matter was governed by the common law, and accordingly, if the prosecution sought to admit such a sample, they should prove genuineness beyond reasonable doubt. The Court was of the opinion that the earlier decision of the Court of Appeal in *Angeli* [1979] 1 WLR 26, that the standard was the civil one, must have been reached *per incuriam*. **F3.42**

Although there is little authority on the point, as a matter of principle, when the burden of proving the admissibility of a particular item of evidence is borne by the defence, the standard to be met should be proof on a balance of probabilities. See, in the case of a defence application under CJA 1988, s. 23 (now repealed), *Mattey* [1995] 2 Cr App R 409.

PRESUMPTIONS

Presumptions without Basic Facts: Generally

Presumptions without basic facts come into operation without the need for proof or admission of any basic or primary fact — they are merely rules that a certain conclusion must be drawn by the court in the absence of any evidence in rebuttal. Thus, although referred to as 'presumptions', in fact they are indistinguishable from the other rules relating to the incidence of the legal or evidential burden. Three examples are considered: the presumption of innocence, the presumption of sanity, and the presumption that mechanical and other instruments of a kind that are usually in working order, were in working order at the time of their use. **F3.43**

Presumption of Innocence

F3.44 The phrase 'the presumption of innocence' is often used as a convenient abbreviation of the common-law rule that, generally speaking, the prosecution bears the burden of proving all the elements in the offence necessary to establish guilt (see *Woolmington v DPP* [1935] AC 462 and generally F3.6).

Presumption of Sanity

F3.45 The presumption of sanity is a convenient abbreviation of the common-law rule that if the accused raises the defence of insanity, he will bear the burden of proving it (on a balance of probabilities) (see *Layton* (1849) 4 Cox CC 149, *M'Naghten's Case* (1843) 10 Cl & F 200, and generally F3.7). The phrase is to be distinguished from 'the presumption of mental capacity' which has been used to refer to the common-law rule that the evidential burden in relation to automatism not due to a disease of the mind is borne by the accused (see *Bratty v A-G for Northern Ireland* [1963] AC 386 at F3.32).

Presumption as to Working of Mechanical and Other Instruments

F3.46 There is a presumption that mechanical and other instruments of a kind that are usually in working order, were in working order at the time of their use. The party against whom the presumption operates bears an evidential burden to adduce some evidence to the contrary. The presumption has been applied in the case of speedometers: see *Nicholas v Penny* [1950] 2 KB 466, in which it was held that justices were entitled to convict of speeding on the evidence of one officer as to the speedometer reading of a police car driven at an even distance behind the accused's car, notwithstanding that no evidence had been adduced as to the accuracy of the speedometer. Traffic lights have likewise been presumed to be in working order: in *Tingle Jacobs & Co. v Kennedy* [1964] 1 WLR 638, Lord Denning MR said (at p. 639) 'when you have a device of this kind set up for public use in active operation . . . the presumption should be that it is in proper working order unless there is evidence to the contrary'. See also, in the case of a public weighbridge, *Kelly Communications Ltd v DPP* (2003) 167 JP 73.

PRESUMPTIONS OF FACT

General Principles

F3.47 The phrase 'presumption of fact' has been used to describe certain frequently recurring varieties of circumstantial evidence, i.e. evidence of relevant facts from which the existence of some fact which is in issue *may* be inferred. Thus, presumptions of fact, sometimes referred to as provisional presumptions, operate in the following manner: on the proof or admission of a basic or primary fact, another fact may be presumed in the absence of sufficient evidence to the contrary. The party against whom the presumption operates bears neither a legal nor an evidential burden in relation to the presumed fact; if he adduces no evidence to the contrary, he runs a risk of losing on that issue, but he is not *bound* to lose on that issue. The following examples are considered: the presumption of continuance of life, the presumption of intention, and the presumption of guilty knowledge in cases of handling, theft, etc.

Continuance of Life

F3.48 On the proof or admission of the basic fact that a person was alive on a certain date, it may be presumed, in the absence of sufficient evidence to the contrary, that he was still alive on some subsequent date (*MacDarmaid v A-G* [1950] P 218; *Re Peete* [1952] 2 All ER 599). Whether or not such an inference should be drawn is a question for the jury, and is entirely dependent upon the facts of the case. Thus, if there is proof that a person was in good health on one day, there would be a strong, almost irresistible, inference that he was alive on the next day, and the jury would in all probability find that he was so; if, on the other hand, it were proved that he was in a dying condition on the first day and nothing further was proved, the jury would probably decline to draw the inference that he was alive on the following day (*Lumley* (1869) LR 1 CCR 196, per Lush J at p. 198, on the question of whether a husband was alive at the date of his wife's allegedly bigamous second marriage, approved in *Morrison* (1938) 27 Cr App R 1).

Intention

Criminal Justice Act 1967, s. 8 F3.49

A court or jury, in determining whether a person has committed an offence—

(a) shall not be bound in law to infer that he intended or foresaw a result of his actions by reason only of its being a natural and probable consequence of those actions; but

(b) shall decide whether he did intend or foresee that result by reference to all the evidence, drawing such inferences from the evidence as appear proper in the circumstances.

Section 8 of the 1967 Act puts on a statutory basis the common-law presumption of fact that a man intends the natural consequences of his acts, and reverses the decision in *DPP v Smith* [1961] AC 290 that in certain circumstances the presumption is a presumption of law (see *Wallett* [1968] 2 QB 367 and *Moloney* [1985] AC 905). In *Moloney*, at p. 929, Lord Bridge, approving the judgment of the Court of Criminal Appeal (Lord Goddard CJ, Atkinson and Cassels JJ) delivered by Lord Goddard CJ in *Steane* [1947] KB 997, at p. 1004, held that in the rare cases in which it is necessary to direct a jury by reference to foresight of consequences, the judge need only invite the jury to consider two questions:

(a) Was the consequence a natural consequence of the defendant's voluntary act?

(b) Did the defendant foresee that consequence as being a natural consequence of his act?

The jury should then be told that if they answer yes to both questions, it is a proper inference for them to draw that the defendant intended that consequence.

Guilty Knowledge in Cases of Handling, Theft etc.

In cases of handling and theft, on proof or admission of the fact that the accused was found in possession of property so shortly after it was stolen that it can fairly be said that he was in recent possession of it, the jury should be directed that such possession calls for explanation, and if none is given, or one is given which they are convinced is untrue, they are entitled to infer, according to the circumstances, that the accused is either the handler or the thief and to convict accordingly (*Schama* (1914) 84 LJ KB 396; *Garth* [1949] 1 All ER 773; *Aves* [1950] 2 All ER 330; *Williams* [1962] Crim LR 54). It is desirable in most cases to direct the jury that the burden of proof remains on the prosecution, and if, therefore, the explanation given by the accused leaves them in doubt as to whether he came by the property honestly, the prosecution have not proved their case and they should acquit (*Aves* and *Hepworth* [1955] 2 QB 600, applied in *Moulding* [1996] Crim LR 440). See also *Aubrey* (1915) 11 Cr App R 182, *Brain* (1918) 13 Cr App R 197 and *Sanders* (1919) 14 Cr App R 11. F3.50

The doctrine of recent possession applies not only in the case of 'receiving', but also in the case of a charge under the second limb of the Theft Act 1968, s. 22 (*Ball* [1983] 1 WLR 801). Apart from handling and theft, the doctrine may also apply to other offences with a theft ingredient, as when the accused is charged with burglary contrary to s. 9(1)(b), and it is proved that shortly after the premises were entered and property stolen therefrom, the accused was found in possession of the property (see *Loughlin* (1951) 35 Cr App R 69 and *Seymour* [1954] 1 WLR 678). There is no general rule of law to the effect that the doctrine has no application in cases in which there is some evidence of the circumstances in which the accused came into possession of the stolen goods (see per Stocker LJ in *Raviraj* (1986) 85 Cr App R 93, commenting on *obiter* remarks made in *Bradley* (1979) 70 Cr App R 200). However, the doctrine cannot be relied upon where the accused failed to give an explanation *after* he was cautioned (*Raviraj*).

F3.51 **'Recent'** Whether possession is 'recent' is a question of fact and degree dependent on all the circumstances of the case in question. Relevant factors include the nature of the property, its saleability, and any evidence, other than that of the accused's possession of the goods, connecting him with the offence charged. In *Smythe* (1980) 72 Cr App R 8, Kilner Brown J said (at p. 11): 'Nearly every reported case is merely a decision of fact as an example of what is no more than a rule of evidence'. The precedents, therefore, are of somewhat limited value.

It is instructive, however, to note that in *Cash* [1985] QB 801, in which the goods were found in the possession of the appellant, C, on 25 February 1983, and none of the property was stolen more recently than 16 February 1983, the Court of Appeal, upholding C's conviction for handling, said that it was not properly open to the jury to infer that C was the burglar or thief. In that case two others were charged in the same indictment: A, who was convicted of burglary and handling offences; and E, who pleaded guilty to burglary and obtaining property by deception. The prosecution case was that C handled goods taken, by A, E and other persons unknown, in the course of a number of separate burglaries which took place between July and October 1982 and January and 16 February 1983. Some of the proceeds of the burglaries were recovered from C's flat on 25 February 1983. A was a lodger in the flat. When arrested, C declined to answer questions, and at the trial elected to give no evidence. In *Smythe* (1980) 72 Cr App R 8 the Court of Appeal said that it would be quite unsafe to infer positive proof of participation in a series of burglaries and robberies from the mere fact of possession, between two and three months after the robberies, of articles stolen in the course of them. See also *Marcus* (1923) 17 Cr App R 191: a period of eight months between the theft and the time when the goods were first seen in the possession of the accused was too long a period for the doctrine to apply.

F3.52 **'Otherwise than in the course of stealing'** In ordinary cases of handling, the prosecution are not required to adduce affirmative proof that the goods were handled 'otherwise than in the course of the stealing' (see the Theft Act 1968, s. 22(1)). This remains the position in recent possession cases, because if the jury draws the inference that the accused is guilty of handling, this includes the inference that he was not the actual thief. However, where the accused is in possession of stolen goods so recently after they are stolen that the inevitable inference is that he is the thief, as when he is found within a few hundred yards of the scene of the theft and minutes after the theft took place, then if he is only charged with handling, the Crown can prove that offence only if it proves affirmatively that the accused was not the thief, and the judge should direct the jury that they must acquit the accused of handling if they take the view that he was the thief (*Cash* [1985] QB 801, applied in *A-G of Hong Kong v Yip Kai-Foon* [1988] AC 642; *Ryan v DPP* (1994) 158 JP 485).

IRREBUTTABLE PRESUMPTIONS OF LAW

General Principles

F3.53 Irrebuttable presumptions of law, or conclusive presumptions, operate in the following way: on the proof or admission of a basic or primary fact another fact must be presumed which no evidence is admissible to rebut. Such presumptions are nothing more than rules of substantive law, as the following example illustrates. (See also the SOA 2003, s. 76, considered at **B3.12**.)

Presumption that Children under 10 Cannot be Guilty of Offence

F3.54 The CYPA 1933, s. 50, provides that: 'It shall be conclusively presumed that no child under the age of 10 years can be guilty of an offence'. It follows from this that a person over the age of 10 who receives property dishonestly acquired by a person under the age of 10 cannot be guilty of receiving stolen property, although if he has the necessary *mens rea*, he may be guilty of theft (*Walters v Lunt* [1951] 2 All ER 645; *McGregor v Benyon* [1957] Crim LR 608).

REBUTTABLE PRESUMPTIONS OF LAW

General Principles

Rebuttable presumptions of law operate in the following manner: on the proof or admission of the basic or primary facts, another fact must be presumed in the absence of sufficient evidence to the contrary. If the defence rely upon a rebuttable presumption of law and adduce prima facie evidence of the basic facts, a legal burden is placed on the prosecution requiring them to disprove or negative the presumed fact beyond reasonable doubt. If the prosecution rely upon a rebuttable presumption of law and adduce prima facie evidence of the basic facts, an evidential burden is placed on the defence which may be discharged by the adduction of such evidence as might leave a jury in reasonable doubt; and if the defence do discharge the evidential burden, the effect is as if the presumption had never come into play — the prosecution are still required to prove the presumed fact beyond reasonable doubt (see *Kay* (1887) 16 Cox CC 292 and *Willshire* (1881) 6 QBD 366 (the presumption of marriage)). **F3.55**

The foregoing relates to common-law presumptions. As to the statutory presumptions which operate to place on the defence a legal burden requiring them to disprove or negative a presumed fact by the adduction of such evidence as will satisfy the jury on a balance of probabilities, see **F3.8** ***et seq.*** As to the statutory presumptions arising under the PACE 1984, s. 74, see **F11.5**. Presumptions relating to the due execution of documents are considered at **F8.32**. The rebuttable presumptions of law that now fall to be considered are the presumptions of regularity, marriage and death.

Presumption of Regularity

The presumption of regularity, expressed in the maxim *omnia praesumuntur rite esse acta*, operates as follows: on proof or admission of the basic or primary fact that a person has acted in a public or official capacity, it is presumed, in the absence of sufficient evidence to the contrary, that that person was regularly and properly appointed and that the act was regularly and properly performed. The presumption cannot be rebutted merely by challenging the presumed fact — evidence must be adduced (*Campbell v Wallsend Slipway and Engineering Co. Ltd* [1978] ICR 1015). Typical examples concern the validity of an official appointment. Thus, on a charge of assaulting a police officer in the course of his duty, evidence that the officer acted in that capacity is sufficient proof of his due appointment (*Gordon* (1789) 1 Leach 515; and see *Cooper v Rowlands* [1971] RTR 291). See also *Borrett* (1833) 6 C & P 124 (a person acting as an officer of the Post Office), *Roberts* (1878) 38 LT 690 (a deputy county court judge), and *Campbell v Wallsend Slipway and Engineering Co. Ltd* (an inspector of the Health and Safety Executive). In *Langton* (1876) 2 QBD 296, the presumption operated to establish the due incorporation of a company which had acted as such. In *Cresswell* (1873) 1 QBD 446, evidence that a marriage had been celebrated in a building in which other marriages had also been celebrated was sufficient to establish that the building was duly consecrated. **F3.56**

The presumption must be applied with caution in cases where commission of an offence is dependent upon compliance with formal statutory conditions. Thus, the Divisional Court has held that it is wrong to presume, on the basis of evidence that a breath test device has been issued to the police, that it was officially approved by the Secretary of State (*Scott v Baker* [1969] 1 QB 659, approved in *Withecombe* [1969] 1 WLR 84). See also *Swift v Barrett* (1940) 163 LT 154, in which the Divisional Court required strict proof that a road sign complied with regulations. Such authorities, it is submitted, are not easily reconciled with *Gibbins v*

Skinner [1951] 2 KB 379, in which it was held that evidence that speed-limit signs had been erected on a road was sufficient to establish that the local authority had performed its statutory duties pursuant to the Road Traffic Acts and given a direction justifying the erection of the signs.

Presumptions of Marriage

F3.57 The civil authorities, although not explicit on the point, suggest that there are three different presumptions of marriage:

(a) a presumption of formal validity (i.e. a presumption of compliance with the formal requirements of the *lex loci celebrationis*, e.g., the requirement, in the case of a Church of England marriage under English law, to obtain a common or special licence);
(b) a presumption of essential validity (i.e. a presumption that each of the parties had the capacity to marry and was not, for example, under the age of 16 or already married); and
(c) a presumption of marriage arising from cohabitation.

Although there is a dearth of criminal authority, it is submitted that the presumptions of formal and essential validity apply in criminal as well as civil proceedings. The presumption of marriage arising from cohabitation, however, would appear to be of limited utility in criminal proceedings; the authorities show that if the prosecution bear the burden of proving the existence of a marriage, the presumption by itself is insufficient to discharge even the evidential burden. Thus in a case of bigamy, the prosecution, in seeking to prove a valid first marriage which subsisted at the date of the second marriage, must adduce some evidence of the celebration of the first marriage; evidence of acknowledgement, cohabitation or repute will not suffice (*Morris v Miller* (1767) 4 Burr 2057). It will suffice, however, if there is not only evidence that the accused had cohabited with a woman and spoken of her as his wife, but also proof from the register of marriages that a person of the same name as the accused married that woman (*Birtles* (1911) 6 Cr App R 177). See also *Umanski* [1961] VR 242.

Presumption of Death

F3.58

> By virtue of a long sequence of judicial statements, which either assert or assume such a rule, it appears accepted that there is a convenient presumption of law applicable to certain cases of seven years' absence where no statute applies. That presumption in its modern shape takes effect (without examining its terms too exactly) substantially as follows. Where as regards 'A.B' there is no acceptable affirmative evidence that he was alive at some time during a continuous period of seven years or more, then if it can be proved first, that there are persons who would be likely to have heard of him over that period, secondly that those persons have not heard of him, and thirdly that all due inquiries have been made appropriate to the circumstances, 'A.B.' will be presumed to have died at some time within that period. (*Chard v Chard* [1956] P 259, per Sachs J at p. 272)

The authorities conflict as to the date on which the fact of death may be presumed; it is either the date of the proceedings in question or the date at the end of the period of absence for seven years (see *Lal Chand Marwari v Mahant Ranrup Gir* (1925) 42 TLR 159, at p. 160, and contrast *Re Westbrook's Trusts* [1873] WN 167 and *Chipchase v Chipchase* [1939] P 31).

Concerning the proviso to the OAPA 1861, s. 57 ('persons [charged with bigamy] marrying a second time whose husband or wife shall have been continually absent for the space of seven years then last past, and shall not have been known by such person to be living within that time'), see **B2.113**.

CONFLICTING PRESUMPTIONS

F3.59 There is civil authority that where two presumptions of equal strength apply in a case with the result that two facts are presumed, the one in conflict with the other, the presumptions neutralise each other and the case falls to be determined without the application of either (see *Monckton v Tarr* (1930) 23 BWCC 504). *Willshire* (1881) 6 QBD 366 is often cited in support of this proposition, although there was no true conflict in that case, which involved two presumptions of unequal strength, a rebuttable presumption of law and a presumption of fact. W was charged with bigamously marrying D in the lifetime of C. W had gone through four ceremonies of marriage, with A in 1864, with B in 1868, with C in 1879, and with D in 1880. The prosecution relied upon the presumption of essential validity in seeking to establish the validity of the marriage of 1879. W sought to show that the marriage of 1879 was void, and accordingly relied upon his previous conviction, in 1868, for marrying B during the lifetime of A: A was alive in 1868 and under the presumption of continuance of life could be presumed to have been alive in 1879, in which case the marriage of 1879 was void. The trial judge did not leave the issue of whether A was alive in 1879 to the jury, directing them that the onus was on W to adduce evidence of her existence on that date. The conviction was quashed. Lord Coleridge CJ, referring to a 'conflict' of presumptions, held that the accused was not bound to do more than set up A's life in 1868, which would be presumed to continue, and it was then for the prosecution to disprove her existence on that date. It is submitted that there was no real conflict of presumptions in this case. The decision reached was correct. The onus of proving the validity of the 1879 marriage was on the prosecution. Their reliance on the presumption of validity placed nothing more than an evidential burden on W, which he had successfully discharged in reliance upon the presumption of continuance of life. The onus remained on the prosecution to establish the validity of the 1879 marriage.

Section F4 Competence and Compellability of Witnesses and Oaths and Affirmations

GENERAL

Meaning of Competence and Compellability

F4.1 A witness is competent if he may lawfully be called to testify, and is compellable if, being competent, he may lawfully be compelled by the court to testify. As to securing the attendance of a witness, whether by witness order or witness summons, see **D14.88** ***et seq*** and **D21.24** ***et seq***.

Determining Competence

F4.2 The question whether a witness is competent to give evidence in criminal proceedings must be determined by the court in accordance with the YJCEA 1999, s. 54 (set out at **F4.23**). It is for the party calling the witness to satisfy the court on a balance of probabilities that the witness is competent (s. 54(2)) and expert evidence may be received on the question (s. 54(5)). In deciding the question, the court must treat the witness as having the benefit of any special measures directions which the court has given or proposes to give in relation to the witness (s. 54(3)). Any proceedings held to decide the question shall take place in the absence of the jury (s. 54(4)) and any questioning of the witness shall be conducted by the court in the presence of the parties (s. 54(6)). See also, in the case of children and persons of unsound mind, **F4.21**.

There are a number of common-law authorities as to the time for determining the competence of a witness. In the case of a prosecution witness, it has been held that the question should be raised and decided at the beginning of the trial (*Yacoob* (1981) 72 Cr App R 313). An objection to the competence of a witness should normally be made before the witness has been examined in chief (*Wollaston v Hakewill* (1841) 3 Man & G 297; *Bartlett v Smith* (1843) 11 M & W 483). An exception exists in cases where the incompetence only becomes apparent during the course of examination-in-chief (*Jacobs v Layborn* (1843) 11 M & W 685). If it only becomes apparent to a judge during the course of the evidence being given by a sworn witness that the witness is of unsound mind, the judge may rule the witness incompetent, direct the jury to ignore his evidence, and continue with the trial (*Whitehead* (1866) LR 1 CCR 33).

Witnesses who Refuse to Take the Oath or Testify

F4.3 Judges of the Crown Court may exercise their power to punish summarily for contempt of court (Supreme Court Act 1981, s. 45(4)) any compellable witness who refuses to take an oath or make an affirmation (*Hennegal v Evance* (1806) 12 Ves Jr 201). Likewise, but subject to public policy or a claim to privilege which the court upholds, a witness who refuses to answer a proper question may be found to be in contempt of court and face the penalty of imprisonment (*Ex parte Fernandez* (1861) 10 CB NS 13). A witness who refuses to testify and runs the risk of committal to prison as a contemnor should be given the opportunity of legal representation (*K* (1984) 78 Cr App R 82). In *Phillips* (1983) 78 Cr App R 88, it was stressed that, on a finding of contempt, sentence need not be passed immediately. The witness may change his mind. It is advisable to sentence at the end of the trial or, at the earliest, at the close of the prosecution case. For the principles to be borne in mind by trial judges, see the observations of Lawton LJ in *Moran* (1985) 81 Cr App R 51 at p. 53 quoted in **B14.76**. For the position in magistrates' courts, see the MCA 1980, s. 97(4), in **B14.73**.

Wards of Court as Witnesses

The leave of the wardship court is not required to call a ward to give evidence at a criminal trial. This is so irrespective of whether (a) the child is interviewed and has made witness statements before or after becoming a ward, (b) it is the prosecution or defence who wish to call the child or (c) the child's failure to give evidence would prevent the prosecution taking place (see *Re K (Minors) (Wardship: Criminal Proceedings)* [1988] Fam 1 and *Re R (A Minor) (Wardship: Criminal Proceedings)* [1991] 2 WLR 912, per Lord Donaldson MR at p. 917). Concerning interviews with wards, see the *Consolidated Criminal Practice Direction*, para. I.5, *Wards of court, Re R (Minors)* [1990] 2 All ER 633 and *Re R (A Minor) (Wardship: Criminal Proceedings)* [1991] 2 WLR 912. **F4.4**

General Rule as to Competence and Compellability

The general rule relating to the competence and compellability of witnesses has two limbs: **F4.5**

(a) The first is that any person is a competent witness in any proceedings. The exceptions to this limb relate to the accused, children, and persons of defective intellect.
(b) The second is that all competent witnesses are compellable. The exceptions to this limb relate to the accused and his or her spouse or civil partner.

The first limb of the general rule has been put on a statutory basis. Under the YJCEA 1999, s. 53(1), which has effect subject to s. 53(3) and s. 53(4), 'At every stage in criminal proceedings all persons are (whatever their age) competent to give evidence'. Under s. 53(3), a person is not competent to give evidence if it appears to the court that he is not a person who is able to (a) understand questions put to him as a witness and (b) give answers to them which can be understood (see **F4.18**). Section 53(4) provides that a person charged is not competent to give evidence for the prosecution (see **F4.8**).

Deaf and Speech Handicapped Witnesses

A deaf mute is competent as a witness, provided that the court is satisfied that he understands the nature of an oath (*Ruston* (1786) 1 Leach 408; *O'Brien* (1845) 1 Cox CC 185). Such a person may take an oath (or make an affirmation) and be examined and cross-examined, through an interpreter, using sign language. The interpreter should also take an oath (or make an affirmation). A witness who cannot speak may be allowed to give his evidence in written form. **F4.6**

No Property in the Evidence of a Witness

No party has any property in the evidence of a witness, so that even if there is a contract between a witness and a party, whereby the latter binds himself not to testify on a matter on which the court can compel him to give evidence, such a contract is contrary to public policy and unenforceable (*Harmony Shipping Co. SA v Saudi Europe Line Ltd* [1979] 1 WLR 1380). However, once a witness in a criminal case has testified on behalf of the prosecution, he cannot be compelled to testify on behalf of the defence (*Kelly* (1985) *The Times*, 27 July 1985). As to expert witnesses, see also **F9.31**. **F4.7**

THE ACCUSED

As a Witness for the Prosecution

F4.8 An accused is incompetent as a witness for the prosecution. Under the YJCEA 1999, s. 53(4), 'A person charged in criminal proceedings is not competent to give evidence in the proceedings for the prosecution (whether he is the only person, or is one of two or more persons, charged in the proceedings)'. A co-accused may only give evidence for the prosecution if he ceases to be a co-accused. Section 53(5) provides that: 'In subsection (4) the reference to a person charged in criminal proceedings does not include a person who is not, or is no longer, liable to be convicted of any offence in the proceedings (whether as a result of pleading guilty or for any other reason)'. 'Other reasons' why a co-accused may not, or may no longer, be liable to be convicted, are that he has been acquitted or is to be tried separately or that the A-G has entered a *nolle prosequi*.

There is a rule of practice, not law, that an accomplice against whom proceedings are pending but who is not an accused in the proceedings in which the prosecution seek to call him, should only be called by the prosecution if they have undertaken to discontinue the proceedings against him. In *Pipe* (1967) 51 Cr App R 17, Pipe was charged with housebreaking and larceny. He was alleged to have stolen a safe and its contents. Swan was called to prove that he had helped Pipe to break open the safe. Swan, before the commencement of Pipe's trial, had been charged with complicity in Pipe's crime in relation to the safe. Swan was not indicted with Pipe. It was intended to try him later. The Court of Appeal held that it was 'wholly irregular' to have called Swan in these circumstances.

In *Turner* (1975) 61 Cr App R 67 it was argued that for some time past there had been a practice for judges not to admit the evidence of accomplices who could still be influenced by continuing inducements, and that in *Pipe* the Court of Appeal had adjudged that this practice had become a rule of law. Rejecting this argument, Lawton LJ said, at p. 78:

> There is nothing in either the arguments [in *Pipe*] or the judgment itself to indicate that the court thought it was changing a rule of law as to the competency of accomplices to give evidence which had been followed ever since the 17th century. The facts of that case must be closely examined....
>
> [*Pipe's*] *ratio decidendi* is confined to a case in which an accomplice, who has been charged, but not tried, is required to give evidence of his own offence in order to secure the conviction of another accused. *Pipe* on its facts was clearly a right decision. The same result could have been achieved by adjudging that the trial judge should have exercised his discretion to exclude Swan's evidence on the ground that there was an obvious and powerful inducement for him to ingratiate himself with the prosecution and the court and that the existence of this inducement made it desirable in the interests of justice to exclude it. See *Noor Mohamed v The King* [1949] AC 182 per Lord du Parcq at p. 192 and followed in *Harris v DPP* [1952] AC 694 per Viscount Simon at p. 707. To have reached the decision on this basis would, we think, have been more in line with the earlier authorities. Lord Parker CJ in *Pipe* seems, however, to have viewed the admission of Swan's evidence in the circumstances of that case as more than a wrong exercise of discretion. He described what happened as being 'wholly irregular'. It does not follow, in our judgment, that in all cases calling a witness who can benefit from giving evidence is 'wholly irregular'. To hold so would be absurd.

As a Witness on his Own Behalf

F4.9 The accused is a competent witness for the defence pursuant to the YJCEA 1999, s. 53(1), whereby 'At every stage in criminal proceedings all persons are . . . competent to give evidence'. The phrase 'at every stage in criminal proceedings' allows the accused to give evidence not only in the trial itself, but also after conviction, in mitigation of sentence (see *Wheeler*

[1917] 1 KB 283, a decision construing a similar phrase used in the Criminal Evidence Act 1898, s. 1, prior to its amendment by the YJCEA 1999). There is some old authority to the effect that the accused is not entitled as of right to give evidence on the *voir dire* (*Baldwin* (1931) 23 Cr App R 62) but that the court may in its discretion allow the accused to give evidence at this stage if the justice of the case makes this desirable (*Cowell* [1940] 2 KB 49). The wording of s. 53(1), however, supports the current practice, which is for the accused to elect whether to give evidence on the *voir dire.*

The accused is not a compellable witness for the defence. Under the Criminal Evidence Act 1898, s. 1(1), 'A person charged in criminal proceedings shall not be called as a witness in the proceedings except upon his own application'.

Giving Evidence from the Witness Box

F4.10 The Criminal Evidence Act 1898, s. 1(4), provides that 'Every person charged in criminal proceedings who is called as a witness in the proceedings shall, unless otherwise ordered by the court, give his evidence from the witness box or other place from which other witnesses give their evidence'. Concerning the statutory precursor to s. 1(4) (s. 1(g) of the 1898 Act), it was held that the intention was that the accused should 'have an opportunity of giving evidence on his own behalf in the same way and from the same place as the witnesses for the prosecution'. Thus the accused should give his evidence from the witness-box unless, for example, he is too infirm to walk there or too violent to be controlled there (*Symonds* (1924) 18 Cr App R 100, per Swift J at p. 101). Section 1(4) does not confer on justices a discretion to direct where evidence should be given from but allows them, in exceptional circumstances of the kind described in *Symonds,* to deny the accused the right he would otherwise have to give evidence from the witnessbox. To offer the accused a choice as to whether they wish to give evidence from the dock or the witness stand is also to fetter that right and any such practice should cease (*Farnham Justices, ex parte Gibson* [1991] RTR 309, where the conviction of a defendant required to give evidence from the dock was quashed, applying the principle that justice must not only be done but must also be seen to be done).

F4.11 **Requirement to Give Evidence on Oath and Liability to Cross-examination** If the accused elects to testify, he must give his evidence on oath and will be liable to cross-examination. This is now expressly stated in the CJA 1982, s. 72, which abolished the accused's right to make an unsworn statement from the dock.

Criminal Justice Act 1982, s. 72

(1) Subject to subsections (2) and (3) below, in any criminal proceedings the accused shall not be entitled to make a statement without being sworn, and accordingly, if he gives evidence he shall do so (subject to sections 55 and 56 of the Youth Justice and Criminal Evidence Act 1999) on oath and be liable to cross-examination; but this section shall not affect the right of the accused, if not represented by counsel or a solicitor, to address the court or jury otherwise than on oath on any matter on which, if he were so represented, counsel or a solicitor could address the court or jury on his behalf.

(2) Nothing in subsection (1) above shall prevent the accused making a statement without being sworn—
   (a) if it is one which he is required by law to make personally; or
   (b) if he makes it by way of mitigation before the court passes sentence upon him.

(3) Nothing in this section applies—
   (a) to a trial; or
   (b) to proceedings before a magistrates' court acting as examining justices,
   which began before the commencement of this section.

The qualification in s. 72(1), ('subject to sections 55 and 56 of the Youth Justice and Criminal Evidence Act 1999') has the effect that the evidence of an accused who is competent to give evidence but who is not permitted to be sworn shall be given unsworn. Section 55

F

Part F Evidence

(determining whether a witness should give sworn evidence) and s. 56 (the reception of unsworn evidence) are set out at **F4.23**.

If the accused does testify, he is liable to cross-examination by the prosecution and, whether or not he has given evidence against a co-accused, by counsel for any co-accused (*Hilton* [1972] 1 QB 421). Subject to the CJA 2003, s. 101 (defendant's bad character), considered at **F12.11**, and to the Criminal Evidence Act 1898, s. 1(4) (above), he will be treated like any other witness. His evidence will be evidence for all the purposes of the case, including the purpose of being evidence against any coaccused (*Rudd* (1948) 32 Cr App R 138, per Humphreys J at p. 140). In *Paul* [1920] 2 KB 183, in which an accused had confined his evidence in chief to an admission of his own guilt, it was held that the prosecution had properly been allowed to cross-examine him and thereby elicit evidence which undermined the defence of his co-accused.

As a Witness for a Co-accused

F4.12 An accused is a competent witness for any co-accused by virtue of the YJCEA 1999, s. 53(1) (see **F4.23**). An accused, however, is not a compellable witness for a co-accused because, under the Criminal Evidence Act 1898, s. 1(1), a person charged in criminal proceedings shall not be called as a witness 'except upon his own application' (see **F4.9**). An accused who does give evidence for a co-accused may be cross-examined to show his own guilt of the offence charged (*Rowland* [1910] 1 KB 458).

A co-accused who ceases to be 'a person charged', and therefore ceases to be on trial, is both competent and compellable as a witness for any 'co-accused'. This may happen in the following ways:

(a) the co-accused pleads guilty;
(b) the co-accused, at the end of the prosecution case, makes a successful submission of no case to answer; or
(c) the co-accused is tried separately as the result of a successful application to sever the indictment.

THE SPOUSE OR CIVIL PARTNER OF THE ACCUSED

F4.13 The competence and compellability of the spouse of an accused is governed by the YJCEA 1999, s. 53(1) (see **F4.23**) and the PACE 1984, s. 80. Section 80 applies in relation to a civil partner of an accused as it applies to a spouse of an accused (Civil Partnership Act 2004, s. 84(1)).

Police and Criminal Evidence Act 1984, s. 80

(2) In any proceedings the wife or husband of a person charged in the proceedings shall, subject to subsection (4) below, be compellable to give evidence on behalf of that person.

(2A) In any proceedings the wife or husband of a person charged in the proceedings shall, subject to subsection (4) below, be compellable—

(a) to give evidence on behalf of any other person charged in the proceedings but only in respect of any specified offence with which that other person is charged; or
(b) to give evidence for the prosecution but only in respect of any specified offence with which any person is charged in the proceedings.

(3) In relation to the wife or husband of a person charged in any proceedings, an offence is a specified offence for the purposes of subsection (2A) above if—

(a) it involves an assault on, or injury or a threat of injury to, the wife or husband or a person who was at the material time under the age of 16;
(b) it is a sexual offence alleged to have been committed in respect of a person who was at the material time under that age; or
(c) it consists of attempting or conspiring to commit, or of aiding, abetting, counselling, procuring or inciting the commission of, an offence falling within paragraph (a) or (b) above.

(4) No person who is charged in any proceedings shall be compellable by virtue of subsection (2) or (2A) above to give evidence in the proceedings.
(4A) References in this section to a person charged in any proceedings do not include a person who is not, or is no longer, liable to be convicted of any offence in the proceedings (whether as a result of pleading guilty or for any other reason).
(5) In any proceedings a person who has been but is no longer married to the accused shall be compellable to give evidence as if that person and the accused had never been married.
(6) Where in any proceedings the age of any person at any time is material for the purposes of subsection (3) above, his age at the material time shall for the purposes of that provision be deemed to be or to have been that which appears to the court to be or to have been his age at that time.
(7) In subsection (3)(b) above 'sexual offence' means an offence under the Protection of Children Act 1978 or part 1 of the Sexual Offences Act 2003.

As a Witness for the Prosecution

The spouse of an accused is competent to give evidence for the prosecution (YJCEA 1999, s. 53(1): see **F4.23**), unless also 'a person charged' in the criminal proceedings (YJCEA 1999, s. 53(4) and (5), considered at **F4.8**). A spouse is competent under s. 53(1) irrespective of whether the evidence to be given will be directed against the accused or any co-accused. **F4.14**

As to compellability, the rule, subject to one exception, is that the spouse shall be compellable to give evidence for the prosecution, but only in respect of any 'specified offence' with which any person is charged in the proceedings (PACE 1984, s. 80(2A)(b)). The exception is where the spouse is also charged in the proceedings (see s. 80(4) and (4A)).

It is submitted that the words 'wife' and 'husband' used in s. 80 refer to persons whose marriage (wherever celebrated) would be recognised by English law. In *Khan* (1987) 84 Cr App R 44, a decision on the common law before the 1984 Act came into force, it was held that a woman who had gone through a Moslem ceremony of marriage with an accused already married under English law to another woman, was in the same position as a mistress, a woman who had not gone through a ceremony of marriage at all or one who had gone through a ceremony of marriage which was void because bigamous. See also *Yacoob* (1981) 72 Cr App R 313. In *Pearce* [2002] 1 WLR 1553 it was held that the words 'wife or husband of the accused' which appeared in s. 80 prior to its amendment by the YJCEA 1999, do not cover a cohabitee of an accused who is not married to the accused, and that proper respect for family life, as envisaged by the ECHR, Article 8, does not require that such a cohabitee should not be compelled to give evidence.

Section 80(3) specifies the offences in respect of which the wife or husband of the accused shall be compellable to give evidence for the prosecution. A spouse is compellable if the offence charged 'involves' an assault on, or injury or a threat of injury to, the wife or husband of the accused or a person who was at the material time under the age of 16. It is unclear, and as yet undecided, whether the 'involvement' must be legal (as a matter of legal definition the offence charged requires an assault on, or injury or a threat of injury to, one of the types of person described in s. 80(3)(a)) or can be factual (as a matter of legal definition the offence charged does not require an assault on or injury or a threat of injury to one of the types of such person but in fact it did involve, or is alleged to have involved, an assault on or injury or a threat of injury to one of the types of such person). See *Lee* [1996] 2 Cr App R 266, construing the similar wording of the CJA 1988, s. 32(2)(a). The phrase 'a threat of injury' may cover not only an uttered threat, but also a threat by conduct, as in *Verolla* [1963] 1 QB 285, where the accused was charged with attempting to murder his wife by poisoning her. A case of that kind, however, is now covered by s. 80(3)(c).

The following propositions, relating to a spouse who is competent but not compellable for the prosecution, derive from *Pitt* [1983] QB 25, at pp. 65–6:

(a) The choice whether to give evidence is that of the spouse, and is not lost because that spouse made a witness statement or gave evidence at the committal proceedings. The spouse retains the right of refusal up to the point when, with full knowledge of that right, he or she takes the oath in the witness-box. Waiver of the right is effective only if made with full knowledge of the right of refusal.
(b) If the spouse waives the right of refusal, he or she becomes an ordinary witness. It follows that if the nature of the evidence then given justifies it, an application may be made to treat the spouse as a hostile witness.
(c) Although not a rule of either law or practice, it is desirable that where a spouse, being competent but not compellable for the prosecution, is called for the prosecution, the judge should explain to the spouse, in the absence of the jury, that before taking the oath, he or she has the right to refuse to give evidence, but that if he or she chooses to give evidence, he or she may be treated like any other witness (but failure to give such an explanation does not necessarily justify interfering with a guilty verdict: *Nelson* [1992] Crim LR 653).

As a Witness for the Accused

F4.15 The spouse of an accused is competent to give evidence for the accused (YJCEA 1999, s. 53(1): see **F4.23**); and shall be compellable to give evidence for the accused (PACE 1984, s. 80(2)), unless also charged in the proceedings (see s. 80(4) and (4A)).

As a Witness for a Co-accused

F4.16 The spouse of an accused is competent to give evidence on behalf of any other person charged in the proceedings, whether or not the accused consents (YJCEA 1999, s. 53(1): see **F4.27**). As to compellability, the rule, subject to one exception, is that the spouse shall be compellable to give evidence on behalf of any such other person, but only in respect of any 'specified offence' with which any person is charged in the proceedings (PACE 1984, s. 80(2A)(a)). The exception is where the spouse is also charged in the proceedings (see s. 80(4) and (4A)).

Competence and Compellability of Former Spouse of the Accused

F4.17 In any proceedings, a person who has been but is no longer married to the accused shall be compellable to give evidence as if they had never been married (PACE 1984, s. 80(5)). Such a person, therefore, is compellable on behalf of the prosecution, the accused or any co-accused, whether the evidence relates to events which occurred before, during or after the terminated marriage. The phrase 'is no longer married' covers the situation where the parties have been divorced and where a voidable marriage has been annulled; but not the situation where the parties have been judicially separated or are merely not cohabiting (whether or not in consequence of an informal arrangement, formal agreement or noncohabitation order). If the marriage of the parties was void *ab initio*, there never was a legally valid marriage, and accordingly a party to such a union will be both competent and compellable on behalf of the accused (the other party to that union), any co-accused or the prosecution. The phrase 'in any proceedings' means any proceedings which take place after s. 80(5) came into effect (1 January 1986); and therefore an ex-wife or an ex-husband is competent and compellable to give evidence in such proceedings about any matter, whether it took place before or after that date (*Cruttenden* [1991] 2 QB 66).

OTHER WITNESSES

Children and Persons of Unsound Mind

F4.18 The competence of a child (or person of unsound mind) to give evidence in criminal proceedings, and the question whether he or she should give sworn or unsworn evidence, are governed by the YJCEA 1999, ss. 53 to 56, which are set out at **F4.23**.

As to competence, the rule is that all persons are (whatever their age) competent to give evidence (s. 53(1)); but a person is not competent if it appears to the court that he is not a person who is able to (a) understand questions put to him as a witness and (b) give answers to them which can be understood (s. 53(2) and (3)). In *MacPherson* [2006] 1 Cr App R 459, it was held that the words 'put to him as a witness' mean the equivalent of 'being asked of him in court'. Accordingly, an infant who can only communicate in baby language with its mother will not ordinarily be competent, but a child who can speak and understand basic English with strangers will be competent. It was also held that there is no requirement that the witness be aware of his status as a witness and that questions of credibility and reliability are not relevant to competence but go to the weight of the evidence and may be considered, if appropriate, on a submission of no case to answer. Equally, a person who has no recollection of an event may be a perfectly competent witness (*DPP v R* [2007] EWHC 1842 (Admin)). The test, in s. 53(3), it is submitted, removes the need to determine whether a child (or person of unsound mind) knows the difference between truth and a lie and the importance of speaking the truth (see *G v DPP* [1997] 2 All ER 755, a decision under the CJA 1988, s. 33A(2A) (the statutory precursor to s. 53(3)), approving Auld J, *obiter*, in *Hampshire* [1995] 3 WLR 260 at p. 268) or is able to distinguish between truth and fiction and between fact and fantasy (see *D* (1995) *The Times*, 15 November 1995, an authority on neither s. 33A(2A) nor s. 53(3)). In *Hampshire* Auld J expressed the view, *obiter*, that although a judge is no longer bound to investigate a child's competence, unless he has reason to doubt it, he may find it appropriate to remind the child, in the presence of the accused and the jury, of the importance of telling the truth, by saying, for example, 'Tell us all you can remember of what happened. Don't make anything up or leave anything out. This is very important' (at p. 269).

Clearly the younger the child, the more likely it is that he or she will be unable to understand questions put and give answers to them which can be understood. However, a court cannot properly conclude that a child is incapable of satisfying the test on the basis of the child's age alone (*MacPherson*; *Powell* [2006] 1 Cr App R 468). The test of competence in s. 53(3) accords with the views of Lord Lane CJ in *Z* [1990] 2 QB 355. In *Wallwork* (1958) 42 Cr App R 153, it was thought to be most undesirable to call as a witness a child as young as five years old. In *Z* Lord Lane CJ held that that decision had been overtaken by events, in particular by the system of video links and by the repeal of the proviso to the CYPA 1933, s. 38(1) (the requirement of corroboration in the case of the unsworn evidence of children), which indicated a change of attitude by Parliament, reflecting in its turn a change of attitude by the public in general to the acceptability of the evidence of young children and an increasing belief that their testimony, when all precautions have been taken, may be just as reliable as that of their elders.

The fact that a child under 10 years of age cannot be prosecuted for the offence of wilfully giving false evidence contrary to the YJCEA 1999, s. 57 (see **B14.16**), is not a reason for excluding the unsworn evidence of a competent child witness (see *N* (1992) 95 Cr App R 256, a decision under the CYPA 1933, s. 38(2), the statutory precursor to s. 57 of the 1999 Act).

Sworn Evidence Whether a child (or person of unsound mind) may be sworn for the purpose of giving evidence on oath is governed by the YJCEA, s. 55. A witness may not be sworn for this purpose unless he has attained the age of 14 and 'has a sufficient appreciation of the solemnity of the occasion and of the particular responsibility to tell the truth which is involved in taking an oath' (s. 55(2)). If the witness is able to give intelligible testimony, i.e. if he is able to understand questions put to him as a witness and give answers to them which can be understood (s. 55(8)), he is presumed to have a sufficient appreciation of those matters unless any party adduces evidence tending to show the contrary (s. 55(3)). If any such evidence is adduced, it is for the party seeking to have the witness sworn to satisfy the **F4.19**

court, on a balance of probabilities, that he has attained the age of 14 and has a sufficient appreciation of the matters in question (s. 55(4)).

F4.20 **Unsworn Evidence** The evidence of a person (of any age) who is competent to give evidence in criminal proceedings but who is not permitted to be sworn for the purpose of giving evidence on oath shall be given unsworn and shall be received in evidence by the court (s. 56(1), (2) and (4)). A deposition of unsworn evidence given by such a person may also be taken for the purposes of criminal proceedings and shall also be received in evidence (s. 56(3) and (4)).

Determining the Competence of Children and Persons of Unsound Mind

F4.21 If a judge has reason to doubt whether a child (or person of unsound mind) is able to understand questions put to him or her as a witness, or to give answers to them which can be understood, because he or she has difficulty in comprehension or expression, the judge will conduct a preliminary investigation under s. 54 (considered at **F4.2**). Such an inquiry should be recorded by the shorthand writer so that it appears in the official transcript (*Khan* (1981) 73 Cr App R 190). The issue of competence should be determined in the ordinary way, i.e. before the witness is sworn, usually as a preliminary issue at the start of the trial, when the judge should watch the video-taped interview of the child and/or ask the child appropriate questions (*MacPherson* [2006] 1 Cr App R 459). In *Hampshire* [1996] QB 1, which was not a decision under s. 54, it was held as follows:

(a) The issue of competence should be dealt with at the earliest possible moment, not as an act of 'ratification' after the evidence has been given.
(b) The judge should conduct the investigation. It is a matter of his perception of the child's understanding as demonstrated in ordinary discourse, not an issue to be resolved by him in response to an adversarial examination and cross-examination.
(c) If there has been an application to use video-recorded evidence (see **F16.47**), the judge's pre-trial view of the recording, if the interview has been properly conducted, will normally enable him to form a view on competence, but if it leaves him in doubt, he should conduct an investigation.

The question of a child's competence to give evidence must be decided at the time of the trial, but should be kept under review, and may need to be revisited when the child's evidence is complete. Thus although at the start of the trial a video-taped interview may indicate competence, a ruling to that effect should be reversed if the child is unable to understand questions at the trial, or to give answers to them which can be understood, which may be the result of lapse of time and lack of memory (*Powell* [2006] 1 Cr App R 468).

Prior to the enactment of the YJCEA 1999, it was held that the question whether a child is capable of giving 'intelligible testimony' does not require any input from experts such as child psychiatrists, because it is a simple test well within the capability of a judge or magistrate (see *G v DPP* [1997] 2 All ER 755). It is submitted that s. 54(5), whereby expert evidence may be received on the question, should be invoked only where necessary.

If a judge conducts an enquiry into the competence of a mentally handicapped person, it is not normally necessary to call that person to give evidence on the subject: the proper course is to adduce expert medical evidence (*Barratt* [1996] Crim LR 495).

Any proceedings held for the determination of the question whether a witness may be sworn for the purpose of giving evidence on oath should take place in the absence of the jury (s. 55(5)). Expert evidence may be received on the question (s. 55(6)) and any questioning of the witness shall be conducted by the court in the presence of the parties (s. 55(7)).

The Weight to be Attached to Evidence given by Persons of Unsound Mind

F4.22 Where a mentally handicapped person gives evidence, it is left to the jury to attach to his evidence such weight as they see fit. If his evidence is so tainted with insanity as to be unworthy of credit, it is the proper function of the jury to disregard it and not to act upon it (*Hill* (1851) 2 Den CC 254). However, a person suffering from a mental illness may be a reliable witness. In *Barratt* [1996] Crim LR 495, in which the witness was suffering from the psychiatric condition known as fixed belief paranoia and held bizarre beliefs about certain aspects of her private life, the court could see no reason for supposing that on matters not affected by her condition, her evidence was not as reliable as that of any other witness.

Youth Justice and Criminal Evidence Act 1999 Part II, Chapter V

F4.23 Youth Justice and Criminal Evidence Act 1999, ss. 53 to 56

53.—(1) At every stage in criminal proceedings all persons are (whatever their age) competent to give evidence.

(2) Subsection (1) has effect subject to subsections (3) and (4).

(3) A person is not competent to give evidence in criminal proceedings if it appears to the court that he is not a person who is able to—

(a) understand questions put to him as a witness, and

(b) give answers to them which can be understood.

(4) A person charged in criminal proceedings is not competent to give evidence in the proceedings for the prosecution (whether he is the only person, or is one of two or more persons, charged in the proceedings).

(5) In subsection (4) the reference to a person charged in criminal proceedings does not include a person who is not, or is no longer, liable to be convicted of any offence in the proceedings (whether as a result of pleading guilty or for any other reason).

54.—(1) Any question whether a witness in criminal proceedings is competent to give evidence in the proceedings, whether raised—

(a) by a party to the proceedings, or

(b) by the court of its own motion,

shall be determined by the court in accordance with this section.

(2) It is for the party calling the witness to satisfy the court that, on a balance of probabilities, the witness is competent to give evidence in the proceedings.

(3) In determining the question mentioned in subsection (1) the court shall treat the witness as having the benefit of any directions under section 19 [special measures directions in the case of vulnerable and intimidated witnesses] which the court has given, or proposes to give, in relation to the witness.

(4) Any proceedings held for the determination of the question shall take place in the absence of the jury (if there is one).

(5) Expert evidence may be received on the question.

(6) Any questioning of the witness (where the court considers that necessary) shall be conducted by the court in the presence of the parties.

55.—(1) Any question whether a witness in criminal proceedings may be sworn for the purpose of giving evidence on oath, whether raised—

(a) by a party to the proceedings, or

(b) by the court of its own motion,

shall be determined by the court in accordance with this section.

(2) The witness may not be sworn for that purpose unless—

(a) he has attained the age of 14, and

(b) he has a sufficient appreciation of the solemnity of the occasion and of the particular responsibility to tell the truth which is involved in taking an oath.

(3) The witness shall, if he is able to give intelligible testimony, be presumed to have a sufficient appreciation of those matters if no evidence tending to show the contrary is adduced (by any party).

(4) If any such evidence is adduced, it is for the party seeking to have the witness sworn to satisfy the court that, on a balance of probabilities, the witness has attained the age of 14 and has a sufficient appreciation of the matters mentioned in subsection (2)(b).

(5) Any proceedings held for the determination of the question mentioned in subsection (1) shall take place in the absence of the jury (if there is one).

(6) Expert evidence may be received on the question.

(7) Any questioning of the witness (where the court considers that necessary) shall be conducted by the court in the presence of the parties.

(8) For the purposes of this section a person is able to give intelligible testimony if he is able to—
  (a) understand questions put to him as a witness, and
  (b) give answers to them which can be understood.

56.—(1) Subsections (2) and (3) apply to a person (of any age) who—
  (a) is competent to give evidence in criminal proceedings, but
  (b) (by virtue of section 55(2)) is not permitted to be sworn for the purpose of giving evidence on oath in such proceedings.

(2) The evidence in criminal proceedings of a person to whom this subsection applies shall be given unsworn.

(3) A deposition of unsworn evidence given by a person to whom this subsection applies may be taken for the purposes of criminal proceedings as if that evidence had been given on oath.

(4) A court in criminal proceedings shall accordingly receive in evidence any evidence given unsworn in pursuance of subsection (2) or (3).

(5) Where a person ('the witness') who is competent to give evidence in criminal proceedings gives evidence in such proceedings unsworn, no conviction, verdict or finding in those proceedings shall be taken to be unsafe for the purposes of any of sections 2(1), 13(1) and 16(1) of the Criminal Appeal Act 1968 (grounds for allowing appeals) by reason only that it appears to the Court of Appeal that the witness was a person falling within section 55(2) (and should accordingly have given his evidence on oath).

The Sovereign and Diplomats

F4.24 The Sovereign is a competent but not a compellable witness. Total or partial immunity from compellability to give evidence is also enjoyed by heads of other sovereign states; diplomatic agents; members of the family of a diplomatic agent forming part of his household; members of the administrative and technical staff of a diplomatic mission and members of their families; persons connected with consular posts; and members of the staff of international organisations. See:

(a) Diplomatic Privileges Act 1964, s. 2(1) and sch. 1, arts. 1, 31, 37, 38(2), and 39;
(b) Consular Relations Act 1968, s. 1(1) and sch. 1, arts. 1(1), 44 and 58(2);
(c) International Organisations Act 1968;
(d) State Immunity Act 1978; and
(e) International Organisations Act 1981.

Bankers

F4.25 Subject to a variety of safeguards, a copy of an entry in a banker's book shall in all legal proceedings be received as prima facie evidence of such entry, and of the matters, transactions and accounts therein recorded (Bankers' Books Evidence Act 1879, ss. 3 and 9). Provision is made for proof that the book was one of the ordinary books of the bank, that the entry was made in the usual and ordinary course of business, that the book is in the custody and control of the bank, and that the copy has been examined with the original entry and is correct (ss. 4 and 5 of the 1879 Act). In any legal proceeding to which the bank is not a party, bank personnel cannot be compelled to produce the originals of such books or to give evidence to prove the matters recorded therein, unless specifically ordered to do so by a judge (see Bankers' Books Evidence Act 1879, s. 6 at **F8.27**).

OATHS AND AFFIRMATIONS

General Rule and Exceptions

F4.26 A witness will normally be sworn for the purpose of giving evidence, i.e. the witness will take the oath or make an affirmation. However, the evidence of a person who is competent to give evidence but who is not permitted to be sworn, shall be given unsworn (see **F4.20**); and at common law a witness called merely for the purpose of producing a document need not be sworn (*Perry v Gibson* (1934) 1 A & E 48). As to the latter situation, the witness, if not sworn, is not liable to cross-examination. However, if the identity of the document is disputed, and must be established, this must be done by sworn evidence.

Where a video recording of an interview with a child is admitted under the YJCEA 1999, s. 27, and the child is then aged 14 or over, the oath should be administered before the start of the cross-examination (*Simmonds* [1996] Crim LR 816, a decision under the CJA 1988, s. 32A, the statutory precursor to s. 27). Where the oath is administered at some later stage, the judge should warn the jury that the earlier answers were not evidence until given subsequent ratification. Without such an explanation, an appeal would be unanswerable (*Simmonds*, applying *Lee* [1988] Crim LR 525). Under the YJCEA 1999, s. 56(5), where a witness who is competent to give evidence in criminal proceedings has given evidence unsworn, no conviction, verdict or finding in those proceedings shall be taken to be unsafe for the purposes of the grounds of appeal in the Criminal Appeal Act 1968, ss. 2(1), 13(1) or 16(1), by reason only that he was a person falling within s. 55(2) of the 1999 Act and therefore should have given his evidence on oath.

Form and Manner of Oath: Christians and Jews

F4.27

Oaths Act 1978, s. 1

(1) Any oath may be administered and taken in England, Wales or Northern Ireland in the following form and manner:—

The person taking the oath shall hold the New Testament, or, in the case of a Jew, the Old Testament, in his uplifted hand, and shall say or repeat after the officer administering the oath the words 'I swear by Almighty God that . . .', followed by the words of the oath prescribed by law.

. . .

(4) In this section 'officer' means any person duly authorised to administer oaths.

The words of s. 1 are directive; therefore failure to comply with them will not necessarily invalidate the taking of an oath, because the efficacy of an oath depends upon it being taken in a way binding, and intended to be binding, upon the conscience of the intended witness (*Chapman* [1980] Crim LR 42, where leave to appeal was refused, the witness in question having failed to take the Testament in his hand).

In the case of a witness in the trial proper, 'the words of the oath prescribed by law', approved by a resolution of the judges of the King's Bench Division on 11 January 1927, are 'the evidence which I shall give shall be the truth, the whole truth and nothing but the truth'. When a witness gives evidence in a trial within a trial, the oath is 'I swear by Almighty God that I will true answer make to all such questions as the Court shall demand of me.' In relation to any oath administered to and taken by any person before a youth court, or administered to and taken by any child or young person before any other court, s. 1 of the Oaths Act 1978 shall have effect as if the words 'I promise before Almighty God' were set out instead of the words 'I swear by Almighty God that' (CYPA 1963, s. 28(1)). Where, in any oath otherwise duly administered and taken, either of the forms mentioned in s. 28 of the CYPA 1963 is used instead of the other, the oath shall nevertheless be deemed to have been duly administered and taken (s. 28(2)).

Form and Manner of Oath: Other Religious Beliefs

F4.28

Oaths Act 1978, s. 1

(2) The officer shall (unless the person about to take the oath voluntarily objects thereto, or is physically incapable of so taking the oath) administer the oath in the form and manner aforesaid without question.

(3) In the case of a person who is neither a Christian nor a Jew, the oath shall be administered in any lawful manner.

(4) In this section 'officer' means any person duly authorised to administer oaths.

Section 1(2) makes it clear that it is incumbent upon a person who is neither a Christian nor a Jew to object to the taking of an oath in the form and manner prescribed by s. 1(1). Such a person may affirm or may take the oath upon such holy book as is appropriate to his or her religious belief. Muslims are sworn on the Koran (*Morgan* (1764) 1 Leach 54). Hindus are sworn on the Vedas or other sacred books. Parsees are sworn on the Zendavesta. The modern practice is to inquire what oath a witness accepts as binding and swear him accordingly.

Whether an oath is administered 'in a lawful manner' for the purposes of s. 1(3) does not depend on what may be the considerable intricacies of the particular religion adhered to by the witness but on (a) whether the oath appears to the court to be binding on the conscience of the witness and (b) whether it is an oath which the witness himself considers to be binding on his conscience (*Kemble* [1990] 1 WLR 1111, where a Muslim, who had taken the oath using the New Testament, was held to have been properly sworn).

In cases in which the ground is properly laid for an expectation that a witness will take the oath on a particular holy book, but the witness affirms, the judge has a discretion to allow the reason why the witness did not take the oath on the holy book to be explored sensitively, but no such questioning should be undertaken without the matter being raised before the judge in the absence of the jury (*Mehrban* [2002] 1 Cr App R 561, where a Muslim witness for the prosecution who had taken the oath on the Koran had challenged one of the accused, also a Muslim, to do likewise).

Swearing with Uplifted Hand

F4.29 **Oaths Act 1978, s. 3**

If any person to whom an oath is administered desires to swear with uplifted hand, in the form and manner in which an oath is usually administered in Scotland, he shall be permitted to do so, and the oath shall be administered to him in such form and manner without further question.

Validity of Oaths

F4.30 **Oaths Act 1978, s. 4**

(1) In any case in which an oath may lawfully be and has been administered to any person, if it has been administered in a form and manner other than that prescribed by law, he is bound by it if it has been administered in such form and with such ceremonies as he may have declared to be binding.

(2) Where an oath has been duly administered and taken, the fact that the person to whom it was administered had, at the time of taking it, no religious belief, shall not for any purpose affect the validity of the oath.

Affirmations

F4.31 **Oaths Act 1978, ss. 5 and 6**

5.—(1) Any person who objects to being sworn shall be permitted to make his solemn affirmation instead of taking an oath.

(2) Subsection (1) above shall apply in relation to a person to whom it is not reasonably practicable without inconvenience or delay to administer an oath in the manner appropriate to his religious belief as it applies in relation to a person objecting to be sworn.

(3) A person who may be permitted under subsection (2) above to make his solemn affirmation may also be required to do so.

(4) A solemn affirmation shall be of the same force and effect as an oath.

6.—(1) Subject to subsection (2) below, every affirmation shall be as follows:—

'I, [name] do solemnly, sincerely and truly declare and affirm,'

and then proceed with the words of the oath prescribed by law, omitting any words of imprecation or calling to witness.

(2) Every affirmation in writing shall commence:—

'I, [name] of [address], do solemnly and sincerely affirm,'

and the form in lieu of the jurat shall be 'Affirmed at this day of 20 , Before me.'

Section F5 Corroboration

GENERAL RULE

The general rule is that there is no requirement that evidence be corroborated and no requirement that the tribunal of fact be warned of the danger of acting on uncorroborated evidence. This section concerns two categories of exception to the general rule: **F5.1**

(a) where corroboration is required by statute; and
(b) where the tribunal of fact should be warned to exercise care before acting on the evidence of certain types of witness, if unsupported.

There is a third category of exception, made up of four cases, confessions by mentally handicapped persons, identification evidence, sudden unexplained infant deaths and unconvincing hearsay evidence, in all of which there is a special need for caution which has led to requirements analogous to but different from those relating to the first two categories. These requirements are considered at **F17.37**, **F18.19** ***et seq.***, **F5.15** and **F16.56** respectively.

CORROBORATION REQUIRED BY STATUTE

Corroboration is required by statute in four cases: treason; perjury (see **B14.14**); offences of speeding (see **C6.47**); and attempts to commit any such offences. As to the first case, treason, the Treason Act 1795, s. 1 provides that a person charged with the offence of treason by compassing the death or restraint of the Queen or her heirs shall not be convicted except on the oaths of two lawful and credible witnesses. As to the last case, under Criminal Attempts Act 1981, s. 2(2)(g), any provision whereby a person may not be convicted or committed for trial on the uncorroborated evidence of one witness (including any provision requiring the evidence of not less than two credible witnesses) shall have effect with respect to an offence under s. 1 of the Act of attempting to commit an offence (see **A6.31**) as it has effect with respect to the offence attempted. Where corroboration is required by statute, a conviction should not be based on uncorroborated evidence and, if it is, will be open to successful appeal. Thus, in the absence of corroboration, the judge should direct an acquittal. **F5.2**

The Meaning of Corroboration

In the case of perjury, corroboration bears the technical meaning it once bore at common law (*Hamid* (1979) 69 Cr App R 324). Corroboration in this technical sense is probably also required in the case of the other three statutory provisions (see per Lord Reading CJ in *Baskerville* [1916] 2 KB 658 at p. 667). Evidence, to be capable of being corroboration in the strict or technical sense, must: **F5.3**

(a) be relevant and admissible (*Scarrott* [1978] QB 1016 at p. 1021);
(b) be credible (*DPP v Kilbourne* [1973] AC 729 at p. 746 and *DPP v Hester* [1973] AC 296 at p. 315);
(c) be independent, i.e. emanate from a source other than the witness requiring corroboration (see *Whitehead* [1929] 1 KB 99); and
(d) implicate the accused.

Corroboration Direction

F5.4 Where a judge directs a jury on corroboration, he should explain what it means, making clear the requirements of credibility, independence and implication (see *Fallon* [1993] Crim LR 591). The judge should also indicate the evidence which is and is not capable of being corroboration (*Charles* [1976] 68 Cr App R 334n; *Cullinane* [1984] Crim LR 420; and *Webber* [1987] Crim LR 412) and, in the case of evidence which is capable of being corroboration, should explain to the jury that it is for them to decide whether the evidence does in fact constitute corroboration (*Tragen* [1956] Crim LR 332; *McInnes* (1989) 90 Cr App R 99).

CARE WARNINGS

General

F5.5 In appropriate circumstances the jury should be warned to exercise caution before acting on the evidence of certain types of witness, if unsupported. Whether a warning is given is a matter of judicial discretion dependent on the particular circumstances of the case, and failure to give a warning therefore will not necessarily furnish grounds for a successful appeal. Equally, if a warning is given, the strength of warning and the extent to which the judge should elaborate upon it, also turn on the particular circumstances of the case. The categories of witness that fall to be considered, for the purposes of considering whether to give a care warning, are:

(a) accomplices giving evidence for the prosecution and complainants in sexual cases (which fall to be considered together);
(b) other witnesses whose evidence may be unreliable;
(c) witnesses whose evidence may be tainted by an improper motive;
(d) children; and
(e) patients at a secure hospital.

Accomplices giving Evidence for the Prosecution and Complainants in Sexual Cases

F5.6 **Position at Common Law** At common law, the jury had to be warned of the danger of acting on the evidence, if not corroborated, of accomplices giving evidence for the prosecution and complainants, whether male or female, in sexual cases. The warning was not required, however, where the evidence of the accomplice was mainly favourable to the accused (*Royce-Bentley* [1974] 1 WLR 535). Nor was a warning required in sexual cases in which identification was in issue, not the commission of the offence. In such cases it normally sufficed to direct the jury in accordance with *Turnbull* [1977] QB 224 (see **F18.19** ***et seq.***: see *Chance* [1988] QB 932. Where a warning was required, it had held to be a 'full' warning, comprising:

(a) a warning to the jury that it was dangerous to convict without corroboration but that they could do so if satisfied of the truth of the evidence of the accomplice or complainant;
(b) an explanation of the technical meaning of corroboration (see **F5.3**);
(c) an indication of what evidence was and was not capable of being corroboration; and
(d) an explanation that it was for them to decide whether evidence did in fact constitute corroboration.

The justification for the full warning in the case of an accomplice giving evidence for the prosecution was that such a witness may have a purpose of his own to serve. Thus he may give false evidence out of spite, or he may exaggerate or invent the accused's role in the crime in order to minimise the extent of his own culpability. The understanding justification for the full warning in the case of sexual offences was the assumption that an allegation of a sexual offence is easy to make but difficult to refute. There is also a danger that a complainant may give false evidence by reason of spite, sexual neurosis, jealousy, fantasy, or a refusal to admit to having consented to an act of which he or she is later ashamed (11th Report, Criminal Law Revision Committee, cmnd 4991, para.186).

Effect of the CJPOA 1994, s. 32 Section 32 of the CJPOA 1994 removed the requirement for full warnings. There were a number of compelling reasons in favour of such reform. They included the following: F5.7

(a) a full warning was required irrespective of the particular circumstances of the case or the credibility of the particular accomplice or complainant;
(b) the highly technical rules relating to the meaning of corroboration had rendered the full warning complex and difficult to understand;
(c) there was an element of contradiction in directing the jury that it was 'dangerous' to convict on evidence if uncorroborated but that they could nonetheless do so;
(d) many sexual offences are committed in circumstances in which it is difficult or impossible to obtain corroboration, and therefore the requirement was capable of allowing the guilty to be acquitted; and
(e) in cases of sexual abuse of children, the requirement compounded the difficulties of convicting the guilty.

Criminal Justice and Public Order Act 1994, s. 32

32.—(1) Any requirement whereby at a trial on indictment it is obligatory for the court to give the jury a warning about convicting the accused on the uncorroborated evidence of a person merely because that person is—
(a) an alleged accomplice of the accused, or
(b) where the offence charged is a sexual offence, the person in respect of whom it is alleged to have been committed,
is hereby abrogated.
. . .
(3) Any requirement that—
(a) is applicable at the summary trial of a person for an offence, and
(b) corresponds to the requirement mentioned in subsection (1) above . . .
is hereby abrogated.

The effect of these provisions is to abrogate the requirements whereby a full warning was obligatory. The judge, however, still retains the discretion to warn the jury to exercise caution whenever he considers it appropriate to do so, whether in respect of an accomplice or a complainant or any other witness. This was made clear in *Makanjuola* [1995] 1 WLR 1348, the leading authority on s. 32, in which Lord Taylor CJ summarised the relevant principles (at p. 1351).

> (1) Section 32(1) abrogated the requirement to give a corroboration direction in respect of an alleged accomplice or a complainant of a sexual offence, simply because a witness falls into one of those categories. (2) It is a matter for the judge's discretion what, if any warning, he considers appropriate in respect of such a witness as indeed in respect of any other witness in whatever type of case. Whether he chooses to give a warning and in what terms will depend on the circumstances of the case, the issues raised and the content and quality of the witness's evidence. (3) In some cases, it may be appropriate for the judge to warn the jury to exercise caution before acting upon the unsupported evidence of a witness. This will not be so simply because the witness is a complainant of a sexual offence nor will it necessarily be so because a witness is alleged to be an accomplice. There will need to be an evidential basis for suggesting that the evidence of the witness may be unreliable. An evidential basis does not include mere suggestion by cross-examining counsel. (4) If any question arises as to whether the judge should give a special warning in respect of a witness, it is desirable that the question be resolved by discussion with counsel in the absence of the jury before final speeches. (5) Where the judge does decide to give some warning in respect of a witness, it will be appropriate to do so as part of the judge's review of the evidence and his comments as to how the jury should evaluate it rather than as a set-piece legal direction. (6) Where some warning is required, it will be for the judge to decide the

strength and terms of the warning. It does not have to be invested with the whole florid regime of the old corroboration rules. (7) It follows that we emphatically disagree with the tentative submission [that if a judge does give a warning, he should give a full warning and should tell the jury what corroboration is in the technical sense and identify the evidence capable of being corroborative]. Attempts to re-impose the straitjacket of the old corroboration rules are strongly to be deprecated. (8) Finally, this court will be disinclined to interfere with a trial judge's exercise of his discretion save in a case where that exercise is unreasonable in the *Wednesbury* sense: see *Associated Provincial Picture Houses Ltd v Wednesbury Corporation* [1948] 1 KB 223.

F5.8 Circumstances in which Warning should be Given As to the circumstances in which it may be appropriate for the judge to give a warning, in *Makanjuola* Lord Taylor said:

> The judge will often consider that no special warning is required at all. Where, however, the witness has been shown to be unreliable, he or she may consider it necessary to urge caution. In a more extreme case, if the witness is shown to have lied, to have made previous false complaints, or to bear the defendant some grudge, a stronger warning may be thought appropriate and the judge may suggest it would be wise to look for some supporting material before acting on the impugned witness's evidence. We stress that these observations are merely illustrative of some, not all, of the factors which the judges may take into account in measuring where a witness stands in the scale of reliability and what response they should make at that level in their directions to the jury.

F5.9 'Supporting Material' In cases in which, after *Makanjuola*, the trial judge decides to direct the jury that 'it would be wise to look for some supporting material' it is incumbent on the judge to identify any 'independent supporting evidence' (*B* [2000] Crim LR 181). It is submitted that such evidence may be furnished by any of the following.

(a) Evidence of an out-of-court confession by the accused.
(b) A damaging admission made by the accused in the course of giving evidence.
(c) Lies told by the accused, whether told in or out of court. In order to constitute 'supporting evidence', however, it is submitted that the lie should meet the criteria formerly employed to determine whether a lie amounted to corroboration in the technical sense, namely that (i) the lie must relate to a material issue (ii) the motive for the lie must be a realisation of guilt and a fear of the truth, as opposed to a lie told, for example, in an attempt to bolster up a just cause or out of shame or a wish to conceal disgraceful behaviour from the family and (iii) the lie must be shown to be such by evidence other than that of the witness whose evidence is to be supported, i.e. by admission or by evidence from an independent witness (see *Lucas* [1981] QB 720 at p. 724; and see also *Credland v Knowler* (1951) 35 Cr App R 48 and *Dawson v McKenzie* [1908] 45 SLR 473).
(d) Evidence of the silence of the accused, where an accusation is made by someone speaking to him on even terms, admissible at common law to show that he accepts the accusation (see **F19.2** and **F19.3**).
(e) Inferences properly drawn under CJPOA, ss. 34 to 37 (see **F19.4** ***et seq.***).
(f) Evidence of refusal to consent to the taking of 'intimate samples' (see **F19.29**).
(g) Similar fact evidence (see **F12.20** ***et seq.***).

It is submitted that in sexual cases in which a special warning is properly given in respect of the evidence of the complainant, the following evidence would not constitute 'supporting material'.

(a) Evidence of a recent complaint admissible by way of exception to the rule against previous consistent statements (see **F6.20**). Such evidence is not truly 'supportive' in that it emanates from the complainant herself (see *Whitehead* [1929] 1 KB 99).
(b) Evidence of the complainant's distress. This evidence also emanates from the complainant herself but, it is submitted, could be 'supportive' when the distress was observed shortly after the offence and there was nothing to suggest that it was simulated

(see *Redpath* [1962] 46 Cr App R 319, *Chauhan* (1981) 73 Cr App R 323 and *Dowley* [1983] Crim LR 168). The weight to be given to evidence of distress varies infinitely and rather than warning juries routinely that little weight should be attached to such evidence, in appropriate cases the judge should alert the jury to the sometimes very real risk that the distress may have been feigned (*Romeo* [2004] Crim LR 302).

(c) Medical evidence, in a case of rape, to show that someone had intercourse with the complainant at a time consistent with her evidence. Such medical evidence, by itself, neither implicates the accused nor proves absence of consent (see *James v R* (1970) 55 Cr App R 299; and cf. per Lord Lane CJ in *Hills* (1987) 86 Cr App R 26 at p. 31. See also *Pountney* [1989] Crim LR 216 and *Franklin* [1989] Crim LR 499).

It may well be that there is properly no desire to revive 'the whole florid regime of the old corroboration rules', but it is submitted that in the 'more extreme case' in which a special warning is thought to be desirable, evidence in the foregoing categories cannot fairly be described as evidence supportive of the evidence of the impugned witness.

Other Witnesses whose Evidence may be Unreliable

Prior to the implementation of CJPOA 1994, s. 32, there were a number of common-law decisions to the effect that a jury should be warned to exercise caution before acting on the evidence of particular types of witness whose evidence might be unreliable for one of a number of reasons. Some of the authorities suggested that the warning was discretionary or desirable as a matter of practice; others suggested that it was sometimes obligatory. In *Muncaster* [1999] Crim LR 409, it was held that all such authorities need to be reconsidered in the light of *Makanjuola* which must be read as applying to all cases in which the evidence of a witness may be suspect because he falls into a particular category. **F5.10**

An Accomplice who is a Co-accused

An accomplice, being an accused who, in giving evidence in his own defence, incriminates another co-accused, may be regarded as having a purpose of his own to serve. For this reason it was held, prior to the implementation of CJPOA 1994, s. 32, that it was desirable to warn the jury of the danger of acting on his unsupported evidence, but that every case should be looked at in the light of its own facts (see *Prater* [1960] 2 QB 464 and *Knowlden* (1983) 77 Cr App R 94; and cf. *Perman* [1995] Crim LR 736, where the evidence incriminated the co-accused in one material respect, but otherwise exonerated him). Where a warning was given, there was no need for a 'full' corroboration warning (see **F5.6**) — the jury simply had to be told that the witness may have had a purpose of his own to serve (*Cheema* [1994] 1 WLR 147). Following *Makanjuola* [1995] 1 WLR 1348, whether a warning is given at all and, if it is, the strength of the warning, continue to be matters of judicial discretion dependent on the particular circumstances of the case (*Muncaster* [1999] Crim LR 409). In *Jones* [2004] 1 Cr App R 60 it was held that in the case of cut-throat defences, even if they are mirror-image cut-throat defences, a warning should normally be considered and given and the judge, in exercising his discretion as to what to say, should at least warn the jury to examine the evidence of each co-accused with care because each has or may have an interest of his own to serve. (Cf. *Burrows* [2000] Crim LR 48 which, according to *Jones*, turned on its own particular facts.) However, failure to give such a warning, where required, will not found a successful appeal if the fact that each of the accused had an axe to grind would have been obvious to the jury (*Petkar* [2004] 1 Cr App R 270). There is a particular need for a warning where one co-accused has refused to answer questions in interview and was therefore able, if he wished, to tailor his defence to the facts in evidence. In many or most cases where a trial judge has to consider what if any warning to give, where co-accused have given evidence against each other, he might consider four points to put to the jury. (1) The jury should consider the case for and against each accused separately. (2) The jury should decide the case on all the evidence, including the evidence of each accused's co-accused. (3) When considering the **F5.11** evidence of a co-accused, the jury should bear in mind that he may have an interest to serve or an axe to grind. (4) The jury should assess the evidence of co-accused in the same way as that of the evidence of any other witness in the case (*Jones* [2004] 1 Cr App R 60).

Witnesses whose Evidence may be Tainted by an Improper Motive

F5.12 At common law, a judge is obliged to advise a jury to proceed with caution where there is material to suggest that a witness' evidence may be tainted by an improper motive, the strength of advice varying according to the facts of the case (*Beck* [1982] 1 WLR 461). Thus where an offender, awaiting sentence, gives evidence for the prosecution in another case, knowing that at the very least he thereby stands a chance of having his sentence reduced, the potential fallibility of his evidence should be put squarely to the jury (*Chan Wai-Keung v R* [1995] 1 WLR 251). *Ashgar* [1995] 1 Cr App R 223 was a murder charge arising out of a fight involving a number of men. Three of the men pleaded guilty to affray and gave evidence against A. The defence case was that they had colluded with others to fabricate a story incriminating A to protect one of their number. It was held that a warning should have been given on the danger of convicting A on the evidence of the three men without some independent supporting evidence.

In *Pringle v R* [2003] UKPC 9, a case of murder which depended in part on the evidence of a cellmate that the accused had confessed to him, the Privy Council held that if there are indications that a cell confession may be tainted by an improper motive — which was thought to be not an exacting test — the judge should draw the jury's attention to these indications and their possible significance. On the facts the judge should have pointed out that the cellmate was an untried prisoner, it was not unknown for persons in his position to wish to ingratiate themselves with the police, that to report a confession was a convenient and obvious way of doing so, and that the jury should therefore be cautious before accepting his evidence. In *Benedetto v R* [2003] 1 WLR 1545 the Privy Council went further and held that evidence from an untried prisoner that a fellow untried prisoner confessed to him that he was guilty of the crime for which he was being held in custody, raises an acute problem which will always call for special attention in view of the danger that it may lead to a miscarriage of justice. It was held that the evidence of prisoner informers is inherently unreliable in view of the personal advantage which such witnesses think they may obtain by providing information to the authorities. Such witnesses, it was said, tend to have no interest whatsoever in the proper course of justice. The prisoner against whom the evidence is given is always at a disadvantage. He is afforded none of the usual protections against the inaccurate recording or invention of words used by him when interviewed by the police and it may be difficult for him to obtain all the information needed to expose fully the informer's bad character. There are two steps which the judge must take, both equally important, first to draw the jury's attention to the indications that may justify the inferences that the prisoner's evidence is tainted and second to advise the jury to be cautious before accepting his evidence. The judge must examine the evidence so that he can instruct the jury fully as to where the indications are to be found and as to their significance. However, in *Stone* [2005] EWCA Crim 105, it was held that not every case involving a cell confession requires the detailed directions discussed in *Pringle* and *Benedetto*. The court held as follows.

(a) Cell confessions prompt the most careful consideration by the trial judge, but it is not trammelled by fixed rules and the judge is best placed to decide the strength of any warning and the necessary extent of any accompanying analysis.

(b) In the case of a standard two-line confession, there is generally a need to point out that such confessions are often easy to concoct and difficult to prove and that experience has shown that prisoners may have many motives to lie. Further, if the prison informant has a significant criminal record or history of lying, this should usually be pointed out, together with an explanation that it gives rise to a need for great care, and why.

(c) However, a summing-up should be tailored by the trial judge to the circumstances of the particular case. Where (as in *Stone* itself) an alleged confession, for whatever reason, would not be easy to invent, then it would be absurd to require a judge to tell the jury that cell confessions are easy to concoct. Similarly, where (as in *Stone* itself) the defence has deliberately not cross-examined the informant about the motive of hope of obtaining advantage, the judge is not required to tell the jury that, merely because the informant was a prisoner, there might, intrinsically, have been such a motive.
(d) There are cases where the prisoner has witnessed the acts constituting the offence in which it is appropriate to treat him as an ordinary witness about whose evidence nothing out of the usual needs to be said and, in relation to those cases, there is no suggestion that a potential motive to gain advantage with the authorities will be absent. Furthermore, indications that the prison informant's evidence may be tainted by an improper motive have to be found in the evidence.
(e) Moreover, it is clear from *Muncaster* [1999] Crim LR 409 (see **F5.13**) and the general language used in *Makanjuola* [1995] 1 WLR 1348 (see **F5.10**) that obligations to give special warnings arising in cases such as *Beck* have to be looked at in the light of the statutory abrogation in relation to accomplices giving evidence for the prosecution and complainants in sexual cases. It would be absurd to suppose that the rules for cases such as *Beck* have survived the statutory abrogation so as to impose obligations more onerous than those now applicable to the original cases.

A warning may be appropriate in the case of the unsupported evidence of a woman upon whose immoral earnings the accused is charged with having lived, even if she is not an accomplice (see *King* (1914) 10 Cr App R 117 and cf. *Hanton* (1985) *The Times*, 14 February 1985) and in the case of a spouse of an accomplice called to give evidence on his or her behalf (see *Allen* [1965] 2 QB 295). A warning may also be appropriate in the case of a witness acting out of malevolence or spite, or with some financial or other personal interest in the outcome of the trial, or who is biased or partial for some other reason.

Children

There was a time when an accused was not liable to be convicted on the unsworn evidence of a child appearing on behalf of the prosecution unless that evidence was corroborated (see CYPA 1933, proviso to s. 38(1)); and when the sworn evidence of a child required a corroboration warning as a matter of law (see, for example, *Cleal* [1942] 1 All ER 203). The former statutory requirement has been repealed (see CJA 1991, s. 101(2)); as to the latter common-law rule, CJA 1988, s. 34(2) now provides that 'Any requirement whereby at a trial on indictment it is obligatory for the court to give the jury a warning about convicting the accused on the uncorroborated evidence of a child is abrogated'. Despite these statutory reforms, in some cases the evidence of some children may remain unreliable, whether by reason of childish imagination, suggestibility or fallibility of memory. In *Pryce* [1991] Crim LR 379, it was held that it was not necessary to give a direction to treat the evidence of a six-year-old with caution, because in effect that would be to reintroduce an abrogated rule, but, after *Makanjuola* [1995] 1 WLR 1348, it is submitted that whether a direction is given, and if so the terms of the direction, are matters of judicial discretion turning on the circumstances of the case (see *L* [1999] Crim LR 489). Circumstances of importance, it is submitted, will include the intelligence of the child and, in the case of unsworn evidence, the extent to which the child understands the duty of speaking the truth. **F5.13**

Patients at a Secure Hospital

In *Spencer* [1987] AC 128, nursing staff of a secure hospital were charged with ill-treating patients who had been convicted of crimes and who were suffering from mental disorders. The prosecution case was made up of the evidence of patients who were characterised as being not only mentally unbalanced and of bad character, but also as anti-authoritarian, prone to **F5.14** lie, and possibly with old scores to settle. The House of Lords held that where the only prosecution evidence comes from a witness who, by reason of his mental condition and criminal connection fulfils criteria analogous to those which (at one time) justified a full corroboration warning, the judge should warn the jury that it is dangerous to convict on such evidence if uncorroborated, although the warning need not amount to the 'full' warning (see **F5.6**). Thus use of the words 'danger' or 'dangerous' is not essential to an adequate warning, provided that the jury is made fully aware of the dangers of convicting on such evidence. Similarly, the extent to which the judge should refer to any corroborative material depends on the facts of each case. It is submitted that 'corroborative material', for these purposes, was not intended to denote material which is corroborative in the strict or technical sense (see **F5.3**) and that notwithstanding the analogy drawn with cases which justified a 'full' corroboration warning, the warning given should reflect the circumstances of the particular case (see *Causley* [1999] Crim LR 572).

SUDDEN UNEXPLAINED INFANT DEATHS

F5.15 Infant deaths are said to be attributable to Sudden Infant Death Syndrome (SIDS), colloquially 'cot deaths', where the deaths are unexplained and the cause or causes, although natural, are, or are as yet, unknown. There is no underlying condition for every SIDS death, but in each case the mechanism of death is the same, namely apnoea, loss of breath or cessation of breathing. In *Cannings* [2004] 1 WLR 2607 the accused was convicted of the murder of two of her four children, J who had died aged 6 weeks and M who had died aged 18 weeks. Her eldest child, G, had also died aged 13 weeks. There was no direct evidence of the crimes alleged. The Crown's case, which was that the accused had smothered J and M, having previously smothered G, depended on specialist evidence about the conclusions to be drawn from the history of three infant deaths and further 'Acute' or 'Apparent Life Threatening Events' in the same family. The defence case was that the deaths were attributable to SIDS. At the appeal reliance was placed on fresh expert evidence, a substantial body of research suggesting that infant deaths occurring in the same family can and do occur naturally, even when they are unexplained. The appeal was allowed. It was held that the correct approach, where three infant deaths have occurred in the same family, each apparently unexplained, and for each of which there is no evidence extraneous to the expert evidence that harm was or must have been inflicted — e.g., indications or admissions of violence, or a pattern of ill-treatment — is to start with the fact that three such deaths were indeed rare, but to proceed on the basis that, if there is nothing to explain them, in our current state of knowledge they remain unexplained and, although some parents do smother their infant children, possible natural deaths. Whether there are one, two or even three deaths, the exclusion of currently known natural causes of infant death does not establish that the death or deaths resulted from the deliberate infliction of harm. Stressing that in many important respects we are still at the frontiers of knowledge in relation to unexplained infant deaths, it was further held, *per curiam*, (at [178]):

> for the time being, where a full investigation into two or more sudden unexplained infant deaths in the same family is followed by a serious disagreement between reputable experts about the cause of death, and a body of such expert opinion concludes that natural causes, whether explained or unexplained, cannot be excluded as a reasonable (and not a fanciful) possibility, the prosecution of a parent or parents for murder should not be started, or continued, unless there is additional cogent evidence, extraneous to the expert evidence, (such as [indications or admissions of violence, or a pattern of ill-treatment]) which tends to support the conclusion that the infant, or where there is more than one death, one of the infants, was deliberately harmed. In cases like the present, if the outcome of the trial depends exclusively or almost exclusively on a serious disagreement between distinguished and reputable experts, it will often be unwise, and therefore unsafe, to proceed.

Cannings was distinguished in *Kai-Whitewind* [2005] 2 Cr App R 457, on the basis that it concerned inferences based upon coincidence or the unlikelihood of two or more infant deaths in the same family, or one death where another child or other children in the family had suffered unexplained 'Apparent Life Threatening Events'. There was a need for additional cogent evidence in such a case because there was essentially no evidence beyond the inferences based upon coincidence which the prosecution experts were prepared to draw but as to which other reputable experts in the same specialist field took a different view. It did not follow that, whenever there was a conflict between expert witnesses, the case for the prosecution had to fail unless the conviction was justified by evidence independent of the expert witnesses. In *Kai-Whitewind* there was a single death, no suggestion that any inference should be drawn against the accused from any previous incident involving any of her other children, and the evidence about the child's condition found on the post-mortem examination — including new and old blood in the lungs consistent with two distinct episodes of upper airway obstruction — was evidence of fact and precisely the kind of material which was sought but not found in *Cannings*. The dispute between the experts about the interpretation of the post-mortem findings did not extinguish the findings themselves and it was therefore for the jury to evaluate the expert evidence, taking account of the facts found at the post-mortem and bearing in mind the additional prosecution evidence against the accused.

Section F6 Examination-in-chief

The object of examination-in-chief (examination of a witness by the party calling him) is to elicit from the witness evidence supportive of the party's case. Examination-in-chief must be conducted in accordance with the exclusionary rules of general application, such as those relating to hearsay, opinion and the character of the accused. This section concerns five other rules governing examination-in-chief:

(a) the rule requiring the prosecution to call all of their evidence before the close of their case; and the rules relating to
(b) leading questions;
(c) refreshing the memory;
(d) previous consistent or self-serving statements; and
(e) impeaching the credit of one's own witness.

RULE REQUIRING PROSECUTION TO CALL ALL THEIR EVIDENCE BEFORE THE CLOSE OF THEIR CASE

General Rule

F6.1 It is a rule of practice, but not law, that all of the evidence which the prosecution intend to rely on as probative of the guilt of the accused should be called before the close of their case (*Rice* [1963] 1 QB 857). The rule applies not only to the adducing of evidence, but also to matters put in cross-examination of the accused (see *Kane* (1977) 65 Cr App R 270). The rule is confined to evidence probative of guilt, and does not extend to evidence going only to the credit of the accused (*Halford* (1978) 67 Cr App R 318). In that case the trial judge had allowed the prosecution to introduce for the first time in cross-examination of the accused, in order to test his credit, two statements made by him at the investigation stage. There was no suggestion that the statements had been made involuntarily, but the judge, in allowing the cross-examination, said that he would also allow the defence to call evidence to show that the statements were improperly obtained or that their admission would result in injustice.

Some of the exceptions to this rule are covered in other sections of this work: as to evidence admissible in rebuttal under exceptions to the rule of finality of answers to questions on collateral matters, see **F7.27** to **F7.34** and as to evidence in rebuttal of evidence of the good character of the accused, see **F13.14**. The three recognised exceptions which call for consideration at this stage are:

(a) evidence not previously available;
(b) failure to call evidence by reason of inadvertence or oversight; and
(c) evidence in rebuttal of matters arising *ex improviso.*

Although these three exceptions are well established, some authorities clearly suggest that there is scope for a more generalised discretionary approach to admissibility, having regard to whether the accused will be unfairly prejudiced (as when the defence would have been conducted differently had the evidence in question been adduced as part of the prosecution case). In *Jolly v DPP* [2000] Crim LR 471, a decision relating to summary trial, it was held that although any trial court had to recognise that it was the duty of the prosecution to call its evidence before closing its case, it was 'beyond argument' that there was a general discretion to permit the calling of evidence at a later stage which, in a magistrates' court, extended up to the time when the Bench retired. Before exercising the discretion, the court would look carefully at the interests of justice overall and in particular the risk of any prejudice whatsoever to the defence. The result would be that the discretion would be sparingly exercised, but it was doubtful whether it assisted a court to speak in terms of 'exceptional circumstances'. Each case, it was said, had to be considered on its own facts. See also *Cook v DPP* [2001] Crim LR 321 and *Khatibi v DPP* (2004) 168 JP 361. However, magistrates, after they have retired to consider their verdict, do have a discretion to receive further evidence in 'special circumstances' (*Malcolm v DPP* [2007] 1 WLR 1230, following *Webb v Leadbetter* [1966] 1 WLR 245, and holding the decision in *R (Travers) v DPP* (2005) 169 JP 421 to have been wrongly decided). In deciding whether special circumstances exist, the magistrates can consider the nature of the defence approach to litigation and, for example, whether there was an ambush of the prosecution in the defence closing speech, and should have regard to the overriding objective in the CrimPR that criminal cases be dealt with justly (*Malcolm v DPP*).

In the Crown Court, once the jury has retired to consider its verdict, no further evidence may be adduced (*Owen* [1952] QB 362).

Evidence Not Previously Available

The question whether or not evidence available for the first time after the close of the prosecution case should be admitted, is a matter to be determined by the trial judge in his discretion, which should be exercised in such a way and subject to such safeguards as seem to him best suited to achieve justice between the Crown and the defendants, and between the defendants. However, the admission of such evidence will be rare (*Rice* [1963] 1 QB 857, per Winn J; and see also *Kane* (1977) 65 Cr App R 270). The evidence may be admitted even if not strictly of a rebutting character, but the court must be vigilant in the exercise of its discretion, in case injustice is done to the accused, and should consider whether it is desirable to grant a defence application for an adjournment (*Doran* (1972) 56 Cr App R 429). In *Doran* the prosecution were allowed to call two witnesses after the close of their case. The witnesses, the existence of whom the prosecution had no prior knowledge, were members of the public, present at the trial, who realised that they could give material evidence. See also *Patel* [1992] Crim LR 739, where the judge gave defence counsel the opportunity to seek an adjournment, take further instructions and call evidence. In *Pilcher* (1974) 60 Cr App R 1, the Court of Appeal, having recognised the general rule and the exception in the case of evidence in rebuttal of matters arising *ex improviso*, i.e. evidence which becomes relevant in circumstances which the prosecution could not have foreseen at the time when they presented their case (see **F6.7**), said (at p. 5): **F6.2**

> We do not say that . . . where the matter has not arisen *ex improviso* the judge had no kind of discretion at all, but we are firmly of opinion that in cases where the matter does not arise *ex improviso* the judge's discretion should not be exercised to allow the late introduction of an additional witness called for the prosecution whose evidence was available before the case for the prosecution closed.

As was pointed out in *Scott* (1984) 79 Cr App R 49, however, the judgment in *Pilcher* seems to narrow the circumstances in which evidence can be called in rebuttal in a way which does not agree with *Doran* (1972) 56 Cr App R 429. It is submitted that *Pilcher* should not be treated as restricting either the exception recognised in *Doran* or the exception, considered at **F6.3**, in the case of failure to call evidence of a formal or technical nature by reason of inadvertence or oversight.

Failure to Call Evidence by Reason of Inadvertence or Oversight

F6.3 **Formal, Technical or Uncontentious Evidence** The judge has a discretion to admit evidence of a formal, technical or uncontentious nature which, by reason of inadvertence or oversight, has not been adduced by the prosecution before the close of their case. Many of the cases relate to the failure to prove a statutory instrument by production of a Stationery Office copy. In *Palastanga v Solman* [1962] Crim LR 334, a case brought under the Motor Vehicles (Construction and Use) Regulations 1955, defence counsel, as a preliminary point, submitted that the burden of proving the regulation in question was on the prosecution, and since a Stationery Office copy had not been produced, the burden had not been discharged. The justices thereupon dismissed the summons. The Divisional Court held that it was a disgraceful point to take. The justices should have adjourned the matter, if the defence had persisted in their submission, to allow the prosecutor to obtain a Stationery Office copy. Failure to produce such a copy did not justify dismissal of the summons. See also *Duffin v Markham* (1918) 88 LJ KB 581, *Royal v Prescott-Clarke* [1966] 1 WLR 788 and *Hammond v Wilkinson* [2001] Crim LR 323. Compare *Tyrell v Cole* (1918) 120 LT 156; and *Ashley* (1967) 52 Cr App R 42: the Prison Rules 1964 require proof by production of a Queen's Printer's Copy. Similarly, evidence may be admitted to make good a failure to prove that leave of the DPP to bring proceedings has been obtained (see *Price v Humphries* [1958] 2 QB 353, in which a submission of no case having succeeded on the basis of the failure to prove such consent, the Divisional Court, applying *Waller* [1910] 1 KB 364 and allowing the appeal, held that unless the defence object before the close of the prosecution case, the court should act on the assumption that the clerk had fulfilled his duty, on the application for issue of the summons, to check that the appropriate consent had been given). A further example is *McKenna* (1956) 40 Cr App R 65, a charge of exporting articles made wholly or mainly of iron or steel, in which a submission of no case was made on the basis that no evidence had been adduced that the articles in question, which included steamrollers, lorries, traction engines and concrete mixers, were made of iron or steel. The judge recalled a prosecution witness to give such evidence. It was held that in the circumstances the judge had a complete discretion whether to allow a witness to be recalled; the appellate courts would not interfere with the exercise of that discretion unless it had resulted in an injustice. On the facts, there was no injustice: it required no great leap of the imagination to think that the objects in question were made of iron or steel, and even in the absence of the additional evidence, there was a case to answer.

F6.4 **Evidence as to Matters of Substance** In appropriate circumstances the prosecution, after the close of their case, may even be permitted to call evidence relating to a matter of substance. Thus, in *Piggott v Simms* [1973] RTR 15, in which the prosecution, after the close of their case, were given leave to admit in evidence an analyst's certificate, the Divisional Court held that, although this was a failure to adduce a vital part of their prosecution case, the justices had an absolute discretion to allow the evidence to be admitted. Likewise in *Matthews v Morris* [1981] Crim LR 495, it was held that justices had correctly permitted the prosecution to reopen their case to put in evidence a statement, made by the owner of the money allegedly stolen, which, although it had been served on the defence under the CJA 1967, s. 9, was omitted from the prosecution case by reason of simple mistake. According to *Middleton v Rowlett* [1954] 1 WLR 831 the court even has a discretion in the case of evidence relating to the identity of the accused. That was a case of dangerous driving, in which the magistrates had refused to allow the prosecution to reopen their case in order to prove the identity of the driver. Although the Divisional Court described the case as 'borderline', it was held that the magistrates were not bound to exercise their discretion in favour of the prosecution.

In *Francis* [1990] 1 WLR 1264, the prosecution called an identification witness to give evidence that at a group identification he had identified the man standing in position number 20 but failed to call any evidence to prove that the man standing at that position was the appellant. The failure was due to a simple misunderstanding between counsel: counsel for the prosecution was under the impression that the name of the person standing at that position was not in issue. After the close of the prosecution case, the trial judge allowed the prosecution to recall the inspector in charge of the identification to say who it was who was standing at position number 20. On appeal, it was held that although the failure was not a mere technicality, but an essential, if minor, link in the chain of identification evidence, the discretion of the judge to admit evidence after the close of the prosecution case is not limited to cases where an issue has arisen *ex improviso* or where what has been omitted is a mere formality. This was one of those rare cases falling outside the two established exceptions and the judge had not erred in the exercise of his discretion. See also, applying *Francis*, *Jackson* [1996] 2 Cr App R 420.

Tendering Evidence After the Start of the Defence Case In *Munnery* [1992] Crim LR 215, where the judge allowed the prosecution to call a witness after the close of its case but before the defence case had begun, it was held that the proposition in *Francis*, that the discretion should only rarely be exercised outside the two exceptions, could be expanded to include the words 'especially when the evidence is tendered after the case for the defendant has begun'. An example of the discretion being exercised at this late stage is *James v South Glamorgan County Council* (1994) 99 Cr App R 321. In that case, in which there had not been a submission of no case to answer, the prosecution were allowed to reopen their case, after the accused had given his evidence-in-chief, to call their main witness, who had arrived late because of transport difficulties and genuine confusion as to the whereabouts of the court. Evidence may also be called, at this late stage, by the judge himself. In *Bowles* [1992] Crim LR 726, the defence case had begun when the trial judge, in answer to a question from the jury, decided in the interests of justice to admit further evidence himself, rather than have the prosecution re-open its case. It was held that the judge was justified in calling the evidence; the defence had not yet closed their case, the evidence was non-controversial and did not contradict that of the accused (although it did support the prosecution case) and it is 'undesirable that a jury should decide a case on a factual basis which may be false and the truth or falsity of which has been raised by the jury and can easily and readily be resolved without injustice to the accused'. See also *Aitken* (1991) 94 Cr App R 85, where the jury was provided with a written summary of a tape-recorded interview during which the accused had made an admission. The accused said that the admission was made under pressure and was untrue. During the defence closing speech, the jury asked to listen to the tape and, when the speech was concluded and after hearing submissions, the judge allowed them to do so. The appeal was dismissed. Where the judge is satisfied that no injustice will be done to the accused, the admission of further evidence is a matter of discretion for the judge. **F6.5**

Late Evidence as to Fundamental Issues The discretion should not be used to allow the prosecution the opportunity to prove the very matter in issue which it has failed to prove. In *Gainsborough Justices, ex parte Green* (1984) 78 Cr App R 9, the prosecution evidence in support of an allegation of a breach of a community service order revealed no such breach. The justices, rejecting a submission of no case to answer, allowed further evidence to be called to establish the breach. The Divisional Court quashed the conviction. **F6.6**

Evidence in Rebuttal of Matters Arising *Ex Improviso*

> There is no doubt that the general rule is that where the Crown begins its case like a plaintiff in a civil suit, they cannot afterwards support their case by calling fresh witnesses, because they are met by certain evidence that contradicts it. They stand or fall by the evidence they have given. They must close their case before the defence begins; but if any matter arises, *ex improviso* which no human ingenuity can foresee, on the part of a defendant in a civil suit, or a prisoner in a criminal case, there seems to me no reason why that matter which so arose *ex improviso* may not be answered by contrary evidence on the part of the Crown. (*Frost* (1839) 4 St Tr NS 85 per Tindal CJ at col. 386) **F6.7**

F

Part F Evidence

Lord Goddard CJ, in *Owen* [1952] 2 QB 362, said of this statement (at p. 367) that it was in 'probably wider language than would be applied at the present day'. Under the modern law, it is for the judge, in the exercise of his discretion, to determine whether the relevance of the evidence in question could *reasonably* have been anticipated (*Scott* (1984) 79 Cr App R 49). If the prosecution can reasonably foresee that certain evidence, available *ab initio*, is relevant to their case, it must be adduced as a part of that case and not to remedy defects in the case after it has been closed (*Day* [1940] 1 All ER 402). In *Day*, a charge of forgery and obtaining money by a forged instrument, the prosecution had in their possession from the start of the proceedings, specimens of the accused's admitted handwriting. The prosecution's case depended on the uncorroborated evidence of an accomplice. After the close of the defence case, the judge allowed the prosecution to call a handwriting expert. Quashing the conviction, the Court of Criminal Appeal held that the judge had wrongly exercised his discretion in admitting the additional evidence, which did not relate to any matter that had arisen *ex improviso* but the possible need for which ought to have been foreseen. *Day* may be contrasted with *Milliken* (1969) 53 Cr App R 330, in which the accused, when giving evidence, for the first time accused certain police officers, some of whom gave evidence that they had seen the accused committing the offence, of a conspiracy to fabricate evidence. The trial judge allowed the prosecution to call evidence in rebuttal, on the basis that such evidence became relevant only when the accused gave evidence, a ruling upheld by the Court of Appeal. (The Court of Appeal also held that the evidence in question was not in any sense probative of the guilt of the accused, since it consisted of no more than denials of the accusations of conspiracy and concoction, but cf. *Busby* (1981) 75 Cr App R 79 and *Mendy* (1976) 64 Cr App R 4, which are considered at **F7.27** and **F7.32**.) See also *Flynn* (1957) 42 Cr App R 15, in which the prosecution were allowed to call evidence in rebuttal of an alibi defence, the details of which became known for the first time when the accused gave evidence; and *Blick* (1966) 50 Cr App R 280.

The *ex improviso* principle requires the prosecution to adduce evidence before the close of its case only if it is clearly relevant. Thus, in *Levy* (1966) 50 Cr App R 198, it was held that there was room for the exercise by the judge of his discretion to admit, in rebuttal, evidence in the possession of the prosecution *ab initio*, which was of marginal relevance. The Court of Criminal Appeal said (at p. 202):

> It is quite clear and long established that the judge has a discretion with regard to the admission of evidence in rebuttal; the field in which that discretion can be exercised is limited by the principle that evidence which is clearly relevant — not marginally, minimally or doubtfully relevant, but clearly relevant — to the issues and within the possession of the Crown should be adduced by the prosecution as part of the prosecution's cases and such evidence cannot properly be admitted after evidence for the defence.

Equally, the *ex improviso* principle has to be applied with a recognition that the prosecution are expected to act reasonably to what may be suggested as pre-trial warnings of evidence likely to be given which calls for denial beforehand, and to suggestions put in cross-examination of their witnesses. 'They are not expected to take notice of fanciful and unreal statements no matter from what source they emanate' (*Hutchinson* (1985) 82 Cr App R 51, per Watkins LJ at p. 59). In this case, the accused was convicted of murder. Before the trial he wrote a letter, passed on to the DPP, containing allegations against a journalist. At the trial he alleged that the journalist was the murderer. The Court of Appeal held that the trial judge, at the close of the defence case, had properly given leave to the prosecution to call the journalist to give evidence in rebuttal; although the letter had alerted them to the possibility of what the accused might say in evidence, it contained many other allegations which were so obviously ridiculous and untrue as to justify the prosecution in regarding the whole of it either as a wicked farrago of lying nonsense or the ravings of a deranged mind. It was unreasonable, therefore, to say that the prosecution should have anticipated that anything said in it would be repeated in court.

It seems that the prosecution may rely upon the *ex improviso* principle to adduce evidence not only in rebuttal of defence *evidence*, but also, in appropriate circumstances, in rebuttal of matters unsupported by evidence but arising by implication from the submissions made by counsel for the defence in his closing speech (*O'Hadhmaill* [1996] Crim LR 509).

LEADING QUESTIONS

Leading Questions Generally Impermissible in Chief

The general rule is that in examination-in-chief a witness may not be asked leading questions, i.e. questions framed in such a way as to suggest the answer sought or to assume the existence of facts yet to be established. Evidence elicited by such questions is not inadmissible, but the weight to be attached to it may be substantially reduced (*Moor v Moor* [1954] 1 WLR 927; *Wilson* (1913) 9 Cr App R 124). 'Leading' is a relative, not an absolute, term (W. M. Best, *The Principles of the Law of Evidence*, 12th ed. by S.L. Phipson (London: Sweet & Maxwell, 1922) at p. 562); and for this reason strict adherence to the rule is not always desirable or possible. Thus leading questions may be allowed, in the interests of justice, at the discretion of the judge. For example, when a magistrate dies in the course of a case in which a witness has given his evidence, the witness, when recalled before a new magistrate, may be asked whether his deposition represents his evidence (*Ex parte Bottomley* [1909] 2 KB 14, at p. 21). It is virtually impossible to ask a witness to identify a person or object in court without the use of leading questions, and accordingly leading questions of this kind are also allowed (see *Watson* (1817) 2 Stark 116, at p. 128). There are two other frequently recurring situations to which the general rule does not apply: **F6.8**

(a) Leading questions may be asked on formal and introductory matters, such as a witness's name, address and occupation; and questions which relate to other relevant facts which are not in dispute, or which are merely introductory to questions about facts which are in dispute, are also generally allowed (*Robinson* (1897) 61 JP 520).
(b) Leading questions may be put to a witness if the party calling him has been given leave to treat him as hostile (see F6.32).

REFRESHING THE MEMORY

General

At common law, a witness in the course of giving his evidence, may refer to a document in order to refresh his memory provided that the document was made or verified by him either at the time of the event in question or so shortly thereafter that the facts were fresh in his memory (see *Simmonds* [1969] 1 QB 685, *Richardson* [1971] 2 QB 484 and *Da Silva* [1990] 1 WLR 31 at p. 32). The common-law rule has been relaxed by the CJA 2003, s.139(1), which substitutes for the requirement of contemporaneity, or that the facts were fresh in the memory, two conditions: (1) that the witness gives evidence that the document records his recollection at the time he made it and (2) that his recollection at that time is likely to have been significantly better than at the time of his oral evidence. Section 139(2), designed to avoid the practical difficulties of refreshing the memory in the witness box from a sound recording, provides for the refreshing of memory from a transcript of a sound recording. **F6.9**

Criminal Justice Act 2003, s. 139

139.—(1) A person giving oral evidence in criminal proceedings about any matter may, at any stage in the course of doing so, refresh his memory of it from a document made or verified by him at an earlier time if—

(a) he states in his oral evidence that the document records his recollection of the matter at that earlier time, and

(b) his recollection of the matter is likely to have been significantly better at that time than it is at the time of his oral evidence.

(2) Where—

(a) a person giving oral evidence in criminal proceedings about any matter has previously given an oral account, of which a sound recording was made, and he states in that evidence that the account represented his recollection of the matter at the time,

(b) his recollection of the matter is likely to have been significantly better at the time of the previous account than it is at the time of his oral evidence, and

(c) a transcript has been made of the sound recording,

he may, at any stage in the course of giving his evidence, refresh his memory of the matter from that transcript.

An application to refresh memory will normally be made by counsel, but it is the proper function of the judge, where the interests of justice demand it, to suggest that a witness, including a prosecution witness, refresh his memory from a document (*Tyagi* (1986) *The Times*, 21 July 1986, *per* Ralph Gibson LJ). Section 139(1) and (2) apply to any person giving oral evidence, including the accused (see, at common law, *Britton* [1987] 1 WLR 539).

Under s. 139(1) and (2), the witness may refresh his memory 'at any stage' in the course of giving his oral evidence. Thus, although a witness refreshing his memory in court will normally do so in examination-in-chief, provided the conditions are met there is nothing wrong in principle in allowing a witness to refresh his memory during re-examination (see, at common law, *Harman* (1984) 148 JP 289 and *Sutton* (1991) 94 Cr App R 70).

Present Recollection Revived and Past Recollection Recorded

F6.10 Both the common-law rule and the statutory rules apply not only in the case of 'present recollection revived' (J.H. Wigmore, *Evidence in Trials at Common Law*, vol. 3 (revised by J. H. Chadbourn) (Boston Mass: Little, Brown & Co, 1970), ch. 28), i.e. where the witness refreshes his memory on sight of the document, but also in the case of 'past recollection recorded' (ibid., *loc. cit.*), i.e. where the witness has no independent recollection of the facts in question but testifies as to the accuracy of the document (see *Maugham v Hubbard* (1828) 8 B&C 14, *Topham v M'Gregor* (1844) 1 Car & Kir 320 and *Bryant* (1946) 31 Cr App R 146). To say that a witness, in the case of 'past recollection recorded' has refreshed his memory is to create a fiction. It would be preferable in principle to treat the out-of-court statement as hearsay admissible for the truth of its contents but, save in exceptional circumstances, at common law it is what the witness says and not the document which constitutes the evidence in the case (see *Maugham v Hubbard*, and see further *Sekhon* (1987) 85 Cr App R 19 and *Virgo* (1978) 67 Cr App R 323, both considered at **F6.13**). However, the common law position has been reversed by the CJA 2003, s. 120(1), (4) and (6).

Criminal Justice Act 2003, s. 120

(1) This section applies where a person (the witness) is called to give evidence in criminal proceedings.

(4) A previous statement by the witness is admissible as evidence of any matter stated of which oral evidence by him would be admissible, if—

(a) any of the following three conditions is satisfied, and

(b) while giving evidence the witness indicates that to the best of his belief he made the statement, and to the best of his belief it states the truth.

(6) The second condition is that the statement was made by the witness when the matters stated were fresh in his memory but he does not remember them, and cannot reasonably be expected to remember them, well enough to give oral evidence of them in the proceedings.

Making or Verification of Document

F6.11 Although under the common-law rule a document includes a tape recording (*Bailey* [2001] EWCA Crim 733), for the purposes of the CJA 2003, s. 139(1), 'document' means anything in which information of any description is recorded, but not including any recording of sounds or moving images (s. 140). Both at common law and under s. 139(1), the document must have been prepared by the witness himself or by another, provided in the latter case that the witness verified the document. For examples of verification, see *Langton* (1876) 2 QBD 296, *Anderson v Whalley* (1852) 3 Car & Kir 54 and *Sekhon* (1987) 85 Cr App R 19. A witness may refresh his memory from his deposition or from a statement to the police taken down by a police officer and then read over by the maker (*Mullins* (1848) 3 Cox CC 528; *Gleed v Stroud* (1962) 26 JCL 161; and *Lau Pak Ngam v R* [1966] Crim LR 443, approved in *Richardson* [1971] 2 QB 484).

In the case of interpreters, see *Attard* (1958) 43 Cr App R 90: at an interview at which an accused is questioned through an interpreter, in the absence of an independent note made by the interpreter of the questions put and the answers given, the interpreter should initial the interview record so that he may use it to refresh his memory when giving evidence.

It is submitted that under s. 139(1), as at common law, verification can be aural or visual. Despite the *obiter dictum* of Winn J in *Mills* [1962] 1 WLR 1152, at p. 1156, that the witness should both *see* and *read* a note made by another, in *Kelsey* (1982) 74 Cr App R 213 the Court of Appeal held that where one person dictates a note to another, hears it read back to him, and confirms its accuracy without reading it himself, the first person may use the note to refresh his memory in court, provided that another witness is called to prove that the note used in court is the same one that was dictated and read back. H, a prosecution witness, refreshed his memory as to the registration number of a car from a note dictated to a police officer. H saw the officer making the note but did not read it himself. The officer read the note back aloud and H confirmed that it was correct. At trial the officer gave evidence that the note used by H was the one that he had made. The Court of Appeal dismissed the appeal on the ground that verification could be aural or visual, the important matter being whether the witness satisfied himself, while the matters were fresh in his mind, that the record was made and that it was accurate. The note in this case, since it was made by a person in the course of a 'profession or other occupation', might be admissible itself as evidence of the facts contained in it under the CJA 2003, s. 117, subject to the discretion to exclude under s. 126: see **F16.56**. The principle of aural verification, however, continues to assist in cases where the note is not made by someone 'in the course of a trade, business, profession or other occupation, or as the holder of a paid or unpaid office'.

Originals and Copies

F6.12 Under the CJA 2003, s. 139(1), there is no requirement that the document be the first or only document made or verified by the witness recording his recollection of the matters in question. Thus, as at common law, a witness may refresh his memory from a document notwithstanding that it is based on original notes or a tape recording made by him. In *Cheng* (1976) 63 Cr App R 20, an officer prepared his committal statement in March from his original notes, which had been made after the accused's arrest in February. By the time of the trial, some three years later, the original notebook had been lost. The Court of Appeal held that, although the committal statement was a partial, and therefore not an exact, copy of the earlier notes from which it had been prepared, it substantially reproduced the notes and could be used by the officer to refresh his memory. Similarly, in *A-G's Ref (No. 3 of 1979)* (1979) 69 Cr App R 411, the Court of Appeal held that a police officer could refresh his memory from a notebook, compiled within two hours of an interview when the facts were still fresh in his memory, on the basis of earlier brief jottings made at the interview, notwithstanding that at the trial he could neither decipher the jottings nor recollect fully the questions put and answers given. In *Mills* [1962] 1 WLR 1152 it was held that a police officer who had heard, and made a tape recording of, a conversation between two accused, could refresh his memory by referring to notes written up with the assistance of the tape recording, which was not itself admitted in evidence.

F

Part F Evidence

It is submitted that where the original of a document has been lost or destroyed, under s. 139(1), as at common law, a witness may use a copy if it is proved to be an accurate copy either by the witness himself or by some other person. Thus, in *Topham v M'Gregor* (1844) 1 Car & Kir 320, the author of an article, written some 14 years earlier, who had no independent recollection of its contents, was allowed to 'refresh his memory' from a copy of the newspaper in which it appeared, evidence having been given by the editor that the original manuscript had been lost and that the newspaper was an accurate copy. See also *Chisnell* [1992] Crim LR 507, where an officer was allowed to refresh his memory from a statement, made nine months after an interview and compiled on the basis of a contemporaneous note, since the court was satisfied that the note, which had been lost, had been accurately transcribed into the statement.

Production for Inspection and Cross-examination

F6.13 A witness who has used a document in court to refresh his memory must produce it for the inspection of the opposing party, who may wish to cross-examine on its contents (*Beech v Jones* (1848) 5 CB 696; *Sekhon* (1987) 85 Cr App R 19). In the majority of cases, the fact that such cross-examination takes place will not make the record evidence in the case, nor will it be necessary for the jury to inspect the document, and it will be inappropriate for the record to become an exhibit (*Sekhon* at p. 22). However, in five situations the document, at the request of the opposing party, may be shown to the jury:

(a) In *Senat v Senat* [1965] P 172, Sir Jocelyn Simon P said (at p. 177, emphasis added):

> Where a document is used to refresh a witness's memory, cross-examining counsel may inspect that document in order to check it, without making it evidence. Moreover he may cross-examine upon it without making it evidence *provided that* his cross-examination does not go further than the parts which are used for refreshing the memory of the witness.

See also *Gregory v Tavernor* (1833) 6 C & P 280 and *Britton* [1987] 1 WLR 539. If cross-examining counsel does go beyond the parts used by the witness to refresh his memory, the document is put in evidence and the jury are allowed to see the document upon which the cross-examination is based. At common law the document is evidence of the witness's consistency or inconsistency going only to his credit (*Virgo* (1978) 67 Cr App R 323 and *Britton* [1987] 1 WLR 539). However, under the CJA 2003, s. 120(1) and (3), the document is also admissible as evidence of any matter stated.

Criminal Justice Act 2003, s. 120

(1) This section applies where a person (the witness) is called to give evidence in criminal proceedings.

. . .

(3) A statement made by the witness in a document—
  (a) which is used by him to refresh his memory while giving evidence,
  (b) on which he is cross-examined, and
  (c) which as a consequence is received in evidence in the proceedings,
  is admissible as evidence of any matter stated of which oral evidence by him would be admissible.

(b) The jury may inspect a memory-refreshing document if it is necessary to their determination of a point in issue. An example is *Bass* [1953] 1 QB 680. In that case the only evidence against the accused was a confession allegedly made to two police officers who, although denying that they had prepared their notes in collaboration, read identical accounts of the interview with the accused. The trial judge rejected a defence application that the jury be allowed to inspect the notebooks. The Court of Criminal Appeal endorsed the practice of officers collaborating in the preparation of their notes after an interview (in order to ensure that they had a correct version of what was said); but, allowing the appeal, held that the jury should have been allowed to inspect the notebooks because it might have assisted them in their evaluation of the credibility and accuracy of the officers. See also *Sekhon* (1986) 85 Cr

App R 19, per Woolf LJ at p. 22: where the nature of the cross-examination involves the suggestion that the witness has subsequently fabricated his evidence, which will usually involve, if not expressly at least by implication, the allegation that the record is concocted, the record may be admissible to rebut this suggestion and, if the nature of the record assists as to this, to show whether or not it is genuine, i.e. whether or not it has the appearance of being a contemporaneous record which has not subsequently been altered.

(c) Where the record is inconsistent with the witness's evidence, it can be admitted as evidence of this inconsistency (*Sekhon* at p. 23).

(d) It is appropriate for the record to be put before the jury where it is difficult for the jury to follow the cross-examination of the witness who has refreshed his memory without having the record or, in practice, copies of the record, before them (*Sekhon*).

(e) There may be cases where it is convenient to use the record as an *aide-mémoire* as to the witness's evidence where that evidence is long and involved. However, care should be exercised in adopting this course in cases where the evidence, and therefore the record, is bitterly contested, because of the danger that the use of the document for this purpose could result in the jury misunderstanding its status, and lead to their wrongly regarding the document as being evidence in itself (*Sekhon*).

Treatment of Memory-refreshing Documents as Exhibits

Where, as is normally the case, a memory-refreshing document is permitted to go before the jury for the limited purpose of assisting them to evaluate the truth of the evidence given in the witness box, it is of no practical importance whether the document is treated as an exhibit, although in a case involving a large number of documents, it may be appropriate to give each one an exhibit number just to identify the document. The exception is the case in which the document provides, because of its nature, material by which its authenticity can be judged: such material can amount to evidence in the case, but only for the purpose of assessing authenticity (*Sekhon* (1986) 85 Cr App R 19, distinguishing *Fenlon* (1980) 71 Cr App R 307 and *Dillon* (1983) 85 Cr App R 29). **F6.14**

The question whether a memory-refreshing document, admitted under s. 120(3) (see **F6.13**) and produced as an exhibit, should accompany the jury when they retire, is governed by the CJA 2003, s. 122.

Criminal Justice Act 2003, s. 122

(1) This section applies if on a trial before a judge and jury for an offence—
  (a) a statement made in a document is admitted in evidence under section 119 or 120, and
  (b) the document or a copy of it is produced as an exhibit.
(2) The exhibit must not accompany the jury when they retire to consider their verdict unless—
  (a) the court considers it appropriate, or
  (b) all the parties to the proceedings agree that it should accompany the jury.

Refreshing Memory out of Court

Prior to Going into the Witness-box The conditions on which a witness may refresh his memory while giving evidence in the witness-box do not apply to a witness who refreshes his memory from a statement before going into the witness-box. In *Richardson* [1971] 2 QB 484 the accused was convicted of burglary offences committed 18 months earlier. Before the trial, four prosecution witnesses were shown their police statements, which they had made some weeks after the alleged offences. On appeal it was argued that the evidence of the four witnesses was, in the circumstances, inadmissible. The appeal was dismissed on the ground that there can be no general rule (which, unlike the rule as to what can be done in the witness-box, would be unenforceable) that witnesses may not before trial see the statements which they made at some period reasonably close to the time of the events which are the subject of the trial. See also, however, *Thomas* [1994] Crim LR 745 where, for reasons that are not **F6.15**

disclosed, it was held to be undesirable for a child aged eight to be shown her signed police statement before giving evidence. In *Richardson*, Sachs LJ, giving the judgment of the Court of Appeal, made the following observations:

(a) It has been recognised in Home Office Circular No. 82–1969 ('Supplies of Copies of Witnesses' Statements'), issued with the approval of the Lord Chief Justice and the judges of the Queen's Bench Division, that witnesses for the prosecution in criminal cases are normally entitled, if they so request, to copies of any statements taken from them by police officers.
(b) It is the practice, normally, for witnesses for the defence to be allowed to have copies of their statements and to refresh their memories from them before going into the witness-box.
(c) The Court agreed with the following two observations of the Supreme Court of Hong Kong in *Lau Pak Ngam v R* [1966] Crim LR 443: 'Testimony in the witness-box becomes more a test of memory than truthfulness if witnesses are deprived of the opportunity of checking their recollection beforehand by reference to statements or notes made at a time closer to the events in question.' 'Refusal of access to statements would tend to create difficulties for honest witnesses but be likely to do little to hamper dishonest witnesses.'
(d) Obviously it would be wrong if several witnesses were handed statements in circumstances which enabled one to compare with another what each had said.

Concerning (d), it is incumbent on prosecuting authorities and judges to ensure that witnesses are informed that they should not discuss cases in which they are involved (*Shaw* [2002] EWCA Crim 3004). As a general rule, discussions between witnesses, particularly just before going into court to give evidence, should not take place, nor should statements or proofs of evidence be read to witnesses in each other's presence (*Skinner* (1994) 99 Cr App R 212). Where such discussions have taken place, each case has to be dealt with on its own facts. If it emerges in cross-examination of the witnesses that the discussion may have led to fabrication, the court may take the view that it would be unsafe to leave any of the evidence of the witnesses concerned to the jury, but in other cases it may suffice to direct the jury on the implications which such conduct might have for the reliability of the evidence of the witnesses concerned (*Arif* (1993) *The Times*, 17 June 1993; and see also *Shaw*).

F6.16 **After Going into the Witness-box** It is also open to the judge, in the exercise of his discretion and in the interests of justice, to permit a witness who has begun to give evidence to refresh his memory from a statement made near to the time of the events in question, even though it is not contemporaneous, provided he is satisfied that:

(a) the witness indicates that he cannot now recall the details of events because of the lapse of time since they took place;
(b) the witness made a statement much nearer the time of the events, and that the contents of the statement represented his recollection at the time he made it;
(c) the witness had not read the statement before coming into the witness-box; and
(d) the witness wished to have an opportunity to read the statement before he continued to give evidence.

It does not matter whether the witness withdraws from the witness-box and reads the statement, or whether he reads it in the witness-box; but it is important, if the former course is adopted, that no communication be had with the witness other than to see that he can read the statement in peace (per Stuart-Smith LJ, delivering the judgment of the Court of Appeal in *Da Silva* [1990] 1 WLR 31, at p. 35). It was also said in *Da Silva* that, whether the witness withdraws from the witness box or not, the statement must be removed from him when he comes to give his evidence and he should not be permitted to refer to it again, because the statement is not contemporaneous. However, this dictum must now be read subject to the terms of the CJA 2003, s. 139, which is considered at **F6.9**.

Da Silva has not laid down as a matter of law that once a witness is in the witness box he can refer to a statement only if all four criteria specified in that case are satisfied, because the court has a real discretion whether to permit a witness to refresh his memory from a non-contemporaneous statement (*South Ribble Magistrates' Court, ex parte Cochrane* [1996] 2 Cr App R 544). In *Ex parte Cochrane*, in which the witness did not satisfy the third criterion (c) above), because he had read his statement before giving evidence but had not taken it in properly it was held to be proper to allow him to refresh his memory. The Divisional Court could see no logical difference between someone in the position of such a witness and someone who has not read his statement at all. See also *Gordon* [2002] EWCA Crim 1, where the witness was dyslexic and could not read his witness statement. Having been examined in the absence of the jury, counsel reading out the statement, he adopted the statement. The Court of Appeal held that there were no fixed and immutable rules to be followed before a witness could refresh his memory by a document prepared by him when his memory was clearer. There was a broad fact-sensitive judicial discretion to be exercised in the interests of fairness and justice.

Informing the Defence If prosecution witnesses have refreshed their memories out of court and before entering the witness-box, it is desirable, but not essential, that the defence should be informed of this (*Worley v Bentley* [1976] 2 All ER 449, affirmed in *Westwell* [1976] 2 All ER 812). (See also, *sed quaere, H* [1992] Crim LR 516, which suggests that child victims of sexual offences should refresh their memory out of court only *with the consent* of the defence.) In some cases the fact that a witness has read his statement out of court may be relevant to the weight which can properly be attached to his evidence, and injustice might be caused to the accused if the jury were left in ignorance of the fact. Accordingly, if the prosecution are aware that statements have been seen by their witnesses, it will be appropriate to inform the defence, although if for any reason this is not done, the omission cannot of itself be a ground for acquittal (*Westwell*). **F6.17**

Cross-examination on Memory-refreshing Document If a witness has refreshed his memory out of court and before entering the witness-box, counsel for the other side is entitled not only to inspect the memory-refreshing document, but also to cross-examine the witness upon the relevant matters contained therein. If counsel cross-examines upon material in the document from which the witness has refreshed his memory, the document is not thereby made evidence in the case; but if he cross-examines upon material which has not been referred to by the witness, this entitles the party calling the witness to put the document in evidence so that the tribunal of fact may see the document upon which the cross-examination is based. In this respect, therefore, the rules are the same as those which apply in the case of a witness refreshing his memory in the witness-box (as to which, see F6.13). See *Owen v Edwards* (1983) 77 Cr App R 191. **F6.18**

PREVIOUS CONSISTENT (SELF-SERVING) STATEMENTS

General Rule against Previous Consistent Statements

Under the rule against previous consistent or self-serving statements, sometimes referred to as the rule against narrative, a witness may not be asked about a previous oral or written statement made by him and consistent with his evidence (*Roberts* [1942] 1 All ER 187; *Larkin* [1943] KB 174; *Oyesiku* (1971) 56 Cr App R 240, at pp. 245–7). Equally, evidence of the previous statement may not be given by any other witness (*Roberts*). The previous statement, which may also be inadmissible as evidence of the facts contained in it under the rule against hearsay, is excluded as evidence of the accused's *consistency*. In *Roberts* [1942] 1 All ER 187, the accused was convicted of the murder of a girl by shooting her. His defence was that the gun went off accidentally when he was trying to make up a quarrel with her. The Court of **F6.19**

F

Part F Evidence

Criminal Appeal held that evidence that two days after the event the accused had told his father that his defence would be accident had been properly excluded. Such evidence is easily manufactured and of no evidential value. The fact that the accused has said the same thing to someone else on a previous occasion does not confirm his evidence (*Roberts*, at p. 191).

The general rule applies in examination-in-chief, cross-examination and re-examination. Thus the credibility of a witness may not be bolstered by evidence of a previous consistent statement merely because his testimony has been impeached in cross-examination, and this remains the case 'even if the impeachment takes the form of contradiction or inconsistency between the evidence given at the trial and something said by the witness on a former occasion' (*Coll* (1889) 24 LR Ir 522, per Holmes J at p. 541. See also *Weekes* [1988] Crim LR 245; *Beattie* (1989) 89 Cr App R 302 per Lord Lane CJ at pp. 306–7; and *P(GR)* [1998] Crim LR 663). Equally, there is no exception to the general rule to the effect that where counsel cross-examines to show inconsistencies, the witness can be re-examined to show consistency (*Beattie* (1989) 89 Cr App R 302 per Lord Lane CJ at p. 307). However, the court does have a residual discretion, necessary in the interests of justice, to permit re-examination to show consistency, to ensure that as a result of the cross-examination the jury is not positively misled as to the existence of some fact or the terms of an earlier statement (*Ali* [2004] 1 Cr App R 501).

Recent Complaints

F6.20 **Common-law Principle** At common law, if the complainant, in a case of rape or some other sexual offence, made a voluntary complaint shortly after the alleged offence, the person to whom the complaint was made may give evidence on behalf of the prosecution of the particulars of the complaint, not as evidence of the facts complained of, but to show the consistency of the conduct of the complainant with the complainant's evidence and, in cases where consent is in issue, as tending to negative consent (see generally *Lillyman* [1896] 2 QB 167). The CJA 2003, s. 120(7), has extended this common-law principle to cover a previous statement by a person against whom any type of offence has been committed, provided that it is an offence to which the proceedings relate, that the statement consists of a complaint about conduct which would, if proved, constitute the offence, and the complainant, in giving evidence, indicates that to the best of her belief, she made the statement and it states the truth. A statement received under s. 120(7) is admissible as evidence of the matters stated and, provided that the evidence is given by the person to whom the complaint was made (see *White v R* [1999] 1 Cr App R 153, below), also goes to the consistency of the witness. Section 120(7) is much wider than the common-law principle, which is likely to be invoked only rarely and is therefore considered in outline only. It is convenient, however, to consider the common-law principle before s. 120(7).

The common-law principle applies in the case of written complaints, as well as oral complaints, and will even cover a private note given to someone by mistake (*B* [1997] Crim LR 220). There is a two-stage test for the jury to follow: to decide first whether a complaint really was made and then whether it is consistent with the complainant's evidence (see *Lillyman* and *Hartley* [2003] All ER (D) 208 (Oct)). It is essential that the jury also be directed that the complaint is not evidence of the facts complained of, but may be of assistance in assessing the veracity of the complainant. Judges should give the Judicial Studies Board standard direction: '[The evidence] may possibly help you to decide whether she has told you the truth. It cannot be independent confirmation of [the complainant's] evidence since it does not come from a source independent of her' (see per Ognall J in *Wright* (1987) 90 Cr App R 91 at p. 97; and *Islam* [1999] 1 Cr App R 22 applied in *NK* [1999] Crim LR 980 and *B* [2003] EWCA Crim 2724).

If the terms of the complaint and the terms of the complainant's testimony are wholly inconsistent, evidence of the complaint will be inadmissible. Evidence of the complaint will be admissible where it is sufficiently consistent that it can, depending on the view of the evidence taken by the jury, support or enhance the credibility of the complainant. Whether the complaint is sufficiently consistent must depend on the facts. It is not necessary that it discloses the ingredients of the offence, but it is usually necessary that it discloses evidence of material and relevant unlawful sexual conduct on the part of the accused that can support the complainant's credibility. Thus it is not usually necessary that the complaint describes the full extent of the unlawful sexual conduct alleged by the complainant in the witness box, provided that it is capable of supporting the credibility of the complainant's evidence. Differences may be accounted for by a variety of matters, for example the complainant's reluctance to disclose the full extent of the conduct at the time of the complaint, but it is for the jury to assess these. Where the complaint is, in part, inconsistent with the evidence given by the complainant, the judge should make clear to the jury the extent and significance of the inconsistency, drawing to their attention any reason given for it and telling them that it is for them to take all these matters into account in deciding whether the complainant is telling the truth (*S* [2004] 1 WLR 2940).

If the complainant does not testify, there will be no evidence with which the complaint may be consistent, and for this reason it should be excluded (*Guttridges* (1840) 9 C & P 471). On this reasoning, in *Wallwork* (1958) 42 Cr App R 153, a charge of incest with a five-year-old, who went into the witness-box but was unable to give evidence, it was held that the child's grandmother had been improperly permitted to give evidence of particulars of a complaint made to her by the child. Lord Goddard CJ was of the opinion that there would have been no objection if the grandmother had given evidence of the bare fact that the girl had made a complaint to her. But see also *Lillyman* [1896] 2 QB 167 per Hawkins J at pp. 178–9 and *Wright* (1987) 90 Cr App R 91 per Ognall J at pp. 96–7. It is submitted that since such evidence could not be admitted, either as evidence of the facts complained of or as evidence of consistency, it would serve only to prejudice the accused and should not be admitted.

The principle is not confined to cases where consent is in issue. A recent complaint is admissible 'whether non-consent is legally a necessary part of the issue or whether on the other hand it is what may be called a collateral issue of fact' (*Osborne*). The principle also extends to sexual offences against males: see *Camelleri* [1922] 2 KB 122 and *Wannell* (1922) 17 Cr App R 53.

In *White v R* [1999] AC 210, it was held that, if the person to whom the complaint was made does not give evidence, the complainant's evidence that she complained cannot show her consistency or negative consent because, in the absence of independent confirmation, her own evidence takes the jury nowhere in deciding whether she is worthy of belief. Lord Hoffmann held that it did not follow that evidence that the complainant spoke to someone after the incident is inadmissible, but she should not be allowed to say that she had told people 'what had happened', because the jury would be bound to infer that she had made statements in substantially the same terms as her evidence, which would be to infringe the spirit of the rule against previous consistent statements. Lord Hoffmann also held that where evidence is given of the bare fact that the complainant spoke to someone after the incident, the judge must give the jury clear instructions that they are not entitled to treat such evidence as confirming her credibility.

In order to be admissible, a complaint must be made 'at the first opportunity after the offence which reasonably offers itself' (*Osborne* [1905] 1 KB 551, per Ridley J at p. 561). This is a matter to be determined by the court in each case (*Cummings* [1948] 1 All ER 551). Thus, although complaints have been excluded if made after a day (*Rush* (1896) 60 JP 777) or three days (*Ingrey* 1900) 64 JP 106), a complaint made after a week has been admitted (*Hedges* (1909) 3 Cr App R 262). Much turns on the circumstances of the case. Account should be taken of the fact that victims, both male and female, often need time before they can bring themselves to tell what has been done to them. Moreover, whereas some victims find it impossible to complain to anyone other than a parent or member of their family, others may feel it quite impossible to tell their parents or members of their family (*Valentine* [1996] 2 Cr

App R 213 at p. 224). However the test is not simply whether the complaint was made on the first occasion that reasonably offered itself: the complaint must also be recent, i.e. it must have been made within a reasonable time of the alleged offence. In *Birks* [2003] 2 Cr App R 122, therefore, it was held, albeit with reluctance, that a complaint made, at the earliest, two months after the alleged offence, was inadmissible notwithstanding that the complainant was only 6 or 7 years old at the time of the offence, that the accused had allegedly threatened her by saying that if she told her mother she would be put in a home, and that the complaint had emerged spontaneously as a result of watching a television programme about child abuse.

A complaint will not be inadmissible merely because there has been an earlier complaint (*Lee* (1912) 7 Cr App R 31 and *Wilbourne* (1917) 12 Cr App R 280; and cf. *Valentine*).

A recent complaint, in order to be admissible, must also have been made voluntarily, and not as a result of leading or intimidating questions. However, the mere fact that the statement was made in answer to a question does not make it inadmissible. Questions of a suggestive or leading character, such as 'Did so-and-so (naming the accused) assault you?' or 'Did he do this and that to you?', will have that effect; but not natural questions put by a person in charge, such as 'What is the matter?' or 'Why are you crying?'. In each case the decision on the character of the question put, as well as other circumstances, such as the relationship of the questioner to the complainant, must be left to the discretion of the judge (*Osborne* [1905] 1 KB 551, per Ridley J at p. 556. See also *Norcott* [1917] 1 KB 347).

F6.21 **Statutory Extension of the Principle** The CJA 2003, s. 120, extends the common-law principle relating to recent complaints in sexual cases to previous statements, whether oral or written, made by a person against whom *any* offence has been committed, provided that it is an offence to which the proceedings relate, and that the statement consists of a complaint about conduct which would, if proved, constitute the offence or part of the offence to which the proceedings relate.

Criminal Justice Act 2003, s. 120

(1) This section applies where a person (the witness) is called to give evidence in criminal proceedings.

. . .

(4) A previous statement by the witness is admissible as evidence of any matter stated of which oral evidence by him would be admissible, if—
   (a) any of the following three conditions is satisfied, and
   (b) while giving evidence the witness indicates that to the best of his belief he made the statement, and that to the best of his belief it states the truth.

. . .

(7) The third condition is that—
   (a) the witness claims to be a person against whom an offence has been committed,
   (b) the offence is one to which the proceedings relate,
   (c) the statement consists of a complaint made by the witness (whether to a person in authority or not) about conduct which would, if proved, constitute the offence or part of the offence,
   (d) the complaint was made as soon as could reasonably be expected after the alleged conduct,
   (e) the complaint was not made as a result of a threat or a promise, and
   (f) before the statement is adduced the witness gives oral evidence in connection with its subject matter.

(8) For the purposes of subsection (7) the fact that the complaint was elicited (for example, by a leading question) is irrelevant unless a threat or a promise was involved.

These provisions, although similar in some respects to the common-law rules, do not codify the law but are freestanding and provide their own criteria (*O* [2006] 2 Cr App R 405). Thus s. 120(7)(d) expresses differently the requirement at common law that a recent complaint (in a sexual case) is admissible only 'when it is made at the first opportunity after the offence which reasonably offers itself' (*Osborne* and *Cummings*). It is submitted that the common-law authorities, including in particular *Valentine*, are nonetheless likely to offer some guidance on the way in which s. 120(7)(d) is applied. As at common law (see *Lee* and *Wilbourne*), there is no limitation in the 2003 Act as to the admission of more than one complaint. In *O* it was held that there is no reason to import such a limitation, although the court added that there is obviously a need to restrict evidence of 'complaint upon complaint', which may merely be self-serving. In that case, a second complaint, made to a person different from the person to whom the first complaint was made, was held to have been properly admitted because of its relevance over and above that of the first complaint. However, s. 120(7) contains no requirement of 'recency' as such, and therefore, depending on all the circumstances, s. 120(7)(d) allows for the admissibility of a complaint made months or even, as in *O*, years after the offence. See also per Rix LJ in *Birks* [2003] 2 Cr App R 122 at [27]–[29], referring to wording identical to s 120(7)(d) in the Criminal Justice Bill. Section 120(7)(e) requires that the complaint was not made as a result of a threat or promise, and under s. 120(8), which does not follow the common-law approach, the fact that the complaint was elicited by a leading question, such as 'Did X (naming the accused) assault you?', is irrelevant unless a threat or promise was made. However, a complaint elicited by way of a leading question is bound to affect the weight to be attached to it. Section 120(7)(f) requires that before the statement is introduced in evidence, the witness 'gives oral evidence in connection with its subject matter', words that suggest that this requirement will be met if the complainant gives some evidence in relation to the conduct referred to in her complaint, even if that evidence does not replicate the complaint or is not wholly consistent with it.

Self-serving Statements Made on Accusation

In *Pearce* (1979) 69 Cr App R 365, at pp. 368 and 370, the Court of Appeal could see no reason for casting doubt on the well-established practice, on the part of the prosecution, to admit in evidence all unwritten, and most written, statements made by an accused person to the police, whether they contain admissions or whether they contain denials of guilt. If such a statement is wholly adverse to the accused, it may be admitted as evidence of the truth of the facts contained in it under the PACE 1984, s. 76 (see **F17.5**). If it is a mixed statement, i.e. a statement containing both inculpatory and exculpatory parts, such as 'I killed X. If I had not done so, X would certainly have killed me there and then', the whole statement is admissible (see principle 2(b) in *Pearce*, below), and both parts are admitted as evidence of the truth of the facts they contain (see *Duncan* (1981) 73 Cr App R 359, *Hamand* (1985) 82 Cr App R 65, *Sharp* [1988] 1 WLR 7 and generally at **F17.61**). However, if the statement is purely exculpatory or self-serving, it is not admitted as evidence of the facts stated in it; it 'is evidence in the trial because of its vital relevance as showing the reaction of the accused when first taxed with the incriminating facts' (*Storey* (1968) 52 Cr App R 334, per Widgery LJ at pp. 337–8). The police having found cannabis in the accused's flat, she told them that it belonged to a man who had brought it there against her will. The Court of Appeal upheld the trial judge's rejection of a submission of no case to answer, on the ground that the accused's statement was not evidence of the facts stated but only evidence of her reaction, which was insufficient to negative evidence of possession. Likewise, in a case where the accused gives no evidence, there is no duty on the judge to remind the jury of voluntary statements made by the accused to the police in exonerating himself (*Barbery* (1975) 62 Cr App R 248; *Tooke* (1989) 90 Cr App R 417). In *Barbery* Eveleigh J said (at p. 250): 'In *Storey*, Widgery LJ . . . pointed out that such a statement, while being admissible for the jury's consideration . . . as to the consistency of an accused's defence, was not admissible as evidence of the truth of the contents . . . and it is therefore no part of the judge's duty to put that statement before the jury as being a factor for their consideration in coming to their conclusion'. But contrast *Donaldson* (1976) 64 Cr App R 59 at p. 69; and see also *Squire* [1990] Crim LR 341. **F6.22**

The Principles as Set Out in *Pearce* The reference in *Storey* to the reaction of the accused 'when first taxed' must not be read as limiting the principle recognised to statements made on **F6.23**

the first encounter with the police (*Pearce* (1979) 69 Cr App R 365). The facts in *Pearce* were as follows. On 6 March the appellant, the manager of a shop, was taxed by his employer's security officer with incriminating facts relating to handling stolen goods, and denied knowledge of them. Two days later he was arrested by the police and made a voluntary statement in the presence of his solicitor. Subsequently, in an interview, he gave certain answers which were relied on by the prosecution. The next day, he made another voluntary statement which was self-serving. The trial judge excluded evidence of all statements made to the police, except those parts of the interview on which the prosecution relied, on the grounds that they were self-serving and therefore inadmissible. On appeal it was argued that the statements had been properly excluded because they were not made when the appellant was first taxed with the incriminating facts on 6 March. Rejecting this argument and quashing the conviction, the Court of Appeal summarised the principles as follows (at p. 369):

(1) A statement which contains an admission is always admissible as a declaration against interest and is evidence of the facts admitted. With this exception a statement made by an accused person is never evidence of the facts in the statement. [It is now clear, however, that the exception encompasses statements which are either wholly or partially adverse to the accused (see *Sharp* [1988] 1 WLR 7 and generally at F17.61)].

(2) (a) A statement that is not an admission is admissible to show the attitude of the accused at the time when he made it. This however is not to be limited to a statement made on the first encounter with the police. The reference in *Storey* to the reaction of the accused 'when first taxed' should not be read as circumscribing the limits of admissibility. The longer the time that has elapsed after the first encounter the less the weight which will be attached to the denial. The judge is able to direct the jury about the value of such statements. (b) A statement that is not in itself an admission is admissible if it is made in the same context as an admission, whether in the course of an interview, or in the form of a voluntary statement. It would be unfair to admit only the statements against interest while excluding part of the same interview or series of interviews. It is the duty of the prosecution to present the case fairly to the jury; to exclude answers which are favourable to the accused while admitting those unfavourable would be misleading. (c) The prosecution may wish to draw attention to inconsistent denials. A denial does not become an admission because it is inconsistent with another denial. There must be many cases however where convictions have resulted from such inconsistencies between two denials.

(3) Although in practice most statements are given in evidence even when they are largely self-serving, there may be a rare occasion when an accused produces a carefully prepared written statement to the police, with a view to it being made part of the prosecution evidence. The trial judge would plainly exclude such a statement as inadmissible.

On the facts, the case fell within principles 2(a) and (b). The first statement was relevant to show the attitude of the appellant at the start of the interview: it set the scene, and when it was decided to admit part of the interview, the only fair course was to admit the statement to put the interview in context. The same principle applied to the questions and answers in the interview which were excluded and to the second voluntary statement on the next day. *Pearce* was applied in *McCarthy* (1980) 71 Cr App R 142.

Principle 2(a) above cannot be relied upon to admit in evidence a statement which adds no weight to other evidence already before the jury as to the accused's reaction to the suggestion that he had committed an offence. In *Tooke* (1989) 90 Cr App R 417, a case of unlawful wounding, the attack took place at 9 p.m. and shortly thereafter, at the scene, T made an exculpatory statement. At 9.40 p.m., T went voluntarily to a police station and made a witness statement setting out his version. The trial judge admitted the statement made at the scene but ruled that the defence were not entitled to cross-examine a police constable in order to prove that T had made the exculpatory statement at the station. It was held that the judge had not erred. The fact that the statement made at the station was a witness statement and not a statement in answer to a charge made no difference, because the same test applied. Furthermore, the statement was spontaneous — it was not suggested that T had time to consult a solicitor or had very much time to think about the matter before the witness statement was made. However, the statement was not relevant since it added nothing to the evidence already before the jury about T's reaction to the suggestion that he had committed an assault.

Principle 2(b) above makes it clear, in the case of a 'mixed statement', that, if the prosecution rely on the parts of the statement unfavourable to the accused, they are obliged to put in evidence the other parts of the statement which are favourable to the accused. However, principle 2(a) is not entirely clear: in the case of a statement which is wholly self-serving, are the prosecution *obliged* to adduce such evidence; and are the defence *entitled* to elicit evidence of such statements in cross-examination of the prosecution witnesses? *McCarthy* (1980) 71 Cr App R 142 supports an affirmative answer. In that case the judge had refused to admit details of an alibi given at a police interview. The Court of Appeal held that the evidence had been *improperly excluded* (although the case against the appellant was strong and the proviso was applied), since it did not come within the exception referred to in *Pearce* (i.e. principle 3). Lawton LJ said (at p. 145):

> One of the best pieces of evidence that an innocent man can produce is his reaction to an accusation of a crime. If he has been told, as the appellant was told, that he was suspected of having committed a particular crime at a particular time and place and he says at once, 'That cannot be right, because I was elsewhere', and gives details of where he was, that is something which the jury can take into account.

Principle 3 is designed to prevent an accused from attempting to take unfair advantage of principle 2(a). An example is *Newsome* (1980) 71 Cr App R 325. On a charge of rape, it was held that a self-serving statement, dictated by the accused to the police after consultation with, and in the presence of, his solicitor, some 13 hours after the alleged offence and subsequent to several interviews with the police, was inadmissible under principle 3. See also *Thatcher* [1967] 1 WLR 1278 (a statement drafted by counsel on instructions and submitted to the officer in charge of the case for his signature). In *Hutton* (1988) *The Times*, 27 October 1988, the police, in exercise of their right to do so under the PACE 1984, s. 58, delayed access to a solicitor and interviewed the accused three times. He refused to sign the notes of those interviews. After being charged, he was allowed access to his solicitor, in whose presence he dictated to the police a self-serving statement consistent with the evidence he gave at the trial. Counsel for the defence submitted that this statement should be put before the jury as a part of the prosecution case, or that in any event he was entitled to cross-examine the officers as to its contents. The judge rejected this submission, ruling that if the accused was cross-examined on the contents of the statement, the whole statement could be admitted, but otherwise the defence were only entitled to elicit, in cross-examination of the officers, the bare facts that after being granted access to his solicitor, the accused made a formal statement of his version of events. On appeal, it was argued that the statement should have been admitted, because the police, in exercising their rights under s. 58, had prevented the accused from making known his reaction to the charge. Rejecting the argument, the Court held that exercise of the s. 58 right did not affect the question whether the statement could properly be described as a spontaneous reaction, and therefore admissible under principle 2(a), or a carefully prepared draft following consultation, and therefore inadmissible under principle 3. The trial judge had properly concluded that the statement fell outside principle 2(a).

Statements in Rebuttal of Allegations of Recent Fabrication

The previous consistent statement of a witness will not become admissible merely because his evidence is impeached in cross-examination (*Fox v General Medical Council* [1960] 1 WLR 1017), even if this takes the form of cross-examination on a previous inconsistent statement (see *Coll* (1889) 24 LR Ir 522 at p. 541 and the other authorities considered at **F6.19**). However, if in cross-examination it is suggested to a witness that his evidence is a recent **F6.24** fabrication, evidence of a previous consistent statement will be admissible in re-examination to negative the suggestion and confirm the witness's credibility (*Y* [1995] Crim LR 155). In a trial for a sexual offence in which the previous statement amounts to a complaint, it may be admissible to rebut the allegation of recent fabrication notwithstanding that it is inadmissible as a recent complaint because not made at the first reasonably practicable opportunity (see *Tyndale* [1999] Crim LR 320 and **F6.20**).

In *Oyesiku* (1971) 56 Cr App R 240, Karminski LJ, giving the judgment of the Court of Appeal (at p. 245), approved the following statement of Dixon CJ in *Nominal Defendant v Clements* (1960) 104 CLR 476, at pp. 479–80:

> If the credit of a witness is impugned as to some material fact to which he deposes upon the ground that his account is a late invention or has been lately devised or reconstructed, even though not with conscious dishonesty, that makes admissible a statement to the same effect as the account he gave as a witness if it was made by the witness contemporaneously with the event or at a time sufficiently early to be inconsistent with the suggestion that his account is a late invention or reconstruction. But, inasmuch as the rule forms a definite exception to the general principle excluding statements made out of court and admits a possibly self-serving statement made by the witness, great care is called for in applying it. The judge at the trial must determine for himself upon the conduct of the trial before him whether a case for applying the rule of evidence has arisen and, from the nature of the matter, if there be an appeal, great weight should be given to his opinion by the appellate court. It is evident however that the judge at the trial must exercise care in assuring himself not only that the account given by the witness in his testimony is attacked on the ground of recent invention or reconstruction or that a foundation for such an attack has been laid by the party but also that the contents of the statement are in fact to the like effect as his account given in his evidence and that having regard to the time and circumstances in which it was made it rationally tends to answer the attack.

In *Oyesiku* the accused was convicted of assaulting a police officer. His wife, who gave evidence that the officer was the aggressor, was cross-examined on the basis that her evidence was a late invention concocted in order to help her husband. The Court of Appeal held that defence counsel, in re-examination, had been properly allowed to adduce evidence of her prior statement, consistent with her evidence, and made to a solicitor after her husband's arrest but before she had seen him. The conviction was quashed, however, because the trial judge had improperly refused to allow the jury to see the previous statement; by inspection of the statement, the jury would have been in a better position to assess the extent to which it rebutted the attack made on the witness's testimony. See also *Sekhon* (1987) 85 Cr App R 19, at **F6.13**. For earlier authority, see *Benjamin* (1913) 8 Cr App R 146 and *Flanagan v Fahy* [1918] 2 IR 361.

Under the CJA 2003, s. 120(1) and (2), a statement by a witness admitted as evidence to rebut a suggestion that his oral evidence has been fabricated will be admissible for the truth of its contents.

Criminal Justice Act 2003, s. 120

(1) This section applies where a person (the witness) is called to give evidence in criminal proceedings.
(2) If a previous statement by the witness is admitted as evidence to rebut a suggestion that his oral evidence has been fabricated, that statement is admissible as evidence of any matter stated of which oral evidence by the witness would be admissible.

Evidence of Previous Identification and Description

F6.25

> In cases where there has been a considerable lapse of time between the offence and the trial, and where there might be a danger of the witness's recollection of the prisoner's features having become dimmed, no doubt it strengthens the value of the evidence if it can be shown that in the meantime, soon after the commission of the offence, the witness saw and recognised the prisoner. (*Fannon* (1922) 22 SR (NSW) 427, per Ferguson J at pp. 429–30).

It is for reasons of this kind that evidence that a witness identified the accused out of court may be given by the witness himself and by any person who witnessed the identification. In *Christie* [1914] AC 545, a case of indecent assault on a small boy, the boy gave unsworn evidence of the assault and identified the accused, but was not questioned as to a previous identification. The boy's mother and a constable were then allowed to give evidence that, shortly after the offence alleged, they saw the boy approach the accused and identify him by saying, 'That is the man'. The House of Lords, by a majority, held that this evidence had been properly admitted. Viscount Haldane LC (who was of the opinion that this evidence *would have been* admissible if the boy had given evidence of his out-of-court identification) described the evidential value of such evidence as follows (at p. 551): 'Its relevancy is to show that the boy was able to identify at the time and to exclude the idea that the identification of the prisoner in the dock was an afterthought or mistake.' See also *Fowkes* (1856) *The Times*, 8 March 1856, at **F6.26**.

As a general rule, a 'dock identification', i.e. an identification of the accused for the first time in court, is undesirable and should be avoided (*Cartwright* (1914) 10 Cr App R 219); and the usual practice is to elicit evidence of a witness's previous out-of-court identification *before* asking him whether that person is in court. As to dock identifications generally and evidence of previous identification, see **F18**. For the position where the witness fails to identify the accused in court, having previously identified him out of court, see *Osbourne* [1973] QB 678, at **F15.11**.

Section 120(5) of the CJA 2003, when read in conjunction with s. 120(1) and (4) of the Act, has extended the common-law principle relating to evidence of *previous identification of the accused* to cover a previous oral or written statement of a witness which *identifies or describes a person, object or place*, provided that the witness, while giving evidence, indicates that to the best of his belief, he made the statement and it states the truth. A statement received under s. 120(5) is admitted as evidence of any matter stated, as well as evidence of the witness's consistency.

Criminal Justice Act 2003, s. 120

(1) This section applies where a person (the witness) is called to give evidence in criminal proceedings.

. . .

(4) A previous statement by the witness is admissible as evidence of any matter stated of which oral evidence by him would be admissible, if—
- (a) any of the following three conditions is satisfied, and
- (b) while giving evidence the witness indicates that to the best of his belief he made the statement, and that to the best of his belief it states the truth.

(5) The first condition is that the statement identifies or describes a person, object or place.

Statements Forming Part of *Res Gestae*

A previous statement of a witness which was so closely associated in time, place and circumstances with some act or event in issue that it can be said to form a part of the *res gestae*, i.e. the same transaction, is admissible as evidence of consistency to confirm evidence given by the witness to the same effect. Such a statement is also admissible for the truth of its contents (see **F16.28** to **F16.32**). In *Fowkes* (1856) *The Times*, 8 March 1856, the accused, commonly known as 'the butcher', was charged with murder. The victim's son gave evidence that he and a police officer were in a room with his father; that a face appeared at the window through which the fatal shot was then fired; and that he thought the face was that of the accused. He was also allowed to give evidence that on seeing the face, he had shouted, 'There's Butcher'; and the officer, who had not seen the face, was also allowed to give evidence as to this exclamation. **F6.26**

UNFAVOURABLE AND HOSTILE WITNESSES

General Rule against Impeaching Credit of Own Witness

F6.27 The general rule is that a party is not entitled to impeach the credit of his own witness by asking questions or adducing evidence concerning such matters as the witness's bad character, previous convictions, bias or previous inconsistent statements. In the case of a witness who is 'unfavourable', i.e. a witness who displays no hostile animus to the party calling him but merely fails to come up to proof or gives evidence unfavourable to that party, the general rule prevails: the only remedy available to the party is to call other witnesses, if available, with a view to proving that which the unfavourable witness failed to establish (*Ewer v Ambrose* (1825) 3 B & C 746). Insofar as this results in two equally credible witnesses directly contradicting each other upon a major fact in issue, it has been said that the party calling them is not entitled to accredit the one and discredit the other; the testimony of both is to be disregarded (*Sumner and Leivesley v John Brown & Co.* (1909) 25 TLR 745, per Hamilton J). However, in *Brent* [1973] Crim LR 295 it was held that this dictum does not apply to criminal proceedings, because of the Crown's duty to call all relevant evidence. In the case of a witness who appears to the judge to be hostile, that is to say not desirous of telling the truth to the court at the instance of the party calling him (Sir James F. Stephen, *A Digest of the Law of Evidence*, 12th ed. by Sir Harry L. Stephen and L. F. Sturge (London: Macmillan, 1936), art. 147), the general rule is modified, but in only two respects:

(a) under the Criminal Procedure Act 1865, s. 3, that party may, by leave of the judge, prove a previous inconsistent statement of the witness (see **F6.31**); and
(b) at common law, the party calling the witness may cross-examine him by asking leading questions (see *Thompson* (1976) 64 Cr App R 96, at **F6.32**).

Calling Witnesses who are Likely to be Hostile

F6.28 The prosecution may call a person as a witness even if he has shown signs that he is likely to be hostile, e.g. by retracting a statement or by making a second statement prior to the trial. Thus if the evidence of a prosecution witness at committal (or transfer) proceedings represents a substantial departure from his police statement, which implicates the accused, the prosecution are not obliged to treat the witness as hostile at that stage but may wait to see what happens at the trial (*Mann* (1972) 56 Cr App R 750). Equally, the fact that a witness has been treated as hostile before the magistrates is not by itself a reason making it improper for the prosecution to call him at the trial and, if necessary, to apply for leave to treat him as hostile again, although each case turns on its own facts (*Vibert* (21 October 1974 unreported)). Further a *voir dire* before a decision on whether to allow the Crown to treat a witness as hostile is only appropriate in exceptional circumstances because a jury may see the witness apparently giving evidence in one frame of mind and then see a complete turn-around after events which have taken place in their absence (*Khan* [2003] Crim LR 428). Similarly, it is only in very exceptional cases that a *voir dire* should be held to decide whether or not a witness who has yet to be called might prove to be hostile (*Olumegbon* [2004] EWCA Crim 2337). However, in cases in which a person indicates that he is no longer in a position to further assist the prosecution or court, or claims to be no longer able to remember anything, it seems that the judge has a discretion to hold a *voir dire* to decide whether to prevent him being called at all (*Honeyghon* [1999] Crim LR 221). The defence are likely to object to the prosecution calling such a person on the basis that it is simply a means to allow the jury to become aware of a previous statement made by him and inconsistent with his testimony. *Dat* [1998] Crim LR 488 provides an alternative but only partial solution to the problem: it was held that the prosecution should cross-examine their own witnesses by degrees, so as to limit the damage which might occur as a result of wide-ranging cross-examination on the previous statement.

Time at which to Apply to Treat Witness as Hostile

The application to treat a witness as hostile should be made when the witness first shows unmistakable signs of hostility (*Pestano* [1981] Crim LR 397). If counsel for the prosecution has a statement directly contradicting one of their witnesses who gives evidence that he is unable to identify the accused, he should at once show the statement to the judge and ask for leave to cross-examine the witness (*Fraser* (1956) 40 Cr App R 160). However, although there may be circumstances where a witness is displaying such an excessive degree of hostility that the only appropriate course is to treat him as hostile, if he gives evidence contrary to an earlier statement (or fails to give the evidence expected) the party calling him and the trial judge should first consider inviting him to refresh his memory from material which it is legitimate to use for that purpose and should not immediately proceed to treat him as hostile (*Maw* [1994] Crim LR 841). In *Powell* [1985] Crim LR 592 it was held that the prosecution, during re-examination, had been properly allowed to treat as hostile a witness who had shown no signs of hostility during examination-in-chief. Although such an application is a little unusual, it is a matter for the judge's discretion (ibid.). See also *Little* (1883) 15 Cox CC 319. F6.29

Role of Judge and Jury

The discretion of the judge, however hostile the witness, is absolute (*Rice v Howard* (1886) 16 QBD 681; *Price v Manning* (1889) 42 ChD 372); and the decision will rarely be open to a successful challenge on appeal (*Manning* [1968] Crim LR 675). F6.30

Although the question whether a witness is hostile is for the judge, the jury should not be excluded from the proceedings while the decision is taken. In *Darby* [1989] Crim LR 817, in which an application to treat a witness as hostile was deferred by the judge, who had him questioned further in the absence of the jury before ruling that he was hostile, it was held that the evidence and demeanour of the witness should have been tested in the presence of the jury.

Criminal Procedure Act 1865, s. 3

Criminal Procedure Act 1865, s. 3 F6.31

> A party producing a witness shall not be allowed to impeach his credit by general evidence of bad character, but he may, in case the witness shall, in the opinion of the judge, prove adverse, contradict him by other evidence, or, by leave of the judge, prove that he has made at other times a statement inconsistent with his present testimony; but before such last mentioned proof can be given the circumstances of the supposed statement, sufficient to designate the particular occasion, must be mentioned to the witness, and he must be asked whether or not he has made such statement.

The first part of this section puts on a statutory basis the common-law rule that a party calling a witness is not entitled to impeach his credit by evidence of bad character, i.e. evidence of previous misconduct, convictions, or other evidence designed to show that the witness is not to be believed on oath. The remaining two rules in the section apply to witnesses who, in the opinion of the judge, prove 'adverse', which means 'hostile' and not merely 'unfavourable' (*Greenough v Eccles* (1859) 5 CB NS 786, a decision on the construction of the Common Law Procedure Act 1854, s. 22, which was repealed but re-enacted by s. 3 of the 1865 Act).

The first rule is that a party may 'contradict' a hostile witness, i.e. call other witnesses to prove that which the hostile witness has failed to establish. Although s. 3 suggests that this rule applies only to hostile witnesses, according to Williams and Willes JJ in *Greenough v Eccles*, it has not affected the common-law rule to the same effect in the case of unfavourable witnesses (see *Ewer v Ambrose* (1825) 3 B & C 746).

The second rule, which does apply only in the case of a witness who is, in the opinion of the judge, hostile, allows the judge to give leave to prove that the witness has made at other times a statement inconsistent with his present testimony. A witness for the defence who is treated as hostile is in the same position as a hostile prosecution witness, and accordingly is open to cross-examination on a previous inconsistent statement (*Booth* (1981) 74 Cr App R 123). The leave of the judge may be given whether the previous inconsistent statement was oral or written (*Prefas* (1986) 86 Cr App R 111). If the witness, when asked, admits that he made the previous statement, this will clearly suffice as proof that he did make it. If the witness does not make such an admission, whether the earlier statement can be used depends on the facts of the particular case. In *Baldwin* [1986] Crim LR 681, where the witness accepted that he had made some parts of a written statement and accepted that the signatures on the statement were his, it was held that this was evidence entitling the judge to conclude that the witness had made the statement, and therefore to rule that cross-examination on it was permissible.

If the nature of the evidence given justifies it, an application may be made to treat as hostile the spouse of an accused who is competent but not compellable for the prosecution, and who has waived his or her right to refuse to testify. However, it is desirable that the judge should explain to the spouse, in the absence of the jury and before the oath is taken, that if the choice is made to give evidence, he or she may be treated like any other witness (*Pitt* [1983] QB 25). See generally, F4.13.

Hostile Witnesses at Common Law

F6.32 The Criminal Procedure Act 1865, s. 3, has not destroyed or removed the common-law right of the judge, in the exercise of his discretion, to allow cross-examination of a hostile witness by asking leading questions about a previous statement. In *Thompson* (1976) 64 Cr App R 96 the appellant was convicted of incest with his daughter. She had made a statement to the police implicating her father but, when sworn as a witness at the trial, she refused to give evidence, and leave was given to treat her as hostile. She was asked leading questions, her previous statement was put to her, and she eventually agreed that its contents were true. It was argued, on appeal, that since the girl had initially given no evidence, there was no 'present testimony' with which her previous statement could be said to be inconsistent, and therefore s. 3 did not apply. Lord Parker CJ found it unnecessary to decide whether s. 3 applied to the facts, since the common-law cases prior to the 1865 Act recognised that pressure could be brought to bear upon witnesses who refused to cooperate. Thus, in *Clarke v Saffery* (1824) Ry & M 126, in which there does not appear to have been evidence contradicting the earlier statement, Best CJ said (at p. 126): 'If a witness, by his conduct in the box, shows himself decidedly adverse, it is always in the discretion of the judge to allow a cross-examination'. In *Bastin v Carew* (1824) cited Ry & M 127, Lord Abbott CJ said: '. . . in each particular case there must be some discretion in the presiding judge as to the mode in which the examination shall be conducted, in order best to answer the purposes of justice'. On this basis, the appeal was dismissed. It is submitted that if the witness in the case had denied making the previous statement and not accepted the truth of its contents, it would not have been open to proof at common law.

Evidential Value of Previous Inconsistent Statement

F6.33 If a hostile witness, on being cross-examined on a previous inconsistent statement, adopts and confirms some of the contents of the statement, then what he says becomes part of his evidence and, subject to the jury assessing his credibility, it is capable of being accepted (*Maw* [1994] Crim LR 841). However, even if he does not admit the truth of the previous statement, under the CJA 2003, s. 119, it is admitted as evidence of the matters stated.

Criminal Justice Act 2003, s. 119

(1) If in criminal proceedings a person gives oral evidence and—
  (a) he admits making a previous inconsistent statement, or
  (b) a previous inconsistent statement made by him is proved by virtue of section 3, 4 or 5 of the Criminal Procedure Act 1865,

> the statement is admissible as evidence of any matter stated of which oral evidence by him would be admissible.

In *Golder* [1960] 1WLR 1169, Lord Parker CJ said (at pp. 1172–3):

> . . . when a witness is shown to have made previous statements inconsistent with the evidence given by that witness at the trial, the jury should . . . be directed that the evidence given at the trial should be regarded as unreliable;

The dictum in *Golder* was cited with approval in *Oliva* [1965] 1 WLR 1028, at pp. 1036–7. However, Lord Parker's dictum was *obiter* and in *Driscoll v The Queen* (1977) 137 CLR 517, at pp. 535–7, the High Court of Australia refused to accept that it was *always* necessary or even appropriate to direct a jury in this way, a view endorsed by the House of Lords in *Governor of Pentonville Prison, ex parte Alves* [1993] AC 284 (at p. 298) and by the Court of Appeal in *Goodway* [1993] 4 All ER 894 (at p. 899). Thus in *Pestano* [1981] Crim LR 397, where the prosecution cross-examined the witness on his deposition, but nonetheless sought to rely upon his evidence insofar as it supported their case, it was held that the evidence was for the jury to consider, subject to a proper warning from the judge as to the weight which could be attached to it. See also *Nelson* [1992] Crim LR 653.

The direction to treat the witness's evidence as 'unreliable' may be inappropriate when a witness gives a rational or convincing explanation for the earlier contradictory statement or gives evidence to the benefit of the accused (see *Thomas* [1985] Crim LR 445 and *Khan* [2003] Crim LR 428). Nonetheless, if a witness has been treated as hostile, it is necessary for the jury to consider whether he should be treated as creditworthy at all, and they should be clearly directed on that point before considering which parts of the evidence are worthy of acceptance and which are to be rejected. It is insufficient to tell the jury to approach the evidence with great caution and reservation. The judge should give a clear warning about the dangers involved in a witness who contradicts himself and should direct them to consider whether they can give any credence to such a witness. It is only if they can, that they may then consider which parts of his evidence they can accept (*Maw* [1994] Crim LR 841).

F

Part F Evidence

Section F7 Cross-examination and Re-examination

CROSS-EXAMINATION: GENERAL CONSIDERATIONS

Nature of Cross-examination

F7.1 Cross-examination is the questioning of a witness by (a) the opponent of the party calling him or (b) any other party to the proceedings. Thus, as to the latter, an accused has the right to cross-examine a co-accused who has chosen to give evidence (and any witnesses called by the co-accused). This applies not only where the co-accused has given evidence unfavourable to the accused (see *Hadwen* [1902] 1 KB 882 and *Paul* [1920] 2 KB 183), but also if the co-accused has merely given evidence in his own defence (*Hilton* [1972] 1 QB 421, per Fenton Atkinson LJ at pp. 423–4). Usually cross-examination follows immediately after examination-in-chief, but witnesses are sometimes merely tendered by the prosecution for cross-examination. Such a witness is called by the prosecution, sworn, asked no questions in chief other than his name and address, and then cross-examined by the defence (see *Brooke* (1819) 2 Stark 472).

Cross-examination by an Accused in Person

F7.2 As a general rule, an accused is entitled to cross-examine in person any witness called by the prosecution. The general rule is subject to a common-law restriction and important statutory exceptions. Concerning the former, a trial judge is not obliged to give an unrepresented accused his head to ask whatever questions, at whatever length, he wishes (*Brown* [1998] 2 Cr App R 364). As to the latter, the YJCEA 1999, ss. 34 to 39, replacing CJA 1988, s. 34A, protect three categories of witness from cross-examination by an accused in person. Under the YJCEA 1999, s. 34, no person charged with a sexual offence as defined in s. 62 of the Act (see **F7.16**) may cross-examine in person the complainant, either in connection with the offence or in connection with any other offence (of whatever nature) with which that person is charged in the proceedings; under s. 35, no person charged with one of a number of specified offences may cross-examine in person a 'protected witness' either in connection with the offence, or in connection with any other offence (of whatever nature) with which that person is charged in the proceedings; and under s. 36, the court has a general power, in cases not covered by ss. 34 and 35, to give a direction prohibiting the accused from cross-examining a witness in person if:

(a) the quality of evidence given by the witness is likely to be diminished by such cross-examination and would be likely to be improved by such a direction; and
(b) it would not be contrary to the interests of justice.

In deciding whether (a) applies in the case of a witness, the court must have regard to the particular matters set out in s. 36(3), including the nature of the questions likely to be asked. The accused should not be denied the opportunity to make representations in relation to the matters set out in s. 36(3) *R (Hillman) v Richmond Magistrates' Court* [2003] EWHC 2580 (Admin).

Section 38 provides that, where an accused is prevented from cross-examining a witness in person, the court must invite him to appoint a legal representative; and that if he fails to do so and the court decides that it is in the interests of justice for the witness to be cross-examined by a legal representative appointed to represent the interests of the accused, the court must choose and appoint such a representative, who shall not be responsible to the accused. Under s. 39, where an accused is prevented from cross-examining a witness in person, the judge must give the jury such warning (if any) as he considers necessary to ensure that the accused is not prejudiced by any inference that might be drawn from the fact that such cross-examination has been prevented or by the fact that the cross-examination was carried out by a court-appointed representative.

For the procedural rules relating to the restriction on cross-examination by an accused see CrimPR, part 31, set out in full in **appendix 1**.

Youth Justice and Criminal Evidence Act 1999, ss. 34 to 39

34. No person charged with a sexual offence may in any criminal proceedings cross-examine in person a witness who is the complainant, either—
(a) in connection with that offence, or
(b) in connection with any other offence (of whatever nature) with which that person is charged in the proceedings.

35.—(1) No person charged with an offence to which this section applies may in any criminal proceedings cross-examine in person a protected witness, either—
(a) in connection with that offence, or
(b) in connection with any other offence (of whatever nature) with which that person is charged in the proceedings.

(2) For the purposes of subsection (1) a 'protected witness' is a witness who—
(a) either is the complainant or is alleged to have been a witness to the commission of the offence to which this section applies, and
(b) either is a child or falls to be cross-examined after giving evidence in chief (whether wholly or in part)—
(i) by means of a video recording made (for the purposes of section 27) at a time when the witness was a child, or
(ii) in any other way at any such time.

(3) The offences to which this section applies are—
(a) any offence under—
(i) the Protection of Children Act 1978; or
(ii) part 1 of the Sexual Offences Act 2003;
(b) kidnapping, false imprisonment or an offence under section 1 or 2 of the Child Abduction Act 1984;
(c) any offence under section 1 of the Children and Young Persons Act 1933;
(d) any offence (not within any of the preceding paragraphs) which involves an assault on, or injury or a threat of injury to, any person.

(4) In this section 'child' means—
(a) where the offence falls within subsection (3)(a), a person under the age of 17; or
(b) where the offence falls within subsection (3)(b), (c) or (d), a person under the age of 14.

(5) For the purposes of this section 'witness' includes a witness who is charged with an offence in the proceedings.

36.—(1) This section applies where, in a case where neither of sections 34 and 35 operates to prevent an accused in any criminal proceedings from cross-examining a witness in person—
(a) the prosecutor makes an application for the court to give a direction under this section in relation to the witness, or
(b) the court of its own motion raises the issue whether such a direction should be given.

(2) If it appears to the court—
(a) that the quality of evidence given by the witness on cross-examination—
(i) is likely to be diminished if the cross-examination (or further cross-examination) is conducted by the accused in person, and
(ii) would be likely to be improved if a direction were given under this section, and

F

Part F Evidence

(b) that it would not be contrary to the interests of justice to give such a direction, the court may give a direction prohibiting the accused from cross-examining (or further cross-examining) the witness in person.

(3) In determining whether subsection (2)(a) applies in the case of a witness the court must have regard, in particular, to—
(a) any views expressed by the witness as to whether or not the witness is content to be cross-examined by the accused in person;
(b) the nature of the questions likely to be asked, having regard to the issues in the proceedings and the defence case advanced so far (if any);
(c) any behaviour on the part of the accused at any stage of the proceedings, both generally and in relation to the witness;
(d) any relationship (of whatever nature) between the witness and the accused;
(e) whether any person (other than the accused) is or has at any time been charged in the proceedings with a sexual offence or an offence to which section 35 applies, and (if so) whether section 34 or 35 operates or would have operated to prevent that person from cross-examining the witness in person;
(f) any direction under section 19 which the court has given, or proposes to give, in relation to the witness.

(4) For the purposes of this section—
(a) 'witness', in relation to an accused, does not include any other person who is charged with an offence in the proceedings; and
(b) any reference to the quality of a witness's evidence shall be construed in accordance with section 16(5).

37.—(1) Subject to subsection (2), a direction has binding effect from the time it is made until the witness to whom it applies is discharged.
In this section 'direction' means a direction under section 36.

(2) The court may discharge a direction if it appears to the court to be in the interests of justice to do so, and may do so either—
(a) on an application made by a party to the proceedings, if there has been a material change of circumstances since the relevant time, or
(b) of its own motion.

(3) In subsection (2) 'the relevant time' means—
(a) the time when the direction was given, or
(b) if a previous application has been made under that subsection, the time when the application (or last application) was made.

(4) [The court must state in open court its reasons for its decision in relation to a direction.]

(5) [Power to make rules of court.]

38.—(1) This section applies where an accused is prevented from cross-examining a witness in person by virtue of section 34, 35 or 36.

(2) Where it appears to the court that this section applies, it must—
(a) invite the accused to arrange for a legal representative to act for him for the purpose of cross-examining the witness; and
(b) require the accused to notify the court, by the end of such period as it may specify, whether a legal representative is to act for him for that purpose.

(3) If by the end of the period mentioned in subsection (2)(b) either—
(a) the accused has notified the court that no legal representative is to act for him for the purpose of cross-examining the witness, or
(b) no notification has been received by the court and it appears to the court that no legal representative is to so act,

the court must consider whether it is necessary in the interests of justice for the witness to be cross-examined by a legal representative appointed to represent the interests of the accused.

(4) If the court decides that it is necessary in the interests of justice for the witness to be so cross-examined, the court must appoint a qualified legal representative (chosen by the court) to cross-examine the witness in the interests of the accused.

(5) A person so appointed shall not be responsible to the accused.

(6) and (7) [Power to make rules of court.]

(8) For the purposes of this section—
(a) any reference to cross-examination includes (in a case where a direction is given under

section 36 after the accused has begun cross-examining the witness) a reference to further cross-examination; and

(b) 'qualified legal representative' means a legal representative who has a right of audience (within the meaning of the Courts and Legal Services Act 1990) in relation to the proceedings before the court.

39.—(1) Where on a trial on indictment with a jury an accused is prevented from cross-examining a witness in person by virtue of section 34, 35 or 36, the judge must give the jury such warning (if any) as the judge considers necessary to ensure that the accused is not prejudiced—

(a) by any inferences that might be drawn from the fact that the accused has been prevented from cross-examining the witness in person;

(b) where the witness has been cross-examined by a legal representative appointed under section 38(4), by the fact that the cross-examination was carried out by such a legal representative and not by a person acting as the accused's own legal representative.

(2) Subsection (8)(a) of section 38 applies for the purposes of this section as it applies for the purposes of section 38.

Object of Cross-examination

The object of cross-examination is: F7.3

(a) to elicit from the witness evidence supporting the cross-examining party's version of the facts in issue;
(b) to weaken or cast doubt upon the accuracy of the evidence given by the witness in chief; and
(c) in appropriate circumstances, to impeach the witness's credibility.

Role of the Judge

In general, when cross-examination is being conducted by competent counsel, a judge should not intervene, save to clarify matters he does not understand or thinks the jury may not understand. If he wishes to ask questions about matters that have not been touched upon, it is generally better to wait until the end of the examination or cross-examination. A judge should not be criticised for occasional transgressions, but there may come a time, depending on the nature and frequency of the interruptions, that the Court of Appeal is of the opinion that defence counsel was so hampered in the way he properly wished to conduct the cross-examination that the judge's conduct amounts to a material irregularity (*Sharp* [1994] QB 261). In rare cases, as when a child complainant becomes truculent during cross-examination and declines to answer any more questions, a judge may take over the questioning, provided that, having unsuccessfully tried to change the witness's mind, he consults with cross-examining counsel as to the questions to be put and gives an appropriate direction to the jury (*Cameron* [2001] Crim LR 587). F7.4

Order of Cross-examination

If there are two or more accused jointly indicted and separately represented by counsel, the order of cross-examination is the order in which the names of the accused appear on the indictment (*Barber* (1844) 1 Car & Kir 434). F7.5

Liability to Cross-examination

All witnesses are liable to cross-examination, except: F7.6

(a) a witness called merely to produce a document, who is not sworn (*Sumners v Moseley* (1834) 2 Cr & M 477) or who is sworn unnecessarily (*Rush v Smith* (1834) 1 Cr M & R 94);
(b) a witness unable to speak as to the matters supposed to be within his knowledge who is called by mistake, provided that the mistake is discovered after the witness has been

sworn but before his examination-in-chief (*Wood v Mackinson* (1840) 2 Mood & R 273); and

(c) a witness called by the judge, who may only be cross-examined with the judge's leave, which should be given if the witness is adverse to either party (*Coulson v Disborough* [1894] 2 QB 316; *Cliburn* (1898) 62 JP 232).

The evidence in chief of a witness who dies before cross-examination remains admissible, although little weight may attach to it (*Doolin* (1832) 1 Jebb CC 123). Similarly, if a witness, during cross-examination, becomes incapable through illness of answering any further questions, the trial may continue on the basis of the evidence already given (*Stretton* (1986) 86 Cr App R 7). In *Stretton*, the witness was the victim of sexual offences and the judge gave a carefully worded direction to the jury to acquit if they felt that the absence of cross-examination prevented them from judging fairly her credibility. See also *Wyatt* [1990] Crim LR 343 in which a seven-year-old girl, the victim of an indecent assault, was cross-examined through video link for about 20 minutes. She became visibly distressed and the judge adjourned the case for about 20 minutes. After the adjournment, the girl continued to cry and the judge decided that her evidence should proceed no further, even though counsel for the defence still had one important question to ask. The appeal was dismissed: the judge had not erred in the exercise of his discretion to adjourn for the length of time that he did and had directed the jury fairly on the girl's evidence and left it to them to determine her credibility. *Stretton* and *Wyatt* were both distinguished in *Lawless* (1994) 98 Cr App R 342. In that case the only direct evidence on one important part of the prosecution case was given by a witness who, at the end of his examination-in-chief, suffered a heart attack and was unable to give further evidence. It was held at least doubtful whether any direction to the jury, however strongly expressed, could have overcome the powerful prejudice of his evidence going wholly untested by cross-examination.

Effect of Failure to Cross-examine

F7.7 In *Wood Green Crown Court, ex parte Taylor* [1995] Crim LR 879, the Divisional Court approved the following principle as stated in the 1995 edition of this work: a party who fails to cross-examine a witness upon a particular matter in respect of which it is proposed to contradict him or impeach his credit by calling other witnesses, tacitly accepts the truth of the witness's evidence in chief on that matter, and will not thereafter be entitled to invite the jury to disbelieve him in that regard. The proper course is to challenge the witness while he is in the witness-box or, at any rate, to make it plain to him at that stage that his evidence is not accepted (*Hart* (1932) 23 Cr App R 202). Thus in *Bircham* [1972] Crim LR 430, counsel for the accused was not permitted to suggest to the jury in his closing speech that the co-accused and a prosecution witness had committed the offence charged, where the allegation had not been put to either in cross-examination.

> . . . nothing would be more absolutely unjust than not to cross-examine witnesses upon evidence which they have given, so as to give them notice, and to give them an opportunity of explanation, and an opportunity very often to defend their own character, and, not having given them such an opportunity, to ask the jury afterwards to disbelieve what they have said, although not one question has been directed either to their credit or to the accuracy of the facts they have deposed to. (*Browne v Dunn* (1893) 6 R 67, per Lord Halsbury at pp. 76–7, followed in *Fenlon* (1980) 71 Cr App R 307.)

See also para. 708(g) of the Code of Conduct of the Bar of England and Wales. Evidence to contradict a witness which was not put to him in cross-examination, may be admitted, provided that the witness is then recalled and cross-examination of him reopened in order to put the new evidence to him (*Cannan* [1998] Crim LR 284).

The rule under discussion is not hard-and-fast or inflexible. Thus where it is proposed to invite the jury to disbelieve a witness on a particular matter, it will not always be necessary to put to him explicitly that he is lying, provided that the overall tenor of the cross-examination is designed to show that his account is incapable of belief (see *Lovelock* [1997] Crim LR 821). Indeed in some cases it may be that the point upon which the witness is to be impeached is manifest, as when the story he tells is incredible, and it is unnecessary to cross-examine him upon it at all: the most effective cross-examination would be to ask him to leave the box (*Browne v Dunn*, per Lords Herschell LC and Morris). Application of the rule may also be unnecessary in the case of a witness whose evidence is purely corroborative of the evidence of another witness whose evidence-in-chief has already been challenged in cross-examination. It is a sensible practice, however, to secure the assurance of the trial judge, and the agreement of the party calling the witness, that failure to cross-examine in such circumstances will not be taken as a tacit acceptance of the witness's evidence. The rule has also been held to be inapplicable in the case of proceedings in magistrates' courts (*O'Connell v Adams* [1973] RTR 150). This may explain *Wilkinson v DPP* [2003] EWHC 865 (Admin), in which the accused was convicted following a summary trial in which the prosecution failed to cross-examine her; it was held that there was nothing to show that the trial was unfair and that the district judge had been entitled to reject her evidence.

RULES GOVERNING CONDUCT OF CROSS-EXAMINATION

Scope of Cross-examination

Questions in cross-examination are not restricted to matters raised in chief, but may relate to any fact in issue (or relevant fact), or to the credibility of the witness. Cross-examination is governed by the following general rules. **F7.8**

Leading Questions

A witness under cross-examination may be asked leading questions. This is so even if he appears to be more favourable to the cross-examining party than to the party calling him (*Parkin v Moon* (1836) 7 C & P 408). **F7.9**

Exclusionary Rules of Evidence

The exclusionary rules of evidence relating to hearsay, opinion, privilege etc. apply to cross-examination as they apply to examination-in-chief. Thus in *Thomson* [1912] 3 KB 19, a charge of using an instrument on a woman with intent to procure a miscarriage, it was held that counsel for the defence had properly been prevented from asking a prosecution witness in cross-examination whether the woman (who had died) had told her that she intended to procure her own miscarriage and, later, that she had done so. The evidence was inadmissible hearsay. See also *Windass* (1988) 89 Cr App R 258 (it is improper for counsel for the prosecution, during cross-examination of the accused, to ask him to explain highly damaging statements contained in a document written by a third party and inadmissible against the accused); *Gray* [1998] Crim LR 570 (it is inappropriate to cross-examine an accused on a co-accused's interview that is inadmissible as against the accused, where the effect is to use what the co-accused said as if it were evidence); and *Re P* [1989] Crim LR 897 (it is improper to cross-examine an accused in a sexual case on a complaint which is otherwise inadmissible because not a 'recent' complaint). **F7.10**

In *Treacy* [1944] 2 All ER 229, a charge of murder, it was held that the accused had been cross-examined improperly upon certain inadmissible confessions made on arrest and inconsistent with his evidence. It has been said that the principle established in this case, that an accused cannot be cross-examined by the prosecution in such a way as to reveal that he made an inadmissible confession, also obtains in favour of any co-accused (*Rice* [1963] 1 QB 857, per Winn J at pp. 868–9). However, see also *Rowson* [1986] QB 174 and other authorities considered in F17.52.

Power of Judge to Restrain Unnecessary or Improper Questions

F7.11 The trial judge has a discretion to prevent any questions in cross-examination which, in his opinion, are unnecessary, improper or oppressive. Cross-examination is a powerful weapon entrusted to counsel, and should be conducted with restraint and a measure of courtesy and consideration which a witness is entitled to expect in a court of law (*Mechanical & General Inventions Co. Ltd v Austin* [1935] AC 346, per Lord Sankey LC at pp. 359–60). Thus, it is no part of the duty of counsel for the defence to embark on lengthy cross-examination on matters which are not really in issue (*Kalia* (1974) 60 Cr App R 200). See also *Simmonds* [1969] 1 QB 685 and *Maynard* (1979) 69 Cr App R 309. Likewise, questions should not be in the nature of comment on the facts; comments should be confined to speeches. Nor should questions be framed in such a way as to invite argument rather than elicit evidence on the facts in issue. Thus counsel should avoid questions such as 'I suggest to you that . . . ' and 'Do you ask the jury to believe that . . . '. Cross-examination should be confined to putting questions of fact. Counsel should not state what somebody else has said or is expected to say. The time for statements such as 'The defendant's recollection is . . . ' or 'The defendant will say . . . ' is the opening speech; such statements should not be made, or put in the form of a question, in cross-examination (*Baldwin* (1925) 18 Cr App R 175, per Lord Hewart CJ at pp. 178–9). The same restrictions apply to questions put by the judge (see *Wilson* [1991] Crim LR 838, where the judge asked the accused 'So this 12-year-old girl has made wicked lies about you?'). See also **F7.13** and **F7.14**.

Power of Judge to Impose Time-limits

F7.12 Although the imposition of time-limits for cross-examination (or examination-in-chief) of witnesses should not become a routine feature of trial management, judges are fully entitled, and indeed obliged, to impose reasonable time-limits where counsel indulge in prolix and repetitious questioning. It is not the duty of counsel to put to a witness every point of an accused's case, however peripheral, or to embark on lengthy cross-examination on matters which are not really in issue. The duty is to discriminate between important and relevant features of a defence case which have to be put to a witness and minor and/or unnecessary matters which do not need to be put. Entitlement to a fair trial is not inconsistent with proper judicial control over the use of court time and the Court of Appeal will not interfere with a decision made by a judge in this respect unless it is plain that it resulted in unfairness. These propositions, which derive from *B* [2005] EWCA Crim 805, may be regarded as specific examples of the general duty of the court to deal with cases efficiently and expeditiously and actively to manage cases to ensure that evidence is presented in the shortest and clearest way, giving any direction appropriate (see CrimPR, rr 1.1(2)(e), 3.2(2)(e) and 3.2(3): see **appendix 1**).

Cross-examination as to Credit

F7.13 'Since the purpose of cross-examination as to credit is to show that the witness ought not to be believed on oath, the matters about which he is questioned must relate to his likely standing after cross-examination with the tribunal which is trying him or listening to his evidence' (*Sweet-Escott* (1971) 55 Cr App R 316 at p. 320; *Hobbs v C.T.Tinling & Co Ltd* [1929] 2 KB 1 per Sankey LJ at p. 51). At common law there is a wide variety of ways in which the cross-examining party may seek to cast doubt upon a witness's evidence-in-chief and to show that he ought not to be believed on his oath. He may cross-examine him about his means of knowledge of the facts to which he has testified, his opportunities for observation, his powers of perception, the quality of his memory, mistakes, omissions and inconsistencies in his evidence, and omissions or inconsistencies in previous statements that relate to his likely standing with the jury after cross-examination but which are not 'relative to the subject matter of the indictment' (see *Funderburk* [1990] 1 WLR 587). As to omissions, where an accused is charged with a sexual offence and asserts fabrication on the part of the complainant, he may be cross-examined as to what facts are known to him that might explain why the complainant would make a false accusation against him (*Brook* [2003] 1 WLR 2809). A witness may also be cross-examined about his previous convictions or bias (if, in either case, it is lawful to do so under the rules relating to evidence of bad character in the CJA 2003, part 11, considered below and at **F12** and **F14**), any mental or physical disability affecting his reliability, and any previous statements made by him 'relative to the subject-matter of the indictment' and inconsistent with his testimony; and if the witness denies any of these matters, the cross-examining party is entitled to prove them (see **F7.32** to **F7.34**). However, cross-examination designed to impugn the witness's credibility should always comply with the rules contained in the Code of Conduct of the Bar (see **F7.14**).

Any questions in cross-examination as to a witness's bad character are subject to the rules set out in the CJA 2003, part 11. Section 99 of the Act abolishes the common-law rules governing the admissibility of evidence of 'bad character' in criminal proceedings and the intention appears to be to abolish not only the rules as to the introduction of such evidence in examination-in-chief, but also the rules governing cross-examination about bad character. Thus such cross-examination is permitted only if it comes within one of the specified categories of admissibility set out in s. 100 (non-defendant's bad character — see **F14**) or 101 (defendant's bad character — see **F12**). Evidence of bad character for the purposes of the Act is defined by s. 98 as evidence of, or of a disposition towards, misconduct, other than evidence which 'has to do with the alleged facts of the offence with which the defendant is charged' or 'evidence of misconduct in connection with the investigation or prosecution of that offence'. Section 108 of the 2003 Act imposes an additional restriction in relation to offences committed by the accused when a child (see **F12.47**). There is a further restriction in the YJCEA 1999, s. 41: in the case of sexual offences, except with the leave of the court, no question may be asked in cross-examination about any sexual behaviour of the complainant (see **F7.16** to **F7.26**).

The Code of Conduct of the Bar

The Code of Conduct of the Bar of England and Wales also regulates the conduct of cross-examination. **F7.14**

Concerning cross-examination, see in particular para. 708 and paras. 5.10, 5.11, 11.1 and 13.5 of the Written Standards. In *McFaden* (1975) 62 Cr App R 187, the Court of Appeal said that the Bar Council Rules (now superseded by the Code), although they had strong persuasive force, did not bind the courts.

In *O'Neill* (1950) 34 Cr App R 108, it was suggested to police officers, in cross-examination, that they had beaten the accused until they made confessions. The accused elected not to testify. Lord Goddard CJ observed that it was 'entirely wrong' to make the suggestions that were made in cross-examination but not subsequently to call the accused to substantiate what they had instructed their counsel to say. The Court of Appeal in *Callaghan* (1979) 69 Cr App R 88 said that it entirely agreed with these observations. However, the observations in *Callaghan* have since been modified by Waller LJ (see *The Times*, 20 February 1980): if the accused declines to give evidence *because of his very bad record*, counsel should warn him that the judge will probably make a very strong comment on his failure to substantiate his allegations on oath. If the client persists with his instructions, however, counsel must carry them out. See also *Brigden* [1973] Crim LR 579, where the accused's case was that the police had 'planted' certain incriminating articles, but he gave no evidence. The Court of Appeal, *without* criticising the conduct of counsel for the defence, held that the trial judge was justified in making a strong comment on the accused's failure to go into the witness-box. See further, para. 708(h) of the Code of Conduct of the Bar.

Inspection of and Cross-examination on Documents

F7.15 As to cross-examination of a witness on a previous inconsistent statement, see the Criminal Procedure Act 1865, ss. 4 and 5, at **F7.28**.

In the case of a document used by a witness to refresh his memory, the cross-examining party may inspect the document without thereby making it evidence (*Gregory v Tavernor* (1833) 6 C & P 280; *Senat v Senat* [1965] P 172). (As to the cross-examination of a witness on a document used by him to refresh his memory, see **F6.13**.) However, if a party calls for and inspects a document in the possession of another party which has *not* been used to refresh a witness's memory, the other party may require him to put it in evidence (*Wharam v Routledge* (1805) 5 Esp 235; and *Calvert v Flower* (1836) 7 C & P 386, applied in *Stroud v Stroud (No. 1)* [1963] 1 WLR 1080). The rule is obscure: it is unclear whether the document is admitted for the truth of its contents or as evidence of the consistency of the witness. In *Stroud v Stroud (No. 1)* Wrangham J observed that the rule had developed at a time when there was no discovery (whereas nowadays all relevant non-privileged documents are, in civil cases, disclosed), and acknowledged, therefore, that occasions for the practical application of the rule are fewer. Nonetheless, he said (at p. 1082): 'the rule itself has never been abrogated, and it may still be of practical importance, for example in criminal proceedings, where there is no discovery.' The Criminal Law Revision Committee recommended abolition of the rule in criminal proceedings, in which it appears never to have been applied (see 11th Report, Cmnd 4991, para. 223).

A document, the contents of which are inadmissible, is not rendered admissible by being put to a witness in cross-examination (see *Treacy* [1944] 2 All ER 229). However, in cross-examination counsel may produce to the witness a document containing an inadmissible hearsay statement and ask him, *without reading it aloud*, whether he accepts the contents as true. If the witness does accept the contents as true, they become evidence in the case; but if not, the contents remain inadmissible hearsay (*Gillespie* (1967) 51 Cr App R 172; applied in *Cross* (1990) 91 Cr App R 115). In *Cooper* (1985) 82 Cr App R 74, a charge of illegally importing drugs (concealed in a television set delivered to the accused's house), customs officers found letters in the house, written by the accused's wife in his and her names, five days before delivery of the television set, which referred to the 'houses' being 'hashless'. The Court of Appeal, applying *Gillespie* held that the proper procedure would have been for the prosecution to prove the finding of the letters as part of their case in order to give notice to the defence of the use to which they might eventually be put; but at this stage there should have been no indication of the contents of the letters to the jury. Then, in cross-examination of the accused, the letters should have been placed before him, and he should have been asked whether he was aware of their contents. Had he said yes, he should have been asked about the passages relating to the shortage of drugs. Similarly, it has been held that it is improper for counsel, when asking a witness to look at a document (the contents of which are inadmissible) and to say whether he still adheres to his answer, to describe to the jury its nature or contents. The proper course is simply to hand the document to the witness, direct him to look at it, and then to ask whether he still adheres to his answer (*Yousry* (1914) 11 Cr App R 13, per Lord Coleridge CJ at p. 18). See also *Tompkins* (1977) 67 Cr App R 181.

In *Hackney* (1982) 74 Cr App R 194, the Court of Appeal considered the growing practice of the defence, during the trial, to call for, and then cross-examine police officers on, records made during the accused's detention at a police station. Noting that entries in such records are often made by a number of police officers, and therefore that any inquiry into the completeness and accuracy of such records would often entail the questioning of many officers, the Court of Appeal said (at p. 198):

> These records, it should be emphasised, do not prove themselves. The prosecution do not have to produce them without some notice which allows proper opportunity of proving and explaining

their contents by the evidence of officers who actually made the records. We think that judges should control the use made of such documents with these factors in mind and also ensure that the use of them is strictly confined to an issue in the case (the credibility of a witness, for example) that time spent exploring them is not inordinate and that indiscriminate use of them is not made either by counsel or by a defendant in person. When deciding what use, if any, should be made of such documents, the judge should take account of whether the defence before the trial began, could have given notice to the prosecution for the production of the documents so that proper steps could have been, at the outset of the trial, taken for the production not only of the documents, but also of witnesses able properly to inform the jury about the contents of them.

PROTECTION OF COMPLAINANTS IN PROCEEDINGS FOR SEXUAL OFFENCES

The Restriction

The circumstances in which, in proceedings for sexual offences, evidence may be adduced, or the complainant cross-examined, by or on behalf of the accused, about any sexual behaviour or experience on his or her part involving the accused or any other person, is governed by the YJCEA 1999, ss. 41 to 43. The intention of these provisions is to counter what in recent Canadian jurisprudence has been described as the twin myths, namely 'that unchaste women were more likely to consent to intercourse and in any event were less worthy of belief' — see *Seaboyer* [1991] 2 SCR 577 at 604, 630 per McLachlin J (per Lords Steyn and Hutton in *A (No. 2)* [2002] 1 AC 45 at [27] and [147] respectively). The provisions are also born of a recognition that to allow victims of sexual offences to be harassed unfairly by questions about their previous sexual experiences is unjust to them and bad for society, because if victims are afraid to complain then the guilty may escape justice. **F7.16**

Under s. 41(1), if at a trial a person is charged with a sexual offence (a) no evidence may be adduced and (b) no question may be asked in cross-examination, by or on behalf of any accused at the trial, about any sexual behaviour of the complainant, except with the leave of the court. Section 41 applies to other proceedings as it applies to a trial, including a hearing held between conviction and sentence for the purposes of deciding matters relevant to the court's decision as to how the accused is to be dealt with (s. 42(3)). A 'sexual offence' is widely defined in s. 62 as any offence under the SOA 2003, part 1. Under s. 42(1)(c), 'sexual behaviour' means 'any sexual behaviour or other sexual experience, whether or not involving any accused or other person, but excluding (except in section 41(3)(c)(i) and (5)(a)) anything alleged to have taken place as part of the event which is the subject matter of the charge against thc accused'. It is submitted that this very wide definition will cover verbal and not merely physical advances of a sexual nature (see, e.g., *Hinds* [1979] Crim LR 111 and *Viola* [1982] 1 WLR 1138, both decisions under the Sexual Offences (Amendment) Act 1976). The phrases 'sexual behaviour' and 'other sexual experience' seem to be referring to acts or events of a sexual character, as opposed to the existence of a relationship, acquaintanceship or familiarity (per Lord Clyde in *A (No. 2)* at [128]). 'Sexual behaviour' it has been said, is a matter of impression and common sense (*Mukadi* [2004] Crim LR 373). However, whether either behaviour or experience is 'sexual' does not depend upon the perception of the complainant, because that would result in many vulnerable people, including children and those with learning difficulties, losing the protection of s. 41.

Section 41 applies only to defence evidence and questions. In *Soroya* [2006] EWCA Crim 1884, a rape case in which the issue was consent, the complainant gave evidence of the fact that during the incident she had said to the appellant that she was a virgin in the hope that this might cause him to desist from the assault on her. The prosecution also produced evidence that what she had said was false because she had had sexual intercourse on a previous occasion. On appeal, it was argued that evidence of the complainant's sexual history had been improperly introduced in circumstances which would not have been permitted had the defence sought to adduce it, which infringed the principle of equality of arms between the defence and prosecution and thereby constituted a breach of the right to a fair trial under ECHR, Article 6. It was further argued that s. 41 should be construed in such a way as to embrace the prosecution. Dismissing the appeal, it was held that what the complainant had said to the appellant had been relevant and admissible evidence bearing on the issue of consent; that the evidence of previous intercourse exposed the falsity of what she had said; and that no justified complaint could be directed at its admission.

It seems that s. 41(1) will apply in the case of evidence or questions about a complainant's false denial of a previous sexual experience, for example a false assertion that she was a virgin at the time of the alleged rape, whereas earlier on the same day she had had sexual intercourse with someone other than the accused (*S* [2003] All ER (D) 408 (Feb)). On the other hand, normally evidence or questions about a complainant's previous false complaints of sexual assaults or about her failure to complain about the assault which is the subject matter of the charge when complaining about other sexual assaults, are not 'about any sexual behaviour of the complainant' under s. 41(1). They relate not to her sexual behaviour, but to her past statements or failure to complain. The purpose of the YJCEA 1999 was not to exclude such evidence. However, if the defence wishes to put questions about previous false complaints, there are two hurdles. First, leave is required under the CJA 2003, s. 100(4) (see **F14.11 *et seq.*)** because such questioning relates to the bad character of the complainant (*V* [2006] EWCA Crim 1901). Second, the defence should seek a ruling from the judge that s. 41 does not exclude the questions.

It would be professionally improper to put such questions in order to elicit evidence about past sexual behaviour as such under the guise of previous false complaints. In any case the defence must have, and the judge is entitled to seek assurances from the defence that it has, a proper evidential basis for asserting that the previous statement was (a) made and (b) untrue. If not, the questions would not be about lies but about the sexual behaviour of the complainant within s. 41(1) (*T* [2002] 1 WLR 632, applied in *E* [2005] Crim LR 227 and *Abdelrahman* [2005] EWCA Crim 1367). See also *H* [2003] All ER (D) 332 (Jul). When there is evidence of a previous complaint, it seems that a complainant's subsequent failure to co-operate with the police may or may not justify a conclusion that it was untrue, depending on the circumstances (*V* [2006] EWCA Crim 1901 and *Garaxo* [2005] EWCA Crim 1170).

The principle established in *T* does not extend to cases in which the accused seeks to rely simply on the fact that the complainant made a statement about her previous sexual experience (as when evidence of the fact is said to be relevant to the defence of belief in consent), rather than the truth or falsity of such a statement. Evidence that such a statement was made falls within s. 41(1) (*W* [2005] EWCA Crim 3103).

Lifting the Restriction

F7.17 The court may give leave in relation to any evidence or question only on an application made by or on behalf of the accused (YJCEA 1999, s. 41(2)). The application shall be heard in private and in the absence of the complainant (s. 43(1)). After the application has been determined, the court must state in open court (but in the absence of the jury, if there is one) its reasons for giving or refusing leave and, if leave is given, the extent to which the evidence may be adduced or questions asked (s. 43(2)). The court may not give leave in relation to any evidence or question unless it is satisfied that s. 41(3) or (5) applies (s. 41(2)(a)) and that a refusal 'might have the result of rendering unsafe a conclusion of the jury or (as the case may be) the court on any relevant issue in the case' (s. 41(2)(b)). A 'relevant issue' means any issue falling to be proved by the prosecution or defence in the trial of the accused (s. 42(1)(a)). The test in s. 41(2)(b) must always be met. The test will be satisfied, it is submitted, when to disallow the evidence or question would be to prevent the jurors (or court) from taking into account material which might cause them to come to a different conclusion on a relevant issue. If this is correct, the test in s. 41(2)(b) is not particularly onerous: the judge need only be satisfied that a refusal might lead the jury to a different conclusion, not that such a consequence is probable. However, the judge is unlikely to be so satisfied, it seems, where there is other evidence before the jury in support of the conclusion advanced by the defence that is stronger and more compelling than the evidence sought to be adduced under s. 41 (see *Bahadoor* [2005] EWCA Crim 396). Under s. 41(6), for the purposes of s. 41(3) and (5), the evidence or question must relate to a specific instance or specific instances of alleged sexual behaviour on the part of the complainant as opposed to, e.g., evidence or a question to the effect that the complainant was promiscuous or a prostitute. Furthermore, in the case of a prostitute, information contained by way of a list of previous convictions for prostitution is incapable of fulfilling the requirements of s. 41(6); otherwise any encounter could fall under s. 41(6) if it could be assigned a date and time (*White* [2004] EWCA Crim 946, a decision under s. 41(3)(c) and considered at **F7.23**).

The operation of s. 41 involves, not the exercise of judicial discretion, but the making of a judgement whether to admit or exclude evidence which is relevant or asserted by the defence to be relevant. If it is relevant, then subject to s. 41(4) (see **F7.18**) and assuming that the criteria for admitting the evidence are established (see **F7.18** to **F7.24**), all the evidence relevant to the issues may be adduced. As part of his control over the case, the judge must ensure that a complainant is not unnecessarily humiliated or cross-examined with inappropriate aggression, or treated otherwise than with proper courtesy, but this does not permit him, by way of a general discretion, to prevent the proper deployment of evidence admissible under s. 41 merely because it comes in a stark, uncompromising form (*F* [2005] 1 WLR 2848, where the evidence included videotapes of the complainant stripping and masturbating).

Section 41(3) and (4): Evidence or a Question Relating to a Relevant Issue

Section 41(3) of the YJCEA 1999 is set out at **F7.25**. In s. 41, 'issue of consent' means any issue whether the complainant in fact consented to the conduct constituting the offence with which the accused is charged and accordingly does not include any issue as to the belief of the accused that the complainant so consented (s. 42(1)(b)). **F7.18**

Section 41(4) provides as follows:

> (4) For the purposes of subsection (3) no evidence or question shall be regarded as relating to a relevant issue in the case if it appears to the court to be reasonable to assume that the purpose (or main purpose) for which it would be adduced or asked is to establish or elicit material for impugning the credibility of the complainant as a witness.

Section 41(4) applies only where 'the purpose (or main purpose)' for which the evidence is adduced or the question is asked is to impugn the credibility of the complainant. In one sense, any evidence which directly challenges the evidence of a complainant, or seeks to demonstrate a malicious motive, involves an attack on her credibility. However, merely because evidence may impugn the complainant's credibility, it does not follow that the purpose or the main purpose for deploying it is to do so (Judge LJ in *F* [2005] 1 WLR 2848 at [27]). In *Martin* [2004] 2 Cr App R 354, a case of indecent assault involving enforced oral sex, M said that the complainant had fabricated her evidence because he had rejected her advances. The trial judge allowed the defence to question her about his allegation that two days earlier she had pestered him for sex. The Court of Appeal held that the defence should also have been allowed to question her about his allegation that on the earlier occasion she had performed an act of oral sex upon him, after which he had rejected her. It was held that, although one purpose of such questioning would have been to impugn the credibility of the complainant, it would also have gone to the accused's credibility and strengthened the defence case of fabrication, because the jury might have interpreted a rejection after the performance of oral sex as more hurtful than rejection after mere verbal advances.

Section 41(4), it is submitted, should not be construed literally. To do so would in large measure seem to defeat the purpose of s. 41(3). It would mean that, if the sole or main purpose of adducing evidence or asking a question is to impugn the complainant's credibility, the evidence or question can never be regarded as relating to a relevant issue in the case, even where it plainly does so relate and where refusal of leave to adduce the evidence or ask the question might have the result of rendering unsafe a conclusion of the jury on a relevant issue. An example under s. 41(3)(c) would be a rape case in which the accused, who says that the complainant consented and after the act of intercourse tried to blackmail him by alleging rape, wishes to cross-examine her about a previous similar attempt to blackmail him (see per Lord Steyn in *A (No. 2)* [2002] 1 AC 45 at [42]). It is submitted that s. 41(4) should be interpreted so as to prevent evidence or questions which go wholly or mainly to credit and which are irrelevant or insufficiently relevant to any relevant issue in the case. As Lord Hutton said, in the context of issues of consent, in *A (No. 2)* (at [138]):

> Issues of consent and issues of credibility may well run so close to each other as almost to coincide. A very sharp knife may be required to separate what may be admitted from what may not. The purpose of subsection (4) may be taken to be the abolition of the false idea that a history of sexual behaviour in some way was relevant to credit. The recognition of that myth as heresy is to be welcomed. But the subsection may have to be carefully handled in order to secure that the myth remains buried in the past and at the same time secure the availability of evidence of sexual behaviour which is properly admissible as bearing on the issue of consent. [cf. Lord Hope at [76] and [95]].

Section 41(3)(a): A Relevant Issue Other than Consent

F7.19 Examples of issues which fall within the YJCEA 1999, s. 41(3)(a), would include (a) the defence of reasonable belief in consent; (b) that the complainant was biased against the accused or had a motive to fabricate the evidence; (c) that there is an alternative explanation for the physical conditions on which the Crown relies to establish that intercourse took place; and (d) especially in the case of young complainants, that the detail of their account must have come from some other sexual activity which provides an explanation for their knowledge of that activity (per Lord Hope in *A (No. 2)* [2002] 1 AC 45 at [79]). However, it seems that the example in (d) above is confined to young complainants. In *M* [2005] EWCA Crim 3376, it was held that an application to cross-examine the 14-year-old complainant about possible sexual intercourse with a boy from school had been properly refused on the basis that, by reason of the complainant's age and the way of children of her age, she could have acquired her knowledge of sexual intercourse through conversations with friends.

In cases of rape, when considering the effect of a complainant's past sexual promiscuity upon the accused's belief that the complainant was consenting to intercourse, there is a difference between believing that the complainant is consenting to intercourse, which is relevant, and believing that the complainant will consent if advances are made, which is not relevant (see *Barton* (1987) 85 Cr App R 5, a decision relating to a defence of *mistaken* belief in consent decided under ss. 1(2) and 2 of the Sexual Offences (Amendment) Act 1976). It is submitted that this distinction remains valid in relation to a defence of *reasonable* belief in consent, for the purposes of the YJCEA 1999, s. 41, and that in each case, therefore, care should be taken to consider whether evidence of the accused's knowledge is relevant to the accused's belief that the complainant was consenting, rather than any belief that the complainant would consent, especially in cases where the knowledge relates to the sexual behaviour or experience of the complainant with another or others (see *Miah* [2006] EWCA Crim 1168).

In *F* [2005] 1 WLR 2848, F was convicted of specimen counts of rape and gross indecency, the evidence of the complainant being that between the ages of 7 and 16 she had been the subject of systematic sexual abuse. F denied any such abuse. The trial judge gave leave to the defence under s. 41 to cross-examine the complainant about the fact, not disputed by the complainant, that as an adult she had shared a full consensual sexual relationship with F. Following that ruling, the complainant's account of the adult relationship was introduced as part of the Crown's case. The defence case was that the adult relationship was inconsistent with the allegations of childhood abuse. The Crown's response was that as an adult the complainant was passive and did what she was pressurised to do, which followed the pattern of the childhood abuse. The complainant said that she had lived with F as an adult because she was scared of what he might do. F said that her complaints were false and motivated by a desire for revenge after he had ended the adult relationship. In his ruling under s. 41, the trial judge had refused to allow the defence to introduce in evidence, or ask questions about, photographs taken and videotapes made during the course of the adult relationship which showed the complainant engaged in erotic and sometimes pornographic behaviour. F's case, in relation to this material, was that it showed that the complainant was at ease and happy in the adult relationship. The complainant's case was that she participated in the making of the material because she thought that sexual intercourse with F would then become less frequent and that, when she had participated, F had told her to look as if she was enjoying herself. The Court of Appeal quashed the convictions. It was held that evidence of the adult relationship was relevant not only to the allegation that the complainant was motivated by a desire for revenge, but also to the critical question whether there had been childhood sexual abuse. The complainant's account of the adult relationship having been elicited as a part of the Crown's case, F was entitled to rebut it under s. 41(5) (see F7.24). He did so, but he was improperly prevented from relying on the photographic and video evidence to support his case that the complainant was not submitting but fully participating, an issue vital to the decision whether there had been childhood abuse. Without the evidence, the jury might have concluded that the adult relationship was one of submission representing the logical conclusion of childhood abuse and that the motive attributed to her by F was itself false.

In *Mokrecovas* [2002] 1 Cr App R 226, a charge of rape in which consent was in issue, it was submitted on an interlocutory appeal that s. 41(3)(a) applied to permit cross-examination of the complainant about an allegation that she had had consensual intercourse with the brother of the accused on two occasions in the 12 hours before the alleged rape, on the basis that such cross-examination went to the issue of the complainant's motive for lying to her father when she first complained of rape. On the facts the complainant had stayed away from home without parental permission; she had drunk excessively; and she had stayed in the flat of the two brothers and her parents may have thought her guilty of sexual behaviour of which they would disapprove. In the circumstances, it was argued, she would want to exonerate herself and therefore had alleged that she had been raped. Rejecting the submission, the court was not satisfied, for the purposes of s. 41(2)(b), that a refusal of leave might have the result of rendering unsafe a conclusion of the jury on any relevant issue in the case. It was held that whether or not sexual intercourse with the brother took place added nothing to the foundations which the defence already had for an allegation of a motive for lying.

Section 41(3)(b) and (c): An Issue of Consent

F7.20 It is plain from the wording of the YJCEA 1999, s. 41(3)(b) and (c) that in a rape case in which consent is in issue leave cannot be given in relation to any evidence or question about sexual behaviour of the complainant which amounts to nothing more than previous voluntary sexual intercourse with the accused. Section 41(3), in this respect, operates to reverse the decision in *Riley* (1887) 18 QBD 481. However, where the complainant and the accused are married or have cohabited, the tribunal of fact may well infer that there has been such voluntary sexual intercourse, and it is submitted that in these circumstances the trial judge, in the spirit of the new legislative framework, should direct the jury that they should draw no such inference because, without more, previous acts of voluntary sexual intercourse can have no bearing on any relevant issue in the case.

F7.21 **Section 41(3)(b)** Section 41(3)(b) covers behaviour such as sexual advances made by the complainant towards the accused or others shortly before or after 'the event which is the subject matter of the charge against the accused' and behaviour indicative of consent at the time of 'the event'. The evidence or question must relate to sexual behaviour of the complainant alleged to have taken place at or about the same time as 'the event', but excluding anything alleged to have taken place as part of the event which is the subject matter of the charge (see s. 42(1)(c)). The distinction between sexual behaviour which took place 'at . . . the same time as the event' and such behaviour which took place 'as part of the event' is far from clear. The phrase 'at or about the same time as the event' introduces an extremely narrow temporal restriction. The use of the words 'or about' provides a degree of elasticity, but cannot be strained to extend the restriction to days, weeks, or months. The explanatory note to the Act prepared by the Home Office states that it is expected that the phrase will generally be interpreted no more widely than 24 hours before or after the offence (see *A (No. 2)* at [9] [40] [82] and [132]). An example of the application of s. 41(3)(b) in a rape case would be where it is alleged that the complainant invited the accused to have sexual intercourse with her earlier in the evening (per Lord Steyn in *A (No. 2)* [2002] 1 AC 45 at [40]). See also, *sed quaere*, *Mukadi* [2004] Crim LR 373.

F7.22 **Section 41(3)(c)** Section 41(3)(c) covers any sexual behaviour of the complainant on another occasion which is, in any respect, so similar in nature to her sexual behaviour which, according to the defence, took place as part of the event which is the subject matter of the charge, or shortly before or after that 'event', that the similarity cannot reasonably be explained as a coincidence. The sexual behaviour could have been with the accused or another and could have taken place before or after the 'event'. See *T* [2004] 2 Cr App R 551, considered below.

As to the requirement that the similarity cannot reasonably be explained as a coincidence, a comparison can be made between s. 41(3)(c) and the concept of similar fact evidence, especially as formulated by Lord Salmon in *DPP v Boardman* [1975] AC 421 at p. 462. The restriction is significantly tighter than the test laid down in *DPP v P* [1991] 2 AC 447 (per Lord Hope in *A (No. 2)* at [83]), but the standard is something short of striking similarity (per Lord Clyde in *A (No. 2)* [2002] 1 AC 45 at [133]). Lord Clyde said (at [135]):

> It is only a similarity that is required, not an identity. Moreover the words 'in any respect' deserve to be stressed. On one view any single factor of similarity might suffice . . . provided that it is not a matter of coincidence. That the behaviour was with the same person, the defendant, must be at least a relevant consideration. But if the identity of the defendant was alone sufficient as the non-coincidental factor, that would seem to open the way in almost every case for a complete enquiry into the whole of the complainant's sexual behaviour with the defendant at least in the recent past, and that can hardly have been the intention of the provision. What must be found is a similarity in some other or additional respect. Further, the similarity must be such as cannot reasonably be explained as coincidence. To my mind that does not necessitate that the similarity has to be in some rare or bizarre conduct. So long as the particular factor is of a significance which goes beyond the realm of what could reasonably be explained as a coincidence, it should suffice.

An example would be a rape case in which the accused, who says that after consensual intercourse the complainant tried to blackmail him by alleging rape, wishes to cross-examine her about a previous similar attempt to blackmail him (per Lord Steyn in *A (No. 2)* at [42]). Section 41(3)(c), however, would not cover, in a case where at the time of the alleged offence and before intercourse kissing or other affectionate behaviour took place, evidence that for a number of months prior to the date of the alleged offence the accused had had frequent consensual intercourse with the complainant, in each case preceded by affectionate behaviour (per Lord Hutton in *A (No. 2)* at [159]). In *T* [2004] 2 Cr App R 551, T was convicted of rape, indecent assault and false imprisonment. The complainant had previously been in a relationship with T. Shortly after the relationship ended they agreed to meet in a park. They went inside a climbing frame, where the sexual acts took place. The issue was consent. The trial judge refused leave to cross-examine on, or adduce evidence of, the fact that three weeks prior to the alleged offences T and the complainant had had consensual sex in the same climbing frame adopting the same positions, both standing and the complainant facing away from the accused. He ruled that the behaviour was insufficiently relevant and that he was constrained by the temporal limitation of s. 41(3)(c)(ii). Allowing the appeal, it was held that the trial judge should have considered the matter under s. 41(3)(c)(i), which had no time constraint, and that had he done so he might have ruled the evidence admissible. As to s. 41(3)(c)(ii), the court observed that although it contained words which at first sight might appear to contain temporal limitations, it was doubtful that that was correct when s. 41(3)(c) was construed as a whole.

Section 41 and the Right to a Fair Trial

In *A (No. 2)* [2002] 1 AC 45, the House of Lords held that although prima facie a sexual relationship between an accused and complainant may be relevant to the issue of consent so as to render its exclusion under s. 41 a contravention of the accused's right to a fair trial under the ECHR, Article 6, it is possible under the HRA 1998, s. 3 to read s. 41, and in particular s. 41(3)(c), as subject to the implied provision that evidence or questioning which is required to ensure a fair trial under Article 6 should not be excluded. In the opinion of Lord Steyn (at [46]), an opinion shared by all of their lordships, if a trial judge finds it necessary to apply the interpretative obligation under s. 3 to the words of s. 41(3)(c), then he should construe those words by applying the following test: **F7.23**

> . . . due regard always being paid to the importance of seeking to protect the complainant from indignity and from humiliating questions, the test of admissibility is whether the evidence (and questioning in relation to it) is nevertheless so relevant to the issue of consent that to exclude it would endanger the fairness of the trial under [ECHR, Article 6].

According to Lord Steyn (at [31]), as a matter of common sense a prior sexual relationship between the complainant and the accused may, depending on the circumstances, be relevant to the issue of consent. Where there has been a recent close and affectionate relationship between the complainant and the accused, it is probable that the evidence will be relevant, not of course to prove consent, but to her show her specific mindset towards the accused, i.e. her affection for him. On the other hand, evidence of the kind which the accused in *A (No. 2)* wished to give, namely evidence of no more than some isolated acts of intercourse, albeit fairly recent, but without the background of an affectionate relationship, is probably not relevant (Lord Hutton at [151]–[154] and Lord Steyn at [31]). Moreover, according to Lord Clyde (at [125]), evidence of the complainant's sexual behaviour with men other than the accused should not be accepted as relevant to the question of consent.

A (No. 2) was followed in *R* [2003] EWCA Crim 2754. The appellants, R and A, were convicted of rape. The complainant said that she had been held on the floor by A when raped by R and that she had also been raped by A. According to R, the complainant had straddled him and the intercourse had been consensual. A simply denied that he had had intercourse. The Court of Appeal held that (1) given the stark contrast between the evidence as to the circumstances of the alleged rape, evidence that R had had a previous relationship with the complainant in which intercourse had occurred on more than one occasion, on the final occasion with both A and R, was relevant to the issue of consent and (2) evidence that R and the complainant had had consensual intercourse some 11 months after the alleged offence was relevant as conduct which might be inconsistent with an allegation of rape. It was held that, although on a strict interpretation of ss. 41(3) and 41(5) the evidence had to be excluded, it was so relevant that its exclusion deprived the appellants of a fair trial. *A (No. 2)* was distinguished in *White* [2004] EWCA Crim 946. W, convicted of rape, said that the complainant had asked him for money, which he had refused to give, and that after consensual intercourse he awoke to find her with his wallet. The trial judge refused an application to cross-examine the complainant on her previous and contemporaneous activities as a prostitute, the fact that she worked as a prostitute being of no relevance to the issue of consent as it was no part of W's case that he had offered payment. Dismissing the appeal, it was held that in the present day a prostitute was as entitled as any other to say 'no' and the fact that she was a prostitute did not mean that she was more likely to say 'yes' to sex. The bare fact that she was a prostitute was irrelevant to the issue of consent: there had to be something about the specific circumstances that had probative force and was so similar to the conduct complained of as to be beyond coincidence.

Section 41(5): Evidence or a Question Relating to Evidence Adduced by the Prosecution

F7.24 Section 41(5) applies if the evidence or question:

(a) relates to any evidence adduced by the prosecution about any sexual behaviour of the complainant (including anything alleged to have taken place as part of the event which is the subject matter of the charge — see s. 42(1)(c)); and
(b) in the opinion of the court, would go no further than is necessary to enable the evidence adduced by the prosecution to be rebutted or explained by or on behalf of the accused.

If, e.g., in a rape case, the complainant gives evidence that she has only ever had consensual sexual intercourse with her husband (A), evidence or questions might be permitted about previous consensual intercourse with the accused (B) or another person (C) before or after the alleged rape. An illustration is furnished by *F* [2005] 1 WLR 2848 (considered at **F7.19**), where the court noted (at [28]) that s. 41(4) applies only for the purposes of s. 41(3) and does not apply for the purposes of s. 41(5).

Statutory Provisions on Protection of Claimants in Sexual Offence Proceedings

F7.25 **Youth Justice and Criminal Evidence Act 1999, ss. 41 to 43**

41.—(1) If at a trial a person is charged with a sexual offence, then, except with the leave of the court—
(a) no evidence may be adduced, and
(b) no question may be asked in cross-examination,
by or on behalf of any accused at the trial, about any sexual behaviour of the complainant.
(2) The court may give leave in relation to any evidence or question only on an application made by or on behalf of an accused, and may not give such leave unless it is satisfied—
(a) that subsection (3) or (5) applies, and
(b) that a refusal of leave might have the result of rendering unsafe a conclusion of the jury or (as the case may be) the court on any relevant issue in the case.
(3) This subsection applies if the evidence or question relates to a relevant issue in the case and either—
(a) that issue is not an issue of consent; or
(b) it is an issue of consent and the sexual behaviour of the complainant to which the evidence or question relates is alleged to have taken place at or about the same time as the event which is the subject matter of the charge against the accused; or
(c) it is an issue of consent and the sexual behaviour of the complainant to which the evidence or question relates is alleged to have been, in any respect, so similar—
(i) to any sexual behaviour of the complainant which (according to evidence adduced or to be adduced by or on behalf of the accused) took place as part of the event which is the subject matter of the charge against the accused, or
(ii) to any other sexual behaviour of the complainant which (according to such evidence) took place at or about the same time as that event,
that the similarity cannot reasonably be explained as a coincidence.
(4) For the purposes of subsection (3) no evidence or question shall be regarded as relating to a

relevant issue in the case if it appears to the court to be reasonable to assume that the purpose (or main purpose) for which it would be adduced or asked is to establish or elicit material for impugning the credibility of the complainant as a witness.

(5) This subsection applies if the evidence or question—

(a) relates to any evidence adduced by the prosecution about any sexual behaviour of the complainant; and

(b) in the opinion of the court, would go no further than is necessary to enable the evidence adduced by the prosecution to be rebutted or explained by or on behalf of the accused.

(6) For the purposes of subsections (3) and (5) the evidence or question must relate to a specific instance (or specific instances) of alleged sexual behaviour on the part of the complainant (and accordingly nothing in those subsections is capable of applying in relation to the evidence or question to the extent that it does not so relate).

(7) Where this section applies in relation to a trial by virtue of the fact that one or more of a number of persons charged in the proceedings is or are charged with a sexual offence—

(a) it shall cease to apply in relation to the trial if the prosecutor decides not to proceed with the case against that person or those persons in respect of that charge; but

(b) it shall not cease to do so in the event of that person or those persons pleading guilty to, or being convicted of, that charge.

(8) Nothing in this section authorises any evidence to be adduced or any question to be asked which cannot be adduced or asked apart from this section.

42.—(1) In section 41—

(a) 'relevant issue in the case' means any issue falling to be proved by the prosecution or defence in the trial of the accused;

(b) 'issue of consent' means any issue whether the complainant in fact consented to the conduct constituting the offence with which the accused is charged (and accordingly does not include any issue as to the belief of the accused that the complainant so consented);

(c) 'sexual behaviour' means any sexual behaviour or other sexual experience, whether or not involving any accused or other person, but excluding (except in section 41(3)(c)(i) and (5)(a)) anything alleged to have taken place as part of the event which is the subject matter of the charge against the accused; and

(d) subject to any order made under subsection (2), 'sexual offence' shall be construed in accordance with section 62.

(2) [Secretary of State's power to add or remove offences.]

(3) Section 41 applies in relation to the following proceedings as it applies to a trial, namely—

(a) proceedings before a magistrates' court inquiring into an offence as examining justices,

(b) the hearing of an application under paragraph 5(1) of schedule 6 to the Criminal Justice Act 1991 (application to dismiss charge following notice of transfer of case to Crown Court),

(c) the hearing of an application under paragraph 2(1) of schedule 3 to the Crime and Disorder Act 1998 (application to dismiss charge by person sent for trial under section 51 or 51A of that Act),

(d) any hearing held, between conviction and sentencing, for the purpose of determining matters relevant to the court's decision as to how the accused is to be dealt with, and

(e) the hearing of an appeal,

and references (in section 41 or this section) to a person charged with an offence accordingly include a person convicted of an offence.

43.—(1) An application for leave shall be heard in private and in the absence of the complainant.

In this section 'leave' means leave under section 41.

(2) Where such an application has been determined, the court must state in open court (but in the absence of the jury, if there is one)—

(a) its reasons for giving, or refusing, leave, and

(b) if it gives leave, the extent to which evidence may be adduced or questions asked in pursuance of the leave,

and, if it is a magistrates' court, must cause those matters to be entered in the register of its proceedings.

(3) [Power to make rules of court.]

Procedure on Applications under s. 41

F7.26 Where an accused wants to introduce evidence or cross-examine a witness about a complainant's sexual behaviour under YJCEA 1999, s. 41, the defence must apply in writing. The CrimPR, part 36 makes provision as to the procedure for making such an application, the time at which such an application should be made and its contents and service. The rules are set out in full in **appendix 1**.

RULE OF FINALITY OF ANSWERS TO QUESTIONS ON COLLATERAL MATTERS

General Rule

F7.27 The general rule, based on the desirability of avoiding a multiplicity of essentially irrelevant issues, is that evidence is not admissible to contradict answers given by a witness to questions put in cross-examination which concern collateral matters, i.e. matters which go merely to credit but which are otherwise irrelevant to the issues in the case (*Harris v Tippett* (1811) 2 Camp 637; *Palmer v Trower* (1852) 8 Exch 247). In *A-G v Hitchcock* (1847) 1 Exch 91, Pollock CB said (at p. 99): 'The test whether a matter is collateral or not is this: if the answer of a witness is a matter which you would be allowed on your own part to prove in evidence — if it have such a connection with the issues that you would be allowed to give it in evidence — then it is a matter on which you may contradict him.' The narrowness and difficulty of this distinction may be illustrated by comparing the decision in *A-G v Hitchcock* with the decisions in *TM* [2004] EWCA Crim 2085 and *Busby* (1981) 75 Cr App R 79. In *A-G v Hitchcock* a maltster was charged with having used a cistern for the making of malt in breach of certain statutory requirements. A prosecution witness, having sworn that the cistern had been used, was asked in cross-examination whether he had not said to one Cook that the Excise officers had offered him £20 to give evidence that the cistern had been used. Upon denial of this allegation, it was held that the defendant was not allowed to call Cook to contradict the witness, because proof that a bribe was offered to the witness and not accepted was irrelevant to the matter in issue. In *TM* certain sexual offences came to light when a private investigator and enquiry agents, being used for the purposes of family proceedings by a man, S, whose wife had been having an affair with M, interviewed the victims of the offences. M denied all the offences and said that S had set out to destroy him and had induced the victims to give evidence against him by offers of financial reward. It was held that M should have been allowed to call a witness to give evidence that she had been approached by the private investigator and when she had refused to give adverse information had been told that S had unlimited funds for the right information. When viewed in isolation, the witness's evidence was collateral, but although 'borderline', it was relevant as showing that the *victims* might have been offered money or been influenced by the offer of money. In *Busby* a prosecution for burglary and handling, police officers were cross-examined to the effect that they had fabricated statements attributed to the accused and indicative of his guilt, and had threatened W, a potential defence witness, to stop him giving evidence. These allegations were denied. The trial judge ruled that the defence could not call W to give evidence that he had been threatened by the officers, because this would go solely to their credit. Allowing the appeal against conviction, the Court of Appeal held that the trial judge had erred: the evidence was relevant to an issue which had to be tried, because, if true, it showed that the police were prepared to go to improper lengths in order to secure a conviction, which would have supported the defence case that the statements attributed to the accused had been fabricated. See also *Marsh* (1985) 83 Cr App R 165 and cf. *Phillips* (1936) 26 Cr App R 17, at F7.32.

In *Funderburk* [1990] 1 WLR 587, at p. 591, *Busby* was treated as having created a new *exception* to the rule of finality. However, in *Edwards* [1991] 1 WLR 207, it was held that the fact that the police were allegedly prepared to prevent the potential witness from giving evidence, came within the exception of bias (see **F7.32**); and that if the decision could not be explained on that basis, it was inconsistent with the general rule and inconsistent with the decision in *Harris v Tippett* itself (where the facts were not dissimilar to those in *Busby*). In *Edwards* a number of officers involved in the case had given evidence in other trials, which had resulted in acquittal, in circumstances which tended to cast doubt on their reliability. In the other trials, evidence showed that some interview notes were inaccurate and that others had seemingly been rewritten to include admissions which did not exist in the originals. It was held that:

(a) it could be put to the officers in cross-examination that they had given evidence in the previous trials, that in each trial there was an issue as to whether alleged confessions had been fabricated and that each trial had ended in acquittal, because there was a sufficient connection between the evidence given by the officers in those trials and their eventual outcome to entitle such cross-examination on the question of their credibility in the instant case; but
(b) if the officers denied such allegations, they could not be proved by evidence in rebuttal, because the questioning would be as to credit alone, a collateral issue, and would not fall within any of the exceptions to the rule of finality.

Whether a particular item of evidence goes to an issue before the court or is merely collateral can be a question of some nicety. It only adds to the difficulty, it is submitted, to suggest that whether the rule of finality applies may turn on whether the matter which the cross-examining party seeks to prove is a single and distinct fact which is easy of proof rather than a broad and complex issue which is difficult of proof (*S* [1992] Crim LR 307). In *Funderburk* the court urged a flexible approach to the rule, on the basis that a general rule designed to serve the interests of justice should not be used to defeat justice by an over-pedantic approach. Henry J observed (at p. 598D), 'The utility of the test may lie in the fact that the answer is an instinctive one based on the prosecutor's and the court's sense of fair play rather than any philosophic or analytic process' (but cf. per Evans LJ in *Neale* [1998] Crim LR 737). Accordingly it has been held that the issue of sufficient relevance is one for the trial judge and that the Court of Appeal will only interfere with a decision to exclude evidence as being insufficiently irrelevant if it is either wrong in principle or plainly wrong as being outside that wide ambit (*Somers* [1999] Crim LR 744).

The Court of Appeal in *Funderburk* also agreed with the editors of *Cross on Evidence* (7th ed., 1990, p. 322) that where the disputed issue is a sexual one between two persons in private, the difference between questions going to credit and questions going to the issue is reduced to vanishing-point because sexual intercourse, whether or not consensual, most often takes place in private and leaves few visible traces of having occurred, so that the evidence is often effectively limited to that of the parties, and much is likely to depend upon the balance of credibility between them. See further at **F7.29**.

Previous Inconsistent Statements

If a witness under cross-examination admits to having made a previous oral or written statement inconsistent with his testimony, no further proof of the statement is required or, it seems, allowed (*P (GR)* [1998] Crim LR 663). However, if the witness denies having made such a statement, and the statement is relevant to an issue in the case, then it may be proved. The statement may be proved even if contained in a letter sent by an accused's solicitor to the CPS suggesting that the accused might plead guilty to a lesser offence, because there is nothing in criminal law akin to without prejudice privilege (*Hayes* [2004] 1 Cr App R 557). **F7.28**

Proof of a previous inconsistent statement is governed by the Criminal Procedure Act 1865, ss. 4 and 5. Section 4 applies to both oral and written statements, but s. 5 applies to written statements only (*Derby Magistrates' Court, ex parte B* [1996] AC 487).

Oral and Written Statements under s. 4

F7.29 **Criminal Procedure Act 1865, s. 4**

> If a witness, upon cross-examination as to a former statement made by him relative to the subject-matter of the indictment or proceeding, and inconsistent with his present testimony, does not distinctly admit that he has made such statement, proof may be given that he did in fact make it; but before such proof can be given the circumstances of the supposed statement, sufficient to designate the particular occasion, must be mentioned to the witness, and he must be asked whether or not he has made such statement.

Section 4 is not confined to previous statements on oath (*Hart* (1957) 42 Cr App R 47, at p. 50; and *O'Neill* [1969] Crim LR 260 — oral statement made to the police). A witness who 'does not distinctly admit' to the making of the previous statement would include, in addition to a witness who denies such a statement, a witness who claims to have no recollection of it, who is equivocal on the subject, or who declines to answer. However, s. 4 does not apply to a party's own hostile witness. Proof of the previous inconsistent statement of a hostile witness requires the leave of the judge under s. 3 of the 1865 Act (see **F6.31**), a requirement which cannot be circumvented by reliance on s. 4 of the Act (*Booth* (1981) 74 Cr App R 123).

Whether a statement is 'relative to the subject-matter of the indictment or proceeding' is a matter within the discretion of the judge (*Bashir* [1969] 1 WLR 1303 per Veale J at p. 1306; and *Hart* (1957) 42 Cr App R 47 per Devlin J at p. 50). For the difficulties to which the issue may give rise, see *Funderburk* [1990] 1 WLR 587. F was convicted on three counts of sexual intercourse with a girl of 13. In her evidence, the girl gave evidence of a number of acts of intercourse with F, the description of the first act clearly describing the loss of her virginity. The defence was that the child was lying and in order to explain how so young a child could, if she were lying, have given such detailed and varied accounts of the acts of intercourse, wished to show that she was sexually experienced and had either transposed to F experiences which she had had with others and/or fantasised about experience with F. For this purpose, the defence wished to put to her that she had told a potential defence witness, P, that before the first incident complained of she had had sexual intercourse with two named men. The defence then wished to call P to give evidence of the conversation. The trial judge, applying the test in s. 4 of the 1865 Act, ruled that the complainant's previous inconsistent statement could not be put to her, nor could P be called, because the complainant's virginity was immaterial to the question whether F had had sexual intercourse with her and therefore was not 'relative to the subject-matter of the indictment'. On the question whether the previous inconsistent statement could be put in cross-examination *to challenge the complainant's credibility*, it was held that there was nothing in s. 4 to prevent this, even if, under s. 4, evidence of the making of that statement would not be allowed because it was not relative to the subject-matter of the indictment. The test for allowing cross-examination *as to credit* was that suggested by Lawton J in *Sweet-Escott* (1971) 55 Cr App R 316: how might the matters put to the witness affect his or her standing with the jury after cross-examination (see **F7.13**). Applying that test, the cross-examination should have been allowed since the jury might reasonably have wished to reappraise her evidence about the loss of her virginity and her credibility if they had heard of her previous statements regarding her earlier sexual experiences. On the question whether, if the complainant had been cross-examined about the conversation with P and she had denied making the previous statements, the defence would have been entitled to call P to prove the conversation, it was held that the previous statements were relative to the subject-matter of the indictment and therefore P could have been called to prove them under s. 4. Where the disputed issue is a sexual one between two persons in private, the difference between questions going to credit and questions going to the issue is reduced to vanishing-point. On the way the prosecution had presented the evidence, the challenge to the loss of virginity went far beyond a mere question of the complainant's credibility and was sufficiently closely related to the subject-matter of the indictment for justice to require investigation for the basis of such a challenge. (Cf. *Neale* [1998] Crim LR

737 and also, *sed quare, Gibson* [1993] Crim LR 453.) See also *Nagrecha* [1997] 2 Cr App R 401. N was accused of indecently assaulting the complainant. There were no witnesses. Under cross-examination, the complainant denied that she had made allegations of sexual impropriety against other men. It was held that evidence of the making of the other allegations was admissible because it went to the central issue of whether or not there had been any indecent assault.

Written Statements under s. 5

Criminal Procedure Act 1865, s. 5 F7.30

> A witness may be cross-examined as to previous statements made by him in writing or reduced into writing relative to the subject matter of the indictment or proceeding, without such writing being shown to him; but if it is intended to contradict such witness by the writing, his attention must, before such contradictory proof can be given, be called to those parts of the writing which are to be used for the purpose of so contradicting him: provided always, that it shall be competent for the judge, at any time during the trial, to require the production of the writing for his inspection, and he may thereupon make such use of it for the purposes of the trial as he may think fit.

The first part of s. 5 expressly allows cross-examination on a previous written statement *without* such writing being shown to the witness. However, if counsel proposes to cross-examine in this way, he must have the writing with him, even if he does not intend to *contradict* the witness with it, because under the proviso to s. 5, the judge may require its production for his inspection, and may thereupon make such use of it as he may think fit (*Anderson* (1929) 21 Cr App R 178). If the writing is shown to the witness, this may be done without putting it in evidence. Thus, counsel may hand the document to the witness, direct him to read the relevant part of it to himself, and then ask whether he wishes to adhere to his testimony. If the witness accepts the truth of the former statement, it becomes part of his evidence; if he adheres to his testimony, there is no obligation on the cross-examining party to contradict the witness and put the document in evidence (a course which it may be wise to avoid, especially if the inconsistency relates to some minor matter, and in all other respects the former statement is *consistent* with the witness's evidence). However, if counsel does wish to contradict the witness, he must put the document in evidence by reading out aloud the contradictory statement. The statement may then be inspected to see how far the suggested contradiction exists; whether the absence of a particular statement is explained by the context; and whether the discrepancy is only a minute point so that, taken as a whole, the document is more in the nature of confirmation rather than contradiction (see generally *Riley* (1866) 4 F & F 964 per Channell B; and *Wright* (1866) 4 F & F 967). It is open to the judge to allow the whole of the written statement to go before the jury, because under s. 5 he may 'make such use of it for the purposes of the trial as he may think fit'. For example, he may call attention to other parts of the statement to which no reference has been made (*Birch* (1924) 18 Cr App R 26, per Avory J at p. 28). However, he has a discretion to allow only part of the statement to go before the jury and therefore, in appropriate circumstances, may permit the jury to see only those parts of the statement upon which the cross-examination was based and not all the other parts relating to other unconnected matters (*Beattie* (1989) 89 Cr App R 302).

Criminal Justice Act 2003, s. 119(1) Under the CJA 2003, s. 119(1), a previous inconsistent statement that a witness admits to having made, or that is proved by virtue of the Criminal Procedure Act 1865, s. 4 or s. 5, is admissible for the truth of its contents. F7.31

Criminal Justice Act 2003, s. 119

> (1) If in criminal proceedings a person gives oral evidence and—
> (a) he admits making a previous inconsistent statement or
> (b) a previous inconsistent statement made by him is proved by virtue of section 3, 4 or 5 of the Criminal Procedure Act 1865,
>
> the statement is admissible as evidence of any matter stated in it of which oral evidence by him would be admissible.

Even where a previous inconsistent statement is admissible under s. 119 on behalf of the prosecution, it may nonetheless be excluded under the PACE 1984, s. 78 (see, e.g., *Coates* [2007] EWCA Crim 1471).

Bias and Partiality

F7.32 Evidence has always been admissible to contradict a witness's denial of bias or partiality towards one of the parties, and to show that he is prejudicial concerning the case being tried (*Mendy* (1976) 64 Cr App R 4, per Geoffrey Lane LJ at p. 6). For earlier authority, see *Yewin* (1811) cited 2 Camp 638 and *Dunn v Aslett* (1838) 2 Mood & R 122. To the extent that this common-law doctrine allows the introduction of evidence of, or of a disposition towards, misconduct on the part of a witness, it has been abolished by the CJA 2003, s. 99. However, much evidence of bias is likely to remain admissible under the doctrine, because it will fall outside the statutory definition of evidence of bad character in s. 98 of the 2003 Act, which excludes 'evidence of, or of a disposition towards misconduct . . . which has to do with the alleged facts of the offence with which the defendant is charged, or is evidence of misconduct in connection with the investigation or prosecution of that offence'. If the evidence in question is not admissible on that basis, it is nonetheless likely to be admitted under the CJA, s. 100(1)(b), i.e. as evidence of the bad character of a person other than the accused that has substantial probative value in relation to a matter which is in issue in the proceedings and is of substantial importance in the context of the case as a whole (see **F14**). For these reasons, each of the following decisions, it is submitted, remains valid.

In *A-G v Hitchcock* (1847) 1 Exch 91 it was held that although evidence is not admissible to contradict a witness's denial that he was *offered* a bribe to give false evidence, because this does not show that he is not a fair and credible witness, evidence is admissible to rebut a witness's denial that he *accepted* such a bribe, because that tends to show his partiality. Pollock CB said: 'A witness may be asked how he stands affected towards one of the parties; and if his relation towards them is such as to prejudice his mind, and fill him with sentiments of revenge and other feelings of a similar kind, and if he denies the fact, evidence may be given to show the state of his mind and feelings.'

In *Shaw* (1888) 16 Cox CC 503 it was held that the accused may call evidence to contradict a prosecution witness who, in cross-examination, denies having threatened to be revenged on the accused following a quarrel with him. See also *Whelan* [1996] Crim LR 423. In *Phillips* (1936) 26 Cr App R 17, a case of incest, the principal prosecution witnesses, the accused's two daughters, were cross-examined on the basis that (a) they had been 'schooled' by their mother into giving false evidence, and (b) they had made admissions that evidence given by them in previous criminal proceedings against their father was false. Both allegations were denied. The trial judge refused to allow the defence to call the woman to whom the admissions were alleged to have been made. Quashing the conviction, the Court of Criminal Appeal held that this evidence should have been admitted because the bias that it would have revealed went to the very foundation of the accused's defence.

In *Mendy* (1976) 64 Cr App R 4, the accused was convicted of assault. At her trial, prospective witnesses were kept out of court in accordance with the normal practice. While a police officer was giving evidence, a man in the public gallery was seen taking notes. He was later seen discussing the case with the accused's husband, apparently describing the officer's evidence to him. The husband, under cross-examination, denied this incident. The Court of Appeal held that the trial judge had properly allowed the prosecution to call evidence in rebuttal: the husband was prepared to lend himself to a scheme, designed to defeat the purpose of keeping prospective witnesses out of court, to enable him the more convincingly to describe how he, and not his wife, had caused the injuries alleged.

Previous Convictions

If a witness, lawfully cross-examined as to a previous conviction, denies it or refuses to answer, it may be proved against him under the Criminal Procedure Act 1865, s. 6. F7.33

Criminal Procedure Act 1865, s. 6

> If, upon a witness being lawfully questioned as to whether he has been convicted of any felony or misdemeanour, he either denies or does not admit the fact, or refuses to answer, it shall be lawful for the cross-examining party to prove such conviction.

Someone other than the accused will only be 'lawfully questioned' as to his previous convictions if the questions are lawful under the CJA 2003, s. 100 (see **F14**), and an accused will only be 'lawfully questioned' as to his previous convictions if the questions are lawful under the CJA 2003, s. 101 (see **F12**). There is an additional restriction in the case of offences committed by the accused when a child (see s. 108 of the 2003 Act, considered at **F12.47**). Furthermore, no reference should be made to a spent conviction if that can be 'reasonably avoided' (see the *Consolidated Criminal Practice Direction*, para. I.6, set out in **appendix** 7 and considered at **D19.49**). However, according to *Corelli* [2001] Crim LR 913, the *Practice Direction* does not operate to remove an unfettered statutory entitlement of a co-accused to cross-examine another co-accused on his previous convictions. (The statutory entitlement in that case arose under the Criminal Evidence Act 1898, s. 1(3)(iii); see now the CJA 2003, s. 101(1)(e), considered at **F12.33**).

Non-compliance with the *Practice Direction* will not necessarily result in a conviction being quashed on appeal (*Smallman* [1982] Crim LR 175). In that case, prosecuting counsel, without seeking the leave of the judge, referred to the spent conviction of a defence witness when cross-examining him. The judge directed the jury to leave out of account the prejudice resulting from the reference. The Court of Appeal held that such a breach of the *Practice Direction* could not be a ground for quashing an otherwise perfectly proper conviction.

Two cases where the charge was wounding and the defence was self-defence can usefully be compared. In *Evans* (1992) 156 JP 539, it was held that the judge should have allowed the defence to cross-examine the victim on her previous but spent convictions for dishonesty and violence because, evidentially, there was a head-on collision between the accused and the victim, and the jury were entitled to know of the victim's criminal record. In *Lawrence* [1995] Crim LR 815, the trial judge refused the defence permission to question the victim in detail on his 20 previous spent convictions, the majority of which were for offences of dishonesty, but only allowed questions on four more recent offences of dishonesty. The Court of Appeal held that the effect of the *Practice Direction* is to give the judge a wide discretion and that although it might have exercised the discretion differently and allowed cross-examination on one of the spent convictions, which involved perverting the course of justice, it was impossible to say that the judge had erred in principle. See also *Whelan* [1996] Crim LR 423.

As to proof of previous convictions, see the PACE 1984, s. 73, at **F11.1**. Where a witness who is cross-examined on a conviction accepts the conviction but claims his innocence, the cross-examining party is not entitled to adduce evidence in rebuttal, such as evidence from the victim of the offence on which the witness stands convicted, because such evidence would go solely to credibility (*Irish* [1995] Crim LR 145, applying *Edwards* [1991] 1 WLR 207, considered at F7.27).

Medical Evidence of Disability Affecting Reliability

> Medical evidence is admissible to show that a witness suffers from some disease or defect or abnormality of mind that affects the reliability of his evidence. Such evidence is not confined to a general opinion of the unreliability of the witness but may give all the matters necessary to show, not only the foundation of and reasons for the diagnosis, but also the extent to which the F7.34

> credibility of the witness is affected. (*Toohey v Metropolitan Police Commissioner* [1965] AC 595, per Lord Pearce at p. 609.)

If the defence adduce such evidence, it may be open to the Crown to call an expert in rebuttal, or even (anticipating the defence expert) as part of the prosecution case. It may even be open to the Crown to rebut by expert evidence a case put only in cross-examination that a prosecution witness is unreliable by reason of mental abnormality. Much may depend on the nature of the abnormality and of the cross-examination. But the rebuttal evidence should be restricted to meeting the specific challenge and should not extend to oath-helping: the Crown cannot call a witness of fact and then, without more, call a psychologist or psychiatrist to give reasons why the jury should regard that witness as reliable (*Robinson* [1994] 3 All ER 346; and see also *Beard* [1998] Crim LR 585). As to oath-helping, however, see also *S* [2006] EWCA Crim 2389, which concerned an autistic girl, aged 13, who was the victim of sexual offences. An expert witness was not allowed to comment directly on the veracity of the complainant, but did give evidence that a child such as the complainant would not easily have been able to invent the story she had told. It was held that this evidence had been properly admitted and that *Robinson* could be distinguished because, whereas the expert evidence in that case had related directly to one particular witness, in the instant case the evidence was of general application and it remained for the jury to decide whether the complainant was to be believed as to the particular allegation she had made. See also *Tobin* [2003] Crim LR 408.

In *Toohey*, T was charged with others with assaulting M with intent to rob. The defence case was that M had been drinking and that the accused were trying to help him, but that he became hysterical and accused them of assaulting him. The trial judge ruled that the medical evidence of a doctor, who had examined M shortly after the alleged assault, that drink could exacerbate hysteria, and that M was more prone to hysteria than a normal person, was inadmissible. The House of Lords quashed the conviction on the grounds that the evidence was admissible, not only because of its relevance to the facts in issue, but also in order to impeach the credibility of M, *qua* witness. Lord Pearce said (at p. 608):

> If a witness purported to give evidence of something which he believed that he had seen at a distance of 50 yards, it must surely be possible to call the evidence of an oculist to the effect that the witness could not possibly see anything at a greater distance than 20 yards, or the evidence of a surgeon who had removed a cataract from which the witness was suffering at the material time and which would have prevented him from seeing what he thought he saw. So, too, must it be allowable to call medical evidence of mental illness which makes a witness incapable of giving reliable evidence . . .

See also *Eades* [1972] Crim LR 99, a charge of causing death by dangerous driving. In his first statement to the police, one week after the accident, the accused said that he had not suffered from any concussion but was unable to remember any details of the accident itself (although he could remember incidents before and after the accident). Six weeks later, in a second statement to the police, he said that a few days earlier he had driven past the *locus in quo* and, as a result of a car emerging from a side road into his path, he had suddenly remembered the circumstances of the accident. Nield J ruled that if the accused gave evidence, the prosecution would be entitled to call a psychiatrist, who, although he had not examined the accused, had heard the prosecution evidence, to contradict the accused by evidence that his account as to how he had recovered his memory was not consistent with medical knowledge. Such evidence would be admissible because it would be not only relevant to a fact in issue, but also would tend to impugn the reliability of the accused as a witness.

The principle established in *Toohey v Metropolitan Police Commissioner* [1965] AC 595, in accordance with the rules governing the use of expert evidence generally, is applicable only in relation to some physical or mental disability calling for expertise, as opposed to matters affecting reliability upon which the jury are capable of forming their own opinion without expert assistance. Thus, expert evidence is generally inadmissible on the issue of an accused's credibility (*Turner* [1975] QB 834, at p. 842). Compare *Lowery v The Queen* [1974] AC 85, and see generally **F10**. In *Toohey*, Lord Pearce said (at p. 608):

> Human evidence shares the frailties of those who give it. It is subject to many cross-currents such as partiality, prejudice, self-interest and, above all, imagination and inaccuracy. Those are matters with which the jury, helped by cross-examination and common sense, must do their best. But when a witness through physical (in which I include mental) disease or abnormality is not capable of giving a true or reliable account to the jury, it must surely be allowable for medical science to reveal this vital hidden fact to them.

In *MacKenney* [2004] 2 Cr App R 32, the accused were convicted of murder. At their trial, in 1980, they alleged that the chief prosecution witness, an accomplice, had fabricated his evidence. The defence sought to call a psychologist, by whom the witness had refused to be examined. The psychologist had watched the witness as he gave his evidence and was of the opinion that he was a psychopath who was likely to be lying and whose mental state meant that his demeanour and behaviour in giving evidence would not betray the usual indications to the jury as to when he was lying. The trial judge ruled the evidence inadmissible and the convictions were upheld on appeal. In 2001 the Criminal Cases Review Commission referred the convictions to the Court of Appeal. There was fresh evidence, from a forensic psychiatrist, who also had not examined the witness, whose opinion was very similar to that of the psychologist which had been ruled inadmissible at the trial. It was held, adopting the approach to the relevance and admissibility of expert evidence set out in *O'Brien* [2000] Crim LR 676 (considered at **F10.11**), that the evidence of the psychologist would today be admissible. The reference was determined on the fresh evidence, on the basis of which the court concluded that the convictions were unsafe and should be quashed. It was held that the absence of an examination by the expert went to the weight to be attached to the opinion, and not to its admissibility. It was also held that the court must be on its guard against any attempt to detract from the jury's task of finding for themselves what evidence to believe: the court should not allow evidence to be put before the jury which does not allege any medical abnormality as the basis for the evidence of a witness being approached with particular caution.

RE-EXAMINATION

After cross-examination, a witness may be re-examined by the party who called him. This applies even in the case of a hostile witness, who may be re-examined on any new matters which arose out of cross-examination (*Wong* [1986] Crim LR 683). Leading questions may not be asked in re-examination. The principal rule of re-examination is that, except with the leave of thc judge, questions should be confined to matters, including any new matters, arising out of cross-examination. This rule applies not only in the case of a witness who has been examined in chief, but also in the case of a witness whose name is notionally on the back of the indictment and who was called by the prosecution merely to allow the defence to cross-examine him (*Beezley* (1830) 4 C & P 220). Where a witness under cross-examination gives evidence of part of a conversation with him on some previous occasion, questions may not be asked in re-examination about everything else that was said at the same time, but only about so much as can be in some way connected with the statement as to which he was cross-examined, such as other statements which qualify or explain it in any way (*Prince v Samo* (1838) 7 A & E 627, per Lord Denman CJ, citing Lord Tenterden in *Queen Caroline's Case* (1820) 2 B & B 284, at p. 297). **F7.35**

A witness may refresh his memory in re-examination: see **F6.9**. As to the admissibility of previous consistent statements in re-examination, see **F6.19** to **F6.26**.

Section F8 Documentary Evidence and Real Evidence

PROOF OF PRIVATE DOCUMENTS

F8.1 Statements contained in documents are subject to the general rules of evidence on admissibility, including those relating to relevance, hearsay, opinion and privilege. Two additional requirements, concerning documents on the contents of which a party seeks to rely, are: (a) proof of the contents and (b) proof of due execution.

Concerning presumptions relating to documents, see **F8.32**. As to stamped documents, see **F8.33**.

PROOF OF CONTENTS: THE BEST EVIDENCE RULE

F8.2 At common law, the general rule, often regarded as the only remaining instance of the best evidence rule, is that a party seeking to rely upon the contents of a document must adduce primary evidence of those contents, i.e. either the original document in question, a copy of an enrolled document, or informal admissions made by parties concerning the contents. Thus if an original document is available in one's hands, one must produce it and one cannot give secondary evidence by producing a copy (*Kajala v Noble* (1982) 75 Cr App R 149 at p. 152). A party having a document available in his hands means a party who has the original of the document with him in court, or could have it in court without any difficulty (*Governor of Pentonville Prison, ex parte Osman* [1990] 1 WLR 277 at p. 308). The rule, in criminal cases, is confined to written documents in the strict sense of the term, and has no relevance to tape recordings and films (*Kajala v Noble* (1982) 75 Cr App R 149). As to the use of tape recordings, see **F8.40**; as to photographs, video recordings and films, see **F8.43**. The general rule does not apply if:

(a) it is unnecessary to place reliance upon the contents because the fact or matter in issue, although recorded in a document, can be proved by other evidence (see, e.g., *Holy Trinity, Kingston-upon-Hull* (*Inhabitants*) (1827) 7 B & C 611: the fact of a tenancy; *Manwaring* (1856) Dears & B 132: proof of a marriage, which may have been registered, by the testimony of a person who had attended the ceremony; and *Seberg* (1870) LR 1 CCR 264: proof by the testimony of eye-witnesses that a ship was British and sailing under the British flag, without production of the register of the vessel); or
(b) the document is tendered merely for the purpose of identifying it or establishing the bare fact of its existence (see *Boyle v Wiseman* (1855) 11 Exch 360, at p. 367 and *Elworthy* (1867) LR 1 CCR 103).

To the general rule there are a number of common-law and statutory exceptions, providing for proof of the contents of documents by secondary evidence. Generally speaking, such secondary evidence may take the form of a copy, a copy of a copy or oral evidence, and 'there are no degrees of secondary evidence' (per Lord Abinger CB in *Doe d Gilbert v Ross* (1840) 7 M & W 102). Thus, an inferior copy may be tendered even if a better copy is available (*Lafone v Griffin* (1909) 25 TLR 308 and *Collins* (1960) 44 Cr App R 170; but contrast *Everingham v Roundell* (1838) 2 Mood & R 138). Likewise, oral evidence of the contents is admissible even if a copy is available (*Brown v Woodman* (1834) 6 C & P 206). The exceptions to the rule that there are no degrees of secondary evidence are the contents of:

(a) a will admitted to probate, which may not be proved by oral evidence if the original or probate copy exists;
(b) judicial documents and bankers' books (see **F8.8** to **F8.30**), which are generally proved by office copies and examined copies respectively; and
(c) various public documents (see **F8.8** to **F8.26**), which may be proved by oral evidence only if examined, certified, or other copies are unavailable.

The law, as set out in the preceding paragraphs, is well-established. However, the Court of Appeal in *Springsteen v Masquerade Music Ltd* [2001] EWCA Civ 563 appears to reject the notion that, at common law, there is a general rule accompanied by a number of exceptions, in favour of a more generalised approach whereby the admissibility of secondary evidence of the contents of a document depends upon the weight to be attached to the secondary evidence. Observing 'with confidence' that the best evidence rule had finally expired, the court held that:

(a) Where the party seeking to adduce the secondary evidence could readily produce the document, it might be expected that, absent some special circumstances, the court would decline to admit the secondary evidence on the ground that it was worthless.
(b) At the other extreme, where that party genuinely could not produce the document, it might be expected that, absent some special circumstances, the court would admit the secondary evidence and attach such weight to it as it considered appropriate in the circumstances.
(c) In cases falling between these two extremes, it was for the court to make a judgment as to whether in all the circumstances any weight should be attached to the secondary evidence.
(d) Thus the admissibility of secondary evidence of the contents of documents is entirely dependent on whether or not any weight was to be attached to the evidence, which was a matter for the court to decide.

It remains to be seen whether this new approach will be followed in the civil courts or adopted in the criminal context.

Statutory Provisions

The common-law authorities have been affected by the CJA 2003, s. 133, and the PACE 1984, s. 71. **F8.3**

Criminal Justice Act 2003, s. 133

Where a statement in a document is admissible as evidence in criminal proceedings, the statement may be proved by producing either—
(a) the document, or
(b) (whether or not the document exists) a copy of the document or of the material part of it,
authenticated in whatever way the court may approve.

A 'statement' for these purposes is any representation of fact or opinion made by a person by whatever means, and includes a representation made in a sketch, photofit or other pictorial form (s. 115(2)); a 'document' means anything in which information of any description is recorded (s. 134(1)); and a 'copy' means anything on to which information recorded in the document has been copied, by whatever means and whether directly or indirectly (s. 134(1)).

Police and Criminal Evidence Act 1984, s. 71

In any proceedings the contents of a document may (whether or not the document is still in existence) be proved by the production of an enlargement of a microfilm copy of that document or of the material part of it, authenticated in such manner as the court may approve.

For the definition of 'proceedings', see s. 72 of the 1984 Act.

Two views are possible with regard to the construction of the CJA 2003, s. 133. On one view, it applies only to hearsay statements contained in documents, and not to the proof of the contents of a document as evidence in their own right. On the other view, it is not confined to the various types of documentary hearsay statement admissible under the 2003 Act itself, but applies to any statement contained in a document and admissible in evidence. Either way, s. 133, which on its wording is permissive rather than mandatory as to the means of proof, must be read subject to:

(a) the exceptions to the general rule at common law, whereby the contents of a document may be proved by secondary evidence which may take the form of *oral* evidence, which is not permitted under s. 133 (see *Nazeer* [1998] Crim LR 750); and, it seems
(b) statutory exceptions to the general rule at common law, principally relating to public and judicial documents and bankers' books, which, although they allow for proof of the contents of such documents by copies, require those copies to take a particular form (which is not the case under s. 133).

In the cases to which s. 133 does apply, it remains to be seen in what manner the courts will require copies to be 'authenticated'. (For the difficulties that can arise in the case of some computer printouts of screen images, see *Skinner* [2005] EWCA 1439, a decision under the CJA 1988, s. 27, the statutory precursor to s. 133.) In the normal case, it is submitted, the court will require the same proof as was necessary when relying upon secondary evidence under one of the common-law exceptions to the general rule, namely proof by the evidence of a person with custody or control of the copy (or some other appropriate person) that it is a true copy of the original. In *Collins* (1960) 44 Cr App R 170, the accused was convicted of obtaining money by false pretences, having cashed a cheque on his bank account which he knew to have been closed. When he failed, after notice to do so, to produce a letter sent to him informing him that the account had been closed, secondary evidence of the contents of the letter became admissible. However, the Court of Criminal Appeal held that a copy of a carbon copy of the letter, produced at the trial by a manager of the bank, had been improperly admitted, there having been no proof that it was a true copy of the carbon copy or that it was in the same terms as the original. Compare *Wayte* (1983) 76 Cr App R 110: the mere fact that it is easy to construct a false document by photocopying techniques does not render a photocopy inadmissible; the fact that the document was a photocopy went to its weight and not its admissibility. The Court of Appeal in that case also gave guidance on the procedure to be adopted when it is sought to produce in evidence photocopies:

(a) Documents should not normally be handed to the jury until questions of admissibility have been determined.
(b) Prior warning of the intention to produce such copies should be given to opposing counsel so that they may have the chance to consider their admissibility.
(c) If the accused is unrepresented, the guidance of the court should be sought before the document is put before the jury.
(d) On very rare occasions, it may be necessary to hold a trial within a trial on the question of admissibility, although ultimately the issue of the genuineness of the copies should be left to the jury.

In relation to copies, the information may have been copied from the original either 'directly or indirectly' (CJA 2003, s. 134(1)). Thus there is no obligation to produce the best copy rather than an inferior copy, even if the best copy, or indeed the original document, is still in existence.

At common law, prior to the decision in *Springsteen v Masquerade Music Ltd* [2001] EWCA Civ 563 (see **F8.2**), there were four established categories of exception to the general rule that a party seeking to rely upon the contents of a document must produce primary evidence of those contents. Since the coming into force of the CJA 2003, s. 133, and on the assumption that the second view of the true construction of that section set forth above is correct, it may only be necessary to rely upon such exceptions if, there being no copy of the document in question, it is sought to adduce *oral* evidence of its contents.

Failure to Produce Original after Notice

A party seeking to rely upon the contents of a document may prove them by secondary evidence if the original is in the possession or control of the other party to the proceedings who, having been served with a notice to produce it, fails to do so (*Hunter* (1829) 3 C & P 591, where secondary evidence was admitted as to the contents of an allegedly forged deed, the deed itself being in the custody of the accused who, despite notice, refused to produce it). See also *Collins* (1960) 44 Cr App R 170, at **F8.3**. Service of a notice to produce is unnecessary where the requirement to produce the original can be implied, as when the indictment gives sufficient notice of the subject of inquiry: see *Aickles* (1784) 1 Leach 294, where on a charge of theft of a bill of exchange, parol evidence concerning it was given without service of a notice; *Clube* (1857) 3 Jur NS 698 and *Hunt* (1820) 3 B & Ald 566. Compare *Kitson* (1853) Dears CC 187, where, on a charge of setting fire to property with intent to defraud an insurance company, secondary evidence as to the contents of the policy of insurance was held to be inadmissible. See also *Elworthy* (1867) LR 1 CCR 103, where, on a charge of perjury, it being alleged that the accused had falsely sworn that there was no draft of a statutory declaration prepared by him, it was held that, although the prosecution could properly adduce parol evidence that such a draft existed and was in the possession of the accused, secondary evidence of the contents of the draft, and of certain alterations made in it was inadmissible, the Crown having given no notice to the accused to produce the original. Notice to produce is also excused where the opponent of the party seeking to rely on the document admits that it has been lost (*Haworth* (1830) 4 C & P 254). **F8.4**

Stranger's Lawful Refusal to Produce Original

If a stranger to the proceedings, having been served with a subpoena *duces tecum, unlawfully* refuses to produce the document in his possession, its contents cannot be proved by secondary evidence, because the stranger is bound to produce it and is punishable for contempt if he refuses to do so (*Llanfaethly* (*Inhabitants*) (1853) 2 E & B 940). However, the contents may be proved by secondary evidence if the stranger *lawfully* refuses to comply with the subpoena: see *Mills v Oddy* (1834) 6 C & P 728 (a claim to privilege); *Kilgour v Owen* (1889) 88 LT Jo 7 (stranger outside the jurisdiction); and *Nowaz* [1976] 1 WLR 830, where the Pakistani consulate having refused, on the grounds of diplomatic immunity, to produce a photograph and an application for a passport, a police officer who had seen the documents was allowed to give oral evidence of their contents. **F8.5**

Original Lost or Destroyed

The contents of a document may be proved by secondary evidence if it can be proved that the original has been destroyed or cannot be found after due search: see *Wayte* (1983) 76 Cr App R 110, where, two letters having been lost, a photocopy of the one and a photocopy of a carbon copy of the other were held to be admissible. The quality of evidence required to show the destruction (or loss and due search) varies according to the nature and value of the document in question (*Brewster v Sewell* (1820) 3 B & Ald 296). See also *Hall* (1872) 12 Cox CC 159. **F8.6**

Production of Original Impossible or Inconvenient

The contents of a document may be proved by secondary evidence if production of the original is physically or legally impossible. As to the former, see *Mortimer v M'Callan* (1840) 6 M & W 58, at p. 72 (inscriptions upon tombstones or on a wall); and *Hunt* (1820) 3 B & Ald **F8.7**

566 (inscriptions on flags or banners). As to the latter, see *Owner v Bee Hive Spinning Co. Ltd* [1914] 1 KB 105 (a notice statutorily required to be constantly affixed at a factory or workshop); and *Alivon v Furnival* (1834) 1 Cr M & R 277 (a document in the custody of a foreign court). In addition to the statutory provisions governing the proof of the contents of public documents by secondary evidence, at common law secondary evidence may also be used to prove the contents of such documents if production of the originals would entail a high degree of public inconvenience. In *Mortimer v M'Callan* (1840) 6 M & W 58, Alderson B said (at p. 72):

> The [books of the Bank of England] are not capable of being produced without so much public inconvenience, that the courts have directed them to remain in the Bank, and copies of them to be received in evidence for the purpose for which the books are receivable. Then, if they are not removable on the ground of public inconvenience, that is upon the same footing in point of principle as in the case of that which is not removable by the physical nature of the thing itself.

PROOF OF PUBLIC AND JUDICIAL DOCUMENTS

Statutory Provisions of General Application

F8.8 A large number of statutes, the most important of which are considered in the following paragraphs, provide for the proof of the contents of various public and judicial documents by secondary evidence, which, for these purposes, is usually required to take the form of an examined, certified, office, Queen's Printer's or Stationery Office copy. An examined copy is a copy proved by oral evidence to correspond with the original. A certified copy is a copy signed and certified to be accurate by an official who has custody of the original. An office copy is a copy made in the office of the High Court and authenticated, with the seal of the Court, by an officer who has custody of the original and the lawful power to provide copies. Two provisions of general importance are the Evidence Act 1845, s. 1, and the Evidence Act 1851, s. 14. Under s. 1 of the 1845 Act, where a statute provides for proof of a document by a certified, sealed or stamped copy, the copy, provided it purports to be signed, sealed or stamped, is admissible without any proof of the signature, seal or stamp, as the case may be.

Evidence Act 1845, s. 1

> Whenever by any Act now in force or hereafter to be in force any certificate, official or public document, or document or proceeding of any corporation or joint-stock or other company, or any certified copy of any document, by-law, entry in any register or other book, or of any other proceeding, shall be receivable in evidence of any particular in any court of justice, or before any legal tribunal, or either House of Parliament, or any committee of either House, or in any judicial proceeding, the same shall respectively be admitted in evidence, provided they respectively purport to be sealed or impressed with a stamp or sealed and signed, or signed alone, as required, or impressed with a stamp and signed, as directed by the respective Acts made or to be hereafter made, without any proof of the seal or stamp, where a seal or stamp is necessary, or of the signature or of the official character of the person appearing to have signed the same, and without any further proof thereof, in every case in which the original record could have been received in evidence.

Under the Evidence Act 1851, s. 14, if no other statute provides for the proof by means of a copy of the contents of a document of such a public nature that it is admissible in evidence on production from proper custody, the contents of such a document may be proved by a certified or examined copy.

Evidence Act 1851, s. 14

> Whenever any book or other document is of such a public nature as to be admissible in evidence on its mere production from the proper custody, and no statute exists which renders its contents provable by means of a copy, any copy thereof or extract therefrom shall be admissible in evidence in any court of justice, or before any person now or hereafter having by law or by consent of parties authority to hear, receive, and examine evidence, provided it be proved to be an

examined copy or extract, or provided it purport to be signed and certified as a true copy or extract by the officer to whose custody the original is entrusted, and which officer is hereby required to furnish such certified copy or extract to any person applying at a reasonable time for the same, upon payment of a reasonable sum for the same.

Acts of Parliament and Journals of Either House

Private and local and personal Acts of Parliament and Journals of either House may be proved by Queen's Printer's or Stationery Office copies. **F8.9**

Evidence Act 1845, s. 3

All copies of private and local and personal Acts of Parliament not public Acts, if purporting to be printed by the Queen's printers, and all copies of the journals of either House of Parliament, and of royal proclamations, purporting to be printed by the printers to the Crown or by the printers to either House of Parliament, or by any or either of them, shall be admitted as evidence thereof by all courts, judges, justices, and others without any proof being given that such copies were so printed.

Documentary Evidence Act 1882, s. 2

Where any enactment, whether passed before or after [19 June 1882] provides that a copy of any Act of Parliament, proclamation, order, regulation, rule, warrant, circular, list, gazette, or document shall be conclusive evidence, or be evidence, or have any other effect, when purporting to be printed by the Government Printer, or the Queen's Printer, or the Queen's printer for Scotland, or a printer authorised by Her Majesty, or otherwise under Her Majesty's authority, whatever may be the precise expression used, such copy shall also be conclusive evidence, or evidence, or have the said effect (as the case may be) if it purports to be printed under the superintendence or authority of Her Majesty's Stationery Office.

As to public Acts, the Interpretation Act 1978, s. 3, provides that 'Every Act is a public Act to be judicially noticed as such unless the contrary is expressly provided by the Act'. Section 3 applies to all Acts passed after 1850. At common law, judicial notice is taken of earlier enactments, if public. See F1.5.

Royal Proclamations and Orders or Regulations issued by Government

These may be proved by Queen's Printer's or Stationery Office copies (see the Documentary Evidence Act 1868, ss. 2 to 6; and the Documentary Evidence Act 1882, s. 2). **F8.10**

Documentary Evidence Act 1868, ss. 2, 3, 5 and 6

2. Prima facie evidence of any proclamation, order, or regulation issued before or after the passing of this Act by Her Majesty or by the Privy Council, also of any proclamation, order, or regulation issued before or after the passing of this Act by or under the authority of any such department of the government or officer or office-holder in the Scottish Administration as is mentioned in the first column of the schedule hereto, may be given in all courts of justice, and in all legal proceedings whatsoever, in all or any of the modes hereinafter mentioned; that is to say:
   (1) By the production of a copy of the Gazette purporting to contain such proclamation, order, or regulation.
   (2) By the production of a copy of such proclamation, order, or regulation purporting to be printed by the government printer, or, where the question arises in a court in any British colony or possession, of a copy purporting to be printed under the authority of the legislature of such British colony or possession.
   (3) By the production, in the case of any proclamation, order, or regulation issued by Her Majesty or by the Privy Council, of a copy or extract purporting to be certified to be true by the Clerk of the Privy Council, or by any one of the lords or others of the Privy Council, and, in the case of any proclamation, order, or regulation issued by or under the authority of any of the said departments or officers or office-holders, by the production of a copy or extract purporting to be certified to be true by the person or persons specified in the second column of the said schedule in connection with such department or officer or office-holder.

Any copy or extract made in pursuance of this Act may be in print or in writing, or partly in print and partly in writing.

No proof shall be required of the handwriting or official position of any person certifying, in pursuance of this Act, to the truth of ant copy of or extract from any proclamation, order, or regulation.

3. Subject to any law that may be from time to time made by the legislature of any British colony or possession, this Act shall be in force in every such colony and possession.

5. The following words shall in this Act have the meaning hereinafter assigned to them, unless there is something in the context repugnant to such construction; (that is to say,)

'British colony and possession' shall for the purposes of this Act include the Channel Islands, the Isle of Man, . . . and all other Her Majesty's dominions.

'Legislature' shall signify any authority other than the Imperial Parliament or Her Majesty in Council competent to make laws for any colony or possession.

'Office-holder in the Scottish Administration' has the same meaning as in the Scotland Act 1998.

'Privy Council' shall include Her Majesty in Council and the Lords and others of Her Majesty's Privy Council, or any of them, and any committee of the Privy Council that is not specially named in the schedule hereto.

'Government printer' shall mean and include the printer to Her Majesty, the Queen's Printer for Scotland and any printer purporting to be the printer authorised to print the statutes, ordinances, acts of State, or other public Acts of the legislature of any British colony or possession, or otherwise to be the government printer of such colony or possession.

'Gazette' shall include the *London Gazette*, the *Edinburgh Gazette*, and the [*Belfast*] *Gazette*, or any of such gazettes.

6. The provisions of this Act shall be deemed to be in addition to, and not in derogation of, any powers of proving documents given by any existing statute or existing at common law.

In *Clarke* [1969] 2 QB 91, at p. 97, the Court of Appeal said that the word 'order' in the 1868 Act should be given a wide meaning, covering 'any executive act of government performed by the bringing into existence of a public document for the purpose of giving effect to an Act of Parliament'; and held that the Breath Test (Approval) (No. 1) Order 1968 (printed by HMSO), although not a statutory instrument, was an 'order' within s. 2 of the Act. As to statutory instruments, see further **F8.12**.

Proclamations, Treaties and Other Acts of State of Foreign States or British Colonies, and Judgments etc. of Courts in Foreign States or British Colonies

F8.11 These may be proved by examined or authenticated copies (see the Evidence Act 1851, s. 7, below; and the Evidence Act 1845, s. 1, at **F8.8**). As to colonial documents, see also the Documentary Evidence Act 1868, s. 3, at **F8.10**.

Evidence Act 1851, s. 7

All proclamations, treaties, and other acts of State of any foreign State or of any British colony, and all judgments, decrees, orders, and other judicial proceedings of any court of justice in any foreign State or in any British colony, and all affidavits, pleadings, and other legal documents filed or deposited in any such court, may be proved in any court of justice, or before any person having by law or by consent of parties authority to hear, receive, and examine evidence, either by examined copies or by copies authenticated as hereinafter mentioned; that is to say, if the document sought to be proved be a proclamation, treaty, or other act of State, the authenticated copy to be admissible in evidence must purport to be sealed with the seal of the foreign State or British colony to which the original document belongs; and if the document sought to be proved be a judgment, decree, order, or other judicial proceeding of any foreign or colonial court, or an affidavit, pleading, or other legal document filed or deposited in any such court, the authenticated copy to be admissible in evidence must purport either to be sealed with the seal of the foreign or colonial court to which the original document belongs, or, in the event of such court having no seal, to be signed by the judge, or, if there be more than one judge, by any one of the judges of the said court; and such judge shall attach to his signature a statement in writing on the said copy that the court whereof he is a judge has no seal; but if any of the aforesaid authenticated copies shall purport to be sealed or signed as hereinbefore respectively directed, the same shall respectively be admitted in evidence in every case in which the original document could have been received in evidence, without any proof of the seal where a seal is necessary, or of the signature, or of the truth of the statement attached thereto, where such signature and statement are necessary, or of the judicial character of the person appearing to have made such signature and statement.

When s. 7 is used to prove a foreign conviction, it still has to be established that the examined copy relates to the person said to have been convicted. This can be proved by any relevant admissible evidence, including evidence of fingerprints (*Mauricia* [2002] 2 Cr App R 377).

Statutory Instruments

Statutory instruments may be proved by Queen's Printer's or Stationery Office copies (see the Documentary Evidence Act 1868, s. 2, and the Documentary Evidence Act 1882, s. 2). However, where a photocopy from a commercial publication is produced instead, and there is no suggestion of any inaccuracy in the version before the court, the proviso to the Criminal Appeal Act 1968, s. 2, may apply (*Koon Cheung Tang* [1995] Crim LR 813). See also *Ashley* (1967) 52 Cr App R 42 and *Palastanga v Solman* [1962] Crim LR 334 (at **F6.3**), and the Statutory Instruments Act 1946, s. 3. **F8.12**

Statutory Instruments Act 1946, s. 3

(1) Regulations made for the purposes of this Act shall make provision for the publication by His Majesty's Stationery Office of lists showing the date upon which every statutory instrument printed and sold by or under the authority of the King's printer of Acts of Parliament was first issued by or under the authority of that office; and in any legal proceedings a copy of any list so published shall be received in evidence as a true copy, and an entry therein shall be conclusive evidence of the date on which any statutory instrument was first issued by His Majesty's Stationery Office.

(2) In any proceedings against any person for an offence consisting of a contravention of any such statutory instrument, it shall be a defence to prove that the instrument had not been issued by or under the authority of His Majesty's Stationery Office at the date of the alleged contravention unless it is proved that at that date reasonable steps had been taken for the purpose of bringing the purport of the instrument to the notice of the public, or of persons likely to be affected by it, or of the person charged.

By-laws

By-laws may be proved by certified printed copies. **F8.13**

Local Government Act 1972, s. 238

The production of a printed copy of a by-law purporting to be made by a local authority, the Greater London Authority or a metropolitan county passenger transport authority upon which is endorsed a certificate purporting to be signed by the proper officer of the authority stating—

(a) that the by-law was made by the authority;
(b) that the copy is a true copy of the by-law;
(c) that on a specified date the by-law was confirmed by the authority named in the certificate or, as the case may require, was sent to the Secretary of State and has not been disallowed;
(d) the date, if any, fixed by the confirming authority for the coming into operation of the by-law;

shall be prima facie evidence of the facts stated in the certificate, and without proof of the handwriting or official position of any person purporting to sign the certificate.

Colonial and Foreign Laws

Colonial statutes may be proved by copies certified by the clerk or other proper officer of the colonial legislative body (the Colonial Laws Validity Act 1865, s. 6), or by copies purporting to be printed by the Government printer of that possession (the Evidence (Colonial Statutes) Act 1907, s. 1). Subject to this, and except where ascertained by the British Law **F8.14**

Ascertainment Act 1859, colonial and foreign law, including Scots law, even if written, cannot be proved in an English court by production of the documents in which it is recorded, or a copy thereof, but generally requires proof by a suitably qualified expert (*Sussex Peerage Case* (1844) 11 Cl & F 85); *Governor of Brixton Prison, ex parte Shuter* [1960] 2 QB 89). See further, **F10.16**.

Public Records

F8.15 Public records in the Public Record Office may be proved by copies which have been examined, certified and sealed or stamped.

Public Records Act 1958, s. 9

(2) A copy of or extract from a public record in the Public Record Office purporting to be examined and certified as true and authentic by the proper officer and to be sealed or stamped with the seal of the Public Record Office shall be admissible as evidence in any proceedings without any further or other proof thereof if the original record would have been admissible as evidence in those proceedings.

(3) An electronic copy of or extract from a public record in the Public Record Office which—
  (a) purports to have been examined and certified as true and authentic by the proper officer; and
  (b) appears on a website purporting to be one maintained by or on behalf of the Public Record Office,

shall, when viewed on the website, be admissible as evidence in any proceedings without further or other proof if the original record would have been admissible as evidence in those proceedings.

(4) In this section any reference to the proper officer is a reference to the Keeper of Public Records or any other officer of the Public Record Office authorised in that behalf by the Keeper of Public Records, and, in the case of copies and extracts made before the commencement of this Act, the deputy keeper of the records or any assistant record keeper appointed under the Public Record Office Act 1838.

Births, Deaths and Marriages

F8.16 An entry in the register of births or deaths may be proved by a certified copy purporting to be sealed or stamped with the seal of the General Register Office, and is admissible evidence of the birth or death to which it relates (see the Births and Deaths Registration Act 1953, s. 34). (As to adopted children, see also the Adoption and Children Act 2002, s. 77(4).) Likewise, proof of the celebration of a marriage or of a civil partnership may be effected by the production of a certified copy of an entry kept at the General Register Office (see the Marriage Act 1949, s. 65(3) and the Civil Partnership (Registration Provisions) Regulations 2005 (SI 2005 No. 3176), reg. 13(4)). In order to prove a birth or death (or the marriage of persons), it is also necessary to adduce some evidence to identify the person in question with the person named in the certified copy (see *Bellis* (1911) 6 Cr App R 283). The same applies where it is sought to prove a person's age by production of a birth certificate. Thus, although age may be proved by other means, e.g., by the testimony of someone present at the time of the birth, by inference from appearance or by hearsay declarations as to pedigree (see *Cox* [1898] 1 QB 179), if a certificate of birth is produced to prove age, evidence must also be adduced to positively identify the person as the person named in the certificate (*Rogers* (1914) 10 Cr App R 276: proof of the age of the complainant on a charge of unlawful sexual intercourse with a girl under 13). A certified copy of an entry in the register of deaths is prima facie evidence of the fact and date of a death; but information contained in the certificate concerning the cause of death, and based on information supplied by a coroner, is inadmissible as evidence of the cause of death (*Bird v Keep* [1918] 2 KB 692, per Swinfen Eady MR, *obiter*).

Births and Deaths Registration Act 1953, s. 34

(1) The following provisions of this section shall have effect in relation to entries in registers under this Act or any enactment repealed by this Act.

(2) An entry or a certified copy of an entry of a birth or death in a register, or in a certified copy of a register, shall not be evidence of the birth or death unless the entry purports to be signed by some person professing to be the informant and to be such a person as might be required or permitted by law at the date of the entry to give to the registrar information concerning that birth or death:
Provided that this subsection shall not apply—
(a) in relation to an entry of a birth which, not being an entry signed by a person professing to be a superintendent registrar, purports to have been made with the authority of the Registrar General; or
(b) in relation to an entry of a death which purports to have been made upon a certificate from a coroner; or
(c) in relation to an entry of a birth or death which purports to have been made in pursuance of the enactments with respect to the registration of births and deaths at sea;
(d) in relation to the re-registration of a birth under section 9(5) of this Act.

(3) Where more than three months have intervened between the date of the birth of any child or the date when any living new-born child or still-born child was found exposed and the date of the registration of the birth of that child, the entry or a certified copy of the entry of the birth of the child in the register, or in a certified copy of the register, shall not be evidence of the birth unless—
(a) if it appears that not more than 12 months have so intervened, the entry purports either to be signed by the superintendent registrar as well as by the registrar or to have been made with the authority of the Registrar General;
(b) if more than 12 months have so intervened, the entry purports to have been made with the authority of the Registrar General:

. . .

(4) Where more than 12 months have intervened between the date of the death or of the finding of the dead body of any person and the date of the registration of that person's death, the entry or a certified copy of the entry of the death in the register, or in a certified copy of the register, shall not be evidence of the death unless the entry purports to have been made with the authority of the Registrar General:
Provided that this subsection shall not apply in any case where the original entry in the register was made before the first day of January, 1875.

(5) A certified copy of an entry in a register or in a certified copy of a register shall be deemed to be a true copy notwithstanding that it is made on a form different from that on which the original entry was made if any differences in the column headings under which the particulars appear in the original entry and the copy respectively are differences of form only and not of substance.

(6) The Registrar General shall cause any certified copy of an entry given in the General Register Office to be sealed or stamped with the seal of that Office; and, subject to the foregoing provisions of this section, any certified copy of an entry purporting to be sealed or stamped with the said seal shall be received as evidence of the birth or death to which it relates without any further or other proof of the entry, and no certified copy purporting to have been given in the said Office shall be of any force or effect unless it is sealed or stamped as aforesaid.

Records of marriages, baptisms and burials entered in parish registers may be proved by an examined copy or by a copy certified as a true copy by the incumbent to whose custody the original is entrusted (see the Evidence Act 1851, s. 14, at **F8.8**).

Births, deaths and marriages out of England may be proved by entries properly and regularly recorded in foreign registers kept under the sanction of public authority (see *Lyell v Kennedy* (1889) 14 App Cas 437, per Lord Selborne at pp. 448–9, and generally **F16.26**). See also the Registration of Births, Deaths and Marriages (Scotland) Act 1854 and the Registration of Births, Deaths and Marriages (Scotland) Amendment Act 1860. Births, deaths and marriages out of England may also be proved by certified copies of registers kept under the local law in any case where the Evidence (Foreign, Dominion and Colonial Documents) Act 1933 has been applied by an Order in Council. As to proof of records kept in an Army Register in respect of an officer or soldier serving overseas, see the Registration of Births, Deaths and Marriages (Army) Act 1879, s. 3. As to returns of births and deaths on ships registered in the UK, and on ships not registered in the UK but calling at a port in the UK, see the Merchant Shipping Act 1995, s. 108, and the Merchant Shipping (Returns of Births and Deaths) Regulations 1979, SI 1979 No. 1577. Returns or reports under s. 72 of the 1970 Act are admissible in evidence (s. 75). As to births, deaths and marriages on Her Majesty's ships at sea and service aircraft, see the Registration of Births, Deaths and Marriages (Special Provisions) Act 1957, s. 2. Ambassadors' or Consular registers of marriages under British law by British subjects are of such a public nature as to be admissible on mere production from proper custody (Foreign Marriages Act 1892, s. 16).

Minute-books of Local Authorities

F8.17 The minutes of the proceedings of local authorities required to be drawn up, entered in a book and signed under the Local Government Act 1972, shall be received in evidence without further proof; and until the contrary is proved, where a minute of such proceedings has been made and signed, the meeting shall be deemed to have been duly convened and held, and all the members present shall be deemed to have been duly qualified (Local Government Act 1972, sch. 12, part VI, para. 41). A document which purports to be a copy of the minutes of the proceedings at a meeting of a local authority (or a committee of a local authority, or a subcommittee of such a committee) or a precursor of a local authority, and which bears a certificate purporting to be signed by the proper officer of the authority and stating that the minutes were signed in accordance with para. 41, shall be evidence in any proceedings of the matters stated in the certificate and of the terms of the minutes in question (Local Government (Miscellaneous Provisions) Act 1976, s. 41(1)).

Professional Lists

F8.18 Various statutes provide for proof that a person is or is not professionally qualified by production of a list, register or certificate of a registrar. Thus, any list purporting to be published by authority of the Law Society and to contain the names of solicitors who have obtained practising certificates for the current year shall, until the contrary is proved, be evidence that the persons so named are solicitors holding such certificates (the Solicitors Act 1974, s. 18(1)). The absence from any such list of the name of any person shall, until the contrary is proved, be evidence that that person is not qualified to practise as a solicitor under a certificate for the current year, but in the case of any such person an extract from the roll certified as correct by the Society shall be evidence of the facts appearing in the extract. See also the Medical Act 1983, s. 34 (registered medical practitioners); the Nursing and Midwifery Order 2002 (SI 2002 No. 253), reg. 8(3); the Health Professions Order 2002 (SI 2002 No. 254), reg. 8(4); the Dentists Act 1984, s. 14(6); the Pharmacy Act 1954, s. 6(2) (registered pharmaceutical chemists); and the Veterinary Surgeons Act 1966, ss. 2 and 9.

Documents Relevant to Insolvency

F8.19 In relation to bankruptcy law, any document purporting to be or to contain any order, direction or certificate issued by the Secretary of State shall be received in evidence and be deemed to be (or contain) that order or certificate or those directions without further proof, unless the contrary is shown; and a certificate signed by the Secretary of State or an officer on his behalf and confirming the making of any order, the issuing of any document or the exercise of any discretion, power or obligation arising or imposed under the Insolvency Act 1986 or the Insolvency Rules 1986 (SI 1986 No. 1925) is conclusive evidence of the matter dealt with in the certificate (Insolvency Rules 1986, r. 12.6). A copy of the Gazette containing any notice required by the Act or the Rules to be gazetted is evidence of any facts stated in the notice; and in the case of an order of the court, notice of which is required to be gazetted, a copy of the Gazette containing the notice may be produced in any proceedings as conclusive evidence that the order was made on the date specified in the notice (Insolvency Rules 1986, r. 12.20).

Company Investigations

A copy of any report of inspectors appointed under part XIV of the Companies Act 1985, certified by the Secretary of State to be a true copy, is admissible in any legal proceedings as evidence of the opinion of the inspectors in relation to any matter contained in the report; and a document purporting to be such a certificate shall be received in evidence and deemed to be such a certificate unless the contrary is proved (Companies Act 1985, s. 441). **F8.20**

Judgments of the House of Lords

Such judgments may be proved by Queen's Printer's or Stationery Office copies (see the Evidence Act 1845, s. 3, and the Documentary Evidence Act 1882, s. 2). **F8.21**

Proceedings in Civil Courts

Under the Civil Procedure Rules 1998, r. 2.6(3), a document purporting to bear the court's seal shall be admissible in evidence without further proof. See also the Supreme Court Act 1981, s. 132: 'Every document purporting to be sealed or stamped with the seal or stamp of the Supreme Court shall be received in evidence in all parts of the UK without further proof.' An official copy of the whole or any part of a will may be obtained under the Supreme Court Act 1981, s. 125, and may be proved under s. 132 of that Act. On a prosecution for perjury (or procuring or suborning the commission of perjury) alleged to have been committed on the trial of any indictment, the fact of that former trial shall be sufficiently proved by a certificate signed by the clerk (or his deputy) of the court where the indictment was tried without proof of the signature (Perjury Act 1911, s. 14). **F8.22**

Proceedings in County Courts

Records of county court proceedings may be proved by certified copies. **F8.23**

County Courts Act 1984, s. 12

(1) The district judge for every district shall keep or cause to be kept such records of and in relation to proceedings in the court for that district as the Lord Chancellor may by regulations made by statutory instrument prescribe.

(2) Any entry in a book or other document required by the said regulations to be kept for the purposes of this section, or a copy of any such entry or document purporting to be signed and certified as a true copy by the registrar, shall at all times without further proof be admitted in any court or place whatsoever as evidence of the entry and of the proceeding referred to by it and of the regularity of that proceeding.

Proceedings in Magistrates' Courts

The CrimPR, r. 6.4, provides that the register of a magistrates' court, or an extract from the register certified by the magistrates' court officer as a true extract, shall be admissible in any legal proceedings as evidence of proceedings of the court entered in the register. **F8.24**

Affidavits

On a prosecution for perjury in an affidavit, the affidavit itself must be produced and proved (*Rees d Howell and Dalton v Bowen* (1825) M'Cle & Yo 383), unless it can be proved to have been lost or destroyed, in which case secondary evidence is admissible of its contents and the signature of the accused (*Milnes* (1860) 2 F & F 10, and see F8.6). **F8.25**

Convictions and Acquittals

F8.26 Provision for the proof of convictions and acquittals is made in the PACE 1984, s. 73. This is dealt with at **F11**.

BANKERS' BOOKS

General

F8.27 In order to facilitate the proof of matters recorded in bankers' books, the Bankers' Books Evidence Act 1879 provides for proof of the contents of such books by the production of examined copies.

Bankers' Books Evidence Act 1879, s. 3

> Subject to the provisions of this Act, a copy of any entry in a banker's book shall in all legal proceedings be received as prima facie evidence of such entry, and of the matters, transactions, and accounts therein recorded.

The expressions 'bank' and 'banker' are defined by s. 9(1) of the Act to mean a deposit-taker (an expression defined by s. 9(1A) to (1C)) and the National Savings Bank.

'Bankers' books' were originally defined to include ledgers, daybooks, cash books, account books, and all other books used in the ordinary business of the bank. Section 9(2) of the 1879 Act, as substituted by the Banking Act 1979, has now extended that definition. It provides that expressions in the Act relating to 'bankers' books' include 'ledgers, daybooks, cash books, account books and other records used in the ordinary business of the bank, whether those records are in written form or are kept on microfilm, magnetic tape or any other form of mechanical or electronic data retrieval mechanism'. In *Williams v Williams* [1988] QB 161, it was held that paid cheques and paying-in slips retained by a bank after the conclusion of a banking transaction to which they relate are not 'bankers' books', because, even if bundles of such documents can be treated as 'records used in the ordinary business of the bank', the act of adding an individual cheque (paying-in slip) cannot be regarded as the making of an 'entry' in the records. It is submitted that similar reasoning may be used to justify the decision reached in *Dadson* (1983) 77 Cr App R 91 prior to the coming into force of the extended definition, that copies of letters written by a bank and contained in a file of its correspondence, were not 'bankers' books'. The words 'other records used in the ordinary business of the bank' are to be construed *eiusdem generis* with ledgers, daybooks, cash books and account books and therefore do not cover records kept by the bank of conversations between its employees and customers or others or internal memoranda (*Re Howglen Ltd* [2001] 1 All ER 376). In the case of documents falling outside the statutory definition, use may be made, in appropriate circumstances, of the hearsay provisions of the CJA 2003, including s. 133 of that Act (see **F8.3**).

Bankers' Books Evidence Act 1879, ss. 4 to 8 and 10

> 4. A copy of an entry in a banker's book shall not be received in evidence under this Act unless it be first proved that the book was at the time of the making of the entry one of the ordinary books of the bank, and that the entry was made in the usual and ordinary course of business, and that the book is in the custody or control of the bank.
>
> Such proof may be given by a partner or officer of the bank, and may be given orally or by an affidavit sworn before any commissioner or person authorised to take affidavits.
>
> Where the proceedings concerned are proceedings before a magistrates' court inquiring into an offence as examining justices, this section shall have effect with the omission of the words 'orally or'.
>
> 5. A copy of an entry in a banker's book shall not be received in evidence under this Act unless it be further proved that the copy has been examined with the original entry and is correct.
>
> Such proof shall be given by some person who has examined the copy with the original entry, and may be given either orally or by an affidavit sworn before any commissioner or person authorised to take affidavits.

Where the proceedings concerned are proceedings before a magistrates' court inquiring into an offence as examining justices, this section shall have effect with the omission of the words 'orally or'.

6. A banker or officer of a bank shall not, in any legal proceeding to which the bank is not a party, be compellable to produce any banker's book the contents of which can be proved under this Act, or to appear as a witness to prove the matters, transactions, and accounts therein recorded, unless by order of a judge made for special cause.

7. On the application of any party to a legal proceeding a court or judge may order that such party be at liberty to inspect and take copies of any entries in a banker's book for any of the purposes of such proceedings. An order under this section may be made either with or without summoning the bank or any other party, and shall be served on the bank three clear days before the same is to be obeyed, unless the court or judge otherwise directs.

8. The costs of any application to a court or judge under or for the purposes of this Act, and the costs of anything done or to be done under an order of a court or judge made under or for the purposes of this Act shall be in the discretion of the court or judge, who may order the same or any part thereof to be paid to any party by the bank, where the same have been occasioned by any default or delay on the part of the bank. Any such order against a bank may be enforced as if the bank was a party to the proceeding.

10. In this Act—

The expression 'legal proceeding' means any civil or criminal proceeding or inquiry in which evidence is or may be given, and includes . . .

The expression 'the court' means the court, judge . . . persons or person before whom a legal proceeding is held or taken;

The expression 'a judge' means with respect to England a judge of the High Court . . .

'A court', for the purposes of s. 7, includes justices before whom criminal proceedings are pending (*Kinghorn* [1908] 2 KB 949). An application under s. 7 in criminal proceedings will not be refused on the grounds that it incriminates the party against whom it is made; but it is a serious interference with the liberty of the subject, and the court should be satisfied, before making an order, that the application is more than a mere 'fishing expedition' by considering whether the prosecution have other evidence to support the charge. The court should also limit the period of disclosure of the bank account to a period in time which is strictly relevant to the charge (*Williams v Summerfield* [1972] 2 QB 512). In *Marlborough Street Stipendiary Magistrate, ex parte Simpson* (1980) 70 Cr App R 290, orders under the Act were quashed on the grounds that they were not limited to a defined period in time. See also *Nottingham City Justices, ex parte Lynn* (1984) 79 Cr App R 238, where, on a charge of drug smuggling, an order for the inspection of accounts over a period of three years was reduced to a period of six months, on the ground that there was insufficient evidence to link the accused with offences during most of the three years.

Bank Accounts of a Non-party An order may be made to inspect the accounts of a person who is not a party to the proceedings, even if not compellable as a witness. Thus in *Andover Justices, ex parte Rhodes* [1980] Crim LR 644, the Divisional Court upheld an order in respect of the account of the husband of an accused, charged with the theft of money, who had told the police that the money was in her husband's account. However, in criminal cases, such an order should be made only in exceptional circumstances, and where the private interest in keeping a bank account confidential is outweighed by the public interest in assisting a prosecution (*Grossman* (1981) 73 Cr App R 302, at p. 307). In that case, an application against the Savings and Investment Bank (registered and licensed as a bank under Manx Law) having been refused by the Manx Court, it was held that an order under s. 7 should not have been made in respect of an account held at a branch of Barclays Bank, which was used as a clearing house by the Savings and Investment Bank. In *MacKinnon v Donaldson, Lufkin and Jenrette Securities Corpn* [1986] Ch 482, *Grossman* was applied, although it was acknowledged that the decision in that case had been given *per incuriam* since the proceedings were criminal, and under the Supreme Court Act 1981, s. 18(1)(a), the Court of Appeal had no jurisdiction. F8.28

F8.29 **Foreign Banks** In *MacKinnon v Donaldson, Lufkin and Jenrette Securities Corpn* [1986] Ch 482 it was held that, save in exceptional circumstances, an order should not be made against a foreign bank which is not a party to the proceedings, even if it carries on business within the jurisdiction and is a recognised bank under the Banking Act 1979, to produce documents outside the jurisdiction concerning business transacted outside the jurisdiction, because an order under the 1879 Act is an exercise of sovereign authority to assist in the administration of justice, and foreign banks owe their customers a duty of confidence regulated by the law of the country where the documents are kept.

F8.30 **Procedure** An application under s. 7 of the 1879 Act may be made *ex parte*, but 'there is much to be said for notice being given' (*Marlborough Street Stipendiary Magistrate, ex parte Simpson* (1980) 70 Cr App R 291, per Widgery LJ at p. 294). See also, in the case of accounts of a person who is not a party to the proceedings, *Grossman* (1981) 73 Cr App R 302, per Oliver LJ at p. 309: either the order should not be made until the person affected has been informed and given an opportunity to be heard, or it should be made in the form of an order *nisi*, allowing a period for that person to show cause why the order should not take effect.

An order under s. 7 of the 1879 Act is not a precondition of adducing evidence under s. 3. The purpose of s. 7 is to enable a banker's books to be inspected and copied despite the duty of confidentiality owed by the banker to the customer, but an order would be unnecessary if, for instance, the customer waived his right to confidentiality and the bank agreed to inspection and copying (see *Wheatley v Commissioner of Police of the British Virgin Islands* [2006] 1 WLR 1683, construing the British Virgin Islands Bankers' Books (Evidence) Act 1881).

PROOF OF DUE EXECUTION

F8.31 The due execution of a document is established by:

(a) proof that it was signed by the person by whom it purports to have been signed; and
(b) if attestation is necessary, proof that it was attested.

In the case of public and judicial documents, the statutory provisions which enable their contents to be proved by copies also dispense with the need to prove due execution (see **F8.8** to **F8.26** and **F1.5**). Where a party seeks to rely upon the contents of a private document, due execution may be formally admitted or presumed. A document which is more than 20 years old, produced from proper custody and otherwise free from suspicion, is presumed to have been duly executed. At common law the period was 30 years, but 20 years was substituted by the Evidence Act 1938, s. 4. A document comes from proper custody even if not found in the best and most proper place of deposit, provided that the court is satisfied that the place in which it was found was custody that was reasonable and natural in the circumstances (*Bishop of Meath v Marquess of Winchester* (1836) 3 Bing NC 183, per Tindal CJ). Proof of due execution is also unnecessary if the document in question is in the possession of an opponent who refuses to comply with a notice to produce it (*Cooke v Tanswell* (1818) 8 Taunt 450). Subject to the foregoing, a party seeking to rely on the contents of a private document must prove its due execution.

Proof that a document was signed or written by the person by whom it purports to have been signed or written may be effected in a variety of ways:

(a) by the admission of the person in question (*Waldridge v Kennison* (1794) 1 Esp 143);
(b) by the testimony (or admissible hearsay assertion) of the signatory identifying his own signature (hand);
(c) by the testimony (or admissible hearsay assertion) of a person who witnessed the execution of the document;

(d) by the opinion evidence of a person acquainted with the signature or handwriting (*Doe d Mudd v Suckermore* (1836) 5 A & E 703, at p. 705, and *Slaney* (1832) 5 C & P 213); or
(e) by comparison of the document in question with another document which is admitted or proved to have been signed or written by the person in question under the Criminal Procedure Act 1865, s. 8. See further **F10.14**.

Any of these methods of proof may also be used in the case of a private document which, although not required by law to be attested, was in fact attested. Under the Criminal Procedure Act 1865, s. 7, 'It shall not be necessary to prove by the attesting witness any instrument to the validity of which attestation is not requisite, and such instrument may be proved as if there had been no attesting witness thereto.'

Where a document requires attestation to be formally valid, it is not strictly necessary to prove attestation by calling an attesting witness, except in the case of wills and other testamentary documents. Under the Evidence Act 1938, s. 3, 'an instrument to the validity of which attestation is requisite may, instead of being proved by an attesting witness, be proved in the manner in which it might be proved if no attesting witness were alive: Provided that nothing in this section shall apply to the proof of wills and other testamentary documents.' Thus, the attestation of private documents other than testamentary documents may be proved by the testimony of an attesting witness; or by evidence as to the handwriting of the attesting witness; or by other evidence, such as the testimony of a non-attesting witness to the execution.

PRESUMPTIONS CONCERNING DOCUMENTS

A document which is more than 20 years old and comes from proper custody is presumed to have been duly executed. It is also presumed that: **F8.32**

(a) a document was made on the date which it bears (*Re Adamson* (1875) LR 3 P & D 253 at p. 256);
(b) a deed was duly sealed (see *Re Sandilands* (1871) LR 6 CP 411); and
(c) an alteration or erasure in a deed was made before execution, but that an alteration or erasure in a will was made after execution (*Doe d Tatum v Catomore* (1851) 16 QB 745).

STAMPED DOCUMENTS

In criminal proceedings, a document required to be stamped for the purposes of stamp duty is admissible even if not duly stamped. **F8.33**

Stamp Act 1891, s. 14

(4) Save as aforesaid, an instrument executed in any part of the United Kingdom, or relating, wheresoever executed, to any property situate, or to any matter or thing done or to be done, in any part of the United Kingdom, shall not, except in criminal proceedings, be given in evidence, or be available for any purpose whatever, unless it is duly stamped in accordance with the law in force at the time when it was first executed.

REAL EVIDENCE

Tangible Objects

Real evidence is usually some material object, the existence, condition or value of which is in issue or relevant to an issue, produced in court for inspection by the tribunal of fact. (As to inspection out of court, see **F8.38**.) Little if any weight can attach to real evidence in the **F8.34** absence of accompanying testimony identifying the object and connecting it with the facts in issue. In some cases the tribunal of fact must not draw its own unaided conclusion without the assistance of expert testimony: see e.g., *Tilley* [1961] 1 WLR 1309 and *Hipson* [1969] Crim LR 85 (comparison of handwriting).

There is no rule of law that an object must be produced, or its non-production excused, before oral evidence may be given about it. In *Hocking v Ahlquist Bros Ltd* [1944] KB 120, proceedings against manufacturers of clothing for non-compliance with restrictions relating to the method of manufacture, in which evidence as to the condition of the garments was received from witnesses who had visited the manufacturer's premises, it was held that the magistrate had been wrong to dismiss the information on the basis that the garments were not produced at the trial. See also *Miller v Howe* [1969] 1 WLR 1510: it is not necessary for the police to produce the very breath test device used by them on a particular occasion. Non-production, however, may give rise to an inference adverse to the party failing to produce the object in question (*Armory v Delamirie* (1722) 1 Str 505), and may go to the weight of the oral evidence adduced. In *Francis* (1874) LR 2 CCR 128, a trial for attempting to pass off a false ring, at which the ring was not produced but witnesses who had seen it gave evidence as to its falsity, Lord Coleridge CJ said (at p. 133): 'though the production of the article may afford ground for observation more or less weighty, according to the circumstances, it only goes to the weight, not the admissibility of the evidence.'

Once an article has become an exhibit, the court has a responsibility, for the purposes of justice, to preserve and retain it until the trial is concluded, or to arrange for its preservation and retention, the usual course being for the court to entrust the exhibits to the police or to the DPP. The duty of the prosecution, if entrusted with exhibits pending trial and after committal, is:

(a) to take all proper care to preserve the exhibits safe from loss or damage;
(b) to cooperate with the defence in order to allow them reasonable access to the exhibits for the purpose of inspection and examination; and
(c) to produce the exhibits at the trial (*Lambeth Metropolitan Stipendiary Magistrate, ex parte McComb* [1983] QB 551). See also *Uxbridge Justices, ex parte Sofaer* (1986) 85 Cr App R 367.

Behaviour, Appearance and Demeanour

F8.35 In addition to material objects, the following may also be regarded as varieties of real evidence:

(a) a person's behaviour, e.g., his misconduct in court for the purposes of contempt of court;
(b) a person's physical appearance, e.g., for the purposes of identification or on the question of the existence or causation of personal injuries;
(c) a person's demeanour or attitude which, in the case of a witness, may be relevant to his credit, the weight to be attached to his evidence, or whether he is to be treated as hostile.

Documents as Real Evidence

F8.36 Documents on the contents of which a party seeks to rely, whether as evidence of their truth, under an exception to the hearsay rule, or as original evidence, are subject to the rules as to proof of contents and due execution, dealt with at **F8.2** to **F8.33**. These rules, however, have no application if:

(a) the contents are referred to merely for the purposes of identifying the document in question or establishing the bare fact of its existence (see *Boyle v Wiseman* (1855) 11 Exch 360, at pp. 367ff); or
(b) the document is tendered as a material object, regardless of its contents, in order to show, e.g., its appearance, that it bears certain fingerprints, that it is made of a particular substance, or that it is in a particular physical condition.

In such cases, a document may be treated as a tangible object to the extent relevant to do so, and becomes a piece of real evidence.

Statements Produced by Computers and Mechanical Devices

Where a computer or mechanical or other device is used as a calculator, i.e. as a tool which does not contribute its own knowledge, but merely performs a sophisticated calculation which could have been done manually, the printout or other reading is not hearsay but an item of real evidence, the proof and relevance of which depends on the evidence of those using the device, such as the computer programmer and other experts involved: see **F15.16**. See also the CJA 2003, s. 129, regarding the admission of representations of fact made otherwise than by a person (see **F15.17**). **F8.37**

There is a rebuttable presumption as to the correct functioning of mechanical and other instruments (see **F3.46**). However, in the case of computer printouts, before the judge can decide whether they are admissible as real evidence or as hearsay pursuant to statute, it is necessary for appropriate authoritative evidence to be called to describe the function and operation of the computer (*Cochrane* [1993] Crim LR 48).

Views

The term 'view' is used to describe both an inspection out of court of some material object which it is inconvenient or impossible to bring to court (see, e.g., *London General Omnibus Co. Ltd v Lavell* [1901] 1 Ch 135 (an omnibus)), and an inspection of the *locus in quo*. **F8.38**

A view should not take place after the summing-up: see *Lawrence* [1968] 1 WLR 341, which was distinguished in *Nixon* [1968] 1 WLR 577, where, the inspection having been at the express request of the defence, the Court applied the proviso and affirmed the conviction. A view should be attended by the judge, the tribunal of fact, the parties, their counsel, and the shorthand writer. In the case of magistrates, as a general rule a visit to the *locus in quo* should take place before the conclusion of the evidence and in the presence of the parties or their representatives, so as to afford them the opportunity of commenting on any feature of the locality which has altered since the time of the incident or any feature not previously noticed by the parties which impresses the magistrates (*Parry v Boyle* (1987) 83 Cr App R 310). The presence of the accused is important because he may be able to point out some important matter of which his legal adviser is ignorant or about which the magistrates are making a mistake (*Ely Justices, ex parte Burgess* [1992] Crim LR 888). See also *Gibbons v DPP* [2000] All ER(D) 2250 (unreported in printed form).

In a trial by jury, the judge should always be present at a view, whether or not any witness is present for the purposes of a demonstration (*Hunter* [1985] 1 WLR 613). The judge should take precautions to prevent any witnesses who are present from communicating, except by way of demonstration, with the jury (*Martin* (1872) LR 1 CCR 378; *Karamat v The Queen* [1956] AC 256). A witness who has already given evidence at the trial may take part in a view; but witnesses taking part in a view should be recalled to be cross-examined, if desired (*Karamat v The Queen*).

It is improper for one juror to attend a view and report back to the others. In *Gurney* [1976] Crim LR 567 the Court of Appeal held that this contravened the principle that the jury should remain together at all times, and quashed the conviction. If the accused declines to attend a view, he cannot afterwards raise the objection that his absence of itself made the view illegal, though he could object if any evidence were given outside the scope of the view as ordered (*Karamat v The Queen*).

Lip-reading

An expert lip-reader who, after viewing a CCTV recording of someone speaking, gives **F8.39** opinion evidence as to what was said, is providing assistance to the jury in their interpretation of a variety of real evidence. Such evidence is capable of passing the ordinary tests of relevance and reliability and is therefore potentially admissible. However, it requires a special warning from the judge as to its limitations and the concomitant risk of error, not least because the expert may not be completely accurate (*Luttrell* [2004] 2 Cr App R 520).

Tape Recordings and Transcripts

F8.40 The contents of tape recordings, produced and played over in court, may be admitted as:

(a) evidence of their truth, under an exception to the hearsay rule (see, e.g., *Senat* (1968) 52 Cr App R 282: tape recordings of incriminating conversations obtained by telephone tapping; and *Maqsud Ali* [1966] 1 QB 688); or

(b) a variety of original evidence, e.g., simply to show that the recording was made.

In either event, the voices recorded must be properly identified (*Maqsud Ali*, at p. 701). At common law, it was held that there is no objection to a properly proved transcript of the recording being put before the jury, provided they are guided by what they *hear* (*Maqsud Ali*, at p. 702). See also *Rampling* [1987] Crim LR 823: the transcript, *not in itself evidence*, may be used as a convenience to the jury. However, a tape recording is a 'document' for the purposes of the CJA 2003, s. 133 (CJA 2003, s. 134(1)). Thus, where a statement contained in a tape is admissible as evidence, it may be proved by production of the tape; or (whether or not the original is still in existence) by the production of a copy of the tape, or of the material part of it, authenticated in whatever way the court may approve; and it is immaterial how many removes there are between a copy and the original. A copy, for these purposes, includes a transcript of the sounds embodied in the tape (CJA 2003, s. 134(1)). As to 'authentication', it is submitted that the courts are likely to require the same kind of proof that was necessary in the case of copies at common law before s. 133 came into force, namely a proper explanation as to why the originals are not available, and proof of the complete accuracy of the copies (*Robson* (June 1973 unreported)).

In the case of tape recordings and transcripts of police interviews, s. 133 must be read in conjunction with the Code of Practice on Tape Recording (PACE Code E: see **appendix** 2), together with the *Consolidated Criminal Practice Direction*, para. IV.43, *Evidence of tape recorded interviews*. The provisions of PACE Code E must be followed in all areas where interviews with suspects are required to be recorded by virtue of the provisions of an order made under s. 60(1)(b) of the PACE 1984. Under s. 67(11) of the 1984 Act, Code E is admissible in evidence, and if any provision thereof appears to the court to be relevant to any question arising in the proceedings, it shall be taken into account in determining that question.

F8.41 **The Common-law Authorities** Section 133 of the CJA 2003 must also be read, it is submitted, in conjunction with the common-law authorities before it came into force. At common law, if the prosecution seek to adduce a tape recording in evidence, the judge must be satisfied, in the absence of the jury, that the prosecution have made out a prima facie case of originality and authenticity, by evidence which defines and describes the provenance and history of the tape up to the moment of its production in court. If such evidence appears to remain intact after cross-examination, it is not incumbent on the judge to hear and weigh other evidence which might controvert the prima facie case. The judge is required to be satisfied to the civil standard, on a balance of probabilities, because application of the criminal standard would amount to an usurpation by the judge of the function of the jury (*Robson* [1972] 1 WLR 651, per Shaw J, a ruling upheld by the Court of Appeal (unreported); cf. *Stevenson* [1971] 1 WLR 1). A better approach, it is submitted, also involving no usurpation of the jury function, would be for the judge to decide the issue as if the party seeking to adduce the evidence bore an evidential burden. The question for the judge would then be whether sufficient evidence had been adduced to justify, as a possibility, a finding by the jury, on the issues of originality and genuineness, favourable to the party seeking to admit the tape.

In *Rampling* [1987] Crim LR 823, the Court of Appeal gave the following general guidance upon the use in trials of tape recordings and transcripts of police interviews:

(a) The tape can be produced and proved by the interviewing officer or any other officer present when it was taken.
(b) The officer should have listened to the tape before the trial so that he can, if required, deal with any objections to its authenticity or accuracy.
(c) As to authenticity, he can, if required, prove who spoke the recorded words.
(d) As to accuracy, he can deal with any challenge, e.g., that the recording has been falsified by addition or omission.
(e) The transcript of the recording can be produced by the officer, who, before the trial, should have checked it against the recording for accuracy. The tape recording is the evidence in the case and can be made an exhibit; the transcript, not in itself evidence, may be used as a convenience to the jury (but see now the CJA 2003, s. 133).
(f) Use of the transcript is an administrative matter to be decided in his discretion by the trial judge. In many cases the accused will agree to its use and will not require the tape to be played at all, in which case the transcript will be read out by the officer who produced it; however, the accused is entitled, if he so wishes, to have any part of the tape played to the jury.
(g) If any part of the tape is played, it is for the judge to decide whether the jury should have the transcript, in order to follow the tape, and have it with them when they retire; the use of the transcript is within the judge's discretion and is not dependent on the consent of the parties; a transcript is usually of very considerable value to the jury, but each case has to be decided on its own facts.

Jury's Access to Tape Where the tape becomes an exhibit (see (e) above), the jury may take it with them when they retire like any other exhibit in the case, and it makes no difference if the tape has already been heard in open court. In most cases, nothing turns on the tone of voice in which an interview was conducted and therefore it will usually be sufficient for the jury to have a transcript, much of which can and should be summarised; but where the tone of voice is all-important, for example when it is alleged that the interviewing officer spoke in a raised voice or in a brusque and intimidating manner, then subject to editing out any inadmissible material, the jury should be given the original tape (*Emmerson* (1991) 92 Cr App R 284). The Court of Appeal, in that case, also gave the following general guidance (at p. 287): **F8.42**

> (1) If the whole of the tape has been played in open court there is no reason why the jury should not have the tape if either side or the jury want it as well as any transcript. It is the tape, after all, which is the evidence. But in order not to waste time the jury should always be directed to the relevant part of the tape. (2) If only part of the tape has been played in open court but the jury have a transcript of the whole tape, then there is no reason why the jury should not have the whole tape. (3) If only part of the tape has been played in open court and the jury have no transcript, then the tape should be edited so as to ensure that the jury do not have anything that has not been given in evidence. (4) We see no advantage, and some disadvantage, in a court being reassembled in order to enable the jury to re-hear a passage of the tape which they have already heard in open court. This would seem to serve no useful purpose and be productive of unnecessary inconvenience.

If the tape is not played during the course of a trial but, after retirement, the jury ask to hear it rather than rely on the written transcript, they are entitled to hear it because the tape is the exhibit and the transcript merely a convenient method of presenting it (*Riaz* (1991) 94 Cr App R 339). However, where the prosecution opt not to play the tape but to provide the jury with an agreed transcript and agreed expert comment on it, the jury should not be allowed to conduct their own enquiry as to what is on the tape (*Hagan* [1997] 1 Cr App R 464). If the jury are entitled to hear the tape, although it is a matter of judicial discretion, the better practice is to bring the jury back into open court to hear the tape because of the difficulties which might arise if they are permitted free access to the tape, including the risk that they might hear matters inadvertently left on the tape which they should not hear (*Riaz*). Equally, however, where the jury ask to hear a tape, of which there is an agreed transcript, which does not contain inadmissible passages and which *has* already been played in court, the judge may, in his discretion, permit them to listen to it in the privacy of their retiring room (*Tonge* [1993] Crim LR 876). As to a jury request to hear a tape during or after closing speeches, but before retirement, see *Aitken* (1991) 94 Cr App R 85 at **F6.5**).

Photographs, Video Recordings and Films

F8.43 A photograph may be admitted in evidence to enable a witness to identify a person or thing. In *Tolson* (1864) 4 F & F 103, a case of bigamy, a photograph was produced, which was admitted to be a photograph of the first husband, and a witness was allowed to testify that he had seen the man in the photograph alive after the date of the allegedly bigamous marriage.

A photograph (or film) the relevance of which can be established by the testimony of someone with personal knowledge of the circumstances in which it was taken (or made), may also be admitted to prove the commission of an offence and the identity of the offender. In *Dodson* [1984] 1 WLR 971, it was held that photographs taken at half-second intervals by security cameras installed at a building society office at which an armed robbery had been attempted, were admissible, on the issue of whether an offence had been committed and, if so, who had committed it, even though no witnesses were called to identify the men in the photographs. However, in a case in which the jury is invited to 'identify' the accused in court from a photograph or video recording of the offender committing the offence, they should be warned of the risk of mistaken identity and of the need to exercise particular care in any identification which they make. They must take into account whether the appearance of the accused has changed since the visual recording was made, but a full *Turnbull* direction (*Turnbull* [1977] QB 224: see **F18.20**) is inappropriate because the process of identifying a person from a photograph is a commonplace event and some things are obvious from the photograph itself. Thus they do not need to be told that the photograph is of good quality or poor, nor whether the person is shown in close-up or was distant from the camera etc. (*Blenkinsop* [1995] 1 Cr App R 7, approving *Downey* [1995] 1 Cr App R 547; cf. *Taylor v Chief Constable of Cheshire* [1986] 1 WLR 1479, below). However, it seems that a request by them that the accused stand up and turn around, in order that they may be given a better view of him, does not have to be met, at least not by an accused who has elected not to testify (*McNamara* [1996] Crim LR 750).

In *Roberts* [1998] Crim LR 682, a police constable made a written statement relating to charges of assault and affray. A video camera had recorded the events in question and the constable later provided a commentary on the video to enable prosecuting counsel to explain to the jury, when viewing it, who was who and where the events took place. The video was then made available to the defence. It was held that it was not wrong in principle that the constable had seen the video. On seeing a video a witness might find that in some respects his recollection had been at fault and might wish to modify earlier evidence. However, nothing should be done which amounted to rehearsing the evidence of a witness or coaching him so as to encourage him to alter the evidence already given. The acid test was whether the procedure adopted was such as to taint the resulting evidence. That was not so in the instant case. The video had been made available to the defence and had been shown to defence witnesses before they gave their evidence, and the constable had been directly challenged on discrepancies between his first statement and his commentary.

In *Thomas* [1986] Crim LR 682, a case of reckless driving, a video recording of the route taken by the accused was admitted to remove the need for maps and still photographs, and to convey a more accurate picture of the roads in question. In *The Statue of Liberty* [1968] 1 WLR 739, a civil action concerning a collision between two ships, Sir Jocelyn Simon P, rejecting a submission that a cinematograph film of radar echoes, recorded by a shore radar station, was inadmissible because produced mechanically without human intervention, said (at p. 740): 'If tape recordings are admissible, it seems that a photograph of radar reception is equally admissible — or indeed, any other type of photograph. It would be an absurd distinction that a photograph should be admissible if the camera were operated manually by a photographer, but not if it were operated by a trip or clock mechanism.' Compare *Wood* (1982) 76 Cr App R 23, at **F15.17**.

Admissibility as Hearsay or Real Evidence Although it is possible to treat a photograph or a film as a hearsay document containing a 'statement' admissible in evidence pursuant to statute, both would appear to be admissible at common law as a variety of real evidence (see *The Statue of Liberty* [1968] 1 WLR 739, where the film, in effect, contained a statement as to the paths taken by the two ships). Moreover, it has been said that a photograph, together with the sketch and the photofit, is in a class of evidence of its own, to which neither the rule against hearsay nor the rule against previous consistent or self-serving statements applies (*Cook* [1987] QB 417 per Watkins LJ; applied in *Constantinou* (1989) 91 Cr App R 74). As to evidence of previous identification of the accused by police photographs, see further at **F18**. **F8.44**

Proof of Contents The contents of photographs and films on which a party seeks to rely may be proved by production of the original; or by production of a copy proved to be an authentic copy; or by the parol evidence of witnesses who have seen the photograph or film. In *Kajala v Noble* (1982) 75 Cr App R 149 Ackner LJ held that the rule, that if an original document is available in a party's hands he must produce it and cannot give secondary evidence of it, was confined to written documents in the strict sense of the term and has no relevance to tapes or films. In *Taylor v Chief Constable of Cheshire* [1986] 1 WLR 1479, a video cassette recording, made by a security camera and showing a person in a shop picking up an item and putting it into his jacket, was played to police officers who identified the person as Taylor. The recording, after it had been returned to the shop, was accidentally erased. Evidence by the officers of what they had seen on the video was held to have been properly admitted, on the ground that what they had seen on the video was no different in principle from the evidence of a bystander who had actually witnessed the incident, and the appeal against conviction was dismissed. The Court of Appeal held that the weight and reliability of the evidence had to be assessed carefully and, because identification was in issue, by reference to the guidelines laid down in *Turnbull* [1977] QB 224, which had to be applied in relation to not only the camera, but also the visual display unit or recorded copy and the officers. See also *Constantinou* (1989) 91 Cr App R 74. **F8.45**

Jury Access Where a video or film has been shown in court and the jury, after retirement, ask to see it again, they may do so, but it is better if they see it again in open court (*Imran* [1997] Crim LR 754, in which the jury had seen a silent video of an attempted robbery). Cf. *Rawlings* [1995] 1 WLR 178 (video recordings of children's evidence), which is considered at **F16.49**. **F8.46**

PACE Code on Video-recording Interviews For the procedures to be followed on video-recording interviews with suspects, see PACE Code F at **appendix 2**. **F8.47**

Section F9 Public Policy and Privilege

EXCLUSION ON GROUNDS OF PUBLIC POLICY

F9.1 This section concerns the principles of law governing the non-disclosure of material on the grounds of public policy. As to the procedure to be followed on an application to the court that unused material should not be disclosed on such grounds, see also **D9.26** ***et seq*** and the CrimPR, part 25. Part I of the CPIA 1996 generally disapplies the common-law rules relating to the prosecution duty of disclosure, but s. 21(2) of that Act preserves the rules of common law as to whether disclosure is in the public interest.

General Principles

F9.2 It is in the public interest to withhold material, the disclosure of which would harm the nation or the proper functioning of the public service. It is also in the public interest that justice should be done, and should be publicly seen to be done, by the reception of all relevant evidence. If there is a conflict between these two interests, whether otherwise admissible evidence should be withheld in the public interest is a question of balance, to be decided by the courts and not by the executive (*Conway v Rimmer* [1968] AC 910). If the evidence is excluded, it is said to be withheld by reason of public interest immunity: see *Lewes Justices, ex parte Secretary of State for the Home Department* [1973] AC 388, per Lord Reid at p. 400, disapproving use of the expression 'Crown privilege'; but contrast *Science Research Council v Nasse'* [1980] AC 1028, per Lord Scarman at p. 1087.

In some cases, the relevant minister (or head of department) or the A-G may intervene to claim immunity. Alternatively, the claim to immunity may be made by the party seeking to withhold the evidence, either on its own initiative or at the request of the relevant government department (see, e.g., *Burmah Oil Co. Ltd v Bank of England* [1980] AC 1090). If necessary, the judge himself should raise the issue, because if there is a public interest to be protected, that should be done regardless of party advantage (*Duncan v Cammell Laird & Co. Ltd* [1942] AC 624, per Viscount Simon LC at p. 642).

A claim to public interest immunity may be supported by affidavit evidence from the relevant minister (or head of department), or by a certificate signed by the minister. However, a minister's affidavit or certificate is not final (except, it seems, in cases concerning national security: see *Balfour v Foreign and Commonwealth Office* [1994] 1 WLR 681, considered at **F9.6**). Although an objection by the Crown to the disclosure of material is entitled to the greatest weight, the court may ask for clarification or amplification of the objection, and has the power to inspect documentary evidence privately and to order its production notwithstanding ministerial objection (*Conway v Rimmer* [1968] AC 910). In *Conway v Rimmer*, it was suggested that certain classes of documents, such as Cabinet papers and Foreign Office despatches should never be disclosed, whatever their contents may be (see per Lords Reid and Upjohn at pp. 952 and 993 respectively). Since then, however, the House of Lords has made it clear that the courts should be prepared to evaluate 'class' claims, even in the case of high-level government papers, and in appropriate circumstances, albeit very rarely, to require their disclosure (see *Burmah Oil Co. Ltd v Bank of England* [1980] AC 1090, per Lord Keith at

p. 1134, and *Air Canada v Secretary of State for Trade* (*No. 2*) [1983] 2 AC 394, per Lord Fraser at p. 432).

In December 1996 the Lord Chancellor issued a statement that the division into class and contents claims would no longer be applied, and that in future ministers would focus directly on the damage that disclosure of sensitive documents would cause. Under this new approach, ministers claim immunity only when they believe that disclosure of a document will cause real damage or harm to the public interest. Damage will normally have to be in the form of a direct or immediate threat to the safety of an individual or to the nation's economic interests or relations with a foreign state, although in some cases the anticipated damage might be indirect or longer term, such as damage to a regulatory process. In any event the nature of the harm will have to be clearly explained, and ministers will no longer be able to claim immunity for internal advice or national security material merely by pointing to the general nature of the document. It is to be hoped that non-governmental bodies claiming public interest immunity, although not bound by the Lord Chancellor's statement, will in practice adopt the same approach.

Decisions as to what should be withheld from disclosure are for the court and should not be made (without reference to the court) by the prosecution, the police, the DPP or counsel (see *Ward* [1993] 1 WLR 619 and, in the case of co-accused, *Adams* [1997] Crim LR 292). The principles are the same whether the proceedings are summary or on indictment, but when, in the case of an either way offence, it is known that a contested issue as to the disclosure of sensitive material is likely to arise, that consideration may sometimes properly found an application by the Crown for trial on indictment, and magistrates would then be well advised to commit (*Bromley Magistrates' Court, ex parte Smith* [1995] 1 WLR 944, distinguishing *DPP, ex parte Warby* [1994] Crim LR 281). The rule established in *Ward* is now reflected in the relevant disclosure provisions of the CPIA 1996. These procedural rules, including the *ex parte* procedure for certain public interest immunity applications and the rules relating to the appointment of a 'special advocate' or 'special counsel', are considered at **D9.26 *et seq.*** As to immunity claims in summary trials, see also **D9.37**. If, in the course of a public interest immunity hearing (whether on the *voire dire* or otherwise) prosecution witnesses lied to the judge, the prosecution would be likely to be tainted beyond redemption, however strong the evidence against the accused might otherwise be (*Early* [2003] 1 Cr App R 288).

In *Keane* [1994] 1 WLR 746 Lord Taylor CJ held that it is for the prosecution to put before the court only those documents which it regards as material but wishes to withhold. It is generally for the prosecution, not the court, to identify the documents and information which are material. However, if, in an exceptional case, the prosecution are in doubt about the materiality of some documents or information, the court may be asked to rule on that issue. When the court is seized of the material, the judge should perform the balancing exercise, balancing the weight of the public interest in non-disclosure against the importance of the documents to the issues of interest to the defence, present and potential, so far as they have been disclosed to him or he can foresee them. However a ruling made prior to the hearing is not necessarily final, because issues may later emerge whereby the public interest in non-disclosure is eclipsed by the accused's need for access (*Bower* [1994] Crim LR 281). The trial judge is under a continuous duty, in the light of the way in which the trial develops, to keep his initial decision under review, and prosecuting counsel must inform himself fully as to the content of any disputed material so as to be in a position to invite the judge to reassess the situation if the previous denial of the material arguably becomes untenable in the light of developments in the trial (*Brown* [1994] 1 WLR 1599 at p. 1608). See also **D9.15**.

Voluntary Disclosure The CPS may voluntarily disclose to the defence documents which would otherwise be in a class covered by public interest immunity, without referring the matter to the court for a ruling, subject to the safeguard of first seeking the express written **F9.3**

approval of the Treasury Solicitor. The CPS should submit to him copies of the documents in question, identify the public interest immunity class into which they fall and indicate the materiality of the documents to the proceedings in which it is proposed to disclose them. The Treasury Solicitor should consult any other relevant government department and satisfy himself that the balance falls clearly in favour of disclosure. He should be more ready to disclose documents likely to assist the defence than those which the CPS wish to disclose with a view to furthering the interests of the prosecution. Before approving disclosure of documents of a particular class sought to be used by the prosecution, he should consider not only their importance to the prosecution's case, but also the importance of the prosecution itself: it may be preferable to abandon the case rather than damage the integrity of the class claim. He should also maintain a permanent record of all approvals given so that any court ruling on disclosure would know how far immunity for that particular class of documents had been weakened by previous voluntary disclosure (*Horseferry Road Magistrates, ex parte Bennett (No. 2)* [1994] 1 All ER 289).

F9.4 **The Balancing Exercise** The principle of public interest immunity is applicable to criminal proceedings, but involves a different balancing exercise to that in civil proceedings. The judge will balance the desirability of preserving the public interest in non-disclosure against the interests of justice. Where the interests of justice arise in a criminal case touching and concerning liberty (or conceivably, on occasion, life), the weight to be attached to the interests of justice is plainly very great; it is a matter of whether the interests of justice outweigh the considerations of public interest as spoken to in the certificate of the Minister. Any prior disclosure of the information in question is a matter to be taken into account in the balance. In assessing the interests of justice, the court must ask whether a document to which the certificate relates is material to the proceedings. Its materiality will depend on the purpose for which it is sought to be deployed. In cases concerning the identity of informers or persons who have allowed their premises to be used for police surveillance (see **F9.9**), there have been observations to the effect that the privilege cannot prevail if the evidence is necessary for the prevention of a miscarriage of justice — no balance is called for (*Governor of Brixton Prison, ex parte Osman* [1991] 1 WLR 281). But see also, in cases concerning the identity of informers, *Keane* [1994] 1 WLR 746, per Lord Taylor CJ (at pp. 751–2):

> We prefer to say that the outcome in the instances given by Lord Esher MR [in *Marks v Beyfus* (1890) 25 QBD 494: see **F9.9**] and Mann LJ [in *Ex parte Osman*] results from performing the balancing exercise, not from dispensing with it. If the disputed material may prove the defendant's innocence or avoid a miscarriage of justice, then the balance comes down resoundingly in favour of disclosing it.

In *Clowes* [1992] 3 All ER 440, the accused were charged with theft and fraud following the collapse of two deposit-taking companies owing investors over £115 million. The liquidators of the company interviewed a number of people in order to establish whether civil claims could be brought on behalf of the investors. Those interviewed attended voluntarily in circumstances of confidence on assurances, express or implied, that any information given to the liquidators would be used solely for the purposes of the liquidation. At the instance of the accused, a witness summons was issued requiring the liquidators to produce the transcripts. The liquidators applied to the Companies Court for directions that they be at liberty to disclose the transcripts to the accused. The judge held that they should claim public interest immunity and refuse to disclose the transcripts unless ordered to do so by the Crown Court. The liquidators then applied to the Crown Court to discharge the summons on the grounds that the transcripts were not 'likely to be material evidence' or should be protected by reason of public interest immunity. Phillips J held that the transcripts were potentially admissible and material. Concerning the claim to public interest immunity, the question arose whether the court should conduct a balancing exercise between the public interest asserted and the interest of the due administration of criminal justice. After reviewing the authorities relating to informers (see **F9.9**) and the decision in *Ex parte Osman*, Phillips J held that he did not find very easy the concept of a balancing exercise between the nature of the public interest on the one hand and the degree and potential consequences of the risk of a miscarriage of justice on the other, but would not readily accept that proportionality between the two is never of relevance. On the facts, he allowed the summons to stand. It did not seem that the public interest in question should carry greater weight than the public interest in concealing the identity of a police informer. Those interviewed inevitably accepted some risk of dissemination of the information they gave and there would be a relatively limited effect on 'the wells of voluntary information'. On the other hand, the accused were charged with grave offences and it was therefore of particular importance that no unnecessary impediment should be put in the way of presenting their defence in the best light. Another significant factor was the complexity of the evidence and the risk of lapse of memory on the part of witnesses.

The Heads of Public Interest Immunity

The heads of public interest immunity which have been recognised by the courts relate to national security, diplomatic relations, international comity, the proper functioning of the public service, informers and information for the detection of crime, judges, jurors, and sources of information contained in publications. Each is considered in the following paragraphs. **F9.5**

National Security, Diplomatic Relations and International Comity

Documents falling within this category are those most readily protected against disclosure; in the case of national security, it seems that a ministerial certificate will be conclusive (*Balfour v Foreign and Commonwealth Office* [1994] 1 WLR 681). That case concerned material relating to the security and intelligence services. It was held that once there is an actual or potential risk to national security demonstrated by an appropriate ministerial certificate, the court should not exercise its right to inspect. See also *Hennessy v Wright* (1888) 21 QBD 509 (communications between the governor of a colony and the colonial secretary); *Chatterton v Secretary of State for India in Council* [1895] 2 QB 189 (communications between the government and the commander-in-chief of forces overseas); *Asiatic Petroleum Co. Ltd v Anglo Persian Oil Co. Ltd* [1916] 1 KB 822 (information relating to the Persian campaign in the First World War); *M. Isaacs & Sons Ltd v Cook* [1925] 2 KB 391 (diplomatic despatches); *Duncan v Cammell Laird & Co. Ltd* [1942] AC 624 (information on the design of a new submarine); and *Buttes Gas and Oil Co. v Hammer (No. 3)* [1981] QB 223 (confidential communications with foreign sovereign states or concerning their interest in international territorial disputes). **F9.6**

Proper Functioning of Public Service

Public interest immunity may be claimed for communications to and from ministers and high-level government officials, regarding the formulation of government policy: see, e.g., *Burmah Oil Co. Ltd v Bank of England* [1980] AC 1090 (memoranda of meetings attended by ministers or government officials relating to government policy on economic matters); and *Air Canada v Secretary of State for Trade (No. 2)* [1983] 2 AC 394 (ministerial papers and inter-departmental communications between senior civil servants concerning government policy in relation to the British Airports Authority). **F9.7**

The public also has an interest in the effective working of non-governmental bodies and agencies performing public functions. However, although the categories of public interest are not closed, the courts can only proceed by analogy with interests which have previously been recognised by the authorities: see *D v National Society for the Prevention of Cruelty to Children* [1978] AC 171, per Lords Diplock, Hailsham, and Simon at pp. 219, 226, and 240 respectively, applied in *Science Research Council v Nassé* [1980] AC 1028 (in which the House rejected a claim in respect of confidential reports on employees seeking promotion). Examples include *Re D (Infants)* [1970] 1 WLR 599 (local authorities); *Lewes Justices, ex parte Secretary of State for the Home Department* [1973] AC 388 (the Gaming Board); *D v National Society for the Prevention of Cruelty to Children* [1978] AC 171 (the NSPCC); and *Buckley v Law Society (No. 2)* [1984] 1 WLR 1101 (the Law Society).

Police Communications

F9.8 Public interest immunity also attaches to police communications relating to the investigation of crime, such as documents or information upon the strength of which search warrants have been obtained (*Taylor v Anderton* (1986) *The Times*, 21 October 1986). Reports sent by the police to the DPP, even if the prosecution has been completed, have also attracted immunity, on the ground that there should be freedom of communication with the DPP, without fear that such reports may be inspected, analysed or investigated in subsequent civil proceedings (see *Evans v Chief Constable of Surrey* [1988] QB 588). Immunity also attaches to international communications between police forces or prosecuting authorities (*Horseferry Road Magistrates' Court, ex parte Bennett (No. 2)* [1994] 1 All ER 289), although in that case the balance favoured disclosure, the documents being relevant to the issue of whether B had been unlawfully returned to the jurisdiction. In appropriate circumstances, immunity may also be claimed for internal police communications other than those relating to the investigation of crime, on the ground that the public has an interest in the proper functioning of the police force (*Conway v Rimmer* [1968] AC 910).

Immunity may also be claimed for police complaints and disciplinary files (*Halford v Sharples* [1992] 1 WLR 736). There is no immunity, however, for written complaints against the police prompting investigations under part IX of the PACE 1984 (*Conerney v Jacklin* [1985] Crim LR 234); and there is no class immunity for statements obtained for the purposes of such investigations, although immunity may be claimed in the case of a particular document by reason of its contents (*Chief Constable of the West Midlands Police, ex parte Wiley* [1995] 1 AC 274, overruling *Neilson v Laugharne* [1981] QB 736 and cases in which it was subsequently applied). However, the working papers and reports prepared by the investigating officers do form a class which is entitled to immunity, and therefore production of such material should be ordered only where the public interest in disclosure of their contents outweighs the public interest in preserving confidentiality (*Taylor v Anderton* [1995] 1 WLR 447).

Public interest immunity does not attach to statements made during the course of a police grievance procedure, initiated by an officer, alleging either racial or sexual discrimination (*Commissioner of Police of the Metropolis v Locker* [1993] 3 All ER 584).

Informers and Information for Detection of Crime

F9.9 There is a long-established rule of law that in public prosecutions witnesses may not be asked, and should not be allowed to disclose, the names of informers or the nature of the information given (*Hardy* (1794) 24 St Tr 199). The rule applies to public prosecutions brought by the DPP and bodies authorised by statute to bring public prosecutions. It also applies to police prosecutions, but not to other private prosecutions. The rationale of the rule was explained by Lawton LJ in *Hennessey* (1978) 68 Cr App R 419 (at p. 425): 'The courts appreciate the need to protect the identity of informers, not only for their own safety but to ensure that the supply of information about criminal activities does not dry up.' See also *D v National Society for the Prevention of Cruelty to Children* [1978] AC 171, per Lord Diplock at p. 218. The judge is obliged to apply the rule even if it is not invoked by the party entitled to object to disclosure (*Marks v Beyfus* (1890) 25 QBD 494, per Lord Esher MR at p. 500, and *Rankine* [1986] QB 861, per Mann J at p. 867).

However, if a witness called at trial is a participating informant in the very instance with which the trial is concerned, there has to be a very strong countervailing interest for his status not to be revealed (*Patel* [2002] Crim LR 304). In that case, it was not for HM Customs to determine the matter in their own favour without putting their own counsel or the court fully in the picture. Nor was it for the judge to have to piece together stray pieces of information in order to decide whether an individual was or was not a participating informant.

As to interception of communications, see **D1.102**.

There is an exception to the common-law rule where the judge is of the opinion that disclosure is necessary to establish the innocence of the accused.

> . . . if upon the trial of a prisoner the judge should be of opinion that the disclosure of the name of the informant is necessary or right in order to show the prisoner's innocence, then one public policy is in conflict with another public policy, and that which says that an innocent man is not to be condemned when his innocence can be proved is the policy that must prevail. (*Marks v Beyfus* (1890) 25 QBD 494, per Lord Esher MR at p. 498)

This outcome, however, results from performing the balancing exercise, not from dispensing with it (*Keane* [1994] 1 WLR 746 — see **F9.2**). Judges should scrutinise applications for disclosure of details about informants with very great care and should be astute to see whether assertions that knowledge of such details is essential to the running of a defence are justified. In some cases, the informant is an informant and no more; but even when the informant has participated in the events constituting, surrounding or following the crime, the judge must consider whether his role so impinges on an issue of interest to the defence, present or potential, as to make disclosure necessary (*Turner* [1995] 1 WLR 264 per Lord Taylor CJ at p. 268).

In *Agar* [1990] 2 All ER 442, the accused alleged that the police had arranged with an informer to ask the accused to go to the informer's house, where drugs allegedly found on him had been planted by the police. It was held that the disclosure of the identity of the informer was necessary to enable the accused to put forward the tenable defence that he had been set up by the police and the informer acting in concert. Therefore, counsel for the accused should have been permitted to cross-examine police witnesses to elicit the fact that the informer had told the police that the accused was coming to his house. (Compare *Slowcombe* [1991] Crim LR 198, where disclosure of the identity of an informer would have contributed little or nothing to the issue which the jury had to consider, and *Menga* [1998] Crim LR 58.) *Agar* was applied in *Langford* [1990] Crim LR 653. See also *Vaillencourt* [1993] Crim LR 311, *Reilly* [1994] Crim LR 279 and *Baker* [1996] Crim LR 55. It is for the accused to show that there is good reason to expect that disclosure is necessary to show his innocence (*Hennessy* (1978) 68 Cr App R 419, per Lawton LJ, and *Hallett* [1986] Crim LR 462). In *Hennessy*, Lawton LJ said (at p. 426): 'This should normally be done, not in the course of a trial, but in any proceedings which may be started to set aside a subpoena or a witness summons served upon a Crown witness who is alleged to be in possession of, or to have control over, tape recordings, transcripts of such recordings and the like.'

Disclosure Relating to Premises The rule also protects the identity of persons who have allowed their premises to be used for police surveillance, and the identity of their premises (*Rankine* [1986] QB 861). If the accused submits that disclosure of the identification of the premises is necessary in order to show his innocence, the judge may nonetheless exclude the evidence, provided that the prosecution have provided a proper evidential basis for such exclusion. In *Johnson* [1988] 1 WLR 1377, Watkins LJ gave the following guidance as to the minimum evidential requirements in this regard (at pp. 1385–6): **F9.10**

(a) The police officer in charge of the observations to be conducted, no one of lower rank than a sergeant should usually be acceptable for this purpose, must be able to testify that beforehand he visited all observation places to be used and ascertained the attitude of occupiers of premises, not only to the use to be made of them, but to the possible disclosure thereafter of the use made and facts which could lead to the identification of the premises thereafter and of the occupiers. He may of course in addition inform the court of difficulties, if any, usually encountered in the particular locality of obtaining assistance from the public.

(b) A police officer of no lower rank than a chief inspector must be able to testify that immediately prior to the trial he visited the places used for observations, the results of which it is proposed to give in evidence, and ascertained whether the occupiers are the same as when the observations took place and whether they are or are not, what the attitude of those occupiers is to the possible disclosure of the use previously made of the premises and of facts which could lead at the trial to identification of premises and occupiers.

Such evidence will of course be given in the absence of the jury when the application to exclude the material evidence is made. The judge should explain to the jury, as this judge did, when summing up or at some appropriate time before that, the effect of his ruling to exclude, if he so rules.

In *Johnson*, the appellant was convicted of supplying drugs. The only evidence against him was given by police officers, who testified that, while stationed in private premises in a known drug-dealing locality, they had observed him selling drugs. The defence applied to cross-examine the officers on the exact location of the observation posts, in order to test what they could see, having regard to the layout of the street and the objects in it. In the jury's absence the prosecution called evidence as to the difficulty of obtaining assistance from the public, and the desire of the occupiers, who were also occupiers at the time of the offence, that their names and addresses should not be disclosed because they feared for their safety. The judge ruled that the exact location of the premises need not be revealed. The appeal was dismissed: although the conduct of the defence was to some extent affected by the restraints placed on it, this led to no injustice. The jury were well aware of the restraints, and were most carefully directed about the very special care they had to give to any disadvantage they may have brought to the defence. *Johnson* was applied and approved in *Hewitt* (1992) 95 Cr App R 81. See also *Grimes* [1994] Crim LR 213. The guidelines in *Johnson* do not require a threat of violence before protection can be afforded to the occupier of an observation post; it suffices if the occupier is in fear of harassment (*Blake v DPP* (1993) 97 Cr App R 169).

The extension of the rule established in *Rankine* [1986] QB 861 is based on the protection of the owner or occupier of the premises, and not on the identity, *simpliciter*, of the observation post. Thus, where officers have witnessed the commission of an offence as part of a surveillance operation conducted from an unmarked police vehicle, information relating to the surveillance and the colour, make and model of the vehicle should not be withheld (*Brown* (1987) 87 Cr App R 52). Hodgson J said (at pp. 59–60):

> We do not rule out the possibility that with the advent of no doubt sophisticated methods of criminal investigation, there may be cases where the public interest immunity may be successfully invoked in criminal proceedings to justify the exclusion of evidence as to police techniques and methods. But if and when such an argument is to be raised, it must, in the judgment of this court, be done properly. The Crown Prosecution Service must at least ensure that counsel is properly instructed to make the application and to identify with precision the evidence sought to be excluded and the reasons for its exclusion. It would seem clear that if such a contention is put forward the judge must be given as much information as possible and the application will have to be supported, not by the instructions of the junior officer in charge of the case, but by the independent evidence of senior officers.

F9.11 **Informer's Wish to Disclose Name** A further exception to the common-law rule against disclosure of the name of an informer was established in *Savage v Chief Constable of Hampshire* [1997] 1 WLR 1061, in which it was held that a police informer who wishes personally to sacrifice his own anonymity will not be precluded from doing so by a claim of immunity, because in such circumstances the primary justification for the claim (that disclosure would endanger the safety of the informer) disappears. The wishes of the informer, however, are not conclusive, and in appropriate cases may be outweighed by other considerations, as when discovery may assist others involved in crime, hamper police operations, or indicate the state of police enquiries into a particular crime.

Informer Called as a Witness In *Patel* [2002] Crim LR 304, the Court of Appeal stated that if a witness called at trial is a participating informer in the very instance in which the trial is concerned, there will have to be a very strong countervailing interest for his status not to be revealed. In this case, it was not for HM Customs to determine the matter in their own favour without putting their own counsel or the court fully in the picture. Nor, the Court stated, was it for the judge to have to piece together stray pieces of information in order to decide whether an individual was or was not a participating informer. F9.12

Judges and Jurors

A judge, including a master of the Supreme Court, cannot be compelled to give evidence of matters of which he became aware relating to, and as a result of, the performance of his judicial functions (as opposed to extraneous matters, such as a crime committed in the face of the court). However, the judge remains competent to give evidence, and if a situation arises where his evidence is vital, the judge should be able to be relied on not to allow his non-compellability to stand in the way of his giving evidence (*Warren v Warren* [1997] QB 488, in which the authorities are reviewed). F9.13

A jury's verdict cannot be impeached by the testimony of a *juror* as to what happened in the jury room. Thus, in *Thompson* [1962] 1 All ER 65, the Court of Criminal Appeal refused to hear evidence that the majority of the jury had been in favour of acquittal until the foreman had produced a list of the appellant's previous convictions which had not been received in evidence. Likewise in *Roads* [1967] 2 QB 108, the Court of Appeal refused to receive affidavit evidence from a juror that she disagreed with the verdict of guilty. See also *Lalchan Nanan v The State* [1986] AC 860 and *Lucas* [1991] Crim LR 844, and compare *Newton* (1912) 7 Cr App R 214, in which a conviction was quashed, where the foreman disclosed to the judge in open court that the jury had decided the case on an impermissible basis. However, misconduct connected with the verdict of a jury may be proved *extrinsically*, for example by the evidence of the officer in charge of the jury or the clerk (*Willmont* (1914) 10 Cr App R 173); and the testimony of a juror may be received as to extraneous matters, i.e. matters extrinsic to the manner in which the verdict was reached and to any occurrence in the jury room (*Hood* [1968] 1 WLR 773).

Sources of Information Contained in Publications

Contempt of Court Act 1981, s. 10 F9.14

> No court may require a person to disclose, nor is any person guilty of contempt of court for refusing to disclose, the source of information contained in a publication for which he is responsible, unless it be established to the satisfaction of the court that disclosure is necessary in the interests of justice or national security or for the prevention of disorder or crime.

Section 10 substitutes for the common-law discretionary protection a rule of law of wide and general application, subject only to the four exceptions specified (*Secretary of State for Defence v Guardian Newspapers Ltd* [1985] AC 339, per Lord Scarman). The section applies to information which has been communicated and received for the purposes of publication, even if it is not 'contained in a publication', because the purpose underlying the statutory protection of sources of information is as much applicable before as after publication (*X Ltd v Morgan-Grampian (Publishers) Ltd* [1991] 1 AC 1 per Lord Bridge of Harwich). It is sufficient, in order to be protected by s. 10, that an order of the court *may*, and not necessarily *will*, result in disclosure of a source of information (*Secretary of State for Defence v Guardian Newspapers Ltd* [1985] AC 339, per Lord Roskill at p. 368). It is a question of fact and not discretion whether an exception applies, and the burden of proof is on the party seeking disclosure (per Lords Diplock and Scarman, at pp. 345 and 364 respectively). Disclosure must be shown to be 'necessary': expediency, however great, will not suffice (per Lord Diplock, at p. 350; *Handmade Films (Productions) Ltd v Express Newspapers plc* [1986] FSR 463). Under s. 10 the judge must first decide whether disclosure is necessary in the interests of justice etc. If he is not so satisfied, he cannot order disclosure; but if he is so satisfied, he must decide whether as a matter of discretion he should order disclosure, which involves weighing the need for disclosure against the need for protection (*John v Express Newspapers plc* [2000] 1 WLR 1931).

F9.15 **Disclosure 'Necessary in the Interests of Justice'** The word 'justice' in the Contempt of Court Act 1981, s. 10, is not used as the antonym of 'injustice', but in the technical sense of the administration of justice in the course of legal proceedings in a court of law or a tribunal, or a body exercising the judicial powers of the state (*Secretary of State for Defence v Guardian Newspapers Ltd* [1985] AC 339, per Lord Diplock at p. 350). It has since been held that the word should not be so confined (see *X Ltd v Morgan Grampian (Publishers) Ltd* [1911] 1 AC 1 below). However, in cases where disclosure is sought for the purposes of legal proceedings, in order to decide whether the exception applies, it is essential first to identify and define the issue in the legal proceedings which requires disclosure, and then to decide whether, looking at the nature of that issue and the circumstances of the case, disclosure is necessary (*Maxwell v Pressdram Ltd* [1987] 1 WLR 298, per Kerr LJ at pp. 308–9). The mere fact that the information in question is relevant to the issue is not sufficient: disclosure must be necessary in the interests of justice (*Maxwell v Pressdram Ltd*, per Parker LJ, at p. 310).

In *X Ltd v Morgan-Grampian (Publishers) Ltd*, the House of Lords agreed with the dictum of Lord Diplock in *Secretary of State for Defence v Guardian Newspapers Ltd* that the word 'justice' is not used as the antonym of 'injustice', but held that the word should not be confined to the technical sense of the administration of justice in the course of legal proceedings in a court of law. It is 'in the interests of justice' that persons should be enabled to exercise important legal rights and to protect themselves from serious legal wrongs whether or not resort to proceedings in a court of law will be necessary to obtain these objectives. This construction emphasises the importance of the balancing exercise. It will not be sufficient, *per se*, for a party seeking disclosure of a source to show merely that he will be unable without disclosure to exercise the legal right or avert the threatened legal wrong. The judge must always weigh in the scales the importance of enabling the ends of justice to be attained in the circumstances of the particular case on the one hand against the importance of protecting the source on the other. It is only if satisfied that disclosure in the interests of justice is of such preponderating importance as to override the statutory privilege against disclosure that the threshold of necessity will be reached. Many factors will be relevant. Lord Bridge of Harwich gave the following illustrations. If the party seeking disclosure shows that his very livelihood depends on it, the case will be near one end of the spectrum; but if he merely seeks to protect a minor interest in property, the case will be at or near the other end of the spectrum. On the other side, one important factor will be the nature of the information obtained: the greater the legitimate public interest in the information, the greater will be the importance of protecting the source. Another perhaps more significant factor is the manner in which the information was obtained by the source: if the information was obtained legitimately this will enhance the importance of protecting the source. Conversely, if the information was obtained illegally, this will diminish the importance of protecting the source unless this factor is counterbalanced by a clear public interest in publication, as when the source has acted to expose iniquity.

Goodwin v UK (1996) 22 EHRR 123, a decision of the European Court of Human Rights, dealt with the same facts as those which were the subject of the decision in *X Ltd v Morgan-Grampian (Publishers) Ltd*, but under the ECHR, Article 10. The tests applied by the European Court and the House of Lords were substantially the same, but the European Court came to a conclusion opposite to that reached by the House of Lords. The explanation may well be that put forward by Thorpe LJ in *Camelot Group plc v Centaur Communications Ltd* [1999] QB 124: the making of a value judgment on competing facts is very close to the exercise of a discretion, and the period of time between the decisions in London and Strasbourg was six years, a period during which standards fundamental to the performance of the balancing exercise may change materially.

Effect of ECHR, Article 10 In *Ashworth Hospital Authority v MGN Ltd* [2001] 1 WLR 515, which concerned the disclosure of confidential medical records to the press, the Court of Appeal considered the proper approach to s. 10 of the Contempt of Court Act 1981 Act in the light of the HRA 1998, s. 3, and the ECHR, Article 10 (see **appendix 6**). The Court held as follows: **F9.16**

(a) Section 10 sets out to give effect to the general requirements of Article 10 in the narrow context of protection of the sources of information of the press. Article 10 permits the right of freedom of expression to be circumscribed where necessary in a democratic society to achieve a number of specified legitimate aims.
(b) The approach to the interpretation of s. 10 should, insofar as possible (i) equate the specific purposes for which disclosure of sources is permitted under s. 10 with 'legitimate aims' under Article 10 and (ii) apply the same test of necessity to that applied by the European Court of Justice when considering Article 10.
(c) The wider interpretation of the 'interests of justice' in *X Ltd v Morgan-Grampian (Publishers) Ltd* [1911] 1 AC 1 (see **F9.15**) accords more happily with the scheme of Article 10 than the interpretation of Lord Diplock in *Secretary of State for Defence v Guardian Newspapers Ltd.* Thus 'interests of justice' in s. 10 means interests that are justiciable. It is difficult to envisage any such interest that would not fall within one or more of the relevant 'legitimate aims' under Article 10.

Affirming the decision, the House of Lords ([2002] 1 WLR 2033) accepted the approach of the European Court in *Goodwin v UK* that, as a matter of general principle, the 'necessity' for any restriction of freedom of expression must be convincingly established and that limits on the confidentiality of journalistic sources call for the most careful scrutiny by the court. It was further held that any restriction of the right to freedom of expression must meet two further requirements: (i) exercise of the disclosure jurisdiction because of Article 10(2) should meet a 'pressing social need' and (ii) the restriction should be proportionate to the legitimate aim which is being pursued.

Material Protected by Legal Professional Privilege It will not inevitably be in the interests of justice to order disclosure of the source of information where the nature of that information suggests that the source has seen material protected by legal professional privilege (*Saunders v Punch Ltd* [1998] 1 WLR 986). In the context of such material it has been held that, before ordering disclosure, the minimum requirement is that the person seeking disclosure has explored other means of identifying the source. It cannot be assumed that it will not be possible to find the source of the information by other means; and when weighing the conflicting public interests involved, it is to be remembered that there is no certainty that ordering a journalist to reveal his sources will be any more successful than the use of other means (*John v Express Newspapers plc* [2000] 1 WLR 1931). **F9.17**

Disclosure 'Necessary for the Prevention of Crime' Concerning the prevention of crime, disclosure will be ordered if shown to be necessary, either for the prevention of crime generally or for the prevention of a particular and identifiable future crime. See *Re an Inquiry under the Company Securities (Insider Dealing) Act 1985* [1988] AC 660. In this case, a journalist who had used confidential price-sensitive information about take-over bids was ordered to disclose his source to inspectors appointed by the Secretary of State to investigate suspected leaks of this kind, on the grounds that they needed the information to expose the leaking of official information and criminal insider trading, and to prevent such behaviour in the future. **F9.18**

However, as in the case of the other exceptions, a claim under this head will succeed only if there is clear and specific evidence of 'necessity'. The party seeking disclosure should adduce evidence on matters such as the extent of his inquiries to identify the sources, whether he referred the matter to the police, and whether criminal investigation is the intended or likely outcome (see *X v Y* [1988] 2 All ER 648).

CONFIDENTIAL BUT NON-PRIVILEGED RELATIONSHIPS

F9.19 At common law no privilege attaches to communications made in confidence except in the case of:

(a) communications between a client and a legal adviser made for the purpose of the obtaining and giving of legal advice; and
(b) communications between a client or his legal adviser and third parties, the dominant purpose of which was preparation for contemplated or pending litigation (see **F9.29** *et seq.*).

Although the courts have an inherent wish to respect the confidences which arise between doctor and patient, bankers and customers etc., if the question to be put to a witness is relevant and necessary in order that justice be done, the witness will be directed to answer (see, e.g., *A-G v Mulholland* [1963] 2 QB 477, per Lord Denning MR at pp. 489–90). Thus, no privilege exists to protect medical records or communications between doctor and patient (*Duchess of Kingston* (1776) 20 St Tr 355; *Gibbons* (1823) 1 C & P 97; *Wheeler v Le Marchant* (1881) 17 Ch D 675, at p. 681; *Hunter v Mann* [1974] QB 767; *McDonald* [1991] Crim LR 122; *Gayle* [1994] Crim LR 679). This remains the case, notwithstanding that the rule is regarded as unsatisfactory and one which the House of Lords has the power to alter (*D v National Society for the Prevention of Cruelty to Children* [1978] AC 171, per Lord Edmund-Davies at pp. 244–5). But see also *K* [1993] Crim LR 281, below. In the case of communications between priest and penitent, there is slender authority in favour of the existence of a privilege: see *Hay* (1860) 2 F & F 4 (in which it was stressed that the priest was asked about a fact and not a communication) and the *obiter dictum* of Best CJ in *Broad v Pitt* (1828) 3 C & P 518: 'I, for one, will never compel a clergyman to disclose communications made to him by a prisoner; but if he chooses to disclose them I shall receive them in evidence.' However, most of such authority as there is, is against the existence of any such privilege (*Normanshaw v Normanshaw* (1893) 69 LT 468; *Wheeler v Le Marchant* (1881) 17 ChD 675, at p. 681; and the authorities cited in Stephen's *Digest of the Law of Evidence* (12th ed.), at p. 220). Similarly, there is no privilege for confidential communications between friends (*Duchess of Kingston's Case* (1776) 20 St Tr 355); or for documents in the possession of an accountant relating to his client's affairs (*Chantrey Martin & Co. v Martin* [1953] 2 QB 286). At common law there is no privilege for journalists who seek to conceal the identities of their sources of information (*A-G v Clough* [1963] 1 QB 773; *A-G v Mulholland* [1963] 2 QB 477). But see now the Contempt of Court Act 1981, s. 10, above. Concerning a court welfare officer's report, the appropriate court may give leave for it to be used in other proceedings if, after evaluating and balancing the need to maintain the confidentiality of the report against the need for its contents to be put in evidence for there to be a fair trial of the action, the court decides that the interests of justice require the confidentiality of the report to be released (*Brown v Matthews* [1990] Ch 662). See also *Elleray* [2003] 2 Cr App R 165: where an offender, during a conversation with a probation officer being held for the purpose of preparing a pre-sentence report, admits to having committed another offence, the prosecution should consider carefully whether it is right to rely on the evidence and should only rely on it if they decide that it is in the public interest to do so. If they do rely on the evidence, the court still has a discretion to exclude it under the PACE 1984, s. 78.

Although at common law no privilege attaches to confidential communications *per se*, in appropriate circumstances a party may be able to rely upon some other head of privilege, such as the privilege which attaches to communications made in the course of matrimonial conciliation (which has also been treated as a limb of public interest immunity: see *D v National Society for the Prevention of Cruelty to Children* [1978] AC 171, per Lords Hailsham and Simon at p. 226 and pp. 236–7 respectively). Alternatively, a claim to public interest immunity may succeed. Thus an interview with a child victim of a sexual offence, which is conducted on a confidential basis for therapeutic purposes, ought not to be disclosed, unless the interests of justice so require, but where the liberty of the subject is an issue and disclosure might be of assistance to an accused, a claim for disclosure will often be strong (*K (T.D.)* (1993) 97 Cr App R 342). Similarly immunity may be claimed for confidential documents relating to abortions carried out under the Abortion Act 1967 (*Morrow v DPP* [1994] Crim LR 58).

In the absence of consent to disclosure by a taxpayer, public interest immunity does attach to documents relating to his tax affairs in the hands of the Inland Revenue, because as a matter of public policy the State should not by compulsory powers obtain information from a citizen for one purpose and then use it for another; but no such immunity attaches to documents held by the taxpayer himself, or his agents, relating to his tax affairs (*Lonrho plc v Fayed (No. 4)* [1994] 1 All ER 870). A claim to public interest immunity may also succeed when the person claiming immunity is exercising a statutory function, the effective performance of which would be impaired by disclosure. See, e.g., *Lonrho Ltd v Shell Petroleum Co. Ltd* [1980] 1 WLR 627 (immunity granted in subsequent litigation for evidence given in confidence to the Bingham Inquiry into the operation of sanctions against Rhodesia) and contrast *Re Arrows Ltd (No. 4)* [1995] 2 AC 75. See also *Re Barlow Clowes Gilt Managers Ltd* [1992] Ch 208. The liquidators of a company are under no duty to assist directors of the company in defending criminal charges, by providing them with information given to the liquidators by third parties in circumstances of confidentiality and by assurances, express or implied, that it would be used only for the purpose of the liquidation. The provision of such information would jeopardise the proper and efficient functioning of the process of compulsory liquidation because of the danger that professional men would no longer cooperate with liquidators on a voluntary basis. However, whether the information in question constitutes 'material evidence' for the purposes of a witness summons is a question for the Crown Court (see further *Clowes* [1992] 3 All ER 440 at **F9.4**). It has also been held, in *Umoh* (1986) 84 Cr App R 138, that although no privilege analogous to that between a lawyer and his client can arise to protect confidential communications about the substance of a legal aid application between a prison legal aid officer and a prisoner, such communications should attract public interest immunity, because a prisoner does not have the freedom to go to a solicitor's office, and if he seeks assistance from such an officer he is likely to disclose and discuss matters connected with the alleged offence. It is in the public interest that such discussions, save in exceptional circumstances, should remain confidential, or otherwise prisoners would be reluctant to take advantage of the scheme.

PRIVILEGED RELATIONSHIPS: GENERAL PRINCIPLES

F9.20 Relevant and otherwise admissible evidence may be excluded on the grounds of either the privilege against self-incrimination (see **F9.21** to **F9.28**) or legal professional privilege (see **F9.29** to **F9.38**). The privilege whereby a married person could refuse to answer questions about communications made to him or her by the spouse during the marriage was abolished for criminal cases by the PACE 1984, s. 80(9) and sch. 7. The privilege whereby, in criminal proceedings, a married person could refuse to answer questions about intercourse with his or her spouse during the marriage, was repealed by s. 80(9) of the 1984 Act.

The following principles are of general application:

(a) A person entitled to claim privilege may refuse to answer the question put or disclose the document sought. The judge should not balance the claim to privilege against the importance of the evidence in relation to the trial. But see *Rank Film Distributors Ltd v Video Information Centre* [1982] AC 380, per Lord Fraser at p. 445.
(b) If a person entitled to claim privilege fails to do so or waives his privilege, no other person may object. The privilege is that of the witness, and neither party can take advantage from it. Thus, if a judge improperly rejects a claim to privilege made by a witness who is not a party to the proceedings, no appeal will lie, for there has been no infringement of the rights of the parties. In *Kinglake* (1870) 11 Cox CC 499, where a claim to privilege made by a prosecution witness on the basis that his evidence would tend to incriminate himself was overruled by the judge, it was not open to the accused to object that the witness's evidence had been improperly admitted.
(c) A party seeking to prove a particular matter in relation to which his opponent or a witness claims privilege, is entitled to prove the matter by other evidence, if available (see **F9.38**).
(d) No adverse inferences may be drawn against a party or witness claiming privilege (*Wentworth v Lloyd* (1864) 10 HL Cas 589).

PRIVILEGE AGAINST SELF-INCRIMINATION

Scope of Privilege

F9.21 Under the Criminal Evidence Act 1898, s. 1(2), 'a person charged in criminal proceedings who is called as a witness in the proceedings may be asked any question in cross-examination notwithstanding that it would tend to criminate him as to any offence with which he is charged in the proceedings'. Subject to s. 1(2), no witness is bound to answer questions in court (or to produce documents or things at trial) if to do so would, in the opinion of the judge, have a tendency to expose him to any criminal charge, penalty or forfeiture (of property) which the judge regards as reasonably likely to be preferred or sued for (*Blunt v Park Lane Hotel Ltd* [1942] 2 KB 253, per Goddard LJ at p. 257). The courts may substitute a different protection in place of the privilege when requiring a person to comply with a disclosure order, provided adequate protection is available, as when the prosecuting authorities unequivocally agree not to make use of the information (*AT&T Istel v Tully* [1993] AC 45). An affidavit sworn by a person in compliance with such an order may then be inadmissible against him in any subsequent criminal trial, but the Crown will not necessarily be prevented from using it to demonstrate his inconsistency and thus to impugn his credit (see *Martin* [1998] 2 Cr App R 385). Penalties arise mainly under statutes relating to the revenue, and under EC regulations (see, e.g., *Rio Tinto Zinc Corporation v Westinghouse Electric Corporation* [1978] AC 547). 'Additional damages', which may be awarded under statutes for breach of copyright, are not penalties (*Rank Film Distributors Ltd v Video Information Centre* [1982] AC 380, at p. 425). A witness may not claim privilege on the basis that his answer to the question put would expose him to civil liability (Witnesses Act 1806). Nor does the privilege extend to answers which would expose the witness to criminal liability under foreign law (*King of the Two Sicilies v Willcox* (1851) 1 Sim NS 301; *Re Atherton* [1912] 2 KB 251, at p. 255). See also *Arab Monetary Fund v Hashim* [1989] 1 WLR 565.

Subject to any statutory exceptions (see **F9.25**), an agent, trustee or other fiduciary of a party may claim the privilege in an action brought against him by that party for breach of that duty (*Bishopsgate Investment Management Ltd v Maxwell* [1993] Ch 1).

Requirement of Real and Appreciable Danger

F9.22 If the fact of the witness being in danger be once made to appear, great latitude should be allowed to him in judging for himself the effect of any particular question, for a question which might appear at first sight a very innocent one, may, by affording a link in the chain of evidence, become the means of bringing home an offence to the witness. Subject to this reservation, the court, before acceding to a claim to privilege, should satisfy itself, from the circumstances of the case and the nature of the evidence which the witness is called to give, that there is a reasonable ground to apprehend real and appreciable danger to the witness with reference to the ordinary operation of the law in the ordinary course of things, and not a danger of an imaginary or insubstantial character. See *Boyes* (1861) 1 B & S 311, per Cockburn CJ. In *R (CPS)* v *Bolton Magistrates' Court* [2004] 1 WLR 835, the Divisional Court, citing with approval the foregoing text, held that it is not sufficient to ascertain that the claim was made on legal advice. The duty of the court is non-delegable: the court cannot simply adopt the conclusion of a solicitor advising the witness, whose conclusion may or may not be correct. In refusing protection, it seems that the court may also take into account the triviality of any charge likely to be brought. In *Rank Film Distributors Ltd v Video Information Centre* [1982] AC 380, a case concerning the application of the privilege to an *Anton Piller* order, Lord Fraser held (at p. 445) that protection should be refused, partly because the likelihood of prosecution under the Copyright Act 1956, s. 21, was too remote, but also because it would be 'unreasonable to allow the possibility of incrimination of such offences to obstruct disclosure of information which would be of much more value to the owners of the infringed copyright than any protection they might obtain from s. 21.' Protection may also be properly refused if the evidence against the witness is already so strong that, if proceedings are to be taken, they will be taken whether or not the witness answers: see, e.g., *Khan v Khan* [1982] 1 WLR 513, where the witness's conduct 'reeked of dishonesty', and evidence as to his use of the proceeds of a stolen cheque did not materially increase the risk of his prosecution for its theft.

Incrimination Must Be of Person Claiming Privilege

In criminal cases, the privilege against self-incrimination is restricted to the person claiming it, and does not extend to questions the answers to which would tend to incriminate a spouse: see *Rio Tinto Zinc Corporation v Westinghouse Electric Corporation* [1978] AC 547, per Lord Diplock at p. 637, and *Pitt* [1983] QB 25, where the Court of Appeal, in holding that an accused's spouse, if she elects to testify, should be treated like any other witness, surely must have assumed that she cannot then claim privilege against the incrimination of her husband; and contrast *All Saints, Worcester (Inhabitants)* (1817) 6 M & S 194, per Bayley J at p. 201. There is no privilege against incriminating strangers (*Minihane* (1921) 16 Cr App R 38). A company may claim privilege in the same way as an individual (*Triplex Safety Glass Co. Ltd v Lancegaye Safety Glass (1934) Ltd* [1939] 2 KB 395). However, the privilege is that of the company and therefore does not extend to incrimination of its office holders (see *Rio Tinto Zinc Corporation v Westinghouse Electric Corporation* per Lord Diplock at pp. 637–8; *Sociedade Nacional de Combustiveis de Angola UEE v Lundqvist* [1991] 2 QB 310 per Beldam LJ at p. 336; and *Tate Access Floors Inc. v Boswell* [1991] Ch 512). **F9.23**

Necessity of Claiming Privilege

A witness may claim the privilege only after he has been sworn and the question put; he is not entitled to refuse to take the oath on the grounds of the privilege (*Boyle v Wiseman* (1855) 1 Exch 647). Although in practice a judge will often warn a witness of his right not to answer a question which might expose him to a criminal charge, in the absence of such a warning, the witness must claim the privilege himself (*Thomas v Newton* (1827) 2 C & P 606). The witness may claim the privilege at any stage of the proceedings, even if he has already answered, without objection, questions which he was not obliged to answer (*Garbett* (1847) 1 Den CC 236). If the witness answers without seeking the protection of the court, his answers may be used in the proceedings in question and in any subsequent criminal proceedings brought against him (*Sloggett* (1856) Dears CC 656; *Coote* (1873) LR 4 PC 599). However, if a judge **F9.24** wrongly denies a witness the protection of privilege, anything the witness is then compelled to say is treated as having been said involuntarily and will be excluded from the subsequent criminal proceedings (*Garbett* (1847) 1 Den CC 236).

Statutory Provisions Requiring Answers to Questions

F9.25 **General** Various statutes and statutory instruments require specified persons in specified circumstances to answer questions or produce documents or information notwithstanding that compliance may incriminate them. Some such provisions abrogate the privilege against self-incrimination impliedly, on the grounds that they would otherwise be largely ineffective (see, e.g., *Bank of England v Riley* [1992] Ch 475, *Re London United Investments plc* [1992] Ch 578 and *Bishopsgate Investment Management Ltd v Maxwell* [1993] Ch 1). In deciding as a matter of construction, under English domestic law, whether such a provision does impliedly abrogate the privilege, the court must consider on the one hand the public interest in obtaining the information, and on the other the 'right to silence' to be affected and the strength of the grounds for preserving it, looking at whether the request forms a part or preliminary part of criminal proceedings, and therefore touches on the rules which prohibit interrogation without caution or after charge, or amounts to a potential abuse of investigatory powers which those rules are designed to prevent (*Hertfordshire County Council, ex parte Green Environmental Industries Ltd* [2000] 2 AC 412). As to the further question whether implied abrogation would amount to a violation of the right to a fair trial under the ECHR, Article 6, under the European jurisprudence the impact of Article 6 is confined to the use of answers in evidence at a criminal trial and is not concerned with extra-judicial inquiries: see *Saunders v United Kingdom* (1997) 23 EHRR 313 at p. 337 (examination by inspectors appointed by the Secretary of State under the Companies Act 1985), *Hertfordshire County Council, ex parte Green Environmental Industries Ltd* (a local authority request for information under the Environmental Protection Act 1990), *Kearns* [2002] 1 WLR 2815 (a demand by the Official Receiver to see a bankrupt's accounting records) and *Brady* [2004] 3 All ER 520 (a requirement by the Official Receiver for information relating to insolvent companies subsequently disclosed to the Inland Revenue for the purpose of investigating possible offences of cheating the public revenue and laying information to obtain search warrants).

Provisions which expressly abrogate the privilege against self-incrimination, typically go on to prevent the answers from being used against the person who answered the question in criminal proceedings in which he is charged with a specified offence. Some examples follow.

F9.26 **Examples** Under the Theft Act 1968, s. 31(1), which requires questions to be answered and orders to be complied with in proceedings for the recovery or administration of any property or dealing with property, notwithstanding that compliance may expose the witness or his spouse to a charge for an offence under the Theft Act 1968, the answers may not be used in proceedings for any such offence. Neither the revocation of the privilege nor the restriction on the use of the answers applies to non-Theft Act offences (*Sociedade Nacional de Combustiveis de Angola UEE v Lundqvist* [1991] 2 WLR 280). However, where to answer the question etc. would expose the relevant person to an offence under the Theft Act 1968 and he claims that it would also expose him to a non-Theft Act offence, the test concerning the latter offence is whether to answer the question etc. would create or increase the risk of proceedings for that offence, separate and distinct from its connection with the Theft Act offence. If the answer is no, there is no privilege, but if it is yes, then the privilege subsists in relation to the latter offence (*Renworth v Stephansen* [1996] 3 All ER 244).

Under the Supreme Court Act 1981, s. 72, whereby the privilege is withdrawn in various proceedings relating to apprehended or actual infringement of rights pertaining to any intellectual property or any apprehended or actual passing off, s. 72(3) provides that answers compelled by reason of such withdrawal of privilege cannot be used in proceedings for certain offences disclosed or for the recovery of certain penalties, liability to which was disclosed.

Under the Children Act 1989, s. 98, in any proceedings in which a court is hearing an application relating to the care, supervision or protection of a child, no one shall be excused from giving evidence on any matter or answering any question put in the course of his giving evidence on the grounds that to do so might incriminate him or his spouse of an offence. Under s. 98(2), a statement or admission made in such proceedings shall not be admissible in evidence against the person making it or his spouse in proceedings for an offence other than perjury. A 'statement or admission', for these purposes, includes a filed statement of the evidence which a party intends to adduce at the hearing, an oral admission made by a parent to a guardian ad litem (*Oxfordshire County Council v P* [1995] Fam 161) and, after the proceedings have started, an oral statement to a social worker carrying out the local authority's duties of investigation in a child protection case (*Cleveland County Council v F* [1995] 1 WLR 785). Both of these decisions, however, have since been doubted (see *Re G (A Minor) (Social Worker: Disclosure)* [1996] 1 WLR 1407).

Under the CJA 1987, s. 2, the Director of the SFO may require someone under investigation for a suspected offence involving serious or complex fraud, or anyone else, to answer questions etc., but a statement in response to such a requirement may be used against its maker only on a prosecution:

(a) for making a false or misleading statement in purported compliance with a requirement under s. 2, or
(b) for some other offence if, in giving evidence, he makes a statement inconsistent with it, and evidence relating to it is adduced, or a question relating to it is asked, by him or on his behalf.

However, it would appear that a statement previously made by an accused in response to questions under the CJA 1987, s. 2, can be used by a *co-accused*, provided it is relevant to his defence, and if this infringes the accused's right to a fair trial, he should be severed from the indictment: see *Wickes*, unreported, NLJ, 25 July 2003, p. 1140.

Under the Companies Act 1985, officers of a company and others possessing relevant information are required to answer questions put by Board of Trade inspectors investigating suspected fraud in the conduct or management of a company, but under s. 434(5A) and (5B) of the Act, in criminal proceedings in which a person who complied with such a requirement is charged with an offence (other than an offence under the Perjury Act 1911, s. 2 or s. 5), no evidence relating to the answer may be adduced and no question relating to it may be asked by or on behalf of the prosecution unless evidence relating to it is adduced, or a question relating to it is asked, by or on behalf of the person charged. For other similar statutory provisions, see the YJCEA 1999, s. 59 and sch. 3.

If a statute revokes the privilege without *any* restriction upon the use that may be made of the answers, the answers will not be treated as having been given involuntarily and may be used in any subsequent criminal proceedings (*Scott* (1856) Dears & B 47). Such use will not invariably amount to a violation of Article 6. In *Brown v Stott* [2003] 1 AC 681, the Privy Council held that at a trial for driving after consuming excess alcohol contrary to the Road Traffic Act 1988, s. 5(1)(a), the introduction of evidence of an admission obtained from the accused under s. 172(2)(a) of the 1988 Act (see **C2.15**) did not infringe her right to a fair hearing under Article 6. Lord Bingham said:

> The jurisprudence of the European Court very clearly establishes that while the overall fairness of a criminal trial cannot be compromised, the constituent rights comprised, whether expressly or implicitly, within Article 6 are not themselves absolute. Limited qualification of these rights is acceptable if reasonably directed by national authorities towards a clear and proper public objective and if representing no greater qualification than the situation calls for.

It was held that there was a clear public interest in enforcement of road traffic legislation and that s. 172, properly applied, did not represent a disproportionate response to this serious social problem. Two main reasons were given:

(a) Section 172 provides for the putting of a single, simple question, the answer to which cannot of itself incriminate the suspect. The penalty for declining to answer the question is moderate and non-custodial. If there were evidence of improper coercion or oppression, the trial judge would have ample power to exclude the evidence.
(b) All who own or drive motor cars know that by doing so they subject themselves to a regulatory regime because the possession and use of cars have the potential to cause grave injury.

Brown v Stott was applied in *Mawdesley v Chief Constable of the Cheshire Constabulary* [2004] 1 WLR 1035 on a charge of driving in excess of the speed limit. The court rejected the argument that it is disproportionate to admit an answer to a s. 172 request in a speeding case, albeit not in a drink-driving case.

In *Allen (No. 2)* [2001] 4 All ER 768, a case of cheating the public revenue of tax, the appellant had provided a schedule of assets in compliance with a notice given by an inspector under the Taxes Management Act 1970, s. 20. A person who fails to comply with such a notice is liable to a penalty (s. 98(1) of the 1970 Act). The House of Lords rejected an argument that the appellant, having been compelled under threat of penalty to incriminate himself, had been denied the right to a fair trial given by the ECHR, Article 6(1). It was held that since the State, for the purpose of collecting tax, is entitled to require a citizen to inform it of his income and to enforce penalties for failure to do so, the s. 20 notice could not constitute a violation of the right against self-incrimination. Allen's application to the European Court of Human Rights was unsuccessful. It was held that the requirement that he declare his assets to the tax authorities did not disclose any issue under Article 6(1), even though there was a penalty for failure to comply. The charge was one of making a false declaration of assets — it was not an example of forced self-incrimination in relation to some previously committed offence (*Allen v United Kingdom* [2003] Crim LR 280; but see also *JB v Switzerland* [2001] Crim LR 748).

F9.27 **Free-standing Material Not Created under Compulsion** In *Saunders v United Kingdom* (1997) 23 EHRR 313, according to the judgment of the majority of the court, the right not to incriminate oneself is primarily concerned with respecting the will of an accused to remain silent and, as understood in Convention countries and elsewhere, it does not extend to the use in criminal proceedings of material obtained by compulsion which has an existence independent of the will of the suspect, such as documents acquired pursuant to a warrant, breath, blood and urine samples, and bodily tissue for the purposes of DNA testing. See also *L v United Kingdom* [2000] 2 FLR 322 and cf. *Funke v France* (1993) 16 EHRR 297 and *Heaney and McGuinness v Ireland* (2001) 33 EHRR 264. This distinction was approved in *A-G's Reference (No. 7 of 2000)* [2001] 1 WLR 1879 in which a bankrupt delivered up to the Official Receiver, pursuant to the duty imposed by the Insolvency Act 1986, s. 291, various documents relating to his estate and affairs, including documents relating to his gambling activities. Under s. 291(6), if he had failed to comply with this duty, he would have been in contempt of court and liable to imprisonment. He was subsequently charged with an offence contrary to s. 362(1)(a) of the 1986 Act, namely material contribution to his insolvency by gambling. The Court of Appeal held that use by the prosecution of the documents relating to his gambling activities would not violate his rights under Article 6. Under domestic law, the documents were admissible in law, subject to the discretion to exclude under s. 78. As to the European jurisprudence, the court approved the distinction made in *Saunders* and did so for the reasons advanced by Justice La Forest in *Thomson Newspapers Ltd v Director of Investigation & Research* (1990) 54 CCC 417 (Supreme Court of Canada), namely that, whereas a compelled statement is evidence that simply would not have existed independently of the exercise of the power of compulsion, evidence which exists independently of the compelled statement could have been found by other means and its quality does not depend on its past connection with the compelled statement. Insofar as there was a difference of view between *Funke* and *Saunders*, the court preferred the approach in *Saunders*. The same principle was applied in *Hundal* [2004] 2 Cr App R 307.

C plc v P [2007] EWCA Civ 493 concerned intellectual property proceedings in which indecent images of children were found on a computer which was the subject of a search order. The Court of Appeal held that the offending material was not privileged from disclosure to the police. A majority of the court regarded itself as bound by *A-G's Reference (No. 7 of 2000)* to reach this conclusion, on the basis that if, in that case, the privilege did not extend to documents which were independent evidence, the same must apply to things which existed independently of a search order. The case was thought to be no different from one in which counterfeit bags of a particular brand, being the subject of a search order, are found to contain drugs or an illegal weapon.

Production Orders under PACE 1984, s. 9 In *R (Bright) v Central Criminal Court* [2001] 1 WLR 662, the majority view was that a trial judge, in his discretion, may make production orders under the PACE 1984, s. 9 (see **D1.84**), even though the subject of the order may incriminate himself by handing over the material. If the subject of the order is prosecuted, the trial judge may consider the ECHR, Article 6 and whether to exclude the evidence under the PACE 1984, s. 78. **F9.28**

LEGAL PROFESSIONAL PRIVILEGE

Scope of Privilege

A client may, and his legal adviser must (subject to the client's waiver), refuse to give oral evidence or to produce documents relating to two types of confidential communication: **F9.29**

(a) communications between the client and his legal adviser made for the purpose of enabling the client to obtain or the adviser to give legal advice about any matter, whether or not litigation was contemplated at the time (*Greenough v Gaskell* (1833) 1 My & K 98); and
(b) communications between the client or his legal adviser and third parties, the sole or dominant purpose of which was to enable the legal adviser to advise or act in relation to litigation that was pending or in the contemplation of the client (*Waugh v British Railways Board* [1980] AC 521).

The privilege also covers items enclosed with or referred to in such communications and brought into existence (i) in connection with the giving of legal advice or (ii) in connection with or in contemplation of legal proceedings and for the purposes of such proceedings: see *R* [1994] 1 WLR 758 and the PACE 1984, s. 10(1)(c). Section 10, which is considered at **F9.34** and **F9.36**, purports to reflect the position at common law.

In *R (Morgan Grenfell & Co Ltd) v Special Commissioner of Income Tax* [2003] 1 AC 563, Lord Hoffmann said (at [7]–[8]):

> Legal professional privilege is a fundamental human right long established in the common law. It is a necessary corollary of the right of any person to obtain skilled advice about the law. Such advice cannot be effectively obtained unless the client is able to put all the facts before the advisor without fear that they may afterwards be disclosed and used to his prejudice. . . . It has been held by the European Court of Human Rights to be part of the right of privacy guaranteed by [the ECHR] Article 8 . . . the courts will ordinarily construe general words in a statute, although literally capable of having some startling or unreasonable consequence, such as overriding fundamental human rights, as not having been intended to do so. An intention to override such rights must be expressly stated or appear by necessary implication.

In that case, it was held that, on its true construction, the Taxes Management Act 1970, s. 20(1), does not entitle an inspector of taxes to require a tax payer to deliver up material that is subject to legal professional privilege. As to the meaning of 'necessary implication', see further *B v Auckland District Law Society* [2003] 2 AC 736. See also *Robinson* [2003] Crim LR 285, in which it was held, *per curiam*, that use of a clerk in a solicitor's office as an informant was not only a serious breach of an accused's right to communicate confidentially with a legal adviser under the seal of legal professional privilege but, on the face of it, and if encouraged by the police, an infringement by them of the accused's rights.

A legal adviser, for the purposes of legal professional privilege, includes, in addition to a solicitor or a barrister, employed advisers (*Alfred Crompton Amusement Machines Ltd v Customs and Excise Commissioners (No. 2)* [1974] AC 405) and overseas advisers (*Re Duncan* [1968] P 306).

Legal Advice Privilege

F9.30 The privilege, in the case of communications between a client and his legal adviser is known as 'legal advice privilege'. The law relating to legal advice privilege is in a state of great flux. It is clear that communications must have been made either in the course of that relationship or with a view to its establishment (*Minter v Priest* [1930] AC 558). The privilege extends to instructions given by the client to the solicitor or by the solicitor to the barrister and to counsel's opinion taken by a solicitor (*Bristol Corporation v Cox* (1884) 26 ChD 678). However, documents emanating from, or prepared by, independent third parties and passed to the lawyer for the purposes of advice are not privileged. In *Three Rivers District Council v Governor and Company of the Bank of England (No. 5)* [2003] QB 1556 it was held that legal advice privilege protects only direct communications between the client and the lawyer and evidence of the content of such communications, and that in the case of a corporate client the privilege covers only communications with those officers or employees expressly designated to act as 'the client'. The privilege will not extend to documents prepared by other employees or ex-employees, even if they were prepared with the dominant purpose of obtaining legal advice, prepared at the lawyer's request, or sent to the lawyer.

The leading authority is *Three Rivers District Council v Governor and Company of the Bank of England (No. 6)* [2005] 1 AC 610. The House of Lords held that the policy basis for legal advice privilege is that it is necessary, in a society in which the restraining and controlling framework was built on a belief in the rule of law, that communications between clients and lawyers, whereby the clients are hoping for the assistance of the lawyers' legal skills in the management of their affairs, should be secure against the possibility of any scrutiny from others. Lord Scott accepted as correct the approach of Taylor LJ in *Balabel v Air India* [1988] Ch 317 at pp. 330–1, where he said that for the purpose of attracting legal advice privilege 'legal advice is not confined to telling the client the law; it must include advice as to what should prudently and sensibly be done in the relevant legal context' but that 'to extend privilege without limit to all solicitor and client communications upon matters within the ordinary business of a solicitor and referable to that relationship [would be] too wide'. Lord Scott said that if a solicitor became the client's 'man of business', responsible for advising him on matters such as investment and finance policy and other business matters, the advice might lack a relevant legal context. The judge would have to ask whether it related to the rights, liabilities, obligations or remedies of the client under either private or public law, and, if so, whether the communication fell within the policy underlying the justification for the privilege, the criterion being an objective one.

Legal advice privilege does not cover records of time spent with a client on attendance notes, time sheets or fee records, because they are not communications between client and legal adviser, or records of appointments, because they are not communications made in connection with legal advice (*Manchester Crown Court, ex parte Rogers* [1999] 1 WLR 832). Nor does it cover a lawyer's records of a client's telephone numbers and of the dates when the client telephoned the lawyer (*R (Miller Gardner Solicitors) v Minshull Street Crown Court* [2002] EWHC 3077 (Admin)). Equally, the privilege does not cover attendance notes made by a solicitor recording what took place in court or in chambers in the presence of the parties on both sides (*Ainsworth v Wilding* [1900] 2 Ch 315); nor does it cover attendance notes recording meetings between the legal advisers of the parties on both sides (with or without their clients in attendance) or attendance notes recording telephone conversations between the parties, because all such notes are not communications between solicitor and client but merely records setting out what passed publicly between the two parties or their advisers (*Parry v News Group Newspapers Ltd* (1990) 140 NLJ 1719). The privilege attaches to communications between the client and his legal adviser for the purposes of obtaining and giving legal advice, and not to *facts* perceived by the legal adviser in the course of that relationship. Thus a solicitor may generally be compelled to give evidence as to his client's identity (*Studdy v Sanders* (1823) 2 Dow & Ry KB 347). In *R (Howe) v South Durham Magistrates' Court* [2005] RTR 55, it was held that a solicitor present in court when an order had been made disqualifying a person from driving could be compelled in a subsequent prosecution to give evidence as to the identity of that person and to produce attendance notes in relation to the disqualification (with anything in the notes attracting privilege blacked out). Equally, a solicitor may be compelled to give evidence as to his client's handwriting (*Dwyer v Collins* (1852) 7 Exch 639) or mental capacity (*James v Godrich* (1844) 5 Moore PCC 16). See also *Brown v Foster* (1857) 1 H & N 736: a barrister who has seen a book produced at his client's trial may give evidence in subsequent proceedings as to its contents.

Litigation Privilege

The privilege, in the case of communications with third parties, is known as 'litigation privilege'. Litigation privilege covers communications between a client or his lawyer and third parties, the sole or dominant purpose of which was to enable the lawyer to advise or act in relation to pending or contemplated litigation. The privilege covers documents created by a party for the purpose of instructing the lawyer and obtaining his advice in the conduct of the litigation (*Anderson v Bank of British Columbia* (1876) 2 Ch D 644, per James LJ at p. 656), but not documents obtained by a party or his adviser for the purpose of litigation that were not created for that purpose (*Ventouris v Mountain* [1991] 1 WLR 607). A copy or translation of an unprivileged document in the control of a party does not become privileged merely because the copy or translation was made for the purpose of the litigation (see, in the case of copies, *Dubai Bank Ltd v Galadari* [1990] Ch 98 and, in the case of translations, *Sumitomo Corp v Credit Lyonnais Rouse Ltd* [2002] 1 WLR 479). However, privilege will attach to a copy of an unprivileged document if the copy was made for the purpose of litigation and the original is not, and has not at any time been, in the control of the party claiming privilege (*The Palermo* (1883) 9 PD 6 and *Watson v Cammell Laird & Co. (Shipbuilders & Engineers) Ltd* [1959] 1 WLR 702). Privilege will also attach where a solicitor has copied or assembled a selection of third-party documents for the purposes of litigation, if its production will betray the trend of the advice he is giving his client (*Lyell v Kennedy (No. 3)* (1884) 27 Ch D 1), but this principle does not extend to a selection of own client documents, or copies or translations representing the fruits of such a selection, made for the purposes of litigation (*Sumitomo Corp v Credit Lyonnais Rouse Ltd*, overruling *Dubai Bank Ltd v Galadari (No. 7)* [1992] 1 WLR 106). F9.31

The dominant purpose for which a document was brought into existence should be ascertained by an objective view of all the evidence, taking into account the intention of not only its author, but also the person or authority under whose direction it was procured (*Guinness Peat Properties Ltd v Fitzroy Robinson Partnership* [1987] 1 WLR 1027). However, it should be noted that in *Secretary of State for Trade and Industry v Baker* [1998] Ch 356, Sir Richard Scott

V-C doubted the correctness of the decisions in both *Re Highgrade Traders Ltd* and *Guinness Peat Properties Ltd v Fitzroy Robinson Partnership.*

If a client communicates with a lawyer via a third party who is not merely an agent for communication, but someone who also has to make a preliminary decision on whether to refer the matter to the lawyer, no privilege will attach to the information supplied to the third party (*Jones v Great Central Railway Co.* [1910] AC 4).

Legal professional privilege survives the death of a client and vests in his or her personal representative or, once administration is complete, the person entitled to the deceased's estate. Such persons, therefore, are entitled to either claim or waive the privilege (*Molloy (Deceased)* [1997] 2 Cr App R 283).

Effect of Rules Governing Disclosure of Expert Evidence

F9.32 The common-law principles relating to communications with third parties must now be read subject to the CrimPR, parts 24 (disclosure of expert evidence) and 33 (expert evidence) (see **D14.73**, **F10.25** to **F10.27**, and **appendix 1**, where the rules are set out). These rules make provision, subject to exceptions, for the disclosure of expert evidence between the parties to Crown Court and summary trials. Under r. 24.3, a party who seeks to adduce expert evidence and who fails to comply with the requirements as to disclosure, shall not adduce that evidence in the proceedings without the leave of the court. Rule 24.3 does not *compel* disclosure: if an expert's report is unhelpful to the party obtaining it, he need not disclose it to his opponent, and the opponent cannot require him, his solicitor or the expert to give evidence as to the instructions given to the expert or the report he prepared. The expert may, however, be called by the opponent to give evidence of facts he has observed and of his opinion on those facts (*Harmony Shipping Co. SA v Saudi Europe Line Ltd* [1979] 1 WLR 1380, applied in *King* [1983] 1 WLR 411), unless his opinion is based on examination of an item which is itself privileged because it was brought into existence for the purpose of obtaining legal advice etc. (*R* [1994] 1 WLR 758, at **F9.34**) or his opinion is inextricably dependent, or based to a material extent, on other privileged material such as communications with an accused (*Davies* (2002) 166 JP 243).

Pre-existing Documents and Items

F9.33 At common law, a legal adviser (or third party) has no greater privilege than his client. Thus, a document that is not privileged in the hands of the client does not become privileged if given into the custody of a lawyer for the purposes of obtaining legal advice (or if sent by the lawyer to a third party in connection with pending or contemplated litigation). In *Peterborough Justice, ex parte Hicks* [1977] 1 WLR 1371, in which the client had sent a forged document to his solicitor for the purposes of obtaining legal advice, a warrant was ordered under the Forgery Act 1913, s. 16, to search the solicitor's premises and seize the document. On an application for certiorari to quash the search warrant, it was held that the document was not privileged in the hands of the solicitor because it would have been open to seizure in the hands of the client. Eveleigh J said (at p. 1374): '. . . it is the privilege of the client . . . . the solicitor holds the document in the right of his client and can assert in respect of its seizure no greater authority than the client himself . . . possesses.' In *Frank Truman Export Ltd v Metropolitan Police Commissioner* [1977] QB 952, Swanwick J expressed views to the contrary, but these dicta were doubted in *King* [1983] 1 WLR 411. In *King*, a case of conspiracy to defraud, an expert instructed by the defence was subpoenaed to produce sample handwriting sent to him by the accused's solicitors for examination (although the instructions sent to him and the report he produced were held to be privileged). But see also *R* [1994] 4 All ER 260, discussed below.

F9.34 **PACE 1984, ss. 9 and 10** The principle established in *Peterborough Justice, ex parte Hicks* [1977] 1 WLR 1371 must now be read subject to the provisions of the PACE 1984. Section

9(2)(a) of the 1984 Act repeals previous legislation insofar as it authorised, by the issue of a warrant, searches for, *inter alia*, 'items subject to legal privilege' and 'special procedure material'. Section 8 of the 1984 Act provides for the issue of warrants of entry and search if, *inter alia*, a justice of the peace is satisfied that the material sought does not consist of or include 'items subject to legal privilege' or 'special procedure material'. Unless 'special procedure material' has been voluntarily disclosed by the person who acquired or created it (see *Singleton* [1995] 1 Cr App R 431), under s. 9(1), a constable may obtain access to such material for the purposes of a criminal investigation by making an application *inter partes* on notice to a circuit judge. Under s. 14(2), 'special procedure material', includes material, other than items subject to legal privilege, in the possession of a person who acquired or created it in the course of any trade, business, profession etc. and holds it subject to an express or implied undertaking to hold it in confidence. The phrase 'items subject to legal privilege' is defined in s. 10 of the Act, which, it has been held, is intended to reflect the position at common law (see the majority view in *Central Criminal Court, ex parte Francis* [1989] AC 346, at **F9.36**).

Police and Criminal Evidence Act 1984, s. 10

(1) Subject to subsection (2) below, in this Act 'items subject to legal privilege' means—
(a) communications between a professional legal adviser and his client or any person representing his client made in connection with the giving of legal advice to the client;
(b) communications between a professional legal adviser and his client or any person representing his client or between such an adviser or his client or any such representative and any other person made in connection with or in contemplation of legal proceedings and for the purposes of such proceedings; and
(c) items enclosed with or referred to in such communications and made—
(i) in connection with the giving of legal advice; or
(ii) in connection with or in contemplation of legal proceedings and for the purposes of such proceedings,
when they are in the possession of a person who is entitled to possession of them.

(2) Items held with the intention of furthering a criminal purpose are not items subject to legal privilege.

In *Guildhall Magistrates' Court, ex parte Primlaks Holdings Co. (Panama) Inc.* [1990] 1 QB 261, it was held that loss of legal privilege by virtue of s. 10(2) does not mean that no express or implied undertaking to hold in confidence can exist. A solicitor's correspondence with his client (and its enclosures) will, if not privileged, fall squarely within s. 14. Thus if, on an application under s. 8, a justice cannot be satisfied that there are reasonable grounds for believing that the material sought does not include any items which are, prima facie, subject to legal privilege or any material which is, prima facie, special procedure material, he should refuse the application and leave the applicant to proceed under s. 9 so that the matter can be fully ventilated before a circuit judge, who will consider the matter *inter partes*. Likewise if the police are aware that what they seek includes items which are, prima facie, the subject of legal privilege, they should proceed under s. 9. It was further observed (at pp. 273–4) that documents of a client sent to a professional legal adviser under cover of privileged correspondence for the purpose of obtaining legal advice would not be within s. 10(1)(c) if they were pre-existing documents and were not made in connection with the giving of legal advice or in connection with or in contemplation of legal proceedings and for the purposes of such proceedings; but such pre-existing documents would be, prima facie, within s. 14(2), and therefore it would be open to the police to make an application under s. 9 of the Act in order to have access to them. However, a document forged by a solicitor or supplied to him by a fraudulent client does not constitute special procedure material because, from its nature, it could not have been acquired or created in the course of the profession of a solicitor (*Leeds Magistrates' Court, ex parte Dumbleton* [1993] Crim LR 866).

In *R* [1994] 1 WLR 758 it was held that the word 'made' in s. 10(1)(c) is used in a general sense and is wide enough to include the meaning 'brought into existence'. It was also held that where an item is protected from production under s. 10(1)(c), oral evidence of opinion based upon the item is also inadmissible. A scientist had carried out DNA tests at the request of the defence solicitors on a blood sample provided by the accused. It was held that s. 10(1)(c) applied not only so as to enable the defence to object to the sample being produced in evidence (because the sample was an item brought into existence for the purposes of legal proceedings), but also so as to prevent the prosecution from calling the scientist to give evidence of opinion based on the sample.

Information Helpful in Establishing Innocence

F9.35 In *Derby Magistrates' Court, ex parte B* [1996] AC 487 the appellant was acquitted of murder. His step-father was subsequently charged with the murder and at his committal proceedings, the appellant was called as a prosecution witness. Counsel for the defence sought to cross-examine the appellant on certain factual instructions that he had given to his solicitors when he had been charged with the offence. The appellant declined to waive his privilege. The magistrates then issued summonses, directing the appellant and his solicitor to produce documentary evidence of the instructions, on the basis that the public interest that all relevant and admissible evidence should be made available to the defence outweighed the public interest which protected confidential communications between a solicitor and a client. An application for judicial review of the decision was refused, but the House of Lords allowed the appeal. It was held that no exception should be allowed to the absolute and permanent nature of 'legal professional privilege' (a phrase used to refer to the privilege attaching to the solicitor-client relationship and not to all other forms of legal professional privilege: see *Re L (A Minor) (Police Investigation: Privilege)* [1997] AC 16) and therefore, overruling *Barton* [1973] 1 WLR 115 and *Ataou* [1988] 2 All ER 321, there could be no question of a balancing exercise of the kind performed by the magistrates. A client must be sure that what he tells his lawyer in confidence will never be revealed without his consent. Once any exception to the general rule is allowed, the client's confidence is necessarily lost. Therefore the documents in question, being protected by legal professional privilege, were immune from production. However, Lord Nicholls, who also rejected any question of a balancing exercise, observed that in cases where the client no longer has any interest in maintaining the privilege, the privilege is spent. His lordship preferred to reserve his final view on the point, being of the opinion that the point did not arise since the appellant had a legitimate interest in not disclosing material which might suggest that he had been improperly acquitted, but in a dictum which, it is submitted, has much to commend it, said (at p. 701):

> I would not expect a law, based explicitly on considerations of the public interest, to protect the right of a client when he has no interest in asserting the right and the enforcement of the right would be seriously prejudicial to another in defending a criminal charge or in some other way.

Communications in Furtherance of Crime or Fraud

F9.36 Communications in furtherance of crime or fraud are a well-recognised exception to the principle of legal professional privilege (*Derby Magistrates' Court, ex parte B* [1996] AC 487, per Lord Lloyd at p. 509). In *Cox* (1884) 14 QBD 153 a solicitor was compelled to disclose communications with the accused, in which the accused had sought his advice in drawing up a bill of sale alleged to be fraudulent. Stephen J, delivering the judgment of the Court for Crown Cases Reserved, held that if a client applies to a legal adviser for advice intended to facilitate or to guide the client in the commission of a crime or fraud, the legal adviser being ignorant of the purpose for which his advice is sought, the communication between the two is not privileged. See also *Hayward* (1846) 2 Car & Kir 234 and *Smith* (1915) 11 Cr App R 229. The principle can be relied upon only if there is prima facie evidence that it was the client's intention to obtain advice in furtherance of his criminal or fraudulent purpose

(*O'Rourke v Darbishire* [1920] AC 581). However, in order to prove the criminal purpose and override the claim to privilege, there is no requirement to produce extraneous evidence, i.e. beyond the communications themselves; if necessary, the court may look at the communications themselves to determine whether they came into existence in furtherance of such a purpose (*Governor of Pentonville Prison, ex parte Osman* [1990] 1 WLR 277 at pp. 309–10). The exception does apply if the legal adviser is aware of or is a party to the crime or fraud, but not if he merely volunteers a warning to his client that certain conduct could result in his being prosecuted (*Butler v Board of Trade* [1971] Ch 680). Fraud, for the purposes of the exception, is not limited to the tort of deceit, and includes all forms of fraud and dishonesty, such as fraudulent breach of trust, fraudulent conspiracy, trickery and sham contrivances, but does not cover the tort of inducing a breach of contract (*Crescent Farm (Sidcup) Sports Ltd v Sterling Offices Ltd* [1972] Ch 553, per Goff J at p. 565) or the torts of trespass and conversion (*Dubai Aluminium Co. Ltd v Al Alawi* [1999] 1 WLR 1964). 'Fraud', in this context, is used in a relatively wide sense. Thus privilege will not attach to legal advice on how to structure a transaction which has been devised to prejudice the interests of a creditor by putting assets beyond his reach (*Barclays Bank Plc v Eustice* [1995] 1 WLR 1238).

The exception is not confined to cases in which solicitors advise on or set up criminal or fraudulent transactions yet to be undertaken, but also covers criminal or fraudulent conduct undertaken for the purposes of acquiring evidence in, or for, litigation. Thus where documents have been generated by, or report on, conduct which constitutes a crime under the data protection legislation, and those documents are relevant to an issue in the proceedings, they will not be protected from disclosure by legal professional privilege (*Dubai Aluminium Co. Ltd v Al Alawi*).

Until recently, there appeared to be no common-law authority to the effect that a criminal intent on the part of a stranger to the relationship of a solicitor and client destroys the privilege of the client (see the speech of Lord Oliver, dissenting, in *Central Criminal Court, ex parte Francis* [1989] AC 346). Such authority as there was suggested the contrary: see, for example, *Banque Keyser Ullman SA v Skandia (UK) Insurance Co. Ltd* [1986] 1 Lloyd's Rep 336, in which it was held that the principle of *Cox* (1884) 14 QBD 153 does not extend to the correspondence between a solicitor and the victim of a fraudster. However, the decision of the majority of the House of Lords in *Ex parte Francis* now provides persuasive authority that the intention of furthering a criminal purpose may be that of the client, the solicitor or any other person. That case concerned the construction of the PACE 1984, s. 10(2), which provides that: 'Items held with the intention of furthering a criminal purpose are not items subject to legal privilege.' In *Snaresbrook Crown Court, ex parte DPP* [1988] QB 532, it was held, giving these words their natural meaning, that what is relevant is the intention of the person holding the items in question. However, in *Ex parte Francis*, a majority of the House, rejecting this construction, held that s. 10(2) was not intended to restrict the principle of *Cox* (1884) 14 QBD 153 to cases in which the legal adviser has the intention of furthering a criminal purpose, but *reflected the position at common law*, and therefore the intention to which it referred could be that of the person holding the document or any other person. On that basis it was held that no privilege attached to documents relating to the purchase of a property by a client and innocently held by a solicitor, because a third party, a relative of the client, intended them to be used to further his criminal purpose in laundering the proceeds of illegal drug trafficking. See also *R (Hallinan, Blackburn Gittings & Notts) (a firm) v Crown Court at Middlesex Guildhall* [2005] 1 WLR 766, where a draft statement, made pursuant to a specific agreement to pervert the course of justice, was forwarded to the accused's solicitors.

In *Leeds Magistrates' Court, ex parte Dumbleton* [1993] Crim LR 866, a warrant was issued to search for and seize documents held by a solicitor and allegedly forged by him and another. It was held that the documents were not covered by s. 10(1) because the phrase 'made in connection with . . . legal proceedings' meant lawfully made, and did not extend to forged documents or copies thereof; in any event the items were held with the intention of furthering a criminal purpose — the word 'held' in s. 10(2) relating to the time at which the documents came into the possession of the person holding them.

Waiver of Privilege and the Criminal Justice and Public Order Act 1994, s. 34

F9.37 In *Condron* [1997] 1 WLR 827, the Court of Appeal gave the following guidance relating to legal professional privilege where an accused refuses to answer police questions on the advice of his solicitor. Communications between an accused and his solicitor prior to interviews by the police are subject to the privilege. If an accused gives as a reason for not answering that he has been advised by his solicitor not to do so, that advice does not amount to a waiver of privilege. But if the accused wishes to invite the court not to draw an adverse inference under the CJPO 1994, s. 34 (see **F19.4**), it is necessary to go further and state the basis or reason for the advice. This may well amount to a waiver of privilege so that the accused, or if his solicitor is also called, the solicitor, can be asked whether there were any other reasons for the advice, and the nature of the advice given, so as to explore whether the advice may also have been given for tactical reasons. However, it should be borne in mind that the information which the prosecution seek to draw from failure to mention facts in interview is that they have been subsequently fabricated. It is open to an accused to attempt to rebut this inference by showing that the relevant facts were communicated to a third party, usually the solicitor, at about the time of the interview. This does not involve waiver of privilege if it is the solicitor to whom the fact is communicated.

It is probably desirable that the judge should warn counsel, or the accused, that the privilege may be taken to have been waived if the accused gives evidence of the nature of the advice.

If the defence reveal the basis or reason for the solicitor's advice to the accused not to answer police questions, this will amount to a waiver of privilege whether the revelation is made by the accused or by the solicitor acting within the scope of his authority as agent on behalf of the accused, and whether the revelation is made in the course of pretrial questioning, in evidence before the jury, or in evidence on the *voir dire* which is *not* repeated before the jury (*Bowden* [1999] 1 WLR 823). *Bowden* was followed in *Loizou* [2006] EWCA Crim 1719, where Hooper LJ said (at [84]):

> There is a distinction between *having* to reveal what was said to a solicitor to rebut an allegation of recent fabrication and *volunteering* information about the legal advice . . . In the former scenario the reason privilege has not been waived is that there is no way of dealing with the allegation other than by revealing what was said. In the latter scenario, while the effect may be to enable an allegation of recent fabrication to be made, this is the consequence of the voluntary provision by or on behalf of the defendant of information which because of its partial nature is misleading.

Waiver of Privilege and Use of Secondary Evidence

F9.38 Legal professional privilege prevents the giving of oral evidence or the production of documents by particular persons, namely the client, the legal adviser (or his clerk or agent) or third parties (in the case of protected communications between the client or his legal adviser and such third parties). If a privilege has been waived, because the contents of a privileged communication have become known to any other person, whether by overhearing a privileged conversation or by obtaining the original or a copy of a privileged document, that person may be compelled to give oral evidence in that regard or to produce the document or copy (see, in the case of copies of privileged documents, *Calcraft v Guest* [1898] 1 QB 759 and, in the case of originals, *Waugh v British Railways Board* [1980] AC 521 per Lord Simon at p. 536 and *Governor of Pentonville Prison, ex parte Osman* [1990] 1 WLR 277 at pp. 309–10). This principle applies not only if the privileged communication was disclosed by accident or error on the part of the client or his legal adviser, but also where it was obtained by improper or even criminal means on the part of his opponent (or some third party). But see also *ITC Film*

Distributors Ltd v Video Exchange Ltd [1982] Ch 431, which is considered at **F2.12**. In *Tompkins* (1977) 67 Cr App R 181, a note from the accused to his counsel had been found on the floor of the court and handed to prosecuting counsel by a representative of his instructing solicitor. The contents of the note being in flat contradiction to an answer given by the accused in cross-examination, prosecuting counsel handed the note to the accused, and without referring to its contents asked the accused whether he adhered to the answer he had given. The judge ruled that the cross-examination was proper but that no direct reference should be made to the note. The accused then admitted the opposite of what he had said. The Court of Appeal held that counsel had been properly allowed to put questions in cross-examination on the basis of the contents of the note. In *Cottrill* [1997] Crim LR 56, applying *Tompkins*, it was held that a statement made by the accused to his solicitors, and voluntarily sent by them to the prosecution without his knowledge or consent, could be used in cross-examination, if his evidence did not accord with the account given in the statement, subject to the provisions of the PACE 1984, s. 78. See also *Willis* [2004] EWCA Crim 3472; and see further the Code of Conduct of the Bar, Written Standards, paras. 7.1 to 7.3.2, discussed at **D15.8**.

In civil proceedings, if the contents of a privileged communication have become known to an opponent otherwise than by waiver of the privilege, then although he may prove them in the litigation by secondary evidence, the court may, at the request of the person in whom the privilege is vested, and in the exercise of its discretion, grant an injunction to restrain the opponent from disclosing or making any use of the confidential information contained in the communication (*Lord Ashburton v Pape* [1913] 2 Ch 469; *Goddard v Nationwide Building Society* [1987] QB 670; *Guinness Peat Properties Ltd v Fitzroy Robinson Partnership* [1987] 1 WLR 1027). Although it has been observed that there is much to be said for allowing the spirit of *Lord Ashburton v Pape* to prevail in criminal as well as civil proceedings (see *Goddard v Nationwide Building Society* per Nourse LJ at p. 686), the principle cannot be used in a *public* prosecution to prevent the prosecution from tendering relevant evidence. In *Butler v Board of Trade* [1971] Ch 680 the plaintiff, who was being prosecuted by the Board of Trade for alleged offences under the Companies Act 1948, sought a declaration that the Board was not entitled to produce in evidence at the criminal trial a copy of a letter from the plaintiff's solicitor to the plaintiff, which had been accidentally included in papers handed over to the Official Receiver. It was held that, although the original letter was privileged, the copy was admissible in the criminal proceedings under the rule in *Calcraft v Guest* [1898] 1 QB 759, the principle established in *Lord Ashburton v Pape* being inapplicable. Goff J said (at p. 690):

> . . . it would not be a right or permissible exercise of the equitable jurisdiction in confidence to make a declaration at the suit of the accused in a public prosecution in effect restraining the Crown from adducing admissible evidence relevant to the crime with which he is charged. It is not necessary for me to decide whether the same result would obtain in the case of a private prosecution, and I expressly leave that point open.

Section F10 Opinion Evidence

GENERAL RULE

F10.1 The general rule is that witnesses may only give evidence of facts they personally perceived and not evidence of their opinion, i.e. evidence of inferences drawn from such facts. The assumption that it is possible to distinguish fact from inference is arguably false (see Thayer, *A Preliminary Treatise on Evidence at the Common Law* (1898), p. 524), but the distinction has given rise to little case law. In *Meads* [1996] Crim LR 519, it was held that evidence of tests showing the speed at which the handwritten notes of disputed interviews had been made, and whether they could have been written in the time claimed by officers, was no more opinion evidence than evidence of the timing of a given journey in order to test an alibi. The inferences to be drawn from such evidence were for the jury.

There are two exceptions to the general rule:

(a) Non-experts. A statement of opinion on any matter not calling for expertise, if made by a witness as a way of conveying relevant facts personally perceived by him, is admissible as evidence of what he perceived.
(b) Experts. Subject to compliance with the CrimPR, parts 24 (disclosure of expert evidence) and 33 (expert evidence) (see **D14.71, F10.25** and **appendix 1**, where the rules are set out), a statement of opinion on any relevant matter calling for expertise may be made by a witness qualified to give such an expert opinion.

NON-EXPERT OPINION EVIDENCE

F10.2 A statement of opinion may be given by a witness, on a matter not calling for expertise, as a compendious means of conveying facts perceived by him. Thus an identification witness is not required to give a description of the offender or some other person, leaving it to the tribunal of fact to decide whether that description fits the accused or other person identified, but may express his opinion that the accused (or other person) is the person he saw on the occasion in question. Likewise, a non-expert may give evidence of opinion to identify an object (see *Lucas v Williams & Sons* [1892] 2 QB 113: a picture), handwriting with which he is familiar (see *Doe d Mudd v Suckermore* (1836) 7 LJ QB 33, *Slaney* (1832) 5 C & P 213, *Rickard* (1918) 13 Cr App R 40) or a voice which he recognises (*Deenik* [1992] Crim LR 578) or with which he is familiar (*Robb* (1991) 93 Cr App R 161). Other examples include evidence of a person's age (*Cox* [1898] 1 QB 179) or the general appearance of his state of health, mind or emotion; the speed of a vehicle (see the Road Traffic Regulation Act 1984, s. 89(2)); the state of the weather; and the passage of time. In *Beckett* (1913) 8 Cr App R 204, in which the value of a plate glass window was in issue, it was held that its value had been established by the evidence of a non-expert, who gave his opinion that it was worth more than five pounds. It is submitted, however, that non-expert opinion evidence should not be received on the value of less commonplace objects or objects such as antiques and works of art, the valuation of which calls for expertise. On a charge of driving when unfit through drink, the fitness of the accused to drive is a matter calling for expertise, though a non-expert may give evidence of his impression as to whether the accused had taken drink, provided he describes the facts on the basis of which he formed that impression (*Davies* [1962] 1 WLR

1111). *Davies* was applied in *Tagg* [2002] 1 Cr App R 22, on a charge of being drunk on an aircraft; members of the cabin crew were allowed to give their opinion that the accused was 'drunk'. See also *Neal* [1962] Crim LR 698. Although scientific evidence is not always required to identify a prohibited drug, police officers' descriptions of a drug must be sufficient to justify the inference that it was the drug alleged (*Hill* (1993) 96 Cr App R 456). The evidence of a non-expert is not admissible in support of an accused's plea of insanity (*Loake* (1911) 7 Cr App R 71, per Lord Alverstone CJ).

In *Davies* [1962] 1 WLR 1111, one of the reasons given by Lord Parker CJ as to why the non-expert could not give his opinion on whether the accused, as a result of the drink he had taken, was unfit to drive a car, was that this was 'the very matter which the court itself has to determine'. However, the common-law rule preventing any witness from expressing his opinion on an ultimate issue, i.e. one of the very issues to be determined by the court, appears to be virtually obsolete (see the Eleventh Report of the Criminal Law Revision Committee 1972 (Cmnd 4991, para. 270)). In *Beckett* (1913) 8 Cr App R 204, the value of the window was the very issue to be decided by the court. As to expert opinion evidence on ultimate issues, see **F10.21**.

EXPERT OPINION EVIDENCE

Competence of Expert Witnesses

Occasionally statute prescribes the qualifications which a person must possess if he is to give expert opinion evidence on a particular matter. For example, a jury shall not acquit on the ground of insanity, or make a determination of unfitness to plead, except on the evidence of two or more registered medical practitioners, at least one of whom is approved by the Secretary of State as having special experience in the diagnosis or treatment of mental disorder (Criminal Procedure (Insanity and Unfitness to Plead) Act 1991, ss. 1(1) and 2). Subject to provisions of this kind, whether a witness is properly qualified in the subject calling for expertise is a question for the court. In rare cases it will be necessary to hold a *voir dire* to decide whether a witness should be allowed to give expert evidence, but in the vast majority of cases the judge will be able to make the decision on the basis of written material (*G* [2004] 2 Cr App R 638). If a witness does give expert evidence, the judge has the power, should the need arise, to remove his expert status and limit his evidence to factual matters (*G*). **F10.3**

The expert's competence or skill may stem from formal study or training, experience, or both. In *Oakley* (1979) 70 Cr App R 7 a police officer with qualifications and experience in accident investigation was allowed to give evidence, on a charge of causing death by dangerous driving, as to how an accident occurred. See also *Hodges* [2003] 2 Cr App R 247 and *Ibrahima* [2005] EWCA Crim 1436, considered at **F10.20**. Compare, *sed quaere*, *Somers* [1963] 1 WLR 1306, in which a doctor was allowed to prove the conversion of figures in an analyst's certificate into the amount of alcohol consumed by the accused, although not an expert in such conversion, and to prove the rate of bodily destruction of alcohol, having refreshed his memory from a BMA publication. See also *Inch* (1989) 91 Cr App R 51, in which it was held that a medical orderly with much experience in the treatment of cuts and lacerations was insufficiently qualified to express an opinion as to whether an inch-long cut to the forehead had been caused by a blunt instrument rather than a head-butt. In *Silverlock* [1894] 2 QB 766 a solicitor, who had for 10 years studied handwriting and on several occasions compared handwriting professionally, was allowed to give expert evidence that an advertisement was in the handwriting of the accused. Affirming the conviction, Lord Russell CJ said (at p. 771):

> There is no decision which requires that the evidence of a man who is skilled in comparing handwriting, and who has formed a reliable opinion from past experience, should be excluded because his experience has not been gained in the way of his business. It is, however, really

> unnecessary to consider this point; for it seems . . . in the present case that the witness was not only *peritus*, but was *peritus* in the way of his business.

In *Robb* (1991) 93 Cr App R 161, an experienced phonetician was allowed to give expert opinion evidence that the voice on two different tapes was the voice of the same person, notwithstanding that his technique, which was one of auditory analysis alone, was not generally respected in the field of phonetics because it was not supplemented and verified by acoustic analysis based on physical measurement of resonance and frequency. However in *O'Doherty* [2003] 1 Cr App R 77, a decision of the Court of Appeal of Northern Ireland which, it is submitted, should be followed in the English jurisdiction, it was held that as a general rule, subject to exceptions, no prosecution should now be brought based on voice identification given by an expert which was solely confined to auditory analysis — there should always be expert evidence of acoustic analysis, including formant analysis.

As to the competence of a witness to give opinion evidence on a point of foreign law, see F10.16.

Conflicts of Interest

F10.4 In *Toth v Jarman* [2006] 4 All ER 1276 it was held that, although a conflict of interest does not automatically disqualify an expert, where the conflict is material or significant the court is likely to decline to act on his evidence or indeed to give permission for his evidence to be adduced. It is therefore important that the party who wishes to call an expert with a potential conflict of interest of any kind — including a financial interest, a personal connection or an obligation (e.g., as a member or officer of some other body) — should disclose the details to the other party and to the court at the earliest possible opportunity. It is for the court and not the parties to decide whether a conflict is material or not. The fact that there is a risk of bias or lack of objectivity that is subliminal, as opposed to conscious, will not prevent an expert from giving his evidence (see *Stubbs* [2006] EWCA Crim 2312). However, if there is a relationship between the proposed expert and the party calling him which a reasonable observer might think was capable of affecting the views of the expert so as to make the expert unduly favourable to that party, his evidence should be excluded, however unbiased his conclusions might be, on the grounds of public policy that justice must not only be done but also must be seen to be done (*Liverpool Roman Catholic Archdiocese Trustees Incorporated v Goldberg (No. 2)* [2001] 1 WLR 2337).

Matters Calling for Expertise

F10.5 Expert opinion evidence may only be received on a subject calling for expertise, which a lay person, such as a magistrate or a juror, could not be expected to possess to a degree sufficient to understand the evidence given in the case unaided. If the tribunal of fact can form its own opinion without the assistance of an expert, the matter being within its own experience and knowledge, expert opinion evidence is inadmissible because it is unnecessary (*Turner* [1975] QB 834, per Lawton LJ at p. 841, applied in *Loughran* [1999] Crim LR 404). Thus a psychologist or other medical expert will not be permitted to give an opinion on the likely deterioration of memory of an ordinary witness (*Browning* [1995] Crim LR 227). On the other hand, in *H (JR) (Childhood Amnesia)* [2006] 1 Cr App R 195, it was held that, although a witness's ability to remember events will ordinarily be well within the experience of jurors, in rare cases in which a witness gives evidence of an event, said to have occurred at an early age, and the evidence is very detailed and contains a number of extraneous facts, an appropriately qualified expert may give evidence that it should be treated with caution and may well be unreliable, because recall of events during 'the period of childhood amnesia', which extends to the age of about seven, will be fragmented, disjointed and idiosyncratic rather than a detailed narrative account. In the absence of such expert evidence, which is likely to be outside the knowledge and experience of the jury, there is a danger that the jury may find the detailed account more convincing than they safely should, because detail normally enhances credibility to the ear of the listener (cf. *Snell* [2006] EWCA Crim 1404). In some cases, it seems that jurors may receive assistance on a matter within their own experience and knowledge if it is provided by someone who has had more time and better facilities to consider that matter than it would be practicable to afford to them (see *Clare* [1995] 2 Cr App R 333, where an officer who did not know the accused but had viewed a video-recording about 40 times, examining it in slow motion and rewinding and replaying it as frequently as was necessary, was permitted to give evidence of identification based on a comparison between the video images and contemporary photographs of the accused).

The subjects calling for expertise, which are so diverse as to defy comprehensive classification, include a variety of medical, psychiatric, scientific and technological matters, and questions relating to standards of professional competence. Specific examples include accident investigation and driver behaviour (*Dudley* [2004] EWCA Crim 3336); age, in the absence of documentary or other reliable evidence (*R (I) v Secretary of State for the Home Department* [2005] EWHC 1025 (Admin) and *Re N (a child) (residence order)* [2006] EWHC 1189 (Fam)); ballistics; blood tests; breath tests and blood/alcohol levels (sometimes including back-calculations thereof, i.e. calculation of the amount of alcohol eliminated in the period between driving and providing a specimen, in order to show that the level was above the prescribed limit at the time of driving: see *Gumbley v Cunningham* [1989] AC 281); forgeries; handwriting identification (including the analysis of indented impressions of handwriting, left on one document as a result of writing on another, and revealed by Electrostatic Detection Apparatus (ESDA): see *Wellington* [1991] Crim LR 543); fingerprint identification; ear print identification (*Dallagher* [2003] 1 Cr App R 195); voice identification; identification by facial mapping (*Stockwell* (1993) 97 Cr App R 260 and *Hookway* [1999] Crim LR 750), expert evidence of which may form the basis of a conviction (*Mitchell* [2005] EWCA Crim 731); facial identification by video superimposition (see *Clarke* [1995] 2 Cr App R 425); genetic fingerprinting (the technique whereby a human cell taken from a sample of blood, saliva, semen or hair is analysed to reveal a person's DNA or genetic 'fingerprint' — see **F18.31**); Sudden Infant Death Syndrome (SIDS): see *Cannings* [2004] 1 WLR 2607, considered at **F5.15**; insanity; automatism; diminished responsibility; and the competence of a medical practitioner (see *Whitehead* (1848) 3 Car & Kir 202: expert opinion evidence as to the state of knowledge and skill of a physician as shown by his treatment of the case in question).

States of Mind

Insanity, Diminished Responsibility and Automatism As to the need for expert evidence to prove insanity, see **A3.13, D12.8, D12.15** and **F10.3**. On the issue of diminished responsibility, the Court of Appeal in *Dix* (1981) 74 Cr App R 306, applying a dictum in *Byrne* [1960] 2 QB 396 at p. 402, said (at p. 311): 'while the Homicide Act 1957, s. 2(1) does not in terms require that medical evidence be adduced in support of a defence of diminished responsibility, it makes it a practical necessity if that defence is to begin to run at all.' As to automatism, see *Smith* [1979] 1 WLR 1445. The accused was convicted of murder by stabbing. The defence was automatism, by sleepwalking. The prosecution, in order to show that this defence was a recently conceived idea, obtained leave to cross-examine the accused about interviews which he had with two psychiatrists while in custody, and to call the psychiatrists to give their views on the defence being run. On appeal it was argued that, since there was no question of insanity or diminished responsibility, the question of automatism should be decided by the jury in the light of their own experience, and unassisted by expert medical evidence. Rejecting this argument, the Court of Appeal held that the type of automatism in question was not something within the realm of the ordinary juror's experience but a matter on which the jury should not be deprived of expert assistance. See also *Hill v Baxter* [1958] 1 QB 277, at p. 285. **F10.6**

F10.7 **Psychiatric Injury** Where psychiatric injury is relied on as the basis for an allegation of assault occasioning actual bodily harm, and the matter is not admitted by the defence, the Crown should call expert evidence to prove the injury; in the absence of such evidence the question whether the assault occasioned such injury should not be left to the jury (*Chan-Fook* [1994] 1 WLR 689, applied in *Morris* [1998] 1 Cr App R 386).

F10.8 **Intent** In appropriate circumstances, expert medical evidence may be admissible on the question of the effect of a medical abnormality upon intent. Thus in *Toner* (1991) 93 Cr App R 382, a physician gave evidence that the accused had been suffering from a minor hypoglycaemic state caused by the ingestion of food after a prolonged fast. It was held that the defence had been improperly prevented from asking the witness what the effect of that minor degree of hypoglycaemia would be on the ability to make judgments or to form specific intents. The Court of Appeal held that there is no distinction between medical evidence relating to hypoglycaemia and its possible effect upon intent, and medical evidence as to the effect of a drug upon intent: both are matters outside the ordinary experience of jurors who cannot bring to bear their own judgment without the assistance of expert evidence. Similarly in *Huckerby* [2004] EWCA Crim 3251, evidence that the accused was suffering from post-traumatic stress disorder, a recognised mental condition with which the jury would not be expected to be familiar, was admissible because it was relevant to an essential issue bearing upon his guilt or innocence, namely whether it had caused him to panic and cooperate with criminals in circumstances in which he would otherwise not have done so. Subject to cases of this kind, however, and except in the case of an accused who comes into the class of mental defective, expert psychiatric evidence is not admissible on the issue of whether the accused did, or did not, have the required *mens rea*. In *Chard* (1971) 56 Cr App R 268 the Court of Appeal held that the judge, in a murder trial, had properly refused a defence application to call a medical witness to give evidence about the accused's intent to kill or do grievous bodily harm. Roskill LJ, giving the judgment of the court, held (at pp. 270–1) that, had the accused been supposedly abnormal, e.g., suffering from insanity or diminished responsibility, the jury would have been entitled to the benefit of expert evidence; but since the accused was entirely normal, the question of his intention was a matter which the jury were well able, by their ordinary experience, to judge for themselves. See also *Reynolds* [1989] Crim LR 220 and, in the case of adolescents, *Coles* [1995] 1 Cr App R 157. Similarly, in *Masih* [1986] Crim LR 395, a case of rape in which the accused suffered from no psychiatric illness, but had an intelligence quotient of 72, just above the level of subnormality, on the question of whether he knew the complainant was not consenting, or was reckless as to whether she consented, psychiatric evidence as to his state of mind, intelligence and ability to appreciate the situation was held to be inadmissible. Upholding the ruling, the Court of Appeal held that, generally speaking, if an accused comes into the class of mental defective, with an IQ of 69 or below, then insofar as the defectiveness is relevant to an issue, expert evidence may be admitted, provided that it is confined to an assessment of the accused's IQ and an explanation of any relevant abnormal characteristics (in order to enlighten the jury on a matter that is abnormal and outside their experience). However, if an accused is within the scale of normality, albeit at the lower end, as was the appellant, expert evidence should generally be excluded. See also *Hall* (1987) 86 Cr App R 159 and *Henry* [2006] 1 Cr App R 118.

In *Wood* [1990] Crim LR 264, the accused, charged with murder, raised the partial defence under Homicide Act 1957, s. 4, of the unsuccessful execution of a suicide pact. In support of this defence, and relying upon an analogy with diminished responsibility, the defence sought unsuccessfully to introduce psychiatric evidence to the effect that the accused suffered from a personality disorder. Refusing leave to appeal, it was held that whereas the defence of diminished responsibility was founded on the existence of some abnormality of mind, in the case of a suicide pact, once the killing had been proved, the questions for the jury are whether there was such a pact and, if so, whether at the time of the killing the accused was acting in pursuance thereof and had the settled intention of dying in pursuance thereof. The Homicide Act 1957, s. 2, introduced no medical or mental tests into the resolution of these questions and therefore psychiatric evidence was no more or less relevant to their solution than it was to the many other questions of fact which juries have to decide. That the applicant had a personality which was to some extent abnormal and liable to give way to excesses of behaviour under stress was not something outside the ordinary experience of the average juror.

Provocation Psychiatric evidence is inadmissible in order to establish that the accused was likely to have been provoked. In *Turner* [1975] QB 834 the Court of Appeal upheld the refusal of a trial judge to allow the defence to call a psychiatrist, on the issues of credibility and provocation, to prove that the accused had had a deep emotional relationship with the victim, which was likely to have caused an explosive release of blind rage after her confession of infidelity to him, and that subsequent to the killing he had behaved like someone suffering from profound grief. The court held that these were matters well within ordinary human experience and upon which the jury required no expert assistance. The evidence was not admissible on the issue of provocation, therefore, and the same reasoning prevented its admission on the issue of credibility. *Sed quaere*, whether expert evidence might not be admitted on an issue of provocation, where the accused suffers from some mental abnormality (*Camplin* [1978] AC 705). *Turner* was distinguished in *McDonald* [1991] Crim LR 122. In that case evidence was adduced of an out-of-court statement made by the accused explaining why he had killed the victim, an explanation which was sufficient to lay a foundation for the defence of provocation. Subsequently, in the course of a psychiatric examination, the accused admitted that the explanation was invented. It was held that it was not unfair for the psychiatrist to give evidence of the admission, because it related to a factual matter, not a medical issue. **F10.9**

Duress In the case of duress, psychiatric evidence may be admissible to show that an accused was suffering from some mental illness, mental impairment or recognised psychiatric condition, if persons generally suffering from such a condition might be more susceptible to pressure and threats, and thus to assist the jury in deciding whether a reasonable person with such a condition might have been impelled to act as the accused had. Psychiatric evidence is not admissible simply to show that an accused not suffering from such a condition, was especially timid, suggestible or vulnerable to pressure and threats (*Walker* [2003] EWCA Crim 1837). **F10.10**

Concerning the defence of duress by threats, expert evidence is admissible for the purposes of the subjective limb of the test, provided that the mental condition or abnormality in question is outside the knowledge and experience of laymen, but inadmissible for the purposes of the objective limb (*Hegarty* [1994] Crim LR 353; cf. *Horne* [1994] Crim LR 584 and *Hurst* [1995] 1 Cr App R 82).

Reliability or Truth of Confessions The expert evidence of a psychiatrist or psychologist is admissible on the issue of the reliability or truth of a confession if it is to the effect that no reliance can be placed on the confession because the accused was suffering from a personality disorder so severe as properly to be categorised as a mental disorder (*Ward* [1993] 1 WLR 619). Admissible evidence from psychiatrists, however, is not confined to evidence of such personality disorders. The test is not whether an abnormality fits into a recognised category such as anti-social personality disorder. That is neither necessary nor sufficient. It is sufficient for the disorder to be of a type which might render a confession or evidence unreliable. However, there must be a very significant deviation from the norm shown, and an independent history, pre-dating the confession or the giving of evidence, which points to or explains the abnormalities. If such evidence is admitted, the jury must be directed that they are not obliged to accept it, but should consider it, if they think it right to do so, as throwing light on the personality of the accused and bringing to their attention aspects of that personality of **F10.11**

F

Part F Evidence

which they might otherwise have been unaware (*O'Brien* [2000] Crim LR 676, applied in *Smith* [2003] EWCA Crim 927). Psychiatric evidence is not admissible in the case of someone with an histrionic personality disorder characterised by emotional superficiality and impulsive behaviour when under stress, but who does not suffer from mental illness and is not below normal intelligence (*Weightman* (1990) 92 Cr App R 291). However, the expert evidence of a psychologist is admissible to show that a confession made by someone not suffering from any personality or abnormal disorder is likely to be unreliable if it was a 'coerced compliant confession', a phenomenon falling outside the experience of the jury. A coerced compliant confession is one brought about by fatigue, together with an inability to control what is happening, which may induce the individual to experience a growing desire to give up resisting suggestions put to him so that eventually he can take no more and is overwhelmed by the need to achieve the immediate goal of bringing the interrogation to an end (*Blackburn* [2005] 2 Cr App R 440). See also, as to the admissibility of psychiatric evidence on a *voir dire* to determine the admissibility of a confession, **F17.10** and **F17.13**.

F10.12 **Psychological Autopsies** The present academic status of 'psychological autopsies' is not such as to allow them to be admitted as a basis for expert opinion evidence (*Gilfoyle* [2001] 2 Cr App R 57). In *Gilfoyle*, a murder trial in which the only other possible explanation for the death was suicide, the Court of Appeal declined to hear the fresh evidence of a distinguished psychologist who had carried out a 'psychological autopsy' of the deceased, relying upon the dictum of Lord President Cooper in *Davie v Magistrates of Edinburgh* 1953 SC 34 at p. 40 that expert witnesses must furnish the court 'with the necessary scientific criteria for testing the accuracy of their conclusions, so as to enable the judge or jury to form their own independent judgment by the application of these criteria to the facts proved in evidence'. Six detailed reasons were given, although the court accepted that the first of these alone would not necessarily be fatal to admissibility.

(a) The psychologist had never before embarked on the task which he set himself in the case.
(b) His reports identified no criteria by reference to which the court could test the quality of his opinions. There was no database comparing real and questionable suicides and no substantial body of academic writing approving his methodology.
(c) His views were based on one-sided information, in particular from the accused and his family.
(d) It was very much doubted whether assessing levels of happiness or unhappiness was a task for an expert rather than jurors.
(e) English, Canadian and United States authority pointed against the admission of the evidence. The principle in *Frye v United States* 293 F. 1013 (1923), that evidence based on a developing new brand of science or medicine is not admissible until accepted by the scientific community as being able to provide accurate and reliable opinion, accorded with the English approach.
(f) If the evidence were admissible, there would be no reason in principle to exclude evidence psychologically profiling an accused, but this would open up unending roads of enquiry of little or no help to a jury.

However, as to the reason set out in (e), see now *Harris* [2006] 1 Cr App R 55, which is considered at **F10.22**.

Credibility

F10.13 Medical evidence is admissible to show that a witness suffers from some disease or defect or abnormality of mind that affects the reliability of his evidence. Such evidence is not confined to a general opinion of the unreliability of the witness but may give all the matters necessary to show, not only the foundation of and reasons for the diagnosis, but also the extent to which the credibility of the witness is affected. (*Toohey v Metropolitan Police Commissioner* [1965] AC 595, per Lord Pearce at p. 609)

See further F7.34. In the case of evidence of 'abnormality of mind', the approach set out in *O'Brien* and considered at **F10.11** applies whether the expert evidence that is being considered relates to a witness or an accused. However, especially in the case of a witness, it is important to take into account the importance of the evidence that the witness gives. If it is of little significance to the issues at the trial, the admission of expert evidence is unlikely to be justified (see *MacKenney* [2004] 2 Cr App R 32, considered at **F7.34**, at [15]). Subject to the principle of *Toohey v Metropolitan Police Commissioner*, it is only in exceptional cases that psychologists and psychiatrists may be called to prove the probability of the veracity of the accused (see *Henry* [2006] 1 Cr App R 118 at [15]) or another witness (see *The Queen v Joyce* [2005] NTSC 21, concerning the credibility of a child, and *S* [2006] EWCA 2389). A rare example is *Lowery v The Queen* [1974] AC 85. L and K were charged with an apparently motiveless murder, the circumstances being that one or both of them must have committed the offence. Each blamed the other for the crime. The Privy Council held that the trial judge had properly permitted K to call a psychologist, who had carried out personality tests on both L and K, to show that K's version of events was more probable than that of L, since, compared to K, L's character and disposition were such that he was more likely to have committed the offence. Commenting upon this decision in *Turner* [1975] QB 834, Lawton LJ said (at p. 842):

> In every case what is relevant and admissible depends on the issues raised in that case. In *Lowery v The Queen* the issues were unusual; and the accused to whose disadvantage the psychologist's evidence went had in effect said before it was called that he was not the sort of man to have committed the offence. . .
>
> We adjudge *Lowery v The Queen* to have been decided on its special facts. We do not consider that it is an authority for the proposition that in all cases psychologists and psychiatrists can be called to prove the probability of the accused's veracity.

In *Rimmer* [1983] Crim LR 250, the two accused were charged with murder, and each blamed the other. On the basis of a medical report, counsel for B cross-examined R, suggesting to him that he had a history of mental illness and that he had killed the victim in a fit of uncontrollable temper to which he was accustomed. The Court of Appeal upheld the ruling of the trial judge that R was not entitled to call medical evidence to establish that he was not, and never had been, mentally ill. See also *Miller* [1952] 2 All ER 667, *Neale* (1977) 65 Cr App R 304, and *Bracewell* (1978) 68 Cr App R 44.

Expert evidence may be admitted as to the dangers of evidence produced through hypnotherapy. In *Clark* [2006] EWCA Crim 231, A, aged 33 at the time of the trial, gave evidence of sexual offences against her when she was aged 10 to 12. The first time she had spoken of the abuse was during a hypnothcrapy session with S shortly before the trial. She said that her subconscious had not previously allowed her to speak of the matter. It was held that A's evidence had been correctly admitted but that the defence should have been allowed to call an expert, not to give his opinion on A's truthfulness, but to criticise S's techniques and to express his opinion about the danger that *if* A's recollection was falsely engendered through the counselling, A would thereafter have regarded it as genuine memory. However, as a matter of principle, evidence produced by the administration of some mechanical, chemical or hypnotic truth test on a witness is inadmissible to show the veracity or otherwise of that witness (*Fennell v Jerome Property Maintenance Ltd* (1986) *The Times*, 26 November 1986). The previous statements of the witness are not only inadmissible hearsay, but insofar as they are consistent with his testimony, inadmissible as evidence of consistency under the rule against previous self-serving statements (see **F6.19**).

Handwriting

Handwriting may be identified by a non-expert familiar with the handwriting in question (see *Doe d Mudd v Suckermore* (1836) 5 A & E 703, and *Slaney* (1832) 5 C & P 213). The witness's **F10.14** knowledge, however, must not have been acquired for the express purpose of qualifying him to testify at the trial (*Crouch* (1850) 4 Cox CC 163). An expert should be called if there is to be a comparison of the 'disputed writing' with specimen handwriting proved or admitted to have been written by the person in question, under the Criminal Procedure Act 1865, s. 8 (*Tilley* [1961] 1 WLR 1309; *Harden* [1963] 1 QB 8). Such expert evidence is admissible under s. 8 even if the expert has not seen the original 'disputed writing' (e.g., because it is lost), but has made his comparison with a photocopy of the original (*Lockheed-Arabia v Owen* [1993] QB 806). See further **F18**. As to the standard of proof required to establish the genuineness of specimen handwriting, see *Ewing* [1983] QB 1039 and *Angeli* [1979] 1 WLR 26.

Obscenity

F10.15 In the normal case, the issues of indecency or obscenity should be determined by the jury without expert assistance. In *Anderson* [1972] 1 QB 304, Lord Widgery CJ said (at p. 313) that in the ordinary run of the mill cases, the issue 'obscene or no' under the Obscene Publications Act 1959 must be tried without the assistance of expert evidence. His lordship said that *DPP v A and BC Chewing Gum Ltd* [1968] 1 QB 159 'should be regarded as highly exceptional and confined to its own circumstances, namely, a case where the alleged obscene matter was directed at very young children, and was of itself of a somewhat unusual kind'. In the latter case the accused were charged with publishing for gain obscene battle cards (which were sold together with packets of bubble gum), contrary to the Obscene Publications Act, s. 2(1) and the Obscene Publications Act 1964, s. 1(1). The Divisional Court held that the magistrates had improperly prevented the prosecution from introducing evidence of experts in child psychiatry as to the likely effect of the cards on children. Lord Parker CJ held that, when considering the effect of something on an adult, an adult jury may be able to judge just as well as an adult witness; but when one is dealing with children of different age groups and children from five upwards, any jury, and any justices, need all the help they can get as to the effect on different children. See also *Skirving* [1985] QB 819, a prosecution arising out of the publication of a book entitled 'Attention Coke Lovers. Free Base. The Greatest Thing Since Sex', which contained explanations, instructions and 'recipes' on how to make use of cocaine to maximum effect. The Court of Appeal held that expert evidence on the characteristics of cocaine and the effects of the various methods of ingesting the drug was admissible, because it was outside the experience of the ordinary person, and only when equipped with such information would the jury be in a position to decide whether the publication had a tendency to deprave and corrupt.

Expert opinion evidence is also admissible on questions of a literary, artistic or scientific nature in relation to the defence of 'public good' under the Obscene Publications Act 1959, s. 4 (see s. 4(2)).

Foreign Law

F10.16 Points of foreign law of any jurisdiction other than that of England and Wales are questions of fact to be decided on the evidence by the judge (Administration of Justice Act 1920, s. 15: see also **F1.28**). Thus, if there has been an English decision on a point of foreign law and the same point subsequently arises again, it must be decided on new evidence (*M'Cormick v Garnett* (1854) 5 De GM & G 278). The general rule is that the law of a foreign country, whether written or not, must be proved by the testimony of a competent expert, by the witnesses statement of such an expert (if admissible), or on the basis of a statement of agreed facts pursuant to CJA 1967, s. 10 (*Ofori* (1994) 99 Cr App R 223). If the expert witnesses agree on a point of foreign law, the court is not entitled to reject their evidence and to conduct its own research by referring to textbooks and foreign law reports (*Bumper Development Corporation Ltd v Commissioner of Police of the Metropolis* [1991] 1 WLR 1362). The expert may refresh his memory from foreign law books, but the law itself is proved by his oral evidence (*Sussex Peerage Case* (1844) 11 Cl & F 85). A witness is competent for these purposes if he is a practitioner in the relevant jurisdiction (*Baron de Bode's Case* (1845) 8 QB 208). There is old authority that a practitioner from the jurisdiction in question should always be called (*Bristow v Sequeville* (1850) 5 Exch 275). However, a witness has been held to be suitably qualified for these purposes if he is:

(a) a former practitioner in the relevant jurisdiction (*Re Duke of Wellington* [1947] Ch 506);
(b) a person qualified to practise in the relevant jurisdiction, even if he has not done so (*Barford v Barford and McLeod* [1918] P 140); or
(c) a person who has acquired the appropriate expertise by academic study (*Brailey v Rhodesia Consolidated Ltd* [1910] 2 Ch 95, reader in Roman-Dutch law to the Council of Legal Education); as an embassy official (*In the Goods of Dost Aly Khan* (1889) 6 PD 6); or in the course of a non-legal business such as banking (*De Beéche v South American Stores (Gath and Chaves) Ltd* [1935] AC 148).

There are two exceptions to the general rule:

(a) The Evidence (Colonial Statutes) Act 1907, s. 1, and the Colonial Laws Validity Act 1865, s. 6, provide for proof of colonial statutes etc.; and English courts may construe such statutes without accompanying expert evidence (see the authorities cited in *Jasiewicz v Jasiewicz* [1962] 1 WLR 1426).
(b) The British Law Ascertainment Act 1859 provides that an English court may state a case on a point of foreign law for the opinion of a superior court in another part of Her Majesty's dominions, and that the opinion thus produced is admissible evidence on the point of law in question.

Competence of Witnesses

Determination of the question whether a child is competent to give evidence for the purposes of the YJCEA 1999, s. 54, does not normally require any input from an expert, but a decision as to the competence of a mentally handicapped person, whether adult or child does require appropriate expert medical evidence (see F4.21). **F10.17**

Proof of Facts upon which Expert Opinion Evidence Based

> Before a court can assess the value of an opinion it must know the facts upon which it is based. If the expert has been misinformed about the facts or has taken irrelevant facts into consideration or has omitted to consider relevant ones, the opinion is likely to be valueless. In our judgment, counsel calling an expert should in examination-in-chief ask his witness to state the facts upon which his opinion is based. It is wrong to leave the other side to elicit the facts by cross-examination. (*Turner* [1975] QB 834 at p. 840) **F10.18**

In some cases, some of the relevant facts upon which the opinion is based can be proved by the expert himself, as when he has examined an exhibit or a fingerprint and therefore has personal or first-hand knowledge of those facts. In other cases, however, the expert will have no personal or first-hand knowledge of the facts, or all of the facts, upon which his opinion is based. For example, in a trial for murder by stabbing, in which the defence is that the victim's injuries were self-inflicted, a medical witness who has not examined the body may be asked whether, assuming that the facts, described by another medical witness who has examined the body, are true, the wound was inflicted by a person other than the deceased (*Mason* (1911) 7 Cr App R 67). Similarly, an expert may give his expert opinion on the basis of preparatory work, such as scientific tests carried out by assistants. Whether or not the expert has personal knowledge of the facts upon which his opinion is based, those facts must be proved. This may be done by calling the person with personal knowledge of them. However, under the CJA 2003, s. 127, a statement made by such a person for the purposes of either a criminal investigation or criminal proceedings may be admitted without the need to call him, and in evidence given in the proceedings the expert may base his opinion on the statement, unless, on an application by a party to the proceedings, the court orders that application of the section is not in the interests of justice.

Criminal Justice Act 2003, s. 127

(1) This section applies if—
  (a) a statement has been prepared for the purposes of criminal proceedings,
  (b) the person who prepared the statement had or may reasonably be supposed to have had personal knowledge of the matters stated,
  (c) notice is given under the appropriate rules that another person (the expert) will in evidence given in the proceedings orally or under section 9 of the Criminal Justice Act 1967 base an opinion or inference on the statement, and
  (d) the notice gives the name of the person who prepared the statement and the nature of the matters stated.
(2) In evidence given in the proceedings the expert may base an opinion or inference on the statement.
(3) If evidence based on the statement is given under subsection (2) the statement is to be treated as evidence of what it says.
(4) This section does not apply if the court, on an application by a party to the proceedings, orders that it is not in the interests of justice that it should apply.
(5) The matters to be considered by the court in deciding whether to make an order under subsection (4) include—
  (a) the expense of calling as a witness the person who prepared the statement;
  (b) whether relevant evidence could be given by that person which could not be given by the expert;
  (c) whether that person can reasonably be expected to remember the matters stated well enough to give oral evidence of them.
(6) Subsections (1) to (5) apply to a statement prepared for the purposes of a criminal investigation as they apply to a statement prepared for the purposes of criminal proceedings, and in such a case references to the proceedings are to criminal proceedings arising from the investigation.

F10.19 **Facts Derived from the Use of a Computer** Where an expert bases his opinion on facts derived from the use of a computer, it seems that there is no obligation to produce the printout (see *Golizadeh* [1995] Crim LR 232, where an expert was allowed to give his opinion that a certain substance was opium on the basis of a printout of a machine used by him to analyse its chemical constituents, the printout itself not having been produced in evidence).

F10.20 **Special Treatment of Hearsay** An expert is not subject to the rule against hearsay in the same way as a non-expert or a witness of fact. Thus, although an expert cannot prove facts upon which his opinion is based, but of which he has no personal or first-hand knowledge, because that would be an infringement of the hearsay rule, he may rely upon such facts as a part of the process of forming an opinion. However, if there is no direct evidence to establish such facts, the weight to be attached to the opinion of the expert is likely to be minimal. In *Bradshaw* (1985) 82 Cr App R 79, a murder trial, the only issue was that of diminished responsibility. (The burden of proof was on the defence: Homicide Act 1957, s. 2(2).) Counsel for the defence sought guidance from the judge as to how far the doctors would be permitted to give evidence as to what the accused had told them during interviews, how far they could express opinions based upon such statements, and whether the judge would make adverse comment if the accused were not to give evidence. The judge replied that, if the truth of what the accused had said to the doctors was in question, the only appropriate course was for the accused to prove the facts upon which the expert opinion was based, or for those facts to be proved by other evidence. The accused, who had recovered from any abnormality of mind at the date of the trial, gave evidence and was cross-examined. He appealed against conviction on the grounds that the ruling of the judge was erroneous. The appeal was dismissed. Lord Lane CJ said (at p. 83):

> Although as a concession to the defence doctors are sometimes allowed to base their opinions on what the defendant has told them (i.e. hearsay) without those matters being proved by admissible evidence, yet the strict (and correct) view is that expressed at p. 446 of *Cross on Evidence*, 5th ed., in the following terms: 'A doctor may not state what a patient told him about past symptoms as evidence of the existence of those symptoms because that would infringe the rule against hearsay, but he may give evidence of what the patient told him in order to explain the grounds on which he came to a conclusion with regard to the patient's condition'.
>
> Thus, if the doctor's opinion is based entirely on hearsay and is not supported by direct evidence, the judge will be justified in telling the jury that the defendant's case (if that is so) is based upon a flimsy or non-existent foundation and that they should reach their conclusion bearing that in mind. In proper cases, for example where, as here, the defendant has completely recovered from any abnormality of mind by the time of the trial, there is no reason why the judge should not comment upon the fact that the defendant could have provided the necessary evidence had he wished to do so, the burden of proof being upon him.

As a part of the process of forming an opinion, expert witnesses may refer not only to their own research, tests and experiments, but also to works of authority, learned articles, research papers, and other similar material written by others and forming part of the general body of knowledge falling within their field of expertise (see generally *Davie v Magistrates of Edinburgh* 1953 SC 34; *Seyfang v G.D. Searle & Co.* [1973] QB 148, at p. 151; and *H v Schering Chemicals Ltd* [1983] 1 WLR 143). In *Abadom* [1983] 1 WLR 126, on the question of whether fragments of glass imbedded in the shoes of the accused had come from a window allegedly broken during a robbery, an expert gave evidence that, based upon his personal analysis of the samples, the glass in the shoes and that from the window bore an identical refractive index; and that, having consulted unpublished statistics compiled by the Home Office Central Research Establishment, which showed that that index occurred in only 4 per cent of all glass samples investigated, in his opinion there was a very strong likelihood that the glass in the shoes came from the window. It was argued, on appeal, that the evidence of the Home Office statistics was inadmissible hearsay, since the expert had no knowledge of the analysis on which the statistics had been based. The appeal was dismissed on the ground that the primary facts, i.e. the refractive indices of the glass samples, had been proved by the expert on the basis of his own analysis; and that once the primary facts upon which an opinion is based have been proved by admissible evidence, an expert is entitled to draw on the work of others as part of the process of arriving at his conclusion, and this involves no breach of the hearsay rule. The Court of Appeal pointed out that part of the experience and expertise of experts lies in their knowledge and evaluation of *unpublished* material; they may draw on such material, provided that they refer to it in their evidence so that the cogency and probative value of their conclusions can be tested and evaluated by reference thereto. Compare *Somers* [1963] 1 WLR 1306, considered at **F10.3**. *Abadom* was applied in *Hodges* [2003] 2 Cr App R 247, a case of conspiracy to supply heroin in which a very experienced drugs officer gave expert evidence, derived in part from what he had been told by others, including other officers, informants and drug users, as to the usual method of supplying heroin, as to its purchase price, and that 14 grammes of heroin was more than would have been for personal use. Similarly, in *Ibrahima* [2005] EWCA Crim 1436, a case of possession of ecstasy tablets with intent to supply, it was held that a person with no medical or psychological qualifications, but with experience and knowledge of drug use as a deputy director of a drug advice charity, was entitled to give evidence, whether for the prosecution or defence, as to what quantities of ecstasy are consistent with personal use, and as to how users acquire an increasing tolerance of the drug, leading to higher consumption, provided that he gave the categories of his sources of information. However, see also *Edwards* [2001] EWCA Crim 2185, where the issue was whether the ecstasy tablets found in the accused's possession were for personal consumption or for supply. 'Experts', neither of whom had any formal medical or toxicological qualifications, were not permitted to give evidence based on their experience, rather than any academic material such as statistical surveys or reports, as to the personal consumption rates of ecstasy tablet users.

Opinions on Ultimate Issues

F10.21 In its Eleventh Report (Cmnd 4991, para. 268), the Criminal Law Revision Committee was of the opinion that the old common-law rule that a witness should not express an opinion on an ultimate issue, i.e. one of the very issues to be determined by the court, probably no longer existed. In practice the rule is largely ignored, or treated as being of only semantic effect, so that an expert *is* allowed to express an opinion on an ultimate issue, provided that the actual words he employs are not noticeably the same as those which will be used when the issue falls to be considered by the court. In *DPP v A and BC Chewing Gum Ltd* [1968] 1 QB 159, Lord Parker CJ said (at p. 164):

> I think it would be wrong to ask the direct question as to whether any particular cards tended to corrupt or deprave, because that final stage was a matter which was entirely for the justices. No doubt, however, in such a case the defence might well put it to the witness that a particular card or cards could not corrupt, and no doubt, whatever the strict position may be, that question coming from the defence would be allowed, if only to give the defence an opportunity of getting an answer 'No' from the expert.
>
> ... I myself would go a little further in that I cannot help feeling that with the advance of science more and more inroads have been made into the old common-law principles. Those who practise in the criminal courts see every day cases of experts being called on the question of diminished responsibility, and although technically the final question 'Do you think he was suffering from diminished responsibility?' is strictly inadmissible, it is allowed time and time again without any objection.

Thus the rule has become 'a matter of form rather than substance' (*Stockwell* (1993) 97 Cr App R 260 at p. 265). For illustrations, see *Mason* 7 Cr App R 67 (whether wounds were self-inflicted), *Holmes* [1953] 1 WLR 686 (insanity), *Silcott* [1987] Crim LR 765 (the unreliability of a confession), *Hookway* [1999] Crim LR 750 (establishing identity by expert evidence of facial mapping) and *Udenze* [2001] EWCA Crim 1381 (in a rape case, the effects of alcohol on the ability to give informed consent). As to possession of drugs with intent to supply, see *Hodges* [2003] 2 Cr App R 247, considered at **F10.20**; but see also *Jeffries* [1997] Crim LR 819.

Duty of Experts

F10.22 In *Harris* [2006] 1 Cr App R 55, it was held that the description of the obligations of an expert witness set out by Creswell J in *National Justice Cia Naviera SA v Prudential Assurance Co Ltd (Ikarian Reefer)* [1993] 2 Lloyd's Rep 68 at p. 81 and the guidance for experts giving evidence involving children provided by Wall J in *In re AB (Child Abuse: Expert Witnesses)* [1995] 1 FLR 181 were both very relevant in criminal proceedings and should be kept well in mind by both prosecution and defence. Some of the factors set out by Creswell J in the former case were summarised in *Harris* (at [271]) as follows:

> (1) Expert evidence presented to the court should be and be seen to be the independent product of the expert uninfluenced as to form or content by the exigencies of litigation.
> (2) An expert witness should provide independent assistance to the court by way of objective unbiased opinion in relation to matters within his expertise. An expert witness in the High Court should never assume the role of the advocate.
> (3) An expert witness should state the facts or assumptions on which his opinion is based. He should not omit to consider material facts which detract from his concluded opinion.
> (4) An expert should make it clear when a particular question or issue falls outside his expertise.
> (5) If an expert's opinion is not properly researched because he considers that insufficient data is available then this must be stated with an indication that the opinion is no more than a provisional one.

(6) If after exchange of reports, an expert witness changes his view on material matters, such changes of view should be communicated to the other side without delay and when appropriate to the court.

In *In re AB (Child Abuse: Expert Witnesses)*, Wall J, referring to cases in which there is a genuine disagreement on a scientific or medical issue or where it is necessary for a party to advance a particular hypothesis to explain a given set of facts, said (at p. 192):

> Where that occurs, the judge [in a criminal case, jury] will have to resolve the issue which is raised. Two points must be made. In my view, the expert who advances such a hypothesis owes a very heavy duty to explain to the court that what he is advancing is a hypothesis, that it is controversial (if it is) and to place before the court all material which contradicts the hypothesis. Secondly, he must make all his material available to the other experts in the case. It is the common experience of the courts that the better the experts the more limited their areas of disagreement, and in the forensic context of a contested case relating to children, the objective of the lawyers and the experts should always be to limit the ambit of disagreement on medical issues to the minimum.

In *Harris* itself it was stressed (at [270]) that developments in scientific thinking should not be kept from the court, simply because they remain at the stage of a hypothesis, but it is of the first importance that the true status of the expert's evidence is frankly indicated to the court. As to limiting the ambit of disagreement, it was further pointed out (at [273]) that CrimPR, r. 24 and para. 15 of the Plea and Case Management form make provision for experts to come together and, if possible, agree points of agreement or disagreement with a summary of reasons. In cases involving allegations of child abuse, it was said that the judge should be prepared to give directions in respect of expert evidence, taking into account the guidance to which the court had referred.

In *B (T)* [2006] 2 Cr App R 22 it was emphasised that the duties of an expert witness as set out in *The Ikarian Reefer* and *Harris* are owed to the court and override any obligation to the person from whom the expert has received instructions, or by whom the expert is paid. Experts should maintain professional objectivity and impartiality at all times.

The duties of an expert, as set out in *Harris* and *B(T)* have been reinforced by the CrimPR, r. 33.2, which provides that an expert must help the court to achieve the overriding objective by giving objective, unbiased opinion on matters within his expertise, that this duty overrides any obligation to the person instructing him or by whom he is paid, and includes an obligation to inform all parties and the court if his opinion changes (see **appendix 1**, where the CrimPR, part 33 is set out in full).

Content of Expert's Report

In *B(T)* [2006] 2 Cr App R 22 it was held that, in addition to the specific factors referred to in *The Ikarian Reefer* [1993] 2 Lloyd's Rep 68 and *Harris* [2006] 1 Cr App R 55, the following are necessary inclusions in an expert report. **F10.23**

(a) Details of the expert's academic and professional qualifications, experience and accreditation relevant to the opinions expressed in the report and the range and extent of the expertise and any limitations upon the expertise.
(b) A statement setting out the substance of all the instructions received, with written or oral questions upon which an opinion is sought, the materials provided and considered, and the documents, statements, evidence, information or assumptions which are material to the opinions expressed or upon which those opinions are based.
(c) Information relating to who has carried out measurements, examinations, tests, etc., and the methodology used, and whether or not such measurements, etc., were carried out under the expert's supervision.
(d) Where there is a range of opinion in the matters dealt with in the report, a summary of the range of opinion and the reasons for the opinion given. In this connection any

material facts or matters which detract from the expert's opinions and any points which should fairly be made against any opinions expressed should be set out.

(e) Relevant extracts of literature or any other material which might assist the court.

(f) A statement to the effect that the expert has complied with his or her duty to the court to provide independent assistance by way of objective, unbiased, opinion in relation to matters within his or her expertise, and an acknowledgement that the expert will inform all parties (and, where appropriate, the court) in the event that his or her opinion changes on any material issues.

Where, on an exchange of experts' reports, matters arise which require a further or supplementary report, the above guidelines should be complied with in that report.

The guidelines on the contents of an expert's report set out in *B(T)* are mirrored, and in some respects amplified, in the CrimPR, r. 33.3, which is set out in full in **appendix 1**.

In *Puaca* [2005] EWCA Crim 3001, a murder conviction was quashed because a review of the development and bases of the views and evidence of the Crown's pathologist, who had undertaken the post-mortem examination, established that his conclusions could not safely be relied on. It was held that the duty of all pathologists is to comply from the start with the obligations imposed on expert witnesses; that it is wholly wrong for a pathologist carrying out the first post-mortem at the request of the police or the coroner merely to leave it to the defence to instruct a pathologist to prepare a report setting out contrary arguments; and that there was also a need, in certain cases, to refer to ante-mortem records.

Function and Weight of Expert Evidence

F10.24 The duty of the expert witness is 'to furnish the judge or jury with the necessary scientific criteria for testing the accuracy of their conclusions, so as to enable the judge or jury to form their own independent judgment by the application of those criteria to the facts proved in evidence'; and it is a misdirection, therefore, to tell the jury that expert evidence should be accepted if uncontradicted (*Davie v Magistrates of Edinburgh* 1953 SC 34, per Lord President Cooper at p. 40). See also *Lanfear* [1968] 2 QB 77 and *Rivett* (1950) 34 Cr App R 87, in which the Court of Appeal refused to interfere with a conviction despite medical evidence of insanity. Equally, it is incumbent on magistrates to approach the evidence of an expert critically, even if no expert is called on the other side, and to be willing to reject the evidence if it leaves questions unanswered (*DPP v Wynne* (2001) *Independent*, 19 February 2001). When expert evidence is given on an ultimate issue, it should be made clear to the jury that they are not bound by the opinion, and that the issue is for them to decide (*Stockwell* (1993) 97 Cr App R 260 per Lord Taylor CJ), but there is no requirement that such a warning be conveyed in any particular way (*Fitzpatrick* [1999] Crim LR 832).

However, it has also been held that it is wrong to direct a jury that they may disregard scientific evidence when the only such evidence adduced on a particular question dictates one answer and only a scientist is qualified to answer that question (*Anderson v The Queen* [1972] AC 100). See also *Matheson* [1958] 1 WLR 474 and *Bailey* (1961) 66 Cr App R 31, in both of which the Court of Criminal Appeal substituted verdicts of manslaughter. In *Matheson* it was held that where the medical evidence of diminished responsibility is uncontradicted and the jury return a verdict of guilty of murder, if there are facts entitling the jury to reject or differ from the expert opinion, the Court of Appeal will not interfere with the verdict; but if there are no facts or circumstances to displace or throw a doubt on the unchallenged medical evidence, such a verdict would not be a true verdict in accordance with the evidence. In *Bailey*, where the defence called expert evidence to prove diminished responsibility and the prosecution adduced no evidence in rebuttal, the Court of Criminal Appeal quashed the jury's verdict of guilty of murder on the ground that, although juries are not bound to accept expert medical evidence, they must act on the evidence, and if there is nothing before them to cast doubt on the medical evidence, it is not open to them to reject it. On the other hand, in *Walton v The Queen* [1978] AC 788, a conviction for murder was upheld despite uncorroborated medical evidence of diminished responsibility. *Matheson* and *Bailey* were distinguished on the basis of the greater weight and quality of the medical evidence in those cases. *Walton* was followed in *Kiszko* (1978) 68 Cr App R 62. In *Sanders* (1991) 93 Cr App R 245, the Court of Appeal held that two clear principles emerged from the cases, on the issue of diminished responsibility:

(a) if there were no other circumstances to consider, unequivocal, uncontradicted medical evidence favourable to an accused should be accepted by a jury and they should be so directed; and
(b) where there were other circumstances to consider, the medical evidence, though it be unequivocal and uncontradicted, must be assessed in the light of the other circumstances.

In deciding what weight, if any, to attach to the evidence of an expert, the jury are entitled to take into account his qualifications and experience, his credibility, and the extent to which his evidence is based on assumed facts which are or are not established.

Pre-trial Disclosure of Expert Evidence

The CrimPR, part 24 (disclosure of expert evidence) makes provision for the pre-trial disclosure of expert evidence between the parties to Crown Court and magistrates' court proceedings (see also **D14.73**). The rules are set out in full in **appendix 1**. **F10.25**

Essentially, part 24 requires a party proposing to rely on expert evidence (whether of fact or opinion) to provide the other parties and the court with a written statement of any finding or opinion of the expert and to notify the expert of this disclosure. If requested to do so, the party must also supply a copy of the record of any observation, test or similar procedure on which the expert evidence is based. The requirement does not apply to evidence relating to sentence and an exception applies where there are reasonable grounds for believing that disclosure might lead to intimidation of a witness. The phrase 'expert evidence (whether of fact or opinion)' in r. 24.1 is sufficiently wide to embrace not only the oral evidence to be given by an expert witness, but also an expert report which it is proposed to adduce under the exception to the hearsay rule contained in the CJA 1988, s. 30(1) (see **F10.28**).

The rules do not supplant or detract from the prosecution's general duty of disclosure in respect of scientific evidence, which exists irrespective of any defence request, extends to anything which may arguably assist the defence, and obliges the prosecution to make full and proper enquiries from forensic scientists in order to ascertain whether there is discoverable material. If an expert has carried out experiments or tests which tend to disprove or cast doubt on the opinion he is expressing (or knows that such experiments or tests have been carried out in his laboratory), he is under a clear obligation to bring the records of such experiments and tests to the attention of the solicitor instructing him (so that it may be disclosed to the other party) or to the expert advising the other party directly (*Ward* [1993] 1 WLR 619). See also *Clark* [2003] EWCA Crim 1020, in which the accused's convictions for the murder of her two infant sons were quashed. A forensic pathologist, in breach of normal practice, had omitted from his autopsy report and had failed to disclose the fact that, in the case of one of the infants, following microbiological examination of certain bodily fluids, a form of bacteria which in some parts of the body can prove lethal had been isolated.

Pre-hearing Discussion of Expert Evidence

Where more than one party wants to introduce expert evidence, the court may direct the experts to discuss the issues and prepare a statement for the court of the matters on which they agree and disagree, giving their reasons; if an expert does not comply with such a **F10.26** direction, his evidence may not be introduced without the leave of the court (CrimPR, rr. 33.5 and 33.6, set out in full in **appendix 1**).

Single Joint Experts

F10.27 Where more than one accused wants to introduce expert evidence, the court may direct that the evidence be given by one expert only (CrimPR, r. 33.7 (1): see **appendix 1**). Provision is also made for selection of an expert where the co-accused cannot agree who should be the expert (r. 33.7 (2)) and for giving instructions and directions to the expert (r. 33.8).

Presentation of Expert and Complicated Evidence

F10.28 **Criminal Justice Act 1988, ss. 30 and 31**

Expert reports

30.—(1) An expert report shall be admissible as evidence in criminal proceedings, whether or not the person making it attends to give oral evidence in those proceedings.

(2) If it is proposed that the person making the report shall not give oral evidence, the report shall only be admissible with the leave of the court.

(3) For the purpose of determining whether to give leave the court shall have regard—

(a) to the contents of the report;

(b) to the reasons why it is proposed that the person making the report shall not give oral evidence;

(c) to any risk, having regard in particular to whether it is likely to be possible to controvert statements in the report if the person making it does not attend to give oral evidence in the proceedings, that its admission or exclusion will result in unfairness to the accused or, if there is more than one, to any of them; and

(d) to any other circumstances that appear to the court to be relevant.

(4) An expert report, when admitted, shall be evidence of any fact or opinion of which the person making it could have given oral evidence.

(4A) Where the proceedings mentioned in subsection (1) above are proceedings before a magistrates' court inquiring into an offence as examining justices this section shall have effect with the omission of—

(a) in subsection (1) the words 'whether or not the person making it attends to give oral evidence in those proceedings'; and

(b) subsections (2) to (4).

(5) In this section 'expert report' means a written report by a person dealing wholly or mainly with matters on which he is (or would if living be) qualified to give expert evidence.

Form of evidence and glossaries

31. For the purpose of helping members of juries to understand complicated issues of fact or technical terms Criminal Procedure Rules may make provision—

(a) as to the furnishing of evidence in any form, notwithstanding the existence of admissible material from which the evidence to be given in that form would be derived; and

(b) as to the furnishing of glossaries for such purposes as may be specified; in any case where the court gives leave for, or requires, evidence or a glossary to be so furnished.

Section F11 Admissibility of Previous Verdicts

PROOF OF CONVICTIONS AND ACQUITTALS

The PACE 1984, s. 73, provides for the proof of convictions and acquittals in the UK by a certificate of conviction or acquittal, together with proof that the person named in the certificate is the person whose conviction or acquittal is in issue. As to the latter issue, although it is for the judge to decide whether there is prima facie evidence fit for the jury's consideration, ultimately it is a question of fact for the jury to decide (*Burns* [2006] 1 WLR 1273 and *Lewendon* [2006] 2 Cr App R 294). **F11.1**

Police and Criminal Evidence Act 1984, ss. 73 and 82

73.—(1) Where in any proceedings the fact that a person has in the United Kingdom been convicted or acquitted of an offence otherwise than by a Service court is admissible in evidence, it may be proved by producing a certificate of conviction or, as the case may be, of acquittal relating to that offence, and proving that the person named in the certificate as having been convicted or acquitted of the offence is the person whose conviction or acquittal of the offence is to be proved.

(2) For the purposes of this section a certificate of conviction or of acquittal—

(a) shall, as regards a conviction or acquittal on indictment, consist of a certificate, signed by the proper officer of the court where the conviction or acquittal took place, giving the substance and effect (omitting the formal parts) of the indictment and of the conviction or acquittal; and

(b) shall, as regards a conviction or acquittal on a summary trial, consist of a copy of the conviction or of the dismissal of the information, signed by the clerk of the court where the conviction or acquittal took place or by the clerk of the court, if any, to which a memorandum of the conviction or acquittal was sent;

and a document purporting to be a duly signed certificate of conviction or acquittal under this section shall be taken to be such a certificate unless the contrary is proved.

(3) In subsection (2) above 'proper officer' means—

(a) in relation to a magistrates' court in England and Wales, the designated officer for the court; and

(b) in relation to any other court, the clerk of the court, his deputy or any other person having custody of the court record.

(4) The method of proving a conviction or acquittal authorised by this section shall be in addition to and not to the exclusion of any other authorised manner of proving a conviction or acquittal.

Part VIII—interpretation

82.—(1) In this part of this Act— . . .

'court-martial' means a court-martial constituted under the Army Act 1955, the Air Force Act 1955 or the Naval Discipline Act 1957;

'proceedings' means criminal proceedings, including—

(a) proceedings in the United Kingdom or elsewhere before a court-martial constituted under the Army Act 1955, the Air Force Act 1955 or the Naval Discipline Act 1957;

(b) proceedings in the United Kingdom or elsewhere before the Courts-Martial Appeal Court—

(i) on an appeal from a court-martial so constituted; or

(ii) on a reference under section 34 of the Courts-Martial (Appeals) Act 1968; and

(c) proceedings before a Standing Civilian Court; and
'Service court' means a court-martial or a Standing Civilian Court.

(2) In this part of this Act references to conviction before a Service court are references to a finding of guilty which is, or falls to be treated as, the finding of the court and 'convicted' shall be construed accordingly.

(b) as regards—
(i) a court-martial; or
(ii) a disciplinary court.

(3) Nothing in this part of this Act shall prejudice any power of a court to exclude evidence (whether by preventing questions from being put or otherwise) at its discretion.

When the Armed Forces Act 2006, s. 378, is brought into force, the following amendments will be made to s. 82 of the 1984 Act: in s. 82(1), the definition of 'court-martial' will be repealed, the words 'service proceedings' will be substituted for sub-paragraphs (a) to (c) and 'Service court' will be re-defined to mean 'the Court Martial or the Service Civilian Court'; and s. 82(2) will be repealed.

Proof of Identity

F11.2 Concerning the requirement, in the PACE 1984, s. 73(1), of proof that the person named in the certificate is the person whose conviction or acquittal is to be proved, in *Pattison v DPP* [2006] 2 All ER 317 it was held that, where s. 73(1) is relied upon by the prosecution to prove the conviction of an accused, the following general principles could be distilled from the authorities:

(a) The prosecution must prove to the criminal standard that the accused is the person named on the certificate.
(b) This proof may be effected by an admission by or on behalf of the accused, by evidence of fingerprints or by the evidence of someone who was present in court at the time.
(c) However, there is no prescribed means of proof; the matter can be proved by any admissible means.
(d) An example of such means is a match between the personal details of the accused and the personal details recorded on the certificate.
(e) Even if the personal details, such as the name of the accused, are not uncommon, a match will be sufficient for a prima facie case.
(f) In the absence of any evidence contradicting such a prima facie case, the evidence will be sufficient.
(g) The failure of the accused to give any contradictory evidence in rebuttal will be a matter to take into account. If it is proper and fair to do so, and a warning has been given, it can additionally give rise to an adverse inference under the CJPOA 1994, s. 35(2) (see F19.20).

Similarity in name and date of birth between a certificate and an accused may or may not amount to prima facie evidence of identity. Each case must depend on its own facts and the material which is available. For example, if an accused has an extremely common name and the date of birth on the certificate is not precisely the same as that of the accused, it may well be that it does not constitute prima facie evidence of identity. On the other hand, if the accused has a highly unusual name with many different component parts, it may constitute prima facie evidence of identity without evidence of an identical date of birth (*Burns*).

Summary Offences, Orders Made by Magistrates and Endorsements

F11.3 To overcome the difficulties, at common law, in seeking to prove the previous convictions of a person convicted of a summary offence, if he does not attend the court, the MCA 1980, s. 104, provides that, if the court is satisfied that, not less than seven days before the hearing, a notice, stating the alleged previous convictions which it is proposed to bring to the attention of the court, has been served on the accused, and the accused is not present before the court, the court may take account of the convictions as if the accused had appeared and admitted them. Orders made by magistrates' courts, such as an order disqualifying a person from holding a driving licence, may be proved under the CrimPR, r. 6.4, which provides that the register of a magistrates' court, or an extract from the register certified by the magistrates' court officer as a true extract, shall be admissible in any legal proceedings as evidence of the proceedings of the court entered in the register. Endorsements on a driving licence of the particulars of a conviction or disqualification may be produced as prima facie evidence of the matters endorsed (see the RTOA 1988, ss. 31(1) and 44(1)).

Convictions Overseas

For the purposes of extradition proceedings, the fact of a conviction overseas may be proved **F11.4**
by a properly certified copy of the court record (see the Extradition Act 1989, sch. 1, para. 12, and *Re Mullin* [1993] Crim LR 390).

CONVICTIONS AS EVIDENCE OF FACTS ON WHICH BASED

At common law, the convictions of one person were not admissible as evidence of the facts **F11.5**
on which they were based at the subsequent trial of another: see *Turner* (1832) 1 Mood CC 347, at p. 349 (one person's conviction for theft inadmissible as evidence of such theft at the trial of another charged with handling the stolen goods); *Hassan* [1970] QB 423 (a woman's convictions for prostitution inadmissible as evidence of such prostitution at the trial of a man charged with living off her immoral earnings); and *Spinks* [1982] 1 All ER 587 (a principal's conviction of wounding inadmissible as evidence of such wounding at the subsequent trial of an alleged accessory). The PACE 1984, s. 74(1), has now reversed the common-law rule, and s. 74(2) has created a persuasive presumption: the person (other than the accused) convicted of an offence shall be taken to have committed that offence unless the contrary is proved. The legal burden is borne by the party against whom the presumption operates; and if borne by the accused, may be discharged by proof on a balance of probabilities (see *Carr-Briant* [1943] KB 607 and generally **F3.40** and **F3.55**). Section 74(3) creates a similar presumption in the case of the previous convictions of *the accused*, provided that evidence is admissible of the fact that the accused has committed the offence in respect of which he has been convicted.

Police and Criminal Evidence Act 1984, s. 74

(1) In any proceedings the fact that a person other than the accused has been convicted of an offence by or before any court in the United Kingdom or by a Service court outside the United Kingdom shall be admissible in evidence for the purpose of proving that that person committed that offence, where evidence of his having done so is admissible, whether or not any other evidence of his having committed that offence is given.

(2) In any proceedings in which by virtue of this section a person other than the accused is proved to have been convicted of an offence by or before any court in the United Kingdom or by a Service court outside the United Kingdom, he shall be taken to have committed that offence unless the contrary is proved.

(3) In any proceedings where evidence is admissible of the fact that the accused has committed an offence, if the accused is proved to have been convicted of the offence—
   (a) by or before any court in the United Kingdom; or
   (b) by a Service court outside the United Kingdom,

   he shall be taken to have committed that offence unless the contrary is proved.

(4) Nothing in this section shall prejudice—
   (a) the admissibility in evidence of any conviction which would be admissible apart from this section; or
   (b) the operation of any enactment whereby a conviction or a finding of fact in any proceedings is for the purposes of any other proceedings made conclusive evidence of any fact.

For the definition of 'proceedings', 'Service court' and 'conviction before a Service court', see s. 82, at **F11.1**.

Police and Criminal Evidence Act 1984, s. 75

(1) Where evidence that a person has been convicted of an offence is admissible by virtue of section 74 above, then without prejudice to the reception of any other admissible evidence for the purpose of identifying the facts on which the conviction was based—
(a) the contents of any document which is admissible as evidence of the conviction; and
(b) the contents of the information, complaint, indictment or charge-sheet on which the person in question was convicted,
shall be admissible in evidence for that purpose.
(2) Where in any proceedings the contents of any document are admissible in evidence by virtue of subsection (1) above, a copy of that document, or of the material part of it, purporting to be certified or otherwise authenticated by or on behalf of the court or authority having custody of that document shall be admissible in evidence and shall be taken to be a true copy of that document or part unless the contrary is shown.
(3) Nothing in any of the following—
(a) section 14 of the Powers of Criminal Courts (Sentencing) Act 2000 (under which a conviction leading to probation or discharge is to be disregarded except as mentioned in that section);
(b) section 247 of the Criminal Procedure (Scotland) Act 1995 (which makes similar provision in respect of convictions on indictment in Scotland); and
(c) section 8 of the Probation Act (Northern Ireland) 1950 (which corresponds to section [13 of the Powers of Criminal Courts Act 1973) or any legislation which is in force in Northern Ireland for the time being and corresponds to that section,
shall affect the operation of section 74 above; and for the purposes of that section any order made by a court of summary jurisdiction in Scotland under section 228 or section 246(3) of the said Act of 1995 shall be treated as a conviction.
(4) Nothing in section 74 above shall be construed as rendering admissible in any proceedings evidence of any conviction other than a subsisting one.

When the Armed Forces Act 2006, s. 378, is brought into force, s. 74(3) of the 1984 Act will be amended by the insertion of '(aa) section 187 of the Armed Forces Act 2006 (which makes similar provision in respect of service convictions);'

A 'subsisting' conviction means either a finding of guilt that has not been quashed on appeal or a formal plea of guilt that has not been withdrawn; whether the accused has been sentenced is irrelevant (*Robertson* [1987] QB 920). It seems that one co-accused may rely upon s. 74(1) to adduce evidence of the convictions of another co-accused, provided that they are relevant to an issue in the proceedings (see *Hendrick* [1992] Crim LR 427, where the convictions were held to be irrelevant). It is possible to envisage situations in which a co-accused pleads guilty to a charge even though the evidence is far from conclusive against him, and in such a case it could well be unfair to allow the prosecution to use the conviction as evidence, on that charge, against the remaining accused (see *Lee* [1996] Crim LR 825). Where one co-accused pleads guilty towards or at the end of the prosecution case and the prosecution make an application to reopen their case to adduce evidence of the guilty plea under s. 74(1), the plea, if relevant to an issue in the proceedings, is admissible, subject to exercise of the discretion to exclude under s. 78, as when it would be unfair because, had the guilty plea been entered and admitted in evidence at an earlier stage, cross-examination might have been conducted differently (*Chapman* [1991] Crim LR 44).

Foreign Convictions

F11.6 Foreign convictions, apart from convictions by Service courts outside the UK, are not covered by PACE 1984, s.74, but may be admissible under the bad character provisions of the CJA 2003 (see **F12** and **F14**) and, if admissible, may be proved under the Evidence Act 1851, s. 7 (see **F8.11**) (*Kordasinski* [2007] 1 Cr App R 238).

Convictions of Persons Other than the Accused

Relevance to an Issue in the Proceedings The wording of the PACE 1984, s. 74(1), was amended by the CJA 2003. The words 'that that person committed that offence, where evidence of his having done so is admissible' were substituted for the original words 'where to do so is relevant to any issue in those proceedings'. The amendment is cosmetic, insofar as evidence of the commission of the offence, in order to be 'admissible', must be relevant to an issue in the proceedings, and it is submitted that such of the following cases in which the court had to decide whether the commission of an offence was 'relevant to any issue in those proceedings' would be decided in the same way under s. 74(1) as amended. **F11.7**

In *Hasson* [1997] Crim LR 579 the accused were charged with being concerned in the supply of drugs. It was held that the previous drug-related convictions of six men with whom the accused had socialised had been improperly admitted because it was not the Crown case that the accused were supplying them with drugs and there was no evidence to show that meetings with them were related to the offence charged.

In some cases proof of the commission of an offence by a person other than the accused will establish an essential ingredient of the offence with which the accused is charged, and therefore will be clearly relevant to an 'issue in those proceedings'. In *Pigram* [1995] Crim LR 808, in which officers had seen H and P transfer goods from H's van to P's lorry and H and P were jointly charged with handling, it was held that H's guilty plea was admissible against P for the purposes of proving that the goods were stolen.

The phrase 'issue in those proceedings', however, was not confined to an issue which was an essential ingredient of the offence charged. In *Robertson* [1987] QB 920, the Court of Appeal held that the phrase also covered less fundamental issues, for example evidential issues arising in the proceedings. The Court also rejected the argument that s. 74(1) applies only to the proof of convictions of offences in which the accused on trial did not participate. Robertson was charged with two co-accused with conspiracy to commit burglary. The co-accused pleaded not guilty to the conspiracy but guilty to some 16 burglaries committed during the period of the conspiracy. Evidence of these convictions was held to be admissible, because it could be inferred from the fact that the co-accused had committed these offences that there was a conspiracy between them, and that was the conspiracy to which, the prosecution alleged, Robertson was a party. In *Golder*, the appeal in which was heard with and is reported with *Robertson* [1987] QB 920, Golder was charged with a robbery committed at garage H. Two of his co-accused pleaded guilty to that robbery, and also to another robbery committed at garage G. The evidence against Golder consisted primarily of a confession statement, which he alleged to have been fabricated by the police, in which he made reference to both robberies. The evidence of the guilty pleas was held to be admissible: proof of the commission of the offences at both garages was relevant, because it showed that the contents of Golder's confession were in accordance with the facts as they were known and the confession was therefore more likely to be true; and proof of the commission of the offence at garage H was relevant, because robbery at that garage was one of the matters which the prosecution had to prove.

The decision in *Robertson* that the phrase 'issue in those proceedings' should be given a wide interpretation so as to include evidentiary matters, was applied in *Castle* [1989] Crim LR 567. C and others, including F, were charged with robbery. The victim, when seeing C and F at the identification parade, said 'yes' in respect of C and 'possibly' in respect of F. F pleaded guilty. It was held that evidence of the guilty plea was admissible because relevant to the issue of the reliability of the identification of C. The evidence, by confirming that the victim was correct in his 'possible' identification of F, tended to corroborate the correctness of his positive identification of C. See also, *sed quaere, Buckingham* (1994) 99 Cr App R 303: evidence of W's conviction of conspiracy to pervert the course of justice by obtaining, as the accused in a previous trial, false evidence of defence witnesses, was admissible at the trial of those witnesses for doing acts intended to pervert the course of justice because, although it was not probative that any of the witnesses had given false evidence, it established the conspiracy.

F11.8 **The Discretion to Exclude** In *O'Connor* (1987) 85 Cr App R 298, B and O'Connor were jointly charged with having conspired together (and with no one else) to obtain property by deception. At the trial of O'Connor, B's plea of guilty was admitted, together with all the detail contained in the conspiracy count (see the PACE 1984, s. 75(1)(b), at **F11.5**). The Court of Appeal upheld O'Connor's conviction by application of the proviso which then applied, but held that the evidence should have been excluded on the ground that it was impossible realistically to exclude the possibility that the jury might infer from B's admission, and the detail contained in the count, that not only had B conspired with O'Connor, but that the converse had also taken place. Furthermore, it was not open to the defence to challenge or test what had been said by B. The court concluded that if it was appropriate within the section to admit the conviction, the judge should have excluded it under s. 78, on the basis that it would have had such an adverse effect on the fairness of the proceedings that it ought not to have been admitted. In *Mattison* [1990] Crim LR 117, M was charged in one count with gross indecency with D. In another count, D was charged with gross indecency with M. D pleaded guilty and at M's trial evidence of that plea was admitted. The judge directed the jury that the evidence of D's plea did not mean that M was guilty, but was before them to make the background accurate. Allowing the appeal, it was held that although D's guilty plea was relevant in the proceedings against M, the judge, bearing in mind M's defence, which was one of complete denial, should have exercised the discretion under s. 78 to exclude the evidence. See also *Fedrick* [1990] Crim LR 403 and *Turpin* [1990] Crim LR 514, discussed below. It seems that evidence of a conviction, which would otherwise be clearly admissible under s. 74, may also be excluded under s. 78 on the basis that it adds little to an already strong case against the accused (see *Warner* (1993) 96 Cr App R 324).

In *Robertson* [1987] QB 920, counsel for the appellant, relying upon *O'Connor*, submitted that the convictions in that case should also have been excluded under s. 78, because the prosecution, in relying on s. 74, had deprived Robertson of the opportunity to cross-examine the co-accused. The Court of Appeal rejected the argument, distinguishing *O'Connor*. Robertson's name did not appear on any of the burglary counts, and even if the co-accused had given evidence in accordance with their guilty pleas, Robertson's counsel would have been unlikely to cross-examine them (or, if he had done so, he would have seriously prejudiced Robertson). (In this respect, see also *Kempster* [1989] 1 WLR 1125, discussed below.) However, the court added (at p. 928): 'Section 74 is a provision which should be sparingly used. There will be occasions where, although the evidence may be technically admissible its effect is likely to be so slight that it will be wiser not to adduce it. This is particularly so when there is a danger of a contravention of section 78.' It was further observed that where the evidence is admitted, the judge should be careful to explain to the jury its effect and limitations.

In *Turner* [1991] Crim LR 57, T and L, in separate cars, were driving at night down a hill. L overtook T, collided with an oncoming vehicle and killed his (L's) passenger. The prosecution alleged that L and T were racing. L pleaded guilty to causing death by reckless driving. T was tried on the same charge and denied that he was racing. It was held that L's guilty plea was relevant to T's trial because the prosecution case was that L had been the principal and T the secondary party who aided and abetted L. The question was whether the plea should have been excluded under s. 78. Provided that the judge made it clear, as he did, that L's plea did not amount to an admission that he was racing, there was nothing unfair in admitting the evidence. In *Bennett* [1988] Crim LR 686, B was charged with theft. Her co-accused, a supermarket cashier, pleaded guilty to theft, the allegation being that she passed goods to B for less than their true price. Evidence of the guilty plea was admitted against B. The Court held that any decision to the contrary would have bewildered the jury. The evidence was adduced to establish that there had been a theft. The issue of whether B had been a party to the theft had been fairly left with the jury, and the judge had properly exercised his discretion under s. 78. See also *Stewart* [1999] Crim LR 746.

Cases of Conspiracy and Joint Enterprise In *Lunnon* [1988] Crim LR 456, in which there were three accused jointly charged with conspiracy, it was held that the guilty plea of one of them had been properly admitted to prove the existence of the conspiracy: the judge had separated two questions for the jury, namely (a) whether there was a conspiracy and (b) who was a party to it, and had made it clear that, despite the evidence of the guilty plea, the jury could acquit the accused. (See also *Garrity* [1994] Crim LR 828; and compare *Humphreys* [1993] Crim LR 288, where it was held that the evidence should have been excluded under the PACE 1984, s. 78, because there was other prosecution evidence of the conspiracy.) In *Chapman* [1991] Crim LR 44, C and seven others were charged with conspiracy to obtain by deception. The pleas of guilty by one of the others to two specific counts of obtaining by deception, being two incidents in which he was involved with C, were held to be relevant; and since there were others in the conspiracy, and since the other co-accused did not plead guilty to conspiracy but to specific obtainings by deception, the evidence of the conviction did not inevitably import the complicity of C. See also *Hunt* [1994] Crim LR 747 and *cf. Curry* [1988] Crim LR 527. The appellant, Curry, was convicted of conspiracy to obtain property by deception. She was charged with two others, one of whom, H, had pleaded guilty. The prosecution case was that Curry, with H's knowledge, had used H's credit card to obtain goods, and that H then intended to report the card as stolen in order to avoid liability to pay for the goods. The other co-accused, W, had driven the women to the shops. Evidence of H's guilty plea was admitted to establish the existence of an unlawful agreement to deceive. The Court of Appeal, distinguishing *Lunnon* (1988) 88 Cr App R 71, quashed the conviction on the grounds that the evidence of the guilty plea clearly implied as a matter of fact that the appellant had been a party to the conspiracy, even though it did not have that effect as a matter of law, and should have been excluded under s. 78. Section 74, it was said, should be sparingly used, particularly in relation to joint offences such as conspiracy and affray. It should not be used where the evidence, expressly or by necessary inference, suggests the complicity of the accused. **F11.9**

This last observation in *Curry* was reiterated in *Kempster* [1989] 1 WLR 1125, in which the Court of Appeal noted that the effect of admitting a conviction as evidence of the complicity of the accused, is that the prosecution will not have to call the person convicted as a witness and the defence will be deprived of any opportunity to cross-examine him, in particular as to the complicity of the accused. Staughton LJ said (at p. 22):

> No doubt such cross-examination may in itself be unlikely in some cases, or else turn out to be a disaster, as the Lord Chief Justice put it in *Robertson*. But one cannot always assume that.

In *Turpin* [1990] Crim LR 514, T, with three others, was charged with violent disorder. Two of the co-accused pleaded guilty. At the trial of T, counsel for the prosecution, in opening the case, told the jury that the guilty pleas were not probative of the case against T in any way. In his defence, T admitted that there had been violent disorder, but denied being involved in it. In the summing-up, the judge did not refer to the pleas of guilty, nor did he repeat what counsel for the prosecution had said in that regard. Dismissing T's appeal, it was held that, although it is desirable to refer to pleas of guilty by co-accused where they necessarily showed complicity with the accused, it is not always necessary for a judge to refer to pleas of guilty by co-accused, and in the present case it was not necessary for the judge to repeat what counsel for the prosecution had said in opening the case. *Turpin* may be compared with *Betterley* [1994] Crim LR 764, where it was held that in a case involving joint enterprise in which one of the co-accused pleads guilty, it is not enough for the judge to direct the jury that they must be sure that each of the accused was a party to the enterprise — they should be told that it is essential that they put the guilty plea out of their minds. See also *Marlow* [1997] Crim LR 457.

F11.10 **Purpose of Adducing Evidence** The Court of Appeal in *Kempster* [1989] 1 WLR 1125 also stressed that it is important to ascertain the purpose for which evidence under the PACE 1984, s. 74, is to be adduced before deciding whether it should be excluded under s. 78; and that if the evidence is admitted, the trial judge should be careful not only to direct the jury about the purpose for which it has been admitted, but also to ensure that counsel do not seek to use it for any other purpose. In that case, evidence of the guilty pleas of a number of co-accused was admitted but not the detailed particulars of the offences committed. At the time of the application to admit, it was unclear whether the prosecution were relying on the evidence in order to prove the guilt of the accused or merely to prevent mystification of the jury, and therefore there was no clear and informed decision by the judge about any adverse effect the evidence might have on the fairness of the proceedings. In the event, the jury were encouraged to rely on the evidence for the purpose of proving the guilt of the accused. The convictions were quashed. In *Mahmood* [1997] 1 Cr App R 414, L, KM and NM were charged with rape. The prosecution case was that the complainant was too drunk to have consented. L pleaded guilty. KM and NM admitted intercourse but alleged consent or alternatively belief in consent. It was held that evidence of L's plea should not have been admitted because, without knowing the basis for it, it was not possible to identify any issue to which it was relevant. There was a real danger that the jury would assume it meant that L knew the complainant could not consent by reason of drink (whereas it is possible that he believed she could consent, but knew she was not consenting or was reckless as to whether she was consenting) and conclude therefore that KM and NM must also have known that she could not consent, an approach which would preclude proper consideration of the state of mind of each accused. Cf. *Skinner* [1995] Crim LR 805. See also *Boyson* [1991] Crim LR 274, where the Court of Appeal held, *per curiam*, that it did not approve of the growing practice of allowing evidence to go before a jury which is irrelevant, inadmissible, prejudicial or unfair simply because it is convenient for the jury to have 'the whole picture', and *Hall* [1993] Crim LR 527.

Convictions of Accused

F11.11 It is clear from the wording of the PACE 1984, s. 74(3), that its purpose is not to define or enlarge the circumstances in which evidence of the fact that the accused has committed an offence is admissible, but is simply to assist in the mode of proof of that fact. The evidence, of course, must also be relevant to an issue in the proceedings and, it is submitted, may be relevant either to an essential ingredient of the offence charged or some less fundamental issue arising in the course of the proceedings (see *Harris* [2001] Crim LR 227, a decision under the original version of s. 74(3), which contained the words 'in so far as that evidence is relevant to any matter in issue in the proceedings . . . '; and cf. *Robertson* [1987] QB 920, considered at **F11.7**).

There are only three situations, it is submitted, in which reliance may be placed on s. 74(3). The first is where the prosecution seek to prove, as an element of the offence with which the accused is charged, the fact that he committed some other offence in respect of which he has been convicted, as when, after the accused's conviction for assault, the victim dies from his injuries, and the accused is then prosecuted for his murder or manslaughter. The second is where the prosecution seek to adduce evidence of the accused's commission of an offence, in respect of which he has been convicted, under the CJA 2003, s. 101 (see **F12.11**). The third situation is where, a conviction having been proved as part of the prosecution case pursuant to statutory provisions such as s. 101 (see **F12.11**) or the Theft Act 1968, s. 27(3)(b) (see **F12.48**), the accused denies having committed the offence in question.

THE RELEVANCE AND ADMISSIBILITY OF ACQUITTALS

Evidence of an earlier acquittal is generally irrelevant and therefore inadmissible, but an exception exists where a witness's credibility is directly in issue and there is a clear inference from the earlier verdict that the jury in that trial rejected his evidence because they did not believe him (*Deboussi* [2007] EWCA Crim 684, which is considered, together with the other authorities, at **F1.15**). **F11.12**

In *Sambasivam v Public Prosecutor of Malaya Federation* [1950] AC 458, S was charged with two offences (a) carrying a revolver, in respect of which a new trial was ordered, and (b) being in possession of ten rounds of ammunition (six of which were loaded in the revolver), of which he was acquitted. At the new trial, the prosecution relied on a statement allegedly made by S in which he admitted both charges. S was convicted. The Privy Council quashed the conviction on the ground that the judge should have directed the tribunal of fact that the accused had been acquitted of being in possession of ammunition, and that the prosecution were bound to accept that the part of the alleged statement relating to the ammunition must be regarded as untrue. Lord MacDermott said (at p. 479):

> The effect of a verdict of acquittal pronounced by a competent court on a lawful charge and after a lawful trial is not completely stated by saying that the person acquitted cannot be tried again for the same offence. To that it must be added that the verdict is binding and conclusive in all subsequent proceedings between the parties to the adjudication.

In *Hay* (1983) 77 Cr App R 70, H made a written confession to two unconnected charges, one of arson and one of burglary. At his trial for the arson charge, his confession was admitted in edited form, excluding references to the burglary. His defence was one of alibi and he alleged that the police had fabricated his confession. He was acquitted. At his subsequent trial for burglary, the judge refused to allow H to adduce evidence of the previous acquittal and alibi evidence, ruling that both were irrelevant to the charge of burglary. On appeal against conviction, the Court of Appeal, having considered the passage (set out above) from Lord MacDermott's judgment in *Sambasivam*, allowed the appeal. O'Connor LJ said (at p. 75):

> The jury ought to have been told of the acquittal and directed that it was conclusive evidence that the accused was not guilty of arson, and that his confession to that offence was untrue. The jury should have been directed that in deciding the contest between the appellant and the police officers as to the part of the statement referring to the burglary, they should keep in mind that the first part must be regarded as untrue.

The decisions in *Sambasivam* and *Hay* must be read subject to the subsequent authorities on the topic.

The decision in *Sambasivam* is not to be regarded as an authority in support of the existence of the doctrine of issue estoppel, which is inapplicable in criminal cases (*DPP v Humphrys* [1977] AC 1 (see **D12.28**)). An acquittal is not conclusive evidence of innocence and does not establish that all relevant issues were resolved in favour of the accused (*Terry* [2005] QB 996, considered below, and *Colman* [2004] EWCA Crim 3252). In *Z* [2000] 2 AC 483, Z was charged with rape, his defence being consent or mistaken belief in consent. The prosecution wished to adduce evidence of four previous incidents, involving four different women, each of which had resulted in a rape trial at which Z's defence had been consent. Z was convicted in one of the cases, but was acquitted in the other three. The judge ruled that the evidence came within the ambit of the similar fact doctrine, but that the evidence of the three women in respect of whom Z had been acquitted was inadmissible by reason of the statement of Lord MacDermott in *Sambasivam* (as set out above), and that by itself the evidence of the woman in respect of whom Z had been convicted did not establish a sufficiently cogent picture of similar facts to be admitted. The Court of Appeal upheld the decision. The prosecution appealed. The House of Lords allowed the appeal on the following grounds:

(a) It had been right to set aside the conviction in *Sambasivam*, but the proper grounds for doing so were those given by Lord Pearce in *Connelly v DPP* [1964] AC 1254 at pp. 1362 and 1364, namely that a man should not be prosecuted a second time where the two offences were in fact founded on one and the same incident (the carrying of the revolver and the ammunition) and that a man should not be tried for a second offence (carrying the revolver in which some of the ammunition was loaded) which was manifestly inconsistent on the facts with a previous acquittal (acquittal of possession of the ammunition).
(b) Provided that an accused is not placed in double jeopardy in the way described by Lord Pearce, evidence which is relevant on a subsequent prosecution is not inadmissible because it shows or tends to show that the accused was, in fact, guilty of an offence of which he had earlier been acquitted. The statement of Lord MacDermott in *Sambasivam* (as set out above) requires to be qualified in this way.
(c) The judgments in *G (an Infant) v Coltart* [1967] 1 All ER 271 should not be followed: a distinction should not be drawn between evidence which shows guilt of an earlier offence of which the accused has been acquitted and evidence which tends to show guilt of such an offence or which appears to relate to one distinct issue rather than the issue of guilt of such an offence.
(d) In the present case, Z would not be placed in double jeopardy and the evidence of the earlier complainants, being relevant and admissible under the similar facts doctrine, should not be inadmissible because it shows that the accused was in fact guilty of the offences of rape of which he had earlier been acquitted.

Evidence of the kind relied on in *Z* is now admissible under the CJA 2003, s. 101(1)(d), whereby evidence of the accused's bad character is admissible 'if it is relevant to an important matter in issue between the defendant and the prosecution', subject to the discretion to exclude it under s. 101(3).

In *Terry* [2005] QB 996, it was observed, concerning the passage in the judgment of O'Connor LJ in *Hay* set out above, that it went further than was necessary to correct the judge's decision on relevance and admissibility and was inconsistent with the rationale of the decision in *Z*, because an acquittal is not conclusive evidence of innocence and does not mean that all relevant issues were resolved in favour of the accused. In *Terry*, Auld LJ also observed (at [45]) that the ruling of the House of Lords in *Z* is not restricted to similar fact evidence: the critical questions are whether the evidence in question is admissible, whatever its species, as relevant to an issue in the case, and whether it is fair to admit it.

Section F12 Character Evidence: Evidence of Bad Character of Accused

CODIFICATION OF EVIDENCE OF BAD CHARACTER BY THE CRIMINAL JUSTICE ACT 2003

The provisions of chapter 1 of part 11 of the CJA 2003 (ss. 98 to 110 and 112) came into force on 15 December 2004 (Criminal Justice Act 2003 (Commencement No. 6 and Transitional Provisions) Order 2004). They now apply in all trials beginning on or after that date (*Bradley* [2005] 1 Cr App R 397), including retrials where the original trial took place before the changes effected by the Act (*Campbell* [2006] EWCA Crim 1305). **F12.1**

The new provisions, with minor exceptions, codify the law governing the admissibility of evidence of bad character, replacing both the common law and the provisions of the Criminal Evidence Act 1898, s. 1(3), which formerly governed the cross-examination of the accused on matters relating to his bad character. In *Bradley*, the Court of Appeal observed that the provisions form part of a 'torrent' of legislation conspicuous more for its quantity than its quality. The courts have had much work to do to interpret the new provisions in a coherent way, but the emergence of a shared approach and common understanding throughout the early judgments of the Court of Appeal has resolved many of the ambiguities in the drafting. The key decisions are *Hanson* [2005] 1 WLR 3169; *Highton* [2005] 1 WLR 3472; *Edwards* [2006]1 WLR 1524; *Weir* [2006] 1 WLR 1855; *Renda* [2006] 1 WLR 2948; and *Lawson* [2007] 1 WLR 1191. For a suggested radical departure from this line of thinking, see *Campbell* [2007] EWCA Crim 1472 at **F12.14**.

The statutory scheme is different from the old law of bad character in many respects. For the purposes of organisation of the materials appearing in this work, the exposition of the statutory principles is most easily dealt with under the categories of admissibility laid down in the CJA 2003, s. 101. For the purposes of comparison, and to assist in the interpretation of some aspect of the new provisions, it may still be helpful to make reference to the 'old' law of character, but subject to the very clear 'health warning' that the new law embodies a different approach to admissibility, which gives effect to Parliament's intention that 'evidence of bad character would be put before juries more frequently than had hitherto been the case' (*Edwards* [2006] 1 WLR 1524). Thus:

> The right way to deal with the new law is not first to ask what would have been the position under the old. In saying that, we do not doubt that some, perhaps many, of the familiar considerations of relevance and fairness which confronted courts before the 2003 Act in cases of multiple allegations where they were said to be of a similar kind will continue to confront them

> dealing with such cases afterwards. Nor do we doubt that the answers may be the same. There has, however, been a sea-change in the law's starting-point (*Chopra* [2007] 1 Cr App R 225).

This observation, though made in the specific context of cases involving multiple allegations (see **F12.30**), is of equal assistance with regard to other cases in which evidence of bad character is in issue. Although the drafting of the CJA 2003 would have admitted of an interpretation preserving far more of the old law, the courts have made sparing reference to previous authorities and have treated the new provisions, in the way that Parliament intended, as a new departure.

It should be noted that the CJA 2003, s. 100, makes separate provision for leave to be obtained before introducing evidence of the bad character of a person other than the accused. This matter is dealt with further at **F14**.

Bad Character

F12.2 The CJA 2003, s. 101, provides that evidence of the bad character of an accused is admissible 'if but only if' it falls within a specific statutory permission, or a 'gateway' as the courts commonly say, in s. 101(a) to (g). Other evidence which does not constitute evidence of bad character within the meaning of the Act, but which nevertheless shows the accused in a bad light, may be admitted on normal principles of relevance, subject to the application of the PACE 1984, s. 78 (*Manister*, heard with *Weir* [2006] 1 WLR 1885).

Criminal Justice Act 2003, s. 98

> References in this chapter to evidence of a person's 'bad character' are to evidence of, or of a disposition towards, misconduct on his part, other than evidence which—
> (a) has to do with the alleged facts of the offence with which the defendant is charged, or
> (b) is evidence of misconduct in connection with the investigation or prosecution of that offence.

Section 99 of the CJA 2003 abolishes 'the common law rules governing the admissibility of evidence of bad character in criminal proceedings'. While it could be argued that the common law regarding what is *inadmissible* evidence of bad character remains intact, this was clearly not the intention.

'Misconduct' means the commission of an offence or other reprehensible behaviour (s. 112(1)).

F12.3 **Convictions** Where convictions are relied upon, it is likely that the value of the evidence will depend on the proof of the circumstances of the offence, not merely upon the actual previous conviction and the matters formally established thereby, and such circumstances will require to be properly proved (*Humphris* (2005) 169 JP 441). *Humphris* was approved in *Ainscough* (2006) 170 JP 517, where the giving of evidence by a police officer based on data held on the Police National Computer was held to be an inappropriate way to settle a dispute between prosecution and defence as to the facts of the previous convictions. It was also observed that the remedy suggested in *Humphris* — procuring a statement by, or evidence from, the victim of an allegedly similar offence — would not be appropriate in cases where D had been dealt with on a plea offered on a different factual basis. The court drew attention to the need for caution and to avoid 'satellite issues' about what did, or did not, happen previously. Where the circumstances of the offence are of the essence, there is an obligation on the party relying upon them to be specific (*Hanson* [2005] 1 WLR 1369); see also the CrimPR, part 35 and, in relation to the admission of such evidence in the Court of Appeal, r. 68.21 (the rules are set out in **appendix 1**).

Note that, while it may be convenient to speak and think of 'previous' convictions, offences occurring subsequent to the offence charged may, as under the old law, be admissible (*Adenusi* (2007) 171 JP 169).

Convictions before a foreign court may be adduced as evidence of bad character under the CJA 2003 (*Kordansinski* [2007] 1 Cr App R 238).

As to the proof that a conviction applies to the individual before the court, see *Lewendon* [2006] 1 WLR 1278 and *Burns* [2006] 1 WLR 1273.

Reprehensible Behaviour The definition of bad character differs from that originally proposed by the Law Commission (*Evidence of Bad Character in Criminal Proceedings*, Law Com No. 273, 2001), which referred to evidence that a person had behaved, or was disposed to behave, in a way that, in the opinion of the court, might be viewed with disapproval by a reasonable person. This was rejected during the Act's passage through Parliament as too vague and potentially too wide, but it is unclear what is gained by the substitution of 'misconduct' defined in terms of 'reprehensible behaviour'. The Government's contention was that this represented a 'tighter formulation'. However, what is 'reprehensible' is surely the same as what is viewed as remiss or as blameworthy by reasonable people — not too far removed, it might be thought, from the Law Commission's original formulation. **F12.4**

In *Renda* [2006] 1 WLR 2948, the Court of Appeal noted that the word 'reprehensible' connoted some element of culpability or blameworthiness. In that case, however, the fact that the accused had been found unfit to plead to the incident in question, which involved gratuitous violence, was not such as to extinguish the element of culpability. In the absence of direct evidence to the contrary, the behaviour was reprehensible. Conduct is not necessarily 'reprehensible' under s. 98 simply because it is morally lax, as in the case of Manister, one of the appeals heard with *Weir* [2006] 1 WLR 1885. In that case it was held wrong to regard the instigation of a sexual relationship by a man in his thirties with a girl of 16 as 'reprehensible'. As it was relevant, the result was that the evidence was admissible (**see F12.2**). In *Edwards* [2006] 1 WLR 1524, the Court of Appeal cautioned against the inclusion in applications to admit evidence under s. 101 of matters which, on proper analysis, did not disclose bad character (in that case the possession of an antique firearm lawfully held by the accused). In *Osbourne* [2007] EWCA Crim 481, the Court of Appeal considered that 'in the context' of a charge of murder, the aggressive, shouting behaviour of one partner towards another over the care of a young child did not constitute reprehensible behaviour. It would, it is submitted, have been preferable to take a more generalised view of what constitutes reprehensible behaviour, and to hold the shouting to be reprehensible but at the same time not relevant to the charge faced by the accused (of murdering a drug dealer). A context-specific test for what is reprehensible will render decision-making unnecessarily complex.

Reputation and Bad Character Section 99(2) of the CJA 2003 preserves the option of proving bad character via reputation at common law, linking with the preserved hearsay exception in s. 118(1) (see **F16.22**). The use of evidence of bad reputation in rebuttal is dealt with at **F13.13**. **F12.5**

'Has to do with' Alleged Facts Excluded from the definition is evidence of misconduct which 'has to do with the alleged facts' of the offence charged, or which is evidence in connection with the investigation or prosecution of that offence. This loose phrase would seem broad enough to cover, for example, the fact that an offence of rape follows on from an assault that is not made the subject of any separate charge, or where it is followed by the theft of items of clothing from the complainant. A difficult line may have to be drawn between evidence of this kind and evidence which falls within the definition of evidence of bad character but is admissible via a specific gateway. In *M* [2006] EWCA Crim 193 the complainant was cross-examined as to why, in the aftermath of an alleged rape, she was passive, made no complaint and got into a car with her alleged attacker. This rendered admissible her account of previous threats to shoot her and her belief that M had a gun. The evidence was thought to 'have to do with' the alleged facts, but if not the court thought it was admissible under gateway (c) as 'explanatory' evidence (see **F12.17**). The expression 'has to do with the **F12.6**

alleged facts' was also considered in relation to s. 100 (bad character of non-defendant: see F14.4) in *Machado* (2006) 170 JP 400, where evidence tending to show the alleged victim of a robbery had taken drugs was held to be within the wording, as providing support for the defence explanation of his sudden collapse (the prosecution having alleged that the accused pushed him over). In *Tirnaveanu* [2007] EWCA Crim 1239 a broad submission that evidence 'has to do' with the facts if it shows the accused was the person who committed the offences was rejected. The court approved the 'fact-specific' analysis applied in *Machado*.

F12.7 **Misconduct in connection with Investigation or Prosecution** A 'gateway' is not necessary in order to admit evidence relating, say, to the telling of lies in interview or the attempted intimidation of witnesses, as this would appear to be 'misconduct in connection with the investigation or prosecution of the offence'.

F12.8 **Bad Character and Cross-examination** Under the CJA 2003, there is no longer a different set of reference points for the definition of bad character evidence according to whether it is to be employed as evidence-in-chief or in cross-examination of the accused. The definition in s. 98 applies for all purposes, as does the qualification that evidence that 'has to do with the alleged facts' of the offence charged or 'is evidence of misconduct in connection with the investigation' is excluded from the definition. Under the Criminal Evidence Act 1898, there was a specific prohibition on the asking of questions of the accused which is not replicated in the CJA 2003, which deals with admissibility of 'evidence' of bad character. However, the evidence that is admissible under s. 101(1)(c) to (g) includes evidence that 'a witness is to be invited to give in cross-examination' (s. 104(2), regarding evidence elicited for the co-accused, and s. 112(1), defining the meaning of 'prosecution evidence' for the purposes of the other provisions). It would appear, therefore, that the putting of a question to which a truthful answer would elicit inadmissible evidence of bad character is normally impermissible — although the matter could have been made clearer.

F12.9 **Previous Allegations as Evidence of Bad Character** It does not appear that the CJA 2003, s. 98, conveys any necessary protection against the revelation of a mere charge (either in the sense of 'charged in court', as in *Stirland v DPP* [1944] AC 315, or in the sense of having been previously suspected) unless the suggestion is that the accused committed the offence with which he was charged, so that the allegation becomes one of the commission of an offence. However, the point made in relation to the previous law in *Maxwell v DPP* [1935] AC 309 continues to hold good: the court should not permit a matter to be raised unless it is demonstrably relevant. The mere making of an allegation will not normally be relevant either to guilt or to the credibility of the accused as a witness (see *Bovell* (2005) 2 Cr App R 401 (decided under s. 100) and *Edwards* [2006] 1 WLR 1524).

F12.10 **Evidence of Matters Already before the Jury** Under the Criminal Evidence Act 1898, s. 1(3), the use of the phrase 'tending to show' matters relating to the accused's bad character was held to import the qualification that matters already before the jury were not covered by the accused's shield (*Jones v DPP* [1962] AC 635). Under the CJA 2003, the prohibition relates to 'evidence of' bad character, and it could be argued that this is a wider prohibition that is not confined to the revelation of previously unmentioned matters. Any additional protection apparently conferred is illusory, however, in that evidence of a relevant matter of the type in issue in *Jones v DPP* (the recycling of a previous alibi) would undoubtedly be rendered admissible by the wide exception in s. 101(1)(d).

The Statutory 'Gateways' — Overview

F12.11 **Criminal Justice Act 2003, s. 101**

(1) In criminal proceedings evidence of the defendant's bad character is admissible if, but only if—

(a) all parties to the proceedings agree to the evidence being admissible,

(b) the evidence is adduced by the defendant himself or is given in answer to a question asked by him in cross-examination and intended to elicit it,
(c) it is important explanatory evidence,
(d) it is relevant to an important matter in issue between the defendant and the prosecution,
(e) it has substantial probative value in relation to an important matter in issue between a defendant and a co-defendant,
(f) it is evidence to correct a false impression given by the defendant, or
(g) the defendant has made an attack on another person's character.

(2) Sections 102 to 106 contain provision supplementing subsection (1).
(3) The court must not admit evidence under subsection (1)(d) or (g) if, on an application by the defendant to exclude it, it appears to the court that the admission of the evidence would have such an adverse effect on the fairness of the proceedings that the court ought not to admit it.
(4) On an application to exclude evidence under subsection (3) the court must have regard, in particular, to the length of time between the matters to which that evidence relates and the matters which form the subject of the offence charged.

Section 101(1)(a) makes it clear that evidence of bad character may be admissible by general consensus of the parties (compare the corresponding provision making hearsay admissible by agreement in the CJA 2003, s. 114(1)(a): see **F15.1**). Thus, for example, in *Kalu* [2007] EWCA Crim 22 a caution for excessive chastisement was admitted by agreement and relied on by both prosecution and defence: by the defence to support a claim that he had learned his lesson, and by the prosecution as part of an alleged history of cruelty to the children in his care. Section 101(1)(b) retains the rule that the accused can elect to tender evidence of his own bad character.

Section 101(1)(c) broadly reflects the common law on 'background' evidence, and is dealt with further at **F12.17**. Section 101(1)(d), however, cuts across much of the thinking of the old law by regarding as admissible evidence that is merely 'relevant' to an important issue between the accused and the prosecution. At common law, the rules on 'similar fact' evidence in particular required a high degree of probative value in order to overcome the prejudicial effect involved in the reception of such evidence (see *DPP v P* [1991] 2 AC 447). The CJA 2003 removes this requirement from the test of admissibility, relegating questions of fairness to the court's power to exclude evidence to avoid prejudice (s. 101(3): see **F12.12**). Although it was initially accepted in *Edwards* [2006] 1 Cr App R 31, following *O'Brien v Chief Constable of South Wales Police* [2005] 2 AC 534, that the CJA 2003 continues to set a standard of 'enhanced relevance' for admissibility of prosecution evidence, the subsequent decision of the Court of Appeal on the facts of Somanathan, one of the appeals, heard with *Weir* [2006] 1 WLR 1885, makes it clear that the CJA 2003 'completely reverses the pre-existing general rule' and that the pre-existing, one-stage test which balanced probative value against prejudicial effect is obsolete'. *O'Brien*, a civil case, is 'capable of being misunderstood' on the point: in other words, clearly wrong.

The most radical aspect of the change brought about by s. 101(1)(d) in combination with s. 103 is that an accused's propensity becomes a matter towards which relevant prosecution evidence may be directed (see **F12.22** ***et seq.***). Section 101(1)(d) has the additional function of admitting evidence to show the untruthfulness of an accused person, and this is dealt with at **F12.23**. Section 101(1)(e) corresponds roughly to the common-law rules permitting a co-accused to adduce evidence of the accused's bad character where it has substantial value in relation to an important issue between them (see **F12.33** and **F12.34**). Section 101(1)(f), evidence to correct a false impression, corresponds broadly to the former category of evidence in rebuttal of evidence of good character adduced by an accused (see **F12.40**) and s. 101(1)(g), evidence to meet an attack on another person, is similar to the previous category of evidence to meet a defence case that involves making imputations on the character of another (see **F12.42**). But see *Campbell* [2007] EWCA Crim 1472 at **F12.14**.

POWERS OF EXCLUSION

F12.12 **Criminal Justice Act 2003, s. 101(3)**

(3) The court must not admit evidence under subsection (1)(d) or (g) if, on an application by the defendant to exclude it, it appears to the court that the admission of the evidence would have such an adverse effect on the fairness of the proceedings that the court ought not to admit it.

The principal mechanism by which the court can ensure that an accused is not prejudiced by revelations of evidence under s. 101(1)(d) or (1)(g) is the exclusionary power under s. 101(3): that it appears to the court that the admission of the evidence would have such an adverse effect on the fairness of the proceedings that the court ought not to admit it.

The power, it should be noted, comes into play on application by the defence to exclude the evidence rather than on the prosecution application to admit it. The power under s. 101(3) does not appear to be exercisable by the court of its own motion (*Highton* [2005] 1 WLR 3472) but, if necessary (for example to protect an unrepresented accused), an application could be prompted by the court.

In *Hanson* [2005] 1 WLR 3169 the Vice-President (Rose LJ) drew attention to the wording 'must not admit', in s. 101(3), with the comment that this was a stronger formula than the one in use in the PACE 1984, s. 78 ('may refuse to allow'). His lordship also expressed the hope that prosecutors would not routinely apply to use evidence of the accused's convictions, but would take into account the particular circumstances of each case. The difference in wording was also noted in *Weir* [2006] 1 WLR 1855, but the currently preferred view is to regard the provision as being on all fours in that a court has no discretion under s. 78 once the conditions for exclusion are satisfied (*Tirnaveanu* [2007] EWCA Crim 1239).

Section 101(3) cannot be used to restrict any of the other five gateways, which appear to lead directly to admissibility. This raises no issues of difficulty in relation to (a) or (b), where the accused has control over the issue. Nor is the absence of discretion a novelty in relation to (e), where it is the co-accused who is entitled to invoke the exception; as at common law there is no discretion to prevent the co-accused taking advantage of the rule permitting him to adduce evidence of the accused's bad character (see *Murdoch v Taylor* [1965] AC 574). In relation to explanatory evidence admitted under s. 101(1)(c), however, and evidence to correct a false impression under s. 101(1)(f), it may be envisaged that there will be cases where the defence will seek to make an argument for exclusion based on unfairness.

As there is no specific provision in chapter 1 of part 11 of the CJA 2003 that excludes the operation of s. 78 of the PACE 1984, it has so far been accepted that it still applies. In *Highton*, a case which did not call directly for the application of s. 78, the inclination of the Court of Appeal was to say that it provided 'an additional protection' to an accused. Judges were encouraged to apply s. 78 pending a definitive ruling to the contrary, so as to avoid any risk of injustice. In considering the appeal of Somanathan, one of the appeals heard with *Weir* [2006] 1 WLR 1885, the court noted that, of the three provisions relied upon by the prosecution, s. 101(3) applied to two, but not to the third, (i.e. s. 101(1)(f)). The Court saw 'no reason to doubt' that s. 78 should be considered where s. 101(1)(f) is relied on, although (as in *Highton*) it did not assist the applicant to do so.

Among the arguments against the application of s. 78 is that, chapter 2 of part 11, which deals with hearsay, includes a provision under which the effect of s. 78 is specifically preserved, together with the operation of any other power of the court to exclude evidence at its discretion (s. 126(2)). In favour of its application is that, where the court sees the exclusion of the evidence as necessary in order to ensure a fair trial under the ECHR, Article 6, this should be sufficient to override any inference arising from the structure of the Act that Parliament's intention was to exclude the general operation of s. 78. In *Highton* Lord Woolf noted that s. 78 serves 'a very similar purpose' to Article 6.

For discretionary exclusion generally, see **F2.13** ***et seq.***

AVOIDING PREJUDICE

The provisions of the CJA 2003, s. 101, are based upon the recommendation of the Law Commission (*Evidence of Bad Character in Criminal Proceedings*, Law Com No. 273, 2001) that the law regarding evidence of bad character was in dire need of an overhaul. Built into the Law Commission's specific proposals, however, were many safeguards designed to ensure that the trial of the accused was not blighted by the introduction of prejudicial evidence. The Government chose instead to legislate by adapting the Law Commission's framework, shorn of most of the safeguards. (See Tapper, 'Criminal Justice Act 2003: Evidence of Bad Character' [2004] Crim LR 533). **F12.13**

The courts in interpreting the provisions have accepted that the CJA 2003 provides a new framework for the wider admissibility of evidence of bad character, making a small but crucial adjustment to the literal wording to ensure that s. 78 of the PACE 1984 can be invoked despite Parliament's apparent intention to restrict its application (see **F12.12**). The key stages are now as set out in *Edwards* [2006] 1 WLR 1524:

(1) The judge determines admissibility under the relevant statutory gateway(s).
(2) Where it is raised, the judge also determines any question of exclusion in respect of prosecution evidence, for example under ss. 101(3) or 103(3) of the CJA 2003, or s. 78 of the PACE 1984.
(3) Once evidence of bad character is admitted, questions of weight are for the jury, subject to the judge's power to stop the case where the evidence is contaminated (under s. 107 at **F12.31**) and the judge's direction as to the use to which the evidence may be put.
(4) The direction on the evidence is of paramount importance. If the ground of the trial has shifted since the evidence was admitted, it may be necessary to tell the jury that it is of little weight.

The Court of Appeal also expressed the view that, if evidence of marginal relevance was tendered under s. 101, it was potentially difficult for the judge to deal with in summing up, and this should be borne in mind by the parties. This reflects observations in the earlier case of *Hanson* [2005] 1 WLR 3169, which was approved in *Edwards*, where the Court of Appeal stated that the purpose of the legislation was 'to assist in the evidence-based conviction of the guilty, without putting those who are not guilty at risk of conviction by prejudice'. As in *Edwards,* much stress was laid on the importance of the direction to the jury, but the hope was also expressed that the prosecution would avoid routine applications wherever an accused has previous convictions, preferring rather to focus on the particular circumstances of each case.

Hanson also outlines the content of a direction on bad character which, though couched in terms of a case involving evidence of propensity, is of more general relevance. A proper direction should:

(1) give the jury a clear warning against the dangers of placing undue reliance on previous convictions;
(2) stress that evidence of bad character cannot be used to bolster a weak case, or to prejudice a jury against the defendant;
(3) emphasise that the jury should not infer guilt from the existence of convictions.

Thus the protection of the accused from prejudice arising from the use of convictions (or it would seem of any other evidence of bad character) under the CJA 2003 depends critically on the ability of the jury to adhere to judicial guidance: under the 'old' law they were prevented from showing prejudice by dint of the evidence being concealed from them. The judicial direction was described in *Eastlake* [2007] EWCA Crim 603 as the 'safety valve' within the new scheme, and in *Isichei* (2006) 170 JP 753 the Court of Appeal noted the dependence of the system on the jury's loyalty to, and understanding of, the judge's directions. This being so, it is important that the directions do not become over-complex and technical, as was frequently the case under the old law.

Evidence Once Admitted is Relevant for All Purposes

F12.14 In *Highton* [2005] 1 WLR 3472 it was held that evidence admitted under the gateway in s. 101(1)(g) of the CJA 2003 (following an attack on another person's character) was thereafter available for any purpose to which it is relevant: 'the use to which [evidence] may be put depends upon the matters to which it is relevant, rather than upon the gateway through which it was admitted.' In *Edwards* [2006] 1 WLR 1524 it was held, following *Highton*, that evidence admitted at the accused's own behest under s. 101(1)(b) could thereafter be used as evidence for any purpose for which it was relevant. This approach, while relieving the judge from the need to point out that relevant evidence is admissible (an outcome the CJA 2003 was designed to avoid) puts a further premium on a careful direction about relevance, and on the judge's ability to predict the uses to which the jury might contemplate putting the evidence. Particular care will be required if evidence admitted under the gateway in s. 101(1)(c) (explanatory evidence) is capable of being considered relevant to the accused's propensity to commit the offence. See **F12.17**. However, the decision in *Campbell* [2007] EWCA Crim 1472 goes further, suggesting that, once evidence is admitted under a particular gateway, it becomes admissible for all relevant purposes. Reference should be made to the transcript in which the Lord Chief Justice also rejects the current JSB directions. Commentary on the case is to be found in the October Bulletin (distributed with this edition).

Reasons for Rulings

F12.15 **Criminal Justice Act 2003, s. 110**

(1) Where the court makes a relevant ruling—
  (a) it must state in open court (but in the absence of the jury, if there is one) its reasons for the ruling;
  (b) if it is a magistrates' court, it must cause the ruling and the reasons for it to be entered in the register of the court's proceedings.
(2) In this section 'relevant ruling' means—
  (a) a ruling on whether an item of evidence is evidence of a person's bad character;
  (b) a ruling on whether an item of such evidence is admissible under section 100 or 101 (including a ruling on an application under section 101(3));
  (c) a ruling under section 107.

Section 107, which codifies the power of the court to stop a case where contaminated evidence of bad character has been admitted, is considered at **F12.31**.

There is now a general duty, in the terms described in s. 110, to give reasons for rulings in relation to bad character. The provision follows a proposal of the Law Commission and is intended to provide for a uniform system applying to all courts, including magistrates' courts. When considering the trial judge's stance in Osbourne, one of the appeals heard with *Renda* [2006] 1 WLR 2948, the Court of Appeal indicated that the mere observation that the jury was entitled to know about character was regarded as an 'over-parsimonious' compliance with s. 110. The point at issue concerned the character of a witness rather than an accused (s. 100: see **F14**) but it is submitted that the principle is the same.

Notice

F12.16 Section 111 of the CJA 2003 permits rules of court to be made in relation to evidence of bad character to supplement the provisions of the Act. Section 111(2) requires provision to be made for the giving of notice by the prosecution of an intention to adduce evidence of an accused's bad character in chief or to elicit such evidence in cross-examination, and permits the making of rules in respect of the giving of notice by a co-accused. The relevant rules are the CrimPR, part 35 and, in relation to the admission of such evidence in the Court of Appeal, r. 68.21; the rules are set out in **appendix 1**. In each case, the rules are applied to all parties wishing to adduce evidence of bad character, and also to an accused's application to exclude bad character evidence: all must be in due form and time limits are set. The accused may waive his entitlement to notice, and the court has power to allow notices to be given in a different form, or at a different time, where to do so is in the interests of justice. Where the rules have not been complied with, the judge's power to exclude evidence should be regarded as a power to prevent unfairness rather than a disciplinary sanction. If unfairness can be cured and the interests of justice require evidence to be admitted then it should not be excluded (*Musone* [2007] EWCA Crim 1237).

Section 111(2) follows a proposal of the Law Commission that the accused should not be unfairly disadvantaged by the presentation of evidence relating to discreditable matters that are not part of the charge. The Commission recognised that other changes to procedure, including the prosecution's duty of disclosure, meant that the use of bad character evidence was unlikely to come as a surprise but the notice requirement will act as a useful long-stop.

EXPLANATORY EVIDENCE

In the CJA 2003, s. 101(1)(c), special provision is made for the admission of 'explanatory' evidence — evidence without which it would be 'impossible or difficult to understand other evidence in the case' — provided that its value for understanding the case as a whole is substantial. It follows that, where the evidence requires no 'footnote or lexicon' but is readily understandable without evidence of bad character, s. 101(1)(c) does not apply (*Beverley* [2006] EWCA Crim 1287). **F12.17**

The operation of the statutory provision is not confined to prosecution evidence. Section 101(1)(c) is supplemented by s. 102.

Criminal Justice Act 2003, ss. 101 and 102

101.—(1) In criminal proceedings evidence of the defendant's bad character is admissible if, but only if—

(a) . . .
(b) . . .
(c) it is important explanatory evidence;
(d) . . .

102 For the purposes of section 101(1)(c) evidence is important explanatory evidence if—

(a) without it, the court or jury would find it impossible or difficult properly to understand other evidence in the case, and
(b) its value for understanding the case as a whole is substantial.

Where an offence is alleged it may be necessary to give evidence of the background against which the offence is committed, even though to do so will reveal facts showing the accused in a discreditable light. The necessity to admit evidence of this kind, for its explanatory as distinct from its probative value, was well-accepted at common law in a line of authorities that continue to be applicable under the CJA 2003 (*Osbourne* [2007] EWCA Crim 481). The most frequently approved statement of principle was that of Purchas LJ in *Pettman* (2 May 1985 unreported) who said:

> Where it is necessary to place before the jury evidence of part of a continual background of history relevant to the offence charged in the indictment and without the totality of which the account placed before the jury would be incomplete or incomprehensible, then the fact that the

whole account involves including evidence establishing the commission of an offence with which the accused is not charged is not of itself a ground for excluding the evidence.

In *Dolan* [2003] 1 Cr App R 281 the court approved the basis for admitting background evidence as explained in the commentary on *Stevens* [1995] Crim LR 649, where it was said that 'it is helpful to have it and difficult for the jury to do their job if events are viewed in total isolation from their history'. Such revelations may be incidental to the offence charged, as in *Neale* (1977) 65 Cr App R 304, where the offence charged was arson of a hostel for boys released from Borstal in which N was an inmate; or germane to the inquiry into guilt, as in *Hagan* (1873) 12 Cox CC 357, where evidence was given of statements made by the accused showing animosity towards the child he was alleged to have murdered. It must be expected that the common-law authorities reviewed above will continue to be illustrative. Explanatory evidence was carefully scrutinised at common law to ensure that it did not become a backdoor method of smuggling in inadmissible evidence of propensity (see, e.g., *Dolan* and *Underwood* [1999] Crim LR 227). Under the CJA 2003, s. 101(1)(d), relevant evidence of propensity becomes admissible and is likely, subject to an argument about exclusion based on prejudice, to be admitted. Even where the admissibility of the evidence is supported only by an argument directed to its explanatory value, the decision in *Highton* [2005] 1 WLR 3472 (see **F12.14**) suggests that evidence admitted under gateway (c) can be used for any purpose for which it is relevant. Such cases will necessitate a particularly careful direction as to the way in which the jury should approach the evidence. Thus, for example, in one of the appeals heard with *Edwards* [2006] 1 Cr App R 31, Chohan, evidence was admitted to support an identification of C as a robber from a person who recognised him from the many occasions on which she had sold him drugs. The separate functions of this background evidence and other evidence of the accused's record which went to his propensity were rightly maintained in the judge's direction.

Where explanatory evidence is admitted, it may be fairest to present it in the form of an agreed statement of facts, for the avoidance of prejudice and to prevent the distraction of the jury (cf. the common law's approach in *Butler* [1999] Crim LR 835).

Discretion and s. 101(1)(c)

F12.18 It should be noted that the court has no explicit statutory discretion to exclude evidence that satisfies the test in the CJA 2003, s. 101(1)(c). Where the evidence is necessary for the proper exposition of the case, in the sense that it would be 'impossible' for the court to manage without it, this makes sense (cf. *Dolan* [2003] 1 Cr App R 281). If, however, it is merely 'difficult', the court will have to consider whether it should have recourse to the general power of exclusion of prosecution evidence in the PACE 1984, s. 78. The observations of the Court of Appeal in *Highton* [2005] 1 WLR 3472 and subsequent authorities (see **F12.12**) would seem to provide some support for this argument. The common law appears to provide for the application of discretion, in cases such as *M (T)* [2000] 1 WLR 421 and *W* [2003] EWCA Crim 3024.

F12.19 **Evidence of Motive or Intention as Explanatory Evidence** Cases in which the previous dealings between the parties are said to show motive or intention sit somewhat uneasily between explanatory evidence and evidence relevant to the issue (CJA 2003, s. 101(1)(d): see **F12.20** ***et seq.***). The sort of evidence described below will undoubtedly continue to be received in trials under the CJA 2003, but it may be that the courts will feel more comfortable invoking s. 101(1)(d) in future. This has the advantage that it will not be necessary to explain why it is 'difficult' to understand the evidence without the additional evidence of intention or motive, or to show the 'substantial' value of the evidence in understanding the case as a whole.

A case illustrating the different emphasis of the two provisions is *Beverley* [2006] EWCA Crim 1287, in which previous convictions for possession of small quantities of cannabis were advanced by the prosecution at the trial of the accused for conspiracy to import a kilo of cocaine. B's appeal was allowed on the ground that the jury would not have been 'disabled or disadvantaged' in understanding the case against B in the absence of evidence of the convictions, so that s. 101(1)(c) was 'entirely unavailable'. Section 101(1)(d) was also discounted on the ground that the previous convictions did not establish a relevant propensity, so as to establish guilty knowledge, in light of the differences in the circumstances, and also the age of the convictions (see **F12.22**).

At common law it was typically under a broad banner of background evidence that courts admitted, for example, evidence given to show prior assaults by the accused on the victim, or menaces or threats uttered to him (*Bond* [1906] 2 KB 389) and evidence of previous acts or words showing enmity as admissible evidence of motive (*Ball* [1911] AC 47 at p. 68). See also *Williams* (1986) 84 Cr App R 299 and *Fulcher* [1995] 2 Cr App R 251, where the previous non-accidental injuries sustained by the baby that F was alleged to have murdered were held to have been relevant to show not only that the child, being in pain, was more likely to be fractious, but also how F was likely to react to the child crying. In *Giannetto* [1997] 1 Cr App R 1, *Ball* and *Williams* were held to justify the admission of the diary of a deceased woman to show a history of threatening and violent behaviour by G towards her, and to form the basis for an inference that G was more likely to have killed her (although it was recognised that a direction that threats and assaults do not always lead to murder was also required). To the same effect are *Phillips* [2003] Crim LR 629, where the unhappy history of the marriage between P and the woman he was charged with murdering was adduced to show motive, and *Shaw* [2003] Crim LR 278, where the history of dealings between S and the police was adduced to shed light on whether S was more likely to have been the aggressor or the innocent victim of an assault by police officers. *Shaw* is a borderline case of relevance, though it may be significant that S chose to adduce something of the history himself in order to show why he believed he was likely to be attacked. In such circumstances, there was a danger that the jury would be left with a misleading picture. Under the CJA 2003 it would appear that s. 101(1)(d) might well provide an alternative route to admissibility in such cases.

In *Sidhu* (1994) 98 Cr App R 59, a video apparently showing S leading the activities of a group of armed rebels in Pakistan was admitted to show his object in participating in a conspiracy to possess explosives in England, which it was alleged was designed to further the interests of the same group. It was held that, provided there was a sufficient nexus in time between S's visit to Pakistan and the offence charged, and provided also that it was necessary to lead the evidence in order to give the jury a complete picture, it was admissible as evidence of a 'continual background of history' relevant to S's part in the conspiracy. As with evidence of motive, such evidence might now be received in the alternative under s. 101(1)(d) on grounds of relevance to the issue.

In *M (T)* [2000] 1 WLR 421, evidence was admitted of the abuse that M and his sister S had suffered at the hands of older members of their family, including instances where M had been forced to abuse his siblings. Without such evidence, the two counts of rape of S could not properly be understood: for example, the jury would inevitably have wondered why S did not turn to other family members for help. See also *M* [2006] EWCA Crim 193, in which previous threats of violence by M towards the girl he was charged with raping were held admissible, either under the CJA 2003, s. 101(1)(c), or as evidence 'having to do' with the alleged facts (see **F12.6**).

In *Sawoniuk* [2000] 2 Cr App R 220, the Court of Appeal upheld the decision of the trial judge to admit evidence that S, charged with four murders in Belarus in 1942, had been a member of a group of policemen involved in a 'search and kill' operation to eliminate Jewish survivors of an earlier massacre. S had claimed not to have been a member but, as the killer was one of the group, it was necessary to the prosecution case to show that he was. Lord Bingham CJ agreed that the evidence was admissible for this purpose, but considered that it could also have been introduced on the broader basis that it was background evidence, as criminal charges 'cannot fairly be judged in a factual vacuum'. Again, the CJA 2003 would seem to provide more than one route for the admissibility of such evidence, and both s. 101(1)(c) and (d) are likely to be canvassed. In terms of outcome, little depends on which of these two routes is chosen (*Tirnaveanu* [2007] EWCA Crim 1239).

EVIDENCE OF BAD CHARACTER ADDUCED BY PROSECUTION TO PROVE GUILT OR UNTRUTHFULNESS

Criminal Justice Act 2003: Admissibility under s. 101(1)(d)

F12.20 **Criminal Justice Act 2003, s. 101**

(1) In criminal proceedings evidence of the defendant's bad character is admissible if, but only if—

. . .

(d) it is relevant to an important matter in issue between the defendant and the prosecution,

The key provision in s. 101(1)(d) is supplemented by s. 103, which fleshes out both the issues to which the provision may apply and the type of evidence that may be rendered admissible thereunder.

Criminal Justice Act 2003, s. 103

(1) For the purposes of section 101(1)(d) the matters in issue between the defendant and the prosecution include—
 (a) the question whether the defendant has a propensity to commit offences of the kind with which he is charged, except where his having such a propensity makes it no more likely that he is guilty of the offence;
 (b) the question whether the defendant has a propensity to be untruthful, except where it is not suggested that the defendant's case is untruthful in any respect.

(2) Where subsection (1)(a) applies, a defendant's propensity to commit offences of the kind with which he is charged may (without prejudice to any other way of doing so) be established by evidence that he has been convicted of—
 (a) an offence of the same description as the one with which he is charged, or
 (b) an offence of the same category as the one with which he is charged.

(3) Subsection (2) does not apply in the case of a particular defendant if the court is satisfied, by reason of the length of time since the conviction or for any other reason, that it would be unjust for it to apply in his case.

(4) For the purposes of subsection (2)—
 (a) two offences are of the same description as each other if the statement of the offence in a written charge or indictment would, in each case, be in the same terms;
 (b) two offences are of the same category as each other if they belong to the same category of offences prescribed for the purposes of this section by an order made by the Secretary of State.

(5) A category prescribed by an order under subsection (4)(b) must consist of offences of the same type.

(6) Only prosecution evidence is admissible under section 101(1)(d).

F12.21 **Relevance to Important Matter** Under the CJA 2003, s. 101(1)(d), the prosecution are required to show that evidence of bad character is relevant to an 'important matter in issue' between prosecution and defence. 'Important matter' means 'a matter of substantial importance in the context of the case as a whole' (s. 112(1)). While the issue must be of substantial importance, however, it is not necessary for the evidence of bad character to be, as it had to be at common law, of substantial probative value. Were it thus, the inclusion in s. 103(1)(a) of evidence of propensity as a matter in issue between the parties would be of very limited effect (*Chopra* [2007] 1 Cr App R 225; *Wallace* [2007] EWCA Crim 1760).

Contrast in this respect s. 100, the parallel provision for evidence of a non-defendant's bad character, where the probative value must be substantial (see F14). Why the threshold for admissibility of the bad character of a witness in the proceedings should be higher than that for the accused is not apparent on the face of the Act, but it arises because the safeguards against the unwarranted revelation of a non-defendant's character proposed by the Law Commission have been enacted, while the more protective provisions recommended to safeguard the accused have been dismantled (see **F12.13**). The effect, as stated in *Weir* [2006] 1 WLR 1885, in relation to the appeal of Somanathan, is that the threshold for admitting an accused's bad character is satisfied if the evidence is merely relevant to an important issue between the prosecution and the defence. Unless there is an application to exclude the evidence, it is admissible.

The (rejected) preference of the Law Commission was for the common-law model of an exclusionary rule with exceptions as being most conducive to a fair trial. The Commission noted that 'it would make for complexity and delay if a judicial discretion had to be exercised in every case where a defendant had a criminal record' (*Evidence of Bad Character in Criminal Proceedings*, Law Com No. 273, (2001) at para. 98). Provided the record is relevant, however, arguments about the proper exercise of the court's judgment under s. 101(3) will now become the prominent feature of cases where evidence of bad character is tendered under s. 101(1)(d) and objected to by the defence. Where evidence is admitted, the accused's protection from unfairness lies in the direction to be given by the trial judge (see **F12.13**). Where there is an appeal, the court is unlikely to interfere unless the judge's judgment as to the capacity of prior events to establish propensity is plainly wrong or his discretion has been exercised unreasonably in the 'Wednesbury' sense (*Hanson* [2005] 1 WLR 3169, applied in the decision of a District Judge in *DPP v Chand* [2007] EWHC 90 (Admin)).

Propensity as an Issue Propensity to commit offences 'of the kind charged' is now to be taken to be an issue between the defence and the prosecution except where it makes it no more likely that the accused is guilty (CJA 2003, s. 103(1)(a)), and propensity to untruthfulness is to be so taken unless it is not suggested that the accused's case is untruthful in any respect (s. 103(1)(b)). This appears to be a 'deeming' provision, given that propensity is not an issue in the normal sense so much as a means of proving what is in issue. The common law was averse to the use of evidence of propensity except where it was strongly probative of guilt, and this was borne out by research: the Law Commission report, *Evidence of Bad Character in Criminal Proceedings*, Law Com No. 273, (2001) at 6.11 makes the point that psychological research supports the common-law approach and that the bare bones of a criminal record do not afford adequate information to deduce whether an accused is likely to have repeated past behaviour. **F12.22**

The inclusion of s. 103(1)(b) marks the merger of the rules of admissibility relating to credit with those relating to the proof of guilt. The Law Commission's recommendation to keep these issues separate was buttressed by safeguards of particular relevance to the maintenance of the balance of fairness at the different stages of the trial at which such issues typically arise (*Evidence of Bad Character in Criminal Proceedings*, Law Com No. 273, (2001), Draft Bill, cls. 8 and 9). The replacement of the safeguards with the exclusionary discretion in s. 101(3) (see **F12.12**) and the more specific power in s. 103(3) facilitates the merger of the two sets of rules, though the courts will be able to exercise the discretions appropriately only by disentangling the factors relating to issue and credit.The steps which have to be followed by the trial judge in determining the use which may be made of evidence of propensity consisting of convictions under s. 101(1)(d) were spelled out in detail in *Hanson* [2005] 1 WLR 3169. In brief these flow as follows:

(1) Does the history of conviction(s) establish a propensity to commit offences of the kind charged?
(2) If so, does the propensity make it more likely that the defendant committed the crime charged? (The example given in the Explanatory Notes to the Criminal Justice Bill of a propensity making it no more likely concerns a homicide case where the accused admits

causing the injuries of the victim but denies that the injuries are the cause of death. In this example the accused's propensity to violence is simply irrelevant).

(3) Where the convictions are for offences of the same category or description (s. 103(2)) is it unjust to rely on them (s. 103(3))? Where the propensity is proved by other means, as permitted by s. 103(1) and (2), is it unfair under s. 101(3) to admit the evidence?

A further elaboration of the second step that will at some stage prove necessary, it is submitted, is that, where the history does not establish a relevant propensity, it may still be the case that the history has relevance to an issue in the case under s. 101(1)(d). In *Beverley* [2006] EWCA Crim 1287, for example, a previous conviction for possession of cannabis was held not to establish a relevant propensity in relation to the importation of cocaine, which is correct. However it is submitted that it might have had significance in showing that the accused understood perfectly well the 'language' of drugs which he claimed not to know, but this was not explored. Propensity evidence is important under s. 101(1)(d), but it is not the only way of using evidence of bad character.

According to *Hanson*, propensity can be demonstrated by one previous event if sufficiently probative, as, for example, where the behaviour would have been regarded as 'strikingly similar' or otherwise admissible at common law (compare *DPP v P* [1991] 2 AC 447). Other examples given were of a single sexual offence (and see Pickstone, heard with *Hanson*) or an offence of fire-setting; see also *Williams* [2006] EWCA Crim 2052 (propensity to strangle). A single offence of shoplifting would not, without more, be enough, but striking similarity of *modus operandi* might make it so. In *Murphy* [2006] EWCA Crim 3408, an old offence of unlawful possession of a firearm was thought at trial to display such a propensity, but the Court of Appeal disagreed. Although a judge is allowed some latitude in making a judgment about relevance, a ruling may be interfered with on appeal where he has 'plainly erred'. In that case the offence was considered to provide 'too slender a basis' upon which any propensity could be founded. See also *Beverley* [2006] EWCA Crim 1287 above). In *Leaver* [2006] EWCA Crim 2988, the accused was charged with rape by continuing with intercourse in a violent manner after the complainant had withdrawn her original consent, and with causing her serious injury with intent when she refused to engage in further sexual activity. It was held that a conviction for indecent exposure, which had not been accompanied by circumstances of any violence, did not bear on the questions for the jury, which were whether the accused reasonably believed the complainant was consenting to intercourse, and whether he had intended to do her serious injury. L's conviction was quashed and a retrial ordered.

Also according to *Hanson*, the calculation over whether to exclude a conviction under s. 101(3) or 103(3) involves a range of issues, including the similarity between the conviction and the offence charged, bearing in mind that offences may be of the same category or description but factually different. The gravity and age of the offence for which the accused has been convicted are also factors, with particular care being addressed to the use of old convictions which are likely to be prejudicial unless they can clearly be shown to demonstrate continuing propensity. (A case near the line is *Ullah* [2006] EWCA Crim 2003, in which a single conviction for a somewhat similar offence of obtaining by deception in 1989 was admitted at U's trial for conspiracy to defraud.) Another cause for concern arises when previous events are disputed, for then the court must be particularly careful to avoid the diversion of the trial into 'satellite' issues not covered by the indictment. See, in addition to *Hanson*, *Lamb* [2006] EWCA Crim 3347. The court should also consider the weight of the other evidence in the case, as it is unlikely to be just to admit convictions where there is very little other evidence. See *DPP v Chand* [2007] EWHC 90 (Admin) in which the District Judge's decision to exclude C's conviction for theft by shoplifting on a charge of stealing a charity box was based both on dissimilarity and the weakness of the prosecution case. The Divisional Court regarded this as a conclusion that could not be condemned as perverse. Where it is foreseeable that the evidence of witnesses might not be as anticipated in their witness statements, and there is in consequence a risk that the use of bad character evidence will overshadow the rest of the prosecution case, it may be desirable to delay a ruling on admissibility until the Crown has called its witnesses (*Gyima* [2007] EWCA Crim 429).

The facts of *Hanson* itself illustrate the careful scrutiny of conviction evidence to determine the existence and possible value of propensity. H was charged with burglary from a room that, it was contended, he alone had opportunity to enter at the relevant time. His various convictions for offences of dishonesty were all within part 1 of the 'Categories of Offences' Schedule (see **F12.24**), but the Court of Appeal nevertheless considered that the judge was obliged to review the relevance to propensity of the individual convictions, as a conviction of the same description or category as the offence charged was not necessarily sufficient in order to show a propensity to commit offences of the kind charged. H's convictions for handling and aggravated vehicle-taking, though of the same 'category' as burglary, were not, without more, such as to demonstrate a propensity to burgle.

Other examples of the use of propensity evidence to prove guilt appear in the following sections, which are arranged according to the function of the evidence: supporting identification, rebutting a defence etc. The use of propensity evidence is not, however, conditional upon the raising of a defence, and may be admissible where the defence is a complete denial (*Wilkinson* [2006] EWCA Crim 1332).

Propensity to Untruthfulness In relation to evidence of propensity to show untruthfulness, *Hanson* [2005] 1 WLR 3169 (see **F12.22**) requires a distinction to be drawn between offences of dishonesty, which may or may not display a propensity to untruthfulness, and evidence which does display such a propensity. The latter category might, for example, include an offence involving lying or making false representations, or the putting forward by the accused of an account in his own defence which can be shown to have been disbelieved. For a fresh and controversial approach to the relationship between untruthfulness and bad character, see *Campbell* [2007] EWCA Crim 1472, where the Lord Chief Justice offered trenchant criticism of the standard direction which then applied. Commentary on the case is to be found in the October Bulletin (distributed with this edition). **F12.23**

The Explanatory Notes that accompanied the Criminal Justice Bill through Parliament indicated that the provision was intended to admit 'evidence such as convictions for perjury or other offences involving deception (for example obtaining property by deception)'. To the extent that the prosecution case generally raises some question as to the truthfulness of some important aspect of the accused's case, such convictions will become routinely admissible unless the courts make wide use of the exclusionary power, along with the other examples of untruthfulness cited in *Hanson* such as the giving of false evidence (although such evidence may also be more likely to give rise to 'satellite issues' of proof if disputed, and thus be more susceptible to exclusion).

In cases where there is a previous conviction for an offence of dishonesty that has a bearing on the issue and that also discloses a relevant propensity to untruthfulness, the two aspects of bad character — evidence going to the issue and evidence of untruthfulness — may be no more than two sides of the same coin (*Ullah* [2006] EWCA Crim 2003). See also *Campbell*.

It should be noted that, paradoxically, evidence of a non-defendant's previous convictions for offences of this type will be admissible under the CJA 2003 only where the court gives leave to adduce it on the ground that it is of substantial probative value and substantial importance to the case (CJA 2003, s. 100: see **F14**). So, for example, a prosecution witness enjoys a higher level of apparent protection than the accused despite the fact that it is only the latter who is in jeopardy of conviction. The proposal to protect witnesses other than the accused is taken wholesale from the Law Commission's recommendations, and the paradox is created by the stripping away of the extra protection that the accused would have enjoyed. It will be for the courts to strike the appropriate balance of fairness using the discretion under s. 101(3).

Examples of the use of evidence of propensity to show untruthfulness are to be found in the following text in relation to s. 101(1)(d).

F12.24 **Prescribed Categories of Offences to Show Propensity** The categories of offences so far prescribed using the power under the CJA 2003, s. 103(4)(b) (see **F12.20**) broadly relate to offences of dishonesty and sexual offences against persons under the age of 16, as contained in the schedule to the Criminal Justice Act 2003 (Categories of Offences) Order 2004 (SI 2004 No. 3346). It should be noted, however, that (under s. 103(1) and (2)) the existence of offences of the same description or category is only one method of proving propensity, so that other relevant evidence may also be relied upon. Thus, for example, a history of separate investigations of the accused for sexual offences against children, which are of probative value in establishing disposition where the investigations had not resulted in prosecution, might be admitted. And in *Weir* [2006] 1 WLR 1885, it was permissible to prove a caution for a non-scheduled offence of taking an obscene photograph of a child; the Court of Appeal pointed out that, while the task of deciding the admissibility of offences within the categories is easier, the opening words of s. 103(2) make clear that the categories do not provide the only route to admissibility. See also *Lamb* [2006] EWCA Crim 3347 at **F12.22** (propensity to stab).

Conversely, the existence of a conviction for a scheduled offence does not, without more, make it admissible: the steps described in *Hanson* [2005] 1 WLR 3169 (see **F12.22**) to ensure relevance and fairness in admitting propensity evidence must also be gone through.

The Criminal Justice Act 2003 (Categories of Offences) Order 2004 (SI 2004 No. 3346), schedule

PRESCRIBED CATEGORIES OF OFFENCES

PART 1

THEFT CATEGORY

1. An offence under section 1 of the Theft Act 1968 (theft).
2. An offence under section 8 of that Act (robbery).
3. An offence under section 9(1)(a) of that Act (burglary) if it was committed with intent to commit an offence of stealing anything in the building or part of a building in question.
4. An offence under section 9(1)(b) of that Act (burglary) if the offender stole or attempted to steal anything in the building or that part of it.
5. An offence under section 10 of that Act (aggravated burglary) if the offender committed a burglary described in paragraph 3 or 4 of this Part of the Schedule.
6. An offence under section 12 of that Act (taking motor vehicle or other conveyance without authority).
7. An offence under section 12A of that Act (aggravated vehicle-taking).
8. An offence under section 22 of that Act (handling stolen goods).
9. An offence under section 25 of that Act (going equipped for stealing).
10. An offence under section 3 of the Theft Act 1978 (making off without payment).
11. An offence of—
    (a) aiding, abetting, counselling, procuring or inciting the commission of an offence specified in this Part of this Schedule; or
    (b) attempting to commit an offence so specified.

PART 2

SEXUAL OFFENCES (PERSONS UNDER THE AGE OF 16) CATEGORY

1. An offence under section 1 of the Sexual Offences Act 1956 (rape) if it was committed in relation to a person under the age of 16.
2. An offence under section 5 of the Sexual Offences Act 1956 (intercourse with a girl under thirteen).
3. An offence under section 6 of that Act (intercourse with a girl under sixteen).
4. An offence under section 7 of that Act (intercourse with a defective) if it was committed in relation to a person under the age of 16.

5. An offence under section 10 of that Act (incest by a man) if it was committed in relation to a person under the age of 16.
6. An offence under section 11 of that Act (incest by a woman) if it was committed in relation to a person under the age of 16.
7. An offence under section 12 of that Act (buggery) if it was committed in relation to a person under the age of 16.
8. An offence under section 13 of that Act (indecency between men) if it was committed in relation to a person under the age of 16.
9. An offence under section 14 of that Act (indecent assault on a woman) if it was committed in relation to a person under the age of 16.
10. An offence under section 15 of that Act (indecent assault on a man) if it was committed in relation to a person under the age of 16.
11. An offence under section 128 of the Mental Health Act 1959 (sexual intercourse with patients) if it was committed in relation to a person under the age of 16.
12. An offence under section 1 of the Indecency with Children Act 1960 (indecent conduct towards young child).
13. An offence under section 54 of the Criminal Law Act 1977 (inciting a girl under 16 to have incestuous sexual intercourse).
14. An offence under section 3 of the Sexual Offences (Amendment) Act 2000 (abuse of a position of trust) if it was committed in relation to a person under the age of 16.
15. An offence under section 1 of the Sexual Offences Act 2003 (rape) if it was committed in relation to a person under the age of 16.
16. An offence under section 2 of that Act (assault by penetration) if it was committed in relation to a person under the age of 16.
17. An offence under section 3 of that Act (sexual assault) if it was committed in relation to a person under the age of 16.
18. An offence under section 4 of that Act (causing a person to engage in sexual activity without consent) if it was committed in relation to a person under the age of 16.
19. An offence under section 5 of the Sexual Offences Act 2003 (rape of a child under 13).
20. An offence under section 6 of that Act (assault of a child under 13 by penetration).
21. An offence under section 7 of that Act (sexual assault of a child under 13).
22. An offence under section 8 of that Act (causing or inciting a child under 13 to engage in sexual activity).
23. An offence under section 9 of that Act (sexual activity with a child).
24. An offence under section 10 of that Act (causing or inciting a child to engage in sexual activity).
25. An offence under section 14 of that Act if doing it will involve the commission of an offence under sections 9 and 10 of that Act (arranging or facilitating the commission of a child sex offence).
26. An offence under section 16 of that Act (abuse of position of trust: sexual activity with a child) if it was committed in relation to a person under the age of 16.
27. An offence under section 17 of that Act (abuse of position of trust: causing or inciting a child to engage in sexual activity) if it was committed in relation to a person under the age of 16.
28. An offence under section 25 of that Act (sexual activity with a child family member) if it was committed in relation to a person under the age of 16.
29. An offence under section 26 of that Act (inciting a child family member to engage in sexual activity) if it was committed in relation to a person under the age of 16.
30. An offence under section 30 of that Act (sexual activity with a person with a mental disorder impeding choice) if it was committed in relation to a person under the age of 16.
31. An offence under section 31 of that Act (causing or inciting a person with a mental disorder impeding choice to engage in sexual activity) if it was committed in relation to a person under the age of 16.
32. An offence under section 34 of that Act (inducement, threat, or deception to procure activity with a person with a mental disorder) if it was committed in relation to a person under the age of 16.
33. An offence under section 35 of that Act (causing a person with a mental disorder to engage in or agree to engage in sexual activity by inducement, threat or deception) if it was committed in relation to a person under the age of 16.

34. An offence under section 38 of that Act (care workers: sexual activity with a person with a mental disorder) if it was committed in relation to a person under the age of 16.
35. An offence under section 39 of that Act (care workers: causing or inciting sexual activity) if it was committed in relation to a person under the age of 16.
36. An offence of—
    (a) aiding, abetting, counselling, procuring or inciting the commission of an offence specified in this Part of this Schedule; or
    (b) attempting to commit an offence so specified.

F12.25 **Presumption of Commission Created by Conviction** To facilitate the operation of the CJA 2003, s. 103(4)(b), and the statutory instrument made under it (see **F12.24**), the PACE 1984, s. 74(3), was amended by the CJA 2003 so that proof of conviction for an offence creates a presumption that the accused committed it, even where its relevance is only to show disposition — a function of the use of previous convictions which was formerly excluded (see **F11.11**). The supplementary provisions of the PACE 1984, s. 75 (see **F11.5**) will also apply, so that regard may be had to a range of documents including the indictment in order to determine the facts on which the conviction adduced in support of propensity was based. These provisions of PACE do not apply to foreign convictions (*Kordansinski* [2007] 1 Cr App R 238).

As to the need to supplement conviction evidence with statements admissible under the hearsay provisions of the CJA 2003 in order to provide evidence of the detail of, for example, the *modus operandi* adopted in relation to previous offences, see *Humphris* (2005) 169 JP 441 and *Ainscough* (2006) 170 JP 517, at **F16.16**.

Identifying the Accused by Evidence of Bad Character under the Criminal Justice Act 2003, s. 101(1)(d)

F12.26 An important function of evidence of bad character at common law was to identify the accused as the perpetrator of an offence, whether by demonstrating that the crime bore his 'signature', or by the more prosaic linkage of matters pointing to his involvement (*W (John)* [1998] 2 Cr App R 289, explaining *DPP v P* [1991] 2 AC 447).

Where a feature is said to be the equivalent of a signature, it is the equivalent of a statement that it possesses to a very high degree the unusual features associated with 'striking similarity' at common law (*DPP v Boardman* [1975] AC 421, *Smith* (1915) 11 Cr App R 229, *Barrington* [1981] 1 WLR 419). When such cases arise under the CJA 2003, the evidence of bad character may support the prosecution case to the extent that very little other evidence is required to convince of guilt. In the old case of *Straffen* [1952] 2 QB 911, the murder of a young girl who was found strangled was considered unusual in that no attempt had been made to assault her sexually or to conceal the body. S came under immediate suspicion because he had previously strangled two other girls, each murder having the same peculiar features, and because he was in the neighbourhood at the time, having just escaped from Broadmoor. Under these circumstances, very little other evidence was required to convict S of the third murder: it bore his 'fingerprints'. See also *Butler* (1986) 84 Cr App R 12 (rapist identified by reference to strikingly similar conduct engaged in, albeit consensually, with his girlfriend) and *Tricoglus* (1976) 65 Cr App R 16, in which the two rapes with which T was charged were sufficiently peculiar to be regarded as the work of the same man, although T's conviction was quashed because further similar fact evidence that had been used to link him with the crimes was inadmissible. Not all 'signature' cases are of a sexual nature. For example, in *Mullen* [1992] Crim LR 735, it was M's distinctive use of a blow-torch to crack glass in order to enter and burgle premises that provided the link between his crimes.

In 'signature' cases under the CJA 2003, the normal direction that evidence of bad character should not be the sole or even the main evidence of guilt (see **F12.12**) may be over-cautious.

Evidence of misconduct may go to support identification without necessarily amounting to 'signature evidence'. Thus for example in *Eastlake* [2007] EWCA Crim 603 two brothers were charged with an offence of street violence. Their propensity (jointly and separately) to commit such offences was admissible to support their disputed identifications, particularly in light of the brothers' defence that they spent the evening together, which strengthened the argument that it would have been a strange coincidence if they had been wrongly identified. See also *Cushing* [2006] EWCA Crim 1221, where the previous offences were for the same crime (burglary) but were factually distinct.

Cases under the common law in which similar fact evidence was admissible as proof of identity without being signature evidence include *Thompson v The King* [1918] AC 221. A man had assaulted two young boys and arranged to meet them again. T kept the appointment but denied being the man who had assaulted the boys. Their identification of him was confirmed by evidence of his possession of powder puffs and indecent photographs, which went to rebut T's claim of mistaken identity.

Bad character may also be relevant (and therefore admissible) to support identification without any similarity between the past and present offences, as in *Isichei* (2006) 170 JP 753, where the fact that a robber, identified as I, had asked for 'coke' was sufficient to admit I's previous convictions for cocaine-related offences.

The impact of the CJA 2003 on the use of bad character evidence for purposes of identification raises particularly difficult issues. It should not be forgotten that the process of detection of crime may, understandably, focus on the accused's convictions for crimes of a particular type, nor that these might be highly prejudicial if relied on in the absence of strong supporting evidence of identification. For example it might appear to a jury that the accused's previous convictions for robbery of taxi-drivers were highly pertinent to whether he committed a similar offence for which no clear evidence of identification exists, yet it might be the case that a number of other individuals with a similar propensity were also operating in the vicinity and that one of them might have committed the offence. In some cases the fair course might be the admission of such evidence against the accused coupled with a strong direction about the need to eliminate the possibility that the offences were the work of others of equally bad character (cf. *Miller* [2003] EWCA Crim 2840). The risk of prejudice is also apparent in the evidence excluded in *Tricoglus*. T, who resembled the general description given of the double rapist, and who drove a car of a similar type, had attempted to pick up two other women in the same city-centre area from which the victims had been taken by the same 'kerb-crawling' method. This evidence was said to prove at most that T had 'unpleasant social habits', and was excluded. Under the CJA 2003, it might be considered relevant evidence of propensity but, in order to combat the risk that the jury would over-value it to the prejudice of the accused, a particularly careful direction would have to be given in respect of it. In *Brima* [2007] 1 Cr App R 316, a man ran up, fatally stabbed the victim in front of several witnesses and ran away. B's defence was that the crime was committed by A, his friend. A positive identification of B by one of the witnesses was supported by some scientific evidence (though in some respects this also pointed to A) and by the evidence of A himself. Propensity evidence in the form of B's two previous convictions for assaults using a knife was held to have been rightly admitted, although in neither of the previous incidents was a serious injury inflicted. The Court of Appeal noted that, in light of B's attack on A, B's convictions would in any event have been brought out under s. 101(1)(g). In *Randall* [2006] EWCA Crim 1413, a 'fleeting glimpse' identification of a burglar was supported by evidence of R's propensity to commit that crime, the judge's pithy direction being that the victim 'had no hesitation in picking [R] out on the video at the identification procedure. She was burgled. She picked out a burglar. Was that pure coincidence?' The risk that it might not have been 'pure' coincidence, but that an accused person might have found himself on the parade because of his previous record, is one the jury also needs to be alerted to where it appears to be relevant.

Where an eye-witness identifies the accused as responsible for one offence, and it is sought to support the correctness of the identification by reference to another eye-witness identification in respect of a separate offence, it was said in *Robinson* [1953] 1 WLR 872 that admissibility could be justified on the basis that it was a remarkable coincidence that R was separately identified by different witnesses as having been involved in two different robberies. Whether such a coincidence is remarkable or not must depend on the facts, but the risk of error inherent in fleeting glimpse identifications is not necessarily counteracted by other purported identifications of the same person. The same logic would point to admissibility under the CJA 203, but the use of s. 101(3) to counter the possible unfairness arising from the linkage of two weak identifications would also require to be considered.

Bad Character Evidence Rebutting Defence

F12.27 A common function that evidence of bad character may be called upon to perform is to show an event involving an accused person in its true light, rebutting an otherwise plausible innocent explanation. An example is given in the Government's White Paper *Justice for All* (2002) of a young man found in possession of a car that has been reported stolen. He claims that he has permission from 'a friend of a friend' to borrow the car, but he has three recent convictions for taking without consent. The convictions would be relevant to an assessment whether it was likely that an informal arrangement of the sort testified to by the accused might have come into being, or that he might have believed that it had, notwithstanding his propensity to take cars without permission when the fancy seized him.

In applying the CJA 2003, s. 101(1)(d), in such instances, it is important to remember that a defence may be rebutted via an inference to be drawn from propensity (as in the illustration above) or because the evidence of bad character has a probative value independent of any inference from propensity (see further as to propensity **F12.22 *et seq.***). In the leading common-law case of *Makin v A-G for New South Wales* [1894] AC 57, the discovery of one child's body in the Makins' backyard was not necessarily (given the social conditions of the time) probative of non-accidental death. It was evidence that many other children had been taken in by the couple and that their bodies too had been discovered in the Makins' gardens that made the inference of murder irresistible. In that case an inference of propensity followed, rather than preceded, the introduction of the evidence.

Many defences that might appear credible if the prosecution is confined to one set of facts may be shown to be unlikely by reference to other instances of misconduct, and common-law examples abound. In *Bond* [1906] 2 KB 389, the prosecution case was that B, a doctor, had operated upon a young woman who was pregnant with his child, with intent to procure her miscarriage. The defence that he was carrying out a lawful medical examination of the girl was held to have been properly rebutted by the evidence of another girl, who claimed that nine months previously B had operated on her when she became pregnant by him, with the intention of terminating her pregnancy, and that he had told her that he had 'put dozens of girls right'. In *Mortimer* (1936) 25 Cr App R 150, M was charged with the murder of a woman cyclist by deliberately driving a motor car at her. To rebut any suggestion that this was a case of manslaughter lacking the element of intention required for murder, evidence was adduced to show that M had, on the evening before the incident, knocked down two other women cyclists in a similar way, that some hours after the incident he had knocked one other woman off her bicycle and that he had attempted to avoid capture by driving his car at police officers who tried to apprehend him. In *Smith* (1915) 11 Cr App R 229, S was charged with the murder of a woman with whom he had been through a ceremony of marriage, and who was found drowned in her bath. Evidence was given that two other women whom S had induced to 'marry' him had met with the same fate. Each death benefited S, who had taken the precaution of insuring the women's lives.

In each of these three common-law examples, the function of the evidence was to put a different complexion on what had occurred; in *Bond* by showing a criminal purpose, in *Mortimer* by showing an intention to cause death or injury, and in *Smith* by showing that the deaths had not occurred through natural causes but through the activities of the accused.

Evidence of the kind deployed in the above cases was relatively freely admissible at common law, and will doubtless continue to be so under s. 101(1)(d). A case similar to *Bond*, for example, is *Adams* [2006] EWCA Crim 2013, where the defence to possession of a large quantity of a controlled drug was that A intended to use it to commit suicide. Previous offences of supply and attempting to supply were properly admitted to rebut the defence and to indicate criminal intent. As at common law, the use of such evidence is easier to justify where the accused already has considerable explaining to do than where it is the mainstay of the case against him. In *Rance* (1975) 62 Cr App R 118, the accused claimed that he signed a particular document authorising a bribe without knowing what it was: an unlikely explanation in any event, but one made incredible by the introduction of evidence of the signing of other similar documents. Where there is little other evidence besides the misconduct, the evidence may be susceptible to exclusion under s. 101(3) unless (as in cases like *Smith*) it has such a strong appeal that not much more is needed to enable an inference of guilt to be drawn.

Evidence of a propensity to untruthfulness may also be of particular importance for the jury in their assessment of the credibility of a defence. In *Malone* [2006] EWCA Crim 1860, M was charged with the murder of his wife, who had been found dead, and who he claimed had been murdered by members of the criminal fraternity who had also threatened him. The prosecution claimed that he had sought to lay a false trail in relation to the wife's disappearance. Evidence that he had, well before his wife's death, falsified a report, claiming to be from a private investigator who had uncovered evidence of the deceased's secret life, was admitted. The Court of Appeal opined that it was relevant to the issue whether he was telling the truth.

Nature of Defence as Factor Affecting Relevance Evidence that is directed to the proof of some fact that is not in issue cannot be received, not because of the prejudicial effect of such evidence but simply because it is irrelevant. It is apparent, therefore, that the nature of the defence or defences reasonably open to the accused may have a bearing on the purpose that evidence of bad character may serve, which bears on its relevance and therefore on its admissibility. This was true of evidence received at common law and remains crucial under the provisions of the CJA 2003. **F12.28**

Under s. 101(1)(d), the criteria to be applied are relevance to an important matter in issue between prosecution and defence and (where application is made by the defence to exclude) unfairness. However, the nature of the defence relied upon continues, to play a major part in determining the relevance, and therefore the admissibility, of evidence of character. Section 103(1) may lend itself to the argument that the accused's propensity is always in issue unless it is clearly irrelevant but it is submitted that it is not an important issue (as required by s. 101(1)(d)) unless the circumstances of the case (which may include the nature of the defence raised) are such as to make it so (see further **F12.22**).

Anticipating Defence to be Raised The reforms to the rule regarding the application of pre-trial disclosure to the defence (see **D9.18**) significantly assist the prosecution in anticipating the issues at trial to which evidence of bad character may be relevant. Where the exact relevance remains unclear, it is better to delay a ruling until the evidence unfolds (see, for example, *M* [2006] EWCA Crim 193, where the defence to a charge of rape involved a suggestion, put to the complainant in cross-examination, that she had neglected an opportunity to complain. This rendered admissible an account by the complainant of her belief, based on a previous incident, that the accused had a gun in his possession). **F12.29**

Multiple Charges and Accusations under the Criminal Justice Act 2003, s. 101(1)(d)

F12.30 Section 112(2) of the CJA 2003 provides that, where an accused faces multiple charges in the same proceedings, the 'bad character' provisions apply as if each was charged in separate proceedings: in other words a 'gateway' is required to support cross-admissibility between charges in the same proceedings in exactly the same way as where only one offence is charged. Where an accused faces more than one charge of a similar nature or where evidence of similar allegations is tendered in support of one charge, the evidence of one accuser may be admissible to support the evidence of another. The principles to be applied to cases of this kind do not differ materially from those applicable where evidence of bad character is used to rebut an explanation otherwise open to the accused: indeed, the function of evidence of multiple accusers is often to rebut such an explanation. Separate exposition is helpful, however, in order to bring out the special problems of collusion that have arisen under this heading, and that will continue to arise now that the governing provisions are those of the CJA 2003. The Act is also constructed in such a way as to anticipate the special problems arising out of contamination of evidence by matters other than collusion.

The underlying principle is that the probative value of multiple accusations may depend in part on their similarity, but also on the unlikely prospect that the same person would find himself falsely accused on different occasions by different and independent individuals. The making of multiple accusations is a coincidence in itself, which has to be taken into account in deciding admissibility. As Lord Cross of Chelsea put it in *DPP v Boardman* [1975] AC 421 (at p. 460):

> . . . the point is not whether what the appellant is said to have suggested would be, as coming from a middle-aged active homosexual, in itself particularly unusual but whether it would be unlikely that two youths who were saying untruly that the appellant had made homosexual advances to them would have put such a suggestion into his mouth.

Similarly under the CJA 2003 in *Chopra* [2007] 1 Cr App R 225 where the three young complainants each separately alleged that C, a dentist, had squeezed their breasts in the course of treatment, there was a sufficient connection to warrant cross-admissibility: the court noted that it was more likely to be true than if only one of them had said it, and was not persuaded by the argument that there were many more patients of C who had made no such allegation. See also *Wallace* [2007] EWCA Crim 1790.

The approach sanctioned at common law stopped short of supporting the conclusion that the mere existence of multiple accusations of similar offences was a *guarantee* of admissibility. As the Court of Appeal previously noted in *Wilmot* (1989) 89 Cr App R 341 (at p. 348), prejudice would result if the jury were to convict on the argument that 'If this many accusations are made, there must be something in each of them'. The risk of prejudice arising in such a case will continue to be the basis of an argument for exclusion under the CJA 2003, s. 101(3) and the court will take into account, among other things, the strength of the other evidence in the case in reaching its decision (see **F12.12**).

The protective value of both the common-law rule of exclusion, and the new rule provided by combining s. 101(1)(d) and 101(3) is weakened in cases involving multiple accusations in consequence of the rules about joinder of counts. These permit charges to be tried together where the evidence in relation to one is similar to, though inadmissible in respect of, another (see as to joinder **D11.56** ***et seq.***). Where this occurs, the efficacy of the decision to regard evidence of bad character as inadmissible depends entirely on the ability of the jury to follow a direction to disregard the evidence on one count when considering another. As the rule of admissibility at common law became more permissive over time, there were fewer cases in which charges could be joined where the evidence was not also cross-admissible (*Christou* [1997] AC 117: see **D11.76**). Under the CJA 2003, the rules on admissibility will be drawn even closer to the rules on joinder, which operate in respect of two or more charges founded on the same facts or forming part of a series of offences of the same or a similar character. Thus the problem, in cases such as *D* [2004] 1 Cr App R 19 (of directing the jury where evidence is not cross-admissible) or *Carman* [2004] EWCA Crim 540 (where some allegations were cross-admissible, some not), becomes thankfully less likely to arise. Cases where the evidence in respect of two offences that are properly joined is not cross-admissible will still arise under the CJA 2003, and the 'remedy' will continue to be a direction to the jury not to carry evidence over from one allegation to another.

Risk of Collusion between Witnesses It is obvious that an apparently strong nexus between accounts of events given by different witnesses does not prove guilt if it can be accounted for by collusion. For some time, controversy surrounded the question whether evidence which carries a real risk of collusion should be excluded, or should be left to the jury with a suitable warning. In *H* [1995] AC 596, the House of Lords decided that, since the credibility of a witness was a matter for the jury, the risk of collusion should normally go to weight not to admissibility. The judge should therefore approach the question of admissibility on the basis that the similar facts alleged are true, with the possible exception of cases where the evidence of collusion was patent, and subject to the power of the judge to withdraw the issue from the jury where no reasonable jury could find the evidence to be genuine. H was charged with sexual offences against his stepdaughter, A, and his adopted daughter, B. If A's account was true, it was possessed of sufficient probative value to be admissible as similar fact evidence in relation to the offence against B, and to corroborate B's evidence, and vice versa. However, the relationship between the girls was such that they could easily have colluded, and the defence contended that they had deliberately conspired to put together a totally false story. The House of Lords unanimously upheld the decision of the trial judge to leave the evidence to the jury, subject to a warning about the risk of collusion. F12.31

The common-law rule as to the assumption of truth stated in *H* is substantially replicated in the CJA 2003, s. 109. Cases under the CJA 2003 have proceeded on the basis that *H* remains good law, and this would seem correct (see e.g., Somanathan, heard with *Weir* [2006] 1 WLR 1855).

Criminal Justice Act 2003, s. 109

(1) Subject to subsection (2), a reference in this chapter to the relevance or probative value of evidence is a reference to its relevance or probative value on the assumption that it is true.

(2) In assessing the relevance or probative value of an item of evidence for any purpose of this chapter, a court need not assume that the evidence is true if it appears, on the basis of any material before the court (including any evidence it decides to hear on the matter), that no court or jury could reasonably find it to be true.

Similarly, the common-law rule as to collusion and other forms of contamination is preserved in s. 107.

Criminal Justice Act 2003, s. 107

(1) If on a defendant's trial before a judge and jury for an offence—
  (a) evidence of his bad character has been admitted under any of paragraphs (c) to (g) of section 101(1), and
  (b) the court is satisfied at any time after the close of the case for the prosecution that—
    (i) the evidence is contaminated, and
    (ii) the contamination is such that, considering the importance of the evidence to the case against the defendant, his conviction of the offence would be unsafe, the court must either direct the jury to acquit the defendant of the offence or, if it considers that there ought to be a retrial, discharge the jury.

(2) Where—
  (a) a jury is directed under subsection (1) to acquit a defendant of an offence, and
  (b) the circumstances are such that, apart from this subsection, the defendant could if acquitted of that offence be found guilty of another offence, the defendant may not be found guilty of that other offence if the court is satisfied as mentioned in subsection (1)(b) in respect of it.

(3) If—
 (a) a jury is required to determine under section 4A(2) of the Criminal Procedure (Insanity) Act 1964 whether a person charged on an indictment with an offence did the act or made the omission charged,
 (b) evidence of the person's bad character has been admitted under any of paragraphs (c) to (g) of section 101(1), and
 (c) the court is satisfied at any time after the close of the case for the prosecution that—
  (i) the evidence is contaminated, and
  (ii) the contamination is such that, considering the importance of the evidence to the case against the person, a finding that he did the act or made the omission would be unsafe, the court must either direct the jury to acquit the defendant of the offence or, if it considers that there ought to be a rehearing, discharge the jury.

(4) This section does not prejudice any other power a court may have to direct a jury to acquit a person of an offence or to discharge a jury.

(5) For the purposes of this section a person's evidence is contaminated where—
 (a) as a result of an agreement or understanding between the person and one or more others, or
 (b) as a result of the person being aware of anything alleged by one or more others whose evidence may be, or has been, given in the proceedings,

the evidence is false or misleading in any respect, or is different from what it would otherwise have been.

The common-law principles described above applied not only to cases of deliberate conspiracy between witnesses, but also to those where there is a risk that one witness may unconsciously have been influenced by the account of another witness (*H* and *Ryder* [1994] 2 All ER 859). The same considerations would seem in theory also to be applicable where the risk of falsity arises not from collusion between witnesses, but from what Lord Wilberforce in *DPP v Boardman* [1975] AC 421 (at p. 444) described as 'a process of infection from media or publicity or simply from fashion'. It would appear that the provisions of s. 107(5) cover both the obvious case of deliberate collusion and the more subtle process of unconscious contamination referred to in the common-law authorities, but the preservation in s. 107(4) of any other common-law powers the court may have makes it certain that, if some cases of unconscious contamination are not caught by the Act, they are subject to the court's common-law jurisdiction. Note that the statutory provisions apply only to trial on indictment (s. 107(1)).

In *C* [2006] 1 WLR 2994, the Court of Appeal suggested that a trial judge should postpone a decision on a plausible submission that there has been contamination until the suggested contaminated evidence has been examined at trial. The judge could then 'have well in mind the precise details of the evidence actually given, with such weaknesses and problems as may have emerged'. This is so, though it also puts a premium on the jury's ability to disregard evidence which the judge decides is contaminated.

Similar Fact Evidence and Acquittals

F12.32 On rare occasions the prosecution contends that D has been guilty of past relevant misconduct despite the fact that he has been acquitted by another court in respect of that conduct. Under the CJA 2003, as at common law, the prosecution would be adducing evidence of 'bad character', despite the acquittal, because the contention is that the accused had been guilty of misconduct on the previous occasion, even though no attempt is made to punish him for it (see **F12.7**). The evidence would be admissible if the prosecution could show its relevance to an important issue under s. 101(1)(d) leaving the accused to contend for the exercise of the specific statutory discretion in s. 101(3).

At common law the use of such evidence was at one time thought to be objectionable under the double jeopardy rule, until the decision of the House of Lords in *Z* [2000] 2 AC 483. Z was charged with the rape of C, and his defence was consent. On four separate occasions Z had been tried for the rape of other women, and on three occasions acquitted. The prosecution contended that evidence from all four previous complainants was admissible to rebut the defence put forward in respect of C. It was conceded that the evidence of the four, taken cumulatively, possessed the degree of probative value required for admissibility at common law, but the question was whether the principle against double jeopardy prevented the prosecution adducing evidence the acceptance of which showed that the accused had been guilty of offences for which he had been acquitted. The House of Lords held that evidence may be adduced to prove the guilt of the accused in relation to the offence for which he is on trial notwithstanding that it shows that he has committed other offences of which he has been acquitted. Provided that the prosecutor does not seek in any way to punish the accused for the other offences, the double jeopardy rule is not infringed. Under *Z*, it remained open for the judge to exercise discretion to prevent the unfair use of such evidence. The vehicle for exclusion under the Act would be s. 101(3).

In Smith, one of the appeals heard with *Edwards* [2006] 1 WLR 1524, the rule in *Z* was applied where the accused had been led to believe that he would not be prosecuted in respect of a particular allegation. This did not prevent the subsequent use of the allegation as evidence of propensity, subject to the application of the court's power to prevent unfair use.

EVIDENCE OF BAD CHARACTER ADDUCED BY A CO-ACCUSED

Criminal Justice Act 2003: Evidence of Bad Character Going to Matter in Issue Between Co-accused

The relevant provision of the Criminal Justice Act 2003 is s. 101(e), which is supplemented by s. 104. **F12.33**

Criminal Justice Act 2003, ss. 101 and 104

101.—(1) In criminal proceedings evidence of the defendant's bad character is admissible if, but only if—

(e) it has substantial probative value in relation to an important matter in issue between the defendant and a co-defendant,

. . .

104.—(1) Evidence which is relevant to the question whether the defendant has a propensity to be untruthful is admissible on that basis under section 101(1)(e) only if the nature or conduct of his defence is such as to undermine the co-defendant's defence.

(2) Only evidence—

(a) which is to be (or has been) adduced by the co-defendant, or

(b) which a witness is to be invited to give (or has given) in cross-examination by the co-defendant,

is admissible under section 101(1)(e).

Section 104(1) is primarily relevant to the cut-throat defence where the evidence of propensity is directed more towards establishing lack of veracity than to the issue of guilt. This is dealt with at **F12.36**. The restriction applied by s. 104(1) does not bite where the evidence of propensity is not directed to untruthfulness but to the issue of commission of the offence. In such cases, s. 101(1)(e) permits propensity evidence to be adduced against an accused by a co-accused whatever the nature of the defence, provided that it is of 'substantial probative value' in relation to an issue between them — though this will frequently occur because one blames the other. Thus in *West* [2006] EWCA Crim 1843, for example, one of the three men accused of the murder of a fourth sought for the first time in giving his evidence to blame W, which created an issue between them which should have allowed W to have recourse to his co-accused's previous convictions for violence. In *De Vos* [2006] EWCA Crim 1688 D's convictions for drugs offences were admissible in relation to his contention that he was an innocent 'mule' duped by his co-accused. In *Land* [2006] EWCA Crim 2856 L, an employee of the CPS, disclosed information to K as a result of which both were charged with offences relating to the administration of justice. L's defence was that he had acted in fear of K, and set about proving K's bad character. Various previous convictions and matters relating to a drugs deal were admitted, but other matters relating, *inter alia,* to the discovery of a sword at K's home were said to have been properly excluded on the grounds that they lacked the necessary 'substantial probative value' in relation to an important issue in the case. The court also endorsed the earlier comment of the court in *Edwards* [2006] 1 WLR 1524 that the trial judge's 'feel' for what is important in the context of the case is most likely to be correct.

Note that there is no discretion to restrain an accused from taking advantage of s. 101(1)(e). Where evidence of propensity satisfies the test for admissibility in s. 101(1)(e) it may be adduced notwithstanding that it is also highly prejudicial: s. 101(3) does not apply. *Musone* [2007] EWCA Crim 1237, where the court also considered and dismissed argument based on the ECHR, Article 6, before concluding that 'The only apparent control on the deployment of evidence by one defendant against another is that which is contained in section 101(1)(e)'. The common law followed the same rule: for example in *Grant* [2004] EWCA Crim 2910, G was charged with murder and was shown by his co-accused to have a relevant propensity by reference to an incident some months earlier for which he was awaiting trial. G relied on his privilege against self-incrimination in respect of the earlier incident, as he was entitled to do, thereby hampering his challenge to the evidence. Provided, however, that G had the opportunity to give the evidence he wanted and to cross-examine the witnesses called for the co-accused, and the matter was summed up fairly, the court was satisfied that there was no unfairness.

Distinguishing the Criminal Justice Act 2003, s. 101(1)(e) from the Common-law Position

F12.34 These provisions were intended to reflect the position at common law, described in detail in previous editions of this work. However, the Act was drafted before the decision of the House of Lords in *Randall* [2004] 1 WLR 56. In that case, R and G were jointly charged with the murder of B, who had been assaulted in the street. Both admitted involvement in persuading B to leave the nearby house of R's aunt, but G denied following B into the street, and R admitted only to inflicting minor injuries on B in self-defence. Each gave evidence blaming the other for inflicting the fatal injuries, so that both were exposed to cross-examination on their records under the Criminal Evidence Act 1898, s. 1(3)(iii), for the purpose of attacking their veracity. G had a 'formidable record' for offences, including serious offences of violence, and it was R's contention that G was more likely to have killed B. The Court of Appeal held that the trial judge wrongly directed the jury that the record of G was relevant only to the truthfulness of the evidence he gave at trial. Where there was a cut-throat defence the 'imbalance' between the record of offending of the two men tended to support the version of events put forward by R. The only issue before the House of Lords was whether G's propensity to use violence was relevant to the issue whether it was R who committed the assault. Lord Steyn, in an opinion in which the other Lords concurred, rejected the argument put forward by the Crown that propensity 'proves nothing' in relation to guilt. The relevance of evidence of propensity was to be determined, like other evidence, by reference to whether 'the evidence is capable of increasing or diminishing the probability of the existence of a fact in issue'. As a matter of common sense, propensity might be relevant:

> Postulate a joint trial involving two accused arising from an assault committed in a pub. Assume it to be clear that one of the two men committed the assault. The one man has a long list of previous convictions involving assaults in pubs. It shows him to be prone to fighting when he had consumed alcohol. The other man has an unblemished record. Relying on experience and common sense one might rhetorically ask why the propensity to violence of one man should not

> be deployed by the other man as part of his defence that he did not commit the assault. Such evidence is capable, depending on the jury's assessment of all the evidence, of making it more probable that the man with the violent disposition when he had consumed alcohol committed the assault. To rule that the jury may use the convictions in regard to his credibility but that convictions revealing his propensity to violence must otherwise be ignored is to ask the jury to put to one side their common sense and experience. It would be curious if the law compelled such an unrealistic result.

Lord Steyn approved as 'high authority' for the proposition that evidence of a co- accused's propensity may be relevant the decision of the Privy Council in *Lowery v The Queen* [1974] AC 85. Lord Morris stated that, where the question is which of two men committed a murder, it would be 'unjust to prevent either of them from calling any evidence of probative value which could point to the probability that the perpetrator was the one rather than the other'.

The major difference that appears to exist between the common law as described in *Randall*, and the statutory provision of the CJA 2003, s. 101(1)(e), is that bad character evidence adduced under the Act must be of 'substantial probative value in relation to an issue' between the accused, rather than being merely relevant. Contrast s. 101(1)(d), which stipulates relevance as the standard for admissibility of prosecution evidence (see **F12.20**). The explanation for applying a harder test for admissibility in respect of evidence from a co-accused is that the court has no discretion to exclude evidence from an accused person (contrast, in relation to prosecution evidence, s. 101(3), supplemented by the PACE 1984, s. 78, at **F12.12**). It appears from the Explanatory Notes which accompanied the Criminal Justice Bill when it was first introduced to Parliament that the reference to 'substantial' is intended only to exclude evidence of 'marginal or trivial value' rather than to impose any specific requirement with regard to the cogency of the evidence. If this is so, there would appear to be no inconsistency with *Randall*, and cases decided under the authority of *Randall* may be of relevance to the construction of the new provision. It appears to have been so considered in *Musone* [2007] EWCA Crim 1237 where, however, the court deliberately refrained from expressing a concluded view as to the meaning of 'substantial' probative value in s. 101(1)(e).

An alternative approach to the new provision might be to cast back to some pre-*Randall* authorities where a stricter approach was preferred, on the ground that these cases more closely approximate to the new test. In *Thompson* [1995] 2 Cr App R 589, in which one accused, S, was held to have been rightly permitted to cross-examine prosecution witnesses with a view to showing that the offence bore the hallmark of his co-accused, T and M, the test for admissibility was said to be one of 'relevance strictly applied'. By this the court appears to have meant that the evidence must be of sufficiently direct relevance, rather than that it should be of the degree of cogency required where such evidence is tendered by the prosecution. In *Randall* the concept of relevance appears to be relevance ordinarily applied, which it is submitted is more consistent with the thrust of the new provisions, which aim to protect the right of the co-accused to adduce evidence tending to show his innocence.

Randall also casts doubt on the correctness of the decision of the Court of Appeal in *Neale* (1977) 65 Cr App R 304. On a charge of arson, N claimed that the fire was started by his co-accused, B, and that N was either not there or not participating when the fire was started. In support of this, N sought to adduce evidence that B had a propensity to start fires. However, it was held that B's propensity to start fires on his own did not logically suggest that he had started the fire in question without the help of N. *Miller* and *Neale* were applied in *Knutton* (1993) 97 Cr App R 114, in which K's formidable list of convictions was held to have been of insufficient relevance where the co-accused's defence was alibi. While the relevance of evidence of propensity is clearly to be determined in light of the defence raised, Lord Steyn stated that *Neale* appeared to be a borderline decision, and he questioned what the outcome would have been had N clearly admitted his presence at the scene.

At common law, when evidence of propensity of an accused was adduced by a co-accused but was also relevant to an issue between the Crown and the accused, although the point was not free from controversy the better view was that it was not necessary for a direction to be given to disregard the evidence as between the accused and the Crown. Justice does not require that such a direction be given, and it would needlessly perplex juries. Thus, as Rix LJ said in *B (C)* [2004] 2 Cr App R 570, where propensity is admitted for the sake of a co-defendant's defence, the Crown becomes the beneficiary of that. The same result would appear to follow under the CJA 2003, s. 101(1)(e): although the prosecution cannot take advantage of the gateway, they may be the beneficiary where a co-accused elects to do so. Decisions under the CJA 2003 have not so far considered the weight to be given to common-law authorities. However, the view which appears to be developing is that the CJA 2003 provides a narrower platform for admissibility for evidence by a co-accused but (in a curious twist on the common law) the co-accused might be the beneficiary of the greater latitude afforded to the prosecution. Thus, in *Lambrou* [2005] EWCA Crim 3595, the trial judge, taken by surprise by the commencement of the new provisions, failed to give sufficient consideration to the terms of s. 101(1)(e) as between L and his co-accused, but the conviction admitted in consequence (for an offence of the same kind) could, the Court considered, have been admitted at the behest of the prosecution under s. 101(1)(d).

Propensity where Character in Issue

F12.35 The doctrine of relevance will operate more favourably towards an accused where his co-accused sets up his own good character, or at least seeks to assert positive aspects of his character, so as to make him seem less likely than the accused to have committed the offence. This was the case at common law, and would seem also to obtain under the CJA 2003, s. 101(1)(e), where the test of 'substantial probative value in relation to an important matter in issue' will more readily be satisfied where a co-accused has chosen to take this line. Relevant common-law authorities include *Bracewell* (1978) 68 Cr App R 44, where B and L were jointly charged with the murder of an old man in the course of a burglary. B was prevented from adducing evidence-in-chief to show L's violent disposition, on the ground of insufficient relevance, but the position changed when it emerged that L's defence was that he was an experienced burglar of a non-violent type, able to keep a cool head, whereas B was inexperienced, nervous, excitable and probably drunk. It was held that by raising this defence L had made an issue of his propensity, and that B should at that stage have been allowed to cross-examine him about his violent nature and to call evidence about it if necessary.

In *Douglass* (1989) Cr App R 264, D and P were charged with causing death by reckless driving, the charges arising out of an incident in which the prosecution alleged that D was trying to prevent P from overtaking him, and that in vying for position P lost control and collided head-on with an oncoming vehicle. P cross-examined a prosecution witness with a view to showing that P had not drunk alcohol in the two years that the witness had known him. The purpose of this was to invite the jury to contrast P with D, who, according to the prosecution evidence, had been drinking, so as to cast the blame on him. It was held that P had put his character in issue, and that D was wrongly prevented from introducing relevant evidence of P's bad record for motoring offences including drink-driving.

Evidence Going to Issue of Untruthfulness between Accused and Co-accused

F12.36 Section 101(1)(e) of the CJA 2003 (**F12.33**) renders admissible evidence that has 'substantial probative value' in relation to an important matter in issue between the defendant and a co-defendant. 'Important matter' means a matter of substantial importance in the context of the case as a whole' (s. 112(1)). Section 101(1)(e) is supplemented by s. 104, under which limited use may be made of the defendant's propensity to untruthfulness. Note that only defence evidence is admissible under this provision (s. 104(2)).

Criminal Justice Act 2003, s. 104

(1) Evidence which is relevant to the question whether the defendant has a propensity to be untruthful is admissible on that basis under section 101(1)(e) only if the nature or conduct of his defence is such as to undermine the co-defendant's defence.

(2) Only evidence—

(a) which is to be (or has been) adduced by the co-defendant, or

(b) which a witness is to be invited to give (or has given) in cross-examination by the co-defendant,

is admissible under section 101(1)(e).

The leading case is *Lawson* [2007] 1 WLR 1191. Three young men were alleged to have participated in the manslaughter of a third by pushing him into deep water, where he drowned. The principal offender pleaded guilty, but there was an issue between the two alleged secondary parties, each of whom denied participation, but alleged that the other had made incriminating remarks as to his own intention to push the victim in. Thus both had undermined the defence of the other. The issue of particular difficulty concerned the conviction of L for an offence of violence. This was held not to establish a relevant propensity to offend, but to go instead to credibility, and to have the necessary 'substantial probative value' in relation to that issue. In so deciding, the Court of Appeal rejected the application to s. 101(1)(e) of *Hanson* [2005] 1 WLR 136 (see **F12.23**), where it was decided that, in relation to s. 101(1)(d), only evidence of direct relevance to veracity, such as a conviction involving lying, is admissible to show untruthfulness. This 'cautious test of admissibility' was held more appropriate to applications by the Crown. An accused should not be so restricted in the evidence of criminal behaviour of a co-accused. The court pointed to the similar outcome in Osbourne, an appeal heard with *Renda* [2006] 1 WLR 2948, in which a propensity to violence had been admitted on the issue of untruthfulness, and rejected the counter-argument based on *M* [2006] EWCA Crim 1126, where such evidence was said not to go to truthfulness, on the ground that the point had not been argued. The distinguishing of *Hanson* is not without difficulty, however, in that both s. 101(1)(d) and (e) deal with an accused having 'a propensity to be untruthful' but it appears that the meaning and content of the propensity is broader in s. 101(1)(e). The inconsistency is aggravated by the acceptance that a propensity to violence can, under s. 101(1)(e), be of 'substantial probative value' when under s. 101(1)(d) it is not even relevant.

More consistent with *Hanson* (though the point in *Lawson* was not argued) is *Reid* [2006] EWCA Crim 2900, where the court applied the *Hanson* distinction between untruthfulness and dishonesty in ruling on the co-accused's admissions of offences involving deception.

Where the conditions of s. 101(1)(e) are fulfilled, the court has no statutory discretion to restrain the co accused from adducing relevant evidence of bad character, as s. 101(3) is inapplicable. This mirrors the law as it was laid down both at common law and under the Criminal Evidence Act 1898 (*Murdoch v Taylor* [1965] AC 574, where it was also held that, notwithstanding the absence of discretion, it was still necessary to seek a ruling from the judge as to admissibility before taking advantage of the provision, a point that must still hold good). See also *McGregor* (1992) 95 Cr App R 240.

The restriction of the provision to cases where the 'nature and conduct of the defence is such as to undermine the co-defendant's defence' would seem to import, in relation to evidence of lack of veracity, much of the previous authority in relation to the Criminal Evidence Act 1898, s. 1(3)(iii), where one co-accused's evidence is said to be 'against' another (so as to let in his character only where the effect is to undermine the defence of that other). The phrase 'nature and conduct' also appears in the 1898 Act, but in relation to s. 1(3)(ii) (imputations on prosecution witnesses etc.); the authorities in relation to that expression may also prove of assistance (see **F12.38**).

F12.37 **'Nature and Conduct of Defence'** Where this phrase occurred in the Criminal Evidence Act 1898, in the slightly different context of a defence involving imputations against the prosecution, it was held that answers given in cross-examination were *prima facie* not to be taken into account in determining the nature or conduct of the defence, as such answers should be taken to form part of the cross-examiner's case (*Jones* (1909) 3 Cr App R 67; *Eidinow* (1932) 23 Cr App R 154). However, answers given in cross-examination which went beyond the scope of the question ran the risk of being held part of the nature and conduct of the defence (*Jones* (1909) 3 Cr App R 67, per Lord Alverstone CJ at p. 69; see also *Courtney* [1995] Crim LR 63). Equally (and more obviously), the accused was exposed to revelations of bad character where his answers in cross-examination did no more than to remove all doubt as to whether the accused was seeking to impugn the character of a prosecution witness (*Selvey v DPP* [1970] AC 304). Where, however, a judge thought that the accused has been trapped into making an imputation by the form of the question put to him, cross-examination on the bad character of the accused was not permitted (*Jones*; *Baldwin* (1925) 18 Cr App R 175). While these authorities cannot be said to be binding on the proper interpretation of s. 104 of the CJA 2003, the use of the same phrase cannot have been accidental.

F12.38 **'Such as to Undermine the Co-defendant's Defence'** The Criminal Evidence Act 1898, s. 1(3)(iii), the forerunner of ss. 101(1)(e) and 104 of the CJA 2003, applied where an accused 'has given evidence against any other person charged in the same proceedings', and authorities dealing with the meaning of the provision may continue to be of relevance. 'Evidence against' meant evidence that supported the prosecution case in a material respect or that undermined the defence of a co-accused (*Murdoch v Taylor* [1965] AC 574, per Lord Donovan at p. 592). His lordship qualified the earlier definition proffered by the Court of Criminal Appeal in *Stannard* [1965] 2 QB 1, in which it was said that the question was whether the evidence 'tended to' support the prosecution case or undermine the defence. This was wrong insofar as it suggested that evidence given by A1 might be evidence against A2 simply because it differed from evidence given by A2.

In *Kirkpatrick* [1998] Crim LR 63, it was held that K's defence to indecent assault (which was that he had been intervening to prevent B and another committing the offence) was not undermined by B's defence, which was that he was asleep and took no part in the events. B did not, merely by providing an inconsistent account, undermine K's defence. It is submitted that the decision is correct, even though a jury which believed B's account could not at the same time believe K's. *A fortiori* if the evidence of A1, if believed, would result in the acquittal of A2, even though it is fundamentally inconsistent with the defence put forward by A2. Thus, in *Bruce* [1975] 1 WLR 1252, B, M and others were charged with robbery, and convicted of stealing cash from a foreigner. M's defence was that there had been a preconceived plan to rob, but he maintained that he was not a party to it, whereas B claimed that there had been no preconceived plan, and indeed that neither he nor M had received any money from the victim. It was held that the inconsistency between their defences did not entitle counsel for M to cross-examine B on his record, because acceptance of B's evidence would have led to the acquittal of M, not his conviction, and: 'The fact that [B's] evidence undermined [M's] defence by supplying him with another does not make it evidence given against him' (per Stephenson LJ at p. 1259). In a situation where A1 provides an alternative explanation, however, it did not take much to persuade a court that A1 had implicated A2 in the offence. Thus, in *Hatton* (1976) 64 Cr App R 88, Hatton's evidence was found on balance to be against that of Hildon who, together with Hatton and Ripley, was charged with theft of scrap metal. Hatton claimed that all three accused acted in pursuance of a plan to take the scrap, but that their intention was not dishonest, because a relation of Hildon had assured them that he had permission to take it. Hildon, on the other hand, claimed that he had happened by the site while Hatton and Ripley were collecting the metal, and had been persuaded to help on the understanding that they had paid for it. Hatton's evidence was held to support 'a material part of the prosecution case' (i.e. a preconceived plan between the three to collect the scrap), and 'although it provided Hildon with another defence, it not merely undermined his credit but on balance did more to undermine his defence than to undermine the prosecution's case' (per Stephenson LJ at p. 91).

It sometimes happens that the only way an accused can assert his innocence is by placing the blame on a co-accused. In this unfortunate situation the shield against cross- examination was lost under the Criminal Evidence Act 1898, and it would appear that in the same situation under the CJA 2003 the defence is inevitably undermined. In *Varley* [1982] 2 All ER 519, V and D were charged with robbery, and D's defence was that he took part in the robbery only because V was present and made threats against D's life. V gave evidence in which he completely denied that he had taken any part in the offence: evidence which clearly undermined D's account, because 'it amounted to saying that not only was [D] telling lies but that [D] would be left as a participant on his own and not acting under duress'. The Court of Appeal summarised the position in the following way (at p. 522):

> Mere denial of participation in a joint venture is not of itself sufficient to rank as evidence against the co-defendant. For the proviso to apply, such denial must lead to the conclusion that if the witness did not participate then it must have been the other who did. . . . Where the one defendant asserts or in due course would assert one view of the joint venture which is directly contradicted by the other such contradiction may be evidence against the co- defendant.

The same result was reached in *Davis* [1975] 1 WLR 345, in which D, under cross- examination, was driven to accuse O, his co-accused, of stealing a gold cross and chain that had disappeared from a house in circumstances such that either D or O must have taken it. Any denial by D in the circumstances necessarily involved undermining the chance of acquittal of O, and was thus evidence against him. A similar case is *Crawford* [1997] 1 WLR 1329, where the prosecution contended that three women entered a public lavatory and robbed the victim. A's defence was that she had been present, along with C and the third woman, but had taken no part in the robbery. C's defence was that she had left the lavatory by the time the robbery occurred. C's account of events was held to be a 'direct contradiction' of A's so as to undermine A's defence and to permit A to cross-examine C on her previous convictions. In *Hendrick* [1992] Crim LR 427, by contrast, co-accused, F and H, were alleged to have been involved in a joint venture to steal a handbag. F's denial of participation did not lead to the loss of his shield against cross-examination as the innocence of F was not incompatible with the innocence of H.

In *Rigot* [2000] 7 Arch News 2, the Court of Appeal held (contrary to what was said in *Varley*) that mere denial of participation in a joint venture with the co-accused could be evidence against him where the effect of the denial was merely to suggest that he 'may' have committed the offence, and not that he 'must' have done so. On the facts of the case, however, R's denial was such as to completely undermine the defence advanced by his co-accused, S, who was claiming in effect to have been an innocent dupe of R and his associates in carrying R's drug-laden suitcase into the country. If, as R said, the suitcase was not his and he was a complete innocent, the only explanation S had advanced for her possession of the drugs was necessarily false. It does not seem necessary to qualify the interpretation in *Varley* to accommodate such facts.

Where evidence undermined a co-accused's defence in the sense described above, it did not matter for the purposes of the Criminal Evidence Act 1898, and should not for the purposes of the CJA 2003, that that the co-accused's defence was already a lost cause, for example because he has effectively admitted his guilt in evidence-in-chief (*Mir* [1989] Crim LR 894).

It was not necessary under the 1898 Act, nor should it be under the CJA 2003, that the evidence of A1 be given with any hostile intent against A2, for 'it is the effect of the evidence upon the minds of the jury which matters, not the state of mind of the person who gives it' (*Murdoch v Taylor* [1965] AC 574, per Lord Donovan at p. 591). Applying this objective test,

F

Part F Evidence

it is obvious that damaging evidence 'would be just as damaging whether given with regret or whether given with relish' (per Lord Morris, at p. 584).

Where A1 is wrongly denied the opportunity to cross-examine A2 on his convictions in a case where each blames the other for the offence, and both are convicted, it was said in relation to the 1898 Act that it does not follow that A1's conviction is unsafe. The jury must necessarily have disbelieved the evidence 'against' A1 to the extent that they disbelieved the denial of A2 (*Boyce* [2001] EWCA Crim 921).

EVIDENCE OF BAD CHARACTER TO CORRECT FALSE IMPRESSION OR COUNTER-ATTACK ANOTHER'S CHARACTER

Uses of Bad Character Evidence Contingent on Nature of Defence

F12.39 The main provisions governing the use of evidence of the accused's bad character to establish the commission of the offence are the CJA 2003, s. 101(1)(d), where the evidence is to be adduced by the prosecution, and s. 101(1)(e), where the evidence is relied upon by a co-accused. These uses of bad character evidence are dealt with at **F12.20** ***et seq.*** and **F12.33** respectively. Both subsections (1)(d) and (e) may also permit the use of evidence of bad character to show untruthfulness. For a controversial approach to the statutory gateways and the relationship between untruthfulness and bad character, see *Campbell* [2007] EWCA Crim 1472. Commentary on the case is to be found in the October Bulletin (distributed with this edition).

In addition, depending on choices made as to the nature of his defence, the accused may also have to meet evidence of bad character designed to correct a false impression he has given (s. 101(1)(f): see **F12.40**), or to repel an attack he has made on the character of another (s. 101(1)(g): see **F12.42**). These methods of deploying bad character evidence are described in the remainder of this section. The first and most obvious difference from the predecessor provision, the Criminal Evidence Act 1898, is that the use of evidence of bad character under the CJA 2003 is not contingent on the decision of the accused to give evidence, as it may be tendered irrespective of whether the accused is called as a witness in the proceedings. This reduces the tactical options open to an accused who wishes to launch an attack upon a prosecution witness or upon a co-accused without exposing his own bad character. It also means that the evidence that is adduced under the provisions, which are considered below, cannot be said, as was frequently the case with evidence adduced under the 1898 Act, to be admissible only in relation to the issue of the credit to be given to the evidence of the accused. Potentially, it is open to a jury to draw on the bad character evidence to prove guilt, unless the judge directs them otherwise. It will be for the courts to decide what use to make of, say, convictions for dishonesty where the accused is charged with a sexual assault, or vice versa. In relation to s. 101(1)(d) (see **F12.20**), it has been held that evidence of untruthfulness is not supplied by evidence of dishonesty simpliciter, but it has been held otherwise in relation to s. 101(1)(e) (see **F12.36**). Neither the gateway under s. 101(1)(g) nor that under s. 101(1)(f) makes explicit reference to evidence of untruthfulness, although evidence under gateway (f) is limited to evidence correcting the false impression so that the authorities under the other provisions may be of limited usefulness.

The CJA 2003 significantly increases the likelihood that evidence of the bad character of the accused will be admitted in criminal proceedings. Whereas the provisions to be considered are recognisably derived from the previous rules, they are far broader in their scope. The recommendations of the Law Commission (*Evidence of Bad Character in Criminal Proceedings*, Law Com No. 273, 2001) would have resulted in a number of changes to protect the accused from the worst excesses of the Criminal Evidence Act 1898, including the need to scrutinise the evidence for substantial relevance to the issues. This would have introduced a measure of 'divisibility' of character not hitherto permitted. However the Act does not take up this proposal, so that there is no improvement, but rather a worsening, in the position of the defence under the new law.

The following provisions, which have already been considered, are of equal application to evidence of bad character admitted under the remaining exceptions: s. 107 (stopping the case where evidence contaminated: **F12.31**), s. 109 (assumption of truth in assessment of relevance or probative value: **F12.30**). The provisions of s. 108, regarding the use which can be made of evidence of convictions when the accused was a child, are also of general relevance and are considered at **F12.47**.

Evidence to Correct a False Impression

Section 101(1)(f) of the CJA 2003 permits evidence of bad character to be adduced by the prosecution to correct a false impression given by the accused. The provision is supplemented by s. 105, which lays down the circumstances in which the accused is regarded as having given such an impression. The provisions of s. 101(3), which exclude evidence having an adverse effect on the fairness of the proceedings, do not apply to evidence tendered under s. 101(1)(f) (see **F12.11**). **F12.40**

Criminal Justice Act 2003, s. 105

(1) For the purposes of section 101(1)(f)—
  (a) the defendant gives a false impression if he is responsible for the making of an express or implied assertion which is apt to give the court or jury a false or misleading impression about the defendant;
  (b) evidence to correct such an impression is evidence which has probative value in correcting it.

(2) A defendant is treated as being responsible for the making of an assertion if—
  (a) the assertion is made by the defendant in the proceedings (whether or not in evidence given by him),
  (b) the assertion was made by the defendant—
    (i) on being questioned under caution, before charge, about the offence with which he is charged, or
    (ii) on being charged with the offence or officially informed that he might be prosecuted for it, and evidence of the assertion is given in the proceedings,
  (c) the assertion is made by a witness called by the defendant,
  (d) the assertion is made by any witness in cross-examination in response to a question asked by the defendant that is intended to elicit it, or is likely to do so, or
  (e) the assertion was made by any person out of court, and the defendant adduces evidence of it in the proceedings.

(3) A defendant who would otherwise be treated as responsible for the making of an assertion shall not be so treated if, or to the extent that, he withdraws it or disassociates himself from it.

(4) Where it appears to the court that a defendant, by means of his conduct (other than the giving of evidence) in the proceedings, is seeking to give the court or jury an impression about himself that is false or misleading, the court may if it appears just to do so treat the defendant as being responsible for the making of an assertion which is apt to give that impression.

(5) In subsection (4) 'conduct' includes appearance or dress.

(6) Evidence is admissible under section 101(1)(f) only if it goes no further than is necessary to correct the false impression.

(7) Only prosecution evidence is admissible under section 101(1)(f).

The Law Commission (*Evidence of Bad Character in Criminal Proceedings*, Law Com No. 273, 2001) recommended that evidence be admissible to correct a false or misleading impression given by the accused, and much of the elaboration of s. 105 follows the pattern set by the Commission. However, the Law Commission's proposal also required the prosecution to satisfy the court that the evidence had 'substantial probative value' in correcting the impression, and that either the evidence was not prejudicial or that, if it was, the interests of justice required it to be admissible (Law Commission draft Bill, cl. 10). None of these safeguards is replicated in s. 101(1)(f) or s. 105: evidence of bad character is admissible provided only that it has 'probative value' in correcting the false impression. This means that the accused is forced back on more slender safeguards: the option to withdraw or dissociate himself from an assertion which would otherwise merit the admission of bad character evidence in rebuttal (s. 105(3)) and the provision that rebuttal evidence is admissible 'only if it goes no further than is necessary to correct the false impression'. The tendency of the courts to permit applications under s. 78 of the PACE 1984 in cases not covered by the specific power of exclusion of evidence of bad character in s. 101(3) of the CJA 2003 is helpful in creating a framework for any further protection the courts may regard as necessary (see **F12.12**).

The CJA 2003 provisions are based on the common-law rule permitting evidence in rebuttal of evidence of good character and the provision of the Criminal Evidence Act 1898, s. 1(3)(ii), permitting cross-examination of the accused who has made an issue of his good character (see the 2005 edition of this work). However, the new provisions apply irrespective of whether witnesses are specifically called as to good character, and whether or not the accused elects to give evidence on his own behalf. Evidence admitted under the provision potentially goes towards correcting the false impression in a manner indicative of guilt, not merely of the credit to be given to any testimony the accused gives. If the accused chooses to make an issue of his good character, in circumstances where to do so would leave the jury with a false impression, the provisions of the CJA 2003, s. 101(1)(f) will bite, but this will in future be just one of the ways in which the accused may render admissible evidence of bad character that would not otherwise have been sufficiently relevant to an issue in the proceedings.

In *Ullah* [2006] EWCA Crim 2003 U's statement in interview that he had never acted dishonestly and that he had been meticulous in his business dealings was sufficient to admit evidence of his previous (similar) conviction for conspiracy to obtain by deception. The CJA 2003 clarifies the position where the accused, as in *Ullah*, makes misleading assertions during questioning or when charged and these are subsequently given in evidence in the proceedings. These constitute assertions for the purposes of the provision (s. 105(2)(b)) and so they may result in the use of evidence to correct any false impression given, even where the prosecution is responsible for placing the original assertion before the court. Where this occurs, the accused would do well, if he does not stand by the assertion, to disassociate himself from it (s. 105(3)).

In *Renda* [2006] 1 WLR 2948, where the issue arose of whether the accused had withdrawn or dissociated himself from a false impression, the Court of Appeal clearly stated that there is a difference between making a positive decision to correct such an impression and being driven in cross-examination to concede its falsity. In the latter case, the accused could derive no benefit from s. 105(3).

Examples of False Impression

F12.41 In *Renda* [2006] 1 WLR 2948, it was said to be 'most unlikely' to be useful to refer to authorities under the Criminal Evidence Act 1898 in deciding whether an accused has given a 'false impression', which was essentially a question of fact. In that case, where R had clearly misrepresented the nature of his previous employment in an attempt to make himself out to be a man of positive good character, there was indeed little to be gained from such an inquiry. Older decisions, even if only as guides to frequently recurring fact situations, may be of some use, and the leading cases are reproduced for what assistance they might offer in that role.

Under the 1898 Act, the shield was not lost where an accused asserted facts relevant to the issue of commission of the offence that incidentally showed him in a good light (*Malindi v The Queen* [1967] AC 439). It was only where he asserted his good character as a separate matter that the shield was down. Under the CJA 2003, the only question is whether he has given a 'false impression' about himself, and it is by no means clear that this leaves the accused the same degree of latitude to present his account of relevant events. Although the statutory definition of 'bad character' is confined to evidence that does not 'have to do with' the facts in issue, there is no corresponding restriction on the meaning of what gives a 'false or misleading impression', though it is submitted that implicitly there must be, for otherwise the judge would have to form a view about the events that are the subject of the charge, and the accused's response to them, in order to decide whether he has given a false impression.

At common law and under the 1898 Act there was doubt as to whether the accused presenting himself as a married man was tantamount to evidence of good character. If the accused is charged with a homosexual offence and chooses to refer to the fact that he has a wife and family (when he has) it would be open to the court to conclude that this is a false impression to the extent that the unspoken but implicit assumption is that he is less likely to have committed the offence charged. This might be sufficient to warrant the admission of evidence of homosexual disposition gleaned from previous convictions. It is also clear that the accused may be held to have given a false impression by means of conduct including dress (s. 105(4) and (5)) but unclear how such a provision permitting rebuttal only to the extent that it is necessary to correct the impression will operate in practice except in the obvious case of a defrocked clergyman (see *D.S.* [1999] Crim LR 911). Similarly in *Robinson* [2001] Crim LR 478 it might be said that an accused who gives evidence waving a Bible is attempting to impress the court with his devotion to the Deity, an impression that might well be false, but only evidence of bad character going directly to the falsity of the impression is admissible in rebuttal.

It would also appear that an accused who adduces evidence of his bad character in order to present himself before the court 'warts and all' may be held to have given a false impression if there are further discreditable revelations to be made. As only prosecution evidence is admissible under s. 101(1)(f), the provision cannot be invoked by a co-accused where one accused is misleadingly trying to present himself, for example, as an experienced burglar with no record for using violence (compare *Bracewell* (1978) 68 Cr App R 44). Such evidence would however appear to be admissible under s. 101(1)(e).

'Attack on Another Person's Character'

The CJA 2003, s. 101(1)(g), permits the prosecution to adduce evidence of bad character to counter an attack on another person. Section 101(1)(g) is supplemented by s. 106, which details the circumstances in which such an attack occurs. An accused may apply to exclude evidence the admission of which under s. 101(1)(g) would have an unfair effect on the fairness of the proceedings (s. 101(3)). **F12.42**

Criminal Justice Act 2003, s. 106

(1) For the purposes of section 101(1)(g) a defendant makes an attack on another person's character if—
  (a) he adduces evidence attacking the other person's character,
  (b) he (or any legal representative appointed under section 38(4) of the Youth Justice and Criminal Evidence Act 1999 to cross-examine a witness in his interests) asks questions in cross-examination that are intended to elicit such evidence, or are likely to do so, or
  (c) evidence is given of an imputation about the other person made by the defendant—
    (i) on being questioned under caution, before charge, about the offence with which he is charged, or
    (ii) on being charged with the offence or officially informed that he might be prosecuted for it.

(2) In subsection (1) 'evidence attacking the other person's character' means evidence to the effect that the other person—
  (a) has committed an offence (whether a different offence from the one with which the defendant is charged or the same one), or

(b) has behaved, or is disposed to behave, in a reprehensible way; and 'imputation about the other person' means an assertion to that effect.

(3) Only prosecution evidence is admissible under section 101(1)(g).

F12.43 **'Attack'** The CJA 2003, s. 106, uses the word 'imputation', which had specific connotations under the Criminal Evidence Act 1898, s. 1(3)(ii). In the context of the CJA 2003, however, the term is more precisely defined. The accused must either adduce evidence or he (or his representative appointed to cross-examine a witness whom the accused may not cross-examine in person) must ask a question, the effect of which is to suggest that another person has committed an offence or is otherwise of bad character within the meaning of the CJA 2003, s. 98. Thus the old law about what constitutes an imputation is of peripheral relevance, though it might assist as to what is 'reprehensible' behaviour or disposition. Questions asked of the accused on behalf of the prosecution do not trigger the provision (cf. *Jones* (1909) 3 Cr App R 67), although it appears, paradoxically perhaps, that questioning at interview may have this effect (s. 106(1)(c)). Perhaps the authorities under the 1898 Act might be brought to bear on an accused who has been driven into making an attack at interview, given that a frightened or blustering suspect might be particularly likely to overstate his case under interrogation.

Evidence of the bad character of a non-defendant is admissible only with the leave of the court under the CJA 2003, s. 100 (see **F14**). It follows that an 'attack' for the purposes of s. 101(1)(g) based on evidence adduced by the defence will have been preceded by the granting of such leave, and therefore the evidence or question must concern a matter that is important explanatory evidence or is of substantial probative value in relation to an important matter in the case. A gratuitous attack designed merely to blacken the non-defendant's character in an attempt to secure an unmeritorious acquittal will not pass muster under this provision — the 'attack' must be merited. It seems therefore to be unnecessarily punitive to provide that it should (subject to the discretion of the court under s. 101(3)) be met with apparently unlimited revelations about the accused's own character, but this appears to be the case. Under the Criminal Evidence Act 1898, a most controversial decision was *Selvey v DPP* [1970] AC 304, wherein the imputation made by the accused, if true, showed that the complainant had invented the allegation. This is clearly an attack, as is the assertion that the other person has committed the offence (also an imputation at common law, *Hudson* [1912] 2 KB 464). The position of the Law Commission (*Evidence of Bad Character in Criminal Proceedings*, Law Com No. 273, 2001) on whose recommendations s. 101(1)(g) was loosely based, was that the accused should not lose his shield where the attack consists of evidence of bad character of the other person that 'has to do with the alleged facts of the offence with which the defendant is charged, or is evidence of misconduct in connection with the investigation or prosecution of that offence' (Law Commission Draft Bill, cl. 9(2)). Thus the accused in *Selvey* and *Hudson* whose imputations were necessary to the development of their defences would have been protected from the use of bad character evidence in rebuttal, and the 'attack' (which would still have had to pass muster under what is now s. 100) would have been more in the nature of an attempt by the accused to discredit the other person by reference, for example to evidence of previous convictions for dishonesty that are claimed to have a bearing on credibility. In that case, to permit evidence of the accused's previous convictions for similar offences would have something to commend it. As it stands, however, s. 101(1)(g) is so widely drawn as to compound all of the unfairness of the old law as described by the Law Commission Report, and turns on its head the draft clause designed to rectify the imbalance for the future. It is indicative of the philosophy of the 2003 Act that an accused who has the temerity to suggest that another person committed the offence with which he is charged should face the revelation of his bad character unless he can persuade a court that this would be unfair. Where the convictions have more apparent bearing on the issue of commission of the offence than on veracity, the accused would appear to be at particular risk of prejudice.

As with s. 101(1)(f) (see **F12.40**), the attack may be made in an out-of-court statement, including an interview in which the accused casts an imputation (s. 106(1)(c)). Again there is no requirement that the evidence of the attack is adduced by the defence, thus in one of the appeals heard with *Renda* [2006] 1 WLR 2948 (that of Ball), B was charged with rape and in the course of interview referred to the complainant as 'a slag', criticising her promiscuity in 'very disparaging terms'. His defence at trial was that she was lying and perhaps motivated by a wish for vengeance for past slights. The trial judge's decision to admit evidence of B's bad character on the strength of the specific slights in the interview which had been adduced as part of the prosecution case was supported by the Court of Appeal as a proper exercise of his discretion. Section 106, unlike s. 105 (which supplements s. 101(1)(f)), does not contain a provision permitting the accused to disassociate himself from the imputation. However, the court's discretion to disallow the admission of evidence of bad character could be invoked where the defence does not seek to maintain the attack. In *Nelson* [2006] EWCA Crim 3412, the court questioned the relevance of statements at interview adduced by the prosecution and expressed the view that such evidence should not be adduced simply to provide a basis for gateway (g).

'On Another Person's Character' Section 101(1)(g) of the CJA 2003, together with the supplementary provision of s. 106, appears to contemplate an attack on a specific person. It would not therefore be sufficient, where a crime has clearly been committed by someone, for the accused to say that he has not done it and to lay the blame on some unknown individual. Where a specific attack is made, however, it does not matter that the person attacked is not a witness in the case. Thus the problems that arose under the Criminal Evidence Act 1898, s. 1(3), which had to be amended in order to include imputations against the deceased in a homicide case, do not arise in relation to the CJA 2003: an attack on any victim may trigger s. 101(1)(g), as may an attack on any other non-witness. Nor is it necessary, for the same reason, to consider whether a person whose hearsay statement is before the court and who is the subject of an attack by the defence is a 'witness': whether he is or not, the attack still triggers the provision (cf. *Miller* [1997] 2 Cr App R 178). In *Nelson* [2006] EWCA Crim 3412, it was, however, suggested that it would be unusual for evidence of an accused's bad character to be admitted where the only basis for doing so was an attack on a non-witness who is also a non-victim. On the facts of that case, however, the person whose character was attacked was alleged to have been conspiring with a prosecution witness, which provided a proper foundation for gateway (g). **F12.44**

Where the Accused Does Not Testify Under the Criminal Evidence Act 1898, s. 1(3), the accused who made an attack could resist the introduction of his own bad character in retaliation because he was not putting his own character in issue, merely that of the witness. It followed that his bad character was admissible only where specifically permitted by the 1898 Act, i.e. where he gave evidence (see *Butterwasser* [1948] 1 KB 4). Under the CJA 2003, however, the accused's bad character may be deployed against him whether he gives evidence or not. This reform was part of the package recommended by the Law Commission, and it is submitted that it is sound in principle. Where the jury have to decide between competing versions of events, the argument that they need to know the character of the person making the attack is as strong where the accused testifies as where he declines to do so. **F12.45**

Discretion Under the CEA 1898, the courts were reluctant to exercise their discretion to exclude evidence of the accused's bad character when he had infringed s. 1(3)(ii) by casting imputations — even necessary imputations — on the character of prosecution witnesses (see, for example, *Selvey v DPP* [1970] AC 304, *Burke* (1985) 82 Cr App R 156 and *Powell* [1985] 1 WLR 1364). If the court adopts the same restrictive approach under the CJA 2003, s. 101(1)(g), the result will be that evidence of bad character will become far more widely admissible, and it has been argued above that the discretion ought to be deployed **F12.46**

more frequently to combat the greater risk of prejudice to individual defendants, where the revelation of bad character would be out of all proportion to the damage done by the attack on the character of another. Previous authorities which might remain of particular assistance include those applicable to the level of detail that it is legitimate to include about earlier offences when the prime purpose of the evidence adduced by the prosecution is to undermine the credibility of the attack made by the defendant (see *McLeod* [1994] 1 WLR 1500).

OFFENCES COMMITTED BY ACCUSED WHEN A CHILD

Criminal Justice Act 2003, s. 108

F12.47 (1) Section 16(2) and (3) of the Children and Young Persons Act 1963 (offences committed by person under 14 disregarded for purposes of evidence relating to previous convictions) shall cease to have effect.

(2) In proceedings for an offence committed or alleged to have been committed by the defendant when aged 21 or over, evidence of his conviction for an offence when under the age of 14 is not admissible unless—

(a) both of the offences are triable only on indictment, and

(b) the court is satisfied that the interests of justice require the evidence to be admissible.

(3) Subsection (2) applies in addition to section 101.

The limitation on admissibility of convictions of offences committed by children was introduced at a late stage of the passage through Parliament of the Criminal Justice Bill to mollify strong opposition to the Bill. Only where the offence is serious (such as rape) and the interests of justice require admissibility should reference be made to offences committed when the accused was a child.

PREVIOUS MISCONDUCT ADMISSIBLE UNDER THE THEFT ACT 1968, s. 27(3)

Theft Act 1968, s. 27

F12.48 (3) Where a person is being proceeded against for handling stolen goods (but not for any offence other than handling stolen goods), then at any stage of the proceedings, if evidence has been given of his having or arranging to have in his possession the goods the subject of the charge, or of his undertaking or assisting in, or arranging to undertake or assist in, their retention, removal, disposal or realisation, the following evidence shall be admissible for the purpose of proving that he knew or believed the goods to be stolen goods—

(a) evidence that he has had in his possession, or has undertaken or assisted in the retention, removal, disposal or realisation of, stolen goods from any theft taking place not earlier than 12 months before the offence charged; and

(b) (provided that seven days' notice in writing has been given to him of the intention to prove the conviction) evidence that he has within the five years preceding the date of the offence charged been convicted of theft or of handling stolen goods.

The Theft Act 1968, s. 27(3), applies to all forms of handling (*Ball* [1983] 1 WLR 801). It can be relied upon by the prosecution only in a case where handling is the only offence involved in the proceedings (*Gardner v New Forest Magistrates' Court* (5 June 1998 unreported)). The provisions of s. 27 are unaffected by the changes made to the admissibility of character evidence at common law by chapter 1 of part 11 of the CJA 2003, although the wider provisions in the CJA for the admissibility of evidence of previous convictions may form an attractive alternative for prosecutors.

Section 27 assists only in the proof of guilty knowledge or belief. It may not assist the prosecution where an issue arises as to dishonesty (*Duffas* (1994) 158 JP 224), nor may it be used to prove possession of the goods in question: indeed, the provision cannot be relied upon unless the prosecution have already adduced evidence of the *actus reus* of the handling offence. The mere fact that possession is disputed is not of itself a bar to the use of s. 27 by the prosecution (*List* [1966] 1 WLR 9, per Roskill J, construing the corresponding provision of the Larceny Act 1916). Where, however, the jury will be faced with a number of counts, in some of which possession is in issue and in some of which the issue is guilty knowledge, it was held in *Wilkins* [1975] 2 All ER 734, that: 'very great care should be exercised by the judge first of all before he allows evidence of the previous convictions to be given at all or, if he does allow that evidence to be admitted, very great care should be exercised in order to ensure that the jury realise the issues to which those previous convictions are relevant'. *Wilkins* was decided under s. 27(3)(b), but it is submitted that precisely the same considerations apply to evidence adduced under s. 27(3)(a).

Restrictive Construction

F12.49 It has been the practice of the courts to construe both limbs of the Theft Act 1968, s. 27(3), in a restrictive way. In *Bradley* (1979) 70 Cr App R 200, the Court of Appeal noted that the section gives the power to introduce evidence that would otherwise not be regarded as relevant, and would therefore be inadmissible, and concluded that it should therefore be construed 'with strict regard to its terms'. In particular, it was held that s. 27(3)(a) does not authorise the giving in evidence of the details of the transaction by which the earlier stolen property had come into the hands of the accused. *Bradley* was applied in *Wood* [1987] 1 WLR 779, in which the Court of Appeal noted a conflict between *Bradley* and the earlier case of *Smith* [1918] 2 KB 415, the decision in *Bradley* being preferred. In *Fowler* (1988) 86 Cr App R 219, *Bradley* was applied to s. 27(3)(b), the Court noting that a 'bare recital of conviction is all that is required, and possibly all that it is permissible to provide the jury with'. However, in *Hacker* [1994] 1 WLR 1659, it was held by the House of Lords that s. 27(3)(b) must be read together with the PACE 1984, s. 73(2), under which a certificate of conviction of an offence on indictment must give 'the substance and effect (omitting the formal parts) of the indictment and of the conviction'. It followed that where H, who was charged with handling the bodyshell of a car, had a previous conviction for receiving a car, the detail of the subject matter of the previous conviction, as it appeared on the certificate, was admissible. A similar proposition was advanced with regard to a previous summary conviction. The House of Lords noted that s. 27 had been extensively criticised, but considered that 'not to be able to show what goods had been stolen or handled on a previous occasion might work in some cases to the disadvantage of the defendant himself' (per Lord Slynn at p. 1665).

Discretion

F12.50 Where evidence is strictly admissible under the Theft Act 1968, s. 27(3), the court has a power to exclude it at common law or under the PACE 1984, s. 78 (*Hacker* [1994] 1 WLR 1659; and see also *Herron* [1967] 1 QB 107, *Smith* (1976) 64 Cr App R 217 and *Perry* [1984] Crim LR 680).

SPENT CONVICTIONS

F12.51 The Rehabilitation of Offenders Act 1974, s. 4(1), lays down a general rule that a person whose conviction is 'spent' under the Act is to be treated as a person who has not committed or been charged with or prosecuted for or convicted of or sentenced for the offence or offences which were the subject of that conviction. Section 7(2)(a) excludes criminal proceedings from the operation of this general rule, although the accused is to an extent protected from the use of spent convictions in cross-examination on his record by the *Consolidated Criminal Practice Direction*, para. I.6, *Spent convictions* (see **appendix** 7 and **D19.49**) which directs the court to have regard to the spirit of the 1974 Act by refusing to allow any mention to be made of a spent conviction, except where it is in the interests of justice to do so. In essence this produces the same test as in civil proceedings that *are* covered by s. 4(1), but in respect of which s. 7(3) provides for evidence of spent convictions to be admitted if justice cannot otherwise be done (*Thomas v Commissioner of Police of the Metropolis* [1997] QB 813, in which careful consideration is given to the relevant criminal authorities). In *Corelli* [2001] Crim LR 913 it was held that the effect of s. 7 in combination with the absence of discretion to restrain one accused from cross-examining another on admissible evidence of bad character is that the *Practice Direction* has no application as between co-accused. As the judge has no discretion to restrain a co-accused, the *Practice Direction* could not be employed to modify the clear words of the 1974 Act. The provisions of the CJA 2003, s. 108 (see **F12.47**), where they apply, constitute an absolute prohibition on the introduction of the criminal record of the accused in respect of offences committed when a child, whether spent or not.

Section F13 Character Evidence: Admissibility of Evidence of Accused's Good Character

History

F13.1 The practice of permitting an accused person to raise evidence of good character as part of his defence has been described as an anomaly (*Rowton* (1865) Le & Ca 520, per Martin B, at p. 537), and so it is, particularly when viewed in the light of the more restrictive rules restraining the prosecution from introducing evidence of bad character as part of the case against him. Nevertheless, the practice has a long pedigree: early examples are *Turner* (1664) 6 St Tr 565, at p. 613, and *Harris* (1680) 7 St Tr 926, at p. 929. The practice is founded on a notion of indulgence rather than of right: Lord Goddard CJ in *Butterwasser* [1948] KB 4, at p. 6 spoke of a practice, stretching over 200 years, of 'allowing' a prisoner to call evidence of good character.

The questions which arise are as to the purpose for which such evidence may be relied upon; the direction which should be given to a jury; the nature of the evidence which may be adduced in support of a claim to good character, and the kind of evidence which may be adduced in rebuttal by the prosecution or, where relevant, by a co-accused.

The provisions of the CJA 2003 do not affect the entitlement of a person of good character to present himself as such: the Act deals only with the admissibility of evidence of bad character in criminal proceedings. To the extent, however, that evidence of bad character may be admitted in rebuttal of an assertion of good character (see **F13.13**), the provisions of the CJA 2003 may come into play.

Purpose of Adducing Evidence of Good Character

F13.2 The accused was entitled to adduce evidence of his good character long before the law treated him as a competent witness in his own defence (*Vye* [1993] 1 WLR 471 at p. 474). Such evidence was said by Patteson J in *Stannard* (1837) 7 C & P 673 (at pp. 674–5) to point to the improbability of guilt:

> I cannot in principle make any distinction between evidence of facts, and evidence of character: the latter is equally laid before the jury as the former, as being relevant to the question of guilty or not guilty: the object of laying it before the jury is to induce them to believe, from the improbability that a person of good character should have conducted himself as alleged, that there is some mistake or misrepresentation in the evidence on the part of the prosecution, and it is strictly evidence in the case.

When the accused became competent to give evidence, evidence of good character acquired the further function of enhancing his credibility as a witness. Although historically a subsidiary purpose, evidence of good character came to be regarded as 'primarily a matter which goes to credibility' (*Bellis* [1966] 1 WLR 234). But good character remained relevant to the issue of guilt, and *Stannard* was approved in *Bryant* [1979] QB 108, in which the judge had taken the view that, as B did not give evidence, his character had 'very little if any part to play' in the jury's deliberations. It was held that, insofar as it had been suggested that character was relevant only to the credibility of an accused who has given evidence, there had been a misdirection. The original function of good character has now reasserted itself, and the tendency is to lay equal emphasis upon both functions of evidence of good character. In *Aziz* [1996] AC 41 Lord Steyn said (at p. 50) 'It has long been recognised that the good character of a defendant is logically relevant to his credibility and to the likelihood that he would commit the offence in question.'

The Need for a Jury Direction

F13.3 In *Aziz* [1996] AC 41, Lord Steyn identifies (at p. 50) a 'veritable sea-change in judicial thinking in regard to the proper way in which a judge should direct a jury on the good character of a defendant'. It was at one time thought, following *Smith* [1971] Crim LR 531, that there was no duty to refer to evidence of good character when summing up, the matter being entirely within the discretion of the judge. In *Hussain* [2005] EWCA Crim 31, which came before the Court of Appeal as a reference from the Criminal Cases Review Commission, the Court observed that a summing up on good character would be delivered in different terms today from those in which it was delivered in 1978 when H was tried. The change is said by Lord Steyn to derive from the modern view that the defence case must be put before the jury in a fair and balanced way and, as evidence of good character is evidence of probative significance, fairness dictates that the judge should direct on it. Failure to direct is likely to be of significance in every case in which it is appropriate for such a direction to be given (*Fulcher* [1995] 2 Cr App R 251, but it is not necessarily decisive: see *Balson v The State* [2005] UKPC 2, in which it was said that any direction would have been 'wholly outweighed' by the circumstantial evidence, and *Jagdeo Singh v The State of Trinididad and Tobago* [2006] 1 WLR 146, where it was said that much might depend on the nature of, and issues in, a case and on the other available evidence). In a case where the accused bears the onus of proof, and credibility is at the forefront of the case, it is of particular importance that an appropriate direction be given (*Soukala-Cacace* [1999] All ER (D) 1120). There is, however, no obligation for the trial judge to deal with good character unless the issue has been raised by the defence (*Thompson v R* [1998] AC 811); and see *Brown v The Queen* [2006] 1 AC 1, where it was noted that a judge would be 'ill-advised' to mention good character unless he had been given information from which he could properly and safely do so. It follows that defence counsel is under an obligation to raise the issue in an appropriate case, so that the accused does not lose the benefit that the direction is designed to confer (*Teeluck v The State of Trinidad and Tobago* [2005] 1 WLR 2421). In the somewhat extreme circumstances of *Gilbert v The Queen* [2006] 1 WLR 2108, in which a bishop was convicted of murdering a teenage girl and his character, if not formally put in issue, was very much in the forefront of the defence case, it was said by Lord Woolf that the judge would have been 'well advised' to clarify the situation before deciding how to direct the jury; nevertheless the omission of a good character direction was not fatal to a conviction based on very substantial evidence.

The purpose of the direction is to convey to the jury that they ought to take account of relevant evidence of good character, although it would be going too far to suggest that they are bound to give it any weight. In *Miah* [1997] 2 Cr App R 12, the Court of Appeal considered it best to avoid telling a jury that it is 'entitled' to consider such evidence: although not strictly inaccurate, the expression conflates the two stages of the process and risks giving the jury the impression that they may choose not to consider the evidence at all. See also *Lloyd* [2000] 2 Cr App R 355 and *Scranage* [2001] EWCA Crim 1171, where it was held that the failure of the judge to express the direction as an affirmative statement (that character was something to be taken into account) was fatal to the conviction. In *Scranage* the issue was whether S had acted dishonestly in transferring a sum wrongly credited to him by his bank, or whether he had, as he said, been trying to teach the bank a lesson. The evidence of good character was of crucial importance. By contrast, in *Sanchez* [2003] EWCA Crim 735 an incorrect direction to the jury that they might (rather than should) consider the evidence of good character in deciding whether S had taken part in drug-smuggling was not fatal to S's conviction, which was based on overwhelming evidence. And in *Rehman* [2006] EWCA Crim 1900 a direction in which the Court of Appeal detected a degree of 'grudging sloppiness' did not affect the safety of the conviction, as the jury would not have construed it as a licence to leave good character out of their deliberations.

Direction on Credibility where Accused Testifies

It has been a settled rule since 1989 that where an accused testifies the judge must give a direction as to the relevance of good character to the accused's credibility. In *Berrada* (1989) 91 Cr App R 131, B was convicted of attempted rape. At his trial there was a direct conflict between the evidence of B on the one hand and of the complainant and police witnesses on the other. The trial judge's direction was held to have been defective in that it made no mention of the relevance of evidence of B's previous good character. Waterhouse J said (at p. 134): **F13.4**

> The striking omission . . . is of any reference to the real and primary relevance of the appellant's previous good character. What the learned judge should have said was that it was primarily relevant to the question of the appellant's credibility. . . . In the judgment of this court, the appellant was entitled to have put to the jury from the judge herself a correct direction about the relevance of his previous good character to his credibility. That is a conventional direction and it is regrettable that it did not appear in the summing-up in this case.

Conventionally, the direction on credibility has become known as the 'first limb' of a character direction, with the 'second limb' consisting of a statement as to the relevance of character to the question whether the accused was likely to have committed the offence. The need for a 'first limb' direction has been reaffirmed in numerous decisions since, culminating in *Vye* [1993] 1 WLR 471, where the authorities are reviewed, and *Aziz* [1996] AC 41, in which the House of Lords treats the point as settled by *Vye*. In *Jagdeo Singh v The State of Trinidad and Tobago* [2006] 1 WLR 146 it was held that a 'first limb' direction should not be implied from a direction on the second limb, or be held to be conveyed by a vague phrase such as that good character is a matter to consider 'when you deal with the evidence of the accused'. In that case, the accused was a lawyer of good character, and the key issue related to the veracity of his account of a meeting with a witness whose character was bad, Lord Bingham opined that a jury could not be assumed to have inferred that the accused was a man of probity without a specific direction to that effect, as 'the belief of lawyers in their own probity is not universally shared'.

Direction on Credibility where Accused Does Not Testify

In *Vye* [1993] 1 WLR 471, the Court of Appeal further decided that where the accused has not given evidence at trial but relies on admissible exculpatory statements made to the police or others, the judge should direct the jury to have regard to the accused's good character when considering the credibility of those statements. The court thought it 'logical' that such evidence should be taken into account, but drew attention also to the judge's entitlement to make observations about the weight to be given to such exculpatory statements in contrast to evidence on oath (see *Duncan* (1981) 73 Cr App R 359 at **F17.62**). In *Aziz* [1996] AC 41, the House of Lords accepted that this 'clearcut' rule in *Vye* represented the best policy. Where an exculpatory statement was evidence in the case, the credibility of the accused who had given that account was a matter of evidential significance requiring a direction (see also *Woodward* [1996] Crim LR 207 and *Garrod* [1997] Crim LR 445). **F13.5**

Vye also decides that, where an accused of good character does not give evidence and has given no pre-trial answers or statements upon which reliance is placed, a 'first limb' direction is not required as no issue as to his credibility arises.

Direction on Propensity

F13.6 The 'second limb' of a character direction deals with the unlikelihood that a person of previous good character would commit the offence charged. In various authorities, including *Berrada* (1990) 91 Cr App R 131, *Thanki* (1991) 93 Cr App R 12n and *Bainbridge* (1991) 93 Cr App R 32, it has been said that the 'second limb' direction is not obligatory. In other cases, however, the omission of such a direction was said to be inappropriate (see e.g., *Marr* (1990) 90 Cr App R 154 and *Anderson* [1990] Crim LR 862). In *Vye* [1993] 1 WLR 471, the Court of Appeal was 'unable to discern any principle or consistent pattern as to when a "second limb" direction should be given and when it need not', and in order to resolve the uncertainty surrounding the issue decided that such a direction should be given in all cases where an accused is of good character, whether he testifies or not. In *Aziz* [1996] AC 41, the House of Lords, while recognising that *Vye* involved a 'policy decision', agreed that the move away from a discretionary system to a settled rule of practice was justified and would reduce the number of appeals.

Vye was applied in *Wren* [1993] Crim LR 952, where it was observed that failure to give a 'second limb' direction might not attract the quashing of a conviction; see also *Anderson* [1995] Crim LR 430. The obligation is, in any event, subject to the judge's entitlement to make observations qualifying the importance of good character, for example by emphasising that it is not in itself a defence and that in some cases the jury may derive limited assistance from the evidence. The example given in *Vye* is where an accused who is charged with murder admits manslaughter, so that the argument that he has never stooped to murder before is countered by the fact that he has never committed manslaughter either. Everything, however, depends on the relevance of the evidence in the circumstances: in *Paria v The State of Trinidad and Tobago* [2004] Crim LR 228 the Privy Council pointed out that a defence of provocation might be supported by the argument that a man of good character would have been unlikely to kill unless provoked into a complete loss of self-control (see also *Langton v The State* (Privy Council Appeal No. 35 of 1999 unreported). In *Fitton* [2001] EWCA Crim 215, the Court of Appeal disagreed with a suggestion that the good character of a nightclub doorman charged with assaulting a customer was less persuasive when the offence was spontaneous: rather the good character of a doorman who is routinely exposed to spontaneous violence may be worth a great deal. More recently, in *Zielinski* [2007] EWCA Crim 704, the Court of Appeal held that a lack of clarity in the second limb of the direction was not fatal where the charge of inflicting grievous bodily harm in a 'road rage' incident involved no more than the reckless use of force: the case was not one in which 'lack of propensity to offend was of such significance as it might have been in many other kinds of alleged offending'.

Where a direction is given about the relevance of good character to guilt it is wrong and unfair to suggest that such evidence comes into play only where the remainder of the evidence leaves the jury in doubt. Evidence of good character is part of the totality of the evidence upon which the jury are to decide whether there is any doubt about guilt (*Handbridge* [1993] Crim LR 287, endorsing the statement of law to this effect in an earlier edition of this work, and see also *Falconer-Atlee* (1973) 58 Cr App R 349 at 357–8). Earlier authorities to the contrary, particularly *Bliss Hill* (1918) 13 Cr App R 125, should, it is submitted, be regarded as wrong on this point.

Where One Accused is of Good Character but Another is Not

F13.7 The difficulty facing a trial judge in the situation where one accused is of good character but another is not is that by commenting on the good character of the one he may be taken to be highlighting the bad character of the other. Nevertheless the Court of Appeal in *Vye* [1993] 1 WLR 471 held, disapproving of compromise solutions suggested in earlier authorities such as *Gibson* (1991) 93 Cr App R 9, that the accused of good character is entitled to the same direction as if he had stood trial alone. This aspect of *Vye* was applied in *Houlden* (1994) 99 Cr App R 244. The possession of disparate characters is said in *Vye* to be a factor to be considered in deciding whether separate trials are needed, but there is no rule in favour of separate trials in such cases. Where no evidence is put in of the record of the accused with bad character, the judge has a discretion whether to comment about that accused when summing up (*Shepherd* [1995] Crim LR 153). Where, however, the jury has been told of his previous convictions, the accused is entitled to an appropriate direction as to the use which may be made of them (*Cain* [1994] 1 WLR 1449). Where a judge mistakenly attributes convictions to the wrong co-accused counsel should be consulted as to the best way to correct the error (*Purdy* [2007] EWCA Crim 295).

Meaning of Good Character

Absence of Previous Convictions, Cautions, etc. An accused may lay claim to a good character not only where he can adduce positive evidence to that effect, but also where he can truthfully assert that he has no previous convictions (*Aziz* [1996] AC 41). However, the jury must not be misled by any claim made by the accused, so where for example he has recently been cautioned for an offence this cannot simply be ignored (*Martin* [2000] 2 Cr App R 42), although it is ultimately a matter of discretion whether the direction is given in whole or (as in *Martin*) in part. If the accused is seeking to conceal a potentially relevant caution, he cannot insist that, as a matter of law, a full direction should be given (*Maillett* [2005] EWCA Crim 3159). Similarly, an accused cannot conceal the fact that he has been found guilty by a foreign court the findings of which are not regarded as 'convictions' until confirmed on appeal (*El Delbi* [2003] EWCA Crim 1767), or that he has admitted some other criminal behaviour (for example, in *Aziz*, where one of the respondents admitted making a false mortgage application). **F13.8**

In *Aziz* the House of Lords held that a trial judge has a limited residual discretion to withhold the directions normally given in accordance with *Vye* [1993] 1 WLR 417 where it would 'make no sense' to give them. The principles stated in *Aziz* and subsequent authorities are helpfully distilled in *Gray* [2004] 2 Cr App R 498. Although the Court of Appeal has since rightly applied the caveat that such distillations should not be taken 'as prescribing precisely what a judge is to do', and that the application of underlying principles so as to ensure fairness is of paramount importance (*Payton* [2006] EWCA Crim 1226), it is nevertheless submitted that the following synopsis, based on *Gray*, provides sound guidance:

(1) The primary rule is that a person of previous good character is entitled to a full direction on both limbs of credibility and propensity. Where there are no further facts to complicate the position the direction is mandatory and should be unqualified.
(2) If an accused has a previous conviction, which, because of its age or its nature, may entitle him to be treated as of effective good character, the trial judge has a discretion so to treat him, and if he does so the accused is entitled to a *Vye* direction.
(3) Where the previous conviction can only be regarded as irrelevant or of no significance in relation to the offence charged, the discretion ought to be exercised in favour of treating the accused as of good character and entitled to a *Vye* direction. Thus a judge who has decided that an accused is, for the purposes of the trial, of good character must confer the benefit on him of a good character direction (*Payton*).
(4) Where an accused of previous good character, whether absolute or (it was suggested in *Gray*) effective, has been shown at trial to be guilty of criminal conduct, the *prima facie* rule of practice is to qualify the *Vye* direction rather than to withhold it.
(5) In such a case there remains a narrowly circumscribed residual discretion to withhold a good character direction, in whole or in part, where it would make no sense or would be meaningless or an insult to common sense to do otherwise (*Zoppola-Barraza* [1994] Crim LR 833, and dicta in *Durbin* [1995] 2 Cr App R 84 and *Aziz*.

(6) Approved examples of the exercise of the residual discretion are not common. *Zoppola Barraza* is one, as is *Shaw* [2001] 1 WLR 1519, and see *Alkaitis* [2004] EWCA 1072 where, paradoxically, it was said that the withholding of the direction would have been less damaging than the modified direction given. Lord Steyn in *Aziz* appears to have considered that a person of previous good character who is shown beyond reasonable doubt to have been guilty of serious criminal behaviour similar to the offence charged would forfeit his right to any direction (at p. 53). On the other hand Lord Taylor's manslaughter/murder example in *Vye* (see **F13.6**), which was cited again in *Durbin*, shows that even in the context of serious crime it may be crucial that a critical intent separates the admitted criminality from that charged.

(7) A direction should never be misleading. Where therefore an accused has withheld something of his record so that otherwise a trial judge is not in a position to refer to it, the accused may forfeit the more ample, if qualified, direction that the judge might have been able to give (*Martin* [2002] 2 Cr App R 42).

It is arguable that in formulating principle (3) above there is a risk of confusion between the lack of evidential significance of bad character and the possession of good character. Thus in *Payton* the accused, who had previous cautions and convictions for possession of cannabis, was charged with possession with intent to supply. The record shed no particular light on the issues for the jury — P had never sought to deny possession when accused of it, so his record was of no use to the prosecution either on the matter of guilt or of credibility. Nevertheless for the court to say, as the current authorities do, that such a person is 'of good character' so as to require a positive *Vye* direction may be a step too far — but it is a matter of policy, rather than of logic, that is at stake.

In *Gray*, the accused, aged 18, was charged with murder following an attack on the victim at his place of work by a group of men, one of whom stabbed him to death. G claimed to have been outside the premises when the fatal assault occurred. He had previous convictions for driving with excess alcohol and (because he was under 17) without licence or insurance. These were minor matters that did not impinge on his right to a direction. He also admitted to minor incidents of violence on the occasion of the murder, including punching a man who was trying to restrain one of the other attackers. The Court of Appeal, having 'wavered' on the question, found that a qualified direction would not have been absurd and that the facts fell within principle (4) rather than (5) above. G should have received a normal credibility direction followed by a modified propensity direction pointing out the difference between the intent required for the crime of murder and that admitted by G.

In cases where the court is considering the exercise of the residual discretion to withhold a direction under (5) above, it would seem that each limb should be separately considered. In some cases, both limbs may be withheld, as in *Akram* [1995] Crim LR 50, where it was held that revelations about A's use of heroin meant that he should not have been treated as of good character on charges relating to the possession of diamorphine. See also *Young* [2004] EWCA Crim 3520, where the fundamental lies told by the accused rendered a credibility direction absurd, and his unlawful possession of firearms made the propensity direction inappropriate on a charge of murder. The appellant would have been entitled, at best, to a partial and qualified direction. Alternatively, one limb only may be withheld, as in *Martin*, where the propensity limb was withheld at M's trial for robbery on the ground of his previous caution for possession of an offensive weapon. In *Sanchez* [2003] EWCA Crim 735, it was held that the trial judge had been entitled to withhold the credibility limb of the direction where S had previously been cautioned for shoplifting, but had never been involved in anything as serious as the cocaine smuggling with which she was charged. Auld LJ said (at para 35):

> As a simple matter of fairness and plain dealing with the jury, a judge may, if circumstances justify it, give only part of the standard good character direction. Whether he does, and, if so, which part he gives, will necessarily turn on the nature and seriousness of the offence, the subject

> of the formal caution or reprimand and the nature and degree of its similarity to the charge being considered by the jury. A direction only as to credibility may be right, as was considered in the case of *Martin*, or, where as here, the earlier offence may be relevant to the defendant's credibility, a direction only as to lack of propensity may be appropriate.

Wherever the judge is minded to give a direction which is not likely to be anticipated by counsel, submissions on the proposed direction should first be invited (*Aziz*).

Failure to raise with the judge the nature of the appropriate direction on character was said in *W* [2004] EWCA Crim 3174 to be 'a very considerable pity', as it would have been likely to result in a direction but with a modified credibility limb when in fact (fatally for the conviction) none was given. In *Gonzales* [2004] EWCA Crim 2117, following discussion that left counsel under the impression that a full direction would be given, the trial judge gave a modified direction that had not been canvassed. The Court of Appeal re-emphasised the importance of discussing with counsel any direction that departs from the normal, full direction, although the conviction was upheld.

Minor or Irrelevant Convictions Where the accused has previous convictions, it has been seen (see **F13.8**) that he may nevertheless be of 'effective' good character. If the convictions are 'spent' under the Rehabilitation of Offenders Act 1974 (see **F12.51**), he may, with the leave of the court, be put forward as a person of good character (*Nye* (1982) 75 Cr App R 247; *Bailey* [1989] Crim LR 723). Judicial discretion should, so far as possible, be exercised favourably to the accused, but 'the jury must not be misled and no lie must be told to them about this matter' (*Nye*, per Talbot J, at p. 251). Where the spent convictions of an accused are regarded as immaterial, he should be entitled to the same directions on good character as an unconvicted accused (*Heath* (1994) *The Times*, 10 February 1994). It is similarly a matter for the judge's discretion whether, and if so to what extent, an unspent conviction prevents an accused from being treated as of good character; it might well not have that effect, particularly if it is of a different kind from the offence charged (*Timson* [1993] Crim LR 59: drink-driving conviction should have been regarded as irrelevant to charges involving dishonesty; *H* [1994] Crim LR 205: conviction for possessing an offensive weapon irrelevant to charges involving indecent assault on stepdaughter; *Burnham* [1995] Crim LR 491: 'unrelated' offence of criminal damage should have led to a qualified good character direction). Convictions which have been disregarded in this context are frequently of a minor nature in addition to being for unrelated offences. For example, an offence of strict liability, such as driving without insurance, should not be assumed to have been committed knowingly where the effect would be to deprive the accused of a good character direction to which he is otherwise entitled (*Goss* (2003) *The Times*, 27 October 2003). In *Gray* [2004] 2 Cr App R 498 (see **F13.8**), where the discretion to withhold the direction was described as 'narrowly circumscribed', the fact that the previous convictions were for relatively minor driving offences was, when the accused was charged with murder, a reason for regarding him as of 'effective' good character and entitled to the directions. By contrast it may be impossible to disregard a conviction, however ancient, if it bears on an issue of character which is before the jury (*Rackham* [1997] 2 Cr App R 222, where R's sexual preference for young girls was in issue and an old conviction for unlawful sexual intercourse with a 13-year-old was properly regarded as preventing R from presenting himself as of good character). And it has already been observed (see **F13.8**) that the decision in *Payton* [2006] EWCA Crim 1226 to disregard convictions for possession of cannabis on a charge of possession with intent may go too far — the fact that convictions do not assist the prosecution to prove their case should not necessarily be regarded as indicating 'good character' on the part of the accused. **F13.9**

In a case where the accused's previous convictions are not of the sort that would debar him from a good character direction, counsel's failure to seek the leave of the court to treat him as of good character may threaten the safety of the conviction (*Kamar* (1999) *The Times*, 14 May 1999).

F13.10 **Effect of Plea of Guilty** A difficult question arises where an accused pleads guilty to one or more of the offences charged at trial. In *Challenger* [1994] Crim LR 202, C was charged with simple possession of cannabis, possession with intent to supply and possession of an offensive weapon, and pleaded guilty to simple possession; a week later he was tried for the two other offences. It was held that the plea meant that C was no longer of good character and that the question of what direction, if any, was appropriate fell to be dealt with in the judge's discretion, taking account of such matters as the nature of the offence and its similarity to the offence charged, and whether the jury would be misled if C was treated as of good character in circumstances where they had not heard about the plea. The judge's decision to give no direction was upheld, despite the presentation of the case by counsel as one where C was of good character apart from the admitted offence. However in *Teasdale* [1993] 4 All ER 290 T, who was charged with causing grievous bodily harm with intent, pleaded guilty to assault occasioning actual bodily harm in respect of the same incident. It was held that T was to be treated as of good character and was entitled to the full direction in *Vye* [1993] 1 WLR 471 (see **F13.4**). In *Challenger* the facts in *Teasdale* were regarded as giving rise to an exception to the general rule applicable wherever a conviction for the offence charged would result in the pleas of guilty being vacated. It is hard to see why this should be so, as the vacation of the plea on the facts in *Teasdale* would not have meant that T had not assaulted the victim and that therefore her character was unblemished: the admitted offence would merely have been swallowed up by proof of the more serious allegation. It is submitted that the same rule should govern all cases involving guilty pleas, and that the approach in *Challenger* is to be preferred.

F13.11 **Other Discreditable Matters** An accused who is otherwise of good character may be shown in a poor light by matters emerging at trial, for example, the fact that he has lied to the police at interview. In such a case the judge has a discretion to qualify the direction on good character by commenting on matters which may adversely affect the jury's impression of him. The mere fact that the accused faces charges in other criminal proceedings which have yet to be heard should not be regarded as depriving him of his right to a positive direction (*Warden* (6 July 2000 unreported)).

Witnesses to Character

F13.12 Since the decision in *Rowton* (1865) Le & Ca 520, it has been the rule that witnesses as to character must testify to the reputation of the accused, and not to specific good acts or individuals' opinions. Lord Cockburn CJ suggested that the true object of the inquiry was in fact the disposition of the accused, but that it was not the practice to inquire into this directly but to arrive at it by 'giving evidence of his general character founded on his general reputation in the neighbourhood in which he lives'. The result was that 'the prisoner cannot give evidence of particular facts, though one fact might weigh more than the opinion of all his friends and neighbours'. Willes J added two further reasons for the exclusion of particular facts: they lack cogency, as even a robber may perform acts of generosity, and they raise issues of which the prosecution have no notice and on which they cannot enter into argument. Although *Rowton* speaks of the accused's reputation within a particular neighbourhood, the concept is capable of an elastic meaning, and it is not uncommon for character witnesses to come from the same workplace as the accused, or the same church or social organisation.

The *Rowton* rule is difficult to apply where character evidence is elicited by the accused in cross-examination of prosecution witnesses, and in cases where evidence of good character is given by the accused himself. Indeed, it may be doubted whether the accused is competent to give evidence of his own reputation. Yet in *Redgrave* (1982) 74 Cr App R 10, it was held that R, charged with importuning for an immoral purpose, was not entitled to raise evidence of his heterosexual disposition to rebut the charge. The effect of *Rowton* was that the accused could 'do no more than say, or call witnesses to prove, that he was not by general repute the kind of young man who would have behaved in the kind of way that the Crown alleged'. The Court noted that a practice had grown up, where allegations of homosexual offences were in issue, of allowing an accused to say that he is happily married and enjoys a normal sexual relationship with his wife, but this was regarded as a special indulgence.

Rebuttal of Good Reputation Where an accused has raised the issue of his good reputation, whether by calling witnesses or giving evidence on his own behalf, the prosecution may seek to respond by calling witnesses in rebuttal, to whom the rule in *Rowton* (1865) Le & CA 520 also applies. Thus such witnesses may speak only to the bad reputation of the accused, not to specific bad acts done by him. Under the CJA 2003, the rules by which the common law allows evidence of reputation to prove character, good and bad, are specifically preserved (CJA 2003, ss. 99(2) and 118(1)). The preservation of evidence of good reputation was necessary only in so far as such evidence would otherwise have been hearsay (see **F16**). The preservation of the rules permitting evidence of bad reputation was also necessitated by the abolition of the common-law rules as to evidence of bad character generally (CJA 2003, s. 99(1)). **F13.13**

Rebuttal of Good Character other than Reputation An accused who refers in favourable terms to his own good disposition in order to strengthen his defence may be held to have made an assertion of good character, which the prosecution are entitled to counter if it is untrue. The reason must be that if the court is prepared to indulge the accused by allowing such evidence to be given, it is only right that it should be open to rebuttal if it is misleading. **F13.14**

Under the provisions of the CJA 2003 regarding evidence of bad character, the right of the prosecution to counter the case put forward by the defence is determined by the provisions of the Act. Section 101(1)(f) of the CJA 2003 provides that evidence of the accused's bad character is admissible 'to correct a false impression given' by the accused. The new law covers similar ground to the previous common-law rules permitting a misleading assertion of good character to be corrected, although it appears to be wider in important respects. Section 101(1)(f) is considered at **F12.40**. (As to the common law, see the 2004 edition of this work.)

Section F14 Character Evidence: Evidence of Bad Character of Persons Other than the Accused

Evidence of Bad Character of Persons other than the Accused at Common Law and under the Criminal Justice Act 2003

F14.1 This section covers the new statutory scheme for the introduction of evidence of the bad character of persons other than the accused. Chapter 1 of part 11 (ss. 98 to 113) of the CJA 2003 abolishes the common-law rules (s. 99(1)), amends the Criminal Procedure Act 1865, s. 6, so that cross-examination on the previous convictions of persons other than the accused becomes subject to the new rules on admissibility (s. 331 and sch. 36, para. 79) and all but codifies the law governing the admissibility of evidence of bad character in criminal cases. The relevant provisions of the CJA 2003 came into force on 15 December 2004 (Criminal Justice Act 2003 (Commencement No. 6 and Transitional Provisions) Order 2004), and apply in all trials beginning on or after that date (*Bradley* [2005] 1 Cr App R 397). However, nothing in the scheme under the CJA 2003 affects the exclusion of evidence under either (a) the rule in the Criminal Procedure Act 1865, s. 3, preventing a party from impeaching the credit of his own witness by general evidence of bad character or (b) the YJCEA 1999, s. 41 (see **F7.16** ***et seq.***), which restricts evidence and questions about the complainant's sexual history in proceedings for sexual offences (s. 112(3) of CJA 2003). Evidence of spent convictions may also continue to be excluded by virtue of the *Consolidated Criminal Practice Direction*, para. I.6 (see **appendix** 7 and **D19.49**).

Overarching common-law rules that now require to be read subject to the scheme of the CJA 2003 are covered in this edition under the headings of the 'General Rule against Impeaching the Credit of Own Witness', considered at **F6.27**, 'Cross-Examination as to Credit' considered at **F7.13** and the 'Rule of Finality of Answers to Questions on Collateral Matters', considered at **F7.27** ***et seq.***

Abolition of the Common-law Rules

F14.2 Section 99(1) of the CJA 2003 abolishes 'the common law rules governing the admissibility of evidence of bad character in criminal proceedings'. Although s. 99(1) refers only to the rules governing the admissibility of evidence of bad character and not, in terms, to the common-law rules governing cross-examination about bad character, it is submitted that the intention is to cover both. As to the questioning of witnesses on their bad character in relation to matters covered by the exceptions to the rule of finality of answers to collateral questions, the common-law rules can certainly be said to 'govern' the admissibility of evidence of bad character, because the matters are put to the witness with a view to eliciting such evidence and, if the matters are denied, they can be proved. The common-law rules permitting the questioning of witnesses on their bad character in relation to matters not covered by the exceptions to the rule of finality may also be said to 'govern' the admissibility of evidence of bad character in that they too are questions put with a view to eliciting such evidence, notwithstanding that if the witness denies the matters put, they cannot be proved. This construction is consistent with the procedural requirements for application to adduce or elicit evidence (see **F14.11**).

'Bad Character'

Criminal Justice Act 2003, s. 98 **F14.3**

References in this Chapter to evidence of a person's 'bad character' are to evidence of, or of a disposition towards, misconduct on his part, other than evidence which—

(a) has to do with the alleged facts of the offence with which the defendant is charged, or
(b) is evidence of misconduct in connection with the investigation or prosecution of that offence.

This wide definition, that generally reflects the common-law concept of bad character, is considered in detail at **F12.2**, as the definition applies equally to evidence of the bad character of an accused. If evidence of bad character does fall within the statutory definition it can be admitted in evidence only if it satisfies the further conditions of admissibility in s. 100 (non-defendant's bad character) or s. 101 (defendant's bad character). Evidence which, though it shows a person in a bad light, is not evidence of bad character within the meaning of the CJA 2003, s. 99, may be given where it is relevant (see **F12.2** ***et seq.***).

Bad Character 'to do with' the Facts of the Offence or in Connection with its Investigation or Prosecution

F14.4 Section 99(1) of the CJA 2003 abolishes the common-law rules governing admissibility of evidence of bad character as defined by s. 98. It follows that the common-law rules continue to operate insofar as they permit evidence to be adduced which, looking to the wording of s. 98(a), 'has to do with the alleged facts of the offence' or, looking to the wording of s. 98(b), 'is evidence of misconduct in connection with the investigation or prosecution of that offence'. The general meaning of these phrases is considered at **F12.6** and **F12.7**. A case specifically decided in relation to the CJA 2003, s. 100, is *Machado* (2006) JP 400, where evidence tending to show the alleged victim of a robbery had taken drugs was held to be within the words 'has to do with the alleged fact of the offence', as providing support for the defence explanation of his sudden collapse (the prosecution having alleged that the accused pushed him over). Section 98(b) would seem apt to cover, for example, evidence that during the investigation the police obtained evidence unlawfully or unfairly (e.g., by fabricating a confession or planting evidence on the accused or in his premises); evidence that during interview the police told lies; and evidence that during the investigation or proceedings the police, or someone on behalf of either the police or accused, had sought to intimidate potential witnesses.

Background to the Criminal Justice Act 2003, s. 100

F14.5 At common law, a witness other than the accused could be cross-examined, in order to impeach his credibility, about his previous misconduct, for example about acts of dishonesty or immorality on his part, about lies he told or false allegations he made, about his drink or drug abuse, and so on. However, insofar as the questions could properly be said to be on collateral matters and the witness denied them, evidence was admissible in rebuttal only exceptionally. The exceptions covered previous convictions, bias and general reputation for untruthfulness (see **F7.27** ***et seq.***). Since the purpose of cross-examination as to credit is to show that a witness ought not to be believed on his oath, at common law the matters about which he is questioned must relate to his likely standing after cross-examination with the tribunal which is trying him (per Lawton LJ in *Sweet-Escott* (1971) 55 Cr App R 316, considered at **F7.13**). Despite this important limitation, the Law Commission expressed its

F

Part F Evidence

concern that those involved in criminal trials should be subject to gratuitous and public attacks on their character (Law Com No. 272, para. 7.2). It was of the view that further restraints were necessary. Three reasons were given: the power of evidence of bad character to distort the fact-finding process, the need to encourage witnesses to give evidence, and the need for courts 'to control gratuitous and offensive cross-examination of little or no purpose other than to intimidate or embarrass the witness or muddy the waters' (para. 9.35). Balancing these factors against the need not to prejudice a fair trial, the Commission recommended a test based on the degree of relevance of bad character evidence to the issues in the case. Evidence of only trivial relevance would be excluded. The views of the Commission are reflected in the terms of the CJA 2003, s. 100.

Criminal Justice Act 2003, s. 100

(1) In criminal proceedings evidence of the bad character of a person other than the defendant is admissible if and only if—
- (a) it is important explanatory evidence,
- (b) it has substantial probative value in relation to a matter which—
  - (i) is a matter in issue in the proceedings, and
  - (ii) is of substantial importance in the context of the case as a whole,

  or
- (c) all parties to the proceedings agree to the evidence being admissible.

Although, on its face, s. 100 governs only the admissibility of evidence of bad character and does not, in terms, govern the asking of questions in cross-examination about bad character (cf., in this regard, YJCEA 1999, s. 41), it is submitted that the intention is to cover both. This would be consistent with the interpretation of s. 99(1) of the Act that it abolishes the common-law rules relating not only to the admissibility of evidence of bad character but also to cross-examination of witnesses about bad character (see **F14.3**). Section 100 covers evidence of the bad character of any person other then the accused, whether or not called as a witness, and whether the evidence is to be adduced or elicited by or on behalf of the prosecution, the accused or any co-accused. The use of s. 100 is not limited to evidence going directly to the issue of guilt or innocence: the undermining of a witness's credibility is a legitimate objective of adducing evidence under s. 100. (Yaxley-Lennon, one of the appeals heard with *Weir* [2006] 1 WLR 1885 at [73]). To decide otherwise, said the Court, would mean that there was a significant lacuna in the legislation, creating the potential for unfairness.

Gateways to Admissibility

(a) Important Explanatory Evidence

F14.6 **Criminal Justice Act 2003, s. 100**

(2) For the purposes of subsection (1)(a) evidence is important explanatory evidence if—
- (a) without it, the court or jury would find it impossible or difficult properly to understand other evidence in the case, and
- (b) its value for understanding the case as a whole is substantial.

Section 100(2) covers evidence of, or a disposition towards, misconduct on the part of someone other than the accused without which the account before the court or jury would be incomplete or incoherent. Thus if the matter to which the evidence relates is largely comprehensible without the explanatory evidence, the evidence will be inadmissible. The wording of s. 100(2)(a) is a marginally different formulation of the common-law rule permitting the use of so-called 'background evidence', notwithstanding that it reveals the bad character or criminal disposition of the accused, where it is part of a continual background or history which is relevant to the offence charged and without the totality of which the account placed before the jury would be incomplete or incomprehensible (per Purchas LJ in *Pettman* (2 May 1985 unreported)). An example, under s. 100(1)(a), given in the Explanatory Notes to the Criminal Justice Bill, is of a case involving the abuse by one person of another over a long period of time. 'For the jury to understand properly the victim's account of the offending and why they (sic) did not seek help from, for example, a parent or other guardian, it might be necessary for evidence to be given of a wider pattern of abuse involving that other person' (para. 360). *Pettman* is considered in relation to s. 101(1)(c) ('explanatory evidence' of defendant's bad character) at **F12.17**. In relation to s. 101(1)(c) it has rightly been held that the phrase 'impossible or difficult to understand' is satisfied only where the jury requires to hear the evidence: if the evidence is readily understandable without evidence of bad character and the jury requires no 'footnote or lexicon', s. 101(1)(c) does not apply (*Beverley* [2006] EWCA Crim 1287). The same must be true of s.100(2)(a).

Explanatory evidence, to be admissible, must also satisfy s. 100(1)(b), i.e. its value for understanding the case as a whole must be 'substantial', as opposed to minor or trivial.

(b) Evidence of Substantial Probative Value in Relation to Matter in Issue

Under the CJA 2003, s. 100(1)(b), the probative value of evidence of bad character of a person other than the accused which is tendered in relation to a matter in issue in the proceedings must be 'substantial' — evidence of only minor probative force should not be admitted. Where an accused is charged with an offence of violence and claims self-defence, a previous instance of violence by the complainant towards the accused using a weapon may be admissible either as explanatory evidence of the accused's state of mind and reason for reacting as he did (see **F14.6**) or to show who was in fact the aggressor under s. 100(1)(b), or indeed as evidence going to the credibility of the complainant (see **F14.8**) (*Riley* [2006] EWCA Crim 2030). **F14.7**

Credibility as a 'matter in issue' A 'matter in issue in the proceedings' covers both issues of disputed fact and issues of credibility (Yaxley-Lennon, one of the appeals heard with *Weir* [2006] 1 WLR 1885 at [73]). In order to be admissible, the evidence must also be of substantial importance in the context of the case as a whole — evidence which goes only to some minor or trivial issue should not be admitted. In Osbourne, one of the appeals heard with *Renda* [2006] 1 WLR 2948 it was held (at [59]) that the conviction of a witness for a serious offence of violence was admissible where without that evidence the jury would have been deprived of 'important evidence of substantial probative value' in relation to his evidence that the complainant had fabricated the robbery which O was alleged to have committed. No attempt is made to justify the suggestion that the commission of an offence of violence bears on testimonial credibility. **F14.8**

In applying the CJA 2003, s. 101(1)(d) (evidence of the defendant's bad character), it has been held that an offence does not display a propensity to untruthfulness within the meaning of s. 103(1)(b) unless it is directly indicative of a propensity to lie, as distinct from a propensity to dishonesty (see *Hanson* [2005] 1 WLR 3169 at **F12.23**). It does not appear, however, that *Hanson* is regarded as establishing a generally applicable meaning of that phrase where it appears elsewhere in the CJA 2003 (see *Lawson* [2007] 1 WLR 1191 at **F12.36**, dealing with s. 101(1)(e)). Because s. 100 does not specifically limit the court to evidence of 'untruthfulness', it follows that it is up to the judge to decide whether evidence of a non-defendant's bad character should be accorded 'substantial' probative value in relation to an 'important' issue of credibility. The distinction applied in *Hanson* has not found favour in relation to s. 100, the courts preferring the common-law notion that bad character of any sort may have a bearing on credibility. Thus in *Stephenson* [2006] EWCA Crim 2325 it was held (by the same court that decided *Lawson*) that a witness's previous cautions in respect of offences of dishonesty ought to have been admitted to support the defence, and the judge was held to have been wrong to exclude them by applying *Hanson*.

Matters Relevant to Assessment of Probative Value Section 100(3) sets out a non-exhaustive list of the factors to which the court must have regard in assessing the probative value of the evidence. **F14.9**

Criminal Justice Act 2003, s. 100

(3) In assessing the probative value of evidence for the purposes of subsection (1)(b) the court must have regard to the following factors (and to any others it considers relevant)—
- (a) the nature and number of the events, or other things, to which the evidence relates;
- (b) when those events or things are alleged to have happened or existed;
- (c) where—
  - (i) the evidence is evidence of a person's misconduct, and
  - (ii) it is suggested that the evidence has probative value by reason of similarity between that misconduct and other alleged misconduct,

  the nature and extent of the similarities and dissimilarities between each of the alleged instances of misconduct;
- (d) where—
  - (i) the evidence is evidence of a person's misconduct,
  - (ii) it is suggested that that person is also responsible for the misconduct charged, and
  - (iii) the identity of the person responsible for the misconduct charged is disputed,

  the extent to which the evidence shows or tends to show that the same person was responsible each time.

As to s. 100(3)(a), the more serious the misconduct on the part of a witness, and the greater the number of instances of misconduct on his part, then the stronger the likely probative value in relation to the issue of his credibility. As to s. 100(3)(b), evidence of misconduct occurring many years ago is usually likely to have less probative value than more recent misconduct, although very serious misconduct in the past may well have a stronger probative force than recent but comparatively minor misconduct.

In *Bovell* [2005] 2 Cr App R 401, B sought to support his defence of self-defence adducing evidence of the bad character of N, the alleged victim, who had convictions for handling and robbery. The convictions were old, and the trial judge declined leave to admit them on that ground and also because there was no evidence of the use of a weapon. Two further matters came to light. First, it transpired that one of the offences involved a knife. The Court of Appeal thought that this added little to the relevance of the evidence, especially as N had pleaded guilty. Second, it was discovered that a more recent allegation of wounding had also been made against N, although subsequently withdrawn. The Court of Appeal thought it unlikely that the mere making of an allegation was capable of being evidence within s. 100 but, even if it was, trial judges should be discouraged from entering into inquiries raising 'satellite matters' such as the credibility of N's alleged victim and the reasons why the charge was dropped (citing *Hanson* [2005] 1 WLR 3169). More recently, in *Edwards* [2006] 1 WLR 1524 (a judgment covering four appeals, including that of *Smith*), the Court of Appeal, while specifically approving the aspect of *Bovell* dealing with the need to guard against satellite litigation, questioned whether all allegations could be excluded from the ambit of the statutory scheme for dealing with evidence of bad character. The context in the case of the appellant, Smith, was that previous untried allegations were tendered against him under s. 101 in order to form the basis of an inference of propensity. The distinction drawn by the court (that *Bovell* applies to allegations against a non-defendant) is surely untenable. The better view is that *Bovell* is dealing with the 'mere making' of an allegation where there is no proof as to its substance, whereas the prosecution case against Smith was that the previous allegations were true and that the evidence, in combination with the evidence of the offences charged, showed that this was so. This conclusion is supported indirectly by *S* v *DPP* (2006) 170 JP 707, in which it was held that magistrates should have adjourned to facilitate, for the purposes of an application under s. 100, the disclosure of the detail of a pending prosecution of the complainant, which had a bearing both on an issue in the case (his propensity to violence) and his credibility (including material suggesting that he had a serious mental health problem). As in *Edwards*, it was in the proof, rather than in the mere making of an allegation, that the meat of the s.100 application lay.

Section 100(3)(c) relates to evidence of a person's misconduct the probative value of which derives from its similarity to other misconduct on his part. Thus, if the accused alleges that a police officer has threatened W, a potential witness for the defence (evidence of which would be admissible under s. 98(b)), and there is evidence that the officer has threatened other potential witnesses for the defence in other cases, then in assessing the probative value of the evidence, the court should have regard to the nature and extent of the similarities and dissimilarities between each of the alleged instances of misconduct.

Section 100(3)(d) relates to evidence, in cases in which the identity of the offender is in dispute, suggesting that a person other than the accused is responsible for the offence charged. Such evidence will often take the form of evidence of similar facts. Thus, although the similar fact rule is now obsolete as the test for adducing the bad character of the accused under s. 101 (see **F12.21** ***et seq.***), its tenets still have some resonance in applying s. 100. For example (and to make use of an illustration provided by Lord Hailsham in *DPP v Boardman* [1975] AC 421 at p. 454) if D is charged with burglary, the prosecution case being that he climbed in through a ground floor window and left a humorous limerick on the walls of the sitting room, the defence being one of mistaken identity, if there is evidence that E has previously committed a number of burglaries in the same vicinity, on each occasion having climbed through a ground floor window and having left the same humorous limerick on the walls of the sitting rooms, then the court, in assessing the probative value of the evidence, must have regard to the extent to which the evidence shows or tends to show that E was responsible for each of the offences. The probative value of similar fact evidence often arises out of the nexus between the spontaneous and independent accounts of two or more witnesses. The probative value of such evidence disappears, therefore, if there is also convincing evidence to suggest that the witnesses have deliberately concocted false evidence by conspiracy or collaboration or that the evidence of each of them has been innocently contaminated. The question whether evidence which carries a real risk of collusion or contamination should be excluded or left to the jury with a suitable warning is governed, under the statutory scheme, by s. 109. Section 109, which applies for the purpose of assessing relevance or probative value under both s. 100 (non-defendant's bad character) and s. 101 (defendant's bad character), is considered at **F12.31**.

(c) Evidence Admitted by Agreement

Under the CJA 2003, s. 100(1)(c), evidence of the bad character of a person other than the accused may be admitted by agreement of 'all parties to the proceedings'. Under s. 100(4), evidence may be admitted under s. 100(1)(c) without the leave of the court. **F14.10**

The Requirement of Leave

Section 100(4) of the CJA 2003 provides that: 'Except where subsection (1)(c) applies, evidence of the bad character of a person other than the defendant must not be given without the leave of the court'. Evidence admissible under s. 100(1)(a) or (b) must not be adduced without leave. Unfortunately, however, the subsection gives no guidance as to what factors, if any, should be taken into account in deciding whether or not to grant leave, apart from the factors set out in s. 100(2) and (3). On one reading s. 100(4) also applies to evidence of bad character of complainants admissible under the YJCEA 1999, s. 41 (see **F7.16** ***et seq.*** and *V* [2006] EWCA Crim 1901, where Crane J acknowledges that both provisions may well be in play, and that 'In many cases s. 41 will be the more formidable obstacle to overcome'). If the leave requirement under s. 100(4) is designed to be additional to the requirements of s. 41, then the issue arises as to what kinds of sexual behaviour on the part of the complainant should be treated as 'bad character' as defined in the CJA 2003. In cases where the defence allege that the complainant has previously made false allegations then, once it appears that there is an evidential basis for suggesting falsity, s. 100 appears to be the dominant provision — the essence of the attack on the complainant is that she is a liar, even if the circumstances **F14.11** also suggest sexual behaviour. In *Stephenson* [2006] EWCA Crim 2325, where S complained on appeal that he had not been permitted sufficient latitude in relation to the complainant's disturbed background and promiscuity as indicative of the likelihood that she had fabricated the case against S, the court made particular reference to the fact that none of the sexual relationships were alleged to have been falsified, and thereafter confined its observations about s. 100 to the effect of the complainant's cautions for offences of dishonesty (see **F14.7**).

F14.12 Section 111 of the CJA 2003 permits rules of court to be made in relation to evidence of bad character to supplement the provisions of the Act. The relevant rules are contained in the CrimPR, part 35, with modifications where the proceedings are before the Court of Appeal which are set out in r. 68.21. See **appendix 1** for the full text.

The rules require application to be made to introduce evidence of a non-defendant's bad character and also for cross-examining a witness with a view to eliciting such evidence; they also set time-limits for any party wishing to adduce evidence of a non-defendant's bad character, and also to an application to oppose the use of such evidence.

Relationship with the Police and Criminal Evidence Act 1984, s. 78

F14.13 It is submitted that, where the prosecution propose to rely upon evidence admissible under the CJA 2003, s. 100, it will be open to the defence to argue that the evidence should be excluded under the PACE 1984, s. 78, i.e. that having regard to all the circumstances, the admission of the evidence would have such an adverse effect on the fairness of the proceedings that the court ought not to admit it. The potential application of s. 78 to evidence of bad character admissible under the CJA 2003 is considered at **F12.12**.

Reasons for Rulings

F14.14 Under the CJA 2003, s. 110, where the court makes a ruling on whether an item of evidence is evidence of a person's bad character and on whether an item of such evidence is admissible under s. 100, it must state in open court (but in the absence of the jury, if there is one), its reasons for the ruling; and, if it is a magistrates' court, it must cause the ruling and the reasons for it to be entered in the register of the court's proceedings. It was stated in *Renda* [2006] 1 WLR 2948 (at [60]), the mere observation that the jury was entitled to know about character was regarded as an 'over-parsimonious' compliance with s. 110.

Section F15 The Rule Against Hearsay: General Principles

Definition of Hearsay Evidence

Criminal Justice Act 2003, s. 114 **F15.1**

(1) In criminal proceedings a statement not made in oral evidence in the proceedings is admissible as evidence of any matter stated if, but only if—
(a) any provision of this chapter or any other statutory provision makes it admissible,
(b) any rule of law preserved by section 118 makes it admissible,
(c) all parties to the proceedings agree to it being admissible, or
(d) the court is satisfied that it is in the interests of justice for it to be admissible.

The new law of hearsay applies to trials and other hearings to which the strict rules of evidence apply, and which commence on or after 4 April 2005 (*H (PG)* [2006] 1 Cr App R 50). Re-trials commencing on or after that date are subject to the new law, even when the accused is being re-tried on the original indictment and the first trial took place before that date (*Sukadave Singh* [2006] 1 WLR 1564). From 4 April 2005, the definition of hearsay in s. 114 of the CJA 2003 supersedes the common-law definition, but the two are in many respects similar. Section 114(1) provides that 'a statement not made in oral evidence in the proceedings is admissible as evidence of any matter stated if, but only if' one of the exceptional cases applies (for exceptions, see **F16.2**). In a leading common-law authority, *Sharp* [1988] 1 WLR 7, Lord Havers adopted the statement in *Cross on Evidence* (6th ed.) that 'an assertion other than one made by a person while giving oral evidence in the proceedings is inadmissible as evidence of any fact asserted'.

The emphasis at common law was on inadmissibility, as hearsay could be admitted only where an exception to the rule applied. Under the CJA 2003 the rule is reformulated in more positive terms. The essence of hearsay — reliance on a statement made otherwise than while giving evidence to prove the truth of a fact asserted — remains constant. It follows that many common-law authorities on the scope of the rule will remain valid. The major exception to this proposition concerns so-called implied assertions (see **F15.13**), some of which are removed from the scope of the hearsay rule by the restrictive definitions of 'statement' and 'matter stated' adopted in the CJA 2003.

Criminal Justice Act 2003, s. 115

(1) In this chapter references to a statement or to a matter stated are to be read as follows.
(2) A statement is any representation of fact or opinion by whatever means; and it includes a representation made in a sketch, photofit or other pictorial form.

. . .

Hearsay and Conduct Whereas most hearsay statements are made (whether orally or in writing) in words, the CJA 2003, s. 115, confirms that a statement may take any form that enables a representation of fact to be made. Thus, as at common law, hearsay may also **F15.2**

F

Part F Evidence

occur in the form of conduct. In *Chandrasekera v The King* [1937] AC 220, a woman's throat had been cut, depriving her of the power of speech. She described C as her attacker using sign language, and nodded when asked whether C had caused her injuries. These communications were likened to the language of a deaf person able to converse only by means of a finger alphabet, and the 'conversation' was admitted under an exception to the hearsay rule.

F15.3 **Hearsay and Statements in Other Proceedings** Under the CJA 2003, s. 114, a statement not made in oral evidence 'in the proceedings' is hearsay. It follows that, as was the case at common law, a statement made on oath in other proceedings is hearsay, and may only be received as evidence of its truth under an exception to the rule (see, e.g., *Berkeley Peerage Case* (1811) 4 Camp 401).

F15.4 **Hearsay and Previous Statements of Witnesses** The out-of-court statements of witnesses who give evidence in the proceedings may be introduced as evidence of consistency or inconsistency without infringing the hearsay rule. (See as to the circumstances in which statements may be used for this purpose **F6.19** to **F6.26** and **F7.27**.) Such statements are, however, hearsay in relation to the 'matters stated' under the CJA 2003, s. 114(1). In the same way, such statements were not evidence of their truth at common law, unless an exception to the hearsay rule applied. At common law there was no general hearsay exception relating to the use of previous statements of witnesses. However, under the CJA 2003, s. 119, a witness's previous inconsistent statement becomes admissible as evidence of the truth of any matter stated by him of which oral evidence by him would be admissible and, under s. 120, evidence of various previous consistent statements likewise may become evidence of the truth of facts stated therein (see further **F6.19**). The reform of this aspect of the hearsay rule was long overdue. The reasons typically given for the exclusion of hearsay (see **F15.6**) do not apply with the same force to the out-of-court statements of those who subsequently appear as witnesses in the proceedings. In many cases a statement made while events were fresher in the witness's mind might provide evidence of better quality than his subsequent evidence in court.

F15.5 **Proof of the Truth of a Matter Stated** Evidence is hearsay under the CJA 2003, s. 114(1), only where it is relied upon as 'evidence of any matter stated': in other words, where it is sought to establish the truth of that matter. In this also, the statutory rule follows the contours of the common law, and the old authorities are illustrative. Thus, where it is sought to establish the registration number of a car involved in an incident, and an eye-witness, A, who has seen the incident, relates the number to B, who has not, it is hearsay for B to tell the court what the number was for the purpose of proving the identity of the car (*McLean* (1967) 52 Cr App R 80; *Jones v Metcalfe* [1967] 1 WLR 1286; *Maher v DPP* [2006] EWCA Crim 1271). (Where B makes a note of the number that A verifies, A may give evidence of the number by refreshing his memory from B's note: *Jones v Metcalfe*; *Kelsey* (1982) 74 Cr App R 213. As to refreshing memory, see **F6.9** to **F6.15**.)

Where goods are imported in bags marked 'Produce of Morocco', the marks are hearsay evidence of the country of origin of the goods (*Patel v Comptroller of Customs* [1966] AC 356). The same result follows even where the information is indelibly stamped into the goods (*Comptroller of Customs v Western Lectric Co. Ltd* [1966] AC 367). Similarly, information stamped on to a document is hearsay evidence of the matters stated, for example of a date: see *Cook* (1980) 71 Cr App R 205, in which is was assumed that such information was admissible only where there was an applicable exception to the hearsay rule. Compare, however, *Miller v Howe* [1969] 1 WLR 1510, in which a police officer was allowed to give evidence identifying a particular device although he had derived his knowledge from the label on the box. A car's vehicle registration document provides only hearsay evidence of its engine number (*Sealby* [1965] 1 All ER 701), as do records compiled in the course of the manufacture of the car

(*Myers v DPP* [1965] AC 1001). A person who relates his own date and place of birth necessarily gives hearsay evidence (*Inhabitants of Rishworth* (1842) 2 QB 476, see also *Day* (1841) 9 C & P 722). A party to a conversation that has been conducted through an interpreter infringes the hearsay rule if he seeks to prove what the other party said by relating to the court what the interpreter told him (*Attard* (1958) 43 Cr App R 90). Similarly, where a police officer testifies that a person receiving a commodity alleged to be heroin from the defendant is a 'known heroin user', he is giving hearsay evidence if the basis of his knowledge is information supplied to him by others, including the recipient in question (*Rothwell* (1994) 99 Cr App R 388). It is submitted that the hearsay rule applies to the above examples with equal force under the CJA 2003. Where, however, the court is satisfied that it is 'in the interests of justice' for hearsay to be admitted, s. 114(1)(d) renders the evidence admissible. Some of the applications of the hearsay rule, which appear to defy common sense, will in future be met by the use of this mechanism (see further **F16**).

Rationale of Hearsay Rule

At common law the hearsay rule operated rigidly to exclude evidence — including evidence of undoubted probative value — unless a specific hearsay exception could be brought to bear. The courts had no power to create exceptions to avoid the exclusion of valuable material, as this was the sole prerogative of Parliament (*Myers v DPP* [1965] AC 1001, in which reliable manufacturing records were rejected). **F15.6**

The reforming strategy of the CJA 2003 is to admit hearsay evidence provided that certain safeguards are met: a more inclusionary approach than at common law. The major feature of the new statutory scheme, which enables the court to break free of the mechanical shackles of the common-law rule, is the general 'interests of justice' exception in s. 114(1)(d), under which evidence may be admitted notwithstanding that it does not conform to a specific exception mentioned in s. 114(1)(a) or (b) and the parties are not agreed on its admission under (c). In deciding whether to admit evidence under s. 114(1)(d), the court is directed to consider such matters as the apparent reliability of the maker of the statement, and the amount of difficulty that there may be in challenging the statement so that the evidence will not be admitted if its hearsay nature poses a genuine threat to the interests of justice (see further **F16.20**) If the courts interpret this new provision widely, the traditional mechanical approach to hearsay will be significantly eroded, but the system will continue to provide safeguards against the use of evidence the reliability of which cannot be properly tested.

In *Sharp* [1988] 1 WLR 7, Lord Havers said (at p. 11) that the principal reason that led the judges to adopt the hearsay rule was 'the fear that juries might give undue weight to evidence the truth of which could not be tested by cross-examination, and possibly also the risk of an account becoming distorted as it was passed from one person to another'. Similarly, in *Blastland* [1986] AC 41, Lord Bridge of Harwich said (at p. 54): 'The rationale of excluding [hearsay] as inadmissible, rooted as it is in the system of trial by jury, is a recognition of the great difficulty, even more acute for a juror than for a trained judicial mind, of assessing what, if any, weight can properly be given to a statement by a person whom the jury have not seen or heard and which has not been subject to any test of reliability by cross-examination'. As Lord Normand most succinctly put it in *Teper v The Queen* [1952] AC 480 (at p. 486) '[Hearsay] is not the best evidence and it is not delivered on oath'.

While the CJA 2003 provides for the wider admissibility of hearsay evidence, the concerns expressed at common law remain significant. Where hearsay evidence is received under the CJA 2003, the safeguards aimed at minimising the dangers identified above include the giving of notice of intention to use hearsay evidence the provision of special rules to scrutinise the credibility of the maker of the statement (CJA 2003, s. 124: see **F16.55**) and the giving of judicial warnings about hearsay (see **F16.21**).

Hearsay Not Rendered Admissible Because Tendered by Defence

F15.7 The CJA 2003 creates no special rule of admissibility favouring the defence. In this also, it reflects the common-law tradition. In *Turner* (1975) 61 Cr App R 67, the Court of Appeal rejected an argument that an accused person should be entitled to rely on hearsay evidence to show that a third party who has not been called as a witness has admitted committing the offence charged. Milmo J added (at p. 88): 'The idea, which may be gaining prevalence in some quarters, that in a criminal trial the defence is entitled to adduce hearsay evidence to establish facts, which if proved would be relevant and would assist the defence, is wholly erroneous.' The existence of any exception in favour of third-party admissions was also denied, *obiter*, by the House of Lords in *Blastland* [1986] AC 41.

In *Sparks v The Queen* [1964] AC 964, a statement made by a child, who was too young to testify, in which she alleged that she had been attacked by a coloured boy, was held inadmissible on behalf of S, a white man. It was argued that it was 'unjust' to leave the jury with the impression that the child had given no clue as to the identity of her attacker, but it was held that the cause of justice was best served by adherence to settled rules, and that, just as the prosecution could not rely on inadmissible hearsay evidence to prove the guilt of S, so also S was unable to rely on such evidence to establish his innocence.

Under the CJA 2003, s. 114(1)(d), evidence of the type rejected in *Sparks* and *Blastland* may in future be admitted where it is in the interests of justice to do so, and the importance of the evidence to the defence will be a factor that the court will consider in deciding where the interests of justice lie. But it remains the case that there is no special hearsay exception for defence evidence.

Statements Tendered for Purpose Other Than as Evidence of Facts Asserted

F15.8 The hearsay rule is not infringed where a statement is tendered for some reason other than to establish the matter stated. This proposition is as true under the CJA 2003 as it was at common law: evidence that was not hearsay before the Act remains non-hearsay (original) evidence after it. The common law authorities remain illustrative.

In *Subramaniam v Public Prosecutor* [1956] 1 WLR 965, S was charged with the capital offence of possession of ammunition. His defence was that he acted under duress. At his trial, he sought to give evidence of threats made to him by certain terrorists who were not called to give evidence, and was prevented from doing so on the ground that such evidence was hearsay. The Privy Council held that this was not the case. The purpose of proving that S had been subjected to threats was not to establish that the threats were true but to show rather that, if they had been believed by S, they might have induced in him an apprehension of instant death if he failed to conform to the terrorists' wishes. The evidence was thus original, non-hearsay evidence, which had been wrongly excluded at trial.

Similar examples may readily be found. In *Davis* [1998] Crim LR 659, D, on being interviewed in connection with theft, failed to reveal facts upon which he afterwards sought to rely in his defence. At trial he wished to give evidence of what his solicitor had said to him prior to the interview, but was prevented from doing so on the grounds that it would infringe the hearsay rule. The Court of Appeal pointed out, correctly, that this was not necessarily the case. It was material for the jury to consider D's reasons for failing to disclose the relevant facts in deciding whether to draw an inference against him under the CJPO 1994, s. 34 (see **F19.4**). If D's purpose in repeating the solicitor's words was simply to show the impact on him of the advice given, the hearsay rule would not have been infringed. It would have been otherwise if D had sought to demonstrate the truth of anything said. See to similar effect *Willis* [1960] 1 WLR 55, *Chapman* [1969] 2 QB 436, and *Woodhouse v Hall* (1980) 72 Cr App R 39. In the latter case, the question to be decided was whether a massage parlour was being run as a brothel. Having defined a brothel as 'an establishment at which two or more women were offering sexual services', the Divisional Court held that it was open to police officers who had attended the premises posing as customers to prove that the women employed there had offered them various sexual services. There was no question of hearsay: the relevant issue was simply whether the offers had been made.

A troublesome question at common law was whether the rule is infringed where a statement is used to show the state of mind of the person making it, as distinct from its effect on the person to whom it is made. According to *Blastland* [1986] AC 41 a statement made to a witness by a third party is not hearsay when put in evidence for this purpose. See to similar effect *Gregson* [2003] 2 Cr App R 521: on the question whether the possession of a large quantity of a drug indicated intent to supply, the fact that the accused told his friends at the time that he had been handed vastly more of the drug than he had asked to purchase from his supplier, and was worried about how to dispose of it safely, was admissible to show a contemporaneous state of mind on his part inconsistent with the prosecution case. Evidence of a relevant state of mind was considered to be first-hand hearsay admissible by way of common-law exception to the rule in *Neill v North Antrim Magistrates' Court* [1992] 1 WLR 1221, considered further at **F16.8** and **F16.36**, but the preponderance of authority suggests that it is not hearsay in the first place. The inconsistency in the authorities was considered in *Gilfoyle* [1996] 1 Cr App R 302. G was convicted of the murder of his wife, P. Notes written by P in which she expressed an intention to take her own life were admitted to support the defence of suicide. The Court of Appeal considered that evidence of further statements made by P showing that she was not in a suicidal frame of mind, and that she had written the notes in the belief that they were required to help G, a nurse, with a project at work was also admissible. It was said (at p. 321) that 'strictly speaking' such evidence fell outside the hearsay rule, but 'in any event, hearsay evidence to prove the declarant's "state of mind" is an exception to the rule which has been accepted by the common law for many years'. Whether hearsay or not, then, such evidence was clearly admissible at common law.

Under the CJA 2003, the statutory definition of hearsay poses the question whether the statement is tendered as evidence 'of any matter stated'. To the extent that a state of mind is asserted by the speaker, the evidence would appear to be hearsay, which may then be fitted within the preserved common-law exception for *res gestae* in s. 118(1) (see **F16.28**). A statement from which a state of mind may be inferred, on the other hand, may fall outside the definition of 'matter stated' in s. 115(3) and be classified, along with many other 'implied assertions' as original evidence (see **F15.13**).

Illustrations of Non-hearsay Evidence

Further illustrations of the use of statements as non-hearsay evidence which it is submitted will survive the CJA 2003, are an admission of bankruptcy tendered to prove not the truth of the assertion (which was proved by other means), but the maker's knowledge of his insolvency (*Thomas v Connell* (1838) 4 M & W 267); an allegation of forgery made against A tendered to show why A had been arrested (*Perkins v Vaughan* (1842) 4 Man & G 988); a cry of 'murder' by the alleged victim of a rape, tendered to prove lack of consent, and a subsequent request by her for money, tendered to prove the contrary (*Guttridges* (1840) 9 C & P 471). Where negligence by omission is alleged, a promise made by a third party to take action on behalf of D may show why D took no action (*The Douglas* (1882) 7 PD 151). Where D denied knowledge that certain premises were being used as a brothel, an advertisement that he had sought to place, referring to the premises and containing a reference to 'many stunning masseuses', was admissible to show that he did know (*Roberts v DPP* [1994] Crim LR 926). **F15.9**

A statement that is demonstrably false may show a consciousness of guilt (*Mawaz Khan v The Queen* [1967] 1 AC 454; *A-G v Good* (1825) M'Cle & Yo 286; *Binham* [1991] Crim LR

774), but see *Malcherek* [1981] 1 WLR 690, in which the telling of lies was thought (*obiter*) to be hearsay evidence of guilt. Under the CJA 2003, it would seem that a lie cannot be hearsay evidence of a matter that it is not intended to assert (see **F15.12**).

Upon application of the test described above, it is perfectly possible that evidence may be admissible, original evidence for one purpose, and inadmissible hearsay for another. Such cases require a very careful judicial direction as to the use to which the evidence may properly be put. Where it happens that the evidence is admissible in relation to one count in an indictment but not another, the inadmissibility is relevant to whether the counts should be tried together (*Watson* [1997] Crim LR 680).

Inferences Founded on Statements

F15.10 Where evidence is inadmissible as hearsay, it is not possible to evade the difficulty by adducing evidence from which it can be inferred that the inadmissible statement was made and that it was true. In *Glinski v McIver* [1962] AC 726, Lord Devlin described the 'customary devices' employed where the hearsay rule is sought to be evaded in this way (at [780–1]):

> The first consists in not asking what was said in a conversation or written in a document but in asking what the conversation or document was about; it is apparently thought that what would be objectionable if fully exposed is permissible if decently veiled. . . . The other device is to ask by means of 'Yes' or 'No' questions what was done. (Just answer 'Yes' or 'No': Did you go to see counsel? Do not tell us what he said but as a result of it did you do something? What did you do?) This device is commonly defended on the ground that counsel is asking only about what was done and not about what was said. But in truth what was done is relevant only because from it there can be inferred something about what was said. Such evidence seems to me to be clearly objectionable. If there is nothing in it, it is irrelevant; if there is something in it, what there is in it is inadmissible.

See also *Saunders* [1899] 1 QB 490.

It is submitted that the same criticism can be made of an attempt to draw a circumstantial inference from a hearsay statement in a document. This occurred in *Rice* [1963] 1 QB 857, where the prosecution relied on an airline ticket in the names of 'Rice and Moore', produced by an airline official whose job it was to deal with used tickets, to give rise to a circumstantial inference that R had travelled on the flight in question. Although the Court of Appeal was agreed that the ticket 'must not be treated as speaking its contents for what it might say could only be hearsay', it was held (at p. 872) that 'the production of the ticket from the place where used tickets would properly be kept was a fact from which the jury might infer that probably two people had flown on the particular flight and that it might or might not seem to them by applying their common knowledge of such matters that the passengers bore the surnames that were written on the ticket'. It is submitted, however, that the production of the ticket proved that the traveller was R only if reliance were placed on its 'contents', i.e. on the statement it bore which showed that it had been issued to one Rice. This is supported by the analysis of the House of Lords in *Myers v DPP* [1965] AC 1001, rejecting the argument that it could be inferred from the efficient manner in which records were compiled by the manufacturers of motor vehicles, that what was stated in the records was inherently likely to be true. Lord Morris said (at p. 1027): 'The circumstances referred to show that evidence of the nature now being considered might with advantage be admitted because there would be every expectation that figures would be correctly recorded. This, however, does not change the character of the evidence. It remains hearsay evidence . . .'

Under the CJA 2003, s. 114(1), it is hard to avoid the conclusion that the statement on the ticket in *Rice* was used as evidence 'of any matter stated'. The broad exception now available for business documents (under s. 117: see **F16.13**) provides a more tenable route to admissibility.

A distinction should, however, be drawn between the permissible use of a statement as an original and independent fact, and the impermissible use of it as evidence of the matter stated. In *Lydon* (1986) 85 Cr App R 221 the prosecution were permitted to tender in evidence a piece of paper found near a weapon believed to have been used in a robbery, and bearing ink of a similar kind to that staining the weapon. On the paper, someone had written 'Sean rules' and 'Sean rules 85'. It was held that the words on the paper created an inferential link with L, whose first name was Sean. *Rice* was distinguished, because '[T]he reference to Sean could be regarded as no more than a statement of fact involving no assertion as to the truth of the contents of the document' (per Woolf LJ at p. 224). *Lydon* was applied in *McIntosh* [1992] Crim LR 651, in which a piece of paper bearing calculations as to the profit and loss made from buying and selling a substance (inferentially a drug) was found on M's premises. The document was not in M's handwriting, but this was immaterial as it was admitted not as evidence of its truth but as purely circumstantial evidence suggesting M's involvement with drug-related offences.

Statements Inextricably Linked to Relevant Acts

Where an issue arises as to the doing of a composite act made up of physical actions and words, the admissibility of the words may be regarded in a different light from the same words standing alone. In *Ratten v The Queen* [1972] AC 378, R was charged with the murder of his wife, and the defence was that she had been shot by accident as R cleaned his gun. The prosecution relied on the evidence of a telephone operator to show that, shortly before she was shot, the victim had telephoned the exchange in a state of hysteria and asked for the police. R denied that any such call had been made. The Privy Council held that, because the making of the call was itself a relevant act, the words used and the state of emotion in which they were spoken were 'relevant and necessary evidence in order to explain and complete the fact of the call being made', and were not hearsay. See also *Blastland* [1986] AC 41, in which it was said (at p. 59) that *Ratten* was authority for the proposition that the admissibility of the telephone call in that case had to be considered as a whole. **F15.11**

Under the CJA 2003, s. 114(1), the position would appear to be that a statement cannot be extricated from the ambit of the hearsay rule merely because it is closely associated with the doing of a relevant act. The association might, however, be relevant to the question whether it is in the interests of justice to admit the statement (see **F16.20**). Where the relevant act is an act of identification that the witness is unable to remember having made (such evidence having been received as non-hearsay in a manner akin to that in *McCay* [1990] 1 WLR 645 or *Osbourne* [1973] QB 678) the admission of the evidence under s. 114(1)(d) might undermine the exception for evidence of identification that the witness *does* remember making and that he believed to be true at the time (s. 120). In some cases the witness's lapse of memory will not be genuine but will be based on fear of repeating the identification, in which case the exception in s. 116 (see **F16.8**) may assist.

Hearsay and 'Matters Stated'

Criminal Justice Act 2003, s. 115 **F15.12**

(1) In this chapter references to a statement or to a matter stated are to be read as follows.
(2) . . .
(3) A matter stated is one to which the chapter applies if (and only if) the purpose, or one of the purposes, of the person making the statement appears to the court to have been—
   (a) to cause another person to believe the matter, or
   (b) to cause another person to act or a machine to operate on the basis that the matter is as stated.

The intended effect of s. 115(3) is to reverse the decision of the House of Lords in *Kearley* [1992] 2 AC 228. K was charged with possession of a controlled drug with intent to supply. The amount found in K's possession being of itself inadequate to warrant an inference of such

F

Part F Evidence

an intent, the prosecution relied upon evidence that, after K's arrest, a number of telephone calls had been made to his home in which the callers asked for K by his nickname and sought to buy drugs, and that a number of individuals had visited the house and asked to be supplied with drugs. None of these persons was called to give evidence at the trial. The House of Lords, by a majority, held that the hearsay rule precluded the use of the callers' requests as implied assertions by them that K was a supplier of drugs. Lord Bridge stated (at p. 665) that the English authorities were both 'clear and unequivocal' in holding that the hearsay rule applies equally to express and to implied assertions. Lord Ackner (whose preferred view was that the evidence was simply irrelevant in that it proved no more than the state of mind of the callers, which was not in issue) considered that, just as a request for drugs containing an express statement that K was a supplier would clearly have been objectionable as hearsay, so a request containing an implied assertion to the same effect would break the hearsay rule. A non-hearsay purpose for adducing the evidence in *Kearley* was thought by the dissenting minority (Lords Griffiths and Browne-Wilkinson) to exist in that the conduct of the callers pointed towards the existence of a 'market' for the supply of drugs, but this argument was thought by the majority to be unsound on the basis that the conduct itself was not relevant except as an implied assertion as to the caller's beliefs, which were hearsay.

On the facts of *Kearley*, the callers whose requests for drugs were tendered in evidence clearly thought that they were speaking to K. There was thus little danger that, in making their requests, they were seeking to mislead the person to whom they were speaking, or to misrepresent or exaggerate the matter on which the prosecution sought to rely, viz. their belief that K was a drug dealer. Under the change in the law brought about by s. 115(3), the 'matter stated' (that K is a dealer) is not one to which the hearsay rule applies unless the person making the request had a purpose either (a) to cause another to believe the matter or (b) to cause another to act as though the matter is as stated. Where the speaker believes that the hearer already knows the matter in question, and is therefore not seeking either to induce a state of belief or to act on the statement as though it were true (whether he believes it or not) the evidence is original, non-hearsay evidence for the future. (It may, of course, be held to be irrelevant if Lord Ackner's preferred view prevails: s. 115(3) provides only that it is not hearsay.)

Implied Statements as Non-hearsay

F15.13 The famous statements in the civil case of *Wright v Doe d. Tatham* (1837) 7 A & E 313 would appear not to be hearsay under the new test encapsulated in the CJA 2003, s. 115(3). The Court of Exchequer Chamber, in a judgment approved in *Kearley* [1992] 2 AC 228, decided that letters written to a deceased testator, being such as one would write to a sane person, were inadmissible as evidence of the testator's sanity. Parke B considered that the hearsay rule would also have been infringed by evidence of conduct tendered to prove the truth of some belief exhibited by the conduct, as where the family of a person takes the same precautions in respect of him as if he were a lunatic. As none of these statements are intended to communicate the relevant information, however, they would appear now to be outside the scope of the hearsay rule.

Section 115(3) enacts the proposal of the Law Commission (Report No. 245, *Evidence in Criminal Proceedings: Hearsay and Related Topics*, Cm 3670). The reason for the change was said to be that, as a class, implied assertions are more reliable than statements made for the purpose of communicating information (para. 4.23). In the majority of cases, the danger is removed if the speaker is not trying to persuade anyone of the matter, and this is covered by s. 115(3)(a). Section 115(3)(b) covers the possibility that the person to whom, or the machine to which, the statement is addressed may be asked simply to act upon it rather than to form a judgement about whether it is true. Because the maker of the statement may have a motive to misrepresent the facts in such a case, the statement is to be treated as hearsay.

The decision in *Kearley* led to some difficult distinctions. In *O'Connell* [2003] EWCA Crim 502, it was stated that, if the accused himself received or heard the call, his response might provide evidence against him (as where he is alleged to have shouted the warning 'Hang up, . . . it's the Old Bill'). However, the calls themselves remained inadmissible at common law. Under the CJA 2003, the result is more consistent with common sense.

However it can with some justification be argued that s. 115(3) has merely replaced one complex set of considerations with another. In *Isichei* (2006) 170 JP 753 the prosecution wished to prove that a member of a party looking for a nightclub had told his colleagues that he would ring 'Marvin'. The purpose of adducing the evidence was to establish a connection between the accused, whose first name this was, and an individual from the club who subsequently assaulted and robbed two female members of the party. While it could be argued that the caller had, as one of his purposes, the intention of causing the other members of the group to know that he was about to call 'Marvin', it was unlikely that he cared what, if anything, they believed as to the name of his contact. The Court of Appeal noted that the level of semantic analysis required by s. 115(3) was, in the circumstances, both highly artificial and disproportionate to the evidential significance of the call. The Court went on to decide that the call would, even if hearsay, have been admissible under the 'interests of justice' provision in s. 114(1)(d). This provides a sensible 'belt and braces' solution wherever the answer under s. 115(3) is unclear (or not worth the effort of pursuing) and the evidence would, if hearsay, be admissible in any event. In retrospect, the route to admissibility provided by s. 114(1)(d) might have provided a simpler and more satisfying legislative solution to the problem of *Kearley*.

In some cases it may be difficult to determine whether a statement is directed at another person, and therefore whether it is intended to be believed. In *N* [2006] EWCA Crim 3309 a statement in a complainant's diary regarding her sexual relationship with her uncle would have been hearsay (but admissible for the defence under an exception) had the statement been intended for another, but had it been intended for the writer's sole use it was not hearsay. The Court of Appeal managed to avoid the conclusion that a non-hearsay diary entry was inadmissible by regarding it as 'real or direct evidence outside the hearsay rule', thus making it (like the evidence in *Isichei*) admissible whether it was hearsay or not. While it is hard to see how the entry could be real evidence of its truth, the argument that it is evidence of the matter contained in it (though not 'stated' for the purposes of the Act) would seem plausible. The only possible objection to the entry was that it was hearsay, which cannot be sustained under the terms of s. 115(3).

In cases where the maker of a statement seeks to use it to convey information, the statement is hearsay evidence of the information he has the purpose to convey, whether the communication is express or implicit. In *Teper v The Queen* [1952] AC 480, T was charged with setting fire to his own business premises with intent to defraud his insurers. A police officer who was on duty near the fire heard an unknown woman shout, 'Your place burning and you going away from the fire', as a man resembling T drove past. This was hearsay at common law, and would continue to be so under the CJA 2003 if the purpose, or one of the purposes, of the woman appeared to the court to be to cause anyone to believe that the matter implicitly stated (that the driver was T) was true. As this seems likely to be the case, a hearsay exception would have to be found.

In *Sukadave Singh* [2006] 1 WLR 1564, the Court of Appeal rejected an argument which would have turned s. 115(3) on its head. By that argument, the provisions of s. 115 qualify only the statutory form of hearsay as described by s. 114; thus, as the rule in *Kearley* subsists only at common law, it remains unaffected. The argument is based on the absence of any express repeal of the common-law hearsay rule. The Court regarded the old rule as effectively abolished by s. 118 (which makes it clear that the only surviving common-law rules are certain preserved exceptions). When read with s. 114, there is no room for any other vestige of common law to remain. What was said by the callers in *Kearley* would now, it was held, be admissible as direct evidence of the fact that there was a ready market for the supply of drugs from the premises, from which could be inferred an intention by the occupier to supply drugs.

Admissions Based on Hearsay

F15.14 Where a person admits something, his own knowledge of which is based on hearsay, the admission does not prove the fact. In *Comptroller of Customs v Western Lectric Co. Ltd* [1966] AC 367, it was held that admissions as to the country of origin of goods, which were based on markings on the goods themselves, were inadmissible. Lord Hodson further described such admissions as being of no real value. See also *Surujpaul v The Queen* [1958] 1 WLR 1050. The same problem frequently arises in handling cases, where there is a dearth of direct evidence to prove that the goods are stolen. In *Hulbert* (1979) 69 Cr App R 243, H admitted that she bought certain goods at very low prices from unnamed sellers in various public houses, and that, in some cases, the sellers told her that the goods were stolen. It was held that H's admission as to facts within her own knowledge (e.g., the price paid, and the circumstances in which the goods were offered for sale) was admissible evidence that the goods might have been stolen, but that her admission as to what she had been told could not be evidence that the goods were stolen. What she had been told would, however, be admissible to prove the state of her knowledge or belief at the time. See also *Sbarra* (1918) 87 LJ KB 1003, *Korniak* (1982) 76 Cr App R 145 and *Overington* [1978] Crim LR 692; and see **F15.8**.

In cases involving the possession of drugs, the accused's admission that the substance in question was a controlled drug would be inadmissible if based on hearsay, and of limited evidential value if based on his own opinion. In some cases the admissions of experienced drug users have been held to be prima facie evidence of the nature of a substance (see *Chatwood* [1980] 1 WLR 874, *Bird v Adams* [1972] Crim LR 174 and *Wells* [1976] Crim LR 518). *Mieras v Rees* [1975] Crim LR 224, which appears to be authority to the contrary, is misreported, the charge was one of attempt, where it was accepted that there was no proof as to the nature of the substance (*Chatwood* [1980] 1 WLR 874).

Statements Tendered to Prove Non-existence of Alleged Facts

F15.15 A difficult question at common law was whether a statement that is hearsay when tendered to prove the truth of a fact asserted in it is equally hearsay when tendered as circumstantial evidence of the non-existence of facts that might have been expected to have been asserted in it if they had been true. The problem arose most acutely with regard to records. In both *Patel* [1981] 3 All ER 94 and *Shone* (1982) 76 Cr App R 72 it was suggested that, provided responsible persons could give evidence of the method of record-keeping, an inference could be drawn about matters not appearing. Thus in *Patel*, which concerned immigration records, evidence as to the method of compilation and custody supported the inference that, if A's name was not recorded, he must be an illegal entrant. Had the CJA 2003, s. 115(3) (see **F15.12**) been applied to the circumstances in *Patel*, it may be argued that, as the purpose of the compiler was not to induce another to believe that A was an illegal entrant, or to cause another to act on the basis that he was, the hearsay rule is not infringed by the use of such records to support circumstantial inferences of a negative nature. Alternatively, to the extent that both the negative and positive use of a record depend on the correctness of the record keeping, negative inferences might be more safely drawn in the same way as positive ones, i.e. within the confines of a hearsay exception. Most records are now admissible under the CJA 2003, s. 117 (see **F16.13**).

When dealing with 'negative hearsay' otherwise than in the context of records, the common law tended towards a relaxed approach. This, it is submitted, is the best explanation of *Muir* (1983) 79 Cr App R 153. M was charged with theft of a video recorder, hired to him by

G Ltd. M's defence was that the video had been taken away by two men who had called at his house. To rebut the suggestion that G Ltd had repossessed the video, S, the district manager of G Ltd, gave evidence that there had been no repossession by the local showroom: a fact within his own knowledge. He was asked in cross-examination about the possibility of repossession by the company's head office, and was allowed to say in response that he had telephoned head office and had been told that they had not ordered the repossession of the video. The Court of Appeal held that, '[I]n the way in which the evidence came out', it was not hearsay, on the ground that S 'was the best person to give the relevant evidence', including informing the court that a check had been made with head office. This analysis ignores the fact that what S had been told during the check was hearsay. On the facts of the case, the only option open to the prosecution if the rule had been strictly applied would have been to call a further witness from head office, and it may have been that expediency dictated the result. However, the decision was noted to have attracted adverse comment in *Coventry Justices, ex parte Bullard* (1992) 95 Cr App R 175. Under the CJA 2003, s. 114(1)(d) might be deployed if it was in the interests of justice to treat the witness S in *Muir* as an acceptable source of information regarding the possibility of repossession by the company's head office.

Mechanically Produced Evidence as Hearsay

Under the CJA 2003, it is apparent from the definition of 'statement' in s. 115(1) (see F15.1) **F15.16**
as a representation of fact or opinion *made by a person* that a purely mechanical generation of an image, say, by CCTV is not hearsay. The provision is equally clear that an image generated by human agency such as a representation in a 'sketch, photofit or other pictorial form' is included.

This follows the common law, whereby juries may be allowed to see still photographs taken by a security camera during an armed robbery (*Dodson* [1984] 1 WLR 971), or a video recording of an incident (*Fowden* [1982] Crim LR 588; *Grimer* [1982] Crim LR 674), and they may hear a tape recording of a relevant conversation (*Maqsud Ali* [1966] 1 QB 688). Furthermore, just as a video recording of the commission of an offence is admissible, so also a witness who has seen the recording may give evidence of what he saw, as he is in effect in the same position as a witness with a 'direct view of the action' (*Taylor v Chief Constable of Cheshire* [1986] 1 WLR 1479). See also, as to computer-produced evidence, F15.17.

In *Cook* [1987] QB 417, the Court of Appeal considered that sketches and photofit likenesses made under the direction of identifying witnesses were analogous to photographs, in that they were not subject to the hearsay rule. The court distinguished between the production of a sketch or photofit, which is not hearsay, and the recital by a witness of the distinguishing features of the person to be identified, which is. There is, however, a difficulty with the analogy preferred by the court, in that photofit likenesses, despite the resemblance of the finished product to a photograph, are compiled at the instigation of a human mind, and are subject to the same dangers as other out-of-court statements. The effect of the CJA 2003, s. 115(1), is to overrule *Cook* and other cases to similar effect such as *Constantinou* (1989) 91 Cr App R 74.

A mechanically generated representation that depends for its accuracy on human input cannot be used in the absence of proof that the input was accurate (see CJA 2003, s. 129, at F15.17).

Computer Evidence and the Hearsay Rule

It follows from the definition of 'statement' in the CJA 2003, s. 115(1), as representation 'by **F15.17**
a person' that computer evidence may or may not be hearsay. To the extent to which a computer is used merely to perform functions of calculation, no question of hearsay is involved in receiving evidence of what the computer 'said', and in this the 2003 Act follows

F

Part F Evidence

the common law (*Minors* [1989] 1 WLR 441, per Steyn J at p. 446). The reason, it is submitted, is that the court, when acting on such information, is not being asked to accept the truth of a matter stated by any person. Thus, in *Wood* (1982) 76 Cr App R 23, the prosecution alleged that metal found at W's premises was stolen. Chemists performed tests on samples of the metal, and used a computer as a tool to perform complicated calculations based on the data they had obtained. At trial, the chemists gave evidence of the outcome of the tests, and produced the computer printout to prove the results of the calculations. It was held that the printout was admissible for this purpose and did not constitute hearsay evidence, being instead real evidence analogous to the reaction of litmus paper as evidence of the acidity of a solution. See also *Golizadeh* [1995] Crim LR 232. In the same way, the printout of an Intoximeter that has performed an analysis of specimens of breath is admissible non-hearsay evidence (*Castle v Cross* [1984] 1 WLR 1372, where the rule regarding admissibility of computer evidence was said to be the same in this respect as in respect of less sophisticated machines; *Castle v Cross* was affirmed by the House of Lords in *DPP v McKeown* [1997] 1 WLR 295). See *The Statue of Liberty* [1968] 1 WLR 739 (automatic record made by radar set at a shore radio station admissible), and see also the rule as it applies to photographs etc. at **F15.16**.

Where a computer is used to record information that is supplied by a person, the hearsay rule will come into play if it is sought to use a printout from the computer to prove that what the person said was true. Thus, documentary records stored on computer are hearsay (*Minors*), and see *Coventry Justices, ex parte Bullard* (1992) 95 Cr App R 175, in which it was held that the crucial distinction was between 'computer printouts containing information implanted by a human, and printouts containing records produced without human intervention'. Similarly, in *Wood*, it was necessary for the chemists who tested the metal to give evidence of the facts on which the tests were based: the computer printout could not have been used to prove that the information fed into the computer was accurate, only that the calculations performed by the computer itself were correct. The CJA 2003 maintains the same distinction.

Criminal Justice Act 2003, s. 129

(1) Where a representation of any fact—
 (a) is made otherwise than by a person, but
 (b) depends for its accuracy on information supplied (directly or indirectly) by a person,
 that representation is not admissible in criminal proceedings as evidence of the fact unless it is proved that the information was accurate.

A more difficult problem of classification arose in *Governor of Brixton Prison, ex parte Levin* [1997] AC 741. L was alleged to have initiated unauthorised payment instructions from his computer terminal in Russia, as a result of which the computerised fund transfer service of an American bank was induced to transfer funds from clients' accounts into accounts controlled by L. The transaction occurred automatically upon receipt of the instruction by L, and was duly copied to the American computer's historical records. L objected to the production of printouts showing the transactions on the grounds that they were hearsay, but the House of Lords held that they were not. Lord Woolf said:

> The printouts are tendered to prove the transfers of funds which they record. They do not assert that such transfers took place. They record the transfers themselves, created by the interaction between whoever purported to request the transfers and the computer program in Parsipanny [New Jersey]. The evidential status of the printouts is no different from that of a photocopy of a forged cheque.

In other words the printout proved the thing done because it was the thing done, or at least a copy of the thing done (commentary by Professor Sir John Smith on *Ewing* [1983] Crim LR 472 at p. 473).

Section F16 Exceptions to the Rule Against Hearsay (Excluding Confessions)

Hearsay Exceptions

The rule against hearsay, as described in F15, has never been an absolute prohibition. However, the various common law and statutory exceptions to the rule which have grown up over time form a complex network, requiring considerable expertise to interpret. The provisions of the CJA 2003, part II, chapter 2, bring about the codification of the rule and of its most important exceptions, together with a considerable and welcome degree of simplification. The new law came into force on 4 April 2005, and applies to all trials taking place after that date (*H (PG)* [2006] 1 Cr App R 50, following *Bradley* [2005] 1 Cr App R 397). **F16.1**

In its construction, the CJA 2003 adopts a template for reform similar to the Civil Evidence Act 1968, drawing up new and broad statutory exceptions, but filling in the cracks with preserved common-law rules. Not all of the common-law rules survive: the exception for dying declarations, for example, is swallowed up in the new provision allowing first-hand oral hearsay from deceased witnesses. The reforms are drawn from the Law Commission Report No. 245, *Evidence in Criminal Proceedings: Hearsay and Related Topics* Cm 3670 (1997) and considered in the Government's White Paper, *Justice for All* (2002). The overall aim, as stated by the Government minister when defending the Criminal Justice Bill in Committee, is to ensure that, subject to the necessary safeguards, relevant evidence should be admitted where that is in the interests of justice.

It is convenient to begin with an overview of the new provisions before embarking on the detail.

Criminal Justice Act 2003: Statutory Regulation of Hearsay

Criminal Justice Act 2003, s. 114 **F16.2**

(1) In criminal proceedings a statement not made in oral evidence in the proceedings is admissible as evidence of any matter stated if, but only if—
   (a) any provision of this chapter or any other statutory provision makes it admissible,
   (b) any rule of law preserved by section 118 makes it admissible,
   (c) all parties to the proceedings agree to it being admissible, or
   (d) the court is satisfied that it is in the interests of justice for it to be admissible.

The CrimPR make provision for the procedure to be followed and other conditions to be fulfilled by a party proposing to tender a hearsay statement in evidence. The relevant rules are the CrimPR, part 34 and, in relation to the admission of such evidence in the Court of Appeal, r. 68.20: the rules are set out in **appendix 1**. The rules are applicable to all parties wishing to introduce hearsay evidence. The court has a wide power to dispense with the notice requirement altogether, or to allow notice to be given in a different form, or orally; the party entitled to notice may also waive the entitlement. The rules do not expressly provide that the failure to oppose a notice of hearsay is to be treated as agreement that the evidence may be given in hearsay form for the purposes of s. 114(1)(c). Section 132(4) stipulates that the rules may so provide, but in fact they do not. The court would thus appear to have a discretion in the matter.

Section 114 is considered at **F15.1**, where the definition of hearsay ('a statement not made in oral evidence') is elaborated. The key change from the common law is that the so-called implied assertion, treated as hearsay at common law, is generally excluded from the definition of 'a matter stated' (see **F15.13**). In order to admit hearsay under the CJA 2003, a party has the options of invoking a statutory rule or a preserved common-law exception, of seeking the agreement of all parties to the use of hearsay, or of persuading the court that the evidence should be received in the interests of justice. There is no definition of 'agreement', but it would appear that failure to object is not necessarily agreement. The inclusion of the 'interests of justice' exception in s. 114(1)(d) (**F16.20**) was described by Lord Cooke of Thorndon in the debates on the Act as the 'great merit' of the whole package of reforms. In effect it modifies the application of the general rule against hearsay — there is no rule against hearsay which it is in the interests of justice to admit — and is thus relevant throughout this section and **F15**. In the Law Commission's original proposals, the modification was described as a 'safety valve', to be used primarily to avoid miscarriages of justice. No such limitation is, however, apparent from the version that appears in the Act.

The principal categories of admissibility dealt with under the new statutory rules concern cases where a witness is unavailable (s. 116: see **F16.4**) and business and other documents (s. 117: see **F16.13**). The preserved common-law rules are contained in s. 118, and concern evidence of public information (see **F16.22**); reputation (see **F16.27**); *res gestae* (see **F16.28**); confessions and admissions (see **F16.38**), common enterprise (see **F16.40**) and expert evidence (see **F16.44**). Sections 119 and 120 respectively make special provision for the previous inconsistent and consistent statements of witnesses in the case, which become more widely admissible as evidence of their truth and not merely of inconsistency or consistency as the case may be (see **F6.19** and **F7.28** respectively). Supplementary provision is made in s. 121 for the problem of multiple hearsay, as to which there is very little authority at common law (see **F16.54**). Section 122 restricts the circumstances in which a jury may take a copy of a hearsay statement produced as an exhibit into the jury room when considering their verdict. Special provision is made in s. 123 to exclude from the operation of the new statutory exceptions statements by persons who lack competence (see **F16.4**) and in s. 124 for testing credibility where the maker of a statement admitted in evidence does not attend to testify (see **F16.55**).

The court acquires a statutory power under s. 125 to stop a case where evidence is unconvincing and a new general discretion, under s. 126, the full extent of which is unclear, but which extends at least to the exclusion of superfluous evidence (see **F16.56**). The new power is in addition to the court's existing range of discretions at common law and under the PACE 1984, s. 78. The power to make rules of court (s. 132) includes the power to establish a regime for giving notice of the intention to use hearsay. Special provision is also made for the use of copies (s. 133), for the use of transcripts at retrial (s. 131: see **F16.46**) and for removing the power of the court to overrule an objection to the reading of depositions (s. 130). Specific reforms are also enacted to regulate the use of confession evidence by one co-accused against another (s. 128: see **F17.19**) and of preparatory work undertaken for criminal proceedings on the basis of which an expert subsequently bases an opinion (s. 127: see **F10.18**).

This section of this work deals with the more important of the various exceptions to the hearsay rule which operate in criminal cases, with the exception of confessions which are dealt with at **F17**. Although the CJA 2003 has significantly simplified the law in this area, it remains the case that the various exceptions overlap: for example the first-hand hearsay statement of a deceased victim of violence admissible under the CJA 2003, s. 116, might, if made under the influence of the event itself, also be received under the *res gestae* exception preserved by s. 118(1).

CRIMINAL JUSTICE ACT 2003: UNAVAILABLE WITNESSES; BUSINESS AND OTHER DOCUMENTS

Scope of CJA 2003, ss. 116 and 117: Automatic Admissibility

The CJA 2003, ss. 116 and 117, replace the provisions of the CJA 1988, ss. 23 to 26. An important change is that the new provisions have been shorn of the discretion and leave requirements that formed a key element of the 1988 Act's provision. The intention is that evidence that satisfies the conditions laid down in either of the two new provisions should be automatically admissible. One reason given by the Law Commission Report No. 245, *Evidence in Criminal Proceedings: Hearsay and Related Topics*, Cm 3670 (1997) was that there was a lack of consistency in the way that courts exercised their powers, and that judges who disliked hearsay evidence were able to find reasons for excluding it. The Government White Paper, *Justice for All* (2002) states (at para. 4.61): **F16.3**

> We believe the right approach is that, if there is a good reason for the original maker not to be able to give the evidence personally (for example through illness or death) or where records have been properly compiled by businesses, then the evidence should automatically go in, rather than its admissibility being judged.

Note, however, that nothing in the hearsay provisions prejudices any power of a court to exclude evidence under the PACE 1984, s. 78 (CJA 2003, s. 126(2)). It follows that courts retain an exclusionary discretion on grounds of fairness in respect of prosecution evidence, so it is critically in relation to hearsay tendered by the defence that the removal of the power afforded by the CJA 1988, ss. 25 and 26, may truly result in 'automatic' admissibility. If, for example, the accused produces a letter from a writer who has made himself scarce, in which an identifiable individual claims full responsibility for the crime with which the accused is charged, the letter qualifies for automatic admissibility under s. 116, leading to concerns that the CJA 2003 will facilitate the manufacture of hearsay evidence for the defence (cf. *James* [2005] EWCA Crim 110, decided under the 1988 Act). A possible solution may lie in the provision of a new general discretion to exclude in s. 126 (see **F16.56**) but this may be limited to superfluous evidence and not be susceptible to manipulation as a discretion based on fairness.

Where evidence was adduced by the prosecution under the previous legislation, the requirement to obtain leave in s. 26 was exercised in such a way as to ensure that the accused's right to a fair trial, guaranteed by the ECHR, Article 6, was not compromised by the use of hearsay evidence. It must be anticipated that the courts will now resort to the PACE 1984, s. 78, to achieve this end (see further **F16.17**).

Unavailable Witnesses

Criminal Justice Act 2003, ss. 116 and 123 **F16.4**

116.—(1) In criminal proceedings a statement not made in oral evidence in the proceedings is admissible as evidence of any matter stated if—
(a) oral evidence given in the proceedings by the person who made the statement would be admissible as evidence of that matter,
(b) the person who made the statement (the relevant person) is identified to the court's satisfaction, and
(c) any of the five conditions mentioned in subsection (2) is satisfied.
(2) The conditions are—
(a) that the relevant person is dead;

Part F Evidence

(b) that the relevant person is unfit to be a witness because of his bodily or mental condition;
(c) that the relevant person is outside the United Kingdom and it is not reasonably practicable to secure his attendance;
(d) that the relevant person cannot be found although such steps as it is reasonably practicable to take to find him have been taken;
(e) that through fear the relevant person does not give (or does not continue to give) oral evidence in the proceedings, either at all or in connection with the subject matter of the statement, and the court gives leave for the statement to be given in evidence.

(3) For the purposes of subsection (2)(e) 'fear' is to be widely construed and (for example) includes fear of the death or injury of another person or of financial loss.

(4) Leave may be given under subsection (2)(e) only if the court considers that the statement ought to be admitted in the interests of justice, having regard—
(a) to the statement's contents,
(b) to any risk that its admission or exclusion will result in unfairness to any party to the proceedings (and in particular to how difficult it will be to challenge the statement if the relevant person does not give oral evidence),
(c) in appropriate cases, to the fact that a direction under section 19 of the Youth Justice and Criminal Evidence Act 1999 (special measures for the giving of evidence by fearful witnesses etc) could be made in relation to the relevant person, and
(d) to any other relevant circumstances.

(5) A condition set out in any paragraph of subsection (2) which is in fact satisfied is to be treated as not satisfied if it is shown that the circumstances described in that paragraph are caused—
(a) by the person in support of whose case it is sought to give the statement in evidence, or
(b) by a person acting on his behalf,
in order to prevent the relevant person giving oral evidence in the proceedings (whether at all or in connection with the subject matter of the statement).

123.—(1) Nothing in section 116, 119 or 120 makes a statement admissible as evidence if it was made by a person who did not have the required capability at the time when he made the statement.

(2) Nothing in section 117 makes a statement admissible as evidence if any person who, in order for the requirements of section 117(2) to be satisfied, must at any time have supplied or received the information concerned or created or received the document or part concerned—
(a) did not have the required capability at that time, or
(b) cannot be identified but cannot reasonably be assumed to have had the required capability at that time.

(3) For the purposes of this section a person has the required capability if he is capable of—
(a) understanding questions put to him about the matters stated, and
(b) giving answers to such questions which can be understood.

(4) Where by reason of this section there is an issue as to whether a person had the required capability when he made a statement—
(a) proceedings held for the determination of the issue must take place in the absence of the jury (if there is one);
(b) in determining the issue the court may receive expert evidence and evidence from any person to whom the statement in question was made;
(c) the burden of proof on the issue lies on the party seeking to adduce the statement, and the standard of proof is the balance of probabilities.

Like its predecessor, s. 23 of the CJA 1988, s. 116 applies only to first-hand hearsay. Where a person makes a statement, but it is not clear whether the statement relates to her own knowledge or to something she has been told, the statement could not be admitted under s. 23 (*JP* [1999] Crim LR 401) and it is submitted that the same holds for s. 116. The 1988 legislation was susceptible to the interpretation that multiple hearsay might have been admissible provided that the statement of what the person had been told was itself admissible under an exception to the hearsay rule, but under the 2003 Act multiple hearsay is admissible only under s. 121 (see **F16.54**). The requirement that the oral evidence of the person who made the statement would have been admissible as evidence of the matter (s. 116(1)(a)) also serves to ensure that hearsay cannot be received if the evidence would have been inadmissible for some other reason, e.g., that it is evidence of bad character that is not admissible under chapter 1 of part 11 of the CJA 2003 (see **F12** and **F14**).

The person who made any hearsay statement must be identifiable (s. 116(1)(b)). If the statement is to be automatically admissible it is important that a party seeking to challenge its credibility must be able to ascertain who made it, and be able where appropriate to invoke s. 124 (see **F16.55**), which is provided by way of a substitute to the right of cross-examination. In *Nkemayang* [2005] EWCA Crim 1937, the Court of Appeal approved of the insistence in the CJA 2003 on strict proof of identity saying that 'any regime controlling the admissibility of evidence must be alert to the danger of fabricated evidence;'. Where identification is not possible, the statement may be admissible in the alternative either under the common law of *res gestae* (see **F16.28**), or under s. 114(1)(d) (see **F16.20**).

Under s. 23 of the CJA 1988, only a statement in a document could be adduced, whereas under s. 116 of the CJA 2003, an oral hearsay statement may be tendered or a statement made by conduct (for the meaning of 'statement' see s. 115(2) (see **F15.1**)). Thus, for example, evidence from a dying victim identifying his assailant could be admissible under s. 116 and proved by one who heard it. In *Musone* [2007] EWCA Crim 1237, a man who had been stabbed was asked 'what's happened, mate?' and replied 'Musone's just stabbed me'. The statement was admitted at M's trial for murder under s. 116. By the same token, a gesture or sign language similarly identifying the guilty party could be received.

Section 116(5) prevents a person from being able to rely on a hearsay statement where he has caused the witness's absence precisely so that he can do so. This provision was included for the sake of completeness: it would seem unlikely to be brought into play very often.

Proof of Unavailability of Maker The reasons specified in the CJA 2003, s. 116(2), for not calling the maker of a statement are disjunctive: provided that the party seeking to rely on the statement can establish that one of the reasons exists, it does not matter that other reasons cannot be made out (*Farrand v Galland* [1989] Crim LR 573, decided under the PACE 1984, s. 68). In *Minors* [1989] 1 WLR 441, the Court of Appeal held that the admissibility of evidence adduced by the prosecution under the PACE 1984, s. 68, had to be established to the criminal standard of proof beyond reasonable doubt. The same result followed in respect of evidence adduced under the CJA 1988 (*Acton Justices, ex parte McMullen* (1990) 92 Cr App R 98, in which Watkins LJ said that he was 'in no doubt that the criminal standard of proof must be applied to subsections (2) and (3) [of s. 23]'); see also *Case* [1991] Crim LR 192. The standard of proof to be achieved by the defence is the ordinary civil standard of proof on a balance of probability (*Mattey* [1995] 2 Cr App R 409). All of these authorities, it is submitted, continue to apply to the new provisions. **F16.5**

Unfitness to be a Witncss Section 116(2)(b) of the CJA 2003 applies not only to the physical act of attending at court, but also to the capacity of the witness when there to give evidence, and includes unfitness through any mental condition. Evidence indicating a medical condition made worse by stress, but not indicating clearly that the witness is unfit, is not sufficient (*McEwan v DPP* (2007) 171 JP 308). Under the previous legislation, which was in similar terms, when a witness was unable to recollect relevant events, and medical evidence established that the cause was a mental disorder giving rise to great anxiety and failure of recall when under stress, the conditions of admissibility were satisfied (*Setz-Dempsey* (1994) 98 Cr App R 23). Other pertinent authorities under the 1988 Act include *Elliott* (2003) *The Times*, 15 May 2003, where it was held that, where the defence can point to proper grounds for wishing to cross-examine a doctor who testifies to the unfitness of a patient, it is right to make an opportunity available for them to do so. The effect of the witness's mental condition at the time the statement was made is, of course, a factor relevant to whether it should be excluded under s. 123 (see **F16.12**). The sudden unfitness of a witness who is hospitalised may be good **F16.6**

reason for refusing an adjournment, but not for refusing to consider an application under s. 116 (*CPS v Uxbridge Magistrates* [2007] EWHC 205 (Admin)).

F16.7 **Outside the UK and Not Reasonably Practicable to Secure Attendance or Cannot be Found after Reasonable Steps** These two conditions also closely follow the provisions of the CJA 1988, s. 23, so that the following authorities, decided under that legislation, continue to be applicable.

In *Castillo* [1996] 1 Cr App R 438 the Court of Appeal held that there were three considerations involved in the issue whether it is reasonably practicable for a witness to attend. The mere fact that it is possible for a witness to come does not answer the question. The court has to consider the importance of the evidence the witness could give, the expense and inconvenience of securing attendance and the weight to be given to the reasons put forward for non-attendance. The court also suggested a consideration of the prejudice to the defence that might arise if prosecution evidence were to be admitted, but this would appear more naturally to be a consideration relevant to the exercise of the court's exclusionary powers (now confined to the PACE 1984, s. 78: see **F16.17** and the powers referred to at **F16.2**). In *French* (1993) 97 Cr App R 421, it was stressed that, in a case where there was a long history of attempts by the prosecution to secure the attendance of the witness, it was not helpful to ask when, if ever, the witness's attendance might be secured; the matter should be considered as it stood at the date of the application. In *Gyima* [2007] EWCA Crim 429, it was held proper to consider where the witness was a child, the refusal of his parents to co-operate with the prosecution's efforts to secure attendance. In *Hurst* [1995] 1 Cr App R 82, the words 'reasonably practicable' were said to involve a consideration of the normal steps that would be taken to secure the attendance of a witness, and that cost was a relevant factor. As to the steps it may be reasonably practicable to take, see also *Maloney* [1994] Crim LR 525, *Gonzalez de Orango* [1992] Crim LR 180 (a case decided under the PACE 1984, s. 68); and *Holman* [1995] Crim LR 80 (in which Bank of Ireland employees declined to attend the trial without an order of the Irish court and it was held that the statutory conditions were plainly made out). The provision is not intended for use where the prosecution have failed to monitor the witness's availability prior to trial and are then taken by surprise by absence abroad of which they should have been aware (*Bray* (1988) 88 Cr App R 354, decided under the PACE 1984, s. 68). In such cases, the question of what is reasonably practicable must be considered over a longer period than what was practicable on the day of the trial.

In *C & K* [2006] EWCA Crim 197, it was held that the expression 'reasonably practicable' in s. 116(2)(c) was to be judged on the basis of the steps taken, or not taken, to secure the attendance of a witness living abroad who was also a suspect in the case and who had suddenly changed his mind about giving evidence for the prosecution. Issues of admissibility under s. 116 were also inextricably linked to questions of fairness in relation to the court's discretionary powers under the PACE 1984, s. 78 (see **F16.17**) and the CJA 2003, s. 126 (see **F16.56**); in such cases there was likely to be a need to consider, in the interests of fairness, the reason for the change of heart and the viability of alternative modes of giving evidence whereby the witness would be subject to cross-examination. (See also *Radak* [1999] 1 Cr App R 187, decided under the 1988 Act.)

The need for the prosecution to satisfy the criminal standard of proof was stressed in *Case* [1991] Crim LR 192, where the only 'evidence' to support the contention that the maker of the statement was out of the country was the statement itself (which was, of course, inadmissible hearsay until proved otherwise), and there was no evidence at all on the issue of whether it would have been practicable to secure the attendance of the maker at the trial. Holding that the statement ought not to have been admitted, the Court of Appeal pointed out that, had the matter been approached properly and with the criminal standard of proof in mind, it was likely that evidence could have been found that would have secured the admissibility of the statement. In *Mattey* [1995] 2 Cr App R 409, where the statement, which was tendered by the defence, had only to satisfy the condition on a balance of probabilities, it was held inadmissible in part because hearsay was relied on in support of it, but the hearsay may have been admissible evidence of the state of mind of the maker, so that *Case* was distinguishable. In any event, it should be noted that there is no bar to the use of a statement by one witness that is itself admissible to prove the inability of another witness to attend the trial (*Castillo* [1996] 1 Cr App R 438). A letter written by a diplomat who is within the UK does not fall within s. 23(2)(b) of the 1988 Act (now s. 116(2)(c)) even though the writer enjoys diplomatic immunity from compulsion to testify (*Jiminez-Paez* (1994) 98 Cr App R 239).

In *Coughlan* [1999] 5 Arch News 2, the court was concerned with the interpretation of s. 23(3)(c) (now s. 116(2)(d)), when a witness cannot be found after taking all reasonable steps. As with a witness who is outside the country, it was said that it was relevant to consider the importance of the evidence and the cost implications, although the seriousness of the offence was said not to be relevant. In reality, of course, the resources devoted to tracing witnesses will necessarily take account of the seriousness of the offence. *Coughlan* was considered in *Henry* [2003] EWCA Crim 1296, where D, an associate of the deceased who had made a statement of apparently marginal relevance regarding her murder, had been deported before the trial, leaving a contact address in Jamaica from which he subsequently disappeared. At trial it emerged for the first time that the defence involved a suggestion that D was involved in the murder; however, what constituted 'reasonable steps' had to be assessed in light of the expected importance of D's evidence. In particular, the prosecution could not be expected to attempt to delay the deportation of an overstayer who has provided an overseas address, unless it ought reasonably to have been apparent that he could have given important evidence.

Fear The condition regarding proof of fear has been significantly reworked from that which originally appeared in the CJA 1988, s. 23. The points of distinction are as follows. First, it is no longer necessary that the statement be made to a person in authority. Secondly, it is made explicit that the condition is satisfied where a witness is called to give oral evidence but does not cover the relevant matter in the statement (cf. *Ashford Magistrates' Court, ex parte Hilden* [1993] 2 WLR 529 and *Waters* (1997) 161 JP 249). The previous statement of a hostile prosecution witness who is motivated simply by the desire to protect the accused, rather than by fear, remains outside the purview of the section, but may be admissible under the CJA 2003, s. 119 (see **F6.19**). Thirdly, s. 116(3) makes it clear that fear is to be 'widely construed', with the result that courts are now 'ill-advised to seek to test the basis of fear by calling witnesses before them' (Davies [2007] 2 All ER 1070). Fourthly, a specific leave requirement is introduced to enable the court to inquire whether the circumstances are such that the statement ought to be admitted in the interests of justice: s. 116(4), a vestige of the leave requirement of the CJA 1988, s. 26. **F16.8**

In *Doherty* (2007) 171 JP 79 a man was injured in a scuffle on a train crowded with football supporters. N, the brother of the injured man, identified the accused as having made an unprovoked attack on the victim, who remembered little of the attack. It was held that leave had properly been given to admit N's statement under s. 116(2)(e), on the strength of further oral and written statements by N that he had received a series of anonymous and implicitly threatening phone calls which appeared to be connected with the trial and in consequence of which he feared for his family's safety. This was sufficient to satisfy the widely drawn 'fear' condition; the question whether the fear was justified was a matter going to the 'interests of justice' test under s. 116(4) (see **F16.9**). Under the previous law, the proof of fear by admissible evidence was a matter which gave rise to difficulty not adverted to in *Doherty*, but it is submitted that the principles remain unchanged. In *Neill v North Antrim Magistrates' Court* [1992] 1 WLR 1221, two boys made statements to the police in which they claimed to have witnessed an assault and to have identified one of the perpetrators. However, they did not attend the subsequent committal proceedings, and evidence was given by a police officer that the boys' mothers had told him that the boys were too afraid to attend. The resident magistrate admitted the boys' statements under art. 3(3)(b) of the Criminal Justice (Evidence, Etc.) (Northern Ireland) Order 1988 (SI 1988 No. 1847), which corresponded to the CJA 1988, s. 23. The House of Lords held that the statements should not have been received because the evidence of the officer was hearsay, being based on what he had been told by the mothers of the boys and not by the boys themselves. If the boys had communicated their fears to him directly he could have given evidence of what they had told him under the 'long-established law that a person's declaration of his contemporaneous state of mind is admissible to prove the existence of that state of mind', per Lord Mustill at p. 1228 following *Blastland* [1986] AC 41 (see now the CJA 2003, s. 118(1)). However, the point was also made that, even had such evidence been available, a court would be cautious about whether it was in the interests of justice to admit documentary evidence of identification or recognition that formed the principal element in the prosecution's case: a point that might now be made with equal force in relation to the risk of unfairness under s. 116(4) (see **F16.9**). The need for due proof of fear was also accepted in *Waters* (1997) 161 JP 249, in which the demeanour of the witness (who testified at a *voir dire* after giving incomplete evidence at trial) was a material factor to which the trial judge rightly had regard. Some of the authorities under the old legislation are in conflict: see, e.g., *Rutherford* [1998] Crim LR 490, *Belmarsh Magistrates' Court, ex parte Gilligan* [1998] 1 Cr App R 14, *Greer* [1998] Crim LR 572.

As to proof of fear by hearsay evidence forming part of the *res gestae*, see **F16.28**. An alternative might be to admit the proof of the witness's fear under the CJA 2003, s. 114(1)(d) ('the interests of justice' exception: see **F16.20**).

The evidence of fear must relate to the relevant time. In *McCoy* [1999] All ER (D) 1410, [2000] 6 Arch News 2, M was charged with 'glassing' B. B failed to attend the trial on the first day. B told a police officer that he had been threatened; although he agreed to attend on the following day, he failed to do so. It was held that there was 'at very least a question mark' whether B's failure to attend on the second day was truly due to fear. To the same effect is *H* [2001] Crim LR 815. The alleged victim of a kidnapping made a statement two months before the trial indicating his fear of reprisals and his intention to abscond, but he in fact remained in the area and was arrested in connection with drugs offences. No evidence of continuing fear was adduced at the trial. Stressing that the fear must be judged at the time of the trial, and that the out-of-date evidence was not by itself sufficient, the Court of Appeal also acknowledged that there might be a 'degree of sensible give and take', for example when a ruling on admissibility was sought in advance of trial to enable counsel for the prosecution to decide how the case should be opened to the jury. Although these are decisions under the CJA 1988, s. 23, they would appear still to be authoritative.

F16.9 **Leave in Fear Cases** In deciding whether to give leave under the CJA 2003, s. 116(4), to admit the statement of a fearful witness, the court is expressly directed to take into account, along with any other circumstances it regards as relevant, the content of the statement, the risk that its admission or exclusion will result in unfairness having regard to the difficulty of challenging the statement if the relevant person does not give oral evidence, and the possibility that a special measures direction under the YJCEA 1999 could be made in relation to that person. This last condition directs the court's attention to the possibility that fear may in some cases be assuaged by the application of special measures, for example, by the use of screens, live-link or video-recorded evidence. These alternatives are preferable to hearsay because the witness is made available to be cross-examined. Thus in *Robinson v Sutton Coldfield Magistrates' Court* [2006] EWHC 307 (Admin), where the complainant in a case of assault (R's former partner) had begun a new life and did not wish R to be able to trace her, it was necessary for the justices, before receiving her evidence, to consider whether any of the 1999 Act's special measures might meet the case. The possibility that special arrangements could have been made to convey her to court without enabling R to discover where she was living might also have been relevant to the overall question of the interests of justice. In *Doherty* (2007) 171 JP 79 (see **F16.8**), the exercise to be undertaken under s. 116(4) was described as 'not strictly an exercise of discretion but something akin to it', and one which the judge is in the best position to perform. Issues of trial fairness, including an alleged infringement of the ECHR, Article 6(3)(d), can conveniently be subsumed within the s. 116(4) inquiry. Thus, in *Doherty,* the court approved the statement in *Sellick* [2005] 1 WLR 3257, that there is no absolute rule that an accused's Article 6(3(d) rights are infringed by the admission of compelling evidence which is the sole or decisive evidence in the case. (See also as to Article 6(3)(d) *Grant v The State* [2007] 1 AC 1 and compare the similar issues which may be raised in respect of other forms of hearsay tendered by the prosecution under s. 116 in respect of which exclusion is sought under the PACE 1984, s. 78 (see **F16.17**)).

Intimidation If the reason for the witness's failure to give evidence in person is that he was intimidated by or on behalf of the accused, who then contests the admissibility of the statement for the prosecution, the strong principle that the accused should not profit from his own wrong has been a factor in the court's decisions under the pre-2003 law in relation to the ECHR, Article 6 (see *Montgomery* [2002] EWCA Crim 1655, *Harvey* [1998] 10 Arch News 2 and *M* [2003] 2 Cr App R 322) and seems likely to continue to do so. In *M* the court considered that to refuse to admit hearsay evidence where an essential or the only witness is kept away by fear would be an intolerable result and would encourage intimidation. On the facts of the case, however, it was wrong, and a breach of Article 6, to admit the hearsay evidence of an essential witness, which was potentially 'completely flawed' and which may have been motivated by the maker's desire to blame M, a person unfit to plead, for an offence in which he was himself implicated. In *Arnold* [2004] EWCA Crim 1293, the Court of Appeal warned prosecutors that the problems posed by intimidation of witnesses by organised criminals did not provide a licence to prosecutors to resort to proof by hearsay: 'Very great care must be taken in each and every case to ensure that attention is paid to the letter and spirit of the Convention and judges should not easily be persuaded that it is in the interests of justice to permit evidence to be read'. The note of caution expressed in *Arnold* was endorsed in *Sellick* [2005] 1 WLR 3257. However, the court in that case felt the need to register an important point which was not fully taken into account in *Arnold,* and took a strong and, it is submitted, welcome line in respect of cases where intimidation is either clearly proved or highly probable. If an accused has been clearly shown to have kept a witness away by fear, he cannot complain that his Article 6(3)(d) right has been infringed, since he is the author of his inability to examine the witness at trial. Even in cases where intimidation is no more than a high probability, it cannot be right to have an absolute rule that, where the evidence adduced is the sole or decisive evidence, it cannot be read without infringing the accused's Article 6 rights. Such a rule would serve to ensure that the more subtle and less easily established forms of intimidation would provide the accused with the opportunity of excluding the most material evidence against them. *Sellick* was approved in *Doherty* (2007) 171 JP 79, decided under the CJA 2003. See also *Boulton* [2007] EWCA Crim 942, where ample evidence of fear was provided by the accused's attempts to 'scupper' the prosecution case by intimidating witnesses. F16.10

Authorities such as *Cole* [1990] 1 WLR 866, decided under the CJA 1988, remain relevant: the presence or absence of other evidence enabling the evidence to be challenged is relevant to the calculation of what has been lost to the party deprived of the opportunity to cross-examine. In *Robinson v Sutton Coldfield Magistrates' Court* [2006] EWHC 307 (Admin), the magistrates were entitled to take account of the unchallenged photographic evidence of the assault, and of a partial admission by R, who further admitted that the complainant was someone who 'does not lie'. Further, although the court cannot require to be told whether the accused intends to give evidence or call witnesses, it is not bound to assess the possibility of challenging the statement upon the basis that the accused will do neither of these things. In *Doherty* (2007) 171 JP 79 the court was influenced not only by the strength of the other evidence of the assault but also by the prospect of witnesses being called who could support the accused's version of events. See also *Price* [1991] Crim LR 707, *Samuel* [1992] Crim LR 189, *Moore* [1992] Crim LR 882 and *Grafton [1995] Crim LR 61.*

F16.11 **Competence** A statement by a witness who lacks testimonial competence at the time the statement was made may not be received under the CJA 2003, s. 116 (s. 123). Contrast *D* [2002] QB 90, where a witness suffering from a degenerative mental condition rendering her unfit to give evidence at trial was also probably incompetent to give evidence at the time when her statement was taken. On the question whether the language in s. 23 of the CJA 1988 required she be competent at this point, the Court of Appeal were doubtful that it did, but were confident that the impact of the witness's illness on the admissibility of her statement could be fully and fairly dealt with by the application of the court's exclusionary powers.

F16.12 **Credibility** Section 124 of the CJA 2003 (see **F16.55**) applies in relation to matters bearing on the credibility of the makers of hearsay statements admissible under s. 116.

Business and Other Documents

F16.13 **Criminal Justice Act 2003, s. 117**

(1) In criminal proceedings a statement contained in a document is admissible as evidence of any matter stated if—
   (a) oral evidence given in the proceedings would be admissible as evidence of that matter,
   (b) the requirements of subsection (2) are satisfied, and
   (c) the requirements of subsection (5) are satisfied, in a case where subsection (4) requires them to be.

(2) The requirements of this subsection are satisfied if—
   (a) the document or the part containing the statement was created or received by a person in the course of a trade, business, profession or other occupation, or as the holder of a paid or unpaid office,
   (b) the person who supplied the information contained in the statement (the relevant person) had or may reasonably be supposed to have had personal knowledge of the matters dealt with, and
   (c) each person (if any) through whom the information was supplied from the relevant person to the person mentioned in paragraph (a) received the information in the course of a trade, business, profession or other occupation, or as the holder of a paid or unpaid office.

(3) The persons mentioned in paragraphs (a) and (b) of subsection (2) may be the same person.

(4) The additional requirements of subsection (5) must be satisfied if the statement—
   (a) was prepared for the purposes of pending or contemplated criminal proceedings, or for a criminal investigation, but
   (b) was not obtained pursuant to a request under section 7 of the Crime (International Co-operation) Act 2003 or an order under paragraph 6 of schedule 13 to the Criminal Justice Act 1988 (which relate to overseas evidence).

(5) The requirements of this subsection are satisfied if—
   (a) any of the five conditions mentioned in section 116(2) is satisfied (absence of relevant person etc), or
   (b) the relevant person cannot reasonably be expected to have any recollection of the matters dealt with in the statement (having regard to the length of time since he supplied the information and all other circumstances).

(6) A statement is not admissible under this section if the court makes a direction to that effect under subsection (7).

(7) The court may make a direction under this subsection if satisfied that the statement's reliability as evidence for the purpose for which it is tendered is doubtful in view of—
   (a) its contents,
   (b) the source of the information contained in it,
   (c) the way in which or the circumstances in which the information was supplied or received, or
   (d) the way in which or the circumstances in which the document concerned was created or received.

Section 117 broadly corresponds to the CJA 1988, s. 24, which it replaces.

Business or Other Documents Section 117 of the CJA 2003 extends, as did its predecessor, s. 24 of the CJA 1998, to documents created or received by a person in the course of a trade, business, profession or other occupation, or as the holder of a paid or unpaid office. Section 117 goes further in that it applies also to parts of documents so created, when the statement in issue is included in that part (for the meaning of 'statement' see s. 115(2) at **F15.1**) In *Clowes* [1992] 3 All ER 440, decided under the CJA 1988, s. 24, transcripts of interviews between the liquidators of companies and persons involved with the companies were held to have been 'received' by the liquidators in the course of their profession and as holders of the office of liquidator. Documents of a non-commercial nature such as a National Health Service hospital's records are clearly admissible, as is the transcript of the evidence given by a witness at an earlier trial, which may be admitted at a retrial even though the court is plainly not a business in any sense (*Lockley* [1995] 2 Cr App R 554). Similarly, a police custody record was admitted under s. 24 in *Hogan* [1997] Crim LR 349. **F16.14**

Because s. 116, like s. 24 before it, applies only to documentary evidence, the compiler of documents for use in criminal proceedings who leaves out important details of information he has gathered from others who do not give evidence cannot simply supplement his record with oral hearsay testimony (*Hinds* [1993] Crim LR 528). Such evidence may however be more readily admissible under the CJA 2003 than under the CJA 1988, either under s. 116 or s. 114(1)(d).

In *Foxley* [1995] 2 Cr App R 523, also decided under the CJA 1988, s. 24, the documents in question were copies of credit notes and payments allegedly made by overseas companies to F, who was accused of receiving them corruptly. They had been obtained by letters of request to the authorities in the relevant countries. It was objected, *inter alia,* that no evidence was available from the creator as to whether these documents had come into existence in the course of a business etc., but it was held to be the intention of the statute that the court be allowed to draw relevant inferences from the documents themselves and from the way in which they had been placed before the court. As Professor Sir John Smith pointed out in his commentary at [1995] Crim LR 637, the court failed to note that the documents in question were not hearsay evidence, so that recourse to s. 24 was not necessary. However, the point made would have been valid in relation to true hearsay evidence. In *Department of Environment, Food and Rural Affairs v Atkinson* [2002] EWHC 2028 (Admin), s. 24 was held, applying *Foxley,* to have been applicable where the label on a bottle was the only proof that it contained a veterinary medicinal product, the possession and supply of which was regulated by statute.

Personal Knowledge The 'supplier' of the information (who must have, etc., personal knowledge of the matters dealt with under the CJA 2003, s. 117(2)(b)) may also be the person who 'creates' the document under s. 117(2)(c) (s. 117(3)). Thus, for example, a note made by an operator working for a paging company that messages had been left for a customer would be admissible (as in *Rock* [1994] Crim LR 843, decided under the 1988 Act) as a first-hand hearsay statement. Where such a document is received in evidence under s. 117, it is not necessary, as it is under s. 116 (see **F16.4**), to prove the unavailability of the maker of the statement. **F16.15**

Section 117 may also be invoked where several degrees of hearsay are involved. Provided each of the persons through whom the information was supplied received it in the course of a trade etc. (s. 117(2)(c)), the facts stated in the document are admissible. In *Maher v DPP* (2006) 170 JP 441 a note which had been made (and lost) of a car number plate could not be adduced as second-hand evidence under s. 117 because a relevant passer-on of information had not received it in the course of their trade etc. The evidence was, however, admitted under s. 121(1)(c) (see **F16.54**) as multiple hearsay, on the ground that the value of the evidence, taking into account its apparent reliability, was so high that the interests of justice required admissibility. This apparent incongruity can be explained on the basis that admissibility under s. 117 is 'automatic', hence the need to demonstrate the degree of reliability inherent in the making of a commercial type of record. The ruling in favour of admissibility in *Maher* is based on the determination that the particular record, though not automatically admissible, was (on investigation of its specific properties) sufficiently reliable and important to be received.

A document produced by a computer without any human intervention cannot be said to contain information 'supplied by a person' with 'personal knowledge' (*Pettigrew* (1980) 71 Cr App R 39). However, as such a document is unlikely to constitute hearsay evidence, it will not matter that the conditions of the exception cannot be satisfied (see *Wood* (1982) 76 Cr App R 23, considered at **F15.17**).

The statement is admissible only as evidence of any matter stated of which 'oral evidence given in the proceedings' would be admissible, and it is submitted that the intention is to prevent the introduction of evidence that contravenes a rule of admissibility other than the hearsay rule, for example, the rule against evidence of bad character. It cannot be a valid objection to the admissibility of evidence under s. 117 that an intermediary through whom the information was supplied could not have given evidence of the fact without contravening the hearsay rule, otherwise the section could not be made to apply to second-hand hearsay, and it is clearly meant to do so (see s. 121 at **F16.54**).

F16.16 **Unavailability of Maker of Statement Prepared for Purposes of Criminal Proceedings or Investigation** It is not generally necessary to show grounds why the maker of a statement should not be called before tendering his statement in evidence under the CJA 2003, s. 117. The only exceptions are those statements prepared for the purposes of pending or contemplated criminal proceedings, or of a criminal investigation (s. 117(4)(a)), which are not obtained pursuant to a request or order specified in s. 117(4)(b). Here, s. 117(5) applies, and it is necessary to establish either:

(1) one of the reasons for not calling the maker that apply in the case of a s. 116 statement (s. 117(5)(a): see **F16.5** ***et seq.***); or
(2) that the maker cannot reasonably be expected (having regard to the time that has elapsed since he made the statement and to all the circumstances) to have any recollection of the matters dealt with in the statement (s. 117(5)(b)).

In *Humphris* (2005) 169 JP 441, an attempt was made to use s. 117 where the prosecution sought to establish the *modus operandi* of previous admissible sexual offences committed by H. The details of the offences were recorded by police officers and other employees all acting under a duty, and the suggestion was that they had the necessary personal knowledge to be the 'relevant person' for the purposes of s. 117(2)(b) and (5). While the court found no difficulty in using s. 117 to establish the fact of conviction, the details of the method used were in each case dependent on information originally supplied by the complainant, who was thus the 'relevant person'. The correct method of proceeding would therefore have been, as it was before the CJA 2003, to take a statement from the complainant. This might, depending on the circumstances, have been admissible under s. 116 (see **F16.4**). See, however, *Ainscough* (2006) 170 JP 517, drawing attention to the fact that a conviction might be complicated by the fact that an accused was sentenced on a different basis as a result of a plea, proferred and accepted by the court at the time. This would affect the fairness of admitting the original complainant's evidence as hearsay and would raise numerous satellite issues about the detail of what occurred (see also **F12.25**).

In *Bedi* (1992) 95 Cr App R 21 the 'lost and stolen' reports maintained by a bank in respect of credit cards it had issued were held not to fall within the equivalent provisions of the CJA 1988. An examination of the reports disclosed that they were kept for the proper conduct of the bank's business, not for criminal proceedings. In *Hogan* [1997] Crim LR 349 it was assumed, surely rightly, that a police custody record fell within the equivalent provisions of the 1988 Act.

Section 117(5)(b) may apply where a witness is unable to recollect one part of a longer statement but is able to give evidence as to the rest (*Carrington* [1994] Crim LR 438, in which the witness's recollection was supplemented in relation to a car registration number that she had forgotten, in circumstances where she was not entitled to refresh her memory from the statement). See as to the evidence that may satisfy this condition, *Crayden* [1978] 1 WLR 604 at p. 608 (decided under the Criminal Evidence Act 1965) and *Feest* [1987] Crim LR 766 (decided under the PACE 1984).

A difficulty in the construction of the CJA 1988 arose because on a literal construction the additional requirements of the equivalent of s. 117(5) appeared to be imposed not on the supplier of the information but (where the two were different) on the creator of the document. It is clear from s. 117(2) and (5) that the 'relevant person' whose absence must be accounted for is the supplier of the information.

Discretionary Exclusion under the PACE 1984, s. 78 of Statements Automatically Admissible under the CJA 2003, ss. 116 and 117

The CJA 2003 repeals the provisions of the CJA 1988, ss. 25 and 26, under which the court controlled the use of otherwise admissible statements in the interests of justice. Under the CJA 2003, the appropriate mechanism for exclusion of prosecution evidence that poses a threat to the interests of justice is most likely to be the PACE 1984, s. 78. In *C &K* [2006] EWCA Crim 197 the Court of Appeal was keen to point out that the satisfaction of (in that case) s. 116 was only 'the first stage in a ruling upon the admissibility of the statement': ultimately the availability of evidence to the prosecution remains subject to the court's discretionary powers. The court referred specifically, though without elaboration, to both s. 78 and the discretion under the CJA 2003, s. 126 (see **F16.56**). The application of the CJA 2003, s. 126, has yet to be tested. Unlike the PACE 1984, s. 78, it applies to both prosecution and defence evidence, but appears to be aimed more at hearsay of trivial import than at the admission of unfair evidence, which is the more important concern. **F16.17**

If this be correct, and s. 78 remains the vehicle for the exclusion of unfair prosecution evidence, there is no corresponding mechanism for the exclusion of unfair defence evidence which is otherwise admissible under s. 116 or s. 117 so that, for example, a first-hand hearsay statement by an identifiable individual who has since disappeared and cannot be found is automatically admissible for the defence under s. 116. There is some reason to fear that the automatic admissibility provisions may lead to the fabrication of hearsay evidence, despite the fact that such fabrications (like false alibis) may rebound on their users.

Fairness-based arguments for the exclusion of hearsay evidence typically emphasise the loss of the important right to cross-examine the absent witness. In *Grant v The State* [2007] 1 AC 1 the Privy Council, rejecting a challenge to the constitutionality of a similar Jamaican scheme for the reception of hearsay evidence, surveyed both the English authorities and the Strasbourg jurisprudence dealing with the ECHR, Article 6(3)(d) and the right of an accused person 'to examine or have examined witnesses against him'. Their lordships emphasised that the hearsay rule had always been subject to exceptions which formed inroads on the normal right to cross-examine; the guiding principle in both jurisdictions was that a new exception must not compromise the overall fairness of the proceedings. The Privy Council endorsed the approach of the English courts in dealing with Article 6(3)(d), namely that it did not impose an absolute prohibition on the admission of hearsay but did require a full consideration of whether the legitimate interests of the accused have been safeguarded in the context of the proceedings as a whole. The role of the judge's discretion to exclude evidence which poses a threat to these interests is of paramount importance, as is, where the evidence is admitted, a proper direction from the trial judge on the correct approach to hearsay evidence. It is submitted that the approach of the English courts to the reconciliation of the strict rules of admissibility with the need to ensure a fair trial, as endorsed in *Grant v The State*, will not (indeed, cannot) change as a result of the introduction of 'automatic admissibility' in ss. 116 and 117. The substitution of the PACE 1984, s. 78, as the vehicle for protecting fairness does not affect the matters of principle at stake.

F16.18 **Hearsay, Loss of Right to Cross-examine and Fair Trial Provisions** Before the implementation of the CJA 2003, the English courts had on a number of occasions addressed the reconciliation of the scheme for receiving hearsay evidence with the ECHR, Article 6(3)(d). The use of hearsay evidence for the prosecution does not of itself contravene the 'fair trial' provisions of the ECHR, provided the court retains the power to assess the interests of justice by reference to the risk of unfairness to the accused (*Gokal* [1997] 2 Cr App R 266, and see *Thomas* [1998] Crim LR 887). As a rule, the accused should be given an adequate and proper opportunity to challenge and question a witness against him, either at the time the statement was made or at some later stage of proceedings (*Thomas, Kostovski v Netherlands* (1990) 12 EHRR 434). Article 6 is most likely to be breached where the result of admitting the evidence would be a conviction resting heavily on a disputed and untested hearsay statement (cf. *Luca v Italy* [2001] Crim LR 747, where it was said that 'where the conviction is both solely or to a decisive degree based on depositions that have been made by a person who the accused has had no opportunity to examine or have examined, whether during the investigation or at the trial, the rights of the defence are restricted to an extent that is incompatible with Article 6'). In *PS v Germany* [2002] Crim LR 312, a violation was found where a conviction of sexual abuse of an eight-year-old was founded on evidence reported to the court by the child's mother and a police officer. Although the decision not to call the child was based on apparently sound concerns for her mental health, the defence were unable effectively to challenge this important evidence. The consequence in many sexual cases will be that, even if the complainant falls within s. 116 on grounds of ill-health (see **F16.6**), it will be inappropriate to allow the evidence to be given under that provision if it is possible instead to afford the defence the right to cross-examine. In some cases this may be achieved by using the 'special measures' of the YJCEA 1999 to protect the complainant while giving evidence. (Compare s. 116(4)(c) (see **F16.9**), requiring appropriate consideration of special measures before leave is given where a witness is in fear.) In *SN v Sweden* [2002] Crim LR 831 the use of special measures was sanctioned provided that the right of the defence to challenge the evidence was also safeguarded. Such alternatives may not always be possible, however. In *D* [2003] QB 90, the evidence of a complainant with Alzheimer's and 'long standing complex delusional problems' was held admissible under the CJA 1988 on charges of attempted rape and indecent assault, one reason being that there was some material upon which the defence could challenge the evidence. The issue of witness competence also raised in *D*, and in the similar case of *Sed* [2004] 1 WLR 3218, would now be a matter going to the admissibility of the statement, not to the power of the court to exclude otherwise admissible evidence (see **F16.11** and the CJA 2003, s. 124 at **F16.55**). The proper vehicle for the admission of the statement of an incompetent person, where this is in the interests of justice, is now s. 114(1)(d) (see **F16.20**).

Where the sole witness to a crime has died, the strong public interest in receiving the evidence may be more significant, on balance, than the interest of the defence in cross-examining. In *Al-Khawaja* [2006] 1 WLR 1078, the deceased complainant was one of two of A's patients who described indecent conduct by him in the course of hypnotherapy. Two other women gave supporting evidence and there was no suggestion of collusion. Given that A was able to attack the deceased's statement on ground of inconsistency with other evidence and by employing expert evidence in relation to the altered mental state brought about by hypnosis, the court held that A's rights under Article 6 were not infringed provided that the judge gave (as he did) an adequate direction about the risks of acting on untested hearsay (see **F16.5**).

The right to challenge hearsay evidence may be particularly important in cases where the weakness of the evidence is generally acknowledged, as with identification or recognition evidence. Where such evidence is hearsay and constitutes the principal element in the prosecution case, the House of Lords has said that courts will be very reluctant to receive the evidence (*Neill v North Antrim Magistrates' Court* [1992] 1 WLR 1221 per Lord Mustill at p. 1229).

Where the prosecutor has delayed proceedings and in consequence a witness is unavailable to testify, the court may exclude the witness's statement on the basis that the prosecution should have proceeded when the witness was available (*French* (1993) 97 Cr App R 421, and see *Radak* [1999] 1 Cr App R 187).

Fairness and Records Where a statement tendered in evidence under the CJA 2003, s. 117, is not a statement prepared for the purpose of criminal proceedings, the absence of any opportunity to cross-examine the maker is likely to be of less importance, even where the statement relied upon is crucial to the case for the prosecution. Thus, in *Schreiber* [1988] Crim LR 112, decided under the Criminal Evidence Act 1965, it was held that customs documents compiled abroad could be given in evidence without calling the maker, even though the documents were the most cogent evidence of fraud by the accused. **F16.19**

CRIMINAL JUSTICE ACT 2003: HEARSAY ADMISSIBLE IN THE INTERESTS OF JUSTICE

Criminal Justice Act 2003, s. 114 **F16.20**

(1) . . . [a] statement not made in oral evidence in the proceedings is admissible as evidence of any matter stated if, but only if—

. . .

(d) the court is satisfied that it is in the interests of justice for it to be admissible.

(2) In deciding whether a statement not made in oral evidence should be admitted under subsection (1)(d), the court must have regard to the following factors (and to any others it considers relevant)—

(a) how much probative value the statement has (assuming it to be true) in relation to a matter in issue in the proceedings, or how valuable it is for the understanding of other evidence in the case;

(b) what other evidence has been, or can be, given on the matter or evidence mentioned in paragraph (a);

(c) how important the matter or evidence mentioned in paragraph (a) is in the context of the case as a whole;

(d) the circumstances in which the statement was made;

(e) how reliable the maker of the statement appears to be;

(f) how reliable the evidence of the making of the statement appears to be;

(g) whether oral evidence of the matter stated can be given and, if not, why it cannot;

(h) the amount of difficulty involved in challenging the statement;

(i) the extent to which that difficulty would be likely to prejudice the party facing it.

Section 114(2) is directed to the assessment of the quality of the evidence as well as the importance of admitting it. It follows that there is less scope for the application of s. 78 of the PACE 1984 or the CJA 2003, s. 126 (see **F16.56**) than in relation to s. 116 (see **F16.3**). For an example of the application of s. 114(2)(d) and multiple hearsay under s. 121, see *Walker* [2007] EWCA Crim 1698.

Where s. 114(2) directs the court to have regard to certain factors, it does not follow that a judge is bound to reach a conclusion on all of them. Proper investigation of all nine factors would be a lengthy process, which the CJA 2003 does not require. All that is required is the exercise of judgment in the light of the factors specifically identified, together with any others considered by the judge to be relevant (*T* [2006] 2 Cr App R 222). An exercise of judgment will be interfered with on appeal only if it has involved the application of incorrect principles or is outside the band of legitimate decision (*Finch* [2007] 1 WLR 1645; *Musone* [2007] EWCA Crim 1237). In considering factors (e) and (f) it is not permissible to reason that the jury may assess matters relating to reliability: the judge is specifically required to make an assessment.

Section 114(1)(d) cannot be used to admit multiple hearsay, which can be adduced only to the extent permitted by s. 121 (see **F16.54**). Section 121(1)(c) makes special provision for multiple hearsay to be admissible in the interests of justice (see, e.g., *Musone*).

Section 114 is most likely to be resorted to where evidence is otherwise unlikely to be admissible, or to provide a supporting argument where it is not clearly so. In *Isichei* (2006) 170 753 the prosecution sought to rely on a contemporaneous statement by a non-witness that he was telephoning 'Marvin' in order to provide a link with the accused, whose first name this was. The statement was argued to be non-hearsay under the CJA 2003, s. 115(3) (see **F15.13**), but, whether it was or not, the court was content that it should be admitted in the interests of justice.

In *Xhabri* [2006] 1 All ER 776, the prosecution case was that L, a Latvian girl, had been abducted and raped by D, and held prisoner for purposes of prostitution. The defence was that her actions were voluntary. The attempts she had made to secure her freedom included a variety of communications with family and friends in which she described her predicament in terms consistent with her evidence in court. The Court noted (at [34]) that:

> Prior to the 2003 Act there might have been some debate as to whether, and on what basis, such evidence could be admitted. Plainly it was in the interests of justice that such evidence should be admitted, not merely as evidence of how L was reacting but as evidence of the truth of the statements that she was making as to her predicament.

Some of the statements were also capable of being received under other exceptions — for example, the extended provision for the reception of evidence of recent complaint in s. 120 (see **F6.20**). In the case of first-hand hearsay statements, however, the alternative of admitting the evidence under s. 114(1)(d) was accepted by the Court. (One statement, which was second-hand, was capable of being received only under s. 121: see **F16.54**.) The Court specifically rejected an argument that s. 114(1)(d) was incompatible with the ECHR, Article 6, for, despite the breadth of the new provision, it remains subject to the duty to ensure the overall fairness of the trial.

Evidence which fails to satisfy the conditions of s. 116 (see **F16.4**) because of lack of diligence by the prosecutor in securing the necessary proof is unlikely to be admitted under s. 114(1)(d) (*McEwan v DPP* (2007) 171 JP 308).

Section 114(1)(d) may benefit either prosecution or defence. A difficult defence case will be that of the third-party confession, currently inadmissible where the maker is available to be called as a witness but neither side chooses to do so (cf. *Blastland* [1986] AC 41). In the absence of evidence that the statement is unreliable, a difficult decision has to be made balancing the probative value of the statement if true against the reason for not calling the maker. In *Finch* the accused sought to rely on a statement made as part of a confession by his erstwhile co-accused, R, who subsequently pleaded guilty. The effect of the plea was that R became a compellable, albeit reluctant, witness for F, and the trial judge's decision that the case was not within s. 114(1)(d) was upheld by the Court of Appeal. Whatever might be the case if R had been unavailable or had demonstrated good reason not to testify, it was said, 'it would not normally be in the interests of justice for evidence which the giver is unprepared to have tested to be put untested before the jury'. An alternative course would have been to invoke the hostile witness provisions of s. 119 (see **F6.33**). It is not clear whether, and if so to what extent, s. 114(1)(d) can be deployed to undermine the common-law rule that the out-of-court statement of one accused, which is not a confession, cannot be admitted. The issue has been considered in *M* [2007] EWCA Crim 219, where the Court of Appeal held that the CJA 2003 had shifted the consideration whether the interests of justice point to admissibility. In other recent decisions, however, the common-law rule has been adhered to (*Williams* [2006] EWCA Crim 3300).

Section 114(1)(d) may provide practical assistance to the prosecution in a range of cases. Thus, for example, in *Lilley* [2003] EWCA Crim 1789, L was arrested for conspiracy to commit benefit fraud. To confirm a visual identification of L as the woman who had encashed benefits from stolen books, an exercise book was produced in which someone had been practising forged signatures and, to exclude the possibility that the book might belong to one of the other accused, the prosecution pointed to the fact that the words 'Sharon's book' were inscribed on the cover. The sole purpose of doing so was to rely on the writer's assertion of ownership: a difficult case at common law, but one that might be resolved in favour of the prosecution under s. 114(1)(d), given that L could easily give evidence to refute ownership. In *T* [2006] 2 Cr App R 222, s. 114(1)(d) was invoked in order to circumvent the common problem whereby the name of a suspect is supplied by a witness who knows it only because he has been told it by another. (If there may be a problem of multiple hearsay in the transmission of the name, the provision in play is s. 121: see **F16.54**.)

Warning as to Quality of Hearsay

As the opportunity to admit evidence under the new statutory exceptions grows, it is of paramount importance that a jury should be made aware of potential weaknesses in hearsay at the point when they come to assess its worth. In *Grant v The State* [2007] 1 AC 1, the Privy Council considered the elements of a direction on hearsay received under a similar statutory scheme to that under the CJA 2003. It is necessary to remind the jury, however obvious it may be to them, that the statement has not been verified on oath nor the author tested by cross-examination. The judge should point out the specific risks of relying on such evidence and invite the jury to scrutinise the evidence with particular care. Instructing the jury to give the statement such weight as they think fit is proper, but it is not very helpful if there is a risk that the jury, when presented with an apparently plausible statement by a person whose reliability and honesty they have no extraneous reason to doubt, may be inclined to give the statement more weight than the oral evidence they have heard. The jury's attention should be drawn to the context of all the other evidence, and if there are discrepancies between the statement and the evidence of other witnesses, the jury's attention should be specifically drawn to them. While failure to give such directions in respect of prosecution evidence will not necessarily render a trial unfair, it may do so, given the importance of the direction as a safeguard of the interests of the defence. **F16.21**

Authorities decided under the statutory schemes that preceded the CJA 2003 also stress the need for the court to assist in the evaluation of the quality of the statement (*Cole* [1990] 1 WLR 866, citing with approval the observations of Lord Griffiths in *Scott v The Queen* [1989] AC 1242). Thus, 'the weight to be attached to the inability to cross-examine and the magnitude of any consequential risk that the admission of the statement will result in unfairness to the accused will depend in part upon the court's assessment of the quality of the evidence shown in the statement'. *Cole* further requires the court to consider whether any potential unfairness may be effectively counterbalanced by a warning to the jury pointing out that the evidence had not been tested by cross-examination and drawing attention to its possible limitations. (In *Cole* the trial judge went even further and commented that the written statement could not possibly have been worth as much as the evidence of other witnesses, but this elaboration was rightly held to be unnecessary in *Greer* [1988] Crim LR 572.) *Cole* was applied in *Kennedy* [1992] Crim LR 64, where the issue was whether K, by fighting with his co-accused, H, was guilty of affray or was acting in self-defence. It was held that a statement by one M, who was the only independent witness to the fight and who had since died, was rightly admitted. It had been contended that M's evidence was flawed in that it was inconsistent with the testimony of both K and H but, as the Court of Appeal rightly pointed out, such inconsistency is not unusual in such cases, and it was sufficient for the trial judge to give the jury a warning of the disadvantages of not having M as a witness in the case. See also *Samuel* [1992] Crim LR 189 and *Kennedy* [1994] Crim LR 50, in which a statement made by W, the victim of an assault (who subsequently died of other causes), was held on balance to have been rightly admitted, notwithstanding that W was very drunk at the time of the incident and that there were important inconsistencies between his version of events and that of other witnesses. However, K's appeal was allowed because the judge had failed to stress these weaknesses when warning the jury how to approach W's statement. Compare *Thompson* [1999] Crim LR 747, in which it was held proper to admit, subject to a warning, the statement of the victim of a robbery notwithstanding that he was awaiting discharge from a hospital to which he had been admitted for drink-related mental problems. It is significant that there was substantial prosecution evidence apart from the victim's statement. In *McCoy* [1999] All ER (D) 1410, [2000] 6 Arch News 2, the statement of the victim of a serious attack, which provided the main evidence identifying his assailant, was held to have been wrongly received under the CJA 1988, s. 23.

The particular difficulty that arises in giving a warning where the evidence is tendered by the defence was considered in *Abiodun* [2003] EWCA Crim 2167, where a 'mild' direction 'which simply reminded the jury of what in any event would have been obvious to them, i.e. that the witnesses had not been cross-examined', was held not to have impinged on the fairness of the proceedings.

CRIMINAL JUSTICE ACT 2003: PRESERVED COMMON-LAW EXCEPTIONS

Admissibility of Public Documents at Common Law and under the Criminal Justice Act 2003

F16.22 The CJA 2003, s. 118, makes express provision to save the common law regarding the issue of certain public documents and information.

Criminal Justice Act 2003, s. 118

(1) The following rules of law are preserved.

Public information etc

Any rule of law under which in criminal proceedings—

(a) published works dealing with matters of a public nature (such as histories, scientific works, dictionaries and maps) are admissible as evidence of facts of a public nature stated in them,

(b) public documents (such as public registers, and returns made under public authority with respect to matters of public interest) are admissible as evidence of facts stated in them,

(c) records (such as the records of certain courts, treaties, Crown grants, pardons and commissions) are admissible as evidence of facts stated in them, or

(d) evidence relating to a person's age or date or place of birth may be given by a person without personal knowledge of the matter.

. . .

A document compiled by a public officer acting under a public duty to inquire and report facts of public interest, which is maintained in order that interested members of the public may have access to the information contained in it, is admissible at common law by way of exception to the hearsay rule as evidence of the facts stated (*Sturla v Freccia* (1880) 5 App Cas 623). Thus, for example, registers of baptisms, marriages and funerals are public documents, as are surveys of Crown Lands, and university records may prove the granting of degrees (*Collins v Carnegie* (1834) 1 A & E 695). Foreign registers may be public documents if the relevant conditions are satisfied (*Lyell v Kennedy* (1889) 14 App Cas 437; *Sturla v Freccia*). See also the Evidence (Foreign Dominion and Colonial Documents) Act 1933, s. 1 of which confers a power to declare that certain foreign registers are public documents.

One reason for the rule is the presumption that entries in such documents made by public officers are to be relied upon (*Irish Society v Bishop of Derry* (1846) 12 Cl & F 641, per Parke B). However, it is also the case that the rule is based on necessity: were it not for the admissibility of public documents, many facts occurring in the distant past would be incapable of proof.

In modern times the importance of the common-law rule has been overshadowed by various statutes rendering particular documents admissible, and (more importantly) by the CJA 2003, s. 117 (see **F16.14**), under which virtually all of the documents which were receivable under the common-law rule, and many that were not, are admissible.

Public Duty

The document must have been made in pursuance of what Lord Blackburn termed 'a judicial, or quasi-judicial, duty to inquire' (*Sturla v Freccia* (1880) 5 App Cas 623, at [643]). The duty must be imposed by virtue of a public office: thus, parish registers of baptisms, marriages and burials are public documents, whereas similar records compiled by other religious groups such as the Quakers are not (*Re Woodward* [1913] 1 Ch 392). Older authority strongly supports the view that the document must be made by the very officer whose duty it is to inquire into the facts, and who would therefore have satisfied himself of the truth of the facts stated (see e.g., *Sturla v Freccia* and *Daniel v Wilkin* (1852) 7 Exch 429). However, in *Halpin* [1975] QB 907 it was held that the functions of inquirer and recorder could be divided, with the result that the statutory returns of a company kept in the Companies Register were admissible where it appeared that the officer making the return had a duty to inquire, and the Registrar of Companies had the duty to record the results of the inquiry. Geoffrey Lane LJ said (at [95]): 'The common law should move with the times and should recognise the fact that the official charged with recording matters of public import can no longer in this highly complicated world . . . have personal knowledge of their accuracy'. The decision has been criticised on the grounds that the House of Lords in *Myers v DPP* [1965] AC 1001 prohibited further judicial extension of the rules admitting hearsay evidence, but, whatever the merits of the criticism, the evidence would now be admissible under the CJA 2003, s. 117 (see **F16.14**). **F16.23**

Where a record is kept by a public officer not for the benefit of others, but simply as a check upon himself, it is not a public document (*Merrick v Wakley* (1838) 8 A & E 170).

Public Matter

The subject-matter of the document need not concern the public as a whole. In *Sturla v Freccia* (1880) 5 App Cas 623, Lord Blackburn said (at [643]): **F16.24**

> I do not think that 'public' . . . is to be taken in the sense of meaning the whole world. I think an entry in the books of a manor is public in the sense that it concerns all the people interested in the manor. And an entry probably in a corporation book concerning a corporate matter, or something in which all the corporation is concerned, would be 'public' within that sense.

> Whether a document deals with a matter of public concern inevitably raises a question of degree, and entries in a corporation's book are not necessarily admissible, despite Lord Blackburn's dictum (see, e.g., *Hill v Manchester & Salford Waterworks Co.* (1833) 5 B & Ad 866). Documents which do not comply with this condition are likely to be admissible under the CJA 1988, s. 24.

Public Reference

Documents which are not maintained for the use of such members of the public as may need to refer to them are not admissible under this exception. In *Lilley v Pettit* [1946] KB 401, **F16.25**

P was prosecuted for falsely stating that her husband was the father of her child. It was held that regimental records showing that the husband was a prisoner of war abroad when the child was conceived were inadmissible because they were not intended for the use of the public. See also *Ioannou v Demetriou* [1952] AC 84.

For the same reason, a record which is maintained for a temporary purpose cannot be received under this exception (*Mercer v Denne* [1905] 2 Ch 538; *Heyne v Fischel & Co.* (1913) 30 TLR 190), although there would be no such objection to its reception in evidence under the CJA 2003, s. 117.

Other Registers etc. Admissible by Statute

F16.26 Some entries in registers are admissible as public documents (see **F16.16**). In many cases, however, statute makes express provision for the admissibility of particular registers. Detailed consideration of such provisions is beyond the scope of this work, and readers are referred to the comprehensive account in Chapter 31 of *Phipson on Evidence*, 16th. ed.

Of particular importance are the provisions of the Births and Deaths Registration Act 1953, s. 34, the text of which is set out at **F8.16**. See also the Non-Parochial Registers Act 1840, s. 6, under which certain records and registers deposited in the General Register Office in accordance with that Act are admissible, and the Births and Deaths Registration Act 1858.

An entry in a register showing that a person has died is admissible evidence of the fact and date of death, but not of the cause of death (*Bird v Keep* [1918] 2 KB 692). Where a birth certificate is relied upon to prove some fact contained in it, the evidence may be of no use unless it can be proved that the person named in it is the same individual with whom the court is concerned. This is difficult to establish without breaking the hearsay rule, for the person named cannot himself give evidence that the certificate appertains to him. A person who was present at the birth may establish identity (*Weaver* (1873) LR 2 CCR 85), though such proof may be hard to come by. It is not surprising that, in some cases, hearsay evidence has been admitted: see, e.g., *Bellis* (1911) 6 Cr App R 283, in which the court admitted evidence of inquiries made about the girl whose age was in issue, which had led the inquirer to be satisfied as to her identity.

Evidence of Reputation

F16.27 The CJA 2003, s. 118(1), makes specific provision for saving the common-law rules admitting evidence of reputation to prove character, and the use of reputation or family tradition to prove or disprove pedigree, the existence of a marriage, any public or general right, or the existence of any person or thing. With the exception of the rules concerning character, which are dealt with at **F13.13**, such evidence is rarely resorted to at common law and is not dealt with in this work.

Note that the preservation of these exceptions in s. 118 operates only to the extent that the common law allows the court to treat such evidence as proving the matter concerned.

Statements Forming Part of *Res Gestae*

F16.28 The CJA 2003, s. 118(1), makes express provision for saving the common-law rules on *res gestae*.

Criminal Justice Act 2003 s. 118

(1) The following rules of law are preserved.

. . .

Res gestae

4. Any rule of law under which in criminal proceedings a statement is admissible as evidence of any matter stated if—

(a) the statement was made by a person so emotionally overpowered by an event that the possibility of concoction or distortion can be disregarded,
(b) the statement accompanied an act which can be properly evaluated as evidence only if considered in conjunction with the statement, or
(c) the statement relates to a physical sensation or a mental state (such as intention or emotion).

The statements most commonly received as evidence under the *res gestae* exception are those referred to in (a) and (c). Statements accompanying relevant acts are rarely admitted in criminal cases (and still more rarely are they properly admitted, cf. *McCay* [1990] 1 WLR 645). The treatment which follows is confined to the two more frequently occurring varieties of *res gestae*: statements made in response to overpowering events, and statements indicative of contemporaneous sensation or state of mind, including intention and emotion).

Statements in Response to Emotionally Overpowering Events

'*Res gestae*' is an inappropriate label for this common-law exception to the hearsay rule, in which admissibility depends on proof of what Lord Ackner in *Andrews* [1987] AC 281 called the 'close and intimate connection' between the exciting events in issue and the making of the statement, the theory being that the spontaneity of the utterance is some guarantee against concoction. The nomenclature has in the past led to confusion and to incorrect decisions, but *Andrews* clarified the law by approving the test for admissibility adopted by the Privy Council in *Ratten v The Queen* [1972] AC 378. In *Mills v The Queen* [1995] 1 WLR 511, the Privy Council praised the changes effected by these decisions, regarding *res gestae* as a modernised exception to the hearsay rule under which the focus was on the probative value of evidence rather than on the question whether it falls within some artificial and rigid category. **F16.29**

In *Ratten v The Queen*, Lord Wilberforce described the rule under which spontaneous statements are admitted in the following way (at [389–90]):

> A hearsay statement is made either by the victim of an attack or by a bystander — indicating directly or indirectly the identity of the attacker. The admissibility of the statement is then said to depend on whether it was made as part of the *res gestae*. A classical instance of this is the much-debated case of *Bedingfield* (1879) 14 Cox CC 341, and there are other instances of its application in reported cases. These tend to apply different standards, and some of them carry less than conviction. The reason why this is so, is that concentration tends to be focused upon the opaque or at least imprecise Latin phrase rather than upon the basic reason for excluding the type of evidence which this group of cases is concerned with. There is no doubt what this reason is: it is twofold. The first is that there may be uncertainty as to the exact words used because of their transmission through the evidence of another person than the speaker. The second is because of the risk of concoction of false evidence by persons who have been victims of assault or accident. The first matter goes to weight. The person testifying to the words used is liable to cross-examination: the accused person (as he could not at the time when earlier reported cases were decided) can give his own account if different. There is no such difference in kind or substance between evidence of what was said and evidence of what was done (for example between evidence of what the victim said as to an attack and evidence that he (or she) was seen in a terrified state or was heard to shriek) as to require a total rejection of one and admission of the other. The possibility of concoction, or fabrication, where it exists, is on the other hand an entirely valid reason for exclusion, and is probably the real test which judges in fact apply. In their lordships' opinion this should be recognised and applied directly as the relevant test: the test should be not the uncertain one whether the making of the statement was in some sense part of the event or transaction. This may often be difficult to establish: such external matters as the time which elapses between the events and the speaking of the words (or vice versa), and differences in location being relevant factors but not, taken by themselves, decisive criteria. As regards statements made after the event it must be for the judge, by preliminary ruling, to satisfy himself that the statement was so clearly made in circumstances of spontaneity or involvement in the event that the possibility of concoction can be disregarded. Conversely, if he considers that the statement was made by way of narrative of a detached prior event so that the speaker was so disengaged from it as to be able to construct or adapt his account, he should exclude it. And the

> same must in principle be true of statements made before the event. The test should be not the uncertain one, whether the making of the statement should be regarded as part of the event or transaction. This may often be difficult to show. But if the drama, leading up to the climax, has commenced and assumed such intensity and pressure that the utterance can safely be regarded as a true reflection of what was unrolling or actually happening, it ought to be received. The expression '*res gestae*' may conveniently sum up these criteria, but the reality of them must always be kept in mind: it is this that lies behind the best reasoned of the judges' rulings.

Lord Wilberforce's reasoning led him to doubt the correctness of the decision in *Bedingfield* (1879) 14 Cox CC 341, in which the statement of a woman whose throat had been cut a few moments before was rejected, on the ground that it was made after the act to which it related was done. Of this, Lord Wilberforce said (at [390]) that 'there could hardly be a case where the speaker's words carried more clearly the mark of spontaneity and intense involvement'. In *Andrews* [1987] AC 281, the House of Lords overruled *Bedingfield*, on the ground that it was inconsistent with the true principle as laid down by Lord Wilberforce in *Ratten v The Queen* [1972] AC 378. *Bedingfield* had previously been approved by the Privy Council in *Teper v The Queen* [1952] AC 480. See also *Christie* [1914] AC 545, per Lord Reading, and *Gibson* (1887) 18 QBD 537. These and other statements of the law involving the application of the discredited test must also be regarded as no longer authoritative.

In *Andrews* [1987] AC 281, the House of Lords accepted and applied the law as stated in *Ratten v The Queen*. A was charged with the murder by stabbing of M, who was attacked by two men in his own home. Within minutes neighbours called the police, who arrived promptly, whereupon M made a statement identifying his attackers. The trial judge admitted the statement and, in a ruling regarded as 'impeccable' both by the Court of Appeal and the House of Lords, he held that there was no possibility in the circumstances of concoction or fabrication of the identification, and that the injuries sustained by M were of such a nature as to drive out any possibility of his being actuated by malice. He also took account of the fact that M correctly identified the other attacker as O, who had subsequently pleaded guilty to manslaughter. Lord Ackner summarised the position which confronts a trial judge when faced in a criminal case with an application under the *res gestae* doctrine to admit evidence of statements, with a view to establishing the truth of some fact thus narrated. He said (at 300–1):

> 1. The primary question which the judge must ask himself is — can the possibility of concoction or distortion be disregarded?
> 2. To answer that question the judge must first consider the circumstances in which the particular statement was made, in order to satisfy himself that the event was so unusual or startling or dramatic as to dominate the thoughts of the victim, so that his utterance was an instinctive reaction to that event, thus giving no real opportunity for reasoned reflection. In such a situation the judge would be entitled to conclude that the involvement or the pressure of the event would exclude the possibility of concoction or distortion, providing that the statement was made in conditions of approximate but not exact contemporaneity.
> 3. In order for the statement to be sufficiently 'spontaneous' it must be so closely associated with the event which has excited the statement, that it can be fairly stated that the mind of the declarant was still dominated by the event. Thus the judge must be satisfied that the event which provided the trigger mechanism for the statement, was still operative. The fact that the statement was made in answer to a question is but one factor to consider under this heading.
> 4. Quite apart from the time factor, there may be special features in the case, which relate to the possibility of concoction or distortion. In the instant appeal the defence relied on evidence to support the contention that the deceased had a motive of his own to fabricate or concoct, namely, a malice which resided in him against O'Neill and the appellant because, so he believed, O'Neill had attacked and damaged his house and was accompanied by the appellant, who ran away on a previous occasion. The judge must be satisfied that the circumstances were such that having regard to the special feature of malice, there was no possibility of any concoction or distortion to the advantage of the maker or the disadvantage of the accused.
> 5. As to the possibility of error in the facts narrated in the statement, if only the ordinary

> fallibility of human recollection is relied upon, this goes to the weight to be attached to and not the admissibility of the statement and is therefore a matter for the jury. However, here again there may be special features that may give rise to the possibility of error. In the instant case there was evidence that the deceased had drunk to excess, well over double the permitted limit for driving a motor car. Another example would be where the identification was made in circumstances of particular difficulty or where the declarant suffered from defective eyesight. In such circumstances the trial judge must consider whether he can exclude the possibility of error.

Some of the difficulties surrounding identification referred to by Lord Ackner arose and were considered in *Turnbull* (1984) 80 Cr App R 104.

Possibility of Error Prior to the decision in *Andrews*, it had been held, in *Nye* (1977) 66 Cr App R 252, that the possibility of error by the maker of the statement was an 'additional factor to be taken into consideration' when determining admissibility. It is now clear from the extract from the speech of Lord Ackner in *Andrews* set out above, that the risk of error bears on the question of admissibility only in cases having 'special features', e.g., an identification in difficult circumstances or by a person with defective eyesight, or by someone who had been drinking. In *Nye*, one Lucas was driving his car when it was struck from behind by another vehicle in which the accused, N and L, were travelling. One of the accused then got out and punched Lucas in the face, while the other tried to put a stop to the assault. Shortly afterwards, when the police arrived, Lucas spontaneously identified L as the man who had hit him. It was argued that Lucas might have made a mistake as to which of the accused had attacked him. On these facts the Court of Appeal considered that there was no chance of an error, stressing in particular that: 'anyone who has been assaulted usually has good reason for remembering what his assailant's face looks like'. It is therefore unlikely that, applying the test in *Andrews*, special circumstances such as the great stress immediately after a motor accident, will be held to affect the admissibility of evidence. The fact that the maker of the statement had been drinking, though capable of being a 'special feature', does not necessarily lead to exclusion. In *Andrews* the deceased had 'drunk to excess', and in *Edwards* [1992] Crim LR 576 the Divisional Court held that a spontaneous allegation of theft of a wallet made against E by A, who was drunk, was admissible. F16.30

Offence Must Generate Statement The event which generates the statement admitted under the rule stated above must be the commission of the offence in question. This is implicit in both *Ratten v The Queen* and *Andrews*, and is expressly stated by Lord Normand in *Teper v The Queen* [1952] AC 480, who said (at [488]): 'for identification purposes in a criminal trial the event with which the words sought to be proved must be so connected as to form part of the *res gestae*, is the commission of the crime itself, the throwing of the stone, the striking of the blow, the setting fire to the building or whatever the criminal act might be'. A *res gestae* statement will typically have been made by the victim of the offence, or a bystander, but may also, if the conditions of admissibility are satisfied, be made by the accused himself (*Glover* [1991] Crim LR 48). F16.31

Statement Not to be Used as Substitute for Available Witness In *Andrews* [1987] AC 281, Lord Ackner observed (at [302]): F16.32

> I would, however, strongly deprecate any attempt in criminal prosecutions to use the doctrine as a device to avoid calling, where he is available, the maker of the statement. Thus to deprive the defence of the opportunity to cross-examine him, would not be consistent with the fundamental duty of the prosecution to place all the relevant material facts before the court, so as to ensure that justice is done.

In *A-G's Ref (No. 1 of 2003)* [2003] Crim LR 547, the court observed that *Andrews* was not authority for the proposition that the *res gestae* exception was to be disapplied if better evidence was available. In that case, the prosecution had used the exception, not as a device to avoid calling the victim of an assault to give evidence against the accused, her son, but because she had later made a formal statement claiming to have sustained the injuries accidentally, which the prosecution believed to be untrue. Nevertheless it was held that the trial judge's decision to exclude the *res gestae* statement could be supported on the basis that it was unfair to admit it when it could not be the subject of cross-examination (applying the PACE 1984, s. 78). The prosecution should have been prepared to tender the mother as a witness: it was not an adequate response that the defence might have called her.

It does not follow from this rule that the *res gestae* exception has no application where the witness is available to give evidence. In *Shickle* (30 July 1997 unreported), S was charged with murder and evidence was given by his teenage son, A, who had witnessed the event. It was held that A's evidence was properly supplemented by spontaneous statements he made at the time, such as 'Mummy's putting needles in the old boy' and 'Hurry up, we've got to stop Mummy'. Although spontaneous statements are often introduced under this exception because the declarant is dead, or is for some other reason unable to give first-hand evidence, the court could find no reason of principle why the evidence should be withheld when the declarant is available. It was further held that the statement, when admitted, goes not only to the truth of the matter but to the consistency of the maker, on the basis that the greater purpose includes the lesser. It is submitted that the court's approach is entirely correct.

F16.33 **Illustrations of Application of the Rule** In *Turnbull* (1984) 80 Cr App R 104, a man who had been mortally wounded staggered into a public house. In the minutes before an ambulance arrived, and in the ambulance on the way to hospital, various witnesses thought that they heard the victim state, in answer to the question who had stabbed him, that it was 'Ronnie Tommo'. The deceased had a strong Scottish accent and the prosecution case was that he in fact said 'Turnbull'. The statements were admitted, and it was held to be irrelevant that the deceased went on to mutter other words which the witnesses were unable to understand, for: 'If a man is asked a straight question . . . and he gives an answer . . . the fact that he mumbles something afterwards, or is trying to say something when he loses consciousness cannot make the completeness of what he has just said incomplete so that it cannot be used in evidence' (per O'Connor LJ, at [111]).

In *O'Shea* (24 July 1986 unreported), which was considered in *Andrews* [1987] AC 281, the elderly occupier of a second-floor flat into which O was trying to break, slipped while trying to escape through a window and sustained injuries which eventually resulted in his death. He was found lying where he had fallen an hour or so after the incident, and the statement which he then made, in which he stated the reason for his injuries, was admitted in evidence. By contrast, in *Newport* [1998] Crim LR 581, a telephone call made by N's wife 20 minutes before he inflicted fatal injuries on her, in which she arranged to take sanctuary in a friend's house if she had to flee in a hurry, was held to have been wrongly admitted. On the facts there was an insufficient connection between the incident and the wife's request: the call was not a spontaneous and unconsidered reaction to an immediately impending emergency. In all probability the evidence might have been admitted if restricted to an account of the wife's contemporaneous state of emotion and agitation, either because such evidence is not within the hearsay rule at all or because, if it is, it falls within the exception for statements of contemporaneous feelings (see **F16.36**).

In *Tobi v Nicholas* [1988] RTR 343, a collision occurred between a car and a stationary motor coach. Some 20 minutes later the driver of the coach, who had summoned the police, identified T as the driver of the car involved. The coach driver was not called to give evidence at the trial, and the Divisional Court held, applying *Andrews* [1987] AC 281, that there were three reasons why his statement should not have been admitted as part of the *res gestae*:

(1) The event which had occurred was not so unusual or dramatic as to dominate the thoughts of the victim. 'Of course anybody whose vehicle has been damaged is annoyed

about it, but there is a world of difference between such an unfortunately commonplace situation and the thoughts of somebody who has been assaulted and stabbed' (per Glidewell LJ, at p. 356).

(2) The statement was not sufficiently contemporaneous with the event.

(3) The *res gestae* doctrine should not be used as a device to avoid calling the maker of the statement where he is available, as the coach driver was, to give evidence.

Where a spontaneous statement includes an element of hearsay in the form of information gleaned from another, the admission of the statement does not of itself warrant the admission of the further element of hearsay. In *Elliott* [2000] Crim LR 51, Y, who had been stabbed, made a statement within minutes in which he said that the man who had attacked him was the same man who previously attacked his brother, and that the name of the man was 'Denrick' (E's first name). Y had been told the name by M, who had witnessed the attack on the brother, and the Court of Appeal held that, once M had given evidence that he had identified E to Y as 'Denrick', there was no hearsay problem involved in admitting the statement of Y in its entirety. While this is true to the extent that it was not necessary to place reliance on that part of Y's statement in which he named E, it would have been better to have stated explicitly that Y's *res gestae* statement could not be evidence of that which he did not know, i.e. the name of his assailant.

Use of Statement itself to Determine Admissibility In *Ratten v The Queen* [1972] AC 378, Lord Wilberforce said (at [391]) that in principle it would not be right for the involvement of the speaker in the pressure of the drama surrounding the event to be proved only by the statement itself, 'otherwise the statement would be lifting itself into the area of admissibility'. However, it was difficult to imagine a case where there was no other evidence to connect the speaker to the event, and it would not be wrong in principle for the judge to take the statement into account, together with other things, in reaching his decision. **F16.34**

Direction to Jury In *Andrews* [1987] AC 281, Lord Ackner said that where a 'spontaneous' statement has been admitted in evidence as part of the *res gestae*, the judge must make it clear to the jury: **F16.35**

(1) That it is for them to decide what was said and to be sure that the witnesses were not mistaken in what they believed had been said to them.

(2) That they must be satisfied that the declarant did not concoct or distort to his advantage or to the disadvantage of the accused the statement relied on, and where there is material to raise the issue, that he was not activated by any malice or ill-will.

(3) Where there are special features that bear on the possibility of mistake, then the jury's attention must be invited to those matters.

In *Mills v The Queen* [1995] 1 WLR 511, the Privy Council rejected an argument that a specific direction must always be given as to the risk of mistaken identification by a dying man in a *res gestae* statement. The jury in that case had been adequately directed about the risks of mistaken identification in relation to the evidence of other witnesses, and fairness did not require a repetition.

Statements of Contemporaneous Bodily or Mental Feelings **F16.36**

The statements of a person in which he relates his contemporaneous bodily feelings are admissible to prove the feelings, but not their cause. Thus, in *Nicholas* (1846) 2 Car & Kir 246, Pollock CB said (at [248]):

> If a man says to his surgeon, 'I have a pain in the head', or in such a part of the body, that is evidence; but, if he says to his surgeon, 'I have a wound'; and was to add, 'I met John Thomas, who had a sword, and ran me through the body with it', that would be no evidence against John Thomas.

Similarly, in *Gloster* (1888) 16 Cox CC 471, statements by a woman who was dying from the effects of an illegal operation, naming the person responsible for her bodily condition, were held inadmissible under this exception. Charles J held (at [473]) that 'the statements must be confined to contemporaneous symptoms, and nothing in the nature of a narrative is admissible as to who caused them, or how they were caused'. *Gloster* was followed in *Thomson* [1912] 3 KB 19, in which the statements of a woman who had recently suffered a miscarriage and who claimed to have operated upon herself were excluded.

What is contemporaneous is a question of fact. In *Black* (1922) 16 Cr App R 118, B was convicted of the murder by poisoning of his wife. It was held on appeal that her descriptions of symptoms she had suffered after taking medicine given to her by B were admissible only because they were made in B's presence in such a way as to demand an answer from him. (See, as to statements made in the presence of the accused, **F17.66** to **F17.68**.) Had the statements been made behind his back it would, per Avory J, have required 'grave consideration whether they could have been admitted', because they concerned her past, rather than her contemporaneous, feelings. However, Salter J in the course of argument said (at [119]):

> . . . 'contemporaneous' cannot be confined to feelings experienced at the actual moment when the patient is speaking; it must include such a statement as 'Yesterday I had a pain after meals'.

In the civil case of *Aveson v Lord Kinnaird* (1805) 6 East 188, statements made by a woman concerning symptoms from which she claimed to have been suffering for some time were admitted, not only to establish her feelings when the statement was made, but also to establish that she had had the same symptoms when seen by a doctor some days previously.

Where a doctor gives expert evidence as to the condition of a patient, he may not give evidence of past symptoms as they have been narrated to him in order to prove that the symptoms existed, although he may be allowed to state what he was told simply in order to explain the conclusion to which he has come. If the existence of past symptoms is in issue, they must be proved by admissible evidence (*Bradshaw* (1985) 82 Cr App R 79).

In some cases statements indicating contemporaneous feelings may be admissible as original evidence. In *Conde* (1867) 10 Cox CC 547, evidence was admitted that a child who died from starvation had begged a neighbour to give him bread. Of this request Channell B is reported as having said that 'it was not so much a statement as an act. A complaint of hunger was an act; although the particulars of the statement might not be receivable, the fact of the complaint was clearly so'. It is also permissible to prove a contemporaneous statement in which the maker claims to be in a particular mental state, such as fear. In *Vincent* (1840) 9 C & P 275, a policeman was allowed to prove statements made by bystanders at a public meeting who claimed that they were frightened by what took place. In *Edwards* (1872) 12 Cox CC 230, E was charged with the murder of his wife, R, and a neighbour testified that a week before R died she came to the neighbour's house bearing a carving knife and a large axe. Quain J allowed the neighbour to state that R had asked her to take care of the implements as 'my husband always threatens me with these and when they're out of the way I feel safer'. In the light of the authorities stated above, it would seem that R's statement should not have been admitted to prove the cause of her fear, but only (if it were relevant to do so) that she was in a state of trepidation when delivering the weapons. Evidence of state of mind may also be used to negate inferences which might otherwise be drawn from conduct. In *Gilfoyle* [1996] 1 Cr App R 302, P died by hanging, leaving suicide notes. Evidence that she was not in a suicidal frame of mind was admissible in order to support the prosecution's contention that P had been tricked by her killer into writing the notes.

In recent times there has been a division of opinion as to whether a statement revealing the maker's state of mind is admissible as non-hearsay evidence from which the state of mind may be inferred (*Blastland* [1986] AC 41; *Kearley* [1992] 2 AC 228) or hearsay admissible under an exception to the rule (*Neill v North Antrim Magistrates' Court* [1992] 1 WLR 1221; *Gilfoyle*). Both views are tenable although the preponderance of modern authority favours the former.

Statements of Present Intention

In various criminal cases, statements indicating the present intention of the speaker have been received in evidence, apparently by way of exception to the hearsay rule. In *Buckley* (1873) 13 Cox CC 293, an inspector of police was permitted to narrate a statement made to him by G, a constable, who said that he intended to go that evening to keep watch on B, whom he suspected of theft. G was later found stabbed to death at some distance from B's cottage, and the statement was relied upon as circumstantial evidence that G had carried out his intention, with fatal consequences. No reason was given for the decision to admit the statement, and it may be that the case is best viewed as involving a declaration made by the deceased G in the course of his duty (a common-law exception not preserved by the CJA 2003, s. 118). **F16.37**

In *Moghal* (1977) 65 Cr App R 56, M was charged with the murder of R, and his defence was that the crime was committed by S. It was held that a statement made by S six months before, in which S declared her intention to murder R, was admissible. However, statements which S made to the police after R had been killed, in which she described her state of mind and feelings before and at the time of the killing, were rejected as inadmissible hearsay on the ground that 'the condition precedent to the admissibility of such statements is that they should relate to the maker's contemporaneous state of mind or emotion'. What is contemporaneous was said to be a question of degree, but what was said in the course of police investigations occurred far too long after the event to be admitted. Where non-contemporaneous declarations are self-serving, there is an additional reason for excluding them, for such declarations might otherwise be used to construct a fraudulent defence (*Petcherini* (1855) 7 Cox CC 79).

Moghal was doubted by the House of Lords in *Blastland* [1986] AC 41, but only on the ground that the isolated declaration of intention made six months before the murder was insufficiently relevant to be admitted. See also *Wainwright* (1875) 13 Cox CC 171, in which W was charged with the murder of a girl, and the prosecution were not allowed to prove that the victim had announced her intention of going to W's premises on the night she died. Cockburn CJ said that the girl's statement was 'only a statement of intention which might or might not be carried out'.

The existence of a hearsay exception for statements of intention seems to have been overlooked in *Thomson* [1912] 3 KB 19, in which the statement of a woman made before she suffered a miscarriage, and in which she declared her intention to operate upon herself, was rejected as inadmissible hearsay. The statement was said not to form part of the *res gestae*, in the sense that it was not a spontaneous statement connected with the operation itself. The possibility that it might be admissible as a declaration of intention does not appear to have been canvassed.

More recently, in *Callender* [1998] Crim LR 337, the Court of Appeal refused to admit statements made by C two weeks before his arrest for conspiring to commit arson, in which he told an acquaintance that his intention was limited to making dummy devices, resembling explosives, which could be used to attract publicity to the cause of animal rights without actually causing damage to property. This mirrored his defence at trial and, if true, was an answer to the charge. C did not give evidence, however, and the court appears to have been concerned that his statement, if admitted, would have permitted C to raise a reasonable doubt about the prosecution case in a manner contrary to the principles of the CJPO 1994, s. 35 (see **F19.20**). But the adverse inferences which the statute permits if an accused fails to testify could still be drawn where his *res gestae* statement is admissible. The reason given for rejection was that the *res gestae* rule was in fact a single principle governed by the decisions in *Andrews* [1987] AC 281 and *Ratten v The Queen* [1972] AC 378 (see **F16.29**). C's statement was thus ruled inadmissible because it was not made in circumstances whereby the possibility of concoction or distortion could be disregarded. It is submitted that this is not the case. The true reason for admitting evidence of a statement revealing the maker's intention or other state of mind, or bodily feelings, is the difficulty of proving the matter by other means. Although C's statement was self-serving, and there was a possibility that he was setting up a defence for himself, it was made when he had no inkling that he was about to be arrested, and might be thought to have had some probative value in relation to his state of mind at the relevant time. Whether it was concocted or not should, under this exception, have been a question for the jury.

Common-law Confessions and Admissions

F16.38 The CJA 2003, s. 118(1), makes express provision for saving the common-law rules on confessions and admissions.

Criminal Justice Act 2003, s. 118

Preservation of certain common law categories of admissibility

(1) The following rules of law are preserved.

. . .

Confessions etc

5. Any rule of law relating to the admissibility of confessions or mixed statements in criminal proceedings.

Admissions by agents etc

6. Any rule of law under which in criminal proceedings—
   (a) an admission made by an agent of a defendant is admissible against the defendant as evidence of any matter stated, or
   (b) a statement made by a person to whom a defendant refers a person for information is admissible against the defendant as evidence of any matter stated.

The common law has little part to play in regulating the admissibility of an accused's confession now the CJA 2003 has taken effect. Confessions tendered by the prosecution are currently governed by the PACE 1984, s. 76 (see **F17**). The CJA 2003, s. 128, extends the coverage of s. 76 to confessions adduced by a co-accused (see **F17.19**). The most important of the vestigial rules retained by paragraph 5 of s. 118(1) is the implied acceptance by the accused of a statement made in his presence (see **F17.66**), which may operate even where the accused is silent in the face of an accusation (see **F19.3**). The latter aspect of the rule was specifically preserved by the CJPO 1994, s. 34(5), and remains of some practical importance despite the statutory inroads on the right to silence made by that Act. To the extent that the admissibility of the self-serving parts of a mixed statement depends on factors not dealt with in the PACE 1984, s. 76, the common law is also preserved by s. 118(1) (see **F17.61**).

Admissions by Agents and Referees

F16.39 An admission made by the agent of an accused person, such as his legal adviser, may be admissible against him (*Turner* (1975) 61 Cr App R 67). Although at first sight such an admission may appear to be a confession, and thus to be governed by the rules of admissibility in the PACE 1984, s. 76 (see **F17**), it is submitted that this is not the case, for the section applies only to a confession made 'by an accused person', and, by s. 82(1), 'confession' includes any statement adverse to 'the person who made it'. It would seem to follow that vicarious admissions continue to be governed by common-law principles.

A statement made by his agent is admissible against the accused only where it is shown that the statement was made within the scope of the agent's authority. The majority of cases dealing with the proof of such authority are civil, and of limited assistance in criminal proceedings, as the few criminal authorities which exist take a more restrictive view as to the extent to which an agent's admissions affect his principal. Thus, in civil cases, admissions made by a solicitor in correspondence on his client's behalf will generally be evidence against the client (see, e.g., *Ellis v Allen* [1914] 1 Ch 904), whereas in criminal cases a client is not bound by statements in letters written by his solicitor in the absence of proof of specific instructions from him (*Downer* (1880) 43 LT 445). Agency may be inferred from the circumstances: thus, in *Turner* (1975) 61 Cr App R 67, it was held that it is permissible to infer from the fact that a barrister makes an admission in court on behalf of and in the presence of his client, that he was authorised to make it. The strength of the inference depends on the circumstances, however, and in *Evans* [1981] Crim LR 699, it was held that agency was not to be inferred simply from the fact that the admission was made by E's solicitor's clerk. An inference of agency will yield to express evidence to the contrary: in *Turner*, the barrister who had made the admissions in previous proceedings against T, gave evidence that he had exceeded his authority in doing so, and the statement was ruled inadmissible.

Evidence of agency must, of course, be admissible in its own right. In *Evans* statements made by the solicitor's clerk indicating that he was acting with E's authority were inadmissible to prove agency, being hearsay. *Evans* was distinguished in *Ungvari* [2003] EWCA Crim 2346, where there was ample evidence in the history of trading between two companies to support the inference that the appellant's sister was acting as his agent.

See, as to the reasons of policy for excluding statements made on behalf of an accused in the course of a pre-trial review, *Hutchinson* (1985) 82 Cr App R 51.

A statement made by a person to whom the accused refers another for information on a particular matter may be evidence against him. Thus, in *Williams v Innes* (1808) 1 Camp 364, an executor referred the plaintiff to a particular individual for information pertaining to the assets of the estate, and it was held that what the referee said was admissible against the executor. Similarly, in *Mallory* (1884) 13 QBD 33, where M told a police officer that his wife would supply a list showing where certain items, suspected of being stolen, were purchased, the list handed over by the wife in M's presence was admissible against him. Coleridge CJ refrained from stating what the outcome would have been had M been absent when the list was handed over, but it is submitted that it would have made no difference.

Statements in Furtherance of Common Enterprise

The CJA 2003, s. 118(1), makes express provision for saving the common-law rules on statements in furtherance of a common enterprise. **F16.40**

Criminal Justice Act 2003, s. 118

(1) The following rules of law are preserved.

. . .

Common enterprise

7. Any rule of law under which in criminal proceedings a statement made by a party to a common enterprise is admissible against another party to the enterprise as evidence of any matter stated.

Scope of the Rule The rule that the acts and statements of one party to a common purpose may be evidence against another is particularly associated with charges of conspiracy. However, it is not confined to such cases, and applies to other offences where complicity is alleged. Thus, in *Jessop* (1877) 16 Cox CC 204, for example, J was charged with the murder of A, with whom he had entered into a suicide pact to die by taking poison. The plan miscarried and J survived. Field J held that evidence of the purchase of poison by A, being an act done in furtherance of the common purpose, was admissible against J. A more modern illustration is **F16.41**

Jones [1997] 2 Cr App R 119, in which it was held that the rule applied to a joint enterprise to evade the prohibition on the importation of drugs, despite the fact that no charge of conspiracy was brought.

The limits of the doctrine were recently considered in *Gray* [1995] 2 Cr App R 100. G and others were each convicted of offences relating to insider dealing. Although there was alleged to be a 'network' between them for the passing of information, each allegation related only to an offence committed by one of them alone. The prosecution case consisted mainly of telephone conversations between the defendants, and the judge told the jury that a statement made in the course of such a conversation, though a particular defendant was not party to it, could nevertheless be evidence against that defendant if there was a joint enterprise between them for the unlawful dissemination of 'inside' information and the statement was made in furtherance of that joint enterprise. The Court of Appeal was inclined to the view that this stated the principle too widely: the acts and declarations of a person engaged in a joint enterprise and made in pursuance of that enterprise might be admissible against another, but only where the evidence shows the complicity of that other in a common offence or series of offences. As none of the offences was alleged to have been committed jointly, the rule did not apply. If, contrary to that view, the principle could be stated in the wider form, the prosecution would have to make clear the limits of the alleged agreement in pursuit of which the specific offences were said to have been committed; as this had not been done the appeals were allowed. Thus it appears that the case for a wider principle could still be made. In *Murray* [1997] 2 Cr App R 136, the Court of Appeal adopted the interpretation of *Gray* in the 1996 edition of this work (which is the same as that set out above) and added that that case is authority primarily for the proposition that the common-law exception cannot be extended to cases where individual defendants are charged with a number of separate substantive offences and the terms of a common enterprise are not provided or are ill-defined. An argument, based on dicta in the case, that *Gray* in fact narrows the scope of the common-law exception was rejected. *Murray* was approved in *Williams* [2002] EWCA Crim 2208, where the true rule was considered to be that 'the acts and declarations by A in furtherance of a sufficiently defined common design are admissible to prove a substantive offence committed alone in pursuance of the same common design, by B'.

The rule permits the actions and declarations of one party, A, to be used in evidence against the other, B, and is thus an exception to the general rule that B is not to be prejudiced by the acts or statements of another, and an exception to the hearsay rule insofar as it may involve reliance on A's statements as evidence of their truth. As an exception to the hearsay rule it defies classification, some writers regarding it as appertaining to the *res gestae* (see *Andrews & Hirst on Criminal Evidence*, 4th ed., at 20.26), others as based on implied agency (see *Cross and Tapper on Evidence*, 10th ed., at p. 611), and others as an independent exception, the justification for which is that such evidence must be used if the 'secret' crime of conspiracy is ever to be proved at all (Gilles, *The Law of Criminal Conspiracy* (1981)).

In order for the act or statement of A to be admissible against B, the rule requires:

(1) that the act or statement of A must be in the course and furtherance of the common purpose; and
(2) that independent evidence be adduced of the existence of the conspiracy and the involvement in it of B.

F16.42 **Meaning of Course and Furtherance of Common Purpose** In the leading case of *Blake* (1844) 6 QB 126, B and T were charged with conspiring to avoid payment of duty on imported goods. B, in the course of his employment at the Customs House, certified that the amount of goods imported by T as an agent was less than was in fact the case. T then charged his principal duty on the full amount, recording the charge in his own day book, and split the proceeds with B. It was held that the entry in T's day book was admissible against B, as being evidence of something done in the course of the transaction, but that the counterfoil of the cheque by which B received his share of the proceeds was not, for it was an act done after the common purpose was effected which had nothing to do with the carrying out of the conspiracy. It will be apparent from Blake that it may be difficult to distinguish precisely where a transaction begins and ends, and whether acts are done in furtherance of it or not. A clearer case of inadmissibility owing to the termination of the criminal purpose is that of the confession of one conspirator made after his apprehension, which is evidence only against the maker (see, e.g., *Walters* (1979) 69 Cr App R 115, at p. 120). And a more obvious example of a statement which cannot be said to be in furtherance of any criminal purpose occurred in *Steward* [1963] Crim LR 697, where one conspirator simply recited to another the various acts of B which had been done in execution of the common purpose, and the statement was held inadmissible against B. See also *Hardy* (1794) 24 St Tr 199, in which a similar recital by a conspirator of his own past acts was held not to be in furtherance of the conspiracy.

In *Devonport* [1996] 1 Cr App R 221, a statement was admitted which may not, in the strict sense, have furthered the conspiracy. The court was concerned with a document drawn up by D concerning the proposed division of spoils between himself and others involved. This was regarded by Judge J as a document in furtherance of the conspiracy, distinguishing *Blake* on the ground that the document was not a record of distribution after the conspiracy but an indication of the intended or prospective distribution of the proceeds of the conspiracy when it has been fulfilled. Even so, as there was no evidence that the document served any purpose other than D's own convenience the decision seems to go further than previous authority. So also does *Ilyas* [1996] Crim LR 810, in which a diary was admitted which was a record of the receipt of stolen car parts by some of the parties to the conspiracy. Nothing was made of the argument that the document was a mere record of what had already occurred and not in furtherance of the enterprise. Latham J, however, asserted that it was 'a document created *in the course of, or furtherance*, of the conspiracy' (emphasis added). This would seem to be a new and alternative ground of admissibility, as a document such as the diary can be said to be created in the course of a conspiracy without being in any way in furtherance of it. It would seem that the rule is in the course of being broadened by the courts. See also *Reeves* [1999] 3 Arch News 2, in which an aide-memoire by one conspirator for his own assistance appears to have been regarded as potentially admissible against co-conspirators under this exception, and *Platten* [2006] EWCA Crim 140, where it was said that 'statements made during the conspiracy and as part of the conspiracy, because they are part of making the natural arrangements to carry out the conspiracy, will be admissible'. In *Platten*, the Court confined the exclusion of statements which are 'mere narrative' to statements made after the conspiracy is concluded. The Court endorsed the rule of thumb adopted by Kennedy LJ in *Barham* [1997] 2 Cr App R 119 of 'the enterprise in operation'.

Where the hearsay statements of co-conspirators in furtherance of the conspiracy implicate an accused, the trial judge must give a careful direction to the jury that the statements cannot be used to provide the link between that accused and the conspiracy (*Blake* (1993) 97 Cr App R 169).

Requirement of Independent Evidence of Common Purpose In *Blake* (1844) 6 QB 126, a case involving conspiracy, Patteson J stated the principle to be that 'you must establish the fact of a conspiracy before you can make the act of one the act of all'. The absence of such independent evidence renders the statement alleged to have been made in furtherance of the conspiracy inadmissible, and it is not possible for the statement itself to provide the evidence of the existence of the conspiracy (*Jenkins* [2003] Crim LR 107, and Commentary by Professor Sir John Smith). This does not mean that such evidence must be brought forward and accepted before the act or statement in question can be proved, for: 'from the nature of this charge [conspiracy] the evidence must necessarily grow up as it proceeds. The acts of the one party must be given in evidence and then the acts of the other, and it may **F16.43**

then be shown that those acts fully prove a conspiracy between them' (*Murphy* (1837) 8 C & P 297, per Coleridge J at [302–3]). See also *Governor of Pentonville Prison, ex parte Osman* [1990] 1 WLR 277 in which Lloyd LJ said (at [316]): '. . . there must always be some evidence other than the hearsay evidence of a fellow conspirator to prove that a particular defendant is party to a conspiracy. Provided there is some other evidence, it does not matter in what order the evidence is adduced.' The principle is thus one of conditional admissibility, in that if, after the evidence has been heard, it transpires that there is no independent evidence of common purpose, the act or statement of A will have to be excluded from the case against B (*Donat* (1985) 82 Cr App R 173. It is submitted that there is no difference in practice between this view and that expressed in *Whittaker* [1914] 3 KB 1283, in which it was said that the act or statement of A, though it may be proved as evidence against him, remains inadmissible against B until the necessary foundation is laid. Insofar as there is a difference, it is submitted that the correct practice is as stated in *Donat.* Failure by the prosecution to satisfy the requirement after evidence of a statement has been admitted *de bene esse* will require a careful direction to the jury, and may require the discharge of the jury and a retrial if the evidence admitted was prejudicial. Where evidence is admitted under the rule it is not necessary for the jury to be directed to convict only if they find evidence against B other than the statement of A. It is for the judge alone to satisfy himself that such evidence exists: if it does, the jury is permitted to look at all the evidence in order to decide guilt. If, however, there is a danger that the jury will rely on the statement by A as primary evidence of B's involvement, 'sweeping away' the other evidence which has led the judge to admit the statement in the first place, the judge should direct the jury as to the shortcomings in the evidence of A, including (if such be the case) the absence of any opportunity to cross-examine A, and the absence of corroborative evidence (*Jones* [1997] 2 Cr App R 119; *Williams* [2002] EWCA Crim 2208).

Common-law Admissibility of Body of Expertise

F16.44 The CJA 2003, s. 118(1), makes express provision for saving the common-law rules allowing an expert to draw on a relevant body of expertise.

Criminal Justice Act 2003, s. 118

(1) The following rules of law are preserved.

. . .

Expert evidence

8. Any rule of law under which in criminal proceedings an expert witness may draw on the body of expertise relevant to his field.

Technically speaking, where an expert draws on the work of others in order to form his opinion, an element of hearsay is necessarily involved. Whether this is objectionable or not depends on the nature of the work referred to. In *Abadom* [1983] 1 WLR 126 (**F10.20**) it was accepted that 'the process of taking account of information stemming from the work of others in the same field is an essential ingredient of the nature of expert evidence', and as such is not subject to the hearsay rule. Where, however, an expert relies on the existence or non-existence of some fact which is basic to the question on which he is asked his opinion, that fact must be proved by admissible evidence. Paragraph 8 of s. 118(1) preserves the effect of *Abadom.* See also, however, s. 127 at **F10.18** which erodes the second part of the rule in *Abadom* by permitting evidence to be given of the preparatory findings on which an expert's opinion is based without the need to call those who made the findings as witnesses in the case.

OTHER STATUTORY EXCEPTIONS

Committal Statements Admissible at Trial

F16.45 The MCA 1980, ss. 5A to 5F, makes far-reaching provision for statements read at committal to be tendered at trial (see **D10.44**). Under the CPIA 1996, sch. 2 (see **D15.16**), statements and depositions which have been admitted at committal are automatically admissible at trial, except that the court has a discretion to exclude the evidence and a party to the proceedings may object to its admission, although the court has a statutory power to order that the objection be of no effect if it is in the interests of justice so to order. These provisions will be repealed upon the coming into force of the CJA 2003, sch. 3. The notice provisions of s. 50 are already defunct (see *CPS v Gil* [2006] EWHC 1153 (Admin)).

Transcript Admissible at Retrial

Criminal Appeal Act 1968, sch. 2, para. 1 **F16.46**

(1) Evidence given at a retrial must be given orally if it was given orally at the original trial, unless—
- (a) all the parties to the retrial agree otherwise;
- (b) section 116 of the Criminal Justice Act 2003 applies (admissibility of hearsay evidence where a witness is unavailable); or
- (c) the witness is unavailable to give evidence, otherwise than as mentioned in subsection (2) of that section, and section 114(1)(d) of that Act applies (admission of hearsay evidence under residual discretion).

(2) Paragraph 5 of schedule 3 to the Crime and Disorder Act 1998 (use of depositions) does not apply at a retrial to a deposition read as evidence at the original trial.

The provisions of sch. 2 reaffirm and clarify a wider common-law rule: see *Thompson* [1982] QB 647, in which it was held that the transcript of evidence of a witness might be read out at a retrial upon proof that she was too ill to travel, notwithstanding that the retrial was not ordered by the Court of Appeal under the 1968 Act. Similarly, in *Hall* [1973] 1 QB 496, it was held that a transcript of evidence is admissible at common law at a retrial if the witness has since died, provided it is authenticated in appropriate manner, e.g., by calling the shorthand writer who took the original note.

The terms of the provision, as substituted by the CJA 2003, s. 131, bring the admissibility of evidence at retrial into line with the range of hearsay exceptions in the 2003 Act. In practical terms, the most important change wrought by s. 131, is the incorporation of the inclusionary discretion ('the safety valve') from s. 114(1)(d).

Video Recordings of Evidence

The CJA 1988, s. 32A, made a significant change to the admissibility of hearsay evidence from child witnesses by providing that a video recording of an interview between an adult and a child witness could be admitted in effect as the evidence-in-chief of the child. Section 32A has now been repealed and replaced by the wider provisions in the YJCEA 1999, part II, the bulk of which were brought into force in July 2002. This brings together a number of special measures for assisting vulnerable and intimidated witnesses when giving their evidence, including a provision under which hearsay evidence in the form of a video recording can be received as evidence-in-chief (s. 27). In the Crown Court, the effect of a complicated procedure of implementation is that s. 27 can be used to assist witnesses eligible for special measures on grounds of youth or physical and mental incapacity (s. 16) but not, for the time being, witnesses eligible on grounds that the giving of evidence will cause fear or distress (s. 17). In magistrates' courts and youth courts, s. 27 will be available only to child witnesses in the limited range of cases covered by the old s. 32A (i.e. sexual cases and those involving violence or cruelty). (The implementation provisions are contained partly in the Youth Justice and Criminal Evidence Act 1999 (Commencement No. 7) Order 2002 (SI 2002 No. 1739) and partly in a letter from the Secretary of State which, by virtue of s. 18(2)(a), constitutes 'notification' of those provisions which are immediately made available to courts.) When resources permit, all witnesses eligible for special measures will be able to benefit from s. 27. **F16.47**

The YJCEA 1999 also introduced the possibility of pre-recorded cross-examination and re-examination where video recording is the medium by which evidence-in-chief is given (s. 28), although this provision has not been brought into force. This will eventually enable the evidence of some children, typically children who are complainants in sexual cases, to be taken before the trial begins. For the time being, however, a witness whose evidence-in-chief is taken under s. 27 must be available for cross-examination at trial unless the parties agree that it is unnecessary (s. 27(4)(a)(ii)). While the YJCEA 1999 makes provision for live-link or the use of screens to minimise the effect of confrontation these measures cannot cushion the witness from the stress of waiting to give evidence, or the delays which may attend the trial process. See **D14.97** ***et seq*** for the full range of 'special measures'.

A video recording admitted under s. 27 is normally made as part of the investigative process and is properly treated as an exception to the hearsay rule, though it differs from hearsay in its classic form because the YJCEA 1999 anticipates that the witness will normally be available for cross-examination at some point before or during the trial except where s. 27(4)(a)(ii) applies. The reception of evidence under s. 27 is unaffected by the enactment of the hearsay provisions of the CJA 2003. However the Act also contains, in s. 137, a general provision admitting a video recording as evidence-in-chief of witnesses to serious offences. This provision is not part of the 'special measures' regime and suggests a preparedness on the part of Government to move towards the wider reception of such evidence provided the witness is available to be cross-examined. Section 137 is not expected to come into force during the currency of this edition of this work.

Youth Justice and Criminal Evidence Act 1999, s. 27

(1) A special measures direction may provide for a video recording of an interview of the witness to be admitted as evidence in chief of the witness.

(2) A special measures direction may, however, not provide for a video recording, or a part of such a recording, to be admitted under this section if the court is of the opinion, having regard to all the circumstances of the case, that in the interests of justice the recording, or that part of it, should not be so admitted.

(3) In considering for the purposes of subsection (2) whether any part of a recording should not be admitted under this section, the court must consider whether any prejudice to the accused which might result from that part being so admitted is outweighed by the desirability of showing the whole, or substantially the whole, of the recorded interview.

(4) Where a special measures direction provides for a recording to be admitted under this section, the court may nevertheless subsequently direct that it is not to be so admitted if—
- (a) it appears to the court that—
  - (i) the witness will not be available for cross-examination (whether conducted in the ordinary way or in accordance with any such direction), and
  - (ii) the parties to the proceedings have not agreed that there is no need for the witness to be so available; or
- (b) any Criminal Procedure Rules requiring disclosure of the circumstances in which the recording was made have not been complied with to the satisfaction of the court.

(5) Where a recording is admitted under this section—
- (a) the witness must be called by the party tendering it in evidence, unless—
  - (i) a special measures direction provides for the witness's evidence on cross-examination to be given otherwise than by testimony in court, or
  - (ii) the parties to the proceedings have agreed as mentioned in subsection (4)(a)(ii); and
- (b) the witness may not give evidence in chief otherwise than by means of the recording—
  - (i) as to any matter which, in the opinion of the court, has been dealt with adequately in the witness's recorded testimony, or
  - (ii) without the permission of the court, as to any other matter which, in the opinion of the court, is dealt with in that testimony.

(6) Where in accordance with subsection (2) a special measures direction provides for part only of a recording to be admitted under this section, references in subsections (4) and (5) to the recording or to the witness's recorded testimony are references to the part of the recording or testimony which is to be so admitted.

(7) The court may give permission for the purposes of subsection (5)(b)(ii) if it appears to the court to be in the interests of justice to do so, and may do so either—

(a) on an application by a party to the proceedings, if there has been a material change of circumstances since the relevant time, or
(b) of its own motion.

(8) In subsection (7) 'the relevant time' means—
(a) the time when the direction was given, or
(b) if a previous application has been made under that subsection, the time when the application (or last application) was made.

(9) The court may, in giving permission for the purposes of subsection (5)(b)(ii), direct that the evidence in question is to be given by the witness by means of a live link; and, if the court so directs, subsections (5) to (7) of section 24 shall apply in relation to that evidence as they apply in relation to evidence which is to be given in accordance with a special measures direction.

(10) A magistrates' court inquiring into an offence as examining justices under section 6 of the Magistrates' Courts Act 1980 may consider any video recording in relation to which it is proposed to apply for a special measures direction providing for it to be admitted at the trial in accordance with this section.

(11) Nothing in this section affects the admissibility of any video recording which would be admissible apart from this section.

In the case of an adult eligible witness the court's power to direct that evidence be received under s. 27 is governed by s. 19; the key issues are whether the special measure would maximise the quality of the witness's evidence (s. 19(3)), bearing in mind the views of the witness (s. 19(3)(a)) and whether the measure might tend to inhibit the evidence being effectively tested (s. 19(3)(b)). Where a witness is under 17 (or was when a relevant recording was made), ss. 21 and 22 (see **D14.102**) erect a presumption that s. 27 will lead to the witness being able to give his best evidence. Where the charge involves violence or the case is of a sexual nature and there is a video recording which is suitable to serve as evidence-in-chief under s. 27, the presumption is particularly strong: the recording must be selected as the appropriate method of giving evidence-in-chief even if the court considers it is not the best way for the witness to give evidence. See also the CrimPR, part 29 (special measures directions), set out in full in **appendix 1** and the Ministry of Justice Circular 25/06/2007 on the extended availability of special measures for complainants in cases involving sexual offences.

The witness who has made the recording must be called as a witness unless he is to be cross-examined otherwise than by 'live' testimony or the parties have agreed that he need not be called (s. 27(5)). This narrow provision appears to qualify the discretion afforded by s. 27(4) to admit a recording where the witness is not available for cross-examination. Section 27 goes further than s. 32A of the CJA 1988 in restricting the circumstances in which a supplementary examination-in-chief may take place at the trial; s. 27(5)(b)(ii) imposes a new requirement to obtain the permission of the court to elaborate on any matter dealt with, albeit inadequately, in the recording.

Section 27 contains many provisions which are similar to those in s. 32A of the CJA 1988, so that reference to earlier authorities may be relevant. Section 32A is considered in the 2000 edition of this work.

Exclusion in the Interests of Justice The court cannot direct that a recording be received in evidence if it is not in the interests of justice to admit it (YJCEA 1999, s. 27(2)). This provision, though cast in similar terms to the earlier legislation, has to be read against the background of strong statutory presumptions in the YJCEA 1999 regarding children's evidence (see **D14.102**), directing the court towards video recorded evidence-in-chief as the way in which children (particularly children in need of 'special protection') should normally give their evidence. To give proper effect to these presumptions it is not open to the court, as it may have been under the previous legislation, to start from a position that 'live' evidence best serves the interests of justice (cf. *R (DPP)* v *Redbridge Youth Court* [2001] 4 All ER 411). The presumptions in the YJCEA 1999 were held in *R (D) v Camberwell Green Youth Court* [2005] 1 WLR 393 not to be susceptible to challenge under the ECHR, Article 6, on the ground of **F16.48**

their generality but rather to be justified in order, *inter alia*, to allow children to know with some certainty the way in which their evidence is to be presented to the court. It thus follows that, in the case of a child, the use of a recording cannot be challenged under s. 27(2) on the ground that the interests of justice would be better served by 'live' evidence unless there exists some specific reason for the contention relating, say, to the individual recording or the circumstances (as in *Parker* [1995] Crim LR 511, where the witness had retracted the statement). In the case of an adult witness, to whom the presumptions do not apply, it is open to the court to consider whether the use of the recording is in any way prejudicial.

In *Powell* [2006] 1 Cr App R 468 (see **F4.21**), where a video recording of an interview with a very young child aged three-and-a-half had been properly admitted but the child proved incompetent when under cross-examination, the judge should have revisited the issue of competence, and this should have led to the withdrawal of the case from the jury.

The court may exclude part only of the recording, but has to balance the possible prejudice to the accused against the desirability of keeping the substance of the recording intact (s. 27(3)). This provision does not render admissible evidence of bad character which would otherwise be excluded (*R (CPS Harrow) v Brentford Youth Court* (2004) 167 JP 614).

In deciding whether to exclude all or part of a recording the court will have regard to relevant provisions of *Achieving Best Evidence in Criminal Proceedings: Guidance for Vulnerable or Intimidated Witnesses, Including Children.* There are sections dealing with the interviewing of children, and of vulnerable and intimidated witnesses (who may or may not be children). Separate sections address the pre-trial and trial stages. Non-compliance does not render an interview inadmissible unless it would be contrary to the interests of justice to admit it under s. 27(2). In *G v DPP* [1998] QB 919, the Divisional Court held that whether failure to comply with the previous guidelines issued in respect of s. 32A should lead to the exclusion of video evidence was not necessarily a question which could be answered simply by considering the nature and extent of the breaches which had occurred. Amongst other factors on which the decision to admit might depend were the extent to which passages in the evidence affected by the breaches were supported by other passages which were not so affected, and the presence or absence of other corroborating evidence. The defence had submitted that the 'substantial and significant' breaches which had allegedly occurred were enough to require exclusion, and the court's rejection of this approach signals a clear (and, it is submitted, correct) distinction between the guidance on pre-recorded evidence on the one hand, and on the other the PACE Codes of Practice, under which such breaches may well lead to discretionary exclusion. In *G* the breaches went only to the weight to be given to the evidence. More recently in *K* [2006] 2 Cr App R 175, the court preferred a differently formulated test, derived from *Hanton* [2005] EWCA Crim 2009: 'could a reasonable jury properly directed be sure that the witness has given a credible and accurate account on the video-tape'. To the extent that this goes beyond the test in *G v DPP* it is submitted that the former is to be preferred.

F16.49 **Replaying the Recording** Where a jury has seen a recording as evidence-in-chief, it has been held in relation to the CJA 1988, s. 32A, that the judge has a discretion to accede to their request to see it again by permitting it to be replayed in court (*Rawlings* [1995] 1 WLR 178), provided that a warning is given that other evidence cannot be replayed, and the jury are reminded of what the child said in cross-examination and in re-examination (safeguards not observed in *M* [1995] Crim LR 336 and *B* [1996] Crim LR 499). *Rawlings* remains good law in relation to the YJCEA 1998, s. 27. A replay may be desirable because the jury requires to be reminded of how the witness gave evidence, rather than of what was said: in the latter case the judge can remind them from his own note. It is only in exceptional circumstances that a video should be replayed otherwise than at the request of the jury (*M* [1996] 2 Cr App R 56). A transcript may be a valuable tool to allow the jury to follow what is said on the tape, provided that it is made clear that the transcript itself is not evidence (*Welstead* [1996] 1 Cr App R 59; *Morris* [1998] Crim LR 416). Similar considerations may affect the replaying of tapes in the youth court. In *L and B v DPP* [1998] 2 Cr App R 69 the Divisional Court declined to lay down the precise procedure to be followed if the tape is to be replayed, but *Rawlings* was cited with approval. It is submitted that the same guidelines should apply, and in particular that nothing should be done which might give the impression that the court has received a double measure of the taped evidence whilst hearing the other side only once. (As to the replaying of a tape which was initially used by the defence to show inconsistencies in the witness's taped evidence-in-chief, see *Eldridge* [1999] Crim LR 166.)

Where a video recording is admitted in evidence, a particularly careful direction may be required concerning any specific problems alleged by the defence to exist in relation to the quality of the evidence (*Springer* [1996] Crim LR 903, where the child's account was alleged to be based on hearsay); see also *DPP v R* [2007] EWHC 1842 (Admin), where the witness no longer had any recollection of the event in question but the video evidence remained admissible.

Consolidated Criminal Practice Direction, para. IV.40, ***Video-recorded evidence-in-chief***

IV.40.1 The procedure for making application for leave to adduce a video recording of testimony from a witness under s. 27 of the Youth Justice and Criminal Evidence Act 1999 is laid down in r. 29.7 of the Criminal Procedure Rules [see **appendix 1**].

IV.40.2 Where a court grants leave to admit a video recording in evidence under s. 27(1) of the 1999 Act it may direct that any part of the recording be excluded (s. 27(2) and (3)). When such a direction is given, the party who made application to admit the video recording must edit the video recording in accordance with the judge's directions and send a copy of the edited recording to the appropriate officer of the Crown Court and to every other party to the proceedings.

IV.40.3 Where a video recording is to be adduced during proceedings before the Crown Court, it should be produced and proved by the interviewer, or any other person who was present at the interview with the witness at which the recording was made. The applicant should ensure that such a person will be available for this purpose, unless the parties have agreed to accept a written statement in lieu of attendance by that person.

IV.40.4 Once a trial has begun if, by reason of faulty or inadequate preparation or for some other cause, the procedures set out above have not been properly complied with and an application is made to edit the video recording, thereby making necessary an adjournment for the work to be carried out, the court may make at its discretion an appropriate award of costs.

Deposition of Child or Young Person

Children and Young Persons Act 1933, s. 43

Where, in any proceedings in respect of any of the offences mentioned in the first schedule to this Act, the court is satisfied by the evidence of a duly qualified medical practitioner that the attendance before the court of any child or young person in respect of whom the offence is alleged to have been committed would involve serious danger to his life or health, any deposition of the child or young person taken under the Indictable Offences Act 1848, or this part of this Act, shall be admissible in evidence either for or against the accused person without further proof thereof if it purports to be signed by the justice by or before whom it purports to be taken: **F16.50**

Provided that the deposition shall not be admissible in evidence against the accused person unless it is proved that reasonable notice of the intention to take the deposition has been served upon him and that he or his counsel or solicitor had, or might have had if he had chosen to be present, an opportunity of cross-examining the child or young person making the deposition.

The relevant provisions of the Indictable Offences Act 1848 have been repealed. For s. 42 of the Children and Young Persons Act 1933, see **D15.38**. The provisions regarding the taking of depositions survive the implementation of the hearsay provisions of the CJA 2003.

The offences to which the provision relates are (CYPA 1933, sch. 1):

(a) the murder or manslaughter of a child or young person, including aiding, abetting, counselling or procuring the suicide of a child or young person, infanticide and an offence under the DVCVA 2004, s. 5 (causing or allowing the death of a child or vulnerable adult), in respect of a child or young person;

(b) any offence under the OAPA 1861, s. 27 or s. 56, and any offence against a child or young person under s. 5 of that Act;

(c) common assault or battery;

(d) any offence under ss. 1, 3, 4, 11, or 23 of the 1933 Act itself;

(e) any offence against a child or young person under the SOA 2003, ss. 1 to 41, 47 to 53, 57 to 61, 66 and 67 and any offence under the SOA 2003, s. 62 or 63, where the intended offence was an offence against a child or young person, or any attempt to commit any such offence; and

(f) any other offence involving bodily injury to a child or young person.

See also the Protection of Children Act 1978, s. 1(5), incorporating offences under s. 1(1)(a) of that Act, and the CJA 1988, sch. 15, incorporating offences under the Child Abduction Act 1984, part I.

Written Statements Admissible under Criminal Justice Act 1967, s. 9

F16.51 For an account of the provisions of the CJA 1967, s. 9, which deal with the admissibility of written statements, see **D21.24**.

Statements Admissible under Miscellaneous Statutory Provisions

F16.52 Various statutes make provision for the admission of hearsay statements. The following are the most commonly invoked.

Under the CJA 1988, s. 30 (see **F10.28**), the report of an expert witness on matters of which he would have been competent to give oral evidence is admissible as evidence of the facts and opinions stated therein. This provision applies only to 'written' reports so that the admissibility of, say, a tape-recorded report may be in doubt. Under the CJA 1972, s. 46(1), written statements made in Scotland or Northern Ireland may be admitted as evidence in other criminal proceedings on the same terms as statements made in England and Wales.

Bankers' Books

F16.53 The Bankers' Books Evidence Act 1879, s. 3 (see **F8.27**) was designed to facilitate proof of bankers' records without bringing the original document to court. As the provision is confined to copies, nothing in s. 3 renders the original banker's book admissible: in most cases, however, the original would be admissible under the CJA 2003, s. 117, and a copy would be admissible by virtue of s. 133 of that Act. Before a copy can be given in evidence under s. 3 of the 1879 Act, s. 4 of that Act requires proof to be given that the banker's book was at the time of the relevant entry one of the ordinary books of the bank, that the entry was made in the usual and ordinary course of business, and that the book is in the custody or control of the bank. If the CJA 2003, s. 117, is relied upon, no such conditions need be satisfied. It should also be noted that the 1879 Act confines itself to the various books and records of a bank. In *Dadson* (1983) 77 Cr App R 91, which concerned events which occurred before the 1879 Act was amended to include records, it was held that a file of correspondence was inadmissible under s. 3 as not being a 'book'. The correspondence would now be admissible under the 1879 Act only if it is held to constitute a 'record', whereas the CJA 2003 imposes no such constraint. It was held in *Re Howglen Ltd* [2001] 1 All ER 376 that a 'record' for this purpose connoted a method by which a bank recorded day-to-day financial transactions: a record of notes of meetings could not be regarded as banker's books within the 1879 Act. A record of a meeting would now be admissible under s. 117 of the 2003 Act.

As to the practice surrounding inspection of bankers' books and their relationship to the best evidence rule, see generally F8.27.

CRIMINAL JUSTICE ACT 2003: ADDITIONAL REQUIREMENT FOR THE USE OF MULTIPLE HEARSAY

The CJA 2003, s. 121, stipulates that only limited use can be made of multiple hearsay. This appears to apply whether the hearsay in question is tendered under the new statutory exceptions contained in the Act itself, or under the preserved common-law exceptions, or under other statutory provisions, given that the new rule is negative in form and defines hearsay evidence in the broadest of terms. **F16.54**

Criminal Justice Act 2003, s. 121

(1) A hearsay statement is not admissible to prove the fact that an earlier hearsay statement was made unless—
- (a) either of the statements is admissible under section 117, 119 or 120,
- (b) all parties to the proceedings so agree, or
- (c) the court is satisfied that the value of the evidence in question, taking into account how reliable the statements appear to be, is so high that the interests of justice require the later statement to be admissible for that purpose.

(2) In this section 'hearsay statement' means a statement, not made in oral evidence, that is relied on as evidence of a matter stated in it.

Under this provision, which was revisited during the passage of the Bill through Parliament, multiple hearsay (such as 'A told me that B told him that D shot V') is not admissible even if both the statement by A and the statement by B fit within one or more of the various exceptions to the hearsay rule (for example B's statement is a spontaneous statement made as part of the *res gestae*, and A's statement is admissible under s. 116 because A has died since making it). The only exceptions to this principle are where one of the statements is admissible as a business document (see s. 117 at **F16.14**) or a previous statement by a witness in the case, or where the court is so convinced by the value of the evidence that it can invoke the special 'safety valve' in s. 121(1)(c). In *Xhabri* [2006] 1 All ER 776 (considered at **F16.20**), the test in s. 121 was satisfied in relation to a complaint of false imprisonment which was relayed by two friends of the victim to a police officer. The complainant and the officer (though not the two friends) were available for cross-examination. The Court considered that both s. 121(1)(a) (admissibility under other provisions) and s. 121(1)(c) (admissibility in the interests of justice) were satisfied. In *Maher v DPP* (2006) 170 JP 441, a note which had been made (and lost) of a car number plate formed the basis of a call to the police in which the number was transmitted. Evidence of the number was received under s. 121(1)(c) although it was inadmissible as a business record under s. 117 (see **F16.15**) on the grounds of reliability. In *Musone* [2007] EWCA Crim 1237, s. 121(1)(c) was invoked to admit the narration by a reluctant witness of the victim's dying declaration. First-hand statements by the same witness were admitted under s. 114(1)(d) (see **F16.20**) and the court noted the similarity of the consideration in play. The difference is that under s. 121(1)(c) the value of the evidence must be 'so high' that its admission is required.

CRIMINAL JUSTICE ACT 2003: EVIDENCE AFFECTING THE CREDIBILITY OF ADMISSIBLE HEARSAY

The CJA 2003, s. 124, governs the admissibility of evidence directed towards the discrediting of a hearsay statement where the maker of the statement does not give oral evidence in connection with the subject-matter of the statement. It does not appear that this provision is limited to hearsay statements admissible under the 2003 Act: on the contrary it appears to be of general effect. **F16.55**

The mixture of materials admissible to discredit the maker is similar to that which previously appeared in the CJA 1988, sch. 2. However, the court has wider powers to admit evidence in order to deny or answer the allegation.

Criminal Justice Act 2003, s. 124

(1) This section applies if in criminal proceedings—
 (a) a statement not made in oral evidence in the proceedings is admitted as evidence of a matter stated, and
 (b) the maker of the statement does not give oral evidence in connection with the subject matter of the statement.
(2) In such a case—
 (a) any evidence which (if he had given such evidence) would have been admissible as relevant to his credibility as a witness is so admissible in the proceedings;
 (b) evidence may with the court's leave be given of any matter which (if he had given such evidence) could have been put to him in cross-examination as relevant to his credibility as a witness but of which evidence could not have been adduced by the cross-examining party;
 (c) evidence tending to prove that he made (at whatever time) any other statement inconsistent with the statement admitted as evidence is admissible for the purpose of showing that he contradicted himself.
(3) If as a result of evidence admitted under this section an allegation is made against the maker of a statement, the court may permit a party to lead additional evidence of such description as the court may specify for the purposes of denying or answering the allegation.
(4) In the case of a statement in a document which is admitted as evidence under section 117 each person who, in order for the statement to be admissible, must have supplied or received the information concerned or created or received the document or part concerned is to be treated as the maker of the statement for the purposes of subsections (1) to (3) above.

UNCONVINCING AND SUPERFLUOUS HEARSAY

F16.56 Under the provisions of the CJA 2003, the Crown Court has a specific power to stop a case where (a) the case depends significantly ('wholly or partly') on a hearsay statement and (b) the evidence is unconvincing to the point where a conviction based on it would be unsafe. In similar circumstances, magistrates are in any event be bound to dismiss a case based on such evidence: the object is to prevent a perverse finding by a jury (and by service courts, to which the power also applies: sch. 7, para. 4).

In addition, any court trying a criminal case has power to exclude hearsay evidence where 'taking account of the danger that to admit it would result in undue waste of time' the case for exclusion outweighs the case for admission. Section 126 operates without prejudice to the common-law power to exclude evidence on the ground that its prejudicial effect outweighs its probative value, or the general discretion to exclude prosecution evidence under the PACE 1984, s. 78. Unlike the preserved powers, however, s. 126 can be invoked in respect of evidence tendered by the defence.

Criminal Justice Act 2003, ss. 125 and 126

125.—(1) If on a defendant's trial before a judge and jury for an offence the court is satisfied at any time after the close of the case for the prosecution that—
 (a) the case against the defendant is based wholly or partly on a statement not made in oral evidence in the proceedings, and
 (b) the evidence provided by the statement is so unconvincing that, considering its importance to the case against the defendant, his conviction of the offence would be unsafe,

the court must either direct the jury to acquit the defendant of the offence or, if it considers that there ought to be a retrial, discharge the jury.
(2) Where—
 (a) a jury is directed under subsection (1) to acquit a defendant of an offence, and

(b) the circumstances are such that, apart from this subsection, the defendant could if acquitted of that offence be found guilty of another offence,

the defendant may not be found guilty of that other offence if the court is satisfied as mentioned in subsection (1) in respect of it.

(3) If—

(a) a jury is required to determine under section 4A(2) of the Criminal Procedure (Insanity) Act 1964 whether a person charged on an indictment with an offence did the act or made the omission charged, and

(b) the court is satisfied as mentioned in subsection (1) above at any time after the close of the case for the prosecution that—

(i) the case against the defendant is based wholly or partly on a statement not made in oral evidence in the proceedings, and

(ii) the evidence provided by the statement is so unconvincing that, considering its importance to the case against the person, a finding that he did the act or made the omission would be unsafe,

the court must either direct the jury to acquit the defendant of the offence or, if it considers that there ought to be a rehearing, discharge the jury.

(4) This section does not prejudice any other power a court may have to direct a jury to acquit a person of an offence or to discharge a jury.

126.—(1) In criminal proceedings the court may refuse to admit a statement as evidence of a matter stated if—

(a) the statement was made otherwise than in oral evidence in the proceedings, and

(b) the court is satisfied that the case for excluding the statement, taking account of the danger that to admit it would result in undue waste of time, substantially outweighs the case for admitting it, taking account of the value of the evidence.

(2) Nothing in this chapter prejudices—

(a) any power of a court to exclude evidence under section 78 of the Police and Criminal Evidence Act 1984 (exclusion of unfair evidence), or

(b) any other power of a court to exclude evidence at its discretion (whether by preventing questions from being put or otherwise).

Section F17 The Rule Against Hearsay: Confessions

Definition

F17.1 **Police and Criminal Evidence Act 1984, s. 82**

(1) In this part of this Act—
'confession', includes any statement wholly or partly adverse to the person who made it, whether made to a person in authority or not and whether made in words or otherwise.

The admissibility of confession evidence is governed by provisions to be found in the PACE 1984, part VII, from which the above definition is taken. At common law, the test for admissibility of confessions was that of voluntariness, and a statement obtained by fear of prejudice or hope of advantage excited or held out by a person in authority was regarded as having been made involuntarily (see, e.g., *Baldry* (1852) 2 Den CC 430, per Baron Parke at p. 444; *Ibrahim v The King* [1914] AC 599; *DPP v Ping Lin* [1976] AC 574). The 1984 Act introduced a new test for admissibility (as to which see **F17.5**) and redefines 'confession'. Section 82(1) makes it clear that the law is no longer concerned with whether the confession was made to a person in authority, such as a police or customs officer, and that the statutory test for admissibility is equally applicable to, for example, an informal admission to a friend or colleague. Dissatisfaction with the common law had been expressed in *Deokinanan v The Queen* [1969] 1 AC 20, in which it was noted that a person who is not in authority may induce an unreliable confession by, for example, offering a bribe. Most confessions will, however, continue to be made to persons in authority such as the police, and the observation made in *Deokinanan v The Queen* that, 'The fact that an inducement is made by a person in authority may make it more likely to operate on the accused's mind and lead him to confess', continues to be true.

It should follow from the definition of 'confession' in s. 82(1), and from the provision in s. 76(1) (see **F17.5**) that only a confession made 'by' an accused may be given in evidence 'against him' and that where the only proof that the accused made the statement comes from the confession itself it should not be admitted. However, in *Ward* [2001] Crim LR 316, the Court of Appeal held that where a passenger in a car gave W's personal details to a police officer when asked for his own, the statement was admissible as a 'confession' by W, who denied being the passenger. It is submitted that while this is a useful device for admitting a common form of evidence of identification it was not a confession 'by' W unless its truth was assumed. A better approach would be to regard the statement as a form of original evidence, unless this option is now precluded by the hearsay provisions of the CJA 2003, in particular s. 115(3) (see **F15.12**).

The result of a literal application of the definition in *Mawdesley v Chief Constable of Cheshire Constabulary* [2004] 1 WLR 1035 was that a statement disclosing the identity of a driver was admissible as a confession if it could be inferred that the accused had written it, even though it was unsigned (and therefore inadmissible under the statutory scheme in the Road Traffic Act 1988).

Guilty Pleas and Pleas in Mitigation A plea of guilty is a confession for the purposes of the PACE 1984, s. 82(1), and as such is admissible in evidence provided that the provisions of s. 76(2) are complied with. At common law a plea of guilty was regarded as an admission of fact and was admissible in evidence against an accused who subsequently changed his plea to 'not guilty', provided that: F17.2

(a) the plea had some probative value; and
(b) the probative value exceeded the prejudicial effect that might be imported by referring to it (*Rimmer* [1972] 1 WLR 268, and see also *Hetherington* [1972] Crim LR 703).

In the vast majority of cases such evidence would not be admitted. Any admission of a guilty plea in evidence would have to be followed by a very careful direction by the trial judge as to exactly how it should be looked at by the jury (*Rimmer*, at p. 272).

An admission made by an accused in other proceedings would similarly constitute a confession for the purposes of the 1984 Act, and could be relied upon provided, as is likely, that it complies with the provisions of s. 76(2). At common law, in *McGregor* [1968] 1 QB 371 there had been a previous trial of M, and at his retrial the prosecution adduced evidence of admissions made at the earlier trial. The Court of Appeal could 'conceive of no ground upon which it could be said that this evidence was inadmissible'.

A plea in mitigation made by counsel on behalf of a client who has been convicted on his plea of 'not guilty' should not be understood as a confession by the convicted person through his counsel. So to regard mitigation would be both unjust and unrealistic, as it is counsel's duty to accept the verdict and seek to mitigate the consequences (*Wu Chun-Piu v The Queen* [1996] 1 WLR 1113). It is submitted that the same must be true if the convicted person advances his mitigation in person.

Confessions Otherwise than in Words

There is no statutory definition of 'statement' for the purposes of part VII of the PACE 1984, but the inclusion in s. 82(1) of the expression 'whether made in words or otherwise' suggests that 'confession' may, in addition to admissions in oral or written form, include conduct such as a nod of acceptance of an accusation or a 'thumbs-up' sign which may be properly regarded as a 'statement' in sign language. In *Li Shu-Ling v The Queen* [1989] AC 270, L, who had previously made a full confession to the police, agreed to take part in a filmed re-enactment of the crime with which he was charged, which was the murder of a woman by strangulation. He gave a running commentary explaining his movements, which he demonstrated on a woman police officer who played the part of the victim. At trial, his account of the killing was entirely different. It was held by the Privy Council (applying common-law principles) that the re-enactment was to be regarded as a confession, and the point was made that it is very much more difficult for an accused to escape from the visual record of his confession than to challenge an oral statement, with the result that a film may constitute most valuable evidence of guilt. Such a film would, it is submitted, constitute a confession under s. 82(1), and may be given in evidence, provided that the conditions of admissibility under the 1984 Act are satisfied. That the conditions of admissibility should be the same for re-enactments or visual demonstrations as for oral or written confessions was confirmed at common law in *Timothy v The State* [2000] 1 WLR 485. Confessions made by two of the accused were excluded following allegations of police misconduct. It was held that the same allegations were relevant to the voluntariness, and therefore to the admissibility, of the conduct of the two in showing the police where they had hidden the murder weapon (see also *Lam Chi Ming v The Queen* [1991] 2 AC 212). F17.3

It is submitted that conduct which is not intended to convey guilt, but which may be interpreted as doing so, is not a 'statement' and hence not a confession. Thus, for example, driving away at speed from the scene of an accident is not a confession to which the 1984 Act applies, though evidence of such conduct would be relevant and admissible.

Partly and Wholly Exculpatory Statements

F17.4 A confession may be 'wholly or partly adverse' to the maker, with the result that a so-called 'mixed statement', which is part confession and part exculpation, is a confession for the purposes of the PACE 1984. (See to the same effect at common law, *Customs and Excise Commissioners v Harz* [1967] 1 AC 760, per Lord Reid at p. 818, and see further as to the use of mixed statements in evidence **F17.61** to **F17.65**).

In *Finch* [2007] 1 WLR 1645, the issue was whether the accused could rely on a statement made by R, an erstwhile co-accused, under the PACE 1984, s. 76A (see **F17.19**). The Court of Appeal identified as suitable for full argument the question whether statements made by R in police interviews which went beyond admissions and were exculpatory of F constituted 'confessions' for the purposes of s. 82(1). A simple solution would be to regard the point at which a statement begins and ends as a question of fact.

Where the part of a mixed statement relied upon by the prosecution also forms part of the defence, it may be easier to set aside errors in the manner by which it was obtained. In *Uddin* [2005] EWCA Crim 464, U, who was of very low IQ, was wrongly interviewed without an independent adult. The only admission U made was of his presence at the scene: in all other respects his statement was self-serving, and consistent with his evidence at trial. In holding that the use of the confession did not lead to an unsafe conviction, the Court of Appeal noted that the purpose of the protection of which U had been deprived was to prevent prejudice arising from his failure to do himself justice at interview. As U's admission of presence was an inherent part of the defence, this had not occurred.

A more difficult issue is whether the PACE 1984, s. 82(1), includes a statement which, when made, is purely self-serving, but which becomes 'adverse' to the interests of the accused because of the way in which it is deployed at trial, typically because it is inconsistent with the defence there put forward. In *Sat-Bhambra* (1988) 88 Cr App R 55, the Court of Appeal (*obiter*) considered that a purely exculpatory statement was not a confession, but noted that such a statement might be excluded under the more general power of the court under s. 78 (see **F17.23** to **F17.35**, and *Jelen* (1989) 90 Cr App R 456). *Sat-Bhambra* was approved by the House of Lords in *Hasan* [2005] 2 AC 467, overturning the decision of the Court of Appeal in the same case, reported as *Z* [2003] 1 WLR 1489. It was argued that the definition in s. 82(1) ('"confession" includes any statement wholly or partly adverse') was apt also to 'include' statements that were not adverse when made. According to Lord Steyn, with whom the other members of the House concurred, the word 'includes' was selected simply in order to extend the core meaning of confession to partly adverse statements. The meaning contended for was strained, and also unnecessary, as s. 78 was available to protect an accused where, for example, the police by oppression secured a wholly exculpatory but false statement by oppression and then sought to use it 'against' an accused so as to damage his credibility. Nor was there (as had been suggested in *Z*) any risk to the fair trial provisions of the ECHR, Article 6, if the accused was denied access to the protection afforded by s. 76, given the 'unrestricted capability of s. 78 to avoid injustice by excluding any evidence obtained by unfairness'. Although s. 78 is formally couched in the language of discretion and s. 76 in the language of judgment, s. 78 'in truth imports a judgment whether in the light of the statutory criteria of fairness the court ought to admit the evidence'. The House therefore concluded that there was no gap in the procedural safeguards provided by the PACE 1984.

Principles of Admissibility under the PACE 1984, s. 76

Police and Criminal Evidence Act 1984, s. 76 **F17.5**

(1) In any proceedings a confession made by an accused person may be given in evidence against him insofar as it is relevant to any matter in issue in the proceedings and is not excluded by the court in pursuance of this section.

(2) If, in any proceedings where the prosecution proposes to give in evidence a confession made by an accused person, it is represented to the court that the confession was or may have been obtained—

(a) by oppression of the person who made it; or

(b) in consequence of anything said or done which was likely, in the circumstances existing at the time, to render unreliable any confession which might be made by him in consequence thereof,

the court shall not allow the confession to be given in evidence against him except insofar as the prosecution proves to the court beyond reasonable doubt that the confession (notwithstanding that it may be true) was not obtained as aforesaid.

(3) In any proceedings where the prosecution proposes to give in evidence a confession made by an accused person, the court may of its own motion require the prosecution, as a condition of allowing it to do so, to prove that the confession was not obtained as mentioned in subsection (2) above.

The CPIA 1996, sch. 1, para. 25, inserted s. 76(9), which provides that, in the case of proceedings before a magistrates' court inquiring into an offence as examining justices, the section shall have effect with the omission in s. 76(1) of the words 'and is not excluded by the court in pursuance of this section' and subsections (2) to (6) and (8).

Section 76 appears not to have been intended as a mechanism for regulating the admissibility of a confession made by one co-accused as evidence for another. In *Myers* [1998] AC 124, the House of Lords declined to decide whether s. 76(1) applied to defence evidence, but the CJA 2003, s. 128, now adds a new s. 76A to the PACE 1984 in order to provide statutory regulation of the admission of the confession of a co-accused (see **F17.19**). For ease of exposition, the position with regard to prosecution evidence will be explained first.

The prosecution do not have to prove the admissibility of a confession upon which they rely unless either (a) the defence 'represents' that it is inadmissible under s. 76(2), or (b) the court of its own motion requires proof of admissibility under s. 76(3). If in either case the prosecution are unable to prove admissibility beyond reasonable doubt, the confession must be excluded, notwithstanding that it may be true: the court has no discretion in the matter (*Paris* (1993) 97 Cr App R 99). A confession may be excluded in part (cf. s. 76(4) and (6) at **F17.53** ***et seq.***). As to procedure, see **F17.39** ***et seq.***

A confession which is inadmissible in criminal proceedings in consequence of s. 76 should not be used as the basis for a formal caution (*Metropolitan Police Commissioner, ex parte Thompson* [1997] 1 WLR 1519).

EXCLUSION FOR OPPRESSION: PACE 1984, s. 76(2)(a)

Definition of Oppression

Police and Criminal Evidence Act 1984, s. 76 **F17.6**

(8) In this section 'oppression' includes torture, inhuman or degrading treatment, and the use or threat of violence (whether or not amounting to torture).

The reference to 'torture' may be interpreted in the light of the offence of torture contained in the CJA 1988, s. 134. 'Torture and inhuman or degrading treatment' is also prohibited by the ECHR, Article 3, and reference may be made to case law under Article 3 (see, e.g., *Republic of Ireland v United Kingdom* (1978) 2 EHRR 25).

Oppression at Common Law

F17.7 At common law, a confession obtained by oppression was regarded as involuntary and therefore inadmissible (see, e.g., *Callis v Gunn* [1964] 1 QB 495; *Prager* [1972] 1 WLR 260). 'Oppression' was understood not only to include physical oppression (*Burut v Public Prosecutor* [1995] 2 AC 579, in which the Privy Council held that the manacling and hooding of suspects under interrogation in Brunei was 'plainly oppressive') but carried a wider sense; it was described by Sachs J in *Priestley* (1965) 51 Cr App R 1 at p. 1 as 'something which tends to sap, and has sapped, that free will which must exist before a confession is voluntary'. This, and other common-law definitions of the term, do not, however, provide reliable indications of the meaning of the word in its present statutory context. In *Fulling* [1987] QB 426 the court held (without referring to the PACE 1984, s. 76(8)) that the 1984 Act does not follow the wording of earlier rules or decisions, nor is it expressed to be a consolidating Act. It is a codifying Act, in the interpretation of which the proper course is to start by ascertaining the natural meaning of the language used, uninfluenced by any considerations derived from the previous state of the law (applying the principles set out by Lord Herschell in *Bank of England v Vagliano Brothers* [1891] AC 107, at pp. 144–5). It was further stated that much of the sort of treatment which would have fallen within the definition of oppression at common law will now fall to be dealt with under the 'reliability' head of exclusion.

Ambit of Oppression

F17.8 In *Fulling* [1987] QB 426 the prosecution tendered a confession by F in which she admitted her part in an insurance fraud initiated by her boyfriend, D. F claimed that the confession was made in order to secure her release from custody after a police officer had revealed, to F's great distress, not only that D had been unfaithful to her, but also that the 'other woman' was being held in the cell next to F's. On the assumption that these revelations were made, the trial judge ruled that there was no oppression in the sense of 'something above and beyond that which is inherently oppressive in police custody . . . [importing] some impropriety . . . actively applied in an improper manner by the police'. The Court of Appeal upheld the ruling of the trial judge. 'Oppression' was to be given its 'ordinary dictionary meaning' of: 'Exercise of authority or power in a burdensome, harsh or wrongful manner; unjust or cruel treatment of subjects, inferiors etc., the imposition of unreasonable or unjust burdens'.

Oppression almost inevitably involves some impropriety on the part of the interrogator (*Fulling* at p. 432). It does not follow that all impropriety necessarily involves oppression; otherwise all wrongful acts, including breaches of the PACE Codes of Practice, could be termed oppressive, which is clearly not so (*Parker* [1995] Crim LR 233; *Re Proulx* [2001] 1 All ER 57). In *Fulling*, the Court drew attention to a quotation which exemplifies the meaning of the term: 'There is not a word in our language that expresses more detestable wickedness than oppression.' In *Emmerson* (1991) 92 Cr App R 284, a police officer had given way to impatience during an interview and had raised his voice and used bad language to the accused. The Court of Appeal ruled that to regard such conduct as oppressive would be to give the word a completely false meaning. Unduly hostile questioning may, however, be oppressive: it is a question of degree. In *Paris* (1993) 97 Cr App R 99 a tape recording of an interview with M revealed that he had been 'bullied and hectored'. The Court of Appeal commented that, short of physical violence, it was hard to conceive of a more hostile and intimidating approach by officers to a suspect. The interview was oppressive and M's later confession ought to have been excluded. However, in *L* [1994] Crim LR 839, tactics similar to those employed in *Paris* appear to have been regarded as acceptable provided the reliability of the confession was not compromised.

A degree of impropriety which is insufficient for oppression may serve to support an argument that a confession should be excluded under the PACE 1984, s. 76(2)(b) or s. 78, considered at **F17.11** *et seq.* and **F17.23** *et seq.* respectively. Thus, in *Samuel* [1988] QB 615, the Court of Appeal, while acknowledging the possibility that oppression might be present where access to legal advice is improperly denied, preferred to quash S's conviction by reference to s. 78. Exclusion for oppression is likely to be reserved for those rare cases where an accused has been subjected to misconduct of a deliberate and serious nature, and where the court is anxious to mark its disquiet at the methods employed. An issue which frequently arises in relation to misconduct is the extent to which the use of similar methods by the same officer in relation to other suspects may figure in cross-examination. This is dealt with at F7.14. In relation to oppression, the court's natural reluctance to exclude on this basis may be overcome by the use of such evidence (see, e.g., *Twitchell* [2000] 1 Cr App R 373, in which the Court of Appeal considered that officers alleged to have tortured D could have been cross-examined to 'potentially devastating' effect had the subsequent findings of a court regarding a similar torture by the same officers on another man been available for use in cross-examination).

Repetition of Confession Originally Obtained by Oppression

Where a confession made in the course of an interview is excluded on grounds of oppression, it may be necessary to consider whether the effect on the accused was such that the repetition by him of the same information at a later, properly conducted interview ought also to be excluded (*Ismail* [1990] Crim LR 109, in which it was held that to accede to the prosecution's submission that misconduct in earlier interviews could be 'cured' by a properly conducted interview would be to condone flouting of the provisions of the Act and codes designed to protect against false confessions). **F17.9**

Relevance of Character and Attributes of Accused

At common law it was held that the nature of oppression varied according to the character and attributes of the accused. Thus, an 'experienced professional criminal' might expect a vigorous interrogation (*Gowan* [1982] Crim LR 821), and in *Dodd* (1981) 74 Cr App 50, O'Connor LJ said (at p. 56) that the trial judge 'was entitled to consider the type of men he was dealing with', all of whom were experienced criminals. O'Connor LJ contrasted the case with that of *Hudson* (1980) 72 Cr App R 163, in which a middle-aged man of previous good character had been subjected to a lengthy, and in certain respects unlawful, interrogation, which was subsequently held to have been oppressive. At the other end of the spectrum, in *Miller* [1986] 1 WLR 1191 Watkins LJ said that it might be oppressive to put questions to an accused who is known to be mentally ill so as 'skilfully and deliberately' to induce a delusionary state in him. Despite the rejection in *Fulling* [1987] QB 426 of common-law rulings on oppression, these cases may still be good law, for the Court of Appeal in *Fulling* was concerned to reject the 'artificially wide' common-law definition of oppression, while the above cases appear to proceed on a meaning which is consistent with the ordinary meaning of oppression as adopted in *Fulling*. This view appears to have been confirmed by *Seelig* [1992] 1 WLR 148, in which Henry J, in a ruling described by the Court of Appeal as 'entirely right', took account of the fact that the person being questioned was 'an experienced merchant banker' and 'intelligent and sophisticated', in determining whether he had been questioned in an oppressive way, and in *Smith* [1994] 1 WLR 1396 the Court of Appeal regarded it as relevant that S, who was questioned by a person in authority within a bank, was himself a chairman and managing director of a substantial financial organisation. Similarly in *Paris* (1993) 97 Cr App R 99 (see **F17.8**) the court, although of the opinion that the bullying and hectoring of M in interview would have been oppressive even with a suspect of normal intelligence, went out of its way to stress that M was on the borderline of mental handicap. **F17.10**

EXCLUSION FOR UNRELIABILITY: PACE 1984, s. 76(2)(b)

Unreliability at Common Law

F17.11 At common law, a confession was regarded as involuntary, and therefore inadmissible, if it was obtained by fear of prejudice or hope of advantage held out or excited by a person in authority (*DPP v Ping Lin* [1976] AC 574). According to a majority of the House of Lords in that case, it did not matter whether the person who induced the confession was behaving improperly or not. Many cases occurred where confessions had to be excluded, notwithstanding that there was no reason to suppose that the threat or inducement concerned had caused the accused to provide an unreliable statement (see, e.g., *Northam* (1967) 52 Cr App R 97, *Zaveckas* [1970] 1 WLR 516). The Criminal Law Revision Committee, in its 11th Report, *Evidence* (1972) Cmnd 4991, proposed that a confession obtained in consequence of a threat or inducement should not be excluded unless the circumstances were such that any confession made by the accused would be likely to be unreliable. This proposal became the PACE 1984, s. 76(2)(b), though the term 'threat or inducement' was replaced by the wider notion of 'anything said or done'.

Application of Statutory Test

F17.12 The PACE 1984 requires the trial judge to consider a hypothetical question: not whether *this* confession is unreliable, but whether *any* confession which the accused might make in consequence of what was said or done was likely to be rendered unreliable. The purport of this provision was considered in *Re Proulx* [2001] 1 All ER 57, where Mance LJ stated (at [46]):

> The test in s. 76 cannot be satisfied by postulating some entirely different confession. There is also no likelihood that anything said or done would have induced any other confession. The word 'any' must thus, I think, be understood as indicating 'any such' or 'such a' confession as the applicant made. The abstract element involved also reflects the fact that the test is not whether the actual confession was untruthful or inaccurate. It is whether whatever was said or done was, in the circumstances existing as at the time of the confession, *likely* to have rendered such a confession unreliable, whether or not it may be seen subsequently — with hindsight and in the light of all the material available at trial — that it did or did not actually do so.

Thus the court must consider whether what happened was likely in the circumstances to induce *an* unreliable confession to the offence in question, and to ignore any evidence suggesting that the *actual* confession was reliable.

In *Cox* [1991] Crim LR 276, a mentally handicapped accused gave evidence at the *voir dire* in the course of which he admitted one of the offences with which he was charged. The trial judge was held to have wrongly based his decision to admit C's out of court confession on the admission by C. The same point was made in *Crampton* (1991) 92 Cr App R 372, where it was said that, if acts are done or words spoken which are likely to induce unreliable confessions, then, whether or not the confession is true, it is inadmissible. Although the judge may not be influenced by evidence that the confession is true in deciding admissibility, he is not precluded from taking into account any other relevant evidence given at trial before the *voir dire* begins which assists him to determine the questions posed by s. 76(2)(b) (*Tyrer* (1989) 90 Cr App R 446 at pp. 449–50). Such evidence must, however, relate to the period before, or at the time when, the confession is made: the judge must 'stop the clock' and consider the issue of reliability at that point in time (a proposition cautiously, but rightly, advanced by Mance LJ in *Re Proulx*).

F17.13 **'Anything Said or Done'** Section 76(2) of PACE 1984 obliges the judge to consider everything said or done (usually, but not inevitably by the police) and not to confine himself to a narrow analysis analogous to offer and acceptance in the law of contract (*Barry* (1992) 95 Cr App R 384; *Wahab* [2003] 1 Cr App R 232). The use of the phrase 'anything said or done', and the inclusion of all the surrounding circumstances, are indications that the new test follows the common law in acknowledging that a confession may be inadmissible, notwithstanding that the police have not behaved improperly. In *Fulling* [1987] QB 426 the Court of Appeal stated, *obiter*, that it was 'abundantly clear' that a confession may be excluded under s. 76(2)(b) where there is no suspicion of any impropriety. Dicta in *Brine* [1992] Crim LR 123, stating that s. 76(2) is 'primarily concerned' with police misconduct, should not be understood to qualify this statement of principle. See also *Harvey* [1988] Crim LR 241, in which a psychopathically disordered woman of low normal intelligence heard her lover confess to a murder. As this experience may have led her to make a false confession out of a child-like desire to protect her lover, her statement was excluded under s. 76(2)(b). *Harvey* was cited with approval in *Raghip* (1991) *The Times*, 9 December 1991 and in *Wahab*. Such a confession might also be excluded under s. 78 (see **F17.23**). In the rather extreme case of *M* [2000] 8 Arch News 2, it was M's solicitor who, by intervening in the interview in an apparent attempt to secure a confession, rendered the resultant confession unreliable. In *Wahab* the Court of Appeal noted that where the solicitor provides proper legal advice to his client this will not normally be a basis for excluding a confession under s. 76(2).

Words or Actions of the Accused It has been held that a confession cannot be rendered inadmissible under the PACE 1984, s. 76(2)(b), by reason only of something said or done by the accused himself (*Goldenberg* (1988) 88 Cr App R 285). In this case G was interviewed on suspicion of conspiracy to supply controlled drugs. The admissions which he made were alleged by the defence to be (a) an attempt by him to get bail, and (b) tainted by the fact that he was a heroin addict who, having been in custody for some time, would have said or done anything, however false, to gain his release so as to feed his addiction. The Court of Appeal considered that this argument was founded entirely 'on what was said or done by the appellant himself and on his state of mind', and that this was beyond the scope of the provision. The wording of the section, and in particular the words 'in consequence' in s. 76(2)(b), imported a causal link between what was said or done and the subsequent confession. **F17.14**

It followed that the provision was looking to something external to the person making the confession and which was likely to have some effect on him. *Goldenberg* was considered in *Crampton* (1991) 92 Cr App R 372, in which police officers interviewed C, a heroin addict, who it subsequently transpired was suffering from withdrawal symptoms. It was noted that in *Goldenberg* it was G himself who had requested the interview, but this was thought not to provide a ground for distinguishing the case, for it was doubtful whether the requirement for something external to be 'said or done' could be satisfied by the mere holding of an interview with an addict in withdrawal. The words of the statute contemplated some words spoken or acts done by the police which were likely to induce unreliable confessions. In *Walker* [1998] Crim LR 211, the Court of Appeal appears to have considered that the issue of whether W had taken cocaine before confessing had a material bearing on admissibility, but this appears to have been achieved by regarding the impairment of the accused as one of the 'circumstances' referred to in s. 76(2)(b).

'Circumstances' The accused's own mental state may be part of the 'circumstances' for the purposes of s. 76(2)(b). In *Re Proulx* [2001] 1 All ER 57, P confessed to a murder to an undercover operative who persuaded him that it was necessary in order to be accepted as a member of a criminal gang anxious to know the truth about his past. Whether this was something likely to induce P to make a false confession was something which could only be determined by an assessment of P (which was easier to make than is usually the case as the confession was video-recorded). It does not matter whether these circumstances were known to the interrogator at the time. In *Everett* [1988] Crim LR 826, E was discovered in a compromising position with a five-year-old boy. On the way to the police station, and while **F17.15**

he was there, he admitted indecently assaulting the child. E was a 42-year-old man with a mental age of eight, and was regarded by a medical witness as being in the bottom 2 per cent of the population. The trial judge regarded the medical evidence as irrelevant provided that he was satisfied (as he was) from listening to the tape recording of the police station interview that E's replies were rational and showed understanding of the questions. The Court of Appeal ruled against this approach, and held that the circumstances to be taken into account 'obviously include' the mental condition of a suspect at the time the confession came into being. The test to be applied was an objective one, i.e. not what the police officers thought (if they thought anything) about the mental condition of the suspect, but instead the actual condition of the suspect as subsequently ascertained from a doctor. The confession ought to have been excluded because the prosecution 'most certainly had not' discharged the burden of proving it admissible. Similarly, in *McGovern* (1991) 92 Cr App R 228, it was said that the physical condition and particular vulnerability of M (she was six months pregnant and of limited intelligence), while not being 'anything said or done' to M, were part of the background against which the submission that she had been wrongly denied access to legal advice had to be judged. The combination of circumstances had the far-reaching result that it was appropriate to exclude both the confession made as a direct consequence of the denial of access and a subsequent confession made in the presence of a solicitor which was tarnished as a result of the earlier confession. In *Souter* [1995] Crim LR 729, a confession was held to be inadmissible where it was made by a soldier who was in a state of extreme emotion and distress to an officer who had been sent to calm him down; other relevant factors were that the conversation between the two had an appearance of confidentiality, and the officer had a very partial recollection of the rest of what had been said. The kind of mental condition which may be taken into account under s. 76(2)(b) is not limited to what might be termed 'impairment of intelligence or social functioning', still less to 'mental impairment' (*Walker* [1998] Crim LR 211). In cases where the mental condition of the accused is a relevant factor, expert evidence is admissible if it demonstrates some form of abnormality relevant to the reliability of a defendant's confession (*O'Brien* [2000] Crim LR 676). In *Ward* [1993] 96 Cr App R 1, it was said that a mental abnormality would have to fall into a recognised category of mental disorder for expert evidence about it to be properly receivable, but in *O'Brien* the court doubted whether this was so, as the operative consideration was simply whether the abnormality might render the confession unreliable. The court added that the abnormality would have to be such as to demonstrate a 'very significant deviation from the norm'. Expert evidence might also be crucial to the understanding of whether an accused of low IQ is abnormally suggestible, bearing in mind that such suggestibility might manifest itself at interview without necessarily being apparent to a jury when the accused testifies at trial with the support of counsel and the protection of the judge (*King* [2000] Crim LR 835; *Smith* [2003] EWCA Crim 927). *O'Brien* was further qualified in *Blackburn* [2005] EWCA Crim 1349, where it was said that expert evidence could be received on the question whether a vulnerable individual, after prolonged questioning, might make a false confession, given that the issue is one falling outside the ken of the normal jury. In *Steel* [2003] EWCA Crim 1640, the Court of Appeal reviewed a conviction for murder in 1979 to assess the effect of fresh psychological evidence of suggestibility and vulnerability in interview which drew on techniques that were unavailable at the time of the trial. Unlike in *King*, the defence could not establish that the confession had been improperly obtained. The court, however, rightly considered that if the new evidence rendered the conviction unsafe it was not necessary to consider whether there had been a breach either of the Judges Rules in force at the time, or of any more thoroughgoing modern safeguards for the protection of suspects and the avoidance of miscarriages of justice. (As to expert evidence, see also **F10.6**.)

F17.16 **Breach of PACE Codes** It is common for the defence to allege that the 'something said or done' includes a breach by the police of an obligation under the PACE 1984 or the Code of Practice for the Detention, Treatment and Questioning of Persons by Police Officers (PACE

Code C). Such a breach will not lead to automatic exclusion of a confession obtained in consequence (*Delaney* (1988) 88 Cr App R 338), though it may, on its own or together with other factors, provide evidence that s. 76(2)(b) has not been complied with. In *Delaney*, D, whose psychological make-up was such that he was likely to feel unusual pressure to escape from interrogation, alleged that he had been induced to confess by a suggestion that the serious indecent assault of which he was suspected was more deserving of treatment than punishment. The interview was not recorded until the following day, in breach of Code C, and the Court of Appeal held that the absence of a reliable record of what occurred 'deprived the court of what was, in all likelihood, the most cogent evidence as to what did indeed happen during those interviews and what did induce the appellant to confess'. The breach was therefore significant, in that, the burden of proof being on the prosecution, the speculation necessarily engendered by the breach was sufficient to tip the scale in favour of the defence. For other cases where confessions were excluded, see, e.g., *Doolan* [1988] Crim LR 747 (failure to caution and to maintain a proper interview record or to show it to D); *Chung* (1991) 92 Cr App R 314 (questioning before allowing access to a solicitor and failure to show note to C or subsequently to his solicitor); *Waters* [1989] Crim LR 62 (improper questioning after charge resulting in ambiguous and potentially unreliable answer); *DPP v Blake* [1989] 1 WLR 432 (the 'spirit of the Code' was broken when a juvenile's estranged father was insisted on by police as the appropriate adult to attend her interview); *Morse* [1991] Crim LR 195 (juvenile's father acting as 'appropriate adult' and subsequently discovered to have low IQ and to be incapable of appreciating the gravity of the situation in which M found himself); *Moss* (1990) 91 Cr App R 371 (suspect of low intelligence interviewed nine times during a lengthy period of detention; access to legal advice improperly denied and no independent person present at interview).

Delaney and *Doolan* serve also to illustrate that 'something said or done' may consist of an omission to fulfil the requirements of the Code, although such an omission might always be described in more positive terms, for example, as interviewing the accused without having cautioned him as the Code requires.

Repetition of Confession Originally Obtained in Breach of PACE Code Where a breach of the PACE 1984 or a PACE Code has occurred which renders a confession inadmissible under s. 76(2)(b), it may be necessary to consider whether a repetition of the confession at a subsequent, properly conducted interview is also inadmissible. In *McGovern* (1991) 92 Cr App R 228, a subsequent interview was held inadmissible as it had been tainted by the matters which had led to the exclusion of an earlier interview, namely breaches of s. 58 and the interviewing provisions of Code C. It was further stated that the very fact that admissions were made at an earlier stage was likely to have an effect on the suspect thereafter, with adverse consequences for the admissibility of any repetition of the confession. In *Glaves* [1993] Crim LR 685 the Court of Appeal, whilst denying that there must necessarily be a 'continuing blight' on confessions obtained subsequent to a confession which is excluded under s. 76(2), nevertheless held that the breaches in the case (which included giving C, a juvenile, the impression that he was bound to answer questions) were not cured by a change of police officers and a caution, particularly as C had received no legal advice between the two interviews. **F17.17**

Section 76 and Causation

At common law a confession which had been obtained following an inducement was admissible provided the prosecution could establish that the inducement was not the cause of the obtaining (*DPP v Ping Lin* [1976] AC 574, per Lord Hailsham of St Marylebone at p. 601: '. . . what excludes evidence is a chain of causation resulting from words or conduct on the part of the person in authority . . . giving rise to a decision by the accused actuated by fear of prejudice or hope of reward'). The PACE 1984, s. 76(2)(a) and (b), imports the same causal **F17.18** link by reason of the words '*by* oppression' and '*in consequence of* anything said or done'. It follows that it may be helpful to consider decisions at common law such as *Rennie* [1982] 1 WLR 64, in which Lord Lane CJ held that the judge should avoid any 'refined analysis of the concept of causation' and 'should approach it much as would a jury. . . . In other words, he should understand the principle and the spirit behind it, and apply his common sense.' See also *Tyrer* (1989) 90 Cr App R 446 and *Barry* (1992) 95 Cr App R 384, in both of which it was accepted that the prosecution may discharge the onus of proof under s. 76(2) by showing that there is no causal link between the confession and things said or done by police officers which might have been conducive to unreliability, and *Crampton* (1991) 92 Cr App R 369 in which *Rennie* was cited in support of the proposition that a confession will not have been caused by anything said or done by an interviewer if a suspect is motivated to confess because he perceives in his own mind that there may be an advantage from doing so. The demeanour of the accused when giving evidence on the *voir dire* may assist the prosecution in showing that he was not affected by threats allegedly made at interview (*Weeks* [1995] Crim LR 52).

CONFESSION TENDERED BY CO-ACCUSED

F17.19 In *Myers* [1998] AC 124, M and Q were charged with murder. Q's defence was that M alone committed the offence, and he sought to rely upon a confession to that effect which M had made. The statement was not relied upon in evidence by the prosecution, in consequence of breaches of the Codes of Practice. However there was no suggestion that the confession was not freely made by M. The House of Lords held that the statement was admissible for Q, although the reasoning behind the decision is somewhat obscure: see previous editions of this work for further discussion. Any such uncertainties have been resolved by the CJA 2003, s. 128. This inserts a new s. 76A which provides that an accused may not give evidence of a co-accused's confession unless the conditions imposed by s. 76A(2) are satisfied. These conditions mirror those imposed on the prosecution except that the burden of proof on the accused is clearly stated to be proof on a burden of probabilities, which must be correct. Note also the provision of s. 128(2), which provides that nothing in the hearsay chapter of the Act makes a confession admissible if it would not be admissible under the PACE 1984, s. 76. This would appear to preclude, for example the use of an otherwise inadmissible confession as a previous inconsistent statement so as to provide evidence that the confession itself is true (previous inconsistent statements have become generally admissible as proof of the truth of the facts stated under s. 119).

Police and Criminal Evidence Act 1984, s. 76A

(1) In any proceedings a confession made by an accused person may be given in evidence for another person charged in the same proceedings (a co-accused) in so far as it is relevant to any matter in issue in the proceedings and is not excluded by the court in pursuance of this section.

(2) If, in any proceedings where a co-accused proposes to give in evidence a confession made by an accused person, it is represented to the court that the confession was or may have been obtained—

(a) by oppression of the person who made it; or

(b) in consequence of anything said or done which was likely, in the circumstances existing at the time, to render unreliable any confession which might be made by him in consequence thereof,

the court shall not allow the confession to be given in evidence for the co-accused except in so far as it is proved to the court on the balance of probabilities that the confession (notwithstanding that it may be true) was not obtained.

(3) Before allowing a confession made by an accused person to be given in evidence for a co-accused in any proceedings, the court may of its own motion require the fact that the confession was not obtained as mentioned in subsection (2) above to be proved in the proceedings on the balance of probabilities.

(4) The fact that a confession is wholly or partly excluded in pursuance of this section shall not affect the admissibility in evidence—
  (a) of any facts discovered as a result of the confession; or
  (b) where the confession is relevant as showing that the accused speaks, writes or expresses himself in a particular way, of so much of the confession as is necessary to show that he does so.

(5) Evidence that a fact to which this subsection applies was discovered as a result of a statement made by an accused person shall not be admissible unless evidence of how it was discovered is given by him or on his behalf.

(6) Subsection (5) above applies—
  (a) to any fact discovered as a result of a confession which is wholly excluded in pursuance of this section; and
  (b) to any fact discovered as a result of a confession which is partly so excluded, if the fact is discovered as a result of the excluded part of the confession.

(7) In this section 'oppression' includes torture, inhuman or degrading treatment, and the use or threat of violence (whether or not amounting to torture).

Nothing in *Myers* or the CJA 2003, s. 128, changes the rule that an accused person may not rely on the out-of-court confession of a third party to the offence charged (*Blastland* [1986] AC 41: see **F15.6**). *Myers* and s. 128 vary the confession rule only where the maker of the confession is a party to the proceedings. Thus in *Finch* [2007] 1 WLR 1645 the accused was unable to rely on a statement, made at interview by R, who subsequently pleaded guilty to his part in the offence, because F and R were not 'charged in the same proceedings'. The Court of Appeal considered the possibility that under the CJA 2003 such evidence might be admitted even where the maker is available to testify under the 'interests of justice' test contained in s. 114(1)(d) (see **F15.6** and **F16.20**), but considered this to be most likely where the maker of the statement was unavailable or had demonstrably good reason not to give evidence. The most appropriate course for F would have been to test the reluctance of R to give evidence, and if R proved hostile to avail himself of the consequent admissibility of R's previous inconsistent statement (under s. 119: see **F6.33**).

THE DISCRETION TO EXCLUDE CONFESSION EVIDENCE

At Common Law

The common-law power of a court to exclude evidence in its discretion is considered in general at **F2.1** *et seq.* The following section is concerned only with the application of the discretion to exclude confession evidence. **F17.20**

Police and Criminal Evidence Act 1984, s. 82

(3) Nothing in this part of this Act shall prejudice any power of a court to exclude evidence (whether by preventing questions from being put or otherwise) at its discretion.

Section 82 applies to part VIII of the 1984 Act, which includes ss. 76 and 78. Prior to the enactment of the Act and the codes of practice made under it, exclusion of confession evidence at common law was recognised in two contexts:

(a) the exclusion of unreliable confessions, the prejudicial effect of which could be said to outweigh their true probative value; and
(b) the exclusion of confession evidence, the admission of which might operate unfairly against the accused.

Exclusion for Unreliability In *Miller* [1986] 1 WLR 1191 the Court of Appeal acknowledged the existence of a discretion to refuse to admit 'a confession which came from a mind which at the time was possibly irrational and [where] what the defendant said may have been the product of delusions and hallucinations'. In *Isequilla* [1975] 1 WLR 716, the court accepted the statement in *Cross on Evidence* (3rd ed., 1967) that 'it would be in accordance **F17.21**

Part F Evidence

with principle to exclude a confession made by someone whose mental state was such as to render his utterances completely unreliable'. See also *Stewart* (1972) 56 Cr App R 272.

F17.22 **Exclusion for Unfairness** In *Sang* [1980] AC 402, [1979] 2 All ER 1222, Lord Diplock said (at p. 437 emphasis added): '*save with regard to admissions and confessions* and generally with regard to evidence obtained from the accused after commission of the offence, he [the trial judge] has no discretion to refuse to admit relevant admissible evidence on the ground that it was obtained by improper or unfair means'. The unfairness discretion was well established at common law with regard to confession evidence. In *Houghton* (1978) 68 Cr App R 197, Lawton LJ held (at p. 206) that evidence 'would operate unfairly against an accused if it had been obtained in an oppressive manner by force or against the wishes of an accused person or by a trick or by conduct of which the Crown ought not to take advantage', and said that trial judges enjoyed a discretion to disallow such evidence. The discretion was recognised to exist, although it was infrequently exercised, with regard to breaches of the Judges' Rules (see, e.g., *Voisin* [1918] 1 KB 531; *Lemsatef* [1977] 1 WLR 812) and where a confession had been extracted following a period of unlawful detention (*Hudson* (1980) 72 Cr App R 163).

The common-law powers, though preserved by the PACE 1984, s. 82(3), are unlikely to be resorted to in practice given the wide ambit of s. 78 (see **F17.23**). The situation in which they are most likely to be used is where a judge becomes aware, after a confession has been admitted in evidence, of circumstances suggesting that it should not have been. Neither s. 76 nor s. 78 applies to this situation (*Sat-Bhambra* (1988) 88 Cr App R 55, discussed in detail at **F17.48**), so the court is thrown back on its common-law powers.

Exclusion under Police and Criminal Evidence Act 1984, s. 78

F17.23 **Police and Criminal Evidence Act 1984, s. 78**

(1) In any proceedings the court may refuse to allow evidence on which the prosecution proposes to rely to be given if it appears to the court that, having regard to all the circumstances, including the circumstances in which the evidence was obtained, the admission of the evidence would have such an adverse effect on the fairness of the proceedings that the court ought not to admit it.
(2) Nothing in this section shall prejudice any rule of law requiring a court to exclude evidence.
(3) This section shall not apply in the case of proceedings before a magistrates' court inquiring into an offence as examining justices.

For the meaning of 'proceedings', see s. 82(1). The power may be used in respect of confession evidence tendered by the prosecution (*Mason* [1988] 1 WLR 139), and numerous instances of its use for this purpose exist. In practice, if not in law, the common-law discretion appears to have been superseded.

The Court of Appeal will not interfere with the exercise of a trial judge's discretion to admit evidence under s. 78 unless satisfied that the decision was perverse (*Dures* [1997] 2 Cr App R 247, applying the general principle stated in *Quinn* [1995] 1 Cr App R 480). It follows that cases in which the discretion is said to have been wrongly exercised are comparatively rare. A recent example is *Miller* [1998] Crim LR 209, in which the judge adverted to an out-of-date version of the PACE Codes of Practice and thereby reached an incorrect conclusion through failure to note serious breaches of the applicable Code.

Section 78 and the PACE Codes of Practice

F17.24 Codes of practice issued under the PACE 1984, s. 66, are admissible in evidence in both criminal and civil proceedings, and any provision of such a code appearing to the court or tribunal conducting the proceedings to be relevant to any question arising in the proceedings, must be taken into account in determining that question by virtue of s. 67(11). Breach of a relevant code provision does not lead to the automatic exclusion of a confession obtained in consequence (see, e.g., *Delaney* (1988) 88 Cr App R 338, where the Court of Appeal heard submissions on ss. 76 and 78, and it was held that '. . . the mere fact that there has been a breach of the PACE Codes does not of itself mean that evidence has to be rejected'; *Parris* (1988) 89 Cr App R 68 at p. 72, where the same point was made). The question is whether the admission of the evidence would have such an adverse effect on the fairness of the proceedings that the court ought not to admit it. Even a plain and admitted breach, though it is to be deplored, may fail to trigger exclusion if it does not operate in a way prejudicial to the accused (*Canale* [1990] 2 All ER 187). See further **F17.25**. In *Roberts* [1997] 1 Cr App R 217, it was held that breach of a PACE Code C provision designed to protect another suspect, could not be prayed in aid by the accused. This was because there was no causal link between the breaches and R's admission. On the facts, however, had the Code been complied with, it might have resulted in a record which would have supported R's contention that the other accused, to whom R subsequently confessed, was acting in the role of police agent in soliciting the confession. It is submitted that the issue is not whether the breach against the other accused caused the confession by R (as plainly it did not) but whether the breach affected the fairness of using R's confession (which it may have done).

Breach of a code of practice is in many cases an important factor in considering whether to exclude evidence. Where confession evidence is concerned, the code most likely to be involved is Code C, dealing with the detention, treatment and questioning of persons by police officers. Certain of the rights guaranteed by Code C, such as the right of access to legal advice, are also to be found in the body of the 1984 Act itself (see PACE Code C, section 6 and s. 58). In *Keenan* [1990] 2 QB 54, the Court of Appeal declined to express a view as to whether a court should differentiate between breaches of the Act and of the codes. It is submitted that, whereas the location of such a right in the body of the Act may be an indication of its importance, the principles to be followed when considering the application of s. 78 are no different.

In *Samuel* [1988] QB 615 the Court of Appeal stated that it was undesirable to give any general guidance on the way in which a judge's discretion under s. 78 or under his inherent powers should be exercised, because circumstances may vary infinitely. Without seeking to give any such general guidance, it is submitted that the following considerations have proved to be of importance where s. 78 is concerned.

Nature and Extent of Breach In *Walsh* (1989) 91 Cr App R 161, W was denied access to legal advice, and it was common ground that there had been a breach of the PACE 1984, s. 58 (see **D1.37**). The Court of Appeal observed (at p. 163): **F17.25**

> The main object of section 58 of the Act and indeed of the codes of practice is to achieve fairness — to an accused or suspected person so as, among other things, to preserve and protect his legal rights; but also fairness for the Crown and its officers so that again, among other things, there might be reduced the incidence or effectiveness of unfounded allegations of malpractice.
>
> To our minds it follows that if there are significant and substantial breaches of section 58 or the provisions of the code, then prima facie at least the standards of fairness set by Parliament have not been met. So far as a defendant is concerned, it seems to us also to follow that to admit evidence against him which has been obtained in circumstances where these standards have not been met, cannot but have an adverse effect on the fairness of the proceedings. This does not mean, of course, that in every case of a significant or substantial breach of section 58 or the code of practice the evidence concerned will automatically be excluded. Section 78 does not so provide. The task of the court is not merely to consider whether there would be an adverse effect on the fairness of the proceedings, but such an adverse effect that justice requires the evidence to be excluded.

Breach of Right to Legal Advice In assessing the effect on the fairness of the proceedings of a breach of the PACE 1984, s. 58, it is relevant to note that it has frequently been stressed that the right of access to legal advice is 'fundamental' (see, e.g., *Samuel* [1988] QB 615) and that **F17.26**

it is regarded as of great importance in the jurisprudence of the European Court of Human Rights (*Murray v UK* (1996) 22 EHRR 29, considered in *Aspinall* [1999] 2 Cr App R 115). However, it does not follow that a breach of s. 58 or the provisions of the code relating to access to legal advice will always be regarded as sufficiently significant or substantial to result in exclusion of evidence. In *Alladice* (1988) 87 Cr App R 380, A was denied access to legal advice by officers who had genuinely misconstrued the provisions of s. 58. A admitted in evidence that he was able to cope with being interviewed, that he had been given and understood the caution, and that he was aware of his legal rights. However, he had requested legal advice in order to have a check on the conduct of the police during interview. The trial judge found that the interviews were properly conducted, and that the only function of legal advice would have been to remind A of rights of which he was already well aware. On these facts, the Court of Appeal held that there was no obligation to exclude the confession. See also *Dunford* (1990) 91 Cr App R 150, *Oliphant* [1992] Crim LR 40 and, by way of contrast, *Sanusi* [1992] Crim LR 43, in which the failure to inform S, a foreigner, of his right to advice was particularly significant in the light of his lack of familiarity with police procedures and meant that his confession ought to have been excluded.

F17.27 **Breach of Interview Procedures** Breaches of the various provisions of Code C regarding the procedures to be followed when interviewing suspects have also tended to lead to the exclusion of evidence under the PACE 1984, s. 78, for reasons similar to those stated in *Walsh* (1989) 91 Cr App R 161. In *Keenan* [1990] 2 QB 54, it was said to be desirable that the provisions of Code C which are designed to ensure that interviews are fully recorded and the suspect afforded an opportunity to contest the record be 'strictly complied with', and that the courts would not be slow to exclude evidence obtained following 'substantial breaches' by the interrogator. Other provisions which have been held capable of requiring or contributing to the exclusion of evidence are those relating to cautioning, and to the right to have an appropriate adult present at interview. In *Aspinall* [1999] 2 Cr App R 115, it was noted that the denial of the right to an appropriate adult might lead to the failure of the accused to recognise the need for legal advice. A waiver in these circumstances would be worthless. In *Kirk* [2000] 1 WLR 567, the right of the accused to know why he has been arrested and 'at least in general terms the level of the offence in respect of which he is suspected' was held sufficient to warrant the exclusion under s. 78 of a confession to theft of a handbag where the suspect was not warned that he was also under suspicion for the more serious offences of robbery from the same victim and of her manslaughter. It was recognised that the accused might reach a view on such matters as whether to seek legal advice, and what to say in response to questions, in the light of his understanding of the seriousness of the matter under investigation. The court's purposive reading of the PACE 1984 and Code C reflects an approach similar to that of the European Court of Human Rights in *Fox, Campbell & Hartley v UK* (1990) 13 EHRR 157 in interpreting the requirement of the ECHR, Article 5(2), that a person arrested be informed promptly of the reasons for his arrest. In similar vein, the Privy Council in *Grant v The State* [2007] 1 AC 1, interpreting the common-law approach to the Judges' Rules in Jamaica, analysed the restrictions on questioning after charge by reference to the increased vulnerability of the accused at that time, and the pressure to speak, before deciding that the essential criterion for admissibility is fairness rather than simply whether the answers were voluntarily given.

(As to the content of the provisions of Code C regarding interrogation, see **D1.52** ***et seq.***)

The failure of the interrogator to appreciate that he is conducting an 'interview' within the meaning of that term in Code C by questioning a suspect about his involvement in an offence has proved an important peg on which to hang arguments for exclusion, as such failure frequently leads to a multiplicity of relevant breaches of Code C. The leading authorities are *Absolam* (1988) 88 Cr App R 332 (breaches including failure to caution, to record, and to offer legal advice prior to impromptu questioning by custody officer: confession should have been excluded); *Cox* (1993) 96 Cr App R 464 (informal questioning in C's own home amounting to interview which ought to have taken place only in a police station, inadequate recording and late caution: confession should have been excluded); *Weekes* (1993) 97 Cr App R 222 (inadequate recording and failure to ensure presence of appropriate adult at conversation in police car amounting to interview: confession should have been excluded); *Okafor* (1994) 99 Cr App R 97 (questioning by customs officer during search of O's bag conducted without caution or other incidents of an interview in order not to excite O's suspicion that the drugs in his luggage had been detected: questioning still an interview and confession should have been excluded for breaches); and *Weedersteyn* [1995] 1 Cr App R 405 (W believed he was assisting officers to find drugs importers and was not aware of the significance of his own incriminating statement, taken without caution, until two months later: statement should have been excluded as arising out of an interview not under caution, and because no record was shown to W). The frequent appearance of cases of this type in applications to exclude under s. 78 may in part be accounted for by the difficulty of applying the definition of interview provided by the first revision of Code C which has now been superseded (see *Cox*, in which the authorities are reviewed). The decision in *Miller* [1998] Crim LR 209, in which a confession made in interview without caution was said to have been wrongly admitted, came to appeal only because the judge mistakenly applied the pre-1995 definition. A more recent example is *Gill* [2003] 1 WLR 469, in which it appears that officers of the Inland Revenue investigating tax fraud did not appreciate that they were required to comply with the code when conducting a 'Hansard' interview. In holding the resultant evidence admissible the court took account of the fact that the defendants were fully aware that their answers might render them liable to criminal proceedings. By contrast, in *Hawkins* [2005] EWCA Crim 1723, a police officer unfamiliar with health and safety legislation spoke to H about an explosion in which H had been burned and another man killed. H was, at the time, in shock and breathing with the assistance of an oxygen mask, having been given the maximum possible dose of morphine. The officer's failure to realise that H was a suspect rather than a mere witness was immaterial: a view to that effect should have been formed, the interview should not have taken place as it did and the fruits of the interview should have been excluded.

Breaches Not Triggering Exclusion Although the provisions regarding the conduct of interviews are of great importance, breaches may nevertheless occur which are insufficiently significant or substantial to trigger the PACE 1984, s. 78. For example, in *Matthews* (1989) 91 Cr App R 43, the decision of the trial judge not to exclude evidence of a confession was upheld where the breach concerned the failure of a police officer to show the suspect a note of a conversation which the suspect had asked to be kept 'off the record'. See also *Courtney* [1995] Crim LR 63 (where the provisions of Code C were 'largely followed'), *RSPCA v Eager* [1995] Crim LR 60 (to similar effect), and *Blackwell* [1995] 2 Cr App R 641 (in which the court's decision that the trial judge was 'perfectly entitled' to admit the evidence was said to be 'highlighted by the technicality of the breaches'. Alternatively, a breach may be more than technical, but in the particular circumstances of the case no unfairness results from admitting the evidence. In *Dunn* (1990) 91 Cr App R 150, the failure of the interviewer to observe the provisions designed to prevent fabrication of the interview record would have been regarded as sufficient to require exclusion but for the fact that D's solicitor's clerk was present during the alleged conversation. It was held that it was legitimate for the trial judge to take account of this factor in exercising his discretion to admit the confession, as the presence of the clerk would have been likely to inhibit fabrication, and provided the accused with a witness as to what was actually said. In *Findlay* [1992] Crim LR 372, two suspects had wrongly been held incommunicado but it was held that the fact that one of them had subsequently had access to a solicitor for half an hour before signing the notes of his interview justified the admission of his confession. In *Ridehalgh v DPP* [2005] RTR 353, it was said that, even if the failure of a police inspector to caution a fellow officer was, on the facts, an error (which it was held not to F17.28

be), it could not have been unfair to admit the incriminating response, both because the person questioned was himself a police officer and because of his willingness to repeat the same matters shortly afterwards under caution. And in *Rehman* [2006] EWCA Crim 1900 the failure to determine at trial whether there was sufficient evidence on which to caution a traveller in whose bags drugs were found at Customs was not fatal — even if a caution had been required, those stopped and questioned in a Customs check are already aware of the formality of the occasion.

Where an interview under caution took place in Scotland without a solicitor, in accordance with Scottish law, there was held to be no breach of s. 78 in using it at trial, notwithstanding that in England there would have been a breach of Code C (*McNab* [2002] Crim LR 129). The court found that there was no bad faith or other unfairness in the way the evidence had been obtained. The emphasis should rather be on how the evidence is used, but the outcome would probably have been unchanged.

F17.29 **Failure to Establish Breach** Where the defence relies on breaches of PACE Code C in constructing a challenge to a confession under the PACE 1984, s. 78, but the court decides that no breach occurred, it follows that it is most unlikely that the discretion will be exercised. For examples see *Hughes* [1988] Crim LR 519 (provisions regarding interviewing in the absence of a solicitor not infringed); *Maguire* (1989) 90 Cr App R 115 (exchange between police officer and M not an 'interview'); *Menard* (1994) *The Times*, 23 March 1994 (meeting sought by M in order to volunteer information not an 'interview').

Where the provisions of Code C have changed in the accused's favour since his interrogation, the court may take account of the new provision as the Code reflects what is considered to be fair (*Ward* (1994) 98 Cr App R 337).

F17.30 **Bad Faith** It is not the function of the court to use the PACE 1984, s. 78, to discipline the police (*Mason* [1988] 1 WLR 139; *Canale* [1990] 2 All ER 187). However, the presence of bad faith where the police have acted in breach of the Act or Code is a factor making it more likely that evidence will be excluded. In *Alladice* (1988) 87 Cr App R 380, the facts of which are stated at **F17.26**, the Court of Appeal held that there is a distinction to be drawn between cases where the police have acted in bad faith, and cases where the police, albeit in good faith, have fallen foul of s. 58. In the former case, a court would have 'little difficulty in ruling any confession inadmissible under s. 78'. In the latter, the evidence would still fall to be excluded in many cases, so that it behoves the police to use their powers of delaying access to a solicitor only with great circumspection, but it was not possible 'to say in advance what would or would not be fair'. A similar distinction was drawn in *Walsh* (1989) 91 Cr App R 160 where it was said (at p. 163) that: 'although bad faith may make substantial or significant that which might not otherwise be so, the contrary does not follow. Breaches which are in themselves significant and substantial are not rendered otherwise by the good faith of the officers concerned.' See also *Samuel* [1988] QB 615, in which a submission was made that, in the absence of impropriety, the discretion should never be exercised to exclude admissible evidence. The Court of Appeal had 'no hesitation in rejecting that submission, although the propriety or otherwise of the way in which the evidence was obtained is something which a court is, in terms, enjoined by the section to take into account'.

Information on which Discretion is to be Exercised

F17.31 The discretion does not fall to be exercised because the judge of his own motion recognises that a serious breach such as might trigger exclusion has taken place: if the accused is represented by an advocate who appears competent, and a particular part of the evidence might be the subject of a tactical or strategic plan on the part of the defence, the judge should not take it upon himself to exclude evidence, though he might consider it appropriate to make pertinent inquiry of counsel in the absence of the jury (*Raphaie* [1996] Crim LR 812).

When the defence seek to exclude evidence obtained by or in circumstances alleged to amount to breaches of the PACE 1984 or a PACE Code, the Court of Appeal in *Keenan* [1990] 2 QB 54 noted that a number of different situations may face the judge:

(a) One or more breaches of a code may be apparent in the custody record itself or from the witness statements.
(b) There may be a prima facie breach which, if objection is taken, must be justified by evidence adduced by the prosecution.
(c) There may be alleged breaches which can probably only be established by the evidence of the accused himself.

Cases under (c) are likely to be rare, and it is likely that in cases under (a) and (b) the judge will have no means of knowing what will ensue after he has made his ruling. If he rules against admissibility, it may be that the accused will exercise his right not to give evidence. To permit the evidence to be given may therefore effectively deprive the accused of a right which he would otherwise have had. If the evidence is admitted, the judge does not know what the response to it may be. The accused may testify that the interview in question never took place at all, or that, though it took place, the questions and answers were fabricated, or that what was said was inaccurately recorded, or he might accept the accuracy of the record. Despite these difficulties, the judge must make his ruling on the information available to him at the time. In *Keenan*, the judge had wrongly assumed that any unfairness which might have been present could be cured by K giving evidence at the trial. Failure to give evidence at the *voir dire* is a different matter, and, in considering whether an accused has been prejudiced by a breach, the judge is entitled to take account of his failure to give evidence at the *voir dire* (*Oni* [1992] Crim LR 183).

The record of interview and the contents of the confession itself may assist on the question whether the admission of the evidence would affect the fairness of the proceedings (*Dunford* (1990) 91 Cr App R 150 at p. 155). However, it was also said that it may be necessary to avoid reference to such material in cases where there is a 'root and branch' challenge by the defence to the contents of the statement.

Unfairness not Arising from Breach of Codes of Practice

In various authorities the significance of conduct not amounting to a breach of a code of practice or of the PACE 1984 has been considered, and it is clear that s. 78 may be invoked in such cases, though instances of the exercise of the discretion are rarer. The principles which have developed in relation to confessions apply also to other forms of prosecution evidence, and reference should be made also to F2.23 to F2.26. **F17.32**

The provisions of Code of Practice C do not apply to conversations between suspects and undercover investigators, unless the undercover pose is deliberately abused as a means of circumventing the code (*Christou* [1992] QB 979; *Bryce* [1992] 4 All ER 569; *Edwards* [1997] Crim LR 348). In deciding whether the code applies the judge should take into account the seriousness of the offence and the potential to put a life at risk (*Rajkuma* [2003] EWCA Crim 1955, where the offence was soliciting to commit murder). Where genuine undercover operations yield evidence, including incriminating statements, the use of subterfuge does not of itself entail a finding of unfairness. Relevant considerations in *Christou* (where undercover police set up as 'shady' jewellers in order to recover stolen property and gather evidence against the thieves and handlers) were that the public interest favoured the operation, that the offences had already been committed and that there was no incitement to crime on the part of the police, and that the suspects had 'applied themselves to the trick' without pressure from the officers. See also *Maclean* [1993] Crim LR 687, a similar operation concerning illegally imported drugs. In *Re Proulx* [2001] 1 All ER 57, an extradition case in which a murder suspect had been induced to confess as a condition of membership of a fictitious criminal gang, Mance LJ (having noted that this was clearly a case where the trick had been applied to P, even though he had willingly fallen in with it) concluded that there would have been 'very considerable difficulty' in upholding a decision to admit such evidence in purely domestic proceedings in the light of decisions such as *Christou, Bryce, Smurthwaite* [1994] 1 All ER 898 (see **F2.28**) and the ruling of Ognall J in *Stagg* (14 September 1994, unreported).

F17.33 Subterfuge in Interrogation and Non-disclosure In *Bailey* [1993] 3 All ER 513 subterfuge in the interrogation process was considered. B and S were arrested and charged with robbery, but maintained their right to silence at interview. They were placed together in a bugged police cell, their suspicions being allayed by play-acting on the part of the police, who pretended to be reluctant to leave them alone together. Their resultant incriminating conversation was admitted, and it was held that the fact that B and S could not, under Code of Practice C, properly have been subjected to further questioning did not mean that they had to be protected from the opportunity to speak incriminatingly to one another if they chose to do so. It was acknowledged to appear odd that, alongside the 'rigorously controlled legislative regime' for questioning it should be considered acceptable for 'parallel covert investigations' legitimately to continue, but, provided such strategems were used only in grave cases and that there was no suggestion of oppression or unreliability, there was nothing unfair about admitting the evidence obtained in consequence. The court distinguished as improper the subterfuge employed in *Mason* [1988] 1 WLR 139 in which a police officer told deliberate lies to M and to M's solicitor regarding the availability of fingerprint evidence connecting M with the offence of which he was suspected, in order to extract a confession from him. The trial judge admitted the confession, but the Court of Appeal held that he had failed to take into account one vital factor, 'namely the deceit practised upon the appellant's solicitor. If he had included that in his consideration . . . he would have been driven to an opposite conclusion.' *Mason* is not, it is submitted, authority for the proposition that lies may safely be told to an accused person provided his legal adviser is not hoodwinked; on the contrary, both aspects of the deception were regarded as equally serious and 'most reprehensible' by the Court of Appeal. The trial judge's failure to take account of the lie told to the solicitor merely provided the ground on which the court was able to review the exercise of his discretion. *Bailey* was applied in *Roberts* [1997] 1 Cr App R 217, in which R was induced to confess by a fellow suspect, C (with whom he had been placed in a bugged cell), to one robbery with which R had already been charged and to another with which he was subsequently charged. The trial judge's conclusion that C was not a police agent and had not been told what to ask R was regarded as 'unassailable', despite breaches of the Code in relation to C which made it hard to determine what precisely had been said to him (see **F17.24**). On the facts as found, the test was said to be whether the conduct of the police, either wittingly or unwittingly, led to unfairness or injustice, and the judge's decision to admit the evidence was upheld. The only difference between this case and *Bailey* was said to be that the police 'had perhaps a rather firmer basis for their expectations' of a confession than in *Bailey*. By contrast, in *Allan* [2004] EWCA Crim 2236 the Court of Appeal, following the reasoning of the European Court of Human Rights in the same case (*Allan v UK* (Application No. 48539/99 (2002) 13 BHRC 652)) held that evidence should be excluded where, the suspect having decided to exercise his right of silence, the authorities use subterfuge to elicit confessions by using an informer as the 'functional equivalent' of an interrogator. In that case there was evidence that police had coached the informer and instructed him to 'pump' the suspect in the cell they shared while A was awaiting trial for murder. Just as a police officer cannot circumvent the protections of the PACE 1984 and the PACE Codes by adopting an undercover pose (*Christou*) so an informer cannot be used to the same end. As the Court of Appeal rightly state, 'allowing an agent of the state to interrogate a suspect in the circumstances of this case bypasses the many necessary protections developed over the last twenty years'. The authorities on eavesdropping do not appear to have been adversely affected. In *Mason* [2002] Cr App R 628, M and others were suspected of joint involvement in a series of burglaries and armed robberies, but there was insufficient evidence to do more than arrest individual members of the group for particular offences. Authorisation was obtained for them to be held together in a bugged cell in the hope that they would, in talking to each other, divulge the full extent of the joint enterprise. The resultant recordings were held to have been rightly admitted, following the reasoning in *Bailey*, notwithstanding that there was a clear breach of the ECHR, Article 8, which could not be justified because the surveillance had not taken place according to any publicly accessible legal structure (cf. *PG and JH v United Kingdom* [2002] Crim LR 308). The court called for clarification of the legal position on surveillance on suspects in custody which may appear inconsistent with the spirit of the PACE 1984, and noted that the Code of Practice provided for by the Regulation of Investigatory Powers Act 2000 was the appropriate vehicle. Compare also *Grant* [2006] QB 60, in which eavesdropping amounting to a deliberate violation of an imprisoned suspect's right to legal professional privilege was held 'so great an affront to the integrity of the justice system' as to render an associated prosecution an abuse of process even if no material is obtained which assists the prosecution.

In *Farrell* [2004] EWCA Crim 597, the court approved as a 'useful guide' the distinction between active lying intended to induce a confession, and the omission or failure by the police to disclose their whole case in advance of interview. The court was not prepared to hold that it was necessarily wrong or misleading for the police to hold back some part of their case before interview. In that case there was no attempt to suggest that the case was stronger than it was, and the evidence (which consisted of lies rather than an outright confession, but the relevant principles are the same) was held to have been properly admitted.

Unfairness Arising from Misunderstanding Unfairness may arise from misunderstanding as well as from subterfuge. In *Smith* [1994] 1 WLR 1396, S was under the impression that R, the bank manager questioning him, was concerned only to obtain information about the impact of a transaction on the market, and not about S's criminal involvement. Although R was guilty of no impropriety, the Court of Appeal held that S's statements should not have been admitted. In *Hayter v L* [1998] 1 WLR 854 the issue was whether it was an abuse of process for a private prosecution to proceed after an offender had been cautioned by the police (a procedure which necessarily involves an admission of guilt). Holding that it was not, the Divisional Court said that any unfairness arising from the use of the cautioned party's admission in the subsequent proceedings could be met by the s. 78 discretion. As a prerequisite of a caution, a party should be made aware that there is the possibility of a private prosecution, but it might still be thought unfair to permit a confession made in hope of escaping a prosecution to be used in order to found one. Similarly in *De Silva* [2003] 2 Cr App R 74 it was held that telephone conversations participated in by D at the instigation of Customs officers following the discovery of drugs in his suitcase should not be used in evidence against D. The purpose of the exercise was to facilitate the arrest of the callers, so it was part of D's role to behave as though he was guilty, whether he was or not. D's agreement to take part in the exercise followed a 'co-operation interview' with the officers, and it was not the purpose of such interviews to gather or initiate further evidence against the interviewee. In *Elleray* [2003] 2 Cr App R 165 the issue was whether a statement made to a probation officer for the purposes of a pre-sentence report could be used as a confession to a more serious offence (rape) than the one to which E had pleaded guilty and for which he was to be sentenced (indecent assault). It was held that such a case required a careful consideration of the public interest, bearing in mind the need for frankness between a probation officer and offender, and the absence of both caution and access to legal advice. In some cases it might be advisable for the officer to terminate the conversation to allow the offender to seek advice. On balance it was not unfair to admit the evidence. **F17.34**

Unfairness arising from Physical Condition of the Accused The discretion may, it seems, be used in respect of evidence which is unreliable as the result of the physical condition of the **F17.35**

suspect, whether or not the interview in which he participates is conducted in breach of the code (see, e.g., *Effik* (1992) 95 Cr App R 427, in which the trial judge, in a ruling endorsed by the Court of Appeal, made it clear that he would have excluded the confession of M, a heroin addict, had it been made at a time when he was suffering acute withdrawal symptoms).

Exclusion of Subsequent Confession

F17.36 Where a confession is excluded, either under s. 76 or under s. 78, for breach of a code, the question may arise as to whether it would be unfair to admit a subsequent confession which has itself been obtained without breaking the rules. In *Gillard* (1991) 92 Cr App R 61, it was held, upholding the admission of subsequent statements by two accused, that there is no universal rule requiring the exclusion of such a subsequent confession. The question is whether, on the facts of a particular case, there is a sufficient nexus between the circumstances in which the two statements were made to render it unfair to admit the subsequent statement, so that, for example, the accused is still affected by some impropriety which took place during the first, excluded interview. Important considerations are whether the objections leading to the exclusion of the first interview were of a fundamental and continuing nature, and whether the arrangements for the subsequent interview gave the accused a sufficient opportunity to exercise an informed and independent choice as to whether he should repeat or retract what he said, or say nothing (*Neil* [1994] Crim LR 441; *Nelson* [1998] 2 Cr App R 399). See also *Canale* (1990) 91 Cr App R 1, in which a subsequent interview was held to have been tainted by an earlier one in which promises were alleged to have been made; *Y v DPP* [1991] Crim LR 917, in which earlier confessions, despite their spontaneous nature, were excluded because of breaches of the code, but a subsequent, properly conducted interview was held to have been rightly admitted; *Wood* [1994] Crim LR 222, in which a multiplicity of breaches at the first interview of a mentally handicapped suspect tainted a later interview; and *Prouse v DPP* [1999] All ER (D) 748, [1999] 10 Arch News 2, in which the provision of legal advice before the later interview rendered it admissible.

Confessions by Mentally Handicapped Persons

F17.37 A confession made by a mentally handicapped person may be admitted in evidence, provided it satisfies the conditions imposed by the PACE 1984, s. 76 (see **F17.5**), and provided also that it is not excluded by the court in the exercise of its discretion to exclude prosecution evidence under s. 78 of the Act. Where such a confession is received in evidence, the provisions of s. 77 come into play and must be complied with.

Police and Criminal Evidence Act 1984, s. 77

(1) Without prejudice to the general duty of the court at a trial on indictment with a jury to direct the jury on any matter on which it appears to the court appropriate to do so, where at such a trial—

(a) the case against the accused depends wholly or substantially on a confession by him; and

(b) the court is satisfied—

(i) that he is mentally handicapped; and

(ii) that the confession was not made in the presence of an independent person,

the court shall warn the jury that there is special need for caution before convicting the accused in reliance on the confession, and shall explain that the need arises because of the circumstances mentioned in paragraphs (a) and (b) above.

(2) In any case where at the summary trial of a person for an offence it appears to the court that a warning under subsection (1) above would be required if the trial were on indictment with a jury, the court shall treat the case as one in which there is a special need for caution before convicting the accused on his confession.

(2A) In any case where at the trial on indictment without a jury of a person for an offence it appears to the court that a warning under subsection (1) above would be required if the trial were with a jury, the court shall treat the case as one in which there is a special need for caution before convicting the accused on his confession.

(3) In this section—
'independent person' does not include a police officer or a person employed for, or engaged on, police purposes;
'mentally handicapped' in relation to a person, means that he is in a state of arrested or incomplete development of mind which includes significant impairment of intelligence and social functioning; and
'police purposes' has the meaning assigned to it by section 101(2) of the Police Act 1996.

In its application to Customs and Excise, s. 77(3) is modified to the extent that the definition of 'independent person' includes, in addition to the persons mentioned therein, an officer or any other person acting under the authority of the Commissioners of Customs and Excise (Police and Criminal Evidence Act 1984) (Application to Customs and Excise) Order 1985 (SI 1985 No. 1800)).

There is no need to give a warning in accordance with s. 77 unless the case for the Crown would be 'substantially less strong' without the confession (*Campbell* [1995] Crim LR 157).

PACE Code C requires the presence at interview of an 'appropriate adult' when the interviewee is a person at risk by reason, *inter alia*, of mental handicap, unless the interview is conducted on an emergency basis. The concept of an 'appropriate adult' is substantially the same as, though not identical to, the 'independent person' mentioned in s. 77. In particular, a solicitor attending the suspect would be an 'independent person', but would be unlikely to be the 'appropriate adult', who would normally be a relative or someone with experience of caring for the suspect (*Lewis* [1996] Crim LR 260). The warning required by s. 77 serves to draw the magistrates' or jury's attention to the potential unreliability of a confession obtained without this safeguard and should be tailored to any specific evidence of unreliability relating to the accused himself (*Campbell*). In *Bailey* [1995] 2 Cr App R 262, it was held to be necessary to give the warning in respect of informal admissions made to members of the public in the absence of an independent third party, but this does not appear to be the mischief at which s. 77 was aimed.

In *Lamont* [1989] Crim LR 813, L was convicted of the attempted murder of his baby son. The only evidence of L's intention came from a confession made in an interview at which no independent person was present. Expert defence evidence indicated mental retardation and impairment of intelligence and social functioning, but the trial judge concluded that L was not mentally handicapped and therefore did not warn the jury in accordance with s. 77. Quashing the conviction, the Court of Appeal held that the required direction under s. 77 was an essential ingredient of a fair summing-up, yet the trial judge had neither suggested to nor directed the jury that if they accepted the expert evidence they should exercise the caution called for by the section. The decision of the Court may, however, be open to doubt in part, in that it is the function of the judge, not the jury, to decide whether the accused is mentally handicapped. In establishing whether a defendant is mentally handicapped within the meaning of s. 77(3) it is not appropriate to take figures produced by intelligence tests in one case and to apply them slavishly in another in order to produce a rigid definition: every case has its individual features (*Kenny* [1994] Crim LR 284).

Practical Application of the Rule In the present climate of opinion, a confession made by a mentally handicapped person otherwise than in the presence of an independent person would be likely to be excluded at trial under either s. 76 or s. 78 of the 1984 Act. It follows that there will be few cases where a court is called on to follow the procedure laid down in s. 77. In *Moss* (1990) 91 Cr App R 371 it was thought that the section was aimed at two possible cases: (a) where a confession has been properly obtained from a mentally handicapped person in the absence of an independent person in the course of an 'urgent interview' as permitted by Code C, (b) where the interview was in breach of Code C but there was only 'one interview during a comparatively short period of custody'. In *Moss*, confessions obtained in the course of nine interviews over a lengthy period of detention were held to have been wrongly admitted **F17.38**

despite the s. 77 direction given by the trial judge: the statements ought to have been excluded under s. 76(2)(b) (see **F17.12**). By contrast, in *Uddin* [2005] EWCA Crim 464, U's appeal failed despite the prosecution's reliance on a confession obtained in the absence of an appropriate adult, and the apparent failure of the judge to give a s. 77 direction (which failure was not noted by the Court of Appeal). The crux of the matter in *Uddin*, however, was that the 'confession' was chiefly composed of self-serving statements. The only element on which the prosecution relied (an admission of presence) was equally an inherent part of the defence case. The Court therefore concluded that the admission of the confession did not threaten the safety of the conviction and would presumably have said the same about the absence of a direction under s. 77. In *Qayyum* [2006] EWCA Crim 1127, the failure of the trial judge to give a formal s. 77 direction following the admission of a confession that, as in *Uddin* was not *per se* damaging to the defence at trial, was held not to render the conviction unsafe, although it was noted that the judge had repeatedly reminded the jury of Q's intellectual shortcomings.

The decision of the Court of Appeal to limit the circumstances in which a case depending on confession evidence of this type should be left to the jury further restricts the ambit of s. 77. In *MacKenzie* (1992) 96 Cr App R 98, the Court of Appeal considered the application of the rule in *Galbraith* [1981] 1 WLR 1039 (see **D15.53**) to the case where the confession of a mentally handicapped person had been admitted at trial, but was unsupported by other evidence. The court laid down the following rules:

> (1) Where the prosecution case depends wholly upon confessions; (2) the defendant suffers from a significant degree of mental handicap; and (3) the confessions are unconvincing to a point where a jury properly directed could not properly convict upon them, then the judge, assuming that he has not excluded the confessions earlier, should withdraw the case from the jury. The confessions may be unconvincing, for example, because they lack the incriminating details to be expected of a guilty and willing confessor, or because they are inconsistent with other evidence, or because they are otherwise inherently improbable.

M, a mentally handicapped man with a personality disorder, was convicted of two offences of manslaughter and two of arson. The prosecution case in respect of the killings depended entirely on unsupported confessions, whereas the proof of arson, though largely dependent on confessions, was supported by other independent evidence. During questioning M had also confessed to twelve other killings, none of which, in the end, the Crown believed he had committed. At the point in the trial when the confessions to the killings were admitted, it was thought that they contained details which only the killer could have known. On a careful review of the confessions, however, the Court of Appeal considered that the knowledge of the basic circumstances of the killings which they contained were of the sort that would not have been confined to the killer, and that they also contained some striking errors and omissions. Bearing in mind that M's credibility was diminished by his false confessions to other killings, and that he may well have been motivated by a desire to stay in the secure hospital at which he had been detained, the court was left with at least a lurking doubt as to whether the verdicts of manslaughter were safe and satisfactory. The convictions for arson, however, were allowed to stand. *MacKenzie* was applied in *Wood* [1994] Crim LR 222, in which the only blow which W had confessed to striking was proved by medical evidence not to have caused the death of the victim.

A confession which falls within the first two limbs of the *MacKenzie* test, but which is admitted because it falls outside the third, may require a very careful judicial direction (*Bailey* [1995] 2 Cr App R 262, where it was held that the judge was obliged, in addition to giving the s. 77 warning, to give the jury a 'full and proper statement' of the defendant's case against the confession being accepted by the jury as true).

DETERMINING THE ADMISSIBILITY OF CONFESSIONS: THE *VOIR DIRE*

The general rules regarding the holding of a *voir dire*, or trial within a trial, in order to determine disputed issues regarding preliminary facts on which the admissibility of evidence depends, are dealt with in detail at D15.20 *et seq.* The principles considered in this section are those which have particular significance with regard to confessions, or are relevant solely to the reception of confession evidence. F17.39

The *Voir Dire* and the PACE 1984, s. 76

At common law, where the admissibility of a confession statement was to be challenged in a trial on indictment, the following practice was followed: F17.40

(a) Defending counsel would notify prosecuting counsel that an objection to admissibility was to be raised.
(b) Prosecuting counsel would then refrain from mentioning the statement in his opening to the jury.
(c) At the appropriate time the judge would conduct a trial on the *voir dire* to decide on the admissibility of the statement (*Ajodha v The State* [1982] AC 204).

The *voir dire* was normally held in the absence of the jury, but only at the request or with the consent of the defence (*Ajodha*, citing *Anderson* (1929) 21 Cr App R 178). See further, as to the obligations of counsel, *Cole* (1941) 28 Cr App R 43, *Patel* [1951] 2 All ER 29 and *Mitchell v The Queen* [1998] AC 695 at p. 704.

The PACE 1984, s. 76(2), follows the common law by providing that where the defence represent that a confession on which the prosecution propose to rely was, or may have been, obtained in such a way as to render it inadmissible in evidence, the court shall not allow the confession to be given in evidence except insofar as the prosecution prove to the court beyond reasonable doubt that the confession was not so obtained. Section 76(3) provides in addition that the court may of its own motion require the prosecution, as a condition of allowing them to give a confession in evidence, to prove that it was not obtained in such a way as to render it inadmissible. Both provisions strongly indicate that a *voir dire* is the correct procedure for determining whether the confession may be given, and the common-law procedure set out above continues to be followed in practice. However it has now been established that the court may require the jury to withdraw whether the defence consents or not (*Davis* [1990] Crim LR 860, and see also *Hendry* [1988] Crim LR 766).

In *Liverpool Juvenile Court, ex parte R* [1988] QB 1, it was held that s. 76 requires magistrates conducting a summary trial to hold a *voir dire* to determine admissibility where the defence, before the close of the prosecution case, represent to the court that the confession was obtained in breach of s. 76(2). The decision represents a significant departure from the common law, which regarded the *voir dire* as inappropriate in summary trials (see further as to summary trials, D21.25). As magistrates are judges of both fact and law, a ruling that a confession is to be excluded will mean that they have to put the objectionable material out of their minds when considering guilt; this is a task with which it has recently been said 'they are well capable of coping both by training and by disposition' (*Hayter v L* [1998] 1 WLR 854, commenting on the comparable situation which arises after the s. 78 discretion to exclude has been exercised).

Unrepresented Accused In *Ajodha v The State* [1982] AC 204 Lord Bridge said (at p. 223): F17.41

> Particular difficulties may arise in the trial of an unrepresented defendant, when the judge must, of course, be especially vigilant to ensure a fair trial. No rules can be laid down, but it may be prudent, if the judge has any reason to suppose that the voluntary character of a statement

F

Part F Evidence

> proposed to be put in evidence by the prosecution is likely to be in issue, that he should speak to the defendant before the trial begins and explain his rights in the matter.

The position appears to be unaltered under the 1984 Act, if for 'voluntary character' is read 'admissibility'. The court also enjoys the power under s. 76(3) to put the prosecutor to his proof on the issue of admissibility, and it is submitted that it would generally be appropriate to exercise that power in the case of an unrepresented accused.

Challenging Admissibility at Trial

F17.42 The position at common law was stated in *Ajodha v The State* [1982] AC 204 by Lord Bridge, who said (at p. 223):

> Though the case for the defence raises an issue as to the voluntariness of a statement . . ., defending counsel may for tactical reasons prefer that the evidence bearing on that issue be heard before the jury, with a single cross-examination of the witnesses on both sides, even though this means that the jury hear the impugned statement whether admissible or not. If the defence adopts this tactic, it will be open to defending counsel to submit at the close of the evidence that, if the judge doubts the voluntariness of the statement, he should direct the jury to disregard it, or, if the statement is essential to sustain the prosecution case, direct an acquittal. Even in the absence of such a submission, if the judge himself forms the view that the voluntariness of the statement is in doubt, he should take the like action *proprio motu.*

In *Liverpool Juvenile Court, ex parte R* [1988] QB 1, at p. 10 it was considered that the defence retained this option:

> There remains a discretion open to the defendant as to the stage at which an attack is to be made upon an alleged confession. A trial within a trial will only take place before the close of the prosecution case if it is represented to the court that the confession was, or may have been, obtained by one or other of the processes set out in subparagraph (a) or (b) of section 76(2). If no such representation is made the defendant is at liberty to raise admissibility or weight of the confession at any subsequent stage of the trial.

It may be argued that this view overlooks the power of the court under the PACE 1984, s. 76(3), to compel the holding of a *voir dire*, apparently irrespective of the defendant's wishes. This power may, however, be intended primarily to enable a court to assist an unrepresented defendant to vindicate his rights, rather than to overrule the wishes of defence counsel where the accused is legally represented. A more fundamental objection to the view taken in *Ex parte R* may be found in *Sat-Bhambra* (1988) 88 Cr App R 55. Certain statements by S had been ruled admissible at the *voir dire*, because there was no evidence to suggest that the statements were likely to be unreliable as a result of the accused's ill health at the time. At the trial, medical evidence was adduced by the defence which came down more strongly in favour of S's contention that he was suffering from hypoglycaemia when he was interviewed. When asked to reconsider his decision on admissibility, the trial judge ruled that the terms of s. 76 prevented him from taking this course. The Court of Appeal agreed, holding (at p. 62):

> The words of section 76 are crucial: 'proposes to be given in evidence' and 'shall not allow the confession to be given' are not, in our judgment, appropriate to describe something which has happened in the past. They are directed solely to the situation before the statement goes before the jury. Once the judge has ruled that it should do so, section 76 (and section 78, for the same reasons) ceases to have effect.

The court went on to consider the powers which the judge may, by virtue of the common law, exercise in this situation, (at p. 62) before concluding: 'If a defendant wishes under section 76 to exclude a confession, the time to make his submission to that effect is before the confession is put in evidence and not afterwards.' It has been noted (see **F17.4**) that the statements in issue in *Sat-Bhambra* were self-serving, and were therefore regarded as not being confessions to which s. 76 applied, as to which, see now *Z* [2003] 1 WLR 1489 at **F17.4**. However, the

Court of Appeal was careful to state that its views on that subsidiary matter were *obiter*, so that the *ratio* of the case appears to be that the admissibility of a confession may not be challenged under s. 76 once the confession has been given in evidence. The contrary view, stated by the Divisional Court in *Liverpool Juvenile Court, ex parte R*, was expressed to apply to summary proceedings only, but it is difficult to see why the interpretation of the Act should vary according to the nature of the trial. Thus, the law, whatever the mode of trial, would appear to be as stated in *Sat-Bhambra*. See also *Davis* [1990] Crim LR 860, in which the Court of Appeal inclined to the view (but without deciding the point) that the language of the section anticipated a *voir dire* taking place before the challenged evidence was heard by the jury.

The *Voir Dire* and the PACE 1984, s. 78

Section 78 is set out at **F17.23**. The view taken, *obiter*, by the Court of Appeal in *Sat-Bhambra* (1988) 88 Cr App R 55 was that the wording of the section suggested that defence objections should be made before the confession is given in evidence. The relevant words are 'the court may refuse to allow evidence *on which the prosecution proposes to rely* to be given'. It does not necessarily follow from this that a *voir dire* should always be held; indeed, it has been said that in a summary trial the defence have no right to a *voir dire* simply in order to determine a preliminary issue under s. 78 (*Vel v Chief Constable of North Wales* (1987) 151 JP 510 and see **D21.25**). However, in many cases it will be convenient to investigate the submission in this way, particularly where the defence also challenge the confession under s. 76, and in *Halawa v Federation Against Copyright Theft* [1995] 1 Cr App R 21 it was said, *obiter*, that if, in connection with an application to exclude evidence under s. 78 alone, the accused wished to proceed by way of a trial within a trial, magistrates might find it necessary to proceed in that way in order to allow the accused to give evidence in relation to the evidential issue without prejudicing his right to silence at trial. **F17.43**

In *R* (2000) *Independent*, 10 April 2000, it was held that a ruling in a preparatory hearing regarding s. 78 was a ruling as to admissibility of evidence under the CPIA 1996, s. 31(3) (see **D14.19** and **D14.21**), and that it was subject to appeal to the Court of Appeal. It seems unlikely that s. 31(3) was intended to apply to questions which are not strictly questions of law, although if the application of s. 78 goes to the heart of the proceedings it may be convenient to deal with it as an interlocutory matter.

Disputes as to Making of Confession

At common law the *voir dire* was inappropriate in trials on indictment where the defence case was simply that no confession was made (*Ajodha v The State* [1982] AC 204). The Board gave as examples cases where the defence allege that an interview never took place, or that no incriminating answers were given, or, in the case of a written statement, that it is a forgery. The issue of fact whether or not the statement was made by the accused is purely for the jury. In the same case, however, the Privy Council recognised that issues of voluntariness might be intertwined with disputes as to the making of the confession, and that it is a fallacy to suppose that the two grounds of challenge are mutually exclusive. Such a case may arise where the accused claims that he was not the author of a written statement which bears his name, and alleges that his signature at the end of the statement was procured by force or by deception. Such cases required the holding of a *voir dire* to determine the issue of voluntariness at common law, leaving the jury to determine the value and weight of the statement if it is admitted. Issues as to admissibility under the PACE 1984, s. 76, are equally capable of arising in combination with disputes as to the making of the statement, and it is submitted that the principles stated in *Ajodha* continue to represent the law. Where the evidence of a person to whom a disputed confession is alleged to have been made may be tainted by an improper motive (as in the case of a 'cell confession') a specific direction to the jury is required as to the need for caution (*Pringle v R* [2003] UKPC 9; *Benedetto v R* [2003] 1 WLR 1545: see **F5.12**). **F17.44**

Where the defence in a trial on indictment challenge the confession under s. 78, they may ultimately wish to assert at the trial that no confession was made. At the point at which the challenge is made, however, the judge may be unaware of the line the defence intend to take at trial, and the defence are under no obligation to disclose their case in this respect (*Keenan* [1990] 2 QB 54). The issue at the *voir dire* is simply whether the introduction of the confession would have such an adverse effect on the fairness of the proceedings that the court ought not to admit it. It is not the function of the judge to decide whether the confession was made (*Keenan*). See, however, *Alladice* (1988) 87 Cr App R 380, in which the trial judge reached such a decision before deciding to admit the statement.

Truth of Confession as Issue on *Voir Dire*

F17.45 It is not the function of the judge or magistrates at a *voir dire* to determine whether a confession is true, but simply whether it should be admitted. The PACE 1984, s. 76, underlines this limitation by providing that the court shall not allow the confession to be admitted 'except insofar as the prosecution proves beyond reasonable doubt that the confession (notwithstanding that it may be true) was not obtained [in breach of s. 76(2)]'.

It does not necessarily follow from this that the truth of the statement is irrelevant to the question whether it should be admitted. At common law there was a conflict of authority on the point. In *Hammond* [1941] 3 All ER 318, H was charged with murder. He gave evidence on the *voir dire*, claiming that he had been knocked about and brutally ill-treated in order to induce a confession. It was held that he was properly cross-examined as to whether his confession was true, as it was relevant to the credit to be given to his assertions, on the basis that: 'If a man says, "I was forced to tell the story . . ." it must be relevant to know whether he was made to tell the truth, or whether he was made to say a number of things which were untrue' (per Humphreys J at p. 321).

In *Wong Kam-ming v The Queen* [1980] AC 247, a majority of the Privy Council disapproved of *Hammond*, and held that it should no longer be followed in Hong Kong. W gave evidence at the *voir dire*, claiming that his confession had been extracted by force. He was cross-examined in detail as to the truth of the statement, which was subsequently excluded. At the trial, prosecuting counsel called evidence to prove that, at the *voir dire*, W had admitted that he was present at the scene of the crime. It was held that the cross-examination was impermissible and that it did not affect the credit of the accused as a witness. Lord Edmund-Davies said (at p. 256) 'If the defendant denies the truth of the confession or some self-incriminating admission contained in it, the question whether his denial is itself true or false cannot be ascertained until after the *voir dire* is over and the defendant's guilt or innocence has been determined by the jury'. If the defendant admits the truth, this tends to show that he is a truthful witness and goes to support his allegations rather than, as *Hammond* supposes, to undermine them. Lord Hailsham of St Marylebone, dissenting on this issue, considered (at p. 262C) that 'the only general limitations on what may be asked or tendered ought to be relevance to the issue to be tried' and concluded that it was not possible 'to say *a priori* that in no circumstances is the truth or falsity of the alleged confession relevant to the question at issue on the *voir dire* or admissible as to credibility of either the prosecution or defence witnesses'. He instanced, *inter alia*, cases in which the defence argue that, because a confession is demonstrably false, it must have been obtained by improper means. It must then be relevant for the prosecution to cross-examine on the truth of the statement.

It is submitted that Lord Hailsham's dissent in *Wong Kam-ming v The Queen* has logic on its side, but that the view of the majority has a sure foundation in policy, being consistent with the rule under which the accused is protected from the consequences of damaging admissions which further his case at the *voir dire* (see **F17.46**).

Precisely the same questions may fall to be considered under s. 76 or s. 78 of the 1984 Act. Although *Hammond* has never been overruled as far as English courts are concerned, in *Liverpool Juvenile Court, ex parte R* [1988] QB 1 the Divisional Court relied on the authority of *Wong Kam-ming v The Queen* for the proposition that a defendant cannot be asked about the truth of a confession during an inquiry as to its admissibility. It should be noted, however, that:

(a) the judgment in that case expressly confined itself to summary proceedings (where it may be thought particularly important that the justices do not confuse the functions of the *voir dire* and the trial); and, more importantly,
(b) the court was not concerned directly with the question under discussion, but was instead engaged in enumerating the advantages to the defendant of the *voir dire* procedure.

In *Davis* [1990] Crim LR 860 the Court of Appeal referred to *Wong Kam-ming v The Queen* as 'strong persuasive authority' for the view that D could not be cross-examined as to the truth of his confession when giving evidence on the *voir dire*, but the point was not decided as the trial judge's ruling to the contrary had had no bearing upon the outcome of the trial.

Admissibility of Evidence Given on *Voir Dire*

In *Wong Kam-ming v The Queen* [1980] AC 247 the Privy Council was unanimously of the opinion that the prosecution could not lead at the trial evidence regarding the testimony given by the defendant at the *voir dire*. Such a rule was necessary (per Lord Hailsham), so that 'the defendant should be able and feel free either by his own testimony or by other means to challenge the voluntary character of the tendered statement'. The rule applies even where the confession is admitted (per Lord Edmund-Davies), because 'it is preferable to maintain a clear distinction between the issue of voluntariness, which is alone relevant to the *voir dire*, and the issue of guilt falling to be decided in the main trial'. **F17.46**

Wong Kam-ming v The Queen was applied in *Brophy* [1982] AC 476. B was tried in Northern Ireland for a large number of offences, including murder, and for being a member of the IRA, a proscribed organisation. At the *voir dire* he succeeded in challenging the admissibility of confessions tendered by the prosecution, on the ground that the statements were extracted from him by extreme misconduct on the part of his interrogators. In support of his case he admitted to membership of the IRA, in order to found an inference that his interrogators would have known of his allegiance and treated him brutally because of it. It was held that the accused's admission, being relevant to the issue at the *voir dire*, was inadmissible for the prosecution at the trial. Furthermore according to Lord Fraser of Tullybelton (at p. 481): 'Where . . . evidence is given at the *voir dire* by an accused person in answer to questions by his counsel, and without objection by counsel for the Crown, his evidence ought . . . to be treated as relevant to the issue at the *voir dire*, unless it is clearly and obviously irrelevant', for example, the accused 'goes out of his way to boast' of his guilt.

Some commentators have argued that the law has altered as a result of the PACE 1984, s. 76, the effect of which is to render such a confession admissible, there being no question of it having been obtained by oppression or in circumstances conducive to unreliability. Even if this is the case, however, the policy behind *Wong Kam-ming v The Queen* and *Brophy* can be preserved and the same result achieved by invoking s. 78 of the 1984 Act to prevent unfairness in the proceedings. It is submitted that the policy is worth preserving, and that the accused would derive no protection from the statutory rules prohibiting the reception of confessions obtained in certain circumstances if the accused could only invoke the rule at the cost of admitting afresh that what he said was true.

Cross-examination on Statements Made on *Voir Dire*

In *Wong Kam-ming v The Queen* [1980] AC 247 W gave evidence at trial and was cross- **F17.47** examined in detail as to statements made on the *voir dire* which were inconsistent with his testimony. The Privy Council held that where, as in the instant case, the confession had been excluded at the *voir dire,* it was not open to the prosecution to conduct such a cross-examination: 'Once a statement has been excluded . . . to adopt the words of Humphreys J in *Treacy* [1944] 2 All ER 229, nothing more should be heard of the *voir dire* unless it gives rise to a prosecution for perjury' (per Lord Hailsham at pp. 260–1).

The rule was otherwise where the confession which was the subject of the *voir dire* was admitted in evidence. In such a case (per Lord Hailsham, at p. 261). '. . . the whole evidence relating to the statement will have to be rehearsed once more . . . in front of the jury', and '. . . the statements on oath by the defendant on the *voir dire* as material for cross-examination do not, from the point of view of public policy, stand in any other situation than any other statements made by him, including the statement which has been admitted'.

The reasons of policy underlying the law as stated in *Wong Kam-ming v The Queen* have not altered since the coming into force of the PACE 1984, and it is submitted that the law remains as stated.

CONFESSION ADMISSIBLE AT TRIAL

Reconsidering Admissibility

F17.48 It has already been noted (**F17.43**) that in *Sat-Bhambra* (1988) 88 Cr App R 55, the Court of Appeal held that, once a confession has been ruled admissible on the *voir dire,* the trial judge has no power under the PACE 1984, s. 76 or s. 78, to reconsider his decision if the evidence given at trial convinces him that he was wrong. To this extent the Act reverses the decision in *Watson* [1980] 1 WLR 991, where it was said that the judge had the power to reconsider the question of admissibility of evidence on which he had already ruled, and had the duty to exclude from the jury's consideration evidence which was inadmissible. However, the court in *Sat-Bhambra* noted that s. 82(3) of the 1984 Act preserved the common-law powers of a court to exclude evidence in its discretion. It followed that the trial judge retained the power, if only under the common law, to take such steps as were necessary to prevent injustice. He might, if he thought that the matter was not capable of remedy by a direction, discharge the jury; he might direct the jury to disregard the statement; or he might by way of direction point out to the jury matters which affect the weight of the confession and leave the matter in their hands. He was not, however, under any obligation to discharge the jury. The change brought about by the Act would seem therefore to be mainly technical, and it is submitted that in any event there is still force in the dictum of the Court of Appeal in *Watson* [1980] 1 WLR 991 that, 'the occasions on which a judge should allow counsel to invite him to reconsider a ruling already made are likely to be extremely rare'.

The problem is perhaps most likely to arise where a decision has been made on the basis that the confession was not obtained pursuant to a breach of the Code of Practice, but it then emerges that a breach may have occurred. In *Hassan* [1995] Crim LR 404, a concession to this effect by a police officer in cross-examination led the trial judge to use his common law powers to reconsider his decision to admit H's confession, although he quite properly did not regard the concession as decisive of whether there had been a breach, and concluded that there had not. It is also possible to reconsider a decision to exclude a statement. In *Allen* [1992] Crim LR 297 the defence sought to cross-examine a police witness to elicit their version of a conversation, the prosecution version of which had been excluded under s. 78. It was held that the judge had correctly exercised his discretion to admit the prosecution version of what had been said.

Role of Jury

F17.49 Under the PACE 1984 as at common law, the admissibility of the confession is a matter for the judge, and the weight to be given to the confession, once it is admitted, is a matter for the jury. In *Mushtaq* [2005] 1 WLR 1513 the House of Lords confirmed the view of the Court of Appeal in the same case that, as the jury is not a 'public authority' within the meaning of the HRA 1998, s. 6(3), it was not necessary in order to protect the accused from the risk of unfair trial that the jury, independently of the judge, should satisfy themselves as to the admissibility of confession evidence. The traditional division of labour between judge and jury thus survives the HRA 1998.

Because the jury are entitled to consider all the circumstances in which a confession is made before deciding whether to act on it, it is the right of counsel for the defence 'to cross-examine again the witnesses who have already given evidence in the absence of the jury; for if he can induce the jury to think that the confession was obtained through some threat or promise, its value will be enormously weakened' (*Murray* [1951] 1 KB 391, decided at common law). The House of Lords in *Mushtaq* confirmed that the jury may be assisted in their function of deciding whether the confession is reliable by hearing the evidence that it was obtained in breach of the PACE 1984, s. 76(2). The House was, however, divided on the issue of the proper direction to be given to a jury in a case where evidence is before them that the confession was obtained by oppression or other improper means (in that case, by alleged threats to exaggerate M's part in the offence if he did not confess). If they conclude that it was so obtained, but is nevertheless reliable, may they act upon it? The traditional direction, given by the trial judge in *Mushtaq*, left the jury free to rely on the confession, if sure that it was true, 'even if it was or may have been made as a result of oppression or other improper circumstances'. A majority of their lordships decided that this direction could not be reconciled with s. 76(2) of the PACE 1984, to the extent that the rejection of an improperly obtained confession is based not solely on its potential unreliability, but on the importance of the defendant's right to avoid self-incrimination (*Lam Chi-ming v The Queen* [1991] AC 212, per Lord Griffiths). To leave the jury with the impression that they could find one or more of these rights to have been improperly infringed, but still rely upon the evidence, would, *per* Lord Roger, have been to contradict the policy:

> The evidence is excluded because, for all the kinds of reasons explained by Lord Griffiths, Parliament considers that it should not play any part in the jury's verdict. It flies in the face of that policy to say that a jury are entitled to rely on a confession even though, as the ultimate arbiters of all matters of fact, they properly consider that it was, or may have been, obtained by oppression or any other improper means.

For the same reasons, the majority considered that the traditional direction contained an invitation to act incompatibly with the accused's right against self-incrimination under Article 6(1). The House therefore departed from previous authorities including *Chan Wei Keung v The Queen* [1967] 2 AC 16. Lord Roger, in a speech with which the majority concurred, concluded that the logic of s. 76(2) of the PACE 1984 requires that the jury should be directed that, if they consider that the confession was or may have been obtained by oppression or in consequence of anything that was likely to render it unreliable, they should disregard it.

If the jury were to be told that the judge had ruled the confession admissible, it is possible that they might be influenced by the judge's view on admissibility in deciding the issues which are for them to decide. Thus it has been the practice in England, both before and after the PACE 1984, for this information to be withheld from them (*Mitchell v The Queen* [1998] AC 695; *Thompson v R* [1998] AC 811).

If a confession is voluntary, the inference that it is also true follows naturally in most cases. On rare occasions, however, the mental condition of the accused may give rise to doubts as to the reliability of his confession. In such a case, expert medical evidence may be admitted to assist the jury in evaluating the reliability of the confession (*Ward* [1993] 1 WLR 619 (severe personality disorder amounting to mental disorder); *MacKenzie* (1992) 96 Cr App R 98 (mentally handicapped accused also suffering personality disorder: Crown conceded jury entitled to the assistance of expert testimony to evaluate confessions: see also **F17.37**).

Confession Implicating Co-accused

F17.50 A confession made by an accused person that is admitted in evidence is evidence against him (PACE 1984, s. 76(1)). It is not, at common law, admissible against any other person implicated in it (*Rhodes* (1959) 44 Cr App R 23) unless it is made in the presence of that person and he acknowledges the incriminating parts so as to make them, in effect, his own. The evidence of a co-accused on oath was, by contrast, admissible for all purposes, including the purpose of being evidence against the accused (*Rudd* (1948) 32 Cr App R 138). The common-law rule has been affected by the enactment of the PACE 1984, s. 74 (**F11.5**). Under that provision there is no doubt that the conviction of A is admissible to establish the guilt of A at B's trial, where it is relevant to do so (the most common example being where B is charged with complicity in a crime that the prosecution contends was committed by A, and of which A has been convicted). In *Hayter* [2005] 1 WLR 605, the House of Lords held, by majority, that the rule where A and B are tried for a joint offence is modified as follows. Where the jury are directed first to consider the case against A, which is based on his out-of-court admissions, they may then be told that their finding as to the guilt of A and the role he played may be used as part of the evidence relevant to the guilt of B. In other words their finding of guilt against A, though based on his confession, becomes a building block in the case against B. This differs only marginally from using the confession of A directly (rather than indirectly through a finding of guilt) as evidence against B, but to hold strictly to the common-law rule would be to open a gulf between cases where A and B are jointly tried and cases where A's guilt is established at a separate trial, where s. 74 applies. Some of the older cases, including *Rhodes* itself, would be decided differently today.

For the circumstances in which a confession may be edited so as to remove incriminating references to a co-accused, see **F17.59**. In exceptional circumstances the existence of a confession by one accused which seriously prejudices another may be grounds for ordering separate trials (*Gunewardene*). Joint offences should generally be tried jointly, however, even though this may involve evidence which is inadmissible in respect of a particular accused being given. The fact that there is some risk of prejudice is not enough, though 'if a case is strong enough, if the prejudice is dangerous enough, if the circumstances are particular enough, all rules of this kind must go in the interests of justice' (*Lake* (1976) 64 Cr App R 172, at p. 175).

CONFESSION EXCLUDED AT TRIAL

Effect of Exclusion on Prosecution

F17.51 In *Treacy* [1944] 2 All ER 229, the prosecution had not sought to put in evidence, as part of their case, a statement made by T to a police officer following T's arrest for murder. Instead it was used in cross-examination of T as a previous inconsistent statement. The statement was assumed by the Court of Appeal to have been inadmissible as part of the prosecution case, and, that being so, it was held that 'nothing more ought to be heard of it, and it is quite a mistake to think that a document can be made admissible in evidence which is otherwise inadmissible simply because it is put to a person in cross-examination'. In *Rice* [1963] 1 QB 857 it was held that the same principle obtains in favour of a co-accused of the maker of the inadmissible statement. The rule prohibits the revelation that the accused has made a statement, 'since evidence of, or revelation of that fact tends in common sense to lend weight to the subsequent evidence'. It does not preclude the use of information derived from the statement as the basis of cross-examination (*Rice*).

Effect of Exclusion on Co-accused

A confession which is inadmissible under the PACE 1984, s. 76(2)(b), on behalf of the prosecution may not be relied upon by a co-accused as evidence of its truth at common law. (*Myers* [1998] AC 124: see **F17.19**). It may, however, be put to the maker in cross-examination, in which case the only limitation is relevancy (*Lui Mei Lin v The Queen* [1989] AC 288). It follows that a co-accused cannot be restrained from cross-examining the accused on the content of any previous statement made by him which is relevant, notwithstanding that that statement may have been ruled inadmissible as part of the prosecution case (*Lui Mei Lin v The Queen*, approving *Rowson* [1986] QB 174), or may have been made in circumstances where it could not be used to prove guilt. In *Hinchcliffe* [2002] EWCA Crim 837 the admission by a company director as part of a 'Carecraft' agreement leading to his disqualification was made on the basis that it could not be used in other proceedings, but this was held to be no bar to its use in cross-examination. Where evidence of an otherwise inadmissible previous statement is elicited by a co-accused in cross-examination, the judge should explain to the jury why the statement has previously been excluded and cannot be relied on by the prosecution to prove their case. It should also be remembered that in cross-examination as to credit the cross-examiner is bound by the answers which he receives, and that it is not legitimate to reopen all the circumstances in which the excluded statement was taken. The trial judge should insist that irrelevant material contained in the statement is not referred to, and that such material is, where necessary, excised from any copies which the jury might see (*Lui Mei Lin v The Queen*). Under the CJA 2003, previous inconsistent statements which are admitted in cross-examination are, generally, evidence of the truth of facts stated (s. 119). This does not, however, permit the introduction of a confession which is inadmissible under the PACE 1984, s. 76 (s. 128(2)). **F17.52**

EVIDENCE YIELDED BY INADMISSIBLE CONFESSIONS

Police and Criminal Evidence Act 1984, s. 76 **F17.53**

(4) The fact that a confession is wholly or partly excluded in pursuance of this section shall not affect the admissibility in evidence—
(a) of any facts discovered as a result of the confession; or
(b) where the confession is relevant as showing that the accused speaks, writes or expresses himself in a particular way, of so much of the confession as is necessary to show that he does so.

(5) Evidence that a fact to which this subsection applies was discovered as a result of a statement made by an accused person shall not be admissible unless evidence of how it was discovered is given by him or on his behalf.

(6) Subsection (5) above applies—
(a) to any fact discovered as a result of a confession which is wholly excluded in pursuance of this section; and
(b) to any fact discovered as a result of a confession which is partly so excluded, if the fact is discovered as a result of the excluded part of the confession.

Discovery of Facts

The PACE 1984, s. 76(4)(a), follows the common-law rule as stated in *Warickshall* (1783) 1 Leach 263. W made a full confession to receiving stolen goods, in consequence of which the goods were found concealed in her bed. The confession was ruled inadmissible, but the prosecution were allowed to prove the discovery of the stolen property. It was held that the principle requiring the rejection of certain confessions in evidence 'has no application whatever as to the admission or rejection of facts, whether the knowledge of them be obtained in **F17.54**

F

Part F Evidence

consequence of an extorted confession, or whether it arises from any other source; for a fact, if it exists at all, must exist invariably in the same manner, whether the confession from which it is derived be in other respects true or false'.

Some difficulty may arise as to where the 'confession' ends and 'facts discovered as a result of it' begin. At common law, in *Barker* [1941] 2 KB 381 documents delivered up by B as a direct result of an inducement were treated as the equivalent of confession evidence, and excluded accordingly. Section 82(1) of the 1984 Act now provides a definition of 'confession' as including 'any statement wholly or partly adverse to the person who made it . . . whether made in words or otherwise'. Words, documents or conduct which come within this definition and which fall foul of the exclusionary rule in s. 76(2) cannot be treated as 'facts' for the purpose of s. 76(4)(a). Thus, for example, a filmed re-enactment of a murder, in which a defendant is shown disposing of the murder weapon, should be regarded as a confession statement rather than as independent facts (*Lam Chi-ming v The Queen* [1991] 2 AC 212). However, it does not seem entirely satisfactory to regard conduct such as that in *Barker* as the equivalent of a 'statement' by him 'in consequence of anything said or done' under s. 76(2)(b) for the purposes of the 1984 Act, and such evidence would seem to be more correctly considered as admissible evidence of facts which, like all prosecution evidence, may in appropriate circumstances be excluded under s. 78 of the 1984 Act.

Confession Relevant to Show Speech, Writing or Expression

F17.55 Section 76(4)(b) of the 1984 Act embodies a principle stated in argument by Lush J in *Voisin* [1918] 1 KB 531. V was charged with the murder of a woman, part of whose body was found in a parcel together with a handwritten note bearing the legend 'Bladie Belgiam'. V, who had not been cautioned, was asked by the police to write the words 'Bloody Belgian', which he did, misspelling them in precisely the same fashion as the writer of the note. The case did not concern an inadmissible confession, but the principle involved in the reception of the note in evidence was said by Lush J to be that 'it cannot make any difference to the admissibility of handwriting whether it is written voluntarily or under compulsion of threats'. The same point was made (*obiter*) in *Nottle* [2004] EWCA Crim 599. Cars had been damaged by scratching an obscene message to the owner, whose name was Justin, but which the vandal had spelt as 'Jutin'. When asked to write down the same message, N also spelt the name incorrectly. On the assumption that the misspelling constituted a confession, the court found that there had been nothing said or done to render the statement inadmissible under s. 76, but that, even if it had been otherwise, s. 76(4)(b) would have rendered the misspelling admissible. Section 76(4)(b) might also be used, for example, in a case of rape, where a tape-recorded confession is ruled inadmissible, but the voice of the accused can be heard speaking with an unusual speech impediment which was also described by the victim, or with a particular local accent. Care must be taken to avoid prejudice to the accused when adducing such evidence; s. 76(4)(b) permits the prosecution to adduce only 'so much of the confession as is necessary to show' the relevant feature, but even this may in some cases be impossible without the jury becoming aware that a confession has been made. In such cases it will have to be considered whether the risk of prejudice can be overcome by a direction as to the purpose for which the evidence has been adduced, or whether the discretion of the court to exclude prosecution evidence, either under s. 78 of the 1984 Act or at common law, should be exercised. In *Nottle* the court held that the failure of the police to disclose to N that the name on the car had been spelled 'Jutin' was not a matter which rendered it unfair for the prosecution subsequently to rely on N's identical misspelling.

Linking Facts to Confession

F17.56 At common law there was some controversy as to the extent to which it was permissible to show that certain facts had come to light as the result of an inadmissible confession by the accused. Section 76(5) and (6) of the 1984 Act confirms the view taken in *Warickshall* (1783) 1 Leach 263, and *Berryman* (1854) 6 Cox CC 388 that no such link can be proved. The only exception is where the defence choose to give evidence of how the facts came to be discovered, in which case, presumably, the prosecution may challenge the account given by the defence, even if to do so involves making reference to the excluded statement.

Evidence Yielded by Confession Excluded under s. 78

The PACE 1984, s. 76(4), applies only to matters coming to light as a result of a confession excluded under s. 76 itself. Where the confession is excluded in the discretion of the court under s. 78, no statutory rule applies, but the common-law principles suggest that evidence discovered in consequence is admissible. **F17.57**

As to the linking of the discovery with the confession, it may be that a court dealing with an application under s. 78 will not feel compelled to follow the principle laid down in s. 76(5), given that the common law on the point was unclear (see, e.g., *Griffin* (1809) Russ & Ry 151; *Gould* (1840) 9 C & P 364, and the views expressed by a majority of the Criminal Law Revision Committee in their 11th Report, *Evidence* (1972) Cmnd 4991, para. 69). It should also be noted that the reasons which led the court to exercise its discretion in respect of the confession may extend also to the subsequently discovered facts, as where an accused discloses information in a confession made after he has been denied access to legal advice by a police officer acting in deliberate and flagrant disregard of s. 58 of the 1984 Act.

Another possibility is that the court will take into account the confirmation of a confession by the discovery of incontrovertible facts in deciding whether to exercise its discretion to exclude the confession statement. Nothing in s. 78 appears to prevent such reasoning, indeed the court is enjoined to have regard to 'all the circumstances' in reaching its conclusion. (Contrast s. 76(2), in which it is clear that the truth of the confession is not a factor to be taken into account in determining admissibility.) The argument is particularly attractive where the defence rely on breach of a provision of a code of practice, the function of which is thought by the court to be to guard against the production of unreliable confession statements, such as the obligation to maintain records of interviews.

EDITING OF CONFESSIONS

Editing at Trial to Protect Accused

Where the confession of an accused person is admitted in evidence against him, the whole confession is admissible, notwithstanding that it includes matter prejudicial to the accused. In *Turner v Underwood* [1948] 2 KB 284 the response of the accused when charged with an offence of indecency was to say 'I have done time for this before', and it was held that the whole confession was admissible in evidence before the magistrates. However, Lord Goddard noted (at p. 286) that: 'It is the practice as a rule in cases which are tried before juries that where the court knows there is something said by a man in his statement which admits a previous conviction, or shows other matter reflecting on his character, the court sees that that is not read out to the jury.' **F17.58**

Similarly, in *Weaver* [1968] 1 QB 353 Sachs LJ said that a statement by an accused ought to be edited at trial to avoid prejudicing him and to eliminate matters which 'it would be better that the jury should not know'. In *Knight* (1946) 31 Cr App R 52 portions of the accused's confessions which related to other offences which were irrelevant to the offence charged were held to have been improperly received in evidence. Quashing the convictions, Lewis J regarded it as 'contrary to the rules of evidence' to admit what was in effect evidence of the bad character of the accused, who had not put their characters in issue. In some cases the material edited out is irrelevant, in others it has a prejudicial effect exceeding its probative value. See also *Hall* [1971] Crim LR 480.

When a statement is to be edited in this way, the proper procedure was said in *Weaver* [1968] 1 QB 353 to be that the statement should not be edited until the trial, at which stage, according to Sachs LJ (at p. 358) 'counsel can confer, and the judge can, if necessary, take his part in ensuring that any "editing" is done, if it is done at all, in the right way and to the right degree'.

Where the matter concerned is relevant and admissible in the trial there is no reason to omit it, even if the jury are made aware of other offences (*Evans* [1950] 1 All ER 601).

In *Pearce* (1979) Cr App R 365, it was said that the rule of practice whereby the courts 'admit in evidence all unwritten and most written statements made by an accused person to the police whether they contain admissions or whether they contain denials of guilt,' was subject to the limitation that any admission of a previous conviction would be excluded.

Editing at Trial to Protect Co-accused

F17.59 Where the confession of an accused person is admitted, it is not, as a general rule, admissible in evidence against a co-accused (see **F17.50**). Where an accused has laid blame, perhaps the greater blame, on his co-accused, the risk of prejudice to the co-accused if the whole statement is heard is obvious. The rule, however, is that the prosecution ought to present the accused's confession as a whole (*Pearce* (1979) 69 Cr App R 365) and the accused could, with good reason, complain if the prosecution picked out certain passages and left out others (*Gunewardene* [1951] 2 KB 600). In *Gunewardene*, G was charged as an accessory to manslaughter arising out of an abortion performed by H, his co-accused. H's confession was read to the jury, including those parts of it which implicated G, the trial judge warning the jury that the statement was not evidence against G. Lord Goddard CJ said (at p. 611) that 'although in many cases counsel do refrain from reading passages which implicate another prisoner and have no real bearing on the case against the prisoner making the statement, we cannot say that anything has been admitted . . . which was not admissible'.

Gunewardene was applied in *Lobban v The Queen* [1995] 1 WLR 877, where the issue before the Privy Council was whether the exculpatory part of a mixed statement made by L's co-accused, R, which incriminated L in a murder, could be excluded or edited in the exercise of the court's discretion to protect L from prejudice, given that the statement was hearsay and inadmissible as against him. The answer was that it could not; the prosecution had placed reliance upon the mixed statement as against R, and the exculpatory parts were therefore admissible evidence for R (see **F17.61**). There was no discretion to restrain a co-accused from defending himself by adducing admissible evidence, and nothing to support the suggestion made in earlier cases that the judge had a discretion to edit a confession so as to deprive one defendant of relevant defence evidence in order to minimise injustice to another (see, e.g., *Rogers* [1971] Crim LR 413). This, while a correct application of principle, may remove what has been an attractive option in some cases (see, e.g., the discussion of earlier authorities in *Jefferson* (1994) 99 Cr App R 14 at p. 26), but it would seem still to leave open the possibility of editing out information irrelevant to the co-accused's case, or of editing with the co-accused's consent.

In *Mitchell* [2005] EWCA Crim 3447, the Court of Appeal was concerned with the editing of two sets of statements. In the first, *Lobban* applied because the prosecution were relying on the whole of the interview and the effect of editing out references to the co-accused would have been to leave the jury with an incomplete and unsatisfactory picture of what the maker had said. In the second, *Lobban* did not apply: the references to the co-accused were made, not by the accused himself, but by a police officer putting forward his opinion that the co-accused had committed another crime which was not the subject of any proceedings. That part of the statement could and should have been removed, and the desire of the accused to use it in order to discredit the co-accused was irrelevant.

Pre-trial Editing of Written Statement Made by Suspect

Consolidated Criminal Practice Direction, para. III.24 **F17.60**

Evidence by written statement

III.24.4 . . . (b) When a suspect is interviewed about more offences than are eventually made the subject of committal charges, a fresh statement should be prepared and signed omitting all questions and answers about the uncharged offences unless either they might appropriately be taken into consideration or evidence about those offences is admissible on the charges preferred, such as evidence of system. It may, however, be desirable to replace the omitted questions and answers with a phrase such as: 'After referring to some other matters, I then said . . .' so as to make it clear that part of the interview has been omitted.

III.24.6 None of the above principles applies, in respect of committal proceedings, to statements which are exhibited (including statements under caution and signed contemporaneous notes). Nor do they apply to oral statements of a defendant which are recorded in the witness statements of interviewing police officers, except in the circumstances referred to in para. 24.4(b) above. All this material should remain in its original state in the committal bundles, any editing being left to prosecuting counsel at the Crown Court (after discussion with defence counsel and, if appropriate, the trial judge).

Where the prosecution tender written statements in evidence, it will frequently be necessary to edit, *inter alia*, statements which contain inadmissible, irrelevant or prejudicial material. The *Practice Direction* recognises that, whereas other written statements may be satisfactorily dealt with by editing, it is preferable in the circumstances identified in para. III.24.4(b), where an interview ranges over more offences than are eventually charged, to prepare a fresh statement. In summary proceedings particularly, there may be a greater need to prepare fresh statements rather than using the method of striking out or bracketing those parts on which no reliance is to be placed by the prosecution in the proceedings (para. III.24.5). See also **D10.29**.

MIXED STATEMENTS

Admissibility of Mixed Statements

The expression 'mixed statement' is used to refer to a statement made by an accused which in part comprises admissions and in part exculpatory or self-serving statements (*Hamand* (1985) 82 Cr App R 65 at p. 67). An example would be 'I admit I hit him, but he was trying to kill me'. A 'partly adverse statement' is a confession by virtue of the PACE 1984, s. 82(1) (see F17.1), and is admissible as such provided that the requirements of s. 76 are complied with. In *Finch* [2007] 1 WLR 1645, the Court of Appeal identified as suitable for full argument the question whether the presence of an admission in a police interview rendered the entire interview a 'confession'. Whether a particular statement is truly 'mixed' is, it is submitted, a question of fact, and both temporal and contextual separation will be relevant to whether two or more propositions form part of the same statement. **F17.61**

Where an admission is made which is qualified by an explanation or excuse, all the authorities agree that it would be unfair to admit the admission without admitting the explanation (*Sharp* [1988] 1 WLR 7 per Lord Havers at p. 12). In *Jones* (1827) 2 C & P 629, the rule was said to be that 'if a prosecutor uses the declaration of a prisoner, he must take the whole of it together, and cannot select one part and leave another'. In *Pearce* (1979) 69 Cr App R 365, it was said that to exclude answers at interview which are favourable to the accused, while admitting those which are unfavourable, would be misleading, and a breach of duty on the part of the prosecutor, whose obligation is to present the case fairly to the jury. See also *McGregor* [1968] 1 QB 371 and *Duncan* (1981) 73 Cr App R 359, at p. 363.

It will be a question for the court in each case to determine whether an excuse or explanation so accompanies an admission as to be part of a mixed statement for the purposes of this rule. In *Pearce* (1979) 69 Cr App R 365, the principle was said to be that a statement which is not an admission is admissible if it is made 'in the same context as an admission', and the Court of Appeal accepted that the two parts of the mixed statement may occur at different places in 'the same interview or series of interviews'.

In many cases, the mixed statement will have been made in the course of questioning of the accused by the police, no distinction being taken in this respect between a written statement and a record of questions and answers at interview (*Polin* [1991] Crim LR 293). It is not, however, a condition of admissibility that the statement was made to a police officer — a point taken by Lord Havers in *Sharp*. Thus, for example, mixed statements have been received which were made by the accused when giving evidence at a previous trial (*McGregor; Higgins* (1829) 3 C & P 603).

Under the CJA 2003, s. 118(1), the common-law rules regarding the admissibility of mixed statements are preserved (see **F16.38**).

Evidential Value of Self-serving Parts of Mixed Statements

F17.62 In *Sharp* [1988] 1 WLR 7, Lord Havers identified two views which had emerged as to the evidential value of the self-serving parts of a mixed statement. The view which the House of Lords accepted is that the whole statement is admissible by way of exception to the hearsay rule, and is thus evidence of the truth of all the facts stated in it. The House expressed approval of the law as stated in *Duncan* (1981) 73 Cr App R 359 by Lord Lane CJ, who said (at p. 365):

> Where a 'mixed' statement is under consideration by the jury in a case where the defendant has not given evidence, it seems to us that the simplest, and, therefore, the method most likely to produce a just result, is for the jury to be told that the whole statement, both the incriminating parts and the excuses or explanations, must be considered by them in deciding where the truth lies. It is, to say the least, not helpful to try to explain to the jury that the exculpatory parts of the statement are something less than evidence of the facts they state.

For examples of earlier decisions to the same effect, see *Clewes* (1830) 4 C & P 221; *McGregor* [1968] 1 QB 371; *Hamand* (1985) 82 Cr App R 65. *Sharp* has been approved by the House of Lords in *Aziz* [1996] AC 41 and by the Privy Council in *Lobban v R* [1995] 1 WLR 877.

The other view which has from time to time been taken, is that the self-serving parts of the statement are not evidence of their truth, but form material which may be of use to the jury in evaluating the admissions. This was said to be the law in, for example, *Sparrow* [1973] 1 WLR 488 and in *Leung Kam-Kwok v The Queen* (1984) 81 Cr App R 83. The House of Lords in *Sharp* [1988] 1 WLR 7 rejected this 'purist' approach:

(a) because the weight of authority supported the contrary view; and
(b) because common sense suggested that the only way in which a jury could use the self-serving parts of the statement to 'evaluate the facts in the admission' would be if they first reached a conclusion as to the truth of the explanation given by the accused.

The question of the evidential value of a mixed statement arises most acutely in cases where the accused does not testify. In both *Duncan* (1981) 73 Cr App R 359 and *Sharp* [1988] 1 WLR 7 the accused gave no evidence, and the statement of Lord Lane CJ which was approved in *Sharp* concerns the direction to be given to a jury in such a case; indeed it incorporates the right to comment on the failure of the accused to repeat the exculpatory statement on oath

(*Downes* (1993) *Independent*, 25 October 1993). Despite this, there is no logical reason why the status of the statement should be any different if the accused testifies.

Weight to be Attached to Self-serving Parts of Mixed Statements

In *Sharp* [1988] 1 WLR 7 the House of Lords approved of the following statement of Lord Lane CJ in *Duncan* (1981) 73 Cr App R 359 at p. 365: **F17.63**

> . . . where appropriate, as it usually will be, the judge may, and should, point out that the incriminating parts are likely to be true (otherwise why say them?), whereas the excuses do not have the same weight. Nor is there any reason why, again where appropriate, the judge should not comment in relation to the exculpatory remarks upon the election of the accused not to give evidence.

In *Donaldson* (1976) 64 Cr App R 59 it was said that the jury, when deciding what weight, if any, to give to those parts of the statement which are favourable to an accused who has elected not to give evidence, should take into account that it was not made on oath and has not been tested by cross-examination. See also *McGregor* [1968] 1 QB 371.

Mixed Statements and the Evidential Burden

Where the accused bears the evidential burden of establishing a sufficient foundation so that a defence such as self-defence or provocation may be left to the jury, he may rely on the self-serving part of a mixed statement which is admitted in evidence under the principles stated above. In *Hamand* (1985) 82 Cr App R 65, H made a statement to the police in which he admitted that he had struck a man in the face, but claimed that the man had acted in such a way as to lead H to believe that he was about to be attacked. The statement was proved in evidence as part of the prosecution case. The Court of Appeal held that the trial judge had been wrong to rule that H's mixed statement was not evidence of self-defence, thus forcing H to testify in his own defence. In assessing the weight to be given to such a statement where it is not supported by any evidence from the accused himself, the comments of Lord Lane CJ in *Duncan* (1981) 73 Cr App R 359 (see **F17.63**) should be borne in mind. **F17.64**

Prosecution Placing No Reliance on Admission Contained in Mixed Statement

The derivation of the rule as stated at **F17.61** and **F17.62** suggests that a mixed statement becomes evidence of the truth of its self-serving parts only where the prosecution elect to rely on it as containing an admission. Some difficulty may arise in cases where the prosecution adduces a mixed statement simply as evidence showing the reaction of the accused when taxed with the offence, and not as evidence of its truth. That this may be done is well established (see, e.g., *Storey* (1968) 52 Cr App R 334; *Donaldson* (1976) 64 Cr App R 59; *Pearce* (1979) 69 Cr App R 365), and may benefit the prosecution by enabling them to draw attention to any inconsistencies between the explanation advanced in the statement and any defence put forward at trial. It seems unlikely that, in such cases, the self-serving passages become evidence of their truth. **F17.65**

For the same reason, it is submitted, a mixed statement which is not relied on by the prosecution for any purpose ought not to be regarded as admissible evidence for the defence of any excuse or explanation asserted in it. This was accepted by the House of Lords in *Aziz* [1996] AC 41 (at p. 50), where the statement to this effect in the 1995 edition of this work was approved. It should, however, be noted that in *Sharp* [1988] 1 WLR 7 the question certified for decision by the House (as amended by Lord Havers) was: 'Where a statement made to a person out of court by a defendant contains both admissions and self-exculpatory parts do the exculpatory parts constitute evidence of the truth of the facts alleged therein?' The question does not confine itself to cases where the prosecution seek to rely on the admissions contained in the statement. It is submitted, however, in the light of *Aziz*, that the answering of this question in the affirmative by the House of Lords does not provide any warrant for qualifying the law as it is stated above.

Recent decisions of lower courts have suggested a wider approach. In *Garrod* [1997] Crim LR 445, the Court of Appeal considered that a statement was properly regarded as 'mixed' if it contained an admission of fact which was capable of adding some degree of weight to the prosecution case, regardless (apparently) of whether the prosecution were relying on it or not. However the statement in that case was purely exculpatory, whichever test was applied. In *Western v DPP* [1997] 1 Cr App R 474, W appealed against conviction for a public order offence on the grounds that the magistrates had wrongly treated as purely self-serving an interview in which W admitted fighting with the victim but claimed to have acted in self-defence. The prosecution resisted the appeal precisely on the grounds that the interview was not a mixed statement unless the prosecution relied on the admission. The appeal was allowed because there was nothing within the stated case to suggest that the prosecution had *not* relied on the admission: on the contrary the circumstances suggested it was highly likely that they had. Butterfield J nevertheless expressed 'grave doubts' about the proposition relied on by the prosecutor, advancing instead the view that whether a statement is mixed should be determined by an examination of its contents, not by the use to which it is put. *Aziz* was not considered. The view of Butterfield J has practical advantages for trial judges, who would not be obliged to draw fine distinctions between apparently similar statements. It is submitted, however, that the current law requires these distinctions to be drawn.

STATEMENTS IN PRESENCE OF ACCUSED

General Rule

F17.66 . . . the rule of law undoubtedly is that a statement made in the presence of an accused person, even upon an occasion which should be expected reasonably to call for some explanation or denial from him, is not evidence against him of the facts stated save so far as he accepts the statement, so as to make it, in effect, his own. (*Christie* [1914] AC 545, per Lord Atkinson at p. 554)

Under the CJA 2003, s. 118(1), the common-law rules regarding the admissibility of confessions are preserved (see **F16.38**). It is submitted that the rules considered in this section will continue to have effect.

Although it is a salutary rule of practice, there is no rule of law requiring the production, before the content of the statement is given in evidence, of some proof of the accused's acceptance of the statement (*Christie*, modifying the stricter rule suggested by the Court of Criminal Appeal in *Norton* [1910] 2 KB 496). Lord Atkinson considered that the procedure suggested by Pickford J in *Norton* was unobjectionable, provided that it was workable. According to that procedure, in a trial on indictment the judge, where it is possible to do so, decides whether there is any evidence of acknowledgement of the statement. Where acknowledgement cannot be deduced, the fact of a statement having been made in the accused's presence may be given in evidence, but not the contents, and the question asked, what the accused said or did on such a statement being made. If the answer is such that acknowledgement may properly be inferred, the contents of the statement become admissible.

If the statement is admitted, the question whether the accused's conduct amounted to an acknowledgement is a question for the jury. If they find that the statement was acknowledged, in whole or in part, then they may take the statement or the relevant part of it into consideration. If they do not so find, they should be directed to disregard the statement altogether (*Norton*). In *Christie*, Lord Atkinson said (at p. 554) that, if the judge is of the view that no evidence has been given on which the jury could reasonably find that the accused had accepted the statement, he should direct the jury to disregard it.

Where the acknowledgement takes the form of a statement by the accused which is wholly or partly adverse to him, he will by virtue of the PACE 1984, s. 82(1), have made a confession for the purposes of part VIII of that Act, and accordingly the conditions of s. 76 must be complied with.

The jury should be given a clear direction as to the inferences to which the accused's conduct may give rise (*Horne* [1990] Crim LR 188; *Chandler* [1976] 1 All ER 585; but see *Black* (1922) 16 Cr App R 118).

Evidence of Acknowledgement

In *Christie* [1914] AC 545, Lord Atkinson considered the various ways in which an accused person might accept an accusation put to him (at p. 554): **F17.67**

> He may accept the statement by word or conduct, action or demeanour, and it is the function of the jury which tries the case to determine whether his words, action, conduct or demeanour at the time when the statement was made amounts to an acceptance of it in whole or in part. It by no means follows, I think, that a mere denial by the accused of the facts mentioned in the statement necessarily renders the statement inadmissible, because he may deny his statement in such a manner and under such circumstances as may lead a jury to disbelieve him, and constitute evidence from which an acknowledgement can be inferred.

See also *Norton* [1910] 2 KB 496. In *Christie*, C was charged with indecent assault on a young boy who, shortly after the alleged offence and in the presence of his mother and of a police officer who was on the spot, confronted C with the words 'That is the man,' and gave details of the assault. C replied 'I am innocent'. Although in the form of a denial, the response was regarded as one from which it was open to the jury to draw an inference of acceptance. Lord Moulton said (at p. 559):

> Going back to first principles . . . the deciding question is whether the evidence of the whole occurrence is relevant or not. If the prisoner admits the charges the evidence is obviously relevant. If he denies it, it may or may not be relevant. For instance, if he is charged with a violent assault and denies that he committed it, that fact might be distinctly relevant if at the trial his defence was that he did commit the act, but that it was in self-defence.

Acceptance by acquiescence was considered sufficient: *O* [2005] EWCA Crim 3082, where the accused stood by, smirking, while his friend explained when asked the reason for an attack that it had been racially motivated.

Where the accused denies the accusation, it must, however, be asked whether the effect on the jury of hearing that an accusation has been made might be to create prejudice on their part which is out of all proportion to the evidential value of the accused's behaviour. If the evidence would have very little or no value, the judge ought to exercise his discretion to exclude it (*Christie*, per Lord Moulton at p. 560).

As to silence in the face of an allegation, see **F19.2**, *et seq.*

Accused Confronted with Statement by Co-accused

The principles set out at F17.66 are of equal application where the accused is confronted with an accusation made by his co-accused. Difficulties may, however, arise if the police show the accused a statement made by a co-accused implicating him, ostensibly to gauge the accused's reaction, but intending also to profit by getting the statement before the court in circumstances where the maker of the statement cannot be called as a witness. The practice was condemned in *Gardner* (1915) 11 Cr App R 265, and although the court was not prepared to say that admissions obtained in this way were inadmissible, it appears to have been regarded as within the discretion of the trial judge to exclude statements put to the accused for the purpose of extracting a confession. See also *Taylor* [1978] Crim LR 92, in which it was said that the prejudicial effect of a co-accused's accusation vastly outweighed its probative value as evidence introducing T's reaction, though it does not appear what the reaction of T was alleged to have been. In *Mills* [1947] KB 297 the Court of Appeal considered that the co- **F17.68** accused's statement ought not to be given in evidence in such circumstances, and the reaction of the accused ought likewise to be excluded unless it could be understood without reference to what the co-accused had said (e.g., where the accused went on to make a full confession).

The practice of the police is now regulated by PACE Code C, para. 16.4 of which provides that, where, after a person has been charged or informed that he may be prosecuted, a police officer wishes to bring to his notice a statement made by, or the content of an interview with, another person, he must give him a true copy of the statement or bring to his attention the content of the interview record whilst doing nothing to invite any reply or comment save to caution him. This should ensure that the only evidence of reaction on which a court is asked to rely will be a voluntary statement under caution. If the co-accused's statement is improperly read, it is likely that the statement will be excluded under the PACE 1984, s. 78, together with the accused's reaction to it, particularly if the latter cannot be made sense of without reference to the statement.

Section F18 Evidence of Identification

Introduction

Evidence of identification may take several different forms. The greater part of this section deals with visual identification by witnesses, but consideration is also given to the use of fingerprints and body impressions, DNA (tissue and hair) samples, voice identification, video images, photographs, composite images (such as EFITS) and artist's sketches. **F18.1**

Most, but not all, identification procedures are regulated by PACE Code D, the latest version of which came into effect in relation to procedures carried out after midnight on 31 December 2005 (see **appendix** 2). There is still nothing in Code D to govern aural identification procedures, although it acknowledges (in para. 1.2) that the use of procedures such as 'voice identification parades' may sometimes be considered appropriate.

VISUAL IDENTIFICATION

The visual identification of suspects or defendants by witnesses has for many years been recognised as problematic and potentially unreliable. It is easy for an honest witness to make a confident, but false, identification of a suspect, even in some cases where the suspect is well known to him. There are several possible reasons for errors of this kind. Some persons may have difficulty in distinguishing between different subjects of only moderately similar appearance, and many witnesses to crimes are able to see the perpetrators only fleetingly, often in stressful circumstances. False identification may even be caused by a process known as unconscious transference, in which the witness confuses a face he recognises from the scene of the crime (perhaps that of an innocent bystander) with that of the offender. Such problems may then be compounded by the understandable, but often misguided, eagerness of many witnesses to help the police by making a positive identification. **F18.2**

The Criminal Law Revision Committee asserted in its Eleventh Report (Cmnd 4991) that cases of mistaken identification 'constitute by far the greatest cause of actual or possible wrong convictions'. Much has been done since then to reduce the dangers posed by such errors. In particular, the Court of Appeal in *Turnbull* [1977] QB 224 laid down rules to guide trial courts faced with contested identification evidence, and PACE Code D attempts to ensure that pre-trial identification procedures are conducted as fairly as possible.

Identification Evidence and Identification Issues

It is important to distinguish between identification evidence and evidence which incriminates by other means. A mere description of the culprit or his clothing is not identification evidence, even if it closely matches the appearance or clothing of the defendant (*Gayle* [1999] 2 Cr App R 130). Nor is it identification evidence where the witness states that the culprit was the driver of a particular vehicle, or the companion of another person, whose own identification is not in dispute (*White* [2000] All ER (D) 602). If there is no identification evidence, the *Turnbull* guidelines will not apply. A witness who has made or who may be able to make an identification, should be invited to view an identification parade or other identification procedure if the police have a known suspect available (Code D, para. 3.12); but inability to **F18.3** make an identification need not prevent the witness giving other evidence that might incriminate the accused, such as a description of the offence or offender (*George* [2003] Crim LR 282).

If the accuracy of a purported identification (as opposed to the honesty of the accusing witness) is not in issue, then neither the *Turnbull* guidelines nor Code D will need to be considered. In such cases any attempt to apply the *Turnbull* guidelines would merely serve to confuse the jury by focusing their attention on the wrong issue (*Courtnell* [1990] Crim LR 115; *Cape* [1996] 1 Cr App R 191). If, for example, the witness claims to have known the accused well and for many years and to have observed him at close range in conditions of perfect visibility for several minutes, or to have conversed with him in the same room, it is unlikely that any identification issue could arise.

On the other hand, identification issues may sometimes arise, even where the witness claims to have recognised the suspect or accused as someone already well known to him, and they are not necessarily excluded even where the principal line of defence involves an attack on the honesty or truthfulness of the witness. This can be seen in *Conway* (1990) 91 Cr App R 143. Two witnesses claimed to have recognised C as the man responsible for a stabbing and he was arrested. He denied that he knew either of the witnesses and asked to be put on an identification parade, but the police took the view that this was unnecessary, as C was a 'named person'. The Court of Appeal held this to be wrong: identification became an issue as soon as C questioned the witnesses' ability to recognise him, and the identification procedures laid down in Code D should have been followed.

The general rule, therefore, is that an appropriate *Turnbull* warning should be given, even in cases of alleged recognition. In *Beckford v The Queen* (1993) 97 Cr App R 409, a witness claimed to have recognised the appellant and others as they committed the alleged offence. He knew them well. The defence alleged that his evidence was wilfully false, but the Privy Council nevertheless held that there was also a possibility of genuine mistake. The witness had been 500 ft from the scene of the crime, and the closest he had come to the perpetrators was 120 ft. Mistakes can be made at such distances, even where known acquaintances are involved, and it was held that a *Turnbull* direction should have been given. See also *Bentley* [1991] Crim LR 620, *Bowden* [1993] Crim LR 379 and *Giga* [2007] EWCA Crim 345. It does not follow, however, that a Code D identification procedure need be held in such cases, because such a procedure will often be considered to serve no useful purpose in a 'recognition' case (see further **F18.6**).

Pre-trial Identification Procedures: Known and Available Suspects

F18.4 In all potential identification cases, Code D, para. 3.1, requires a record to be made of the description of the 'suspect' (meaning the person allegedly seen at the scene of the crime etc.) as first given by the witness. This must where practicable be disclosed to the 'suspect' (meaning the potential defendant) or his solicitor before any identification procedures are undertaken, and any discrepancies between the original description and the actual appearance of any person identified will be a matter for judicial comment under the *Turnbull* guidelines.

Where the ability of a witness to make a positive visual identification is in issue, and there is a known suspect who is available to take part in an identification procedure, one of the procedures laid down in Code D, paras. 3.5 to 3.10 should normally be arranged as soon as possible (para. 3.4). Such procedures may also be held if the officer in charge of the investigation considers that this would be useful (para. 3.13).

The current version of Code D (para. 3.12) provides that formal identification procedures should be followed both in cases where there is already some disputed identification evidence of the suspect and in cases where there is a witness who may be able to make an identification, provided in either case that such procedures would be practicable and might conceivably serve a useful purpose. See also (*Rutherford* (1993) 98 Cr App R 191; *Forbes* [2001] 1 AC 473). If, for example, the police have arrested a suspect on the basis of other evidence, and there are witnesses who indicate that they might be able to make an identification, then an identification procedure should be followed. A positive identification would strengthen the case for the prosecution; whilst a defendant should not be deprived of the opportunity to have witnesses to the crime declare that the offender they saw is not in front of them.

The Identification Officer and his Delegates

The arrangements for, and conduct of, identification procedures under Code D are the responsibility of the 'identification officer': an officer not below the rank of inspector who is not otherwise involved with the investigation (see para. 3.11). Code D nevertheless permits substantial delegation of this officer's duties (and those of the custody officer) to other officers or to civilian police employees (para. 2.21). Certain duties may also be performed by the custody officer, in respect of the 'notice to suspect' requirements under paras. 3.17 to 3.19, where the identification procedure is to be carried out at a later date, and an inspector is not available to act as identification officer. This flexibility is intended to avoid or reduce delay in arranging identification procedures by enabling the required information and warnings to be given at the earliest opportunity. F18.5

Where Identification Procedures may be Unnecessary

Code D, para. 3.12, provides that an identification procedure need not be held if, in all the circumstances, it would serve no useful purpose: as for example where the suspect is already well known to the witnesses, or where there is no reasonable possibility that a witness would be able to make an identification at all. This provision was first added to Code D in April 2002 but merely confirms existing practice. See for example *Montgomery* [1996] Crim LR 507, *Nicholson* [1999] 1 Cr App R 182 and *Forbes* [2001] 1 AC 473. In *Forbes* Lord Bingham said: F18.6

> If an eye-witness of a criminal incident makes plain to the police that he cannot identify the culprit, it will very probably be futile to invite that witness to attend an identification [procedure]. If an eye-witness may be able to identify clothing worn by a culprit, but not the culprit himself, it will probably be futile to mount an identification [procedure] rather than simply inviting the witness to identify the clothing. If a case is one of pure recognition of someone well known to the eye-witness, it may again be futile to hold an identification [procedure]. But save in cases such as these, or other exceptional circumstances, the effect of [Code D] is clear: if (a) the police have sufficient information to justify the arrest of a particular person for suspected involvement in an offence, and (b) an eye-witness has identified or may be able to identify that person, and (c) the suspect disputes his identification as a person involved in the commission of that offence, an identification [procedure] must be held. . .

Forbes was followed in *Muhidinz* [2005] EWCA Crim 2464.

Code D was not designed to apply to situations in which the police seek to connect a suspect with events that occurred many years previously, when his appearance was markedly different. Other procedures may then be permissible. In *Folan* [2003] EWCA Crim 908, the Court of Appeal upheld the conviction of the appellant (F) who was alleged to have murdered his wife some 20 years earlier. Her remains were found beneath a concrete floor at the site of a disused hospital that was being demolished, and the police had to establish whether he had worked on the site at the time of her disappearance. No identify parade or group identification was held, as would have been required if Code D had applied. Instead, persons connected with the site at the time were shown a photograph of F dating from the relevant period, and were asked whether they recognised him: a procedure that Code D (if applicable) would have prohibited.

Breaches of Code D: General Principles

As with the other codes of practice issued under the PACE 1984, breaches of Code D need not inevitably lead to the exclusion of evidence (*Khan* [1997] Crim LR 584; *McEvoy* [1997] F18.7

Crim LR 887), but it is essential that the trial court or judge determines whether any alleged breaches have occurred, and whether they may have caused any prejudice to the accused (*Grannell* (1989) 90 Cr App R 149; *Ryan* [1992] Crim LR 187; *Quinn* [1995] 1 Cr App R 480; and *Hickin* [1996] Crim LR 584). In *Beveridge* (1987) 85 Cr App R 255, the Court of Appeal stated that the determination of such facts can usually be accomplished without the need for a trial within a trial, but this cannot be an absolute rule. The holding of a trial within a trial was not questioned in *Willoughby* [1999] 2 Cr App R 82.

If it is clear that no prejudice resulted then there will be no case for excluding the evidence. If, on the other hand, some prejudice may have been caused, it will be necessary to determine, under the PACE 1984, s. 78, whether the adverse effect would be such that justice requires the evidence to be excluded. Cases will, to a large extent, turn on their own facts. A trial court or judge should nevertheless give reasons for any decision to admit identification evidence obtained in breach of Code D (*Allen* [1995] Crim LR 643) and in a trial on indictment the jury must ordinarily be told 'that an identification procedure enables suspects to put the reliability of an eye-witness's identification to the test, that the suspect has lost the benefit of that safeguard, and that they should take account of that fact in their assessment of the whole case, giving it such weight as they think fit' (*H* [2003] EWCA Crim 174, per Potter LJ).

Identification evidence will usually be excluded where important provisions have been flouted. In *Nagah* [1991] Grim LR 55, N's conviction was quashed after evidence had been admitted at his trial of a deliberately staged encounter outside the police station, in which he had been confronted by the identifying witness as he left, after having being told that there was insufficient evidence to charge him. He had previously agreed to stand on an identification parade, but this was never held. See also *Finley* [1993] Crim LR 50 and *Gall* (1989) 90 Cr App R 64.

Failure to comply with Code D may also give rise to issues under the ECHR, notably in cases involving covert videotaping of suspects, which may be open to challenge under Article 8 if not performed in strict accordance with domestic law (see *Perry v United Kingdom* (2003) 39 EHRR 76).

Identification of Known and Available Suspects

F18.8 Code D provides for four possible procedures by which a known suspect may be placed before witnesses in order to establish if they can identify him. Under earlier versions of Code D, the identification parade was the preferred procedure, assuming the suspect was available and willing to take part. The 2002 revisions to Code D changed this hierarchy by giving equal status to video identification (in which the witness is shown moving images of the suspect together with images of other people who resemble him), and the current version goes one step further by specifying video identification as the normal first-choice procedure (see para. 3.14). The identification officer and the officer in charge of the investigation may consult with each other and choose between offering video identification or an identification parade, the latter being offered where it seems both practicable and more suitable than a video parade.

Group identification is now only the third-choice procedure, but may be used where it is considered more suitable than a video identification or identification parade (para. 3.16). Confrontation remains the last resort, to be used only if all others (including covertly recorded video, etc.) are impracticable (see para. 3.23). Whichever procedure is adopted, it must be carried out in accordance with the appropriate annex to Code D.

Where the Suspect Refuses to Consent to an Identification Procedure

F18.9 Code D, para. 3.15, gives detailed guidance as to the procedures to adopt where a suspect refuses to consent to the suggested identification procedure. Where a suspect refuses the identification procedure which is first offered he (or his solicitor or appropriate adult) may make representations as to why another procedure should be used. The identification officer 'shall, if appropriate,' arrange for him to be offered a suitable and practicable alternative. The words, 'if appropriate' indicate that the police need not give in to objections that appear to be merely obstructive, misguided or petulant. If for any reason the identification officer decides that it is not suitable and practicable to offer an alternative procedure, the reasons for that decision must be recorded.

Some procedures are viable only with the suspect's co-operation. Under para. 3.21, the identification officer may arrange a covert video identification or a covert group identification in cases where the suspect's lack of co-operation makes the usual procedures impracticable. The identification officer has discretion to use for this purpose any suitable images of the suspect, whether moving or still, which are available or can be obtained. Force may not be used in order to facilitate an identification where the suspect attempts to hide his face (see *Jones* (1999) *The Times*, 26 March 1999 and Code D, Annex D, para. 3) but where there are reasonable grounds to suspect that, if forewarned, the suspect would take steps to avoid being identified, para. 3.20 permits the identification officer to arrange for images to be obtained for use in a video identification procedure before the usual information and notice is given to the suspect under paras. 3.17 and 3.18.

Video Identification

Annex A to Code D deals with video identification, which was originally covered by annex B. **F18.10**
It does not however apply to cases in which suspects are identified from closed circuit security videotapes or from any other scene-of-crime recordings made before the emergence of a suspect (*Jones* (1995) 159 JP 293). The rules deal not only with the conduct of 'video parades' but also with documentation and with image security and destruction. The current annex A is largely identical to the old, but paras. 2A to 2C are new and there are also changes to paras. 2 and 10.

Identification Parades

Annex B deals with the holding of parades and with related documentation (including **F18.11**
a video or colour photograph of the parade). Paragraph 10 gives formal approval to the established practice of concealing any distinctive scar, tattoo, hairstyle or hair colour of the suspect that cannot be replicated on other members of the identification parade, as long as the suspect and his solicitor etc. agree. All members of the parade may for example wear a similar adhesive plaster or hat, so that all resemble each other in general appearance. The witness may however require such articles to be removed. See para. 19, and *Marrin* (2002) *The Times*, 5 March 2002.

Regrettably, some deficiencies revealed in past cases have not been addressed by the revised Code D. Annex B lays down strict rules to prevent contact between witnesses, or between witnesses and investigating officers, during a parade or immediately before it (see paras. 14 to 16) but still says nothing about the propriety of such contact once the witnesses in question have viewed the parade. See *Willoughby* [1999] 2 Cr App R 82 and **F18.4**.

Group Identification

Annex C deals with group identification. It seeks to ensure that, as far as possible, such **F18.12**
procedures follow the same principles as identification parades so that the conditions are fair to the suspect in the way they test the witness's ability to make an identification. The conditions under which group identifications take place cannot, of course, be controlled to the same degree as parades or video parades, but under para. 6 the identification officer must reasonably expect that over the period the witness observes the group they will be able to see, from time to time, a number of others (in addition to the suspect) whose appearance is

broadly similar. In *Jamel* [1993] Crim LR 52, a group identification was arranged on the basis that a parade was impracticable. J was of mixed race, and the identification was held in a street where one might have expected a variety of individuals of various races to pass by. In the event, nobody of mixed race but J appeared, and he was identified by the witness. The Court of Appeal declined to find fault with this procedure, but indicated that they would have taken a different view had it been held in an overwhelmingly white neighbourhood.

A group identification must ordinarily be conducted with the suspect's consent, but may in certain circumstances be conducted covertly (see Code D, para. 3.21 and note 3D). It may be held in either a public place or a secure environment (such as a prison or police station) and the suspect may be part of either a moving or a stationary group. Annex C makes provision for each type of case. An identification carried out in accordance with Annex C remains a group identification notwithstanding that at the time of being seen by the witness the suspect was on his or her own rather than in a group (see para. 10).

Confrontation

F18.13 Confrontation of a suspect by a witness is governed by annex D. Force may not be used even if the suspect attempts to hide his face (see para. 3, which confirms the rule previously applied in *Jones* (1999) *The Times*, 26 March 1999) nor may confrontation ordinarily take place in the absence of the suspect's legal adviser etc. (para. 4). Confrontation is in some respects little better than dock identification, and the courts will almost certainly exclude such evidence if the limited safeguards required under annex D have been breached. See, for example, *Powell v DPP* [1992] RTR 270 and *Samms* [1991] Crim LR 197. Judicial mistrust of confrontation can most clearly be seen in *Joseph* [1994] Crim LR 48, where the police had done their best to arrange for a parade, group identification or video identification, but without success (J being tall, black and bearded, with shoulder length dreadlocks). The prosecution sought to proceed on the basis of other evidence, but J demanded a confrontation before the trial, in the misguided hope that the witnesses would not identify him. He was in fact identified by two witnesses, and the trial judge admitted that evidence on the basis that J had asked for the confrontation, but the Court of Appeal considered that the weakness of this evidence required its exclusion under the PACE 1984, s. 78.

Qualified Identification

F18.14 In some cases, a witness may qualify his identification of the suspect by indicating that he cannot be quite certain', or that he is only '90 per cent sure'. A defendant cannot properly be convicted on qualified identification evidence alone (*George* [2003] Crim LR 282) but it may still have some probative value when added to support other more positive evidence. Counsel should take care not to question a witness who has given a qualified identification so as to suggest that, but for some detail or other, it would have been a positive one (*ibid*) and although Code D remains largely silent on the subject, it would clearly be improper for the police to encourage a witness to be more positive once the initial parade or video identification process has been concluded (e.g., by telling him that he has 'got the right one'). As Lord Bingham CJ observed in *Willoughby* [1999] 2 Cr App R 82:

> There . . . would be the utmost ground for concern if there were any question of the police nudging, prompting or encouraging any witness . . . to make a more positive identification of a suspect. . . . It would seem to us important that a witness should not be told whether an identification is right or wrong until after the witness has made any further statement that the witness may wish.

No Identified Suspect

F18.15 Where there is no identified suspect available to take part in an identification procedure, Code D (paras. 3.2 and 3.3) allows witnesses to be shown photographs, or to be taken to a particular neighbourhood or place, in the hope that they will recognise the offender. Paragraph 3.2 governs cases in which witnesses are taken to a particular neighbourhood or place to see whether they can identify the person whom they saw on the relevant occasion. The showing of photographs should be done in accordance with annex E to Code D. Once one witness has made a positive identification from photographs then, unless the person identified can be eliminated from the enquiry, no further witnesses should be shown photographs; instead, an identification or video parade etc. should be arranged as soon as possible. Similarly, if the use of an artist's sketch or composite likeness points to a known suspect who can be asked to participate in an identification procedure, the likeness must not then be shown to other witnesses (annex E, para. 8).

Identification from police photographs indicates that the defendant must have a criminal record, or be known to the police, and the prosecution should not ordinarily reveal this fact (*Lamb* (1979) 71 Cr App R 198), unless the defendant's record is already before the jury (*Allen* [1996] Crim LR 426). If, however, the defence choose to make an issue of the witness's ability to make an identification at that time, it may be necessary to admit such evidence to prevent the jury being misled. In *Bleakley* [1993] Crim LR 203, B had been identified by a witness, first from photographs and subsequently at a parade. The defence suggested that the witness identified B at the parade only because B had visited his premises the night before. Evidence of the earlier identification by photographs was held to have been properly admitted to rebut this suggestion. This does not mean that the jury should be told all about the accused's criminal record. Care should be taken to minimise any prejudice to him (*Campbell* [1994] Crim LR 357).

Code D does not seek to inhibit the showing of videos or photographs to the public through national or local media, or to police officers for the purposes of recognition and tracing suspects, but when such material is shown to potential witnesses (including police officers) for the purpose of obtaining identification evidence, it must be shown on an individual basis so as to avoid collusion, and in broad accordance with annex A (if the suspect is known) or otherwise in accordance with annex E (Code D, paras. 3.28 and 3.29; but see the discussion of *Folan* [2003] EWCA Crim 908 at **F18.6**).

Videotape showing the commission of a crime must ordinarily be kept as evidence at trial. Should the tape accidentally be lost or erased, testimony from those who viewed it may be admissible in lieu, although such evidence would require a *Turnbull* warning and would be inferior to the video itself. It may in some cases be proper to exclude such evidence under the PACE 1984, s. 78. In *Taylor v Chief Constable of Cheshire* [1986] 1 WLR 1479, Ralph Gibson LJ said:

> The weight and reliability of the evidence will depend upon assessment of all relevant considerations, including the clarity of the recording, its length and . . . the witness's prior knowledge of the person said to be identified.

See also (as to the loss or erasure of video-taped evidence generally) *R (Ebrahim) v Feltham Magistrates' Court* [2001] 1 WLR 1293.

Dock Identification

The 'dock identification' of an accused for the first time during the course of the trial itself has long been considered an unfair and unsatisfactory procedure (see *Edwards v The Queen* [2006] UKPC 29. The A-G and the DPP therefore undertook in 1976 that in cases tried on indictment: **F18.16**

> The [prosecution] at committal proceedings, or Crown Counsel at any subsequent trial, will not invite a witness to identity, who has not previously identified the accused at an identity parade, to make a dock identification unless the witness's attendance at a parade was unnecessary or impracticable, or there are exceptional circumstances.

This is a statement of policy, rather than a rule of law and dock identification remains legally admissible, but a judge would ordinarily prohibit any such identification during the course of a trial on indictment (see *Fergus* (1993) 98 Cr App R 313). Different considerations may apply in respect of minor summary offences, where the holding of an identity parade or similar Code D procedure may often appear impracticable. In *Barnes v Chief Constable of Durham* [1997] 2 Cr App R 505, Popplewell J suggested that the rule of practice that applies to trials on indictment 'has singularly little application to the everyday activities of the magistrates' court'. In *Karia v DPP* (2002) 166 JP 753, Stanley Burnton J adopted a more cautious stance, observing merely that: 'It cannot be sensible to require identity parades to be held in all motoring cases, in circumstances where there is no reason to believe that identity is in issue', but both rulings appear to conflict with *North Yorkshire Trading Standards Dept v Williams* (1994) 159 JP 383 in which the court rejected the notion that less strict identification rules should apply in respect of summary offences. See further T. Watkin, 'In the Dock — an Overview of Decisions of the High Court on Dock Identifications in the Magistrates' Court' [2003] Crim LR 463. Whether dock identification infringes the right to a fair trial under the ECHR, Article 6, depends on all the circumstances of the case. Such a procedure cannot be said to be unfair *per se* (*Holland v HM Advocate* [2005] HRLR 25).

There is a danger that a witness may sometimes make a dock identification even where none has been solicited by the prosecution. If that happens (as in *Thomas* [1994] Crim LR 128), it may be necessary for the trial judge to warn the jury against giving it any weight or credence. It would not suffice merely to observe (as did the trial judge in *Thomas*) that an identification of that sort would not ordinarily take place.

There is also a risk, if the accused is not in custody and no identification has previously been arranged, that a witness will identify him as he arrives or waits outside the court. In *Tiplady* (1995) 159 JP 548, the prosecution actually arranged for a group identification in the foyer of the court building as the defendant arrived and this evidence was properly admitted at trial. It is unlikely, however, that the circumstances of such an identification would be wholly satisfactory (especially where a considerable time has elapsed since the alleged offence), and it may prove necessary in some cases to exclude such evidence (*Martin* [1994] Crim LR 218, but cf. *Campbell* [1996] Crim LR 500).

Recognition cases, such as *Reid* [1994] Crim LR 442, appear to be different. The Court of Appeal in *Reid* were anxious not to encourage dock identification, but saw no reason to interfere with the trial judge's decision to admit recognition evidence in that case, notwithstanding that no identification parade or group identification had been held. A *Turnbull* direction was still needed but it was not a case in which the witness's ability to make a leisurely identification was in doubt. See also *Gardner* [2004] EWCA Crim 1639.

Pre-trial Identification: Admissibility

F18.17 In the ordinary course of events, where the identifying witness testifies adequately against the accused at trial, the pre-trial identification serves to prove his consistency and his ability to make an identification under fair and objective circumstances.

At common law, such evidence was admissible by way of an exception to the rule against previous consistent statements (*Christie* [1914] AC 545). If the police officer who supervised the identification parade was called to testify as to the identification, he could do so only in support of the identifying witness. His testimony could not go to the issue of the accused's guilt, because he would have no first-hand knowledge of it. Without the evidence of the original witness, his testimony would ordinarily be inadmissible hearsay (*Sparks v The Queen* [1964] AC 964; *Sealey v The State* [2002] UKPC 52).

This basic principle was overlooked by the Court of Appeal in *Osbourne* [1973] QB 678, but appears to have been applied in *Smith* (1987) 85 Cr App R 197.

The position was different where the witness could recall making an identification, and assert that it was correct, but was unable for some reason to swear that the accused is the person he identified on that occasion. (One possible explanation might be a change in the accused's appearance in the intervening period; another might be the fading of visual memory in the months between identification and trial.) In such a case, an officer who conducted or witnessed the parade would be permitted to testify (on the basis of his own first-hand knowledge) that the person identified was indeed the accused (or one of them).

Pre-trial Identification under the Criminal Justice Act 2003

The CJA 2003 provides (in s. 120(4) and (5)) that a previous statement by a witness will be admissible as evidence of any matter stated of which oral evidence by him would be admissible, if the statement identifies or describes a person, object or place and while giving evidence the witness indicates that to the best of his belief he made the statement, and that to the best of his belief it states the truth. This appears to make no significant change to the common-law position as stated in **F18.17**. **F18.18**

There are, however, further circumstances in which out-of-court statements may be now admissible as hearsay under the CJA 2003 (e.g., in cases where the witness is not available to testify in court) or under common-law rules (such as the rules concerning *res gestae*) and these may include statements involving evidence of identification. See further **F16.6** and **F16.24** ***et seq.***

The *Turnbull* Guidelines

In response to widespread concern over the problems posed by cases of mistaken identification, the Court of Appeal in *Turnbull* [1977] QB 224 laid down important guidelines for judges in trials that involve disputed identification evidence. The guidelines are also applicable, *mutatis mutandis*, in summary trials, and are reproduced (with slight abridgement) below: **F18.19**

> First, whenever the case against an accused depends wholly or substantially on the correctness of one or more identifications of the accused which the defence alleges to be mistaken, the judge should warn the jury of the special need for caution before convicting the accused in reliance on the correctness of the identification or identifications. In addition he should instruct them as to the reason for the need for such a warning and should make some reference to the possibility that a mistaken witness can be a convincing one and that a number of such witnesses can all be mistaken. Provided this is done in clear terms the judge need not use any particular form of words.
>
> Secondly, the judge should direct the jury to examine closely the circumstances in which the identification by each witness came to be made. How long did the witness have the accused under observation? At what distance? In what light? Was the observation impeded in any way, as for example, by passing traffic or a press of people? Had the witness ever seen the accused before? How often? If only occasionally, had he any special reason for remembering the accused? How long elapsed between the original observation and the subsequent identification to the police? Was there any material discrepancy between the description of the accused given to the police by the witness when first seen by them and his actual appearance? If in any case, whether it is being dealt with summarily or on indictment, the prosecution have reason to believe that there is such a material discrepancy they should supply the accused or his legal advisers with particulars of the description the police were first given. In all cases if the accused asks to be given particulars of such descriptions, the prosecution should supply them. Finally, he should remind the jury of any specific weaknesses which had appeared in the identification evidence.
>
> Recognition may be more reliable than identification of a stranger; but even when the witness is purporting to recognise someone whom he knows, the jury should be reminded that mistakes in recognition of close relatives and friends are sometimes made.
>
> All these matters go to the quality of the identification evidence. If the quality is good and remains good at the close of the accused's case, the danger of a mistaken identification is lessened; but the poorer the quality, the greater the danger.

> In our judgment when the quality is good, as for example when the identification is made after a long period of observation, or in satisfactory conditions by a relative, a neighbour, a close friend, a workmate and the like, the jury can safely be left to assess the value of the identifying evidence even though there is no other evidence to support it; provided always, however, that an adequate warning has been given about the special need for caution. Were the Courts to adjudge otherwise, affronts to justice would frequently occur. . . .
>
> When, in the judgment of the trial judge, the quality of the identifying evidence is poor, as for example when it depends solely on a fleeting glance or on a longer observation made in difficult conditions, the situation is very different. The judge should then withdraw the case from the jury and direct an acquittal unless there is other evidence which goes to support the correctness of the identification. This may be corroboration in the sense lawyers use that word; but it need not be so if its effect is to make the jury sure that there has been no mistaken identification. . . .
>
> The trial judge should identify to the jury the evidence which he adjudges is capable of supporting the evidence of identification. If there is any evidence or circumstances which the jury might think was supporting when it did not have this quality, the judge should say so.

Scope of the *Turnbull* Guidelines

F18.20 A *Turnbull* direction need not be provided unless the prosecution case depends wholly or substantially on visual identification (see *McMillan* [2005] EWCA Crim 1774 and **F18.3**), but where such a direction is required the specimen direction from the Judicial Studies Board is the briefest permissible (*Nash* [2005] Crim LR 232). Juries must therefore be warned that the warning is based on past experience (*ibid*). The absence of an adequate *Turnbull* direction, tailored to the facts of the particular case, will usually require a conviction to be quashed as unsafe (*Beckford v The Queen* (1993) 97 Cr App R 409; *Bowden* [1993] Crim LR 379; *Farquharson v The Queen* (1993) 98 Cr App R 398) although it may be condonable if the other evidence is overwhelming (see *Freemantle v The Queen* [1994] 1 WLR 437). Where the principal or sole means of defence is a challenge to the credibility of the identifying witness, there may be exceptional cases in which a full *Turnbull* warning is unnecessary or may be given more briefly than in a case where the accuracy of identification is challenged (*Shand v The Queen* [1996] 1 All ER 511; *Giga* [2007] EWCA Crim 345).

Paying lip service to the guidelines will not be enough (*Graham* [1994] Crim LR 212), nor will it suffice to give a general warning without detailed references to any particular circumstances that may have affected the accuracy of the witness's observation (*Reid v The Queen* [1990] 1 AC 363). See for example *Keane* (1977) 65 Cr App R 247, where the Court of Appeal criticised the trial judge for failing to identify possible supporting evidence or specific weaknesses, and for appearing 'more anxious to reassure the jury than to warn them'. On the other hand, the guidelines do not require the slavish use of a rigid form of words in every case (*Mills v The Queen* [1995] 1 WLR 511; *Qadir* [1998] Crim LR 828) and a judge may properly point out that a mistaken identification (as where a witness has identified a volunteer at a parade) does not necessarily prove that the accused is innocent or that the witness is untrustworthy in other respects, especially if his view of the crime was imperfect (*Trew* [1996] Crim LR 441).

The guidelines may also need to be followed in cases involving the disputed identification of an alleged accomplice (*Bath* (1990) 154 JP 849) and an inadequate direction in respect of the evidence against one accused may render unsafe the conviction of another (*Elliott* (1986) *The Times*, 8 August 1986), although this will depend on the circumstances of the particular case.

The guidelines are not applicable to cases involving the identification of motor vehicles. The reliability of a vehicle identification may however depend, *inter alia*, on the witness having had a satisfactory opportunity to see the vehicle and on his ability to distinguish between one model and another. This should be drawn to the jury's attention (*Browning* (1991) 94 Cr App R 109).

It was held in *Oakwell* [1978] 1 All ER 1223 that the guidelines were 'intended primarily to deal with the ghastly risk run in cases of fleeting encounters' and were not applicable to a case in which the witness may merely have been mistaken as to which person in a well identified group had struck him. In that case the judge had drawn the jury's attention to the possibility that the witness may have been momentarily unsighted, and this was held to be sufficient. *Oakwell* was followed in *Curry* [1983] Crim LR 737 and *Beckles* [1999] Crim LR 148; but in *Bowden* the Court of Appeal held that this principle was applicable only to situations in which the accused's presence at the scene of the crime is admitted. A *Turnbull* warning was accordingly held to have been necessary in *Bowden*, even though a police officer claimed to have had a long and careful look at the offender; see also *B* [2004] EWCA Crim 1481.

It does not follow from *Oakwell* that no *Turnbull* direction would ever be necessary if the accused's presence at the scene is admitted. There will be some circumstances in which it will be appropriate to give such a direction and some in which it will not (contrast *Thornton* [1995] 1 Cr App R 578 with *Slater* [1995] 1 Cr App R 584 and see also *Pattinson* [1996] 1 Cr App R 51).

The applicability of the *Turnbull* guidelines to cases of alleged recognition is discussed at **F18.3**. As the guidelines themselves explain, recognition evidence will often be more reliable than identification of a stranger, but may still be erroneous. Lord Lane CJ elaborated on this point in *Bentley* [1991] Crim LR 620:

> Many people have experienced seeing someone in the street whom they knew, only to discover that they were wrong. The expression, 'I could have sworn it was you' indicated the sort of warning which a judge should give, because that was exactly what a testifying witness did — he swore that it was the person he thought it was. But he may have been mistaken . . .

Supporting Evidence

Evidence capable of supporting a disputed identification may take any admissible form, including self-incrimination by the accused, similar fact evidence and other evidence of identification. The judge must identify evidence that is capable of providing such support and warn the jury against reliance on anything that might appear supportive without really having that capability. A prior discussion between judge and counsel is strongly advisable in this context, 'if only so that the judge knows on what points counsel will seek to rely in their speeches to support or undermine the identifications and that counsel will know the judge's view as to whether any particular piece of evidence is capable of having either effect' (*Stanton* (2004) *The Times*, 28 April 2004). **F18.21**

Where a judge decides that the identification evidence in a given case is of such poor quality that he would not have left the case to the jury in the absence of supporting evidence, there is no obligation on him to warn the jury that they should not convict on the basis of the evidence of identification alone, should they reject the supporting evidence. There might be some cases where, in the light of the evidence that has unfolded, a direction of that kind might be appropriate, but it is not required as a general rule (*Ley* [2007] 1 Cr App R 325).

Mutually Supportive Identifications It is permissible in appropriate cases for two or more disputed identifications of the accused to be treated as mutually supportive (*Weeder* (1980) 71 Cr App R 228; *Shelton* [1981] Crim LR 776) but only if the identifications are 'of a quality that a jury can safely be left to assess' (*Weeder*). It does not matter that both witnesses may have made their identifications from the same spot (*Tyler* (1992) 96 Cr App R 332) and in some cases the identifications may relate to separate incidents (see *Barnes* [1995] 2 Cr App R 491). **F18.22**

Self-incrimination Disputed identification evidence can clearly be supported by an admissible confession, but careful consideration must be given to cases in which the defendant is alleged to have incriminated himself by lies or false alibis. In *Turnbull* [1977] QB 224, Lord Widgery CJ said (at p. 230): **F18.23**

> Care should be taken by the judge when directing the jury about the support for an identification which may be derived from the fact that they have rejected an alibi. False alibis may be put forward for many reasons; an accused, for example, who has only his own truthful evidence to rely on may stupidly fabricate an alibi and get lying witnesses to support it out of fear that his own evidence will not be enough. Further, alibi witnesses can make genuine mistakes about dates and occasions like any other witnesses can. It is only when the jury is satisfied that the sole reason for the fabrication was to deceive them and there is no other explanation for its being put forward can fabrication provide any support fort identification evidence. The jury should be reminded that proving the accused has told lies about where he was at the material time does not by itself prove that he was where the identifying witness says he was.

This guidance remains valid, but the governing principles in relation to self-incrimination by false alibis or other lies, as set out by the Court of Appeal in *Lucas* [1981] QB 720, have now been held applicable in identification cases (*Goodway* [1993] 4 All ER 894). Before such lies can be regarded as supporting an identification, they must accordingly be shown to be deliberate and material; the court or jury must be able to discount any possible innocent motive for the lies and they must be proved to be lies by evidence other than the identification(s) that they are to support.

F18.24 **The Accused's Silence** Lord Widgery CJ warned in *Turnbull* [1977] QB 277 that an accused's failure to testify must not be viewed as capable of supporting the evidence against him. This must now be reconsidered in the light of recent legislation. Under the CJPO 1994, ss. 34 to 38, the failure of the accused:

(a) to mention facts when questioned or charged which are later relied upon in his defence;
(b) to account for objects in his possession or substances or marks on his body or clothing;
(c) to account for his presence at a particular place; or
(d) to testify at his trial,

may each, in appropriate cases, entitle the court or jury to 'draw such inferences as appear proper'. They do not, in themselves, constitute evidence of guilt and should not be seen as a substitute for satisfactory identification evidence, but the absence of testimony or explanation from the accused may legitimately enable a court or jury to infer, in appropriate cases, that the prosecution evidence is correct and that the accused has no answer to it. See F19.

The Quality of the Witness

F18.25 There is no doubt that some witnesses may be capable of providing more reliable identification evidence than others in the same position. A witness with perfect vision may clearly be expected to do better than a myopic witness who has lost his spectacles. More controversial is the suggestion that police officers may, by virtue of their training, be more observant than ordinary witnesses, or at least better at noting features or details that may be significant. That suggestion was rejected by the Privy Council in *Reid v The Queen* [1990] AC 363, but was subsequently held to be quite proper by the Court of Appeal in *Ramsden* [1991] Crim LR 295, where Lord Lane CJ opined that it would be wrong for a trial judge not to direct the jury as to the potentially greater reliability of police identification. See also *Tyler* (1992) 96 Cr App R 332; *Williams* (1994) *The Times*, 7 October 1994.

Stopping a Trial Based on Inadequate Identification

F18.26 The *Turnbull* guidelines require the trial judge to direct an acquittal in cases where identification evidence is both deficient and unsupported by alternative evidence. If necessary, the trial judge should invite the defence to make submissions to that effect (*Fergus* (1993) 98 Cr App R 313). In such cases, the Court of Appeal may quash a conviction, even though the judge's direction on the evidence was otherwise impeccable (see for example *Pope* (1986) 85 Cr App R 201).

This does not involve any conflict with the principles laid down by the Court of Appeal in

Galbraith [1981] 1 WLR 1039 (**D15.32** *et seq.*) because, in stopping the trial, the judge does not purport to determine whether prosecution witnesses are telling the truth. He merely decides that there is insufficient evidence on which a jury could properly convict (*Daley v The Queen* [1994] 1 AC 117; *Macmath* [1997] Crim LR 586).

PHOTOGRAPHS, PHOTOFITS AND VIDEOTAPE

The use of photographs or video footage in order to help witnesses identify possible offenders is dealt with at **F18.15**. What follows is concerned with the photographing of suspects and the use of visual images as evidence at trial.

Photographing Suspects

Section 64A of the PACE 1984 provides for the photographing of suspects at police stations (with or without their consent) and for the retention and use of photographs or other images taken of detained suspects. It also permits the police to require the removal of items (such as hats, face paint, masks or dark glasses) worn over the head or face, and to remove such items themselves if necessary. Section 64A has been amended, *inter alia*, by the SOCPA 2005, s. 116, the Police and Justice Act 2006 and the VCRA 2006, s. 27. These amendments enable a person to be photographed elsewhere if arrested by a constable for an offence, taken into custody by a constable after arrest by some other person, required to wait by a community support officer, given a direction by a constable under s. 27 of the VCRA 2006, given a notice in relation to a relevant fixed penalty offence (within the meaning of sch. 5A to the Police Reform Act 2002) by an accredited inspector by virtue of accreditation specifying that para. 1 of sch. 5A applies to him, or issued with a fixed penalty notice by a constable, CSO or accredited person. Section 64A says nothing about the destruction of such photographs if any charges are dropped, etc., but Code D, paras. 3.31 to 3.33 contains provisions addressing that issue. **F18.27**

What then if the police retain and use photographs that they ought to have destroyed in accordance with Code D? As with almost any breach of a PACE Code, evidence obtained as a result of such a breach is not thereby rendered inadmissible, but the breach may be taken into account when a court or judge is considering whether it would be in the interests of justice to admit such evidence under the PACE 1984 s. 78. See generally *A-G's Ref (No. 3 of 1999)* [2001] 2 AC 91.

The search or examination of a suspect with a view to finding, and if necessary photographing, any distinguishing marks or injuries is governed by the PACE 1984, s. 54A and Code D, paras. 5.1 to 5.11.

Use of Visual Images as Evidence at Trial

In *A-G's Ref (No. 2 of 2002)* [2003] 1 Cr App R 321, Rose LJ said (at [19]): **F18.28**

> In our judgment, on the authorities, there are . . . at least four circumstances in which, subject to the judicial discretion to exclude . . . and subject to appropriate directions in the summing-up, a jury can be invited to conclude that the defendant committed the offence on the basis of a photographic image from the scene of the crime:
>
> (i) where the photographic image is sufficiently clear, the jury can compare it with the defendant sitting in the dock (*Dodson & Williams* (1984) 79 Cr App R 220);
>
> (ii) where a witness knows the defendant sufficiently well to recognise him as the offender depicted in the photographic image, he can give evidence of this *Fowden* [1982] Crim LR 588, *Kajala v Noble* (1982) 75 Cr App R 149, *Grimer* [1982] Crim LR 674, *Caldwell* (1994) 99 Cr App R 73 and *Blenkinsop* [1995] 1 Cr App R 7; and this may be so even if the photographic image is no longer available for the jury (*Taylor v Chief Constable of Cheshire* (1987) 84 Cr App R 191);

(iii) where a witness who does not know the defendant spends substantial time viewing and analysing photographic images from the scene, thereby acquiring special knowledge which the jury does not have, he can give evidence of identification based on a comparison between those images and a reasonably contemporary photograph of the defendant, provided that the images and the photograph are available to the jury (*Clare* [1995] 2 Cr App R 333);

(iv) a suitably qualified expert with facial mapping skills can give opinion evidence of identification based on a comparison between images from the scene (whether expertly enhanced or not) and a reasonably contemporary photograph of the defendant, provided the images and the photograph are available for the jury (*Stockwell* (1993) 97 Cr App R 260, *Clarke* [1995] 2 Cr App R 425 and *Hookway* [1999] Crim LR 750).

In the first kind of case, photographs or video recordings (whether originals or copies) may be shown as real evidence and may provide the court with the equivalent of a direct view of the incident in question. A full *Turnbull* warning might not be appropriate in such cases, but the jury should still be warned of the dangers of mistaken identification, and should be reminded of the need to exercise great care when attempting to make an identification from photographs or video recordings (*Blenkinsop*). As to the use of witness evidence to assist the jury in identifying the offender from a photograph, see also *West* [2005] EWCA Crim 3034. In many cases, however, the quality of security videos is so poor that juries may need expert assistance. Evidence of facial mapping may, in such a case, enhance the value of poor quality images, but concerns have sometimes been expressed as to the proper scope and function of such evidence.

In *Hookway*, security video footage showed a robbery being committed by a group of stocking-masked men, one of whom was alleged to be H. There was no way in which the jury itself could be expected to identify H under such conditions, but evidence was admitted from two experts in facial mapping, who had studied the masked video images and compared them with photographs of H, so as to establish whether key facial features, such as the distance between the eyes, corresponded. They were satisfied that these features did indeed correspond, and opined that this provided 'very powerful support for the assertion that the offender was the appellant'. On the other hand, they 'could not be 100% certain' that H was one of the raiders. Notwithstanding the total absence of any other incriminating evidence, the jury convicted H, and his conviction was upheld on appeal. See also *Mitchell* [2005] EWCA Crim 731.

With respect, the expert evidence seems to have established only that H could have been one of the robbers. As the Court of Appeal admitted, there was no statistical evidence as to the significance of such similarities as were identified, because without an appropriate database it is impossible to know how many persons share the same features. How then could a jury properly convict on such evidence alone? Contrast the much stricter rule applied to qualified identification evidence in *George* [2003] Crim LR 282. Note also the concerns expressed by the Court of Appeal in *Gray* [2003] EWCA Crim 1001 and *Gardner* [2004] EWCA Crim 1639, although in *Gardner* the court rejected the suggestion that expert witnesses should be prevented from expressing opinions as to probabilities based on facial mapping evidence; and in *Ciantar* [2005] EWCA Crim 3559, the Court rejected arguments that expert evidence of facial mapping should have been discounted or excluded merely because other experts had expressed doubts as to its quality and sufficiency. (As to the weight to be attached to expert evidence generally, see **F10.24**.)

The third of Rose LJ's examples in *A-G's Ref (No. 2 of 2002)* was considered in *Abnett* [2006] EWCA Crim 3320. A police officer, who had spent some time interviewing the appellant and repeatedly viewing CCTV footage of a robbery, together with still images from that film, was permitted to state that he was '100 per cent sure' that one of the robbers pictured was the appellant. He had no specialist training in facial mapping or any other such technique, and (with respect) it is not obvious how or why his repeated viewing of the images would have equipped him to make a significantly more reliable identification than the jury, who had access to the same footage and images. Contrast *Clare* [1995] 2 Cr App R 333, in which the police officer had spent hours analysing footage of crowd violence and was able (*inter alia*) to explain to the jury how the incident in question had developed.

Artist's sketches or 'photofits' (which now use computer-based EFIT or CD-FIT technology) are fundamentally different in principle, in that they depend on the fallible (and potentially mendacious) assertions of the witnesses who help to compile them. An EFIT showing a bald or bearded suspect is manifestly a product of a witness's assertion that the suspect was bald or bearded, and should logically be categorised as a kind of statement, albeit one in visual form. In *Cook* [1987] QB 417, the Court of Appeal nevertheless held that such images should be regarded not as statements but as analogous to photographs, and thus free from the limitations which would otherwise be imposed on them under the hearsay rule. *Cook* was, with respect, a demonstrably flawed decision, but it was followed in *Constantinou* (1989) 91 Cr App R 74, in which a photofit picture compiled by the victim of a robbery was admitted in evidence against the appellant. Although the victim could have had only a partially obscured view of the robber through the sunroof of his car, no *Turnbull* warning was deemed necessary. This seems most unsatisfactory. The error in the reasoning adopted in *Cook* has been recognised in the CJA 2003, s. 115, which defines a 'statement' for the purpose of the hearsay rule as: ' . . . any representation of fact or opinion made by a person by whatever means; and it includes a representation made in a sketch, photofit or other pictorial form'.

VOICE IDENTIFICATION

At trial, evidence may be admissible from persons who claim to have recognised the accused's voice. There are few English guidelines, however, as to the procedures which should be followed in voice identification cases. Only the briefest of references to voice identification may be found in Code D, namely in para. 1.2 (which states that nothing in that Code precludes the use of aural identification procedures) and in annex B, para. 18, which provides that a witness may ask any member of a normal visual identity parade to speak. The witness should first be asked if he can make a purely visual identification, and must be reminded that participants will have been chosen on the basis of their appearance only). Code D makes no direct provision for cases in which the attempted identification is to be made on the basis of voice alone. This is unfortunate, because there is clear evidence that the risks of mistaken identification are very great. See *Roberts* [2000] Crim LR 183 and *Chenia* [2003] 2 Cr App R 83. For a detailed examination of the issues see David Ormerod, 'Sounds Familiar? — Voice Identification Evidence' [2001] Crim LR 595 and 'Sounding out Expert Voice Identification' [2002] Crim LR 771. One possible approach is to adapt the usual Code D procedures, so as to hold what is in effect a 'voice identification parade'. In *Hersey* [1998] Crim LR 281, the Court of Appeal upheld a conviction based largely on evidence derived from such a parade. The victim of a masked robbery claimed that he had recognised the voice of one of the robbers as being that of H, and was then able to identify H's voice on a 'parade' in which H and 11 volunteers each read out a passage from an earlier interview with H himself. It will clearly be necessary in such cases for the 'parade' to be composed of persons with broadly similar accents to that of the suspect, but it may not be helpful or realistic to assemble an entire parade of similarly-pitched voices. In *Hersey* the trial judge refused to admit expert evidence from the defence, to the effect that most of the volunteers on the parade had higher pitched voices than H. It was acknowledged in *Hersey* that voice identification shares many of the dangers of visual identification, and should be subject at trial to analogous warnings derived or adapted from the *Turnbull* guidelines. See also *Gummerson* [1999] Crim LR 680, *Neal* [2003] EWCA Crim 3465, *Davies* [2004] EWCA Crim 2521 and *Robinson* [2006] 1 Cr App R 221. F18.29

If there are tape recordings of the offender's voice, expert evidence may also be admissible on the question of whether this matches the voice of the defendant. Most phoneticians use acoustic analysis techniques for this purpose, but it was held in *Robb* (1991) 93 Cr App R 161 that an expert who uses only auditory phonetic techniques may still be competent to testify, even though the rejection of such methods by other phoneticians might mean that a jury would possibly give his views less weight, but the adequacy of unsupported auditory phonetic evidence must be in doubt after *Dallagher* [2003] 1 Cr App R 195, in which Kennedy LJ observed that 'technology has moved on' since *Robb* and noted that the courts in Northern Ireland have already held (in *O'Doherty* [2003] 1 Cr App R 77) that auditory phonetic analysis cannot suffice on its own to prove identity. This suggests that any prosecution evidence of that kind must be supported by expert evidence of acoustic analysis, save only where the issue is which voice out of a known group spoke which words, or where the speaker's voice has unusual and identifiable characteristics, or where the only issue relates to the speaker's accent or dialect.

The jury should be allowed to hear any admissible voice recordings for themselves, so that they may form their own judgment of the opinions expressed (*Bentum* (1989) 153 JP 538) but should be warned of the dangers of relying on their own untrained ears.

DENTAL OR SKIN IMPRESSIONS AND BODY SAMPLES

F18.30 The obtaining of body samples, skin impressions (including footprints) and dental impressions is governed by the PACE 1984, ss. 62 to 63A (as amended by the CJPA 2001, the Police Reform Act 2002, the CJA 2003, s. 10 and the SOCPA 2005, ss. 117 and 119), and by Code D, para. 6 (see **appendix** 2). A distinction is made between intimate and non-intimate samples, as defined in the PACE 1984, s. 65. Intimate samples are defined as blood, semen or tissue fluid; urine; pubic hair; dental impressions and swabs taken from the genitals or pubic hair or from orifices other than the mouth. Hair samples (other than pubic hair) are non-intimate, even if plucked with roots for DNA testing (s. 63A(2)).

Dental impressions may be taken only by a registered dentist; other intimate samples (except urine) may be taken only by a registered medical practitioner or a registered health care professional (s. 62(9)). Intimate samples may be taken only on the authority of an officer of at least the rank of inspector, and with the 'appropriate consent' (i.e. the consent in writing of the suspect, if he has reached 17; that of his parent or guardian if he is a child aged under 14; and the consent of both suspect and parent or guardian where the suspect is aged between 14 and 17: PACE 1984, s. 65). The authorising officer must have reasonable grounds for suspecting involvement in a recordable offence, (as to which see Code D, note 4A) and for believing that the sample will tend to confirm or disprove involvement. Under the PACE 1984, s. 62(10), a refusal, without good cause, to consent to the taking of an intimate sample may entitle a court or jury to 'draw such inferences as appear proper'. The suspect should be warned of this in accordance with PACE Code D, para. 6.3. See also **F19.30**.

Under the PACE 1984, s. 63, non-intimate samples must usually be taken with the appropriate consent (see above), but may be taken without consent in a number of circumstances provided for in s. 63(2A) to (3C) (see also Code D, paras. 6.5 to 6.6).

Police and Criminal Evidence Act 1984, s. 63

(2A) A non-intimate sample may be taken from a person without the appropriate consent if two conditions are satisfied.

(2B) The first is that the person is in police detention in consequence of his arrest for a recordable offence.

(2C) The second is that—

(a) he has not had a non-intimate sample of the same type and from the same part of the body taken in the course of the investigation of the offence by the police, or

(b) he has had such a sample taken but it proved insufficient.

(3) A non-intimate sample may be taken from a person without the appropriate consent if—

(a) he is being held in custody by the police on the authority of a court; and

(b) an officer of at least the rank of inspector authorises it to be taken without the appropriate consent.

(3A) A non-intimate sample may be taken from a person (whether or not he is in police detention or held in custody by the police on the authority of a court) without the appropriate consent if—

(a) he has been charged with a recordable offence or informed that he will be reported for such an offence; and

(b) either he has not had a non-intimate sample taken from him in the course of the investigation of the offence by the police or he has had a non-intimate sample taken from him but either it was not suitable for the same means of analysis or, though so suitable, the sample proved insufficient.

(3B) A non-intimate sample may be taken from a person without the appropriate consent if he has been convicted of a recordable offence.

(3C) A non-intimate sample may also be taken from a person without the appropriate consent if he is a person to whom section 2 of the Criminal Evidence (Amendment) Act 1997 applies (persons detained following acquittal on grounds of insanity or finding of unfitness to plead).

Authorisation may be given under s. 63(3) only where the officer has reasonable grounds for suspecting the subject's involvement in a recordable offence and for believing that the sample will tend to confirm or disprove his involvement (s. 63(4)). It may be given orally at first, but if so it must then be confirmed in writing (s. 63(5)).

Section 63(3A) also applies where the original sample has been lost, contaminated or damaged, or where analysis was unsatisfactory (s. 65(2)).

Section 63(3B) does not apply where the person concerned was convicted of a recordable offence before 10 April 1995 unless he is serving a sentence of imprisonment (or of detention under the Mental Health Act 1983, part III) for an offence listed in the Criminal Evidence (Amendment) Act 1997, sch. 1 (see PACE 1984, s. 63(9A)).

Intimate or non-intimate samples (or fingerprints) may be used for 'speculative searches' (as to which see **F18.33**). Suspects must be told of this possibility before samples are taken (ss. 62(7A) and 63(8B)).

See also the Serious Organised Crime and Police Act 2006 (Application and Modification of Certain Enactments to Designated Staff of SOCA) Order 2006 (SI 2006 No. 987), arts. 2 and 3 and sch. 1, para. 16.

Some of the problems that may arise where attempts are made to identify offenders by relying on unusual types of skin impression (such as earprint evidence) were examined by the Court of Appeal in *Kempster* [2003] EWCA Crim 3555. See also *Dallagher* [2003] 1 Cr App R 195.

Presentation and Evaluation of DNA Evidence

DNA evidence is becoming increasingly specific and precise, but it still depends on statistical evaluation and juries must not be given the impression that it is more cogent than it really is. It is also essential that admissible evidence is given as to each stage of the process by which a DNA match was obtained. Evidence from an expert who has compared DNA profiles must be supported by admissible evidence as to the procedures by which those profiles were obtained and as to the sources of the samples themselves (*Loveridge* [2001] EWCA Crim 734). **F18.31**

DNA extracted from blood or semen stains, or even from body hairs, etc., found at the scene of the crime or on the victim is compared with samples (typically derived from mouth swabs) taken from the suspect. The process has been refined in recent years, but the underlying principles are essentially similar to those described by Lord Taylor CJ in *Deen* (1994) *The Times*, 10 January 1994 and *Gordon* [1995] 1 Cr App R 290. It is not necessary that a court or jury fully understands the technicalities of the process, but it is vital that they understand the significance of matches or mismatches between DNA profiles taken from the crime stain and the accused. Some margin of error must be allowed for in the process, but a clear mismatch between specific bands will prove that the samples came from different persons. If it is certain that the crime stain contains the real offender's DNA, any such mismatch will be conclusive of the accused's innocence.

A positive match between the two profiles does not necessarily provide comparable proof of guilt. Assuming that the matching process was accurate (which may be a matter for conflicting expert opinion), there remains the problem of evaluating the significance of the match. As Lord Taylor explained in *Deen*, this partly depends on the number of matching bands and on the frequency of such matches amongst the relevant population. Some matches may be more significant than others. It is essential that the jury are not confused between the 'match probability' (or random occurrence ratio) on the one hand and the 'likelihood ratio' on the other. The odds against an innocent individual, chosen at random, matching the DNA profile of the crime stain might be estimated in a given case at five million to one; but if the only evidence against a given suspect is a match between his DNA profile and that of the crime stain, one cannot conclude, on that evidence alone, that the odds against him being innocent (the likelihood ratio) are five million to one. On the contrary, one would expect there to be a number of unrelated individuals in the UK with similar profiles. In *Deen*, the prosecution misled the jury by confusing the two questions, and the conviction was quashed.

The procedure to be followed in respect of the disclosure and presentation of DNA evidence has more recently been laid down by the Court of Appeal in *Doheny* [1997] 1 Cr App R 369. Prosecution experts should adduce the evidence of the DNA comparisons together with their calculations of the random occurrence ratio. The Crown should serve upon the defence details as to how the calculations have been carried out, sufficient for the defence to scrutinise the basis of the calculations; and the forensic science service should make available to a defence expert, if requested, the databases upon which the calculations are based. An expert witness should not express opinions as to the likelihood of the accused being the source of a crime stain, because this requires consideration of factors other than those within his area of expertise. Phillips LJ suggested in *Doheny* that juries be directed along the following lines:

> If you accept the scientific evidence called by the Crown, that indicates that there are probably only four or five white males in the United Kingdom from whom that semen stain could have come. The defendant is one of them. The decision you have to reach, on all the evidence, is whether you are sure that it was the defendant who left that stain or whether it is possible that it was one of that other small group of men who share the same DNA characteristics.

Recent advances in DNA profiling may yield random occurrence ratios of, say, a billion to one (see *Weir* (2000) *The Times*, 16 June 2000). Given that the entire population of the UK is only about 60 million, this may provide very powerful evidence of guilt, even in the absence of other evidence. In practice, there will almost always be more evidence against the accused than the results of DNA profiling. If it can be proved not only that his DNA matches that of the crime stain but also that his fingerprints were found on a weapon used in the crime, his involvement in that crime may be almost impossible to deny.

As to the presentation and evaluation of evidence of partial or incomplete DNA profiles, see *Bates* [2006] EWCA Crim 1395, in which Moore-Bick LJ said (at [30]):

> We can see no reason why partial profile DNA evidence should not be admissible provided that the jury are made aware of its inherent limitations and are given a sufficient explanation to enable them to evaluate it. There may be cases where the match probability in relation to all the samples tested is so great that the judge would consider its probative value to be minimal and decide to

exclude the evidence in the exercise of his discretion, but this gives rise to no new question of principle and can be left for decision on a case by case basis. However, the fact that there exists in the case of all partial profile evidence the possibility that a 'missing' allele might exculpate the accused altogether does not provide sufficient grounds for rejecting such evidence. In many cases there is a possibility (at least in theory) that evidence exists which would assist the accused and perhaps even exculpate him altogether, but that does not provide grounds for excluding relevant evidence that is available and otherwise admissible, though it does make it important to ensure that the jury are given sufficient information to enable them to evaluate that evidence properly

Conversely, evidence derived from DNA profiling may be contradicted by an alibi or other 'non-scientific' defence evidence. When evaluating DNA evidence alongside other such evidence, juries should use their common sense knowledge of the world. They should not (at least in the absence of special features or circumstances) be invited to use complex mathematical formulae, such as Bayes' Theorem, in doing so (*Doheny*; and see also *Adams* [1996] 2 Cr App R 467). Such an approach has been labelled a 'recipe for confusion, misunderstanding and misjudgment' (*Adams (No. 2)* [1998] 1 Cr App R 377 at p. 384).

FINGERPRINTS AND FOOTWEAR IMPRESSIONS

The taking of fingerprints (which include palm prints) is governed by the PACE 1984, ss. 27, 61 and 63A, and by PACE Code D, para. 4 (see **appendix 2**). Section 61(6A) to (7A) and (8A) has not yet been brought into force. Section 61(8A) will, when in force, provide for prints to be taken electronically in accordance with regulations; but no such regulations have yet been made. The SOCPA 2005, s. 118, inserts new provisions (including s. 61A) making similar provision in respect of impressions of footwear, which are reflected in the revised Code D. **F18.32**

Police and Criminal Evidence Act 1984, ss. 61 and 61A

61.—(1) Except as provided by this section no person's fingerprints may be taken without the appropriate consent.

(2) Consent to the taking of a person's fingerprints must be in writing if it is given at a time when he is at a police station.

(3) The fingerprints of a person detained at a police station may be taken without the appropriate consent if—

(a) he is detained in consequence of his arrest for a recordable offence; and

(b) he has not had his fingerprints taken in the course of the investigation of the offence by the police.

(3A) Where a person mentioned in paragraph (a) of subsection (3) or (4) has already had his fingerprints taken in the course of the investigation of the offence by the police, that fact shall be disregarded for the purposes of that subsection if—

(a) the fingerprints taken on the previous occasion do not constitute a complete set of his fingerprints; or

(b) some or all of the fingerprints taken on the previous occasion are not of sufficient quality to allow satisfactory analysis, comparison or matching (whether in the case in question or generally).

(4) The fingerprints of a person detained at a police station may be taken without the appropriate consent if—

(a) he has been charged with a recordable offence or informed that he will be reported for such an offence; and

(b) he has not had his fingerprints taken in the course of the investigation of the offence by the police.

(4A) The fingerprints of a person who has answered to bail at a court or police station may be taken without the appropriate consent at the court or station if—

(a) the court, or

(b) an officer of at least the rank of inspector,

authorises them to be taken.

(4B) A court or officer may only give an authorisation under subsection (4A) if—

(a) the person who has answered to bail has answered to it for a person whose fingerprints were taken on a previous occasion and there are reasonable grounds for believing that he is not the same person; or

(b) the person who has answered to bail claims to be a different person from a person whose fingerprints were taken on a previous occasion

(5) An officer may give an authorisation under subsection (4A) above orally or in writing but, if he gives it orally, he shall confirm it in writing as soon as is practicable.

(6) Any person's fingerprints may be taken without the appropriate consent if—

(a) he has been convicted of a recordable offence;

(b) he has been given a caution in respect of a recordable offence which, at the time of the caution, he has admitted; or

(c) he has been warned or reprimanded under section 65 of the Crime and Disorder Act 1998 for a recordable offence.

(6A) A constable may take a person's fingerprints without the appropriate consent if—

(a) the constable reasonably suspects that the person is committing or attempting to commit an offence, or has committed or attempted to commit an offence; and

(b) either of the two conditions mentioned in subsection (6B) is met.

(6B) The conditions are that—

(a) the name of the person is unknown to, and cannot be readily ascertained by, the constable;

(b) the constable has reasonable grounds for doubting whether a name furnished by the person as his name is his real name.

(6C) The taking of fingerprints by virtue of subsection (6A) does not count for any of the purposes of this Act as taking them in the course of the investigation of an offence by the police.

(7) In a case where by virtue of subsection (3), (4), (6) or (6A) above a person's fingerprints are taken without the appropriate consent—

(a) he shall be told the reason before his fingerprints are taken; and

(b) the reason shall be recorded as soon as is practicable after the fingerprints are taken.

(7A) If a person's fingerprints are taken at a police station or by virtue of subsection (6A) at a place other than a police station, whether with or without the appropriate consent—

(a) before the fingerprints are taken, an officer (or, in a subsection (6A) case, the constable) shall inform him that they may be the subject of a speculative search; and

(b) the fact that the person has been informed of this possibility shall be recorded as soon as is practicable after the fingerprints have been taken.

(8) If he is detained at a police station when the fingerprints are taken, the reason for taking them and, in the case falling within subsection 7A above, the fact referred to in paragraph (b) of that subsection shall be recorded on his custody record.

(8A) Where a person's fingerprints are taken electronically, they must be taken only in such manner, and using such devices, as the Secretary of State has approved for the purposes of electronic fingerprinting.

(8B) The power to take the fingerprints of a person detained at a police station without the appropriate consent shall be exercisable by any constable.

(9) Nothing in this section—

(a) affects any power conferred by paragraph 18(2) of schedule 2 to the Immigration Act 1971, section 141 of the Immigration and Asylum Act 1999 or regulations made under section 144 of that Act; or

(b) applies to a person arrested or detained under the terrorism provisions.

(10) Nothing in this section applies to a person arrested under an extradition arrest power.

61A.—(1) Except as provided by this section, no impression of a person's footwear may be taken without the appropriate consent.

(2) Consent to the taking of an impression of a person's footwear must be in writing if it is given at a time when he is at a police station.

(3) Where a person is detained at a police station, an impression of his footwear may be taken without the appropriate consent if—

(a) he is detained in consequence of his arrest for a recordable offence, or has been charged with a recordable offence, or informed that he will be reported for a recordable offence; and

(b) he has not had an impression taken of his footwear in the course of the investigation of the offence by the police.

(4) Where a person mentioned in paragraph (a) of subsection (3) above has already had an impression taken of his footwear in the course of the investigation of the offence by the police, that fact shall be disregarded for the purposes of that subsection if the impression of his footwear taken previously is—

(a) incomplete; or

(b) is not of sufficient quality to allow satisfactory analysis, comparison or matching (whether in the case in question or generally).

(5) If an impression of a person's footwear is taken at a police station, whether with or without the appropriate consent—

(a) before it is taken, an officer shall inform him that it may be the subject of a speculative search; and

(b) the fact that the person has been informed of this possibility shall be recorded as soon as is practicable after the impression has been taken, and if he is detained at a police station, the record shall be made on his custody record.

(6) In a case where, by virtue of subsection (3) above, an impression of a person's footwear is taken without the appropriate consent—

(a) he shall be told the reason before it is taken; and

(b) the reason shall be recorded on his custody record as soon as is practicable after the impression is taken.

(7) The power to take an impression of the footwear of a person detained at a police station without the appropriate consent shall be exercisable by any constable.

(8) Nothing in this section applies to any person—

(a) arrested or detained under the terrorism provisions;

(b) arrested under an extradition arrest power.

For the meaning of 'appropriate consent', see **F18.30**.

See also the Serious Organised Crime and Police Act (Application and Modification of Certain Enactments to Designated Staff of SOCA) Order 2006 (SI 2006 No. 987), arts. 2 and 3 and sch. 1, paras. 14 and 15.

Fingerprint evidence should be presented by a qualified expert, with appropriate experience in the examination and comparison of such evidence (see *Barnes* [2005] EWCA Crim 1158). Properly presented fingerprint evidence may provide sufficient identification, even if unsupported by other evidence, but the accused must be linked to the relevant prints by admissible evidence (*Chappell v DPP* (1988) 89 Cr App R 82). In *Buckley* (1999) 163 JP 561, Rose LJ said:

> Fingerprint evidence, like any other evidence, is admissible . . . if it tends to prove the guilt of the accused. It may so tend, even if there are only a few similar ridge characteristics, but it may, in such a case, have little weight. It may be excluded in the exercise of judicial discretion, if its prejudicial effect outweighs its probative value. . . .

He added that courts or judges would have to consider the experience and expertise of the witness presenting it, the number of similar ridge characteristics identified, the presence of any dissimilar characteristics, the size of the crime print (a given number of matches in a fragment of a print may be more compelling than a similar number in a complete print) and the quality and clarity of that print (including any evidence of injury to the person who left the print, and any smearing or contamination of the print). The latest guidelines on fingerprint analysis similarly emphasise the primacy of subjective evaluation when comparing prints, and no longer rely on any particular number of matching characteristics.

Speculative Searches

F18.33 Under the PACE 1984, s. 63A (as amended by the SOCPA 2005), fingerprints, impressions of footwear, samples or the information derived from samples may be used for the purpose of speculative searches as prescribed in that section. Section 63A (1ZA) is not yet in force.

The PACE 1984, s. 64, specifies the circumstances in which fingerprints, impressions of footwear, samples or the information derived from samples may be retained and used and the circumstances in which they must be destroyed (or may be retained but not searched against or used in evidence against the person from whom they were taken). Amendments made by the CJPA 2001 provide that samples, etc., taken from suspects who have later been acquitted (or against whom charges have been dropped) no longer have to be destroyed (but as to persons other than suspects, see s. 64(3)). Section 64(1BA) is not yet in force.

In *R (S) v Chief Constable of South Yorkshire Police* [2004] 1 WLR 2196, the House of Lords examined the relevant provisions and upheld the wider retention of such data, unanimously dismissing challenges to the practice based on the ECHR, Articles 8 and 14.

Police and Criminal Evidence Act 1984, ss. 63A and 64

63A.—(1) Where a person has been arrested on suspicion of being involved in a recordable offence or has been charged with such an offence or has been informed that he will be reported for such an offence, fingerprints, impressions of footwear or samples or the information derived from samples taken under any power conferred by this part of this Act from the person may be checked against—

(a) other fingerprints, impressions of footwear or samples to which the person seeking to check has access and which are held by or on behalf of any one or more relevant law-enforcement authorities or which are held in connection with or as a result of an investigation of an offence;

(b) information derived from other samples if the information is contained in records to which the person seeking to check has access and which are held as mentioned in paragraph (a) above.

(1ZA) Fingerprints taken by virtue of section 61(6A) above may be checked against other fingerprints to which the person seeking to check has access and which are held by or on behalf of any one or more relevant law-enforcement authorities or which are held in connection with or as a result of an investigation of an offence.

[(1A) and (1B) define 'relevant law-enforcement authorities']

(1C) Where—

(a) Fingerprints, impressions of footwear or samples have been taken from any person in connection with the investigation of an offence but otherwise than in circumstances to which subsection (1) above applies, and

(b) that person has given his consent in writing to the use in a speculative search of the fingerprints, of the impressions of footwear or of the samples and of information derived from them,

the fingerprints or impressions of footwear or impressions of footwear or, as the case may be, those samples and that information may be checked against any of the fingerprints, impressions of footwear, samples or information mentioned in paragraph (a) or (b) of that subsection.

(1D) A consent given for the purposes of subsection (1C) above shall not be capable of being withdrawn.

(2) Where a sample of hair other than pubic hair is to be taken the sample may be taken either by cutting hairs or by plucking hairs with their roots so long as no more are plucked than the person taking the sample reasonably considers to be necessary for a sufficient sample.

(3) Where any power to take a sample is exercisable in relation to a person the sample may be taken in a prison or other institution to which the Prison Act 1952 applies.

(3A) Where—

(a) the power to take a non-intimate sample under section 63(3B) above is exercisable in relation to any person who is detained under part III of the Mental Health Act 1983 in pursuance of—

(i) a hospital order or interim hospital order made following his conviction for the recordable offence in question, or

(ii) a transfer direction given at a time when he was detained in pursuance of any sentence or order imposed following that conviction, or

(b) the power to take a non-intimate sample under section 63(3C) above is exercisable in relation to any person, the sample may be taken in the hospital in which he is detained under that Part of that Act. Expressions used in this subsection and in the Mental Health Act 1983 have the same meaning as in that Act.

(3B) Where the power to take a non-intimate sample under section 63(3B) above is exercisable in relation to a person detained in pursuance of directions of the Secretary of State under section 92 of the Powers of Criminal Courts (Sentencing) Act 2000 the sample may be taken at the place where he is so detained.

(4) Any constable may, within the allowed period, require a person who is neither in police detention nor held in custody by the police on the authority of a court to attend a police station in order to have a sample taken where—

(a) the person has been charged with a recordable offence or informed that he will be reported for such an offence and either he has not had a sample taken from him in the course of the investigation of the offence by the police or he has had a sample so taken from him but either it was not suitable for the same means of analysis or, though so suitable, the sample proved insufficient; or

(b) the person has been convicted of a recordable offence and either he has not had a sample taken from him since the conviction or he has had a sample taken from him (before or after his conviction) but either it was not suitable for the same means of analysis or, though so suitable, the sample proved insufficient.

(5) The period allowed for requiring a person to attend a police station for the purpose specified in subsection (4) above is—

(a) in the case of a person falling within paragraph (a), one month beginning with the date of the charge or of his being informed as mentioned in that paragraph or one month beginning with the date on which the appropriate officer is informed of the fact that the sample is not suitable for the same means of analysis or has proved insufficient, as the case may be;

(b) in the case of a person falling within paragraph (b), one month beginning with the date of the conviction or one month beginning with the date on which the appropriate officer is informed of the fact that the sample is not suitable for the same means of analysis or has proved insufficient, as the case may be.

(6) A requirement under subsection (4) above—

(a) shall give the person at least 7 days within which he must so attend; and

(b) may direct him to attend at a specified time of day or between specified times of day.

(7) Any constable may arrest without a warrant a person who has failed to comply with a requirement under subsection (4) above.

(8) In this section 'the appropriate officer' is—

(a) in the case of a person falling within subsection (4)(a), the officer investigating the offence with which that person has been charged or as to which he was informed that he would be reported;

(b) in the case of a person falling within subsection (4)(b), the officer in charge of the police station from which the investigation of the offence of which he was convicted was conducted.

64.—(1A) Where—

(a) Fingerprints, impressions of footwear or samples are taken from a person in connection with the investigation of an offence, and

(b) subsection (3) below does not require them to be destroyed,

the fingerprints, impressions of footwear or samples may be retained after they have fulfilled the purposes for which they were taken but shall not be used by any person except for purposes related to the prevention or detection of crime, the investigation of an offence, the conduct of a prosecution or the identification of a deceased person or of the person from whom a body part came.

(1B) In subsection (1A) above—

(a) the reference to using a fingerprint or an impression of footwear includes a reference to allowing any check to be made against it under section 63A(1) or (1C) above and to disclosing it to any person;

(b) the reference to using a sample includes a reference to allowing any check to be made under section 63A(1) or (1C) above against it or against information derived from it and to disclosing it or any such information to any person;

(c) the reference to crime includes a reference to any conduct which—
(i) constitutes one or more criminal offences (whether under the law of a part of the United Kingdom or of a country or territory outside the United Kingdom); or
(ii) is, or corresponds to, any conduct which, if it all took place in any one part of the United Kingdom, would constitute one or more criminal offences;
and
(d) the references to an investigation and to a prosecution include references, respectively, to any investigation outside the United Kingdom of any crime or suspected crime and to a prosecution brought in respect of any crime in a country or territory outside the United Kingdom.

(1BA) Fingerprints taken from a person by virtue of section 61(6A) above must be destroyed as soon as they have fulfilled the purpose for which they were taken.

(3) If—
(a) fingerprints, impressions of footwear or samples are taken from a person in connection with the investigation of an offence; and
(b) that person is not suspected of having committed the offence,
they must, except as provided in the following provisions of this section, be destroyed as soon as they have fulfilled the purpose for which they were taken.

(3AA) Samples, fingerprints and impressions of footwear are not required to be destroyed under subsection (3) above if—
(a) they were taken for the purposes of the investigation of an offence of which a person has been convicted; and
(b) a sample, fingerprint, (or as the case may be) an impression of footwear was also taken from the convicted person for the purposes of that investigation.

(3AB) Subject to subsection (3AC) below, where a person is entitled under subsection (1BA) or (3) above to the destruction of any fingerprint, impression of footwear or sample taken from him (or would be but for subsection (3AA) above), neither the fingerprint, nor the impression of footwear, nor any information derived from the sample, shall be used—
(a) in evidence against the person who is or would be entitled to the destruction of that fingerprint, impression of footwear or sample; or
(b) for the purposes of the investigation of any offence;
and subsection (1B) above applies for the purposes of this subsection as it applies for the purposes of subsection (1A) above.

(3AC) Where a person from whom a fingerprint, impression of footwear or sample has been taken consents in writing to its retention—
(a) that fingerprint, impression of footwear or sample need not be destroyed under subsection (3) above;
(b) subsection (3AB) above shall not restrict the use that may be made of the fingerprint, impression of footwear or sample or, in the case of a sample, of any information derived from it; and
(c) that consent shall be treated as comprising a consent for the purposes of section 63A(1C) above;
and a consent given for the purpose of this subsection shall not be capable of being withdrawn.
This subsection does not apply to fingerprints taken from a person by virtue of section 61(6A) above.

(3AD) For the purposes of subsection (3AC) above it shall be immaterial whether the consent is given at, before or after the time when the entitlement to the destruction of the fingerprint, impression of footwear or sample arises.

(4) Repealed

(5) If fingerprints or impressions of footwear are destroyed—
(a) any copies of the fingerprints shall also be destroyed; and
(b) any chief officer of police controlling access to computer data relating to the fingerprints shall make access to the data impossible, as soon as it is practicable to do so.

(6) A person who asks to be allowed to witness the destruction of his fingerprints or impressions of footwear or copies of them shall have a right to witness it.

(6A) If—
(a) subsection (5)(b) above falls to be complied with; and
(b) the person to whose fingerprints or impressions of footwear the data relate asks for a certificate that it has been complied with,

such a certificate shall be issued to him, not later than the end of the period of three months beginning with the day on which he asks for it, by the responsible chief officer of police or a person authorised by him or on his behalf for the purposes of this section.

(6B) In this section—

'the responsible chief officer of police' means the chief officer of police in whose police area the computer data were put on to the computer.

(7) Nothing in this section—

(a) affects any power conferred by paragraph 18(2) of Schedule 2 to the Immigration Act 1971 or section 20 of the Immigration and Asylum Act 1999 (c. 33) (disclosure of police information to the Secretary of State for use for immigration purposes);

(b) applies to a person arrested or detained under the terrorism provisions.

See also the Serious Organised Crime and Police Act (Application and Modification of Certain Enactments to Designated Staff of SOCA) Order 2006 (SI 2006 No. 987), arts. 2 and 3 and sch. 1, paras. 17 and 19.

What then if the police obtain a sample from D in the course of a mass screening programme, unlawfully retain a DNA profile obtained from it, contrary to s. 64(3), and then unlawfully access it when investigating another offence thereby identifying D as the perpetrator? This would raise the same kind of issues as those considered by the House of Lords in *A-G's Ref (No. 3 of 1999)* [2001] 2 AC 91, in which it was held that the unlawful retention and use of such material during the investigation did not preclude the admission of fresh samples (or other evidence) taken from D after he had been identified, although such evidence would be subject to possible discretionary exclusion under the PACE 1984, s. 78 (see **F2.21** ***et seq.***).

Section F19 Inferences from Silence and the Non-production of Evidence

THE RIGHT TO SILENCE

F19.1 An accused person in a criminal trial has traditionally been accorded a 'right to silence', sometimes termed a privilege against self-incrimination. These concepts are not specifically mentioned in the rights guaranteed by the ECHR, Article 6, but it has been held that they constitute 'generally recognised international standards which lie at the heart of the notion of a fair procedure under Article 6' (*Murray v UK* (1996) 22 EHRR 29; *Saunders v UK* (1996) 23 EHRR 313). Although the right is said in *Murray* not to be an absolute right, the extent to which the provisions of the CJPO 1994, ss. 34 to 38 operate consistently with the right to a fair trial is still a matter of some debate.

Aspects of the right to silence which are recognised in domestic law are that the accused is not a compellable witness at trial (see **F4.9**) and that he is under no general duty to assist the police with their inquiries (*Rice v Connolly* [1966] 2 QB 414). In recent years it has become fashionable to confer statutory powers upon certain individuals charged with the duty of inquiring into various commercial or financial activities by virtue of which a person who refuses to answer their questions incurs a penalty. In *Saunders v UK*, the European Court of Human Rights held that the right to a fair trial was contravened where evidence obtained by these methods was used at trial. The YJCEA 1999, s. 59 and sch. 3, respond to the decision in *Saunders v UK* by restricting the use which can be made of evidence obtained under compulsion under a variety of statutory provisions including the Companies Act 1985, s. 434 (the provision in issue in *Saunders v UK*). The powers of investigation themselves are not affected: only the use of evidence obtained under them. The effect of the amendments to s. 434 is that, in criminal proceedings, the prosecution will not be able to adduce evidence, or put questions, about the accused's answers to inspectors conducting an investigation using their powers of compulsion unless the evidence is first adduced, or a question asked, by or on behalf of the accused in the proceedings. The other provisions which are amended to similar effect are the Insurance Companies Act 1982, ss. 43A and 44; the Companies Act 1985, s. 447; the Insolvency Act 1986, s. 433; the Company Directors Disqualification Act 1986, s. 20; the Building Societies Act 1986, s. 57; the Financial Services Act 1986, ss. 105 and 177; the Companies (Northern Ireland) Order 1986, arts. 427 and 440; the Criminal Justice Act 1987, s. 2; the Companies Act 1989, s. 83; the Companies (Northern Ireland) Order 1989, art. 23; the Insolvency (Northern Ireland) Order 1989, art. 375; the Friendly Societies Act 1992, s. 67; the Criminal Law (Consolidation) (Scotland) Act 1995, s. 28 and the Proceeds of Crime (Northern Ireland) Order 1996, sch. 2, para. 6.

At common law, the right to silence was supplemented by a further right: no inferences were generally permitted to be drawn from the exercise of the right to silence either by a suspect under investigation or by an accused person at his trial. This right has been substantially eroded by the CJPO 1994, ss. 34 to 38, which specify the circumstances in which adverse inferences may be drawn from the exercise of the primary right. Where the statutory scheme does not apply, the common-law rule still applies (*McGarry* [1999] 1 WLR 1500 and **F19.7**). Where the statutory scheme comes into play, the court is under an obligation to ensure that the jury are properly directed regarding the limited inferences which can be drawn (*Condron v UK* [2001] 31 EHRR 1). In *Condron v UK*, the European Court of Human Rights accepted that the right to silence could not of itself prevent the accused's silence, in cases which clearly call for an explanation by him, being taken into account in assessing the persuasiveness of the prosecution evidence, but also stressed that a fair procedure (under Article 6) required 'particular caution' on the part of a domestic court before invoking the accused's silence against him. Whether the statutory scheme, as supplemented by the decisions of domestic courts, fulfils this requirement is a matter that is likely to continue to figure in criminal appeals.

OUT-OF-COURT SILENCE AT COMMON LAW

Accused and Accuser on 'even terms'

The conduct of the accused when an accusation is made against him may form the basis of an inference that he accepts the accusation (see **F17.65**). In the authorities which follow, it was the silence of the accused which was relied upon as the basis for such an inference. The CJPO 1994, s. 34(5) (see **F19.4**), makes it clear that insofar as these authorities permit inferences to be drawn they remain good law. Even if none of the statutory inferences is in play, therefore, the trial judge needs to have the possibility of a common-law inference in mind before resorting to the standard direction (in accordance with *McGarry* [1999] 1 WLR 1500: see **F19.7**) that no inference should be drawn. **F19.2**

In *Norton* [1910] 2 KB 496 it was accepted that the silence of the accused 'on an occasion which demanded an answer' might be conduct from which an inference of acknowledgement might be drawn. In *Mitchell* (1892) 17 Cox CC 503, Cave J described more fully the circumstances in which silence in the face of an accusation might be tantamount to an admission of guilt. He said (at p. 508):

> Now the whole admissibility of statements of this kind rests upon the consideration that if a charge is made against a person in that person's presence it is reasonable to expect that he or she will immediately deny it, and that the absence of such a denial is some evidence of an admission on the part of the person charged, and of the truth of the charge. Undoubtedly, when persons are speaking on even terms, and a charge is made, and the person charged says nothing, and expresses no indignation, and does nothing to repel the charge, that is some evidence to show that he admits the charge to be true.

It follows that silence does not constitute an acknowledgement of guilt if the circumstances are such that a reasonable person would not be expected to counter the allegation. In *Mitchell* the accusation was made by a woman on her deathbed. M and her solicitor were present to hear the statement, which was recorded by a magistrate for use at M's trial for manslaughter. The statement proved to be inadmissible either as a dying declaration or a deposition, and the prosecution sought instead to admit the accusation as a statement made in M's presence. Cave J refused the application, holding that it would be 'monstrous' to say that, because M had not 'started up and denied' the charge, she must have accepted it. In all the circumstances, including the woman's condition, the formality of the proceedings, and the presence of a solicitor to represent M's interests, it was unreasonable to expect any response from M.

Mitchell was approved by the Privy Council in *Parkes v The Queen* [1976] 1 WLR 1251. A girl was stabbed to death, and P was charged with her murder. The girl's mother gave evidence that, on finding her daughter injured, she immediately accused P, who made no reply. When she threatened to detain him until the police arrived, he tried to stab her. It was held that P's reactions to the accusations, including his silence, were matters to be taken into account by the jury in deciding whether P had committed the offence charged. It is not entirely clear whether the outcome would have been the same had silence alone been relied on as evidence

F

Part F Evidence

of guilt, for the Board made a particular point of noting that P's reaction was 'not one of mere silence', but it is submitted that the difference is that mere silence might be entitled to less weight than silence coupled with positive conduct, depending on the circumstances.

Where silence may be attributable to a variety of factors it is for the jury to decide what inference to draw. In *Coll* [2005] EWCA Crim 3675, C was attending to the wounds of the dying victim when her co-accused allegedly made a remark suggesting that C should offer to be a witness 'so they can't tell we did it'. The failure of C to react adversely to the use of 'we' rather than 'I' (her defence being that the co-accused alone was responsible) was held to have been properly left to the jury, along with C's explanation that she was not listening properly and was in shock. See also *O* [2005] EWCA Crim 3082, where the accused's acquiescence while his friend gave a racial motive for an attack constituted an admission (see **F17.67**).

Accusations by or in the Presence of Police Officers

F19.3 It is not clear whether the principles stated above apply to accusations by or in the presence of police officers. In *Hall v The Queen* [1971] 1 WLR 298, H was charged jointly with T and G with unlawful possession of drugs. Premises occupied by the three had been searched by the police in H's absence and a quantity of drugs found in a bag which T said belonged to H. Shortly afterwards the police brought H to the premises, where he was told of the allegation made by T. H, who had not been cautioned, said nothing. It was held that the principle that a person is entitled to refrain from answering a question put to him for the purpose of discovering whether he has committed a crime meant that, 'exceptional circumstances' apart, 'silence alone on being informed by a police officer that someone else has made an accusation against him cannot give rise to an inference that the person to whom this information is communicated accepts the truth of the accusation'. The fact that H was not under caution was irrelevant as the 'caution merely serves to remind the accused of a right which he already possesses at common law. The fact that in a particular case he has not been reminded of it is no ground for inferring that his silence was not in exercise of that right, but was an acknowledgement of the truth of the accusation'.

The law stated in *Hall* must now be read subject to the CJPO 1994, ss. 34, 36 and 37 (see **F19.4** *et seq.*). Silence in the face of the sort of questioning to which those provisions apply may clearly give rise to specific adverse inferences arising out of the failure to mention facts subsequently relied upon (s. 34) or to account for various matters including the possession of incriminating material and presence at the scene of an offence (ss. 36 and 37); the caution and warnings to be given to suspects makes this clear (see PACE Code C, paras. 10.5 and 10.10 and annex C).

The decision in *Hall*, however, would seem still to be authority for the principle that a suspect, whether cautioned or not, should not be regarded as accepting the truth of a charge which he does not deny. In *Chandler* [1976] 1 WLR 585, however, the Court of Appeal expressed reservations about the correctness of the law as stated in *Hall*, regarding it as in conflict with the general rule laid down in *Christie* [1914] AC 545 (see **F17.66**), a criticism reiterated in *Raviraj* (1986) 85 Cr App R 93. The right of a person not to incriminate himself was well accepted, but it 'does not follow that a failure to answer an accusation or question when an answer could reasonably be expected may not provide some evidence in support of an accusation' (*Chandler*, at p. 589). If *Chandler* is right about this, and *Hall* is wrong, the inferences which may be drawn from silence under police questioning may, subject to what is said below, go beyond what is expressly permitted by the 1994 Act. *Chandler* does, however, accept two important limitations: an inference of acceptance cannot be drawn (a) where the parties are not on even terms and (b) where the suspect has been cautioned that he does not have to say anything.

In *Parkes v The Queen* [1976] 1 WLR 1251 the decision in *Hall* was distinguished on the ground that the person by whom the accusation was communicated to the accused was a police officer whom he knew was investigating an offence, whereas in *Parkes* the accusation was made spontaneously by a mother about an injury done to her daughter. In other words, in *Parkes* the parties were, while in *Hall* they were not, on even terms. In *Chandler* C was interviewed in connection with a fraud involving rented television sets. His solicitor was present. In the early stages of questioning, and before he had been cautioned, C refused to answer certain questions, including one which concerned his acquaintance with a man, A, who later stood trial with C. The Court of Appeal regarded *Mitchell* (1892) 17 Cox CC 503 as the applicable authority: the presence of C's solicitor meant that the parties were on 'even terms'. On the facts, however, the trial judge was wrong to suggest that an inference of guilt might be drawn directly from C's failure to answer the questions put, for the most that could be concluded, for example from C's silence when asked if he knew A, was that he did indeed know A. *Chandler* was applied in *Horne* [1990] Crim LR 188, in which police officers brought about a confrontation between H and a man he was suspected of having wounded. The man, still bleeding from his wounds, accused H of having caused them, and H refrained from making any reply. As in *Chandler*, the jury were not given a sufficiently full direction with regard to the use which could be made of the accused's silence, as nothing was said by the trial judge as to the circumstances in which silence might constitute an acknowledgement, or as to how the jury should approach the question of whether those circumstances existed in the case before them.

The principles stated in the cases at **F19.3** and **F19.4** were held in *Collins* [2004] 1 WLR 1705 to be of equal application where a lie is told in the presence and hearing of the accused (in this instance by a co-accused) and the question is whether the accused, by his silence, has adopted the untrue statement as his own. On the facts of the case, where the lie was told in response to a question asked by a police officer and the parties were not on equal terms, there was no evidential basis for an inference other than that C's silence was an exercise by him of his right to silence.

It was accepted in *Chandler* that the drawing of inferences after a suspect has been cautioned that he need say nothing is inappropriate. Since the coming into force of the PACE 1984 and its Codes of Practice, the questioning of a suspect otherwise than under caution which occurred in *Chandler* would rarely be permissible. For this reason the decision has been of limited effect in recent years, but it is arguable that the caution and warnings relating to the inferences which may be drawn under the 1994 Act will, because they put the accused on notice that specific inferences may be drawn, open the door to an argument that wider inferences are also possible, at least where the suspect's legal adviser is also present. However the caution before interview continues to include the words 'You do not have to say anything'. This being so, it is submitted that the appropriate inference from failure to deny an accusation under caution is still that the suspect is relying on his right to silence.

OUT-OF-COURT SILENCE UNDER THE 1994 ACT

Failure to Reveal Facts Afterwards Relied upon in Court

A strong argument for drawing an adverse inference from silence occurs where the accused withholds his defence under interrogation but presents it at trial when it may be too late for it **F19.4**
to be countered. At common law it was improper to invite the jury to draw an adverse inference. In *Gilbert* (1977) 66 Cr App R 237, G, who was suspected of murdering a colleague, declined to answer questions put to him under caution, but on the following day proffered a statement which dealt only with his business relationship with the deceased and not with the circumstances surrounding the killing. At trial, G relied on self-defence. The trial judge correctly directed the jury that no inferences could be drawn from G's refusal to

answer questions, but went on to suggest that, so far as the statement was concerned, it was 'remarkable' that nothing was said about self-defence. This was held to be misdirection. The authorities (some of which were considered to be in conflict) established that the jury should not be invited to form an adverse opinion against an accused on account of his exercise of the right to silence.

Section 34 of the CJPO 1994 addresses this problem. It follows the recommendations of the Criminal Law Revision Committee *11th Report: Evidence* (Cmnd 4991, 1972), previously implemented in Northern Ireland (Criminal Evidence (Northern Ireland) Order 1988). In so doing it disregards the recommendations of a majority of the Royal Commission on Criminal Justice (the Runciman Commission) (Cm. 2263, 1993), who considered that no inferences should be drawn from silence at the police station, and that it was when and only when the prosecution case had been fully disclosed that defendants should be required to offer an answer to the charges or risk adverse comment at trial on any new line of defence.

Criminal Justice and Public Order Act 1994, s. 34

(1) Where, in any proceedings against a person for an offence, evidence is given that the accused—

(a) at any time before he was charged with the offence, on being questioned under caution by a constable trying to discover whether or by whom the offence had been committed, failed to mention any fact relied on in his defence in those proceedings; or

(b) on being charged with the offence or officially informed that he might be prosecuted for it, failed to mention any such fact,

being a fact which in the circumstances existing at the time the accused could reasonably have been expected to mention when so questioned, charged or informed, as the case may be, subsection (2) below applies.

(2) Where this subsection applies—

(a) a magistrates' court, in deciding whether to grant an application for dismissal made by the accused under section 6 of the Magistrates' Courts Act 1980 (application for dismissal of charge in course of proceedings with a view to transfer for trial);

(b) a judge, in deciding whether to grant an application made by the accused under—

(i) section 6 of the Criminal Justice Act 1987 (application for dismissal of charge of serious fraud in respect of which notice of transfer has been given under section 4 of that Act); or

(ii) paragraph 5 of schedule 6 to the Criminal Justice Act 1991 (application for dismissal of charge of violent or sexual offence involving child in respect of which notice of transfer has been given under section 53 of that Act);

(c) the court, in determining whether there is a case to answer; and

(d) the court or jury, in determining whether the accused is guilty of the offence charged,

may draw such inferences from the failure as appear proper.

(2A) Where the accused was at an authorised place of detention at the time of the failure, subsections (1) and (2) above do not apply if he had not been allowed an opportunity to consult a solicitor prior to being questioned, charged or informed as mentioned in subsection (1) above.

(3) Subject to any directions by the court, evidence tending to establish the failure may be given before or after evidence tending to establish the fact which the accused is alleged to have failed to mention.

(4) This section applies in relation to questioning by persons (other than constables) charged with the duty of investigating offences or charging offenders as it applies in relation to questioning by constables; and in subsection (1) above 'officially informed' means informed by a constable or any such person.

(5) This section does not—

(a) prejudice the admissibility in evidence of the silence or other reaction of the accused in the face of anything said in his presence relating to the conduct in respect of which he is charged, in so far as evidence thereof would be admissible apart from this section; or

(b) preclude the drawing of any inference from any such silence or other reaction of the accused which could properly be drawn apart from this section.

(6) This section does not apply in relation to a failure to mention a fact if the failure occurred before the commencement of this section.

The function of this provision is to permit the tribunal of fact to draw 'such inferences as appear proper' (s. 34(2)) from the accused's silence, provided that the various conditions set forth in s. 34(1) are made out and any questions of fact arising thereunder are resolved against the accused (*Argent* [1997] 2 Cr App R 27). The provision applies only where a particular fact is advanced by the defence which is suspicious by reason of not being put forward at an early opportunity. Thus *Gilbert* (1977) 66 Cr App R 237 is reversed to the extent that G's reticence about his defence, and the reasons for it, could now be explored with a view (if no plausible explanation appears) to drawing an inference of guilt. The section is, however, capable of far wider application, in that a direction may properly be given in relation to any fact relied on at trial which the accused might have been expected to mention earlier. The Court of Appeal has expressed concern that prosecutors might too readily resort to s. 34, and has suggested that they bear in mind that the mischief at which it is primarily directed is 'the positive defence following a "no comment" interview and/or the "ambush" defence': *Brizzalari* (2004) *The Times*, 3 March 2004. Counsel should not complicate trials and summings-up by invoking the section unless the merits of the individual case require it. This is, it is submitted, entirely sound advice which should be followed not only in the interests of simplicity but also of fairness.

It is now accepted that the adverse inference which may be drawn under s. 34 includes a general inference of guilt. The current Judicial Studies Board Direction tells the jury that they may take the failure to mention the fact into account as 'some additional support' for the prosecution case.

Decisions of the European Court of Human Rights have confirmed that the mere fact that a trial judge leaves a jury with the option of drawing an adverse inference from silence in interview is not incompatible with the requirements of a fair trial. Whether the drawing of adverse inferences infringes the ECHR, Article 6 is a matter to be determined in light of all the circumstances of the case, having regard to the situations where inferences may be drawn, the weight attached to them by the national court, and the degree of compulsion inherent in the situation. Of particular importance are the terms of the judge's direction to the jury on the drawing of adverse inferences (*Condron v UK* [2001] 31 EHRR 1; *Beckles v UK* [2002] 36 EHRR 162).

The domestic cases show that s. 34 has given rise to much more difficulty in directing the jury than s. 35 (failure to testify at trial see **F19.19**). Although each case requires a direction tailored to its own facts, trial judges should follow closely the Judicial Studies Board specimen direction which was accepted by the European Court of Human Rights in *Beckles v UK* (*Chenia* [2003] 2 Cr App R 83). Failure to give a proper direction will not, however, necessarily involve a breach of Article 6, nor render a conviction unsafe (*Chenia*, where earlier authorities are considered). In *Chenia*, the factors which persuaded the court that C had received a fair trial included the strength of the evidence, the fact that his failure to mention relevant facts was not consequent upon legal advice (as to which, see **F19.10**) and the clear and accurate direction given on the failure of C to give evidence in the case.

Access to Legal Advice Section 34(2A) of the CJPO 1994 was added by the YJCEA 1999, s. 58, to bring the law into line with the judgment of the European Court of Human Rights in *Murray v United Kingdom* (1996) 22 EHRR 29. The Court considered that even the lawful exercise of a power to delay access to legal advice could, where the accused was at risk of adverse inferences under the statutory scheme, be sufficient to deprive the accused of a fair procedure under Article 6. The accused was faced with a 'fundamental dilemma' at the outset of the investigation, in that his silence might lead to adverse inferences being drawn against him, while breaking his silence might prejudice his defence without necessarily removing the possibility of inferences being drawn against him. Under the amended scheme, the dilemma is resolved by postponing the prospect that inferences will be drawn until the accused has had the option of consulting with a legal adviser. The postponement occurs in exactly the same **F19.5**

way whether access to legal advice is delayed lawfully or unlawfully. An 'authorised place of detention' is defined by s. 38(2A) to include police stations and any other place prescribed by order. The caution to be given to a person to whom a restriction on drawing inferences applies is specified by PACE Code C, annex C.

No Conviction etc. Wholly or Mainly on Silence

F19.6 **Criminal Justice and Public Order Act 1994, s. 38**

(3) A person shall not have the proceedings against him transferred to the Crown Court for trial, have a case to answer or be convicted of an offence solely on an inference drawn from such a failure or refusal as is mentioned in section 34(2), 35(3), 36(2) or 37(2).

(4) A judge shall not refuse to grant such an application as is mentioned in section 34(2)(b), 36(2)(b) and 37(2)(b) solely on an inference drawn from such a failure as is mentioned in section 34(2), 36(2) or 37(2).

Section 38(3) applies to all four of the provisions of the 1994 Act which operate to permit the drawing of inferences from silence, and s. 38(4) to the three appertaining to out-of-court silence. Neither provision is of great consequence with regard to inferences drawn under s. 34, which could hardly in practice form the *sole* reason for any of the outcomes referred to in s. 38(3) or (4). With regard to those outcomes which occur before the defence calls any evidence, there is the further problem that it may be impossible at that stage to determine whether the defence had placed reliance on any particular fact which had not been revealed at the investigation stage (see, e.g., *Hart* [1998] 6 Arch News 1).

Where the issue is whether the jury should be at liberty to convict in reliance on an inference drawn under s. 34, it is essential that they be directed that such an inference cannot standing alone prove guilt (*Abdullah* [1999] 3 Arch News 3). A more pressing question is whether the courts should go beyond the rule laid down in s. 38(3) in order to ensure that no conviction is based *mainly* on one or more of the statutory inferences. In *Murray v UK* (1996) 22 EHRR 29, there is a very strong statement that it would be incompatible with the accused's rights to base a conviction 'solely or mainly on the accused's silence or on a refusal to answer questions or to give evidence himself'; see also *Condron v UK* [2001] 31 EHRR 1. To the extent that the statutory scheme does not expressly prevent a conviction founded 'mainly' on silence, therefore, it may be defective. In *Doldur* [2000] Crim LR 178, the Court of Appeal held that there was no need for a judge to direct a jury that, before they could draw an inference under s. 34, they must be satisfied that there was a case to answer. Such a direction has been held to be required in relation to s. 35 (see **F19.21**) where the accused does not testify, but the court regarded the two cases as distinguishable in that, under s. 35, there was a logical reason for confining the jury to considering whether the prosecution had established a *prima facie* case as a prerequisite to drawing an inference, whereas under s. 34 the jury would need to have regard to evidence adduced by the defence in order to decide whether s. 34 applied. This is true, but the need to honour *Murray* may well require some further elaboration. The current specimen direction of the Judicial Studies Board makes reference to the need for the jury to be satisfied that there is a case to meet, and in *Milford* [2001] Crim LR 330, the Court of Appeal noted that *Doldur*, although based on compelling logic, had failed to address 'the European dimension', and considered that both *Condron* [1997] 1 WLR 827 and *Birchall* [1999] Crim LR 311 were to the contrary. In *Beckles v UK* [2002] 36 EHRR 162, the European Court of Human Rights, after considering the above authorities, confirmed that the correct principle was, as stated in *Murray v UK*, that a conviction based solely or mainly on silence or a refusal to answer questions would be incompatible with the right to silence. More recently, in *Chenia* [2003] 2 Cr App R 83, the Court of Appeal confirmed that a direction which omitted reference to the need to consider whether there was a case to answer is 'deficient', but on the facts did not consider it was fatal to a conviction where the existence of a prima facie case is beyond dispute. Further, in *Petkar* [2004] 1 Cr App R 270, it was held that the jury should be told in terms not to convict 'wholly or mainly' on an adverse inference, and that the words 'or mainly' were required to 'buttress' the requirement for proof of a case to answer otherwise than by means of the inference. In *Parchment* [2003] EWCA Crim 2428, it was said that where the case against an accused was weak it was crucial that the limited function of the failure to mention something in interview was clearly spelled out to the jury, and accordingly the conviction of one of the accused for murder was quashed where the appropriate direction had not been given.

Fact Relied On

Section 34 of the CJPO 1994 does not apply where the accused makes no attempt to put forward at trial some previously undisclosed fact (e.g., where he simply contends that the prosecution has failed to prove its case). In *Moshaid* [1998] Crim LR 420, M, acting on legal advice, declined to answer any questions. At trial he did not give or call any evidence. It was held that s. 34 did not bite in these circumstances. It goes too far, however, to suggest that s. 34 applies only where the accused gives evidence: a fact relied on may be established by a witness called by the accused, or may be elicited from a prosecution witness (*Bowers* 1988] Crim LR 817). In *Webber* [2004] 1 WLR 404, where the authorities are reviewed by Lord Bingham, it was held that an accused 'relies on' a fact or matter in his defence not only where he gives or adduces evidence of it but also where counsel, acting on his instructions, puts a specific and positive case to prosecution witnesses, as opposed to asking questions intended to probe or test the prosecution case. The effect of specific and positive suggestions from counsel, whether or not accepted, is to plant in the jury's mind the accused's version of events. This may be so even if the witness rejects the suggestion, since the jury may mistrust the witness's evidence. If the judge is in doubt whether counsel is merely testing the prosecution case or putting a positive case, counsel should be asked, in the absence of the jury, to make the position clear. However, the positive case ought to be apparent from the defence statement made in advance of trial. The same reasoning also led the House of Lords to conclude that the adoption by counsel of evidence given by a co-defendant may amount to reliance on the relevant facts or matters. Following *Webber* it has been held that the putting forward by an accused of a possible explanation for his fingerprints being on a car number plate is a 'fact' as broadly construed in that case (*Esimu* [2007] EWCA Crim 1380). F19.7

In *Betts* [2001] 2 Cr App R 257, a bare admission at trial of a part of the prosecution case was held incapable of constituting a 'fact' for the purposes of s. 34. The alternative construction would effectively have removed the accused's right to silence by requiring him to make admissions at interview, an obligation which would have conflicted with the ECHR, Article 6. A direction under s. 34 will rarely, if ever, be appropriate in relation to the failure to mention an admittedly true fact, since the adverse inference under s. 34 is that a matter not mentioned at interview is unlikely to be true (*Webber* [2004] 1 WLR 404, approving *Wisdom* (10 December 1999 unreported).

If the prosecution fail to establish that the accused has failed to mention a fact, the jury should be directed to draw no inference (*B (MT)* [2000] Crim LR 181). Where the judge directs the jury on the basis that s. 34 applies, it is important that the facts relied on should be identified in the course of the direction (*Chenia, Lewis* [2003] EWCA Crim 223 and *Backwell* (2003) *The Times*, 15 December 2003). The identification of the specific fact or facts is required by the Judicial Studies Board Direction, which also suggests that any proposed direction should be discussed with counsel before closing speeches. In *B* the Court of Appeal stated:

> In our view it is particularly important that judges should take this course in relation to directions as to the application of section 34. That section is a notorious minefield. Discussion with counsel will reduce the risk of mistakes.

Where the prosecution is able to identify a specific fact or fact relied upon within the meaning of s. 34, it does not necessarily follow that the point should be taken at trial: prosecutors should remember that the twin mischiefs at which the section is aimed are the positive defence following a 'no comment' interview and the 'ambush' defence. Consideration should therefore be given in other cases to whether the withholding of the fact is sufficient to justify the sanction of s. 34, given the weight juries are likely to give to being directed as to adverse inferences (*Brizzalari* (2004) *The Times*, 3 March 2004).

F19.8 **Prepared Statements** Where the accused at the relevant time gives a prepared statement in which certain facts are set forth, it cannot subsequently be said that he has failed to mention those facts. The aim of s. 34 of the CJPO 1994 was to encourage a suspect to disclose his factual defence, not to sanction inferences from the accused's failure to respond to questions (*Knight* [2004] 1 WLR 340). A prepared statement may, however, be a dangerous device for an innocent accused who later discovers that something significant has been omitted (*Knight* and *Turner* [2004] 1 All ER 1025). In *Turner* it was noted that, as inconsistencies between the prepared statement and the defence at trial do not necessarily amount to reliance on unmentioned facts, the judge must be particularly careful to pinpoint any fact that might properly be the subject of a s. 34 direction. Alternatively, the jury might more appropriately be directed to regard differences between the prepared statement and the accused's evidence as constituting a previous lie rather than as the foundation for a direction under s. 34.

Caution or Charge

F19.9 Inferences before a suspect is charged under the CJPO 1994, s. 34, may not be drawn except 'on being questioned under caution by a constable' (s. 34(1)(a)). If no questions have been put, for example because the accused refuses to leave his cell for questioning, the section cannot apply, as the statutory language cannot be ignored (*Johnson* [2005] EWCA Crim 971). It does not however follow that a fact can only be 'mentioned' in the form of an answer to a question: in *Ali* [2001] EWCA Crim 863, the accused handed over a prepared statement in which the relevant facts were mentioned and this was sufficient to prevent an inference, although he subsequently declined to answer questions: see also *Knight* [2004] 1 WLR 340. (The reference to 'constable' includes others charged with investigating offences: s. 34(4).)

The caution makes clear the risks that attend the failure to mention facts which later form part of the defence. It is set out in Code C, para. 10.5 and runs as follows:

> You do not have to say anything. But it may harm your defence if you do not mention when questioned something which you later rely on in court. Anything you do say may be given in evidence.

Minor deviations from the formula are not a breach of the code as long as the sense is preserved (para. 10.7), and an officer is permitted to paraphrase if it appears that the person with whom he is dealing does not understand what the caution means (Note for Guidance 10D). A suspect who has been arrested should not normally be questioned about his involvement in an offence except in an interview at a police station, and it is envisaged that questioning to which s. 34 applies should occur in the course of such an interview which, being properly recorded, will then allow the court to make reliable deductions about the nature and extent of any silence. Clearly, if the accused alleges that he did mention the relevant fact when questioned, the prosecution will have to prove the contrary before any adverse inference can be drawn. Where it is alleged that a 'significant silence' (i.e. one which appears capable of being used in evidence against the suspect) has occurred before his arrival at a police station, then at the beginning of an interview at the station the interviewing officer should put the matter to the suspect, under caution, and ask him whether he confirms or denies that earlier silence and whether he wishes to add anything (para. 11.4). The consequence of failing to go through this procedure (which applies to evidentially significant statements as it does to silences) must be to increase significantly the likelihood that the evidence in question will be excluded under s. 78 if the suspect denies that the earlier statement was made or that the silence occurred. Furthermore if the suspect is questioned improperly in circumstances prohibited by Code C, e.g., where sufficient evidence for the accused to be charged already exists, s. 34 should not be brought to bear on the suspect's failure to respond (*Pointer* [1997] Crim LR 676; *Gayle* [1999] 2 Cr App R 130). There is a lack of consistency in the authorities on when there is sufficient evidence for this purpose (see *McGuinness* [1999] Crim LR 318; *Ioannou* [1999] Crim LR 586; *Odeyemi* [1999] Crim LR 828; *Flynn* [2001] EWCA Crim 1633; *Elliott* [2002] EWCA Crim 931), but no doubt about the principle.

The drawing of inferences from the withholding of a fact at the point of charge under s. 34(1)(b) is a distinct process from that under s. 34(1)(a). Where, therefore, no inference could be drawn from silence at interview because the interview itself had been excluded under the PACE 1984, s. 78, it did not follow that an inference could not be drawn from silence at the point of charge as long as there is no unfairness in doing so (*Dervish* [2002] 2 Cr App R 105). In that case D had the opportunity 'in a single sentence' to put the essence of his defence following charge, and the police would thereafter have been precluded from questioning him about it. Since he declined to do so, it was rightly left to the jury to decide whether an inference should be drawn.

Facts which Should Have Been Mentioned

Adverse inferences may be drawn from a fact subsequently relied on in defence only where the fact is one which, in the circumstances existing at the time, the accused could reasonably have been expected to mention (s. 34(1)). It follows that any explanation advanced by the accused for non-disclosure must be considered in deciding what inferences, if any, should be drawn (*Webber* [2004] 1 WLR 404, where the House of Lords considered that the jury was 'very much concerned' with the truth or otherwise of an explanation from the accused as, if they accept it as true or possibly so, no adverse inference should be drawn from his failure to mention it). Ultimately an adverse inference is appropriate only where the jury concludes that the silence can only sensibly be attributed to the defendant's having no answer, or none that would stand up to questioning (*Condron* [1997] 1 WLR 827; *Betts* [2001] 2 Cr App R 257; *Daly* [2002] 2 Cr App R 201; *Petkar* [2004] 1 Cr App R 270). Similar formulae appear also in *Condron v UK* [2001] 31 EHRR 1, and *Beckles v UK* [2002] 36 EHRR 162). In *Barnes* (4 July 2003 unreported), B's contention was that he thought that he had mentioned the fact in issue during his interview. As this was not advanced as a reason for non-disclosure, it was said that it provided no impediment to the drawing of an adverse inference. While this may be so, if B genuinely believed that he had mentioned the fact, then his state of mind at interview was not that of a guilty person withholding information. It is important that any direction given should reflect this. In *Hilliard* [2004] EWCA Crim 837, H's only chance to mention a fact was when a witness's statement had been read to him in interview. He had not been told that he should correct any statement with which he disagreed. It was held that it would be 'wholly unsafe' to seek to draw an adverse inference since H had never had the opportunity to deal with the matter (which was not central) even if he ought to have identified it as something that was important enough to mention. **F19.10**

The specific references to the accused and to the circumstances indicates that a range of factors may be relevant to what might have been expected to be forthcoming, including age, experience, mental capacity, health, sobriety, tiredness and personality. A restrictive approach would not be appropriate (*Argent* [1997] 2 Cr App R 27).

The failure of the interviewer to disclose relevant information when asked to do so by the accused or his legal adviser is another factor bearing upon the propriety of drawing an inference. If little information is forthcoming a legal adviser may well counsel silence until a better assessment of the case to answer can be made (*Roble* [1997] Crim LR 449).

F19.11 **Legal Advice to Remain Silent** The difficult issue of what use, if any, can be made of a failure to advance facts following legal advice to remain silent has been the subject of numerous decisions, both by domestic courts and Strasbourg. In *Beckles* [2005] 1 WLR 2829, Lord Woolf CJ, commented that the position in such cases is 'singularly delicate'. On the one hand, the courts not unreasonably seek to avoid having the accused drive a coach and horses through s. 34 by advancing an explanation for silence that is easy to make and difficult to investigate because of legal professional privilege. On the other hand, 'it is of the greatest importance that defendants should be able to be advised by their lawyer without their having to reveal the terms of that advice if they act in accordance with that advice'. Perhaps because of this, the authorities have not all spoken with one voice, although now a consistent theme seems to be emerging. In *Condron* [1997] 1 WLR 827, C and his wife, admitted heroin addicts, were convicted of offences relating to the supply of the drug. At interview both remained silent, on the advice of their solicitor who (despite medical advice to the contrary) considered that their drug withdrawal symptoms rendered them unfit to be interviewed. At trial, the defence relied upon detailed innocent explanations of prosecution evidence which could have been put forward at the time of interview. It was held that the giving of legal advice to remain silent did not of itself preclude the drawing of inferences: all depends on the view the jury takes of the reason advanced by the accused, after having been directed in accordance with the formula (above) that they should consider whether the silence can only sensibly be attributed to the accused having no answer, or none that would stand up to questioning. (Such a direction was said to be 'desirable' in *Condron*, but the European Court of Human Rights subsequently considered that fairness required a direction to be given which left the jury in no doubt in this important matter (*Condron v UK*).) In *Beckles* [2005] 1 WLR 2829, the Court of Appeal reviewed a number of post-*Condron* authorities, including the earlier decision of the European Court of Human Rights in *Beckles* itself ((2002) 36 EHRR 162). Two strands of authority, one proceeding from *Betts* [2001] 2 Cr App R 257, and the other from *Howell* [2005] 1 Cr App R 1 and *Knight* [2003] EWCA Crim 1977 had been regarded as in conflict, with *Betts* favouring a subjective test (did the accused genuinely rely on legal advice?) and *Howell* and *Knight* an objective test (did the accused reasonably rely on legal advice?). The Court in *Beckles* adopted the reconciliation of the two strands proposed by Auld LJ in *Hoare* [2005] 1 WLR 1804, which accepts that 'genuine reliance by a defendant on his solicitor's advice to remain silent is not in itself enough to preclude adverse comment'. Auld LJ went on:

> It is not the purpose of section 34 to exclude a jury from drawing an adverse inference against a defendant because he genuinely or reasonably believes that, regardless of his guilt or innocence, he is entitled to take advantage of that advice to impede the prosecution case against him. In such a case the advice is not truly the reason for not mentioning the facts. The section 34 inference is concerned with flushing out innocence at an early stage, or supporting other evidence of guilt at a later stage, not simply with whether a guilty defendant is entitled, or genuinely or reasonably believes that he is entitled, to rely on legal rights of which his solicitor has advised him. Legal entitlement is one thing. An accused's reason for exercising it is another. His belief in his entitlement may be genuine, but it does not follow that his reason for exercising it is . . .

In *Hoare*, the defence produced at trial for producing a Class B drug was that H believed he was involved in the secret production of a cure for cancer. H had given a 'no comment' interview following legal advice, the solicitor apparently having thought that there was insufficient disclosure of the evidence against H at that stage. Under cross-examination, H said that, while he could have given his explanation at the time, he had been stunned and surprised, had not had much sleep, and 'most people would act on the advice of their lawyer'. The true question, however, according to *Hoare*, is not whether H's solicitors rightly or wrongly believed that H was not required to answer the questions, nor whether H genuinely relied on the advice in the sense that he believed he had the right to do so. The true question is whether H remained silent 'not because of that advice but because he had no or no satisfactory explanation to give'.

Waiver of Privilege and Statements The accused who wishes to give an account of his reasons for silence following legal advice may find it hard to do so without waiving privilege. While no waiver is involved in a bare assertion that he had been advised to remain silent, little weight in likely to attach to such an assertion unless the reasons for it are before the court (*Condron* [1997] 1 WLR 827; *Robinson* [2003] EWCA Crim 2219). In *Bowden* [1999] 1 WLR 823 a waiver was held to have occurred where B called evidence in his defence of a statement made by his solicitor at interview, namely that he had advised B to remain silent because of the lack of evidence against him. B was held to have been properly cross-examined about the extent to which he had disclosed to the solicitor the facts that subsequently formed the basis of his defence. Lord Bingham CJ stated, *obiter*, that the giving of evidence at a *voir dire* as to the reasons for legal advice for silence would operate as a waiver of privilege at trial even if the evidence was not repeated before the jury: the accused cannot 'have his cake and eat it' where privilege is concerned. The same point is also made, though in less emphatic terms, by the European Court of Human Rights in *Condron v UK* [2000] Crim LR 679, where it is said that there was no compulsion on C to disclose the advice given, other than the indirect compulsion to provide a convincing explanation for silence, and that because C chose to make the content of the solicitor's advice part of his defence he could not complain that the CJPO 1994 overrode the confidentiality of discussions with his legal adviser. Voluntariness is also cited as a reason for holding that a waiver has occurred in *Loizou* [2006] EWCA Crim 1719. F19.12

Where the accused's solicitor, following a consultation with his client, makes a statement to the officers conducting the interview with regard to the accused's reasons for silence (in the presence of the accused who says nothing in dissent), the statement may be given in evidence and may form the basis of an adverse inference (*Fitzgerald* [1998] 4 Arch News 2). It would appear that the Court of Appeal had in mind by way of exception to the hearsay rule either the doctrine of admission by an agent, or implied admission by silence where a statement is made in the presence of the accused (see **F16.38** and **F19.2** respectively). In *Bowden* the Court of Appeal expressed a preference for the explanation based on agency, which it is submitted is correct. In this connection it is relevant to note that privilege should not be regarded as waived if the accused merely seeks to demonstrate the fact that he communicated relevant exculpatory facts to his legal adviser prior to the interview (cf. *Wilmot* (1988) 89 Cr App R 341). Nor is it hearsay for the accused to tell the court what advice the solicitor gave him, provided that his purpose in doing so is not to establish the truth of any fact narrated by the solicitor. It is the accused's reason for withholding facts that is in issue so, provided that, for example, he merely wishes to explain the impact upon him of the advice given, there is no hearsay problem (*Davis* [1998] Crim LR 659). In *Hill* [2003] EWCA Crim 1179, H contended that an interview conducted in the presence of a solicitor should have been excluded (and therefore unavailable as the basis for an inference) on the ground that her solicitor was affected by a conflict of interest as the representative of a co-accused. It was held that the proper course would have been to waive privilege and consider the matter fully on a *voire dire*: the court should not be asked to speculate that the solicitor had acted improperly.

In some cases the reasons for the advice given to the accused may be difficult to explain to a jury without descending into legal complexity, or revealing that the accused is no stranger to the legal process. The point was raised (but not answered) in *Beard* [2002] Crim LR 684, where it was considered that there was on the facts no such difficulty in leaving the issue to the jury. Where it is otherwise, it will be necessary to consider whether to exclude evidence relating to the interview on the ground of unfairness.

A frequent outcome of consultation with a legal adviser is that the accused volunteers a prepared statement which is subsequently relied upon as demonstrating that he has 'mentioned' those facts which form the basis of his defence at trial. If the statement proves incomplete, a particularly careful direction may be required (see **F19.7**) which may be complicated further by the fact that the statement was originally crafted on legal advice.

Direction as to Permissible Inferences

F19.13 Where the fact is one which the accused could reasonably have been expected to mention it will be permissible to draw 'such inferences from the failure as appear proper' (s. 34(2)) in a variety of contexts including the determination of guilt (s. 34(2)(d), and whether there is a case to answer (s. 34(2)(c)), bearing in mind always that an inference drawn under the subsection is not by itself sufficient to sustain either determination (s. 38(3): see **F19.6**). Although the most common inference from failure to reveal facts which are subsequently relied on is that the facts have been invented after the interview, it may equally appear to the jury that the accused had the facts in mind at the time of interview, but was unwilling to expose his account to scrutiny (*Milford* [2001] Crim LR 330). Similarly, the jury may deduce that the accused was faced with a choice between on the one hand silence, and on the other either lying or incriminating himself further with the truth. Again, this is a permissible inference under s. 34 (*Daniel* [1998] 2 Cr App R 373). It follows that, even if it is common ground that an accused spoke to his solicitor about a proposed defence of alibi before any interview took place, his failure to reveal the alibi in interview was still a matter from which inferences could be drawn if the jury were unconvinced by the accused's explanation (*Taylor* [1999] Crim LR 77). Nothing in *Condron* or *Cowan* should be read as indicating that the only adverse inference to be drawn is one of recent fabrication (*Beckles* [1999] Crim LR 148). Where the inference which the prosecution suggests should be drawn is not the standard inference of late fabrication but is less severe, the judge should make this clear when summing up (*Petkar* [2004] 1 Cr App R 270).

In cases where the accused explains his failure to mention facts on the ground that he was acting on legal advice, but without explaining the reasons behind the advice, the trial judge should be particularly careful to avoid directing the jury in such a way as to indicate that the silence is necessarily a guilty one (*Bresa* [2005] EWCA Crim 1414 and see **F19.11** as to the construction of a possible inference following legal advice).

In some cases an inference cannot logically be drawn without first concluding that the accused is guilty, and in such cases, s. 34 has been said to be of no assistance (*Mountford* [1999] Crim LR 575). M, charged with possession of heroin with intent to supply, put forward the defence that the actual dealer was W, the main prosecution witness, while he was merely a customer. M gave as his explanation for failing to reveal this defence at interview his reluctance to expose W to prosecution. The Court of Appeal held that the jury could not properly reject M's reason for not mentioning this fact without first concluding that the fact was untrue: the very issue on which M's guilt turned. In these (somewhat unusual) circumstances the judge should not have left s. 34 to the jury. (See also *Gill* [2001] 1 Cr App R 160, a case on similar facts.) In *Daly* [2002] 2 Cr App R 201, however, the decision in *Mountford* was doubted on the ground that there is nothing in s. 34 which requires that the issue be one which is capable of separate resolution in the case. While this is true, there is much to be said for the view that the judge should steer the jury in the direction of a logical resolution to the issues. However a differently-constituted later court made the same point in *Gowland-Wynn* [2002] 1 Cr App R 569, and it may be that the qualification in *Mountford* is too subtle. In *Chenia* [2003] 2 Cr App R 83, the approach in *Mountford* was said to be appropriate in the 'rare case' only and in *Webber* [2004] 1 WLR 404 the House of Lords (while not specifically overruling *Mountford*) considered that the s. 34 direction was rightly given in that case, which is tantamount to outright rejection. *Webber* was a very different type of case, however, and did not involve the problem of circularity in *Mountford*.

F19.14 **Direction where s. 34 Applicable** In all cases where the CJPO 1994, s. 34, is to be relied upon, it is submitted that a clear judicial direction will be required as to the nature of the inference that may properly be drawn. Where prosecution counsel had not sought to rely upon s. 34, and had not raised the matter with the accused in cross-examination, the Court of Appeal in *Khan* [1999] 2 Arch News 2 rightly 'deprecated' the decision of the trial judge to direct the jury that they might draw an inference under s. 34 without first raising the matter with counsel. It was held, however, that (as there would have been no basis upon which the judge could have been deterred from giving the direction had the matter been argued) K had suffered no disadvantage. It is submitted that this is a dangerous approach. A trial judge ought not, in fairness, to leave it open to the jury to make use of silence which, because the defence did not expect to have to explain it away, has not been the subject of any comment by the accused or the defence witnesses. If the judge thinks that s. 34 might come into play, the matter should be raised in time for it to be the subject of evidence not speculation. If, on the other hand, there has been no discussion with counsel of the intended direction in circumstances where it is clear to the defence that the prosecution are relying on the accused's failure to mention a specific fact, it is unlikely that the omission will render the trial unfair (*Barnes* 4 July 2003 unreported). In *Brooks* [2004] EWCA Crim 3021, the direction had been discussed with counsel, who were left with the impression that no direction of the kind that was in due course given would be given. The importance of following and adapting the Judicial Studies Board Specimen Direction is frequently mentioned in connection with s. 34, and although it need not be slavishly adhered to in every case (*Salami* [2003] EWCA Crim 3831) it affords particularly useful guidance in this difficult area.

A direction may be called for where there is more than one accused. If A has failed to mention a relevant fact so as to attract a s. 34 direction, it is desirable in the case of co-accused B whose case stands or falls with A's to give a direction not to draw any inference against B.

A direction may also be called for in relation to something said by the accused which the prosecution claim both conceals a fact later relied on and constitutes a positive lie. In such a case both a s. 34 direction and a *Lucas* direction (see **F1.19**) should be given; see *Turner* [2004] 1 All ER 1025.

As to the circumstances in which a conviction may be safe notwithstanding the significant misdirection of a jury under s. 34, see *Boyle* [2006] EWCA Crim 2101 and *Lowe* [2007] EWCA Crim 833.

As to the 'unfair' use of silence, see **F19.18**.

Direction where s. 34 Not Applicable to Accused's Silence Where the judge concludes that the requirements of the CJPO 1994, s. 34, have not been met, but the jury have been made aware of the accused's failure to answer questions, it was held in *McGarry* [1999] 1 WLR 1500 that a direction should be given to the jury that they should not hold the accused's silence against him. If that were not done, the jury would be left in 'no-man's land' between the common-law rule and the statutory exception, without any guidance as to how to regard the accused's silence. This was qualified in *La Rose* [2003] EWCA Crim 1471, where it was held that the omission of the so-called 'counterweight' direction was not fatal where L had never given any explanation for his conduct and had declined to give evidence at trial, thus attracting a s. 35 direction (see **F19.14**). It was 'fanciful' to suggest that an adverse inference which would not otherwise have been drawn would have arisen from the failure to give a counterweight direction. In *McGarry*, by contrast, M gave evidence and a (belated) explanation for his conduct. In such circumstances there was a real risk of prejudice arising from a failure to direct. **F19.15**

Failure to Account for Objects, Substances, Marks and Presence

Criminal Justice and Public Order Act 1994, ss. 36 and 37 **F19.16**

36.—(1) Where—
(a) a person is arrested by a constable, and there is—
(i) on his person; or

(ii) in or on his clothing or footwear; or
(iii) otherwise in his possession; or
(iv) in any place in which he is at the time of his arrest,
any object, substance or mark, or there is any mark on any such object; and
(b) that or another constable investigating the case reasonably believes that the presence of the object, substance or mark may be attributable to the participation of the person arrested in the commission of an offence specified by the constable; and
(c) the constable informs the person arrested that he so believes, and requests him to account for the presence of the object, substance or mark; and
(d) the person fails or refuses to do so,
then if, in any proceedings against the person for the offence so specified, evidence of those matters is given, subsection (2) below applies.

(2) Where this subsection applies—
(a) a magistrates' court, in deciding whether to grant an application for dismissal made by the accused under section 6 of the Magistrates' Courts Act 1980 (application for dismissal of charge in course of proceedings with a view to transfer for trial);
(b) a judge, in deciding whether to grant an application made by the accused under—
(i) section 6 of the Criminal Justice Act 1987 (application for dismissal of charge of serious fraud in respect of which notice of transfer has been given under section 4 of that Act); or
(ii) paragraph 5 of schedule 6 to the Criminal Justice Act 1991 (application for dismissal of charge of violent or sexual offence involving child in respect of which notice of transfer has been given under section 53 of that Act);
(c) the court, in determining whether there is a case to answer; and
(d) the court or jury, in determining whether the accused is guilty of the offence charged,
may draw such inferences from the failure or refusal as appear proper.

(3) Subsections (1) and (2) above apply to the condition of clothing or footwear as they apply to a substance or mark thereon.

(4) Subsections (1) and (2) above do not apply unless the accused was told in ordinary language by the constable when making the request mentioned in subsection (1)(c) above what the effect of this section would be if he failed or refused to comply with the request.

(4A) Where the accused was at an authorised place of detention at the time of the failure or refusal, subsections (1) and (2) do not apply if he had not been allowed an opportunity to consult a solicitor prior to the request being made.

(5) This section applies in relation to officers of customs and excise as it applies in relation to constables.

(6) This section does not preclude the drawing of any inference from a failure or refusal of the accused to account for the presence of an object, substance or mark or from the condition of clothing or footwear which could properly be drawn apart from this section.

(7) This section does not apply in relation to a failure or refusal which occurred before the commencement of this section.

37.—(1) Where—
(a) a person arrested by a constable was found by him at a place at or about the time the offence for which he was arrested is alleged to have been committed; and
(b) that or another constable investigating the offence reasonably believes that the presence of the person at that place and at that time may be attributable to his participation in the commission of the offence; and
(c) the constable informs the person that he so believes, and requests him to account for that presence; and
(d) the person fails or refuses to do so,
then if, in any proceedings against the person for the offence, evidence of those matters is given, subsection (2) below applies.

(2) Where this subsection applies—
(a) a magistrates' court, in deciding whether to grant an application for dismissal made by the accused under section 6 of the Magistrates' Courts Act 1980 (application for dismissal of charge in course of proceedings with a view to transfer for trial);
(b) a judge, in deciding whether to grant an application made by the accused under—
(i) section 6 of the Criminal Justice Act 1987 (application for dismissal of charge of

serious fraud in respect of which notice of transfer has been given under section 4 of that Act); or

(ii) paragraph 5 of schedule 6 to the Criminal Justice Act 1991 (application for dismissal of charge of violent or sexual offence involving child in respect of which notice of transfer has been given under section 53 of that Act);

(c) the court, in determining whether there is a case to answer; and

(d) the court or jury, in determining whether the accused is guilty of the offence charged, may draw such inferences from the failure or refusal as appear proper.

(3) Subsections (1) and (2) do not apply unless the accused was told in ordinary language by the constable when making the request mentioned in subsection (1)(c) above what the effect of this section would be if he failed or refused to comply with the request.

(3A) Where the accused was at an authorised place of detention at the time of the failure or refusal, subsection (1) and (2) do not apply if he had not been allowed an opportunity to consult a solicitor prior to the request being made.

(4) This section applies in relation to officers of customs and excise as it applies in relation to constables.

(5) This section does not preclude the drawing of any inference from a failure or refusal of the accused to account for his presence at a place which could properly be drawn apart from this section.

(6) This section does not apply in relation to a failure or refusal which occurred before the commencement of this section.

Sections 36(4A) and 37(3A) were added by the YJCEA 1999, s. 58. They are designed to bring the law into line with the judgment of the European Court of Human Rights in *Murray v United Kingdom* (1996) 22 EHRR 29. An 'authorised place of detention' is defined by s. 38(2A) to include police stations and any other place prescribed by order.

Sections 36 and 37 are based on the Irish Criminal Justice Act 1984. They go further than s. 34, which relates to the weight to be given to D's defence, and amount to positive evidence to support the prosecution case.

Basis for Inference

Neither s. 36 nor s. 37 of the CJPO 1994 permits an inference to be drawn unless four conditions are satisfied: **F19.17**

(a) the accused is arrested;

(b) a constable (not necessarily the arresting officer) reasonably believes that the object, substance or mark, or the presence of the accused at the relevant place, may be attributable to the accused's participation in a crime (in s. 36 an offence 'specified by the constable'; in s. 37 the offence for which he was arrested);

(c) the constable informs the accused of his belief and requests an explanation of the matter in question;

(d) the constable tells the suspect in ordinary language the effect of a failure or refusal to comply with the request.

The four conditions may, on their face, be satisfied where an arrested person is confronted with incriminating circumstances before he is taken to the police station for interview. However, a request for information under the two sections would appear to be a form of questioning, and because an arrested suspect should not normally be questioned about his involvement in an offence except in interview at a police station (PACE Code C, para. 11.1) the tendering in evidence of an unproductive request for information 'on the beat' should be the exception rather than the norm. If such a request is made and is alleged to have yielded a silence from which inferences can properly be drawn, the procedure for putting the silence to the suspect in a subsequent interview at the police station will apply (para. 11.4: see **F19.9**). The 'special warnings' to be given at interview in connection with ss. 36 and 37 are dealt with in PACE Code C, paras. 10.10 and 10.11).

As with s. 34 (see **F19.4**), only 'proper' inferences may be drawn. The jury must be satisfied that the accused has failed to 'account' for the relevant matter (*Compton* [2002] EWCA Crim 2835) and that any explanation advanced by the accused should be rejected as implausible before an inference can be said to be proper (see **F19.10**). Clearly the strength of the inference increases with the suspicious nature of the circumstances, so that if the accused is arrested when in possession of a car with explosive devices in full view on the back seat, his failure to give an account is more suggestive of guilt than if he refuses to account for a dirty mark on his clothing following a fight in which he is alleged to have fallen to the ground. In some cases a strong inference is proper. In *Connolly* (10 June 1994 unreported), C had been given an opportunity to account for an incriminating receipt found in his pocket, and his presence near the scene of the crime, but had maintained complete silence. The Court of Appeal for Northern Ireland accepted the trial judge's inference, drawn under provisions equivalent to ss. 36 and 37, that C was determined to sit out interrogation, assess the strength of the case against him and, if charged, to present a version of his activities unembarrassed by any statements to which he might have committed himself during interview.

Sections 36 and 37 are somewhat restrictively drawn. Section 36 is concerned with the state of the suspect at the time of his arrest, and not with his state at other relevant times, e.g., when seen by an eye-witness at the time of the crime. Section 37 is similarly concerned only with the suspect's location at the time of arrest, and applies only when he was found at the location of the crime at or about the relevant time. No mention is made of his presence at the scene at other relevant times: what if he gave the police the slip at the scene and was arrested elsewhere? If the intention is to build upon already suspicious circumstances by allowing an additional guilty inference if the accused fails to explain them, it is not clear why the provisions are so restrictive: a suspected rapist may have inferences drawn for failing to explain away stains on his trousers, but not for refusing to explain why he is not wearing any (unless he has discarded them nearby).

Section 38(3) (see **F19.6**) provides that an inference drawn under these provisions may, *inter alia*, form part of the case to answer or contribute to a verdict of guilty, though neither outcome may be based 'solely' upon such an inference. It is not clear what this means. An inference drawn under ss. 36 and 37 can never exist 'solely', in the sense of independently of the proof of the suspicious circumstances for which the accused refuses to account. In some cases, such circumstances may be sufficient to convict, as in the case of the man arrested with two bombs on the back seat of his car. The fact that the accused gave no explanation cannot prevent the circumstances having this effect: on the contrary, it strengthens the inference to be drawn from them. Perhaps the intention behind the provision is to prompt the judge to tell the jury not to convict just because the accused has been unhelpful.

It is not clear how frequently these two provisions will function independently of ss. 34 and 35. If D goes on to present a defence relying on facts he could have mentioned earlier, as in *Connolly*, it is likely that s. 34 will also apply. If he gives no evidence, then s. 35 (see **F19.20**) may come into play.

Unfair Use of Pre-trial Silence

F19.18 Failure or refusal to respond to questioning relevant to ss. 34, 36 and 37 seems unlikely to be regarded as a 'statement', and is thus incapable of being a confession within s. 82 of the PACE 1984 for the purposes of s. 76 of that Act (see **F17.5**). Silence obtained by oppression or in circumstances conducive to unreliability would not therefore be automatically inadmissible, as would a confession similarly obtained. It would however be subject to exclusion under the discretion conferred by the PACE 1984, s. 78, in respect of all prosecution evidence, to the extent that it would be unfair to make use of it.

Extensive use has also been made of s. 78 in rejecting confession evidence which, while admissible under s. 76, has been obtained in breach of the 1984 Act or Codes of Practice, or by other unfair means (see **F17.20**). These authorities would seem to apply also to silence, with the result that, e.g., failure to make proper records of an interrogation, may lead to exclusion.

FAILURE OF ACCUSED TO TESTIFY

The CJPO 1994 repealed the Criminal Evidence Act 1898, s. 1(b). The 1898 Act provided that the failure of the accused to testify was not to be made the subject of any comment by the prosecution. Comment by the judge was permissible but the scope for it was limited, and it had always to be accompanied with a reminder that the accused was not bound to give evidence and that, while the jury had been deprived of the opportunity of hearing his story tested in cross-examination, they were not to assume that he was guilty because he had not gone into the witness-box (*Bathurst* [1968] 2 QB 99). Stronger comment was permitted where the defence case involved the assertion of facts which were at variance with the prosecution evidence, or additional to it and exculpatory, and which, if true, would have been within the accused's own knowledge (*Martinez-Tobon* [1994] 1 WLR 388). **F19.19**

Failure to Testify following the 1994 Act

Under the CJPO 1994, s. 35, it is submitted that the common-law authorities will continue to provide useful guidance as to the type of case in which the strongest inferences are permissible. (See further **F19.21** to **F19.27**.) A careful direction will be required in all cases where the accused does not testify, in order to make the jury aware of the inferences which may properly be drawn, not least because of the need to comply with the 'fair trial' provisions of the ECHR, Article 6 (*Birchall* [1999] Crim LR 311). **F19.20**

Criminal Justice and Public Order Act 1994, s. 35

(1) At the trial of any person for an offence, subsections (2) and (3) below apply unless—
(a) the accused's guilt is not in issue; or
(b) it appears to the court that the physical or mental condition of the accused makes it undesirable for him to give evidence;
but subsection (2) below does not apply if, at the conclusion of the evidence for the prosecution, his legal representative informs the court that the accused will give evidence or, where he is unrepresented, the court ascertains from him that he will give evidence.
(2) Where this subsection applies, the court shall, at the conclusion of the evidence for the prosecution, satisfy itself (in the case of proceedings on indictment, in the presence of the jury) that the accused is aware that the stage has been reached at which evidence can be given for the defence and that he can, if he wishes, give evidence and that, if he chooses not to give evidence, or having been sworn, without good cause refuses to answer any question, it will be permissible for the court or jury to draw such inferences as appear proper from his failure to give evidence or his refusal, without good cause, to answer any question.
(3) Where this subsection applies, the court or jury, in determining whether the accused is guilty of the offence charged, may draw such inferences as appear proper from the failure of the accused to give evidence or his refusal, without good cause, to answer any question.
(4) This section does not render the accused compellable to give evidence on his own behalf, and he shall accordingly not be guilty of contempt of court by reason of a failure to do so.
(5) For the purposes of this section a person who, having been sworn, refuses to answer any question shall be taken to do so without good cause unless—
(a) he is entitled to refuse to answer the question by virtue of any enactment, whenever passed or made, or on the ground of privilege; or
(b) the court in the exercise of its general discretion excuses him from answering it.
(6) [Repealed by CDA 1998, s. 35.]
(7) This section applies—
(a) in relation to proceedings on indictment for an offence, only if the person charged with the offence is arraigned on or after the commencement of this section;

(b) in relation to proceedings in a magistrates' court, only if the time when the court begins to receive evidence in the proceedings falls after the commencement of this section.

Consolidated Criminal Practice Direction, para. IV.44

Defendant's right to give or not to give evidence

IV.44.1 At the conclusion of the evidence for the prosecution, section 35(2) of the Criminal Justice and Public Order Act 1994 requires the court to satisfy itself that the accused is aware that the stage has been reached at which evidence can be given for the defence and that he can, if he wishes, give evidence and that, if he chooses not to give evidence or, having been sworn, without good cause refuses to answer any question, it will be permissible for the jury to draw such inferences as appear proper from his failure to give evidence of his refusal, without good cause, to answer any question.

If the accused is legally represented

IV.44.2 Section 35(1) provides that section 35(2) does not apply if at the conclusion of the evidence for the prosecution the accused's legal representative informs the court that the accused will give evidence. This should be done in the presence of the jury. If the representative indicates that the accused will give evidence, the case should proceed in the usual way.

IV.44.3 If the court is not so informed, or if the court is informed that the accused does not intend to give evidence, the judge should in the presence of the jury inquire of the representative in these terms:

'Have you advised your client that the stage has now been reached at which he may give evidence and, if he chooses not to do so or, having been sworn, without good cause refuses to answer any question, the jury may draw such inferences as appear proper from his failure to do so?'

IV.44.4 If the representative replies to the judge that the accused has been so advised, then the case shall proceed. If counsel replies that the accused has not been so advised then the judge shall direct the representative to advise his client of the consequences set out in paragraph 44.3 and should adjourn briefly for this purpose before proceeding further.

If the accused is not legally represented

IV.44.5 If the accused is not represented, the judge shall at the conclusion of the evidence for the prosecution and in the presence of the jury say to the accused:

'You have heard the evidence against you. Now is the time for you to make your defence. You may give evidence on oath, and be cross-examined like any other witness. If you do not give evidence or, having been sworn, without good cause refuse to answer any question the jury may draw such inferences as appear proper. That means they may hold it against you. You may also call any witness or witnesses whom you have arranged to attend court. Afterwards you may also, if you wish, address the jury by arguing your case from the dock. But you cannot at that stage give evidence. Do you now intend to give evidence?'

The court's obligation in s. 35(2) to satisfy itself that the accused knows that he can, if he wishes, give evidence is mandatory and cannot be overlooked even where the accused has, by absconding, put himself beyond the reach of the warning (*Gough* [2002] 2 Cr App R 121).

It has long been the recommended practice, and is of great importance in light of s. 35, for counsel to record the decision of the accused not to give evidence, and to sign it and indicate that it was made voluntarily (see **D16.3** and *Bevan* (1994) 98 Cr App R 354 and *Chatroodi* [2001] EWCA Crim 585).

The DVCVA 2004, s. 6, makes special provision for the inferences to be drawn where a person fails to testify when charged with an offence under s. 5 of that Act (causing or allowing the death of a child or vulnerable adult: see **B1.45**).

Domestic Violence, Crime and Victims Act 2004, s. 6

(2) Where by virtue of section 35(3) of the Criminal Justice and Public Order Act 1994 a court or jury is permitted, in relation to the section 5 offence, to draw such inferences as appear

proper from the defendant's failure to give evidence or refusal to answer a question, the court or jury may also draw such inferences in determining whether he is guilty—
(a) of murder or manslaughter, or
(b) of any other offence of which he could lawfully be convicted on the charge of murder or manslaughter,
even if there would otherwise be no case for him to answer in relation to that offence.

'Proper' Inferences of Guilt

Under the CJPO 1994, s. 35, the 'proper' inferences come about as a result of the failure of the accused to give evidence or his refusal without good cause to answer any question (s. 35(3)). Defendants whose 'physical or mental condition make it undesirable' for them to give evidence are excluded from the operation of the section, together with those whose 'guilt is not in issue' (s. 35(1)). By virtue of s. 35(5), privilege is a valid ground for refusing to answer, as is a statutory entitlement such as the Criminal Evidence Act 1898, s. 1(3) (see **F12.45** ***et seq.***). In *McManus* [2001] EWCA Crim 2455 it was held that a s. 35 direction was inappropriate where the facts were not in dispute and the only issue was as to whether they were such as to fall within the offence of keeping a disorderly house. There being nothing the accused could have said to throw light on the issue before the jury, the direction was prejudicial. Subject to these exceptions, the accused must answer all proper questions or risk the drawing of inferences, and a judge may remind him of his duty in this regard, though he should avoid doing so in an oppressive way (*Ackinclose* [1996] Crim LR 747). The court is obliged to satisfy itself that defendants who have not indicated that they intend to give evidence understand the consequences of declining to do so (s. 35(2) and (3) and the *Consolidated Criminal Practice Direction*, para. IV.44, *Defendant's right to give or not to give evidence*). The *Practice Direction* makes clear that the burden of explaining the option to testify and the consequences of failing to do so to the defendant rests, in the case of a legally represented defendant, with the legal representative. This accords with the position at common law (cf. *Sankar v State of Trinidad and Tobago* [1995] 1 WLR 194). **F19.21**

Accused with Physical or Mental Limitations The meaning of s. 35(1)(b) of the CJPO 1994 was considered in *Friend* [1997] 1 WLR 1433. F was tried for murder. He had a physical age of 15, a mental age of 9, and an IQ of 63. Expert evidence suggested that, although not suggestible, his powers of comprehension were limited and he might find it difficult to do justice to himself in the witness box. Nevertheless F had given a clear account of his defence at various stages prior to trial. Taking all of these matters into account, the trial judge ruled that F's mental condition did not make it 'undesirable' for him to give evidence, so that his failure to do so led to the jury being directed that they might draw inferences under s. 35(3). The Court of Appeal agreed, noting that it would only be in a rare case that the judge would be called upon to arrive at a decision under s. 35(1)(b); generally an accused who was unable to comprehend proceedings so as to make a proper defence would be unfit to plead, so the issue would not arise. Section 35(1)(b) was intended to mitigate any injustice to a person whose physical or mental handicap was less severe, and it gave a wide discretion to a trial judge which did not require to be circumscribed by any further judicial test. The trial judge had been right not to base his conclusion on the mental age of F: a person with a mental age of less than 14 did not automatically qualify for the protection which before 1998 applied to a person of that physical age. Nor was he bound to determine the issue on the expert evidence alone, but was entitled to take account of the behaviour of F before and after the commission of the offence including the way in which he had put his defence in interview. (The conduct of F at the time of the offence, which was hotly disputed, was rightly not considered by the judge.) The trial judge in *Friend* seems to have been much influenced by the fact that young children regularly appear as witnesses in criminal cases, and that measures can be taken by which they and other vulnerable witnesses can, if their needs are correctly assessed, be protected from unfair or oppressive cross-examination. Thus, as the main reason for questioning the desirability of F testifying was that he might give a poor account of himself unless care **F19.22**

were taken to ensure that he understood and had time to respond to questions, the fact that the court itself could respond sensitively to F's needs was a factor militating against the defence argument. The outcome suggests that the discretion will be exercised against the background of an assumption that it is generally desirable for an accused to testify, so that cases in which it can be said to be 'undesirable' will be rare indeed.

Both *Friend* and the later decision in *A* [1997] Crim LR 883 require there to be an evidential basis for a ruling that s. 35(1)(b) applies. A *voir dire* may be required to determine the issue, although the judge is, according to *A*, under no obligation to initiate the procedure if defence counsel does not seek to do so. In *R (DPP) Kavanagh* [2005] EWHC 820 (Admin), it was doubted whether, even in summary trial, non-expert evidence (such as that of a family member) as to the mental condition of the accused could be sufficient. In that case K's mother had testified to his history of depression, but even her evidence taken at its highest fell short of disclosing a subsisting condition making it undesirable for him to give evidence.

F19.23 **Nature of Inference under s. 35** The adverse inference which it may be proper to draw under s. 35(3) of the CJPO 1994 is that the accused 'is guilty of the offence charged'. As s. 35 does not come into play until after the close of the evidence for the prosecution, it presupposes that a prima facie case has already been established against the accused. In *Murray v DPP* [1994] 1 WLR 1, a decision concerning the equivalent provision in the Criminal Evidence (Northern Ireland) Order 1988, M was convicted of attempted murder and possession of a firearm with intent to endanger life. Scientific evidence linked M with a car used in the attack: the situation was one calling for 'confession and avoidance'. M advanced various explanations during interrogation, but gave no evidence at trial, from which failure the trial judge drew a strong adverse inference. The House of Lords considered that the inference was justified. The 1988 Order was intended to change the law and practice and to lay down new rules as to the comments which could be made and inferences which could be drawn. The accused is not compellable to testify, but he must risk the consequences if he does not do so. These consequences are not simply that specific inferences may be drawn from specific facts, but include in a proper case the inference that the accused is guilty. As to what is proper, Lord Slynn said (at p. 11):

> If there is no prima facie case shown by the prosecution there is no case to answer. Equally, if parts of the prosecution case had so little evidential value that they called for no answer, a failure to deal with those specific matters cannot justify an inference of guilt.
>
> On the other hand, if aspects of the evidence taken alone or in combination with other facts clearly call for an explanation which the accused ought to be in a position to give, if an explanation exists, then a failure to give any explanation may as a matter of common sense allow the drawing of an inference that there is no explanation and that the accused is guilty.

F19.24 **No Conviction Solely on Inference from s. 35** As with ss. 34, 36 and 37 of the CJPO 1994, the accused cannot be convicted solely on an inference drawn from a failure or refusal (s. 38(3): see **F19.6**). In *Cowan* [1996] QB 373 the Court of Appeal emphasised that the prosecution remains under an obligation to establish a prima facie case before any question of the accused testifying is raised. Their lordships took this to mean not only that the case should be fit to be left to the jury, but also that the judge should make clear to the jury that *they* must be convinced of the existence of a prima facie case before drawing an adverse inference from silence. This may seem to go beyond the strict requirement of the statute, but serves to ensure conformity with the principle in *Murray v UK* (1996) 22 EHRR 29 that the accused should not be convicted 'solely or mainly' on an inference from silence (*Burchill* [1999] Crim LR 311: see also **F19.6**). In a case where there is a compelling case for the accused to answer it has been held that the failure to direct in accordance with this aspect of *Cowan* could not affect the safety of the conviction (*Bromfield* [2002] EWCA Crim 195). In *Whitehead* [2006] EWCA Crim 1486, where the case for the prosecution in a sexual offence depended on the credibility of a complainant who had delayed making a complaint for more than ten years, the

Criminal Cases Review Commission referred the case to the Court of Appeal on the basis that the omission to direct the jury that they should first find a case to answer might have led to them using the accused's failure to testify to 'shore up' the deficiencies in the complainant's evidence. The Court of Appeal dismissed this possibility as 'fanciful' in light of the very clear directions that had been given to the jury that they had to be 'sure' the complainant was not lying, and that the accused's silence was not by itself proof of guilt. The Court considered that the direction to the jury to find a prima facie case before considering the implications of the accused's silence 'amplifies and spells out' what is already implicit in the separate injunction that failure to give evidence cannot by itself prove guilt.

Inference not Confined to 'Exceptional' Cases In *Cowan* [1996] QB 373, the Court of Appeal rejected an argument that s. 35 should be permitted to operate in exceptional cases only. The argument was based first on the extent to which the section breached a long-established principle by inhibiting the exercise of the right to silence, and secondly on the effect it was alleged to have of 'watering down' the burden of proof. The court held that even before the 1994 Act the accused had been in certain respects inhibited from exercising the right to silence (for example out of fear that the jury might draw adverse inferences even where the classic direction in *Bathurst* was given) and that the burden of proof, far from being altered or watered down, remained on the prosecution. The effect of s. 35 was simply to add a further evidential factor in support of the prosecution case. The court also stressed that the plain wording of s. 35 indicated that it was not limited to exceptional cases: on the contrary, the exceptional cases were those dealt with in s. 35(1) in which the provisions were *not* to be invoked. However, it was open to a court in any case to which the exceptions in s. 35(1) did not apply to decline to draw an inference from silence, though for a judge to advise a jury against drawing such an inference would require either 'some evidential basis for doing so or some exceptional factors in the case making that a fair course to take'. The Court of Appeal gave no example of the situation in which it would be improper to draw an inference from silence, although it stipulated that an inference could not be drawn unless the jury decides that the silence 'can only sensibly be attributed' to the accused having no answer, or none that would stand up to cross-examination. F19.25

Cowan was applied in *Napper* (1997) 161 JP 16. N claimed that the failure of the police to interview him while the frauds with which he was charged were reasonably fresh in his mind should have led the judge to direct the jury to draw no adverse inferences from his silence at trial. It was held that this was not, under *Cowan*, an exceptional case where such a direction would have been justified in the interests of justice. Nothing prevented N from making his own record from which to refresh his memory, and the crucial issues were in any case sufficiently memorable to present him with no difficulty of recollection. More recently in *Becouarn* [2003] EWCA Crim 1154 it was held (on facts similar to those before the court in *Cowan*) that the normal s. 35 direction should be given notwithstanding that B's reason for not testifying was that his criminal record would have been revealed because his defence consisted of an assertion that prosecution witnesses had committed the crime with which he was charged. That practice was endorsed by the House of Lords (*Becouarn* [2005] 1 WLR 2589), although it was not to be an invariable practice having regard to the trial judge's overriding discretion to avoid unfairness by declining to give a direction in a particular case, the decision is effectively superseded by the CJA 2003, s. 101. Under s. 101(1)(g), an accused who has attacked another person's character renders himself liable to the disclosure of his own bad character whether he testifies or not, so that the option of not testifying now entails the likelihood of both disclosure of the record and a s. 35 direction and the dilemma facing the accused in *Becouarn* no longer obtains.

No Inference where Prosecution Case is Weak It seems from the observations of Lord Slynn in *Murray v DPP* [1994] 1 WLR 1 (see **F19.23**) that inferences of guilt should not be drawn from failure to give evidence to contradict a prosecution case of 'little evidential value'. F19.26

This accords with the position at common law, where it was considered improper for a judge to bolster a weak prosecution case by making comments on an accused's failure to give evidence (*Waugh v The King* [1950] AC 203). W had been convicted of murder on very weak evidence. The only evidence of any strength was a statement made by the deceased shortly before his death. The police accepted the appellant's explanation as to what had happened, but a coroner ordered his prosecution. At the trial the appellant did not testify. In his summing-up the trial judge commented nine times on the fact. The Privy Council disapproved of these comments. Lord Oaksey said (at pp. 211–12):

> . . . in the present case their lordships think that the prisoner's counsel was fully justified in not calling the prisoner, and that the judge, if he made any comment on the matter at all, ought at least have pointed out to the jury that the prisoner was not bound to give evidence and that it was for the prosecution to make out the case beyond reasonable doubt.

F19.27 **Strong Inference where Facts Clearly Call for Explanation or are Within the Accused's Knowledge** In *Mutch* [1973] 1 All ER 178, the Court of Appeal identified exceptional cases at common law in which stronger comment was justified. They were those in which an inference could be drawn from uncontested or clearly established facts which point so strongly to guilt as to call for an explanation. *Corrie* (1904) 20 TLR 365 and *Bernard* (1908) 1 Cr App R 218 are cited in *Mutch* as exceptional examples of the kind of case in which such an inference may properly be drawn. So also is *Brigden* [1973] Crim LR 579. The accused gave no evidence, but alleged that the police had planted incriminating evidence on him and cross-examined a prosecution witness on a conviction. It is submitted that such a case would support a strong inference under the CJPO 1994 that the defence was untrue. The same may be said of other cases concerning facts within the accused's own knowledge which were said to justify strong comment at common law in *Martinez-Tobon* [1994] 1 WLR 388 (see **F19.13**).

Burden on Accused

F19.28 A different form of comment was required at common law in cases in which the accused bears the burden of proof, namely 'that he is not bound to go into the witness box, nobody can force him to go into the witness box, but the burden is upon him, and if he does not, he runs the risk of not being able to prove his case' (*Bathurst* [1968] 2 QB 99: see **F19.19**). The same situation under the CJPO 1994 would seem to justify a strong adverse inference if the defence is one which, if true, could be proved by the accused's own evidence (e.g., that his possession of an offensive weapon was lawful: Prevention of Crime Act 1953, s. 1(1), see **B12.128**).

In cases in which there is a defence of diminished responsibility, only rarely was it proper for a comment to be made (*Bathurst*). A defence such as diminished responsibility or insanity can be made out without the accused's contribution. Under the 1994 Act the position appears to be the same: s. 35(1)(b) provides that no inference may be drawn if the mental condition of the accused makes it undesirable for him to give evidence.

ACCUSED FAILING TO PROVIDE SAMPLES ETC.

F19.29 At common law, an adverse inference could be drawn from unhelpful conduct other than silence while under interrogation. In *Smith* (1985) 81 Cr App R 286, S was asked in the presence of his solicitor if he was willing to provide a sample of hair. When he asked why, S was told that it was for comparison with hairs found at the scene of the robbery of which he was suspected. He replied 'In that case, no I am not'. It was held that the fact that, at that time, such samples could not lawfully be taken without S's consent did not mean that no inferences could be drawn from his refusal. Leonard J considered that it would be 'contrary to good sense' to prohibit the drawing of inferences and that the case was 'in a wholly different category' from evidence of a failure to answer questions under caution. Nevertheless the court borrowed from the rules regarding silence when it stressed the fact that the presence of S's solicitor rendered the parties 'on even terms' (see **F19.2**). (See also *McVeigh v Beattie* [1988] Fam 69, in which it was held that the refusal of the respondent in affiliation proceedings to submit to a blood test which might have excluded the possibility that he had fathered the child in question could, in the absence of a reasonable explanation, amount to corroboration of the evidence of the complainant.)

Under the PACE 1984, s. 63, a sample of hair can now be taken from a suspect without his consent. The taking of intimate samples continues to require consent (s. 62) (see **F18.30** for detailed discussion of ss. 62 and 63). The rule in *Smith* has found statutory expression in s. 62(10), which permits 'such inferences as appear proper' to be drawn 'where the appropriate consent to the taking of an intimate sample from a person was refused without good cause' in a variety of circumstances including the determination of whether the person is guilty of the offence charged.

FAILURE TO CALL WITNESSES OR PROVIDE EVIDENCE

If the accused fails to call a particular person as a witness, then, if appropriate, as when the prosecution had no possible means of knowing that that person had any relevant evidence to give until the accused himself gave evidence at the trial, the judge may direct the jury that they may take into account the fact that the potential witness was not called, but should exercise a degree of care. In particular he should avoid the suggestion that the failure is something of importance where there may be a valid reason for not calling the witness (Megaw LJ in *Gallagher* [1974] 1 WLR 1204, affirmed in *Couzens* [1992] Crim LR 822). Comment may also be justified if there is a very strong case for suggesting that an account which an accused is giving has recently been fabricated and where, if it has not, there would be another witness or other witnesses of any description who could substantiate the accused's story if it were true (*Wilmot* (1988) 89 Cr App R 341 per Glidewell LJ at p. 352). However, comment in this area has to be made with circumspection and reserve (*Weller* [1994] Crim LR 856). In *Weller* the Court of Appeal held that it could not envisage any case in which it would be appropriate to make a comment to the effect that if there were any truth in the accused's story, he would have been expected to have called a particular witness. In the somewhat extreme case of *Forsyth* [1997] 2 Cr App R 299, the witness, J, was not one whom the defence might have been expected to call in the light of the issues raised by prosecution or defence at trial, but his absence was the subject of comment by prosecuting counsel in his closing address, and the jury subsequently asked the judge for guidance. It was held that the judge should have made it clear to the jury that they should draw no inference from the absence of J, and that they should decide the case on the evidence and without speculating on what J might have said. See also *Wright* [2000] Crim LR 510, where it was said that comments on the failure to call a particular witness may amount to a reversal of the burden of proof, and *Rodenhurst* (2001) *Independent*, 23 July 2001, where the court approved the trial judge's warning that 'the danger of speculating about a witness's absence is precisely that you may impute some motive that may be entirely wrong'. **F19.30**

Comment on Failure of Spouse or Civil Partner of Accused to Testify

The failure of the spouse or civil partner of the accused to give evidence shall not be made the subject of any comment by the prosecution (PACE 1984, s. 80A). In *Brown* [1983] Crim LR 38, it was held with respect to the forerunner of s. 80A that the wording was mandatory, and that breach of the prohibition would amount to a material irregularity in the course of the trial. However, whether a breach would lead to a conviction being quashed depended upon all the circumstances, and in particular whether the trial judge corrected the breach in his summing-up. In *Dickman* (1910) 5 Cr App R 135, in which counsel inadvertently commented upon the failure of the spouse of the accused to testify but the jury were told to **F19.31** dismiss the comment from their minds, the appeal against conviction was dismissed. Likewise in *Hunter* [1969] Crim LR 262, where a comment was made in breach of the prohibition but the judge, refusing to discharge the jury, warned them about the comment, the conviction was upheld. These cases may be contrasted with *Naudeer* [1984] 3 All ER 1036. N, a man of good character, was convicted of theft. At the trial, counsel for the prosecution suggested that the failure of N's wife to give evidence had deprived the jury of what would probably have been material evidence, and the judge failed in his summing-up to give any direction to repair the breach of the prohibition on such comment. The Court of Appeal quashed the conviction on the grounds that the breach was central to the overall justice of the case, particularly since the accused was a man of good character (which he had put before the jury), and the question of his bona fides was central to the offence itself. It was the duty of the judge, depending upon the circumstances of each case, to remedy any breach of the prohibition on such comment in his summing-up.

Section 80A of the PACE 1984 does not prevent comment by the judge on the failure of the spouse or civil partner of the accused to testify. In *Naudeer*, Purchas LJ said (at p. 1039) that 'if a judge in the exercise of his discretion decides to comment upon the failure of the accused to call his spouse or to give evidence himself he must, except in exceptional circumstances, do this with a great deal of circumspection'. The same degree of circumspection would also appear to be required in the case of failure to call cohabitees, who are not covered by s. 80(8) (see *Weller* [1994] Crim LR 856). In *Whitton* [1998] Crim LR 492, prosecuting counsel commented on the failure of W's husband, who had been present when she allegedly assaulted a neighbour, to give evidence. This clear breach was, however, held to have been subsumed in the summing-up in which the trial judge quite properly elected to make a comment of his own. It was not possible in the circumstances to argue that counsel's comment undermined the safety of W's conviction, though this should clearly not be read as an invitation to counsel to disregard the statutory provision, however strong the case for judicial comment.

Appendix 1 Criminal Procedure Rules 2005 (SI 2005 No. 384)

Part 1 The Overriding Objective

The overriding objective

1.1 (1) The overriding objective of this new code is that criminal cases be dealt with justly.
(2) Dealing with a criminal case justly includes—
(a) acquitting the innocent and convicting the guilty;
(b) dealing with the prosecution and the defence fairly;
(c) recognising the rights of a defendant, particularly those under Article 6 of the European Convention on Human Rights;
(d) respecting the interests of witnesses, victims and jurors and keeping them informed of the progress of the case;
(e) dealing with the case efficiently and expeditiously;
(f) ensuring that appropriate information is available to the court when bail and sentence are considered; and
(g) dealing with the case in ways that take into account—
(i) the gravity of the offence alleged,
(ii) the complexity of what is in issue,
(iii) the severity of the consequences for the defendant and others affected, and
(iv) the needs of other cases.

The duty of the participants in a criminal case

1.2 (1) Each participant, in the conduct of each case, must—
(a) prepare and conduct the case in accordance with the overriding objective;
(b) comply with these Rules, practice directions and directions made by the court; and
(c) at once inform the court and all parties of any significant failure (whether or not that participant is responsible for that failure) to take any procedural step required by these Rules, any practice direction or any direction of the court. A failure is significant if it might hinder the court in furthering the overriding objective.
(2) Anyone involved in any way with a criminal case is a participant in its conduct for the purposes of this rule.

The application by the court of the overriding objective

1.3 The court must further the overriding objective in particular when—
(a) exercising any power given to it by legislation (including these Rules);
(b) applying any practice direction; or
(c) interpreting any rule or practice direction.

Part 2 Understanding and Applying the Rules

When the Rules apply

2.1 (1) In general, the Criminal Procedure Rules apply—
(a) in all criminal cases in magistrates' courts and in the Crown Court; and
(b) in all cases in the criminal division of the Court of Appeal.
(2) If a rule applies only in one or two of those courts, the rule makes that clear.
(3) The Rules apply on and after 4th April, 2005, but do not affect any right or duty existing under the rules of court revoked by the coming into force of these Rules.
(4) The Rules in Part 33 apply in all cases in which the defendant is charged on or after 6 November 2006 and in other cases if the court so orders.
(5) The rules in Part 14 apply in cases in which one of the events listed in sub-paragraphs (a) to (d) of rule 14.1(1) takes place on or after 2nd April 2007. In other cases the rules of court replaced by those rules apply.
(6) The rules in Part 28 apply in cases in which an application under rule 28.3 is made on or after 2nd April 2007. In other cases the rules replaced by those rules apply.

Definitions

2.2 (1) In these Rules, unless the context makes it clear that something different is meant:
'court' means a tribunal with jurisdiction over criminal cases. It includes a judge, recorder, District Judge (Magistrates' Courts), lay justice and, when exercising their judicial powers, the Registrar of Criminal Appeals, a justices' clerk or assistant clerk;
'court officer' means the appropriate member of the staff of a court; and
'Practice Direction' means the Lord Chief Justice's Consolidated Criminal Practice Direction, as amended.
(2) Definitions of some other expressions are in the rules in which they apply.

References to Acts of Parliament and to Statutory Instruments

2.3 In these Rules, where a rule refers to an Act of Parliament or to subordinate legislation by title and year, subsequent references to that Act or to that legislation in the rule are shortened: so, for example, after a reference to the Criminal Procedure and Investigations Act 1996 that Act is called 'the 1996 Act'; and after a reference to the Criminal Procedure and Investigations Act 1996 (Defence Disclosure Time Limits) Regulations 1997 those Regulations are called 'the 1997 Regulations'.

The glossary

2.4 The glossary at the end of the Rules is a guide to the meaning of certain legal expressions used in them.

Part 3 Case Management

The scope of this Part

3.1 This Part applies to the management of each case in a magistrates' court and in the Crown Court (including an appeal to the Crown Court) until the conclusion of that case.

The duty of the court

3.2 (1) The court must further the overriding objective by actively managing the case.
(2) Active case management includes—
(a) the early identification of the real issues;
(b) the early identification of the needs of witnesses;
(c) achieving certainty as to what must be done, by whom, and when, in particular by the early setting of a timetable for the progress of the case;
(d) monitoring the progress of the case and compliance with directions;
(e) ensuring that evidence, whether disputed or not, is presented in the shortest and clearest way;
(f) discouraging delay, dealing with as many aspects of the case as possible on the same occasion, and avoiding unnecessary hearings;
(g) encouraging the participants to co-operate in the progression of the case; and
(h) making use of technology.
(3) The court must actively manage the case by giving any direction appropriate to the needs of that case as early as possible.

The duty of the parties

3.3 Each party must—
(a) actively assist the court in fulfilling its duty under rule 3.2, without or if necessary with a direction; and
(b) apply for a direction if needed to further the overriding objective.

Case progression officers and their duties

3.4 (1) At the beginning of the case each party must, unless the court otherwise directs—
(a) nominate an individual responsible for progressing that case; and
(b) tell other parties and the court who he is and how to contact him.
(2) In fulfilling its duty under rule 3.2, the court must where appropriate—
(a) nominate a court officer responsible for progressing the case; and
(b) make sure the parties know who he is and how to contact him.
(3) In this Part a person nominated under this rule is called a case progression officer.
(4) A case progression officer must—
(a) monitor compliance with directions;

(b) make sure that the court is kept informed of events that may affect the progress of that case;
(c) make sure that he can be contacted promptly about the case during ordinary business hours;
(d) act promptly and reasonably in response to communications about the case; and
(e) if he will be unavailable, appoint a substitute to fulfil his duties and inform the other case progression officers.

The court's case management powers

3.5 (1) In fulfilling its duty under rule 3.2 the court may give any direction and take any step actively to manage a case unless that direction or step would be inconsistent with legislation, including these Rules.
(2) In particular, the court may—
(a) nominate a judge, magistrate, justices' clerk or assistant to a justices' clerk to manage the case;
(b) give a direction on its own initiative or on application by a party;
(c) ask or allow a party to propose a direction;
(d) for the purpose of giving directions, receive applications and representations by letter, by telephone or by any other means of electronic communication, and conduct a hearing by such means;
(e) give a direction without a hearing;
(f) fix, postpone, bring forward, extend or cancel a hearing;
(g) shorten or extend (even after it has expired) a time limit fixed by a direction;
(h) require that issues in the case should be determined separately, and decide in what order they will be determined; and
(i) specify the consequences of failing to comply with a direction.
(3) A magistrates' court may give a direction that will apply in the Crown Court if the case is to continue there.
(4) The Crown Court may give a direction that will apply in a magistrates' court if the case is to continue there.
(5) Any power to give a direction under this Part includes a power to vary or revoke that direction.

Application to vary a direction

3.6 (1) A party may apply to vary a direction if—
(a) the court gave it without a hearing;
(b) the court gave it at a hearing in his absence; or
(c) circumstances have changed.
(2) A party who applies to vary a direction must—
(a) apply as soon as practicable after he becomes aware of the grounds for doing so; and
(b) give as much notice to the other parties as the nature and urgency of his application permits.

Agreement to vary a time limit fixed by a direction

3.7 (1) The parties may agree to vary a time limit fixed by a direction, but only if—
(a) the variation will not—
(i) affect the date of any hearing that has been fixed, or
(ii) significantly affect the progress of the case in any other way;
(b) the court has not prohibited variation by agreement; and
(c) the court's case progression officer is promptly informed.
(2) The court's case progression officer must refer the agreement to the court if he doubts the condition in paragraph (1)(a) is satisfied.

Case preparation and progression

3.8 (1) At every hearing, if a case cannot be concluded there and then the court must give directions so that it can be concluded at the next hearing or as soon as possible after that.
(2) At every hearing the court must, where relevant—
(a) if the defendant is absent, decide whether to proceed nonetheless;
(b) take the defendant's plea (unless already done) or if no plea can be taken then find out whether the defendant is likely to plead guilty or not guilty;

(c) set, follow or revise a timetable for the progress of the case, which may include a timetable for any hearing including the trial or (in the Crown Court) the appeal;
(d) in giving directions, ensure continuity in relation to the court and to the parties' representatives where that is appropriate and practicable; and
(e) where a direction has not been complied with, find out why, identify who was responsible, and take appropriate action.

Readiness for trial or appeal

3.9 (1) This rule applies to a party's preparation for trial or (in the Crown Court) appeal, and in this rule and rule 3.10 trial includes any hearing at which evidence will be introduced.
(2) In fulfilling his duty under rule 3.3, each party must—
(a) comply with directions given by the court;
(b) take every reasonable step to make sure his witnesses will attend when they are needed;
(c) make appropriate arrangements to present any written or other material; and
(d) promptly inform the court and the other parties of anything that may—
(i) affect the date or duration of the trial or appeal, or
(ii) significantly affect the progress of the case in any other way.
(3) The court may require a party to give a certificate of readiness.

Conduct of a trial or an appeal

3.10 In order to manage the trial or (in the Crown Court) appeal, the court may require a party to identify—
(a) which witnesses he intends to give oral evidence;
(b) the order in which he intends those witnesses to give their evidence;
(c) whether he requires an order compelling the attendance of a witness;
(d) what arrangements, if any, he proposes to facilitate the giving of evidence by a witness;
(e) what arrangements, if any, he proposes to facilitate the participation of any other person, including the defendant;
(f) what written evidence he intends to introduce;
(g) what other material, if any, he intends to make available to the court in the presentation of the case;
(h) whether he intends to raise any point of law that could affect the conduct of the trial or appeal; and
(i) what timetable he proposes and expects to follow.

Case management forms and records

3.11 (1) The case management forms set out in the Practice Direction must be used, and where there is no form then no specific formality is required.
(2) The court must make available to the parties a record of directions given.

PART 4 SERVICE OF DOCUMENTS

When this Part applies

4.1 The rules in this Part apply to the service of every document in a case to which these Rules apply, subject to any special rules in other legislation (including other Parts of these Rules) or in the Practice Direction.

Methods of service

4.2 A document may be served by any of the methods described in rules 4.3 to 4.6 (subject to rule 4.7), or in rule 4.8.

Service by handing over a document

4.3 (1) A document may be served on—
(a) an individual by handing it to him or her;
(b) a corporation by handing it to a person holding a senior position in that corporation;
(c) an individual or corporation who is legally represented in the case by handing it to that representative;
(d) the prosecution by handing it to the prosecutor or to the prosecution representative;
(e) the court officer by handing it to a court officer with authority to accept it at the relevant court office; and

(f) the Registrar of Criminal Appeals by handing it to a court officer with authority to accept it at the Criminal Appeal Office.

(2) If an individual is 17 or under, a copy of a document served under paragraph (1)(a) must be handed to his or her parent, or another appropriate adult, unless no such person is readily available.

Service by leaving or posting a document

4.4 (1) A document may be served by leaving it at the appropriate address for service under this rule or by sending it to that address by first class post or by the equivalent of first class post.

(2) The address for service under this rule on—

(a) an individual is an address where it is reasonably believed that he or she will receive it;

(b) a corporation is its principal office in England and Wales, and if there is no readily identifiable principal office then any place in England and Wales where it carries on its activities or business;

(c) an individual or corporation who is legally represented in the case is that representative's office;

(d) the prosecution is the prosecutor's office;

(e) the court officer is the relevant court office; and

(f) the Registrar of Criminal Appeals is the Criminal Appeal Office, Royal Courts of Justice, Strand, London WC2A 2LL.

Service through a document exchange

4.5 A document may be served by document exchange (DX) where—

(a) the writing paper of the person to be served gives a DX box number; and

(b) that person has not refused to accept service by DX.

Service by fax, e-mail or other electronic means

4.6 (1) A document may be served by fax, e-mail or other electronic means where—

(a) the person to be served has given a fax, e-mail or other electronic address; and

(b) that person has not refused to accept service by that means.

(2) Where a document is served under this rule the person serving it need not provide a paper copy as well.

Documents that must be served only by handing them over, leaving or posting them

4.7 (1) The documents listed in this rule may be served—

(a) on an individual only under rule 4.3(1)(a) or rule 4.4(1) and (2)(a); and

(b) on a corporation only under rule 4.3(1)(b) or rule 4.4(1) and (2)(b).

(2) Those documents are—

(a) a summons, requisition or witness summons;

(b) notice of an order under section 25 of the Road Traffic Offenders Act 1988;

(c) a notice of registration under section 71(6) of that Act;

(d) a notice of discontinuance under section 23(4) of the Prosecution of Offences Act 1985;

(e) notice under rule 37.3(1) of the date, time and place to which the trial of an information has been adjourned, where it was adjourned in the defendant's absence;

(f) a notice of fine or forfeited recognizance required by rule 52.1(1);

(g) notice under section 86 of the Magistrates' Courts Act 1980 of a revised date to attend a means inquiry;

(h) notice of a hearing to review the postponement of the issue of a warrant of commitment under section 77(6) of the Magistrates' Courts Act 1980;

(i) a copy of the minute of a magistrates' court order required by rule 52.7(1);

(j) an invitation to make observations or attend a hearing under rule 53.1(2) on the review of a compensation order under section 133 of the Powers of Criminal Courts (Sentencing) Act 2000;

(k) any notice or document served under Part 19.

Service by person in custody

4.8 (1) A person in custody may serve a document by handing it to the custodian addressed to the person to be served.

(2) The custodian must—

(a) endorse it with the time and date of receipt;

(b) record its receipt; and
(c) forward it promptly to the addressee.

Service by another method

4.9 (1) The court may allow service of a document by a method other than those described in rules 4.3 to 4.6 and in rule 4.8.
(2) An order allowing service by another method must specify—
(a) the method to be used; and
(b) the date on which the document will be served.

Date of service

4.10 (1) A document served under rule 4.3 or rule 4.8 is served on the day it is handed over.
(2) Unless something different is shown, a document served on a person by any other method is served—
(a) in the case of a document left at an address, on the next business day after the day on which it was left;
(b) in the case of a document sent by first class post or by the equivalent of first class post, on the second business day after the day on which it was posted or despatched;
(c) in the case of a document served by document exchange, on the second business day after the day on which it was left at the addressee's DX or at a correspondent DX;
(d) in the case of a document transmitted by fax, e-mail or other electronic means, on the next business day after it was transmitted; and
(e) in any case, on the day on which the addressee responds to it if that is earlier.
(3) Unless something different is shown, a document produced by a court computer system is to be taken as having been sent by first class post or by the equivalent of first class post to the addressee on the business day after the day on which it was produced.
(4) In this Part 'business day' means any day except Saturday, Sunday, Christmas Day, Boxing Day, Good Friday, Easter Monday or a bank holiday.
(5) Where a document is served on or by the court officer, 'business day' does not include a day on which the court office is closed.

Proof of service

4.11 The person who serves a document may prove that by signing a certificate explaining how and when it was served.

Court's power to give directions about service

4.12 (1) The court may specify the time as well as the date by which a document must be—
(a) served under rule 4.3 or rule 4.8; or
(b) transmitted by fax, e-mail or other electronic means if it is served under rule 4.6.
(2) The court may treat a document as served if the addressee responds to it even if it was not served in accordance with the rules in this Part.

Part 5 Forms

Forms

5.1 The forms set out in the Practice Direction shall be used as appropriate in connection with the rules to which they apply.

Magistrates' court forms in Welsh

5.2 (1) Subject to the provisions of this rule, the Welsh language forms set out in the Practice Direction or forms to the like effect may be used in connection with proceedings in magistrates' courts in Wales.
(2) Both a Welsh form and an English form may be used in the same document.
(3) When only a Welsh form set out in the Practice Direction accompanying this rule, or only the corresponding English form, is used in connection with proceedings in magistrates' courts in Wales, there shall be added the following words in Welsh and English:

'Darperir y ddogfen hon yn Gymraeg/Saesneg os bydd arnoch ei heisiau. Dylech wneud cais yn ddi-oed i (Glerc Llys yr Ynadon) (rhodder yma'r cyfeiriad) ....

This document will be provided in Welsh/English if you require it. You should apply immediately to (the Justices' Clerk to the Magistrates' Court) (address)................

If a person other than a justices' clerk is responsible for sending or giving the document, insert that person's name.'

(4) The justices' clerk or other person responsible for the service of a form bearing the additional words set out in paragraph (3) above shall, if any person upon whom the form is served so requests, provide him with the corresponding English or Welsh form.

(5) In this rule any reference to serving a document shall include the sending, giving or other delivery of it.

(6) In the case of a discrepancy between an English and Welsh text the English text shall prevail.

Signature of magistrates' court forms by justices' clerk

5.3 (1) Subject to paragraph (2) below, where any form prescribed by these Rules contains provision for signature by a justice of the peace only, the form shall have effect as if it contained provision in the alternative for signature by the justices' clerk.

(2) This rule shall not apply to any form of information, complaint, statutory declaration or warrant, other than a warrant of commitment or of distress.

(3) In this rule where a signature is required on a form or warrant other than an arrest, remand or commitment warrant, an electronic signature incorporated into the document will satisfy this requirement.

Part 6 Court Records

Magistrates' court register

6.1 (1) A magistrates' court officer shall keep a register in which there shall be entered—

(a) a minute or memorandum of every adjudication of the court; and

(b) a minute or memorandum of every other proceeding or thing required by these Rules or any other enactment to be so entered.

(2) The register may be stored in electronic form on the court computer system and entries in the register shall include, where relevant, the following particulars—

(a) the name of the informant, complainant or applicant;

(b) the name and date of birth (if known) of the defendant or respondent;

(c) the nature of offence, matter of complaint or details of the application;

(d) the date of offence or matter of complaint;

(e) the plea or consent to order; and

(f) the minute of adjudication.

(3) Particulars of any entry relating to a decision about bail or the reasons for any such decisions or the particulars of any certificate granted under section 5(6A) of the Bail Act 1976 may be made in a book separate from that in which the entry recording the decision itself is made, but any such separate book shall be regarded as forming part of the register.

(4) Where, by virtue of section 128(3A) of the Magistrates' Courts Act 1980, an accused gives his consent to the hearing and determination in his absence of any application for his remand on an adjournment of the case under sections 5, 10(1) or 18(4) of that Act, the court shall cause the consent of the accused, and the date on which it was notified to the court, to be entered in the register.

(5) Where any consent mentioned in paragraph (4) is withdrawn, the court shall cause the withdrawal of the consent and the date on which it was notified to the court to be entered in the register.

(6) On the summary trial of an information the accused's plea shall be entered in the register.

(7) Where a court tries any person summarily in any case in which he may be tried summarily only with his consent, the court shall cause his consent to be entered in the register and, if the consent is signified by a person representing him in his absence, the court shall cause that fact also to be entered in the register.

(8) Where a person is charged before a magistrates' court with an offence triable either way the court shall cause the entry in the register to show whether he was present when the proceedings for determining the mode of trial were conducted and, if they were conducted in his absence, whether they were so conducted by virtue of section 18(3) of the 1980 Act (disorderly conduct on his part) or by virtue of section 23(1) of that Act (consent signified by person representing him).

(9) In any case to which section 22 of the 1980 Act (certain offences triable either way to be tried summarily if value involved is small) applies, the court shall cause its decision as to the value

involved or, as the case may be, the fact that it is unable to reach such a decision to be entered in the register.

(10) Where a court has power under section 53(3) of the 1980 Act to make an order with the consent of the defendant without hearing evidence, the court shall cause any consent of the defendant to the making of the order to be entered in the register.

(11) In the case of conviction or dismissal, the register shall clearly show the nature of the offence of which the accused is convicted or, as the case may be, the nature of the offence charged in the information that is dismissed.

(12) An entry of a conviction in the register shall state the date of the offence.

(13) Where a court is required under section 130(3) of the Powers of Criminal Courts (Sentencing) Act 2000 to give reasons for not making a compensation order the court shall cause the reasons given to be entered in the register.

(14) Where a court passes a custodial sentence, the court shall cause a statement of whether it obtained and considered a pre-sentence report before passing sentence to be entered in the register.

(15) Every register shall be open to inspection during reasonable hours by any justice of the peace, or any person authorised in that behalf by a justice of the peace or the Lord Chancellor.

(16) A record of summary conviction or order made on complaint required for an appeal or other legal purpose may be in the form of certified extract from the court register.

(17) Such part of the register as relates to proceedings in a youth court may be recorded separately and stored in electronic form on the court computer system.

Registration of endorsement of licence under section 57 of the Road Traffic Offenders Act 1988

6.2 A magistrates' court officer or justices' clerk who, as a fixed penalty clerk within the meaning of section 69(4) of the Road Traffic Offenders Act 1988, endorses a driving licence under section 57(3) or (4) of that Act (endorsement of licences without hearing) shall register the particulars of the endorsement in a book separate from the register kept under rule 6.1 but any such book shall be regarded as forming part of the register.

Registration of certificate issued under section 70 of the Road Traffic Offenders Act 1988

6.3 A magistrates' court officer shall register receipt of a registration certificate issued under section 70 of the Road Traffic Offenders Act 1988 (sum payable in default of fixed penalty to be enforced as a fine) in a book separate from the register kept under rule 6.1 but any such book shall be regarded as forming part of the register.

Proof of proceedings in magistrates' courts

6.4 The register of a magistrates' court, or an extract from the register certified by the magistrates' court officer as a true extract, shall be admissible in any legal proceedings as evidence of the proceedings of the court entered in the register.

Part 7 Commencing Proceedings in Magistrates' Courts

Information and complaint

7.1 (1) An information may be laid or complaint made by the prosecutor or complainant in person or by his counsel or solicitor or other person authorised in that behalf.

(2) Subject to any provision of the Magistrates' Courts Act 1980 and any other enactment, an information or complaint need not be in writing or on oath.

Statement of offence

7.2 (1) Every written charge issued by a public prosecutor and every information, summons or warrant laid in or issued by a magistrates' court shall be sufficient if it—

(a) describes the offence with which the accused is charged, or of which he is convicted, in ordinary language avoiding as far as possible the use of technical terms; and

(b) gives such particulars as may be necessary to provide reasonable information about the nature of the charge.

(2) It shall not be necessary for any of those documents to—

(a) state all the elements of the offence; or

(b) negative any matter upon which the accused may rely.

(3) If the offence charged is one created by or under any Act, the description of the offence shall contain a reference to the section of the Act, or, as the case may be, the rule, order, regulation, bylaw or other instrument creating the offence.

Information or written charge to be for one offence only

7.3 (1) Subject to any Act passed after 2nd October 1848, a magistrates' court shall not proceed to the trial of an information or written charge that charges more than one offence.

(2) Nothing in this rule shall prohibit two or more informations or written charges being set out in one document.

(3) If, notwithstanding paragraph (1), it appears to the court at any stage in the trial of an information or written charge that the information or written charge charges more than one offence, the court shall call upon the prosecutor to elect on which offence he desires the court to proceed, whereupon the offence or offences on which the prosecutor does not wish to proceed shall be struck out of the information or written charge; and the court shall then proceed to try that information or written charge afresh.

(4) If a prosecutor who is called upon to make an election under paragraph (3) fails to do so, the court shall dismiss the information or written charge.

(5) Where, after an offence has or offences have been struck out of the information or written charge under paragraph (3), the accused requests an adjournment and it appears to the court that he has been unfairly prejudiced, it shall adjourn the trial.

Duty of court officer receiving statutory declaration under section 14(1) of the Magistrates' Courts Act 1980

7.4 Where a magistrates' court officer receives a statutory declaration which complies with section 14(1) of the Magistrates' Courts Act 1980 (accused did not know of proceedings), he shall—

(a) note the receipt of the declaration in the register; and

(b) inform the prosecutor and, if the prosecutor is not a constable, the chief officer of police of the receipt of the declaration.

Notice of order under section 25 of the Road Traffic Offenders Act 1988

7.5 (1) Where a magistrates' court makes an order under section 25 of the Road Traffic Offenders Act 1988 that an offender shall inform the court of his date of birth or sex or both and the offender is not present in court, the court officer shall serve notice in writing of the order on the offender.

Statutory declaration under section 72 and 73 of the Road Traffic Offenders Act 1988

7.6 Where a magistrates' court officer receives a statutory declaration under section 72 and 73 of the Road Traffic Offenders Act 1988 (fixed penalty notice or notice fixed to vehicle invalid) he shall send a copy of it to the appropriate chief officer of police.

Form of summons or requisition

7.7 (1) A summons or requisition must state the name of the justice or public prosecutor issuing it.

(2) A summons or requisition requiring a person to appear before a magistrates' court to answer to an information, written charge or complaint shall state shortly the matter of the information, written charge or complaint and shall state the time and place at which the defendant is required by the summons or requisition to appear.

(3) A single summons or requisition may be issued against a person in respect of several informations, written charges or complaints; but the summons or requisition shall state the matter of each information, written charge or complaint separately and shall have effect as several summonses or requisitions, each issued in respect of one information, written charge or complaint.

(4) In this rule where a signature is required, an electronic signature incorporated into the document shall satisfy this requirement.

Summons or warrant to secure attendance of a parent or guardian at a youth court

7.8 Where a child or young person is charged with an offence, or is for any other reason brought before a court, a summons or warrant may be issued by a court to enforce the attendance of a parent or guardian under section 34A of the Children and Young Persons Act 1933, in the same manner as if an information were laid upon which a summons or warrant could be issued against a defendant under the Magistrates' Courts Act 1980 and a summons to the child or young person may include a summons to the parent or guardian to enforce his attendance for the said purpose.

Magistrates' court officer to have copies of documents sent to accused under section 12(1) of the Magistrates' Courts Act 1980

7.9 Where the prosecutor notifies a magistrates' court officer that the documents mentioned in section 12(1)(a) and 12(1)(b) of the Magistrates' Courts Act 1980 have been served upon the accused, the prosecutor shall send to the court officer a copy of the document mentioned in section 12(1)(b).

Part 8 Objecting to the Discontinuance of Proceedings in a Magistrates' Court

Time for objecting

8.1 The period within which an accused person may give notice under section 23(7) of the Prosecution of Offences Act 1985 that he wants proceedings against him to continue is 35 days from the date when the proceedings were discontinued under that section.

Form of notice

8.2 Notice under section 23(3), (4) or (7) of the Prosecution of Offences Act 1985 shall be given in writing and shall contain sufficient particulars to identify the particular offence to which it relates.

Duty of Director of Public Prosecutions

8.3 On giving notice under section 23(3) or (4) of the Prosecution of Offences Act 1985 the Director of Public Prosecutions shall inform any person who is detaining the accused person for the offence in relation to which the notice is given that he has given such notice and of the effect of the notice.

Duty of magistrates' court

8.4 On being given notice under section 23(3) of the Prosecution of Offences Act 1985 in relation to an offence for which the accused person has been granted bail by a court, a magistrates' court officer shall inform—

(a) any sureties of the accused; and

(b) any persons responsible for securing the accused's compliance with any conditions of bail

that he has been given such notice and of the effect of the notice.

Part 9 Pre-trial Hearings in Magistrates' Courts

[There are currently no rules in this part.]

Part 10 Committal for Trial

Restrictions on reports of committal proceedings

10.1 (1) Except in a case where evidence is, with the consent of the accused, to be tendered in his absence under section 4(4)(b) of the Magistrates' Courts Act 1980 (absence caused by ill health), a magistrates' court acting as examining justices shall before admitting any evidence explain to the accused the restrictions on reports of committal proceedings imposed by section 8 of that Act and inform him of his right to apply to the court for an order removing those restrictions.

(2) Where a magistrates' court has made an order under section 8(2) of the 1980 Act removing restrictions on the reports of committal proceedings, such order shall be entered in the register.

(3) Where the court adjourns any such proceedings to another day, the court shall, at the beginning of any adjourned hearing, state that the order has been made.

Committal for trial without consideration of the evidence

10.2 (1) This rule applies to committal proceedings where the accused has a solicitor acting for him in the case and where the court has been informed that all the evidence falls within section 5A(2) of the Magistrates' Courts Act 1980.

(2) A magistrates' court inquiring into an offence in committal proceedings to which this rule applies shall cause the charge to be written down, if this has not already been done, and read to the accused and shall then ascertain whether he wishes to submit that there is insufficient evidence to put him on trial by jury for the offence with which he is charged.

(3) If the court is satisfied that the accused or, as the case may be, each of the accused does not wish to make such a submission as is referred to in paragraph (2) it shall, after receiving any written evidence falling within section 5A(3) of the 1980 Act, determine whether or not to commit the accused for trial without consideration of the evidence, and where it determines not to so commit the accused it shall proceed in accordance with rule 10.3.

Consideration of evidence at committal proceedings

10.3 (1) This rule does not apply to committal proceedings where under section 6(2) of the Magistrates' Courts Act of 1980 a magistrates' court commits a person for trial without consideration of the evidence.

(2) A magistrates' court inquiring into an offence as examining justices, having ascertained—

(a) that the accused has no legal representative acting for him in the case; or

(b) that the accused's legal representative has requested the court to consider a submission that there is insufficient evidence to put the accused on trial by jury for the offence with which he is charged, as the case may be,

shall permit the prosecutor to make an opening address to the court, if he so wishes, before any evidence is tendered.

(3) After such opening address, if any, the court shall cause evidence to be tendered in accordance with sections 5B(4), 5C(4), 5D(5) and 5E(3) of the 1980 Act, that is to say by being read out aloud, except where the court otherwise directs or to the extent that it directs that an oral account be given of any of the evidence.

(4) The court may view any exhibits produced before the court and may take possession of them.

(5) After the evidence has been tendered the court shall hear any submission which the accused may wish to make as to whether there is sufficient evidence to put him on trial by jury for any indictable offence.

(6) The court shall permit the prosecutor to make a submission—

(a) in reply to any submission made by the accused in pursuance of paragraph (5); or

(b) where the accused has not made any such submission but the court is nevertheless minded not to commit him for trial.

(7) After hearing any submission made in pursuance of paragraph (5) or (6) the court shall, unless it decides not to commit the accused for trial, cause the charge to be written down, if this has not already been done, and, if the accused is not represented by counsel or a solicitor, shall read the charge to him and explain it in ordinary language.

Court's reminder to a defendant of right to object to evidence being read at trial without further proof

10.4 A magistrates' court which commits a person for trial shall forthwith remind him of his right to object, by written notification to the prosecutor and the Crown Court within 14 days of being committed unless that court in its discretion permits such an objection to be made outside that period, to a statement or deposition being read as evidence at the trial without oral evidence being given by the person who made the statement or deposition, and without the opportunity to cross-examine that person.

Material to be sent to court of trial

10.5 (1) As soon as practicable after the committal of any person for trial, and in any case within 4 days from the date of his committal (not counting Saturdays, Sundays, Good Friday, Christmas Day or Bank Holidays), the magistrates' court officer shall, subject to the provisions of section 7 of the Prosecution of Offences Act 1985 (which relates to the sending of documents and things to the Director of Public Prosecutions), send to the Crown Court officer—

(a) the information, if it is in writing;

(b)

(i) the evidence tendered in accordance with section 5A of the Magistrates' Courts Act 1980 and, where any of that evidence consists of a copy of a deposition or documentary exhibit which is in the possession of the court, any such deposition or documentary exhibit, and

(ii) a certificate to the effect that that evidence was so tendered;

(c) any notification by the prosecutor under section 5D(2) of the 1980 Act regarding the admissibility of a statement under section 23 or 24 of the Criminal Justice Act 1988 (first hand hearsay; business documents);

(d) a copy of the record made in pursuance of section 5 of the Bail Act 1976 relating to the grant or withholding of bail in respect of the accused on the occasion of the committal;
(e) any recognizance entered into by any person as surety for the accused together with a statement of any enlargement thereof under section 129(4) of the 1980 Act;
(f) a list of the exhibits produced in evidence before the justices or treated as so produced;
(g) such of the exhibits referred to in paragraph (1)(f) as have been retained by the justices;
(h) the names and addresses of any interpreters engaged for the defendant for the purposes of the committal proceedings, together with any telephone numbers at which they can be readily contacted, and details of the languages or dialects in connection with which they have been so engaged;
(i) if the committal was under section 6(2) of the 1980 Act (committal for trial without consideration of the evidence), a statement to that effect;
(j) if the magistrates' court has made an order under section 8(2) of the 1980 Act (removal of restrictions on reports of committal proceedings), a statement to that effect;
(k) the certificate of the examining justices as to the costs of the prosecution under the Costs in Criminal Cases (General) Regulations 1986;
(l) if any person under the age of 18 is concerned in the committal proceedings, a statement whether the magistrates' court has given a direction under section 39 of the Children and Young Persons Act 1933 (prohibition of publication of certain matter in newspapers);
(m) a copy of any representation order previously made in the case;
(n) a copy of any application for a representation order previously made in the case which has been refused; and
(o) any documents relating to an appeal by the prosecution against the granting of bail.

(2) The period of 4 days specified in paragraph (1) may be extended in relation to any committal for so long as the Crown Court officer directs, having regard to the length of any document mentioned in that paragraph or any other relevant circumstances.

Part II Transfer for Trial of Serious Fraud Cases or Cases Involving Children

Interpretation of this part

11.1 (1) In this Part:
'notice of transfer' means a notice referred to in section 4(1) of the Criminal Justice Act 1987 or section 53(1) of the Criminal Justice Act 1991.
(2) Where this Part requires a document to be given or sent, or a notice to be communicated in writing, it may, with the consent of the addressee, be sent by electronic communication.
(3) Electronic communication means a communication transmitted (whether from one person to another, from one device to another or from a person to a device or vice versa)—
(a) by means of an electronic communications network (within the meaning of the Communications Act 2003); or
(b) by other means but while in an electronic form.

Transfer on bail

11.2 (1) Where a person in respect of whom notice of transfer has been given—
(a) is granted bail under section 5(3) or (7A) of the Criminal Justice Act 1987 by the magistrates' court to which notice of transfer was given; or
(b) is granted bail under paragraph 2(1) or (7) of Schedule 6 to the Criminal Justice Act 1991 by the magistrates' court to which notice of transfer was given,
the magistrates' court officer shall give notice thereof in writing to the governor of the prison or remand centre to which the said person would have been committed by that court if he had been committed in custody for trial.
(2) Where notice of transfer is given under section 4(1) of the 1987 Act in respect of a corporation the magistrates' court officer shall give notice thereof to the governor of the prison to which would be committed a male over 21 committed by that court in custody for trial.

Notice where person removed to hospital

11.3 Where a transfer direction has been given by the Secretary of State under section 47 or 48 of the Mental Health Act 1983 in respect of a person remanded in custody by a magistrates' court and,

before the direction ceases to have effect, notice of transfer is given in respect of that person, the magistrates' court officer shall give notice thereof in writing—
(a) to the governor of the prison to which that person would have been committed by that court if he had been committed in custody for trial; and
(b) to the managers of the hospital where he is detained.

Variation of arrangements for bail

11.4 (1) A person who intends to make an application to a magistrates' court under section 3(8) of the Bail Act 1976 as that subsection has effect under section 3(8A) of that Act shall give notice thereof in writing to the magistrates' court officer, and to the designated authority or the defendant, as the case may be, and to any sureties concerned.
(2) Where, on an application referred to in paragraph (1), a magistrates' court varies or imposes any conditions of bail, the magistrates' court officer shall send to the Crown Court officer a copy of the record made in pursuance of section 5 of the 1976 Act relating to such variation or imposition of conditions.

Documents etc to be sent to Crown Court

11.5 As soon as practicable after a magistrates' court to which notice of transfer has been given has discharged the functions reserved to it under section 4(1) of the Criminal Justice Act 1987 or section 53(3) of the Criminal Justice Act 1991, the magistrates' court officer shall send to the Crown Court officer—
(a) a list of the names, addresses and occupations of the witnesses;
(b) a copy of the record made in pursuance of section 5 of the Bail Act 1976 relating to the grant of withholding of bail in respect of the accused;
(c) any recognizance entered into by any person as surety for the accused together with a statement of any enlargement thereof;
(d) a copy of any representation order previously made in the case; and
(e) a copy of any application for a representation order previously made in the case which has been refused.

Part 12 Sending for Trial

Documents to be sent to the Crown Court

12.1 (1) As soon as practicable after any person is sent for trial (pursuant to section 51 of the Crime and Disorder Act 1998), and in any event within 4 days from the date on which he is sent (not counting Saturdays, Sundays, Good Friday, Christmas Day or Bank Holidays), the magistrates' court officer shall, subject to section 7 of the Prosecution of Offences Act 1985 (which relates to the sending of documents and things to the Director of Public Prosecutions), send to the Crown Court officer—
(a) the information, if it is in writing;
(b) the notice required by section 51(7) of the 1998 Act;
(c) a copy of the record made in pursuance of section 5 of the Bail Act 1976 relating to the granting or withholding of bail in respect of the accused on the occasion of the sending;
(d) any recognizance entered into by any person as surety for the accused together with any enlargement thereof under section 129(4) of the Magistrates' Courts Act 1980;
(e) the names and addresses of any interpreters engaged for the defendant for the purposes of the appearance in the magistrates' court, together with any telephone numbers at which they can be readily contacted, and details of the languages or dialects in connection with which they have been so engaged;
(f) if any person under the age of 18 is concerned in the proceedings, a statement whether the magistrates' court has given a direction under section 39 of the Children and Young Persons Act 1933 (prohibition of publication of certain matter in newspapers);
(g) a copy of any representation order previously made in the case;
(h) a copy of any application for a representation order previously made in the case which has been refused; and
(i) any documents relating to an appeal by the prosecution against the granting of bail.
(2) The period of 4 days specified in paragraph (1) may be extended in relation to any sending for trial for so long as the Crown Court officer directs, having regard to any relevant circumstances.

Time for first appearance of accused sent for trial

12.2 A Crown Court officer to whom notice has been given under section 51(7) of the Crime and Disorder Act 1998, shall list the first Crown Court appearance of the person to whom the notice relates in accordance with any directions given by the magistrates' court.

Part 13 Dismissal of Charges Transferred or Sent to the Crown Court

Interpretation of this Part

13.1 In this Part:

'notice of transfer' means a notice referred to in section 4(1) of the Criminal Justice Act 1987 or section 53(1) of the Criminal Justice Act 1991; and

'the prosecution' means the authority by or on behalf of whom notice of transfer was given under the 1987 or 1991 Acts, or the authority by or on behalf of whom documents were served under paragraph 1 of Schedule 3 to the Crime and Disorder Act 1998.

Written notice of oral application for dismissal

13.2 (1) Where notice of transfer has been given under the Criminal Justice Act 1987 or the Criminal Justice Act 1991, or a person has been sent for trial under the Crime and Disorder Act 1998, and the person concerned proposes to apply orally—

(a) under section 6(1) of the 1987 Act;

(b) under paragraph 5(1) of Schedule 6 to the 1991 Act; or

(c) under paragraph 2(1) of Schedule 3 to the 1998 Act

for any charge in the case to be dismissed, he shall give notice of his intention in writing to the Crown Court officer at the place specified by the notice of transfer under the 1987 or 1991 Acts or the notice given under section 51(7) of the 1998 Act as the proposed place of trial. Notice of intention to make an application under the 1987 or 1991 Acts shall be in the form set out in the Practice Direction.

(2) Notice of intention to make an application shall be given—

(a) in the case of an application to dismiss charges transferred under the 1987 Act, not later than 28 days after the day on which notice of transfer was given;

(b) in the case of an application to dismiss charges transferred under the 1991 Act, not later than 14 days after the day on which notice of transfer was given; and

(c) in the case of an application to dismiss charges sent under the 1998 Act, not later than 14 days after the day on which the documents were served under paragraph 1 of Schedule 3 to that Act,

and a copy of the notice shall be given at the same time to the prosecution and to any person to whom the notice of transfer relates or with whom the applicant for dismissal is jointly charged.

(3) The time for giving notice may be extended, either before or after it expires, by the Crown Court, on an application made in accordance with paragraph (4).

(4) An application for an extension of time for giving notice shall be made in writing to the Crown Court officer, and a copy thereof shall be given at the same time to the prosecution and to any other person to whom the notice of transfer relates or with whom the applicant for dismissal is jointly charged. Such an application made in proceedings under the 1987 or 1991 Acts shall be in the form set out in the Practice Direction.

(5) The Crown Court officer shall give notice in the form set out in the Practice Direction of the judge's decision on an application under paragraph (3)—

(a) to the applicant for dismissal;

(b) to the prosecution; and

(c) to any other person to whom the notice of transfer relates or with whom the applicant for dismissal is jointly charged.

(6) A notice of intention to make an application under section 6(1) of the 1987 Act, paragraph 5(1) of Schedule 6 to the 1991 Act or paragraph 2(1) of Schedule 3 to the 1998 Act shall be accompanied by a copy of any material on which the applicant relies and shall—

(a) specify the charge or charges to which it relates;

(b) state whether the leave of the judge is sought under section 6(3) of the 1987 Act, paragraph 5(4) of Schedule 6 to the 1991 Act or paragraph 2(4) of Schedule 3 to the 1998 Act to adduce oral evidence on the application, indicating what witnesses it is proposed to call at the hearing; and

(c) in the case of a transfer under the 1991 Act, confirm in relation to each such witness that he is not a child to whom paragraph 5(5) of Schedule 6 to that Act applies.

(7) Where leave is sought from the judge for oral evidence to be given on an application, notice of his decision, indicating what witnesses are to be called if leave is granted, shall be given in writing by the Crown Court officer to the applicant for dismissal, the prosecution and to any other person to whom the notice of transfer relates or with whom the applicant for dismissal is jointly charged. Notice of a decision in proceedings under the 1987 or 1991 Acts shall be in the form set out in the Practice Direction.

(8) Where an application for dismissal under section 6(1) of the 1987 Act, paragraph 5(1) of Schedule 6 to the 1991 Act or paragraph 2(1) of Schedule 3 to the 1998 Act is to be made orally, the Crown Court officer shall list the application for hearing before a judge of the Crown Court and the prosecution shall be given the opportunity to be represented at the hearing.

Written application for dismissal

13.3 (1) Application may be made for dismissal under section 6(1) of the Criminal Justice Act 1987, paragraph 5(1) of Schedule 6 to the Criminal Justice Act 1991 or paragraph 2(1) of Schedule 3 to the Crime and Disorder Act 1998 without an oral hearing. Such an application shall be in writing, and in proceedings under the 1987 or 1991 Acts shall be in the form set out in the Practice Direction.

(2) The application shall be sent to the Crown Court officer and shall be accompanied by a copy of any statement or other document, and identify any article, on which the applicant for dismissal relies.

(3) A copy of the application and of any accompanying documents shall be given at the same time to the prosecution and to any other person to whom the notice of transfer relates or with whom the applicant for dismissal is jointly charged.

(4) A written application for dismissal shall be made—

(a) not later than 28 days after the day on which notice of transfer was given under the 1987 Act;

(b) not later than 14 days after the day on which notice of transfer was given under the 1991 Act; or

(c) not later than 14 days after the day on which documents required by paragraph 1 of Schedule 3 to the 1998 Act were served

unless the time for making the application is extended, either before or after it expires, by the Crown Court; and rule 13.2(4) and (5) shall apply for the purposes of this paragraph as if references therein to giving notice of intention to make an oral application were references to making a written application under this rule.

Prosecution reply

13.4 (1) Not later than seven days from the date of service of notice of intention to apply orally for the dismissal of any charge contained in a notice of transfer or based on documents served under paragraph 1 of Schedule 3 to the Crime and Disorder Act 1998, the prosecution may apply to the Crown Court under section 6(3) of the Criminal Justice Act 1987, paragraph 5(4) of Schedule 6 to the Criminal Justice Act 1991 or paragraph 2(4) of Schedule 3 to the 1998 Act for leave to adduce oral evidence at the hearing of the application, indicating what witnesses it is proposed to call.

(2) Not later than seven days from the date of receiving a copy of an application for dismissal under rule 13.3, the prosecution may apply to the Crown Court for an oral hearing of the application.

(3) An application under paragraph (1) or (2) shall be served on the Crown Court officer in writing and, in the case of an application under paragraph (2), shall state whether the leave of the judge is sought to adduce oral evidence and, if so, shall indicate what witnesses it is proposed to call. Where leave is sought to adduce oral evidence under paragraph 5(4) of Schedule 6 to the 1991 Act, the application should confirm in relation to each such witness that he is not a child to whom paragraph 5(5) of that Schedule applies. Such an application in proceedings under the 1987 or 1991 Acts shall be in the form set out in the Practice Direction.

(4) Notice of the judge's determination upon an application under paragraph (1) or (2), indicating what witnesses (if any) are to be called shall be served in writing by the Crown Court officer on the prosecution, on the applicant for dismissal and on any other party to whom the notice of transfer relates or with whom the applicant for dismissal is jointly charged. Such a notice in proceedings under the 1987 or 1991 Acts shall be in the form set out in the Practice Direction.

(5) Where, having received the material specified in rule 13.2 or, as the case may be, rule 13.3, the prosecution proposes to adduce in reply thereto any written comments or any further evidence, the prosecution shall serve any such comments, copies of the statements or other documents outlining the evidence of any proposed witnesses, copies of any further documents and, in the case of an application to dismiss charges transferred under the 1991 Act, copies of any video recordings which it is proposed to tender in evidence, on the Crown Court officer not later than 14 days from the date of receiving the said material, and shall at the same time serve copies thereof on the applicant for dismissal and any other person to whom the notice of transfer relates or with whom the applicant is jointly charged. In the case of a defendant acting in person, copies of video recordings need not be served but shall be made available for viewing by him.

(6) The time for—

(a) making an application under paragraph (1) or (2) above; or

(b) serving any material on the Crown Court officer under paragraph (5) above

may be extended, either before or after it expires, by the Crown Court, on an application made in accordance with paragraph (7) below.

(7) An application for an extension of time under paragraph (6) above shall be made in writing and shall be served on the Crown Court officer, and a copy thereof shall be served at the same time on to the applicant for dismissal and on any other person to whom the notice of transfer relates or with whom the applicant for dismissal is jointly charged. Such an application in proceedings under the 1987 or 1991 Acts shall be in the form set out in the Practice Direction.

Determination of applications for dismissal—procedural matters

13.5 (1) A judge may grant leave for a witness to give oral evidence on an application for dismissal notwithstanding that notice of intention to call the witness has not been given in accordance with the foregoing provisions of this Part.

(2) Where an application for dismissal is determined otherwise than at an oral hearing, the Crown Court officer shall as soon as practicable, send to all the parties to the case written notice of the outcome of the application. Such a notice in proceedings under the 1987 and 1991 Acts shall be in the form set out in the Practice Direction.

Part 14 The Indictment

Signature and service of indictment

14.1 (1) The prosecutor must serve a draft indictment on the Crown Court officer not more than 28 days after—

(a) service on the defendant and on the Crown Court officer of copies of the documents containing the evidence on which the charge or charges are based, in a case where the defendant is sent for trial;

(b) a High Court judge gives permission to serve a draft indictment;

(c) the Court of Appeal orders a retrial; or

(d) the committal or transfer of the defendant for trial.

(2) The Crown Court may extend the time limit, even after it has expired.

(3) Unless the Crown Court otherwise directs, the court officer must—

(a) sign and date the draft, which then becomes an indictment; and

(b) serve a copy of the indictment on all parties.

Form and content of indictment

14.2 (1) An indictment must be in one of the forms set out in the Practice Direction and must contain, in a paragraph called a "count"—

(a) a statement of the offence charged that—

(i) describes the offence in ordinary language, and

(ii) identifies any legislation that creates it; and

(b) such particulars of the conduct constituting the commission of the offence as to make clear what the prosecutor alleges against the defendant.

(2) More than one incident of the commission of the offence may be included in a count if those incidents taken together amount to a course of conduct having regard to the time, place or purpose of commission.

(3) An indictment may contain more than one count if all the offences charged—

(a) are founded on the same facts; or
(b) form or are a part of a series of offences of the same or a similar character.

(4) The counts must be numbered consecutively.

(5) An indictment may contain—
(a) any count charging substantially the same offence as one—
(i) specified in the notice of the offence or offences for which the defendant was sent for trial,
(ii) on which the defendant was committed for trial, or
(iii) specified in the notice of transfer given by the prosecutor; and
(b) any other count based on the prosecution evidence already served which the Crown Court may try.

Part 15 Preparatory Hearings in Cases of Serious Fraud and other Complex or Lengthy Cases in the Crown Court

Application for a preparatory hearing

15.1 (1) A party who wants the court to order a preparatory hearing under section 7(2) of the Criminal Justice Act 1987 or under section 29(4) of the Criminal Procedure and Investigations Act 1996 must—
(a) apply in the form set out in the Practice Direction;
(b) include a short explanation of the reasons for applying; and
(c) serve the application on the court officer and all other parties.

(2) A prosecutor who wants the court to order that—
(a) the trial will be conducted without a jury under section 43 or section 44 of the Criminal Justice Act 2003; or
(b) the trial of some of the counts included in the indictment will be conducted without a jury under section 17 of the Domestic Violence, Crime and Victims Act 2004,

must apply under this rule for a preparatory hearing, whether or not the defendant has applied for one.

Time for applying for a preparatory hearing

15.2 (1) A party who applies under rule 15.1 must do so not more than 28 days after—
(a) the committal of the defendant;
(b) the consent to the preferment of a bill of indictment in relation to the case;
(c) the service of a notice of transfer; or
(d) where a person is sent for trial, the service of copies of the documents containing the evidence on which the charge or charges are based.

(2) A prosecutor who applies under rule 15.1 because he wants the court to order a trial without a jury under section 44 of the Criminal Justice Act 2003 (jury tampering) must do so as soon as reasonably practicable where the reasons do not arise until after that time limit has expired.

(3) The court may extend the time limit, even after it has expired.

Representations concerning an application

15.3 (1) A party who wants to make written representations concerning an application made under rule 15.1 must—
(a) do so within 7 days of receiving a copy of that application; and
(b) serve those representations on the court officer and all other parties.

(2) A defendant who wants to oppose an application for an order that the trial will be conducted without a jury under section 43 or section 44 of the Criminal Justice Act 2003 must serve written representations under this rule, including a short explanation of the reasons for opposing that application.

Determination of an application

15.4 (1) Where an application has been made under rule 15.1(2), the court must hold a preparatory hearing.

(2) Other applications made under rule 15.1 should normally be determined without a hearing.

(3) The court officer must serve on the parties in the case, in the form set out in the Practice Direction—
(a) notice of the determination of an application made under rule 15.1; and

(b) an order for a preparatory hearing made by the court of its own initiative, including one that the court is required to make.

Orders for disclosure by prosecution or defence

15.5 (1) Any disclosure order under section 9 of the Criminal Justice Act 1987, or section 31 of the Criminal Procedure and Investigations Act 1996, must identify any documents that are required to be prepared and served by the prosecutor under that order.

(2) A disclosure order under either of those sections does not require a defendant to disclose who will give evidence, except to the extent that disclosure is required—

(a) by section 6A(2) of the 1996 Act (disclosure of alibi); or

(b) by Part 24 of these Rules (disclosure of expert evidence).

(3) The court officer must serve notice of the order, in the relevant form set out in the Practice Direction, on the parties.

Part 16 Restrictions on Reporting and Public Access

Application for a reporting direction under section 46(6) of the Youth Justice and Criminal Evidence Act 1999

16.1 (1) An application for a reporting direction made by a party to any criminal proceedings, in relation to a witness in those proceedings, must be made in the form set out in the Practice Direction or orally under rule 16.3.

(2) If an application for a reporting direction is made in writing, the applicant shall send that application to the court officer and copies shall be sent at the same time to every other party to those proceedings.

Opposing an application for a reporting direction under section 46(6) of the Youth Justice and Criminal Evidence Act 1999

16.2 (1) If an application for a reporting direction is made in writing, any party to the proceedings who wishes to oppose that application must notify the applicant and the court officer in writing of his opposition and give reasons for it.

(2) A person opposing an application must state in the written notification whether he disputes that the—

(a) witness is eligible for protection under section 46 of the Youth Justice and Criminal Evidence Act 1999; or

(b) granting of protection would be likely to improve the quality of the evidence given by the witness or the level of co-operation given by the witness to any party to the proceedings in connection with that party's preparation of its case.

(3) The notification under paragraph (1) must be given within five business days of the date the application was served on him unless an extension of time is granted under rule 16.6.

Urgent action on an application under section 46(6) of the Youth Justice and Criminal Evidence Act 1999

16.3 (1) The court may give a reporting direction under section 46 of the Youth Justice and Criminal Evidence Act 1999 in relation to a witness in those proceedings, notwithstanding that the five business days specified in rule 16.2(3) have not expired if—

(a) an application is made to it for the purposes of this rule; and

(b) it is satisfied that, due to exceptional circumstances, it is appropriate to do so.

(2) Any party to the proceedings may make the application under paragraph (1) whether or not an application has already been made under rule 16.1.

(3) An application under paragraph (1) may be made orally or in writing.

(4) If an application is made orally, the court may hear and take into account representations made to it by any person who in the court's view has a legitimate interest in the application before it.

(5) The application must specify the exceptional circumstances on which the applicant relies.

Excepting direction under section 46(9) of the Youth Justice and Criminal Evidence Act 1999

16.4 (1) An application for an excepting direction under section 46(9) of the Youth Justice and Criminal Evidence Act 1999 (a direction dispensing with restrictions imposed by a reporting direction) may be made by—

(a) any party to those proceedings; or

(b) any person who, although not a party to the proceedings, is directly affected by a reporting direction given in relation to a witness in those proceedings.

(2) If an application for an excepting direction is made, the applicant must state why—
   (a) the effect of a reporting direction imposed places a substantial and unreasonable restriction on the reporting of the proceedings; and
   (b) it is in the public interest to remove or relax those restrictions.

(3) An application for an excepting direction may be made in writing, pursuant to paragraph (4), at any time after the commencement of the proceedings in the court or orally at a hearing of an application for a reporting direction.

(4) If the application for an excepting direction is made in writing it must be in the form set out in the Practice Direction and the applicant shall send that application to the court officer and copies shall be sent at the same time to every party to those proceedings.

(5) Any person served with a copy of an application for an excepting direction who wishes to oppose it, must notify the applicant and the court officer in writing of his opposition and give reasons for it.

(6) The notification under paragraph (5) must be given within five business days of the date the application was served on him unless an extension of time is granted under rule 16.6.

Variation or revocation of a reporting or excepting direction under section 46 of the Youth Justice and Criminal Evidence Act 1999

16.5 (1) An application for the court to—
   (a) revoke a reporting direction; or
   (b) vary or revoke an excepting direction,

may be made to the court at any time after the commencement of the proceedings in the court.

(2) An application under paragraph (1) may be made by a party to the proceedings in which the direction was issued, or by a person who, although not a party to those proceedings, is in the opinion of the court directly affected by the direction.

(3) An application under paragraph (1) must be made in writing and the applicant shall send that application to the officer of the court in which the proceedings commenced, and at the same time copies of the application shall be sent to every party or, as the case may be, every party to the proceedings.

(4) The applicant must set out in his application the reasons why he seeks to have the direction varied or, as the case may be, revoked.

(5) Any person served with a copy of an application who wishes to oppose it, must notify the applicant and the court officer in writing of his opposition and give reasons for it.

(6) The notification under paragraph (5) must be given within five business days of the date the application was served on him unless an extension of time is granted under rule 16.6.

Application for an extension of time in proceedings under section 46 of the Youth Justice and Criminal Evidence Act 1999

16.6 (1) An application may be made in writing to extend the period of time for notification under rule 16.2(3), rule 16.4(6) or rule 16.5(6) before that period has expired.

(2) An application must be accompanied by a statement setting out the reasons why the applicant is unable to give notification within that period.

(3) An application must be sent to the court officer and a copy of the application must be sent at the same time to the applicant.

Decision of the court on an application under section 46 of the Youth Justice and Criminal Evidence Act 1999

16.7 (1) The court may—
   (a) determine any application made under rules 16.1 and rules 16.3 to 16.6 without a hearing; or
   (b) direct a hearing of any application.

(2) The court officer shall notify all the parties of the court's decision as soon as reasonably practicable.

(3) If a hearing of an application is to take place, the court officer shall notify each party to the proceedings of the time and place of the hearing.

(4) A court may hear and take into account representations made to it by any person who in the court's view has a legitimate interest in the application before it.

Proceedings sent or transferred to the Crown Court with direction under section 46 of the Youth Justice and Criminal Evidence Act 1999 in force

16.8 Where proceedings in which reporting directions or excepting directions have been ordered are sent or transferred from a magistrates' court to the Crown Court, the magistrates' court officer shall forward copies of all relevant directions to the Crown Court officer at the place to which the proceedings are sent or transferred.

Hearings in camera and applications under section 46 of the Youth Justice and Criminal Evidence Act 1999

16.9 If in any proceedings, a prosecutor or defendant has served notice under rule 16.10 of his intention to apply for an order that all or part of a trial be held in camera, any application under this Part relating to a witness in those proceedings need not identify the witness by name and date of birth.

Application to hold a Crown Court trial in camera

16.10 (1) Where a prosecutor or a defendant intends to apply for an order that all or part of a trial be held in camera for reasons of national security or for the protection of the identity of a witness or any other person, he shall not less than 7 days before the date on which the trial is expected to begin serve a notice in writing to that effect on the Crown Court officer and the prosecutor or the defendant as the case may be.

(2) On receiving such notice, the court officer shall forthwith cause a copy thereof to be displayed in a prominent place within the precincts of the Court.

(3) An application by a prosecutor or a defendant who has served such a notice for an order that all or part of a trial be heard in camera shall, unless the Court orders otherwise, be made in camera, after the defendant has been arraigned but before the jury has been sworn and, if such an order is made, the trial shall be adjourned until whichever of the following shall be appropriate—

(a) 24 hours after the making of the order, where no application for leave to appeal from the order is made; or

(b) after the determination of an application for leave to appeal, where the application is dismissed; or

(c) after the determination of the appeal, where leave to appeal is granted.

Crown Court hearings in chambers

16.11 (1) The criminal jurisdiction of the Crown Court specified in the following paragraph may be exercised by a judge of the Crown Court sitting in chambers.

(2) The said jurisdiction is—

(a) hearing applications for bail;

(b) issuing a summons or warrant;

(c) hearing any application relating to procedural matters preliminary or incidental to criminal proceedings in the Crown Court, including applications relating to legal aid;

(d) jurisdiction under rules 12.2 (listing first appearance of accused sent for trial), 28.3 (application for witness summons), 63.2(5) (extending time for appeal against decision of magistrates' court), and 64.7 (application to state case for consideration of High Court);

(e) hearing an application under section 41(2) of the Youth Justice and Criminal Evidence Act 1999 (evidence of complainant's previous sexual history);

(f) hearing applications under section 22(3) of the Prosecution of Offences Act 1985 (extension or further extension of custody time limit imposed by regulations made under section 22(1) of that Act);

(g) hearing an appeal brought by an accused under section 22(7) of the 1985 Act against a decision of a magistrates' court to extend, or further extend, such a time limit, or brought by the prosecution under section 22(8) of the same Act against a decision of a magistrates' court to refuse to extend, or further extend, such a time limit;

(h) hearing appeals under section 1 of the Bail (Amendment) Act 1993 (against grant of bail by magistrates' court); and

(i) hearing appeals under section 16 of the Criminal Justice Act 2003 (against condition of bail imposed by magistrates' court).

Part 17 Extradition

Refusal to make an order of committal

17.1 (1) Where a magistrates' court refuses to make an order of committal in relation to a person in respect of the offence or, as the case may be, any of the offences to which the authority to proceed relates and the state, country or colony seeking the surrender of that person immediately informs the court that it intends to make an application to the court to state a case for the opinion of the High Court, if the magistrates' court makes an order in accordance with section 10(2) of the Extradition Act 1989 releasing that person on bail, the court officer shall forthwith send a copy of that order to the Administrative Court Office.

(2) Where a magistrates' court refuses to make an order of committal in relation to a person in respect of the offence or, as the case may be, any of the offences to which the authority to proceed relates and the state, country or colony seeking his surrender wishes to apply to the court to state a case for the opinion of the High Court under section 10(1) of the 1989 Act, such application must be made to the magistrates' court within the period of 21 days following the day on which the court refuses to make the order of committal unless the court grants a longer period within which the application is to be made.

(3) Such an application shall be made in writing and shall identify the question or questions of law on which the opinion of the High Court is sought.

(4) Within 21 days after receipt of an application to state a case under section 10(1) of the 1989 Act, the magistrates' court officer shall send a draft case to the solicitor for the state, country or colony and to the person whose surrender is sought or his solicitor and shall allow each party 21 days within which to make representations thereon; within 21 days after the latest day on which such representations may be made the court of committal shall, after considering any such representations and making such adjustments, if any, to the draft case as it thinks fit, state and sign the case which the court officer shall forthwith send to the solicitor for the state, country or colony.

Notice of waiver

17.2 (1) A notice given under section 14 of, or paragraph 9 of Schedule 1 to, the Extradition Act 1989 (notice of waiver under the simplified procedure) shall be in the form set out in the Practice Direction or a form to the like effect.

(2) Such a notice shall be signed in the presence of the Senior District Judge (Chief Magistrate) or another District Judge (Magistrates' Courts) designated by him for the purposes of the Act, a justice of the peace or a justices' clerk.

(3) Any such notice given by a person in custody shall be delivered to the Governor of the prison in whose custody he is.

(4) If a person on bail gives such notice he shall deliver it to, or send it by post in a registered letter or by recorded delivery service addressed to, the Under Secretary of State, Home Office, London SW1H 9AT.

Notice of consent

17.3 (1) A person arrested in pursuance of a warrant under section 8 of or paragraph 5 of Schedule 1 to the Extradition Act 1989 may at any time consent to his return; and where such consent is given in accordance with the following provisions of this rule, the Senior District Judge (Chief Magistrate) or another District Judge (Magistrates' Courts) designated by him for the purposes of the Act may order the committal for return of that person in accordance with section 14(2) of that Act or, as the case may be, paragraph 9(2) of Schedule 1 to the Act.

(2) A notice of consent for the purposes of this rule shall be given in the form set out in the Practice Direction and shall be signed in the presence of the Senior District Judge (Chief Magistrate) or another District Judge (Magistrates' Courts) designated by him for the purposes of the 1989 Act.

Notice of consent (parties to 1995 Convention)

17.4 (1) This rule applies as between the United Kingdom and states other than the Republic of Ireland that are parties to the Convention drawn up on the basis of Article 31 of the Treaty on European Union on Simplified Extradition Procedures between the Member States of the European Union, in relation to which section 14A of the Extradition Act 1989 applies by virtue of section 34A and Schedule 1A of that Act.

(2) Notice of consent for the purposes of section 14A(3) of the 1989 Act shall be given in the form set out in the Practice Direction and shall be signed in the presence of the Senior District Judge (Chief Magistrate) or another District Judge (Magistrates' Courts) designated by him for the purposes of that Act.

(3) A Senior District Judge (Chief Magistrate) or another District Judge (Magistrates' Courts) designated by him for the purposes of the Act may order the committal for return of a person

if he gives consent under section 14A of the 1989 Act in accordance with paragraph (2) above before he is committed under section 9 of that Act.

Consent to early removal to Republic of Ireland

17.5 (1) A notice given under section 3(1)(a) of the Backing of Warrants (Republic of Ireland) Act 1965 (consent to surrender earlier than is otherwise permitted) shall be signed in the presence of a justice of the peace or a justices' clerk.

(2) Any such notice given by a person in custody shall be delivered to the Governor of the prison in whose custody he is.

(3) If a person on bail gives such notice, he shall deliver it to, or send it by post in a registered letter or by recorded delivery service addressed to, the police officer in charge of the police station specified in his recognizance.

(4) Any such notice shall be attached to the warrant ordering the surrender of that person.

Bail pending removal to Republic of Ireland

17.6 (1) The person taking the recognizance of a person remanded on bail under section 2(1) or 4(3) of the Backing of Warrants (Republic of Ireland) Act 1965 shall furnish a copy of the recognizance to the police officer in charge of the police station specified in the recognizance.

(2) The court officer for a magistrates' court which ordered a person to be surrendered and remanded him on bail shall deliver to, or send by post in a registered letter or by recorded delivery service addressed to, the police officer in charge of the police station specified in the recognizance the warrant ordering the person to be surrendered.

(3) The court officer for a magistrates' court which refused to order a person to be delivered under section 2 of the 1965 Act but made an order in accordance with section 2A(2) of that Act releasing that person on bail, upon the chief officer of police immediately informing the court that he intended to make an application to the court to state a case for the opinion of the High Court, shall forthwith send a copy of that order to the Administrative Court Office.

Delivery of warrant issued in Republic of Ireland

17.7 (1) The court officer for a magistrates' court which ordered a person to be surrendered under section 2(1) of the Backing of Warrants (Republic of Ireland) Act 1965 shall deliver to, or send by post in a registered letter or by recorded delivery service addressed to—

(a) if he is remanded in custody under section 5(1)(a) of the 1965 Act, the prison Governor to whose custody he is committed;

(b) if he is remanded on bail under section 5(1)(b) of the 1965 Act, the police officer in charge of the police station specified in the recognizance; or

(c) if he is committed to the custody of a constable pending the taking from him of a recognizance under section 5(1) of the 1965 Act, the police officer in charge of the police station specified in the warrant of commitment,

the warrant of arrest issued by a judicial authority in the Republic of Ireland and endorsed in accordance with section 1 of the 1965 Act.

(2) The Governor or police officer to whom the said warrant of arrest is delivered or sent shall arrange for it to be given to the member of the police force of the Republic into whose custody the person is delivered when the person is so delivered.

Verification of warrant etc. issued in Republic of Ireland

17.8 (1) A document purporting to be a warrant issued by a judicial authority in the Republic of Ireland shall, for the purposes of section 7(a) of the Backing of Warrants (Republic of Ireland) Act 1965, be verified by a certificate purporting to be signed by a judicial authority, a clerk of a court or a member of the police force of the Republic and certifying that the document is a warrant and is issued by a judge or justice of a court or a peace commissioner.

(2) A document purporting to be a copy of a summons issued by a judicial authority in the Republic shall, for the purposes of section 7(a) of the 1965 Act, be verified by a certificate purporting to be signed by a judicial authority, a clerk of a court or a member of the police force of the Republic and certifying that the document is a true copy of such a summons.

(3) A deposition purporting to have been made in the Republic, or affidavit or written statement purporting to have been sworn therein, shall, for the purposes of section 7(c) of the 1965

Act, be verified by a certificate purporting to be signed by the person before whom it was sworn and certifying that it was so sworn.

Application to state a case where court declines to order removal to Republic of Ireland

17.9 (1) Where a magistrates' court refuses to make an order in relation to a person under section 2 of the Backing of Warrants (Republic of Ireland) Act 1965, any application to the court under section 2A(1) of that Act to state a case for the opinion of the High Court on any question of law arising in the proceedings must be made to the court by the chief officer of police within the period of 21 days following the day on which the order was refused, unless the court grants a longer period within which the application is to be made.

(2) Such an application shall be made in writing and shall identify the question or questions of law on which the opinion of the High Court is sought.

Draft case where court declines to order removal to Republic of Ireland

17.10 Within 21 days after receipt of an application to state a case under section 2A(1) of the Backing of Warrants (Republic of Ireland) Act 1965, the magistrates' court officer shall send a draft case to the applicant or his solicitor and to the person to whom the warrant relates or his solicitor and shall allow each party 21 days within which to make representations thereon; within 21 days after the latest day on which such representations may be made the court shall, after considering such representations and making such adjustments, if any, to the draft case as it thinks fit, state and sign the case which the court officer shall forthwith send to the applicant or his solicitor.

Forms for proceedings for removal to Republic of Ireland

17.11 Where a requirement is imposed by the Backing of Warrants (Republic of Ireland) Act 1965 for the use of a form, and an appropriate form is contained in the Practice Direction, that form shall be used.

Part 18 Warrants

Scope of this Part and interpretation

18.1 (1) This Part applies to any warrant issued by a justice of the peace.

(2) Where a rule applies to some of those warrants and not others, it says so.

(3) In this Part, the 'relevant person' is the person against whom the warrant is issued.

Warrants must be signed

18.2 Every warrant under the Magistrates' Courts Act 1980 must be signed by the justice issuing it, unless rule 5.3 permits the justices' clerk to sign it.

Warrants issued when the court office is closed

18.3 (1) If a warrant is issued when the court office is closed, the applicant must—

(a) serve on the court officer any information on which that warrant is issued; and

(b) do so within 72 hours of that warrant being issued.

(2) In this rule, the court office is the officc foı the local justice area in which the justice is acting when he issues the warrant.

Commitment to custody must be by warrant

18.4 A justice of the peace must issue a warrant of commitment when committing a person to—

(a) a prison;

(b) a young offender institution;

(c) a remand centre;

(d) detention at a police station under section 128(7) of the Magistrates' Courts Act 1980; or

(e) customs detention under section 152 of the Criminal Justice Act 1988.

Terms of a warrant of arrest

18.5 A warrant of arrest must require the persons to whom it is directed to arrest the relevant person.

Terms of a warrant of commitment or detention: general rules

18.6 (1) A warrant of commitment or detention must require—

(a) the persons to whom it is directed to—

(i) arrest the relevant person, if he is at large,

(ii) take him to the prison or place specified in the warrant, and

(iii) deliver him with the warrant to the governor or keeper of that prison or place; and

(b) the governor or keeper to keep the relevant person in custody at that prison or place—

(i) for as long as the warrant requires, or

(ii) until he is delivered, in accordance with the law, to the court or other proper place or person.

(2) Where the justice issuing a warrant of commitment or detention is aware that the relevant person is already detained in a prison or other place of detention, the warrant must be delivered to the governor or keeper of that prison or place.

Terms of a warrant committing a person to customs detention

18.7 (1) A warrant committing a person to customs detention under section 152 of the 1988 Act must—

(a) be directed to the officers of Her Majesty's Revenue and Customs; and

(b) require those officers to keep the person committed in their custody, unless in the meantime he be otherwise delivered, in accordance with the law, to the court or other proper place or person, for a period (not exceeding 192 hours) specified in the warrant.

(2) Rules 18.6(1), 18.10 and 18.12 do not apply where this rule applies.

Form of warrant where male aged 15 or 16 is committed

18.8 (1) This rule applies where a male aged 15 or 16 years is remanded or committed to—

(a) local authority accommodation, with a requirement that he be placed and kept in secure accommodation;

(b) a remand centre; or

(c) a prison.

(2) The court must include in the warrant of commitment a statement of any declaration that is required in connection with that remand or committal.

Information to be included in a warrant

18.9 A warrant of arrest, commitment or detention must contain the following information—

(a) the name or a description of the relevant person; and

(b) either—

(i) a statement of the offence with which the relevant person is charged,

(ii) a statement of the offence of which the person to be committed or detained was convicted; or

(iii) any other ground on which the warrant is issued.

Persons who may execute a warrant

18.10 A warrant of arrest, commitment or detention may be executed by—

(a) the persons to whom it is directed; or

(b) by any of the following persons, whether or not it was directed to them—

(i) a constable for any police area in England and Wales, acting in his own police area, and

(ii) any person authorised under section 125A (civilian enforcement officers) or section 125B (approved enforcement agencies) of the Magistrates' Courts Act 1980.

Making an arrest under a warrant

18.11 (1) The person executing a warrant of arrest, commitment or detention must, when arresting the relevant person—

(a) either—

(i) show the warrant (if he has it with him) to the relevant person, or

(ii) tell the relevant person where the warrant is and what arrangements can be made to let that person inspect it;

(b) explain, in ordinary language, the charge and the reason for the arrest; and

(c) (unless he is a constable in uniform) show documentary proof of his identity.

(2) If the person executing the warrant is one of the persons referred to in rule 18.10(b)(ii) (civilian enforcement officers or approved enforcement agencies), he must also show the relevant person a written statement under section 125A(4) or section 125B(4) of the Magistrates' Courts Act 1980, as appropriate.

Place of detention

18.12 (1) This rule applies to any warrant of commitment or detention.

(2) The person executing the warrant is required to take the relevant person to the prison or place of detention specified in the warrant.
(3) But where it is not immediately practicable to do so, or where there is some other good reason, the relevant person may be taken to any prison or place where he may be lawfully detained until such time when he can be taken to the prison or place specified in the warrant.
(4) If (and for as long as) the relevant person is detained in a place other than the one specified in the warrant, the warrant will have effect as if it specified the place where he is in fact being detained.
(5) The court must be kept informed of the prison or place where the relevant person is in fact being detained.
(6) The governor or keeper of the prison or place, to which the relevant person is delivered, must give a receipt on delivery.

Duration of detention where bail is granted subject to pre-release conditions

18.13 (1) This rule applies where a magistrates' court—
(a) grants bail to a person subject to conditions which must be met prior to release on bail; and
(b) commits that person to custody until those conditions are satisfied.
(2) The warrant of commitment must require the governor or keeper of the prison or place of detention to bring the relevant person to court either before or at the end of a period of 8 clear days from the date the warrant was issued, unless section 128(3A) or section 128A of the Magistrates' Courts Act 1980 applies to permit a longer period.

Validity of warrants that contain errors

18.14 A warrant of commitment or detention will not be invalidated on the ground that it contains an error, provided that the warrant—
(a) is issued in relation to a valid—
(i) conviction, or
(ii) order requiring the relevant person to do, or to abstain from doing, something; and
(b) it states that it is issued in relation to that conviction or order.

Circumstances in which a warrant will cease to have effect

18.15 (1) A warrant issued under any of the provisions listed in paragraph (2) will cease to have effect when—
(a) the sum in respect of which the warrant is issued (together with the costs and charges of commitment, if any) is paid to the person who is executing the warrant;
(b) that sum is offered to, but refused by, the person who is executing the warrant; or
(c) a receipt for that sum given by—
(i) the court officer for the court which issued the warrant, or
(ii) the charging or billing authority,
is produced to the person who is executing the warrant.
(2) Those provisions are—
(a) section 76 (warrant to enforce fines and other sums);
(b) section 83(1) and (2) (warrant to secure attendance of offender for purposes of section 82);
(c) section 86(4) (warrant to arrest offender following failure to appear on day fixed for means inquiry);
(d) section 136 (committal to custody overnight at police station), of the Magistrates' Courts Act 1980.
(3) No person may execute, or continue to execute, a warrant that ceases to have effect under this rule.

Warrant endorsed for bail (record to be kept)

18.16 A person executing a warrant of arrest that is endorsed for bail under section 117 of the Magistrates' Courts Act 1980 must—
(a) make a record stating—
(i) the name of the person arrested,
(ii) the charge and the reason for the arrest,
(iii) the fact that the person is to be released on bail,
(iv) the date, time and place at which the person is required to appear before the court, and

(v) any other details which he considers to be relevant; and

(b) after making the record—

(i) sign the record,

(ii) invite the person arrested to sign the record and, if they refuse, make a note of that refusal on the record,

(iii) make a copy of the record and give it to the person arrested, and

(iv) send the original record to the court officer for the court which issued the warrant.

Part 19 Bail in Magistrates' Courts and the Crown Court

Application to a magistrates' court to vary conditions of police bail

19.1 (1) An application under section 43B(1) of the Magistrates' Courts Act of 1980 or section 47(1E) of the Police and Criminal Evidence Act 1984 shall—

(a) be made in writing;

(b) contain a statement of the grounds upon which it is made;

(c) specify the offence with which the applicant was charged before his release on bail;

(d) where the applicant has been bailed following charge, specify the offence with which he was charged and, in any other case, specify the offence under investigation; and

(e) specify the name and address of any surety provided by the applicant before his release on bail to secure his surrender to custody.

(2) Any such application shall be sent to the court officer for—

(a) the magistrates' court appointed by the custody officer as the court before which the applicant has a duty to appear; or

(b) if no such court has been appointed, a magistrates' court acting for the local justice area in which the police station at which the applicant was granted bail or at which the conditions of his bail were varied, as the case may be, is situated.

(3) The court officer to whom an application is sent under paragraph (2) above shall serve notice in writing of the date, time and place fixed for the hearing of the application on—

(a) the applicant;

(b) the prosecutor or, if the applicant has not been charged, the chief officer of police or other investigator, together with a copy of the application; and

(c) any surety in connection with bail in criminal proceedings granted to, or the conditions of which were varied by a custody officer in relation to, the applicant.

(4) The time fixed for the hearing shall be not later than 72 hours after receipt of the application. In reckoning for the purposes of this paragraph any period of 72 hours, no account shall be taken of Christmas Day, Boxing Day, Good Friday, any bank holiday, or any Saturday or Sunday.

(5) [Revoked.]

(6) If the magistrates' court hearing an application under section 43B(1) of the 1980 Act or section 47(1E) of the 1984 Act discharges or enlarges any recognizance entered into by any surety or increases or reduces the amount in which that person is bound, the court officer shall forthwith give notice thereof to the applicant and to any such surety.

(7) In this rule, 'the applicant' means the person making an application under section 43B(1) of the 1980 Act or section 47(1E) of the 1984 Act.

Application to a magistrates' court to reconsider grant of police bail

19.2 (1) The appropriate court for the purposes of section 5B of the Bail Act 1976 in relation to the decision of a constable to grant bail shall be—

(a) the magistrates' court appointed by the custody officer as the court before which the person to whom bail was granted has a duty to appear; or

(b) if no such court has been appointed, a magistrates' court acting for the local justice area in which the police station at which bail was granted is situated.

(2) An application under section 5B(1) of the 1976 Act shall—

(a) be made in writing;

(b) contain a statement of the grounds on which it is made;

(c) specify the offence which the proceedings in which bail was granted were connected with, or for;

(d) specify the decision to be reconsidered (including any conditions of bail which have been imposed and why they have been imposed)

(e) specify the name and address of any surety provided by the person to whom the application relates to secure his surrender to custody; and

(f) contain a notice of the powers available to the court under section 5B of the 1976 Act.

(3) The court officer to whom an application is sent under paragraph (2) above shall serve notice in writing of the date, time and place fixed for the hearing of the application on—

(a) the prosecutor who made the application;

(b) the person to whom bail was granted, together with a copy of the application; and

(c) any surety specified in the application.

(4) The time fixed for the hearing shall be not later than 72 hours after receipt of the application. In reckoning for the purpose of this paragraph any period of 72 hours, no account shall be taken of Christmas Day, Good Friday, any bank holiday or any Sunday.

(5) [Revoked.]

(6) At the hearing of an application under section 5B of the 1976 Act the court shall consider any representations made by the person affected (whether in writing or orally) before taking any decision under that section with respect to him; and, where the person affected does not appear before the court, the court shall not take such a decision unless it is proved to the satisfaction of the court, on oath or in the manner set out by rule 4.2(1), that the notice required to be given under paragraph (3) of this rule was served on him before the hearing.

(7) Where the court proceeds in the absence of the person affected in accordance with paragraph (6)—

(a) if the decision of the court is to vary the conditions of bail or impose conditions in respect of bail which has been granted unconditionally, the court officer shall notify the person affected;

(b) if the decision of the court is to withhold bail, the order of the court under section 5B(5)(b) of the 1976 Act (surrender to custody) shall be signed by the justice issuing it or state his name and be authenticated by the signature of the clerk of the court.

Notice of change of time for appearance before magistrates' court

19.3 Where—

(a) a person has been granted bail under the Police and Criminal Evidence Act 1984 subject to a duty to appear before a magistrates' court and the court before which he is to appear appoints a later time at which he is to appear; or

(b) a magistrates' court further remands a person on bail under section 129 of the Magistrates' Courts Act 1980 in his absence,

it shall give him and his sureties, if any, notice thereof.

Directions by a magistrates' court as to security, etc

19.4 Where a magistrates' court, under section 3(5) or (6) of the Bail Act 1976, imposes any requirement to be complied with before a person's release on bail, the court may give directions as to the manner in which and the person or persons before whom the requirement may be complied with.

Requirements to be complied with before release on bail granted by a magistrates' court

19.5 (1) Where a magistrates' court has fixed the amount in which a person (including any surety) is to be bound by a recognizance, the recognizance may be entered into—

(a) in the case of a surety where the accused is in a prison or other place of detention, before the governor or keeper of the prison or place as well as before the persons mentioned in section 8(4)(a) of the Bail Act 1976;

(b) in any other case, before a justice of the peace, a justices' clerk, a magistrates' court officer, a police officer who either is of the rank of inspector or above or is in charge of a police station or, if the person to be bound is in a prison or other place of detention, before the governor or keeper of the prison or place; or

(c) where a person other than a police officer is authorised under section 125A or 125B of the Magistrates' Courts Act 1980 to execute a warrant of arrest providing for a recognizance to be entered into by the person arrested (but not by any other person), before the person executing the warrant.

(2) The court officer for a magistrates' court which has fixed the amount in which a person (including any surety) is to be bound by a recognizance or, under section 3(5), (6) or (6A) of the 1976 Act imposed any requirement to be complied with before a person's release on bail or any condition of bail shall issue a certificate showing the amount and conditions, if any, of the recognizance, or as the case may be, containing a statement of the requirement or

condition of bail; and a person authorised to take the recognizance or do anything in relation to the compliance with such requirement or condition of bail shall not be required to take or do it without production of such a certificate as aforesaid.

(3) If any person proposed as a surety for a person committed to custody by a magistrates' court produces to the governor or keeper of the prison or other place of detention in which the person so committed is detained a certificate to the effect that he is acceptable as a surety, signed by any of the justices composing the court or the clerk of the court and signed in the margin by the person proposed as surety, the governor or keeper shall take the recognizance of the person so proposed.

(4) Where the recognizance of any person committed to custody by a magistrates' court or of any surety of such a person is taken by any person other than the court which committed the first-mentioned person to custody, the person taking the recognizance shall send it to the court officer for that court:

Provided that, in the case of a surety, if the person committed has been committed to the Crown Court for trial or under any of the enactments mentioned in rule 43.1(1), the person taking the recognizance shall send it to the Crown Court officer.

Notice to governor of prison, etc, where release from custody is ordered by a magistrates' court

19.6 Where a magistrates' court has, with a view to the release on bail of a person in custody, fixed the amount in which he or any surety of such a person shall be bound or, under section 3(5), (6) or (6A) of the Bail Act 1976, imposed any requirement to be complied with before his release or any condition of bail—

(a) the magistrates' court officer shall give notice thereof to the governor or keeper of the prison or place where that person is detained by sending him such a certificate as is mentioned in rule 19.5(2); and

(b) any person authorised to take the recognizance of a surety or do anything in relation to the compliance with such requirement shall, on taking or doing it, send notice thereof by post to the said governor or keeper and, in the case of a recognizance of a surety, shall give a copy of the notice to the surety.

Release when notice received by governor of prison that recognizances have been taken or requirements complied with

19.7 Where a magistrates' court has, with a view to the release on bail of a person in custody, fixed the amount in which he or any surety of such a person shall be bound or, under section 3(5) or (6) of the Bail Act 1976, imposed any requirement to be complied with before his release and given notice thereof in accordance with this Part to the governor or keeper of the prison or place where that person is detained, the governor or keeper shall, when satisfied that the recognizances of all sureties required have been taken and that all such requirements have been complied with, and unless he is in custody for some other cause, release him.

Notice from a magistrates' court of enlargement of recognizances

19.8 (1) If a magistrates' court before which any person is bound by a recognizance to appear enlarges the recognizance to a later time under section 129 of the Magistrates' Courts Act 1980 in his absence, it shall give him and his sureties, if any, notice thereof.

(2) If a magistrates' court, under section 129(4) of the 1980 Act, enlarges the recognizance of a surety for a person committed for trial on bail, it shall give the surety notice thereof.

Further remand of minors by a youth court

19.9 Where a child or young person has been remanded, and the period of remand is extended in his absence in accordance with section 48 of the Children and Young Persons Act 1933, notice shall be given to him and his sureties (if any) of the date at which he will be required to appear before the court.

Notes of argument in magistrates' court bail hearings

19.10 Where a magistrates' court hears full argument as to bail, the clerk of the court shall take a note of that argument.

Bail records to be entered in register of magistrates' court

19.11 Any record required by section 5 of the Bail Act 1976 to be made by a magistrates' court (together with any note of reasons required by section 5(4) to be included and the particulars set out in any certificate granted under section 5(6A)) shall be made by way of an entry in the register.

Notification of bail decision by magistrate after arrest while on bail

19.12 Where a person who has been released on bail and is under a duty to surrender into the custody of a court is brought under section 7(4)(a) of the Bail Act 1976 before a justice of the peace, the justice shall cause a copy of the record made in pursuance of section 5 of that Act relating to his decision under section 7(5) of that Act in respect of that person to be sent to the court officer for that court:

Provided that this rule shall not apply where the court is a magistrates' court acting for the same local justice area as that for which the justice acts.

Transfer of remand hearings

19.13 (1) Where a magistrates' court, under section 130(1) of the Magistrates' Courts Act 1980, orders that an accused who has been remanded in custody be brought up for any subsequent remands before an alternate magistrates' court, the court officer for the first-mentioned court shall, as soon as practicable after the making of the order and in any case within 2 days thereafter (not counting Sundays, Good Friday, Christmas Day or bank holidays), send to the court officer for the alternate court—

(a) a statement indicating the offence or offences charged;

(b) a copy of the record made by the first-mentioned court in pursuance of section 5 of the Bail Act 1976 relating to the withholding of bail in respect of the accused when he was last remanded in custody;

(c) a copy of any representation order previously made in the same case;

(d) a copy of any application for a representation order;

(e) if the first-mentioned court has made an order under section 8(2) of the 1980 Act (removal of restrictions on reports of committal proceedings), a statement to that effect.

(f) a statement indicating whether or not the accused has a solicitor acting for him in the case and has consented to the hearing and determination in his absence of any application for his remand on an adjournment of the case under sections 5, 10(1) and 18(4) of the 1980 Act together with a statement indicating whether or not that consent has been withdrawn;

(g) a statement indicating the occasions, if any, on which the accused has been remanded under section 128(3A) of the 1980 Act without being brought before the first-mentioned court; and

(h) if the first-mentioned court remands the accused under section 128A of the 1980 Act on the occasion upon which it makes the order under section 130(1) of that Act, a statement indicating the date set under section 128A(2) of that Act.

(2) Where the first-mentioned court is satisfied as mentioned in section 128(3A) of the 1980 Act, paragraph (1) shall have effect as if for the words 'an accused who has been remanded in custody be brought up for any subsequent remands before' there were substituted the words 'applications for any subsequent remands of the accused be made to'.

(3) The court officer for an alternate magistrates' court before which an accused who has been remanded in custody is brought up for any subsequent remands in pursuance of an order made as aforesaid shall, as soon as practicable after the order ceases to be in force and in any case within 2 days thereafter (not counting Sundays, Good Friday, Christmas Day or bank holidays), send to the court officer for the magistrates' court which made the order—

(a) a copy of the record made by the alternate court in pursuance of section 5 of the 1976 Act relating to the grant or withholding of bail in respect of the accused when he was last remanded in custody or on bail;

(b) a copy of any representation order made by the alternate court;

(c) a copy of any application for a representation order made to the alternate court;

(d) if the alternate court has made an order under section 8(2) of the 1980 Act (removal of restrictions on reports of committal proceedings), a statement to that effect;

(e) a statement indicating whether or not the accused has a solicitor acting for him in the case and has consented to the hearing and determination in his absence of any application for his remand on an adjournment of the case under sections 5, 10(1) and 18(4) of the 1980 Act together with a statement indicating whether or not that consent has been withdrawn; and

(f) a statement indicating the occasions, if any, on which the accused has been remanded by the alternate court under section 128(3A) of the 1980 Act without being brought before that court.

(4) Where the alternate court is satisfied as mentioned in section 128(3A) of the 1980 Act paragraph (2) above shall have effect as if for the words 'an accused who has been remanded in custody is brought up for any subsequent remands' there shall be substituted the words 'applications for the further remand of the accused are to be made'.

Notice of further remand in certain cases

19.14 Where a transfer direction has been given by the Secretary of State under section 47 of the Mental Health Act 1983 in respect of a person remanded in custody by a magistrates' court and the direction has not ceased to have effect, the court officer shall give notice in writing to the managers of the hospital where he is detained of any further remand under section 128 of the Magistrates' Courts Act 1980.

Cessation of transfer direction

19.15 Where a magistrates' court directs, under section 52(5) of the Mental Health Act 1983, that a transfer direction given by the Secretary of State under section 48 of that Act in respect of a person remanded in custody by a magistrates' court shall cease to have effect, the court officer shall give notice in writing of the court's direction to the managers of the hospital specified in the Secretary of State's direction and, where the period of remand has not expired or the person has been committed to the Crown Court for trial or to be otherwise dealt with, to the Governor of the prison to which persons of the sex of that person are committed by the court if remanded in custody or committed in custody for trial.

Lodging an appeal against a grant of bail by a magistrates' court

19.16 (1) Where the prosecution wishes to exercise the right of appeal, under section 1 of the Bail (Amendment) Act 1993, to a judge of the Crown Court against a decision to grant bail, the oral notice of appeal must be given to the justices' clerk and to the person concerned, at the conclusion of the proceedings in which such bail was granted and before the release of the person concerned.

(2) When oral notice of appeal is given, the justices' clerk shall announce in open court the time at which such notice was given.

(3) A record of the prosecution's decision to appeal and the time the oral notice of appeal was given shall be made in the register and shall contain the particulars set out.

(4) Where an oral notice of appeal has been given the court shall remand the person concerned in custody by a warrant of commitment.

(5) On receipt of the written notice of appeal required by section 1(5) of the 1993 Act, the court shall remand the person concerned in custody by a warrant of commitment, until the appeal is determined or otherwise disposed of.

(6) A record of the receipt of the written notice of appeal shall be made in the same manner as that of the oral notice of appeal under paragraph (3).

(7) If, having given oral notice of appeal, the prosecution fails to serve a written notice of appeal within the two hour period referred to in section 1(5) of the 1993 Act the justices' clerk shall, as soon as practicable, by way of written notice (served by a court officer) to the persons in whose custody the person concerned is, direct the release of the person concerned on bail as granted by the magistrates' court and subject to any conditions which it imposed.

(8) If the prosecution serves notice of abandonment of appeal on a court officer, the justices' clerk shall, forthwith, by way of written notice (served by the court officer) to the governor of the prison where the person concerned is being held, or the person responsible for any other establishment where such a person is being held, direct his release on bail as granted by the magistrates' court and subject to any conditions which it imposed.

(9) A court officer shall record the prosecution's failure to serve a written notice of appeal, or its service of a notice of abandonments.

(10) Where a written notice of appeal has been served on a magistrates' court officer, he shall provide as soon as practicable to a Crown Court officer a copy of that written notice, together with—

(a) the notes of argument made by the court officer for the court under rule 19.10; and

(b) a note of the date, or dates, when the person concerned is next due to appear in the magistrates' court, whether he is released on bail or remanded in custody by the Crown Court.

(11) References in this rule to 'the person concerned' are references to such a person within the meaning of section 1 of the 1993 Act.

Crown Court procedure on appeal against grant of bail by a magistrates' court

19.17 (1) This rule shall apply where the prosecution appeals under section 1 of the Bail (Amendment) Act 1993 against a decision of a magistrates' court granting bail and in this rule 'the person concerned' has the same meaning as in that Act.

(2) The written notice of appeal required by section 1(5) of the 1993 Act shall be in the form set out in the Practice Direction and shall be served on—

(a) the magistrates' court officer; and

(b) the person concerned.

(3) The Crown Court officer shall enter the appeal and give notice of the time and place of the hearing to—

(a) the prosecution;

(b) the person concerned or his legal representative; and

(c) the magistrates' court officer.

(4) The person concerned shall not be entitled to be present at the hearing of the appeal unless he is acting in person or, in any other case of an exceptional nature, a judge of the Crown Court is of the opinion that the interests of justice require his to be present and gives him leave to be so.

(5) Where a person concerned has not been able to instruct a solicitor to represent him at the appeal, he may give notice to the Crown Court requesting that the Official Solicitor shall represent him at the appeal, and the court may, if it thinks fit, assign the Official Solicitor to act for the person concerned accordingly.

(6) At any time after the service of written notice of appeal under paragraph (2), the prosecution may abandon the appeal by giving notice in writing in the form set out in the Practice Direction.

(7) The notice of abandonment required by the preceding paragraph shall be served on—

(a) the person concerned or his legal representative;

(b) the magistrates' court officer; and

(c) the Crown Court officer.

(8) Any record required by section 5 of the Bail Act 1976 (together with any note of reasons required by subsection (4) of that section to be included) shall be made by way of an entry in the file relating to the case in question and the record shall include the following particulars, namely—

(a) the effect of the decision;

(b) a statement of any condition imposed in respect of bail, indicating whether it is to be complied with before or after release on bail; and

(c) where bail is withheld, a statement of the relevant exception to the right to bail (as provided in Schedule 1 to the 1976 Act) on which the decision is based.

(9) The Crown Court officer shall, as soon as practicable after the hearing of the appeal, give notice of the decision and of the matters required by the preceding paragraph to be recorded to—

(a) the person concerned or his legal representative;

(b) the prosecution;

(c) the police;

(d) the magistrates' officer; and

(e) the governor of the prison or person responsible for the establishment where the person concerned is being held.

(10) Where the judge hearing the appeal grants bail to the person concerned, the provisions of rule 19.18(9) (informing the Court of any earlier application for bail) and rule 19.22 (conditions attached to bail granted by the Crown Court) shall apply as if that person had applied to the Crown Court for bail.

(11) The notices required by paragraphs (3), (5), (7) and (9) of this rule may be served under rule 4.6 (service by fax, e-mail or other electronic means) and the notice required by paragraph (3) may be given by telephone.

Applications to Crown Court relating to bail

19.18 (1) This rule applies where an application to the Crown Court relating to bail is made otherwise than during the hearing of proceedings in the Crown Court.

(2) Subject to paragraph (7) below, notice in writing of intention to make such an application to the Crown Court shall, at least 24 hours before it is made, be given to the prosecutor and if the prosecution is being carried on by the Crown Prosecution Service, to the appropriate Crown Prosecutor or, if the application is to be made by the prosecutor or a constable under section 3(8) of the Bail Act 1976, to the person to whom bail was granted.

(3) On receiving notice under paragraph (2), the prosecutor or appropriate Crown Public Prosecutor or, as the case may be, the person to whom bail was granted shall—

(a) notify the Crown Court officer and the applicant that he wishes to be represented at the hearing of the application;

(b) notify the Crown Court officer and the applicant that he does not oppose the application; or

(c) give to the Crown Court officer, for the consideration of the Crown Court, a written statement of his reasons for opposing the application, at the same time sending a copy of the statement to the applicant.

(4) A notice under paragraph (2) shall be in the form set out in the Practice Direction or a form to the like effect, and the applicant shall give a copy of the notice to the Crown Court officer.

(5) Except in the case of an application made by the prosecutor or a constable under section 3(8) of the 1976 Act, the applicant shall not be entitled to be present on the hearing of his application unless the Crown Court gives him leave to be present.

(6) Where a person who is in custody or has been released on bail desires to make an application relating to bail and has not been able to instruct a solicitor to apply on his behalf under the preceding paragraphs of this rule, he may give notice in writing to the Crown Court of his desire to make an application relating to bail, requesting that the Official Solicitor shall act for him in the application, and the Court may, if it thinks fit, assign the Official Solicitor to act for the applicant accordingly.

(7) Where the Official Solicitor has been so assigned the Crown Court may, if it thinks fit, dispense with the requirements of paragraph (2) and deal with the application in a summary manner.

(8) Any record required by section 5 of the 1976 Act (together with any note of reasons required by section 5(4) to be included) shall be made by way of an entry in the file relating to the case in question and the record shall include the following particulars, namely—

(a) the effect of the decision;

(b) a statement of any condition imposed in respect of bail, indicating whether it is to be complied with before or after release on bail;

(c) where conditions of bail are varied, a statement of the conditions as varied; and

(d) where bail is withheld, a statement of the relevant exception to the right to bail (as provided in Schedule 1 to the 1976 Act) on which the decision is based.

(9) Every person who makes an application to the Crown Court relating to bail shall inform the Court of any earlier application to the High Court or the Crown Court relating to bail in the course of the same proceedings.

Notice to governor of prison of committal on bail

19.19 (1) Where the accused is committed or sent for trial on bail, a magistrates' court officer shall give notice thereof in writing to the governor of the prison to which persons of the sex of the person committed or sent are committed or sent by that court if committed or sent in custody for trial and also, if the person committed or sent is under 21, to the governor of the remand centre to which he would have been committed or sent if the court had refused him bail.

(2) Where a corporation is committed or sent for trial, a magistrates' court officer shall give notice thereof to the governor of the prison to which would be committed or sent a man committed or sent by that court in custody for trial.

Notices on committal of person subject to transfer direction

19.20 Where a transfer direction has been given by the Secretary of State under section 48 of the Mental Health Act 1983 in respect of a person remanded in custody by a magistrates' court and, before the direction ceases to have effect, that person is committed or sent for trial, a magistrates' court officer shall give notice—

(a) to the governor of the prison to which persons of the sex of that person are committed or sent by that court if committed or sent in custody for trial; and
(b) to the managers of the hospital where he is detained.

Variation of arrangements for bail on committal to Crown Court

19.21 Where a magistrates' court has committed or sent a person on bail to the Crown Court for trial or under any of the enactments mentioned in rule 43.1(1) and subsequently varies any conditions of the bail or imposes any conditions in respect of the bail, the magistrates' court officer shall send to the Crown Court officer a copy of the record made in pursuance of section 5 of the Bail Act 1976 relating to such variation or imposition of conditions.

Conditions attached to bail granted by the Crown Court

19.22 (1) Where the Crown Court grants bail, the recognizance of any surety required as a condition of bail may be entered into before an officer of the Crown Court or, where the person who has been granted bail is in a prison or other place of detention, before the governor or keeper of the prison or place as well as before the persons specified in section 8(4) of the Bail Act 1976.

(2) Where the Crown Court under section 3(5) or (6) of the 1976 Act imposes a requirement to be complied with before a person's release on bail, the Court may give directions as to the manner in which and the person or persons before whom the requirement may be complied with.

(3) A person who, in pursuance of an order made by the Crown Court for the grant of bail, proposes to enter into a recognizance or give security must, unless the Crown Court otherwise directs, give notice to the prosecutor at least 24 hours before he enters into the recognizance or gives security as aforesaid.

(4) Where, in pursuance of an order of the Crown Court, a recognizance is entered into or any requirement imposed under section 3(5) or (6) of the 1976 Act is complied with (being a requirement to be complied with before a person's release on bail) before any person, it shall be his duty to cause the recognizance or, as the case may be, a statement of the requirement to be transmitted forthwith to the court officer; and a copy of the recognizance or statement shall at the same time be sent to the governor or keeper of the prison or other place of detention in which the person named in the order is detained, unless the recognizance was entered into or the requirement was complied with before such governor or keeper.

(5) Where, in pursuance of section 3(5) of the 1976 Act, security has been given in respect of a person granted bail with a duty to surrender to the custody of the Crown Court and either—
(a) that person surrenders to the custody of the Court; or
(b) that person having failed to surrender to the custody of the Court, the Court decides not to order the forfeiture of the security,

the court officer shall as soon as practicable give notice of the surrender to custody or, as the case may be, of the decision not to forfeit the security to the person before whom the security was given.

Estreat of recognizances in respect of person bailed to appear before the Crown Court

19.23 (1) Where a recognizance has been entered into in respect of a person granted bail to appear before the Crown Court and it appears to the Court that a default has been made in performing the conditions of the recognizance, other than by failing to appear before the Court in accordance with any such condition, the Court may order the recognizance to be estreated.

(2) Where the Crown Court is to consider making an order under paragraph (1) for a recognizance to be estreated, the court officer shall give notice to that effect to the person by whom the recognizance was entered into indicating the time and place at which the matter will be considered; and no such order shall be made before the expiry of 7 days after the notice required by this paragraph has been given.

Forfeiture of recognizances in respect of person bailed to appear before the Crown Court

19.24 (1) Where a recognizance is conditioned for the appearance of an accused before the Crown Court and the accused fails to appear in accordance with the condition, the Court shall declare the recognizance to be forfeited.

(2) Where the Crown Court declares a recognizance to be forfeited under paragraph (1), the court officer shall issue a summons to the person by whom the recognizance was entered into

requiring him to appear before the Court at a time and place specified in the summons to show cause why the Court should not order the recognizance to be estreated.

(3) At the time specified in the summons the Court may proceed in the absence of the person by whom the recognizance was entered into if it is satisfied that he has been served with the summons.

Part 20 Custody Time Limits

Appeal to the Crown Court against a decision of a magistrates' court in respect of a custody time limit

20.1 (1) This rule applies—

(a) to any appeal brought by an accused, under section 22(7) of the Prosecution of Offences Act 1985, against a decision of a magistrates' court to extend, or further extend, a custody time limit imposed by regulations made under section 22(1) of the 1985 Act; and

(b) to any appeal brought by the prosecution, under section 22(8) of the 1985 Act, against a decision of a magistrates' court to refuse to extend, or further extend, such a time limit.

(2) An appeal to which this rule applies shall be commenced by the appellant's giving notice in writing of appeal—

(a) to the court officer for the magistrates' court which took the decision;

(b) if the appeal is brought by the accused, to the prosecutor and, if the prosecution is to be carried on by the Crown Prosecution Service, to the appropriate Crown Prosecutor;

(c) if the appeal is brought by the prosecution, to the accused; and

(d) to the Crown Court officer.

(3) The notice of an appeal to which this rule applies shall state the date on which the custody time limit applicable to the case is due to expire and, if the appeal is brought by the accused under section 22(7) of the 1985 Act, the date on which the custody time limit would have expired had the court decided not to extend or further extend that time limit.

(4) On receiving notice of an appeal to which this rule applies, the Crown Court officer shall enter the appeal and give notice of the time and place of the hearing to—

(a) the appellant;

(b) the other party to the appeal; and

(c) the court officer for the magistrates' court which took the decision.

(5) Without prejudice to the power of the Crown Court to give leave for an appeal to be abandoned, an appellant may abandon an appeal to which this rule applies by giving notice in writing to any person to whom notice of the appeal was required to be given by paragraph (2) of this rule not later than the third day preceding the day fixed for the hearing of the appeal:

Provided that, for the purpose of determining whether notice was properly given in accordance with this paragraph, there shall be disregarded any Saturday and Sunday and any day which is specified to be a bank holiday in England and Wales under section 1(1) of the Banking and Financial Dealings Act 1971.

Part 21 Advance Information

Scope of procedure for furnishing advance information

21.1 This Part applies in respect of proceedings against any person ('the accused') for an offence triable either way.

Notice to accused regarding advance information

21.2 As soon as practicable after a person has been charged with an offence in proceedings in respect of which this Part applies or a summons has been served on a person in connection with such an offence, the prosecutor shall provide him with a notice in writing explaining the effect of rule 21.3 and setting out the address at which a request under that section may be made.

Request for advance information

21.3 (1) If, in any proceedings in respect of which this Part applies, either before the magistrates' court considers whether the offence appears to be more suitable for summary trial or trial on indictment or, where the accused has not attained the age of 18 years when he appears or is brought before a magistrates' court, before he is asked whether he pleads guilty or not guilty, the accused or a person representing the accused requests the prosecutor to furnish him with advance information, the prosecutor shall, subject to rule 21.4, furnish him as soon as practicable with either—

(a) a copy of those parts of every written statement which contain information as to the facts and matters of which the prosecutor proposes to adduce evidence in the proceedings; or

(b) a summary of the facts and matters of which the prosecutor proposes to adduce evidence in the proceedings.

(2) In paragraph (1) above, 'written statement' means a statement made by a person on whose evidence the prosecutor proposes to rely in the proceedings and, where such a person has made more than one written statement one of which contains information as to all the facts and matters in relation to which the prosecutor proposes to rely on the evidence of that person, only that statement is a written statement for purposes of paragraph (1) above.

(3) Where in any part of a written statement or in a summary furnished under paragraph (1) above reference is made to a document on which the prosecutor proposes to rely, the prosecutor shall, subject to rule 21.4, when furnishing the part of the written statement or the summary, also furnish either a copy of the document or such information as may be necessary to enable the person making the request under paragraph (1) above to inspect the document or a copy thereof.

Refusal of request for advance information

21.4 (1) If the prosecutor is of the opinion that the disclosure of any particular fact or matter in compliance with the requirements imposed by rule 21.3 might lead to any person on whose evidence he proposes to rely in the proceedings being intimidated, to an attempt to intimidate him being made or otherwise to the course of justice being interfered with, he shall not be obliged to comply with those requirements in relation to that fact or matter.

(2) Where, in accordance with paragraph (1) above, the prosecutor considers that he is not obliged to comply with the requirements imposed by rule 21.3 in relation to any particular fact or matter, he shall give notice in writing to the person who made the request under that section to the effect that certain advance information is being withheld by virtue of that paragraph.

Duty of court regarding advance information

21.5 (1) Subject to paragraph (2), where an accused appears or is brought before a magistrates' court in proceedings in respect of which this Part applies, the court shall, before it considers whether the offence appears to be more suitable for summary trial or trial on indictment, satisfy itself that the accused is aware of the requirements which may be imposed on the prosecutor under rule 21.3.

(2) Where the accused has not attained the age of 18 years when he appears or is brought before a magistrates' court in proceedings in respect of which this rule applies, the court shall, before the accused is asked whether he pleads guilty or not guilty, satisfy itself that the accused is aware of the requirements which may be imposed on the prosecutor under rule 21.3.

Adjournment pending furnishing of advance information

21.6 (1) If, in any proceedings in respect of which this Part applies, the court is satisfied that, a request under rule 21.3 having been made to the prosecutor by or on behalf of the accused, a requirement imposed on the prosecutor by that section has not been complied with, the court shall adjourn the proceedings pending compliance with the requirement unless the court is satisfied that the conduct of the case for the accused will not be substantially prejudiced by non-compliance with the requirement.

(2) Where, in the circumstances set out in paragraph (1) above, the court decides not to adjourn the proceedings, a record of that decision and of the reasons why the court was satisfied that the conduct of the case for the accused would not be substantially prejudiced by non-compliance with the requirement shall be entered in the register kept under rule 6.1.

Part 22 Disclosure by the Prosecution

[There are currently no rules in this part.]

Part 23 Disclosure by the Defence

[There are currently no rules in this part.]

Part 24 Disclosure of Expert Evidence

Requirement to disclose expert evidence

24.1 (1) Following—

(a) a plea of not guilty by any person to an alleged offence in respect of which a magistrates' court proceeds to summary trial;

(b) the committal for trial of any person;

(c) the transfer to the Crown Court of any proceedings for the trial of a person by virtue of a notice of transfer given under section 4 of the Criminal Justice Act 1987;

(d) the transfer to the Crown Court of any proceedings for the trial of a person by virtue of a notice of transfer served on a magistrates' court under section 53 of the Criminal Justice Act 1991;

(e) the sending of any person for trial under section 51 of the Crime and Disorder Act 1998;

(f) the preferring of a bill of indictment charging a person with an offence under the authority of section 2(2)(b) of the Administration of Justice (Miscellaneous Provisions) Act 1933; or

(g) the making of an order for the retrial of any person,

if any party to the proceedings proposes to adduce expert evidence (whether of fact or opinion) in the proceedings (otherwise than in relation to sentence) he shall as soon as practicable, unless in relation to the evidence in question he has already done so or the evidence is the subject of an application for leave to adduce such evidence in accordance with section 41 of the Youth Justice and Criminal Evidence Act 1999—

(i) furnish the other party or parties and the court with a statement in writing of any finding or opinion which he proposes to adduce by way of such evidence and notify the expert of this disclosure, and

(ii) where a request in writing is made to him in that behalf by any other party, provide that party also with a copy of (or if it appears to the party proposing to adduce the evidence to be more practicable, a reasonable opportunity to examine) the record of any observation, test, calculation or other procedure on which such finding or opinion is based and any document or other thing or substance in respect of which any such procedure has been carried out.

(2) A party may by notice in writing waive his right to be furnished with any of the matters mentioned in paragraph (1) and, in particular, may agree that the statement mentioned in paragraph (1)(a) may be furnished to him orally and not in writing.

(3) In paragraph (1), 'document' means anything in which information of any description is recorded.

Withholding evidence

24.2 (1) If a party has reasonable grounds for believing that the disclosure of any evidence in compliance with the requirements imposed by rule 24.1 might lead to the intimidation, or attempted intimidation, of any person on whose evidence he intends to rely in the proceedings, or otherwise to the course of justice being interfered with, he shall not be obliged to comply with those requirements in relation to that evidence.

(2) Where, in accordance with paragraph (1), a party considers that he is not obliged to comply with the requirements imposed by rule 24.1 with regard to any evidence in relation to any other party, he shall give notice in writing to that party to the effect that the evidence is being withheld and the grounds for doing so.

Effect of failure to disclose

24.3 A party who seeks to adduce expert evidence in any proceedings and who fails to comply with rule 24.1 shall not adduce that evidence in those proceedings without the leave of the court.

Part 25 Applications for Public Interest Immunity and Specific Disclosure

Public interest: application by prosecutor

25.1 (1) This rule applies to the making of an application by the prosecutor under section 3(6), 7A(8) or 8(5) of the Criminal Procedure and Investigations Act 1996.

(2) Notice of such an application shall be served on the court officer and shall specify the nature of the material to which the application relates.

(3) Subject to paragraphs (4) and (5) below, a copy of the notice of application shall be served on the accused by the prosecutor.

(4) Where the prosecutor has reason to believe that to reveal to the accused the nature of the material to which the application relates would have the effect of disclosing that which the prosecutor contends should not in the public interest be disclosed, paragraph (3) above shall not apply but the prosecutor shall notify the accused that an application to which this rule applies has been made.

(5) Where the prosecutor has reason to believe that to reveal to the accused the fact that an application is being made would have the effect of disclosing that which the prosecutor contends should not in the public interest be disclosed, paragraph (3) above shall not apply.

(6) Where an application is made in the Crown Court to which paragraph (5) above applies, notice of the application may be served on the trial judge or, if the application is made before the start of the trial, on the judge, if any, who has been designated to conduct the trial instead of on the court officer.

Public interest: hearing of application by prosecutor

25.2 (1) This rule applies to the hearing of an application by the prosecutor under section 3(6), 7A(8) or 8(5) of the Criminal Procedure and Investigations Act 1996.

(2) Where notice of such an application is served on the Crown Court officer, the officer shall on receiving it refer it—

(a) if the trial has started, to the trial judge; or

(b) if the application is received before the start of the trial either—

(i) to the judge who has been designated to conduct the trial, or

(ii) if no judge has been designated for that purpose, to such judge as may be designated for the purposes of hearing the application.

(3) Where such an application is made and a copy of the notice of application has been served on the accused in accordance with rule 25.1(3), then subject to paragraphs (4) and (5) below—

(a) the court officer shall on receiving notice of the application give notice to—

(i) the prosecutor,

(ii) the accused, and

(iii) any person claiming to have an interest in the material to which the application relates who has applied under section 16(b) of the 1996 Act to be heard by the court,

of the date and time when and the place where the hearing will take place and, unless the court orders otherwise, such notice shall be given in writing;

(b) the hearing shall be inter partes; and

(c) the prosecutor and the accused shall be entitled to make representations to the court.

(4) Where the prosecutor applies to the court for leave to make representations in the absence of the accused, the court may for that purpose sit in the absence of the accused and any legal representative of his.

(5) Subject to rule 25.5(4) (interested party entitled to make representations), where a copy of the notice of application has not been served on the accused in accordance with rule 25.1(3)—

(a) the hearing shall be ex parte;

(b) only the prosecutor shall be entitled to make representations to the court;

(c) the accused shall not be given notice as specified in paragraph (3)(a)(ii) of this rule; and

(d) where notice of the application has been served in the Crown Court in pursuance of rule 25.1(6), the judge on whom it is served shall take such steps as he considers appropriate to ensure that notice is given as required by paragraph (3)(a)(i) and (iii) of this rule.

Public interest: non-disclosure order

25.3 (1) This rule applies to an order under section 3(6), 7A(8) or 8(5) of the Criminal Procedure and Investigations Act 1996.

(2) On making an order to which this rule applies, the court shall state its reasons for doing so. Where such an order is made in the Crown Court, a record shall be made of the statement of the court's reasons.

(3) In a case where such an order is made following—

(a) an application to which rule 25.1(4) (nature of material not to be revealed) applies; or

(b) an application notice of which has been served on the accused in accordance with rule 25.1(3) but the accused has not appeared or been represented at the hearing of that application,

the court officer shall notify the accused that an order has been made. No notification shall be given in a case where an order is made following an application to which rule 25.1(5) (fact of application not to be revealed) applies.

Review of non-disclosure order: application by accused

25.4 (1) This rule applies to an application by the accused under section 14(2) or section 15(4) of the Criminal Procedure and Investigations Act 1996.

(2) Such an application shall be made by notice in writing to the court officer for the court that made the order under section 3(6), 7A(8) or 8(5) of the 1996 Act and shall specify the reason why the accused believes the court should review the question whether it is still not in the public interest to disclose the material affected by the order.

(3) A copy of the notice referred to in paragraph (2) shall be served on the prosecutor at the same time as it is sent to the court officer.

(4) Where such an application is made in a magistrates' court, the court officer shall take such steps as he thinks fit to ensure that the court has before it any document or other material which was available to the court which made the order mentioned in section 14(2) of the 1996 Act.

(5) Where such an application is made in the Crown Court, the court officer shall refer it—

(a) if the trial has started, to the trial judge; or

(b) if the application is received before the start of the trial either—

(i) to the judge who has been designated to conduct the trial, or

(ii) if no judge has been designated for that purpose, to the judge who made the order to which the application relates.

(6) The judge to whom such an application has been referred under paragraph (5) shall consider whether the application may be determined without a hearing and, subject to paragraph (7), may so determine it if he thinks fit.

(7) No application to which this rule applies shall be determined by the Crown Court without a hearing if it appears to the judge that there are grounds on which the court might conclude that it is in the public interest to disclose material to any extent.

(8) Where a magistrates' court considers that there are no grounds on which it might conclude that it is in the public interest to disclose material to any extent it may determine an application to which this rule applies without hearing representations from the accused, the prosecutor or any person claiming to have an interest in the material to which the application relates.

(9) Subject to paragraphs (10) and (11) of this rule and to rule 25.5(4) (interested party entitled to make representations), the hearing of an application to which this rule applies shall be inter partes and the accused and the prosecutor shall be entitled to make representations to the court.

(10) Where after hearing the accused's representations the prosecutor applies to the court for leave to make representations in the absence of the accused, the court may for that purpose sit in the absence of the accused and any legal representative of his.

(11) Subject to rule 25.5(4), where the order to which the application relates was made following an application of which the accused was not notified under rule 25.1(3) or (4), the hearing shall be ex parte and only the prosecutor shall be entitled to make representations to the court.

(12) The court officer shall give notice in writing to—

(a) the prosecutor;

(b) except where a hearing takes place in accordance with paragraph (11), the accused; and

(c) any person claiming to have an interest in the material to which the application relates who has applied under section 16(b) of the 1996 Act to be heard by the court,

of the date and time when and the place where the hearing of an application to which this rule applies will take place and of any order which is made by the court following its determination of the application.

(13) Where such an application is determined without a hearing in pursuance of paragraph (6), the court officer shall give notice in writing in accordance with paragraph (12) of any order which is made by the judge following his determination of the application.

Public interest applications: interested persons

25.5 (1) Where the prosecutor has reason to believe that a person who was involved (whether alone or with others and whether directly or indirectly) in the prosecutor's attention being brought to any material to which an application under section 3(6), 7A(8), 8(5), 14(2) or 15(4) of the Criminal Procedure and Investigations Act 1996 relates may claim to have an interest in that material, the prosecutor shall—

(a) in the case of an application under section 3(6), 7A(8) or 8(5) of the 1996 Act, at the same time as notice of the application is served under rule 25.1(2) or (6); or

(b) in the case of an application under section 14(2) or 15(4) of the 1996 Act, when he receives a copy of the notice referred to in rule 25.4(2),

give notice in writing to—

(i) the person concerned of the application, and

(ii) the court officer or, as the case may require, the judge of his belief and the grounds for it.

(2) An application under section 16(b) of the 1996 Act shall be made by notice in writing to the court officer or, as the case may require, the judge as soon as is reasonably practicable after receipt of notice under paragraph (1)(i) above or, if no such notice is received, after the person concerned becomes aware of the application referred to in that sub-paragraph and shall specify the nature of the applicant's interest in the material and his involvement in bringing the material to the prosecutor's attention.

(3) A copy of the notice referred to in paragraph (2) shall be served on the prosecutor at the same time as it is sent to the court officer or the judge as the case may require.

(4) At the hearing of an application under section 3(6), 7A(8), 8(5), 14(2) or 15(4) of the 1996 Act a person who has made an application under section 16(b) in accordance with paragraph (2) of this rule shall be entitled to make representations to the court.

Disclosure: application by accused and order of court

25.6 (1) This rule applies to an application by the accused under section 8(2) of the Criminal Procedure and Investigations Act 1996.

(2) Such an application shall be made by notice in writing to the court officer and shall specify—

(a) the material to which the application relates;

(b) that the material has not been disclosed to the accused;

(c) the reason why the material might be expected to assist the applicant's defence as disclosed by the defence statement given under section 5 or 6 of the 1996 Act; and

(d) the date of service of a copy of the notice on the prosecutor in accordance with paragraph (3).

(3) A copy of the notice referred to in paragraph (2) shall be served on the prosecutor at the same time as it is sent to the court officer.

(4) Where such an application is made in the Crown Court, the court officer shall refer it—

(a) if the trial has started, to the trial judge, or

(b) if the application is received before the start of the trial—

(i) to the judge who has been designated to conduct the trial, or

(ii) if no judge has been designated for that purpose, to such judge as may be designated for the purposes of determining the application.

(5) A prosecutor receiving notice under paragraph (3) of an application to which this rule applies shall give notice in writing to the court officer within 14 days of service of the notice that—

(a) he wishes to make representations to the court concerning the material to which the application relates; or

(b) if he does not so wish, that he is willing to disclose that material,

and a notice under paragraph 5(a) shall specify the substance of the representations he wishes to make.

(6) A court may determine an application to which this rule applies without hearing representations from the applicant or the prosecutor unless—

(a) the prosecutor has given notice under paragraph (5)(a) and the court considers that the representations should be made at a hearing; or

(b) the court considers it necessary to hear representations from the applicant or the prosecutor in the interests of justice for the purposes of determining the application.

(7) Subject to paragraph (8), where a hearing is held in pursuance of this rule—

(a) the court officer shall give notice in writing to the prosecutor and the applicant of the date and time when and the place where the hearing will take place;
(b) the hearing shall be inter partes; and
(c) the prosecutor and the applicant shall be entitled to make representations to the court.

(8) Where the prosecutor applies to the court for leave to make representations in the absence of the accused, the court may for that purpose sit in the absence of the accused and any legal representative of his.

(9) A copy of any order under section 8(2) of the 1996 Act shall be served on the prosecutor and the applicant.

Disclosure: application for extension of time limit and order of the court

25.7 (1) This rule applies to an application under regulation 3(2) of the Criminal Procedure and Investigations Act 1996 (Defence Disclosure Time Limits) Regulations 1997, including that regulation as applied by regulation 4(2).

(2) An application to which this rule applies shall be made by notice in writing to the court officer and shall, in addition to the matters referred to in regulation 3(3)(a) to (c) of the 1997 Regulations, specify the date of service of a copy of the notice on the prosecutor in accordance with paragraph (3) of this rule.

(3) A copy of the notice referred to in paragraph (2) of this rule shall be served on the prosecutor at the same time as it is sent to the court officer.

(4) The prosecutor may make representations to the court concerning the application and if he wishes to do so he shall do so in writing within 14 days of service of a notice under paragraph (3) of this rule.

(5) On receipt of representations under paragraph (4) above, or on the expiration of the period specified in that paragraph if no such representations are received within that period, the court shall consider the application and may, if it wishes, do so at a hearing.

(6) Where a hearing is held in pursuance of this rule—
(a) the court officer shall give notice in writing to the prosecutor and the applicant of the date and time when and the place where the hearing will take place;
(b) the hearing shall be inter partes; and
(c) the prosecutor and the applicant shall be entitled to make representations to the court.

(7) A copy of any order under regulation 3(1) or 4(1) of the 1997 Regulations shall be served on the prosecutor and the applicant.

Public interest and disclosure applications: general

25.8 (1) Any hearing held under this Part may be adjourned from time to time.

(2) Any hearing referred to in paragraph (1) other than one held under rule 25.7 may be held in private.

(3) Where a Crown Court hearing, or any part thereof, is held in private under paragraph (2), the court may specify conditions subject to which the record of its statement of reasons made in pursuance of rule 25.3(2) is to be kept.

(4) Where an application or order to which any provision of this rule applies is made after the start of a trial in the Crown Court, the trial judge may direct that any provision of this rule requiring notice of the application or order to be given to any person shall not have effect and may give such direction as to the giving of notice in relation to that application or order as he thinks fit.

Part 26 Confidential Material

Application for permission to use or disclose object or information

26.1 (1) This rule applies to an application under section 17(4) of the Criminal Procedure and Investigations Act 1996.

(2) Such an application shall be made by notice in writing to the court officer for the court which conducted or is conducting the proceedings for whose purposes the applicant was given, or allowed to inspect, the object to which the application relates.

(3) The notice of application shall—
(a) specify the object which the applicant seeks to use or disclose and the proceedings for whose purposes he was given, or allowed to inspect, it;
(b) where the applicant seeks to use or disclose any information recorded in the object specified in pursuance of paragraph (3)(a), specify that information;

(c) specify the reason why the applicant seeks permission to use or disclose the object specified in pursuance of paragraph (3)(a) or any information specified in pursuance of paragraph (3)(b);
(d) describe any proceedings in connection with which the applicant seeks to use or disclose the object or information referred to in paragraph (3)(c); and
(e) specify the name and address of any person to whom the applicant seeks to disclose the object or information referred to in paragraph (3)(c).

(4) Where the court officer receives an application to which this rule applies, the court officer or the clerk of the magistrates' court shall fix a date and time for the hearing of the application.

(5) The court officer shall give the applicant and the prosecutor at least 28 days' notice of the date fixed in pursuance of paragraph (4) and shall at the same time send to the prosecutor a copy of the notice given to him in pursuance of paragraph (2).

(6) Where the prosecutor has reason to believe that a person may claim to have an interest in the object specified in a notice of application in pursuance of paragraph (3)(a), or in any information so specified in pursuance of paragraph (3)(b), he shall, as soon as reasonably practicable after receipt of a copy of that notice under paragraph (5), send a copy of the notice to that person and inform him of the date fixed in pursuance of paragraph (4).

Prosecutor or interested party wishing to be heard

26.2 (1) This rule applies to an application under section 17(6)(b) of the Criminal Procedure and Investigations Act 1996.

(2) An application to which this rule applies shall be made by notice in writing to the court officer of the court referred to in rule 26.1(2) not less than 7 days before the date fixed in pursuance of rule 26.1(4).

(3) The applicant shall at the same time send to the person whose application under section 17(4) of the 1996 Act is concerned a copy of the notice given in pursuance of paragraph (2).

Decision on application for use or disclosure

26.3 (1) Where no application to which rule 26.2 applies is made in accordance with paragraph (2) of that rule, the court shall consider whether the application under section 17(4) of the Criminal Procedure and Investigations Act 1996 may be determined without hearing representations from the accused, the prosecutor or any person claiming to have an interest in the object or information to which the application relates, and may so determine it if the court thinks fit.

(2) Where an application to which rule 26.1 applies is determined without hearing any such representations the court officer shall give notice in writing to the person who made the application and to the prosecutor of any order made under section 17(4) of the 1996 Act or, as the case may be, that no such order has been made.

Unauthorised use or disclosure

26.4 (1) This rule applies to proceedings to deal with a contempt of court under section 18 of the Criminal Procedure and Investigations Act 1996.

(2) In such proceedings before a magistrates' court the Magistrates' Courts Act 1980 shall have effect subject to the modifications contained in paragraphs (3) to (7) (being provisions equivalent to those in Schedule 3 to the Contempt of Court Act 1981 subject to modifications which the Lord Chancellor considered appropriate after consultation with the rule committee for magistrates' courts).

(3) Where proceedings to which this rule applies are taken of the court's own motion the provisions of the 1980 Act listed in paragraph (4) shall apply as if a complaint had been made against the person against whom the proceedings are taken and subject to the modifications specified in paragraphs (5) and (6).

(4) The provisions referred to in paragraph (3) are—
(a) section 51 (issue of summons);
(b) section 53(1) and (2) (procedure on hearing);
(c) section 54 (adjournment);
(d) section 55 (non-appearance of defendant);
(e) section 97(1) (summons to witness);
(f) section 101 (onus of proving exceptions etc);

(g) section 121(1) and (3)(a) (constitution and place of sitting of court); and
(h) section 123 (defect in process).

(5) In—
(a) section 55(1) for the words 'the complainant appears but the defendant does not' there shall be substituted the words 'the defendant does not appear'; and
(b) section 55(2) the words 'if the complaint has been substantiated on oath, and' shall be omitted.

(6) In section 123(1) and (2) the words 'adduced on behalf of the prosecutor or complainant' shall be omitted.

(7) Where proceedings to which this rule applies are taken by way of complaint for an order—
(a) section 127 of the 1980 Act (limitation of time) shall not apply to the complaint;
(b) the complaint may be made by the prosecutor or by any other person claiming to have an interest in the object, or in any information recorded in an object, the use or disclosure of which is alleged to contravene section 17 of the 1996 Act; and
(c) the complaint shall be made to the magistrates' court officer for the magistrates' court which conducted or is conducting the proceedings for whose purposes the object mentioned in paragraph (7)(b) was given or inspected.

(8) An application to the Crown Court for an order of committal or for the imposition of a fine in proceedings to which this rule applies may be made by the prosecutor or by any other person claiming to have an interest in the object, or in any information recorded in an object, the use or disclosure of which is alleged to contravene section 17 of the 1996 Act. Such an application shall be made in accordance with paragraphs (9) to (20).

(9) An application such as is referred to in paragraph (8) shall be made by notice in writing to the court officer at the same place as that in which the Crown Court sat or is sitting to conduct the proceedings for whose purposes the object mentioned in paragraph (2) was given or inspected.

(10) The notice referred to in paragraph (9) shall set out the name and a description of the applicant, the name, description and address of the person sought to be committed or fined and the grounds on which his committal or the imposition of a fine is sought and shall be supported by an affidavit verifying the facts.

(11) Subject to paragraph (12), the notice referred to in paragraph (9), accompanied by a copy of the affidavit in support of the application, shall be served personally on the person sought to be committed or fined.

(12) The court may dispense with service of the notice under this rule if it is of the opinion that it is necessary to do so in order to protect the applicant or for another purpose identified by the court.

(13) Nothing in the foregoing provisions of this rule shall be taken as affecting the power of the Crown Court to make an order of committal or impose a fine of its own motion against a person guilty of a contempt under section 18 of the 1996 Act.

(14) Subject to paragraph (15), proceedings to which this rule applies shall be heard in open court.

(15) Proceedings to which this rule applies may be heard in private where—
(a) the object, the use or disclosure of which is alleged to contravene section 17 of the 1996 Act, is; or
(b) the information, the use or disclosure of which is alleged to contravene that section, is recorded in,

an object which is, or forms part of, material in respect of which an application was made under section 3(6), 7A(8) or 8(5) of the 1996 Act, whether or not the court made an order that the material be not disclosed:

Provided that where the court hears the proceedings in private it shall nevertheless, if it commits any person to custody or imposes a fine on him in pursuance of section 18(3) of the 1996 Act, state in open court the name of that person, the period specified in the order of committal or, as the case may be, the amount of the fine imposed, or both such period and such amount where both are ordered.

(16) Except with the leave of the court hearing an application for an order of committal or for the imposition of a fine no grounds shall be relied upon at the hearing except the grounds set out in the notice referred to in paragraph (9).

(17) If on the hearing of the application the person sought to be committed or fined expresses a wish to give oral evidence on his own behalf, he shall be entitled to do so.

(18) The court by whom an order of committal is made may by order direct that the execution of the order of committal shall be suspended for such period or on such terms or conditions as it may specify.

(19) Where execution of an order of committal is suspended by an order under paragraph (18), the applicant for the order of committal must, unless the court otherwise directs, serve on the person against whom it was made a notice informing him of the making and terms of the order under that paragraph.

(20) The court may, on the application of any person committed to custody for a contempt under section 18 of the 1996 Act, discharge him.

Forfeiture of object used or disclosed without authority

26.5 (1) Where the Crown Court finds a person guilty of contempt under section 18 of the Criminal Procedure and Investigations Act 1996 and proposes to make an order under section 18(4) or (7), the court may adjourn the proceedings.

(2) Where the court adjourns the proceedings under paragraph (1), the court officer shall give notice to the person found guilty and to the prosecutor—

(a) that the court proposes to make such an order and that, if an application is made in accordance with paragraph (5), it will before doing so hear any representations made by the person found guilty, or by any person in respect of whom the prosecutor gives notice to the court under paragraph (3); and

(b) of the time and date of the adjourned hearing.

(3) Where the prosecutor has reason to believe that a person may claim to have an interest in the object which has been used or disclosed in contravention of section 17 of the 1996 Act he shall, on receipt of notice under paragraph (2), give notice of that person's name and address to the court office for the court which made the finding of guilt.

(4) Where the court officer receives a notice under paragraph (3), he shall, within 7 days of the finding of guilt, notify the person specified in that notice—

(a) that the court has made a finding of guilt under section 18 of the 1996 Act, that it proposes to make an order under section 18(4) or, as the case may be, 18(7) and that, if an application is made in accordance with paragraph (5), it will before doing so hear any representations made by him; and

(b) of the time and date of the adjourned hearing.

(5) An application under section 18(6) of the 1996 Act shall be made by notice in writing to the court officer not less than 24 hours before the time set for the adjourned hearing.

Part 27 Witness Statements

Witness statements in magistrates' courts

27.1 (1) Written statements to be tendered in evidence in accordance with section 5B of the Magistrates' Courts Act 1980 or section 9 of the Criminal Justice Act 1967 shall be in the form set out in the Practice Direction.

(2) When a copy of any of the following evidence, namely—

(a) evidence tendered in accordance with section 5A of the 1980 Act (committal for trial); or

(b) a written statement tendered in evidence under section 9 of the 1967 Act (proceedings other than committal for trial),

is given to or served on any party to the proceedings a copy of the evidence in question shall be given to the court officer as soon as practicable thereafter, and where a copy of any such statement as is referred to in sub-paragraph (b) is given or served by or on behalf of the prosecutor, the accused shall be given notice by or on behalf of the prosecutor of his right to object to the statement being tendered in evidence.

(3) Where—

(a) a statement or deposition to be tendered in evidence in accordance with section 5A of the 1980 Act; or

(b) a written statement to be tendered in evidence under section 9 of the 1967 Act,

refers to any document or object as an exhibit, that document or object shall wherever possible be identified by means of a label or other mark of identification signed by the maker of the statement or deposition, and before a magistrates' court treats any document or object referred to as an exhibit in such a statement or deposition as an exhibit produced and identified in court by the maker of the statement or deposition, the court shall be satisfied that the document or object is sufficiently described in the statement or deposition for it to be identified.

(4) If it appears to a magistrates' court that any part of any evidence tendered in accordance with section 5A of the 1980 Act or a written statement tendered in evidence under section 9 of the 1967 Act is inadmissible there shall be written against that part—
  (a) in the case of any evidence tendered in accordance with section 5A of the 1980 Act, but subject to paragraph (5) of this rule, the words 'Treated as inadmissible' together with the signature and name of the examining justice or, where there is more than one examining justice, the signature and name of one of the examining justices by whom the evidence is so treated;
  (b) in the case of a written statement tendered in evidence under section 9 of the 1967 Act the words 'Ruled inadmissible' together with the signature and name of one of the justices who ruled the statement to be inadmissible.

(5) Where the nature of the evidence referred to in paragraph (4)(a) is such that it is not possible to write on it, the words set out in that sub-paragraph shall instead be written on a label or other mark of identification which clearly identifies the part of the evidence to which the words relate and contains the signature and name of an examining justice in accordance with that sub-paragraph.

(6) Where, before a magistrates' court—
  (a) a statement or deposition is tendered in evidence in accordance with section 5A of the 1980 Act; or
  (b) a written statement is tendered in accordance with section 9 of the 1967 Act,

the name of the maker of the statement or deposition shall be read aloud unless the court otherwise directs.

(7) Where—
  (a) under section 5B(4), 5C(4), 5D(5) or 5E(3) of the 1980 Act; or
  (b) under section 9(6) of the 1967 Act,

in any proceedings before a magistrates' court any part of the evidence has to be read out aloud, or an account has to be given orally of so much of any evidence as is not read out aloud, the evidence shall be read or the account given by or on behalf of the party which has tendered the evidence.

(8) Statements and depositions tendered in evidence in accordance with section 5A of the 1980 Act before a magistrates' court acting as examining justices shall be authenticated by a certificate signed by one of the examining justices.

(9) Where, before a magistrates' court—
  (a) evidence is tendered as indicated in paragraph (2)(a) of this rule, retained by the court, and not sent to the Crown Court under rule 10.5; or
  (b) a written statement is tendered in evidence as indicated in paragraph (2)(b) of this rule and not sent to the Crown Court under rule 43.1 or 43.2,

all such evidence shall, subject to any direction of the court in respect of non-documentary exhibits falling within paragraph (9)(a), be preserved for a period of three years by the magistrates' court officer for the magistrates' court.

Right to object to evidence being read in Crown Court trial

27.2 (1) The prosecutor shall, when he serves on any other party a copy of the evidence to be tendered in committal proceedings, notify that party that if he is committed for trial he has the right to object, by written notification to the prosecutor and the Crown Court within 14 days of being so committed unless the court in its discretion permits such an objection to be made outside that period, to a statement or deposition being read as evidence at the trial without oral evidence being given by the person who made the statement or deposition and without the opportunity to cross-examine that person.

(2) The prosecutor shall, on notifying a party as indicated in paragraph (1), send a copy of such notification to the magistrates' court officer.

(3) Any objection under paragraph 1(3)(c) or paragraph 2(3)(c) of Schedule 2 to the Criminal Procedure and Investigations Act 1996 to the reading out at the trial of a statement or deposition without further evidence shall be made in writing to the prosecutor and the Crown Court within 14 days of the accused being committed for trial unless the court at its discretion permits such an objection to be made outside that period.

Part 28 Witness Summonses and Orders

When this Part applies

28.1 (1) This Part applies in magistrates' courts and in the Crown Court where—
(a) a party wants the court to issue a witness summons, warrant or order under—
(i) section 97 of the Magistrates' Courts Act 1980,
(ii) section 2 of the Criminal Procedure (Attendance of Witnesses) Act 1965, or
(iii) section 7 of the Bankers' Books Evidence Act 1879;
(b) the court considers the issue of such a summons, warrant or order on its own initiative as if a party had applied; or
(c) one of those listed in rule 28.7 wants the court to withdraw such a summons, warrant or order.
(2) A reference to a 'witness' in this Part is a reference to a person to whom such a summons, warrant or order is directed.

Issue etc. of summons, warrant or order with or without a hearing

28.2 (1) The court may issue or withdraw a witness summons, warrant or order with or without a hearing.
(2) A hearing under this Part must be in private unless the court otherwise directs.

Application for summons, warrant or order: general rules

28.3 (1) A party who wants the court to issue a witness summons, warrant or order must apply as soon as practicable after becoming aware of the grounds for doing so.
(2) The party applying must—
(a) identify the proposed witness;
(b) explain—
(i) what evidence the proposed witness can give or produce,
(ii) why it is likely to be material evidence, and
(iii) why it would be in the interests of justice to issue a summons, order or warrant as appropriate.
(3) The application may be made orally unless—
(a) rule 28.5 applies; or
(b) the court otherwise directs.

Written application: form and service

28.4 (1) An application in writing under rule 28.3 must be in the form set out in the Practice Direction, containing the same declaration of truth as a witness statement.
(2) The party applying must serve the application—
(a) in every case, on the court officer and as directed by the court; and
(b) as required by rule 28.5, if that rule applies.

Application for summons to produce a document, etc.: special rules

28.5 (1) This rule applies to an application under rule 28.3 for a witness summons requiring the proposed witness—
(a) to produce in evidence a document or thing; or
(b) to give evidence about information apparently held in confidence, that relates to another person.
(2) The application must be in writing in the form required by rule 28.4.
(3) The party applying must serve the application—
(a) on the proposed witness, unless the court otherwise directs; and
(b) on one or more of the following, if the court so directs—
(i) a person to whom the proposed evidence relates,
(ii) another party.
(4) The court must not issue a witness summons where this rule applies unless—
(a) everyone served with the application has had at least 14 days in which to make representations, including representations about whether there should be a hearing of the application before the summons is issued; and
(b) the court is satisfied that it has been able to take adequate account of the duties and rights, including rights of confidentiality, of the proposed witness and of any person to whom the proposed evidence relates.

(5) This rule does not apply to an application for an order to produce in evidence a copy of an entry in a banker's book.

Application for summons to produce a document, etc.: court's assessment of relevance and confidentiality

28.6 (1) This rule applies where a person served with an application for a witness summons requiring the proposed witness to produce in evidence a document or thing objects to its production on the ground that—

(a) it is not likely to be material evidence; or

(b) even if it is likely to be material evidence, the duties or rights, including rights of confidentiality, of the proposed witness or of any person to whom the document or thing relates outweigh the reasons for issuing a summons.

(2) The court may require the proposed witness to make the document or thing available for the objection to be assessed.

(3) The court may invite—

(a) the proposed witness or any representative of the proposed witness; or

(b) a person to whom the document or thing relates or any representative of such a person,

to help the court assess the objection.

Application to withdraw a summons, warrant or order

28.7 (1) The court may withdraw a witness summons, warrant or order if one of the following applies for it to be withdrawn—

(a) the party who applied for it, on the ground that it no longer is needed;

(b) the witness, on the grounds that—

(i) he was not aware of any application for it, and

(ii) he cannot give or produce evidence likely to be material evidence, or

(iii) even if he can, his duties or rights, including rights of confidentiality, or those of any person to whom the evidence relates outweigh the reasons for the issue of the summons, warrant or order; or

(c) any person to whom the proposed evidence relates, on the grounds that—

(i) he was not aware of any application for it, and

(ii) that evidence is not likely to be material evidence, or

(iii) even if it is, his duties or rights, including rights of confidentiality, or those of the witness outweigh the reasons for the issue of the summons, warrant or order.

(2) A person applying under the rule must—

(a) apply in writing as soon as practicable after becoming aware of the grounds for doing so, explaining why he wants the summons, warrant or order to be withdrawn; and

(b) serve the application on the court officer and as appropriate on—

(i) the witness,

(ii) the party who applied for the summons, warrant or order, and

(iii) any other person who he knows was served with the application for the summons, warrant or order.

(3) Rule 28.6 applies to an application under this rule that concerns a document or thing to be produced in evidence.

Court's power to vary requirements under this Part

28.8 (1) The court may—

(a) shorten or extend (even after it has expired) a time limit under this Part; and

(b) where a rule or direction requires an application under this Part to be in writing, allow that application to be made orally instead.

(2) Someone who wants the court to allow an application to be made orally under paragraph (1)(b) of this rule must—

(a) give as much notice as the urgency of his application permits to those on whom he would otherwise have served an application in writing; and

(b) in doing so explain the reasons for the application and for wanting the court to consider it orally.

Part 29 Special Measures Directions

Application for special measures directions

29.1 (1) An application by a party in criminal proceedings for a magistrates' court or the Crown Court to give a special measures direction under section 19 of the Youth Justice and Criminal Evidence Act 1999 must be made in writing in the form set out in the Practice Direction.

(2) If the application is for a special measures direction—

(a) enabling a witness to give evidence by means of a live link, the information sought in Part B of that form must be provided;

(b) providing for any examination of a witness to be conducted through an intermediary, the information sought in Part C of that form must be provided; or

(c) enabling a video recording of an interview of a witness to be admitted as evidence in chief of the witness, the information sought in Part D of that form must be provided.

(3) The application under paragraph (1) above must be sent to the court officer and at the same time a copy thereof must be sent by the applicant to every other party to the proceedings.

(4) The court officer must receive the application—

(a) in the case of an application to a youth court, within 28 days of the date on which the defendant first appears or is brought before the court in connection with the offence;

(b) in the case of an application to a magistrates' court, within 14 days of the defendant indicating his intention to plead not guilty to any charge brought against him and in relation to which a special measures direction may be sought; and

(c) in the case of an application to the Crown Court, within 28 days of—

(i) the committal of the defendant, or

(ii) the consent to the preferment of a bill of indictment in relation to the case, or

(iii) the service of a notice of transfer under section 53 of the Criminal Justice Act 1991, or

(iv) where a person is sent for trial under section 51 of the Crime and Disorder Act 1998, the service of copies of the documents containing the evidence on which the charge or charges are based under paragraph 1 of Schedule 3 to that Act, or

(v) the service of a Notice of Appeal from a decision of a youth court or a magistrates' court.

(5) A party to whom an application is sent in accordance with paragraph (3) may oppose the application for a special measures direction in respect of any, or any particular, measure available in relation to the witness, whether or not the question whether the witness is eligible for assistance by virtue of section 16 or 17 of the 1999 Act is in issue.

(6) A party who wishes to oppose the application must, within 14 days of the date the application was served on him, notify the applicant and the court officer, as the case may be, in writing of his opposition and give reasons for it.

(7) Paragraphs (5) and (6) do not apply in respect of an application for a special measures direction enabling a child witness in need of special protection to give evidence by means of a live link if the opposition is that the special measures direction is not likely to maximise the quality of the witness's evidence.

(8) In order to comply with paragraph (6)—

(a) a party must in the written notification state whether he—

(i) disputes that the witness is eligible for assistance by virtue of section 16 or 17 of the 1999 Act,

(ii) disputes that any of the special measures available would be likely to improve the quality of evidence given by the witness or that such measures (or a combination of them) would be likely to maximise the quality of that evidence, and

(iii) opposes the granting of a special measures direction; and

(b) where the application relates to the admission of a video recording, a party who receives a recording must provide the information required by rule 29.7(7) below.

(9) Except where notice is received in accordance with paragraph (6), the court (including, in the case of an application to a magistrates' court, a single justice of the peace) may—

(a) determine the application in favour of the applicant without a hearing; or

(b) direct a hearing.

(10) Where a party to the proceedings notifies the court in accordance with paragraph (6) of his

opposition to the application, the justices' clerk or the Crown Court must direct a hearing of the application.

(11) Where a hearing of the application is to take place in accordance with paragraph (9) or (10) above, the court officer shall notify each party to the proceedings of the time and place of the hearing.

(12) A party notified in accordance with paragraph (11) may be present at the hearing and be heard.

(13) The court officer must, within 3 days of the decision of the court in relation to an application under paragraph (1) being made, notify all the parties of the decision, and if the application was made for a direction enabling a video recording of an interview of a witness to be admitted as evidence in chief of that witness, the notification must state whether the whole or specified parts only of the video recording or recordings disclosed are to be admitted in evidence.

(14) In this Part:
'an intermediary' has the same meaning as in section 29 of the 1999 Act; and
'child witness in need of protection' shall be construed in accordance with section 21(1) of the 1999 Act.

Application for an extension of time

29.2 (1) An application may be made in writing for the period of 14 days or, as the case may be, 28 days specified in rule 29.1(4) to be extended.

(2) The application may be made either before or after that period has expired.

(3) The application must be accompanied by a statement setting out the reasons why the applicant is or was unable to make the application within that period and a copy of the application and the statement must be sent to every other party to the proceedings.

(4) An application for an extension of time under this rule shall be determined by a single justice of the peace or a judge of the Crown Court without a hearing unless the justice or the judge otherwise directs.

(5) The court officer shall notify all the parties of the court's decision.

Late applications

29.3 (1) Notwithstanding the requirements of rule 29.1—

(a) an application may be made for a special measures direction orally at the trial; or

(b) a magistrates' court or the Crown Court may of its own motion raise the issue whether a special measures direction should be given.

(2) Where an application is made in accordance with paragraph (1)(a)—

(a) the applicant must state the reasons for the late application; and

(b) the court must be satisfied that the applicant was unable to make the application in accordance with rule 29.1.

(3) The court shall determine before making a special measures direction—

(a) whether to allow other parties to the proceedings to make representations on the question;

(b) the time allowed for making such representations (if any); and

(c) whether the question should be determined following a hearing at which the parties to the proceedings may be heard.

(4) Paragraphs (2) and (3) do not apply in respect of an application made orally at the trial for a special measures direction—

(a) enabling a child witness in need of special protection to give evidence by means of a live link; or

(b) enabling a video recording of such a child to be admitted as evidence in chief of the witness,

if the opposition is that the special measures direction will not maximise the quality of the witness's evidence.

Discharge or variation of a special measures direction

29.4 (1) An application to a magistrates' court or the Crown Court to discharge or vary a special measures direction under section 20(2) of the Youth Justice and Criminal Evidence Act 1999 must be in writing and each material change of circumstances which the applicant alleges has occurred since the direction was made must be set out.

(2) An application under paragraph (1) must be sent to the court officer as soon as reasonably practicable after the change of circumstances occurs.

(3) The applicant must also send copies of the application to each party to the proceedings at the same time as the application is sent to the court officer.

(4) A party to whom an application is sent in accordance with paragraph (3) may oppose the application on the ground that it discloses no material change of circumstances.

(5) Rule 29.1(6) to (13) shall apply to an application to discharge or vary a special measures direction as it applies to an application for a direction.

Renewal application following a material change of circumstances

29.5 (1) Where an application for a special measures direction has been refused by a magistrates' court or the Crown Court, the application may only be renewed ('renewal application') where there has been a material change of circumstances since the court refused the application.

(2) The applicant must—

(a) identify in the renewal application each material change of circumstances which is alleged to have occurred; and

(b) send the renewal application to the court officer as soon as reasonably practicable after the change occurs.

(3) The applicant must also send copies of the renewal application to each of the parties to the proceedings at the same time as the application is sent to the court officer.

(4) A party to whom the renewal application is sent in accordance with paragraph (3) above may oppose the application on the ground that it discloses no material change of circumstances.

(5) Rules 29.1(6) to (13), 29.6 and 29.7 apply to a renewal application as they apply to the application which was refused.

Application for special measures direction for witness to give evidence by means of a live television link

29.6 (1) Where the application for a special measures direction is made, in accordance with rule 29.1(2)(a), for a witness to give evidence by means of a live link, the following provisions of this rule shall also apply.

(2) A party who seeks to oppose an application for a child witness to give evidence by means of a live link must, in order to comply with rule 29.1(5), state why in his view the giving of a special measures direction would not be likely to maximise the quality of the witness's evidence.

(3) However, paragraph (2) does not apply in relation to a child witness in need of special protection.

(4) Where a special measures direction is made enabling a witness to give evidence by means of a live link, the witness shall be accompanied at the live link only by persons acceptable to the court.

(5) If the special measures directions combine provisions for a witness to give evidence by means of a live link with provision for the examination of the witness to be conducted through an intermediary, the witness shall be accompanied at the live link only by—

(a) the intermediary; and

(b) such other persons as may be acceptable to the court.

Video recording of testimony from witnesses

29.7 (1) Where an application is made to a magistrates' court or the Crown Court for a special measures direction enabling a video recording of an interview of a witness to be admitted as evidence in chief of the witness, the following provisions of this rule shall also apply.

(2) The application made in accordance with rule 29.1(1) must be accompanied by the video recording which it is proposed to tender in evidence and must include—

(a) the name of the defendant and the offence to be charged;

(b) the name and date of birth of the witness in respect of whom the application is made;

(c) the date on which the video recording was made;

(d) a statement as to whether, and if so at what point in the video recording, an oath was administered to, or a solemn declaration made by, the witness;

(e) a statement that, in the opinion of the applicant, either—

(i) the witness is available for cross-examination, or

(ii) the witness is not available for cross-examination and the parties have agreed that there is no need for the witness to be so available;

(f) a statement of the circumstances in which the video recording was made which complies with paragraph (4) of this rule; and
(g) the date on which the video recording was disclosed to the other party or parties.

(3) Where it is proposed to tender part only of a video recording of an interview with the witness, the application must specify that part and be accompanied by a video recording of the entire interview, including those parts which it is not proposed to tender in evidence, and by a statement of the circumstances in which the video recording of the entire interview was made which complies with paragraph (4) of this rule.

(4) The statement of the circumstances in which the video recording was made referred to in paragraphs (2)(f) and (3) of this rule shall include the following information, except in so far as it is contained in the recording itself—
(a) the times at which the recording commenced and finished, including details of interruptions;
(b) the location at which the recording was made and the usual function of the premises;
(c) in relation to each person present at any point during, or immediately before, the recording—
(i) their name, age and occupation,
(ii) the time for which each person was present, and
(iii) the relationship, if any, of each person to the witness and to the defendant;
(d) in relation to the equipment used for the recording—
(i) a description of the equipment,
(ii) the number of cameras used,
(iii) whether the cameras were fixed or mobile,
(iv) the number and location of the microphones,
(v) the video format used; and
(vi) whether it offered single or multiple recording facilities and, if so, which were used; and
(e) the location of the mastertape if the video recording is a copy and details of when and by whom the copy was made.

(5) If the special measures directions enabling a video recording of an interview of a witness to be admitted as evidence in chief of the witness with provision for the examination of the witness to be conducted through an intermediary, the information to be provided under paragraph (4)(c) shall be the same as that for other persons present at the recording but with the addition of details of the declaration made by the intermediary under rule 29.9.

(6) If the special measures directions enabling a video recording of an interview of a witness to be admitted as evidence in chief of the witness with provision for the witness, in accordance with section 30 of the Youth Justice and Criminal Evidence Act 1999, to be provided with a device as an aid to communication during the video recording of the interview the information to be included under paragraph (4)(d) shall include also details of any such device used for the purposes of recording.

(7) A party who receives a recording under paragraph (2) must within 14 days of its receipt, notify the applicant and the court officer, in writing—
(a) whether he objects to the admission under section 27 of the 1999 Act of any part of the video recording or recordings disclosed, giving his reasons why it would not be in the interests of justice for the recording or any part of it to be admitted;
(b) whether he would agree to the admission of part of the video recording or recordings and, if so, which part or parts; and
(c) whether he wishes to be represented at any hearing of the application.

(8) A party who seeks to oppose an application for a special measures direction enabling a video recording of an interview of a child witness to be admitted as evidence in chief of the witness must, in order to comply with rule 29.1(6), state why in his view the giving of a special measures direction would not be likely to maximise the quality of the witness's evidence.

(9) However, paragraph (8) does not apply if the witness is a child witness in need of special protection.

(10) Notwithstanding the provisions of rule 29.1 and this rule, any video recording which the defendant proposes to tender in evidence need not be sent to the prosecution until the close of the prosecution case at the trial.

(11) The court may determine an application by the defendant to tender in evidence a video

recording even though the recording has not, in accordance with paragraph (10), been served upon the prosecution.

(12) Where a video recording which is the subject of a special measures direction is sent to the prosecution after the direction has been made, the prosecutor may apply to the court for the direction to be varied or discharged.

(13) An application under paragraph (12) may be made orally to the court.

(14) A prosecutor who makes an application under paragraph (12) must state—

(a) why he objects to the admission under section 27 of the 1999 Act of any part of the video recording or recordings disclosed, giving his reasons why it would not be in the interests of justice for the recording or any part of it to be admitted; and

(b) whether he would agree to the admission of part of the video recording or recordings and, if so, which part or parts.

(15) The court must, before determining the application—

(a) direct a hearing of the application; and

(b) allow all the parties to the proceedings to be present and be heard on the application.

(16) The court officer must notify all parties to the proceedings of the decision of the court as soon as may be reasonable after the decision is given.

(17) Any decision varying a special measures direction must state whether the whole or specified parts of the video recording or recordings subject to the application are to be admitted in evidence.

Expert evidence in connection with special measures directions

29.8 Any party to proceedings in a magistrates' court or the Crown Court who proposes to adduce expert evidence (whether of fact or opinion) in connection with an application or renewal application for, or for varying or discharging, a special measures direction must, not less than 14 days before the date set for the trial to begin—

(a) furnish the other party or parties to those proceedings and the court with a statement in writing of any finding or opinion which he proposes to adduce by way of such evidence and notify the expert of this disclosure; and

(b) where a request is made to him in that behalf by any other party to those proceedings, provide that party also with a copy of (or if it appears to the party proposing to adduce the evidence to be more practicable, a reasonable opportunity to examine) the record of any observation, test, calculation or other procedure on which such finding or opinion is based and any document or other thing or substance in respect of which any such procedure has been carried out.

Intermediaries

29.9 The declaration required to be made by an intermediary in accordance with section 29(5) of the Youth Justice and Criminal Evidence Act 1999 shall be in the following form:

'I solemnly, sincerely and truly declare that I will well and faithfully communicate questions and answers and make true explanation of all matters and things as shall be required of me according to the best of my skill and understanding.'

Part 30 Use of Live Television Link Other than for Vulnerable Witnesses

Evidence by live television link in the Crown Court where witness is outside the United Kingdom

30.1 (1) Any party may apply for leave under section 32(1) of the Criminal Justice Act 1988 for evidence to be given through a live television link by a witness who is outside the United Kingdom.

(2) An application under paragraph (1), and any matter relating thereto which, by virtue of the following provisions of this rule, falls to be determined by the Crown Court, may be dealt with in chambers by any judge of the Crown Court.

(3) An application under paragraph (1) shall be made by giving notice in writing, which shall be in the form set out in the Practice Direction.

(4) An application under paragraph (1) shall be made within 28 days after the date of the committal of the defendant or, as the case may be, of the giving of a notice of transfer under section 4(1)(c) of the Criminal Justice Act 1987, or of the service of copies of the documents containing the evidence on which the charge or charges are based under paragraph 1 of Schedule 3 to the Crime and Disorder Act 1998, or of the preferring of a bill of indictment in relation to the case.

(5) The period of 28 days in paragraph (4) may be extended by the Crown Court, either before or after it expires, on an application made in writing, specifying the grounds of the application. The court officer shall notify all the parties of the decision of the Crown Court.

(6) The notice under paragraph (3) or any application under paragraph (5) shall be sent to the court officer and at the same time a copy thereof shall be sent by the applicant to every other party to the proceedings.

(7) A party who receives a copy of a notice under paragraph (3) shall, within 28 days of the date of the notice, notify the applicant and the court officer, in writing—

(a) whether or not he opposes the application, giving his reasons for any such opposition; and

(b) whether or not he wishes to be represented at any hearing of the application.

(8) After the expiry of the period referred to in paragraph (7), the Crown Court shall determine whether an application under paragraph (1) is to be dealt with—

(a) without a hearing; or

(b) at a hearing at which the applicant and such other party or parties as the court may direct may be represented;

(c) and the court officer shall notify the applicant and, where necessary, the other party or parties, of the time and place of any such hearing.

(9) The court officer shall notify all the parties of the decision of the Crown Court in relation to an application under paragraph (1) and, where leave is granted, the notification shall state—

(a) the country in which the witness will give evidence;

(b) if known, the place where the witness will give evidence;

(c) where the witness is to give evidence on behalf of the prosecutor, or where disclosure is required by section 5(7) of the Criminal Procedure and Investigations Act 1996 (alibi) or by rules under section 81 of the Police and Criminal Evidence Act 1984 (expert evidence), the name of the witness;

(d) the location of the Crown Court at which the trial should take place; and

(e) any conditions specified by the Crown Court in accordance with paragraph (10).

(10) The Crown Court dealing with an application under paragraph (1) may specify that as a condition of the grant of leave the witness should give the evidence in the presence of a specified person who is able and willing to answer under oath or affirmation any questions the trial judge may put as to the circumstances in which the evidence is given, including questions about any persons who are present when the evidence is given and any matters which may affect the giving of the evidence.

Part 31 Restriction on Cross-Examination by a Defendant Acting in Person

Restrictions on cross-examination of witness

31.1 (1) This rule and rules 31.2 and 31.3 apply where an accused is prevented from cross-examining a witness in person by virtue of section 34, 35 or 36 of the Youth Justice and Criminal Evidence Act 1999.

(2) The court shall explain to the accused as early in the proceedings as is reasonably practicable that he—

(a) is prevented from cross-examining a witness in person; and

(b) should arrange for a legal representative to act for him for the purpose of cross-examining the witness.

(3) The accused shall notify the court officer within 7 days of the court giving its explanation, or within such other period as the court may in any particular case allow, of the action, if any, he has taken.

(4) Where he has arranged for a legal representative to act for him, the notification shall include details of the name and address of the representative.

(5) The notification shall be in writing.

(6) The court officer shall notify all other parties to the proceedings of the name and address of the person, if any, appointed to act for the accused.

(7) Where the court gives its explanation under paragraph (2) to the accused either within 7 days of the day set for the commencement of any hearing at which a witness in respect of whom a prohibition under section 34, 35 or 36 of the 1999 Act applies may be cross-examined or after such a hearing has commenced, the period of 7 days shall be reduced in accordance with any directions issued by the court.

(8) Where at the end of the period of 7 days or such other period as the court has allowed, the court has received no notification from the accused it may grant the accused an extension of time, whether on its own motion or on the application of the accused.

(9) Before granting an extension of time, the court may hold a hearing at which all parties to the proceedings may attend and be heard.

(10) Any extension of time shall be of such period as the court considers appropriate in the circumstances of the case.

(11) The decision of the court as to whether to grant the accused an extension of time shall be notified to all parties to the proceedings by the court officer.

Appointment of legal representative by the Crown Court

31.2 (1) Where the court decides, in accordance with section 38(4) of the Youth Justice and Criminal Evidence Act 1999, to appoint a qualified legal representative, the court officer shall notify all parties to the proceedings of the name and address of the representative.

(2) An appointment made by the court under section 38(4) of the 1999 Act shall, except to such extent as the court may in any particular case determine, terminate at the conclusion of the cross-examination of the witness or witnesses in respect of whom a prohibition under section 34, 35 or 36 of the 1999 Act applies.

Appointment arranged by the accused

31.3 (1) The accused may arrange for the qualified legal representative, appointed by the court under section 38(4) of the Youth Justice and Criminal Evidence Act 1999, to be appointed to act for him for the purpose of cross-examining any witness in respect of whom a prohibition under section 34, 35 or 36 of the 1999 Act applies.

(2) Where such an appointment is made—

(a) both the accused and the qualified legal representative appointed shall notify the court of the appointment; and

(b) the qualified legal representative shall, from the time of his appointment, act for the accused as though the arrangement had been made under section 38(2)(a) of the 1999 Act and shall cease to be the representative of the court under section 38(4).

(3) Where the court receives notification of the appointment either from the qualified legal representative or from the accused but not from both, the court shall investigate whether the appointment has been made, and if it concludes that the appointment has not been made, paragraph (2)(b) shall not apply.

(4) An accused may, notwithstanding an appointment by the court under section 38(4) of the 1999 Act, arrange for a legal representative to act for him for the purpose of cross-examining any witness in respect of whom a prohibition under section 34, 35 or 36 of the 1999 Act applies.

(5) Where the accused arranges for, or informs the court of his intention to arrange for, a legal representative to act for him, he shall notify the court, within such period as the court may allow, of the name and address of any person appointed to act for him.

(6) Where the court is notified within the time allowed that such an appointment has been made, any qualified legal representative appointed by the court in accordance with section 38(4) of the 1999 Act shall be discharged.

(7) The court officer shall, as soon as reasonably practicable after the court receives notification of an appointment under this rule or, where paragraph (3) applies, after the court is satisfied that the appointment has been made, notify all the parties to the proceedings—

(a) that the appointment has been made;

(b) where paragraph (4) applies, of the name and address of the person appointed; and

(c) that the person appointed by the court under section 38(4) of the 1999 Act has been discharged or has ceased to act for the court.

Prohibition on cross-examination of witness

31.4 (1) An application by the prosecutor for the court to give a direction under section 36 of the Youth Justice and Criminal Evidence Act 1999 in relation to any witness must be sent to the court officer and at the same time a copy thereof must be sent by the applicant to every other party to the proceedings.

(2) In his application the prosecutor must state why, in his opinion—

(a) the evidence given by the witness is likely to be diminished if cross-examination is undertaken by the accused in person;

(b) the evidence would be improved if a direction were given under section 36(2) of the 1999 Act; and

(c) it would not be contrary to the interests of justice to give such a direction.

(3) On receipt of the application the court officer must refer it—

(a) if the trial has started, to the court of trial; or

(b) if the trial has not started when the application is received—

(i) to the judge or court designated to conduct the trial, or

(ii) if no judge or court has been designated for that purpose, to such judge or court designated for the purposes of hearing that application.

(4) Where a copy of the application is received by a party to the proceedings more than 14 days before the date set for the trial to begin, that party may make observations in writing on the application to the court officer, but any such observations must be made within 14 days of the receipt of the application and be copied to the other parties to the proceedings.

(5) A party to whom an application is sent in accordance with paragraph (1) who wishes to oppose the application must give his reasons for doing so to the court officer and the other parties to the proceedings.

(6) Those reasons must be notified—

(a) within 14 days of the date the application was served on him, if that date is more than 14 days before the date set for the trial to begin;

(b) if the trial has begun, in accordance with any directions issued by the court; or

(c) if neither paragraph (6)(a) nor (b) applies, before the date set for the trial to begin.

(7) Where the application made in accordance with paragraph (1) is made before the date set for the trial to begin and—

(a) is not contested by any party to the proceedings, the court may determine the application without a hearing;

(b) is contested by a party to the proceedings, the court must direct a hearing of the application.

(8) Where the application is made after the trial has begun—

(a) the application may be made orally; and

(b) the court may give such directions as it considers appropriate to deal with the application.

(9) Where a hearing of the application is to take place, the court officer shall notify each party to the proceedings of the time and place of the hearing.

(10) A party notified in accordance with paragraph (9) may be present at the hearing and be heard.

(11) The court officer must, as soon as possible after the determination of an application made in accordance with paragraph (1), give notice of the decision and the reasons for it to all the parties to the proceedings.

(12) A person making an oral application under paragraph (8)(a) must—

(a) give reasons why the application was not made before the trial commenced; and

(b) provide the court with the information set out in paragraph (2).

PART 32 INTERNATIONAL CO-OPERATION

Notice required to accompany process served outside the United Kingdom and translations

32.1 (1) The notice which by virtue of section 3(4)(b) of the Crime (International Co-operation) Act 2003 (general requirements for service of process) must accompany any process served outside the United Kingdom must give the information specified in paragraphs (2) and (4) below.

(2) The notice must—

(a) state that the person required by the process to appear as a party or attend as a witness can obtain information about his rights in connection therewith from the relevant authority; and

(b) give the particulars specified in paragraph (4) about that authority.

(3) The relevant authority where the process is served—

(a) at the request of the prosecuting authority, is that authority; or

(b) at the request of the defendant or the prosecutor in the case of a private prosecution, is the court by which the process is served.

(4) The particulars referred to in paragraph (2) are—

(a) the name and address of the relevant authority, together with its telephone and fax numbers and e-mail address; and
(b) the name of a person at the relevant authority who can provide the information referred to in paragraph (2)(a), together with his telephone and fax numbers and e-mail address.

(5) The justices' clerk or Crown Court officer must send, together with any process served outside the United Kingdom—
(a) any translation which is provided under section 3(3)(b) of the 2003 Act; and
(b) any translation of the information required to be given by this rule which is provided to him.

(6) In this rule 'process' has the same meaning as in section 51(3) of the 2003 Act.

Proof of service outside the United Kingdom

32.2 (1) A statement in a certificate given by or on behalf of the Secretary of State—
(a) that process has been served on any person under section 4(1) of the Crime (International Co-operation) Act 2003 (service of process otherwise than by post);
(b) of the manner in which service was effected; and
(c) of the date on which process was served;
shall be admissible as evidence of any facts so stated.

(2) In this rule 'process' has the same meaning as in section 51(3) of the 2003 Act.

Supply of copy of notice of request for assistance abroad

32.3 Where a request for assistance under section 7 of the Crime (International Co-operation) Act 2003 is made by a justice of the peace or a judge exercising the jurisdiction of the Crown Court and is sent in accordance with section 8(1) of the 2003 Act, the justices' clerk or the Crown Court officer shall send a copy of the letter of request to the Secretary of State as soon as practicable after the request has been made.

Persons entitled to appear and take part in proceedings before a nominated court and exclusion of public

32.4 A court nominated under section 15(1) of the Crime (International Co-operation) Act 2003 (nominating a court to receive evidence) may—
(a) determine who may appear or take part in the proceedings under Schedule 1 to the 2003 Act before the court and whether a party to the proceedings is entitled to be legally represented; and
(b) direct that the public be excluded from those proceedings if it thinks it necessary to do so in the interests of justice.

Record of proceedings to receive evidence before a nominated court

32.5 (1) Where a court is nominated under section 15(1) of the Crime (International Co-operation) Act 2003 the justices' clerk or Crown Court officer shall enter in an overseas record—
(a) details of the request in respect of which the notice under section 15(1) of the 2003 Act was given;
(b) the date on which, and place at which, the proceedings under Schedule 1 to the 2003 Act in respect of that request took place;
(c) the name of any witness who gave evidence at the proceedings in question;
(d) the name of any person who took part in the proceedings as a legal representative or an interpreter;
(e) whether a witness was required to give evidence on oath or (by virtue of section 5 of the Oaths Act 1978) after making a solemn affirmation; and
(f) whether the opportunity to cross-examine any witness was refused.

(2) When the court gives the evidence received by it under paragraph 6(1) of Schedule 1 to the 2003 Act to the court or authority that made the request or to the territorial authority for forwarding to the court or authority that made the request, the justices' clerk or Crown Court officer shall send to the court, authority or territorial authority (as the case may be) a copy of an extract of so much of the overseas record as relates to the proceedings in respect of that request.

Interpreter for the purposes of proceedings involving a television or telephone link

32.6 (1) This rule applies where a court is nominated under section 30(3) (hearing witnesses in the UK through television links) or section 31(4) (hearing witnesses in the UK by telephone) of the Crime (International Co-operation) Act 2003.

(2) Where it appears to the justices' clerk or the Crown Court officer that the witness to be heard in the proceedings under Part 1 or 2 of Schedule 2 to the 2003 Act ('the relevant proceedings') is likely to give evidence in a language other than English, he shall make arrangements for an interpreter to be present at the proceedings to translate what is said into English.

(3) Where it appears to the justices' clerk or the Crown Court officer that the witness to be heard in the relevant proceedings is likely to give evidence in a language other than that in which the proceedings of the court referred to in section 30(1) or, as the case may be, 31(1) of the 2003 Act ('the external court') will be conducted, he shall make arrangements for an interpreter to be present at the relevant proceedings to translate what is said into the language in which the proceedings of the external court will be conducted.

(4) Where the evidence in the relevant proceedings is either given in a language other than English or is not translated into English by an interpreter, the court shall adjourn the proceedings until such time as an interpreter can be present to provide a translation into English.

(5) Where a court in Wales understands Welsh—

(a) paragraph (2) does not apply where it appears to the justices' clerk or Crown Court officer that the witness in question is likely to give evidence in Welsh;

(b) paragraph (4) does not apply where the evidence is given in Welsh; and

(c) any translation which is provided pursuant to paragraph (2) or (4) may be into Welsh instead of English.

Record of television link hearing before a nominated court

32.7 (1) This rule applies where a court is nominated under section 30(3) of the Crime (International Co-operation) Act 2003.

(2) The justices' clerk or Crown Court officer shall enter in an overseas record—

(a) details of the request in respect of which the notice under section 30(3) of the 2003 Act was given;

(b) the date on which, and place at which, the proceedings under Part 1 of Schedule 2 to that Act in respect of that request took place;

(c) the technical conditions, such as the type of equipment used, under which the proceedings took place;

(d) the name of the witness who gave evidence;

(e) the name of any person who took part in the proceedings as a legal representative or an interpreter; and

(f) the language in which the evidence was given.

(3) As soon as practicable after the proceedings under Part 1 of Schedule 2 to the 2003 Act took place, the justices' clerk or Crown Court officer shall send to the external authority that made the request a copy of an extract of so much of the overseas record as relates to the proceedings in respect of that request.

Record of telephone link hearing before a nominated court

32.8 (1) This rule applies where a court is nominated under section 31(4) of the Crime (International Co-operation) Act 2003.

(2) The justices' clerk or Crown Court officer shall enter in an overseas record—

(a) details of the request in respect of which the notice under section 31(4) of the 2003 Act was given;

(b) the date, time and place at which the proceedings under Part 2 of Schedule 2 to the 2003 Act took place;

(c) the name of the witness who gave evidence;

(d) the name of any interpreter who acted at the proceedings; and

(e) the language in which the evidence was given.

Overseas record

32.9 (1) The overseas records of a magistrates' court shall be part of the register (within the meaning of section 150(1) of the Magistrates' Courts Act 1980) and shall be kept in a separate book.

(2) The overseas records of any court shall not be open to inspection by any person except—

(a) as authorised by the Secretary of State; or

(b) with the leave of the court.

Part 33 Expert Evidence

Reference to expert

33.1 A reference to an 'expert' in this Part is a reference to a person who is required to give or prepare expert evidence for the purpose of criminal proceedings, including evidence required to determine fitness to plead or for the purpose of sentencing.

Expert's duty to the court

33.2 (1) An expert must help the court to achieve the overriding objective by giving objective, unbiased opinion on matters within his expertise.

(2) This duty overrides any obligation to the person from whom he receives instructions or by whom he is paid.

(3) This duty includes an obligation to inform all parties and the court if the expert's opinion changes from that contained in a report served as evidence or given in a statement under Part 24 or Part 29.

Content of expert's report

33.3 (1) An expert's report must—

(a) give details of the expert's qualifications, relevant experience and accreditation;

(b) give details of any literature or other information which the expert has relied on in making the report;

(c) contain a statement setting out the substance of all facts given to the expert which are material to the opinions expressed in the report or upon which those opinions are based;

(d) make clear which of the facts stated in the report are within the expert's own knowledge;

(e) say who carried out any examination, measurement, test or experiment which the expert has used for the report and—

(i) give the qualifications, relevant experience and accreditation of that person,

(ii) say whether or not the examination, measurement, test or experiment was carried out under the expert's supervision, and

(iii) summarise the findings on which the expert relies;

(f) where there is a range of opinion on the matters dealt with in the report—

(i) summarise the range of opinion, and

(ii) give reasons for his own opinion;

(g) if the expert is not able to give his opinion without qualification, state the qualification;

(h) contain a summary of the conclusions reached;

(i) contain a statement that the expert understands his duty to the court, and has complied and will continue to comply with that duty; and

(j) contain the same declaration of truth as a witness statement.

(2) Only sub-paragraphs (i) and (j) of rule 33.3(1) apply to a summary by an expert of his conclusions served in advance of that expert's report.

Expert to be informed of service of report

33.4 A party who serves on another party or on the court a report by an expert must, at once, inform that expert of that fact.

Pre-hearing discussion of expert evidence

33.5 (1) This rule applies where more than one party wants to introduce expert evidence.

(2) The court may direct the experts to—

(a) discuss the expert issues in the proceedings; and

(b) prepare a statement for the court of the matters on which they agree and disagree, giving their reasons.

(3) Except for that statement, the content of that discussion must not be referred to without the court's permission.

Failure to comply with directions

33.6 A party may not introduce expert evidence without the court's permission if the expert has not complied with a direction under rule 33.5.

Court's power to direct that evidence is to be given by a single joint expert

33.7 (1) Where more than one defendant wants to introduce expert evidence on an issue at trial, the court may direct that the evidence on that issue is to be given by one expert only.

(2) Where the co-defendants cannot agree who should be the expert, the court may—
(a) select the expert from a list prepared or identified by them; or
(b) direct that the expert be selected in such other manner as the court may direct.

Instructions to a single joint expert

33.8 (1) Where the court gives a direction under rule 33.7 for a single joint expert to be used, each of the co-defendants may give instructions to the expert.
(2) When a co-defendant gives instructions to the expert he must, at the same time, send a copy of the instructions to the other co-defendant(s).
(3) The court may give directions about—
(a) the payment of the expert's fees and expenses; and
(b) any examination, measurement, test or experiment which the expert wishes to carry out.
(4) The court may, before an expert is instructed, limit the amount that can be paid by way of fees and expenses to the expert.
(5) Unless the court otherwise directs, the instructing co-defendants are jointly and severally liable for the payment of the expert's fees and expenses.

Part 34 Hearsay Evidence

When this Part applies

34.1 This Part applies in a magistrates' court and in the Crown Court where a party wants to introduce evidence on one or more of the grounds set out in section 114(1)(a) to (d) of the Criminal Justice Act 2003, and in this Part that evidence is called 'hearsay evidence'.

Notice of hearsay evidence

34.2 The party who wants to introduce hearsay evidence must give notice in the form set out in the Practice Direction to the court officer and all other parties.

When the prosecutor must give notice of hearsay evidence

34.3 The prosecutor must give notice of hearsay evidence—
(a) in a magistrates' court, at the same time as he complies or purports to comply with section 3 of the Criminal Procedure and Investigations Act 1996 (disclosure by prosecutor); or
(b) in the Crown Court, not more than 14 days after—
(i) the committal of the defendant, or
(ii) the consent to the preferment of a bill of indictment in relation to the case, or
(iii) the service of a notice of transfer under section 4 of the Criminal Justice Act 1987 (serious fraud cases) or under section 53 of the Criminal Justice Act 1991 (certain cases involving children), or
(iv) where a person is sent for trial under section 51 of the Crime and Disorder Act 1998 (indictable-only offences sent for trial), the service of copies of the documents containing the evidence on which the charge or charges are based under paragraph 1 of Schedule 3 to the 1998 Act.

When a defendant must give notice of hearsay evidence

34.4 A defendant must give notice of hearsay evidence not more than 14 days after the prosecutor has complied with or purported to comply with section 3 of the Criminal Procedure and Investigations Act 1996 (disclosure by prosecutor).

Opposing the introduction of hearsay evidence

34.5 A party who receives a notice of hearsay evidence may oppose it by giving notice within 14 days in the form set out in the Practice Direction to the court officer and all other parties.

Methods of giving notice

34.6 [Revoked.]

Court's power to vary requirements under this Part

34.7 The court may—
(a) dispense with the requirement to give notice of hearsay evidence;
(b) allow notice to be given in a different form, or orally; or
(c) shorten a time limit or extend it (even after it has expired).

Waiving the requirement to give a notice of hearsay evidence

34.8 A party entitled to receive a notice of hearsay evidence may waive his entitlement by so informing the court and the party who would have given the notice.

Part 35 Evidence of Bad Character

When this Part applies

35.1 This Part applies in a magistrates' court and in the Crown Court when a party wants to introduce evidence of bad character as defined in section 98 of the Criminal Justice Act 2003.

Introducing evidence of non-defendant's bad character

35.2 A party who wants to introduce evidence of a non-defendant's bad character or who wants to cross-examine a witness with a view to eliciting that evidence, under section 100 of the Criminal Justice Act 2003 must apply in the form set out in the Practice Direction and the application must be received by the court officer and all other parties to the proceedings—

(a) not more than 14 days after the prosecutor has—

(i) complied or purported to comply with section 3 of the Criminal Procedure and Investigations Act 1996 (disclosure by the prosecutor), or

(ii) disclosed the previous conviction of that non-defendant; or

(b) as soon as reasonably practicable, where the application concerns a non-defendant who is to be invited to give (or has given) evidence for a defendant.

Opposing introduction of evidence of non-defendant's bad character

35.3 A party who receives a copy of an application under rule 35.2 may oppose that application by giving notice in writing to the court officer and all other parties to the proceedings not more than 14 days after receiving that application.

Prosecutor introducing evidence of defendant's bad character

35.4 (1) A prosecutor who wants to introduce evidence of a defendant's bad character or who wants to cross-examine a witness with a view to eliciting that evidence, under section 101 of the Criminal Justice Act 2003 must give notice in the form set out in the Practice Direction to the court officer and all other parties to the proceedings.

(2) Notice under paragraph (1) must be given—

(a) in a case to be tried in a magistrates' court, at the same time as the prosecutor complies or purports to comply with section 3 of the Criminal Procedure and Investigations Act 1996; and

(b) in a case to be tried in the Crown Court, not more than 14 days after—

(i) the committal of the defendant, or

(ii) the consent to the preferment of a bill of indictment in relation to the case, or

(iii) the service of notice of transfer under section 4(1) of the Criminal Justice Act 1987 (notices of transfer) or under section 53(1) of the Criminal Justice Act 1991 (notices of transfer in certain cases involving children), or

(iv) where a person is sent for trial under section 51 of the Crime and Disorder Act 1998 (sending cases to the Crown Court) the service of copies of the documents containing the evidence on which the charge or charges are based under paragraph 1 of Schedule 3 to that Act.

Co-defendant introducing evidence of defendant's bad character

35.5 A co-defendant who wants to introduce evidence of a defendant's bad character or who wants to cross-examine a witness with a view to eliciting that evidence under section 101 of the Criminal Justice Act 2003 must give notice in the form set out in the Practice Direction to the court officer and all other parties to the proceedings not more than 14 days after the prosecutor has complied or purported to comply with section 3 of the Criminal Procedure and Investigations Act 1996.

Defendant applying to exclude evidence of his own bad character

35.6 A defendant's application to exclude bad character evidence must be in the form set out in the Practice Direction and received by the court officer and all other parties to the proceedings not more than 14 days after receiving a notice given under rules 35.4 or 35.5.

Methods of giving notice

35.7 [Revoked.]

Court's power to vary requirements under this Part

35.8 The court may—
(a) allow a notice or application required under this rule to be given in a different form, or orally; or
(b) shorten a time-limit under this rule or extend it even after it has expired.

Defendant waiving right to receive notice

35.9 A defendant entitled to receive a notice under this Part may waive his entitlement by so informing the court and the party who would have given the notice.

Part 36 Evidence about a Complainant's Sexual Behaviour

When this Part applies

36.1 This Part applies in magistrates' courts and in the Crown Court where a defendant wants to—
(a) introduce evidence; or
(b) cross-examine a witness about a complainant's sexual behaviour despite the prohibition in section 41 of the Youth Justice and Criminal Evidence Act 1999.

Application for permission to introduce evidence or cross-examine

36.2 The defendant must apply for permission to do so—
(a) in writing; and
(b) not more than 28 days after the prosecutor has complied or purported to comply with section 3 of the Criminal Procedure and Investigations Act 1996 (disclosure by prosecutor).

Content of application

36.3 The application must—
(a) identify the issue to which the defendant says the complainant's sexual behaviour is relevant;
(b) give particulars of—
(i) any evidence that the defendant wants to introduce, and
(ii) any questions that the defendant wants to ask;
(c) identify the exception to the prohibition in section 41 of the Youth Justice and Criminal Evidence Act 1999 on which the defendant relies; and
(d) give the name and date of birth of any witness whose evidence about the complainant's sexual behaviour the defendant wants to introduce.

Service of application

36.4 The defendant must serve the application on the court officer and all other parties.

Reply to application

36.5 A party who wants to make representations about an application under rule 36.2 must—
(a) do so in writing not more than 14 days after receiving it; and
(b) serve those representations on the court officer and all other parties.

Application for special measures

36.6 If the court allows an application under rule 36.2 then—
(a) a party may apply not more than 14 days later for a special measures direction or for the variation of an existing special measures direction; and
(b) the court may shorten the time for opposing that application.

Court's power to vary requirements under this Part

36.7 The court may shorten or extend (even after it has expired) a time limit under this Part.

Part 37 Summary Trial

Order of evidence and speeches: information

37.1 (1) On the summary trial of an information, where the accused does not plead guilty, the prosecutor shall call the evidence for the prosecution, and before doing so may address the court.

(2) At the conclusion of the evidence for the prosecution, the accused may address the court, whether or not he afterwards calls evidence.

(3) At the conclusion of the evidence, if any, for the defence, the prosecutor may call evidence to rebut that evidence.

(4) At the conclusion of the evidence for the defence and the evidence, if any, in rebuttal, the accused may address the court if he has not already done so.

(5) Either party may, with the leave of the court, address the court a second time, but where the court grants leave to one party it shall not refuse leave to the other.

(6) Where both parties address the court twice the prosecutor shall address the court for the second time before the accused does so.

Procedure on information where accused is not legally represented

37.2 (1) The court shall explain to an accused who is not legally represented the substance of the charge in simple language.

(2) If an accused who is not legally represented, instead of asking a witness in support of the charge questions by way of cross-examination, makes assertions, the court shall then put to the witness such questions as it thinks necessary on behalf of the accused and may for this purpose question the accused in order to bring out or clear up any point arising out of such assertions.

Adjournment of trial of information

37.3 (1) Where in the absence of the accused a magistrates' court adjourns the trial of an information, the court officer shall give to the accused notice in writing of the time and place at which the trial is to be resumed.

Formal admissions

37.4 Where under section 10 of the Criminal Justice Act 1967 a fact is admitted orally in court by or on behalf of the prosecutor or defendant for the purposes of the summary trial of an offence the court shall cause the admission to be written down and signed by or on behalf of the party making the admission.

Notice of intention to cite previous convictions

37.5 Service on any person of a notice of intention to cite previous convictions under section 104 of the Magistrates' Courts Act 1980 or section 13 of the Road Traffic Offenders Act 1988 may be effected by delivering it to him or by sending it by post in a registered letter or by recorded delivery service, or by first class post addressed to him at his last known or usual place of abode.

Preservation of depositions where offence triable either way is dealt with summarily

37.6 The magistrates' court officer for the magistrates' court by which any person charged with an offence triable either way has been tried summarily shall preserve for a period of three years such depositions as have been taken.

Order of evidence and speeches: complaint

37.7 (1) On the hearing of a complaint, except where the court determines under section 53(3) of the Magistrates' Courts Act 1980 to make the order with the consent of the defendant without hearing evidence, the complainant shall call his evidence, and before doing so may address the court.

(2) At the conclusion of the evidence for the complainant the defendant may address the court, whether or not he afterwards calls evidence.

(3) At the conclusion of the evidence, if any, for the defence, the complainant may call evidence to rebut that evidence.

(4) At the conclusion of the evidence for the defence and the evidence, if any, in rebuttal, the defendant may address the court if he has not already done so.

(5) Either party may, with the leave of the court, address the court a second time, but where the court grants leave to one party it shall not refuse leave to the other.

(6) Where the defendant obtains leave to address the court for a second time his second address shall be made before the second address, if any, of the complainant.

Part 38 Trial of Children and Young Persons

Application of this Part

38.1 (1) This Part applies, subject to paragraph (3) of this rule, where proceedings to which paragraph (2) applies are brought in a magistrates' court in respect of a child or young person ('the relevant minor').

(2) This paragraph applies to proceedings in which the relevant minor is charged with an offence, and, where he appears or is brought before the court, to proceedings under—

(a) Paragraphs 1, 2, 5 and 6 of Schedule 7 to the Powers of Criminal Courts (Sentencing) Act 2000 (breach, revocation and amendment of supervision orders);

(b) Part II, III or IV of Schedule 3 to the 2000 Act (breach, revocation and amendment of certain community orders);

(c) Paragraphs 4, 5, 6 and 7 of Schedule 5 to the 2000 Act (breach, revocation and amendment of attendance centre orders); and

(d) Schedule 8 to the 2000 Act (breach, revocation and amendment of action plan orders and reparation orders).

(3) Where the court is inquiring into an offence as examining justices, only rules 38.2, 38.3 and 38.5(3) apply, and where the proceedings are of a kind mentioned in paragraph (2)(a), (b) or (c) rule 38.4 does not apply.

Assistance in conducting case

38.2 (1) Except where the relevant minor is legally represented, the magistrates' court shall allow his parent or guardian to assist him in conducting his case.

(2) Where the parent or guardian cannot be found or cannot in the opinion of the court reasonably be required to attend, the court may allow any relative or other responsible person to take the place of the parent or guardian for the purposes of this Part.

Duty of court to explain nature of proceedings etc

38.3 (1) The magistrates' court shall explain to the relevant minor the nature of the proceedings and, where he is charged with an offence, the substance of the charge.

(2) The explanation shall be given in simple language suitable to his age and understanding.

Duty of court to take plea to charge

38.4 Where the relevant minor is charged with an offence the magistrates' court shall, after giving the explanation required by rule 38.3, ask him whether he pleads guilty or not guilty to the charge.

Evidence in support of charge

38.5 (1) Where—

(a) the relevant minor is charged with an offence and does not plead guilty, or

(b) the proceedings are of a kind mentioned in rule 38.1(2)(a), (b) or (c),

the magistrates' court shall hear the witnesses in support of the charge or, as the case may be, the application.

(2) Except where—

(a) the proceedings are of a kind mentioned in rule 38.1(2)(a), (b) or (c), and

(b) the relevant minor is the applicant,

each witness may at the close of his evidence-in-chief be cross-examined by or on behalf of the relevant minor.

(3) If in any case where the relevant minor is not legally represented or assisted as provided by rule 38.2, the relevant minor, instead of asking questions by way of cross-examination, makes assertions, the court shall then put to the witness such questions as it thinks necessary on behalf of the relevant minor and may for this purpose question the relevant minor in order to bring out or clear up any point arising out of any such assertions.

Evidence in reply

38.6 If it appears to the magistrates' court after hearing the evidence in support of the charge or application that a prima facie case is made out, the relevant minor shall, if he is not the applicant and is not legally represented, be told that he may give evidence or address the court, and the evidence of any witnesses shall be heard.

Part 39 Trial on Indictment

Time limits for beginning of trials

39.1 The periods set out for the purposes of section 77(2)(a) and (b) of the Supreme Court Act 1981 shall be 14 days and 8 weeks respectively and accordingly the trial of a person committed by a magistrates' court—

(a) shall not begin until the expiration of 14 days beginning with the date of his committal, except with his consent and the consent of the prosecution; and

(b) shall, unless the Crown Court has otherwise ordered, begin not later than the expiration of 8 weeks beginning with the date of his committal.

Appeal against refusal to excuse from jury service or to defer attendance

39.2 (1) A person summoned under the Juries Act 1974 for jury service may appeal in accordance with the provisions of this rule against any refusal of the appropriate court officer to excuse him under section 9(2), or to defer his attendance under section 9A(1), of that Act.

(2) Subject to paragraph (3), an appeal under this rule shall be heard by the Crown Court.

(3) Where the appellant is summoned under the 1974 Act to attend before the High Court in Greater London the appeal shall be heard by a judge of the High Court and where the appellant is summoned under that Act to attend before the High Court outside Greater London or before a county court and the appeal has not been decided by the Crown Court before the day on which the appellant is required by the summons to attend, the appeal shall be heard by the court before which he is summoned to attend.

(4) An appeal under this rule shall be commenced by the appellant's giving notice of appeal to the appropriate court officer of the Crown Court or the High Court in Greater London, as the case may be, and such notice shall be in writing and shall specify the matters upon which the appellant relies as providing good reason why he should be excused from attending in pursuance of the summons or why his attendance should be deferred.

(5) The court shall not dismiss an appeal under this rule unless the appellant has been given an opportunity of making representations.

(6) Where an appeal under this rule is decided in the absence of the appellant, the appropriate court officer of the Crown Court or the High Court in Greater London, as the case may be, shall notify him of the decision without delay.

Part 40 Tainted Acquittals

Time of certification

40.1 Where a person is convicted of an offence as referred to in section 54(1)(b) of the Criminal Procedure and Investigations Act 1996 and it appears to the court before which the conviction has taken place that the provisions of section 54(2) are satisfied, the court shall make the certification referred to in section 54(2) at any time following conviction but no later than—

(a) immediately after the court sentences or otherwise deals with that person in respect of the offence; or

(b) where the court, being a magistrates' court, commits that person to the Crown Court, or remits him to another magistrates' court, to be dealt with in respect of the offence, immediately after he is so committed or remitted, as the case may be; or

(c) where that person is a child or young person and the court, being the Crown Court, remits him to a youth court to be dealt with in respect of the offence, immediately after he is so remitted.

Form of certification in the Crown Court

40.2 A certification referred to in section 54(2) of the Criminal Procedure and Investigations Act 1996 by the Crown Court shall be drawn up in the form set out in the Practice Direction.

Service of a copy of the certification

40.3 (1) Where a magistrates' court or the Crown Court makes a certification as referred to in section 54(2) of the Criminal Procedure and Investigations Act 1996, the court officer shall, as soon as practicable after the drawing up of the form, serve a copy on the acquitted person referred to in the certification, on the prosecutor in the proceedings which led to the acquittal, and, where the acquittal has taken place before a court other than, or at a different place to, the court where the certification has been made, on—

(a) the clerk of the magistrates' court before which the acquittal has taken place; or

(b) the Crown Court officer at the place where the acquittal has taken place.

(2) to (4) [Revoked.]

Entry in register or records in relation to the conviction which occasioned certification

40.4 A clerk of a magistrates' court or an officer of a Crown Court which has made a certification under section 54(2) of the Criminal Procedure and Investigations Act 1996 shall enter in the register or records, in relation to the conviction which occasioned the certification, a note of the fact that certification has been made, the date of certification, the name of the acquitted person referred to in the certification, a description of the offence of which the acquitted person has been acquitted, the date of the acquittal, and the name of the court before which the acquittal has taken place.

Entry in the register or records in relation to the acquittal

40.5 The court officer of the court before which an acquittal has taken place shall, as soon as practicable after receipt of a copy of a form recording a certification under section 54(2) of the Criminal Procedure and Investigations Act 1996 relating to the acquittal, enter in the register or records a note that the certification has been made, the date of the certification, the name of the court which has made the certification, the name of the person whose conviction occasioned the making of the certification, and a description of the offence of which that person has been convicted. Where the certification has been made by the same court as the court before which the acquittal has occurred, sitting at the same place, the entry shall be made as soon as practicable after the making of the certification. In the case of an acquittal before a magistrates' court the entry in the register shall be signed by the clerk of the court.

Display of copy certification form

40.6 (1) Where a court makes a certification as referred to in section 54(2) of the Criminal Procedure and Investigations Act 1996, the court officer shall, as soon as practicable after the drawing up of the form, display a copy of that form at a prominent place within court premises to which place the public has access.

(2) Where an acquittal has taken place before a court other than, or at a different place to, the court which has made the certification under section 54(2) of the 1996 Act in relation to the acquittal, the court officer at the court where the acquittal has taken place shall, as soon as practicable after receipt of a copy of the form recording the certification, display a copy of it at a prominent place within court premises to which place the public has access.

(3) The copy of the form referred to in paragraph (1), or the copy referred to in paragraph (2), shall continue to be displayed as referred to, respectively, in those paragraphs at least until the expiry of 28 days from, in the case of paragraph (1), the day on which the certification was made, or, in the case of paragraph (2), the day on which the copy form was received at the court.

Entry in the register or records in relation to decision of High Court

40.7 (1) The court officer at the court where an acquittal has taken place shall, on receipt from the Administrative Court Office of notice of an order made under section 54(3) of the Criminal Procedure and Investigations Act 1996 quashing the acquittal, or of a decision not to make such an order, enter in the register or records, in relation to the acquittal, a note of the fact that the acquittal has been quashed by the said order, or that a decision has been made not to make such an order, as the case may be.

(2) The court officer of the court which has made a certification under section 54(2) of the 1996 Act shall, on receipt from the Administrative Court Office of notice of an order made under section 54(3) of that Act quashing the acquittal referred to in the certification, or of a decision not to make such an order, enter in the register or records, in relation to the conviction which occasioned the certification, a note that the acquittal has been quashed by the said order, or that a decision has been made not to make such an order, as the case may be.

(3) The entries in the register of a magistrates' court referred to, respectively, in paragraphs (1) and (2) above shall be signed by the magistrates' court officer.

Display of copy of notice received from High Court

40.8 (1) Where the court officer of a court which has made a certification under section 54(2) of the Criminal Procedure and Investigations Act 1996 or before which an acquittal has occurred to which such a certification refers, receives from the Administrative Court Office notice of an order quashing the acquittal concerned, or notice of a decision not to make such an order, he shall, as soon as practicable after receiving the notice, display a copy of it at a prominent place within court premises to which place the public has access.

(2) The copy notice referred to in paragraph (1) shall continue to be displayed as referred to in that paragraph at least until the expiry of 28 days from the day on which the notice was received at the court.

Part 41 Retrial Following Acquittal for Serious Offence

Interpretation

41.1 In this Part:

'business day' means any day other than a Saturday, Sunday, Christmas Day, Good Friday or a bank holiday under the Banking and Financial Dealings Act 1971, in England and Wales; and

'section 76 application' means an application made by a prosecutor under section 76(1) or (2) of the Criminal Justice Act 2003.

Notice of a section 76 application

41.2 (1) A prosecutor who wants to make a section 76 application must serve notice of that application in the form set out in the Practice Direction on the Registrar and the acquitted person.

(2) That notice shall, where practicable, be accompanied by—

(a) relevant witness statements which are relied upon as forming new and compelling evidence of guilt of the acquitted person as well as any relevant witness statements from the original trial;

(b) any unused statements which might reasonably be considered capable of undermining the section 76 application or of assisting an acquitted person's application to oppose that application under rule 41.3;

(c) a copy of the indictment and paper exhibits from the original trial;

(d) copies of the transcript of the summing up and any other relevant transcripts from the original trial; and

(e) any other documents relied upon to support the section 76 application.

(3) The prosecutor must, as soon as practicable after service of that notice on the acquitted person, file with the Registrar a witness statement or certificate of service which exhibits a copy of that notice.

Response of the acquitted person

41.3 (1) An acquitted person who wants to oppose a section 76 application must serve a response in the form set out in the Practice Direction on the Registrar and the prosecutor which—

(a) indicates if he is also seeking an order under section 80(6) of the Criminal Justice Act 2003 for—

(i) the production of any document, exhibit or other thing, or

(ii) a witness to attend for examination and to be examined before the Court of Appeal; and

(b) exhibits any relevant documents.

(2) The acquitted person must serve that response not more than 28 days after receiving notice under rule 41.2.

(3) The Court of Appeal may extend the period for service under paragraph (2), either before or after that period expires.

Examination of witnesses or evidence by the Court of Appeal

41.4 (1) Prior to the hearing of a section 76 application, a party may apply to the Court of Appeal for an order under section 80(6) of the Criminal Justice Act 2003 for—

(a) the production of any document, exhibit or other thing; or

(b) a witness to attend for examination and to be examined before the Court of Appeal.

(2) An application under paragraph (1) must be in the form set out in the Practice Direction and must be sent to the Registrar and a copy sent to each party to the section 76 application.

(3) An application must set out the reasons why the order was not sought from the Court when—

(a) the notice was served on the Registrar under rule 41.2, if the application is made by the prosecutor; or

(b) the response was served on the Registrar under rule 41.3, if the application is made by the acquitted person.

(4) An application must be made at least 14 days before the day of the hearing of the section 76 application.

(5) If the Court of Appeal makes an order under section 80(6) of the 2003 Act on its own motion or on application from the prosecutor, it must serve notice and reasons for that order on all parties to the section 76 application.

Bail or custody hearings in the Crown Court

41.5 (1) Rules 19.18, 19.22 and 19.23 shall apply where a person is to appear or be brought before the Crown Court pursuant to sections 88 or 89 of the Criminal Justice Act 2003 (with the modification as set out in paragraph (2)), as if they were applications under rule 19.18(1).

(2) Substitute the following for Rule 19.18:

'Where a person is to appear or be brought before the Crown Court pursuant to sections 88 or 89 of the Criminal Justice Act 2003, the prosecutor must serve notice of the need for such a hearing on the court officer.'

(3) Where a person is to appear or be brought before the Crown Court pursuant to sections 88 or 89 of the 2003 Act the Crown Court may order that the person shall be released from custody on entering into a recognizance, with or without sureties, or giving other security before—

(a) the Crown Court officer; or

(b) any other person authorised by virtue of section 119(1) of the Magistrates' Courts Act 1980 to take a recognizance where a magistrates' court having power to take the recognizance has, instead of taking it, fixed the amount in which the principal and his sureties, if any, are to be bound.

(4) The court officer shall forward to the Registrar a copy of any record made in pursuance of section 5(1) of the Bail Act 1976.

Further provisions regarding bail and custody in the Crown Court

41.6 (1) The prosecutor may only apply to extend or further extend the relevant period before it expires and that application must be served on the Crown Court officer and the acquitted person.

(2) A prosecutor's application for a summons or a warrant under section 89(3)(a) or (b) of the Criminal Justice Act 2003 must be served on the court officer and the acquitted person.

Bail or custody orders in the Court of Appeal

41.7 Rules 68.8 and 68.9 shall apply to bail or custody orders made in the Court of Appeal under section 90 of the Criminal Justice Act 2003 as if they were orders made pursuant to an application under rule 68.7.

Application for restrictions on publication

41.8 (1) An application by the Director of Public Prosecutions, under section 82 of the Criminal Justice Act 2003, for restrictions on publication must be in the form set out in the Practice Direction and be served on the Registrar and the acquitted person.

(2) If notice of a section 76 application has not been given and the Director of Public Prosecution has indicated that there are reasons why the acquitted person should not be notified of the application for restrictions on publication, the Court of Appeal may order that service on the acquitted person is not to be effected until notice of a section 76 application is served on that person.

(3) If the Court of Appeal makes an order for restrictions on publication of its own motion or on application of the Director of Public Prosecutions, the Registrar must serve notice and reasons for that order on all parties, unless paragraph (2) applies.

Variation or revocation of restrictions on publication

41.9 (1) A party who wants to vary or revoke an order for restrictions on publication, under section

82(7) of the Criminal Justice Act 2003, may apply to the Court of Appeal in writing at any time after that order was made.

(2) A copy of the application to vary or revoke shall be sent to all parties to the section 76 application unless paragraph (3) applies.

(3) If the application to vary or revoke is made by the Director of Public Prosecutions and—

(a) the notice of a section 76 application has not been given under rule 41.2; and

(b) the Director of Public Prosecutions has indicated that there are reasons why the acquitted person should not be notified of an application for restrictions on publication,

the Court of Appeal may order that service on the acquitted person is not to be effected until notice of a section 76 application is served on that person.

(4) If the Court of Appeal varies or revokes an order for restrictions on publication of its own motion or on application, it must serve notice and reasons for that order on all parties, unless paragraph (3) applies.

Powers exercisable by a single judge of the Court of Appeal

41.10 (1) The following powers under the Criminal Justice Act 2003 and under this Part may be exercised by a single judge in the same manner as they may be exercised by the Court of Appeal and subject to the same provisions, namely to—

(a) order the production of any document, exhibit or thing under section 80(6)(a) of the 2003 Act;

(b) order any witness who would be a compellable witness in proceedings pursuant to an order or declaration made on the application to attend for examination and be examined before the Court of Appeal under section 80(6)(b) of the 2003 Act;

(c) extend the time for service under rule 41.3(2); and

(d) delay the requirement of service on the acquitted person of an application for restrictions on publication under rules 41.8(2) and 41.9(3).

(2) A single judge may, for the purposes of exercising any of the powers specified in paragraph (1), sit in such place as he appoints and may sit otherwise than in open court.

(3) Where a single judge exercises one of the powers set out in paragraph (1), the Registrar must serve notice of the single judge's decision on all parties to the section 76 application.

Powers exercisable by the Registrar

41.11 (1) The Registrar may require the Crown Court at the place of original trial to provide the Court of Appeal with any assistance or information which it may require for the purposes of exercising its jurisdiction under Part 10 of the Criminal Justice Act 2003 or this Part.

(2) The following powers may be exercised by the Registrar in the same manner as the Court of Appeal and subject to the same provisions

(a) order the production of any document, exhibit or thing under section 80(6)(a) of the 2003 Act;

(b) order any witness who would be a compellable witness in proceedings pursuant to an order or declaration made on the application to attend for examination and be examined before the Court of Appeal under section 80(6)(b) of the 2003 Act; and

(c) extend the time for service under rule 41.3(2).

(3) Where the Registrar exercises one of the powers set out in paragraph (2) the Registrar must serve notice of that decision on all parties to the section 76 application.

(4) Where the Registrar has refused an application to exercise any of the powers referred to in paragraph (2), the party making the application may have it determined by a single judge by serving a renewal in the form set out in the Practice Direction within 14 days of the day on which notice of the Registrar's decision is served on the party making the application, unless that period is extended by the Court of Appeal.

Determination by full court

41.12 (1) Where a single judge has refused an application to exercise any of the powers referred to in rule 41.10, the applicant may have that application determined by the Court of Appeal by serving a notice of renewal in the form set out in the Practice Direction.

(2) A notice under paragraph (1) must be served on the Registrar within 14 days of the day on which notice of the single judge's decision is served on the party making the application, unless that period is extended by the Court of Appeal.

(3) If a notice under paragraph (1) is not served on the Registrar within the period specified in

paragraph (2) or such extended period as the Court of Appeal has allowed, the application shall be treating as having been refused by the Court of Appeal.

Notice of the determination of the application

41.13 (1) The Court of Appeal may give its determination of the section 76 application at the conclusion of the hearing.

(2) If determination is reserved, the Registrar shall as soon as practicable, serve notice of the determination on the parties to the section 76 application.

(3) If the Court of Appeal orders under section 77 of the Criminal Justice Act 2003 that a retrial take place, the Registrar must as soon as practicable, serve notice on the Crown Court officer at the appropriate place of retrial.

Notice of application to set aside order for retrial

41.14 (1) If an acquitted person has not been arraigned before the end of 2 months after the date of an order under section 77 of the Criminal Justice Act 2003 he may apply in the form set out in the Practice Direction to the Court of Appeal to set aside the order.

(2) An application under paragraph (1) must be served on the Registrar and the prosecutor.

Leave to arraign

41.15 (1) If the acquitted person has not been arraigned before the end of 2 months after the date of an order under section 77 of the Criminal Justice Act 2003, the prosecutor may apply in the form set out in the Practice Direction to the Court of Appeal for leave to arraign.

(2) An application under paragraph (1) must be served on the Registrar and the acquitted person.

Abandonment of the application

41.16 (1) A section 76 application may be abandoned by the prosecutor before the hearing of that application by serving a notice in the form set out in the Practice Direction on the Registrar and the acquitted person.

(2) The Registrar must, as soon as practicable, after receiving a notice under paragraph (1) send a copy of it endorsed with the date of receipt to the prosecutor and acquitted person.

Part 42 Remittal from one Magistrates' Court to Another for Sentence

Remittal for sentence

42.1 (1) Where a magistrates' court remits an offender to some other magistrates' court under section 10 of the Powers of Criminal Courts (Sentencing) Act 2000 after convicting him of an offence, the court officer for the convicting court shall send to the court officer for the other court—

(a) a copy signed by the court officer for the convicting court of the minute or memorandum of the conviction and remittal entered in the register;

(b) a copy of any note of the evidence given at the trial of the offender, any written statement tendered in evidence and any deposition;

(c) such documents and articles produced in evidence before the convicting court as have been retained by that court;

(d) any report relating to the offender considered by the convicting court;

(e) if the offender is remitted on bail, a copy of the record made by the convicting court in pursuance of section 5 of the Bail Act 1976 relating to such bail and also any recognizance entered into by any person as his surety;

(f) if the convicting court makes an order under section 148 of the 2000 Act (restitution orders), a copy signed by the court officer for the convicting court of the minute or memorandum of the order entered in the register;

(g) a copy of any representation order previously made in the same case; and

(h) a copy of any application for a representation order.

(2) Where a magistrates' court remits an offender to some other magistrates' court as aforesaid and the other court remits him back to the convicting court under section 10(5) of the 2000 Act, the court officer for the other court shall send to the court officer for the convicting court—

(a) a copy signed by the court officer for the other court of the minute or memorandum of the remittal back entered in the register;

(b) if the offender is remitted back on bail, a copy of the record made by the other court in pursuance of section 5 of the Bail Act 1976 relating to such bail and also any recognizance entered into by any person as his surety; and

(c) all documents and articles sent in pursuance of paragraph (1) of this rule.

(3) In this rule 'the offender', 'the convicting court' and 'the other court' have the same meanings as in section 10 of the 2000 Act.

Part 43 Committal to the Crown Court for Sentence

Committals for sentence, etc

43.1 (1) Where a magistrates' court commits an offender to the Crown Court under the Vagrancy Act 1824, sections 3, 6, 116(3)(b) or 120(2)(a) of the Powers of Criminal Courts (Sentencing) Act 2000 or section 6 of the Bail Act 1976 after convicting him of an offence, the magistrates' court officer shall send to the Crown Court officer—

(a) a copy signed by the magistrates' court officer of the minute or memorandum of the conviction entered in the register;

(b) copy of any note of the evidence given at the trial of the offender, any written statement tendered in evidence and any deposition;

(c) such documents and articles produced in evidence before the court as have been retained by the court;

(d) any report relating to the offender considered by the court;

(e) if the offender is committed on bail, a copy of the record made in pursuance of section 5 of the 1976 Act relating to such bail and also any recognizance entered into by any person as his surety;

(f) if the court imposes under section 26 of the Road Traffic Offenders Act 1988 an interim disqualification for holding or obtaining a licence under Part III of the Road Traffic Act 1988, a statement of the date of birth and sex of the offender;

(g) if the court makes an order under section 148 of the 2000 Act (restitution orders), a copy signed by the clerk of the convicting court of the minute or memorandum of the order entered in the register; and

(h) any documents relating to an appeal by the prosecution against the granting of bail.

(2) Where a magistrates' court commits an offender to the Crown Court under the Vagrancy Act 1824 or sections 3, 6 or 120(2) of the 2000 Act and the magistrates' court on that occasion imposes, under section 26 of the Road Traffic Offenders Act 1988, an interim disqualification for holding or obtaining a licence under Part III of the Road Traffic Act 1988, the magistrates' court officer shall give notice of the interim disqualification to the Crown Court officer.

(3) Where a magistrates' court commits a person on bail to the Crown Court under any of the enactments mentioned in paragraph (2) of this rule or under section 6 of the Bail Act 1976 the magistrates' court officer shall give notice thereof in writing to the governor of the prison to which persons of the sex of the person committed are committed by that court if committed in custody for trial and also, if the person committed is under the age of 21, to the governor of the remand centre to which he would have been committed if the court had refused him bail.

Committal to Crown Court for order restricting discharge, etc

43.2 Where a magistrates' court commits an offender to the Crown Court either—

(a) under section 43 of the Mental Health Act 1983 with a view to the making of a hospital order with an order restricting his discharge; or

(b) under section 3 of the Powers of Criminal Courts (Sentencing) Act 2000, as modified by section 43(4) of the 1983 Act, with a view to the passing of a more severe sentence than the magistrates' court has power to inflict if such an order is not made,

the magistrates' court officer shall send to the Crown Court officer—

(i) the copies, documents and articles specified in rule 43.1,

(ii) any written evidence about the offender given by a medical practitioner under section 37 of the 1983 Act or a copy of a note of any oral evidence so given,

(iii) the name and address of the hospital the managers of which have agreed to admit the offender if a hospital order is made, and

(iv) if the offender has been admitted to a hospital under section 37 of the 1983 Act, the name and address of that hospital.

Part 44 Sentencing Children and Young Persons

Procedure after finding against minor in a magistrates' court

44.1 (1) This rule applies where—

(a) the relevant minor (as defined in rule 38.1) is found guilty by a magistrates' court of an offence, whether after a plea of guilty or otherwise; or

(b) in proceedings of a kind mentioned in rule 38.1(2)(a), (b) or (c) the court is satisfied that the case for the applicant—

(i) if the relevant minor is not the applicant, has been made out, or

(ii) if he is the applicant, has not been made out.

(2) Where this rule applies—

(a) the relevant minor and his parent or guardian, if present, shall be given an opportunity of making a statement;

(b) the court shall take into consideration all available information as to the general conduct, home surroundings, school record and medical history of the relevant minor and, in particular, shall take into consideration such information as aforesaid which is provided in pursuance of section 9 of the Children and Young Persons Act 1969;

(c) if such information as aforesaid is not fully available, the court shall consider the desirability of adjourning the proceedings for such inquiry as may be necessary;

(d) any written report of a probation officer, local authority, local education authority, educational establishment or registered medical practitioner may be received and considered by the court without being read aloud; and

(e) if the court considers it necessary in the interests of the relevant minor, it may require him or his parent or guardian, if present, to withdraw from the court.

(3) The court shall arrange for copies of any written report before the court to be made available to—

(a) the legal representative, if any, of the relevant minor;

(b) any parent or guardian of the relevant minor who is present at the hearing; and

(c) the relevant minor, except where the court otherwise directs on the ground that it appears to it impracticable to disclose the report having regard to his age and understanding or undesirable to do so having regard to potential serious harm which might thereby be suffered by him.

(4) In any case in which the relevant minor is not legally represented and where a report which has not been made available to him in accordance with a direction under paragraph (3)(c) has been considered without being read aloud in pursuance of paragraph (2)(d) or where he or his parent or guardian has been required to withdraw from the court in pursuance of paragraph (2)(e), then—

(a) the relevant minor shall be told the substance of any part of the information given to the court bearing on his character or conduct which the court considers to be material to the manner in which the case should be dealt with unless it appears to it impracticable so to do having regard to his age and understanding; and

(b) the parent or guardian of the relevant minor, if present, shall be told the substance of any part of such information which the court considers to be material as aforesaid and which has reference to his character or conduct or to the character, conduct, home surroundings or health of the relevant minors, and if such a person, having been told the substance of any part of such information, desires to produce further evidence with reference thereto, the court, if it thinks the further evidence would be material, shall adjourn the proceedings for the production thereof and shall, if necessary in the case of a report, require the attendance at the adjourned hearing of the person who made the report.

Duty of magistrates' court to explain manner in which it proposes to deal with case and effect of order

44.2 (1) Before finally disposing of the case or before remitting the case to another court in pursuance of section 8 of the Powers of Criminal Courts (Sentencing) Act 2000, the magistrates' court shall inform the relevant minor and his parent or guardian, if present, or any person assisting him in his case, of the manner in which it proposes to deal with the case and allow any of those persons so informed to make representations; but the relevant minor shall not be informed as aforesaid if the court considers it undesirable so to do.

(2) On making any order, the court shall explain to the relevant minor the general nature and

effect of the order unless, in the case of an order requiring his parent or guardian to enter into a recognizance, it appears to it undesirable so to do.

Part 45 Deferred Sentence

Further conviction in magistrates' court after sentence deferred

45.1 Where under section 1 of the Powers of Criminal Courts (Sentencing) Act 2000 a court has deferred passing sentence on an offender and before the expiration of the period of deferment he is convicted of any offence by a magistrates' court, the court officer for the convicting court shall, if the court which deferred passing sentence on the earlier occasion was another magistrates' court or the Crown Court, give notice of the conviction to the court officer for that court.

Part 46 Custodial Sentences

[There are currently no rules in this part.]

Part 47 Suspended Sentences of Imprisonment

Entries in magistrates' court register in respect of suspended sentences

47.1 (1) Where under section 119 of the Powers of Criminal Courts (Sentencing) Act 2000 a magistrates' court deals with a person in respect of a suspended sentence otherwise than by making an order under section 119(1)(a), the court shall cause to be entered in the register its reasons for its opinion that it would be unjust to make such an order.

(2) Where an offender is dealt with under section 119 of the 2000 Act in respect of a suspended sentence passed by a magistrates' court, the court officer shall note this in the register, or where the suspended sentence was not passed by that court, shall notify the court officer for the court by which it was passed who shall note it in the register.

Suspended sentence supervision orders

47.2 (1) Where a magistrates' court makes an order under section 119(1)(a) or (b) of the Powers of Criminal Courts (Sentencing) Act 2000 in respect of a person who is subject to a suspended sentence supervision order, the court officer shall note this in the register, or where that order was not made by that court, shall—

(a) if the order was made by another magistrates' court, notify the court officer for that court who shall note the court register accordingly; or

(b) if the order was made by the Crown Court, notify the Crown Court officer.

(2) Where a magistrates' court discharges a suspended sentence supervision order under section 124(1) of the 2000 Act, the court officer shall note this in the register, or where that order was not made by that court, shall—

(a) if the order was made by another magistrates' court, notify the court officer for that court who shall note the court register accordingly; or

(b) if the order was made by the Crown Court, notify the Crown Court officer.

(3) Where a magistrates' court fines a person under section 123 of the 2000 Act for breach of the requirements of a suspended sentence supervision order which was not made by that court, the court officer shall—

(a) if the order was made by another magistrates' court, notify the court officer for that court; or

(b) if the order was made by the Crown Court, notify the Crown Court officer.

Part 48 Community Penalties

Curfew order or requirement with electronic monitoring requirement

48.1 (1) This rule applies where the Crown Court makes—

(a) a curfew order with an electronic monitoring requirement under section 35 of the Crime (Sentences) Act 1997 or under sections 37 and 36B of the Powers of Criminal Courts (Sentencing) Act 2000; or

(b) a community rehabilitation order with curfew and electronic monitoring requirements under section 41 of and paragraph 7 of Schedule 2 to the 2000 Act.

(2) The court officer shall serve notice of the order on the person in respect of whom it is made by way of pages 1 and 2 of the form set out in the Practice Direction.

(3) The court officer shall serve notice of the order on the person responsible for electronically monitoring compliance with it by way of the form set out in the Practice Direction.

(4) Where any community order additional to the curfew order has been made in respect of the offender, the court officer shall serve a copy of the notice required by paragraph (3) on the local probation board or Youth Offending Team responsible for the offender.

Part 49 Hospital and Guardianship Orders

Remand by magistrates' court for medical inquiries

49.1 On exercising the powers conferred by section 11 of the Powers of Criminal Courts (Sentencing) Act 2000 a magistrates' court shall—

(a) where the accused is remanded in custody, send to the institution or place to which he is committed; or

(b) where the accused is remanded on bail, send to the institution or place at which, or the person by whom, he is to be examined,

a statement of the reasons why the court is of opinion that an inquiry ought to be made into his physical or mental condition and of any information before the court about his physical or mental condition.

Hospital or guardianship order imposed by a magistrates' court

49.2 (1) The magistrates' court by which a hospital order is made under section 37 of the Mental Health Act 1983 shall send to the hospital named in the order such information in the possession of the court as it considers likely to be of assistance in dealing with the patient to whom the order relates, and in particular such information about the mental condition, character and antecedents of the patient and the nature of the offence.

(2) The magistrates' court by which a guardianship order is made under section 37 of the 1983 Act shall send to the local health authority named therein as guardian or, as the case may be, the local health authority for the area in which the person so named resides, such information in the possession of the court as it considers likely to be of assistance in dealing with the patient to whom the order relates and in particular such information about the mental condition, character and antecedents of the patient and the nature of the offence.

(3) The magistrates' court by which an offender is ordered to be admitted to hospital under section 44 of the 1983 Act shall send to the hospital such information in the possession of the court as it considers likely to assist in the treatment of the offender until his case is dealt with by the Crown Court.

Part 50 Supplementary Orders Made on Conviction

Sexual offences prevention orders made by a magistrates' court on conviction

50.1 (1) A sexual offences prevention order made by a magistrates' court under section 104 of the Sexual Offences Act 2003 shall be in the form set out in the Practice Direction.

(2) An interim sexual offences prevention order made by a magistrates' court under section 109 of the 2003 Act shall be in the form set out in the Practice Direction.

(3) As soon as reasonably practicable after a sexual offences prevention order or an interim sexual offences prevention order has been made, the court officer shall serve a copy of that order on the defendant. Any copy of an order required to be sent under this rule to the defendant shall be either given to him in person or sent by post to his last known address and, if so given or sent, shall be deemed to have been received by him, unless the defendant proves that it was not received by him.

Parenting orders made by a magistrates' court on conviction

50.2 (1) A parenting order made by a magistrates' court under section 8 of the Crime and Disorder Act 1998 shall be in the form set out in the Practice Direction.

(2) A parenting order made by a magistrates' court under paragraph 9D of Schedule 1 to the Powers of Criminal Courts (Sentencing) Act 2000 shall be in the form set out in the Practice Direction.

Variation of certain orders by a magistrates' court

50.3 (1) An application to a magistrates' court for variation or discharge of any of the following orders shall be by complaint:

(a) A parenting order made under section 9(5) of the Crime and Disorder Act 1998;

(b) A parenting order made under paragraph 9D of Schedule 1 to the Powers of Criminal Courts (Sentencing) Act 2000;

(c) a reparation order, under paragraph 5 of Schedule 8 to the Powers of Criminal Courts (Sentencing) Act 2000; or

(d) an action plan order, under that paragraph.

(2) An application under paragraph (1)(b) above shall be made to the magistrates' court which made the order, and shall specify the reason why the applicant for variation or discharge believes the court should vary or discharge the order, as the case may be.

Anti-social behaviour orders made by the Crown Court on conviction

50.4 An order made by the Crown Court under section 1C of the Crime and Disorder Act 1998 on conviction in criminal proceedings shall be in the form set out in the Practice Direction.

PART 51 FINES

[There are currently no rules in this part.]

PART 52 ENFORCEMENT OF FINES

Notice to defendant of fine or forfeited recognizance

52.1 (1) Where under section 140(1) of the Powers of Criminal Courts (Sentencing) Act 2000 or section 67(2) of the Criminal Justice Act 1988 a magistrates' court is required to enforce payment of a fine imposed or recognizance forfeited by the Crown Court or where a magistrates' court allows time for payment of a sum adjudged to be paid by a summary conviction, or directs that the sum be paid by instalments, or where the offender is absent when a sum is adjudged to be paid by a summary conviction, the magistrates' court officer shall serve on the offender notice in writing stating the amount of the sum and, if it is to be paid by instalments, the amount of the instalments, the date on which the sum, or each of the instalments, is to be paid and the places and times at which payment may be made; and a warrant of distress or commitment shall not be issued until the preceding provisions of this rule have been complied with.

Payment of fine to be made to magistrates' court officer

52.2 (1) A person adjudged by the conviction of a magistrates' court to pay any sum shall, unless the court otherwise directs, pay that sum, or any instalment of that sum, to the court officer.

(2) Where payment of any sum or instalment of any sum adjudged to be paid by the conviction or order of a magistrates' court is made to any person other than the court officer, that person, unless he is the person to whom the court has directed payment to be made or, in the case of a child, is the person with whom the child has his home, shall, as soon as may be, account for and, if the court officer so requires, pay over the sum or instalment to the court officer.

(3) Where payment of any sum adjudged to be paid by the conviction or order of a magistrates' court, or any instalment of such a sum, is directed to be made to the court officer for another court, the court officer for the court that adjudged the sum to be paid shall pay over any sums received by him on account of the said sum or instalment to the court officer for that other court.

Duty of magistrates' court officer to give receipt

52.3 The court officer for a magistrates' court shall give or send a receipt to any person who makes a payment to him in pursuance of a conviction or order of a magistrates' court and who asks for a receipt.

Application to magistrates' court for further time

52.4 An application under section 75(2) of the Magistrates' Courts Act 1980 (further time to pay) may, unless the court requires the applicant to attend, be made in writing.

Notice of date of hearing of means inquiry, etc in magistrates' court

52.5 [Revoked.]

Review of terms of postponement of warrant of commitment by magistrates' court

52.6 An application under section 77(5) of the Magistrates' Courts Act 1980 may be made in writing or in person.

Notice to defendant before enforcing magistrates' court order

52.7 (1) A warrant of commitment shall not be issued for disobedience to an order of a magistrates' court unless the defendant has been previously served with a copy of the minute of the order, or the order was made in his presence and the warrant is issued on that occasion:
Provided that this paragraph shall not apply to an order to pay money.

Execution of magistrates' court distress warrant

52.8 (1) A warrant of distress issued for the purpose of levying a sum adjudged to be paid by a summary conviction or order—
(a) shall name or otherwise describe the person against whom the distress is to be levied;
(b) shall be directed to the constables of the police area in which the warrant is issued or to the civilian enforcement officers for the area in which they are employed, or to a person named in the warrant and shall, subject to, and in accordance with, the provisions of this rule, require them to levy the said sum by distress and sale of the goods belonging to the said person; and
(c) may where it is directed to the constables of a police area, instead of being executed by any of those constables, be executed by any person under the direction of a constable.

(2) The warrant shall authorise the person charged with the execution of it to take as well any money as any goods of the person against whom the distress is levied; and any money so taken shall be treated as if it were the proceeds of the sale of goods taken under the warrant.

(3) The warrant shall require the person charged with the execution to pay the sum to be levied to the court officer for the court that issued the warrant.

(4) A warrant to which this rule applies may be executed by the persons to whom it was directed or by any of the following persons, whether or not the warrant was directed to them—
(a) a constable for any police area in England and Wales, acting in his own police area;
(b) where the warrant is one to which section 125A of the Magistrates' Courts Act 1980 applies, a civilian enforcement officer within the meaning of section 125A of the 1980 Act; and
(c) where the warrant is one to which section 125A of the 1980 Act applies, any of the individuals described in section 125B(1) of the 1980 Act;

and in this rule any reference to the person charged with the execution of a warrant includes any of the above persons who is for the time being authorised to execute the warrant, whether or not they have the warrant in their possession at the time.

(5) A person executing a warrant of distress shall—
(a) either—
(i) if he has the warrant with him, show it to the person against whom the distress is levied, or
(ii) otherwise, state where the warrant is and what arrangements may be made to allow the person against whom distress is levied to inspect it;
(b) explain, in ordinary language, the sum for which distress is levied and the reason for the distress;
(c) where the person executing the warrant is one of the persons referred to in paragraph (4)(b) or (c) above, show the person against whom distress is levied a written statement under section 125A(4) or 125B(4) as appropriate; and
(d) in any case, show documentary proof of his identity.

(6) There shall not be taken under the warrant the clothing or bedding of any person or his family or the tools, books, vehicles or other equipment which he personally needs to use in his employment, business or vocation, provided that in this paragraph the word 'person' shall not include a corporation.

(7) The distress levied under any such warrant as aforesaid shall be sold within such period beginning not earlier than the 6th day after the making of the distress as may be specified in

the warrant, or if no period is specified in the warrant, within a period beginning on the 6th day and ending on the 14th day after the making of the distress:

Provided that with the consent in writing of the person against whom the distress is levied the distress may be sold before the beginning of the said period.

(8) The clerk of the court which issued the warrant may, on the application of the person charged with the execution of it, extend the period within which the distress must be sold by any number of days not exceeding 60; but following the grant of such an application there shall be no further variation or extension of that period.

(9) The said distress shall be sold by public auction or in such other manner as the person against whom the distress is levied may in writing allow.

(10) Notwithstanding anything in the preceding provisions of this rule, the said distress shall not be sold if the sum for which the warrant was issued and the charges of taking and keeping the distress have been paid.

(11) Subject to any direction to the contrary in the warrant, where the distress is levied on household goods, the goods shall not, without the consent in writing of the person against whom the distress is levied, be removed from the house until the day of sale; and so much of the goods shall be impounded as is in the opinion of the person executing the warrant sufficient to satisfy the distress, by affixing to the articles impounded a conspicuous mark.

(12) The person charged with the execution of any such warrant as aforesaid shall cause the distress to be sold, and may deduct out of the amount realised by the sale all costs and charges incurred in effecting the sale; and he shall return to the owner the balance, if any, after retaining the amount of the sum for which the warrant was issued and the proper costs and charges of the execution of the warrant.

(13) The person charged with the execution of any such warrant as aforesaid shall as soon as practicable send to the court officer for the court that issued it a written account of the costs and charges incurred in executing it; and the court officer shall allow the person against whom the distress was levied to inspect the account within one month after the levy of the distress at any reasonable time to be appointed by the court.

(14) If any person pays or tenders to the person charged with the execution of any such warrant as aforesaid the sum mentioned in the warrant, or produces a receipt for that sum given by the court officer for the court that issued the warrant, and also pays the amount of the costs and charges of the distress up to the time of the payment or tender or the production of the receipt, the person as aforesaid shall not execute the warrant, or shall cease to execute it, as the case may be.

Payment after imprisonment imposed by magistrates' court

52.9 (1) The persons authorised for the purposes of section 79(2) of the Magistrates' Courts Act 1980 to receive a part payment are—

(a) unless there has been issued a warrant of distress or commitment, the court officer for the court enforcing payment of the sum, or any person appointed under section 88 of that Act to supervise the offender;

(b) where the issue of a warrant of commitment has been suspended on conditions which provide for payment to be made to the court officer for another magistrates' court, that court officer;

(c) any constable holding a warrant of distress or commitment or, where the warrant is directed to some other person, that person; and

(d) the governor or keeper of the prison or place in which the defaulter is detained, or other person having lawful custody of the defaulter:

provided that—

(i) the said governor or keeper shall not be required to accept any sum tendered in part payment under the said section 79(2) of the 1980 Act except on a week-day between 9 o'clock in the morning and 5 o'clock in the afternoon, and

(ii) no person shall be required to receive in part payment under the said subsection (2) an amount which, or so much of an amount as, will not procure a reduction of the period for which the defaulter is committed or ordered to be detained.

(2) Where a person having custody of a defaulter receives payment of any sum he shall note receipt of the sum on the warrant of commitment.

(3) Where the magistrates' court officer for a court other than the court enforcing payment of

the sums receives payment of any sum he shall inform the magistrates' court officer for the other court.

(4) Where a person appointed under section 88 of the 1980 Act to supervise an offender receives payment of any sum, he shall send it forthwith to the magistrates' court officer for the court which appointed him.

Order for supervision made by magistrates' court

52.10 (1) Unless an order under section 88(1) of the Magistrates' Courts Act 1980 is made in the offender's presence, the court officer for the court making the order shall deliver to the offender, or serve on him by post, notice in writing of the order.

(2) It shall be the duty of any person for the time being appointed under the said section to advise and befriend the offender with a view to inducing him to pay the sum adjudged to be paid and thereby avoid committal to custody and to give any information required by a magistrates' court about the offender's conduct and means.

Transfer of magistrates' court fine order

52.11 (1) The court officer for a magistrates' court which has made a transfer of fine order under section 89 or 90 or section 90 as applied by section 91 of the Magistrates' Courts Act 1980 shall send to the clerk of the court having jurisdiction under the order a copy of the order.

(2) Where a magistrates' court has made a transfer of fine order in respect of a sum adjudged to be paid by a court in Scotland or in Northern Ireland the court officer shall send a copy of the order to the clerk of the Scottish court or to the clerk of the Northern Irish court, as the case may be.

(3) Where a court officer receives a copy of a transfer of fine order (whether made in England and Wales, or in Scotland or in Northern Ireland) specifying his court as the court by which payment of the sum in question is to be enforceable, he shall thereupon, if possible, deliver or send by post to the offender notice in writing.

(4) Where under a transfer of fine order a sum adjudged to be paid by a Scottish court or by a Northern Irish court is enforceable by a magistrates' court—

(a) if the sum is paid, the court officer shall send it to the clerk of the Scottish court or to the clerk of the Northern Irish court, as the case may be; or

(b) if the sum is not paid, the court officer shall inform the clerk of the Scottish court or the clerk of the Northern Irish court, as the case may be, of the manner in which the adjudication has been satisfied or that the sum, or any balance thereof, appears to be irrecoverable.

Directions by magistrates' court that money found on defaulter shall not be applied in satisfaction of debt

52.12 Where the defaulter is committed to, or ordered to be detained in, a prison or other place of detention, any direction given under section 80(2) of the Magistrates' Courts Act 1980 shall be endorsed on the warrant of commitment.

Particulars of fine enforcement to be entered in magistrates' court register

52.13 (1) Where the court on the occasion of convicting an offender of an offence issues a warrant of commitment for a default in paying a sum adjudged to be paid by the conviction or, having power to issue such a warrant, fixes a term of imprisonment under section 77(2) of the Magistrates' Courts Act 1980, the reasons for the court's action shall be entered in the register, or any separate record kept for the purpose of recording particulars of fine enforcement.

(2) There shall be entered in the register, or any such record, particulars of any—

(a) means inquiry under section 82 of the 1980 Act;

(b) hearing under subsection (5) of the said section 82;

(c) allowance of further time for the payment of a sum adjudged to be paid by a conviction;

(d) direction that such a sum shall be paid by instalments including any direction varying the number of instalments payable, the amount of any instalments payable and the date on which any instalment becomes payable;

(e) distress for the enforcement of such a sum;

(f) attachment of earnings order for the enforcement of such a sum;

(g) decision of the Secretary of State to make deductions from income support under section 24 of the Criminal Justice Act 1991;

(h) order under the 1980 Act placing a person under supervision pending payment of such a sum;
(i) order under section 85(1) of the 1980 Act remitting the whole or any part of a fine;
(j) order under section 120(4) of the 1980 Act remitting the whole or any part of any sum enforceable under that section (forfeiture of recognizance);
(k) authority granted under section 87(3) of the 1980 Act authorising the taking of proceedings in the High Court or county court for the recovery of any sum adjudged to be paid by a conviction;
(l) transfer of fine order made by the court;
(m) order transferring a fine to the court;
(n) order under section 140(1) of the Powers of Criminal Courts (Sentencing) Act 2000 specifying the court for the purpose of enforcing a fine imposed or a recognizance forfeited by the Crown Court; and
(o) any fine imposed or recognizance forfeited by a coroner which has to be treated as imposed or forfeited by the court;
(p) reference by a justice of the peace of an application under section 77(5) of the 1980 Act for a review of the terms on which a warrant of commitment is postponed; or
(q) order under section 77(3) of the 1980 Act varying the time for which or the conditions subject to which a warrant of commitment is postponed.

Attendance Centre Order imposed by magistrates' court in default of payment of a financial penalty

52.14 (1) Where any person is ordered, under section 60 of the Powers of Criminal Courts (Sentencing) Act 2000, to attend at an attendance centre in default of payment of a sum of money, payment may thereafter be made—
(a) of the whole of the said sum, to the court officer for the magistrates' court which made the order, or
(b) of the whole or, subject to paragraph (2), any part of the said sum, to the officer in charge of the attendance centre specified in the order ('the officer in charge').

(2) The officer in charge may not accept a part payment that would not secure the reduction by one or more complete hours of the period of attendance specified in the order.

(3) On receiving a payment under paragraph (1) the court officer shall forthwith notify the officer in charge.

(4) The officer in charge shall pay any money received by him under paragraph (1) above to the court officer and shall note the receipt of the money in the register maintained at the attendance centre.

Part 53 Compensation Orders

Review of compensation order made by a magistrates' court

53.1 (1) An application under section 133 of the Powers of Criminal Courts (Sentencing) Act 2000 for the review of a compensation order shall be by complaint.

(2) The court officer for the magistrates' court to which the complaint is made shall send a letter post to the person for whose benefit the compensation order was made, inviting him to make observations and to attend any hearing of the complaint and advising him of his right to be heard.

Part 54 Conditional Discharge

Further offence committed after offender conditionally discharged by a magistrates' court

54.1 (1) Where a magistrates' court deals with a person under section 13 of the Powers of Criminal Courts (Sentencing) Act 2000 in relation to an order for conditional discharge which was not made by that court the court officer shall give notice of the result of the proceedings to the court officer for the court by which the order was made.

(2) The court officer for a magistrates' court receiving a notice under this rule shall note the decision of the other court in the register.

Part 55 Road Traffic Penalties

Endorsement of driving licence by magistrates' court

55.1 (1) Where a magistrates' court convicts a person of an offence and, under section 44 of the Road

Traffic Offenders Act 1988 orders that particulars of the conviction, and, if the court orders him to be disqualified, particulars of the disqualification, shall be endorsed on any licence held by him, the particulars to be endorsed shall include—

(a) the name of the local justice area for which the court is acting;

(b) the date of the conviction and the date on which sentence was passed (if different);

(c) particulars of the offence including the date on which it was committed; and

(d) particulars of the sentence of the court (including the period of disqualification, if any).

(2) Where a magistrates' court orders that the licence of an offender be endorsed as mentioned in paragraph (1) or imposes an interim disqualification as mentioned in rule 43.1(1)(f) and the court officer knows or is informed of the date of birth and sex of the offender, the court officer shall send the information to the licensing authority which granted the licence.

Application to magistrates' court for removal of disqualification

55.2 (1) An application under section 42 of the Road Traffic Offenders Act 1988 or paragraph 7 of Schedule 4 to the Road Traffic (Consequential Provisions) Act 1988 for an order removing a disqualification or disqualifications for holding or obtaining a licence shall be by complaint.

(2) The justice to whom the complaint is made shall issue a summons directed to the chief officer of police requiring him to appear before a magistrates' court to show cause why an order should not be made on the complaint.

(3) Where a magistrates' court makes an order under either of the provisions mentioned in paragraph (1) the court shall cause notice of the making of the order and a copy of the particulars of the order endorsed on the licence, if any, previously held by the applicant for the order to be sent to the licensing authority to which notice of the applicant's disqualification was sent.

Application to magistrates' court for review of course organiser's refusal to issue certificate of satisfactory completion of driving course

55.3 (1) An application to the supervising court under section 34B(6) or (7) of the Road Traffic Offenders Act 1988 shall be served on the court officer within 28 days after the date specified in an order under section 34A(2) of the 1988 Act, where that date falls on or after 24th May 1993.

(2) An application under section 34B(6) of the 1988 Act shall be accompanied by the notice under section 34B(5) of the 1988 Act.

(3) Where such an application is served on the court officer—

(a) he shall fix a date and time for the hearing of the application; and

(b) he shall—

(i) serve a copy of the application on the course organiser, and

(ii) serve notice of the hearing on the applicant and course organiser.

(4) If the course organiser fails to appear or be represented at the hearing of the application without reasonable excuse, the court may proceed to decide the application in his absence.

(5) In this rule, 'course organiser' and 'supervising court' have the meanings assigned to them in England and Wales by section 34C of the 1988 Act.

Part 56 Confiscation Proceedings under the Criminal Justice Act 1988 and the Drug Trafficking Act 1994

Statements etc, relevant to making confiscation orders

56.1 (1) Where a prosecutor or defendant—

(a) tenders to a magistrates' court any statement or other document under section 73 of the Criminal Justice Act 1988 in any proceedings in respect of an offence listed in Schedule 4 to that Act; or

(b) tenders to the Crown Court any statement or other document under section 11 of the Drug Trafficking Act 1994 or section 73 of the 1988 Act in any proceedings in respect of a drug trafficking offence or in respect of an offence to which Part VI of the 1988 Act applies,

he must serve a copy as soon as practicable on the defendant or the prosecutor, as the case may be.

(2) Any statement tendered by the prosecutor to the magistrates' court under section 73 of the 1988 Act or to the Crown Court under section 11(1) of the 1994 Act or section 73(1A) of the 1988 Act shall include the following particulars—

(a) the name of the defendant;

(b) the name of the person by whom the statement is made and the date on which it was made;
(c) where the statement is not tendered immediately after the defendant has been convicted, the date on which and the place where the relevant conviction occurred; and
(d) such information known to the prosecutor as is relevant to the determination as to whether or not the defendant has benefited from drug trafficking or relevant criminal conduct and to the assessment of the value of his proceeds of drug trafficking or, as the case may be, benefit from relevant criminal conduct.

(3) Where, in accordance with section 11(7) of the 1994 Act or section 73(1C) of the 1988 Act, the defendant indicates the extent to which he accepts any allegation contained within the prosecutor's statement, if he indicates the same in writing to the prosecutor, he must serve a copy of that reply on the court officer.

(4) Expressions used in this rule shall have the same meanings as in the 1994 Act or, where appropriate, the 1988 Act.

Postponed determinations

56.2 (1) Where an application is made by the defendant or the prosecutor—
(a) to a magistrates' court under section 72A(5)(a) of the Criminal Justice Act 1988 asking the court to exercise its powers under section 72A(4) of that Act; or
(b) to the Crown Court under section 3(5)(a) of the Drug Trafficking Act 1994 asking the Court to exercise its powers under section 3(4) of that Act, or under section 72A(5)(a) of the 1988 Act asking the court to exercise its powers under section 72A(4) of the 1988 Act,

the application must be made in writing and a copy must be served on the prosecutor or the defendant, as the case may be.

(2) A party served with a copy of an application under paragraph (1) shall, within 28 days of the date of service, notify the applicant and the court officer, in writing, whether or not he proposes to oppose the application, giving his reasons for any opposition.

(3) After the expiry of the period referred to in paragraph (2), the court shall determine whether an application under paragraph (1) is to be dealt with—
(a) without a hearing; or
(b) at a hearing at which the parties may be represented.

Confiscation orders—revised assessments

56.3 (1) Where the prosecutor makes an application under section 13, 14 or 15 of the Drug Trafficking Act 1994 or section 74A, 74B or 74C of the Criminal Justice Act 1988, the application must be in writing and a copy must be served on the defendant.

(2) The application must include the following particulars—
(a) the name of the defendant;
(b) the date on which and the place where any relevant conviction occurred;
(c) the date on which and the place where any relevant confiscation order was made or, as the case may be, varied;
(d) the grounds on which the application is made; and
(e) an indication of the evidence available to support the application.

Application to Crown Court to discharge or vary order to make material available

56.4 (1) Where an order under section 93H of the Criminal Justice Act 1988 (order to make material available), section 55 of the Drug Trafficking Act 1994 (order to make material available), or section 345 of the Proceeds of Crime Act 2002 (production orders) has been made by the Crown Court, any person affected by it may apply in writing to the court officer for the order to be discharged or varied, and on hearing such an application a circuit judge or, in the case of an order under the 2002 Act, a judge entitled to exercise the jurisdiction of the Crown Court may discharge the order or make such variations to it as he thinks fit.

(2) Subject to paragraph (3), where a person proposes to make an application under paragraph (1) for the discharge or variation of an order, he shall give a copy of the application, not later than 48 hours before the making of the application—
(a) to a constable at the police station specified in the order; or
(b) where the application for the order was made under the 2002 Act and was not made by a constable, to the office of the appropriate officer who made the application, as specified in the order,

in either case together with a notice indicating the time and place at which the application for discharge or variation is to be made.

(3) A circuit judge or, in the case of an order under the 2002 Act, a judge entitled to exercise the jurisdiction of the Crown Court may direct that paragraph (2) need not be complied with if he is satisfied that the person making the application has good reason to seek a discharge or variation of the order as soon as possible and it is not practicable to comply with that paragraph.

(4) In this rule:

'appropriate officer' has the meaning given to it by section 378 of the 2002 Act;

'constable' includes a person commissioned by the Commissioners of Customs and Excise;

'police station' includes a place for the time being occupied by Her Majesty's Customs and Excise.

Application to Crown Court for increase in term of imprisonment in default of payment of a confiscation order

56.5 (1) This rule applies to applications made, or that have effect as made, to the Crown Court under section 10 of the Drug Trafficking Act 1994 and section 75A of the Criminal Justice Act 1988 (interest on sums unpaid under confiscation orders).

(2) Notice of an application to which this rule applies to increase the term of imprisonment or detention fixed in default of payment of a confiscation order by a person ('the defendant') shall be made by the prosecutor in writing to the court officer.

(3) A notice under paragraph (2) shall—

(a) state the name and address of the defendant;

(b) specify the grounds for the application;

(c) give details of the enforcement measures taken, if any; and

(d) include a copy of the confiscation order.

(4) On receiving a notice under paragraph (2), the court officer shall—

(a) forthwith send to the defendant and the magistrates' court required to enforce payment of the confiscation order under section 140(1) of the Powers of Criminal Courts (Sentencing) Act 2000, a copy of the said notice; and

(b) notify in writing the applicant and the defendant of the date, time and place appointed for the hearing of the application.

(5) Where the Crown Court makes an order pursuant to an application mentioned in paragraph (1) above, the court officer shall send forthwith a copy of the order—

(a) to the applicant;

(b) to the defendant;

(c) where the defendant is at the time of the making of the order in custody, to the person having custody of him; and

(d) to the magistrates' court mentioned in paragraph (4)(a).

Drug trafficking—compensation on acquittal in Crown Court

56.6 Where a Crown Court cancels a confiscation order under section 22(2) of the Drug Trafficking Act 1994, the court officer shall serve notice to that effect on the High Court and on the magistrates' court which has responsibility for enforcing the order.

Part 57 Proceeds of Crime Act 2002—Rules Applicable to all Proceedings

Interpretation

57.1 In this Part and in Parts 58, 59, 60 and 61:

'business day' means any day other than a Saturday, Sunday, Christmas Day or Good Friday, or a bank holiday under the Banking and Financial Dealings Act 1971, in England and Wales;

'document' means anything in which information of any description is recorded;

'hearsay evidence' means evidence consisting of hearsay within the meaning of section 1(2) of the Civil Evidence Act 1995;

'restraint proceedings' means proceedings under sections 42 and 58(2) and (3) of the Proceeds of Crime Act 2002;

'receivership proceedings' means proceedings under sections 48, 49, 50, 51, 52, 53, 54(4), 56(4), 59(2) and (3), 60(2) and (3), 62 and 63 of the 2002 Act;

'witness statement' means a written statement signed by a person which contains the evidence, and only that evidence, which that person would be allowed to give orally; and words and expressions used have the same meaning as in Part 2 of the 2002 Act.

Calculation of time

57.2 (1) This rule shows how to calculate any period of time for doing any act which is specified by this Part and Parts 58, 59, 60 and 61 for the purposes of any proceedings under Part 2 of the Proceeds of Crime Act 2002 or by an order of the Crown Court in restraint proceedings or receivership proceedings.

(2) A period of time expressed as a number of days shall be computed as clear days.

(3) In this rule 'clear days' means that in computing the number of days—

(a) the day on which the period begins; and

(b) if the end of the period is defined by reference to an event, the day on which that event occurs are not included.

(4) Where the specified period is five days or less and includes a day which is not a business day that day does not count.

Court office closed

57.3 When the period specified by this Part or Parts 58, 59, 60 and 61, or by an order of the Crown Court under Part 2 of the Proceeds of Crime Act 2002, for doing any act at the court office falls on a day on which the office is closed, that act shall be in time if done on the next day on which the court office is open.

Application for registration of Scottish or Northern Ireland Order

57.4 (1) This rule applies to an application for registration of an order under article 6 of the Proceeds of Crime Act 2002 (Enforcement in different parts of the United Kingdom) Order 2002.

(2) The application may be made without notice.

(3) The application must be in writing and may be supported by a witness statement which must—

(a) exhibit the order or a certified copy of the order; and

(b) to the best of the witness's ability, give full details of the realisable property located in England and Wales in respect of which the order was made and specify the person holding that realisable property.

(4) If the court registers the order, the applicant must serve notice of the registration on—

(a) any person who holds realisable property to which the order applies; and

(b) any other person whom the applicant knows to be affected by the order.

(5) The permission of the Crown Court under rule 57.13 is not required to serve the notice outside England and Wales.

Application to vary or set aside registration

57.5 (1) An application to vary or set aside registration of an order under article 6 of the Proceeds of Crime Act 2002 (Enforcement in different parts of the United Kingdom) Order 2002 may be made to the Crown Court by—

(a) any person who holds realisable property to which the order applies; and

(b) any other person affected by the order.

(2) The application must be in writing and may be supported by a witness statement.

(3) The application and any witness statement must be lodged with the Crown Court.

(4) The application must be served on the person who applied for registration at least seven days before the date fixed by the court for hearing the application, unless the Crown Court specifies a shorter period.

(5) No property in England and Wales may be realised in pursuance of the order before the Crown Court has decided the application.

Register of orders

57.6 (1) The Crown Court must keep, under the direction of the Lord Chancellor, a register of the orders registered under article 6 of the Proceeds of Crime Act 2002 (Enforcement in different parts of the United Kingdom) Order 2002.

(2) The register must include details of any variation or setting aside of a registration under rule 57.5 and of any execution issued on a registered order.

(3) If the person who applied for registration of an order which is subsequently registered

notifies the Crown Court that the court which made the order has varied or discharged the order, details of the variation or discharge, as the case may be, must be entered in the register.

Statements of truth

57.7 (1) Any witness statement required to be served by this Part or by Parts 58, 59, 60 or 61 must be verified by a statement of truth contained in the witness statement.

(2) A statement of truth is a declaration by the person making the witness statement to the effect that the witness statement is true to the best of his knowledge and belief and that he made the statement knowing that, if it were tendered in evidence, he would be liable to prosecution if he wilfully stated in it anything which he knew to be false or did not believe to be true.

(3) The statement of truth must be signed by the person making the witness statement.

(4) If the person making the witness statement fails to verify the witness statement by a statement of truth, the Crown Court may direct that it shall not be admissible as evidence.

Use of witness statements for other purposes

57.8 (1) Except as provided by this rule, a witness statement served in proceedings under Part 2 of the Proceeds of Crime Act 2002 may be used only for the purpose of the proceedings in which it is served.

(2) Paragraph (1) does not apply if and to the extent that—

(a) the witness gives consent in writing to some other use of it;

(b) the Crown Court gives permission for some other use; or

(c) the witness statement has been put in evidence at a hearing held in public.

Expert evidence

57.9 (1) A party to proceedings under Part 2 of the Proceeds of Crime Act 2002 who wishes to adduce expert evidence (whether of fact or opinion) in the proceedings must, as soon as practicable—

(a) serve on the other parties a statement in writing of any finding or opinion which he proposes to adduce by way of such evidence; and

(b) serve on any party who requests it in writing, a copy of (or if it appears to the party proposing to adduce the evidence to be more practicable, a reasonable opportunity to examine)—

(i) the record of any observation, test, calculation or other procedure on which the finding or opinion is based, and

(ii) any document or other thing or substance in respect of which the observation, test, calculation or other procedure mentioned in paragraph (1)(b)(i) has been carried out.

(c) A party may serve notice in writing waiving his right to be served with any of the matters mentioned in paragraph (1) and, in particular, may agree that the statement mentioned in paragraph (1)(a) may be given to him orally and not served in writing.

(d) If a party who wishes to adduce expert evidence in proceedings under Part 2 of the 2002 Act fails to comply with this rule he may not adduce that evidence in those proceedings without the leave of the court, except where rule 57.10 applies.

Exceptions to procedure for expert evidence

57.10 (1) If a party has reasonable grounds for believing that the disclosure of any evidence in compliance with rule 57.9 might lead to the intimidation, or attempted intimidation, of any person on whose evidence he intends to rely in the proceedings, or otherwise to the course of justice being interfered with, he shall not be obliged to comply with those requirements in relation to that evidence, unless the Crown Court orders otherwise.

(2) Where, in accordance with paragraph (1), a party considers that he is not obliged to comply with the requirements imposed by rule 57.9 with regard to any evidence in relation to any other party, he must serve notice in writing on that party stating—

(a) that the evidence is being withheld; and

(b) the reasons for withholding the evidence.

Service of documents

57.11 (1) Part 4 and rule 32.1 (notice required to accompany process served outside the United Kingdom and translations) shall not apply in restraint proceedings and receivership proceedings.

(2) Where this Part or Parts 58, 59, 60 or 61 requires service of a document, then, unless the Crown Court directs otherwise, the document may be served by any of the following methods—
(a) in all cases, by delivering the document personally to the party to be served;
(b) if no solicitor is acting for the party to be served by delivering the document at, or by sending it by first class post to, his residence or his last-known residence; or
(c) if a solicitor is acting for the party to be served—
(i) by delivering the document at, or sending it by first class post to, the solicitor's business address, or
(ii) where the solicitor's business address includes a numbered box at a document exchange, by leaving the document at that document exchange or at a document exchange which transmits documents on every business day to that document exchange, or
(iii) if the solicitor has indicated that he is willing to accept service by facsimile transmission, by sending a legible copy of the document by facsimile transmission to the solicitor's office.

(3) A document shall, unless the contrary is proved, be deemed to have been served—
(a) in the case of service by first class post, on the second business day after posting;
(b) in the case of service in accordance with paragraph (2)(c)(ii), on the second business day after the day on which it is left at the document exchange; and
(c) in the case of service in accordance with paragraph (2)(c)(iii), where it is transmitted on a business day before 4 p.m., on that day and in any other case, on the next business day.

(4) An order made in restraint proceedings or receivership proceedings may be enforced against the defendant or any other person affected by it notwithstanding that service of a copy of the order has not been effected in accordance with this rule if the Crown Court is satisfied that the person had notice of the order by being present when the order was made.

Service by an alternative method

57.12 (1) Where it appears to the Crown Court that there is a good reason to authorise service by a method not otherwise permitted by rule 57.11, the court may make an order permitting service by an alternative method.
(2) An application for an order permitting service by an alternative method—
(a) must be supported by evidence; and
(b) may be made without notice.
(3) An order permitting service by an alternative method must specify—
(a) the method of service; and
(b) the date when the document will be deemed to be served.

Service outside the jurisdiction

57.13 (1) Where this Part requires a document to be served on someone who is outside England and Wales, it may be served outside England and Wales with the permission of the Crown Court.
(2) Where a document is to be served outside England and Wales it may be served by any method permitted by the law of the country in which it is to be served.
(3) Nothing in this rule or in any court order shall authorise or require any person to do anything in the country where the document is to be served which is against the law of that country.
(4) Where this Part requires a document to be served a certain period of time before the date of a hearing and the recipient does not appear at the hearing, the hearing must not take place unless the Crown Court is satisfied that the document has been duly served.

Certificates of service

57.14 (1) Where this Part requires that the applicant for an order in restraint proceedings or receivership proceedings serve a document on another person, the applicant must lodge a certificate of service with the Crown Court within seven days of service of the document.
(2) The certificate must state—
(a) the method of service;
(b) the date of service; and

(c) if the document is served under rule 57.12, such other information as the court may require when making the order permitting service by an alternative method.

(3) Where a document is to be served by the Crown Court in restraint proceedings and receivership proceedings and the court is unable to serve it, the court must send a notice of non-service stating the method attempted to the party who requested service.

External requests and orders

57.15 (1) The rules in this Part and in Parts 59 to 61 and 71 apply with the necessary modifications to proceedings under the Proceeds of Crime Act 2002 (External Requests and Orders) Order 2005 in the same way that they apply to corresponding proceedings under Part 2 of the Proceeds of Crime Act 2002.

(2) This table shows how provisions of the 2005 Order correspond with provisions of the 2002 Act.

Article of the Proceeds of Crime Act 2002 (External Requests and Orders) Order 2005	*Section of the Proceeds of Crime Act 2002*
B3	41
B4	42
B5	43
B6	44
B10	48
B11	49
B12	58
B18	31
B22	50
B24	51
B25	52
B26	53
B29	55
B31	57
B36	62
B37	63
B39	65
B40	66

Part 58 Proceeds of Crime Act 2002—Rules Applicable only to Confiscation Proceedings

Statements in connection with confiscation orders

58.1 (1) When the prosecutor or the Director is required, under section 16 of the Proceeds of Crime Act 2002, to give a statement to the Crown Court, the prosecutor or the Director, as the case may be, must also, as soon as practicable, serve a copy of the statement on the defendant.

(2) Any statement given to the Crown Court by the prosecutor or the Director under section 16 of the 2002 Act must, in addition to the information required by the 2002 Act, include the following information—

(a) the name of the defendant;

(b) the name of the person by whom the statement is made and the date on which it is made; and

(c) where the statement is not given to the Crown Court immediately after the defendant has been convicted, the date on which and the place where the relevant conviction occurred.

(3) Where, under section 17 of the 2002 Act, the Crown Court orders the defendant to indicate the extent to which he accepts each allegation in a statement given by the prosecutor or the Director, the defendant must indicate this in writing to the prosecutor or the Director (as the case may be) and must give a copy to the Crown Court.
(4) Where the Crown Court orders the defendant to give to it any information under section 18 of the 2002 Act, the defendant must provide the information in writing and must, as soon as practicable, serve a copy of it on—
(a) the prosecutor, if the prosecutor asked the court to proceed under section 6 of the 2002 Act; or
(b) the Director, if the Director asked the court to proceed under section 6 of the 2002 Act.

Postponement of confiscation proceedings

58.2 The Crown Court may grant a postponement under section 14(1)(b) of the Proceeds of Crime Act 2002 without a hearing.

Application for reconsideration of decision to make confiscation order or benefit assessed for purposes of confiscation order

58.3 (1) This rule applies where the prosecutor or Director makes an application under section 19, 20 or 21 of the Proceeds of Crime Act 2002.
(2) The application must be in writing and give details of—
(a) the name of the defendant;
(b) the date on which and the place where any relevant conviction occurred;
(c) the date on which and the place where any relevant confiscation order was made or varied;
(d) the grounds for the application; and
(e) an indication of the evidence available to support the application.
(3) The application must be lodged with the Crown Court.
(4) The application must be served on the defendant at least seven days before the date fixed by the court for hearing the application, unless the Crown Court specifies a shorter period.

Application for reconsideration of available amount

58.4 (1) This rule applies where the prosecutor, the Director or a receiver makes an application under section 22 of the Proceeds of Crime Act 2002 for a new calculation of the available amount.
(2) The application must be in writing and may be supported by a witness statement.
(3) The application and any witness statement must be lodged with the Crown Court.
(4) The application and any witness statement must be served on—
(a) the defendant;
(b) the receiver, if the prosecutor or the Director is making the application and a receiver has been appointed under section 50 or 52 of the 2002 Act; and
(c) if the receiver is making the application—
(i) the prosecutor, or
(ii) if the Director is appointed as the enforcement authority under section 34 of the 2002 Act, the Director,
at least seven days before the date fixed by the court for hearing the application, unless the Crown Court specifies a shorter period.

Variation of confiscation order due to inadequacy of available amount

58.5 (1) This rule applies where the defendant or a receiver makes an application under section 23 of the Proceeds of Crime Act 2002 for the variation of a confiscation order.
(2) The application must be in writing and may be supported by a witness statement.
(3) The application and any witness statement must be lodged with the Crown Court.
(4) The application and any witness statement must be served on—
(a) the prosecutor, or if the Director is appointed as the enforcement authority under section 34 of the 2002 Act, the Director;
(b) the defendant, if the receiver is making the application; and
(c) the receiver, if the defendant is making the application and a receiver has been appointed under section 50 or 52 of the 2002 Act,
at least seven days before the date fixed by the court for hearing the application, unless the Crown Court specifies a shorter period.

Application by magistrates' court officer to discharge confiscation order

58.6 (1) This rule applies where a magistrates' court officer makes an application under section 24 or 25 of the Proceeds of Crime Act 2002 for the discharge of a confiscation order.

(2) The application must be in writing and give details of—

(a) the confiscation order;

(b) the amount outstanding under the order; and

(c) the grounds for the application.

(3) The application must be served on—

(a) the defendant;

(b) the prosecutor; and

(c) any receiver appointed under section 50 of the 2002 Act.

(4) The Crown Court may determine the application without a hearing unless a person listed in paragraph (3) indicates, within seven days after the application was served on him, that he would like to make representations.

(5) If the Crown Court makes an order discharging the confiscation order, the court must, at once, send a copy of the order to—

(a) the magistrates' court officer who applied for the order;

(b) the defendant;

(c) the prosecutor; and

(d) any receiver appointed under section 50 of the 2002 Act.

Application for variation of confiscation order made against an absconder

58.7 (1) This rule applies where the defendant makes an application under section 29 of the Proceeds of Crime Act 2002 for the variation of a confiscation order made against an absconder.

(2) The application must be in writing and supported by a witness statement which must give details of—

(a) the confiscation order made against an absconder under section 6 of the 2002 Act as applied by section 28 of the 2002 Act;

(b) the circumstances in which the defendant ceased to be an absconder;

(c) the defendant's conviction of the offence or offences concerned; and

(d) the reason why he believes the amount required to be paid under the confiscation order was too large.

(3) The application and witness statement must be lodged with the Crown Court.

(4) The application and witness statement must be served on the prosecutor or, if the Director is appointed as the enforcement authority under section 34 of the 2002 Act, the Director at least seven days before the date fixed by the court for hearing the application, unless the Crown Court specifies a shorter period.

Application for discharge of confiscation order made against an absconder

58.8 (1) This rule applies if the defendant makes an application under section 30 of the Proceeds of Crime Act 2002 for the discharge of a confiscation order.

(2) The application must be in writing and supported by a witness statement which must give details of—

(a) the confiscation order made under section 28 of the 2002 Act;

(b) the date on which the defendant ceased to be an absconder;

(c) the acquittal of the defendant if he has been acquitted of the offence concerned; and

(d) if the defendant has not been acquitted of the offence concerned—

(i) the date on which the defendant ceased to be an absconder,

(ii) the date on which the proceedings taken against the defendant were instituted and a summary of steps taken in the proceedings since then, and

(iii) any indication given by the prosecutor that he does not intend to proceed against the defendant.

(3) The application and witness statement must be lodged with the Crown Court.

(4) The application and witness statement must be served on the prosecutor or, if the Director is appointed as the enforcement authority under section 34 of the 2002 Act, the Director at least seven days before the date fixed by the court for hearing the application, unless the Crown Court specifies a shorter period.

(5) If the Crown Court orders the discharge of the confiscation order, the court must serve notice on the magistrates' court responsible for enforcing the order if the Director has not been appointed as the enforcement authority under section 34 of the 2002 Act.

Application for increase in term of imprisonment in default

58.9 (1) This rule applies where the prosecutor or the Director makes an application under section 39(5) of the Proceeds of Crime Act 2002 to increase the term of imprisonment in default of payment of a confiscation order.

(2) The application must be made in writing and give details of—

(a) the name and address of the defendant;

(b) the confiscation order;

(c) the grounds for the application; and

(d) the enforcement measures taken, if any.

(3) On receipt of the application, the court must—

(a) at once, send to the defendant and, if the Director has not been appointed as the enforcement authority under section 34 of the 2002 Act, the magistrates' court responsible for enforcing the order, a copy of the application; and

(b) fix a time, date and place for the hearing and notify the applicant and the defendant of that time, date and place.

(4) If the Crown Court makes an order increasing the term of imprisonment in default, the court must, at once, send a copy of the order to—

(a) the applicant;

(b) the defendant;

(c) where the defendant is in custody at the time of the making of the order, the person having custody of the defendant; and

(d) if the Director has not been appointed as the enforcement authority under section 34 of the 2002 Act, the magistrates' court responsible for enforcing the order.

Compensation—general

58.10 (1) This rule applies to an application for compensation under section 72 of the Proceeds of Crime Act 2002.

(2) The application must be in writing and may be supported by a witness statement.

(3) The application and any witness statement must be lodged with the Crown Court.

(4) The application and any witness statement must be served on—

(a) the person alleged to be in default; and

(b) the person by whom the compensation would be payable under section 72(9) of the 2002 Act (or if the compensation is payable out of a police fund under section 72(9)(a), the chief officer of the police force concerned),

at least seven days before the date fixed by the court for hearing the application, unless the Crown Court directs otherwise.

Compensation—confiscation order made against absconder

58.11 (1) This rule applies to an application for compensation under section 73 of the Proceeds of Crime Act 2002.

(2) The application must be in writing and supported by a witness statement which must give details of—

(a) the confiscation order made under section 28 of the 2002 Act;

(b) the variation or discharge of the confiscation order under section 29 or 30 of the 2002 Act;

(c) the realisable property to which the application relates; and

(d) the loss suffered by the applicant as result of the confiscation order.

(3) The application and witness statement must be lodged with the Crown Court.

(4) The application and witness statement must be served on the prosecutor or, if the Director is appointed as the enforcement authority under section 34 of the 2002 Act, the Director at least seven days before the date fixed by the court for hearing the application, unless the Crown Court specifies a shorter period.

Payment of money in bank or building society account in satisfaction of confiscation order

58.12 (1) An order under section 67 of the Proceeds of Crime Act 2002 requiring a bank or building society to pay money to a magistrates' court officer ('a payment order') shall—

(a) be directed to the bank or building society in respect of which the payment order is made;

(b) name the person against whom the confiscation order has been made;

(c) state the amount which remains to be paid under the confiscation order;

(d) state the name and address of the branch at which the account in which the

money ordered to be paid is held and the sort code of that branch, if the sort code is known;
(e) state the name in which the account in which the money ordered to be paid is held and the account number of that account, if the account number is known;
(f) state the amount which the bank or building society is required to pay to the court officer under the payment order;
(g) give the name and address of the court officer to whom payment is to be made; and
(h) require the bank or building society to make payment within a period of seven days beginning on the day on which the payment order is made, unless it appears to the court that a longer or shorter period would be appropriate in the particular circumstances.

(2) The payment order shall be served on the bank or building society in respect of which it is made by leaving it at, or sending it by first class post to, the principal office of the bank or building society.

(3) A payment order which is served by first class post shall, unless the contrary is proved, be deemed to have been served on the second business day after posting.

(4) In this rule 'confiscation order' has the meaning given to it by section 88(6) of the Proceeds of Crime Act 2002.

Part 59 Proceeds of Crime Act 2002—Rules Applicable only to Restraint Proceedings

Application for restraint order

59.1 (1) This rule applies where the prosecutor, the Director or an accredited financial investigator makes an application for a restraint order under section 42 of the Proceeds of Crime Act 2002.

(2) The application may be made without notice.

(3) The application must be in writing and supported by a witness statement which must—
(a) give the grounds for the application;
(b) to the best of the witness's ability, give full details of the realisable property in respect of which the applicant is seeking the order and specify the person holding that realisable property;
(c) give the grounds for, and full details of, any application for an ancillary order under section 41(7) of the 2002 Act for the purposes of ensuring that the restraint order is effective; and
(d) where the application is made by an accredited financial investigator, include a statement that he has been authorised to make the application under section 68 of the 2002 Act.

Restraint orders

59.2 (1) The Crown Court may make a restraint order subject to exceptions, including, but not limited to, exceptions for reasonable living expenses and reasonable legal expenses, and for the purpose of enabling any person to carry on any trade, business or occupation.

(2) But the Crown Court must not make an exception for legal expenses where this is prohibited by section 41(4) of the Proceeds of Crime Act 2002.

(3) An exception to a restraint order may be made subject to conditions.

(4) The Crown Court must not require the applicant for a restraint order to give any undertaking relating to damages sustained as a result of the restraint order by a person who is prohibited from dealing with realisable property by the restraint order.

(5) The Crown Court may require the applicant for a restraint order to give an undertaking to pay the reasonable expenses of any person, other than a person who is prohibited from dealing with realisable property by the restraint order, which are incurred in complying with the restraint order.

(6) A restraint order must include a statement that disobedience of the order, either by a person to whom the order is addressed, or by another person, may be contempt of court and the order must include details of the possible consequences of being held in contempt of court.

(7) Unless the Crown Court directs otherwise, a restraint order made without notice has effect until the court makes an order varying or discharging the restraint order.

(8) The applicant for a restraint order must—
(a) serve copies of the restraint order and of the witness statement made in support of the

application on the defendant and any person who is prohibited from dealing with realisable property by the restraint order; and

(b) notify any person whom the applicant knows to be affected by the restraint order of the terms of the restraint order.

Application for discharge or variation of restraint order by person affected by order

59.3 (1) This rule applies where a person affected by a restraint order makes an application to the Crown Court under section 42(3) of the Proceeds of Crime Act 2002 to discharge or vary the restraint order or any ancillary order made under section 41(7) of the Act.

(2) The application must be in writing and may be supported by a witness statement.

(3) The application and any witness statement must be lodged with the Crown Court.

(4) The application and any witness statement must be served on the person who applied for the restraint order and any person who is prohibited from dealing with realisable property by the restraint order (if he is not the person making the application) at least two days before the date fixed by the court for hearing the application, unless the Crown Court specifies a shorter period.

Application for variation of restraint order by the person who applied for the order

59.4 (1) This rule applies where the applicant for a restraint order makes an application under section 42(3) of the Proceeds of Crime Act 2002 to the Crown Court to vary the restraint order or any ancillary order made under section 41(7) of the 2002 Act (including where the court has already made a restraint order and the applicant is seeking to vary the order in order to restrain further realisable property).

(2) The application may be made without notice if the application is urgent or if there are reasonable grounds for believing that giving notice would cause the dissipation of realisable property which is the subject of the application.

(3) The application must be in writing and must be supported by a witness statement which must—

(a) give the grounds for the application;

(b) where the application is for the inclusion of further realisable property in the order give full details, to the best of the witness's ability, of the realisable property in respect of which the applicant is seeking the order and specify the person holding that realisable property; and

(c) where the application is made by an accredited financial investigator, include a statement that he has been authorised to make the application under section 68 of the 2002 Act.

(4) The application and witness statement must be lodged with the Crown Court.

(5) Except where, under paragraph (2), notice of the application is not required to be served, the application and witness statement must be served on any person who is prohibited from dealing with realisable property by the restraint order at least 2 days before the date fixed by the court for hearing the application, unless the Crown Court specifies a shorter period.

(6) If the court makes an order for the variation of a restraint order, the applicant must serve copies of the order and of the witness statement made in support of the application on—

(a) the defendant;

(b) any person who is prohibited from dealing with realisable property by the restraint order (whether before or after the variation); and

(c) any other person whom the applicant knows to be affected by the order.

Application for discharge of a restraint order by the person who applied for the order

59.5 (1) This rule applies where the applicant for a restraint order makes an application under section 42(3) of the Proceeds of Crime Act 2002 to discharge the order or any ancillary order made under section 41(7) of the 2002 Act.

(2) The application may be made without notice.

(3) The application must be in writing and must state the grounds for the application.

(4) If the court makes an order for the discharge of a restraint order, the applicant must serve copies of the order on—

(a) the defendant;

(b) any person who is prohibited from dealing with realisable property by the restraint order (whether before or after the discharge); and

(c) any other person whom the applicant knows to be affected by the order.

Part 60 Proceeds of Crime Act 2002—Rules Applicable only to Receivership Proceedings

Application for appointment of a management or enforcement receiver

60.1 (1) This rule applies to an application for the appointment of a management receiver under section 48(1) of the Proceeds of Crime Act 2002 and an application for the appointment of an enforcement receiver under section 50(1) of the 2002 Act.

(2) The application may be made without notice if—
(a) the application is joined with an application for a restraint order under rule 59.1;
(b) the application is urgent; or
(c) there are reasonable grounds for believing that giving notice would cause the dissipation of realisable property which is the subject of the application.

(3) The application must be in writing and must be supported by a witness statement which must—
(a) give the grounds for the application;
(b) give full details of the proposed receiver;
(c) to the best of the witness's ability, give full details of the realisable property in respect of which the applicant is seeking the order and specify the person holding that realisable property;
(d) where the application is made by an accredited financial investigator, include a statement that he has been authorised to make the application under section 68 of the 2002 Act; and
(e) if the proposed receiver is not a member of staff of the Assets Recovery Agency, the Crown Prosecution Service or the Commissioners of Customs and Excise and the applicant is asking the court to allow the receiver to act—
(i) without giving security, or
(ii) before he has given security or satisfied the court that he has security in place,
explain the reasons why that is necessary.

(4) Where the application is for the appointment of an enforcement receiver, the applicant must provide the Crown Court with a copy of the confiscation order made against the defendant.

(5) The application and witness statement must be lodged with the Crown Court.

(6) Except where, under paragraph (2), notice of the application is not required to be served, the application and witness statement must be lodged with the Crown Court and served on—
(a) the defendant;
(b) any person who holds realisable property to which the application relates; and
(c) any other person whom the applicant knows to be affected by the application,
at least seven days before the date fixed by the court for hearing the application, unless the Crown Court specifies a shorter period.

(7) If the court makes an order for the appointment of a receiver, the applicant must serve copies of the order and of the witness statement made in support of the application on—
(a) the defendant;
(b) any person who holds realisable property to which the order applies; and
(c) any other person whom the applicant knows to be affected by the order.

Application for conferral of powers on management receiver, enforcement receiver or director's receiver

60.2 (1) This rule applies to an application for the conferral of powers on a management receiver under section 49(1) of the Proceeds of Crime Act 2002, an enforcement receiver under section 51(1) of the 2002 Act or a Director's receiver under section 53(1) of the 2002 Act.

(2) The application may be made without notice if the application is to give the receiver power to take possession of property and—
(a) the application is joined with an application for a restraint order under rule 59.1;
(b) the application is urgent; or
(c) there are reasonable grounds for believing that giving notice would cause the dissipation of the property which is the subject of the application.

(3) The application must be made in writing and supported by a witness statement which must—
(a) give the grounds for the application;
(b) give full details of the realisable property in respect of which the applicant is seeking the order and specify the person holding that realisable property; and

(c) where the application is made by an accredited financial investigator, include a statement that he has been authorised to make the application under section 68 of the 2002 Act.

(4) Where the application is for the conferral of powers on an enforcement receiver or Director's receiver, the applicant must provide the Crown Court with a copy of the confiscation order made against the defendant.

(5) The application and witness statement must be lodged with the Crown Court.

(6) Except where, under paragraph (2), notice of the application is not required to be served, the application and witness statement must be served on—

(a) the defendant;

(b) any person who holds realisable property in respect of which a receiver has been appointed or in respect of which an application for a receiver has been made;

(c) any other person whom the applicant knows to be affected by the application; and

(d) the receiver (if one has already been appointed), at least seven days before the date fixed by the court for hearing the application, unless the Crown Court specifies a shorter period.

(7) If the court makes an order for the conferral of powers on a receiver, the applicant must serve copies of the order on—

(a) the defendant;

(b) any person who holds realisable property in respect of which the receiver has been appointed; and

(c) any other person whom the applicant knows to be affected by the order.

Applications for discharge or variation of receivership orders and applications for other orders

60.3 (1) This rule applies to applications under section 62(3) of the Proceeds of Crime Act 2002 for orders (by persons affected by the action of receivers) and applications under section 63(1) of the 2002 Act for the discharge or variation of orders relating to receivers.

(2) The application must be made in writing and lodged with the Crown Court.

(3) The application must be served on the following persons (except where they are the person making the application)—

(a) the person who applied for appointment of the receiver;

(b) the defendant;

(c) any person who holds realisable property in respect of which the receiver has been appointed;

(d) the receiver; and

(e) any other person whom the applicant knows to be affected by the application, at least seven days before the date fixed by the court for hearing the application, unless the Crown Court specifies a shorter period.

(4) If the court makes an order for the discharge or variation of an order relating to a receiver under section 63(2) of the 2002 Act, the applicant must serve copies of the order on any persons whom he knows to be affected by the order.

Sums in the hands of receivers

60.4 (1) This rule applies where the amount payable under a confiscation order has been fully paid and any sums remain in the hands of an enforcement receiver or Director's receiver.

(2) The receiver must make an application to the Crown Court for directions as to the distribution of the sums in his hands.

(3) The application and any evidence which the receiver intends to rely on in support of the application must be served on—

(a) the defendant; and

(b) any other person who held (or holds) interests in any property realised by the receiver, at least seven days before the date fixed by the court for hearing the application, unless the Crown Court specifies a shorter period.

(4) If any of the provisions listed in paragraph (5) (provisions as to the vesting of funds in a trustee in bankruptcy) apply, then the Crown Court must make a declaration to that effect.

(5) These are the provisions—

(a) section 31B of the Bankruptcy (Scotland) Act 1985;

(b) section 306B of the Insolvency Act 1986; and

(c) article 279B of the Insolvency (Northern Ireland) Order 1989.

Security

60.5 (1) This rule applies where the Crown Court appoints a receiver under section 48, 50 or 52 of the Proceeds of Crime Act 2002 and the receiver is not a member of staff of the Assets Recovery Agency, the Crown Prosecution Service or of the Commissioners of Customs and Excise (and it is immaterial whether the receiver is a permanent or temporary member or he is on secondment from elsewhere).

(2) The Crown Court may direct that before the receiver begins to act, or within a specified time, he must either—

(a) give such security as the Crown Court may determine; or

(b) file with the Crown Court and serve on all parties to any receivership proceedings evidence that he already has in force sufficient security,

to cover his liability for his acts and omissions as a receiver.

(3) The Crown Court may terminate the appointment of a receiver if he fails to—

(a) give the security; or

(b) satisfy the court as to the security he has in force, by the date specified.

Remuneration

60.6 (1) This rule applies where the Crown Court appoints a receiver under section 48, 50 or 52 of the Proceeds of Crime Act 2002 and the receiver is not a member of staff of the Assets Recovery Agency, the Crown Prosecution Service or of the Commissioners of Customs and Excise (and it is immaterial whether the receiver is a permanent or temporary member or he is on secondment from elsewhere).

(2) The receiver may only charge for his services if the Crown Court—

(a) so directs; and

(b) specifies the basis on which the receiver is to be remunerated.

(3) Unless the Crown Court orders otherwise, in determining the remuneration of the receiver, the Crown Court shall award such sum as is reasonable and proportionate in all the circumstances and which takes into account—

(a) the time properly given by him and his staff to the receivership;

(b) the complexity of the receivership;

(c) any responsibility of an exceptional kind or degree which falls on the receiver in consequence of the receivership;

(d) the effectiveness with which the receiver appears to be carrying out, or to have carried out, his duties; and

(e) the value and nature of the subject matter of the receivership.

(4) The Crown Court may refer the determination of a receiver's remuneration to be ascertained by the taxing authority of the Crown Court and rules 78.4 to 78.7 shall have effect as if the taxing authority was ascertaining costs.

(5) A receiver appointed under section 48 of the 2002 Act is to receive his remuneration by realising property in respect of which he is appointed, in accordance with section 49(2)(d) of the 2002 Act.

(6) A receiver appointed under section 50 of the 2002 Act is to receive his remuneration by applying to the magistrates' court officer for payment under section 55(4)(b) of the 2002 Act.

(7) A receiver appointed under section 52 of the 2002 Act is to receive his remuneration by applying to the Director for payment under section 57(4)(b) of the 2002 Act.

Accounts

60.7 (1) The Crown Court may order a receiver appointed under section 48, 50 or 52 of the Proceeds of Crime Act 2002 to prepare and serve accounts.

(2) A party to receivership proceedings served with such accounts may apply for an order permitting him to inspect any document in the possession of the receiver relevant to those accounts.

(3) Any party to receivership proceedings may, within 14 days of being served with the accounts, serve notice on the receiver—

(a) specifying any item in the accounts to which he objects;

(b) giving the reason for such objection; and

(c) requiring the receiver within 14 days of receipt of the notice, either—

(i) to notify all the parties who were served with the accounts that he accepts the objection, or
(ii) if he does not accept the objection, to apply for an examination of the accounts in relation to the contested item.

(4) When the receiver applies for the examination of the accounts he must at the same time lodge with the Crown Court—
(a) the accounts; and
(b) a copy of the notice served on him under this section of the rule.

(5) If the receiver fails to comply with paragraph (3)(c) of this rule, any party to receivership proceedings may apply to the Crown Court for an examination of the accounts in relation to the contested item.

(6) At the conclusion of its examination of the accounts the court will certify the result.

Non-compliance by receiver

60.8 (1) If a receiver appointed under section 48, 50 or 52 of the Proceeds of Crime Act 2002 fails to comply with any rule, practice direction or direction of the Crown Court, the Crown Court may order him to attend a hearing to explain his non-compliance.

(2) At the hearing, the Crown Court may make any order it considers appropriate, including—
(a) terminating the appointment of the receiver;
(b) reducing the receiver's remuneration or disallowing it altogether; and
(c) ordering the receiver to pay the costs of any party.

Part 61 Proceeds of Crime Act 2002—Rules Applicable to Restraint and Receivership Proceedings

Distress and forfeiture

61.1 (1) This rule applies to applications under sections 58(2) and (3), 59(2) and (3) and 60(2) and (3) of the Proceeds of Crime Act 2002 for leave of the Crown Court to levy distress against property or exercise a right of forfeiture by peaceable re-entry in relation to a tenancy, in circumstances where the property or tenancy is the subject of a restraint order or a receiver has been appointed in respect of the property or tenancy.

(2) The application must be made in writing to the Crown Court.

(3) The application must be served on—
(a) the person who applied for the restraint order or the order appointing the receiver; and
(b) any receiver appointed in respect of the property or tenancy,

at least seven days before the date fixed by the court for hearing the application, unless the Crown Court specifies a shorter period.

Joining of applications

61.2 An application for the appointment of a management receiver or enforcement receiver under rule 60.1 may be joined with—
(a) an application for a restraint order under rule 59.1; and
(b) an application for the conferral of powers on the receiver under rule 60.2.

Applications to be dealt with in writing

61.3 Applications in restraint proceedings and receivership proceedings are to be dealt with without a hearing, unless the Crown Court orders otherwise.

Business in chambers

61.4 Restraint proceedings and receivership proceedings may be heard in chambers.

Power of court to control evidence

61.5 (1) When hearing restraint proceedings and receivership proceedings, the Crown Court may control the evidence by giving directions as to—
(a) the issues on which it requires evidence;
(b) the nature of the evidence which it requires to decide those issues; and
(c) the way in which the evidence is to be placed before the court.

(2) The court may use its power under this rule to exclude evidence that would otherwise be admissible.

(3) The court may limit cross-examination in restraint proceedings and receivership proceedings.

Evidence of witnesses

61.6 (1) The general rule is that, unless the Crown Court orders otherwise, any fact which needs to be proved in restraint proceedings or receivership proceedings by the evidence of a witness is to be proved by their evidence in writing.

(2) Where evidence is to be given in writing under this rule, any party may apply to the Crown Court for permission to cross-examine the person giving the evidence.

(3) If the Crown Court gives permission under paragraph (2) but the person in question does not attend as required by the order, his evidence may not be used unless the court gives permission.

Witness summons

61.7 (1) Any party to restraint proceedings or receivership proceedings may apply to the Crown Court to issue a witness summons requiring a witness to—

(a) attend court to give evidence; or

(b) produce documents to the court.

(2) Rule 28.3 applies to an application under this rule as it applies to an application under section 2 of the Criminal Procedure (Attendance of Witnesses) Act 1965.

Hearsay evidence

61.8 Section 2(1) of the Civil Evidence Act 1995 (duty to give notice of intention to rely on hearsay evidence) does not apply to evidence in restraint proceedings and receivership proceedings.

Disclosure and inspection of documents

61.9 (1) This rule applies where, in the course of restraint proceedings or receivership proceedings, an issue arises as to whether property is realisable property.

(2) The Crown Court may make an order for disclosure of documents.

(3) Part 31 of the Civil Procedure Rules 1998 as amended from time to time shall have effect as if the proceedings were proceedings in the High Court.

Court documents

61.10 (1) Any order which the Crown Court issues in restraint proceedings or receivership proceedings must—

(a) state the name and judicial title of the person who made it;

(b) bear the date on which it is made; and

(c) be sealed by the Crown Court.

(2) The Crown Court may place the seal on the order—

(a) by hand; or

(b) by printing a facsimile of the seal on the order whether electronically or otherwise.

(3) A document purporting to bear the court's seal shall be admissible in evidence without further proof.

Consent orders

61.11 (1) This rule applies where all the parties to restraint proceedings or receivership proceedings agree the terms in which an order should be made.

(2) Any party may apply for a judgment or order in the terms agreed.

(3) The Crown Court may deal with an application under paragraph (2) without a hearing.

(4) Where this rule applies—

(a) the order which is agreed by the parties must be drawn up in the terms agreed;

(b) it must be expressed as being 'By Consent'; and

(c) it must be signed by the legal representative acting for each of the parties to whom the order relates or by the party if he is a litigant in person.

(5) Where an application is made under this rule, then the requirements of any other rule as to the procedure for making an application do not apply.

Slips and omissions

61.12 (1) The Crown Court may at any time correct an accidental slip or omission in an order made in restraint proceedings or receivership proceedings.

(2) A party may apply for a correction without notice.

Supply of documents from court records

61.13 (1) No document relating to restraint proceedings or receivership proceedings may be supplied from the records of the Crown Court for any person to inspect or copy unless the Crown Court grants permission.

(2) An application for permission under paragraph (1) must be made on notice to the parties to the proceedings.

Disclosure of documents in criminal proceedings

61.14 (1) This rule applies where—

(a) proceedings for an offence have been started in the Crown Court and the defendant has not been either convicted or acquitted on all counts; and

(b) an application for a restraint order under section 42(1) of the Proceeds of Crime Act 2002 has been made.

(2) The judge presiding at the proceedings for the offence may be supplied from the records of the Crown Court with documents relating to restraint proceedings and any receivership proceedings.

(3) Such documents must not otherwise be disclosed in the proceedings for the offence.

Preparation of documents

61.15 (1) Every order in restraint proceedings or receivership proceedings will be drawn up by the Crown Court unless—

(a) the Crown Court orders a party to draw it up;

(b) a party, with the permission of the Crown Court, agrees to draw it up; or

(c) the order is made by consent under rule 61.10.

(2) The Crown Court may direct that—

(a) an order drawn up by a party must be checked by the Crown Court before it is sealed; or

(b) before an order is drawn up by the Crown Court, the parties must lodge an agreed statement of its terms.

(3) Where an order is to be drawn up by a party—

(a) he must lodge it with the Crown Court no later than seven days after the date on which the court ordered or permitted him to draw it up so that it can be sealed by the Crown Court; and

(b) if he fails to lodge it within that period, any other party may draw it up and lodge it.

(4) Nothing in this rule shall require the Crown Court to accept a document which is illegible, has not been duly authorised, or is unsatisfactory for some other similar reason.

Change of solicitor

61.16 (1) This rule applies where—

(a) a party for whom a solicitor is acting in restraint proceedings or receivership proceedings wants to change his solicitor;

(b) a party, after having represented himself in such proceedings, appoints a solicitor to act on his behalf (except where the solicitor is appointed only to act as an advocate for a hearing); or

(c) a party, after having been represented by a solicitor in such proceedings, intends to act in person.

(2) Where this rule applies, the party or his solicitor (where one is acting) must—

(a) lodge notice of the change at the Crown Court; and

(b) serve notice of the change on every other party and, where paragraph (1)(a) or (c) applies, on the former solicitor.

(3) The notice lodged at the Crown Court must state that notice has been served as required by paragraph (2)(b).

(4) Subject to paragraph (5), where a party has changed his solicitor or intends to act in person, the former solicitor will be considered to be the party's solicitor unless and until—

(a) notice is served in accordance with paragraph (2); or

(b) the Crown Court makes an order under rule 61.17 and the order is served as required by paragraph (3) of that rule.

(5) Where the certificate of a LSC funded client is revoked or discharged—

(a) the solicitor who acted for that person will cease to be the solicitor acting in the proceedings as soon as his retainer is determined under regulation 4 of the Community Legal Service (Costs) Regulations 2000; and

(b) if that person wishes to continue, where he appoints a solicitor to act on his behalf paragraph (2) will apply as if he had previously represented himself in the proceedings.

(6) 'Certificate' in paragraph (5) means a certificate issued under the Funding Code (approved under section 9 of the Access to Justice Act 1999) and 'LSC funded client' means an individual who receives services funded by the Legal Services Commission as part of the Community Legal Service within the meaning of Part I of the 1999 Act.

Application by solicitor for declaration that solicitor has ceased to act

61.17 (1) A solicitor may apply to the Crown Court for an order declaring that he has ceased to be the solicitor acting for a party to restraint proceedings or receivership proceedings.

(2) Where an application is made under this rule—

(a) notice of the application must be given to the party for whom the solicitor is acting, unless the Crown Court directs otherwise; and

(b) the application must be supported by evidence.

(3) Where the Crown Court makes an order that a solicitor has ceased to act, the solicitor must serve a copy of the order on every party to the proceedings.

Application by other party for declaration that solicitor has ceased to act

61.18 (1) Where—

(a) a solicitor who has acted for a party to restraint proceedings or receivership proceedings—

(i) has died,

(ii) has become bankrupt,

(iii) has ceased to practise, or

(iv) cannot be found, and

(b) the party has not given notice of a change of solicitor or notice of intention to act in person as required by rule 61.16,

any other party may apply to the Crown Court for an order declaring that the solicitor has ceased to be the solicitor acting for the other party in the proceedings.

(2) Where an application is made under this rule, notice of the application must be given to the party to whose solicitor the application relates unless the Crown Court directs otherwise.

(3) Where the Crown Court makes an order under this rule, the applicant must serve a copy of the order on every other party to the proceedings.

Order for costs

61.19 (1) This rule applies where the Crown Court is deciding whether to make an order for costs under rule 78.1 in restraint proceedings or receivership proceedings.

(2) The court has discretion as to—

(a) whether costs are payable by one party to another;

(b) the amount of those costs; and

(c) when they are to be paid.

(3) If the court decides to make an order about costs—

(a) the general rule is that the unsuccessful party will be ordered to pay the costs of the successful party; but

(b) the court may make a different order.

(4) In deciding what order (if any) to make about costs, the court must have regard to all of the circumstances, including—

(a) the conduct of all the parties; and

(b) whether a party has succeeded on part of an application, even if he has not been wholly successful.

(5) The orders which the court may make under rule 78.1 include an order that a party must pay—

(a) a proportion of another party's costs;

(b) a stated amount in respect of another party's costs;

(c) costs from or until a certain date only;

(d) costs incurred before proceedings have begun;

(e) costs relating to particular steps taken in the proceedings;

(f) costs relating only to a distinct part of the proceedings; and

(g) interest on costs from or until a certain date, including a date before the making of an order.

(6) Where the court would otherwise consider making an order under paragraph (5)(f), it must instead, if practicable, make an order under paragraph (5)(a) or (c).

(7) Where the court has ordered a party to pay costs, it may order an amount to be paid on account before the costs are assessed.

Assessment of costs

61.20 (1) Where the Crown Court has made an order for costs in restraint proceedings or receivership proceedings it may either—
(a) make an assessment of the costs itself; or
(b) order assessment of the costs under rule 78.3.
(2) In either case, the Crown Court or the taxing authority, as the case may be, must—
(a) only allow costs which are proportionate to the matters in issue; and
(b) resolve any doubt which it may have as to whether the costs were reasonably incurred or reasonable and proportionate in favour of the paying party.
(3) The Crown Court or the taxing authority, as the case may be, is to have regard to all the circumstances in deciding whether costs were proportionately or reasonably incurred or proportionate and reasonable in amount.
(4) In particular, the Crown Court or the taxing authority must give effect to any orders which have already been made.
(5) The Crown Court or the taxing authority must also have regard to—
(a) the conduct of all the parties, including in particular, conduct before, as well as during, the proceedings;
(b) the amount or value of the property involved;
(c) the importance of the matter to all the parties;
(d) the particular complexity of the matter or the difficulty or novelty of the questions raised;
(e) the skill, effort, specialised knowledge and responsibility involved;
(f) the time spent on the application; and
(g) the place where and the circumstances in which work or any part of it was done.

Time for complying with an order for costs

61.21 (1) A party to restraint proceedings or receivership proceedings must comply with an order for the payment of costs within 14 days of—
(a) the date of the order if it states the amount of those costs;
(b) if the amount of those costs is decided later under rule 78.3, the date of the taxing authority's decision; or
(c) in either case, such later date as the Crown Court may specify.

Application of costs rules

61.22 Rules 61.19, 61.20 and 61.21 do not apply to the assessment of costs in proceedings to the extent that section 11 of the Access to Justice Act 1999 applies and provisions made under that Act make different provision.

Part 62 Proceeds of Crime Act 2002—Rules Applicable to Investigations

Account monitoring orders under the Terrorism Act 2000 and the Proceeds of Crime Act 2002

62.1 (1) Where a circuit judge makes an account monitoring order under paragraph 2(1) of Schedule 6A to the Terrorism Act 2000 the court officer shall give a copy of the order to the financial institution specified in the application for the order.
(2) Where any person other than the person who applied for the account monitoring order proposes to make an application under paragraph 4(1) of Schedule 6A to the 2000 Act or section 375(2) of the Proceeds of Crime Act 2002 for the discharge or variation of an account monitoring order he shall give a copy of the proposed application, not later than 48 hours before the application is to be made—
(a) to a police officer at the police station specified in the account monitoring order; or
(b) where the application for the account monitoring order was made under the 2002 Act and was not made by a constable, to the office of the appropriate officer who made the application, as specified in the account monitoring order,
in either case together with a notice indicating the time and place at which the application for discharge or variation is to be made.
(3) In this rule:
'appropriate officer' has the meaning given to it by section 378 of the 2002 Act; and

references to the person who applied for an account monitoring order must be construed in accordance with section 375(4) and (5) of the 2002 Act.

Customer information orders under the Proceeds of Crime Act 2002

62.2 (1) Where any person other than the person who applied for the customer information order proposes to make an application under section 369(3) of the Proceeds of Crime Act 2002 for the discharge or variation of a customer information order, he shall, not later than 48 hours before the application is to be made, give a copy of the proposed application—

(a) to a police officer at the police station specified in the customer information order; or

(b) where the application for the customer information order was not made by a constable, to the office of the appropriate officer who made the application, as specified in the customer information order,

in either case together with a notice indicating the time and place at which the application for a discharge or variation is to be made.

(2) In this rule:

'appropriate officer' has the meaning given to it by section 378 of the 2002 Act; and

references to the person who applied for the customer information order must be construed in accordance with section 369(5) and (6) of the 2002 Act.

Proof of identity and accreditation

62.3 (1) This rule applies where—

(a) an appropriate officer makes an application under section 345 (production orders), section 363 (customer information orders) or section 370 (account monitoring orders) of the Proceeds of Crime Act 2002 for the purposes of a confiscation investigation or a money laundering investigation; or

(b) the Director of the Assets Recovery Agency makes an application under section 357 of the 2002 Act (disclosure orders) for the purposes of a confiscation investigation.

(2) Subject to section 449 of the 2002 Act (which makes provision for members of staff of the Assets Recovery Agency to use pseudonyms), the appropriate officer or the Director of the Assets Recovery Agency, as the case may be, must provide the judge with proof of his identity and, if he is an accredited financial investigator, his accreditation under section 3 of the 2002 Act.

(3) In this rule:

'appropriate officer' has the meaning given to it by section 378 of the 2002 Act; and

'confiscation investigation' and 'money laundering investigation' have the meanings given to them by section 341 of the 2002 Act.

Part 63 Appeal to the Crown Court Against Conviction or Sentence

Application of this Part

63.1 This Part shall apply to any appeal under section 108(1) of the Magistrates' Courts Act 1980 (conviction and sentence), section 45(1) of the Mental Health Act 1983 (hospital or guardianship order in the absence of conviction) and paragraph 11 of Schedule 3 to the Powers of Criminal Courts (Sentencing) Act 2000 (re-sentencing on failure to comply with supervision order).

Notice of appeal

63.2 (1) An appeal shall be commenced by the appellant's giving notice of appeal in accordance with the following provisions of this rule.

(2) The notice required by the preceding paragraph shall be in writing and shall be given to a court officer for the magistrates' court and to any other party to the appeal.

(3) Notice of appeal shall be given not later than 21 days after the day on which the decision appealed against is given and, for this purpose, where the court has adjourned the trial of an information after conviction, that day shall be the day on which the court sentences or otherwise deals with the offender:

Provided that, where a court exercises its power to defer sentence under section 1(1) of the Powers of Criminal Courts (Sentencing) Act 2000, that day shall, for the purposes of an appeal against conviction, be the day on which the court exercises that power.

(4) A notice of appeal shall state the grounds of appeal.

(5) The time for giving notice of appeal may be extended, either before or after it expires, by the Crown Court, on an application made in accordance with paragraph (6).

(6) An application for an extension of time shall be made in writing, specifying the grounds of the application and sent to a Crown Court officer.

(7) Where the Crown Court extends the time for giving notice of appeal, the Crown Court officer shall give notice of the extension to—

(a) the appellant; and

(b) the magistrates' court officer,

and the appellant shall give notice of the extension to any other party to the appeal.

Documents to be sent to Crown Court

63.3 (1) The magistrates' court officer shall as soon as practicable send to the Crown Court officer any notice of appeal to the Crown Court given to the magistrates' court officer.

(2) The magistrates' court officer shall send to the Crown Court officer, with the notice of appeal, a copy of the extract of the magistrates' court register relating to that decision and of the last known or usual place of abode of the parties to the appeal.

(3) Where any person, having given notice of appeal to the Crown Court, has been granted bail for the purposes of the appeal the magistrates' court officer for the court from whose decision the appeal is brought shall before the day fixed for the hearing of the appeal send to the Crown Court officer a copy of the record made in pursuance of section 5 of the Bail Act 1976.

(4) Where a notice of appeal is given in respect of a hospital order or guardianship order made under section 37 of the Mental Health Act 1983 (powers of courts to order hospital admission or guardianship), a magistrates' court officer for the court from which the appeal is brought shall send with the notice to the Crown Court officer any written evidence considered by the court under section 37(2) of the 1983 Act.

(5) Where a notice of appeal is given in respect of an appeal against conviction by a magistrates' court the magistrates' court officer shall send with the notice to the Crown Court officer any admission of facts made for the purposes of the summary trial under section 10 of the Criminal Justice Act 1967 (proof by formal admission).

(6) Where a notice of appeal is given in respect of an appeal against sentence by a magistrates' court, and where that sentence was a custodial sentence, the magistrates' court officer shall send with the notice to the Crown Court officer a statement of whether the magistrates' court obtained and considered a pre-sentence report before passing such sentence.

Entry of appeal and notice of hearing

63.4 On receiving notice of appeal, the Crown Court officer shall enter the appeal and give notice of the time and place of the hearing to—

(a) the appellant;

(b) any other party to the appeal; and

(c) the magistrates' court officer.

Abandonment of appeal—notice

63.5 (1) Without prejudice to the power of the Crown Court to give leave for an appeal to be abandoned, an appellant may abandon an appeal by giving notice in writing, in accordance with the following provisions of this rule, not later than the third day before the day fixed for hearing the appeal.

(2) The notice required by the preceding paragraph shall be given—

(a) to the magistrates' court officer;

(b) to the Crown Court officer; and

(c) to any other party to the appeal.

(3) For the purposes of determining whether notice of abandonment was given in time there shall be disregarded any Saturday, Sunday and any day which is specified to be a bank holiday in England and Wales under section 1(1) of the Banking and Financial Dealings Act 1971.

Abandonment of appeal—bail

63.6 Where notice to abandon an appeal has been given by the appellant, any recognizance conditioned for the appearance of the appellant at the hearing of the appeal shall have effect as if conditioned for the appearance of the appellant before the court from whose decision the appeal was brought at a time and place to be notified to the appellant by the court officer for that court.

Number and qualification of justices—appeals from youth courts

63.7 Subject to the provisions of rule 63.8 and to any directions under section 74(4) of the Supreme Court Act 1981 (directions disapplying the set out number and qualifications of justices), on the hearing of an appeal from a youth court the Crown Court shall consist of a judge sitting with two justices each of whom is a member of a youth court panel and who are chosen so that the Court shall include a man and a woman.

Number and qualification of justices—dispensation for special circumstances

63.8 (1) The Crown Court may enter on any appeal notwithstanding that the Court is not constituted as required by section 74(1) of the Supreme Court Act 1981 or rule 63.7 if it appears to the judge that the Court could not be constituted without unreasonable delay and the Court includes one justice who is a member of a youth court panel.

(2) The Crown Court may at any stage continue with any proceedings with a Court from which any one or more of the justices initially comprising the Court has withdrawn, or is absent for any reason.

Disqualifications

63.9 A justice of the peace shall not sit in the Crown Court on the hearing of an appeal in a matter on which he adjudicated.

Part 64 Appeal to the High Court by Way of Case Stated

Application to a magistrates' court to state a case

64.1 (1) An application under section 111(1) of the Magistrates' Courts Act 1980 shall be made in writing and signed by or on behalf of the applicant and shall identify the question or questions of law or jurisdiction on which the opinion of the High Court is sought.

(2) Where one of the questions on which the opinion of the High Court is sought is whether there was evidence on which the magistrates' court could come to its decision, the particular finding of fact made by the magistrates' court which it is claimed cannot be supported by the evidence before the magistrates' court shall be specified in such application.

(3) Any such application shall be sent to a court officer for the magistrates' court whose decision is questioned.

Consideration of a draft case by a magistrates' court

64.2 (1) Within 21 days after receipt of an application made in accordance with rule 64.1, a court officer for the magistrates' court whose decision is questioned shall, unless the justices refuse to state a case under section 111(5) of the Magistrates' Courts Act 1980, send a draft case in which are stated the matters required under rule 64.6 (content of case stated) to the applicant or his legal representative and shall send a copy thereof to the respondent or his legal representative.

(2) Within 21 days after receipt of the draft case under paragraph (1), each party may make representations thereon. Any such representations shall be in writing and signed by or on behalf of the party making them and shall be sent to the magistrates' court officer.

(3) Where the justices refuse to state a case under section 111(5) of the 1980 Act and they are required by a mandatory order of the High Court under section 111(6) to do so, this rule shall apply as if in paragraph (1)—

(a) for the words 'receipt of an application made in accordance with rule 64.1' there were substituted the words 'the date on which a mandatory order under section 111(6) of the 1980 Act is made'; and

(b) the words 'unless the justices refuse to state a case under section 111(5) of the 1980 Act' were omitted.

Preparation and submission of final case to a magistrates' court

64.3 (1) Within 21 days after the latest day on which representations may be made under rule 64.2, the justices whose decision is questioned shall make such adjustments, if any, to the draft case prepared for the purposes of that rule as they think fit, after considering any such representations, and shall state and sign the case.

(2) A case may be stated on behalf of the justices whose decision is questioned by any 2 or more of them and may, if the justices so direct, be signed on their behalf by the justices' clerk.

(3) Forthwith after the case has been stated and signed a court officer for the court shall send it to the applicant or his legal representative, together with any statement required by rule 64.4.

Extension of time limits by a magistrates' court

64.4 (1) If a magistrates' court officer is unable to send to the applicant a draft case under rule 64.2(1) within the time required by that paragraph, he shall do so as soon as practicable thereafter and the provisions of that rule shall apply accordingly; but in that event a court officer shall attach to the draft case, and to the final case when it is sent to the applicant or his legal representative under rule 64.3(3), a statement of the delay and the reasons for it.

(2) If a magistrates' court officer receives an application in writing from or on behalf of the applicant or the respondent for an extension of the time within which representations on the draft case may be made under rule 64.2(2), together with reasons in writing for it, the justices' clerk may, by notice in writing sent to the applicant, or respondent as the case may be, by the magistrates' court officer, extend the time and the provisions of that paragraph and of rule 64.3 shall apply accordingly; but in that event the court officer shall attach to the final case, when it is sent to the applicant or his legal representative under rule 64.3(3), a statement of the extension and the reasons for it.

(3) If the justices are unable to state a case within the time required by rule 64.3(1), they shall do so as soon as practicable thereafter and the provisions of that rule shall apply accordingly; but in that event a court officer shall attach to the final case, when it is sent to the applicant or his legal representative under rule 64.3(3), a statement of the delay and the reasons for it.

Service of documents where application made to a magistrates' court

64.5 [Revoked.]

Content of case stated by a magistrates' courts

64.6 (1) A case stated by the magistrates' court shall state the facts found by the court and the question or questions of law or jurisdiction on which the opinion of the High Court is sought.

(2) Where one of the questions on which the opinion of the High Court is sought is whether there was evidence on which the magistrates' court could come to its decision, the particular finding of fact which it is claimed cannot be supported by the evidence before the magistrates' court shall be specified in the case.

(3) Unless one of the questions on which the opinion of the High Court is sought is whether there was evidence on which the magistrates' court could come to its decision, the case shall not contain a statement of evidence.

Application to the Crown Court to state a case

64.7 (1) An application under section 28 of the Supreme Court Act 1981 to the Crown Court to state a case for the opinion of the High Court shall be made in writing to a court officer within 21 days after the date of the decision in respect of which the application is made.

(2) The application shall state the ground on which the decision of the Crown Court is questioned.

(3) After making the application, the applicant shall forthwith send a copy of it to the parties to the proceedings in the Crown Court.

(4) On receipt of the application, the Crown Court officer shall forthwith send it to the judge who presided at the proceedings in which the decision was made.

(5) On receipt of the application, the judge shall inform the Crown Court officer as to whether or not he has decided to state a case and that officer shall give notice in writing to the applicant of the judge's decision.

(6) If the judge considers that the application is frivolous, he may refuse to state a case and shall in that case, if the applicant so requires, cause a certificate stating the reasons for the refusal to be given to him.

(7) If the judge decides to state a case, the procedure to be followed shall, unless the judge in a particular case otherwise directs, be the procedure set out in paragraphs (8) to (12) of this rule.

(8) The applicant shall, within 21 days of receiving the notice referred to in paragraph (5), draft a case and send a copy of it to the Crown Court officer and to the parties to the proceedings in the Crown Court.

(9) Each party to the proceedings in the Crown Court shall, within 21 days of receiving a copy of the draft case under paragraph (8), either—

(a) give notice in writing to the applicant and the Crown Court officer that he does not intend to take part in the proceedings before the High Court;

(b) indicate in writing on the copy of the draft case that he agrees with it and send the copy to a court officer; or

(c) draft an alternative case and send it, together with the copy of the applicant's case, to the Crown Court officer.

(10) The judge shall consider the applicant's draft case and any alternative draft case sent to the Crown Court officer under paragraph (9)(c).

(11) If the Crown Court so orders, the applicant shall, before the case is stated and delivered to him, enter before the Crown Court officer into a recognizance, with or without sureties and in such sum as the Crown Court considers proper, having regard to the means of the applicant, conditioned to prosecute the appeal without delay.

(12) The judge shall state and sign a case within 14 days after either—

(a) the receipt of all the documents required to be sent to a court officer under paragraph (9); or

(b) the expiration of the period of 21 days referred to in that paragraph,

whichever is the sooner.

(13) A case stated by the Crown Court shall state the facts found by the Crown Court, the submissions of the parties (including any authorities relied on by the parties during the course of those submissions), the decision of the Crown Court in respect of which the application is made and the question on which the opinion of the High Court is sought.

(14) Any time limit referred to in this rule may be extended either before or after it expires by the Crown Court.

(15) If the judge decides not to state a case but the stating of a case is subsequently required by a mandatory order of the High Court, paragraphs (7) to (14) shall apply to the stating of the case save that—

(a) in paragraph (7) the words 'If the judge decides to state a case' shall be omitted; and

(b) in paragraph (8) for the words 'receiving the notice referred to in paragraph (5)' there shall be substituted the words 'the day on which the mandatory order was made'.

Part 65 Appeal to the Court of Appeal Against Ruling in Preparatory Hearing

Notice of appeal

65.1 (1) An application to the judge of the Crown Court for leave to appeal under section 9(11) of the Criminal Justice Act 1987 or section 35(1) of the Criminal Procedure and Investigations Act 1996 shall be made orally within two days of the making of the order or ruling to which it relates.

(2) Unless the application is made on the occasion of the order or ruling to which it relates, the appellant shall serve notice in writing thereof, specifying the grounds of the application, on the Crown Court officer and on all parties to the hearing directly affected by the order or ruling in question.

(3) The appellant shall no later than the day referred to in paragraph (4) serve notice of appeal from an order or ruling under section 9(11) of the 1987 Act or section 31(3) of the 1996 Act or, as the case may be, of an application to the Court of Appeal for leave to appeal from such a ruling on—

(a) the Registrar;

(b) the Crown Court officer; and

(c) all parties to the preparatory hearing directly affected by the said order or ruling.

(4) The day referred to is—

(a) the day which occurs seven days after the making of the order or ruling; or

(b) where an application is made to the judge of the Crown Court for leave to appeal under section 31(3) of the 1996 Act as in paragraph (1), the day which occurs 7 days after such application is determined or withdrawn.

(5) The time for giving notice under paragraph (3) may be extended, before or after it expires, by the Court of Appeal.

(6) A notice of appeal or of an application for leave to appeal, or an application to the Court of Appeal for an extension of time as referred to in paragraph (5), shall be in the form set out in the Practice Direction.

(7) If notice in writing of an application for leave to appeal was, under paragraph (2), served on the Crown Court, a copy thereof shall accompany the notice of appeal or, as the case may be,

of an application for leave to appeal required under paragraph (3) to be served on the Registrar.

(8) Notice of appeal or of an application for leave to appeal may be given either in respect of the whole or any part of the order to which it relates and shall—
(a) specify any question of law in respect of which the appeal is brought and, where appropriate, such facts of the case as are necessary for its proper consideration;
(b) summarise the arguments intended to be put to the Court of Appeal; and
(c) specify any authorities intended to be cited.

(9) Where the judge of the Crown Court has given leave to appeal the notice of appeal shall state that fact and specify the grounds on which leave is given.

(10) Notice of appeal or of an application for leave to appeal shall be accompanied by any documents or other things (or copies thereof) necessary for the proper determination of the appeal or application.

Respondent's notice

65.2 (1) Upon receiving notice of appeal or of an application for leave to appeal, the respondent if he desires to oppose the appeal, shall, within seven days of receipt of the notice, serve a notice in the form set out in the Practice Direction on the Registrar—
(a) stating the date on which the appellant's notice was received by the respondent;
(b) summarising his response to the arguments of the appellant; and
(c) specifying the authorities which he intends to cite,
and shall at the same time serve a copy thereof on the appellant and any other party to the proceedings directly affected by the order or ruling and on the Crown Court officer.

(2) The time for giving notice under this rule may be extended, either before or after it expires, by the Court of Appeal.

Persons in custody

65.3 (1) A person in custody shall be entitled to be present on the hearing of an appeal, or an application for leave to appeal, under section 9(11) of the Criminal Justice Act 1987 or section 35(1) of the Criminal Procedure and Investigations Act 1996, to which he is a party.

(2) Except as provided by paragraph (1) above, a person in custody shall not be entitled to be present on the hearing of an appeal, or an application for leave to appeal, under section 9(11) of the 1987 Act or section 35(1) of the 1996 Act except—
(a) on an application to the Crown Court for leave to appeal, with the leave of the judge; or
(b) on an appeal, or an application to the Court of Appeal for leave to appeal, with the leave of that Court.

(3) An application for leave to be present under paragraph (2) shall be made—
(a) where paragraph (2)(a) applies, orally to the judge;
(b) where paragraph (2)(b) applies, by serving notice in the form set out in the Practice Direction on the Registrar, or orally to the Court.

Supply of documentary and other exhibits

65.4 Rule 68.11 (supply of documentary and other exhibits) shall apply in relation to an appellant and a respondent under section 9(11) of the Criminal Justice Act 1987 or section 35(1) of the Criminal Procedure and Investigations Act 1996 as it applies in relation to an appellant and a respondent under Part I of the Criminal Appeal Act 1968.

Abandonment of proceedings

65.5 Rule 68.22 (abandonment of proceedings) shall apply for the purposes of an appeal or an application for leave to appeal by an appellant under section 9(11) of the Criminal Justice Act 1987 or section 35(1) of the Criminal Procedure and Investigations Act 1996 as it applies to an appeal or application for leave under Part I of the Criminal Appeal Act 1968, except that—
(a) notice thereof shall be served on the Registrar in the alternative form set out in the Practice Direction; and
(b) the requirement under rule 68.22(3) for the Registrar to send a copy of a notice of abandonment of proceedings to the Secretary of State shall be omitted.

Powers exercisable by single judge

65.6 (1) The following powers may be exercised by a judge of the court in the same manner as they may be exercised by the court and subject to the same provisions, namely—
(a) to give leave to appeal under section 9(11) of the Criminal Justice Act 1987 or section 35(1) of the Criminal Procedure and Investigations Act 1996;
(b) to extend, under rule 65.1, the time within which notice of appeal or of an application for leave to appeal must be given;
(c) to extend the time within which a notice under rule 65.2 of opposition to an appeal or application for leave to appeal must be given by the respondent; and
(d) to give leave, in pursuance of rule 65.3, for a person in custody to be present at any proceedings.
(2) A judge of the court shall, for the purpose of exercising any of the powers specified above, sit in such place as he appoints, and may sit otherwise than in open court.

Determination by full court

65.7 (1) Where a judge of the court has refused an application on the part of an applicant to exercise in his favour any of the powers referred to in rule 65.6, the applicant may have the application determined by the court by serving a notice in the form set out in the Practice Direction on the Registrar within 7 days, or such longer period as a judge of the court may fix, from the date on which notice of the refusal was served on him by the Registrar.
(2) The notice shall be signed by, or on behalf of, the applicant.
(3) If the notice is not signed by the applicant and the applicant is in custody, the Registrar shall, as soon as practicable after receiving the notice, send a copy of it to the applicant.
(4) If such a notice is not served on the Registrar within the said 7 days or such longer period as a judge of the court may fix, the application shall be treated as having been refused by the court.

Notice of determination of court

65.8 (1) The Registrar shall, as soon as practicable, serve notice of any determination by the Court of Appeal or by any judge of the court under rule 65.6 on—
(a) the applicant;
(b) the respondent; and
(c) and any other party who is directly affected by the ruling to which the appeal or application relates,
and notice of a determination by a single judge under rule 65.6 shall be served in the form set out in the Practice Direction.
(2) The Registrar shall, as soon as practicable, serve notice on the Crown Court officer at the place of trial of the order of the Court of Appeal disposing of an appeal or application for leave to appeal.

Service of documents

65.9 [Revoked.]

The Registrar

65.10 (1) The Registrar may require the Crown Court at the place of trial to furnish the Court of Appeal with any assistance or information which it may require for the purpose of exercising its jurisdiction.
(2) Subject to paragraphs (3) and (4) the Registrar shall give as long notice in advance as reasonably possible of the date of hearing of any appeal or application—
(a) to the appellant; and
(b) to the respondent and any other party directly affected by the order or ruling to which the appeal or application relates.
(3) Paragraph (2) shall not apply to proceedings before a judge of the court under rule 65.6.
(4) Where a party to whom notice is required to be given by this rule is at the material time in custody, notice shall instead be given to the person having custody of him.

Appeal against order following discharge of jury because of jury tampering

65.11 The rules in this Part apply with the necessary modifications to an appeal under section 47 of the Criminal Justice Act 2003.

Part 66 Appeal to the Court of Appeal Against Ruling Adverse to Prosecution

Interpretation

66.1 In this Part:

'appeal' means an appeal against a ruling under section 58 of the Criminal Justice Act 2003 and 'application for leave to appeal' should be construed accordingly;

'business day' means any day other than a Saturday, Sunday, Christmas Day or Good Friday or a bank holiday under the Banking and Financial Dealings Act 1971 in England and Wales;

'defendant' means a party in whose favour the ruling was made which is the subject of the appeal;

'interested party' means a person other than the defendant who—

(a) is a party to the proceedings in the Crown Court;

(b) may be affected by the decision of the trial judge under section 59(1) of the 2003 Act as to whether or not the appeal should be expedited; and

(c) is permitted by the trial judge or the Court of Appeal to make representations on that issue;

'judge of the court' means the judge of the Crown Court with conduct of the proceedings; and

'public interest ruling' means a ruling under section 3(6), 7A(8) or 8(5) of the Criminal Procedure and Investigations Act 1996 that it is in the public interest to disclose material in the possession of the prosecutor.

Request for adjournment

66.2 (1) A request by the prosecutor for an adjournment under section 58(4)(a)(ii) of the Criminal Justice Act 2003 must be made to the judge of the court immediately following the making of a ruling to which section 58 of that Act refers, unless paragraph (2) applies.

(2) If that ruling is a ruling of no case to answer, an application by the prosecutor under paragraph (1) must be made immediately following that ruling of no case to answer notwithstanding that the prosecutor may also nominate earlier rulings to be the subject of an appeal.

(3) The judge of the court shall grant the request unless it is in the interests of justice for the prosecutor to indicate immediately whether or not he intends to seek leave to appeal.

(4) The adjournment shall be until the next business day after the day on which the ruling was given, unless the interests of justice require a longer adjournment.

(5) Subject to rule 66.8, as soon as is reasonably practicable after the prosecutor informs the judge of the court that he intends to seek leave to appeal or requests an adjournment to consider whether to do so, the court officer shall provide a transcript of the ruling which is the subject of the proposed appeal to—

(a) the prosecutor;

(b) the defendant; and

(c) any interested party.

Application to the judge of the court for leave to appeal

66.3 (1) The prosecutor must inform the judge of the court immediately after the ruling or the adjournment if he intends to seek leave to appeal against a ruling and at the same time he may apply orally for leave to appeal.

(2) Before deciding whether or not to grant leave to appeal, the judge of the court shall hear oral representations from the defendant.

(3) The judge of the court shall decide whether or not to give leave to appeal on the same day on which an oral application for leave to appeal is made to that judge.

(4) The judge of the court may extend the period under paragraph (3) only if it is in the interests of justice to do so.

(5) If the judge of the court gives leave to appeal he must issue a certificate in the form set out in the Practice Direction and the court officer must forward that certificate to the Registrar.

Expedited appeal

66.4 (1) At the time when the prosecutor informs the judge of the court that he intends to seek leave to appeal against a ruling, he must also make oral representations as to whether or not that appeal should be expedited under section 59(1) of the Criminal Justice Act 2003.

(2) Before deciding whether or not the appeal should be expedited, the judge of the court shall hear oral representations from the defendant or any interested party.

(3) The court officer must provide a copy of the reasons given by the judge of the court, for his decision whether or not the appeal should be expedited, to the prosecutor, the defendant and all interested parties.

(4) The judge of the court may reverse his decision that the appeal should be expedited at any time before notice of appeal or application for leave to appeal is served on the Crown Court under rule 66.5(1) and must provide reasons for that reversal in writing to the prosecutor, the defendant and all interested parties.

(5) At any time after notice of appeal or application for leave to appeal has been served on the Registrar under rule 66.5(1), the prosecutor or defendant may invite the Court of Appeal to reverse a judge's decision that the appeal should be expedited under section 59(4) of the 2003 Act and written notice of such an application must be served on—

(a) the Registrar;
(b) the court officer;
(c) the prosecutor
(d) the defendant; and
(e) any interested party.

Notice of appeal or application for leave to appeal

66.5 (1) Subject to rule 66.8, a notice of appeal (where the judge of the court has granted leave) or notice of application for leave to appeal shall be in the form prescribed in the Practice Direction and must be served by the prosecutor on—

(a) the Registrar;
(b) the court officer;
(c) the defendant; and
(d) any interested party.

(2) Notice of appeal or application for leave to appeal must be served—

(a) where the judge of the court has decided that the appeal should be expedited under section 59(1) of the Criminal Justice Act 2003 and that decision has not been subsequently reversed, before 5.00 p.m. on the day on which the prosecutor informs the judge of the court that he intends to seek leave to appeal or, if the prosecutor demonstrates to that judge that it is not practical to do so, before 5.00 p.m. on the next business day; or
(b) in any other case, within seven business days of the day on which the prosecutor informs the judge of the court that he intends to seek leave to appeal.

(3) The Court of Appeal may extend the period for service under paragraph (2), either before or after it expires, on application by the prosecutor.

(4) Notice of appeal or application for leave to appeal must be accompanied by any documents necessary for the proper determination of the appeal or application for leave to appeal including—

(a) transcript of the ruling which is the subject of the appeal;
(b) the skeleton arguments provided to the judge of the court by the parties in respect of the issue which gave rise to the ruling; and
(c) if the appeal is to be expedited, a copy of the reasons given by the judge of the court under rule 66.4(3).

(5) Subject to rule 66.8, the notice of appeal or application for leave to appeal served on the defendant must be accompanied by the form set out in the Practice Direction for the defendant to complete if he wishes to oppose the appeal or application.

Defendant's response

66.6 (1) Upon receiving notice of an appeal or application for leave to appeal, the defendant if he wishes to oppose the appeal or application, must serve his response in the form set out in the Practice Direction on the—

(a) Registrar;
(b) court officer;
(c) prosecutor; and
(d) any interested party.

(2) A defendant's response must be served on those listed in paragraph (1)—

(a) on the next business day after the day on which the notice of appeal or application for leave to appeal is served on the defendant, where the judge of the court has decided that the appeal should be expedited under section 59(1) of the Criminal

Justice Act 2003 and that decision has not been subsequently reversed under section 59(4) of that Act; or

(b) within seven business days of the day on which notice of the appeal or application for leave to appeal is served on the defendant in any other case.

(3) The Court of Appeal may extend the period of service under paragraph (2) either before or after it expires.

Defendants in custody

66.7 (1) A defendant in custody is not entitled to be present in person at the hearing of an appeal or application for leave to appeal, unless the Court of Appeal so directs.

(2) However, a defendant in custody may participate in such a hearing, without a direction of the Court of Appeal, by way of live television link if he is able to see and hear the court and to be seen and heard by it.

(3) In directing whether a defendant in custody shall be present in person under paragraph (1) the Court of Appeal must take into account—

(a) any representations of the prosecutor and the defendant;

(b) the availability and reliability of live television link facilities;

(c) any practical difficulties with the physical attendance of the defendant; and

(d) whether or not the appeal is expedited under section 59 of the Criminal Justice Act 2003.

Public interest rulings

66.8 (1) This rule applies where a public interest ruling is the subject of an appeal or application for leave to appeal.

(2) In any appeal or application for leave to appeal against a public interest ruling, the prosecutor need not describe the material that is the subject of the ruling in the notice of appeal or application for leave to appeal under rule 66.5.

(3) Where the prosecutor has reason to believe that to reveal to the defendant or any interested party the category of material that is the subject of the public interest ruling would have the effect of disclosing that which the prosecutor considers should not be disclosed, the prosecutor need not describe the category of the material in the notice of appeal or application for leave to appeal under rule 66.5.

(4) Where the prosecutor has reason to believe that to reveal to the defendant or to any other interested party the fact that a public interest ruling has been made would have the effect of disclosing that which the prosecutor considers should not be disclosed, the prosecutor need not serve notice of appeal or application for leave to appeal on the defendant or any interested party as otherwise required under rule 66.5, unless the Court of Appeal otherwise directs.

(5) Where the prosecutor has taken the measures set out in paragraphs (2), (3) or (4), the notice of appeal or application for leave to appeal served on the Registrar under rule 66.5(1)(a), must be accompanied by a confidential annexe indicating that the measures have been taken and giving the prosecutor's reasons for taking them.

(6) Where the prosecutor has taken the measures set out in paragraph (4), the defendant shall not be entitled to be present in person at the hearing by the Court of Appeal of the appeal or application for leave to appeal, or appear by way of live television link, unless the Court of Appeal otherwise directs.

Supply of documentary and other exhibits

66.9 (1) The Registrar must, on request, supply to the prosecutor, the defendant or any interested party copies of documents or other exhibits required for the appeal or application for leave to appeal and may make charges in accordance with scales and rates fixed for the time being by the Treasury.

(2) The Registrar must, on request, make arrangements for the prosecutor, the defendant or any interested party to inspect any document or other exhibit required for the appeal.

(3) This rule shall not apply to the supply of transcripts of proceedings.

(4) This rule shall not require the Registrar to supply to the defendant or any interested party, or allow the defendant or any interested party to inspect—

(a) material that is the subject of a public interest ruling;

(b) a notice of appeal served by the prosecutor on the Registrar in accordance with rule 66.8(4); or

(c) a confidential annexe served by the prosecutor on the Registrar in accordance with rule 66.8(5),

unless the Court of Appeal otherwise directs.

Abandonment of proceedings

66.10 An appeal or application for leave to appeal (including an application for leave to appeal to the House of Lords) may be abandoned by the prosecutor before it is heard by the Court of Appeal by serving notice in writing on the Registrar in the form set out in the Practice Direction.

Powers exercisable by a single judge

66.11 (1) The following powers may be exercised by a single judge in the same manner as they may be exercised by the Court of Appeal and subject to the same provisions—

(a) to give leave to appeal under section 57(4) of the Criminal Justice Act 2003;

(b) to reverse a decision of the judge of the court that an appeal should be expedited under section 59(4) of that Act;

(c) to extend the time for service of the notice of appeal or of an application for leave to appeal under rule 66.5(3);

(d) to extend time for service of the defendant's response under rule 66.6(3);

(e) to direct that the defendant in custody be present in person at the hearing of the appeal or application for leave to appeal under rule 66.7(1); and

(f) to order the acquittal of the defendant and, where appropriate, his release from custody and order payment of his costs where the prosecution has served a notice of abandonment under rule 66.10.

(2) A single judge may, for the purposes of exercising any of the powers specified in paragraph (1), sit in such place as he appoints and may sit otherwise than in open court.

Powers exercisable by the Registrar

66.12 (1) The following powers may be exercised by the Registrar in the same manner as they may be exercised by the Court of Appeal and subject to the same provisions—

(a) to extend the time for service of the notice of appeal or of an application for leave to appeal under rule 66.5(3); and

(b) to extend time for service of the defendant's response under rule 66.6(3).

(2) Where the Registrar has refused an application to exercise any of the powers referred to in paragraph (1), the party making the application may have it determined by a single judge by serving a renewal in the form set out in the Practice Direction within seven business days of the day on which notice of the Registrar's decision is served on that party.

Determination by full court

66.13 (1) Where a single judge has refused an application to exercise any of the powers referred to in rule 66.11, the party making the application may have it determined by the Court of Appeal by serving a notice of renewal in the form set out in the Practice Direction.

(2) Notice of renewal must be served on the Registrar within seven business days of the day on which notice of the single judge's decision is served on the party making the application.

(3) The Court of Appeal may extend the period for service under paragraph (2) either before or after it expires.

(4) A notice of renewal must be signed by, or on behalf of, the person making the application. If the notice is not signed by the party making the application and that party is in custody, the Registrar shall, as soon as practicable after receiving the notice, send a copy of it to that party.

(5) If the notice of renewal is not served on the Registrar within the period specified in paragraph (2) or such extended period as the Court of Appeal has allowed under paragraph (3), the application shall be treated as having been refused by the court.

Notice of hearing and determination of the Court, single judge or Registrar

66.14 (1) The Registrar must give notice, as far in advance as reasonably practicable, of the date fixed for the hearing by the Court of Appeal of an appeal or application to—

(a) the prosecutor;

(b) the defendant;

(c) any interested party; and

(d) the court officer.

(2) The Registrar must, as soon as reasonably practicable, serve notice of—
(a) a decision of the Court of Appeal on an appeal or application;
(b) a decision of a single judge exercising one of the powers referred to in rule 66.11(1); or
(c) a decision of the Registrar exercising one of the powers referred to in rule 66.12(1); on those parties listed in paragraph (1).

(3) Where a party to whom notice is required to be given under this rule is in custody, notice must instead be given to the person having custody of him.

(4) But where rule 66.8 (public interest rulings) applies the Registrar must not give or serve any notice under this rule on the defendant or any interested party, unless a judge or the Court of Appeal otherwise directs.

Assistance from the Crown Court

66.15 The Registrar may require the court officer to furnish the Court of Appeal with any assistance or information which it may require for the purposes of exercising its jurisdiction under Part 9 of the Criminal Justice Act 2003.

Appeal to the House of Lords

66.16 (1) An application to the Court of Appeal for leave to appeal to the House of Lords under Part 9 of the Criminal Justice Act 2003 may be made—
(a) orally after the decision of the Court of Appeal from which an appeal lies to the House of Lords; or
(b) in writing and served on the Registrar within seven business days of the reasons for the decision.

(2) If leave to appeal to the House of Lords is granted by the Court of Appeal, or a party has made an application to the House of Lords for leave, in a case where the judge of the court has decided that the appeal should be expedited under section 59(1) of the 2003 Act and that decision has not subsequently been reversed under section 59(4) of that Act, the Registrar must inform the court officer that the jury must be discharged from giving a verdict in respect of that defendant.

Part 67 Appeal to the Court of Appeal against Order Restricting Reporting or Public Access

Appeal against order restricting reporting of proceedings

67.1 (1) An application for leave to appeal under section 159(1)(a), (aa) or (c) of the Criminal Justice Act 1988 shall be made within 14 days after the date on which the order was made by serving on the Registrar a notice which shall be in the form set out in the Practice Direction.

(2) The applicant shall at the same time serve a copy of the application under paragraph (1) on the Crown Court officer at the place where the order was made, on the prosecutor and the defendant and on any other interested person.

(3) A prosecutor or a defendant or any interested person may, not later than 3 days after service of the application, notify the Registrar in writing that he wishes to be made a respondent to the appeal if leave is granted, and shall serve a copy of such notice on the applicant.

(4) The period of 14 days in paragraph (1) may be extended by the Court or a judge of the Court, before or after it expires, on an application which shall be made in writing, specifying the grounds of the application, and served on the Registrar, and a copy of the application shall be served by the applicant on every person who is to be served under paragraph (2).

(5) An application under paragraph (4) shall be determined without a hearing, unless the Court or a judge of the Court, as the case may be, directs otherwise.

(6) An application under paragraph (1) may be determined without a hearing.

(7) Where the Court grants leave to appeal—
(a) the notice of application for leave shall stand as the notice of appeal, unless the Court otherwise orders;
(b) without prejudice to the generality of its powers under section 159(3) of the 1988 Act, the Court shall direct that the person in whose favour the order was made is to be a respondent to the appeal and determine what, if any, other persons are to be respondents or may be respondents if they wish;
(c) the evidence of any witness shall be given in writing, unless the Court otherwise orders;

(d) rule 68.11 (supply of documentary and other exhibits) shall apply, with the necessary modifications; and

(e) the Registrar shall notify the parties of the time and place of the hearing of the appeal.

Appeal against order restricting public access to proceedings

67.2 (1) This rule applies to proceedings in which a prosecutor or a defendant has served a notice under rule 16.10(1) of his intention to apply for an order that all or part of a trial be held in camera for reasons of national security or for the protection of a witness or any other person.

(2) Where a notice has been displayed under rule 16.10(2), a person aggrieved may serve notice on the Registrar in the form set out in the Practice Direction that he intends to appeal against any order that may be made on the prosecutor's or defendant's application, and he shall serve a copy of such notice on the Crown Court officer at the place where the trial is to take place, on the prosecutor and the defendant and on any other interested person.

(3) Subject to paragraph (4) a notice shall be served on the Registrar under paragraph (2) within 7 days of the display of the notice under rule 16.10(2) and where such an order is made at the trial, the notice shall be treated as the application for leave to appeal against the order.

(4) Where an order is made at the trial, a person aggrieved who has not served a notice under paragraph (2) may apply for leave to appeal against the order by serving notice in the form set out in the Practice Direction on the Registrar within 24 hours after the making of the order, and he shall forthwith serve a copy of such notice on each of the persons who are to be served under paragraph (2).

(5) Where an order has been made, and a person aggrieved has served a notice under paragraph (2) or (4), the Crown Court officer shall forthwith upon the making of the order notify the Registrar of its making, and the applicant for the order shall, as soon as practicable, send the Registrar a copy of any transcript or note of the application for the order and of any documents that were in evidence in the Crown Court.

(6) An application for leave to appeal shall be determined by a judge of the Court, or the Court as the case may be, without a hearing.

(7) Where leave to appeal is granted, the appeal shall be determined without a hearing.

(8) The Registrar shall, as soon as practicable, serve notice of the order of the court disposing of an appeal or application for leave to appeal on the person aggrieved and on each of the persons specified in paragraph (2).

(9) Section 159(4) of the Criminal Justice Act 1988 shall not apply to proceedings to which this rule applies.

Part 68 Appeal to the Court of Appeal against Conviction, Sentence or Sentence Review Decision

Service of documents

68.1 [Revoked.]

Certificate of trial judge

68.2 (1) The certificate of the judge of the court of trial under section 1(2), 12 or 15(2) of the Criminal Appeal Act 1968 that a case is a fit case for appeal shall be in the form set out in the Practice Direction.

(2) The certificate shall be forwarded forthwith to the Registrar, whether or not the person to whom the certificate relates has applied for a certificate.

(3) A copy of the certificate shall be forwarded forthwith to the person to whom the certificate relates or to his legal representative.

Notice of appeal and application for extension of time

68.3 (1) Notice of appeal or of an application for leave to appeal under Part I of the Criminal Appeal Act 1968 or notice of appeal under section 13 (appeal in cases of contempt of court) of the Administration of Justice Act 1960 (as required by section 18A of the 1968 Act) against an order or decision of the Crown Court shall be given by completing the form set out in the Practice Direction and serving it on a Crown court officer.

(1A) Notice of an application for leave to appeal under paragraph 14 of schedule 22 to the Criminal Justice Act 2003 shall be given by completing the form set out in the Practice Direction and serving it on the Registrar.

(1B) Notice of an application for leave to appeal under section 74(8) of the Serious Organised

Crime and Police Act 2005 shall be given by completing the form set out in the Practice Direction and serving it on a Crown officer.

(1C) A document to be served on a Crown Court officer under this Part must be served on a court officer at the Crown Court centre at which the conviction, verdict, finding, decision or sentence appealed against was given or passed.

(2) A notice of appeal or of an application for leave to appeal shall be accompanied by a notice in the form set out in the Practice Direction containing the grounds of the appeal or application.

(3) A notice of the grounds of appeal or application in the form set out in the Practice Direction shall include notice—

(a) of any application to be made to the court for a declaration of incompatibility under section 4 of the Human Rights Act 1998; or

(b) of any issue for the court to decide which may lead to the court making such a declaration.

(4) Where the grounds of appeal or application include notice in accordance with paragraph (3)(b) above, a copy of the notice shall be served on the prosecutor by the appellant.

(5) If the appellant has been convicted of more than one offence, the notice of appeal or of an application for leave, referred to in paragraph (2), shall specify the convictions or sentences against which the appellant is appealing or applying for leave to appeal.

(6) The grounds of an appeal or application, referred to in paragraph (2), may, with the consent of the court, be varied or amplified within such time as the court may allow.

(7) Notice of an application to extend the time within which notice of appeal or of an application for leave to appeal may be given under—

(a) Part I of the 1968 Act;

(b) article 3 of the Criminal Justice Act 2003 (Mandatory Life Sentences: Appeals in Transitional Cases) Order 2005; or

(c) article 5 of the Serious Organised Crime and Police Act 2005 (Appeals under section 74) Order 2006,

by completing so much of Part 2 of the form, referred to in paragraph (2), as relates to the application and by giving notice of appeal or of an application for leave to appeal in accordance with the foregoing provisions of this rule.

(8) Notice of an application to extend the time within which notice of appeal or of an application for leave to appeal may be given under—

(a) Part I of the 1968 Act;

(b) article 3 of the 2005 Order; or

(c) article 5 of the 2006 Order,

[and] shall specify the grounds of the application.

(9) An appellant who is appealing or applying for leave to appeal against conviction shall specify in the form, referred to in paragraph (2), any exhibit produced at the trial which he wishes to be kept in custody for the purposes of his appeal.

(10) The forms to which this rule relates, shall be signed by, or on behalf of, the appellant.

(11) If a form is not signed by the appellant and the appellant is in custody, the Registrar shall, as soon as practicable after receiving the form from the Crown Court, send a copy of it to the appellant.

(12) Where an appellant does not require leave to appeal, a notice of application for leave to appeal shall be treated as a notice of appeal; and where an appellant requires leave to appeal but serves only a notice of appeal, the notice of appeal shall be treated as an application for leave to appeal.

Appeal following reference by Criminal Cases Review Commission

68.4 (1) In this rule:

'the Commission' means the Criminal Cases Review Commission, and

'reference' means the reference of a conviction, verdict, finding or sentence to the Court of Appeal by the Commission under section 9 of the Criminal Appeal Act 1995.

(2) The Registrar must serve on the appellant written notice of receipt of a reference.

(3) The appellant must give notice of appeal under rule 68.3 by serving it on the Registrar within—

(a) 28 days of the date of the notice served under paragraph (2), in the case of an appeal against sentence; or

(b) 56 days of the date of that notice, in the case of an appeal against conviction, verdict of not guilty by reason of insanity, finding that the appellant was under a disability, or finding that the appellant did the act or made the omission charged.

(4) The court may extend the time for giving notice of appeal, either before or after it expires.

(5) The grounds of appeal accompanying a notice of appeal must include—

(a) where a ground of appeal is said to relate to a reason given by the Commission for making the reference, an explanation of how it is related; and

(b) where a ground of appeal is said not to be so related, notice of application for leave to appeal on that ground.

(6) If a notice of appeal is not received within the time specified in paragraph (3), or within such longer period as the court allows under paragraph (4), the reasons given by the Commission for making the reference shall stand as the grounds of appeal.

(7) On receiving a notice of appeal the Registrar must serve a copy on the prosecutor and on any other party to the appeal.

Exercise of court's powers to give leave to appeal, etc: general rules

68.5 (1) This rule and rule 68.6 apply when the Registrar or a single judge exercises a power conferred by one of the following provisions—

(a) section 31 of the Criminal Appeal Act 1968, article 8 of the Criminal Justice Act 2003 (Mandatory life Sentences: Appeals in Transitional Cases) Order 2005 (powers exercisable by a single judge) or article 11 of the Serious Organised Crime and Police Act 2005 (Appeals under section 74) Order 2006;

(b) section 31A of the 1968 Act, article 9 of the 2005 Order (powers exercisable by the Registrar) or article 12 of the 2006 Order;

(c) section 31B of the 1968 Act, article 10 of the 2005 Order (procedural directions by a single judge or the Registrar) or article 13 of the 2006 Order; or

(d) section 31C of the 1968 Act, article 11 of the 2005 Order (appeals against procedural directions) or article 14 of the 2006 Order.

(2) An application to the Registrar, a single judge or the court for the exercise of any of the powers referred to in paragraph (1) should be in the relevant form set out in the Practice Direction or in the form required by the Registrar.

(3) An application by an appellant must be signed by him or on his behalf. If it is not signed by him and he is in custody, the Registrar must send him a copy as soon as practicable after receiving it.

(4) If an appellant makes an application for the exercise of any of the powers under the 1968 Act and he makes it when he gives notice of appeal or notice of an application for leave to appeal, the application must be served on the Crown Court officer. In all other cases, the application must be served on the Registrar.

(5) Neither a single judge nor the Registrar need sit in court to exercise any of the powers referred to in paragraph (1) of this rule.

Further applications to a judge or to the court: additional rules

68.6 (1) Where—

(a) an appellant renews an application for the exercise of a power conferred by section 31 of the 1968 Act, article 8 of the Criminal Justice Act 2003 (Mandatory Life Sentences: Appeals in Transitional Cases) Order 2005 (powers exercisable by a single judge) or article 11 of the Serious Organised Crime and Police Act 2005 (Appeals under section 74) Order 2006; or

(b) an appellant renews an application for the exercise of a power conferred by section 31A of the 1968 Act, article 9 of the 2005 Order (powers exercisable by the Registrar) or article 12 of the 2006 Order; or

(c) an appellant or a respondent applies for procedural directions under section 31C of the 1968 Act, article 11 of the 2005 Order (appeals against procedural directions) or article 14 of the 2006 Order,

then he must do so within 14 days. That period begins when the Registrar serves on him notice of the decision that prompts his further application. That period may be extended before or after it expires by the Registrar, by a single judge or by the court. The general rule is that an application for an extension of that period will be considered at the same time as the further application itself.

(2) Where—

(a) an appellant may renew to the court an application for the exercise of a power conferred by section 31 of the 1968 Act, article 8 of the 2005 Order or article 11 of the 2006 Order; but

(b) he does not do so within the period fixed by this rule or extended under it,
then his application shall be treated as having been refused by the court.

Application for bail pending appeal

68.7 (1) Notice of an application by the appellant to be granted bail pending the determination of his appeal or pending his retrial shall be in the form set out in the Practice Direction and, unless notice of appeal or of an application for leave to appeal has previously been given, shall be accompanied by such a notice and shall be served on the Registrar; save that where notice of such an application is given together with a notice of appeal or notice of application for leave to appeal, it shall be served on the Crown Court officer.

(2) An application as aforesaid may be made to the court orally.

(3) Notice in writing of intention to make an application relating to bail to the court shall, unless the court or a judge thereof otherwise directs, at least 24 hours before it is made be served on the prosecutor and on the Director of Public Prosecutions, if the prosecution was carried on by him or, if the application is to be made by the prosecutor or a constable under section 3(8) of the Bail Act 1976, on the appellant.

Bail with condition of surety

68.8 (1) Where the court grants bail to the appellant or, in an appeal brought by a specified prosecutor under section 74(8) of the Serious Organised Crime and Police Act 2005, in respect of an offender, the recognizance of any surety required as a condition of bail may be entered into before the Registrar or, where the person who has been granted bail is in a prison or other place of detention, before the governor or keeper of the prison or place as well as before the persons specified in section 8(4) of the Bail Act 1976.

(2) The recognizance of a surety shall be in the form set out in the Practice Direction, there being an alternative form for use in relation to an appellant granted bail pending his retrial or on the issue of a writ of venire de novo.

(3) Where, under section 3(5) or (6) of the 1976 Act, the court imposes a requirement to be complied with before a person's release on bail, the court may give directions as to the manner in which and the person or persons before whom the requirement may be complied with.

(4) A person who, in pursuance of an order for the grant of bail made by the court, proposes to enter into a recognizance as a surety or give security shall, unless the court or a judge thereof otherwise directs, give notice to the prosecutor at least 24 hours before he enters into the recognizance or gives security as aforesaid.

(5) Where the court has fixed the amount in which a surety is to be bound by a recognizance or, under section 3(5) or (6) of the 1976 Act, has imposed any requirement to be complied with before the appellant's release on bail, the Registrar shall issue a certificate in the form set out in the Practice Direction showing the amount and conditions, if any, of the recognizance or, as the case may be, containing a statement of the requirement; and a person authorised to take the recognizance or do anything in relation to the compliance with such requirement shall not be required to take or do it without production of such a certificate as aforesaid.

(6) Where, in pursuance of an order for the grant of bail made by the court, a recognizance is entered into or requirement complied with before any person, it shall be the duty of that person to cause the recognizance or, as the case may be, a statement that the requirement has been complied with, to be transmitted forthwith to the Registrar; and a copy of such recognizance or statement shall at the same time be sent to the governor or keeper of the prison or other place of detention in which the appellant is detained, unless the recognizance was entered into or the requirement complied with before such governor or keeper.

(7) A person taking a recognizance in pursuance of such an order shall give a copy thereof to the person entering into the recognizance.

(8) Where the court has fixed the amount in which a surety is to be bound by a recognizance or, under section 3(5) or (6) of the 1976 Act, has imposed any requirement to be complied with before the appellant's release on bail, the governor or keeper of the prison or other place of detention in which the appellant is detained shall, on receipt of a certificate in the appropriate form stating that the recognizances of all sureties required have been taken and that all such requirements have been complied with or on being otherwise so satisfied, release the appellant.

(9) Where the court has granted bail pending retrial or on ordering the issue of a writ of venire de novo, the Registrar shall forward to the Crown Court officer a copy of any record made in

pursuance of section 5 of the 1976 Act relating to such bail and also all recognizances and statements sent to the Registrar under paragraph (6) of this rule.

(10) Any record required by section 5 of the 1976 Act shall be made by including in the file relating to the case in question—

(a) where bail is granted, a copy of the form issued under paragraph (5) of this rule and a statement of the day on which, and the time and place at which, the appellant is notified to surrender to custody; and

(b) in any other case, a copy of the notice served under rule 68.29(1) (notice of determination of court).

Forfeiture of recognizances in respect of person bailed to appear

68.9 (1) Where a recognizance has been entered into in respect of an appellant and it appears to the court that a default has been made in performing the conditions of the recognizance, the court may order the recognizance to be forfeited and such an order may—

(a) allow time for the payment of the amount due under the recognizance;

(b) direct payment of that amount by instalments of such amounts and on such dates respectively as may be specified in the order; or

(c) discharge the recognizance or reduce the amount due thereunder.

(2) Where the court is to consider making an order under paragraph (1) for a recognizance to be forfeited, the Registrar shall give notice to that effect to the person by whom the recognizance was entered into indicating the time and place at which the matter will be considered; and no such order shall be made before the expiry of seven days after the notice required by this paragraph has been given.

Custody of exhibits

68.10 (1) On a conviction on indictment or on a coroner's inquisition a court officer of the court of trial shall, subject to any directions of the judge of the court of trial, make arrangements for any exhibit at the trial which in his opinion may be required for the purposes of an appeal against conviction to be kept in the custody of the court, or given into the custody of the person producing it at the trial or any other person for retention, until the expiration of 35 days from the date of conviction.

(2) Where an appellant has given notice of appeal, or of an application for leave to appeal, against conviction, the Registrar shall inform a court officer of the notice and give directions concerning the continued retention in custody of any exhibit which appears necessary for the proper determination of the appeal or application.

(3) Where the court orders an appellant to be retired, it shall make arrangements pending his retrial for the continued retention in custody of exhibits.

(4) Any arrangements under this rule may include arrangements for the inspection of an exhibit by an interested party.

Supply of documentary and other exhibits

68.11 (1) Unless the court otherwise directs, the Registrar shall, on request, supply to the appellant or respondent copies of documents or other things required for the appeal and in such case may make charges in accordance with scales and rates fixed for the time being by the Treasury.

(2) Unless the court otherwise directs, the Registrar shall, on request, make arrangements for the appellant or respondent to inspect any document or other thing required for the appeal.

(3) This rule shall not apply to the supply of the transcripts of any proceedings or part thereof.

Record of proceedings

68.12 (1) Except as provided by this rule, the whole of any proceedings in respect of which an appeal lies (with or without leave) to the court shall be recorded by means of shorthand notes or, with the permission of the Lord Chancellor, by mechanical means.

(2) Where such proceedings are recorded by means of shorthand notes, it shall not be necessary to record—

(a) the opening or closing addresses to the jury on behalf of the prosecution or an accused person unless the judge of the court of trial otherwise directs; or

(b) any other part of such proceedings which the judge of the court of trial directs need not be recorded.

(3) Where it is not practicable for such proceedings to be recorded by means of shorthand notes or by mechanical means, the judge of the court of trial shall direct how and to what extent the proceedings shall be recorded.

(4) The permission of the Lord Chancellor may contain conditions concerning the custody, and supply of transcripts, of a recording made by mechanical means.

Transcripts

68.13 (1) A transcript of the record of any proceedings or part thereof in respect of which an appeal lies, with or without leave, to the court and which are recorded in accordance with the provisions of rule 68.12—

(a) shall, on request be supplied to the Registrar; and

(b) shall, on request, be supplied to any other person on payment of such charge as may be fixed for the time being by the Treasury, unless the court otherwise directs.

(2) Without prejudice to the provisions of paragraph (1) of this rule, the Registrar may, on request, supply to any interested party a transcript of the record of any proceedings or part thereof which is in his possession for the purposes of the appeal or application in question and in such case may make charges in accordance with scales and rates fixed for the time being by the Treasury:

Provided that in the case of an interested party who has been granted a right to representation by the Criminal Defence Service under Schedule 3 to the Access to Justice Act 1999 for the purpose of the appeal or any proceedings preliminary or incidental thereto such a transcript shall be supplied free.

Verification of record of proceedings

68.14 (1) An official shorthand writer who takes shorthand notes of any proceedings or part thereof in respect of which an appeal lies (with or without leave) to the court shall—

(a) at the beginning of the notes state the name of the parties to the proceedings;

(b) in the case of shorthand notes of part of any proceedings, state the part concerned;

(c) record his name in the notes; and

(d) retain the shorthand notes for not less than five years.

(2) Verification of a transcript of the shorthand notes taken by an official shorthand writer of any proceedings or part thereof in respect of which an appeal lies (with or without leave) to the court shall be by a certificate by the person making the transcript that—

(a) he has made a correct and complete transcript of the notes to the best of his skill and ability; and

(b) the notes were either taken by him and were to the best of his skill and ability a complete and correct account of those proceedings or part thereof or were taken by another official shorthand writer.

(3) Verification of a transcript of the record of the proceedings or part thereof if recorded by mechanical means shall be by—

(a) a certificate by the person making the transcript that he has made a correct and complete transcript of the recording to the best of his skill and ability; and

(b) a certificate by a person responsible for the recording or a successor that the recording records so much of the proceedings as is specified in the certificate.

(4) Verification of a transcript of the record of the proceedings or part thereof if recorded in any other way shall be by—

(a) a certificate by the person who made the record that he recorded the proceedings or part thereof to the best of his ability; and

(b) a certificate by the person making the transcript that he has made a correct and complete transcript of the record to the best of his skill and ability.

Application for a witness order and for evidence to be received

68.15 (1) Notice of an application by the appellant, or, in an appeal brought by a specified prosecutor under section 74(8) of the Serious Organised Crime and Police Act 2005, by the appellant or the offender —

(a) that a witness who would have been a compellable witness at the trial be ordered to attend for examination by the court; or

(b) that the evidence of a witness be received by the court;

shall be in the form set out in the Practice Direction and shall be served on the Registrar; save that where a notice of an application under sub-paragraph (a) or (b) is given together with a notice of appeal or notice of application for leave to appeal, it shall be served on the Crown Court officer.

(2) An application as aforesaid may be made to the court orally.

Examination of witnesses by the court

68.16 (1) An order of the court to a person to attend for examination as a witness shall be in the form set out in the Practice Direction and shall specify the time and place of attendance.

(2) The examination of a witness shall be conducted by the taking of a deposition and, unless the court directs otherwise, shall take place in public.

Vulnerable witness giving video recorded testimony

68.17 (1) A party to an appeal who applies for leave to call a witness may also apply for leave under section 32A of the Criminal Justice Act 1988 to tender in evidence a video recording of testimony from a witness where—

(a) the offence charged is one to which section 32(2) of the 1988 Act applies;

(b) in the case of an offence falling within section 32(2)(a) or (b) of the 1988 Act, the proposed witness is under the age of 14 or, if he was under 14 when the video recording was made, is under the age of 15;

(c) in the case of an offence falling within section 32(2)(c) of the 1988 Act, the proposed witness is under the age of 17 or, if he was under 17 when the video recording was made, is under the age of 18; and

(d) the video recording is of an interview conducted between an adult and a person coming within sub-paragraph (b) or (c) above (not being the accused or one of the accused) which relates to any matter in issue in the proceedings;

and references in this rule to an offence include references to attempting or conspiring to commit, or aiding, abetting, counselling, procuring or inciting the commission of, that offence.

(2) An application under paragraph (1) shall be made by serving a notice in writing on the Registrar. The application shall be accompanied by the video recording which it is proposed to tender in evidence and shall include the following, namely—

(a) the name of the appellant or, in an appeal brought by a specified prosecutor under section 74(8) of the Serious Organised Crime and Police Act 2005, the name of the offender, and the offence or offences charged;

(b) the name and date of birth of the witness in respect of whom the application is made;

(c) the date on which the video recording was made;

(d) a statement that in the opinion of the applicant the witness is willing and able to attend the appeal for cross-examination; and

(e) a statement of the circumstances in which the video recording was made which complies with paragraph (4).

(3) Where it is proposed to tender part only of a video recording of an interview with the witness, an application under paragraph (1) must specify that part and be accompanied by a video recording of the entire interview, including those parts which it is not proposed to tender in evidence, and by a statement of the circumstances in which the video recording of the entire interview was made which complies with paragraph (4).

(4) The statement of the circumstances in which the video recording was made referred to in paragraphs (2)(e) and (3) shall include the following information, except in so far as it is contained in the recording itself, namely—

(a) the times at which the recording commenced and finished, including details of any interruptions;

(b) the location at which the recording was made and the usual function of the premises;

(c) the name, age and occupation of any person present at any point during the recording, the time for which he was present, his relationship (if any) to the witness and to the appellant;

(d) a description of the equipment used including the number of cameras used and whether they were fixed or mobile, the number and location of microphones, the video format used and whether there were single or multiple recording facilities; and

(e) the location of the mastertape if the video recording is a copy and details of when and by whom the copy was made.

(5) An application under paragraph (1) shall be made at the same time as the application for leave to call the witness or at any time thereafter, but no less than 14 days before the date fixed for the hearing of the appeal except with the leave of the court.

(6) The Registrar shall, as soon as practicable after receiving an application under paragraph (1), send a copy of the notice to the other parties to the appeal. Copies of any video recording required by paragraph (2) or (3) to accompany the notice shall be provided by the applicant and sent by the Registrar to any party to the appeal not already served with a copy. In the case of an appellant acting in person, a copy shall be made available for viewing by him.

(7) An application under paragraph (1) shall be determined without a hearing, unless the Court otherwise directs, and the Registrar shall notify the applicant and the other parties of the time and place of any hearing.

(8) Without prejudice to rule 68.29, the Registrar shall notify all the parties of the decision of the Court in relation to an application under paragraph (1) and, where leave is granted, the notification shall state whether the whole or specified parts only of the video recording or recordings disclosed are to be admitted in evidence.

Vulnerable witness giving evidence by live television link

68.18 (1) A party to an appeal who applies for leave to call a witness may also apply for leave under section 32(1)(b) of the Criminal Justice Act 1988 for the evidence of that witness to be given through a live television link where—

(a) the offence charged is one to which section 32(2) of the 1988 Act applies; and

(b) the evidence is to be given by a witness who is either—

(i) in the case of an offence falling within section 32(2)(a) or (b) of the 1988 Act, under the age of 14,

(ii) in the case of an offence falling within section 32(2)(c) of the 1988 Act, under the age of 17, or

(iii) a person who is to be cross-examined following the admission under section 32A of the 1988 Act of a video recording of testimony from him,

and references in this rule to an offence include references to attempting or conspiring to commit, or aiding, abetting, counselling, procuring or inciting the commission of, that offence.

(2) An application under paragraph (1) shall be made by serving a notice in writing on the Registrar which shall state—

(a) the grounds of the application;

(b) the date of birth of the witness;

(c) the name of the witness; and

(d) the name, occupation and relationship (if any) to the witness of any person proposed to accompany the witness and the grounds for believing that person should accompany the witness.

(3) An application under paragraph (1) shall be made at the same time as the application for leave to call the witness or at any time thereafter, but no less than 14 days before the date fixed for the hearing of the appeal except with the leave of the court.

(4) The Registrar shall, as soon as practicable after receiving an application under paragraph (1), send a copy of the notice to the other parties to the appeal.

(5) An application under paragraph (1) shall be determined without a hearing, unless the Court otherwise directs, and the Registrar shall notify the applicant and the other parties of the time and place of any hearing.

(6) Without prejudice to rule 68.29, the Registrar shall notify all the parties and the person who is to accompany the witness (if known) of the decision of the court in relation to an application under paragraph (1). Where leave is granted, the notification shall state the name of the witness, and, if known, the name, occupation and relationship (if any) to the witness of the person who is to accompany the witness.

(7) A witness giving evidence through a television link pursuant to leave granted in accordance with this rule shall be accompanied by a person acceptable to the Court and, unless the Court otherwise directs, by no other person.

Evidence through live television link where witness is outside the United Kingdom

68.19 (1) A party to an appeal who applies for leave to call a witness may also apply for leave under section 32(1) of the Criminal Justice Act 1988 for the evidence of that witness to be given through a live television link where the witness is outside the United Kingdom.

(2) An application under paragraph (1) shall be made by serving a notice in writing on the Registrar which shall state—

(a) the grounds of the application;
(b) the name of the witness;
(c) the country and place where it is proposed the witness will be when giving evidence; and
(d) the name and occupation of any person who it is proposed should be available for the purpose specified in paragraph (3).

(3) The purpose referred to in paragraph (2)(d) is that of answering any questions the court may put, before or after the evidence of the witness is given, as to the circumstances in which the evidence is given, including questions about any persons who are present when the evidence is given and any matters which may affect the giving of the evidence.

(4) An application under paragraph (1) shall be made at the same time as the application for leave to call the witness or at any time thereafter, but no less than 14 days before the date fixed for the hearing of the appeal except with the leave of the court.

(5) The Registrar shall, as soon as practicable after receiving an application under paragraph (1), send a copy of the notice to the other parties to the appeal.

(6) An application under paragraph (1) shall be determined without a hearing, unless the court otherwise directs, and the Registrar shall notify the applicant and the other parties of the time and place of any such hearing.

(7) Without prejudice to rule 68.29, the Registrar shall notify all the parties of the decision of the court in relation to an application under paragraph (1), and, where leave is granted, the notification shall state the name of the witness and, where applicable, the name and occupation of any person specified by the court for the purpose set out in paragraph (3).

Procedure for the admission of hearsay evidence

68.20 (1) Part 34 applies where a party wants to introduce hearsay evidence in an appeal or application for leave to appeal, except for rules 34.2, 34.3 and 34.4 (relating to the notice of hearsay evidence).

(2) An appellant who wants to introduce hearsay evidence to support a ground of appeal contained in his notice under rule 68.3(2)—
(a) must give notice in the form set out in the Practice Direction to the Crown Court officer with his notice of application for leave to appeal under rule 68.3(1); but
(b) need not give a separate notice of application under rule 68.15(1) for that same evidence to be received by the court.

(3) A party who wants to introduce hearsay evidence in any other circumstances must give notice in the form set out in the Practice Direction to the Registrar and all other parties not more than 28 days after—
(a) leave to appeal is given; or
(b) notice of appeal is given, if leave is not required.

Procedure for the admission of evidence of bad character

68.21 Part 35 applies to the introduction of evidence of bad character in proceedings before the Court of Appeal, except for rule 35.1 and with the following modifications—
(a) a reference to a defendant should be read as a reference to an appellant or, where the appeal is brought by a specified prosecutor under section 74(8) of the Serious Organised Crime and Police Act 2005, as a reference to an offender, and 'non-defendant' and 'co-defendant' read accordingly;
(b) a reference to a court officer should be read as a reference to the Registrar; and
(c) an application under rule 35.2 (non-defendant's bad character) must be received, and a notice under rule 35.4 or 35.5 (defendant's bad character) must be given, not more than 28 days after—
(i) leave to appeal is given, or
(ii) notice of appeal is given, if leave is not required.

Abandonment of proceedings

68.22 (1) An appeal or an application for leave to appeal under part I of the Criminal Appeal Act 1968, under paragraph 14 of schedule 22 to the Criminal Justice Act 2003 or under section 74(8) of the Serious Organised Crime and Police Act 2005 may be abandoned before the hearing of the appeal or application by serving on the Registrar notice thereof in the form set out in the Practice Direction.

(2) The notice shall be signed by, or on behalf of, the appellant.

(3) The Registrar shall, as soon as practicable after receiving a notice under this rule, send a copy of it, endorsed with the date of receipt, to the appellant, to the Secretary of State and to a court officer of the Crown Court.

(4) Where an appeal or an application for leave to appeal is abandoned, the appeal or application shall be treated as having been dismissed or refused by the court.

The Registrar

68.23 (1) The Registrar may require the Crown Court to furnish the court with any assistance or information which it may require for the purpose of exercising its jurisdiction.

(2) The Registrar shall give as long notice in advance as reasonably possible of the date on which the court will hear any appeal or application by an appellant to—

(a) the appellant;

(b) any person having custody of the appellant; and

(c) any other interested party whom the court requires to be represented at the hearing.

(3) This paragraph shall not apply to proceedings before a single judge of the court under section 31 of the Criminal Appeal Act 1968.

Sittings in vacation

68.24 The Lord Chief Justice shall determine the days on which the court shall, if necessary, sit during vacations; and the court shall sit on such days in accordance with arrangements made by the Lord Chief Justice after consultation with the Master of the Rolls.

Opinion of court on point referred by Criminal Cases Review Commission

68.25 Where the Criminal Cases Review Commission refers a point to the court under section 14(3) of the Criminal Appeal Act 1995 the court may consider the point in private if appropriate.

Application to the Court of Appeal for leave to be present

68.26 (1) Notice of an application by the appellant to be given leave by the court to be present at proceedings for which such leave is required shall be in the form set out in the Practice Direction and shall be served on the Registrar; save that where a notice of such an application is given together with a notice of appeal or notice of application for leave to appeal, it shall be served on a Crown Court officer.

(2) An application as aforesaid may be made to the court orally.

Declaration of Incompatibility

68.27 (1) The court shall not consider making a declaration of incompatibility under section 4 of the Human Rights Act 1998 unless it has given written notice to the Crown.

(2) Where notice has been given to the Crown, a Minister, or other person entitled under the 1998 Act to be joined as a party, shall be so joined on giving written notice to the court.

(3) A notice given under paragraph (1) above shall be given to—

(a) the person named in the list published under section 17(1) of the Crown Proceedings Act 1947; or

(b) in the case of doubt as to whether any and if so which of those departments is appropriate, the Treasury Solicitor.

(4) A notice given under paragraph (1) above, shall provide an outline of the issues in the case and specify—

(a) the prosecutor and appellant;

(b) the date, judge and court of the trial in the proceedings from which the appeal lies; and

(c) the provision of primary legislation and the Convention right under question.

(5) Any consideration of whether a declaration of incompatibility should be made, shall be adjourned for—

(a) 21 days from the date of the notice given under paragraph (1) above; or

(b) such other period (specified in the notice), as the court shall allow in order that the relevant Minister or other person, may seek to be joined and prepare his case.

(6) Unless the court otherwise directs, the Minister or other person entitled under the 1998 Act to be joined as a party shall, if he is to be joined, give written notice to the court and every other party.

(7) Where a Minister of the Crown has nominated a person to be joined as a party by virtue of section 5(2)(a) of the 1998 Act, a notice under paragraph (6) above shall be accompanied by a written nomination signed by or on behalf of the Minister.

Dismissal of appeal against hospital order

68.28 If the court dismisses an appeal or an application for leave to appeal by an appellant who is subject to a hospital order under the Mental Health Act 1983 or an order under section 5(1) of the Criminal Procedure (Insanity) Act 1964 (power to deal with persons not guilty by reason of insanity or unfit to plead etc.) or the court affirms the order and the appellant has been released on bail pending his appeal, the court shall give such directions as it thinks fit for his conveyance to the hospital from which he was released on bail and for his detention, if necessary, in a place of safety as defined in section 55 of the 1983 Act pending his admission to the said hospital.

Notice of determination of court

68.29 (1) The Registrar shall, as soon as practicable, serve notice of any determination by the court or by any judge of the court under section 31 of the Criminal Appeal Act 1968, under article 8 of the Criminal Justice Act 2003 (Mandatory Life Sentences: Appeals in Transitional Cases) Order 2005 or under article 11 of the Serious Organised Crime and Police Act 2005 (Appeals under section 74) Order 2006 (powers exercisable by a single judge) on any appeal or application by an appellant on—

(a) the appellant;

(b) the Secretary of State;

(c) any person having custody of the appellant;

(d) in the case of an appellant detained under the Mental Health Act 1983 the responsible authority;

(e) in the case of a declaration of incompatibility under section 4 of the Human Rights Act 1998, the declaration shall be served on—

(i) all of the parties to the proceedings, and

(ii) where a Minister of the Crown has not been joined as a party, the Crown (in accordance with rule 68.27(3) above);

(f) in the case of an appeal under section 74(8) of the Serious Organised Crime and Police Act 2005, on the specified prosecutor and on the offender.

(2) The Registrar shall, as soon as practicable[,] serve notice of the order of the court disposing of an appeal or application for leave to appeal on a court officer of the Crown Court.

(3) In this rule the expression 'responsible authority' means—

(a) in relation to a patient liable to be detained under the 1983 Act in a hospital or mental nursing home, the managers of the hospital or home as defined in section 145(1) of that Act; and

(b) in relation to a patient subject to guardianship, the responsible local health authority as defined in section 34(3) of the 1983 Act.

Enforcement of fines

68.30 (1) Where the court imposes a fine on an appellant or, in an appeal brought by a specified prosecutor under section 74(8) of the Serious Organised Crime and Police Act 2005, on the offender, the court shall make an order fixing a term of imprisonment, not exceeding 12 months, which the appellant is to undergo if the fine is not duly paid or recovered.

(2) Such an order may—

(a) allow time for the payment of the fine; or

(b) direct payment of the fine by instalments of such amounts and on such dates respectively as may be specified in the order.

Notice of application after order for retrial

68.31 Notice of an application under section 8(1) of the Criminal Appeal Act 1968 for leave to arraign, and notice of an application under section 8(1A) of that Act to set aside an order for retrial shall be in the form set out in the Practice Direction and shall be served on the prosecutor or the person ordered to be retried as the case may be, and on the Registrar.

Part 69 Reference to the Court of Appeal of Point of Law

References

69.1 (1) Every reference under section 36 of the Criminal Justice Act 1972 shall be in writing and shall—

(a) specify the point of law referred and, where appropriate, such facts of the case as are necessary for the proper consideration of the point of law;

(b) summarise the arguments intended to be put to the court; and

(c) specify the authorities intended to be cited:

Provided that no mention shall be made in the reference of the proper name of any person or place which is likely to lead to the identification of the respondent.

(2) A reference shall be entitled 'Reference under section 36 of the Criminal Justice Act 1972' together with the year and number of the reference.

Registrar's notice to respondent

69.2 (1) The Registrar shall cause to be served on the respondent notice of the reference which shall also—

(a) inform the respondent that the reference will not affect the trial in relation to which it is made or any acquittal in that trial; and

(b) invite the respondent, within such period as may be specified in the notice (being not less than 28 days from the date of service of the notice), to inform the Registrar if he wishes to present any argument to the court and, if so, whether he wishes to present such argument in person or by counsel on his behalf.

(2) The court shall not hear argument by or on behalf of the Attorney General until the period specified in the notice has expired unless the respondent agrees or has indicated that he does not wish to present any argument to the court.

Withdrawal or amendment of reference

69.3 The Attorney General may withdraw or amend the reference at any time before the court have begun the hearing, or, after that, and until the court have given their opinion, may withdraw or amend the reference by leave of the court, and notice of such withdrawal or amendment shall be served on the respondent on behalf of the Attorney General.

Anonymity of respondent

69.4 The court shall ensure that the identity of the respondent is not disclosed during the proceedings on a reference except where the respondent has given his consent to the use of his name in the proceedings.

Reference to House of Lords

69.5 An application under section 36(3) of the Criminal Justice Act 1972 (reference to the House of Lords) may be made orally immediately after the court give their opinion or by notice served on the Registrar within the 14 days next following.

Part 70 Reference to the Court of Appeal of Unduly Lenient Sentence

Applications

70.1 (1) Every application for a reference under section 36 of the Criminal Justice Act 1988 shall be in writing and shall—

(a) specify—

(i) the name of the offender,

(ii) the date on which, and the offence of which, he was convicted,

(iii) the sentence passed on him in respect of that offence,

(iv) the date on which the sentence was passed (if later than the date under sub-paragraph (ii)), and

(v) the judge by whom, and the location of the Crown Court at which, the sentence was passed; and

(b) state the reason why it appears to the Attorney General that the sentencing of the offender was unduly lenient.

(2) An application shall be entitled 'Reference under section 36 of the Criminal Justice Act 1988' together with the year and number of the application and the name of the offender.

Notice of application

70.2 The sending of the application to the Registrar shall constitute the giving of notice of the application for the purpose of paragraph 1 of Schedule 3 to the Criminal Justice Act 1988 (notice to be given within 28 days of passing of sentence).

Registrar's notice to offender

70.3 (1) The Registrar shall, as soon as practicable after receiving the application, cause to be served on the offender a copy of it together with a notice which—

(a) informs him that the result of any reference could be that the court would quash the sentence passed on him in the proceeding and in place of it pass such sentence as they thought appropriate for the case and as the court below had power to pass when dealing with him (including a greater punishment);

(b) informs him of the effect of paragraph 6 (entitlement of offender to be present at hearing of reference, although he may be in custody), 7 (offender in custody requires leave of court to be present at hearing of application), 8 (power of court to pass sentence on offender who is not present) and 11 (entitlement of offender to reasonable costs out of central funds) of Schedule 3 to the Criminal Justice Act 1988;

(c) invites him, within such period as the Registrar may specify (being not less than 14 days from the date of service on him of the notice), to serve notice on the Registrar if he wishes—

(i) to apply to the court for leave to be present under paragraph 7 of Schedule 3 to the 1988 Act, and

(ii) to present any argument to the court on the hearing of the application or, if leave is given, of the reference, and whether to present it in person or by counsel on his behalf;

(d) draws to his attention the effect of rule 70.7 (supply of documentary and other exhibits); and

(e) advises him to consult a solicitor as to his position as soon as possible.

(2) The court shall not hear argument by or on behalf of the Attorney General until the period specified by the Registrar has expired unless the offender agrees or has indicated that he does not wish to present any argument to the Court.

References

70.4 (1) Every reference shall be in writing and shall—

(a) contain the information required by rule 70.1(1)(a) to be specified in an application;

(b) summarise the arguments intended to be put to the court; and

(c) specify the authorities intended to be cited.

(2) The reference shall bear the same title as the application.

(3) Subject to paragraph (4), the reference shall be sent on behalf of the Attorney General to the Registrar, who shall, as soon as practicable after receiving it, cause to be served a copy of it on the offender.

(4) Where the court gives leave for a case to be referred to it and is satisfied that the document comprising the application also contains the material required by paragraph (1) to be contained in a reference, the court may order that the document be treated for the purpose of this Part as the reference; and in that case paragraph (3) shall not apply.

Withdrawal or amendment of application or reference

70.5 The Attorney General may withdraw or amend an application or reference at any time before the court have begun the hearing of the application or reference as the case may be, or, after that, and until the court have given their decision, may withdraw or amend the application or reference by leave of the court, and notice of such withdrawal or amendment shall be served on the Registrar and on the offender on behalf of the Attorney General.

Registrar's power to require information from court of trial

70.6 The Registrar may require the court of trial to furnish the Court with any assistance or information which they may require for the purpose of exercising their jurisdiction.

Supply of documentary and other exhibits

70.7 (1) The Registrar shall, on request, supply to the offender copies or reproductions of documents or other things required for the application or reference and in such case may make charges in accordance with scales and rates fixed from time to time by the Treasury.

(2) The Registrar shall, on request, make arrangements for the offender to inspect any document or other thing required for the application or reference.

(3) This rule shall not apply to the supply of transcripts of any proceedings or part of proceedings.

Part 71 Appeal to the Court of Appeal under the Proceeds of Crime Act 2002—General Rules

Extension of time

71.1 (1) An application to extend the time limit for giving notice of application for leave to appeal under Part 2 of the Proceeds of Crime Act 2002 must—

(a) be included in the notice of appeal; and

(b) state the grounds for the application.

(2) The parties may not agree to extend any date or time limit set by this Part, Part 72 or Part 73, or by the Proceeds of Crime Act 2002 (Appeals under Part 2) Order 2003.

Other applications

71.2 Rules 68.15 (application for witness order or for court to receive evidence) and 68.26 (application for leave to be present) shall apply in relation to an application—

(a) by a party to an appeal under Part 2 of the Proceeds of Crime Act 2002 that, under article 7 of the Proceeds of Crime Act 2002 (Appeals under Part 2) Order 2003, a witness be ordered to attend or that the evidence of a witness be received by the Court of Appeal; or

(b) by the defendant to be given leave by the court to be present at proceedings for which leave is required under article 6 of the 2003 Order,

as they apply in relation to applications under Part I of the Criminal Appeal Act 1968 and the form in which rules 68.15 and 68.26 require notice to be given may be modified as necessary.

Examination of witness by court

71.3 (1) Rule 68.16 (examination of witness by court) shall apply in relation to an order of the court under article 7 of the Proceeds of Crime Act 2002 (Appeals under Part 2) Order 2003 to require a person to attend for examination as it applies in relation to such an order of the court under Part I of the Criminal Appeal Act 1968.

(2) The form set out in the Practice Direction, which relates to rule 68.16, may be modified as necessary.

Supply of documentary and other exhibits

71.4 Rule 68.11 (supply of documentary and other exhibits) shall apply in relation to an appellant or respondent under Part 2 of the Proceeds of Crime Act 2002 as it applies in relation to an appellant and respondent under Part I of the Criminal Appeal Act 1968.

Registrar's power to require information from court of trial

71.5—The Registrar may require the Crown Court to provide the Court of Appeal with any assistance or information which they may require for the purposes of exercising their jurisdiction under Part 2 of the Proceeds of Crime Act 2002, the Proceeds of Crime Act 2002 (Appeals under Part 2) Order 2003, this Part or Parts 72 and 73.

Hearing by single judge

71.6 (1) Rule 68.5 (exercise of court's power to give leave) shall apply in relation to a judge exercising any of the powers referred to in article 8 of the Proceeds of Crime Act 2002 (Appeals under Part 2) Order 2003 or the powers in rules 71.12(1), (2) and (4) (service of documents), 72.2(3) and (4) (respondent's notice), 73.2(2) (notice of appeal) and 73.3(6) (respondent's notice), as it applies in relation to a judge exercising the powers referred to in section 31(2) of the Criminal Appeal Act 1968.

(2) The form in which rule 68.5 requires an application to be made may be modified as necessary.

Determination by full court

71.7 Rule 68.6 (further application to the court) shall apply where a single judge has refused an application by a party to exercise in his favour any of the powers listed in article 8 of the Proceeds of Crime Act 2002 (Appeals under Part 2) Order 2003 or the power in rule 72.2(3) or (4) as it applies where the judge has refused to exercise the powers referred to in section 31(2) of the Criminal Appeal Act 1968.

Notice of determination

71.8 (1) This rule applies where a single judge or the Court of Appeal has determined an application or appeal under the Proceeds of Crime Act 2002 (Appeals under Part 2) Order 2003 or under Part 2 of the Proceeds of Crime Act 2002.

(2) The Registrar must, as soon as practicable, serve notice of the determination on all of the parties to the proceedings.

(3) Where a single judge or the Court of Appeal has disposed of an application for leave to appeal or an appeal under section 31 of the 2002 Act, the registrar must also, as soon as practicable, serve the order on a court officer of the court of trial and any magistrates' court responsible for enforcing any confiscation order which the Crown Court has made.

Record of proceedings and transcripts

71.9 (1) Rules 68.12 (record of proceedings at trial), 68.13 (transcripts) and 68.14 (verification of record of proceedings) shall apply in relation to proceedings in respect of which an appeal lies to the Court of Appeal under Part 2 of the Proceeds of Crime Act 2002 as they apply in relation to proceedings in respect of which an appeal lies to the Court of Appeal under Part I of the Criminal Appeal Act 1968.

(2) The Director of the Assets Recovery Agency shall be treated as an interested party for the purposes of rule 68.13 as it applies by virtue of this rule.

Appeal to House of Lords

71.10 (1) An application to the Court of Appeal for leave to appeal to the House of Lords under Part 2 of the Proceeds of Crime Act 2002 must be made—

(a) orally after the decision of the Court of Appeal from which an appeal lies to the House of Lords; or

(b) in the form set out in the Practice Direction, in accordance with article 12 of the Proceeds of Crime Act 2002 (Appeals under Part 2) Order 2003 and served on the Registrar.

(2) The application may be abandoned at any time before it is heard by the Court of Appeal by serving notice in writing on the Registrar.

(3) Rule 68.5(5) (hearing by single judge or Registrar) applies in relation to a single judge exercising any of the powers referred to in article 15 of the 2003 Order, as it applies in relation to a single judge exercising the powers referred to in section 31(2) of the Criminal Appeal Act 1968.

(4) Rules 68.5 (exercise of court's power to give leave to appeal, etc: general rules) and 68.6 (further applications to a judge or to the Court of Appeal: additional rules) apply where a single judge has refused an application by a party to exercise in his favour any of the powers listed in article 15 of the 2003 Order as they apply where the judge has refused to exercise the powers referred to in section 31(2) of the 1968 Act.

(5) The form in which rule 68.5 requires an application to be made may be modified as necessary.

Part 72 Appeal to the Court of Appeal under Proceeds of Crime Act 2002—Prosecutor's Appeal Regarding Confiscation

Notice of appeal

72.1 (1) Where an appellant wishes to apply to the Court of Appeal for leave to appeal under section 31 of the Proceeds of Crime Act 2002, he must serve a notice of appeal in the form set out in the Practice Direction on—

(a) the Crown Court officer; and

(b) the defendant.

(2) When the notice of the appeal is served on the defendant, it must be accompanied by a respondent's notice in the form set out in the Practice Direction for the defendant to complete and a notice which—

(a) informs the defendant that the result of an appeal could be that the Court of Appeal would increase a confiscation order already imposed on him, make a confiscation order itself or direct the Crown Court to hold another confiscation hearing;

(b) informs the defendant of any right he has under article 6 of the Proceeds of Crime Act 2002 (Appeals under Part 2) Order 2003 to be present at the hearing of the appeal, although he may be in custody;

(c) invites the defendant to serve notice on the registrar if he wishes—

(i) to apply to the Court of Appeal for leave to be present at proceedings for which leave is required under article 6 of the 2003 Order, or

(ii) to present any argument to the Court of Appeal on the hearing of the application

or, if leave is given, the appeal, and whether he wishes to present it in person or by means of a legal representative;
- (d) draws to the defendant's attention the effect of rule 71.4 (supply of documentary and other exhibits); and
- (e) advises the defendant to consult a solicitor as soon as possible.

(3) The appellant must provide a Crown Court officer with a certificate of service stating that he has served the notice of appeal on the defendant in accordance with paragraph (1) or explaining why he has been unable to effect service.

Respondent's notice

72.2 (1) This rule applies where a defendant is served with a notice of appeal under rule 72.1.

(2) If the defendant wishes to oppose the application for leave to appeal, he must, not later than 14 days after the date on which he received the notice of appeal, serve on the Registrar and on the appellant a notice in the form set out in the Practice Direction—
- (a) stating the date on which he received the notice of appeal;
- (b) summarising his response to the arguments of the appellant; and
- (c) specifying the authorities which he intends to cite.

(3) The time for giving notice under this rule may be extended by the Registrar, a single judge or by the Court of Appeal.

(4) Where the Registrar refuses an application under paragraph (3) for the extension of time, the defendant shall be entitled to have his application determined by a single judge.

(5) Where a single judge refuses an application under paragraph (3) or (4) for the extension of time, the defendant shall be entitled to have his application determined by the Court of Appeal.

Amendment and abandonment of appeal

72.3 (1) The appellant may amend a notice of appeal served under rule 72.1 or abandon an appeal under section 31 of the Proceeds of Crime Act 2002—
- (a) without the permission of the Court at any time before the Court of Appeal have begun hearing the appeal; and
- (b) with the permission of the Court after the Court of Appeal have begun hearing the appeal,

by serving notice in writing on the Registrar.

(2) Where the appellant serves a notice abandoning an appeal under paragraph (1), he must send a copy of it to—
- (a) the defendant;
- (b) a court officer of the court of trial; and
- (c) the magistrates' court responsible for enforcing any confiscation order which the Crown Court has made.

(3) Where the appellant serves a notice amending a notice of appeal under paragraph (1), he must send a copy of it to the defendant.

(4) Where an appeal is abandoned under paragraph (1), the application for leave to appeal or appeal shall be treated, for the purposes of section 85 of the 2002 Act (conclusion of proceedings), as having been refused or dismissed by the Court of Appeal.

Part 73 Appeal to the Court of Appeal under Poca 2002—Restraint or Receivership Orders

Leave to appeal

73.1 (1) Leave to appeal to the Court of Appeal under section 43 or section 65 of the Proceeds of Crime Act 2002 will only be given where—
- (a) the Court of Appeal considers that the appeal would have a real prospect of success; or
- (b) there is some other compelling reason why the appeal should be heard.

(2) An order giving leave may limit the issues to be heard and be made subject to conditions.

Notice of appeal

73.2 (1) Where an appellant wishes to apply to the Court of Appeal for leave to appeal under section 43 or 65 of the Proceeds of Crime Act 2002 Act, he must serve a notice of appeal in the form set out in the Practice Direction on the Crown Court officer.

(2) Unless the Registrar, a single judge or the Court of Appeal directs otherwise, the appellant must serve the notice of appeal, accompanied by a respondent's notice in the form set out in the Practice Direction for the respondent to complete, on—
(a) each respondent;
(b) any person who holds realisable property to which the appeal relates; and
(c) any other person affected by the appeal,
as soon as practicable and in any event not later than 7 days after the notice of appeal is served on a Crown Court officer.

(3) The appellant must serve the following documents with his notice of appeal—
(a) four additional copies of the notice of appeal for the Court of Appeal;
(b) four copies of any skeleton argument;
(c) one sealed copy and four unsealed copies of any order being appealed;
(d) four copies of any witness statement or affidavit in support of the application for leave to appeal;
(e) four copies of a suitable record of the reasons for judgment of the Crown Court; and
(f) four copies of the bundle of documents used in the Crown Court proceedings from which the appeal lies.

(4) Where it is not possible to serve all of the documents referred to in paragraph (3), the appellant must indicate which documents have not yet been served and the reasons why they are not currently available.

(5) The appellant must provide a Crown Court officer with a certificate of service stating that he has served the notice of appeal on each respondent in accordance with paragraph (2) and including full details of each respondent or explaining why he has been unable to effect service.

Respondent's notice

73.3 (1) This rule applies to an appeal under section 43 or 65 of the Proceeds of Crime Act 2002.

(2) A respondent may serve a respondent's notice on the Registrar.

(3) A respondent who—
(a) is seeking leave to appeal from the Court of Appeal; or
(b) wishes to ask the Court of Appeal to uphold the decision of the Crown Court for reasons different from or additional to those given by the Crown Court,
must serve a respondent's notice on the Registrar.

(4) A respondent's notice must be in the form set out in the Practice Direction and where the respondent seeks leave to appeal to the Court of Appeal it must be requested in the respondent's notice.

(5) A respondent's notice must be served on the Registrar not later than 14 days after—
(a) the date the respondent is served with notification that the Court of Appeal has given the appellant leave to appeal; or
(b) the date the respondent is served with notification that the application for leave to appeal and the appeal itself are to be heard together.

(6) Unless the Registrar, a single judge or the Court of Appeal directs otherwise, the respondent serving a respondent's notice must serve the notice on the appellant and any other respondent—
(a) as soon as practicable; and
(b) in any event not later than seven days,
after it is served on the Registrar.

Amendment and abandonment of appeal

73.4 (1) The appellant may amend a notice of appeal served under rule 73.2 or abandon an appeal under section 43 or 65 of the Proceeds of Crime Act 2002—
(a) without the permission of the Court at any time before the Court of Appeal have begun hearing the appeal; and
(b) with the permission of the Court after the Court of Appeal have begun hearing the appeal,
by serving notice in writing on the Registrar.

(2) Where the appellant serves a notice under paragraph (1), he must send a copy of it to each respondent.

Stay

73.5 Unless the Court of Appeal or the Crown Court orders otherwise, an appeal under section 43 or 65 of the Proceeds of Crime Act 2002 shall not operate as a stay of any order or decision of the Crown Court.

Striking out appeal notices and setting aside or imposing conditions on leave to appeal

73.6 (1) The Court of Appeal may—
(a) strike out the whole or part of a notice of appeal served under rule 73.2; or
(b) impose or vary conditions upon which an appeal under section 43 or 65 of the Proceeds of Crime Act 2002 may be brought.
(2) The Court of Appeal will only exercise its powers under paragraph (1) where there is a compelling reason for doing so.
(3) Where a party is present at the hearing at which leave to appeal was given, he may not subsequently apply for an order that the Court of Appeal exercise its powers under paragraph (1)(b).

Hearing of appeals

73.7 (1) This rule applies to appeals under section 43 or 65 of the Proceeds of Crime Act 2002.
(2) Every appeal will be limited to a review of the decision of the Crown Court unless the Court of Appeal considers that in the circumstances of an individual appeal it would be in the interests of justice to hold a re-hearing.
(3) The Court of Appeal will allow an appeal where the decision of the Crown Court was—
(a) wrong; or
(b) unjust because of a serious procedural or other irregularity in the proceedings in the Crown Court.
(4) The Court of Appeal may draw any inference of fact which it considers justified on the evidence.
(5) At the hearing of the appeal a party may not rely on a matter not contained in his notice of appeal unless the Court of Appeal gives permission.

Part 74 Appeal to the House of Lords

Application for leave to appeal from the Criminal Division of the Court of Appeal to the House of Lords

74.1 (1) An application to the criminal division of the Court of Appeal—
(a) for leave to appeal to the House of Lords under Part II of the Criminal Appeal Act 1968 or section 13 of the Administration of Justice Act 1960 or Part 3 of the Criminal Justice Act 2003 (Mandatory Life Sentences: Appeals in Transitional Cases) Order 2005;
(b) to extend the time within which an application may be made by the defendant to the House of Lords or the court under section 34(1) of the 1968 Act or that subsection as applied by section 13(4) of the 1960 Act or article 13(2) of the 2005 Order;
(c) by the defendant to be given leave to be present on the hearing of the appeal or of any proceedings preliminary or incidental thereto; or
(d) by the defendant to be granted bail pending the appeal,
shall either be made orally immediately after the decision of the court from which an appeal lies to the House of Lords or notice thereof shall be in the form set out in the Practice Direction and shall be served on the Registrar.
(2) The recognizance of a surety shall be in the form set out in the Practice Direction.
(3) Rules 68.8 (bail with condition of surety) and 68.9 (forfeiture of recognizances) shall apply with respect to a defendant pending his appeal to the House of Lords as they apply with respect to an appellant with the necessary modifications.
(4) An application to the court for leave to appeal to the House of Lords under Part II of the 1968 Act or section 13 of the 1960 Act, or Part 3 of the 2005 Order may be abandoned before the hearing of the application by serving on the Registrar notice to that effect.
(5) For the purpose of having an application determined by the court in pursuance of section 44 of the 1968 Act, rules 68.5 (exercise of court's power to give leave) and 68.6 (further application to the court) shall apply with the necessary modifications.
(6) Rule 68.29 (notice if determination of court) shall apply to a determination under Part II of the 1968 Act or section 13 of the 1960 Act with the necessary modifications.

(7) Rules 68.11 (supply of documentary and other exhibits), 68.13(2) (transcripts) and 68.23 (the Registrar) shall apply in relation to an appeal under Part II of the 1968 Act or section 13 of the 1960 Act as they apply in relation to an appeal under Part I of the 1968 Act, except that any reference to section 31 of the 1968 Act shall be construed as a reference to section 44 of the 1968 Act.

(8) In this rule any reference to a defendant includes an appellant under section 13 of the 1960 Act or under the 2005 Order.

Part 75 Reference to the European Court

Reference to the European Court

75.1 (1) In this rule 'order' means an order referring a question to the European Court for a preliminary ruling under Article 234 of the Treaty establishing the European Community, Article 150 of the Treaty establishing Euratom or Article 41 of the Treaty establishing the Coal and Steel Community.

(2) An order may be made—

(a) by the Crown Court of its own motion or on application by a party to proceedings in the Crown Court; or

(b) by the Court of Appeal, on application or otherwise, at any time before the determination of an appeal or application for leave to appeal under Part I of the Criminal Appeal Act 1968.

(3) An order shall set out in a schedule the request for the preliminary ruling of the European Court, and the court making the order may give directions as to the manner and form in which the schedule is to be prepared.

(4) When an order has been made, a copy shall be sent to the senior master of the Supreme Court (Queen's Bench Division) for transmission to the Registrar of the European Court.

(5) The Crown Court proceedings in which an order is made shall, unless the Crown Court otherwise determines, be adjourned until the European Court has given a preliminary ruling on the question referred to it.

(6) Nothing in paragraph (5) above shall be taken as preventing the Crown Court from deciding any preliminary or incidental question that may arise in the proceedings after an order is made and before a preliminary ruling is given by the European Court.

(7) No appeal or application for leave to appeal, in the course of which an order is made, shall, unless the Court of Appeal otherwise orders, be determined until the European Court has given a preliminary ruling on the question referred to it.

Part 76 Representation Orders

[There are currently no rules in this part.]

Part 77 Recovery of Defence Costs Orders

[There are currently no rules in this part.]

Part 78 Costs Orders against the Parties

Crown Court's jurisdiction to award costs in appeal from magistrates' court

78.1 (1) Subject to the provisions of section 109(1) of the Magistrates' Courts Act 1980 (power of magistrates' courts to award costs on abandonment of appeals from magistrates' courts), no party shall be entitled to recover any costs of any proceedings in the Crown Court from any other party to the proceedings except under an order of the Court.

(2) Subject to the following provisions of this rule, the Crown Court may make such order for costs as it thinks just.

(3) No order for costs shall be made on the abandonment of an appeal from a magistrates' court by giving notice under rule 63.5.

(4) Without prejudice to the generality of paragraph (2), the Crown Court may make an order for costs on dismissing an appeal where the appellant has failed to proceed with the appeal or on the abandonment of an appeal not being an appeal to which paragraph (3) applies.

Crown Court's jurisdiction to award costs in magistrates' court proceedings from which appeal is brought

78.2 Where an appeal is brought to the Crown Court from the decision of a magistrates' court and the appeal is successful, the Crown Court may make any order as to the costs of the proceedings in the magistrates' court which that court had power to make.

Taxation of Crown Court costs

78.3 (1) Where under these Rules the Crown Court has made an order for the costs of any proceedings to be paid by a party and the Court has not fixed a sum, the amount of the costs to be paid shall be ascertained as soon as practicable by the Crown Court officer (hereinafter referred to as the taxing authority).

(2) On a taxation under the preceding paragraph there shall be allowed the costs reasonably incurred in or about the prosecution and conviction or the defence, as the case may be.

Review of Crown Court costs by taxing authority

78.4 (1) Any party dissatisfied with the taxation of any costs by the taxing authority under rule 78.3 may apply to the taxing authority to review his decision.

(2) The application shall be made by giving notice to the taxing authority and to any other party to the taxation within 14 days of the taxation, specifying the items in respect of which the application is made and the grounds of objection.

(3) Any party to whom notice is given under the preceding paragraph may within 14 days of the service of the notice deliver to the taxing authority answers in writing to the objections specified in that notice to the taxing authority and, if he does, shall send copies to the applicant for the review and to any other party to the taxation.

(4) The taxing authority shall reconsider his taxation in the light of the objections and answers, if any, of the parties and any oral representations made by or on their behalf and shall notify them of the result of his review.

Further review of Crown Court costs by taxing master

78.5 (1) Any party dissatisfied with the result of a review of taxation under rule 78.4 may, within 14 days of receiving notification thereof, request the taxing authority to supply him with reasons in writing for his decision and may within 14 days of the receipt of such reasons apply to the Chief Taxing Master for a further review and shall, in that case, give notice of the application to the taxing authority and to any other party to the taxation, to whom he shall also give a copy of the reasons given by the taxing authority.

(2) Such application shall state whether the application wishes to appear or be represented, or whether he will accept a decision given in his absence and shall be accompanied by a copy of the notice given under rule 78.4, of any answer which may have been given under paragraph (3) thereof and of the reasons given by the taxing authority for his decision, together with the bill of costs and full supporting documents.

(3) A party to the taxation who receives notice of an application under this rule shall inform the Chief Taxing Master whether he wishes to appear or be represented at a further review, or whether he will accept a decision given in his absence.

(4) The further review shall be conducted by a Taxing Master and if the applicant or any other party to the taxation has given notice of his intention to appear or be represented, the Taxing Master shall inform the parties (or their agents) of the date on which the further review will take place.

(5) Before reaching his decision the Taxing Master may consult the judge who made the order for costs and the taxing authority and, unless the Taxing Master otherwise directs, no further evidence shall be received on the hearing of the further review; and no ground of objection shall be valid which was not raised on the review under rule 78.4.

(6) In making his review, the Taxing Master may alter the assessment of the taxing authority in respect of any sum allowed, whether by increase or decrease.

(7) The Taxing Master shall communicate the result of the further review to the parties and to the taxing authority.

Appeal to High Court judge after review of Crown Court costs

78.6 (1) Any party dissatisfied with the result of a further review under rule 78.5 may, within 14 days of receiving notification thereof, appeal by originating summons to a judge of the Queen's Bench Division of the High Court if, and only if, the Taxing Master certifies that the question to be decided involves a point of principle of general importance.

(2) On the hearing of the appeal the judge may reverse, affirm or amend the decision appealed against or make such other order as he thinks appropriate.

Supplementary provisions on Crown Court costs

78.7 (1) On a further review or an appeal to a judge of the High Court the Taxing Master or judge may make such order as he thinks just in respect of the costs of the hearing of the further review or the appeal, as the case may be.

(2) The time set out by rules 78.4, 78.5 and 78.6 may be extended by the taxing authority, Taxing Master or judge of the High Court on such terms as he thinks just.

Glossary

This glossary is a guide to the meaning of certain legal expressions as used in these rules.

Expression	Meaning
account monitoring order	an order requiring certain types of financial institution to provide certain information held by them relating to a customer for the purposes of an investigation
action plan order	a type of community sentence requiring a child or young person to comply with a three month plan relating to his actions and whereabouts and to comply with the directions of a responsible officer (e.g. probation officer)
admission of evidence	acceptance by the court of the evidence into proceedings (not all evidence tendered by the parties may be allowable in court)
to adduce	to put forward (in evidence)
to adjourn	to suspend or delay the hearing of a case until another day
advance information	information about the case against an accused, to which the accused may be entitled before he or she enters a plea
affidavit	a written, sworn statement of evidence
affirmation	a non-religious alternative to the oath sworn by someone about to give evidence in court or swearing a statement
appellant	person who is appealing against a decision of the court
to arraign	to put charges to the defendant in open court in the Crown Court
arraignment	the formal process of putting charges to the defendant in the Crown Court which consists of three parts: (1) calling him to the bar by name, (2) putting the charges to him by reading from the indictment and (3) asking him whether he pleads guilty or not guilty
authorities	judicial decisions or opinions of authors of repute used as grounds of statements of law
bill of indictment	a written accusation of a crime against one or more persons—a criminal trial in the Crown Court cannot start without a valid indictment
in camera (trial)	proceedings which are held in private
case stated	an appeal to the High Court against the decision of a magistrates court on the basis that the decision was wrong in law or in excess of the magistrates' jurisdiction
in chambers	proceedings which may be held in private
child safety order	an order made by a magistrates' court placing a child under the supervision of a responsible officer where the child has committed acts which could, had he been over 10 years old at the time, have constituted an offence or which have or are likely to cause harassment, alarm or distress
committal	sending someone to a court (usually from a magistrates' court to the Crown court) or to prison
committal for sentence	procedure whereby a person convicted in a magistrates' court is sent to the Crown Court for sentencing when the sentencing powers of the magistrates' court are not considered sufficient
committal proceedings	preliminary hearing in a magistrates' court before a case is sent to be tried before a jury in the Crown Court
compellable witness	a witness who can be forced to give evidence against an accused (not all witnesses are compellable)
compensation order	an order that a convicted person must pay compensation for loss or damage caused by the convicted person
complainant	a person who makes a formal complaint—in relation to an offence of rape or other sexual offences the complainant is the person against whom the offence is alleged to have been committed
complaint	document used to start certain types of proceedings in a magistrates' court, or the process of using such a document to start proceedings

Expression	Meaning
conditional discharge	an order which does not impose any immediate punishment on a person convicted of an offence, subject to the condition that he does not commit an offence in a specified period
confiscation order	an order that private property be taken into possession by the state
Convention right	a right under the European Convention on Human Rights
costs	the expenses involved in a court case, including the fees of the solicitors and barristers and of the court
counsel	a barrister
cross examination	questioning of a witness by a party other than the party who called the witness
custody time limit	the maximum period, as set down in statute, for which a person may be kept in custody before being brought to trial—these maximum periods may only be extended by an order of the judge
customer information order	an order requiring a financial institution to provide certain information held by them relating to a customer for the purposes of an investigation into the proceeds of crime
declaration of incompatibility	a declaration by a court that a piece of UK legislation is incompatible with the provisions of the European Convention of Human Rights
deferred sentence	a sentence which is determined after a delay to allow the court to assess any change in the person's conduct or circumstances after his or her conviction
deposition	written record of a witness' written evidence
estreatment (of recognizance)	forfeiture
evidence in chief	the evidence given by a witness for the party who called him
examining justice	a magistrate carrying out his or her function of checking that a case appears on the face of the prosecution case papers to exist against an accused before the case is put forward for trial in the Crown Court—see committal and sending for trial
exhibit	a document or thing presented as evidence in court
ex parte	a hearing where only one party is allowed to attend and make submissions
forfeiture by peaceable re-entry	the re-possession by a landlord of premises occupied by tenants
guardianship order	an order appointing someone to take charge of a child's affairs and property
hearsay evidence	oral or written statements made by someone who is not a witness in the case but which the court is asked to accept as proving what they say—this expression is defined further by rule 34.1 for the purposes of Part 34, and by rule 57.1 for the purposes of Parts 57–61
hospital order	an order that an offender be admitted to and detained in a specified hospital
indictment	the document containing the formal charges against a defendant—a trial in the Crown Court cannot start without this
informant	someone who lays an information
information	statement by which a magistrate is informed of the offence for which a summons or warrant is required—the procedure by which this statement is brought to the magistrates' attention is known as laying an information
interested party	a person or organisation who is not the prosecutor or defendant but who has some other legal interest in a criminal case—this expression is defined further in rule 66.1, for the purposes of Part 66 only
intermediary	a person who asks a witness (particularly a child) questions posed by the cross-examining legal representative
inter partes	a hearing where both parties attend and can make submissions
justice of the peace	a lay magistrate or District Judge (Magistrates' Courts);
justices' clerk	post in the magistrates' court of person who has various powers and duties in a magistrates' court, including giving advice to the magistrates on law and procedure
leave of the court	permission granted by the court
leave to appeal	permission granted to appeal the decision of a court
letter of request	letter issued to a foreign court asking a judge to take the evidence of some person within that court's jurisdiction
live link	audio and/or video equipment set up in order to enable evidence to be given from outside the court room in which a case is being heard
to levy distress	to seize property from a debtor or a wrongdoer
local justice area	an area established for the purposes of the administration of magistrates' courts

Expression	Meaning
mandatory order	order from the divisional Court of the Queen's Bench Division ordering a body (such as a magistrates' court) to do something (such as rehear a case)
nominated court	a court nominated to take evidence pursuant to a request by a foreign court
notice of transfer	procedure used in cases of serious and complex fraud, and in certain cases involving child witnesses, whereby the prosecution can, without seeking judicial approval, have the case sent direct to the Crown Court without the need to have the accused committed for trial
offence triable only summarily	an offence which can be tried only in a magistrates' court
offence triable either way	an offence which may be tried either in the magistrates' court or in the Crown Court
offence triable only on indictment	an offence which can be tried only in the Crown Court
in open court	in a courtroom which is open to the public
order of committal	an order sending someone to prison for contempt of court
order restricting discharge	an order restricting the discharge from hospital of patients who have been sent there for psychiatric treatment
parenting order	an order which can be made in certain circumstances where a child has been convicted of an offence which may require parents of the offender to comply with certain requirements including attendance of counselling or guidance sessions
party	a person or organisation directly involved in a criminal case, either as prosecutor or defendant
practice direction	direction relating to the practice and procedure of the courts
to prefer, preferment	to bring or lay a charge or indictment
preparatory hearing	a hearing forming part of the trial sometimes used in long and complex cases to settle various issues without requiring the jury to attend
prima facie case	a prosecution case which is strong enough to require the defendant to answer it
primary legislation	Acts of Parliament
realisable property	property which can be sold for money
receiver	a person appointed with certain powers in respect of the property and affairs of a person who has obtained such property in the course of criminal conduct and who has been convicted of an offence—there are various types of receiver (management receiver, director's receiver, enforcement receiver)
receivership order	an order that a person's assets be put into the hands of an official with certain powers and duties to deal with that property
recognizance	formal undertaking to pay the crown a specified sum if an accused fails to surrender to custody
register	the formal records kept by a magistrates' court
to remand	to send a person away when a case is adjourned until another date—the person may be remanded on bail (when he can leave, subject to conditions) or in custody
reparation order	an order made against a child or young person who has been convicted of an offence, requiring him or her to make specific reparations to the victim or to the community at large
representation order	an order authorising payment of legal aid for a defendant
requisition	a document issued under section 29 of the Criminal Justice Act 2003 requiring a person to appear before a magistrates' court to answer a written charge
respondent	the other party (to the appellant) in a case which is the subject of an appeal
restraint order	an order prohibiting a person from dealing with any realisable property held by him
seal	a formal mark which the court puts on a document to indicate that the document has been issued by the court
security	money deposited to ensure that the defendant attends court
sending for trial	procedure whereby indictable offences are transferred to the Crown Court without the need for a committal hearing in the magistrates' court
skeleton argument	a document prepared by a party or their legal representative setting out the basis of the party's argument, including any arguments based on law—the court may require such documents to be served on the court and on the other party prior to a trial
special measures	measures which can be put in place to provide protection and/or anonymity to a witness (e.g. a screen separating witness from the accused)
statutory declaration	a declaration made before a Commissioner for Oaths in a prescribed form

Expression	Meaning
to stay	to halt proceedings, apart from taking any steps allowed by the Rules or the terms of the stay—proceedings may be continued if a stay is lifted
summons	a document signed by a magistrate after an information is laid before him which sets out the basis of the accusation against the accused and the time and place when he must appear
surety	a person who guarantees that a defendant will attend court
suspended sentence	sentence which takes effect only if the offender commits another offence punishable with imprisonment within the specified period
supervision order	an order placing a person who has been given a suspended sentence under the supervision of a local officer
tainted acquittal	an acquittal affected by interference with a witness or a juror
taxation of costs	the assessment of the expenses involved in a court case
taxing authority	a body which assesses costs
Taxing Master	a judge who assesses costs
territorial authority	the UK authority which has power to do certain things in connection with co-operation with other countries and international organisations in relation to the collection of or hearing of evidence etc
transfer direction (mental health)	a direction that a person who is serving a sentence of imprisonment who is suffering from a mental disorder be transferred to a hospital and be detained there for treatment
warrant of arrest	court order to arrest a person
warrant of commitment	court order sending someone to prison
warrant of distress	court order giving the power to seize goods from a debtor to pay his debts
warrant of detention	a court order authorising someone's detention
wasted costs order	an order that a barrister or solicitor is not to be paid fees that they would normally be paid by the Legal Services Commission
witness	a person who gives evidence, either by way of a written statement or orally in court
witness summons	a document served on a witness requiring him or her to attend court to give evidence
writ of venire de novo	an order directing a new trial after a mistrial involving a fundamental irregularity
written charge	a document issued by a public prosecutor under section 29 of the Criminal Justice Act 2003 which institutes criminal proceedings by charging a person with an offence
youth court	magistrates' courts exercising jurisdiction over offences committed by and other matters related to, children and young persons.

Appendix 2 Codes of Practice Under the Police and Criminal Evidence Act 1984

PACE CODE A
CODE OF PRACTICE FOR THE EXERCISE BY: POLICE OFFICERS OF STATUTORY POWERS OF STOP AND SEARCH
POLICE OFFICERS AND POLICE STAFF OF REQUIREMENTS TO RECORD PUBLIC ENCOUNTERS

Commencement—transitional arrangements

This code applies to any search by a police officer and the requirement to record public encounters taking place after midnight on 31 December 2005.

General

This code of practice must be readily available at all police stations for consultation by police officers, police staff, detained persons and members of the public.
The notes for guidance included are not provisions of this code, but are guidance to police officers and others about its application and interpretation. Provisions in the annexes to the code are provisions of this code.

This code governs the exercise by police officers of statutory powers to search a person or a vehicle without first making an arrest. The main stop and search powers to which this code applies are set out in Annex A, but that list should not be regarded as definitive. [See Note 1] In addition, it covers requirements on police officers and police staff to record encounters not governed by statutory powers. This code does not apply to:

(a) the powers of stop and search under;
   (i) Aviation Security Act 1982, section 27(2);
   (ii) Police and Criminal Evidence Act 1984, section 6(1) (which relates specifically to powers of constables employed by statutory undertakers on the premises of the statutory undertakers).

(b) searches carried out for the purposes of examination under Schedule 7 to the Terrorism Act 2000 and to which the Code of Practice issued under paragraph 6 of Schedule 14 to the Terrorism Act 2000 applies.

1. Principles governing stop and search

1.1 Powers to stop and search must be used fairly, responsibly, with respect for people being searched and without unlawful discrimination. The Race Relations (Amendment) Act 2000 makes it unlawful for police officers to discriminate on the grounds of race, colour, ethnic origin, nationality or national origins when using their powers.

1.2 The intrusion on the liberty of the person stopped or searched must be brief and detention for the purposes of a search must take place at or near the location of the stop.

1.3 If these fundamental principles are not observed the use of powers to stop and search may be drawn into question. Failure to use the powers in the proper manner reduces their effectiveness. Stop and search can play an important role in the detection and prevention of crime, and using the powers fairly makes them more effective.

1.4 The primary purpose of stop and search powers is to enable officers to allay or confirm suspicions about individuals without exercising their power of arrest. Officers may be required to justify the use or authorisation of such powers, in relation both to individual searches and the overall pattern of their activity in this regard, to their supervisory officers or in court. Any misuse of the powers is likely to be harmful to policing and lead to mistrust of the police. Officers must also be able to explain their actions to the member of the public searched. The misuse of these powers can lead to disciplinary action.

1.5 An officer must not search a person, even with his or her consent, where no power to search is applicable. Even where a person is prepared to submit to a search voluntarily, the person must not be searched unless the necessary legal power exists, and the search must be in accordance with the relevant power and the provisions of this Code. The only exception, where an officer does not require a specific power, applies to searches of persons entering sports grounds or other premises carried out with their consent given as a condition of entry.

2. Explanation of powers to stop and search

2.1 This code applies to powers of stop and search as follows:

(a) powers which require reasonable grounds for suspicion, before they may be exercised; that articles unlawfully obtained or possessed are being carried, or under Section 43 of the Terrorism Act 2000 that a person is a terrorist;

(b) authorised under section 60 of the Criminal Justice and Public Order Act 1994, based upon a reasonable belief that incidents involving serious violence may take place or that people are carrying dangerous instruments or offensive weapons within any locality in the police area;

(c) authorised under section 44(1) and (2) of the Terrorism Act 2000 based upon a consideration that the exercise of one or both powers is expedient for the prevention of acts of terrorism;

(d) powers to search a person who has not been arrested in the exercise of a power to search premises (see Code B paragraph 2.4).

Searches requiring reasonable grounds for suspicion

2.2 Reasonable grounds for suspicion depend on the circumstances in each case. There must be an objective basis for that suspicion based on facts, information, and/or intelligence which are relevant to the likelihood of finding an article of a certain kind or, in the case of searches under section 43 of the Terrorism Act 2000, to the likelihood that the person is a terrorist. Reasonable suspicion can never be supported on the basis of personal factors alone without reliable supporting intelligence or information or some specific behaviour by the person concerned. For example, a person's race, age, appearance, or the fact that the person is known to have a previous conviction, cannot be used alone or in combination with each other as the reason for searching that person. Reasonable suspicion cannot be based on generalisations or stereotypical images of certain groups or categories of people as more likely to be involved in criminal activity. A person's religion cannot be considered as reasonable grounds for suspicion and should never be considered as a reason to stop or stop and search an individual.

2.3 Reasonable suspicion can sometimes exist without specific information or intelligence and on the basis of some level of generalisation stemming from the behaviour of a person. For example, if an officer encounters someone on the street at night who is obviously trying to hide something, the officer may (depending on the other surrounding circumstances) base such suspicion on the fact that this kind of behaviour is often linked to stolen or prohibited articles being carried. Similarly, for the purposes of section 43 of the Terrorism Act 2000, suspicion that a person is a terrorist may arise from the person's behaviour at or near a location which has been identified as a potential target for terrorists.

2.4 However, reasonable suspicion should normally be linked to accurate and current intelligence or information, such as information describing an article being carried, a suspected offender, or a person who has been seen carrying a type of article known to have been stolen recently from premises in the area. Searches based on accurate and current intelligence or information are more likely to be effective. Targeting searches in a particular area at specified crime problems increases their effectiveness and minimises inconvenience to law-abiding members of the public. It also helps in justifying the use of searches both to those who are searched and to the public. This does not however prevent stop and search powers being exercised in other locations where such powers may be exercised and reasonable suspicion exists.

2.5 Searches are more likely to be effective, legitimate, and secure public confidence when reasonable suspicion is based on a range of factors. The overall use of these powers is more likely to be effective when up to date and accurate intelligence or information is communicated to officers and they are well-informed about local crime patterns.

2.6 Where there is reliable information or intelligence that members of a group or gang habitually carry knives unlawfully or weapons or controlled drugs, and wear a distinctive item of clothing or other means of identification to indicate their membership of the group or gang, that distinctive item of clothing or other means of identification may provide reasonable grounds to stop and search a person. [See *Note 9*]

2.7 A police officer may have reasonable grounds to suspect that a person is in innocent possession of a stolen or prohibited article or other item for which he or she is empowered to search. In that case the officer may stop and search the person even though there would be no power of arrest.

2.8 Under section 43(1) of the Terrorism Act 2000 a constable may stop and search a person whom the officer reasonably suspects to be a terrorist to discover whether the person is in possession of anything which may constitute evidence that the person is a terrorist. These searches may only be carried out by an officer of the same sex as the person searched.

2.9 An officer who has reasonable grounds for suspicion may detain the person concerned in order to carry out a search. Before carrying out a search the officer may ask questions about the person's behaviour or presence in circumstances which gave rise to the suspicion. As a result of questioning the detained person, the reasonable grounds for suspicion necessary to detain that person may be confirmed or, because of a satisfactory explanation, be eliminated. [See *Notes 2* and *3*] Questioning may also reveal reasonable grounds to suspect the possession of a different kind of unlawful article from that originally suspected. Reasonable grounds for suspicion however cannot be provided retrospectively by such questioning during a person's detention or by refusal to answer any questions put.

2.10 If, as a result of questioning before a search, or other circumstances which come to the attention of the officer, there cease to be reasonable grounds for suspecting that an article is being carried of a kind for which there is a power to stop and search, no search may take place. [See *Note 3*] In the absence of any other lawful power to detain, the person is free to leave at will and must be so informed.

2.11 There is no power to stop or detain a person in order to find grounds for a search. Police officers have many encounters with members of the public which do not involve detaining people against their will. If reasonable grounds for suspicion emerge during such an encounter, the officer may search the person, even though no grounds existed when the encounter began. If an officer is detaining someone for the purpose of a search, he or she should inform the person as soon as detention begins.

Searches authorised under section 60 of the Criminal Justice and Public Order Act 1994

2.12 Authority for a constable in uniform to stop and search under section 60 of the Criminal Justice and Public Order Act 1994 may be given if the authorising officer reasonably believes:

(a) that incidents involving serious violence may take place in any locality in the officer's police area, and it is expedient to use these powers to prevent their occurrence, or

(b) that persons are carrying dangerous instruments or offensive weapons without good reason in any locality in the officer's police area.

2.13 An authorisation under section 60 may only be given by an officer of the rank of inspector or above, in writing, specifying the grounds on which it was given, the locality in which the powers may be exercised and the period of time for which they are in force. The period authorised shall be no longer than appears reasonably necessary to prevent, or seek to prevent incidents of serious violence, or to deal with the problem of carrying dangerous instruments or offensive weapons. It may not exceed 24 hours. [See *Notes 10–13*]

2.14 If an inspector gives an authorisation, he or she must, as soon as practicable, inform an officer of or above the rank of superintendent. This officer may direct that the authorisation shall be extended for a further 24 hours, if violence or the carrying of dangerous instruments or offensive weapons has occurred, or is suspected to have occurred, and the continued use of the powers is considered necessary to prevent or deal with further such activity. That direction must also be given in writing at the time or as soon as practicable afterwards. [See *Note 12*]

Powers to require removal of face coverings

2.15 Section 60AA of the Criminal Justice and Public Order Act 1994 also provides a power to demand the removal of disguises. The officer exercising the power must reasonably believe that someone is wearing an item wholly or mainly for the purpose of concealing identity. There is also a power to seize such items where the officer believes that a person intends to wear them for this purpose. There is no power to stop and search for disguises. An officer may seize any such item which is discovered when exercising a power of search for something else, or which is being carried, and which the officer reasonably believes is intended to be used for concealing anyone's identity. This power can only be used if an authorisation under section 60 or an authorisation under section 60AA is in force.

2.16 Authority for a constable in uniform to require the removal of disguises and to seize them under section 60AA may be given if the authorising officer reasonably believes that activities may take place in any locality in the officer's police area that are likely to involve the commission of offences and it is expedient to use these powers to prevent or control these activities.

2.17 An authorisation under section 60AA may only be given by an officer of the rank of inspector or above, in writing, specifying the grounds on which it was given, the locality in which the powers may be exercised and the period of time for which they are in force. The period authorised shall be no longer than appears reasonably necessary to prevent, or seek to prevent the commission of offences. It may not exceed 24 hours. [See *Notes 10–13*]

2.18 If an inspector gives an authorisation, he or she must, as soon as practicable, inform an officer of or above the rank of superintendent. This officer may direct that the authorisation shall be extended for a further 24 hours, if crimes have been committed, or is suspected to have been committed, and the continued use of the powers is considered necessary to prevent or deal with further such activity. This direction must also be given in writing at the time or as soon as practicable afterwards. [See *Note 12*]

Searches authorised under section 44 of the Terrorism Act 2000

2.19 An officer of the rank of assistant chief constable (or equivalent) or above, may give authority for the following powers of stop and search under section 44 of the Terrorism Act 2000 to be exercised in the whole or part of his or her police area if the officer considers it is expedient for the prevention of acts of terrorism:

(a) under section 44(1) of the Terrorism Act 2000, to give a constable in uniform power to stop and search any vehicle, its driver, any passenger in the vehicle and anything in or on the vehicle or carried by the driver or any passenger; and

(b) under section 44(2) of the Terrorism Act 2000, to give a constable in uniform power to stop and search any pedestrian and anything carried by the pedestrian.

An authorisation under section 44(1) may be combined with one under section 44(2).

2.20 If an authorisation is given orally at first, it must be confirmed in writing by the officer who gave it as soon as reasonably practicable.

2.21 When giving an authorisation, the officer must specify the geographical area in which the power may be used, and the time and date that the authorisation ends (up to a maximum of 28 days from the time the authorisation was given). [See *Notes 12* and *13*]

2.22 The officer giving an authorisation under section 44(1) or (2) must cause the Secretary of State to be informed, as soon as reasonably practicable, that such an authorisation has been given. An authorisation which is not confirmed by the Secretary of State within 48 hours of its having been given, shall have effect up until the end of that 48 hour period or the end of the period specified in the authorisation (whichever is the earlier). [See *Note 14*]

2.23 Following notification of the authorisation, the Secretary of State may:

(i) cancel the authorisation with immediate effect or with effect from such other time as he or she may direct;

(ii) confirm it but for a shorter period than that specified in the authorisation; or

(iii) confirm the authorisation as given.

2.24 When an authorisation under section 44 is given, a constable in uniform may exercise the powers:

(a) only for the purpose of searching for articles of a kind which could be used in connection with terrorism (see paragraph 2.25);

(b) whether or not there are any grounds for suspecting the presence of such articles.

2.24A When a Community Support Officer on duty and in uniform has been conferred powers under Section 44 of the Terrorism Act 2000 by a Chief Officer of their force, the exercise of this power must comply with the requirements of this Code of Practice, including the recording requirements.

2.25 The selection of persons stopped under section 44 of Terrorism Act 2000 should reflect an objective assessment of the threat posed by the various terrorist groups active in Great Britain. The powers must not be used to stop and search for reasons unconnected with terrorism. Officers must take particular care not to discriminate against members of minority ethnic groups in the exercise of these powers. There may be circumstances, however, where it is appropriate for officers to take account of a person's ethnic origin in selecting persons to be stopped in response to a specific terrorist threat (for example, some international terrorist groups are associated with particular ethnic identities). [See *Notes 12* and *13*]

2.26 The powers under sections 43 and 44 of the Terrorism Act 2000 allow a constable to search only for articles which could be used for terrorist purposes. However, this would not prevent a search being carried out under other powers if, in the course of exercising these powers, the officer formed reasonable grounds for suspicion.

Powers to search in the exercise of a power to search premises

2.27 The following powers to search premises also authorise the search of a person, not under arrest, who is found on the premises during the course of the search:

(a) section 139B of the Criminal Justice Act 1988 under which a constable may enter school premises and search the premises and any person on those premises for any bladed or pointed article or offensive weapon; and
(b) under a warrant issued under section s.23(3) of the Misuse of Drugs Act 1971 to search premises for drugs or documents but only if the warrant specifically authorises the search of persons found on the premises.

2.28 Before the power under section 139B of the Criminal Justice Act 1988 may be exercised, the constable must have reasonable grounds to believe that an offence under section 139A of the Criminal Justice Act 1988 (having a bladed or pointed article or offensive weapon on school premises) has been or is being committed. A warrant to search premises and persons found therein may be issued under section s.23(3) of the Misuse of Drugs Act 1971 if there are reasonable grounds to suspect that controlled drugs or certain documents are in the possession of a person on the premises.

2.29 The powers in paragraph 2.27(a) or (b) do not require prior specific grounds to suspect that the person to be searched is in possession of an item for which there is an existing power to search. However, it is still necessary to ensure that the selection and treatment of those searched under these powers is based upon objective factors connected with the search of the premises, and not upon personal prejudice.

3. Conduct of searches

3.1 All stops and searches must be carried out with courtesy, consideration and respect for the person concerned. This has a significant impact on public confidence in the police. Every reasonable effort must be made to minimise the embarrassment that a person being searched may experience. [See *Note 4*]

3.2 The co-operation of the person to be searched must be sought in every case, even if the person initially objects to the search. A forcible search may be made only if it has been established that the person is unwilling to co-operate or resists. Reasonable force may be used as a last resort if necessary to conduct a search or to detain a person or vehicle for the purposes of a search.

3.3 The length of time for which a person or vehicle may be detained must be reasonable and kept to a minimum. Where the exercise of the power requires reasonable suspicion, the thoroughness and extent of a search must depend on what is suspected of being carried, and by whom. If the suspicion relates to a particular article which is seen to be slipped into a person's pocket, then, in the absence of other grounds for suspicion or an opportunity for the article to be moved elsewhere, the search must be confined to that pocket. In the case of a small article which can readily be concealed, such as a drug, and which might be concealed anywhere on the person, a more extensive search may be necessary. In the case of searches mentioned in paragraph 2.1(b), (c), and (d), which do not require reasonable grounds for suspicion, officers may make any reasonable search to look for items for which they are empowered to search. [See *Note 5*]

3.4 The search must be carried out at or near the place where the person or vehicle was first detained. [See *Note 6*]

3.5 There is no power to require a person to remove any clothing in public other than an outer coat, jacket or gloves except under section 45(3) of the Terrorism Act 2000 (which empowers a constable conducting a search under section 44(1) or 44(2) of that Act to require a person to remove headgear and footwear in public) and under section 60AA of the Criminal Justice and Public Order Act 1994 (which empowers a constable to require a person to remove any item worn to conceal identity). [See *Notes 4* and *6*] A search in public of a person's clothing which has not been removed must be restricted to superficial examination of outer garments. This does not, however, prevent an officer from placing his or her hand inside the pockets of the outer clothing, or feeling round the inside of collars, socks and shoes if this is reasonably necessary in the circumstances to look for the object of the search or to remove and examine any item reasonably suspected to be the object of the search. For the same reasons, subject to the restrictions on the removal of headgear, a person's hair may also be searched in public (see paragraphs 3.1 and 3.3).

3.6 Where on reasonable grounds it is considered necessary to conduct a more thorough search (e.g. by requiring a person to take off a T-shirt), this must be done out of public view, for example, in a police van unless paragraph 3.7 applies, or police station if there is one nearby. [See *Note 6*] Any search involving the removal of more than an outer coat, jacket, gloves, headgear or footwear, or any other item concealing identity, may only be made by an officer of the same sex as the person searched and may not be made in the presence of anyone of the opposite sex unless the person being searched specifically requests it. [See *Notes 4, 7* and *8*]

3.7 Searches involving exposure of intimate parts of the body must not be conducted as a routine extension of a less thorough search, simply because nothing is found in the course of the initial search. Searches involving exposure of intimate parts of the body may be carried out only at a nearby police station or other nearby location which is out of public view (but not a police vehicle). These searches must be conducted in accordance with paragraph 11 of Annex A to Code C except that an intimate search mentioned in paragraph 11(f) of Annex A to Code C may not be authorised or carried out under any stop and search powers. The other provisions of Code C do not apply to the conduct and recording of searches of persons detained at police stations in the exercise of stop and search powers. [See *Note 7*]

Steps to be taken prior to a search

3.8 Before any search of a detained person or attended vehicle takes place the officer must take reasonable steps to give the person to be searched or in charge of the vehicle the following information:

(a) that they are being detained for the purposes of a search

(b) the officer's name (except in the case of enquiries linked to the investigation of terrorism, or otherwise where the officer reasonably believes that giving his or her name might put him or her in danger, in which case a warrant or other identification number shall be given) and the name of the police station to which the officer is attached;

(c) the legal search power which is being exercised; and

(d) a clear explanation of:

(i) the purpose of the search in terms of the article or articles for which there is a power to search; and

(ii) in the case of powers requiring reasonable suspicion (see paragraph 2.1(a)), the grounds for that suspicion; or

(iii) in the case of powers which do not require reasonable suspicion (see paragraph 2.1(b), and (c)), the nature of the power and of any necessary authorisation and the fact that it has been given.

3.9 Officers not in uniform must show their warrant cards. Stops and searches under the powers mentioned in paragraphs 2.1(b), and (c) may be undertaken only by a constable in uniform.

3.10 Before the search takes place the officer must inform the person (or the owner or person in charge of the vehicle that is to be searched) of his or her entitlement to a copy of the record of the search, including his entitlement to a record of the search if an application is made within 12 months, if it is wholly impracticable to make a record at the time. If a record is not made at the time the person should also be told how a copy can be obtained (see section 4). The person should also be given information about police powers to stop and search and the individual's rights in these circumstances.

3.11 If the person to be searched, or in charge of a vehicle to be searched, does not appear to understand what is being said, or there is any doubt about the person's ability to understand English, the officer must take reasonable steps to bring information regarding the person's rights and any relevant provisions of this Code to his or her attention. If the person is deaf or cannot understand English and is accompanied by someone, then the officer must try to establish whether that person can interpret or otherwise help the officer to give the required information.

4. Recording requirements

4.1 An officer who has carried out a search in the exercise of any power to which this Code applies, must make a record of it at the time, unless there are exceptional circumstances which would make this wholly impracticable (e.g. in situations involving public disorder or when the officer's presence is urgently required elsewhere). If a record is not made at the time, the officer must do so as soon as practicable afterwards. There may be situations in which it is not practicable to obtain the information necessary to complete a record, but the officer should make every reasonable effort to do so. [See *Note 21*]

4.2 A copy of a record made at the time must be given immediately to the person who has been searched. The officer must ask for the name, address and date of birth of the person searched, but there is no obligation on a person to provide these details and no power of detention if the person is unwilling to do so.

4.3 The following information must always be included in the record of a search even if the person does not wish to provide any personal details:

(i) the name of the person searched, or (if it is withheld) a description;

(ii) a note of the person's self-defined ethnic background; [See *Note 18*]

(iii) when a vehicle is searched, its registration number; [See *Note 16*]

(iv) the date, time, and place that the person or vehicle was first detained;

(v) the date, time and place the person or vehicle was searched (if different from (iv));

(vi) the purpose of the search;
(vii) the grounds for making it, or in the case of those searches mentioned in paragraph 2.1(b) and (c), the nature of the power and of any necessary authorisation and the fact that it has been given; [See *Note 17*]
(viii) its outcome (e.g. arrest or no further action);
(ix) a note of any injury or damage to property resulting from it;
(x) subject to paragraph 3.8(b), the identity of the officer making the search. [See *Note 15*]

4.4 Nothing in paragraph 4.3 (x) or 4.10A requires the names of police officers to be shown on the search record or any other record required to be made under this code in the case of enquiries linked to the investigation of terrorism or otherwise where an officer reasonably believes that recording names might endanger the officers. In such cases the record must show the officers' warrant or other identification number and duty station.

4.5 A record is required for each person and each vehicle searched. However, if a person is in a vehicle and both are searched, and the object and grounds of the search are the same, only one record need be completed. If more than one person in a vehicle is searched, separate records for each search of a person must be made. If only a vehicle is searched, the name of the driver and his or her self-defined ethnic background must be recorded, unless the vehicle is unattended.

4.6 The record of the grounds for making a search must, briefly but informatively, explain the reason for suspecting the person concerned, by reference to the person's behaviour and/or other circumstances.

4.7 Where officers detain an individual with a view to performing a search, but the search is not carried out due to the grounds for suspicion being eliminated as a result of questioning the person detained, a record must still be made in accordance with the procedure outlined in Paragraph 4.12.

4.8 After searching an unattended vehicle, or anything in or on it, an officer must leave a notice in it (or on it, if things on it have been searched without opening it) recording the fact that it has been searched.

4.9 The notice must include the name of the police station to which the officer concerned is attached and state where a copy of the record of the search may be obtained and where any application for compensation should be directed.

4.10 The vehicle must if practicable be left secure.

4.10A When an officer makes a record of the stop electronically and is unable to produce a copy of the form at the time, the officer must explain how the person can obtain a full copy of the record of the stop or search and give the person a receipt which contains:

- a unique reference number and guidance on how to obtain a full copy of the stop or search;
- the name of the officer who carried out the stop or search (unless paragraph 4.4 applies); and
- the power used to stop and search them. [See *Note 21*]

Recording of encounters not governed by Statutory Powers

4.11 Not used.

4.12 When an officer requests a person in a public place to account for themselves, i.e. their actions, behaviour, presence in an area or possession of anything, a record of the encounter must be completed at the time and a copy given to the person who has been questioned. The record must identify the name of the officer who has made the stop and conducted the encounter. This does not apply under the exceptional circumstances outlined in paragraph 4.1 of this code.

4.13 This requirement does not apply to general conversations such as when giving directions to a place, or when seeking witnesses. It also does not include occasions on which an officer is seeking general information or questioning people to establish background to incidents which have required officers to intervene to keep the peace or resolve a dispute.

4.14 A separate record need not be completed when:

- stopping a person in a vehicle when an HORT/1 form, a Vehicle Defect Rectification Scheme Notice, or aFixed Penalty Notice is issued. It also does not apply when a specimen of breath is required under Section 6 of the Road Traffic Act 1988.
- stopping a person when a Penalty Notice is issued for an offence.

4.15 Officers must inform the person of their entitlement to a copy of a record of the encounter.

4.16 The provisions of paragraph 4.4 of this code apply equally when the encounters described in 4.12 and 4.13 are recorded.

4.17 The following information must be included in the record
(i) the date, time and place of the encounter;
(ii) if the person is in a vehicle, the registration number;
(iii) the reason why the officer questioned that person; [See *Note 17*]

(iv) a note of the person's self-defined ethnic background; [See *Note 18*]
(v) the outcome of the encounter.

4.18 There is no power to require the person questioned to provide personal details. If a person refuses to give their self-defined ethnic background, a form must still be completed, which includes a description of the person's ethnic background. [See Note 18]

4.19 A record of an encounter must always be made when the criteria set out in 4.12 have been met. If the criteria are not met but the person requests a record, the officer should provide a copy of the form but record on it that the encounter did not meet the criteria. The officer can refuse to issue the form if he or she reasonably believes that the purpose of the request is deliberately aimed at frustrating or delaying legitimate police activity. [See *Note 20*]

4.20 All references to officers in this section include police staff designated as Community Support Officers under section 38 of the Police Reform Act 2002.

5. Monitoring and supervising the use of stop and search powers

5.1 Supervising officers must monitor the use of stop and search powers and should consider in particular whether there is any evidence that they are being exercised on the basis of stereotyped images or inappropriate generalisations. Supervising officers should satisfy themselves that the practice of officers under their supervision in stopping, searching and recording is fully in accordance with this Code. Supervisors must also examine whether the records reveal any trends or patterns which give cause for concern, and if so take appropriate action to address this

5.2 Senior officers with area or force-wide responsibilities must also monitor the broader use of stop and search powers and, where necessary, take action at the relevant level.

5.3 Supervision and monitoring must be supported by the compilation of comprehensive statistical records of stops and searches at force, area and local level. Any apparently disproportionate use of the powers by particular officers or groups of officers or in relation to specific sections of the community should be identified and investigated.

5.4 In order to promote public confidence in the use of the powers, forces in consultation with police authorities must make arrangements for the records to be scrutinised by representatives of the community, and to explain the use of the powers at a local level. [See *Note 19*]

Notes for Guidance

Officers exercising stop and search powers

1 This code does not affect the ability of an officer to speak to or question a person in the ordinary course of the officer's duties without detaining the person or exercising any element of compulsion. It is not the purpose of the code to prohibit such encounters between the police and the community with the co-operation of the person concerned and neither does it affect the principle that all citizens have a duty to help police officers to prevent crime and discover offenders. This is a civic rather than a legal duty; but when a police officer is trying to discover whether, or by whom, an offence has been committed he or she may question any person from whom useful information might be obtained, subject to the restrictions imposed by Code C. A person's unwillingness to reply does not alter this entitlement, but in the absence of a power to arrest, or to detain in order to search, the person is free to leave at will and cannot be compelled to remain with the officer.

2 In some circumstances preparatory questioning may be unnecessary, but in general a brief conversation or exchange will be desirable not only as a means of avoiding unsuccessful searches, but to explain the grounds for the stop/search, to gain cooperation and reduce any tension there might be surrounding the stop/search.

3 Where a person is lawfully detained for the purpose of a search, but no search in the event takes place, the detention will not thereby have been rendered unlawful.

4 Many people customarily cover their heads or faces for religious reasons—for example, Muslim women, Sikh men, Sikh or Hindu women, or Rastarfarian men or women. A police officer cannot order the removal of a head or face covering except where there is reason to believe that the item is being worn by the individual wholly or mainly for the purpose of disguising identity, not simply because it disguises identity. Where there may be religious sensitivities about ordering the removal of such an item, the officer should permit the item to be removed out of public view. Where practicable, the item should be removed in the presence of an officer of the same sex as the person and out of sight of anyone of the opposite sex.

5 A search of a person in public should be completed as soon as possible.

6 A person may be detained under a stop and search power at a place other than where the person was first detained, only if that place, be it a police station or elsewhere, is nearby. Such a place should be located within a reasonable travelling distance using whatever mode of travel (on foot or by car) is

appropriate. This applies to all searches under stop and search powers, whether or not they involve the removal of clothing or exposure of intimate parts of the body (see paragraphs 3.6 and 3.7) or take place in or out of public view. It means, for example, that a search under the stop and search power in section 23 of the Misuse of Drugs Act 1971 which involves the compulsory removal of more than a person's outer coat, jacket or gloves cannot be carried out unless a place which is both nearby the place they were first detained and out of public view, is available. If a search involves exposure of intimate parts of the body and a police station is not nearby, particular care must be taken to ensure that the location is suitable in that it enables the search to be conducted in accordance with the requirements of paragraph 11 of Annex A to Code C.

7 A search in the street itself should be regarded as being in public for the purposes of paragraphs 3.6 and 3.7 above, even though it may be empty at the time a search begins. Although there is no power to require a person to do so, there is nothing to prevent an officer from asking a person voluntarily to remove more than an outer coat, jacket or gloves (and headgear or footwear under section 45(3) of the Terrorism Act 2000) in public.

8 Where there may be religious sensitivities about asking someone to remove headgear using a power under section 45(3) of the Terrorism Act 2000, the police officer should offer to carry out the search out of public view (for example, in a police van or police station if there is one nearby).

9 Other means of identification might include jewellery, insignias, tattoos or other features which are known to identify members of the particular gang or group.

Authorising officers

10 The powers under section 60 are separate from and additional to the normal stop and search powers which require reasonable grounds to suspect an individual of carrying an offensive weapon (or other article). Their overall purpose is to prevent serious violence and the widespread carrying of weapons which might lead to persons being seriously injured by disarming potential offenders in circumstances where other powers would not be sufficient. They should not therefore be used to replace or circumvent the normal powers for dealing with routine crime problems. The purpose of the powers under section 60AA is to prevent those involved in intimidatory or violent protests using face coverings to disguise identity.

11 Authorisations under section 60 require a reasonable belief on the part of the authorising officer. This must have an objective basis, for example: intelligence or relevant information such as a history of antagonism and violence between particular groups; previous incidents of violence at, or connected with, particular events or locations; a significant increase in knife-point robberies in a limited area; reports that individuals are regularly carrying weapons in a particular locality; or in the case of section 60AA previous incidents of crimes being committed while wearing face coverings to conceal identity.

12 It is for the authorising officer to determine the period of time during which the powers mentioned in paragraph 2.1 (b) and (c) may be exercised. The officer should set the minimum period he or she considers necessary to deal with the risk of violence, the carrying of knives or offensive weapons, or terrorism. A direction to extend the period authorised under the powers mentioned in paragraph 2.1(b) may be given only once. Thereafter further use of the powers requires a new authorisation. There is no provision to extend an authorisation of the powers mentioned in paragraph 2.1(c); further use of the powers requires a new authorisation.

13 It is for the authorising officer to determine the geographical area in which the use of the powers is to be authorised. In doing so the officer may wish to take into account factors such as the nature and venue of the anticipated incident, the number of people who may be in the immediate area of any possible incident, their access to surrounding areas and the anticipated level of violence. The officer should not set a geographical area which is wider than that he or she believes necessary for the purpose of preventing anticipated violence, the carrying of knives or offensive weapons, acts of terrorism, or, in the case of section 60AA, the prevention of commission of offences. It is particularly important to ensure that constables exercising such powers are fully aware of where they may be used. If the area specified is smaller than the whole force area, the officer giving the authorisation should specify either the streets which form the boundary of the area or a divisional boundary within the force area. If the power is to be used in response to a threat or incident that straddles police force areas, an officer from each of the forces concerned will need to give an authorisation.

14 An officer who has authorised the use of powers under section 44 of the Terrorism Act 2000 must take immediate steps to send a copy of the authorisation to the National Joint Unit, Metropolitan Police Special Branch, who will forward it to the Secretary of State. The Secretary of State should be informed of the reasons for the authorisation. The National Joint Unit will inform the force

concerned, within 48 hours of the authorisation being made, whether the Secretary of State has confirmed or cancelled or altered the authorisation.

Recording

15 Where a stop and search is conducted by more than one officer the identity of all the officers engaged in the search must be recorded on the record. Nothing prevents an officer who is present but not directly involved in searching from completing the record during the course of the encounter.

16 Where a vehicle has not been allocated a registration number (e.g. a rally car or a trials motorbike) that part of the requirement under 4.3(iii) does not apply.

17 It is important for monitoring purposes to specify whether the authority for exercising a stop and search power was given under section 60 of the Criminal Justice and Public Order Act 1994, or under section 44(1) or 44(2) of the Terrorism Act 2000.

18 Officers should record the self-defined ethnicity of every person stopped according to the categories used in the 2001 census question listed in Annex B. Respondents should be asked to select one of the five main categories representing broad ethnic groups and then a more specific cultural background from within this group. The ethnic classification should be coded for recording purposes using the coding system in Annex B. An additional 'Not stated' box is available but should not be offered to respondents explicitly. Officers should be aware and explain to members of the public, especially where concerns are raised, that this information is required to obtain a true picture of stop and search activity and to help improve ethnic monitoring, tackle discriminatory practice, and promote effective use of the powers. If the person gives what appears to the officer to be an 'incorrect' answer (e.g. a person who appears to be white states that they are black), the officer should record the response that has been given. Officers should also record their own perception of the ethnic background of every person stopped and this must be done by using the PNC/Phoenix classification system. If the 'Not stated' category is used the reason for this must be recorded on the form.

19 Arrangements for public scrutiny of records should take account of the right to confidentiality of those stopped and searched. Anonymised forms and/or statistics generated from records should be the focus of the examinations by members of the public.

20 Where an officer engages in conversation which is not pertinent to the actions or whereabouts of the individual (e.g. does not relate to why the person is there, what they are doing or where they have been or are going) then issuing a form would not meet the criteria set out in paragraph 4.12. Situations designed to impede police activity may arise, for example, in public order situations where individuals engage in dialogue with the officer but the officer does not initiate or engage in contact about the person's individual circumstances.

21 In situations where it is not practicable to provide a written record of the stop or stop and search at that time, the officer should consider providing the person with details of the station to which the person may attend for a record. This may take the form of a simple business card, adding the date of the stop or stop and search.

Annex A
Summary of Main Stop and Search Powers

This Table Relates to Stop and Search Powers only. Individual Statutes Below May Contain other Police Powers of Entry, Search and Seizure

Power	Object of Search	Extent of Search	Where Exercisable
Unlawful articles general			
1. Public Stores Act 1875, s6	HM Stores stolen or unlawfully obtained	Persons, vehicles and vessels	Anywhere where the constabulary powers are exercisable
2. Firearms Act 1968, s47	Firearms	Persons and vehicles	A public place, or anywhere in the case of reasonable suspicion of offences of carrying firearms with criminal intent or trespassing with firearms

Power	Object of Search	Extent of Search	Where Exercisable
3. Misuse of Drugs Act 1971, s23	Controlled drugs	Persons and vehicles	Anywhere
4. Customs and Excise Management Act 1979, s163	Goods: (a) on which duty has not been paid; (b) being unlawfully removed, imported or exported; (c) otherwise liable to forfeiture to HM Customs and Excise	Vehicles and vessels only	Anywhere
5. Aviation Security Act 1982, s27(1)	Stolen or unlawfully obtained goods	Airport employees and vehicles carrying airport employees or aircraft or any vehicle in a cargo area whether or not carrying an employee	Any designated airport
6. Police and Criminal Evidence Act 1984, s1	Stolen goods; articles for use in certain Theft Act offences; offensive weapons, including bladed or sharply-pointed articles (except folding pocket knives with a bladed cutting edge not exceeding 3 inches); prohibited possession of a category 4 (display grade) firework, any person under 18 in possession of an adult firework in a public place.	Persons and vehicles	Where there is public access
	Criminal Damage: Articles made, adapted or intended for use in destroying or damaging property	Persons and vehicles	Where there is public access
Police and Criminal Evidence Act 1984, s6(3) (by a constable of the United Kingdom Atomic Energy Authority Constabulary in respect of property owned or controlled by British Nuclear Fuels plc	HM Stores (in the form of goods and chattels belonging to British Nuclear Fuels plc)	Persons, vehicles and vessels	Anywhere where the constabulary powers are exercisable
7. Sporting events (Control of Alcohol etc.) Act 1985, s7	Intoxicating liquor	Persons, coaches and trains	Designated sports grounds or coaches and trains travelling to or from a designated sporting event
8. Crossbows Act 1987, s4	Crossbows or parts of crossbows (except crossbows with a draw weight of less than 1.4 kilograms)	Persons and vehicles	Anywhere except dwellings
9. Criminal Justice Act 1988 s139B	Offensive weapons, bladed or sharply pointed article	Persons	School premises
Evidence of game and wildlife offences			
10. Poaching Prevention Act 1862, s2	Game or poaching equipment	Persons and vehicles	A public place

Power	Object of Search	Extent of Search	Where Exercisable
11. Deer Act 1991, s12	Evidence of offences under the Act	Persons and vehicles	Anywhere except dwellings
12. Conservation of Seals Act 1970, s4	Seals or hunting equipment	Vehicles only	Anywhere
13. Badgers Act 1992, s11	Evidence of offences under the Act	Persons and vehicles	Anywhere
14. Wildlife and Countryside Act 1981, s19	Evidence of wildlife offences	Persons and vehicles	Anywhere except dwellings
Other			
15. Terrorism Act 2000, s.43	*Evidence of liability to arrest under section 14 of the Act*	Persons	Anywhere
16. Terrorism Act 2000, s.44(1)	Articles which could be used for a purpose connected with the commission, preparation or instigation of acts of terrorism	*Vehicles, driver and passengers*	Anywhere within the area or locality authorised under subsection (1)
17. Terrorism Act 2000, s.44(2)	*Articles which could be used for a purpose connected with the commission, preparation or instigation of acts of terrorism*	*Pedestrians*	Anywhere within the area of locality authorised
18. Paragraphs 7 and 8 of Schedule 7 to the Terrorism Act 2000	*Anything relevant to determining if a person being examined falls within paragraph 2(1)(a) to (c) of Schedule 5*	Persons, vehicles, vessels etc.	*Ports and airports*
19. Section 60 Criminal Justice and Public Order Act 1994, *as amended by s.8 of the Knives Act 1997*	Offensive weapons or dangerous instruments to prevent incidents of serious violence *or to deal with the carrying of such items*	Persons and vehicles	Anywhere within a locality authorised under subsection (1)

Annex B

Self-defined Ethnic Classification Categories

White	W
A. White—British	W1
B. White—Irish	W2
C. Any other White background	W9
Mixed	M
D. White and Black Caribbean	M1
E. White and Black African	M2
F. White and Asian	M3
G. Any other Mixed Background	M9
Asian / Asian—British	A
H. Asian—Indian	A1
I. Asian—Pakistani	A2
J. Asian—Bangladeshi	A3
K. Any other Asian background	A9
Black / Black—British	B
L. Black—Caribbean	B1
M. Black African	B2
N. Any other Black background	B9

Other	O
O. Chinese	O1
P. Any other	O9
Not Stated	NS

Annex C
Summary of Powers of Community Support Officers to Search and Seize

The following is a summary of the search and seizure powers that may be exercised by a community support officer (CSO) who has been designated with the relevant powers in accordance with Part 4 of the Police Reform Act 2002.

When exercising any of these powers, a CSO must have regard to any relevant provisions of this Code, including section 3 governing the conduct of searches and the steps to be taken prior to a search.

1. Power to stop and search not requiring consent

Designation	Power conferred	Object of Search	Extent of Search	Where Exercisable
Police Reform Act 2002, Schedule 4, paragraph 15	*(a) Terrorism Act 2000, s.44(1)(a) and (d) and 45(2);*	Items intended to be used in connection with terrorism.	(a) Vehicles or anything carried in or on the vehicle and anything carried by driver or passenger.	Anywhere within area of locality authorised and in the company and under the supervision of a constable.
	(b) Terrorism Act 2000, s.44 (2)(b) and 45(2).		(b) Anything carried by a pedestrian.	

2. Powers to search requiring the consent of the person and seizure

A CSO may detain a person using reasonable force where necessary as set out in Part 1 of Schedule 4 to the Police Reform Act 2002. If the person has been lawfully detained, the CSO may search the person provided that person gives consent to such a search in relation to the following:

Designation	Powers conferred	Object of Search	Extent of Search	Where Exercisable
Police Reform Act 2002, Schedule 4, paragraph 7A	(a) Criminal Justice and Police Act 2001, s12(2)	a) Alcohol or a container for alcohol	a) Persons	a) Designated public place
	(b) Confiscation of Alcohol (Young Persons) Act 1997, s1	b) Alcohol	b) Persons under 18 years old	b) Public place
	(c) Children and Young Persons Act 1933, section 7(3)	(c) Tobacco or cigarette papers	(c) Persons under 16 years old found smoking	(c) Public place

3. Powers to search not requiring the consent of the person and seizure

A CSO may detain a person using reasonable force where necessary as set out in Part 1 of Schedule 4 to the Police Reform Act 2002. If the person has been lawfully detained, the CSO may search the person without the need for that person's consent in relation to the following:

Designation	Power conferred	Object of Search	Extent of Search	Where Exercisable
Police Reform Act 2002, Schedule 4, paragraph 2A	Police and Criminal Evidence Act 1984, s.32	a) Objects that might be used to cause physical injury to the person or the CSO. b) Items that might be used to assist escape.	Persons made subject to a requirement to wait.	Any place where the requirement to wait has been made.

4. Powers to seize without consent

This power applies when drugs are found in the course of any search mentioned above.

Designation	Power conferred	Object of Seizure	Where Exercisable
Police Reform Act 2002, Schedule 4, paragraph 7B	*Police Reform Act 2002, Schedule 4, paragraph 7B*	Controlled drugs in a person's possession.	Any place where the person is in possession of the drug.

PACE CODE B

CODE OF PRACTICE FOR SEARCHES OF PREMISES BY POLICE OFFICERS AND THE SEIZURE OF PROPERTY FOUND BY POLICE OFFICERS ON PERSONS OR PREMISES

Commencement—transitional arrangements

This Code applies to applications for warrants made after midnight 31 December 2005 and to searches and seizures taking place after midnight on 31 December 2005.

1. Introduction

1.1 This Code of Practice deals with police powers to:
- search premises
- seize and retain property found on premises and persons

1.1A These powers may be used to find:
- property and material relating to a crime
- wanted persons
- children who abscond from local authority accommodation where they have been remanded or committed by a court

1.2 A justice of the peace may issue a search warrant granting powers of entry, search and seizure, e.g. warrants to search for stolen property, drugs, firearms and evidence of serious offences. Police also have powers without a search warrant. The main ones provided by the Police and Criminal Evidence Act 1984 (PACE) include powers to search premises:
- to make an arrest
- after an arrest

1.3 The right to privacy and respect for personal property are key principles of the Human Rights Act 1998. Powers of entry, search and seizure should be fully and clearly justified before use because they may significantly interfere with the occupier's privacy. Officers should consider if the necessary objectives can be met by less intrusive means.

1.4 In all cases, police should:
- exercise their powers courteously and with respect for persons and property
- only use reasonable force when this is considered necessary and proportionate to the circumstances

1.5 If the provisions of PACE and this Code are not observed, evidence obtained from a search may be open to question.

2. General

2.1 This Code must be readily available at all police stations for consultation by:

- police officers
- police staff
- detained persons
- members of the public

2.2 The *Notes for Guidance* included are not provisions of this Code.

2.3 This Code applies to searches of premises:

(a) by police for the purposes of an investigation into an alleged offence, with the occupier's consent, other than:
- routine scene of crime searches;
- calls to a fire or burglary made by or on behalf of an occupier or searches following the activation of fire or burglar alarms or discovery of insecure premises;
- searches when *paragraph 5.4* applies;
- bomb threat calls;

(b) under powers conferred on police officers by PACE, sections 17, 18 and 32;

(c) undertaken in pursuance of search warrants issued to and executed by constables in accordance with PACE, sections 15 and 16. See *Note 2A*;

(d) subject to *paragraph 2.6*, under any other power given to police to enter premises with or without a search warrant for any purpose connected with the investigation into an alleged or suspected offence. See *Note 2B*.

For the purposes of this Code, 'premises' as defined in PACE, section 23, includes any place, vehicle, vessel, aircraft, hovercraft, tent or movable structure and any offshore installation as defined in the Mineral Workings (Offshore Installations) Act 1971, section 1. See *Note 2D*

2.4 A person who has not been arrested but is searched during a search of premises should be searched in accordance with Code A. See *Note 2C*

2.5 This Code does not apply to the exercise of a statutory power to enter premises or to inspect goods, equipment or procedures if the exercise of that power is not dependent on the existence of grounds for suspecting that an offence may have been committed and the person exercising the power has no reasonable grounds for such suspicion.

2.6 This Code does not affect any directions of a search warrant or order, lawfully executed in England or Wales that any item or evidence seized under that warrant or order be handed over to a police force, court, tribunal, or other authority outside England or Wales. For example, warrants and orders issued in Scotland or Northern Ireland, see *Note 2B(f)* and search warrants issued under the Criminal Justice (International Co-operation) Act 1990, section 7.

2.7 When this Code requires the prior authority or agreement of an officer of at least inspector or superintendent rank, that authority may be given by a sergeant or chief inspector authorised to perform the functions of the higher rank under PACE, section 107.

2.8 Written records required under this Code not made in the search record shall, unless otherwise specified, be made:
- in the recording officer's pocket book ('pocket book' includes any official report book issued to police officers) or
- on forms provided for the purpose

2.9 Nothing in this Code requires the identity of officers, or anyone accompanying them during a search of premises, to be recorded or disclosed:

(a) in the case of enquiries linked to the investigation of terrorism; or

(b) if officers reasonably believe recording or disclosing their names might put them in danger.

In these cases officers should use warrant or other identification numbers and the name of their police station. Police staff should use any identification number provided to them by the police force. See *Note 2E*

2.10 The 'officer in charge of the search' means the officer assigned specific duties and responsibilities under this Code.Whenever there is a search of premises to which this Code applies one officer must act as the officer in charge of the search. See *Note 2F*

2.11 In this Code:

(a) 'designated person' means a person other than a police officer, designated under the Police Reform Act 2002, Part 4 who has specified powers and duties of police officers conferred or imposed on them. See *Note 2G*.

(b) any reference to a police officer includes a designated person acting in the exercise or performance of the powers and duties conferred or imposed on them by their designation.

(c) a person authorised to accompany police officers or designated persons in the execution of a warrant has the same powers as a constable in the execution of the warrant and the search and seizure of anything related to the warrant. These powers must be exercised in the company and under the supervision of a police officer. See *Note 3C*.

2.12 If a power conferred on a designated person:
   (a) allows reasonable force to be used when exercised by a police officer, a designated person exercising that power has the same entitlement to use force;
   (b) includes power to use force to enter any premises, that power is not exercisable by that designated person except:
      (i) in the company and under the supervision of a police officer; or
      (ii) for the purpose of:
         • saving life or limb; or
         • preventing serious damage to property.

2.13 Designated persons must have regard to any relevant provisions of the Codes of Practice.

Notes for Guidance

2A PACE sections 15 and 16 apply to all search warrants issued to and executed by constables under any enactment, e.g. search warrants issued by a:
   (a) justice of the peace under the:
      • Theft Act 1968, section 26—stolen property;
      • Misuse of Drugs Act 1971, section 23—controlled drugs;
      • PACE, section 8—evidence of an indictable offence;
      • Terrorism Act 2000, Schedule 5, paragraph 1;
   (b) judge of the High Court, a Circuit judge, a Recorder or a District Judge under:
      • PACE, Schedule 1;
      • Terrorism Act 2000, Schedule 5, paragraph 11.

   [Until the Courts Act 2003, s. 65 and sch. 4, para. 16(5) are brought into force, applications under the PACE 1984, sch. 1 or the Terrorism Act 2000, sch. 5 must continue to be made to a Circuit Judge: see Home Office Circular 56/2005.]

2B Examples of the other powers in paragraph 2.3(d) include:
   (a) Road Traffic Act 1988, section 6E(1) giving police power to enter premises under section 6E(1) to:
      • require a person to provide a specimen of breath; or
      • arrest a person following
         — a positive breath test;
         — failure to provide a specimen of breath;
   (b) Transport and Works Act 1992, section 30(4) giving police powers to enter premises mirroring the powers in (a) in relation to specified persons working on transport systems to which the Act applies;
   (c) Criminal Justice Act 1988, section 139B giving police power to enter and search school premises for offensive weapons, bladed or pointed articles;
   (d) Terrorism Act 2000, Schedule 5, paragraphs 3 and 15 empowering a superintendent in urgent cases to give written authority for police to enter and search premises for the purposes of a terrorist investigation;
   (e) Explosives Act 1875, section 73(b) empowering a superintendent to give written authority for police to enter premises, examine and search them for explosives;
   (f) search warrants and production orders or the equivalent issued in Scotland or Northern Ireland endorsed under the Summary Jurisdiction (Process) Act 1881 or the Petty Sessions (Ireland) Act 1851 respectively for execution in England and Wales.

2C The Criminal Justice Act 1988, section 139B provides that a constable who has reasonable grounds to believe an offence under the Criminal Justice Act 1988, section 139A has or is being committed may enter school premises and search the premises and any persons on the premises for any bladed or pointed article or offensive weapon. Persons may be searched under a warrant issued under the Misuse of Drugs Act 1971, section 23(3) to search premises for drugs or documents only if the warrant specifically authorises the search of persons on the premises.

2D The Immigration Act 1971, Part III and Schedule 2 gives immigration officers powers to enter and search premises, seize and retain property, with and without a search warrant. These are similar to the powers available to police under search warrants issued by a justice of the peace and without a warrant under PACE, sections 17, 18, 19 and 32 except they only apply to specified offences under the Immigration Act 1971 and immigration control powers. For certain types of investigations and enquiries these powers avoid the need for the Immigration Service to rely on police officers becoming directly involved. When exercising these powers, immigration officers are required by the

Immigration and Asylum Act 1999, section 145 to have regard to this Code's corresponding provisions. When immigration officers are dealing with persons or property at police stations, police officers should give appropriate assistance to help them discharge their specific duties and responsibilities.

2E The purpose of paragraph 2.9(b) is to protect those involved in serious organised crime investigations or arrests of particularly violent suspects when there is reliable information that those arrested or their associates may threaten or cause harm to the officers or anyone accompanying them during a search of premises. In cases of doubt, an officer of inspector rank or above should be consulted.

2F For the purposes of paragraph 2.10, the officer in charge of the search should normally be the most senior officer present. Some exceptions are:

(a) a supervising officer who attends or assists at the scene of a premises search may appoint an officer of lower rank as officer in charge of the search if that officer is:
- more conversant with the facts;
- a more appropriate officer to be in charge of the search;

(b) when all officers in a premises search are the same rank. The supervising officer if available must make sure one of them is appointed officer in charge of the search, otherwise the officers themselves must nominate one of their number as the officer in charge;

(c) a senior officer assisting in a specialist role. This officer need not be regarded as having a general supervisory role over the conduct of the search or be appointed or expected to act as the officer in charge of the search.

Except in (c), nothing in this Note diminishes the role and responsibilities of a supervisory officer who is present at the search or knows of a search taking place.

2G An officer of the rank of inspector or above may direct a designated investigating officer not to wear a uniform for the purposes of a specific operation.

3. Search warrants and production orders

(a) Before making an application

3.1 When information appears to justify an application, the officer must take reasonable steps to check the information is accurate, recent and not provided maliciously or irresponsibly. An application may not be made on the basis of information from an anonymous source if corroboration has not been sought. See *Note 3A*

3.2 The officer shall ascertain as specifically as possible the nature of the articles concerned and their location.

3.3 The officer shall make reasonable enquiries to:

(i) establish if:
- anything is known about the likely occupier of the premises and the nature of the premises themselves;
- the premises have been searched previously and how recently;

(ii) obtain any other relevant information.

3.4 An application:

(a) to a justice of the peace for a search warrant or to a judge of the High Court, a Circuit judge, a Recorder or a District Judge for a search warrant or production order under PACE, Schedule 1

must be supported by a signed written authority from an officer of inspector rank or above:

Note: If the case is an urgent application to a justice of the peace and an inspector or above is not readily available, the next most senior officer on duty can give the written authority.

[Until the Courts Act 2003, s. 65 and sch. 4, para. 16(5) are brought into force, applications under the PACE 1984, sch. 1 or the Terrorism Act 2000, sch. 5 must continue to be made to a Circuit Judge: see Home Office Circular 56/2005.]

(b) to a circuit judge under the Terrorism Act 2000, Schedule 5 for
- a production order;
- search warrant; or
- an order requiring an explanation of material seized or produced under such a warrant or production order

must be supported by a signed written authority from an officer of superintendent rank or above.

3.5 Except in a case of urgency, if there is reason to believe a search might have an adverse effect on relations between the police and the community, the officer in charge shall consult the local police/community liaison officer:

- before the search; or
- in urgent cases, as soon as practicable after the search

(b) *Making an application*

3.6 A search warrant application must be supported in writing, specifying:
 (a) the enactment under which the application is made, see *Note 2A;*
 (b) (i) whether the warrant is to authorise entry and search of:
  - one set of premises; or
  - if the application is under PACE section 8, or Schedule 1, paragraph 12, more than one set of specified premises or all premises occupied or controlled by a specified person, and

  (ii) the premises to be searched;
 (c) the object of the search, see *Note 3B;*
 (d) the grounds for the application, including, when the purpose of the proposed search is to find evidence of an alleged offence, an indication of how the evidence relates to the investigation;
 (da) where the application is under PACE section 8, or Schedule 1, paragraph 12 for a single warrant to enter and search:
  (i) more than one set of specified premises, the officer must specify each set of premises which it is desired to enter and search
  (ii) all premises occupied or controlled by a specified person, the officer must specify;
  - as many sets of premises which it is desired to enter and search as it is reasonably practicable to specify
  - the person who is in occupation or control of those premises and any others which it is desired to search
  - why it is necessary to search more premises than those which can be specified
  - why it is not reasonably practicable to specify all the premises which it is desired to enter and search

 (db) whether an application under PACE section 8 is for a warrant authorising entry and search on more than one occasion, and if so, the officer must state the grounds for this and whether the desired number of entries authorised is unlimited or a specified maximum.
 (e) there are no reasonable grounds to believe the material to be sought, when making application to a:
  (i) justice of the peace or a judge of the High Court, a Circuit judge, a Recorder or a District Judge, consists of or includes items subject to legal privilege;
  (ii) justice of the peace, consists of or includes excluded material or special procedure material;

 Note: this does not affect the additional powers of seizure in the Criminal Justice and Police Act 2001, Part 2 covered in paragraph 7.7, see Note 3B;
 [Until the Courts Act 2003, s. 65 and sch. 4, para. 16(5) are brought into force, applications under the PACE 1984, sch. 1 or the Terrorism Act 2000, sch. 5 must continue to be made to a Circuit Judge: see Home Office Circular 56/2005.]
 (f) if applicable, a request for the warrant to authorise a person or persons to accompany the officer who executes the warrant, see *Note 3C.*

3.7 A search warrant application under PACE, Schedule 1, paragraph 12(a), shall if appropriate indicate why it is believed service of notice of an application for a production order may seriously prejudice the investigation. Applications for search warrants under the Terrorism Act 2000, Schedule 5, paragraph 11 must indicate why a production order would not be appropriate.

3.8 If a search warrant application is refused, a further application may not be made for those premises unless supported by additional grounds.

Notes for Guidance

3A The identity of an informant need not be disclosed when making an application, but the officer should be prepared to answer any questions the magistrate or judge may have about:
- the accuracy of previous information from that source
- any other related matters

3B The information supporting a search warrant application should be as specific as possible, particularly in relation to the articles or persons being sought and where in the premises it is suspected they may be found. The meaning of 'items subject to legal privilege', 'excluded material' and 'special procedure material' are defined by PACE, sections 10, 11 and 14 respectively.

3C Under PACE, section 16(2), a search warrant may authorise persons other than police officers to accompany the constable who executes the warrant. This includes, e.g. any suitably qualified or skilled person or an expert in a particular field whose presence is needed to help accurately identify the material sought or to advise where certain evidence is most likely to be found and how it should be dealt with. It does not give them any right to force entry, but it gives them the right to be on the premises during the search and to search for or seize property without the occupier's permission.

4. Entry without warrant—particular powers

(a) Making an arrest etc

4.1 The conditions under which an officer may enter and search premises without a warrant are set out in PACE, section 17. It should be noted that this section does not create or confer any powers of arrest. See other powers in *Note 2B(a).*

(b) Search of premises where arrest takes place or the arrested person was immediately before arrest

4.2 When a person has been arrested for an indictable offence, a police officer has power under PACE, section 32 to search the premises where the person was arrested or where the person was immediately before being arrested.

(c) Search of premises occupied or controlled by the arrested person

4.3 The specific powers to search premises occupied or controlled by a person arrested for an indictable offence are set out in PACE, section 18. They may not be exercised, except if section 18(5) applies, unless an officer of inspector rank or above has given written authority. That authority should only be given when the authorising officer is satisfied the necessary grounds exist. If possible the authorising officer should record the authority on the Notice of Powers and Rights and, subject to *paragraph 2.9*, sign the Notice. The record of the grounds for the search and the nature of the evidence sought as required by section 18(7) of the Act should be made in:

- the custody record if there is one, otherwise
- the officer's pocket book, or
- the search record

5. Search with consent

5.1 Subject to *paragraph 5.4*, if it is proposed to search premises with the consent of a person entitled to grant entry the consent must, if practicable, be given in writing on the Notice of Powers and Rights before the search. The officer must make any necessary enquiries to be satisfied the person is in a position to give such consent. See *Notes 5A* and *5B*

5.2 Before seeking consent the officer in charge of the search shall state the purpose of the proposed search and its extent. This information must be as specific as possible, particularly regarding the articles or persons being sought and the parts of the premises to be searched. The person concerned must be clearly informed they are not obliged to consent and anything seized may be produced in evidence. If at the time the person is not suspected of an offence, the officer shall say this when stating the purpose of the search.

5.3 An officer cannot enter and search or continue to search premises under *paragraph 5.1* if consent is given under duress or withdrawn before the search is completed.

5.4 It is unnecessary to seek consent under *paragraphs 5.1* and *5.2* if this would cause disproportionate inconvenience to the person concerned. See *Note 5C*

Notes for Guidance

5A In a lodging house or similar accommodation, every reasonable effort should be made to obtain the consent of the tenant, lodger or occupier. A search should not be made solely on the basis of the landlord's consent unless the tenant, lodger or occupier is unavailable and the matter is urgent.

5B If the intention is to search premises under the authority of a warrant or a power of entry and search without warrant, and the occupier of the premises co-operates in accordance with paragraph 6.4, there is no need to obtain written consent.

5C Paragraph 5.4 is intended to apply when it is reasonable to assume innocent occupiers would agree to, and expect, police to take the proposed action, e.g. if:

- a suspect has fled the scene of a crime or to evade arrest and it is necessary quickly to check surrounding gardens and readily accessible places to see if the suspect is hiding
- police have arrested someone in the night after a pursuit and it is necessary to make a brief check of gardens along the pursuit route to see if stolen or incriminating articles have been discarded

6. Searching premises—general considerations

(a) Time of searches

6.1 Searches made under warrant must be made within three calendar months of the date of the warrant's issue.

6.2 Searches must be made at a reasonable hour unless this might frustrate the purpose of the search.

6.3 When the extent or complexity of a search mean it is likely to take a long time, the officer in charge of the search may consider using the seize and sift powers referred to in *section 7*.

6.3A A warrant under PACE, section 8 may authorise entry to and search of premises on more than one occasion if, on the application, the justice of the peace is satisfied that it is necessary to authorise multiple entries in order to achieve the purpose for which the warrant is issued. No premises may be entered or searched on any subsequent occasions without the prior written authority of an officer of the rank of inspector who is not involved in the investigation. All other warrants authorise entry on one occasion only.

6.3B Where a warrant under PACE section 8, or Schedule 1, paragraph 12 authorises entry to and search of all premises occupied or controlled by a specified person, no premises which are not specified in the warrant may be entered and searched without the prior written authority of an officer of the rank of inspector who is not involved in the investigation.

(b) Entry other than with consent

6.4 The officer in charge of the search shall first try to communicate with the occupier, or any other person entitled to grant access to the premises, explain the authority under which entry is sought and ask the occupier to allow entry, unless:

(i) the search premises are unoccupied;
(ii) the occupier and any other person entitled to grant access are absent;
(iii) there are reasonable grounds for believing that alerting the occupier or any other person entitled to grant access would frustrate the object of the search or endanger officers or other people.

6.5 Unless *sub-paragraph 6.4(iii)* applies, if the premises are occupied the officer, subject to *paragraph 2.9*, shall, before the search begins:

(i) identify him or herself, show their warrant card (if not in uniform) and state the purpose of and grounds for the search;
(ii) identify and introduce any person accompanying the officer on the search (such persons should carry identification for production on request) and briefly describe that person's role in the process.

6.6 Reasonable and proportionate force may be used if necessary to enter premises if the officer in charge of the search is satisfied the premises are those specified in any warrant, or in exercise of the powers described in *paragraphs 4.1* to *4.3*, and if:

(i) the occupier or any other person entitled to grant access has refused entry;
(ii) it is impossible to communicate with the occupier or any other person entitled to grant access; or
(iii) any of the provisions of *paragraph 6.4* apply.

(c) Notice of Powers and Rights

6.7 If an officer conducts a search to which this Code applies the officer shall, unless it is impracticable to do so, provide the occupier with a copy of a Notice in a standard format:

(i) specifying if the search is made under warrant, with consent, or in the exercise of the powers described in *paragraphs 4.1* to *4.3*. Note: the notice format shall provide for authority or consent to be indicated, see *paragraphs 4.3* and *5.1;*
(ii) summarising the extent of the powers of search and seizure conferred by PACE;
(iii) explaining the rights of the occupier, and the owner of the property seized;
(iv) explaining compensation may be payable in appropriate cases for damages caused entering and searching premises, and giving the address to send a compensation application, see *Note 6A;*
(v) stating this Code is available at any police station.

6.8 If the occupier is:

- present, copies of the Notice and warrant shall, if practicable, be given to them before the search begins, unless the officer in charge of the search reasonably believes this would frustrate the object of the search or endanger officers or other people
- not present, copies of the Notice and warrant shall be left in a prominent place on the premises or

appropriate part of the premises and endorsed, subject to *paragraph 2.9* with the name of the officer in charge of the search, the date and time of the search

the warrant shall be endorsed to show this has been done.

(d) Conduct of searches

6.9 Premises may be searched only to the extent necessary to achieve the object of the search, having regard to the size and nature of whatever is sought.

6.9A A search may not continue under:

- a warrant's authority once all the things specified in that warrant have been found
- any other power once the object of that search has been achieved

6.9B No search may continue once the officer in charge of the search is satisfied whatever is being sought is not on the premises. See *Note 6B.* This does not prevent a further search of the same premises if additional grounds come to light supporting a further application for a search warrant or exercise or further exercise of another power. For example, when, as a result of new information, it is believed articles previously not found or additional articles are on the premises.

6.10 Searches must be conducted with due consideration for the property and privacy of the occupier and with no more disturbance than necessary. Reasonable force may be used only when necessary and proportionate because the co-operation of the occupier cannot be obtained or is insufficient for the purpose. See *Note 6C*

6.11 A friend, neighbour or other person must be allowed to witness the search if the occupier wishes unless the officer in charge of the search has reasonable grounds for believing the presence of the person asked for would seriously hinder the investigation or endanger officers or other people. A search need not be unreasonably delayed for this purpose. A record of the action taken should be made on the premises search record including the grounds for refusing the occupier's request.

6.12 A person is not required to be cautioned prior to being asked questions that are solely necessary for the purpose of furthering the proper and effective conduct of a search, see Code C, *paragraph 10.1(c).* For example, questions to discover the occupier of specified premises, to find a key to open a locked drawer or cupboard or to otherwise seek co-operation during the search or to determine if a particular item is liable to be seized.

6.12A If questioning goes beyond what is necessary for the purpose of the exemption in Code C, the exchange is likely to constitute an interview as defined by Code C, *paragraph 11.1A* and would require the associated safeguards included in Code C, *section 10.*

(e) Leaving premises

6.13 If premises have been entered by force, before leaving the officer in charge of the search must make sure they are secure by:

- arranging for the occupier or their agent to be present
- any other appropriate means

(f) Searches under PACE Schedule 1 or the Terrorism Act 2000, Schedule 5

6.14 An officer shall be appointed as the officer in charge of the search, see *paragraph 2.10,* in respect of any search made under a warrant issued under PACE Act 1984, Schedule 1 or the Terrorism Act 2000, Schedule 5. They are responsible for making sure the search is conducted with discretion and in a manner that causes the least possible disruption to any business or other activities carried out on the premises.

6.15 Once the officer in charge of the search is satisfied material may not be taken from the premises without their knowledge, they shall ask for the documents or other records concerned. The officer in charge of the search may also ask to see the index to files held on the premises, and the officers conducting the search may inspect any files which, according to the index, appear to contain the material sought. A more extensive search of the premises may be made only if:

- the person responsible for them refuses to:
  — produce the material sought, or
  — allow access to the index
- it appears the index is:
  — inaccurate, or
  — incomplete
- for any other reason the officer in charge of the search has reasonable grounds for believing such a search is necessary in order to find the material sought

Notes for Guidance

6A Whether compensation is appropriate depends on the circumstances in each case. Compensation for damage caused when effecting entry is unlikely to be appropriate if the search was lawful, and the force used can be shown to be reasonable, proportionate and necessary to effect entry. If the wrong premises are searched by mistake everything possible should be done at the earliest opportunity to allay any sense of grievance and there should normally be a strong presumption in favour of paying compensation.

6B It is important that, when possible, all those involved in a search are fully briefed about any powers to be exercised and the extent and limits within which it should be conducted.

6C In all cases the number of officers and other persons involved in executing the warrant should be determined by what is reasonable and necessary according to the particular circumstances.

7. Seizure and retention of property

(a) Seizure

7.1 Subject to *paragraph 7.2*, an officer who is searching any person or premises under any statutory power or with the consent of the occupier may seize anything:

(a) covered by a warrant

(b) the officer has reasonable grounds for believing is evidence of an offence or has been obtained in consequence of the commission of an offence but only if seizure is necessary to prevent the items being concealed, lost, disposed of, altered, damaged, destroyed or tampered with

(c) covered by the powers in the Criminal Justice and Police Act 2001, Part 2 allowing an officer to seize property from persons or premises and retain it for sifting or examination elsewhere

See *Note 7B*

7.2 No item may be seized which an officer has reasonable grounds for believing to be subject to legal privilege, as defined in PACE, section 10, other than under the Criminal Justice and Police Act 2001, Part 2.

7.3 Officers must be aware of the provisions in the Criminal Justice and Police Act 2001, section 59, allowing for applications to a judicial authority for the return of property seized and the subsequent duty to secure in section 60, see *paragraph 7.12(iii)*.

7.4 An officer may decide it is not appropriate to seize property because of an explanation from the person holding it but may nevertheless have reasonable grounds for believing it was obtained in consequence of an offence by some person. In these circumstances, the officer should identify the property to the holder, inform the holder of their suspicions and explain the holder may be liable to civil or criminal proceedings if they dispose of, alter or destroy the property.

7.5 An officer may arrange to photograph, image or copy, any document or other article they have the power to seize in accordance with *paragraph 7.1*. This is subject to specific restrictions on the examination, imaging or copying of certain property seized under the Criminal Justice and Police Act 2001, Part 2. An officer must have regard to their statutory obligation to retain an original document or other article only when a photograph or copy is not sufficient.

7.6 If an officer considers information stored in any electronic form and accessible from the premises could be used in evidence, they may require the information to be produced in a form:

- which can be taken away and in which it is visible and legible; or
- from which it can readily be produced in a visible and legible form

(b) Criminal Justice and Police Act 2001: Specific procedures for seize and sift powers

7.7 The Criminal Justice and Police Act 2001, Part 2 gives officers limited powers to seize property from premises or persons so they can sift or examine it elsewhere. Officers must be careful they only exercise these powers when it is essential and they do not remove any more material than necessary. The removal of large volumes of material, much of which may not ultimately be retainable, may have serious implications for the owners, particularly when they are involved in business or activities such as journalism or the provision of medical services. Officers must carefully consider if removing copies or images of relevant material or data would be a satisfactory alternative to removing originals. When originals are taken, officers must be prepared to facilitate the provision of copies or images for the owners when reasonably practicable. See *Note 7C*

7.8 Property seized under the Criminal Justice and Police Act 2001, sections 50 or 51 must be kept securely and separately from any material seized under other powers. An examination under section 53 to determine which elements may be retained must be carried out at the earliest practicable time, having due regard to the desirability of allowing the person from whom the property was seized, or a person with an interest in the property, an opportunity of being present or represented at the examination.

7.8A All reasonable steps should be taken to accommodate an interested person's request to be present, provided the request is reasonable and subject to the need to prevent harm to, interference with, or unreasonable delay to the investigatory process. If an examination proceeds in the absence of an interested person who asked to attend or their representative, the officer who exercised the relevant seizure power must give that person a written notice of why the examination was carried out in those circumstances. If it is necessary for security reasons or to maintain confidentiality officers may exclude interested persons from decryption or other processes which facilitate the examination but do not form part of it. See *Note 7D*

7.9 It is the responsibility of the officer in charge of the investigation to make sure property is returned in accordance with sections 53 to 55. Material which there is no power to retain must be:
- separated from the rest of the seized property
- returned as soon as reasonably practicable after examination of all the seized property

7.9A Delay is only warranted if very clear and compelling reasons exist, e.g. the:
- unavailability of the person to whom the material is to be returned
- need to agree a convenient time to return a large volume of material

7.9B Legally privileged, excluded or special procedure material which cannot be retained must be returned:
- as soon as reasonably practicable
- without waiting for the whole examination

7.9C As set out in section 58, material must be returned to the person from whom it was seized, except when it is clear some other person has a better right to it. See *Note 7E*

7.10 When an officer involved in the investigation has reasonable grounds to believe a person with a relevant interest in property seized under section 50 or 51 intends to make an application under section 59 for the return of any legally privileged, special procedure or excluded material, the officer in charge of the investigation should be informed as soon as practicable and the material seized should be kept secure in accordance with section 61. See *Note 7C*

7.11 The officer in charge of the investigation is responsible for making sure property is properly secured. Securing involves making sure the property is not examined, copied, imaged or put to any other use except at the request, or with the consent, of the applicant or in accordance with the directions of the appropriate judicial authority. Any request, consent or directions must be recorded in writing and signed by both the initiator and the officer in charge of the investigation. See *Notes 7F* and *7G*

7.12 When an officer exercises a power of seizure conferred by sections 50 or 51 they shall provide the occupier of the premises or the person from whom the property is being seized with a written notice:

(i) specifying what has been seized under the powers conferred by that section;
(ii) specifying the grounds for those powers;
(iii) setting out the effect of sections 59 to 61 covering the grounds for a person with a relevant interest in seized property to apply to a judicial authority for its return and the duty of officers to secure property in certain circumstances when an application is made;
(iv) specifying the name and address of the person to whom:
  - notice of an application to the appropriate judicial authority in respect of any of the seized property must be given;
  - an application may be made to allow attendance at the initial examination of the property.

7.13 If the occupier is not present but there is someone in charge of the premises, the notice shall be given to them. If no suitable person is available, so the notice will easily be found it should either be:
- left in a prominent place on the premises
- attached to the exterior of the premises

(c) Retention

7.14 Subject to *paragraph 7.15*, anything seized in accordance with the above provisions may be retained only for as long as is necessary. It may be retained, among other purposes:

(i) for use as evidence at a trial for an offence;
(ii) to facilitate the use in any investigation or proceedings of anything to which it is inextricably linked, see *Note 7H*;
(iii) for forensic examination or other investigation in connection with an offence;
(iv) in order to establish its lawful owner when there are reasonable grounds for believing it has been stolen or obtained by the commission of an offence.

7.15 Property shall not be retained under *paragraph 7.14(i), (ii)* or *(iii)* if a copy or image would be sufficient.

(d) Rights of owners etc

7.16 If property is retained, the person who had custody or control of it immediately before seizure must, on request, be provided with a list or description of the property within a reasonable time.

7.17 That person or their representative must be allowed supervised access to the property to examine it or have it photographed or copied, or must be provided with a photograph or copy, in either case within a reasonable time of any request and at their own expense, unless the officer in charge of an investigation has reasonable grounds for believing this would:

(i) prejudice the investigation of any offence or criminal proceedings; or

(ii) lead to the commission of an offence by providing access to unlawful material such as pornography;

A record of the grounds shall be made when access is denied.

Notes for Guidance

7A Any person claiming property seized by the police may apply to a magistrates' court under the Police (Property) Act 1897 for its possession and should, if appropriate, be advised of this procedure.

7B The powers of seizure conferred by PACE, sections 18(2) and 19(3) extend to the seizure of the whole premises when it is physically possible to seize and retain the premises in their totality and practical considerations make seizure desirable. For example, police may remove premises such as tents, vehicles or caravans to a police station for the purpose of preserving evidence.

7C Officers should consider reaching agreement with owners and/or other interested parties on the procedures for examining a specific set of property, rather than awaiting the judicial authority's determination. Agreement can sometimes give a quicker and more satisfactory route for all concerned and minimise costs and legal complexities.

7D What constitutes a relevant interest in specific material may depend on the nature of that material and the circumstances in which it is seized. Anyone with a reasonable claim to ownership of the material and anyone entrusted with its safe keeping by the owner should be considered.

7E Requirements to secure and return property apply equally to all copies, images or other material created because of seizure of the original property.

7F The mechanics of securing property vary according to the circumstances; 'bagging up', i.e. placing material in sealed bags or containers and strict subsequent control of access is the appropriate procedure in many cases.

7G When material is seized under the powers of seizure conferred by PACE, the duty to retain it under the Code of Practice issued under the Criminal Procedure and Investigations Act 1996 is subject to the provisions on retention of seized material in PACE, section 22.

7H Paragraph 7.14 (ii) applies if inextricably linked material is seized under the Criminal Justice and Police Act 2001, sections 50 or 51. Inextricably linked material is material it is not reasonably practicable to separate from other linked material without prejudicing the use of that other material in any investigation or proceedings. For example, it may not be possible to separate items of data held on computer disk without damaging their evidential integrity. Inextricably linked material must not be examined, imaged, copied or used for any purpose other than for proving the source and/or integrity of the linked material.

8. Action after searches

8.1 If premises are searched in circumstances where this Code applies, unless the exceptions in *paragraph 2.3(a)* apply, on arrival at a police station the officer in charge of the search shall make or have made a record of the search, to include:

(i) the address of the searched premises;

(ii) the date, time and duration of the search;

(iii) the authority used for the search:

- if the search was made in exercise of a statutory power to search premises without warrant, the power which was used for the search:
- if the search was made under a warrant or with written consent;

— a copy of the warrant and the written authority to apply for it, see paragraph 3.4; or
— the written consent;

shall be appended to the record or the record shall show the location of the copy warrant or consent.

(iv) subject to *paragraph 2.9*, the names of:
- the officer(s) in charge of the search;
- all other officers and any authorised persons who conducted the search;

(v) the names of any people on the premises if they are known;
(vi) any grounds for refusing the occupier's request to have someone present during the search, see *paragraph 6.11;*
(vii) a list of any articles seized or the location of a list and, if not covered by a warrant, the grounds for their seizure;
(viii) whether force was used, and the reason;
(ix) details of any damage caused during the search, and the circumstances;
(x) if applicable, the reason it was not practicable;
(a) to give the occupier a copy of the Notice of Powers and Rights, see *paragraph 6.7*;
(b) before the search to give the occupier a copy of the Notice, see *paragraph 6.8*;
(xi) when the occupier was not present, the place where copies of the Notice of Powers and Rights and search warrant were left on the premises, see *paragraph 6.8*.

8.2 On each occasion when premises are searched under warrant, the warrant authorising the search on that occasion shall be endorsed to show:
(i) if any articles specified in the warrant were found and the address where found;
(ii) if any other articles were seized;
(iii) the date and time it was executed and if present, the name of the occupier or if the occupier is not present the name of the person in charge of the premises:
(iv) subject to paragraph 2.9, the names of the officers who executed it and any authorised persons who accompanied them;
(v) if a copy, together with a copy of the Notice of Powers and Rights was:
- handed to the occupier; or
- endorsed as required by paragraph 6.8; and left on the premises and where.

8.3 Any warrant shall be returned within three calendar months of its issue or sooner on completion of the search(es) authorised by that warrant, if it was issued by a:
- justice of the peace, to the designated officer for the local justice area in which the justice was acting when issuing the warrant; or
- judge, to the appropriate officer of the court concerned,

9. Search registers

9.1 A search register will be maintained at each sub-divisional or equivalent police station. All search records required under *paragraph 8.1* shall be made, copied, or referred to in the register. See *Note 9A*

Note for Guidance

9A Paragraph 9.1 also applies to search records made by immigration officers. In these cases, a search register must also be maintained at an immigration office. See also *Note 2D*

PACE CODE C
CODE OF PRACTICE FOR THE DETENTION, TREATMENT AND QUESTIONING OF PERSONS BY POLICE OFFICERS

Commencement—transitional arrangements

This Code applies to people in police detention after midnight on 24 July 2006, notwithstanding that their period of detention may have commenced before that time.

1. General

1.1 All persons in custody must be dealt with expeditiously, and released as soon as the need for detention no longer applies.

1.1A A custody officer must perform the functions in this Code as soon as practicable. A custody officer will not be in breach of this Code if delay is justifiable and reasonable steps are taken to prevent unnecessary delay. The custody record shall show when a delay has occurred and the reason. See *Note 1H*

1.2 This Code of Practice must be readily available at all police stations for consultation by:
- police officers
- police staff
- detained persons
- members of the public.

1.3 The provisions of this Code:
- include the *Annexes*
- do not include the *Notes for Guidance.*

1.4 If an officer has any suspicion, or is told in good faith, that a person of any age may be mentally disordered or otherwise mentally vulnerable, in the absence of clear evidence to dispel that suspicion, the person shall be treated as such for the purposes of this Code. See *Note 1G*

1.5 If anyone appears to be under 17, they shall be treated as a juvenile for the purposes of this Code in the absence of clear evidence that they are older.

1.6 If a person appears to be blind, seriously visually impaired, deaf, unable to read or speak or has difficulty orally because of a speech impediment, they shall be treated as such for the purposes of this Code in the absence of clear evidence to the contrary.

1.7 'The appropriate adult' means, in the case of a:

(a) juvenile:
- (i) the parent, guardian or, if the juvenile is in local authority or voluntary organisation care, or is otherwise being looked after under the Children Act 1989, a person representing that authority or organisation;
- (ii) a social worker of a local authority social services department;
- (iii) failing these, some other responsible adult aged 18 or over who is not a police officer or employed by the police.

(b) person who is mentally disordered or mentally vulnerable: See *Note 1D*
- (iv) a relative, guardian or other person responsible for their care or custody;
- (v) someone experienced in dealing with mentally disordered or mentally vulnerable people but who is not a police officer or employed by the police;
- (vi) failing these, some other responsible adult aged 18 or over who is not a police officer or employed by the police.

1.8 If this Code requires a person be given certain information, they do not have to be given it if at the time they are incapable of understanding what is said, are violent or may become violent or in urgent need of medical attention, but they must be given it as soon as practicable.

1.9 References to a custody officer include any:–
- police officer; or
- designated staff custody officer acting in the exercise or performance of the powers and duties conferred or imposed on them by their designation,

performing the functions of a custody officer. See *Note 1J.*

1.9A When this Code requires the prior authority or agreement of an officer of at least inspector or superintendent rank, that authority may be given by a sergeant or chief inspector authorised to perform the functions of the higher rank under the Police and Criminal Evidence Act 1984 (PACE), section 107.

1.10 Subject to *paragraph 1.12,* this Code applies to people in custody at police stations in England and Wales, whether or not they have been arrested, and to those removed to a police station as a place of safety under the Mental Health Act 1983, sections 135 and 136. *Section 15* applies solely to people in police detention, e.g. those brought to a police station under arrest or arrested at a police station for an offence after going there voluntarily.

1.11 People detained under the Terrorism Act 2000, Schedule 8 and section 41 and other provisions of that Act are not subject to any part of this Code. Such persons are subject to the Code of Practice for detention, treatment and questioning of persons by police officers detained under that Act.

1.12 This Code's provisions do not apply to people in custody:
- (i) arrested on warrants issued in Scotland by officers under the Criminal Justice and Public Order Act 1994, section 136(2), or arrested or detained without warrant by officers from a police force in Scotland under section 137(2). In these cases, police powers and duties and the person's rights and entitlements whilst at a police station in England or Wales are the same as those in Scotland;
- (ii) arrested under the Immigration and Asylum Act 1999, section 142(3) in order to have their fingerprints taken;
- (iii) whose detention is authorised by an immigration officer under the Immigration Act 1971;
- (iv) who are convicted or remanded prisoners held in police cells on behalf of the Prison Service under the Imprisonment (Temporary Provisions) Act 1980;
- (v) not used;
- (vi) detained for searches under stop and search powers except as required by Code A.

The provisions on conditions of detention and treatment in *sections 8* and *9* must be considered as the minimum standards of treatment for such detainees.

1.13 In this Code:

(a) 'designated person' means a person other than a police officer, designated under the Police Reform Act 2002, Part 4 who has specified powers and duties of police officers conferred or imposed on them;

(b) reference to a police officer includes a designated person acting in the exercise or performance of the powers and duties conferred or imposed on them by their designation.

1.14 Designated persons are entitled to use reasonable force as follows:–

(a) when exercising a power conferred on them which allows a police officer exercising that power to use reasonable force, a designated person has the same entitlement to use force; and

(b) at other times when carrying out duties conferred or imposed on them that also entitle them to use reasonable force, for example:

- when at a police station carrying out the duty to keep detainees for whom they are responsible under control and to assist any other police officer or designated person to keep any detainee under control and to prevent their escape.
- when securing, or assisting any other police officer or designated person in securing, the detention of a person at a police station.
- when escorting, or assisting any other police officer or designated person in escorting, a detainee within a police station.
- for the purpose of saving life or limb; or
- preventing serious damage to property.

1.15 Nothing in this Code prevents the custody officer, or other officer given custody of the detainee from allowing police staff who are not designated persons to carry out individual procedures or tasks at the police station if the law allows. However, the officer remains responsible for making sure the procedures and tasks are carried out correctly in accordance with the Codes of Practice. Any such person must be:

(a) a person employed by a police authority maintaining a police force and under the control and direction of the Chief Officer of that force;

(b) employed by a person with whom a police authority has a contract for the provision of services relating to persons arrested or otherwise in custody.

1.16 Designated persons and other police staff must have regard to any relevant provisions of the Codes of Practice.

1.17 References to pocket books include any official report book issued to police officers or other police staff.

Notes for Guidance

1A Although certain sections of this Code apply specifically to people in custody at police stations, those there voluntarily to assist with an investigation should be treated with no less consideration, e.g. offered refreshments at appropriate times, and enjoy an absolute right to obtain legal advice or communicate with anyone outside the police station.

1B A person, including a parent or guardian, should not be an appropriate adult if they:

- are
  - — suspected of involvement in the offence
  - — the victim
  - — a witness
  - — involved in the investigation
- received admissions prior to attending to act as the appropriate adult.

Note: If a juvenile's parent is estranged from the juvenile, they should not be asked to act as the appropriate adult if the juvenile expressly and specifically objects to their presence.

1C If a juvenile admits an offence to, or in the presence of, a social worker or member of a youth offending team other than during the time that person is acting as the juvenile's appropriate adult, another appropriate adult should be appointed in the interest of fairness.

1D In the case of people who are mentally disordered or otherwise mentally vulnerable, it may be more satisfactory if the appropriate adult is someone experienced or trained in their care rather than a relative lacking such qualifications. But if the detainee prefers a relative to a better qualified stranger or objects to a particular person their wishes should, if practicable, be respected.

1E A detainee should always be given an opportunity, when an appropriate adult is called to the police station, to consult privately with a solicitor in the appropriate adult's absence if they want. An appropriate adult is not subject to legal privilege.

1F A solicitor or independent custody visitor (formerly a lay visitor) present at the police station in that capacity may not be the appropriate adult.

1G 'Mentally vulnerable' applies to any detainee who, because of their mental state or capacity, may not understand the significance of what is said, of questions or of their replies. 'Mental disorder' is defined in the Mental Health Act 1983, section 1(2) as 'mental illness, arrested or incomplete development of mind, psychopathic disorder and any other disorder or disability of mind'. When the custody officer has any doubt about the mental state or capacity of a detainee, that detainee should be treated as mentally vulnerable and an appropriate adult called.

1H Paragraph 1.1A is intended to cover delays which may occur in processing detainees e.g. if:
- a large number of suspects are brought into the station simultaneously to be placed in custody;
- interview rooms are all being used;
- there are difficulties contacting an appropriate adult, solicitor or interpreter.

1I The custody officer must remind the appropriate adult and detainee about the right to legal advice and record any reasons for waiving it in accordance with section 6.

1J The designation of police staff custody officers applies only in police areas where an order commencing the provisions of the Police Reform Act 2002, section 38 and Schedule 4A, for designating police staff custody officers is in effect.

1K This Code does not affect the principle that all citizens have a duty to help police officers to prevent crime and discover offenders. This is a civic rather than a legal duty; but when a police officer is trying to discover whether, or by whom, an offence has been committed he is entitled to question any person from whom he thinks useful information can be obtained, subject to the restrictions imposed by this Code. A person's declaration that he is unwilling to reply does not alter this entitlement

2. Custody records

2.1A When a person is brought to a police station:
- under arrest;
- is arrested at the police station having attended there voluntarily; or
- attends a police station to answer bail

they should be brought before the custody officer as soon as practicable after their arrival at the station or, if appropriate, following arrest after attending the police station voluntarily. This applies to designated and non-designated police stations. A person is deemed to be 'at a police station' for these purposes if they are within the boundary of any building or enclosed yard which forms part of that police station.

2.1 A separate custody record must be opened as soon as practicable for each person brought to a police station under arrest or arrested at the station having gone there voluntarily or attending a police station in answer to street bail. All information recorded under this Code must be recorded as soon as practicable in the custody record unless otherwise specified. Any audio or video recording made in the custody area is not part of the custody record.

2.2 If any action requires the authority of an officer of a specified rank, subject to *paragraph 2.6A*, their name and rank must be noted in the custody record.

2.3 The custody officer is responsible for the custody record's accuracy and completeness and for making sure the record or copy of the record accompanies a detainee if they are transferred to another police station. The record shall show the:
- time and reason for transfer;
- time a person is released from detention.

2.4 A solicitor or appropriate adult must be permitted to consult a detainee's custody record as soon as practicable after their arrival at the station and at any other time whilst the person is detained. Arrangements for this access must be agreed with the custody officer and may not unreasonably interfere with the custody officer's duties.

2.4A When a detainee leaves police detention or is taken before a court they, their legal representative or appropriate adult shall be given, on request, a copy of the custody record as soon as practicable. This entitlement lasts for 12 months after release.

2.5 The detainee, appropriate adult or legal representative shall be permitted to inspect the original custody record after the detainee has left police detention provided they give reasonable notice of their request. Any such inspection shall be noted in the custody record.

2.6 Subject to *paragraph 2.6A*, all entries in custody records must be timed and signed by the maker. Records entered on computer shall be timed and contain the operator's identification.

2.6A Nothing in this Code requires the identity of officers or other police staff to be recorded or disclosed:
(a) not used;
(b) if the officer or police staff reasonably believe recording or disclosing their name might put them in danger.
In these cases, they shall use their warrant or other identification numbers and the name of their police station. See *Note 2A*

2.7 The fact and time of any detainee's refusal to sign a custody record, when asked in accordance with this Code, must be recorded.

Note for Guidance

2A The purpose of paragraph 2.6A(b) is to protect those involved in serious organised crime investigations or arrests of particularly violent suspects when there is reliable information that those arrested or their associates may threaten or cause harm to those involved. In cases of doubt, an officer of inspector rank or above should be consulted.

3. Initial action

(a) Detained persons—normal procedure

3.1 When a person is brought to a police station under arrest or arrested at the station having gone there voluntarily, the custody officer must make sure the person is told clearly about the following continuing rights which may be exercised at any stage during the period in custody:
(i) the right to have someone informed of their arrest as in *section 5*;
(ii) the right to consult privately with a solicitor and that free independent legal advice is available;
(iii) the right to consult these Codes of Practice. See *Note 3D*

3.2 The detainee must also be given:
- a written notice setting out:
  — the above three rights;
  — the arrangements for obtaining legal advice;
  — the right to a copy of the custody record as in *paragraph 2.4A*;
  — the caution in the terms prescribed in *section 10*.
- an additional written notice briefly setting out their entitlements while in custody, see *Notes 3A* and *3B*.

Note: The detainee shall be asked to sign the custody record to acknowledge receipt of these notices. Any refusal must be recorded on the custody record.

3.3 A citizen of an independent Commonwealth country or a national of a foreign country, including the Republic of Ireland, must be informed as soon as practicable about their rights of communication with their High Commission, Embassy or Consulate. See *section 7*

3.4 The custody officer shall:
- record the offence(s) that the detainee has been arrested for and the reason(s) for the arrest on the custody record. See paragraph 10.3 and Code G paragraphs 2.2 and 4.3.
- note on the custody record any comment the detainee makes in relation to the arresting officer's account but shall not invite comment. If the arresting officer is not physically present when the detainee is brought to a police station, the arresting officer's account must be made available to the custody officer remotely or by a third party on the arresting officer's behalf. If the custody officer authorises a person's detention the detainee must be informed of the grounds as soon as practicable and before they are questioned about any offence;
- note any comment the detainee makes in respect of the decision to detain them but shall not invite comment;
- not put specific questions to the detainee regarding their involvement in any offence, nor in respect of any comments they may make in response to the arresting officer's account or the decision to place them in detention. Such an exchange is likely to constitute an interview as in *paragraph 11.1A* and require the associated safeguards in *section 11*.

See *paragraph 11.13* in respect of unsolicited comments.

3.5 The custody officer shall:
(a) ask the detainee, whether at this time, they:
  (i) would like legal advice, see *paragraph 6.5*;
  (ii) want someone informed of their detention, see *section 5*;
(b) ask the detainee to sign the custody record to confirm their decisions in respect of (*a*);
(c) determine whether the detainee:
  (iii) is, or might be, in need of medical treatment or attention, see *section 9*;

(iv) requires:
- an appropriate adult;
- help to check documentation;
- an interpreter;

(d) record the decision in respect of (*c*).

3.6 When determining these needs the custody officer is responsible for initiating an assessment to consider whether the detainee is likely to present specific risks to custody staff or themselves. Such assessments should always include a check on the Police National Computer, to be carried out as soon as practicable, to identify any risks highlighted in relation to the detainee. Although such assessments are primarily the custody officer's responsibility, it may be necessary for them to consult and involve others, e.g. the arresting officer or an appropriate health care professional, see *paragraph 9.13*. Reasons for delaying the initiation or completion of the assessment must be recorded.

3.7 Chief Officers should ensure that arrangements for proper and effective risk assessments required by *paragraph 3.6* are implemented in respect of all detainees at police stations in their area.

3.8 Risk assessments must follow a structured process which clearly defines the categories of risk to be considered and the results must be incorporated in the detainee's custody record. The custody officer is responsible for making sure those responsible for the detainee's custody are appropriately briefed about the risks. If no specific risks are identified by the assessment, that should be noted in the custody record. See *Note 3E* and *paragraph 9.14*

3.9 The custody officer is responsible for implementing the response to any specific risk assessment, e.g.:
- reducing opportunities for self harm;
- calling a health care professional;
- increasing levels of monitoring or observation.

3.10 Risk assessment is an ongoing process and assessments must always be subject to review if circumstances change.

3.11 If video cameras are installed in the custody area, notices shall be prominently displayed showing cameras are in use. Any request to have video cameras switched off shall be refused.

(b) Detained persons—special groups

3.12 If the detainee appears deaf or there is doubt about their hearing or speaking ability or ability to understand English, and the custody officer cannot establish effective communication, the custody officer must, as soon as practicable, call an interpreter for assistance in the action under *paragraphs 3.1–3.5*. See *section 13*

3.13 If the detainee is a juvenile, the custody officer must, if it is practicable, ascertain the identity of a person responsible for their welfare. That person:
- may be:
  - — the parent or guardian;
  - — if the juvenile is in local authority or voluntary organisation care, or is otherwise being looked after under the Children Act 1989, a person appointed by that authority or organisation to have responsibility for the juvenile's welfare;
  - — any other person who has, for the time being, assumed responsibility for the juvenile's welfare.
- must be informed as soon as practicable that the juvenile has been arrested, why they have been arrested and where they are detained. This right is in addition to the juvenile's right in *section 5* not to be held incommunicado. See *Note 3C*

3.14 If a juvenile is known to be subject to a court order under which a person or organisation is given any degree of statutory responsibility to supervise or otherwise monitor them, reasonable steps must also be taken to notify that person or organisation (the 'responsible officer'). The responsible officer will normally be a member of a Youth Offending Team, except for a curfew order which involves electronic monitoring when the contractor providing the monitoring will normally be the responsible officer.

3.15 If the detainee is a juvenile, mentally disordered or otherwise mentally vulnerable, the custody officer must, as soon as practicable:
- inform the appropriate adult, who in the case of a juvenile may or may not be a person responsible for their welfare, as in *paragraph 3.13*, of:
  - — the grounds for their detention;
  - — their whereabouts.
- ask the adult to come to the police station to see the detainee.

3.16 It is imperative that a mentally disordered or otherwise mentally vulnerable person, detained under the Mental Health Act 1983, section 136, be assessed as soon as possible. If that assessment is to take place at the police station, an approved social worker and a registered medical practitioner shall be called to the station as soon as possible in order to interview and examine the detainee. Once the detainee has been interviewed, examined and suitable arrangements made for their treatment or care, they can no longer be detained under section 136. A detainee must be immediately discharged from detention under section 136 if a registered medical practitioner, having examined them, concludes they are not mentally disordered within the meaning of the Act.

3.17 If the appropriate adult is:
- already at the police station, the provisions of *paragraphs 3.1* to *3.5* must be complied with in the appropriate adult's presence;
- not at the station when these provisions are complied with, they must be complied with again in the presence of the appropriate adult when they arrive.

3.18 The detainee shall be advised that:
- the duties of the appropriate adult include giving advice and assistance;
- they can consult privately with the appropriate adult at any time.

3.19 If the detainee, or appropriate adult on the detainee's behalf, asks for a solicitor to be called to give legal advice, the provisions of *section 6* apply.

3.20 If the detainee is blind, seriously visually impaired or unable to read, the custody officer shall make sure their solicitor, relative, appropriate adult or some other person likely to take an interest in them and not involved in the investigation is available to help check any documentation. When this Code requires written consent or signing the person assisting may be asked to sign instead, if the detainee prefers. This paragraph does not require an appropriate adult to be called solely to assist in checking and signing documentation for a person who is not a juvenile, or mentally disordered or otherwise mentally vulnerable (see *paragraph 3.15*).

(c) Persons attending a police station voluntarily

3.21 Anybody attending a police station voluntarily to assist with an investigation may leave at will unless arrested. See *Note 1K*. If it is decided they shall not be allowed to leave, they must be informed at once that they are under arrest and brought before the custody officer, who is responsible for making sure they are notified of their rights in the same way as other detainees. If they are not arrested but are cautioned as in *section 10*, the person who gives the caution must, at the same time, inform them they are not under arrest, they are not obliged to remain at the station but if they remain at the station they may obtain free and independent legal advice if they want. They shall be told the right to legal advice includes the right to speak with a solicitor on the telephone and be asked if they want to do so.

3.22 If a person attending the police station voluntarily asks about their entitlement to legal advice, they shall be given a copy of the notice explaining the arrangements for obtaining legal advice. See *paragraph 3.2*

(d) Documentation

3.23 The grounds for a person's detention shall be recorded, in the person's presence if practicable.

3.24 Action taken under *paragraphs 3.12* to *3.20* shall be recorded.

(e) Persons answering street bail

3.25 When a person is answering street bail, the custody officer should link any documentation held in relation to arrest with the custody record. Any further action shall be recorded on the custody record in accordance with *paragraphs 3.23* and *3.24* above.

Notes for Guidance

3A The notice of entitlements should:
- list the entitlements in this Code, including:
  - visits and contact with outside parties, including special provisions for Commonwealth citizens and foreign nationals;
  - reasonable standards of physical comfort;
  - adequate food and drink;
  - access to toilets and washing facilities, clothing, medical attention, and exercise when practicable.
- mention the:
  - provisions relating to the conduct of interviews;
  - circumstances in which an appropriate adult should be available to assist the detainee and their statutory rights to make representation whenever the period of their detention is reviewed.

3B In addition to notices in English, translations should be available in Welsh, the main minority ethnic languages and the principal European languages, whenever they are likely to be helpful. Audio versions of the notice should also be made available.

3C If the juvenile is in local authority or voluntary organisation care but living with their parents or other adults responsible for their welfare, although there is no legal obligation to inform them, they should normally be contacted, as well as the authority or organisation unless suspected of involvement in the offence concerned. Even if the juvenile is not living with their parents, consideration should be given to informing them.

3D The right to consult the Codes of Practice does not entitle the person concerned to delay unreasonably any necessary investigative or administrative action whilst they do so. Examples of action which need not be delayed unreasonably include:
- procedures requiring the provision of breath, blood or urine specimens under the Road Traffic Act 1988 or the Transport and Works Act 1992;
- searching detainees at the police station;
- taking fingerprints, footwear impressions or non-intimate samples without consent for evidential purposes.

3E Home Office Circular 32/2000 provides more detailed guidance on risk assessments and identifies key risk areas which should always be considered.

4. Detainee's property

(a) Action

4.1 The custody officer is responsible for:
(a) ascertaining what property a detainee:
(i) has with them when they come to the police station, whether on:
- arrest or re-detention on answering to bail;
- commitment to prison custody on the order or sentence of a court;
- lodgement at the police station with a view to their production in court from prison custody;
- transfer from detention at another station or hospital;
- detention under the Mental Health Act 1983, section 135 or 136;
- remand into police custody on the authority of a court

(ii) might have acquired for an unlawful or harmful purpose while in custody;
(b) the safekeeping of any property taken from a detainee which remains at the police station.

The custody officer may search the detainee or authorise their being searched to the extent they consider necessary, provided a search of intimate parts of the body or involving the removal of more than outer clothing is only made as in *Annex A.* A search may only be carried out by an officer of the same sex as the detainee. See *Note 4A*

4.2 Detainees may retain clothing and personal effects at their own risk unless the custody officer considers they may use them to cause harm to themselves or others, interfere with evidence, damage property, effect an escape or they are needed as evidence. In this event the custody officer may withhold such articles as they consider necessary and must tell the detainee why.

4.3 Personal effects are those items a detainee may lawfully need, use or refer to while in detention but do not include cash and other items of value.

(b) Documentation

4.4 It is a matter for the custody officer to determine whether a record should be made of the property a detained person has with him or had taken from him on arrest. Any record made is not required to be kept as part of the custody record but the custody record should be noted as to where such a record exists. Whenever a record is made the detainee shall be allowed to check and sign the record of property as correct. Any refusal to sign shall be recorded.

4.5 If a detainee is not allowed to keep any article of clothing or personal effects, the reason must be recorded.

Notes for Guidance

4A PACE, Section 54(1) and paragraph 4.1 require a detainee to be searched when it is clear the custody officer will have continuing duties in relation to that detainee or when that detainee's behaviour or offence makes an inventory appropriate. They do not require every detainee to be searched, e.g. if it is clear a person will only be detained for a short period and is not to be placed in a cell, the custody officer may decide not to search them. In such a case the custody record will be endorsed 'not searched', paragraph 4.4 will not apply, and the detainee will be invited to sign the entry. If the detainee refuses, the custody officer will be obliged to ascertain what property they have in accordance with paragraph 4.1.

4B Paragraph 4.4 does not require the custody officer to record on the custody record property in the detainee's possession on arrest if, by virtue of its nature, quantity or size, it is not practicable to remove it to the police station.

4C Paragraph 4.4 does not require items of clothing worn by the person be recorded unless withheld by the custody officer as in paragraph 4.2.

5. Right not to be held incommunicado

(a) Action

5.1 Any person arrested and held in custody at a police station or other premises may, on request, have one person known to them or likely to take an interest in their welfare informed at public expense of their whereabouts as soon as practicable. If the person cannot be contacted the detainee may choose up to two alternatives. If they cannot be contacted, the person in charge of detention or the investigation has discretion to allow further attempts until the information has been conveyed. See *Notes 5C* and *5D*

5.2 The exercise of the above right in respect of each person nominated may be delayed only in accordance with *Annex B*.

5.3 The above right may be exercised each time a detainee is taken to another police station.

5.4 The detainee may receive visits at the custody officer's discretion. See *Note 5B*

5.5 If a friend, relative or person with an interest in the detainee's welfare enquires about their whereabouts, this information shall be given if the suspect agrees and *Annex B* does not apply. See *Note 5D*

5.6 The detainee shall be given writing materials, on request, and allowed to telephone one person for a reasonable time, see *Notes 5A* and *5E*. Either or both these privileges may be denied or delayed if an officer of inspector rank or above considers sending a letter or making a telephone call may result in any of the consequences in:

(a) *Annex B paragraphs 1* and *2* and the person is detained in connection with an indictable offence;

(b) Not used.

Nothing in this paragraph permits the restriction or denial of the rights in *paragraphs 5.1* and *6.1*.

5.7 Before any letter or message is sent, or telephone call made, the detainee shall be informed that what they say in any letter, call or message (other than in a communication to a solicitor) may be read or listened to and may be given in evidence. A telephone call may be terminated if it is being abused. The costs can be at public expense at the custody officer's discretion.

5.7A Any delay or denial of the rights in this section should be proportionate and should last no longer than necessary.

(b) Documentation

5.8 A record must be kept of any:

(a) request made under this section and the action taken;

(b) letters, messages or telephone calls made or received or visit received;

(c) refusal by the detainee to have information about them given to an outside enquirer. The detainee must be asked to countersign the record accordingly and any refusal recorded.

Notes for Guidance

5A A person may request an interpreter to interpret a telephone call or translate a letter.

5B At the custody officer's discretion, visits should be allowed when possible, subject to having sufficient personnel to supervise a visit and any possible hindrance to the investigation.

5C If the detainee does not know anyone to contact for advice or support or cannot contact a friend or relative, the custody officer should bear in mind any local voluntary bodies or other organisations who might be able to help. Paragraph 6.1 applies if legal advice is required.

5D In some circumstances it may not be appropriate to use the telephone to disclose information under paragraphs 5.1 and 5.5.

5E The telephone call at paragraph 5.6 is in addition to any communication under paragraphs 5.1 and 6.1.

6. Right to legal advice

(a) Action

6.1 Unless *Annex B* applies, all detainees must be informed that they may at any time consult and communicate privately with a solicitor, whether in person, in writing or by telephone, and that free independent legal advice is available from the duty solicitor. See *paragraph 3.1, Note 6B* and *Note 6J*

6.2 Not used

6.3 A poster advertising the right to legal advice must be prominently displayed in the charging area of every police station. See *Note 6H*

6.4 No police officer should, at any time, do or say anything with the intention of dissuading a detainee from obtaining legal advice.

6.5 The exercise of the right of access to legal advice may be delayed only as in *Annex B*. Whenever legal advice is requested, and unless *Annex B* applies, the custody officer must act without delay to secure the provision of such advice. If, on being informed or reminded of this right, the detainee declines to speak to a solicitor in person, the officer should point out that the right includes the right to speak with a solicitor on the telephone. If the detainee continues to waive this right the officer should ask them why and any reasons should be recorded on the custody record or the interview record as appropriate. Reminders of the right to legal advice must be given as in *paragraphs 3.5, 11.2, 15.4, 16.4, 2B of Annex A, 3 of Annex K* and *16.5* and Code D, *paragraphs 3.17(ii)* and *6.3*. Once it is clear a detainee does not want to speak to a solicitor in person or by telephone they should cease to be asked their reasons. See *Note 6K*

6.5A In the case of a juvenile, an appropriate adult should consider whether legal advice from a solicitor is required. If the juvenile indicates that they do not want legal advice, the appropriate adult has the right to ask for a solicitor to attend if this would be in the best interests of the person. However, the detained person cannot be forced to see the solicitor if he is adamant that he does not wish to do so.

6.6 A detainee who wants legal advice may not be interviewed or continue to be interviewed until they have received such advice unless:

(a) *Annex B* applies, when the restriction on drawing adverse inferences from silence in *Annex C* will apply because the detainee is not allowed an opportunity to consult a solicitor; or

(b) an officer of superintendent rank or above has reasonable grounds for believing that:

(i) the consequent delay might:

- lead to interference with, or harm to, evidence connected with an offence;
- lead to interference with, or physical harm to, other people;
- lead to serious loss of, or damage to, property;
- lead to alerting other people suspected of having committed an offence but not yet arrested for it;
- hinder the recovery of property obtained in consequence of the commission of an offence.

(ii) when a solicitor, including a duty solicitor, has been contacted and has agreed to attend, awaiting their arrival would cause unreasonable delay to the process of investigation.

Note: In these cases the restriction on drawing adverse inferences from silence in *Annex C* will apply because the detainee is not allowed an opportunity to consult a solicitor;

(c) the solicitor the detainee has nominated or selected from a list:

(i) cannot be contacted;

(ii) has previously indicated they do not wish to be contacted; or

(iii) having been contacted, has declined to attend; and

the detainee has been advised of the Duty Solicitor Scheme but has declined to ask for the duty solicitor.

In these circumstances the interview may be started or continued without further delay provided an officer of inspector rank or above has agreed to the interview proceeding.

Note: The restriction on drawing adverse inferences from silence in *Annex C* will not apply because the detainee is allowed an opportunity to consult the duty solicitor;

(d) the detainee changes their mind, about wanting legal advice.

In these circumstances the interview may be started or continued without delay provided that:

(i) the detainee agrees to do so, in writing or on the interview record made in accordance with Code E or F; and

(ii) an officer of inspector rank or above has inquired about the detainee's reasons for their change of mind and gives authority for the interview to proceed.

Confirmation of the detainee's agreement, their change of mind, the reasons for it if given and, subject to *paragraph 2.6A*, the name of the authorising officer shall be recorded in the written interview record or the interview record made in accordance with Code E or F. See *Note 6I*

Note: In these circumstances the restriction on drawing adverse inferences from silence in *Annex C* will not apply because the detainee is allowed an opportunity to consult a solicitor if they wish.

6.7 If *paragraph 6.6(b)(i)* applies, once sufficient information has been obtained to avert the risk, questioning must cease until the detainee has received legal advice unless *paragraph 6.6(a), (b)(ii), (c)* or *(d)* applies.

6.8 A detainee who has been permitted to consult a solicitor shall be entitled on request to have the solicitor present when they are interviewed unless one of the exceptions in *paragraph 6.6* applies.

6.9 The solicitor may only be required to leave the interview if their conduct is such that the interviewer is unable properly to put questions to the suspect. See *Notes 6D and 6E*

6.10 If the interviewer considers a solicitor is acting in such a way, they will stop the interview and consult an officer not below superintendent rank, if one is readily available, and otherwise an officer not below inspector rank not connected with the investigation. After speaking to the solicitor, the officer consulted will decide if the interview should continue in the presence of that solicitor. If they decide it should not, the suspect will be given the opportunity to consult another solicitor before the interview continues and that solicitor given an opportunity to be present at the interview. See *Note 6E*

6.11 The removal of a solicitor from an interview is a serious step and, if it occurs, the officer of superintendent rank or above who took the decision will consider if the incident should be reported to the Law Society. If the decision to remove the solicitor has been taken by an officer below superintendent rank, the facts must be reported to an officer of superintendent rank or above who will similarly consider whether a report to the Law Society would be appropriate. When the solicitor concerned is a duty solicitor, the report should be both to the Law Society and to the Legal Services Commission.

6.12 'Solicitor' in this Code means:

- a solicitor who holds a current practising certificate
- an accredited or probationary representative included on the register of representatives maintained by the Legal Services Commission.

6.12A An accredited or probationary representative sent to provide advice by, and on behalf of, a solicitor shall be admitted to the police station for this purpose unless an officer of inspector rank or above considers such a visit will hinder the investigation and directs otherwise. Hindering the investigation does not include giving proper legal advice to a detainee as in *Note 6D*. Once admitted to the police station, *paragraphs 6.6* to *6.10* apply.

6.13 In exercising their discretion under *paragraph 6.12A*, the officer should take into account in particular:

- whether:
  - — the identity and status of an accredited or probationary representative have been satisfactorily established;
  - — they are of suitable character to provide legal advice, e.g. a person with a criminal record is unlikely to be suitable unless the conviction was for a minor offence and not recent.
- any other matters in any written letter of authorisation provided by the solicitor on whose behalf the person is attending the police station. See *Note 6F*

6.14 If the inspector refuses access to an accredited or probationary representative or a decision is taken that such a person should not be permitted to remain at an interview, the inspector must notify the solicitor on whose behalf the representative was acting and give them an opportunity to make alternative arrangements. The detainee must be informed and the custody record noted.

6.15 If a solicitor arrives at the station to see a particular person, that person must, unless *Annex B* applies, be so informed whether or not they are being interviewed and asked if they would like to see the solicitor. This applies even if the detainee has declined legal advice or, having requested it, subsequently agreed to be interviewed without receiving advice. The solicitor's attendance and the detainee's decision must be noted in the custody record.

(b) Documentation

6.16 Any request for legal advice and the action taken shall be recorded.

6.17 A record shall be made in the interview record if a detainee asks for legal advice and an interview is begun either in the absence of a solicitor or their representative, or they have been required to leave an interview.

Notes for Guidance

6A In considering if paragraph 6.6(b) applies, the officer should, if practicable, ask the solicitor for an estimate of how long it will take to come to the station and relate this to the time detention is permitted, the time of day (i.e. whether the rest period under paragraph 12.2 is imminent) and the requirements of other investigations. If the solicitor is on their way or is to set off immediately, it will not normally be appropriate to begin an interview before they arrive. If it appears necessary to begin an interview before the solicitor's arrival, they should be given an indication of how long the police would be able to wait before 6.6(b) applies so there is an opportunity to make arrangements for someone else to provide legal advice.

6B A detainee who asks for legal advice should be given an opportunity to consult a specific solicitor or another solicitor from that solicitor's firm or the duty solicitor. If advice is not available by these means, or they do not want to consult the duty solicitor, the detainee should be given an opportunity to choose a solicitor from a list of those willing to provide legal advice. If this solicitor is unavailable, they may choose up to two alternatives. If these attempts are unsuccessful, the custody officer has discretion to allow further attempts until a solicitor has been contacted and agrees to provide legal advice. Apart from carrying out these duties, an officer must not advise the suspect about any particular firm of solicitors.

6C Not used

6D A detainee has a right to free legal advice and to be represented by a solicitor. The solicitor's only role in the police station is to protect and advance the legal rights of their client. On occasions this may require the solicitor to give advice which has the effect of the client avoiding giving evidence which strengthens a prosecution case. The solicitor may intervene in order to seek clarification, challenge an improper question to their client or the manner in which it is put, advise their client not to reply to particular questions, or if they wish to give their client further legal advice. Paragraph 6.9 only applies if the solicitor's approach or conduct prevents or unreasonably obstructs proper questions being put to the suspect or the suspect's response being recorded. Examples of unacceptable conduct include answering questions on a suspect's behalf or providing written replies for the suspect to quote.

6E An officer who takes the decision to exclude a solicitor must be in a position to satisfy the court the decision was properly made. In order to do this they may need to witness what is happening.

6F If an officer of at least inspector rank considers a particular solicitor or firm of solicitors is persistently sending probationary representatives who are unsuited to provide legal advice, they should inform an officer of at least superintendent rank, who may wish to take the matter up with the Law Society.

6G Subject to the constraints of Annex B, a solicitor may advise more than one client in an investigation if they wish. Any question of a conflict of interest is for the solicitor under their professional code of conduct. If, however, waiting for a solicitor to give advice to one client may lead to unreasonable delay to the interview with another, the provisions of paragraph 6.6(b) may apply.

6H In addition to a poster in English, a poster or posters containing translations into Welsh, the main minority ethnic languages and the principal European languages should be displayed wherever they are likely to be helpful and it is practicable to do so.

6I Paragraph 6.6(d) requires the authorisation of an officer of inspector rank or above to the continuation of an interview when a detainee who wanted legal advice changes their mind. It is permissible for such authorisation to be given over the telephone, if the authorising officer is able to satisfy themselves about the reason for the detainee's change of mind and is satisfied it is proper to continue the interview in those circumstances.

6J Whenever a detainee exercises their right to legal advice by consulting or communicating with a solicitor, they must be allowed to do so in private. This right to consult or communicate in private is fundamental. If the requirement for privacy is compromised because what is said or written by the detainee or solicitor for the purpose of giving and receiving legal advice is overheard, listened to, or read by others without the informed consent of the detainee, the right will effectively have been denied. When a detainee chooses to speak to a solicitor on the telephone, they should be allowed to do so in private unless this is impractical because of the design and layout of the custody area or the location of telephones. However, the normal expectation should be that facilities will be available, unless they are being used, at all police stations to enable detainees to speak in private to a solicitor either face to face or over the telephone.

6K A detainee is not obliged to give reasons for declining legal advice and should not be pressed to do so.

7. Citizens of independent Commonwealth countries or foreign nationals

(a) Action

7.1 Any citizen of an independent Commonwealth country or a national of a foreign country, including the Republic of Ireland, may communicate at any time with the appropriate High Commission, Embassy or Consulate. The detainee must be informed as soon as practicable of:
- this right;
- their right, upon request, to have their High Commission, Embassy or Consulate told of their whereabouts and the grounds for their detention. Such a request should be acted upon as soon as practicable.

7.2 If a detainee is a citizen of a country with which a bilateral consular convention or agreement is in force requiring notification of arrest, the appropriate High Commission, Embassy or Consulate shall be informed as soon as practicable, subject to *paragraph 7.4*. The countries to which this applies as at 1 April 2003 are listed in *Annex F.*

7.3 Consular officers may visit one of their nationals in police detention to talk to them and, if required, to arrange for legal advice. Such visits shall take place out of the hearing of a police officer.

7.4 Notwithstanding the provisions of consular conventions, if the detainee is a political refugee whether for reasons of race, nationality, political opinion or religion, or is seeking political asylum, consular officers shall not be informed of the arrest of one of their nationals or given access or information about them except at the detainee's express request.

(b) Documentation

7.5 A record shall be made when a detainee is informed of their rights under this section and of any communications with a High Commission, Embassy or Consulate.

Note for Guidance

7A The exercise of the rights in this section may not be interfered with even though Annex B applies.

8. Conditions of detention

(a) Action

8.1 So far as it is practicable, not more than one detainee should be detained in each cell.

8.2 Cells in use must be adequately heated, cleaned and ventilated. They must be adequately lit, subject to such dimming as is compatible with safety and security to allow people detained overnight to sleep. No additional restraints shall be used within a locked cell unless absolutely necessary and then only restraint equipment, approved for use in that force by the Chief Officer, which is reasonable and necessary in the circumstances having regard to the detainee's demeanour and with a view to ensuring their safety and the safety of others. If a detainee is deaf, mentally disordered or otherwise mentally vulnerable, particular care must be taken when deciding whether to use any form of approved restraints.

8.3 Blankets, mattresses, pillows and other bedding supplied shall be of a reasonable standard and in a clean and sanitary condition. See *Note 8A*

8.4 Access to toilet and washing facilities must be provided.

8.5 If it is necessary to remove a detainee's clothes for the purposes of investigation, for hygiene, health reasons or cleaning, replacement clothing of a reasonable standard of comfort and cleanliness shall be provided. A detainee may not be interviewed unless adequate clothing has been offered.

8.6 At least two light meals and one main meal should be offered in any 24 hour period. See *Note 8B.* Drinks should be provided at meal times and upon reasonable request between meals. Whenever necessary, advice shall be sought from the appropriate health care professional, see *Note 9A*, on medical and dietary matters. As far as practicable, meals provided shall offer a varied diet and meet any specific dietary needs or religious beliefs the detainee may have. The detainee may, at the custody officer's discretion, have meals supplied by their family or friends at their expense. See *Note 8A*

8.7 Brief outdoor exercise shall be offered daily if practicable.

8.8 A juvenile shall not be placed in a police cell unless no other secure accommodation is available and the custody officer considers it is not practicable to supervise them if they are not placed in a cell or that a cell provides more comfortable accommodation than other secure accommodation in the station. A juvenile may not be placed in a cell with a detained adult.

(b) Documentation

8.9 A record must be kept of replacement clothing and meals offered.

8.10 If a juvenile is placed in a cell, the reason must be recorded.

8.11 The use of any restraints on a detainee whilst in a cell, the reasons for it and, if appropriate, the arrangements for enhanced supervision of the detainee whilst so restrained, shall be recorded. See *paragraph 3.9*

Notes for Guidance

8A The provisions in paragraph 8.3 and 8.6 respectively are of particular importance in the case of a person likely to be detained for an extended period. In deciding whether to allow meals to be supplied by family or friends, the custody officer is entitled to take account of the risk of items being concealed in any food or package and the officer's duties and responsibilities under food handling legislation.

8B Meals should, so far as practicable, be offered at recognised meal times, or at other times that take account of when the detainee last had a meal.

9. Care and treatment of detained persons

(a) General

9.1 Nothing in this section prevents the police from calling the police surgeon or, if appropriate, some other health care professional, to examine a detainee for the purposes of obtaining evidence relating to any offence in which the detainee is suspected of being involved. See *Note 9A*

9.2 If a complaint is made by, or on behalf of, a detainee about their treatment since their arrest, or it comes to notice that a detainee may have been treated improperly, a report must be made as soon as practicable to an officer of inspector rank or above not connected with the investigation. If the matter concerns a possible assault or the possibility of the unnecessary or unreasonable use of force, an appropriate health care professional must also be called as soon as practicable.

9.3 Detainees should be visited at least every hour. If no reasonably foreseeable risk was identified in a risk assessment, see *paragraphs 3.6–3.10*, there is no need to wake a sleeping detainee. Those suspected of being intoxicated through drink or drugs or having swallowed drugs, see *Note 9CA*, or whose level of consciousness causes concern must, subject to any clinical directions given by the appropriate health care professional, see *paragraph 9.13*:

- be visited and roused at least every half hour
- have their condition assessed as in *Annex H*
- and clinical treatment arranged if appropriate

See *Notes 9B, 9C* and *9H*

9.4 When arrangements are made to secure clinical attention for a detainee, the custody officer must make sure all relevant information which might assist in the treatment of the detainee's condition is made available to the responsible health care professional. This applies whether or not the health care professional asks for such information. Any officer or police staff with relevant information must inform the custody officer as soon as practicable.

(b) Clinical treatment and attention

9.5 The custody officer must make sure a detainee receives appropriate clinical attention as soon as reasonably practicable if the person:

(a) appears to be suffering from physical illness; or
(b) is injured; or
(c) appears to be suffering from a mental disorder;
(d) appears to need clinical attention.

9.5A This applies even if the detainee makes no request for clinical attention and whether or not they have already received clinical attention elsewhere. If the need for attention appears urgent, e.g. when indicated as in *Annex H*, the nearest available health care professional or an ambulance must be called immediately.

9.5B The custody officer must also consider the need for clinical attention as set out in Note for Guidance 9C in relation to those suffering the effects of alcohol or drugs.

9.6 *Paragraph 9.5* is not meant to prevent or delay the transfer to a hospital if necessary of a person detained under the Mental Health Act 1983, section 136. See *Note 9D*. When an assessment under that Act takes place at a police station, see *paragraph 3.16*, the custody officer must consider whether an appropriate health care professional should be called to conduct an initial clinical check on the detainee. This applies particularly when there is likely to be any significant delay in the arrival of a suitably qualified medical practitioner.

9.7 If it appears to the custody officer, or they are told, that a person brought to a station under arrest may be suffering from an infectious disease or condition, the custody officer must take reasonable steps to safeguard the health of the detainee and others at the station. In deciding what action to take, advice must be sought from an appropriate health care professional. See *Note 9E*. The custody officer has discretion to isolate the person and their property until clinical directions have been obtained.

9.8 If a detainee requests a clinical examination, an appropriate health care professional must be called as soon as practicable to assess the detainee's clinical needs. If a safe and appropriate care plan cannot be provided, the police surgeon's advice must be sought. The detainee may also be examined by a medical practitioner of their choice at their expense.

9.9 If a detainee is required to take or apply any medication in compliance with clinical directions prescribed before their detention, the custody officer must consult the appropriate health care professional before the use of the medication. Subject to the restrictions in *paragraph 9.10*, the custody officer is responsible for the safekeeping of any medication and for making sure the detainee is given the opportunity to take or apply prescribed or approved medication. Any such consultation and its outcome shall be noted in the custody record.

9.10 No police officer may administer or supervise the self-administration of medically prescribed controlled drugs of the types and forms listed in the Misuse of Drugs Regulations 2001, Schedule 2 or 3. A detainee may only self-administer such drugs under the personal supervision of the registered medical practitioner authorising their use. Drugs listed in Schedule 4 or 5 may be distributed by the custody officer for self-administration if they have consulted the registered medical practitioner authorising their use, this may be done by telephone, and both parties are satisfied self-administration will not expose the detainee, police officers or anyone else to the risk of harm or injury.

9.11 When appropriate health care professionals administer drugs or other medications, or supervise their self-administration, it must be within current medicines legislation and the scope of practice as determined by their relevant professional body.

9.12 If a detainee has in their possession, or claims to need, medication relating to a heart condition, diabetes, epilepsy or a condition of comparable potential seriousness then, even though *paragraph 9.5* may not apply, the advice of the appropriate health care professional must be obtained.

9.13 Whenever the appropriate health care professional is called in accordance with this section to examine or treat a detainee, the custody officer shall ask for their opinion about:

- any risks or problems which police need to take into account when making decisions about the detainee's continued detention;
- when to carry out an interview if applicable; and
- the need for safeguards.

9.14 When clinical directions are given by the appropriate health care professional, whether orally or in writing, and the custody officer has any doubts or is in any way uncertain about any aspect of the directions, the custody officer shall ask for clarification. It is particularly important that directions concerning the frequency of visits are clear, precise and capable of being implemented. See *Note 9F*.

(c) Documentation

9.15 A record must be made in the custody record of:

(a) the arrangements made for an examination by an appropriate health care professional under *paragraph 9.2* and of any complaint reported under that paragraph together with any relevant remarks by the custody officer;

(b) any arrangements made in accordance with *paragraph 9.5*;

(c) any request for a clinical examination under *paragraph 9.8* and any arrangements made in response;

(d) the injury, ailment, condition or other reason which made it necessary to make the arrangements in *(a)* to *(c)*, see *Note 9G*;

(e) any clinical directions and advice, including any further clarifications, given to police by a health care professional concerning the care and treatment of the detainee in connection with any of the arrangements made in *(a)* to *(c)*, see *Note 9F*;

(f) if applicable, the responses received when attempting to rouse a person using the procedure in *Annex H*, see *Note 9H*.

9.16 If a health care professional does not record their clinical findings in the custody record, the record must show where they are recorded. See *Note 9G*. However, information which is necessary to custody staff to ensure the effective ongoing care and well being of the detainee must be recorded openly in the custody record, see *paragraph 3.8* and *Annex G, paragraph 7*.

9.17 Subject to the requirements of *Section 4*, the custody record shall include:

- a record of all medication a detainee has in their possession on arrival at the police station;
- a note of any such medication they claim to need but do not have with them.

Notes for Guidance

9A A 'health care professional' means a clinically qualified person working within the scope of practice as determined by their relevant professional body. Whether a health care professional is 'appropriate' depends on the circumstances of the duties they carry out at the time.

9B Whenever possible juveniles and mentally vulnerable detainees should be visited more frequently.

9C A detainee who appears drunk or behaves abnormally may be suffering from illness, the effects of drugs or may have sustained injury, particularly a head injury which is not apparent. A detainee needing or dependent on certain drugs, including alcohol, may experience harmful effects within a short time of being deprived of their supply. In these circumstances, when there is any doubt, police should always act urgently to call an appropriate health care professional or an ambulance. Paragraph 9.5 does not apply to minor ailments or injuries which do not need attention. However, all such ailments or injuries must be recorded in the custody record and any doubt must be resolved in favour of calling the appropriate health care professional.

9CA Paragraph 9.3 would apply to a person in police custody by order of a magistrates' court under the Criminal Justice Act 1988, section 152 (as amended by the Drugs Act 2005, section 8) to facilitate the recovery of evidence after being charged with drug possession or drug trafficking and suspected of having swallowed drugs. In the case of the health care needs of a person who has swallowed drugs, the custody officer subject to any clinical directions, should consider the necessity for rousing every half hour. This does not negate the need for regular visiting of the suspect in the cell.

9D Whenever practicable, arrangements should be made for persons detained for assessment under the Mental Health Act 1983, section 136 to be taken to a hospital. There is no power under that Act to transfer a person detained under section 136 from one place of safety to another place of safety for assessment.

9E It is important to respect a person's right to privacy and information about their health must be kept confidential and only disclosed with their consent or in accordance with clinical advice when it is necessary to protect the detainee's health or that of others who come into contact with them.

9F The custody officer should always seek to clarify directions that the detainee requires constant observation or supervision and should ask the appropriate health care professional to explain precisely what action needs to be taken to implement such directions.

9G Paragraphs 9.15 and 9.16 do not require any information about the cause of any injury, ailment or condition to be recorded on the custody record if it appears capable of providing evidence of an offence.

9H The purpose of recording a person's responses when attempting to rouse them using the procedure in Annex H is to enable any change in the individual's consciousness level to be noted and clinical treatment arranged if appropriate.

10. Cautions

(a) When a caution must be given

10.1 A person whom there are grounds to suspect of an offence, see *Note 10A*, must be cautioned before any questions about an offence, or further questions if the answers provide the grounds for suspicion, are put to them if either the suspect's answers or silence, (i.e. failure or refusal to answer or answer satisfactorily) may be given in evidence to a court in a prosecution. A person need not be cautioned if questions are for other necessary purposes, e.g.:

(a) solely to establish their identity or ownership of any vehicle;

(b) to obtain information in accordance with any relevant statutory requirement, see *paragraph 10.9*;

(c) in furtherance of the proper and effective conduct of a search, e.g. to determine the need to search in the exercise of powers of stop and search or to seek cooperation while carrying out a search;

(d) to seek verification of a written record as in *paragraph 11.13*;

(e) not used.

10.2 Whenever a person not under arrest is initially cautioned, or reminded they are under caution, that person must at the same time be told they are not under arrest and are free to leave if they want to. See *Note 10C*

10.3 A person who is arrested, or further arrested, must be informed at the time, or as soon as practicable thereafter, that they are under arrest and the grounds for their arrest, see *paragraph 3.4, Note 10B* and *Code G, paragraphs 2.2* and *4.3*.

10.4 As per *Code G, section 3*, a person who is arrested, or further arrested, must also be cautioned unless:

(a) it is impracticable to do so by reason of their condition or behaviour at the time;
(b) they have already been cautioned immediately prior to arrest as in *paragraph 10.1*.

(b) Terms of the cautions

10.5 The caution which must be given on:
(a) arrest;
(b) all other occasions before a person is charged or informed they may be prosecuted, see *section 16*,
should, unless the restriction on drawing adverse inferences from silence applies, see *Annex C*, be in the following terms:

'You do not have to say anything. But it may harm your defence if you do not mention when questioned something which you later rely on in Court. Anything you do say may be given in evidence.'

See *Note 10G*

10.6 *Annex C, paragraph 2* sets out the alternative terms of the caution to be used when the restriction on drawing adverse inferences from silence applies.

10.7 Minor deviations from the words of any caution given in accordance with this Code do not constitute a breach of this Code, provided the sense of the relevant caution is preserved. See *Note 10D*

10.8 After any break in questioning under caution, the person being questioned must be made aware they remain under caution. If there is any doubt the relevant caution should be given again in full when the interview resumes. See *Note 10E*

10.9 When, despite being cautioned, a person fails to co-operate or to answer particular questions which may affect their immediate treatment, the person should be informed of any relevant consequences and that those consequences are not affected by the caution. Examples are when a person's refusal to provide:
- their name and address when charged may make them liable to detention;
- particulars and information in accordance with a statutory requirement, e.g. under the Road Traffic Act 1988, may amount to an offence or may make the person liable to a further arrest.

(c) Special warnings under the Criminal Justice and Public Order Act 1994, sections 36 and 37

10.10 When a suspect interviewed at a police station or authorised place of detention after arrest fails or refuses to answer certain questions, or to answer satisfactorily, after due warning, see *Note 10F*, a court or jury may draw such inferences as appear proper under the Criminal Justice and Public Order Act 1994, sections 36 and 37. Such inferences may only be drawn when:
(a) the restriction on drawing adverse inferences from silence, see *Annex C*, does not apply; and
(b) the suspect is arrested by a constable and fails or refuses to account for any objects, marks or substances, or marks on such objects found:
- on their person;
- in or on their clothing or footwear;
- otherwise in their possession; or
- in the place they were arrested;

(c) the arrested suspect was found by a constable at a place at or about the time the offence for which that officer has arrested them is alleged to have been committed, and the suspect fails or refuses to account for their presence there.

When the restriction on drawing adverse inferences from silence applies, the suspect may still be asked to account for any of the matters in (*b*) or (*c*) but the special warning described in *paragraph 10.11* will not apply and must not be given.

10.11 For an inference to be drawn when a suspect fails or refuses to answer a question about one of these matters or to answer it satisfactorily, the suspect must first be told in ordinary language:
(a) what offence is being investigated;
(b) what fact they are being asked to account for;
(c) this fact may be due to them taking part in the commission of the offence;
(d) a court may draw a proper inference if they fail or refuse to account for this fact;
(e) a record is being made of the interview and it may be given in evidence if they are brought to trial.

(d) Juveniles and persons who are mentally disordered or otherwise mentally vulnerable

10.12 If a juvenile or a person who is mentally disordered or otherwise mentally vulnerable is cautioned in the absence of the appropriate adult, the caution must be repeated in the adult's presence.

(e) Documentation

10.13 A record shall be made when a caution is given under this section, either in the interviewer's pocket book or in the interview record.

Notes for Guidance

10A There must be some reasonable, objective grounds for the suspicion, based on known facts or information which are relevant to the likelihood the offence has been committed and the person to be questioned committed it.

10B An arrested person must be given sufficient information to enable them to understand that they have been deprived of their liberty and the reason they have been arrested, e.g. when a person is arrested on suspicion of committing an offence they must be informed of the suspected offence's nature, when and where it was committed. The suspect must also be informed of the reason or reasons why the arrest is considered necessary. Vague or technical language should be avoided.

10C The restriction on drawing inferences from silence, see Annex C, paragraph 1, does not apply to a person who has not been detained and who therefore cannot be prevented from seeking legal advice if they want, see paragraph 3.21.

10D If it appears a person does not understand the caution, the person giving it should explain it in their own words.

10E It may be necessary to show to the court that nothing occurred during an interview break or between interviews which influenced the suspect's recorded evidence. After a break in an interview or at the beginning of a subsequent interview, the interviewing officer should summarise the reason for the break and confirm this with the suspect.

10F The Criminal Justice and Public Order Act 1994, sections 36 and 37 apply only to suspects who have been arrested by a constable or Customs and Excise officer and are given the relevant warning by the police or customs officer who made the arrest or who is investigating the offence. They do not apply to any interviews with suspects who have not been arrested.

10G Nothing in this Code requires a caution to be given or repeated when informing a person not under arrest they may be prosecuted for an offence. However, a court will not be able to draw any inferences under the Criminal Justice and Public Order Act 1994, section 34, if the person was not cautioned.

11. Interviews—general

(a) Action

11.1A An interview is the questioning of a person regarding their involvement or suspected involvement in a criminal offence or offences which, under *paragraph 10.1,* must be carried out under caution. Whenever a person is interviewed they must be informed of the nature of the offence, or further offence. Procedures under the Road Traffic Act 1988, section 7 or the Transport and Works Act 1992, section 31 do not constitute interviewing for the purpose of this Code.

11.1 Following a decision to arrest a suspect, they must not be interviewed about the relevant offence except at a police station or other authorised place of detention, unless the consequent delay would be likely to:

(a) lead to:
- interference with, or harm to, evidence connected with an offence;
- interference with, or physical harm to, other people; or
- serious loss of, or damage to, property;

(b) lead to alerting other people suspected of committing an offence but not yet arrested for it; or

(c) hinder the recovery of property obtained in consequence of the commission of an offence.

Interviewing in any of these circumstances shall cease once the relevant risk has been averted or the necessary questions have been put in order to attempt to avert that risk.

11.2 Immediately prior to the commencement or re-commencement of any interview at a police station or other authorised place of detention, the interviewer should remind the suspect of their entitlement to free legal advice and that the interview can be delayed for legal advice to be obtained, unless one of the exceptions in *paragraph 6.6* applies. It is the interviewer's responsibility to make sure all reminders are recorded in the interview record.

11.3 Not used.

11.4 At the beginning of an interview the interviewer, after cautioning the suspect, see *section 10,* shall put to them any significant statement or silence which occurred in the presence and hearing of a police officer or other police staff before the start of the interview and which have not been put to the suspect in the course of a previous interview. See *Note 11A.* The interviewer shall ask the suspect whether they confirm or deny that earlier statement or silence and if they want to add anything.

11.4A A significant statement is one which appears capable of being used in evidence against the suspect, in particular a direct admission of guilt. A significant silence is a failure or refusal to answer a question or answer satisfactorily when under caution, which might, allowing for the restriction on drawing adverse inferences from silence, see *Annex C*, give rise to an inference under the Criminal Justice and Public Order Act 1994, Part III.

11.5 No interviewer may try to obtain answers or elicit a statement by the use of oppression. Except as in *paragraph 10.9*, no interviewer shall indicate, except to answer a direct question, what action will be taken by the police if the person being questioned answers questions, makes a statement or refuses to do either. If the person asks directly what action will be taken if they answer questions, make a statement or refuse to do either, the interviewer may inform them what action the police propose to take provided that action is itself proper and warranted.

11.6 The interview or further interview of a person about an offence with which that person has not been charged or for which they have not been informed they may be prosecuted, must cease when:

(a) the officer in charge of the investigation is satisfied all the questions they consider relevant to obtaining accurate and reliable information about the offence have been put to the suspect, this includes allowing the suspect an opportunity to give an innocent explanation and asking questions to test if the explanation is accurate and reliable, e.g. to clear up ambiguities or clarify what the suspect said;

(b) the officer in charge of the investigation has taken account of any other available evidence; and

(c) the officer in charge of the investigation, or in the case of a detained suspect, the custody officer, see paragraph 16.1, reasonably believes there is sufficient evidence to provide a realistic prospect of conviction for that offence. See *Note 11B*

This paragraph does not prevent officers in revenue cases or acting under the confiscation provisions of the Criminal Justice Act 1988 or the Drug Trafficking Act 1994 from inviting suspects to complete a formal question and answer record after the interview is concluded.

(b) Interview records

11.7 (a) An accurate record must be made of each interview, whether or not the interview takes place at a police station

(b) The record must state the place of interview, the time it begins and ends, any interview breaks and, subject to *paragraph 2.6A*, the names of all those present; and must be made on the forms provided for this purpose or in the interviewer's pocket book or in accordance with the Codes of Practice E or F;

(c) Any written record must be made and completed during the interview, unless this would not be practicable or would interfere with the conduct of the interview, and must constitute either a verbatim record of what has been said or, failing this, an account of the interview which adequately and accurately summarises it.

11.8 If a written record is not made during the interview it must be made as soon as practicable after its completion.

11.9 Written interview records must be timed and signed by the maker.

11.10 If a written record is not completed during the interview the reason must be recorded in the interview record.

11.11 Unless it is impracticable, the person interviewed shall be given the opportunity to read the interview record and to sign it as correct or to indicate how they consider it inaccurate. If the person interviewed cannot read or refuses to read the record or sign it, the senior interviewer present shall read it to them and ask whether they would like to sign it as correct or make their mark or to indicate how they consider it inaccurate. The interviewer shall certify on the interview record itself what has occurred. See *Note 11E*

11.12 If the appropriate adult or the person's solicitor is present during the interview, they should also be given an opportunity to read and sign the interview record or any written statement taken down during the interview.

11.13 A written record shall be made of any comments made by a suspect, including unsolicited comments, which are outside the context of an interview but which might be relevant to the offence. Any such record must be timed and signed by the maker. When practicable the suspect shall be given the opportunity to read that record and to sign it as correct or to indicate how they consider it inaccurate. See *Note 11E*

11.14 Any refusal by a person to sign an interview record when asked in accordance with this Code must itself be recorded.

(c) Juveniles and mentally disordered or otherwise mentally vulnerable people

11.15 A juvenile or person who is mentally disordered or otherwise mentally vulnerable must not be interviewed regarding their involvement or suspected involvement in a criminal offence or offences, or asked to provide or sign a written statement under caution or record of interview, in the absence of the appropriate adult unless *paragraphs 11.1, 11.18* to *11.20* apply. See *Note 11C*

11.16 Juveniles may only be interviewed at their place of education in exceptional circumstances and only when the principal or their nominee agrees. Every effort should be made to notify the parent(s) or other person responsible for the juvenile's welfare and the appropriate adult, if this is a different person, that the police want to interview the juvenile and reasonable time should be allowed to enable the appropriate adult to be present at the interview. If awaiting the appropriate adult would cause unreasonable delay, and unless the juvenile is suspected of an offence against the educational establishment, the principal or their nominee can act as the appropriate adult for the purposes of the interview.

11.17 If an appropriate adult is present at an interview, they shall be informed:

- they are not expected to act simply as an observer; and
- the purpose of their presence is to:
  — advise the person being interviewed;
  — observe whether the interview is being conducted properly and fairly;
  — facilitate communication with the person being interviewed.

(d) Vulnerable suspects—urgent interviews at police stations

11.18 The following persons may not be interviewed unless an officer of superintendent rank or above considers delay will lead to the consequences in *paragraph 11.1(a)* to *(c)*, and is satisfied the interview would not significantly harm the person's physical or mental state (see *Annex G*):

(a) a juvenile or person who is mentally disordered or otherwise mentally vulnerable if at the time of the interview the appropriate adult is not present;

(b) anyone other than in *(a)* who at the time of the interview appears unable to:
- appreciate the significance of questions and their answers; or
- understand what is happening because of the effects of drink, drugs or any illness, ailment or condition;

(c) a person who has difficulty understanding English or has a hearing disability, if at the time of the interview an interpreter is not present.

11.19 These interviews may not continue once sufficient information has been obtained to avert the consequences in *paragraph 11.1(a)* to *(c)*.

11.20 A record shall be made of the grounds for any decision to interview a person under *paragraph 11.18*.

Notes for Guidance

11A Paragraph 11.4 does not prevent the interviewer from putting significant statements and silences to a suspect again at a later stage or a further interview.

11B The Criminal Procedure and Investigations Act 1996 Code of Practice, paragraph 3.4 states 'In conducting an investigation, the investigator should pursue all reasonable lines of enquiry, whether these point towards or away from the suspect. What is reasonable will depend on the particular circumstances.' Interviewers should keep this in mind when deciding what questions to ask in an interview.

11C Although juveniles or people who are mentally disordered or otherwise mentally vulnerable are often capable of providing reliable evidence, they may, without knowing or wishing to do so, be particularly prone in certain circumstances to provide information that may be unreliable, misleading or self-incriminating. Special care should always be taken when questioning such a person, and the appropriate adult should be involved if there is any doubt about a person's age, mental state or capacity. Because of the risk of unreliable evidence it is also important to obtain corroboration of any facts admitted whenever possible.

11D Juveniles should not be arrested at their place of education unless this is unavoidable. When a juvenile is arrested at their place of education, the principal or their nominee must be informed.

11E Significant statements described in paragraph 11.4 will always be relevant to the offence and must be recorded. When a suspect agrees to read records of interviews and other comments and sign them as correct, they should be asked to endorse the record with, e.g. 'I agree that this is a correct record of what was said' and add their signature. If the suspect does not agree with the record, the interviewer should record the details of any disagreement and ask the suspect to read these details and sign them to the effect that they accurately reflect their disagreement. Any refusal to sign should be recorded.

12. Interviews in police stations

(a) Action

12.1 If a police officer wants to interview or conduct enquiries which require the presence of a detainee, the custody officer is responsible for deciding whether to deliver the detainee into the officer's custody.

12.2 Except as below, in any period of 24 hours a detainee must be allowed a continuous period of at least 8 hours for rest, free from questioning, travel or any interruption in connection with the investigation concerned. This period should normally be at night or other appropriate time which takes account of when the detainee last slept or rested. If a detainee is arrested at a police station after going there voluntarily, the period of 24 hours runs from the time of their arrest and not the time of arrival at the police station. The period may not be interrupted or delayed, except:

(a) when there are reasonable grounds for believing not delaying or interrupting the period would:
   (i) involve a risk of harm to people or serious loss of, or damage to, property;
   (ii) delay unnecessarily the person's release from custody;
   (iii) otherwise prejudice the outcome of the investigation;

(b) at the request of the detainee, their appropriate adult or legal representative;

(c) when a delay or interruption is necessary in order to:
   (i) comply with the legal obligations and duties arising under *section 15*;
   (ii) to take action required under *section 9* or in accordance with medical advice.

If the period is interrupted in accordance with *(a)*, a fresh period must be allowed. Interruptions under *(b)* and *(c)*, do not require a fresh period to be allowed.

12.3 Before a detainee is interviewed the custody officer, in consultation with the officer in charge of the investigation and appropriate health care professionals as necessary, shall assess whether the detainee is fit enough to be interviewed. This means determining and considering the risks to the detainee's physical and mental state if the interview took place and determining what safeguards are needed to allow the interview to take place. See *Annex G.* The custody officer shall not allow a detainee to be interviewed if the custody officer considers it would cause significant harm to the detainee's physical or mental state.Vulnerable suspects listed at *paragraph 11.18* shall be treated as always being at some risk during an interview and these persons may not be interviewed except in accordance with *paragraphs 11.18* to *11.20.*

12.4 As far as practicable interviews shall take place in interview rooms which are adequately heated, lit and ventilated.

12.5 A suspect whose detention without charge has been authorised under PACE, because the detention is necessary for an interview to obtain evidence of the offence for which they have been arrested, may choose not to answer questions but police do not require the suspect's consent or agreement to interview them for this purpose. If a suspect takes steps to prevent themselves being questioned or further questioned, e.g. by refusing to leave their cell to go to a suitable interview room or by trying to leave the interview room, they shall be advised their consent or agreement to interview is not required. The suspect shall be cautioned as in *section 10,* and informed if they fail or refuse to co-operate, the interview may take place in the cell and that their failure or refusal to co-operate may be given in evidence. The suspect shall then be invited to co-operate and go into the interview room.

12.6 People being questioned or making statements shall not be required to stand.

12.7 Before the interview commences each interviewer shall, subject to *paragraph 2.6A,* identify themselves and any other persons present to the interviewee.

12.8 Breaks from interviewing should be made at recognised meal times or at other times that take account of when an interviewee last had a meal. Short refreshment breaks shall be provided at approximately two hour intervals, subject to the interviewer's discretion to delay a break if there are reasonable grounds for believing it would:

(i) involve a:
   - risk of harm to people;
   - serious loss of, or damage to, property;

(ii) unnecessarily delay the detainee's release;

(iii) otherwise prejudice the outcome of the investigation.

See *Note 12B*

12.9 If during the interview a complaint is made by or on behalf of the interviewee concerning the provisions of this Code, the interviewer should:

(i) record it in the interview record;

(ii) inform the custody officer, who is then responsible for dealing with it as in *section 9.*

(b) Documentation

12.10 A record must be made of the:
- time a detainee is not in the custody of the custody officer, and why
- reason for any refusal to deliver the detainee out of that custody

12.11 A record shall be made of:
(a) the reasons it was not practicable to use an interview room; and
(b) any action taken as in *paragraph 12.5*.
The record shall be made on the custody record or in the interview record for action taken whilst an interview record is being kept, with a brief reference to this effect in the custody record.

12.12 Any decision to delay a break in an interview must be recorded, with reasons, in the interview record.

12.13 All written statements made at police stations under caution shall be written on forms provided for the purpose.

12.14 All written statements made under caution shall be taken in accordance with *Annex D*. Before a person makes a written statement under caution at a police station they shall be reminded about the right to legal advice. See *Note 12A*

Notes for Guidance

12A It is not normally necessary to ask for a written statement if the interview was recorded in writing and the record signed in accordance with paragraph 11.11 or audibly or visually recorded in accordance with Code E or F. Statements under caution should normally be taken in these circumstances only at the person's express wish. A person may however be asked if they want to make such a statement.

12B Meal breaks should normally last at least 45 minutes and shorter breaks after two hours should last at least 15 minutes. If the interviewer delays a break in accordance with paragraph 12.8 and prolongs the interview, a longer break should be provided. If there is a short interview, and another short interview is contemplated, the length of the break may be reduced if there are reasonable grounds to believe this is necessary to avoid any of the consequences in paragraph 12.8(i) to (iii).

13. Interpreters

(a) General

13.1 Chief officers are responsible for making sure appropriate arrangements are in place for provision of suitably qualified interpreters for people who:
- are deaf;
- do not understand English.

Whenever possible, interpreters should be drawn from the National Register of Public Service Interpreters (NRPSI) or the Council for the Advancement of Communication with Deaf People (CADCP) Directory of British Sign Language/English Interpreters.

(b) Foreign languages

13.2 Unless *paragraphs 11.1, 11.18* to *11.20* apply, a person must not be interviewed in the absence of a person capable of interpreting if:
(a) they have difficulty understanding English;
(b) the interviewer cannot speak the person's own language;
(c) the person wants an interpreter present.

13.3 The interviewer shall make sure the interpreter makes a note of the interview at the time in the person's language for use in the event of the interpreter being called to give evidence, and certifies its accuracy. The interviewer should allow sufficient time for the interpreter to note each question and answer after each is put, given and interpreted. The person should be allowed to read the record or have it read to them and sign it as correct or indicate the respects in which they consider it inaccurate. If the interview is audibly recorded or visually recorded, the arrangements in Code E or F apply.

13.4 In the case of a person making a statement to a police officer or other police staff other than in English:
(a) the interpreter shall record the statement in the language it is made;
(b) the person shall be invited to sign it;
(c) an official English translation shall be made in due course.

(c) Deaf people and people with speech difficulties

13.5 If a person appears to be deaf or there is doubt about their hearing or speaking ability, they must not be interviewed in the absence of an interpreter unless they agree in writing to being interviewed without one or *paragraphs 11.1, 11.18* to *11.20* apply.

13.6 An interpreter should also be called if a juvenile is interviewed and the parent or guardian present as the appropriate adult appears to be deaf or there is doubt about their hearing or speaking ability, unless they agree in writing to the interview proceeding without one or *paragraphs 11.1, 11.18* to *11.20* apply.

13.7 The interviewer shall make sure the interpreter is allowed to read the interview record and certify its accuracy in the event of the interpreter being called to give evidence. If the interview is audibly recorded or visually recorded, the arrangements in Code E or F apply.

(d) Additional rules for detained persons

13.8 All reasonable attempts should be made to make the detainee understand that interpreters will be provided at public expense.

13.9 If *paragraph 6.1* applies and the detainee cannot communicate with the solicitor because of language, hearing or speech difficulties, an interpreter must be called. The interpreter may not be a police officer or any other police staff when interpretation is needed for the purposes of obtaining legal advice. In all other cases a police officer or other police staff may only interpret if the detainee and the appropriate adult, if applicable, give their agreement in writing or if the interview is audibly recorded or visually recorded as in Code E or F.

13.10 When the custody officer cannot establish effective communication with a person charged with an offence who appears deaf or there is doubt about their ability to hear, speak or to understand English, arrangements must be made as soon as practicable for an interpreter to explain the offence and any other information given by the custody officer.

(e) Documentation

13.11 Action taken to call an interpreter under this section and any agreement to be interviewed in the absence of an interpreter must be recorded.

14. Questioning—special restrictions

14.1 If a person is arrested by one police force on behalf of another and the lawful period of detention in respect of that offence has not yet commenced in accordance with PACE, section 41 no questions may be put to them about the offence while they are in transit between the forces except to clarify any voluntary statement they make.

14.2 If a person is in police detention at a hospital they may not be questioned without the agreement of a responsible doctor. See *Note 14A*

Note for Guidance

14A If questioning takes place at a hospital under paragraph 14.2, or on the way to or from a hospital, the period of questioning concerned counts towards the total period of detention permitted.

15. Reviews and extensions of detention

(a) Persons detained under PACE

15.1 The review officer is responsible under PACE, section 40 for periodically determining if a person's detention, before or after charge, continues to be necessary. This requirement continues throughout the detention period and except as in *paragraph 15.10*, the review officer must be present at the police station holding the detainee. See *Notes 15A* and *15B*

15.2 Under PACE, section 42, an officer of superintendent rank or above who is responsible for the station holding the detainee may give authority any time after the second review to extend the maximum period the person may be detained without charge by up to 12 hours. Further detention without charge may be authorised only by a magistrates' court in accordance with PACE, sections 43 and 44. See *Notes 15C, 15D* and *15E*

15.2A Section 42(1) of PACE as amended extends the maximum period of detention for indictable offences from 24 hours to 36 hours. Detaining a juvenile or mentally vulnerable person for longer than 24 hours will be dependent on the circumstances of the case and with regard to the person's:

(a) special vulnerability;
(b) the legal obligation to provide an opportunity for representations to be made prior to a decision about extending detention;
(c) the need to consult and consider the views of any appropriate adult; and
(d) any alternatives to police custody.

15.3 Before deciding whether to authorise continued detention the officer responsible under *paragraphs 15.1* or *15.2* shall give an opportunity to make representations about the detention to:

(a) the detainee, unless in the case of a review as in *paragraph 15.1*, the detainee is asleep;

(b) the detainee's solicitor if available at the time; and
(c) the appropriate adult if available at the time.

15.3A Other people having an interest in the detainee's welfare may also make representations at the authorising officer's discretion.

15.3B Subject to *paragraph 15.10*, the representations may be made orally in person or by telephone or in writing. The authorising officer may, however, refuse to hear oral representations from the detainee if the officer considers them unfit to make representations because of their condition or behaviour. See *Note 15C*

15.3C The decision on whether the review takes place in person or by telephone or by video conferencing (see *Note 15G*) is a matter for the review officer. In determining the form the review may take, the review officer must always take full account of the needs of the person in custody. The benefits of carrying out a review in person should always be considered, based on the individual circumstances of each case with specific additional consideration if the person is:
(a) a juvenile (and the age of the juvenile); or
(b) mentally vulnerable; or
(c) has been subject to medical attention for other than routine minor ailments; or
(d) there are presentational or community issues around the person's detention.

15.4 Before conducting a review or determining whether to extend the maximum period of detention without charge, the officer responsible must make sure the detainee is reminded of their entitlement to free legal advice, see *paragraph 6.5*, unless in the case of a review the person is asleep.

15.5 If, after considering any representations, the officer decides to keep the detainee in detention or extend the maximum period they may be detained without charge, any comment made by the detainee shall be recorded. If applicable, the officer responsible under *paragraph 15.1* or *15.2* shall be informed of the comment as soon as practicable. See also *paragraphs 11.4* and *11.13*

15.6 No officer shall put specific questions to the detainee:
- regarding their involvement in any offence; or
- in respect of any comments they may make:
  — when given the opportunity to make representations; or
  — in response to a decision to keep them in detention or extend the maximum period of detention.

Such an exchange could constitute an interview as in *paragraph 11.1A* and would be subject to the associated safeguards in *section 11* and, in respect of a person who has been charged, *paragraph 16.5*. See also *paragraph 11.13*

15.7 A detainee who is asleep at a review, see *paragraph 15.1,* and whose continued detention is authorised must be informed about the decision and reason as soon as practicable after waking.

15.8 Not used.

(b) Telephone review of detention

15.9 PACE, section 40A provides that the officer responsible under section 40 for reviewing the detention of a person who has not been charged, need not attend the police station holding the detainee and may carry out the review by telephone.

15.9A PACE, section 45A(2) provides that the officer responsible under section 40 for reviewing the detention of a person who has not been charged, need not attend the police station holding the detainee and may carry out the review by video conferencing facilities (see *Note 15G*).

15.9B A telephone review is not permitted where facilities for review by video conferencing exist and it is practicable to use them.

15.9C The review officer can decide at any stage that a telephone review or review by video conferencing should be terminated and that the review will be conducted in person. The reasons for doing so should be noted in the custody record.
See *Note 15F*

15.10 When a telephone review is carried out, an officer at the station holding the detainee shall be required by the review officer to fulfil that officer's obligations under PACE section 40 or this Code by:
(a) making any record connected with the review in the detainee's custody record;
(b) if applicable, making a record in (*a*) in the presence of the detainee; and
(c) giving the detainee information about the review.

15.11 When a telephone review is carried out, the requirement in *paragraph 15.3* will be satisfied:
(a) if facilities exist for the immediate transmission of written representations to the review officer, e.g. fax or email message, by giving the detainee an opportunity to make representations:

(i) orally by telephone; or
(ii) in writing using those facilities; and

(b) in all other cases, by giving the detainee an opportunity to make their representations orally by telephone.

(c) Documentation

15.12 It is the officer's responsibility to make sure all reminders given under *paragraph 15.4* are noted in the custody record.

15.13 The grounds for, and extent of, any delay in conducting a review shall be recorded.

15.14 When a telephone review is carried out, a record shall be made of:
(a) the reason the review officer did not attend the station holding the detainee;
(b) the place the review officer was;
(c) the method representations, oral or written, were made to the review officer, see *paragraph 15.11*.

15.15 Any written representations shall be retained.

15.16 A record shall be made as soon as practicable about the outcome of each review or determination whether to extend the maximum detention period without charge or an application for a warrant of further detention or its extension. If *paragraph 15.7* applies, a record shall also be made of when the person was informed and by whom. If an authorisation is given under PACE, section 42, the record shall state the number of hours and minutes by which the detention period is extended or further extended. If a warrant for further detention, or extension, is granted under section 43 or 44, the record shall state the detention period authorised by the warrant and the date and time it was granted.

Notes for Guidance

15A Review officer for the purposes of:
- PACE, sections 40 and 40A means, in the case of a person arrested but not charged, an officer of at least inspector rank not directly involved in the investigation and, if a person has been arrested and charged, the custody officer;

15B The detention of persons in police custody not subject to the statutory review requirement in paragraph 15.1 should still be reviewed periodically as a matter of good practice. Such reviews can be carried out by an officer of the rank of sergeant or above. The purpose of such reviews is to check the particular power under which a detainee is held continues to apply, any associated conditions are complied with and to make sure appropriate action is taken to deal with any changes. This includes the detainee's prompt release when the power no longer applies, or their transfer if the power requires the detainee be taken elsewhere as soon as the necessary arrangements are made. Examples include persons:
(a) arrested on warrant because they failed to answer bail to appear at court;
(b) arrested under the Bail Act 1976, section 7(3) for breaching a condition of bail granted after charge;
(c) in police custody for specific purposes and periods under the Crime (Sentences) Act 1997, Schedule 1;
(d) convicted, or remand prisoners, held in police stations on behalf of the Prison Service under the Imprisonment (Temporary Provisions) Act 1980, section 6;
(e) being detained to prevent them causing a breach of the peace;
(f) detained at police stations on behalf of the Immigration Service.
(g) detained by order of a magistrates' court under the Criminal Justice Act 1988, section 152 (as amended by the Drugs Act 2005, section 8) to facilitate the recovery of evidence after being charged with drug possession or drug trafficking and suspected of having swallowed drugs.

The detention of persons remanded into police detention by order of a court under the Magistrates' Courts Act 1980, section 128 is subject to a statutory requirement to review that detention. This is to make sure the detainee is taken back to court no later than the end of the period authorised by the court or when the need for their detention by police ceases, whichever is the sooner.

15C In the case of a review of detention, but not an extension, the detainee need not be woken for the review. However, if the detainee is likely to be asleep, e.g. during a period of rest allowed as in paragraph 12.2, at the latest time a review or authorisation to extend detention may take place, the officer should, if the legal obligations and time constraints permit, bring forward the procedure to allow the detainee to make representations. A detainee not asleep during the review must be present when the grounds for their continued detention are recorded and must at the same time be informed of those grounds unless the review officer considers the person is incapable of understanding what is said, violent or likely to become violent or in urgent need of medical attention.

15D An application to a Magistrates' Court under PACE, sections 43 or 44 for a warrant of further detention or its extension should be made between 10am and 9pm, and if possible during normal court hours. It will not usually be practicable to arrange for a court to sit specially outside the hours of 10am to 9pm. If it appears a special sitting may be needed outside normal court hours but between 10am and 9pm, the clerk to the justices should be given notice and informed of this possibility, while the court is sitting if possible.

15E In paragraph 15.2, the officer responsible for the station holding the detainee includes a superintendent or above who, in accordance with their force operational policy or police regulations, is given that responsibility on a temporary basis whilst the appointed long-term holder is off duty or otherwise unavailable.

15F The provisions of PACE, section 40A allowing telephone reviews do not apply to reviews of detention after charge by the custody officer. When video conferencing is not required, they allow the use of a telephone to carry out a review of detention before charge. The procedure under PACE, section 42 must be done in person.

15G The use of video conferencing facilities for decisions about detention under section 45A of PACE is subject to the introduction of regulations by the Secretary of State.

16. Charging detained persons

(a) Action

16.1 When the officer in charge of the investigation reasonably believes there is sufficient evidence to provide a realistic prospect of conviction for the offence (see *paragraph 11.6*), they shall without delay, and subject to the following qualification, inform the custody officer who will be responsible for considering whether the detainee should be charged. See *Notes 11B* and *16A.* When a person is detained in respect of more than one offence it is permissible to delay informing the custody officer until the above conditions are satisfied in respect of all the offences, but see *paragraph 11.6.* If the detainee is a juvenile, mentally disordered or otherwise mentally vulnerable, any resulting action shall be taken in the presence of the appropriate adult if they are present at the time. See *Notes 16B* and *16C*

16.1A Where guidance issued by the Director of Public Prosecutions under section 37A is in force the custody officer must comply with that Guidance in deciding how to act in dealing with the detainee. See *Notes 16AA* and *16AB*

16.1B Where in compliance with the DPP's Guidance the custody officer decides that the case should be immediately referred to the CPS to make the charging decision, consultation should take place with a Crown Prosecutor as soon as is reasonably practicable. Where the Crown Prosecutor is unable to make the charging decision on the information available at that time, the detainee may be released without charge and on bail (with conditions if necessary) under section 37(7)(a). In such circumstances, the detainee should be informed that they are being released to enable the Director of Public Prosecutions to make a decision under section 37B.

16.2 When a detainee is charged with or informed they may be prosecuted for an offence, see *Note 16B*, they shall, unless the restriction on drawing adverse inferences from silence applies, see *Annex C*, be cautioned as follows:

> 'You do not have to say anything. But it may harm your defence if you do not mention now something which you later rely on in court. Anything you do say may be given in evidence.'

Annex C, paragraph 2 sets out the alternative terms of the caution to be used when the restriction on drawing adverse inferences from silence applies.

16.3 When a detainee is charged they shall be given a written notice showing particulars of the offence and, subject to *paragraph 2.6A*, the officer's name and the case reference number. As far as possible the particulars of the charge shall be stated in simple terms, but they shall also show the precise offence in law with which the detainee is charged. The notice shall begin:

'*You are charged with the offence(s) shown below.*' Followed by the caution.

If the detainee is a juvenile, mentally disordered or otherwise mentally vulnerable, the notice should be given to the appropriate adult.

16.4 If, after a detainee has been charged with or informed they may be prosecuted for an offence, an officer wants to tell them about any written statement or interview with another person relating to such an offence, the detainee shall either be handed a true copy of the written statement or the content of the interview record brought to their attention. Nothing shall be done to invite any reply or comment except to:

(a) caution the detainee, '*You do not have to say anything, but anything you do say may be given in evidence.*'; and

(b) remind the detainee about their right to legal advice.

16.4A If the detainee:

- cannot read, the document may be read to them
- is a juvenile, mentally disordered or otherwise mentally vulnerable, the appropriate adult shall also be given a copy, or the interview record shall be brought to their attention

16.5 A detainee may not be interviewed about an offence after they have been charged with, or informed they may be prosecuted for it, unless the interview is necessary:

- to prevent or minimise harm or loss to some other person, or the public
- to clear up an ambiguity in a previous answer or statement
- in the interests of justice for the detainee to have put to them, and have an opportunity to comment on, information concerning the offence which has come to light since they were charged or informed they might be prosecuted

Before any such interview, the interviewer shall:

(a) caution the detainee, '*You do not have to say anything, but anything you do say may be given in evidence.*';

(b) remind the detainee about their right to legal advice.

See *Note 16B*

16.6 The provisions of *paragraphs 16.2* to *16.5* must be complied with in the appropriate adult's presence if they are already at the police station. If they are not at the police station then these provisions must be complied with again in their presence when they arrive unless the detainee has been released.

See *Note 16C*

16.7 When a juvenile is charged with an offence and the custody officer authorises their continued detention after charge, the custody officer must try to make arrangements for the juvenile to be taken into the care of a local authority to be detained pending appearance in court unless the custody officer certifies it is impracticable to do so or, in the case of a juvenile of at least 12 years old, no secure accommodation is available and there is a risk to the public of serious harm from that juvenile, in accordance with PACE, section 38(6). See *Note 16D*

(b) Documentation

16.8 A record shall be made of anything a detainee says when charged.

16.9 Any questions put in an interview after charge and answers given relating to the offence shall be recorded in full during the interview on forms for that purpose and the record signed by the detainee or, if they refuse, by the interviewer and any third parties present. If the questions are audibly recorded or visually recorded the arrangements in Code E or F apply.

16.10 If it is not practicable to make arrangements for a juvenile's transfer into local authority care as in *paragraph 16.7*, the custody officer must record the reasons and complete a certificate to be produced before the court with the juvenile. See *Note 16D*

Notes for Guidance

16A The custody officer must take into account alternatives to prosecution under the Crime and Disorder Act 1998, reprimands and warning applicable to persons under 18, and in national guidance on the cautioning of offenders, for persons aged 18 and over.

16AA When a person is arrested under the provisions of the Criminal Justice Act 2003 which allow a person to be re-tried after being acquitted of a serious offence which is a qualifying offence specified in Schedule 5 to that Act and not precluded from further prosecution by virtue of section 75(3) of that Act the detention provisions of PACE are modified and make an officer of the rank of superintendent or above who has not been directly involved in the investigation responsible for determining whether the evidence is sufficient to charge.

16AB Where Guidance issued by the Director of Public Prosecutions under section 37B is in force, a custody officer who determines in accordance with that Guidance that there is sufficient evidence to charge the detainee, may detain that person for no longer than is reasonably necessary to decide how that person is to be dealt with under PACE, section 37(7)(a) to (d), including, where appropriate, consultation with the Duty Prosecutor. The period is subject to the maximum period of detention before charge determined by PACE, sections 41 to 44. Where in accordance with the Guidance the case is referred to the CPS for decision, the custody officer should ensure that an officer involved in the investigation sends to the CPS such information as is specified in the Guidance.

16B The giving of a warning or the service of the Notice of Intended Prosecution required by the Road Traffic Offenders Act 1988, section 1 does not amount to informing a detainee they may be prosecuted for an offence and so does not preclude further questioning in relation to that offence.

16C There is no power under PACE to detain a person and delay action under paragraphs 16.2 to 16.5 solely to await the arrival of the appropriate adult. After charge, bail cannot be refused, or release on bail delayed, simply because an appropriate adult is not available, unless the absence of that adult provides the custody officer with the necessary grounds to authorise detention after charge under PACE, section 38.

16D Except as in paragraph 16.7, neither a juvenile's behaviour nor the nature of the offence provides grounds for the custody officer to decide it is impracticable to arrange the juvenile's transfer to local authority care. Similarly, the lack of secure local authority accommodation does not make it impracticable to transfer the juvenile. The availability of secure accommodation is only a factor in relation to a juvenile aged 12 or over when the local authority accommodation would not be adequate to protect the public from serious harm from them. The obligation to transfer a juvenile to local authority accommodation applies as much to a juvenile charged during the daytime as to a juvenile to be held overnight, subject to a requirement to bring the juvenile before a court under PACE, section 46.

17. Testing persons for the presence of specified Class A drugs

(a) Action

17.1 This section of Code C applies only in selected police stations in police areas where the provisions for drug testing under section 63B of PACE (as amended by section 5 of the Criminal Justice Act 2003 and section 7 of the Drugs Act 2005) are in force and in respect of which the Secretary of State has given a notification to the relevant chief officer of police that arrangements for the taking of samples have been made. Such a notification will cover either a police area as a whole or particular stations within a police area. The notification indicates whether the testing applies to those arrested or charged or under the age of 18 as the case may be and testing can only take place in respect of the persons so indicated in the notification. Testing cannot be carried out unless the relevant notification has been given and has not been withdrawn. See *Note 17F*

17.2 A sample of urine or a non-intimate sample may be taken from a person in police detention for the purpose of ascertaining whether he has any specified Class A drug in his body only where they have been brought before the custody officer and:

(a) either the arrest condition, see *paragraph 17.3*, or the charge condition, see *paragraph 17.4* is met;

(b) the age condition see *paragraph 17.5*, is met;

(c) the notification condition is met in relation to the arrest condition, the charge condition, or the age condition, as the case may be. (Testing on charge and/or arrest must be specifically provided for in the notification for the power to apply. In addition, the fact that testing of under 18s is authorised must be expressly provided for in the notification before the power to test such persons applies.). See *paragraph 17.1*; and

(d) a police officer has requested the person concerned to give the sample (the request condition).

17.3 The arrest condition is met where the detainee:

(a) has been arrested for a trigger offence, see *Note 17E*, but not charged with that offence; or

(b) has been arrested for any other offence but not charged with that offence and a police officer of inspector rank or above, who has reasonable grounds for suspecting that their misuse of any specified Class A drug caused or contributed to the offence, has authorised the sample to be taken.

17.4 The charge condition is met where the detainee:

(a) has been charged with a trigger offence, or

(b) has been charged with any other offence and a police officer of inspector rank or above, who has reasonable grounds for suspecting that the detainee's misuse of any specified Class A drug caused or contributed to the offence, has authorised the sample to be taken.

17.5 The age condition is met where:

(a) in the case of a detainee who has been arrested but not charged as in *paragraph 17.3*, they are aged 18 or over;

(b) in the case of a detainee who has been charged as in *paragraph 17.4*, they are aged 14 or over.

17.6 Before requesting a sample from the person concerned, an officer must:
(a) inform them that the purpose of taking the sample is for drug testing under PACE. This is to ascertain whether they have a specified Class A drug present in their body;
(b) warn them that if, when so requested, they fail without good cause to provide a sample they may be liable to prosecution;
(c) where the taking of the sample has been authorised by an inspector or above in accordance with *paragraph 17.3(b)* or *17.4(b)* above, inform them that the authorisation has been given and the grounds for giving it;
(d) remind them of the following rights, which may be exercised at any stage during the period in custody:
(i) the right to have someone informed of their arrest [see *section 5*];
(ii) the right to consult privately with a solicitor and that free independent legal advice is available [see *section 6*]; and
(iii) the right to consult these Codes of Practice [see *section 3*].

17.7 In the case of a person who has not attained the age of 17—
(a) the making of the request for a sample under *paragraph 17.2(d)* above;
(b) the giving of the warning and the information under *paragraph 17.6* above; and
(c) the taking of the sample, may not take place except in the presence of an appropriate adult. (See *Note 17G*

17.8 Authorisation by an officer of the rank of inspector or above within *paragraph 17.3(b)* or *17.4(b)* may be given orally or in writing but, if it is given orally, it must be confirmed in writing as soon as practicable.

17.9 If a sample is taken from a detainee who has been arrested for an offence but not charged with that offence as in *paragraph 17.3*, no further sample may be taken during the same continuous period of detention. If during that same period the charge condition is also met in respect of that detainee, the sample which has been taken shall be treated as being taken by virtue of the charge condition, see *paragraph 17.4*, being met.

17.10 A detainee from whom a sample may be taken may be detained for up to six hours from the time of charge if the custody officer reasonably believes the detention is necessary to enable a sample to be taken. Where the arrest condition is met, a detainee whom the custody officer has decided to release on bail without charge may continue to be detained, but not beyond 24 hours from the relevant time (as defined in section 41(2) of PACE), to enable a sample to be taken.

17.11 A detainee in respect of whom the arrest condition is met, but not the charge condition, see *paragraphs 17.3* and *17.4*, and whose release would be required before a sample can be taken had they not continued to be detained as a result of being arrested for a further offence which does not satisfy the arrest condition, may have a sample taken at any time within 24 hours after the arrest for the offence that satisfies the arrest condition.

(b) Documentation

17.12 The following must be recorded in the custody record:
(a) if a sample is taken following authorisation by an officer of the rank of inspector or above, the authorisation and the grounds for suspicion;
(b) the giving of a warning of the consequences of failure to provide a sample;
(c) the time at which the sample was given; and
(d) the time of charge or, where the arrest condition is being relied upon, the time of arrest and, where applicable, the fact that a sample taken after arrest but before charge is to be treated as being taken by virtue of the charge condition, where that is met in the same period of continuous detention. See *paragraph 17.9*

(c) General

17.13 A sample may only be taken by a prescribed person. See *Note 17C*

17.14 Force may not be used to take any sample for the purpose of drug testing.

17.15 The terms 'Class A drug' and 'misuse' have the same meanings as in the Misuse of Drugs Act 1971. 'Specified' (in relation to a Class A drug) and 'trigger offence' have the same meanings as in Part III of the Criminal Justice and Court Services Act 2000.

17.16 Any sample taken:

(a) may not be used for any purpose other than to ascertain whether the person concerned has a specified Class A drug present in his body; and
(b) must be retained until the person concerned has made their first appearance before the court.

(d) Assessment of misuse of drugs

17.17 Under the provisions of Part 3 of the Drugs Act 2005, where a detainee has tested positive for a specified Class A drug under section 63B of PACE a police officer may, at any time before the person's release from the police station, impose a requirement for them to attend an initial assessment of their drug misuse by a suitably qualified person and to remain for its duration. The requirement may only be imposed on a person if:
(a) they have reached the age of 18;
(b) notification has been given by the Secretary of State to the relevant chief officer of police that arrangements for conducting initial assessments have been made for those from whom samples for testing have been taken at the police station where the detainee is in custody.

17.18 When imposing a requirement to attend an initial assessment the police officer must:
(a) inform the person of the time and place at which the initial assessment is to take place;
(b) explain that this information will be confirmed in writing; and
(c) warn the person that he may be liable to prosecution if he fails without good cause to attend the initial assessment and remain for its duration

17.19 Where a police officer has imposed a requirement to attend an initial assessment in accordance with *paragraph 17.17*, he must, before the person is released from detention, give the person notice in writing which:
(a) confirms that he is required to attend and remain for the duration of an initial assessment; and
(b) confirms the information and repeats the warning referred to in *paragraph 17.18*.

17.20 The following must be recorded in the custody record:
(a) that the requirement to attend an initial assessment has been imposed; and
(b) the information, explanation, warning and notice given in accordance with *paragraphs 17.17* and *17.19*.

17.21 Where a notice is given in accordance with *paragraph 17.19*, a police officer can give the person a further notice in writing which informs the person of any change to the time or place at which the initial assessment is to take place and which repeats the warning referred to in *paragraph 17.18(c)*.

17.22 Part 3 of the Drugs Act 2005 also requires police officers to have regard to any guidance issued by the Secretary of State in respect of the assessment provisions.

Notes for Guidance

17A When warning a person who is asked to provide a urine or non-intimate sample in accordance with paragraph 17.6(b), the following form of words may be used:

'You do not have to provide a sample, but I must warn you that if you fail or refuse without good cause to do so, you will commit an offence for which you may be imprisoned, or fined, or both'.

17B A sample has to be sufficient and suitable. A sufficient sample is sufficient in quantity and quality to enable drug-testing analysis to take place. A suitable sample is one which by its nature, is suitable for a particular form of drug analysis.

17C A prescribed person in paragraph 17.13 is one who is prescribed in regulations made by the Secretary of State under section 63B(6) of the Police and Criminal Evidence Act 1984. [The regulations are currently contained in regulation SI 2001 No. 2645, the Police and Criminal Evidence Act 1984 (Drug Testing Persons in Police Detention) (Prescribed Persons) Regulations 2001.]

17D The retention of the sample in paragraph 17.16(b) allows for the sample to be sent for confirmatory testing and analysis if the detainee disputes the test. But such samples, and the information derived from them, may not be subsequently used in the investigation of any offence or in evidence against the persons from whom they were taken.

17E Trigger offences are:
1. Offences under the following provisions of the Theft Act 1968:

section 1	(theft)
section 8	(robbery)
section 9	(burglary)
section 10	(aggravated burglary)
section 12	(taking a motor vehicle or other conveyance without authority)
section 12A	(aggravated vehicle-taking)

section 15 (obtaining property by deception)
section 22 (handling stolen goods)
section 25 (going equipped for stealing etc.)

2. Offences under the following provisions of the Misuse of Drugs Act 1971, if committed in respect of a specified Class A drug:–
section 4 (restriction on production and supply of controlled drugs)
section 5(2) (possession of a controlled drug)
section 5(3) (possession of a controlled drug with intent to supply)

3. An offence under section 1(1) of the Criminal Attempts Act 1981 if committed in respect of an offence under any of the following provisions of the Theft Act 1968:
section 1 (theft)
section 8 (robbery)
section 9 (burglary)
section 15 (obtaining property by deception)
section 22 (handling stolen goods)

4. Offences under the following provisions of the Vagrancy Act 1824:
section 3 (begging)
section 4 (persistent begging)

17F The power to take samples is subject to notification by the Secretary of State that appropriate arrangements for the taking of samples have been made for the police area as a whole or for the particular police station concerned for whichever of the following is specified in the notification:
(a) persons in respect of whom the arrest condition is met;
(b) persons in respect of whom the charge condition is met;
(c) persons who have not attained the age of 18.

Note: Notification is treated as having been given for the purposes of the charge condition in relation to a police area, if testing (on charge) under section 63B(2) of PACE was in force immediately before section 7 of the Drugs Act 2005 was brought into force; and for the purposes of the age condition, in relation to a police area or police station, if immediately before that day, notification that arrangements had been made for the taking of samples from persons under the age of 18 (those aged 14–17) had been given and had not been withdrawn.

17G Appropriate adult in paragraph 17.7 means the person's:–
(a) parent or guardian or, if they are in the care of a local authority or voluntary organisation, a person representing that authority or organisation; or
(b) a social worker of, in England, a local authority or, in Wales, a local authority social services department; or
(c) if no person falling within (a) or (b) above is available, any responsible person aged 18 or over who is not a police officer or a person employed by the police.

Annex A
Intimate and Strip Searches

A. Intimate search

1. An intimate search consists of the physical examination of a person's body orifices other than the mouth. The intrusive nature of such searches means the actual and potential risks associated with intimate searches must never be underestimated.

(a) Action

2. Body orifices other than the mouth may be searched only:
(a) if authorised by an officer of inspector rank or above who has reasonable grounds for believing that the person may have concealed on themselves:
(i) anything which they could and might use to cause physical injury to themselves or others at the station; or
(ii) a Class A drug which they intended to supply to another or to export;
and the officer has reasonable grounds for believing that an intimate search is the only means of removing those items; and
(b) if the search is under *paragraph 2(a)(ii)* (a drug offence search), the detainee's appropriate consent has been given in writing.

2A Before the search begins, a police officer, designated detention officer or staff custody officer, must tell the detainee:–

(a) that the authority to carry out the search has been given;
(b) the grounds for giving the authorisation and for believing that the article cannot be removed without an intimate search.

2B Before a detainee is asked to give appropriate consent to a search under *paragraph 2(a)(ii)* (a drug offence search) they must be warned that if they refuse without good cause their refusal may harm their case if it comes to trial, see *Note A6*. This warning may be given by a police officer or member of police staff. A detainee who is not legally represented must be reminded of their entitlement to have free legal advice, see *Code C, paragraph 6.5*, and the reminder noted in the custody record.

3. An intimate search may only be carried out by a registered medical practitioner or registered nurse, unless an officer of at least inspector rank considers this is not practicable and the search is to take place under *paragraph 2(a)(i)*, in which case a police officer may carry out the search. See *Notes A1* to *A5*

3A Any proposal for a search under *paragraph 2(a)(i)* to be carried out by someone other than a registered medical practitioner or registered nurse must only be considered as a last resort and when the authorising officer is satisfied the risks associated with allowing the item to remain with the detainee outweigh the risks associated with removing it. See *Notes A1* to *A5*

4. An intimate search under:
   - *paragraph 2(a)(i)* may take place only at a hospital, surgery, other medical premises or police station
   - *paragraph 2(a)(ii)* may take place only at a hospital, surgery or other medical premises and must be carried out by a registered medical practitioner or a registered nurse

5. An intimate search at a police station of a juvenile or mentally disordered or otherwise mentally vulnerable person may take place only in the presence of an appropriate adult of the same sex, unless the detainee specifically requests a particular adult of the opposite sex who is readily available. In the case of a juvenile the search may take place in the absence of the appropriate adult only if the juvenile signifies in the presence of the appropriate adult they do not want the adult present during the search and the adult agrees. A record shall be made of the juvenile's decision and signed by the appropriate adult.

6. When an intimate search under *paragraph 2(a)(i)* is carried out by a police officer, the officer must be of the same sex as the detainee. A minimum of two people, other than the detainee, must be present during the search. Subject to *paragraph 5*, no person of the opposite sex who is not a medical practitioner or nurse shall be present, nor shall anyone whose presence is unnecessary. The search shall be conducted with proper regard to the sensitivity and vulnerability of the detainee.

(b) Documentation

7. In the case of an intimate search, the following shall be recorded as soon as practicable, in the detainee's custody record:
   (a) for searches under paragraphs *2(a)(i)* and *(ii)*;
   - the authorisation to carry out the search;
   - the grounds for giving the authorisation;
   - the grounds for believing the article could not be removed without an intimate search;
   - which parts of the detainee's body were searched;
   - who carried out the search;
   - who was present;
   - the result.

   (b) for searches under paragraph 2(a)(ii):
   - the giving of the warning required by *paragraph 2B*;
   - the fact that the appropriate consent was given or (as the case may be) refused, and if refused, the reason given for the refusal (if any).

8. If an intimate search is carried out by a police officer, the reason why it was impracticable for a registered medical practitioner or registered nurse to conduct it must be recorded.

B. Strip search

9. A strip search is a search involving the removal of more than outer clothing. In this Code, outer clothing includes shoes and socks.

(a) Action

10. A strip search may take place only if it is considered necessary to remove an article which a detainee

would not be allowed to keep, and the officer reasonably considers the detainee might have concealed such an article. Strip searches shall not be routinely carried out if there is no reason to consider that articles are concealed.

The conduct of strip searches

11. When strip searches are conducted:
   (a) a police officer carrying out a strip search must be the same sex as the detainee;
   (b) the search shall take place in an area where the detainee cannot be seen by anyone who does not need to be present, nor by a member of the opposite sex except an appropriate adult who has been specifically requested by the detainee;
   (c) except in cases of urgency, where there is risk of serious harm to the detainee or to others, whenever a strip search involves exposure of intimate body parts, there must be at least two people present other than the detainee, and if the search is of a juvenile or mentally disordered or otherwise mentally vulnerable person, one of the people must be the appropriate adult. Except in urgent cases as above, a search of a juvenile may take place in the absence of the appropriate adult only if the juvenile signifies in the presence of the appropriate adult that they do not want the adult to be present during the search and the adult agrees. A record shall be made of the juvenile's decision and signed by the appropriate adult. The presence of more than two people, other than an appropriate adult, shall be permitted only in the most exceptional circumstances;
   (d) the search shall be conducted with proper regard to the sensitivity and vulnerability of the detainee in these circumstances and every reasonable effort shall be made to secure the detainee's co-operation and minimise embarrassment. Detainees who are searched shall not normally be required to remove all their clothes at the same time, e.g. a person should be allowed to remove clothing above the waist and redress before removing further clothing;
   (e) if necessary to assist the search, the detainee may be required to hold their arms in the air or to stand with their legs apart and bend forward so a visual examination may be made of the genital and anal areas provided no physical contact is made with any body orifice;
   (f) if articles are found, the detainee shall be asked to hand them over. If articles are found within any body orifice other than the mouth, and the detainee refuses to hand them over, their removal would constitute an intimate search, which must be carried out as in *Part A*;
   (g) a strip search shall be conducted as quickly as possible, and the detainee allowed to dress as soon as the procedure is complete.

(b) Documentation

12. A record shall be made on the custody record of a strip search including the reason it was considered necessary, those present and any result.

Notes for Guidance

A1 Before authorising any intimate search, the authorising officer must make every reasonable effort to persuade the detainee to hand the article over without a search. If the detainee agrees, a registered medical practitioner or registered nurse should whenever possible be asked to assess the risks involved and, if necessary, attend to assist the detainee.

A2 If the detainee does not agree to hand the article over without a search, the authorising officer must carefully review all the relevant factors before authorising an intimate search. In particular, the officer must consider whether the grounds for believing an article may be concealed are reasonable.

A3 If authority is given for a search under paragraph 2(a)(i), a registered medical practitioner or registered nurse shall be consulted whenever possible. The presumption should be that the search will be conducted by the registered medical practitioner or registered nurse and the authorising officer must make every reasonable effort to persuade the detainee to allow the medical practitioner or nurse to conduct the search.

A4 A constable should only be authorised to carry out a search as a last resort and when all other approaches have failed. In these circumstances, the authorising officer must be satisfied the detainee might use the article for one or more of the purposes in paragraph 2(a)(i) and the physical injury likely to be caused is sufficiently severe to justify authorising a constable to carry out the search.

A5 If an officer has any doubts whether to authorise an intimate search by a constable, the officer should seek advice from an officer of superintendent rank or above.

A6 In warning a detainee who is asked to consent to an intimate drug offence search, as in paragraph 2B, the following form of words may be used:

'You do not have to allow yourself to be searched, but I must warn you that if you refuse without good cause, your refusal may harm your case if it comes to trial.'

Annex B

Delay in Notifying Arrest or Allowing Access to Legal Advice

A. Persons detained under PACE

1. The exercise of the rights in *Section 5* or *Section 6*, or both, may be delayed if the person is in police detention, as in PACE, section 118(2), in connection with an indictable offence, has not yet been charged with an offence and an officer of superintendent rank or above, or inspector rank or above only for the rights in *Section 5*, has reasonable grounds for believing their exercise will:
   (i) lead to:
   - interference with, or harm to, evidence connected with an indictable offence; or
   - interference with, or physical harm to, other people; or

   (ii) lead to alerting other people suspected of having committed an indictable offence but not yet arrested for it; or
   (iii) hinder the recovery of property obtained in consequence of the commission of such an offence.
2. These rights may also be delayed if the officer has reasonable grounds to believe that:
   (i) the person detained for an indictable offence has benefited from their criminal conduct (decided in accordance with Part 2 of the Proceeds of Crime Act 2002); and
   (ii) the recovery of the value of the property constituting that benefit will be hindered by the exercise of either right.
3. Authority to delay a detainee's right to consult privately with a solicitor may be given only if the authorising officer has reasonable grounds to believe the solicitor the detainee wants to consult will, inadvertently or otherwise, pass on a message from the detainee or act in some other way which will have any of the consequences specified under *paragraphs 1 or 2*. In these circumstances the detainee must be allowed to choose another solicitor. See *Note B3*
4. If the detainee wishes to see a solicitor, access to that solicitor may not be delayed on the grounds they might advise the detainee not to answer questions or the solicitor was initially asked to attend the police station by someone else. In the latter case the detainee must be told the solicitor has come to the police station at another person's request, and must be asked to sign the custody record to signify whether they want to see the solicitor.
5. The fact the grounds for delaying notification of arrest may be satisfied does not automatically mean the grounds for delaying access to legal advice will also be satisfied.
6. These rights may be delayed only for as long as grounds exist and in no case beyond 36 hours after the relevant time as in PACE, section 41. If the grounds cease to apply within this time, the detainee must, as soon as practicable, be asked if they want to exercise either right, the custody record must be noted accordingly, and action taken in accordance with the relevant section of the Code.
7. A detained person must be permitted to consult a solicitor for a reasonable time before any court hearing.

B. Not used

C. Documentation

13. The grounds for action under this Annex shall be recorded and the detainee informed of them as soon as practicable.
14. Any reply given by a detainee under *paragraphs 6* or *11* must be recorded and the detainee asked to endorse the record in relation to whether they want to receive legal advice at this point.

D. Cautions and special warnings

When a suspect detained at a police station is interviewed during any period for which access to legal advice has been delayed under this Annex, the court or jury may not draw adverse inferences from their silence.

Notes for Guidance

B1 Even if Annex B applies in the case of a juvenile, or a person who is mentally disordered or otherwise mentally vulnerable, action to inform the appropriate adult and the person responsible for a juvenile's welfare if that is a different person, must nevertheless be taken as in paragraph 3.13 and 3.15.

B2 In the case of Commonwealth citizens and foreign nationals, see Note 7A.

B3 A decision to delay access to a specific solicitor is likely to be a rare occurrence and only when it can be shown the suspect is capable of misleading that particular solicitor and there is more than a substantial risk that the suspect will succeed in causing information to be conveyed which will lead to one or more of the specified consequences.

Annex C

Restriction on Drawing Adverse Inferences from Silence and Terms of the Caution when the Restriction Applies

(a) The restriction on drawing adverse inferences from silence

1. The Criminal Justice and Public Order Act 1994, sections 34, 36 and 37 as amended by the Youth Justice and Criminal Evidence Act 1999, section 58 describe the conditions under which adverse inferences may be drawn from a person's failure or refusal to say anything about their involvement in the offence when interviewed, after being charged or informed they may be prosecuted. These provisions are subject to an overriding restriction on the ability of a court or jury to draw adverse inferences from a person's silence. This restriction applies:
   (a) to any detainee at a police station, see *Note 10C* who, before being interviewed, see *section 11* or being charged or informed they may be prosecuted, see *section 16,* has:
      (i) asked for legal advice, see *section 6, paragraph 6.1;*
      (ii) not been allowed an opportunity to consult a solicitor, including the duty solicitor, as in this Code; and
      (iii) not changed their mind about wanting legal advice, see *section 6, paragraph 6.6(d)*

      Note the condition in (ii) will
      — apply when a detainee who has asked for legal advice is interviewed before speaking to a solicitor as in *section 6, paragraph 6.6(a)* or *(b).*
      — not apply if the detained person declines to ask for the duty solicitor, see *section 6, paragraphs 6.6(c)* and *(d).*
   (b) to any person charged with, or informed they may be prosecuted for, an offence who:
      (i) has had brought to their notice a written statement made by another person or the content of an interview with another person which relates to that offence, see *section 16, paragraph 16.4;*
      (ii) is interviewed about that offence, see *section 16, paragraph 16.5;* or
      (iii) makes a written statement about that offence, see *Annex D, paragraphs 4* and *9.*

(b) Terms of the caution when the restriction applies

2. When a requirement to caution arises at a time when the restriction on drawing adverse inferences from silence applies, the caution shall be:

   'You do not have to say anything, but anything you do say may be given in evidence.'

3. Whenever the restriction either begins to apply or ceases to apply after a caution has already been given, the person shall be re-cautioned in the appropriate terms. The changed position on drawing inferences and that the previous caution no longer applies shall also be explained to the detainee in ordinary language. See *Note C2*

Notes for Guidance

C1 The restriction on drawing inferences from silence does not apply to a person who has not been detained and who therefore cannot be prevented from seeking legal advice if they want to, see paragraphs 10.2 and 3.15.

C2 The following is suggested as a framework to help explain changes in the position on drawing adverse inferences if the restriction on drawing adverse inferences from silence:
   (a) begins to apply:

   'The caution you were previously given no longer applies. This is because after that caution:
      (i) you asked to speak to a solicitor but have not yet been allowed an opportunity to speak to a solicitor'. See paragraph 1(a); or
      (ii) 'you have been charged with/informed you may be prosecuted.' See paragraph 1(b).

   'This means that from now on, adverse inferences cannot be drawn at court and your defence will not be harmed just because you choose to say nothing. Please listen carefully to the caution I am about to give you because it will apply from now on. You will see that it does not say anything about your defence being harmed.'

(b) ceases to apply before or at the time the person is charged or informed they may be prosecuted, see paragraph 1(a);

'The caution you were previously given no longer applies. This is because after that caution you have been allowed an opportunity to speak to a solicitor. Please listen carefully to the caution I am about to give you because it will apply from now on. It explains how your defence at court may be affected if you choose to say nothing.'

ANNEX D
WRITTEN STATEMENTS UNDER CAUTION

(a) Written by a person under caution

1. A person shall always be invited to write down what they want to say.
2. A person who has not been charged with, or informed they may be prosecuted for, any offence to which the statement they want to write relates, shall:
   (a) unless the statement is made at a time when the restriction on drawing adverse inferences from silence applies, see *Annex C,* be asked to write out and sign the following before writing what they want to say:

   'I make this statement of my own free will. I understand that I do not have to say anything but that it may harm my defence if I do not mention when questioned something which I later rely on in court. This statement may be given in evidence.';

   (b) if the statement is made at a time when the restriction on drawing adverse inferences from silence applies, be asked to write out and sign the following before writing what they want to say;

   'I make this statement of my own free will. I understand that I do not have to say anything. This statement may be given in evidence.'
3. When a person, on the occasion of being charged with or informed they may be prosecuted for any offence, asks to make a statement which relates to any such offence and wants to write it they shall:
   (a) unless the restriction on drawing adverse inferences from silence, see *Annex C,* applied when they were so charged or informed they may be prosecuted, be asked to write out and sign the following before writing what they want to say:

   'I make this statement of my own free will. I understand that I do not have to say anything but that it may harm my defence if I do not mention when questioned something which I later rely on in court. This statement may be given in evidence.';

   (b) if the restriction on drawing adverse inferences from silence applied when they were so charged or informed they may be prosecuted, be asked to write out and sign the following before writing what they want to say:

   'I make this statement of my own free will. I understand that I do not have to say anything. This statement may be given in evidence.'
4. When a person, who has already been charged with or informed they may be prosecuted for any offence, asks to make a statement which relates to any such offence and wants to write it they shall be asked to write out and sign the following before writing what they want to say:

   'I make this statement of my own free will. I understand that I do not have to say anything. This statement may be given in evidence.'
5. Any person writing their own statement shall be allowed to do so without any prompting except a police officer or other police staff may indicate to them which matters are material or question any ambiguity in the statement.

(b) Written by a police officer or other police staff

6. If a person says they would like someone to write the statement for them, a police officer, or other police staff shall write the statement.
7. If the person has not been charged with, or informed they may be prosecuted for, any offence to which the statement they want to make relates they shall, before starting, be asked to sign, or make their mark, to the following:
   (a) unless the statement is made at a time when the restriction on drawing adverse inferences from silence applies, see *Annex C*:

   'I, ..., wish to make a statement. I want someone to write down what I say. I understand that I do not have to say anything but that it may harm my defence if I do not mention when questioned something which I later rely on in court. This statement may be given in evidence.';

(b) if the statement is made at a time when the restriction on drawing adverse inferences from silence applies:

'I, ..., wish to make a statement. I want someone to write down what I say. I understand that I do not have to say anything. This statement may be given in evidence.'

8. If, on the occasion of being charged with or informed they may be prosecuted for any offence, the person asks to make a statement which relates to any such offence they shall before starting be asked to sign, or make their mark to, the following:

(a) unless the restriction on drawing adverse inferences from silence applied, see *Annex C*, when they were so charged or informed they may be prosecuted:

'I, ..., wish to make a statement. I want someone to write down what I say. I understand that I do not have to say anything but that it may harm my defence if I do not mention when questioned something which I later rely on in court. This statement may be given in evidence.';

(b) if the restriction on drawing adverse inferences from silence applied when they were so charged or informed they may be prosecuted:

'I, ..., wish to make a statement. I want someone to write down what I say. I understand that I do not have to say anything. This statement may be given in evidence.'

9. If, having already been charged with or informed they may be prosecuted for any offence, a person asks to make a statement which relates to any such offence they shall before starting, be asked to sign, or make their mark to:

'I, ..., wish to make a statement. I want someone to write down what I say. I understand that I do not have to say anything. This statement may be given in evidence.'

10. The person writing the statement must take down the exact words spoken by the person making it and must not edit or paraphrase it. Any questions that are necessary, e.g. to make it more intelligible, and the answers given must be recorded at the same time on the statement form.

11. When the writing of a statement is finished the person making it shall be asked to read it and to make any corrections, alterations or additions they want. When they have finished reading they shall be asked to write and sign or make their mark on the following certificate at the end of the statement:

'I have read the above statement, and I have been able to correct, alter or add anything I wish. This statement is true. I have made it of my own free will.'

12. If the person making the statement cannot read, or refuses to read it, or to write the above mentioned certificate at the end of it or to sign it, the person taking the statement shall read it to them and ask them if they would like to correct, alter or add anything and to put their signature or make their mark at the end. The person taking the statement shall certify on the statement itself what has occurred.

Annex E
Summary of Provisions Relating to Mentally Disordered and Otherwise Mentally Vulnerable People

1. If an officer has any suspicion, or is told in good faith, that a person of any age may be mentally disordered or otherwise mentally vulnerable, or mentally incapable of understanding the significance of questions or their replies that person shall be treated as mentally disordered or otherwise mentally vulnerable for the purposes of this Code. See *paragraph 1.4*

2. In the case of a person who is mentally disordered or otherwise mentally vulnerable, 'the appropriate adult' means:

(a) a relative, guardian or other person responsible for their care or custody;

(b) someone experienced in dealing with mentally disordered or mentally vulnerable people but who is not a police officer or employed by the police;

(c) failing these, some other responsible adult aged 18 or over who is not a police officer or employed by the police.

See *paragraph 1.7(b)* and *Note 1D*

3. If the custody officer authorises the detention of a person who is mentally vulnerable or appears to be suffering from a mental disorder, the custody officer must as soon as practicable inform the appropriate adult of the grounds for detention and the person's whereabouts, and ask the adult to come to the police station to see them. If the appropriate adult:

- is already at the station when information is given as in *paragraphs 3.1* to *3.5* the information must be given in their presence
- is not at the station when the provisions of *paragraphs 3.1* to *3.5* are complied with these provisions must be complied with again in their presence once they arrive.

See *paragraphs 3.15* to *3.17*

4. If the appropriate adult, having been informed of the right to legal advice, considers legal advice should be taken, the provisions of *section 6* apply as if the mentally disordered or otherwise mentally vulnerable person had requested access to legal advice. See *paragraph 3.19* and *Note E1*
5. The custody officer must make sure a person receives appropriate clinical attention as soon as reasonably practicable if the person appears to be suffering from a mental disorder or in urgent cases immediately call the nearest health care professional or an ambulance. It is not intended these provisions delay the transfer of a detainee to a place of safety under the Mental Health Act 1983, section 136 if that is applicable. If an assessment under that Act is to take place at a police station, the custody officer must consider whether an appropriate health care professional should be called to conduct an initial clinical check on the detainee. See *paragraphs 9.5* and *9.6*
6. It is imperative a mentally disordered or otherwise mentally vulnerable person detained under the Mental Health Act 1983, section 136 be assessed as soon as possible. If that assessment is to take place at the police station, an approved social worker and registered medical practitioner shall be called to the station as soon as possible in order to interview and examine the detainee. Once the detainee has been interviewed, examined and suitable arrangements been made for their treatment or care, they can no longer be detained under section 136. A detainee should be immediately discharged from detention if a registered medical practitioner having examined them, concludes they are not mentally disordered within the meaning of the Act. See *paragraph 3.16*
7. If a mentally disordered or otherwise mentally vulnerable person is cautioned in the absence of the appropriate adult, the caution must be repeated in the appropriate adult's presence. See *paragraph 10.12*
8. A mentally disordered or otherwise mentally vulnerable person must not be interviewed or asked to provide or sign a written statement in the absence of the appropriate adult unless the provisions of *paragraphs 11.1* or *11.18* to *11.20* apply. Questioning in these circumstances may not continue in the absence of the appropriate adult once sufficient information to avert the risk has been obtained. A record shall be made of the grounds for any decision to begin an interview in these circumstances. See *paragraphs 11.1, 11.15* and *11.18* to *11.20*
9. If the appropriate adult is present at an interview, they shall be informed they are not expected to act simply as an observer and the purposes of their presence are to:
   - advise the interviewee
   - observe whether or not the interview is being conducted properly and fairly
   - facilitate communication with the interviewee

   See *paragraph 11.17*
10. If the detention of a mentally disordered or otherwise mentally vulnerable person is reviewed by a review officer or a superintendent, the appropriate adult must, if available at the time, be given an opportunity to make representations to the officer about the need for continuing detention. See *paragraph 15.3*
11. If the custody officer charges a mentally disordered or otherwise mentally vulnerable person with an offence or takes such other action as is appropriate when there is sufficient evidence for a prosecution this must be done in the presence of the appropriate adult. The written notice embodying any charge must be given to the appropriate adult. See *paragraphs 16.1* to *16.4A*
12. An intimate or strip search of a mentally disordered or otherwise mentally vulnerable person may take place only in the presence of the appropriate adult of the same sex, unless the detainee specifically requests the presence of a particular adult of the opposite sex. A strip search may take place in the absence of an appropriate adult only in cases of urgency when there is a risk of serious harm to the detainee or others. See *Annex A, paragraphs 5* and *11(c)*
13. Particular care must be taken when deciding whether to use any form of approved restraints on a mentally disordered or otherwise mentally vulnerable person in a locked cell. See *paragraph 8.2*

Notes for Guidance

E1 The purpose of the provision at paragraph 3.19 is to protect the rights of a mentally disordered or otherwise mentally vulnerable detained person who does not understand the significance of what is said to them. If the detained person wants to exercise the right to legal advice, the appropriate action should be taken and not delayed until the appropriate adult arrives. A mentally disordered or otherwise mentally vulnerable detained person should always be given an opportunity, when an appropriate adult is called to the police station, to consult privately with a solicitor in the absence of the appropriate adult if they want.

E2 Although people who are mentally disordered or otherwise mentally vulnerable are often capable of providing reliable evidence, they may, without knowing or wanting to do so, be particularly prone in certain circumstances to provide information that may be unreliable, misleading or self-incriminating. Special care should always be taken when questioning such a person, and the appropriate adult should be involved if there is any doubt about a person's mental state or capacity. Because of the risk of unreliable evidence, it is important to obtain corroboration of any facts admitted whenever possible.

E3 Because of the risks referred to in Note E2, which the presence of the appropriate adult is intended to minimise, officers of superintendent rank or above should exercise their discretion to authorise the commencement of an interview in the appropriate adult's absence only in exceptional cases, if it is necessary to avert an immediate risk of serious harm. See paragraphs 11.1, 11.18 to 11.20

Annex F

Countries with which Bilateral Consular Conventions or Agreements Requiring Notification of the Arrest and Detention of their Nationals are in Force as at 1 April 2003

Armenia
Austria
Azerbaijan
Belarus
Belgium
Bosnia-Herzegovina
Bulgaria
China*
Croatia
Cuba
Czech Republic
Denmark
Egypt
France
Georgia
German Federal Republic
Greece
Hungary
Italy
Japan
Kazakhstan
Macedonia
Mexico
Moldova
Mongolia
Norway
Poland
Romania
Russia
Slovak Republic
Slovenia
Spain
Sweden
Tajikistan
Turkmenistan
Ukraine
USA
Uzbekistan
Yugoslavia

* Police are required to inform Chinese officials of arrest/detention in the Manchester consular district only. This comprises Derbyshire, Durham, Greater Manchester, Lancashire, Merseyside, North South and West Yorkshire, and Tyne and Wear.

Annex G

Fitness to be Interviewed

1. This Annex contains general guidance to help police officers and health care professionals assess whether a detainee might be at risk in an interview.
2. A detainee may be at risk in an interview if it is considered that:
   (a) conducting the interview could significantly harm the detainee's physical or mental state;
   (b) anything the detainee says in the interview about their involvement or suspected involvement in the offence about which they are being interviewed **might** be considered unreliable in subsequent court proceedings because of their physical or mental state.
3. In assessing whether the detainee should be interviewed, the following must be considered:
   (a) how the detainee's physical or mental state might affect their ability to understand the nature and purpose of the interview, to comprehend what is being asked and to appreciate the significance of any answers given and make rational decisions about whether they want to say anything;

(b) the extent to which the detainee's replies may be affected by their physical or mental condition rather than representing a rational and accurate explanation of their involvement in the offence;
(c) how the nature of the interview, which could include particularly probing questions, might affect the detainee.

4. It is essential health care professionals who are consulted consider the functional ability of the detainee rather than simply relying on a medical diagnosis, e.g. it is possible for a person with severe mental illness to be fit for interview.
5. Health care professionals should advise on the need for an appropriate adult to be present, whether reassessment of the person's fitness for interview may be necessary if the interview lasts beyond a specified time, and whether a further specialist opinion may be required.
6. When health care professionals identify risks they should be asked to quantify the risks. They should inform the custody officer:
   - whether the person's condition:
     — is likely to improve
     — will require or be amenable to treatment; and
   - indicate how long it may take for such improvement to take effect
7. The role of the health care professional is to consider the risks and advise the custody officer of the outcome of that consideration. The health care professional's determination and any advice or recommendations should be made in writing and form part of the custody record.
8. Once the health care professional has provided that information, it is a matter for the custody officer to decide whether or not to allow the interview to go ahead and if the interview is to proceed, to determine what safeguards are needed. Nothing prevents safeguards being provided in addition to those required under the Code. An example might be to have an appropriate health care professional present during the interview, in addition to an appropriate adult, in order constantly to monitor the person's condition and how it is being affected by the interview.

Annex H
Detained Person: Observation List

1. If any detainee fails to meet any of the following criteria, an appropriate health care professional or an ambulance must be called.
2. When assessing the level of rousability, consider:
   Rousability—can they be woken?
   - go into the cell
   - call their name
   - shake gently

   Response to questions—can they give appropriate answers to questions such as:
   - What's your name?
   - Where do you live?
   - Where do you think you are?

   Response to commands—can they respond appropriately to commands such as:
   - Open your eyes!
   - Lift one arm, now the other arm!
3. Remember to take into account the possibility or presence of other illnesses, injury, or mental condition, a person who is drowsy and smells of alcohol may also have the following:
   - Diabetes
   - Epilepsy
   - Head injury
   - Drug intoxication or overdose
   - Stroke

Annex I

Not used

Annex J

Not used

Annex K
X-Rays and Ultrasound Scans

(a) Action

1. PACE, section 55A allows a person who has been arrested and is in police detention to have an X-ray taken of them or an ultrasound scan to be carried out on them (or both) if:
   (a) authorised by an officer of inspector rank or above who has reasonable grounds for believing that the detainee:
      (i) may have swallowed a Class A drug; and
      (ii) was in possession of that Class A drug with the intention of supplying it to another or to export; and
   (b) the detainee's appropriate consent has been given in writing.
2. Before an X-ray is taken or an ultrasound scan carried out, a police officer, designated detention officer or staff custody officer must tell the detainee:–
   (a) that the authority has been given; and
   (b) the grounds for giving the authorisation.
3. Before a detainee is asked to give appropriate consent to an X-ray or an ultrasound scan, they must be warned that if they refuse without good cause their refusal may harm their case if it comes to trial, see *Notes K1* and *K2*. This warning may be given by a police officer or member of police staff. A detainee who is not legally represented must be reminded of their entitlement to have free legal advice, see *Code C, paragraph 6.5*, and the reminder noted in the custody record.
4. An X-ray may be taken, or an ultrasound scan may be carried out, only by a registered medical practitioner or registered nurse, and only at a hospital, surgery or other medical premises.

(b) Documentation

5. The following shall be recorded as soon as practicable in the detainee's custody record:
   (a) the authorisation to take the X-ray or carry out the ultrasound scan (or both);
   (b) the grounds for giving the authorisation;
   (c) the giving of the warning required by paragraph 3; and
   (d) the fact that the appropriate consent was given or (as the case may be) refused, and if refused, the reason given for the refusal (if any); and
   (e) if an X-ray is taken or an ultrasound scan carried out:
      - where it was taken or carried out
      - who took it or carried it out
      - who was present
      - the result

   Paragraphs 1.4–1.7 of this Code apply and an appropriate adult should be present when consent is sought to any procedure under this Annex

Notes for Guidance

K1 If authority is given for an X-ray to be taken or an ultrasound scan to be carried out (or both), consideration should be given to asking a registered medical practitioner or registered nurse to explain to the detainee what is involved and to allay any concerns the detainee might have about the effect which taking an X-ray or carrying out an ultrasound scan might have on them. If appropriate consent is not given, evidence of the explanation may, if the case comes to trial, be relevant to determining whether the detainee had a good cause for refusing.

K2 In warning a detainee who is asked to consent to an X-ray being taken or an ultrasound scan being carried out (or both), as in paragraph 3, the following form of words may be used:

'You do not have to allow an X-ray of you to be taken or an ultrasound scan to be carried out on you, but I must warn you that if you refuse without good cause, your refusal may harm your case if it comes to trial.'

PACE CODE D
CODE OF PRACTICE FOR THE IDENTIFICATION OF PERSONS BY POLICE OFFICERS

Commencement—transitional arrangements

This code has effect in relation to any identification procedure carried out after midnight on 31 December 2005

1. Introduction

1.1 This Code of Practice concerns the principal methods used by police to identify people in connection with the investigation of offences and the keeping of accurate and reliable criminal records.

1.2 Identification by witnesses arises, e.g., if the offender is seen committing the crime and a witness is given an opportunity to identify the suspect in a video identification, identification parade or similar procedure. The procedures are designed to:
- test the witness' ability to identify the person they saw on a previous occasion
- provide safeguards against mistaken identification.

While this Code concentrates on visual identification procedures, it does not preclude the police making use of aural identification procedures such as a 'voice identification parade', where they judge that appropriate.

1.3 Identification by fingerprints applies when a person's fingerprints are taken to:
- compare with fingerprints found at the scene of a crime
- check and prove convictions
- help to ascertain a person's identity.

1.3A Identification using footwear impressions applies when a person's footwear impressions are taken to compare with impressions found at the scene of a crime.

1.4 Identification by body samples and impressions includes taking samples such as blood or hair to generate a DNA profile for comparison with material obtained from the scene of a crime, or a victim.

1.5 Taking photographs of arrested people applies to recording and checking identity and locating and tracing persons who:
- are wanted for offences
- fail to answer their bail.

1.6 Another method of identification involves searching and examining detained suspects to find, e.g., marks such as tattoos or scars which may help establish their identity or whether they have been involved in committing an offence.

1.7 The provisions of the Police and Criminal Evidence Act 1984 (PACE) and this Code are designed to make sure fingerprints, samples, impressions and photographs are taken, used and retained, and identification procedures carried out, only when justified and necessary for preventing, detecting or investigating crime. If these provisions are not observed, the application of the relevant procedures in particular cases may be open to question.

2. General

2.1 This Code must be readily available at all police stations for consultation by:
- police officers and police staff
- detained persons
- members of the public

2.2 The provisions of this Code:
- include the *Annexes*
- do not include the *Notes for guidance.*

2.3 Code C, paragraph 1.4, regarding a person who may be mentally disordered or otherwise mentally vulnerable and the *Notes for guidance* applicable to those provisions apply to this Code.

2.4 Code C, paragraph 1.5, regarding a person who appears to be under the age of 17 applies to this Code.

2.5 Code C, paragraph 1.6, regarding a person who appears blind, seriously visually impaired, deaf, unable to read or speak or has difficulty orally because of a speech impediment applies to this Code.

2.6 In this Code:
- 'appropriate adult' means the same as in Code C, paragraph 1.7,
- 'solicitor' means the same as in Code C, paragraph 6.12

and the *Notes for guidance* applicable to those provisions apply to this Code.

2.7 References to custody officers include those performing the functions of custody officer, see *paragraph 1.9* of Code C.

2.8 When a record of any action requiring the authority of an officer of a specified rank is made under this Code, subject to *paragraph 2.18*, the officer's name and rank must be recorded.

2.9 When this Code requires the prior authority or agreement of an officer of at least inspector or superintendent rank, that authority may be given by a sergeant or chief inspector who has been authorised to perform the functions of the higher rank under PACE, section 107.

2.10 Subject to *paragraph 2.18*, all records must be timed and signed by the maker.

2.11 Records must be made in the custody record, unless otherwise specified. References to 'pocket book' include any official report book issued to police officers or police staff.

2.12 If any procedure in this Code requires a person's consent, the consent of a:

- mentally disordered or otherwise mentally vulnerable person is only valid if given in the presence of the appropriate adult
- juvenile, is only valid if their parent's or guardian's consent is also obtained unless the juvenile is under 14, when their parent's or guardian's consent is sufficient in its own right. If the only obstacle to an identification procedure in *section 3* is that a juvenile's parent or guardian refuses consent or reasonable efforts to obtain it have failed, the identification officer may apply the provisions of *paragraph 3.21*. See *Note 2A*.

2.13 If a person is blind, seriously visually impaired or unable to read, the custody officer or identification officer shall make sure their solicitor, relative, appropriate adult or some other person likely to take an interest in them and not involved in the investigation is available to help check any documentation. When this Code requires written consent or signing, the person assisting may be asked to sign instead, if the detainee prefers. This paragraph does not require an appropriate adult to be called solely to assist in checking and signing documentation for a person who is not a juvenile, or mentally disordered or otherwise mentally vulnerable (see *Note 2B* and *Code C paragraph 3.15*).

2.14 If any procedure in this Code requires information to be given to or sought from a suspect, it must be given or sought in the appropriate adult's presence if the suspect is mentally disordered, otherwise mentally vulnerable or a juvenile. If the appropriate adult is not present when the information is first given or sought, the procedure must be repeated in the presence of the appropriate adult when they arrive. If the suspect appears deaf or there is doubt about their hearing or speaking ability or ability to understand English, and effective communication cannot be established, the information must be given or sought through an interpreter.

2.15 Any procedure in this Code involving the participation of a suspect who is mentally disordered, otherwise mentally vulnerable or a juvenile must take place in the presence of the appropriate adult. See *Code C paragraph 1.4*.

2.15A Any procedure in this Code involving the participation of a witness who is or appears to be mentally disordered, otherwise mentally vulnerable or a juvenile should take place in the presence of a pre-trial support person. However, the support-person must not be allowed to prompt any identification of a suspect by a witness. See *Note 2AB*.

2.16 References to:

- 'taking a photograph', include the use of any process to produce a single, still or moving, visual image
- 'photographing a person', should be construed accordingly
- 'photographs', 'films', 'negatives' and 'copies' include relevant visual images recorded, stored, or reproduced through any medium
- 'destruction' includes the deletion of computer data relating to such images or making access to that data impossible.

2.17 Except as described, nothing in this Code affects the powers and procedures:

(i) for requiring and taking samples of breath, blood and urine in relation to driving offences, etc, when under the influence of drink, drugs or excess alcohol under the:
- Road Traffic Act 1988, sections 4 to 11
- Road Traffic Offenders Act 1988, sections 15 and 16
- Transport and Works Act 1992, sections 26 to 38;

(ii) under the Immigration Act 1971, Schedule 2, paragraph 18, for taking photographs and fingerprints from persons detained under that Act, Schedule 2, paragraph 16 (Administrative Controls as to Control on Entry etc.); for taking fingerprints in accordance with the Immigration and Asylum Act 1999; sections 141 and 142(3), or other methods for collecting information about a person's external physical characteristics provided for by regulations made under that Act, section 144;

(iii) under the Terrorism Act 2000, Schedule 8, for taking photographs, fingerprints, skin impressions, body samples or impressions from people:
- arrested under that Act, section 41,
- detained for the purposes of examination under that Act, Schedule 7, and to whom the Code of Practice issued under that Act, Schedule 14, paragraph 6, applies ('the terrorism provisions')

See *Note 2C*;

(iv) for taking photographs, fingerprints, skin impressions, body samples or impressions from people who have been:
- arrested on warrants issued in Scotland, by officers exercising powers under the Criminal Justice and Public Order Act 1994, section 136(2)
- arrested or detained without warrant by officers from a police force in Scotland exercising their powers of arrest or detention under the Criminal Justice and Public Order Act 1994, section 137(2), (Cross Border powers of arrest etc.).

Note: In these cases, police powers and duties and the person's rights and entitlements whilst at a police station in England and Wales are the same as if the person had been arrested in Scotland by a Scottish police officer.

2.18 Nothing in this Code requires the identity of officers or police staff to be recorded or disclosed:
(a) in the case of enquiries linked to the investigation of terrorism;
(b) if the officers or police staff reasonably believe recording or disclosing their names might put them in danger.

In these cases, they shall use warrant or other identification numbers and the name of their police station. See *Note 2D*

2.19 In this Code:
(a) 'designated person' means a person other than a police officer, designated under the Police Reform Act 2002, Part 4, who has specified powers and duties of police officers conferred or imposed on them;
(b) any reference to a police officer includes a designated person acting in the exercise or performance of the powers and duties conferred or imposed on them by their designation.

2.20 If a power conferred on a designated person:
(a) allows reasonable force to be used when exercised by a police officer, a designated person exercising that power has the same entitlement to use force;
(b) includes power to use force to enter any premises, that power is not exercisable by that designated person except:
(i) in the company, and under the supervision, of a police officer; or
(ii) for the purpose of:
- saving life or limb; or
- preventing serious damage to property.

2.21 Nothing in this Code prevents the custody officer, or other officer given custody of the detainee, from allowing police staff who are not designated persons to carry out individual procedures or tasks at the police station if the law allows. However, the officer remains responsible for making sure the procedures and tasks are carried out correctly in accordance with the Codes of Practice. Any such person must be:
(a) a person employed by a police authority maintaining a police force and under the control and direction of the Chief Officer of that force;
(b) employed by a person with whom a police authority has a contract for the provision of services relating to persons arrested or otherwise in custody.

2.22 Designated persons and other police staff must have regard to any relevant provisions of the Codes of Practice.

Notes for Guidance

2A For the purposes of paragraph 2.12, the consent required from a parent or guardian may, for a juvenile in the care of a local authority or voluntary organisation, be given by that authority or organisation. In the case of a juvenile, nothing in paragraph 2.12 requires the parent, guardian or representative of a local authority or voluntary organisation to be present to give their consent, unless they are acting as the appropriate adult under paragraphs 2.14 or 2.15. However, it is important that a parent or guardian not present is fully informed before being asked to consent. They must be given the same information about the procedure and the juvenile's suspected involvement in the offence as the juvenile and appropriate adult. The parent or guardian must also be allowed to speak to the juvenile and the appropriate adult if they wish. Provided the consent is fully informed and is not withdrawn, it may be obtained at any time before the procedure takes place.

2AB The Youth Justice and Criminal Evidence Act 1999 guidance 'Achieving Best Evidence in Criminal Proceedings' indicates that a pre-trial support person should accompany a vulnerable witness during any identification procedure. It states that this support person should not be (or not be likely to be) a witness in the investigation.

2B People who are seriously visually impaired or unable to read may be unwilling to sign police documents. The alternative, i.e. their representative signing on their behalf, seeks to protect the interests of both police and suspects.

2C Photographs, fingerprints, samples and impressions may be taken from a person detained under the terrorism provisions to help determine whether they are, or have been, involved in terrorism, as well as when there are reasonable grounds for suspecting their involvement in a particular offence.

2D The purpose of paragraph 2.18(b) is to protect those involved in serious organised crime investigations or arrests of particularly violent suspects when there is reliable information that those arrested or their associates may threaten or cause harm to the officers. In cases of doubt, an officer of inspector rank or above should be consulted.

3. Identification by witnesses

3.1 A record shall be made of the suspect's description as first given by a potential witness. This record must:

(a) be made and kept in a form which enables details of that description to be accurately produced from it, in a visible and legible form, which can be given to the suspect or the suspect's solicitor in accordance with this Code; and

(b) unless otherwise specified, be made before the witness takes part in any identification procedures under *paragraphs 3.5* to *3.10, 3.21* or *3.23.*

A copy of the record shall where practicable, be given to the suspect or their solicitor before any procedures under *paragraphs 3.5* to *3.10, 3.21* or *3.23* are carried out. See *Note 3E*

(a) Cases when the suspect's identity is not known

3.2 In cases when the suspect's identity is not known, a witness may be taken to a particular neighbourhood or place to see whether they can identify the person they saw. Although the number, age, sex, race, general description and style of clothing of other people present at the location and the way in which any identification is made cannot be controlled, the principles applicable to the formal procedures under *paragraphs 3.5* to *3.10* shall be followed as far as practicable. For example:

(a) where it is practicable to do so, a record should be made of the witness' description of the suspect, as in paragraph 3.1(a), before asking the witness to make an identification;

(b) care must be taken not to direct the witness' attention to any individual unless, taking into account all the circumstances, this cannot be avoided. However, this does not prevent a witness being asked to look carefully at the people around at the time or to look towards a group or in a particular direction, if this appears necessary to make sure that the witness does not overlook a possible suspect simply because the witness is looking in the opposite direction and also to enable the witness to make comparisons between any suspect and others who are in the area; See *Note 3F*

(c) where there is more than one witness, every effort should be made to keep them separate and witnesses should be taken to see whether they can identify a person independently;

(d) once there is sufficient information to justify the arrest of a particular individual for suspected involvement in the offence, e.g., after a witness makes a positive identification, the provisions set out from paragraph 3.4 onwards shall apply for any other witnesses in relation to that individual. Subject to *paragraphs 3.12* and *3.13,* it is not necessary for the witness who makes such a positive identification to take part in a further procedure;

(e) the officer or police staff accompanying the witness must record, in their pocket book, the action taken as soon as, and in as much detail, as possible. The record should include: the date, time and place of the relevant occasion the witness claims to have previously seen the suspect; where any identification was made; how it was made and the conditions at the time (e.g., the distance the witness was from the suspect, the weather and light); if the witness's attention was drawn to the suspect; the reason for this; and anything said by the witness or the suspect about the identification or the conduct of the procedure.

3.3 A witness must not be shown photographs, computerised or artist's composite likenesses or similar likenesses or pictures (including 'E-fit' images) if the identity of the suspect is known to the police and the suspect is available to take part in a video identification, an identification parade or a group identification. If the suspect's identity is not known, the showing of such images to a witness to obtain identification evidence must be done in accordance with *Annex E.*

(b) Cases when the suspect is known and available

3.4 If the suspect's identity is known to the police and they are available, the identification procedures set out in paragraphs 3.5 to 3.10 may be used. References in this section to a suspect being 'known' mean there is sufficient information known to the police to justify the arrest of a particular person for suspected involvement in the offence. A suspect being 'available' means they are immediately available or will be within a reasonably short time and willing to take an effective part in at least one of the following which it is practicable to arrange:

- video identification;
- identification parade; or
- group identification.

Video identification

3.5 Change to: 'A 'video identification' is when the witness is shown moving images of a known suspect, together with similar images of others who resemble the suspect. Moving images must be used unless:

- the suspect is known but not available (see *paragraph 3.21* of this Code); or
- in accordance with *paragraph 2A of Annex A* of this Code, the identification officer does not consider that replication of a physical feature can be achieved or that it is not possible to conceal the location of the feature on the image of the suspect.

The identification officer may then decide to make use of video identification but using still images.

3.6 Video identifications must be carried out in accordance with *Annex A*.

Identification parade

3.7 An 'identification parade' is when the witness sees the suspect in a line of others who resemble the suspect.

3.8 Identification parades must be carried out in accordance with *Annex B*.

Group identification

3.9 A 'group identification' is when the witness sees the suspect in an informal group of people.

3.10 Group identifications must be carried out in accordance with *Annex C*.

Arranging identification procedures

3.11 Except for the provisions in *paragraph 3.19*, the arrangements for, and conduct of, the identification procedures in paragraphs 3.5 to 3.10 and circumstances in which an identification procedure must be held shall be the responsibility of an officer not below inspector rank who is not involved with the investigation, 'the identification officer'. Unless otherwise specified, the identification officer may allow another officer or police staff, see *paragraph 2.21*, to make arrangements for, and conduct, any of these identification procedures. In delegating these procedures, the identification officer must be able to supervise effectively and either intervene or be contacted for advice. No officer or any other person involved with the investigation of the case against the suspect, beyond the extent required by these procedures, may take any part in these procedures or act as the identification officer. This does not prevent the identification officer from consulting the officer in charge of the investigation to determine which procedure to use. When an identification procedure is required, in the interest of fairness to suspects and witnesses, it must be held as soon as practicable.

Circumstances in which an identification procedure must be held

3.12 Whenever:

(i) a witness has identified a suspect or purported to have identified them prior to any identification procedure set out in paragraphs 3.5 to 3.10 having been held; or

(ii) there is a witness available, who expresses an ability to identify the suspect, or where there is a reasonable chance of the witness being able to do so, and they have not been given an opportunity to identify the suspect in any of the procedures set out in paragraphs 3.5 to 3.10,

and the suspect disputes being the person the witness claims to have seen, an identification procedure shall be held unless it is not practicable or it would serve no useful purpose in proving or disproving whether the suspect was involved in committing the offence. For example, when it is not disputed that the suspect is already well known to the witness who claims to have seen them commit the crime.

3.13 Such a procedure may also be held if the officer in charge of the investigation considers it would be useful.

Selecting an identification procedure

3.14 If, because of paragraph 3.12, an identification procedure is to be held, the suspect shall initially be offered a video identification unless:

a) a video identification is not practicable; or

b) an identification parade is both practicable and more suitable than a video identification; or
c) paragraph 3.16 applies.

The identification officer and the officer in charge of the investigation shall consult each other to determine which option is to be offered. An identification parade may not be practicable because of factors relating to the witnesses, such as their number, state of health, availability and travelling requirements. A video identification would normally be more suitable if it could be arranged and completed sooner than an identification parade.

3.15 A suspect who refuses the identification procedure first offered shall be asked to state their reason for refusing and may get advice from their solicitor and/or if present, their appropriate adult. The suspect, solicitor and/or appropriate adult shall be allowed to make representations about why another procedure should be used. A record should be made of the reasons for refusal and any representations made. After considering any reasons given, and representations made, the identification officer shall, if appropriate, arrange for the suspect to be offered an alternative which the officer considers suitable and practicable. If the officer decides it is not suitable and practicable to offer an alternative identification procedure, the reasons for that decision shall be recorded.

3.16 A group identification may initially be offered if the officer in charge of the investigation considers it is more suitable than a video identification or an identification parade and the identification officer considers it practicable to arrange.

Notice to suspect

3.17 Unless *paragraph 3.20* applies, before a video identification, an identification parade or group identification is arranged, the following shall be explained to the suspect:

(i) the purposes of the video identification, identification parade or group identification;
(ii) their entitlement to free legal advice; see Code C, paragraph 6.5;
(iii) the procedures for holding it, including their right to have a solicitor or friend present;
(iv) that they do not have to consent to or co-operate in a video identification, identification parade or group identification;
(v) that if they do not consent to, and co-operate in, a video identification, identification parade or group identification, their refusal may be given in evidence in any subsequent trial and police may proceed covertly without their consent or make other arrangements to test whether a witness can identify them, see *paragraph 3.21;*
(vi) whether, for the purposes of the video identification procedure, images of them have previously been obtained, see *paragraph 3.20,* and if so, that they may co-operate in providing further, suitable images to be used instead;
(vii) if appropriate, the special arrangements for juveniles;
(viii) if appropriate, the special arrangements for mentally disordered or otherwise mentally vulnerable people;
(ix) that if they significantly alter their appearance between being offered an identification procedure and any attempt to hold an identification procedure, this may be given in evidence if the case comes to trial, and the identification officer may then consider other forms of identification, see *paragraph 3.21* and *Note 3C*;
(x) that a moving image or photograph may be taken of them when they attend for any identification procedure;
(xi) whether, before their identity became known, the witness was shown photographs, a computerised or artist's composite likeness or similar likeness or image by the police, see *Note 3B;*
(xii) that if they change their appearance before an identification parade, it may not be practicable to arrange one on the day or subsequently and, because of the appearance change, the identification officer may consider alternative methods of identification, see *Note 3C;*
(xiii) that they or their solicitor will be provided with details of the description of the suspect as first given by any witnesses who are to attend the video identification, identification parade, group identification or confrontation, see *paragraph 3.1.*

3.18 This information must also be recorded in a written notice handed to the suspect. The suspect must be given a reasonable opportunity to read the notice, after which, they should be asked to sign a second copy to indicate if they are willing to co-operate with the making of a video or take part in the identification parade or group identification. The signed copy shall be retained by the identification officer.

3.19 The duties of the identification officer under *paragraphs 3.17* and *3.18* may be performed by the custody officer or other officer not involved in the investigation if:

(a) it is proposed to release the suspect in order that an identification procedure can be arranged and carried out and an inspector is not available to act as the identification officer, see *paragraph 3.11*, before the suspect leaves the station; or

(b) it is proposed to keep the suspect in police detention whilst the procedure is arranged and carried out and waiting for an inspector to act as the identification officer, see *paragraph 3.11*, would cause unreasonable delay to the investigation.

The officer concerned shall inform the identification officer of the action taken and give them the signed copy of the notice. See *Note 3C*

3.20 If the identification officer and officer in charge of the investigation suspect, on reasonable grounds that if the suspect was given the information and notice as in *paragraphs 3.17* and *3.18*, they would then take steps to avoid being seen by a witness in any identification procedure, the identification officer may arrange for images of the suspect suitable for use in a video identification procedure to be obtained before giving the information and notice. If suspect's images are obtained in these circumstances, the suspect may, for the purposes of a video identification procedure, co-operate in providing new images which if suitable, would be used instead, see *paragraph 3.17(vi)*.

(c) Cases when the suspect is known but not available

3.21 When a known suspect is not available or has ceased to be available, see *paragraph 3.4*, the identification officer may make arrangements for a video identification (see Annex A). If necessary, the identification officer may follow the video identification procedures but using **still** images. Any suitable moving or still images may be used and these may be obtained covertly if necessary. Alternatively, the identification officer may make arrangements for a group identification. See *Note 3D*. These provisions may also be applied to juveniles where the consent of their parent or guardian is either refused or reasonable efforts to obtain that consent have failed (see *paragraph 2.12*).

3.22 Any covert activity should be strictly limited to that necessary to test the ability of the witness to identify the suspect.

3.23 The identification officer may arrange for the suspect to be confronted by the witness if none of the options referred to in paragraphs 3.5 to 3.10 or 3.21 are practicable. A 'confrontation' is when the suspect is directly confronted by the witness. A confrontation does not require the suspect's consent. Confrontations must be carried out in accordance with Annex D.

3.24 Requirements for information to be given to, or sought from, a suspect or for the suspect to be given an opportunity to view images before they are shown to a witness, do not apply if the suspect's lack of co-operation prevents the necessary action.

(d) Documentation

3.25 A record shall be made of the video identification, identification parade, group identification or confrontation on forms provided for the purpose.

3.26 If the identification officer considers it is not practicable to hold a video identification or identification parade requested by the suspect, the reasons shall be recorded and explained to the suspect.

3.27 A record shall be made of a person's failure or refusal to co-operate in a video identification, identification parade or group identification and, if applicable, of the grounds for obtaining images in accordance with *paragraph 3.20*.

(e) Showing films and photographs of incidents and information released to the media

3.28 Nothing in this Code inhibits showing films or photographs to the public through the national or local media, or to police officers for the purposes of recognition and tracing suspects. However, when such material is shown to potential witnesses, including police officers, see *Note 3A*, to obtain identification evidence, it shall be shown on an individual basis to avoid any possibility of collusion, and, as far as possible, the showing shall follow the principles for video identification if the suspect is known, see *Annex A*, or identification by photographs if the suspect is not known, see *Annex E*.

3.29 When a broadcast or publication is made, see *paragraph 3.28*, a copy of the relevant material released to the media for the purposes of recognising or tracing the suspect, shall be kept. The suspect or their solicitor shall be allowed to view such material before any procedures under *paragraphs 3.5* to *3.10, 3.21* or *3.23* are carried out, provided it is practicable and would not unreasonably delay the investigation. Each witness involved in the procedure shall be asked, after they have taken part, whether they have seen any broadcast or published films or photographs relating to the offence or any description of the suspect and their replies shall be recorded. This paragraph does not affect any separate requirement under the Criminal Procedure and Investigations Act 1996 to retain material in connection with criminal investigations.

(f) Destruction and retention of photographs taken or used in identification procedures

3.30 PACE, section 64A, see *paragraph 5.12*, provides powers to take photographs of suspects and allows these photographs to be used or disclosed only for purposes related to the prevention or detection of crime, the investigation of offences or the conduct of prosecutions by, or on behalf of, police or other law enforcement and prosecuting authorities inside and outside the United Kingdom or the enforcement of a sentence. After being so used or disclosed, they may be retained but can only be used or disclosed for the same purposes.

3.31 Subject to *paragraph 3.33*, the photographs (and all negatives and copies), of suspects not taken in accordance with the provisions in *paragraph 5.12* which are taken for the purposes of, or in connection with, the identification procedures in *paragraphs 3.5* to *3.10, 3.21* or *3.23* must be destroyed unless the suspect:

(a) is charged with, or informed they may be prosecuted for, a recordable offence;

(b) is prosecuted for a recordable offence;

(c) is cautioned for a recordable offence or given a warning or reprimand in accordance with the Crime and Disorder Act 1998 for a recordable offence; or

(d) gives informed consent, in writing, for the photograph or images to be retained for purposes described in *paragraph 3.30.*

3.32 When *paragraph 3.31* requires the destruction of any photograph, the person must be given an opportunity to witness the destruction or to have a certificate confirming the destruction if they request one within five days of being informed that the destruction is required.

3.33 Nothing in *paragraph 3.31* affects any separate requirement under the Criminal Procedure and Investigations Act 1996 to retain material in connection with criminal investigations.

Notes for Guidance

3A Except for the provisions of Annex E, paragraph 1, a police officer who is a witness for the purposes of this part of the Code is subject to the same principles and procedures as a civilian witness.

3B When a witness attending an identification procedure has previously been shown photographs, or been shown or provided with computerised or artist's composite likenesses, or similar likenesses or pictures, it is the officer in charge of the investigation's responsibility to make the identification officer aware of this.

3C The purpose of paragraph 3.19 is to avoid or reduce delay in arranging identification procedures by enabling the required information and warnings, see sub-paragraphs 3.17(ix) and 3.17(xii), to be given at the earliest opportunity.

3D Paragraph 3.21 would apply when a known suspect deliberately makes themself 'unavailable' in order to delay or frustrate arrangements for obtaining identification evidence. It also applies when a suspect refuses or fails to take part in a video identification, an identification parade or a group identification, or refuses or fails to take part in the only practicable options from that list. It enables any suitable images of the suspect, moving or still, which are available or can be obtained, to be used in an identification procedure. Examples include images from custody and other CCTV systems and from visually recorded interview records, see Code F Note for Guidance 2D.

3E When it is proposed to show photographs to a witness in accordance with Annex E, it is the responsibility of the officer in charge of the investigation to confirm to the officer responsible for supervising and directing the showing, that the first description of the suspect given by that witness has been recorded. If this description has not been recorded, the procedure under Annex E must be postponed. See Annex E paragraph 2

3F The admissibility and value of identification evidence obtained when carrying out the procedure under paragraph 3.2 may be compromised if:

(a) before a person is identified, the witness' attention is specifically drawn to that person; or

(b) the suspect's identity becomes known before the procedure.

4. Identification by fingerprints and footwear impressions

A. *Taking fingerprints in connection with a criminal investigation*

(a) General

4.1 References to 'fingerprints' means any record, produced by any method, of the skin pattern and other physical characteristics or features of a person's:

(i) fingers; or

(ii) palms.

(b) Action

4.2 A person's fingerprints may be taken in connection with the investigation of an offence only with their consent or if *paragraph 4.3* applies. If the person is at a police station consent must be in writing.

4.3 PACE, section 61, provides powers to take fingerprints without consent from any person over the age of ten years:

(a) under section 61(3), from a person detained at a police station in consequence of being arrested for a recordable offence, see Note 4A, if they have not had their fingerprints taken in the course of the investigation of the offence unless those previously taken fingerprints are not a complete set or some or all of those fingerprints are not of sufficient quality to allow satisfactory analysis, comparison or matching.

(b) under section 61(4), from a person detained at a police station who has been charged with a recordable offence, see Note 4A, or informed they will be reported for such an offence if they have not had their fingerprints taken in the course of the investigation of the offence unless those previously taken fingerprints are not a complete set or some or all of those fingerprints are not of sufficient quality to allow satisfactory analysis, comparison or matching.

(c) under section 61(4A), from a person who has been bailed to appear at a court or police station if the person:

(i) has answered to bail for a person whose fingerprints were taken previously and there are reasonable grounds for believing they are not the same person; or

(ii) who has answered to bail claims to be a different person from a person whose fingerprints were previously taken;

and in either case, the court or an officer of inspector rank or above, authorises the fingerprints to be taken at the court or police station;

(d) under section 61(6), from a person who has been:

(i) convicted of a recordable offence;

(ii) given a caution in respect of a recordable offence which, at the time of the caution, the person admitted; or

(iii) warned or reprimanded under the Crime and Disorder Act 1998, section 65, for a recordable offence.

4.4 PACE, section 27, provides power to:

(a) require the person as in *paragraph 4.3(d)* to attend a police station to have their fingerprints taken if the:

(i) person has not been in police detention for the offence and has not had their fingerprints taken in the course of the investigation of that offence; or

(ii) fingerprints that were taken from the person in the course of the investigation of that offence, do not constitute a complete set or some, or all, of the fingerprints are not of sufficient quality to allow satisfactory analysis, comparison or matching; and

(b) arrest, without warrant, a person who fails to comply with the requirement.

Note: The requirement must be made within one month of the date the person is convicted, cautioned, warned or reprimanded and the person must be given a period of at least 7 days within which to attend. This 7 day period need not fall during the month allowed for making the requirement.

4.5 A person's fingerprints may be taken, as above, electronically.

4.6 Reasonable force may be used, if necessary, to take a person's fingerprints without their consent under the powers as in *paragraphs 4.3* and *4.4*.

4.7 Before any fingerprints are taken with, or without, consent as above, the person must be informed:

(a) of the reason their fingerprints are to be taken;

(b) of the grounds on which the relevant authority has been given if the power mentioned in *paragraph 4.3 (c) applies*;

(c) that their fingerprints may be retained and may be subject of a speculative search against other fingerprints, see *Note 4B*, unless destruction of the fingerprints is required in accordance with *Annex F, Part (a)*; and

(d) that if their fingerprints are required to be destroyed, they may witness their destruction as provided for in *Annex F, Part (a)*.

(c) Documentation

4.8 A record must be made as soon as possible, of the reason for taking a person's fingerprints without consent. If force is used, a record shall be made of the circumstances and those present.

4.9 A record shall be made when a person has been informed under the terms of *paragraph 4.7(c)*, of the possibility that their fingerprints may be subject of a speculative search.

B. *Taking fingerprints in connection with immigration enquiries*

Action

4.10 A person's fingerprints may be taken for the purposes of Immigration Service enquiries in accordance with powers and procedures other than under PACE and for which the Immigration Service (not the police) are responsible, only with the person's consent in writing or if *paragraph 4.11* applies.

4.11 Powers to take fingerprints for these purposes without consent are given to police and immigration officers under the:

(a) Immigration Act 1971, Schedule 2, paragraph 18(2), when it is reasonably necessary for the purposes of identifying a person detained under the Immigration Act 1971, Schedule 2, paragraph 16 (Detention of person liable to examination or removal);

(b) Immigration and Asylum Act 1999, section 141(7)(a), from a person who fails to produce, on arrival, a valid passport with a photograph or some other document satisfactorily establishing their identity and nationality if an immigration officer does not consider the person has a reasonable excuse for the failure;

(c) Immigration and Asylum Act 1999, section 141(7)(b), from a person who has been refused entry to the UK but has been temporarily admitted if an immigration officer reasonably suspects the person might break a condition imposed on them relating to residence or reporting to a police or immigration officer, and their decision is confirmed by a chief immigration officer;

(d) Immigration and Asylum Act 1999, section 141(7)(c), when directions are given to remove a person:

- as an illegal entrant,
- liable to removal under the Immigration and Asylum Act 1999, section 10,
- who is the subject of a deportation order from the UK;

(e) Immigration and Asylum Act 1999, section 141(7)(d), from a person arrested under UK immigration laws under the Immigration Act 1971, Schedule 2, paragraph 17;

(f) Immigration and Asylum Act 1999, section 141(7)(e), from a person who has made a claim:

- for asylum
- under Article 3 of the European Convention on Human Rights; or

(g) Immigration and Asylum Act 1999, section 141(7)(f), from a person who is a dependant of someone who falls into (b) to (f) above.

4.12 The Immigration and Asylum Act 1999, section 142(3), gives a police and immigration officer power to arrest, without warrant, a person who fails to comply with a requirement imposed by the Secretary of State to attend a specified place for fingerprinting.

4.13 Before any fingerprints are taken, with or without consent, the person must be informed:

(a) of the reason their fingerprints are to be taken;

(b) the fingerprints, and all copies of them, will be destroyed in accordance with *Annex F, Part B.*

4.14 Reasonable force may be used, if necessary, to take a person's fingerprints without their consent under powers as in *paragraph 4.11.*

4.15 *Paragraphs 4.1* and *4.8* apply.

C. *Taking footwear impressions in connection with a criminal investigation*

(a) Action

4.16 Impressions of a person's footwear may be taken in connection with the investigation of an offence only with their consent or if *paragraph 4.17* applies. If the person is at a police station consent must be in writing.

4.17 PACE, section 61A, provides power for a police officer to take footwear impressions without consent from any person over the age of ten years who is detained at a police station:

(a) in consequence of being arrested for a recordable offence, see *Note 4A*; or if the detainee has been charged with a recordable offence, or informed they will be reported for such an offence; and

(b) the detainee has not had an impression of their footwear taken in the course of the investigation of the offence unless the previously taken impression is not complete or is not of sufficient quality to allow satisfactory analysis, comparison or matching (whether in the case in question or generally).

4.18 Reasonable force may be used, if necessary, to take a footwear impression from a detainee without consent under the power in *paragraph 4.17.*

4.19 Before any footwear impression is taken with, or without, consent as above, the person must be informed:

(a) of the reason the impression is to be taken;

(b) that the impression may be retained and may be subject of a speculative search against other impressions, see *Note 4B*, unless destruction of the impression is required in accordance with *Annex F, Part (a)*; and

(c) that if their footwear impressions are required to be destroyed, they may witness their destruction as provided for in *Annex F, Part (a)*.

(b) Documentation

4.20 A record must be made as soon as possible, of the reason for taking a person's footwear impressions without consent. If force is used, a record shall be made of the circumstances and those present.

4.21 A record shall be made when a person has been informed under the terms of *paragraph 4.19(b)*, of the possibility that their footwear impressions may be subject of a speculative search.

Notes for Guidance

4A References to 'recordable offences' in this Code relate to those offences for which convictions, cautions, reprimands and warnings may be recorded in national police records. See PACE, section 27(4). The recordable offences current at the time when this Code was prepared, are any offences which carry a sentence of imprisonment on conviction (irrespective of the period, or the age of the offender or actual sentence passed) as well as the non-imprisonable offences under the Vagrancy Act 1824 sections 3 and 4 (begging and persistent begging), the Street Offences Act 1959, section 1 (loitering or soliciting for purposes of prostitution), the Road Traffic Act 1988, section 25 (tampering with motor vehicles), the Criminal Justice and Public Order Act 1994, section 167 (touting for hire car services) and others listed in the National Police Records (Recordable Offences) Regulations 2000 as amended.

4B Fingerprints, footwear impressions or a DNA sample (and the information derived from it) taken from a person arrested on suspicion of being involved in a recordable offence, or charged with such an offence, or informed they will be reported for such an offence, may be subject of a speculative search. This means the fingerprints, footwear impressions or DNA sample may be checked against other fingerprints, footwear impressions and DNA records held by, or on behalf of, the police and other law enforcement authorities in, or outside, the UK, or held in connection with, or as a result of, an investigation of an offence inside or outside the UK. Fingerprints, footwear impressions and samples taken from a person suspected of committing a recordable offence but not arrested, charged or informed they will be reported for it, may be subject to a speculative search only if the person consents in writing. The following is an example of a basic form of words:

'I consent to my fingerprints, footwear impressions and DNA sample and information derived from it being retained and used only for purposes related to the prevention and detection of a crime, the investigation of an offence or the conduct of a prosecution either nationally or internationally.

I understand that my fingerprints, footwear impressions or DNA sample may be checked against other fingerprint, footwear impressions and DNA records held by or on behalf of relevant law enforcement authorities, either nationally or internationally.

I understand that once I have given my consent for my fingerprints, footwear impressions or DNA sample to be retained and used I cannot withdraw this consent.'

See Annex F regarding the retention and use of fingerprints and footwear impressions taken with consent for elimination purposes.

5. Examinations to establish identity and the taking of photographs

A. *Detainees at police stations*

(a) Searching or examination of detainees at police stations

5.1 PACE, section 54A (1), allows a detainee at a police station to be searched or examined or both, to establish:

(a) whether they have any marks, features or injuries that would tend to identify them as a person involved in the commission of an offence and to photograph any identifying marks, see *paragraph 5.5*; or

(b) their identity, see *Note 5A*.

A person detained at a police station to be searched under a stop and search power, see Code A, is not a detainee for the purposes of these powers.

5.2 A search and/or examination to find marks under section 54A (1) (a) may be carried out without the detainee's consent, see *paragraph 2.12*, only if authorised by an officer of at least inspector rank when consent has been withheld or it is not practicable to obtain consent, see *Note 5D*.

5.3 A search or examination to establish a suspect's identity under section 54A (1) (b) may be carried out without the detainee's consent, see *paragraph 2.12*, only if authorised by an officer of at least inspector rank when the detainee has refused to identify themselves or the authorising officer has reasonable grounds for suspecting the person is not who they claim to be.

5.4 Any marks that assist in establishing the detainee's identity, or their identification as a person involved in the commission of an offence, are identifying marks. Such marks may be photographed with the detainee's consent, see *paragraph 2.12*; or without their consent if it is withheld or it is not practicable to obtain it, see *Note 5D*.

5.5 A detainee may only be searched, examined and photographed under section 54A, by a police officer of the same sex.

5.6 Any photographs of identifying marks, taken under section 54A, may be used or disclosed only for purposes related to the prevention or detection of crime, the investigation of offences or the conduct of prosecutions by, or on behalf of, police or other law enforcement and prosecuting authorities inside, and outside, the UK. After being so used or disclosed, the photograph may be retained but must not be used or disclosed except for these purposes, see *Note 5B*.

5.7 The powers, as in *paragraph 5.1*, do not affect any separate requirement under the Criminal Procedure and Investigations Act 1996 to retain material in connection with criminal investigations.

5.8 Authority for the search and/or examination for the purposes of *paragraphs 5.2* and *5.3* may be given orally or in writing. If given orally, the authorising officer must confirm it in writing as soon as practicable. A separate authority is required for each purpose which applies.

5.9 If it is established a person is unwilling to co-operate sufficiently to enable a search and/or examination to take place or a suitable photograph to be taken, an officer may use reasonable force to:

(a) search and/or examine a detainee without their consent; and

(b) photograph any identifying marks without their consent.

5.10 The thoroughness and extent of any search or examination carried out in accordance with the powers in section 54A must be no more than the officer considers necessary to achieve the required purpose. Any search or examination which involves the removal of more than the person's outer clothing shall be conducted in accordance with Code C, Annex A, paragraph 11.

5.11 An intimate search may not be carried out under the powers in section 54A.

(b) Photographing detainees at police stations and other persons elsewhere than at a police station

5.12 Under PACE, section 64A, an officer may photograph:

(a) any person whilst they are detained at a police station; and

(b) any person who is elsewhere than at a police station and who has been:—

(i) arrested by a constable for an offence;

(ii) taken into custody by a constable after being arrested for an offence by a person other than a constable;

(iii) made subject to a requirement to wait with a community support officer under *paragraph 2(3) or (3B)* of Schedule 4 to the Police Reform Act 2002;

(iv) given a penalty notice by a constable in uniform under Chapter 1 of Part 1 of the Criminal Justice and Police Act 2001, a penalty notice by a constable under section 444A of the Education Act 1996, or a fixed penalty notice by a constable in uniform under section 54 of the Road Traffic Offenders Act 1988;

(v) given a notice in relation to a relevant fixed penalty offence (within the meaning of paragraph 1 of Schedule 4 to the Police Reform Act 2002) by a community support officer by virtue of a designation applying that paragraph to him; or

(vi) given a notice in relation to a relevant fixed penalty offence (within the meaning of paragraph 1 of Schedule 5 to the Police Reform Act 2002) by an accredited person by virtue of accreditation specifying that that paragraph applies to him.

5.12A Photographs taken under PACE, section 64A:

(a) may be taken with the person's consent, or without their consent if consent is withheld or it is not practicable to obtain their consent, see *Note 5E*; and

(b) may be used or disclosed only for purposes related to the prevention or detection of crime, the investigation of offences or the conduct of prosecutions by, or on behalf of, police or other law enforcement and prosecuting authorities inside and outside the United Kingdom or the enforcement of any sentence or order made by a court when dealing with an offence. After being so used or disclosed, they may be retained but can only be used or disclosed for the same purposes. see *Note 5B.*

5.13 The officer proposing to take a detainee's photograph may, for this purpose, require the person to remove any item or substance worn on, or over, all, or any part of, their head or face. If they do not comply with such a requirement, the officer may remove the item or substance.

5.14 If it is established the detainee is unwilling to co-operate sufficiently to enable a suitable photograph to be taken and it is not reasonably practicable to take the photograph covertly, an officer may use reasonable force, see *Note 5F.*

(a) to take their photograph without their consent; and

(b) for the purpose of taking the photograph, remove any item or substance worn on, or over, all, or any part of, the person's head or face which they have failed to remove when asked.

5.15 For the purposes of this Code, a photograph may be obtained without the person's consent by making a copy of an image of them taken at any time on a camera system installed anywhere in the police station.

(c) Information to be given

5.16 When a person is searched, examined or photographed under the provisions as in *paragraph 5.1* and *5.12*, or their photograph obtained as in *paragraph 5.15*, they must be informed of the:

(a) purpose of the search, examination or photograph;

(b) grounds on which the relevant authority, if applicable, has been given; and

(c) purposes for which the photograph may be used, disclosed or retained.

This information must be given before the search or examination commences or the photograph is taken, except if the photograph is:

(i) to be taken covertly;

(ii) obtained as in *paragraph 5.15*, in which case the person must be informed as soon as practicable after the photograph is taken or obtained.

(d) Documentation

5.17 A record must be made when a detainee is searched, examined, or a photograph of the person, or any identifying marks found on them, are taken. The record must include the:

(a) identity, subject to paragraph 2.18, of the officer carrying out the search, examination or taking the photograph;

(b) purpose of the search, examination or photograph and the outcome;

(c) detainee's consent to the search, examination or photograph, or the reason the person was searched, examined or photographed without consent;

(d) giving of any authority as in *paragraphs 5.2* and *5.3*, the grounds for giving it and the authorising officer.

5.18 If force is used when searching, examining or taking a photograph in accordance with this section, a record shall be made of the circumstances and those present.

B. *Persons at police stations not detained*

5.19 When there are reasonable grounds for suspecting the involvement of a person in a criminal offence, but that person is at a police station **voluntarily** and not detained, the provisions of *paragraphs 5.1* to *5.18* should apply, subject to the modifications in the following paragraphs.

5.20 References to the 'person being detained' and to the powers mentioned in *paragraph 5.1* which apply only to detainees at police stations shall be omitted.

5.21 Force may not be used to:

(a) search and/or examine the person to:

(i) discover whether they have any marks that would tend to identify them as a person involved in the commission of an offence; or

(ii) establish their identity, see *Note 5A*;

(b) take photographs of any identifying marks, see *paragraph 5.4*; or

(c) take a photograph of the person.

5.22 Subject to *paragraph 5.24*, the photographs of persons or of their identifying marks which are not taken in accordance with the provisions mentioned in *paragraphs 5.1* or *5.12*, must be destroyed (together with any negatives and copies) unless the person:

(a) is charged with, or informed they may be prosecuted for, a recordable offence;

(b) is prosecuted for a recordable offence;

(c) is cautioned for a recordable offence or given a warning or reprimand in accordance with the Crime and Disorder Act 1998 for a recordable offence; or

(d) gives informed consent, in writing, for the photograph or image to be retained as in *paragraph 5.6*.

5.23 When *paragraph 5.22* requires the destruction of any photograph, the person must be given an opportunity to witness the destruction or to have a certificate confirming the destruction provided they so request the certificate within five days of being informed the destruction is required.

5.24 Nothing in *paragraph 5.22* affects any separate requirement under the Criminal Procedure and Investigations Act 1996 to retain material in connection with criminal investigations.

Notes for Guidance

5A The conditions under which fingerprints may be taken to assist in establishing a person's identity, are described in Section 4.

5B Examples of purposes related to the prevention or detection of crime, the investigation of offences or the conduct of prosecutions include:

(a) checking the photograph against other photographs held in records or in connection with, or as a result of, an investigation of an offence to establish whether the person is liable to arrest for other offences;

(b) when the person is arrested at the same time as other people, or at a time when it is likely that other people will be arrested, using the photograph to help establish who was arrested, at what time and where;

(c) when the real identity of the person is not known and cannot be readily ascertained or there are reasonable grounds for doubting a name and other personal details given by the person, are their real name and personal details. In these circumstances, using or disclosing the photograph to help to establish or verify their real identity or determine whether they are liable to arrest for some other offence, e.g. by checking it against other photographs held in records or in connection with, or as a result of, an investigation of an offence;

(d) when it appears any identification procedure in section 3 may need to be arranged for which the person's photograph would assist;

(e) when the person's release without charge may be required, and if the release is:

(i) on bail to appear at a police station, using the photograph to help verify the person's identity when they answer their bail and if the person does not answer their bail, to assist in arresting them; or

(ii) without bail, using the photograph to help verify their identity or assist in locating them for the purposes of serving them with a summons to appear at court in criminal proceedings;

(f) when the person has answered to bail at a police station and there are reasonable grounds for doubting they are the person who was previously granted bail, using the photograph to help establish or verify their identity;

(g) when the person arrested on a warrant claims to be a different person from the person named on the warrant and a photograph would help to confirm or disprove their claim;

(h) when the person has been charged with, reported for, or convicted of, a recordable offence and their photograph is not already on record as a result of (a) to (f) or their photograph is on record but their appearance has changed since it was taken and the person has not yet been released or brought before a court.

5C There is no power to arrest a person convicted of a recordable offence solely to take their photograph. The power to take photographs in this section applies only where the person is in custody as a result of the exercise of another power, e.g. arrest for fingerprinting under PACE, section 27.

5D Examples of when it would not be practicable to obtain a detainee's consent, see paragraph 2.12, to a search, examination or the taking of a photograph of an identifying mark include:

(a) when the person is drunk or otherwise unfit to give consent;

(b) when there are reasonable grounds to suspect that if the person became aware a search or examination was to take place or an identifying mark was to be photographed, they would take steps to prevent this happening, e.g. by violently resisting, covering or concealing the mark etc and it would not otherwise be possible to carry out the search or examination or to photograph any identifying mark;

(c) in the case of a juvenile, if the parent or guardian cannot be contacted in sufficient time to allow the search or examination to be carried out or the photograph to be taken.

5E Examples of when it would not be practicable to obtain the person's consent, see paragraph 2.12, to a photograph being taken include:

(a) when the person is drunk or otherwise unfit to give consent;

(b) when there are reasonable grounds to suspect that if the person became aware a photograph, suitable to be used or disclosed for the use and disclosure described in paragraph 5.6, was to be taken, they would take steps to prevent it being taken, e.g. by violently resisting, covering or distorting their face etc, and it would not otherwise be possible to take a suitable photograph;
(c) when, in order to obtain a suitable photograph, it is necessary to take it covertly; and
(d) in the case of a juvenile, if the parent or guardian cannot be contacted in sufficient time to allow the photograph to be taken.

5F The use of reasonable force to take the photograph of a suspect elsewhere than at a police station must be carefully considered. In order to obtain a suspect's consent and co-operation to remove an item of religious headwear to take their photograph, a constable should consider whether in the circumstances of the situation the removal of the headwear and the taking of the photograph should be by an officer of the same sex as the person. It would be appropriate for these actions to be conducted out of public view.

6. Identification by body samples and impressions

A. *General*

6.1 References to:
(a) an 'intimate sample' mean a dental impression or sample of blood, semen or any other tissue fluid, urine, or pubic hair, or a swab taken from any part of a person's genitals or from a person's body orifice other than the mouth;
(b) a 'non-intimate sample' means:
(i) a sample of hair, other than pubic hair, which includes hair plucked with the root, see *Note 6A*;
(ii) a sample taken from a nail or from under a nail;
(iii) a swab taken from any part of a person's body other than a part from which a swab taken would be an intimate sample;
(iv) saliva;
(v) a skin impression which means any record, other than a fingerprint, which is a record, in any form and produced by any method, of the skin pattern and other physical characteristics or features of the whole, or any part of, a person's foot or of any other part of their body.

B. *Action*

(a) Intimate samples

6.2 PACE, section 62, provides that intimate samples may be taken under:
(a) section 62(1), from a person in police detention only:
(i) if a police officer of inspector rank or above has reasonable grounds to believe such an impression or sample will tend to confirm or disprove the suspect's involvement in a recordable offence, see *Note 4A*, and gives authorisation for a sample to be taken; and
(ii) with the suspect's written consent;
(b) section 62(1A), from a person not in police detention but from whom two or more non-intimate samples have been taken in the course of an investigation of an offence and the samples, though suitable, have proved insufficient if:
(i) a police officer of inspector rank or above authorises it to be taken; and
(ii) the person concerned gives their written consent. See *Notes 6B* and *6C*

6.3 Before a suspect is asked to provide an intimate sample, they must be warned that if they refuse without good cause, their refusal may harm their case if it comes to trial, see *Note 6D*. If the suspect is in police detention and not legally represented, they must also be reminded of their entitlement to have free legal advice, see Code C, *paragraph 6.5*, and the reminder noted in the custody record. If *paragraph 6.2(b)* applies and the person is attending a station voluntarily, their entitlement to free legal advice as in Code C, *paragraph 3.21* shall be explained to them.

6.4 Dental impressions may only be taken by a registered dentist. Other intimate samples, except for samples of urine, may only be taken by a registered medical practitioner or registered nurse or registered paramedic.

(b) Non-intimate samples

6.5 A non-intimate sample may be taken from a detainee only with their written consent or if *paragraph 6.6* applies.

6.6 (a) under section 63, a non-intimate sample may not be taken from a person without consent and the consent must be in writing (aa) A non-intimate sample may be taken from a person without the appropriate consent in the following circumstances:

(i) under section 63(2A) where the person is in police detention as a consequence of his arrest for a recordable offence and he has not had a non-intimate sample of the same type and from the same part of the body taken in the course of the investigation of the offence by the police or he has had such a sample taken but it proved insufficient.

(ii) Under section 63(3) (a) where he is being held in custody by the police on the authority of a court and an officer of at least the rank of inspector authorises it to be taken.

(b) under section 63(3A), from a person charged with a recordable offence or informed they will be reported for such an offence: and

(i) that person has not had a non-intimate sample taken from them in the course of the investigation; or

(ii) if they have had a sample taken, it proved unsuitable or insufficient for the same form of analysis, see *Note 6B*; or

(c) under section 63(3B), from a person convicted of a recordable offence after the date on which that provision came into effect. PACE, section 63A, describes the circumstances in which a police officer may require a person convicted of a recordable offence to attend a police station for a non-intimate sample to be taken.

6.7 Reasonable force may be used, if necessary, to take a non-intimate sample from a person without their consent under the powers mentioned in *paragraph 6.6.*

6.8 Before any intimate sample is taken with consent or non-intimate sample is taken with, or without, consent, the person must be informed:

(a) of the reason for taking the sample;

(b) of the grounds on which the relevant authority has been given;

(c) that the sample or information derived from the sample may be retained and subject of a speculative search, see *Note 6E,* unless their destruction is required as in *Annex F,* Part A.

6.9 When clothing needs to be removed in circumstances likely to cause embarrassment to the person, no person of the opposite sex who is not a registered medical practitioner or registered health care professional shall be present, (unless in the case of a juvenile, mentally disordered or mentally vulnerable person, that person specifically requests the presence of an appropriate adult of the opposite sex who is readily available) nor shall anyone whose presence is unnecessary. However, in the case of a juvenile, this is subject to the overriding proviso that such a removal of clothing may take place in the absence of the appropriate adult only if the juvenile signifies, in their presence, that they prefer the adult's absence and they agree.

(c) Documentation

6.10 A record of the reasons for taking a sample or impression and, if applicable, of its destruction must be made as soon as practicable. If force is used, a record shall be made of the circumstances and those present. If written consent is given to the taking of a sample or impression, the fact must be recorded in writing.

6.11 A record must be made of a warning given as required by *paragraph 6.3.*

6.12 A record shall be made of the fact that a person has been informed as in *paragraph 6.8(c)* that samples may be subject of a speculative search.

Notes for Guidance

6A When hair samples are taken for the purpose of DNA analysis (rather than for other purposes such as making a visual match), the suspect should be permitted a reasonable choice as to what part of the body the hairs are taken from. When hairs are plucked, they should be plucked individually, unless the suspect prefers otherwise and no more should be plucked than the person taking them reasonably considers necessary for a sufficient sample.

6B (a) An insufficient sample is one which is not sufficient either in quantity or quality to provide information for a particular form of analysis, such as DNA analysis. A sample may also be insufficient if enough information cannot be obtained from it by analysis because of loss, destruction, damage or contamination of the sample or as a result of an earlier, unsuccessful attempt at analysis.

(b) An unsuitable sample is one which, by its nature, is not suitable for a particular form of analysis.

6C Nothing in paragraph 6.2 prevents intimate samples being taken for elimination purposes with the consent of the person concerned but the provisions of paragraph 2.12 relating to the role of the appropriate adult, should be applied. Paragraph 6.2(b) does not, however, apply where the non-intimate samples were previously taken under the Terrorism Act 2000, Schedule 8, paragraph 10.

6D In warning a person who is asked to provide an intimate sample as in paragraph 6.3, the following form of words may be used:

'You do not have to provide this sample/allow this swab or impression to be taken, but I must warn you that if you refuse without good cause, your refusal may harm your case if it comes to trial.'

6E Fingerprints or a DNA sample and the information derived from it taken from a person arrested on suspicion of being involved in a recordable offence, or charged with such an offence, or informed they will be reported for such an offence, may be subject of a speculative search. This means they may be checked against other fingerprints and DNA records held by, or on behalf of, the police and other law enforcement authorities in or outside the UK or held in connection with, or as a result of, an investigation of an offence inside or outside the UK. Fingerprints and samples taken from any other person, e.g. a person suspected of committing a recordable offence but who has not been arrested, charged or informed they will be reported for it, may be subject to a speculative search only if the person consents in writing to their fingerprints being subject of such a search. The following is an example of a basic form of words:

'I consent to my fingerprints/DNA sample and information derived from it being retained and used only for purposes related to the prevention and detection of a crime, the investigation of an offence or the conduct of a prosecution either nationally or internationally.

I understand that this sample may be checked against other fingerprint/DNA records held by or on behalf of relevant law enforcement authorities, either nationally or internationally.

I understand that once I have given my consent for the sample to be retained and used I cannot withdraw this consent.'

See Annex F regarding the retention and use of fingerprints and samples taken with consent for elimination purposes.

6F Samples of urine and non-intimate samples taken in accordance with sections 63B and 63C of PACE may not be used for identification purposes in accordance with this Code. See Code C note for guidance 17D.

Annex A

Video Identification

(a) General

1. The arrangements for obtaining and ensuring the availability of a suitable set of images to be used in a video identification must be the responsibility of an identification officer, who has no direct involvement with the case.

2. The set of images must include the suspect and at least eight other people who, so far as possible, resemble the suspect in age, general appearance and position in life. Only one suspect shall appear in any set unless there are two suspects of roughly similar appearance, in which case they may be shown together with at least twelve other people.

2A If the suspect has an unusual physical feature, e.g., a facial scar, tattoo or distinctive hairstyle or hair colour which does not appear on the images of the other people that are available to be used, steps may be taken to:

(a) conceal the location of the feature on the images of the suspect and the other people; or

(b) replicate that feature on the images of the other people.

For these purposes, the feature may be concealed or replicated electronically or by any other method which it is practicable to use to ensure that the images of the suspect and other people resemble each other. The identification officer has discretion to choose whether to conceal or replicate the feature and the method to be used. If an unusual physical feature has been described by the witness, the identification officer should, if practicable, have that feature replicated. If it has not been described, concealment may be more appropriate.

2B If the identification officer decides that a feature should be concealed or replicated, the reason for the decision and whether the feature was concealed or replicated in the images shown to any witness shall be recorded.

2C If the witness requests to view an image where an unusual physical feature has been concealed or replicated without the feature being concealed or replicated, the witness may be allowed to do so.

3. The images used to conduct a video identification shall, as far as possible, show the suspect and other people in the same positions or carrying out the same sequence of movements. They shall also show the suspect and other people under identical conditions unless the identification officer reasonably believes:

(a) because of the suspect's failure or refusal to co-operate or other reasons, it is not practicable for the conditions to be identical; and
(b) any difference in the conditions would not direct a witness' attention to any individual image.

4. The reasons identical conditions are not practicable shall be recorded on forms provided for the purpose.
5. Provision must be made for each person shown to be identified by number.
6. If police officers are shown, any numerals or other identifying badges must be concealed. If a prison inmate is shown, either as a suspect or not, then either all, or none of, the people shown should be in prison clothing.
7. The suspect or their solicitor, friend, or appropriate adult must be given a reasonable opportunity to see the complete set of images before it is shown to any witness. If the suspect has a reasonable objection to the set of images or any of the participants, the suspect shall be asked to state the reasons for the objection. Steps shall, if practicable, be taken to remove the grounds for objection. If this is not practicable, the suspect and/or their representative shall be told why their objections cannot be met and the objection, the reason given for it and why it cannot be met shall be recorded on forms provided for the purpose.
8. Before the images are shown in accordance with *paragraph 7*, the suspect or their solicitor shall be provided with details of the first description of the suspect by any witnesses who are to attend the video identification. When a broadcast or publication is made, as in *paragraph 3.28*, the suspect or their solicitor must also be allowed to view any material released to the media by the police for the purpose of recognising or tracing the suspect, provided it is practicable and would not unreasonably delay the investigation.
9. The suspect's solicitor, if practicable, shall be given reasonable notification of the time and place the video identification is to be conducted so a representative may attend on behalf of the suspect. If a solicitor has not been instructed, this information shall be given to the suspect. The suspect may not be present when the images are shown to the witness(es). In the absence of the suspect's representative, the viewing itself shall be recorded on video. No unauthorised people may be present.

(b) Conducting the video identification

10. The identification officer is responsible for making the appropriate arrangements to make sure, before they see the set of images, witnesses are not able to communicate with each other about the case, see any of the images which are to be shown, see, or be reminded of, any photograph or description of the suspect or be given any other indication as to the suspect's identity, or overhear a witness who has already seen the material. There must be no discussion with the witness about the composition of the set of images and they must not be told whether a previous witness has made any identification.
11. Only one witness may see the set of images at a time. Immediately before the images are shown, the witness shall be told that the person they saw on a specified earlier occasion may, or may not, appear in the images they are shown and that if they cannot make a positive identification, they should say so. The witness shall be advised that at any point, they may ask to see a particular part of the set of images or to have a particular image frozen for them to study. Furthermore, it should be pointed out to the witness that there is no limit on how many times they can view the whole set of images or any part of them. However, they should be asked not to make any decision as to whether the person they saw is on the set of images until they have seen the whole set at least twice.
12. Once the witness has seen the whole set of images at least twice and has indicated that they do not want to view the images, or any part of them, again, the witness shall be asked to say whether the individual they saw in person on a specified earlier occasion has been shown and, if so, to identify them by number of the image. The witness will then be shown that image to confirm the identification, see *paragraph 17*.
13. Care must be taken not to direct the witness' attention to any one individual image or give any indication of the suspect's identity. Where a witness has previously made an identification by photographs, or a computerised or artist's composite or similar likeness, the witness must not be reminded of such a photograph or composite likeness once a suspect is available for identification by other means in accordance with this Code. Nor must the witness be reminded of any description of the suspect.
14. After the procedure, each witness shall be asked whether they have seen any broadcast or published films or photographs, or any descriptions of suspects relating to the offence and their reply shall be recorded.

(c) Image security and destruction

15. Arrangements shall be made for all relevant material containing sets of images used for specific identification procedures to be kept securely and their movements accounted for. In particular, no-one involved in the investigation shall be permitted to view the material prior to it being shown to any witness.
16. As appropriate, *paragraph 3.30* or *3.31* applies to the destruction or retention of relevant sets of images.

(d) Documentation

17. A record must be made of all those participating in, or seeing, the set of images whose names are known to the police.
18. A record of the conduct of the video identification must be made on forms provided for the purpose. This shall include anything said by the witness about any identifications or the conduct of the procedure and any reasons it was not practicable to comply with any of the provisions of this Code governing the conduct of video identifications.

Annex B
Identification Parades

(a) General

1. A suspect must be given a reasonable opportunity to have a solicitor or friend present, and the suspect shall be asked to indicate on a second copy of the notice whether or not they wish to do so.
2. An identification parade may take place either in a normal room or one equipped with a screen permitting witnesses to see members of the identification parade without being seen. The procedures for the composition and conduct of the identification parade are the same in both cases, subject to *paragraph 8* (except that an identification parade involving a screen may take place only when the suspect's solicitor, friend or appropriate adult is present or the identification parade is recorded on video).
3. Before the identification parade takes place, the suspect or their solicitor shall be provided with details of the first description of the suspect by any witnesses who are attending the identification parade. When a broadcast or publication is made as in *paragraph 3.28*, the suspect or their solicitor should also be allowed to view any material released to the media by the police for the purpose of recognising or tracing the suspect, provided it is practicable to do so and would not unreasonably delay the investigation.

(b) Identification parades involving prison inmates

4. If a prison inmate is required for identification, and there are no security problems about the person leaving the establishment, they may be asked to participate in an identification parade or video identification.
5. An identification parade may be held in a Prison Department establishment but shall be conducted, as far as practicable under normal identification parade rules. Members of the public shall make up the identification parade unless there are serious security, or control, objections to their admission to the establishment. In such cases, or if a group or video identification is arranged within the establishment, other inmates may participate. If an inmate is the suspect, they are not required to wear prison clothing for the identification parade unless the other people taking part are other inmates in similar clothing, or are members of the public who are prepared to wear prison clothing for the occasion.

(c) Conduct of the identification parade

6. Immediately before the identification parade, the suspect must be reminded of the procedures governing its conduct and cautioned in the terms of Code C, paragraphs 10.5 or 10.6, as appropriate.
7. All unauthorised people must be excluded from the place where the identification parade is held.
8. Once the identification parade has been formed, everything afterwards, in respect of it, shall take place in the presence and hearing of the suspect and any interpreter, solicitor, friend or appropriate adult who is present (unless the identification parade involves a screen, in which case everything said to, or by, any witness at the place where the identification parade is held, must be said in the hearing and presence of the suspect's solicitor, friend or appropriate adult or be recorded on video).
9. The identification parade shall consist of at least eight people (in addition to the suspect) who, so far as possible, resemble the suspect in age, height, general appearance and position in life. Only

one suspect shall be included in an identification parade unless there are two suspects of roughly similar appearance, in which case they may be paraded together with at least twelve other people. In no circumstances shall more than two suspects be included in one identification parade and where there are separate identification parades, they shall be made up of different people.

10. If the suspect has an unusual physical feature, e.g., a facial scar, tattoo or distinctive hairstyle or hair colour which cannot be replicated on other members of the identification parade, steps may be taken to conceal the location of that feature on the suspect and the other members of the identification parade if the suspect and their solicitor, or appropriate adult, agree. For example, by use of a plaster or a hat, so that all members of the identification parade resemble each other in general appearance.
11. When all members of a similar group are possible suspects, separate identification parades shall be held for each unless there are two suspects of similar appearance when they may appear on the same identification parade with at least twelve other members of the group who are not suspects. When police officers in uniform form an identification parade any numerals or other identifying badges shall be concealed.
12. When the suspect is brought to the place where the identification parade is to be held, they shall be asked if they have any objection to the arrangements for the identification parade or to any of the other participants in it and to state the reasons for the objection. The suspect may obtain advice from their solicitor or friend, if present, before the identification parade proceeds. If the suspect has a reasonable objection to the arrangements or any of the participants, steps shall, if practicable, be taken to remove the grounds for objection. When it is not practicable to do so, the suspect shall be told why their objections cannot be met and the objection, the reason given for it and why it cannot be met, shall be recorded on forms provided for the purpose.
13. The suspect may select their own position in the line, but may not otherwise interfere with the order of the people forming the line. When there is more than one witness, the suspect must be told, after each witness has left the room, that they can, if they wish, change position in the line. Each position in the line must be clearly numbered, whether by means of a number laid on the floor in front of each identification parade member or by other means.
14. Appropriate arrangements must be made to make sure, before witnesses attend the identification parade, they are not able to:
    (i) communicate with each other about the case or overhear a witness who has already seen the identification parade;
    (ii) see any member of the identification parade;
    (iii) see, or be reminded of, any photograph or description of the suspect or be given any other indication as to the suspect's identity; or
    (iv) see the suspect before or after the identification parade.
15. The person conducting a witness to an identification parade must not discuss with them the composition of the identification parade and, in particular, must not disclose whether a previous witness has made any identification.
16. Witnesses shall be brought in one at a time. Immediately before the witness inspects the identification parade, they shall be told the person they saw on a specified earlier occasion may, or may not, be present and if they cannot make a positive identification, they should say so. The witness must also be told they should not make any decision about whether the person they saw is on the identification parade until they have looked at each member at least twice.
17. When the officer or police staff (see paragraph 3.11) conducting the identification procedure is satisfied the witness has properly looked at each member of the identification parade, they shall ask the witness whether the person they saw on a specified earlier occasion is on the identification parade and, if so, to indicate the number of the person concerned, see *paragraph 28*.
18. If the witness wishes to hear any identification parade member speak, adopt any specified posture or move, they shall first be asked whether they can identify any person(s) on the identification parade on the basis of appearance only. When the request is to hear members of the identification parade speak, the witness shall be reminded that the participants in the identification parade have been chosen on the basis of physical appearance only. Members of the identification parade may then be asked to comply with the witness' request to hear them speak, see them move or adopt any specified posture.
19. If the witness requests that the person they have indicated remove anything used for the purposes of *paragraph 10* to conceal the location of an unusual physical feature, that person may be asked to remove it.
20. If the witness makes an identification after the identification parade has ended, the suspect and, if

present, their solicitor, interpreter or friend shall be informed. When this occurs, consideration should be given to allowing the witness a second opportunity to identify the suspect.

21. After the procedure, each witness shall be asked whether they have seen any broadcast or published films or photographs or any descriptions of suspects relating to the offence and their reply shall be recorded.
22. When the last witness has left, the suspect shall be asked whether they wish to make any comments on the conduct of the identification parade.

(d) Documentation

23. A video recording must normally be taken of the identification parade. If that is impracticable, a colour photograph must be taken. A copy of the video recording or photograph shall be supplied, on request, to the suspect or their solicitor within a reasonable time.
24. As appropriate, *paragraph 3.30* or *3.31*, should apply to any photograph or video taken as in *paragraph 23*.
25. If any person is asked to leave an identification parade because they are interfering with its conduct, the circumstances shall be recorded.
26. A record must be made of all those present at an identification parade whose names are known to the police.
27. If prison inmates make up an identification parade, the circumstances must be recorded.
28. A record of the conduct of any identification parade must be made on forms provided for the purpose. This shall include anything said by the witness or the suspect about any identifications or the conduct of the procedure, and any reasons it was not practicable to comply with any of this Code's provisions.

Annex C
Group Identification

(a) General

1. The purpose of this Annex is to make sure, as far as possible, group identifications follow the principles and procedures for identification parades so the conditions are fair to the suspect in the way they test the witness' ability to make an identification.
2. Group identifications may take place either with the suspect's consent and cooperation or covertly without their consent.
3. The location of the group identification is a matter for the identification officer, although the officer may take into account any representations made by the suspect, appropriate adult, their solicitor or friend.
4. The place where the group identification is held should be one where other people are either passing by or waiting around informally, in groups such that the suspect is able to join them and be capable of being seen by the witness at the same time as others in the group. For example people leaving an escalator, pedestrians walking through a shopping centre, passengers on railway and bus stations, waiting in queues or groups or where people are standing or sitting in groups in other public places.
5. If the group identification is to be held covertly, the choice of locations will be limited by the places where the suspect can be found and the number of other people present at that time. In these cases, suitable locations might be along regular routes travelled by the suspect, including buses or trains or public places frequented by the suspect.
6. Although the number, age, sex, race and general description and style of clothing of other people present at the location cannot be controlled by the identification officer, in selecting the location the officer must consider the general appearance and numbers of people likely to be present. In particular, the officer must reasonably expect that over the period the witness observes the group, they will be able to see, from time to time, a number of others whose appearance is broadly similar to that of the suspect.
7. A group identification need not be held if the identification officer believes, because of the unusual appearance of the suspect, none of the locations it would be practicable to use satisfy the requirements of *paragraph 6* necessary to make the identification fair.
8. Immediately after a group identification procedure has taken place (with or without the suspect's consent), a colour photograph or video should be taken of the general scene, if practicable, to give a general impression of the scene and the number of people present. Alternatively, if it is practicable, the group identification may be video recorded.

9. If it is not practicable to take the photograph or video in accordance with *paragraph 8*, a photograph or film of the scene should be taken later at a time determined by the identification officer if the officer considers it practicable to do so.
10. An identification carried out in accordance with this Code remains a group identification even though, at the time of being seen by the witness, the suspect was on their own rather than in a group.
11. Before the group identification takes place, the suspect or their solicitor shall be provided with details of the first description of the suspect by any witnesses who are to attend the identification. When a broadcast or publication is made, as in *paragraph 3.28*, the suspect or their solicitor should also be allowed to view any material released by the police to the media for the purposes of recognising or tracing the suspect, provided that it is practicable and would not unreasonably delay the investigation.
12. After the procedure, each witness shall be asked whether they have seen any broadcast or published films or photographs or any descriptions of suspects relating to the offence and their reply recorded.

(b) Identification with the consent of the suspect

13. A suspect must be given a reasonable opportunity to have a solicitor or friend present. They shall be asked to indicate on a second copy of the notice whether or not they wish to do so.
14. The witness, the person carrying out the procedure and the suspect's solicitor, appropriate adult, friend or any interpreter for the witness, may be concealed from the sight of the individuals in the group they are observing, if the person carrying out the procedure considers this assists the conduct of the identification.
15. The person conducting a witness to a group identification must not discuss with them the forthcoming group identification and, in particular, must not disclose whether a previous witness has made any identification.
16. Anything said to, or by, the witness during the procedure about the identification should be said in the presence and hearing of those present at the procedure.
17. Appropriate arrangements must be made to make sure, before witnesses attend the group identification, they are not able to:
    (i) communicate with each other about the case or overhear a witness who has already been given an opportunity to see the suspect in the group;
    (ii) see the suspect; or
    (iii) see, or be reminded of, any photographs or description of the suspect or be given any other indication of the suspect's identity.
18. Witnesses shall be brought one at a time to the place where they are to observe the group. Immediately before the witness is asked to look at the group, the person conducting the procedure shall tell them that the person they saw may, or may not, be in the group and that if they cannot make a positive identification, they should say so. The witness shall be asked to observe the group in which the suspect is to appear. The way in which the witness should do this will depend on whether the group is moving or stationary.

Moving group

19. When the group in which the suspect is to appear is moving, e.g. leaving an escalator, the provisions of *paragraphs 20* to *24* should be followed.
20. If two or more suspects consent to a group identification, each should be the subject of separate identification procedures. These may be conducted consecutively on the same occasion.
21. The person conducting the procedure shall tell the witness to observe the group and ask them to point out any person they think they saw on the specified earlier occasion.
22. Once the witness has been informed as in *paragraph 21* the suspect should be allowed to take whatever position in the group they wish.
23. When the witness points out a person as in *paragraph 21* they shall, if practicable, be asked to take a closer look at the person to confirm the identification. If this is not practicable, or they cannot confirm the identification, they shall be asked how sure they are that the person they have indicated is the relevant person.
24. The witness should continue to observe the group for the period which the person conducting the procedure reasonably believes is necessary in the circumstances for them to be able to make comparisons between the suspect and other individuals of broadly similar appearance to the suspect as in *paragraph 6*.

Stationary groups

25. When the group in which the suspect is to appear is stationary, e.g. people waiting in a queue, the provisions of *paragraphs 26* to *29* should be followed.
26. If two or more suspects consent to a group identification, each should be subject to separate identification procedures unless they are of broadly similar appearance when they may appear in the same group. When separate group identifications are held, the groups must be made up of different people.
27. The suspect may take whatever position in the group they wish. If there is more than one witness, the suspect must be told, out of the sight and hearing of any witness, that they can, if they wish, change their position in the group.
28. The witness shall be asked to pass along, or amongst, the group and to look at each person in the group at least twice, taking as much care and time as possible according to the circumstances, before making an identification. Once the witness has done this, they shall be asked whether the person they saw on the specified earlier occasion is in the group and to indicate any such person by whatever means the person conducting the procedure considers appropriate in the circumstances. If this is not practicable, the witness shall be asked to point out any person they think they saw on the earlier occasion.
29. When the witness makes an indication as in *paragraph 28*, arrangements shall be made, if practicable, for the witness to take a closer look at the person to confirm the identification. If this is not practicable, or the witness is unable to confirm the identification, they shall be asked how sure they are that the person they have indicated is the relevant person.

All cases

30. If the suspect unreasonably delays joining the group, or having joined the group, deliberately conceals themselves from the sight of the witness, this may be treated as a refusal to co-operate in a group identification.
31. If the witness identifies a person other than the suspect, that person should be informed what has happened and asked if they are prepared to give their name and address. There is no obligation upon any member of the public to give these details. There shall be no duty to record any details of any other member of the public present in the group or at the place where the procedure is conducted.
32. When the group identification has been completed, the suspect shall be asked whether they wish to make any comments on the conduct of the procedure.
33. If the suspect has not been previously informed, they shall be told of any identifications made by the witnesses.

(c) Identification without the suspect's consent

34. Group identifications held covertly without the suspect's consent should, as far as practicable, follow the rules for conduct of group identification by consent.
35. A suspect has no right to have a solicitor, appropriate adult or friend present as the identification will take place without the knowledge of the suspect.
36. Any number of suspects may be identified at the same time.

(d) Identifications in police stations

37. Group identifications should only take place in police stations for reasons of safety, security or because it is not practicable to hold them elsewhere.
38. The group identification may take place either in a room equipped with a screen permitting witnesses to see members of the group without being seen, or anywhere else in the police station that the identification officer considers appropriate.
39. Any of the additional safeguards applicable to identification parades should be followed if the identification officer considers it is practicable to do so in the circumstances.

(e) Identifications involving prison inmates

40. A group identification involving a prison inmate may only be arranged in the prison or at a police station.
41. When a group identification takes place involving a prison inmate, whether in a prison or in a police station, the arrangements should follow those in *paragraphs 37* to *39*. If a group identification takes place within a prison, other inmates may participate. If an inmate is the suspect, they do not have to wear prison clothing for the group identification unless the other participants are wearing the same clothing.

(f) Documentation

42. When a photograph or video is taken as in *paragraph 8* or *9*, a copy of the photograph or video shall be supplied on request to the suspect or their solicitor within a reasonable time.
43. *Paragraph 3.30* or *3.31*, as appropriate, shall apply when the photograph or film taken in accordance with *paragraph 8* or *9* includes the suspect.
44. A record of the conduct of any group identification must be made on forms provided for the purpose. This shall include anything said by the witness or suspect about any identifications or the conduct of the procedure and any reasons why it was not practicable to comply with any of the provisions of this Code governing the conduct of group identifications.

Annex D
Confrontation by a Witness

1. Before the confrontation takes place, the witness must be told that the person they saw may, or may not, be the person they are to confront and that if they are not that person, then the witness should say so.
2. Before the confrontation takes place the suspect or their solicitor shall be provided with details of the first description of the suspect given by any witness who is to attend. When a broadcast or publication is made, as in *paragraph 3.28*, the suspect or their solicitor should also be allowed to view any material released to the media for the purposes of recognising or tracing the suspect, provided it is practicable to do so and would not unreasonably delay the investigation.
3. Force may not be used to make the suspect's face visible to the witness.
4. Confrontation must take place in the presence of the suspect's solicitor, interpreter or friend unless this would cause unreasonable delay.
5. The suspect shall be confronted independently by each witness, who shall be asked 'Is this the person?'. If the witness identifies the person but is unable to confirm the identification, they shall be asked how sure they are that the person is the one they saw on the earlier occasion.
6. The confrontation should normally take place in the police station, either in a normal room or one equipped with a screen permitting a witness to see the suspect without being seen. In both cases, the procedures are the same except that a room equipped with a screen may be used only when the suspect's solicitor, friend or appropriate adult is present or the confrontation is recorded on video.
7. After the procedure, each witness shall be asked whether they have seen any broadcast or published films or photographs or any descriptions of suspects relating to the offence and their reply shall be recorded.

Annex E
Showing Photographs

(a) Action

1. An officer of sergeant rank or above shall be responsible for supervising and directing the showing of photographs. The actual showing may be done by another officer or police staff, see *paragraph 3.11*.
2. The supervising officer must confirm the first description of the suspect given by the witness has been recorded before they are shown the photographs. If the supervising officer is unable to confirm the description has been recorded they shall postpone showing the photographs.
3. Only one witness shall be shown photographs at any one time. Each witness shall be given as much privacy as practicable and shall not be allowed to communicate with any other witness in the case.
4. The witness shall be shown not less than twelve photographs at a time, which shall, as far as possible, all be of a similar type.
5. When the witness is shown the photographs, they shall be told the photograph of the person they saw may, or may not, be amongst them and if they cannot make a positive identification, they should say so. The witness shall also be told they should not make a decision until they have viewed at least twelve photographs. The witness shall not be prompted or guided in any way but shall be left to make any selection without help.
6. If a witness makes a positive identification from photographs, unless the person identified is otherwise eliminated from enquiries or is not available, other witnesses shall not be shown photographs. But both they, and the witness who has made the identification, shall be asked to attend a video identification, an identification parade or group identification unless there is no dispute about the suspect's identification.
7. If the witness makes a selection but is unable to confirm the identification, the person showing the

photographs shall ask them how sure they are that the photograph they have indicated is the person they saw on the specified earlier occasion.

8. When the use of a computerised or artist's composite or similar likeness has led to there being a known suspect who can be asked to participate in a video identification, appear on an identification parade or participate in a group identification, that likeness shall not be shown to other potential witnesses.
9. When a witness attending a video identification, an identification parade or group identification has previously been shown photographs or computerised or artist's composite or similar likeness (and it is the responsibility of the officer in charge of the investigation to make the identification officer aware that this is the case), the suspect and their solicitor must be informed of this fact before the identification procedure takes place.
10. None of the photographs shown shall be destroyed, whether or not an identification is made, since they may be required for production in court. The photographs shall be numbered and a separate photograph taken of the frame or part of the album from which the witness made an identification as an aid to reconstituting it.

(b) Documentation

11. Whether or not an identification is made, a record shall be kept of the showing of photographs on forms provided for the purpose. This shall include anything said by the witness about any identification or the conduct of the procedure, any reasons it was not practicable to comply with any of the provisions of this Code governing the showing of photographs and the name and rank of the supervising officer.
12. The supervising officer shall inspect and sign the record as soon as practicable.

ANNEX F
FINGERPRINTS, FOOTWEAR IMPRESSIONS AND SAMPLES—DESTRUCTION AND SPECULATIVE SEARCHES

(a) Fingerprints, footwear impressions and samples taken in connection with a criminal investigation

1. When fingerprints, footwear impressions or DNA samples are taken from a person in connection with an investigation and the person is not suspected of having committed the offence, see *Note F1*, they must be destroyed as soon as they have fulfilled the purpose for which they were taken unless:
   (a) they were taken for the purposes of an investigation of an offence for which a person has been convicted; and
   (b) fingerprints, footwear impressions or samples were also taken from the convicted person for the purposes of that investigation.

   However, subject to *paragraph 2*, the fingerprints, footwear impressions and samples, and the information derived from samples, may not be used in the investigation of any offence or in evidence against the person who is, or would be, entitled to the destruction of the fingerprints, footwear impressions and samples, see *Note F2*.
2. The requirement to destroy fingerprints, footwear impressions and DNA samples, and information derived from samples, and restrictions on their retention and use in paragraph 1 do not apply if the person gives their written consent for their fingerprints, footwear impressions or sample to be retained and used after they have fulfilled the purpose for which they were taken, see *Note F1*.
3. When a person's fingerprints, footwear impressions or sample are to be destroyed:
   (a) any copies of the fingerprints and footwear impressions must also be destroyed;
   (b) the person may witness the destruction of their fingerprints, footwear impressions or copies if they ask to do so within five days of being informed destruction is required;
   (c) access to relevant computer fingerprint data shall be made impossible as soon as it is practicable to do so and the person shall be given a certificate to this effect within three months of asking; and
   (d) neither the fingerprints, footwear impressions, the sample, or any information derived from the sample, may be used in the investigation of any offence or in evidence against the person who is, or would be, entitled to its destruction.
4. Fingerprints, footwear impressions or samples, and the information derived from samples, taken in connection with the investigation of an offence which are not required to be destroyed, may be retained after they have fulfilled the purposes for which they were taken but may be used only for purposes related to the prevention or detection of crime, the investigation of an offence or the

conduct of a prosecution in, as well as outside, the UK and may also be subject to a speculative search. This includes checking them against other fingerprints, footwear impressions and DNA records held by, or on behalf of, the police and other law enforcement authorities in, as well as outside, the UK.

(b) Fingerprints taken in connection with Immigration Service enquiries

5. Fingerprints taken for Immigration Service enquiries in accordance with powers and procedures other than under PACE and for which the Immigration Service, not the police, are responsible, must be destroyed as follows:
   (a) fingerprints and all copies must be destroyed as soon as practicable if the person from whom they were taken proves they are a British or Commonwealth citizen who has the right of abode in the UK under the Immigration Act 1971, section 2(1)(b);
   (b) fingerprints taken under the power as in *paragraph 4.11(g)* from a dependant of a person in *4.11 (b)* to *(f)* must be destroyed when that person's fingerprints are to be destroyed;
   (c) fingerprints taken from a person under any power as in *paragraph 4.11* or with the person's consent which have not already been destroyed as above, must be destroyed within ten years of being taken or within such period specified by the Secretary of State under the Immigration and Asylum Act 1999, section 143(5).

Notes for Guidance

F1 Fingerprints, footwear impressions and samples given voluntarily for the purposes of elimination play an important part in many police investigations. It is, therefore, important to make sure innocent volunteers are not deterred from participating and their consent to their fingerprints, footwear impressions and DNA being used for the purposes of a specific investigation is fully informed and voluntary. If the police or volunteer seek to have the fingerprints, footwear impressions or samples retained for use after the specific investigation ends, it is important the volunteer's consent to this is also fully informed and voluntary.

Examples of consent for:

- DNA/fingerprints/footwear impressions—to be used only for the purposes of a specific investigation;
- DNA/fingerprints/footwear impressions—to be used in the specific investigation **and** retained by the police for future use.

To minimise the risk of confusion, each consent should be physically separate and the volunteer should be asked to sign **each consent**.

(a) DNA:

(i) DNA sample taken for the purposes of elimination or as part of an intelligence-led screening and to be used only for the purposes of that investigation and destroyed afterwards:

'I consent to my DNA/mouth swab being taken for forensic analysis. I understand that the sample will be destroyed at the end of the case and that my profile will only be compared to the crime stain profile from this enquiry. I have been advised that the person taking the sample may be required to give evidence and/or provide a written statement to the police in relation to the taking of it'.

(ii) DNA sample to be retained on the National DNA database and used in the future:

'I consent to my DNA sample and information derived from it being retained and used only for purposes related to the prevention and detection of a crime, the investigation of an offence or the conduct of a prosecution either nationally or internationally.'

'I understand that this sample may be checked against other DNA records held by, or on behalf of, relevant law enforcement authorities, either nationally or internationally'.

'I understand that once I have given my consent for the sample to be retained and used I cannot withdraw this consent.'

(b) Fingerprints:

(i) Fingerprints taken for the purposes of elimination or as part of an intelligence-led screening and to be used only for the purposes of that investigation and destroyed afterwards:

'I consent to my fingerprints being taken for elimination purposes. I understand that the fingerprints will be destroyed at the end of the case and that my fingerprints will only be compared to the fingerprints from this enquiry. I have been advised that the person taking the fingerprints may be required to give evidence and/or provide a written statement to the police in relation to the taking of it.'

(ii) Fingerprints to be retained for future use:

'I consent to my fingerprints being retained and used only for purposes related to the prevention and detection of a crime, the investigation of an offence or the conduct of a prosecution either nationally or internationally'.

'I understand that my fingerprints may be checked against other records held by, or on behalf of, relevant law enforcement authorities, either nationally or internationally.'

'I understand that once I have given my consent for my fingerprints to be retained and used I cannot withdraw this consent.'

(c) Footwear impressions:

(i) Footwear impressions taken for the purposes of elimination or as part of an intelligence-led screening and to be used only for the purposes of that investigation and destroyed afterwards:

'I consent to my footwear impressions being taken for elimination purposes. I understand that the footwear impressions will be destroyed at the end of the case and that my footwear impressions will only be compared to the footwear impressions from this enquiry. I have been advised that the person taking the footwear impressions may be required to give evidence and/or provide a written statement to the police in relation to the taking of it.'

(ii) Footwear impressions to be retained for future use:

'I consent to my footwear impressions being retained and used only for purposes related to the prevention and detection of a crime, the investigation of an offence or the conduct of a prosecution, either nationally or internationally'.

'I understand that my footwear impressions may be checked against other records held by, or on behalf of, relevant law enforcement authorities, either nationally or internationally.'

'I understand that once I have given my consent for my footwear impressions to be retained and used I cannot withdraw this consent.'

F2 The provisions for the retention of fingerprints, footwear impressions and samples in paragraph 1 allow for all fingerprints, footwear impressions and samples in a case to be available for any subsequent miscarriage of justice investigation.

PACE CODE E
CODE OF PRACTICE ON AUDIO RECORDING INTERVIEWS WITH SUSPECTS

Commencement—transitional arrangements

This code applies to interviews carried out after midnight on 31 December 2005, notwithstanding that the interview may have commenced before that time.

1. General

1.1 This Code of Practice must be readily available for consultation by:
- police officers
- police staff
- detained persons
- members of the public.

1.2 The *Notes for Guidance* included are not provisions of this Code.

1.3 Nothing in this Code shall detract from the requirements of Code C, the Code of Practice for the detention, treatment and questioning of persons by police officers.

1.4 This Code does not apply to those people listed in Code C, *paragraph 1.12*.

1.5 The term:
- 'appropriate adult' has the same meaning as in Code C, *paragraph 1.7*
- 'solicitor' has the same meaning as in Code C, *paragraph 6.12*.

1.6 In this Code:

(aa) 'recording media' means any removable, physical audio recording medium (such as magnetic type, optical disc or solid state memory) which can be played and copied.

(a) 'designated person' means a person other than a police officer, designated under the Police Reform Act 2002, Part 4 who has specified powers and duties of police officers conferred or imposed on them;

(b) any reference to a police officer includes a designated person acting in the exercise or performance of the powers and duties conferred or imposed on them by their designation.

1.7 If a power conferred on a designated person:

(a) allows reasonable force to be used when exercised by a police officer, a designated person exercising that power has the same entitlement to use force;

(b) includes power to use force to enter any premises, that power is not exercisable by that designated person except:

(i) in the company, and under the supervision, of a police officer; or

(ii) for the purpose of:

- saving life or limb; or
- preventing serious damage to property.

1.8 Nothing in this Code prevents the custody officer, or other officer given custody of the detainee, from allowing police staff who are not designated persons to carry out individual procedures or tasks at the police station if the law allows. However, the officer remains responsible for making sure the procedures and tasks are carried out correctly in accordance with these Codes. Any such police staff must be:

(a) a person employed by a police authority maintaining a police force and under the control and direction of the Chief Officer of that force; or

(b) employed by a person with whom a police authority has a contract for the provision of services relating to persons arrested or otherwise in custody.

1.9 Designated persons and other police staff must have regard to any relevant provisions of the Codes of Practice.

1.10 References to pocket book include any official report book issued to police officers or police staff.

1.11 References to a custody officer include those performing the functions of a custody officer as in *paragraph 1.9* of Code C.

2. Recording and sealing master recordings

2.1 Recording of interviews shall be carried out openly to instil confidence in its reliability as an impartial and accurate record of the interview.

2.2 One recording, the master recording, will be sealed in the suspect's presence. A second recording will be used as a working copy. The master recording is either of the two recordings used in a twin deck/drive machine or the only recording in a single deck/drive machine. The working copy is either the second/third recording used in a twin/triple deck/drive machine or a copy of the master recording made by a single deck/drive machine. See *Notes 2A* and *2B*

2.3 Nothing in this Code requires the identity of officers or police staff conducting interviews to be recorded or disclosed:

(a) in the case of enquiries linked to the investigation of terrorism; or

(b) if the interviewer reasonably believes recording or disclosing their name might put them in danger.

In these cases interviewers should use warrant or other identification numbers and the name of their police station. See Note 2C

Notes for Guidance

2A The purpose of sealing the master recording in the suspect's presence is to show the recording's integrity is preserved. If a single deck/drive machine is used the working copy of the master recording must be made in the suspect's presence and without the master recording leaving their sight. The working copy shall be used for making further copies if needed.

2B Not used.

2C The purpose of paragraph 2.3(b) is to protect those involved in serious organised crime investigations or arrests of particularly violent suspects when there is reliable information that those arrested or their associates may threaten or cause harm to those involved. In cases of doubt, an officer of inspector rank or above should be consulted.

3. Interviews to be audio recorded

3.1 Subject to *paragraphs 3.3* and *3.4*, audio recording shall be used at police stations for any interview:
(a) with a person cautioned under Code C, *section 10* in respect of any indictable offence, including an offence triable either way; see *Note 3A*
(b) which takes place as a result of an interviewer exceptionally putting further questions to a suspect about an offence described in *paragraph 3.1(a)* after they have been charged with, or told they may be prosecuted for, that offence, see Code C, *paragraph 16.5*
(c) when an interviewer wants to tell a person, after they have been charged with, or informed they may be prosecuted for, an offence described in *paragraph 3.1(a)*, about any written statement or interview with another person, see Code C, *paragraph 16.4*.

3.2 The Terrorism Act 2000 makes separate provision for a Code of Practice for the audio recording of interviews of those arrested under Section 41 or detained under Schedule 7 of the Act. The provisions of this Code do not apply to such interviews.

3.3 The custody officer may authorise the interviewer not to audio record the interview when it is:
(a) not reasonably practicable because of equipment failure or the unavailability of a suitable interview room or recorder and the authorising officer considers, on reasonable grounds, that the interview should not be delayed; or
(b) clear from the outset there will not be a prosecution.
Note: In these cases the interview should be recorded in writing in accordance with Code C, *section 11*. In all cases the custody officer shall record the specific reasons for not audio recording. See *Note 3B*

3.4 If a person refuses to go into or remain in a suitable interview room, see Code C *paragraph 12.5*, and the custody officer considers, on reasonable grounds, that the interview should not be delayed the interview may, at the custody officer's discretion, be conducted in a cell using portable recording equipment or, if none is available, recorded in writing as in Code C, *section 11*. The reasons for this shall be recorded.

3.5 The whole of each interview shall be audio recorded, including the taking and reading back of any statement.

Notes for Guidance

3A Nothing in this Code is intended to preclude audio recording at police discretion of interviews at police stations with people cautioned in respect of offences not covered by paragraph 3.1, or responses made by persons after they have been charged with, or told they may be prosecuted for, an offence, provided this Code is complied with.

3B A decision not to audio record an interview for any reason may be the subject of comment in court. The authorising officer should be prepared to justify that decision.

4. The interview

(a) General

4.1 The provisions of Code C:
• *sections 10 and 11*, and the applicable *Notes for Guidance* apply to the conduct of interviews to which this Code applies
• *paragraphs 11.7 to 11.14* apply only when a written record is needed.

4.2 Code C, *paragraphs 10.10, 10.11* and Annex C describe the restriction on drawing adverse inferences from a suspect's failure or refusal to say anything about their involvement in the offence when interviewed or after being charged or informed they may be prosecuted, and how it affects the terms of the caution and determines if and by whom a special warning under sections 36 and 37 can be given.

(b) Commencement of interviews

4.3 When the suspect is brought into the interview room the interviewer shall, without delay but in the suspect's sight, load the recorder with new recording media and set it to record. The recording media must be unwrapped or opened in the suspect's presence.

4.4 The interviewer should tell the suspect about the recording process. The interviewer shall:
(a) say the interview is being audibly recorded
(b) subject to *paragraph 2.3*, give their name and rank and that of any other interviewer present
(c) ask the suspect and any other party present, e.g. a solicitor, to identify themselves
(d) state the date, time of commencement and place of the interview
(e) state the suspect will be given a notice about what will happen to the copies of the recording.
See *Note 4A*

4.5 The interviewer shall:
- caution the suspect, see Code C, *section 10*
- remind the suspect of their entitlement to free legal advice, see Code C, *paragraph 11.2.*

4.6 The interviewer shall put to the suspect any significant statement or silence; see Code C, *paragraph 11.4.*

(c) Interviews with deaf persons

4.7 If the suspect is deaf or is suspected of having impaired hearing, the interviewer shall make a written note of the interview in accordance with Code C, at the same time as audio recording it in accordance with this Code. See *Notes 4B* and *4C*

(d) Objections and complaints by the suspect

4.8 If the suspect objects to the interview being audibly recorded at the outset, during the interview or during a break, the interviewer shall explain that the interview is being audibly recorded and that this Code requires the suspect's objections to be recorded on the audio recording. When any objections have been audibly recorded or the suspect has refused to have their objections recorded, the interviewer shall say they are turning off the recorder, give their reasons and turn it off. The interviewer shall then make a written record of the interview as in Code C, *section 11*. If, however, the interviewer reasonably considers they may proceed to question the suspect with the audio recording still on, the interviewer may do so. This procedure also applies in cases where the suspect has previously objected to the interview being visually recorded, see *Code F 4.8*, and the investigating officer has decided to audibly record the interview. See *Note 4D*

4.9 If in the course of an interview a complaint is made by or on behalf of the person being questioned concerning the provisions of this Code or Code C, the interviewer shall act as in Code C, *paragraph 12.9.* See *Notes 4E* and *4F*

4.10 If the suspect indicates they want to tell the interviewer about matters not directly connected with the offence and they are unwilling for these matters to be audio recorded, the suspect should be given the opportunity to tell the interviewer at the end of the formal interview.

(e) Changing recording media

4.11 When the recorder shows the recording media only has a short time left, the interviewer shall tell the suspect the recording media are coming to an end and round off that part of the interview. If the interviewer leaves the room for a second set of recording media, the suspect shall not be left unattended. The interviewer will remove the recording media from the recorder and insert the new recording media which shall be unwrapped or opened in the suspect's presence. The recorder should be set to record on the new media. To avoid confusion between the recording media, the interviewer shall mark the media with an identification number immediately after they are removed from the recorder.

(f) Taking a break during interview

4.12 When a break is taken, the fact that a break is to be taken, the reason for it and the time shall be recorded on the audio recording.

4.12A When the break is taken and the interview room vacated by the suspect, the recording media shall be removed from the recorder and the procedures for the conclusion of an interview followed, see *paragraph 4.18.*

4.13 When a break is a short one and both the suspect and an interviewer remain in the interview room, the recording may be stopped. There is no need to remove the recording media and when the interview recommences the recording should continue on the same recording media. The time the interview recommences shall be recorded on the audio recording.

4.14 After any break in the interview the interviewer must, before resuming the interview, remind the person being questioned that they remain under caution or, if there is any doubt, give the caution in full again. See *Note 4G*

(g) Failure of recording equipment

4.15 If there is an equipment failure which can be rectified quickly, e.g. by inserting new recording media, the interviewer shall follow the appropriate procedures as in *paragraph 4.11*. When the recording is resumed the interviewer shall explain what happened and record the time the interview recommences. If, however, it will not be possible to continue recording on that recorder and no replacement recorder is readily available, the interview may continue without being audibly recorded. If this happens, the interviewer shall seek the custody officer's authority as in *paragraph 3.3.* See *Note 4H*

(h) Removing recording media from the recorder

4.16 When recording media is removed from the recorder during the interview, they shall be retained and the procedures in *paragraph 4.18* followed.

(i) Conclusion of interview

4.17 At the conclusion of the interview, the suspect shall be offered the opportunity to clarify anything he or she has said and asked if there is anything they want to add.

4.18 At the conclusion of the interview, including the taking and reading back of any written statement, the time shall be recorded and the recording shall be stopped. The interviewer shall seal the master recording with a master recording label and treat it as an exhibit in accordance with force standing orders. The interviewer shall sign the label and ask the suspect and any third party present during the interview to sign it. If the suspect or third party refuse to sign the label an officer of at least inspector rank, or if not available the custody officer, shall be called into the interview room and asked, subject to *paragraph 2.3*, to sign it.

4.19 The suspect shall be handed a notice which explains:
- how the audio recording will be used
- the arrangements for access to it
- that if the person is charged or informed they will be prosecuted, a copy of the audio recording will be supplied as soon as practicable or as otherwise agreed between the suspect and the police.

Notes for Guidance

4A For the purpose of voice identification the interviewer should ask the suspect and any other people present to identify themselves.

4B This provision is to give a person who is deaf or has impaired hearing equivalent rights of access to the full interview record as far as this is possible using audio recording.

4C The provisions of Code C, section 13 on interpreters for deaf persons or for interviews with suspects who have difficulty understanding English continue to apply. However, in an audibly recorded interview the requirement on the interviewer to make sure the interpreter makes a separate note of the interview applies only to paragraph 4.7 (interviews with deaf persons).

4D The interviewer should remember that a decision to continue recording against the wishes of the suspect may be the subject of comment in court.

4E If the custody officer is called to deal with the complaint, the recorder should, if possible, be left on until the custody officer has entered the room and spoken to the person being interviewed. Continuation or termination of the interview should be at the interviewer's discretion pending action by an inspector under Code C, paragraph 9.2.

4F If the complaint is about a matter not connected with this Code or Code C, the decision to continue is at the interviewer's discretion. When the interviewer decides to continue the interview, they shall tell the suspect the complaint will be brought to the custody officer's attention at the conclusion of the interview. When the interview is concluded the interviewer must, as soon as practicable, inform the custody officer about the existence and nature of the complaint made.

4G The interviewer should remember that it may be necessary to show to the court that nothing occurred during a break or between interviews which influenced the suspect's recorded evidence. After a break or at the beginning of a subsequent interview, the interviewer should consider summarising on the record the reason for the break and confirming this with the suspect.

4H Where the interview is being recorded and the media or the recording equipment fails the officer conducting the interview should stop the interview immediately. Where part of the interview is unaffected by the error and is still accessible on the media, that media shall be copied and sealed in the suspect's presence and the interview recommenced using new equipment/media as required. Where the content of the interview has been lost in its entirety the media should be sealed in the suspect's presence and the interview begun again. If the recording equipment cannot be fixed or no replacement is immediately available the interview should be recorded in accordance with Code C, section 11.

5. After the interview

5.1 The interviewer shall make a note in their pocket book that the interview has taken place, was audibly recorded, its time, duration and date and the master recording's identification number.

5.2 If no proceedings follow in respect of the person whose interview was recorded, the recording media must be kept securely as in *paragraph 6.1* and *Note 6A*.

Note for Guidance

5A Any written record of an audibly recorded interview should be made in accordance with national guidelines approved by the Secretary of State.

6. Media security

6.1 The officer in charge of each police station at which interviews with suspects are recorded shall make arrangements for master recordings to be kept securely and their movements accounted for on the same basis as material which may be used for evidential purposes, in accordance with force standing orders. See *Note 6A*

6.2 A police officer has no authority to break the seal on a master recording required for criminal trial or appeal proceedings. If it is necessary to gain access to the master recording, the police officer shall arrange for its seal to be broken in the presence of a representative of the Crown Prosecution Service. The defendant or their legal adviser should be informed and given a reasonable opportunity to be present. If the defendant or their legal representative is present they shall be invited to reseal and sign the master recording. If either refuses or neither is present this should be done by the representative of the Crown Prosecution Service. See *Notes 6B* and *6C*

6.3 If no criminal proceedings result or the criminal trial and, if applicable, appeal proceedings to which the interview relates have been concluded, the chief officer of police is responsible for establishing arrangements for breaking the seal on the master recording, if necessary.

6.4 When the master recording seal is broken, a record must be made of the procedure followed, including the date, time, place and persons present.

Notes for Guidance

6A This section is concerned with the security of the master recording sealed at the conclusion of the interview. Care must be taken of working copies of recordings because their loss or destruction may lead to the need to access master recordings.

6B If the recording has been delivered to the crown court for their keeping after committal for trial the crown prosecutor will apply to the chief clerk of the crown court centre for the release of the recording for unsealing by the crown prosecutor.

6C Reference to the Crown Prosecution Service or to the crown prosecutor in this part of the Code should be taken to include any other body or person with a statutory responsibility for prosecution for whom the police conduct any audibly recorded interviews.

PACE CODE F

CODE OF PRACTICE ON VISUAL RECORDING WITH SOUND OF INTERVIEWS WITH SUSPECTS

Commencement—transitional arrangements

The contents of this code should be considered if an interviewing officer decides to make a visual recording with sound of an interview with a suspect after midnight on 31 December 2005.

There is no statutory requirement to visually record interviews

1. General

1.1 This code of practice must be readily available for consultation by police officers and other police staff, detained persons and members of the public.

1.2 The notes for guidance included are not provisions of this code. They form guidance to police officers and others about its application and interpretation.

1.3 Nothing in this code shall be taken as detracting in any way from the requirements of the Code of Practice for the Detention, Treatment and Questioning of Persons by Police Officers (Code C). [See *Note 1A*].

1.4 The interviews to which this Code applies are set out in paragraphs 3.1–3.3.

1.5 In this code, the term 'appropriate adult', 'solicitor' and 'interview' have the same meaning as those set out in Code C. The corresponding provisions and Notes for Guidance in Code C applicable to those terms shall also apply where appropriate.

1.6 Any reference in this code to visual recording shall be taken to mean visual recording with sound.

1.7 References to 'pocket book' in this Code include any official report book issued to police officers.

Note for Guidance

1A As in paragraph 1.9 of Code C, references to custody officers include those carrying out the functions of a custody officer.

2. Recording and sealing of master tapes

2.1 The visual recording of interviews shall be carried out openly to instil confidence in its reliability as an impartial and accurate record of the interview. [See *Note 2A*].

2.2 The camera(s) shall be placed in the interview room so as to ensure coverage of as much of the room as is practicably possible whilst the interviews are taking place.

2.3 The certified recording medium will be of a high quality, new and previously unused. When the certified recording medium is placed in the recorder and switched on to record, the correct date and time, in hours, minutes and seconds, will be superimposed automatically, second by second, during the whole recording. [See *Note 2B*].

2.4 One copy of the certified recording medium, referred to in this code as the master copy, will be sealed before it leaves the presence of the suspect. A second copy will be used as a working copy. [See *Note 2C and 2D*].

2.5 Nothing in this code requires the identity of an officer to be recorded or disclosed if:

(a) the interview or record relates to a person detained under the Terrorism Act 2000; or

(b) otherwise where the officer reasonably believes that recording or disclosing their name might put them in danger.

In these cases, the officer will have their back to the camera and shall use their warrant or other identification number and the name of the police station to which they are attached. Such instances and the reasons for them shall be recorded in the custody record. [See *Note 2E*]

Notes for Guidance

2A Interviewing officers will wish to arrange that, as far as possible, visual recording arrangements are unobtrusive. It must be clear to the suspect, however, that there is no opportunity to interfere with the recording equipment or the recording media.

2B In this context, the certified recording media will be of either a VHS or digital CD format and should be capable of having an image of the date and time superimposed upon them as they record the interview.

2C The purpose of sealing the master copy before it leaves the presence of the suspect is to establish their confidence that the integrity of the copy is preserved.

2D The recording of the interview may be used for identification procedures in accordance with paragraph 3.21 or Annex E of Code D.

2E The purpose of the paragraph 2.5 is to protect police officers and others involved in the investigation of serious organised crime or the arrest of particularly violent suspects when there is reliable information that those arrested or their associates may threaten or cause harm to the officers, their families or their personal property.

3. Interviews to be visually recorded

3.1 Subject to paragraph 3.2 below, if an interviewing officer decides to make a visual recording these are the areas where it might be appropriate:

(a) with a suspect in respect of an indictable offence (including an offence triable either way) [see *Notes 3A and 3B*];

(b) which takes place as a result of an interviewer exceptionally putting further questions to a suspect about an offence described in sub-paragraph (a) above after they have been charged with, or informed they may be prosecuted for, that offence [see *Note 3C*];

(c) in which an interviewer wishes to bring to the notice of a person, after that person has been charged with, or informed they may be prosecuted for an offence described in sub-paragraph (a) above, any written statement made by another person, or the content of an interview with another person [see *Note 3D*]

(d) with, or in the presence of, a deaf or deaf/blind or speech impaired person who uses sign language to communicate;

(e) with, or in the presence of anyone who requires an 'appropriate adult'; or

(f) in any case where the suspect or their representative requests that the interview be recorded visually.

3.2 The Terrorism Act 2000 makes separate provision for a code of practice for the video recording of interviews in a police station of those detained under Schedule 7 or section 41 of the Act. The provisions of this code do not therefore apply to such interviews [see *Note 3E*].

3.3 The custody officer may authorise the interviewing officer not to record the interview visually:

(a) where it is not reasonably practicable to do so because of failure of the equipment, or the non-availability of a suitable interview room, or recorder, and the authorising officer considers on reasonable grounds that the interview should not be delayed until the failure has been rectified or a suitable room or recorder becomes available. In such cases the custody officer may authorise the interviewing officer to audio record the interview in accordance with the guidance set out in Code E;

(b) where it is clear from the outset that no prosecution will ensue; or

(c) where it is not practicable to do so because at the time the person resists being taken to a suitable interview room or other location which would enable the interview to be recorded, or otherwise fails or refuses to go into such a room or location, and the authorising officer considers on reasonable grounds that the interview should not be delayed until these conditions cease to apply.

In all cases the custody officer shall make a note in the custody records of the reasons for not taking a visual record. [See *Note 3F*].

3.4 When a person who is voluntarily attending the police station is required to be cautioned in accordance with Code C prior to being interviewed, the subsequent interview shall be recorded, unless the custody officer gives authority in accordance with the provisions of paragraph 3.3 above for the interview not to be so recorded.

3.5 The whole of each interview shall be recorded visually, including the taking and reading back of any statement.

3.6 A visible illuminated sign or indicator will light and remain on at all times when the recording equipment is activated or capable of recording or transmitting any signal or information

Notes for Guidance

3A Nothing in the code is intended to preclude visual recording at police discretion of interviews at police stations with people cautioned in respect of offences not covered by paragraph 3.1, or responses made by interviewees after they have been charged with, or informed they may be prosecuted for, an offence, provided that this code is complied with.

3B Attention is drawn to the provisions set out in Code C about the matters to be considered when deciding whether a detained person is fit to be interviewed.

3C Code C sets out the circumstances in which a suspect may be questioned about an offence after being charged with it.

3D Code C sets out the procedures to be followed when a person's attention is drawn after charge, to a statement made by another person. One method of bringing the content of an interview with another person to the notice of a suspect may be to play him a recording of that interview.

3E When it only becomes clear during the course of an interview which is being visually recorded that the interviewee may have committed an offence to which paragraph 3.2 applies, the interviewing officer should turn off the recording equipment and the interview should continue in accordance with the provisions of the Terrorism Act 2000.

3F A decision not to record an interview visually for any reason may be the subject of comment in court. The authorising officer should therefore be prepared to justify their decision in each case.

4. The interview

(a) General

4.1 The provisions of Code C in relation to cautions and interviews and the Notes for Guidance applicable to those provisions shall apply to the conduct of interviews to which this Code applies.

4.2 Particular attention is drawn to those parts of Code C that describe the restrictions on drawing adverse inferences from a suspect's failure or refusal to say anything about their involvement in the offence when interviewed, or after being charged or informed they may be prosecuted and how those restrictions affect the terms of the caution and determine whether a special warning under Sections 36 and 37 of the Criminal Justice and Public Order Act 1994 can be given.

(b) Commencement of interviews

4.3 When the suspect is brought into the interview room the interviewer shall without delay, but in sight of the suspect, load the recording equipment and set it to record. The recording media must be unwrapped or otherwise opened in the presence of the suspect. [See *Note 4A*]

4.4 The interviewer shall then tell the suspect formally about the visual recording. The interviewer shall:

(a) explain the interview is being visually recorded;
(b) subject to paragraph 2.5, give his or her name and rank, and that of any other interviewer present;
(c) ask the suspect and any other party present (e.g. his solicitor) to identify themselves.
(d) state the date, time of commencement and place of the interview; and
(e) state that the suspect will be given a notice about what will happen to the recording.

4.5 The interviewer shall then caution the suspect, which should follow that set out in Code C, and remind the suspect of their entitlement to free and independent legal advice and that they can speak to a solicitor on the telephone.

4.6 The interviewer shall then put to the suspect any significant statement or silence (i.e. failure or refusal to answer a question or to answer it satisfactorily) which occurred before the start of the interview, and shall ask the suspect whether they wish to confirm or deny that earlier statement or silence or whether they wish to add anything. The definition of a 'significant' statement or silence is the same as that set out in Code C.

(c) Interviews with the deaf

4.7 If the suspect is deaf or there is doubt about their hearing ability, the provisions of Code C on interpreters for the deaf or for interviews with suspects who have difficulty in understanding English continue to apply.

(d) Objections and complaints by the suspect

4.8 If the suspect raises objections to the interview being visually recorded either at the outset or during the interview or during a break in the interview, the interviewer shall explain the fact that the interview is being visually recorded and that the provisions of this code require that the suspect's objections shall be recorded on the visual recording. When any objections have been visually recorded or the suspect has refused to have their objections recorded, the interviewer shall say that they are turning off the recording equipment, give their reasons and turn it off. If a separate audio recording is being maintained, the officer shall ask the person to record the reasons for refusing to agree to visual recording of the interview. Paragraph 4.8 of Code E will apply if the person objects to audio recording of the interview. The officer shall then make a written record of the interview. If the interviewer reasonably considers they may proceed to question the suspect with the visual recording still on, the interviewer may do so. See *Note 4G.*

4.9 If in the course of an interview a complaint is made by the person being questioned, or on their behalf, concerning the provisions of this code or of Code C, then the interviewer shall act in accordance with Code C, record it in the interview record and inform the custody officer. [See *4B and 4C*].

4.10 If the suspect indicates that they wish to tell the interviewer about matters not directly connected with the offence of which they are suspected and that they are unwilling for these matters to be recorded, the suspect shall be given the opportunity to tell the interviewer about these matters after the conclusion of the formal interview.

(e) Changing the recording media

4.11 In instances where the recording medium is not of sufficient length to record all of the interview with the suspect, further certified recording medium will be used. When the recording equipment indicates that the recording medium has only a short time left to run, the interviewer shall advise the suspect and round off that part of the interview. If the interviewer wishes to continue the interview but does not already have further certified recording media with him, they shall obtain a set. The suspect should not be left unattended in the interview room. The interviewer will remove the recording media from the recording equipment and insert the new ones which have been unwrapped or otherwise opened in the suspect's presence. The recording equipment shall then be set to record. Care must be taken, particularly when a number of sets of recording media have been used, to ensure that there is no confusion between them. This could be achieved by marking the sets of recording media with consecutive identification numbers.

(f) Taking a break during the interview

4.12 When a break is to be taken during the course of an interview and the interview room is to be vacated by the suspect, the fact that a break is to be taken, the reason for it and the time shall be recorded. The recording equipment must be turned off and the recording media removed. The procedures for the conclusion of an interview set out in paragraph 4.19, below, should be followed.

4.13 When a break is to be a short one, and both the suspect and a police officer are to remain in the interview room, the fact that a break is to be taken, the reasons for it and the time shall be recorded on the recording media. The recording equipment may be turned off, but there is no need to remove the recording media. When the interview is recommenced the recording shall continue on the same recording media and the time at which the interview recommences shall be recorded.

4.14 When there is a break in questioning under caution, the interviewing officer must ensure that the person being questioned is aware that they remain under caution. If there is any doubt, the caution must be given again in full when the interview resumes. [See *Notes 4D and 4E*].

(g) Failure of recording equipment

4.15 If there is a failure of equipment which can be rectified quickly, the appropriate procedures set out in paragraph 4.12 shall be followed. When the recording is resumed the interviewer shall explain what has happened and record the time the interview recommences. If, however, it is not possible to continue recording on that particular recorder and no alternative equipment is readily available, the interview may continue without being recorded visually. In such circumstances, the procedures set out in paragraph 3.3 of this code for seeking the authority of the custody officer will be followed. [See *Note 4F*].

(h) Removing used recording media from recording equipment

4.16 Where used recording media are removed from the recording equipment during the course of an interview, they shall be retained and the procedures set out in paragraph 4.18 below followed.

(i) Conclusion of interview

4.17 Before the conclusion of the interview, the suspect shall be offered the opportunity to clarify anything he or she has said and asked if there is anything that they wish to add.

4.18 At the conclusion of the interview, including the taking and reading back of any written statement, the time shall be recorded and the recording equipment switched off. The master tape or CD shall be removed from the recording equipment, sealed with a master copy label and treated as an exhibit in accordance with the force standing orders. The interviewer shall sign the label and also ask the suspect and any appropriate adults or other third party present during the interview to sign it. If the suspect or third party refuses to sign the label, an officer of at least the rank of inspector, or if one is not available, the custody officer, shall be called into the interview room and asked to sign it.

4.19 The suspect shall be handed a notice which explains the use which will be made of the recording and the arrangements for access to it. The notice will also advise the suspect that a copy of the tape shall be supplied as soon as practicable if the person is charged or informed that he will be prosecuted.

Notes for Guidance

4A The interviewer should attempt to estimate the likely length of the interview and ensure that an appropriate quantity of certified recording media and labels with which to seal the master copies are available in the interview room.

4B Where the custody officer is called immediately to deal with the complaint, wherever possible the recording equipment should be left to run until the custody officer has entered the interview room and spoken to the person being interviewed. Continuation or termination of the interview should be at the discretion of the interviewing officer pending action by an inspector as set out in Code C.

4C Where the complaint is about a matter not connected with this code of practice or Code C, the decision to continue with the interview is at the discretion of the interviewing officer. Where the interviewing officer decides to continue with the interview, the person being interviewed shall be told that the complaint will be brought to the attention of the custody officer at the conclusion of the interview. When the interview is concluded, the interviewing officer must, as soon as practicable, inform the custody officer of the existence and nature of the complaint made.

4D In considering whether to caution again after a break, the officer should bear in mind that he may have to satisfy a court that the person understood that he was still under caution when the interview resumed.

4E The officer should bear in mind that it may be necessary to satisfy the court that nothing occurred during a break in an interview or between interviews which influenced the suspect's recorded evidence. On the re-commencement of an interview, the officer should consider summarising on the tape or CD the reason for the break and confirming this with the suspect.

4F If any part of the recording media breaks or is otherwise damaged during the interview, it should be sealed as a master copy in the presence of the suspect and the interview resumed where it left off.

The undamaged part should be copied and the original sealed as a master tape in the suspect's presence, if necessary after the interview. If equipment for copying is not readily available, both parts should be sealed in the suspect's presence and the interview begun again.

4G The interviewer should be aware that a decision to continue recording against the wishes of the suspect may be the subject of comment in court.

5. After the interview

5.1 The interviewer shall make a note in his or her pocket book of the fact that the interview has taken place and has been recorded, its time, duration and date and the identification number of the master copy of the recording media.

5.2 Where no proceedings follow in respect of the person whose interview was recorded, the recording media must nevertheless be kept securely in accordance with paragraph 6.1 and Note 6A.

Note for Guidance

5A Any written record of a recorded interview shall be made in accordance with national guidelines approved by the Secretary of State, and with regard to the advice contained in the Manual of Guidance for the preparation, processing and submission of files.

6. Master copy security

(a) General

6.1 The officer in charge of the police station at which interviews with suspects are recorded shall make arrangements for the master copies to be kept securely and their movements accounted for on the same basis as other material which may be used for evidential purposes, in accordance with force standing orders [See *Note 6A*].

(b) Breaking master copy seal for criminal proceedings

6.2 A police officer has no authority to break the seal on a master copy which is required for criminal trial or appeal proceedings. If it is necessary to gain access to the master copy, the police officer shall arrange for its seal to be broken in the presence of a representative of the Crown Prosecution Service. The defendant or their legal adviser shall be informed and given a reasonable opportunity to be present. If the defendant or their legal representative is present they shall be invited to reseal and sign the master copy. If either refuses or neither is present, this shall be done by the representative of the Crown Prosecution Service. [See *Notes 6B and 6C*].

(c) Breaking master copy seal: other cases

6.3 The chief officer of police is responsible for establishing arrangements for breaking the seal of the master copy where no criminal proceedings result, or the criminal proceedings, to which the interview relates, have been concluded and it becomes necessary to break the seal. These arrangements should be those which the chief officer considers are reasonably necessary to demonstrate to the person interviewed and any other party who may wish to use or refer to the interview record that the master copy has not been tampered with and that the interview record remains accurate. [See *Note 6D*]

6.4 Subject to paragraph 6.6, a representative of each party must be given a reasonable opportunity to be present when the seal is broken, the master copy copied and resealed.

6.5 If one or more of the parties is not present when the master copy seal is broken because they cannot be contacted or refuse to attend or paragraph 6.6 applies, arrangements should be made for an independent person such as a custody visitor, to be present. Alternatively, or as an additional safeguard, arrangement should be made for a film or photographs to be taken of the procedure.

6.6 Paragraph 6.5 does not require a person to be given an opportunity to be present when:

(a) it is necessary to break the master copy seal for the proper and effective further investigation of the original offence or the investigation of some other offence; and

(b) the officer in charge of the investigation has reasonable grounds to suspect that allowing an opportunity might prejudice any such an investigation or criminal proceedings which may be brought as a result or endanger any person. [See *Note 6E*]

(d) Documentation

6.7 When the master copy seal is broken, copied and re-sealed, a record must be made of the procedure followed, including the date time and place and persons present.

Notes for Guidance

6A This section is concerned with the security of the master copy which will have been sealed at the conclusion of the interview. Care should, however, be taken of working copies since their loss or destruction may lead unnecessarily to the need to have access to master copies.

6B If the master copy has been delivered to the Crown Court for their keeping after committal for trial the Crown Prosecutor will apply to the Chief Clerk of the Crown Court Centre for its release for unsealing by the Crown Prosecutor.

6C Reference to the Crown Prosecution Service or to the Crown Prosecutor in this part of the code shall be taken to include any other body or person with a statutory responsibility for prosecution for whom the police conduct any recorded interviews.

6D The most common reasons for needing access to master copies that are not required for criminal proceedings arise from civil actions and complaints against police and civil actions between individuals arising out of allegations of crime investigated by police.

6E Paragraph 6.6 could apply, for example, when one or more of the outcomes or likely outcomes of the investigation might be: (i) the prosecution of one or more of the original suspects, (ii) the prosecution of someone previously not suspected, including someone who was originally a witness; and (iii) any original suspect being treated as a prosecution witness and when premature disclosure of any police action, particularly through contact with any parties involved, could lead to a real risk of compromising the investigation and endangering witnesses.

PACE CODE G
CODE OF PRACTICE FOR THE STATUTORY POWER OF ARREST BY POLICE OFFICERS

Commencement

This Code applies to any arrest made by a police officer after midnight on 31 December 2005

1. Introduction

1.1 This Code of Practice deals with statutory power of police to arrest persons suspected of involvement in a criminal offence.

1.2 The right to liberty is a key principle of the Human Rights Act 1998. The exercise of the power of arrest represents an obvious and significant interference with that right.

1.3 The use of the power must be fully justified and officers exercising the power should consider if the necessary objectives can be met by other, less intrusive means. Arrest must never be used simply because it can be used. Absence of justification for exercising the powers of arrest may lead to challenges should the case proceed to court. When the power of arrest is exercised it is essential that it is exercised in a nondiscriminatory and proportionate manner.

1.4 Section 24 of the Police and Criminal Evidence Act 1984 (as substituted by section 110 of the Serious Organised Crime and Police Act 2005) provides the statutory power of arrest. If the provisions of the Act and this Code are not observed, both the arrest and the conduct of any subsequent investigation may be open to question.

1.5 This code of practice must be readily available at all police stations for consultation by police officers and police staff, detained persons and members of the public.

1.6 The notes for guidance are not provisions of this code.

2. Elements of arrest under section 24 PACE

2.1 A lawful arrest requires two elements:

A person's involvement or suspected involvement or attempted involvement in the commission of a criminal offence;

AND

Reasonable grounds for believing that the person's arrest is necessary.

2.2 Arresting officers are required to inform the person arrested that they have been arrested, even if this fact is obvious, and of the relevant circumstances of the arrest in relation to both elements and to inform the custody officer of these on arrival at the police station. See Code C paragraph 3.4.

Involvement in the commission of an offence

2.3 A constable may arrest without warrant in relation to any offence, except for the single exception listed in Note for Guidance 1. A constable may arrest anyone:
- who is about to commit an offence or is in the act of committing an offence
- whom the officer has reasonable grounds for suspecting is about to commit an offence or to be committing an offence
- whom the officer has reasonable grounds to suspect of being guilty of an offence which he or she has reasonable grounds for suspecting has been committed
- anyone who is guilty of an offence which has been committed or anyone whom the officer has reasonable grounds for suspecting to be guilty of that offence.

Necessity criteria

2.4 The power of arrest is only exercisable if the constable has reasonable grounds for believing that it is necessary to arrest the person. The criteria for what may constitute necessity are set out in paragraph 2.9. It remains an operational decision at the discretion of the arresting officer as to:
- what action he or she may take at the point of contact with the individual;
- the necessity criterion or criteria (if any) which applies to the individual; and
- whether to arrest, report for summons, grant street bail, issue a fixed penalty notice or take any other action that is open to the officer.

2.5 In applying the criteria, the arresting officer has to be satisfied that at least one of the reasons supporting the need for arrest is satisfied.

2.6 Extending the power of arrest to all offences provides a constable with the ability to use that power to deal with any situation. However applying the necessity criteria requires the constable to examine and justify the reason or reasons why a person needs to be taken to a police station for the custody officer to decide whether the person should be placed in police detention.

2.7 The criteria below are set out in section 24 of PACE as substituted by section 110 of the Serious Organised Crime and Police Act 2005. The criteria are exhaustive. However, the circumstances that may satisfy those criteria remain a matter for the operational discretion of individual officers. Some examples are given below of what those circumstances may be.

2.8 In considering the individual circumstances, the constable must take into account the situation of the victim, the nature of the offence, the circumstances of the suspect and the needs of the investigative process.

2.9 The criteria are that the arrest is necessary:

(a) to enable the name of the person in question to be ascertained (in the case where the constable does not know, and cannot readily ascertain, the person's name, or has reasonable grounds for doubting whether a name given by the person as his name is his real name)

(b) correspondingly as regards the person's address

an address is a satisfactory address for service of summons if the person will be at it for a sufficiently long period for it to be possible to serve him or her with a summons; or, that some other person at that address specified by the person will accept service of the summons on their behalf.

(c) to prevent the person in question—

(i) causing physical injury to himself or any other person;

(ii) suffering physical injury ;

(iii) causing loss or damage to property;

(iv) committing an offence against public decency (only applies where members of the public going about their normal business cannot reasonably be expected to avoid the person in question); or

(v) causing an unlawful obstruction of the highway;

(d) to protect a child or other vulnerable person from the person in question

(e) to allow the prompt and effective investigation of the offence or of the conduct of the person in question.

This may include cases such as:

(i) Where there are reasonable grounds to believe that the person:
- has made false statements;
- has made statements which cannot be readily verified;
- has presented false evidence;
- may steal or destroy evidence;
- may make contact with co-suspects or conspirators;

- may intimidate or threaten or make contact with witnesses;
- where it is necessary to obtain evidence by questioning; or

(ii) when considering arrest in connection with an indictable offence, there is a need to:
- enter and search any premises occupied or controlled by a person
- search the person
- prevent contact with others
- take fingerprints, footwear impressions, samples or photographs of the suspect

(iii) ensuring compliance with statutory drug testing requirements.

(f) to prevent any prosecution for the offence from being hindered by the disappearance of the person in question.

This may arise if there are reasonable grounds for believing that
- if the person is not arrested he or she will fail to attend court
- street bail after arrest would be insufficient to deter the suspect from trying to evade prosecution

3. Information to be given on arrest

(a) Cautions—when a caution must be given (taken from Code C section 10)

3.1 A person whom there are grounds to suspect of an offence (see Note 2) must be cautioned before any questions about an offence, or further questions if the answers provide the grounds for suspicion, are put to them if either the suspect's answers or silence, (i.e. failure or refusal to answer or answer satisfactorily) may be given in evidence to a court in a prosecution. A person need not be cautioned if questions are for other necessary purposes e.g.:
(a) solely to establish their identity or ownership of any vehicle;
(b) to obtain information in accordance with any relevant statutory requirement;
(c) in furtherance of the proper and effective conduct of a search, e.g. to determine the need to search in the exercise of powers of stop and search or to seek cooperation while carrying out a search;
(d) to seek verification of a written record as in *Code C paragraph 11.13*;
(e) when examining a person in accordance with the Terrorism Act 2000, Schedule 7 and the Code of Practice for Examining Officers issued under that Act, Schedule 14, paragraph 6.

3.2 Whenever a person not under arrest is initially cautioned, or reminded they are under caution, that person must at the same time be told they are not under arrest and are free to leave if they want to.

3.3 A person who is arrested, or further arrested, must be informed at the time, or as soon as practicable thereafter, that they are under arrest and the grounds for their arrest, see *Note 3*.

3.4 A person who is arrested, or further arrested, must also be cautioned unless:
(a) it is impracticable to do so by reason of their condition or behaviour at the time;
(b) they have already been cautioned immediately prior to arrest as in *paragraph 3.1*.
(c) Terms of the caution (Taken from Code C section 10)

3.5 The caution, which must be given on arrest, should be in the following terms:

'You do not have to say anything. But it may harm your defence if you do not mention when questioned something which you later rely on in Court. Anything you do say may be given in evidence.'

See *Note 5*

3.6 Minor deviations from the words of any caution given in accordance with this Code do not constitute a breach of this Code, provided the sense of the relevant caution is preserved. See *Note 6*

3.7 When, despite being cautioned, a person fails to co-operate or to answer particular questions which may affect their immediate treatment, the person should be informed of any relevant consequences and that those consequences are not affected by the caution. Examples are when a person's refusal to provide:
- their name and address when charged may make them liable to detention;
- particulars and information in accordance with a statutory requirement, e.g. under the Road Traffic Act 1988, may amount to an offence or may make the person liable to a further arrest.

4. Records of arrest

(a) General

4.1 The arresting officer is required to record in his pocket book or by other methods used for recording information:
- the nature and circumstances of the offence leading to the arrest
- the reason or reasons why arrest was necessary
- the giving of the caution
- anything said by the person at the time of arrest

4.2 Such a record should be made at the time of the arrest unless impracticable to do. If not made at that time, the record should then be completed as soon as possible thereafter.

4.3 On arrival at the police station, the custody officer shall open the custody record (see paragraph 1.1A and section 2 of Code C). The information given by the arresting officer on the circumstances and reason or reasons for arrest shall be recorded as part of the custody record. Alternatively, a copy of the record made by the officer in accordance with paragraph 4.1 above shall be attached as part of the custody record. See *paragraph 2.2* and *Code C paragraphs 3.4 and 10.3*.

4.4 The custody record will serve as a record of the arrest. Copies of the custody record will be provided in accordance with paragraphs 2.4 and 2.4A of Code C and access for inspection of the original record in accordance with paragraph 2.5 of Code C.

(b) Interviews and arrests

4.5 Records of interview, significant statements or silences will be treated in the same way as set out in sections 10 and 11 of Code C and in Code E (tape recording of interviews).

Notes for Guidance

1 The powers of arrest for offences under sections 4(1) and 5(1) of the Criminal Law Act 1967 require that the offences to which they relate must carry a sentence fixed by law or one in which a first time offender aged 18 or over could be sentenced to 5 years or more imprisonment

2 There must be some reasonable, objective grounds for the suspicion, based on known facts or information which are relevant to the likelihood the offence has been committed and the person to be questioned committed it.

3 An arrested person must be given sufficient information to enable them to understand they have been deprived of their liberty and the reason they have been arrested, e.g. when a person is arrested on suspicion of committing an offence they must be informed of the suspected offence's nature, when and where it was committed. The suspect must also be informed of the reason or reasons why arrest is considered necessary. Vague or technical language should be avoided.

4 Nothing in this Code requires a caution to be given or repeated when informing a person not under arrest they may be prosecuted for an offence. However, a court will not be able to draw any inferences under the Criminal Justice and Public Order Act 1994, section 34, if the person was not cautioned.

5 If it appears a person does not understand the caution, the people giving it should explain it in their own words.

6 The powers available to an officer as the result of an arrest—for example, entry and search of premises, holding a person incommunicado, setting up road blocks—are only available in respect of indictable offences and are subject to the specific requirements on authorisation as set out in the 1984 Act and relevant PACE Code of Practice.

PACE CODE H

CODE OF PRACTICE IN CONNECTION WITH THE DETENTION, TREATMENT AND QUESTIONING BY POLICE OFFICERS OF PERSONS UNDER SECTION 41 OF, AND SCHEDULE 8 TO, THE TERRORISM ACT 2000

Code H applies to people in police detention following their arrest under the Terrorism Act 2000, s. 41; it took effect from midnight on 24 July 2006 notwithstanding that the person may have been arrested before that time.

Code H is not reproduced here but its main provisions are summarised below and Section 14 (Reviews and extensions of detention), which contains significant changes from the equivalent provisions in PACE Code C owing to the changes made to maximum detention times by the Terrorism Act 2006, is set out in full. The provisions of Code H are based on, and closely follow, those of Code C as the issues faced by officers conducting detention under the Terrorism Act 2000, s. 41 and sch. 8 are the same as for other forms of police detention. The full text of Code H is freely available at http://

police.homeoffice.gov.uk/news-and-publications/publication/operational-policing/PACECodeCH.pdf? or via a link from the *Blackstone's Criminal Practice* companion website (http://www.oup.com/uk/booksites/content/0199275297/).

Section 1—General

This section covers the scope and applicability of the Code (which are, by definition, different from the equivalent provisions of Code C); it also covers the availability of the Code, definitions, applicability to the deaf, blind and speech impaired and the use of reasonable force, and in these respects follows Code C.

Section 2—Custody records

This section follows Code C. It covers general requirements for making custody records, including the exemption for counter terrorism officers from disclosing their identities on custody records and provisions as to access to custody records by detainees' solicitors and disclosure of those records to them.

Section 3—Initial action in respect of arrested individuals

Code H broadly follows Code C in respect of detainees' rights and arrangements for exercising them but differs in a number of respects:

(a) the record will indicate that the arrest was under s. 41 as opposed to indicating the offence in respect of which the arrest was made—Note 3G indicates that, where an arrest is made on grounds of sensitive information which cannot be disclosed, the recorded grounds 'may be given in terms of the interpretation of "terrorist"' set out in s. 40(1)(a) or 40(1)(b);

(b) there is a specific provision to the effect that risk assessments do not form part of the custody record and should not be shown to the detainee or their legal representative;

(c) there are provisions relating to the initial steps that may be taken in connection with the identification of suspects.

Section 4—Detainees' property

This section of Code H includes a simplification of the circumstances in which a custody officer should search a detainee to ascertain what they have in their possession but there is no material change in comparison with Code C.

Section 5—Right not to be held incommunicado

The detainee's right to have someone informed of his whereabouts closely follows the equivalent section of Code C but there is much more detailed guidance on visiting rights. A requirement is imposed for custody officers to liaise with the investigation team to ascertain the risks presented by visits. Where visits from relatives etc. present a risk, consideration of more frequent visits from independent visitor schemes is suggested. Visits from official visitors ('official visitors' may include accredited faith representatives and MPs) may be allowed subject to consultation with the officer in charge of the investigation. Note 5B indicates that custody officers should bear in mind the effects of prolonged detention under the Act and consider the health and welfare benefits that visits bring to detainees who are held for extended periods. However, Note 5G reminds officers that the nature of terrorist investigations means that they need to have 'particular regard to the possibility of suspects attempting to pass information which may be detrimental to public safety, or to an investigation'. It should also be noted that the provisions in Annex B relating to delaying notification of arrest allow for delay in many more instances than under the new Code C (they follow section B of Annex B to the old Code C).

Section 6—Right to legal advice

The principal difference from Code C is that there is provision for an authorisation to be given whereby a detainee may only consult a solicitor within sight and hearing of a qualified officer (a uniformed officer of at least the rank of inspector who has no connection with the investigation). It should however be noted that the provisions in Annex B relating to delaying access to legal advice allow for delay in many more instances than under the new Code C (they follow section B of Annex B to the old code C).

Section 7—Citizens of independent commonwealth countries or foreign nationals

Section 7 shows no material change from the equivalent Code C provisions.

Section 8—Conditions of detention

The main differences from Code C are that there is specific reference to allowing detainees to practice religious observance and to the provision of reading material, including religious texts. Police should consult with representatives of religious communities on provision of facilities for religious observance and handling of religious texts and other articles. The benefits of exercise for detainees, particularly in the cases of prolonged detention, are emphasised. If facilities exist, indoor exercise is to be offered if requested or if outdoor exercise is not practicable. Although the same restrictions on putting a juvenile in a cell apply as under Code C, there is no requirement to include occasions when a juvenile is so confined on the custody record.

Section 9—Care and treatment of detained persons

Section 9 of Code H begins by requiring that, notwithstanding other requirements for medical attention, 'detainees who are held for more than 96 hours must be visited by a healthcare professional at least once every 24 hours'. In all other material respects, the provisions are the same as under Code C.

Section 10—Cautioning

Insofar as relevant, the provisions on cautions closely follow those of Code C.

Section 11—Interviews (general)

There are no material differences from Code C under this section. The Code H equivalent is however much shorter, reflecting the fact that not all instances covered by the Code C equivalent are relevant to detention of terrorist suspects

Section 12—Interviews in police stations

The only material difference here is set out at para. 12.9:

12.9 During extended periods where no interviews take place, because of the need to gather further evidence or analyse existing evidence, detainees and their legal representative shall be informed that the investigation into the relevant offence remains ongoing. If practicable, the detainee and legal representative should also be made aware in general terms of any reasons for long gaps between interviews. Consideration should be given to allowing visits, more frequent exercise, or for reading or writing materials to be offered *see paragraph 5.4, section 8* and *Note 12C.*

Note 12C indicates that consideration should be given to the matters referred to in para. 12.9 after a period of over 24 hours without questioning.

Section 13—Interpreters

The requirements for accredited interpreters to be provided for deaf or non-English speakers, for both general custody procedures and interviews are the same as under Code C.

Section 14—Reviews and extensions of detention

This section contains significant changes from the equivalent provisions in PACE Code C (PACE Code C, s. 15), owing to the changes made to maximum detention times by the Terrorism Act 2006. It is set out in full below.

14 Reviews and extensions of Detention

(a) Reviews and Extensions of detention

14.1 The powers and duties of the review officer are in the Terrorism Act 2000, Schedule 8, Part II. See *Notes 14A* and *14B*. A review officer should carry out his duties at the police station where the detainee is held, and be allowed such access to the detainee as is necessary for him to exercise those duties.

14.2 For the purposes of reviewing a person's detention, no officer shall put specific questions to the detainee:
- regarding their involvement in any offence; or
- in respect of any comments they may make:
  —when given the opportunity to make representations; or
  —in response to a decision to keep them in detention or extend the maximum period of detention.

Such an exchange could constitute an interview as in *paragraph 11.1* and would be subject to the associated safeguards in *section 11* and, in respect of a person who has been charged see *PACE Code C Section 16.8.*

14.3 If detention is necessary for longer than 48 hours, a police officer of at least superintendent rank, or a Crown Prosecutor may apply for warrants of further detention under the Terrorism Act 2000, Schedule 8, Part III.

14.4 When an application for a warrant of further or extended detention is sought under Paragraph 29 or 36 of Schedule 8, the detained person and their representative must be informed of their rights in respect of the application. These include:
- (a) the right to a written or oral notice of the warrant See *Note 14G*.
- (b) the right to make oral or written representations to the judicial authority about the application.
- (c) the right to be present and legally represented at the hearing of the application, unless specifically excluded by the judicial authority.
- (d) their right to free legal advice (see section 6 of this Code).

(b) Transfer of detained persons to prison

14.5 Where a warrant is issued which authorises detention beyond a period of 14 days from the time of arrest (or if a person was being detained under TACT Schedule 7, from the time at which the examination under Schedule 7 began), the detainee must be transferred from detention in a police station to detention in a designated prison as soon as is practicable, unless:
- (a) the detainee specifically requests to remain in detention at a police station and that request can be accommodated, or
- (b) there are reasonable grounds to believe that transferring a person to a prison would:
  - (i) significantly hinder a terrorism investigation;
  - (ii) delay charging of the detainee or his release from custody, or
  - (iii) otherwise prevent the investigation from being conducted diligently and expeditiously.

If any of the grounds in (b)(i) to (iii) above are relied upon, these must be presented to the judicial authority as part of the application for the warrant that would extend detention beyond a period of 14 days from the time of arrest (or if a person was being detained under TACT Schedule 7, from the time at which the examination under Schedule 7 began) *See Note 14J*.

14.6 If a person remains in detention at a police station under a warrant of further detention as described at section 14.5, they must be transferred to a prison as soon as practicable after the grounds at (b)(i) to (iii) of that section cease to apply.

14.7 Police should maintain an agreement with the National Offender Management Service (NOMS) that stipulates named prisons to which individuals may be transferred under this section. This should be made with regard to ensuring detainees are moved to the most suitable prison for the purposes of the investigation and their welfare, and should include provision for the transfer of male, female and juvenile detainees. Police should ensure that the Governor of a prison to which they intend to transfer a detainee is given reasonable notice of this. Where practicable, this should be no later than the point at which a warrant is applied for that would take the period of detention beyond 14 days.

14.8 Following a detained person's transfer to a designated prison, their detention will be governed by the terms of Schedule 8 and Prison Rules, and this Code of Practice will not apply during any period that the person remains in prison detention. The Code will once more apply if a detained person is transferred back from prison detention to police detention. In order to enable the Governor to arrange for the production of the detainee back into police custody, police should give notice to the Governor of the relevant prison as soon as possible of any decision to transfer a detainee from prison back to a police station. Any transfer between a prison and a police station should be conducted by police, and this Code will be applicable during the period of transit See *Note 14K*. A detainee should only remain in police custody having been transferred back from a prison, for as long as is necessary for the purpose of the investigation.

14.9 The investigating team and custody officer should provide as much information as necessary to enable the relevant prison authorities to provide appropriate facilities to detain an individual. This should include, but not be limited to:
- (i) medical assessments
- (ii) security and risk assessments
- (iii) details of the detained person's legal representatives
- (iv) details of any individuals from whom the detained person has requested visits, or who have requested to visit the detained person.

14.10 Where a detainee is to be transferred to prison, the custody officer should inform the detainee's legal adviser beforehand that the transfer is to take place (including the name of the prison). The custody officer should also make all reasonable attempts to inform:

- family or friends who have been informed previously of the detainee's detention; and
- the person who was initially informed of the detainee's detention as at *paragraph 5.1.*

(c) Documentation

14.11 It is the responsibility of the officer who gives any reminders as at *paragraph 14.4,* to ensure that these are noted in the custody record, as well any comments made by the detained person upon being told of those rights.

14.12 The grounds for, and extent of, any delay in conducting a review shall be recorded.

14.13 Any written representations shall be retained.

14.14 A record shall be made as soon as practicable about the outcome of each review or determination whether to extend the maximum detention period without charge or an application for a warrant of further detention or its extension.

14.15 Any decision not to transfer a detained person to a designated prison under paragraph *14.5,* must be recorded, along with the reasons for this decision. If a request under paragraph *14.5(a)* is not accommodated, the reasons for this should also be recorded.

Notes for guidance

14A TACT Schedule 8 Part II sets out the procedures for review of detention up to 48 hours from the time of arrest under TACT section 41 (or if a person was being detained under TACT Schedule 7, from the time at which the examination under Schedule 7 began). These include provisions for the requirement to review detention, postponing a review, grounds for continued detention, designating a review officer, representations, rights of the detained person and keeping a record. The review officer's role ends after a warrant has been issued for extension of detention under Part III of Schedule 8.

14B Section 24(1) of the Terrorism Act 2006, amended the grounds contained within the 2000 Act on which a review officer may authorise continued detention. Continued detention may be authorised if it is necessary-

(a) to obtain relevant evidence whether by questioning him or otherwise
(b) to preserve relevant evidence
(c) while awaiting the result of an examination or analysis of relevant evidence
(d) for the examination or analysis of anything with a view to obtaining relevant evidence
(e) pending a decision to apply to the Secretary of State for a deportation notice to be served on the detainee, the making of any such application, or the consideration of any such application by the Secretary of State
(f) pending a decision to charge the detainee with an offence.

14C Applications for warrants to extend detention beyond 48 hours, may be made for periods of 7 days at a time (initially under TACT Schedule 8 paragraph 29, and extensions thereafter under TACT Schedule 8, Paragraph 36), up to a maximum period of 28 days from the time of arrest (or if a person was being detained under TACT Schedule 7, from the time at which the examination under Schedule 7 began). Applications may be made for shorter periods than 7 days, which must be specified. The judicial authority may also substitute a shorter period if he feels a period of 7 days is inappropriate.

14D Unless Note 14F applies, applications for warrants that would take the total period of detention up to 14 days or less should be made to a judicial authority, meaning a *District Judge (Magistrates' Court) designated by the Lord Chancellor to hear such applications.*

14E Any application for a warrant which would take the period of detention beyond 14 days from the time of arrest (or if a person was being detained under TACT Schedule 7, from the time at which the examination under Schedule 7 began), must be made to a High Court Judge.

14F If an application has been made to a High Court judge for a warrant which would take detention beyond 14 days, and the High Court judge instead issues a warrant for a period of time which would not take detention beyond 14 days, further applications for extension of detention must also be made to a High Court judge, regardless of the period of time to which they refer.

14G TACT Schedule 8 Paragraph 31 requires a notice to be given to the detained person if a warrant is sought for further detention. This must be provided before the judicial hearing of the application for that warrant and must include:

(a) notification that the application for a warrant has been made
(b) the time at which the application was made
(c) the time at which the application is to be heard
(d) the grounds on which further detention is sought.

A notice must also be provided each time an application is made to extend an existing warrant.

14H An officer applying for an order under TACT Schedule 8 Paragraph 34 to withhold specified information on which he intends to rely when applying for a warrant of further detention, may make the application for the order orally or in writing. The most appropriate method of application will depend on the circumstances of the case and the need to ensure fairness to the detainee.

14I Where facilities exist, hearings relating to extension of detention under Part III of Schedule 8 may take place using video conferencing facilities provided that the requirements set out in Schedule 8 are still met. However, if the judicial authority requires the detained person to be physically present at any hearing, this should be complied with as soon as practicable. Paragraphs 33(4) to 33(9) of TACT Schedule 8 govern the relevant conduct of hearings.

14J Transfer to prison is intended to ensure that individuals who are detained for extended periods of time are held in a place designed for longer periods of detention than police stations. Prison will provide detainees with a greater range of facilities more appropriate to longer detention periods.

14K The Code will only apply as is appropriate to the conditions of detention during the period of transit. There is obviously no requirement to provide such things as bed linen or reading materials for the journey between prison and police station.

General

There are no equivalents to PACE Code C, ss. 16 and 17, which cannot apply in the context of a terrorist investigation. The annexes to Code H are in terms which closely follow Code C. While the changes are mainly to remove or amend references that are not applicable to terrorism detention, it should be noted that the provisions in Annex B relating to delaying notification of arrest or access to legal advice allow for delay in many more instances than under the new Code C (they follow section B of Annex B to the old code C).

* The complete PACE Code H can be found on *Blackstone's Criminal Practice 2007* CD Rom.

Appendix 3 Attorney-General's Guidelines

EXERCISE BY THE CROWN OF ITS RIGHT OF STAND-BY

1. Although the law has long recognised the right of the Crown to exclude a member of a jury panel from sitting as a juror by the exercise in open court of the right to request a stand-by or, if necessary, by challenge for cause, it has been customary for those instructed to prosecute on behalf of the Crown to assert that right only sparingly and in exceptional circumstances. It is generally accepted that the prosecution should not use its right in order to influence the overall composition of a jury or with a view to tactical advantage.
2. The approach outlined above is founded on the principles that (a) the members of a jury should be selected at random from the panel subject to any rule of law as to right of challenge by the defence, and (b) the Juries Act 1974 together with the Juries (Disqualification) Act 1984 identified those classes of persons who alone are disqualified from or ineligible for service on a jury. No other class of person may be treated as disqualified or ineligible.
3. The enactment by Parliament of s. 118 of the Criminal Justice Act 1988 abolishing the right of defendants to remove jurors by means of peremptory challenge makes it appropriate that the Crown should assert its right to stand by only on the basis of clearly defined and restrictive criteria. Derogation from the principle that members of a jury should be selected at random should be permitted only where it is essential.
4. Primary responsibility for ensuring that an individual does not serve on a jury if he is not competent to discharge properly the duties of a juror rests with the appropriate court officer and, ultimately, the trial judge. Current legislation provides, in ss. 9 and 10 of the Juries Act 1974, fairly wide discretions to excuse or discharge jurors either at the person's own request, where he offers 'good reason why he should be excused', or where the judge determines that 'on account of physical disability or insufficient understanding of English there is doubt as to his capacity to act effectively as a juror'.
5. The circumstances in which it would be proper for the Crown to exercise its right to stand by a member of a jury panel are: (a) where a jury check authorised in accordance with the Attorney-General's guidelines on jury checks reveals information justifying exercise of the right to stand by in accordance with para. 9 of the guidelines and the Attorney-General personally authorises the exercise of the right to stand by; or (b) where a person is about to be sworn as a juror who is manifestly unsuitable and the defence agree that, accordingly, the exercise by the prosecution of the right to stand by would be appropriate. An example of the sort of *exceptional* circumstances which might justify stand-by is where it becomes apparent that, despite the provisions mentioned in para. 4 above, a juror selected for service to try a complex case is in fact illiterate.

JURY CHECKS

1. The principles which are generally to be observed are (a) that members of a jury should be selected at random from the panel, (b) the Juries Act 1974 together with the Juries (Disqualification) Act 1984 identified those classes of persons who alone are either disqualified from or ineligible for service on a jury; no other class of person may be treated as disqualified or ineligible, and (c) the correct way for the Crown to seek to exclude a member of the panel from sitting as a juror is by the exercise in open court of the right to request a stand-by or, if necessary, to challenge for cause.
2. Parliament has provided safeguards against jurors who may be corrupt or biased. In addition to the provision for majority verdicts, there is the sanction of a criminal offence for a disqualified person to serve on a jury. The omission of a disqualified person from the panel is a matter for court officials but any search of criminal records for the purpose of ascertaining whether or not a jury panel includes any disqualified person is a matter for the police as the only authority able to carry out such a search and as part of their usual function of preventing the commission of offences. The recommendations of the Association of Chief Police Officers respecting checks on criminal records for disqualified persons are annexed to these guidelines.
3. There are, however, certain exceptional types of case of public importance for which the provisions as to majority verdicts and the disqualification of jurors may not be sufficient to ensure the proper

administration of justice. In such cases it is in the interests of both justice and the public that there should be further safeguards against the possibility of bias and in such cases checks which go beyond the investigation of criminal records may be necessary.

4. These classes of case may be defined broadly as (a) cases in which national security is involved and part of the evidence is likely to be heard in camera, and (b) terrorist cases.
5. The particular aspects of these cases which may make it desirable to seek extra precautions are (a) in security cases a danger that a juror, either voluntarily or under pressure, may make an improper use of evidence which, because of its sensitivity, has been given in camera, (b) in both security and terrorist cases the danger that a juror's political beliefs are so biased as to go beyond normally reflecting the broad spectrum of views and interests in the community to reflect the extreme views of sectarian interest or pressure group to a degree which might interfere with his fair assessment of the facts of the case or lead him to exert improper pressure on his fellow jurors.
6. In order to ascertain whether in exceptional circumstances of the above nature either of these factors might seriously influence a potential juror's impartial performance of his duties or his respecting the secrecy of evidence given in camera, it may be necessary to conduct a limited investigation of the panel. In general, such further investigation beyond one of criminal records made for disqualifications may only be made with the records of police Special Branches. However, in cases falling under para. 4(a) above (security cases), the investigation may, additionally, involve the security services. No checks other than on these sources and no general inquiries are to be made save to the limited extent that they may be needed to confirm the identity of a juror about whom the initial check has raised serious doubts.
7. No further investigation, as described in para. 6 above, should be made save with the personal authority of the Attorney-General on the application of the Director of Public Prosecutions and such checks are hereafter referred to as 'authorised checks'. When a chief officer of police has reason to believe that it is likely that an authorised check may be desirable and proper in accordance with these guidelines he should refer the matter to the Director of Public Prosecutions with a view to his having the conduct of the prosecution from an early stage. The Director will make any appropriate application to the Attorney-General.
8. The result of any authorised check will be sent to the Director of Public Prosecutions. The Director will then decide, having regard to the matters set out in para. 5 above, what information ought to be brought to the attention of prosecuting counsel.
9. No right of stand-by should be exercised by counsel for the Crown on the basis of information obtained as a result of an authorised check save with the personal authority of the Attorney-General and unless the information is such as, having regard to the facts of the case and the offences charged, to afford strong reason for believing that a particular juror might be a security risk, be susceptible to improper approaches or be influenced in arriving at a verdict for the reasons given above.
10. Where a potential juror is asked to stand by for the Crown, there is no duty to disclose to the defence the information on which it was founded; but counsel may use his discretion to disclose it if its nature and source permit it.
11. When information revealed in the course of an authorised check is not such as to cause counsel for the Crown to ask for a juror to stand by but does give reason to believe that he may be biased against the accused, the defence should be given, at least, an indication of why that potential juror may be inimical to their interests; but because of its nature and source it may not be possible to give the defence more than a general indication.
12. A record is to be kept by the Director of Public Prosecutions of the use made by counsel of the information passed to him and of the jurors stood by or challenged by the parties to the proceedings. A copy of this record is to be forwarded to the Attorney-General for the sole purpose of enabling him to monitor the operation of these guidelines.
13. No use of the information obtained as a result of an authorised check is to be made except as may be necessary in direct relation to or arising out of the trial for which the check was authorised.

Annex: Recommendations of the Association of Chief Police Officers

1. The Association of Chief Police Officers recommends that in the light of observations made in *Mason* [1981] QB 881 the police should undertake a check of the names of potential jurors against records of previous convictions in any case when the Director of Public Prosecutions or a chief constable considers that in all the circumstances it would be in the interests of justice so to do, namely (i) in any case in which there is reason to believe that attempts are being made to circumvent the statutory provisions excluding disqualified persons from service on a jury, including any case when there is reason to believe that a particular juror may be disqualified, (ii) in any case in

which it is believed that in a previous related abortive trial an attempt was made to interfere with a juror or jurors, and (iii) in any other case in which in the opinion of the Director of Public Prosecutions or the chief constable it is particularly important to ensure that no disqualified person serves on the jury.

2. The association also recommends that no further checks should be made unless authorised by the Attorney-General under his guidelines and no inquiries carried out save to the limited extent that they may be needed to confirm the identity of a juror about whom the initial check has raised serious doubts.
3. The association further recommends that chief constables should agree to undertake checks of jurors on behalf of the defence only if requested to do so by the Director of Public Prosecutions acting on behalf of the Attorney-General. Accordingly if the police are approached directly with such a request they will refer it to the Director.
4. When, as a result of any checks of criminal records, information isobtained which suggests that, although not disqualified under the terms of the Juries Act 1974, a person may be unsuitable to sit as a member of a particular jury the police or the Director may pass the relevant information to prosecuting counsel, who will decide what use to make of it.

ACCEPTANCE OF PLEAS AND THE PROSECUTOR'S ROLE IN THE SENTENCING EXERCISE

A Foreword

A1. Prosecutors have an important role in protecting the victim's interests in the criminal justice process, not least in the acceptance of pleas and the sentencing exercise. The basis of plea, particularly in a case that is not contested, is the vehicle through which the victim's voice is heard. Factual inaccuracies in pleas in mitigation cause distress and offence to victims, the families of victims and witnesses. This can take many forms but may be most acutely felt when the victim is dead and the family hears inaccurate assertions about the victim's character or lifestyle. Prosecution advocates are reminded that they are required to adhere to the standards set out in the Victim's Charter, which places the needs of the victim at the heart of the criminal justice process, and that they will be subject to a similar obligation in respect of the Code of Practice for Victims of Crime when it comes into force.

A2. The principle of fairness is central to the administration of justice. The implementation of Human Rights Act 1998 in October 2000 incorporated into domestic law the principle of fairness to the accused articulated in the European Convention on Human Rights. Accuracy and reasonableness of plea plays an important part in ensuring fairness both to the accused and to the victim.

A3. The Attorney General's Guidelines on the Acceptance of Pleas issued on December 7, 2000 highlighted the importance of transparency in the conduct of justice. The basis of plea agreed by the parties in a criminal trial is central to the sentencing process. An illogical or unsupported basis of plea can lead to the passing of an unduly lenient sentence and has a consequential effect where consideration arises as to whether to refer the sentence to the Court of Appeal under section 36 of the Criminal Justice Act 1988.

A4. These Guidelines, which expand upon and now replace the Guidelines issued on the 7 December 2000, give guidance on how prosecutors should meet these objectives of protection of victims' interests and of securing fairness and transparency in the process. They take into account the guidance issued by the Court of Appeal (Criminal) Division in *R* v *Beswick* [1996] 1 Cr App R 343, *R* v *Tolera* [1999] 1 Cr App R 25 and *R* v *Underwood* [2005] 1 Cr App R 178. They complement the Bar Council Guidance on Written Standards for the Conduct of Professional Work issued with the 7th edition of the Code of Conduct for the Bar of England and Wales and the Law Society's Professional Conduct Rules. When considering the acceptance of a guilty plea prosecution advocates are also reminded of the need to apply 'The Farquharson Guidelines on The Role and Responsibilities of the Prosecution Advocate'.

A5. The Guidelines should be followed by all prosecutors and those persons designated under section 7 of the Prosecution of Offences Act 1985 (designated caseworkers) and apply to prosecutions conducted in England and Wales.

B General Principles

B1. Justice in this jurisdiction, save in the most exceptional circumstances, is conducted in public. This includes the acceptance of pleas by the prosecution and sentencing.

B2. The Code for Crown Prosecutors governs the prosecutor's decision-making prior to the commencement of the trial hearing and sets out the circumstances in which pleas to a reduced number of charges, or less serious charges, can be accepted.

B3. When a case is listed for trial and the prosecution form the view that the appropriate course is to accept a plea before the proceedings commence or continue, or to offer no evidence on the indictment or any part of it, the prosecution should whenever practicable speak to the victim or the victim's family, so that the position can be explained. The views of the victim or the family may assist in informing the prosecutor's decision as to whether it is the public interest, as defined by the Code for Crown Prosecutors, to accept or reject the plea. The victim or victim's family should then be kept informed and decisions explained once they are made at court.

B4. The appropriate disposal of a criminal case after conviction is as much a part of the criminal justice process as the trial of guilt or innocence. The prosecution advocate represents the public interest, and should be ready to assist the court to reach its decision as to the appropriate sentence. This will include drawing the court's attention to:

— any victim personal statement or other information available to the prosecution advocate as to the impact of the offence on the victim;
— where appropriate, any evidence of the impact of the offending on a community;
— any statutory provisions relevant to the offender and the offences under consideration;
— any relevant sentencing guidelines and guideline cases; and the aggravating and mitigating factors of the offence under consideration;

The prosecution advocate may also offer assistance to the court by making submissions, in the light of all these factors, as to the appropriate sentencing range.

In all cases, it is the prosecution advocate's duty to apply for appropriate ancillary orders, such as anti-social behaviour orders and confiscation orders. When considering which ancillary orders to apply for, prosecution advocates must always have regard to the victim's needs, including the question of his or her future protection.

C The Basis of Plea

C1. The basis of a guilty plea must not be agreed on a misleading or untrue set of facts and must take proper account of the victim's interests. An illogical or insupportable basis of plea will inevitably result in the imposition of an inappropriate sentence and is capable of damaging public confidence in the criminal justice system.

C2. When the defendant indicates an acceptable plea, the defence advocate should reduce the basis of the plea to writing. This should be done in all cases save for those in which the issue is simple or where the defendant has indicated that the guilty plea has been or will be tendered on the basis of the prosecution case.

C3. The written basis of plea must be considered with great care, taking account of the position of any other relevant defendant where appropriate. The prosecution should not lend itself to any agreement whereby a case is presented to the sentencing judge on a misleading or untrue set of facts or on a basis that is detrimental to the victim's interests. There will be cases where a defendant seeks to mitigate on the basis of assertions of fact which are outside the scope of the prosecution's knowledge. A typical example concerns the defendant's state of mind. If a defendant wishes to be sentenced on this basis, the prosecution advocate should invite the judge not to accept the defendant's version unless he or she gives evidence on oath to be tested in cross-examination.

C4. The prosecution advocate should show the prosecuting authority any written record relating to the plea and agree with them the basis on which the case will be opened to the court.

C5. It is the responsibility of the prosecution advocate thereafter to ensure that the defence advocate is aware of the basis on which the plea is accepted by the prosecution and the way in which the prosecution case will be opened to the court.

C6. (1) In all cases before the Crown Court, and in cases before the magistrates' court where the issues are complex or there is scope for misunderstanding, the prosecution must commit to writing the aggravating and mitigating factors that will form the opening of the prosecution case as well as any statutory limitations on sentencing. The prosecution will address, where relevant, the factors outlined at B4 including the matters set out in the next sub-paragraph.

(2) The matters to be dealt with are:

- the aggravating and mitigating factors of the offence (not personal mitigation);
- any statutory provisions relevant to the offender and the offence under consideration so that the judge is made aware of any statutory limitations on sentencing;
- any relevant sentencing Guidelines and guideline cases;

- identifying any victim personal statement or other information available to the prosecution advocate as to the impact of the offence on the victim;
- where appropriate, any evidence of the impact of the offending on a community;
- an indication, where applicable, of an intention to apply for any ancillary orders, such as anti-social behaviour orders and confiscation orders, and so far as possible, indicating the nature of the order to be sought.

C7. When the prosecution advocate has agreed the written basis of plea submitted by the defence advocate, he or she should endorse the document accordingly. If the prosecution advocate takes issue with all or part of the written basis of plea, he or she should set out in writing what is accepted and what is rejected or not accepted. Where there is a dispute about a particular fact which the defence advocate believes to be effectively immaterial to the sentencing decision, the difference should be recorded so that the judge can make up his or her own mind. The signed original document should be made available to the trial judge and thereafter lodged with the court papers, as it will form part of the record of the hearing.

C8. Where a defendant declines to admit an offence that he or she previously indicated should be taken into consideration, the prosecution advocate should indicate to the defence advocate and the court that, subject to further review, the offence may now form the basis of a new prosecution.

C9. Where the basis of plea cannot be agreed and the discrepancy between the two accounts is such as to have a potentially significant effect on the level of sentence, it is the duty of the defence advocate so to inform the court before the sentencing process begins. There remains an overriding duty on the prosecution advocate to ensure that the sentencing judge is made aware of the discrepancy and of the consideration which must be given to the holding of a Newton hearing to resolve the issue. The court should be told where a derogatory reference to a victim, witness or third party is not accepted, even though there may be no effect on sentence.

C10. Whenever an agreement as to the basis of plea is made between the prosecution and defence, any such agreement will be subject to the approval of the trial judge, who may of his or her own motion disregard the agreement and direct that a *Newton* hearing should be held to determine the proper basis on which sentence should be passed.

D Sentence Indications

D1. Only in the Crown Court may sentence indications be sought. Advocates there are reminded that indications as to sentence should not be sought from the trial judge unless issues between the prosecution and defence have been addressed and resolved. Therefore, in difficult or complicated cases, no less than seven days notice in writing of an intention to seek an indication should normally be given to the prosecution and the court. When deciding whether the circumstances of a case require such notice to be given, defence advocates are reminded that prosecutors should not agree a basis of plea unless and until the necessary consultation has taken place first with the victim and/or the victim's family and second, in the case of an independent prosecution advocate, with the prosecuting authority.

D2. If there is no final agreement about the plea to the indictment, or the basis of plea, and the defence nevertheless proceeds to seek an indication of sentence, which the judge appears minded to give, the prosecution advocate should remind him or her of the guidance given in *R* v *Goodyear (Karl)* [2005] EWCA 888 that normally speaking an indication of sentence should not be given until the basis of the plea has been agreed or the judge has concluded that he or she can properly deal with the case without the need for a trial of the issue.

D3. If an indication is sought, the prosecution advocate should normally enquire whether the judge is in possession of or has access to all the evidence relied on by the prosecution, including any victim personal statement, as well as any information about relevant previous convictions recorded against the defendant.

D4. Before the judge gives the indication, the prosecution advocate should draw the judge's attention to any minimum or mandatory statutory sentencing requirements. Where the prosecution advocate would be expected to offer the judge assistance with relevant guideline cases or the views of the Sentencing Guidelines Council, he or she should invite the judge to allow them to do so. Where it applies, the prosecution advocate should remind the judge that the position of the Attorney General to refer any sentencing decision as unduly lenient is unaffected. In any event, the prosecution advocate should not say anything which may create the impression that the sentence indication has the support or approval of the Crown.

E Pleas in Mitigation

E1. The prosecution advocate must challenge any assertion by the defence in mitigation which is derogatory to a person's character, (for instance, because it suggests that his or her conduct is or has been criminal, immoral or improper) and which is either false or irrelevant to proper sentencing considerations. If the defence advocate persists in that assertion, the prosecution advocate should invite the court to consider holding a *Newton* hearing to determine the issue.

E2. The defence advocate must not submit in mitigation anything that is derogatory to a person's character without giving advance notice in writing so as to afford the prosecution advocate the opportunity to consider their position under paragraph E1. When the prosecution advocate is so notified they must take all reasonable steps to establish whether the assertions are true. Reasonable steps will include seeking the views of the victim. This will involve seeking the views of the victim's family if the victim is deceased, and the victim's parents or legal guardian where the victim is a child. Reasonable steps may also include seeking the views of the police or other law enforcement authority, as appropriate. An assertion which is derogatory to a person's character will rarely amount to mitigation unless it has a causal connection to the circumstances of the offence or is otherwise relevant to proper sentencing considerations.

E3. Where notice has not been given in accordance with paragraph E2, the prosecution advocate must not acquiesce in permitting mitigation which is derogatory to a person's character. In such circumstances, the prosecution advocate should draw the attention of the court to the failure to give advance notice and seek time, and if necessary, an adjournment to investigate the assertion in the same way as if proper notice had been given. Where, in the opinion of the prosecution advocate, there are substantial grounds for believing that such an assertion is false or irrelevant to sentence, he or she should inform the court of their opinion and invite the court to consider making an order under section 58(8) of the Criminal Procedure and Investigations Act 1996, preventing publication of the assertion.

E4. Where the prosecution advocate considers that the assertion is, if true, relevant to sentence, or the count has so indicated, he or she should seek time, and if necessary an adjournment, to establish whether the assertion is true. If the matter cannot be resolved to the satisfaction of the parties, the prosecution advocate should invite the court to consider holding a *Newton* hearing to determine the issue.

GUIDANCE ON THE USE OF THE COMMON LAW OFFENCE OF CONSPIRACY TO DEFRAUD

Summary

1. This guidance concerns the issues which the Attorney General asks prosecuting authorities in England and Wales to consider before using the common law offence of conspiracy to defraud, in the light of the implementation of the Fraud Act 2006. It may be supplemented by Departmental-specific guidance issued by individual Directors of the prosecuting authorities.

Background

2. When the Fraud Act 2006 comes into force on 15 January 2007, the prosecution will be able to use modern and flexible statutory offences of fraud. The 2006 Act replaces the deception offences contained in the Theft Acts 1968–1996 with a general offence of fraud that can be committed in three ways:
   - fraud by false representation;
   - fraud by failing to disclose information; and
   - fraud by abuse of position.

   It also introduces other offences which can be used in particular circumstances, notably:
   - new offences to tackle the possession and supply of articles for use in fraud; and
   - a new offence of fraudulent trading applicable to sole traders and other businesses not caught by the existing offence in section 458 of the Companies Act 1985.
3. The new offences are designed to catch behaviour that previously fell through gaps in the Theft Acts and could only be prosecuted as conspiracy to defraud. Indeed the Act is based on a Law Commission report (Cm 5560) which also recommended the abolition of the common law offence of conspiracy to defraud. The argument is that the offence is unfairly uncertain, and wide enough to have the potential to catch behaviour that should not be criminal. Furthermore it can seem anomalous that what is legal if performed by one person should be criminal if performed by many.
4. However, consultations showed a widespread view in favour of retention of common law conspiracy to defraud, and the Government decided to retain it for the meantime, but accepted the

case for considering repeal in the longer term. Whether there is a continuing need for retention of the common law offence is one of the issues that will be addressed in the Home Office review of the operation of the Fraud Act 2006, which will take place 3 years after its implementation.

5. In 2003, 14,928 defendants were proceeded against in England and Wales for crimes of fraud; 1018 of these were charged with the common law crime of conspiracy to defraud of which 44% were found guilty (compared with 71% for the statutory fraud offences). The expectation now is that the common law offence will be used to a significantly lesser extent once the Fraud Act 2006 has come into force.

Issues to be considered in using the common law offence

6. In selecting charges in fraud cases, the prosecutor should first consider:
   - whether the behaviour could be prosecuted under statute—whether under the Fraud Act 2006 or another Act or as a statutory conspiracy; and
   - whether the available statutory charges adequately reflect the gravity of the offence.
7. Statutory conspiracy to commit a substantive offence should be charged if the alleged agreement satisfies the definition in section 1 of the Criminal Law Act 1977, provided that there is no wider dishonest objective that would be important to the presentation of the prosecution case in reflecting the gravity of the case.
8. Section 12 of the Criminal Justice Act 1987 provides that common law conspiracy to defraud may be charged even if the conduct agreed upon will involve the commission of a statutory offence. However, Lord Bingham said in *R v Rimmington and R v Goldstein* [(2005) UKHL 63]:

   'I would not go to the length of holding that conduct may never be lawfully prosecuted as a generally-expressed common law crime where it falls within the terms of a specific statutory provision, *but good practice and respect for the primacy of statute do in my judgment require that conduct falling within the terms of a specific statutory provision should be prosecuted under that provision unless there is good reason for doing otherwise.*'
9. In the Attorney General's view the common law charge may still be appropriate in the type of cases set out in paragraphs 12–15, but in order to understand the circumstances under which conspiracy to defraud is used *prosecutors should make a record of the reasons for preferring that charge.*

Records of decisions

10. Where a charge of common law conspiracy to defraud is proposed the case lawyer must consider and set out in writing in the review note:
    - how much such a charge will add to the amount of evidence likely to be called both by the prosecution and the defence; and
    - the justification for using the charge, and why specific statutory offences are inadequate or otherwise inappropriate.

    Thereafter, and before charge, the use of this charge should be specifically approved by a supervising lawyer experienced in fraud cases. Equivalent procedures to ensure proper consideration of the charge and recording of the decision should be applied by all prosecuting authorities in their case review processes.
11. Information from these records will be collected retrospectively for the review to be conducted in 3 years. It will enable the identification of where and why the common law offence has been used. It could then also form the basis for any future work on whether, and if so how, to replace the common law or whether it can simply and safely be repealed. It is expected that in 3 years the Government will be able to review the situation in the light of the practical operation not only of the new fraud offences, but of other relevant changes. These include the Lord Chief Justice's protocol on the control and management of heavy fraud cases, and the sample count provisions in the Domestic Violence, Crime and Victims Act 2004. Any actual or proposed changes to the law on assisting and encouraging crime in the light of the Law Commission's study of that issue [Cm 6878, published in July 2006] will also be taken into account.

A Conduct that can more effectively be prosecuted as conspiracy to defraud

12. There may be cases where the interests of justice can only be served by presenting to a court an overall picture which cannot be achieved by charging a series of substantive offences or statutory conspiracies. Typically, such cases will involve some, but not necessarily all of the following:
    - evidence of several significant but different kinds of criminality;
    - several jurisdictions;
    - different types of victims, e.g. individuals, banks, web site administrators, credit card companies;
    - organised crime networks.

13. The proper presentation of such cases as statutory conspiracies could lead to:
    - large numbers of separate counts to reflect the different conspiracies;
    - severed trials for single or discrete groups of conspiracies;
    - evidence in one severed trial being deemed inadmissible in another.
14. If so, the consequences might be that no one court would receive a cohesive picture of the whole case which would allow sentencing on a proper basis. In contrast a single count of common law conspiracy to defraud might, in such circumstances, reflect the nature and extent of criminal conduct in a way that prosecuting the underlying statutory offences or conspiracies would fail to achieve.

B Conduct that can only be prosecuted as conspiracy to defraud

15. Examples of such conduct might include but are not restricted to agreements to the following courses of action:
    - The dishonest obtaining of land and other property which cannot be stolen such as intellectual property not protected by the Copyright, Designs and Patents Act 1988 and the Trademarks Act 1994, and other confidential information. The Fraud Act will bite where there is intent to make a gain or cause a loss through false representation, failure to disclose information where there is a legal obligation to do so, or the abuse of position;
    - Dishonestly infringing another's right; for example the dishonest exploitation of another's patent in the absence of a legal duty to disclose information about its existence;
    - Where it is intended that the final offence be committed by someone outside the conspiracy; and
    - Cases where the accused cannot be proved to have had the necessary degree of knowledge of the substantive offence to be perpetrated;

SECTION 18 RIPA: PROSECUTORS INTERCEPT GUIDELINES

1. These guidelines concern the approach to be taken by prosecutors in applying section 18 of the Regulation of Investigatory Powers Act (RIPA) in England and Wales.

Background

2. It has been long-standing Government policy that the fact that interception of communications has taken place in any particular case should remain secret and not be disclosed to the subject. This is because of the need to protect the continuing value of interception as a vital means of gathering intelligence about serious crime and activities which threaten national security. The Government judges that if the use of the technique in particular cases were to be confirmed, the value of the technique would be diminished because targets would either know, or could deduce, when their communications might be intercepted and so could take avoiding action by using other, more secure means of communication.
3. In the context of legal proceedings, the policy that the fact of interception should remain secret is implemented by section 17 of RIPA. Section 17 provides that no evidence shall be adduced, question asked, assertion or disclosure made or other thing done in, for the purposes of, or in connection with, any legal proceedings which discloses the contents of a communication which has been obtained following the issue of an interception warrant or a warrant under the Interception of Communications Act 1985, or any related communications data ('protected information'), or tends to suggest that certain events have occurred.
4. The effect of section 17 is that the fact of interception of the subject's communications and the product of that interception cannot be relied upon or referred to by either party to the proceedings. This is given further effect by sections 3(7), 7(6), 7A(9) and 9(9) of the Criminal Procedure and Investigations Act 1996 (as amended). This protects the continuing value of interception whilst also creating a 'level playing-field', in that neither side can gain any advantage from the interception. In the context of criminal proceedings, this means that the defendant cannot be prejudiced by the existence in the hands of the prosecution of intercept material which is adverse to his interests.

Detailed Analysis

First Stage: action to be taken by the prosecutor

5. Section 18(7)(a) of RIPA provides:

   'Nothing in section 17(1) shall prohibit any such disclosure of any information that continues to be available for disclosure as is confined to . . . a disclosure to a person conducting a criminal prosecution for the purpose only of enabling that person to determine what is required of him by his duty to secure the fairness of the prosecution'.

If protected information is disclosed to a prosecutor, as permitted by section 18(7)(a), the first step that should be taken by the prosecutor is to review any information regarding an interception that remains extant at the time that he or she has conduct of the case.[1] In reviewing it, the prosecutor should seek to identify any information whose existence, if no action was taken by the Crown, might result in unfairness. Experience suggests that the most likely example of such potential unfairness is where the evidence in the case is such that the jury may draw an inference which intercept shows to be wrong, and to leave this uncorrected will result in the defence being disadvantaged.

6. If in the view of the prosecutor to take no action would render the proceedings unfair, the prosecutor should, first consulting with the relevant prosecution agency, take such steps as are available to him or her to secure the fairness of the proceedings provided these steps do not contravene section 18(10). In the example given above, such steps could include:
   (i) putting the prosecution case in such a way that the misleading inference is not drawn by the jury; or
   (ii) not relying upon the evidence which makes the information relevant; or
   (iii) discontinuing that part of the prosecution case in relation to which the protected information is relevant, by amending a charge or count on the indictment or offering no evidence on such a charge or count; or
   (iv) making an admission of fact.[2]

   There is no requirement for the prosecutor to notify the judge of the action that he or she has taken or proposes to take. Such a course should only be taken by the prosecutor if he considers it essential in the interests of justice to do so (see below).

Second Stage: disclosure to the judge

7. There may be some cases (although these are likely to be rare) where the prosecutor considers that he cannot secure the fairness of the proceedings without assistance from the relevant judge. In recognition of this, section 18(7)(b) of RIPA provides that in certain limited circumstances, the prosecutor may invite the judge to order a disclosure of the protected information to him.
8. If the prosecutor considers that he requires the assistance of the trial judge to ensure the fairness of the proceedings, or he is in doubt as to whether the result of taking the steps outlined at para 6 above would ensure fairness, he must apply to see the judge *ex parte*. Under section 18(8), a judge shall not order a disclosure to him except where he is satisfied that the exceptional circumstances of the case make that disclosure essential in the interests of justice. Before the judge is in a position to order such disclosure the prosecutor will need to impart to the judge such information, but only such information, as is necessary to demonstrate that exceptional circumstances mean that the prosecutor acting alone cannot secure the fairness of the proceedings. Experience suggests that exceptional circumstances in the course of a trial justifying disclosure to a judge arise only in the following two situations:

   (1) where the judge's assistance is necessary to ensure the fairness of the trial

   This situation may arise in the example given at paragraph 5 above, where there is a risk that the jury might draw an inference from certain facts, which protected information shows would be the wrong inference, and the prosecutor is unable to ensure that the jury will not draw this inference by his actions alone. The purpose in informing the judge is so that the judge will then be in a position to ensure fairness by:
   (i) summing up in a way which will ensure that the wrong inference is not drawn; or
   (ii) giving appropriate directions to the jury; or

[1] Section 15(1) of RIPA provides that it is the duty of the Secretary of State to ensure that arrangements are in place to ensure that (amongst other matters) intercept material is retained by the intercepting agencies only for as long as is necessary for any of the authorised purposes. The authorised purposes include retention which:

'is necessary to ensure that a person conducting a criminal prosecution has the information he needs to determine what is required of him by his duty to secure the fairness of the prosecution'. (section 15(4)(d))

[2] This is acceptable as long as to do so would not contravene section 17 i.e. reveal the existence of an interception warrant. Prosecutors must bear in mind that such a breach might conceivably occur not only from the factual content of the admission, but also from the circumstances in which it is made.

(iii) requiring the Crown to make an admission of fact which the judge thinks *essential in the interests of justice* if he is of the opinion that *exceptional circumstances* require him to make such a direction (section 18(9)). However, such a direction ***must not*** authorise or require anything to be done which discloses any of the contents of an intercepted communication or related data or tends to suggest that anything falling within section 17(2) has or may have occurred or be going to occur (section 18(10)). Situations where an admission of fact is required are likely to be rare. The judge must be of the view that proceedings could not be continued unless an admission of fact is made (and the conditions in section 18(9) are satisfied). There may be other ways in which it is possible for a judge to ensure fairness, such as those outlined at (i) and (ii) above.

In practice, no question of taking the action at (i)–(iii) arises if the protected information is already contained in a separate document in another form that has been or can be disclosed without contravening section 17(1), and this disclosure will secure the fairness of the proceedings.

(2) where the judge requires knowledge of the protected material for some other purpose

This situation may arise where, usually in the context of a PII application, the true significance of, or duty of disclosure in relation to, other material being considered for disclosure by a judge, cannot be appraised by the judge without reference to protected information. Disclosure to the judge of the protected information without more may be sufficient to enable him to appraise the material, but once he has seen the protected information the judge may also conclude that the conditions in section 18(9) are satisfied so that an admission of fact by the Crown is required in addition to or instead of disclosure of the non-protected material.

Another example is a case where protected information underlies operational decisions which are likely to be the subject of cross-examination and it is necessary to inform the judge of the existence of the protected information to enable him to deal with the issue when the questions are first posed in a way which ensures section 17(1) is not contravened.

What if the actions of the prosecutor and/or the judge cannot ensure the fairness of the proceedings?

9. There may be very rare cases in which no action taken by the prosecutor and/or judge can prevent the continuation of the proceedings being unfair, e.g. where the requirements of fairness could only be met if the Crown were to make an admission, but it cannot do so without contravening section 18(10). In that situation the prosecutor will have no option but to offer no evidence on the charge in question, or to discontinue the proceedings in their entirety.

Responding to questions about interception

10. Prosecutors are sometimes placed in a situation in which they are asked by the court or by the defence whether interception has taken place or whether protected information exists. Whether or not interception has taken place or protected information exists, an answer in the following terms, or similar should be given:

> 'I am not in a position to answer that, but I am aware of sections 17 and 18 of the Regulation of Investigatory Powers Act 2000 and the Attorney General's Guidelines on the Disclosure of Information in Exceptional Circumstances under section 18'.

In a case where interception has taken place or protected information exists, an answer in these terms will avoid a breach of the prohibition in section 17 while providing assurance that the prosecutor is aware of his obligations.

11. For the avoidance of doubt, any notification or disclosure of information to the judge in accordance with paragraphs 7–10 must be *ex parte*. It will never be appropriate for prosecutors to volunteer, either *inter partes* or to the Court *ex parte*, that interception has taken place or that protected information exists, save in accordance with section 18 as elaborated in these Guidelines.

Further Assistance

12. Should a prosecutor be unsure as to the application of these guidelines in any particular case, further guidance should be sought from those instructing him or her. In those cases where a prosecutor has been instructed by the Crown Prosecution Service, the relevant CPS prosecutor must seek appropriate guidance from Casework Directorate, CPS Headquarters, Ludgate Hill.

DISCLOSURE

The Attorney-General's Guidelines on Disclosure of Information in Criminal Proceedings are reproduced in **appendix** 5.

Appendix 4 The Code for Crown Prosecutors

1 Introduction

1.1 The decision to prosecute an individual is a serious step. Fair and effective prosecution is essential to the maintenance of law and order. Even in a small case a prosecution has serious implications for all involved — victims, witnesses, and defendants. The Crown Prosecution Service applies the Code for Crown Prosecutors so that it can make fair and consistent decisions about prosecutions.

1.2 The Code helps the Crown Prosecution Service to play its part in making sure that justice is done. It contains information that is important to police officers and others who work in the criminal justice system and to the general public. Police officers should apply the provisions of this Code whenever they are responsible for deciding whether to charge a person with an offence.

1.3 The Code is also designed to make sure that everyone knows the principles that the Crown Prosecution Service applies when carrying out its work. By applying the same principles, everyone involved in the system is helping to treat victims, witnesses, and defendants fairly, while prosecuting cases effectively.

2 General Principles

2.1 Each case is unique and must be considered on its own facts and merits. However, there are general principles that apply to the way in which Crown Prosecutors must approach every case.

2.2 Crown Prosecutors must be fair, independent, and objective. They must not let any personal views about ethnic or national origin, disability, sex, religious beliefs, political views or the sexual orientation of the suspect, victim, or witness influence their decisions. They must not be affected by improper or undue pressure from any source.

2.3 It is the duty of Crown Prosecutors to make sure that the right person is prosecuted for the right offence. In doing so, Crown Prosecutors must always act in the interests of justice and not solely for the purpose of obtaining a conviction.

2.4 Crown Prosecutors should provide guidance and advice to investigators throughout the investigative and prosecuting process. This may include lines of inquiry, evidential requirements, and assistance in any pre-charge procedures. Crown Prosecutors will be proactive in identifying and, where possible, rectifying evidential deficiencies and in bringing to an early conclusion those cases that cannot be strengthened by further investigation.

2.5 It is the duty of Crown Prosecutors to review, advise on, and prosecute cases, ensuring that the law is properly applied, that all relevant evidence is put before the court, and that obligations of disclosure are complied with, in accordance with the principles set out in this Code.

2.6 The Crown Prosecution Service is a public authority for the purposes of the Human Rights Act 1998. Crown Prosecutors must apply the principles of the European Convention on Human Rights in accordance with the Act.

3 The Decision to Prosecute

3.1 In most cases, Crown Prosecutors are responsible for deciding whether a person should be charged with a criminal offence, and if so, what that offence should be. Crown Prosecutors make these decisions in accordance with this Code and the Director's Guidance on Charging. In those cases where the police determine the charge, which are usually more minor and routine cases, they apply the same provisions.

3.2 Crown Prosecutors make charging decisions in accordance with the Full Code Test (see section 5 below), other than in those limited circumstances where the Threshold Test applies (see section 6 below).

3.3 The Threshold Test applies where the case is one in which it is proposed to keep the suspect in custody after charge, but the evidence required to apply the Full Code Test is not yet available.

3.4 Where a Crown Prosecutor makes a charging decision in accordance with the Threshold Test, the case must be reviewed in accordance with the Full Code Test as soon as reasonably practicable, taking into account the progress of the investigation.

4 Review

4.1 Each case the Crown Prosecution Service receives from the police is reviewed to make sure that it is right to proceed with a prosecution. Unless the Threshold Test applies, the Crown Prosecution

Service will only start or continue with a prosecution when the case has passed both stages of the Full Code Test.

4.2 Review is a continuing process and Crown Prosecutors must take account of any change in circumstances. Wherever possible, they should talk to the police first if they are thinking about changing the charges or stopping the case. Crown Prosecutors should also tell the police if they believe that some additional evidence may strengthen the case. This gives the police the chance to provide more information that may affect the decision.

4.3 The Crown Prosecution Service and the police work closely together, but the final responsibility for the decision whether or not a charge or a case should go ahead rests with the Crown Prosecution Service.

5 The Full Code Test

5.1 The Full Code Test has two stages. The first stage is consideration of the evidence. If the case does not pass the evidential stage it must not go ahead no matter how important or serious it may be. If the case does pass the evidential stage, Crown Prosecutors must proceed to the second stage and decide if a prosecution is needed in the public interest. The evidential and public interest stages are explained below.

The Evidential Stage

5.2 Crown Prosecutors must be satisfied that there is enough evidence to provide a 'realistic prospect of conviction' against each defendant on each charge. They must consider what the defence case may be, and how that is likely to affect the prosecution case.

5.3 A realistic prospect of conviction is an objective test. It means that a jury or bench of magistrates or judge hearing a case alone, properly directed in accordance with the law, is more likely than not to convict the defendant of the charge alleged. This is a separate test from the one that the criminal courts themselves must apply. A court should only convict if satisfied so that it is sure of a defendant's guilt.

5.4 When deciding whether there is enough evidence to prosecute, Crown Prosecutors must consider whether the evidence can be used and is reliable. There will be many cases in which the evidence does not give any cause for concern. But there will also be cases in which the evidence may not be as strong as it first appears. Crown Prosecutors must ask themselves the following questions:

Can the evidence be used in court?

(a) Is it likely that the evidence will be excluded by the court? There are certain legal rules which might mean that evidence which seems relevant cannot be given at a trial. For example, is it likely that the evidence will be excluded because of the way in which it was gathered? If so, is there enough other evidence for a realistic prospect of conviction?

Is the evidence reliable?

(b) Is there evidence which might support or detract from the reliability of a confession? Is the reliability affected by factors such as the defendant's age, intelligence, or level of understanding?

(c) What explanation has the defendant given? Is a court likely to find it credible in the light of the evidence as a whole? Does it support an innocent explanation?

(d) If the identity of the defendant is likely to be questioned, is the evidence about this strong enough?

(e) Is the witness's background likely to weaken the prosecution case? For example, does the witness have any motive that may affect his or her attitude to the case, or a relevant previous conviction?

(f) Are there concerns over the accuracy or credibility of a witness? Are these concerns based on evidence or simply information with nothing to support it? Is there further evidence which the police should be asked to seek out which may support or detract from the account of the witness?

5.5 Crown Prosecutors should not ignore evidence because they are not sure that it can be used or is reliable. But they should look closely at it when deciding if there is a realistic prospect of conviction.

The Public Interest Stage

5.6 In 1951, Lord Shawcross, who was Attorney General, made the classic statement on public interest, which has been supported by Attorneys General ever since: 'It has never been the rule in this country — I hope it never will be — that suspected criminal offences must automatically be the subject of prosecution'. (House of Commons Debates, volume 483, column 681, 29 January 1951.)

5.7 The public interest must be considered in each case where there is enough evidence to provide a realistic prospect of conviction. Although there may be public interest factors against prosecution in a particular case, often the prosecution should go ahead and those factors should be put to the court for consideration when sentence is being passed. A prosecution will usually take place unless there are public interest factors tending against prosecution which clearly outweigh those tending in favour, or it appears more appropriate in all the circumstances of the case to divert the person from prosecution (see section 8 below).

5.8 Crown Prosecutors must balance factors for and against prosecution carefully and fairly. Public interest factors that can affect the decision to prosecute usually depend on the seriousness of the offence or the circumstances of the suspect. Some factors may increase the need to prosecute but others may suggest that another course of action would be better.

The following lists of some common public interest factors, both for and against prosecution, are not exhaustive. The factors that apply will depend on the facts in each case.

Some common public interest factors in favour of prosecution

5.9 The more serious the offence, the more likely it is that a prosecution will be needed in the public interest. A prosecution is likely to be needed if:

(a) a conviction is likely to result in a significant sentence;
(b) a conviction is likely to result in a confiscation or any other order;
(c) a weapon was used or violence was threatened during the commission of the offence;
(d) the offence was committed against a person serving the public (for example, a police or prison officer, or a nurse);
(e) the defendant was in a position of authority or trust;
(f) the evidence shows that the defendant was a ringleader or an organizer of the offence;
(g) there is evidence that the offence was premeditated;
(h) there is evidence that the offence was carried out by a group;
(i) the victim of the offence was vulnerable, has been put in considerable fear, or suffered personal attack, damage, or disturbance;
(j) the offence was committed in the presence of, or in close proximity to, a child;
(k) the offence was motivated by any form of discrimination against the victim's ethnic or national origin, disability, sex, religious beliefs, political views or sexual orientation, or the suspect demonstrated hostility towards the victim based on any of those characteristics;
(l) there is a marked difference between the actual or mental ages of the defendant and the victim, or if there is any element of corruption;
(m) the defendant's previous convictions or cautions are relevant to the present offence;
(n) the defendant is alleged to have committed the offence while under an order of the court;
(o) there are grounds for believing that the offence is likely to be continued or repeated, for example, by a history of recurring conduct;
(p) the offence, although not serious in itself, is widespread in the area where it was committed; or
(q) a prosecution would have a significant positive impact on maintaining community confidence.

Some common public interest factors against prosecution

5.10 A prosecution is less likely to be needed if:

(a) the court is likely to impose a nominal penalty;
(b) the defendant has already been made the subject of a sentence and any further conviction would be unlikely to result in the imposition of an additional sentence or order, unless the nature of the particular offence requires a prosecution or the defendant withdraws consent to have an offence taken into consideration during sentencing;
(c) the offence was committed as a result of a genuine mistake or misunderstanding (these factors must be balanced against the seriousness of the offence);
(d) the loss or harm can be described as minor and was the result of a single incident, particularly if it was caused by a misjudgement;
(e) there has been a long delay between the offence taking place and the date of the trial, unless:
- the offence is serious;
- the delay has been caused in part by the defendant;
- the offence has only recently come to light; or
- the complexity of the offence has meant that there has been a long investigation;

(f) a prosecution is likely to have a bad effect on the victim's physical or mental health, always bearing in mind the seriousness of the offence;
(g) the defendant is elderly, or is, or was at the time of the offence, suffering from significant mental or physical ill health, unless the offence is serious or there is real possibility that it may be repeated. The Crown Prosecution Service, where necessary, applies Home Office guidelines about how to deal with mentally disordered offenders. Crown Prosecutors must balance the

desirability of diverting a defendant who is suffering from significant mental or physical ill health with the need to safeguard the general public;

(h) the defendant has put right the loss or harm that was caused (but defendants must not avoid prosecution or diversion solely because they pay compensation); or

(i) details may be made public that could harm sources of information, international relations, or national security.

5.11 Deciding on the public interest is not simply a matter of adding up the number of factors on each side. Crown Prosecutors must decide how important each factor is in the circumstances of each case and go on to make an overall assessment.

The relationship between the victim and the public interest

5.12 The Crown Prosecution Service does not act for victims or the families of victims in the same way as solicitors act for their clients. Crown Prosecutors act on behalf of the public and not just in the interests of any particular individual. However, when considering the public interest, Crown Prosecutors should always take into account the consequences for the victim of whether or not to prosecute, and any views expressed by the victim or the victim's family.

5.13 It is important that a victim is told about a decision which makes a significant difference to the case in which they are involved. Crown Prosecutors should ensure that they follow any agreed procedures.

6 The Threshold Test

6.1 The Threshold Test requires Crown Prosecutors to decide whether there is at least a reasonable suspicion that the suspect has committed an offence, and if there is, whether it is in the public interest to charge that suspect.

6.2 The Threshold Test is applied to those cases in which it would not be appropriate to release a suspect on bail after charge, but the evidence to apply the Full Code Test is not yet available.

6.3 There are statutory limits that restrict the time a suspect may remain in police custody before a decision has to be made whether to charge or release the suspect. There will be cases where the suspect in custody presents a substantial bail risk if released, but much of the evidence may not be available at the time the charging decision has to be made. Crown Prosecutors will apply the Threshold Test to such cases for a limited period.

6.4 The evidential decision in each case will require consideration of a number of factors including:

- the evidence available at the time;
- the likelihood and nature of further evidence being obtained;
- the reasonableness for believing that evidence will become available;
- the time it will take to gather that evidence and the steps being taken to do so;
- the impact the expected evidence will have on the case;
- the charges that the evidence will support.

6.5 The public interest means the same as under the Full Code Test, but will be based on the information available at the time of charge which will often be limited.

6.6 A decision to charge and withhold bail must be kept under review. The evidence gathered must be regularly assessed to ensure the charge is still appropriate and that continued objection to bail is justified. The Full Code Test must be applied as soon as reasonably practicable.

7 Selection of Charges

7.1 Crown Prosecutors should select charges which:

(a) reflect the seriousness and extent of the offending;

(b) give the court adequate powers to sentence and impose appropriate post-conviction orders; and

(c) enable the case to be presented in a clear and simple way.

This means that Crown Prosecutors may not always choose or continue with the most serious charge where there is a choice.

7.2 Crown Prosecutors should never go ahead with more charges than are necessary just to encourage a defendant to plead guilty to a few. In the same way, they should never go ahead with a more serious charge just to encourage a defendant to plead guilty to a less serious one.

7.3 Crown Prosecutors should not change the charge simply because of the decision made by the court or the defendant about where the case will be heard.

8 Diversion from Prosecution

Adults

8.1 When deciding whether a case should be prosecuted in the courts, Crown Prosecutors should consider the alternatives to prosecution. Where appropriate, the availability of suitable rehabilitative, reparative, or restorative justice processes can be considered.

8.2 Alternatives to prosecution for adult suspects include a simple caution and a conditional caution.

Simple caution

8.3 A simple caution should only be given if the public interest justifies it and in accordance with Home Office guidelines. Where it is felt that such a caution is appropriate, Crown Prosecutors must inform the police so they can caution the suspect. If the caution is not administered, because the suspect refuses to accept it, a Crown Prosecutor may review the case again.

Conditional caution

8.4 A conditional caution may be appropriate where a Crown Prosecutor considers that while the public interest justifies a prosecution, the interests of the suspect, victim, and community may be better served by the suspect complying with suitable conditions aimed at rehabilitation or reparation. These may include restorative processes.

8.5 Crown Prosecutors must be satisfied that there is sufficient evidence for a realistic prospect of conviction and that the public interest would justify a prosecution should the offer of a conditional caution be refused or the offender fail to comply with the agreed conditions of the caution.

8.6 In reaching their decision, Crown Prosecutors should follow the Conditional Cautions Code of Practice and any guidance on conditional cautioning issued or approved by the Director of Public Prosecutions.

8.7 Where Crown Prosecutors consider a conditional caution to be appropriate, they must inform the police, or other authority responsible for administering the conditional caution, as well as providing an indication of the appropriate conditions so that the conditional caution can be administered.

Youths

8.8 Crown Prosecutors must consider the interests of a youth when deciding whether it is in the public interest to prosecute. However, Crown Prosecutors should not avoid prosecuting simply because of the defendant's age. The seriousness of the offence or the youth's past behaviour is very important.

8.9 Cases involving youths are usually only referred to the Crown Prosecution Service for prosecution if the youth has already received a reprimand and final warning, unless the offence is so serious that neither of these were appropriate or the youth does not admit committing the offence. Reprimands and final warnings are intended to prevent re-offending, and the fact that a further offence has occurred indicates that attempts to divert the youth from the court system have not been effective. So the public interest will usually require a prosecution in such cases, unless there are clear public interest factors against prosecution.

9 Mode of Trial

9.1 The Crown Prosecution Service applies the current guidelines for magistrates who have to decide whether cases should be tried in the Crown Court when the offence gives the option and the defendant does not indicate a guilty plea. Crown Prosecutors should recommend Crown Court trial when they are satisfied that the guidelines require them to do so.

9.2 Speed must never be the only reason for asking for a case to stay in the magistrates' courts. But Crown Prosecutors should consider the effect of any likely delay if they send a case to the Crown Court, and any possible stress on victims and witnesses if the case is delayed.

10 Accepting Guilty Pleas

10.1 Defendants may want to plead guilty to some, but not all, of the charges. Alternatively, they may want to plead guilty to a different, possibly less serious, charge because they are admitting only part of the crime. Crown Prosecutors should only accept the defendant's plea if they think the court is able to pass a sentence that matches the seriousness of the offending, particularly where there are aggravating features. Crown Prosecutors must never accept a guilty plea just because it is convenient.

10.2 In considering whether the pleas offered are acceptable, Crown Prosecutors should ensure that the interests of the victim and, where possible, any views expressed by the victim or victim's family, are taken into account when deciding whether it is in the public interest to accept the plea. However, the decision rests with the Crown Prosecutor.

10.3 It must be made clear to the court on what basis any plea is advanced and accepted. In cases where a defendant pleads guilty to the charges but on the basis of facts that are different from the prosecution case, and where this may significantly affect sentence, the court should be invited to hear evidence to determine what happened, and then sentence on that basis.

10.4 Where a defendant has previously indicated that he or she will ask the court to take an offence into consideration when sentencing, but then declines to admit that offence at court, Crown Prosecutors will consider whether a prosecution is required for that offence. Crown Prosecutors should explain to the defence advocate and the court that the prosecution of that offence may be subject to further review.

10.5 Particular care must be taken when considering pleas which would enable the defendant to avoid the imposition of a mandatory minimum sentence. When pleas are offered, Crown Prosecutors must bear in mind the fact that ancillary orders can be made with some offences but not with others.

11 Prosecutors' Role in Sentencing

11.1 Crown Prosecutors should draw the court's attention to:

- any aggravating or mitigating factors disclosed by the prosecution case;
- any victim personal statement;
- where appropriate, evidence of the impact of the offending on a community;
- any statutory provisions or sentencing guidelines which may assist;
- any relevant statutory provisions relating to ancillary orders (such as anti-social behaviour orders).

11.2 The Crown Prosecutor should challenge any assertion made by the defence in mitigation that is inaccurate, misleading, or derogatory. If the defence persist in the assertion, and it appears relevant to the sentence, the court should be invited to hear evidence to determine the facts and sentence accordingly.

12 Re-Starting a Prosecution

12.1 People should be able to rely on decisions taken by the Crown Prosecution Service. Normally, if the Crown Prosecution Service tells a suspect or defendant that there will not be a prosecution, or that the prosecution has been stopped, that is the end of the matter and the case will not start again. But occasionally there are special reasons why the Crown Prosecution Service will re-start the prosecution, particularly if the case is serious.

12.2 These reasons include:

(a) rare cases where a new look at the original decision shows that it was clearly wrong and should not be allowed to stand;

(b) cases which are stopped so that more evidence which is likely to become available in the fairly near future can be collected and prepared. In these cases, the Crown Prosecutor will tell the defendant that the prosecution may well start again; and

(c) cases which are stopped because of a lack of evidence but where more significant evidence is discovered later.

12.3 There may also be exceptional cases in which, following an acquittal of a serious offence, the Crown Prosecutor may, with the written consent of the Director of Public Prosecutions, apply to the Court of Appeal for an order quashing the acquittal and requiring the defendant to be retried, in accordance with Part 10 of the Criminal Justice Act 2003.

Appendix 5 Disclosure

CRIMINAL PROCEDURE AND INVESTIGATIONS ACT 1996: CODE OF PRACTICE UNDER PART II

Preamble

This code of practice is issued under part II of the Criminal Procedure and Investigations Act 1996 ('the Act'). It sets out the manner in which police officers are to record, retain and reveal to the prosecutor material obtained in a criminal investigation and which may be relevant to the investigation, and related matters.

Introduction

1.1 This code of practice applies in respect of criminal investigations conducted by police officers which begin on or after the day on which this code comes into effect. Persons other than police officers who are charged with the duty of conducting an investigation as defined in the Act are to have regard to the relevant provisions of the code, and should take these into account in applying their own operating procedures.

1.2 This code does not apply to persons who are not charged with the duty of conducting an investigation as defined in the Act.

1.3 Nothing in this code applies to material intercepted in obedience to a warrant issued under section 2 of the Interception of Communications Act 1985 or section 5 of the Regulation of Investigatory Powers Act 2000, or to any copy of that material as defined in section 10 of the 1985 Act or section 15 of the 2000 Act.

1.4 This code extends only to England and Wales.

Definitions

2.1 In this code:

— a *criminal investigation* is an investigation conducted by police officers with a view to it being ascertained whether a person should be charged with an offence, or whether a person charged with an offence is guilty of it. This will include

— investigations into crimes that have been committed;

— investigations whose purpose is to ascertain whether a crime has been committed, with a view to the possible institution of criminal proceedings; and

— investigations which begin in the belief that a crime may be committed, for example when the police keep premises or individuals under observation for a period of time, with a view to the possible institution of criminal proceedings;

— charging a person with an offence includes prosecution by way of summons;

— an *investigator* is any police officer involved in the conduct of a criminal investigation. All investigators have a responsibility for carrying out the duties imposed on them under this code, including in particular recording information, and retaining records of information and other material;

— the *officer in charge of an investigation* is the police officer responsible for directing a criminal investigation. He is also responsible for ensuring that proper procedures are in place for recording information, and retaining records of information and other material, in the investigation;

— the *disclosure officer* is the person responsible for examining material retained by the police during the investigation; revealing material to the prosecutor during the investigation and any criminal proceedings resulting from it, and certifying that he has done this; and disclosing material to the accused at the request of the prosecutor;

— the *prosecutor* is the authority responsible for the conduct, on behalf of the Crown, of criminal proceedings resulting from a specific criminal investigation;

— *material* is material of any kind, including information and objects, which is obtained in the course of a criminal investigation and which may be relevant to the investigation. This includes not only material coming into the possession of the investigator (such as documents seized in the course of searching premises) but also material generated by him (such as interview records);

— material may be *relevant to an investigation* if it appears to an investigator, or to the officer in charge of an investigation, or to the disclosure officer, that it has some bearing on any offence under investigation or any person being investigated, or on the surrounding circumstances of the case, unless it is incapable of having any impact on the case;

— *sensitive material* is material the disclosure of which, the disclosure officer believes would give rise to a real risk of serious prejudice to an important public interest;
— references to *prosecution disclosure* are to the duty of the prosecutor under sections 3 and 7A of the Act to disclose material which is in his possession or which he has inspected in pursuance of this code, and which might reasonably be capable of undermining the case against the accused, or of assisting the case for the accused;
— references to the disclosure of material to a person accused of an offence include references to the disclosure of material to his legal representative;
— references to police officers and to the chief officer of police include those employed in a police force as defined in section 3(3) of the Prosecution of Offences Act 1985.

General responsibilities

3.1 The functions of the investigator, the officer in charge of an investigation and the disclosure officer are separate. Whether they are undertaken by one, two or more persons will depend on the complexity of the case and the administrative arrangements within each police force. Where they are undertaken by more than one person, close consultation between them is essential to the effective performance of the duties imposed by this code.

3.2 In any criminal investigation, one or more deputy disclosure officers may be appointed to assist the disclosure officer, and a deputy disclosure officer may perform any function of a disclosure officer as defined in paragraph 2.1.

3.3 The chief officer of police for each police force is responsible for putting in place arrangements to ensure that in every investigation the identity of the officer in charge of an investigation and the disclosure officer is recorded. The chief officer of police for each police force shall ensure that disclosure officers and deputy disclosure officers have sufficient skills and authority, commensurate with the complexity of the investigation, to discharge their functions effectively. An individual must not be appointed as disclosure officer, or continue in that role, if that is likely to result in a conflict of interest, for instance, if the disclosure officer is the victim of the alleged crime which is the subject of the investigation. The advice of a more senior officer must always be sought if there is doubt as to whether a conflict of interest precludes an individual acting as disclosure officer. If thereafter the doubt remains, the advice of a prosecutor should be sought.

3.4 The officer in charge of an investigation may delegate tasks to another investigator, to civilians employed by the police force, or to other persons participating in the investigation under arrangements for joint investigations, but he remains responsible for ensuring that these have been carried out and for accounting for any general policies followed in the investigation. In particular, it is an essential part of his duties to ensure that all material which may be relevant to an investigation is retained, and either made available to the disclosure officer or (in exceptional circumstances) revealed directly to the prosecutor.

3.5 In conducting an investigation, the investigator should pursue all reasonable lines of inquiry, whether these point towards or away from the suspect. What is reasonable in each case will depend on the particular circumstances. For example, where material is held on computer, it is a matter for the investigator to decide which material on the computer it is reasonable to inquire into, and in what manner.

3.6 If the officer in charge of an investigation believes that other persons may be in possession of material that may be relevant to the investigation, and if this has not been obtained under paragraph 3.5 above, he should ask the disclosure officer to inform them of the existence of the investigation and to invite them to retain the material in case they receive a request for its disclosure. The disclosure officer should inform the prosecutor that they may have such material. However, the officer in charge of an investigation is not required to make speculative enquiries of other persons: there must be some reason to believe that they may have relevant material. That reason may come from information provided to the police by the accused or from other inquiries made or from some other source.

3.7 If, during a criminal investigation, the officer in charge of an investigation or disclosure officer for any reason no longer has responsibility for the functions falling to him, either his supervisor or the police officer in charge of criminal investigations for the police force concerned must assign someone else to assume that responsibility. That person's identity must be recorded, as with those initially responsible for these functions in each investigation.

Recording of information

4.1 If material which may be relevant to the investigation consists of information which is not recorded in any form, the officer in charge of an investigation must ensure that it is recorded in a durable or retrievable form (whether in writing, on video or audio tape, or on computer disk).

4.2 Where it is not practicable to retain the initial record of information because it forms part of a larger record which is to be destroyed, its contents should be transferred as a true record to a durable and more easily-stored form before that happens.

4.3 Negative information is often relevant to an investigation. If it may be relevant it must be recorded. An example might be a number of people present in a particular place at a particular time who state that they saw nothing unusual.

4.4 Where information which may be relevant is obtained, it must be recorded at the time it is obtained or as soon as practicable after that time. This includes, for example, information obtained in house-to-house enquiries, although the requirement to record information promptly does not require an investigator to take a statement from a potential witness where it would not otherwise be taken.

Retention of material

(a) Duty to retain material

5.1 The investigator must retain material obtained in a criminal investigation which may be relevant to the investigation. Material may be photographed, video-recorded, captured digitally or otherwise retained in the form of a copy rather than the original at any time, if the original is perishable, the original was supplied to the investigator rather than generated by him and is to be returned to its owner; or the retention of a copy rather than the original is reasonable in all the circumstances.

5.2 Where material has been seized in the exercise of the powers of seizure conferred by the Police and Criminal Evidence Act 1984, the duty to retain it under this code is subject to the provisions on the retention of seized material in section 22 of that Act.

5.3 If the officer in charge of an investigation becomes aware as a result of developments in the case that material previously examined but not retained (because it was not thought to be relevant) may now be relevant to the investigation, he should, wherever practicable, take steps to obtain it or ensure that it is retained for further inspection or for production in court if required.

5.4 The duty to retain material includes in particular the duty to retain material falling into the following categories, where it may be relevant to the investigation:

— crime reports (including crime report forms, relevant parts of incident report books or police officers' notebooks);

— custody records;

— records which are derived from tapes of telephone messages (for example, 999 calls) containing descriptions of an alleged offence or offender;

— final versions of witness statements (and draft versions where their content differs from the final version), including any exhibits mentioned (unless these have been returned to their owner on the understanding that they will be produced in court if required);

— interview records (written records, or audio or video tapes, of interviews with actual or potential witnesses or suspects);

— communications between the police and experts such as forensic scientists, reports of work carried out by experts, and schedules of scientific material prepared by the expert for the investigator, for the purposes of criminal proceedings;

— records of the first description of a suspect by each potential witness who purports to identify or describe the suspect, whether or not the description differs from that of subsequent descriptions by that or other witnesses;

— any material casting doubt on the reliability of a witness.

5.5 The duty to retain material, where it may be relevant to the investigation, also includes in particular the duty to retain material which may satisfy the test for prosecution disclosure in the Act, such as:

— information provided by an accused person which indicates an explanation for the offence with which he has been charged;

— any material casting doubt on the reliability of a confession;

— any material casting doubt on the reliability of a prosecution witness.

5.6 The duty to retain material falling into these categories does not extend to items which are purely ancillary to such material and possess no independent significance (for example, duplicate copies of records or reports).

(b) Length of time for which material is to be retained

5.7 All material which may be relevant to the investigation must be retained until a decision is taken whether to institute proceedings against a person for an offence.

5.8 If a criminal investigation results in proceedings being instituted, all material which may be relevant must be retained at least until the accused is acquitted or convicted or the prosecutor decides not to proceed with the case.

5.9 Where the accused is convicted, all material which may be relevant must be retained at least until:
— the convicted person is released from custody, or discharged from hospital, in cases where the court imposes a custodial sentence or a hospital order;
— six months from the date of conviction, in all other cases.

If the court imposes a custodial sentence or hospital order and the convicted person is released from custody or is discharged from hospital earlier than six months from the date of conviction, all material which may be relevant must be retained at least until six months from the date of conviction.

5.10 If an appeal against conviction is in progress when the release or discharge occurs, or at the end of the period of six months specified in paragraph 5.9, all material which may be relevant must be retained until the appeal is determined. Similarly, if the Criminal Cases Review Commission is considering an application at that point in time, all material which may be relevant must be retained at least until the Commission decides not to refer the case to the Court of Appeal, or until the Court determines the appeal resulting from the reference by the Commission.

5.11 Material need not be retained by the police as required in paragraph 5.9 if it was seized and is to be returned to its owner.

Preparation of material for prosecutor

(a) Introduction

6.1 The officer in charge of the investigation, the disclosure officer or an investigator may seek advice from the prosecutor about whether any particular item of material may be relevant to the investigation.

6.2 Material which may be relevant to an investigation, which has been retained in accordance with this code, and which the disclosure officer believes will not form part of the prosecution case, must be listed on a schedule.

6.3 Material which the disclosure officer does not believe is sensitive must be listed on a schedule of non-sensitive material. The schedule must include a statement that the disclosure officer does not believe the material is sensitive.

6.4 Any material which is believed to be sensitive must be either listed on a schedule of sensitive material or, in exceptional circumstances, revealed to the prosecutor separately.

6.5 Paragraphs 6.6 to 6.11 below apply to both sensitive and non-sensitive material. Paragraphs 6.12 to 6.14 apply to sensitive material only.

(b) Circumstances in which a schedule is to be prepared

6.6 The disclosure officer must ensure that a schedule is prepared in the following circumstances:
— the accused is charged with an offence which is triable only on indictment;
— the accused is charged with an offence which is triable either way, and it is considered either that the case is likely to be tried on indictment or that the accused is likely to plead not guilty at a summary trial;
— the accused is charged with a summary offence, and it is considered that he is likely to plead not guilty.

6.7 In respect of either way and summary offences, a schedule may not be needed if a person has admitted the offence, or if a police officer witnessed the offence and that person has not denied it.

6.8 If it is believed that the accused is likely to plead guilty at a summary trial, it is not necessary to prepare a schedule in advance. If, contrary to this belief, the accused pleads not guilty at a summary trial, or the offence is to be tried on indictment, the disclosure officer must ensure that a schedule is prepared as soon as is reasonably practicable after that happens.

(c) Way in which material is to be listed on schedule

6.9 The disclosure officer should ensure that each item of material is listed separately on the schedule, and is numbered consecutively. The description of each item should make clear the nature of the item and should contain sufficient detail to enable the prosecutor to decide whether he needs to inspect the material before deciding whether or not it should be disclosed.

6.10 In some enquiries it may not be practicable to list each item of material separately. For example, there may be many items of a similar or repetitive nature. These may be listed in a block and described by quantity and generic title.

6.11 Even if some material is listed in a block, the disclosure officer must ensure that any items among that material which might meet the test for primary prosecution disclosure are listed and described individually.

(d) Treatment of sensitive material

6.12 Subject to paragraph 6.13 below, the disclosure officer must list on a sensitive schedule any material, the disclosure of which would give a real risk of serious prejudice to an important public interest, and the reason for that belief. The schedule must include a statement that the disclosure officer believes the material is sensitive. Depending on the circumstances, examples of such material may include the following among others:

— material relating to national security;
— material received from the intelligence and security agencies;
— material relating to intelligence from foreign sources which reveals sensitive intelligence gathering methods;
— material given in confidence;
— material relating to the identity or activities of informants, or under-cover police officers, or witnesses, or other persons supplying information to the police who may be in danger if their identities are revealed;
— material revealing the location of any premises or other place used for police surveillance, or the identity of any person allowing a police officer to use them for surveillance;
— material revealing, either directly or indirectly, techniques and methods relied upon by a police officer in the course of a criminal investigation, for example covert surveillance techniques, or other methods of detecting crime;
— material whose disclosure might facilitate the commission of other offences or hinder the prevention and detection of crime;
— material upon the strength of which search warrants were obtained;
— material containing details of persons taking part in identification parades;
— material supplied to an investigator during a criminal investigation which has been generated by an official of a body concerned with the regulation or supervision of bodies corporate or of persons engaged in financial activities, or which has been generated by a person retained by such a body;
— material supplied to an investigator during a criminal investigation which relates to a child or young person and which has been generated by a local authority social services department, an Area Child Protection Committee or other party contacted by an investigator during the investigation;
— material relating to the private life of a witness.

6.13 In exceptional circumstances, where an investigator considers that material is so sensitive that its revelation to the prosecutor by means of an entry on the sensitive schedule is inappropriate, the existence of the material must be revealed to the prosecutor separately. This will apply where compromising the material would be likely to lead directly to the loss of life, or directly threaten national security.

6.14 In such circumstances, the responsibility for informing the prosecutor lies with the investigator who knows the detail of the sensitive material. The investigator should act as soon as is reasonably practicable after the file containing the prosecution case is sent to the prosecutor. The investigator must also ensure that the prosecutor is able to inspect the material so that he can assess whether it is disclosable and, if so, whether it needs to be brought before a court for a ruling on disclosure.

Revelation of material to prosecutor

7.1 The disclosure officer must give the schedules to the prosecutor. Wherever practicable this should be at the same time as he gives him the file containing the material for the prosecution case (or as soon as is reasonably practicable after the decision on mode of trial or the plea, in cases to which paragraph 6.8 applies).

7.2 The disclosure officer should draw the attention of the prosecutor to any material an investigator has retained (including material to which paragraph 6.13 applies) which may satisfy the test for prosecution disclosure in the Act, and should explain why he has come to that view.

7.3 At the same time as complying with the duties in paragraphs 7.1 and 7.2, the disclosure officer must give the prosecutor a copy of any material which falls into the following categories (unless such material has already been given to the prosecutor as part of the file containing the material for the prosecution case):

— information provided by an accused person which indicates an explanation for the offence with which he has been charged;

— any material casting doubt on the reliability of a confession;
— any material casting doubt on the reliability of a witness;
— any other material which the investigator believes may fall within the test for primary prosecution disclosure in the Act.

7.4 If the prosecutor asks to inspect material which has not already been copied to him, the disclosure officer must allow him to inspect it. If the prosecutor asks for a copy of material which has not already been copied to him, the disclosure officer must give him a copy. However, this does not apply where the disclosure officer believes, having consulted the officer in charge of the investigation, that the material is too sensitive to be copied and can only be inspected.

7.5 If material consists of information which is recorded other than in writing, whether it should be given to the prosecutor in its original form as a whole, or by way of relevant extracts recorded in the same form, or in the form of a transcript, is a matter for agreement between the disclosure officer and the prosecutor.

Subsequent action by disclosure officer

8.1 At the time a schedule of non-sensitive material is prepared, the disclosure officer may not know exactly what material will form the case against the accused, and the prosecutor may not have given advice about the likely relevance of particular items of material. Once these matters have been determined, the disclosure officer must give the prosecutor, where necessary, an amended schedule listing any additional material:
— which may be relevant to the investigation,
— which does not form part of the case against the accused,
— which is not already listed on the schedule, and
— which he believes is not sensitive,
unless he is informed in writing by the prosecutor that the prosecutor intends to disclose the material to the defence.

8.2 Section 7A of the Act imposes a continuing duty on the prosecutor, for the duration of criminal proceedings against the accused, to disclose material which satisfies the test for disclosure (subject to public interest considerations). To enable him to do this, any new material coming to light should be treated in the same way as the earlier material.

8.3 In particular, after a defence statement has been given, the disclosure officer must look again at the relevant material which has been retained and must draw the attention of the prosecutor to any material which might reasonably be expected to assist the defence disclosed by the accused; and he must reveal it to him in accordance with paragraphs 7.4 and 7.5 above.

Certification by disclosure officer

9.1 The disclosure officer must certify to the prosecutor that, to the best of his knowledge and belief, all relevant material which has been retained and made available to him has been revealed to the prosecutor in accordance with this code. He must sign and date the certificate. It will be necessary to certify not only at the time when the schedule and accompanying material is submitted to the prosecutor, and when relevant material which has been retained is reconsidered after the accused has given a defence statement, but also whenever a schedule is otherwise given or material is otherwise revealed to the prosecutor.

Disclosure of material to accused

10.1 If material has not already been copied to the prosecutor, and he requests its disclosure to the accused on the ground that:
— it falls within the test for prosecution disclosure, **or**
— the court has ordered its disclosure after considering an application from the accused,
the disclosure officer must disclose it to the accused.

10.2 If material has been copied to the prosecutor, and it is to be disclosed, whether it is disclosed by the prosecutor or the disclosure officer is a matter for agreement between the two of them.

10.3 The disclosure officer must disclose material to the accused either by giving him a copy or by allowing him to inspect it. If the accused person asks for a copy of any material which he has been allowed to inspect, the disclosure officer must give it to him, unless in the opinion of the disclosure officer that is either not practicable (for example because the material consists of an object which cannot be copied, or because the volume of material is so great), or not desirable (for example because the material is a statement by a child witness in relation to a sexual offence).

10.4 If material which the accused has been allowed to inspect consists of information which is recorded other than in writing, whether it should be given to the accused in its original form or in the form of a transcript is a matter for the discretion of the disclosure officer. If the material is transcribed, the disclosure officer must ensure that the transcript is certified to the accused as a true record of the material which has been transcribed.

10.5 If a court concludes that an item of sensitive material satisfies the prosecution disclosure test and that the interests of the defence outweigh the public interest in withholding disclosure, it will be necessary to disclose the material if the case is to proceed. This does not mean that sensitive documents must always be disclosed in their original form: for example, the court may agree that sensitive details still requiring protection should be blocked out, or that documents may be summarised, or that the prosecutor may make an admission about the substance of the material under section 10 of the Criminal Justice Act 1967.

ATTORNEY-GENERAL'S GUIDELINES: DISCLOSURE OF INFORMATION IN CRIMINAL PROCEEDINGS

Introduction

1. Every accused person has a right to a fair trial, a right long embodied in our law and guaranteed under Article 6 of the European Convention on Human Rights (ECHR). A fair trial is the proper object and expectation of all participants in the trial process. Fair disclosure to an accused is an inseparable part of a fair trial.
2. What must be clear is that a fair trial consists of an examination not just of all the evidence the parties wish to rely on but also all other relevant subject matter. A fair trial should not require consideration of irrelevant material and should not involve spurious applications or arguments which serve to divert the trial process from examining the real issues before the court.
3. The scheme set out in the Criminal Procedure and Investigations Act 1996 (as amended by the Criminal Justice Act 2003) (the Act) is designed to ensure that there is fair disclosure of material which may be relevant to an investigation and which does not form part of the prosecution case. Disclosure under the Act should assist the accused in the timely preparation and presentation of their case and assist the court to focus on all the relevant issues in the trial. Disclosure which does not meet these objectives risks preventing a fair trial taking place.
4. This means that the disclosure regime set out in the Act must be scrupulously followed. These Guidelines build upon the existing law to help to ensure that the legislation is operated more effectively, consistently and fairly.
5. Disclosure must not be an open ended trawl of unused material. A critical element to fair and proper disclosure is that the defence play their role to ensure that the prosecution are directed to material which might reasonably be considered capable of undermining the prosecution case or assisting the case for the accused. This process is key to ensuring prosecutors make informed determinations about disclosure of unused material.
6. Fairness does recognise that there are other interests that need to be protected, including those of victims and witnesses who might otherwise be exposed to harm. The scheme of the Act protects those interests. It should also ensure that material is not disclosed which overburdens the participants in the trial process, diverts attention from the relevant issues, leads to unjustifiable delay, and is wasteful of resources.
7. Whilst it is acknowledged that these Guidelines have been drafted with a focus on Crown Court proceedings the spirit of the Guidelines must be followed where they apply to proceedings in the magistrates' court.

General principles

8. Disclosure refers to providing the defence with copies of, or access to, any material which might reasonably be considered capable of undermining the case for the prosecution against the accused, or of assisting the case for the accused, and which has not previously been disclosed.
9. Prosecutors will only be expected to anticipate what material might weaken their case or strengthen the defence in the light of information available at the time of the disclosure decision, and this may include information revealed during questioning.
10. Generally, material which can reasonably be considered capable of undermining the prosecution case against the accused or assisting the defence case will include anything that tends to show a fact inconsistent with the elements of the case that must be proved by the prosecution. Material can fulfil the disclosure test:
    (a) by the use to be made of it in cross-examination; or
    (b) by its capacity to support submissions that could lead to:

(i) the exclusion of evidence; or
(ii) a stay of proceedings; or
(iii) a court or tribunal finding that any public authority had acted incompatibly with the accused 's rights under the ECHR, or

(c) by its capacity to suggest an explanation or partial explanation of the accused's actions.

11. In deciding whether material may fall to be disclosed under paragraph 10, especially (b)(ii), prosecutors must consider whether disclosure is required in order for a proper application to be made. The purpose of this paragraph is not to allow enquiries to support speculative arguments or for the manufacture of defences.
12. Examples of material that might reasonably be considered capable of undermining the prosecution case or of assisting the case for the accused are:
    i. Any material casting doubt upon the accuracy of any prosecution evidence.
    ii. Any material which may point to another person, whether charged or not (including a co-accused) having involvement in the commission of the offence.
    iii. Any material which may cast doubt upon the reliability of a confession.
    iv. Any material that might go to the credibility of a prosecution witness.
    v. Any material that might support a defence that is either raised by the defence or apparent from the prosecution papers.
    vi. Any material which may have a bearing on the admissibility of any prosecution evidence.
13. It should also be borne in mind that while items of material viewed in isolation may not be reasonably considered to be capable of undermining the prosecution case or assisting the accused, several items together can have that effect.
14. Material relating to the accused's mental or physical health, intellectual capacity, or to any ill treatment which the accused may have suffered when in the investigator's custody is likely to fall within the test for disclosure set out in paragraph 8 above.

Defence statements

15. A defence statement must comply with the requirements of section 6A of the Act. A comprehensive defence statement assists the participants in the trial to ensure that it is fair. The trial process is not well served if the defence make general and unspecified allegations and then seek far-reaching disclosure in the hope that material may turn up to make them good. The more detail a defence statement contains the more likely it is that the prosecutor will make an informed decision about whether any remaining undisclosed material might reasonably be considered capable of undermining the prosecution case or of assisting the case for the accused, or whether to advise the investigator to undertake further enquiries. It also helps in the management of the trial by narrowing down and focussing on the issues in dispute. It may result in the prosecution discontinuing the case. Defence practitioners should be aware of these considerations when advising their clients.
16. Whenever a defence solicitor provides a defence statement on behalf of the accused it will be deemed to be given with the authority of the solicitor's client.

Continuing duty of prosecutor to disclose

17. Section 7A of the Act imposes a continuing duty upon the prosecutor to keep under review at all times the question of whether there is any unused material which might reasonably be considered capable of undermining the prosecution case against the accused or assisting the case for the accused and which has not previously been disclosed. This duty arises after the prosecutor has complied with the duty of initial disclosure or purported to comply with it and before the accused is acquitted or convicted or the prosecutor decides not to proceed with the case. If such material is identified, then the prosecutor must disclose it to the accused as soon as is reasonably practicable.
18. As part of their continuing duty of disclosure, prosecutors should be open, alert and promptly responsive to requests for disclosure of material supported by a comprehensive defence statement. Conversely, if no defence statement has been served or if the prosecutor considers that the defence statement is lacking specificity or otherwise does not meet the requirements of section 6A of the Act, a letter should be sent to the defence indicating this. If the position is not resolved satisfactorily, the prosecutor should consider raising the issue at a hearing for directions to enable the court to give a warning or appropriate directions.
19. When defence practitioners are dissatisfied with disclosure decisions by the prosecution and consider that they are entitled to further disclosure, applications to the court should be made pursuant to section 8 of the Act and in accordance with the procedures set out in the Criminal Procedure Rules. Applications for further disclosure should not be made as ad hoc applications but dealt with under the proper procedures.

Applications for non-disclosure in the public interest

20. Before making an application to the court to withhold material which would otherwise fall to be disclosed, on the basis that to disclose would give rise to a real risk of serious prejudice to an important public interest, prosecutors should aim to disclose as much of the material as they properly can (for example, by giving the defence redacted or edited copies or summaries). Neutral material or material damaging to the defendant need not be disclosed and must *not* be brought to the attention of the court. It is only in truly borderline cases that the prosecution should seek a judicial ruling on the disclosability of material in its possession.
21. Prior to or at the hearing, the court must be provided with full and accurate information. Prior to the hearing the prosecutor and the prosecution advocate must examine all material, which is the subject matter of the application and make any necessary enquiries of the investigator. The prosecutor (or representative) and/or investigator should attend such applications.
22. The principles set out at paragraph 36 of *R* v *H & C* should be rigorously applied firstly by the prosecutor and then by the court considering the material. It is essential that these principles are scrupulously attended to to ensure that the procedure for examination of material in the absence of the accused is compliant with Article 6 of ECHR.

Responsibilities

Investigators and disclosure officers

23. Investigators and disclosure officers must be fair and objective and must work together with prosecutors to ensure that disclosure obligations are met. A failure to take action leading to inadequate disclosure may result in a wrongful conviction. It may alternatively lead to a successful abuse of process argument, an acquittal against the weight of the evidence or the appellate courts may find that a conviction is unsafe and quash it.
24. Officers appointed as disclosure officers must have the requisite experience, skills, competence and resources to undertake their vital role. In discharging their obligations under the Act, code, common law and any operational instructions, investigators should always err on the side of recording and retaining material where they have any doubt as to whether it may be relevant.
25. An individual must not be appointed as disclosure officer, or continue in that role, if that is likely to result in a conflict of interest, for instance, if the disclosure officer is the victim of the alleged crime which is the subject of investigation. The advice of a more senior investigator must always be sought if there is doubt as to whether a conflict of interest precludes an individual acting as the disclosure officer. If thereafter a doubt remains, the advice of a prosecutor should be sought.
26. There may be a number of disclosure officers, especially in large and complex cases. However, there must be a lead disclosure officer who is the focus for enquiries and whose responsibility it is to ensure that the investigator's disclosure obligations are complied with. Disclosure officers, or their deputies, must inspect, view or listen to all relevant material that has been retained by the investigator, and the disclosure officer must provide a personal declaration to the effect that this task has been undertaken.
27. Generally this will mean that such material must be examined in detail by the disclosure officer or the deputy, but exceptionally the extent and manner of inspecting, viewing or listening will depend on the nature of material and its form. For example, it might be reasonable to examine digital material by using software search tools, or to establish the contents of large volumes of material by dip sampling. If such material is not examined in detail, it must nonetheless be described on the disclosure schedules accurately and as clearly as possible. The extent and manner of its examination must also be described together with justification for such action.
28. Investigators must retain material that may be relevant to the investigation. However, it may become apparent to the investigator that some material obtained in the course of an investigation because it was considered potentially relevant, is in fact incapable of impact. It need not then be retained or dealt with in accordance with these Guidelines, although the investigator should err on the side of caution in coming to this conclusion and seek the advice of the prosecutor as appropriate.
29. In meeting the obligations in paragraph 6.9 and 8.1 of the Code, it is crucial that descriptions by disclosure officers in non-sensitive schedules are detailed, clear and accurate. The descriptions may require a summary of the contents of the retained material to assist the prosecutor to make an informed decision on disclosure. Sensitive schedules must contain sufficient information to enable the prosecutor to make an informed decision as to whether or not the material itself should be viewed, to the extent possible without compromising the confidentiality of the information.
30. Disclosure officers must specifically draw material to the attention of the prosecutor for

consideration where they have any doubt as to whether it might reasonably be considered capable of undermining the prosecution case or of assisting the case for the accused.

31. Disclosure officers must seek the advice and assistance of prosecutors when in doubt as to their responsibility as early as possible. They must deal expeditiously with requests by the prosecutor for further information on material, which may lead to disclosure.

Prosecutors

32. Prosecutors must do all that they can to facilitate proper disclosure, as part of their general and personal professional responsibility to act fairly and impartially, in the interests of justice and in accordance with the law. Prosecutors must also be alert to the need to provide advice to, and where necessary probe actions taken by, disclosure officers to ensure that disclosure obligations are met.

33. Prosecutors must review schedules prepared by disclosure officers thoroughly and must be alert to the possibility that relevant material may exist which has not been revealed to them or material included which should not have been. If no schedules have been provided, or there are apparent omissions from the schedules, or documents or other items are inadequately described or are unclear, the prosecutor must at once take action to obtain properly completed schedules. Likewise schedules should be returned for amendment if irrelevant items are included. If prosecutors remain dissatisfied with the quality or content of the schedules they must raise the matter with a senior investigator, and if necessary, persist, with a view to resolving the matter satisfactorily.

34. Where prosecutors have reason to believe that the disclosure officer has not discharged the obligation in paragraph 26 to inspect, view or listen to relevant material, they must at once raise the matter with the disclosure officer and, if it is believed that the officer has not inspected, viewed or listened to the material, request that it be done.

35. When prosecutors or disclosure officers believe that material might reasonably be considered capable of undermining the prosecution case or assisting the case for the accused, prosecutors must always inspect, view or listen to the material and satisfy themselves that the prosecution can properly be continued having regard to the disclosability of the material reviewed. Their judgement as to what other material to inspect, view or listen to will depend on the circumstances of each case.

36. Prosecutors should copy the defence statement to the disclosure officer and investigator as soon as reasonably practicable and prosecutors should advise the investigator if, in their view, reasonable and relevant lines of further enquiry should be pursued.

37. Prosecutors cannot comment upon, or invite inferences to be drawn from, failures in defence disclosure otherwise than in accordance with section 11 of the Act. Prosecutors may cross-examine the accused on differences between the defence case put at trial and that set out in his or her defence statement. In doing so, it may be appropriate to apply to the judge under section 6E of the Act for copies of the statement to be given to a jury, edited if necessary to remove inadmissible material. Prosecutors should examine the defence statement to see whether it points to other lines of enquiry. If the defence statement does point to other reasonable lines of inquiry further investigation is required and evidence obtained as a result of these enquiries may be used as part of the prosecution case or to rebut the defence.

38. Once initial disclosure is completed and a defence statement has been served requests for disclosure should ordinarily only be answered if the request is in accordance with and relevant to the defence statement. If it is not, then a further or amended defence statement should be sought and obtained before considering the request for further disclosure.

39. Prosecutors must ensure that they record in writing all actions and decisions they make in discharging their disclosure responsibilities, and this information is to be made available to the prosecution advocate if requested or if relevant to an issue.

40. If the material does not fulfil the disclosure test there is no requirement to disclose it. For this purpose, the parties' respective cases should not be restrictively analysed but must be carefully analysed to ascertain the specific facts the prosecution seek to establish and the specific grounds on which the charges are resisted. Neutral material or material damaging to the defendant need not be disclosed and must not be brought to the attention of the court. Only in truly borderline cases should the prosecution seek a judicial ruling on the disclosability of material in its hands.

41. If prosecutors are satisfied that a fair trial cannot take place where material which satisfies the disclosure test cannot be disclosed, and that this cannot or will not be remedied including by, for example, making formal admissions, amending the charges or presenting the case in a different way so as to ensure fairness or in other ways, they must not continue with the case.

Prosecution advocates

42. Prosecution advocates should ensure that all material that ought to be disclosed under the Act is disclosed to the defence. However, prosecution advocates cannot be expected to disclose material if they are not aware of its existence. As far as is possible, prosecution advocates must place themselves in a fully informed position to enable them to make decisions on disclosure.
43. Upon receipt of instructions, prosecution advocates should consider as a priority all the information provided regarding disclosure of material. Prosecution advocates should consider, in every case, whether they can be satisfied that they are in possession of all relevant documentation and that they have been instructed fully regarding disclosure matters. Decisions already made regarding disclosure should be reviewed. If as a result, the advocate considers that further information or action is required, written advice should be promptly provided setting out the aspects that need clarification or action. Prosecution advocates must advise on disclosure in accordance with the Act. If necessary and where appropriate a conference should be held to determine what is required.
44. The prosecution advocate must keep decisions regarding disclosure under review until the conclusion of the trial. The prosecution advocate must in every case specifically consider whether he or she can satisfactorily discharge the duty of continuing review on the basis of the material supplied already, or whether it is necessary to inspect further material or to reconsider material already inspected. Prosecution advocates must not abrogate their responsibility under the Act by disclosing material which could not be considered capable of undermining the prosecution case or of assisting the case for the accused.
45. Prior to the commencement of a trial, the prosecuting advocate should always make decisions on disclosure in consultation with those instructing him or her and the disclosure officer. After a trial has started, it is recognised that in practice consultation on disclosure issues may not be practicable; it continues to be desirable, however, whenever this can be achieved without affecting unduly the conduct of the trial.
46. There is no basis in law or practice for disclosure on a 'counsel to counsel' basis.

Involvement of other agencies

Material held by Government departments or other Crown bodies

47. Where it appears to an investigator, disclosure officer or prosecutor that a Government department or other Crown body has material that may be relevant to an issue in the case, reasonable steps should be taken to identify and consider such material. Although what is reasonable will vary from case to case, the prosecution should inform the department or other body of the nature of its case and of relevant issues in the case in respect of which the department or body might possess material, and ask whether it has any such material.
48. It should be remembered that investigators, disclosure officers and prosecutors cannot be regarded to be in constructive possession of material held by Government departments or Crown bodies simply by virtue of their status as Government departments or Crown bodies.
49. Departments in England and Wales should have identified personnel as established Enquiry Points to deal with issues concerning the disclosure of information in criminal proceedings.
50. Where, after reasonable steps have been taken to secure access to such material, access is denied the investigator, disclosure officer or prosecutor should consider what if any further steps might be taken to obtain the material or inform the defence.

Material held by other agencies

51. There may be cases where the investigator, disclosure officer or prosecutor believes that a third party (for example, a local authority, a social services department, a hospital, a doctor, a school, a provider of forensic services) has material or information which might be relevant to the prosecution case. In such cases, if the material or information might reasonably be considered capable of undermining the prosecution case or of assisting the case for the accused prosecutors should take what steps they regard as appropriate in the particular case to obtain it.
52. If the investigator, disclosure officer or prosecutor seeks access to the material or information but the third party declines or refuses to allow access to it, the matter should not be left. If despite any reasons offered by the third party it is still believed that it is reasonable to seek production of the material or information, and the requirements of section 2 of the Criminal Procedure (Attendance of Witnesses) Act 1965 or as appropriate section 97 of the Magistrates' Courts Act 1980 are satisfied, then the prosecutor or investigator should apply for a witness summons causing a representative of the third party to produce the material to the Court.

53. Relevant information which comes to the knowledge of investigators or prosecutors as a result of liaison with third parties should be recorded by the investigator or prosecutor in a durable or retrievable form (for example potentially relevant information revealed in discussions at a child protection conference attended by police officers).
54. Where information comes into the possession of the prosecution in the circumstances set out in paragraphs 51–53 above, consultation with the other agency should take place before disclosure is made: there may be public interest reasons which justify withholding disclosure and which would require the issue of disclosure of the information to be placed before the court.

Other disclosure

Disclosure prior to initial disclosure

55. Investigators must always be alive to the potential need to reveal and prosecutors to the potential need to disclose material, in the interests of justice and fairness in the particular circumstances of any case, after the commencement of proceedings but before their duty arises under the Act. For instance, disclosure ought to be made of significant information that might affect a bail decision or that might enable the defence to contest the committal proceedings.
56. Where the need for such disclosure is not apparent to the prosecutor, any disclosure will depend on what the accused chooses to reveal about the defence. Clearly, such disclosure will not exceed that which is obtainable after the statutory duties of disclosure arise

Summary trial

57. The prosecutor should, in addition to complying with the obligations under the Act, provide to the defence all evidence upon which the Crown proposes to rely in a summary trial. Such provision should allow the accused and their legal advisers sufficient time properly to consider the evidence before it is called.

Material relevant to sentence

58. In all cases the prosecutor must consider disclosing in the interests of justice any material, which is relevant to sentence (e.g. information which might mitigate the seriousness of the offence or assist the accused to lay blame in part upon a co-accused or another person).

Post-conviction

59. The interests of justice will also mean that where material comes to light after the conclusion of the proceedings, which might cast doubt upon the safety of the conviction, there is a duty to consider disclosure. Any such material should be brought immediately to the attention of line management.
60. Disclosure of any material that is made outside the ambit of Act will attract confidentiality by virtue of *Taylor* v *SFO* [1998].

Applicability of these guidelines

61. Although the relevant obligations in relation to unused material and disclosure imposed on the prosecutor and the accused are determined by the date on which the investigation began, these Guidelines should be adopted with immediate effect in relation to all cases submitted to the prosecuting authorities in receipt of these Guidelines save where they specifically refer to the statutory or Code provisions of the Criminal Justice Act 2003 that do not yet apply to the particular case.

DISCLOSURE: A PROTOCOL FOR THE CONTROL AND MANAGEMENT OF UNUSED MATERIAL IN THE CROWN COURT

[This Protocol was drafted by a team led by Mr Justice Fulford and Mr Justice Openshaw and was published under the auspices of the Court of Appeal. It applies to all trials on indictment from 20 February 2006.]

Introduction

1. Disclosure is one of the most important—as well as one of the most abused—of the procedures relating to criminal trials. There needs to be a sea-change in the approach of both judges and the parties to all aspects of the handling of the material which the prosecution do not intend to use in support of their case. For too long, a wide range of serious misunderstandings has existed, both as to the exact ambit of the unused material to which the defence is entitled, and the role to be played by the judge in ensuring that the law is properly applied. All too frequently applications by the parties

and decisions by the judges in this area have been made based either on misconceptions as to the true nature of the law or a general laxity of approach (however well intentioned). This failure properly to apply the binding provisions as regards disclosure has proved extremely and unnecessarily costly and has obstructed justice. It is, therefore, essential that disclosure obligations are properly discharged—by both the prosecution and the defence—in all criminal proceedings, and the court's careful oversight of this process is an important safeguard against the possibility of miscarriages of justice.

2. The House of Lords stated in *R v H and C* [2004] 2 AC 134, at 147:

> Fairness ordinarily requires that any material held by the prosecution which weakens its case or strengthens that of the defendant, if not relied on as part of its formal case against the defendant, should be disclosed to the defence. Bitter experience has shown that miscarriages of justice may occur where such material is withheld from disclosure. The golden rule is that full disclosure of such material should be made.

3. However, it is also essential that the trial process is not overburdened or diverted by erroneous and inappropriate disclosure of unused prosecution material, or by misconceived applications in relation to such material.
4. The overarching principle is therefore that unused prosecution material will fall to be disclosed if, and only if, it satisfies the test for disclosure applicable to the proceedings in question, subject to any overriding public interest considerations. The relevant test for disclosure will depend on the date the criminal investigation in question commenced (see the section on Sources below), as this will determine whether the common law disclosure regime applies, or either of the two disclosure regimes under the *Criminal Procedure and Investigations Act 1996 (CPIA)*.
5. There is very clear evidence that, without active judicial oversight and management, the handling of disclosure issues in general, and the disclosure of unused prosecution material in particular, can cause delays and adjournments.
6. The failure to comply fully with disclosure obligations, whether by the prosecution or the defence, may disrupt and in some cases even frustrate the course of justice.
7. Consideration of irrelevant unused material may consume wholly unjustifiable and disproportionate amounts of time and public resources, undermining the overall performance and efficiency of the criminal justice system. The aim of this Protocol is therefore to assist and encourage judges when dealing with all disclosure issues, in the light of the overarching principle set out in paragraph 4 above. This guidance is intended to cover all Crown Court cases (including cases where relevant case management directions are made at the Magistrates' Court). It is not, therefore, confined to a very few high profile and high cost cases.
8. Unused material which has been gathered during the course of a criminal investigation and disclosed by the prosecution pursuant to their duties (as set out elsewhere in this Protocol) is received by the defence subject to a prohibition not to use or disclose the material for any purpose which is not connected with the proceedings for whose purposes they were given it (s. 17 CPIA). The common law, which applies to all disclosure not made under the CPIA, achieves the same result by the creation of an implied undertaking not to use the material for any purposes other than the proper conduct of the particular case (see *Taylor v Director of the Serious Fraud Office* I IL [1999] 2 AC 177). A breach of that undertaking would constitute a contempt of court. These provisions are designed to ensure that the privacy and confidentiality of those who provided the material to the investigation (as well as those who are mentioned in the material) is protected and is not invaded any more than is absolutely necessary. However, neither statute nor the common law prevents any one from using or disclosing such material if it has been displayed or communicated to the public in open court (unless the evidence is subject to continuing reporting restriction), and moreover, an application can be made to the court for permission to use or disclose the object or information.

Sources

9. It is not the purpose of this Protocol to rehearse the law in detail; however, some of the principal sources are set out here.
10. The correct test for disclosure will depend upon the date the relevant criminal investigation commenced:
    (a) In relation to offences in respect of which the criminal investigation began prior to 1 April 1997, the common law will apply, and the test for disclosure is that set out in *R v Keane* [1994] 1 WLR 746; (1994) 99 Cr App R 1.
    (b) If the criminal investigation commenced on or after 1 April 1997, but before 4 April 2005, then the CPIA in its original form will apply, with separate tests for disclosure of unused prosecution material at the primary and secondary disclosure stages (the latter following service

of a defence statement by the accused). The disclosure provisions of the Act are supported by the 1997 edition of the Code of Practice issued under section 23(1) of the CPIA (Statutory Instrument 1997 No. 1033)

(c) Where the criminal investigation has commenced on or after 4 April 2005, the law is set out in the CPIA as amended by Part V of the Criminal Justice Act 2003. There is then a single test for disclosure of unused prosecution material and the April 2005 edition of the Code of Practice under section 23(1) of the CPIA will apply (see SI 2005 No. 985).

The CPIA also identifies the stage(s) at which the prosecution is required to disclose material, and the formalities relating to defence statements. The default time limit for prosecution disclosure is set out in section 13 of the Act (see further at paragraph 13 below). The time limits applicable to defence disclosure are set out in the Criminal Procedure and Investigations Act 1996 (Defence Disclosure Regulations) 1997 (S.I. 1997 No. 684).

11. Regard must be had to the Attorney General's Guidelines on Disclosure (April 2005). Although these do not have the force of law (*R v Winston Brown* [1995] 1 Cr App R 191; [1994] 1 WLR 1599) they should be given due weight.

12. Part 25 of the Criminal Procedure Rules 2005 (see SI 2005 No. 384) sets out the procedures to be followed for applications to the court concerning both sensitive and non-sensitive unused material. Part 3 of the Rules is also relevant in respect of the court's general case management powers, and parties should also have regard to the Consolidated Criminal Practice Direction.

13. Parts 22 and 23 of the Criminal Procedure Rules are set aside to make provision for other rules concerning disclosure by the prosecution and the defence, although at the date of this Protocol there are no rules under those Parts.

The Duty to Gather and Record Unused Material

14. For the statutory scheme to work properly, investigators and disclosure officers responsible for the gathering, inspection, retention and recording of relevant unused prosecution material must perform their tasks thoroughly, scrupulously and fairly. In this, they must adhere to the appropriate provisions of the CPIA Code of Practice.

15. It is crucial that the police (and indeed all investigative bodies) implement appropriate training regimes and appoint competent disclosure officers, who have sufficient knowledge of the issues in the case. This will enable them to make a proper assessment of the unused prosecution material in the light of the test for relevance under paragraph 2.1 of the CPIA Code of Practice, with a view to preparing full and accurate schedules of the retained material. In any criminal investigation, the disclosure officer must retain material that may be relevant to an investigation. This material must be listed on a schedule. Each item listed on the schedule should contain sufficient detail to enable the prosecutor to decide whether or not the material falls to be disclosed. The schedules must be sent to the prosecutor. Wherever possible this should be at the same time as the file containing the material for the prosecution case but the duty to disclose does not end at this point and must continue while relevant material is received even after conviction.

16. Furthermore, the scheduling of the relevant material must be completed expeditiously, so as to enable the prosecution to comply promptly with the duty to provide primary (or, when the amended CPIA regime applies) initial disclosure as soon as practicable after:

- the case has been committed for trial under section 6(1) or 6(2) of the Magistrates' Courts Act 1980; or
- the case has been transferred to the Crown Court under section 4 of the Criminal Justice Act 1987, or section 53 of the Criminal Justice Act 1991; or
- copies of documents containing the evidence are served on the accused in according with the Crime and Disorder Act 1998 (Service of Prosecution Evidence) Regulations 2005 (S.I. 2005 No. 902), where the matter has been sent to the Crown Court pursuant to section 51 or 51A of the Crime and Disorder Act 1998; or
- a matter has been added to an indictment in accordance with section 40 of the Criminal Justice Act 1988; or
- a bill of indictment has been preferred under section 2(2)(b) of the Administration of Justice (Miscellaneous Provisions) Act 1933 or section 22B(3)(a) of the Prosecution of Offences Act 1985.

17. Investigators, disclosure officers and prosecutors must promptly and properly discharge their responsibilities under the Act and statutory Code, in order to ensure that justice is not delayed, denied or frustrated. In this context, under paragraph 3.5 of the Code of Practice, it is provided 'an investigator should pursue all reasonable lines of inquiry, whether these point towards or away from the suspect'.

18. CPS lawyers advising the police pre-charge at police stations should consider conducting a preliminary review of the unused material generated by the investigation, where this is practicable, so as to give early advice on disclosure issues. Otherwise, prosecutors should conduct a preliminary review of disclosure at the same time as the initial review of the evidence. It is critical that the important distinction between the evidence in the case, on the one hand, and any unused material, on the other, is not blurred. Items such as exhibits should be treated as such and the obligation to serve them is not affected by the disclosure regime.
19. Where the single test for disclosure applies under the amended CPIA disclosure regime, the prosecutor is under a duty to consider, at an early stage of proceedings, whether there is any unused prosecution material which is reasonably capable of assisting the case for the accused. What a defendant has said by way of defence or explanation either in interview or by way of a prepared statement can be a useful guide to making an objective assessment of the material which would satisfy this test.
20. There may be some occasions when the prosecution, pursuant to surviving common law rules of disclosure, ought to disclose an item or items of unused prosecution material, even in advance of primary or initial disclosure under section 3 of the CPIA. This may apply, for instance, where there is information which might affect a decision as to bail; where an abuse of process is alleged; where there is material which might assist the defence to make submissions as to the particular charge or charges, if any, the defendant should face at the Crown Court; and when it is necessary to enable particular preparation to be undertaken at an early stage by the defence. Guidance as to occasions where such disclosure may be appropriate is provided in *R v DPP ex parte Lee* (1999) 2 Cr App R 304. However, once the CPIA is triggered (for instance, by committal, or service of case papers following a section 51 sending) it is the CPIA which determines what material should be disclosed.

The Judge's Duty to Enforce the Statutory Scheme

21. When cases are sent to the Crown Court under section 51 of the Crime and Disorder Act 1998, the Crime and Disorder Act 1998 (Service of Prosecution Evidence) Regulations 2005 allow the prosecution 70 days from the date the matter was sent (50 days, where the accused is in custody) within which to serve on the defence and the court copies of the documents containing the evidence upon which the charge or charges are based (in effect, sufficient evidence to amount to a prima facie case). These time limits may be extended and varied at the court's direction. Directions for service of these case papers may be given at the Magistrates' Court.
22. While it is important to note that this time limit applies to the service of evidence, rather than unused prosecution material, the court will need to consider at the Magistrates' Court or preliminary hearing whether it is practicable for the prosecution to comply with primary or initial disclosure at the same time as service of such papers, or whether disclosure ought to take place after a certain interval, but before the matter is listed for a PCMH.
23. If the nature of the case does not allow service of the evidence and initial or primary disclosure within the 70, or if applicable 50, days (or such other period as directed by the Magistrates' Court), the investigator should ensure that the prosecution advocate at the Magistrates' Court, preliminary Crown Court hearing, or further hearing prior to the PCMH, is aware of the problems, knows why and how the position has arisen and can assist the court as to what revised time limits are realistic.
24. It would be helpful if the prosecution advocate could make any foreseeable difficulties clear as soon as possible, whether this is at the Magistrates' Court or in the Crown Court at the preliminary hearing (where there is one).
25. Failing this, where such difficulties arise or have come to light after directions for service of case papers and disclosure have been made, the prosecution should notify the court and the defence promptly. This should be done in advance of the PCMH date, and prior to the date set by the court for the service of this material.
26. It is important that this is done in order that the listing for the PCMH is an effective one, as the defence must have a proper opportunity to read the case papers and to consider the initial or primary disclosure, with a view to timely drafting of a defence case statement (where the matter is to be contested), prior to the PCMH.
27. In order to ensure that the listing of the PCMH is appropriate, Judges should not impose time limits for service of case papers or initial/primary disclosure unless and until they are confident that the prosecution advocate has taken the requisite instructions from those who are actually going to do the work specified. It is better to impose a realistic timetable from the outset than to set unachievable limits. Reference should be made to Part 3 of the Criminal Procedure Rules and the Consolidated Practice Direction in this respect.

28. This is likewise appropriate where directions, or further directions, are made in relation to prosecution or defence disclosure at the PCMH. Failure to consider whether the timetable is practicable may dislocate the court timetable and can even imperil trial dates. At the PCMH, therefore, all the advocates—prosecution and defence—must be fully instructed about any difficulties the parties may have in complying with their respective disclosure obligations, and must be in a position to put forward a reasonable timetable for resolution of them.
29. Where directions are given by the court in the light of such inquiry, extensions of time should not be given lightly or as a matter of course. If extensions are sought, then an appropriately detailed explanation must be given. For the avoidance of doubt, it is not sufficient merely for the CPS (or other prosecutor) to say that the papers have been delivered late by the police (or other investigator): the court will need to know why they have been delivered late. Likewise, where the accused has been dilatory in serving a defence statement (where the prosecution has complied with the duty to make primary or initial disclosure of unused material, or has purported to do so), it is not sufficient for the defence to say that insufficient instructions have been taken for service of this within the 14-day time limit: the court will need to know why sufficient instructions have not been taken, and what arrangements have been made for the taking of such instructions.
30. Delays and failures by the defence are as damaging to the timely, fair and efficient hearing of the case as delays and failures by the prosecution, and judges should identify and deal with all such failures firmly and fairly.
31. Judges should not allow the prosecution to abdicate their statutory responsibility for reviewing the unused material by the expedient of allowing the defence to inspect (or providing the defence with copies of) everything on the schedules of non-sensitive unused prosecution material, irrespective of whether that material, or all of that material, satisfies the relevant test for disclosure. Where that test is satisfied it is for the prosecutor to decide the form in which disclosure is made. Disclosure need not be in the same form as that in which the information was recorded. Guidance on case management issues relating to this point was given by Rose LJ in *R v CPS (Interlocutory Application under sections 35/36 CPIA)* [2005] EWCA Crim 2342.
32. Indeed, the larger and more complex the case, the more important it is for the prosecution to adhere to the overarching principle in paragraph 4 and ensure that sufficient prosecution resources are allocated to the task. Handing the defence the 'keys to the warehouse' has been the cause of many gross abuses in the past, resulting in huge sums being run up by the defence without any proportionate benefit to the course of justice. These abuses must end.

The Defence Case Statement

33. Reference has been made above to defence disclosure obligations. After the provision of primary or initial disclosure by the prosecution, the next really critical step in the preparation for trial is the service of the defence statement. It is a mandatory requirement for a defence statement to be served, where section 5(5) of the CPIA applies to the proceedings. This is due within 14 days of the date upon which the prosecution has complied with, or purported to comply with, the duty of primary or initial disclosure. Service of the defence statement is a critical stage in the disclosure process, and timely service of the statement will allow for the proper consideration of disclosure issues well in advance of the trial date.
34. There may be some cases where it is simply not possible to serve a proper defence case statement within the 14-day time limit; well founded defence applications for an extension of time under paragraph (2) of regulation 3 of the Criminal Procedure and Investigations Act 1996 (Defence Disclosure Time Limits) Regulations 1997 may therefore be granted. In a proper case, it may be appropriate to put the PCMH back by a week or so, to enable a sufficient defence case statement to be filed and considered by the prosecution.
35. In the past, the prosecution and the court have too often been faced with a defence case statement that is little more than an assertion that the Defendant is not guilty. As was stated by the Court of Appeal in *R v Patrick Bryant* [2005] EWCA Crim 2079 (per Judge LJ, paragraph 12), such a reiteration of the defendant's plea is not the purpose of a defence statement. Defence statements must comply with the requisite formalities set out in section 5(6) and (7), or section 6A, of the CPIA, as applicable.
36. Where the enhanced requirements for defence disclosure apply under section 6A of the CPIA (namely, where the case involves a criminal investigation commencing on or after 4 April 2005) the defence statement must spell out, in detail, the nature of the defence, and particular defences relied upon; it must identify the matters of fact upon which the accused takes issue with the prosecution, and the reason why, in relation to each disputed matter of fact. It must further identify any point of

law (including points as to the admissibility of evidence, or abuse of process) which the accused proposes to take, and identify authorities relied on in relation to each point of law. Where an alibi defence is relied upon, the particulars given must comply with section 6(2)(a) and (b) of the CPIA. Judges will expect to see defence case statements that contain a clear and detailed exposition of the issues of fact and law in the case.

37. Where the pre-4 April 2005 CPIA disclosure regime applies, the accused must, in the defence statement, set out the nature of the defence in general terms, indicate the matters upon which the defendant takes issue with the prosecution and set out (in relation to each such matter) why issue is taken. Any alibi defence relied upon should comply with the formalities in section 5(7)(a) and (b) of the Act.

38. There must be a complete change in the culture. The defence must serve the defence case statement by the due date. Judges should then examine the defence case statement with care to ensure that it complies with the formalities required by the CPIA. As was stated in paragraph 35 of *R v H and C* [2004]:

> If material does not weaken the prosecution case or strengthen that of the defendant, there is no requirement to disclose it. For this purpose the parties' respective cases should not be restrictively analysed. But they must be carefully analysed, to ascertain the specific facts the prosecution seek to establish and the specific grounds on which the charges are resisted. The trial process is not well served if the defence are permitted to make general and unspecified allegations and then seek far-reaching disclosure in the hope that material may turn up to make them good. Neutral material or material damaging to the defendant need not be disclosed and should not be brought to the attention of the court.

39. If no defence case statement—or no sufficient case statement—has been served by the PCMH, the judge should make a full investigation of the reasons for this failure to comply with the mandatory obligation of the accused, under section 5(5) of the CPIA.

40. If there is no—or no sufficient—defence statement by the date of PCMH, or any pre-trial hearing where the matter falls to be considered, the judge must consider whether the defence should be warned, pursuant to section 6E(2) of the CPIA, that an adverse inference may be drawn at the trial. In the usual case, where section 6E(2) applies and there is no justification for the deficiency, such a warning should be given.

41. Judges must, of course, be alert to ensure that defendants do not suffer because of the faults and failings of their lawyers, but there must be a clear indication to the professions that if justice is to be done, and if disclosure to be dealt with fairly in accordance with the law, a full and careful defence case statement is essential.

42. Where there are failings by either the defence or the prosecution, judges should, in exercising appropriate oversight of disclosure, pose searching questions to the parties and, having done this and explored the reasons for default, give clear directions to ensure that such failings are addressed and remedied well in advance of the trial date.

43. The ultimate sanction for a failure in disclosure by the accused is the drawing of an inference under section 11 of the CPIA. Where the amended CPIA regime applies, the strict legal position allows the prosecution to comment upon any failure of defence disclosure, with a view to seeking such an inference (except where the failure relates to identifying a point of law), without leave of the court, but often it will be helpful to canvass the matter with the judge beforehand. In suitable cases, the prosecution should consider commenting upon failures in defence disclosure, with a view to such an inference, more readily than has been the practice under the old CPIA regime, subject to any views expressed by the judge.

44. It is vital to a fair trial that the prosecution are mindful of their continuing duty of disclosure, and they must particularly review disclosure in the light of the issues identified in the defence case statement. As part of the timetabling exercise, the judge should set a date by which any application under section 8 (if there is to be one) should be made. While the defence may indicate, in advance of the cut-off date, what items of unused material they are interested in and why, such requests must relate to matters raised in the accused's defence statement. The prosecution should only disclose material in response to such requests if the material meets the appropriate test for disclosure, and the matter must proceed to a formal section 8 hearing in the event that the prosecution declines to make disclosure of the items in question. Paragraphs 4(iv)—(vi)(a) of the Lord Chief Justice's March 2005 Protocol for the Control and Management of Heavy Fraud and Other Complex Criminal Cases should be construed accordingly.

45. If, after the prosecution have complied with, or purported to comply with, primary or initial disclosure, and after the service of the defence case statement and any further prosecution disclosure

flowing there from, the defence have a reasonable basis to claim disclosure has been inadequate, they must make an application to the court under section 8 of the CPIA. The procedure for the making of such an application is set out in the Criminal Procedure Rules, Part 25, r 25.6. This requires written notice to the prosecution in the form prescribed by r 25.6(2). The prosecution is then entitled (r 25.6(5)) to 14 days within which to agree to provide the specific disclosure requested or to request a hearing in order to make representations in relation to the defence application. As part of the timetabling exercise, the judge should set a date by which any applications under section 8 are to be made and should require the defence to indicate in advance of the cut-off date for specific disclosure applications what documents they are interested in and from what source; in appropriate cases, the judge should require justification of such requests.

46. The consideration of detailed defence requests for specific disclosure (socalled 'shopping lists') otherwise than in accordance with r 25.6, is wholly improper. Likewise, defence requests for specific disclosure of unused prosecution material in purported pursuance of section 8 of the CPIA and r 25.6, which are not referable to any issue in the case identified by the defence case statement, should be rejected. Judges should require an application to be made under section 8 and in compliance with r 25.6 before considering any order for further disclosure.

47. It follows that the practice of making blanket orders for disclosure in all cases should cease, since such orders are inconsistent with the statutory framework of disclosure laid down by the CPIA, and which was endorsed by the House of Lords in *R v H and C* (supra).

Listing

48. It will be clear that the conscientious discharge of a judge' s duty at the PCMH requires a good deal more time than under the old PDH regime; furthermore a good deal more work is required of the advocate. The listing of PCMHs must take this into account. Unless the court can sit at 10am and finish the PCMH by 10.30am, it will not therefore usually be desirable for a judge who is partheard on a trial to do a PCMH.

49. It follows that any case which raises difficult issues of disclosure should be referred to the Resident Judge for directions. Cases of real complexity should, if possible, be allocated to a specific trial judge at a very early stage, and usually before the PCMH.

50. Although this Protocol is addressed to the issues of disclosure, it cannot be seen in isolation; it must be seen in the context of general case management.

Public Interest Immunity

51. Recent authoritative guidance as to the proper approach to PII is provided by the House of Lords in *R v H and C* (supra). It is clearly appropriate for PII applications to be considered by the trial judge. No judge should embark upon a PII application without considering that case and addressing the questions set out in paragraph 36, which for ease of reference we reproduce here:

> '36. When any issue of derogation from the golden rule of full disclosure comes before it, the court must address a series of questions:
>
> (1) What is the material which the prosecution seek to withhold? This must be considered by the court in detail.
>
> (2) Is the material such as may weaken the prosecution case or strengthen that of the defence? If No, disclosure should not be ordered. If Yes, full disclosure should (subject to (3), (4) and (5) below be ordered.
>
> (3) Is there a real risk of serious prejudice to an important public interest (and, if so, what) if full disclosure of the material is ordered? If No, full disclosure should be ordered.
>
> (4) If the answer to (2) and (3) is Yes, can the defendant's interest be protected without disclosure or disclosure be ordered to an extent or in a way which will give adequate protection to the public interest in question and also afford adequate protection to the interests of the defence?
>
> This question requires the court to consider, with specific reference to the material which the prosecution seek to withhold and the facts of the case and the defence as disclosed, whether the prosecution should formally admit what the defence seek to establish or whether disclosure short of full disclosure may be ordered. This may be done in appropriate cases by the preparation of summaries or extracts of evidence, or the provision of documents in an edited or anonymised form, provided the documents supplied are in each instance approved by the judge. In appropriate cases the appointment of special counsel may be a necessary step to ensure that the contentions of the prosecution are tested and the interests of the defendant protected (see paragraph 22

above). In cases of exceptional difficulty the court may require the appointment of special counsel to ensure a correct answer to questions (2) and (3) as well as (4).

(5) Do the measures proposed in answer to (4) represent the minimum derogation necessary to protect the public interest in question? If No, the court should order such greater disclosure as will represent the minimum derogation from the golden rule of full disclosure.

(6) If limited disclosure is ordered pursuant to (4) or (5), may the effect be to render the trial process, viewed as a whole, unfair to the defendant? If Yes, then fuller disclosure should be ordered even if this leads or may lead the prosecution to discontinue the proceedings so as to avoid having to make disclosure.

(7) If the answer to (6) when first given is No, does that remain the correct answer as the trial unfolds, evidence is adduced and the defence advanced? It is important that the answer to (6) should not be treated as a final, once-and-for-all, answer but as a provisional answer which the court must keep under review.'

52. In this context, the following matter are emphasised:

(a) The procedure for making applications to the Court is as set out in the Criminal Procedure Rules 2005, Part 25 (r 25.1—r 25.5);

(b) Where the PII application is a Type 1 or Type 2 application, proper notice to the defence is necessary to allow them to make focused submissions to the court before hearing an application to withhold material; the notice should be as specific as the nature of the material allows. It is appreciated that in some cases only the generic nature of the material can properly be identified. In some wholly exceptional cases (Type 3 cases) it may even be justified to give no notice at all. The judge should always ask the prosecution to justify the form of notice given (or the decision to give no notice at all).

(c) The prosecution should be alert to the possibility of disclosing a statement in redacted form by, for example simply removing personal details. This may obviate the need for a PII application, unless the redacted material in itself would also satisfy the test for disclosure.

(d) Except where the material is very short (say a few sheets only), or where the material is of such sensitivity that do so would be inappropriate, the prosecution should have supplied securely sealed copies to the judge beforehand, together with a short statement of the reasons why each document is said to be relevant and fulfils the disclosure test and why it is said that its disclosure would cause a real risk of serious prejudice to an important public interest; in undertaking this task, the use of merely formulaic expressions is to be discouraged. In any case of complexity a schedule of the material should be provided showing the specific objection to disclosure in relation to each item, leaving a space for the decision.

(e) The application, even if held in private or in secret, should be recorded. The judge should give some short statement of reasons; this is often best done document by document as the hearing proceeds.

(f) The tape, copies of the judge's orders (and any copies of the material retained by the court) should be clearly identified, securely sealed and kept in the court building in a safe or stout lockable cabinet consistent with its security classification, and there should be a proper register of all such material kept. Some arrangement should be made between the court and the prosecution authority for the periodic removal of such material once the case is concluded and the time for an appeal has passed.

Third Party Disclosure

53. The disclosure of unused material that has been gathered or generated by a third party is an area of the law that has caused some difficulties: indeed, a Home Office Working Party has been asked to report on it. This is because there is no specific procedure for the disclosure of material held by third parties in criminal proceedings, although the procedure under section 2 of the Criminal Procedure (Attendance of Witnesses) Act 1965 or section 97 of the Magistrates' Courts Act 1980 is often used in order to effect such disclosure. It should, however, be noted that the test applied under both Acts is not the test to be applied under the CPIA, whether in the amended or unamended form. These two provisions require that the material in question is material evidence, ie, immediately admissible in evidence in the proceedings (see in this respect *R v Reading Justices ex parte: Berkshire County Council* [1996] 1 Cr App R 239, *R v Derby Magistrates' Court ex parte B* [1996] AC 487; [1996] 1 Cr App R 385 and *R v Alibhai and others* [2004] EWCA Crim 681).

54. Material held by other government departments or other Crown agencies will not be prosecution material for the purposes of section 3(2) or section 8(4) of the CPIA, if it has not been inspected,

recorded and retained during the course of the relevant criminal investigation. The Attorney General's Guidelines on Disclosure, however, impose a duty upon the investigators and the prosecution to consider whether such departments or bodies have material which may satisfy the test for disclosure under the Act. Where this is the case, they must seek appropriate disclosure from such bodies, who should themselves have an identified point for such enquiries (see paragraphs 47 to 51, Attorney General's Guidelines on Disclosure).

55. Where material is held by a third party such as a local authority, a social services department, hospital or business, the investigators and the prosecution may seek to make arrangements to inspect the material with a view to applying the relevant test for disclosure to it and determining whether any or all of the material should be retained, recorded and, in due course, disclosed to the accused. In considering the latter, the investigators and the prosecution will establish whether the holder of the material wishes to raise PII issues, as a result of which the material may have to be placed before the court. Section 16 of the CPIA gives such a party a right to make representations to the court.

56. Where the third party in question declines to allow inspection of the material, or requires the prosecution to obtain an order before handing over copies of the material, the prosecutor will need to consider whether it is appropriate to obtain a witness summons under either section 2 of the Criminal Procedure (Attendance of Witnesses) Act 1965 or section 97 of the Magistrates' Court Act 1980. However, as stated above, this is only appropriate where the statutory requirements are satisfied, and where the prosecutor considers that the material may satisfy the test for disclosure. *R v Alibhai and others* supra makes it clear that the prosecutor has a 'margin of consideration' in this regard.

57. It should be understood that the third party may have a duty to assert confidentiality, or the right to privacy under article 8 of the ECHR, where requests for disclosure are made by the prosecution, or anyone else. Where issues are raised in relation to allegedly relevant third party material, the judge must ascertain whether inquiries with the third party are likely to be appropriate, and, if so, identify who is going to make the request, what material is to be sought, from whom is the material to be sought and within what time scale must the matter be resolved.

58. The judge should consider what action would be appropriate in the light of the third party failing or refusing to comply with a request, including inviting the defence to make the request on its own behalf and, if necessary, to make an application for a witness summons. Any directions made (for instance, the date by which an application for a witness summons with supporting affidavit under section 2 of the 1965 should be served) should be put into writing at the time. Any failure to comply with the timetable must immediately be referred back to the court for further directions, although a hearing will not always be necessary.

59. Where the prosecution do not consider it appropriate to seek such a summons, the defence should consider doing so, where they are of the view (notwithstanding the prosecution assessment) that the third party may hold material which might undermine the prosecution case or assist that for the defendant, and the material would be likely to be 'material evidence' for the purposes of the 1965 Act. The defence must not sit back and expect the prosecution to make the running. The judge at the PCMH should specifically enquire whether any such application is to be made by the defence and set out a clear timetable. The objectionable practice of defence applications being made in the few days before trial must end.

60. It should be made clear, though, that 'fishing' expeditions in relation to third party material—whether by the prosecution or the defence—must be discouraged, and that, in appropriate cases, the court will consider making an order for wasted costs where the application is clearly unmeritorious and ill-conceived.

61. Judges should recognise that a summons can only be issued where the document(s) sought would be admissible in evidence. While it may be that the material in question may be admissible in evidence as a result of the hearsay provisions of the CJA (sections 114 to 120), it is this that determines whether an order for production of the material is appropriate, rather than the wider considerations applicable to disclosure in criminal proceedings: see *R v Reading Justices* (supra), upheld by the House of Lords in *R v Derby Magistrates' Court* (supra).

62. A number of Crown Court centres have developed local protocols, usually in respect of sexual offences and material held by social services and health and education authorities. Where these protocols exist they often provide an excellent and sensible way to identify relevant material that might assist the defence or undermine the prosecution.

63. Any application for third party disclosure must identify what documents are sought and why they are said to be material evidence. This is particularly relevant where attempts are made to access the

medical reports of those who allege that they are victims of crime. Victims do not waive the confidentiality of their medical records, or their right to privacy under article 8 of the ECHR, by the mere fact of making a complaint against the accused. Judges should be alert to balance the rights of victims against the real and proven needs of the defence. The court, as a public authority, must ensure that any interference with the article 8 rights of those entitled to privacy is in accordance with the law and necessary in pursuit of a legitimate public interest. General and unspecified requests to trawl through such records should be refused. If material is held by any person in relation to family proceedings (eg, where there have been care proceedings in relation to a child, who has also complained to the police of sexual or other abuse) then an application has to be made by that person to the family court for leave to disclose that material to a third party, unless the third party, and the purpose for which disclosure is made, is approved by Rule 10.20A(3) of the Family Proceedings Rules 1991 (SI 1991 No. 1247). This would permit, for instance, a local authority, in receipt of such material, to disclose it to the police for the purpose of a criminal investigation, or to the CPS, in order for the latter to discharge any obligations under the CPIA.

Conclusion

64. The public rightly expects that the delays and failures which have been present in some cases in the past where there has been scant adherence to sound disclosure principles will be eradicated by observation of this Protocol. The new regime under the Criminal Justice Act and the Criminal Procedure Rules gives judges the power to change the culture in which such cases are tried. It is now the duty of every judge actively to manage disclosure issues in every case. The judge must seize the initiative and drive the case along towards an efficient, effective and timely resolution, having regard to the overriding objective of the Criminal Procedure Rules (Part 1). In this way the interests of justice will be better served and public confidence in the criminal justice system will be increased.

Appendix 6 Human Rights

CONVENTION FOR THE PROTECTION OF HUMAN RIGHTS AND FUNDAMENTAL FREEDOMS, ARTICLES 5 TO 7 AND 10

Article 5
Right to liberty and security

1. Everyone has the right to liberty and security of the person. No one shall be deprived of his liberty save in the following cases and in accordance with a procedure prescribed by law:
   (a) the lawful detention of a person after conviction by a competent court;
   (b) the lawful arrest or detention of a person for non-compliance with the lawful order of a court or in order to secure the fulfilment of any obligation prescribed by law;
   (c) the lawful arrest or detention of a person effected for the purpose of bringing him before the competent legal authority on reasonable suspicion of having committed an offence or when it is reasonably considered necessary to prevent his committing an offence or fleeing after having done so;
   (d) the detention of a minor by lawful order for the purpose of educational supervision or his lawful detention for the purpose of bringing him before the competent legal authority;
   (e) the lawful detention of persons for the prevention of spreading of infectious diseases, of persons of unsound mind, alcoholics or drug addicts or vagrants;
   (f) the lawful arrest or detention of a person to prevent his effecting an unauthorised entry into the country or of a person against whom action is being taken with a view to deportation or extradition.
2. Everyone who is arrested shall be informed promptly, in a language which he understands, of the reasons for his arrest and of any charge against him.
3. Everyone arrested or detained in accordance with the provisions of paragraph (1)(c) of this Article shall be brought promptly before a judge or other officer authorised by law to exercise judicial power and shall be entitled to trial within a reasonable time or to release pending trial. Release may be conditioned by guarantees to appear for trial.
4. Everyone who is deprived of his liberty by arrest or detention shall be entitled to take proceedings by which the lawfulness of his detention shall be decided speedily by a court and his release ordered if the detention is not lawful.
5. Everyone who has been the victim of arrest or detention in contravention of the provisions of this Article shall have an enforceable right to compensation.

Article 6
Right to a fair trial

1. In the determination of his civil rights and obligations or of any criminal charge against him, everyone is entitled to a fair and public hearing within a reasonable time by an independent and impartial tribunal established by law. Judgment shall be pronounced publicly but the press and public may be excluded from all or part of the trial in the interests of morals, public order or national security in a democratic society, where the interests of juveniles or the protection of the private life of the parties so require, or to the extent strictly necessary in the opinion of the court in special circumstances where publicity would prejudice the interests of justice.
2. Everyone charged with a criminal offence shall be presumed innocent until proved guilty according to law.
3. Everyone charged with a criminal offence has the following minimum rights:
   (a) to be informed promptly, in a language which he understands and in detail, of the nature and cause of the accusation against him;
   (b) to have adequate time and facilities for the preparation of his defence;
   (c) to defend himself in person or through legal assistance of his own choosing or, if he has not sufficient means to pay for legal assistance, to be given it free when the interests of justice so require;
   (d) to examine or have examined witnesses against him and to obtain the attendance and examination of witnesses on his behalf under the same conditions as witnesses against him;
   (e) to have the free assistance of an interpreter if he cannot understand or speak the language used in court.

Article 7
No punishment without law

1. No one shall be held guilty of any criminal offence on account of any act or omission which did not constitute a criminal offence under national or international law at the time when it was committed. Nor shall a heavier penalty be imposed than the one that was applicable at the time the criminal offence was committed.
2. This Article shall not prejudice the trial and punishment of any person for any act or omission which, at the time when it was committed, was criminal according to the general principles of law recognised by civilised nations.

Article 10
Freedom of expression

1. Everyone has the right to freedom of expression. This right shall include freedom to hold opinions and to receive and impart information and ideas without interference by public authority and regardless of frontiers. This Article shall not prevent States from requiring the licensing of broadcasting, television or cinema enterprises.
2. The exercise of these freedoms, since it carries with it duties and responsibilities, may be subject to such formalities, conditions, restrictions or penalties as are prescribed by law and are necessary in a democratic society, in the interests of national security, territorial integrity or public safety, for the prevention of disorder or crime, for the protection of health or morals, for the protection of the reputation or rights of others, for preventing the disclosure of information received in confidence, or for maintaining the authority and impartiality of the judiciary.

HUMAN RIGHTS ACT 1998, SS. 2 TO 4, 6 AND 10

2. Interpretation of Convention Rights

(1) A court or tribunal determining a question which has arisen under this Act in connection with a Convention right must take into account any—
- (a) judgment, decision, declaration or advisory opinion of the European Court of Human Rights,
- (b) opinion of the Commission given in a report adopted under Article 31 of the Convention,
- (c) decision of the Commission in connection with Article 26 or 27(2) of the Convention, or
- (d) decision of the Committee of Ministers taken under Article 46 of the Convention, whenever made or given, so far as, in the opinion of the court or tribunal, it is relevant to the proceedings in which that question has arisen.

(2) Evidence of any judgment, decision, declaration or opinion of which account may have to be taken under this section is to be given in proceedings before any court or tribunal in such manner as may be provided by rules.

(3) In this section 'rules' means rules of court or, in the case of proceedings before a tribunal, rules made for the purposes of this section—
- (a) by the Lord Advocate or Secretary of State, in relation to proceedings in Scotland; or
- (b) by the Lord Chancellor or Secretary of State, in relation to any other proceedings.

(4) Where a court or tribunal is determining a question which has arisen under this Act in connection with a Convention right it shall be a defence for a person to show that he has acted in pursuance of a manifestation of religious belief in accordance with the historic teaching and practices of a christian or other principal religious tradition represented in Great Britain.

(5) For the avoidance of doubt, the teaching and practices referred to in subsection (4) above do not include any teaching or practice which contravenes the criminal law.

(6) Subject to subsection (5) above, the teaching and practices referred to in subsection (4) above shall include teaching or practice in accordance with a relevant historic creed, canon, confession of faith, catechism or formulary.

(7) In this section 'manifestation of religious belief' shall be taken to include actions such as worship, observance, conformity to a moral or ethical principle, practice, teaching and employment policies.

3. Interpretation of Legislation

(1) So far as it is possible to do so, primary legislation and subordinate legislation must be read and given effect in a way which is compatible with the Convention rights.

(2) This section—

(a) applies to primary legislation and subordinate legislation whenever enacted;
(b) does not affect the validity, continuing operation or enforcement of any incompatible primary legislation; and
(c) does not affect the validity, continuing operation or enforcement of any incompatible subordinate legislation if (disregarding any possibility of revocation) primary legislation prevents removal of the incompatibility.

4. Declaration of Incompatibility

(1) Subsection (2) applies in any proceedings in which a court determines whether a provision of primary legislation is compatible with a Convention right.
(2) If the court is satisfied that the provision is incompatible with a Convention right, it may make a declaration of that incompatibility.
(3) Subsection (4) applies in any proceedings in which a court determines whether a provision of subordinate legislation, made in the exercise of a power conferred by primary legislation, is compatible with a Convention right.
(4) If the court is satisfied—
(a) that the provision is incompatible with a Convention right, and
(b) that (disregarding any possibility of revocation) the primary legislation concerned prevents removal of the incompatibility, it may make a declaration of that incompatibility.
(5) In this section 'court' means—
(a) the House of Lords;
(b) the Judicial Committee of the Privy Council;
(c) the Courts-Martial Appeal Court;
(d) in Scotland, the High Court of Justiciary sitting otherwise than as a trial court or the Court of Session;
(e) in England and Wales or Northern Ireland, the High Court or the Court of Appeal.
(6) A declaration under this section ('a declaration of incompatibility')—
(a) does not affect the validity, continuing operation or enforcement of the provision in respect of which it is given; and
(b) is not binding on the parties to the proceedings in which it is made.

6. Acts of Public Authorities

(1) It is unlawful for a public authority to act in a way which is incompatible with a Convention right.
(2) Subsection (1) does not apply to an act if—
(a) as the result of one or more provisions of primary legislation, the authority could not have acted differently; or
(b) in the case of one or more provisions of, or made under, primary legislation which cannot be read or given effect in a way which is compatible with the Convention rights, the authority was acting so as to give effect to or enforce those provisions.
(3) In this section 'public authority' includes—
(a) a court or tribunal, and
(b) any person certain of whose functions are functions of a public nature, but does not include either House of Parliament or a person exercising functions in connection with proceedings in Parliament.

10. Power to take remedial action

(1) This section applies if—
(a) a provision of legislation has been declared under section 4 to be incompatible with a Convention right and, if an appeal lies—
(i) all persons who may appeal have stated in writing that they do not intend to do so;
(ii) the time for bringing an appeal has expired and no appeal has been brought within that time; or
(iii) an appeal brought within that time has been determined or abandoned; or
(b) it appears to a Minister of the Crown or Her Majesty in Council that, having regard to a finding of the European Court of Human Rights made after the coming into force of this section in proceedings against the United Kingdom, a provision of legislation is incompatible with an obligation of the United Kingdom arising from the Convention.
(2) If a Minister of the Crown considers that there are compelling reasons for proceeding under this section, he may by order make such amendments to the legislation as he considers necessary to remove the incompatibility.

(3) If, in the case of subordinate legislation, a Minister of the Crown considers—
  (a) that it is necessary to amend the primary legislation under which the subordinate legislation in question was made, in order to enable the incompatibility to be removed, and
  (b) that there are compelling reasons for proceeding under this section, he may by order make such amendments to the primary legislation as he considers necessary.

Appendix 7 The Consolidated Criminal Practice Direction

This is a consolidation, with some amendments, of existing Practice Directions, Practice Statements and Practice Notes as they affect proceedings in the Court of Appeal (Criminal Division), the Crown Court and the magistrates' courts, with the exception of the Practice Directions which relate to costs. Practice Directions relating to costs are consolidated in the Practice Direction on Costs in Criminal Proceedings, handed down on 18 May 2004.

The following Practice Directions are included by way of cross-reference only:

(a) The Practice Direction relating to References to the European Court of Justice by the Court of Appeal and the High Court under Article 177 of the European Communities Treaty [1999] 1 WLR 260; [1999] 1 Cr App R 452.
(b) The Practice Direction relating to Devolution Issues [1999] 1 WLR 1592; [1999] 3 All ER 466; [1999] 2 Cr App R 486.
(c) The Practice Direction (Court of Appeal (Civil Division)) [1999] 1 WLR 1027; [1999] 2 All ER 490, paragraph 9 (relating to the availability of judgments given in the Court of Appeal and the High Court) and paragraph 10.1 (relating to the citation of judgments in court).

Guidelines issued by the Attorney General are not included.

Also excluded is the guidance given by the Court of Appeal (Civil Division) in *C v S (Money Laundering: Discovery of Documents) (Practice Direction)* [1991] 1 WLR 1551, which deals with the conflict which can arise between the interests of the state in combating crime on the one hand and, on the other hand, the entitlement of private bodies to obtain redress from the courts and the principles that justice should be administered in public and that a party should know the case advanced against him, should have the opportunity to reply to it and should know the reasons for the decision of the court. Though arising from crime, this was civil litigation.

Reference should also be made to the following Civil Procedure Practice Directions:

(a) Such parts of the Practice Direction—Addition and Substitution of Parties, supplementary to CPR Part 19, as may apply where a defendant makes a claim for a declaration of incompatibility in accordance with section 4 of the Human Rights Act 1998.
(b) The Practice Direction—Court Sittings, supplementary to CPR Part 39.

This consolidation is not a comprehensive statement of the practice and procedure of the criminal courts. For this reference must be made to the relevant Acts and Rules to which this Direction is supplementary and to the Attorney General's guidelines.

A list of the Practice Directions which are consolidated *for the purpose of criminal proceedings* is at Appendix A. Where appropriate, these Practice Directions have been brought up to date. Any changes were of a relatively minor nature.

The consolidation does not affect proceedings in the Court of Appeal (Civil Division) or in any division of the High Court. So, for example, in the Family Division, reference should still be made to such directions, etc as affect proceedings there. Some criminal cases come before the Administrative Court. These form a small part of the work of that court and are not affected by this consolidation. The Administrative Court Office has a list of the relatively few Practice Directions which apply there.

This Practice Direction is divided into the following Parts:

Part I	Directions of General Application
Part II	Further Directions applying in the Court of Appeal (Criminal Division)
Part III	Further Directions applying in the Crown Court and in magistrates' courts
Part IV	Further Directions applying in the Crown Court
Part V	Further Directions applying in magistrates' courts
Annex A	List of Practice Directions, Practice Notes and Practice Statements included in this consolidation [omitted].
Annex B	List of Practice Directions, Practice Notes and Practice Statements not included in this consolidation, but no longer applicable in criminal proceedings [omitted].
Annex C	Form of words recommended for use in explanations for the imposition of custodial sentences.

Annex D Forms for use in criminal proceedings.

Annex E Forms to facilitate case management [reproduced as appendix 5]

NOTE: Throughout this document words connoting the masculine include the feminine.

Part I Directions of General Application

I.1. Court dress

I.1.1 In magistrates' courts, advocates appear without robes or wigs. In all other courts, Queen's Counsel wear a short wig and a silk (or stuff) gown over a court coat with bands, junior counsel wear a short wig and stuff gown with bands, and solicitors and other advocates authorised under the Courts and Legal Services Act 1990 wear a black stuff gown with bands.

I.2. Unofficial tape recording of proceedings

I.2.1 Section 9 of the Contempt of Court Act 1981 contains provisions governing the unofficial use of tape recorders in court. Section 9(1) provides that it is a contempt of court (a) to use in court, or bring into court for use, any tape recorder or other instrument for recording sound, except with the leave of the Court; (b) to publish a recording of legal proceedings made by means of any such instrument, or any recording derived directly or indirectly from it, by playing it in the hearing of the public or any section of the public, or to dispose of it or any recording so derived, with a view to such publication; (c) to use any such recording in contravention of any conditions of leave granted under paragraph (a). These provisions do not apply to the making or use of sound recordings for purposes of official transcripts of the proceedings, upon which the Act imposes no restriction whatever.

I.2.2 The discretion given to the Court to grant, withhold or withdraw leave to use tape recorders or to impose conditions as to the use of the recording is unlimited, but the following factors may be relevant to its exercise: (a) the existence of any reasonable need on the part of the applicant for leave, whether a litigant or a person connected with the press or broadcasting, for the recording to be made; (b) the risk that the recording could be used for the purpose of briefing witnesses out of court; (c) any possibility that the use of the recorder would disturb the proceedings or distract or worry any witnesses or other participants.

I.2.3 Consideration should always be given whether conditions as to the use of a recording made pursuant to leave should be imposed. The identity and role of the applicant for leave and the nature of the subject matter of the proceedings may be relevant to this.

I.2.4 The particular restriction imposed by section 9(1)(b) applies in every case, but may not be present to the mind of every applicant to whom leave is given. It may therefore be desirable on occasion for this provision to be drawn to the attention of those to whom leave is given.

I.2.5 The transcript of a permitted recording is intended for the use of the person given leave to make it and is not intended to be used as, or to compete with, the official transcript mentioned in section 9(4).

I.3. Restrictions on reporting proceedings

I.3.1 Under section 4(2) of the Contempt of Court Act 1981 a court may, where it appears necessary for avoiding a substantial risk of prejudice to the administration of justice in the proceedings before it or in any others pending or imminent, order that publication of any report of the proceedings or part thereof be postponed for such time as the court thinks necessary for that purpose. Section 11 of the Act provides that a court may prohibit the publication of any name or other matter in connection with the proceedings before it which it has allowed to be withheld from the public.

I.3.2 When considering whether to make such an order there is nothing which precludes the court from hearing a representative of the press. Indeed it is likely that the court will wish to do so.

I.3.3 It is necessary to keep a permanent record of such orders for later reference. For this purpose all orders made under section 4(2) must be formulated in precise terms having regard to the decision in *R* v *Horsham Justices ex parte Farquharson* [1982] QB 762; 76 Cr App R 87, and orders under both sections must be committed to writing either by the judge personally or by the clerk of the court under the judge's directions. An order must state (a) its precise scope, (b) the time at which it shall cease to have effect, if appropriate, and (c) the specific purpose of making the order. Courts will normally give notice to the press in some form that an order has been made under either section of the Act and the court staff should be prepared to answer any enquiry about a specific case, but it is, and will remain, the responsibility of those reporting cases, and their editors, to ensure that no breach of any orders occurs and the onus rests on them to make enquiry in any case of doubt.

I.4. Availability of judgments given in the Court of Appeal and the High Court

I.4.1 Reference should be made to paragraph 9 of Practice Direction (Court of Appeal (Civil Division)) [1999] 1 WLR 1027; [1999] 2 All ER 490.

I.5. Wards of court

I.5.1 Where a child has been interviewed by the police in connection with contemplated criminal proceedings and the child subsequently becomes a ward of court, no leave of the wardship court is required for the child to be called as a witness in those proceedings. Where, however, the police desire to interview a child who is already a ward of court, application must, other than in the exceptional cases referred to in paragraph I.5.3, be made to the wardship court, on summons and on notice to all parties, for leave for the police to do so. Where, however, a party may become the subject of a criminal investigation and it is considered necessary for the ward to be interviewed without that party knowing that the police are making inquiries, the application for leave may be made ex parte to a judge without notice to that party. Notice, should, where practicable, be given to the reporting officer.

I.5.2 Where leave is given the order should, unless some special reason requires the contrary, give leave for any number of interviews which may be required by the prosecution or the police. If it is desired to conduct any interview beyond what has been permitted by the order, a further application should be made.

I.5.3 The exceptional cases are those where the police need to deal with complaints or alleged offences concerning wards and it is appropriate, if not essential, for action to be taken straight away without the prior leave of the wardship court. Typical examples may be: (a) serious offences against the ward, such as rape, where medical examination and the collection of scientific evidence ought to be carried out promptly; (b) where the ward is suspected by the police of having committed a criminal act and the police wish to interview him about it; (c) where the police wish to interview the ward as a potential witness. The list is not exhaustive; there will inevitably be other instances where immediate action is appropriate. In such cases the police should notify the parent or foster parent with whom the ward is living or other 'appropriate adult' within the Code of Practice for the Detention, Treatment and Questioning of Persons by Police Officers, so that that adult has the opportunity of being present when the police interview the child. Additionally, if practicable, the reporting officer (if one has been appointed) should be notified and invited to attend the police interview or to nominate a third party to attend on his behalf. A record of the interview or a copy of any statement made by the ward should be supplied to the reporting officer. Where the ward has been interviewed without the reporting officer's knowledge, he should be informed at the earliest opportunity. So too, if it be the case that the police wish to conduct further interviews. The wardship court should be appraised of the situation at the earliest possible opportunity thereafter by the reporting officer, the parent, foster parent (through the local authority) or other responsible adult.

I.5.4 No evidence or documents in the wardship proceedings or information about the proceedings should be disclosed in the criminal proceedings without leave of the wardship court.

I.6. Spent convictions

I.6.1 The effect of section 4(1) of the Rehabilitation of Offenders Act 1974 is that a person who has become a rehabilitated person for the purpose of the Act in respect of a conviction (known as a 'spent' conviction) shall be treated for all purposes in law as a person who has not committed or been charged with or prosecuted for or convicted of or sentenced for the offence or offences which were the subject of that conviction.

I.6.2 Section 4(1) of the 1974 Act does not apply, however, to evidence given in criminal proceedings: section 7(2)(a). Convictions are often disclosed in such criminal proceedings. When the Bill was before the House of Commons on 28 June 1974 the hope was expressed that the Lord Chief Justice would issue a Practice Direction for the guidance of the Crown Court with a view to reducing disclosure of spent convictions to a minimum and securing uniformity of approach. The direction is set out in the following paragraphs. The same approach should be adopted in all courts of criminal jurisdiction.

I.6.3 During the trial of a criminal charge, reference to previous convictions (and therefore to spent convictions) can arise in a number of ways. The most common is when the character of the accused or a witness is sought to be attacked by reference to his criminal record, but there are, of course, cases where previous convictions are relevant and admissible as, for instance, to prove system.

I.6.4 It is not possible to give general directions which will govern all these different situations, but it is recommended that both court and advocates should give effect to the general intention of Parliament by never referring to a spent conviction when such reference can reasonably be avoided.

I.6.5 After a verdict of guilty the court must be provided with a statement of the defendant's record for the purposes of sentence. The record supplied should contain all previous convictions, but those which are spent should, so far as practicable, be marked as such.

I.6.6 No one should refer in open court to a spent conviction without the authority of the judge, which authority should not be given unless the interests of justice so require.

I.6.7 When passing sentence the judge should make no reference to a spent conviction unless it is necessary to do so for the purpose of explaining the sentence to be passed.

I.7. Explanations for the imposition of custodial sentences

I.7.1 The practical effect of custodial sentences imposed by the courts is almost entirely governed by statutory provisions. Those statutory provisions, changed by Parliament from time to time, are not widely understood by the general public. It is desirable that when sentence is passed the practical effect of the sentence should be understood by the defendant, any victim and any member of the public who is present in court or reads a full report of the proceedings.

I.7.2 Whenever a custodial sentence is imposed on an offender the court should explain the practical effect of the sentence in addition to complying with existing statutory requirements. This will be no more than an explanation; the sentence will be that pronounced by the court.

I.7.3 Sentencers should give the explanation in terms of their own choosing, taking care to ensure that the explanation is clear and accurate. No form of words is prescribed. Annexed to this Practice Direction are short statements which may, adapted as necessary, be of value as models (see Annex C). These statements are based on the statutory provisions in force on 1 January 1998 and will, of course, require modification if those provisions are materially amended.

I.7.4 Sentencers will continue to give such explanation as they judge necessary of ancillary orders relating to matters such as disqualification, compensation, confiscation, costs and so on.

I.7.5 The power of the Secretary of State to release a prisoner early under supervision is not part of the sentence. The judge is therefore not required in his sentencing remarks to provide an explanation of this power. However, in explaining the effect of custodial sentences the judge should not say anything which conflicts with the existence of this power.

I.8. Words to be used when passing sentence

I.8.1 Where a court passes on a defendant more than one term of imprisonment the court should state in the presence of the defendant whether the terms are to be concurrent or consecutive. Should this not be done the court clerk should ask the court, before the defendant leaves court, to do so.

I.8.2 If a prisoner is, at the time of sentence, already serving two or more consecutive terms of imprisonment and the court intends to increase the total period of imprisonment, it should use the expression 'consecutive to the total period of imprisonment to which you are already subject' rather than 'at the expiration of the term of imprisonment you are now serving', lest the prisoner be not then serving the last of the terms to which he is already subject.

I.9. Substitution of suspended sentences for immediate custodial sentences

I.9.1 Where an appellate court substitutes a suspended sentence of imprisonment for one having immediate effect, the court should have in mind any period the appellant has spent in custody. If the court is of the opinion that it would be fair to do so, an approximate adjustment to the term of the suspended sentence should be made. Whether or not the court makes such adjustment, it should state that it had that period in mind. The court should further indicate that the operational period of suspension runs from the date the court passes the suspended sentence.

I.10. References to the European Court of Justice

I.10.1 These are the subject of Practice Direction: References to the European Court of Justice by the Court of Appeal and the High Court under Article 177 of the EC Treaty [1999] 1 WLR 260; [1999] 1 Cr App R 452, to which reference should be made.

I.11. Devolution issues

I.11.1 These are the subject of Practice Direction: (Supreme Court)(Devolution Issues) [1999] 1 WLR 1592; [1999] 3 All ER 466; [1999] 2 Cr App R 486, to which reference should be made.

I.12. Preparation of judgments: neutral citation

I.12.1 Since 11 January 2001 every judgment of the Court of Appeal, and of the Administrative Court, and since 14 January 2002 every judgment of the High Court, has been prepared and issued as approved with single spacing, paragraph numbering (in the margins) and no page numbers. In courts with more than one judge the paragraph numbering continues sequentially through each judgment and does not start again at the beginning of each judgment. Indented paragraphs are not numbered. A unique reference number is given to each judgment. For judgments of the Court of Appeal this number is given by the official shorthand writers. For judgments of the High Court it is provided by the Mechanical Recording Department at the Royal Courts of Justice. Such a number will also be furnished, on request to the Mechanical Recording Department, Royal Courts of Justice, Strand, London WC2A 2LL (Tel: 020 7947 7771), to High Court judgments delivered outside London.

I.12.2 Each Court of Appeal judgment starts with the year, followed by EW (for England and Wales), then CA (for Court of Appeal), followed by Civ or Crim and finally the sequential number. For example *Smith v Jones* [2001] EWCA Civ 10.

I.12.3 In the High Court, represented by HC, the number comes before the divisional abbreviation and, unlike Court of Appeal judgments, the latter is bracketed: (Ch), (Pat), (QB), (Admin), (Comm), (Admlty), (TCC) or (Fam) as appropriate. For example, [2002] EWHC 123 (Fam) or [2002] EWHC 124 (QB) or [2002] EWHC 125 (Ch).

I.12.4 This 'neutral citation', as it is called, is the official number attributed to the judgment and must always be used at least once when the judgment is cited in a later judgment. Once the judgment is reported this neutral citation appears in front of the familiar citation from the law reports series. Thus: *Smith v Jones* [2001] EWCA (Civ) 10; [2001] QB 124; [2001] 2 All ER 364, etc.

I.12.5 Paragraph numbers are referred to in square brackets. When citing a paragraph from a High Court judgment it is unnecessary to include the descriptive word in brackets: (Admin), (QB) or whatever. When citing a paragraph from a Court of Appeal judgment, however, Civ or Crim is included. If it is desired to cite more than one paragraph of a judgment each numbered paragraph should be enclosed with a square bracket. Thus paragraph 59 in *Green v White* [2002] EWHC 124 (QB) would be cited: *Green v White* [2002] EWHC 124 at [59]; paragraphs 30–35 in *Smith v Jones* would be *Smith v Jones* [2001] EWCA Civ 10 at [30]–[35]; similarly, where a number of paragraphs are cited: *Smith v Jones* [2001] EWCA Civ 10 at [30], [35] and [40–43].

I.12.6 If a judgment is cited more than once in a later judgment it is helpful if only one abbreviation is used, e.g. *Smith v Jones* or Smith's case, but preferably not both (in the same judgment).

I.13. Bail: failure to surrender and trials in absence

I.13.1 The following directions take effect immediately.

I.13.2 The failure of the defendants to comply with the terms of their bail by not surrendering can undermine the administration of justice. It can disrupt proceedings. The resulting delays impact on victims, witnesses and other court users and also waste costs. A defendant's failure to surrender affects not only the case with which he is concerned, but also the courts' ability to administer justice more generally by damaging the confidence of victims, witnesses and the public in the effectiveness of the court system and the judiciary. It is therefore most important that defendants who are granted bail appreciate the significance of the obligation to surrender to custody in accordance with the terms of their bail and that courts take appropriate action if they fail to do so.

I.13.3 There are at least three courses of action for the courts to consider taking:—

[A] imposing penalties for the failure to surrender;

[B] revoking bail or imposing more stringent bail conditions; and

[C] conducting trials in the absence of the defendant.

Penalties for Failure to Surrender

I.13.4 A defendant who commits a section 6(1) or section 6(2) Bail Act 1976 offence commits an offence that stands apart from the proceedings in respect of which bail was granted. The seriousness of the offence can be reflected by an appropriate penalty being imposed for the Bail Act offence.

I.13.5 The common practice at present of courts automatically deferring disposal of a section 6(1) or section 6(2) Bail Act 1976 offence (failure to surrender) until the conclusion of the proceedings in respect of which bail was granted should no longer be followed. Instead, courts should now deal with defendants as soon as is practicable. In deciding what is practicable, the Court must take into account when the proceedings in respect of which bail was granted are expected to conclude, the seriousness of the offence for which the defendant is already being prosecuted, the type of penalty that might be imposed for the breach of bail and the original offence as well as any other relevant circumstances. If there is no good reason for postponing dealing with the breach until after the trial, the breach should be dealt with as soon as practicable. If the disposal of the breach of bail is deferred, then it is still necessary to consider imposing a separate penalty at the trial and the sentence for the breach of the bail should usually be custodial and consecutive to any other custodial sentence (as to which see I.13.13). In addition, bail should usually be revoked in the meantime (see I.13.14 to 16). In the case of offences which cannot, or are unlikely to, result in a custodial sentence, trial in the absence of the defendant may be a pragmatic sensible response to the situation (see I.13.17 to I.13.19). This is not a penalty for the Bail Act offence and a penalty may also be imposed for the Bail Act offence.

Initiating proceedings—bail granted by a police officer

I.13.6 When a person has been granted bail by a police officer to attend court and subsequently fails to surrender to custody, the decision whether to initiate proceedings for a section 6(1) or section 6(2) offence will be for the police/prosecutor.

I.13.7 The offence in this form is a summary offence and should be initiated as soon as practicable after the offence arises in view of the six month time limit running from the failure to surrender. It should be dealt with on the first appearance after arrest, unless an adjournment is necessary, as it will be relevant in considering whether to grant bail again.

Initiating proceedings—bail granted by a court

I.13.8 When a person has been granted bail by a court and subsequently fails to surrender to custody, on arrest that person should normally be brought as soon as appropriate before the court at which the proceedings in respect of which bail was granted are to be heard. (The six months time limit does not apply where bail was granted by the court.) Should the defendant commit another offence outside the jurisdiction of the bail court, the Bail Act offence should, where practicable, be dealt with by the new court at the same time as the new offence. If impracticable, the defendant may, if this is appropriate, be released formally on bail by the new court so that the warrant may be executed for his attendance before the first court in respect of the substantive and Bail Act offences.

I.13.9 Given that bail was granted by a court, it is more appropriate that the court itself should initiate the proceedings by its own motion. The court will be invited to take proceedings by the prosecutor, if the prosecutor considers proceedings are appropriate.

Conduct of proceedings

I.13.10 Proceedings under section 6 Bail Act 1976 may be conducted either as a summary offence or as a criminal contempt of court. Where the court is invited to take proceedings by the prosecutor, the prosecutor will conduct the proceedings and, if the matter is contested, call the evidence. Where the court initiates proceedings without such an invitation the same role can be played by the prosecutor at the request of the court, where this is practicable.

I.13.11 The burden of proof is on the defendant to prove that he had reasonable cause for his failure to surrender to custody (s 6(3) Bail Act 1976).

Proceedings to be progressed to disposal as soon as is practicable

I.13.12 If the court decides to proceed, the section 6 Bail Act offence should be concluded as soon as practicable.

Sentencing for a Bail Act offence

I.13.13 In principle, a custodial sentence for the offence of failing to surrender should be ordered to be served consecutively to any other sentence imposed at the same time for another offence unless there are circumstances that make this inappropriate (see *White & McKinnon*).

Relationship between the Bail Act Offence and Further Remands on Bail or in Custody

I.13.14 When a defendant has been convicted of a Bail Act offence, the court should review the remand status of the defendant, including the conditions of that bail, in respect of the main proceedings for which bail had been granted.

I.13.15 Failure by the defendant to surrender or a conviction for failing to surrender to bail in connection with the main proceedings will be significant factors weighing against the re-granting of bail or, in the case of offences which do not normally give rise to a custodial sentence, in favour of trial in the absence of the offender.

I.13.16 Whether or not an immediate custodial sentence has been imposed for the Bail Act offence, the court may, having reviewed the defendant's remand status, also remand the defendant in custody in the main proceedings.

Trials in Absence

I.13.17 A defendant has a right, in general, to be present and to be represented at his trial. However, a defendant may choose not to exercise those rights by voluntarily absenting himself and failing to instruct his lawyers adequately so that they can represent him and, in the case of proceedings before the magistrates' court, there is an express statutory power to hear trials in the defendant's absence (s11 of the Magistrates' Courts Act 1980). In such circumstances, the court has discretion whether the trial should take place in his/her absence.

I.13.18 The court must exercise its discretion to proceed in the absence of the defendant with the utmost care and caution. The overriding concern must be to ensure that such a trial is as fair as circumstances permit and leads to a just outcome.

I.13.19 Due regard should be had to the judgment of Lord Bingham in *R* v *Jones* [2003] AC 1, [2002] 2 AER 113 in which Lord Bingham identified circumstances to be taken into account before proceeding, which include: the conduct of the defendant, the disadvantage to the defendant, public interest, the effect of any delay and whether the attendance of the defendant could be secured at a later hearing. Other relevant considerations are the seriousness of the offence and likely outcome if the defendant is found guilty. If the defendant is only likely to be fined for a summary offence this can be relevant since the costs that a defendant might otherwise be ordered to pay as a result of an adjournment could be disproportionate. In the case of summary proceedings the fact that there can be an appeal that is a complete rehearing is also relevant, as is the power to re-open the case under s 142 of the Magistrates' Courts Act 1980.

I.14. Forms

I.14.1 This Practice Direction supplements Part 5 (forms) of the Criminal Procedure Rules.

I.14.2 The forms set out in Annex D, or forms to that effect, are to be used in the criminal courts on or after 4th April 2005, when the Criminal Procedure Rules come into force. Almost all are identical to those in use before that date, and accordingly a form in use before that date which corresponds with one set out in Annex D may still be used in connection with the rule to which it applies.

I.14.3 The table at the beginning of Annex D lists the forms set out in that Annex and—

- shows the rule in connection with which each form applies
- describes each form
- in the case of a form in use before the Criminal Procedure Rules came into force, shows the legislation by which the form was prescribed and by what number (if any) it was known.

Part II Further Directions Applying in the Court of Appeal (Criminal Division)

II.1. Appeals against sentence—the provision of notice to the prosecution

II.1.1 The Registrar of Criminal Appeals will notify the relevant prosecution authority in the event that:

(a) leave to appeal against sentence is granted by the single Judge; or

(b) the single Judge or the Registrar refers an application for leave to appeal against sentence to the Full Court for determination; or

(c) the Registrar becomes aware that Counsel for the applicant will be appearing at a renewed application for leave to appeal against sentence.

II.1.2 The Prosecution will have 7 days from the grant of leave by the single Judge or the referral by the Registrar to notify the Registrar if they wish to be represented at the hearing OR to request sight of the grounds of appeal and/or any comments made by the single Judge when granting leave or referring the case to the Full Court. Upon such a request, the prosecution will have a further 7 days from receipt to notify the Registrar if they wish to be represented at the hearing.

II.1.3 Occasionally, for example, where the single Judge fixes a hearing date at short notice, the Registrar may have to foreshorten the period specified in II.1.2 above.

II.1.4 In relation to (c) in paragraph II.1.1, the prosecution will have 72 hours or, if the case is listed, 48 hours, to notify the Registrar that they wish to be represented at the hearing. Should the prosecution require sight of the grounds of appeal and the single Judge's comments, such a request should be made as expeditiously as possible.

II.1.5 If the prosecution wishes to be represented at any hearing, the notification should include details of Counsel instructed, a time estimate and an indication whether a skeleton argument will be lodged no later than 14 days before the hearing (or such shorter period as may be necessary). If a skeleton argument is to be lodged, it must be served on the Court and the applicant/appellant.

II.1.6 An application by the prosecution to remove a case from the list for Counsel's convenience, or to allow further preparation time, will rarely be granted.

II.1.7 There may be occasions when the Court of Appeal Criminal Division will grant leave to appeal to an unrepresented applicant and proceed forthwith with the appeal in the absence of the appellant and Counsel. In those circumstances there will be no opportunity to notify the prosecution.

II.1.8 As a Court of Review, the Court of Appeal Criminal Division would expect the prosecution to have raised any specific matters of relevance with the sentencing Judge in the first instance.

II.1.9 When the prosecution attend a hearing as a result of this Practice Direction, the prosecution should not volunteer assistance in relation to any unrepresented applicant.

II.1.10 This Direction will come into force as from 10 November 2003.

II.1.11 The Prosecution are already invited to appear and respond, as a matter of course, in appeals against Confiscation Orders and where the Court is considering issuing sentencing guidelines. This practice will continue without change.

II.1.12 This Practice Direction replaces the existing protocol whereby the prosecution were responsible for lodging a letter of interest with the Registrar of Criminal Appeals via the Crown Court.

II.2. Listing of appeals against conviction and sentence in the CACD

II.2.1 Arrangements for the fixing of dates for the hearing of appeals will be made by the Criminal Appeal Office Listing Officer, under the superintendence of the Registrar of Criminal Appeals who may give such directions as he deems necessary.

II.2.2 Where possible, regard will be had to an advocate's existing commitments. However, in relation to the listing of appeals, the Court of Appeal takes precedence over all lower courts, including the Crown Court. Wherever practicable a lower court will have regard to this principle when making arrangements to release an advocate to appear in the Court of Appeal. In case of difficulty the lower court should communicate with the Registrar. In general an advocate's commitment in a lower court will not be regarded as a good reason for failing to accept a date proposed for a hearing in the Court of Appeal.

II.2.3 The copy of the Criminal Appeal Office summary provided to advocates will contain the summary writer's time estimate for the whole hearing including delivery of judgment. The Listing Officer will rely on that estimate unless the advocate for the appellant or the Crown provides a different time estimate to the Listing Officer, in writing, within 7 days of the receipt of the summary by the advocate. Where the time estimate is considered by an advocate to be inadequate, or where the estimate has been altered because, for example, a ground of appeal has been abandoned, it is the duty of the advocate to inform the Court promptly, in which event the Registrar will reconsider the time estimate and inform the parties accordingly.

II.2.4 In furtherance of the Court's aim of continuing to improve the service provided to appellants and respondents the following target times will be set for the hearing of appeals. Target times will run from the receipt of the appeal by the Listing Officer, as being ready for hearing. These arrangements will apply to appeals so received on and after 22nd March 2004.

II.2.5

Nature of appeal	From receipt by listing officer to fixing of hearing date	From fixing of hearing date to hearing	Total time from receipt by listing officer to hearing
Sentence Appeal	14 days	14 days	28 days
Conviction Appeal	21 days	42 days	63 days
Conviction Appeal where witness to attend	28 days	52 days	80 days

II.2.6 Where legal vacations impinge these periods may be extended. Where expedition is required, the Registrar may direct that these periods be abridged.

II.2.7 'Appeal' includes an application for leave to appeal which requires an oral hearing.

II.13. Mode of addressing the court

II.13.1 Judges of the Court of Appeal and of the High Court are addressed as 'My Lord' or 'My Lady'; so are Circuit Judges sitting as judges of the High Court under section 9 of the Supreme Court Act 1981.

II.14. Notices of appeal and of applications for leave to appeal

II.14.1 These are to be served on the Crown Court at the centre where the proceedings took place. The Crown Court will forward them to the Criminal Appeal Office together with the trial documents and any others which may be required.

II.15. Grounds of appeal

II.15.1 Advocates should not settle grounds or support them with written advice unless they consider that they are properly arguable. Grounds should be carefully drafted and properly particularised. Advocates should not assume that the Court will entertain any ground of appeal not set out and properly particularised. Should leave to amend the grounds be granted it is most unlikely that further grounds will be entertained.

II.15.2 A copy of the advocate's positive advice about the merits should be attached as part of the grounds.

II.16. Loss of time

II.16.1 Both the Court and the single judge have power in their discretion to direct that part of the time during which an applicant is in custody after putting in his notice of application for leave to appeal should not count towards sentence. Those who contemplate putting in such a notice and their legal advisers should bear this in mind. It is important that those contemplating an appeal should seek advice and should remember that it is useless to appeal without grounds and that grounds should be substantial and particularised and not a mere formula. Where an application devoid of merit has been refused by the single judge and a direction for loss of time has been made, the Full Court, on renewal of the application, may direct that additional time shall be lost if it, once again, thinks it right so to exercise its discretion in all the circumstances of the case.

II.17. Skeleton arguments

II.17.1 In all appeals against conviction a skeleton argument from the advocate for the appellant is to be lodged with the Registrar of Criminal Appeals and served on the prosecuting authority within 14 days of receipt by the advocate of the notification of the grant of leave to appeal against conviction or such longer period as the Registrar or the Court may direct. The skeleton may refer to an advice, which should be annexed with an indication of which parts of it are relied upon, and should include any additional arguments to be advanced.

II.17.2 The advocate for the prosecuting authority should lodge with the Registrar and the advocate for the appellant his skeleton argument within 14 days of the receipt of the skeleton argument for the appellant or such longer (or, in exceptional cases, shorter) period as the Registrar or the Court may direct.

II.17.3 Practitioners should ensure that, where reliance is placed upon unreported cases in skeleton arguments, short head notes are included.

II.17.4 Advocates should ensure that the correct Criminal Appeal Office number appears at the beginning of their skeleton arguments and that their names are at the end.

II.17.5 A skeleton argument should contain a numbered list of the points the advocate intends to argue, grouped under each ground of appeal, and stated in no more than one or two sentences. It should be as succinct as possible, the object being to identify each point, not to argue it or elaborate on it. Each listed point should be followed by full references to the material to which the advocate will refer in support of it, i.e. the relevant passages in the transcripts, authorities, etc. It should also contain anything the advocate would expect to be taken down by the Court during the hearing, such as propositions of law, chronologies, etc. If more convenient, these can be annexed to the skeletons rather than included in it. For points of law, the skeleton should state the point and cite the principal authority or authorities in support with reference to the passages where the principle is enunciated. Chronologies should, if possible, be agreed with the opposing advocate before the hearing. Respondents' skeletons should follow the same principles.

II.18. Criminal Appeal Office summaries

II.18.1 To assist the Court the Criminal Appeal Office prepares summaries of the cases coming before it. These are entirely objective and do not contain any advice about how the Court should deal with the case or any view about its merits. They consist of two Parts.

II.18.2 Part I, which is provided to all of the advocates in the case, generally contains (a) particulars of the proceedings in the Crown Court, including representation and details of any co-accused, (b) particulars of the proceedings in the Court of Appeal (Criminal Division), (c) the facts of the case, as drawn from the transcripts, advice of the advocates, witness statements and/or the exhibits, (d) the submissions and rulings, summing up and sentencing remarks. Should an advocate not want any factual material in his advice taken into account this should be stated in the advice.

II.18.3 The contents of the summary are a matter for the professional judgment of the writer, but an advocate wishing to suggest any significant alteration to Part I should write to the Registrar of Criminal Appeals. If the Registrar does not agree, the summary and the letter will be put to the Court for decision. The Court will not generally be willing to hear oral argument about the content of the summary.

II.18.4 Advocates may show Part I of the summary to their professional or lay clients (but to no one else) if they believe it would help to check facts or formulate arguments, but summaries are not to be copied or reproduced without the permission of the Criminal Appeal Office; permission for this will not normally be given in cases involving children or sexual offences or where the Crown Court has made an order restricting reporting.

II.18.5 Unless a judge of the High Court or the Registrar of Criminal Appeals gives a direction to the contrary in any particular case involving material of an explicitly salacious or sadistic nature, Part I will also be supplied to appellants who seek to represent themselves before the full court or who renew to the full court their applications for leave to appeal against conviction or sentence.

II.18.6 Part II, which is supplied to the Court alone, contains (a) a summary of the grounds of appeal and (b) in appeals against sentence (and applications for such leave), summaries of the antecedent histories of the parties and of any relevant pre-sentence, medical or other reports.

II.18.7 All of the source material is provided to the Court and advocates are able to draw attention to anything in it which may be of particular relevance.

II.19. Citation of judgments in court

II.19.1 Reference should be made to paragraph 10.1 of Practice Direction (Court of Appeal (Civil Division)) [1999] 1 WLR 1027; [1999] 2 All ER 490.

II.20. Citation of Hansard

II.20.1 Where any party intends to refer to the reports of Parliamentary proceedings as reported in the Official Reports of either House of Parliament ('Hansard') in support of any such argument as is permitted by the decisions in *Pepper* v *Hart* [1993] AC 593 and *Pickstone* v *Freeman* [1989] AC 66 or otherwise he must, unless the Court otherwise directs, serve upon all other parties and the Court copies of any such extract together with a brief summary of the argument intended to be based upon such extract. No other report of Parliamentary proceedings may be cited.

II.20.2 Unless the Court otherwise directs, service of the extract and summary of the argument shall be effected not less than 5 clear working days before the first day of the hearing, whether or not it has a fixed date. Advocates must keep themselves informed as to the state of the lists where no fixed date has been given. Service on the Court shall be effected by sending three copies to the Registrar of Criminal Appeals, Room C212, Royal Courts of Justice, Strand, London WC2A 2LL. If any party fails to do so the Court may make such order (relating to costs or otherwise) as is in all the circumstances appropriate.

Part III Further Directions Applying in the Crown Court and Magistrates' Courts

III.21.1 Classification of Crown Court business and allocation to Crown Court Centres

Classification

III.21.1 For the purposes of trial in the Crown Court offences are classified as follows:

Class 1: (a) Misprision of treason and treason felony; (b) Murder; (c) Genocide; (d) Torture, hostage-taking and offences under the War Crimes Act 1991; (e) An offence under the Official Secrets Acts; (f) Manslaughter; (g) Infanticide; (h) Child destruction; (i) Abortion (section 58 of the Offences against the Person Act 1861); (j) Sedition; (k) An offence under section 1 of the Geneva Conventions Act 1957; (l) Mutiny; (m) Piracy; (n) Soliciting, incitement, attempt or conspiracy to commit any of the above offences.

Class 2: (a) Rape; (b) Sexual intercourse with a girl under 13; (c) Incest with a girl under 13; (d) Assault by penetration; (e) Causing a person to engage in sexual activity, where penetration is involved; (f) Rape of a child under 13; (g) Assault of a child under 13 by penetration; (h) Causing or inciting a child under 13 to engage in sexual activity, where penetration is involved; (i) Sexual activity with a person with a mental disorder, where penetration is involved; (j)

Inducement to procure sexual activity with a mentally disordered person where penetration is involved; (k) Paying for sexual services of a child where child is under 13 and penetration is involved; (l) Committing an offence with intent to commit a sexual offence, where the offence is kidnapping or false imprisonment; (m) Soliciting, incitement, attempt or conspiracy to commit any of the above offences.

Class 3: All other offences not listed in classes 1 or 2.

III.21.2 The magistrates' court, upon either committing a person for trial under section 6 of the Magistrates' Courts Act 1980, or sending a person under section 51 of the Crime and Disorder Act 1998, shall:

(a) if the offence or any of the offences is included in Class 1, specify the most convenient location of the Crown Court where a High Court Judge, or, where a Circuit Judge duly authorised by the Lord Chief Justice to try class 1 cases, regularly sits.

(b) if the offence or any of the offences is included in Class 2, specify the most convenient location of the Crown Court where a Judge duly authorised to try Class 2 regularly sits. These courts on each Circuit will be identified by the Presiding Judges, with the concurrence of the Lord Chief Justice.

(c) where an offence is in Class 3 the magistrates' court shall specify the most convenient location of the Crown Court.

Where a case is transferred under section 4 of the Criminal Justice Act 1987 or section 53 of the Criminal Justice Act 1991, the authority shall, in specifying the proposed place of trial in the notice of transfer, comply with the provisions of this paragraph.

III.21.3 In selecting the most convenient location of the Crown Court the justices shall have regard to the considerations referred to in section 7 of the Magistrates' Courts Act 1980 and section 51(10) of the Crime and Disorder Act 1998 and the location or locations of the Crown Court designated by a Presiding Judge as the location to which cases should normally be committed from their court.

III.21.4 Where on one occasion a person is committed in respect of a number of offences all the committals shall be to the same location of the Crown Court and that location shall be the one where a High Court Judge regularly sits if such a location is appropriate for any of the offences.

Committals following breach

III.21.5 Where, in the Crown Court, a community order or an order for conditional discharge has been made, or a suspended sentence has been passed, and the offender is subsequently found or alleged to be in breach before a magistrates' court which decides to commit the offender to the Crown Court, he shall be committed in accordance with paragraphs III.21.6, III.21.7 or III.21.8

III.21.6 He shall be committed to the location of the Crown Court where the order was made or the suspended sentence was passed, unless it is inconvenient, impracticable or inappropriate to do so in all the circumstances.

III.21.7 If, for whatever reason, he is not so committed and the order was made or sentence passed by a High Court Judge, he shall be committed to the most convenient location of the Crown Court where a High Court Judge regularly sits.

III.21.8 In all other cases he shall be committed to the most convenient location of the Crown Court.

III.21.9 In selecting the most convenient location of the Crown Court, the justices shall have regard to the locations of the Crown Court designated by a Presiding Judge as the locations to which cases should normally be committed from their court.

Notice of transfer in cases of serious or complex fraud

III.21.10 Where a notice of transfer is served under section 4 of the Criminal Justice Act 1987 the proposed place of trial to be specified in the notice shall be one of the Crown Court centres designated by the Senior Presiding Judge.

Notice of transfer in child witness cases

III.21.11 Where a notice of transfer is served under section 53 of the Criminal Justice Act 1991 (child witness cases) the proposed place of trial to be specified in accordance with paragraph 1(1) of schedule 6 to the Act shall be a Crown Court centre which is equipped with live television link facilities.

III.22. Applications for evidence to be given in Welsh

III.22.1 If a defendant in a court in England asks to give or call evidence in the Welsh language the case should not be transferred to Wales. In ordinary circumstances interpreters can be provided on request.

III.23. Use of the Welsh language in courts in Wales

III.23.1 The purpose of this direction is to reflect the principle of the Welsh Language Act 1993 that in the administration of justice in Wales the English and Welsh languages should be treated on a basis of equality.

General

III.23.2 It is the responsibility of the legal representatives in every case in which the Welsh language may be used by any witness or party or in any document which may be placed before the court to inform the court of that fact so that appropriate arrangements can be made for the listing of the case.

III.23.3 If the possible use of the Welsh language is known at the time of committal, transfer or appeal to the Crown Court, the court should be informed immediately after committal or transfer or when the notice of appeal is lodged. Otherwise the court should be informed as soon as possible use of the Welsh language becomes known.

III.23.4 If costs are incurred as a result of failure to comply with these directions, a wasted costs order may be made against the defaulting party and/or his legal representatives.

III.23.5 The law does not permit the selection of jurors in a manner which enables the court to discover whether a juror does or does not speak Welsh or to secure a jury whose members are bilingual to try a case in which the Welsh language may be used.

Plea and directions hearings

III.23.6 An advocate in a case in which the Welsh language may be used must raise that matter at the plea and directions hearing and endorse details of it on the judge's questionnaire so that appropriate directions may be given for the progress of the case.

Listing

III.23.7 The listing officer, in consultation with the resident judge, should ensure that a case in which the Welsh language may be used is listed (a) wherever practicable before a Welsh speaking judge, and (b) in a court in Wales with simultaneous translation facilities.

Interpreters

III.23.8 Whenever an interpreter is needed to translate evidence from English into Welsh or from Welsh into English, the court manager in whose court the case is to be heard shall ensure that the attendance is secured of an interpreter whose name is included in the list of approved court interpreters.

Jurors

III.23.9 The jury bailiff when addressing the jurors at the start of their period of jury service shall inform them that each juror may take an oath or affirm in Welsh or English as he wishes.

III.23.10 After the jury has been selected to try a case, and before it is sworn, the court officer swearing in the jury shall inform the jurors in open court that each juror may take an oath or affirm in Welsh or English as he wishes.

Witnesses

III.23.11 When each witness is called the court officer administering the oath or affirmation shall inform the witness that he may be sworn or affirm Welsh or English as he wishes.

Opening/closing of courts

III.23.12 Unless it is not reasonably practicable to do so, the opening and closing of the court should be performed in Welsh and English.

Role of liaison judge

III.23.13 If any question or problem arises concerning the implementation of paragraphs III.23.1–III.23.12, contact should in the first place be made with the liaison judge for Welsh language matters on circuit.

III.24. Evidence by written statement

III.24.1 Where the prosecution proposes to tender written statements in evidence either under sections 5A and 5B of the Magistrates' Courts Act 1980 or section 9 of the Criminal Justice Act 1967 it will frequently be not only proper, but also necessary for the orderly presentation of the evidence, for certain statements to be edited. This will occur either because a witness has made more than one statement whose contents should conveniently be reduced into a single, comprehensive statement or where a statement contains inadmissible, prejudicial or irrelevant material. Editing of statements should in all circumstances be done by a Crown Prosecutor (or by a legal representative, if any, of the prosecutor if the case is not being conducted by the Crown Prosecution Service) and not by a police officer.

Composite statements

III.24.2 A composite statement giving the combined effect of two or more earlier statements or settled by a person referred to in paragraph III.24.1 must be prepared in compliance with the requirements of sections 5A and 5B of the 1980 Act or section 9 of the 1967 Act as appropriate and must then be signed by the witness.

Editing single statements

III.24.3 There are two acceptable methods of editing single statements.

(a) By marking *copies* of the statement in a way which indicates the passages on which the prosecution will not rely. This merely indicates that the prosecution will not seek to adduce the evidence so marked. The *original signed statement* to be tendered to the court is not marked in any way. The marking on the copy statement is done by lightly striking out the passages to be edited so that what appears beneath can still be read, or by bracketing, or by a combination of both. It is not permissible to produce a photocopy with the deleted material obliterated, since this would be contrary to the requirement that the defence and the court should be served with copies of the signed original statement. Whenever the striking out/bracketing method is used, it will assist if the following words appear at the foot of the frontispiece or index to any bundle of copy statements to be tendered: 'The prosecution does not propose to adduce evidence of those passages of the attached copy statements which have been struck out and/or bracketed (nor will it seek to do so at the trial unless a notice of further evidence is served).'

(b) By obtaining a fresh statement, signed by the witness, which omits the offending material, applying the procedure in paragraph III.24.2.

III.24.4 In most cases where a single statement is to be edited, the striking out/bracketing method will be the more appropriate, but the taking of a fresh statement is preferable in the following circumstances:

(a) When a police (or other investigating) officer's statement contains details of interviews with more suspects than are eventually charged, a fresh statement should be prepared and signed omitting all details of interview with those not charged except, insofar as it is relevant, for the bald fact that a certain named person was interviewed at a particular time, date and place.

(b) When a suspect is interviewed about more offences than are eventually made the subject of committal charges, a fresh statement should be prepared and signed omitting all questions and answers about the uncharged offences unless either they might appropriately be taken into consideration or evidence about those offences is admissible on the charges preferred, such as evidence of system. It may, however, be desirable to replace the omitted questions and answers with a phrase such as: 'After referring to some other matters, I then said . . .', so as to make it clear that part of the interview has been omitted.

(c) A fresh statement should normally be prepared and signed if the only part of the original on which the prosecution is relying is only a small proportion of the whole, although it remains desirable to use the alternative method if there is reason to believe that the defence might itself wish to rely, in mitigation or for any other purpose, on at least some of those parts which the prosecution does not propose to adduce.

(d) When the passages contain material which the prosecution is entitled to withhold from disclosure to the defence.

III.24.5 Prosecutors should also be aware that, where statements are to be tendered under section 9 of the 1967 Act in the course of *summary* proceedings, there will be a need to prepare fresh statements excluding inadmissible or prejudicial material rather than using the striking out or bracketing method.

III.24.6 None of the above principles applies, in respect of committal proceedings, to documents which are exhibited (including statements under caution and signed contemporaneous notes). Nor do they apply to oral statements of a defendant which are recorded in the witness statements of interviewing police officers, except in the circumstances referred to in paragraph III.24.4(b). All this material should remain in its original state in the committal bundles, any editing being left to prosecuting counsel at the Crown Court (after discussion with defence counsel and, if appropriate, the trial judge).

III.24.7 Whenever a fresh statement is taken from a witness, a copy of the earlier, unedited statement(s) of that witness will be given to the defence in accordance with the Attorney General's guidelines on the disclosure of unused material (Practice Note [1982] 1 All ER 734) unless there are grounds under paragraph 6 of the guidelines for withholding such disclosure.

III.25. Bail during trial

III.25.1 Paragraphs III.25.2 to III.25.5 are to be read subject to the Bail Act 1976, especially section 4.

III.25.2 Once a trial has begun the further grant of bail, whether during the short adjournment or overnight, is in the discretion of the trial judge. It may be a proper exercise of this discretion to refuse bail during the short adjournment if the accused cannot otherwise be segregated from witnesses and jurors.

III.25.3 An accused who was on bail while on remand should not be refused overnight bail during the trial unless in the opinion of the judge there are positive reasons to justify this refusal. Such reasons are likely to be:

(a) that a point has been reached where there is a real danger that the accused will abscond, either because the case is going badly for him, or for any other reason;

(b) that there is a real danger that he may interfere with witnesses or jurors.

III.25.4 There is no universal rule of practice that bail shall not be renewed when the summing-up has begun. Each case must be decided in the light of its own circumstances and having regard to the judge's assessment from time to time of the risks involved.

III.25.5 Once the jury has returned a verdict a further renewal of bail should be decided in the light of the gravity of the offence and the likely sentence to be passed in all the circumstances of the case.

III.26. Facts to be stated on pleas of guilty

III.26.1 To enable the press and the public to know the circumstances of an offence of which an accused has been convicted and for which he is to be sentenced, in relation to each offence to which an accused has pleaded guilty the prosecution shall state those facts in open court before sentence is imposed.

III.27. Antecedents

Standard for the provision of information of antecedents in the Crown Court and magistrates' courts

III.27.1 In the Crown Court the police will provide brief details of the circumstances of the last three similar convictions and/or of convictions likely to be of interest to the court, the latter being judged on a case by case basis. This information should be provided separately and attached to the antecedents as set out below.

III.27.2 Where the current alleged offence could constitute a breach of an existing community order, e.g. community rehabilitation order, and it is known that that order is still in force then, to enable the court to consider the possibility of revoking that order, details of the circumstances of the offence leading to the community order should be included in the antecedents as set out below.

Preparation of antecedents and standard formats to be used

III.27.3 In magistrates' courts and the Crown Court:

Personal details and summary of convictions and cautions—Police National Computer ['PNC'] Court/Defence/Probation Summary Sheet;

Previous convictions—PNC Court/Defence/Probation printout, supplemented by Form MG16 if the police force holds convictions not shown on PNC;

Recorded cautions—PNC Court/Defence/Probation printout, supplemented by Form MG17 if the police force holds cautions not shown on PNC.

and, in addition, in the Crown Court:

Circumstances of the last three similar convictions;

Circumstances of offence leading to a community order still in force;

Form MG(c). The detail should be brief and include the date of the offence.

Provision of antecedents to the court and parties

Crown Court

III.27.4 The Crown Court antecedents will be prepared by the police immediately following committal proceedings, including committals for sentence, transfers under section 4 of the Criminal Justice

Act 1987 or section 53 of the Criminal Justice Act 1991 or upon receipt of a notice of appeal, excluding non-imprisonable motoring offences.

III.27.5 Seven copies of the antecedents will be prepared in respect of each defendant. Two copies are to be provided to the Crown Prosecution Service ['CPS'] direct, the remaining five to be sent to the Crown Court. The court will send one copy to the defence and one to the Probation Service. The remaining copies are for the court's use. Where following conviction a custodial order is made one copy is to be attached to the order sent to the prison.

III.27.6 The antecedents must be provided, as above, within 21 days of committal or transfer in each case. Any points arising from them are to be raised with the police by the defence solicitor as soon as possible and, where there is time, at least seven days before the hearing date so that the matter can be resolved prior to that hearing.

III.27.7 Seven days before the hearing date the police will check the record of convictions. Details of any additional convictions will be provided using the standard format above. These will be provided as above and attached to the documents already supplied. Details of any additional outstanding cases will also be provided at this stage.

Magistrates' courts

III.27.8 The magistrates' court antecedents will be prepared by the police and submitted to the CPS with the case file.

III.27.9 Five copies of the antecedents will be prepared in respect of each defendant and provided to the CPS who will be responsible for distributing them to others at the sentencing hearing. Normally two copies will be provided to the court, one to the defence and one to the Probation Service when appropriate. Where following conviction a custodial order is made, one of the court's copies is to be attached to the order sent to the prison.

III.27.10 In instances where antecedents have been provided to the court some time before the hearing the police will, if requested to do so by the CPS, check the record of convictions. Details of any additional convictions will be provided using the standard format above. These will be provided as above and attached to the documents already supplied. Details of any additional outstanding cases will also be provided at this stage.

III.27.11 The above arrangements whereby the police provide the antecedents to the CPS for passing on to others will apply unless there is a local agreement between the CPS and the court that alters that arrangement.

III.28. Personal statements of victims

III.28.1 This section draws attention to a scheme, which started on 1 October 2001, to give victims a more formal opportunity to say how a crime has affected them. It may help to identify whether they have a particular need for information, support and protection. It will also enable the court to take the statement into account when determining sentence.

III.28.2 When a police officer takes a statement from a victim the victim will be told about the scheme and given the chance to make a victim personal statement. A victim personal statement may be made or updated at any time prior to the disposal of the case. The decision about whether or not to make a victim personal statement is entirely for the victim. If the court is presented with a victim personal statement the following approach should be adopted:

(a) The victim personal statement and any evidence in support should be considered and taken into account by the court prior to passing sentence.

(b) Evidence of the effects of an offence on the victim contained in the victim personal statement or other statement, must be in proper form, that is a witness statement made under section 9 of the Criminal Justice Act 1967 or an expert's report, and served upon the defendant's solicitor or the defendant, if he is not represented, prior to sentence. Except where inferences can properly be drawn from the nature of or circumstances surrounding the offence, a sentencer must not make assumptions unsupported by evidence about the effects of an offence on the victim.

(c) The court must pass what it judges to be the appropriate sentence having regard to the circumstances of the offence and of the offender, taking into account, so far as the court considers it appropriate, the consequences to the victim. The opinions of the victim or the victim's close relatives as to what the sentence should be are therefore not relevant, unlike the consequence of the offence on them. Victims should be advised of this. If, despite the advice, opinions as to sentence are included in the statement, the court should pay no attention to them.

(d) The court should consider whether it is desirable in its sentencing remarks to refer to the evidence provided on behalf of the victim.

III.29. Support for witnesses giving evidence by live television link

III.29.1 This section of the Practice Direction is made pursuant to [rule 29.6 of the Criminal Procedure Rules 2005] and supersedes previous guidance given by the Senior Presiding Judges, Lord Justice Tasker Watkins in 1991 and Lord Justice Auld in 1998.

III.29.2 An increased degree of flexibility is now appropriate as to who can act as supporter of a witness giving evidence by live television link. Where a special measures direction is made enabling a vulnerable, intimidated or child witness to give evidence by means of a live television link, the trial judge will make a direction as to the identity of the witness supporter. Where practical, the direction will be made before the trial commences. In giving the direction, the trial judge will balance all relevant interests—see paragraph 1.11 of the guidance '*Achieving Best Evidence*'. The witness supporter should be completely independent of the witness and his or her family and have no previous knowledge of or personal involvement in the case. The supporter should also be suitably trained so as to understand the obligations of, and comply with, the National Standards relating to witness supporters. Providing these criteria are met, the witness supporter need not be an usher or court official. Thus, for example, the functions of the witness supporter may be performed by a representative of the Witness Service.

III.29.3 Where the witness supporter is someone other than the court usher, the usher should continue to be available both to assist the witness and the witness supporter, and to ensure that the judge's requirements are properly complied with in the CCTV room.

III.30 Treatment of vulnerable defendants

III.30.1 This direction applies to proceedings in the Crown Court and in magistrates' courts on the trial, sentencing or (in the Crown Court) appeal of (a) children and young persons under 18 or (b) adults who suffer from a mental disorder within the meaning of the Mental Health Act 1983 or who have any other significant impairment of intelligence and social function. In this direction such defendants are referred to collectively as "vulnerable defendants". The purpose of this direction is to extend to proceedings in relation to such persons in the adult courts procedures analogous to those in use in youth courts.

III.30.2 The steps which should be taken to comply with paragraphs III.30.3 to III.30.17 should be judged, in any given case, taking account of the age, maturity and development (intellectual, social and emotional) of the defendant concerned and all other circumstances of the case.

The overriding principle

III.30.3 A defendant may be young and immature or may have a mental disorder within the meaning of the Mental Health Act 1983 or some other significant impairment of intelligence and social function such as to inhibit his understanding of and participation in the proceedings. The purpose of criminal proceedings is to determine guilt, if that is in issue, and decide on the appropriate sentence if the defendant pleads guilty or is convicted. All possible steps should be taken to assist a vulnerable defendant to understand and participate in those proceedings. The ordinary trial process should, so far as necessary, be adapted to meet those ends. Regard should be had to the welfare of a young defendant as required by section 44 of the Children and Young Persons Act 1933, and generally to parts 1 and 3 of the Criminal Procedure Rules (the overriding objective and the court's powers of case management).

Before the trial, sentencing or appeal

III.30.4 If a vulnerable defendant, especially one who is young, is to be tried jointly with one who is not, the court should consider at the plea and case management hearing, or at a case management hearing in a magistrates' court, whether the vulnerable defendant should be tried on his own and should so order unless of the opinion that a joint trial would be in accordance with part 1 of the Criminal Procedure Rules (the overriding objective) and in the interests of justice. If a vulnerable defendant is tried jointly with one who is not, the court should consider whether any of the modifications set out in this direction should apply in the circumstances of the joint trial and so far as practicable make orders to give effect to any such modifications.

III.30.5 At the plea and case management hearing, or at a case management hearing in a magistrates' court, the court should consider and so far as practicable give directions on the matters covered in paragraphs III.30.9 to III.30.17.

III.30.6 It may be appropriate to arrange that a vulnerable defendant should visit, out of court hours and before the trial, sentencing or appeal hearing, the courtroom in which that hearing is to take place so that he can familiarise himself with it.

III.30.7 If any case against a vulnerable defendant has attracted or may attract widespread public or media interest, the assistance of the police should be enlisted to try and ensure that the defendant is not, when attending the court, exposed to intimidation, vilification or abuse. Section 41 of the Criminal Justice Act 1925 prohibits the taking of photographs of defendants and witnesses (among others) in the court building or in its precincts, or when entering or leaving those precincts. A direction informing media representatives that the prohibition will be enforced may be appropriate.

III.30.8 The court should be ready at this stage, if it has not already done so, where relevant to make a reporting restriction under section 39 of the Children and Young Persons Act 1933 or, on an appeal to the Crown Court from a youth court, to remind media representatives of the application of section 49 of that Act. Any such order, once made, should be reduced to writing and copies should on request be made available to anyone affected or potentially affected by it.

The trial, sentencing or appeal hearing

III.30.9 Subject to the need for appropriate security arrangements the proceedings should, if practicable, be held in a courtroom in which all the participants are on the same or almost the same level.

III.30.10 A vulnerable defendant, especially if he is young, should normally, if he wishes, be free to sit with members of his family or others in a like relationship, and with some other suitable supporting adult such as a social worker, and in a place which permits easy, informal communication with his legal representatives. The court should ensure that a suitable supporting adult is available throughout the course of the proceedings.

III.30.11 At the beginning of the proceedings the court should ensure that what is to take place has been explained to a vulnerable defendant in terms he can understand, and at trial in the Crown Court it should ensure in particular that the role of the jury has been explained. It should remind those representing the vulnerable defendant and the supporting adult of their responsibility to explain each step as it takes place, and at trial to explain the possible consequences of a guilty verdict. Throughout the trial the court should continue to ensure, by any appropriate means, that the defendant understands what is happening and what has been said by those on the bench, the advocates and witnesses.

III.30.12 A trial should be conducted according to a timetable which takes full account of a vulnerable defendant's ability to concentrate. Frequent and regular breaks will often be appropriate. The court should ensure, so far as practicable, that the trial is conducted in simple, clear language that the defendant can understand and that cross-examination is conducted by questions that are short and clear.

III.30.13 A vulnerable defendant who wishes to give evidence by live link in accordance with section 33A of the Youth Justice and Criminal Evidence Act 1999 may apply for a direction to that effect. Before making such a direction the court must be satisfied that it is in the interests of justice to do so, and that the use of a live link would enable the defendant to participate more effectively as a witness in the proceedings. The direction will need to deal with the practical arrangements to be made, including the room from which the defendant will give evidence, the identity of the person or persons who will accompany him, and how it will be arranged for him to be seen and heard by the court.

III.30.14 In the Crown Court robes and wigs should not be worn unless the court for good reason orders that they should. It may be appropriate for the court to be robed for sentencing in a grave case even though it has sat without robes for trial. It is generally desirable that those responsible for the security of a vulnerable defendant who is in custody, especially if he is young, should not be in uniform, and that there should be no recognisable police presence in the courtroom save for good reason.

III.30.15 The court should be prepared to restrict attendance by members of the public in the court room to a small number, perhaps limited to those with an immediate and direct interest in the outcome. The court should rule on any challenged claim to attend.

III.30.16 Facilities for reporting the proceedings (subject to any restrictions under section 39 or 49 of the Children and Young Persons Act 1933) must be provided. But the court may restrict the number of reporters attending in the courtroom to such number as is judged practicable and desirable. In ruling on any challenged claim to attend in the court room for the purpose of reporting the court should be mindful of the public's general right to be informed about the administration of justice.

III.30.17 Where it has been decided to limit access to the courtroom, whether by reporters or generally, arrangements should be made for the proceedings to be relayed, audibly and if possible visually, to another room in the same court complex to which the media and the public have access if it appears that there will be a need for such additional facilities. Those making use of such a facility should be reminded that it is to be treated as an extension of the court room and that they are required to conduct themselves accordingly.

III.30.18 Where the court is called upon to exercise its discretion in relation to any procedural matter falling within the scope of this practice direction but not the subject of specific reference, such discretion should be exercised having regard to the principles in paragraph III.30.3.

III.31 Binding over orders and conditional discharges

III.31.1 This direction takes into account the judgments of the European Court of Human Rights in *Steel v United Kingdom* (1999) 28 EHRR 603, [1998] Crim LR 893 and in *Hashman and Harrup v United Kingdom* (2000) 30 EHRR 241, [2000] Crim LR 185. Its purpose is to give practical guidance, in the light of those two judgments, on the practice of imposing binding over orders. The direction applies to orders made under the court's common law powers, under the Justices of the Peace Act 1361, under section 1(7) of the Justices of the Peace Act 1968 and under section 115 of the Magistrates' Courts Act 1980. This direction also gives guidance concerning the court's power to bind over parents or guardians under section 150 of the Powers of Criminal Courts (Sentencing) Act 2000 and the Crown Court's power to bind over to come up for judgment. The court's power to impose a conditional discharge under section 12 of the Powers of Criminal Courts (Sentencing) Act 2000 is also covered by this direction.

Binding over to keep the peace

III.31.2 Before imposing a binding over order, the court must be satisfied that a breach of the peace involving violence or an imminent threat of violence has occurred or that there is a real risk of violence in the future. Such violence may be perpetrated by the individual who will be subject to the order or by a third party as a natural consequence of the individual's conduct.

III.31.3 In light of the judgment in *Hashman and Harrup*, courts should no longer bind an individual over 'to be of good behaviour'. Rather than binding an individual over to "keep the peace" in general terms, the court should identify the specific conduct or activity from which the individual must refrain.

Written order

III.31.4 When making an order binding an individual over to refrain from specified types of conduct or activities, the details of that conduct or those activities should be specified by the court in a written order served on all relevant parties. The court should state its reasons for the making of the order, its length and the amount of the recognisance. The length of the order should be proportionate to the harm sought to be avoided and should not generally exceed 12 months.

Evidence

III.31.5 Sections 51 to 57 of the Magistrates' Courts Act 1980 set out the jurisdiction of the magistrates' court to hear an application made on complaint and the procedure which is to be followed. This includes a requirement under section 53 to hear evidence and the parties before making any order. This practice should be applied to all cases in the magistrates' court and the Crown Court where the court is considering imposing a binding over order. The court should give the individual who would be subject to the order and the prosecutor the opportunity to make representations, both as to the making of the order and as to its terms. The court should also hear any admissible evidence the parties wish to call and which has not already been heard in the proceedings. Particularly careful consideration may be required where the individual who would be subject to the order is a witness in the proceedings.

III.31.6 Where there is an admission which is sufficient to found the making of a binding over order and/or the individual consents to the making of the order, the court should nevertheless hear sufficient representations and, if appropriate, evidence, to satisfy itself that an order is appropriate in all the circumstances and to be clear about the terms of the order.

III.31.7 Where there is an allegation of breach of a binding over order and this is contested, the court should hear representations and evidence, including oral evidence, from the parties before making a finding.

Burden of proof

III.31.8 The court should be satisfied beyond reasonable doubt of the matters complained of before a binding over order may be imposed. Where the procedure has been commenced on complaint, the burden of proof rests on the complainant. In all other circumstances, the burden of proof rests upon the prosecution.

III.31.9 Where there is an allegation of breach of a binding over order, the court should be satisfied beyond reasonable doubt that a breach has occurred before making any order for forfeiture of a recognisance. The burden of proof shall rest on the prosecution.

Recognisance

III.31.10 The court must be satisfied on the merits of the case that an order for binding over is appropriate and should announce that decision before considering the amount of the recognisance. The individual who is made subject to the binding over order should be told he has a right of appeal from the decision.

III.31.11 When fixing the amount of the recognisance, courts should have regard to the individual's financial resources and should hear representations from the individual or his legal representatives regarding finances.

Refusal to enter into a recognisance

III.31.12 If there is any possibility that an individual will refuse to enter a recognisance, the court should consider whether there are any appropriate alternatives to a binding over order (for example, continuing with a prosecution). Where there are no appropriate alternatives and the individual continues to refuse to enter into the recognisance, the magistrates' court may use its power under section 115(3) of the Magistrates Court Act 1980, and the Crown Court may use its common law power, to commit the individual to custody.

III.31.13 Before the court exercises a power to commit the individual to custody, the individual should be given the opportunity to see a duty solicitor or another legal representative and be represented in proceedings if the individual so wishes. Public funding should generally be granted to cover representation.

III.31.14 In the event that the individual does not take the opportunity to seek legal advice, the court shall give the individual a final opportunity to comply with the request and shall explain the consequences of a failure to do so.

Antecedents

(III.31.15) Courts are reminded of the provisions of section 7(5) of the Rehabilitation of Offenders Act 1974 which excludes from a person's antecedents any order of the court 'with respect to any person otherwise than on a conviction'.

Binding over to come up for judgment

III.31.16 If the Crown Court is considering binding over an individual to come up for judgment, the court should specify any conditions with which the individual is to comply in the meantime and not specify that the individual is to be of good behaviour.

Binding over of parent or guardian

III.31.17 Where a court is considering binding over a parent or guardian under section 150 of the Powers of Criminal Courts (Sentencing) Act 2000 to enter into a recognisance to take proper care of and exercise proper control over a child or young person, the court should specify the actions which the parent or guardian is to take.

Security for good behaviour

III.31.18 Where a court is imposing a conditional discharge under section 12 of the Powers of Criminal Courts (Sentencing) Act 2000, it has the power, under section 12(6) to make an order that a person who consents to do so give security for the good behaviour of the offender. When making such an order, the court should specify the type of conduct from which the offender is to refrain.

Part IV Further Directions Applying in the Crown Court

IV.30. Modes of address and titles of judges

Mode of address

IV.30.1 The following judges, when sitting in court, should be addressed as 'My Lord' or 'My Lady', as the case may be, whatever their personal status:

(a) any Circuit Judge sitting as a judge of the High Court under section 9(1) of the Supreme Court Act 1981;

(b) any judge sitting at the Central Criminal Court;

(c) any Senior Circuit Judge who is the Honorary Recorder of the city in which he sits.

IV.30.2 Subject to paragraph 30.1, Circuit Judges, Recorders and Deputy Circuit Judges should be addressed as 'Your Honour' when sitting in court.

Description

IV.30.3 In cause lists, forms and orders members of the judiciary should be described as follows:

(d) Circuit Judges, as 'His [or Her] Honour Judge A' (when the judge is sitting as a judge of the High Court under section 9(1) of the Supreme Court Act 1981 the words 'sitting as a judge of the High Court' should be added);

(e) Recorders, as 'Mr [or Mrs] Recorder B'. This style is appropriate irrespective of any honour or title which the recorder might possess, but if in any case it is desired to include an honour or title the alternative description 'Sir CD, Recorder' or 'The Lord D, Recorder' may be used;

(f) Deputy Circuit Judges, as 'His [or Her] Honour EF, sitting as a Deputy Circuit Judge'.

IV.31. Transfer of cases from one circuit to another

IV.31.1 An application that a case be transferred from one Circuit to another should not be granted unless the judge is satisfied that:

(a) the approval of the Presiding Judges and Regional Director for each Region/Circuit has been obtained, or

(b) the case may be transferred under general arrangements approved by the Presiding Judges and Regional Directors.

IV.32. Transfer of proceedings between locations of the Crown Court

IV.32.1 Without prejudice to the provisions of section 76 of the Supreme Court Act 1981 (committal for trial: alteration of place of trial) directions may be given for the transfer from one location of the Crown Court to another of: (a) appeals; (b) proceedings on committal for sentence or to be dealt with.

IV.32.2 Such directions may be given in a particular case by an officer of the Crown Court, or generally, in relation to a class or classes of case, by the Presiding Judge or a judge acting on his behalf.

IV.32.3 If dissatisfied with such directions given by an officer of the Crown Court, any party to the proceedings may apply to a judge of the Crown Court who may hear the application in chambers.

IV.33. Allocation of business within the Crown Court

General

IV.33.1 Cases in Class 1 may only be tried by:

(1) a High Court Judge, or

(2) a Circuit Judge or Deputy High Court Judge or Deputy Circuit Judge provided (a) that, in all cases save attempted murder, such judge is authorised by the Lord Chief Justice to try murder cases, or in the case of attempted murder, to try murder or attempted murder, and (b) the Presiding Judge has released the case for trial by such a judge.

IV.33.2 Cases in Class 2 may be tried by:

(1) a High Court Judge

(2) a Circuit Judge or Deputy High Court Judge or Deputy Circuit Judge or a Recorder, provided that in all cases such judge is authorised to try class 2 cases by the Lord Chief Justice and the case has been assigned to the judge by or under the direction of either the Presiding Judge or Resident Judge in accordance with guidance given by the Presiding Judges.

IV.33.3 Cases in Class 3 may be tried by a High Court Judge, or in accordance with guidance given by the Presiding Judges, a Circuit Judge, a Deputy Circuit Judge or a Recorder. A case in Class 3 shall not be listed for trial by a High Court Judge except with the consent of a Presiding Judge.

IV.33.4 Appeals from decisions of magistrates shall be heard by:

(a) a Resident Judge, or

(b) a Circuit Judge, nominated by the Resident Judge, who regularly sits at the Crown Court centre, or

(c) an experienced Recorder or Deputy Circuit Judge specifically approved by or under the direction of the Presiding Judges for the purpose, or

(d) where no Circuit Judge or Recorder satisfying the requirements above is available and it is not practicable to obtain the approval of the Presiding Judges, by a Circuit Judge, Recorder or Deputy Circuit Judge selected by the Resident Judge to hear a specific case or cases listed on a specific day.

IV.33.5 Committals following breach (such as a matter in which a community order has been made, or a suspended sentence passed) should, where possible, be listed before the judge who originally dealt with the matter, or, if not, before a judge of the same or higher level.

Applications for removal of a driving disqualification

IV.33.6 Application should be made to the location of the Crown Court where the order of disqualification was made.

Absence of Resident Judge

IV.33.7 A Resident Judge must appoint a deputy to exercise his functions when he is absent from his centre.

Guidance issued by the Senior Presiding Judge and the Presiding Judges

IV.33.8 For the just, speedy and economical disposal of the business of the Circuits or a Circuit, the Senior Presiding Judge or the Presiding Judges, with the approval of the Senior Presiding Judge, may issue guidance to Resident Judges in relation to the allocation and management of the work at their court.

IV.33.9 With the approval of the Senior Presiding Judge, general directions may be given by the Presiding Judges of the South Eastern Circuit concerning the distribution and allocation of business of all classes of case at the Central Criminal Court.

IV.34. Settling the indictment

IV.34.1 Rule 14.1 of the Criminal Procedure Rules requires the prosecutor to serve a draft indictment not more than 28 days after service of the evidence in a case sent for trial, after the committal of the defendant for trial, or after one of the other events listed in that rule. Rule 14.2(5) provides that an indictment may contain any count charging substantially the same offence as one sent or committed for trial and any other count based on the prosecution evidence already served which the Crown Court has jurisdiction to try. Where the prosecutor intends to include in the draft indictment counts which differ materially from, or are additional to, those on which the defendant was sent or committed for trial then the defendant should be given as much notice as possible, usually by service of a draft indictment, or a provisional draft indictment, at the earliest possible opportunity.

IV.34.2 There is no rule of law or practice which prohibits two indictments being in existence at the same time for the same offence against the same person and on the same facts. But the court will not allow the prosecution to proceed on both indictments. They cannot be tried together and the court will require the prosecution to elect the one on which the trial will proceed. Where different defendants have been separately sent or committed for trial for offences which can lawfully be charged in the same indictment then it is permissible to join in one indictment counts based on the separate sendings or committals for trial even if an indictment based on one of them already has been signed. Where necessary the court should be invited to exercise its powers of amendment under section 5 of the Indictments Act 1915.

IV.34.3 Save in the special circumstances described in the following paragraphs of this Practice Direction, it is undesirable that a large number of counts should be contained in one indictment. Where defendants on trial have a variety of offences alleged against them then in the interests of effective case management it is the court's responsibility to exercise its powers in accordance with the overriding objective set out in part 1 of the Criminal Procedure Rules. The prosecution may be required to identify a selection of counts on which the trial should proceed, leaving a decision to be taken later whether to try any of the remainder. Where an indictment contains substantive counts and one or more related conspiracy counts the court will expect the prosecution to justify the joinder. Failing justification the prosecution should be required to choose whether to proceed on the substantive counts or on the conspiracy counts. In any event, if there is a conviction on any counts that are tried then those that have been postponed can remain on the file marked 'not to be proceeded with without the leave of the court'. In the event that a conviction is later quashed on appeal, the remaining counts can be tried. Where necessary the court has power to order that an indictment be divided and some counts removed to a separate indictment.

Multiple offending: trial by jury and then by judge alone

IV.34.4 Under sections 17 to 21 of the Domestic Violence, Crime and Victims Act 2004 the court may order that the trial of certain counts will be by jury in the usual way and, if the jury convicts, that other associated counts will be tried by judge alone. The use of this power is likely to be appropriate where justice cannot be done without charging a large number of separate offences and the allegations against the defendant appear to fall into distinct groups by reference to the identity of the victim, by reference to the dates of the offences, or by some other distinction in the nature of the offending conduct alleged.

IV.34.5 In such a case it is essential to make clear from the outset the association asserted by the prosecutor between those counts to be tried by a jury and those counts which it is proposed should be tried by judge alone, if the jury convict on the former. A special form of indictment is prescribed for this purpose.

IV.34.6 An order for such a trial may be made only at a preparatory hearing. It follows that where the prosecutor intends to invite the court to order such a trial it will normally be appropriate to proceed as follows. The draft indictment served under Criminal Procedure Rule 14.1(1) should be in the form appropriate to such a trial. It should be accompanied by an application under Criminal Procedure Rule 15.1 for a preparatory hearing. On receipt of such a draft indictment Crown Court staff should not sign it before consulting a judge, who is likely to direct under Criminal Procedure Rule 14.1(3) that it should not be signed before the prosecutor's application is heard. This will ensure that the defendant is aware at the earliest possible opportunity of what the prosecution propose and of the proposed association of counts in the indictment. It is undesirable for a draft indictment in the usual form to be served where the prosecutor expects to apply for a two stage trial and hence, of necessity, for permission to amend the indictment at a later stage in order that it may be in the special form.

IV.34.7 If the court allows the prosecutor's application for a two stage trial then it will direct the Crown Court officer to sign the draft indictment accordingly. If the court refuses the application then it will give such directions for the preparation and signature of an indictment as may be appropriate.

Multiple offending: count charging more than one incident

IV.34.8 Rule 14.2(2) of the Criminal Procedure Rules allows a single count to allege more than one incident of the commission of an offence in certain circumstances. Each incident must be of the same offence. The circumstances in which such a count may be appropriate include, but are not limited to, the following:

(a) the victim on each occasion was the same, or there was no identifiable individual victim as, for example, in a case of the unlawful importation of controlled drugs or of money laundering;
(b) the alleged incidents involved a marked degree of repetition in the method employed or in their location, or both;
(c) the alleged incidents took place over a clearly defined period, typically (but not necessarily) no more than about a year;
(d) in any event, the defence is such as to apply to every alleged incident without differentiation. Where what is in issue differs between different incidents, a single 'multiple incidents' count will not be appropriate, though it may be appropriate to use two or more such counts according to the circumstances and to the issues raised by the defence.

IV.34.9 Even in circumstances such as those set out in paragraph IV.34.8, there may be occasions on which a prosecutor chooses not to use such a count, in order to bring the case within section 75(3)(a) of the Proceeds of Crime Act 2002 (criminal lifestyle established by conviction of three or more offences in the same proceedings) for example, because section 75(2)(c) of that Act does not apply (criminal lifestyle established by an offence committed over a period of at least six months). Where the prosecutor proposes such a course it is unlikely that part 1 of the Criminal Procedure Rules (the overriding objective) will require an indictment to contain a single 'multiple incidents' count in place of a larger number of counts, subject to the general principles set out in paragraph IV.34.3.

IV.34.10 For some offences, particularly sexual offences, the penalty for the offence may have changed during the period over which the alleged incidents took place. In such a case, additional 'multiple incidents' counts should be used so that each count only alleges incidents to which the same maximum penalty applies.

IV.34.11 In some cases, such as money laundering or theft, there will be documented evidence of individual incidents but the sheer number of these will make it desirable to cover them in a single count. Where the indictment contains a count alleging multiple incidents of the commission of such offences, and during the course of the trial it becomes clear that the jury may bring in a verdict in relation to a lesser amount than that alleged by the prosecution, it will normally be desirable to direct the jury that they should return a partial verdict with reference to that lesser amount.

IV.34.12 In other cases, such as sexual or physical abuse, a complainant may be in a position only to give evidence of a series of similar incidents without being able to specify when or the precise circumstances in which they occurred. In these cases, a 'multiple incidents' count may be desirable. If on the other hand, the complainant is able to identify particular incidents of the offence by reference to a date or other specific event, but alleges that in addition there were other incidents which the complainant is unable to specify, then it may be desirable to include separate counts for the identified incidents and a 'multiple incidents' count or counts alleging that incidents of the same offence occurred 'many' times. Using a 'multiple incidents' count may be an appropriate alternative to using 'specimen' counts in some cases where repeated sexual or physical abuse is alleged. The choice of count will depend on the particular circumstances of the case and should be determined bearing in mind the implications for sentencing set out in *R v Canavan; R v Kidd; R v Shaw* [1998] 1 Cr App R 79.

IV.35. Voluntary bills of indictment

IV.35.1 Section 2(2)(b) of the Administration of Justice (Miscellaneous Provisions) Act 1933 allows the preferment of a bill of indictment by the direction or with the consent of a judge of the High Court. Bills so preferred are known as voluntary bills.

IV.35.2 Applications for such consent must not only comply with each paragraph of the Indictments (Procedure) Rules 1971, SI 1971/2084, but must also be accompanied by:

(a) a copy of any charges on which the defendant has been committed for trial;
(b) a copy of any charges on which his committal for trial was refused by the magistrates' court;
(c) a copy of any existing indictment which has been preferred in consequence of his committal;
(d) a summary of the evidence or other document which (i) identifies the counts in the proposed indictment on which he has been committed for trial (or which are substantially the same as charges on which he has been so committed), and (ii) in relation to each other count in the proposed indictment, identifies the pages in the accompanying statements and exhibits where the essential evidence said to support that count is to be found;
(e) marginal markings of the relevant passages on the pages of the statements and exhibits identified under (d)(ii).

These requirements should be complied with in relation to each defendant named in the indictment for which consent is sought, whether or not it is proposed to prefer any new count against him.

IV.35.3 The preferment of a voluntary bill is an exceptional procedure. Consent should only be granted where good reason to depart from the normal procedure is clearly shown and only where the interests of justice, rather than considerations of administrative convenience, require it.

IV.35.4 Neither the 1933 Act nor the 1971 Rules expressly require a prosecuting authority applying for consent to the preferment of a voluntary bill to give notice of the application to the prospective defendant or to serve on him a copy of documents delivered to the judge; nor is it expressly required that the prospective defendant have any opportunity to make any submissions to the judge, whether in writing or orally.

IV.35.5 The prosecuting authorities for England and Wales have issued revised guidance to prosecutors on the procedures to be adopted in seeking judicial consent to the preferment of voluntary bills. These procedures direct prosecutors:

(a) on the making of application for consent to preferment of a voluntary bill, forthwith to give notice to the prospective defendant that such application has been made;
(b) at about the same time, to serve on the prospective defendant a copy of all the documents delivered to the judge (save to the extent that these have already been served on him);
(c) to inform the prospective defendant that he may make submissions in writing to the judge, provided that he does so within nine working days of the giving of notice under (a) above. Prosecutors will be directed that these procedures should be followed unless there are good grounds for not doing so, in which case prosecutors will inform the judge that the procedures have not been followed and seek his leave to dispense with all or any of them. Judges should not give leave to dispense unless good grounds are shown.

IV.35.6 A judge to whom application for consent to the preferment of a voluntary bill is made will, of course, wish to consider carefully the documents submitted by the prosecutor and any written submissions timeously made by the prospective defendant, and may properly seek any necessary amplification. The judge may invite oral submissions from either party, or accede to a request for an opportunity to make such oral submissions, if the judge considers it necessary or desirable to receive such oral submissions in order to make a sound and fair decision on the application. Any such oral submissions should be made on notice to the other party, who should be allowed to attend.

IV.36. Abuse of process stay applications

IV.36.1 In all cases where a defendant in the Crown Court proposes to make an application to stay an indictment on the grounds of abuse of process, written notice of such application must be given to the prosecuting authority and to any co-defendant not later than 14 days before the date fixed or warned for trial ('the relevant date'). Such notice must:

(a) give the name of the case and the indictment number;
(b) state the fixed date or the warned date as appropriate;
(c) specify the nature of the application;
(d) set out in numbered sub-paragraphs the grounds upon which the application is to be made;
(e) be copied to the chief listing officer at the court centre where the case is due to be heard.

IV.36.2 Any co-defendant who wishes to make a like application must give a like notice not later than seven days before the relevant date, setting out any additional grounds relied upon.

IV.36.3 In relation to such applications, the following automatic directions shall apply:

(a) the advocate for the applicant(s) must lodge with the court and serve on all other parties a skeleton argument in support of the application at least five clear working days before the relevant date. If reference is to be made to any document not in the existing trial documents, a paginated and indexed bundle of such documents is to be provided with the skeleton argument;
(b) the advocate for the prosecution must lodge with the court and serve on all other parties a responsive skeleton argument at least two clear working days before the relevant date, together with a supplementary bundle if appropriate.

IV.36.4 All skeleton arguments must specify any propositions of law to be advanced (together with the authorities relied upon in support, with page references to passages relied upon) and, where appropriate, include a chronology of events and a list of dramatis personae. In all instances where reference is made to a document, the reference in the trial documents or supplementary bundle is to be given.

IV.36.5 The above time limits are minimum time limits. In appropriate cases the court will order longer lead times. To this end in all cases where defence advocates are, at the time of the plea and directions hearing, considering the possibility of an abuse of process application, this must be raised with the judge dealing with the matter, who will order a different timetable if appropriate, and may wish, in any event, to give additional directions about the conduct of the application.

IV.37. Citation of Hansard

IV.37.1 Where any party intends to refer to the reports of Parliamentary proceedings as reported in the Official Reports of either House of Parliament ('Hansard') in support of any such argument as is permitted by the decisions in *Pepper* v *Hart* [1993] AC 593 and *Pickstone* v *Freeman* [1989] AC 66 or otherwise must, unless the court otherwise directs, serve upon all other parties and the court copies of any such extract together with a brief summary of the argument intended to be based upon such extract. No other report of Parliamentary proceedings may be cited.

IV.37.2 Unless the court otherwise directs, service of the extract and summary of the argument shall be effected not less than 5 clear working days before the first day of the hearing, whether or not it has a fixed date. Advocates must keep themselves informed as to the state of the lists where no fixed date has been given. Service on the court shall be effected by sending three copies to the chief clerk of the relevant Crown Court centre. If any party fails to do so the court may make such order (relating to costs or otherwise) as is in all the circumstances appropriate.

IV.38. Applications for representation orders

IV.38.1 Applications for representation by a Queen's Counsel alone or by more than one advocate under Part IV of the Criminal Defence Service (General) (No 2) Regulations 2001 SI 2001/1437 made to the Crown Court shall be placed before the Resident Judge of that Crown Court (or, in his absence, a judge nominated for that purpose by a Presiding Judge of the circuit) who shall determine the application, save that, where the application relates to a case which is to be heard before a named High Court judge or a named Circuit Judge, he should refer the application to the named judge for determination.

IV.38.2 This does not apply where an application is made in the course of a trial or of a preliminary hearing, pre-trial review, or plea and directions hearing by the judge presiding at that trial or hearing.

IV.38.3 In the event of any doubt as to the proper application of this direction, reference shall be made by the judge concerned to a Presiding Judge of the circuit, who shall give such directions as he thinks fit.

IV.39. Trial of children and young persons

IV.39.1 This direction applies to trials of children and young persons in the Crown Court. In it children and young persons are together called 'young defendants'.

IV.39.2 The steps which should be taken to comply with paragraphs IV.39.3 to IV.39.17 should be judged, in any given case, taking account of the age, maturity and development (intellectual and emotional) of the young defendant on trial and all other circumstances of the case.

The overriding principle

IV.39.3 Some young defendants accused of committing serious crimes may be very young and very immature when standing trial in the Crown Court. The purpose of such trial is to determine guilt (if that is in issue) and decide the appropriate sentence if the young defendant pleads guilty or is convicted. The trial process should not itself expose the young defendant to avoidable intimidation, humiliation or distress. All possible steps should be taken to assist the young defendant to understand and participate in the proceedings. The ordinary trial process should, so far as necessary, be adapted to meet those ends. Regard should be had to the welfare of the young defendant as required by section 44 of the Children and Young Persons Act 1933.

Before trial

IV.39.4 If a young defendant is indicted jointly with an adult defendant, the court should consider at the plea and directions hearing whether the young defendant should be tried on his own and should ordinarily so order unless of opinion that a joint trial would be in the interests of justice and would not be unduly prejudicial to the welfare of the young defendant. If a young defendant is tried jointly with an adult the ordinary procedures will apply subject to such modifications (if any) as the court may see fit to order.

IV.39.5 At the plea and directions hearing before trial of a young defendant, the court should consider and so far as practicable give directions on the matters covered in paragraphs IV.39.9–IV.39.15.

IV.39.6 It may be appropriate to arrange that a young defendant should visit, out of court hours and before the trial, the courtroom in which the trial is to be held so that he can familiarise himself with it.

IV.39.7 If any case against a young defendant has attracted or may attract widespread public or media interest, the assistance of the police should be enlisted to try and ensure that a young defendant is not, when attending for the trial, exposed to intimidation, vilification or abuse.

IV.39.8 The court should be ready at this stage (if it has not already done so) to give a direction under section 39 of the 1933 Act or, as the case may be, section 45 of the Youth Justice and Criminal Evidence Act 1999. Any such order, once made, should be reduced to writing and copies should on request be made available to anyone affected or potentially affected by it.

The trial

IV.39.9 The trial should, if practicable, be held in a courtroom in which all the participants are on the same or almost the same level.

IV.39.10 A young defendant should normally, if he wishes, be free to sit with members of his family or others in a like relationship and in a place which permits easy, informal communication with his legal representatives and others with whom he wants or needs to communicate.

IV.39.11 The court should explain the course of proceedings to a young defendant in terms he can understand, should remind those representing a young defendant of their continuing duty to explain each step of the trial to him and should ensure, so far as practicable, that the trial is conducted in language which the young defendant can understand.

IV.39.12 The trial should be conducted according to a timetable which takes full account of a young defendant's inability to concentrate for long periods. Frequent and regular breaks will often be appropriate.

IV.39.13 Robes and wigs should not be worn unless the young defendant asks that they should or the court for good reason orders that they should. Any person responsible for the security of a young defendant who is in custody should not be in uniform. There should be no recognisable police presence in the courtroom save for good reason.

IV.39.14 The court should be prepared to restrict attendance at the trial to a small number, perhaps limited to some of those with an immediate and direct interest in the outcome of the trial. The court should rule on any challenged claim to attend.

IV.39.15 Facilities for reporting the trial (subject to any direction given under section 39 of the 1933 Act or section 45 of the 1999 Act) must be provided. But the court may restrict the number of those attending in the courtroom to report the trial to such number as is judged practicable and desirable. In ruling on any challenged claim to attend the courtroom for the purpose of reporting the trial the court should be mindful of the public's general right to be informed about the administration of justice in the Crown Court. Where access to the courtroom by reporters is restricted, arrangements should be made for the proceedings to be relayed, audibly and if possible visually, to another room in the same court complex to which the media have free access if it appears that there will be a need for such additional facilities.

IV.39.16 Where the court is called upon to exercise its discretion in relation to any procedural matter falling within the scope of this Practice Direction but not the subject of specific reference, such discretion should be exercised having regard to the principles in paragraph IV.39.3.

Appeal and committals for sentence

IV.39.17 This practice direction does not in terms apply to appeals and committals for sentence, but regard should be paid to the effect of it if the arrangements for hearing any appeal or committal might otherwise be prejudicial to the welfare of a young defendant.

IV.40. Video recorded evidence in chief

IV.40.1 The procedure for making application for leave to adduce a video recording of testimony from a witness under section 27 of the Youth Justice and Criminal Evidence Act 1999 is laid down in rule [29.7 of the Criminal Procedure Rules].

IV.40.2 Where a court, on application by a party to the proceedings or of its own motion, grants leave to admit a video recording in evidence under section 27(1) of the 1999 Act it may direct that any part of the recording be excluded (section 27(2) and (3)). When such direction is given, the party who made application to admit the video recording must edit the recording in accordance with the judge's directions and send a copy of the edited recording to the appropriate officer of the Crown Court and to every other party to the proceedings.

IV.40.3 Where a video recording is to be adduced during proceedings before the Crown Court, it should be produced and proved by the interviewer, or any other person who was present at the interview with the witness at which the recording was made. The applicant should ensure that such a person will be available for this purpose, unless the parties have agreed to accept a written statement in lieu of attendance by that person.

IV.40.4 Once a trial has begun if, by reason of faulty or inadequate preparation or for some other cause, the procedures set out above have not been properly complied with and an application is made to edit the video recording, thereby making necessary an adjournment for the work to be carried out, the court may make at its discretion an appropriate award of costs.

IV.41. Management of cases to be heard in the Crown Court

IV.41.1 This section of the practice direction supplements the rules in part 3 of the Criminal Procedure Rules as they apply to the management of cases to be heard in the Crown Court. Where time limits or other directions in the Consolidated Criminal Practice Direction appear inconsistent with this section, the directions in this section take precedence.

IV.41.2 The case details form set out in annex E should be completed by the Crown Court case progression officer in all cases to be tried on indictment.

Cases sent for trial

IV.41.3 A preliminary hearing ('PH') is not required in every case sent for trial under section 51 of the Crime and Disorder Act 1998: see rule 12.2 (which altered the Crown Court rule from which it derived). A PH should normally only be ordered by the magistrates' court or by the Crown Court where:

(i) there are case management issues which call for such a hearing;
(ii) the case is likely to last for more than 4 weeks;
(iii) it would be desirable to set an early trial date;
(iv) the defendant is a child or young person;
(v) there is likely to be a guilty plea and the defendant could be sentenced at the preliminary hearing; or
(vi) it seems to the court that it is a case suitable for a preparatory hearing in the Crown Court (see sections 7 and 9 of the Criminal Justice Act 1987 and sections 29–32 of the Criminal Procedure and Investigations Act 1996).

A PH, if there is one, should be held about 14 days after sending.

IV.41.4 The case progression form to be used in the magistrates' court and the PH form to be used in the Crown Court are set out in annex E with guidance notes. The forms provide a detailed timetable to enable the subsequent plea and case management hearing ('PCMH') to be effective.

IV.41.5 Where the magistrates' court does not order a PH it should order a PCMH to be held within about 14 weeks after sending for trial where a defendant is in custody and within about 17 weeks after sending for trial where a defendant is on bail. Those periods accommodate the periods fixed by the relevant rules for the service of the prosecution case papers and for making all potential preparatory applications. Where the parties realistically expect to have completed their preparation for the PCMH in less time than that then the magistrates' court should order it to be held earlier. But it will not normally be appropriate to order that the PCMH be held on a date before the expiry of at least 4 weeks from the date on which the prosecutor expects to serve the prosecution case papers, to allow the defence a proper opportunity to consider them. To order that a PCMH be held before the parties have had a reasonable opportunity to complete their preparation in accordance with the Criminal Procedure Rules risks compromising the effectiveness of this most important pre-trial hearing and risks wasting their time and that of the court.

Cases committed for trial

IV.41.6 For cases committed to the Crown Court for trial under section 6 of the Magistrates' Courts Act 1980 the case progression form to be used in the magistrates' court is set out in annex E with guidance notes. A PCMH should be ordered by the magistrates' court in every case, to be held within about 7 weeks after committal. That period accommodates the periods fixed by the relevant rules for making all potential preparatory applications. Where the parties realistically expect to have completed their preparation for the PCMH in less time than that then the magistrates' court should order it to be held earlier. However, to order that a PCMH be held before the parties have had a reasonable opportunity to complete their preparation in accordance with the Criminal Procedure Rules risks compromising the effectiveness of this most important pre-trial hearing and risks wasting their time and that of the court.

Cases transferred for trial

IV.41.7 In a case transferred to the Crown Court for trial under section 4(1) of the Criminal Justice Act 1987 or under section 53(1) of the Criminal Justice Act 1991 the directions contained in the case progression form used in cases for committal for trial apply as if the case had been committed on the date of the notice of transfer. A PCMH should be listed by the Crown Court to be held within about 7 weeks after transfer. That period accommodates the periods fixed by the relevant rules for making all potential preparatory applications. Where the parties realistically expect to have completed their preparation for the PCMH in less time than that then the magistrates' court should order it to be held earlier. However, to order that a PCMH be held before the parties have had a reasonable opportunity to complete their preparation in accordance with the Criminal Procedure Rules risks compromising the effectiveness of this most important pre-trial hearing and risks wasting their time and that of the court.

Plea and case management hearing

IV.41.8 Active case management at the PCMH is essential to reduce the number of ineffective and cracked trials and delays during the trial to resolve legal issues. The effectiveness of a PCMH hearing in a contested case depends in large measure upon preparation by all concerned and upon the presence of the trial advocate or an advocate who is able to make decisions and give the court the assistance which the trial advocate could be expected to give. Resident Judges in setting the listing policy should ensure that list officers fix cases as far as possible to enable the trial advocate to conduct the PCMH and the trial.

IV.41.9 In Class 1 and Class 2 cases, and in all cases involving a serious sexual offence against a child, the PCMH must be conducted by a High Court judge; by a circuit judge or by a recorder to whom the case has been assigned in accordance with paragraph IV.33 (allocation of business within the Crown Court); or by a judge authorised by the Presiding Judges to conduct such hearings. In the event of a guilty plea before such an authorised judge, the case will be adjourned for sentencing by a High Court judge or by a circuit judge or recorder to whom the case has been assigned.

Use of the PCMH form

IV.41.10 The PCMH form as set out in annex E must be used in accordance with the guidance notes.

Further pre-trial hearings after the PCMH

IV.41.11 Additional pre-trial hearings should be held only if needed for some compelling reason. Such hearings — often described informally as 'mentions' — are expensive and should actively be discouraged. Where necessary the power to give, vary or revoke a direction without a hearing should be used. Rule 3.9(3) of the Criminal Procedure Rules enables the Court to require the parties' case progression officers to inform the Crown Court case progression officer that the case is ready for trial, that it will proceed as a trial on the date fixed and will take no more or less time than that previously ordered.

IV.42. Juries

Jury service

IV.42.1 The effect of section 321 Criminal Justice Act 2003 was to remove certain categories of persons from those previously ineligible for jury service (the judiciary and others concerned with the administration of justice) and certain other categories ceased to be eligible for excusal as of right, (such as members of Parliament and medical professionals). Jury service is an important public duty which individual members of the public are chosen at random to undertake. The normal presumption is that everyone, unless mentally disordered or disqualified, will be required to serve when summoned to do so. This legislative change has, however, meant an increase in the number of jurors with professional and public service commitments. One of the results of this change is that trial judges must continue to be alert to the need to exercise their discretion to adjourn a trial, excuse or discharge a juror should the need arise. Whether or not an application has already been made to the jury summoning officer for deferral or excusal it is also open to the person summoned to apply to the court to be excused. Such applications must be considered with common sense and according to the interests of justice. An explanation should be required for an application being much later than necessary.

IV.42.2 Where a juror appears on a jury panel, it may be appropriate for a judge to excuse the juror from that particular case where the potential juror is personally concerned with the facts of the particular case or is closely connected with a prospective witness. Where the length of the trial is estimated to be significantly longer than the normal period of jury service, it is good practice for the trial judge to enquire whether the potential jurors on the jury panel foresee any difficulties with the length and if the judge is satisfied that the jurors concerns are justified he may say that they are not required for that particular jury. This does not mean that the judge must excuse the juror from sitting at that court altogether as it may well be possible for the juror to sit on a shorter trial at the same court.

IV.42.3 Where a juror unexpectedly finds him or herself in difficult professional or personal circumstances during the course of the trial, jurors should be encouraged to raise such problems with the trial judge. This might apply, for example, to a parent whose childcare arrangements unexpectedly fail or a worker who is engaged in the provision of services the need for which can be critical or Member of Parliament who has deferred their jury service to an apparently more convenient time, but is unexpectedly called back to work for a very important reason. Such difficulties would normally be raised through a jury note in the normal manner. In such circumstances, the judge must exercise his or her discretion according to the interests of justice and the requirements of each individual case. The judge must decide for himself whether the juror has presented a sufficient reason to interfere with the course of the trial. If the juror has presented a sufficient reason, in longer trials it may well be possible to adjourn for a short period in order to allow the juror to overcome the difficulty. In shorter cases it may be more appropriate to discharge the juror and to continue the trial with a reduced number of jurors. The power to do this is implicit in section 16(1) Juries Act 1974. In unusual cases (such as an unexpected emergency arising over night) a juror need not be discharged in open court. The good administration of justice depends on the cooperation of jurors who perform an essential public service. All such applications should be dealt with sensitively and sympathetically and the trial judge should always seek to meet the interests of justice without unduly inconveniencing any juror.

Jury oath

IV.42.4 The wording of the oath to be taken by jurors is: 'I swear by Almighty God that I will faithfully try the defendant and give a true verdict according to the evidence.' Any person who objects to being sworn shall be permitted to make his solemn affirmation instead. The wording of the affirmation is 'I do solemnly, sincerely and truly declare and affirm that I will faithfully try the defendant and give a true verdict according to the evidence.'

Guidance to jurors

IV.42.5 The following directions take effect immediately.

IV.42.6 Trial judges should ensure that the jury is alerted to the need to bring any concerns about fellow jurors to the attention of the judge at the time, and not to wait until the case is concluded. At the same time, it is undesirable to encourage inappropriate criticism of fellow jurors, or to threaten jurors with contempt of court.

IV.42.7 Judges should therefore take the opportunity, when warning the jury of the importance of not discussing the case with anyone outside the jury, to add a further warning. It is for the trial judge to tailor the further warning to the case, and to the phraseology used in the usual warning. The effect of the further warning should be that it is the duty of jurors to bring to the judge's attention, promptly, any behaviour among the jurors or by others affecting the jurors, that causes concern. The point should be made that, unless that is done while the case is continuing, it may be impossible to put matters right.

IV.42.8 The Judge should consider, particularly in a longer trial, whether a reminder on the lines of the further warning is appropriate prior to the retirement of the jury.

IV.42.9 In the event that such an incident does occur, trial judges should have regard to the remarks of Lord Hope at paras 127 and 128 in *R* v *Connors and Mirza* [2004] 2 WLR 201 and consider the desirability of preparing a statement that could be used in connection with any appeal arising from the incident to the Court of Appeal Criminal Division. Members of the Court of Appeal Criminal Division should also remind themselves of the power to request the judge to furnish them with any information or assistance under rule [68.23(1) of the Criminal Procedure Rules 2005] and section 87(4) of the Supreme Court Act 1981.

IV.43. Evidence of tape recorded interviews

IV.43.1 Where a suspect is to be interviewed by the police, the Code of Practice on Tape Recording of Interviews with Suspects effective from 10th April 1995 and issued under section 60 of the Police and Criminal Evidence Act 1984 applies. Where a record of the interview is to be prepared this should be in accordance with the national guidelines approved by the Secretary of State, as envisaged by Note E:5A of the Code.

IV.43.2 Where the prosecution intends to adduce evidence of the interview in evidence, and agreement between the parties has not been reached about the record, sufficient notice must be given to allow consideration of any amendment to the record or the preparation of any transcript of the interview or any editing of a tape for the purpose of playing it back in court. To that end, the following practice should be followed.

(a) Where the defence is unable to agree a record of interview or transcript (where one is already available) the prosecution should be notified no more than 21 days from the date of committal or date of transfer, or at the PDH if earlier, with a view to securing agreement to amend. The notice should specify the part to which objection is taken or the part omitted which the defence consider should be included. A copy of the notice should be supplied to the court within the period specified above.

(b) If agreement is not reached and it is proposed that the tape or part of it be played in court, notice should be given to the prosecution by the defence no more than 14 days after the expiry of the period in (a), or as ordered at the PDH, in order that counsel for the parties may agree those parts of the tape that should not be adduced and that arrangements may be made, by editing or in some other way, to exclude that material. A copy of the notice should be supplied to the court within the period specified above.

(c) Notice of any agreement reached under (a) or (b) should be supplied to the court by the prosecution as soon as is practicable.

(d) Alternatively, if, in any event, prosecuting counsel proposes to play the tape or part of it, the prosecution should, within 28 days of the date of committal or date of transfer or, if earlier, at the PDH, notify the defence and the court. The defence should notify the prosecution and the court within 14 days of receiving the notice if they object to the production of the tape on the basis that a part of it should be excluded. If the objections raised by the defence are accepted, the prosecution should prepare an edited tape or make other arrangements to exclude the material part and should notify the court of the arrangements made.

(e) Whenever editing or amendment of a record of interview or of a tape or of a transcript takes place, the following general principles should be followed:

  (i) Where a defendant has made a statement which includes an admission of one or more other offences, the portion relating to other offences should be omitted unless it is or becomes admissible in evidence;

  (ii) Where the statement of one defendant contains a portion which is partly in his favour and partly implicatory of a co-defendant in the trial, the defendant making the statement has the right to insist that everything relevant which is in his favour goes before the jury.

In such a case the judge must be consulted about how best to protect the position of the co-defendant.

IV.43.3 If there is a failure to agree between counsel under paragraph IV.43.2(a) to (e), or there is a challenge to the integrity of the master tape, notice and particulars should be given to the court and to the prosecution by the defence as soon as is practicable. The court may then, at its discretion, order a pretrial review or give such other directions as may be appropriate.

IV.43.4 If a tape is to be adduced during proceedings before the Crown Court it should be produced and proved by the interviewing officer or any other officer who was present at the interview at which the recording was made. The prosecution should ensure that such an officer will be available for this purpose.

IV.43.5 Where such an officer is unable to act as the tape machine operator it is for the prosecution to make some other arrangement.

IV.43.6 In order to avoid the necessity for the court to listen to lengthy or irrelevant material before the relevant part of a tape recording is reached, counsel shall indicate to the tape machine operator those parts of a recording which it may be necessary to play. Such an indication should, so far as possible, be expressed in terms of the time track or other identifying process used by the interviewing police force and should be given in time for the operator to have located those parts by the appropriate point in the trial.

IV.43.7 Once a trial has begun, if, by reason of faulty preparation or for some other cause, the procedures above have not been properly complied with, and an application is made to amend the record of interview or transcript or to edit the tape, as the case may be, thereby making necessary an adjournment for the work to be carried out, the court may make at its discretion an appropriate award of costs.

IV.43.8 Where a case is listed for hearing on a date which falls within the time limits set out above, it is the responsibility of the parties to ensure that all the necessary steps are taken to comply with this Practice Direction within such shorter period as is available.

IV.43.9 In paragraph IV.43.2(a) and (d), 'date of transfer' is the date on which notice of transfer is given in accordance with the provisions of section 4(1)(c) of the Criminal Justice Act 1987.

IV.43.10 This direction should be read in conjunction with the Code of Practice on Tape Recording referred to in paragraph IV.43.1 and with Home Office Circular 26/1995.

IV.44. Defendant's right to give or not to give evidence

IV.44.1 At the conclusion of the evidence for the prosecution, section 35(2) of the Criminal Justice and Public Order Act 1994 requires the court to satisfy itself that the accused is aware that the stage has been reached at which evidence can be given for the defence and that he can, if he wishes, give evidence and that, if he chooses not to give evidence, or having been sworn, without good cause refuses to answer any question, it will be permissible for the jury to draw such inferences as appear proper from his failure to give evidence or his refusal, without good cause, to answer any question.

If the accused is legally represented

IV.44.2 Section 35(1) provides that section 35(2) does not apply if at the conclusion of the evidence for the prosecution the accused's legal representative informs the court that the accused will give evidence. This should be done in the presence of the jury. If the representative indicates that the accused will give evidence the case should proceed in the usual way.

IV.44.3 If the court is not so informed, or if the court is informed that the accused does not intend to give evidence, the judge should in the presence of the jury inquire of the representative in these terms: 'Have you advised your client that the stage has now been reached at which he may give evidence and, if he chooses not to do so or, having been sworn, without good cause refuses to answer any question, the jury may draw such inferences as appear proper from his failure to do so ?'

IV.44.4 If the representative replies to the judge that the accused has been so advised, then the case shall proceed. If counsel replies that the accused has not been so advised, then the judge shall direct the representative to advise his client of the consequences set out in paragraph IV.44.3 and should adjourn briefly for this purpose before proceeding further.

If the accused is not legally represented

IV.44.5 If the accused is not represented, the judge shall at the conclusion of the evidence for the prosecution and in the presence of the jury say to the accused:

'You have heard the evidence against you. Now is the time for you to make your defence. You may give evidence on oath, and be cross-examined like any other witness. If you do not give evidence or, having been sworn, without good cause refuse to answer any question the jury may draw such inferences as appear proper. That means they may hold it against you. You may also call any witness or witnesses whom you have arranged to attend court. Afterwards you may also, if you wish, address the jury by arguing your case from the dock. But you cannot at that stage give evidence. Do you now intend to give evidence?'

IV.45. Discussions about sentence

IV.45.1 An advocate must be free to do what is his duty, namely to give the accused the best advice he can and, if need be, in strong terms. It will often include advice that a guilty plea, showing an element of remorse, is a mitigating factor which may well enable the court to give a lesser sentence than would otherwise be the case. The advocate will, of course, emphasise that the accused must not plead guilty unless he has committed the acts constituting the offence(s) charged.

IV.45.2 The accused, having considered the advocate's advice, must have complete freedom of choice whether to plead guilty or not guilty.

IV.45.3 There must be freedom of access between advocate and judge. Any discussion must, however, be between the judge and the advocates on both sides. If counsel is instructed by a solicitor who is in court, he too should be allowed to attend the discussion. This freedom of access is important because there may be matters calling for communication or discussion of such a nature that the advocate cannot, in his client's interest, mention them in open court, e.g. the advocate, by way of mitigation, may wish to tell the judge that the accused has not long to live because he is suffering may be from cancer of which he is and should remain ignorant. Again, the advocates on both sides may wish to discuss with the judge whether it would be proper, in a particular case, for the prosecution to accept a plea to a lesser offence. It is imperative that, so far as possible, justice must be administered in open court. Advocates should, therefore, only ask to see the judge when it is felt to be really necessary. The judge must be careful only to treat such communications as private where, in fairness to the accused, this is necessary.

IV.45.4 The judge should, subject to one exception, never indicate the sentence he is minded to impose. The exception is that it should be permissible for a judge to say, if it be the case, that, whatever happens, whether the accused pleads guilty or not guilty, the sentence will or will not take a particular form. Where any such discussion on sentence has taken place, the advocate for the defence should disclose it to the accused and, subject to the exception of those matters of which he should remain ignorant, such as cancer, of which he is unaware, inform him of what took place.

IV.45.5 Where any such discussion takes place it should be recorded either by a tape recorder or a shorthand writer.

IV.46. Majority verdicts

IV.46.1 It is important that all those trying indictable offences should so far as possible adopt a uniform practice when complying with section 17 of the Juries Act 1974, both in directing the jury in summing-up and also in receiving the verdict or giving further directions after retirement. So far as the summing-up is concerned, it is inadvisable for the judge, and indeed for advocates, to attempt an explanation of the section for fear that the jury will be confused. Before the jury retire, however, the judge should direct the jury in some such words as the following:

'As you may know, the law permits me, in certain circumstances, to accept a verdict which is not the verdict of you all. Those circumstances have not as yet arisen, so that when you retire I must ask you to reach a verdict upon which each one of you is agreed. Should, however, the time come when it is possible for me to accept a majority verdict, I will give you a further direction.'

IV.46.2 Thereafter the practice should be as follows: Should the jury return *before* two hours and ten minutes since the last member of the jury left the jury box to go to the jury room (or such longer time as the judge thinks reasonable) has elapsed (see section 17(4)), they should be asked: (a) 'Have you reached a verdict upon which you are all agreed? Please answer Yes or No'; (b) (i) If unanimous, 'What is your verdict?'; (ii) If not unanimous, the jury should be sent out again for further deliberation with a further direction to arrive if possible at an unanimous verdict.

IV.46.3 Should the jury return (whether for the first time or subsequently) or be sent for *after* the two hours and ten minutes (or the longer period) has elapsed, questions (a) and (b)(i) in paragraph IV.46.2 should be put to them and, if it appears that they are not unanimous, they should be asked to retire once more and told that they should continue to endeavour to reach an unanimous verdict but that, if they cannot, the judge will accept a majority verdict as in section 17(1).

IV.46.4 When the jury finally return they should be asked: (a) 'Have at least ten (or nine as the case may be) of you agreed on your verdict?'; (b) If 'Yes', 'What is your verdict? Please only answer Guilty or

Not Guilty'; (c) (i) If 'Not Guilty', accept the verdict without more ado; (ii) If 'Guilty', 'Is that the verdict of you all or by a majority?'; (d) If 'Guilty' by a majority, 'How many of you agreed to the verdict and how many dissented?'

IV.46.5 At whatever stage the jury return, before question (a) is asked, the senior officer of the court present shall state in open court, for each period when the jury was out of court for the purpose of considering their verdict(s), the time at which the last member of the jury left the jury box to go to the jury room and the time of their return to the jury box and will additionally state in open court the total of such periods.

IV.46.6 The reason why section 17(3) is confined to a majority verdict of guilty and for the somewhat complicated procedure set out in paragraph IV.46.3 and paragraph IV.46.4 is to prevent it being known that a verdict of 'Not Guilty' is a majority verdict. If the final direction in paragraph IV.46.3 continues to require the jury to arrive, if possible, at an unanimous verdict and the verdict is received as in paragraph IV.46.4, it will not be known for certain that the acquittal is not unanimous.

IV.46.7 Where there are several counts (or alternative verdicts) left to the jury the above practice will, of course, need to be adapted to the circumstances. The procedure will have to be repeated in respect of each count (or alternative verdict), the verdict being accepted in those cases where the jury are unanimous and the further direction in paragraph IV.46.3 being given in cases in which they are not unanimous. Should the jury in the end be unable to agree on a verdict by the required majority (i.e. if the answer to the question in paragraph IV.46.4(a) be in the negative) the judge in his discretion will either ask them to deliberate further or discharge them.

IV.46.8 Section 17 will, of course, apply also to verdicts other than 'Guilty' or 'Not Guilty', e.g. to special verdicts under the Criminal Procedure (Insanity) Act 1964, verdicts under that Act as to fitness to be tried, and special verdicts on findings of fact. Accordingly in such cases the questions to jurors will have to be suitably adjusted.

IV.47. Imposition of discretionary life sentences

IV.47.1 Section 82A of the Powers of Criminal Courts (Sentencing) Act 2000 empowers a judge when passing a sentence of life imprisonment, where such a sentence is not fixed by law, to specify by order such part of the sentence ('the relevant part') as shall be served before the prisoner may require the Secretary of State to refer his case to the Parole Board.

IV.47.2 Thus the discretionary life sentence falls into two parts:

(a) the relevant part, which consists of the period of detention imposed for punishment and deterrence, taking into account the seriousness of the offence, and

(b) the remaining part of the sentence, during which the prisoner's detention will be governed by considerations of risk to the public.

IV.47.3 The judge is not obliged by statute to make use of the provisions of section 82A when passing a discretionary life sentence. However, the judge should do so, save in the very exceptional case where the judge considers that the offence is so serious that detention for life is justified by the seriousness of the offence alone, irrespective of the risk to the public. In such a case, the judge should state this in open court when passing sentence.

IV.47.4 In cases where the judge is to specify the relevant part of the sentence under section 82A, the judge should permit the advocate for the defendant to address the court as to the appropriate length of the relevant part. Where no relevant part is to be specified, the advocate for the defendant should be permitted to address the court as to the appropriateness of this course of action.

IV.47.5 In specifying the relevant part of the sentence, the judge should have regard to the specific terms of section 82A and should indicate the reasons for reaching his decision as to the length of the relevant part.

IV.47.6 Whether or not the court orders that section 82A should apply, the judge shall not, following the imposition of a discretionary life sentence, make a written report to the Secretary of State through the Lord Chief Justice as was the practice until 8 February 1993.

NOTE: Reference should also be made to the section on life sentences below.

IV.48. Life sentences for juveniles convicted of murder

IV.48.1 When a person is convicted of a murder committed when under the age of 18 the determination of the minimum term (previously tariff) applicable to his sentence has since 30 November 2000 been set by the trial judge, as it was and is for adults subject to discretionary life sentences: see section 82A of the Powers of Criminal Courts (Sentencing) Act 2000.

IV.49. Life sentences

IV.49.1 This direction replaces amendment number 6 to the Consolidated Criminal Practice Direction handed down on 18 May 2004 (previously inserted at paragraphs IV.49.1 to IV.49.25 of the Consolidated Criminal Practice Direction). Its purpose is to give practical guidance as to the procedure for passing a mandatory life sentence under section 269 of and schedule 21 to the Criminal Justice Act 2003 ('the Act'). This direction also gives guidance as to the transitional arrangements under section 276 of and schedule 22 to the Criminal Justice Act 2003 ('the Act'). It clarifies the correct approach to looking at the practice of the Secretary of State prior to December 2002 for the purposes of schedule 22 to the Act, in the light of the judgment in *R* v *Sullivan, Gibbs, Elener and Elener* [2004] EWCA Crim. 1762 ('*Sullivan*').

IV.49.2 Section 269 of the Act came into force on 18 December 2003. Under section 269 all courts passing a mandatory life sentence must either announce in open court the minimum term the prisoner must serve before the Parole Board can consider release on licence under the provisions of section 28 of the Crime (Sentences) Act 1997 (as amended by section 275 of the Act) or announce that the seriousness of the offence is so exceptionally high that the early release provisions should not apply at all (a 'whole life order').

IV.49.3 In setting the minimum term the court must set the term it considers appropriate taking into account the seriousness of the offence. In considering the seriousness of the offence the court must have regard to the general principles set out in schedule 21 to the Act and any other guidelines issued by the Sentencing Guidelines Council which are relevant to the case and not incompatible with the provisions of schedule 21. Although it is necessary to have regard to the guidance, it is always permissible not to apply the guidance if a judge considers there are reasons for not following it. It is always necessary to have regard to the need to do justice in the particular case. However, if a court departs from any of the starting points given in schedule 21 the court is under a duty to state its reasons for doing so.

IV.49.4 The guidance states that, where the offender is 21 or over, the first step is to choose one of three starting points: 'whole life', 30 years or 15 years. Where the 15 year starting point has been chosen, judges should have in mind that this starting point encompasses a very broad range of murders. At para.35 of *Sullivan* the court found that it should not be assumed that Parliament intended to raise all minimum terms that would previously have had a lower starting point to 15 years.

IV.49.5 Where the offender was 21 or over at the time of the offence, and the court takes the view that the murder is so grave that the offender ought to spend the rest of his life in prison, the appropriate starting point is a 'whole life order'. The effect of such an order is that the early release provisions in section 28 of the Crime (Sentences) Act 1997 will not apply. Such an order should only be specified where the court considers that the seriousness of the offence (or the combination of the offence and one or more other offences associated with it) is exceptionally high. Paragraph 4(2) of schedule 21 to the Act sets out examples of cases where it would normally be appropriate to take the 'whole life order' as the appropriate starting point.

IV.49.6 Where the offender is aged 18 to 20 and commits a murder that is so serious that it would require a whole life order if committed by an offender aged 21 or over, the appropriate starting point will be 30 years.

IV.49.7 Where a case is not so serious as to require a 'whole life order' but where the seriousness of the offence is particularly high and the offender was aged 18 or over when he committed the offence, the appropriate starting point is 30 years. Paragraph 5(2) of schedule 21 to the Act sets out examples of cases where a 30 year starting point would normally be appropriate (if they do not require a 'whole life order').

IV.49.8 Where the offender was aged 18 or over when he committed the offence and the case does not fall within paragraph 4(1) or 5(1) of schedule 21 the appropriate starting point is 15 years.

IV.49.9 18 to 20 year olds are only the subject of the 30 year and 15 year starting points.

IV.49.10 The appropriate starting point when setting a sentence of detention during Her Majesty's pleasure for offenders aged under 18 when they committed the offence is always 12 years.

IV.49.11 The second step after choosing a starting point is to take account of any aggravating or mitigating factors which would justify a departure from the starting point. Additional aggravating factors (other than those specified in paragraphs 4(1) and 5(1)) are listed at paragraph 10 of schedule 21. Examples of mitigating factors are listed at paragraph 11 of schedule 21. Taking into account the aggravating and mitigating features the court may add to or subtract from the starting point to arrive at the appropriate punitive period.

IV.49.12 The third step is that the court should consider the effect of section 151(1) of the Powers of Criminal Courts (Sentencing) Act 2000 (or, when it is in force, section 143(2) of the Act) in relation to previous convictions and section 151(2) of the Powers of Criminal Courts (Sentencing) Act 2000 (or, when it is in force, section 143(3) of the Act) where the offence was committed whilst the offender was on bail. The court should also consider the effect of section 152 of the Powers of Criminal Courts (Sentencing) Act 2000 (or, when it is in force, section 144 of the Act) where the offender has pleaded guilty. The court should then take into account what credit the offender would have received for a remand in custody under section 240 of the Act, but for the fact that the mandatory sentence is one of life imprisonment. Where the offender has been remanded in custody in connection with the offence or a related offence, the court should have in mind that no credit will otherwise be given for this time when the prisoner is considered for early release. The appropriate time to take it into account is when setting the minimum term. The court should normally subtract the time for which the offender was remanded in custody in connection with the offence or a related offence from the punitive period it would otherwise impose in order to reach the minimum term.

IV.49.13 Following these calculations the court should have arrived at the appropriate minimum term to be announced in open court. As paragraph 9 of schedule 21 makes clear, the judge retains ultimate discretion and the court may arrive at any minimum term from any starting point. The minimum term is subject to appeal by the offender under section 271 of the Act and subject to review on a reference by the Attorney-General under section 272 of the Act.

Transitional arrangements for new sentences where the offence was committed before 18 December 2003

IV.49.14 Where the court is passing a sentence of mandatory life imprisonment for an offence committed before 18 December 2003, the court should take a fourth step in determining the minimum term in accordance with section 276 of and schedule 22 to the Act.

IV.49.15 The purpose of those provisions is to ensure that the sentence does not breach the principle of non-retroactivity by ensuring that a lower minimum term would not have been imposed for the offence when it was committed. Before setting the minimum term the court must check whether the proposed term is greater than that term which the Secretary of State would probably have notified under the practice followed by the Secretary of State before December 2002.

IV.49.16 The decision in *Sullivan, Gibbs, Elener and Elener* [2004] EWCA Crim. 1762 gives detailed guidance as to the correct approach to this practice and judges passing mandatory life sentences where the murder was committed prior to 18 December 2003 are well advised to read that judgment before proceeding.

IV.49.17 The practical result of that judgment is that, in sentences where the murder was committed before 31 May 2002, the best guide to what would have been the practice of the Secretary of State is the letter sent to judges by Lord Bingham CJ on 10th February 1997, the relevant parts of which are set out at paras. IV.49.18 to IV.49.21 below.

IV.49.18 The practice of Lord Bingham, as set out in his letter of 10 February 1997, was to take 14 years as the period actually to be served for the 'average', 'normal' or 'unexceptional' murder. Examples of factors he outlined as capable, in appropriate cases, of mitigating the normal penalty were:

1. Youth.
2. Age (where relevant to physical capacity on release or the likelihood of the defendant dying in prison).
3. Subnormality or mental abnormality.
4. Provocation (in a non-technical sense), or an excessive response to a personal threat.
5. The absence of an intention to kill.
6. Spontaneity and lack of premeditation (beyond that necessary to constitute the offence: e.g. a sudden response to family pressure or to prolonged and eventually insupportable stress).
7. Mercy killing.
8. A plea of guilty, or hard evidence of remorse or contrition.

IV.49.19 Lord Bingham then listed the following factors as likely to call for a sentence more severe than the norm:

1. Evidence of a planned, professional, revenge or contract killing.
2. The killing of a child or a very old or otherwise vulnerable victim.
3. Evidence of sadism, gratuitous violence, or sexual maltreatment, humiliation or degradation before the killing.
4. Killing for gain (in the course of burglary, robbery, blackmail, insurance fraud, etc.).
5. Multiple killings.
6. The killing of a witness or potential witness to defeat the ends of justice.
7. The killing of those doing their public duty (policemen, prison officers, postmasters, firemen, judges, etc.).

8. Terrorist or politically motivated killings.
9. The use of firearms or other dangerous weapons, whether carried for defensive or offensive reasons.
10. A substantial record of serious violence.
11. Macabre attempts to dismember or conceal the body.

IV.49.20 Lord Bingham further stated that the fact that a defendant was under the influence of drink or drugs at the time of the killing is so common he would be inclined to treat it as neutral. But in the not unfamiliar case in which a married couple, or two derelicts, or two homosexuals, inflamed by drink, indulge in a violent quarrel in which one dies, often against a background of longstanding drunken violence, then he would tend to recommend a term somewhat below the norm.

IV.49.21 Lord Bingham went on to say that given the intent necessary for proof of murder, the consequences of taking life and the understandable reaction of relatives of the deceased, a substantial term will almost always be called for, save perhaps in a truly venial case of mercy killing. While a recommendation of a punitive term longer than, say, 30 years will be very rare indeed, there should not be any upper limit. Some crimes will certainly call for terms very well in excess of the norm.

IV.49.22 For the purposes of sentences where the murder was committed after 31 May 2002 and before 18 December 2003, the judge should apply the Practice Statement handed down on 31 May 2002 reproduced at paras. 49.23 to 49.33 below.

IV.49.23 This Statement replaces the previous single normal tariff of 14 years by substituting a higher and a normal starting point of respectively 16 (comparable to 32 years) and 12 years (comparable to 24 years). These starting points have then to be increased or reduced because of aggravating or mitigating factors such as those referred to below. It is emphasised that they are no more than starting points.

The normal starting point of 12 years

IV.49.24 Cases falling within this starting point will normally involve the killing of an adult victim, arising from a quarrel or loss of temper between two people known to each other. It will not have the characteristics referred to in paragraph 49.26. Exceptionally, the starting point may be reduced because of the sort of circumstances described in the next paragraph.

IV.49.25 The normal starting point can be reduced because the murder is one where the offender's culpability is significantly reduced, for example, because:
(a) the case came close to the borderline between murder and manslaughter; or
(b) the offender suffered from mental disorder, or from a mental disability which lowered the degree of his criminal responsibility for the killing, although not affording a defence of diminished responsibility, or
(c) the offender was provoked (in a non-technical sense), such as by prolonged and eventually unsupportable stress; or
(d) the case involved an over reaction in self-defence; or
(e) the offence was a mercy killing.

These factors could justify a reduction to 8/9 years (equivalent to 16/18 years).

The higher starting point of 15/16 years

IV.49.26 The higher starting point will apply to cases where the offender's culpability was exceptionally high or the victim was in a particularly vulnerable position. Such cases will be characterised by a feature which makes the crime especially serious, such as:
(a) the killing was 'professional' or a contract killing;
(b) the killing was politically motivated;
(c) the killing was done for gain (in the course of a burglary, robbery etc.);
(d) the killing was intended to defeat the ends of justice (as in the killing of a witness or potential witness);
(e) the victim was providing a public service;
(f) the victim was a child or was otherwise vulnerable;
(g) the killing was racially aggravated;
(h) the victim was deliberately targeted because of his or her religion or sexual orientation;
(i) there was evidence of sadism, gratuitous violence or sexual maltreatment, humiliation or degradation of the victim before the killing;
(j) extensive and/or multiple injuries were inflicted on the victim before death;
(k) the offender committed multiple murders.

Variation of the starting point

IV.49.27 Whichever starting point is selected in a particular case, it may be appropriate for the trial judge to vary the starting point upwards or downwards, to take account of aggravating or mitigating factors, which relate to either the offence or the offender, in the particular case.

IV.49.28 Aggravating factors relating to the offence can include:
(a) the fact that the killing was planned;
(b) the use of a firearm;
(c) arming with a weapon in advance;
(d) concealment of the body, destruction of the crime scene and/or dismemberment of the body;
(e) particularly in domestic violence cases, the fact that the murder was the culmination of cruel and violent behaviour by the offender over a period of time.

IV.49.29 Aggravating factors relating to the offender will include the offender's previous record and failures to respond to previous sentences, to the extent that this is relevant to culpability rather than to risk.

IV.49.30 Mitigating factors relating to the offence will include:
(a) an intention to cause grievous bodily harm, rather than to kill;
(b) spontaneity and lack of pre-meditation.

IV.49.31 Mitigating factors relating to the offender may include:
(a) the offender's age;
(b) clear evidence of remorse or contrition;
(c) a timely plea of guilty.

Very serious cases

IV.49.32 A substantial upward adjustment may be appropriate in the most serious cases, for example, those involving a substantial number of murders, or if there are several factors identified as attracting the higher starting point present. In suitable cases, the result might even be a minimum term of 30 years (equivalent to 60 years) which would offer little or no hope of the offender's eventual release. In cases of exceptional gravity, the judge, rather than setting a whole life minimum term, can state that there is no minimum period which could properly be set in that particular case.

IV.49.33 Among the categories of case referred to in paragraph IV.49.26 some offences may be especially grave. These include cases in which the victim was performing his duties as a prison officer at the time of the crime or the offence was a terrorist or sexual or sadistic murder or involved a young child. In such a case, a term of 20 years and upwards could be appropriate.

IV.49.34 In following this guidance; judges should bear in mind the conclusion of the Court in *Sullivan* that the general effect of both these statements is the same. While Lord Bingham does not identify as many starting points, it is open to the judge to come to exactly the same decision irrespective of which was followed. Both pieces of guidance give the judge a considerable degree of discretion.

Procedure for announcing the minimum term in open court

IV.49.35 Having gone through the three or four steps outlined above, the court is then under a duty under section 270 of the Act, to state in open court, in ordinary language, its reasons for deciding on the minimum term or for passing a whole life order.

IV.49.36 In order to comply with this duty the court should state clearly the minimum term it has determined. In doing so, it should state which of the starting points it has chosen and its reasons for doing so. Where the court has departed from that starting point due to mitigating or aggravating features it must state the reasons for that departure and any aggravating or mitigating features which have led to that departure. At that point the court should also declare how much, if any, time is being deducted for time spent in custody. The court must then explain that the minimum term is the minimum amount of time the prisoner will spend in prison, from the date of sentence, before the Parole Board can order early release. If it remains necessary for the protection of the public, the prisoner will continue to be detained after that date. The court should also state that where the prisoner has served the minimum term and the Parole Board has decided to direct release the prisoner will remain on licence for the rest of his life and may be recalled to prison at any time.

IV.49.37 Where the offender was 21 or over when he committed the offence and the court considers that the seriousness of the offence is so exceptionally high that a 'whole life order' is appropriate, the court should state clearly its reasons for reaching this conclusion. It should also explain that the early release provisions will not apply.

IV.50. Bail pending appeal

IV.50.1 The procedure for granting bail by a judge of the Crown Court pending an appeal to the Court of Appeal (Criminal Division) (see sections 1(2) and 11(1A) of the Criminal Appeal Act 1968, and section 81(1B) of the Supreme Court Act 1981) is described in the *Guide to Proceedings in the Court of Appeal Criminal Division.* This is available at Crown Courts and is to be found at (1983) 77 Cr App R 138 and [1983] Crim LR 145.

IV.50.2 The procedure is also set out in outline on Criminal Appeal Office Form C (Crown Court Judge's Certificate of fitness for appeal) and Form BC (Crown Court Judge's Order granting bail), copies of which are held by the Crown Court. The court clerk will ensure that these forms are always available when a judge hears an application under these provisions.

IV.50.3 The judge may well think it right (a) to hear the application for a certificate in chambers with a shorthand writer present; (b) to invite the defendant's advocate to submit before the hearing of the application a draft of the grounds of appeal which he will ask the judge to certify on Form C. The advocate for the Crown will be better able to assist the judge at the hearing if the draft ground is sent beforehand to him also.

IV.50.4 The first question for the judge is then whether there exists a particular and cogent ground of appeal. If there is no such ground there can be no certificate, and if there is no certificate there can be no bail. A judge should not grant a certificate with regard to sentence merely in the light of mitigation to which he has, in his opinion, given due weight, nor in regard to conviction on a ground where he considers the chance of a successful appeal is not substantial. The judge should bear in mind that, where a certificate is refused, application may be made to the Court of Appeal for leave to appeal and for bail.

IV.50.5 The length of the period which might elapse before the hearing of any appeal is not relevant to the grant of a certificate, but, if the judge does decide to grant a certificate, it may be one factor in the decision whether or not to grant bail. A judge who is minded to take this factor into account may find it advisable to have the court clerk contact the Criminal Appeal Office Listing Co-ordinator in order that he may have an accurate and up-to-date assessment of the likely waiting time. This can be very short. The Co-ordinator will require a general account of the weight and urgency of the case.

IV.50.6 Where the defendant's representative considers that bail should be applied for as a matter of urgency, the application should normally be made, in the first instance, to the trial judge, and the Court of Appeal may decline to treat such an application as urgent if there is no good reason why it has not been made to the trial judge.

Part V Further Directions Applying in the Magistrates' Courts

V.51. Mode of trial

V.51.1 The purpose of these guidelines is to help magistrates decide whether or not to commit defendants charged with 'either way' offences for trial in the Crown Court. Their object is to provide guidance not direction. They are not intended to impinge on a magistrate's duty to consider each case individually and on its own particular facts. These guidelines apply to all defendants aged 18 and above.

General mode of trial considerations

V.51.2 Section 19 of the Magistrates' Courts Act 1980 requires magistrates to have regard to the following matters in deciding whether an offence is more suitable for summary trial or trial on indictment:

(a) the nature of the case;
(b) whether the circumstances make the offence one of a serious character;
(c) whether the punishment which a magistrates' court would have power to inflict for it would be adequate;
(d) any other circumstances which appear to the court to make it more suitable for the offence to be tried in one way rather than the other;
(e) any representations made by the prosecution or the defence.

V.51.3 Certain general observations can be made:

(a) the court should never make its decision on the grounds of convenience or expedition;
(b) the court should assume for the purpose of deciding mode of trial that the prosecution version of the facts is correct;
(c) the fact that the offences are alleged to be specimens is a relevant consideration (although, it has to be borne in mind that difficulties can arise in sentencing in relation to specimen counts see *R* v *Clark* [1996] 2 Cr App R (S) 351 and *R* v *Canavan and others* [1998] 1 Cr App

R (S) 243); the fact that the defendant will be asking for other offences to be taken into consideration, if convicted, is not;

(d) where cases involve complex questions of fact or difficult questions of law, including difficult issues of disclosure of sensitive material, the court should consider committal for trial;

(e) where two or more defendants are jointly charged with an offence each has an individual right to elect his mode of trial;

(f) in general, except where otherwise stated, either way offences should be tried summarily unless the court considers that the particular case has one or more of the features set out in paragraphs V.51.4 to V.51.18 and that its sentencing powers are insufficient;

(g) the court should also consider its power to commit an offender for sentence under sections 3 and 4 of the Powers of Criminal Courts (Sentencing) Act 2000, if information emerges during the course of the hearing which leads it to conclude that the offence is so serious, or the offender such a risk to the public, that its powers to sentence him are inadequate. This means that committal for sentence is no longer determined by reference to the character and antecedents of the offender.

Features relevant to individual offences

V.51.4 Where reference is made in these guidelines to property or damage of 'high value' it means a figure equal to at least twice the amount of the limit (currently £5,000) imposed by statute on a magistrates' court when making a compensation order.

Burglary: Dwelling-house

V.51.5 Cases should be tried summarily unless the court considers that one or more of the following features is present in the case *and* that its sentencing powers are insufficient. Magistrates should take account of their powers under sections 3 and 4 of the Powers of Criminal Courts (Sentencing) Act 2000 to commit for sentence, see paragraph V.51.3(l).

(a) Entry in the daytime when the occupier (or another) is present;
(b) Entry at night of a house which is normally occupied, whether or not the occupier (or another) is present;
(c) The offence is alleged to be one of a series of similar offences;
(d) When soiling, ransacking, damage or vandalism occurs;
(e) The offence has professional hallmarks;
(f) The unrecovered property is of high value: see paragraph V.51.4 for definition of high value;
(g) The offence is racially motivated.

Note: Attention is drawn to paragraph 28(c) of schedule 1 to the Magistrates' Courts Act 1980 by which offences of burglary in a dwelling cannot be tried summarily if any person in the dwelling was subjected to violence or the threat of violence.

Burglary: Non-dwelling

V.51.6 Cases should be tried summarily unless the court considers that one or more of the following features is present in the case *and* that its sentencing powers are insufficient. Magistrates should take account of their powers under sections 3 and 4 of the Powers of Criminal Courts (Sentencing) Act 2000 to commit for sentence, see paragraph V.51.3(g).

(a) Entry of a pharmacy or doctor's surgery;
(b) Fear is caused or violence is done to anyone lawfully on the premises (e.g. night-watchman, security guard);
(c) The offence has professional hallmarks;
(d) Vandalism on a substantial scale;
(e) The unrecovered property is of high value: see paragraph V.51.4 for definition of high value;
(f) The offence is racially motivated.

Theft and fraud

V.51.7 Cases should be tried summarily unless the court considers that one or more of the following features is present in the case *and* that its sentencing powers are insufficient. Magistrates should take account of their powers under sections 3 and 4 of the Powers of Criminal Courts (Sentencing) Act 2000 to commit for sentence, see paragraph V.51.3(g).

Breach of trust by a person in a position of substantial authority, or in whom a high degree of trust is placed;
Theft or fraud which has been committed or disguised in a sophisticated manner;
Theft or fraud committed by an organised gang;

The victim is particularly vulnerable to theft or fraud, e.g. the elderly or infirm;
The unrecovered property is of high value: see paragraph V.51.4 for definition of high value.

Handling

V.51.8 Cases should be tried summarily unless the court considers that one or more of the following features is present in the case *and* that its sentencing powers are insufficient. Magistrates should take account of their powers under sections 3 and 4 of the Powers of Criminal Courts (Sentencing) Act 2000 to commit for sentence, see paragraph V.51.3(g).

(a) Dishonest handling of stolen property by a receiver who has commissioned the theft;
(b) The offence has professional hallmarks;
(c) The property is of high value: see paragraph V.51.4 for definition of high value.

Social security frauds

V.51.9 Cases should be tried summarily unless the court considers that one or more of the following features is present in the case *and* that its sentencing powers are insufficient. Magistrates should take account of their powers under sections 3 and 4 of the Powers of Criminal Courts (Sentencing) Act 2000 to commit for sentence, see paragraph V.51.3(g).

(a) Organised fraud on a large scale;
(b) The frauds are substantial and carried out over a long period of time.

Violence (sections 20 and 47 of the Offences against the Person Act 1861)

V.51.10 Cases should be tried summarily unless the court considers that one or more of the following features is present in the case *and* that its sentencing powers are insufficient. Magistrates should take account of their powers under sections 3 and 4 of the Powers of Criminal Courts (Sentencing) Act 2000 to commit for sentence, see paragraph V.51.3(g).

(a) The use of a weapon of a kind likely to cause serious injury;
(b) A weapon is used and serious injury is caused;
(c) More than minor injury is caused by kicking or head-butting;
(d) Serious violence is caused to those whose work has to be done in contact with the public or are likely to face violence in the course of their work;
(e) Violence to vulnerable people, e.g. the elderly and infirm;
(f) The offence has clear racial motivation.

Note: the same considerations apply to cases of domestic violence.

Public order act offences

V.51.11 Cases should be tried summarily unless the court considers that one or more of the following features is present in the case *and* that its sentencing powers are insufficient. Magistrates should take account of their powers under sections 3 and 4 of the Powers of Criminal Courts (Sentencing) Act 2000 to commit for sentence, see paragraph V.51.3(g).

(a) Cases of *violent disorder* should generally be committed for trial;
(b) *Affray*;
  (i) Organised violence or use of weapons;
  (ii) Significant injury or substantial damage;
  (iii) The offence has clear racial motivation;
  (iv) An attack on police officers, ambulance staff, fire-fighters and the like.

Violence to and neglect of children

V.51.12 Cases should be tried summarily unless the court considers that one or more of the following features is present in the case *and* that its sentencing powers are insufficient. Magistrates should take account of their powers under sections 3 and 4 of the Powers of Criminal Courts (Sentencing) Act 2000 to commit for sentence, see paragraph V.51.3(g):

(a) Substantial injury;
(b) Repeated violence or serious neglect, even if the physical harm is slight;
(c) Sadistic violence, e.g. deliberate burning or scalding.

Indecent assault

V.51.13 Cases should be tried summarily unless the court considers that one or more of the following features is present in the case *and* that its sentencing powers are insufficient. Magistrates should take account of their powers under sections 3 and 4 of the Powers of Criminal Courts (Sentencing) Act 2000 to commit for sentence, see paragraph V.51.3(g).

(a) Substantial disparity in age between victim and defendant, and a more serious assault;

(b) Violence or threats of violence;
(c) Relationship of trust or responsibility between defendant and victim;
(d) Several more serious similar offences;
(e) The victim is particularly vulnerable;
(f) Serious nature of the assault.

Unlawful sexual intercourse

V.51.14 Cases should be tried summarily unless the court considers that one or more of the following features is present in the case *and* that its sentencing powers are insufficient. Magistrates should take account of their powers under sections 3 and 4 of the Powers of Criminal Courts (Sentencing) Act 2000 to commit for sentence, see paragraph V.51.3(g).
(a) Wide disparity of age;
(b) Breach of position of trust;
(c) The victim is particularly vulnerable.

Note: Unlawful sexual intercourse with a girl *under 13* is triable only on indictment.

Drugs

V.51.15 Class A:
(a) Supply; possession with intent to supply:
These cases should be committed for trial.
(b) Possession:
Should be committed for trial unless the amount is consistent only with personal use.

V.51.16 Class B:
(a) Supply; possession with intent to supply:
Should be committed for trial unless there is only small scale supply for no payment.
(b) Possession:
Should be committed for trial when the quantity is substantial and not consistent only with personal use.

Dangerous driving and aggravated vehicle taking

V.51.17 Cases should be tried summarily unless the court considers that one or more of the following features is present in the case *and* that its sentencing powers are insufficient. Magistrates should take account of their powers under sections 3 and 4 of the Powers of Criminal Courts (Sentencing) Act 2000 to commit for sentence, see paragraph V.51.3(g).
(a) Alcohol or drugs contributing to the dangerous driving;
(b) Grossly excessive speed;
(c) Racing;
(d) Prolonged course of dangerous driving;
(e) Other related offences;
(f) Significant injury or damage sustained.

Criminal damage

V.51.18 Cases should be tried summarily unless the court considers that one or more of the following features is present in the case *and* that its sentencing powers are insufficient. Magistrates should take account of their powers under sections 3 and 4 of the Powers of Criminal Courts (Sentencing) Act 2000 to commit for sentence, see paragraph V.51.3(g).
(a) Deliberate fire-raising;
(b) Committed by a group;
(c) Damage of a high value;
(d) The offence has clear racial motivation.

Note: Offences set out in schedule 2 to the Magistrates' Courts Act 1980 (which includes offences of criminal damage which do not amount to arson) *must* be tried summarily if the value of the property damaged or destroyed is £5,000 or less.

V.52. Committal for sentence and appeals to Crown Court

V.52.1 Any case notes should be sent to the Crown Court when there is an appeal, thereby making them available to the judge if the judge requires them in order to decide before the hearing questions of listing or representation or the like. They will also be available to the court during the hearing if it becomes necessary or desirable for the court to see what happened in the lower court. On a committal for sentence or an appeal, any reasons given by the magistrates for their decision should be included with the notes.

V.53. Bail before committal for trial

V.53.1 [Rules 19.18 and 19.22 of the Criminal Procedure Rules 2005] apply to these applications.

V.53.2 Before the Crown Court can deal with an application it must be satisfied that the magistrates' court has issued a certificate under section 5(6A) of the Bail Act 1976 that it heard full argument on the application for bail before it refused the application. A copy of the certificate will be issued to the applicant and not sent directly to the Crown Court. It will therefore be necessary for the applicant's solicitors to attach a copy of the certificate to the bail application form. If the certificate is not enclosed with the application form it will be difficult to avoid some delay in listing.

Venue

V.53.3 Applications should be made to the court to which the defendant will be or would have been committed for trial. In the event of an application in a purely summary case, it should be made to the Crown Court centre which normally receives class [3] work. The hearing will be listed as a chambers matter unless a judge has directed otherwise.

V.54. Contempt in the face of the magistrates' court

General

V.54.1 Section 12 of the Contempt of Court Act 1981 gives magistrates' courts the power to detain until the court rises, someone, whether a defendant or another person present in court, who wilfully insults anyone specified in section 12 or who interrupts proceedings. In any such case, the court may order any officer of the court, or any constable, to take the offender into custody and detain him until the rising of the court; and the court may, if it thinks fit, commit the offender to custody for a specified period not exceeding one month or impose a fine not exceeding level 4 on the standard scale or both. This power can be used to stop disruption of their proceedings. Detention is until the person can be conveniently dealt with without disruption of the proceedings. Prior to the court using the power the offender should be warned to desist or face the prospect of being detained.

V.54.2 Magistrates' courts also have the power to commit to custody any person attending or brought before a magistrates' court who refuses without just cause to be sworn or to give evidence under section 97(4) of the Magistrates' Courts Act 1980, until the expiration of such period not exceeding one month as may be specified in the warrant or until he sooner gives evidence or produces the document or thing, or impose on him a fine not exceeding £2,500, or both.

V.54.3 In the exercise of any of these powers, as soon as is practical, and in any event prior to an offender being proceeded against, an offender should be told of the conduct which it is alleged to constitute his offending in clear terms. When making an order under section 12 the justices should state their findings of fact as to the contempt.

V.54.4 Exceptional situations require exceptional treatment. While this direction deals with the generality of situations, there will be a minority of situations where the application of the direction will not be consistent with achieving justice in the special circumstances of the particular case. Where this is the situation, the compliance with the direction should be modified so far as is necessary so as to accord with the interests of justice.

V.54.5 The power to bind persons over to be of good behaviour in respect of their conduct in court should cease to be exercised.

Contempt consisting of wilfully insulting anyone specified in section 12 or interrupting proceedings

V.54.6 In the case of someone who wilfully insults anyone specified in section 12 or interrupts proceedings, if an offender expresses a willingness to apologise for his misconduct, he should be brought back before the court at the earliest convenient moment in order to make the apology and to give undertakings to the court to refrain from further misbehaviour.

V.54.7 In the majority of cases, an apology and a promise as to future conduct should be sufficient for justices to order an offender's release. However, there are likely to be certain cases where the nature and seriousness of the misconduct require the justices to consider using their powers under section 12(2) of the Contempt of Court 1981 Act either to fine or to order the offender's committal to custody.

Where an offender is detained for contempt of court

V.54.8 Anyone detained under either of these provisions in paragraphs V.54.1 or V.54.2 should be seen by the duty solicitor or another legal representative and be represented in proceedings if they so wish. Public funding should generally be granted to cover representation. The offender must be afforded adequate time and facilities in order to prepare his case. The matter should be resolved the same day if at all possible.

V.54.9 The offender should be brought back before the court before the justices conclude their daily business. The justices should ensure that he understands the nature of the proceedings, including his opportunity to apologise or give evidence and the alternative of them exercising their powers.

V.54.10 Having heard from the offender's solicitor, the justices should decide whether to take further action.

Sentencing of an offender who admits being in contempt

V.54.11 If an offence of contempt is admitted the justices should consider whether they are able to proceed on the day or whether to adjourn to allow further reflection. The matter should be dealt with on the same day if at all possible. If the justices are of the view to adjourn they should generally grant the offender bail unless one or more of the exceptions to the right to bail in the Bail Act 1976 are made out.

V.54.12 When they come to sentence the offender where the offence has been admitted, the justices should first ask the offender if he has any objection to them dealing with the matter. If there is any objection to the justices dealing with the matter a differently constituted panel should hear the proceedings. If the offender's conduct was directed to the justices, it will not be appropriate for the same bench to deal with the matter.

V.54.13 The justices should consider whether an order for the offender's discharge is appropriate, taking into account any time spent on remand, whether the offence was admitted and the seriousness of the contempt. Any period of committal should be for the shortest time commensurate with the interests of preserving good order in the administration of justice.

Trial of the issue where the contempt is not admitted

V.54.14 Where the contempt is not admitted the justices' powers are limited to making arrangements for a trial to take place. They should not at this stage make findings against the offender.

V.54.15 In the case of a contested contempt the trial should take place at the earliest opportunity and should be before a bench of justices other than those before whom the alleged contempt took place. If a trial of the issue can take place on the day such arrangements should be made taking into account the offender's rights under Article 6 of the European Convention for the Protection of Human Rights and Fundamental Freedoms (Rome, 4 November 1950; TS 71 (1953); Cmd 8969). If the trial cannot take place that day the justices should again bail the offender unless there are grounds under the Bail Act 1976 to remand him in custody.

V.54.16 The offender is entitled to call and examine witnesses where evidence is relevant. If the offender is found by the court to have committed contempt the court should again consider first whether an order for his discharge from custody is sufficient to bring proceedings to an end. The justices should also allow the offender a further opportunity to apologise for his contempt or to make representations. If the justices are of the view that they must exercise their powers to commit to custody under section 12(2) of the 1981 Act, they must take into account any time spent on remand and the nature and seriousness of the contempt. Any period of committal should be for the shortest period of time commensurate with the interests of preserving good order in the administration of justice.

V.55. Clerk retiring with justices

V.55.1 A justices' clerk is responsible for:

(a) the legal advice tendered to the justices within the area;

(b) the performance of any of the functions set out below by any member of his staff acting as legal adviser;

(c) ensuring that competent advice is available to justices when the justices' clerk is not personally present in court; and

(d) the effective delivery of case management and the reduction of unnecessary delay.

V.55.2 Where a person other than the justices' clerk (a 'legal adviser'), who is authorised to do so, performs any of the functions referred to in this direction he will have the same responsibilities as the justices' clerk. The legal adviser may consult the justices' clerk or other person authorised by the justices' clerk for that purpose before tendering advice to the bench. If the justices' clerk or that person gives any advice directly to the bench, he should give the parties or their advocates an opportunity of repeating any relevant submissions prior to the advice being given.

V.55.3 It shall be the responsibility of the legal adviser to provide the justices with any advice they require properly to perform their functions, whether or not the justices have requested that advice, on:

(a) questions of law (including European Court of Human Rights jurisprudence and those matters set out in section 2(1) of the Human Rights Act 1998);
(b) questions of mixed law and fact;
(c) matters of practice and procedure;
(d) the range of penalties available;
(e) any relevant decisions of the superior courts or other guidelines;
(f) other issues relevant to the matter before the court; and
(g) the appropriate decision-making structure to be applied in any given case.

In addition to advising the justices it shall be the legal adviser's responsibility to assist the court, where appropriate, as to the formulation of reasons and the recording of those reasons.

V.55.4 A justices' clerk or legal adviser must not play any part in making findings of fact, but may assist the bench by reminding them of the evidence, using any notes of the proceedings for this purpose.

V.55.5 A justices' clerk or legal adviser may ask questions of witnesses and the parties in order to clarify the evidence and any issues in the case. A legal adviser has a duty to ensure that every case is conducted fairly.

V.55.6 When advising the justices the justices' clerk or legal adviser, whether or not previously in court, should:
(a) ensure that he is aware of the relevant facts; and
(b) provide the parties with the information necessary to enable the parties to make any representations they wish as to the advice before it is given.

V.55.7 At any time justices are entitled to receive advice to assist them in discharging their responsibilities. If they are in any doubt as to the evidence which has been given, they should seek the aid of their legal adviser, referring to his notes as appropriate. This should ordinarily be done in open court. Where the justices request their adviser to join them in the retiring room, this request should be made in the presence of the parties in court. Any legal advice given to the justices other than in open court should be clearly stated to be provisional and the adviser should subsequently repeat the substance of the advice in open court and give the parties an opportunity to make any representations they wish on that provisional advice. The legal adviser should then state in open court whether the provisional advice is confirmed or if it is varied the nature of the variation.

V.55.8 The performance of a legal adviser may be appraised by a person authorised by the magistrates' courts committee to do so. For that purpose the appraiser may be present in the justices' retiring room. The content of the appraisal is confidential, but the fact that an appraisal has taken place, and the presence of the appraiser in the retiring room, should be briefly explained in open court.

V.55.9 The legal adviser is under a duty to assist unrepresented parties to present their case, but must do so without appearing to become an advocate for the party concerned.

V.55.10 The role of legal advisers in fine default proceedings or any other proceedings for the enforcement of financial orders, obligations or penalties is to assist the court. They must not act in an adversarial or partisan manner. With the agreement of the justices a legal adviser may ask questions of the defaulter to elicit information which the justices will require to make an adjudication, for example to facilitate his explanation for the default. A legal adviser may also advise the justices in the normal way as to the options open to them in dealing with the case. It would be inappropriate for the legal adviser to set out to establish wilful refusal or neglect or any other type of culpable behaviour, to offer an opinion on the facts, or to urge a particular course of action upon the justices. The duty of impartiality is the paramount consideration for the legal adviser at all times, and this takes precedence over any role he may have as a collecting officer. The appointment of other staff to 'prosecute' the case for the collecting officer is not essential to ensure compliance with the law, including the Human Rights Act 1998. Whether to make such appointments is a matter for the justices' chief executive.

V.56. Case management in magistrates' courts

V.56.1 This section of the practice direction supplements the rules in Part 3 of the Criminal Procedure Rules as they apply to the management of cases in magistrates' courts. Where time limits or other directions in the Consolidated Criminal Practice Direction appear inconsistent with this section, the directions in this section take precedence. To avoid unnecessary and wasted hearings the parties should be allowed adequate time to prepare the case, having regard to the time limits for applications and notices set by the Criminal Procedure Rules and by other legislation. When those time limits have expired the parties will be expected to be fully prepared.

Cases to be tried summarily by the magistrates' court

V.56.2 The case progression form to be used is set out in annex E with guidance notes. The form, read with the notes, constitutes a case progression timetable for the effective preparation of a case.

Cases sent, committed or transferred to the Crown Court for trial

V.56.3 The case progression forms set out in annex E with guidance notes are to be used in connection with cases that are sent to the Crown Court for trial under section 51 of the Crime and Disorder Act 1998 and cases that are committed to the Crown Court for trial under section 6 of the Magistrates' Courts Act 1980. In a case transferred to the Crown Court for trial under section 4(1) of the Criminal Justice Act 1987 or under section 53(1) of the Criminal Justice Act 1991 the directions contained in the case progression form used for committal for trial apply as if the case had been committed on the date of the notice of transfer.

V.56.4 A preliminary hearing ('PH') is not required in every case sent for trial under section 51 of the Crime and Disorder Act 1998: see rule 12.2 (which altered the Crown Court rule from which it derived). A PH should be ordered only where such a hearing is considered necessary. The PH should be held about 14 days after sending.

V.56.5 Whether or not a magistrates' court orders a PH, a plea and case management hearing ('PCMH') should be ordered in every case sent or committed to the Crown Court for trial. The PCMH should be held within about 7 weeks after committal for trial, within about 14 weeks after sending for trial where a defendant is in custody and within about 17 weeks after sending for trial where a defendant is on bail.

Use of the forms: directions that apply by default

V.56.6 The case progression forms to be used in magistrates' courts contain directions some of which are determined by Criminal Procedure Rules or by other legislation and some of which are discretionary, as explained in the guidance notes. All those directions apply in every case unless the court otherwise orders.

The Lord Chief Justice of England and Wales 8 July 2002, as amended 25 April 2007

Annex A

[This annex consists of a List of Practice Directions, Practice Notes and Practice Statements included in the consolidation. It is omitted.]

Annex B

[This annex consists of a List of Practice Directions, Practice Notes and Practice Statements not included in the consolidation, but no longer applicable in criminal proceedings. It is omitted.]

Annex C

Explanations for the imposition of custodial sentences: forms of words

The following forms may need to be adapted in the light of such provisions or practices as are in force affecting possible earlier release.

Forms of words are provided for use where the offender (a) will be a short term prisoner not subject to licence; (b) will be a short term prisoner subject to licence; (c) will be a long term prisoner; (d) will be subject to a discretionary sentence of life imprisonment.

Sentencers will bear in mind that where an offender is sentenced to terms which are consecutive, or wholly or partly concurrent, they are to be treated as a single term: section 51(2) of the Criminal Justice Act 1991.

(a) Total term less than 12 months

The sentence is () months.

Unless you are released earlier under supervision, you will serve half that sentence in prison/a young offender institution. After that time you will be released.

Your release will not bring this sentence to an end. If after your release and before the end of the period covered by the sentence you commit any further offence, you may be ordered to return to custody to serve the balance of the original sentence outstanding at the date of the further offence, as well as being punished for that new offence.

Any time you have spent on remand in custody in connection with the offence(s) for which you are now being sentenced will count as part of the sentence to be served, unless it has already been counted.

(b) Total term of 12 months and less than 4 years

The sentence is () (months/years).

Unless you are released earlier under supervision, you will serve half that sentence in a prison/a young offender institution. After that time you will be released.

Your release will not bring this sentence to an end. If after your release and before the end of the period covered by the sentence you commit any further offence you may be ordered to return to custody to serve the balance of the original sentence outstanding at the date of the further offence, as well as being punished for that new offence.

Any time you have spent on remand in custody in connection with the offence(s) for which you are now being sentenced will count as part of the sentence to be served, unless it has already been counted.

After your release you will also be subject to supervision on licence until the end of three-quarters of the total sentence. (If an order has been made under section 85 of the Powers of Criminal Courts (Sentencing) Act 2000: After your release you will also be subject to supervision on licence for the remainder of the licence period.) If you fail to comply with any of the requirements of your licence then again you may be brought before a court which will have power to suspend your licence and order your return to custody.

(c) Total term of 4 years or more

The sentence is () (years/months).

Your case will not be considered by the Parole Board until you have served at least half that period in custody. Unless the Parole Board recommends earlier release, you will not be released until you have served two-thirds of that sentence.

Your release will not bring the sentence to an end. If after your release and before the end of the period covered by the sentence you commit any further offence you may be ordered to return to custody to serve the balance of the original sentence outstanding at the date of the new offence, as well as being punished for that new offence.

Any time you have spent in custody on remand in connection with the offence(s) for which you are now being sentenced will count as part of the sentence to be served, unless it has already been counted.

After your release you will also be subject to supervision on licence until the end of three-quarters of the total sentence. (If an order has been made under section 85 of the Powers of Criminal Courts (Sentencing) Act 2000: After your release you will also be subject to supervision on licence for the remainder of the licence period. You will be liable to be recalled to prison if your licence is revoked, either on the recommendation of the Parole Board, or, if it is thought expedient in the public interest, by the Secretary of State).

(d) Discretionary life sentence

The sentence of the court is life imprisonment/custody for life/detention for life under section 91 of the Powers of Criminal Courts (Sentencing) Act 2000. For the purposes of section 82A of that Act the court specifies a period of (x) years. That means that your case will not be considered by the Parole Board until you have served at least (x) years in custody. After that time the Parole Board will be entitled to consider your release. When it is satisfied that you need no longer be confined in custody for the protection of the public it will be able to direct your release. Until it is so satisfied you will remain in custody.

If you are released, it will be on terms that you are subject to a licence for the rest of your life and liable to be recalled to prison at any time if your licence is revoked, either on the recommendation of the Parole Board, or, if it is thought expedient in the public interest, by the Secretary of State.

Annex D

[This annex consists of a list of forms for use in criminal proceedings and is omitted.]

Annex E

[This annex contains the forms to be used to facilitate case management and is omitted.]

Appendix 8 Sentencing Guidelines Council Guidelines

PART 1 REDUCTION IN SENTENCE FOR A GUILTY PLEA

Foreword

One of the first guidelines to be issued by the Sentencing Guidelines Council related to the statutory obligation to take account of any guilty plea when determining sentence. As set out in the Foreword to that guideline,[1] the intention was 'to promote consistency in sentencing by providing clarity for courts, court users and victims so that everyone knows exactly what to expect'. Prior to that guideline there had been different understandings of the purpose of the reduction and the extent of any reduction given.

Since the guideline was issued, there has been much greater clarity but there still remain concerns about some of the content of the guideline and about the extent to which the guideline has been consistently applied. Accordingly the Council has undertaken a review of the guideline (in accordance with the statutory obligation placed upon it to do so from time to time[2]); it has also requested that the Judicial Studies Board consider further ways in which judicial training can incorporate the guideline.

The Council is extremely grateful to the Sentencing Advisory Panel for the speed and thoroughness with which it has prepared its Advice following extensive consultation. The Council has accepted almost all the recommendations of the Panel; the issues and arguments are set out fully in the Panel's advice (see www.sentencing-guidelines.gov.uk). This revised guideline applies to all cases sentenced on or after *23 July 2007*.

The Council has agreed with the Panel that the general approach of the guideline is correct in setting out clearly the purpose of the reduction for a guilty plea, in settling for a reduction no greater than one third (with lower levels of reduction where a plea is entered other than at the first reasonable opportunity) and in continuing to provide for a special approach when fixing the minimum term for a life sentence imposed following conviction for murder.

The Council has agreed with the Panel that some discretion should be introduced to the approach where the prosecution case is 'overwhelming'. The Council has not accepted the Panel's recommendation in relation to circumstances where a magistrates' court is sentencing an offender for a number of offences where the overall maximum imprisonment is 6 months. The Council continues to consider that there must be some incentive to plead guilty in such circumstances; this is consistent with other aspects of the guideline.

The Council has not accepted the Panel's recommendation in relation to the 'capping' of the effect of reduction on very large fines. The number of such fines is very low and the Council was not convinced that the arguments were strong enough to justify a departure from the general approach in the guideline not to 'cap' the effect of the reduction.

In addition, the revised guideline provides guidance as to when the 'first reasonable opportunity' is likely to occur in relation to indictable only offences; emphasises that remorse and material assistance provided to prosecuting authorities are separate issues from those to which the guideline applies and makes clear that the approach to calculation of the reduction where

[1] Published December 2004

[2] Criminal Justice Act 2003, s.170(4)

an indeterminate sentence is imposed (other than that following conviction for murder) should be the same as that for determinate sentences.

Since the guideline was issued in 2004, there have been changes in the statutory provisions governing the reduction for guilty plea and in those relating to sentences for public protection. The review has provided an opportunity to bring the guideline up to date and those changes have been incorporated.

A. Statutory Provision

Section 144 Criminal Justice Act 2003 provides:

(1) In determining what sentence to pass on an offender who has pleaded guilty to an offence in proceedings before that or another court, a court must take into account:
   (a) the stage in the proceedings for the offence at which the offender indicated his intention to plead guilty, and
   (b) the circumstances in which this indication was given.

(2) In the case of an offence the sentence for which falls to be imposed under subsection (2) of section 110 or 111 of the Sentencing Act,[3] nothing in that subsection prevents the court, after taking into account any matter referred to in subsection (1) of this section, from imposing any sentence which is not less than 80 per cent of that specified in that subsection.

Section 174(2) Criminal Justice Act 2003 provides:

(2) In complying with subsection (1)(a), the court must:
   (a) . . .,
   (b) . . .,
   (c) . . .,
   (d) where as a result of taking into account any matter referred to in section 144(1), the court imposes a punishment on the offender which is less severe than the punishment it would otherwise have imposed, state that fact, . . .
   (e) . . .

1.1 This guideline applies whether a case is dealt with in a magistrates' court or in the Crown Court and whenever practicable in the youth court (taking into account legislative restrictions such as those relevant to the length of Detention and Training orders).

1.2 The application of this guideline to sentencers when arriving at the appropriate minimum term for the offence of murder is set out in Section F.

1.3 This guideline can also be found at www.sentencing-guidelines.gov.uk or can be obtained from the Council's Secretariat at Room G11, Allington Towers, 19 Allington Street, London SW1E 5EB.

B. Statement of Purpose

2.1 When imposing a custodial sentence, statute requires that a court must impose the shortest term that is commensurate with the seriousness of the offence(s).[4] Similarly, when imposing a community order, the restrictions on liberty must be commensurate with the seriousness of the offence(s).[5] Once that decision is made, a court is required to give consideration to the reduction for any guilty plea. As a result, the final sentence after the reduction for a guilty plea will be less than the seriousness of the offence requires.

2.2 A reduction in sentence is appropriate because a guilty plea avoids the need for a trial (thus enabling other cases to be disposed of more expeditiously), shortens the gap between charge and sentence, saves considerable cost, and, in the case of an early plea, saves victims and witnesses from the concern about having to give evidence. The reduction principle derives from the need for the effective administration of justice and not as an aspect of mitigation.

2.3 Where a sentencer is in doubt as to whether a custodial sentence is appropriate, the reduction attributable to a guilty plea will be a relevant consideration. Where this is amongst the factors leading to the imposition of a non-custodial sentence, there will be no need to apply a further

[3] These provisions prescribe minimum mandatory sentences in certain circumstances.
[4] Criminal Justice Act 2003, s.153(2)
[5] Criminal Justice Act 2003, s.148(2)

reduction on account of the guilty plea. A similar approach is appropriate where the reduction for a guilty plea is amongst the factors leading to the imposition of a financial penalty or discharge instead of a community order.

2.4 When deciding the most appropriate length of sentence, the sentencer should address separately the issue of remorse, together with any other mitigating features, before calculating the reduction for the guilty plea. Similarly, assistance to the prosecuting or enforcement authorities is a separate issue which may attract a reduction in sentence under other procedures; care will need to be taken to ensure that there is no 'double counting'.

2.5 The implications of other offences that an offender has asked to be taken into consideration should be reflected in the sentence before the reduction for guilty plea has been applied.

2.6 A reduction in sentence should only be applied to the *punitive elements* of a penalty.[6] The guilty plea reduction has no impact on sentencing decisions in relation to ancillary orders, including orders of disqualification from driving.

C. Application of the Reduction Principle

3.1 Recommended Approach

The court decides sentence for the offences taking into account other offences that have been formally admitted (TICs),

↓

The court selects the amount of the reduction by reference to the sliding scale,

↓

The court applies the reduction,

↓

When pronouncing sentence the court should usually state what the sentence would have been if there had been no reduction as a result of the guilty plea.

D. Determining the Level of Reduction

4.1 The level of reduction should be *a proportion of the total sentence* imposed, with the proportion calculated by reference to the circumstances in which the guilty plea was indicated, in particular the stage in the proceedings. The greatest reduction will be given where the plea was indicated at the 'first reasonable opportunity'.

4.2 Save where section 144(2) of the 2003 Act[7] applies, the level of the reduction will be gauged on a *sliding scale* ranging from a recommended *one third* (where the guilty plea was entered at the first reasonable opportunity in relation to the offence for which sentence is being imposed), reducing to a recommended *one quarter* (where a trial date has been set) and to a recommended *one tenth* (for a guilty plea entered at the 'door of the court' or after the trial has begun). See diagram below.

4.3 The level of reduction should reflect the stage at which the offender indicated a *willingness to admit guilt* to the offence for which he is eventually sentenced:

(i) the largest recommended reduction will not normally be given unless the offender indicated willingness to admit guilt at the *first reasonable opportunity*; when this occurs will vary from case to case. (*see Annex 2 for illustrative examples*);

(ii) where the admission of guilt comes later than the first reasonable opportunity, the reduction for guilty plea will be less than one third;

(iii) where the plea of guilty comes very late, it is still appropriate to give some reduction;

(iv) if after pleading guilty there is a *Newton* hearing and the offender's version of the circumstances of the offence is rejected, this should be taken into account in determining the level of reduction;

(v) if the not guilty plea was entered and maintained for tactical reasons (such as to retain privileges whilst on remand), a late guilty plea should attract very little, if any, discount.

[6] Where a court imposes an indeterminate sentence for public protection, the reduction principle applies in the normal way to the determination of the minimum term (see para. 5.1, footnote and para. 7 below) but release from custody requires the authorisation of the Parole Board once that minimum term has been served.

[7] See section A above.

In each category, there is a presumption that the recommended reduction will be given unless there are good reasons for a lower amount.

First reasonable opportunity	After trial date is set	Door of the court/ after trial has begun
=======|	==============|	===============|
recommended 1/13	**recommended 1/4**	**recommended 1/10**

E. Withholding a Reduction

On the basis of dangerousness

5.1 Where a sentence for a 'dangerous offender' is imposed under the provisions in the Criminal Justice Act 2003, whether the sentence requires the calculation of a minimum term or is an extended sentence, the approach will be the same as for any other determinate sentence (see also section G below).[8]

Where the prosecution case is overwhelming

5.2 The purpose of giving credit is to encourage those who are guilty to plead at the earliest opportunity. Any defendant is entitled to put the prosecution to proof and so every defendant who is guilty should be encouraged to indicate that guilt at the first reasonable opportunity.

5.3 Where the prosecution case is overwhelming, it may not be appropriate to give the full reduction that would otherwise be given. Whilst there is a presumption in favour of the full reduction being given where a plea has been indicated at the first reasonable opportunity, the fact that the prosecution case is overwhelming without relying on admissions from the defendant may be a reason justifying departure from the guideline.

5.4 Where a court is satisfied that a lower reduction should be given for this reason, a recommended reduction of 20% is likely to be appropriate where the guilty plea was indicated at the first reasonable opportunity.

5.5 A Court departing from a guideline must state the reasons for doing so.[9]

Where the maximum penalty for the offence is thought to be too low

5.6 The sentencer is bound to sentence for the offence with which the offender has been charged, and to which he has pleaded guilty. The sentencer cannot remedy perceived defects (for example an inadequate charge or maximum penalty) by refusal of the appropriate discount.

Where jurisdictional issues arise

(i) *Where sentencing powers are limited to 6 months imprisonment despite multiple offences*

5.7 When the total sentence for both or all of the offences is 6 months imprisonment, a court may determine to impose consecutive sentences which, even allowing for a reduction for a guilty plea where appropriate on each offence, would still result in the imposition of the maximum sentence available. In such circumstances, in order to achieve the purpose for which the reduction principle has been established,[10] some modest allowance should normally be given against the total sentence for the entry of a guilty plea.

(ii) *Where a maximum sentence might still be imposed*

5.8 Despite a guilty plea being entered which would normally attract a reduction in sentence, a magistrates' court may impose a sentence of imprisonment of 6 months for a single either-way offence where, but for the plea, that offence would have been committed to the Crown Court for sentence.

5.9 Similarly, a detention and training order of 24 months may be imposed on an offender aged under 18 if the offence is one which would but for the plea have attracted a sentence of long-term detention in excess of 24 months under the Powers of Criminal Courts (Sentencing) Act 2000, section 91.

---

[8] There will be some cases arising from offences committed before the commencement of the relevant provisions of the Criminal Justice Act 2003 in which a court will determine that a longer than commensurate, extended, or indeterminate sentence is required for the protection of the public. In such a case, the minimum custodial term (but not the protection of public element of the sentence) should be reduced to reflect the plea.

[9] Criminal Justice Act 2003, s. 174(2)(a)

[10] See section B above.

F. Application to Sentencing for Murder

6.1 Murder has always been regarded as the most serious criminal offence and the sentence prescribed is different from other sentences. By law, the sentence for murder is imprisonment (detention) for life and an offender will remain subject to the sentence for the rest of his/her life.

6.2 The decision whether to release the offender from custody during this sentence will be taken by the Parole Board which will consider whether it is safe to release the offender on licence. The Court that imposes the sentence is required by law to set a minimum term that has to be served before the Parole Board may start to consider whether to authorise release on licence. If an offender is released, the licence continues for the rest of the offender's life and recall to prison is possible at any time.

6.3 Uniquely, Parliament has set starting points[11] (based on the circumstances of the killing) which a Court will apply when it fixes the minimum term. Parliament has further prescribed that, having identified the appropriate starting point, the Court must then consider whether to increase or reduce it in the light of aggravating or mitigating factors, some of which are listed in statute. Finally, Parliament specifically provides[12] that the obligation to have regard to any guilty plea applies to the fixing of the minimum term, by making the same statutory provisions that apply to other offences apply to murder without limiting the courts discretion (as it did with other sentences under the Powers of Criminal Courts (Sentencing) Act 2000).

6.4 There are important differences between the usual fixed term sentence and the minimum term set following the imposition of the mandatory life sentence for murder. The most significant of these, from the sentencer's point of view, is that a reduction for a plea of guilty in the case of murder will have double the effect on time served in custody when compared with a determinate sentence. This is because a determinate sentence will provide (in most circumstances) for the release of the offender[13] on licence half way through the total sentence whereas in the case of murder a minimum term is the period in custody before consideration is given by the Parole Board to whether release is appropriate.

6.5 Given this difference, the special characteristic of the offence of murder and the unique statutory provision of starting points, careful consideration will need to be given to the extent of any reduction and to the need to ensure that the minimum term properly reflects the seriousness of the offence. Whilst the general principles continue to apply (both that a guilty plea should be encouraged and that the extent of any reduction should reduce if the indication of plea is later than the first reasonable opportunity), the process of determining the level of reduction will be different.

6.6 *Approach*

1. Where a Court determines that there should be a *whole life* minimum term, there will be no reduction for a guilty plea.
2. In other circumstances,
   a) the Court will weigh carefully the overall length of the minimum term taking into account other reductions for which offenders may be eligible so as to avoid a combination leading to an inappropriately short sentence;
   b) where it is appropriate to reduce the minimum term having regard to a plea of guilty, the reduction will not exceed one sixth and will never exceed 5 years;
   c) the sliding scale will apply so that, where it is appropriate to reduce the minimum term on account of a guilty plea, the maximum reduction (one sixth or five years whichever is the less) is only available where there has been an indication of willingness to plead guilty at the first reasonable opportunity, with a recommended 5% for a late guilty plea.
   d) the Court should then review the sentence to ensure that the minimum term accurately reflects the seriousness of the offence taking account of the statutory starting point, all aggravating and mitigating factors and any guilty plea entered.

G. Application to other Indeterminate Sentences

7.1 There are other circumstances in which an indeterminate sentence will be imposed. This may be a discretionary life sentence or imprisonment for public protection.

7.2 As with the mandatory life sentence imposed following conviction for murder, the Court will be

[11] Criminal Justice Act 2003, schedule 21
[12] Criminal Justice Act 2003, schedule 1 para 12(c)
[13] In accordance with the provisions of the Criminal Justice Act 2003

obliged to fix a minimum term to be served before the Parole Board is able to consider whether the offender can be safely released.

7.3 However, the process by which that minimum term is fixed is different from that followed in relation to the mandatory life sentence and requires the Court first to determine what the equivalent determinate sentence would have been. Accordingly, the approach to the calculation of the reduction for any guilty plea should follow the process and scale adopted in relation to determinate sentences, as set out in section D above.

ANNEX 1
FIRST REASONABLE OPPORTUNITY

1. The critical time for determining the reduction for a guilty plea is the first reasonable opportunity for the defendant to have indicated a willingness to plead guilty. This opportunity will vary with a wide range of factors and the Court will need to make a judgement on the particular facts of the case before it.
2. The key principle is that the purpose of giving a reduction is to recognise the benefits that come from a guilty plea both for those directly involved in the case in question but also in enabling Courts more quickly to deal with other outstanding cases.
3. This Annex seeks to help Courts to adopt a consistent approach by giving examples of circumstances where a determination will have to be made.
   (a) the first reasonable opportunity may be the first time that a defendant appears before the court and has the opportunity to plead guilty;
   (b) but the court may consider that it would be reasonable to have expected an indication of willingness even earlier, perhaps whilst under interview;
   Note: For a) and b) to apply, the Court will need to be satisfied that the defendant (and any legal adviser) would have had sufficient information about the allegations
   (c) where an offence triable either way is committed to the Crown Court for trial and the defendant pleads guilty at the first hearing in that Court, the reduction will be less than if there had been an indication of a guilty plea given to the magistrates' court (recommended reduction of one third) but more than if the plea had been entered after a trial date had been set (recommended reduction of one quarter), and is likely to be in the region of 30%;
   (d) where an offence is triable only on indictment, it may well be that the first reasonable opportunity would have been during the police station stage; where that is not the case, the first reasonable opportunity is likely to be at the first hearing in the Crown Court;
   (e) where a defendant is convicted after pleading guilty to an alternative (lesser) charge to that to which he/she had originally pleaded not guilty, the extent of any reduction will be determined by the stage at which the defendant first formally indicated to the court willingness to plead guilty to the lesser charge, and the reason why that lesser charge was proceeded with in preference to the original charge.

PART 2 NEW SENTENCES: CRIMINAL JUSTICE ACT 2003

FOREWORD

In accordance with the provisions of section 170(9) Criminal Justice Act 2003, the Sentencing Guidelines Council issues this guideline as a definitive guideline. By virtue of section 172 of the Act, every court must have regard to a relevant guideline.

The Council was created in 2004 in order to frame Guidelines to assist Courts as they deal with criminal cases across the whole of England and Wales.

This guideline relates to the new sentencing framework introduced by the Criminal Justice Act 2003, which affects the nature of community and custodial sentences. Only those sentences and related provisions which are expected to come into force by April 2005 are dealt with in this guideline. It will be followed by further guidelines in due course. This is an unusual guideline since it covers a range of sentences outside the context of individual offences and does so in readiness for the coming into force of the statutory provisions creating the sentences. It is designed with the object of ensuring a consistent approach when the sentences become available.

This guideline applies only to sentences passed under the sentencing framework applicable to those aged 18 or over.

The guideline is divided into two sections:

- Sections 1 covers the practical aspects of implementing the non-custodial powers namely the new community sentence and the new form of deferred sentence;
- Section 2 deals with the new custodial sentence provisions relating to suspended sentences, prison sentences of 12 months or more, and intermittent custody.[14]

The Act also contains an extensive range of provisions to protect the public from dangerous offenders. These will be dealt with separately.

. . .

Chairman of the Council

December 2004

Section 1
Part 1—Community Sentences

A. Statutory Provisions

(i) *The Thresholds for Community Sentences*

1.1.1 Seriousness—Section 148 Criminal Justice Act 2003:

(1) A court must not pass a community sentence on an offender unless it is of the opinion that the offence, or the combination of the offence and one or more offences associated with it, was serious enough to warrant such a sentence.

1.1.2 Persistent Offenders—Section 151 Criminal Justice Act 2003:

(1) Subsection (2) applies where—

(a) a person aged 16 or over is convicted of an offence ('the current offence'),

(b) on three or more previous occasions he has, on conviction by a court in the United Kingdom of any offence committed by him after attaining the age of 16, had passed on him a sentence consisting only of a fine, and

(c) despite the effect of section 143(2), the court would not (apart from this section) regard the current offence, or the combination of the current offence and one or more offences associated with it, as being serious enough to warrant a community sentence.

(2) The court may make a community order in respect of the current offence instead of imposing a fine if it considers that, having regard to all the circumstances including the matters mentioned in subsection (3), it would be in the interests of justice to make such an order.

(ii) *The Sentences Available*

1.1.3 Meaning of Community Sentence—Section 147 Criminal Justice Act 2003

(1) In this Part 'community sentence' means a sentence which consists of or includes—

(a) a community order (as defined by section 177), or

(b) one or more youth community orders.

1.1.4 Offenders aged 16 or over—Section 177 Criminal Justice Act 2003:

(1) Where a person aged 16 or over is convicted of an offence, the court by or before which he is convicted may make an order (in this Part referred to as a 'community order') imposing on him any one or more of the following requirements—

(a) an unpaid work requirement (as defined by section 199),

(b) an activity requirement (as defined by section 201),

(c) a programme requirement (as defined by section 202),

(d) a prohibited activity requirement (as defined by section 203),

(e) a curfew requirement (as defined by section 204),

(f) an exclusion requirement (as defined by section 205),

(g) a residence requirement (as defined by section 206),

(h) a mental health treatment requirement (as defined by section 207),

(i) a drug rehabilitation requirement (as defined by section 209),

(j) an alcohol treatment requirement (as defined by section 212),

(k) a supervision requirement (as defined by section 213), and

(l) in a case where the offender is aged under 25, an attendance centre requirement (as defined by section 214).

[14] References to the Probation Service reflect current roles and responsibilities. By the time these provisions come into force, some or all of those roles and responsibilities may be those of the National Offender Management Service (NOMS).

(2) Subsection (1) has effect subject to sections 150 and 218 and to the following provisions of Chapter 4 relating to particular requirements—
(a) section 199(3) (unpaid work requirement),
(b) section 201(3) and (4) (activity requirement),
(c) section 202(4) and (5) (programme requirement),
(d) section 203(2) (prohibited activity requirement),
(e) section 207(3) (mental health treatment requirement),
(f) section 209(2) (drug rehabilitation requirement), and
(g) section 212(2) and (3) (alcohol treatment requirement).

(3) Where the court makes a community order imposing a curfew requirement or an exclusion requirement, the court must also impose an electronic monitoring requirement (as defined by section 215) unless—
(a) it is prevented from doing so by section 215(2) or 218(4), or
(b) in the particular circumstances of the case, it considers it inappropriate to do so.

(4) Where the court makes a community order imposing an unpaid work requirement, an activity requirement, a programme requirement, a prohibited activity requirement, a residence requirement, a mental health treatment requirement, a drug rehabilitation requirement, an alcohol treatment requirement, a supervision requirement or an attendance centre requirement, the court may also impose an electronic monitoring requirement unless prevented from doing so by section 215(2) or 218(4).

(iii) *Determining Which Orders to make & Requirements to Include*

1.1.5 Suitability—Section 148 Criminal Justice Act 2003

(2) Where a court passes a community sentence which consists of or includes a community order—
(a) the particular requirement or requirements forming part of the community order must be such as, in the opinion of the court, is, or taken together are, the most suitable for the offender, and
(b) the restrictions on liberty imposed by the order must be such as in the opinion of the court are commensurate with the seriousness of the offence, or the combination of the offence and one or more offences associated with it.

1.1.6 Restrictions on liberty—Section 149 Criminal Justice Act 2003

(1) In determining the restrictions on liberty to be imposed by a community order or youth community order in respect of an offence, the court may have regard to any period for which the offender has been remanded in custody in connection with the offence or any other offence the charge for which was founded on the same facts or evidence.

1.1.7 Compatibility—Section 177 Criminal Justice Act 2003

(6) Before making a community order imposing two or more different requirements falling within subsection (1), the court must consider whether, in the circumstances of the case, the requirements are compatible with each other.

(iv) *Electronic Monitoring*

1.1.8 Section 177 Criminal Justice Act 2003

(3) Where the court makes a community order imposing a curfew requirement or an exclusion requirement, the court must also impose an electronic monitoring requirement (as defined by section 215) unless—
(a) it is prevented from doing so by section 215(2) or 218(4), or
(b) in the particular circumstances of the case, it considers it inappropriate to do so.

(4) Where the court makes a community order imposing an unpaid work requirement, an activity requirement, a programme requirement, a prohibited activity requirement, a residence requirement, a mental health treatment requirement, a drug rehabilitation requirement, an alcohol treatment requirement, a supervision requirement or an attendance centre requirement, the court may also impose an electronic monitoring requirement unless prevented from doing so by section 215(2) or 218(4).

B. Imposing a Community Sentence—The Approach

1.1.9 On pages 8 and 9 of the Seriousness guideline the two thresholds for the imposition of a community sentence are considered. Sentencers must consider all of the disposals available (within or below the threshold passed) at the time of sentence, and reject them before reaching the provisional decision to make a community sentence, so that even where the threshold for a community sentence has been passed a financial penalty or discharge may still be an appropriate penalty. Where an offender has a low risk of reoffending, particular care needs to be taken in the light of evidence that indicates that there are circumstances where inappropriate intervention can increase the risk of re-offending rather than decrease it. In addition, recent improvements in enforcement of financial penalties make them a more viable sentence in a wider range of cases.

1.1.10 Where an offender is being sentenced for a non-imprisonable offence or offences, great care will be needed in assessing whether a community sentence is appropriate since failure to comply could result in a custodial sentence.

1.1.11 Having decided (in consultation with the Probation Service where appropriate) that a community sentence is justified, the court must decide which requirements should be included in the community order. The requirements or orders imposed will have the effect of restricting the offender's liberty, whilst providing punishment in the community, rehabilitation for the offender, and/or ensuring that the offender engages in reparative activities.

The key issues arising are:
(i) which requirements to impose;
(ii) how to make allowance for time spent on remand; and
(iii) how to deal with breaches.

(i) *Requirements*

1.1.12 When deciding which requirements to include, the court must be satisfied on three matters—
(i) that the *restriction on liberty is commensurate with the seriousness* of the offence(s);[15]
(ii) that the *requirements are the most suitable* for the offender;[16] and
(iii) that, where there are two or more requirements included, they are *compatible with each other.*[17]

1.1.13 Sentencers should have the possibility of breach firmly in mind when passing sentence for the original offence. If a court is to reflect the seriousness of an offence, there is little value in setting requirements as part of a community sentence that are not demanding enough for an offender. On the other hand, there is equally little value in imposing requirements that would 'set an offender up to fail' and almost inevitably lead to sanctions for a breach.

In community sentences, the guiding principles are proportionality and suitability. Once a court has decided that the offence has crossed the community sentence threshold and that a community sentence is justified, the *initial* factor in defining which requirements to include in a community sentence should be the seriousness of the offence committed.

1.1.14 This means that 'seriousness' is an important factor in deciding whether the Court chooses the low, medium or high range (see below) but, having taken that decision, selection of the content of the order within the range will be determined by a much wider range of factors.

- **Sentencing ranges must remain flexible enough to take account of the suitability of the offender, his or her ability to comply with particular requirements and their availability in the local area.**
- **The justification for imposing a community sentence in response to persistent petty offending is the persistence of the offending behaviour rather than the seriousness of the offences being committed. The requirements imposed should ensure that the restriction on liberty is proportionate to the seriousness of the offending, to reflect the fact that the offences, of themselves, are not sufficiently serious to merit a community sentence.**

(a) *Information for Sentencers*

1.1.15 In many cases, a pre-sentence report[18] will be pivotal in helping a sentencer decide whether to impose a custodial sentence or whether to impose a community sentence and, if so, whether particular requirements, or combinations of requirements, are suitable for an individual offender. The court must always ensure (especially where there are multiple requirements) that the restriction on liberty placed on the offender is proportionate to the seriousness of the offence committed.[19] The court must also consider the likely effect of one requirement on another, and that they do not place conflicting demands upon the offender.[20]

[15] Criminal Justice Act 2003 section 148(2)(b)
[16] ibid section 148(2)(a)
[17] ibid section 177(6)
[18] Under the Act, a pre-sentence report includes a full report following adjournment, a specific sentence report, a short format report or an oral report. The type of report supplied will depend on the level of information requested. Wherever it appears, the term 'pre-sentence report' includes all these types of report.
[19] Criminal Justice Act 2003 section 148(2)
[20] ibid section 177(6)

1.1.16 The Council supports the approach proposed by the Panel at paragraph 78 of its Advice that, having reached the provisional view that a community sentence is the most appropriate disposal, the sentencer should request a pre-sentence report, indicating which of the three sentencing ranges is relevant and the purpose(s) of sentencing that the package of requirements is required to fulfil. Usually the most helpful way for the court to do this would be to produce a written note for the report writer, copied on the court file. If it is known that the same tribunal and defence advocate will be present at the sentencing hearing and a probation officer is present in court when the request for a report is made, it may not be necessary to commit details of the request to writing. However, events may change during the period of an adjournment and it is good practice to ensure that there is a clear record of the request for the court. These two factors will guide the Probation Service in determining the nature and combination of requirements that may be appropriate and the onerousness and intensity of those requirements. A similar procedure should apply when ordering a pre-sentence report when a custodial sentence is being considered.

1.1.17 There will be occasions when any type of report may be unnecessary despite the intention to pass a community sentence though this is likely to be infrequent. A court could consider dispensing with the need to obtain a pre-sentence report for adult offenders—

- where the offence falls within the **LOW** range of seriousness (see [below]) and
- where the sentencer was minded to impose a single requirement, such as an exclusion requirement (where the circumstances of the case mean that this would be an appropriate disposal without electronic monitoring) *and*
- where the sentence will not require the involvement of the Probation Service, for example an electronically monitored curfew (subject to the court being satisfied that there is an appropriate address at which the curfew can operate).

(b) *Ranges of Sentence Within the Community Sentence Band*

1.1.18 To enable the court to benefit from the flexibility that community sentences provide and also to meet its statutory obligations, any structure governing the use of community requirements must allow the courts to choose the most appropriate sentence for each individual offender.

1.1.19 Sentencers have a statutory obligation to pass sentences that are commensurate with the seriousness of an offence. However, within the range of sentence justified by the seriousness of the offence(s), courts will quite properly consider those factors that heighten the risk of the offender committing further offences or causing further harm with a view to lessening that risk. The extent to which requirements are imposed must be capable of being varied to ensure that the restriction on liberty is commensurate with the seriousness of the offence.

1.1.20 The Council recognises that it would be helpful for sentencers to have a framework to help them decide on the most appropriate use of the new community sentence. While there is no single guiding principle, the seriousness of the offence that has been committed is an important factor. Three sentencing ranges (low, medium and high) within the community sentence band can be identified. It is not possible to position particular types of offence at firm points within the three ranges because the seriousness level of an offence is largely dependent upon the culpability of the offender and this is uniquely variable. The difficulty is particularly acute in relation to the medium range where it is clear that requirements will need to be tailored across a relatively wide range of offending behaviour.

1.1.21 In general terms, the lowest range of community sentence would be for those offenders whose offence was relatively minor within the community sentence band and would include persistent petty offenders whose offences only merit a community sentence by virtue of failing to respond to the previous imposition of fines. Such offenders would merit a 'light touch' approach, for example, normally a single requirement such as a short period of unpaid work, or a curfew, or a prohibited activity requirement or an exclusion requirement (where the circumstances of the case mean that this would be an appropriate disposal without electronic monitoring).

1.1.22 The top range would be for those offenders who have only just fallen short of a custodial sentence and for those who have passed the threshold but for whom a community sentence is deemed appropriate.

1.1.23 In all three ranges there must be sufficient flexibility to allow the sentence to be varied to take account of the suitability of particular requirements for the individual offender and whether a particular requirement or package of requirements might be more effective at reducing any identified risk of re-offending. It will fall to the sentencer to ensure that the sentence strikes the right balance between proportionality and suitability.

There should be three sentencing ranges (low medium and high) within the community sentence band based upon seriousness.

It is not intended that an offender necessarily progress from one range to the next on each sentencing occasion. The decision as to the appropriate range each time is based upon the seriousness of the new offence(s).

The decision on the nature and severity of the requirements to be included in a community sentence should be guided by:

(i) the assessment of offence seriousness (LOW, MEDIUM OR HIGH);
(ii) the purpose(s) of sentencing the court wishes to achieve;
(iii) the risk of re-offending;
(iv) the ability of the offender to comply, and
(v) the availability of requirements in the local area.

The resulting restrictions on liberty must be a proportionate responde to the offence that was committed.

1.1.24 Below we set out a non-exhaustive description of examples of requirements that might be appropriate in the three sentencing ranges. These examples focus on punishment in the community, although it is recognised that not all packages will necessarily need to include a punitive requirement. There will clearly be other requirements of a rehabilitative nature, such as a treatment requirement or an accredited programme, which may be appropriate depending on the specific needs of the offender and assessment of suitability. Given the intensity of such interventions, it is expected that these would normally only be appropriate at medium and high levels of seriousness, and where assessed as having a medium or high risk of re-offending. In addition, when passing sentence in any one of the three ranges, the court should consider whether a rehabilitative intervention such as a programme requirement, or a restorative justice intervention might be suitable as an additional or alternative part of the sentence.

LOW

1.1.25 For offences only just crossing the community sentence threshold (such as persistent petty offending, some public order offences, some thefts from shops, or interference with a motor vehicle, where the seriousness of the offence or the nature of the offender's record means that a discharge or fine is inappropriate).

1.1.26 Suitable requirements might include:

- 40 to 80 hours of unpaid work or
- a curfew requirement within the lowest range (e.g. up to 12 hours per day for a few weeks) or
- an exclusion requirement (where the circumstances of the case mean that this would be an appropriate disposal without electronic monitoring) lasting a few months or
- a prohibited activity requirement or
- an attendance centre requirement (where available).

1.1.27 Since the restriction on liberty must be commensurate with the seriousness of the offence, particular care needs to be taken with this band to ensure that this obligation is complied with. In most cases, only one requirement will be appropriate and the length may be curtailed if additional requirements are necessary.

MEDIUM

1.1.28 For offences that obviously fall within the community sentence band such as handling stolen goods worth less than £1000 acquired for resale or somewhat more valuable goods acquired for the handler's own use, some cases of burglary in commercial premises, some cases of taking a motor vehicle without consent, or some cases of obtaining property by deception.

1.1.29 Suitable requirements might include:

- a greater number (e.g. 80 to 150) of hours of unpaid work or
- an activity requirement in the middle range (20 to 30 days) or
- a curfew requirement within the middle range (e.g. up to 12 hours for 2–3 months) or
- an exclusion requirement lasting in the region of 6 months or
- a prohibited activity requirement.

1.1.30 Since the restriction on liberty must be commensurate with the seriousness of the offence, particular care needs to be taken with this band to ensure that this obligation is complied with.

HIGH

1.1.31 For offences that only just fall below the custody threshold or where the custody threshold is crossed but a community sentence is more appropriate in all the circumstances, for example some cases displaying the features of a standard domestic burglary committed by a first-time offender.

1.1.32 More intensive sentences which combine two or more requirements may be appropriate at this level. Suitable requirements might include an unpaid work order of between 150 and 300 hours; an activity requirement up to the maximum 60 days; an exclusion order lasting in the region of 12 months; a curfew requirement of up to 12 hours a day for 4–6 months.

(c) *Electronic Monitoring*

1.1.33 The court must also consider whether an electronic monitoring requirement[21] should be imposed which is mandatory[22] in some circumstances.

Electronic monitoring should be used with the primary purpose of promoting and monitoring compliance with other requirements, in circumstances where the punishment of the offender and/or the need to safeguard the public and prevent re-offending are the most important concerns.

(d) *Recording the Sentence Imposed*

1.1.34 Under the new framework there is only one (generic) community sentence provided by statute. This does not mean that offenders who have completed a community sentence and have then re-offended should be regarded as ineligible for a second community sentence on the basis that this has been tried and failed. Further community sentences, perhaps with different requirements, may well be justified.

1.1.35 Those imposing sentence will wish to be clear about the 'purposes' that the community sentence is designed to achieve when setting the requirements. Sharing those purposes with the offender and Probation Service will enable them to be clear about the goals that are to be achieved.

1.1.36 Any future sentencer must have full information about the requirements that were inserted by the court into the previous community sentence imposed on the offender (including whether it was a low/medium/high level order) and also about the offender's response. This will enable the court to consider the merits of imposing the same or different requirements as part of another community sentence. The requirements should be recorded in such a way as to ensure that they can be made available to another court if another offence is committed.

When an offender is required to serve a community sentence, the court records should be clearly annotated to show which particular requirements have been imposed.

(ii) *Time Spent on Remand*

1.1.37 The court will need to consider whether to give any credit for time spent in custody on remand.[23] (For further detail from the Panel's Advice, see Annex A)

The court should seek to give credit for time spent on remand (in custody or equivalent status) in all cases. It should make clear, when announcing sentence, whether or not credit for time on remand has been given (bearing in mind that there will be no automatic reduction in sentence once section 67 of the Criminal Justice Act 1967 is repealed) and should explain its reasons for not giving credit when it considers either that this is not justified, would not be practical, or would not be in the best interests of the offender.

1.1.38 Where an offender has spent a period of time in custody on remand, there will be occasions where a custodial sentence is warranted but the length of the sentence justified by the seriousness of the offence would mean that the offender would be released immediately. Under the present framework, it may be more appropriate to pass a community sentence since that will ensure supervision on release.

1.1.39 However, given the changes in the content of the second part of a custodial sentence of 12 months or longer, a court in this situation where the custodial sentence would be 12 months or more should, under the new framework, pass a custodial sentence in the knowledge that licence requirements will be imposed on release from custody. This will ensure that the sentence imposed properly reflects the seriousness of the offence.

1.1.40 Recommendations made by the court at the point of sentence will be of particular importance in influencing the content of the licence. This will properly reflect the gravity of the offence(s) committed.

---

[21] ibid section 177(3) and (4)

[22] unless the necessary facilities are not available or, in the particular circumstances of the case, the court considers it inappropriate.

[23] Criminal Justice Act 2003 section 149

(iii) *Breaches*

1.1.41 Where an offender fails, without reasonable excuse, to comply with one or more requirements, the 'responsible officer'[24] can either give a warning or initiate breach proceedings. Where the offender fails to comply without reasonable excuse for the second time within a 12-month period, the 'responsible officer' must initiate proceedings.

1.1.42 In such proceedings the court must[25] either *increase the severity of the existing sentence* (i.e. impose more onerous conditions including requirements aimed at enforcement, such as a curfew or supervision requirement) or *revoke the existing sentence and proceed as though sentencing for the original offence.* The court is required to take account of the circumstances of the breach,[26] which will inevitably have an impact on its response.

1.1.43 In certain circumstances (where an offender has wilfully and persistently failed to comply with an order made in respect of an offence that is not itself punishable by imprisonment), the court can *impose a maximum of 51 weeks custody.*[27]

1.1.44 When increasing the onerousness of requirements, the court must consider the impact on the offender's ability to comply and the possibility of precipitating a custodial sentence for further breach. For that reason, and particularly where the breach occurs towards the end of the sentence, the court should take account of compliance to date and may consider that extending the supervision or operational periods will be more sensible; in other cases it might choose to add punitive or rehabilitative requirements instead. In making these changes the court must be mindful of the legislative restrictions on the overall length of community sentences and on the supervision and operational periods allowed for each type of requirement.

1.1.45 The court dealing with breach of a community sentence should have as its primary objective ensuring that the requirements of the sentence are finished, and this is important if the court is to have regard to the statutory purposes of sentencing. A court that imposes a custodial sentence for breach without giving adequate consideration to alternatives is in danger of imposing a sentence that is not commensurate with the seriousness of the original offence and is solely a punishment for breach. This risks undermining the purposes it has identified as being important. Nonetheless, courts will need to be vigilant to ensure that there is a realistic prospect of the purposes of the order being achieved.

Having decided that a community sentence is commensurate with the seriousness of the offence, the *primary* objective when sentencing for breach of requirements is to ensure that those requirements are completed.

1.1.46 A court sentencing for breach must take account of the extent to which the offender has complied with the requirements of the community order, the reasons for breach and the point at which the breach has occurred. Where a breach takes place towards the end of the operational period and the court is satisfied that the offender's appearance before the court is likely to be sufficient in itself to ensure future compliance, then given that it is not open to the court to make no order, an approach that the court might wish to adopt could be to re-sentence in a way that enables the original order to be completed properly — for example, a differently constructed community sentence that aims to secure compliance with the purposes of the original sentence.

1.1.47 If the court decides to increase the onerousness of an order, it must give careful consideration, with advice from the Probation Service, to the offender's ability to comply. A custodial sentence should be the last resort, where all reasonable efforts to ensure that an offender completes a community sentence have failed.

- **The Act allows for a custodial sentence to be imposed in response to breach of a community sentence. Custody should be the last resort, reserved for those cases of deliberate and repeated breach where all reasonable efforts to ensure that the offender complies have failed.**
- **Before increasing the onerousness of requirements, sentencers should take account of the offender's ability to comply and should avoid precipitating further breach by overloading the offender with too many or conflicting requirements.**
- **There may be cases where the court will need to consider re-sentencing to a differently constructed community sentence in order to secure compliance with the purposes of the original sentence, perhaps where there has already been partial compliance or where events since the sentence was imposed have shown that a different course of action is likely to be effective.**

[24] Criminal Justice Act 2003 schedule 8, paragraphs 5–6
[25] ibid paragraphs 9–10
[26] ibid paragraph 9(2)
[27] ibid paragraph 9(1)(c)

Section 1
Part 2—Deferred Sentences

A. Statutory Provisions

1.2.1 Under the existing legislation,[28] a court can defer a sentence for up to six months, provided the offender consents and the court considers that deferring the sentence is in the interests of justice.

1.2.2 The new provisions[29] continue to require the consent of the offender and that the court be satisfied that the making of such a decision is in the interests of justice. However, it is also stated that the power to defer sentence can only be exercised where:
'the offender undertakes to comply with any requirements as to his conduct during the period of the deferment that the court considers it appropriate to impose;'[30]

1.2.3 This enables the court to impose a wide variety of conditions (including a residence requirement).[31] The Act allows the court to appoint the probation service or other responsible person to oversee the offender's conduct during this period and prepare a report for the court at the point of sentence i.e. the end of the deferment period.

1.2.4 As under the existing legislation, if the offender commits another offence during the deferment period the court may have the power to sentence for both the original and the new offence at once. Sentence cannot be deferred for more than six months and, in most circumstances, no more than one period of deferment can be granted.[32]

1.2.5 A significant change is the provision enabling a court to deal with an offender before the end of the period of deferment.[33] For example if the court is satisfied that the offender has failed to comply with one or more requirements imposed in connection with the deferment, the offender can be brought back before the court and the court can proceed to sentence.

B. Use of Deferred Sentences

1.2.6 Under the new framework, there is a wider range of sentencing options open to the courts, including the increased availability of suspended sentences, and deferred sentences are likely to be used in very limited circumstances. A deferred sentence enables the court to review the conduct of the defendant before passing sentence, having first prescribed certain requirements. It also provides several opportunities for an offender to have some influence as to the sentence passed—

a) it tests the commitment of the offender not to re-offend;

b) it gives the offender an opportunity to do something where progress can be shown within a short period;

c) it provides the offender with an opportunity to behave or refrain from behaving in a particular way that will be relevant to sentence.

1.2.7 Given the new power to require undertakings and the ability to enforce those undertakings before the end of the period of deferral, the decision to defer sentence should be predominantly for a small group of cases at either the custody threshold or the community sentence threshold where the sentencer feels that there would be particular value in giving the offender the opportunities listed because, if the offender complies with the requirements, a different sentence will be justified at the end of the deferment period. This could be a community sentence instead of a custodial sentence or a fine or discharge instead of a community sentence. It may, rarely, enable a custodial sentence to be suspended rather than imposed immediately.

The use of deferred sentences should be predominantly for a small group of cases close to a significant threshold where, should the defendant be prepared to adapt his behaviour in a way clearly specified by the sentencer, the court may be prepared to impose a lesser sentence.

1.2.8 A court may impose any conditions during the period of deferment that it considers appropriate.[34] These could be specific requirements as set out in the provisions for community sentences,[35] or requirements that are drawn more widely. These should be specific, measurable conditions so that the offender knows exactly what is required and the court can assess compliance; the restriction

---

[28] Powers of Criminal Courts (Sentencing) Act 2000 sections 1 and 2
[29] Criminal Justice Act 2003 schedule 23 repealing and replacing sections 1 and 2 of the 2000 Act
[30] ibid new section 1(3)(b) as inserted by schedule 23 to the Criminal Justice Act 2003
[31] ibid new section 1A(1)
[32] ibid new section 1(4)
[33] ibid new section 1B
[34] ibid new section 1 (3)(b) as inserted by schedule 23 to the Criminal Justice Act 2003
[35] Criminal Justice Act 2003 section 177

on liberty should be limited to ensure that the offender has a reasonable expectation of being able to comply whilst maintaining his or her social responsibilities.

1.2.9 Given the need for clarity in the mind of the offender and the possibility of sentence by another court, the court should give a clear indication (and make a written record) of the type of sentence it would be minded to impose if it had not decided to defer and ensure that the offender understands the consequences of failure to comply with the court's wishes during the deferral period.

When deferring sentence, the sentencer must make clear the consequence of not complying with any requirements and should indicate the type of sentence it would be minded to impose. Sentencers should impose specific, measurable conditions that do not involve a serious restriction on liberty.

SECTION 2—CUSTODIAL SENTENCES
PART 1—CUSTODIAL SENTENCES OF 12 MONTHS OR MORE

A. Statutory Provisions

2.1.1 Under existing legislation:

- an adult offender receiving a custodial sentence of at least 12 months and below 4 years will automatically be released at the halfway point and will then be supervised under licence until the three-quarter point of the sentence. [For some, the actual release date may be earlier as a result of release on Home Detention Curfew (HDC).]
- an adult offender receiving a determinate sentence of 4 years or above will be eligible for release from the halfway point and, if not released before, will automatically be released at the two-thirds point. After release, the offender will be supervised under licence until the three-quarter point of the sentence.

2.1.2 Under the new framework, the impact of a custodial sentence will be more severe since the period in custody and under supervision will be for the whole of the sentence term set by the court. Additionally, separate provisions for the protection of the public will be introduced for those offenders designated as 'dangerous' under the Act which are designed to ensure that release only occurs when it is considered safe to do so.

2.1.3 Where a prison sentence of 12 months or more is imposed on an offender who is not classified as 'dangerous', that offender will be entitled to be released from custody after completing half of the sentence. The whole of the second half of the sentence will be subject to licence requirements. These requirements will be set shortly before release by the Secretary of State (with advice from the Governor responsible for authorising the prisoner's release in consultation with the Probation Service) but a court will be able to make recommendations at the sentencing stage on the content of those requirements.[36] The conditions that the Secretary of State may attach to a licence are to be prescribed by order.[37]

2.1.4 The Act requires that a custodial sentence for a fixed term should be for the shortest term that is commensurate with the seriousness of the offence.[38]

B. Imposition of Custodial Sentences of 12 Months or More

(i) *Length of Sentence*

2.1.5 The requirement that the second half of a prison sentence will be served in the community subject to conditions imposed prior to release is a major new development and will require offenders to be under supervision for the full duration of the sentence prescribed by the court. The Probation Service will be able to impose a number of complementary requirements on the offender during the second half of a custodial sentence and these are expected to be more demanding and involve a greater restriction on liberty than current licence conditions.

2.1.6 As well as restricting liberty to a greater extent, the new requirements will last until the very end of the sentence, rather than to the three-quarter point as at present, potentially making a custodial sentence significantly more demanding than under existing legislation. Breach of these requirements at any stage is likely to result in the offender being returned to custody and this risk continues, therefore, for longer under the new framework than under the existing legislation.

[36] Criminal Justice Act 2003 section 238(1)
[37] ibid section 250
[38] ibid section 153(2)

Transitional arrangements

2.1.7 In general, a fixed term custodial sentence of 12 months or more under the new framework will increase the sentence actually served (whether in custody or in the community) since it continues to the end of the term imposed. Existing guidelines issued since 1991 have been based on a different framework and so, in order to maintain consistency between the lengths of sentence under the current and the new framework, there will need to be some adjustment to the starting points for custodial sentences contained in those guidelines (subject to the special sentences under the 2003 Act where the offender is a 'dangerous' offender).

2.1.8 This aspect of the guideline will be temporary to overcome the short-term situation where sentencing guidelines (issued since implementation of the reforms to custodial sentences introduced by the Criminal Justice Act 1991) are based on a different framework and the new framework has made those sentences more demanding. As new guidelines are issued they will take into account the new framework in providing starting points and ranges of appropriate sentence lengths for offences and an adjustment will not be necessary.

2.1.9 Since there are so many factors that will vary, it is difficult to calculate precisely how much more demanding a sentence under the new framework will be. The Council's conclusion is that the sentencer should seek to achieve the best match between a sentence under the new framework and its equivalent under the old framework so as to maintain the same level of punishment. As a guide, the Council suggests the sentence length should be reduced by in the region of 15%.

2.1.10 The changes in the nature of a custodial sentence will require changes in the way the sentence is announced. Sentencers will need to continue[39] to spell out the practical implications of the sentence being imposed so that offenders, victims and the public alike all understand that the sentence does not end when the offender is released from custody. The fact that a breach of the requirements imposed in the second half of the sentence is likely to result in a return to custody should also be made very clear at the point of sentence.

- **When imposing a fixed term custodial sentence of 12 months or more under the new provisions, courts should consider reducing the overall length of the sentence that would have been imposed under the current provisions by in the region of 15%.**
- **When announcing sentence, sentencers should explain the way in which the sentence has been calculated, how it will be served and the implications of non-compliance with licence requirements. In particular, it needs to be stated clearly that the sentence is in two parts, one in custody and one under supervision in the community.**
- **This proposal does not apply to sentences for dangerous offenders, for which separate provision has been made in the Act.**

(ii) *Licence conditions*

2.1.11 Under the Act, a court imposing a prison sentence of 12 months or more may recommend conditions that should be imposed by the Secretary of State (with advice from the Governor responsible for authorising the prisoner's release in consultation with the Probation Service) on release from custody.[40] Recommendations do not form part of the sentence and they are not binding on the Secretary of State.[41]

2.1.12 When passing such a sentence, the court will not know with any certainty to what extent the offender's behaviour may have been addressed in custody or what the offender's health and other personal circumstances might be on release and so it will be extremely difficult, especially in the case of longer custodial sentences, for sentencers to make an informed judgement about the most appropriate licence conditions to be imposed on release. However, in most cases, it would be extremely helpful for sentencers to indicate areas of an offender's behaviour about which they have the most concern and to make suggestions about the types of intervention whether this, in practice, takes place in prison or in the community.

2.1.13 The involvement of the Probation Service at the pre-sentence stage will clearly be pivotal. A recommendation on the likely post-release requirements included in a presentence report will assist the court with the decision on overall sentence length, although any recommendation would still have to be open to review when release is being considered. A curfew, exclusion requirement or prohibited activity requirement might be suitable conditions to recommend for the licence period. A court might also wish to suggest that the offender should complete a rehabilitation programme, for example for drug abuse, anger management, or improving skills

[39] having reference to the *Consolidated Criminal Practice Direction* [see **appendix 8**], Annex C, as suitably amended
[40] Criminal Justice Act 2003 section 238(1)
[41] ibid section 250

such as literacy and could recommend that this should be considered as a licence requirement if the programme has not been undertaken or completed in custody.

2.1.14 The Governor responsible for authorising the prisoner's release, in consultation with the Probation Service, is best placed to make recommendations at the point of release; this is the case at present and continues to be provided for in the Act. *Specific* court recommendations will only generally be appropriate in the context of relatively short sentences, where it would not be unreasonable for the sentencer to anticipate the relevance of particular requirements at the point of release. Making recommendations in relation to longer sentences (other than suggestions about the types of intervention that might be appropriate at some point during the sentence) would be unrealistic. The Governor and Probation Service should have due regard to any recommendations made by the sentencing court and the final recommendation to the Secretary of State on licence conditions will need to build upon any interventions during the custodial period and any other changes in the offender's circumstances.

- **A court may sensibly suggest interventions that could be useful when passing sentence, but should only make *specific* recommendations about the requirements to be imposed on licence when announcing short sentences and where it is reasonable to anticipate their relevance at the point of release. The Governor and Probation Service should have due regard to any recommendations made by the sentencing court but its decision should be contingent upon any changed circumstances during the custodial period.**
- **The court should make it clear, at the point of sentence, that the requirements to be imposed on licence will ultimately be the responsibility of the Governor and Probation Service and that they are entitled to review any recommendations made by the court in the light of any changed circumstances.**

Section 2—Custodial Sentences
Part 2—Suspended Sentences of Imprisonment

A. Statutory Provisions

2.2.1 *Section 189 Criminal Justice Act 2003*

(1) A court which passes a sentence of imprisonment for a term of at least 28 weeks but not more than 51 weeks[42] in accordance with section 181 may—
  (a) order the offender to comply during a period specified for the purposes of this paragraph in the order (in this Chapter referred to as 'the supervision period') with one or more requirements falling within section 190(1)and specified in the order, and
  (b) order that the sentence of imprisonment is not to take effect unless either—
    (i) during the supervision period the offender fails to comply with a requirement imposed under paragraph (a), or
    (ii) during a period specified in the order for the purposes of this subparagraph (in this Chapter referred to as 'the operational period') the offender commits in the United Kingdom another offence (whether or not punishable with imprisonment), and (in either case) a court having power to do so subsequently orders under paragraph 8 of Schedule 12 that the original sentence is to take effect.

(2) Where two or more sentences imposed on the same occasion are to be served consecutively, the power conferred by subsection (1) is not exercisable in relation to any of them unless the aggregate of the terms of the sentences does not exceed 65 weeks.

(3) The supervision period and the operational period must each be a period of not less than six months and not more than two years beginning with the date of the order.

(4) The supervision period must not end later than the operational period.

(5) A court which passes a suspended sentence on any person for an offence may not impose a community sentence in his case in respect of that offence or any other offence of which he is convicted by or before the court or for which he is dealt with by the court.

(6) Subject to any provision to the contrary contained in the Criminal Justice Act 1967, the Sentencing Act or any other enactment passed or instrument made under any enactment after 31st December 1967, a suspended sentence which has not taken effect under paragraph 8 of Schedule 12 is to be treated as a sentence of imprisonment for the purposes of all enactments and instruments made under enactments.

[42] Since 'custody plus' is not expected to be brought into force until a later date, it is likely that transitional provisions will provide for this power to be used for any sentence of imprisonment of less than 12 months.

(7) In this Part—
(a) 'suspended sentence order' means an order under subsection (1),
(b) 'suspended sentence' means a sentence to which a suspended sentence order relates, and
(c) 'community requirement', in relation to a suspended sentence order, means a requirement imposed under subsection (1)(a).

2.2.2 *Imposition of requirements*—Section 190 Criminal Justice Act 2003

(1) The requirements falling within this subsection are—
(a) an unpaid work requirement (as defined by section 199),
(b) an activity requirement (as defined by section 201),
(c) a programme requirement (as defined by section 202),
(d) a prohibited activity requirement (as defined by section 203),
(e) a curfew requirement (as defined by section 204),
(f) an exclusion requirement (as defined by section 205),
(g) a residence requirement (as defined by section 206),
(h) a mental health treatment requirement (as defined by section 207),
(i) a drug rehabilitation requirement (as defined by section 209),
(j) an alcohol treatment requirement (as defined by section 212),
(k) a supervision requirement (as defined by section 213), and
(l) in a case where the offender is aged under 25, an attendance centre requirement (as defined by section 214).

(2) Section 189(1)(a) has effect subject to section 218 and to the following provisions of Chapter 4 relating to particular requirements—
(a) section 199(3) (unpaid work requirement),
(b) section 201(3)and (4) (activity requirement),
(c) section 202(4)and (5) (programme requirement),
(d) section 203(2) (prohibited activity requirement),
(e) section 207(3) (mental health treatment requirement),
(f) section 209(2) (drug rehabilitation requirement), and
(g) section 212(2) and (3) (alcohol treatment requirement).

(3) Where the court makes a suspended sentence order imposing a curfew requirement or an exclusion requirement, it must also impose an electronic monitoring requirement (as defined by section 215) unless—
(a) the court is prevented from doing so by section 215(2) or 218(4), or
(b) in the particular circumstances of the case, it considers it inappropriate to do so.

(4) Where the court makes a suspended sentence order imposing an unpaid work requirement, an activity requirement, a programme requirement, a prohibited activity requirement, a residence requirement, a mental health treatment requirement, a drug rehabilitation requirement, an alcohol treatment requirement, a supervision requirement or an attendance centre requirement; the court may also impose an electronic monitoring requirement unless the court is prevented from doing so by section 215(2) or 218(4).

(5) Before making a suspended sentence order imposing two or more different requirements falling within subsection (1), the court must consider whether, in the circumstances of the case, the requirements are compatible with each other.

2.2.3 *Power to provide for review*—Section 191 Criminal Justice Act 2003

(1) A suspended sentence order may—
(a) provide for the order to be reviewed periodically at specified intervals,
(b) provide for each review to be made, subject to section 192(4), at a hearing held for the purpose by the court responsible for the order (a 'review hearing'),
(c) require the offender to attend each review hearing, and
(d) provide for the responsible officer to make to the court responsible for the order, before each review, a report on the offender's progress in complying with the community requirements of the order.

(2) Subsection (1) does not apply in the case of an order imposing a drug rehabilitation requirement (provision for such a requirement to be subject to review being made by section 210).

(3) In this section references to the court responsible for a suspended sentence order are references—
(a) where a court is specified in the order in accordance with subsection (4), to that court;
(b) in any other case, to the court by which the order is made.

(4) Where the area specified in a suspended sentence order made by a magistrates' court is not the area for which the court acts, the court may, if it thinks fit, include in the order provision specifying for the purpose of subsection (3) a magistrates' court which acts for the area specified in the order.

(5) Where a suspended sentence order has been made on an appeal brought from the Crown Court or from the criminal division of the Court of Appeal, it is to be taken for the purposes of subsection (3)(b) to have been made by the Crown Court.

2.2.4 *Periodic reviews*—Section 192 Criminal Justice Act 2003

(1) At a review hearing (within the meaning of subsection (1) of section 191) the court may, after considering the responsible officer's report referred to in that, subsection, amend the community requirements of the suspended sentence order, or any provision of the order which relates to those requirements.

(2) The court—

(a) may not amend the community requirements of the order so as to impose a requirement of a different kind unless the offender expresses his willingness to comply with that requirement,

(b) may not amend a mental health treatment requirement, a drug rehabilitation requirement or an alcohol treatment requirement unless the offender expresses his willingness to comply with the requirement as amended,

(c) may amend the supervision period only if the period as amended complies with section 189(3) and (4),

(d) may not amend the operational period of the suspended sentence, and

(e) except with the consent of the offender, may not amend the order while an appeal against the order is pending.

(3) For the purposes of subsection (2)(a)—

(a) a community requirement falling within any paragraph of section 190(1) is of the same kind as any other community requirement falling within that paragraph, and

(b) an electronic monitoring requirement is a community requirement of the same kind as any requirement falling within section 190(1) to which it relates.

(4) If before a review hearing is held at any review the court, after considering the responsible officer's report, is of the opinion that the offender's progress in complying with the community requirements of the order is satisfactory, it may order that no review hearing is to be held at that review; and if before a review hearing is held at any review, or at a review hearing, the court, after considering that report, is of that opinion, it may amend the suspended sentence order so as to provide for each subsequent review to be held without a hearing.

(5) If at a review held without a hearing the court, after considering the responsible officer's report, is of the opinion that the offender's progress under the order is no longer satisfactory, the court may require the offender to attend a hearing of the court at a specified time and place.

(6) If at a review hearing the court is of the opinion that the offender has without reasonable excuse failed to comply with any of the community requirements of the order, the court may adjourn the hearing for the purpose of dealing with the case under paragraph 8 of Schedule 12.

(7) At a review hearing the court may amend the suspended sentence order so as to vary the intervals specified under section 191(1).

(8) In this section any reference to the court, in relation to a review without a hearing is to be read—

(a) in the case of the Crown Court, as a reference to a judge of the court, and

(b) in the case of a magistrates ' court, as a reference to a justice of the peace acting for the commission area for which the court acts.

2.2.5 *Breach, revocation or amendment of orders, and effect of further conviction—Section 193 Criminal Justice Act 2003*

Schedule 12 (which relates to the breach, revocation or amendment of the community requirements of suspended sentence orders, and to the effect of any further conviction) shall have effect.

B. Imposing a Suspended Sentence

2.2.6 A suspended sentence is a sentence of imprisonment. It is subject to the same criteria as a sentence of imprisonment which is to commence immediately. In particular, this requires a court to be satisfied that the custody threshold has been passed and that the length of the term is the shortest term commensurate with the seriousness of the offence.

2.2.7 A court which passes a prison sentence of less than 12 months may suspend it for between 6 months and 2 years (the operational period).[43] During that period, the court can impose one or more requirements for the offender to undertake in the community. The requirements are identical to those available for the new community sentence.

2.2.8 The period during which the offender undertakes community requirements is 'the supervision period' when the offender will be under the supervision of a 'responsible officer'; this period may be shorter than the operational period. The court may periodically review the progress of the offender in complying with the requirements and the reviews will be informed by a report from the responsible officer.

2.2.9 If the offender fails to comply with a requirement during the supervision period, or commits a further offence during the operational period, the suspended sentence can be activated in full or in part or the terms of the supervision made more onerous. There is a presumption that the suspended sentence will be activated either in full or in part.

(i) *The decision to suspend*

2.2.10 There are many similarities between the suspended sentence and the community sentence. In both cases, requirements can be imposed during the supervision period and the court can respond to breach by sending the offender to custody. The crucial difference is that the suspended sentence is a prison sentence and is appropriate only for an offence that passes the custody threshold and for which imprisonment is the only option. A community sentence may also be imposed for an offence that passes the custody threshold where the court considers that to be appropriate.

2.2.11 The full decision making process for imposition of custodial sentences under the new framework (including the custody threshold test) is set out in paragraphs 1.31–1.33 of the Seriousness guideline. For the purposes of suspended sentences the relevant steps are:

(a) has the custody threshold been passed?
(b) if so, is it unavoidable that a custodial sentence be imposed?
(c) if so, can that sentence be suspended? (sentencers should be clear that they would have imposed a custodial sentence if the power to suspend had not been available)
(d) if not, can the sentence be served intermittently?
(e) if not, impose a sentence which takes immediate effect for the term commensurate with the seriousness of the offence.

(ii) *Length of sentence*

2.2.12 Before making the decision to suspend sentence, the court must already have decided that a prison sentence is justified and should also have decided the length of sentence that would be the shortest term commensurate with the seriousness of the offence if it were to be imposed immediately. The decision to suspend the sentence should not lead to a longer term being imposed than if the sentence were to take effect immediately.

A prison sentence that is suspended should be for the same term that would have applied if the offender were being sentenced to immediate custody.

2.2.13 When assessing the length of the operational period of a suspended sentence, the court should have in mind the relatively short length of the sentence being suspended and the advantages to be gained by retaining the opportunity to extend the operational period at a later stage (see below).

The operational period of a suspended sentence should reflect the length of the sentence being suspended. As an approximate guide, an operational period of up to 12 months might normally be appropriate for a suspended sentence of up to 6 months and an operational period of up to 18 months might normally be appropriate for a suspended sentence of up to 12 months.

(iii) *Requirements*

2.2.14 The court will set the requirements to be complied with during the supervision period. Whilst the offence for which a suspended sentence is imposed is generally likely to be more serious than one for which a community sentence is imposed, the imposition of the custodial sentence is a clear punishment and deterrent. In order to ensure that the overall terms of the sentence are commensurate with the seriousness of the offence, it is likely that the requirements to be undertaken during the supervision period would be less onerous than if a community sentence had been imposed. These requirements will need to ensure that they properly address those factors that are most likely to reduce the risk of re-offending.

[43] The power to suspend a sentence is expected to come into force earlier than the provisions implementing 'custody plus' and transitional provisions are expected to enable any sentence of imprisonment of under 12 months to be suspended. This guideline therefore is written in the language of the expected transitional provisions.

Because of the very clear deterrent threat involved in a suspended sentence, requirements imposed as part of that sentence should generally be less onerous than those imposed as part of a community sentence. A court wishing to impose onerous or intensive requirements on an offender should reconsider its decision to suspend sentence and consider whether a community sentence might be more appropriate.

C. Breaches

2.2.15 The essence of a suspended sentence is to make it abundantly clear to an offender that failure to comply with the requirements of the order or commission of another offence will almost certainly result in a custodial sentence. Where an offender has breached any of the requirements without reasonable excuse for the first time, the responsible officer must either give a warning or initiate breach proceedings.[44] Where there is a further breach within a twelve-month period, breach proceedings must be initiated.[45]

2.2.16 Where proceedings are brought the court has several options, including extending the operational period. However, the presumption (which also applies where breach is by virtue of the commission of a further offence) is that the suspended prison sentence will be activated (either with its original custodial term or a lesser term) unless the court takes the view that this would, in all the circumstances, be unjust. In reaching that decision, the court may take into account both the extent to which the offender has complied with the requirements and the facts of the new offence.[46]

2.2.17 Where a court considers that the sentence needs to be activated, it may activate it in full or with a reduced term. Again, the extent to which the requirements have been complied with will be very relevant to this decision.

2.2.18 If a court amends the order rather than activating the suspended prison sentence, it must either make the requirements more onerous, or extend the supervision or operational periods (provided that these remain within the limits defined by the Act).[47] In such cases, the court must state its reasons for not activating the prison sentence,[48] which could include the extent to which the offender has complied with requirements or the facts of the subsequent offence.

2.2.19 If an offender near the end of an operational period (having complied with the requirements imposed) commits another offence, it may be more appropriate to amend the order rather than activate it.

2.2.20 If a new offence committed is of a less serious nature than the offence for which the suspended sentence was passed, it may justify activating the sentence with a reduced term or amending the terms of the order.

2.2.21 It is expected that any activated suspended sentence will be consecutive to the sentence imposed for the new offence.

2.2.22 If the new offence is non-imprisonable, the sentencer should consider whether it is appropriate to activate the suspended sentence at all.

Where the court decides to amend a suspended sentence order rather than activate the custodial sentence, it should give serious consideration to extending the supervision or operational periods (within statutory limits) rather than making the requirements more onerous.

SECTION 2 CUSTODIAL SENTENCES
PART 3—INTERMITTENT CUSTODY

A. Statutory Provisions

2.3.1 *Section 183 Criminal Justice Act 2003*

(1) A court may, when passing a sentence of imprisonment for a term complying with subsection (4)—
 (a) specify the number of days that the offender must serve in prison under the sentence before being released on licence for the remainder of the term, and
 (b) by order—
  (i) specify periods during which the offender is to be released temporarily on licence before he has served that number of days in prison, and

[44] Criminal Justice Act 2003 schedule 12, para 4
[45] ibid para 5
[46] ibid para 8(4)
[47] ibid section 189 (3) and (4)
[48] ibid schedule 12, para. 8(3)

(ii) require any licence to be granted subject to conditions requiring the offender's compliance during the licence periods with one or more requirements falling within section 182(1) and specified in the order.

(2) In this Part 'intermittent custody order' means an order under subsection (1)(b).

(3) In this Chapter—

'licence period', in relation to a term of imprisonment to which an intermittent custody order relates, means any period during which the offender is released on licence by virtue of subsection (1)(a) or (b)(i); 'the number of custodial days', in relation to a term of imprisonment to which an intermittent custody order relates, means the number of days specified under subsection (1)(a).

(4) The term of the sentence—

(a) must be expressed in weeks,

(b) must be at least 28 weeks,

(c) must not be more than 51 weeks in respect of any one offence, and

(d) must not exceed the maximum term permitted for the offence.

(5) The number of custodial days—

(a) must be at least 14, and

(b) in respect of any one offence, must not be more than 90.

(6) A court may not exercise its powers under subsection (1) unless the offender has expressed his willingness to serve the custodial part of the proposed sentence intermittently, during the parts of the sentence that are not to be licence periods.

(7) Where a court exercises its powers under subsection (1) in respect of two or more terms of imprisonment that are to be served consecutively—

(a) the aggregate length of the terms of imprisonment must not be more than 65 weeks, and

(b) the aggregate of the numbers of custodial days must not be more than 180.

(8) The Secretary of State may by order require a court, in specifying licence periods under subsection (1)(b)(i), to specify only—

(a) periods of a prescribed duration,

(b) periods beginning or ending at prescribed times, or

(c) periods including, or not including, specified parts of the week.

(9) An intermittent custody order which specifies two or more requirements may, in relation to any requirement, refer to compliance within such licence period or periods, or part of a licence period, as is specified in the order.

2.3.2 *Restrictions on power to make orders—Section 184 Criminal Justice Act 2003*

(1) A court may not make an intermittent custody order unless it has been notified by the Secretary of State that arrangements for implementing such orders are available in the area proposed to be specified in the intermittent custody order and the notice has not been withdrawn.

(2) The court may not make an intermittent custody order in respect of any offender unless—

(a) it has consulted an officer of a local probation board,

(b) it has received from the Secretary of State notification that suitable prison accommodation is available for the offender during the custodial periods, and

(c) it appears to the court that the offender will have suitable accommodation available to him during the licence periods.

(3) In this section 'custodial period', in relation to a sentence to which an intermittent custody order relates, means any part of the sentence that is not a licence period.

2.3.3 *Licence conditions—Section 185 Criminal Justice Act 2003*

(1) Section 183(1)(b) has effect subject to section 218 and to the following provisions of Chapter 4 limiting the power to require the licence to contain particular requirements—

(a) section 199(3) (unpaid work requirement),

(b) section 201(3) and (4) (activity requirement),

(c) section 202(4) and (5) (programme requirement), and

(d) section 203(2) (prohibited activity requirement).

(2) Subsections (3) to (5) of section 182 have effect in relation to an intermittent custody order as they have effect in relation to a custody plus order.

2.3.4 *Further provisions—Section 186 Criminal Justice Act 2003*

(1) Section 21 of the 1952 Act (expenses of conveyance to prison) does not apply in relation to the conveyance to prison at the end of any licence period of an offender to whom an intermittent custody order relates.

(2) The Secretary of State may pay to any offender to whom an intermittent custody order relates the whole or part of any expenses incurred by the offender in travelling to and from prison during licence periods.

(3) In section 49 of the 1952 Act (persons unlawfully at large) after subsection (4) there is inserted—

'(4A) For the purposes of this section a person shall also be deemed to be unlawfully at large if, having been temporarily released in pursuance of an intermittent custody order made under section 183 of the Criminal Justice Act 2003, he remains at large at a time when, by reason of the expiry of the period for which he was temporarily released, he is liable to be detained in pursuance of his sentence.'

(4) In section 23 of the Criminal Justice Act 1961 (prison rules), in subsection (3) for 'The days' there is substituted 'Subject to subsection (3A), the days' and after subsection (3) there is inserted—

'(3A) In relation to a prisoner to whom an intermittent custody order under section 183 of the Criminal Justice Act 2003 relates, the only days to which subsection (3) applies are Christmas Day, Good Friday and any day which under the Banking and Financial Dealings Act 1971 is a bank holiday in England and Wales.'

(5) In section 1 of the Prisoners (Return to Custody) Act 1995 (remaining at large after temporary release) after subsection (1) there is inserted—

'(1A) A person who has been temporarily released in pursuance of an intermittent custody order made under section 183 of the Criminal Justice Act 2003 is guilty of an offence if, without reasonable excuse, he remains unlawfully at large at any time after becoming so at large by virtue of the expiry of the period for which he was temporarily released.'

(6) In this section 'the 1952 Act' means the Prison Act 1952.

2.3.5 *Revocation or amendment—Section 187 Criminal Justice Act 2003*
Schedule 10 (which contains provisions relating to the revocation or amendment of custody plus orders and the amendment of intermitten custody orders) shall have effect.

B. Imposing an Intermittent Custody Order

2.3.6 Intermittent custody must be used only for offences that have crossed the custodial threshold. It is an alternative to immediate full-time custody and so must meet all the criteria that apply to such a sentence, in particular the need to pass the custody threshold and the need to ensure that the sentence is for the shortest term commensurate with the seriousness of the offence.

2.3.7 The prison sentence is not continuous but is interspersed by periods when the offender is released on temporary licence in the community. A court may only impose intermittent custody if the offender consents to serving the custodial part of the sentence intermittently. The court must also make sure that the relevant resources are available in the local area and must consult the Probation Service[49] to confirm that the offender is an appropriate candidate for such a sentence.

2.3.8 This sentence is currently being piloted and this guidance will be reviewed and may need to be developed further in the light of the outcome.

(i) *Circumstances when intermittent custody may be appropriate*

2.3.9 Guidance supporting the pilots[50] states that intermittent custody is not intended to be used for sex offenders or those convicted of *serious* offences of either violence or burglary. There may be other offences which by their nature would make intermittent custody inappropriate and public safety should always be the paramount consideration.

2.3.10 The circumstances of the offender are likely to be the determining factor in deciding whether an intermittent custody order is appropriate. It is only appropriate where the custody threshold has been crossed and where suspending the custodial sentence or imposing a non-custodial sentence have been ruled out. Suitable candidates for weekend custody might include offenders who are: full-time carers; employed; or in education.

2.3.11 The full decision making process for imposition of custodial sentences under the new framework (including the custody threshold test) is set out in paragraphs 1.31–1.33 of the Seriousness guideline. For the purposes of intermittent custody the relevant steps are:

(a) has the custody threshold been passed?
(b) if so, is it unavoidable that a custodial sentence be imposed?
(c) if so, can that sentence be suspended? (sentencers should be clear that they would have imposed a custodial sentence if the power to suspend had not been available)

[49] Criminal Justice Act 2003 section 184(2)
[50] IC Pilot Project 'A Brief Guide to Intermittent Custody' 02/03/04 HMPS

(d) if not, can it be served intermittently?
(e) if not, impose a sentence which takes immediate effect for the term commensurate with the seriousness of the offence.

- **Courts must be satisfied that a custodial sentence of less than 12 months is justified and that neither a community sentence nor a suspended sentence is appropriate before considering whether to make an intermittent custody order.**
- **When imposing a custodial sentence of less than 12 months, the court should always consider whether it would be appropriate to sentence an offender to intermittent custody; primary considerations will be public safety, offender suitability and sentence availability.**
- **Courts should strive to ensure that the intermittent custody provisions are applied in a way that limits discrimination and they should, in principle, be considered for all offenders.**

(ii) *Licence requirements*

2.3.12 As a primary objective of being able to serve a custodial sentence intermittently is to enable offenders to continue to fulfil existing obligations in the community, and since the time spent in custody is utilised extensively for activities, experience has so far shown that additional, similar, requirements to be completed whilst on licence are not practical. However, requirements such as curfews, prohibited activity and exclusion requirements might be appropriate in a particular case.

The practical workings of an intermittent custody sentence will effectively rule out the use of some of the longer or more intensive community requirements. Requirements such as curfews, prohibited activity and exclusion requirements might be appropriate in a particular case.

(iii) *Sentence length*

2.3.13 The demands made on the offender by this sentence will generally be considerably greater than for a custodial sentence to be served immediately in full. The disruptive effect on family life, the psychological impact of going in and out of custody and the responsibility on the offender to travel to and from the custodial establishment on many occasions all make the sentence more onerous.

Once a court has decided that an offender should be sent to prison and has determined the length of the sentence, it should reduce the overall length of the sentence because it is to be served intermittently.

Annex A
Time Spent on Remand—Sentencing Advisory Panel's Advice

The Act makes provision for a sentencer to give credit for time spent on remand in custody where a custodial sentence is passed.[51] It also empowers the court to have regard to time spent on remand in custody when determining the restrictions on liberty to be imposed by a community order or youth community order.[52] Where an offender has spent several weeks in custody, this may affect the nature of the sentence that is passed. For example, where the court decides that a custodial sentence is justified some sentencers may decide to pass a community sentence instead, on the basis that the offender has already completed the equivalent of a punitive element in a sentence. The Panel takes the view that, given the changes in the content of the second part of a custodial sentence, in such cases it will be more appropriate to pass a custodial sentence knowing that licence requirements will be imposed on release from custody (which may be immediate). Recommendations made by the court at the point of sentence will then be of particular importance in influencing the content of the licence. This will help to ensure that the record clearly shows the assessment of seriousness of the offending behaviour.

Whereas the Act clearly states that time spent on remand is to be regarded as part of a custodial sentence unless the Court considers it unjust,[53] it states that sentencers passing a community sentence *may* have regard to time spent on remand, but no further information is given on how this discretion should be exercised. The Panel recognises that giving credit for time spent on remand is likely to be easier to apply in relation to punitive requirements rather than the rehabilitative elements of a community sentence. For example, reducing the number of unpaid work hours could be fairly easy, whereas reducing the length of a rehabilitation programme might not be appropriate as it could undermine its effectiveness. Where an offender has been kept on remand, one could take the view that this action was justified by

[51] Criminal Justice Act 2003 section 240
[52] ibid section 149
[53] ibid section 240 (which will, at a future date, replace Criminal Justice Act 1967, section 67, by which such period is now deducted automatically).

the bail provisions and that the sentencer should not, therefore, feel obliged to adjust the terms of the community sentence. However, in principle, the Panel recommends that the court should seek to give credit for time spent on remand in all cases and should explain its reasons for not doing so when it considers either that this is not justified, would not be practical, or would not be in the best interests of the offender.

The court should seek to give credit for time spent on remand in all cases. It should make clear, when announcing sentence, whether or not credit for time on remand has been given and should explain its reasons for not giving credit when it considers either that this is not justified, would not be practical, or would not be in the best interests of the offender.

Where, following a period of time spent in custody on remand, the court decides that a custodial sentence is justified then, given the changes in the content of the second part of a custodial sentence, the court should pass a custodial sentence in the knowledge that licence requirements will be imposed on release from custody. Recommendations made by the court at the point of sentence will be of particular importance in influencing the content of the licence.[54]

PART 3 OVERARCHING PRINCIPLES: SERIOUSNESS

Foreword

In accordance with the provisions of section 170(9) Criminal Justice Act 2003, the Sentencing Guidelines Council issues this guideline as a definitive guideline. By virtue of section 172 of the Act, every court must have regard to a relevant guideline.

The Council was created in 2004 in order to frame Guidelines to assist Courts as they deal with criminal cases across the whole of England and Wales.

The Council has stated that it intends to follow a principled approach to the formulation of guidelines to assist sentencers which will include consideration of overarching and general principles relating to the sentencing of offenders. Following the planned implementation of many of the sentencing provisions in the 2003 Act in April 2005, this guideline deals with the general concept of seriousness in the light of those provisions and considers how sentencers should determine when the respective sentencing thresholds have been crossed when applying the provisions of the Act.

This guideline applies only to sentences passed under the sentencing framework applicable to those aged 18 or over although there are some aspects that will assist courts assessing the seriousness of offences committed by those under 18. The Council has commissioned separate advice from the Sentencing Advisory Panel on the sentencing of young offenders.

. . .

Chairman of the Council

December 2004

Seriousness

A. Statutory provisions

1.1 In every case where the offender is aged 18 or over at the time of conviction, the court must have regard to the five purposes of sentencing contained in section 142(1) Criminal Justice Act 2003:
   (a) the punishment of offenders
   (b) the reduction of crime (including its reduction by deterrence)
   (c) the reform and rehabilitation of offenders
   (d) the protection of the public
   (e) the making of reparation by offenders to persons affected by their offence

1.2 The Act does not indicate that any one purpose should be more important than any other and in practice they may all be relevant to a greater or lesser degree in any individual case—the sentencer has the task of determining the manner in which they apply.

1.3 The sentencer must start by considering the *seriousness* of the offence, the assessment of which will:
   - determine which of the sentencing thresholds has been crossed;
   - indicate whether a custodial, community or other sentence is the most appropriate;

[54] This recommendation only applies to sentences of 12 months and above pending the implementation of 'custody plus'.

- be the key factor in deciding the length of a custodial sentence, the onerousness of requirements to be incorporated in a community sentence and the amount of any fine imposed.

1.4 A court is required to pass a sentence that is commensurate with the seriousness of the offence. The *seriousness* of an offence is determined by two main parameters; the *culpability* of the offender and the *harm* caused or risked being caused by the offence.

1.5 Section 143(1) Criminal Justice Act 2003 provides:
'In considering the seriousness of any offence, the court must consider the offender's culpability in committing the offence and any harm which the offence caused, was intended to cause or might foreseeably have caused.'

B. Culpability

1.6 Four levels of criminal culpability can be identified for sentencing purposes:

1.7 Where the offender;

(i) has the *intention* to cause harm, with the highest culpability when an offence is planned. The worse the harm intended, the greater the seriousness.

(ii) is *reckless* as to whether harm is caused, that is, where the offender appreciates at least some harm would be caused but proceeds giving no thought to the consequences even though the extent of the risk would be obvious to most people.

(iii) has *knowledge* of the specific risks entailed by his actions even though he does not intend to cause the harm that results.

(iv) is guilty of *negligence.*

Note: *There are offences where liability is strict and no culpability need be proved for the purposes of obtaining a conviction, but the degree of culpability is still important when deciding sentence. The extent to which recklessness, knowledge or negligence are involved in a particular offence will vary.*

C. Harm

1.8 The relevant provision is widely drafted so that it encompasses those offences where harm is caused but also those where neither individuals nor the community suffer harm but a risk of harm is present.

To Individual Victims

1.9 The types of harm caused or risked by different types of criminal activity are diverse and victims may suffer physical injury, sexual violation, financial loss, damage to health or psychological distress. There are gradations of harm within all of these categories.

1.10 The nature of harm will depend on personal characteristics and circumstances of the victim and the court's assessment of harm will be an effective and important way of taking into consideration the impact of a particular crime on the victim.

1.11 In some cases no actual harm may have resulted and the court will be concerned with assessing the relative dangerousness of the offender's conduct; it will consider the likelihood of harm occurring and the gravity of the harm that could have resulted.

To the Community

1.12 Some offences cause harm to the community at large (instead of or as well as to an individual victim) and may include economic loss, harm to public health, or interference with the administration of justice.

Other Types of harm

1.13 There are other types of harm that are more difficult to define or categorise. For example, cruelty to animals certainly causes significant harm to the animal but there may also be a human victim who also suffers psychological distress and/or financial loss.

1.14 Some conduct is criminalised purely by reference to public feeling or social mores. In addition, public concern about the damage caused by some behaviour, both to individuals and to society as a whole, can influence public perception of the harm caused, for example, by the supply of prohibited drugs.

D. The Assessment of Culpability and Harm

1.15 Section 143(1) makes clear that the assessment of the seriousness of any individual offence must take account not only of any harm actually caused by the offence, but also of any harm that was intended to be caused or might foreseeably be caused by the offence.

1.16 Assessing seriousness is a difficult task, particularly where there is an imbalance between culpability and harm:

- sometimes the harm that actually results is greater than the harm intended by the offender;
- in other circumstances, the offender's culpability may be at a higher level than the harm resulting from the offence.

1.17 Harm must always be judged in the light of culpability. The precise level of culpability will be determined by such factors as motivation, whether the offence was planned or spontaneous or whether the offender was in a position of trust.

Culpability will be greater if:

- an offender deliberately causes more harm than is necessary for the commission of th offence, or
- where an offender targets a vulnerable victim (because of their old age or youth, disability or by virtue of the job they do).

1.18 Where unusually serious harm results and was unintended and beyond the control of the offender, culpability will be significantly influenced by the extent to which the harm could have been foreseen.

1.19 If much *more* harm, or much *less* harm has been caused by the offence than the offender intended or foresaw, the culpability of the offender, depending on the circumstances, may be regarded as carrying greater or lesser weight as appropriate.

The culpability of the offender in the particular circumstances of an individual case should be the initial factor in determining the seriousness of an offence.

(i) Aggravating Factors

1.20 Sentencing guidelines for a particular offence will normally include a list of aggravating features which, if present in an individual instance of the offence, would indicate *either* a higher than usual level of culpability on the part of the offender, *or* a greater than usual degree of harm caused by the offence (or sometimes both).

1.21 The lists below bring together the most important aggravating features with potential application to more than one offence or class of offences. They include some factors (such as the vulnerability of victims or abuse of trust) which are integral features of certain offences; in such cases, the presence of the aggravating factor is already reflected in th penalty for the offence and *cannot be used as justification for increasing the sentence further.* The lists are not intended to be comprehensive and the aggravating factors are not listed in any particular order of priority. On occasions, two or more of the factors listed will describe the same feature of the offence and care needs to be taken to avoid 'doublecounting'. Those factors starred with an asterisk are statutory aggravating factors where the statutory provisions are in force. Those marked with a hash are yet to be brought into force but as factors in an individual case are still relevant and should be taken into account.

1.22 *Factors indicating higher culpability:*

- Offence committed whilst on bail for other offences*
- Failure to respond to previous sentences#
- Offence was racially or religiously aggravated*
- Offence motivated by, or demonstrating, hostility to the victim based on his or her sexual orientation (or presumed sexual orientation)#
- Offence motivated by, or demonstrating, hostility based on the victim's disability (or presumed disability)#
- Previous conviction(s), particularly where a pattern of repeat offending is disclosed #
- Planning of an offence
- An intention to commit more serious harm than actually resulted from the offence
- Offenders operating in groups or gangs
- 'Professional' offending
- Commission of the offence for financial gain (where this is not inherent in the offence itself)
- High level of profit from the offence
- An attempt to conceal or dispose of evidence
- Failure to respond to warnings or concerns expressed by others about the offender's behaviour
- Offence committed whilst on licence
- Offence motivated by hostility towards a minority group, or a member or members of it
- Deliberate targeting of vulnerable victim(s)
- Commission of an offence while under the influence of alcohol or drugs
- Use of a weapon to frighten or injure victim
- Deliberate and gratuitous violence or damage to property, over and above what is needed to carry out the offence
- Abuse of power
- Abuse of a position of trust

1.23 *Factors indicating a more than usually serious degree of harm:*

- Multiple victims
- An especially serious physical or psychological effect on the victim, even if unintended
- A sustained assault or repeated assaults on the same victim
- Victim is particularly vulnerable
- Location of the offence (for example, in an isolated place)
- Offence is committed against those working in the public sector or providing a service to the public
- Presence of others e.g. relatives, especially children or partner of the victim
- Additional degradation of the victim (e.g. taking photographs of a victim as part of a sexual offence)
- In property offences, high value (including sentimental value) of property to the victim, or substantial consequential loss (e.g. where the theft of equipment causes serious disruption to a victim's life or business)

(ii) Mitigating factors

1.24 Some factors may indicate that an offender's culpability is *unusually* low, or that the harm caused by an offence is less than usually serious.

1.25 *Factors indicating significantly lower culpability:*

- A greater degree of provocation than normally expected
- Mental illness or disability
- Youth or age, where it affects the responsibility of the individual defendant
- The fact that the offender played only a minor role in the offence

(iii) Personal mitigation

1.26 Section 166(1) Criminal Justice Act 2003 makes provision for a sentencer to take account of any matters that 'in the opinion of the court, are relevant in mitigation of sentence'.

1.27 When the court has formed an initial assessment of the seriousness of the offence, then it should consider any offender mitigation. The issue of remorse should be taken into account at this point along with other mitigating features such as admissions to the police in interview.

(iv) Reduction for a guilty plea

1.28 Sentencers will normally reduce the severity of a sentence to reflect an early guilty plea. This subject is covered by a separate guideline and provides a sliding scale reduction with a normal maximum one-third reduction being given to offenders who enter a guilty plea at the first reasonable opportunity.

1.29 Credit may also be given for ready co-operation with the authorities. This will depend on the particular circumstances of the individual case.

E. The Sentencing Thresholds

1.30 Assessing the seriousness of an offence is only the first step in the process of determining the appropriate sentence in an individual case. Matching the offence to a type and level of sentence is a separate and complex exercise assisted by the application of the respective threshold tests for custodial and community sentences.

The Custody Threshold

1.31 Section 152(2) Criminal Justice Act 2003 provides:

'The court must not pass a custodial sentence unless it is of the opinion that the offence, or the combination of the offence and one or more offences associated with it, was so serious that neither a fine alone nor a community sentence can be justified for the offence.'

1.32 In applying the threshold test, sentencers should note:

- the clear intention of the threshold test is to reserve prison as a punishment for the most serious offences;
- it is impossible to determine definitively which features of a particular offence make it serious enough to merit a custodial sentence;
- passing the custody threshold does *not* mean that a custodial sentence should be deemed inevitable, and custody can still be avoided in the light of personal mitigation or where there is a suitable intervention in the community which provides sufficient restriction (by way of punishment) while addressing the rehabilitation of the offender to prevent future crime. For example, a prolific offender who currently could expect a short custodial sentence (which, in advance of custody plus, would have no provision for supervision on release) might more appropriately receive a suitable community sentence.

1.33 The approach to the imposition of a custodial sentence under the new framework should be as follows:
- (a) has the custody threshold been passed?
- (b) if so, is it unavoidable that a custodial sentence be imposed?
- (c) if so, can that sentence be suspended? (sentencers should be clear that they would have imposed a custodial sentence if the power to suspend had not been available)
- (d) if not, can the sentence be served intermittently?
- (e) if not, impose a sentence which takes immediate effect for the term commensurate with the seriousness of the offence.

The Threshold for Community Sentences

1.34 Section 148(1) Criminal Justice Act 2003 provides:

'A court must not pass a community sentence on an offender unless it is of the opinion that the offence, or the combination of the offence and one or more offences associated with it, was serious enough to warrant such a sentence.'

1.35 In addition, the threshold for a community sentence can be crossed even though the seriousness criterion is not met. Section 151 Criminal Justice Act 2003 provides that, in relation to an offender aged 16 or over on whom, on 3 or more previous occasions, sentences had been passed consisting only of a fine, a community sentence may be imposed (if it is in the interests of justice) despite the fact that the seriousness of the current offence (and others associated with it) might not warrant such a sentence.

1.36 Sentencers should consider all of the disposals available (within or below the threshold passed) at the time of sentence before reaching the provisional decision to make a community sentence, so that, even where the threshold for a community sentence has been passed, a financial penalty or discharge may still be an appropriate penalty.

Summary

1.37 It would not be feasible to provide a form of words or to devise any formula that would provide a general solution to the problem of where the custody threshold lies. Factors vary too widely between offences for this to be done. It is the task of *guidelines for individual offences* to provide more detailed guidance on what features within that offence point to a custodial sentence, and also to deal with issues such as sentence length, the appropriate requirements for a community sentence or the use of appropriate ancillary orders.

Having assessed the seriousness of an individual offence, sentencers must consult the sentencing guidelines for an offence of that type for guidance on the factors that are likely to indicate whether a custodial sentence or other disposal is most likely to be appropriate.

F. Prevalence

1.38 The seriousness of an individual case should be judged on its own dimensions of harm and culpability rather than as part of a collective social harm. It is legitimate for the overall approach to sentencing levels for particular offences to be guided by their cumulative effect. However, it would be wrong to further penalise individual offenders by increasing sentence length for committing an individual offence of that type.

1.39 There may be exceptional local circumstances that arise which may lead a court to decide that prevalence should influence sentencing levels. The pivotal issue in such cases will be the harm being caused to the community. It is essential that sentencers both have supporting evidence from an external source (for example the local Criminal Justice Board) to justify claims that a particular crime is prevalent in their area and are satisfied that there is a compelling need to treat the offence more seriously than elsewhere.

The key factor in determining whether sentencing levels should be enhanced in response to prevalence will be the level of harm being caused in the locality. Enhanced sentences should be exceptional and in response to exceptional circumstances. Sentencers must sentence within the sentencing guidelines once the prevalence has been addressed.

PART 4 MANSLAUGHTER BY REASON OF PROVOCATION

Foreword

In accordance with section 170(9) of the Criminal Justice Act 2003, the Sentencing Guidelines Council issues this guideline as a definitive guideline. By virtue of section 172 of the Act, every court must have regard to a relevant guideline. This guideline applies to offenders convicted of manslaughter by reason of provocation who are sentenced after 28 November 2005.

This guideline stems from a reference from the Home Secretary for consideration of the issue of sentencing where provocation is argued in cases of homicide, and, in particular, domestic violence homicides. For the purpose of describing 'domestic violence', the Home Secretary adopted the Crown Prosecution Service definition.[55] The guideline applies to sentencing of an adult offender for this offence in whatever circumstances it occurs. It identifies the widely varying features of both the provocation and the act of retaliation and sets out the approach to be adopted in deciding both the sentencing range and the starting point within that range.

This guideline is for use where the conviction for manslaughter is clearly founded on provocation alone. There will be additional, different and more complicated matters to be taken into account where the other main partial defence, diminished responsibility, is a factor.

The Council's Guideline *New Sentences: Criminal Justice Act 2003* recognised the potentially more demanding nature of custodial sentences of 12 months or longer imposed under the new framework introduced by the Criminal Justice Act 2003. Consequently the sentencing ranges and starting points in this guideline take that principle into account.

. . .

Chairman of the Council

November 2005

Manslaughter by Reason of Provocation

A. Statutory Provision

1.1 Murder and manslaughter are common law offences and there is no complete statutory definition of either. 'Provocation' is one of the partial defences by which an offence that would otherwise be murder may be reduced to manslaughter.

1.2 Before the issue of provocation can be considered, the Crown must have proved beyond reasonable doubt that all the elements of murder were present, including the necessary intent (i.e. the offender must have intended either to kill the victim or to cause grievous bodily harm). The court must then consider section 3 of the Homicide Act 1957, which provides:

Where on a charge of murder there is evidence on which the jury can find that the person charged was provoked (whether by things done or by things said or by both together) to lose his self-control, the question whether the provocation was enough to make a reasonable man do as he did shall be left to be determined by the jury; and in determining that question the jury shall take into account everything both done and said according to the effect which, in their opinion, it would have on a reasonable man.

Although both murder and manslaughter result in death, the difference in the level of culpability creates offences of a distinctively different character. Therefore the approach to sentencing in each should start from a different basis.

B. Establishing the Basis for Sentencing

2.1 The Court of Appeal in *Attorney General's Reference (Nos. 74, 95 and 118 of 2002) (Suratan and others)*,[56] set out a number of assumptions that a judge must make in favour of an offender found not

[55] 'Any criminal offence arising out of physical, sexual, psychological, emotional or financial abuse by one person against a current or former partner in a close relationship, or against a current or former family member.' A new definition of domestic violence was agreed in 2004 (and appears in the CPS Policy on Prosecuting cases of Domestic Violence, 2005) 'any incident of threatening behaviour, violence or abuse [psychological, physical, sexual, financial or emotional] between adults who are or have been intimate partners or family members, regardless of gender or sexuality'

[56] [2003] 2 Cr App R (S) 42

guilty of murder but guilty of manslaughter by reason of provocation. The assumptions are required in order to be faithful to the verdict and should be applied equally in all cases whether conviction follows a trial or whether the Crown has accepted a plea of guilty to manslaughter by reason of provocation:

- first, that the offender had, at the time of the killing, lost self-control; mere loss of temper or jealous rage is not sufficient
- second, that the offender was caused to lose self-control by things said or done, normally by the person killed
- third, that the offender's loss of control was reasonable in all the circumstances, even bearing in mind that people are expected to exercise reasonable control over their emotions and that, as society advances, it ought to call for a higher measure of self control.
- fourth, that the circumstances were such as to make the loss of self-control sufficiently excusable to reduce the gravity of the offence from murder to manslaughter.

Bearing in mind the loss of life caused by manslaughter by reason of provocation, the starting point for sentencing should be a custodial sentence. Only in a very small number of cases involving very exceptional mitigating factors should a judge consider that a non-custodial sentence is justified.

The same general sentencing principles should apply in all cases of manslaughter by reason of provocation irrespective of whether or not the killing takes place in a domestic context.

C. Factors Influencing Sentence

3.1 A number of elements must be considered and balanced by the sentencer. Some of these are common to all types of manslaughter by reason of provocation; others have a particular relevance in cases of manslaughter in a domestic context.

3.2 ***The degree of provocation as shown by its nature and duration*** – An assessment of the *degree* of the provocation as shown by its nature and duration is the critical factor in the sentencing decision.

(a) *In assessing the* degree *of provocation, account should be taken of the following factors:*

- if the provocation (which does not have to be a wrongful act) involves gross and extreme conduct on the part of the victim, it is a more significant mitigating factor than conduct which, although significant, is not as extreme
- the fact that the victim presented a threat not only to the offender, but also to children in his or her care
- the offender's previous experiences of abuse and/or domestic violence either by the victim or by other people
- any mental condition which may affect the offender's perception of what amounts to provocation
- the nature of the conduct, the period of time over which it took place and its cumulative effect
- discovery or knowledge of the fact of infidelity on the part of a partner does not necessarily amount to *high* provocation. The gravity of such provocation depends entirely on all attendant circumstances.

(b) *Whether the provocation was suffered over a* long or short *period is important to the assessment of gravity. The following factors should be considered:*

- the impact of provocative behaviour on an offender can build up over a period of time
- consideration should not be limited to acts of provocation that occurred immediately before the victim was killed. For example, in domestic violence cases, cumulative provocation may eventually become intolerable, the latest incident seeming all the worse because of what went before.

(c) *When looking at the* nature *of the provocation the court should consider both the type of provocation and whether, in the particular case, the actions of the victim would have had a particularly marked effect on the offender:*

- actual (or anticipated) violence from the victim will generally be regarded as involving a higher degree of provocation than provocation arising from abuse, infidelity or offensive words unless that amounts to psychological bullying
- in cases involving actual or anticipated violence, the culpability of the offender will therefore generally be less than in cases involving verbal provocation
- where the offender's actions were motivated by fear or desperation, rather than by anger, frustration, resentment or a desire for revenge, the offender's culpability will generally be lower.

3.3 ***The extent and timing of the retaliation*** – It is implicit in the verdict of manslaughter by reason of provocation that the killing was the result of a loss of self-control because of things said and/or done. The intensity, extent and nature of that loss of control must be assessed in the context of the provocation that preceded it.

3.4 The *circumstances of the killing* itself will be relevant to the offender's culpability, and hence to the appropriate sentence:

- in general, the offender's violent response to provocation is likely to be less culpable the shorter the time gap between the provocation (or the last provocation) and the killing – as evidenced, for example, by the use of a weapon that happened to be available rather than by one that was carried for that purpose or prepared for use in advance
- conversely, it is not necessarily the case that greater culpability will be found where there has been a significant lapse of time between the provocation (or the last provocation) and the killing. Where the provocation is cumulative, and particularly in those circumstances where the offender is found to have suffered domestic violence from the victim over a significant period of time, the required loss of self-control may not be sudden as some experience a 'slow-burn' reaction and appear calm
- choosing or taking advantage of favourable circumstances for carrying out the killing (so that the victim was unable to resist, such as where the victim was not on guard, or was asleep) may well be an aggravating factor – unless this is mitigated by the circumstances of the offender, resulting in the offender being the weaker or vulnerable party.

3.5 The *context of the relationship* between the offender and the victim must be borne in mind when assessing the nature and degree of the provocation offered by the victim before the crime and the length of time over which the provocation existed. In cases where the parties were still in a relationship at the time of the killing, it will be necessary to examine the balance of power between one party and the other and to consider other family members who may have been drawn into, or been victims of, the provocative behaviour.

Although there will usually be less culpability when the retaliation to provocation is sudden, it is not always the case that greater culpability will be found where there has been a significant lapse of time between the provocation and the killing.

It is for the sentencer to consider the impact on an offender of provocative behaviour that has built up over a period of time.

An offence should be regarded as aggravated where it is committed in the presence of a child or children or other vulnerable family member, whether or not the offence takes place in a domestic setting.

3.6 *Post-offence behaviour* – The behaviour of the offender after the killing can be relevant to sentence:

- immediate and genuine remorse may be demonstrated by the summoning of medical assistance, remaining at the scene, and co-operation with the authorities
- concealment or attempts to dispose of evidence or dismemberment of the body may aggravate the offence.

Post-offence behaviour is relevant to the sentence. It may be an aggravating or mitigating factor. When sentencing, the judge should consider the motivation behind the offender's actions.

3.7 *Use of a weapon*

(a) In relation to this offence, as in relation to many different types of offence, the carrying and use of a weapon is an aggravating factor. Courts must consider the type of weapon used and, importantly, whether it was to hand or carried to the scene and who introduced it to the incident.

(b) The use or not of a weapon is a factor heavily influenced by the gender of the offender. Whereas men can and do kill using physical strength alone, women often cannot and thus resort to using a weapon. The issue of key importance is whether the weapon was to hand or carried deliberately to the scene, although the circumstances in which the weapon was brought to the scene will need to be considered carefully.

Although there will usually be less culpability when the retaliation to provocation is sudden, it is not always the case that greater culpability will be found where there has been a significant lapse of time between the provocation and the killing.

It is for the sentencer to consider the impact on an offender of provocative behaviour that has built up over a period of time.

An offence should be regarded as aggravated where it is committed in the presence of a child or children or other vulnerable family member, whether or not the offence takes place in a domestic setting.

The use of a weapon should not necessarily move a case into another sentencing bracket.

In cases of manslaughter by reason of provocation, use of a weapon may reflect the imbalance in strength between the offender and the victim and how that weapon came to hand is likely to be far more important than the use of the weapon itself.

It will be an aggravating factor where the weapon is brought to the scene in contemplation of use *before* the loss of self-control (which may occur some time before the fatal incident).

D. Sentence Ranges and Starting Points

4.1 **Manslaughter is a 'serious offence' for the purposes of the provisions in the Criminal Justice Act 2003[57] for dealing with dangerous offenders. It is possible that a court will be required to use the sentences for public protection prescribed in the Act when sentencing an offender convicted of the offence of manslaughter by reason of provocation. An alternative is a discretionary life sentence. In accordance with normal practice, when setting the minimum term to be served within an indeterminate sentence under these provisions, that term will usually be half the equivalent determinate sentence.**

4.2 *Identifying sentence ranges* – The key factor that will be relevant in every case is the nature and the duration of the provocation.

(a) The process to be followed by the court will be:

identify the sentence range by reference to the degree of provocation

adjust the starting point within the range by reference to the length of time over which the provocation took place

take into consideration the circumstances of the killing (e.g. the length of time that had elapsed between the provocation and the retaliation and the circumstances in which any weapon was used)

(b) This guideline establishes that:

- there are three sentencing ranges defined by the degree of provocation – low, substantial and high
- within the three ranges, the starting point is based on provocation taking place over a short period of time.
- the court will move from the starting point (based upon the degree of provocation) by considering the length of time over which the provocation has taken place, and by reference to any aggravating and mitigating factors

Manslaughter by Reason of Provocation

Factors to take into consideration

1. The sentences for public protection must be considered in all cases of manslaughter.
2. The presence of any of the general aggravating factors identified in the Council's Guideline *Overarching Principles: Seriousness* or any of the additional factors identified in this Guideline will indicate a sentence above the normal starting point.
3. This offence will not be an initial charge but will arise following a charge of murder. The Council Guideline *Reduction in Sentence for a Guilty Plea* will need to be applied with this in mind. In particular, consideration will need to be given to the time at which it was indicated that the defendant would plead guilty to manslaughter by reason of provocation.
4. An assessment of the *degree* of the provocation as shown by its nature and duration is the critical factor in the sentencing decision.
5. The intensity, extent and nature of the loss of control must be assessed in the context of the provocation that preceded it.
6. Although there will usually be less culpability when the retaliation to provocation is sudden, it is not always the case that greater culpability will be found where there has been a significant lapse of time between the provocation and the killing.
7. It is for the sentencer to consider the impact on an offender of provocative behaviour that has built up over a period of time.
8. The use of a weapon should not necessarily move a case into another sentencing bracket.
9. Use of a weapon may reflect the imbalance in strength between the offender and the victim and how that weapon came to hand is likely to be far more important than the use of the weapon itself.
10. It will be an aggravating factor where the weapon is brought to the scene in contemplation of use *before* the loss of self-control (which may occur some time before the fatal incident).
11. Post-offence behaviour is relevant to the sentence. It may be an aggravating or mitigating factor. When sentencing, the judge should consider the motivation behind the offender's actions.

[57] Sections 224–230

Manslaughter by Reason of Provocation

This is a serious offence for the purposes of section 224 of the Criminal Justice Act 2003

Maximum penalty: Life imprisonment

Type/Nature of Activity	Sentence Ranges & Starting Points
Low degree of provocation: A low degree of provocation occurring over a short period	Sentence Range: 10 years–life Starting Point–12 years custody
Substantial degree of provocation: A substantial degree of provocation occurring over a short period	Sentence Range: 4–9 years Starting Point – 8 years custody
High degree of provocation: A high degree of provocation occurring over a short period	Sentence Range: if custody is necessary, up to 4 years Starting Point–3 years custody

Additional aggravating factors	Additional mitigating factors
1. Concealment or attempts to dispose of evidence*	1. The offender was acting to protect another
2. Dismemberment or mutilation of the body*	2. Spontaneity and lack of premeditation
3. Offence committed in the presence of a child/children or other vulnerable family member	3. Previous experiences of abuse and/or domestic violence
	4. Evidence that the victim presented an ongoing danger to the offender or another
*subject to para 3.6 above.	5. Actual (or reasonably anticipated) violence from the victim

The Council Guideline New Sentences: Criminal Justice Act 2003 recognised the potentially more demanding nature of custodial sentences of 12 months or longer imposed under the new framework introduced by the Criminal Justice Act 2003. The sentencing ranges and starting points in the above guideline take account of this.

PART 5 ROBBERY

In accordance with section 170(9) of the Criminal Justice Act 2003, the Sentencing Guidelines Council issues this guideline as a definitive guideline. By virtue of section 172 of the Act, every court must have regard to a relevant guideline. This guideline applies to the sentencing of offenders convicted of robbery who are sentenced on or after 1 August 2006.

Part 1 of this guideline provides starting points and sentencing ranges that are applicable to three types of robbery; street robbery or 'mugging', robberies of small businesses and less sophisticated commercial robberies. For other types of robbery, relevant guidance from the Court of Appeal should be applied; this is summarised in Part 2 of this guideline.

The guideline makes clear that robbery will usually merit a custodial sentence but that exceptional circumstances may justify a non-custodial penalty for an adult and, more frequently, for a young offender. In this way it is not intended to make a significant change to current practice. Over the past ten years the majority of young offenders sentenced for robbery have been given a non-custodial sentence. This contrasts with adult offenders where the majority sentenced for robbery have been given a custodial sentence.[58]

[58] In 2004 37% of youths and 87% of adults sentenced for robbery were given custodial sentences.

The Council Guideline *New Sentences: Criminal Justice Act 2003* recognised the potentially more demanding nature of custodial sentences of 12 months or longer imposed under the new framework introduced by the Criminal Justice Act 2003. Consequently the sentencing ranges and starting points in this guideline take that principle into account . . .

Chairman of the Council
July 2006

A. Statutory Provision

Section 8(1) Theft Act 1968 provides:

> A person is guilty of robbery if he steals, and immediately before or at the time of doing so, and in order to do so, he uses force on any person or puts or seeks to put any person in fear of being then and there subjected to force.

B. Forms of Robbery and Structure of the Guideline

For the purposes of this guideline, five categories of robbery have been identified and established from sentencing ranges and previous guidance. They are:

1. Street robbery or 'mugging'
2. Robberies of small businesses
3. Less sophisticated commercial robberies
4. Violent personal robberies in the home
5. Professionally planned commercial robberies

The guideline is divided into two parts.

Part 1—This part covers categories 1-3 above.

For each of the three categories, three levels of seriousness have been identified based on the extent of force used or threatened.

For each level of seriousness a sentencing range and a starting point within that range have been identified.

Adult and youth offenders are distinguished and the guideline provides for them as separate groups.

Part 2—No guideline is provided for categories 4 and 5.Violent personal robberies are often accompanied by other serious offences which affect sentencing decisions. For professionally planned commercial robberies, existing case authority is still valid and this is summarised in Part 2.

C. Part 1

Street robbery or 'mugging'

Street robberies will usually involve some physical force (or threat) to steal modest sums, although in some cases there is significant intimidation or violence. The victim may or may not be physically injured.

Robberies of small businesses

This category covers robberies of businesses such as a small shop or post office, petrol station or public transport/taxi facility which may well lack the physical and electronic security devices available to banks or building societies and larger businesses.

Less sophisticated commercial robberies

This category covers a wide range of locations, extent of planning and degree of violence including less sophisticated bank robberies or where larger commercial establishments are the target but without detailed planning or high levels of organisation.

D. Assessing Seriousness

(i) Levels of Seriousness

Three levels of seriousness are identified by reference to the features or type of activity that characterise an offence at each level and the degree of force or threat present. The levels apply to all three categories of robbery but it will be very rare for robberies of small businesses or less sophisticated commercial robberies to have the features of the lowest level of seriousness.

Level 1—Threat and/or use of minimal force

The offence includes the threat or use of force and removal of property such as snatching from a persons grasp causing bruising/pain and discomfort.

The relative seriousness of a level 1 offence depends on:

(a) the nature and duration of any force, threat or intimidation
(b) the extent of injury (if any) to the victim
(c) the value of the property taken
(d) the number and degree of aggravating factors

Level 2—Use of weapon to threaten and/or use of significant force

A weapon is produced and used to threaten, and/or force is used which results in injury to the victim.

The relative seriousness of a level 2 offence depends on:

(a) the nature and duration of the threat or intimidation
(b) the extent of injury (if any) to the victim
(c) the nature of the weapon used, whether it was real and, if it was a real firearm, whether it was loaded
(d) the value of the property taken
(e) the number and degree of aggravating factors

Level 3—Use of weapon and/or significant force and serious injury caused

The victim is caused serious physical injury, such as a broken limb, stab wound or internal injury, by the use of significant force and/or use of a weapon. Offences at this level are often accompanied by the presence of additional aggravating factors such as a degree of planning or the targeting of large sums of money or valuable goods.

The relative seriousness of a level 3 offence depends on:

(a) the extent of injury (if any) to the victim
(b) the nature of the weapon used
(c) the value of the property taken
(d) the number and degree of aggravating factors

(ii) Aggravating & Mitigating Factors

The presence of one or more aggravating features will indicate a more severe sentence within the suggested range. If the aggravating feature(s) are exceptionally serious, the case may move to the next level of seriousness.

Aggravating factors particularly relevant to robbery

(a) Degree of force or violence

- Use of a particular degree of force is more serious than the threat (which is not carried into effect) to use that same degree of force.
- Depending on the facts, however, a threat to use a high degree of force might properly be regarded as more serious than actual use of a lesser degree of force.

(b) Use of a weapon

- Possession of a weapon during the course of an offence will be an aggravating factor, even if it is not used, because it indicates planning.
- Possession of a firearm which is loaded is more serious than possession of a firearm which is unloaded.
- Whether the weapon is real or imitation is not a major factor in determining sentence because the amount of fear created in the victim is likely to be the same.
- In cases of robbery in which a firearm is carried by the offender, a separate offence of possession of a firearm may be charged. In such circumstances, sentencers should consider, where appropriate, the use of consecutive sentences which properly reflect the totality of the offending.

(c) Vulnerability of the victim

- Targeting the elderly, the young, those with disabilities and persons performing a service to the public, especially outside normal working hours, will aggravate an offence.

(d) Number involved in the offence and roles of offenders

- Group offending will aggravate an offence because the level of intimidation and fear caused to the victim is likely to be greater.
- It may also indicate planning or 'gang' activity.
- The precise role of each offender will be important. Being the ringleader in a group is an aggravating factor. However, an offender may have played a peripheral role in the offence and, rather than having planned to take part, may have become involved spontaneously through the influence of others (see Mitigating Factors below).

(e) Value of items taken

- Property value may be more important in planned/sophisticated robberies.
- The value of the property capable of being taken should be taken into account as well as the amount/value of the property actually taken.

(f) Offence committed at night/in hours of darkness

- A victim is more vulnerable while in darkness than during daylight, all other things being equal.
- The degree of fear experienced by the victim is likely to be greater if an offence is committed at night or during hours of darkness.

(g) Wearing of a disguise

- The wearing of a disguise in order to commit an offence of robbery usually indicates a degree of planning on the part of the offender.
- The deliberate selection of a particular type of disguise in advance of the offence, for example, a balaclava or a mask, will be more serious than the improvised use of items of clothing such as a hat or hood.

Mitigating factors particularly relevant to robbery:

(a) Unplanned/opportunistic

- Many street robberies are unplanned or opportunistic by their nature so the extent of the mitigation in such cases may be limited.

(b) Peripheral Involvement

- Where, as part of a group robbery, the offender has played a peripheral role in the offence this should be treated as a mitigating factor although it should be borne in mind that by participating as part of a group, even in a minor role, the offender is likely to have increased the degree of fear caused to the victim (see Aggravating Factors above).

(c) Voluntary return of property taken

- The point at which the property is returned will be important and, in general, the earlier the property is returned the greater the degree of mitigation the offender should receive.

The court will also take account of the presence or absence of other factors including:

- **Personal mitigation**
- **First offence of violence**
- **Clear evidence of remorse**
- **Ready co-operation with the police**
- **Response to previous sentences**

7

A list of the most important general aggravating and mitigating factors can be found in the Guideline *Overarching Principles: Seriousness.*[59] These factors are reproduced at Annex A for ease of reference.

Young Offenders

- Young offenders may have characteristics relevant to their offending behaviour which are different from adult offenders. Also, by statute, the youth justice system has the principal aim of preventing offending by children and young persons.[60] Because of this, there may be factors which are of greater significance in cases involving young offenders including:

[59] Paragraphs 1.22-1.25
[60] Crime and Disorder Act 1998, s. 37

- **Age of the offender**
- **Immaturity of the offender**
- **Group Pressure**

Sentencers should recognise the varying significance of these factors for different ages.

(iii) Reduction in Sentence for Guilty Plea

Having taking account of aggravating and mitigating factors the court should consider whether the sentence should be reduced to take account of a guilty plea and by how much, in accordance with the Guideline: *Reduction in Sentence for a Guilty Plea.*

E. Public Protection Sentences—Dangerous Offenders

Robbery is a serious offence for the purposes of section 225 of the Criminal Justice Act 2003 and sentencers should consider whether a life sentence or sentence for public protection should be imposed.

F. Ancillary Orders

In all cases, courts should consider making the following orders:

- Restitution Order[61]—requiring the return of property
- Compensation Order[62]—for injury, loss or damage suffered.

Where a non-custodial sentence is imposed, courts may also consider making:

- Anti-social behaviour order[63]—to protect the public from behaviour causing harassment, alarm or distress. This order may be particularly appropriate where the offence of robbery forms part of a pattern of behaviour but such an order may be unnecessary if it will simply prohibit what is already criminal conduct. It may be used to prevent some offenders associating with other offenders with whom offences of robbery have been committed.

G. Factors to take into consideration—Adult Offenders

1. Robbery is a serious offence for the purposes of section 225 of the Criminal Justice Act 2003 and sentencers should consider whether a life sentence or sentence for public protection should be imposed. The following guidelines apply to offenders who have not been assessed as dangerous.
2. The sentencing ranges and presumptive starting points apply to all three categories of robbery detailed above:
   - **Street robbery or 'mugging'**
   - **Robberies of small businesses**
   - **Less sophisticated commercial robberies**
3. The 'starting points' are based upon a first time offender who pleaded not guilty.
4. A reduction to the appropriate sentence, taking account of seriousness and aggravating and mitigating factors, will need to be made if an offender has pleaded guilty. The effect of applying the reduction may be that the sentence imposed for an offence at one level of seriousness may fall within the range suggested for the next lowest level of seriousness.
5. The relative seriousness of each offence will be determined by the following factors:
   - **Degree of force and/or nature and duration of threats**
   - **Degree of injury to the victim**
   - **Degree of fear experienced by the victim**
   - **Value of property taken**
6. Use of a particular degree of force is more serious than the threat (which is not carried into effect) to use that same degree of force. Depending on the facts, however, a threat to use a high degree of force might properly be regarded as more serious than actual use of a lesser degree of force.
7. If a weapon is involved in the use or threat of force, the offence will be more serious. Possession of a weapon during the course of an offence will be an aggravating factor, even if it is not used, because it indicates planning. If the offence involves a real firearm it will be more serious if that firearm is loaded. Whether the weapon is real or imitation is not a major factor in determining sentence because the amount of fear created in the victim is likely to be the same.

[61] Powers of Criminal Courts (Sentencing) Act 2000, ss. 148-149
[62] ibid. s. 130
[63] Crime & Disorder Act 1998, s. 1 as amended

8. The value of the property capable of being taken as well as the actual amount taken is important.
9. The presence of one or more aggravating features will indicate a more severe sentence within the suggested range and, if the aggravating feature(s) are exceptionally serious, the case will move up to the next level.
10. In all cases, courts should consider making a restitution order and/or a compensation order. Where a non-custodial sentence is imposed, the court may also consider making an anti-social behaviour order.
11. Passing the custody threshold does not mean that a custodial sentence should be deemed inevitable.[64]

Street Robbery or 'Mugging' Robberies of Small Businesses Less Sophisticated Commercial Robberies

Robbery is a serious offence for the purposes of sections 225 and 227 Criminal Justice Act 2003
Maximum Penalty: **Life imprisonment**

ADULT OFFENDERS

Type/nature of activity	**Starting point**	**Sentencing Range**
The offence includes custody the threat or use of minimal force and removal of property.	12 months custody	Up to 3 years
A weapon is produced and used to threaten, and/or force is used which results in injury to the victim.	4 years custody	2-7 years custody
The victim is caused serious physical injury by the use of significant force and/or use of a weapon.	8 years custody	7-12 years custody

Additional aggravating factors	**Additional mitigating factors**
1. More than one offender involved.	1. Unplanned/opportunistic.
2. Being the ringleader of a group of offenders.	2. Peripheral involvement.
3. Restraint, detention or additional degradation, taken.	3. Voluntary return of property of the victim.
4. Offence was pre-planned.	4. Clear evidence of remorse.
5. Wearing a disguise.	5. Ready co-operation with the police.
6. Offence committed at night.	
7. Vulnerable victim targeted.	
8. Targeting of large sums of money or valuable goods.	
9. Possession of a weapon that was not used.	

H. Factors to take into consideration—Young Offenders

1. A youth court cannot impose a custodial sentence on an offender aged 10 or 11. If the offender is aged 12, 13 or 14, a detention and training order can only be imposed by a youth court in the case of persistent young offenders. In the Crown Court, however, long term detention in accordance with the Powers of Criminal Courts (Sentencing) Act 2000 can be ordered on any young offender without the requirement of persistence. The Crown Court may also impose an extended sentence, detention for public protection or detention for life where the young offender meets the criteria for being a "dangerous offender." **The following guidelines apply to offenders who have *not* been assessed as dangerous.**

[64] Guideline *Overarching Principles: Seriousness,* para 1.32

2. If a youth court is considering sending a case to the Crown Court, the court must be of the view that it is such a serious case that detention above two years is required, or that the appropriate sentence is a custodial sentence approaching the two year limit which is normally applicable to older offenders.[65]
3. The sentencing ranges and presumptive starting points apply to all three categories of robbery detailed above:
   - **Street robbery or 'mugging'**
   - **Robberies of small businesses**
   - **Less sophisticated commercial robberies**
4. The 'starting points' are based upon a first-time offender, aged 17 years old, who pleaded not guilty. For younger offenders sentencers should consider whether a lower starting point is justified in recognition of the offender's age or immaturity.
5. Young offenders may have characteristics relevant to their offending behaviour which are different from adult offenders. Also, by statute, the youth justice system has the principal aim of preventing offending by children and young persons.[66] Because of this, there may be factors which are of greater significance in cases involving young offenders. Sentencers should recognise the varying significance of such factors for different ages.
6. A reduction to the appropriate sentence, taking account of seriousness, and aggravating and mitigating factors, will need to be made if an offender has pleaded guilty. The effect of applying the reduction may be that the sentence imposed for an offence at one level of seriousness may fall within the range suggested for the next lowest level of seriousness.
7. The relative seriousness of each offence will be determined by the following factors:
   - **Degree of force and/or nature and duration of threats**
   - **Degree of injury to the victim**
   - **Degree of fear experienced by the victim**
   - **Value of property taken**
8. Use of a particular degree of force is more serious than the threat (which is not carried into effect) to use that same degree of force. Depending on the facts, however, a threat to use a high degree of force might properly be regarded as more serious than actual use of a lesser degree of force.
9. If a weapon is involved in the use or threat of force, the offence will be more serious. Possession of a weapon during the course of an offence will be an aggravating factor, even if it is not used, because it indicates planning. If the offence involves a real firearm it will be more serious if that firearm is loaded. Whether the weapon is real or imitation is not a major factor in determining sentence because the amount of fear created in the victim is likely to be the same.
10. The value of the property capable of being taken as well as the actual amount taken is important.
11. The presence of one or more aggravating features will indicate a more severe sentence within the suggested range and, if the aggravating feature(s) are exceptionally serious, the case will move up to the next level.
12. In all cases, courts should consider making a restitution order and/or a compensation order. Where a non-custodial sentence is imposed, the court may also consider making an anti-social behaviour order.
13. Courts are required by section 44(1) of the Children and Young Persons Act 1933 to have regard to the welfare of the child, and under section 37 of the Crime and Disorder Act 1998 to have regard to the overall aim of the youth justice system of preventing re-offending.
14. Passing the custody threshold does not mean that a custodial sentence should be deemed inevitable.[67]

[65] *W v Southampton Youth Court, K v Wirral Borough Magistrates' Court* [2003] 1 Cr App R (S) 87
[66] Crime and Disorder Act 1998, s. 37
[67] Guideline *Overarching Principles:* Seriousness, para 1.32

15. Where there is evidence that the offence has been committed to fund a drug habit and that treatment for this could help tackle the offender's offending behaviour, sentencers should consider a drug treatment requirement as part of a supervision order or action plan order.

Street Robbery or 'Mugging' Robberies of Small Businesses Less Sophisticated Commercial Robberies

Robbery is a serious offence for the purposes of sections 226 and 228 Criminal Justice Act 2003

Maximum Penalty: **Life imprisonment**

YOUNG OFFENDERS*

Type/nature of activity	Starting point	Sentencing Range
The offence includes the threat or use of minimal force and removal of property.	Community Order	Community Order—12 months detention and training order
A weapon is produced and used to threaten, and/or force is used which results in injury to the victim.	3 years detention	1-6 years detention
The victim is caused serious physical injury by the use of significant force and/or use of a weapon.	7 years detention	6-10 years detention

* The 'starting points' are based upon a first-time offender aged 17 years old who pleaded not guilty. For younger offenders, sentencers should consider whether a lower starting point is justified in recognition of the offender's age or immaturity.

Additional aggravating factors	Additional mitigating factors
1. More than one offender involved.	1. Unplanned/opportunistic.
2. Being the ringleader of a group of offenders.	2. Peripheral involvement
3. Restraint, detention or additional degradation, taken.	3. Voluntary return of property of the victim.
4. Offence was pre-planned.	4. Clear evidence of remorse.
5. Wearing a disguise.	5. Ready co-operation with the police.
6. Offence committed at night.	6. Age of the offender.
7. Vulnerable victim targeted.	7. Immaturity of the offender.
8. Targeting of large sums of money or valuable goods.	8. Peer group pressure.
9. Possession of a weapon that was not used.	

* The 'starting points' are based upon a first-time offender aged 17 years old who pleaded not guilty. For younger offenders, sentencers should consider whether a lower starting point is justified in recognition of the offender's age or immaturity.

I. Part 2

Relevant guidance from the Court of Appeal (which is summarised below for ease of reference) should apply to cases falling within the final two categories of robbery.

Violent personal robberies in the home

The sentencing range for robbery in the home involving physical violence is 13-16 years for a first time offender pleading not guilty. In this type of case, the starting point reflects the high level of violence, although it is clear that longer terms will be appropriate where extreme violence is used.[68]

This category overlaps with some cases of aggravated burglary (an offence which also carries a maximum of life imprisonment) where comparable sentences are passed. Consideration will need to be given as to whether the offender is a 'dangerous offender' for the purposes of the Criminal Justice Act 2003.

Professionally planned commercial robberies

The leading Court of Appeal decision on sentencing for robbery is the 1975 case of *Turner*.[69] This focuses on serious commercial robberies at the upper end of the sentencing range but just below the top level—planned professional robberies of banks and security vehicles, involving firearms and high value theft, but without the additional elements that characterise the most serious cases. The Court of Appeal said it had 'come to the conclusion that the normal sentence for anyone taking part in a bank robbery or in the hold-up of a security or a Post Office van should be 15 years if firearms were carried and no serious injury done.'

The Court also said that 18 years should be about the maximum for crimes which are not 'wholly abnormal' (such as the Great Train Robbery).[70]

In cases involving the most serious commercial robberies the Court has imposed 20-30 years (15-20 years after a plea of guilty).

Consideration will need to be given as to whether the offender is a 'dangerous offender' for the purposes of the Criminal Justice Act 2003.

Annex A

[Annex A consists of extracts from the SGC Guideline, *Overarching Principles: Seriousness*, which is reproduced in full in part 3 of this appendix.]

PART 6 BREACH OF A PROTECTIVE ORDER

Foreword

In accordance with section 170(9) of the Criminal Justice Act 2003, the Sentencing Guidelines Council issues this guideline as a definitive guideline. By virtue of section 172 of the Act, every court must have regard to a relevant guideline. This guideline applies to offenders convicted of breach of an order who are sentenced on or after 18 December 2006.

This guideline deals specifically with the sentencing of offenders who have breached either a restraining order imposed in order to prevent future conduct causing harassment or fear of violence, or a non- molestation order which prohibits a person from molesting another person.

It highlights the particular factors that courts should take into account when dealing with the criminal offence of breaching an order and includes starting points based on the different types of activity which can constitute a breach. It also identifies relevant aggravating and mitigating factors.

Advice from the Sentencing Advisory Panel covered both domestic violence and the offences of breach of a restraining order or a non- molestation order. The Council is issuing two separate guidelines which are published simultaneously.

. . .

Chairman of the Council
December 2006

[68] *O'Driscoll* (1986) 8 Cr App R (S) 121
[69] (1975) 61 Cr App R 67
[70] *Wilson and others* (1964) 48 Cr App R 329

A. Statutory Provisions

1.1 For the purposes of this guideline, two protective orders are considered:

(i) Restraining Order

1.2 It is an offence contrary to the Protection from Harassment Act 1997 to behave in a way which a person knows (or ought to know) causes someone else harassment (section 2) or fear of violence (section 4). When imposing sentence on an offender, a court may also impose a restraining order to prevent future conduct causing harassment or fear of violence.

1.3 An offence under these provisions may have occurred in a domestic context or may have occurred in other contexts. The Domestic Violence, Crime and Victims Act 2004 provides for such orders also to be made on conviction for any offence or following acquittal.[71]

1.4 It is an offence contrary to section 5(5) of the Act to fail to comply with the restraining order without reasonable excuse. That offence is punishable with a maximum of five years imprisonment.

(ii) Non- Molestation Order

1.5 Section 42 of the Family Law Act 1996 provides that, during family proceedings, a court may make a non- molestation order containing either or both of the following provisions:

(a) provision prohibiting a person ('the respondent') from molesting another person who is associated with the respondent;

(b) provision prohibiting the respondent from molesting a relevant child.

1.6 Section 1 of the Domestic Violence, Crime and Victims Act 2004[72] inserts a new section 42A into the 1996 Act. Section 42A (1) will provide that it is an offence to fail to comply with the order without reasonable excuse. That offence is punishable with a maximum of five years imprisonment.

1.7 In addition, breach of a non- molestation order may be dealt with as a contempt of court.

B. Sentencing for Breach

2.1 The facts that constitute a breach of a protective order may or may not also constitute a substantive offence. Where they do constitute a substantive offence, it is desirable that the substantive offence and the breach of the order should be charged as separate counts. Where necessary, consecutive sentences should be considered to reflect the seriousness of the counts and achieve the appropriate totality.

2.2 Sometimes, however, only the substantive offence or only the breach of the order will be charged. The basic principle is that the sentence should reflect all relevant aspects of the offence so that, provided the facts are not in issue, the result should be the same, regardless of whether one count or two has been charged. For example:

(i) **if the substantive offence only has been charged, the fact that it constitutes breach of a protective order should be treated as an aggravating factor;**

(ii) **if breach of the protective order only has been charged, the sentence should reflect the nature of the breach, namely, the conduct that amounts to the substantive offence, aggravated by the fact that it is also breach of an order.**

2.3 If breach of a protective order has been charged where no substantive offence was involved, the sentence should reflect the circumstances of the breach, including whether it was an isolated breach, or part of a course of conduct in breach of the order; whether it was planned or unpre-meditated; and any consequences of the breach, including psychiatric injury or distress to the person protected by the order.

C. Factors Influencing Sentencing

3.1 **In order to ensure that a protective order achieves the purpose it is intended for – protecting the victim from harm – it is important that the terms of the order are necessary and proportionate.**

3.2 The circumstances leading to the making of one of the protective orders will vary widely. Whilst a restraining order will be made in criminal proceedings, it will almost certainly result from offences of markedly different levels of seriousness or even acquittal. A nonmolestation order will have been made in civil proceedings and, again, may follow a wide variety of conduct by the subject of the order.

3.3 **In all cases the order will have been made to protect an individual from harm and action in response to breach should have as its primary aim the importance of ensuring that the order is complied with and that it achieves the protection that it was intended to achieve.**

[71] When in force, s. 12 of the 2004 Act amends s. 5 of the 1997 Act and inserts a new s. 5A to that Act.
[72] When in force.

3.4 **When sentencing for a breach of an order, the main aim should be to achieve future compliance with that order where that is realistic.**

The nature and context of the originating conduct or offence

3.5 The nature of the original conduct or offence is relevant in so far as it allows a judgement to be made on the level of harm caused to the victim by the breach and the extent to which that harm was intended by the offender.

3.6 If the original offence was serious, conduct which breaches the order might have a severe effect on the victim where in other contexts such conduct might appear minor. Even indirect contact, such as telephone calls, can cause significant harm or anxiety for a victim.

3.7 However, sentence following a breach is for the breach alone and must avoid punishing the offender again for the offence or conduct as a result of which the order was made.

The nature and context of the conduct that caused the breach

3.8 **The protective orders are designed to protect a victim. When dealing with a breach, a court will need to consider the extent to which the conduct amounting to breach put the victim at risk of harm.**

3.9 There may be exceptional cases where the nature of the breach is particularly serious but has not been dealt with by a separate offence being charged. In these cases, the risk posed by the offender and the nature of the breach will be particularly significant in determining the response. Where the order is breached by the use of physical violence, the starting point should normally be a custodial sentence.

3.10 Non-violent behaviour and/or indirect contact can also cause (or be intended to cause) a high degree of harm and anxiety. In such circumstances, it is likely that the custody threshold will have been crossed.

3.11 Where an order was made in civil proceedings, its purpose may have been to cause the subject of the order to modify behaviour rather than to imply that the conduct was especially serious. If so, it is likely to be disproportionate to impose a custodial sentence for a breach of the order if the breach did not involve threats or violence.

3.12 In some cases where a breach might result in a short custodial sentence but the court is satisfied that the offender genuinely intends to reform his or her behaviour and there is a real prospect of rehabilitation, the court may consider it appropriate to impose a sentence that will allow this. This may mean imposing a suspended sentence order or a community order (where appropriate with a requirement to attend an accredited domestic violence programme).

3.13 **Breach of a protective order will generally be more serious than breach of a conditional discharge.** Not only is a breach of a protective order an offence in its own right but it also undermines a specific prohibition imposed by the court. Breach of a conditional discharge amounts to an offender failing to take a chance that has been provided by the court.

D. Aggravating and Mitigating Factors

4.1 Many of the aggravating factors which apply to an offence of violence in a domestic context will apply also to an offence arising from breach of a protective order.

Aggravating Factors

(i) Victim is particularly vulnerable

4.2 For cultural, religious, language, financial or any other reasons, some victims may be more vulnerable than others. This vulnerability means that the terms of a protective order are particularly important and a violation of those terms will warrant a higher penalty than usual.

4.3 Age, disability or the fact that the victim was pregnant or had recently given birth at the time of the offence may make a victim particularly vulnerable.

4.4 Any steps taken to prevent the victim reporting an incident or obtaining assistance will usually aggravate the offence.

(ii) Impact on children

4.5 If a protective order is imposed in order to protect children, either solely or in addition to another victim, then a breach of that order will generally be more serious.[73]

(iii) A proven history of violence or threats by the offender

4.6 Of necessity, a breach of a protective order will not be the first time an offender has caused fear or

[73] The definition of 'harm' in s. 31(9) of the Children Act 1989 as amended by s. 120 of the Adoption and Children Act 2002 includes 'impairment suffered from seeing or hearing the ill-treatment of another'.

harassment towards a victim. However, the offence will be more serious if the breach is part of a series of prolonged violence or harassment towards the victim or the offender has a history of disobedience to court orders.

4.7 Where an offender has previously been convicted of an offence involving domestic violence, either against the same or a different person, or has been convicted for a breach of an order, this is likely to be a statutory aggravating factor.[74]

(iv) Using contact arrangements with a child to instigate an offence

4.8 An offence will be aggravated where an offender exploits contact arrangements with a child in order to commit an offence.

(v) Victim is forced to leave home

4.9 A breach will be aggravated if, as a consequence, the victim is forced to leave home.

(vi) Additional aggravating factors

4.10 In addition to the factors listed above, the following will aggravate a breach of an order:
- the offence is a further breach, following earlier breach proceedings;
- the breach was committed immediately or shortly after the order was made.

Mitigating Factors

(i) Breach was committed after a long period of compliance

4.11 If the court is satisfied that the offender has complied with a protective order for a substantial period before a breach is committed, the court should take this into account when imposing sentence for the breach. The history of the relationship and the specific nature of the contact will be relevant in determining its significance as a mitigating factor.

(ii) Victim initiated contact

4.12 If the conditions of an order are breached following contact from the victim, this should be considered as mitigation. It is important to consider the history of the relationship and the specific nature of the contact in determining its significance as a mitigating factor.

4.13 Nonetheless it is important for the court to make clear that it is the responsibility of the offender and not the victim to ensure that the order is complied with.

E. Factors to take into Consideration

Aims of sentencing

(a) When sentencing for a breach of a protective order (which would have been imposed to protect a victim from further harm), the main aim should be to achieve future compliance with that order.

(b) A court will need to assess the level of risk posed by the offender. If the offender requires treatment or assistance for mental health or other issues, willingness to undergo treatment or accept help may influence sentence.

1. Key Factors

(a) The nature of the conduct that caused the breach of the order, in particular, whether the contact was direct or indirect, although it is important to recognise that indirect contact is capable of causing significant harm or anxiety.

(b) **There may be exceptional cases where the nature of the breach is particularly serious but has not been dealt with by a separate offence being charged. In these cases the risk posed by the offender and the nature of the breach will be particularly significant in determining the response.**

(c) The nature of the original conduct or offence is relevant to sentencing for the breach in so far as it allows a judgement to be made on the level of harm caused to the victim by the breach, and the extent to which that harm was intended by the offender.

(d) The sentence following a breach is for the breach alone and must avoid punishing the offender again for the offence or conduct as a result of which the order was made.

(e) Where violence is used to breach a restraining order or a molestation order, custody is the starting point for sentence.

(f) Non- violent conduct in breach may cross the custody threshold where a high degree of harm or anxiety has been caused to the victim.

[74] Criminal Justice Act 2003, s. 143(2).

(g) Where an order was made in civil proceedings, its purpose may have been to cause the subject of the order to modify behaviour rather than to imply that the conduct was especially serious. If so, it is likely to be disproportionate to impose a custodial sentence for a breach of the order if the breach did not involve threats or violence.

(h) In some cases where a breach might result in a short custodial sentence but the court is satisfied that the offender genuinely intends to reform his or her behaviour and there is a real prospect of rehabilitation, the court may consider it appropriate to impose a sentence that will allow this. This may mean imposing a suspended sentence order or a community order (where appropriate with a requirement to attend an accredited domestic violence programme).

(i) While, in principle, consecutive sentences may be imposed for each breach of which the offender is convicted, the overall sentence should reflect the totality principle.

2. General

(a) Breach of a protective order should be considered more serious than a breach of a conditional discharge.

(b) The principle of reduction in sentence for a guilty plea should be applied as set out in the Council guideline *Reduction in Sentence for a Guilty Plea.*

3. Non-custodial sentences

(a) It is likely that all breaches of protective orders will pass the threshold for a community sentence. The reference in the starting points to medium and low range community orders refers to the Council guideline *New Sentences: Criminal Justice Act 2003* paragraphs 1.1.18–1.1.32.

(b) In accordance with general principle, the fact that the seriousness of an offence crosses a particular threshold does not preclude the court from imposing another type of sentence of a lower level where appropriate.

BREACH OF A PROTECTIVE ORDER

Breach of a Restraining Order
Section 5(5) Protection from Harassment Act 1997

Breach of a Non-Molestation Order
*Section 42A Family Law Act 1996**

Maximum Penalty: **5 years imprisonment**

Where the conduct is particularly serious, it would normally be charged as a separate offence. These starting points are based on the premise that the activity has either been prosecuted separately as an offence or is not of a character sufficient to justify prosecution of it as an offence in its own right.

Nature of activity	Starting points
	Custodial Sentence
Breach (whether one or more) involving significant physical violence and significant physical or psychological harm to the victim	More than 12 months The length of the custodial sentence imposed will depend on the nature and seriousness of the breach(es).
More than one breach involving some violence and/or significant physical or psychological harm to the victim	26–39 weeks custody [Medium/High Custody Plus order]**
Single breach involving some violence and/or significant physical or psychological harm to the victim	13–26 weeks custody [Low/ Medium Custody Plus order]**
	Non-Custodial Sentence
More than one breach involving no/minimal contact or some direct contact	MEDIUM range community order
Single breach involving no/minimal direct contact	LOW range community order

Additional aggravating factors	Additional mitigating factors
1. Victim is particularly vulnerable. 2. Impact on children. 3. A proven history of violence or threats by the offender. 4. Using contact arrangements with a child to instigate an offence. 5. Victim is forced to leave home. 6. Offence is a further breach, following earlier breach proceedings. 7. Offender has a history of disobedience to court orders. 8. Breach was committed immediately or shortly after the order was made.	1. Breach occurred after a long period of compliance. 2. Victim initiated contact.

* When in force.
** When the relevant provisions of the Criminal Justice Act 2003 are in force.

PART 7 OVERARCHING PRINCIPLES: DOMESTIC VIOLENCE

Foreword

In accordance with section 170(9) of the Criminal Justice Act 2003, the Sentencing Guidelines Council issues this guideline as a definitive guideline. By virtue of section 172 of the Act, every court must have regard to a relevant guideline. This guideline applies to offences sentenced on or after 18 December 2006.

This guideline stems from a reference from the Home Secretary for consideration of sentencing in cases of domestic violence. The referral suggested that 'domestic violence' should be described in terms of the Crown Prosecution Service definition (described on page 3) and this suggestion was adopted by the Council.

Consequently this guideline is for use for all cases that fall within the Crown Prosecution Service definition of domestic violence.

There is no specific offence of domestic violence. The definition covers a broad set of circumstances and allows conduct amounting to domestic violence to be covered by a wide range of offences. The guideline identifies the principles relevant to the sentencing of cases involving violence that has occurred in a domestic context and includes details of particular aggravating and mitigating factors.

This guideline makes clear that offences committed in a domestic context should be regarded as being no less serious than offences committed in a non-domestic context. Indeed, because an offence has been committed in a domestic context, there are likely to be aggravating factors present that make it more serious.

In many situations of domestic violence, the circumstances require the sentence to demonstrate clearly that the conduct is unacceptable. However, there will be some situations where all parties genuinely and realistically wish the relationship to continue as long as the violence stops. In those situations, and where the violence is towards the lower end of the scale of seriousness, it is likely to be appropriate for the court to impose a sentence that provides the support necessary.

Advice from the Sentencing Advisory Panel covered both domestic violence and the offences of breach of a restraining order or a non-molestation order. The Council is issuing two guidelines which are published simultaneously.

. . .

Chairman of the Council
December 2006

A. Definition of Domestic Violence

1.1 There is no specific offence of domestic violence and conduct amounting to domestic violence is covered by a number of statutory provisions. For the purposes of this guideline, wherever such offending occurs, domestic violence is:

> 'Any incident of threatening behaviour, violence or abuse [psychological, physical, sexual, financial or emotional] between adults who are or have been intimate partners or family members, regardless of gender or sexuality.'[75]

1.2 Most incidents of domestic violence can be charged as one of a wide range of offences including physical assault (with or without a weapon), harassment, threats to cause injury or to kill, destroying or damaging property, false imprisonment (locking the victim in a room or preventing that person from leaving the house), and sexual offences.

1.3 This guideline covers issues which are relevant across the range of offences that might be committed in a domestic context. Under the above definition, the domestic context includes relationships involving intimate partners who are living together, intimate partners who do not live together and former intimate partners. It is also wide enough to include relationships between family members, for example between a father and a daughter, or a mother and a daughter, perhaps where the daughter is the mother's carer.

B. Assessing Seriousness

2.1 **As a starting point for sentence, offences committed in a domestic context should be regarded as being no less serious than offences committed in a non-domestic context.**

2.2 Thus, the starting point for sentencing should be the same irrespective of whether the offender and the victim are known to each other (whether by virtue of being current or former intimate partners, family members, friends or acquaintances) or unknown to each other.

2.3 A number of aggravating factors may commonly arise by virtue of the offence being committed in a domestic context and these will increase the seriousness of such offences. These are described in more detail in C below.

C. Aggravating and Mitigating Factors

3.1 Since domestic violence takes place within the context of a current or past relationship, the history of the relationship will often be relevant in assessing the gravity of the offence. Therefore, a court is entitled to take into account anything occurring within the relationship as a whole, which may reveal relevant aggravating or mitigating factors.

3.2 The following aggravating and mitigating factors (which are not intended to be exhaustive) are of particular relevance to offences committed in a domestic context, and should be read alongside the general factors set out in the Council guideline *Overarching Principles: Seriousness.*[76]

Aggravating Factors

(i) Abuse of trust and abuse of power

3.3 The guideline *Overarching Principles: Seriousness* identifies abuse of a position of trust and abuse of power as factors that indicate higher culpability. Within the nature of relationship required to meet the definition of domestic violence set out above, trust implies a mutual expectation of conduct that shows consideration, honesty, care and responsibility. In some such relationships, one of the parties will have the power to exert considerable control over the other.

3.4 In the context of domestic violence:

- an *abuse of trust*, whether through direct violence or emotional abuse, represents a violation of this understanding;
- an *abuse of power* in a relationship involves restricting another individual's autonomy which is sometimes a specific characteristic of domestic violence. This involves the exercise of control over an individual by means which may be psychological, physical, sexual, financial or emotional.

3.5 Where an abuse of trust or abuse of power is present, it will aggravate the seriousness of an offence. These factors are likely to exist in many offences of violence within a domestic context.

3.6 However, the breadth of the definition of domestic violence (set out in **1.1** above) encompasses offences committed by a former spouse or partner. Accordingly, there will be circumstances where the abuse of trust or abuse of power may be a very minor feature of an offence or may be deemed no longer to exist – for example, where the offender and victim have been separated for a long period of time.

[75] This is the Government definition of domestic violence agreed in 2004. It is taken from *Policy on Prosecuting cases of Domestic Violence*, Crown Prosecution Service, 2005.

[76] Published December 2004. The lists of aggravating factors from the guideline are reproduced at Annex A for ease of reference. See also www.sentencing-guidelines.gov.uk

(ii) Victim is particularly vulnerable

3.7 For cultural, religious, language, financial or any other reasons, some victims of domestic violence may be more vulnerable than others, not least because these issues may make it almost impossible for the victim to leave a violent relationship.

3.8 Where a perpetrator has exploited a victim's vulnerability (for instance, when the circumstances have been used by the perpetrator to prevent the victim from seeking and obtaining help), an offence will warrant a higher penalty.

3.9 Age, disability or the fact that the victim was pregnant or had recently given birth at the time of the offence may make a victim particularly vulnerable.

3.10 Any steps taken to prevent the victim reporting an incident or obtaining assistance will usually aggravate the offence.

(iii) Impact on children

3.11 Exposure of children to an offence (either directly or indirectly) is an aggravating factor.

3.12 Children are likely to be adversely affected by directly witnessing violence or other abuse and by being aware of it taking place while they are elsewhere in the home.[77]

(iv) Using contact arrangements with a child to instigate an offence

3.13 An offence will be aggravated where an offender exploits contact arrangements with a child in order to commit an offence.

(v) A proven history of violence or threats by the offender in a domestic setting

3.14 It is important that an assessment of the seriousness of an offence recognises the cumulative effect of a series of violent incidents or threats over a prolonged period, where such conduct has been proved or accepted.

3.15 Where an offender has previously been convicted of an offence involving domestic violence either against the same or a different partner, this is likely to be a statutory aggravating factor.[78]

(vi) A history of disobedience to court orders

3.16 A breach of an order that has been imposed for the purpose of protecting a victim can cause significant harm or anxiety. Where an offender's history of disobedience has had this effect, it will be an aggravating factor.

3.17 Commission of the offence in breach of a non-molestation order imposed in civil proceedings, in breach of a sentence (such as a conditional discharge) imposed for similar offending, or while subject to an ancillary order, such as a restraining order, will aggravate the seriousness of the offence.

3.18 The appropriate response to breach of a civil order is dealt with in a separate guideline *Breach of a Protective Order*.

(vii) Victim forced to leave home

3.19 An offence will be aggravated if, as a consequence, the victim is forced to leave home.

Mitigating Factors

(i) Positive good character

3.20 As a general principle of sentencing, a court will take account of an offender's positive good character. However, it is recognised that one of the factors that can allow domestic violence to continue unnoticed for lengthy periods is the ability of the perpetrator to have two personae. In respect of an offence of violence in a domestic context, an offender's good character in relation to conduct outside the home should generally be of no relevance where there is a proven pattern of behaviour.

3.21 Positive good character is of greater relevance in the rare case where the court is satisfied that the offence was an isolated incident.

(ii) Provocation

3.22 It may be asserted that the offence, at least in part, has been provoked by the conduct of the victim. Such assertions need to be treated with great care, both in determining whether they have a

[77] The definition of 'harm' in s. 31(9) of the Children Act 1989 as amended by s. 120 of the Adoption and Children Act 2002 includes 'impairment suffered from seeing or hearing the ill- treatment of another'.

[78] Criminal Justice Act 2003, s. 143(2).

factual basis and in considering whether in the circumstances the alleged conduct amounts to provocation sufficient to mitigate the seriousness of the offence.

3.23 For provocation to be a mitigating factor, it will usually involve actual or anticipated violence including psychological bullying. Provocation is likely to have more of an effect as mitigation if it has taken place over a significant period of time.

D. Other factors influencing sentence

Wishes of the victim and effect of the sentence

4.1 As a matter of general principle, a sentence imposed for an offence of violence should be determined by the seriousness of the offence, not by the expressed wishes of the victim.

4.2 There are a number of reasons why it may be particularly important that this principle is observed in a case of domestic violence:
- it is undesirable that a victim should feel a responsibility for the sentence imposed;
- there is a risk that a plea for mercy made by a victim will be induced by threats made by, or by a fear of, the offender;
- the risk of such threats will be increased if it is generally believed that the severity of the sentence may be affected by the wishes of the victim.

4.3 Nonetheless, there may be circumstances in which the court can properly mitigate a sentence to give effect to the expressed wish of the victim that the relationship be permitted to continue. The court must, however, be confident that such a wish is genuine, and that giving effect to it will not expose the victim to a real risk of further violence. Critical conditions are likely to be the seriousness of the offence and the history of the relationship. It is vitally important that the court has up-to-date information in a pre- sentence report and victim personal statement.

4.4 Either the offender or the victim (or both) may ask the court to take into consideration the interests of any children and to impose a less severe sentence. The court will wish to have regard not only to the effect on the children if the relationship is disrupted but also to the likely effect on the children of any further incidents of domestic violence.

E. Factors to Take into Consideration

The following points of principle should be considered by a court when imposing sentence for any offence of violence committed in domestic context.

1. Offences committed in a domestic context should be regarded as being no less serious than offences committed in a non-domestic context.
2. Many offences of violence in a domestic context are dealt with in a magistrates' court as an offence of common assault or assault occasioning actual bodily harm because the injuries sustained are relatively minor. Offences involving serious violence will warrant a custodial sentence in the majority of cases.
3. Some offences will be specified offences for the purposes of the dangerous offender provisions.[79] In such circumstances, consideration will need to be given to whether there is a significant risk of serious harm to members of the public, which include, of course, family members. If so, the court will be required to impose a life sentence, imprisonment for public protection or an extended sentence.
4. Where the custody threshold is only just crossed, so that if a custodial sentence is imposed it will be a short sentence, the court will wish to consider whether the better option is a suspended sentence order or a community order, including in either case a requirement to attend an accredited domestic violence programme. Such an option will only be appropriate where the court is satisfied that the offender genuinely intends to reform his or her behaviour and that there is a real prospect of rehabilitation being successful. Such a situation is unlikely to arise where there has been a pattern of abuse.

Annex A

Extracts from Guideline *Overarching Principles: Seriousness*

[Omitted: the relevant Guideline is set out in full in part 3 of this appendix.]

[79] Criminal Justice Act 2003, part 12, chapter 5.

PART 8 SEXUAL OFFENCES ACT 2003

Foreword

In accordance with section 170(9) of the Criminal Justice Act (CJA) 2003, the Sentencing Guidelines Council issues this guideline as a definitive guideline. By virtue of section 172 of the CJA 2003, every court must have regard to a relevant guideline. This guideline applies to the sentencing of offenders convicted of any of the sexual offences covered by this guideline who are sentenced on or after 14 May 2007.

The Sexual Offences Act 2003 contains a large number of new or amended offences for which there was no sentencing case law. Following implementation of this Act in May 2004, a number of cases have been considered by the Court of Appeal and guidance from those judgments has been incorporated into this guideline.

The guideline uses the starting point of 5 years for the rape of an adult with no aggravating or mitigating factors (derived from *Millberry and others*[80]) as the baseline from which all other sentences for offences in this guideline have been calculated. Since the judgment in *Millberry*, changes introduced by the CJA 2003 have both affected the structure of custodial sentences of 12 months and above and introduced new sentences for those convicted of many of the offences in this guideline where the court considers that the offender provides a significant risk of serious harm in the future.

The sentencing ranges and starting points in this guideline take account of both these changes. Accordingly, the transitional arrangements set out in paragraphs 2.1.7–2.1.10 of the Council guideline *New Sentences: Criminal Justice Act 2003* do not apply.

Sexual offences can be committed in a domestic context and so come within the definition of 'domestic violence' used in the Council guideline *Overarching Principles: Domestic Violence* published in December 2006. In such circumstances, reference should also be made to this guideline to identify additional principles and factors that should also be taken into account in assessing the seriousness of an offence and determining the appropriate sentence.

. . .

Chairman of the Council
April 2007

Part 1: General Principles

Introduction

1.1 The Sexual Offences Act (SOA) 2003 came into force on 1 May 2004.Part 1 creates a number of new sexual offences. It also includes a large number of pre-existing offences, some of which have been redefined and/ or have revised maximum penalties.

1.2 The Criminal Justice Act (CJA) 2003 provides[81] that the seriousness of an offence should be determined by two main parameters: the *culpability* of the offender and the *harm* caused, or risked, by the offence, including the impact on the victim(s). The Sentencing Guidelines Council guideline on seriousness[82] provides that the seriousness of an offence is to be determined according to the relative impact of the culpability of the offender and the actual or foreseeable harm caused to the victim. Where there is an imbalance between culpability and harm, the culpability of the offender in the particular circumstances of an individual case should be the primary factor in determining the seriousness of the offence.

1.3 The guideline has been formulated on the basis of the sentencing framework that is currently in force. **For these types of offence more than for many others, the sentencing process must allow for flexibility and variability. The suggested starting points and sentencing ranges contained in the offence guidelines are not rigid, and movement within and between ranges will be dependent upon the circumstances of individual cases and, in particular, the aggravating and mitigating factors that are present.**

---

[80] [2003] 2 Cr App R (S) 31
[81] s. 143(1)
[82] *Overarching Principles: Seriousness*, published 16 December 2004 – www.sentencing-guidelines.gov.uk

In order to assist in developing consistency of approach, a decision making process is set out at page 17.

1.4 In the guideline published by the Council to support the new sentencing framework introduced by the CJA 2003,[83] in relation to custodial sentences of 12 months or more it is stated that, generally, a court should only make *specific* recommendations about the requirements to be included in the licence conditions when announcing shorter sentences where it is reasonable to anticipate the relevance of the requirement at the point of release. However, sentencing for a sexual offence is an example of an occasion where the court may sensibly suggest interventions that could be useful, either during the custodial period or on release. The court's recommendation will not form part of the sentence, but will be a helpful guide for the probation service.

1.5 Apart from the offence of rape which, when charged as a primary offence, is confined to male defendants, the SOA 2003 makes no distinction in terms of liability or maximum penalties for male and female offenders. The guidelines are proposed on the basis that they should apply irrespective of the gender of the victim or of the offender, except in specified circumstances where a distinction is justified by the nature of the offence.

Seriousness

1.6 The guidelines for sentencing for serious sexual offences have been based on the guideline judgment on rape – *Millberry and others*[84] – in which the Court of Appeal stated that:

> '... there are, broadly, three dimensions to consider in assessing the gravity of an individual offence of rape. The first is the degree of harm to the victim; the second is the level of culpability of the offender; and the third is the level of risk posed by the offender to society.'

1.7 In the subsequent *Attorney General's Reference (Nos. 91, 119, 120 of 2002)*,[85] the Court of Appeal held that 'similar dimensions should apply to other categories of sexual offences', and added that there would also be a need to deter others from acting in a similar fashion.

1.8 These statements established the general principles for assessing the seriousness of sexual offences that are now encapsulated in the provisions of the CJA 2003.

1.9 The maximum penalty and mode of trial prescribed by Parliament for each sexual offence give a general indication of the relative seriousness of different offences and these have also acted as a broad guide for the proposed sentencing starting points.

The harm caused by sexual offences

1.10 All sexual offences where the activity is non-consensual, coercive or exploitative result in harm. Harm is also inherent where victims ostensibly consent but where their capacity to give informed consent is affected by their youth or mental disorder.

1.11 The effects of sexual offending may be physical and/ or psychological. The physical effects – injury, pregnancy or sexually transmitted infections – may be very serious. The psychological effects may be equally or even more serious, but much less obvious (even unascertainable) at the time of sentencing. They may include any or all of the following (although this list is not intended to be comprehensive and items are not listed in any form of priority):

- *Violation of the victim's sexual autonomy*
- *Fear*
- *Humiliation*
- *Degradation*
- *Shame*
- *Embarrassment*
- *Inability to trust*
- *Inability to form personal or intimate relationships in adulthood*
- *Self harm or suicide*

The offender's culpability in sexual offences

1.12 According to the Council's guideline on seriousness, culpability is determined by the extent to which the offender intends to cause harm – the worse the harm intended, the greater the offender's culpability. Sexual offences are somewhat different in that the offender's intention may be to obtain sexual gratification, financial gain or some other result, rather than to harm the victim. However, where the activity is in any way non-consensual, coercive or exploitative, the offence is inherently

---

[83] *New Sentences: Criminal Justice Act 2003*, published 16 December 2004 – www.sentencing-guidelines.gov.uk
[84] [2003] 2 Cr App R (S) 31
[85] [2003] 2 Cr App R (S) 338

harmful and therefore the offender's culpability is high. Planning an offence makes the offender more highly culpable than engaging in opportunistic or impulsive offending.

1.13 In general, the difficulty of assessing seriousness where there is an imbalance between culpability and harm does not arise in relation to sexual offences. However, some offences in the SOA 2003 are defined in terms of the offender's intention to commit an offence that does not, in fact, take place, for example the 'incitement offences', the 'preparatory offences' and the new offence of 'meeting a child following sexual grooming etc'. In such cases, the level of actual harm to the victim may be lower than in cases involving the commission of a physical sexual offence. Here the level of culpability will be the primary factor in determining the seriousness of the offence, with the degree of harm that could have been caused to an individual victim, and the risk posed to others by the offender, being integral to the sentencing decision.

The culpability of young offenders

1.14 The SOA 2003 makes special provision for young offenders found guilty of certain sexual offences – namely those in the 'ostensibly consensual' category – by providing that offenders aged under 18 will face a maximum penalty of 5 years' detention, as opposed to the maximum 14 years for offenders aged 18 or over. These are dealt with in Part 7 of the guideline.

1.15 The age of the offender will also be significant in the sentencing exercise in relation to non-consensual offences, where no special sentencing provisions have been provided for in the legislation. Its significance is particularly acute in relation to the strict liability offences such as 'rape of a child under 13', where the maximum penalty is life imprisonment, especially if an offender is very young and the disparity in age between the offender and the victim is very small.

1.16 Section 44(1) of the Children and Young Persons Act 1933 provides that every court dealing with a child or young person, as an offender or otherwise, 'shall have regard to the welfare of the child or young person'.

1.17 The youth and immaturity of an offender must always be potential mitigating factors for the courts to take into account when passing sentence. However, where the facts of a case are particularly serious, the youth of the offender will not necessarily mitigate the appropriate sentence.[86]

The nature of the sexual activity

1.18 The nature of the sexual activity covered by some offences in the SOA 2003 (such as 'rape' and 'assault by penetration') is quite precisely defined whilst others – for example, 'sexual activity with a child', 'sexual activity with a child family member', 'abuse of a position of trust' – are drawn very widely and cover all forms of intentional activity involving sexual touching, including penetration.

- Sexual activity involves varying types and degrees of touching ranging from genital or oral penetration through to non-genital touching of the victim's clothed body.
- Penetrative acts are more serious than non-penetrative acts. The fact that the offender or victim (especially the victim) is totally or partially naked makes the activity more serious.
- The touching may be consensual, ostensibly consensual or non-consensual. Where the victim's ability to consent is impaired by, for example, youth or mental incapacity, this makes the activity, regardless of its nature, more serious.

Aggravating and mitigating factors

1.19 The Council guideline on seriousness sets out aggravating and mitigating factors that are applicable to a wide range of cases. Care needs to be taken to ensure that there is no double counting where an essential element of the offence charged might, in other circumstances, be an aggravating factor.

1.20 Sentencers should refer to paragraphs 1.20–1.27 of the Council guideline. For ease of reference, extracts from the guideline are provided below. The fact that a victim was vulnerable will be of particular relevance in cases involving sexual offences.

[86] *R v Paiwant Asi- Akram* [2005] EWCA Crim 1543, *R v Patrick M* [2005] EWCA Crim 1679

THESE FACTORS APPLY TO A WIDE RANGE OF OFFENCES AND NOT ALL WILL BE RELEVANT TO SEXUAL OFFENCES.

Factors indicating higher culpability:

- Offence committed whilst on bail for other offences
- Failure to respond to previous sentences
- Offence was racially or religiously aggravated
- Offence motivated by, or demonstrating, hostility to the victim based on his or her sexual orientation (or presumed sexual orientation)
- Offence motivated by, or demonstrating, hostility based on the victim's disability (or presumed disability)
- Previous conviction(s), particularly where a pattern of repeat offending is disclosed
- Planning of an offence
- An intention to commit more serious harm than actually resulted from the offence
- Offenders operating in groups or gangs
- 'Professional' offending
- Commission of the offence for financial gain (where this is not inherent in the offence itself)
- High level of profit from the offence
- An attempt to conceal or dispose of evidence
- Failure to respond to warnings or concerns expressed by others about the offender's behaviour
- Offence committed whilst on licence
- Offence motivated by hostility towards a minority group, or a member or members of it
- Deliberate targeting of vulnerable victim(s)
- Commission of an offence while under the influence of alcohol or drugs
- Use of a weapon to frighten or injure victim
- Deliberate and gratuitous violence or damage to property, over and above what is needed to carry out the offence
- Abuse of power
- Abuse of a position of trust

Factors indicating a more than usually serious degree of harm:

- Multiple victims
- An especially serious physical or psychological effect on the victim, even if unintended
- A sustained assault or repeated assaults on the same victim
- Victim is particularly vulnerable
- Location of the offence (for example, in an isolated place)
- Offence is committed against those working in the public sector or providing a service to the public
- Presence of others e.g. relatives, especially children or partner of the victim
- Additional degradation of the victim (e.g. taking photographs of a victim as part of a sexual offence)
- In property offences, high value (including sentimental value) of property to the victim, or substantial consequential loss (e.g. where the theft of equipment causes serious disruption to a victim's life or business)

Factors indicating significantly lower culpability:

- A greater degree of provocation than normally expected
- Mental illness or disability
- Youth or age, where it affects the responsibility of the individual defendant
- The fact that the offender played only a minor role in the offence

Personal mitigation

Section 166(1) Criminal Justice Act 2003 makes provision for a sentencer to take account of any matters that 'in the opinion of the court, are relevant in mitigation of sentence'. When the court has formed an initial assessment of the seriousness of the offence, then it should consider any offender mitigation. The issue of remorse should be taken into account at this point along with other mitigating features such as admissions to the police in interview.

The risk of re-offending

1.21 One of the purposes of sentencing set out in the CJA 2003[87] is 'the protection of the public'. Part 2 of the Sexual Offences Act 2003 strengthens the current system of registration for sex offenders and also introduces a number of new orders, some of which are available on conviction and others by application in civil proceedings to a magistrates' court. There are also a number of sentencing options, custodial and non-custodial, open to sentencers where the risk of re-offending is high.

1.22 The arrangements for registration of sex offenders (see also paragraph 1.29 below) follow automatically on conviction, and are not part of the sentencing process. The duty to give reasons for, and to explain the effect of, sentencing is now set out in the CJA 2003.[88]

1.23 If a victim personal statement has not been produced, the court should enquire whether the victim has been given the opportunity to make one. In the absence of a victim personal statement, the court should not assume that the offence had no impact on the victim. A pre-sentence report should normally be prepared before sentence is passed for any sexual offence, as this may contain important information about the sexually deviant tendencies of an offender and an assessment of the likelihood of re-offending; a psychiatric report may also be appropriate. It is clearly in the interests of public protection to provide effective treatment for sex offenders at the earliest opportunity.

Dangerous offenders

1.24 In relation to custodial sentences, the starting point will be the assessment of dangerousness as set out in section 229 of the CJA 2003; since the majority of the offences in the SOA 2003 are 'specified' offences (as defined in section 224 and listed in schedule 15, part 2). There are three sentencing options for offenders aged 18 or over: discretionary life sentences, indeterminate sentences of 'imprisonment for public protection', and the redefined extended sentences.[89]

1.25 The criterion for the assessment of dangerousness in all cases falling within the provisions for dangerous offenders is whether the court considers that there is a significant risk to members of the public of serious harm occasioned by the commission by the offender of further specified offences.[90] If the criterion is met, the options available depend on whether the offence is a 'serious' offence.

1.26 Where a specified offence carries a maximum penalty of life imprisonment or 10 years' imprisonment or more, it is a 'serious' offence for the purposes of section 225. In such cases, if the risk criterion is met in respect of an adult offender, a life sentence or imprisonment for public protection must be imposed.

1.27 In setting the minimum term to be served within an indeterminate sentence under these provisions, in accordance with normal practice that term will usually be half the equivalent determinate sentence. Such period will normally be reduced by time spent on remand in custody.

1.28 In relation to 'specified' offences that are not 'serious' offences, where the risk criterion is met in relation to an adult offender, under section 227 the court is required to extend the period for which the offender will be subject to a licence on release from custody; the custodial element in such cases must be for a minimum of 12 months. Within the statutory limits, the period of licence must be of such length as the court considers necessary for the purposes of protecting members of the public from serious harm occasioned by the commission of further specified offences.

Other orders

1.29 There are a number of orders and requirements relevant to those convicted of sexual offences. Some follow automatically on conviction and others can be applied for:

- inclusion of an offender's name on a *Sex Offenders' Register* – used for risk management by local authorities and other statutory agencies to indicate that an individual may pose an ongoing risk to children – follows automatically on conviction or caution for a sexual offence;[91] and
- *notification orders* which impose sex offender registration requirements on offenders living in the UK who have been convicted of a sexual offence overseas – available on application by complaint to a magistrates' court.[92]

1.30 A court has a duty to consider making two ancillary orders that require the intervention of the

[87] s. 142(1)
[88] s. 174
[89] Criminal Justice Act 2003, ss. 225–228
[90] Ibid. 225(1)
[91] Children and Young Persons Act 1933, schedule 1 – currently subject to a cross-government review, in light of the alternative provisions that now exist to prohibit working with children
[92] Sexual Offences Act 2003, s. 97

sentencer, namely sexual offences prevention orders (SOPO)[93] and orders disqualifying an offender from working with children:[94]

- *sexual offences prevention orders* – civil preventative orders that can be made either at the point of sentence in the Crown Court or a magistrates' court, or by complaint to a magistrates' court in respect of someone previously convicted of a sexual offence where that person's behaviour suggests the possibility of re-offending; and
- *disqualification orders* – an order disqualifying an offender convicted of an offence against a child from working with children, which *must* (or in defined circumstances *may*) be imposed unless the court is satisfied that the offender is unlikely to commit a further offence against a child.

When passing sentence for a sexual offence, the court must always consider whether or not it would be appropriate to make a sexual offences prevention order or an order disqualifying the offender from working with children.

Community orders

1.31 The availability of requirements able to be included within a community order, and the suitability of them for an individual offender, will be detailed in a pre-sentence report. Some options of direct relevance to sex offenders are considered below.

Sex offender treatment programmes

1.31.1 These are available both in prisons and in the community. Participation in a programme whilst in custody is voluntary, but programmes in the community can be a mandatory requirement of a community order where a PSR writer has made a recommendation and commented on the suitability of the offender for such a requirement.

- Accredited treatment programmes are targeted at males, who form the overwhelming majority of sex offenders, but individual programmes are devised for female offenders.
- Treatment programmes are usually only available to those who are given a long community order (normally 3 years), and may not always be available for those sentenced to shorter custodial sentences.

Before imposing sentence, the court should investigate the content and availability of such programmes and will wish to be satisfied that a programme will be able to commence within a realistic timeframe.

Curfews

1.31.2 A curfew requirement, usually associated with electronic monitoring, may be helpful in restricting an offender's right to be out in public at the same time as, for example, schoolchildren. A curfew requirement is most likely to be effective when used in conjunction with a residence requirement requiring an offender to live in approved accommodation where behaviour and compliance can be monitored. Such a requirement can be for between 2 and 12 hours per day and last up to 6 months.

When a court imposes a community order for a sexual offence, it should always consider imposing a requirement to attend a special treatment programme designed to help the offender recognise and control any sexually deviant tendencies.

Financial orders

1.32 In addition to the sentence imposed for the offence(s), the following supplementary penalties should be considered.

Confiscation orders

1.32.1 Depending on the date of the offence, the CJA 1988 or Proceeds of Crime Act 2002 set out the circumstances in which the courts are entitled or required to make a confiscation order to recover some of the proceeds of an offender's crime. The prosecution may suggest consideration of a confiscation order but, where appropriate, the court should consider making such an order of its own volition.

Deprivation orders

1.32.2 The courts should also consider whether, in the particular circumstances of the case, it would be

[93] Sexual Offences Act 2003, s. 104

[94] Criminal Justice and Courts Services Act 2000, ss. 28 and 29, as amended by the Criminal Justice Act 2003, s. 299 and schedule 30

appropriate to make an order depriving an offender of property used for the purposes of crime.[95] This will be a particularly relevant consideration where, for example, someone convicted of a voyeurism or child pornography offence possesses a camera or a computer used to make, store or circulate sexual material connected to the offence, or where a pimp convicted of controlling prostitution uses a car to drive prostitutes to their 'patch'. A Crown Court can also make a restraint order[96] in respect of realisable property held by an offender who is believed to have benefited from criminal conduct, prohibiting them from dealing with it.

Whenever an offender has profited in some way from the sexual exploitation of others, the court should give serious consideration to the making of a confiscation order to recover the proceeds of the crime.

The court should also, especially in relation to offences involving voyeurism, prostitution, pornography and trafficking, consider whether it would be appropriate to make an order depriving an offender of property used, or intended to be used, in connection with the offence.

Compensation orders

1.32.3 The court must consider making a compensation order, in accordance with the provisions of the Powers of Criminal Courts (Sentencing) Act 2000, in respect of any personal injury, loss or damage occasioned to a victim. Compensation should benefit, not inflict further harm on, the victim. Any financial recompense from the offender for a sexual offence may cause the victim additional humiliation, degradation and distress. The victim's views are properly obtained through sensitive discussion with the victim by the police or witness care unit, when it can be explained that the offender's ability to pay will ultimately determine whether, and how much, compensation is ordered. The views of the victim regarding compensation should be made known to the court and respected and, if appropriate, acknowledged at the time of sentencing. A victim may not want compensation from the offender, but this should not be assumed.

Summary of general principles

(i) Except where otherwise indicated, the offence guidelines all relate to sentencing on conviction for a first-time offender after a plea of not guilty.

(ii) Starting points are based on a basic offence[97] of its category. Aggravating and mitigating factors that are particularly relevant to each offence are listed in the individual offence guidelines. The list of aggravating factors is not exhaustive and the factors are not ranked in any particular order. A factor that is an ingredient of an offence cannot also be an aggravating factor. Sexual offences will often involve some form of violence as an essential element of the offence and this has been included in fixing the starting points. Where harm is inflicted over and above that necessary to commit the offence, that will be an aggravating factor.

(iii) In relation to sexual offences, the presence of generic and offence-specific aggravating factors will significantly influence the type and length of sentence imposed. The generic list of aggravating and mitigating factors identified by the Sentencing Guidelines Council in its guideline on seriousness is reproduced at paragraph 1.20 above but *not* for each offence. **These factors apply to a wide range of offences and not all will be relevant to sexual offences.**

(iv) Unless specifically stated, the starting points assume that the offender is an adult. Sentences will normally need to be reduced where the offender is sentenced as a youth, save in the most serious cases (see paragraph 1.17 above).

(v) Specific guidance on sentencing youths for one of the child sex offences that attracts a lower statutory maximum penalty where the offender is under 18 can be found in Part 7.

(vi) There are a large number of new or amended offences in the SOA 2003 for which there is no sentencing case law. The guidelines use the starting point of 5 years for the rape of an adult with no aggravating or mitigating factors (derived from *Millberry and others*[98]) as the baseline from which all other sentences have been calculated.

(vii) Where a community order is the recommended starting point, the requirements to be imposed are left for the court to decide according to the particular facts of the individual case. Where a

[95] Powers of Criminal Courts (Sentencing) Act 2000, s. 143

[96] Proceeds of Crime Act 2002, s. 41

[97] A 'basic offence' is one in which the ingredients of the offence as defined are present, and assuming no aggravating or mitigating factors

[98] [2003] 2 Cr App R (S) 31

community order is the proposed starting point for different levels of seriousness of the same offence or for a second or subsequent offence of the same level of seriousness, this should be reflected by the imposition of more onerous requirements.[99]

(viii) Treatment programmes are not specifically mentioned in the guidelines. A sentencer should always consider whether, in the circumstances of the individual case and the profile of the offending behaviour, it would be sensible to require the offender to take part in a programme designed to address sexually deviant behaviour.

(ix) Reference to 'non-custodial sentence' in any of the offence guidelines (save for those in Part 7) suggests that the court consider a community order or a fine. In most instances, an offence will have crossed the threshold for a community order. However, in accordance with normal sentencing practice, even in those circumstances a court is not precluded from imposing a financial penalty where that is determined to be the appropriate sentence.

(x) In all cases, the court must consider whether it would be appropriate to make any ancillary orders, such as an order banning the offender from working with children, an order requiring the offender to pay compensation to a victim, or an order confiscating an offender's assets or requiring the forfeiture of equipment used in connection with an offence.

The decision making process

The process set out below is intended to show that the sentencing approach for sexual offences is fluid and requires the structured exercise of discretion.

1. Identify dangerous offenders

Most sexual offences are specified offences for the purposes of the public protection provisions in the CJA 2003. The court must determine whether there is a significant risk of serious harm by the commission of a further specified offence. The starting points in the guidelines are a) for offenders who do not meet the dangerous offender criteria and b) as the basis for the setting of a minimum term within an indeterminate sentence for those who do meet the criteria.

2. Identify the appropriate starting point

Because many acts can be charged as more than one offence, consideration will have to be given to the appropriate guideline once findings of fact have been made. The sentence should reflect the facts found to exist and not just the title of the offence of which the offender is convicted.

3. Consider relevant aggravating factors, both general and those specific to the type of offence

This may result in a sentence level being identified that is higher than the suggested starting point, sometimes substantially so.

4. Consider mitigating factors and personal mitigation

There may be general or offence-specific mitigating factors and matters of personal mitigation which could result in a sentence that is lower than the suggested starting point (possibly substantially so), or a sentence of a different type.

5. Reduction for guilty plea

The court will then apply any reduction for a guilty plea following the approach set out in the Council's guideline *Reduction in Sentence for a Guilty Plea.*

6. Consider ancillary orders

The court should consider whether ancillary orders are appropriate or necessary. These are referred to in some of the offence guidelines.

7. The totality principle

The court should review the total sentence to ensure that it is proportionate to the offending behaviour and properly balanced.

8. Reasons

When a court moves from the suggested starting points and sentencing ranges identified in the guidelines, it should explain its reasons for doing so.

[99] For further information, see the Council guideline *New Sentences: Criminal Justice Act 2003,* section B: 'Imposing a Community Sentence – The Approach'

Sentencing ranges and starting points

1. Typically, a guideline will apply to an offence that can be committed in a variety of circumstances with different levels of seriousness. It will apply to a first-time offender who has been convicted after a trial. Within the guidelines, a first-time offender is a person who does not have a conviction which, by virtue of section 143(2) of the CJA 2003, must be treated as an aggravating factor.
2. As an aid to consistency of approach, the guidelines describe a number of types of activity which would fall within the broad definition of the offence. These are set out in a column headed 'Type/ nature of activity'.
3. The expected approach is for a court to identify the description that most nearly matches the particular facts of the offence for which sentence is being imposed. This will identify a starting point from which the sentencer can depart to reflect aggravating or mitigating factors affecting the seriousness of the offence (beyond those contained within the column describing the type or nature of offence activity) to reach a provisional sentence.
4. The *sentencing range* is the bracket into which the provisional sentence will normally fall after having regard to factors which aggravate or mitigate the seriousness of the offence. The particular circumstances may, however, make it appropriate that the provisional sentence falls outside the range.
5. Where the offender has previous convictions which aggravate the seriousness of the current offence, that may take the provisional sentence beyond the range given, particularly where there are significant other aggravating factors present.
6. Once the provisional sentence has been identified by reference to those factors affecting the seriousness of the offence, the court will take into account any relevant factors of personal mitigation, which may take the sentence outside the range indicated in the guideline.
7. Where there has been a guilty plea, any reduction attributable to that plea will be applied to the sentence at this stage. This reduction may take the sentence below the range provided.
8. A court must give its reasons for imposing a sentence of a different kind or outside the range provided in the guidelines.[100]

Part 2: Non-consensual Offences

2.1 The offences in this category include 'rape', 'assault by penetration', 'sexual assault' and causing a victim to take part in sexual activity without consent. Some offences are generic; others protect victims who are under 13 or who have a mental disorder impeding choice.

2.2 **The SOA 2003 creates a rule of law that there is no defence of consent where sexual activity is alleged in relation to a child under 13 years of age or a person who has a mental disorder impeding choice.[101]**

The harm caused by non-consensual offences

2.3 All non-consensual offences involve the violation of the victim's sexual autonomy and will result in harm.

2.4 The seriousness of the violation may depend on a number of factors, but the nature of the sexual behaviour will be the primary indicator of the degree of harm caused in the first instance.

2.5 The principle that offences involving sexual penetration are more serious than non-penetrative sexual assault is reflected in the higher maximum penalty accorded in statute to these offences.

The relationship between the victim and the offender

2.6 The guideline judgment in *Millberry and others*[102] established the principle that sentencers should adopt the same starting point for 'relationship rape' or 'acquaintance rape' as for 'stranger rape'. The Council has determined that the same principle should apply to all non-consensual offences. Any rape is a traumatic and humiliating experience and, although the particular circumstances in which the rape takes place may affect the sentence imposed, the starting point for sentencing should be the same.

The age of the victim

2.7 The extreme youth or old age of a victim should be an aggravating factor.

2.8 In addition, in principle, the younger the child and the greater the age gap between the offender and the victim, the higher the sentence should be.

[100] Criminal Justice Act 2003, s. 174(2)(a)
[101] See, for example, the offences set out in the Sexual Offences Act 2003, ss. 5–8 and 30–33
[102] [2003] 2 Cr App R (S) 31

2.9 However, the youth and immaturity of the offender must also be taken into account in each case.

2.10 The court in *Millberry* adopted the principle that a sexual offence against a child is more serious than the same offence perpetrated against an adult and attracts a higher starting point. No distinction was made between children aged 13 and over but under 16, and those aged under 13.

2.11 Special weight has subsequently been accorded to the protection of very young children by the introduction of a range of strict liability offences in the SOA 2003 specifically designed to protect children under 13:

- The offences of 'rape of a child under 13', 'assault by penetration of a child under 13' and 'causing a child under 13 to engage in sexual activity' where the activity included sexual penetration carry the maximum life penalty.
- The maximum penalty for the new offence of 'sexual assault of a child under 13' is 14 years, as opposed to a maximum of 10 years for the generic 'sexual assault' offence.

2.12 In keeping with the principles of protection established in the SOA 2003, the Council has determined that:

- **higher starting points in cases involving victims under 13 should normally apply, but there may be exceptions;**
- **particular care will need to be taken when applying the starting points in certain cases, such as those involving young offenders or offenders whose judgement is impaired by a mental disorder; and**
- **proximity in age between a young victim and an offender is also a relevant consideration.**

Victims with a mental disorder

2.13 The SOA 2003 introduces three groups of offences specifically designed to protect vulnerable adults who have a mental disorder. The aim is to protect all victims with a mental disorder, whether or not they have the capacity to consent to sexual activity, but the legislation has been drafted to make a distinction between:

(i) those persons who have a mental disorder 'impeding choice' – persons whose mental functioning is so impaired at the time of the sexual activity that they are 'unable to refuse';

(ii) those who have a mental disorder (but not falling within (i) above[103]) such that any ability to choose is easily overridden and agreement to sexual activity can be secured through relatively low levels of inducement, threat or deception; and

(iii) those who have a mental disorder, regardless of their ability to choose whether or not to take part in sexual activity, whose actions may be influenced by their familiarity with, or dependence upon, a care worker.

The latter two groups are considered in Part 3 of the guideline, which relates to offences involving ostensible consent.

2.14 The maximum penalty for non-consensual offences involving victims with a mental disorder is high, indicating the relative seriousness of such offending behaviour.

2.15 In line with the thinking relating to the protection of children under 13, the fact that the victim has a mental disorder impeding choice should always aggravate an offence, bearing in mind that it will have been proven that the offender knew, or could reasonably have been expected to know, that the victim had a mental disorder impeding choice.

The starting points for sentencing for offences involving victims with a mental disorder impeding choice should be higher than in comparable cases where the victim has no such disability.

The offender's culpability in non-consensual offences

2.16 All the non-consensual offences involve a high level of culpability on the part of the offender, since that person will have acted either deliberately without the victim's consent or without giving due consideration to whether the victim was able to or did, in fact, consent.

2.17 Notwithstanding paragraph 2.11 above, there will be cases involving victims under 13 years of age where there was, *in fact*, consent where, *in law*, it cannot be given. In such circumstances, presence of consent may be material in relation to sentence, particularly in relation to a young offender where there is close proximity in age between the victim and offender or where the mental capacity or maturity of the offender is impaired.

2.18 Where there was reasonable belief on the part of a young offender that the victim was 16, this can be taken into consideration as a mitigating factor.

[103] That is, it is not of such a character that it 'impedes choice' within the meaning of the SOA 2003

2.19 The planning of an offence indicates a higher level of culpability than an opportunistic or impulsive offence.

2.20 In *Millberry*, the Court of Appeal established that the offender's culpability in a case of rape would be 'somewhat less' in cases where the victim had consented to sexual familiarity with the offender on the occasion in question than in cases where the offender had set out with the intention of committing rape.

2.21 Save in cases of breach of trust or grooming, an offender's culpability may be reduced if the offender and victim engaged in consensual sexual activity on the same occasion and immediately before the offence took place. Factors relevant to culpability in such circumstances include the type of consensual activity that occurred, similarity to what then occurs, and timing. However, the seriousness of the non-consensual act may overwhelm any other consideration.

2.22 The same principle should apply to the generic offences of 'assault by penetration' and 'sexual assault'. However, it should not apply to the equivalent offences relating to victims who are under 13 or who have a mental disorder impeding choice, given the presumption inherent in these offences that the victim cannot in law consent to any form of sexual activity, save where there is close proximity of age between the offender and the victim, or where the mental capacity or maturity of the offender is impaired.

Part 2A: Rape and Assault by Penetration

2A.1 The SOA 2003 has redefined the offence of rape so that it now includes nonconsensual penile penetration of the mouth and has also introduced a new offence of 'assault by penetration'. Parliament agreed the same maximum penalty of life imprisonment for these offences.

2A.2 It is impossible to say that any one form of non-consensual penetration is inherently a more serious violation of the victim's sexual autonomy than another. The Council therefore has determined that the sentencing starting points established in *Millberry* should apply to all non-consensual offences involving penetration of the anus or vagina or penile penetration of the mouth.

- **5 years** is intended to be the starting point for a case involving an adult victim raped by a single offender in a case that involves *no aggravating factors at all.*
- **8 years** is the suggested starting point where any of the particular aggravating factors identified in the offence guidelines are involved.

2A.3 In addition:

- where identified aggravating factors exist and the victim is a child aged 13 or over but under 16, the recommended starting point is 10 years;
- for the rape of a child under 13 where there are no aggravating factors, a starting point of 10 years is recommended, rising to 13 years for cases involving any of the particular aggravating factors identified in the guideline.

2A.4 These are starting points. The existence of aggravating factors may significantly increase the sentence. The new sentences for public protection are designed to ensure that sexual offenders are not released into the community if they present a significant risk of serious harm.

Rape

Factors to take into consideration:

1. The sentences for public protection *must* be considered in all cases of rape.
   a) As a result, imprisonment for life or an order of imprisonment for public protection will be imposed in some cases. Both sentences are designed to ensure that sexual offenders are not released into the community if they present a significant risk of serious harm.
   b) Life imprisonment is the maximum for the offence. Such a sentence may be imposed either as a result of the offence itself where a number of aggravating factors are present, or because the offender meets the dangerousness criterion.
   c) Within any indeterminate sentence, the minimum term will generally be half the appropriate determinate sentence. The starting points will be relevant, therefore, to the process of fixing any minimum term that may be necessary.
2. Rape includes penile penetration of the mouth.
3. There is no distinction in the starting points for penetration of the vagina, anus or mouth.
4. All the non-consensual offences involve a high level of culpability on the part of the offender, since that person will have acted either deliberately without the victim's consent or without giving due care to whether the victim was able to or did, in fact, consent.

5. The planning of an offence indicates a higher level of culpability than an opportunistic or impulsive offence.
6. An offender's culpability may be reduced if the offender and victim engaged in consensual sexual activity on the same occasion and immediately before the offence took place. Factors relevant to culpability in such circumstances include the type of consensual activity that occurred, similarity to what then occurs, and timing. However, the seriousness of the non-consensual act may overwhelm any other consideration.
7. The seriousness of the violation of the victim's sexual autonomy may depend on a number of factors, but the nature of the sexual behaviour will be the primary indicator of the degree of harm caused in the first instance.
8. The presence of any of the general aggravating factors identified in the Council guideline on seriousness or any of the additional factors identified in the guidelines will indicate a sentence above the normal starting point.

Rape

THESE ARE SERIOUS OFFENCES FOR THE PURPOSES OF SECTION 224 CJA 2003

1. **Rape** (section 1): Intentional non-consensual penile penetration of the vagina, anus or mouth
2. **Rape of a child under 13** (section 5): Intentional penile penetration of the vagina, anus or mouth of a person under 13

Maximum penalty for both offences: **Life imprisonment**

Type/nature of activity	Starting points	Sentencing ranges
Repeated rape of same victim over a course of time or rape involving multiple victims	**15 years custody**	**13–19 years custody**
Rape accompanied by any one of the following: abduction or detention; offender aware that he is suffering from a sexually transmitted infection; more than one offender acting together; abuse of trust; offence motivated by prejudice (race, religion, sexual orientation, physical disability); sustained attack	**13 years custody** if the victim is under 13 **10 years custody** if the victim is a child aged 13 or over but under 16 **8 years custody** if the victim is 16 or over	**11–17 years custody** **8–13 years custody** **6–11 years custody**
Single offence of rape by single offender	**10 years custody** if the victim is under 13 **8 years custody** if the victim is 13 or over but under 16 **5 years custody** if the victim is 16 or over	**8–13 years custody** **6–11 years custody** **4–8 years custody**

Additional aggravating factors	Additional mitigating factors
1. Offender ejaculated or caused victim to ejaculate 2. Background of intimidation or coercion 3. Use of drugs, alcohol or other substance to facilitate the offence 4. Threats to prevent victim reporting the incident 5. Abduction or detention 6. Offender aware that he is suffering from a sexually transmitted infection 7. Pregnancy or infection results	*Where the victim is aged 16 or over* Victim engaged in consensual sexual activity with the offender on the same occasion and immediately before the offence *Where the victim is under 16* • Sexual activity between two children (one of whom is the offender) was mutually agreed and experimental • Reasonable belief (by a young offender) that the victim was aged 16 or over

An offender convicted of these offences is automatically subject to notification requirements.[104]

[104] In accordance with the SOA 2003, s. 80 and schedule 3

Assault by penetration

Factors to take into consideration:

1. The sentences for public protection *must* be considered in all cases of assault by penetration. They are designed to ensure that sexual offenders are not released into the community if they present a significant risk of serious harm. Within any indeterminate sentence, the minimum term will generally be half the appropriate determinate sentence. The starting points will be relevant, therefore, to the process of fixing any minimum term that may be necessary.
2. This offence involves penetration of the vagina or anus only, with objects or body parts. It may include penile penetration where the means of penetration is only established during the trial.
3. All the non-consensual offences involve a high level of culpability on the part of the offender, since that person will have acted either deliberately without the victim's consent or without giving due care to whether the victim was able to or did, in fact, consent.
4. The planning of an offence indicates a higher level of culpability than an opportunistic or impulsive offence.
5. An offender's culpability may be reduced if the offender and victim engaged in consensual sexual activity on the same occasion and immediately before the offence took place. Factors relevant to culpability in such circumstances include the type of consensual activity that occurred, similarity to what then occurs, and timing. However, the seriousness of the non-consensual act may overwhelm any other consideration.
6. The seriousness of the violation of the victim's sexual autonomy may depend on a number of factors, but the nature of the sexual behaviour will be the primary indicator of the degree of harm caused in the first instance.
7. The presence of any of the general aggravating factors identified in the Council guideline on seriousness or any of the additional factors identified in the guidelines will indicate a sentence above the normal starting point.
8. Brief penetration with fingers, toes or tongue may result in a significantly lower sentence where no physical harm is caused to the victim.

Assault by penetration

THESE ARE SERIOUS OFFENCES FOR THE PURPOSES OF SECTION 224 CJA 2003

1. **Assault by penetration** (section 2): Non-consensual penetration of the vagina or anus with objects or body parts
2. **Assault of a child under 13 by penetration** (section 6): Intentional penetration of the vagina or anus of a person under 13 with objects or body parts

Maximum penalty for both offences: **Life imprisonment**

Type/nature of activity	Starting points	Sentencing Ranges
Penetration with an object or body part, accompanied by any one of the following: abduction or detention; more than one offender acting together; abuse of trust; offence motivated by prejudice (race, religion, sexual orientation, physical disability); sustained attack	**13 years custody** if the victim is under 13	**11–17 years custody**
	10 years custody if the victim is 13 or over but under 16	**8–13 years custody**
	8 years custody if the victim is 16 or over	**6–11 years custody**
Penetration with an object – in general, the larger or more dangerous the object, the higher the sentence should be	**7 years custody** if the victim is under 13	**5–10 years custody**
	5 years custody if the victim is 13 or over but under 16	**4–8 years custody**
	3 years custody if the victim is 16 or over	**2–5 years custody**
Penetration with a body part (fingers, toes or tongue) where no physical harm is sustained by the victim	**5 years custody** if the victim is under 13	**4–8 years custody**
	4 years custody if the victim is 13 or over but under 16	**3–7 years custody**
	2 years custody if the victim is 16 or over	**1–4 years custody**

Additional aggravating factors	Additional mitigating factors
1. Background of intimidation or coercion 2. Use of drugs, alcohol or other substance to facilitate the offence 3. Threats to prevent victim reporting the incident 4. Abduction or detention 5. Offender aware that he is suffering from a sexually transmitted infection 6. Physical harm arising from the penetration 7. Offender ejaculated or caused the victim to ejaculate	*Where the victim is aged 16 or over* Victim engaged in consensual sexual activity with the offender on the same occasion and immediately before the offence *Where the victim is under 16* • Sexual activity between two children (one of whom is the offender) was mutually agreed and experimental • Reasonable belief (by a young offender) that the victim was aged 16 or over Penetration is minimal or for a short duration

An offender convicted of these offences is automatically subject to notification requirements.[105]

Part 2B: Sexual Assault

2B.1 Various activities previously covered by the offence of 'indecent assault' now fall within the definitions of other offences in the SOA 2003:
- Forcible penile penetration of the mouth now comes within the definition of 'rape'.
- Penetration of the vagina or anus with a body part or other object is covered by the offence of 'assault by penetration'.
- All forms of ostensibly consensual sexual activity involving children under 16 (who cannot in law give any consent to prevent an act being an assault) now fall within a range of child sex offences.
- Vulnerable adults subjected to a sexual assault are now protected by the offences of 'sexual activity with a person with a mental disorder impeding choice' and 'causing or inciting a person with a mental disorder impeding choice to engage in sexual activity'.

2B.2 The offence of 'sexual assault' covers all forms of sexual touching and will largely be used in relation to the lesser forms of assault that would have previously fallen at the lower end of the penalty scale.

2B.3 The exact nature of the sexual activity should be the key factor in assessing the seriousness of a sexual assault and should be used as the starting point from which to begin the process of assessing the overall seriousness of the offending behaviour.

2B.4 The presence of aggravating factors can make an offence significantly more serious than the nature of the activity alone might suggest.

- **The nature of the sexual activity will be the *primary* factor in assessing the seriousness of an offence of sexual assault.**
- **In all cases, the fact that the offender has ejaculated or has caused the victim to ejaculate will increase the seriousness of the offence.**

Sexual assault

Factors to take into consideration:

1. The sentences for public protection *must* be considered in all cases of sexual assault. They are designed to ensure that sexual offenders are not released into the community if they present a significant risk of serious harm.
2. The offence of 'sexual assault' covers all forms of sexual touching and therefore covers a wide range of offending behaviour. Some offences may justify a lesser sentence where the actions were more offensive than threatening and comprised a single act rather than more persistent behaviour.
3. The nature of the sexual activity will be the *primary* factor in assessing the seriousness of an offence and should be use as the starting point from which to begin the process of assessing the overall seriousness of the offending behaviour.
4. The presence of aggravating factors can make an offence significantly more serious than the nature of the activity alone might suggest.
5. For the purpose of the guideline, types of sexual touching are broadly grouped in terms of seriousness. An offence may involve activities from more than one group. In all cases, the fact that the offender has ejaculated or has caused the victim to ejaculate will increase the seriousness of the offence.

105 In accordance with the SOA 2003, s. 80 and schedule 3

6. An offender's culpability may be reduced if the offender and victim engaged in consensual sexual activity on the same occasion and immediately before the offence took place. Factors relevant to culpability in such circumstances include the type of consensual activity that occurred, similarity to what then occurs, and timing. However, the seriousness of the non-consensual act may overwhelm any other consideration.
7. Where this offence is being dealt with in a magistrates' court, more detailed guidance is provided in the Magistrates' Court Sentencing Guidelines (MCSG).

Sexual assault

THESE ARE SERIOUS OFFENCES FOR THE PURPOSES OF SECTION 224 CJA 2003

1. **Sexual assault** (section 3): Non-consensual sexual touching

Maximum penalty: **10 years**

2. **Sexual assault of a child under 13** (section 7): Intentional sexual touching of a person under 13

Maximum penalty: **14 years**

Type/ nature of activity	Starting points	Sentencing ranges
Contact between naked genitalia of offender and naked genitalia, face or mouth of the victim	**5 years custody** if the victim is under 13 **3 years custody** if the victim is aged 13 or over	**4–8 years custody** **2–5 years custody**
Contact between naked genitalia of offender and another part of victim's body Contact with genitalia of victim by offender using part of his or her body other than the genitalia, or an object Contact between either the clothed genitalia of offender and naked genitalia of victim or naked genitalia of offender and clothed genitalia of victim	**2 years custody** if the victim is under 13 **12 months custody** if the victim is aged 13 or over	**1–4 years custody** **26 weeks–2 years custody**
Contact between part of offender's body (other than the genitalia) with part of the victim's body (other than the genitalia)	**26 weeks custody** if the victim is under 13 **Community order** if the victim is aged 13 or over	**4 weeks–18 months custody** **An appropriate non-custodial sentence***

* 'Non-custodial sentence' in this context suggests a community order or a fine. In most instances, an offence will have crossed the threshold for a community order. However, in accordance with normal sentencing practice, a court is not precluded from imposing a financial penalty where that is determined to be the appropriate sentence.

Additional aggravating factors	Additional mitigating factors
1. Offender ejaculated or caused victim to ejaculate 2. Background of intimidation or coercion 3. Use of drugs, alcohol or other substance to facilitate the offence 4. Threats to prevent victim reporting the incident 5. Abduction or detention 6. Offender aware that he or she is suffering from a sexually transmitted infection 7. Physical harm caused 8. Prolonged activity or contact	*Where the victim is aged 16 or over* Victim engaged in consensual sexual activity with the offender on the same occasion and immediately before the offence *Where the victim is under 16* • Sexual activity between two children (one of whom is the offender) was mutually agreed and experimental • Reasonable belief (by a young offender) that the victim was aged 16 or over Youth and immaturity of the offender Minimal or fleeting contact

An offender convicted of these offences is automatically subject to notification requirements.[106]

[106] In accordance with the SOA 2003, s. 80 and schedule 3

Part 2C: Causing or Inciting Sexual Activity

2C.1 There are three offences in this category covering a wide range of sexual activity:

- Causing a person to engage in sexual activity without consent
- Causing or inciting a child under 13 to engage in sexual activity
- Causing or inciting a person with a mental disorder impeding choice to engage in sexual activity

2C.2 The maximum penalty for the second and third of these offences is the same whether the sexual activity is *caused* or *incited*. This recognises that, with vulnerable victims, incitement to indulge in sexual activity is, of itself, likely to result in harm.

2C.3 Deciding sentence may be complex where an incited offence did not actually take place. Whilst the effect of the incitement is of no relevance to whether or not the offence incited was *committed*, it is likely to be relevant to the sentence imposed.

2C.4 Accordingly, the starting point should be the same whether or not the sexual activity takes place. Where it does not take place, the harm (and sometimes the culpability) is likely to be less, and the sentence should be reduced appropriately to reflect this.

2C.5 If the activity does not take place because the offender desists of his or her own accord, culpability (and sometimes harm) will be reduced. This should be treated as a mitigating factor for sentencing purposes and does not affect the principle that starting points for 'causing' or 'inciting' an activity should be the same.

2C.6 If the offender is prevented from achieving his or her aim by reasons outside their control, culpability may not be reduced, but it is possible that the harm will be less than if the activity had taken place.

2C.7 Culpability must be the primary indicator for sentencing in such cases, but it would make no sense for courts to pass the same sentence for an incited offence that did not actually take place as it would for the substantive offence itself. In these circumstances, the sentence should be calculated using the starting point for the substantive offence, taking account of the nature of the harm that would have been caused had the offence taken place, and the degree to which an intended victim may have suffered as a result of knowing or believing that the incited offence would take place, but nevertheless reflecting the facts if no actual harm has been caused to a victim.

- **The starting point should be the same whether an offender causes an act to take place or incites an act which does not take place.**
- **A reduction will generally be appropriate where the incited activity does not take place.**
- **Where an offender voluntarily desists from any action taken to incite a sexual act, or personally and of their own volition intervenes to prevent a sexual act from taking place, this will be an additional mitigating factor.**
- **Whether or not the sexual activity takes place, the degree of harm done to the victim will be a material consideration when considering the sentence.**

2C.8 The offence of 'causing a person to engage in sexual activity without consent' covers situations where, for example, a victim is forced to carry out a sexual act involving his or her own person, such as self-masturbation, or to engage in sexual activity with a third party, or situations in which the victim is forced to engage in sexual activity with the offender.

2C.9 The underlying purpose is to create offences that carry the same level of penalties for what amounts to the same type of offending behaviour, regardless of the gender or sexual orientation of the offender. This is reflected in the recommended starting points for penetrative acts charged within this category.

2C.10 The two main factors determining the seriousness of an offence of causing or inciting sexual activity without consent will be the nature of the sexual activity (as an indication of the degree of harm caused, or likely to be caused, to the victim) and the level of the offender's culpability. Culpability will be higher if the victim is forced to engage in sexual activity with the offender, or with another victim, than in cases where there is no sexual contact between the victim and the offender or anyone else. In all cases, the degree of force or coercion used by the offender will be an indication of the offender's level of culpability and may also exacerbate the harm suffered by the victim.

2C.11 The same sentencing starting points for offences involving non-consensual penetration of the vagina or anus of another person will apply regardless of whether the offender is male or female. There should be no differentiation between the starting point for 'rape' and an offence where a female offender causes or incites a non-consenting male to penetrate her vagina, anus or mouth. Similarly, where a victim is caused or incited to take part in penetrative activities with a third party or where the offender causes or incites other forms of sexual activity, there is no reason to differentiate sentence for male and female offenders.

The starting points for sentencing for sexual activity that is caused or incited by the offender without the consent of the victim(s) should mirror those for similar activity perpetrated within the offences of 'rape', 'assault by penetration' and 'sexual assault'.

Causing sexual activity without consent

Factors to take into consideration:

1. The sentences for public protection *must* be considered in all cases of causing sexual activity. They are designed to ensure that sexual offenders are not released into the community if they present a significant risk of serious harm. Within any indeterminate sentence, the minimum term will generally be half the appropriate determinate sentence. The starting points will be relevant, therefore, to the process of fixing any minimum term that may be necessary.
2. The same degree of seriousness applies whether an offender causes an act to take place, incites an act that actually takes place, or incites an act that does not take place only because it is prevented by factors beyond the control of the offender.
3. The same starting points apply whether the activity was caused or incited and whether or not the incited activity took place, but some reduction will generally be appropriate when the incited activity does not, in fact, take place.
4. Where an offender voluntarily desists from any action taken to incite a sexual act or personally, and of their own volition, intervenes to prevent from taking place a sexual act that he or she has incited, this should be treated as a mitigating factor.
5. The effect of the incitement is relevant to the length of the sentence to be imposed. A court should take into account the degree to which the intended victim may have suffered as a result of knowing or believing that an offence would take place.

Causing sexual activity without consent

THESE ARE SERIOUS OFFENCES FOR THE PURPOSES OF SECTION 224 CJA 2003

1. **Causing a person to engage in sexual activity without consent** (section 4): Forcing someone else to perform a sexual act on him or herself or another person

Maximum penalty: **Life imprisonment** if the activity involves penetration; **10 years** if the activity does not involve penetration

2. **Causing or inciting a child under 13 to engage in sexual activity** (section 8): Causing or inciting a person under 13 to perform a sexual act on him or herself or another person

Maximum penalty: **Life imprisonment** if the activity involves penetration; **14 years** if the activity does not involve penetration

3. **Causing or inciting a person with a mental disorder impeding choice to engage in sexual activity** (section 31): Intentionally causing or inciting a person with a mental disorder impeding choice to engage in sexual activity.

Maximum penalty: **Life imprisonment** if the activity involves penetration; **14 years** if penetration not involved

Type/ nature of activity	Starting points:	Sentencing ranges
Penetration with any one of the following aggravating factors: abduction or detention; offender aware that he or she is suffering from a sexually transmitted infection; more than one offender acting together; abuse of trust; offence motivated by prejudice (race, religion, sexual orientation, physical disability); sustained attack	**13 years custody** if the victim is a child under 13 or a person with a mental disorder **10 years custody** if the victim is 13 or over but under 16 **8 years custody** if the victim is 16 or over	**11–17 years custody** **8–13 years custody** **6–11 years custody**
Single offence of penetration of/ by single offender with no aggravating or mitigating factors	**7 years custody** if the victim is a child under 13 or a person with a mental disorder **5 years custody** if the victim is 13 or over but under 16 **3 years custody** if the victim is 16 or over	**5–10 years custody** **4–8 years custody** **2–5 years custody**

Type/ nature of activity	Starting points:	Sentencing ranges
Contact between naked genitalia of offender and naked genitalia of victim, *or* causing two or more victims to engage in such activity with each other, *or* causing victim to masturbate him/herself	**5 years custody** if the victim is a child under 13 or a person with a mental disorder **3 years custody**	**4–8 years custody** **2–5 years custody**
Contact between naked genitalia of offender and another part of victim's body, *or* causing two or more victims to engage in such activity with each other Contact with naked genitalia of victim by offender using part of the body other than the genitalia or an object, *or* causing two or more victims to engage in such activity with each other Contact between either the clothed genitalia of offender and naked genitalia of victim, between naked genitalia of offender and clothed genitalia of victim, *or* causing two or more victims to engage in such activity with each other	**2 years custody** if the victim is a child under 13 or a person with a mental disorder **12 months custody**	**1–4 years custody** **26 weeks– 2 years custody**
Contact between part of offender's body (other than the genitalia) with part of victim's body (other than the genitalia)	**26 weeks custody** if the victim is a child under 13 or a person with a mental disorder **Community order**	**4 weeks–18 months custody** **An appropriate non-custodial sentence***

* 'Non-custodial sentence' in this context suggests a community order or a fine. In most instances, an offence will have crossed the threshold for a community order. However, in accordance with normal sentencing practice, a court is not precluded from imposing a financial penalty where that is determined to be the appropriate sentence.

Additional aggravating factors	Additional mitigating factors
1. Offender ejaculated or caused victim to ejaculate 2. History of intimidation or coercion 3. Use of drugs, alcohol or other substance to facilitate the offence 4. Threats to prevent victim reporting the incident 5. Abduction or detention 6. Offender aware that he or she is suffering from a sexually transmitted infection	

An offender convicted of these offences is automatically subject to notification requirements.[107]

Part 2D: Other Non-Consensual Offences

2D.1 Four other offences fall within the general category of non-consensual offences:

- Engaging in sexual activity in the presence of a child
- Engaging in sexual activity in the presence of a person with a mental disorder impeding choice
- Causing a child to watch a sexual act
- Causing a person with a mental disorder impeding choice to watch a sexual act

2D.2 These are offences that relate to lesser forms of offending behaviour than offences that involve

[107] In accordance with the SOA 2003, s. 80 and schedule 3

physical touching of the victim, but they nevertheless attract maximum penalties of 10 years' imprisonment in recognition of the fact that the victims are particularly vulnerable.

2D.3 The guidelines are predicated on the principle that the more serious the nature of the sexual activity a victim is forced to witness, the higher the sentencing starting point should be.

2D.4 These offences can cover a very wide range of sexual activity and an equally wide range of circumstances in which a victim is subjected to witnessing it.

2D.5 However, any form of sexual activity in the presence of a child or person with a mental disorder impeding choice may well be serious enough to merit a custodial starting point. It is always within the power of the court in an individual case to consider whether there are particular factors that mitigate sentence and should move it back below the custodial threshold.

- **The same starting points for sentencing should apply in relation to the various levels of activity falling within the offences of 'engaging in sexual activity in the presence of a child' and 'engaging in sexual activity in the presence of a person with a mental disorder impeding choice'. Similarly, the same starting points should apply in relation to the offences of 'causing a child to watch a sexual act' and 'causing a person with a mental disorder impeding choice to watch a sexual act'.**
- **An offence involving an offender who intentionally commits a sexual act in the presence of a child or a person with a mental disorder impeding choice in order to obtain sexual gratification will potentially be serious enough to merit a custodial sentence. In an individual case the court will need to consider whether there are particular mitigating factors that move the sentence below the custodial threshold.**

Sexual activity in the presence of another person

Factors to take into consideration:

1. The sentences for public protection *must* be considered in all cases of engaging in sexual activity in the presence of another person. They are designed to ensure that sexual offenders are not released into the community if they present a significant risk of serious harm.
2. These offences involve intentionally, and for the purpose of obtaining sexual gratification, engaging in sexual activity in the presence of a person under 16, or a person with a mental disorder, knowing or believing that person to be aware of the activity.
3. The guidelines are predicated on the principle that the more serious the nature of the sexual activity a victim is forced to witness, the higher the sentencing starting point should be.
4. These offences will potentially be serious enough to merit a custodial sentence. In an individual case the court will need to consider whether there are particular mitigating factors that move the sentence below the custodial threshold.

Sexual activity in the presence of another person

THESE ARE SERIOUS OFFENCES FOR THE PURPOSES OF SECTION 224 CJA 2003

1. **Engaging in sexual activity in the presence of a child** (section 11)

Maximum penalty: **10 years (5 years if offender is under 18)**

2. **Engaging in sexual activity in the presence of a person with a mental disorder impeding choice** (section 32)

Maximum penalty: **10 years**

Type/nature of activity	Starting points	Sentencing ranges
Consensual intercourse or other forms of consensual penetration	**2 years custody**	**1–4 years custody**
Masturbation (of oneself or another person)	**18 months custody**	**12 months–2 years** **6 months custody**
Consensual sexual touching involving naked genitalia	**12 months custody**	**26 weeks–18 months custody**
Consensual sexual touching of naked body parts but not involving naked genitalia	**26 weeks custody**	**4 weeks–18 months custody**

Additional aggravating factors	Additional mitigating factors
1. Background of intimidation or coercion 2. Use of drugs, alcohol or other substance to facilitate the offence 3. Threats to prevent victim reporting the incident 4. Abduction or detention	

An offender convicted of these offences is automatically subject to notification requirements.[108]

Causing or inciting another person to watch a sexual act

Factors to take into consideration:

1. The sentences for public protection *must* be considered in all cases. They are designed to ensure that sexual offenders are not released into the community if they present a significant risk of serious harm.
2. These offences include intentionally causing or inciting, for the purpose of sexual gratification, a person under 16, or a person with a mental disorder, to watch sexual activity or look at a photograph or pseudo-photograph of sexual activity.
3. The guidelines are predicated on the principle that the more serious the nature of the sexual activity a victim is caused to witness, the higher the sentencing starting point should be.
4. These offences will potentially be serious enough to merit a custodial sentence. In an individual case the court will need to consider whether there are particular mitigating factors that should move the sentence below the custodial threshold.
5. The same starting points apply whether the activity was caused or incited and whether or not the incited activity took place.

Causing or inciting another person to watch a sexual act

THESE ARE SERIOUS OFFENCES FOR THE PURPOSES OF SECTION 224 CJA 2003

1. Causing a child to watch a sexual act (section 12)

Maximum penalty: **10 years (5 years if offender is under 18)**

2. Causing a person with a mental disorder impeding choice, to watch a sexual act (section 33)

Maximum penalty: **10 years**

Type/nature of activity	Starting points	Sentencing ranges
Live sexual activity	**18 months custody**	**12 months–2 years custody**
Moving or still images of people engaged in sexual activity involving penetration	**32 weeks custody**	**26 weeks–12 months custody**
Moving or still images of people engaged in sexual activity other than penetration	**Community order**	**Community order–26 weeks custody**

Additional aggravating factors	Additional mitigating factors
1. Background of intimidation or coercion 2. Use of drugs, alcohol or other substance to facilitate the offence 3. Threats to prevent victim reporting the incident 4. Abduction or detention 5. Images of violent activity	

An offender convicted of these offences is automatically subject to notification requirements.[109]

[108] In accordance with the SOA 2003, s. 80 and schedule 3
[109] In accordance with the SOA 2003, s. 80 and schedule 3

Part 3: Offences Involving Ostensible Consent

3.1 There are several groups of offences in the SOA 2003 that involve a compliant or willing partner. Any sexual activity involving a person below the age of consent is unlawful notwithstanding any ostensible consent. In addition, there are circumstances where sexual activity takes place with the ostensible consent of both parties but where one of the parties is in such a great position of power over the other that the sexual activity is wrong.

3.2 There are two categories of offence within this broad grouping:

- Part 3A – sexual activity with children under 16 – or under 18 where there is an imbalance of power (for example, within the family unit) or an abuse of trust (for example, between a teacher and a pupil); and
- Part 3B – sexual activity with adults who have the capacity to consent but who, by reason of, or for reasons related to, a mental disorder are susceptible to coercion and exploitation.

Part 3A: Offences Involving Children

3A.1 In addition to the range of non-consensual sexual offences designed to protect children under 13, there are three further groups of offences that cover all forms of ostensibly consensual sexual activity involving children under 16 and also provide additional protection for older children:

(i) 'child sex offences' (covering unlawful sexual activity with children under 16) including 'arranging or facilitating the commission of a child sex offence';

(ii) 'familial child sex offences' (relating to offences committed by members of the child's family or household and primarily intended to ensure that charges can be brought in relation to victims aged 16 or 17); and

(iii) 'abuse of a position of trust' (another offence that enables the prosecution of sexual activity involving victims aged 16 or 17, in this case where the offender has a relationship of trust with the child, such as that of a teacher or care worker).

3A.2 A 'reasonable' belief that the child was aged 16 or over is a defence to all the child sex offences, provided the child was, in fact, aged 13 or over. With the same proviso, a reasonable belief that the victim was aged 18 or over is a defence to the familial child sex offences and the abuse of trust offences.

3A.3 The maximum penalties for the offences in these groups give some indication of their relative seriousness and of the factors that increase the seriousness of an offence.

3A.4 Conversely, the lower maximum penalties for offenders aged under 18 indicate that the offence is less serious when the age gap between the victim and the offender is relatively narrow. The young age of an offender may often be seen as a mitigating factor for sentencing. This principle has already largely been catered for in the child sex offences by the provision in statute of lower maximum penalties for young offenders, which are designed to take account of their immaturity (see Part 7). However, the extreme youth of an offender and close proximity in age between the offender and the victim are both factors that will still be relevant for the court to consider when deciding sentence.

The significance of family relationships

3A.5 Family relationships, as defined in the SOA 2003 in relation to the offences of sexual activity with a child family member and inciting a child family member to engage in sexual activity, are not restricted to blood relationships and include relationships formed through adoption, fostering, marriage or partnership.

3A.6 Some relationships, such as parents and siblings, are automatically covered. Others, such as step-parents and cousins, fall within the definition of 'family member' only if they live, or have lived, in the same household as the child or if they are, or have been, regularly involved in caring for, training, supervising or being in sole charge of the child.

3A.7 More distant 'relationships', such as lodgers and au pairs, are covered only if they were living in the same household as the child at the time of the offence and were regularly involved in caring for, training, supervising or being in sole charge of the child at that time.

3A.8 These offences bring ostensibly consensual sexual activity between persons over the age of consent (which would not otherwise be unlawful) within the scope of the criminal law.

All children, even those aged 16 or 17, are potentially vulnerable to exploitation within the family unit and the offences attract the same maximum penalty regardless of the age of the victim. The Council's view is that the worst aspect of child sexual abuse within the family is that the offender is one of the very people to whom the child would normally expect to turn for support and protection.

3A.9 Victims aged 16 or 17 may have been 'groomed' by a family member from a very young age before sexual activity takes place. Evidence of grooming can be treated as an aggravating factor for sentencing purposes, as can the extreme youth of a victim. However, the closeness of the relationship in such cases increases the seriousness of the offence regardless of the age of the victim and should be reflected in the sentencing starting points.

3A.10 There is a clear difference between a young person being coerced into sexual activity by an adult who holds a position of trust in his or her life outside the family unit and being coerced into a sexual relationship by someone (adult or child) who holds a position of trust within the family unit.

3A.11 The starting points for sentencing where the child is aged 13 or over but under 16 should be higher than for the equivalent child sex offences, to reflect the inherent abuse of trust. The amount of enhancement should vary to reflect the wide range of 'familial' relationships covered by this offence –on the basis that abuse by a parent is more serious than abuse by, for example, a foster sibling or lodger.

The starting points for sentencing for the familial child sex offences should be between 25% and 50% higher than those for the generic child sex offences in all cases where the victim is aged 13 or over but under 16; the closer the familial relationship, using the statutory definitions as a guide, the higher the increase that should be applied.

3A.12 Where a victim is over the age of consent, the starting points should only be significant where the offender is a close relative and where the abuse of a familial relationship is most serious. Where the activity is commenced when the victim is already aged 16 or 17 and the sexual relationship is unlawful only because it takes place within a familial setting (e.g. the activity is between foster siblings or involves an au pair or lodger), the starting points for sentencing should be lower than those for 'sexual activity with a child' and should be matched with the starting points for the 'abuse of trust' offences.

- **Where the victim of a familial child sex offence is aged 16 or 17 when the sexual activity is commenced and the sexual relationship is unlawful only because it takes place within a familial setting, the starting points for sentencing should be in line with those for the generic abuse of trust offences.**
- **Evidence that a victim has been 'groomed' by the offender to agree to take part in sexual activity will aggravate sentence.**

Abuse of a position of trust

3A.13 These offences criminalise sexual activity by adults over 18 with children under 18 in situations where the adults are looking after the children in educational establishments or in various residential settings, or where their duties involve them in the regular unsupervised contact of children in the community.

3A.14 The maximum penalty for the offences of abuse of trust (5 years) is relatively low because the offences are primarily designed to protect young people who are over the legal age of consent (i. e. aged 16 or 17) from being persuaded to engage in sexual activity that would not be criminal except for the offender's position of trust in relation to the victim.

3A.15 In view of the fact that these offences will only be charged where the victim is aged 16 or 17, the sentencing starting points in the guidelines are significantly lower than those for a child sex offence involving the same type of sexual activity. The potential harm caused to victims who have been coerced and manipulated into undesirable sexual relationships has not been underestimated, and evidence of serious coercion, threats or trauma would all be aggravating factors that would move a sentence well beyond the starting point. However, some relationships caught within the scope of these offences, although unlawful, will be wholly consensual. The length of time over which a relationship has been sustained and the proximity in age between the parties could point to a relationship born out of genuine affection. Each case must be considered carefully on its own facts.

When sentencing for an abuse of trust offence, serious coercion, threats or trauma are aggravating factors that should move a sentence well beyond the starting point.

Assessing the seriousness of sexual offences against children

3A.16 The culpability of the offender will be the primary indicator of offence seriousness, and the nature of the sexual activity will provide a guide as to the seriousness of the harm caused to the victim, for any of the offences in the three categories involving ostensibly consensual activity with children. Other factors will include:

- the age and degree of vulnerability of the victim –as a general indication, the younger the child,

the more vulnerable he or she is likely to be, although older children may also suffer serious and long-term psychological damage as a result of sexual abuse;
- the age gap between the child and the offender;
- the youth and immaturity of the offender; and
- except where it is inherent in an offence, any breach of trust arising from a family relationship between the child and the offender, or from the offender's professional or other responsibility for the child's welfare, will make an offence more serious.

Sexual activity with a child

Factors to take into consideration:

1. The sentences for public protection *must* be considered in all cases. They are designed to ensure that sexual offenders are not released into the community if they present a significant risk of serious harm.
2. The culpability of the offender will be the primary indicator of offence seriousness, and the nature of the sexual activity will provide a guide as to the seriousness of the harm caused to the victim. Other factors will include:
   - the age and degree of vulnerability of the victim –as a general indication, the younger the child, the more vulnerable he or she is likely to be, although older children may also suffer serious and long-term psychological damage as a result of sexual abuse;
   - the age gap between the child and the offender;
   - the youth and immaturity of the offender; and
   - except where it is inherent in an offence, any breach of trust arising from a family relationship between the child and the offender, or from the offender's professional or other responsibility for the child's welfare, will make an offence more serious.
3. The same starting points apply whether the activity was caused or incited. Where an offence was incited but did not take place as a result of the voluntary intervention of the offender, that is likely to reduce the severity of the sentence imposed.

Sexual activity with a child

THESE ARE SERIOUS OFFENCES FOR THE PURPOSES OF SECTION 224 CJA 2003

1. **Sexual activity with a child** (section 9): Intentional sexual touching of a person under 16
2. **Causing or inciting a child to engage in sexual activity** (section 10): Intentionally causing or inciting a person under 16 to engage in sexual activity

Maximum penalty for both offences: **14 years (5 years if offender is under 18)**

Type/nature of activity	**Starting points**	**Sentencing ranges**
Penile penetration of the vagina, anus or mouth *or* penetration of the vagina or anus with another body part or an object	**4 years custody**	**3–7 years custody**
Contact between naked genitalia of offender and naked genitalia or another part of victim's body, particularly face or mouth	**2 years custody**	**1–4 years custody**
Contact between naked genitalia of offender *or* victim and clothed genitalia of victim or offender or contact with naked genitalia of victim by offender using part of his or her body other than the genitalia or an object	**12 months custody**	**26 weeks–2 years custody**
Contact between part of offender's body (other than the genitalia) with part of the victim's body (other than the genitalia)	**Community order**	**An appropriate non-custodial sentence***

* 'Non-custodial sentence' in this context suggests a community order or a fine. In most instances, an offence will have crossed the threshold for a community order. However, in accordance with normal sentencing practice, a court is not precluded from imposing a financial penalty where that is determined to be the appropriate sentence.

Additional aggravating factors	Additional mitigating factors
1. Offender ejaculated or caused victim to ejaculate 2. Threats to prevent victim reporting the incident 3. Offender aware that he or she is suffering from a sexually transmitted infection	1. Offender intervenes to prevent incited offence from taking place 2. Small disparity in age between the offender and the victim

An offender convicted of these offences is automatically subject to notification requirements.[110]

Familial child sex offences

Factors to take into consideration:

1. The new sentences for public protection *must* be considered in all cases. They are designed to ensure that sexual offenders are not released into the community if they present a significant risk of serious harm.
2. The culpability of the offender will be the primary indicator of offence seriousness, and the nature of the sexual activity will provide a guide as to the seriousness of the harm caused to the victim. Other factors will include:
   - the age and degree of vulnerability of the victim –as a general indication, the younger the child, the more vulnerable he or she is likely to be, although older children may also suffer serious and long-term psychological damage as a result of sexual abuse;
   - the age gap between the child and the offender; and
   - the youth and immaturity of the offender.
3. The starting points for sentencing for the familial child sex offences should be between 25% and 50% higher than those for the generic child sex offences in all cases where the victim is aged 13 or over but under 16; the closer the familial relationship, using the statutory definitions as a guide, the higher the increase that should be applied.
4. Where a victim is over the age of consent, the starting points assume that the offender is a close relative.
5. Where the victim of a familial child sex offence is aged 16 or 17 when the sexual activity is commenced and the sexual relationship is unlawful only because it takes place within a familial setting, the starting points for sentencing should be in line with those for the generic abuse of trust offences.
6. Evidence that a victim has been 'groomed' by the offender to agree to take part in sexual activity will aggravate the seriousness of the offence.

Familial child sex offences

THESE ARE SERIOUS OFFENCES FOR THE PURPOSES OF SECTION 224 CJA 2003

1. **Sexual activity with a child family member** (section 25)
2. **Inciting a child family member to engage in sexual activity** (section 26)

Maximum penalty for both offences: **14 years (5 years if offender is under 18)**

For use in cases where:

(a) the victim is 13 or over but under 16, regardless of the familial relationship with the offender; (b) he victim is 16 or 17 but the sexual relationship commenced when the victim was under 16; or (c) the victim is aged 16 or 17 and the offender is a blood relative.

Type/nature of activity	Starting points	Sentencing ranges
Penile penetration of the vagina, anus or mouth *or* penetration of the vagina or anus with another body part or an object	**5 years custody**	**4–8 years custody**
Contact between naked genitalia of offender and naked genitalia of victim	**4 years custody**	**3–7 years custody**

[110] In accordance with the SOA 2003, s. 80 and schedule 3

Contact between naked genitalia of offender or victim and clothed genitalia of the victim or offender	**18 months custody**	**12 months–2 years 6 months custody**
Contact between naked genitalia of victim by another part of the offender's body or an object, *or* between the naked genitalia of offender and another part of victim's body		
Contact between part of offender's body (other than the genitalia) with part of the victim's body (other than the genitalia)	**Community order**	**An appropriate non-custodial sentence***

* 'Non-custodial sentence' in this context suggests a community order or a fine. In most instances, an offence will have crossed the threshold for a community order. However, in accordance with normal sentencing practice, a court is not precluded from imposing a financial penalty where that is determined to be the appropriate sentence.

For use in cases where the victim was aged 16 or 17 when the sexual relationship commenced and the relationship is only unlawful because of the abuse of trust implicit in the offence.

Type/nature of activity	Starting points	Sentencing ranges
Penile penetration of the vagina, anus or mouth *or* penetration of the vagina or anus with another body part or an object	**2 years custody**	**1–4 years custody**
Any other form of nonpenetrative sexual activity involving the naked contact between the offender and victim	**12 months custody**	**26 weeks–2 years custody**
Contact between clothed part of offender's body (other than the genitalia) with clothed part of victim's body (other than the genitalia)	**Community order**	**An appropriate non-custodial sentence***

* 'Non-custodial sentence' in this context suggests a community order or a fine. In most instances, an offence will have crossed the threshold for a community order. However, in accordance with normal sentencing practice, a court is not precluded from imposing a financial penalty where that is determined to be the appropriate sentence.

Additional aggravating factors	Additional mitigating factors
1. Background of intimidation or coercion 2. Use of drugs, alcohol or other substance 3. Threats deterring the victim from reporting the incident 4. Offender aware that he or she is suffering from a sexually transmitted infection 5. Closeness of familial relationship	1. Small disparity in age between victim and offender

An offender convicted of these offences is automatically subject to notification requirements.[111]

[111] In accordance with the SOA 2003, s. 80 and schedule 3

Abuse of trust: sexual activity with a person under 18

Factors to take into consideration:

1. The sentences for public protection *must* be considered in all cases. They are designed to ensure that sexual offenders are not released into the community if they present a significant risk of serious harm.
2. The culpability of the offender will be the primary indicator of offence seriousness, and the nature of the sexual activity will provide a guide as to the seriousness of the harm caused to the victim. Other factors will include:
   - the age and degree of vulnerability of the victim –as a general indication, the younger the child, the more vulnerable he or she is likely to be, although older children may also suffer serious and long-term psychological damage as a result of sexual abuse;
   - the age gap between the child and the offender; and
   - the youth and immaturity of the offender.
3. These offences will only be charged where the victim is aged 16 or 17. Therefore, the sentencing starting points in the guidelines are only intended for those cases and are significantly lower than those for a child sex offence involving the same type of sexual activity, which should be applied in all other cases.
4. When sentencing for an abuse of trust offence, evidence of serious coercion, threats or trauma are aggravating factors that should move a sentence well beyond the starting point.
5. Some relationships caught within the scope of these offences, although unlawful, will be wholly consensual. The length of time over which a relationship has been sustained and the proximity in age between the parties could point to a relationship born out of genuine affection. Each case must be considered carefully on its own facts.
6. The same starting points apply whether the activity was caused or incited. Where an offence was incited but did not take place as a result of the voluntary intervention of the offender, that is likely to reduce the severity of the sentence imposed.

Abuse of trust: sexual activity with a person under 18

THESE ARE SPECIFIED OFFENCES FOR THE PURPOSES OF SECTION 224 CJA 2003

1. **Abuse of position of trust: sexual activity with a child** (section 16): Intentional sexual touching of a child under 18 by a person aged 18 or over who is in a position of trust in relation to the child
2. **Abuse of position of trust: Causing or inciting a child to engage in sexual activity** (section 17): Intentional causing or inciting of a child under 18 to engage in sexual activity, by a person aged 18 or over who is in a position of trust in relation to the child

Maximum penalty for both offences: 5 years

The starting points shown below are intended to be used only in relation to victims aged 16 or 17. Where the victim is a child under 16, one of the child sex offences in sections 9 to 13 should normally be charged. If one of the abuse of trust offences has nevertheless been charged, the starting points should be the same as they would be for the relevant child sex offence.

Type/nature of activity	Starting points	Sentencing ranges
Penile penetration of the vagina, anus or mouth *or* penetration of the vagina or anus with another body part or an object	**18 months custody**	**12 months–2 years** **6 months custody**
Other forms of non-penetrative activity	**26 weeks custody**	**4 weeks–18 months custody**
Contact between part of offender's body (other than the genitalia) with part of the victim's body (other than the genitalia)	**Community order**	**An appropriate non-custodial sentence***

* 'Non-custodial sentence' in this context suggests a community order or a fine. In most instances, an offence will have crossed the threshold for a community order. However, in accordance with normal sentencing practice, a court is not precluded from imposing a financial penalty where that is determined to be the appropriate sentence.

Additional aggravating factors	Additional mitigating factors
1. Background of intimidation or coercion 2. Offender ejaculated or caused the victim to ejaculate 3. Use of drugs, alcohol or other substance to facilitate the offence 4. Offender aware that he or she is suffering from a sexually transmitted infection	1. Small disparity in age between victim and offender 2. Relationship of genuine affection 3. No element of corruption

An offender convicted of these offences is automatically subject to notification requirements.[112]

Abuse of trust: sexual activity in presence of a person under 18

Factors to take into consideration:

1. The sentences for public protection *must* be considered in all cases. They are designed to ensure that sexual offenders are not released into the community if they present a significant risk of serious harm.
2. The guidelines are predicated on the principle that the more serious the nature of the sexual activity a victim is forced to witness, the higher the sentencing starting point should be.
3. These offences will only be charged where the victim is aged 16 or 17. Therefore, the sentencing starting points in the guidelines are only intended for those cases and are significantly lower than those for a child sex offence involving the same type of sexual activity, which should be applied in all other cases.
4. These offences will potentially be serious enough to merit a custodial sentence. In an individual case, the court will need to consider whether there are particular mitigating factors that should move the sentence below the custodial threshold.

Abuse of trust: sexual activity in presence of a person under 18

THIS IS A SPECIFIED OFFENCE FOR THE PURPOSES OF SECTION 224 CJA 2003

Abuse of trust: sexual activity in the presence of a child (section 18): Intentionally, and for the purpose of obtaining sexual gratification, engaging in sexual activity in the presence of a person under 18 (abuse of trust), knowing or believing that person to be aware of the activity

Maximum penalty: **5 years**

Type/nature of activity	Starting points	Sentencing ranges
Consensual intercourse or other forms of consensual penetration	**2 years custody**	**1–4 years custody**
Masturbation (of oneself or another person)	**18 months custody**	**12 months–2 years 6 months custody**
Consensual sexual touching involving naked genitalia	**12 months custody**	**26 weeks–2 years custody**
Consensual sexual touching of naked body parts but not involving naked genitalia	**26 weeks custody**	**4 weeks–18 months custody**

Additional aggravating factors	Additional mitigating factors
1. Background of intimidation or coercion 2. Use of drugs, alcohol or other substance to facilitate the offence 3. Threats to prevent victim reporting the incident 4. Abduction or detention	

An offender convicted of this offence is automatically subject to notification requirements.[113]

[112] In accordance with the SOA 2003, s. 80 and schedule 3
[113] In accordance with the SOA 2003, s. 80 and schedule 3

Abuse of trust: cause a person under 18 to watch a sexual act

Factors to take into consideration:

1. The sentences for public protection *must* be considered in all cases. They are designed to ensure that sexual offenders are not released into the community if they present a significant risk of serious harm.
2. The culpability of the offender will be the primary indicator of offence seriousness, and the nature of the sexual activity will provide a guide as to the seriousness of the harm caused to the victim. Other factors will include:
   - the age and degree of vulnerability of the victim –as a general indication, the younger the child, the more vulnerable he or she is likely to be, although older children may also suffer serious and long-term psychological damage as a result of sexual abuse;
   - the age gap between the child and the offender; and
   - the youth and immaturity of the offender.
3. Serious coercion, threats, corruption or trauma are aggravating factors that should move a sentence well beyond the starting point.
4. Some relationships caught within the scope of these offences, although unlawful, will be wholly consensual. The length of time over which a relationship has been sustained and the proximity in age between the parties could point to a relationship born out of genuine affection. Each case must be considered carefully on its own facts.
5. These offences will only be charged where the victim is aged 16 or 17.Therefore, the sentencing starting points in the guidelines are only intended for those cases and are significantly lower than those for a child sex offence involving the same type of sexual activity, which should be applied in all other cases.
6. The guideline is predicated on the principle that the more serious the nature of the sexual activity a victim is forced to witness, the higher the sentencing starting point should be.
7. The offence will potentially be serious enough to merit a custodial sentence. In an individual case, the court will need to consider whether there are particular mitigating factors that should move the sentence below the custodial threshold.

Abuse of trust: cause a person under 18 to watch a sexual act

THIS IS A SPECIFIED OFFENCE FOR THE PURPOSES OF SECTION 224 CJA 2003

Abuse of position of trust: causing a child to watch a sexual act (section 19): Intentionally causing or inciting, for the purpose of sexual gratification, a person under 18 (abuse of trust) to watch sexual activity or look at a photograph or pseudo-photograph of sexual activity

Maximum penalty: **5 years**

Type/nature of activity	Starting points	Sentencing ranges
Live sexual activity	**18 months custody**	**12 months–2 years custody**
Moving or still images of people engaged in sexual activity involving penetration	**32 weeks custody**	**26 weeks–12 months custody**
Moving or still images of people engaging in sexual activity other than penetration	**Community order**	**Community order–26 weeks custody**

Additional aggravating factors	Additional mitigating factors
1. Background of intimidation or coercion 2. Use of drugs, alcohol or other substance to facilitate the offence 3. Threats to prevent victim reporting the incident 4. Abduction or detention 5. Images of violent activity	1. Small disparity in age between victim and offender

An offender convicted of this offence is automatically subject to notification requirements.[114]

[114] In accordance with the SOA 2003, s. 80 and schedule 3

Arranging a child sex offence

Factors to take into consideration:

1. The sentences for public protection *must* be considered in all cases. They are designed to ensure that sexual offenders are not released into the community if they present a significant risk of serious harm.
2. Sentencers should refer to the individual guideline for the substantive offence under sections 9–13 of the SOA 2003 that was arranged or facilitated.
3. In cases where there is no commercial exploitation, the range of behaviour within, and the type of offender charged with, this offence will be wide. In some cases, a starting point below the suggested starting point for the substantive child sex offence may be appropriate.

Arranging a child sex offence

THIS IS A SERIOUS OFFENCE FOR THE PURPOSES OF SECTION 224 CJA 2003

Arranging or facilitating commission of a child sex offence (section 14): Intentionally arranging or facilitating the commission of a child sex offence by the defendant or another person, anywhere in the world

Maximum penalty: **14 years**

Type/nature of activity	Starting points and sentencing ranges
Where the activity is arranged or facilitated as part of a commercial enterprise, even if the offender is under 18	As this offence is primarily aimed at persons organising the commission of relevant sexual offences for gain, and sometimes across international borders, this is the most likely aggravating factor. Starting points and sentencing ranges should be increased above those for the relevant substantive offence under sections 9–13.
Basic offence as defined in the SOA 2003 assuming no aggravating or mitigating factors.	The starting point and sentencing range should be commensurate with that for the relevant substantive offence under sections 9–13.

Additional aggravating factors	Additional mitigating factors
1. Background of intimidation or coercion 2. Use of drugs, alcohol or other substance to facilitate the offence 3. Threats to prevent victim reporting the incident 4. Abduction or detention 5. Number of victims involved	

An offender convicted of this offence is automatically subject to notification requirements.[115]

Part 3B: Offences Against Vulnerable Adults

3B.1 The offences in the SOA 2003 that are designed to protect those who have a mental disorder impeding choice are referred to in Part 1.

3B.2 In addition, the Act includes a group of offences designed to protect adults whose mental impairment is not so severe that they are unable to make a choice, but who are nevertheless vulnerable to relatively low levels of inducement, threats or deception.

3B.3 The structure of these offences broadly parallels that of the offences against children, but the maximum penalties for the offences are higher and mirror those for the offences relating to persons with a mental disorder impeding choice. Charges brought under these offences relate to ostensibly consensual activity, but cases will be brought in circumstances where there is clear evidence to suggest that agreement has been secured unlawfully.

3B.4 Although the level of mental impairment of the victim is different between the offences in Part 1 and those in this part, the prosecution is required in all cases to prove that the offender knew of the victim's mental disorder. Thus the victim's capacity to consent will be irrelevant to a finding of guilt, and the level of offender culpability is high.

[115] In accordance with the SOA 2003, s. 80 and schedule 3

3B.5 Where a victim is unable to refuse, the sexual activity may, or may not, have been forced upon the victim. Where a victim has the capacity to consent but is vulnerable to coercion, the activity will be ostensibly consensual, but the level of trauma and harm caused, or risked, to the victim may be very high.

3B.6 The level of protection accorded to the victim should be the same, and sentencing starting points for the two groups of offences should also be comparable.

The starting points for sentencing for a sexual offence should be the same whether the victim has a mental disorder impeding choice, or has a mental disorder and the activity has been procured by inducement, threat or deception.

3B.7 There is a further group of offences designed to protect those with a mental disorder, which consists of four offences relating to sexual activity by care workers. As with the abuse of trust offences protecting children, these offences primarily relate to ostensibly consensual sexual activity with persons over 16 that is only criminal because of the care worker relationship.

3B.8 These offences are primarily designed to be charged where victims have the capacity to choose and where there is no clear evidence of inducement, threat or deception. The maximum penalties, therefore, are lower than those arising from the other two groups of 'mental disorder' offences and it follows that starting points for sentencing should be proportionately lower. The maximum penalties, however, are more significant than those for the range of abuse of trust offences, in recognition of the fact that these offences are designed to protect a particularly vulnerable group of victims, and this has been taken into account in the guideline.

3B.9 The nature of the sexual activity and the degree of vulnerability of the victim will be the main determinants of the seriousness of an offence in these categories. The aggravating factors identified in the Council guideline on seriousness and in Part 1 are relevant to these offences.

3B.10 The period of time during which sexual activity has taken place will be relevant in determining the seriousness of an offender's behaviour but could, depending on the particular circumstances, be considered as either an aggravating or a mitigating factor. The fact that an offender has repeatedly involved a victim in exploitative behaviour over a period of time will normally be an aggravating feature for sentencing purposes. However, in cases involving ostensibly consensual sexual activity with a person over the age of consent who has a low-level mental disorder that does not impair his or her ability to choose, evidence of a long-term relationship between the parties may indicate the existence of genuine feelings of love and affection that deserve to be treated as a mitigating factor for sentencing. As with the abuse of trust offences, each case must be carefully considered on its facts.

Sexual activity with a person who has a mental disorder

Factors to take into consideration:

1. The sentences for public protection *must* be considered in all cases. They are designed to ensure that sexual offenders are not released into the community if they present a significant risk of serious harm. Within any indeterminate sentence, the minimum term will generally be half the appropriate determinate sentence. The starting points will be relevant, therefore, to the process of fixing any minimum term that may be necessary.
2. The starting points for sentencing for a sexual offence should be the same whether the victim has a mental disorder impeding choice, or has a mental disorder that makes him or her vulnerable to inducement, threat or deception.
3. The same starting points apply whether the activity was caused or incited. Where an offence was incited but did not take place as a result of the voluntary intervention of the offender, that is likely to reduce the severity of the sentence imposed.

Sexual activity with a person who has a mental disorder

THESE ARE SERIOUS OFFENCES FOR THE PURPOSES OF SECTION 224 CJA 2003

1. **Sexual activity with a person with a mental disorder impeding choice** (section 30): Intentional sexual touching of a person with a mental disorder
2. **Inducement, threat or deception to procure sexual activity with a person with a mental disorder** (section 34): Intentional sexual touching of someone with a mental disorder whose agreement has been obtained by the giving or offering of an inducement, the making of a threat or the practice of a deception
3. **Causing a person with a mental disorder to engage in, or agree to engage in, sexual activity by inducement, threat or deception** (section 35): Using inducement, threat or deception to secure the

agreement of a person with a mental disorder impeding choice to perform a sexual act on him or herself or another person.

Maximum penalty: Life if activity involves penetration; 14 years if no penetration

Type/nature of activity	Starting points	Sentencing ranges
Penetration with any of the aggravating factors: abduction or detention; offender aware that he or she is suffering from a sexually transmitted infection; more than one offender acting together; offence motivated by prejudice (race, religion, sexual orientation, physical disability); sustained or repeated activity	**13 years custody**	**11–17 years custody**
Single offence of penetration of/by single offender with no aggravating or mitigating factors	**10 years custody**	**8–13 years custody**
Contact between naked genitalia of offender and naked genitalia of victim	**5 years custody**	**4–8 years custody**
Contact between naked genitalia of offender and another part of victim's body *or* naked genitalia of victim by offender using part of his or her body other than the genitalia Contact between clothed genitalia of offender and naked genitalia of victim *or* naked genitalia of offender and clothed genitalia of victim	**15 months custody**	**36 weeks–3 years custody**
Contact between part of offender's body (other than the genitalia) with parts of victim's body (other than the genitalia)	**26 weeks custody**	**4 weeks–18 months custody**

Additional aggravating factors	Additional mitigating factors
1. Background of intimidation or coercion 2. Offender ejaculated or caused the victim to ejaculate 3. Use of drugs, alcohol or other substance to facilitate the offence 4. Threats to prevent the victim reporting the incident 5. Abduction or detention 6. Offender is aware that he or she is suffering from a sexually transmitted infection	1. Relationship of genuine affection 2. Offender had a mental disorder at the time of the offence that significantly affected his or her culpability

An offender convicted of these offences is automatically subject to notification requirements.[116]

Care workers: sexual activity with a person who has a mental disorder

Factors to take into consideration:

1. The sentences for public protection *must* be considered in all cases. They are designed to ensure that sexual offenders are not released into the community if they present a significant risk of serious harm.

[116] In accordance with the SOA 2003, s. 80 and schedule 3

2. The starting points for sentencing are predicated on the fact that these offences are designed to be charged where victims have the capacity to choose and where there is no clear evidence of inducement, threat or deception.

Care workers: sexual activity with a person who has a mental disorder

THESE ARE SERIOUS OFFENCES FOR THE PURPOSES OF SECTION 224 CJA 2003

1. **Care workers: sexual activity with a person with a mental disorder** (section 38): Intentional sexual touching of a person with a mental disorder by someone involved in his or her care
2. **Care workers: causing or inciting sexual activity** (section 39): Someone involved in the care of a person with a mental disorder intentionally causing or inciting that person to engage in sexual activity

Maximum penalty: **14 years** if activity involves penetration; **10 years** if activity does not involve penetration

Type/nature of activity	Starting points	Sentencing ranges
Basic offence of sexual activity involving penetration, assuming no aggravating or mitigating factors	**3 years custody**	**2–5 years custody**
Other forms of nonpenetrative activity	**12 months custody**	**26 weeks–2 years custody**
Naked contact between part of the offender's body with part of the victim's body	**Community order**	**An appropriate non-custodial sentence***

* 'Non-custodial sentence' in this context suggests a community order or a fine. In most instances, an offence will have crossed the threshold for a community order. However, in accordance with normal sentencing practice, a court is not precluded from imposing a financial penalty where that is determined to be the appropriate sentence.

Additional aggravating factors	Additional mitigating factors
1. History of intimidation 2. Use of drugs, alcohol or other substance to facilitate the offence 3. Threats to prevent victim reporting the incident 4. Abduction or detention 5. Offender aware that he or she is suffering from a sexually transmitted infection	1. Relationship of genuine affection

An offender convicted of these offences is automatically subject to notification requirements.[117]

Sexual activity in the presence of a person with a mental disorder

Factors to take into consideration:

1. The sentences for public protection *must* be considered in all cases. They are designed to ensure that sexual offenders are not released into the community if they present a significant risk of serious harm.
2. The starting points for sentencing for a sexual offence should be the same whether the victim has a mental disorder impeding choice, or has a mental disorder that makes him or her vulnerable to inducement, threat or deception.
3. The guidelines are predicated on the principle that the more serious the nature of the sexual activity a victim is forced to witness, the higher the sentencing starting point should be.
4. These offences will potentially be serious enough to merit a custodial sentence. In an individual case, the court will need to consider whether there are particular mitigating factors that should move the sentence below the custodial threshold.

[117] In accordance with the SOA 2003, s. 80 and schedule 3

Sexual activity in the presence of a person with a mental disorder

OFFENCES UNDER SECTION 36 ARE SERIOUS OFFENCES FOR THE PURPOSES OF SECTION 224 CJA 2003

OFFENCES UNDER SECTION 40 ARE SPECIFIED OFFENCES FOR THE PURPOSES OF SECTION 224 CJA 2003

1. **Engaging in sexual activity in the presence, secured by inducement, threat or deception, of a person with a mental disorder** (section 36): Intentionally, and for the purpose of obtaining sexual gratification, engaging in sexual activity in the presence of a person with a mental disorder, knowing or believing that person to be aware of the activity

Maximum penalty: 10 years

2. **Care workers: sexual activity in the presence of a person with a mental disorder** (section 40): Care worker intentionally, and for the purpose of obtaining sexual gratification, engaging in sexual activity in the presence of a person with a mental disorder, knowing or believing that person to be aware of the activity

Maximum penalty: 7 years

Type/nature of activity	Starting points	Sentencing ranges
Consensual intercourse or other forms of consensual penetration	2 years custody	1–4 years custody
Masturbation (of oneself or another person)	18 months custody	12 months–2 years 6 months custody
Consensual sexual touching involving naked genitalia	12 months custody	26 weeks–2 years custody
Consensual sexual touching of naked body parts but not involving naked genitalia	26 weeks custody	4 weeks–18 months custody

Additional aggravating factors	Additional mitigating factors
1. Background of intimidation or coercion 2. Use of drugs, alcohol or other substance to facilitate the offence 3. Threats to prevent victim reporting the incident 4. Abduction or detention	

An offender convicted of these offences is automatically subject to notification requirements.[118]

Causing or inciting a person with a mental disorder to watch a sexual act

Factors to take into consideration:

1. The sentences for public protection *must* be considered in all cases. They are designed to ensure that sexual offenders are not released into the community if they present a significant risk of serious harm.
2. The starting points for sentencing for a sexual offence should be the same whether the victim has a mental disorder impeding choice, or has a mental disorder that makes him or her vulnerable to inducement, threat or deception.
3. The guidelines are predicated on the principle that the more serious the nature of the sexual activity a victim is forced to witness, the higher the sentencing starting point should be.
4. These offences will potentially be serious enough to merit a custodial sentence. In an individual case, the court will need to consider whether there are particular mitigating factors that move the sentence below the custodial threshold.
5. The same starting points apply whether the activity was caused or incited. Where an offence was incited but did not take place as a result of the voluntary intervention of the offender, that is likely to reduce the severity of the sentence imposed.

[118] In accordance with the SOA 2003, s. 80 and schedule 3

Causing or inciting a person with a mental disorder to watch a sexual act

OFFENCES UNDER SECTION 37 ARE SERIOUS OFFENCES FOR THE PURPOSES OF SECTION 224 CJA 2003

OFFENCES UNDER SECTION 41 ARE SPECIFIED OFFENCES FOR THE PURPOSES OF SECTION 224 CJA 2003

1. **Causing a person with a mental disorder to watch a sexual act by inducement, threat or deception** (section 37): Intentionally causing by inducement, threat or deception, for the purpose of sexual gratification, a person with a mental disorder to watch sexual activity or look at a photograph or pseudo-photograph of sexual activity

Maximum penalty: **10 years**

2. **Care workers: causing a person with a mental disorder to watch a sexual act** (section 41): Intentionally causing, for the purpose of sexual gratification, a person with a mental disorder to watch sexual activity or look at a photograph or pseudo-photograph of sexual activity

Maximum penalty: **7 years**

Type/nature of activity	Starting points	Sentencing ranges
Live sexual activity	18 months custody	**12 months–2 years custody**
Moving or still images of people engaged in sexual activity involving penetration	**32 weeks custody**	**26 weeks–12 months custody**
Moving or still images of people engaging in sexual activity other than penetration	**Community order**	**Community order–26 weeks**

Additional aggravating factors	Additional mitigating factors
1. Background of intimidation or coercion 2. Use of drugs, alcohol or other substance to facilitate the offence 3. Threats to prevent victim reporting the incident 4. Abduction or detention 5. Images of violent activity	

An offender convicted of this offence is automatically subject to notification requirements.[119]

Part 4: Preparatory Offences

4.1 The characteristic feature of this group of offences is that the offender intended to commit a sexual offence that was not, in fact, carried out, either because the act was interrupted or because of a change of mind.

4.2 In some circumstances, an offender may be charged with both the preparatory and the substantive offence.

4.3 The new offence of 'meeting a child following sexual grooming etc' has been included within this category.

The following offences are covered in this section:

- Sexual grooming
- Committing another offence with intent
- Trespass with intent
- Administering a substance with intent

Sexual grooming

Factors to take into consideration:

1. The sentences for public protection *must* be considered in all cases. They are designed to ensure that sexual offenders are not released into the community if they present a significant risk of serious harm.

[119] In accordance with the SOA 2003, s. 80 and schedule 3

2. In a case where no substantive sexual offence has in fact been committed, the main dimension of seriousness will be the offender's *intention* –the more serious the offence intended, the higher the offender's culpability.
3. The *harm* to the victim in such cases will invariably be less than that resulting from a completed offence, although the *risk* to which the victim has been put is always a relevant factor.
4. In some cases, where the offender has come quite close to fulfilling his or her intention, the victim may have been put in considerable fear, and physical injury to the victim is a possible feature.
5. In addition to the generic aggravating factors identified in the Council guideline on seriousness, the main factors determining the seriousness of a preparatory offence are:
   - the seriousness of the intended offence (which will affect both the offender's culpability and the degree of risk to which the victim has been exposed);
   - the degree to which the offence was planned;
   - the sophistication of the grooming;
   - the determination of the offender;
   - how close the offender came to success;
   - the reason why the offender did not succeed, i. e. whether it was a change of mind or whether someone or something prevented the offender from continuing; and
   - any physical or psychological injury suffered by the victim.
6. The starting point should be commensurate with that for the preparatory offence actually committed, with an enhancement to reflect the nature and severity of the intended sexual offence.

Sexual grooming

THIS IS A SERIOUS OFFENCE FOR THE PURPOSES OF SECTION 224 CJA 2003

Meeting a child following sexual grooming etc (section 15): An offender aged 18 or over meeting, or travelling to meet, a child under 16 (having met or communicated with the child on at least two previous occasions) with the intention of committing a sexual offence against the child

Maximum penalty: **10 years**

Type/nature of activity	Starting points	Sentencing ranges
Where the intent is to commit an assault by penetration or rape	**4 years custody** if the victim is under 13 **2 years custody** if the victim is 13 or over but under 16	**3–7 years custody** **1–4 years custody**
Where the intent is to coerce the child into sexual activity	**2 years custody** if the victim is under 13 **18 months custody** if the victim is 13 or over but under 16	**1–4 years custody** **12 months–1 years** **6 months custody**

Additional aggravating factors	Additional mitigating factors
1. Background of intimidation or coercion 2. Use of drugs, alcohol or other substance to facilitate the offence 3. Offender aware that he or she is suffering from a sexually transmitted infection 4. Abduction or detention	

An offender convicted of this offence is automatically subject to notification requirements.[120]

Committing another offence with intent

Factors to take into consideration:

This guideline assumes that the intended sexual offence was not committed.

1. The sentences for public protection *must* be considered in all cases. They are designed to ensure that sexual offenders are not released into the community if they present a significant risk of serious harm. Within any indeterminate sentence, the minimum term will generally be half the appropriate

[120] In accordance with the SOA 2003, s. 80 and schedule 3

determinate sentence. The starting points will be relevant, therefore, to the process of fixing any minimum term that may be necessary.
2. In a case where no substantive sexual offence has in fact been committed, the main dimension of seriousness will be the offender's *intention* –the more serious the offence intended, the higher the offender's culpability.
3. The *harm* to the victim in such cases will invariably be less than that resulting from a completed offence, although the *risk* to which the victim has been put is always a relevant factor.
4. In some cases, where the offender has come quite close to fulfilling his or her intention, the victim may have been put in considerable fear, and physical injury to the victim is a possible feature.
5. In addition to the generic aggravating factors identified in the Council guideline on seriousness, the main factors determining the seriousness of a preparatory offence are:
   - the seriousness of the intended offence (which will affect both the offender's culpability and the degree of risk to which the victim has been exposed);
   - the degree to which the offence was planned;
   - the determination of the offender;
   - how close the offender came to success;
   - the reason why the offender did not succeed, i. e. whether it was a change of mind or whether someone or something prevented the offender from continuing; and
   - any physical or psychological injury suffered by the victim.
6. The starting point should be commensurate with that for the preparatory offence actually committed, with an enhancement to reflect the nature and severity of the intended sexual offence.

Committing another offence with intent

THIS IS A SERIOUS OFFENCE FOR THE PURPOSES OF SECTION 224 CJA 2003

Committing an offence with intent to commit a sexual offence (section 62)

Maximum penalty: **Life imprisonment** if offence is kidnapping or false imprisonment; **10 years** for any other criminal offence

Type/nature of activity	Starting points and Sentencing ranges
Any offence committed with intent to commit a sexual offence, e.g. assault (see item 4 of 'Factors to take into consideration' above)	The starting point and sentencing range should be commensurate with that for the preliminary offence actually committed, but with an enhancement to reflect the intention to commit a sexual offence. The enhancement will need to be varied depending on the nature and seriousness of the intended sexual offence, but **2 years** is suggested as a suitable enhancement where the intent was to commit rape or an assault by penetration.

Additional aggravating factors	Additional mitigating factors
1. Use of drugs, alcohol or other substance to facilitate the offence 2. Offender aware that he or she is suffering from a sexually transmitted infection (where the intended offence would have involved penile penetration)	1. Offender decides, of his or her own volition, not to proceed with the intended sexual offence 2. Incident of brief duration

An offender convicted of this offence is automatically subject to notification requirements.[121]

Trespass with intent

Factors to take into consideration:
1. The sentences for public protection *must* be considered in all cases. They are designed to ensure that sexual offenders are not released into the community if they present a significant risk of serious harm.
2. In a case where no substantive sexual offence has in fact been committed, the main dimension of seriousness will be the offender's *intention* –the more serious the offence intended, the higher the offender's culpability.

[121] In accordance with the SOA 2003, s. 80 and schedule 3

3. The *harm* to the victim in such cases will invariably be less than that resulting from a completed offence, although the *risk* to which the victim has been put is always a relevant factor.
4. In some cases, where the offender has come quite close to fulfilling his or her intention, the victim may have been put in considerable fear, and physical injury to the victim is a possible feature.
5. In addition to the generic aggravating factors identified in the Council guideline on seriousness, the main factors determining the seriousness of a preparatory offence are:
   - the seriousness of the intended offence (which will affect both the offender's culpability and the degree of risk to which the victim has been exposed);
   - the degree to which the offence was planned;
   - the determination of the offender;
   - how close the offender came to success;
   - the reason why the offender did not succeed, i. e. whether it was a change of mind or whether someone or something prevented the offender from continuing; and
   - any physical or psychological injury suffered by the victim.
6. The starting point should be commensurate with that for the preparatory offence actually committed, with an enhancement to reflect the nature and severity of the intended sexual offence.

Trespass with intent

THIS IS A SERIOUS OFFENCE FOR THE PURPOSES OF SECTION 224 CJA 2003

Trespass with intent to commit a sexual offence (section 63): Knowingly or recklessly trespassing on any premises with intent to commit a sexual offence on those premises

Maximum penalty: **10 years**

Type/nature of activity	Starting points	Sentencing ranges
The intention is to commit rape or an assault by penetration	**4 years custody**	**3–7 years custody**
The intended sexual offence is other than rape or assault by penetration	**2 years custody**	**1–4 years custody**

Additional aggravating factors	Additional mitigating factors
1. Offender aware that he or she is suffering from a sexually transmited infection (where intended offence would have involved penile penetration) 2. Targeting of a vulnerable victim 3. Significant impact on persons present in the premises	1. Offender decides, of his or her own volition, not to commit the intended sexual offence

An offender convicted of this offence is automatically subject to notification requirements.[122]

Administering a substance with intent

Factors to take into consideration:

1. The sentences for public protection *must* be considered in all cases. They are designed to ensure that sexual offenders are not released into the community if they present a significant risk of serious harm.
2. In a case where no substantive sexual offence has in fact been committed, the main dimension of seriousness will be the offender's *intention* –the more serious the offence intended, the higher the offender's culpability. This is equally so where the offence is committed by an offender for the benefit of another.
3. The *harm* to the victim in such cases will invariably be less than that resulting from a completed offence, although the *risk* to which the victim has been put is always a relevant factor.
4. In some cases, where the offender has come quite close to fulfilling his or her intention, the victim may have been put in considerable fear, and physical injury to the victim is a possible feature, in particular for this offence.

[122] In accordance with the SOA 2003, s. 80 and schedule 3

5. In addition to the generic aggravating factors identified in the Council guideline on seriousness, the main factors determining the seriousness of a preparatory offence are:
   - the seriousness of the intended offence (which will affect both the offender's culpability and the degree of risk to which the victim has been exposed);
   - the degree to which the offence was planned;
   - the determination of the offender;
   - how close the offender came to success;
   - the reason why the offender did not succeed, i. e. whether it was a change of mind or whether someone or something prevented the offender from continuing; and
   - any physical or psychological injury suffered by the victim.
6. The starting point should be commensurate with that for the preparatory offence actually committed, with an enhancement to reflect the nature and severity of the intended sexual offence.

Administering a substance with intent

THIS IS A SERIOUS OFFENCE FOR THE PURPOSES OF SECTION 224 CJA 2003

Administering a substance with intent (section 61): Administering a substance, without the consent of the victim, with the intention of overpowering or stupefying the victim in order to enable any person to engage in sexual activity involving the victim

Maximum penalty: **10 years**

Type/nature of activity	**Starting points**	**Sentencing ranges**
If intended offence is rape or assault by penetration	**8 years custody** if the victim is under 13 **6 years custody** otherwise	**6–9 years custody** **4–9 years custody**
If intended offence is any sexual offence other than rape or assault by penetration **6 years custody** if the victim is under 13	**6 years custody** if the victim is under 13 **4 years custody** otherwise	**4–9 years custody** **3–7 years custody**

Additional aggravating factors	**Additional mitigating factors**
1. Threats to prevent the victim reporting an offence 2. Abduction or detention 3. Offender aware that he or she, or the person planning to commit the sexual offence, is suffering from a sexually transmitted infection 4. Targeting of the victim	1. Offender intervenes to prevent the intended sexual offence from taking place

An offender convicted of this offence is automatically subject to notification requirements.[123]

Part 5: Other Offences

5.1 This category covers a small number of relatively minor offences, none of which involves direct sexual contact with a person who was not consenting:
   - Prohibited adult sexual relationships: sex with an adult relative
   - Sexual activity in a public lavatory
   - Exposure
   - Voyeurism
   - Intercourse with an animal
   - Sexual penetration of a corpse

[123] In accordance with the SOA 2003, s. 80 and schedule 3

Prohibited adult sexual relationships: sex with an adult relative

Factors to take into consideration:

1. The sentences for public protection *must* be considered in all cases. They are designed to ensure that sexual offenders are not released into the community if they present a significant risk of serious harm.
2. The two offences within this category are triable either way and carry a maximum penalty of 2 years' imprisonment on conviction on indictment. The relatively low maximum penalty for these offences reflects the fact that they involve sexual relationships between consenting adults.
3. For these offences, unlike those against child family members, the relationship between offender and victim is narrowly defined in terms of close blood relationships only: 'a parent, grandparent, child, grandchild, brother, sister, half-brother, half-sister, uncle, aunt, nephew or niece'.
4. It is a defence to both offences that the offender was unaware of the blood relationship, unless it is proved that he or she could reasonably have been expected to be aware of it.
5. These offences could be charged in a wide range of circumstances and the most important issue for the sentencer to consider is the particular circumstances in which an offence has taken place and the harm that has been caused or risked:
    - Where an offence involves no harm to a victim (other than the offensiveness of the conduct to society at large), the starting point for sentencing should normally be a community order.
    - Where there is evidence of the exploitation of a victim or significant aggravation, the normal starting point should be a custodial sentence.
    - The presence of certain aggravating factors should merit a higher custodial starting point.
6. Examples of aggravating factors especially relevant to these offences include:
    - high level of coercion or humiliation of the victim;
    - imbalance of power;
    - evidence of grooming;
    - age gap between the parties;
    - history of sexual offending;
    - sexual intercourse with the express intention of conceiving a child or resulting in the conception of a child; and
    - no attempt taken to prevent the transmission of a sexual infection.

Prohibited adult sexual relationships: sex with an adult relative

THESE ARE SPECIFIED OFFENCES FOR THE PURPOSES OF SECTION 224 CJA 2003

1. **Sex with an adult relative: penetration** (section 64): Intentional penetration of the vagina or anus of an adult blood relative with a body part or object; or penetration of the vagina, anus or mouth with the penis
2. **Sex with an adult relative: consenting to penetration** (section 65): Consenting to intentional penetration of the vagina or anus by an adult blood relative with a body part or object; or penetration of the vagina, anus or mouth with the penis

Maximum penalty for both offences: 2 years

Type/nature of activity	Starting points	Sentencing ranges
Where there is evidence of long-term grooming that took place at a time when the person being groomed was under 18	**12 months custody** if offender is 18 or over	**26 weeks–2 years custody**
Where there is evidence of grooming of one party by the other at a time when both parties were over the age of 18	**Community order**	**An appropriate non-custodial sentence***
Sexual penetration with no aggravating factors	**Community order**	**An appropriate non-custodial sentence***

* 'Non-custodial sentence' in this context suggests a community order or a fine. In most instances, an offence will have crossed the threshold for a community order. However, in accordance with normal sentencing practice, a court is not precluded from imposing a financial penalty where that is determined to be the appropriate sentence.

Additional aggravating factors	Additional mitigating factors
1. Background of intimidation or coercion 2. Use of drugs, alcohol or other substance to facilitate the offence 3. Threats to prevent the victim reporting an offence 4. Evidence of long-term grooming 5. Offender aware that he or she is suffering from a sexually transmitted infection 6. Where there is evidence that no effort was made to avoid pregnancy or the sexual transmission of infection	1. Small disparity in age between victim and offender 2. Relationship of genuine affection

An offender convicted of these offences is automatically subject to notification requirements.[124]

Sexual activity in a public lavatory

Factors to take into consideration:

1. This offence has been introduced to give adults and children the freedom to use public lavatories for the purpose for which they are designed, without the fear of being an unwilling witness to overtly sexual behaviour of a kind that most people would not expect to be conducted in public.
2. This offence, being a public order offence rather than a sexual offence, carries the lowest maximum penalty in the SOA 2003–6 months' imprisonment – and the starting point for sentencing reflects this.
3. More detailed guidance is provided in the Magistrates' Court Sentencing Guidelines (MCSG).

Sexual activity in a public lavatory

Sexual activity in a public lavatory (section 71): Intentionally engaging in sexual activity in a public lavatory

Maximum penalty: **6 months**

Type/nature of activity	Starting points	Sentencing ranges
Repeat offending and/or aggravating factors	**Community order**	**An appropriate non-custodial sentence***
Basic offence as defined in the SOA 2003, assuming no aggravating or mitigating factors	**Fine**	**An appropriate non-custodial sentence***

* 'Non-custodial sentence' in this context suggests a community order or a fine. In most instances, an offence will have crossed the threshold for a community order. However, in accordance with normal sentencing practice, a court is not precluded from imposing a financial penalty where that is determined to be the appropriate sentence.

Additional aggravating factors	Additional mitigating factors
1. Intimidating behaviour/threats of violence to member(s) of the public	

Exposure

Factors to take into consideration:

1. The sentences for public protection *must* be considered in all cases. They are designed to ensure that sexual offenders are not released into the community if they present a significant risk of serious harm.
2. The offence replaces section 4 of the Vagrancy Act 1824 and section 28 of the Town Police Clauses Act 1847. It is gender neutral (covering exposure of male or female genitalia to a male or female witness) and carries a maximum penalty of 2 years' imprisonment.
3. These offences are sometimes more serious than they may, at first, appear. Although there is no

[124] In accordance with the SOA 2003, s. 80 and schedule 3

physical contact with the victim, the offence may cause serious alarm or distress, especially when the offender behaves aggressively or uses obscenities.
4. A pre-sentence report,[125] which can identify sexually deviant tendencies, will be extremely helpful in determining the most appropriate disposal. It will also help determine whether an offender would benefit from participation in a programme designed to help them address those tendencies.
5. A person convicted of this offence is subject to notification requirements.[126]
6. Where this offence is being dealt with in a magistrates' court, more detailed guidance is provided in the Magistrates' Court Sentencing Guidelines (MCSG).

Exposure

THIS IS A SPECIFIED OFFENCE FOR THE PURPOSES OF SECTION 224 CJA 2003

Exposure (section 66): Intentional exposure of the offender's genitals, intending that someone will see them and be caused alarm or distress

Maximum penalty: 2 years

Type/nature of activity	Starting points	Sentencing ranges
Repeat offender	**12 weeks custody**	**4 weeks– 26 weeks custody**
Basic offence as defined in the SOA 2003, assuming no aggravating or mitigating factors, or some offences with aggravating factors	**Community order**	**An appropriate non-custodial sentence***

* 'Non-custodial sentence' in this context suggests a community order or a fine. In most instances, an offence will have crossed the threshold for a community order. However, in accordance with normal sentencing practice, a court is not precluded from imposing a financial penalty where that is determined to be the appropriate sentence.

Additional aggravating factors	Additional mitigating factors
1. Threats to prevent the victim reporting an offence 2. Intimidating behaviour/threats of violence 3. Victim is a child	

An offender convicted of this offence is automatically subject to notification requirements.[127]

Voyeurism

Factors to take into consideration:
1. The sentences for public protection *must* be considered in all cases. They are designed to ensure that sexual offenders are not released into the community if they present a significant risk of serious harm.
2. The offence of voyeurism covers cases where someone who has a reasonable expectation of privacy is secretly observed. The offence may be committed in a number of ways:
   - by direct observation on the part of the offender;
   - by operating equipment with the intention of enabling someone else to observe the victim;
   - by recording someone doing a private act, with the intention that the recorded image will be viewed by the offender or another person; or
   - by installing equipment or constructing or adapting a structure with the intention of enabling the offender or another person to observe a private act.
3. In all cases the observation, or intended observation, must be for the purpose of obtaining sexual gratification and must take place, or be intended to take place, without the consent of the person observed.
4. The SOA 2003 defines a 'private act', in the context of this offence, as an act carried out in a place which, in the circumstances, would reasonably be expected to provide privacy, and where the victim's genitals, buttocks or breasts are exposed or covered only in underwear; *or* the victim is using a lavatory; *or* the person is 'doing a sexual act that is not of a kind ordinarily done in public'.

[125] 2 As defined in the Criminal Justice Act 2003, s. 158
[126] In accordance with the Sexual Offences Act 2003, s. 80 and schedule 3
[127] In accordance with the SOA 2003, s. 80 and schedule 3

5. The harm inherent in this offence is intrusion of the victim's privacy. Whilst less serious than non-consensual touching, it may nevertheless cause severe distress, embarrassment or humiliation to the victim, especially in cases where a private act is not simply observed by one person, but where an image of it is disseminated for wider viewing. A higher sentencing starting point is recommended for cases where the offender records and shares images with others.
6. For offences involving the lowest level of offending behaviour, i. e. spying on someone for private pleasure, a non-custodial sentence is recommended as the starting point.
7. A pre-sentence report,[128] which can identify sexually deviant tendencies, will be extremely helpful in determining the most appropriate disposal. It will also help determine whether an offender would benefit from participation in a programme designed to help them address those tendencies.
8. Where this offence is being dealt with in a magistrates' court, more detailed guidance is provided in the Magistrates' Court Sentencing Guidelines (MCSG).

Voyeurism

THIS IS A SPECIFIED OFFENCE FOR THE PURPOSES OF SECTION 224 CJA 2003

Voyeurism (section 67): For the purpose of obtaining sexual gratification, and knowing that the other person does not consent to being observed, observing another person engaged in a private act

Maximum penalty: 2 years

Type/nature of activity	Starting points	Sentencing ranges
Offence with serious aggravating factors such as recording sexual activity and placing it on a website or circulating it for commercial gain	**12 months custody**	**26 weeks–2 years custody**
Offence with aggravating factors such as recording sexual activity and showing it to others	**26 weeks custody**	**4 weeks–18 months custody**
Basic offence as defined in the SOA 2003, assuming no aggravating or mitigating factors, e.g. the offender spies through a hole he or she has made in a changing room wall	**Community order**	**An appropriate non-custodial sentence***

* 'Non-custodial sentence' in this context suggests a community order or a fine. In most instances, an offence will have crossed the threshold for a community order. However, in accordance with normal sentencing practice, a court is not precluded from imposing a financial penalty where that is determined to be the appropriate sentence.

Additional aggravating factors	Additional mitigating factors
1. Threats to prevent the victim reporting an offence 2. Recording activity and circulating pictures/videos 3. Circulating pictures or videos for commercial gain – particularly if victim is vulnerable, e.g. a child or person with a mental or physical disorder 4. Distress to victim, e.g. where the pictures/videos are circulated to people known to the victim	

An offender convicted of this offence is automatically subject to notification requirements.[129]

Intercourse with an animal

Factors to take into consideration:

1. The sentences for public protection *must* be considered in all cases. They are designed to ensure that sexual offenders are not released into the community if they present a significant risk of serious harm.

[128] As defined in the Criminal Justice Act 2003, s. 158

[129] In accordance with the SOA 2003, s. 80 and schedule 3

2. This replaces the previous offence of 'buggery' with an animal, for which the maximum penalty was life imprisonment. The maximum penalty of 2 years' imprisonment attached to this offence is sufficient to recognise an offender's predisposition towards unnatural sexual activity.
3. A custodial sentence for an adult for this offence will result in an obligation to comply with notification requirements and this seems to be the most appropriate course of action for a repeat offender. The offence can be charged in addition to existing offences relating to cruelty to animals.
4. A pre-sentence report,[130] which can identify sexually deviant tendencies, will be extremely helpful in determining the most appropriate disposal. It will also help determine whether an offender would benefit from participation in a programme designed to help them address those tendencies.

Intercourse with an animal

THIS IS A SPECIFIED OFFENCE FOR THE PURPOSES OF SECTION 224 CJA 2003

Intercourse with an animal (section 69): Intentionally penetrating a live animal's anus or vagina with the offender's penis; or intentionally causing or allowing a person's anus or vagina to be penetrated by the penis of a live animal

Maximum penalty: 2 years

Type/nature of activity	Starting points	Sentencing ranges
Basic offence as defined in the SOA 2003, assuming no aggravating or mitigating factors	**Community order**	**An appropriate non-custodial sentence***

* 'Non-custodial sentence' in this context suggests a community order or a fine. In most instances, an offence will have crossed the threshold for a community order. However, in accordance with normal sentencing practice, a court is not precluded from imposing a financial penalty where that is determined to be the appropriate sentence.

Additional aggravating factors	Additional mitigating factors
1. Recording activity and/or circulating pictures or videos	1. Symptom of isolation rather than depravity

An offender convicted of this offence is automatically subject to notification requirements.[131]

Sexual penetration of a corpse

Factors to take into consideration:

1. The sentences for public protection *must* be considered in all cases. They are designed to ensure that sexual offenders are not released into the community if they present a significant risk of serious harm.
2. Necrophilia is associated with 'other very deviant behaviour', and killers who use the bodies of their victims for sexual gratification cannot, under the existing law, be formally recognised as, or treated as, sexual offenders.
3. A pre-sentence report[132] (and in some cases a psychiatric report), which can identify sexually deviant tendencies, will be extremely helpful in determining the most appropriate disposal. It will also help determine whether an offender would benefit from participation in a programme designed to help them address those tendencies.

Sexual penetration of a corpse

THIS IS A SPECIFIED OFFENCE FOR THE PURPOSES OF SECTION 224 CJA 2003

Sexual penetration of a corpse (section 70): Intentional sexual penetration of part of the body of a dead person with a part of the offender's body or an object

[130] As defined in the Criminal Justice Act 2003, s. 158
[131] In accordance with the SOA 2003, s. 80 and schedule 3
[132] As defined in the Criminal Justice Act 2003, s. 158

Maximum penalty: 2 years

Type/nature of activity	Starting points	Sentencing ranges
Repeat offending and/or aggravating factors	**26 weeks custody**	**4 weeks–18 months custody**
Basic offence as defined in the SOA 2003, assuming no aggravating or mitigating factors	**Community order**	**An appropriate non-custodial sentence***

* 'Non-custodial sentence' in this context suggests a community order or a fine. In most instances, an offence will have crossed the threshold for a community order. However, in accordance with normal sentencing practice, a court is not precluded from imposing a financial penalty where that is determined to be the appropriate sentence.

Additional aggravating factors	Additional mitigating factors
1. Distress caused to relatives or friends of the deceased 2. Physical damage caused to body of the deceased 3. The corpse was that of a child 4. The offence was committed in a funeral home or mortuary	

An offender convicted of this offence is automatically subject to notification requirements.[133]

Part 6: Exploitation Offences

6.1 Whilst all sexual offences involve, to a greater or lesser degree, the exploitation or abuse of a victim or victims, the specific sexual exploitation offences involve a high degree of offender culpability, with offenders intentionally exploiting vulnerable individuals. In some cases, for example the prostitution offences, the sexual acts themselves may not be unlawful, but the purpose of the legislation is to address the behaviour of those who are prepared to exploit others by causing, inciting or controlling their sexual activities, whether or not for gain.

The harm caused by the offences

6.2 Section 54 of the SOA 2003 defines 'gain' as:

(a) *any financial advantage, including the discharge of an obligation to pay or the provision of goods or services (including sexual services) gratuitously or at a discount; or*

(b) the goodwill of any person which is, or appears likely, in time, to bring financial advantage.

6.3 The sexual exploitation offences cover a range of offending behaviour that is broken down into four groups in the SOA 2003:

(i) indecent photographs of children;
(ii) abuse of children through prostitution and pornography;
(iii) exploitation of prostitution; and
(iv) trafficking.

6.4 Groups (i) and (ii) specifically relate to the exploitation and abuse of children; for the purposes of these offences, 'child' means anyone under the age of 18.

6.5 The 'exploitation of prostitution' offences relate to adult victims. The offences in group (iii) include the specific element that the activity was carried out 'for gain'. However, whether or not it is implicit in the offence that the prosecution is seeking to prove, in most cases someone will secure an advantage from the exploitation.

6.6 The 'trafficking' offences are designed to protect victims of all ages.

6.7 The term 'prostitution', which is used in most of the offences in these groups, is defined as 'providing sexual services for payment or promise of payment' and 'payment' is defined as being 'any financial advantage'.

6.8 The offences that do not require the prosecution to prove that the offender acted 'for gain' have the effect that offenders cannot avoid prosecution by claiming that they did not stand to benefit by their involvement. For these offences, the starting points for sentencing are based solely on the

[133] In accordance with the SOA 2003, s. 80 and schedule 3

criminality of taking part in sexual exploitation without taking into account any benefits, financial or otherwise, that the defendant may receive.

Where a sexual exploitation offence does not require the prosecution to prove that the offender acted for gain, the degree of personal involvement of the offender and the levels of personal or financial gain should be treated as aggravating factors for sentencing.

6.9 Confiscation and compensation orders have particular relevance in the context of exploitation offences, where it is extremely likely both that there will be property that can be seized from the offender and also that exploited victims will have been caused a degree of harm that might merit compensation.

6.10 The 'for gain' element is inherent in the 'exploitation of prostitution' offences; therefore, it cannot be treated as an aggravating factor and is reflected in the starting points for sentencing. This group of offences relates to offenders who control the activities of those over the age of consent, and the maximum penalties are lower than for offences where the prosecution is not required to prove that the defendant acted 'for gain'. However, the commercial sexual exploitation of another person's vulnerability is serious and socially unacceptable offending behaviour, and the starting point for these offences should still be significant.

Where a sexual exploitation offence requires the prosecution to prove that the offender acted for personal gain and this is already reflected in the starting point for sentencing, evidence of substantial financial or other advantage to a value in the region of £5000 and upwards (in line with the provisions of section 75(4) of the Proceeds of Crime Act 2002) should be treated as an aggravating factor.

6.11 Although the courts must bear in mind the actual 'recoverable amount'[134] when making a confiscation order, they can legitimately take into account, as an aggravating factor for sentencing purposes, not only the benefits secured by the offender in fact, but also the benefits that he or she would have accrued from the offence had the activity not been intercepted or disrupted. Courts should also take into account non-monetary profits such as payment in kind, gifts or favours, which will need to be carefully assessed in each individual case.[135]

The offender's culpability

6.12 In the Council's guideline on seriousness, it is stated that, in broad terms, an intention to cause harm is at the highest level of criminal culpability – the worse the harm intended, the higher the offender's culpability – and planning an offence makes the offender more highly culpable than impulsive offending.

6.13 The common thread of the exploitation offences is the planned abuse of vulnerable victims, with the main purpose of the offender being to secure some form of personal advantage, whether this is financial gain or reward, sexual services or personal sexual gratification (as in the offence of 'paying for sexual services of a child').

6.14 As the combination of culpability with harm determines the seriousness of an offence, it follows that the offences covered in this section are at the higher end of the scale of seriousness, and robust sentencing provisions are needed.

Evidence of an offender's involvement in, or management of, a well-planned or large-scale commercial operation resulting in sexual exploitation should be treated as an aggravating factor for sentencing: the greater the offender's degree of involvement, the more serious the offence.

The age of the victim

- **In general, the younger the age of the child, the higher the sentence should be for an offence involving the sexual exploitation of a child.**
- **In particular, the starting points for sentencing should be higher where the victim is under 13. The starting points for offences involving victims aged 16 or 17 should be lower than those for victims aged 13 or over but under 16, to recognise that they are over the legal age of consent, but any evidence of grooming, coercion, threats or intimidation should increase a sentence in line with that which would apply if the victim were aged 13 or over but under 16.**

[134] Proceeds of Crime Act 2002, s. 9
[135] ibid. ss. 79–81

The risk of re-offending

6.15 The sexual exploitation offences are of a level of seriousness that suggests a custodial sentence will normally be appropriate, but the way in which the risk of re-offending should be addressed will depend on the nature of, and the motivation for, the offences committed.

6.16 A person found guilty of, for example, 'paying for sexual services of a child' or, in some cases, 'causing or inciting child prostitution or pornography' may very well benefit from taking part in a sex offender treatment programme, which will help the offender to recognise and control sexually deviant tendencies. There is a need to ensure that offenders are assessed for their suitability to take part in such programmes and that periods spent on licence in the community are of a sufficient length to enable such programmes to take place.

6.17 However, different issues arise where the courts are sentencing someone whose behaviour has nothing to do with personal sexual deviance but instead involves the exploitation of the sexual appetites or deviancies of others, whether or not for gain. In such cases, sex offender treatment programmes are unlikely to be appropriate. The use of fines or community orders containing requirements such as a curfew, residence, unpaid work and prohibited activity may be effective in discouraging future offending.

Part 6A: Indecent Photographs of Children

6A.1 The SOA 2003 makes amendments to the Protection of Children Act 1978 and the Criminal Justice Act 1988. It is now a crime to take, make, permit to take, distribute, show, possess, possess with intent to distribute, or to advertise indecent photographs or pseudo-photographs of any person below the age of 18.

6A.2 The levels for sentencing of offences involving pornographic images were established in the case of *R v Oliver, Hartrey and Baldwin.*[136] These levels have been reviewed in terms of the nature of the images falling into each level:

- Images depicting non-penetrative activity are less serious than images depicting penetrative activity.
- Images of non-penetrative activity between children are generally less serious than images depicting non-penetrative activity between adults and children.
- All acts falling within the definitions of rape and assault by penetration, which carry the maximum life penalty, should be classified as level 4.

The levels of seriousness (in ascending order) for sentencing for offences involving pornographic images are:

Level 1 Images depicting erotic posing with no sexual activity
Level 2 Non-penetrative sexual activity between children, or solo masturbation by a child
Level 3 Non-penetrative sexual activity between adults and children
Level 4 Penetrative sexual activity involving a child or children, or both children and adults
Level 5 Sadism or penetration of, or by, an animal

Offences involving any form of sexual penetration of the vagina or anus, or penile penetration of the mouth (except where they involve sadism or intercourse with an animal, which fall within level 5), should be classified as activity at level 4.

6A.3 Pseudo-photographs should generally be treated as less serious than real images. However, they can be just as serious as photographs of a real child, for example where the imagery is particularly grotesque and beyond the scope of normal photography.

6A.4 The aggravating and mitigating factors set out in the case of *Oliver* remain relevant and are included in the guideline for this offence.

6A.5 An adult (aged 18 or over) who is given any sentence (including a conditional discharge) in relation to offences involving a victim or victims aged under 16 will be subject to registration requirements.[137] Where the offences involved a victim or victims aged 16 or 17, the requirement to register is triggered by a sentence other than an absolute or conditional discharge. Where the imposition of a conditional discharge would not result in registration, it should not be imposed purely to avoid the requirement for registration.

[136] [2003] 2 Cr App R(S) 15
[137] Sexual Offences Act 2003, s. 134

6A.6 Courts have the discretion to make an order disqualifying an offender (adult or juvenile) from working with children regardless of the sentence imposed.[138]

Possession of indecent photographs where the child depicted is aged 16 or 17

6A.7 The starting points for sentencing should reflect the fundamental facts of a case, including that the victim is over the legal age of consent.

Sentences should be lower than those involving photographs of children under 16 where:
- **an offender possesses only a few indecent photographs, none of which includes sadism or penetration of, or by, an animal; and**
- **the images are of children aged 16 or 17; and**
- **the photographs are retained solely for the use of the offender.**

6A.8 The presence of any aggravating factors will substantially increase a sentence, and the principle of lower sentences should not be applied where an offender possesses images at level 5 as these will involve either non-consensual or unlawful activity.

6A.9 Where it cannot be established that a victim was under 13, penalties will need to be based on the sentencing starting points for children aged 13 or over but under 16. In many cases, however, the extreme youth of the child in a photograph or pseudo-photograph will either be a matter of proven fact or will be a question that is beyond reasonable doubt. Where the nature of the image indicates that the victim is likely to have suffered particularly serious harm, this should always aggravate the sentence.

Starting points for sentencing for possession of indecent photographs should be higher where the victim is a child under 13.

6A.10 The court cannot make inferences about the status of unknown material, because of the fundamental principle that a person may only be convicted and sentenced according to the facts that have been proved. However, if an offender has used devices to destroy or hide material then it falls within the general aggravating factor 'An attempt to conceal or dispose of evidence'.

Showing or distributing and the element of financial gain

6A.11 The starting points in the guideline reflect the differences in terms of relative seriousness and maximum penalty available for possessing indecent photographs or pseudo-photographs (5 years) and taking or making, distributing or showing, etc such photographs (10 years).

6A.12 Showing or distributing indecent photographs or pseudo-photographs, even on a very small scale, is regarded as serious offending behaviour. Wide-scale distribution is in the most serious category of offending behaviour.

6A.13 Where the material is shown or distributed without the victim's consent, the fact that the victim is over the age of consent should not have any bearing on sentencing levels, even if the material was originally taken and possessed with his or her consent.

6A.14 Where the offence involves a victim aged 16 or 17, the starting points for sentencing should reflect the fact that the victim is above the age of consent. The fact that the victim was not coerced or forced into the activity must be relevant for sentencing purposes, and starting points should be lower to encourage consistency. Any evidence of threats or intimidation to induce consent should have the effect of increasing sentence in an individual case.

6A.15 Any profit for the victim, financial or otherwise, actual or anticipated, should be neutral for sentencing purposes.

The showing or distribution of pornographic images of children under 16, or of children aged 16 or 17 without their consent, is an aggravating factor for sentencing purposes.

Indecent photographs of children

Factors to take into consideration:

1. The levels of seriousness (in ascending order) for sentencing for offences involving pornographic images are:

[138] Criminal Justice and Court Services Act 2000, s. 29A as inserted by the Criminal Justice Act 2003, schedule 30

Level 1 Images depicting erotic posing with no sexual activity
Level 2 Non-penetrative sexual activity between children, or solo masturbation by a child
Level 3 Non-penetrative sexual activity between adults and children
Level 4 Penetrative sexual activity involving a child or children, or both children and adults
Level 5 Sadism or penetration of, or by, an animal

2. Offences involving any form of sexual penetration of the vagina or anus, or penile penetration of the mouth (except where they involve sadism or intercourse with an animal, which fall within level 5), should be classified as activity at level 4.
3. Pseudo-photographs generally should be treated less seriously than real photographs.
4. Sentences should be lower than those involving photographs of children under 16 where:
   - an offender possesses only a few indecent photographs, none of which includes sadism or penetration of, or by, an animal; and
   - the images are of children aged 16 or 17; and
   - the photographs are retained solely for the use of the offender.
5. The fact that the subject of the indecent photograph(s) is aged 16 or 17 has *no* impact on sentencing starting points where the activity depicted is at level 5.
6. Starting points for sentencing for possession of indecent photographs should be higher where the subject of the indecent photograph(s) is a child under 13.
7. Registration requirements attach to a conviction for this offence dependent upon the age of the subject portrayed in the indecent photograph(s) and the sentence imposed.
8. Courts should consider making an order disqualifying an offender (adult or juvenile) from working with children regardless of the sentence imposed.
9. Courts should consider making an order for the forfeiture of any possessions (for example, computers or cameras) used in connection with the commission of the offence.

Indecent photographs of children

THESE OFFENCES ARE SERIOUS OFFENCES FOR THE PURPOSES OF SECTION 224 CJA 2003, EXCEPT WHERE THEY INVOLVE ONLY POSSESSION, WHEN THEY ARE SPECIFIED OFFENCES FOR THE PURPOSES OF SECTION 227

Indecent photographs of children (section 1 of the Protection of Children Act 1978 and section 160 of the Criminal Justice Act 1988, as amended by section 45 of the SOA 2003): Taking, making, permitting to take, possessing, possessing with intent to distribute, distributing or advertising indecent photographs or pseudo-photographs of children under 18.

Maximum penalty: **5 years** for possession; otherwise **10 years**

Type/nature of activity	Starting points	Sentencing ranges
Offender commissioned or encouraged the production of level 4 or 5 images Offender involved in the production of level 4 or 5 images	**6 years custody**	**4–9 years custody**
Level 4 or 5 images shown or distributed	**3 years custody**	**2–5 years custody**
Offender involved in the production of, or has traded in, material at levels 1–3	**2 years custody**	**1–4 years custody**
Possession of a large quantity of level 4 or 5 material for personal use only Large number of level 3 images shown or distributed	**12 months custody**	**26 weeks–2 years custody**

Type/nature of activity	Starting points	Sentencing ranges
Possession of a large quantity of level 3 material for personal use Possession of a small number of images at level 4 or 5 Large number of level 2 images shown or distributed Small number of level 3 images shown or distributed	**26 weeks custody**	**4 weeks–18 months custody**
Offender in possession of a large amount of material at level 2 or a small amount at level 3 Offender has shown or distributed material at level 1 or 2 on a limited scale Offender has exchanged images at level 1 or 2 with other collectors, but with no element of financial gain	**12 weeks custody**	**4 weeks–26 weeks custody**
Possession of a large amount of level 1 material and/or no more than a small amount of level 2, and the material is for personal use and has not been distributed or shown to others	**Community order**	**An appropriate non-custodial sentence***

* 'Non-custodial sentence' in this context suggests a community order or a fine. In most instances, an offence will have crossed the threshold for a community order. However, in accordance with normal sentencing practice, a court is not precluded from imposing a financial penalty where that is determined to be the appropriate sentence.

Additional aggravating factors	Additional mitigating factors
1. Images shown or distributed to others, especially children 2. Collection is systematically stored or organised, indicating a sophisticated approach to trading or a high level of personal interest 3. Images stored, made available or distributed in such a way that they can be inadvertently accessed by others 4. Use of drugs, alcohol or other substance to facilitate the offence of making or taking 5. Background of intimidation or coercion 6. Threats to prevent victim reporting the activity 7. Threats to disclose victim's activity to friends or relatives 8. Financial or other gain	1. A few images held solely for personal use 2. Images viewed but not stored 3. A few images held solely for personal use and it is established both that the subject is aged 16 or 17 and that he or she was consenting

An offender convicted of this offence is automatically subject to notification requirements.[139]

Part 6B: Abuse of Children Through Prostitution and Pornography

6B.1 The four offences in this category are:
- Paying for sexual services of a child
- Causing or inciting child prostitution or pornography

[139] In accordance with the SOA 2003, s. 80 and schedule 3

- Controlling a child prostitute or a child involved in pornography
- Arranging or facilitating child prostitution or pornography

Paying for sexual services of a child

Factors to take into consideration:

1. The sentences for public protection *must* be considered in all cases. They are designed to ensure that sexual offenders are not released into the community if they present a significant risk of serious harm. Within any indeterminate sentence, the minimum term will generally be half the appropriate determinate sentence. The starting points will be relevant, therefore, to the process of fixing any minimum term that may be necessary.
2. The offence of 'paying for sexual services of a child' is the only offence in this group that involves actual physical sexual activity between an offender and a victim.
3. It carries staged maximum penalties according to the age of the victim (in this case under 16, or over 16 but under 18) and also, specifically in relation to victims under 13, whether the sexual services provided or offered involved penetrative activity.
4. The starting points for sentencing for the offence of 'paying for sexual services of a child', where the victim is aged 13 or over but under 16, are higher than those for the offence of 'sexual activity with a child', to reflect the fact that the victim has been commercially exploited.
5. Starting points for victims aged 16 or 17 are lower than the equivalent starting points for victims aged 13 to 15, in line with the difference in the maximum penalty, to reflect the fact that the victim is above the legal age of consent.
6. The starting points where the victim is aged 13 or over but under 16 are higher than those for the offence of 'sexual activity with a child', to reflect the fact that the victim has been commercially exploited.
7. The starting points for sentencing for the offence of 'paying for sexual services of a child' where the victim is under 13 are higher than those for the specific 'under 13' offences covering the same type of sexual activity, to reflect the fact that the victim has been commercially exploited.
8. The offence of 'paying for sexual services of a child' includes higher maximum penalties to cater for those (albeit rare) cases where the age of the victim is only established during the course of a trial. The same principle has been applied to the starting points for sentencing.

Paying for sexual services of a child

THIS IS A SERIOUS OFFENCE FOR THE PURPOSES OF SECTION 224 CJA 2003

Paying for sexual services of a child (section 47): Intentionally obtaining the sexual services of a child having made or promised payment or knowing that another person has made or promised payment

Maximum penalty: **Life imprisonment** for offences involving penetration where the child is under 13, otherwise **14 years; 14 years** where the child is aged 13 or over but under 16; **7 years** where the child is aged 16 or 17

Type/nature of activity	Starting points	Sentencing ranges
History of paying for penetrative sex with children under 18	If the victim is under 13, the offence of 'rape of a child under 13' or 'assault of a child under 13 by penetration' would normally be charged. Any commercial element to the offence and any history of repeat offending would be aggravating factors. However, if this offence is charged – **15 years custody**	**13–19 years custody**
	7 years custody if the victim is 13 or over but under 16	**5–10 years custody**
	3 years custody if the victim is aged 16 or 17	**2–5 years custody**

Type/nature of activity	Starting points	Sentencing ranges
Penile penetration of the vagina, anus or mouth *or* penetration of the vagina or anus with another body part or an object	If the victim is under 13, the offence of 'rape of a child under 13' or 'assault of a child under 13 by penetration' would normally be charged. Any commercial element to the offence would be an aggravating factor. However, if this offence is charged – **12 years custody**	**10–16 years custody**
	5 years custody if the victim is 13 or over but under 16	**4–8 years custody**
	2 years custody if the victim is aged 16 or 17	**1–4 years custody**
Sexual touching falling short of penetration	If the victim is under 13, the offence of 'sexual assault of a child under 13' would normally be charged. Any commercial element to the offence would be an aggravating factor. However, if this offence is charged – **5 years custody**	**4–8 years custody**
	4 years custody if the victim is 13 or over but under 16	**3–7 years custody**
	12 months custody if the victim is aged 16 or 17	**26 weeks– 2 years custody**

Additional aggravating factors	Additional mitigating factors
1. Use of drugs, alcohol or other substance to secure the victim's compliance 2. Abduction or detention 3. Threats to prevent victim reporting the activity 4. Threats to disclose victim's activity to friends or relatives 5. Offender aware that he or she is suffering from a sexually transmitted infection	

An offender convicted of this offence is automatically subject to notification requirements.[140]

Child prostitution or pornography

Factors to take into consideration:

1. The sentences for public protection *must* be considered in all cases. They are designed to ensure that sexual offenders are not released into the community if they present a significant risk of serious harm.
2. Three offences fall within this group:
   - Causing or inciting child prostitution or child pornography
   - Controlling a child prostitute or a child involved in pornography
   - Arranging or facilitating child prostitution or pornography
3. The level of involvement of the offender is a fundamental element of the 'abuse of children through prostitution and pornography' offences.
4. Financial reward may not always be a factor in someone's involvement in these offences. Thus the offences cover anyone who takes part in any way, for whatever reason, in a child's involvement in prostitution or pornography. However, most offenders will stand to gain in some way from their involvement, and sentencing starting points need to be relatively high, in line with established principles about the serious nature of commercial exploitation.
5. The courts should consider making an order confiscating any profits stemming from the offender's criminal lifestyle or forfeiting any possessions (for example cameras, computers, property) used in connection with the commission of the offence.

[140] In accordance with the SOA 2003, s. 80 and schedule 3

6. Evidence of an offender's involvement in, or management of, a well-planned or large-scale commercial operation resulting in sexual exploitation should be treated as an aggravating factor for sentencing: the greater the offender's degree of involvement, the more serious the offence.
7. The starting point for the child prostitution and pornography offences will always be a custodial sentence.
8. The same starting points apply whether the activity was caused or incited. Where an offence was incited but did not take place as a result of the voluntary intervention of the offender, that is likely to reduce the severity of the sentence imposed.
9. The presence of any of the general aggravating factors identified in the Council guideline on seriousness or any of the additional factors identified in the guidelines will indicate a sentence above the normal starting point.
10. In cases where a number of children are involved, consecutive sentences may be appropriate, leading to cumulative sentences significantly higher than the suggested starting points for individual offences.
11. In cases where the offender is, to a degree, another victim, a court may wish to take a more lenient stance. A court might consider whether the circumstances of the offender should mitigate sentence. This will depend on the merits of each case.

Child prostitution and pornography

THESE ARE SERIOUS OFFENCES FOR THE PURPOSES OF SECTION 224 CJA 2003

1. **Causing or inciting child prostitution or pornography** (section 48): Intentionally causing or inciting a child to become a prostitute, or to be involved in pornography, anywhere in the world
2. **Controlling a child prostitute or a child involved in pornography** (section 49): Intentionally controlling any of the activities of a child under 18 where those activities relate to child's prostitution, or involvement in pornography, anywhere in the world
3. **Arranging or facilitating child prostitution or pornography** (section 50): Intentionally arranging or facilitating the prostitution of a child, or the child's involvement in pornography, anywhere in the world

Maximum penalty for all offences: **14 years**

Type/nature of activity: Penetrative activity	Starting points	Sentencing ranges
Organised commercial exploitation	If the victim is under 13, the offence of 'causing or inciting a child under 13 to engage in sexual activity' would normally be charged. The commercial element of the offence would be an aggravating factor. However, if this offence is charged – **10 years custody**	**8–13 years custody**
	8 years custody if the victim is 13 or over but under 16	**6–11 years custody**
	4 years custody if the victim is aged 16 or 17	**3–7 years custody**
Offender's involvement is minimal and not perpetrated for gain	If the victim is under 13, the offence of 'causing or inciting a child under 13 to engage in sexual activity' would normally be charged. The commercial element of the offence would be an aggravating factor. However, if this offence is charged – **8 years custody**	**6–11 years custody**
	5 years custody if the victim is 13 or over but under 16	**4–8 years custody**
	2 years custody if the victim is aged 16 or 17	**1–4 years custody**

Type/nature of activity: Penetrative activity	Starting points	Sentencing ranges
Organised commercial exploitation	If the victim is under 13, the offence of 'causing or inciting a child under 13 to engage in sexual activity' would normally be charged. The commercial element of the offence would be an aggravating factor. However, if this offence is charged – **8 years custody**	**6–11 years custody**
	6 years custody if the victim is 13 or over but under 16	**4–9 years custody**
	3 years custody if the victim is aged 16 or 17	**2–5 years custody**
Offender's involvement is minimal and not perpetrated for gain	If the victim is under 13, the offence of 'causing or inciting a child under 13 to engage in sexual activity' would normally be charged. The commercial element of the offence would be an aggravating factor. However, if this offence is charged – **6 years custody**	**4–9 years custody**
	3 years custody if the victim is aged 13 or over but under 16	**2–5 years custody**
	12 months custody if the victim is aged 16 or 17	**26 weeks–2 years custody**

Additional aggravating factors	Additional mitigating factors
1. Background of threats or intimidation 2. Large-scale commercial operation 3. Use of drugs, alcohol or other substance to secure the victim's compliance 4. Induced dependency on drugs 5. Forcing a victim to violate another person 6. Victim has been manipulated into physical and emotional dependence on the offender 7. Abduction or detention 8. Threats to prevent victim reporting the activity 9. Threats to disclose victim's activity to friends or relatives 10. Storing, making available or distributing images in such a way that they can be inadvertently accessed by others 11. Images distributed to other children or persons known to the victim 12. Financial or other gain	1. Offender also being controlled in prostitution or pornography and subject to threats or intimidation

An offender convicted of this offence is automatically subject to notification requirements.[141]

[141] In accordance with the SOA 2003, s. 80 and schedule 3

Part 6C: Exploitation of Prostitution

6C.1 The offences in this section relate to the exploitation of adults who work as prostitutes, replacing gender-specific offences in the Sexual Offences Act 1956. Offenders who cause, incite or control the activities of a prostitute for their own gain, or for the gain of a third person, can be prosecuted under two new offences.

6C.2 The offences 'causing or inciting prostitution for gain' and 'controlling prostitution for gain' cover two levels of criminal activity:

(i) the coercion of another person into prostitution; and
(ii) controlling his or her activities for gain.

Exploitation of prostitution

Factors to take into consideration:

1. The sentences for public protection *must* be considered in all cases. They are designed to ensure that sexual offenders are not released into the community if they present a significant risk of serious harm.
2. The degree of coercion, both in terms of recruitment and subsequent control of a prostitute's activities, is highly relevant to sentencing.
3. The degree to which a victim is exploited or controlled, the harm suffered as a result, the level of involvement of the offender, the scale of the operation and the timescale over which it has been run will all be relevant in terms of assessing the seriousness of the offence.
4. Where an offender has profited from his or her involvement in the prostitution of others, the courts should always consider making a confiscation order approximately equivalent to the profits enjoyed.
5. The presence of any of the general aggravating factors identified in the Council guideline on seriousness or any of the additional factors identified in the guidelines will indicate a sentence above the normal starting point.
6. Where there is evidence that an offender convicted of an exploitation of prostitution offence is not actively involved in the coercion or control of the victim(s), that he or she acted through fear or intimidation and that he or she is trying to exit prostitution, the courts may wish to consider whether, in the particular circumstances of the case, this should mitigate sentence.
7. The starting points are the same whether prostitution was caused or incited and whether or not the incited activity took place. Where the offence was incited, the sentencer should begin from the starting point that the offence was incited, taking account of the nature of the harm that would have been caused had the offence taken place and calculating the final sentence to reflect that no actual harm was occasioned to the victim, but being mindful that the intended victim may have suffered as a result of knowing or believing the offence would take place.
8. The starting point for the exploitation of prostitution offences where an offender's involvement was minimal, and he or she has not actively engaged in the coercion or control of those engaged in prostitution, is a non-custodial sentence.
9. A fine may be more appropriate for very minimal involvement.
10. Where an offender has profited from his or her involvement in the prostitution of others, the court should consider making a confiscation order[142] approximately equivalent to the profits enjoyed.
11. Where this offence is being dealt with in a magistrates' court, more detailed guidance is provided in the Magistrates' Court Sentencing Guidelines (MCSG).

Exploitation of prostitution

THESE ARE SPECIFIED OFFENCES FOR THE PURPOSES OF SECTION 227 CJA 2003

1. **Causing or inciting prostitution for gain** (section 52): Intentionally causing or inciting another person to become a prostitute anywhere in the world
2. **Controlling prostitution for gain** (section 53): Intentionally controlling any of the activities of another person relating to that person's prostitution in any part of the world

[142] Criminal Justice Act 1988 as amended by the Proceeds of Crime Act 2002

Maximum penalty for both offences: 7 years

Type/nature of activity	Starting points	Sentencing ranges
Evidence of physical and/or mental coercion	**3 years custody**	**2–5 years custody**
No coercion or corruption, but the offender is closely involved in the victim's prostitution	**12 months custody**	**26 weeks–2 years custody**
No evidence that the victim was physically coerced or corrupted, and the involvement of the offender was minimal	**Community order**	**An appropriate non-custodial sentence***

* 'Non-custodial sentence' in this context suggests a community order or a fine. In most instances, an offence will have crossed the threshold for a community order. However, in accordance with normal sentencing practice, a court is not precluded from imposing a financial penalty where that is determined to be the appropriate sentence.

Additional aggravating factors	Additional mitigating factors
1. Background of threats, intimidation or coercion 2. Large-scale commercial operation 3. Substantial gain (in the region of £5000 and upwards) 4. Use of drugs, alcohol or other substance to secure the victim's compliance 5. Induced dependency on drugs 6. Abduction or detention 7. Threats to prevent victim reporting the activity 8. Threats to disclose victim's activity to friends or relatives	1. Offender also being controlled in prostitution and subject to threats or intimidation

Keeping a brothel used for prostitution

Factors to take into consideration:

1. The sentences for public protection *must* be considered in all cases. They are designed to ensure that sexual offenders are not released into the community if they present a significant risk of serious harm.
2. The offence covers anyone who keeps, manages or acts or assists in the management of a brothel. The degree of coercion, both in terms of recruitment and subsequent control of a prostitute's activities, is highly relevant to sentencing.
3. The degree to which a victim is exploited or controlled, the harm suffered as a result, the level of involvement of the offender, the scale of the operation and the timescale over which it has been run will all be relevant in terms of assessing the seriousness of the offence.
4. The presence of any of the general aggravating factors identified in the Council guideline on seriousness or any of the additional factors identified in the guidelines will indicate a sentence above the normal starting point.
5. Where there is evidence that an offender convicted of an exploitation of prostitution offence is not actively involved in the coercion or control of the victim(s), that he or she acted through fear or intimidation and that he or she is trying to exit prostitution, the courts may wish to consider whether, in the particular circumstances of the case, this should mitigate sentence.
6. The starting points are the same whether prostitution was caused or incited and whether or not the incited activity took place. Where the offence was incited, the sentencer should begin from the starting point that the offence was incited, taking account of the nature of the harm that would have been caused had the offence taken place and calculating the final sentence to reflect that no actual harm was occasioned to the victim, but being mindful that the intended victim may have suffered as a result of knowing or believing the offence would take place.
7. A non-custodial sentence may be appropriate for very minimal involvement.
8. Where an offender has profited from his or her involvement in the prostitution of others, the courts should always consider making a confiscation order approximately equivalent to the profits enjoyed.

9. Where this offence is being dealt with in a magistrates' court, more detailed guidance is provided in the Magistrates' Court Sentencing Guidelines (MCSG).

Keeping a brothel used for prostitution (section 33A of the Sexual Offences Act 1956 as inserted by section 55 of the SOA 2003): Keeping, managing, or acting or assisting in the management of a brothel

Maximum penalty: 7 **years**

Type/nature of activity	Starting points	Sentencing ranges
Offender is the keeper of a brothel and has made substantial profits in the region of £5000 and upwards	2 years custody	1–4 years custody
Offender is the keeper of the brothel and is personally involved in its management	12 months custody	26 weeks–2 years custody
Involvement of the offender was minimal	Community order	An appropriate non-custodial sentence*

* 'Non-custodial sentence' in this context suggests a community order or a fine. In most instances, an offence will have crossed the threshold for a community order. However, in accordance with normal sentencing practice, a court is not precluded from imposing a financial penalty where that is determined to be the appropriate sentence.

Additional aggravating factors	Additional mitigating factors
1. Background of threats, intimidation or coercion 2. Large-scale commercial operation 3. Personal involvement in the prostitution of others 4. Abduction or detention 5. Financial or other gain	1. Using employment as a route out of prostitution and not actively involved in exploitation 2. Coercion by third party

SENTENCERS ARE REMINDED THAT A NUMBER OF FINANCIAL ORDERS CAN BE MADE IN ADDITION TO THE SENTENCE IMPOSED FOR THIS OFFENCE (see Part 1, paragraph 1.32 above).

Part 6D: Trafficking

Factors to take into consideration:

1. The sentences for public protection *must* be considered in all cases. They are designed to ensure that sexual offenders are not released into the community if they present a significant risk of serious harm.
2. The type of activity covered by the various trafficking offences in the SOA 2003 is broadly the same, the only difference being the geographical area within which the trafficked persons are moved. The harm being addressed is sexual exploitation, but here either children or adults may be involved as victims.
3. The offences are designed to cover anyone involved in any stage of the trafficking operation, whether or not there is evidence of gain. This is serious offending behaviour, which society as a whole finds repugnant, and a financial or community penalty would rarely be an appropriate disposal.
4. The degree of coercion used and the level of control over the trafficked person's liberty will be relevant to assessing the seriousness of the offender's behaviour. The nature of the sexual exploitation to which the victim is exposed will also be relevant, as will the victim's age and vulnerability.
5. In general terms the greater the level of involvement, the more serious the crime. Those at the top of an organised trafficking chain may have very little personal involvement with day-to-day operations and may have no knowledge at all of individual victims. However, being in control of a money-making operation that is based on the degradation, exploitation and abuse of vulnerable people may be equally, if not more, serious than the actions of an individual who is personally involved at an operational level.
6. The presence of any of the general aggravating factors identified in the Council guideline on seriousness or any of the additional factors identified in the guidelines will indicate a sentence above the normal starting point.
7. Circumstances such as the fact that the offender is also a victim of trafficking and that their actions were governed by fear could be a mitigating factor if not accepted as a defence.

8. The starting point for sentencing for offences of trafficking for sexual exploitation should be a custodial sentence. Aggravating factors such as participation in a large-scale commercial enterprise involving a high degree of planning, organisation or sophistication, financial or other gain, and the coercion and vulnerability of victims should move sentences towards the maximum 14 years.
9. In cases where a number of children are involved, consecutive sentences may be appropriate, leading to cumulative sentences significantly higher than the suggested starting points for individual offences.
10. Where an offender has profited from his or her involvement in the prostitution of others, the court should consider making a confiscation order[143] approximately equivalent to the profits enjoyed.
11. The court may order the forfeiture of a vehicle used, or intended to be used, in connection with the offence.[144]

Trafficking

THESE ARE SERIOUS OFFENCES FOR THE PURPOSES OF SECTION 224 CJA 2003

Trafficking into/within/out of the UK for sexual exploitation (sections 57, 58 and 59): Intentionally arranging or facilitating a person's arrival/travel within/departure from the UK, intending or believing that a sexual offence will be committed

Maximum penalty for all offences: **14 years**

Type/nature of activity	Starting points	Sentencing ranges
Involvement at any level in any stage of the trafficking operation where the victim was coerced	**6 years custody**	**4–9 years custody**
Involvement at any level in any stage of the trafficking operation where there was no coercion of the victim	**2 years custody**	**1–4 years custody**

Note: if the victim us under 13, one of the specific under-13 offfences would normally be charged. Any commercial exploitation element would be an aggravating factor.

Additional aggravating factors	Additional mitigating factors
1. Large-scale commercial operation 2. High degree of planning or sophistication 3. Large number of people trafficked 4. Substantial financial (in the region of £5000 and upwards) or other gain 5. Fraud 6. Financial extortion of the victim 7. Deception 8. Use of force, threats of force or other forms of coercion 9. Threats against victim or members of victim's family 10. Abduction or detention 11. Restriction of victim's liberty 12. Inhumane treatment 13. Confiscation of victim's passport	1. Coercion of the offender by a third party 2. No evidence of personal gain 3. Limited involvement

143 Proceeds of Crime Act 2002, part 2
144 Sexual Offences Act 2003, s. 60A as inserted by the Violent Crime Reduction Act 2006, s. 54 and schedule 4

Part 7: Sentencing Young Offenders – Offences with a Lower Statutory Maximum

7.1 The SOA 2003 makes special provision in respect of the maximum sentence that can be imposed for certain offences where committed by a person under the age of 18 (a young offender). The sentencing framework that applies to the sentencing of young offenders is also different.

7.2 This section deals with those offences within the context of the framework that currently applies. Many cases will be sentenced in the youth court, but a significant proportion may also be dealt with in the Crown Court. The essential elements of each offence, relevant charging standards and any other general issues pertaining to the offence are set out in the offence guidelines at pages 135–139.

7.3 The offences with which Part 7 is concerned are:
- (i) Sexual activity with a child
- (ii) Causing or inciting a child to engage in sexual activity
- (iii) Engaging in sexual activity in the presence of a child
- (iv) Causing a child to watch a sexual act
- (v) Sexual activity with a child family member
- (vi) Inciting a child family member to engage in sexual activity

7.4 In relation to each offence, the maximum sentence for an offence committed by a young offender is 5 years' custody compared with a maximum of 14 years or 10 years for an offender aged 18 or over. Offences under (i), (ii), (v) and (vi) above can be committed to the Crown Court where it is considered that sentencing powers greater than those available in a magistrates' court may be needed.[145]

7.5 The provisions relating to the sentencing of dangerous offenders apply to young offenders with some variation and, where appropriate, cases should be sent for trial or committed for sentence in the Crown Court. The offences in this section are 'serious' offences for the purposes of the provisions. Where the significant harm criterion is met, the court is required[146] to impose one of the sentences for public protection, which in the case of those under 18 are discretionary detention for life, indeterminate detention for public protection or an extended sentence.

7.6 The following guidelines are for those offences where the court considers that the facts found by the court justify the involvement of the criminal law – these findings may be different from those on which the decision to prosecute was made.

7.7 The sentencing framework that applies to young offenders is different from that for adult offenders. The significant factors are set out below.

7.8 For each offence, the circumstances that would suggest that a custodial sentence should be passed where it is available to the court and those that would suggest that a case should be dealt with in the Crown Court (as 'grave crimes') are set out. As for adult offenders, these guidelines relate to sentencing on conviction for a first-time offender after a plea of not guilty.

7.9 The principal aim for all involved in the youth justice system is to prevent offending by children and young persons.[147]

7.10 A court imposing sentence on a youth must have regard to the welfare,[148] maturity, sexual development and intelligence of the youth. These are always important factors.

7.11 Where a young offender pleads guilty to one of these offences and it is the first offence of which they are convicted, a youth court may impose an absolute discharge, a mental health disposal, a custodial sentence, or make a referral order.

7.12 Except where the dangerous offender provisions apply:
- (i) Where the young offender is aged 12, 13 or 14, a custodial sentence may only be imposed if the youth is a 'persistent offender' or has committed a 'grave crime' warranting detention for a period in excess of 2 years.[149]
- (ii) Where a young offender is aged 10 or 11, no custodial sentence is available in the youth court.
- (iii) Where a custodial sentence is imposed in the youth court, it must be a Detention and Training Order (DTO), which can only be for 4/6/8/10/12/18 or 24 months.
- (iv) Where a custodial sentence is imposed in the Crown Court, it may be a DTO or it may be detention for a period up to the maximum for the offence.

---

145 Powers of Criminal Courts (Sentencing) Act 2000, s. 91
146 Criminal Justice Act 2003, ss. 226 and 228
147 Crime and Disorder Act 1998, s. 37
148 Children and Young Persons Act 1933, s. 44
149 Powers of Criminal Courts (Sentencing) Act 2000, s. 100

Sexual activity with a child
(when committed by a person under the age of 18)

THIS IS A SPECIFIED OFFENCE FOR THE PURPOSES OF SECTION 224 CJA 2003

Intentional sexual touching of a person under 16 (sections 9 and 13)
Maximum penalty: 5 years (14 years if offender is 18 or over)

The starting points below are based upon a first-time offender aged 17 years old who pleaded not guilty. For younger offenders, sentencers should consider whether a lower starting point is justified in recognition of the offender's age or immaturity.

Type/nature of activity	Starting points	Sentencing ranges
Offence involving penetration where one or more aggravating factors exist or where there is a substantial age gap between the parties	**Detention and Training Order 12 months**	**Detention and Training Order 6–24 months**
CUSTODY THRESHOLD		
Any form of sexual activity (non-penetrative or penetrative) not involving any aggravating factors	**Community order**	**An appropriate non-custodial sentence***

* 'Non-custodial sentence' in this context suggests a youth community order (as defined in the Criminal Justice Act 2003, section 147(2)) or a fine. In most instances, an offence will have crossed the threshold for a community order. However, in accordance with normal sentencing practice, a court is not precluded from imposing a financial penalty where that is determined to be the appropriate sentence.

Aggravating factors	Mitigating factors
1. Background of intimidation or coercion 2. Use of drugs, alcohol or other substance to facilitate the offence 3. Threats to prevent victim reporting the incident 4. Abduction or detention 5. Offender aware that he or she is suffering from a sexually transmitted infection	1. Relationship of genuine affection 2. Youth and immaturity of offender

An offender convicted of this offence is automatically subject to notification requirements when sentenced to imprisonment for a term of at least 12 months.[150]

Causing or inciting a child to engage in sexual activity
(when committed by a person under the age of 18)

THIS IS A SPECIFIED OFFENCE FOR THE PURPOSES OF SECTION 224 CJA 2003

Intentional causing/inciting of person under 16 to engage in sexual activity (sections 10 and 13)

Maximum penalty: 5 years (14 years if offender is 18 or over)

The same starting points apply whether the activity was caused or incited and whether or not the incited activity took place.

The starting points below are based upon a first-time offender aged 17 years old who pleaded not guilty. For younger offenders, sentencers should consider whether a lower starting point is justified in recognition of the offender's age or immaturity.

[150] In accordance with the SOA 2003, s. 80 and schedule 3

Type/nature of activity	Starting points	Sentencing ranges
Offence involving penetration where one or more aggravating factors exist or where there is a substantial age gap between the parties	**Detention and Training Order 12 months**	**Detention and Training Order 6–24 months**
CUSTODY THRESHOLD		
Any form of sexual activity (non-penetrative or penetrative) not involving any aggravating factors	**Community order**	**An appropriate non-custodial sentence***

* 'Non-custodial sentence' in this context suggests a youth community order (as defined in the Criminal Justice Act 2003, section 147(2)) or a fine. In most instances, an offence will have crossed the threshold for a community order. However, in accordance with normal sentencing practice, a court is not precluded from imposing a financial penalty where that is determermed to be the appropriate sentence.

Aggravating factors	Mitigating factors
1. Background of intimidation or coercion 2. Use of drugs, alcohol or other substance to facilitate the offence 3. Threats to prevent victim reporting the incident 4. Abduction or detention 5. Offender aware that he or she is suffering from a sexually transmitted infection	1. Relationship of genuine affection 2. Offender intervenes to prevent incited offence from taking place 3. Youth and immaturity of offender

An offender convicted of this offence is automatically subject to notification requirements when sentenced to imprisonment for a term of at least 12 months.[151]

Engaging in sexual activity in the presence of a child
(when committed by a person under the age of 18)

THIS IS A SPECIFIED OFFENCE FOR THE PURPOSES OF SECTION 224 CJA 2003

Intentionally, and for the purpose of obtaining sexual gratification, engaging in sexual activity in the presence of a person under 16, knowing or believing that the child is aware of the activity (sections 11 and 13)

Maximum penalty: **5 years (10 years** if offender is 18 or over)

The starting points below are based upon a first-time offender aged 17 years old who pleaded not guilty. For younger offenders, sentencers should consider whether a lower starting point is justified in recognition of the offender's age or immaturity.

Type/nature of activity	Starting points	Sentencing ranges
Sexual activity involving penetration where one or more aggravating factors exist	**Detention and Training Order 12 months**	**Detention and Training Order 6–24 months**
CUSTODY THRESHOLD		
Any form of sexual activity (non-penetrative or penetrative) not involving any aggravating factors	**Community order**	**An appropriate non-custodial sentence***

* 'Non-custodial sentence' in this context suggests a youth community order (as defined in the Criminal Justice Act 2003, section 147(2)) or a fine. In most instances, an offence will have crossed the threshold for a community order. However, in accordance with normal sentencing practice, a court is not precluded from imposing a financial penalty where that is determined to be the appropriate sentence.

[151] In accordance with the SOA 2003, s. 80 and schedule 3

Aggravating factors	Mitigating factors
1. Background of intimidation or coercion 2. Use of drugs, alcohol or other substance to facilitate the offence 3. Threats to prevent victim reporting the incident 4. Abduction or detention	1. Youth and immaturity of offender

An offender convicted of this offence is automatically subject to notification requirements when sentenced to imprisonment for a term of at least 12 months.[152]

Causing a child to watch a sexual act
(when committed by a person under the age of 18)

THIS IS A SPECIFIED OFFENCE FOR THE PURPOSES OF SECTION 224 CJA 2003

Intentionally causing a person under 16 to watch sexual activity or look at a photograph or pseudo-photograph of sexual activity, for the purpose of obtaining sexual gratification (sections 12 and 13)
Maximum penalty: **5 years (10 years** if offender is 18 or over)

The starting points below are based upon a first-time offender aged 17 years old who pleaded not guilty. For younger offenders, sentencers should consider whether a lower starting point is justified in recognition of the offender's age or immaturity.

Type/nature of activity	Starting points	Sentencing ranges
Live sexual activity	**Detention and Training Order 8 months**	**Detention and Training Order 6–12 months**
CUSTODY THRESHOLD		
Moving or still images of people engaged in sexual acts involving penetration	**Community order**	**An appropriate non-custodial sentence***
Moving or still images of people engaged in sexual acts other than penetration	**Community order**	**An appropriate non-custodial sentence***

* 'Non-custodial sentence' in this context suggests a youth community order (as defined in the Criminal Justice Act 2003, section 147(2)) or a fine. In most instances, an offence will have crossed the threshold for a community order. However, in accordance with normal sentencing practice, a court is not precluded from imposing a financial penalty where that is determined to be the appropriate sentence.

Aggravating factors	Mitigating factors
1. Background of intimidation or coercion 2. Use of drugs, alcohol or other substance to facilitate the offence 3. Threats to prevent victim reporting the incident 4. Abduction or detention 5. Images of violent activity	1. Youth and immaturity of offender

An offender convicted of this offence is automatically subject to notification requirements when sentenced to imprisonment for a term of at least 12 months.[153]

[152] In accordance with the SOA 2003, s. 80 and schedule 3
[153] In accordance with the SOA 2003, s. 80 and schedule 3

Sexual activity with a child family member and Inciting a child family member to engage in sexual activity
(when committed by a person under the age of 18)

THIS IS A SERIOUS OFFENCE FOR THE PURPOSES OF SECTION 224 CJA 2003

Intentional sexual touching with a child family member (section 25)

Intentionally inciting sexual touching by a child family member (section 26)

Maximum penalty for both offences: 5 years (14 years if offender is 18 or over)

The starting points below are based upon a first-time offender aged 17 years old who pleaded not guilty. For younger offenders, sentencers should consider whether a lower starting point is justified in recognition of the offender's age or immaturity.

Type/nature of activity	Starting points	Sentencing ranges
Offence involving penetration where one or more aggravating factors exist or where there is a substantial age gap between the parties	**Detention and Training Order 18 months**	**Detention and Training Order 6–24 months**
CUSTODY THRESHOLD		
Any form of sexual activity that does not involve any aggravating factors	**Community order**	**An appropriate non-custodial sentence***

* 'Non-custodial sentence' in this context suggests a youth community order (as defined in the Criminal Justice Act 2003, section 147(2)) or a fine. In most instances, an offence will have crossed the threshold for a community order. However, in accordance with normal sentencing practice, a court is not precluded from imposing a financial penalty where that is determined to be the appropriate sentence.

Aggravating factors	Mitigating factors
1. Background of intimidation or coercion 2. Use of drugs, alcohol or other substance 3. Threats deterring the victim from reporting the incident 4. Offender aware that he or she is suffering from a sexually transmitted infection	1. Small disparity in age between victim and offender 2. Relationship of genuine affection 3. Youth and immaturity of offender

An offender convicted of this offence is automatically subject to notification requirements when sentenced to imprisonment for a term of at least 12 months.[154]

[154] In accordance with the SOA 2003, s. 80 and schedule 3

Appendix 9 Control and Management of Heavy Fraud and other Complex Criminal Cases

A PROTOCOL ISSUED BY THE LORD CHIEF JUSTICE OF ENGLAND AND WALES – 22 March 2005

Introduction

There is a broad consensus that the length of fraud and trials of other complex crimes must be controlled within proper bounds in order:

(i) To enable the jury to retain and assess the evidence which they have heard. If the trial is so long that the jury cannot do this, then the trial is not fair either to the prosecution or the defence.

(ii) To make proper use of limited public resources: see *Jisl* [2004] EWCA Crim 696 at [113]–[121].

There is also a consensus that no trial should be permitted to exceed a given period, save in exceptional circumstances; some favour 3 months, others an outer limit of 6 months. Whatever view is taken, it is essential that the current length of trials is brought back to an acceptable and proper duration.

This Protocol supplements the Criminal Procedure Rules and summarises good practice which experience has shown may assist in bringing about some reduction in the length of trials of fraud and other crimes that result in complex trials. Flexibility of application of this Protocol according to the needs of each case is essential; it is designed to inform but not to prescribe.

This Protocol is primarily directed towards cases which are likely to last eight weeks or longer. It should also be followed, however, in all cases estimated to last more than four weeks. This Protocol applies to trials by jury, but many of the principles will be applicable if trials without a jury are permitted under s. 43 of the Criminal Justice Act 2003.

The best handling technique for a long case is continuous management by an experienced Judge nominated for the purpose.

It is intended that this Protocol be kept up to date; any further practices or techniques found to be successful in the management of complex cases should be notified to the office of the Lord Chief Justice.

1. The Investigation

(i) The role of the prosecuting authority and the judge

(a) Unlike other European countries, a judge in England and Wales does not directly control the investigative process; that is the responsibility of the Investigating Authority, and in turn the Prosecuting Authority and the prosecution advocate. Experience has shown that a prosecution lawyer (who must be of sufficient experience and who will be a member of the team at trial) and the prosecution advocate, if different, should be involved in the investigation as soon as it appears that a heavy fraud trial or other complex criminal trial is likely to ensue. The costs that this early preparation will incur will be saved many times over in the long run.

(b) The judge can and should exert a substantial and beneficial influence by making it clear that, generally speaking, trials should be kept within manageable limits. In most cases 3 months should be the target outer limit, but there will be cases where a duration of 6 months, or in exceptional circumstances, even longer may be inevitable.

(ii) Interviews

(a) At present many interviews are too long and too unstructured. This has a knock-on effect on the length of trials. Interviews should provide an opportunity for suspects to respond to the allegations against them. They should not be an occasion to discuss every document in the case. It should become clear from judicial rulings that interviews of this kind are a waste of resources.

(b) The suspect must be given sufficient information before or at the interview to enable them to meet the questions fairly and answer them honestly; the information is not provided to give the suspect the opportunity to manufacture a false story which fits undisputable facts.

(c) It is often helpful if the principal documents are provided either in advance of the interview or shown as the interview progresses; asking detailed questions about events a considerable period in the past without reference to the documents is often not very helpful.

(iii) The prosecution and defence teams

(a) *The Prosecution Team*
While instructed, it is for the lead advocate for the prosecution to take all necessary decisions in the presentation and general conduct of the prosecution case in court. The prosecution lead advocate will be treated by the court as having that responsibility.
However, in relation to policy decisions, the lead advocate for the prosecution must not give an indication or undertaking which binds the prosecution without first discussing the issue with the Director of the Prosecuting authority or other senior officer.
'Policy' decisions should be understood as referring to non-evidential decisions on: the acceptance of pleas of guilty to lesser counts or groups of counts or available alternatives: offering no evidence on particular counts; consideration of a re-trial; whether to lodge an appeal; certification of a point of law; and the withdrawal of the prosecution as a whole (for further information see the 'Farquharson Guidelines' on the role and responsibilities of the prosecution advocate).

(b) *The Defence Team*
In each case, the lead advocate for the defence will be treated by the court as having responsibility to the court for the presentation and general conduct of the defence case.

(c) In each case, a case progression officer must be assigned by the court, prosecution and defence from the time of the first hearing when directions are given (as referred to in paragraph 3 (iii)) until the conclusion of the trial.

(d) In each case where there are multiple defendants, the LSC will need to consider carefully the extent and level of representation necessary.

(iv) Initial consideration of the length of a case

If the prosecutor in charge of the case from the Prosecuting Authority or the lead advocate for the prosecution consider that the case as formulated is likely to last more than 8 weeks, the case should be referred in accordance with arrangements made by the Prosecuting Authority to a more senior prosecutor. The senior prosecutor will consider whether it is desirable for the case to be prosecuted in that way or whether some steps might be taken to reduce its likely length, whilst at the same time ensuring that the public interest is served.

Any case likely to last 6 months or more must be referred to the Director of the Prosecuting Authority so that similar considerations can take place.

(v) Notification of cases likely to last more than 8 weeks

Special arrangements will be put in place for the early notification by the CPS and other Prosecuting Authorities, to the LSC and to a single designated officer of the Court in each Region (Circuit) of any case which the CPS or other Prosecuting Authority consider likely to last over 8 weeks.

(vi) Venue

The court will allocate such cases and other complex cases likely to last 4 weeks or more to a specific venue suitable for the trial in question, taking into account the convenience to witnesses, the parties, the availability of time at that location, and all other relevant considerations.

2. Designation of the Trial Judge

(i) The assignment of a judge

(a) In any complex case which is expected to last more than four weeks, the trial judge will be assigned under the direction of the Presiding Judges at the earliest possible moment.

(b) Thereafter the assigned judge should manage that case 'from cradle to grave'; it is essential that the same judge manages the case from the time of his assignment and that arrangements are made for him to be able to do so. It is recognised that in certain court centres with a large turnover of heavy cases (e.g. Southwark) this objective is more difficult to achieve. But in those court centres there are teams of specialist judges, who are more readily able to handle cases which the assigned judge cannot continue with because of unexpected events; even at such courts, there must be no exception to the principle that one judge must handle all the pre-trial hearings until the case is assigned to another judge.

3. Case Management

(i) Objectives

(a) The number, length and organisation of case management hearings will, of course, depend critically on the circumstances and complexity of the individual case. However, thorough, well-prepared and extended case management hearings will save court time and costs overall.

(b) Effective case management of heavy fraud and other complex criminal cases requires the judge to have a much more detailed grasp of the case than may be necessary for many other Plea and Case Management Hearings (PCMHs). Though it is for the judge in each case to decide how much pre-reading time he needs so that the judge is on top of the case, it is not always a sensible use of judicial time to allocate a series of reading days, during which the judge sits alone in his room, working through numerous boxes of ring binders.
See paragraph 3 (iv) (e) below.

(ii) Fixing the trial date

Although it is important that the trial date should be fixed as early as possible, this may not always be the right course. There are two principal alternatives:

(a) The trial date should be fixed at the first opportunity – i.e. at the first (and usually short) directions hearing referred to in subparagraph (iii). From then on everyone must work to that date. All orders and pre-trial steps should be timetabled to fit in with that date. All advocates and the judge should take note of this date, in the expectation that the trial will proceed on the date determined.
(b) The trial date should not be fixed until the issues have been explored at a full case management hearing (referred to in subparagraph (iv), after the advocates on both sides have done some serious work on the case. Only then can the length of the trial be estimated.

Which is apposite must depend on the circumstances of each case, but the earlier it is possible to fix a trial date, by reference to a proper estimate and a timetable set by reference to the trial date, the better. It is generally to be expected that once a trial is fixed on the basis of the estimate provided, that it will be **increased** if, and only if, the party seeking to extend the time justifies why the original estimate is no longer appropriate.

(iii) The first hearing for the giving of initial directions

At the first opportunity the assigned judge should hold a short hearing to give initial directions. The directions on this occasion might well include:

(a) That there should be a full case management hearing on, or commencing on, a specified future date by which time the parties will be properly prepared for a meaningful hearing and the defence will have full instructions.
(b) That the prosecution should provide an outline written statement of the prosecution case at least one week in advance of that case management hearing, outlining in simple terms:
    (i) The key facts on which it relies.
    (ii) The key evidence by which the prosecution seeks to prove the facts.
    The statement must be sufficient to permit the judge to understand the case and for the defence to appreciate the basic elements of its case against each defendant. The prosecution may be invited to highlight the key points of the case orally at the case management hearing by way of a short mini-opening. The outline statement should not be considered binding, but it will serve the essential purpose in telling the judge, and everyone else, what the case is really about and identifying the key issues.
(c) That a core reading list and core bundle for the case management hearing should be delivered at least one week in advance.
(d) Preliminary directions about disclosure: see paragraph 4.

(iv) The first case management hearing

(a) At the first case management hearing:
    (i) The prosecution advocate should be given the opportunity to highlight any points from the prosecution outline statement of case (which will have been delivered at least a week in advance).
    (ii) Each defence advocate should be asked to outline the defence.
    If the defence advocate is not in a position to say what is in issue and what is not in issue, then the case management hearing can be adjourned for a short and limited time and to a fixed date to enable the advocate to take instructions; such an adjournment should only be necessary in exceptional circumstances, as the defence advocate should be properly instructed by the time of the first case management hearing and in any event is under an obligation to take sufficient instructions to fulfil the obligations contained in S 33–39 of Criminal Justice Act 2003.
(b) There should then be a real dialogue between the judge and all advocates for the purpose of identifying:
    (i) The focus of the prosecution case.
    (ii) The common ground.
    (iii) The real issues in the case. (Rule 3.2 of the Criminal Procedure Rules.)

(c) The judge will try to generate a spirit of co-operation between the court and the advocates on all sides. The expeditious conduct of the trial and a focussing on the real issues must be in the interests of **all** parties. It cannot be in the interests of any defendant for his good points to become lost in a welter of uncontroversial or irrelevant evidence.

(d) In many fraud cases the primary facts are not seriously disputed. The real issue is what each defendant knew and whether that defendant was dishonest. Once the judge has identified what is in dispute and what is not in dispute, the judge can then discuss with the advocate how the trial should be structured, what can be dealt with by admissions or agreed facts, what uncontroversial matters should be proved by concise oral evidence, what timetabling can be required under Rule 3.10 Criminal Procedure Rules, and other directions.

(e) In particularly heavy fraud or complex cases the judge may possibly consider it necessary to allocate a whole week for a case management hearing. If that week is used wisely, many further weeks of trial time can be saved. In the gaps which will inevitably arise during that week (for example while the advocates are exploring matters raised by the judge) the judge can do a substantial amount of informed reading. The case has come 'alive' at this stage. Indeed, in a really heavy fraud case, if the judge fixes one or more case management hearings on this scale, there will be need for fewer formal reading days. Moreover a huge amount can be achieved in the pre-trial stage, if all trial advocates are gathered in the same place, focussing on the case **at the same time**, for several days consecutively.

(f) Requiring the defence to serve proper case statements may enable the court to identify:
(i) what is common ground and
(ii) the real issues.
It is therefore important that proper defence case statements be provided as required by the Criminal Procedure Rules; Judges will use the powers contained in ss 28–34 of the [CPIA 1996] (and the corresponding provisions of the CJA 1987, ss. 33 and following of the Criminal Justice Act 2003) and the Criminal Procedure Rules to ensure that realistic defence case statements are provided.

(g) Likewise this objective may be achieved by requiring the prosecution to serve draft admissions by a specified date and by requiring the defence to respond within a specified number of weeks.

(v) Further case management hearings

(a) The date of the next case management hearing should be fixed at the conclusion of the hearing so that there is no delay in having to fix the date through listing offices, clerks and others.

(b) If one is looking at a trial which threatens to run for months, pre-trial case management on an intensive scale is essential.

(vi) Consideration of the length of the trial

(a) Case management on the above lines, the procedure set out in paragraph 1 (iv), may still be insufficient to reduce the trial to a manageable length; generally a trial of 3 months should be the target, but there will be cases where a duration of 6 months or, in exceptional circumstances, even longer may be inevitable.

(b) If the trial is not estimated to be within a manageable length, it will be necessary for the judge to consider what steps should be taken to reduce the length of the trial, whilst still ensuring that the prosecution has the opportunity of placing the full criminality before the court.

(c) To assist the judge in this task,
(i) The lead advocate for the prosecution should be asked to explain why the prosecution have rejected a shorter way of proceeding; they may also be asked to divide the case into sections of evidence and explain the scope of each section and the need for each section.
(ii) The lead advocates for the prosecution and for the defence should be prepared to put forward in writing, if requested, ways in which a case estimated to last more than three months can be shortened, including possible severance of counts or defendants, exclusions of sections of the case or of evidence or areas of the case where admissions can be made.

(d) One course the judge may consider is pruning the indictment by omitting certain charges and/or by omitting certain defendants. The judge must not usurp the function of the prosecution in this regard, and he must bear in mind that he will, at the outset, know less about the case than the advocates. The aim is achieve fairness to all parties.

(e) Nevertheless, the judge does have two methods of pruning available for use in appropriate circumstances:
(i) Persuading the prosecution that it is not worthwhile pursuing certain charges and/or certain defendants.
(ii) Severing the indictment. Severance for reasons of case management alone is perfectly proper,

although judges should have regard to any representations made by the prosecution that severance would weaken their case. Indeed the judge's hand will be strengthened in this regard by rule 1.1 (2) (g) of the Criminal Procedure Rules. However, before using what may be seen as a blunt instrument, the judge should insist on seeing full defence statements of all affected defendants. Severance may be unfair to the prosecution if, for example, there is a cut-throat defence in prospect. For example, the defence of the principal defendant may be that the defendant relied on the advice of his accountant or solicitor that what was happening was acceptable. The defence of the professional may be that he gave no such advice. Against that background, it might be unfair to the prosecution to order separate trials of the two defendants.

(vii) The exercise of the powers

(a) The Criminal Procedure Rules require the court to take a more active part in case management. These are salutary provisions which should bring to an end interminable criminal trials of the kind which the Court of Appeal criticised in *Jisl* [2004] EWCA 696 at [113]–[121].

(b) Nevertheless these salutary provisions do not have to be used on every occasion. Where the advocates have done their job properly, by narrowing the issues, pruning the evidence and so forth, it may be quite inappropriate for the judge to 'weigh in' and start cutting out more evidence or more charges of his own volition. It behoves the judge to make a careful assessment of the degree of judicial intervention which is warranted in each case.

(c) The note of caution in the previous paragraph is supported by certain experience which has been gained of the Civil Procedure Rules (on which the Criminal Procedure Rules are based). The CPR contain valuable and efficacious provisions for case management by the judge on his own initiative which have led to huge savings of court time and costs. Surveys by the Law Society have shown that the CPR have been generally welcomed by court users and the profession, but there have been reported to have been isolated instances in which the parties to civil litigation have faithfully complied with both the letter and the spirit of the CPR, and have then been aggrieved by what was perceived to be unnecessary intermeddling by the court.

(viii) Expert evidence

(a) Early identification of the subject matter of expert evidence to be adduced by the prosecution and the defence should be made as early as possible, preferably at the directions hearing.

(b) Following the exchange of expert evidence, any areas of disagreement should be identified and a direction should generally be made requiring the experts to meet and prepare, after discussion, a joint statement identifying points of agreement and contention and areas where the prosecution is put to proof on matters of which a positive case to the contrary is not advanced by the defence. After the statement has been prepared it should be served on the court, the prosecution and the defence. In some cases, it might be appropriate to provide that to the jury.

(ix) Surveillance evidence

(a) Where a prosecution is based upon many months' observation or surveillance evidence and it appears that it is capable of effective presentation based on a shorter period, the advocate should be required to justify the evidence of such observations before it is permitted to be adduced, either substantially or in its entirety.

(b) Schedules should be provided to cover as much of the evidence as possible and admissions sought.

4. Disclosure

In fraud cases the volume of documentation obtained by the prosecution is liable to be immense. The problems of disclosure are intractable and have the potential to disrupt the entire trial process.

(i) The prosecution lawyer (and the prosecution advocate if different) brought in at the outset, as set out in paragraph 1 (i)(a), each have a continuing responsibility to discharge the prosecution's duty of disclosure, either personally or by delegation, in accordance with the Attorney General's Guidelines on Disclosure.

(ii) The prosecution should only disclose those documents which are relevant (i.e. likely to assist the defence or undermine the prosecution – see s. 3 (1) of CPIA 1996 and the provisions of the CJA 2003).

(iii) It is almost always undesirable to give the 'warehouse key' to the defence for two reasons:

(a) This amounts to an abrogation of the responsibility of the prosecution;

(b) The defence solicitors may spend a disproportionate amount of time and incur disproportionate costs trawling through a morass of documents.

The Judge should therefore try and ensure that disclosure is limited to what is likely to assist the defence or undermine the prosecution.

(iv) At the outset the judge should set a timetable for dealing with disclosure issues. In particular, the judge should fix a date by which all defence applications for specific disclosure must be made. In this regard, it is relevant that the defendants are likely to be intelligent people, who know their own business affairs and who (for the most part) will know what documents or categories of documents they are looking for.

(v) At the outset (and before the cut-off date for specific disclosure applications) the judge should ask the defence to indicate what documents they are interested in and from what source. A general list is not an acceptable response to this request. The judge should insist upon a list which is specific, manageable and realistic. The judge may also require justification of any request.

(vi) In non-fraud cases, the same considerations apply, but some may be different:

(a) It is not possible to approach many non-fraud cases on the basis that the defendant knows what is there or what they are looking for. But on the other hand this should not be turned into an excuse for a 'fishing expedition'; the judge should insist on knowing the issue to which a request for disclosure applies.

(b) If the bona fides of the investigation is called into question, a judge will be concerned to see that there has been independent and effective appraisal of the documents contained in the disclosure schedule and that its contents are adequate. In appropriate cases where this issue has arisen and there are grounds which show there is a real issue, consideration should be given to receiving evidence on oath from the senior investigating officer at an early case management hearing.

5. Abuse of Process

(i) Applications to stay or dismiss for abuse of process have become a normal feature of heavy and complex cases. Such applications may be based upon delay and the health of defendants.

(ii) Applications in relation to absent special circumstances tend to be unsuccessful and not to be pursued on appeal. For this reason there is comparatively little Court of Appeal guidance: but see: *Harris and Howells* [2003] EWCA Crim 486. It should be noted that abuse of process is not there to discipline the prosecution or the police.

(iii) The arguments on both sides must be reduced to writing. Oral evidence is seldom relevant.

(iv) The judge should direct full written submissions (rather than 'skeleton arguments') on any abuse application in accordance with a timetable set by him; these should identify any element of prejudice the defendant is alleged to have suffered.

(v) The Judge should normally aim to conclude the hearing within an absolute maximum limit of one day, if necessary in accordance with a timetable. The parties should therefore prepare their papers on this basis and not expect the judge to allow the oral hearing to be anything more than an occasion to highlight concisely their arguments and answer any questions the court may have of them; applications will not be allowed to drag on.

6. The Trial

(i) The particular hazard of heavy fraud trials

A heavy fraud or other complex trial has the potential to lose direction and focus. This is a disaster for three reasons:

(a) The jury will lose track of the evidence, thereby prejudicing both prosecution and defence.

(b) The burden on the defendants, the judge and indeed all involved will become intolerable.

(c) Scarce public resources are wasted. Other prosecutions are delayed or – worse – may never happen. Fraud which is detected but not prosecuted (for resource reasons) undermines confidence.

(ii) Judicial mastery of the case

(a) It is necessary for the judge to exercise firm control over the conduct of the trial at all stages.

(b) In order to do this the judge must read the witness statements and the documents, so that the judge can discuss case management issues with the advocates on – almost – an equal footing.

(c) To this end, the judge should not set aside weeks or even days for pre-reading (see paragraph 3 (i)(b) above). Hopefully the judge will have gained a good grasp of the evidence during the case management hearings. Nevertheless, realistic reading time must be provided for the judge in advance of trial.

(d) The role of the judge in a heavy fraud or other complex criminal trial is different from his/her role in a 'conventional' criminal trial. So far as possible, the judge should be freed from other duties and burdens, so that he/she can give the high degree of commitment which a heavy fraud trial requires. This will pay dividends in terms of saving weeks or months of court time.

(iii) The order of the evidence

(a) By the outset of the trial at the latest (and in most cases very much earlier) the judge must be provided with a schedule, showing the sequence of prosecution (and in an appropriate case defence) witnesses and the dates upon which they are expected to be called. This can only be prepared by discussion between prosecution and defence which the judge should expect, and say he/she expects, to take place: See: Criminal Procedure Rule 3.10. The schedule should, in so far as it relates to Prosecution witnesses, be developed in consultation with the witnesses, via the Witness Care Units, and with consideration given to their personal needs. Copies of the schedule should be provided for the Witness Service.

(b) The schedule should be kept under review by the trial judge and by the parties. If a case is running behind or ahead of schedule, each witness affected must be advised by the party who is calling that witness at the earliest opportunity.

(c) If an excessive amount of time is allowed for any witness, the judge can ask why. The judge may probe with the advocates whether the time envisaged for the evidence-in-chief or cross-examination (as the case may be) of a particular witness is really necessary.

(iv) Case management sessions

(a) The order of the evidence may have legitimately to be departed from. It will, however, be a useful for tool for monitoring the progress of the case. There should be periodic case management sessions, during which the judge engages the advocates upon a stock-taking exercise: asking, amongst other questions, 'where are we going?' and 'what is the relevance of the next three witnesses?'. This will be a valuable means of keeping the case on track. Rule 3.10 of the Criminal Procedure Rules will again assist the judge.

(b) The judge may wish to consider issuing the occasional use of 'case management notes' to the advocates, in order to set out the judge's tentative views on where the trial may be going off track, which areas of future evidence are relevant and which may have become irrelevant (e.g. because of concessions, admissions in cross-examination and so forth). Such notes from the judge plus written responses from the advocates can, cautiously used, provide a valuable focus for debate during the periodic case management reviews held during the course of the trial.

(v) Controlling prolix cross-examination

(a) Setting **rigid** time limits in advance for cross-examination is rarely appropriate – as experience has shown in civil cases; but a timetable is essential so that the judge can exercise control and so that there is a clear target to aim at for the completion of the evidence of each witness. Moreover the judge can and should indicate when cross-examination is irrelevant, unnecessary or time wasting. The judge may limit the time for further cross-examination of a particular witness.

(vi) Electronic presentation of evidence

(a) Electronic presentation of evidence (EPE) has the potential to save huge amounts of time in fraud and other complex criminal trials and should be used more widely.

(b) HMCS is providing facilities for the easier use of EPE with a standard audio visual facility. Effectively managed, the savings in court time achieved by EPE more than justify the cost.

(c) There should still be a core bundle of those documents to which frequent reference will be made during the trial. The jury may wish to mark that bundle or to refer back to particular pages as the evidence progresses. EPE can be used for presenting all documents not contained in the core bundle.

(d) Greater use of other modern forms of graphical presentations should be made wherever possible.

(vii) Use of interviews

The Judge should consider extensive editing of self serving interviews, even when the defence want the jury to hear them in their entirety; such interviews are not evidence of the truth of their contents but merely of the defendant's reaction to the allegation.

(viii) Jury management

(a) The jury should be informed as early as possible in the case as to what the issues are in a manner directed by the Judge.

(b) The jury must be regularly updated as to the trial timetable and the progress of the trial, subject to warnings as to the predictability of the trial process.

(c) Legal argument should be heard at times that causes the least inconvenience to jurors.
(d) It is useful to consider with the advocates whether written directions should be given to the jury and, if so, in what form.

(ix) Maxwell hours

(a) Maxwell hours should only be permitted after careful consideration and consultation with the Presiding Judge.
(b) Considerations in favour include:
 (i) Legal argument can be accommodated without disturbing the jury;
 (ii) There is a better chance of a representative jury;
 (iii) Time is made available to the judge, advocates and experts to do useful work in the afternoons.
(c) Considerations against include:
 (i) The lengthening of trials and the consequent waste of court time;
 (ii) The desirability of making full use of the jury once they have arrived at court;
 (iii) Shorter trials tend to diminish the need for special provisions e.g. there are fewer difficulties in empanelling more representative juries;
 (iv) They are unavailable if any defendant is in custody.
(d) It may often be the case that a maximum of one day of Maxwell hours a week is sufficient; if so, it should be timetabled in advance to enable all submissions by advocates, supported by skeleton arguments served in advance, to be dealt with in the period after 1:30 pm on that day.

(x) Livenote

If Livenote is used, it is important that all users continue to take a note of the evidence, otherwise considerable time is wasted in detailed reading of the entire daily transcript.

7. Other Issues

(i) Defence representation and defence costs

(a) Applications for change in representation in complex trials need special consideration; the ruling of HH Judge Wakerley QC (as he then was) in *Asghar Ali* has been circulated by the JSB.
(b) Problems have arisen when the Legal Services Commission have declined to allow advocates or solicitors to do certain work; on occasions the matter has been raised with the judge managing or trying the case.
(c) The Legal Services Commission has provided guidance to judges on how they can obtain information from the LSC as to the reasons for their decisions; further information in relation to this can be obtained from *Nigel Field, Head of the Complex Crime Unit, Legal Services Commission, 29–37 Red Lion Street, London, WC1R 4PP.*

(ii) Assistance to the judge

Experience has shown that in some very heavy cases, the judge's burden can be substantially offset with the provision of a Judicial Assistant or other support and assistance.

Index

Useful References

PRINCIPLES—PART A

ROAD TRAFFIC OFFENCES —PART C

CONTEMPT OF COURT —PARTS B & D

POLICE POWERS —PART D

TRIAL PRELIMINARIES — PART D

CASE MANAGEMENT —PART D

REMAND AND BAIL —PART D

ASSETS RECOVERY—PART D

DISCLOSURE—PART D

SENDING CASES TO THE CROWN COURT—PART D

INDICTMENTS—PART D

PLEAS—PART D

CUSTODY—PART D

TRIAL ON INDICTMENT — PART D

SUMMARY TRIAL—PART D

TRIAL OF JUVENILES —PART D

SENTENCING AND FINES —PART E

EVIDENCE—PART F